DICTIONARY
AND ENCYCLOPEDIA

COLLINS

Double Book

DICTIONARY AND ENCYCLOPEDIA

WITH 293 COLOUR PHOTOGRAPHS

COLLINS
LONDON AND GLASGOW

GENERAL EDITOR: J. B. FOREMAN, M.A.

Dictionary, first published, 1959
In this edition, 1968
Reprinted 1969 (twice)
Reprinted 1970
Reprinted 1972

ACKNOWLEDGMENTS

Colour Photographs in this volume by kind permission of:

Ackermanns Kunstverlag, Munich; A.D.A.G.P., Paris; Prof. Adam-Laborde, Paris; Anthony-Verlag, Starnberg; Baege, Wiesbaden; Battelle-Institut, Frankfurt; Bavaria-Verlag, München-Gauting; Bettermann, Giessen; Bibliothèque Nationale, Paris; Blauel, Munich; Dr. Bonn, Stuttgart; Bötzl, Dorfen; Bresgen, Lucerne; Renate Braun, Bonn; British Museum, London; Buckup, Munich; California Institute of Technology, Pasadena; Chem. Werke Hüls AG, Marl; Christiansen, Copenhagen; Collignon, Munich; Deutsche Fotothek, Dresden; Doeser, Holland; Deutsche Presseagentur; Dr. Dorff, Helmstedt; Farbwerke Hoechst AG, Frankfurt; Erich Fischer, Hamburg-Blankenese; Fried, F. A. Brockhaus, Wiesbaden; Gartner, Brussels; Gangkofner, Munich; Gerken, Oldenburg; Giraudon, Paris; Dr. Grunow, Hohenpeissenberg; Dr. Haefelfinger, Basle; Hahn, Bad Wildungen; Hanfstaengl, Munich; Dr. Heineck, Weisbaden; Held, Lausanne; Hinz, Basle; Hirmer-Verlag, Munich; Kalle AG, Weisbaden-Biebrich; Prof. Kayser, Cologne; Prof. Keylwerth, Reinbek; Klein-Verlag, Baden-Baden; Prof. Dr. A. Kolb, Hamburg; Krainz, Zürich; Kunsthistor. Museum, Wien; Kunstverlag Berger, Köln; Kunstverlag Fingerle & Co., Esslingen; Kusch, Nürnberg; Laborde, Paris; Land-u. Hausw. Auswertungs-u. Informations-dienst, Bad Godesberg; Lauterwasser, Überlingen; Prof. Lehmann, Frankfurt; Mariani, Como, Italy; Dr. Melchers, Kassel; Möhrs, Geisenheim; Münch, Ratingen; Museum f. Kunsthandwerk, Frankfurt; Musem f. Kunst u. Gewerbe, Hamburg; Museum of Fine Arts, Boston, U.S.A.; Okapia, Frankfurt; Österr. Museum f. angewandte Kunst; Philippi, Bad Dürkheim; Photographic Agency Paul Popper, London; Piperdrucke, Munich; Dr. Quitter, F. A. Brockhaus; Reitz, Hanover; Rhein. Landesmuseum Trier; Rijksmuseum, Leyden, Holland; Roubier, Paris; Scala, Florence; Schacht, Munich; Schranner, Würzburg; Schuler-Verlag, Stuttgart; Werner Schulz, Dallas; Senfft, Darmstadt; Skira, Geneva; Prof. Speiser, Cologne; Staatl. Kunstsammlungen Kassel; Süssmuth, Immenhausen; The Tate Gallery, London; Dr. Thutewohl, F. A. Brockhaus; Dr. Valentin, Berlin; Verlag Schroll, Vienna; Weber, Würzburg; Prof. Wilhelmy, Tübingen; Wissenbach, Herborn; Wolf i. v. Schweinitz, Wiesbaden; Zentrale Farbbild-Agentur GmbH, Heidelberg.

PRINTED IN GREAT BRITAIN
COLLINS CLEAR-TYPE PRESS

DICTIONARY

Contents

PLAN OF THE TEXT

The words in this Dictionary are arranged in groups, derived and related words being placed under the word chosen as the main-entry.

Each main-entry is given a simple phonetic re-spelling to assist in pronunciation, and where a word of more than one syllable occurs, a mark is made to indicate where the stress should lie. Sub-entries are given separate spellings only where the pronunciation differs from that of the main-entry, or where, by reason of length, it may give difficulty to the reader.

The part of speech of each word is given immediately after its phonetic spelling, and the derivation appears at the end of each paragraph.

The following example will help to make these arrangements clear:

main (mān) *a.* principal; first in size, importance, etc.; essential; sheer;—*n.* the chief part; strength, as in *might and main*; a wide expanse of land or ocean; the principal pipe in water, gas, or electricity system.—**main′brace** *n.* the brace of the main-yard.—**to splice the main-brace**, to hand out a double ration of rum.—**main′chance** *n.* self-interest.—**main′door** *n.* a front door giving access to ground-floor house.—**main′land** *n.* a continent as distinct from islands.—**main′ly** *adv.*—**main′mast** *n.* the principal mast of a ship.—**main′road** *n.* a highway, esp. between two towns.—**main′sail** *n.* the principal sail on the main-mast.—**main′stay** *n.* the rope from the maintop to the deck; (*Fig.*) the chief support [O.E. *maegen*, strong, powerful].

ABBREVIATIONS USED IN THIS DICTIONARY

a. adjective
abbrev. abbreviation
ablat. ablative; ablatival
Aborig. Aboriginal
acc. accusative
A.D. Anno Domini (in the year of Our Lord)
adv. adverb
Aero. Aeronautics
Afr. Africa; African
Agric. Agriculture
Alg. Algebra
Amer. America; American
Anat. Anatomy
Anglo-Ind. Anglo-Indian
Anthropol. Anthropology
Ar. Arabic
Arch. Archaic
Archaeol. Archaeology
Archit. Architecture
Arith. Arithmetic
Astrol. Astrology
Astron. Astronomy
aux. auxiliary
Aviat. Aviation.

Bacter. Bacteriology
B.C. before Christ
Bib. Biblical
Biol. Biology
Bot. Botany
Br. British
Braz. Brazilian
Bret. Breton
Build. Building

c. about (Lat. = *Circa*)
C. Centigrade; Central
Can. Canada; Canadian
cap. capital
Carib. Caribbean
Carp. Carpentry
Celt. Celtic
cent. century
Cent. Central
cf. compare (Lat. = *confer*)
ch. chapter
Chem. Chemistry
Chin. Chinese
Class. Myth. Classical Mythology
Colloq. Colloquial; Colloquialism
Comm. Commerce; Commercial
comp. comparative
conj. conjunction
conn. connected
contr. contraction
corrupt. corruption

Dan. Danish
dat. dative
def. art. definite article
demons. demonstrative
der. derivation; derived
Dial. Dialect; Dialectal
Dict. Dictionary
dim. diminutive
Dut. Dutch
Dyn. Dynamics

E. East; English
Eccl. Ecclesiastical
e.g. for example (Lat. = *exemplia gratia*)
E.Ind. East Indian
Elect. Electricity
Embryol. Embryology
Engin. Engineering
Entom. Entomology
esp. especially
Ethnol. Ethnology
etym. etymology

F., Fahr. Fahrenheit
fem. feminine
fig. figuratively
Finn. Finnish
Flem. Flemish
Fort. Fortification
fr. from
Fr. French

Gael. Gaelic
gen. genitive
Geog. Geography
Geol. Geology
Geom. Geometry
Ger. German
Gk. Greek
Gk. Myth. Greek Mythology
Gram. Grammar

Heb. Hebrew
Her. Heraldry
Hind. Hindustani
Hist. History
Hort. Horticulture
Hung. Hungarian

i. intransitive
Ice. Icelandic
i.e. that is (Lat. = *id est*)
imit. imitation; imitative
imper. imperative
impers. impersonal
Ind. Indian
indef. art. indefinite article
indic. indicative
infin. infinitive
interj. interjection
interrog. interrogative
Ir. Irish
It. Italian

Jap. Japanese

L. Latin
L.Ger. Low German
lit. literally
Lit. Literature
L.L. Low (Late) Latin

masc. masculine
Math. Mathematics
M.E. Middle English
Mech. Mechanics
Med. Medicine
Metal. Metallurgy
Meteor. Meteorology
Mex. Mexican
M.H.Ger. Middle High German
Mil. Military
Min. Mineralogy
Mod. Modern
Mus. Music
Myth. Mythology

n. noun
N. North; Norse
Nat.Hist. Natural History
Naut. Nautical
neg. negative
neut. neuter
nom. nominative
Norw. Norwegian
n.pl. noun plural
n.sing. noun singular
N.T. New Testament

obj. object; objective
obs. obsolete
O.E. Old English
O.Fr. Old French
O.H.Ger. Old High German
O.L.Ger. Old Low German
O.N. Old Norse
Onomat. Onomatopoeic
opp. opposite; opposed
Opt. Optics
orig. originally
Ornith. Ornithology
O.T. Old Testament

Paint. Painting
pa.p. past participle
pass. passive
pa.t. past tense
Path. Pathology
perh. perhaps
pers. person
Pers. Persian
pert. pertaining
Peruv. Peruvian
Pharm. Pharmacy
Philol. Philology
Philos. Philosophy
Phon. Phonetics
Photog. Photography
Phys. Physics
Physiol. Physiology
pl. plural
Poet. Poetry; poetical
Pol. Polish
Port. Portuguese
poss. possessive
pref. prefix
prep. preposition
pres. present
Print. Printing
prob. probably
pron. pronoun
Pros. Prosody
Prov. Provincial
pr.p. present participle
Psych. psychology

q.v. which see (Lat. *quod vide*)

ABBREVIATIONS USED IN THIS DICTIONARY

R. River
R.C. Roman Catholic
recip. reciprocal
redup. reduplication
ref. reference; referring
refl. reflexive
rel. related; relative
Rhet. Rhetoric
Rom. Roman
Rom.Myth. Roman Mythology
Russ. Russian

S. South
S.Afr. South African
S.Amer. South American
Sans. Sanskrit
Scand. Scandinavian
Scot. Scots; Scottish
Sculp. Sculpture
sing. singular
Singh. Singhalese
Slav. Slavonic
Sp. Spanish
St. Saint
superl. superlative
Surg. Surgery
Sw. Swedish
Syn. Synonym

t. transitive
Teleg. Telegraphy
Teut. Teutonic
Theat. Theatre
Theol. Theology
Trig. Trigonometry
Turk. Turkish

U.S.(A.) United States (of America)

v. verb
var. variant; variation
v.i. verb intransitive
v.t. verb transitive
vulg. vulgar

W. Welsh; West

Zool. Zoology

KEY TO PRONUNCIATION

(a) Apart from " g " (always hard as in *get*) the consonants retain their name-sounds.

(b) All unmarked vowels are sounded as in *pat*, *pet*, *pit*, *pot*, *nut*.

(c) Special symbols used are:—

(i)	ā	as in	l*a*te	ō	as in	v*o*te
	ȧ	,,	f*a*r	ȯȯ	,,	m*oo*n
	ạ	,,	*a*do	oo	,,	g*oo*d
	ē	,,	m*e*	ū	,,	t*u*ne
	ẹ	,,	h*e*r	aw	,,	f*a*ll
	ī	,,	m*i*te	ou	,,	f*ou*l
(ii)	th	,,	*th*in	hw	,,	*wh*en
	TH	,,	*th*en	ch	,,	*ch*ur*ch*
	H	,,	lo*ch*	j	,,	*j*am
	zh	,,	lei*s*ure	y	,,	*y*et

(d) The French nasal vowels (*an*, *on*, *in*, *un*), so difficult to interpret accurately, have been reduced to the following simple approximations:—

an, am, en, em = ong
on, om = ōng
in = ang
un = ung

For example: embonpoint = (ong-bōng-pwang)

DICTIONARY
OF THE ENGLISH LANGUAGE

A

A (ā, ạ) *a.* the indefinite article, meaning *one.* It is a contraction of *an* (fr. O.E. *an,* one), still used before vowels.

AI (ā wun) denotes a ship listed as " first-class" in Lloyd's Register of Shipping; hence, first-rate; excellent; physically fit.

aabec (à´bek) *n.* an Australian bark used as a sweat-producing medicine [Native].

aardvark (ȧrd´vȧrk) *n.* animal resembling the ant-eater, found in parts of Africa; the earth-pig [Dut. *aarde,* earth; *vark,* a pig].

aardwolf (ȧrd´wŏŏlf) *n.* a S. African carnivorous animal, resembling a hyaena; earth-wolf [Dut. *aarde,* earth, and *wolf*].

Aaron (ā´ron) *n.* (*Bib.*) the elder brother of Moses, and first high-priest of the Jews.—**Aaron's beard,** *Hypericum calycinum* (St. John's Wort, or Rose of Sharon).—**Aaron's rod,** *Verbascum thapsus,* a plant with flowers on a long stem; (*Archit.*) a rod with a serpent twisted round it.

aasvogel (ȧs-vō´gel) *n.* the S. African vulture [Dut. *aas,* carrion; *vogel,* a bird].

ab- (ab) L. prefix meaning from, away, off.

abaca (ab´ạ-ka) *n.* Manila hemp, or the plant producing it [Malay].

aback (ạ-bak') *adv.* backward; on the back; (*Naut.*) against the masts, of sails pressed back by the wind.—**taken aback,** taken by surprise; disconcerted [O.E. *on baec*].

abacus (ab´ạ-kus) *n.* an instrument with parallel wires on which arithmetical calculations are made with sliding balls or beads; a counting-frame; (*Archit.*) a tablet crowning a column and its capital [L., from Gk. *abax,* a reckoning-board].

abaft (ạ-baft) *adv.* and *prep.* (*Naut.*) at or towards the stern; behind [O.E. *aeftan,* behind].

abalone (ab-ạ-lōn´ē) *n.* the name of several species of limpet-like molluscs or " ear-shells," yielding mother-of-pearl [Sp.].

abandon (ạ-ban´don) *v.t.* to give up wholly and finally; to relinquish; to surrender;—*n.* careless freedom; a yielding to unrestrained impulse; dash.—**aban'doned** *a.* deserted; forsaken; unrestrained; given up entirely to, esp. wickedness.—**aban'donedly** *adv.*—**aban'donment** *n.* the act of abandoning, or state of being abandoned; (*Law*) the relinquishing of an interest or claim [Fr. *abandonner,* to give up].

abase (ạ-bās') *v.t.* to bring low; to cast down; to humble.—**abase'ment** *n.* humiliation [L. *ad,* to; L.L. *bassare,* to lower].

abash (ạ-bash') *v.t.* to strike with shame or fear; to excite a consciousness of guilt, inferiority, etc.—**abash'ment** *n.* confusion from shame, etc. [Fr. *ébahir,* to astound].

abate (ạ-bāt') *v.t.* to beat down, lessen; (*Law*) to put an end to, as a nuisance; to annul, as a writ;—*v.i.* to decrease, subside, decline.—**abat'able** *a.*—**abate'ment** *n.*—**abat'er** *n.* [L. *ad,* and *batere,* for *batuere,* to strike].

abatis, abattis (a´ba-tis) *n.* a barricade of felled trees for defence [Fr. fr. *abattre,* to fell].

abattoir (a-ba-twȧr') *n.* a slaughter-house, esp. one under a local government authority [Fr. *abattre,* to fell].

Abba (ab´a) *n.* (*Bib.*) father; used in the phrase ' Abba, Father,' an invocation used in fervent prayer [Heb. *ab,* father].

abbacy (ab´ạ-si) *n.* the office or dignity of an abbot; the building under the control of an abbot; an abbey.—**abbatial** (ạ-bā´shạl) *a.* pert to an abbot, or an abbey.—**abbé** (ab´ā) *n.* designation of and mode of address for an R.C. priest in France; an abbot.—**abb'ey** *n.* a church establishment forming the dwelling-place of a community of monks or nuns.—**abb'ot** (*fem.* **abb'ess**) *n.* the head of an abbey or monastery.—**abb'otship** *n.* [Syriac *abba,* father; Heb. *ab,* father].

abbreviate (ạ-brē´vi-āt) *v.t.* to shorten, reduce by contraction or omission.—**abbrevia'tion** *n.* the act of abbreviating; a shortened form.—**abbre'viator** *n.*—**abbre'viatory** *a.* [L. *abbreviare,* fr. *brevis,* short].

Abc (ā-bē-sē') *n.* the first three letters of the alphabet; the alphabet; the rudiments of any subject; a primer.

abdicate (ab´di-kāt) *v.t.* and *i.* formally to give up power or office.—**abdica'tion** *n.* [L. *ab,* from; *dicare,* to proclaim].

abdomen (ab-dō´men, ab´dō-men) *n.* the lower part of the trunk of the body; the belly.—**abdom'inal** *a.* pert. to abdomen.—**abdom'inous** *a.* having a big belly; paunchy [L.].

abduct (ab-dukt') *v.t.* to take away by fraud or force; to kidnap; (*Anat.*) to draw, e.g. a limb, away from its natural position.—**abducent** (ab-dū´sent) *a.* (*Anat.*) abducting.—**abduc'tion** *n.* [L. *ab,* from; *ducere, ductum,* to lead].

abeam (ạ-bēm') *adv.* (*Naut.*) at right angles to a ship's length; hence, straight across a ship; abreast [E. *beam*].

abecedarian (ā-bē-sē-dā´ri-ạn) *a.* pert. to the a,b,c; alphabetical; rudimentary;—*n.* one who teaches or learns the alphabet; a beginner.

abed (ạ-bed') *adv.* in bed [E. *on bed*].

abele (a-bēl') *n.* the white poplar-tree [L. *albus,* white].

aberrate (ab´ẹr-āt) *v.i.* to deviate from the right path or normal course.—**aber'rant** *a.* deviating from the normal.—**aberra'tion** *n.* a wandering, esp. mental disorder, forgetfulness; mental instability or peculiarity; moral lapse [L. *ab,* from; *errare,* to wander].

abet (ạ-bet') *v.t.* to encourage or aid, esp. in doing wrong.—*pr.p.* **abet'ting.**—*pa.p.* and *pa.t.* **abet'ted.**—**abet'ment** *n.*—**abet'ter, abet'tor** *n.* [O.Fr. *abeter,* to incite].

abeyance (ạ-bā´ạns) *n.* a state of suspension or temporary inactivity; the condition of not being in use or action. Also **abey'ancy** [O.Fr. *abeer,* to gape at].

abhor (ab-hor') *v.t.* to hate extremely.—*pr.p.* **abhor'ring.**—*pa.p.* and *pa.t.* **abhorred'.**—**abhor'rence** *n.* detestation; loathing.—**abhor'rent** *a.* detestable; abominable; repugnant.—**abhor'rer** *n.* [L. *ab,* from; *horrere,* to shiver].

abide (ạ-bīd') *v.i.* to stay; reside; continue firm or stable;—*v.t.* to tolerate; bear; wait for.—*pa.p.* and *pa.t.* **abode'.**—**abid'ance** *n.*—**abid'ing** *a.* lasting; enduring [O.E. *abidan*].

Abies (ab´i-ēz) *n.* (*Bot.*) a genus of coniferous trees, containing the firs, larches, spruces, and cedars [L.].

Abigail (ab´i-gāl) *n.* (*Bib.*) the wife of David (See I Sam. 25); also the name of a sister of David.—**ab'igail** *n.* a waiting-maid; a lady's maid.

ability (ạ-bil´i-ti) *n.* quality, state, or condition of being able; power to act; skill; capacity; competence. [L. *habilitas,* cleverness].

abiogenesis (ab-i-ō-jen´e-sis) *n.* (*Biol.*) the theory of spontaneous generation from non-living matter [Gk. *a-*; neg.; *bios,* life; *genesis,* birth].

abject (ab´jekt) *a.* base; degraded; mean and

worthless; contemptible; miserable.—**ab'jectly** *adv.*—**abjec'tion, ab'jectness** *n.* degradation; abasement; servility [L. *ab*, away; *jacere, jactum*, to throw].

abjure (ab-jŏŏr') *v.t.* to renounce upon oath; to abandon allegiance to a cause, doctrine, or principle; repudiate; forswear.—**abjura'tion** *n.* [L. *abjurare*, to deny on oath].

ablation (ab-lā'shun) *n.* a wasting or carrying away.—**ablati'tious** *a.* [L. *ab*, from; *ferre, latum*, to carry].

ablative (ab'lą-tiv) *a.* (used as *n.*) the sixth case of Latin nouns and pronouns expressing *time when*; originally implied *separation from*. —**ablati'val** *a.* [L. *ab*, from; *ferre, latum*, to carry].

ablaut (ab'lout) *n.* (*Philol.*) variation of root vowel in certain related words, as *sink, sank, sunk* [Ger. *ab*, from; *Laut*, sound].

ablaze (ą-blāz') *a.* on fire; aglow; gleaming.

able (ā'bl) *a.* (*comp.* **a'bler**; *superl.* **a'blest**) having skill, strength to perform a task; competent; talented; vigorous.—**a'ble-bod'ied** *a.* of sound body; robust; (of a seaman, *abbrev.* **A.B.**) having all-round knowledge of seamanship.—**a'bleness, abil'ity** *n.*—**a'bly** *adv.* competently [L. *habilis*, manageable].

ablen (ab'len) *n.* a small whitish fresh-water fish; the bleak. Also **ab'let** [L. *albus*, white].

ablepsy (a-blep'si) *n.* blindness. Also **ablep'sia** [Gk. *ablepsia*, blindness].

ablocate (ab'lō-kāt) *v.t.* to let out; lease [L. *ab*, from; *locare, locatum*, let out].

abloom (ą-blŏŏm') *adv.* or *a.* in bloom.

abluent (ab'lŏŏ-ent) *a.* cleansing.—*n.* a detergent [L. *ab*, from; *luere*, to wash].

ablution (ab-lŏŏ'shun) *n.* cleansing or washing; (usually plural) the purification of the body or of sacred vessels before certain religious ceremonies, e.g. Eucharist; the wine and water used.—**ablu'tionary** *a.* pert. to cleansing.—**ablu'vion** *n.* that which is washed off (L. *ab*, from; *luere, lutum*, to wash].

abnegate (ab'ne-gāt) *v.t.* to deny; surrender; relinquish.—**abnega'tion** *n.* denying; renunciation [L. *ab*, away; *negare*, to deny].

abnormal (ab-nor'mąl) *a.* contrary to rule, or system; deviating from a recognised standard; exceptional; psychologically maladjusted. Also **abnor'mous.**—**abnor'malism** *n.* the state of being abnormal; something freakish.—**abnormal'ity** *n.* the state of being abnormal; deformity; idiosyncrasy.—**abnor'mally** *adv.*—**abnor'mity** *n.* abnormality; monstrosity [L. *ab*, from; *norma*, rule].

aboard (ą-bōrd') *adv.* and *prep.* (*Naut.*) on board; within a vessel; (*U.S.*) on a train.

abode (ą-bōd') *n.* residence, permanent or temporary; a dwelling-place [from *abide*].

abolish (ą-bol'ish) *v.t.* to do away with; to repeal; to obliterate.—**abol'ishment** *n.*—**aboli'tion** *n.* the act of abolishing, as of laws, taxes, etc.—**aboli'tional** *a.*—**aboli'tionism** *n.* the policy of an abolitionist [L. *abolescere*, to decay].

abominate (ą-bom'i-nāt) *v.t.* to loathe; detest extremely; abhor.—**abom'inable** *a.* loathsome; morally detestable; odious.—**abom'inableness** *n.*—**abom'inably** *adv.*—**abomina'tion** *n.* the act or object of loathing; a despicable practice [L. *abominari*, to detest].

aborigines (ab-o-rij'i-nēz) *n.pl.* the original inhabitants of a country, e.g. "blackfellows" of Australia or Maoris of New Zealand.—**aborig'inal** *a.* [L. *ab origine*, from the beginning].

abort (ab-ort') *v.i.* to miscarry in giving birth; (*Fig.*) to fail to come to fruition.—**abortifac'ient** *n.* a drug causing abortion;—*a.* capable of producing abortion.—**abor'tion** *n.* miscarriage; one born prematurely.—**abor'tionist** *n.*—**abor'tive** *a.* prematurely produced; undeveloped; imperfect; rudimentary.—**abor'tively** *adv.* [L. *aboriri, abortus*, to miscarry].

abound (ą-bound') *v.i.* to be in great plenty (used with preps. *with* and *in*).—**abound'ing** *a.* plentiful [L. *abundare*, to overflow].

about (ą-bout') *adv.* and *prep.* on every side; concerning; approximately; (before an infin.) on the point of.—**to bring about,** to effect [O.E. *būtan*, outside].

above (ą-buv') *adv.* and *prep.* and *a.* higher than; more in number, quantity or degree.—**above board,** open or openly; honourably [O.E. *abufan*, upwards].

abracadabra (ab'rą-ką-dab'rą) *n.* corrupt. of sacred Gnostic term, derived from ancient Egyptian magical formula; a catchword; gibberish.

abrade (ab-rād') *v.t.* to rub or wear off; to scrape or grate off; to graze (of skin).—**abra'dant** *n.* a substance, e.g. emery powder, for polishing.—**abra'ding** *n.* soil-erosion.—**abra'sion** *n.* a rubbing or scraping off; a grazing of the skin.—**abra'sive** *a.* tending to abrade; scouring.—*n.* something used for scouring [L. *ab*, from; *radere, rasum*, to scrape].

abranchiate, abranchial (ą-brang'ki-āt, -ąl) *a.* (*Zool.*) having no gills [Gk. *a-*, neg.; *branchia*, gills].

abreaction (ab-rē-ak'shun) *n.* in psycho-analysis, elimination of a morbid complex by expression through conscious association with the original cause.—**abreact'** *v.t.* [L. *ab*, from; and *reaction*].

abreast (ą-brest') *adv.* side by side; on a line with [E.].

abreption (ab-rep'shun) *n.* carrying off by force; separation [L. *ab*, from; *rapere, raptum*, to seize].

abridge (ą-brij') *v.t.* to shorten; curtail; reduce; diminish; epitomise.—**abridg'ment, abridge'ment** *n.* a cutting-off; a summary; a précis; an abstract of evidence.—**abridg'er** *n.* [Fr. *abréger*; L. *abbreviare*, to shorten].

abroad (ą-brawd') *adv.* and *a.* at large, over a wide space; beyond or out of a house, camp, or other enclosure; in foreign countries; overseas; perplexed; quite wrong [E.].

abrogate (ab'rō-gāt) *v.t.* to annul; repeal (a law); do away with; put an end to; cancel.—**abroga'tion** *n.* [L. *ab*, away; *rogare*, to ask].

abrupt (ą-brupt') *a.* broken off; steep; precipitous; describing a sudden change of subject, etc. in speech or writing; curt; unceremonious; brusque; (*Bot.*) without a terminal leaf.—**abrup'tion** *n.* a breaking off; wrenching asunder.—**abrupt'ly** *adv.*—**abrupt'ness** *n.* [L. *ab*, away; *rumpere, ruptum*, to break].

abscess (ab'ses) *n.* a gathering of pus in any infected organ or tissue of the body [L. *abscessus*, a going away].

abscind (ab-sind') *v.t.* to cut off; pare away; separate; rend apart.—**ab'sciss, abscis'sa** *n.* (*Geom.*) the distance of a point from a fixed line measured horizontally; one of the elements of reference by which a point, as of a curve, is referred to a system of fixed rectilineal co-ordinate axes;—*pl.* **abscis'ses, absciss'ae.**—**abscis'sion** *n.* act or process of cutting off [L. *ab*, away; *scindere, scissum*, to cut].

absconce (ab'skons) *n.* a small dark-lantern holding a wax candle used in the R.C. Church [L. *abs*, away; *condere*, to hide].

abscond (ab-skond') *v.i.* to take oneself off; to flee from justice.—**abscon'dence** *n.*—**abscon'der** *n.* [L. *abs*, away; *condere*, to hide].

absence (ab'sens) *n.* being absent; failure to appear when cited to a court of law; inattention to prevailing conditions.—**ab'sent** *a.* not present; inattentive.—**absent'** *v.t.* to withdraw (oneself); deliberately to fail to appear.—**absentee'** *n.* one who is not present.—**ab'sently** *adv.* casually; forgetfully.—**ab'sent-mind'ed** *a.* abstracted; absorbed; pre-occupied [L. *ab*, away; *esse*, to be].

absinth, absinthe (ab'sinth) *n.* a green-coloured liqueur flavoured with wormwood and other aromatics [L. *absinthium*, wormwood].

absolute (ab'sō-lòòt, (-lūt)) *a.* uncontrolled; unconditional; without restraint; (*Gram.*) not dependent; pure.—**ab'solutely** *adv.* positively; very; entirely.—**ab'soluteness** *n.*—**absolu'tion** *n.* a remission of sin after confession, pronounced by the R.C. Church; formal acquittal by a judge.—**ab'solutism** *n.* unrestricted and unlimited rule; arbitrary government.—**ab'solutist** *n.*—**absol'utory, absolv'atory** *a.*—**absolute alcohol,** alcohol free from water.—**absolute pressure** (*Phys.*) pressure of gas, steam, or liquid measured as excess over zero pressure, i.e. over atmospheric pressure.—**absolute zero** (*Phys.*) the lowest possible temperature − 273.1° C.—**nominative (ablative) absolute,** a grammatical construction consisting of a substantive and a participle independent of the main sentence [L. *absolutus*, freed].

absolve (ab-solv') *v.t.* to set free from an obligation, guilt, debt, penalty; to pardon; acquit.—**absolv'er** *n.* [L. *ab*, away; *solvere*, to loosen].

absorb (ab-sorb') *v.t.* to swallow up; drink in; suck up; to engage one's whole attention.—**absorbabil'ity** *n.*—**absorb'able** *a.*—**absorbefac'ient** *n.* that which causes absorption; a drying up; —*a.* absorbing rapidly.—**absorb'ent** *a.* absorbing;—*n.* anything which absorbs [L. *ab*, away; *sorbere, sorptum*, to suck].

absorption (ab-sorp'shun) *n.* the act of absorbing.—**absorp'tive** *a.* able to absorb.—**absorptiv'ity** *n.* the power of absorbing [fr. *absorb*].

abstain (ab-stān') *v.i.* to forbear; to refrain.—**abstain'er** *n.* one who abstains, esp. from alcohol [L. *abs*, from; *tenere*, to hold].

abstemious (ab-stēm'i-us) *a.* showing moderation in the use of food and drink.—**abstem'iously** *adv.*—**abstem'iousness** *n.* [L. *abs*, from; *temetum*, strong drink].

abstention (ab-sten'shun) *n.* the act of abstaining or refraining from.—**absten'tionist** *n.* [L. *abs*, from; *tenere*, to hold].

absterge (ab-stẹrj') *v.t.* to clean by wiping; to cleanse.—**abster'gent** *a.* cleansing.—*n.* a cleansing substance.—**abster'sion** *n.*—**abster'sive** *a.* [L. *abs*, away; *tergere, tersum*, to wipe].

abstinence (abs'tin-ens) *n.* voluntary forbearance from using or doing something. Also **abs'tinency.**—**abs'tinent** *a.* temperate; refraining from.—**abs'tinently** *adv.* [L. *abs*, from; *tenere*, to hold].

abstract (ab-strakt') *v.t.* to separate from; remove, esp. secretly, for one's own use; summarise; reduce.—**ab'stract** *a.* not concrete; theoretical;—*n.* that which comprises in itself the essential qualities of a larger thing, or of several things; a summary.—**abstrac'tion** *n.* abstracting or separating; a theoretical idea;—**in the abstract,** without reference to particular cases [L. *abs*, from; *trahere, tractum*, to draw].

abstruse (ab-stròòs') *a.* hidden; difficult or hard to be understood.—**abstruse'ly** *adv.*—**abstruse'ness** *n.* [L. *abs*, from; *trudere, trusum*, to thrust].

absurd (ab-surd') *a.* contrary to reason; ridiculous; silly.—**absurd'ly** *adv.*—**absurd'ity** *n.* that which is absurd. Also **absurd'ness** [L. *absurdus*, out of tune].

abundance (ạ-bun'dạns) *n.* ample sufficiency; great plenty.—**abun'dant** *a.* fully sufficient; plentiful.—**abun'dantly** *adv.* [L. *abundare*, to overflow].

abuse (ạ-būz') *v.t.* to make a wrong use of; to ill-treat; to violate; revile; malign.—**abuse** (ạ-būs') *n.* ill-usage; improper treatment; a corrupt practice; rude language.—**abu'sive** *a.* practising abuse; rude; insulting.—**abu'siveness** *n.* [Fr. *abuser*].

abut (ạ-but') *v.i.* to end; to touch with one end; to border on; to adjoin.—*pr.p.* **abut'ting.**—*pa.p.* **abut'ted.**—**abut'ment** *n.* (*Archit.*) the support at end of an arch or bridge [O.Fr. *abouter*, to join at the end].

abyss (ạ-bis') *n.* any deep chasm; a gulf.—formerly, **abysm** (ạ-bizm') *n.*—**aby'smal** *a.* bottomless; vast; profound.—**abys'mally** *adv.*—**abyss'al** *a.* inhabiting, or characteristic of, the depths of the ocean; abysmal [Gk. *abussos*, bottomless].

acacia (ạ-kā'shi-ạ) *n.* thorny, leguminous tree or shrub, yielding gum arabic [Gk. *akakia*, from *akē*, a sharp point].

academy (ạ-kad'e-mi) *n.* a garden or grove near Athens, where Plato and his followers held their conferences; a place of education or specialised training; popularly a school; a society of men united for the promotion of the arts and sciences.—**academ'ic, academ'ical** *a.* belonging to an academy or other institution of learning.—**academician** (ạ-kad-ẹ-mish'ạn) *n.* a member of an academy or society for promoting the arts and sciences [Gk. *akadēmeia*].

acanthus (a-kan'thus) *n.* a prickly plant, also called 'bear's breech' or 'brank-ursine'; (*Archit.*) an ornament like this leaf, esp. on the capitals of Corinthian pillars [Gk. *akē*, a point; *anthos*, a flower].

acarpous (ạ-kār'pus) *a.* (*Bot.*) not producing fruit [Gk. *a-*, neg.; *karpos*, fruit].

acatalectic (ạ-kat-ạ-lek'tik) *a.* not stopping short; complete in syllables;—*n.* a verse that has the complete number of syllables.

acatalepsy (ạ-kat-ạ-lep'si) *n.* incomprehensibility; (*Med.*) uncertainty in the diagnosis of a disease.—**acatalep'tic** *a.* [Gk. *a-*, neg.; *kata*, down,; *lēpsis*, a seizing].

acataphasia (ạ-kat-ạ-fā'zi-ạ) *n.* difficulty or inability in expressing ideas logically.

accede (ak-sēd') *v.i.* to agree; assent; consent; to arrive at a certain state or condition; to succeed as heir.—**acced'er** *n.* [L. *ad*, to; *cedere*, to go].

accelerando (ak-sel-e-ran'dō) *a.* and *n.* (*Mus.*) a direction to quicken the time [It. fr. L. *celer*, swift].

accelerate (ak-sel'e-rāt) *v.t.* and *i.* to cause to move faster; to become swifter.—**accelera'tion** *n.* an increase in speed, action, etc.; the rate of increase in the velocity of a moving body.—**accel'erative** *a.* quickening.—**accel'erator** *n.* a mechanism for increasing speed.—**accel'eratory** *a.* [L. *celer*, swift].

accend (ak-send') *v.i.* to kindle.—**accend'ible** *a.* capable of being kindled.—**accendibil'ity** *n.*—**accen'sion** *n.*—**accen'sor** *n.* [L. *accendere*, burn].

accent (ak'sent) *n.* stress on a syllable or syllables of a word; a mark to show this; inflection of the voice; manner of speech; pronunciation and inflection of the voice peculiar to a country, town, or individual.—**accent** (ak-sent') *v.t.* to utter, pronounce, or mark with accent; to emphasise; to stress.—**accent'ual** *a.*—**accent'uate** *v.t.* to accent; to stress; to make more prominent.—**accentua'tion** *n.* [Fr. fr. L. *accentus*, a tone].

accept (ak-sept') *v.t.* to take; receive; admit; believe; to agree to; (*Comm.*) to agree to meet a bill.—**accept'able** *a.* welcome; pleasing; agreeable.—**accept'ably** *adv.*—**accept'ance** *n.* the act of accepting.—**accepta'tion** *n.* a kind reception; the usual meaning of a word, statement, etc. —**accept'ed** *a.*—**accept'er, accept'or** *n.* [L. *acceptare*].

access (ak'ses) *n.* a coming to the means or way of approach; admission; entrance; attack; fit.—**access'ary** *a.* (See **accessory**).—**access'ible** *a.* easy of access or approach; approachable.—**accessibil'ity** *n.*—**acces'sion** *n.* increase; a coming to, esp. to a throne, office, or dignity.—**accessory** (ak-ses'o-ri, ak'-ses-or-i), **access'ary** *a.* aiding; contributing; additional;—*n.* an additional, secondary piece of equipment; an accompaniment; (*Law*) one implicated in a felony (though not as a principal); a confederate [L. *accedere, accessum*, to go to].

accidence (ak'si-dens) *n.* the part of grammar dealing with changes in the form of words, e.g. plurals, etc. [fr. *accidents*].

accident (ak′si-dent) *n.* chance; a mishap; a casualty; contingency; a quality not essential.—**accident'ally** *adv.* [L. *ad*, to; *cadere*, to fall].

acclaim (ạ-klām′) *v.t.* and *i.* to receive with applause, etc.; cheer; to hail as;—**acclama'tion** *n.* general applause.—**acclam'atory** *a.* [L. *acclamare*, to shout to].

acclimatise (ạ-klī′mạ-tīz) *v.t.* to accustom to a new climate. Also **accli'mate.**—**acclimatisa'tion** *n.* Also **acclima'tion, acclimata'tion** *n.* [fr. *climate*].

acclivity (ạ-kliv′i-ti) *n.* an upward slope [L. *ad*, to; *clivus*, a slope].

accolade (ak′ō-lād) *n.* a ceremony used in conferring knighthood, consisting now of a tap given on the shoulder with the flat of a sword [L. *ad*, to; *collum*, the neck].

accommodate (ạ-kom′ō-dāt) *v.t.* to render fit or suitable; adapt; adjust; reconcile; provide room for.—**accom'modating** *a.* obliging.—**accommoda'tion** *n.* convenience; room or space for; lodgings; a loan of money.—**accom'modative** *a.* obliging; supplying accommodation; adaptive [L. *accommodare*, to fit].

accompany (ạ-kum′pạ-ni) *v.t.* to go with; (*Mus.*) to play the accompaniment.—**accom'paniment** *n.* that which goes with; (*Mus.*) the instrumental parts played with a vocal or other instrumental part.—**accom'panist** *n.* [Fr. *accompagner*].

accomplice (ạ-kom′plis) *n.* a companion in evil deeds; an associate in crime [Earlier *complice*, fr. L. *complex*, woven together].

accomplish (ạ-kom′plish) *v.t.* to carry out; to finish; to complete; to perform.—**accom'plished** *a.* complete; perfect; having accomplishments; hence, talented.—**accom'plishment** *n.* completion; finish; that which makes for culture, elegant manners, etc. [L. *ad*, to; *complere*, to complete].

accord (ạ-kord′) *n.* agreement; harmony;—*v.t.* to grant; settle; compose;—*v.i.* to agree; to agree in pitch and tone.—**accord'ance** *n.*—**accord'ant** *a.* corresponding.—**accord'ing** *a.* in accordance; agreeing; suitable.—**accord'ingly** *adv.*—**of one's own accord**, of one's own free will; voluntarily [L. *ad*, to; *cor, cordis*, the heart].

accordion (ạ-kor′di-on) *n.* wind instrument fitted with bellows and button keyboards; in the **piano-accordion** the right hand keyboard is like that of a piano.—**accor'dion-pleat'ed** *a.* having narrow folds like those of the bellows of an accordion.

accost (ạ-kost′) *v.t.* to speak first to; to address [L. *ad*, to; *costa*, a rib].

accouchement (ạ-kòòsh′mong) *n.* delivery in childbed; confinement.—**accoucheuse** (ạ-kòòsh-ẹz) *n.fem.* midwife [Fr. fr. *coucher*, put to bed].

account (ạ-kount′) *n.* a reckoning; a record; a report; a description; a statement of debts and credits in money transactions; value; advantage; profit;—*v.t.* to reckon, judge;—*v.i.* to give a reason; to give a financial reckoning.—**account'able** *a.* liable to be held responsible; able to be explained.—**account'ably** *adv.*—**accountabil'ity** *n.*—**account'ancy** *n.* the profession of an accountant.—**account'ant** *n.* one skilled in recording financial transactions, esp. as a profession [O.Fr. *aconter*, to reckon].

accoutre (ạ-kòò′tẹr) *v.t.* to furnish with dress or equipment, esp. military; to equip.—**accou'trements** *n.pl.* dress; military dress and equipment [Fr. *accoutrer*, to dress].

accredit (ạ-kred′it) *v.t.* to give trust or confidence to; to vouch for; to recommend; to furnish with credentials, as an envoy or ambassador [Fr. *accréditer*].

accrescent (ạ-kres′ent) *a.* growing; accumulating.—**accres'cence** *n.* growth; increase.—**accretion** (ạ-krē′shun) *n.* an increase in growth, esp. by an addition of parts externally.—**accre'tive** *a.* [L. *ad*, to; *crescere*, to grow].

accrue (ạ-kròò′) to increase; to result naturally; to come as an addition, e.g. interest, profit, etc. [Fr. *accrue*, an extension, from L. *ad*, to; *crescere*, to grow].

accumulate (ạ-kū′mū-lāt) *v.t.* to heap up; to collect;—*v.i.* to grow into a mass; to increase.—**accumula'tion** *n.* a collection; a mass; a pile.—**accu'mulative** *a.*—**accu'mulatively** *adv.*—**accu'mulator** *n.* one who, or that which, collects; an apparatus for the storage of electricity [L. *ad*, to; *cumulus*, a heap].

accurate (ak′ū-rāt) *a.* correct.—**ac'curately** *adv.*—**ac'curacy** *n.* correctness; exactness; precision [L. *ad*, to; *cura*, care].

accurse (a-kurs′) *v.t.* to doom to destruction; to curse.—**accurs'ed** *a.* under a curse.

accuse (a-kūz′) *v.t.* to charge with a crime or fault; to blame.—**accused'** *a.* charged with a crime;—*n.* one so charged.—**accus'er** *n.*—**accusa'tion** *n.* a charge.—**accus'ative** *a.* producing or containing accusations; (*Gram.*) of the case which forms the direct object of a transitive verb (the objective case);—*n.* the accusative case.—**accus'atory** *a.* [L. *accusare*].

accustom (ạ-kus′tom) *v.t.* to make familiar by use; to familiarise; to habituate.—**accus'tomed** *a.* often practised; usual; ordinary [O.Fr. *acostumer*].

ace (ās) *n.* a card, domino, etc. with only one spot; a single point; a particle; the best, highest; an outstanding fighter airman; an expert player of any game; an unreturnable service in tennis [L. *as*, a unit].

acerbate (ạ-sẹr′bāt, as′ẹr-bāt) *v.t.* to make bitter; to exasperate;—*a.* embittered; severe; exasperated.—**acer'bitude** *n.* bitterness.—**acer'bity** *n.* sourness of taste, with bitterness and astringency.—hence bitterness, or severity in persons [L. *acerbus*, bitter].

acetic (ạ-set′ik, ạ-sē′tik) *a.* pert. to acetic acid, the acid in vinegar.—**a'cetate** *n.* (*Chem.*) a salt formed by acetic acid.—**acet'ify** *v.t.* and *v.i.* to turn into vinegar.—**acetifica'tion** *n.*—**acetous** (ạ-sē′tus) *a.* sour.—**acetylene** (ạ-set′i-lēn) *n.* a highly inflammable gas used as an illuminant [L. *acetum*, vinegar].

ache (āk) *n.* a continuous pain; a dull, heavy pain; often found compounded in such words as *earache, headache*;—*v.i.* to be in pain.—**ach'ing** *a.* and *n.* [O.E. *acan*].

achieve (ạ-chēv′) *v.t.* to bring to a successful end; to accomplish.—**achiev'able** *a.*—**achieve'ment** *n.* performing; a performance; an exploit; a feat [O.Fr. *à chef*, to a head].

achromasia (ak-rō-mā′zi-ạ) *n.* (*Med.*) absence of colour.—**achro'mate** *a.* without colour; showing colour-blindness.—**achromatop'sia** *n.* (*Med.*) colour-blindness, usually the inability to distinguish red or green [Gk. *a-*, neg.; *chroma*, colour].

achromatic (ak-rō-mat′ik) *a.* (*Opt.*) free from colour; transmitting light without decomposing it; of a lens, giving an image free from colour round the edges.—**achromati'city, achro'matism** *n.*—**achro'matise** *v.t.* to deprive of colour [Gk. *a-*, neg.; *chroma*, colour].

acicular (ạ-sik′ū-lar) *a.* needle-shaped. Also **acic'ulate** [L. *acicula*, a small needle].

acid (as′id) *a.* sour; sharp to the taste; having the taste of vinegar;—*n.* a sour substance; (*Chem.*) a substance which contains hydrogen replaceable by a metal, is generally sour and reacts with a base to form salt and water.—**acid'ify** *v.t.* and *i.* to make or become sour; to turn into an acid.—**acid'ity** *n.* the state or quality of being acid; sourness; sharpness.—**acidosis** (as-i-dō′sis) *n.* (*Med.*) fatty-acid poisoning in the blood, due to over-production of acids in it.—**acid'ulate** *v.t.* to make slightly acid or sour; (*Fig.*) to embitter.—**acid'ulated, acid'ulous** *a.* slightly sour; sourish; severe.—**acid test** (*Fig.*) a conclusive proof of genuineness (referring to the test of gold by acid) [L. *acidus*, sour].

ack-ack (ak′ak) *a.* (*Mil. slang*) anti-aircraft;—*n.* anti-aircraft fire.—**ack′em'ma** *n.* of time, a.m. (before noon); (*R.A.F.*) air mechanic [fr.

army signallers' names for letters A and M].

acknowledge (ak-nol´ej) *v.t.* to admit as true; to give a receipt for; to give thanks for; to reward.—**acknowl'edgment, acknowl'edgement** *n.* [M.E. *knowlechen*, to perceive].

acme (ak´mē) *n.* the highest point, the top; perfection; (*Med.*) the crisis of an illness [Gk. *akmē*, the top].

acne (ak´nē) *n.* a skin disease characterised by hard, reddish pimples often appearing as blackheads [fr. Gk. *akmē*, a point].

acolyte (ak´ō-līt) *n.* a candidate for priesthood in the R.C. Church; a lesser church officer; an assistant; a novice (Gk. *akolouthos*, a follower].

aconite (ak´o-nīt) *n.* (*Bot.*) wolf's-bane or monk's-hood; a poisonous drug extracted from it.—**acon'itine** *n.* the poisonous substance in aconite [Gk. *akoniton*].

acorn (ā´korn) *n.* the seed or fruit of the oak [O.E. *aecern*, fruit of the open country].

acotyledon (ạ-kot-i-lē´don) *n.* (*Bot.*) a plant in which the seed-lobes, or cotyledons, are not present (Gk. *a-*, neg.; *kotulē*, a cup].

acoustic (ạ-kóò´stik, ạ-kou´stik) *a.* pert. to the sense of hearing.—**acou'stics** *n.pl.* the science of sounds; the estimation of audibility in a theatre, etc. [Gk. *akouein*, to hear].

acquaint (ạ-kwānt) *v.t.* to make fully known or familiar; to inform.—**acquaint'ance** *n.* familiar knowledge; a person known slightly.—**acquaint'anceship** *n.* [O. Fr. *acointier*; L. *cognoscere, cognitum*, to know].

acquiesce (ak-wi-es') *v.i.* to agree in silence; to assent without objection.—**acquies'cence** *n.* silent assent.—**acquies'cent** *a.* submissive; consenting [L. *ad*, to; *quiescere*, to keep quiet].

acquire (ạ-kwīr') *v.t.* to gain; to obtain; to get.—**acquir'able** *a.*—**acquire'ment** *n.*—**acquisi'tion** *n.* the act of acquiring; the thing acquired.—**acquisitive** (ạ-kwiz´i-tiv) *a.* grasping; greedy for gain.—**acquis'itiveness** *n.* [L. *ad.* to; *quaerere*, to seek].

acquit (ạ-kwit') *v.t.* to set free; release; declare innocent; to conduct oneself; to discharge a debt.—*pr.p.* **acquitt'ing**.—*pa.p.* and *pa.t.* **acquitt'ed**.—**acquitt'al** *n.* judicial release; declaration of 'not guilty.'—**acquitt'ance** *n.* [Fr. *acquitter*, fr. L. *quies*, rest].

acre (ā´kẹr) *n.* a measure of land containing 4840 square yards.—**a'creage** *n.* extent of a piece of land in acres. [O.E. *aecer*, a field].

acrid (ak´rid) *a.* bitter; sharp; pungent; harsh; ill-tempered.—**ac'ridly** *adv.*—**acrid'ity, ac'ridness** *n.* [L. *acer*, sharp].

acrimony (ak´ri-mon-i) *n.* bitterness of temper or of language.—**acrimonious** (ak-ri-mō´ni-us) *a.* sharp; bitter; stinging; sarcastic.—**acrimo'niously** *adv.* [L. *acer*, sharp].

acrobat (ak´rō-bat) *n.* one skilled in gymnastic feats; a rope-dancer; a tumbler.—**acrobat'ic** *a.* [Gk. *akrobatein*, to walk on tiptoe].

acrophobia (ak-rō-fō´bi-ạ) *n.* a morbid fear of heights [Gk. *akros*, extreme; *phobia*, fear].

acropolis (ạ-krop´ō-lis) *n.* the fortified summit of a Greek city; a citadel, esp. the citadel of Athens, on which stands the Parthenon [Gk. *akros*, topmost; *polis*, city].

across (ạ-kros') *adv.* and *prep.* from side to side; transversely; athwart; at an angle with [*a*, and *cross*].

acrostic (ạ-kros´tik) *n.* a composition in verse, in which the first, and sometimes last, letters of the lines read in order form a name, a sentence, or title [Gk. *akros*, extreme; *stichos*, a line].

act (akt) *v.t.* to perform, esp. upon stage; to behave as;—*v.i.* to exert energy; to fulfil a function; to operate.—*n.* deed; performance; actuality; a decree, law, edict, or judgment; principal division of a play.—**act'ing** *a.* performing a duty; performing on the stage; deputising for, as *Acting Captain.*—*n.* action.—**act'or** *n.* one who performs on a stage; one who plays a part in outstanding event.—**act'ress** *n.* a female actor.—**Act of Parliament**, the written law of a country [L. *agere, actum*, to do].

ACTH Adreno-corticotropic-hormone used in the treatment of rheumatic diseases.

actinia (ak-tin´i-ạ) *n.* the sea anemone.—*pl.* **actin'iae** [Gk. *aktis*, a ray].

actinism (ak´ti-nizm) *n.* the radiation of light or heat; the property possessed by the sun's rays, of producing chemical changes, as in photography.—**actin'ic** *a.* pert. to actinism.—**actin'iform** *a.* having a ray-like structure [Gk. *aktis*, a ray].

actinium (ak-tin´i-um) *n.* a radio-active element; symbol **Ac** [Gk. *aktis*, a ray].

actinology (ak-ti-nol´o-ji) *n.* that branch of science concerned with chemical action of light [Gk. *aktis*, a ray; *logos*, word].

actinotherapy (ak-tin-ō-ther´ap-i) *n.* the treatment of disease by natural or artificial light rays; often known as 'sunlight treatment.' [Gk. *aktis*, a ray; *therapeia*, service].

action (ak´shun) *n.* a thing done; behaviour; physical movement; function; a battle; the development of events in a play, etc.; legal proceedings; (*Chem.*) effect.—**ac'tionable** *a.* affording grounds for legal proceedings.—**ac'tionably** *adv.*—**ac'tive** *a.* having the power to act; agile; busy; alert; (*Gram.*) implying action by the subject.—**ac'tively** *adv.* vigorously.—**ac'tivism** *n.* policy of those who, by energetic action, seek to fulfil the promises of a political programme.—**ac'tivist** *n.* worker who succeeds in increasing own production or that of his group.—**activ'ity, ac'tiveness** *n.*—**reflex action**, an involuntary motor reaction to a sensory impulse [L. *agere, actum*, to do].

actual (ak´tū-ạl) *a.* existing now or as a fact; real; effectual.—**act'ualise** *v.t.* to make real in fact or by vivid description.—**act'ualist** *n.* a realist.—**actual'ity** *n.* reality, existence.—**act'ually** *adv.* [L. *actualis*, active].

actuary (ak'-tū-ar-i) *n.* registrar or clerk; an official who calculates for insurance companies.—**actua'rial** *a.*—**actua'rially** *adv.* [L. *actuarius*, a clerk].

actuate (ak'-tū-āt) *v.t.* to put into action; incite; motivate; influence.—**actua'tion** *n.* [L. *actus*, action].

acumen (ạ-kū'-men) *n.* quickness of perception or discernment; sharpness; penetration.—**acu'minous** *a.* [L. *acumen*, a point].

acushla (ạ-kóòsh'-lạ) *n.* sweetheart [Ir.].

acute (ạ-kūt') *a.* sharp; pointed; sagacious; subtle; penetrating; shrill; (*Med.*) of disease with severe symptoms and sharp crisis; (*Geom.*) less than a right angle.—**acute'ly** *adv.*—**acute'ness** *n.*—**acute accent**, a mark (') over a letter, as in French, to indicate pronunciation [L. *acutus*, sharp].

adage (ad'-āj) *n.* saying or maxim that has obtained credit by long use; a proverb; a byword.—**adag'ial** *a.* [L. *adagium*, proverb].

adagio (ạ-dà'-jō) *adv.* (*Mus.*) slowly and expressively;—*n.* a slow movement, in a symphony or sonata.—**adagio cantabile**, slowly and in a singing manner [It.].

adamant (ad'-ạ-mant) *n.* a stone of impenetrable hardness; the diamond.—*a.* very hard; unyielding.—**adaman'tine** *a.* (Gk. *a-*, neg.; *damaein*, subdue].

adapt (ạ-dapt') *v.t.* to make fit or suitable; to make to correspond.—**adaptabil'ity, adapt'ableness** *n.* the quality of being adaptable.—**adapt'able** *a.* may be adapted; versatile.—**adapta'tion** *n.* the gradual process of adjustment to new physical conditions exhibited by living organisms.—**adap'ter** *n.* any appliance which makes possible a union of two different parts of an apparatus.—**adap'tive** *a.*—**adap'tively** *adv.*—**adap'tiveness** *n.*—**adap'tor** *n.* a device to make possible the use of plates or films in a camera designed for one type only; a device for readily interchanging lenses in a camera [L. *ad*, to; *aptare*, to fit].

add (ad) *v.t.* to join, unite to form one sum or

whole; to annex; to increase; to say further.—**add'able, add'ible** *a.*—**add'er** *n.* a machine which adds; a comptometer.—**addibil'ity** *n.*—**addi'tion** *n.* the act of adding; anything added; the branch of arithmetic which deals with adding.—**addi'tional** *a.* supplementary; extra.—**addi'tionally** *adv.*—**add'itive** *a.* to be added; of the nature of an addition [L. *ad*, to; *dare*, to give].

addendum (a-den'dum) *n.* a thing to be added; an appendix.—*pl.* **adden'da** [L.].

adder (ad'er) *n.* a venomous serpent. The only poisonous reptile found in Britain.—**adder's-tongue**, a form of fern.—**adder's-wort**, snakeweed, a cure for snake bites [M.E. *an addere* for *a naddere*, fr. O.E. *naeddre*, snake].

addict (a-dikt') *v.t.* to apply habitually; habituate.—**ad'dict** *n.* one addicted to evil habit, e.g. drug-taking.—**addict'ed** *a.* devoted, wholly given over to.—**addic'tion, addict'ness**, *n.* [L. *addicere*, to assign].

Addison's disease (ad'i-sunz diz-ēz') *n.* tuberculosis of the adrenal capsules or glands [Dr. Thos. *Addison*].

addle (ad'l) *v.t.* to corrupt; putrify; confuse; to make addled.—**add'le, add'led**, *a.* diseased, e.g. an egg; putrid; unfruitful; barren.—**add'le-brained, -head'ed, -pa'ted** *a.* muddle-headed [O.E. *adela*, filth].

address (a-dres') *v.t.* to direct in writing, as a letter; to apply (oneself); to make a speech; to present a congratulatory message or petition; accost;—*n.* a formal speech; manner of speaking; direction of a letter; skill.—**address'es** *n. pl.* attentions in courtship.—**addressee'** *n.* person to whom a communication is sent.—**address'er** *n.*—**address'ograph** *n.* a machine for addressing envelopes, etc. [Fr. *adresser*].

adduce (a-dūs') *v.t.* to bring forward as proof; to cite; to quote.—**adduc'er** *n.*—**adduc'ible** *a.*—**adduc'tion** *n.* drawing together or bringing forward.—**adduc'tive** *a.* tending to bring together.—**adduc'tor** *n.* adducent muscle [L. *ad*, to; *ducere*, to lead].

ademption (a-demp'shun) *n.* (*Law*) the revocation of a grant or bequest [L. *ademptio*, taking away].

aden (o) - (a'den- (o)) a combining form (fr. Gk. *aden*, a gland).—**adeni'tis** *n.* inflammation of the lymphatic glands.—**ad'enoid, ad'enoidal** *a.* glandular; gland-shaped.—**ad'enoids** *n.pl.* a swelling of tissue between nose and throat.

adept (a-dept') *n.* one skilled in any art; an expert;—*a.* well skilled; expert [L. *adeptus*, having attained].

adequate (ad'e-kwāt) *a.* equal to; sufficient.—**ad'equacy, ad'equateness** *n.*—**ad'equately** *adv.* [L. *adaequatus*, made equal to].

adhere (ad-hēr') *v.i.* to stick fast; to be devoted to; to hold to (an opinion).—**adher'ence** *n.* state of adhering; steady attachment.—**adher'ent** *a.* united with or to;—*n.* supporter of person or cause.—**adhe'sion** *n.* act of adhering.—**adhes'ive** *a.* sticky; tenacious;—*n.* an agent which sticks things together.—**adhes'ively** *adv.*—**adhes'iveness** *n.* [L. *ad*, to; *haerere*, to stick].

adhibit (ad-hib'it) *v.t.* to use or apply; to attach [L. *adhibitus*, added to].

adiabatic (ad-i-a-bat'ik) *a.* without gain or loss of heat [Gk. *adiabatos*, not to be passed through].

adieu (a-dū') *interj.* good-bye; farewell.—*n.* a farewell; a leave-taking.—*pl.* **adieus, adieux** (a-dūz') [Fr. meaning, "*to God*"].

adipose (ad'i-pōs) *a.* pert. to animal fat; fatty.—**adiposity** (ad-i-pos'i-ti) *n.* fatness.—**adip'ic** *a.* pert. to, or derived from, fatty substances. [L. *adeps*, soft fat].

adit (ad'it) *n.* horizontal or inclined entrance into a mine [L. *aditus*, an entrance].

adjacent (a-jā'sent) *a.* lying close to; adjoining; bordering on.—**adja'cently** *adv.*—**adja'cency** *n.* [L. *ad*, to; *jacere*, to lie].

adjective (ad'jek-tiv) *n.* a word used with a noun to qualify, limit, or define it;—*a.* pert. to an adjective.—**adjecti'val** *a.*—**adjecti'vally** *adv.* [L. *adjicere*, to add].

adjoin (a-join') *v.t.* to join or unite to; to be next or contiguous to;—*v.i.* to be next to.—**adjoin'ing** *a.* [L. *adjungere*, to join to].

adjourn (a-jurn') *v.t.* to put off to another day.—**adjourn'ment** *n.* postponing; deferring of business [L. *diurnus*, daily].

adjudge (a-juj') *v.t.* to settle judicially; to pronounce judgment; to award; to regard or deem.—**adjudg'ment** *n.*—**adjudicate** (a-jóó'di-kāt) *v.t.* to settle judicially;—*v.i.* to pronounce judgment.—**adjudica'tion** *n.*—**adju'dicator** *n.* a judge [L. *adjudicare*, to award as a judge].

adjunct (ad'jungkt) *n.* something joined to another thing, but not essential to it; (*Gram.*) a word or phrase added to modify meaning;—*a.* added to; united with.—**adjunc'tive** —**adjunc'tively** *adv.* [L. *adjunctus*, united to].

adjure (ad-jóór') *v.t.* to charge or bind, under oath; to entreat earnestly.—**adjura'tion** *n.* a solemn command on oath; an earnest appeal.—**adjur'atory** *a.* [L. *adjurare*, to confirm by oath].

adjust (a-just') *v.t.* to adapt; to put in order; to accommodate.—**adjust'able** *a.*—**adjust'ment** *n.* arrangement; settlement; adaptation [L. *ad*, to; *justus*, just].

adjutant (ad'jóó-tant) *n.* an assistant; executive officer to a battalion commander, army, or to a station commander, R.A.F.—**ad'jutancy** *n.* the office of an adjutant.—**adjutant bird**, a species of Indian stork [L. *ad*, to; *juvare*, to help].

admeasure (ad-mezh'ūr) *v.t.* to take the dimensions of; (*Law*) to apportion.—**admeas'urement** *n.*—**admensura'tion** *n.* [L. *ad*, to; *mensura*, measure].

administer (ad-min'is-ter) *v.t.* to manage public affairs or an estate; to dispense, as justice or relief; to give, as medicine; to apply, as punishment or reproof; (*Law*) to settle the estate of one who has died intestate;—*v.i.* to give aid (to).—**admin'istrable** *a.*—**admin'istrant** *a.* executive;—*n.* one who administers.—**administra'tion** *n.* the executive part of a government; dispensation; direction.—**admin'istrative** *a.*—**administra'tor** *n.* (*fem.* **administra'trix**) one who directs, executes affairs of any kind [L. *ad*, to; *ministrare*, to give service].

admiral (ad'mi-ral) *n.* a naval officer of the highest rank (graded as—admiral, vice-admiral, or rear-admiral).—**Admiral of the Fleet**, a title corresponding to field-marshal in the army.—**The Lord High Admiral** used to have charge of naval affairs.—**Admiralty** *n.* the Lords Commissioners appointed for the management of naval affairs [Fr. *amiral*, fr. Ar. *amir-al-bahr*, prince of the sea].

admiral (ad'mi-ral) *n.* a species of butterfly, esp. the red admiral.

admire (ad-mīr') *v.t.* to regard with wonder and approval, esteem, or affection; to prize highly.—*v.i.* to wonder; to marvel.—**admir'er** *n.*—**admir'ing** *a.*—**admir'ingly** *adv.*—**ad'mirable** *a.* excellent; praiseworthy.—**ad'mirably** *adv.*—**admira'tion** *n.* wonder mingled with esteem, love, or veneration [L. *ad*, to; *mirari*, to wonder].

admissible (ad-mis'i-bl) *a.* allowable.—**admis'sibly** *adv.*—**admissibil'ity** *n.*—**admis'sion** *n.* permission to enter; the price paid for this [L. (part.) *admissus*, allowed to go].

admit (ad-mit') *v.t.* to grant entrance; to concede as true; to acknowledge.—**admit'tance** *n.* permission to enter [L. *ad*, to; *mittere*, to send].

admix (ad-miks') *v.t.* to mingle with something else.—**admix'ture** *n.*

admonish (ad-mon'ish) *v.t.* to reprove gently; to instruct or direct.—**admon'isher** *n.*—**admoni'tion** *n.* rebuke.—**admon'itory** *a.* [L. *ad*, to; *monere*, *monitum*, to warn].

ado (a-dóó') *n.* fuss; bustle; trouble.

adobe (ạ-dō'bi) *n.* sun-dried brick made of clay, common in Texas and New Mexico; a house made of such bricks [Sp.].

adolescence (ạd-ō-les'ens) *n.* stage between childhood and manhood; youth.—**adoles'cent** *a.* growing up; advancing towards maturity. —*n.* a young man or woman [L. *adolescere*, to grow up].

adopt (ạ-dopt') *v.t.* to receive the child of another and treat it as one's own; to select and accept as one's own, e.g. a view.—**adopt'er** *n.*—**adop'table** *a.*—**adop'tion** *n.*—**adop'tive** *a.* that adopts or is adopted [L. *ad*, to; *optare*, to choose].

adore (ạ-dōr') *v.t.* to worship; to love deeply; to idolise; to venerate.—**ador'er** *n.* a lover.—**ador'able** *a.*—**ador'ably** *adv.*—**ador'ableness** *n.*—**adora'tion** *n.* worship paid to the Divine Being; profound veneration; ardent devotion [L. *ad*, to; *orare*, to pray].

adorn (ạ-dorn') *v.t.* to decorate; to deck or ornament; to dignify; to set off to advantage. —**adorn'ing** *a.* beautifying; ornamental.—**adorn'ment** *n.* ornament; embellishment; [L. *ad*, to; *ornare*, to deck].

adrenal (ạd-rē'nạl) *n.* a small, ductless gland situated close to upper end of each kidney (same as *supra-renal*).—**adre'nalin** *n.* the hormone of the adrenal glands; the most effective haemostatic agent known [L. *ad*, to; *renes*, kidneys].

adrift (ạ-drift') *adv.* and *a.* floating at random; at mercy of the wind and tide; (*Fig.*) at a loss.

adroit (ạ-droit') *a.* dexterous; skilful; ingenious; resourceful; adept.—**adroit'ly** *adv.*—**adroit'ness** *n.* [Fr.].

adscititious (ad-si-tish'us) *a.* added; additional; supplementary; not essential [L. *adsciscere*, *adscitum*, to take to oneself].

adsorb (ad-sorb') *v.t.* said of solids, to condense and hold a gas on the surface. [L. *ad*, to; *sorbere*, to drink in].

adstriction (ạd-strik'shun) *n.* costiveness; constipation [L. *ad*, to; *stringere*, to draw].

adulate (ad'ū-lāt) *v.t.* to praise or flatter in a servile manner; to fawn; to cringe.—**adula'tion** *n.*—**adula'tor** *n.*—**ad'ulatory** *a.* excessively [L. *adulari*, to flatter].

adult (a-dult', a'dult) *a.* grown to maturity, or to full size and strength; appropriate for a grown-up.—*n.* a grown-up person.—**adult'ness** *n.* [L. *adultus*, grown up].

adulterate (ạ-dul'tẹr-āt) *v.t.* to debase by addition of inferior materials; to vitiate; to corrupt.—*a.* debased; guilty of adultery.—**adult'erant** *n.* person or thing that adulterates. —**adultera'tion** *n.* being debased; the act of debasing a substance [L. *adulterare*, to defile].

adultery (ạ-dul'tẹr-i) *n.* violation of the marriage vows; sexual intercourse between married person and one who is not the legal wife or husband.—**adult'erer** *n.* (*fem.* **adult'eress**)—**adult'erine** *a.* born of adultery; spurious; illicit; illegal.—**adult'erous** *a.* pert. to or guilty of adultery.—**adult'erously** *adv.* [L. *adulterare*, to defile].

adumbrate (ạd-um'brāt) *v.t.* to shadow forth; to give faint outline of; to forecast; to typify. —**adum'bral** *a.* shady.—**adum'brant** *a.* showing a slight resemblance.—**adum'brative** *a.*—**adumbra'tion** *n.* [L. *ad*, to; *umbra*, a shade].

advance (ạd-vans') *v.t.* to bring or push forward; to raise in status, price, or value; to propose as a claim; to supply beforehand, esp. money;—*v.i.* to go forward; to improve; to rise in rank, etc.—*a.* before the time, as in *advance-booking*.—*n.* a forward movement; gradual approach; a paying out of money before due; an increase in price; expansion of knowledge.—**advanced'** *a.* in the front rank; progressive; well on in years; beyond the elementary stage (in education).—**advance'ment** *n.* promotion; improvement; success; the state of being progressive in opinion; a loan of money; provision made for a child in event of parent's death.—**advanc'er** *n.* a promoter.—**advanc'ive** *a.* capable of being advanced.—**to make advances**, to solicit the friendship (of another) [Fr. *avancer*, to go forward].

advantage (ạd-van'tāj) *n.* any state or means favourable to some desired end; upperhand; profit; in tennis, a point gained after deuce;—*v.t.* to benefit, to promote the interests of; to profit.—**advan'tageable** *a.* able to be turned to advantage.—**advanta'geous** *a.* beneficial; opportune; convenient.—**advanta'geously** *adv.*—**to advantage**, with good results; most effectively [Fr. *avantage*].

advent (ad'vent) *n.* arrival; approach; the anticipated coming of Christ; the four weeks from the Sunday nearest to St. Andrew's Day (30th Nov.) to Christmas.—**advent'ual** *adv.* pertaining to the season of Advent [L. *ad*, to; *venire*, to come].

adventitious (ad-ven-tish'us) *a.* accidental; out of the proper place; extraneous.—**adventi'tiously** *adv.* [L. *ad*, to; *venire*, to come].

adventure (ạd-ven'tūr) *n.* risk; bold undertaking; chance; trading enterprise of a speculative nature;—*v.t.* to risk;—*v.i.* to venture; to dare.—**adven'turer** *n.* (*fem.* **adven'turess**).—**(ad)vent'uresome** *a.* bold; daring; enterprising; facing risk.—**advent'uresomeness** *n.*—**advent'urous** *a.* inclined to take risks; perilous; hazardous.—**advent'urously** *adv.* [L. *adventurus*, about to arrive].

adverb (ad'vẹrb) *n.* a word used to modify the sense of a verb, adjective, or other adverb.—**adverb'ial** *a.*—**adverb'ially** *adv.* [L. *ad*, to; *verbum*, a word].

adversaria (ạd-vẹrs-ār'i-ạ) *n.pl.* a common-place-book [L. *adversus*, opposite to].

adversary (ad'vẹr-sar-i) *n.* an opponent; one who strives against us; an enemy [L. *adversus*, opposite to].

adversative (ạd-vẹrs'ạ-tiv) *a.* expressing opposition; not favourable [L. *adversus*].

adverse (ad'vẹrs) *a.* contrary; opposite in position; unfortunate; opposed.—**ad'versely** *adv.*—**ad'verseness** *n.*—**advers'ity** *n.* adverse circumstances; misfortune; distress; calamity [L. *adversus*, opposite to].

advert (ạd-vẹrt') *v.i.* to turn the mind or attention to; to remark upon; allude; refer.—**advert'ance, advert'ency** *n.* [L. *ad*, to; *vertere*, to turn].

advertise (ad'vẹr-tīz) *v.t.* and *v.i.* to give public notice of; to inform; to make known through agency of the press.—**adver'tisement** *n.* a public intimation in the press; legal notification.—**adverti'ser** *n.* one who advertises; an advertising sheet or newspaper.—**adverti'sing** *n.* and *a.* [Fr. *avertir*, from L. *ad*, to; *vertere*, to turn].

advice (ạd-vīs') *n.* opinion offered as to what one should do; counsel; information;—*pl.* notification regarding mercantile transactions, especially despatch of goods [Fr. *avis*].

advise (ạd-vīz') *v.t.* to give advice to; to counsel; to give information to; to consult (with).—*v.i.* to deliberate.—**advisabil'ity, advis'ableness** *n.* expediency.—**advis'able** *a.* prudent; expedient.—**advis'ably** *adv.*—**advised'** *a.* acting with due deliberation; cautious; prudent; judicious.—**advis'edly** *adv.* purposely; deliberately.—**advis'edness** *n.* deliberate consideration; expediency.—**advis'er** *n.*—**advis'ory** *a.* having power to advise; containing advice [Fr. *avis*].

advocaat (ad'-vō-kȧt) *n.* a liqueur, originally made in Holland, compounded of eggs, brandy and various flavourings. Also **ad'vokaat** (Dut. *advokaat*, an advocate).

advocate (ad'vō-kāt) *n.* a vocal supporter of any cause; one who pleads or speaks for another; (*Law*) in Scotland and France, a barrister.—*v.t.* to plead in favour of; to recommend; to maintain by argument.—**ad'vocacy** *n.* a pleading for; judicial pleading. —**ad'vocator** *n.* an intercessor; a pleader [L. *ad*, to; *vocare*, to call].

advowee (ạd-vou'ē) *n.* a person possessed of

an advowson.—**advow'son** *n.* the right of presenting a clergyman to a benefice in the Church of England [O.Fr. *avoeson*, fr. L. *advocare*, to call in].

adze, adz (adz) *n.* a carpenter's tool for chipping, having a thin arching blade set at right angles to the handle [O.E. *adesa*].

aegis (ē′jis) *n.* originally the shield of Jupiter; (*Fig.*) protection [Gk. *aigis*].

Aeolian (ē-ō′li-ạn) *a.* pert. to Aeolia (or Aeolis), in Asia Minor; pert. to *Aeolus*, the god of the winds; pert. to, or produced by, the wind. Also **Aeo'lic.**—**Aeolian harp,** a stringed instrument played by the wind.

aeon, eon (ē′on) *n.* an infinitely long period of time; a kalpa or age [Gk. *aion*, an age].

aerate (ā′ẹ-rāt) *v.t.* to charge with carbonic acid or other gas; to supply with air.—**aera'tion** *n.* the act of exposing to the action of the air; saturation with a gas.—**a'erator** *n.*—**aerated waters,** beverages charged with carbonic acid [Gk. *aēr*, air].

aerial (ā′ẹr-i-ạl) *a.* pert. to, consisting of, air;—*n.* and *a.* (*Wireless*) an insulated wire or wires, generally elevated above the ground and connected to a wireless transmitting or receiving set.—**ae'rially** *adv.* [Gk. *aēr*, air].

aerie, aery (ā′ri, ē′ri) *n.* the nest of a bird of prey, esp. of the eagle or hawk. Also **ey'rie, ey'ry** [O.Fr. *aire*].

aeriferous (ā-ẹr-if′ẹr-us) *a.* conveying or containing air.—**a'eriform** *a.* having the form or nature of air; gaseous.—**a'erify** *v.t.* to fill with air; to change a solid or liquid into a gas.—**aerifica'tion** *n.* [Gk. *aēr*, air; L. *ferre*, to carry; *facere*, to make].

aero- (ā′ẹr-ō) a combining form from Gk. *aēr*, air, used in many derivatives.—**a'ero-ca'mera** *n.* a camera used in taking photographs of the ground from aircraft.—**a'ero-en'gine (-mo'tor)** *n.* an internal-combustion engine for aircraft.—**-gun** *n.* anti-aircraft gun.

aerobatics (ā-ẹr-ō-ba′tiks) *n.pl.* aerial acrobatics, performed by an aeroplane.

aerodrome (ā′ẹr-ō-drōm) *n.* a stretch of ground or water, prepared for ascents and descents of aircraft; an aircraft station; an aviation terminus [Gk. *aēr*, air; *dromos*, a course].

aerodynamics (ā-ẹr-ō-dī-nam′iks) *n.* the science that treats of gases in motion.—**aerodyne** (ā′ẹr-ō-dīn) *n.* a term applied to all types of aircraft which derive their lifting power from aerodynamic forces [Gk. *aēr*, air; *dunamis*, power].

aerofoil (ā′ẹr-ō-foil) *n.* an aeroplane wing; a tailplane [Gk. *aēr*, air; L. *folium*,, a leaf].

aerolite (ā′ẹr-ō-līt) *n.* a meteorite; a meteoric stone. Also **a'erolith.**—**aerolith'ic** *a.*—**aerolithol'ogy** *n.* the study of meteorites.—**aerol'ogy** *n.* the science which treats of the air and its phenomena [Gk. *aēr*, air; *lithos*, stone; *logos*, discourse].

aerometer (ā-ẹr-om′e-tẹr) *n.* an instrument for measuring the weight or density of air and other gases.—**aerom'etry** *n.* this science [Gk. *aēr*, air; *metron*, a measure].

aeronaut (ā′ẹr-ō-nawt) *n.* an air-ship navigator; a balloonist.—**aeronaut'ic** *a.* pert. to aeronautics.—**aeronaut'ics** *n.* the science of air-navigation in general [Gk. *aēr*, air; *nautes*, a sailor].

aerophobia (ā-ẹr-ō-fō′bi-ạ) *n.* a morbid dread of currents of air. Also **a'erophoby** [Gk. *aēr*, air; *phobos*, fear].

aeroplane (ā′ẹr-ō-plān) *n.* a flying-machine. Also **air'plane,** esp. in America.—(*abbrev.*) **plane** [Gk. *aēr*, air; L. *planus*, flat].

aerostat (ā′ẹr-ō-stat) *n.* a generic term for all lighter-than-air flying-machines.—**aerostat'ics** *n.* the science that treats of the equilibrium of gases, or of the buoyancy of bodies sustained in them; the science of air-navigation [Gk. *aēr*, air; *statos*, standing].

aesthetics (ēs-, es-thet′iks) *n.* the laws and principles determining the beautiful in nature, art, taste, etc.—**aesthet'ic, aesthet'ical** *a.*—**aesthet'ically** *adv.*—**aesthete** (ēs′, es′thēt) *n.* a disciple of aestheticism; a lover of the beautiful (sometimes to an extravagant degree).—**aesthet'icism** *n.* the cult of the beautiful in nature and the fine arts [Gk. *aisthanesthai*, to perceive].

aestival (es′ti-vạl) *a.* pert. to, or produced in, summer.—Also **es'tival.**—**aes'tivate** *v.i.* to pass the summer [L. *aestas*, summer].

aetiology (ē-ti-ol′o-ji) *n.* the doctrine of causation; the science of the causes of a disease.—**aetiolog'ical** *a.* [Gk. *aitia*, cause; *logos*, discourse].

afar (ạ-fạr′) *adv.* from, at, or to a distance; far away [E. *far*].

affable (af′ạ-bl) *a.* ready to converse; easy to speak to; courteous; friendly.—**af'ably** *adv.*—**affabil'ity** *n.* [L. *ad*, to; *fari*, to speak].

affair (ạ-fār′) what is to be done; a business or matter; a concern; a thing; (*Mil.*) a minor engagement.—**affairs'** *n.pl.* public or private business; finances.—**affair of honour,** a duel [L. *ad*, to; *facere*, to do].

affect (ạ-fekt′) *v.t.* to act upon; to produce a change in; to put on a pretence of; to influence.—**affect'ed** *a.* inclined or disposed; not natural.—**affect'edly** *adv.*—**affect'edness** *n.*—**affect'ing** *a.* moving; pathetic.—**affect'ingly** *adv.*—**affecta'tion** *n.* a striving after artificial appearance or manners.—**affec'tion** *n.* disposition of mind; good-will; tender attachment; disease.—**affec'tionate** *a.* loving; proceeding from love.—**affec'tionately** *adv.*—**affec'tionateness** *n.*—**affec'tioned** *a.* inclined; disposed.—**affec'tive** *a.* pertaining to the affections.—**affec'tively** *adv.* [L. *affectare*, to apply oneself to].

affeer (ạ-fēr′) *v.i.* to fix the price of; to confirm; (*Law*) to settle a fine [L. *ad*, to; *forum*, a market].

afferent (af′ẹr-ent) *a.* conveying to, esp. of nerves carrying sensations to the centres [L. *ad*, to; *ferre*, to carry].

affiance (ạ-fī′ạns) *n.* plighted faith; betrothal; the marriage contract; reliance; confidence;—*v.t.* to betroth.—**affi'anced** *a.* and *n.* [O.Fr. *afiance*, trust].

affidavit (af-i-dā′vit) *n.* (*Law*) a written statement of evidence on oath [L.L. = he pledged his faith, from L. *ad*, to; *fides*, faith].

affiliate (ạ-fil′i-āt) *v.t.* to adopt as a son; to receive into fellowship; to unite a society, firm, or political party with another, but without loss of identity.—**affilia'tion** *n.* a legal process whereby the father of a child born out of wedlock is made responsible for its maintenance [L. *ad*, to; *filius*, a son].

affinity (ạ-fin′i-ti) *n.* relationship by marriage; close agreement; resemblance; attraction; likeness of nature or disposition; similarity; (*Biol.*) resemblance in structure.—**affined'** *a.* related to; bound; obliged.—**affin'itive** *a.* by affinity [L. *affinis*, related].

affirm (ạ-fẹrm′) *v.t.* to assert positively; to confirm; to aver; to strengthen; to ratify a judgment; to affirm;—*v.i.* (*Law*) to make a solemn promise to tell the truth without oath; to ratify a law.—**affirm'able** *a.*—**affirm'ably** *adv.*—**affirm'ance** *n.* assertion; confirmation; (*Law*) ratification of a voidable act.—**affirm'ant, affirm'er** *n.* one who affirms.—**affirma'tion** *n.*—**affirm'ative** *a.* affirming; dogmatic; ratifying;—*n.* positive; speaking in favour of a motion or subject of debate.—**in the affirmative, yes.**—**affirm'atively** *adv.* [L. *affirmare*, to assert].

affix (ạ-fiks′) *v.t.* to fasten to; to attach; to append to.—**af'fix** *n.* addition to either end of word to modify meaning or use (includes *prefix* and *suffix*) [L. *affigere*].

afflation (ạ-flā′shun) *n.* act of blowing or breathing on.—**affla'ted** *a.* inspired.—**affla'tus** *n.* inspiration [L. *ad*, to; *flare*, to blow].

afflict (ạ-flikt′) *v.t.* to give continued pain to;

to cause distress or grief to.—**afflict'ed** *a.* distressed in mind; diseased.—**afflict'ing** *a.* distressing.—**afflict'ingly** *adv.*—**afflic'tion** *n.* a cause of continued pain of body or mind.—**afflict'ive** *a.* causing distress.—**afflict'ively** *adv.* [L. *affligere*].

affluence (af'lòò-ens) *n.* abundance, esp. riches.—**af'fluent** *a.* wealthy; flowing to;—*n.* tributary of river.—**af'fluently** *adv.*—**af'flux, afflux'ion** *n.* flowing to; that which flows to [L. *ad*, towards; *fluere*, to flow].

afford (a-fōrd') *v.t.* to yield, supply, or produce; to be able to bear expense [O.E. *geforthian*, to further].

afforest (a-for'est) *v.t.* to plant trees on a big scale.—**affoesta'tion** *n.* [from *forest*].

affranchise (a-fran'chīz) *v.t.* to enfranchise; to free from slavery; to liberate.—**affran'chisement** *n.* [Fr. *affranchir*, make free].

affray (a-frā') *n.* a noisy quarrel or fight in public;—*v.t.* to frighten; to startle [Fr. *effrayer*, to frighten].

affreight (a-frāt') *v.t.* to hire or freight a ship for the transportation of goods [Fr. *affréter*, to hire].

affright, affrighten (a-frīt', -en) *v.t.* to impress with sudden and lively fear [O.E. *āfyrhtan*, to terrify].

affront (a-frunt') *v.t.* to confront; to meet face to face; to insult one to the face; to abash.—**affront'ed** *a.* insulted [L. *ad*, to; *frons, frontis*, forehead].

afield (a-fēld') *adv.* to or in the field; abroad; off the beaten track; astray [E].

afire (a-fīr') *adv.* and *a.* on fire.

aflame (a-flām') *adv.* and *a.* flaming; in or into flame; on fire; glowing; ablaze [E.].

afloat (a-flōt') *adv.* and *a.* borne on the water; not aground or anchored.

afoot (a-foot') *adv.* on foot; astir [E.].

afore (a-fōr') *adv.* and *prep.* before.—**afore'hand** *adv.* beforehand; before;—*a.* provided; prepared.—**afore'mentioned** *a.* spoken of, or named, before.—**afore'said** *a.* said or mentioned before.—**afore'thought** *a.* thought of beforehand; premeditated.—**afore'time** *adv.* in times past; at a former time; previously [O.E. *on foran*, in front].

afraid (a-frād') *a.* filled with fear; frightened [orig. *affrayed*].

afresh (a-fresh') *adv.* anew; over again.

African (af'ri-kan) *a.* (*Geog.*) pert. or belonging to Africa;—*n.* a native of Africa.—**African'der** *n.* a native of S. Africa, born of white parents esp. of Dutch descent. Also **Afrikan'der.**—**Afrikaans** (af-ri-kàns') *n.* S. African Dutch; Taal.

aft (aft) *adv.* or *a.* (*Naut.*) toward, or at, the stern.—**fore and aft**, lengthwise [O.E. *afta*, behind].

after (af'ter) *prep.* behind; later; in pursuit of; in imitation of; according to;—*adv.* behind;—*a.* in the rear; succeeding.—**af'terbirth** *n.* (*Med.*) the placenta etc. expelled from uterus after childbirth.—**af'tercrop** *n.* a later crop in same year from same soil.—**af'ter-damp** *n.* a gas formed in a mine after an explosion of fire-damp; choke-damp.—**af'terglow** *n.* a glow in the sky after sunset.—**af'termath** *n.* a second crop of grass after first mowing; (*Fig.*) result; consequence.—**af'termost** *a.* hindmost; nearest to stern.—**af'ternoon** *n.* time from noon to evening.—**af'ter-pains** *n.pl.* pains succeeding childbirth.—**af'terthought** *n.* reflection after an act; an idea occurring later.—**af'terward(s)** *adv.* later; subsequently [O.E. *aefter*, farther away].

aga, agha (à'ga) *n.* a Turkish civil or military officer of high rank [*Turk.*].

again (a-gen') *adv.* another time; once more; in return; moreover [O.E. *ongean*].

against (a-genst') *prep.* in contact with; opposite to; in opposition to; in preparation for; in exchange for [fr. *again*].

agape (a-gāp') *a.* or *adv.* open-mouthed, as in wonder, expectation, etc.; gaping.

agape (ag'a-pē) *n.* a love-feast among the early Christians [Gk. *agapē*, love].

agar-agar (ā-gàr-ā'gàr) *n.* an East-Indian sea-weed used for the culture of bacteria; when dried, used in Malay for the making of soups, jellies, etc. [Malay].

agaric (ag'a-rik) *n.* a name of various fungi, including mushrooms and toadstools;—*a.* fungoid [Gk. *agarikon*].

agate (ag'āt) *n.* a precious stone, composed of layers of quartz of different colours [Gk. *Achatēs*, so called because found near the river *Achates*, in Sicily].

Agave (a-gā'vē) *n.* a genus of plants, including the American aloe or century plant [Gk. *agauos*, noble].

age (āj) *n.* the length of time a person or thing has existed; a period of time; periods of history; maturity; (*Colloq.*) a long time;—*v.t.* to cause to grow old;—*v.i.* to grow old;—*pr.p.* **aging**—*pa.p.* and *pa.t.* **aged**; also *a.* of the age of.—**aged** (āj'ed) *a.* old; having lived long.—**ag'edness** *n.*—**age'less** *a.*—**age'long** *a.*—**to come of age**, to attain one's 21st birthday. [Fr. *âge*, from L. *aetas*, age].

agee, ajee (a-jē') *adv.* off the straight, ajar [Scot.]

agenda (a-jen'da) *n.* literally, things to be done; the items of business to be discussed at a meeting [L. *pl.* of *agendum*].

agene (ā'jēn) *n.* commercial name for nitrogen trichloride used to whiten and preserve flour.—**a'genise** *v.t.*

agent (ā'jent) *n.* a person or thing that exerts power or has the power to act; one entrusted with the business of another; a deputy or substitute.—**a'gency** *n.* instrumentality; a mode of exerting power; office or duties of an agent. [L. *agere*, to do].

agglomerate (a-glom'e-rāt) *v.t.* and *i.* to collect into a mass;—*a.* heaped up;—*n.* (*Geol.*) a mass of compacted volcanic debris.—**agglomera'tion** *n.*—**agglom'erative** *a.* [L. *ad*, to; *glomus*, mass or ball].

agglutinate (a-glòò'ti-nāt) *v.t.* to unite with glue;—*a.* united, as with glue;—**agglutina'tion** *n.*—**agglut'inative** *a.* having a tendency to cause adhesion; (*Phil.*) applied to languages which are non-inflectional [L. *ad*, to; *gluten*, glue].

aggrandise (ag'ran-dīz) *v.t.* to make greater in size, power, rank, wealth, etc.; to promote; to increase; to exalt.—**aggran'disement** *n.* [L. *ad*, to; *grandis*, great].

aggravate (ag'ra-vāt) *v.t.* to make more grave, worse; (*Colloq*). to irritate.—**ag'gravating** *a.* making worse; provoking.—**ag'gravatingly** *adv.*—**aggrava'tion** *n.* [L. *aggravare*, to make heavier].

aggregate (ag're-gāt) *v.t.* to collect into a total; to accumulate into a heap;—*n.* a sum or assemblage of particulars; the sum total;—*a.* collected together.—**aggrega'tion** *n.* the act of aggregating; a combined whole.—**ag'gregative** *a.* collective; accumulative [L. *aggregare*, to form into a flock, fr. *grex, gregis*, a flock].

aggress (a-gres') *v.i.* to attack; to start a quarrel.—**aggres'sion** *n.* a first act of hostility; an unprovoked attack.—**aggres'sive** *a.*—**aggres'sively** *adv.*—**aggres'siveness** *n.*—**aggres'sor** *n.* the one who first attacks, who provokes a quarrel [L. *aggredi*, to attack].

aggrieve (a-grēv') *v.t.* to give pain or sorrow to; to bear heavily upon; to vex; to afflict.—**aggrieved'** *a.* [L. *aggravare*, to make heavier].

aghast (a-gàst') *a.* struck with amazement, horror, terror; transfixed with fright [earlier *agast*, fr. O.E. *gaestan*, to terrify].

agile (aj'il, aj'il) *a.* having the power of quick motion; nimble.—**ag'ilely** *adv.*—**ag'ileness, agil'ity** *n.* [L. *agilis*, fr. *agere*, to do].

agitate (aj'i-tāt) *v.t.* to throw into violent motion; to stir up; to disturb, excite, upset; to debate earnestly;—*v.i.* to cause a disturbance.—**agita'tion** *n.* violent and irregular motion; perturbation; inciting to public disturbance.—**ag'itator** *n.* [L. *agitare,* to keep in motion].

agnail (ag'nāl) *n.* an inflammation round the nail; a whitlow; a hangnail; a corn [O.E. *ang,* tight; *naegel,* a nail].

agname (ag'nām) *n.* an additional name over and above Christian and surname; a nickname [L. *ad,* to; *nomen,* name].

agnate (ag'nāt) *n.* any male relation on the father's side.—*a.* related on the father's side; akin; allied.—**agnat'ic** *a.*—**agna'tion** *n.* [L. *ad,* to; *natus,* born].

agnomen (ag-nō'men) *n.* an additional name given by the Romans, generally because of some famous exploit, as Scipio *Africanus.* [L. *ad,* to; *nomen,* name].

agnostic (ag-nos'tik) *n.* one who believes that God, life hereafter, etc., can neither be proved nor disproved, and who accepts material phenomena only;—*a.* pert. to agnosticism.—**agnos'ticism** *n.* [Gk. *a-,* neg.; *gnostikos,* knowing].

ago, agone (a-gō,' a-gon') *adv.* and *a.* past; gone; in time past [O.E. *agan,* to pass away].

agog (a-gog') *a.* and *adv.* eagerly excited; expectantly [etym. unknown].

agonic (a-gon'ik) *a.* not forming an angle [Gk. *a-,* neg.; *gonia,* an angle].

agonism (ag'on-izm) *n.* the striving after a prize.—**ag'onist** *n.* one who contends for a prize in public games [Gk. *agon,* contest].

agony (ag'o-ni) *n.* extreme physical or mental pain; the death struggle; throes; pang.—**ag'onise** *v.t.* to distress with great pain; to torture.—*v.i.* to writhe in torment.—**ag'onising** *a.*—**ag'onisingly** *adv.*—**agony column,** section of newspaper containing advertisements for lost relatives, personal messages, etc. [Gk. *agon,* a contest].

agora (ag'or-a) *n.* forum, public square, or market of ancient Greek towns.—**agoraphobia** *n.* fear of open spaces [Gk. *agora,* a market place; *phobia,* fear].

agouti (a-gōō'ti) *n.* a genus of rodents or gnawing animals, natives of S. America, allied to the guinea-pig [Native].

agrarian (a-grā'ri-an) *a.* relating to lands, their management and distribution; (*Bot.*) growing in a field.—*n.* one who favours an equal division of property.—**agra'rianise** *v.t.*—**agra'rianism** *n.* an equal division of land or property. [L. *ager,* a field].

agree (a-grē') *v.i.* to be of one mind; to acquiesce; to resemble; (*Gram.*) to correspond in gender, case, or number.—*pr.p.* **agree'ing.**—*pa.p.* **agreed'.**—**agree'able** *a.* consenting; favourable; suitable; pleasant; congenial.—**agree'ably** *adv.*—**agree'ableness** *n.*—**agree'ment** *n.* agreeing; bargain; a written statement accepting certain conditions [L. *ad,* to; *gratus,* pleasing].

agrestic (a-gres'tik) *a.* rural; uncouth; countrified [L. *agrestis,* rustic].

agriculture (ag'ri-kul-tūr) *n.* the science and practice of the cultivation of the soil.—**agricul'tural** *a.*—**agricul'turist** or **agricul'turalist** *n.* one skilled in agriculture; a farmer [L. *ager,* a field; *colere, cultum,* to till].

agriology (ag-ri-ol'o-ji) *n.* the comparative study of primitive man.—**agriol'ogist** *n.* [Gk. *agrios,* wild; *logos,* discourse].

agronomy (a-gron'om-i) *n.* rural economy; husbandry.—**agronom'ial, agronom'ic, agronom'ical** *a.*—**agronom'ics** *n.pl.* the science of management of farms.—**agron'omist** *n.* [Gk. *agros,* field; *nemein,* to deal out].

aground (a-ground') *adv.* and *a.* on the ground; stranded; run ashore; beached.

ague (ā'gū) *n.* (*Med.*) intermittent malarial fever, marked by fits of shivering, burning, sweating.—**a'gued, a'guish** *a.* [L. *acuta febris,* acute fever].

ahead (a-hed') *adv.* farther forward; in advance; in front; head foremost [E.].

aheap (a-hēp') *adv.* in a heap [E.].

ahoy (a-hoi') *interj.* used in hailing, as in *ship ahoy* [form of interj. *hoy*].

ahull (a-hul') *adv.* and *a.* with sails furled and helm lashed on lee-side [*hull*].

ai (à'ē) *n.* the three-toed sloth of S. America, named from its cry [Braz.].

aid (ād) *v.t.* and *v.i.* to help; to relieve.—*n.* help; assistance; the person or thing which aids; auxiliary; assistant.—**aids** *n.pl.* subsidies or moneys granted to a king [Fr. *aider*].

aide-de-camp (ād-de-kong') *n.* an officer attached to the personal staff of a general to assist him in his military routine.—*pl.* **aides-de-camp'** [Fr.].

aigrette (ā'gret) *n.* a tuft or spray, as of feathers, diamonds, etc.; the small white heron; an egret [Fr.].

aiguille (ā-gwēl') *n.* (*Geol.*) a sharp, slender rock; a drill for boring rock.—**aiguillette', aiguillet** (ā-gwē-let') *n.* the tag of a shoe-lace;—*pl.* ornamental spangles of a dancer's dress [Fr. = a needle].

ail (āl) *v.t.* to trouble; disturb; to pain; afflict.—*v.i.* to feel pain; to be ill.—**ail'ing** *pr.p.*—**ail'ment** *n.* illness; morbid disease; sickness [O.E. *eglan,* to pain].

aileron (ā'le-ron) *n.* adjustable flaps near the tips of the wings of an aeroplane for balance and lateral control [Fr.].

aim (ām) *v.t.* to point at; to direct; to endeavour after; to intend;—*n.* direction; end; purpose; intention.—**aim'less** *a.* without aim or purpose.—**aim'lessly** *adv.*—**aim'lessness** *n.* [O.Fr. *esmer,* esteem].

ain't (ānt) (*Colloq.*) contracted form of *am not, is not,* or *are not.*

air (ār) *n.* the atmosphere; a gas; a light breeze; a tune; manner, bearing of a person; carriage; appearance; mien.—*v.t.* to expose to air or heat, for drying or warming; to parade before the public.—**airs** *n.pl.* an affected manner.—**air'ing** *n.* a ride or walk in the open air.—**air'y** *a.* of air; exposed to the air; light-hearted.—**air'ily** *adv.* gaily; merrily; lightly.—**air'iness** *n.* openness to the air; gaiety.—**air'-base** *n.* a place for housing, or directing operations of, aircraft.—**air'-blad'der** *n.* a swimming bladder.—**air'-borne** *a.* carried by aircraft; supported by the air (of aircraft).—**air'-brake** *n.* brake worked by compressed air.—**air'-chief-marsh'al** *n.* R.A.F. rank corresponding to admiral or general.—**air'-comm'odore** *n.* R.A.F. rank equivalent to commodore in navy or brigadier in army.—**air'-condens'er** *n.* an electrical condenser insulated between the plates by air.—**air'-condi'tion** *v.t.* to provide a building, etc. with air through a filtering apparatus.—**air'-course** *n.* (*Mining*) a passage for ventilation.—**air'-craft** *n.* all kinds of flying-machines.—**air'craft(s)man** *n.* a rank in the R.A.F.—**air-craft carrier,** an armed vessel built to carry aircraft.—**air'-cush'ion** *n.* a rubber cushion which can be inflated.—**air'-en'gine** *n.* an engine driven by compression and expansion of air.—**air'field** *n.* tract of land, used for accommodation and maintenance of aircraft.—**air force,** the whole of a nation's aircraft; in the British Empire, the R.A.F.—**air'-gas** *n.* illuminating gas made by charging air with petroleum vapour, etc.—**air'graph** *n.* airmail in which letters are photographed on reduced scale.—**air'-gun** *n.* a gun discharged by elastic force of air.—**air'-lift** *n.* large-scale transport operation by aircraft.—**air'-line** *n.* a service of aircraft plying regularly; a telephone line above ground level.—**air'-li'ner** *n.* a large passenger aeroplane flying on an air-line.—**air'-load** *n.* cargo carried by aircraft.—**air'-lock** *n.* the stoppage of the flow of liquid in a pipe caused by the presence of air; a small chamber to allow the passage of men or materials at the top of a caisson.—**air'-mail** *n.* the transport of letters, parcels, etc., by aeroplane.—**air'-man** *n.* an aviator.—**air'-park** *n.* a private aerodrome. **-air'-pi'lot** *n.* a person granted a certificate as pilot of an aeroplane. —**air'plane** *n.* (*U.S.*) an aeroplane.—**air'port** *n.* a terminal station for passenger aeroplanes.—**air'-pump** *n.* a machine for exhausting the air from a closed vessel.—**air'-raid** *n.* an attack by hostile aircraft.—**air-raid precautions** (*abbrev.* **A.R.P.**) protection for towns and the civilian population against explosive, incendiary, and gas attack by hostile aircraft.—**air'-sacs** *n. pl.* air-cells in the bodies of birds.—**air'-screw** *n.* the propeller of an aeroplane or airship.—**air'ship** *n.* lighter-than-air machine, developed from balloon.—**air'stop** *n.* a helicopter passenger station.—**air'-strip** *n.* concrete runway on an airfield; aerodrome.—**air'-tight** *a.* admitting no air.—**air'-trap** *n.* a contrivance to prevent or facilitate the escape of foul air from sewers, etc.—**air-vice-marshal**, a rank in the R.A.F. equivalent to rear-admiral.—**air'way** *n.* a prepared route for travel by aeroplane; a ventilating passage. [Gk. *aēr*, air].

airedale (ār'dāl) *n.* a kind of large terrier, with a close, wiry coat of tan and black [originally fr. *Airedale*, Yorkshire].

aisle (īl) *n.* the wing of a building; any lateral division of a church; (incorrectly) the passage-ways between pews [L. *ala*, a wing].

ait (āt) *n.* a small flat island in a lake or river [a form of *eyot*].

aitchbone (āch'bōn) *n.* the rump bone of an ox; the cut of beef surrounding it [L. *natis*, the rump; E. *bone*].

ajar (a-jàr') *adv.* partly open, as a door [M.E. *on char*, on the turn].

akimbo (a-kim'bō) *adv.* with a crook; bent. —**with arms akimbo**, with hands on hips and elbows turned outward [M.E. *in kenebow*, into a crooked bend].

akin (a-kin') *a.* related by blood; allied by nature; having the same properties.

alabaster (al'a-bas-ter) *n.* gypsum; a semi-transparent kind of soft marble-like mineral; —*a.* made of, or white as, alabaster.—**alabas'trian, alabas'trine** *a.* [Gk. *alabastros*].

alack (a-lak') *interj.* (*Arch.*) an exclamation expressive of sorrow.—**alack-a-day** (a-lak' a-dā) *interj.* an exclamation of regret [E.].

alacrity (a-lak'ri-ti) *n.* cheerful readiness; eagerness; briskness [L. *alacer*, brisk].

alar (ā'jàr) *a.* wing-like; pert. to wings; having wings [L. *ala*, a wing].

alarm (a-làrm') *n.* sound giving notice of danger; a mechanical contrivance to rouse from sleep; a summons to arms; sudden fear or apprehension; dismay; trepidation.—*v.t.* to fill with apprehension; to call to arms.—**alarm clock**, a clock made to ring loudly at a set time.—**alarm'ingly** *adv.*—**alarm'ist** *n.* one given to exciting alarm, esp. needlessly. —**alar'um** *n.* an old spelling of 'alarm' [O.Fr. *a l'arme*, to arms].

alas (a-las') *interj.* an exclamation of sorrow, pity, etc. [O.Fr. *a las*, ah weary].

alate (al'āt) *a.* having wings; winged. Also **al'ated** *a.* [L. *ala*, a wing].

alb (alb) *n.* a vestment of white linen, reaching to the feet, worn by R.C. clergy officiating at the Eucharist [L. *albus*, white].

albacore (al'ba-kōr) *n.* tunny fish [Ar. *al*, the; *bukr*, a young camel].

albatross (al'ba-tros) *n.* a large web-footed sea-bird commonest in the South Seas [fr. obsolete *alcatras*, a frigate-bird].

albeit (awl-bē'it) *conj.* although; even though; notwithstanding that [E. *al* = although, *be*, and *it*].

albert (al'bert) *n.* a kind of short watch-chain [named after Prince *Albert*].

albino (al-bī'no, bē'no) *n.* a person, or animal, with an abnormal whiteness of the skin and hair, and a pink colour in the eyes. —**al'binism** *n.* [L. *albus*, white].

Albion (al'bi-on) *n.* an old and poetic name for Britain [Gael. *alp*, a height].

album (al'bum) *n.* a book for autographs, photographs, stamps, etc.; a book of selections [L. *album*, a white tablet].

albumen (al-bū'men) *n.* white of egg; a similar substance found in the tissues of animals and plants.—**albu'min** *n.* any of a class of proteins, necessary for growth in the body.—**albu'minise** *v.t.* to convert into albumen.—**albu'minoid** *n.* a substance resembling albumen.—**albu'minous** *a.* [L. *albumen*, white of egg].

alburnum (al-bur'-num) *n.* sapwood, part of tree under bark and outside heart up which sap rises [L. *albus*, white].

alchemy (al'ke-mi) *n.* the forerunner of modern chemistry. Its chief aims were (*a*) transmuting the baser metals into gold, and (*b*) discovery of an elixir of life.— **alchem'ic** *a.*—**al'chemist** *n.* [Ar. *al*, the; *kimia* fr. Gk. *chumeia*, alloying of metals].

alcohol (al'kō-hol) *n.* pure spirit; a liquid of strong pungent taste, the intoxicating element in fermented or distilled liquor.— **al'coholism** *n.* a morbid condition caused by over-indulgence in alcoholic liquor.—**alcohol'ic** *a.* pert. to alcohol;—*n.* one addicted to the immoderate use of alcohol; a habitual drunkard.—**absolute alcohol**, alcohol entirely free from water [Ar. *al-koh'l*, powder of antimony to stain the eyelids].

Alcoran (al'kō-ràn, or al-kō-ràn') *n.* the sacred book of the Mohammedans. Also **Koran'** [Ar. *al*, the; *qoran*, reading].

alcove (al'kōv) *n.* a recess in a room; a covered seat in a garden [Sp. *alcoba*].

aldehyde (al'de-hīd) *n.* a liquid produced by the oxidation of alcohol [fr. letters of *al*cohol *dehyd*rogenatum, i.e. alcohol without hydrogen].

alder (awl'der) *n.* a tree of birch family, growing in marshy soil [O.F. *alor*].

alderman (awl'der-man) *n.* a civic dignitary, next in rank to the mayor.—**alderman'ic** *a.* [O.E. *ealdorman*, chief man].

Aldine (awl'dīn) *a.* (of books) printed by *Aldus* Manutius, of Venice, in 16th cent.

Aldis lamp (awl'dis) *n.* signalling lamp used in the services. [W. *Aldis*, inventor].

ale (āl) *n.* liquor made from malt by fermentation; a festivity (from the amount of ale drunk at it) [O.E. *ealu*].

alembic (a-lem'bik) *n.* a vessel of glass or metal formerly used in distillation; (*Fig.*) a refining medium, as in the *alembic of the mind* [Ar. *al-ambig*, a cup].

alert (a-lert') *a.* watchful; vigilant; brisk; nimble; active;—*n.* a signal by sirens of air attack; period of air-raid.—**alert'ly** *adv.* —**alert'ness** *n.* [It. *all' erta*, on the look-out].

Alexandrine (al-eg-zan'-drīn) *n.* a verse of six iambic feet, probably from O.Fr. poems dealing with Alexander the Great; found as ninth line of Spenserian Stanza.

alfa (al'fa) *n.* N. African name for esparto grass [etym. unknown].

alfalfa (al-fal'fa) *n.* plant of the pea family, valued as fodder, esp. in U.S. [Sp. *alfalfa*, three-leaved grass].

alfresco (al-fres'kō) *a.* and *adv.* in the fresh air, as an *alfresco meal* [It.].

alga (al'ga) *n.* (*Bot.*) one of the **algae** (al'jē), plants found in sea-water, and in slow-moving fresh or stagnant water.—**al'gal, al'goid, al'gous** *a.*—**algol'ogy** *n.* scientific study of marine plants [L. *alga*, seaweed].

algebra (al'je-bra) *n.* a branch of mathematics in which calculations are made by using letters to represent numbers or quantities and symbols to denote arithmetical operations of these numbers; a kind of abstract arithmetic used in almost all branches of science.—**algebra'ic(al)** *a.*—**algebra'ically** *adv.* —**algebra'ist** *n.* [Ar. *al'jebr*, joining together of fragments].

algid (al'jid) *a.* cold.—**algid cholera** Asiatic cholera.—**algid'ity, al'gidness** *n.* coldness.—

algif'ic *a.* causing cold [L.*algere*, to be cold].
alias (ā'li-as) *adv.* otherwise;—*n.* an assumed name;—*n.pl.* **a'liases** [L. *alias*, at another time].
alibi (al'i-bī) *n.* (*Law*) a plea that the prisoner was elsewhere when the crime was committed [L. *alibi*, elsewhere].
alien (āl'yen) *a.* of another country; foreign; different in nature; estranged;—*n.* a non-naturalised foreigner.—**al'ienable** *a.* (of property) capable of being sold or handed over.—**alienabil'ity** *n.*—**al'ienate** *v.t.* to transfer to another; estrange.—**aliena'tion** *n.* (*Med*). insanity.—**al'ienator** *n.*—**al'ienism** *n.* study of mental diseases.—**al'ienist** *n.* specialist in treatment of mental diseases, a psychiatrist [L. *alienus*, belonging to another].
aliferous (al-if'ẹr-us) *a.* having wings.—**al'iform** *a.* wing-shaped.—**aligerous** (a-lij'ẹr-us) *a.* winged (L. *ala*, a wing].
alight (ạ-līt') *adv.* or *a.* on fire; illuminated; kindled [O.E. *on*; *lēoht*, light].
alight (ạ-līt') *v.i.* to dismount; to finish one's journey; to fall; to descend.—**alight'ing** *n.* [O.E. *alihtan*, to descend].
align (ạ-līn') *v.t.* to adjust by a line; to line up; to range;—*v.i.* to form in a line; to fall in, as troops. Also **aline'.**—**align'ment** *n.* [Fr. *aligner*, to put in line].
alike (ạ-līk') *a.* having likeness; similar;—*adv.* similarly; equally [O.E. *gelic*, like].
aliment (al'i-ment) *n.* nourishment; nutriment; (*Law*) provision for maintenance.—*v.t.* to maintain.—**aliment'al** *a.*—**aliment'ally** *adv.*—**aliment'ary** *a.* pert. to food; nutritive.—**alimenta'tion** *n.* the process of introducing nutriment into the body.—**alimentary canal,** the great intestine [L. *alimentum*, nourishment].
alimony (al'i-mon-i) *n.* means of living, esp. an allowance made to a wife out of her husband's income, after legal separation [L. *alimonia*, sustenance].
aliquant (a'li-kwant) *a.* (of a number) not dividing without remainder [L. *aliquantus*, considerable].
aliquot (al'i-kwot) *a.* dividing exactly, or without remainder [L. *aliquot*, some].
alive (ạ-līv') *a.* having life; existent; active; alert; thronged with [O.E. *on life*, living].
alkali (al'kạ-lī) *n.* one of a class of chemical compounds which combine with acids to form salts—used with fats to form soap.—*pl.* **al'kalis, al'kalies.**—**al'kalify** *v.t.* to render alkaline;—*v.i.* to become alkaline;—*pa.p.* **al'kalified.**—**alkalifi'able** *a.* capable of being converted into an alkali.—**alkalim'etry** *n.* the quantitative estimation of the strength of alkalies.—**al'kaline** *a.* pert. to alkali; with qualities of alkali.—**alkalin'ity** *n.*—**al'kaloid** *n.* nitrogenous organic compound which acts chemically like an alkali;—*a.* resembling an alkali in properties [Ar. *al*, the; *qaliy*, calcined ashes].
Alkathene (al'ka-thēn) *n.* a thermoplastic; the I.C.I. brand of polythene.
Alkoran See **Alcoran.**
all (awl) *a.* the whole of; every one of;—*n.* whole amount; whole duration of;—*adv.* wholly; entirely.—**all'-fours** *n.* hands and feet; a card-game.—**all'-hail!** *interj.* welcome! good health!—**all'-in** *a.* (of wrestling) no style debarred.—**all'-pow'erful** *a.* omnipotent.—**all but,** nearly; almost.—**all in all,** in all respects [O.E. *all. eall*].
Allah (al'ạ) *n.* Mohammedan God [Ar.].
allay (ạ-lā') *v.t.* to lighten; to make quiet; to lessen grief or pain.—**allay'er** *n.*—**allay'ment** *n.* [O.E. *alecgan*, to put down].
allegation (al-e-gā'shun) *n.* affirmation; that which is positively asserted; the act of alleging [L. *allegare*, to allege].
allege (a-lej') *v.t.* to bring forward with positiveness; to assert as an argument, plea, or excuse; to declare; affirm; cite [L. *allegare*, to allege].
allegiance (ạ-lē'jạns) *n.* the duty of a subject to his liege, sovereign, or government; loyalty; an oath of homage.—**alle'giant** *a.* loyal;—*n.* one who owes allegiance [fr. O.Fr. *ligeance*].
allegory (al'e-gor-i) *n.* a narrative in which abstract ideas are personified; a description to convey a different meaning from that which is expressed; a continued metaphor.—**allegor'ic, -al** *a.*—**allegor'ically** *adv.*—**al'legorise** *v.t.* to write in allegorical form;—*v.i.* to use figurative language.—**al'legorist** *n.* [Gk. *allos*, other; *agoreuein*, to speak].
allegretto (al-le-gret'tō) *a.* (*Mus.*) livelier than *andante* but not so quick as *allegro* [It. dim. of *allegro*, gay].
allegro (al-lā-grō) *a.* (*Mus.*) brisk, gay, sprightly (movement).—**allegro vivace** (vē-vàtch'e), allegro in an even more spirited manner [It. *allegro*, gay].
alleluiah (al-e-lòò'ya) *interj.* hallelujah;—*n.* song of praise to the Almighty [Heb.].
allergy (al'ẹr-ji) *n.* hyper-sensitivity to particular substances; susceptibility to ill-effects from eating some foods.—**al'lergen** *n.* a substance which induces allergy.—**aller'gic** *a.* [Gk. *allos*, other; *ergon*, work]
alleviate (a-lēv'i-āt) *v.t.* to make light; to lighten; to ease; to afford relief; to mitigate.—**allevia'tion** *n.*—**alle'viative** *a.*—**alle'viator** *n.* [L. *alleviare*. fr. *levis*, light].
alley (al'i) *n.* a narrow passage between buildings; a garden path; a long, narrow passage adapted for playing bowls or skittles.—*pl.* **all'eys** [Fr. *aller*, to go].
alliance (ạ-lī'ạns) *n.* persons, parties, or states allied together for a common purpose; union by marriage [Fr. *allier*].
alligate (al'i-gāt) *v.t.* to conjoin [L. *ad*, to; *ligare*, to bind].
alligator (al'i-gā-tor) *n.* a reptile of America, distinguished from crocodile by a broad flat head, depressed muzzle and unequal teeth [Sp. *el lagarto*, the lizard].
allineate (ạl-in'e-āt) *v.t.* to regulate by a line [L. *ad*, to; *linea*, a line].
alliterate (al-it'ẹr-āt) *v.i.* to begin each word with the same letter or sound.—**allitera'tion** *n.* recurrence of a letter or letters at the beginning of words in close succession; head rhyme [L. *ad*, to; *littera*, letter].
all-mains (awl-mānz') *n.* or *a.* in wireless, (of) a receiver obtaining its power entirely from electric supply mains.
allocate (al'ō-kāt) *v.t.* to distribute; to assign to each his share; to place.—**alloca'tion** *n.*—**alloca'tur** *n.* (*Law*) a certificate that costs have been allowed [L. *ad*, to; *locus*, a place].
allocution (al-ō-kū'shun) *n.* a formal address, esp. of the Pope to his clergy [L. *ad*, to; *locutio*, a speech].
allodium (ạ-lō'di-um) *n.* a freehold estate.—**allo'dial** *a.* [Late L. *allodium*].
allot (ạ-lot') *v.t.* to divide by lot; to distribute as shares.—**allot'ment** *n.* allotting; what is allotted; distribution; a share; a portion of a field divided among many holders for vegetable gardens, etc. [L. *ad*, to; O.E. *hlot*, a share].
allotropy (ạ-lot'rō-pi) *n.* property of some chemical substances of being found in two or more different forms, e.g. coal, graphite, and diamond are all carbon.—**allotrop'ic** *a.*—**allot'ropism** *n.* [Gk. *allos*, other; *tropos*, manner].
allow (ạ-lou') *v.t.* to acknowledge; to permit; to give; to set apart;—*v.i.* to provide.—**allow'able** *a.* permissible; lawful; acceptable.—**allow'ance** *n.* what is allowed; permission; a stated quantity to be added or deducted; a rebate; a grant.—**allow'edly** *adv.*—**to make allowance for,** to take into consideration [O.Fr. *allouer*].
alloy (ạ-loi') *v.t.* to melt together two or more metals; to reduce the purity of a metal by mixing with a less valuable one; to debase.—**alloy** (ạ-loi', al'oi) *n.* any mixture of metals,

e.g. copper and zinc to form brass; a combination; an amalgam; (*Fig.*) evil mixed with good [L. *ad*, to; *ligare*, to join].

allspice (awl′spīs) *n.* the berry of the pimento, or Jamaica pepper; a spice made from it [E. *all*, and *spice*].

allude (a-lūd′) *v.i.* to refer indirectly to; to hint at; to suggest; to mention lightly [L. *ad*, at; *ludere*, to play].

allure (a-lūr′) *v.t.* to tempt by a lure, offer, or promise.—**allure′ment** *n.* that which allures.—**allur′ing** *a.* enticing; attractive; fascinating.—**allur′ingly** *adv.* [L. *ad*, to; Fr. *leurre*, bait].

allusion (a-lū′zhun) *n.* a passing or indirect reference; a hint; a suggestion.—**allus′ive** *a.* referring to indirectly; marked by allusions; symbolical.—**allus′ively** *adv.* [fr. *allude*].

alluvion (a-lū′vi-on) *n.* land formed by washed-up earth and sand.—**allu′vium** *n.* water-borne matter deposited on low-lying lands.—*pl.* **allu′viums**, or **allu′via**.—**allu′vial** *a.* [L. *alluvio*, an overflowing].

ally (a-lī′) *v.t.* to join by treaty, marriage, or friendship;—*pr.p.* **ally′ing**;—*pa.p.* and *pa.t.* **allied**.—**ally** (a-lī′, or a′lī) *n.* a person, family, country, etc., bound to another, esp. of nations in war-time; a partner.—*pl.* **allies** (a-līz′, or a′līz) [L. *ad*, to; *ligare*, to bind].

almanac (al′ma-nak) *n.* a calendar of days, weeks, and months, to which astronomical and other information is added [etym. uncertain].

almighty (awl-mīt′i) *a.* all-powerful; omnipotent.—**The Almighty**, the Supreme Being; God.—**almight′iness** *n.* [O.E. *ealmihtig*].

almond (á′mond) *n.* the kernel of the nut of the almond-tree; a tonsil, from its resemblance in shape to an almond [Gk. *amugdalē*, an almond].

almoner (á′, al′mon-er) *n.* one who distributes alms or bounty; a paid official attached to a hospital to supervise Social Service workers.—**al′monry** *n.* a place for distributing alms [O.Fr. *almosnier*].

almost (awl′mōst) *adv.* very nearly; all but [O.E. *eallmoest*].

alms (ámz) *n.* gifts offered to relieve the poor; a charitable donation.—**alms′-house** *n.* a building, usually erected and endowed by private charity, for housing the aged poor [Gk. *eleēmosunē*, pity].

aloe (al′ō) *n.* a bitter plant used in medicine.—*pl.* **al′oes**, a purgative drug, made from the juice of several species of aloe.—**aloes wood**, the heart of the Asiatic tree *Aquilaria Agallocha* [Gk. *aloē*, a bitter herb].

aloft (a-loft′) *adv.* on high; (*Naut.*) on the yards or rigging [O.N. *a lopt*, in the air].

alone (a-lōn′) *a.* solitary; single;—*adv.* by oneself; singly [E. *all* and *one*].

along (a-long′) *adv.* in a line with; throughout the length of; lengthwise; onward; in the company of (followed by *with*);—*prep.* by the side of.—**along′side** *adv.* by the side of, esp. of a ship [O.E. *andlang*].

aloof (a-lòòf′) *a.* reserved in manner, almost unsociable;—*adv.* at a distance; apart.—**aloof′ness** *n.* [fr. Dut. *to loef*, to windward].

alopecia (al-ō-pē′si-a) *n.* disease causing loss of hair [Gk. *alopekia*, fox-mange].

aloud (a-loud′) *adv.* with a loud voice or noise; loudly; audibly [fr. E. *loud*].

alp (alp) *n.* a high mountain; mountain pasture-land.—**Alps** *n.pl.* the mountains of Switzerland.—**al′pine** *a.* pert. to the Alps;—*n.* a plant that grows on high ground.—**alpinist** (al′pin-ist) *n.* [L. *Alpes*].

alpaca (al-pak′a) *n.* a sheeplike animal of Peru; a species of llama; a thin kind of cloth made of the wool of the alpaca [Sp.].

alpenhorn, alphorn (al′pen-horn, alp′horn) *n.* a long wooden horn curving towards a wide mouth-piece, used by Swiss herds.—**al′penstock** *n.* a long, stout staff, shod with iron, used by mountaineers [Ger.=horn (stick) of the Alps].

alpha (al′fȧ) *n.* the first letter of Greek alphabet.—**alpha and omega**, the first and the last.—**alpha particle**, a helium nucleus travelling at high speed, given out when atoms of Uranium, Radium, etc., undergo radioactive breakdown.—**alpha rays**, streams of alpha particles [Gk.].

alphabet (al′fa-bet) *n.* letters of a language arranged in order; first principles.—**alphabet′ic, -al** *a.*—**alphabet′ically** *adv.* [Gk. *alpha*, *bēta*, the first two Greek letters].

already (awl-red′i) *adv.* before this; even now; even then; previously to the time specified [E. *all ready*, prepared].

alright (awl-rīt) a common but incorrect spelling of **all right**.

also (awl′sō) *adv.* and *conj.* in like manner; likewise; further.

alt (alt) *n.* (*Mus.*) a high tone.—**in alt**, in octave above treble stave [It. *alto*, high].

altar (awl′tar) *n.* a table or raised structure in a place of worship, on which gifts and sacrifices are offered to a deity; the communion table [L. *altare*].

alter (awl′ter) *v.t.* to change;—*v.i.* to become different.—**al′terably** *adv.*—**alterabil′ity** *n.*—**altera′tion** *n.* the act of altering; change; modification [L. *alter*, other].

altercate (awl′ter-kāt) *v.i.* to contend in words; to wrangle.—**alterca′tion** *n.* a dispute; a controversy [L. *altercari*, to wrangle].

alternate (a(w)l-ter′nāt) *a.* occurring by turns; one following the other in succession.—**al′ternately** *adv.* by turns.—**alternate** (a(w)l′ter-nāt) *v.t.* to cause to follow by turns;—*v.i.* to happen by turns.—**alternation** (a(w)l-ter-nā′shun) *n.*—**alter′native** *a.* offering a choice of two things.—*n.* a choice of two things—**alter′natively** *adv.*—**al′ternator** *n.* (*Elect.*) a dynamo for producing alternating current.—**alternating current** (*Elect.*) a current which reverses its direction of flow at fixed periods.—*Abbrev.* **A.C.** [L. *alternare*, fr. *alter*, other].

although (awl-thō′) *conj.* admitting that; notwithstanding that [E. *all* and *though*].

altimeter (al-tim′e-ter) *n.* an instrument for taking altitudes; in aviation, barometer to show height [L. *altus*, high; Gk. *metron*, a measure].

altitude (al′ti-tūd) *n.* height; perpendicular elevation above a given level [L. *altitudo*].

alto (al′tō) *n.* (*Mus.*) part once sung by highest male voice or counter-tenor, now sung by lowest female voice; singer with voice higher than tenor, lower than soprano; contralto [L. *altus*, high].

altogether (awl-tòò-geTH′er) *adv.* wholly, entirely, quite; on the whole [E.].

altometer (al-tom′e-ter) *n.* an instrument for measuring altitude; a theodolite [L. *altus*, high; Gk. *metron*, a measure].

alto-rilievo (al′to-ril-yā′vō) *n.* high relief; sculpture in which figures project prominently from their background. Contrasted with *bas-relief* [It.].

altruism (al′tròò-izm) *n.* the principle of living for the good of others (opp. to *egoism*).—**al′truist** *n.*—**altruis′tic** *a.* unselfish.—**altruis′tically** *adv.* [L. *alter*, another].

alum (al′um) *n.* a double sulphate of alumina and potash; a mineral salt used as a styptic, astringent, etc., as a mordant in dyeing, and in tanning [L. *alumen*].

aluminium (al-ū-min′i-um) *n.* a whitish metal produced largely from bauxite; it is strong, light, malleable.—**alu′mina, al′umine** *n.* an oxide of aluminium; the clay, loam, etc., from which alum is obtained.—**alu′minate** *v.t.* to impregnate with alum.—**alu′minic** *a.*—**aluminif′erous** *a.* containing alum or alumina.—**alu′minite** *n.* a sulphate of alumina. [L. *alumen*, alum].

alumnus (a-lum′nus) *n.* (*fem.* **alum′na**.—*pl.* **alum′nae**) a pupil; a graduate or undergraduate of a college or university.—*pl.* **alum′ni** [L. *alumnus*, foster-child].

alveolar (al-vē´ō-lar) *a.* pert. to or resembling the sockets of the teeth.—**alve'olate** *a.* pitted; honeycombed.—**alve'olus** *n.* (*pl.* **alve'oli**) a tooth socket; a cell in a honeycomb. [L. *alveolus,* a small cavity].

alway, always (awl´wā, -wāz) *adv.* at all times; perpetually; invariably; regularly [O.E. *ealne weg,* the whole way].

alyssum (a´li-sum) *n.* a species of rock plant with white or yellow flowers; madwort [Gk. *alussos,* curing madness].

am (am) the *first person sing. pres. indic.* of the verb **to be.**

amain (ą-mąn') *adv.* with all strength or force [E. *on; main,* strength].

amalgam (ą-mal´gam) *n.* a compound of mercury with another metal; a mixture of different substances.—**amal'gamate** *v.t.* to mix a metal with quicksilver; to compound; to consolidate; to combine (esp. of business firms);—*v.i.* to coalesce; to blend; to fuse.—**amalgama'tion** *n.* the act of amalgamating.—**amalgama'tive** *a.*—**amalgama'tor** *n.* [Gk. *malagma,* an emollient].

amanuensis (ą-man-ū-en´sis) *n.* one who writes what another dictates, or copies what another has written; a secretary.—*pl.* **amanuen'ses** [L. *ab,* from; *manus,* hand].

amaranth (am´a-ranth) *n.* an imaginary purple flower which never fades; 'love-lies-bleeding'; a purplish colour.—**amaran'thine** *a.* never-fading; purplish [Gk. *amaranthos,* never-fading].

amass (ą-mas') *v.t.* to heap up; to collect; accumulate [L. *ad,* to; *massa,* a lump].

amateur (am´a-tęr) *n.* one who cultivates any study, art, or sport for the love of it, and not for money;—*a.* like an amateur.—**amateur'ish** *a.* unskilled; clumsy.—**am'ateurism, amateur'ishness** *n.* [L. *amare,* to love].

amative (am´ą-tiv) *a.* pert. to love; amorous [L. *amare,* to love].

amatol (am´ą-tol) *n.* explosive of ammonium nitrate of trinitrotoluene (T.N.T.) [name from parts of names of ingredients].

amatory (am´ą-tor-i) *a.* pert. to or causing love.—**amato'rial** *a.* amorous; affectionate.—**amato'rially** *adv.* [L. *amare,* to love].

amaze (ą-māz') *v.t.* to fill with astonishment or wonder; to confound; to perplex.—**amaze'ment** *n.* astonishment, surprise.—**amaz'ing** *a.* causing amazement, wonder, or surprise.—**amaz'ingly** *adv.* [O.E. *amasian,* to confound].

Amazon (am´az-on) *n.* one of a mythical race of female warriors of Scythia; a masculine woman.—**Amazo'nian** *a.* [Gk. *a-,* neg. and *mazos,* breast].

ambage (am´bāj) *n.* a circumlocution; subterfuge; evasion; used in *pl.* **am'bages** [L. *ambages,* a winding].

ambassador (am-bas´a-dor) *n.* an envoy of highest rank sent to a foreign country; (*Fig.*) an intermediary; a messenger;—**ambass'adress** *n. fem.*—**ambassado'rial** *a.*—**ambass'adorship** *n.*—**am'bassage** *n.* now *embassage* (cf. *embassy*), business of an ambassador or diplomatic mission [L. *ambactus,* vassal].

amber (am´bęr) *n.* a yellowish, brittle fossil resin of vegetable origin, used in making beads, brooches, mouthpieces of pipes, etc.;—*a.* of, or like, amber [Ar. *anbar,* ambergris].

ambergris (am´bęr-grēs) *n.* a fragrant, ash-coloured, waxy substance, derived from a biliary secretion of the spermaceti whale [Fr. *ambre gris,* grey amber].

ambidexter (am-bi-deks´tęr) *n.* one able to use either hand with equal dexterity; a double-dealer.—**ambidexter'ity** *n.*—**ambidex'trous** *a.* able to use either hand equally skilfully.—**ambidex'trously** *adv.* [L. *ambo,* both; *dexter,* right hand].

ambient (am´bi-ent) *a.* encompassing on all sides [L. *ambire,* to go round].

ambiguity (am-bi-gū´i-ti) *n.* any statement that may be interpreted in more than one way.—**ambig'uous** *a.* doubtful or uncertain; equivocal; susceptible of two or more meanings.—**ambig'uously** *adv.*—**ambig'uousness** *n.* [L. *ambigere,* to waver].

ambit (am´bit) *n.* circuit or compass; sphere of action; scope [L. *ambire,* to go round].

ambition (am-bish´un) *n.* an eager desire for the attainment of honour, fame, or power; aim; aspiration.—**ambi'tious** *a.* ardently desirous of acquiring power, rank, office, etc.—**ambi'tiously** *adv.* [L. *ambitio,* going about for votes].

ambivalence, ambivalency (am-biv´ą-lens, -i) *n.* in psycho-analysis, the simultaneous operation in the mind of two irreconcilable wishes.—**ambiv'alent** *a.* [L. *ambo,* both; *valere,* to be strong].

amble (am´bl) *v.i.* to move along, easily and gently;—*n.* a peculiar gait of a horse; a stroll.—**am'bler** *n.*—**am'bling** *a.*—**am'blingly** *adv.* [L. *ambulare,* to walk].

ambo (am´bō) *n.* a reading-desk in medieval churches [Gk. *ambon,* rising].

ambrosia (am-brō´zi-a) *n.* (*Myth.*) the food of the Ancient Greek gods which conferred immortality; an exquisite dish.—**ambro'sial** *a.*—**ambro'sially** *adv.* [Gk. *a-,* neg.; *brotos,* mortal].

ambulance (am´bū-ląns) *n.* a covered vehicle for the transport of the injured or sick; a hospital unit in the field.—**ambulan'cier** *n.* an ambulance man [Fr. *ambulance*].

ambulant (am´bū-ląnt) *a.* walking.—**am'bulate** *v.i.* to walk backwards and forwards.—**ambula'tion** *n.* walking.—**ambula'tor** *n.* instrument for measuring distances.—**am'bulatory** *a.* having power of walking; used for walking; moving from place to place;—*n.* a cloister for walking exercise [L. *ambulare,* to walk].

ambuscade (am-bus-kād') *n.* ambush; the place of ambush; the force concealed;—*v.i.* to lie in wait;—*v.t.* to attack from a concealed position [*ambush*].

ambush (am´boosh) *n.* and *v.t.* same as **ambuscade** [L. *in;* Late L. *boscus,* a wood].

ameer, amir (ą-mēr') *n.* a prince; a chief in Mohammedan countries; an emir [Ar.].

ameliorate (ą-mēl´yur-āt) *v.t.* and *v.i.* to make better; to improve.—**ameliora'tion** *n.*—**amel'iorative** *a.* [L. *ad,* to; *melior,* better].

Amen (ā-men', á´men) *adv,* or *interj.* so be it; truly; verily (uttered at the end of a prayer) [Heb=certainly].

amenable (ą-men´ą-bl, ą-mē´ną-bl) *a.* liable to be brought to account; easily led; willing to yield or obey.—**amenabil'ity, amen'ableness** *n.* the state of being amenable.—**amen'ably** *adv.* [Fr. *amener,* to lead near].

amend (ą-mend') *v.t.* to change for the better; to improve; to alter in detail as a bill in parliament, etc.;—*v.i.* to grow better.—**amend'able** *a.*—**amend'atory** *a.*—**amend'ment** *n.* the act of amending; a change for the better.—**amends'** *n.pl.* reparation for loss or injury; compensation [L. *emendare,* to remove a fault].

amenity (ą-men´i-ti, ą-mē´ni-ti) *n.* pleasantness in situation, climate, manners, or disposition.—**amen'ities** *n.pl.* pleasant ways or manners; agreeable surroundings [L. *amoenus,* agreeable].

amerce (ą-męrs') *v.t.* to punish by a fine.—**amerce'able** *a.* liable to a fine.—**amerce'ment** *n.* a pecuniary penalty [L. *merces,* a fine].

American (ą-mer´i-kąn) *a.* pert. to America;—*n.* a native or citizen of America.—**Amer'icanese** *n.* writing or introducing words, phrases, and idioms peculiar to America.—**Amer'icanise** *v.t.* and *i.* to make American in manners, customs, etc. [fr. *Amerigo* Vespucci, an Italian navigator, 1451-1512].

amethyst (am´e-thist) *n.* a kind of quartz, of violet, purple, or blue colour, formerly supposed to prevent intoxication.—**amethys'tine** *a.* pert. to amethyst; bluish-violet [Gk. *a-,* neg.; *methuein,* to be drunken].

amiable (ā´mi-ą-bl) *a.* worthy of love or affection; sweet-tempered.—**a'miably** *adv.*—

amiabil'ity *n.* Also **a'miableness** [L. *amicabilis*, friendly].
amicable (am′i-ka-bl) *a.* friendly; peaceable.—**am'icably** *adv.*—**amicabil'ity** *n.* Also **am'icableness** [L *amicabilis*, friendly].
amice (am′is) *n.* a loose, flowing garment worn by pilgrims; an oblong of white, embroidered linen worn under alb by R.C. priests; a college hood [L. *amictus*, dress].
amid, amidst (a-mid', a-mid′st) *prep.* in the middle of; among [O.E. *on middan*].
amir (a-mēr') *n.* See **ameer.**
amiss (a-mis') *a.* wrong; faulty; improper;—*adv.* in a faulty manner.—**amiss'ing** *a.* missing; lost; wanting [E. *miss*, a failure].
amity (am′i-ti) *n.* friendship [Fr. *ami*, a friend, fr. L. *amicus*].
ammeter (am′e-tẹr) *n.* an instrument used to measure the strength of an electric current in amperes [fr. *ampere*, and Gk. *metron*, a measure].
ammo (am′ō) *n.* (*Army Slang*) ammunition.
ammonal (am′ō-nal) *n.* a mixture of ammonium nitrate, aluminium, and charcoal, used as a high explosive [fr. *ammonia*].
ammonia (a-mō′ni-a) *n.* a pungent, alkaline gas, very soluble in water; a solution of this gas in water, for household use.—**ammo'niac, ammoni'acal** *a.*—**ammo'niated** *a.* combined with, containing, ammonia.—**ammo'nium** *n.* hypothetical base of ammonia [fr. *sal ammoniac*, a salt said to have been first obtained in a region named after the Egyptian god Jupiter *Ammon*].
ammonite (am′on-īt) *n.* one of the fossil shells of a genus of extinct cuttle-fishes; a high explosive used in coal mines for blasting [fr. *Ammon*; and *ammonia*].
ammunition (am-ū-nish′un) *n.* military projectiles and missiles of all kinds; originally, military stores; often used adjectivally, e.g. *ammunition dump* [O.Fr. *l'amunition*, for *la munition*].
amnesia (am-nē′zi-a) *n.* loss of memory [Gk.].
amnesty (am′nes-ti) *n.* an act of oblivion; a general pardon of political offenders [Gk. *amnēsia*, a forgetting].
amoeba (a-mē′ba) *n.* a minute animalcule of the simplest structure constantly changing in shape.—*pl.* **amoe'bae, amoe'bas.**—**amoe'boid** *a.* [Gk. *amoibē*, change].
amok (a-mok') See **amuck.**
among, amongst (a-mung', a-mungst') *prep.* mixed with; making part of; amidst [M.E. *amonge*].
Amontillado (a-mon-til-yá′dō) *n.* a dry sherry, light in colour and body [Sp.].
amoral (a-mor′al) *a.* non-moral; heedless of morals [Gk. *a-*, neg.; and E. *moral*].
amorous (am′or-us) *a.* having a propensity for love and sexual enjoyment; in love; pert. to love.—**am'orously** *adv.*—**am'orousness** *n.*—**am'orist** *n.* [L. *amor*, love].
amorphous (a-mor′fus) *a.* without regular shape; shapeless; irregular; uncrystallised, as glass [Gk. *a-*, neg.; *morphē*, form].
amount (a-mount') *v.i.* to rise to; to result in; to come to (in value or meaning); to be equal to;—*n.* the sum total; the whole, or aggregate [O.Fr. *amonter*, to mount up].
ampere (am-per') *n.* the unit of electric current; (*Abbrev.*) **amp** [named after André *Ampère*, a French physicist, 1775-1836].
ampersand (am′per-sand) *n.* the name formerly given to the sign &. Also **am'perzand, am'pussyand, am'passy** [fr. *and per se and*, i.e. 'and' by itself='and.'].
Amphibia (am-fib′i-a) *n.pl.* animals that can live either on land or in water, as frogs, toads, newts, etc.—**amphib'ian** *a.* pert. to Amphibia;—*n.* an animal of the class Amphibia.—**amphib'ious** *a.* [Gk. *amphi*, on both sides; *bios*, life].
amphibrach (am′fi-brak) *n.* in prosody, a foot of three syllables, the middle one long, the first and last short (⏑—⏑). In English the term is applied to a foot of three syllables of which only the middle one is stressed.—**am'phibrachic** *a.* [Gk. fr. *amphi*, on both sides; *brachus*, short].
amphitheatre (am-fi-thē′a-tẹr) *n.* an edifice, having tiers of seats, encircling an arena, used for sports or spectacles; a rising gallery in a theatre, concert-hall, etc. [Gk. *amphi*, on both sides; *theatron*, a theatre].
amphora (am′fō-ra) *n.* a two-handled earthenware vessel or jar, used by the ancient Greeks and Romans; as a measure, about 6 gallons [Gk. *amphi*, on both sides; *pherein*, to bear].
ample (am′pl) *a.* of full dimensions; of adequate size; of sufficient quantity; abundant; copious.—**am'ply** *adv.*—**am'pleness** *n.* [L. *amplus*].
amplify (am′pli-fī) *v.t.* to make larger; to extend; to enlarge;—*v.i.* to dilate; to expatiate upon.—**amplifica'tion** *n.*—**am'plifier** *n.* an apparatus which increases the volume of sound in wireless reception [L. *amplus*, large; *facere*, to make].
amplitude (am′pli-tūd) *n.* largeness; extent; abundance; (*Radio*) (of a wave) vertical distance between its highest and lowest levels; (*Elect.*) maximum value of an alternating current [L. *amplus*, large].
ampoule (am′pòòl) *n.* a small sealed glass container holding hypodermic dose [Fr.].
ampulla (am-pūl′a) *n.* a sacred vessel for holding oil, used in ceremonies such as coronation; a kind of cruet holding wine and water for Mass [L. *ampulla*].
amputate (am′pū-tāt) *v.t.* to cut off, as a limb of the body, or bough of a tree.—**amputa'tion** *n.* [L. *amputare*, to cut off].
amuck, amok (a-muk', a-mok') *adv.* as in phrase, *to run amuck*. to rush about frantically attacking and committing murder indiscriminately [Malay *amuq*, rushing in frenzy].
amulet (am′ū-let) *n.* a talisman; a charm worn to ward off disease or evil spells.—**amulet'ic** *a.* [Fr. *amulette*, fr. L. *amuletum*].
amuse (a-mūz') *v.t.* to entertain agreeably; to occupy pleasantly; to divert.—**amuse'ment** *n.* anything which entertains or pleases; a pastime.—**amus'ing** *a.* pleasing; diverting.—**amus'ingly** *adv.* [Fr. *amuser*, to entertain].
amyl (a′mil) *n.* (*Chem.*) hypothetical radical, thought to exist in many compounds such as *amyl alcohol* [Gk. *amulon*, starch].
an (an) *a.* the form of the indefinite article used before a vowel sound. See **a.** Also *conj.* if=a form of *and* [O.E. *ān*, one].
anabaptist (an-a-bap′tist) *n.* one who denies the validity of infant baptism and advocates re-baptism of adults (by immersion) [Gk. *ana*, again; *baptizein*, to dip].
anabolism (an-ab′ol-izm) *n.* (*Physiol.*) the constructive form of metabolism; the building-up of tissues by plant or animal from carbohydrates, fats, proteins, etc., in its food, which process alternates with the breaking down (katabolism) in the chemical routine [Gk. *ana*, up; *bolē*, a throwing].
anachronism (an-ak′ron-ism) *n.* a chronological error; post- or ante-dating of an event or thing.—**anachronist'ic** *a.*—**ana'chronous** *a.*—**anachronist'ically** [Gk. *ana*, back; *chronos*, time].
anaconda (an-a-kon′da) *n.* a gigantic, non-venomous snake of tropical S. America, allied to boa species; orig. name given to python of Ceylon [etym. uncertain].
anadrom (an′a-drom) *n.* a fish which migrates up a river e.g. salmon.—**anad'romous** *a.* [Gk. *ana*, up; *dromos*, a running].
anaemia (a-nē′mi-a) *n.* disease characterised by a deficiency of blood or of haemoglobin, leading to pallor of skin and mucous membranes.—**anae'mic.**—**anaemot'rophy** *n.* under-nourishment due to anaemia [Gk. *an-*, neg.; *haima*, blood].
anaesthesia, anesthesia (an-es-thē′zi-a) *n.* absence of sensibility to external impressions

particularly touch. Also **anaesthe'sis**.—**anaesthet'ic, anesthet'ic** *n.* a drug which induces insensibility to pain;—*a.* producing loss of feeling and sensation.—**anaesthet'ically, anesthet'ically** *adv.* — **anaes'thetise, anes'thetise** *v.t.*—**anaesthet'ist** *n.* [Gk. *an-*, not; *aisthesis*, feeling].

anaglyph (an'ą-glif) *n.* a figure or ornament cut in low relief; a cameo; a picture printed in red and green with a slight overlap, which when viewed through spectacles with a red and a green eye-piece, appears stereoscopic; the spectacles for this.—**anaglyph'ic** *a.* [Gk. *ana*, up; *gluphein*, to engrave].

anagram (an'ą-gram) *n.* a transposition of the letters of a word or phrase to form a new word or phrase.—**anagrammat'ic, -al** *a.*—**anagrammat'ically** *adv.*—**anagram'matise** *v.t.* to form anagrams.—**anagram'matism** *n.*—**anagram'matist** *n.* [Gk. *ana-*, again; *gramma*, letter].

anal (ā'nąl) *a.* pert. to or near the anus.

analects, analecta (an'ą-lekts, an-ą-lek'tą) *n.pl.* an anthology of short literary fragments. —**analec'tic** *a.* [Gk. *analektos*, choice].

analepsis (an-ą-lep'sis) *n.* (*Med.*) restoration of strength after disease. Also **analep'sy**.—**analep'tic** *a.* restorative [Gk. *ana*, up; *lēpsis*, a taking].

analgesia (an-al-jē'zi-ą) *n.* (*Med.*) absence of pain while retaining tactile sense; painlessness. —**analge'sic** *a.* insensible to or alleviating pain;—*n.* a drug which relieves pain; an anodyne [Gk. *an-*, neg.; *algēsis*, pain].

analogy (a-nal'o-ji) *n.* resemblance in essentials between things or statements otherwise different; relationship; likeness; parallelism; correspondence.—**analog'ic,-al** *a.* —**analog'ically** *adv.*—**anal'ogise** *v.t.* to explain by analogy.—**anal'ogism** *n.* an argument proceeding from cause to effect; investigation by, or reasoning from, analogy.—**anal'ogist** *n.*—**anal'ogous** *a.* having analogy. —**anal'ogously** *adv.*—**an'alogue** *n.* a word or thing resembling another [Gk. *analogia*, proportion].

analysis (ą-nal'i-sis) *n.* the resolution, separating, or breaking up of anything into its constituent elements; a synopsis; (*Chem.*) determination of elements comprising a compound or mixture; (*Gram.*) logical arrangement of a sentence into its component parts; (*Math.*) theory of real and complex numbers.—*pl.* **anal'yses**,—**analys'able** *a.* —**analysa'tion** *n.*—**an'alyse** *v.t.* to take to pieces; to examine critically part by part. —**an'alyst** *n.* one skilled in analysis; an analytical chemist.—**analyt'ic,-al** *a.*—**analyt'ically** *adv.*—**analyt'ics** *n. pl.* the technique of logical analysis [Gk. *ana*, up; *lusis*, a loosening].

ananas (an-an'as) *n.* the pine-apple. Also **an'ana** [Guiana].

anapaest, anapest (an'a-pēst, -pest) *n.* in prosody, a foot of three syllables, two short or unaccented followed by one long or accented syllable (◡◡—).—**anapaes'tic** *a.* [Gk. *anapaistos*, reversed, because it may be considered the reverse of a dactyl].

anarchy (an'ar-ki) *n.* want of government in society; lawless disorder in a country; a political theory, which would dispense with all laws, founding authority on the individual conscience.—**anarch'ic, anarch'ically** *adv.* —**an'archise** *v.t.*—**an'archism** *n.* confusion, chaos, lawlessness, disorder.—**an'archist** *n.* [Gk. *an-*, neg.; *archein*, to rule].

anathema (ą-nath'e-ma) *n.* the word used in the R.C. church as part of the formula in excommunication; something highly distasteful to one; accursed thing.—**anathemat'ic** *a.*—**anathemat'ically** *adv.*—**anathematisa'tion** *n.*—**anath'ematise** *v.t.* to pronounce a curse against; to excommunicate (See 1 Cor. 16) [Gk.].

anatomy (ą-nat'o-mi) *n.* art of dissecting an animal or a plant; study of form or structure of an animal; the body; a skeleton.—**anatom'ic (al)** *a.*—**anatom'ically** *adv.*—**anat'omise** *v.t.* to dissect; to lay open the interior structure for examining each part.—**anat'omist** *n.* one skilled in anatomy [Gk. *ana*, up; *tomē*, cutting].

ancestor (an'ses-tor) *n.* (*fem.* **an'cestress**) forefather; progenitor; forebear;—**ances'tral** *a.* —**an'cestry** *n.* lineage. [L. *ante*, before; *cedere, cessum*, to go].

anchor (ang'kor) *n.* a heavy iron instrument by which a ship is held fast to the sea-bottom; a moulder's chaplet;—*v.t.* to place at anchor;—*v.i.* to cast anchor; to stop.—**anch'orage** *n.* a sheltered place where a ship may anchor; dues chargeable on ships which wish to anchor in harbour.—**anch'ored** *a.* at anchor; firmly fixed.—**to cast anchor,** to let down anchor.—**to weigh anchor,** to raise anchor preparatory to sailing [L. *ancora*].

anchorite, anchoret (ang'ko-rīt, -ret) *n.* one who lives apart, renouncing the world for religious reasons; a hermit.—**anch'oress, anch'oritess** *n.* a female hermit.—**anch'orage** *n.* home of anchorite [Gk. *anachorētēs*, one who retires].

anchovy (an-chō'vi, an'chō-vi) *n.* a small sea-fish of the herring family, caught in the Mediterranean, and eaten pickled or prepared as a sauce. [Sp. *anchova*].

ancient (ān'shęnt) *a.* very old; antique; venerable; former;—*n.* an aged or venerable person; one who lived in olden times.—**an'ciently** *adv.*—**an'cientness** *n.*—**an'cientry** *n.* ancientness; ancestry; seniority.—**the Ancient of Days,** a biblical title for God [L. *ante*, before].

ancillary (an-sil'ąr-i) *a.* giving help to; attending upon; auxiliary; subordinate [L. *ancilla*, a maid-servant].

and (and) *conj.* added to; together with; a word that joins words, clauses, or sentences [O.E.].

andante (an-dan'te) *a.* or *adv.* (*Mus.*) moving rather slowly, but in a steady, flowing manner, faster than *larghetto*, but slower than *allegretto*;—*n.* a moderately slow, flowing movement [It. *andare*, to go].

Anderson shelter (an'dęr-son, shel'tęr) *n.* the name given to a small shelter in 1939 to give protection during air-raids [named after Sir John *Anderson*, Home Secretary].

andiron (and'ī-ęrn) *n.* a utensil for supporting logs or fire-irons in a fireplace; a fire-dog [O.Fr. *andier*].

androgynous (an-droj'i-nus) *a.* having the characteristics of both sexes; hermaphrodite. —also **androg'ynal**.—**androg'yny** *n.* [Gk. *anēr, andros*, a man; *kephalē*, the head; *gunē*, a woman].

anecdote (an'ek-dōt) *n.* a biographical incident; a brief account of any fact or happening (often amusing);—**an'ecdotage** *n.* anecdotes collectively.—**an'ecdotal** *a.*—**an'ecdotist** *n.* a writer or teller of anecdotes [Gk. *anekdotos*, not published].

anele, aneal (ą-nēl') *v.t.* to anoint with holy oil; to give extreme unction [O.E. *an*, on; *ele*, oil].

anelectric (an-e-lek'trik) *a.* non-electric;—*n.* a body that does not become electric; a conductor of electricity.—**anelec'trode** *n.* the positive pole of a galvanic battery [Gk. *an-*, neg., and *electric*].

anemograph (ą-nem'ō-graf) *n.* an instrument for recording force and direction of wind.—**anemom'eter** *n.* an instrument for measuring force or velocity of wind; a wind-gauge [Gk. *anemos*, wind; *graphein*, to write; *metron*, a measure].

anemone (ą-nem'ō-nē) *n.* plant of crow-foot family; wind-flower.—**sea'-anem'one** *n.* name given to certain plant-like marine animals [Gk. *anemos*, wind].

anent (ạ-nent') *prep.* concerning; about; in respect of; as to [O.E. *on; efen*, even].

aneroid (an'e-roid) *a.* denoting a barometer depending for its action on the pressure of the atmosphere on a metallic box almost exhausted of air, without the use of mercury or other fluid [Gk. *a-*, neg.; *nēros*, wet; *eidos*, form].

aneurism (an'ū-rizm) *n.* (*Med.*) a local widening or dilatation in the course of an artery [Gk. *ana*, up; *eurus*, wide].

anew (ạ-nū') *adv.* in a new form or manner; newly; over again; afresh [M.E. *of newe*].

angel (ān'jel) *n.* a heavenly messenger; a spirit who conveys God's will to man; a guardian spirit; an old English coin worth about 10s. bearing the figure of archangel Michael; (*Colloq.*) a lovable person; a dear.—**angelic(al)** (an-jel'ic, -i-kạl) *a.* like an angel.—**angel'ically** *adv.* [Gk. *angelos*, a messenger].

angelica (an-jel'i-kạ) *n.* (*Bot.*) a genus of umbelliferous plants having white flowers tinged with pink; a candied confection prepared from its aromatic stem [Gk. *angelikos*, angelic].

angelus (an'je-lus) *n.* a short devotional service in the R.C. Church held morning, noon, and sunset. The opening words are '*Angelus* Domini nuntiavit Mariae '; the bell rung to remind the faithful to recite the prayer [L.].

anger (ang'gẹr) *n.* a strong passion or emotion excited by injury; rage;—*v.t.* to excite to wrath; to enrage.—**angry** (ang'gri) *a.* roused to anger; displeased; enraged; inflamed.—**ang'rily** *adv.*—**ang'riness** *n.* [O.N. *angr*, trouble].

Angevin (an'jẹ-vin) *a.* pert. to Anjou, an ancient province of France.

angina (an-jī'na, an'ji-na) *n.* (*Med.*) inflammation of the throat, e.g. quinsy.—**angina pectoris**, a heart disease characterised by attacks of agonising pain [L.].

angiosperm (an'ji-ō-spẹrm) *n.* (*Bot.*) a plant whose seeds are enclosed in a seed-vessel, e.g. the chestnut, as opposed to a *gymnosperm*, which bears naked seeds [Gk. *angeion*, a vessel; *sperma*, a seed].

angle (ang'gl) *n.* a fish-hook; a rod and line for fishing;—*v.i.* to fish with rod, line, and hook; (*Fig.*) to use artifice.—**ang'ler** *n.* one who angles.—**ang'ling** *n.* [O.E. *angul*].

angle (ang'gl) *n.* a corner; the point at which two lines meet; (*Geom.*) the amount of turning made by revolving a straight line in a plane, round a point in itself, from one direction to another; (*Fig.*) a point of view.—**ang'ular** *a.* having angles; forming an angle; pointed; stiff; formal.—**ang'ularly** *adv.*;—**angular'ity** *n.* —**acute angle**, one less than 90°.—**obtuse angle**, is greater than 90°, but less than 180°.—**right angle**, is a quarter of a complete revolution, i.e. 90° [L. *angulus*, a corner].

Angle (ang'gl) *n.* a member of a Teutonic tribe which, along with the Jutes and Saxons, invaded England in the 5th cent. and gave their name to this country.

Anglican (ang'gli-cạn) *a.* English; of, or belonging to, Church of England;—*n.* a member of Church of England.—**Ang'licanism** *n.* [L. *Angli*, the Angles].

anglice (ang'gli-sē) *adv.* in English; in plain terms; sometimes written **anglicé**, or **anglicè**. —**ang'licise** *v.t.* to make or express in English idiom.—**ang'licism** *n.* an English idiom; an English custom or characteristic.—**ang'lify** *v.t.* to make English [L. *Angli*, the Angles].

Anglo- (ang'glo) *prefix* fr. L. *Anglus*, an Angle, combining to form many compound words.—**Ang'lo-Amer'ican** *a.* involving English and Americans.—**Ang'lo-Cath'olic** *a.* belonging or pert. to a very ritualistic section of the Church of England;—*n.* a High-Churchman.—**Ang'lo-In'dian** *n.* a person whose father, or any male progenitor was of European descent, and who was born in India; earlier meaning, a native of Britain resident in India; often applied in India to one of mixed European and Asiatic parentage.—**Ang'lo-Sax'on** *a.* pert. to Anglo-Saxons or their language;—*n.* one of the nations formed by the union of the Angles, Saxons, and other early Teutonic settlers in Britain; one of the English race; the earliest form of the English language, now more correctly named Old English.—**Angloma'nia** *n.* excessive fondness for, or imitation of, everything English.—**Anglophile** (ang'glō-fil) *a.* favouring anything English;—*n.* a supporter of English customs, manners, or policy.—**Anglophobia** (ang-glō-fō'bi-ạ) *n.* an intense dislike or fear of England, or of what is English.—**Ang'lophobe** *n.*

Angora (ang-gō'rạ) *n.* a Turkish province in Asia Minor, famous for a breed of goats, whose long, white silky hair is used in the manufacture of mohair; cloth made from this hair.

angostura (ang-gos-tòó'rạ) *n.* an aromatic bark used as a febrifuge and tonic. Also **angustu'ra** [fr. *Angostura*, a town of Venezuela, now called *Ciudad Bolivar*].

anguish (ang'gwish) *n.* acute pain of body or of mind; grief; anxiety; moral torment.—**ang'uishment** *n.* [L. *angustia*, straitness].

angular (ang'gū-lạr) *a.* having angles; sharp-cornered; (of people) not plump; gawky; irascible.—**angular'ity** *n.*—**ang'ularly** *adv.*—**ang'ulate** *a.* having angles [L. *angulus*, a corner].

anhydride (an-hī'drīd) *n.* (*Chem.*) a compound formed from an acid by evaporation of water.—**anhy'drite** *n.* anhydrous sulphate of lime found in Austria.—**anhydro'sis** *n.* (*Med.*) a loss of sweat.—**anhy'drous** *a.* entirely without water [Gk. *an-*, neg.; *hudor*, water].

anil (an'il) *n.* a West Indian shrub from the leaves and stalks of which indigo is made.—**aniline** (an'il-īn) *n.* a product, orig. obtained from indigo, now got mainly from coal-tar, and used in the manufacture of brilliant dyes, coloured inks, soaps, explosives, etc. ;—*a.* pert. to anil or aniline [Fr. fr. Sans. *nila*, dark blue].

anile (an'īl) *a.* like an old woman; imbecile. —**anil'ity** *n.* senility [L. *anus*, an old woman].

animadvert (an-i-mad-vẹrt') *v.t.* to turn the mind to; to consider disparagingly; to comment on censoriously; to reprove,—**animadver'sion** *n.* [L. *animus*, the mind; *vertere*, to turn].

animal (an'i-mạl) *n.* a living creature having sensation and power of voluntary motion; a living organism, distinct from plants;—*a.* pert. to or got from animals.—**animal'cule** *n.* a very minute animal (*pl.* **animal'cules** or **animal'cula**)—**animal'culine** *a.* pert. to animalcula.—**animal magnetism**, mesmerism, hypnotism.—**animal spirits**, natural buoyancy [L. *anima*, breath].

animate (an'i-māt) *v.t.* to give natural life to; to endow with spirit or vigour; to energise; to inspire;—*a.* living or organic.—**an'imated** *a.* alive; spirited.—**an'imatedly** *adv.*—**an'imating** *a.* inspiring.—**an'imatingly** *adv.*—**anima'tion** *n.* the state of possessing life or spirit; vivacity.—**an'imator** *n.* one who or that which animates; a cinema cartoonist [L. *animatus*, filled with life].

animism (an'i-mizm) *n.* the belief that all forms of organic life have their origin in the soul.—**an'imist** *n.*—**animis'tic** *a.* [L. *anima*, life or soul].

animosity (an-i-mos'i-ti) *n.* violent hatred; active enmity; acrimony; orig. meant *courage* [L. *animosus*, full of spirit].

animus (an'i-mus) *n.* animosity; temper; grudge; (*Law*) intention, purpose [L. *animus*, spirit, temper].

anise (an'is) *n.* an umbelliferous plant with pungent smell, and bearing aromatic seeds. —**an'iseed** *n.* seed of anise used for flavouring and in manufacture of liqueurs [Gk. *anis*].

anker (ang'kẹr) *n.* a Dutch liquid measure,

at one time used in England, containing 8½ gallons; a keg containing this amount.

ankle (ang´kl) *n.* the joint connecting the foot with the leg.—**ank'let** *n.* an ornament, support, or fetter for the ankle [M.E. *ancle*].

anna (an´a) *n.* in the East Indies, a copper coin worth one-sixteenth of a rupee, i.e. about 1d. or 1⅓d. [Hind.].

annals (an´ạlz) *n.pl.* history of events recorded each year; a yearly chronicle.—**ann'alise** *v.t.* to write annals; to record chronologically.—**ann'alist** *n.* [L. *annus*, a year].

anneal (ạ-nēl') *v.t.* to heat, and then cool slowly, for the purpose of rendering less brittle; to heat in order to fix colours.—**anneal'ing** *n.* [O.E. *an*; *aelan*, to kindle].

annelid (an´e-lid) *n.* a class of red-blooded invertebrates which includes segmented worms found in earth, fresh and sea water [L. *annellus*, a small ring].

annex (ạ-neks') *v.t.* to unite at the end; to subjoin; to bind to; to take additional territory under control.—**annexa'tion** *n.* the taking over by one power of territory without consent of the other state ; what is annexed.—**annexa'tionist** *n.*—**annexe** (an´eks) *n.* something joined on; building attached to, or sufficiently near, main building to be considered part of it.—**annex'ion, annex'ment** *n.* [L. *ad*, to; *nectere*, to bind].

annihilate (ạ-nī´hil-āt) *v.t.* to reduce to nothing; to destroy; to make null and void.—**anni'hilable** *a.*—**annihila'tion** *n.*—**annihila'tor** *n.* [L. *ad*, to; *nihil*, nothing].

anniversary (an-i-vẹr´sạ-ri) *a.* yearly; annual; —*n.* day on which event is yearly celebrated [L. *annus*, year; *vertere*, to turn].

annotate (an´ō-tāt) *v.t.* to mark in writing; to write explanatory notes, esp. upon literary text.—**annota'tion** *n.* a written commentary. —**an'notator** *n.*—**annota'tory** *a.* [L. *annatotus*, marked with notes].

annotine (an´ō-tīn) *a.* one year old [L. *annotinus*, a year old].

announce (ạ-nouns') *v.t.* to give first public notice of; to proclaim; to promulgate; to publish.—**announce'ment** *n.* giving public notice; proclamation; declaration.—**announc'er** *n.* a broadcasting official who gives the news, etc. [L. *ad*, to; *nuntiare*, to announce].

annoy (ạ-noi') *v.t.* to injure, disturb continually; to torment; tease; vex; pester; molest; trouble.—**annoy'ance** *n.*—**annoy'ingly** *adv.* [fr. L. *in odio*, in hatred].

annual (an´ū-ạl) *a.* returning or happening every year; to be renewed each year; performed in the course of a year;—*n.* a periodical published once a year; plants which complete their life-cycle within a year.—**ann'ually** *adv.* [L. *annus*, a year].

annuity (ạ-nū´i-ti) *n.* a fixed sum of money payable each year for a number of years, or for life.—**annu'itant** *n.* one in receipt of an annuity [L. *annus*, a year].

annul (ạ-nul') *v.t.* to make void; to nullify; repeal; cancel;—*pr.p.* **annul'ling**; *pa.t.* and *pa.p.* **annulled'**.—**annul'ment** *n.* [L. *ad*, to; *nullus*, none].

annular (an´ū-lạr) *a.* ring-shaped; like a ring. —**ann'ulated,** *a.* having rings or belts.—**ann'ulet** *n.* a little ring.—**ann'ularly** *adv.*—**ann'ulose** *a.* ringed.—**annula'tion** *n.* ring-like formation [L. *annulus*, a ring].

annunciate (ạ-nun´shi-āt) *v.t.* to announce; to make known; to proclaim.—**annuncia'tion** *n.* an announcing; a festival (25th March) in memory of the angel's announcement to the Virgin Mary; Lady Day.—**annuncia'tor** *n.* —**annuncia'tory** *a.* [L. *ad*, to; *nuntiare*, to announce].

anode (an´ōd) *n.* positive electrode of a voltaic current; (*Radio*) plate in a thermionic valve to which high tension voltage is applied to collect electrons from filament [Gk. *anodos*, way up].

anodyne (an´ō-dīn) *n.* a drug or measures which procure relief from pain.—**anod'ynous** *a.* [Gk. *an-*, neg.; *odunē*, pain].

anoint (ạ-noint') *v.t.* to pour oil upon; to rub over with an ointment or oil; to consecrate by unction.—**anoin'ted** *a.* consecrated;—*n.* a consecrated person.—**anoint'ment** *n.* consecration; a salve.—**the Lord's anointed,** Christ [L. *in*, on; *ungere*, to anoint].

anomaly (ạ-nom´a-li) *n.* deviation from the common rule or type; irregularity;—*pl.* **anom'alies.**—**anom'alism** *n.* anomaly; irregularity.—**anomalis'tic** *a.* irregular.—**anom'alous** *a.* irregular; abnormal; incongruous.—**anom'alously** *adv.* [Gk. *anomalos*, not even].

anon (ạ-non') *adv.* quickly; at once; forthwith. —**ever and anon,** every now and then [O.E. *on*, in; *an*, one].

anonymous (ạ-non´i-mus) *a.* applied to a writing or work of which the author is not named.—**an'onym** *n.* one who remains anonymous.—**anon'ymously** *adv.*—**anonym'ity** *n.* [Gk. *an*,- neg; *onoma*, name].

anopheles (ạn-of´el-ēz) *n.* the mosquito carrying the parasite which causes malaria [Gk. *an-*, neg.; *ophelein*, benefit].

another (ạ-nuTH´ẹr) *a.* not the same; different; one more;—*pron.* any one else [E.].

anserine (an´se-rīn) *a.* pert. to a goose; silly [L. *anser*, a goose].

answer (an´sẹr) *v.t.* to speak or write in return; to vindicate; to witness for;—*v.i.* to reply; to suit; to suffer the consequence of;—*n.* something said or written in return to a question, etc.; the solution of a problem; response.—**an'swerable** *a.* capable of being answered; responsible.—**an'swerer** *n.*—**to answer for,** to be responsible for [O.E. *andswarian*, to swear back].

ant (ant) *n.* a small membranous-winged insect; applied also to nerve-winged white ant or termite though not a true ant; an emmet.—**ant'-bear** *n.* the great ant-eater of South America.—**ant'-eat'er** *n.* one of several edentate quadrupeds, e.g. ant-bear, aardvark, that feed chiefly on ants.—**ant'-egg** *n.* the egg, or larva of an ant, sold as food for goldfish.—**ant'-hill** *n.* a mound raised by a colony of ants or termites [O.E. *aemette*].

ant- (ant) a combining form fr. Gk. *anti*, against, used to form compounds.—**antacid** (ant-as´id) *a.* counteracting acidity;—*n.* a remedy for acidity of the stomach.—**antal'gic** *a.* alleviating pain;—*n.* an anodyne.

antagonise (an-tag´o-nīz) *v.t.* to contend violently against; to act in opposition; to oppose; to make hostile.—**antag'onism** *n.* opposition; hostility; hatred; dislike.—**antag'onist** *n.*—**antagonist'ic** *a.*—**antagonist'ically** *adv.* [Gk. *anti*, against; *agon*, a contest].

antarctic (ant-ärk´tic) *a.* opposite to arctic pole; relating to southern pole or region near it [Gk. *anti*, against; E. *arctic*].

ante (an´te) *n.* in poker, a player's stake [L. *ante*, before].

ante- (an´te) *prefix* fr. L. *ante*, meaning *before* (place, time, or order), combining to form derivatives.—**antecedent** (an-te-sēd´ent) *a.* going before in time, place, rank, etc.; preceding; prior;—*n.* that which goes before; (*Gram.*) the noun or pronoun to which a relative refers.—**an'techamber** *n.* a chamber leading to the chief apartment.—**an'tecursor** *n.* a forerunner [L. *cedere*, to go; *camera*, a room; *currere*, to run].

antedate (an´te-dāt) *v.t.* to date before the true time [L. *ante*, before; E. *date*].

antediluvian (an-te-di-lū´vi-ạn) *a.* pert. to before the Flood; ancient; antiquated [L. *ante*, before; *diluvium*, a flood].

antelope (an´te-lōp) *n.* a hoofed ruminant, notable for its graceful and agile movement [Gk. *antholops*].

antemeridian (an-te-mẹr-id´i-ạn) *a.* before noon (abbrev. a.m.) [L.=before midday, the period of time between midnight and noon].

antenatal (an-te-nā´tạl) *a.* pertaining to

period before birth [L. *ante*, before; *natus*, born].
antenna (an-ten′a) *n.* feeler of an insect, crustacean, etc.—*pl.* **antennae** (an-ten′ē).—**antenn'a** *n.* (*Wireless*) a wire for sending or receiving electric waves; an aerial.—*pl.* **antenn'as.**—**antenn'al, antenn'ary** *a.* [L. *antenna*, a sail-yard].
antenuptial (an-te-nup′shal) *a.* before marriage [L. *ante*, before; *nuptiae*, marriage].
antepenult (an-te-pe-nult′) *n.* last syllable but two of word.—**antepenult'imate** *a.* last but two [L. *ante*, before; *paene*, almost; *ultimus*, last].
anterior (an-tē′ri-or) *a.* before; occurring earlier.—**anterior'ity** *n.* [L. *ante*, before].
ante-room (an′te-ròòm) *n.* a room giving entry to another; [L. *ante*, before; E. *room*].
anthem (an′them) *n.* a hymn sung in alternate parts; any Church music adapted to passages from the Scriptures; any song of praise [Gk. *antiphonon*, a response sung].
anther (an′ther) *n.* the little sac in a flower, containing the pollen or fertilising dust.—**an'theral** *a.*—**antherif'erous** *a.* bearing anthers.—**an'theroid** *a.* resembling an anther [Gk. *antherōs*, flowery].
anthology (an-thol′o-ji) *n.* orig. a collection of flowers; a collection of literary passages or poetry.—**anthol'ogist** *n.* [Gk. *anthos*, a flower; *legein*, to gather].
anthracene (an′thra-sēn) *n.* product from distillation of coal-tar, used in manufacture of dyes.—**an'thracite** *n.* coal, nearly pure carbon, burning without smoke or flame [Gk. *anthrax*, coal].
anthrax (an′thrax) *n.* a carbuncle; a malignant disease in cattle and sheep, communicable to man; a malignant pustule [Gk. *anthrax*, coal].
anthropo- (an′thrō-pō) *prefix* fr. Gk. *anthropos*, meaning man, combining to form derivatives.—**anthropogeny** (-poj′en-i) *n.* science of development of man .—**anthropog'raphy** *n.* science that treats of geographical distribution of man.—**an'thropoid** *a.* man-like [Gk. *genesthai*, to be born; *graphein*, to write; *eidos*, form; *lithos*, a stone].
anthropology (an-thrō-pol′ō-ji) *n.* study of man, including all aspects of his evolution, physical and social.—**anthropolog'ical** *a.*—**anthropolog'ically** *adv.*—**anthropol'ogist** *n.* [Gk. *anthropos*, man; *logos*, discourse].
anthropometry (an-thrō-pom′e-tri) *n.* the scientific measurement of the human body.—**anthropomet'ric** *a.* [Gk. *anthropos*, man; *metron*, a measure].
anthropomorphism (an-thrō-pō-mor′fizm) *n.* the conception of God as a human being with human attributes.—**anthropomor'phist** *n.*—**anthropomor'phise** *v.t.* to invest with human qualities.—**anthropomor'phic** *a.* [Gk. *anthropos*, man; *morphe*, form].
anthropomorphosis (an-thrō-pō-mor-fō′sis, or -morf′ō-sis) *n.* transformation into human shape.—**anthropomor'phous** *a.* [Gk. *anthropos*, man; *morphé*, form].
anthropopathy (an-thrō-pop′a-thi) *n.* the ascription of human feelings and emotions to the Supreme Being [Gk. *anthropos*, man; *pathos*, feeling].
anti- (an′ti) *prefix* fr. Gk. *anti*, meaning *against, opposite, instead of*, combining to form derivatives; contracted to **ant-** before a vowel.—**an'ti-air'craft** *a.* used against aircraft.
antibiotic (an-ti-bī-ot′ik) *n.* substance (e.g. penicillin) elaborated by micro-organisms and acting as an antibacterial agent.—**antibio'sis** *n.* an association between organisms which is injurious to one of them [Gk. *anti*, against; *bios*, life].
antibody (an′ti-bod-i) *n.* a substance in blood which counteracts growth and harmful action of bacteria; anti-toxin.
antic (an′tik) *a.* odd; fanciful; fantastic; grotesque; —*n.* a buffoon; a comical trick or action [L. *antiquus*, old].
Antichrist (an′ti-krīst) *n.* a name given in the New Testament to various incarnations of opposition to Christ.
anticipate (an-tis′i-pāt) *v.t.* to be before another; to be beforehand in thought or action; to enjoy prematurely; to forestall.—**antic'ipant** *a.* anticipating; (*Med.*) occurring before the regular time.—**anticipa'tion** *n.* the act of anticipating.—**antic'ipative** *a.* full of expectation.—**antic'ipatively, antic'ipatorily** *adv.*—**antic'ipatory** *a.* happening in advance [L. *ante*, before; *capere*, to take].
anticlimax (an-ti-klī′maks) *n.* a sentence or figure of speech in which ideas are arranged in descending order of importance; opp. of *climax*; a sudden drop from the dignified to the trivial.
anticyclone (an′ti-sī′klōn) *n.* an outward flow of air in a spiral movement (clockwise in N. Hemisphere, anti-clockwise in S. Hemisphere) from an atmospheric area of high pressure, tending to produce steady weather, frosty in winter, hot in summer.
antidisestablishmentarianism (an′ti-dis-es tab-lish-ment-ār′i-an-izm) *n.* opposition to the movement to disestablish the Church.
antidote (an′ti-dōt) *n.* a remedy which counteracts the effects of a poison; (*Fig.*) anything which counteracts evil.—**an'tidotal** *a.* [Gk. *anti*, against; *doton*, given].
antifreeze (an-ti-frēz′) *n.* a substance added to water in motor car radiators to prevent freezing in very cold weather.
antigen (an′ti-jen) *n.* a substance, such as an anti-toxin, which can produce the formation of antibodies in the blood-stream [Gk. *anti*, against; *genesthai*, to be born].
antilogarithm (an-ti-log′a-rithm) *n.* the complement of a logarithm or of a sine, tangent, or secant; the number corresponding to a logarithm. (*Abbrev.*) **antilog.**
antilogy (an-til′o-ji) *n.* a contradiction in terms, or in two separate passages of a book.—**antil'ogous** *a.* [Gk. *logos*, a discourse].
antimacassar (an-ti-ma-kas′ar) *n.* an ornamental covering for chair backs, etc., to keep them from being soiled (by hair oil) [Gk. *Macassar oil* from Celebes].
antimony (an′ti-mon-i) *n.* a whitish, brittle chemical element; a bad conductor of heat, it is used as an alloy in medicine and the arts.—**antimon'ial** *a.*—**antimon'iate** *n.* a salt of antimonic acid.—**antimon'ic, antimon'ious** *a.* of or containing antimony.—**an'timonite** *n.* stibnite [L. *antimonium*, antimony].
antipathy (an-tip′a-thi) *n.* aversion; dislike; enmity; hatred.—**antipathet'ical** *a.*—**antipath'ic** *a.* hostile to; having an opposite nature.—**antip'athist** *n.* [Gk. *anti*, against; *pathos*, feeling].
antiphlogistic (an-ti-flō-jis′tik) *a.* counteracting inflammation; cooling;—*n.* anything that allays inflammation.
antiphon, antiphony (an′ti-fōn, -fon) (an-tif′ō-ni) *n.* the chant, or alternate singing, in choirs; an anthem; a response.—**antiph'onal** *a.*—*n.* a book of antiphons.—**antiph'onally** *adv.*—**antiphon'ic, antiphon'ical** *a.*—**antiphon'ically** *adv.* [doublet of *anthem*].
antiphrasis (an-tif′ra-sis) *n.* (*Rhet.*) use of words in a sense opposite to their proper meaning.—**antiphras'tic, antiphras'tical** *a.* pert. to antiphrasis.—**antiphras'tically** *adv.* [Gk. *anti*, against; *phrazein*, speak].
antipodes (an-tip′ō-dēz) *n.pl.* those living on opposite side of globe; regions directly opposite any given point on globe; (*Fig.*) anything diametrically opposed to anything else.—**antipodal, antipodean** (an-tip′ō-dal, an-tip-ō-dē′an) *a.* [Gk. *anti*, against; *pous*, a foot].
antipope (an′ti-pōp) *n.* one who usurps the papal office; rival to Pope properly elected by Cardinals.—**antipa'pal** *a.* opposing Pope or Popery.

antipyrin (an-ti-pī′rin) *n.* derivative of coal-tar products used to counteract fever or give relief in migraine, etc.—**antipyret′ic** *n.* any agent which lowers temperature in fevers; a febrifuge;—*a.* counteracting fever [Gk. *anti*, against; *puretos*, fever].

antique (an-tēk′) *a.* ancient; old-fashioned; obsolete; aged;—*n.* relic of bygone times; ancient work of art; the style of ancient art.—**antiqua′rian** *n.* student of antiquity or antiquities; a collector of relics of former times;—*a.* pert. to old times or objects; out-of-date; obsolete.—**antiquar′ianism** *n.* study of antiquities.—**an′tiquary** *n.* an antiquarian.—**an′tiquate** *v.t.* to render obsolete.—**an′tiquated** *a.* very old; out of date.—**antique′ly** *adv.*—**antique′ness** *n.* the condition of being antique.—**antiq′uity** *n.* ancient times; former ages; great age; the people of ancient times.—**antiq′uities**, *n.pl.* the remains and relics of ancient times; manners and customs of ancient times [Fr. fr. L. *antiquus*, ancient].

antirrhinum (an-tir-rī′num) *n.* the snap-dragon, a common flowering plant [Gk. *anti*, opposite; *rhis*, the nose].

antisabbatarian (an-ti-sa-ba-tār′i-ạn) *n.* one who refuses to acknowledge the strictness of the Jewish Sabbath as being applicable to the Christian Sabbath.

antiscorbutic (an-ti-skor-bū′tik) *n.* an agent which prevents or cures scurvy, e.g. lime juice, lemons;—*a.* opposed to scurvy.

anti-semitism (an-ti-sem′i-tizm) *n.* wide-spread outburst of hatred against members of the Hebrew race leading to persecution.—**antisem′ite** *n.* one animated with hatred against the Jews.—**anti-semit′ic** *a.*

antisepsis (an-ti-sep′sis) *n.* prevention of sepsis; destruction or arresting of growth of living micro-organisms which cause putrefaction.—**antisep′tic** *n.* a disinfectant; a substance which destroys bacteria;—*a.* [Gk. *anti*, against; *sepsis*, putrefaction].

anti-social (an-ti-sō′shạl) *a.* averse to social intercourse; opposed to social order.

antitheism (an-ti-thē′izm) *n.* opposition to the belief in the existence of God.—**antithe′ist** *n.*—**antitheist′ic** *a.*

antithesis (an-tith′e-sis) *n.* a direct opposition of words or ideas; a figure in rhetoric in which words or thoughts are set in contrast.—*pl.* **antith′eses**.—**antithet′ic**, **antithet′ical** *a.*—**antithet′ically** *adv.* [Gk. *anti*, opposite; *thesis*, placing].

antitoxin (an-ti-tox′in) *n.* a toxin which neutralises another toxin in the blood serum.—**antitox′ic** *a.* [Gk. *anti*, against; *toxikon*, arrow-poison].

antivivisection (an-ti-vi-vi-sek′shun) *n.* agitation against vivisection [Gk. *anti*, against].

antler (ant′lẹr) *n.* the annual horny outgrowth of the frontal bone found in male animals of the deer family and in female reindeer.—**ant′lered** *a.* furnished with antlers [L. *ante*, before; *oculus*, the eye].

antonomasia (an-ton-ō-mā′zi-ạ) *n.* a figure whereby an epithet or phrase stands for a proper name; or conversely, the use of a proper name to express a general idea [Gk. *anti*, against; *onoma*, a name].

antonym (an′tō-nim) *n.* a word of contrary meaning.—the opposite of *synonym* [Gk. *anti*, against; *onoma*, a name].

anus (ā′nus) *n.* the lower orifice of the alimentary canal [L.].

anvil (an′vil) *n.* an iron block, usually steel-faced, upon which blacksmith's forgings are hammered and shaped.—**an′villed** *a.* [O.E. *anfilte*].

anxiety (ang-zī′et-i) *n.* distress of mind; disquietude; uneasiness; eagerness (to serve, etc.).—**anxious** (angk′shus) *a.* uneasy; eager.—**an′xiously** *adv.*—**an′xiousness** *n.* [L. *anxius*, anxious].

any (en′i) *a.* one out of many; some;—*adv.* to any extent; at all.—**an′ybody** *n.* any person; an ordinary person.—**an′yhow** *adv.* at any rate; in a careless manner; in any case.—**an′ything** *n.* any one thing, no matter what.—**an′ywhere** *adv.* in any place [O.E. *an*, one].

Anzac (an′zak) *a.* (*World War* 1) pert. to the Australian and New Zealand expeditionary force;—*n.* a soldier of that army [fr. the initials of Australian and New Zealand Army Corps].

aorist (ā′ō-rist) *n.* (*Gram.*) a Greek tense expressing indefinite past time.—**aoris′tic** *a.* [Gk. *aoristos*, indefinite].

aorta (ā-or′tạ) *n.* the great artery leading from the left ventricle of the heart.—*pl.* **aortae** (ā-or′tē)—**aor′tal**, **aor′tic** *a.* [Gk. *aortē*].

apace (ạ-pās′) *adv.* at a quick pace; hastily; swiftly; fast [*a-* and *pace*, at a walk].

Apache (ạ-pȧ′chā) *n.* one of a tribe of N. American Indians.—**apache** (ạ-pȧsh′) *n.* a bandit of the Paris underworld; a street hooligan [Amer. Ind. *e patch*, an enemy].

apanage (ap′ạ-nāj) *n.* See **appanage**.

apart (ạ-pȧrt′) *adv.* separately; aside; asunder; at a distance [Fr. *à part*, aside].

apartheid (a-pȧrt′hād) *n.* word of Afrikaans origin to indicate a political, economic, cultural, spiritual and racial separateness, as apart from mere physical (or geographical) separateness.

apartment (ạ-part′ment) *n.* a room in a house;—*pl.* a suite of rooms; lodgings [Fr. *appartement*, a suite of rooms].

apathy (ap′ath-i) *n.* want of feeling; indifference.—**apathet′ic** *a.* void of feeling; indifferent; insensible; passionless.—**apathet′ically** *adv.* [Gk. *a-*, neg.; *pathos*, feeling].

ape (āp) *n.* a monkey, esp. one without a tail; one of the larger species, e.g. chimpanzee, gorilla, etc.; a mimic;—*v.t.* to imitate; to mimic.—**a′per** *n.* one who apes; a servile imitator.—**a′pery** *n.* an ape-house; mimicry.—**a′pish** *a.* ape-like; inclined to imitate in a foolish manner.—**a′pishly** *adv.*—**a′pishness** *n.* [O.E. *apa*].

apeak (ạ-pēk′) *adv.* (*Naut.*) in a vertical position, or nearly so [*a* and *peak*].

apepsia (ạ-pep′si-ạ) *n.* (*Med.*) indigestion; dyspepsia. Also **apep′sy** [Gk. *a-*, neg.; *peptein*, to digest].

aperient (a-pē′ri-ent) *a.* opening;—*n.* a laxative; a purgative.—**aperitif** (a-pā′rē-tēf) *n.* alcoholic drink taken before meals, to stimulate appetite [L. *aperire*, to open].

aperture (a′pẹr-tūr) *n.* an opening; a hole [L. *aperire*, to open].

apex (ā′peks) *n.* the top, peak, or summit of anything.—*pl.* **a′pexes** or **a′pices**.

aphasia (ạ-fā′zi-ạ) *n.* loss of power of expressing ideas in words, often due to brain disease; loss of power of remembering words.—**aphas′ic** *a.* [Gk. *a-*, neg.; *phasis*, speech].

aphelion (ạ-fē′li-on) *n.* point of planet's orbit most distant from sun.—*pl.* **aphe′lia** [Gk. *apo*, away; *hēlios*, the sun].

aphis (a′fis) *n.* a genus of lice, including the vine phylloxera, green-fly, etc., injurious to plant life.—*pl.* **aphides** (af′i-dēz).—**aphid′ian** *a.* and *n.* [etym. unknown].

aphonia, aphony (ạ-fō′ni-ạ, af′ō-ni) *n.* loss of voice [Gk. *a-*, neg.; *phōnē*, voice].

aphorism (af′or-izm) *n.* a pithy saying; a maxim.—**aphoris′tic** *a.*—**aphoris′tically** *adv.*—**aph′orise** *v.t.* and *i.* to make or use aphorisms.—**aph′oriser**, **aph′orist** *n.* [Gk. *aphorismos*, a definition].

aphrasia (ạ-frā′zi-ạ) *n.* inability to use connected language; speechlessness [Gk. *a-*, neg.; *phrasis*, speech].

Aphrodite (af-rō-dī′tē) *n.* (*Myth.*) the Greek goddess of love and beauty.—**aphrodisiac** (af-rō-diz′i-ak) *a.* exciting sexual desire;—*n.* anything which so excites, e.g. cantharidin.

apiary (ā′pi-ạr-i) *n.* place where bees are kept.—**apiarian** (ā-pi-ā′ri-ạn) *a.* pert. to bees or to bee-keeping.—**a′piarist** *n.* one who keeps or studies bees.—**a′piculture** *n.* bee-keeping [L. *apis*, a bee].

apiece (a-pēs) *adv.* for each one; to each one [orig. two words].
aplomb (a-plōng') *n.* perpendicularity; uprightness; (*Fig.*) self-assurance; coolness [L. *ad*, to; *plumbum*, lead].
apocalypse (a-pok'a-lips) *n.* an unveiling of hidden things; revelation; disclosure.—**Apoc'alypse** *n.* (*Bib.*) the last book of the New Testament, called the Revelation of St. John.—**apocalypt'ic(al)** pert. to revelation; of style, allegorical; obscure.—**apocalypt'ically** *adv.* [Gk. *apokalupsis*, unveiling].
apocrypha (a-pok'ri-fa) *n.pl.* originally, hidden or secret things not suitable to be seen by the uninitiated.—**Apoc'rypha** *n.pl.* (*Bib.*) the collective name for the fourteen books originally included in the Old Testament, and still incorporated in the Vulgate of the R.C. Church.—**apoc'ryphal** *a.* spurious; unauthentic; pert. to the Apocrypha [Gk. *apo*, away; *kruptein*, to hide].
apodosis (a-pod'o-sis) *n.* (*Gram.*) the clause, in a conditional sentence, which expresses result as distinct from the *protasis* [Gk. *apo*, back; *didonai*, to give].
apogee (ap'ō-jē) *n.* that point in the orbit of a heavenly body at the greatest distance from the earth (opposed to *perigee*); the culmination; climax; highest point; zenith.—**apogeal** (ap-ō-jē'al), **apog'ean** *a.* [Gk. *apo*, from; *gē*, the earth].
apologue (ap'o-log) *n.* a short story used to convey a moral truth; a parable; a fable [Gk. *apo*, from; *logos*, speech].
apology (a-pol'o-ji) *n.* something spoken in defence; expression of regret at offence; an excuse; a poor substitute (with for).—**apol'ogise** *v.i.* to make an apology, or excuse; to express regret.—**apol'ogist** *n.* one who makes an apology; a defender of a cause.—**apologet'ic** (a-pol-ō-jet'ik), **apologet'ical** *a.*—**apologet'ically** *adv.*—**apologet'ics** *n.* the branch of theology charged with the defence of Christianity.—**apolo'gia** *n.* a defence in writing of the author's principles, etc. [Gk. *apologia*, a speaking away].
apophthegm, apothegm (a'pō-them) *n.* a short, pithy, saying; a maxim; a proverb.—**apophthegmatic** (a-pō-theg-mat'ik), **apophthegmat'ical** *a.* [Gk. *apo*, from; *phthengesthai*, to utter].
apoplexy (ap'ō-plek-si) *n.* a sudden loss of consciousness, sensation, and voluntary motion, due generally to rupture of a blood-vessel in the brain.—**apoplec'tic** *a.* [Gk. *apoplēxia*].
apostasy, apostacy (a-pos'ta-si) *n.* the act of renouncing one's faith, principles, or party; desertion of a cause.—**apost'ate** *n.* renegade; traitor; deserter;—*a.* false; traitorous.—**apostat'ic(al)** *a.*—**apost'atise** *v.i.* to abandon one's faith [Gk. *apo*, apart; *stasis*, a standing].
apostle (a-pos'l) *n.* one sent out to preach or advocate a cause; one of the twelve disciples of Christ sent to preach the Gospel.—**apost'olate** *n.* the office or dignity or mission of an apostle.—**apostol'ic**, **apostol'ical** *a.*—**apostol'ically** *adv.*—**apostol'icism** *n.*—**Apostles' Creed**, creed supposedly used by apostles, summarising Christian faith.—**Apostolic Church**, church derived from, and incorporating the spirit of, the apostles.—**Apostolic see**, the jurisdiction of the Pope.—**Apostolic succession**, the derivation of spiritual authority in an unbroken line from the Apostles, through bishops [Gk. *apo*, away; *stellein*, to send].
apostrophe (a-pos'trō-fe) *n.* an address delivered to the absent or the dead, or to an inanimate thing, as if present; a mark (') indicating possessive case, or omission of one or more letters of a word.—**apostroph'ic** *a.*—**apos'trophise** *v.t.* and *i.* to address by, or to use, apostrophe [Gk. *apostrophē*, a turning away].
apothecary (a-poth'e-kar-i) *n.* one who prepares or sells drugs for medicines [Gk. *apothēkē*, a store house].
apothegm See **apophthegm.**
apotheosis (a-po-thē'ō-sis, or a-po-the-ō'sis) *n.* the act of raising a mortal to the rank of the gods; deification.—**apoth'eosise** *v.t.* to exalt to the dignity of a god [Gk. *apo*, apart; *theos*, a god].
appal (a-pawl') *v.t.* to overwhelm with sudden fear; to confound; to scare; to terrify;—*pr.p.* **appal'ling**;—*pa.p.* **appalled'**.—**appal'ling** *a.* shocking.—**appal'lingly** *adv.* [O.Fr. *apalir*, to make pale].
appanage, apanage (a'pan-āj) *n.* the granting of lands from Crown property to younger sons of the Royal house; a dependency; adjunct; attribute; perquisite—orig. a subsistence allowance for bread.—**ap'panaged** *a.*—**ap'panagist** *n.* [L. *ad*, to; *panis*, bread].
apparatus (ap-a-rā'tus) *n.* things provided as a means to an end; collection of implements or utensils for effecting an experiment, or given work [L. *ad*, to; *parare*, to prepare].
apparel (a-par'el) *n.* clothing; dress; garments; (*Naut.*) rigging, etc.;—*v.t.* to dress;—*pr.p.* **appar'elling, appar'eling'**—*pa.p.* **appar'el(l)ed** [O.Fr. *apareiller*, to dress].
apparent (a-pār'ent) *a.* visible; evident; obvious.—**appar'ently** *adv.*—**appar'entness** *n.* [L. *apparere*, to appear].
apparition (ap-a-rish'un) *n.* appearance (esp. inexplicable); spectre.—**appari'tional** *a.* [Fr. fr. L. *apparitio*, appearance].
appeal (a-pēl') *v.i.* to invoke; to call to witness; to solicit aid; (*Law*) to reopen a case before a higher court; to be pleasing to mind or senses.—*pr.p.* **appeal'ing**;—*pa.p.* **appealed'**;—*n.* an urgent call for sympathy or aid; personal attraction.—**appeal'able, appeal'ing** *a.*—**appeal'ingly** *adv.*—**appeal'ingness** *n.* [O.Fr. *apeler*, to call].
appear (a-pēr') *v.i.* to come in sight; to become visible; to seem; to be obvious or manifest.—**appear'ance** *n.* a coming in sight; semblance; outward look or show; likeness; personal presence.—**appear'er** *n.* one who puts in an appearance [L. *apparere*, to appear].
appease (a-pēz') *v.t.* to quiet; to calm; to pacify; to satisfy (hunger, etc.); to dispel anger or hatred.—**appeas'able** *a.*—**appease'ment** *n.* pacifying; policy of making substantial concessions in order to preserve peace.—**appeas'er** *n.*—**appeas'ive** *a.* having power to appease [Fr. *apaiser*; O.Fr. *a pais*, at peace].
appellant (a-pel'ant) *n.* (*Law*) one who appeals to a higher court against the verdict of a lower tribunal; one who makes any appeal. **appell'ancy**, *n.* an appeal.—**appell'ate** *a.* (*Law*) pert. to appeals; having power to hear and give decision on appeals.—**appella'tion** *n.* name; title; designation.—**appella'tional** *a.*—**appell'ative** *a.* naming; common to many; pert. to the common noun;—*n.* *common* noun as distinct from *proper* noun.—**appell'atively** *adv.*—**appellee** *n.* (*Law*) the defendant in an appeal [L. *appellare*, to call].
append (a-pend') *v.t.* to hang or attach to; to add.—**append'age** *n.* something added.—**append'ant** *n.* an adjunct or unessential thing;—*a.* hanging to; annexed [L. *appendere*, to hang on].
appendicitis (a-pen-di-sī'tis) *n.* (*Path.*) inflammation of the appendix vermiformis [fr. *appendix*].
appendicle (a-pen'di-kl) *n.* a small appendage.—**appendic'ular** *a.* [L. *appendicula*].
appendix (a-pen'diks) *n.* thing added; an adjunct; supplement at end of book; (*Med.*) the blind tube extending from caecum into pelvis.—*pl.* **appen'dixes, appen'dices** [L. *ad*, to; *pendere*, to hang].
apperception (ap-er-sep'shun) *n.* (*Philos.*) an act of voluntary consciousness; a mental perception of self as a conscious agent; spontaneous thought [L. *ad*, to; *percipere*, *perceptum*, to perceive].
appertain (ap-er-tān') *v.i.* to belong by

nature; to relate.—**appertain'ing** *a.*—**appertain'ment** *n.*—**apper'tinent** *a.* belonging to [L. *ad*, to; *pertinere*, to belong].

appetite (ap′e-tīt) *n.* desire as for food, drink, rest, etc.—**appet'itive** *a.*—**ap'petise** *v.t.* to create an appetite.—**appetis'er** *n.* something taken before a meal to create appetite.—**appetis'ing** *a.* [L. *ad*, to; *petere*, to seek].

applaud (a̧-plawd′) *v.t.* and *v.i.* to praise by clapping; to acclaim; commend; extol.—**applaud'er** *n.*—**applause'** *n.* approval publicly expressed [L. *ad*, to; *plaudere*, to clap].

apple (ap′l) *n.* fruit of the apple-tree; the apple-tree.—**ap'ple-faced, ap'ple-cheeked** *a.* of rosy hue; chubby.—**apple-pie order,** perfect order.—**ap'ple-sauce** *n.* (*slang*) flattery [O.E. *aeppel*].

appliance See under **apply.**

applicant (ap′li-ka̧nt) *n.* one who applies; a candidate; a petitioner.—**applicabil'ity** *n.* the quality of being suitable.—**ap'plicable** *a.* suitable; adapted.—**ap'plicableness** *n.*—**ap'plicably** *adv.*—**ap'plicate** *a.* applied or put to some use.—**applica'tion** *n.* the act of applying; the thing applied; close attention.—**ap'plicative** *a.* may be applied; useful.—**ap'plicatory** *a.* [L. *applicare*, to attach to].

applied (a-plīd′) *pa.p.* and *pa.t.* of **apply.**

appliqué (ap-lē-kā′) *n.* any ornamentation, sewn or fixed on a material or metal [Fr.].

apply (a̧-plī′) *v.t.* to place one thing upon another; to employ for a particular purpose; to fix the attention upon; to administer a remedy;—*v.i.* to agree with; to be relevant; to have recourse to; to become a candidate.—**appli'ance** *n.* act of applying; thing applied; an instrument or tool [L. *ad*, to; *plicare*, to fold].

appoint (a̧-point′) *v.t.* to set apart; to assign; to ordain; to decree; to designate for an office; to fix (a date); to equip.—**appoint'ed** *a.* established, furnished.—**appoint'ee** *n.* the person appointed.—**appoint'ment** *n.* act of appointing; a new situation or post.—**appoint'ments** *n.pl.* equipments; furnishings; fittings. [Fr. *à point*, fitly].

apport (ap′or) *n.* in spiritualism, alleged moving of material objects without material agency [Fr. from *apporter*, to bring to].

apportion (a̧-pōr′shun) *v.t.* to divide and share in just proportion.—**appor'tionment** *n.* [L. *ad*, to; *portio*, a share].

apposite (ap′ō-zit) *a.* appropriate; well adapted.—**ap'positely** *adv.*—**ap'positeness** *n.*—**apposition** (ap-ō-zish′un) *n.* the act of placing beside; (*Gram.*) the relation to a noun (or pronoun) of a noun, adjective, or clause, added by way of explanation.—**apposi'tional** *a.* [L. *appositus*, put near].

appraise (a̧-prāz′) *v.t.* to put a price upon; to fix the value of.—**apprais'al** *n.* the act of appraising; a valuation.—**appraise'ment** *n.*—**apprais'er** *n.* [L. *ad*, to; *pretium*, price].

appreciate (a̧-prē′shi-āt) *v.t.* to value justly —*v.i.* to rise in value.—**appreciation** (a̧-prē-shi-ā′shun) *n.* the setting of a value on; a just estimate; rise in value.—**appre'ciative, appre'ciatory** *a.*—**appre'ciatively** *adv.*—**appre'ciable** *a.* that may be estimated.—**appre'ciably** *adv.* [L. *ad*, to; *pretium*, price].

apprehend (ap-re-hend′) *v.t.* to seize; to arrest; to understand; to fear.—**apprehens'ible** *a.*—**apprehen'sion** *n.*—**apprehen'sive** *a.* filled with dread; suspicious.—**apprehen'sively** *adv.*—**apprehen'siveness** *n.* [L. *ad*, to; *prehendere*, to grasp].

apprentice (a̧-pren′tis) *n.* one bound to another to learn a trade or art; beginner;—*v.t.* to bind as apprentice.—**appren'ticeship** *n.* [L. *ad*, to; *prehendere*, to grasp].

apprise (a̧-prīz) *v.t.* to inform; to tell; to give notice [Fr. *apprendre*, to inform].

approach (a̧-prōch′) *v.i.* to come near;—*v.t.* to come near to; to enter into negotiations with; to resemble; (*Golf*) to play a shot intended to reach the green;—*n.* the act of drawing near; access; a road; approximation; negotiation.—**approach'es** *n. pl.* the works thrown up by besiegers in their advances towards a fortress.—**approach'able** *a.* accessible.—**approachabil'ity** *n.* [L. *ad*, to; *prope*, near].

approbation (ap-rō-bā′shun) *n.* approval; sanction.—**ap'probate** *v.t.* to approve of.—**ap'probative, ap'probatory** *a.* approving [L. *ad*, to; *probare*, to test].

appropriate (a̧-prō′pri-āt) *v.t.* to take as one's own; to set apart for a particular purpose; to claim;—*a.* suitable; fitting.—**appro'priately** *adv.*—**appro'priateness** *n.*—**appropria'tion** *n.* the act of setting apart.—**appro'priative** *a.*—**appro'priator** *n.* [L. *ad*, to; *proprius*, one's own].

approve (a̧-prȯȯv′) *v.t.* to be pleased with; to commend; to accept; to sanction officially.—**approv'al** *n.* the act of approving. [L. *ad*, to; *probare*, to test].

approximate (a̧-prok′si′māt) *v.t.* to come near to; to bring near;—*a.* near to; nearly correct; not quite exact.—**approx'imately** *adv.*—**approxima'tion** *n.* a coming near; a close estimate [L. *ad*, to; *proximus*, near].

appurtenance (a̧-pur′te-na̧ns) *n.* that which appertains or is annexed to another thing; adjunct; accessory.—**appur'tenant** *a.* [O.Fr. *apartenance*, a belonging].

apricot (ā′pri-kot) *n.* an oval, orange-yellow fruit like a plum, but resembling a peach in taste [L. *praecox*, early ripe].

April (ā′pril) *n.* the fourth month of the year. —**April fool,** one who is the victim of a playful hoax on 1st April (All Fools' Day) [L. *Aprilis*, fr. *aperire*, to open].

apron (ā′pron) *n.* a covering or protection worn in front to protect the clothes; concrete-surfaced area in front of hangar of aerodrome. —**apron stage,** a theatre stage, with a movable extension jutting out into auditorium [O.Fr. *naperon*, a cloth].

apse (aps) *n.* semi-circular recess at east end of church.—**ap'sidal** *a.* [Gk. *hapsis*, loop].

apsis (ap′sis) *n.* the point at which a planet is nearest to, or farthest from, the sun.—*pl.* **apsides** (ap′si-dēz).—**ap'sidal** *a.* [Gk. *hapsis*, a loop, a vault].

apt (apt) *a.* fit; suitable; prompt; quick-witted.—**apt'ly** *adv.*—**ap'titude** *n.* natural capacity for; suitableness; faculty for learning; talent.—**apt'ness** *n.* fitness; appropriateness [L. *aptus*, fit].

apteral (ap′ter-a̧l) *a.* without wings; (*Archit.*) having no lateral columns.—**ap'terous** *a.* (*Zool.*) wingless.—**ap'teryx** *n.* the kiwi [Gk. *a-*, neg.; *pteron*, a wing].

aqua (ā′kwa̧, ak′wa̧) *n.* L.=water.—**aqua fortis** *n.* 'strong water', nitric acid, esp. as used by etchers and engravers.—**aquafor'tist** *n.* etcher who uses aqua fortis.—**aqua pura,** pure water. —**aqua vitae,** 'water of life', any distilled alcoholic liquor, esp. brandy or whisky.

aquamarine (ak-wa̧-ma̧-rēn′, ā-kwa̧′ma̧-rēn′) *n.* a semi-precious stone, the sea-green coloured beryl;—*a.* of a sea-green colour [L. *aqua*, water; *mare*, the sea].

aquaplane (ak′wa̧-plān) *n.* a plank or boat towed by a fast motor-boat [L. *aqua*, water; *planus*, flat].

aquarium (a̧-kwā′ri-um) *n.* a glass tank in which is kept living specimens of water animals and plants.—*pl.* **aqua'riums,** or **aqua'ria** [L. *aqua*, water].

Aquarius (a̧-kwā′ri-us) *n.* (*Astron.*) the Waterbearer, the 11th sign of the Zodiac which the sun enters about 20th Jan.

aquatic (a̧-kwat′ik) *a.* growing or living in water; of sports, practised on, or in, water [L. *aqua*, water].

aquatint (ak′wa-tint, ā′kwa̧-tint) *n.* an etching process by which engravings, resembling Indian-ink drawings, are produced;—*v.i.* [L. *aqua*, water, and *tint*].

aqueduct (ak′we-dukt) *n.* a course, channel, or bridge for conveying water either under or above ground [L. *aqua*, water; *ducere*, to lead].

aqueous (ā´kwe-us) *a.* watery; made of, or from, water.—**a'queously** *adv.*—**aquiferous** (a-kwif´e-rus) *a.* conveying water, as the canals of sponges and many molluscs.—**aquiform** (ak´wi-form) *a.* in the form of water (L. *aqua*, water; *ferre*, to bear].

aquiline (ak´wi-lin, -līn) *a.* belonging to the eagle; curving; hooked like the beak of an eagle [L. *aquila*, an eagle].

Arab (ar´ab) *n.* native of Arabia; an Arab horse.—**street arab**, a homeless urchin of the streets.—**Arab'ian** *n.* native of Arabia;—*a.* relating to Arabia.—**Ar'abic** *n.* the language of the Arabians.—**gum arabic**, resinous gum from a kind of acacia plant.

arabesque (ar-a-besk') *n.* an ornament after the Arabian manner, with intricate interlacing of foliage, fruits, etc.;—*a.* **ar'abesqued** [It. *Arabesco*, Arabian-like].

arable (ar´ a-bl) *a.* fit for ploughing or tillage; cultivable [L. *arāre*, to plough].

Arachis (ar´a-kis) *n.* a genus of plants to which the ground nut belongs. [Gk. *arachos*, wild vetch].

arachnid (a-rak´nid) *n.* one of the *Arachnida*, the spiders, scorpions, mites, etc.—**arach'noid** *a.* resembling *Arachnida*; cobweb-like.—**arachnoid'al** *a.* [Gk. *arachnē*, a spider].

araucaria (ar-aw-kā´ri-a) *n.* a genus of cone-bearing trees, including the monkey-puzzle [*Araucanos*, a tribe of Indians in Chile].

arbalist (ar´ba-list) *n.* a powerful type of crossbow. Also **ar'balest, ar'blast.**—**ar'balister, ar'balester** *n.* crossbow man [L. *arcus*, a bow; *ballista*, an engine for throwing large missiles].

arbiter (år´bi-ter) *n.* (*fem.* **ar'bitress**) an umpire; a judge in a dispute; one who has supreme control.—**ar'bitrable** *a.* capable of settlement by discussion.—**ar'bitrage** *n.*—**arbit'rament** *n.* decision; authoritative judgment; award of arbitration.—**ar'bitrary** *a.* guided by will only; high-handed; despotic; absolute.—**ar'bitrarily** *adv.*—**ar'bitrariness** *n.*—**ar'bitrate** *v.t.* and *v.i.* to hear and give an authoritative decision in a dispute.—**arbitra'tion** *n.* a method of settling disputes between persons, parties and nations by an agreement on both sides to accept the findings of a third party.—**ar'bitrator** *n.* (*fem.* **ar'bitratrix**) a referee; an umpire. [L. *arbiter*, a judge].

arbor (år´bor) *n.* the Latin word for a *tree*.—**arbora'ceous** *a.* tree-like; wooded.—**arbor'eal** *a.* living in trees.—**arbor'eous** *a.* wooded.—**arboresc'ent** *a.* growing like a tree.—**arbore'tum** *n.* botanical garden for special planting and growing of trees.—(*pl.* **arbore'ta**).—**arboricul'ture** *n.* scientific cultivation of trees; forestry.—**ar'boriculturist** *n.*—**ar'borous** *a.* formed by trees [L. *arbor*, a tree].

arbour (år´bur) *n.* a garden seat sheltered or enclosed by trees; a bower; a shady retreat [L. *arbor*, a tree].

arbutus, arbute (år-bū´tus, år´būt) *n.* evergreen shrub with scarlet berries of strawberry type [L. *arbutus*, the wild strawberry tree].

arc (ark) *n.* a curved line or any part of a curve forming segment of a circle; the arc-shaped band of light formed by passage of an electric current between two carbon points.—**arc'-lamp**, *n.* an electric lamp making use of electric arc, used in spotlights, searchlights, etc.—**arc'-weld'ing**, *n.* a method of joining metals by use of electric arc [L. *arcus*, bow].

arcade (år-kād') *n.* a series of arches, generally supported by pillars; a walk, arched above; a covered street, usually with shops on both sides [L. *arcus*, bow].

Arcadia (år-kā´di-a) *n.* region in the Peloponnesus conceived by poets to be a land of shepherds and shepherdesses.—**Arcad'ian** *a.* simple; ideally rustic; innocent.—**Ar'cady** *n.* an ideal rustic place.

arcanum (år-kā´num) *n.* a secret; mystery (**arcan'a** *pl.*) [L. *arcanum*, secret].

arch (årch) *a.* cunning; sly; mischievous; roguish.—**arch'ly** *adv.*—**arch'ness** *n.* [Gk. *archein*, to rule].

arch (årch, årk) *prefix* used as *a.* chief; first of a class, as in *arch-bishop*, etc.—**archan'gel** *n.* an angel of supreme order.—**archbish'op** *n.* a chief bishop in a Church province.—**archdea'con** *n.* a Church dignitary next below bishop.—**archdea'conate** *n.* jurisdiction of an archdeacon.—**archdea'conship** *n.* office of an archdeacon.—**archduke'** *n.* a grand duke; son of Emperor of Austria.—**archduch'ess** *n.*—**arch'duch'y** *n.* the territory of an archduke.—**archdu'cal** *a.* [Gk. *archein*, to rule].

arch (årch) *n.* an arc of a circle; a structure of stone, brickwork, or steel ribs in the form of an arc, over an open space or river, whereby a load is supported equally at all points and designed to sustain a super-incumbent load;—*v.t.* or *v.i.* to form an arch; to bend into an arch.—**arched** *a.* in the form of an arch; containing arches.—**arch'way** *n.* arched passage into a castle or courtyard [L. *arca*, a chest, and *arcus*, a bow].

archaean (år-kē´an) *a.* pert. to the oldest period of geological time [Gk. *archaios*, ancient].

archaeology (år-kē-ol´o-ji) *n.* the study of human antiquities [Gk. *archaios*, ancient; *logos*, a discourse].

archaic, archaical (år-kā´ik, -al) *a.* antiquated; ancient; antique; obsolete; primitive.—**archa'ically** *adv.*—**ar'chaism** *n.* a word, expression or idiom out of date.—**ar'chaist** *n.* an antiquary; one who revives the use of archaisms in his writings.—**archais'tic** *a.* [Gk. *archaios*, ancient].

archeion (ark´ī-on) *n.* sanctuary; a building where archives are kept [Gk.].

archer (årch´er) *n.* one who shoots with a bow; a bowman [L. *arcus*, a bow].

archetype (år´kē-tīp) *n.* the original pattern or model from which a thing is made or copied; prototype.—**archetyp'al** *a.* [Gk. *archi-*, chief; *tupos*, a model].

archidiaconal (ark-i-dī-ak´on-al) *a.* pert. to an archdeacon.

archiepiscopacy (årk-i-e-pis´ko-pas-i) *n.* the office or jurisdiction of an archbishop. Also **archiepis'copate.**—**archiepis'copal**, *a.*

Archimedean (årk-i-mē´dē-an) *a.* pert. to the celebrated mathematician of antiquity, *Archimedes* of Syracuse (287-212 B.C.).

archipelago (år-ki-pel´a-gō) *n.* name originally of Aegean Sea; a group of islands; a stretch of water scattered with isles.—*pl.* **archipel'agoes.**—**archipelag'ic** (-aj´ik) *a.* [Gk. *archi-*, chief; *pelagos*, the sea].

architect (år´ki-tekt) *n.* one skilled in the art of building; designer or contriver.—**architecton'ics** *n.pl.* the science or art of architecture.—**architect'ural** *a.*—**architect'urally** *adv.*—**architect'ure** *n.* the art of building; a distinct style of designing buildings [Gk. *archi-*, chief; *tekton*, worker].

architrave (år´ki-trāv) *n.* (*Archit.*) epistyle; the lower division of an entablature, which rests the chief beam of a building on the column; the ornamental band of mouldings running round a door or window opening [Gk. *archi-*, chief; L. *trabs*, a beam].

archives (år´kīvz) *n.pl.* place in which public or historical records, charters and documents are stored and preserved; public records.—**archi'val** *a.*—**ar'chivist** *n.* a keeper of archives [Gk. *archeion*, a town-hall].

archon (årk´on) *n.* one of the nine chief magistrates in Ancient Athens.—**arch'onship** *n.*—**arch'ontate** *n.* duration in office as an archon [Gk. *archon*, ruler].

arctic (årk´tik) *a.* pert. to the regions near the N. Pole; northern; extremely cold; frigid [Gk. *arktos*, a bear].

arcuate (år´kū-āt) *a.* bent like a bow. Also **ar'cuated.**
ardent (år-dent) *a.* burning; passionate; eager. —**ar'dently** *adv.*—**ar'dency** *n.* warmth of passion; zeal.—**ardour** (år´dẹr) *n.* heat; warmth of affection; eagerness; enthusiasm; zeal [L. *ardere,* to burn].
Ardil (ar´dil) *n.* a wool-like textile fibre manufactured from groundnuts [made at *Ardeer,* Scotland.—Protected Trade Name].
arduous (år´dū-us) *a.* high and lofty; steep; difficult to overcome; laborious; strenuous. —**ar'duously** *adv.* [L. *arduus,* steep].
are (år) present indicative plural of the verb **to be** [O.E. *aron*].
are (ar) *n.* the French unit of land measure containing 100 square metres, about 119.6 square yards [Fr. fr. L. *area*].
area (ā´re-ạ) *n.* an open space; a tract of land; a region; scope; a sunken yard round basement of building; superficial extent [L. *area,* open space].
areca (ar´ē-kạ) *n.* a genus of plants of the palm family, including the betel-nut palm and the cabbage palm [Native].
arefaction (ar-e-fak´shun) *n.* the act of drying; dryness.—**arefy** (ar´e-fī) *v.t.* and *i.* to dry up [L. *arefacere,* to make dry].
arena (ạ-rē´nạ) *n.* the sand-strewn central space of a Roman amphitheatre, in which the gladiators fought; any place of public contest; a battlefield.—**arenaceous** (ar-e-nā'-shus) *a.* like sand; sandy [L. *arena,* sand].
areometer (ā-re-om´e-tẹr) *n.* an instrument for measuring the specific gravity of fluids [Gk. *araios,* rare; *metron,* a measure].
arete (a-ret') *n.* a sharp mountain ridge; a rocky spur [Fr.=a fish-bone].
argent (ar´jent) *a.* made of, or like, silver; silvery;—*n.* white or silver colour in heraldry. —**argentif'erous** *a.* bearing silver.—**ar'gentine** *a.* pert. to, or like, silver; sounding like silver; —*n.* a variety of carbonate of lime, having a silvery-white lustre; white metal coated with silver.—**ar'gentite** *n.* natural silver sulphide, an ore of silver [L. *argentum,* silver].
argil (ar´jil) *n.* pure clay; potters' earth.—**argillaceous** (år-ji-lā´shus) *a.* like clay; clayey. —**argillif'erous** *a.* producing clay [L. *argilla,* white clay].
argillo- (år-jil´ō) a combining form fr. L. *argilla,* meaning *clay,* found in compound words;—**argill'o-arena'ceous** *a.* consisting of clay and sand.—**argill'o-calca'reous** *a.* consisting of clay and lime.
argon (år´gon) *n.* an inert gas used for filling electric light bulbs [Gk. *argos,* inactive].
Argonaut (år´gō-nawt) *n.* (*Myth.*) one of the band of heroes who sailed in the *Argo* in quest of the Golden Fleece.—**Argonaut'ic** *a.* [Gk. *Argo,* and *nautēs,* a sailor].
argosy (år´go-si) *n.* a large, richly-laden merchant ship [earlier *ragusye,* a ship of *Ragusa,* a Dalmatian port].
argot (år´gō, år´got) *n.* orig. the slang used as a kind of secret language by thieves in France; slang; cant [Fr.].
argue (år´gū) *v.t.* to prove by reasoning; to discuss; to persuade by debate;—*v.i.* to prove; to offer reasons; to dispute;—**arg'uable** *a.* capable of being argued.—**arg'uer** *n.* one who argues.—**arg'ument** *n.* a reason offered in proof for or against a thing; the subject of a speech, etc.—**argumenta'tion** *n.* arguing, reasoning.—**argument'ative** *a.* given to arguing; contentious.—**argument'atively** *adv.*—**argument'ativeness** *n.* [L. *arguere,* to chide].
Argus (år´gus) *n.* (*Myth.*) a fabulous creature with a hundred eyes; hence, an ever-watchful person; a faithful guardian.
aria (å´ri-ạ, ā´ri-ạ) *n.* (*Mus.*) a melody as distinct from harmony; a solo part in a cantata, opera, oratorio, etc., with musical accompaniment.—**ariet'ta, ariette'** *n.* a short air or song [It. *aria,* an air].
Arian (ā´ri-ạn) *a.* pert. to *Arius* of Alexandria (A.D. 280-336), who denied Christ's divinity; —*n.* a follower of Arius.—**A'rianism** *n.* the heretical doctrine of the Arians.
arid (ar´id) *a.* dry; parched; barren; (*Fig.*) uninteresting.—**arid'ity** *n.* absence of moisture; dryness; barrenness [L. *aridus*].
aright (ạ-rīt') *adv.* rightly [E. *on right*].
arise (ạ-rīz') *v.t.* to come up; to stand up; to get up; to come into view; to spring up; to occur;—*pr.p.* **aris'ing.**—*pa.p.* **arisen** (ạ-rizn'). —*pa.t.* **arose'** [O.E. *arisan*].
aristocracy (ar-is-tok´rạ-si) *n.* originally the rule of the best; later, the rule of an hereditary upper class; privileged class in a state; the nobility; upper classes.—**aristocrat** (a-ris´to-krat, or ar´ist-ō-krat) *n.* a member of the aristocracy.—**aristocrat'ic** *a.*—**aristocrat'ically** *adv.*—**aristoc'ratism** *n.* [Gk. *aristos,* best; *kratos,* power].
Aristotle (ar-is-tot´l) *n.* (384-322 B.C.), a great Greek philosopher, pupil and disciple of Plato. —**Aristotelian** (ar-is-tō-tē´li-ạn) *a.* pert. to Aristotle, his works, or his disciples.—*n.* a follower of Aristotle.
arithmetic (ạ-rith´met-ik) *n.* the science of numbers; the art of reckoning by figures; a work on this subject.—**arithmet'ical** *a.*—**arithmet'ically** *adv.*—**arithmetician** (ạ-rith-mẹ-tish´ạn) *n.* one skilled in arithmetic.—**arithmetical progression,** a series of numbers which increase or decrease by a common difference, e.g. 2, 4, 6, 8, or 21, 18, 15, 12 [Gk. *arithmos,* number].
ark (årk) *n.* the large floating vessel in which Noah lived during the Flood (Genesis 6-8); vessel of bulrushes in which the infant Moses was placed (Exodus 2)—**ark of the Covenant,** the chest containing the two Tables of the Law, a pot of manna, and Aaron's rod (Exodus 25); a chest; a coffer [O.E. *arc,* a box].
arles (år´lz) *n.* in Scotland and N. England, earnest-money given as a token that a bargain has been confirmed. Also **earles'-penn'y** [L. *arrha,* earnest-money].
arm (årm) *n.* the limb extending from shoulders to hand; anything projecting from main body, as a branch;—*v.t.* to give an arm to for support.—**arm'less** *a.* without arms.—**arm'ful** *n.* as much as the arms can hold of anything.—**arm'-chair** *n.* a chair with arms.—**arm'let** *n.* a small arm, as of the sea; a bracelet; a band round the arm, often as official badge.—**arm'-pit** *n.* the cavity under the shoulder.—**at arm's length,** at a safe distance. —**with open arms,** cordially [O.E. *earm*].
arm (årm) *n.* a weapon; a branch of the army, e.g. infantry, artillery, etc.;—*pl.* all weapons; war; warlike; exploits; military profession; armour; heraldic bearings;—*v.t.* to equip with weapons;—*v.i.* to take up arms.—**armed** (armd, or arm'-ed) *a.* equipped with, or supported by, arms; fortified; strengthened.—**armed neutrality,** the condition of holding aloof from a contest, while ready to repel attack.—**small arms,** weapons that can be carried by hand, e.g. pistols, revolvers, shotguns, rifles, etc.—**under arms,** enlisted for military service; fully equipped for battle.—**up in arms,** eager to give battle; roused to anger.—**to lay down arms,** to surrender [L. *arma,* weapons].
armada (år-mā´dạ, år-må´dạ) *n.* a fleet of armed ships [Sp. *armar,* to arm].
armadillo (år-mạ-dil´ō) *n.* an animal, having the body encased in armour-like covering of small, bony shell plates [Sp. dimin. of *armado* a man-in-armour].
Armageddon (ar-ma-ged´on) *n.* the scene of the last battle between the powers of good and evil, before Day of Judgment; final decisive battle between great nations. [Origin doubtful; may be from *Megiddo,* in Palestine, scene of many battles (Rev. 19).]
armament (år´ma-ment) *n.* land, naval, or

Mosaic in Galla Placidia, Ravenna

EUROPEAN ART pre 1400

Giotto: The Betrayal

Miniature, St Louis Psalter (1256)

Purse clasp, Sutton Hoo treasure

Memlinc: detail, Shepherds receiving news of the birth of Christ (1480)

ART 15th and 16th Centuries

Fra Filippo Lippi: detail, Madonna painting

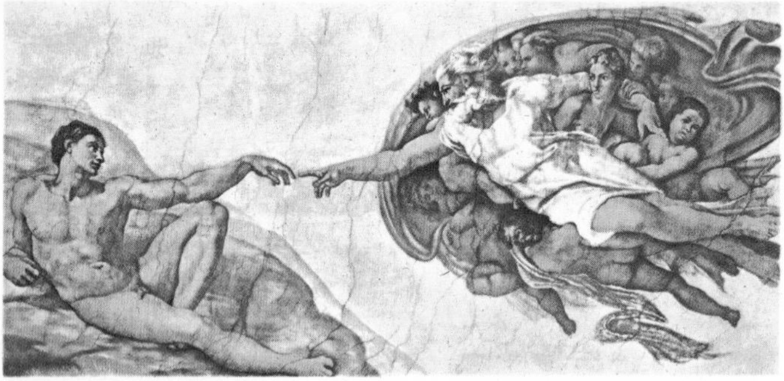

Michelangelo: Creation of Adam

Leonardo da Vinci: Self portrait

A. Dürer: Maximilian I (1519)

air forces equipped for war; the munitions of a ship of war, esp. guns, torpedoes, etc.; the process of equipping forces in time of war [L. pl. *armamenta*, equipment].

armature (år′ma-tūr) *n.* armour; protective covering (of plants); the 'keeper' of a horse-shoe magnet; part of magnet or dynamo which rotates in electrical generator; coil of wire in electric motor which breaks magnetic field [L. *armare*, to arm].

Armenian (år-mē′ni-ạn) *a.* pert. to Armenia;—*n.* native or language of Armenia.

armiger (år′mi-jẹr) *n.* one who is entitled to bear coat-of-arms.—**armi'gerous** *a.* [L. *arma*, weapons; *gerere*, to bear].

armipotence (år-mip′ō-tens) *n.* power in arms.—**armi'potent** *a.* all powerful in arms [L. *arma*, arms; *potens*, powerful].

armistice (år′mis-tis) *n.* a temporary or lasting cessation of hostilities; a truce [L. *arma*, weapons; *sistere*, to cause to stop].

armlet (årm′let) *n.* a small arm, as of sea; band worn round arm [O.E. *earm*].

armoire (arm′wår) *n.* a cupboard [Fr.].

armory (ar′mor-i) *n.* science of heraldry.—**armor'ial** *a.* pert. to heraldic bearings.—**ar'morist** *n.* an expert in heraldry [L. *arma*, weapons or arms].

armour (år′mor) *n.* defensive covering for the body in battle; orig. chain-mail etc.; steel plates used to protect ships of war, tanks, cars, etc.—**arm'our-bear'er** *n.* one who carried arms of a superior.—**arm'our-clad** *a.*—**armoured car,** a metal-plated car with machine-gun in revolving turret.—**armoured division,** a mobile unit with tanks, armoured cars, etc.—**arm'ourer** *n.* a maker or repairer of weapons; one in charge of small arms.—**arm'ouring** *n.* the external steel wiring on submarine cables to combat abnormal strain.—**arm'our-plat'ed** *a.* protected by steel plates against shells, mines, etc.—**arm'oury** *n.* a place where weapons are stored [L. *armare*, to arm].

army (år′mi) *n.* a body of men trained and equipped for war; a military force commanded by a general; an organised body for some special purpose, e.g. *Salvation Army*; large number of people. -**army corps,** a division comprising various branches of the service commanded by lieutenant-general.—**standing army,** the regular army in peacetime [L. *arma*, weapons].

arnica (år′ni-kạ) *n.* (*Bot.*) a genus of hardy perennials of the order of Compositae.—**arnica montana,** mountain tobacco used for wounds and bruises [etym. unknown].

arnot, arnut (år′not, -nut) *n.* the pig-nut or earth-nut [E.].

aroma (ạ-rō′mạ) *n.* fragrance in plants; perfume or flavour; charm; atmosphere.—**aromat'ic** *a.* fragrant; spicy;—*n.* a plant, drug with fragrant smell. [Gk. *aroma*, spice].

around (ạ-round′) *adv.* in a circle; near;—*prep.* on all sides of; about [E. *a*, on; *round*].

arouse (ạ-rouz′) *v.t.* to excite to action; to awaken;—*v.i.* to wake; to become active [E. *a*, on and *rouse*].

arow (ạ-rō′) *adv.* in a row.

arpeggio (år-ped′jē-ō) *n.* (*Mus.*) the sounding of notes of a chord in quick succession [It. *arpeggiare*, to play the harp].

arquebus (år′kwē-bus) *n.* an ancient form of handgun. Also **har'quebus.**—**arquebusier'** *n.* [O.H.Ger. *Haken*, hook; *Büchse*, a gun].

arrack (år′ak) *n.* a spirit distilled in E. Indies from rice or juice of coconut tree [Ar. *arak*, juice of date-palm].

arraign (ạ-rān′) *v.t.* to call or set a prisoner at the bar; to call to account; to accuse publicly.—**arraign'er** *n.*—**arraign'ment** *n.* [L. *ad*, to; *ratio*, account].

arrange (ạ-rānj′) *v.t.* to put into order; to settle terms; to prepare; to adapt; to adjust;—*v.i.* to make agreement; to take steps.—**arrange'ment** *n.* act of arranging; the way or manner in which things are placed; needful preparation; (*Mus.*) transcription or adaptation of a piece of music to an instrument other than that for which it was originally composed.—**arrang'er** *n.* [Fr. *rang*, rank].

arrant (ar′ạnt) *a.* notorious; unmitigated; utter—**ar'rantly** *adv.* (doublet of *errant*).

arras (ar′ạs) *n.* tapestry; large tapestries, ornamented with figures, used as wall hangings.—**ar'rased** *a.* hung with arras (fr. the city of *Arras*, France, where first woven].

array (ạr-rā′) *v.t.* to set in order; to draw up, as troops for battle; to dress; to equip;—*n.* order; equipment; fine apparel; raiment [O.Fr. *areer*].

arrear (ạ-rēr′) *n.* the state of being behind.—**arrears'** *n.pl.* moneys still owing; work still to be overtaken.—**arrear'age** *n.* arrears [Fr. *arrière*, behind].

arrect (ạ-rekt′) *v.t.* to raise; set upright;—*a.* erect [L. *arrectus*, set upright].

arrest (ạ-rest′) *v.t.* to stop; to check; to hinder; to seize by authority of law; to engage the attention;—*n.* the apprehending of a person by the authority of law; any seizure, physical or moral; stoppage.—**arresta'tion** *n.* act of arresting.—**arrest'er, arrest'or** *n.* one who, or that which, arrests.—**arrest'ing** *a.* impressive; striking.—**arrest'ive** *a.*calculated to draw attention.—**arrest'ment** *n.* an arrest of a criminal; the seizure of a person's wages, etc. in debt claims [O.Fr. *arester*].

arris (ar′is) *n.* (*Archit.*) the edge formed by two surfaces meeting each other.

arrive (ạ-rīv′) *v.i.* to reach a point; to come to; to attain to any aim or object.—**arriv'al** *n.* act of arriving [Fr. *arriver*, to arrive].

arrogance, arrogancy (ar′o-gans, -gan-si) *n.* insolent pride; intolerable presumption; over-bearing manner.—**ar'rogant** *a.* presuming on one's rank or power; haughty; proud.—**ar'rogantly** *adv.*—**ar'rogate** *v.t.* to claim unduly; to take upon one's self without authority; to demand overbearingly; to presume; to assume; to usurp.—**arroga'tion** *n.* [L. *ad*, for; *rogare*, to ask].

arrondissement (a-rōng-dēs′mong) *n.* the largest civil sub-division of a French department [Fr.].

arrosion (ạ-rō′zhun) *n.* the act of gnawing; the state of being gnawed away or corroded [L. *arrodere, arrosum*, to gnaw at].

arrow (ar′ō) *n.* a painted, barbed missile shot from a bow; a sign ➳→ to show direction.—**ar'rowy** *a.* of, like an arrow.—**ar'row-grass** *n.* small, erect, grass-like plants.—**ar'rowhead** *n.* pointed end of an arrow; a plant with arrow-shaped leaves [O.E. *arwe*].

arrowroot (ar′ō-ròòt) *n.* a highly nutritious, farinaceous starch obtained from the roots and tubers of various West Indian plants [So-called because used to counteract the poison of arrows].

arse (ars) *n.* the buttocks [O.E. *aers*].

arsenal (år′sen-ạl) *n.* factory for military and naval arms and stores; an armoury [It. *arsenale*, fr. Ar. *al-sina'ah*, workshop].

arsenic (ar′se-nik) *n.* a semi-metallic element; the poisonous, whitish, or steel-grey powder of white oxide of arsenic.—**ar'senic, arsen'ical** *a.* pert. to arsenic.—**ar'senate, arsen'iate** *n.* a salt of arsenic acid.—**arsen'icate** *v.t.* to combine with arsenic; to treat with arsenic [Gk. *arsēn*, male. The alchemists classed metals as male and female].

arson (år-son) *n.* the crime of intentionally setting on fire houses, buildings, ships or other property [L. *ardere, arsum*, to burn].

art (årt) second person singular, present indicative, of the verb **to be.**

art (årt) *n.* skill; human skill as opposed to nature; skill applied to music, painting, poetry, etc.; any of the subjects of this skill; a system of rules; a profession or craft; cunning; trick.—**arts** *n.pl.* certain branches of learning, languages, history, etc. as distinct from natural science.—**art'ful** *a.* exhibiting art or skill; crafty; cunning.—**art'fully** *adv.*—**art'fulness** *n.*—**art'less** *a.* free from art; guileless.—**art'lessly** *adv.*—**art'lessness** *n.*—**art'y** *a.* (*Colloq.*) affectedly artistic.—**art and part** (*Scots Law*) participation.—**black art,** magic.—**fine arts,** painting, sculpture, architecture, music.—**useful arts,** those in which the hands, rather than the mind, are used [L. *ars, artis*].

artery (ár′-tẹ-ri) *n.* a vessel carrying blood from the heart; (*Fig.*) any essential channel of communication.—**arterial** (ár-tē′-ri-ạl) *a.* pert. to an artery; pert. to a first-class road.—**arte'rialise** *v.t.* to change venous blood into arterial blood by oxygenisation.—**arterialisa'tion** *n.*—**arte'riole** *n.* a small artery.—**arteriol'ogy** *n.* the study of the arteries.—**arte'rio-sclero'sis** *n.* (*Med.*) a hardening of the arteries [Gk. *arteria,* the windpipe, an artery; *logos,* discourse; *skleros,* hard].

Artesian (ár-tē′-zhạn) *a.* belonging to *Artois,* in France.—**artesian well,** a well bored deep enough so that water rises to the surface of the ground by internal pressure (the first such well was sunk at *Artois* in the 12th cent.) [Fr. *Artésien*].

arthralgia (ár-thral′-ji-ạ) *n.* (*Med.*) pain in the joints.—**arthritis** (ár-thrī′-tis) *n.* inflammation of a joint; gout.—**arthritic** (ár-thrit′-ik), **arthrit'ical** *a.*—**arthro'dia** *n.* a gliding joint.—**arthrodyn'ia** *n.* pain in a joint [Gk. *arthron,* a joint; *algos,* pain; *eidos,* form; *odunē,* pain].

arthropod (ár′-thrō-pod) *n.* an animal with segmented body and jointed limbs, e.g. a spider, crustacean, etc.—**arthrop'odal** *a.* [Gk. *arthron,* a joint; *pous, podos,* a foot].

artichoke (ár′-ti-chōk) *n.* a plant with thistle-like head, which can be cooked and the fleshy base eaten.—**Jerusalem artichoke** *n.* an entirely different plant, bearing edible tubers which resemble the potato in appearance [It. *articiocco,* fr. Ar., Jerusalem is corrupt. of It. *girasole,* sun-flower].

article (ár′-ti-kl) *n.* a clause or term in a contract, treaty, etc.; a literary composition in a journal, etc.; a paragraph or section; a point of faith; a rule or condition; an item; a commodity or object; (*Gram.*) one of the words *a, an* (the indefinite article) and *the* (the definite article); *-v.t.* to bind as an apprentice; to accuse specifically [L. *articulus,* a little joint].

articular (ár-tik′-ū-lạr) *a.* pert. to the joints [L. *articulus,* a little joint].

articulate (ár-tik′-ū-lāt) *v.t.* to connect by a joint; to utter clearly-defined sounds;—*v.i.* to be connected by joints; to speak in distinct syllables or words;—*a.* jointed; of speech, clear, distinct.—**artic'ulately** *adv.*—**artic'ulateness** *n.*—**articula'tion** *n.* the act of articulating; a consonant; a joint between two or more bones [L. *articulus,* a little joint, fr. *artus,* a limb].

artifact (ár′-ti-fakt) *n.* something shaped by the art of man and not by nature. Also *artefact* [L. *ars, artis,* art; *facere,* to make].

artifice (ár′-ti-fis) *n.* an artful or skilful contrivance; a ruse; a trick; cunning.—**artif'icer** *n.* a skilled workman; an inventor; (*Navy*) term denoting ranks in the engine-room.—**artific'ial** (ár-ti-fish′-ạl) *a.* made by art; manufactured; affected in manners.—**artific'ially** *adv.*—**artificial'ity** *n.* [L. *artificium,* a trade, fr. *ars,* art; *facere,* to make].

artillery (ár-til′-ẹ-ri) *n.* cannon; troops trained in the use of guns; a branch of the armed forces, e.g. the Royal Field Artillery, etc.—**artillerist** (ár-til′-ẹ-rist) *n.* one skilled in the design, construction, or use of artillery.—**artill'eryman** *n.* a soldier serving in the artillery [Fr. *artillerie,* fr. O.Fr. *artillier,* to equip].

artisan (ár′-ti-zan *n.* a craftsman; a mechanic; a workman skilled in any trade [Fr. fr. L. *ars, artis,* art].

artist (ár′-tist) *n.* one who practises one of the fine arts, e.g. painting, sculpture, etc.; applicable to any craftsman whose work is of high standard.—**artis'tic, artis'tical** *a.*—**artis'tically** *adv.*—**artistry** (ár′-tis-tri) *n.* artistic ability or effect; beauty of work [L. *ars, artis,* art].

artiste (ar-tēst′) *n.* an expert in some art, not one of the fine arts; often applied to a member of the theatrical profession, esp. a music-hall performer [L. *ars, artis,* art].

arum (ā′-rum) *n.* a genus of plants, including the wake-robin or cuckoo-pint.—**arum lily,** a kind of large white lily [Gk. *aron*].

Aryan (ā′-ri-ạn) *n.* early race of pure Hindu stock, thought to have originated in plains of Northern India, the progenitors of the Indo-European group, i.e. Celtic, Teutonic, etc. [Sans. *Arya,* noble].

as (az) *adv.* like; in like manner; similar to; for example;—*conj.* since; because; when; while;—*pron.* that [form of *also*].

asa (as′-ạ) *n.* a resinous gum.—**asadul'cis** *n.* benzoin.—**asafoetida** (as-ạ-fēt′-i-dạ) *n.* gum-resin with offensive odour, much used in medicine [Pers. *aza,* mastic; L. *dulcis,* sweet; *fetidus,* stinking].

asbestos (as-bes′-tos) *n.* a fibrous non-inflammable mineral, used in manufacture of fire-proof materials.—**asbes'tic, asbes'tiform, asbes'tine, asbes'toid** *a.* pert. to, like, or made of asbestos; non-inflammable [Gk. *a-,* neg.; *sbestos,* to be quenched].

ascarides (as-kar′-i-dēz) *n.pl.* thread-worms which commonly infest the canals of the intestines [Gk. *ascaris*].

ascend (ạ-send′) *v.t.* to climb, to mount; to walk up;—*v.i.* to rise; to arise; to soar; to climb; to mount; to go back in time.—**ascen'dable, ascen'dible** *a.*—**ascen'dancy, ascen'dency** *n.* superior or controlling influence; authority; domination;—**ascen'dant, ascen'dent** *a.* rising; just above the horizon; predominant; surpassing;—*n.* ascendancy; superiority [L. *ad,* to; *scandere,* to climb].

ascension (ạ-sen′-shun) *n.* the act of ascending or rising;—(*Bib.*) the visible rising of Christ to heaven.—**ascen'sional** *a.* pert. to ascension.—**ascen'sive** *a.* rising.—**Ascension Day,** a church festival (Holy Thursday), falling 10 days before Whit sunday, in commemoration of Christ's ascent to heaven after the Resurrection.—**ascent** (ạ-sent′) *n.* the act of rising; the way by which one rises; a slope; a way up [L. *ad,* to; *scandere,* to climb].

ascertain (as-ẹr-tān′) *v.t.* to get to know; to find out for a certainty.—**ascertain'able** *a.*—**ascertain'ment** *n.* [L. *ad,* to; *certus,* sure].

ascetic (a-set′-ik) *a.* sternly self-denying; austere; strict;—*n.* one who practises rigorous self-denial; a hermit; an anchorite.—**ascet'icism** *n.* [Gk. *askein,* to exercise].

ascribe (as-krīb′) *v.t.* to attribute; to impute; to assign.—**ascrib'able** *a.*—**ascrip'tion** *n.* [L. *ascribere,* to add in writing].

asdic (as′-dik) *n.* electrical detector apparatus invented during World War 2, for locating enemy submarines. [from the initial letters of *A*llied *S*ubmarine *D*etective *I*nvestigation *C*ommittee]. Also **A.S.D.I.C.**

aseity (a-sē′-it-i) *n.* independent existence, esp. of God [L. *a.* from; *se,* oneself].

asepsis (a-sep′-sis) *n.* freedom from putrefaction; freeing from bacteria by use of antiseptics.—**asep'tic** *a.* not liable to putrefaction; sterilised.—**asep'ticise** *v.t.* to make surgically clean.—**asep'ticism** *n.* process of sterilising a wound, etc. [Gk. *a-,* neg.; *sepsis,* decay].

asexual (ạ-sek′-sū-ạl) *a.* without sex; lacking sexual instinct or reproductive organs.—**asexual'ity** *n.* [L. *a,* away; *sexus,* sex].

ash (ash) *n.* a genus of trees of the olive family having a tough, hard, elastic wood.—**mountain ash,** the rowan tree.—**ash'en** *a.* [O.E. *aesce,* the ash-tree].

ash (ash) *n.* the dry white or greyish dust left after a substance has been burned.—**ash'es** *n.pl.* the remains of a human body after cremation or disintegration; (*Fig.*) a dead body; (*Chem.*) potash.—**ash'-bin** *n.* a bucket for ashes and refuse.—**ash'-can** *n.* an ashbin; (*Naval Slang*) a depth-charge; a multiple arc-lamp used in cinemas.—**ash'en** *a.* of the colour of ashes; pale.—**ash'ery** *n.* a place where potash is made from wood-ashes.—**ash'-pan** *n.* a removable receptacle for ashes under grate.—**ash'-tray** *n.* receptacle for cigarette ash.—**ash'y** *a.*—**the Ashes,** (ash'ez) the mythical trophy for which England and Australia compete in cricket Test matches.—**sackcloth and ashes,** symbols of abject humiliation.—**Ash Wednesday,** the first day of Lent, when a cross is traced with *ashes* on the forehead of worshippers [M.E. *asche,* ash].

ashamed (a-shāmd') *a.* affected by shame; covered with confusion, caused by awareness of guilt.—**asham'edly** *adv.* [O.E. *ascamian,* to be ashamed].

ashet (ash'et) *n.* a large flat dish, oval in shape, for serving meat [Fr. *assiette*].

ashlar, ashler (ash'lar, -lẹr) *n.* freestones hewn for facing.—**ash'laring, ash'lering** *n.* upright pieces to which laths are nailed in garrets; ashlar masonry [L. *axilla,* dim. of *axis,* a board or plank].

ashore (a-shōr') *adv.* on or to shore; on land, opp. to *aboard* [E. *a,* on; M.E. *shore* fr. O.E. *sciran,* to cut].

Asian, Asiatic (ā'shi-ạn, ā'shi-at'ik) *a.* pert. to Asia or to the people of Asia [Gk. *Asia,* a part of Lydia].

aside (a-sīd') *n.* something said in an undertone, esp. on stage by an actor and supposed not to be heard by the other actors.—*adv.* on or to one side; apart; dismissed from use [O.E. *a,* on; *sid,* broad].

asiderite (a-sidẹr-rīt) *n.* a meteorite containing no iron [Gk. *a-,* neg.; *sideros,* iron].

asinine (as'in-īn) *a.* pert. to an ass; stupid.—**asinin'ity** *n.* [L. *asinus,* an ass].

ask (ask) *v.t.* to seek information; to interrogate;—*v.i.* (*for, about*) to request; to inquire.—**ask'er** *n.* [O.E. *ascian,* to seek].

askance, askant (ạ-skans', ạ-skant') *adv.* towards one corner of the eye; awry; with disdain or suspicious; not straightforward; sideways [etym. uncertain].

askari (as-kå'ri) *n.* a native soldier employed in the service of a European power in E. Africa [Ar. *askas,* army].

askew (ạ-skū') *adv.* askant; aside; awry; obliquely; off the straight [See **skew**].

aslant (ạ-slant') *adv.* in a slanting direction.

asleep (ạ-slēp') *adv.* and *a.* in a state of sleep; at rest; benumbed; dormant; dead.

aslope (ạ-slōp') *a.* sloping; tilted; oblique.—*adv.* with a slope [O.E. *slūpan,* to slip].

asomatous (ạ-sō'mạ-tus) *a.* destitute of a body [Gk. *a-,* neg.; *soma,* a body].

asp, aspic (asp, asp'ik) *n.* a small, hooded, poisonous serpent [Gk. *aspis*].

asparagin, asparagine (ạs-par'ạ-jin) *n.* a crystalline substance with a diuretic action found in asparagus [fr. *asparagus*].

asparagus (ạs-par'ạ-gus) *n.* a succulent vegetable with tender shoots [Gk.].

aspect (as'pekt) *n.* look; appearance; position or situation; view [L. *aspicere,* look at].

aspen (as'pen) *n.* a British tree known also as the trembling poplar because of its quivering leaves;—*a.* pert. to the aspen [O.E. *aespe*].

asper (as'per) *a.* rough; harsh;—*n.* a sign of aspiration in Greek grammar.—**as'perate** *v.t.* to make harsh or uneven; to roughen [L.].

asperity (as-per'i-ti) *n.* roughness of surface, taste, or speech; harshness; bitterness; tartness; crabbedness; sharpness; acrimony [L. *asper,* rough].

aspermia (ạ-sper'mi-ạ) *n.* (*Bot.*) state of not producing seed; (*Med.*) absence of semen [Gk. *a-,* neg.; *sperma,* seed].

asperse (as-pers') *v.t.* to slander; to defame; to vilify; to calumniate; to bespatter (with).—**asper'ser** *n.*—**asper'sion** *n.* slander.—**aspers'ive, aspers'ory** *a.* [L. *ad,* to; *spargere,* to sprinkle].

asphalt (as'falt, as-falt') *n.* a black, hard, tar-like substance, used for paving, roofing, etc.;—**asphalt'** *v.t.* to cover with asphalt.—**asphal'tic** *a.* bituminous [Gk. *asphaltos*].

asphodel (as'fō-del) *n.* any plant of the genus Asphodelus; a kind of lily; a daffodil; (*Myth.*) the immortal flower that grew in the Elysian fields [Gk. *asphodelos*].

asphyxia, asphyxy (ạs-fik'si-ạ, -si) *n.* suspended animation due to lack of oxygen in the blood; it is caused by obstructed breathing, as in drowning, inhalation of gases, etc.—**asphyx'ial** *a.*—**asphyx'iant** *n.* a substance that produces asphyxia.—**asphyx'iate** *v.t.* to produce asphyxia; to suffocate.—**asphyxia'tion** *n.* [Gk. *asphuxia,* pulse stoppage].

aspic (as'pik) *n.* the asp; (*Bot.*) the great lavender [L. *spica,* a spike].

aspic (as'pik) *n.* savoury meat jelly containing pieces of fish, fowl, egg, etc. [Fr.].

aspidistra (ạs-pi-dis'trạ) *n.* a plant with large, broad leaves, often grown in pots [Gk. *aspis,* a shield; *astron,* a star].

aspirate (as'pi-rāt) *v.t.* to pronounce with a full breathing sound; to prefix the sound *h* to a word or letter;—*n.* a letter marked with a note of breathing; a breathed sound;—*a.* pronounced with a rough breathing.—**aspira'tion** *n.* (*Med.*) the removal of fluids from a cavity in the body by suction [L. *aspiratus,* breathed upon].

aspire (ạs-pīr') *v.i.* to desire with eagerness; to strive towards something higher (usually followed by *to* or *after*).—**aspir'ant** *a.* ambitious;—*n.* one who aspires; a candidate.—**aspiration** (ạs-pi-rā'shun) *n.* the act of aspiring *adv.* [L. *ad,* to; *spirare,* to breathe].

Aspirin (as'pi-rin) *n.* a drug, acetylsalicylic acid, used as a febrifuge and for relief of headache, etc. [Protected Trade Name].

ass (as) *n.* a quadruped of the horse family but smaller and with longer ears; a donkey; (*Fig.*) a stupid person [L. *asinus,* an ass].

assagai (ass'ạ-gī) *n.* Same as **assegai.**

assail (ạ-sāl') *v.t.* to leap or fall on; to attack; to assault; to ply with arguments, reproaches, etc.—**assail'able** *a.*—**assail'ant** *a.* and *n.* [L. *ad,* to; *salire,* to leap].

assassin (ạ-sas'in) *n.* one who murders by secret or treacherous assault, esp. a hired murderer.—**assas'sinate** *v.t.* to murder by guile or by sudden violence.—**assassina'tion** *n.*—**assas'sinator** *n.*—**the assassins,** a fanatical Moslem sect (11th cent.), who murdered enemies of the Moslem faith. They nerved themselves with *hashish,* an intoxicating drug, hence their name.

assault (ạ-sawlt') *n.* a violent onset or attack;—*v.t.* to attack violently, both physically and with words or arguments; to storm.—**assault'able** *a.*—**assault'er** *n.*—**assault at arms,** an exhibition of military exercises.—**assault and battery** (*Law*) the crime of violently attacking and beating a person [L. *ad,* to; *salire,* to leap].

assay (ạ-sā') *n.* trial; test; examination; analysis of the amount of metal in ores or coins, or of ingredients in drugs;—*v.t.* to test, esp. with a view to determining the presence or amount of metals in ores.—**assay'er** *n.* [Fr. *essayer,* to try].

assegai (as'e-gī) *n.* a light, slender spear used by S. African natives [Port. *azagaia,* a spear].

assemble (ạ-sem'bl) *v.t.* to bring or call together; to collect; to fit together the parts, e.g. of a machine;—*v.i.* to meet together.—**assem'blage** *n.* the act of assembling.—**assem'bly** *n.* a meeting; a company gathered; the putting together of all the different parts to make a complete machine.—**assem'bly-line** *n.* line of machines and workers handling a product to be assembled [L. *ad,* to; *simul,* together].

assent (ạ-sent') *v.i.* to agree; to admit; to

concur;—*n.* acquiescence; approval.—**assenta'tion** *n.* servile assent; obsequiousness.—**assent'er, assent'or** *n.* one who assents.—**assentient** (ạ-sen'shent) *a.* giving assent;—*n.* one who assents [L. *ad*, to; *sentire*, to think].

assert (ạ-sert') *v.t.* to declare strongly; to maintain or defend by argument.—**assert'er, assert'or** *n.*—**asser'tion** *n.* the act of asserting; affirmation; declaration.—**assert'ive** *a.* positive; self-confident.—**assert'ively** *adv.*—**assert'iveness** *n.*—**assert'ory** *a.* affirmative [L. *asserere*, to claim].

assess (ạ-ses') *v.t.* to fix the amount (of a tax or fine); to tax or fine; to estimate for damage, taxation, etc; to rate; to appraise.—**assess'able** *a.*—**assess'ment** *n.* assessing; valuation for taxation; a tax; evaluation of merits.—**assess'or** *n.* a legal adviser who sits beside a lay magistrate to advise him; official who assesses taxes; one appointed by the holder of an office of dignity, e.g. the Chancellor's assessor in certain universities.—**assesso'rial** *a.*—**assess'orship** *n.* the office of an assessor [L. *assidere, assessum*, to sit by a judge].

assets (as'ets) *n.pl.* funds or property available for payment of debts, etc.; the estate of an insolvent or deceased person; the entire property of a business company, association, society, etc.;—*n.sing.* an item of such property; a thing of value [Fr. *assez*, enough].

asseverate (ạ-sev'ẹr-āt) *v.t.* and *i.* to assert positively or solemnly; to aver.—**assevera'tion** *n.* a positive or solemn assertion [L. *asseverare*, fr. *severus*, serious].

assiduous (ạ-sid'ū-us) *a.* constant in application or attention; diligent; hard-working.—**assid'uously** *adv.*—**assid'uousness, assiduity** (as-i-dū'i-ti) *n.* close application; unremitting attention; devotion [L. *assiduus*, constantly near].

assign (ạ-sīn') *v.t.* to allot; to apportion; to give out; to fix; to transfer; to ascribe.—**assign'able** *a.*—**assignation** (a-sig-nā'shun) *n.* the act of assigning; an appointment, esp. if made by lovers; a tryst; (*Law*) an assignment, or the deed by which it is made.—**assignee** (a-sī-nē') *n.* one to whom something is assigned; a person appointed to act for another.—**assign'ment** *n.* an allotting to a particular person or use; a transfer of legal title or interest.—**assign'er, assign'or** *n.* [L. *assignare*, to allot by sign (*signum*)].

assimilate (ạ-sim'i-lāt) *v.t.* to make similar; to change into a like substance; to absorb into the system; to digest;—*v.i.* to become similar; to be absorbed.—**assim'ilable** *a.*—**assimilabil'ity** *n.* the quality of being assimilable.—**assimila'tion** *n.* the act of assimilating; (*Fig.*) full comprehension of anything.—**assim'ilative** *a.* capable of assimilating.—**assim'ilatory** *a.* tending to assimilate [L. *assimilare*, to make like].

assist (ạ-sist') *v.t.* to help; to aid; to give support to;—*v.i.* to lend aid; to be present.—**assist'ance** *n.* help; aid.—**assist'ant** *a.* helping; acting under the direction of a superior;—*n.* one who assists; a helper; a subordinate [L. *assistere*, to stand by].

assize (ạ-sīz') *v.t.* to fix the rate of; to assess;—*n.* orig. the regulation of a court fixing selling price of bread, ale, etc.; a sitting of a court of justice; (*Scot.*) trial before a jury; the jury.—**assiz'es** *n.pl.* courts held three, sometimes four, times per annum in the counties of England and Wales (except Middlesex) by the judges of the Supreme Court on circuit, and dealing with criminal and serious civil cases, before a jury.—**assize'ment** *n.* inspection of weights and measures.—**assiz'er** *n.* [O.Fr. *assise*, an assembly of judges].

associate (a-sō'shi-āt) *v.t.* to join with as a friend, colleague, confederate or partner; to class together; (*reflex.*) to express agreement with;—*v.i.* (foll. by *with*) to keep company; to combine;—*n.* a companion; a coadjutor; a member of a group; a junior member of an academy lower in status than an Academician;—*a.* affiliated.—**asso'ciable** *a.* companionable.—**asso'ciableness, associabil'ity,** *n.* friendly, companionable quality; sympathy.—**asso'ciateship** *n.*—**associa'tion** *n.* act of associating; connection; bond; union of persons for some special cause or purpose, e.g. Liberal Association.—**asso'ciative** *a.* [L. *associare*, fr. *socius*, an ally].

assonance (as'ō-nạns) *n.* a resemblance of sounds; imperfect rhyme in which vowel sounds are same, but consonants following are different, e.g. *blunder, slumber*.—**as'sonant(al)** *a.*—**as'sonate** *v.t.* to correspond in sound [L. *ad*, to; *sonare*, to sound].

assort (a-sort') *v.t.* to classify; to arrange;—*v.i.* to suit or agree or match (foll. by *with*).—**assort'ed** *a.* classified; varied.—**assort'edness, assort'ment** *n.* act of arranging in groups; a miscellaneous collection [Fr. *assortir*, to match].

assuage (a-swāj') *v.t.* to soften; to allay; to mitigate.—**assuage'ment** *n.*—**assuag'er** *n.*—**assua'sive** *a.* mitigating; softening; soothing [L. *ad*, to; *suavis*, sweet].

assuetude (as'wē-tūd) *n.* custom; habit [L. *ad*, to; *suescere*, to become accustomed].

assume (a-sūm') *v.t.* to take upon oneself; to take for granted; to appropriate; to usurp;—*v.i.* to claim unduly; to be pretentious or arrogant.—**assum'able** *a.*—**assumed'** *a.* supposed; feigned; hypothetical.—**assum'edly** *adv.*—**assum'ing** *a.* arrogant.—**assum'ingly** *adv.*—**assum'ption** *n.* the act of taking to or upon oneself by force or right; the act of taking for granted; the thing supposed to be true, or to have happened.—**assump'tive** *a.* capable of being assumed or taken for granted.—**assump'tively** *adv.*—**Feast of the Assumption,** the festival in honour of the translation to heaven of the Virgin Mary—celebrated on August 15th. [L. *ad*, to; *sumere*, to take].

assure (a-shóór') *v.t.* to make sure or certain; to affirm; to ensure; to convince.—**assur'able** *a.*—**assur'ance** *n.* the act of assuring; promise; self-confidence; presumption; insurance, in sense of life assurance; a contract for the payment of a sum of money on a person's death.—**assured'** *a.* certain; safe; confident.—**assur'edly** *adv.*—**assur'edness** *n.* certainty.—**assur'er** *n.*—**assur'ingly** *adv.* confidently [L. *ad*, to; *securus*, safe].

aster (as'tẹr) *n.* a genus of plants of the order of Compositae, so called because the expanded flowers of various hues are like stars [Gk. *astēr*, star].

asterisk (as'te-risk) *n.* the mark (*) used in printing to indicate words for reference or words omitted.—**as'terism** *n.* small cluster of stars, three asterisks (⁂), indicating in books, point or passage of special interest [Gk. *asterikos*, a little star].

astern (ạ-stern') *adv.* in, at, or toward the hinder part of a ship; behind.

asteroid (as'ter-oid) *a.* star-shaped;—*n.* one of the smaller planets; (*Zool.*) star-fish.—**asteroid'al** *a.* [Gk. *aster*, a star; *eidos*, a form].

asthenia (as-then'i-ạ) *n.* (*Med.*) absence or loss of muscular strength; weakness [Gk. *asthenia*, weakness].

asthma (ast'mạ, as'mạ, asth'mạ) *n.* a chronic disorder of the respiratory organs, marked by cough, laboured breathing and feeling of suffocation.—**asthmat'ic(al)** *a.*—**asthmat'ically** *adv.* [Gk. *asthma*, panting].

astigmatism (a-stig'mạ-tizm) *n.* a defect of eye, attended with dimness of vision, due to malformation of lens of eye.—**astigmat'ic** *a.* [Gk. *a-*, neg.; *stigma*, point].

astir (ạ-stẹr') *adv.* or *a.* on the move; alert; stirring [E.].

astonish (ạs-ton'ish) *v.t.* to impress with sudden surprise, wonder or admiration; to strike with sudden terror; to amaze; to astound.—**aston'ished** *a.* greatly surprised;

dazed; stunned; dismayed.—**aston'ishing** *a.* amazing; remarkable.—**aston'ishingly** *adv.*—**aston'ishment** *n.* amazement; surprise [Formerly, also *astony*, fr. O.Fr. *astoner*].

astound (ạs-tound') *v.t.* to strike dumb with terror or amazement; to astonish greatly; to stun.—**astound'ing** *a.* [By-form of *astony, astonish*].

astragal (as'trạ-gạl) *n.* (*Archit.*) a small semi-circular moulding or bead at the upper end of the shaft of a column or at its base to bind the column and entablature together; the small moulding, usually applied to the bars in windows which carry the glass [Gk. *astragalos*, ankle bone].

astrakhan (as'trạ-kan) *n.* the skin of the young Persian lamb with soft, curling ringlets of wool; a cheap fabric, made in imitation [*Astrakhan*, city on the Caspian Sea].

astral (as'tral) *a.* pert. to the stars;—*n.* in Theosophy, the astral sphere connected with our earth and its inhabitants.—**astral body**, a body built of matter of the astral plane, i.e. an octave higher than that of the physical [Gk. *astron*, star].

astray (ạ-strā') *adv.* out of the right way; in the wrong direction.

astrict (ạ-strikt') *v.t.* to bind fast; to confine; to restrict; to contract.—**astric'tion** *n.* restriction; (*Med.*) constipation.—**astric'tive** *a.* astringent [L. *astrictus*, drawn close].

astride (ạ-strīd') *adv.* straddling; with the legs apart;—*prep.* with one foot on each side of an object.

astringe (as-trinj') *v.t.* to bind together; to draw together; to astrict; to constipate.—**astrin'gency** *n.* the condition of being astringent.—**astrin'gent** *a.* binding; strengthening; constricting; contracting;—*n.* a drug which causes contraction of the muscular fibre-tissues.—**astrin'gently** *adv.* [L. *ad*, to; *stringere*, to bind].

astro- (as'trō) *prefix* used in the construction of compound words having some reference to stars [Gk. *astron*, star].

astro-hatch (as'trō-hach) *n.* the overhead window in the cockpit of an aeroplane.

astrology (as-trol'o-ji) *n.* the science, originally identical with astronomy, which interprets celestial phenomena as having a bearing upon mundane affairs, thus affording a means of predicting the course of future events.—**astrol'oger** *n.*—**astrolog'ic, astrolog'ical** *a.*—**astrolog'ically** *adv.* [Gk. *astron*, a star; *logos*, a discourse].

astrometry (as-trom'e-tri) *n.* the determination of the magnitudes of the fixed stars [Gk. *astron*, a star; *metron*, measure].

astronomy (ạs-tron'ō-mi) *n.* the science which treats of the heavenly bodies, describing their magnitudes, positions, motions, etc. and all the phenomena therewith connected.—**astron'omer** *n.* one versed in astronomy.—**astrono'mic, -al** *a.* pert. to astronomy; boundless, countless, prodigious.—**astronom'ically** *adv.*—**astron'omise** *v.i.* [Gk. *astron*, a star; *nomos*, law].

astrophysics (ạs-trō-fiz'iks) *n.* (*Astron.*) the study of the physical components of the stars by means of the spectroscope [Gk. *astron*, a star; *phusis*, nature].

astute (as-tūt') *a.* cunning; shrewd; sagacious; crafty; wily; sly; subtle; keen.—**astute'ly** *adv.*—**astute'ness** *n.* [L. *astutus*].

asunder (ạ-sun'dẹr) *adv.* apart; into different pieces; in a divided state.

asylum (ạ-sī'lum) *n.* a sanctuary; refuge for criminals, debtors and others liable to be pursued; any place of refuge; an institution for the deaf and dumb, the blind, or the insane; the protection afforded by such places [Gk. *asulon*, inviolate].

asymmetry (ạ-sim'e-tri] *n.* want of symmetry—**asymmet'ric, -al** *a.*

asymptote (as'im-tōt) *n.* (*Math.*) a straight line that continually approaches a curve, but never meets it within a finite distance.—**asympto'tic, asympto'tical** *a.* [Gk. *a-*, neg.; *sun*, with; *ptosis*, a falling].

asynchronism (ạ-sin'krō-nizm) *n.* lack of synchronism; want of correspondence in time.—**asyn'chronous** *a.* not simultaneous.

asyntactic (as-in-tak'tik) *a.* not syntactical.

At (at) *n.* (*Colloq.*) a member of the A.T.S. (Women's) Auxiliary Territorial Service.

at (at) *prep.* denoting rest in a place, presence, or nearness; near to, by, in; engaged on; in the direction of [O.E. *aet*].

atabrine (at'a-brīn) *n.* an anti-malarial drug.

ataraxia (at-ạ-rak'si-ạ) *n.* freedom from the passions. Also **atarax'y** [Gk. *a-*, neg.; *tarassein*, to disturb].

atavism (at'ạ-vizm) *n.* the recurrence in human beings, animals, or plants of hereditary characteristics, diseases, etc. which have skipped one or more generations; reversion to type.—**atavist'ic** [L. *atavus*, a great-grandfather's grandfather].

ataxia, ataxy (a-tak'si-ạ, -si) *n.* (*Med.*) irregularity of bodily functions; irregularity of movement, due to defective muscular control, especially pronounced in **locomotor ataxy**.—**atax'ic** *a.* [Gk. *a-*, neg.; *taxis*, order].

ate (et) past tense of the verb **eat**.

atelier (at-el-yā') *n.* a workshop, esp. of an artist; hence, a studio [Fr. a workshop].

atheism (ā'thē-izm) *n.* disbelief in the existence of God.—**a'theist** *n.* one who denies the existence of God.—**atheis'tic, atheis'tical** *a.* pert. to atheism; godless.—**atheis'tically** *adv.* [Gk. *a-*, neg.; *theos*, a god].

atheling (ath'el-ing) *n.* in Anglo-Saxon times, a member of a noble family; a prince royal [O.E. *aetheling*].

Athena, Athene (a-thē'na, -nē) *n.* (*Myth.*) Greek goddess of wisdom (Minerva of the Romans), and tutelar deity of philosophers, orators, poets, painters, etc.—**athenaeum, atheneum** (ath-ẹ-nē'um) *n.* originally, her temple at Athens, the meeting-place of philosophers, orators, and poets; a name often given to literary institutions.—**Athe'nian** *a.* pert. to Athens—*n.* native of Athens.

athirst (ạ-therst') *a.* thirsty [fr. *thirst*].

athlete (ath'lēt) *n.* one trained to physical exercises, feats or contests of strength, etc.; a man strong and active by training.—**athletic** (ath-let'ik) *a.* pert. to physical exercises, contests, etc.; strong; vigorous; muscular.—**athlet'ics** *n.pl.* athletic sports [Gk. *athlētēs*, a contestant for a prize].

athwart (ạ-thwort') *prep.* across; from side to side;—*adv.* crosswise [O.N. *a*, and *thvert*, across].

Atlantes (at-lan'tēz) *n.pl.* (*Archit.*) male figures used instead of columns [Gk. *pl.* of *Atlas*].

Atlantic (at-lan'tik) *a.* pert. to the ocean (named after Mt. *Atlas*) separating Europe and Africa from America;—*n.* the ocean itself.

Atlas (at'las) *n.* (*Myth.*) a Titan, condemned by Zeus to carry the world on his shoulders.—**at'las** *n.* a book of maps, so called because the figure of Atlas often embellished the title-page of old atlases.

atmosphere (at'mos-fēr) *n.* the mass of air, clouds, gases, and vapour, surrounding the earth or other heavenly body; any similar mass; atmospheric pressure; the air in any place, esp. if enclosed, e.g. in a theatre; (*Fig.*) any surrounding influence.—**atmospher'ic, atmospher'ical** *a.* pert. to, or depending on, the atmosphere.—**atmospher'ically** *adv.*—**atmospher'ics** *n.pl.* electrical disturbances in atmosphere, causing interference in a radio receiving set [Gk. *atmos*, vapour; *sphaira*, a ball].

atoll (at'ol, ạ-tol') *n.* a ring-shaped coral reef surrounding a lagoon [Native].

atom (at'om) *n.* the smallest unit of an element that retains the characteristics of that element and cannot be decomposed by chemical means, shown by nuclear physicists to be made up of three fundamental particles, protons, neutrons (forming the nucleus) and electrons; (*Fig.*) anything very small; a tiny bit.—**atom'ic, atom'ical** *a.* pert. to the atom.—**atomi'city** *n.* the number of atoms in the molecule of an element.—**atomisa'tion** *n.* the changing of any liquid into the form of fine spray.—**at'omiser** *n.* an instrument for reducing a liquid to the form of spray.—**at'omy** *n.* an atom; a tiny being; (*Anat.*) a skeleton.—**atom (atomic) bomb,** a bomb of unimaginable destructive power, whose energy is derived from the nuclear disintegration of atoms of elements of high atomic mass, e.g. uranium 235.—**atomic energy,** energy derived from the disintegration of the nucleus of an atom.—**atomic fission,** the action of disintegrating; the disintegration of the atom.—**atomic pile,** apparatus for producing energy by the disintegration of atoms.—**atomic weight,** the weight of an atom of an element, taking the weight of the hydrogen atom as 1, e.g. oxygen=16, nitrogen=14, sulphur=32, etc. [Gk. *a-*, neg; *tomē*, a cutting].

atonal (a-tō'nal) *a.* (*Mus.*) without tone; unreferred to any scale or tonic.—**atonal'ity** *n.*—**atonic** (a-ton'ik) *a.* without tone; unaccented; (*Med.*) lacking tone or energy.—**atony** (at'ō-ni) *n.* lack of tone or accent [Gk. *a-*, neg; *tonos*, tone].

atone (a-tōn') *v.t.* to appease; to expiate (*rare*);—*v.i.* to make amends or reparation for an offence; to satisfy by giving an equivalent (with *for*).—**atone'ment** *n.* amends; reconciliation, esp. the reconciliation of God and man by the sufferings and death of Christ [E. (to set) *at one*].

atrabiliar (at-ra-bil'i-ar) *a.* affected by black bile; hypochondriac, melancholy. Also **atrabil'ious** [L. *ater*, black; *bilis*, bile].

atrip (a-trip') *adv.* (*Naut.*) said of the anchor when lifted just clear of the ground.

atrium (ā'tri-um) *n.* the entrance-hall, the principal room of an ancient Roman house; (*Anat.*) an auricle of the heart [L.=a hall].

atrocious (a-trō-shus) *a.* savagely brutal; extremely cruel; very wicked; grievous; (*Colloq.*) of work, etc., of very poor quality.—**atro'ciously** *adv.*—**atro'ciousness** *n.*—**atrocity** (a-tros'i-ti) *n.* extreme wickedness; a cruel and brutal act [L. *atrox*, fierce].

atrophy (at'rō-fi) *n.* a wasting away through lack of nutrition or use; emaciation; Also *v.t.* and *i.* to waste away; to cause to waste away.—**atroph'ic, at'rophied** *a.* [Gk. *a-*, neg.; *trophē*, nourishment].

atropin, atropine (at'rō-pin) *n.* a poisonous alkaloid obtained from the deadly nightshade, used as a drug to dilate the pupil of the eye [Gk. *Atropos*, one of the *Fates*].

attach (a-tach') *v.t.* to bind, fasten, or tie; to take by legal authority; to bind by affection; to assign, e.g. an officer to a regiment;—*v.i.* to adhere; to be ascribed to.—**attach'able** *a.*—**attached'** *a.* fixed; fastened; bound by affection; fond of.—**attach'ment** *n.* [Fr. *attacher*].

attaché (a-ta'shā) *n.* one attached to the suite of an ambassador.—**attaché-case,** *n.* small leather hand-case [Fr. *attacher*].

attack (a-tak') *v.t.* to fall on with force; to assail with hostile criticism in words or writing; to set to work on; to begin to affect (of illness);—*n.* a violent onset or assault [Fr. *attaquer*].

attain (a-tān') *v.t.* to reach by exertion; to obtain by effort; to accomplish; to achieve;—*v.i.* to arrive at (generally foll. by *to*).—**attain'able** *a.*—**attainabil'ity, attain'ableness** *n.*—**attain'ment** *n.* the act of attaining; that which is attained [L. *attingere*, to reach].

attaint (a-tānt') *v.t.* to stain or disgrace; to accuse of; to find guilty; to deprive of civil rights for treason;— *n.* a taint or disgrace.—**attain'der** *n.* loss of civil rights after sentence of death or outlawry for treason or felony.—**attaint'ment** *n.* [O.Fr. *ataint*, convicted].

attar (at'ar) *n.* a fragrant volatile oil obtained from rose-petals. Also **ot'to, ot'tar** [Pers. *atar*].

attempt (a-temt') *v.t.* to try; to endeavour to do; to attack; to tempt;—*n.* trial; an effort, esp. unsuccessful; an assault.—**attempt'able** *a.* [L. *ad*, to; *temptare*, to try].

attend (a-tend') *v.t.* to take part in; to accompany as companion or servant; to be present with or at; to give medical care to;—*v.i.* to pay attention; to take care of; to wait or be in waiting.—**attend'ance** *n.* the act of attending; persons present.—**attend'ant** *a.* being present; consequent;—*n.* one who accompanies as friend or servant; a caretaker.—**atten'tion** *n.* careful observation; watching; act of civility; command issued, as in a military sense, to ensure readiness to act.—**atten'tions** *n. pl.* courtship.—**attent'ive** *a.* full of attention.—**attent'ively** *adv.*—**attent'iveness** *n.* [L. *ad*, to; *tendere*, to stretch].

attenuate (a-ten'ū-āt) *v.t.* to make thin or fine; to make slender; to weaken the potency of;—*a.* slender; thin; (*Bot.*) tapering.—**atten'uant** *a.* tending to make thin, esp. of liquids; diluting.—**atten'uated** *a.*—**attenua'tion** *n.* [L. *ad*, to; *tenuis*, thin].

attest (a-test') *v.t.* and *v.i.* to bear witness to; to vouch for; to certify; (*Law*) to witness officially (a signature).—**attest'able, attest'ative** *a.*—**attesta'tion** *n.* [L. *attestari*, to bear witness].

Attic (a'tik) *a.* pert. to *Attica* or Athens; resembling the refined and elegant style of the Athenian writers.—**att'ic** *n.* a room under the roof of a house where ceiling follows line of the roof (common in Greek archit.);—a garret.—**Attic wit** or **salt,** delicate, subtly sharp wit [Gk. *Attikos*, pert. to Attica].

attire (a-tīr') *v.t.* to dress; to array in splendid garments;—*n.* apparel; dress.—**attire'ment, attir'ing** *n.* [O.Fr. *atirier*, to put in order].

attitude (at'i-tūd) *n.* posture of a person; pose (in portrait); (*Fig.*) mental or moral disposition;—**attitud'inal** *a.* pert. to attitude.—**attitudina'rian** *n.* one who studies or affects attitudes.—**attitud'inise** *v.i.*—**attitudini'ser** [L. *aptus*, fit].

attorney (a-ter'ni) *n.* one put in the *turn* or place of another; one legally authorised by another to transact business; a solicitor.—**attorn'** *v.t.* to transfer;—*v.i.* to transfer homage; to acknowledge a new landlord.—**attor'neyship** *n.*—**attor'neydom** *n.*—**power, letter** or **warrant of attorney,** a legal authorisation by which one person may act for another [O.Fr. *atorner*, to direct].

attract (a-trakt') *v.t.* and *v.i.* to draw toward; to cause to approach; (*Fig.*) to allure; to provoke notice.—**attractabil'ity** *n.* the quality of being attractable.—**attract'able** *a.*—**attract'ile** *a.* attractive.—**attrac'tion** *n.* the act of drawing to; the force which draws together bodies or particles; the affinity existing between one chemical body and another; (*Fig.*) that which allures, or fascinates.—**attract'ive** *a.* having the power to attract.—**attract'ively** *adv.*—**attract'iveness** *n.* [L. *ad*, to; *trahere*, *tractum*, to draw].

attribute (a-trib'ūt) *v.t.* to consider as belonging to; to ascribe to.—**attribute** (at'ri-būt) *n.* something inherent in a person or thing; an inseparable property; (*Gram.*) a qualifying word used, not as part of predicate, but adjectivally, as in *red* hair.—**attrib'utable** *a.* that may be ascribed to.—**attribu'tion** *n.* the act of ascribing to; the quality attributed.—*a.* **attrib'utive** [L. *ad*, to; *tribuere*, to bestow].

attrition (a-trish'un) *n.* the act of wearing away by friction; state of being worn; (*Mil.*) deliberate exhaustion of enemy's men and resources before making an attack.—**attrite'** *a.* worn away by rubbing or friction; (*Theol.*)

penitent through fear [L. *attritus*, rubbed away].

attune (a-tūn') *v.t.* to put in tune; to make musical; to make one instrument accord with another; (*Fig.*) to bring into spiritual harmony; to fit for a purpose.—**attune'ment** *n.* [L. *ad*, to; *tune*].

aubade (ō-bȧd') *n.* a morning song [Fr. *aube*, dawn].

aubergine (ō'ber-zhēn) *n.* edible, white, egg-shaped fruit of the egg-plant, used as a vegetable [Fr.].

aubrietia (aw-bri-ē'sha) *n.* or *Purple Rock Cress*, a hardy, evergreen trailing plant [fr. *Aubriet* (1665-1742), a naturalist].

auburn (aw'burn) *a.* reddish brown;—*n.* rich chestnut colour [L.L. *alburnus*, blond].

auction (awk'shun) *n.* a method of public sale whereby the object for sale is secured by highest bidder.—*v.t.* to sell by auction.—**auc'tionary** *a.*—**auctioneer'** *n.* one licensed to sell by auction;—*v.i.* to sell by auction.—**Dutch auction**, an auction at which the upset price is very high, and is gradually lowered [L. *augere, auctum*, to increase].

auction bridge (awk'shun brij') *n.* a card game for four players.

auctorial (awk'tōr-i-al) *a.* pertaining to authorship [L. *auctor*, author].

audacious (aw-dā'shus) *a.* bold, fearless; impudent; insolent.—**auda'ciously** *adv.*—**auda'ciousness** *n.*—**audac'ity** *n.* boldness, effrontery, impudence. [L. *audax*, bold].

audible (aw'di-bl) *a.* capable of being heard. —**aud'ibly** *adv.*—**audibil'ity, aud'ibleness** *n.* [L. *audire*, to hear].

audience (aw'di-ens) *n.* the act of hearing; an assembly of hearers; a ceremonial reception or interview; a judicial hearing.—**aud'ient** *a.* listening [L. *audire*, to hear].

audit (aw'dit) *n.* an examination, by qualified persons, of accounts of a business, public office, or undertaking;—*v.t.* to test and vouch for the accuracy of accounts.—**audi'tion** *n.* the act, or sense, of hearing; hearing given to a performer as test.—**aud'itor** *n.* a hearer; one authorised to investigate the financial condition of a company or society.—**auditor'ium** *n.* the body of a concert hall or theatre where the audience are seated; the nave of a church. —**aud'itorship** *n.*—**aud'itory** *a.* pert. to the sense of hearing;—*n.* a lecture room; an audience. [L. *audire*, to hear].

auger (aw'ger) *n.* a boring tool for woodwork, like a large gimlet. [*An auger* for *a nauger*, fr. O.E. *nafu*, nave; *gār*, dart].

aught (awt) *n.* anything; any part; a whit;—*adv.* to any extent [O.E. *awiht*, fr. *a*, ever, and *wiht*, thing].

augment (awg-ment') *v.t.* to increase; to add to; to make larger; to enlarge;—*v.i.* to grow larger.—**aug'ment** *n.* an increase; a prefix added to the past tense of verbs to distinguish them from other tenses.—**augment'able** *a.*—**augmenta'tion** *n.* act of enlarging; an increase.—**augmen'tative** *a.* increasing;—*n.* a word which expresses with increased force the idea conveyed by the simpler word, e.g. *arch*, chief, as in *arch-duke*, etc.—**augment'er** *n.* [L. *augmentum*, an increase].

augur (aw'gur) *n.* a soothsayer; a diviner; a member of a college of priests in Rome who claimed to be able to foretell events by observing the flight or other actions of birds; —*v.t.* to foretell; to presage; to prognosticate. —**au'gural** *a.*—**au'gurship** *n.*—**au'gury** *n.* art of an augur; omen [L.].

august (aw-gust') *a.* majestic; imposing; sublime; grand; magnificent; sacred [a title first bestowed on the Emperor Octavianus by the Roman Senate, fr. L. *augere*, to increase].

August (aw'gust) *n.* the eighth month of the year [named in honour of the Emperor *Augustus* as being the month identified with memorable events in his career].

Augustan (aw-gus'tan) *a.* classic; refined; pertaining to the Emperor *Augustus*, 31 B.C.-A.D. 14;—*n.* a writer of the Augustan age.

Augustine (aw-gus'tin) *n.* a member of a monastic order which follows rules framed by St. Augustine (354-430) or deduced from his writings; a Black Friar.

auk (awk) *n.* a marine bird, of the Arctic regions, with short wings, webbed feet and heavy body. The **great auk** (extinct since 1884) was flightless. The **little auk** is a winter visitor to Britain [Icel. *alka*].

aunt (ȧnt) *n.* a father's or a mother's sister; also applied to an uncle's wife.—**Aunt Sally**, a game at fairs, which consists in throwing balls or sticks at a woman's head on a pole [L. *amita*, a father's sister].

aura (aw'ra) *n.* a subtle invisible essence or fluid said to emanate from human and animal bodies, and even from things; (*Fig.*) the atmosphere surrounding a person; character; personality; (*Path.*) a premonitory symptom of epilepsy and hysteria, as of cold air rising to the head.—**aur'al** *a.* pert. to the air, or to an aura [L. *aura*, a breeze].

aural (aw'ral) *a.* pert. to the ear, or sense of hearing.—**aur'ally** *adv.* [L. *auris*, the ear].

aureola, aureole (aw-rē'o-la, aw'rē-ōl) *n.* a radiance round a sacred figure, in art; also a gold disc round the head, as a symbol of holiness; a halo; a nimbus [L. *aureus*, golden].

aureomycin (aw'rē-ō-mī'sin) *n.* an antibiotic, similar to penicillin and streptomycin. [L. *aureus*, Gk. *mukēs*, mushroom].

auric (aw'rik) *a.* pert. to gold; (*Chem*). applied to compounds in which gold is trivalent [L. *aurum*, gold].

auricle (aw'ri-kl) *n.* the external ear; each of the two upper cavities of the heart.—**auricula** (aw-rik'ū-la) *n.* (*Bot.*) a kind of primula, 'dusty miller' or 'bear's ear.'—**auric'ular** *a.* pert. to ear, or to hearing; told in the ear (of confession).—**auric'ulate, au'riform** *a.* ear-shaped [L. *auris*, the ear].

auriferous (aw-rif'e-rus) *a.* yielding gold [L. *aurum*, gold; *ferre*, to bear].

Aurora (aw-ro'ra) *n.* (*Myth.*) the Roman goddess of the dawn.—**auro'ra** *n.* the dawn; the rosy tint in the sky before the sun rises; an orange-red colour.—**aurora borealis** (bō-rē-ā'lis), a luminous phenomenon, supposed to be of electrical origin, seen at night in the northern sky. Also called 'northern lights.'—**aurora australis**, the corresponding phenomenon in the southern sky.

auscultation (aws-kul-tā'shun) *n.* (*Med.*) listening to the movement of heart and lungs either directly with the ear, or with a stethoscope.—**aus'culate** *v.t.* and *i.* to examine thus [L. *auscultare*, to listen to].

auspice (aw'spis) *n.* an omen based on observing birds; augury; divination; *n.pl.*—**au'spices**, protection; patronage, esp. **under the auspices of**, under the protection or patronage of.—**au'spicate** *v.t.* to predict; to inaugurate in favourable conditions.—**auspi'cious** (aw-spi'shus) *a.* giving promise of success; favourable; propitious.—**auspi'ciously** *adv.*—**auspi'ciousness** *n.* [L. *auspicium*, fr. *avis*, a bird; *specere*, to behold].

austere (aws-tēr') *a.* harsh; severe; strict; simple and without luxury.—**austere'ly** *adv.* —**austere'ness, austerity** *n.* severity; extreme simplicity; asceticism [Gk. *austēros*, harsh].

austral (aws'tral) *a.* southern.—**Australasian** (aws-tral-ā'shi-an) *a.* pert. to Australia and the neighbouring islands;—*n.* a native there. —**Australian** (aws-trāl'yan) *a.* pert. to Australia;—*n.* a native of Australia [L. *auster*, the south wind].

autarchy (awt'ar-ki) *n.* absolute power; despotism; dictatorship [Gk. *autos*, self; *archein*, to rule].

authentic (aw-thent'ik) *a.* genuine; real; not of doubtful origin; trustworthy; of attested authority. Also **authent'ical.—authent'ically** *adv.*—**authent'icate** *v.t.* to prove to be genuine; to confirm.—**authentica'tion** *n.*—**authenticity** *n.* (aw-then-tis'i-ti) the quality of genuineness [Gk. *authentikos*, warranted, fr. *authentein*, to have full power].

author (aw'thor) *n.* (*fem.* **au'thoress**) the beginner or originator of anything; the writer of a book, article etc.—**autho'rial** *a.* pert. to an author.—**au'thorship** *n.* the quality or function of being an author; source; origin [L. *auctor*].

authorise (aw'thor-īz) *v.t.* to clothe with authority; to empower; to sanction; to make legal; to justify.—**authoris'able** *a.*—**authorisa'tion** *n.* [L. *auctorari*].

authority (aw-thor'i-ti) *n.* legal power or right; influence exercised by virtue of character, office, or mental or moral qualities; one who is appealed to in support of actions or measures; a writing by an expert on a particular subject; the writer himself; justification; influence; permission; a body or group of persons in control (often *pl.*).—**authorita'rian** *a.* advocating obedience to authority as opposed to individual liberty;—*n.* an advocate of authority.—**author'itative** *a.* having the weight of authority; justified.—**author'itatively** *adv.*—**author'itativeness** *n.* [L. *auctoritas*].

auto- (aw'tō) a combining form fr. Gk. *autos*, self, used in many derivatives and meaning *self, oneself, by oneself*, etc.

auto (aw'tō) *n.* (*Colloq.*) abbrev. for automobile.—**au'tobus** *n.* an automobile omnibus; a motor-bus.—**au'tocar** *n.* a motor-car.—**au'toist** *n.* (*U.S.*) a motorist.—**automobile** (aw-tō-mō'bil, aw'tō-mō-bēl) *n.* a road vehicle driven by mechanical power; a motor-car;—*a.* pert. to motor cars. [Gk. *autos*, self; L. *mobilis*, mobile].

autobahn (ou'tō-bân) in Germany, a trunk road specially constructed for motor traffic [Ger. *Bahn*, a road].

autobiography (aw-tō-bī-og'ra-fi) *n.* the story of a person's life, written by himself.—**autobiog'rapher** *n.*—**autobiograph'ic**, *a.*—**autobiograph'ically** *adv.* [Gk. *autos*, self; *bios*, life; *graphein*, to write].

autochthon (aw-tok'thon) *n.* an original inhabitant, an aboriginal; a native.—**autoch'thonous** *a.*—**autoch'thony** *n.* [Gk. *autos*, self; *chthon*, the land].

autocrat (aw'tō-krat) *n.* a monarch who rules by his own absolute right; despot. -**autocrat'ic** *a.*—**autocrat'ically** *adv.*—**autocracy** (aw-tok'ra-si) *n.* uncontrolled power; a state, the ruler of which has absolute power [Gk. *autos*, self; *kratein*, to rule].

auto-da-fé (aw'tō-dâ-fā') *n.* the ceremony accompanying the sentence and execution (generally by burning) of heretics by the Inquisition;—*pl.* **au'tos-da-fé** [Port. fr. L. *actum*, an act; *de*, of; *fides*, faith].

auto-erotism (aw'tō-er'ot-izm) *n.* sexual emotion self-produced [Gk. *autos*, self; *eros*, love].

autograph (aw'tō-graf) *n.* a person's own handwriting or signature; an original manuscript;—*a.* written in one's own handwriting;—*v.t.* to write one's own hand; to write one's signature in [Gk. *autos*, self; *graphein*, to write].

autogyro (aw-tō-jī'rō) *n.* aeroplane using horizontal airscrew for vertical ascent and descent [Gk. *autos*, self; *guros*, a ring].

automatic (aw-to-mat'ik) *a.* self-acting; mechanical; not voluntary; done unconsciously;—*n.* an automatic pistol—**automat'ical** *a.*—**automat'ically** *adv.* mechanically.—**automation** (o-tō-mā'shon) *n.* the automatic control of production processes by electronic apparatus.—**autom'atism** *n.* involuntary action; power of self-movement without external stimulus.—**autom'aton** *n.* a mechanical contrivance, having its m tive power within itself; a robot.—*pl.* **autom'ata** [Gk. *automatso*, self-acting].

autonomy (aw-ton'ō-mi) *n.* the right of self-government; independence.—**auton'omous, autonom'ic** *a.* self-governing; independent [Gk. *autos*, self; *nomos*, a law].

autopsy (aw'top-si) *n.* the dissection and examination of a dead body; a post-mortem examination; personal observation.—**autop'tic(al)** *a.* self-observed.—**autop'tically** *adv.* [Gk. *autos*, self; *opsis*, sight].

auto-suggestion (aw'tō-su-jest'yun) *n.* a mental process similar to hypnotism but applied by the subject to himself.

autotomy (aw-tot'-o-mi) *n.* self-mutilation of some animals [GK. *tomé*, cut].

autumn (aw'tum) *n.* the third season of the year, generally applied to August, September, October; the season of decay; the time of declining powers.—**autum'nal** *a.* [L. *autumnus*].

auxiliary (awg-zil'ya-ri) *a.* helping; assisting; subsidiary;—*n.* a helper; (*Gram.*) a verb which helps to form moods, tenses, or voice of another verb, e.g. *be, have, shall, will, may* [L. *auxilium*, help].

avail (a-vāl') *v.i.* to profit by; to take advantage of;—*v.t.* to benefit; to profit;—*n.* advantage; profit; benefit; utility.—**avail'able** *a.* capable of being used to advantage; procurable.—**avail'ableness, availabil'ity** *n.* [L. *ad*, to; *valere*, to be strong].

aval (âv'al) *a.* belonging to a grandfather [L. *avus*, grandfather].

avalanche (av'a-lansh) *n.* mass of snow and ice moving down from a height and gathering momentum in its descent; a snowslip; (*Fig.*) tremendous downpour [O.Fr. *a val*, into the valley].

avarice (av'a-ris) *n.* excessive love of money; greed; miserliness; cupidity.—**avari'cious** *a.* covetous; grasping.—**avari'ciously** *adv.*—**avari'ciousness** *n.* [L. *avarus*, greedy].

avast (a-vast') *interj.* cease! hold! stop! enough! [Dut. *houd vast*, hold fast].

Avatar (av-a-tar') *n.* Divine incarnation; the descent to earth of a god or some exalted being [Sans. descent].

ave (ā'vā, ā'vē) *interj.* hail! farewell!—*n.* an Ave Maria or Hail Mary, an invocation to the Virgin Mary. (Luke 1) [L.].

avenge (a-venj') *v.t.* and *v.i.* to take satisfaction for an injury; to punish a wrong-doer; to seek retribution.—**avenge'ful** *a.* desiring retribution.—**avenge'ment** *n.*—**aveng'er** *n.* (*fem.* **aveng'eress**) one who avenges [O.Fr. *avengier*, to seek retribution].

avenue (av'e-nū) *n.* principal approach bordered with trees to a mansion; any road in park bordered with trees; a wide street with houses and row of trees down each side; (*Fig.*) a means towards, as in *avenue to fame* [L. *ad*, to; *venire*, to come].

aver (a-ver') *v.t.* to declare positively; to avouch; to assert; to allege.—*pr.p.* **aver'ring**;—*pa.p.* **averred'**.—**aver'ment** *n.* the act of averring; a positive assertion; (*Law*) proof of a plea [L. *ad*, to; *verus*, true].

average (av'e-rāj) *a.* containing a mean proportion; ordinary; normal;—*n.* a medial estimate obtained by dividing the sum of a number of quantities by the number of quantities.—*v.t.* to reduce to a mean [O.Fr. *average*, cattle or possessions; fr. L. *habere*, to have].

averse (a-vers') *a.* reluctant (to do) or disinclined for; unwilling; set against (foll. by *to*).—**averse'ly** *adv.* with repugnance.—**averse'ness** *n.*—**aver'sion** *n.* a strong dislike; instinctive antipathy; object of dislike [L. *aversus*, turned away].

avert (a-vert') *v.t.* to turn away from or aside; to ward off.—**avert'ed** *a.*—**avert'edly** *adv.*—**avert'ible** *a.* capable of being avoided [L. *a*, from; *vertere*, to turn].

avian (ā'vi-an) *a.* pert. to birds.—**av'iary** *n.* an enclosed space for breeding, rearing and keeping of birds.—**av'iculture** *n.* the scientific breeding of birds [L. *avis*, a bird].

aviation (ā-vi-ā′shun) *n.* the art of flying aircraft.—**a'viate** *v.i.* to fly.—**a'viator** *n.*—(*fem.* **a'viatress, a'viatrix.**) a qualified pilot of an aircraft [L. *avis*, a bird].

avid (av′id) *a.* eager; greedy; desirous (foll. by *of* or *for*).—**avid'ity** *n.* greediness; eagerness; hunger; (*Fig.*) zest; burning desire [L. *avidus*, greedy].

avital (av′i-tạl) *a.* pert. to a grandfather [L. *avus*, a grandfather].

avizandum (av-i-zan′dum) *n.* (*Scots Law*) the suspension of a case for the judge's private consideration. Also **avisan'dum** [L.L. *avisare*, to consider].

avocado (av-ō-ka′dō) *n.* the alligator pear; the juicy edible fruit of a West Indian tree of the laurel family [Mex.].

avocation (av-ō-kā′shun) *n.* originally the business which diverted or distracted one from the pleasures of life, now used for one's primary vocation in life; a distraction.—**avoc'ative** *a.* calling off;—*n.* a dissuasion; that which calls off.—**avoc'atory** *a.* recalling, especially of letters recalling subjects to their native countries in time of war [L. *a*, away; *vocare*, to call].

avocet, avoset (av′ō-set) *n.* a genus of wading-birds related to the snipe [Fr.].

avoid (ạ-void′) *v.t.* to shun; to elude; to keep clear of; to eschew; to abstain from; to escape; (*Law*) to invalidate; to annul.—**avoid'able** *a.*—**avoid'ance** *n.* act of shunning; a vacant church benefice [L. *ex*, out; and *void*].

avoirdupois (av-ur-dū-poiz′) *n.* a common system of weights [corrupt. of O.Fr. *avoir de pois*, goods by weight, i.e. not by numbers].

avoset See **avocet.**

avouch (ạ-vouch′) *v.t.* to declare positively; to avow; to guarantee; [L. *ad*, to; *vocare*, to call].

avow (ạ-vou′) *v.t.* to declare openly; to own; to confess freely; to acknowledge.—**avow'able** *a.*—**avow'al** *n.* an open declaration or admission.—**avow'ance,** evidence; testimony.—**avow'edly** *adv.* [Fr. *avouer*].

avowee Same as **advowee.**

avulsion (ạ-vul′shun) *n.* (*Med.*) a tearing asunder; a fragment torn off [L. *avulsus*, plucked off].

avuncular (ạ-vung′kū-lạr) *a.* pert. to an uncle [L. *avunculus*, a maternal uncle].

await (ạ-wāt′) *v.t.* to wait for; be in store for; attend; be ready for.

awake (ạ-wāk′) *v.t.* to rouse from sleep; to stir up;—*v.i.* to cease from sleep; to bestir oneself;—*pa.t.* **awoke'**; *pa.p.* **awoke', awaked'**;—*a.* not asleep; alert; vigilant; alive.—**awak'en** *v.t.* and *v.i.* to rouse from sleep; to awake; to excite.—**awak'enment, awak(en)'ing** *n.* the art of awaking; a revival of interest or conscience [O.E. *awacian*].

award (ạ-wawrd′) *v.t.* to adjudge; to determine (a point submitted); to decide authoritatively; to assign judicially;—*n.* judgment; the recorded decision of an arbitrator in a court of law; thing awarded; prize.—**award'ment** *n.* the promulgating of an award [fr. O.Fr. *eswarder*].

aware (ạ-wār) *a.* watchful; mindful; conscious of; possessing knowledge of; sensible.—**aware'ness** *n.* [O.E. *gewaer*, conscious].

awash (ạ-wosh′) *adv.* (*Naut.*) level with the surface of the water; washed by the waves.

away (ạ-wā) *adv.* absent; at a distance; on the way; apart; be gone! [O.E. *onweg*, on the way].

awe (aw) *n.* great fear mingled with veneration and apprehension of danger; dread; terror;—*v.t.* to inspire with awe.—**awe'some** *a.* inspiring awe.—**awestruck', awe'stricken** *a.* overwhelmed with awe.—**aw'ful** *a.* full of awe; filling with fear and admiration; impressive; venerable; majestic; dreadful; terrible; horrible; ugly; unsightly.—**aw'fulness** *n.* [O.E. *ege*, awe].

aweigh (ạwā′) *adv.* (*Naut.*) when a ship's anchor is just broken out of the ground by the initial strain on the cable; atrip.

awful See under **awe.**

awhile (ạ-whīl′) *adv.* for a while.

awkward (awk′ward) *a.* unskilful; ungainly; clumsy; difficult to manage; inconvenient; embarrassing; perverted; sinister.—**awk'wardly** *adv.*—**awk'wardness** *n.* [M.E. *awk*, wrong; and *ward*].

awl (awl) *n.* a small pointed instrument for boring holes in leather [O.E. *awel*].

awn (awn) *n.* the bristle-like growth, popularly known as the beard, of cereals (oats, barley) and grasses; a scale or husk.—**awned', awn'y** *a.* having awns, full of beard. [Scand.].

awning (aw′ning) *n.* a covering of canvas, etc. to shelter from the sun's rays.—**awning deck,** a superstructure deck; the top deck of a two-deck ship [etym. unknown].

awoke See **awake.**

awry (a-ri′) *adv.* and *a.* twisted to one side; crooked [See **wry**]. [earlier, *on wry*].

axe, ax (aks) *n.* a cutting instrument with a blade in line with the handle, used with both hands for hewing down trees or chopping wood.—**an axe to grind,** a private end or purpose to serve [O.E. *aex*].

axes (ak′ses) plural form of **axe** and **axis.**

axiom (ak′si-om) *n.* a necessary and self-evident proposition, requiring no proof.—**axiomat'ic, -al** *a.* self-evident.—**axiomat'ically** *adv.* [Gk. *axioma*. fr. *axioein*, to require].

axis (ak′sis) *n.* the imaginary line round which a solid body rotates or a geometrical figure is symmetrically disposed.—*pl.* **ax'es.**—**Axis Powers,** Germany, Italy and Japan previous to the Second World War.—**ax'ial** *a.* forming the axis.—**ax'ially** *adv.* [L. *axis*, an axle].

axle, axle-tree (ak′sl-trē) *n.* a bar of wood or iron rod on which a wheel, or a system of wheels, turns.—**ax'le-arm** *n.* the portion of the axle passing through the hub of the wheel.—**ax'le-bed,** *n.* the portion of the axle between the wheels.—**ax'led** *a.* having an axle.—**ax'le-pin** *n.* a pin or bolt securing the axle to the body of a vehicle [O.N. *oxul-tre*].

Axminster (aks′min-stẹr) *n.* a rich machine-made carpet [orig. woven in *Axminster*].

ay, aye (ī) *adv.* yes; yea.—**ayes** (īz) *n.pl.* affirmative votes or voters [*yea*].

ayah (ī′ya) *n.* a native Indian nurse-maid or lady's maid [Port. *aia*, a governess].

aye, ay (ā) *adv.* always; ever; [O.N. *ei*].

azalea (a-zā′le-ạ) *n.* a genus of plants allied to the rhododendron [Gk. *azaleos*, dry].

azimuth (az′i-muth) *n.* of a heavenly body, the arc of the horizon comprehended between the meridian of the observer and a vertical circle passing through the centre of the body.—**az'imuthal** [Ar. *al*, the; *samt*, direction].

azoic (ạ-zō′ik) *a.* pert. to that part of geologic time before animal life existed [Gk. *a-*, neg.; *zoē*, life].

Aztec (az′tek) *n.* a member of the race which founded the Mexican Empire centuries before their conquest by the Spaniards;—their language;—*a.* pert. to the race or its language.

azure (azh′ūr) *n.* sky blue; the sky;—*a.* sky-blue [Fr. *azur*, from Ar.].

B

Baal (bā′al) *n.* a false deity.—*pl.* **Ba'alim.**—**Ba'alist** *n.* a worshipper of Baal.—**Ba'alism** *n.* [Heb.].

baas (bȧs) *n.* in S. Africa, the master or head-man, usually a white man [Dut.].

Babbitt metal (bab′it met′ạl) *n.* a soft alloy used to reduce friction in machine bearings.—

babb'itt *v.t.* to line, fill or face with this [Isaac *Babbitt*, inventor].

babble (ba′-bl) *v.t.* and *i.* to chatter senselessly; to prate; to reveal secrets;—*n.* prattling; idle talk; murmuring of running water.—**bab'bler** *n.*—**bab'bling** *n.* [Onomat].

babel (bā′-bel) *n.* a confusion of unintelligible sounds; noisy babble of many people talking at the one time; uproar, at a public meeting. —**ba'beldom** *n.* uproar. [Heb.=confusion].

baboo, babu (bȧ′-bȯȯ) *n.* the Hindu word of respect for Mr., but often used contemptuously of anglicised Hindus.—**baboo English,** a mongrel form of English.

baboon (bạ-bȯȯn′) *n.* a species of monkey with large body, big canine teeth and capacious cheek-pouches. [Fr. *babouin*].

baby (bā′-bi) *n.* an infant; a young child;—*a.* pert. to a baby; small, as in **ba'by-car, ba'by-grand** (piano), etc.—**ba'by-farm'er** *n.* one who, for a fee, accepts care of infants.—**ba'byhood** *n.* the period of infancy.—**ba'byish** *a.* infantile; behaving like a young child.—**ba'byishness** *n.*—**ba'byism** *n.* the characteristics or qualities of a baby.—**ba'by-sitt'er** *n.* one who takes over duties of parents for an evening. [earlier *baban*, imit. of baby speech].

Babylonian (bab-i-lō′-ni-ạn) *n.* an inhabitant of Babylon; a papist;—*a.* pert. to ancient Babylonia; magnificent; luxurious; dissolute; vicious.

baccalaureate (bak-ạ-law′-rē-āt) *n.* the university degree of bachelor; (*U.S.*) an address to a graduating class.—**baccalau'rean** *a.* [fr. L.L. *baccalarius*, a small farmer].

baccarat, baccara (bak-ạ-rȧ′) *n.* a card game of chance [Fr.].

Bacchus (bak′-us)*n.* (*Myth.*) the god of wine.—**bacch'anal** *n.* a worshipper of Bacchus; a drunken reveller; an orgy in honour of Bacchus;—*a.* pert. to Bacchus; riotous; drunken.—**bacchana'lia** *n.pl.* feasts in honour of Bacchus; drunken revels.—**bacchana'lian** *n.* and *a.* bacchanal.—**bacch'ant** *n.* a priest or worshipper of Bacchus; a reveller.—(**bacchan'te** *n. fem.*).—**bacc'hic** *a.* relating to Bacchus; jovial due to intoxication [L.].

bachelor (bach′-e-lor) *n.* an unmarried man; a celibate; formerly, a young knight who fought under the aegis of another; one who has taken the first degree at a university; a monk who performed menial duties.—**bach'elorhood, bach'elorism, bach'elorship** *n.* the state of being a bachelor; celibacy.—**bach'elordom** *n.* bachelors collectively.—**bachelor's buttons,** the small yellow double flowers of buttercups or the red double flowers of the daisy [L.L. *baccalarius*, a small farmer].

bacillus (bạ-sil′-us) *n.* microscopic, rod-like organisms capable of causing certain diseases. —*pl.* **bacil'li**.—**bacil'lar, bacil'lary** *a.*—**bacil'licide** *n.* a substance used to destroy bacilli; a disinfectant.—**bacil'liform** *a.* of a rod-like shape [L. *baculus*, a rod].

back (bak) *n.* the upper or hinder part of the trunk of an animal; the hinder part of an object; a footballer whose position is in front of goal-keeper;—*a.* of the back; at the rear of; not current (as a magazine); reversed; remote;—*adv.* to or toward a former place, state, condition, or time; away from the front; in return;—*v.t.* to get, or ride, upon the back of; to provide with a back; to force backward; to place a bet on; to support; to endorse (a cheque, etc.);—*v.i.* to move or go back; of the wind, to change direction counter-clockwise.—**back'ache** *n.* continuous pain in the back.—**back'ben'cher** *n.* a member of parliament not entitled to sit on the front benches.—**back'bite** *v.t.* to speak evil of someone in his absence.—**back'biter** *n.*—**back'-blocks** *n.pl.* the far interior of Australia.—**back'-bone** *n.* the spine or vertebral column; firmness; courage.—**back'-boned** *a.* staunch.—**back'-chat** *n.* perky reply; insolence; impertinence.—**back'-cloth** *n.* painted cloth at back of stage, depicting scenery.—**back'-door** *n.* a back entrance; an indirect approach.—**back'-end** *n.* latter part; towards end of season.—**back'er** *n.* supporter; one who bets on a horse, greyhound, or the like; a punter.—**back'-fire** *n.* in internal combustion engines, an explosion in the cylinder occurring before the piston has reached the top of the stroke; —*v.i.* to do this.—**back'-ground** *n.* ground at the back; a situation not readily noticed; part behind foreground of a picture or stage setting; knowledge gained by experience.—**back'-hand** *n.* writing sloped from left to right; a stroke in tennis with the hand turned backwards.—**back'-hand'ed** *a.* with the back of the hand; deceitful; indirect; sarcastic; doubtful.—**back'hander** *n.* a blow with the back of the hand; a bribe.—**back'ing** *n.* support; sympathy; providing anything with a support; a wind-change in a counter-clockwise direction.—**back'lash** *n.* the jarring reaction of a machine due to the degree of play between two or more cogs on a wheel-train.—**back'-num'ber** *n.* a copy of an out-of-date publication; one behind the times or unprogressive.—**back'-room** *n.* a room at the back of a building; a room where secret devices are tried out.—**back-room boys,** experts esp. during time of war, conducting secret experiments.—**back'side** *n.* back or hinder part; the rear side; the buttocks; the rump.—**back'-sight** *n.* the rear sight of a rifle. —**back'slide** *v.i.* to slide backwards; to lapse from a high moral standard.—**back'slider** *n.*—**back'sliding** *n.*—**back'stairs** *n.pl.* stairs at the back of a house;—*a.* not straightforward; underhand.—**back'stays** *n.pl.* ropes supporting the upper mast, secured to the gunwale abaft the same to counteract the strain of the sails. —**back'ward** *adv.* with the back in advance; towards, or on, the back; to a worse state; in a reverse direction;—*a.* directed to the back or rear; dull; behind in one's education; shy; unwilling; late.—**back'wardness** *n.*—**back'wards** *adv.*—**back'wash** *n.* backward current; (*Slang*) the dire consequences.—**back'water** *n.* water held back by a dam; water thrown back by a paddle-wheel; a by-way in a river or creek.—**back'woods** *n.pl.* outlying forest districts or remote undeveloped country.—**backwoods'-man** *n.*—**behind one's back,** clandestinely; not openly.—**to back out,** to retract; to recede from a promise.—**to back up,** to support.—**to break the back of,** to lay too onerous a burden on; to perform successfully the most difficult part of.—**to put one's back into,** to work with a will.—**to put one's back up,** to annoy or irritate [O.E. *baec*].

backgammon (bak-gam′-un) *n.* a game played by two with 15 pieces each on a special board, the moves depending on the throw of a dice [E. fr. *back* and M.E. *gamen*, play].

backsheesh, backshish (bak′-shēsh) *n.* word used in the East for a present of money; a gratuity; a tip.—Army pronunciation=buk-shē′ [Pers.].

bacon (bā′-kn) *n.* the finished product of the flesh of pigs and hogs after being salted and smoked; a rustic, or chawbacon.—**to save one's bacon** (*Colloq.*) to escape bodily injury or loss [O.Fr.].

bacterium (bak-tē′-ri-um) *n.* minute unicellular living organisms of the group of Schizomycetes or split fungi. The active cause of fermentations, putrefaction and disease; micro-organisms in general.—*pl.* **bacte'ria**.—**bacteriaem'ia** *n.* the presence of bacteria in the blood.—**bacte'rial** *a.*—**bacte'ricide** *n.* any agent capable of destroying bacteria.—**bactericid'al** *a.*—**bacte'riocyte** *n.* a phagocytic cell which engulfs bacteria.—**bacteriol'ogy** *n.* the study of bacteria.—**bacteriolog'ical** *a.*—**bacteriol'ogist** *n.* [Gk. *baktērion*, a little stick].

bad (bad) *a.* ill or evil; wicked.—**bad'dish** *a.* rather bad.—**bad'ly** *adv.*—**bad'ness** *n.*—**bad blood,** ill feeling.—**to go bad,** to rot or decay.—**to go to the bad,** to become worthless; to stray from moral rectitude [M.E. *badde*].

bade (bad) past tense of the verb **bid.**

badge (baj) *n.* an emblem, usually symbolic, worn to distinguish members of societies, regiments, etc.; token; mark; symbol [M.E. *bage*].

badger (baj'ẹr) *n.* a greyish-brown hibernating animal;—*v.t.* to follow hotly as dogs the badger; to tease, by persistent questioning; to pester or annoy [from the white stripe or *badge* on the animal's forehead].

badinage (bad-i-nàzh) *n.* playful or sportive talk; banter [Fr. *badin,* frivolous].

badminton (bad'min-tun) *n.* a game similar to tennis with the substitution of shuttlecocks for tennis balls; a summer-beverage compounded of claret, sugar and soda-water [fr. *Badminton* House in Gloucestershire where the game was invented].

baffle (baf'l) *v.t.* to check by shifts and turns; to treat with insult or mockery; to defeat in any way.—**baf'fler** *n.* -**baf'fling** *a.* disconcerting; confusing; bewildering;—**baf'flingly** *adv.* [etym. uncertain].

baffle (baf'l) *n.* a plate for regulating the flow of a liquid or gas; a metal plate used between the cylinders of an air-cooled motor engine to break up a stream of heated gases; a baffle-plate; a rigid mounting usually of wood, holding the reproducing diaphragm of a wireless receiver in order to diminish distortion and improve the bass tones [etym. uncertain].

baffy (baf'i) *n.* a wooden-headed golf-club with an oblique hitting surface.

bag (bag) *n.* a sack or pouch; content of a sack; results of one's fishing or hunting; an udder; —*v.t.* to put into a bag; to seize;—*v.i.* to hang loosely; to bulge or swell out.—*pr.p.* **bag'ging.** —*pa.p.* **bagged.**—**bag'gage,** *n.* tents and stores of an army; luggage; a dissolute woman.—**bag and baggage,** with all one's belongings.—**bag'ging** *n.* cloth or material for bags.—**bag'giness** *n.* the state of being baggy (as trousers).—**bag'git** *n.* a female salmon after spawning.—**bag'gy** *a.* hanging loosely; puffy. —**bag'man** *n.* (*Colloq.*) a commercial traveller. —**bags** *n.pl.* trousers;—(*Colloq.*) plenty.—**to let the cat out of the bag,** to reveal a secret unwittingly [O.N. *baggi*].

bagatelle (bag-ạ-tel') *n.* a trifle; a thing of little worth or importance; a game played with balls and a cue on a board; a short piece of music in light style [Fr.].

bagnio (ban'yō) *n.* a bathing establishment; a bath; a brothel; a place of detention in Turkey for slaves [It.].

bagpipe (bag'pīp) *n.* musical instrument, fitted with a wind-bag, a chanter on which the melody is played, and the drones which furnish the ground bass.—**bag'-pip'er** *n.* [M.E. *baggepipe*].

bail (bāl) *n.* (*Law*) security taken by the court that a person charged will attend at a future date to answer to the charge; one who furnishes this security;—*v.t.* to obtain the release of a person from prison by giving security against his reappearance.—**bail'able** *a.*—**bail'-bond** *n.* a bond given by a person who is being bailed and his surety.—**bail'ee** *n.* the holder of goods in trust who must obey the direction with which the delivery to him is made.—**bail out** *v.i.* to jump from an aircraft and descend by parachute.—**to admit to bail,** to release upon security [O.Fr. *bailler,* to keep secure].

bail, bale (bāl) *n.* a scoop; a shallow vessel for clearing water out of a boat;—*v.t.* to empty of water with some kind of water scoop.—**bail'er** *n.* [perh. Dut.].

bail (bāl) *n.* a little cross-piece bar laid on the tops of stumps in cricket; a pole separating horses in a stable [O.Fr. *baille,* barrier; perh. fr. L. *baculum,* a stick].

bailey (bā'li) *n.* the outer walls of a feudal castle; the enclosed spaces, lying between the outward wall and the central keep [perh. from *bail,* a little bar].

Bailey bridge (bāl'i brij) *n.* an extending bridge built up of panel units of steel trusses and designed for rapid construction [fr. the inventor].

bailie, baillie (bāl'i) *n.* a magistrate of a Scottish burgh with certain judicial and administrative authority within the burgh [O.Fr. *baillif,* a justice].

bailiff (bā'lif) *n.* an under-officer of a sheriff employed to prosecute directions and orders of the court as to ejectment and distress for rent; land-owner's agent [O.Fr. *baillif,* a a justice].

bailiwick (bāl'i-wik) *n.* the district over which the sheriff, as king's bailiff, has jurisdiction; bailiff's jurisdiction [O.Fr., *baillif,* a justice; O.E. *wik,* a village].

baillie See **bailie.**

bairn (bārn) *n.* (*Scot.*) a child [O.E. *bearn*].

bait (bāt) *n.* food, set to entice fish or an animal; food taken on a journey for refreshment; provender for horses at a regular stopping-place; a lure; snare;—*v.t.* to put food on a hook or in a trap as a lure; to give refreshment on a journey; to set dogs on an animal, such as the badger, the bear, etc.; to harass; to tease.—**bait'er** *n.*—**bait'ing** *a.* and *n.* [Icel. *beita,* to cause to bite].

baize (bāz) *n.* a woollen or cotton cloth with long nap, usually dyed in plain colours and mainly used for curtains, table-coverings and linings [O.Fr.].

bake (bāk) *v.t.* to harden by heat; to cook in an oven or over a fire;—*v.i.* to work at baking; to be baked.—**bake'house** *n.*—**bak'er** *n.*—**bak'ery** *n.* a bakehouse.—**bak'ing** *n.* a batch of bread, etc.—**a baker's dozen,** thirteen.—**baking powder,** a mixture of tartaric acid and bicarbonate of soda as a substitute for yeast [O.E. *bacan*].

Bakelite (bāk'ẹ-līt) *n.* a hard, strong, synthetic resin used as a substitute for wood, bone, celluloid, etc. [L.H. *Baekeland,* the inventor].

baksheesh See **backsheesh.**

Balaclava helmet (bal'ạ-klav'ạ) *n.* a woollen covering for the whole head, only the face being exposed [Crimean war].

balaena (ba-lē'nạ) *n.* the true whale, distinguished by having no dorsal fin [L.].

balalaika (bal-a-lī'kạ) *n.* an old Slavic musical instrument, having a triangular base with two or three strings [Russ.].

balance (bal'ạns) *n.* an apparatus for determining the weight, or comparing the masses, of bodies; a poised beam with two opposite scales; any condition of equilibrium; part of a watch or clock which regulates the beats; a sense of proportion and discretion; poise; payment still due, or cash in hand;—*v.t.* to weigh, as in a balance; to render equal in proportion, etc.; to adjust, as an account; —*v.i.* to be of the same weight; to be in equipoise; to hesitate.—**balance sheet,** a statement of the assets and liabilities of a company.—**bal'ance-wheel** *n.* the wheel regulating the beat in watches [L. *bis,* twice; *lanx,* a plate].

balcony (bal'ko-ni) *n.* a platform or gallery projecting from a building; a lower gallery in a theatre or concert hall.—**balconet'** *n.* the railing round a balcony or a window-sill.—**balconette'** *n.* a small balcony [It. *balcone*].

bald (bawld) *a.* destitute of hair or feathers on the crown of the head; bare; unadorned; undisguised; without literary style; monotonous.—**bald'head, bald'pate** *n.* one destitute of hair.—**bald'ly** *adv.*—**bald'ness** *n.* [M.E. *balled*].

balderdash (bawl'dẹr-dash) *n.* a jargon of

meaningless words jumbled together; senseless talk; nonsense [etym. uncertain].

baldicoot (bawld′i-kōōt) *n.* the common coot, so called from its white frontal plate; a monk, probably because of his shaven crown; a bald person.

baldric, baldrick (bawl′drik) *n.* a broad belt, usually of ornate design, worn hanging over the shoulder, across the body diagonally with a sword, dagger, or horn suspended from it [L. *balteus*, a belt].

bale (bāl) *n.* that which causes sorrow or ruin; evil; misery; mischief; injury; woe.—**bale′ful** *a.* full of grief and misery, hurtful.—**bale′fully** *adv.*—**bale′fulness** *n.* perniciousness [O.E. *bealu*, evil].

bale (bāl) *n.* a funeral pyre; a large fire; a bonfire [O.E. *bael*, a fire].

bale (bāl) *n.* a package, compactly compressed, and wrapped in a protecting cover;—*v.t.* to pack in bales.—**bal′er** *n.* one employed in baling goods [M.E. *bale*].

bale (bāl) *v.t.* See **bail**.—**to bale out,** to jump from an aeroplane by parachute.

baleen (ba-lēn′) *n.* the whalebone of commerce [L. *balaena*, a whale].

baline (bā-lēn′) *n.* coarse canvas, used for packing [Fr.].

balista (ba-lis′ta) *n.* See **ballista.**

balister (bạl-is′tẹr) *n.* an arbalest; a cross-bow; a cross-bowman [L. *ballista*, a cross-bow].

balk, baulk (bawk) *n.* a great beam or rafter, of squared timber, stretching from wall to wall; an unploughed ridge of land; a barrier or check; a disappointment; a part of a billiard table;—*v.t.* to frustrate; to bar the way;—*v.i.* to stop abruptly; to jib.—**balk′y** *a.* [O.E. *balca*, a ridge].

ball (bawl) *n.* any round body; a sphere; a globe; the earth; bullet or shot; a delivery by a bowler in cricket; the heavy piece of a pendulum;—*v.t.* and *i.* to form into a ball.—**ball′bear′ings** *n.* hardened steel balls interposed in channels or 'races' between the rotating and stationary surfaces of a bearing to lessen friction.—**ball′-cock** *n.* automatic contrivance in a cistern which controls the flow of water by means of a floating ball and valve.—**ball-point pen** *n.* fountain pen with a tiny ball point leaving a fine trace of ink on the paper.—**ball′-race** *n.* the grooves in which the balls of a ball-bearing run.—**ball and socket,** a joint formed by a ball partly enclosed in a cup and so adjusted that it can move freely in all directions.—**no ball,** in cricket, a ball improperly delivered [Fr. *balle*, of Scand. origin].

ball (bawl) *n.* a social gathering for the purpose of dancing; an assembly.—**ball′-room** *n.* [L.L. *ballare*, to dance].

ballad (bal′ạd) *n.* a story in verse, of popular origin, generally patriotic and sung orig. to the harp; a concert-room melody, usually sentimental.—**bal′ladist** *n.* a composer or singer of ballads.—**bal′lad-mon′ger,** *n.* a ballad-writer.—**ball′adry** *n.* collected ballads; folk songs [L.L. *ballare*, to dance].

ballade (ba-lād′) *n.* a short poem of one to three triplet stanzas of eight lines, each with the same rhymes and refrain, and an envoi of four or five lines [Fr.].

ballast (bal′ạst) *n.* heavy material taken on board ship to increase the vessel's draft and steadiness; sandy material dredged from river beds used for concrete; that which renders anything steady;—*v.t.* to load with ballast; to steady [obs. *last*, burden].

ballerina (ba-lẹr-ē′nạ) *n.* a ballet girl; a female dancer [It.].

ballet (bal′ā) *n.* a spectacular representation, consisting of dancing and miming, aiming to express an idea or tell a story, to the accompaniment of music.—**ball′etomane** *n.* an enthusiast for ballet [Fr.].

ballista, balista (bạ-lis′tạ) *n.* an ancient military contrivance for hurling huge stones—**ballis′tic** *a.* pert. to a projectile and its flight.—**ballis′tics** *n.pl.* scientific study of motion of projectiles [Gk. *ballein*, to throw].

balloon (bạ-lōōn′) *n.* an aerostat consisting of a gas-filled envelope, not equipped for mechanical propulsion; anything inflated.—**balloon′ing** *n.*—**balloon′ist** *n.*—**balloon barrage,** a defensive system of captive balloons whereby enemy aircraft are forced to fly too high for accurate aim [Fr. *ballon*].

ballot (bal′ot) *n.* secret voting, usually by marking a ballot-paper and inserting it in a ballot-box; a little ball or slip of paper used in secret voting;—*v.t.* to draw lots [Fr. *ballotte*, a little ball].

bally (ba′li) *a.* a slang expression of disapproval, contempt or disgust; confounded.—**bal′lyhoo** *n.* U.S. slang term for exaggerated advertising; bombast [*var.* of *bloody*].

balm (bâm) a fragrant plant; any fragrant or healing ointment; anything which soothes pain.—**balm′iness** *n.*—**balm′y** *a.* fragrant; bearing balm [fr. *balsam*].

balmoral (bạl-mor′ạl) *n.* a round cap like a beret; a long laced boot; a petticoat [*Balmoral*, in Aberdeenshire].

baloney, boloney (bạ-, bō-lōn′i) *n.* (*Slang*) misleading talk; humbug; nonsense [etym. unknown].

balsa, balza (bawl′sạ, -zạ) *n.* the extremely light wood of a W. Indian tree, used in aeroplane construction and for aeroplane models; a raft made of this wood [Sp.].

balsam (bawl′sạm) *n.* a name applied to many aromatic resins and oils with stimulant and tonic properties; a soothing ointment; a healing agent.—**balsam′ic** *n.* soothing, oily medicine;—*a.* having fragrance of balsam.—**balsamif′erous,** *a.* yielding balsam.—**bal′samous** *a.* soothing.—**bal′samy** *a.* [Gk. *balsamon*].

baluster (bal′us-tẹr) *n.* a short stone shaft turned and moulded, used to support a hand-rail or a coping.—**bal′ustered** *a.* provided with balusters.—**bal′ustrade** *n.* a row of balusters with continuous base and capping, forming an ornamental parapet to a bridge or balcony [Gk. *balaustion*, the pomegranate, whose flowers it resembles].

bambino (bam-bē′nō) *n.* a child or baby [It.].

bamboo (bam-bōō′) *n.* a genus of immense grasses in the tropics, the stems hollow and partitioned at the nodes. [Malay].

bamboozle (bam-bōō′zl) *v.t.* (*Slang*) to mystify; to trick; hoax; cheat; swindle.—**bambooz′ler** *n.* [etym. unknown].

ban (ban) *n.* proclamation; a sentence of outlawry; excommunication; a curse; a prohibition; *v.t.* to prohibit; to curse;—*pr.p.* **ban′ning.**—*pa.t.* and *pa.p.* **banned** [O.E. *bannan*, to curse].

banal (bān′al, ban-al′, ban′al) *a.* trite, trivial, petty, vulgar, commonplace.—**banal′ity** *n.* triteness, triviality [Fr.].

banana (bạ-nâ′na) *n.* a large herbaceous plant, the edible fruit of which is a long, seedless berry with soft skin over edible pulp. [Sp.].

banbury (ban′ber-i) *n.* a special kind of cake first made at *Banbury*, Oxfordshire.

band (band) *n.* a cord, tie, or fillet; part of a clerical, legal, or university vestment consisting of two pieces of cambric or linen joined together and worn under the chin; an ornamental strip separating mouldings on a building or dividing a wall space; an endless belt used for driving wheels or rollers.—**band′-box** *n.* a light cardboard box for millinery.—**band′-saw,** *n.* an endless steel belt, with a serrated edge, used for sawing [O.E. *bindan*, to bind].

band (band) *n.* players of musical instruments in combined performance; a company united for common purpose; a number of armed men;—*v.t.* to bind together;—*v.i.* to associate, join together.—**band′master** *n.* director of a military or brass band.—**bands′man** *n.* a member of a brass band.—**band'stand** *n.* an open-air structure suitable for musical performances. —**to join the band-wagon,** to participate in a movement when its success is assured.—**Band of Hope,** a society for promoting temperance principles among the young [Fr.].

bandage (band'āj) *n.* a swathe of cloth, used for binding up wounds, etc.—*v.t.* to bind with a bandage.—**ban'daging** *n.* material for bandages [O.E. *bindan*, to bind].

bandana, bandanna (ban-dan'ạ) *n.* a silk or cotton handkerchief, orig. made in India, with pattern of diamonds or spots upon a red or dark ground [Hind.].

bandeau (ban'dō) *n.* a narrow band or fillet worn by women to bind the hair;—*pl.* **ban'deaux.** [Fr.].

banderilla (ban-dā-rēl'yạ) *n.* a small decorated dart used to goad the bull in a bull-ring [Sp.].

banderol, banderole (ban'dẹ-rōl) *n.* a small streamer attached to a mast, lance, or spear; a scroll on engravings containing a title or description of the picture [Fr.].

bandicoot (ban'di-kòòt) *n.* a small insectivorous marsupial, indigenous to Australia; the great rat of India [Telugu, *pandi-kokku*, a pig-rat].

bandied, bandiness See **bandy.**

bandit (ban'dit) *n.* desperate robber, prepared to use firearms if resisted; brigand; outlaw; highwayman;—*pl.* **ban'dits, bandit'ti** *n.* [It. *bandito*, fr. *bandire*, to outlaw].

bandoleer, bandolier (band-dō-lēr') *n.* a broad leathern belt fitted with pockets to hold cartridges [It. *bandoliera*].

bandolero (band-o-lār'ō) *n.* a robber; a bandit; a highwayman [Sp.].

bandy (ban'di) *a.* crooked; bent; bandied; bandy-legged;—*v.t.* to beat to and fro; to toss from one to another, as 'to bandy words.' —**ban'died** *a.* bandy.—**ban'diness** *n.*—**ban'dy-leg'ged** *a.* having crooked legs, bending outwards [Fr. *bander*, to bend].

bandy (ban'di) *n.* name applied in U.S. to the game of ice-hockey; a club for hitting a ball in ice-hockey [etym. unknown].

bane (bān) *n.* any cause of ruin; destruction; mischief; noxious substance; poison.—**bane'ful** *a.* having poisonous qualities.—**bane'fully** *adv.* —**bane'fulness** *n.* [O.E. *bana*, a murderer].

bang (bang) *v.t.* to beat, as with a club; to handle roughly; to make a loud noise;—*n.* a blow with a club or a fist; a loud noise; an explosion.—**bang'ing** *n.* [Scand. *banga*, to hammer].

bang (bang) *v.t.* to cut the front hair square across;—*n.* a straight fringe over the forehead or at the end of a horse's tail [N. Amer.].

bang See **bhang.**

bangle (bang'gl) *n.* an ornamental ring worn round arm or ankle; bracelet [Urdu, *bangri*, a bracelet].

banian See **banyan,** the Indian fig-tree.

banish (ban'ish) *v.t.* to condemn to exile; to drive away; to expel; to cast from the mind. —**ban'ishment** *n.* exile [fr. *ban*].

banister (ban'is-tẹr) *n.* Same as **baluster.**

banjo (ban'jō) *n.* a musical instrument with long neck and tambourine-like body. [Gk. *pandoura*, a musical instrument].

bank (bangk) *n.* a ridge of earth; a shoal; a sandbank; the edge of a stream or lake; the raised edge of a road, etc.; a mass of heavy clouds or fog;—*v.t.* to raise a mound; to dike; to cover a fire with small coal to procure slow combustion; to tilt an aeroplane about the longitudinal axis when turning.—**to bank on** *v.t.* to be depending on [O.E. *banc*, a bench].

bank (bangk) *n.* a bench on which rowers sit; a tier of oars; the bench on which judges sat [Fr. *banc*].

bank (bangk) *n.* an establishment where money is received for custody and repaid on demand; money-box; the money at stake in card games of hazard; a pool;—*v.t.* to deposit money in a bank.—**bank'-book** *n.* a pass-book in which a customer's dealings with a bank are recorded.—**bank cheque,** an order to pay, issued upon a bank.—**bank'er** *n.* one employed in banking; in games of chance the proprietor against whom the other players stake; a card game of chance.—**bank'-note** *n.* a promissory note on bank of issue promising to pay its face value to bearer on demand.—**bank'-rate** *n.* the rate of discount, fixed weekly, at the Bank of England. [Fr. *banque*].

bankrupt (bangk'rupt) *n.* insolvent person compelled to place his affairs in the hands of creditors;—*v.t.* to cause to go bankrupt;— *a.* insolvent, unable to pay debts; lacking in (ideas, etc.).—**bank'ruptcy** *n.* [E. *bank*; *ruptus*, broken].

banner (ban'ẹr) *n.* a flag or ensign.—**ban'nered** *a.* provided with banners.—**ban'neret** *n.* a small banner, or streamer. Also **ban'nerette.**— **banner headline,** a prominent head-line in a newspaper, extending the whole width of the paper [Fr. *bannière*].

bannerol Same as **banderol.**

bannock (ban'ok) *n.* (*Scot.*) a flat, thick, cake of oatmeal, barley, or pease-meal, baked on a griddle [Gael. *bonnach*].

banns (banz) *n.pl.* proclamation of intended marriage [fr. *ban*].

banquet (bang'kwet) *n.* a feast; a rich repast; something specially delicious;—*v.t.* to entertain to a banquet.—**banq'ueting** *n.* [Fr. dim. of *banc*, bench].

banshee (ban'shē) *n.* in Ireland and W. Highlands of Scotland, a fairy-elf who, by shrieks and wailing, foretells the approaching death of a member of a family [Ir. *bean sidhe*, woman of the fairies].

bantam (ban'tạm) *n.* a variety of the small common domestic fowl;—*a.* of very light weight; plucky.—**bantam-weight,** a boxer weighing less than 8 stones, 6 lbs. [fr. *Bantam*, a village in Java].

banter (ban'tẹr) *v.i.* to make good-natured fun of someone; to joke, jest; to rally;—*n.* wit at expense of another; chaff; pleasantry. —**bant'erer** *n.*—**ban'tering** *n.*—**ban'teringly** *adv.* [etym. unknown].

banting (bant'ing) *n.* a system of dieting for keeping down superfluous fat.—**bant'ingism** *n.* [fr. Wm. *Banting*, a London undertaker, who advocated the system].

bantling (bant'ling) *n.* an infant; a brat [E. *band*, and *-ling* (dim.)=one wrapped in swaddling bands].

Bantu (ban'tòò) *n.* a generic name applied to the native languages and natives of Africa from 6° N. lat. to 20° S. [*ntu*, human being, man; *ba*, pl. prefix].

banyan, banian (ban'yan) *n.* the Indian fig; a tree whose branches, bending to the ground, take root and form new stocks, till they become a forest. Hence—**to flourish like the banyan-tree** [Port.].

baobab (bā'ō-bab) *n.* one of the largest of trees, found in tropical Africa [African].

baptise (bap-tīz') *v.t.* to administer the sacrament of baptism to; to christen; give a name to.—**bap'tism** *n.* sacrament by which a person is initiated into the membership of the Christian Church, either by sprinkling of water or by immersion.—**baptis'mal** *a.*— **bap'tist** *n.* one who baptises; one who insists that the rite of initiation is duly administered only by immersion and only to adults.— **bap'tistery, bap'tistry** *n.* an ancient circular building in which baptisms took place [Gk. *baptein*, to dip].

bar (bàr) *n.* a long piece of any solid material, used especially for preventing ingress or egress; the bolt of a door; a boom across a river; a sand-bank; part of a tavern with a counter for the sale of liquor; a public-house; the rail before the judge's seat where prisoners appear; members of the legal profession allowed to plead in court; (*Her.*) a band crossing the shield; (*Mus.*) a perpendicular line drawn across the stave immediately before the primary accent;—*v.t.* to fasten or mark with a bar; to obstruct; to prevent; to exclude;—*prep.* except.—**bar'-ir'on** *n.* iron wrought into malleable bars.—**bar'-mag'net** *n.* a permanent magnet in the form of a bar.—**bar'maid, bar'man, bar'tender** *n.* a bar attendant.—**bar'ring** *prep.* excepting;—*n.* exclusion of any kind.—**to call to the Bar,** to admit as a barrister [Fr. *barre*].

barathea (ba-ra-thē'-ạ) *n.* a worsted twill cloth [etym. unknown].

barb (bȧrb) *n.* a hooked hair; the spike of an arrow, fish-hook, etc.; a horse of great speed and endurance, originally from Barbary —*v.t.* to furnish with barbs or prongs, as an arrow; to trim the beard.—**barbed** *a.* bearded; furnished with a barb or barbs.—**barbed'-wire** *n.* a wire armed with sharp points used for defensive purposes [L. *barba,* a beard].

barbacan See **barbican.**

barbarian (bar-bā'-ri-ạn) *n.* orig. one who could not speak Greek, now an uncivilised being without culture; a cruel, brutal man;—*a.* savage; rude.—**barbar'ic** *a.* uncivilised; rude; nobly savage.—**bar'barise** *v.t.* to render barbarous.—**bar'barism** *n.* incorrect use of idiom or word; want of civilisation.—**barbar'ity** *n.* cruelty; savagery.—**bar'barous** *a.* uncivilised or savage.—**bar'barously** *adv.*—**bar'barousness** *n.* [Gk. *barbaros,* foreign].

barbecue (bȧr'-be-kū) *n.* a grid-iron on which an animal is roasted whole; an animal so roasted; upper storey of a house where grain or coffee is stored; (*U.S.*) a lavish open-air feast [Haytian].

barbel (bȧr'-bel) *n.* a small, beard-like process, appended to the mouth of certain fishes; a large fresh-water fish.—**bar'bellate** *a.* having barbed or bearded bristles [L. *barba,* beard].

barber (bȧrb'-ẹr) *n.* one who shaves or trims and dresses the hair; a hair-dresser [L. *barba,* beard].

barberry (bȧr'-ber-i) *n.* (*Bot.*) a species of Berberidaceae, common in the hedge-rows of England [L.L. *berberis*].

barbette (bar-bet') *n.* a platform on which guns are mounted [L. *barba,* a beard].

barbican (bȧr'-bi-kạn) *n.* an outwork to protect the approaches to a castle or fortified town; a loop-hole through which fire-arms were discharged [etym. unknown].

barbitone (bȧr'-bi-tōn) *n.* the synthetic soporific drug known as veronal.

barbiturates (bar-bit'-ū-rātz) *n.* (*Med.*) derivatives of barbituric acid, non-habit forming, hypnotic drugs, e.g. evipan, luminal and pentothal [Fr. *barbitone*].

barbule (bȧrb'-ūl) *n.* (*Bot.*) a small barb or beard [var. of *barbel*].

barcarolle, barcarole (bȧr'-kạ-rōl) *n.* a musical composition written in imitation of the gondoliers' songs of Venice. [It. *barca,* a boat].

bard (bȧrd) *n.* a Celtic minstrel who celebrated in song the great deeds of heroes; a poet.—**bard'ic** *a.* pert. to bards or their poetry [Celt.].

bare (bār) *a.* without covering; naked; empty; open to view; paltry;—*v.t.* to strip off or uncover.—**bare'ly** *adv.* openly; poorly; scarcely.—**bare'ness** *n.*—**bare'backed** *a.* with bare back; having no saddle.—**bare'faced** *a.* shameless, downright.—**bare'facedness** *n.* sheer impudence.—**bare'footed** *a.* and *adv.* unshod.—**bare'headed** *a.* [O.E. *baer*].

bargain (bȧr'-gin) *n.* an agreement between parties in buying and selling; a profitable transaction; something purchased cheaply.—*v.i.* to make a contract; to chaffer.—**bar'gainer** *n.* one who haggles over the price.—**into the bargain,** over and above what is agreed upon [O.Fr. *bargaigner*].

barge (barj) *n.* flat-bottomed boat, designed for transporting merchandise on rivers, canals; a naval commander's boat;—*v.i.* to push forward roughly.—**bar'gee, barge'man** *n.* one who manages or is employed working a barge [L. *barca,* a boat].

barge-board (barj'-bōrd) *n.* a verge-board, an inclined projecting board on the gable of a building to hide and protect the ends of the roof timbers and for ornamental purposes [corruption of *verge*].

baritone, barytone (bar'-i-tōn) *n.* the male human voice between tenor and bass [Gk. *barus,* heavy; *tonos,* tone].

barium (bā'-ri-um) *n.* metallic element (symbol *Ba.*), compounds poisonous, nitrate used for making green flares for fireworks.—**ba'ric** *a.* pert. to barium [See **baryta**].

bark (bȧrk) *n.* the outer covering of a tree; rind; waste tan used in manufacturing white-lead;—*v.t.* to strip off bark; to graze the skin.—**bark'en** *v.i.* to become dry like bark [Scand.].

bark (bȧrk) *v.t.* to utter a cry like a dog; to yelp; to snarl (at);—*n.* sound emitted by a dog; coughing; sound of a gun.—**to bark up the wrong tree,** to be on the wrong trail [O.E. *beorcan*].

bark, barque (bȧrk) *n.* a sailing-ship with not less than three masts, having her fore and main masts rigged square, and the last (the mizzen in a three-masted vessel) fore-and-aft rigged; a small sailing-ship; (*Poet.*) a ship [Fr. *barque*].

barley (bȧr'-li) *n.* an important cereal of very ancient culture, the grain being used for malt-making, bread, and food for cattle.—**bar'ley-corn** *n.* a grain of barley; the third part of an inch.—**John Barleycorn** (*Fig.*) whisky.—**bar'ley-flour** *n.* flour made by grinding barley.—**bar'ley-su'gar** *n.* a confection made from sugar boiled till brittle in barley water.—**bar'ley-wat'er** *n.* an infusion of pearl barley.—**pearl'-bar'ley** *n.* the grain of the barley.—**pot'-bar'ley** *n.* grain which has been husked [O.E. *bere,* barley].

barm (bȧrm) *n.* the froth on fermenting malt liquors, used in making bread; yeast.—**barm'y** *a.* pert. to barm; light-headed, flighty, or giddy [O.E. *beorma,* yeast].

barmecide (bȧr'-me-sīd) *n.* one who invites to an imaginary repast;—*a.* imaginary; non-existent.—**Barmecide Feast,** so called from the story in the *Arabian Nights* where a hungry beggar was invited to imaginary banquet [Pers. family of 8th cent.].

barn (bȧrn) *n.* a covered farm-building for storing grain, hay, etc.;—*v.t.* to store in a barn.—**barn'-dance** *n.* a lively dance in pointed 4-4 time, resembling the schottische.—**barn'-yard** *a.* pert. to domestic fowls.—*n.* open enclosure attached to barn.—**barn'-owl** *n.* bird of prey which takes up permanent residence in steeples, barns, etc.—**barn'-storm'er** *n.* a strolling-player [O.E. *bere,* barley; *ern,* a place].

barnacle (bȧr'-nạ-kl) *n.* a shell-fish which attaches itself to the bottoms of ships and to rocks.—**bar'nacles** *n.pl.* spectacles [O.Fr. *bernaque*].

barney (bar'-ni) *n.* (*Slang*) humbug; a prize-fight.

barogram (bar'-ō-gram) *n.* the record made by a barograph.—**bar'ograph** *n.* a self-registering barometer of the aneroid type for recording on a revolving drum variations of atmospheric pressure.—**barograph'ic** *a.* [Gk. *baros,* weight; *gramma,* a writing].

barometer (bạ-rom'-e-tẹr) *n.* an instrument for recording the weight or pressure of the atmosphere, for indicating impending weather changes. -**baromet'ric, baromet'rical** *a.*—**baromet'rically** *adv.*—**barom'etry** *n.* [Gk. *baros,* weight; *metron,* measure].

baron (bar'-on) *n.* a title of nobility, the lowest of the British peerage to sit in the House of Lords; a judge of the Court of Exchequer; a commercial magnate in U.S.—**bar'onage** *n.* the whole body of barons.—**bar'oness** *n.* a baron's wife; a woman holding a barony.—**baron'ial** *a.*

pert. to a barony.—**bar'ony** *n.* the lordship of a baron; the domain of a baron; in Ireland, a division of a county; in Scotland, a large freehold estate.—**baron of beef,** a joint consisting of both sides of the back; a double sirloin [L.L. *baro,* a man].

baronet (bar'ō-net) *n.* hereditary title ranking below a baron and above a knight but without privilege of peerage.—**bar'onetcy** *n.* the rank of a baronet [dim. of *baron*].

baroque (ba-rok') *n.* orig. a jeweller's trade term for ill-shaped pearls; (*Archit.*) a decadent, bizarre and florid style of late Renaissance; rococo;—*a.* over-lavish; bizarre; odd [Port. *barrocco*].

baroscope (bar'ō-skōp) *n.* an instrument giving rough indications of variations in the atmospheric pressure [Gk. *baros,* weight; *skopein,* to see].

barouche (ba-rōōsh') *n.* a double-seated, four-wheeled horse-driven carriage, with a folding top [L. *bis.* double; *rota,* a wheel].

barque (bårk) *n.* See **bark.**

barrack (bar'ak) *n.* a building for the accommodation of soldiers (generally used in the plural) [Sp. *barraca,* a tent].

barracking (bar'ak-ing) *n.* shouting and cheering in chorus with a view to encouraging or discouraging one of the participants in a game, such as cricket [Austral. aborig. *borak,* chaff at another's expense].

barracuda, barracouta, barracoota (barakōō'da, -ta) *n.* a large edible pike-like fish, found in the Atlantic [Sp.].

barrage (bår'āj) *n.* an artificial bar erected across a stream to regulate its flow; a screen of continuous military fire produced to protect the advance of troops or to stop hostile attacks. See **balloon** [Fr.].

barratry (bar'a-tri) *n.* fraudulent breach of duty by the master of a ship entailing loss on the owners or insurers of ship or cargo; habitually inciting subjects of the king to riot or stirring up suits and quarrels at law [O.Fr. *barat,* fraud].

barrel (bar'el) *n.* a cylindrical wooden container consisting of staves bound by hoops; a measure of capacity, of ale, 36 gall., of wine 31½ gall; anything cylindrical, as a gun-barrel;—*v.t.* to stow in barrels.—**bar'rel-or'gan** *n.* street-organ played by rotating a wooden barrel [Fr. *baril*].

barren (bar'en) *a.* incapable of producing offspring or fruit.—**bar'renly** *adv.*—**bar'renness** *n.* sterility [O.Fr.].

barricade (bar'i-kād) *n.* a make-shift fortification, built as an obstruction; any erection which hinders free passage;—*v.t.* to build this; formerly **barrica'do** [Fr. *barrique,* a cask].

barrier (bar'i-ẹr) *n.* a chain of military posts to protect frontiers; a railing, fence, or wall; any obstruction; a line of separation [O.Fr. *barrière*].

barrister (bar'is-tẹr) *n.* a member of the highest branch of the legal profession, with exclusive right of practising in the superior courts of England.—**barrister'ial** *a.*—**bar'ristership** *n.* [fr. *bar*].

barrow (bar'ō) *n.* a small kind of light frame provided with two shafts, for carrying loads. —**bar'row-tram,** *n.* the shaft of a barrow [O.E. *beran,* to bear].

barrow (bar'ō) *n.* an artificial mound of stone, wood, or earth, piled up in prehistoric times over the remains of the dead; a hillock [O.E. *beorg,* a mound].

barter (bår'tẹr) *v.t.* to exchange or give in exchange;—*v.i.* to traffic by exchange of one kind of goods for another;—*n.* direct exchange of commodities [O.Fr. *barater,* to haggle].

barton (bår'tun) *n.* back part of country-house where stables, etc., are housed; farmyard [O.E. *bere,* barley; *tūn,* enclosure].

barycentric (bar-i-sen'trik) *a.* pert. to the centre of gravity [Gk. *baros,* weight; *kentron,* centre].

barytes (ba-rī'tēz) *n.* heavy spar or barium sulphate.—**bary'ta,** *n.* an earth occurring in the mineral, heavy spar [Gk. *barus,* heavy].

barytone See **baritone.**

basal See **base.**

basalt (ba-sawlt') *n.* an igneous rock of a greenish-black colour.—**basalt'ic** *a.*—**basal'tiform** *a.* columnar; having the form of basalt [L. *basaltes,* black basalt].

bascule (bas'kūl) *n.* a balancing lever.—**bas'cule-bridge** *n.* a counterpoise bridge [Fr. *bas,* down; *cul,* the posterior].

base (bās) *a.* of humble birth or of low degree; morally low.—**base'ly** *adv.*—**base'born** *a.* illegitimate.—**base metal,** *a.* metal such as copper, lead, zinc, tin as distinct from the precious metals [Fr. *bas,* low].

base (bās) *n.* bottom; part of a thing on which it rests; foundation; support; starting-place; fixed point; supply point of an army; station at base-ball; main ingredient; (*Chem.*) a substance capable of combining with an acid to form a salt;—*v.t.* to put on a base; to found.—**bas'al** *a.* situated at the base.—**base'less** *a.* having no foundation.—**base'lessness** *n.*—**base'ly** *adv.*—**base'ment** *n.* the lowest storey of a building.—**bas'ic** *a.*—**base'board** *n.* a skirting board covering the lower part of a wall to conceal the join with the flooring [Gk. *basis*].

base (bās) (*Mus.*). See **bass.**

baseball (bās'bawl) *n.* the American game of ball, bearing a resemblance to both rounders and cricket; the ball used.

bash (bash) *v.t.* (*Colloq.*) to smash in; to beat in; to knock out of shape; to beat;—*n.* a severe blow; a dent.—**bash'ing** *n.* a thrashing [Scand.].

bashful (bash'fool) *a.* easily confused; not desiring to attract notice.—**bash'fully** *adv.*—**bash'fulness** *n.* [fr. *abashfull*].

bashi-bazouks (bash'i-ba-zōōks) *n.pl.* irregular Turkish troops, formerly notorious for violence and plundering.—**bash'ibazouk'ery** *n.* heinous cruelty and rapine [Turk.].

basic (bā'sik) *a.* relating to or serving as a base; primary; containing a small amount of silica.—**basic dyes,** colour bases with hydrochloric acid.—**basic English,** simplification of English for foreigners by reducing number of essential key-words.—**bas'ic-slag** *n.* a by-product in the manufacture of steel, now widely used as a manure [Gk. *basis,* a base].

basil (baz'il) *n.* aromatic culinary plant; sweet basil [Gk. *basilikos,* royal].

basil, bazil (baz'il) *n.* the skin of a sheep; skin which has been roughly tanned in larch or oak bark for shoe-linings, book-binding, etc. Also **bas'an** [Fr. *basane*].

basilica (ba-sil'i-ka) *n.* a public building or hall of the Romans, later often converted into a church by early Christians; a spacious church built on the model of the original basilicas.—**basil'ican** *a.* [Gk. *basilikos,* royal].

basilisk (bas'i-lisk) *n.* an animal fabled to have been hatched by a toad from the egg of an old cock; possessed of a white spot on its head like a royal crown, its glance and breath were fatal to living things; a cockatrice (*Zool.*) a harmless tree-dwelling American lizard; an ancient brass piece of ordnance [Gk. *basilikos,* royal].

basin (bā'sn) *n.* a wide, hollow, bowl-shaped vessel; a land-locked bay with a good anchorage; the whole tract of country drained by a river [Fr. *bassin*].

basis (bā'sis) *n.* that on which a thing rests; foundation.—*pl.* **ba'ses** [Gk.].

bask *v.i.* to sun oneself; to lie in warmth or sunshine [Scand.].

basket (bas'ket) *n.* a vessel made of willow, cane, rushes, or other flexible materials, interwoven.—**bas'ket-ball** *n.* a game where ball has to be propelled into a basket.—**bas'ketful** *n.*—**bas'ket-hilt** *n.* a steel, basket-shaped hilt of a sword or fencing-stick.—**bas'ketry, bas'ket-work** *n.* wickerwork [etym. unknown].

Basque (bȧsk) *n.* a native or the language of the Basque country (Western Pyrenees); part of a lady's dress, resembling a jacket with a short skirt;—*a.* relating to the Basques [Fr.].

bas-relief, bass-relief (bȧs *or* bȧ-re-lēf') *n.* or *a.* low relief, sculpture in which figures or objects are raised slightly upon a flat surface, like embossed work [Fr.].

bass (bȧs) *n.* name applied to any perch-like fish [M.E. *barse, bace*].

bass (bȧs) *n.* the lime-tree or its inner bark; fibre; matting [O.E. *baest*].

bass, base (bās) *n.* (*Mus.*) the lowest part of harmony, whether vocal or instrumental; the deepest quality of the human voice or a stringed instrument;—*a.* low.—**bass'-clef** *n.* the sign on the fourth line of the bass stave.—**doub'le-bass'** *n.* the largest of the stringed instruments [It. *basso*, low].

basset (bas'et) *n.* a hound formerly used in badger hunting; a card game resembling the modern faro; (*Geol.*) emergence of strata at the surface; out-crop.—**bass'et-horn** *n.* a rich-toned wind instrument [Fr. *bas*, low].

bassinet, bassinette (bas-i-net') *n.* a baby's basket with a hood; a perambulator [Fr. dim. fr. *bassin*].

basso (bas'ō) *n.* a bass singer; the bass part of a harmony [It.=low].

bassoon (bạ-sōōn') *n.* a wood-wind musical instrument with a double reed mouthpiece; organ reed stop of that name.—**double bassoon,** one which sounds an octave lower.—**bassoon'-ist** *n.* [It. *basso*, low].

bast (bast) *n.* inner bark of a tree, often specially applied to that of the lime; flexible fibre of bark of some trees used for binding purposes; raffia, matting, cordage, etc., made of the bark [O.E. *baest*].

bastard (bas'tard) *n.* a child born out of wedlock; an impure, coarse brown refuse product of sugar-refining, used to colour beer;—*a.* illegitimate; false; counterfeit;—**bas'-tardy** *n.* act of begetting a bastard; being a bastard.—**bas'tardise** *v.t.* to render illegitimate. [O.Fr. *bastard*, from *fils de bast*, son of a pack-saddle].

baste (bāst) *v.t.* to beat with a cudgel; to drop fat on meat when roasting [etym. unknown].

baste (bāst) *v.t.* to sew loosely with long stitches [O.Fr. *bastir*, to stitch loosely].

bastille (bas-tēl') *n.* originally a tower or bastion; a state prison.—**The Bastille,** the famous state prison of Paris, demolished by the revolutionary mob on July 14, 1789 [Fr. *bastille*, a building].

bastinado (bas-ti-nā'dō) *n.* an Oriental form of punishment by beating the soles of the feet [Sp. *baston*, a stick].

bastion (bast'yun) *n.* a stronghold of defence [Fr.].

bat (bat) *n.* a club or stick; a shaped club used in cricket or baseball; a batsman; a piece of a brick larger than a closer;—*v.i.* to face the bowling in cricket;—*pr.p.* **bat'ting**; *pa.p.* **bat'ted** —**bat'ter, bats'man** *n.* one who is batting at cricket.—**bat'ting** *n.* the act of wielding a bat. —**off one's own bat,** alone, without any assistance [O.E. *batt*, club].

bat (bat) *n.* an animal, related to the hedgehog and shrew and able to fly as the long fingers are united by a membrane to the hind legs and tail.—**bat'ty** *a.* (*Slang*) crazy. Also **bats.**—**to have bats in the belfry,** to be crazy or eccentric [M.E. *batte*].

bat (bat) *v.t.* (*Colloq.*) to wink.—(*U.S.*) **never batted an eyelid,** showed no emotion whatever; never slept.

batch (bach) *n.* the quantity of bread baked at one time; a number of articles received or despatched at one time; a set of similar articles [M.E. *bache*, fr. *bake*].

bate (bāt) *v.t.* to lessen; to abate [form of *abate*].

bath (bȧth) *n.* a vessel or place to bathe in; the water in which to bathe; a solution in which photographic plates are immersed;—*v.t.* to wash oneself.—**baths** *n.pl.* hot or mineral springs resorted to by invalids.—**bath'-chair** *n.* a wheeled chair for invalids, first used at Bath.—**bath'-house** *n.*—**bath'room** *n.*—**Bath'-stone** *n.* a soft, easily worked limestone quarried near Bath.—**blood'-bath** *n.* a massacre.—**Turkish bath,** a bath in which, after being sweated in hot air, the patient is massaged and conducted through a series of cooling chambers.—**sitz bath,** a shallow bath, for bathing hips and buttocks [O.E. *baeth*].

bathe (bāTH) *v.t.* to wash by immersion;—*v.i.* to be immersed; to enter sea or fresh-water for recreation;—*pr.p.* **bath'ing.**—**bath'er** *n.*—**bath'ing** *n.*—**bath'ing-machine** *n.* a wheeled vehicle for bathers.—**bath'ing-pool** *n.* [O.E. *bathian*].

bathetic See under **bathos.**

bathometer (bạ-thom'e-tẹr) *n.* a spring balance for determining the depth of water [Gk. *bathos*, depth; *metron*, measure].

bathos (bā'thos) *n.* a term which indicates a ludicrous descent from the sublime to the ridiculous in speech or writing; anti-climax. —**bathet'ic** *a.* [Gk. *bathos*, depth].

bathy- (bath-i) *prefix.* from Gk. *bathus*, deep, used in the construction of compound terms relating to sea-depths.—**bathyal zone,** the floor of the sea at a depth of 600-3000 feet.—**bathym'etry** *n.* science of deep-sea sounding (*cf.* **bathom'eter**).—**bath'y-orograph'ical** *a.* term applied to maps which by suitable colouring indicate both the land altitudes and the sea depths.—**bath'ysphere** *n.* a form of deep-sea diving-bell [Gk. *bathus*, deep; *metron*, to measure; *sphaira*, a ball].

batik (bȧ'tēk) *n.* ancient Javanese method of designing in colour on fabrics by waxing parts not to be dyed [Malay *'mbatik*].

batiste (ba-tēst') *n.* a fine kind of linen cloth from Flanders; a variety of cambric [Fr.].

batman (bȧt'man) *n.* officer's servant or runner [Fr. *bât*, a pack-saddle].

baton (ba'ton) *n.* a short staff or club; a truncheon, symbolic of authority or used as an offensive weapon; in music, wand used by conductor in beating time; a marshal's staff.—*v.t.* to strike with a baton.—**bat'on-sin'ister** *n.* in heraldry, to indicate illegitimacy [Fr. *baton*].

batrachia (ba-trā'ki-ạ) *n.pl.* an order of amphibians, the group of vertebrates which includes the frogs, toads, newts, etc.—**batrach'ian** *n.* and *a.* [Gk. *batrachos*, a frog].

battalion (bạ-tal'yun) *n.* a military tactical and administrative unit of command. As infantry, consists of about 1000 men under a lieut.-colonel.—**battal'ions** *n.pl.* great numbers, swarms [Fr. *bataillon*, cf. **battle**].

batten (bat'n) *v.t.* to fatten;—*v.i.* to grow fat in luxury [Icel. *batna*, to grow better].

batten (bat'n) *n.* a piece of wood nailed on a surface to give it strength; a cleat; a row of lamps used for stage-lighting; board used on ships to fasten down the hatch-covers in stormy weather;—*v.t.* to fasten or form with battens [a form of *bâton*].

batter (bat'ẹr) *v.t.* to strike or beat continuously; to assault; to wear by hard use; —*n.* a mixture moistened to a paste and briskly beaten up.—**batt'ering-ram,** *n.* a suspended beam, with a head like a ram's, formerly used to breach walls [Fr. *battre*, to beat].

battery (bat'ẹr-i) *n.* act of battering; a place where cannon are mounted; a division of artillery; electric cells which store electric current [Fr. *battre*, to beat].

battle (bat'l) *n.* an encounter between enemies; struggle of any kind;—*v.i.* to fight on a large scale.—**bat'tle-axe** *n.* primitive weapon of warfare, consisting of a blade and a handle.—**bat'tle-crui'ser** *n.* large warship combining the heavy armament of a battleship and the speed of a cruiser.—**bat'tle-cry** *n.* a war-shout; a slogan.—**bat'tle-dress** *n.* standardised uniform, adopted universally in the British Army in 1939.—**bat'tle-field, bat'tle-ground** *n.* scene of battle.—**bat'tler** *n.* one who takes part in a battle.—**bat'tle-roy'al** *n.* a regular melée where fists are freely used.—**bat'tle-ship** *n.* the largest and most heavily armed of fast warships [Fr. *bataille*].

battledore, battledoor (bat'-l-dōr) *n.* a circular wooden bat for beating clothes in laundries; a baker's utensil with a very long handle for handling loaves in an oven; an old game, akin to badminton [etym. uncertain].

battlement (bat'-l-ment) *n.* a protective parapet on a wall with embrasures or crenelles at regular intervals for the discharge of fire-arms [M.E. *batilment*].

battue (ba'-tòò) *n.* a method of killing game by employing beaters to drive them out of cover towards the sportsmen; indiscriminate slaughter [Fr. *battre*, to beat].

bauble (baw'-bl) *n.* a trifling piece of finery; a gew-gaw; a stick with a fool's head attached carried by jesters of former times;—*a.* trifling [O.Fr. *baubel*, a toy].

baulk (bawk) See **balk**.

bauxite (bō'-zīt, bok-sīt) *n.* a hydrated oxide of aluminium and ferric oxide valuable for the production of aluminium and alumina [fr. *Baux*, near Arles, S. France].

bawd (bawd) *n.* a procurer or procuress of women for immoral purposes.—**bawd'ily** *adv.* —**bawd'iness** *n.*—**bawd'ry** *n.*—**bawd'y** *a.* obscene filthy; unchaste.—**bawd'y-house,** *n.* a brothel [O.Fr. *baud*, gay].

bawl (bawl) *v.t.* to shout, to proclaim;—*v.i.* to shout out with a loud voice;—*n.* a loud, prolonged cry [L.L. *baulare*, to bark].

bay (bā) *a.* reddish-brown;—*n.* a chestnut horse.—**bay'ard** *n.* a bay horse; a spirited horse; one foolishly self-confident; a knight of good fame [L. *badius*, chestnut-coloured].

bay (bā) *n.* an inlet of the sea, wider at the mouth than a gulf [Fr. *baie*].

bay (bā) *n.* the subdivision longitudinally of a building by piers, arches, girders, etc.—**bay'-win'dow** *n.* a window projecting beyond the wall.—**sick'-bay,** ship's hospital [Fr. *baie*].

bay (bā) *n.* the laurel tree.—**bays** *n.pl.* the victor's garland or crown.—**bay'-rum** *n.* an aromatic liquid used as a perfume and cosmetic for the hair [Fr. *baie*, berry].

bay (bā) *n.* barking, esp. of hounds in pursuit of prey;—*v.t.* to bark at.—**at bay,** said of a hunted animal, when all escape is cut off [O.Fr. *abaier*, to bark].

bayberry (bā'-ber-i) *n.* evergreen shrub, used for making bay-rum [*bay* and *berry*].

bayonet (bā'-ō-net) *n.* a short spear-like weapon for fixing to the muzzle of a rifle; —*v.t.* to stab with a bayonet. [fr. *Bayonne*, the town where first made].

bazaar, bazar (bạ-zàr') *n.* an Oriental market-place; a sale of work where articles given are sold for charity; shop selling miscellaneous goods [Pers.].

bazil See **basil**.

bazooka (ba-zoo'-ka) *n.* an American light rocket-gun; (*Slang*) the face.

be (bē) *v.i.* and *aux.* (*pres. indic.* **am**; *past indic.* **was**; *past part.* **been**), to exist; to live; to have a state, existence, or quality; to remain.—**let be,** leave alone [O.E. *beōn*].

be- (bē) *prefix* used in the construction of compound words, as *becalm*, etc.

beach (bēch) *n.* the shore of the sea or of a lake, esp. where sandy or pebbly; the shore;—*v.t.* to run or haul a boat up on to a beach.—**beach'-comb'er** *n.* a long, rolling wave; a lounger who frequents wharves of seaports; scrounger.—**beach'-head** *n.* a footing gained on hostile shores by an opposing army.—**beach'y** *a.* consisting of a beach; pebbly [etym. uncertain].

beacon (bē'-kn) *n.* a fire lit on a high eminence, usually as a warning; a warning; a floating buoy; traffic sign indicating a pedestrian crossing;—*v.t.* to mark a channel by beacons [O.E. *beacn*].

bead (bēd) *n.* a little ball pierced for stringing; any small spherical object.—*v.t.* to furnish with beads;—*v.i.* to string beads.—**beads** *n.pl.* a rosary, a necklace; an astragal; flange of a tyre;—**bead'ed** *a.* in bead form.—**bead'ing** *n.* a small rounded moulding imitating beads.—**bead'roll** *n.* a list of the dead to be prayed for; a rosary.—**beads'man, bedes'man** *n.* an almsman in Cathedrals of Henry VIII's foundation, residing in a bede-house under an obligation to pray for the soul of the founder.—**bead'y** *a.* bead-like.—**to draw a bead on,** to aim a gun at. —**to tell one's beads,** to recite the rosary [O.E. *gebed*, a prayer].

beadle (bē'-dl) *n.* a functionary who carries out ceremonial duties at Oxford and Cambridge; in Scotland, an attendant on the minister.—**bead'ledom** *n.* stupid officiousness [O.E. *bydel*].

beagle (bē'-gl) *n.* the smallest hound used in hunting; a spy or informer; a sheriff's officer, bailiff [etym. unknown].

beak (bēk) *n.* the horny bill of a bird, turtle, etc.; anything shaped like a beak; (*Slang*) magistrate or school-master [Fr. *bec*.].

beaker (bē'-kẹr) *n.* a large drinking-cup or vessel; a tumbler-shaped vessel of thin glass used by chemists [Scand. *bikarr*].

beam (bēm) *n.* a strong, horizontal piece of timber or reinforced concrete for spanning and supporting weights; the part of a balance from which the scales hang; the cross-timber of a ship; the extreme width, measured athwartships, of a ship; wooden cylinder on which the warp is wound in a loom; the pole of a carriage; the shaft of an anchor; a sharply defined ray of light; the sparkle in a person's eyes manifesting extreme pleasure or interest;—*v.t.* to emit beams of light;—*v.i.* to send forth rays of light; to shine; to smile benignly.—**beam'-ends** *n.* position when a ship lies on her side with her cross-beams upright; (*Fig.*) the last of a person's resources.—**beam'ing** *a.* radiantly happy; shining;—*n.* rays of light; manifestation of pleasure by smiling.—**beam'less** *a.*

beam-tree (bēm'-trē) *n.* the white-beam, a species of Rosaceae with wood hard and suitable for turning [O.E. *beam*, a tree].

bean (bēn) *n.* the flat, kidney-shaped seed of various plants, chiefly of the order Leguminosae.—**bean'-feast** *n.* a feast where food is abundant; a jollification.—**bean'o** *n.* (*Slang*) jollification; festivity.—**full of beans,** in good fettle; energetic.—**without a bean,** penniless [O.E. *bean*].

bear (bār) *v.t.* to support or to carry; to endure; to suffer; to behave; to give birth to; —*v.i.* to produce (as fruit); to endure; to press;—*pa.t.* **bore**; *pa.p.* **borne** or **born**.—**bear'able** *a.* able to be borne; tolerable.—**bear'ably** *adv.*—**bear'er** *n.* carrier or messenger; a person who helps to carry a coffin; a presenter of a cheque; a body-servant.—**bear'ing** *n.* the manner in which a person acts or behaves; the direction in which one thing lies from another; relation to or connection with;—**bear'ings** *n.pl.* machine surfaces carrying a moving part and bearing friction.—**to bear out,** to corroborate.—**to bear one's cross,** to endure suffering.—**to bear with,** to endure patiently.—**to bring to bear,** to apply pressure. —**to lose one's bearings,** to lose all sense of direction [O.E. *beran*].

bear (bār) *n.* a carnivorous mammal of the Ursidae order; a rough, boorish person; one who sells stocks before he has bought them, in the hope of a fall in price before settlement,

(*Astron.*) one of two constellations in the northern hemisphere, called respectively the **Great Bear** and the **Lesser Bear**.—**bear'-bait'ing** *n.* a form of sport where dogs were employed to worry the animal.—**bear'-gar'den** *n.* an enclosure for bears; a turbulent, noisy gathering.—**bear'ish** *a.* bear-like.—**bear'-lead'er** *n.* one who exhibits a bear at fairs, etc.; a tutor specially attached to a student.—**bear'like** *a.* resembling a bear; gruff.—**bear'skin** *n.* skin of bear; tall fur cap worn by Guards on ceremonial occasions.—**bear'ward** *n.* a warden or keeper of bears [O.E. *bera*].

bear, bere (bār) *n.* a coarse form of barley, used in malting [O.E. *bere*, barley].

beard (bērd) *n.* the hair that grows on the chin and cheeks; the awns or prickles of an ear of corn; the gills of oysters; the barb of an arrow;—*v.t.* to pluck the beard of; to confront or defy someone.—**beard'ed** *a.*—**beard'less** *a.* [O.E.].

beast (bēst) *n.* any inferior animal as opposed to man; a four-footed animal especially if wild; cattle; person of brutal nature or of dirty habits.—**beast'ly** *a.* like a beast in form or nature; filthy; displeasing.—**beast'liness** *n.* [L. *bestia*].

beat (bēt) *v.t.* to strike or hit repeatedly; to pommel; to crush; to defeat; to be too difficult for; to spread flat and thin with a tool, as gold leaf; to drive game out of cover; to mark time in music;—*v.i.* to throb; to dash against, as waves, wind, etc.—*pa.t.* **beat**; *pa.p.* **beat'en**;—*n.* a recurrent stroke; a pulse throb; (*Mus.*) the divisions in a bar, the movement of a conductor's baton; zig-zag sailing of a ship working up against the wind; the round or course followed repeatedly by someone, e.g. a policeman, a postman; a place of resort.—**beat'en** *a.* hammered into shape by a tool; worn by continual use.—**beat'er** *n.*—**beat'ing** *n.* act of giving blows; a thrashing; throbbing; driving out game.—**to beat about the bush**, to approach a subject in a roundabout way.—**to beat hollow**, to surpass someone completely.—**to beat the air**, to contend uselessly.—**to beat a tattoo**, to sound the drums at roll-call.—**dead beat**, absolutely exhausted [O.E. *bēatan*].

beatify (bē-at'-i-fī) *v.t.* to render supremely blessed or happy; to bless with celestial enjoyment (preliminary to canonisation in R.C. Church).—**beatif'ic(al)** *a.* having power of making happy or blessed.—**beatif'ically** *adv.*—**beatifica'tion** *n.* act of the Pope in permitting one, after death, to be declared blessed [L. *beatus*, happy].

beatitude (bē-at'-i-tūd) *n.* highest form of heavenly happiness; supreme blessedness.—**the beatitudes** (*Bib.*) blessings spoken by our Saviour in regard to particular virtues (Matt. 5) [L. *beatus*, happy].

beau (bō) *n.* a fop; dandy; lady's man; suitor.—*pl.* **beaux** (bōz).—**beau'-monde** *n.* the fashionable world and its people [Fr.].

Beaune (bōn) *n.* a red Burgundy wine [a town in Burgundy, France].

beauty (bū'-ti) *n.* the inherent quality in an object of pleasing the eye, ear, or mind; a particular grace or excellence; a beautiful woman; a fine specimen.—**beau'teous** *a.* full of beauty; very handsome.—**beau'teously** *adv.*—**beau'teousness** *n.*—**beautic'ian** *n.* expert in use of cosmetics.—**beau'tifier** *n.* a cosmetic; a decorator.—**beau'tiful** *a.* highly pleasing to eye, ear, or mind; handsome; lovely; fine; excellent.—**beau'tifully** *adv.*—**beau'tifulness** *n.*—**beau'tify** *v.t.* to make beautiful.—**beau'tiless** *a.* lacking beauty.—**beau'ty-cul'ture** *n.* use of cosmetics to improve a person's appearance.—**beauty parlour**, the establishment of a beautician.—**beau'ty-spot** *n.* a place noted for its attractive surroundings; a patch placed on the face to heighten beauty [Fr. *beauté*].

beaver (bēv'-er) *n.* an amphibious, four-footed rodent valued for its fur and for castoreum, an extract from its glands used in medicine; the fur of the beaver; a beaver hat;—*a.* made of beaver fur. [O.E. *beofor*].

beaver (bēv'-er) *n.* lower part of medieval helmet which could be drawn over face [O.Fr. *baviere*, a child's bib].

bebop (bē'-bop) *n.* (*U.S. Slang*) jazz music of a certain type.

becalm (bē-kȧm') *v.t.* to make calm or quiet.—**becalmed'** *a.*

became (be-kām') past tense of **become**.

because (be-kawz') *adv.* and *conj.* for the reason that; since [E. *by*, and *cause*].

beck (bek) *n.* sign or gesture of the head or hand; a nod;—*v.i.* to make such a gesture;—*v.t.* to call by a nod or a sign; to beckon.—**at one's beck and call**, entirely at someone's disposal [fr. *beckon*].

beck (bek) *n.* a small brook, or the valley in which it runs [Scand. *bekkr*].

becket (bek'-et) *n.* a rope with knot and eye, for securing tackles, spars, etc.; a hook; a cleat [etym. unknown].

beckon (bek'-n) *v.t.* and *v.i.* to make a sign with the hand or head; to summon with hand or finger [O.E. *becnan*].

become (bē-kum') *v.t.* to pass from one state to another; to suit or be suitable to;—*pa.t.* **became'**; *pa.p.* **become'**.—**becom'ing** *a.* appropriate or fit.—**becom'ingly** *adv.*—**becom'ingness** *n.* [O.E. *becuman*].

bed (bed) *n.* a couch on which to sleep or take rest; a plot of ground in which plants are cultivated; channel of a stream; the bearing surface of anything; a thin layer of mortar between two surfaces; a layer of rock; stratum;—*v.t.* to place in bed; to plant out; to arrange in layers;—*pr.p.* **bed'ding**; *pa.p.* **bed'ded**.—**bed'-bug** *n.* brown, wingless insect which sucks blood of human beings.—**bed'-cham'ber** *n.* a bedroom.—**bed'der** *n.* a plant for the garden bed.—**bed'ding** *n.* materials of a bed—**bed'-fast** *a.* confined to bed; bed-ridden.—**bed'-fel'low** *n.* one who sleeps in the same bed with another.—**bed'-pan** *n.* a pan for warming a bed; a chamber-pot.—**bed'-plate** *n.* the foundation plate of an engine, lathe, etc.—**bed'post** *n.* one of the upright supports of a bedstead.—**bed'rid, bed'ridden** *a.* permanently confined to bed by age or infirmity.—**bed'-rock** *n.* the solid rock beneath loose material as sand, etc.; fundamentals.—**bed'room** *n.* a room for sleeping in.—**bed'-sore** *n.* ulcer caused by constant pressure on a part of the body of a bed-ridden patient.—**bed'-spread** *n.* a covering of fine material for a bed.—**bed'-stead** *n.* the framework, of iron or wood, of a bed.—**bed'straw** *n.* (*Bot.*) popular name of the genus Galium of the order Rubiaceae, comprising some 200 species.—**bed'-tick** *n.* the cloth case for holding the feathers, hair, etc. of a mattress.—**bed and board** (or **breakfast**), food and lodging [O.E. *bedd*].

bedaggle (bē-dag'-l) *v.t.* to soil one's clothes by falling in mud [fr. *bedraggle*].

bedash (bē-dash') *v.t.* to wet by throwing water on; to bespatter with water.

bedazzle (bē-daz'-l) *v.t.* to overpower by employing too strong a light or by a magnificent show.

bede (bēd) *n.* a prayer. [See **bead**].

bedeck (bē-dek') *v.t.* to deck, adorn, ornament.

bedel (bē'-dl), **bedell** (be-del'), **bedellus** (be-del'-us) *n.* a beadle; a university officer. See **beadle**.

bedesman See under **bead**.

bedevil (bē-dev'-l) *v.t.* to beat with devilish malignity; to torment; to throw into confusion, to confound; to bewitch.

bedew (bē-dū') *v.t.* to moisten with dew.

bedight (bē-dīt') *a.* decked out with ornaments; adorned; arrayed (*Poet.*).

bedim (bē-dim') *v.t.* to make dim; to darken.—**bedimmed'** *a.*

bedizen (bē-diz'-n, bē-dī'-zn) *v.t.* to dress gaudily or with false taste.—**bedi'zened** *a.*

bedlam (bed´lam) *n.* a mad-house; a lunatic asylum; a mental institution; a scene of uproar; pandemonium.—**bed'lamite** *n.* a lunatic [corrupt. of *Bethlehem,* a priory in Bishopsgate converted into an asylum].

bedlington (bed´ling-tun) *n.* a rough, stiff-coated terrier [*Bedlington,* Northumberland, where bred by miners].

Bedouin (bed´òò-in) *n.* the name given to the Arabs who live a nomadic life in the desert [Ar. *bādāwin,* dwellers in the desert].

bedraggle (bē-drag´l) *v.t.* to soil by trailing in the wet or mud. Also **bedagg'le.**

bee (bē) *n.* highest form of insect belonging to the order Hymenoptera, having two pairs of membranous wings; the honey-bee; a social gathering for amusement or mutual help, e.g. a spelling-bee; a busy person.—**bee'-bread** *n.* a brownish substance, the pollen of flowers gathered by bees as food for their young.—**bee'-cul'ture** *n.* the rearing of bees, apiculture.—**bee'-eat'er** *n.* brightly coloured bird of the king-fisher family.—**bee'-glue** *n.* the gummy matter with which bees fix their combs to the hive.—**bee'-hive** *n.* a case or box where the bees are housed;—*a.* shaped like a bee-hive.—**bee'-keep'er, bee'-mas'ter** *n.* one who keeps bees.—**bee'-line** *n.* the shortest route from one place to another.—**bee´-orc'his** *n.* a wall-flower, part of whose flower resembles a bee.—**bees'wax** *n.* the wax secreted by bees; a floor-polish;—*v.t.* to polish with beeswax.—**bees'wing** *n.* a thin film which forms on old port, indicating its age; a beverage formed with yeast.—**to have a bee in one's bonnet,** to be hare-brained; to be cranky on some subject [O.E. *bēo*].

beech (bēch) *n.* a tree of the temperate and sub-frigid zones, greatly valued for its wood.—**beech'coal** *n.* charcoal made from beech-wood.—**beech'en** *a.* made of beech.—**beech'-finch** *n.* the chaffinch.—**beech'mast** *n.* the nuts of the beech-tree.—**beech'nut** *n.* the triangular, edible nut of the beech [O.E. *bece*].

beef (bēf) *n.* the flesh of an ox, bull, or cow; flesh and muscle; muscular strength; vigour;—*a.* consisting of beef;—*v.i.* (*Slang*) to make finicky complaints.—**beeves** (bēvz) *n.pl.* oxen.—**beef'eater** *n.* one of the Yeomen of the Guard; a Warder of the Tower of London.—**beef'iness** *n.* tendency to put on flesh.—**beef'-steak** *n.* a thick slice of rump-beef for grilling.—**beef'-tea** *n.* an extract of beef used as a stimulating drink.—**beef'y** *a.* stolid; fat; stout [Fr. *boeuf,* ox].

been (bēn) *pa.p.* of the verb **be.**

beer (bēr) *n.* an alcoholic beverage made by fermentation from malted barley, hops, sugar and water with the aid of yeast.—**beer'shop** *n.* a beer-house; a tavern.—**beer'y** *a.* pert. to the taste or smell of beer; discoloured with beer slops; under the influence of beer.—**not all beer and skittles,** not all pleasure and easy living.—**small beer,** beer of poor quality, hence a person of little or no importance in the scheme of things [O.E. *beor*].

beestings, biestings (bēs´tingz) *n.* the first milk taken from a cow after calving, thicker than ordinary milk [O.E. *bysting*].

beet (bēt) *n.* a garden or field plant having a succulent tap root, the red variety being used as a salad, the white yielding sugar. —**beet'root** *n.* the root of the beet plant.—**beet'-sugar** *n.* crystallised sugar extracted from beetroot [O.E. *bēte,* fr. L. *bēta*].

beetle (bē´tl) *n.* heavy wooden mallet for beating down paving-stones or driving in piles; wooden utensil for beating linen, mashing potatoes or stirring porridge, etc. [O.E. *bytel,* a mallet].

beetle (bē´tl) *n.* name of a large order of insects, Coleoptera [O.E. *bitel,* a biter].

beetle (bē´tl) *v.i.* to be prominent; to jut out; to overhang.—**beet'ling** *a.* overhanging.—**beet'le-browed** *a.* with overhanging brows; scowling.—**beet'le-head** *n.* a dull, stupid person.—**beet'le-head'ed** *a.* [O.E. *bitel*].

beeves (bēvz) *n.pl.* cattle, oxen [See **beef**].

befall (bē-fawl') *v.t.* to happen to;—*v.i.* to come to pass; to happen;—*pr.p.* **befall'ing;** *pa.t.* **befell';** *pa.p.* **befall'en** [O.E. *befeallan*].

befit (bē-fit') *v.t.* to fit or be suitable to; to become; be right for;—*pr.p.* **befit'ting;** *pa.t. pa.p.* **befit'ted.**—**befit'ting** *a.*—**befit'tingly** *adv.*

befog (bē-fog') *v.t.* to envelop in a fog; perplex.

before (bē-fōr') *prep.* in front of; preceding; in the presence of; prior to; previous to; superior to;—*adv.* in front; in advance; a short time ago; already.—*conj.* sooner than; rather than.—**before'hand** *adv.* previously.—**before'time** *adv.* of old; formerly.—**before the mast,** to be an ordinary seaman [O.E. *beforan*].

befoul (bē-foul') *v.t.* to foul, soil, dirty.

befriend (bē-frend') *v.t.* to act as a friend to; to favour; to help a stranger.

beg (beg) *v.t.* to ask earnestly and humbly; to ask for alms; to practise begging; to beseech;—*pr.p.* **beg'ging;** *pa.t.* and *pa.p.* **begged.**—**beg'gar** *n.* one who solicits alms; a mendicant;—*v.t.* to reduce to beggary; to ruin financially.—**beg'garliness** *n.*—**beg'garly** *a.* like a beggar; poor; mean; squalid; worthless; meagre; trifling;—*adv.* meanly.—**beg'gary** *n.* extreme poverty.—**beg'ging** *n.* soliciting alms;—*a.* pert. to begging; imploring; soliciting.—**beg'gingly** *adv.*—**to beg off,** to solicit pardon or a favour.—**to beg the question,** to assume truth of thing to be proved.—**to go a-begging,** not to be in demand [etym. unknown].

began (bē-gan') *pa.t.* of **begin.**

beget (bē-get') *v.t.* to generate; to procreate; to produce or to cause; to get; give rise to.—*pr.p.* **beget'ting;** *pa.t.* **begot', begat';** *pa.p.* **begot', begot'ten** [O.E. *begitan,* fr. *get*].

begin (bē-gin') *v.t.* to enter on; to set on foot;—*v.i.* to take rise; to set about.—*pr.p.* **begin'ning;** *pa.t.* **began';** *pa.p.* **begun'.**—**begin'ner** *n.* one who begins; novice.—**begin'-ning** *n.* what comes first [O.E. *beginnan*].

begird (bē-gird') *v.t.* to gird or bind with a girdle or band.—*pa.t.* **begirt'** or **begird'ed.**

begone (bē-gon') *interj.* go away! depart!—**woe'begone** *a.* gloomy and miserable.

begonia (bē-gōn´ya) *n.* a genus of tropical plants [Michel *Bégon,* Fr. botanist].

begot (bē-got'), **begotten** *pa.p.* of **beget.**

begrime (bē-grīm') *v.t.* to soil with grime.

begrudge (bē-gruj') *v.t.* to grudge; to allow reluctantly.

beguile (bē-gīl') *v.t.* to cheat or deceive by trickery; to ensnare; to delude; to while away (time); to amuse or divert.—**beguile'-ment** *n.*—**beguil'er** *n.*—**beguil'ingly** *adv.*

beguine (bā-gēn') *n.* a dance tune in common time with broken chord accompaniments [Fr.].

begum (bē´gum) *n.* the Hindustani name given to a Moslem princess.

begun (bē-gun') *pa.p.* of **begin.**

behalf (bē-hâf') *n.* favour; advantage; benefit; support; vindication; defence [O.E. *be healfe,* by the side].

behave (bē-hāv') *v.t.* and *v.i.* to conduct oneself; to act.—**behav'iour** *n.* bearing or conduct; deportment.—**behav'iourism** *n.* theory that man's actions are automatic responses to stimuli and not dictated by consciousness.—**behav'iourist** *n.*—**behaviouris'tic** *a.*

behead (bē-hed') *v.t.* to sever the head from the body.—**behead'al, behead'ing** *n.*

beheld (bē-held') *pa.p.* of **behold.**

behemoth (bē´hē-moth) *n.* (*Bib.*) a large animal, real or imaginary (Job. 40), identified with the hippopotamus [Heb.].

behest (bē-hest') *n.* that which is willed or ordered [O.E. *behaes*].

behind (bē-hīnd') *prep.* at the back of; in the rear (of); after; late; farther back than; in an inferior position;—*n.* rump; buttocks; posterior.—**behind'hand** *adv.* and *a.* late; backward; in arrears; clandestine.

behold (bē-hōld′) *v.t.* to look at; to fix the eyes upon; to observe carefully;—*v.i.* to look; fix the attention.—*pa.t.* and *pa.p.* **beheld′**.—**behold′en** *a.* obliged (to); owing a debt of gratitude (to).—**behold′er** *n.* an onlooker; spectator [O.E. *behealdan*].

behoof (bē-hòóf′) *n.* need; necessity; advantage; benefit; profit; use.—**behove′**, **behoove′** *v.t.* to be necessary, convenient for; to befit [O.E. *behofian*, to need].

beige (bezh, bāzh) *n.* a woollen cloth made of undyed wool; hence the greyish colour of unbleached wool [Fr.].

being (bē′ing) *n.* existence; that which exists; an animal [fr. *to be*].

bel (bel) *n.* (*Elect.*) ten transmission units or decibels, used as a measure of intensity of current in all types of electrical communication circuits [Graham *Bell*].

belabour (bē-lā′bur) *v.t.* to beat soundly; to cudgel; to exert much labour upon.

belate (bē-lāt′) *v.t.* to cause to be late; to retard.—**belat′ed** *a.* benighted; abroad late at night.—**belat′edness** *n.*

belaud (bē′lawd′) *v.t.* to praise highly.

belay (bē-lā′) *v.t.* to make fast a rope, by winding it round a fixed pin or cleat;—*n.* in mountaineering, a rock to which a climber anchors himself by a rope.—**belay′ing-pin** *n.* a pin or cleat, to which running rigging may be belayed [Dut. *beleggen*].

belch (belsh, belch) *v.t.* to emit wind from the stomach by way of the mouth; to cast forth;—*n.* eructation [O.E. *bealcan*].

beldame (bel′dąm) *n.* a grandmother; an ugly, old woman; a hag; an irate woman [orig. *grandmother*, Fr. *belle dame*].

beleaguer (bē-lē′gẹr) *v.t.* to surround with an army so as to preclude escape.—**beleag′uerment** *n.* [Dut. *belegeren*, to besiege].

belfry (bel′fri) *n.* a bell-tower, or a part of a steeple, where bells are hung. Orig. a watch-tower, a bell being the signal.—**bel′fried** *a.* having a belfry [Fr. *beffroi*].

Belgian (bel′jąn) *a.* pert. to Belgium.—*n.* a native or inhabitant of Belgium.—**Bel′gic** *a.* pert. to Belgians or to the *Belgae*, the ancient inhabitants of Belgium.

Belial (bēl′yąl) *n.* Satan; the devil [Heb.=that which is without profit or worth].

belibel (bē-lī′bel) *v.t.* to pronounce a libel against; to slander; to calumniate.

belie (bē-lī′) *v.t.* to give the lie to; to falsify; to speak falsely of; to misrepresent;—*pr.p.* **bely′ing** [O.E. *beleogan*, to deceive].

believe (bē-lēv′) *v.t.* to regard as true; to trust; —*v.i.* to have faith (in); to think; to suppose. —**belief′** *n.* that which is believed; full acceptance of a thing as true; faith; a firm persuasion of the truth of a body of religious tenets. —**believ′able** *a.* credible.—**believ′er** *n.*—**to make believe**, to pretend; to fancy [M.E. *beleven*].

belittle (bē-lit′l) *v.t.* to make small; to think lightly of; to disparage.—**belit′tlement** *n.* disparagement.—**belit′tling** *a.*

bell (bel) *n.* a hollow, cup-shaped metal vessel which gives forth a clear, musical note when struck; anything shaped like a bell;—*v.t.* to provide with a bell.—**bells** *n.pl.* (*Naut.*) half hours of a watch at sea, struck on a ship's bell.—**bell′-boy** *n.* page-boy in hotel.—**bell′-buoy** *n.* a buoy which by its swaying rings a bell attached.—**bell′-flow′er** *n.* the balloon flower.—**bell′-glass** *n.* a bell-shaped glass for protection of plants from frost.—**bell′-hang′er** *n.* one who hangs and fixes bells.—**bell′man** *n.* a town crier who attracts attention by first ringing a hand-bell.—**bell′-punch** *n.* a punch which rings a bell when a ticket is punched.—**bell′push** *n.* a switch which when pressed, operates an electric bell.—**bell′-tur′ret** *n.* a turret containing a bell-chamber, crowned with a spire.—**bell′-weth′er** *n.* a sheep which leads the flock with a bell hung from his neck; a noisy mob-orator.—**to bell the cat**, to hazard one's safety for the sake of others, by challenging a superior in any way (from the fable of the mice which decided to put a bell on the cat) [O.E. *belle*].

bell (bel) *n.* the cry of an animal; the bellow of the stag in rutting time. Also **bell′ing**;—*v.i.* to bellow; to roar [O.E. *bellan*, to roar].

belladonna (bel-ą-don′ą) *n.* deadly nightshade from which drugs, hyoscine and atropine, are obtained [It.=fair lady].

belle (bel) *n.* a particularly beautiful woman [Fr. *belle*, fair].

belles-lettres (bel-let′r) *n.pl.* polite literature, i.e. literature which includes poetry, the drama, criticism, aesthetics, etc. [Fr.].

bellicose (bel′i-kōs) *a.* pugnacious; contentious; war-like; quarrelsome.—**bel′licosely** *adv.* —**bellicos′ity** *n.* [L. *bellum*, war].

belligerence (bel-ij′er-ens) *n.* the state of being at war.—**bellig′erency** *n.* a state of war. —**bellig′erent** *n.* a nation, party, or person taking part in war; a contending party;—*a.* carrying on legalised war; pugnacious; bellicose [L. *bellum*, war; *gerere*, to carry on].

bellow (bel′ō) *v.i.* to roar like a bull; to shout loudly; to make an outcry; to roar, as of cannon;—*n.* a loud hollow roar, as of a bull, cannon, etc.; any deep cry.—**bell′ower** *n.* [O.E. *bellan*, to bellow].

bellows (bel′ōz, bel′us) *n.pl.* an instrument for producing a strong blast of air (to stimulate a fire, to work an organ, etc.) [fr. O.E. *bielg*, belly; the full O.E. name was *blaestbelg*, blast-bag].

belly (bel′i) *n.* part of the body which contains bowels; abdomen; stomach; part of anything bulging like a paunch;—*a.* ventral; abdominal;—*v.i.* to swell out; to bulge.—**bel′lied** *a.* swelled out; bulging; pot-bellied.—**bel′ly-ache** *n.* abdominal pains.—**bel′ly-band** *n.* a band under the belly of a horse to secure saddle.—**bel′ly-board** *n.* the top plate, usually of pine wood, of a violin.—**bel′lyful** *n.* sufficiency of food, etc.—**bel′lying** *a.* bulging; distended; bloated; puffed out [O.E. *belg*].

belong (bē-long′) *v.i.* to pertain to; to be connected with; to be property or attribute of; to be resident or native of.—**belong′ings** *n.pl.* what belongs to one; possessions [M.E. *belongen*].

beloved (bē-luv′ed, bē-luvd′) *a.* greatly loved;—*n.* one very dear to others.

below (bē-lō′) *prep.* under; beneath; of inferior rank or status; on a lower level than; unworthy of;—*adv.* in a lower place; beneath; on earth or hell, as opposed to heaven [*by*, and *low*].

belt (belt) *n.* a band, girdle, or zone, used for encircling; a zone given over to the raising of one plant, e.g. wheat;—*v.t.* to encircle, as with a belt; to thrash with a belt.—**belt′ed** *a.* wearing a belt, esp. as a mark of honour, as in 'a belted knight'; thrashed with a belt.—**belt′-convey′or** *n.* an endless belt used for conveying material from one place to another.—**belt′ing** *n.* material for skirt or bodice bands; a thrashing [E.].

belvedere (bel-ve-dēr′) *n.* a small pavilion or turret on top of building, open at one or more sides; summer-house commanding extensive view [It.=fine view].

bemoan (bē-mōn′) *v.t.* to express deep grief for, by moaning; to lament; to mourn for.

bemuse (bē-mūz′) *v.t.* to put into a state of confusion; to stupefy; to daze.—**bemused′** *a.* lost in thought; stupefied; dazed; in a trance-like state; confused.

ben (ben) *n.* a geographical term, a mountain peak, as Ben Lomond [Gael].

bench (bensh) *n.* a long seat or form; a table on which woodwork is done; the seat in court of a judge or magistrate; collective name for the body of judges sitting in judgment;—*v.t.* to furnish with benches; to place, for exhibit, on a bench.—**bench′er** *n.* (*Law*) a senior member of the Inns of Court.—**bench′ing** *n.* row of benches.—**Front Bench**, in parliament

the leaders of the party in power [M.E. *benche* fr. O.E. *benc*].
bench-mark (bensh'-mark) *n.* in ordnance surveying a fixed point of reference for use in levelling. The mark is in the form of a broad arrow and a short horizontal line.
bend (bend) *v.t.* to curve; to arch; to turn out of direct course; to incline; to sway; to apply earnestly; to subdue or make submissive; to tie, make fast—of ropes and sails;—*v.i.* to be moved out of a straight line; to stoop; to lean, to incline; to bow; to yield;—*pa.t.* **bent**, *pa.p.* **bent** or **bend'ed**;—*n.* a curve; crook; curvature; turn.—**bend'er** *n.* an instrument for bending; a hard drinker; (*U.S.*) a drinking debauch; (*Slang*) a sixpence.—**to be bent upon**, to be determined upon [O.E. *bendan*].
beneath (bē-nēth') *prep.* under; below; lower than; unworthy of; below the level of;—*adv.* below [O.E. *beneothan*].
benedict (ben'-e-dikt) *n.* a man newly married, esp. if long considered a confirmed bachelor. Also **Ben'edick** [a character in *Much Ado About Nothing*].
Benedict (ben'e-dikt) *n.* name of the saint (c. 480-543), the founder of Western monachism.—**Benedic'tine** *a.* pert. to St. Benedict or his monastic order;—*n.* a Black Friar; a cordial or liqueur originally distilled by the Benedictine monks.
benediction (ben-e-dik'-shun) *n.* a blessing of a formal character; the blessing uttered by the priest at the end of a religious service.—**benedict'ory** *a.* imparting a blessing [L. *bene*, well; *dicere*, to speak].
benefaction (ben-e-fak'-shun) *n.* act of doing good; a benefit conferred; donation.—**benefac'tor** *n.* (*fem.* **benefac'tress**) one who helps others; a donor; a patron.—**benefac'tory** *a.* [L. *bene*, well; *facere*, *factum*, to do].
benefice (ben'-e-fis) *n.* an ecclesiastical living or preferment in the Church of England, generally held by vicars and perpetual curates.—**beneficed'** *a.* in enjoyment of a benefice [L. *beneficium*].
beneficence (be-nef'-i-sens) *n.* habitual practice of doing good; charity.—**benef'icent** *a.* kindly disposed; generous; doing good.—**benef'icently** *adv.* [L. *beneficium*].
beneficial (ben-e-fish'-al) *a.* conferring benefits; receiving or entitled to receive advantages; advantageous; helpful.—**benefic'ially** *adv.*—**benefic'ialness** *n.*—**benefic'iary** *n.* one who benefits from the act of another; a holder of an ecclesiastical benefice [L.L. *beneficialis*].
benefit (ben'-e-fit) *n.* an act of kindness; a favour conferred; an advantage; profit; interest; a theatrical or other exhibition, the proceeds of which go to charity or an individual; an allowance under a national scheme of Health Service, Unemployment Insurance, etc.;—*v.t.* to do good to; to be useful to; to profit;—*v.i.* to gain advantage (from) [L. *bene*, well; *facere*, to do].
Benelux (ben'-el-uks) *n.* the economic bloc of the three countries *Be*lgium, the *Ne*therlands, and *Lux*emburg.
benevolence (ben-ev'-o-lens) *n.* disposition to do good; love of mankind; an act of kindness; generosity.—**benev'olent** *a.* of a kindly nature; beneficent;—**benev'olently** *adv.* [L. *bene*, well; *velle*, to wish].
Bengal (ben-gawl') *n.* a province of India.—**Bengal'i** *a.* of or belonging to Bengal.—*n.* a native of Bengal; one of the languages comprising eastern group of Indo-Aryan tongues.—**bengal'-light** *n.* a coloured fire, used at sea as a signal and in firework displays.
benighted (bē-nīt'-ed) *a.* overtaken by night; enveloped in moral or mental darkness; ignorant; unenlightened; lost.
benign (be-nīn') *a.* of a kindly disposition; mild (of disease); propitious (of climate).—**benignancy** (be-nig'-nan-si) *n.* benignant quality.—**benig'nant** *a.* kind; gracious; favourable; beneficial.—**benig'nantly** *adv.*—**benig'nity** *n.*—**benign'ly** *adv.* in benign fashion.—**benign'ness** *n.* benignity [L. *benignus*, kind].
benison (ben'-i-zn) *n.* benediction; blessing [L. *benedictio*. Doublet of *benediction*].
Benjamin (ben'-ja-min) *n.* (*Bib.*) a youngest son; a favourite child [Heb.= son of the right hand].
benjamin (ben'-ja-min) *n.* benzoin, a kind of resin or gum used as a medicine [corrupt. of *benzoin*].
benjamin (ben'-ja-min) *n.* a kind of overcoat worn by men [*Benjamin*, a tailor].
bent (bent) *pa.t.* and *pa.p.* of **bend**.
bent (bent) *n.* (of mind), leaning, bias, or inclination for; a tendency; a gouge [fr. *bend*].
bent (bent) *n.* bent grass; any stiff, wiry, coarse grass.—**bent'y** *a.* overrun with bent [O.E. *beonet*].
benumb (bē-num') *v.t.* to make numb, through cold or fear; to deprive of all sensation; to deaden.—**benumbed'** *a.* [O.E. *beniman*, to deprive].
Benzedrine (ben'-ze-drēn) *n.* amphetamine, a synthetic drug used to relieve nasal congestion, or to stimulate the central nervous system (Protected Trade Name).
benzene (ben'-zēn) *n.* a colourless, volatile, inflammable liquid derived from coal-tar and coke-oven gas, a solvent for fats and grease. [Ar. *luban jawi*, Java frankincense].
benzine (ben'-zēn) *n.* a mixture of low-boiling-point paraffins forming a colourless volatile, inflammable liquid used as a solvent and as a motor fuel. Also known as benzoline, gasoline, or light petroleum.
benzoin (ben'-zō-in) *n.* an aromatic gum obtained from the Eastern tree, *Styrax benzoin* used in medicine and perfumery and as an incense. On heating it yields **benzoic acid.** [See **benjamin**].
benzol (ben'-zol) *n.* a trade name for crude benzene mixed with petrol.
benzolin (ben'-zō-lin) *n.* the trade name for impure benzene.
bequeath (bē-kwēTH') *v.t.* to leave by will, said of personal property; to leave to those who follow on, as a problem, trouble, etc.—**bequest'** *n.* that which is devised by will, esp. to a public body or institute [O.E. *becwethan*].
berate (bē-rāt') *v.t.* to rate or chide vehemently; to scold vigorously.
Berber (ber'-ber) *n.* a native or the language of Barbary, in Africa;—*a.* pert. to the Berbers or their language [perh. fr. L. *barbari*]. [See **barbarian**].
berceuse (ber-sez') *n.* a lullaby or cradle song; [a slumber song [Fr.].
bere (bēr) *n.* barley. See **bear**.
bereave (bē-rēv') *v.t.* to make destitute; to deprive of;—*pa.p.* **bereaved'** or **bereft'**.—**bereaved'** *a.* robbed by death, esp. of a relative.—**bereave'ment** *n.* loss, esp. by death [E. pref. *be*; O.E. *rēafian*, to spoil].
beret, berret (ber'-ā, ber'-et) *n.* a soft, round tight-fitting cap without any peak [Fr. fr. L.L. *birretum*, a cap].
berg (berg) *n.* a large mass or mountain of ice; an iceberg; a hill or mountain, as in S. Africa [Ger.=a mountain].
bergamask (ber'-ga-mask) *n.* a dance in imitation of the clownish rustics of *Bergamo*, in Lombardy. Also **ber'gomask**.
bergamot (ber'-ga-mot) *n.* a variety of sweet orange, from the rind of which a fragrant essential oil, essence of bergamot, is obtained [*Bergamo*, town in Lombardy].
bergamot (ber'-ga-mot) *n.* a luscious variety of pear [Turk. *berg-armudi*, prince's pear].
bergomask See **bergamask**.
beri-beri (ber'-i-ber'-i) *n.* a nervous disease due to deficiency of vitamin B, prevalent in tropical countries [Singh.].
berlin (ber'-lin) *n.* a four-wheeled carriage with a hooded sheltered seat behind the body.—**berlin wool**, a fine wool, dyed in colours which merge into one another, used in fancy worsted work [fr. *Berlin*, Germany].

berry (ber'i) *n.* a small, pulpy, juicy fruit; strictly, a simple fruit with succulent pericarp.—**ber'ried** *a.* [O.E. *berie*].

berserk, berserker (ber'serk, -ker) *n.* a battle-frenzied Norse warrior;—*a.* frenzied.—**to go berserk,** to go mad with fury [Scand. = bare of sark or shirt of mail].

berth (berth) *n.* the place where a ship is anchored or moored; a sleeping-place on a ship, etc.; a situation or job;—*v.t.* to bring to anchorage.—**berth'age** *n.* dock or harbour dues.—**to give a wide berth to,** to steer clear of; to shun; to avoid [Doublet of *birth*].

beryl (ber'il) *n.* a group of green or bluish-green precious stones of exceptional hardness, includes the emerald and aquamarine;—*a.* beryl-like in colour.—**ber'ylline** *a.* resembling beryl.—**beryl'lium** *n.* a rare metal of the magnesium group, silver white and stable; glucinum [Gk. *bērullos*].

beseech (bē-sēch') *v.t.* to ask or entreat earnestly; to solicit; beg; implore;—*pa.t.* and *pa.p.* **besought'**.—**beseecher** *n.*—**beseech'ing** *a.* imploring.—**beseech'ingly** *adv.*—**beseech'ment** *n.* [M.E. *sechen*, to seek].

beseem (bē-sēm') *v.t.* to be fit for; to befit; to suit; to become.—**beseem'ing** *a.*

beset (bē'set') *v.t.* to place on, in, or around; to hem in on all sides; to surround; to enclose; to assail;—*pr.p.* **beset'ting** *pa.t.* and *pa.p.* **beset'**.—**beset'ment** *n.*—**beset'ter** *n.*—**beset'ting** *a.* customary; habitual, as in 'besetting sin' [O.E. *besettan*].

beshrew (bē-shrōō') *v.t.* to wish some slight evil to befall one; to curse; to rate.

beside (bē-sīd') *prep.* and *adv.* at the side of; over and above; in addition to; apart from; distinct from.—**besides'** *adv.* moreover;—*prep.* over and above.—**beside oneself,** out of one's wits [O.E. *bi sidan*].

besiege (bē-sēj') *v.t.* to lay siege to; to surround with armed forces; to pay court to; to beleaguer.—**besiege'ment** *n.*—**besieg'er** *n.*—**besieg'ing** *a.*—**besieg'ingly** *adv.* [M.E. *asege*, fr. Fr. *assiéger*].

besmear (bē-smēr') *v.t.* to smear over with any sticky, gluey matter; to soil; to bedaub.

besmirch (bē-smerch') *v.t.* to soil; to sully; to tarnish one's reputation, etc.

besom (bē'zum, bez'um) *n.* a brush of twigs for sweeping; a broom; a troublesome woman or girl; a hussy [O.E. *besema*].

besot (bē-sot') *v.t.* to make sottish by drink; to make stupid.—**besot'ted** *a.* [O.E.].

besought (bē-sawt') *pa.t.* and *pa.p.* of **beseech**.

bespatter (bē-spat'er) *v.t.* to sprinkle or splash with mud, ink, etc.; to defame.

bespeak (bē-spēk') *v.t.* to order, speak for, or engage beforehand; to betoken;—*pa.t.* **bespoke'**.—*pa.p.* **bespoke'** and **bespok'en**.—*n.* a benefit performance.—**bespoke', bespok'en** *a.* ordered beforehand; of goods, made to measure, esp. shoes and clothes [*speak*].

bespeckle (bē-spek'l) *v.t.* to mark with speckles or spots; to variegate.

Bessemer (bes'em-er) *a.* applied to steel prepared by the Bessemer process of forcing atmospheric air into molten cast iron [Sir H. *Bessemer*, (1813-98), the inventor].

best (best) *a. superl.* good in the highest degree; excellent beyond all others; most suitable, advantageous, advisable, or appropriate;—*adv.* in the most excellent manner; —*n.* utmost; highest endeavour; perfection.—**best man,** a groomsman at a wedding.—**best seller,** a current popular book with an enormous sale.—**to make the best of,** to resign oneself to conditions, etc. [O.E. *bet(e)st*].

bestead (bē-sted') *v.t.* to help; to avail; to be of use to.

bestial (bes-ti-al) *a.* pert. to a beast; having the instincts of a beast; like a repulsive beast. —**bestial'ity** *n.* beastly depravity.—**bes'tially** *adv.* [Fr. fr. L. *bestialis*].

bestir (bē-ster') *v.t.* to rouse into vigorous action; to exert (oneself); to stimulate.

bestow (bē-stō') *v.t.* to lay up in store; to expend, as energy; to give ceremoniously; to confer; to award; grant; present; impart.—**bestow'al** *n.*—**bestow'er** *n.*—**bestow'ment** *n.* bestowing; what is bestowed [M.E. *bestowen*, to place].

bestraddle (bē-strad'l) *v.t.* to bestride.

bestrew (bē-strōō') *v.t.* to scatter over; to besprinkle.—*pa.p.* **bestrewed', bestrewn'**.

bestride (bē'strīd') *v.t.* to stride over; to stand or sit with the legs extended across.—*pr.p.* **bestrid'ing**; *pa.t.* **bestrode', bestrid'**; *pa.p.* **bestrid', bestrid'den**.

bet (bet) *n.* a stake or wager on some problematical event;—*v.t.* to stake money upon some contingency;—*pr.p.* **bet'ting**; *pa.t.* and *pa.p.* **bet** or **bet'ted**.—**bet'ter, bet'tor** *n.* one who lays a bet [fr. *abet*].

beta (bē'ta, bā-ta) *n.* the second letter of the Greek alphabet, printed thus, β.—**beta particles,** fast electrons emitted when certain atoms undergo radio-active breakdown.—**beta rays,** streams of beta particles emanated by radio-active substances.

betake (bē-tāk') *v.t.* to have recourse to; to apply; (with reflexive) to go, to repair to; to make one's way;—*pr.p.* **betak'ing**; *pa.t.* **betook'**; *pa.p.* **betak'en** [M.E. *betaken*].

betatron (bā-ta-tron') *n.* an arrangement for accelerating electrons which, emitted from a hot metal filament, are constrained to move in circles in a powerful magnetic field and are accelerated by an alternating high frequency potential [Gk. *bēta*, letter B.].

betel (bē'tl) *n.* a species of pepper, the leaves of which are prepared as a stimulant, and chewed by inhabitants of India, staining the saliva a brilliant red.—**be'tel-nut,** *n.* the nut of the areca palm [Port. *betle*].

Bethel (beth'el) *n.* Palestine; a hallowed spot; a non-conformist chapel [Heb. *bēth-el*, house of God].

Bethell's Process (beth'elz prō'ses) *n.* process of preserving timber by drying in a partial vacuum and forcing creosote into the timber under pressure (*Bethell*, the inventor).

bethink (bē-thingk') *v.t.* to call to mind; to remind oneself; to cogitate.

betide (bē-tīd') *v.t.* to happen to;—*v.i.* to occur; happen [M.E. *betiden*, to happen].

betimes (bē-tīmz') *adv.* in good time; seasonably; soon; early; forward.

betoken (bē-tō'kn) *v.t.* to show by some visible sign; to foreshow [M.E. *betacnien*].

betony (bet'o-ni) *n.* a perennial herb used for dyeing wool a fine dark-yellow shade and formerly regarded as a remedy for coughs [L. *betonica*].

betook (bē-tòòk') *pa.t.* of **betake**.

betray (bē-trā') *v.t.* to give up treacherously; to be disloyal to; to disclose (a secret); to seduce; to show signs of; deceive.—**betray'al** *n.* act of betraying.—**betray'er** *n.* a traitor; a seducer [L. *tradere*, to give up].

betroth (bē-trōTH') *v.t.* to promise to give or take in marriage; to affiance.—**betroth'al** *n.* an agreement with a view to marriage.—**betrothed'** *n.* a person engaged to be married; fiancé, (*fem*). fiancée.—**betroth'ment** *n.* the state of being betrothed [M.E. *bitreuthien*].

better (bet'er) *a.* (compar. of *good*), showing a greater degree of excellence; improved in health;—*adv.* (compar. of *well*), in a more excellent or superior manner; more fully;— *v.t.* and *i.* to make better; to amend; to raise one's worldly position.—**bet'terment** *n.* improvement; enhanced value of property due to local improvements.—**bet'ters** *n.pl.* one's superiors in rank or wealth.—**better half,** a jocular term for wife.—**better off,** in more prosperous circumstances.—**to get the better of,** to gain an advantage over.—**to think better of,** to reconsider [O.E. *betera*].

betting, better, bettor. See under **bet**.

between (bē-twēn') *prep.* in the middle of two

(of space, time, etc.); in the middle or intermediate space; shared by two;—*adv.* midway.—**betwixt'** *prep.* between; midway.—**go'-between'** *n.* an intermediary.—**between'-maid** *n.* a young maid-servant who assists both cook and housemaid; (*Colloq.*) a tweeny [O.E. *betweonum*, by twain].

bevel (bev'l) *n.* an angle, not being a right angle, formed by two surfaces; an adjustable instrument used in building, etc. for testing angles;—*a.* having the form of a bevel; slanting;—*v.t.* to cut to a bevel angle.—*pr.p.* **bev'elling**;—*pa.t.* and *pa.p.* **bev'elled**.—**bev'elled** *a.* cut to a slope or bevel.—**bev'elling, bev'elment** *n.* [Fr. *biveau*, carpenter's rule].

beverage (bev'e-rāj) *n.* a refreshing liquid suitable for drinking [O.Fr. *bevrage*].

bevy (bev'i) *n.* a flock of birds, esp. quails or larks; an assembly, esp. of young ladies; a collection or group [etym. unknown].

bewail (bē-wāl') *v.t.* to express grief for; to lament; deplore; mourn over.

beware (bē-wār') *v.i.* to be wary of; to be on one's guard; to be alive to impending danger; to take care (lest).

bewilder (bē-wil'dęr) *v.t.* to lead astray or into confusion; to confound; perplex; puzzle.—**bewil'dered** *a.* in a state of mental confusion; confounded.—**bewil'dering** *a.* confusing.—**bewil'derment** *n.* [fr. obs. *wildern*, wilderness].

bewitch (bē-wich') *v.t.* to gain power over, by sorcery; to charm; captivate; entrance.—**bewitch'er** *n.*—**bewitch'ery, bewitch'ment** *n.* power to bewitch; enchantment.—**bewitch'ing** *a.* charming; alluring.—**bewitch'ingly** *adv.* [M.E. *bewicchen*].

bewray (bē-rā') *v.t.* to divulge; to disclose; to reveal; to betray without intent [O.E. *wregan*, to accuse].

bey (bā) *n.* a governor of a town, sanjak, or district in Turkish dominions [Turk. *beg*, a governor].

beyond (bē-yond') *prep.* on the farther side of; out of reach of; above; past in time; later than; superior to;—*adv.* farther off; at a distance;—*n.* the future life [O.E. *geond*, across].

bezel (bez'el) *n.* the piece of metal under the setting holding the jewel of a ring; the groove in which the glass of a watch is set; the sloped cutting edge of a tool; the sloping facets of a cut gem. Also **bas'il** or **bez'il** [O.Fr. *bisel*].

bezique (bę-zēk') *n.* a card game played with two packs (all cards under seven being omitted) by two players [Fr.].

bhang (bang) *n.* narcotic, prepared leaf of Indian hemp; called hashish when strained in water [Hind.].

bi-, bis- (bī, bis) *prefix.* used in the construction of compound nouns, indicating two, twice, or double [L. *bis*, twice].

bias (bī'as) *n.* the weight on one side of a bowl (in game of *Bowls*), which gives it a tendency to diverge from straight line when running; prejudice; prepossession that sways the mind;—*v.t.* to influence; to prejudice; to prepossess (often unduly);—*pa.t.* and *pa.p.* **bi'assed** or **bi'ased** [Fr. *biais*, oblique].

bib (bib) *n.* piece of cloth worn mainly by children over the breast when eating; part of a workman's overalls to protect chest;—*v.t.* and *v.i.* to sip; tipple; drink frequently.—*pr.p.* **bib'bing**;—*pa.t.* and *pa.p.* **bibbed**.—**biba'cious** *a.* addicted to tippling.—**bib'ber** *n.* a person given to frequent and excessive imbibing of liquor or wines; a tippler [L. *bibere*, to drink].

Bible (bī'bl) *n.* the volume which contains the Scriptures of the Old and New Testaments; an authoritative book on a specific subject.—**bib'lical** *a.* pert. to the Bible; scriptural [Gk. *biblia*, books].

biblio- (bib'li-ō) *prefix* from Gk. *biblion*, a book, used in the formation of compound words referring to books.—**bibliog'raphy** *n.* expert knowledge of history of books; a list of books on a specific subject.—**biblio'grapher** *n.* one who compiles lists of books for further study of a subject; one interested in various editions of certain books.—**bibliograph'ic(al)** *a.*—**bibliol'atry** *n.* extreme regard for the letter of Scripture.—**bibliol'atrist, bibliol'ater** *n.* one who regards the Bible as authoritative in all matters.—**bibliol'atrous** *a.*—**bibliol'ogy** *n.* knowledge of the production and distribution of books.—**biblioman'cy** *n.* a means of divining the future by opening the Bible at random.—**biblioma'nia** *n.* a mania for possessing rare books.—**biblioman'iac** *n.*—**bib'liophile** *n.* a lover of books.—**bib'liopole, bibliop'olist** *n.* a dealer in books, esp. rare books.—**bibliop'oly** *n.*—**bibliothec'a** *n.* a bookcase; a library.—**bibliothec'ary** *n.* a librarian [Gk. *biblion*, a book].

bibulous (bib'ū-lus) *a.* given to excessive or frequent drinking; absorbent; spongy.—**bib'ulously** *adv.* [L. *bibere*, to drink].

bicameral (bī-kam'e-ręl) *a.* pert. to or containing two legislative or other chambers [L. *bis*, twice; *camera*, chamber].

bicarbonate (bī-kár'bo-nāt) *n.* a salt or compound containing two equivalents of carbonic acid to one of a base—usually applied loosely for 'bicarbonate of soda.'

bice (bīs) *n.* a pigment [Fr. *bis*].

bicentenary (bī-sen'te-nę-ri, bī-sen-tē'nę-ri) *a.* pert. to the two hundredth year;—*n.* the two hundredth anniversary. Also **bicentennial** (bī-sen-ten'i-ęl) *a.*

biceps (bī'seps) *n.* two-headed muscle of arm or leg; a flexor muscle.—**bicip'ital** *a.* [L. *bis*, twice; *caput*, head].

bicker (bik'ęr) *v.i.* to bandy words; to wrangle; to move quickly and lightly.—**bick'ering** *n.*—**bick'erment** *n.* [origin uncertain].

bicuspid (bī-kus'pid) *n.* a tooth with two fangs;—*a.* having two cusps or fangs. Also **bicus'pidate** [L. *bis*, twice; *cuspis*, a point].

bicycle (bī'si-kl) *n.* a vehicle with two wheels, one in front of the other, propelled by pedals; *v.i.* to cycle.—**bi'cyclist** *n.* one who rides a bicycle.—**bike** *n.* (*Colloq.*) [L. *bis*, twice; Gk. *kuklos*, a wheel].

bid (bid) *v.t.* to ask; to invite; to order or direct; to offer a price; to give, as good-bye;—*pr.p.* **bid'ding**; *pa.t.* **bid** or **bade**; *pa.p.* **bid**, **bid'den**;—*n.* an offer of a price, esp. at auctions; an attempt.—**bid'dable** *a.* compliant; docile; obedient; submissive; willing; (*Cards*) that may be bid without undue risk.—**bid'der** *n.*—**bid'ding** *n.* invitation; command; offer at an auction; series of bids at cards [confusion of O.E. *beodan*, offer, and *biddan*, request].

biddy (bid'i) *n.* a young servant girl, esp. Irish.—**red biddy**, intoxicating drink from methylated spirit and red wine [dim. of *Bridget*].

bide (bīd) *v.i.* to dwell permanently; abide; remain; continue; tarry; sojourn; reside;—*v.t.* to endure; put up with; suffer; tolerate; bear [O.E. *bidan*, to remain].

biennial (bī-en'i-ęl) *a.* happening once in two years; lasting for only two years;—*n.* a plant which requires two seasons to produce its flowers and fruit.—**bienn'ially** *adv.* [L. *bis*, twice; *annus*, a year].

bier (bēr) *n.* a frame or carriage for conveying the dead to the grave; a coffin; grave; tomb [O.E. *baer*].

biestings See **beestings**.

bifacial (bī-fāsh'yęl) *a.* having two like faces or opposite surfaces.

biflorate (bī-flō'rāt) *a.* (*Bot.*) bearing two flowers on the one stem. Also **biflo'rous**.

bifocal (bī-fō'kal) *a.* having two foci;—*n.pl.* spectacles with a small lens for reading, set into a larger lens for distant vision [L. *bis*, twice; E. *focal*].

bifoliate (bī-fō'li-āt) *a.* (*Bot.*) having two leaflets springing from the same point. Also **bifol'iolate** [L. *bis*, twice; *folium*, leaf].

bifurcate (bī-fur'kāt) *v.t.* to divide into two branches;—*v.i.* to fork.—**bifur'cate, bifur'cated**

a. divided into two prongs, forks, or branches.—**bifurca'tion** *n.*—**bifur'cous** *a.* bifurcate [L. *bis*, twice; *furca*, a fork].

big (big) *a.* bulky; massive; huge; great; pregnant; generous; magnanimous; important.—**big'-bell'ied** *a.* corpulent; pregnant.—**big'-bug** *n.* (*Slang*) an important person; a bigwig.—**big'-end** *n.* the crank-pin end of a connecting rod at its point of attachment in a reciprocating engine.—**big'gish** *a.*—**big'-heart'ed** *a.*—**big'ness** *n.* size; bulk; largeness; importance.—**big'-noise** *n.* (*Colloq.*) a person of much authority.—**big'wig** *n.* (*Colloq.*) a person of great importance or influence [etym. unknown].

bigamy (big'ạ-mi) *n.* the crime of having two wives or husbands at one time.—**big'amist** *n.*—**big'amous** *a.*—**big'amously** *adv.* [L. *bis*, twice; Gk. *gamos*, marriage].

bight (bīt) *n.* a curve; a loop of a rope when folded; a bend in the sea-coast; an open bay [O.E. *byht*].

bigot (big'ot) *n.* one obstinately and unreasonably wedded to a particular belief or creed; dogmatist.—**big'oted** *a.* obstinate in belief.—**big'otedly** *adv.*—**big'otry** *n.* the blind zeal of a bigot [Fr. of unknown origin].

bijou (bē-zhòó') *n.* a gem; a trinket of precious material or workmanship.—*pl.* **bijoux** (bē-zhòó').—**bijou'terie**, **bijou'try** *n.* jewellery; trinkets; articles of vertu [Fr.].

bike (bīk) *n.* (*Colloq.*) a bicycle.

bikini (bi-kē'ni) *n.* a scanty two-piece bathing suit [*Bikini*, Pacific island].

bilateral (bī-lat'e-rạl) *a.* having two sides; affecting two parties.—**bilat'erally** *adv.* [L. *bis*, twice; *latus*, *lateris*, side].

bilberry (bil'ber-i) *n.* the whortleberry; in Scotland, blaeberry (=blueberry).

bilbo (bil'bō) *n.* a rapier or sword.—**bil'boes** *n.pl.* shackles for the feet, formerly used on Spanish ships [fr. *Bilbao*].

bile (bīl) *n.* a greenish, viscous, bitter fluid secreted by the liver; gall; general disorder of health due to faulty secretion of bile; bad temper.—**biliary** (bil'i-ar-i) *a.* pert. to the bile.—**bil'ious** *a.* pert. to the bile; affected by bile; choleric; peevish; crabbed; ill-humoured.—**bil'iousness** *n.* a disturbance of the digestive system associated with an excess of bile [L. *bilis*].

bilge (bilj) *n.* the swelling part of a cask; the broadest part of a ship's bottom nearest the keel, acting as a sump; (*Colloq.*) nonsense;—*v.i.* to spring a leak.—**bilge'-wa'ter** *n.* evil-smelling water which gathers in a ship's bottom [form of *bulge*].

bilingual (bī-ling'gwạl) *a.* speaking, or written in, two languages. Also **biling'uar**.—**biling'uist** *n.* a person who can speak fluently in two languages [L. *bis*, twice; *lingua*, tongue].

bilious, biliousness See **bile**.

bilk (bilk) *v.t.* to defraud, to swindle.—**bilk'er** *n.* [origin uncertain].

bill (bil) *n.* the horny, toothless and lipless jaw of a bird; beak; a promontory;—*v.i.* to stroke bills, as birds; to caress; to fondle.—**to bill and coo**, to make love [O.E. *bile*].

bill (bil) *n.* a kind of axe with two sharp pointed spikes mounted on a long staff; a hook-shaped pruning instrument.—**bill'-hook** *n.* a small bill with a hooked end for lopping branches [O.E. *bil*].

bill (bil) *n.* printed notice for public display; an account of money; a written engagement to pay money under the hand of the granter; a declaration of certain facts in legal proceedings; the draft of a proposed law;—*v.t.* to announce by posters; to cover with posters; to placard.—**bill'-bro'ker** *n.* one who negotiates the discount of bills.—**bill'head** *n.* the printed matter at the top of stationery; an invoice form.—**bill'ing** *n.* advertising by use of posters; (*U.S.*) invoicing.—**bill'-post'er**, **bill'-stick'er** *n.* one who posts up bills.—**bill of entry**, a statement to customs officials giving particulars of goods imported or shipped.—**bill of exchange**, written order, signed by drawer and addressed to drawee, requiring the latter to pay sum of money to the drawer, or anyone appointed by him, by a given date.—**bill of fare**, menu.—**bill of health**, an official document required from the authorities of a port by a captain of a ship showing the sanitary condition and health of the port and on board ship, when clearing.—**bill of indictment**, a statement setting forth the charges against an accused person.—**bill of lading**, a written acknowledgment of goods received for shipment issued by the captain of a ship, and regarded as a contract to deliver the goods safely.—**bill of sale**, a legal document by which property is transferred from the vendor to the purchaser, or goods and chattels are assigned by way of security.—**to fill the bill**, to be satisfactory in all respects [L.L. *billa*=*bulla*, a seal].

billabong, bilabong (bil'a-bong) *n.* a backwater; a branch from a stream [Aborig. *billa*, river; *beong*, dead].

billet (bil'et) *n.* a short note; an order requisitioning accommodation for soldiers; the quarters occupied by soldiers in private houses, etc.; a situation, job, or post;—*v.t.* to quarter or lodge troops.—**billet-doux** (bil-e-dòó') *n.* a love letter [Fr.=a note].

billet (bil'et) *n.* a small log used as fuel [Fr. *bille*, a log].

billiard (bil'yard) *a.* pert. to billiards.—**bill'iards**, *n.* a table game played with three balls which are hit by a leather-tipped cue [Fr. *bille*, a ball].

Billingsgate (bil'ingz-gāt) *n.* a fish-market in London, a byword for foul language.

billion (bil'yun) *n.* a million millions (10^{12}); in U.S. a thousand millions (10^{9}).—**bill'ionaire** *n.* a fabulously wealthy person.—**bill'ionth** *a.* [L. *bis*, twice; *million*].

billow (bil'ō) *n.* a great, swelling wave of the sea; a surge of flame, smoke, cloud, etc.; a breaker.—*v.i.* to swell or roll, as waves.—**bill'owed**, **bill'owy** *a.* [O.N. *bylga*].

billy (bil'i) *n.* in Australia, a round tin-can with a loose handle, used as a kettle [*abbrev.* fr. *billycan*, fr. Fr. *bouilli* and *can*].

billycock (bil'i-kok) *n.* a low-crowned felt hat with a broad rim [etym. doubtful].

billygoat (bil'i-gōt) a he-goat; a tufted beard [*billy*=*Willie*].

biltong (bil'tong) *n.* thin strips of lean meat dried in the sun [S. Afr.].

bimetallism (bī-met'ạl-izm) *n.* in currency, the use of both gold and silver coins at a fixed relative value.—**bimet'allist** *n.* one who advocates the policy of bimetallism.

bimonthly (bī-munth'li) *a.* properly once in two months, but often means, erroneously, twice in a month;—*n.* a periodical which appears once in two months.

bin (bin) *n.* a box or enclosed place with a lid, for corn, bread, etc.; a receptacle for bottles of wine;—*v.t.* to store in a bin [O.E. *binn*, crib].

binary (bī'nạ-ri) *a.* composed of two; twofold; double; dual;—*n.* a double star.—**bi'nate** *a.* growing in pairs [L. *bini*, two by two].

bind (bīnd) *v.t.* to tie together as with a band, cord, etc.; to constrain by moral influence; to secure together and enclose in a cover; to place under legal obligation; to be obligatory; to apprentice; to constipate;—*pa.t.* and *pa.p.* **bound**.—**bind'er** *n.* a person who binds; a machine for binding, as sheaves, books, etc.; a transfer case in filing and loose-leaf systems; a bandage.—**bind'ery** *n.* a book-binding establishment.—**bind'ing** *a.* obligatory; constipating;—*n.* act of fastening; anything which binds; partial locking of a sliding part of a machine due to faulty lubrication.—**bind'weed** *n.* a plant with twining stems; convolvulus [O.E. *bindan*].

bing (bing) *n.* a heap of grain; a bin; a weight

of lead ore, 8 cwt.; the refuse of a mine built up to a considerable height [Scand. *bingr*, a heap].

binge (binj) *n.* concerted eating and especially drinking, to celebrate an occasion; a spree [University slang].

binnacle (bin´ạ-kl) *n.* the box containing the compass of a ship [earlier *bittacle*, fr. L. *habitaculum*, little dwelling].

binocle (bin´o-kl) *n.* a telescope fitted with two tubes.—**binoc'ular,** *a.* adapted for the use of both eyes;—*n.* a binocular telescope.—**binoc'ulars** *n.pl.* field-glasses.—**binoc'ulate,** *a.* having two eyes; adapted for the use of two eyes [L. *bini*, two by two; *oculus*, eye].

binomial (bī-nō´mi-ạl) *n.* an algebraic expression involving two terms connected by the sign plus (+) or minus (—), e.g. a + b, or c — d;—*a.* pert. to binomials.—**binomial theorem,** an algebraic formula for expressing any power of a binomial by a converging infinite series [L. *bis*, twice; *nomen*, name].

binominal (bī-nom´i-nạl) *a.* (*Bot.*) having two names, the first indicating the genus, the second indicating the species.

bio- (bī´ō) a *prefix* used in the construction of compound terms, to express having organic life [Gk. *bios*, life].

biochemistry (bī-ō-kem´is-tri) *n.* physiology considered from the chemical point of view; the chemistry of living things.

biodynamics (bī-ō-dī-nam´iks) *n.pl.* the science which investigates the vital forces; the energy of living functions.

biogen (bī´o-jen) *n.* a hypothetical protein molecule assumed to be the primary source of all living matter.—**biogen'esis** *n.* the theory that life develops only from living organisms, as opposed to abiogenesis.—**biogenet'ic** *a.* pert. to biogenesis.—**biogenet'ically** *adv.* [Gk. *bios*, life; *genesis*, beginning].

biograph, bioscope (bī´ō-graf, -skōp) *n.* early cinematograph [Gk. *bios*, life; *graphein*, to write; *skopein*, to see].

biography (bī-og´rạ-fi) *n.* the detailed story of a person's life and achievements; the section of literature devoted to the writing of the life-stories of individuals.—**biograph'ic, biograph'ical** *a.*—**biograph'ically** *adv.* [Gk. *bios*, life; *graphein*, to write].

biology (bī-ol´o-ji) *n.* the science of life, whether animal or vegetable.—**biolog'ic, biolog'ical** *a.*—**biolog'ically** *adv.*—**biol'ogist** *n.*—**biological warfare,** a method of fighting in which disease bacteria would be used [Gk. *bios*, life; *logos*, a discourse].

bionomics (bī-on-om´iks) *n.* study of influence of environment on organisms; oecology [Gk. *bios*, life; *nomos*, law]. [organisms.

biophysics (bī-ō-fiz´iks) *n.* physics of living

bioscope See **biograph.**

biotic (bī-ot´ik) *a.* (*Biol.*) relating to life; vital.—**biot'ics** *n.* the functions, properties, and activities of living animals or plants [Gk. *bios*, life].

biotin (bī´ō-tin) *n.* a constituent of the vitamin B_2 complex, formerly known as vitamin H, essential to many forms of plant and animal life [Gk. *bios*, life].

bipartient (bī-par´ti-ent) *n.* a number which divides another into two equal parts, e.g. 16 is a bipartient of 32 [L. *bis*, twice; *partire*, to divide].

bipartisan (bī-par´ti-zạn) *a.* pert. to, representing, or composed of, members of two parties [L. *bis*, twice; *partire*, to divide].

bipartite (bī-par´tīt) *a.* divided or split into two parts as far as the base, as a leaf; consisting of two corresponding parts; shared by the two parties concerned.—**biparti'tion** *n.* [L. *bis*, twice; *partire*, to divide].

biped (bī´ped) *n.* an animal with two feet.—**bi'ped, biped'al** *a.* [L. *bis*, twice; *pes*, a foot].

biplane (bī´plān) *n.* an aeroplane or glider having two main plane surfaces.

bipod (bī´pod) *n.* a two-legged stand.—cf. **tripod.**

bipolar (bī-pōl´ạr) *a.* having two poles [L.].

biquadrate (bī-kwod´rāt) *n.* (*Math.*) the value of the fourth power of a number, e.g. 81, equivalent to 3^4.—**biquadrat'ic** *a.*—*n.* the fourth power [L. *bis*, twice; *quadratus*, squared].

birch (bẹrch) *n.* a tree with slim branches and silvery bark-scales; the hard, close-grained wood of the birch;—*v.t.* flog with a birch-rod.—**birch, birch'en** *a.* of birch.—**birch'rod,** *n.* a rod of birch twigs for inflicting corporal punishment on young offenders [O.E. *birce*].

bird (bẹrd) *n.* a feathered animal.—**bird'-cage** *n.* a cage made of wire and wood for keeping birds.—**bird'-call** *n.* instrument used to allure birds by imitating their notes.—**bird'-eyed** *a.* keen of vision.—**bird'-fan'cier** *n.* one who breeds birds for show or sale.—**bird'like** *a.* dainty.—**bird'-lime** *n.* a sticky substance used to catch birds.—**bird'-man** *n.* an airman or balloonist.—**bird'-net** *n.* a net used for catching birds.—**bird's'-eye** *n.* kind of tobacco.—**bird's eye view,** a comprehensive view as would be seen by a bird.—**to get the bird,** to be hissed off the stage [O.E. *brid*, a bird].

birdie (bẹrd´i) *n.* (*Golf*) holing a ball in one stroke below par; a term of endearment.

bireme (bī´rēm) *n.* a Roman galley with two tiers or banks of oars [L. *bis*, twice; *remus*, an oar].

biretta (bi-ret´a) *n.* a flat, square, stiff cap worn by Catholic clergy, the colour varying with rank of wearer [It. *berretta*].

birr (bir) *n.* a whirring noise like that of a revolving wheel; an energetic push; a pronounced accent; strongly trilling the consonant *r*. Also **burr** [Scand. *byrr*].

birth (bẹrth) *n.* act of coming into life or of being born; the delivery of a newly born child alive; descent; origin.—**birth'-control'** *n.* restriction of conception.—**birth'day** *n.* the day on which one is born; the anniversary of that day.—**birth'mark** *n.* peculiar mark on the body at birth.—**birth'-place** *n.* the place where a person is born.—**birth'-rate** *n.* the ratio of births to the total population.—**birth'right** *n.* anything to which one is entitled by birth [M.E. *birthe*, perh. fr. Scand.].

bis (bis) *adv.* twice; (*Mus.*) to show that the bar or passage is to be performed twice:—*n.* a form of applause in France.

biscuit (bis´kit) *n.* small thin cake; stoneware, earthenware, porcelain, etc. after firing but before being glazed [L. *bis*, twice; *coctus*, cooked].

bisect (bī-sekt') *v.t.* to divide into two equal parts.—**bisec'tion** *n.* one of two equal parts.—**bisec'tor** *n.* a bisecting line.—**biseg'ment** *n.* one of the two segments of a bisected line [L. *bis*, twice; *secare*, to cut].

bisexual (bī-seks´ū-ạl) *a.* having the organs of both sexes in one individual; hermaphroditic [L. *bis*, twice].

bishop (bish´op) *n.* a clergyman of highest rank, head of diocese, himself under archbishop; chess man moving diagonally; a beverage of red wine, oranges and sugar.—**bish'opric** *n.* diocese, jurisdiction, or office of a bishop.—**bishop's lawn,** a fine kind of linen.—**bish'opweed** *n.* the grab-weed, a hedge plant. Also **bishop's weed** [fr. Gk. *episkopos*, overseer].

bishop (bish´op) *v.t.* to tamper with a horse, esp. teeth, to deceive as to its age [*Bishop*, a horse-dealer].

bismuth (biz´muth) *n.* a reddish-white metal —one of the elementary bodies, the salts of which are used extensively in medicine.—**bis'muthal, bis'muthic** *a.* pert. to bismuth.—**bismuth meal,** carbonate of bismuth, added to bread and milk, given to a patient about to be X-rayed [etym. unknown].

bison (bī´son, bīs´on) *n.* the large wild ox or buffalo of the Rocky Mountains [L.].

bisque (bisk] *n.* a soup, also known as bisk; unglazed porcelain.
bisque (bisk) *n.* (*Golf, Tennis*, etc.) odds given to a weaker player, to be taken when it best suits him [Fr.].
bistre (bis′tėr) *n.* a dark-brown pigment consisting of the soot of beech-wood, or of other woods, ground in oil [Fr.].
bisulphate (bī-sul′fāt) *n.* a salt of sulphuric acid in which one-half of the hydrogen in the acid is replaced by a metal.
bit (bit) *pa.t.* of **bite.**
bit (bit) *n.* a mouthful; a morsel; small piece of anything; a fragment; a small coin, as a threepenny bit; (*Slang*) a woman; a boring tool generally for use in a brace; part of bridle which is placed in a horse's mouth;—*v.t.* to put the bit in the mouth of a horse;—**to take the bit between the teeth,** to become unmanageable [See **bite**].
bitch (bich) *n.* the female of the dog, wolf, or fox; (*Colloq.*) an opprobious term for a woman [O.E. *bicce*].
bite (bīt) *v.t.* to cut, crush, seize, or wound with the teeth; to pinch with cold; to eat into, as acid; to corrode; to gnaw; to champ; to nip; to defraud; to cheat.—*v.i.* to be given to biting; to be pungent;—*pr.p.* **bit′ing;** *pa.t.* **bit;** *pa.p.* **bit** or **bit′ten;**—act of biting; a portion bitten off; food; morsel; sharp, pungent taste; the nibble of a fish at a hook; the grip of an edged tool on metal.—**bi′ter** *n.*—**bi′ting** *a.* sharp; severe; sarcastic; caustic; pungent; chilling [O.E. *bitan*].
bitt (bit) *n.* a post for securing cables, etc., usually *pl.*—*v.t.* to put around a bitt [Scand.].
bittacle See **binnacle.**
bitter (bit′ėr) *a.* biting or acrid to the taste; causing pain or smart to the feelings;—*n.* bitter beer.—**bitt′erly** *adv.*—**bitt′erness** *n.* the quality of being bitter to the taste; animosity.—**bitt′ers** *n.* alcoholic liquor containing bitter flavourings, e.g. angostura.—**bitt′er-sweet** *n.* the woody nightshade whose root, when chewed, tastes first bitter then sweet; the meadow-sweet [O.E. *biter*].
bittern (bit′ėrn) *n.* a wading marsh-bird of the heron family [O. Fr. *butor*].
bitumen (bi-tū′men, bit′ū-men) *n.* an inflammable, mineral pitch, as asphalt, petroleum, etc.—**bitu′minise** *v.t.* to cover roads with bitumen preparations to render them dustless.—**bitu′minous** *a.* resembling, or containing, bitumen [L.].
bivalve (bī′valv) *a.* having two valves;—*n.* an animal with a shell of two parts opening like a hinge; a seed case of this kind.—**bival′vous** *a.* having bivalve shells.—**bivalv′ular** *a.* having two valves; bivalved.
bivouac (biv′ōō-ak) *n.* an encampment in the open air, without any cover;—*v.i.* to encamp without covering.—*pr.p.* **biv′ouacking;** *pa.t.* and *pa.p.* **biv′ouacked** [Fr.].
bi-weekly (bī′wēk′li) *a.* occurring once in every two weeks; occurring twice in each week;—*n.* a periodical issued twice a week or once in two weeks [L. *bis*, twice].
bizarre (bi-zâr′) *a.* odd; eccentric; grotesque [Fr.].
Bizonia (bī-zō′ni-ạ) *n.* after World War II, two zones of occupied Germany, esp. those under British and American control when considered together.—**bizo′nal** *a.* [L. *bis*, twice; Gk. *zōnē*, a girdle].
blab (blab) *v.t.* to reveal imprudently secrets entrusted to one;—*v.i.* to tell tales;—*pr.p.* **blab′bing;** *pa.t.* and *pa.p.* **blabbed.**—*n.* a chatterer; a gossip; a tell-tale. Also **blab′ber** [Scand. *blabbra*, to babble].
black (blak) *a.* of the darkest colour; dark; night-like; destitute of light; funereal; ominous;—*n.* the darkest colour; Negro; mourning;—*v.t.* to make black.—**blacks** *n.pl.* black clothes;—**black′en** *v.t.* to make black; to polish with blacking; to defame;—*v.i.* to grow or turn black.—**black′ly** *adv.*—**black′ness** *n.*—**black′amoor** *n.* a Negro or Moor.—**black art,** magic; necromancy.—**black and tan** (Manchester) terrier.—**Black and Tans,** a semi-military police force raised in 1920 for suppression of I.R.A. in Ireland, uniform being khaki with a black hat.—**black′-ball,** *v.t.* to reject a candidate for admission to a club by putting a black ball in the ballot box.—**black′-beet′le** *n.* a cockroach found indoors.—**black′berry** *n.* a fruit-bearing shrub, the bramble.—**black′-bird** *n.* a song-bird of the thrush family.—**black′-bird′ing** *n.* the kidnapping of Negroes for slaves.—**black′-board** *n.* a board painted black for writing on.—**black′-book** *n.* a record of offenders.—**black′-bread** *n.* rye bread.—**black′-browed** *a.* having black eyebrows; dour; sullen.—**black′-cap** *n.* a small British song-bird, allied to thrush, the male of which has a jet-black head; a cap assumed by judges when a sentence of death is being imposed.—**black′-coat** *n.* a clergyman or a professional man.—**black′-cock** *n.* the male bird of the common black grouse.—**black′-cur′rant** *n.* the fruit of a garden bush or the bush itself.—**black′-damp** *n.* a suffocating mixture, in mines, of carbon dioxide and air; choke damp.—**black diamonds** (*Colloq.*) coal.—**black dog,** sulking.—**black′-draught** *n.* a purgative of senna and Epsom salts.—**black′-eye** *n.* discolouration due to a blow.—**black′-faced** *n.* a breed of sheep.—**black′-fel′low** *n.* an Australian aborigine.—**black′-flag** *n.* flag popularly associated with pirates.—**black′-fri′ar** *n.* a Dominican friar, from his black mantle.—**black′-frost** *n.* frost without rime.—**blackguard** (blag′ârd) *n.* orig. a menial of the scullery; a low scoundrel;—*a.* low; vile;—*v.t.* to treat as a blackguard; to revile;—*v.i.* to act in a vile manner.—**black′guardism** *n.*—**black′guardly** *a.*—**black′head** *n.* a small black-topped mass which plugs the mouths of the follicles of the skin.—**black′ing** *n.* an old form of boot-polish.—**black′jack** *n.* a can, originally of leather, now of tin, for liquids; the flag of a pirate; a miner's name for zinc-blende; black bituminous mixtures used for roof repairs.—**black′-lead** *n.* graphite, a form of nearly pure carbon obtained from plumbago, and used in the manufacture of stove-polish and lead pencils.—**black′-leg** *n.* one who works during an industrial dispute; a gambler and a cheat.—**black′-list** *n.* any list of undesirable persons;—*v.t.* to place on such a list.—**black′mail** *n.* extortion of money by threats of exposure or denunciation; hush-money; orig. moneys paid over to robbers to obviate constant pillaging.—**Black Maria,** a prison-van used for the conveyance of prisoners between court and prison.—**black′-mar′ket** *n.* in war-time, a clandestine market for the sale of essential goods whose distribution is regulated, and which are not on free sale.—**black′-out** *n.* temporary loss of vision or memory; a total cutting off of all lights.—**black′-pud′ding** *n.* a mixture of ox-blood, oatmeal, suet and seasoning enclosed in a sausage-skin.—**Black Rod,** the usher of the Order of the Garter and of the House of Lords.—**black′-sheep** *n.* a loose, dissolute member of a respectable family.—**Black Shirt,** a member of the Italian Fascisti; a fascist.—**black′smith** *n.* a smith who works in iron.—**black′thorn** *n.* the sloe; a stout cudgel cut from the tree.—**Black Watch,** a Highland regiment, so called from the dark colour of the tartan.—**blackwater fever,** intermittent fever of malarial origin, characterised by dark coloured urine.—**black and blue,** to describe a bruise [O.E. *blac*].
bladder (blad′ėr) *n.* a thin musculo-membranous bag, in the pelvis, serving as a reservoir for urine; the windbag of a bagpipe; any membranous sac.—**bladd′ered** *a.* swollen like a bladder.—**bladd′er-wort** *n.* water-plant with floating leaves.—**bladd′ery** *a.* thin and inflated; blistered [O.E. *blaedre*, a blister].
blade (blād) *n.* the leaf, or flat part of the

leaf, of a plant; the cutting part of a knife, or tool; the broad part of an oar; a sword; (*Colloq.*) a dashing fellow.—**blade'-bone** *n.* the upper bone in shoulder; scapula.—**blad'ed** *a.* [O.E. *blaed*].

blae (blā) *a.* bluish-black in colour; livid (of skin); bleak.—**blae'ber'ry** *n.* (*Scot.*) bilberry; whortleberry [Scand. *blaa*, blue].

blaes (blāz) *n.* the bituminous shale of coal measures, which, when burnt, turns from blue to red, and is used for covering garden-paths, etc. [Scand. *blaa*, blue].

blague (blag) *n.* nonsense; humbug; bounce; swagger; conceited talk [Fr.].

blah (blȧ) *n.* (*Slang*) brag; silly talk [origin unknown].

blain (blān) *n.* an inflamed eruption on the skin [O.E. *blegen*, a boil].

blame (blām) *v.t.* to express disapprobation of; to censure;—*n.* fault.—**blam'able** *a.*—**blam'ableness** *n.*—**blam'ably** *adv.*—**blame'ful** *a.*—**blame'fully** *adv.*—**blame'fulness** *n.*—**blame'less** *a.*—**blame'lessness** *n.*—**blame'worthy** *a.* worthy of blame.—**blame'worthiness** *n.* [O.Fr. *blasmer*= Fr. *blâmer*. Doublet of *blaspheme*].

blanch (blansh) *v.t.* to whiten; to bleach; to strip (the husk).—*v.i.* to become white; to turn pale; to gloss over.—**blanch'ing** *n.* [Fr. *blanc*, white].

blanc-mange (blạ-mawngzh') *n.* a pudding made of cornflour, milk, etc. [Fr. *blanc*, white; *manger*, to eat].

bland (bland) *a.* mild; gentle; affable.—**bland'ly** *adv.*—**bland'ness** *n.* [L. *blandus*, flattering].

blandish (blan'dish) *v.t.* to flatter and coax; to wheedle; to caress.—**bland'isher** *n.*—**bland'ishing, bland'ishment** *n.* [L. *blandus*].

blank (blangk) *a.* without writing or any marks; empty; confused.—*n.* an empty space; a lottery ticket not drawing a prize; the white disc of a target.—**blank'ly** *adv.*—**blank verse**, unrhymed heroic verse consisting of iambic-pentameters.—**pointblank, a** direct aim [Fr. *blanc*, white].

blanket (blang'ket) *n.* a loosely woven woollen bedcover; a horse-covering; a thick canopy of cloud;—*v.t.* to cover with a blanket; to toss in a blanket.—**blank'eting** *n.* thick material for blankets; tossing in a blanket.—**blanket vote**, collective vote of enfranchised natives.—**to be born on the wrong side of the blanket**, to be illegitimate.—**a wet blanket**, one who depresses others; kill-joy [Fr. *blanc*, white].

blare (blār) *v.t.* and *v.i.* to sound loudly; to trumpet;—*n.* a long, prolonged noise [O.E. *blaesan*, to blow].

blarney (blȧr'ni) *n.* coaxing, cajoling talk; outrageous flattery; blandishing [fr. *Blarney*-stone in Castle Blarney, near Cork, reputed to give any one who kisses it the gift of persuasive eloquence].

blasé (blȧ'zā) *a.* surfeited with everything; absolutely bored; sophisticated [Fr.].

blaspheme (blas-fēm') *v.t.* to speak irreverently of God; to desecrate by impious talk;—*v.i.* to take God's name in vain; to curse and swear.—**blasphem'er** *n.*—**blasphem'ing** *n.* impious talk.—**blas'phemous** *a.*—**blas'phemously** *adv.*—**blas'phemy** *n.* irreverence in speaking of sacred matters; profane talk [Gk. *blasphēmein*].

blast (blast) *n.* a gust or puff of air; a forced stream of air; the blowing of a wind instrument; an explosion of gunpowder in rending rocks; a blight, affecting plants or cattle.—*v.t.* to injure, as by a noxious wind; to blight; to split, as by gunpowder; to abuse vehemently.—**blast'ed** *a.* blighted; accursed; (*Colloq.*) confounded; infernal.—**blast'er** *n.* -**blast'-fur'nace** *n.* a smelting-furnace in which a hot draught is furnished by bellows or other apparatus.—**blast'ing** *n.* a blast; explosion; withering effect; blaring of loud trumpets; (*Radio*) distortion due to over-loading [O.E. *blaest*].

blasto- (blas'to) *prefix* from Gk. *blastos*, a bud, used in the construction of compound biological terms.

blastoderm (blas'tō-dẹrm) *n.* the rudimentary structure of primitive cells which forms round the protoplasm in the ovum [Gk. *blastos*, a bud; *derma*, skin].

blatant (blā'tant) *a.* offensively noisy; loud-(voiced); brawling; obtrusive.—**blat'ancy** *n.*—**blat'antly** *adv.* [origin unknown].

blate (blāt) *a.* bashful; modest; timid [O.E. *blat*, pale].

blather, blatherskite See **blether.**

blatter (blat'ẹr) *v.i.* to talk boastfully, and incessantly [L. *blaterare*, to prattle].

blaze (blāz) *n.* bright flame; a big conflagration; outburst of activity or zeal; display; white mark upon a horse's forehead; a mark on a tree made by pathfinders;—*v.t.* to mark a tree by chipping off pieces of bark;—*v.i.* to burn brightly; to glow with anger.—**blaz'er** *n.* sporting jacket of bright colour.—**blaz'es** *pl.* hell, as in **'Go to blazes'** [O.E. *blaese*, a flame].

blaze (blāz) *n.* wide publicity;—*v.t.* to proclaim; spread abroad [O.E. *blaesan*, to blow].

blazon (blā'zn) *v.t.* to make known to everybody; to display armorial bearings in their proper colours; to embellish;—*n.* art of drawing or explaining coats of arms.—**blaz'oner** *n.*—**blaz'onment** *n.*—**blaz'onry** *n.* art of describing or explaining coats of arms in heraldic terms [Fr. *blason*, shield].

bleach (blēch) *v.t.* to whiten by exposure to sunlight and air, or by chemical action;—*v.i.* to become whiter or paler.—*n.* a decolourising, chemical agent.—**bleach'er** *n.* one who, or that which, bleaches; (*U.S. Slang*) outdoor, uncovered seat for a spectator in a stadium.—**bleach'ing-pow'der** *n.* calcium hydroxide saturated with chlorine; chloride of lime [O.E. *blaecan*, fr. *blaec*, pale).

bleak (blēk) *a.* without colour; pale; desolate and exposed.—**bleak'ly** *adv.*—**bleak'ness** *n.* [O.E. *blaec*, pale].

blear (blēr) *a.* dim or watery, due to inflammation of the eye;—*v.t.* to dim or blur.—**blear'edness** *n.*—**blear'y** *a.* dim [M.E. *bleren*, to have sore eyes].

bleat (blēt) *v.i.* to cry as a sheep; to talk in a complaining, whining fashion;—*n.* the sound made by a sheep [O.E. *blaetan*].

bleed (blēd) *v.t.* to draw blood surgically; to extort money from someone;—*v.i.* to lose blood; to die in battle;—*pa.t.* and *pa.p.* **bled.**—**bleed'er** *n.* a person who is afflicted by haemophilia, excessive bleeding (confined to males).—**bleed'ing** *n.* [O.E. *bledan*].

blemish (blem'ish) *n.* any deformity, physical or moral; flaw; disfigurement;—*v.t.* to mark with a flaw; to mar or disfigure.—**blem'ishment,** *n.* [Fr. *blêmir*, to turn pale].

blench (blensh) *v.i.* to start back from lack of courage; to flinch [O.E. *blencan*, to deceive].

blend (blend) *v.t.* to mix two allied articles together to improve quality or change the colour shade;—*v.i.* to intermix (as in marriage); to mingle well;—*pa.p.* **blend'ed** or **blent**;—*n.* a mixture.—**blend'er** *n.*—**blend'ing** *n.* [Scand. *blanda*, to mix].

blende (blend) *n.* an ore of zinc, consisting of zinc and sulphur; name given to certain lustrous minerals [Ger. *blenden*, to dazzle].

blenheim (blen'em) *n.* a miniature breed of spaniel.—**blenheim orange,** an orange-red variety of apple [fr. *Blenheim*, Marlborough's residence].

blenny (blen'i) *n.* a fish common in deep pools —so called from the shining mucus covering the skin [Gk. *blenna*, mucus].

blent (blent) *pa.p.* of **blend.**

bless (bles) *v.t.* to consecrate; glorify; sanctify; praise; to give thanks to; invoke happiness on; magnify.—*pa.p.* **blessed** or **blest.**—**blessed** (bles'id), **blest** *a.* happy; favoured with blessings; hallowed; heavenly; (*Colloq.*) confounded.—**bless'edly** *adv.*—**bless'edness** *n.* happiness; heavenly joy; bliss; felicity.—**bless'ing** *n.* a source of happiness or gratitude; benefaction; boon; benediction; prayer invoking Divine protection; benison.—**to ask a blessing,** to say grace [O.E. *bletsian,* to consecrate (with blood)].

blether (bleTH′er) *n.* one who talks nonsense.—*v.i.* to talk nonsense.—**bleth'ers** *n.pl.* nonsensical, foolish talk.—**bleth'ering** *n.*—**bleth'erskate, blath'erskite** *n.* one who talks sheer nonsense [Scand. *blathra,* to talk nonsense].

blew (blòò) *pa.t.* of **blow.**

blight (blīt) *n.* disease of plants caused by certain fungi or parasitic bacteria; anything which has an adverse effect, injures, or destroys;—*v.t.* to affect with blight; to arrest the growth of.—**blight'ing** *n.* and *a.* [etym. uncertain].

blighter (blīt′er) *n.* scamp; cad; rascal (*Slang term,* the significance of which varies from hatred to endearment).

blighty (blīt′i) *n.* (*Army Slang*) soldier's name for Britain, or for a wound involving a return to Britain [fr. Hind. *bilati,* home].

blimp (blimp) *n.* a small non-rigid airship used for observing [form of limp].

blind (blīnd) *a.* destitute of sight; ignorant; undiscerning; reckless; unaware of; heedless; at random; invisible; concealed; closed at one end; (*Slang*) drunk—*v.t.* to deprive of sight; to dazzle; to darken or obscure; to hide; to deceive;—*n.* a window-covering or screen; something intended to mislead; a pretext; (*sl.*) a drinking bout.—**blind alley, a cul-de-sac;**—*a.* employment, esp. juvenile, without prospects.—**blind'ed** *a.* rendered sightless; dazzled; oblivious to all other factors.—**blind'ers** *n.pl.* a horse's blinkers.—**blind'fold** *a.*—*v.t.* to cover the eyes with something; to mislead.—**blind'ing** *a.* causing temporary loss of sight; making blind.—**blind'-lan'ding** *n.* grounding an aircraft by depending on radio signals.—**blind'ly** *adv.*—**blind'ness** *n.* lacking power of sight; ignorance; obstinacy.—**col'our-blind'ness** *n.* inability to distinguish certain colours.—**night'-blind'ness** *n.* vision subnormal at night.—**snow'-blind'ness** *n.* defective vision, due to glare of sunlight upon snow.—**blind'worm** *n.* the slow worm, a legless lizard with very tiny eyes.—**blindman's buff,** a game where blindfolded person tries to catch others [O.E. *blind*].

blink (blingk) *v.i.* to wink; to look with the eyes half-shut; to glimmer, as a candle;—*v.t.* to shut out of sight, as a fact or question; to ignore;—*n.* a glimpse; a glance.—**blink'ard** *n.* one who blinks; that which twinkles, as a dim star.—**blink'ers** *n.pl.* pieces of leather preventing a horse from seeing to either side [M.E. *blenken,* to shine].

bliss (blis) *n.* the acme of happiness; perfect felicity; heavenly rapture.—**bliss'ful** *a.* supremely happy; enjoyable.—**bliss'fully** *adv.*—**bliss'fulness** *n.*—**bliss'less** *a.* [O.E. *bliths,* fr. *blithe*].

blister (blis′ter) *n.* a vesicle of the skin filled with a clear or blood-stained serum; a pustule; any like swelling as on plants, paint or steel; a plaster applied to skin to raise a blister;—*v.t.* to raise blisters upon; to wither up with scorn and sarcasm;—*v.i.* to rise in blisters.—**blis'ter-fly** *n.* the Spanish fly or cantharis, a powder used in the preparation of a blistering medium.—**blis'tery** *a.* [O.Fr. *blestre*].

blithe (blīth) *a.* gay; happy; gladsome; jolly; merry; sprightly.—**blithe'ly** *adv.*—**blithe'ness** *n.*—**blithe'some** *a.* merry; cheerful.—**blithe'someness** *n.* [O.E. *blithe,* joyous].

blitz (blits) *n.* a heavy, sudden attack by enemy bombers;—*v.t.* to bomb from the air.—**blitzed** *a.* wrecked or demolished by bombs or gunfire [Ger. *Blitz,* lightning].

blizzard (bliz′ard) *n.* a blinding snowstorm [imit.].

bloat (blōt) *v.t.* to cause to have an unsound, swollen appearance; to swell or puff out; to cure fish by salting and smoking.—**bloat'ed** *a.* swollen with self-indulgence; pampered and insolent.—**bloat'edness** *n.*—**bloat'er** *n.* a Yarmouth smoked herring [fr. Scand. *blautr,* soft].

blob (blob) *n.* anything small and globular, as a dewdrop; (*Colloq.*) a duck at cricket [var. of *bleb*].

bloc (blok) *n.* a combination of two or more countries or political parties [Fr.].

block (blok) *n.* a solid mass of matter; a roughly squared piece of wood, stone, etc.; the large piece of wood on which persons were beheaded; the wheel of a pulley with its case of wood; a number of buildings forming one compact mass; an obstruction, esp. on roads; mounted plate for printing;—*v.t.* to shut in, to enclose; to obstruct; to shape (a hat); to sketch out roughly.—**block'-bus'ter** *n.* a heavy high explosive bomb.—**block'ing** *n.* the process of stamping book-covers with a decorative pattern.—**block'ish** *a.* like a block; stupid; dull.—**block'-head** *n.* a stupid dolt; a dullard.—**block'house** *n.* an improvised fort made of logs; a fortified place.—**block'-let'ters** *n.* a form of script where the letters are printed instead of in the usual cursive style.—**block and fall,** the rope tackle used in lifting heavy loads.—**block and tackle,** a pulley enclosed in a block used for lifting weights, with small muscular effort [Fr. *bloc*].

blockade (blo-kād′) *n.* prevention of imports into enemy countries during a war;—*v.t.* to shut up hostile troops in a town by surrounding it; to prevent trade with a hostile country.—**blockade'-runn'er** *n.* a vessel employed to slip through with goods to a blockaded country.—**blockade'-runn'ing** *n.* [fr. *block*].

bloke (blōk) *n.* (*Colloq.*) a fellow; a chap.

blond (blond) *n.* (*fem.* **blonde**) a person of fair complexion and generally, light blue eyes;—*a.* fair; light golden-brown [Fr.].

blood (blud) *n.* the red, viscid fluid which circulates in the body of men and animals; relationship, consanguinity, kindred; honourable birth; descent; a rake, man about town; a sensational tale;—*v.t.* (*Med.*) to let blood, to bleed; (*Fig.*) to initiate.—**blood'-bank** *n.* a store of blood for use in transfusion.—**blood'-corpus'cle** *n.* a cell normally contained in suspension in the blood.—**blood'-curd'ling** *a.* terrifying to the extent of making the blood appear to curdle.—**blood'ed** *a.* initiated; of good stock; pedigreed.—**blood'-feud** *n.* a vendetta, involving the shedding of blood.—**blood'-group** *n.* one of four groups into which the blood of human beings may fall.—**blood'-guil'ty** *a.* guilty of murder.—**blood′-heat** *n.* heat approximating to 98° F.—**blood'-horse** *n.* a thoroughbred horse of the purest blood or origin.—**blood'-hound** *n.* a large hound, prized for its keen scent and perseverance.—**blood'ily** *adv.*—**blood'less** *a.* without blood; anaemic; spiritless.—**blood'lessness** *n.*—**blood'letting** *n.* the withdrawal of blood to allay fever; phlebotomy; venesection.—**blood′-mon'ey** *n.* money paid for betraying another on a capital charge; wages earned at a sweated rate of labour.—**blood plasma,** the fluid part of blood.—**blood'-pois'oning** *n.* a morbid condition due to circulation of bacteria in blood stream; pyaemia; septicaemia.—**blood'-press'ure** *n.* the pressure exerted by the blood on the walls of the arteries.—**blood'-pud'ding** *n.* a black pudding, a mixture of blood, suet and other materials.—**blood'-red** *a.* crimson, red as blood.—**blood'-se'rum** *n.* the fluid part of the blood after the fibrin and the corpuscles have been eliminated.—**blood'shed** *n.* the shedding of blood; slaughter.—**blood'shot** *a.* of the eyes, red or congested with blood.—**blood'-sports** *n.pl.* fox-hunting and similar sports where an animal is hunted.—**blood'-stain** *n.* the dried and darkened stain left on clothing, floors, etc.

after contact with blood.—**blood'-stock** *n.* thoroughbred horses.—**blood'-stone** *n.* a semi-precious stone, a variety of crystalline silica, dark green in colour with red spots. Also called heliotrope.—**blood'-suck'er** *n.* an animal which sucks blood, esp. the leech; an extortioner.—**blood'-test** *n.* an examination of the blood to determine to which of the four groups it belongs.—**blood'-thirst'y** *a.* eager to shed blood.—**blood'-transfu'sion** *n.* the transference of blood from one person to another. —**blood'-ves'sel** *n.* an artery or vein through which blood flows.—**blood'y** *a.* pert. to blood; stained with or containing blood; ruthless in shedding blood; vulgarly used as an expletive to add an intensive force;—*v.t.* to make bloody.—**bad blood,** a state of ill-feeling and enmity.—**flesh and blood,** human frame or nature.—**his blood is up,** he is in a state of rage.—**in cold blood,** coolly and deliberately [O.E. *blod*].

bloom (blòòm) *n.* a flower; a blossom; state of freshness and vigour; flush of youth; velvety bluish colour of grapes and plums; vigorous youth.—**bloom'ing** *a.* [Scand. *bloma*].

bloomer (blòòm'ẹr) *n.* (*Slang*) a faux-pas; a ludicrous mistake; a blunder.

bloomers (blòò'merz) *n.pl.* women's knickers; a costume for ladies, consisting of short skirt and bodice, with loosely made knickerbockers, gathered round the ankle [Mrs. *Bloomer*, of New York, who introduced it in 1849].

blossom (blos'um) *n.* the flower of a plant, esp. a tree;—*v.i.* to put forth blossoms; to flourish.—**bloss'omed** *a.*—**bloss'omy** *a.* rich in blossoms [O.E. *blostm*].

blot (blot) *v.t.* to spot or bespatter, esp. with ink; to stain with infamy; to obliterate; to dry with blotting-paper;—*pr.p.* **blot'ting**; *pa.p.* **blot'ted**;—*n.* a spot or stain, as of ink; blemish; disgrace.—**blot'ter** *n.* a blotting-pad. —**blot'ting-pa'per** *n.* a kind of unsized paper for drying ink [Scand.].

blotch (bloch) *n.* an irregular, coloured spot; an eruption upon the skin; a pustule; pimple;—*v.t.* to mark with blotches; to make spotted.—**blotch'y** *a.* [O.Fr. *bloche*].

blotto (blot'ō) *a.* (*Slang*) very drunk.

blouse (blouz, blous) *n.* a light, loose upper garment, fitted to the waist by a belt [Fr.].

blow (blō) *n.* a mass or bed of flowers;—*v.i.* to blossom [O.E. *blowan*, to blossom].

blow (blō) *n.* a stroke; a knock; a thump; a smack; a rap; sudden calamity or misfortune [etym. doubtful].

blow (blō) *v.i.* to produce a current of air; to move, as air; to breathe hard or quickly; to puff; to pant; (*Slang*) to brag; (*Slang*) to squander; to spout (of whales); to deposit eggs; —*v.t.* to direct a current of air on; to sound a wind instrument; to put out of breath;—*pa.t.* **blew**; *pa.p.* **blown**;—*n.* a high wind; a short walk in the open air.—**blow'er** *n.* (*Slang*) the telephone.—**blow'-fly** *n.* insect, e.g. bluebottle, which blows eggs in meat.—**blow'-lamp** *n.* a portable lamp for applying intense local heat.—**blown'** *a.* swelled; tired; out of breath; tainted.—**blow'-out** *n.* (*Slang*) a feast or big meal; a burst tyre.—**blow'-pipe** *n.* an instrument for concentrating the heat of a flame on some point, by blowing.—**blow'y** *a.* windy, breezy.—**to blow hot and cold,** to be inconsistent.—**to blow off steam,** to get rid of superfluous energy.—**to blow one's horn or trumpet,** to praise oneself; to brag [O.E. *blawan*].

blowze (blouz) *n.* a ruddy, fat-faced wench.—**blowzed** *a.* bloated; slatternly.—**blow'zy** *a.* coarse and ruddy-faced; slovenly; dishevelled [origin uncertain].

blubber (blub'ẹr) *n.* the fat of whales and other marine animals;—*v.i.* to weep unrestrainedly.—**blubb'ered** *a.* swollen by weeping. —**blubb'ering** *n.* [imit. formation, with first meaning of *bubble*].

blucher (blòòch'ẹr) *n.* a strong leather half-boot or high shoe, named after the Prussian field-marshal, *Blücher* (1742-1819).

bludgeon (bluj'un) *n.* a short cudgel with one end loaded;—*v.t.* to knock out with a club [Celt., fr. *plug*].

blue (blòò) *n.* the colour of the clear sky; one of the seven primary colours; a dye or pigment; indigo powder used in laundering; the sea; one who has represented his university in a sport.—**blues** *n.pl.* (*Slang*) a fit of depression; a very slow jazz dance of Negro origin.—**The Blues,** the Royal Horse Guards. —**blue** *a.* of the colour blue; azure; livid; learned; pedantic; melancholy; glum; aristocratic; indecent or obscene.—*v.t.* to make or dye blue; to dip linen in a blue solution; (*Slang*) to squander.—**blu'ish** *a.* slightly blue.—**blue'-bell** *n.* the wild hyacinth; in Scotland, the harebell.—**blue'-berry** *n.* a heath plant, with small berries.—**blue'-bird** *n.* a migratory bird of N. America belonging to the thrush family.—**blue'-blood** *n.* an aristocrat.—**blue'-bonn'et** *n.* Scottish trooper, from the blue woollen cap at one time in general use in Scotland.—**blue'-book** *n.* a government publication issued in blue covers.—**blue'-bottle** *n.* the corn-flower; a large fly which lays its eggs in meat.—**blue'-coat** *n.* a 16th cent. cut of coat, now worn by boys at Blue Coat School (Christ's Hospital).—**blue ensign,** a blue flag of the Royal Naval Reserve.—**blue'-grass** *n.* meadow grass of Kentucky, U.S., which forms thick turf.—**blue heat,** about 550° F.—**blue'-jack'et** *n.* a sailor, as distinguished from a marine, in the Royal Navy.—**blue'-mould** *n.* a fungus found on cheese, jams, paste, etc.—**blue'ness** *n.* the quality of being blue; a blue hue or colour.—**blue'-nose,** a nickname for a Nova-Scotian, from a variety of potato.—**blue'-pet'er** *n.* a flag with a blue ground and a white square in the centre, hoisted when ship is about to sail.—**blue'-print** *n.* a simple photographic reproduction of technical drawings leaving white lines of plan on a blue background; (*Fig.*) any projected political or social plan with its details.—**blue ribbon,** broad, dark blue ribbon worn by a Knight of the Garter; an emblem of temperance; the winning of some great prize.—**blue'-stock'ing** *n.* a female pedant, especially if she airs her knowledge.—**blue'-stone** *n.* blue copperas, sulphate of copper; a durable basaltic rock used for buildings, road-making, etc.—**blue'-tit** *n.* a bird with blue wings and tail.—**blue vitriol,** crystals of sulphate of copper.—**blue water,** deep sea.—**true blue,** faithful; staunch; unwavering; a supporter of Conservative party.—**once in a blue moon,** a rare occurrence [Fr. *bleu*].

bluff (bluf) *a.* steep and broad; rough and ready; frank and hearty in manner;—*n.* a high bank or cliff presenting a steep front; a headland; a cluster of trees on the prairie.—**bluff'ness** *n.* steepness; a frank, blunt manner of speech [etym. uncertain].

bluff (bluf) *n.* an attempt to mislead in regard to one's real purpose;—*v.t.* to mislead one by giving a wrong impression.—**bluff'er** *n.* one who bluffs [etym. uncertain].

blunder (blun'der) *v.i.* to make a gross mistake; to err through thoughtlessness; to flounder about;—*n.* a gross mistake.—**blun'derer** *n.*—**blun'derhead** *n.* one continually blundering.—**blun'dering** *n.* and *a.* continually making mistakes; bungling; clumsy; fumbling—**blun'deringly** *adv.* [M.E. *blondren*, to confuse].

blunderbuss (blun'der-bus) *n.* an obsolete short gun with a bell-shaped muzzle and a wide bore [Dut. *donderbus*, thunder-box].

blunt (blunt) *a.* having a dull edge or point; dull; brusque in speech;—*v.t.* to render less sharp; to weaken appetite or desire.—**blunt'ly** *adv.*—**blunt'ness** [origin unknown].

blur (blur) *n.* a spot; stain; smudge; whatever dims without effacing;—*v.t.* to smear; to

make indistinct;—*pr.p.* **blur'ring**; *pa.t.* and *pa.p.* **blurred** [etym. unknown].
blurb (blerb) *n.* fulsome praise and synopsis of a book printed on its outside wrapper; a publisher's puff [invented word].
blurt (blurt) *n.* a sudden outburst.—**to blurt out** *v.t.* to give information suddenly, indiscreetly, or tactlessly [imit.].
blush (blush) *v.i.* to redden in the face, from shame, modesty, or confusion;—*n.* a rosy tint; a red colour suffusing the face; first glance or view.—**blush'ing** *n.* a rosy glow on the face;—*a.* modest; coy; bashful.—**blush'ingly** *adv.* [O.E *blyscan*, to shine].
bluster (blus'ter) *v.i.* to blow in boisterous gusts, of wind; to talk with violence and noise; to bully or swagger;—*n.* fitful noise and violence.—**blus'terer** *n.*—**blus'tering** *n.* noisy, menacing language;—*a.* boisterous; roaring; storming; bullying; vapouring; bragging.—**blus'teringly** *adv.*—**blus'terous** *a.* boisterous; blustering.—**blus'tery** *a.* stormy; blowing in fitful gusts [etym. uncertain].
boa (bō'a) *n.* a genus of constricting, non-venomous serpents; a long round coil of fur or feathers for the neck.—**bo'a-constrict'or** *n.* a serpent which crushes its victims by compression [L.].
boar (bōr) *n.* the male of the swine.—**boar'-hound** *n.* a great mastiff used in hunting boars [O.E. *bar*].
board (bōrd) *n.* a long, narrow strip of timber less than 2 in. thick; a table, hence food or diet; council-table; council itself; a thick paper made by pasting together several layers (card-board, paste-board, etc.);—*v.t.* to cover with boards; to supply with meals and lodging for payment; to embark on a ship;—*v.i.* to be a lodger.—**boards** *n.pl.* the stage in a theatre; the covers of a book.—**board'er** *n.* one who boards a ship; one receiving food and lodging.—**board'ing** *n.* a wooden fence, floor, etc.; entering a ship; obtaining food and lodging.—**board'ing-house** *n.* a house in which boarders are accommodated.—**board'ing-out** *n.* a system by which Local Authorities send children under their charge to be cared for in private houses for payment.—**board'ing-school** *n.* a school in which the scholars are in residence.—**board'school** *n.* a school, formerly under the control of a school-board; in Scotland, a public elementary school.—**board wages**, wages given to domestic servants in lieu of food.—**to go by the board**, to be abandoned.—**to sweep the board**, to take all the stakes or prizes [O.E. *bord*, ship's side].
boast (bōst) *v.t.* to speak with vanity of; to be unduly proud of;—*v.i.* to brag; to vaunt; to praise extravagantly oneself;—*n.* a statement, expressive of pride or vain glory; that which is boasted of.—**boast'er** *n.*—**boast'ful** *a.*—**boast'fully** *adv.* — **boast'fulness**, **boast'ing** *n.* indulging in boasting.—**boast'ingly** *adv.* [M.E. *bost*].
boat (bōt) *n.* a small vessel, generally undecked, moved by oars or sails or small motor; a ship; anything resembling a boat, e.g. a sauce-boat;—*v.t.* to carry in a boat;—*v.i.* to row or sail about in a boat.—**boat'-bridge** *n.* a bridge resting on pontoons.—**boat'er** *n.* one who boats; a straw hat.—**boat'-hook** *n.* a pole with an iron hook for holding on to a boat.—**boat'-house** *n.* a shed for boats.—**boatswain** (bō'sun) *n.* a warrant officer in the navy who had particular charge of boats, sails, rigging, cables and anchors.—**boat'-man** *n.* a man in charge of a boat.—**to burn one's boats**, to be committed irrevocably to some course of action [O.E. *bāt*].
bob (bob) *n.* a short, jerking motion; anything which swings when suspended; a jerk; a pendant; the weight of a pendulum; hair cut short and square across; a docked tail;—*v.t.* to move with a jerk; to cut hair semi-short;—*v.i.* to dangle; to move up and down or in and out;—*pr.p.* **bob'bing**; *pa.p.* **bobbed**.—**bob'stays** *n.pl.* ropes or chains to confine the bowsprit of a ship downward to the stem or cut water.—**bob'-wig** *n.* a short-tailed wig (etym. unknown].
bob (bob) *n.* (*Slang*) a shilling.
bobbin (bob'in) *n.* a small wooden cylinder on which thread is wound [Fr. *bobine*].
bobby (bob'i) *n.* (*Slang*) a policeman [fr. Sir *Robert* Peel who established the police force in 1829].
bobby-sox (bob'i-soks) *n.* (*U.S. Slang*) ankle socks, usually worn by girls in their teens;—**bob'by-sox'er** *n.* a girl in her teens.
bobsleigh, bobsled (bob'slā, -sled), *n.* two small sleighs coupled together by means of a top plank;—*v.i.* to use a bobsleigh.
bobstays See under **bob**.
Boche (bosh) *n.* and *a.* German [war-time slang, fr. Fr. slang, *caboche*, head, a reference to shape of German head].
bode (bōd) *v.t.* and *v.i.* to portend; to presage; to foretell; to foreshadow; to be an omen of.—**bode'ful** *a.*—**bode'ment** *n.* an omen; portent; presentiment.—**bod'ing** *a.* ominous;—*n.* an omen; a presentiment [O.E. *bodian*, to announce].
bodega (bō-dē'ga) *n.* a wine-shop [Sp.].
bodge Same as **botch**.
bodice (bod'is) *n.* that part of a woman's dress above the waist, with or without sleeves, and close-fitting [orig. *pl. bodies*].
bodkin (bod'kin) *n.* a short, sharp dagger or stiletto; an instrument for piercing holes in material; a large blunt needle; a pin for dressing hair [M.E. *boidekin*].
body (bod'i) *n.* the frame of a human being or of an animal; the main part of anything; coachwork, seating and upholstery of a car; an assemblage of things or persons; a solid substance; strength or consistency of a liquid;—*v.t.* to produce in definite shape;—*pa.t.* and *pa.p.* **bod'ied**.—**bod'ied** *a.* used in compounds, e.g. able-bodied.—**bod'iless** *a.* possessing no body.—**bod'ily** *a.* pert. to the body;—*adv.* physically, in the body, in the flesh; altogether; completely; in the mass.—**bod'yguard** *n.* life-guard of a sovereign or an important individual; an escort.—**body politic**, the mass of the members of a nation considered as an organised political body.—**bod'y-ser'vant** *n.* a personal attendant; a valet; a retainer.—**bod'y-snatch'er** *n.* one who robs graves of dead bodies for the purpose of disposing of them for dissection [O.E. *bodig*].
Boeotian (bē-ō'shan) *a.* pert. to *Boeotia* in ancient Greece; boorish, dull, stupid, as the inhabitants were so considered.
Boer (bòòr) *n.* a Dutch farmer of S. Africa; a person of Dutch descent [Dut. cf. *boor*].
boffin (bof'in) *n.* (*World War* 2) a civilian scientist or expert attached to Royal Air Force headquarters (*R.A.F. Slang*).
bog (bog) *n.* wet soft ground; a deep soft marsh;—*v.t.* to engulf in a bog.—**bogg'y** *a.* full of bogs; marshy.—**bog'-land** *n.* marsh-land.—**bog'-moss** *n.* sphagnum, found in damp places, and of great value as a surgical dressing.—**bog'-myr'tle** *n.* a shrub found in swamps.—**bog'-trott'er** *n.* a dweller in a boggy country; an Irishman [Ir. Gael. *bogach*, fr. *bog*, soft].
bogey (bō'gi) *n.* (*Golf*) standard score for a hole or course expected of a good player [fr. imaginary partner, Colonel *Bogey*].
bogey See **bogie**, or **bogle**.
boggle (bog'l) *v.i.* to stop at; to make difficulties; to shrink back through fear; to equivocate.—**bogg'ler** *n.* See **bogle**.
bogie, bogey (bō'gi) *n.* a small low truck on four or six wheels, free to move on a central pivot for easy turning; the undercarriage of a railway-carriage or locomotive [etym. unknown].
bogle (bō'gl) *n.* a ghost or demon; a fearsome apparition, imp, or hobgoblin associated with the nursery.—**bog'ey**, **bog'y** *n.* the devil;

a bug-bear; a goblin.—**bogey'man, bogg'ard** *n.* [fr. *bug*].

bogus (bō'gus) *a.* sham; counterfeit; spurious; false [etym. unknown].

bohea (bō-hē') *n.* an inferior kind of black tea [fr. Chinese].

Bohemian (bō-hē'mi-an) *a.* pert. to Bohemia or its inhabitants; pert. to the gipsies; unconventional;—*n.* a native of Bohemia; a gipsy; one who leads a loose and unsettled life [Fr. *bohémien*, gipsy].

boil (boil) *v.t.* to bring to a seething condition, by heating; to cook, by boiling;—*v.i.* to be agitated by the action of heat; to seethe; to reach boiling-point.—**boil'er** *n.* one who boils; a vessel for boiling.—**boil'ings** *n.pl.* sweets made by boiling sugar.—**boiling point,** the temperature at which a liquid boils.—of water 212° Fahr.—**boiled'-shirt** *n.* (*Slang*) the starched shirt worn with evening dress; evening dress [Fr. *bouillir*, to boil].

boil (boil) *n.* local inflammation of the skin round a hair follicle [O.E. *byle*, sore].

boisterous (bois'tẹr-us) *a.* wild; noisy; hearty; turbulent; stormy; windy.—**bois'terously** *adv.*—**bois'terousness** *n.* [M.E. *boistous*].

bolas (bol'as) *n.* a missile used by S. American cowboys, consisting of two or three stone balls attached to the ends of a rope, to entangle the feet of cattle [Sp.].

bold (bōld) *a.* daring; ready to meet danger; courageous; brave; intrepid; valorous; fearless; cheeky.—**bold'-faced** *a.* impudent; forward; brazen; of letters, printed with heavy thick strokes.—**bold'ly** *adv.*—**bold'ness** *n.* [O.E. *bald*].

bole (bōl) *n.* the trunk of a tree.—**boll'ing** *n.* a tree with the top and branches cut off; a pollard [Scand. *bolr.*].

bolero (bo-lā'rō) *n.* a national Spanish dance, in triple time; the music for this dance; a lady's short jacket, usually without sleeves, worn over a blouse [Sp.].

boll (bōl) *n.* a seed capsule of cotton, flax, etc. **boll weevil, boll worm,** larvae of various moths destructive of cotton crops [O.E. *bolla*].

bollard (bol'ard) *n.* a strong post on a wharf, etc., for making fast hawsers [fr. *bole*].

bolling See **bole.**

boloney See **baloney.**

Bolshevik (bol'she-vik) *n.* a member of the Russian Majority, or Extreme, Communist Party; a violent revolutionary.—**bol'shevism** *n.* theory and practice of Russian Bolsheviki; Russian or other communism.—**bol'shevist** *n.* and *a.*—**bolshevis'tic** *a.*—**bol'shevise** *v.t.*—**bol'shie** *n.* (*Slang*) bolshevik [Russ. *bolshe*, comp. of *veliki*, great].

bolster (bōl'stẹr) *n.* a long round bed-pillow; anything designated as a support.—*v.t.* to sustain; to support; to prop.—**bol'sterer** *n.*—**to bolster up,** to support a weak case or person [O.E.].

bolt (bōlt) *n.* a bar for fastening a door, window, etc.; part of a lock which engages with the keeper; pin for holding objects together; a narrow roll of cloth; a thunderbolt; an arrow; a shackle for prisoners; a sudden rush;—*v.t.* to fasten with a bolt; to swallow food hurriedly; to expel suddenly.—*v.i.* to rush away; to start suddenly forward, as of a horse.—**bolt'-hole** *n.* an underground shelter; an emergency exit.—**bolt'-up'right** *adv.* straight up, as a bolt or arrow [E.].

bolt (bōlt) *v.t.* to sift through a sieve.—**bolt'er** *n.* a sieve.—**bolt'ing-hutch, bolt'ing-tub,** *n.* a receptacle into which flour is bolted [formerly *boult*, O.Fr. *bulter*].

bolus (bō'lus) *n.* a rounded mass of medicine; a large pill [Gk. *bolos*, a clod].

bomb (bom) *n.* a cast-iron container filled with high explosives, gas, incendiary contents, or smoke-producing substances exploding by percussion or by a timing mechanism.—**bomb'er** *n.* an aeroplane for bombs.—**bomb'-proof** *a.* secure against small bomb splinters.—**bomb'shell** *n.* a bomb; something devastating and quite unexpected.—**atom(ic) bomb,** a bomb depending on the release of atomic energy [Gk. *bombos*, a booming sound].

bombard (bom'bard) *n.* an early mortar with a wide bore, using stone-shot; a large vat for liquor; a powerful organ stop.—**bombard** (bom-bard') *v.t.* to prolong heavy artillery fire on a selected objective; to ply with many questions.—**bombardier'** *n.* a gunner in the artillery.—**bombard'ment** *n.* a sustained attack with guns, bombs, etc. [O.Fr. *bombarde*].

bombardon (bom-bàr'dun) *n.* a brass wind-instrument [Fr. fr. Gk. *bombas*, a booming sound].

bombast (bom', bum'bast) *n.* cotton-wool; wadding; padding; inflated, high-sounding language.—**bombas'tic** *a.*—**bombas'tically** *adv.* [O.Fr. *bombace*, cotton-wool].

Bombay-duck (bom-bā'duk) *n.* a marine, salmon-like fish, salted, dried and exported as a delicacy from Bombay.

bombazine, bombasine (bom-bạ-zēn') *n.* a twilled fabric of silk and worsted or cotton [Fr. *bombasin*].

bombe (bōmb) *n.* a cone-shaped dish [Fr.].

bombic (bom'bik) *a.* of, or pert. to, the silk-worm [Gk. *bombux*, silkworm].

bon (bōng) *a.* fr. Fr. *bon*, good, used in words and phrases not yet Anglicised.—**bon-bon** (bōng'bōng) *n.* a sweetmeat; a sugar plum.

bonanza (bō'nan'zạ) *n.* an exceptionally rich and persistent vein of ore; a profitable enterprise; a large shop or store [Sp.].

bona roba (bō'nạ rō'bạ) *n.* a showy wanton woman; a courtesan [It.].

bond (bond) *n.* that which binds, a band, a link, a tie; an oath or promise; obligation; duty; the arrangement of bricks or stones in a wall so that successive courses interlock and give stability.—**bonds** *n.pl.* fetters; chains; captivity.—**bond'age** *n.* a state of being bound; slavery; political subjection.—**bond'er, bond'-stone** *n.* a stone which penetrates into the backing of a wall to assist bonding.—**bond'maid, bond'man, bonds'man, bond'ser'vant, bond'wom'an, bonds'wom'an** *n.* a serf [O.E. *bindan*, to bind].

bond (bond) *n.* a legal engagement in writing to fulfil certain conditions; a certificate of ownership of capital lent to a government, municipality, etc.; a mortgage on a house, etc.;—*v.t.* to put dutiable articles in a customs store till the duties are paid.—**bond'ed** *a.* placed in bond; mortgaged.—**bonded warehouse,** a customs store for bonded goods. —**in bond,** in a bonded store [O.E. *bindan*, to bind].

bone (bōn) *n.* the hard tissue which forms the skeleton of mammals, birds, reptiles and fishes;—*v.t.* to remove the bones; to fillet (fish); to stiffen corsets with whale-bone, etc.; (*Slang*) to filch.—**bones** *n.pl.* human remains; corpse; dice; castanets.—**bone'-ash** *n.* calcined bones.—**bone'-black** *n.* finely ground animal charcoal.—**bone'-break'er** *n.* the osprey.—**bone'-dry** *a.* absolutely dry.—**bone'-earth** *n.* ash left when bones are reduced in a furnace. —**bone'less** *a.* without bones.—**bone'-meal** *n.* a fertiliser for dry soils, made from ground bones.—**bone'-set'ter** *n.* one skilled in the manipulation of dislocated bones of the limbs.—**bone'shak'er** *n.* an early form of safety bicycle with solid tyres.—**bon'iness** *n.*—**bon'y** *a.* full of, or consisting of, bones.—**bone of contention,** the subject in dispute [O.E. *ban*].

bonfire (bon'fīr) *n.* orig. a fire for burning bones; a large fire specially built and lit to express public joy [fr. *bone* and *fire*].

bonhomie (bon'o-mē) *n.* frank and simple good-nature; geniality [Fr.].

boning (bōn'ing) *n.* in surveying, obtaining

the levels by means of **bon'ing rods**, T-shaped appliances made of deal wood [fr. *bone*].

bonito (bō-nē'-tō) *n.* a fish of the striped tunny kind [Sp.].

bonnet (bon'-et) *n.* a flat cap; a woman's head-gear, of various shapes; a movable protecting cover, as of a valve-box, a motor-engine, etc.;—*v.t.* to put on a bonnet; to crush a person's hat over his eyes in order to rob him.—**bonn'eted** *a.* wearing, or covered by, a bonnet.—**bonn'et-laird** *n.* one who farms his own property [etym. uncertain].

bonny (bon'-i) *a.* pretty; beautiful; handsome; comely; considerable.—**bonn'ily** *adv.*—**bonn'iness** *n.* [Fr. *bon, bonne*].

bonspiel (bon'-spēl) *n.* a grand curling match [etym. uncertain].

bonus (bō'-nus) *n.* an extra dividend given to shareholders in a public company; an extra gratuity paid to workmen [L. *bonus*, good].

bonze (bonz) *n.* a priest of different Oriental sects [Jap. *bonzo*, a pious man].

bonzer (bon'-zẹr) *n.* in Australia, a stroke of good fortune; something especially good;—*a.* fine, first-rate; excellent. Also **bon'za** [fr. *bonze*, considered as a lucky emblem].

boo (bòò) *interj.* an exclamation of disapproval or contempt.—**booes** *n.pl.*—**boo** *v.t.* and *v.i.* to hoot; to show disapproval.—*pr.t.* (he) **booes**; *pa.t.* **booed** [imit.].

boob See under **booby**.

booby (bòò'-bi) *n.* a sea-bird of the gannet type, said to be easily caught; a dunce; numskull; blockhead.—**boob** *n.* (*Slang*) a simpleton; a stupid, clumsy fellow.—**boo'by-prize** *n.* a prize to the worst performer.—**boo'by-trap** *n.* (*World War* 2) an apparently innocent object which explodes when handled [Sp. *bobo*, a dolt].

boogie woogie (bòò'-gi wòò'-gi) *n.* a style of dance music based upon contrasted rhythm [imit.].

book (bòòk) *n.* a number of sheets of paper, etc. bound together; a literary composition or treatise, written or printed; a record of betting transactions; the words of a play, the libretto;—*v.t.* to put into a book; to obtain, or give, a business order, ticket (theatre, etc.)—**books** *n.pl.* record of business transactions, especially financial; ledgers.—**book'-bin'der** *n.* one who binds books.—**book'-bin'ding** *n.*—**book'-case** *n.* a case with shelving for books.—**book'-club** *n.* a club to distribute specially chosen books to subscribers.—**book'-ends** *n.pl.* weighted props to keep books upright on a shelf.—**book'ie** *n.* (*Slang*) a bookmaker.—**book'ing** *n.* entering in a book a business transaction; recording field observations in surveying.—**book'ing-clerk** *n.* a clerk who issues railway, etc., tickets or registers orders.—**book'ing-hall, book'ing-off'ice** *n.* a place where tickets are issued.—**book'ish** *a.* fond of books and study.—**book'ishness** *n.*—**book'-jack'et** *n.* an attractively printed outer paper wrapper of a book.—**book'-keep'er** *n.*—**book'-keep'ing** *n.* the art of keeping a systematic account of financial transactions.—**book'-know'ledge, book'-learn'ing, book'-lore** *n.* knowledge acquired by extensive reading.—**book'let** *n.* a small book; a pamphlet.—**book'-mak'er** *n.* one who compiles a book from various sources; a professional betting-man who accepts bets; a turf accountant.—**book'-mark** *n.* something placed in a book to mark a particular page.—**the Book of Books**, the Holy Bible.—**book'-plate** *n.* a label, often illustrated, pasted on the front end-papers of a book to denote ownership.—**book'-sell'er** *n.* one who sells books.—**book'-sell'ing** *n.*—**book'-shelf** *n.* a shelf for displaying books.—**book'-shop, book'-stall, book'-stand,** *n.* a place for exhibiting books and periodicals for sale.—**book'work** *n.* theory as opposed to practice.—**book'worm** *n.* one who reads intensively; larvae of insects which bore holes through the pages and bindings.—**reference book,** a book which gives information in a condensed form.—**to be upon the books,** to have one's name included in an official list.—**to bring to book,** to call to account.—**to take a leaf out of his book,** to follow his example [O.E. *boc*, a book, the beech].

boom (bòòm) *n.* light spar for stretching bottom of a sail; an obstruction across a harbour, etc.—**boom'-ir'ons** *n.pl.* rings of iron attached to the yard through which the studding sail-booms are projected [Dut.].

boom (bòòm) *v.i.* to make a deep hollow sound; to be extremely popular and successful; to be in great demand;—*n.* a hollow roar; the cry of the bittern; a sudden advance in popular favour; a sudden demand for an article.—**boom'er** *n.*—**boom'ing** *a.* [M.E. *bommen*].

boomerang (bòò'-mẹ-rang) *n.* a curved wooden missile used by the natives of Australia (thrown forward from the hand, it finally takes a backward direction, towards the thrower) [Native].

boon (bòòn) *n.* some good thing given or asked for; a benefaction [Fr. *bon*, good].

boon (bòòn) *a.* gay; merry; jolly [Fr. *bon*].

boor (bòòr) *n.* a peasant; a rustic; a churl; lout; clown, bumpkin, clodpole.—**boor'ish** *a.* rude, clownish.—**boor'ishly** *adv.*—**boor'ishness** *n.* [Dut. *boer*, peasant].

boost (bòòst) *v.t.* to hoist; to give a lift to; to help forward; to advertise on a big scale; to increase the output or power of a machine;—*n.* a push up; a shove; (*Elect*). the amount by which the pressure obtained in an induction manifold is increased by a super-charger.—**boost'er** *n.* [Amer.].

boot (bòòt) *n.* a covering for the foot and ankle; an instrument of judicial torture in which the leg was crushed; a luggage-box in a coach, motor-car, etc.;—*v.t.* to put on boots; to kick.—**boot'black** *n.* one who polishes the boots of casual passers-by for hire.—**boot'ee** *n.* a knitted boot for an infant.—**boot'ikin** *n.* the instrument of torture known as 'the boot.'—**boot'-jack** *n.* an appliance for pulling off long-legged boots.—**boot'lace** *n.* a lace or thong for fastening boots.—**boot'-last, boot'-tree** *n.* an instrument to stretch, or preserve the shape of, a boot.—**boot'leg** *n.* leather cut out for the leg of a boot;—*v.t.* to import or sell illicitly alcoholic liquor; to smuggle.—**boot'legger** *n.*—**boot'legging** *n.*—**boot'-lick'er** *n.* (*Colloq.*) a hanger-on; a toady; a flatterer; a sycophant.—**boot'-lick'ing** *n.*—**boot'maker** *n.* one who makes or deals in foot-wear.—**boots** *n.* the male servant in a hotel who cleans boots and acts as a handy-man [Fr. *botte*].

boot (bòòt) *v.t.* to profit or advantage;—*n.* profit; avail; advantage; (*Law*) compensation paid for injuries.—**boot'less** *a.* useless; without profit.—**boot'lessly** *adv.*—**boot'lessness** *n.*—**to boot,** in addition [O.E. *bot*, profit].

booth (bòòth) *n.* a temporary hut of boards or other slight materials; a covered stall at a market or fair.—**poll'ing-booth** *n.* a place for casting votes [O.N. *buth*, a dwelling].

booty (bòò'-ti) *n.* spoil taken in war; plunder; pillage [Fr. *butin*].

booze, boose (bòòz) *n.* a drinking-bout;—*v.i.* to drink excessively.—**boo'zer, boo'ser** *n.* one who drinks to excess; a tippler.—**boo'zy, boo'sy** *a.* a little intoxicated [Dut.].

boracic See under **borax**.

borage (bor'-āj) *n.* a herb formerly esteemed as a cordial [Fr. *bourrache*].

borak (bō'-rak) *n.* banter, chaff.—**to poke borak at,** to make fun of [Austral.].

borax (bō'-raks) *n.* hydrated sodium borate, used in the manufacture of enamels and glazes, as a softener for hard water, an antiseptic, a soldering flux, etc.—**borac'ic** *a.*—**boracic acid,** white powder used as an antiseptic or for checking excessive perspiration.—**bo'rate** *n.* a salt of boracic acid [Ar. *būraq*].

bordeaux (bor-dō') *n.* red or white wines

Hals: Gypsy Girl

Rubens: Self portrait with Isabella Brant (c. 1609)

PAINTING
17th Century

P. de Hooch: Mother and Child (c. 1660)

Murillo: Urchin

Velasquez: Las Meninas

Watteau: L'Indifferent

David: Mme Sérizat and her son

PAINTING
18th Century

Constable: Salisbury Cathedral

Reynolds: Portrait of a Young Lady

Goya: The Colossus

of *Bordeaux,* France.—**bordeaux mixture,** copper sulphate in limewater used against blight on fruit-trees [Fr.].

bordel (bor'del) *n.* a brothel [O.Fr.].

border (bord'ẹr) *n.* the outer part or edge of anything; the exterior limit of a place; a frontier; an ornamental design round the outside edge of anything; a flower-bed;—*v.t.* to adorn with a border; to adjoin;—*v.i.* to touch at the edge; to come near.—**bord'erer** *n.* one who lives near a frontier, esp. that between England and Scotland.—**bord'ering** *n.* material for a border.—**bor'der-land** *n.* land contiguous to a frontier; an indeterminate state or condition [Fr. *bordure*].

bore (bōr) *v.t.* to make a hole in; to pierce; to drill; to weary by uninteresting talk; to fatigue.—*n.* the hole made by boring; the inside diameter measurement of a cylinder; the hollow interior part of a gun barrel; a thing or person that wearies one.—**bore'dom** *n.* the state of being bored; ennui.—**bor'er** *n.* [O.E. *borian,* to pierce].

bore (bōr) *n.* a tidal wave of great force in some rivers; an eagre [O.N. *bara,* a wave].

bore (bōr) *pa.t.* of **bear.**

Boreas (bō're-ạs) *n.* (*Myth.*) the god of the North wind.—**bo'real** *a.* northern [Gk.].

boric (bōr'ik) *a.* pert. to boron [shortened form of *boracic*].

born (born) *pa.p.* of **bear,** to bring forth;—*a.* natural; innate; perfect.

borne (bōrn) *pa.p.* of **bear,** to carry.

boron (bō'ron) *n.* a non-metallic element whose compounds are useful in the arts and medicine [fr. *borax*].

borough (bur'ō) *n.* an incorporated town; a town represented in Parliament.—**close'-, pock'et-,** or **rot'ten-bor'ough** *n.* a borough whose parliamentary representation was in the hands of an individual or family [O.E. *burg, burh,* a fort, a manor-house].

borrow (bor'ō) *v.t.* to obtain on loan or trust; to adopt from abroad.—**borr'owed** *a.*—**borr'ower** *n.*—**borr'owing** *n.* [O.E. *borgian,* fr. *borg,* a pledge].

Borstal (bors'tạl) *n.* a system of reformatory schools for youthful offenders (16-21 yrs.), aiming at teaching self-reliance and self-respect [*Borstal,* Kent].

borzoi (bor'zoi) *n.* the Russian wolf-hound, remarkable for grace and swiftness [Russ.].

boscage, boskage (bos'kāj) *n.* a wood; underwood; a thicket [O.Fr. *boscage*].

bosh (bosh) *n.* empty talk; nonsense [Turk.].

bosk (bosk) *n.* a thicket or small wood.—**bosk'y** *a.* bushy; covered with underwood.—**bosk'iness** *n.* [See **boscage**].

bosom (bòò'zum) *n.* the breast of a human being; part of the dress over the breast; the heart; embrace; enclosure; expanse; a shirt-front;—*v.t.* to press to the bosom;—*a.* intimate; cherished [O.E. *bosm*].

boss (bos) *n.* a prominent circular projection on any article; a stud; a knob; a round, slightly raised ornament.—*v.t.* to emboss; to provide with bosses.—**bossed** *a.* embossed.—**boss'-eyed** *a.* (*Colloq.*) having a squint; cross-eyed.—**boss'y** *a.* containing, or ornamented with, bosses [Fr. *bosse,* a hump].

boss (bos) *n.* (*Colloq.*) master; employer; one in charge;—*v.t.* to manage; to supervise; (*Colloq.*) to browbeat.—**boss'iness** *n.*—**boss'y** *a.* fussy and masterful [Dut. *baas,* master].

boss (bos) *a.* hollow; empty [E.].

bos'un See **boatswain** (under **boat**).

bot, bott (bot) *n.* usually *pl.* **bots, botts,** larvae of species of gad-fly found in intestines of horses, etc., causing tumour-like swellings [Gael. *botus,* belly-worm].

botany (bot'ạ-ni) *n.* that branch of biology which is concerned with the structure and growth of plants.—**botan'ic, botan'ical** *a.* pert. to botany.—**botan'ically** *adv.*—**botanic garden,** a garden where plants are scientifically studied.—**bot'anist** *n.*—**bot'anise** *v.i.* to study plants; to search for and collect plants for further study [Gk. *botanē,* herb].

botch (boch) *n.* a large ulcerous affection; a clumsy patch of a garment; bungled work;—*v.t.* to bungle; to patch clumsily; to blunder; spoil. Also **bodge.**—**botch'er** *n.* a bungler.—**botch'ery, botch'work** *n.* clumsy workmanship.—**botch'ily** *adv.* in a botchy manner.—**botch'y** *a.* [M.E. *bocchen,* to patch].

botfly See **bot.**

both (bōth) *a.* and *pron.* the one and the other;—*conj.* (foll. by *and*) as well [O.E. *bā*].

bother (boTH'ẹr) *v.t.* to annoy; worry; trouble; vex; perplex; flurry; tease; plague;—*v.i.* to fuss; to be troublesome;—*n.* trouble; annoyance; fuss; worry;—*interj.* an exclamation of annoyance.—**bothera'tion** *n.* trouble and worry; a mild imprecation.—**both'ersome** *a.* troublesome; annoying [etym. unknown].

bothie, bothy (both'i) *n.* (*Scot.*) the quarters allotted to ploughmen, usually unmarried, on a farm in Scotland; a poorly furnished hovel [cf. *booth*].

bott See **bot.**

bottle (bot'l) *n.* a vessel with a narrow neck for holding liquids; its contents; hard drinking; a thermionic valve;—*v.t.* to put into bottles; to restrain; to curb.—**bott'led** *a.* enclosed in bottles; of a bottle shape.—**bott'led-up** *a.* confined; not allowed to speak.—**bott'le-glass** *n.* a coarse, green variety of glass.—**bott'le-green** *a.* of a dark-green colour.—**bott'le-head** *n.* the bottle-nose whale.—**bott'ling** *n.* and *a.*—**bott'le-neck** *n.* a narrow outlet which impedes the smooth flow of traffic or production of goods.—**bott'le-nose** *n.* a whale with a beaked snout.—**bott'le-par'ty,** *n.* one where the guests provide the liquid refreshments; a night-club.—**bott'ler** *n.* one who bottles beer, etc. [O.Fr. *botel,* fr. *botte,* a truss].

bottom (bot'um) *n.* the lowest part of anything; the posterior of human body; the base; bed or channel of a river or lake; foundation or groundwork; stamina; origin;—*a.* to put a bottom on an article; to lay a foundation for a road, etc.—**bott'oms** *n.pl.* the deepest workings of a mine; the heavy material left in smelting.—**bott'omed** *a.*—**bott'om-fish'ing** *n.* trawling.—**bott'omless** *a.*—**bott'omry** *n.* pledging a ship, its freight and cargo as security for a loan to be repaid when the vessel reaches its destination.—**bottomless pit,** hell [O.E. *botm*].

botulism (bot'ū-lizm) *n.* a rare and dangerous form of food poisoning caused by canned goods [L. *botulus,* a sausage].

bouclé (bòò'klā') *n.* a woven material with raised pile.—*a.* pert. to such material [Fr.].

boudoir (bòò'dwár) *n.* a lady's small private room; a kind of private notepaper, measuring 6 in. by 3 in. [Fr. *bouder,* to sulk].

bougainvillea (bòò'gān-vil'e-ạ) *n.* a S. American plant with great masses of red or lilac bracts, grown in British gardens [Louis *Bougainville* (1729-1814)].

bough (bou) *n.* an arm or large branch of a tree [O.E. *bog, boh*].

bought (bawt) *pa.t.* and *pa.p.* of **buy.**

bouillabaisse (bòò-ya-bes') *n.* a Provençal fish soup or stew.—**bouilli** (bòò-yē') *n.* boiled meat.—**bouillon** (bòò-ē-yōng') *n.* broth; stock [Fr. *bouillir,* to boil].

boulder (bōl'dẹr) *n.* a rock torn from its bed, and rounded by water.—**boul'der-clay** *n.* a stiff clay of the glacial or ice-drift age [M.E. *bulderston*].

boule (bòòl) See **buhl.**

boulevard (bòòl'ẹ-var) *n.* a street or promenade (orig. on the site of the ramparts) planted with trees.—**boul'evardier** *n.* one who haunts the boulevards; a man-about-town [Fr. fr. Ger. *Bollwerk*].

bounce (bouns) *v.i.* to leap or spring suddenly; to come or go suddenly; to boast; to brag;—*v.t.* to cause to rebound, as a ball; to eject;—*n.* a sudden fall; rebound; a boast; a boaster;

—bounc'er *n.* (*U.S. Slang*) a chucker-out.—bounc'ing *a.* lusty; boastful.—bounc'ingly *adv.* [Dut. *bonzen*, to strike].

bound (bound) *pa.t.* and *pa.p.* of **bind**.—**bound, boun'den** *a.* imposed as a duty.

bound (bound) *v.i.* to leap; jump; spring; skip; frisk.—*n.* a leap; jump [Fr. *bondir*, to leap].

bound (bound) *a.* prepared for going; intending to go, etc.; direction, as in *homeward bound* [Scand.].

bound (bound) *n.* usually in *pl.* limit or boundary; confines; precincts;—*v.t.* to restrain; to form the boundary of; to set bounds to.—**bound'ed** *a.* restricted; bordered; cramped.—**bound'er** *n.* (*Slang*) an objectionable, vulgar person.—**bound'less** *a.* without limits; wide and spacious; vast; infinite.—**bound'lessness** *n.*—**out of bounds**, not allowed to enter [O.E. *bindan*, to bind].

boundary (bound'ar-i) *n.* a border or limit; a dividing line; barrier; precincts; march-line; termination; the line which circumscribes the playing-pitch at cricket [*bound*].

bounty (boun'ti) *n.* liberality; generosity; munificence; gratuity; a payment formerly made to men enlisting voluntarily in the army or navy; a grant or premium to assist certain branches of industry, agriculture, etc. —**boun'teous, boun'tiful** *a.* generous; liberal; ample; plentiful.—**boun'teously, boun'tifully** *adv.* **boun'teousness, boun'tifulness** *n.*—**King's (Queen's) bounty**, grant of money made to the parents of triplets [Fr. *bonté*, goodness].

bouquet (bòò'kā) *n.* a nosegay; a bunch of flowers; a perfume; the aromatic flavour and aroma of wine; a compliment [Fr.].

bourbon (bòòr'bon) *n.* a coarse whisky distilled in U.S. from Indian corn and rye [*Bourbon*, town in Kentucky, U.S.A.].

bourg (bòòrg) *n.* See **borough, burgh**.

bourgeois (boor-zhwaw') *n.* a member of middle-class society.—*a.* of commercial or non-manual classes; middle-class; conventional; humdrum; stodgy.—**bourgeoisie** (bòòrzh'waw-zē) *n.* [Fr.].

bourgeon (bur'jun) *v.i.* to sprout; to bud; to put forth branches [Fr.].

bourn (burn) *n.* a stream; a burn [O.E. *burna*].

bourn, bourne (bōrn, bòòrn) *n.* a boundary; a limit; a realm; a domain; goal.—**last bourne**, the grave [Fr. *borne*, limit].

bourse (bòòrs) *n.* the stock exchange, esp. in Paris [Fr.]. [See **purse**].

bout (bout) *n.* a turn; a conflict; contest; continuous drinking [Doublet of *bight*].

boviform (bō'vi-form) *a.* having the form of an ox [L. *bos, bovis*, ox; *forma*, shape].

bovine (bō'vīn) *a.* pert. to cattle; ox-like; dull; stupid; stolid; obtuse [L. *bovinus*].

bow (bou) *v.i.* to bend body in respect, assent, etc.; to submit;—*v.t.* to bend downwards; to cause to stoop; to crush; to subdue;—*n.* an inclination of head or body; the rounded forward part of a ship; the stem or prow.—**bow-line** (bō'lin) *n.* a rope used to keep the weather edge of the sail tight forward; knot used for tying a rope to a post.—**bow'-man** *n.* the one who rows the foremost oar in a boat.—**bow'-oar** *n.* the oar or rower nearest the bow. —**bowsprit** (bō'sprit) *n.* a large spar projecting over the stem of a vessel [O.E. *bugan*, to bend].

bow (bō) *n.* anything bent or curved; weapon from which an arrow is discharged; any curved instrument, as a fiddle-stick; a lace or ribbon tied in a slip-knot; a rainbow; any metal ring used as an attachment;—*v.t.* to manipulate the bow of a violin, etc.—**bow'-backed** *a.* having a bent back.—**bow'-brace** *n.* a covering to protect the left arm of a bowman.—**bowed** *a.* bent like a bow; crooked.—**bow'er** *n.* a bow-maker; one who bows.—**bow'-file** *n.* a curved file; a riffler.—**bow'-legged** *a.* having crooked legs.—**bow'man** *n.* an archer.—**bow'-saw** *n.* a thin-bladed saw kept taut by a bow-shaped frame.—**bow'-shot** *n.* the distance an arrow may carry.—**bow'-string** *n.* the string of a bow. —**bow'-win'dow** *n.* a curved, bay window.—**to draw the long bow**, to exaggerate [O.E. *boga*].

bowdlerise (bōd-, boud'lęr'īz) *v.t.* to leave out indelicate words or passages in a book in the alleged interest of moral purity.—**bowd'lerism** *n.* [fr. T. *Bowdler's* expurgated edition of Shakespeare, 1818].

bowel (bou'el) *n.* an entrail; the entrails; the inside of everything; (*Fig.*) the seat of pity, tenderness, etc.—**bowels** *n.pl.* the intestines [O.Fr. *boel*].

bower (bou'ęr) *n.* a boudoir; a shady recess; an arbour; a small country dwelling.—**bow'ery** *a.* shady [O.E. *bur*, dwelling].

bowie-knife (bō'e-nīf) *n.* a long hunting-knife, the point double-edged, the blade, straight and single-edged to the hilt [invented by Col. James *Bowie*].

bowl (bōl) *n.* a round vessel; a deep basin; a drinking-cup; the hollow part of anything, as a pipe for smoking [O.E. *bolle*].

bowl (bōl) *n.* anything rounded by art; a ball rolled along the ground in certain games; a ball with bias;—*pl.* a game played on a bowling-green with bowls;—*v.t.* to roll, as a bowl;—*v.i.* to play with bowls; to move rapidly and smoothly; to deliver a ball.—**bowl'er** *n.* one who bowls.—**bowl'ing** *n.*—**bowl'ing-all'ey** *n.* a covered place for playing at bowls.—**bowl'ing-green** *n.* a pitch, for bowling [O.Fr. *boule*].

bowler (bōl'ęr) *n.* a hard, felt hat [fr. name of original maker].

bowsprit (bō'sprit) *n.* See **bow**.

box (boks) *n.* a small case or chest, generally with a lid; its contents; a compartment in a law-court for witnesses; a small wooden hut for a sentry; the driver's seat on a carriage; a gratuity at Christmas time;—*v.t.* to enclose in a box.—**box'-bed** *n.* a bed in the kitchen of old Scottish houses, fitted into a recess, and concealed by sliding panels.—**box'-board** *n.* thin card-board, made from waste paper, used for cartons.—**box'-car** *n.* a closed railway-car used for transporting perishable goods.—**Boxing Day**, day after Christmas, when Christmas 'boxes' were given.—**box'-kite** *n.* a kite consisting of a square frame and four braces placed diagonally to give strength.—**box'-off'ice** *n.* ticket office at a theatre.—**box'-pleat** *n.* a double fold in a dress-cloth with a knife edge.—**to box the compass**, to name the 32 points of the compass in their order and backwards [O.E.].

box (boks) *n.* a small evergreen shrub.—**box'-ber'ry** *n.* the wintergreen.—**box'en** *a.* made of or like box-wood.—**box'-tree** *n.* the tree variety of box.—**box'-wood** *n.* [L. *buxus*].

box (boks) *n.* a buffet on the head or the ears; —*v.t.* to buffet; to mix up playing-cards while shuffling so as to show their faces;—*v.i.* to fight in an arena with the fists.—**box'er** *n.* a pugilist.—**box'ing** *n.* the sport of scientific fighting, with fists.—**box'ing-booth** *n.* place where boxing exhibitions were held in old-time fairs.—**box'ing-glove** *n.* a padded glove worn by boxers.

boxhaul (boks'hawl) *v.t.* to veer a ship, when close hauled, round to the other tack by throwing back the head-sails, putting the helm alee and then rounding to.

boy (boi) *n.* a male child; a lad; generally in the Colonies, a native servant or labourer.—**boy'hood** *n.* the state of a boy.—**boy'ish** *a.* boy-like; puerile.—**boy'ishly** *adv.*—**boy'ishness** *n.* the natural actions of a boy [M.E. *boi, boy*].

boycott (boi'kot) *n.* a method of coercion by conspiracy, whereby all dealings cease with an undesirable individual;—*v.t.* to act as above; to ostracise.—**boy'cotter** *n.*—**boy'cotting** *n.* [fr. Capt. *Boycott*, a land-agent in Co. Mayo, Ireland, the first victim, in 1880].

brace (brās) *n.* a rod or bar crossing a space diagonally to connect two structural parts;

a carpenter's tool for boring; a printer's mark (⟨) used in bracketing words; (*Naut.*) a rope passing through a block at the end of a yard for regulating its movements;—*v.t.* to furnish with braces; to support; to tighten; to nerve or strengthen.—**brac'es** *n.pl.* straps which support trousers, etc.; suspenders; an arm guard.—**brace bit,** the small interchangeable boring tool fitted into the socket of a brace.—**brac'er** *n.* a wrist-guard of leather or metal, used esp. by archers; (*Colloq.*) stimulating drink.—**brac'ing** *a.* strengthening; invigorating; stimulating; refreshing [Fr. *bras*, arm].

bracelet (brās'let) *n.* an ornament for the wrist;—**brace'lets** *n.pl.* (*Colloq.*) handcuffs.

brach (brak, brach) *n.* a bitch hound; a hunting-dog with a keen scent [O.Fr.].

brachial (brak'i-al, brā'ki-al) *a.* belonging to the arm; of the nature of an arm; resembling an arm [L. *brachium*, arm].

bracken (brak'en) *n.* a large coarse species of fern [M.E. *braken*].

bracket (brak'et) *n.* a projecting support fastened to a wall; one of two hooks, [ ], ⟨ ⟩, or ( ), used to enclose explanatory words;—*v.t.* to place within brackets; to couple names together as of equal merit, etc. [Fr. *braguette*, fr. L. *bracae*, breeches].

brackish (brak'ish) *a.* somewhat salty; of fresh water which has been mixed with salt water.—**brack'ishness** *n.* [Dut. *brak*, briny].

bract (brakt) *n.* a leaf in the axil of which a flower or inflorescence arises.—**brac'teal** *a.* of the nature of a bract.—**brac'teate** *a.* formed of metal beaten thin; (*Bot.*) having bracts; bracteal;—*n.* a thin silver coin formerly current; a thin metal plaque of silver or gold [L. *bractea*, a thin plate].

brad (brad) *n.* a cut nail tapering in width with a small head projecting on one side.—**brad'-awl** *n.* a small hand-boring tool [Scand.].

brae (brā) *n.* (*Scot.*) the side of a hill; a stretch of sloping ground.

brag (brag) *v.i.* to boast; to praise oneself or one's belongings;—*pr.p.* **brag'ging**; *pa.t.* and *pa.p.* **bragged**;—*n.* boasting; bragging; a gambling game of cards, depending mainly on bluff.—**braggadocio** (brag-a-dō'shi-ō) *n.* a boasting fellow.—**bragg'art** *a.* boastful;—*n.* a boaster.—**bragg'ing** *a.* boastful;—*n.* boastful language; vainglory.—**bragg'ingly** *adv.* [origin uncertain].

Brahma (brȧ'ma) *n.* the 1st aspect of the Trimurti, or Hindu Trinity, the Creator.—**brah'min** *n.* a person of the highest or priestly caste among the Hindus.—**brah'minism** *n.* the religion and philosophy of the Brahmins.

braid (brād) *v.t.* to plait, entwine, or interweave; to bind with braid;—*n.* a narrow ribbon or tape used as a dress-trimming or in upholstery; a tress of hair.—**braid'ed** *a.* —**braid'ing** *n.* [O.E. *bregdan*].

braille (brāl) *n.* a system of printing books in relief to be read by the blind; also the letters used, consisting of raised dots in combination [Louis *Braille*, inventor].

brain (brān) *n.* the whitish, soft mass in the skull in which are the nerve centres; intellect; mental capacity; understanding; intelligence; —*v.t.* to dash out the brains of.—**brained** *a.* having the brains beaten out; used in compound terms as *feather-brained*, etc.—**brain'-fev'er** *n.* inflammation of the brain; meningitis.—**brain'less** *a.* witless; stupid; doltish.—**brain'lessness** *n.*—**brain'-pan** *n.* the skull.—**brain'-storm** *n.* a sudden attack of insanity.—**brains trust,** a group of persons prepared to give impromptu rational answers to questions of current or topical interest, either on the radio or at a public meeting; a body of experts engaged on research or planning.—**brain'-wave** *n.* (*Colloq.*) an unexpected, spontaneous bright idea.—**brain'y** *a.* highly intellectual; clever [O.E. *braegen*].

braise (brāz) *v.t.* to stew with vegetables, etc., and then bake;—*n.* the roach.—**brais'er** *n.* a covered pot used in braising [Fr.].

brake (brāk) *n.* a place overgrown with ferns, etc.; a thicket; brushwood [Scand.].

brake (brāk) *n.* instrument for breaking flax or hemp; a harrow; a vehicle consisting of the underpart of a carriage and a driver's seat used for breaking-in and training carriage-horses; a large wagonette; any device for checking speed by friction on a wheel or rail; any restraining influence or curb;—*v.t.* to pound or crush flax, hemp, etc., by beating; to check by applying a brake.—**brak'ing** *n.* act of applying brakes to a moving object; mechanism for applying brakes.—**brake'man, brakes'man** *n.* one who works the brakes on railway rolling-stock.—**brake'-shoe** *n.* the surface of a block brake; a device for halting wagons during shunting.—**brake'-van** *n.* a railway carriage containing the brake [etym. uncertain].

bramble (bram'bl) *n.* a prickly hedge-plant; the wild blackberry; the small, dark purple fruit of the bramble [O.E. *brembel*].

bran (bran) *n.* the husk of wheat and other grain, separated in milling from the flour.—**bran'-tub** *n.* a lucky dip in which parcels are concealed in bran [O.Fr.].

branch (bransh) *n.* a limb of a tree or shrub; a bough; a department of a business, etc.; a line of family descent; an off-shoot; ramification; section; part; sub-division;—*a.* pert. to a subsidiary section of any business;—*v.t.* to divide, as into branches;—*v.i.* to spread, in branches; to diverge.—**branched** *a.*—**branch'ing** *a.* shooting out; starting from.—**branch'y** *a.* having spreading branches.—**root and branch,** thoroughly [Fr. *branche*].

branchiae (brang'ki-ē) *n.pl.* the breathing organs of fishes, the gills.—**bran'chial** *a.* pert. to gills.—**bran'chiate** *a.* furnished with gills [Gk. *branchia*, gills].

brand (brand) *n.* a burning, or partly burnt, piece of wood; an iron used for burning marks on; a mark made by a hot iron; an article with a trade-mark; a grade; a sword; a mark of infamy; stigma;—*v.t.* to burn a mark on; to fix a stamp on; to designate a commodity by a special name or trade-mark; to stigmatise; to reproach.—**brand'ed** *a.*—**brand'er** *n.* a gridiron;—*v.t.* to broil on a gridiron; to grill.—**brand'ing-i'ron** *n.* an iron used to brand with; a trivet for holding a pot. —**brand'-new, bran'-new** *a.* quite new [O.E.].

brand-goose Same as **brant-goose**.

brandish (bran'dish) *v.t.* to flourish or wave, as a weapon [Fr. *brand*, sword].

brandy (bran'di) *n.* an ardent spirit distilled from wine.—**bran'dy-ball** *n.* a sweet in the shape of a ball.—**bran'dy-snap,** *n.* a thin, round, ginger-bread [Dut. *brandewijn*, burnt wine].

brank (brangk) *v.t.* to bridle; restrain;—*v.i.* to toss (the head); to prance; to dress oneself in one's best.—**branks** *n.pl.* a bridle for horses and cows; a scolding bridle for refractory women, consisting of a hoop with hinges to enclose the head, and a gag to render speech impossible or painful [var. of *prank*].

bran-new Var. of **brand-new**. [See **brand**].

brant-goose See **brent-goose**.

brash (brash) *n.* a slight indisposition; a rash on the skin; a clear watery eructation from stomach due to acidity; a sudden downpour of rain; a military attack;—*a.* sudden; hasty; insolent [etym. uncertain].

brass (bras) *n.* a yellow alloy of two parts of copper to one of zinc; (*Colloq.*) money; effrontery; impudence; obstinacy;—*a.* brazen; made of brass.—**brass'es** *n.pl.* monumental plates in a church to commemorate deceased persons; the brass instruments of an orchestra.—**brass'-band** *n.* musicians who perform on brass instruments; (*Colloq.*) a military band. —**brass'et** *n.* a brassard; a casque or headpiece of armour.—**brass'-faced** *a.* impudent; brazen.

—**brass′founder** *n.* one who casts articles of brass.—**brass′-hat** *n.* (*Colloq.*) staff-officer (from gold braid on hat).—**brass′iness** *n.*—**brass′-plate** *n.* a large name-plate beside an outer door.—**brass′y** *a.* pert. to brass;—**brass′y, brass′ie** *n.* a wooden golf-club with a brass sole.—**to get down to brass tacks** (*Colloq.*) to return to essentials, fundamentals [O.E. *braes*].

brassard (bras′ard) *n.* a band worn round arm to signify special duty; armour for upper arm [Fr. *bras*, arm].

brassière (bras-i-er′) *n.* a woman's undergarment supporting the breasts [Fr.].

brat (brat) *n.* an apron of coarse cloth; a child (used contemptuously); offspring [O.E. *bratt*, a pinafore].

bravado (brạ-vå′dō) *n.* a swaggerer; showy bravery;—*pl.* **brava′does** [Sp.].

brave (brāv) *a.* courageous; noble; finely-dressed;—*n.* a Red Indian warrior;—*v.t.* to encounter with courage.—**brave′ly** *adv.*—**brav′ery** *n.* courage; heroism; elaborate personal attire [Fr.].

bravo (bra′vō) *n.* a bandit; a hired assassin; *interj.* an expression of applause, well done! —*pl.* **bra′voes** [It.].

bravura (bra-vòò′rạ) *n.* a spirited air with florid graces;—*a.* florid; brilliant [It.].

brawl (brawl) *v.i.* to flow noisily, as water; to squabble noisily;—*n.* a noisy quarrel.—**brawl′er** *n.* [Fr. fr. Scand.].

brawn (brawn) *n.* thick flesh; muscular strength, esp. of the arms and legs; muscles; the flesh of a boar; a preparation of meat made from pigs' head, salted, boiled, and allowed to settle in its own jelly.—**brawn′er** *n.* a boar fattened for the table.—**brawn′iness** *n.* —**brawn′y** *a.* muscular; sinewy; athletic; robust; stout [O.Fr. *braon*, fleshy part].

braxy (brak′si) *n.* (*Scot.*) a fatal disease of sheep; the flesh of such a sheep;—*a.* affected with braxy.

bray (brā) *n.* the harsh noise of an ass; any harsh, strident noise; continual complaining; —*v.i.* to utter a harsh noise, like an ass [Fr. *braire*]. [O.Fr. *breier*].

bray (brā) *v.t.* to pound; to powder; to pulverise; to grind small.

braze (brāz) *v.t.* to solder metals with spelter, brass, or silver.—**braz′ing** *n.* [Fr. *braser*, to solder].

brazen (brā′zn) *a.* pert. to, or made of, brass; impudent; shameless; sounding like a brass instrument;—*v.t.* to face a situation in a bold, impudent manner when clearly in the wrong, as in 'to brazen it out.'—**bra′zenly** *adv.* [M.E. *brasen*].

brazier (brāzh′yẹr) *n.* a portable iron container to hold burning coke; a worker in brass [Fr. *brasier*].

Brazilian (brạ-zil′i-ạn) *n.* a native of *Brazil*, in S. America;—*a.* pert. to Brazil.—**brazil nut**, the hard-shelled edible seed of a large S. American fruit-tree.—**brazil wood**, heavy red wood of a tropical tree, used for dyeing and the manufacture of red ink.

breach (brēch) *n.* a break or opening, esp. in a wall; a hole or gap; non-fulfilment of a contract, promise, etc.; an infringement of a rule, duty, etc.; a quarrel;—*v.t.* to make a breach or gap in something.—**breach of promise**, the non-fulfilment of a promise of marriage [Fr. *brèche*].

bread (bred) *n.* form of food prepared by baking from dough made from a cereal; food in general.—**bread′-bas′ket** *n.* (*Slang*) the stomach.—**bread′less** *a.* starving.—**bread′-win′ner** *n.* one who earns a living for his dependants.—**one's bread and butter**, one's means of livelihood.—**to break bread**, to partake of Holy Communion [O.E.].

breadth (bredth) *n.* distance from side to side; width; freedom from narrowness of mind [O.E. *braedu*].

break (brāk) *v.t.* to shatter by force; to divide into two; to mitigate (a blow, a fall); to tame (a horse, etc.); to wean from (a habit); to dismiss from office; to bankrupt; to weaken or impair (health); to subdue (a person's temper); to violate (promises, etc.); to interrupt (friendship, silence, monotony, etc.);—*v.i.* to divide into several parts; to open (as an abscess); curl over (as waves); to burst forth (as a storm); to dawn (as an idea, day, etc.); to crack or falter (as the voice); to change direction (as a cricket ball); to make the first stroke at billiards; to change pace (as a horse);—*pa.t.* **broke**; *pa.p.* **brok′en.** —**to break cover**, to start from a hiding-place (as a fox).—**to break down**, to crush opposition etc.; to lose control of one's feelings.—**to break new ground**, to change one's activities. —**to break the bank**, to overstrain the financial resources [O.E. *brecan*, to break].

break (brāk) *n.* the act or state of being broken; a fracture; a gap; an opening; dawn; separation; interruption; a breathing space; (*Slang*) a chance; a sudden fall in price; a scoring sequence at billiards.—**break′able** *a.* fragile.—**break′age** *n.* act of breaking; an allowance for articles broken.—**break′away** *n.* an animal which darts away from the herd; panic rush; leaving a parent body to start a new movement.—**break′down** *n.* loss of health; an accident to machinery; suspension of negotiations;—*v.t.* to divide into small categories.—**break′er** *n.* one who breaks; a long wave or crest as it breaks into foam.—**break′fast** *n.* the first meal of the day.—**break′ing** *n.* forming wool fibres in long lengths.—**break′neck** *a.* dangerous to life and limb.—**break′-wat′er** *n.* a strong structure to break the force of the waves.—**break′-of-day** *n.* the dawn.—**a bad break**, a period of misfortune [O.E. *brecan*, to break].

bream (brēm) *n.* fresh-water fish of the carp family [fr. *brême*].

breast (brest) *n.* the external part of the thorax or chest between neck and abdomen; bosom; seat of the affections and passions; —*v.t.* to bear the breast against; to oppose, face, or meet boldly (a wave); to mount (a hill, etc.).—**breasts** *n.pl.* the milk or mammary glands of women and female animals.—**breast′-bone** *n.* the sternum, the flat narrow bone to which the first seven ribs are attached.—**breast′-deep, breast′-high** *adv.* reaching as far as the breast.—**breast′-plate** *n.* a metal plate or piece of armour for protecting the chest.—**breast′-stroke** *n.* a long-distance stroke in swimming.—**breast′work** *n.* a parapet on a building; a hastily constructed earthwork, faced with sods, etc., to afford protection against attack.—**to make a clean breast**, to confess [E.O. *brēost*].

breath (breth) *n.* air respired by the lungs; the act of breathing freely; life; respite; a single respiration, or the time of making it; a very slight breeze; whisper; fragrance.—**breath′less** *a.* out of breath; panting; dead; eager and excited; expectant.—**breath′lessness** *n.*—**to catch the breath**, to stop breathing momentarily from excitement.—**with bated breath**, breath held from fear or excitement [O.E. *braeth*, exhalation].

breathe (brēTH) *v.t.* to draw in and give out air from the lungs; to infuse or inspire, as life, courage, etc.;—*v.i.* to inhale and emit air—hence to live; to take breath.—**breath′able** *a.*—**breathed** (brēTHd) *a.* out of breath; (*Phil.*) uttered with breath only.—**breath′er** *n.* in motoring, a vent to allow pressure in crankcase, gearbox, etc., to remain normal; a short spell of rest.—**breath′er-pipe**, *n.* a pipe usually cowled, fitted on breather.—**breath′ing** *n.* respiration; gentle breeze; a mark (ʻ) placed over a vowel in Greek grammar giving it the sound of *h*.—**breath′ing-space, breath′ing-time**, *n.* pause; relaxation; a short respite [fr. *breath*].

bred *pa.t.* and *pa.p.* of **breed.**

breech (brēch) *n.* the buttocks; the hinder part, esp. of a gun-barrel;—*v.t.* to put (a young child for the first time) into breeches; to whip; to flog.—**breech'es** *n.pl.* trousers, esp. those which fit tightly round knees.—**breech'-buoy, breech'es-buoy** *n.* an apparatus consisting of a canvas bag slung along a rope, used for saving persons from a wreck.—**breech'ing** *n.* that part of the harness which passes round a horse's haunches.—**breech'-load'er** *n.* a gun or howitzer, loaded at the breech [O.E. *brec*].

breed (brēd) *v.t.* to beget; to engender; to generate; to propagate; to hatch; to train or bring up;—*v.i.* to be produced; to be with young; to increase in number;—*pa.t.* and *pa.p.* **bred**;—*n.* a race of animals from the same stock; kind; sort.—**breed'er** *n.* one who breeds cattle or other live stock.—**breed'ing** *n.* producing; the rearing of live stock; manners; deportment; courtesy [O.E. *bredan*, to nourish].

breeks (brēks) *n.pl.* (*Scot.*) breeches; trousers.

breeze (brēz) *n.* a wind of moderate strength; a quarrel; a disturbance.—**breez'y** *a.* windy; gusty; of a person, with animation and bluffness [Fr. *brise*].

breeze (brēz) *n.* a fly of various species which sucks the blood of animals.—**breeze'-fly** *n.* the cleg [O.E. *briosa*].

breeze (brēz) *n.* finely broken coke; furnace ashes; clinkers; house-sweepings [Fr. *braise*, cinders].

bren gun (bren gun) *n.* a light, rapid-fire machine gun [*Brno*, town in Czechoslovakia, where first made].

brent, brent-goose (brent gôôs) *n.* a small goose, dark in neck and whitish-grey or brown below [=brindled].

Brer (brer) *n.* brother; used in the Negro animal stories of Uncle Remus.

brethren (breTH'ren) *n.pl.* members of the same society or profession.—**Plymouth Brethren**, a Christian sect [See **brother**].

Breton (bret'on) *n.* pert. to Brittany;—*a.* one of the Celtic dialects, spoken in Brittany; a native of Brittany [O.Fr.].

breve (brēv) *n.* the longest note now used in music, ‖O‖; a mark; (ᴗ) distinguishing short vowels [It. fr. L. *brevis*, short].

brevet (brev'et) *a.* a commission, which entitles an officer to an honorary rank in the army above his actual rank.—**brev'etcy** *n.* brevet rank [Fr. fr. L. *brevis*, short].

breviary (brēv'i-a-ri) *n.* an abridgment; a book containing the daily service of the R.C. Church [L. *brevis*, short].

brevity (brev'i-ti) *n.* shortness; conciseness; briefness; terseness [L. *brevis*, short].

brew (brôô) *v.t.* to prepare a fermented liquor, from malt, hops, etc.; to infuse (tea); to plot; concoct; mix; season;—*v.i.* to perform the operations of brewing; to be impending;—*n.* something brewed; a particular brand or quality of beer.—**brew'er** *n.*—**brew'ery** *n.* a place where brewing is carried on.—**brew'ster** *n.* a brewer; a female brewer [O.E. *breowan*].

briar (brī'ar) *n.* the common heath-plant of S. France; a pipe made from the root of this briar [Fr. *bruyère*, heather].

briar, brier (brī'ar) *n.* the wild rose; any prickly bush; a thorn.—**sweet-bri'ar, sweet-bri'er** *n.* the wild rose [earlier *brere*, O.E. *braer*].

bribe (brīb) *n.* anything bestowed, with a view to influence judgment and conduct;—*v.t.* to influence by gifts;—*v.i.* to practise bribery.—**brib'able** *a.*—**brib'ery** *n.* [Fr. *bribe*, fragment].

bric-à-brac (brik'a-brak) *n.* fancy ware; curios of slight artistic value [Fr.].

brick (brik) *n.* special clay moulded into a rectangular block and hardened by burning; one of the wooden blocks used in kindergarten instruction; (*Colloq.*) a sterling friend;—*v.t.* to lay, or pave, with bricks.—**brick'bat** *n.* a fragment of a brick.—**brick'bats** *n.pl.* angry comments.—**brick'-field** *n.* a place where bricks are made.—**brick'-kiln** *n.* a kiln in which bricks are baked or burnt.—**brick'layer** *n.* one who is skilled in building with bricks.—**brick'-lay'ing** *n.*—**brick'-red** *a.* of a dull scarlet colour like brick.—**brick'work** *n.* any structure built of bricks as distinguished from other materials.—**brick'-yard** *n.* a place where bricks are made.—**to drop a brick** (*Slang*) to be tactless [Fr. *brique*].

bride (brīd) *n.* a woman about to be, or just, married.—**bri'dal** *n.* wedding; orig. bride-ale, the ale-drinking at a wedding;—*a.* pert. to a bride or a wedding; nuptial; connubial; conjugal.—**bri'dal-suite** *n.* apartments set aside for a honeymoon couple.—**bride'groom** *n.* a man newly-married, or about to be married.—**brides'maid** *n.* an unmarried woman who acts as attendant on a bride; best maid.—**brides'man** *n.* a man who attends the bride-groom; best man [O.E. *bryd*].

bridge (brij) *n.* a roadway over arches spanning a river or a valley; a support for the strings of a violin; the hurricane deck or bridge deck of a vessel; the bone of the nose, etc.;—*v.t.* to build a bridge or bridges over.—**bridge'-head** *n.* a work protecting the end of a bridge nearest the enemy; a footing gained by an attacking force on the far bank of a river.—**pontoon bridge**, a bridge made across a stream upon boats or metal pontoons.—**suspension bridge**, a bridge hung on chains or cables stretched over piers.—**swing bridge**, a bridge which moves on a pivot and opens for vessels to pass.—**tubular bridge**, a series of tubes supported on piers, the roadway being in the interior [O.E. *brycg*].

bridge (brij) *n.* a card game for four players; a development of whist, *auction bridge*, *contract bridge*, variant forms of this.

bridle (brī'dl) *n.* the headgear of a beast of burden, of a horse; a curb; constraint;—*v.t.* to put a bridle upon; to check; subdue; curb; control.—**bri'dle-path, bri'dle-road** *n.* a narrow track used by riders on horseback [O.E. *bridel*].

brief (brēf) *a.* short in duration; using few words;—*n.* an abridged statement of a client's case, prepared by a solicitor for study and examination by a counsel;—*v.t.* to instruct or retain counsel by giving him a brief; to inform personnel of the details of an impending military or air action.—**brief'ly** *adv.*—**brief'ness** *n.* [Fr. *bref*, fr. L. *brevis*, short].

brier *n.* See **briar**.

brig (brig) *n.* a sailing-ship with two masts, both square-rigged [shortened *brigantine*, q.v. but not to be confused with it].

brigade (bri-gād') *n.* a sub-division of an army under the command of a general officer.—**armoured brigade**, a brigade with mobile guns and tanks.—**brigade'-maj'or** *n.* a staff officer attached to a general.—**brigadier'**, **brigadier'-gen'eral** *n.* officer in command of a brigade [It. *brigata*, a troop].

brigand (brig'and) *n.* a lawless fellow who lives by plunder; bandit; freebooter; highwayman.—**brig'andage** *n.* [O.Fr. *brigand*, a foot-soldier].

brigantine (brig'an-tēn) *n.* a light, two-masted vessel, the foremast with square sails and the other with a triangular sail [Fr. *brigantin*, a piratical vessel].

bright (brīt) *a.* shining; full of light or splendour; cheerful; vivacious; sparkling; luminous; radiant; clear; clever; intelligent.—**bright'en** *v.t.* to make bright;—*v.i.* to grow bright.—**bright'ly** *adv.*—**bright'ness** *n.*—**bright'-some** *a.* brilliant [O.E. *beorht*].

brill (bril) *n.* a flat fish of the turbot family, though smaller [etym. unknown].

brilliant (bril'yant) *a.* glittering; sparkling; radiant; shining; illustrious; distinguished; splendid; very clever;—*n.* a polished diamond cut to a definite pattern.—**brill'-**

iantly *adv.*—**brill'iantness** *n.*—**brill'iance** *n.*—**brill'iancy** *n.* [Fr. *brillant*].
brilliantine (bril'-yan-tēn) *n.* a hairdresser's preparation to give the hair a glossy appearance and for fixing it in position [Fr. *briller*, to shine].
brim (brim) *n.* rim or border; the rim of a hat;—*v.i.* to be full to the brim.—**brim'ful** *a.* full to the brim.—**brimmed** *a.* brimful.—**brimm'er** *n.* a drinking vessel, full to the brim; a bumper.—**brimm'ing** *a.* full to overflowing [M.E. *brimme*].
brimstone (brim'-stōn) *n.* sulphur; hellfire;—*a.* lemon-coloured [M.E. *brenston*=burning-stone].
brinded, brindled (brin'-ded, -dld) *a.* streaked with coloured stripes; spotted [Scand.].
brine (brīn) *n.* water containing an admixture of salt; sea-water; the sea; tears.—**brin'ish** *a.* salty, like brine.—**brin'y** *a.* pert. to brine or the sea; saltish.—**the briny** (*Colloq.*) the sea.—**brine'-spring** *n.* a spring of salt water [O.E. *bryne*].
bring (bring) *v.t.* to carry; to fetch; to convey from one person or place to another; to transfer; to transport; to draw; to lead; to prevail on;—*pa.t.* and *pa.p.* **brought** (brawt).—**to bring about,** to effect; to cause to happen.—**to bring down the house,** to earn great applause.—**to bring forth,** to produce, give birth to.—**to bring home to,** to prove; to make realise.—**to bring round,** to restore to consciousness.—**to bring to,** to resuscitate; to check the course of a ship.—**to bring to bear,** to apply pressure.—**to bring up,** to rear; to educate; to raise in discussion; to vomit; to cast anchor [O.E. *bringan*].
brink (bringk) *n.* edge, margin of a steep slope; verge [M.E. *brenk*].
brio (brē'-ō) *n.* (*Mus.*) liveliness; vivacity [It.]
briony (brī'-o-ni) *n.* See **bryony.**
briquette (bri-ket') *n.* a brick of compressed coal dust [Fr.].
brisk (brisk) *a.* full of activity;—*v.t.* and *i.* to enliven; to cheer up.—**brisk'ly** *adv.*—**brisk'ness** *n.* [Celt.].
brisket (bris'-ket) *a.* part of animal's breast which lies next to ribs [O.Fr.].
brisling (bris'-ling) *n.* a Norwegian sprat, somewhat similar to sardines [Scand.].
bristle (bris'-l) *n.* a very stiff, erect, coarse hair, as of swine; a quill;—*v.t.* to erect the bristles of;—*v.i.* to stand up erect, like bristles; to show anger; to be surrounded with.—**bristled** (bris'-ld) *a.* provided with bristles.—**brist'liness** *n.*—**brist'ly** *a.* thick set with bristles.—**to bristle up,** to flare up in a temper.—**to bristle with,** to abound in [O.E. *byrst*].
Bristol-board (bris'-tol-bōrd) *n.* a pasteboard with a smooth, glazed surface.—**Bristol fashion** (*Naut.*) in good order; well [fr. *Bristol*, in England].
Britannia (bri-tan'-ya) *n.* Great Britain personified; a female figure forming an emblem of Great Britain.—**Britan'nia-met'al** *n.* an alloy of tin, antimony, bismuth, and copper.—**Britan'nic** *a.* pert. to Great Britain [L.].
British (brit'-ish) *a.* of or pertaining to Britain;—*n.* the inhabitants of Britain.—**Brit'icism** *n.* a British idiom.—**Brit'isher** *n.* a British subject [fr. *Briton*].
Briton (brit'-un) *n.* one of the Brythons, or ancient Celtic inhabitants of Britain; a native of Britain [L. *Brito*].
brittle (brit'-l) *a.* easily broken; apt to break; frail; frangible; fragile;—**britt'leness** *n.* [fr. O.E. *breotan*, to break].
broach (brōch) *n.* a roasting-spit; a tapered, hardened-steel bit for enlarging holes in metal; the guiding-pin of a lock into which the barrel of a key fits;—*v.t.* to pierce; to tap, as a cask; to open; to approach a subject.—**to broach to** (*Naut.*) to turn to windward [Fr. *broche*, a roasting-spit].
broad (brawd) *a.* wide, ample, open; outspoken, unrestrained; coarse, indelicate, gross; tolerant, liberal-minded; with a marked local dialect; plain, unmistakable (hint); full (daylight).—**broad, broad'ly** *adv.*—**broad'-ar'row** *n.* the official mark on British Government property.—**broad'-bean** *n.* the common bean of Europe.—**broad'bill** *n.* the spoon-bill or shoveller duck.—**broad'-brim** *n.* a wide-brimmed hat, much affected by Quakers, and so a Quaker.—**broad'cast** *v.t.* to scatter seed;—*n.* a casting of seed from the hand in sowing [See **broadcast**].—**broad'cloth** *n.* a finely woven woollen cloth for men's wear.—**broad'en** *v.t.* and *v.i.* to make or grow broad.—**broad gauge,** a railway gauge which is wider than 4 ft. 8½ in.—**broad'-mind'ed** *a.* tolerant.—**broad'ness** *n.*—**broad'-sheet** *n.* a sheet of paper printed on one side of the paper only; ballad, political squib, popular in 18th and 19th cents.—**broad'side** *n.* the whole side of a ship above water-line; a volley from the guns on one side of a naval craft; broad-sheet.—**broad'sword** *n.* a cutting sword with a short, flat blade as used by Highlanders [O.E. *brad*].
broadcast See under **broad.**
broadcast (brawd'-kast) *n.* a transmission by wireless telephony of lectures, music, etc.; a programme;—*a.*;—*v.t.* to disseminate by radio-telephone transmitter, news, plays, music, etc., for reception by receiving apparatus.—**broadcast'er** *n.* a person or organisation broadcasting [O.E. *brad*, and Dan. *kaste*].
Brobdingnagian (brob-ding-nag'-i-an) *a.* gigantic;—*n.* a person of extraordinary size [fr. *Gulliver's Travels*].
brocade (brō-kād') *n.* a fabric of silk, rayon, cotton, etc., variegated with gold and silver thread or raised ornamentations;—*v.t.* to make brocade; to ornament a fabric with raised designs.—**broca'ded** *a.* [Sp. *brocado*].
broccoli (brok'-o-li) *n.* a variety of the cauliflower [It. pl. dim. fr. *brocco*, a shoot].
broch (broH) *n.* a prehistoric, dry-stone circular tower. Found in N. of Scotland. Also known as Duns or Pictish-towers [O.N. *borg*, a castle].
brochure (bro-shŏŏr') *n.* a printed work of a few sheets of paper; a booklet; a pamphlet [Fr. *brocher*, to stitch].
brock (brok) *n.* a badger [O.E. *broc*, fr. Celt.].
broderie anglaise (bro-drē' ong-glez') *n.* open embroidery on white linen [Fr. = English embroidery].
brog (brog) *n.* a pointed steel instrument used by joiners for piercing holes in woods; a brad-awl;—*v.t.* to prick; to pierce.
brogan (brō'-gan) *n.* in N. America, a strong shoe worn by fieldworkers.
brogue (brōg) *n.* a stout, coarse kind of shoe, of one entire piece and gathered round the foot by a thong [Ir. *brog*].
brogue (brōg) *n.* a mode of pronunciation peculiar to Irish speakers.—**brog'uish** *a.* having a trace of the brogue [Ir. *brog*, shoe].
broider (broi'-der) *v.t.* to adorn with figured needlework; to embroider [Fr. *broder*].
broil (broil) *n.* a noisy quarrel; contention; altercation [Fr. *brouiller*, to trouble].
broil (broil) *v.t.* to cook by roasting over a hot fire, or on a gridiron; to grill;—*v.i.* to suffer discomfort through heat; to be overheated [Fr. *brûler*, to burn].
broke (brōk) *pa.t.* and old *pa.p.* of **break;**—*a.* (*Colloq.*) penniless; ruined; degraded.—**brok'en** *pa.p.* of **break;**—*a.* shattered; fractured; severed; separated; parted; abrupt; rough; impaired; exhausted; spent.—**broken English,** imperfect English, as spoken by a non-native.—**brok'en-heart'ed** *a.* crushed with grief; inconsolable.—**brok'enly** *adv.* intermittently.—**brok'enness** *n.* [*break*].
broke (brōk) *v.i.* to act for another on a

commission basis.—**brok'er** *n.* a person employed in the negotiation of commercial transactions between other parties in the interests of one of the principals; a pawn-broker; a dealer in second-hand goods; an agent.—**brok'erage, brok'age,** *n.* the business of a broker; the commission charged by a broker.—**brok'ery** *n.* the business of a broker. —**brok'ing** *a.* [M.E. *brocour*].

broma (brō'ma) *n.* a preparation of chocolate; (*Med.*) solid food.—**bromatog'raphy** *n.* disquisition on food [Gk. *broma,* food].

bromide (brō'mīd) *n.* a compound of bromine with some other elements; a sedative drug, employed to induce sleep [See **bromine**].

bromine (brō'min, -mīn) *n.* one of the elements, related to chlorine, iodine, and fluorine.—**brom'ic** *a.* [Gk. fr. *bromos,* stench].

bronchi, bronchia (brong'kī, -ią) *n.pl.* the two tubes forming the lower end of the trachea.—**bron'chial** *a.* pert. to the bronchi.—**bronchi'tis** *n.* inflammation of the bronchial tubes.—**bronch'ial-catarrh'** *n.* inflammation of the mucous membrane of small bronchi.—**bronch'o-pneumon'ia** *n.* patchy inflammation of the lobules of the lungs [Gk. *bronchia*].

broncho (brong'kō) *n.* a half-broken native horse in America [Sp.=rough, crabbed].

bronchus (brong'kus) *n.* one of the bifurcations of the windpipe;—*pl.* **bronc'hi** [Gk. *bronchos,* windpipe].

bronco See **broncho.**

brontosaurus (bron-tō-saw'rus) *n.* a large dinosaur, a giant lizard, the fossil remains of which have been found in Wyoming, U.S.A.; —*pl.* **brontosau'ri** [Gk. *brontē,* thunder; *sauros,* a lizard].

bronze (bronz) *n.* an alloy of copper, tin and zinc; a work of art cast in bronze; the colour of bronze;—*a.* made of or coloured like bronze;—*v.t.* to give the appearance of bronze to; to sunburn; to harden.—**Bronze Age,** pre-historic period between the Stone and Iron Ages [It. *bronzo*].

brooch (brōch) *n.* an ornamental clasp with a pin for attaching it to a garment [Fr. *broche,* a spike, a brooch].

brood (brôôd) *v.t.* to sit upon, as a hen on eggs; to brood over;—*v.i.* to sit upon to hatch; to meditate moodily.—*n.* off-spring; a family of young, esp. of birds; a tribe; a race. —**brood'er** *n.* an appliance for rearing incubator-hatched chickens by artificial heat.—**brood'-mare** *n.* a mare kept for breeding.—**brood'y** *a.* wishing to sit, as a hen; moody; sullen [O.E. *brod*].

brook (brook) *n.* a small stream.—**brook'let** *n.* a streamlet [O.E. *broc*].

brook (brook) *v.t.* to bear; to endure; to support [O.E. *brucan,* use, enjoy].

broom (brôôm) *n.* a wild evergreen shrub producing yellow flowers and pods; a besom made of broom.—**broom'stick** *n.* the handle of a broom [O.E. *brom*].

brose (brōz) *n.* a Scottish dish made of oat or pease meal with the addition of butter.—**Athole brose,** a mixture of whisky and honey [O.Fr. *broez*].

broth (broth) *n.* water in which flesh has been boiled with vegetables [O.E. *brodh*].

brothel (broth'el) *n.* house of prostitution [O.E. *brothen,* degenerate].

brother (bruTH'ẹr) *n.* a male born of the same parents; one closely resembling another in manner or character; an associate or fellow-member of a corporate body;—*pl.* **broth'ers, breth'ren.**—**broth'er-ger'man,** *n.* a full brother as distinguished from a half-brother.—**broth'erhood** *n.* the state of being a brother; an association of men of the same religious order, profession, or society; the mutual regard resulting from this association.—**broth'er-in-law** *n.* the brother of one's husband or wife; a sister's husband.—**broth'er-like, broth'erly** *a.* like a brother, affectionate.—**broth'erliness** *n.*—**broth'er-u'terine** *n.* one born of the same mother but of a different father [O.E. *brothor*].

brougham (brôôm-, brō'am) *n.* a closed horse-carriage with two or four wheels, with an elevated seat for the driver [fr. Lord *Brougham,* d. 1868].

brought (brawt) *pa.t.* and *pa.p.* of **bring.**

brow (brou) *n.* the ridge over the eyes; the eyebrow; the forehead; the rounded top of a hill.—**brow'-beat** *v.t.* to bully or over-rule a person by vehement over-bearing speech.—**brow'-beat'er** *n.* [O.E. *bru*].

brown (broun) *n.* a dark colour inclining to red or yellow; a mixture of black, red and yellow; (*Slang*) a penny;—*a.* of a brown colour; swarthy; sunburnt;—*v.t.* to make or give a brown colour to; to sunbathe; to grill or roast brown.—**brown'-coal** *n.* lignite, an intermediate form between peat and true coal.—**brown'ish** *a.*—**brown'ness** *n.*—**brown'-shirt** *n.* a member of the German Nazi party.—**brown'-stout** *n.* good quality porter.—**brown study,** absent-minded reverie.—**brown sugar,** sugar made from molasses.—**browned off** (*Slang*) in a state of indifference; depressed; bored [O.E. *brun*].

brownie (broun'i) *n.* a good-natured household elf; a member of the junior section of the Girl Guides.

browse (brouz) *v.t.* and *i.* to nibble the tender shoots and leaves of plants; to graze; to pore over a book.—**brows'ing** *n.* [O.Fr. *broust,* a shoot].

bruise (brôôz) *v.t.* to injure or crush by contact with a solid body; to contuse; to pound or pulverise; to fight with the fists; —*n.* a contusion, caused by injury from a blow or pressure, without breaking the skin and accompanied by discolouration of the skin.—**bruis'er** *n.* a prize-fighter; a rough.—**bruising mill,** a small hand-mill for coarse grinding of grain for feeding-stuffs [O.E. *brysan,* to break].

bruit (brôôt) *n.* report; rumour; fame; a noise;—*v.t.* to report; to noise abroad [Fr.].

brumal (brôô'mal) *a.* relating to winter [L. *bruma,* winter].

brume (brôôm) *n.* mist, fog, vapour.—**brum'ous** *a.* foggy [Fr. *brume,* fog].

Brummagem (brum'ą-jem) *a.* made in Birmingham; sham, and of little value [a mispronunciation].

brunch (brunsh) *n.* (*Colloq.*) breakfast and lunch combined (Portmanteau word].

brunette (brôô-net') *n.* a woman with dark brown hair or brown complexion [Fr.].

brunt (brunt) *n.* the main shock of onset; the force of a blow [E., conn. with *burn*].

brush (brush) *n.* an implement made of bristles, twigs, feathers, etc., bound together and used for removing dust, dressing the hair, applying paint, and the like; the smaller trees of a forest, brushwood; a sharp skirmish; the bushy tail of a fox or squirrel; in electricity, the stationary contact-pieces which collect current from the commutator of a dynamo;—*v.t.* to remove dust, etc., from; to touch lightly in the passing;—*v.i.* to touch with light contact.—**brush'-off** *n.* (*U.S. Slang*) an abrupt refusal.—**brush'wood** *n.* low scrubby bushes; a thicket or coppice; undergrowth.—**brush'y** *a.* rough, shaggy.—**to brush up,** to brighten or revive; to recall what has been partly forgotten [O.Fr. *brosse,* brushwood].

brusque (brusk, broosk') *a.* blunt; abrupt in speech.—**brusque'ness** *n.*—**brusquerie** (brôôs'kerē) *n.* a brusque expression or act [Fr.].

Brussels (brus'ẹlz) *n.*—**Brussels carpet,** a kind of carpet with a thick-looped pile.—**Brussels sprouts,** a cultivated variety of cabbage with small clustering heads like miniature cabbages [*Brussels,* in Belgium].

brute (brôôt) *a.* irrational; ferocious; brutal; —*n.* a beast; one of lower animals; a low-bred, unfeeling person.—**brut'al** *a.* savage; inhuman. —**brut'alism** *n.* brutality.—**brutal'ity** *n.* in humanity; savagery.—**brut'alise** *v.t.* to make brutal, cruel, or coarse;—*v.i.* to become brutal.—**brut'ally** *adv.*—**brut'ish** *a.* resembling a brute.—**brut'ishly** *adv.*—**brut'ishness** *n.* bestiality; grossness [L. *brutus*, dull; stupid].

bryology (brī-ol′o-ji) *n.* the science of mosses.—**bryol'ogist** *n.* [Gk. *bruon*, moss; *logos*, discourse].

bryony (brī′ō-ni) *n.* a wild climbing plant with red poisonous berries [Gk. *bruonia*].

Brythonic (brith-on′ik) *a.* term embracing the Welsh, Cornish and Breton group of Celtic languages [W. *Brython*, a Briton].

bubble (bub′l) *n.* a hollow globe of water or other liquid blown out with air or gas; a small bladder-like excrescence on surface of paint, metals, etc.; anything fragile or empty; a swindle;—*a.* deceptive; not solid; unsubstantial;—*v.i.* to rise in bubbles; to effervesce; to make a noise like bubbles; to gurgle; to boil; (*Colloq.*) to weep noisily.—**bubble and squeak,** cold potatoes, cabbage and meat fried together.—**bubb'ly** *a.* abounding in bubbles;—*n.* (*Slang*) champagne.—**bubb'ly-jock** *n.* (*Scot.*) a turkey [earlier *burble*, of imit. origin].

bubo (bū′bō) *n.* lymphatic swelling of the glands in the groin or armpit.—**bubon'ic** *a.* pert. to buboes.—**bubonic plague,** the Black Death of the 14th cent [Gk. *boubon*, the groin].

buccaneer, buccanier (buk-a-nēr′) *n.* a pirate, esp. one who infested W. Indies;—*v.i.* to play the buccaneer [Fr. *boucanier*, fr. Carib. *boucan*, a grill, used by colonists].

bucentaur (bū-sen′tawr) *n.* a fabulous monster, half bull, half man; state barge of Doge of Venice [Gk. *bous*, ox; *centaur*].

Buchmanism (bóóch′man-izm) *n.* an evangelical movement, stressing the Scriptures, which originated in America in the 1930's.—**Buch'manite** *n.* a follower of this; a member of the 'Oxford Group' [Frank *Buchman*, the founder].

buck (buk) *n.* a he-goat; the male of the rabbit, hare and the deer, esp. the fallow deer; a gay, spirited young dandy; (*U.S.*) a male Indian;—*v.i.* to attempt to unseat a rider by jumping vertically with arched back and head down; to foil all attempts at improvement.—**buck'er** *n.* a bucking horse.—**buck'-hound** *n.* dog resembling stag-hound, used for buck-hunting.—**buck'ish** *a.* gay; frivolous; lively.—**buck'-shot** *n.* large leaden shot for killing big game.—**buck'-skin** *n.* a soft leather made of deerskin or sheepskin; a twilled fabric of fine quality wool, with the nap cropped off very finely.—**buck'-tooth** *n.* a tooth which protrudes.—**buck up!** (*Colloq.*) hurry up! cheer up! [M.E. *bukke*, a he-goat].

buck (buk) *n.* lye in which cloth is bleached; linen in the first stage of bleaching;—*v.t.* to wash in suds.—**buck'-bas'ket** *n.* a basket in which clothes are carried to the washing [etym. unknown].

buck (buk) *n.* an object which marks the place where the dealer at cards sits.—**to pass the buck** (*Slang*) to evade responsibility by passing the matter on to another.

buck (buk) *n.* the body of a farm cart in U.S.—**buck'-board** *n.* a four-wheeled vehicle in which a long elastic board takes the place of steel springs.

buck (buk) *n.* (*U.S. Slang*) a dollar.

bucket (buk′et) *n.* a vessel for carrying water, etc.; a pail; holder for a whip; the piston of a reciprocating pump;—*v.t.* to ride a horse almost beyond endurance; to splash much water by hurrying the stroke in rowing.—**bucket'ful** *n.* the quantity held by a bucket.—**buck'et-seat** *n.* a small round-backed seat for one.—**buck'et-shop** *n.* the office of an outside stockbroker who engages in highly speculative transactions.—**to kick the bucket** (*Slang*) to die [O.E. *buc*, pitcher].

buckle (buk′l) *n.* a metal clasp with a rim and tongue, for fastening straps, bands, etc.; a state of unequal tension in metal plates;—*v.t.* and *v.i.* to fasten or clasp with a buckle; to twist out of shape; to bend; to put on mail-clad armour; to gird with a shield and sword.—**buck'ler** *n.* a small, round shield, with a boss, for parrying a stroke [M.E. *bokel*].

buckram (buk′ram) *n.* a coarse linen cloth stiffened with glue, used in bookbinding;—*a.* made of buckram; stiff [O.Fr. *boucaran*, goat's skin, fr. *bouc*, he-goat].

buckshee (buk′shē) *n.* an extra allowance; a windfall;—*a.* free of charge; unexpected but welcome [var. of *baksheesh*].

buckthorn (buk′thorn) *n.* a genus of plants, yielding a sap-green pigment.

buckwheat (buk′hwēt) *n.* a plant, allied to the rhubarb, yielding grain like beechnuts [O.E. *boc*, beech tree].

bucolic (bū-kol′ik) *a.* rustic; countrified;—*n.* a pastoral poem [Gk. *boukolos*, cowherd].

bud (bud) *n.* the shoot or sprout on a plant containing an unexpanded leaf, branch, or flower;—*v.i.* to put forth buds; to begin to grow;—*v.t.* to graft by budding.—**bud'ding** *n.* the act of inserting the bud of one tree under the bark of another, for propagation.—**bud'let** *n.* a little bud.—**to nip in the bud,** to destroy at the beginning [M.E. *budde*].

Buddhism (bóó′dizm) *n.* the philosophical and religious system of Gautama, named *Buddha*, 'The Enlightened' (6th cent. B.C.); the chief religion of E. Asia.—**Bud'dhist** *n.* a worshipper of Buddha [Sans. *buddha*, wise].

buddy (bud′i) *n.* a person; a bosom friend; a comrade [fr. *body*].

budge (buj) *v.t.* and *i.* to move; to stir [Fr. *bouger*, to move].

budgerigar (buj-er-e-gar′) *n.* a small parrakeet known as a 'love-bird' [Austral. *budgeree*, good; *gar*, cockatoo].

budget (buj′et) *n.* a bag with its contents; a store; the annual financial estimates of the Chancellor of the Exchequer; a plan for systematic spending [Fr. *bougette*].

buff (buf) *n.* a soft, yellow leather prepared from the skin of the buffalo, elk, and other animals; a rough strong felt; a revolving wooden disc covered with layers of leather or cloth used with an abrasive for polishing; a buff-wheel; a polishing pad or stick; a light yellow-pink colour;—*a.* made of, or coloured like, buff leather; (*Scot.*) the lights of animals;—*v.t.* to polish with a buff.—**buff'y** *a.* of a buff colour.—**The Buffs** *n.* the third regiment of the line, The East Kents, so called from the facings of their uniforms [Fr. *buffle*, buffalo].

buff (buf) *n.* a blow as in blind-man's-*buff* [O.Fr. *bouffe*, a slap].

buffalo (buf′a-lō) *n.* a ruminating horned animal, resembling an ox, but larger and more powerful; name given in America to the bison [Port. *bufalo*].

buffer (buf′er) *n.* a resilient cushion or apparatus to deaden the concussion between a moving body and one on which it strikes, as railway carriages.—**buffer-state,** a country lying between two powerful and rival nations [fr. *buff*].

buffer (buf′er) *n.* a silly or stupid fellow; a familiar term of address [O.Fr. *buffer*, to puff out the cheeks].

buffet (buf′et, buf′ā, bóóf-ā′) *n.* a cupboard for displaying fine china, plate, etc.; a refreshment bar; a low three-legged stool.—**buffet'-car** *n.* a railway dining-car in which snacks are served [Fr.].

buffet (buf′et) *n.* a blow with the fist; a slap; a cuff on the ears;—*v.t.* to strike with the fist; to contend against.—**buff'ets** *n.pl.* hardships [O.Fr. *buffet*, a slap].

buffoon (bu-fóón′) *n.* a person who acts the clown by his clumsy attempts at humour; a fool.—**buffoon'ery** *n.* the silly, vulgar, antics or practical jokes of a buffoon.—**buffoon'ish** *a.* [Fr. *bouffon*].

bug (bug) *n.* a parasitic insect, of which there

are thousands of species, that feeds on the juice of plants or blood of animals, best known of the latter being the **bed'-bug** [corrupt. of O.E. *budda*, beetle].

bug (bug) *n.* an object of terror.—**bug'aboo** *n.* a terrifying object; an imaginary fear.—**bug'bear** *n.* anything which frightens or annoys.—**bug'gy** *a.* crazy.—**a big bug** (*Slang*) someone of importance [M.E. *bugge*].

buggy (bug'i) *n.* a word applied to various types of carriages [etym. unknown].

bugle (bū'gl) *n.* a wind instrument, bell-mouthed, of copper with brass mouthpiece, used because of its penetrating note for conveying orders by certain calls;—*v.i.* to sound a call.—**bu'gler** *n.* [for *bugle-horn* fr. L. *buculus*, dim. of *bos*, ox].

bugle (bū'gl) *n.* a creeping plant belonging to the order Labiates [L. *bugillo*]

bugloss (bū'glos) *n.* the popular name for many common English plants which have rough, bristly leaves resembling an ox tongue [Gk. *bous*, ox; *glossa*, tongue].

buhl, boule (bŏŏl) *n.* term applied to furniture and ornamental pieces consisting of an inlay of tortoise-shell, enamel, rosewood and brass strips [André *Boule* (1642-1732), who invented the process].

build (bild) *v.t.* to erect a structure; to construct a public work, as a railway, etc.; to fabricate; to establish (a reputation, etc.); to raise (hopes);—*v.i.* to exercise the art or work of building; to depend (with *on, upon*);—*pa.t.* and *pa.p.* **built**;—*n.* form; construction; physique; style of construction.—**build'er** *n.* one who supervises the erection of a building.—**build'ing** *n.* the act of constructing; any substantial structure; an edifice.—**built'-in** *a.* applied to furniture and fittings, usually movable, but which are an integral part of the building.—**built up area**, a piece of land which is taken up by roads and buildings [O.E. *byldan*].

bulb (bulb) *n.* a modified leaf-bud emitting roots from its base and formed of fleshy leaf scales containing a reserve supply of food; any globular form, shaped like a bulb; a dilated glass tube containing filament for electric lighting;—*v.i.* to form bulbs; to bulge.—**bulba'ceous, bul'bar, bulbed, bul'bose, bul'by** *a.* pert. to bulbs.—**bulb'iform** *a.* shaped like a bulb.—**bulbos'ity** *n.* the state of being bulbous.—**bul'bous** *a.* having the appearance of a bulb; growing from bulbs [L. *bulbus*].

bulbul (bŏŏl'bŏŏl) *n.* the Persian nightingale [Pers.].

bulge (bulj) *n.* anything rounded which juts out; the part of a cask which swells out; an outer protective hull, below the water-line;—*v.i.* to swell out.—**bul'gy** *a.* swollen out [O.Fr. *boulge*].

bulk (bulk) *n.* size; the main body; the majority; the largest portion; the cargo stowed in a ship's hold;—*v.t.* to pile up;—*v.i.* to be of some importance.—**bulk'age** *n.* roughage.—**bulk'iness** *n.*—**bulk'y** *a.* voluminous and clumsy in shape, so difficult to handle.—**to break bulk**, to begin to unload a cargo [O.N. *bulki*, heap, cargo].

bulkhead (bulk'hed) *n.* a partition in a ship made with boards, etc., to form separate compartments.

bull (bŏŏl) *n.* the male of any bovine, esp. the ox; the male of numerous animals as elephant, whale, seal, moose, elk, deer; a sign of the zodiac, the constellation Taurus; a speculator who buys stocks or shares to make a profit by selling at a higher rate before time of settlement arrives; score gained by hitting a target in the centre ring;—*v.t.* to attempt to bring about a rise in the price of stocks and shares;—*a.* to denote a male animal.—**bull'-bait'ing** *n.* an ancient sport of setting ferocious dogs on to attack a bull tied to a stake.—**bull'-calf** *n.* male calf; a stupid person; a booby.—**bull'dog** *n.* a breed of dog formerly used for bull-baiting; a person who displays obstinate courage; a proctor's attendant at Oxford and Cambridge who secures offenders against university regulations; a short revolver.—**bull'dozer** *n.* a machine which forces metal work into dies by means of a ram; a tractor, with an attached horizontal blade in front for moving, levelling, or spreading earth, etc.—**bull'-fight** *n.* the national sport of certain Latin races, esp. in Spain and consisting of a combat between men and specially bred bulls.—**bull'-finch** *n.* a common bird in England, of the thrush family but with a thicker head and neck.—**bull'-frog** *n.* a large, dusky-brown, N. American frog.—**bull'-head'ed** *a.* acting in a reckless manner; taking unnecessary risks.—**bull'-head'edness** *n.*—**bull'ish** *a.*—**bull'-mas'tiff** *n.* a large size, fawn-coated dog of English breed, developed by crossing the bulldog and the mastiff.—**bull'ock** *n.* an ox or castrated bull.—**bull'-ring** *n.* the arena in which a bull-fight is held; the ring to which straining wires of overhead electric tramway wires are attached.—**bull's'-eye,** *n.* a small circular or elliptical window; the boss or lump of glass in the centre of a plate of glass; a ball-shaped sweet with coloured stripes.—**bull'-ter'rier** *n.* a cross between bulldog and terrier.—**bull'-trout** *n.* a fish allied to salmon, also known as *gray trout*.—**to take the bull by the horns,** to face a difficulty resolutely [M.E. *bole*].

bull (bŏŏl) *n.* the seal appended to the edicts of the pope; papal edict.—**bull'ary** *n.* a collection of papal bulls [L. *bulla*, a bubble, a seal].

bull (bŏŏl) *n.* a ludicrous contradiction in speech, associated with Irishmen [etym. uncertain].

bull (bŏŏl) *n.* (*Mil. Slang*) any activity which is, or appears, unnecessary, e.g. too much 'spit and polish,' ceremonial drill, etc.

bullet (bool'et) *n.* a small projectile consisting of a lead core enclosed in a pointed case of harder metal, discharged from a gun, rifle or revolver.—**-head'ed** *a.* round-headed; stubborn.—**-proof** *a.* not able to be pierced by bullets [L. *bulla*, a bubble, a knob].

bulletin (bool'e-tin) *n.* a daily report; an official medical report; a brief statement of facts issued by authority [Fr.].

bullion (bool'yun) *n.* uncoined, refined gold or silver, generally in ingots; the precious metals, including coined metal, when exported or imported [etym. uncertain].

bully (bool'i) *n.* a noisy, over-bearing person who tyrannises over the weak; a man who lives on the immoral earnings of a woman; a hired ruffian;—*v.t.* to domineer; intimidate; overawe; ill-treat;—*v.i.* to bluster;—*interj.* (*Slang*) fine! well-done!—**bull'yrag** *v.t.* to act as a bully towards someone;—*v.i.* to be continually noisy and quarrelsome.

bully (bool'i) *n.* canned or corned meat. Also **bull'y-beef** [Fr. *bouilli*, boiled].

bully (bool'i) *v.t.* (*Hockey*) to start the game (or restart it after each goal and half-time) by *bullying* the ball in the centre of the ground;—*n.* the start (or restart) of play.

bulrush (bŏŏl'rush) *n.* name applied to several species of marsh plants [O.E. *bulrysche*].

bulwark (bool'wark) *n.* an outwork for defence; sea defence wall;—*pl.* a railing round the deck of a ship; any defence of a ship.—*v.t.* to fortify with a rampart; to protect [Ger. *Bollwerk*].

bum (bum) *n.* the buttocks; (*Colloq.*) a bum-bailiff.—**bum'-boat** *n.* a small boat which plies between vessels and the shore, carrying provisions, stores, etc. [M.E. not a contr. fr. *bottom*].

bum (bum) *n.* in N. America, a person who idles about hotels; a loafer;—*v.i.* to loaf, cadge [Ger. *bummeln*, to loaf].

bum (bum) *v.i.* to hum like a bee; (*Colloq.*) to

brag.—**bum'blebee** *n.* the humble-bee [E. *bumble*=keep bumming] [See **boom**].
bumbailiff (bum-bā́-lif) *n.* an under-bailiff [perhaps for *bound-bailiff*].
bumble-bee. See **bum.**
bumbledom (buḿ-bl-dom) *n.* fussy, petty officialdom [fr. *Bumble* in *Oliver Twist*].
bummaree (buḿ-ar-ē) *n.* salesman in fish-market; (*Slang*) money-lender [cf. *bottomry*].
bump (bump) *n.* a dull, heavy blow; a thump; a swelling resulting from a bump or blow; one of the protuberances on the skull, said by phrenologists to give an indication of mental qualities, character, etc.;—*v.t.* to strike against;—*v.i.* to rise abruptly (of a cricket ball).—**bump off** *v.t.* (*Colloq.*) to murder; get rid of.—**bump'y** *a.* covered with bumps [imit.].
bumper (buḿ-per) *n.* a cup or glass filled to the brim, esp. when toasting a guest; anything large and satisfying; in motoring, a bar, usually spring steel, carried in front and rear of car to minimise danger of damaging mudguards, etc., in minor collisions; in U.S., a buffer;—*a.* very large; excellent, as 'a bumper crop' [fr. *bump*].
bumpkin (bumṕ-kin) *n.* an awkward, stupid person; a country lout; yokel; clodpole [E=*bumkin*, a thick log, fr. Dut.].
bumptious (bumṕ-shus) *a.* rudely self-assertive; quarrelsome; self-important.—**bump'tiousness** *n.* [fr. *bump*].
bun (bun) *n.* a kind of small cake, light in texture and well sweetened; hair twisted into a knot at the back of a woman's head [O.Fr. *bugne*].
bun (bun) *n.* a rabbit; a squirrel; a flat-bottomed boat, square at each end [Amer.].
buna (bū́n-a) *n.* synthetic rubber.
bunch (bunsh) *n.* a cluster of similar things, tied or growing together; a tuft or knot; a bouquet of flowers; (*U.S. Slang*) a group, gang, or party;—*v.t.* to tie up or gather together; to crowd;—*v.i.* to swell out like a bunch.—**bunched** *a.* crowded together.—**bunch'y** *a.* growing in bunches [Dan. *bunke*, a heap].
buncombe See **bunkum.**
Bund *n.* (bŏŏnd) a confederation, league, or confederacy, esp. that of the German States [Ger.].
bundle (buń-dl) *n.* a number of things bound together; a package; a definite number of things;—*v.t.* to make up into a bundle or roll;—*v.i.* to hurry off.—**bun'dling** *n.* an old pre-nuptial custom of putting betrothed couples in bed, fully dressed, before marriage [O.E. *byndel*].
bung (bung) *n.* the stopper for an opening in a cask; a large cork; a pick-pocket; (*Slang*) a publican;—*v.t.* to close or stop up with a bung [origin uncertain].
bungalow (bunǵ-ga-lō) *n.* the house of a European in India, of a single floor; small detached modern, one-storied house [Hind. *bangla*, fr. *Banga*, Bengalese].
bungle (bunǵ-gl) *v.t.* to make or mend clumsily; to manage clumsily; to botch;—*v.i.* to act awkwardly;—*n.* a blundering performance.—**bung'ler** *n.*—**bung'ling** *a.* [etym. uncertain].
bunion (buń-yun) *n.* an inflamed swelling occurring on the foot, esp. on the large toe joint [etym. uncertain].
bunk (bungk) *n.* a box-like structure used as a seat by day and a bed at night; a sleeping-berth on board ship, in a camp, etc.;—*v.i.* to lodge or sleep with a person in a small, confined space containing bunks.—**to do or make a bunk** (*Slang*) to vanish rapidly from sight [Scand.].
bunk (bungk) *n.* (*Colloq.*) humbug; nonsense; rubbish [fr. *bunkum*].
bunker (bunǵ-ker) *n.* a large hopper or bin for holding coal, etc.; storage room on board hips for coal or oil fuel; a sand-pit placed as an obstacle on a golf course;—*v.t.* to load up a ship with coal; to confound or perplex [Scand.].
bunkum, buncombe (bunǵ-kum) *n.* nonsense; claptrap; bombastic oratory [fr. *Buncombe*, county in N. Carolina, U.S.A., the member for which in Congress insisted on 'making a speech for Buncombe,' i.e. for effect on his constituents].
bunny (buń-i) *n.* a pet name for a rabbit.—**bunn'yhug** *n.* a kind of jazz dance [etym. unknown].
Bunsen burner (bŏŏń-sen, buń-sen buŕ-ner) *n.* a gas burner in which a strong current of air produces a weakly luminous, but very hot, flame [fr. the inventor, Prof. *Bunsen*, the German chemist].
bunt (bunt) *n.* the middle or furled part of a sail.—**bunt'line** *n.* a rope fastened to the bottom of a sail, used to haul it up [Scand.].
bunt (bunt) *n.* a parasitic fungus or smut, destructive to wheat and other cereals [etym. unknown].
bunter (buń-ter) *n.* a female rag-picker; a low, vulgar woman [See **bunt**].
bunting (buń-ting) *n.* a group of birds of the finch family, including the corn-, yellow-, reed-, and snow-buntings; coarse woollen fabric of which flags are made; flags in general [etym. unknown].
buoy (boi) *n.* any floating body of wood or iron employed to point out the particular situation of a ship's anchor, a shoal, a navigable channel, etc.; a life-buoy;—*v.t.* to fix buoys.—**to buoy up,** to keep afloat; to sustain (hopes, etc.).—**buoy'age** *n.* a series of buoys in position; the providing of buoys.—**buoy'ancy** *n.* capacity for floating in water or air; cheerfulness.—**buoy'ant** *a.* floating lightly; lighthearted; hopeful; of stocks and shares, tending to increase in price.—**buoy'antly** *adv.* [Dut. *boei*].
bur See **burr.**
burble (buŕ-bl) *v.i.* to bubble up; to froth up; to gurgle, as of running water; (*Colloq.*) to talk idly.—**burb'ling** *n.* [imit.].
burbot (buŕ-bot) *n.* large fresh-water fish, resembling cod [L. *barba*, beard].
burden (buŕ-dn) *n.* that which is borne or carried; anything difficult to bear, as care, sorrow, etc.; capacity of a vessel stated in tons; (*Scots Law*) an encumbrance or restriction on property;—*v.t.* to load; to oppress; to encumber. Also **burth'en.**—**bur'denous, bur'densome, burth'ensome** *a.* heavy, onerous; felt as a burden.—**bur'densomeness** *n.* [O.E. *byrthen*]
burden (buŕ-dn) *n.* the refrain of a song; a chorus; the main theme; the drone of a bagpipe [Fr. *bourdon*, deep murmur].
burdock (buŕ-dok) *n.* a roadside plant, of the Compositae order, with hooked leaves which cling to animals [Dan. *borre*, a bur].
bureau (bū-rō', bū́-rō) *n.* a writing-desk; a small chest of drawers; a display-cabinet; an office, esp. for public business; a government department in U.S.;—*pl.* **bureaux** (būŕ-ō), **bureaus** (būŕ-ōz) [Fr.].
bureaucracy (bū-rọ́-kra-si) *n.* a highly centralised form of administration in which officials control every detail of public and private life, subject only to their superior officers; identified with officialism and 'red tape.'—**bu'reaucrat** *n.* one who advocates or takes part in such a system of government.—**bureaucrat'ic** *a.* [Fr. *bureau*; Gk. *kratein*, to govern].
burette (bū-ret') *n.* a graduated glass tube provided with a stop-cock at the lower end, used for delivering accurately measured quantities of liquid [Fr.].
burg (burg') *n.* (*U.S.*) a town or village; a common ending of the names of continental cities; a borough.—**burgess** (buŕ-jes) *n.* an inhabitant, citizen, or freeman of a borough.—**burg'omas'ter** *n.* chief magistrate of a town in Holland or Germany [O.E. *burh*].

burgee (bur-jē') *n.* a pennant of a yacht club, ending in two points; small coal for furnaces [etym. unknown].
burgeon See **bourgeon.**
burgess See under **burg.**
burgh (bur'ạ) *n.* a Scots word corresponding to 'borough'; a town with certain privileges resting upon charter, prescription or legislative enactment. — **bur'ghal** *a.* — **burgher** (bur'ger) *n.* a citizen or freeman [O.E. *burh*].
burglar (burg'lar) *n.* one who is guilty of house-breaking by night.—**burg'lary** *n.* breaking and entering into a dwelling-house between 9 p.m. and 6 a.m. with intent to commit a felony.—**burglar'ious** *a.*—**bur'gle** *v.t.* [etym. doubtful].
burgomaster See under **burg.**
Burgundy (bur'gun-di) *n.* name given to various wines, red or white, produced in *Burgundy*, a district in France.
burial (ber'i-ạl) *n.* the act of burying; interment; sepulture; funeral; entombment. —**bur'ial-mound** *n.* a barrow [O.E. *byrgels*, tomb]. [See **bury**].
burin (būr'in) *n.* a tool of tempered steel used for engraving on copper or steel.—**bur'inist** *n.* an engraver [Fr.].
burke (burk) *v.t.* to murder, esp. by smothering; to put an end to quietly.—**to burke the issue,** to avoid the implications [fr. notorious criminal, William *Burke*, *c.* 1828, who provided thus bodies for anatomists].
burlap (bur'lap) *n.* gunny sacking; a coarsely woven canvas of flax, hemp, or jute, used for packing and as a wall covering, etc. [etym. unknown].
burlesque (bur-lesk') *n.* distorting, exaggerating, and ridiculing a work of art; travesty; parody;—*a.* comical; ludicrous; jocular;—*v.t.* to turn into burlesque [It. *burlesco*].
burly (bur'li) *a.* of stout build; big and sturdy; boisterous; lusty.—**bur'liness** *n.* [M.E. *borlich*, massive].
Burmese (bur'mēz) *n.* a native of Burma; the language;—*a.* pert. to Burma.
burn (burn) *n.* a small stream; a brook; a rivulet [O.E. *burna*, brook].
burn (burn) *v.t.* to consume with fire; to subject to the action of fire; to char; to scorch;—*v.i.* to be on fire; to flame; flare; blaze; glow; be excited or inflamed with passion;—*pa.t.* and *pa.p.* **burned** or **burnt**;—*n.* injury or damage caused by heat; a lesion of the skin caused by burning.—**burn'er** *n.* part of a lamp or gas jet from which the flame issues.—**burn'ing** *n.* act of consuming by fire; inflammation;—*a.* flaming; scorching; parching; ardent; excessive.—**burn'ing-glass** *n.* a convex lens which causes intense heat by bending the rays of the sun and concentrating them upon a single point.—**burn'ing-house** *n.* a miner's kiln.—**burning question,** a topic of universal discussion.—**burnt'-ear** *n.* a fungus disease destructive to corn.—**burnt'-off'ering** *n.* a sacrifice of a living person or animal by burning.—**burnt sienna,** a fine, reddish-brown pigment from calcined Sienna earth.—**burnt umber,** a brown pigment obtained from calcined umber.—**to burn one's boats,** to act so that there can be no question of retreat [O.E. *baernan*].
burnish (bur'nish) *v.t.* to polish by continual rubbing;—*n.* polish; gloss; lustre [O.Fr. *burnisant*, polishing].
burnous (bur-nóōs') *n.* a hooded cloak worn by Arabs. Also **burnoose'** [Ar.].
burnt *pa.t.* and *pa.p.* of **burn.**
burr (bur) *n.* the rough, sticky seed-case of certain plants with hooked spines to help in its distribution; a rough edge left on metal by a cutting tool [Dan. *borre*].
burr (bur) *n.* the trilled guttural sound of *r*, as heard in Northumberland and Scotland; —*v.t.* and *i.* to roll the 'r' sound [imit.].
burro (bur'ō) *n.* in U.S., a donkey [Sp.].
burrow (bur'ō) *n.* a hole dug in the ground by certain small animals to serve as an abode or for concealment;—*v.i.* to tunnel through earth; to search assiduously; to live in a burrow [var. of *borough*].
bursar (bur'sạr) *n.* one who holds the purse; a treasurer of a college; a registrar; in Scotland, the holder of a scholarship at school or university.—**bur'sary** *n.* a scholarship gained in open competition or by presentation.—**bursic'ulate, burs'iform** *a.* purse-shaped; pouch-shaped [L.L. *bursa*, Fr. *bourse*, a purse].
burst (burst) *v.t.* to fly asunder; to break into pieces; to break open violently; to break suddenly into some expression of feeling; to split;—*v.i.* to shatter; to break violently;—*pa.t.* and *pa.p.* **burst**;—*n.* a bursting; an explosion; an outbreak; spurt; (*Slang*) a drunken spree [O.E. *berstan*].
burthen (burth'n) *n.* and *a.* obs. *burden.*
burton (bur'tun) *n.* a light tackle formed by two or three blocks or pulleys.—(*Air Force Slang*) gone for a **burton,** missing in action, dead [origin unknown].
bury (ber'i) *v.t.* to inter in a grave; to put underground; to hide or conceal by covering; —*pa.p.* **bur'ied.**—**bur'ying** *n.* burial; interment.—**to bury the hatchet,** to cease from strife; to restore friendly relations [O.E. *byrigan*].
bus, 'bus (bus) *n.* a popular contraction for *omnibus*; a vehicle for public conveyance of passengers on the roads; (*Slang*) a motor car or aeroplane;—*pl.* **bus'es.**—**a busman's holiday,** one spent in a similar environment to one's regular vocation [L. *omnibus*, for all and sundry].
busby (buz'bi) *n.* a bearskin cap, part of the dress uniform of the hussars and horse artillery of the British Army [Hung.].
bush (boosh) *n.* a shrub; a low woody plant with numerous branches near ground-level; a thicket of small trees and shrubs; the interior of a country; the backwoods;—*v.i.* to grow thick or bushy;—*v.t.* to plant bushes about.—**bush'craft** *n.* skilled knowledge of conditions of life in the bush.—**bush'-fight'ing** *n.* guerilla warfare where advantage is taken of trees and bushes.—**bush'iness** *n.* the quality of being bushy.—**bush'man** *n.* a member of an aboriginal, negroid race of S.W. Africa; a settler in the backwoods or bush country of the colonies; a woodsman.—**bush'-rang'er** *n.* in Australia, a desperado, usually an escaped convict who lived the life of a highwayman on the edge of the gold-fields.—**bush'y** *a.* full of bushes; thick and spreading.—**to beat about the bush,** to approach a matter in a roundabout way; unwilling to come to the point [M.E. *busch*].
bush (boosh) *n.* the internal lining of a bearing, to form a plain bearing surface for a pin or shaft [Dut. *bus*, a box].
bushel (boosh'el) *n.* a dry measure of 8 gallons, for corn, fruit, etc.—**to hide one's light under a bushel,** to be unduly modest [O.Fr. *boissel*, a little box].
business (biz'nes) *n.* employment; profession; vocation; any occupation for a livelihood; trade; firm; concern; action on the stage, apart from dialogue.—**bus'iness-like** *a.* practical; systematic; methodical [fr. *busy*].
busk (busk) *v.t.* and *i.* to make ready; to dress or attire [O.N. *buask*].
busk (busk) *v.i.* to hurry; to hasten; to cruise along a shore; to seek.—**busk'er** *n.* entertainer who depends on voluntary contributions from audiences; itinerant musician [Sp. *buscar*, to seek].
buskin (busk'in) *n.* a kind of half-boot, part of the costume of actors in tragic drama on the ancient Greek stage; a synonym for 'tragedy.'—**busk'ined** *a.* dressed in buskins; tragic [etym. uncertain].
buss (bus) *n.* a hearty kiss;—*v.t.* to kiss, esp. boisterously [Fr. *baiser*, to kiss].
bust (bust) *n.* sculptured representation of

a person from the waist upwards; the upper part of the human body; a woman's bosom.—**bust'ed** *a.* breasted [Fr. *buste*].

bust (bust) *v.i.* and *v.t.* (*Slang*) to burst; to break;—*n.* a drinking bout.

bustard (bus'tard) *n.* one of a group of very large birds, somewhat similar to the ostrich, but powerful in flight [O.Fr. fr. L. *avis tarda*, slow bird].

bustle (bus'l) *v.i.* to busy oneself with much stir and movement; to be ostentatiously active;—*n.* great stir and hurried activity.—**bust'ler** *n.* [O.E. *bysig*, busy].

bustle (bus'l) *n.* a stuffed pad worn by ladies to support and elevate the back of the skirt just below the waist [Fr. *buste*].

busy (biz'i) *a.* having plenty to do; active and earnest in work; diligent; industrious; officious; meddling;—*n.* (*Slang*) a detective;—*v.t.* to make or keep busy; to occupy (oneself);—*pr.p.* **bus'ying**; *pa.p.* **bus'ied**.—**bus'ily** *adv.*—**bus'ybod'y** *n.* a person who meddles in other people's business.—**bus'yness** *n.* state of being busy [O.E. *bysig*].

but (but) *conj.* yet; unless; that not; nevertheless; notwithstanding;—*prep.* except; without;—*adv.* only.—**all but**, nearly; almost [O.E. *butan*, outside].

but (but) *a.* (*Scot.*) outside.—**but and ben**, a two-roomed cottage, with outer and inner room [O.E. *butan*, outside].

butane (bū'tān) *n.* a paraffin hydrocarbon forming the principal constituent of liquid cymogene used in freezing machines [L. *butyrum*, butter].

butcher (booch'er) *n.* one who slaughters animals for food or retails the flesh; one who recklessly destroys human life;—*v.t.* to slaughter animals for food; to murder in cold blood; to spoil work.—**butch'er-bird** *n.* a shrike.—**butch'ering, butch'ing** *n.* killing for food or lust of blood.—**butcher meat, butcher's meat**, flesh of domestic animals exposed for sale.—**butch'ery** *n.* wanton slaughter [O.Fr. *bochier*, one who kills goats].

butler (but'ler) *n.* a male servant who has charge of the liquors, plate, etc. and who exercises general supervision over the members of the house-staff.—**but'lery** *n.* a butler's pantry [O.Fr. *bouteillier*, a bottler].

butment See **abutment**.

butt (but) *n.* the lower end of a tree-trunk providing the strongest timber; a hinge with square edges intended to be sunk into the edge of a door or casement; one continually subject to ridicule;—*v.t.* to strike by thrusting the head downwards.—**butts** *n.pl.* a mound with targets where shooting is practised.—**butt'-end** *n.* the thick or large end, as of a rifle.—**butt'er** *n.* an animal, e.g. the goat, which butts.—**to butt in** (*Colloq.*) to intervene without permission [Fr. *but*, end].

butt (but) *n.* a large cask [Fr. *botte*].

butter (but'er) *n.* the fatty ingredients of milk, emulsified by churning; gross flattery;—*v.t.* to spread with butter; to flatter; to fail to accept a catch at cricket.—**butt'er-bean** *n.* a large, dried haricot bean.—**butt'ercup** *n.* plant of Ranunculus family with cup-shaped, glossy, yellow flowers.—**butt'er-fin'gers** *n.* (*Colloq*) one who has failed to hold a catch at cricket.—**butt'er-milk** *n.* the fluid residue after butter has been churned from cream.—**butt'er-mus'lin** *n.* thin, loosely woven cotton fabric used for backing maps, etc.—**butt'er-scotch** *n.* a kind of toffee with butter as an ingredient.—**butt'ery** *a.* like butter [O.E. *butere*].

butterfly (but'er-flī) *n.* the common name of all diurnal, lepidopterous insects; a gay, flighty woman [O.E. *buter-flege*].

buttery (but'er-i) *n.* a pantry for the storage of food and wine.—**butt'ery-bar** *n.* a ledge for holding tankards [O.Fr. *boterie*, a place for keeping casks or butts].

buttock (but'ok) *n.* the rump; rounded prominence at the lower posterior part of the body; hip; haunch (usually in *pl.*) [prob. dim. of *butt*. thick end].

button (but'n) *n.* a knob or stud for fastening clothing; a bud; the safety knob at the end of a fencing foil; a small round protuberance, e.g. that of an electric bell; the winding knob of a keyless-watch;—*v.t.* to fasten with buttons;—*v.i.* to be fastened by a button.—**butt'ons** *n.pl.* a jocular term for a page-boy.—**butt'on-hole** *n.* the hole or loop in which a button is fastened; a flower or spray worn in a button-hole;—*v.t.* to detain a person in talk against his will.—**butt'on-hook** *n.* a hook for pulling a button through a button-hole.—**butt'on-stick** *n.* a strip of brass with a slit used for polishing metal buttons.—**butt'on-weed** *n.* the knapweed [Fr. *bouton*, bud].

buttress [but'res) *n.* a projecting support to a wall; any prop or support;—*v.t.* to support [O.Fr. *bouterez*, supports, fr. *bouter*, to thrust].

butyl (bū'til) *n.* an alcohol radical; a highly elastic synthetic rubber, made from butane, a natural gas [L. *butyrum*, butter].

butyraceous (bu-ti-rā'shus) *a.* buttery; having the consistency of butter [L. *butyrum*, butter].

buxom (buks'um) *a.* full of health; lively; cheery; plump; gay; comely; winsome.—**bux'omness** *n.* [O.E. *bugan*, to bend].

buy (bī) *v.t.* to obtain by payment; to purchase; to pay a price for; to bribe;—*pa.t.* and *pa.p.* **bought**.—**buy'er** *n.* a purchaser; one who buys [O.E. *bycgan*].

buzz (buz) *v.i.* to make a humming or hissing sound;—*v.t.* to spread news abroad secretly; to tap out signals by means of a buzzer.—**buzz'er** *n.* one who buzzes; an apparatus used for telephonic signalling by Morse; an apparatus for testing wireless receiving sets.—**buzz'ingly** *adv.*—**buzz-bomb** (buz'bom) *n.* a jet-propelled bomb used by the Nazis in their bombardment of England in World War 2.—**buzz off!** (*Slang*) get away! [imit. word].

buzzard (buz'ard) *n.* a genus of birds of the hawk family; a dunce or blockhead [O.Fr. *busard*].

by (bī) *prep.* near; beside; in the neighbourhood of; past; through the agency of; according to;—*adv.* near; in the neighbourhood; close; out of the way; beyond.—**by and by**, soon; in the near future.—**by'-blow** *n.* an illegitimate child.—**by'-elec'tion** *n.* a parliamentary election at any time but a general election.—**by'name** *n.* a nick-name.—**by'-pass** *n.* a road for the diversion of traffic from crowded centres;—*v.t.* to avoid a place by going round it.—**by'-path** *n.* a side path.—**by'-play** *n.* action carried on apart from the main part of a play; diversion.—**by'-pro'duct** *n.* secondary product obtained during manufacture of principal commodity.—**by'-road** *n.* a less frequented side road.—**by'stander** *n.* an onlooker.—**by'-street** *n.* a less important street.—**by'way** *n.* a secluded path or road.—**by'word** *n.* a common saying; a proverb; a name which has become notorious.—**by the by, by the bye, by the way**, phrases used for introducing a new topic of conversation [O.E. *bi*].

bye (bī) *n.* anything subordinate; a walk-over in a round of a competition due to an odd number of competitors; the holes still remaining to be played at golf after the game has been won; a run made at cricket without ball having been hit by batsman; a goal in lacrosse.—**bye-bye** (*Colloq.*) good-bye; bed; sleep [var. of *by*].

bylaw, bye-law (bī'law) *n.* a local law made by a subordinate authority [M.E. *bilaw*, fr. *bi*, a borough].

byre (bīr) *n.* a cow-house or -shed [O.E.].

Byzantine (biz-an'tīn, biz') *a.* relating to *Byzantium*, the original name for Constantinople; pert. to Asiatic architecture with Grecian characteristics;—*n.* a dweller in Byzantium; a bezant.

C

cab (kab) *n.* a light carriage drawn by one horse; a public carriage; the covered part of a locomotive; driver's accommodation on a motor-lorry or 'bus.—**cab'man** *n.* the driver of a cab.—**cab'-rank** *n.* an official stance for taxis.—**cabb'y** *n.* (*Colloq.*) a cabman [short for Fr. *cabriolet*, a light carriage].
cabal (ka-bal') *n.* a secret intriguing faction in a state [Heb. *gabbalah*, mystical interpretation].
caballero (ka-bål-yā'rō) *n.* a Spanish gentleman [Sp.].
cabaret (ka'ba-rā, -ret) *n.* restaurant providing entertainment; the entertainment itself [Fr. *cabaret*, a tavern].
cabbage (kab'āj) *n.* a garden vegetable of Brassica family.—**cabbage-butterfly**, a large white butterfly whose larvae are injurious to cabbage [L. *caput*, the head].
cabbala, cabala (kab'a-la) *n.* a secret science by which the Rabbis interpreted the mystic sense of the Hebrew scriptures.—**cabb'alism, cab'alism** *n.*—**cabb'alist, cab'alist** *n.*—**cabbalis'tic(al), cabalis'tic(al)** *a.* pert. to Jewish cabbala; mysterious [Heb. *gabbalah*, mystical interpretation].
caber (kā'ber) *n.* a stout pole or stem of a tree, used in the Highland game of 'tossing the caber' [Gael. *cabar*, a pole].
cabin (kab'in) *n.* a small room; a hut; an apartment in a ship;—*v.t.* to confine in a cabin;—*v.i.* to live in a cabin; to lodge.—**cabin boy**, a boy who waits on the officers of a ship [Fr. *cabine*, a cabin; *cabane*, a hut].
cabinet (kab'i-net) *n.* a small room; a closet; a council of ministers; a chest, box, or case.—**the Cabinet**, in Gt. Britain, the centre of executive power, the Prime Minister and his Ministers.—**cab'inet-mak'er** *n.* a maker of cabinets and other furniture [Fr. *cabinet*, fr. *cabine*].
cable (kā'bl) *n.* a large, strong rope or chain, to retain a vessel at anchor, etc.; a submarine telegraph line; a message sent by such line;—*v.t.* to fasten with a cable; to send a message by cable.—**ca'blegram** *n.* a telegram sent by cable; a cable.—**cable's length**, a measure equal to 100 fathoms (a fathom=6 feet) [fr. L.L. *capulum*, a halter].
caboodle (ka-bŏŏ'dl) *n.* (*Slang*) collection; lot; **the whole caboodle**, the whole lot.
caboose (ka-bŏŏs') *n.* the kitchen of a ship; in N. America, a car attached to a freight train for conductor [Dut. *kombuis*].
cabriolet (kab-ri-ō-lā') *n.* a light one-horse carriage with a hood; a cab; a type of motor car body with a folding hood [Fr. fr. L. *caper*, a goat].
cacao (ka-kā'ō) *n.* a tropical tree from the seeds of which cocoa and chocolate are prepared [Mex.].
cachalot (kash'a-lot) *n.* the sperm-whale, the largest of the toothed whales [Fr.].
cache (kash) *n.* orig. a hole in the ground for storing or hiding provisions, etc.; any hiding-place [Fr. *cacher*, to hide].
cachet (ka'shā) *n.* a seal, as on a letter; distinctive mark or character.—**lettre de cachet** (i.e. sealed letter) a warrant ordering the imprisonment of an individual without trial, issued by former kings of France [Fr. *cacher*, to hide].
cachinnation (kak-i-nā'shun) *n.* loud, immoderate, or hysterical laughter.—**cach'innate** *v.i.* to laugh thus.—**cachinn'atory** *a.* [L. *cachinnare*, to laugh loudly].
cachou (ka-shŏŏ') *n.* an aromatic preparation in the form of a tablet or pellet, used to perfume the breath [Fr.].
cackle (kak'l) *v.i.* to make a noise like a hen or goose; to gossip noisily;—*n.* the noise of a hen; prattle; silly talk [imit.].
caco- (kak'ō) a combining form fr. Gk. *kakos*, bad, used in derivatives.
cacogastric (kak-ō-gas'trik) *a.* having bad digestion; dyspeptic [Gk. *kakos*, bad; *gastēr*, the stomach].
cacography (ka-kog'ra-fi) *n.* bad writing or spelling [Gk. *kakos*, bad; *graphia*, writing].
cacophony (ka-kof'ō-ni) *n.* a harsh or disagreeable sound; a discord; a use of ill-sounding words.—**cacoph'onous** *a.* [Gk. *kakos*, bad; *phōnē*, sound].
cactus (kak'tus) *n.* a plant of S. America and Mexico; thick, fleshy, prickly stems, and generally no leaves.—*pl.* **cac'tuses**, or **cac'ti.**—**cacta'ceous, cac'tal** *a.* allied to the cactus [Gk. *kaktos*, a cardoon].
cad (kad) *n.* a low, mean, vulgar fellow; a townsman (at Oxford).—**cadd'ish** *a.* ill-bred, mean [short for Fr. *cadet*, junior].
cadastre (ka-das'tre) *n.* a register of lands for purposes of taxation.—**cadas'tral** *a.* [Fr.].
cadaver (ka-dá'ver) *n.* (*Med.*) a corpse.—**cada'verous** *a.* corpse-like; gaunt; sickly-looking [L. *cadaver*, a dead body].
caddie, caddy (kad'i) *n.* an attendant who carries a golfer's clubs;—*v.i.* to carry clubs [fr. Fr. *cadet*].
caddis, caddice (kad'is) *n.* worm-like aquatic larva of caddis-fly [etym. unknown].
caddy (kad'i) *n.* a small box for holding tea [Malay, *kati*, a weight, 1⅓ lbs. (for tea)].
cade (kād) *a.* tame [etym. unknown].
cadence (kā'dens) *n.* a fall of the voice in reading or speaking; a modulation; the rhythmical beat of any rhythmical action; (*Mus.*) the subsiding of a melody towards a close.—**ca'denced** *a.* rhythmical.—**ca'dency** *n.* rhythmical flow [L. *cadere*, to fall].
cadenza (ka-den'za) *n.* (*Mus.*) an ornamental passage for a voice or solo instrument in an aria or concerto, intended to show off the soloist's virtuosity [It.].
cadet (ka-det') *n.* a younger, or youngest son of a noble family; (*Mil.*) a youth in training for commissioned rank; a member of a Cadet Corps.—**cadet'ship** *n.*—**Cadet Corps**, an organisation for the training of boys on military lines [Fr. *cadet*, younger].
cadge (kaj) *v.t.* and *i.* to hawk goods; to beg.—**cadg'er** *n.* a hawker; a beggar; a loafer; a sponger [origin unknown].
cadmium (kad'mi-um) *n.* (*Chem.*) a soft, bluish-white metal of zinc group.—**cad'mia** *n.* an oxide of zinc [Gk. *kadmeia*].
cadre (kà'dr) *n.* the framework of a regiment or corps [Fr.=a frame].
caducous (ka-dū'kus) *a.* (*Bot.*) falling off early, as leaves or flowers.—**cadu'cean** *a.*—**cadu'city** *n.* tendency to fall early; (*Fig.*) transitoriness; feebleness of old age [L. *caducus*, falling].
caecum (sē'kum) *n.* (*Med.*) the first part of the large intestine, opening into the colon; the blind gut.—*pl.* **cae'ca.**—**cae'cal** *a.* [L. *caecus*, blind].
Caesar (sē'zar) *n.* one who acts like Julius Caesar (100-44 B.C.), Roman emperor and dictator; hence, autocrat; dictator.—**Caesa'rean, Caesa'rian** *a.* pert. to Julius Caesar.—**Caesarean section** (*Med.*) delivery of child through an opening cut in abdominal wall (Julius Caesar is said to have been born thus).
caesium (sē'zi-um) *n.* a silver-white alkaline metal, belonging to the sodium and potassium family.—**cae'sious** *a.* bluish-grey [L. *caesius*, bluish-grey].
caesura, cesura (sē-zū'ra) *n.* a break or division in a line of poetry; in English prosody, the natural pause of the voice.—**caesu'ral** *a.* [L. *caedere*, *caesum*, to cut].
café (ka-fā, kaf'e) *n.* a coffee-house; a restaurant, usually licensed for the sale of light refreshments only [Fr. *café*, coffee].
cafeteria (kaf-i-tēr'i-a) *n.* a restaurant where the customers help themselves [Amer.-Sp.= a coffee-shop].
caffeine (kaf'e-in, -ē'in, -ēn) *n.* the stimu-

lating alkaloid in coffee and tea.—**caffe'ic** *a.* pert. to coffee or caffeine [Fr. *café*, coffee].
caftan (kaf'tan) *n.* a long Eastern gown, with long, wide sleeves [Turk. *qaftan*].
cage (kāj) *n.* a place of confinement; a box-like enclosure, with bars of iron or wire, for keeping animals or birds;—*v.t.* to confine in a cage; to imprison.—**cage'ling** *n.* a bird kept in a cage.—**cage'work,** *n.* open frame-work.—**ca'gey** *a.* cautious, wary [L. *cavea*, hollow].
cahoot (ka-hòòt') *n.* (*U.S. Slang*) league or partnership.
caiman See **cayman.**
cainozoic (kā-nō-zō'ik) *a.* (*Geol.*) belonging to the third or Tertiary period, in which were deposited the rocks containing fossils of the early forms of mammals [Gk. *kainos*, recent; *zōē*, life].
caique (ką-ēk') *n.* a Turkish skiff or light boat [Fr. fr. Turk.].
cairn (kārn) *n.* a rounded or conical pile of stones.—**cairngorm'** *n.* a yellowish-brown variety of rock-crystal from the *Cairngorm* Mts., Scotland.—**Cairn terrier,** a type of short-haired Scottish terrier [Gael. *carn.* a heap]
caisson (kā'son) *n.* an ammunition chest or waggon; (*Engineering*) a water-tight chamber of sheet-iron or wood, used in laying the foundations of piers or bridges, quay-walls, etc.; an apparatus for raising sunken vessels [Fr. *caisse*, a case].
caitiff (kā'tif) *n.* a captive; a mean, despicable person;—*a.* base; vile; mean [L. *captivus*; doublet of *captive*].
cajole (ką-jōl') *v.t.* to delude by flattery; to coax; to deceive.—**cajol'er** *n.*—**cajol'ery** *n.* the act of cajoling [Fr. *cajoler*].
cake (kāk) *n.* a piece of dough baked; fancy bread; a flattish mass of matter, esp. soap, tobacco, etc.;—*v.t.* to make into a cake;—*v.i.* to become a flat, doughy mass.—**cak'y** *a.*—**cake'walk** *n.* an American Negro dance [O.N. *kaka*].
calabash (kȧl'ą-bash) *n.* the bottle-gourd tree of India and W. Africa; the fruit of this tree; a vessel made from the gourd, or the gourd itself; a species of pear [Ar.].
calaboose (kal'ą-bòòs) *n.* (*Slang*) a prison; a jail [Sp.].
calamary (kal'ą-ma-ri) *n.* a kind of cuttle-fish; a squid [L. *calamus*, a pen].
calamine (kal'ą-mīn) *n.* zinc carbonate; native silicate of zinc, used as a pigment in painting pottery; an alloy of zinc, lead, and tin [Gk. *kadmeia*].
calamity (ką-lam'i-ti) *n.* any great misfortune; disaster; affliction; mischance.—**calam'itous** *a.* producing distress and misery.—**calam'itously** *adv.*—**calam'itousness** *n.* [Fr. *calamité*].
calamus (kal'ą-mus) *n.* a reed used in ancient times as a pen, or made into a musical instrument; the sweet flag, or its aromatic root, used in medicine [L. fr. Gk.].
calash (ką-lash') *n.* a light carriage with low wheels, and a top or hood that can be raised or lowered; a silk hood formerly worn by ladies [Fr. *calèche*].
calcar (kal'kȧr) *n.* (*Bot.*) a spur or hollow tube at the base of a petal.—**cal'carate** *a.* spurred.—**calcar'iform** *a.* spur-shaped [L.= a spur].
calcareous (kal-kā'rē-us) *a.* having the nature of limestone; containing chalk or lime [L. *calx, calcis*, lime].
calceolaria (kal-sē-ō-lā'ri-ą) *n.* kinds of plants producing a slipper-shaped flower [L. *calceolus*, dim. of *calceus*, a shoe].
calciferol (kal-sif'ę-rol) *n.* crystalline vitamin D. used in fortifying margarine.—**calcif'erous** *a.* containing carbonate of lime [L. *calx, calcis*, lime; *ferre.* to bear].
calcify (kal'si-fī) *v.t.* and *i.* to turn into lime; to harden or petrify, by a deposit of lime.—**calcifica'tion** *n.* [L. *calx*, lime; *facere*, to make].
calcine (kal'sin, -sīn, kal-sīn') *v.t.* to reduce to powder by heat; to expel water and other volatile substances by heat;—*v.i.* to be turned into powder.—**cal'cinable** *a.*—**calcina'tion** *n.*—**calcin'atory** *n.* a vessel used in calcination [Fr. *calciner*, to calcify].
calcium (kal'si-um) *n.* the metallic base of lime.—**cal'cic** *a.* containing calcium.—**cal'cite** *n.* native carbonate of lime [L. *calx, calcis*, lime].
calculate (kal'kū-lāt) *v.t.* to count; to estimate; to compute; (*U.S.*) to plan; to expect;—*v.i.* to make a calculation.—**cal'culable** *a.*—**cal'culated** *a.* adapted to a purpose; intended to produce a certain effect.—**cal'culating** *a.* capable of performing calculations; shrewd in matters of self-interest; scheming.—**calcula'tion** *n.*—**cal'culative** *a.* tending to calculate.—**cal'culator** *n.*[L. *calculare*, to count with the help of pebbles, fr. *calculus*, a pebble].
calculus (kal'kū-lus) *n.* (*Med.*) a hard concretion which forms, esp. in kidney, bladder, etc. usually called stone or gravel;—*pl.* **cal'culi.**—**cal'culose, cal'culous** *a.* hard like stone; gritty [L].
calculus (kal'kū-lus) *n.* a higher branch of mathematics concerned with the properties of continuously varying quantities.—**differential calculus,** the branch of the calculus dealing with the differentials, i.e. increments and decrements of varying quantities.—**integral calculus** is the process of summation or integration of these differentials [L. *calculus*, a pebble].
caldron, cauldron (kawl'dron) *n.* a large metal kettle or boiler [L. *caldarium*, fr. *calidus*, hot].
Caledonia (kal-e-dō'ni-ą) *n.* the Roman name for Scotland.—**Caledo'nian** *a.*
calefaction (kal-e-fak'shun) *n.* the act of heating, the state of being heated.—**calefacient** (kal-e-fā'shi-ent) *a.* making warm;—*n.* a heat-giving remedy.—**calefac'tor** *n.* that which gives heat.—**calefac'tory** *a.* [L. *calere*, to be warm; *facere*, to make].
calendar (kal'en-dąr) *n.* a table of days, months or seasons; an almanack; a list of criminal cases; a list of saints;—*v.t.* to enter in a list; to index documents [L. *Calendae*, the calends].
calender (kal'en-dęr) *n.* a hot press with rollers, used to make cloth, etc. smooth and glossy [Fr. *calandre*, a cylinder].
calends (kal'endz) *n.pl.* the first day of each month, among the Romans.—**at the Greek calends,** never (because the Greeks had no calends). Also **kal'ends** [L. *Calendae*].
calf (kȧf) *n.* the young of the cow, and of some other mammals, such as elephant, whale, etc.; a fine, light-coloured leather used for binding books;—*pl.* **calves** (kȧvz).—**calf-love,** a youthful, transitory attachment to one of the opposite sex.—**calf's-foot jelly,** a palatable jelly made from calves' feet.—**calve** *v.i.* to bring forth a calf [O.E. *cealf*].
calf (kȧf) *n.* the thick, fleshy part of the leg below the knee;—*pl.* **calves** [O.N. *kalfi*].
calibre (kal'i-bęr) *n.* the diameter of the bore of a cannon, gun, etc.; the internal diameter of a tube or cylinder; (*Fig.*) capacity; quality of mind; character.—**cal'ibrate** *v.t.* to determine the calibre of a firearm, tube, or other cylindrical object.—**calibra'tion** *n.* [Fr. *calibre*].
calico (kal'i-kō) *n.* white cotton cloth, first made in *Calicut* in India; coarse printed cotton cloth; -*a.* made of calico.
calipers See **callipers.**
caliph, calif (kal'if, kā'lif) *n.* a title given to the successors of Mahomet in the high priesthood.—**cal'iphate, cal'ifate** *n.* the office of a caliph [Ar. *khalifah*, a successor].
calix See **calyx.**
calk, in shipbuilding. See **caulk.**
calk (kawk) *n.* a pointed stud on a horse-shoe to prevent slipping. Also **calk'er** or **calk'in;**—*v.t.* to furnish with a calk [L. *calcar*, a spur].

call (kawl) *v.t.* to announce; to name; to summon; to name, as for office; to utter in a loud voice;—*v.i.* to speak in a loud voice; to cry out; to make a brief visit;—*v.t.* and *v.i.* (in the game of Bridge, etc.) to bid;—*n.* a vocal address of summons or invitation; a short visit; a public claim; a requisition; authorised command; an invitation, as to be minister of a church; a note blown on a horn, bugle, etc.; in the game of Bridge, etc. a bid. —**call'er** *n.* one who calls.—**call'ing** *n.* a person's usual occupation.—**at call,** on demand.—**on call,** of a person, ready if summoned.—**within call,** within hearing; close at hand.—**call'-bird,** *n.* a decoy-bird.—**call'-boy** *n.* (*Theatre*) a boy who calls actors to go on the stage.—**call'-off'ice,** *n.* a public telephone kiosk.—**to call down,** to rebuke sharply.—**to call in question,** to impugn; to challenge a statement.—**to call to account,** to demand an explanation of.—**to call to the bar,** to admit as a barrister.—**to call up** (*Mil.*) to summon to military service [O.E. *ceallian*].

calligraphy (ka-lig′-rạ-fi) *n.* the art of beautiful writing; penmanship.—**callig'rapher, callig'raphist** *n.*—**calligraph'ic** *a.* [Gk. *kallos*, beauty; *graphein*, to write].

callipers (kal′-i-pẹrz) *n.* a two-legged instrument for measuring diameters.—**walking callipers** (*Med.*) a surgical appliance, with steel supports, fitted to a boot and strapped to the knee or thigh, to take the weight of the body off an injured leg. Also **calipers** [Fr. *calibre*].

callisthenics (kal-is-then′-iks) *n.pl.* light gymnastic exercises to promote beauty and grace of movement.—**callisthen'ic** *a.* [Gk. *kallos*, beauty; *sthenos*, strength].

callous (kal′-us) *a.* hardened; hardened in mind; unfeeling.—**call'ously** *adv.*—**call'ousness** *n.*—**callos'ity** *n.* a horny hardness of the skin [L. *callus*, hard skin].

callow (kal′-o) *a.* pert. to the condition of a young bird; unfledged; (*Fig.*) inexperienced; raw.—**cal'lowness** *n.* [L. *calvus*, bald].

callus (kal′-us) *n.* a hardened or thickened part of the skin [L.=hard skin].

calm (kȧm) *a.* still; quiet; at rest;—*n.* the state of being calm;—*v.t.* to make calm; to pacify; to quiet;—*v.i.* to become calm.—**calm'ly** *adv.*—**calm'ness** *n.* [Fr. *calme*].

calomel (kal′-ō-mel) *n.* (*Med.*) sub-chloride of mercury, used as a purgative, and in the treatment of syphylis [Gk. *kalos*, fair; *melas*, black].

caloric (kạ-lor′-ik) *n.* heat;—*a.* pert. to heat; heat-producing.—**caloric'ity** *n.* the power of animals to develop heat.—**calorifacient** (kal-ō-ri-fā′-shi-ent) *a.* heat-producing.—**calorif'ic** *a.* pert. to heat; heat-producing.—**calorifica'-tion** *n.* the production of heat [L. *calor*, heat].

calorie, calory (kal′-or-i) *n.* (*Phys.*) the unit of heat; the unit of heat or energy produced by any food substance.—**large calorie,** the amount of heat required to raise the temperature of 1,000 grams (i.e. 1 kilogram) of water by 1° centigrade.—**small calorie,** the amount of heat required to raise the temperature of 1 gram of water by 1° centigrade.—**calorim'eter** *n.* a scientific instrument for determining the amount of heat produced by any substance.—**calorim'etry** *n.* [L. *calor*, heat].

caltrop (kal′-trop) *n.* an instrument with four iron spikes used to impede an enemy's cavalry; a name given to several plants [L. *calx*, heel; E. *trap*].

calumet (kal′-ū-met) *n.* the 'pipe of peace' of the N. American Indians [L. *calamus*, a reed].

calumniate (kạ-lum′-ni-āt) *v.t.* to accuse falsely; to slander;—*v.i.* to utter slanders.—**calumnia'tion** *n.* false and slanderous representations. — **calum'niator** *n.* — **calum'niatory, calum'nious** *a.* slanderous.—**calum'niously** *adv.* —**cal'umny** *n.* a false accusation; malicious slander; libel [L. *calumnia*].

Calvary (kal′-vạ-ri) *n.* the place of Christ's crucifixion; (*R.C.*) a series of representations of the Passion (e.g. in a chapel) [L. *calvaria*, a skull].

calve (kȧv) See **calf.**

Calvinism (kal′-vin-izm) *n.* the doctrines of John *Calvin*, a Genevan Protestant Reformer (1509-1564), which lay special stress on the sovereignty of God in the conferring of grace. —**cal'vinist** *n.*

calx (kalks) *n.* the crumbly substance that remains after the calcination of a metal or mineral;—*pl.* **calxes, calces** (kalk′-sēz, kal′-sēz) [L.=lime].

calypso (kalip′-sō) *n.* an improvised song in native rhythm from the West Indies.

calyx, calix (kā′-liks) *n.* a cup-shaped cavity; the outer covering or leaf-like envelope of a flower, its segments being called *sepals* [Gk. *kalux*, a husk, a cup].

cam (kam) *n.* a projecting part of a wheel, or moving piece, so shaped as to give an alternating or variable motion to another wheel or piece.—**cam'shaft** *n.* the shaft on which cams are formed for opening the valves [Dut. *kam*, a comb].

caman (kam′-an) *n.* a shinty stick.—**camanachd** (kam-an-aH′) *n.* shinty [Gael.].

camaraderie (kam-a-rad′-ẹ-rē) *n.* good-fellowship; comradeship; loyalty to one's fellows [Fr. *camarade*, a companion].

camarilla (kam-ạ-ril′-ạ) *n.* a secret council; a body of political intriguers; a clique; a cabal [Sp. *camarilla*, a little chamber].

camber (kam′-bẹr) *n.* slight convexity of an upper surface, as of a ship's deck, a bridge, a road surface [Fr. *cambrer*, to arch, fr. L. *camera*, a vault].

Cambrian (kam′-bri-ạn) *a.* Welsh; pert. to Cambria or Wales;—*n.* a Welshman.—**the Cambrian rocks** are the lowest stratum of rocks in which fossils are found below the Silurian [L. fr. *Cymru*, Wales].

cambric (kām′-brik) *n.* a fine white linen fabric first made at *Cambrai*, in N. France.

came (kām) *pa.t.* of the verb **come.**

camel (kam′-el) *n.* a large ruminant animal of Asia and Africa, with one or two humps, used as a beast of burden.—**cam'eleer** *n.* a camel driver [Gk. *kamēlos*].

cameleon (kạ-mēl′-yun) *n.* See **chamel'eon.**

camellia (kạ-mēl′-yạ) *a.* a species of Asiatic shrub with showy flowers and elegant dark-green, laurel-like leaves [fr. *Kamel*, a Jesuit and botanist of the 18th cent.].

camelopard (kạ-mel′-ō-pȧrd, kam′-el-ō-pard) *n.* the giraffe [fr. *camel*, and *pard*].

Camembert (ka′-mam-ber) *n.* a small, soft, rich cheese [fr. name of a village in Normandy].

cameo (kam′-ē-ō) *n.* a stone of two layers cut in ornamental relief;—*pl.* **cam'eos** [etym. unknown].

camera (kam′-e-rạ) *n.* a box used in photography, fitted with a film or sensitive plate at one end and a lens and focusing apparatus at the other; a development of the camera obscura.—**cam'era-man** *n.* a professional cinema-film or press photographer.—**camera obscura,** an optical contrivance by means of which the images of external objects are made to appear on a light-coloured surface in a darkened room [L. *camera*, a vault].

camera (kam′-e-rạ) *n.* a vaulted room; a judge's private room; hence (*Law*) 'to hear a case' **in camera,** to hear the evidence in private [L. *camera*, a room].

cami-knickers (kam′-i-nik-ers) *n.* a woman's undergarment, combining a *cami*-sole and *knickers*. Also **cam'iknicks.**

camisole (kam′-i-sōl) *n.* a lady's under-bodice; a lady's light dressing-jacket [Fr.].

camomile, chamomile (kam′-ō-mīl) *n.* an aromatic creeping plant whose flowers are used medicinally for making infusions [Gk. *chamaimēlon*, the earth-apple].

camouflage (kȧ′-mȯȯ-flazh) *n.* (*Mil.*) a method of visual deception of the enemy by disguising; any form of disguise;—*v.t.* to cover with camouflage material; to disguise [Fr.].
camp (kamp) *n.* the area of ground where soldiers are lodged in huts or tents; permanent barracks near a suitable exercise ground; an encampment;—*v.t.* and *i.* to encamp; to pitch tents.—**camp'er** *n.* one who lives in a camp in open country, esp. a holiday-maker, etc. living in a tent.—**camp'ing** *n.* the act of living in camp.—**camp'-bed** *n.* a light, portable bed with folding legs.—**camp'-chair** *n.* a light, portable chair with folding legs.—**camp'-fe'ver** *n.* typhoid-fever.—**camp'-foll'ower** *n.* a non-combatant attached to a body of troops, usually for provisioning purposes.—**camp'-meet'ing** *n.* a religious meeting in the open air [L. *campus*, a field].
campaign (kam-pān') *n.* an extensive tract of level country; a large plain; (*Mil.*) a series of operations in a particular theatre of war; hence, in Politics, Social Economics, etc. an organised series of operations (meetings, canvassing, etc.);—*v.i.* to serve in a war; to conduct, or assist in political, etc. operations.—**campaign'er** *n.* [L. *campus*, a plain].
campanile (kam-pạ-nē′-le, kam′-pạ-nīl) *n.* a bell-tower constructed beside a church, but not attached to it;—*pl.* **campani'les.**—**campanol'ogy** *n.* the art of bell-ringing, or of bell-founding; bell-lore.—**campanol'ogist** *n.* [It. *campana*, a bell].
campanula (kam-pan′-ū-lạ) *n.* a genus of plants bearing bell-shaped flowers, a common species being the harebell.—**campan'iform, campan'ular, campan'ulate** *a.* bell-shaped [It. *campana*, a bell].
camphor (kam′-for) *n.* a whitish substance with an aromatic taste and smell, obtained from the camphor laurel-tree.—**camphoraceous** (kam-for-ā′-shus) *a.* resembling camphor.—**cam'phorate** *v.t.* to impregnate with camphor.—**cam'phorate, camphor'ic** *a.* pert. to camphor [Malay, *kapur*, chalk].
campion (kam′-pi-un) *n.* plant of the Pink family [L. *campus*, a field].
campus (kam′-pus) *n.* (*U.S.*) the grounds of a college or school [L. *campus*, a plain].
can (kan) *pres. indic.* of a defective, intransitive verb meaning, to be able, to have the power, to be allowed [O.E. *cunnan*, to know].
can (kan) *n.* a metal vessel or container for holding liquids, etc.;—*v.t.* to put into a tin or can for the purpose of preserving;—*pr.p.* **can'ning.**—*pa.p.* and *pa.t.* **canned.**—**can'nery** *n.* a factory where foods are preserved by canning [O.E. *canne*].
Canadian (kạ-nā′-di-ạn) *n.* an inhabitant of *Canada*;—*a.* pert. to Canada.—**Canadian,** or **Canada balsam,** a transparent liquid resin, obtained from the balsam-fir.
canaille (kạ-nȧ′-yẹ) *n.* the dregs of society; the mob; rabble [Fr. fr. L. *canis*, a dog].
canal (kạ-nal') *n.* an artificial watercourse for transport, drainage or irrigation purposes; a duct in the body; a groove.—**can'alise** *v.t.* to make a canal through; to convert into a canal [L. *canalis*].
canapé (ka′-nạ-pā) *n.* a piece of toast or fried bread, with anchovies, etc. on it [Fr. *canapé*, a sofa].
canard (ka-nȧr(d)') *n.* a false rumour; an absurd or extravagant piece of news [Fr.].
canary (kạ-nā′-ri) *n.* a yellow singing bird, a species of finch; a pale-yellow colour; a light wine made in the Canary Islands [Fr. *canari*].
Canasta (ka-nas′-ta) *n.* a card game resembling Bridge played with two packs.
can-can (kan-kan') *n.* a kind of dance, once popular in music-halls in France [Fr.].
cancel (kan′-sel) *v.t.* to cross out; to blot out; to annul; to suppress; (*Math.*) to strike out common factors; to balance; to offset;—*pr.p.* **can'celling.**—*pa.p.* and *pa.t.* **can'celled.**—**can'cellate, can'cellated** *a.* marked with cross-lines.—**cancella'tion** *n.* the act of cancelling [L. *cancellatus*, latticed].
cancer (kan′-sẹr) *n.* (*Med.*) a malignant growth or tumour.—**can'cerate** *v.i.* to grow into a cancer.—**cancera'tion** *n.*—**can'cerous** *a.* pert. to or resembling cancer.—**can'croid** *a.* like cancer.—**cancėropho'bia** *n.* a morbid dread of cancer [L. *cancer*, a crab].
candelabrum (kan-dẹ-lā′-brum) *n.* a tall stand for a lamp; a branched and highly ornamented candle-stick; a chandelier.—*pl.* **candela'bra.** Also **candela'bra** *n.sing.* and **candela'bras** *n.pl.* [L. fr. *candela*, a candle].
candid (kan′-did) *a.* fair; open; frank.—**can'didly** *adv.*—**can'didness** *n.* frankness; ingenuousness [L. *candidus*, white].
candidate (kan′-di-dāt) *n.* one who seeks an appointment, office, honour, etc.—**can'didature** (*U.S.* **can'didacy**) *n.* the position of being a candidate [L. *candidus*, white (one wearing a white toga)].
candle (kan′-dl) *n.* a stick of tallow, wax, etc. with a wick inside, used for giving light.—**candle power,** the unit of luminosity.—**can'dlestick** *n.* an instrument of wood, iron, brass, etc. for holding a candle.—**not fit to hold a candle to (a person),** very inferior to.—**not worth the candle,** not worth the pains, trouble, or expense [L. *candela*].
Candlemas (kan′-dl-mas) *n.* a religious festival, held on Feb. 2 in Catholic and Anglican churches, to commemorate the Purification of the Blessed Virgin [*candle* and *mass*].
candour (kan′-dur) *n.* candidness; sincerity; frankness [L. *candor*, whiteness].
candy (kan′-di) *n.* a kind of sweetmeat made of sugar;—*v.t.* to preserve in sugar; to form into crystals, as sugar;—*v.i.* to become candied.—**candied** (kan′-did) *a.* preserved or coated with sugar; (*Fig.*) flattering [Ar. *qand*, sugar].
candytuft (kan′-di-tuft) *n.* a large genus of annual, biennial, and perennial herbs or shrubs of the order Cruciferae [fr. *Candia*].
cane (kān) *n.* the stem of a small palm or long, strong reed; the bamboo, etc.; the sugar-cane; a walking-stick;—*v.t.* to beat with a cane; to fix a cane bottom to, e.g. a chair.—**cane'-su'gar** *n.* sugar obtained from the sugar-cane [Gk. *kanna*, a reed].
canine (ka-nīn', kā′-nīn) *a.* of, or pert. to, a dog.—**canine teeth,** the two pointed teeth in each jaw, one on each side, between the incisors and the molars [L. *canis*, a dog].
canister (kan′-is-tẹr) *n.* a small case or box for holding tea, coffee, etc.—**can'ister-shot,** *n.* a number of small iron balls enclosed in a case of a size to fit the gun-barrel (an early form of shrapnel) [L. *canistrum*, a wicker basket].
canker (kang′-kẹr) *n.* an eating sore; ulceration of the mouth; a disease of trees, esp. apple-trees, due to a fungus; a disease of the ear of dogs and cats; (*Fig.*) anything that eats away, corrupts, etc.;—*v.t.* to consume; to gnaw at; to corrupt;—*v.i.* to decay, to become cankered.—**can'kered** *a.* corrupted; crabbed; malignant.—**can'kerous** *a.* corrupting like a canker.—**can'kery** *a.* cankered.—**can'ker-worm** *n.* a destructive caterpillar [L, *cancer*, a crab].
cannel-coal (kan′-el-kōl) *n.* a kind of coal, burning with a clear, smokeless flame, used in the manufacture of gas. Also **can'dle-coal** [prob. fr. *candle*].
cannibal (kan′-i-bạl) *n.* one who eats human flesh;—*a.* relating to this practice.—**cann'ibalism** *n.* the practice of eating human flesh.—**cannibalist'ic** *a.*—**cann'ibalise** *v.t.* to dismantle in the hope of getting spare parts to be used for re-conditioning. [Sp. *canibal* = *Caribal*, a Carib].
cannon (kan′-on) *n.* a large gun; guns which

fire small shells from aircraft;—*v.i.* to cannonade.—**cannonade′** *n.* an attack with cannon; the firing of cannon;—*v.t.* to bombard.—**cannoneer, cannonier** (kan-on-ēr′) *n.* one who loads or fires cannon; an artilleryman.—**cann′on-ball,** *n.* an iron ball to be discharged by cannon.—**cann′on-shot** *n.* a cannon-ball; the range of a cannon [L. *canna,* a reed, a tube].

cannon (kan′on) *n.* a billiard stroke, hitting both object balls in succession with one's own;—*v.t.* to make this stroke;—*v.i.* to collide; to rebound [earlier *carom,* fr. Sp. *carambola,* the red ball].

cannot (kan′ot) combination of *can* and *not,* therefore,=not to be able.

canny (kan′i) *a.* (*Scot.*) cautious; thrifty.

canoe (kạ-nōō′) *n.* a boat propelled by a hand paddle; a skiff; a light boat.—**canoe′ist** *n.* [Hayti, *canoa*].

canon (kan′on) *n.* a law or rule, esp. of the church; the books of the Scriptures accepted by the Church as of divine authority; rules of faith; a standard; the list of saints; a church dignitary, esp. one connected with a cathedral; (*Mus.*) a form of composition in which the melody is repeated at set intervals by the other parts.—**can′oness** *n.* a member of a religious association of women, vowed to obedience and chastity.—**canon′ic, canon′ical** *a.*—**canon′icals** *n.pl.* official dress worn by a clergyman officiating at a church service; vestments.—**canon′ically** *adv.*—**canonisa′tion** *n.* —**can′onise** *v.t.* to place in the list of saints.—**can′onist** *n.* one skilled in canon law.—**can′onry** *n.* the office of canon.—**canon law,** the ecclesiastical laws of the Greek, Roman, and Anglican Catholics [Gk. *kanōn,* a rule; L. *canonicus,* a regular priest].

canon (kan′yon) *n.* See **canyon.**

canopy (kan′ō-pi) *n.* a covering fixed above a bed, or a dais, or carried on poles above the head; any overhanging shelter;—*v.t.* to cover with canopy [Gk. *kōnōpion,* a couch with mosquito curtains].

cant (kant) *n.* an inclination from the level; a tilted position;—*v.t.* to tilt; to jerk; to toss;—*v.i.* to have, or take a leaning position [O.Fr.].

cant (kant) *n.* an insincere or conventional mode of speaking; an expression peculiar to a class, as *thieves' cant;* slang;—*v.i.* to speak hypocritically with affected piety [L. *cantare,* to sing].

can't (kant) *v.* contr. of **cannot.**

Cantab (kan′tab) *n.* a member of Cambridge University;—*a.* pert. to Cambridge [abbrev. of L. *Cantabrigiensis,* fr. *Cantabrigia,* Cambridge].

cantabile (kan-tà′bē-lā) *adv.* (*Mus*) in a flowing, graceful, style, like singing [It.].

cantaloup, cantaloupe (kan′tạ-loop) *n.* a variety of musk-melon, having a furrowed rind [*Cantalupo,* a town in Italy].

cantankerous (kan-tang′kẹ-rus) *a.* perverse; ill-natured; cross-grained; quarrelsome.—**cantan′kerously** *adv.*—**cantan′kerousness** *n.* [orig. uncertain].

cantata (kan-tà′tạ) *n.* a short musical composition in oratorio or lyric drama form.—**cantatrice** (kan′tạ-trēs, kan-tā-trē′chā) a professional female singer [It.].

canteen (kan-tēn′) *n.* a store and refreshment-room in camps and barracks for soldiers, sailors, etc.; a similar place in a social or institutional club; a mess-tin; a case of cutlery [It. *cantina,* a cellar].

canter (kan′tẹr) *v.i.* to move at an easy gallop;—*n.* an easy gallop or gait [fr. *Canterbury gallop,* the easy pace of the pilgrims riding to Canterbury].

canterbury (kan′tẹr-ber-i) *n.* a stand with divisions to hold music, papers, etc.—**Canterbury bell** (*Bot.*) a kind of Campanula, with fine bell-shaped flowers.

cantharis (kan′thạ-ris) *n.* the Spanish fly.—*pl.* **cantharides** (kan-thar′i-dēz), a preparation of Spanish fly used as a blistering agent [L.].

canticle (kan′ti-kl) *n.* a little song; a non-metrical hymn.—**Canticles** (*Bib.*) the Song of Songs, or Song of Solomon [L. *canticulum,* a little song].

cantilever (kan′ti-lēv-ẹr) *n.* a bracket for supporting a cornice or balcony.—**cantilever bridge,** a bridge built on the same principle with two long arms or brackets projecting towards each other from opposite banks or piers [fr. E. *cant,* an angle; Fr. *lever,* to raise].

canto (kan′tō) *n.* a division or part of a poem.—**can′tor** *n.* a precentor; the leader of the singing, esp. in a synagogue.—**canto′rial** *a.* [It. fr. L. *canere,* to sing.].

canton (kan′ton) *n.* a small district (in Switzerland, administered by a separate government); a section of something;—*v.t.* to divide into districts, as territory; to allot quarters to troops.—**can′tonal** *a.*—**canton′ment** *n.* quarters for troops [Fr.].

Canuck (kạ-nuk′) *n.* and *a.* a (French-) Canadian; a small breed of horse [Amer.].

canvas (kan′vas) *n.* a coarse cloth made of hemp, for sails, tents, etc.; the sails of a vessel; a specially prepared material for painting on; hence, an oil-painting [O.Fr. *canevas;* L. *cannabis,* hemp].

canvass (kan′vas) *v.t.* to sift; to examine thoroughly; to solicit support, or votes, or contributions;—*v.i.* to solicit votes;—*n.* a close examination (by discussion); a scrutiny; solicitation; a seeking to obtain votes.—**can′vasser** *n.* [fr. *canvas*=to sift, as through canvas].

canyon (kan′yon) *n.* a ravine; a deep gorge. Also **cañon** [Sp.].

canzone (kant-sō′nā) *n.* (*Mus.*) a light air in two or three parts; a short Italian poem divided into stanzas.—**canzonet′, canzonet′ta** *n.* a short part-song [It. *canzone,* a song].

caoutchouc (kout′chŏŏk) *n.* india-rubber; gum-elastic [S. Amer. *cahuchu*].

cap (kap) *n.* a brimless covering, for the head; the top or highest point; a small lid used as a cover;—*v.t.* to cover the top or end of; to raise one's cap in salutation or out of respect; to surpass; (*University, etc.*) to confer a degree on;—*pr.p.* **cap′ping.**—*pa.p.* and *pa.t.* **capped.**—**cap and bells,** the insignia of the professional jester in medieval times.—**black cap,** the cap put on by a judge before he pronounces the death sentence.—**to set one's cap at,** said of a woman who tries to attract a suitor.—**if the cap fits,** if the remark applies [O.E. *cappe,* a hood].

capable (kā′pạ-bl) *a.* competent; gifted; skilful.—**ca′pably** *adv.*—**ca′pableness** *n.*—**capabil′ity** *n.* power [L. *capere,* to hold].

capacious (kạ-pā′shus) *a.* roomy; spacious; comprehensive.—**capa′ciously** *adv.*—**capa′ciousness** *n.* [L. *capere,* to hold].

capacity (ka-pas′i-ti) *n.* power of holding or grasping; room; volume; power of mind; character; ability; cubic content.—**capac′itate** *v.t.* to render capable [L. *capacitas*].

cap-à-pie (kap-a-pē′) *adv.* from head to foot [O.Fr. fr. L. *caput,* the head; *pes,* the foot].

caparison (kạ-par′i-son) *n.* a covering laid over a horse; trappings; harness;—*v.t.* to cover with a decorated cloth; to adorn with rich dress [O.Fr. *caparasson,* preparation].

cape (kāp) *n.* a covering for the shoulders [L.L. *cappa*].

cape (kāp) *n.* a point of land running out into the sea; a headland [L. *caput,* the head].

caper (kā′pẹr) *v.i.* to leap about like a goat, in a sprightly manner; to skip; to dance; to frolic;—*n.* a frolicsome skip [L. *caper,* a goat].

caper (kā′pẹr) *n.* a herb or shrub whose flower-buds when pickled in vinegar are used in sauces [Gk. *kapparis*].

capercailzie (ka-pẹr-kāl′i) *n.* a large game-bird, the wood-grouse [Gael. *capull,* a mare; *coille,* a wood].

capillary (kap´i-lar-i, ka-pil´a-ri) *a.* resembling a hair; as fine as a hair; descriptive of the very fine bore of a tube or similar passage;—*n.* one of the microscopic blood-vessels connecting the arteries and veins.—**capillar'ity** *n.* name given to the phenomenon that liquids rise in very narrow tubes against the force of gravity, owing to surface tension.—**capill'iform** *a.* hair-shaped.—**cap'illose** *a.* hairy; rough;—*n.* a sulphide of nickel [L. *capillus*, hair].

capital (kap´i-tal) *a.* pert. to the head; involving the forfeiture of life; first in importance; chief; principal; excellent;—*n.* (*Archit.*) the head of a column, pilaster, etc.; the chief city; a metropolis; (*Print.*) type larger than that used in body of page; the estimated total value of a business, property, stock, etc.; ready money.—**cap'itally** *adv.* in a capital manner; splendidly [L. *caput*, the head].

capitalism (kap´i-tal-ism) *n.* form of economic, industrial, and social organisation of society involving ownership, control, and direction of production by privately owned business organisations.—**cap'italist** *n.* one who has capital.—**cap'italise** *v.t.* to convert into capital or ready money.

capitation (kap-i-tā´shun) *n.* a census; a tax or grant per head.—**capitation fee,** under the National Health Service, a sum paid to a doctor for each patient under his care [L. *capitatio*, a poll-tax].

Capitol (kap´i-tol) *n.* the temple of Jupiter in Rome; the buildings of the U.S. Congress in Washington [L. *Capitolium*].

capitulate (ka-pit´ū-lāt) *v.i.* to surrender on conditions; to draw up terms of an agreement.—**capitula'tion** *n.*—**capit'ulator** *n.* [L.L. *capitulare*, to draw up a treaty].

capon (kā´pon) *n.* a young castrated cock fed for the table.—**ca'ponise** *v.t.* [O.E. *capun*].

capote (ka-pot') *n.* a kind of long cloak, generally with a hood; a leather top or hood for a vehicle [Fr., dim. of *cape*, a cloak].

capric (kap´rik) *a.* pert. to goats [L. *caper*, a goat].

caprice (ka-prēs') *n.* illogical change of feeling or opinion; a whim; a fancy.—**capricious** (ka-pri´shus) *a.*—**capri'ciously** *adv.*—**capric'iousness** *n.* [L. *caper*, a goat].

caprid (kap´rid) *a.* pert. to goats.—**cap'rine** *a.* pert. to or like a goat [L. *caper*, a goat].

capriole (kap´ri-ōl) *n.* a caper or gambol; a leap that a horse makes off all fours and without advancing [L. *caper*, a goat].

Capsicum (kap´si-kum) *n.* a genus of tropical plants, whose fruits when dried and ground give Cayenne pepper [L. *capsa*, a box].

capsize (kap-sīz') *v.t.* and *i.* to upset; to overturn [etym. uncertain].

capstan (kap´stan) *n.* a heavy cable-holder revolving on an upright spindle [L. *capistrum*, a halter].

capsule (kap´sūl) *n.* the seed-vessel of a plant; a small gelatinous case containing medicine; a metal cap placed over the mouth of a corked bottle.—**cap'sular** *a.* hollow like a capsule [L. *capsa*, a box].

captain (kap´tin) *n.* in the army, an officer commanding a company of infantry; in the navy, an officer in command of a man-of-war; the master of a merchant ship; in sport, the leader of a team; in school, the head boy or girl;—*v.t.* to command; to lead.—**cap'taincy** *n.* the rank or commission of a captain [L. *caput*, the head].

caption (kap´shun) *n.* the heading of a newspaper, chapter, page, etc.; the title of an illustration [fr. L. *capere*, to take].

captious (kap´shus) *a.* apt to find fault; difficult to please.—**cap'tiously** *adv.*—**cap'tiousness** *n.* fault-finding [L. *captiosus*, deceiving].

captivate (kap´ti-vāt) *v.t.* to capture the fancy of.—**cap'tivating** *a.* winning, charming.—**captiva'tion** *n.* [L. *captivus*, captive].

captive (kap´tiv) *n.* one taken prisoner by force, surprise, or stratagem; one held in captivity;—*a.* made prisoner.—**captiv'ity** *n.* imprisonment; bondage; servitude.—**cap'tor** *n.* (*fem.* **cap'tress**) one who takes a prisoner or a prize.—**cap'ture** *n.* the act of seizing by force or stratagem; arrest; the thing seized; the prize;—*v.t.* to take captive; to take possession of by force [L. *capere*, to take].

Capuchin (kap´ū-chin, kap-òò-shēn') *n.* a Franciscan monk (from the hood he wears); a hooded cloak for women; a hooded pigeon; a long-tailed S. American monkey.—**capuche** (ka-pòòsh') *n.* a hood; a cowl, esp. of a Capuchin [It. *cappucino*, a cowl].

car (kâr) *n.* any kind of vehicle on wheels; abbrev. for motor-car; the part of a balloon in which the aeronauts sit [L. *carrus*].

carabine, carabineer See **carbine.**

caracole (kâr´a-kol) *n.* a prancing half-turn right or left by a spirited horse; a wheeling movement of cavalry; a spiral staircase;—*v.i.* to wheel [Sp.].

carafe (ka-râf') *n.* a glass water-bottle or decanter [Fr.].

caramel (kar´a-mel) *n.* burnt sugar, used for colouring spirits, wines, etc. and in cooking; a kind of sweetmeat [Sp. *caramelo*].

carapace (kar´a-pās) *n.* the shell that covers the back of the tortoise, lobster, etc. [Fr.].

carat (kar´at) *n.* a measure of weight for gold and precious stones, the standard carat being 3.16 grains troy; a proportional measure of 24ths, used to express the fineness of gold, e.g. 22 parts of pure gold in a mass of 24=22 carat gold [Gk. *keration*, a carob-tree seed (of very light weight)].

caravan (kar´a-van, kar-a-van') *n.* parties of merchants or pilgrims travelling together for greater security, esp. across deserts; a sort of house on wheels used by gipsies, showmen, etc.—**caravaneer'** *n.* the leader of a caravan.—**caravan'sary, caravan'serai** *n.* a large unfurnished Eastern inn, with a court in the middle for the accommodation of caravans [Pers. *karwan*].

caravel (kar´a-vel) *n.* a light sailing-ship. Also **car'vel** [L. *carabus*, a wicker boat].

caraway (kar´a-wā) *n.* a biennial aromatic plant; its seed, used as a flavouring for bread, cakes, etc. [Gk. *karon*].

carbide (kâr´bīd) *n.* a compound of carbon with certain elements, including calcium, manganese, iron, etc.—**calcium carbide,** produces acetylene when water is added to it [L. *carbo*, coal].

carbine, carabine (kâr´(a)-bīn) *n.* a short cavalry rifle.—**carbineer', carabineer'** *n.* a soldier armed with a carbine; a light horseman [etym. uncertain].

carbohydrate (kâr-bō-hī´drāt) *n.* a substance, such as sugar, starch, cellulose, etc. composed of carbon, hydrogen, and oxygen [L. *carbo*, coal; Gk. *hudōr*, water].

carbolic (kâr-bol´ik) *a.* derived from carbon,—*n.* carbolic acid.—**car'bolated** *a.* treated with, or containing, carbolic acid.—**carbolic acid,** a poisonous acid distilled from coal-tar and used as an antiseptic and disinfectant [L. *carbo*, coal].

carbon (kâr´bon) *n.* a non-metallic element existing pure in nature as diamond, graphite, charcoal, etc. and as a compound of animal and vegetable substances; a thin rod of hard carbon used in an electric arc-lamp; a copy made by using carbon paper.—**carbonaceous** (kar-bon-ā´shus) *a.* pert. to, or composed of, coal.—**car'bonate** *n.* a salt of carbonic acid.—**carbon'ic** *a.* pert. to, or coming from, carbon.—**carbonif'erous** *a.* producing carbon or coal.—**car'bonise** *v.t.* to make into carbon; to coat with carbon.—**carbonisa'tion** *n.*—**carbon paper,** a thin paper coated with colouring-matter on one side, used for duplicating written or type-written work [L. *carbo*, coal].

Carborundum (kȧr-bō-run′dum) *n.* silicon carbide, a black, crystalline substance, of exceptional hardness [Protected Trade Name, fr. *carbon* and *corundum*].

carboy (kȧr′boi) *n.* a large, globular glass bottle, encased in basket-work [Pers. *qarabah*].

carbuncle (kȧr′bung-kl) *n.* a gem of a deep red colour; a variety of garnet; an inflamed bunion or boil.—**carbun′cular** *a.* [L. *carbunculus*, a small coal].

carburet (kȧr′bū-ret) *v.t.* to combine or impregnate with carbon;—*pr.p.* **car′buretting;** —*pa.p.* and *pa.t.* **car′buretted.**—**car′burettor, car′buretter** *n.* an apparatus in an internal-combustion engine to convert liquid petrol into vaporised form.—**carbura′tion** *n.* [L. *carbo*, coal].

carcanet (kȧr′kạ-net) *n.* a collar of jewels [Fr. *carcan*, a convict's collar].

carcase, carcass (kȧr′kạs) *n.* the dead body of man or animal, esp. of the latter; the framework or shell of anything [It. *carcassa*, the framework of a ship, etc.].

card (kȧrd) *n.* pasteboard; a small piece of pasteboard often with figures, pictures, etc. on it for playing games; a piece of pasteboard having on it a person's name and address; (*Slang*) a queer or humorous fellow.—**card′-board** *n.* finely finished pasteboard.—**card′-case** *n.* case for visiting-cards.—**card′-in′dex** *n.* an index in which each entry is made on a separate card.—**card′sharper** *n.* one who cheats at cards.—**on the cards,** possible; likely to happen [L. *charta*, paper].

card (kȧrd) *n.* a toothed instrument for combing wool, flax, etc.;—*v.t.* to comb, as wool, flax, etc.—**card′er** *n.* one who cards [L. *carduus*, a thistle].

cardigan (kȧr′dig-ạn) *n.* a kind of knitted waistcoat [fr. an Earl of *Cardigan*].

cardinal (kȧr′di-nạl) *a.* chief; main; of great importance; fundamental; (*Colour*) deep scarlet.—**car′dinally** *adv.*—**cardinal numbers,** 1, 2 3, 4, 5, etc.—**cardinal points** (of the compass), north, south, east, west.—**cardinal signs** (of the Zodiac), Aries, Libra, Cancer, Capricorn.—**cardinal virtues,** justice, prudence, temperance, fortitude [L. *cardo*, a hinge].

cardinal (kȧr′di-nạl) *n.* the highest rank next to the Pope, in the Catholic Church.—**car′dinalate, car′dinalship** *n.* the office of a cardinal [L. *cardo*, a hinge].

cardio- (kȧr′di-ō) *prefix* from Gk. *kardia*, the heart, combining to form derivatives.—**car′diac** *a.* pert. to the heart;—*n.* a heart stimulant.—**car′diogram** *n.* the graphic tracing of the movements of the heart as recorded by an instrument called the **cardiograph.**—**cardiol′ogy** *n.* (*Med.*) the branch of medicine which deals with the functions and diseases of the heart.

care (kār) *n.* concern or anxiety; an object of anxiety; pains or heed; caution; charge or oversight; trouble; grief (formerly);—*v.i.* to be anxious, concerned; to be affected with solicitude; to have a fondness (with *for*).—**care′ful** *a.* full of care or solicitude; cautious or watchful; painstaking.—**care′fully** *adv.*—**care′fulness** *n.*—**care′less** *a.* heedless; thoughtless; regardless.—**care′lessly** *adv.*—**care′lessness** *n.*—**care′worn** *a.* showing the wearing effects of care.—**care′taker** *n.* one who takes over the care of unoccupied premises [O.E. *caru*].

careen (kạ-rēn′) *v.t.* to turn a ship over on one side to repair the keel;—*v.i.* to lie or heel over [L. *carina*, a keel].

career (kạ-rēr) *n.* rapid motion; a course of action; profession; conduct in life, or progress through life;—*v.i.* to speed along; to rush wildly.—**career′ist** *n.* one who makes his personal advancement his one aim in life [Fr. *carrière*, orig. a chariot course].

caress (kạ-res′) *v.t.* to treat with affection; to fondle; to kiss;—*n.* a loving touch; an embrace.—**caress′ing** *a.* [L. *carus*, dear].

caret (kar′et, kā′ret) *n.* a mark (‸) which shows where something that has been omitted is to be inserted [L. *caret*, is wanting].

cargo (kȧr′gō) *n.* the freight of a ship; the goods or merchandise carried in a vessel.—*pl.* **car′goes** [Sp. fr. *cargar*, to load].

caribou (kar′i-bòò) *n.* the N. American reindeer. Also **car′iboo** [Canadian Fr.].

Caribs (ka′ribs) *n.pl.* fierce tribes of Indians found by early explorers in W. Indies and S. America [Sp.].

caricature (kar′i-kạ-tūr) *n.* a ludicrous exaggeration (usually in picture form) of peculiar personal characteristics;—*v.t.* to exaggerate or distort, in words or in pictorial form.—**caricatur′ist** *n.* [It. *caricare*, to load].

carillon (kar′i-lon, kạ-ril′yon) *n.* a set or peal of bells of different tones; a melody played on such bells [Fr.].

cariole (kar′i-ōl) *n.* a small open carriage or light cart. Also **car′riole** [L. *carrus*].

cark (kȧrk) *n.* care or solicitude; distress;—*v.t.* to burden; to make anxious;—*v.i.* to be anxious [O.E. *cearig*, anxious, fr. *caru*, care].

carl, carle (kȧrl) *n.* a rustic or churl; a boor or low-bred fellow.—**carline** (kar′lin) *n.* an old woman; a witch [O. Scand.].

Carlovingian (kȧr-lō-vin′ji-ạn) *a.* pert. to, or descended from, *Charlemagne.*

Carmelite (kȧr′mel-īt) *n.* a begging friar of the order of Our Lady of Mount Carmel, established in the 12th cent.; also called White Friar, from the white cloak worn [fr. Mount *Carmel*, in N.W. Palestine].

carminative (kȧr′min-at-iv) *n.* a remedy, for relieving pain and flatulence. Also *a.* [L. *carminare*, to card wool].

carmine (kȧr′mīn) *n.* a brilliant crimson, prepared from cochineal. Also *a.* [Fr. or Sp. *carmin*].

carnage (kȧr′nāj) *n.* slaughter; massacre; bloodshed [L. *caro, carnis*, flesh].

carnal (kȧr′nạl) *a.* pert. to the flesh; sensual; animal; worldly; material, as opposed to spiritual.—**car′nalise** *v.t.* to make carnal.—**carna′lity** *n.* fleshly lust; sensuality.—**car′nally** *adv.*—**carnal knowledge,** sexual intercourse [L. *caro, carnis*, flesh].

carnation (kȧr-nā′shun) *n.* a flesh-colour; a variety of the clove-pink, noted for its beauty and sweet scent [L. *carnatio*, fleshiness].

carnelian (kȧr-nēl′yạn) *n.* See **cornel′ian.**

carnival (kȧr′ni-vạl) *n.* in R.C. countries a season of feasting and revelry preceding Lent; any feasting or merrymaking [L. *carnem levare*, to take away flesh].

carnivora (kȧr-niv′ō-ra) *n.pl.* animals that feed on flesh.—**carnivore** (kar′ni-vōr) *n.* a flesh-eating animal.—**carniv′orous** *a.* flesh-eating.—**carniv′orously** *adv.*—**carniv′orousness** *n.* [L. *caro, carnis*, flesh; *vorare*, to devour].

carol (kar′ol) *n.* a song of joy, esp. a Christmas hymn;—*v.i.* to sing a carol; to sing joyfully [O.Fr. *carole*].

Caroline (kar′ō-līn) *a.* pert. to the time of Charles I or II of England [L.L. *Carolus*, Charles].

carotid (kạ-rot′id) *n.* each of the two main arteries in the neck conveying blood to the head;—*a.* pert. to these [Gk. *karōtides*].

carouse (kạ-rouz′) *v.i.* to revel; to drink deep; to hold a drinking-party.—**carou′sal** *n.* a noisy drinking-party.—**carou′ser** *n.* a reveller [O.Fr. *carous*, fr. Ger. *gar aus* (drink) right to the bottom (of the glass)].

carousel (kar′òò-zel) *n.* a merry-go-round; a roundabout; military tournament [Fr.].

carp (kȧrp) *v.i.* to catch at small faults or errors; to find fault petulantly and without reason [O.N. *karpa*, to chatter].

carp (kȧrp) *n.* a fresh-water fish [Fr. *carpe*].

carpel (kȧr′pel) *n.* (*Bot.*) the seed-bearing part of a plant; part of a compound ovary.—**car′pellary** *a.* [Gk. *karpos*, fruit].

carpenter (kȧr′pen-tẹr) *n.* a worker in

timber as used in building of houses, ships, etc.—**car'pentry** *n.* a carpenter's trade or his work [L.L. *carpentarius*, a cartwright].

carpet (kår'-pet) *n.* a woven, tufted or felted cover for floors, etc.;—*v.t.* cover with this; (*Fig.*) to strew.—**car'pet-bag** *n.* a 19th cent. travelling bag made of carpet.—**car'pet-bag'ger** *n.* a political adventurer.—**on the carpet,** under consideration; (*Slang*) awaiting a probable reprimand from a superior [L.L. *carpita*, patchwork].

carrageen (kar'-a-gēn) *n.* an edible seaweed which when dried is known as Irish moss; used for making soups, jellies, size, etc. [fr. *Carragheen*, Ireland].

carraway See **caraway.**

carriage (kar'-ij) *n.* the act of carrying passengers or goods; the cost of carrying; a vehicle for passengers; a railway coach; bearing; demeanour; conduct.—**carriageable** (kar'-ij-a-bl) *a.* carriable; passable for carriages. -**carriage forward,** cost of transport to be paid by the receiver.—**carriage paid,** cost of transport paid by the sender [O.Fr. *cariage*, luggage].

carrier (kar'-i-er) *n.* one who carries; one who carries goods for hire, often called a 'common carrier'; a receptacle for carrying objects; a pigeon used for carrying messages; (*Med.*) one who, without showing symptoms of disease, can convey infection to others [O.Fr. *carier*, to load].

carriole See **cariole.**

carrion (kar'-i-on) *n.* dead, rotting flesh; anything putrid.—**carr'ion-crow** *n.* a crow which feeds on carrion [L. *caro*, flesh].

carrot (kar'-ot) *n.* a plant cultivated for its edible root.—**carr'oty** *a.* reddish-yellow; red-haired [L. *carota*].

carry (kar'-i) *v.t.* to convey; to transport; to impel; to transfer, as from one column, page, or book to another; to accomplish; to obtain possession of by force; to behave;—*v.i.* to reach, of a projectile;—*n.* range.—**to carry all before one,** to overcome all difficulties; to win triumphantly.—**to carry off,** to win; to gain.—**a carry-on** (*Colloq.*) unusual conduct; unnecessary fuss.—**to carry one's bat** (*Cricket*) not to be out at the end of the innings.—**to carry weight,** to exert an influence; to impress; to have power.—**to be carried away,** to be very greatly excited [O.Fr. *carier* fr. *car*, a vehicle].

carse (kårs) *n.* in Scotland a stretch of low fertile land along the banks of a river [etym. uncertain].

cart (kårt) *n.* a two-wheeled vehicle used for the transport of heavy goods;—*v.t.* to convey in a cart.—**car'tage** *n.* carting; the price paid for carting.—**car'ter** *n.* one who drives a cart. —**cartwright** (kårt'-rīt) *n.* a builder or maker of carts.—**to be in the cart** (*Slang*) to be in a fix [O.N. *kartr*, a cart].

cartel (kår'-tel) *n.* a challenge; an agreement between states at war for exchange of prisoners; an industrial combination for regulating volume and price of output; a trust [Fr. fr. L. *cartello*].

Cartesian (kår-tē'-zi-an) *a.* pert. to the French philosopher René *Descartes* (17th cent.), or to his philosophy.

Carthusian (kår-thū'-zi-an) *n.* one of a very austere religious order founded in the 11th cent. at *Chartreuse* in France; this monastery; a scholar of Charterhouse School (orig. a Carthusian monastery) [L. *Cartusianus*].

cartilage (kår'-ti-lāj) *n.* (*Anat.*) gristle; a strong, transparent tissue in the body, very elastic and softer than bone.—**cartilaginous** (kår-ti-la'-ji-nus) *a.* [L. *cartilago*, gristle].

cartography (kår-tog'-ra-fi) *n.* the art of making charts or maps.—**cartog'rapher** *n.* [L. *charta*, chart; Gk. *graphein*, to draw].

cartomancy (kår'-tō-man-si) *n.* divination by means of playing-cards [L. *charta*, a card; Gk. *manteia*, divination].

carton (kår'-ton *n.* thin pasteboard; a pasteboard box; a white disc on the bull's-eye of a target; a shot which strikes this [Fr. *carton*, pasteboard].

cartoon (kår-tòòn') *n.* a design drawn on strong paper for transference to mosaics, tapestries, frescoes, etc.; any large illustration, esp. one treating current affairs in an amusing fashion; a pictorial caricature.—**cartoon'ist** *n.* [Fr. *carton*, pasteboard].

cartridge (kår'-trij) *n.* a case made of metal, cardboard, etc. to contain the charge for a gun.—**blank cartridge,** one without ball, bullet, or shot, for use in peace-time manoeuvres, etc.—**ball cartridge,** a live cartridge, i.e. one with the bullet not extracted.—**cartridge paper,** stout, thick paper [Fr. *cartouche*, fr. L. *charta*, paper].

carve (kårv) *v.t.* and *i.* to fashion artistically by cutting; to hew out, as a path, a career, etc.; to cut in pieces or slices, as meat, etc.; to divide.—**car'ver** *n.* one who carves; a large knife for carving [O.E. *ceorfan*].

carvel (kår'-vel) *n.* carvel-built craft.—**car'vel-built** *a.* with planks meeting flush at the seams, instead of overlapping as in clinker-built [L. *carabus*, a wicker boat].

caryatid (kar-i-at'-id) *n.* (*Archit.*) a draped, female figure used in place of a column.—*pl.* **caryatides** (kar-i-at'-i-dēz) [Gk. *Karuatis*, a woman of *Caryae* in Laconia].

cascade (kas'-kād) *n.* a waterfall; anything resembling this; a wavy fall of lace;—*v.i.* to fall in cascades [L. *cadere*, to fall].

cascara (kas'-ka-ra, ka-ka'-ra) *n.* **cascara sagrada,** a fluid extracted from dried Californian bark and used as a laxative [Sp. *cascara*, bark; *sagrada*, sacred].

case (kās) *n.* a receptacle; a covering; a sheath; anything which encloses or contains; a box and its contents; a set; (*Print.*) a frame for holding type;—*v.t.* to put in a case.—**cas'ing** *n.* a case or covering.—**case'room** *n.* (*Print.*) the room in which type is set up.—**case'-shot** *n.* canister shot; small projectiles put in cases or canisters, to be shot from cannon.—**case'-harden** *v.t.* to heat soft steel in contact with carbonaceous material, so that carbon is absorbed, and a surface of harder steel produced.—**lower case** (*Print.*) denoting the small letters in distinction from capitals.—**upper case** (*Print.*) denoting capital letters [O.Fr. *casse*].

case (kās) *n.* an event, occurrence, or circumstance; a state or condition of things or persons; a question of facts or principles requiring investigation or solution; (*Med.*) a patient under treatment; (*Gram.*) an inflection or terminal change in nouns, pronouns, etc.—**cas'al** *a.* (*Gram.*) pert. to case.—**in case,** lest.—**to make out a good case,** to give good reasons for [L. *casus*, fr. *cadere*, to fall].

casein (kā'-sē-in) *n.* the curd or cheesy part of milk, a protein [L. *caseus*, cheese].

casemate (kās'-māt) *n.* (*Mil.*) in fortifications, a shell-proof vault built into the rampart of a fortress, with loopholes through which guns may be fired; (*Naval*) a similar armoured protection on warships; (*Archit.*) a hollow moulding [Fr.].

casement (kās'-ment) *n.* a window-frame; a window, or part of a window, opening on hinges [fr. *encase*].

cash (kash) *n.* money, esp. ready money; coin; also, paper-money, bank-notes, etc.;—*v.t.* to turn into, or exchange for, money.—**cash-reg'ister** *n.* an automatic money-till which registers and indicates the amount paid for goods sold [O.Fr. *casse*, a box]

cashew (ka-shòò') *n.* a tropical American tree whose fruit, the cashew-nut, is eaten raw or roasted [Fr. *acajou*].

cashier (kash-ēr') *n.* one who has charge of the cash [O.Fr. *casse*, a box].

cashier (kash-ēr') *v.t.* to dismiss from office in disgrace; to discard; to annul [Fr. *casser*, to annul, to dismiss].

cashmere (kash´mēr) *n.* a shawl made from the hair of the Cashmere goat; the material;—*a.* [fr. *Kashmir*, in India].

casino (ką-sē´nō) *n.* a public assembly-room or building for dancing, gambling, etc. [It. *casino*, a little house].

cask (kȧsk) *n.* a large wooden vessel for holding liquor; a barrel;—*v.t.* to put in a cask [Sp. *casco*, a potsherd, a cask].

casket (kȧs´ket) *n.* a small cask or case; a small box for jewels, etc.; the container for ashes of cremated person; (*U.S.*) a coffin [Sp. *casco*, a potsherd, a cask].

casque (kask) *n.* a sort of military helmet [Sp. *casco*, a helmet].

casserole (kas´e-rōl) *n.* a stew-pan; a vessel in which food is cooked and served without transfer to a dish; a kind of stew [Fr.].

cassia (kash´yą) *n.* a genus of plants, including the senna, whose pods are used medicinally as an aperient drug; a cheap kind of cinnamon [L. *casia*].

cassimere (kas´i-mēr) *n.* a thin twilled, woollen cloth [form of *cashmer*].

cassock (kas´ok) *n.* a long, close-fitting black gown worn by clergymen under the gown [Fr. *casaque*].

cassowary (kas´ō-wą-ri) *n.* a large swift-running bird of Malaya [Malay].

cast (kȧst) *v.t.* to fling; to hurl; to direct or bestow, as a glance; to project, as a shadow; to shed, as a skin; to reckon or compute (with *up*); to shape in a mould (as metal); to distribute the parts of a play among the actors; to throw a line in angling; to forecast (to cast a horoscope); to let down (an anchor); to give (a vote); to bring to birth prematurely;—*n.* the act of casting; a throw; the distance a thing is thrown; a mould or form; a change of direction; that which is shed or ejected (skin of insect, excrement of earthworm); a reckoning; a forecast; assignment of parts in a play; the actors appearing in the play; expression (of the face); squint (of the eye).—**cast'ing** *n.* a piece of metal cast in a mould; the act of founding and moulding metal.—**cast'ing-vote** *n.* the vote of a chairman, which decides a question when votes are equally divided.—**cast'-i'ron** *a.* made of cast iron; rigid; indefatigable; unshakable; (*Slang*) irrefutable.—**cast'-steel** *n.* steel melted, cast, and rolled out into bars.—**cast'-off** *a.* discarded;—*n.* the thing discarded.—**to cast away,** to wreck.—**to cast up,** to cast ashore; to add; to bring up as a reproach against a person [O.N. *kasta*].

castanets (kas´tą-nets) *n.pl.* two small concave shells of ivory or hard wood, fastened to the thumb and clicked in time to dances and music of a Spanish type [L. *castanea*, a chestnut-tree].

castaway (kȧst´ą-wā) *n.* a shipwrecked person; an outcast [fr. to *cast away*].

caste (kȧst) *n.* one of the four hereditary classes into which society in India is divided; any exclusive social order in other countries.—**to lose caste,** to lose social standing [L. *castus*, pure].

castellated (kas´te-lā-ted) *a.* adorned with turrets and battlements like a castle [L. *castellatus*].

caster, castor (kas´tẹr, -tor) *n.* a small bottle with perforated top for sugar, pepper, etc.; a small swivelled wheel on the foot of a chair-leg, etc.—**cas'ter-, cas'tor- su'gar** *n.* finely-powdered sugar [fr. *cast*].

castigate (kas´ti-gāt) *v.t.* to correct; to rebuke severely; to chastise; to punish.—**castiga'tion** *n.* severe chastisement; discipline.—**cas'tigator** *n.* [L. *castigare*, to punish].

castle (kas´l) *n.* a fortified residence; a stronghold, esp. of nobleman; any imposing mansion; a piece (also called 'rook') in chess.—**cas'tled** *a.* having a castle; built like a castle [L. *castellum*].

castor (kas´tor) *n.* the beaver; a hat made of beaver fur. Also **cast'er** [Gk. *kastōr*].

castor-oil (kas´tor-oil) *n.* an oil extracted from the seeds of the castor-oil plant, or *Palma Christi* [origin uncertain].

castrate (kas´trāt) *v.t.* to deprive of the testicles; to emasculate; to render incapable of generation; to render imperfect.—**castra'tion** *n.* [L. *castrare*].

casual (kazh´ū-al) *a.* accidental; incidental; occasional; offhand or careless;—*n.* a casual or occasional worker, etc.—**cas'ually** *adv.*—**cas'ualty** *n.* an accident, mishap.—**cas'ualties** *n.pl.* (*Mil.*) losses caused by death, wounds, capture, etc. [L. *casus*, accident, chance].

casuist (kazh´ū-ist) *n.* one versed in casuistry.—**cas'uistry** *n.* the science of dealing with problems of right or wrong conduct by applying principles drawn from the Scriptures, etc.; the use of specious reasoning and fallacious argument to reconcile right and wrong; quibbling, esp. on matters of morals.—**casuist'ic, casuist'ical** *a.*—**casuist'ically** *adv.* [Fr. *casuiste*].

cat (kat) *n.* a small domestic quadruped, of the family of felines; the undomesticated cat, usually called wild-cat; a spiteful woman; a small tapering block of wood used in the game of tipcat; strong tackle used to hoist an anchor; a whip;—*v.t.* and *i.* to hoist an anchor; (*Colloq.*) to vomit.—**cat'ty, cat'tish** *a.* spiteful.—**cat burg·lar,** a burglar who makes his entry by climbing to windows, roofs, etc.—**cat'-call** *n.* a cat-like cry, used by audiences to express disapproval.—**cat'-eyed** *a.* able to see in the dark.—**cat'-ice** *n.* thin, brittle ice.—**cat'-lap** *n.* any thin, weak drink.—**cat'-nap** *n.* a very short, light sleep.—**cat's'-cra'dle** *n.* a game which consists in making varying designs with string looped over the fingers.—**cat's'-eye** *n.* a gem with light-reflections like those from a cat's eye.—**cat's eyes,** discs or studs of glass fixed into traffic signs, danger posts, etc. which when illuminated by the lights of vehicles act as reflectors.—**cat's'-paw** *n.* a dupe of another; (*Naut.*) a light breeze.—**cat'-o'-nine-tails** *n.* a whip with nine thongs or lashes.—**tabby cat,** a female cat; a striped cat.—**tom cat,** a male cat [O.E. *catt*].

cat (kat) *n.* on the coast of England, a deep-waisted coal and timber boat.

cata- (kat´ą) a combining form fr. Gk. *kata*, meaning down, away, against, fully, used to form derivatives.

catachresis (kat-ą-krē´sis) (*Rhet.*) a figure by which one word is wrongly put for another [Gk. *katachresis*, misuse].

cataclysm (kat´ą-klizm) *n.* a deluge; a catastrophe; a sudden and violent alteration in earth's surface.—**cataclys'mal** *a.* [Gk. *kata*, down; *kluzein*, to wash over].

catacombs (kat´ą-kōmz) *n.pl.* underground galleries with niches for tombs [Gr. *kata*, down; *kumbē*, a cavity].

catafalque (kat´ą-falk) *n.* a structure on which a coffin is placed for a lying-in-state [origin uncertain].

catalectic (kat-ą-lek´tik) *a.* wanting a syllable at the end of a verse; applied to an incomplete foot in prosody [Gk. *kata*, down; *legein*, to stop].

catalepsy (kat´ą-lep-si) *n.* (*Med.*) suspension of senses and bodily powers, with muscular rigidity; a trance.—**catalep'tic** *a.* [Gk. *kata*, down; *lēpsis*, a seizure].

catalogue (kat´ą-log) *n.* a list, usually alphabetical, of names, books, goods, etc.; a descriptive price-list;—*v.t.* to make such a list.—**cat'aloguer** *n.* [Gk. *kata*, throughout; *legein*, to choose].

catalysis (ką-tal´i-sis) *n.* (*Chem.*) the chemical change effected in one substance by the aid of another which itself undergoes no change.—**cat'alyst** *n.* a substance producing such a change.—**catalyt'ic** *a.* [Gk. *kata*, down; *lusis*, a loosening].

catamaran (kat-ą-mą-ran′) *n.* a raft consisting of pieces of wood lashed together [Tamil=a tied tree].

catapult (kat′ą-pult) *n.* a siege engine for hurling stones, arrows, etc.; a forked piece of wood, with elastic attached to the two points, for propelling small stones, etc. through the air;—*v.t.* to hurl by means of a catapult [Gk. *kata,* against; *pallein,* to hurl].

cataract (kat′ą-rakt) *n.* a waterfall; the flow of a large body of water over a precipice; a torrent; (*Med.*) a disease of the eye, characterised by opaque state in the lens of the eye [Gk. *katarrhaktēs*].

catarrh (ką-tàr′) *n.* (*Med.*) inflammation of the mucous membranes of the body; particularly applied to such inflammation of the nose (nasal catarrh).—**catarrh′al, catarrh′ous** *a.* [Gk. *katarrhein,* to flow down].

catastasis (ka-tas′tą-sis) *n.* part of drama where action has reached its height; explanatory preface of a speech [Gk.].

catastrophe (ką-tas′trō-fe) *n.* a disaster; a calamity; a decisive event in drama; the denouement; the culmination.—**catastroph′ic** *a.* [Gk. *katastrophē,* an overturning].

catatonic (kat-a-ton′ik) *a.* pertaining to abnormal postural qualities [Gk. *kata,* throughout; *tonos,* a stretching].

catch (kach) *v.t.* to take hold of; to seize; to grasp; to arrest; to trap; to take a disease by infection or contagion; to detect; to understand; to come upon unexpectedly;—*v.i.* to seize, and keep hold, as a hook; to grasp at; to be spread by infection;—*n.* a seizure; anything that holds, stops, etc.; that which is caught; a sudden advantage; gain; the total amount of fish taken by a fisherman; a form of musical composition (a round).—**catch′able** *a.* able to be caught.—**catch′er** *n.* —**catch′y** *a.* containing a hidden difficulty; (*Mus.*) (usually of light music) captivating; attractive.—**catch′-crop** *v.* to snatch a crop off ground which is only vacant for a short period;—*n.* a crop gained in such a manner.—**catch′-land** *n.* land without an owner and regarded as public.—**to catch it** (*Colloq.*) to be scolded or punished.—**to catch a Tartar,** to get more than one bargained for, esp. from an opponent.—**catch-as-catch-can,** a Lancashire style of wrestling [L. *capere,* to take].

catchfly (kach′flī) *n.* the name of certain plants to whose stems insects adhere.

catchment (kach′ment) *n.* the area in which water, from rainfall or otherwise, collects, to form the supply of a river, stream, or drainage area [fr. *catch*].

catchpenny (kach′pen-i) *n.* something of little value and usually showy, made to sell quickly;—*a.* cheap and showy.

catchpoll, catchpole (kach′pōl) *n.* a sheriff's officer, esp. one who arrests for debt [O.Fr. *chacepol,* a tax-gatherer].

catchup, catsup, ketchup (kach′up, kat′sup, kech′up) *n.* a bottled sauce made from tomatoes, mushrooms, walnuts, etc., with vinegar, sugar and spices [E. Ind.].

catchword (kach′wurd) *n.* a word or short phrase that takes the popular fancy; a slogan; (*Theat.*) an actor's cue; the first word in the column of a dictionary, etc., repeated above the column as a reference.

catechise (kat′e-kīz) *v.t.* to instruct by question and answer, esp. in Christian doctrine; to question; to examine orally.—**catechism** (kat′e-kizm) *n.* a set form of question and answer to teach the tenets of religion; a book containing this system.—**cat′echist** *n.* one who catechises.—**catechet′ical** *a.* consisting of question and answer.—**catechet′ically** *adv.*—**catechesis** (kat′e-kē′sis) *n.* oral instruction as given to catechumens [Gk. *katēchizein,* to teach by word of mouth].

category (kat′e-gor-i) *n.* a class, group, or order; in logic, any fundamental conception. —**categor′ical** *a.* pert. to a category; admitting no conditions; absolute; precise.—**categor′ically** *adv.*—**cat′egorise** *v.t.* to place in a category [Gk. *katēgoria,* an assertion].

catena (ką-tē′ną) *n.* a chain; a series of connected things.—**ca′tenate** *v.t.* to connect in a series of links.—**catena′tion** *n.* [L.=a chain].

cater (kā′tęr) *v.i.* to buy or procure food; to provide food, entertainment, etc.; to purvey. —**ca′terer** *n.* [O.Fr. *acat,* a purchase].

cateran (kat′ęr-an) *n.* a Highland reiver or marauder; an irregular soldier (Ir. or Scot.); any freebooter [Gael. *ceatharnach*].

caterpillar (kat′ęr-pil-ąr) *n.* the grub or larva of butterflies and moths. It has a long segmented body and feeds on fruits and the leaves of plants [O.Fr. *chatepelose,* lit. a hairy cat].

caterwaul (kat′ęr-wawl) *v.i.* to cry like cats in heat [E. *cat,* and imit. sound].

catfish (kat′fish) *n.* a species of fish, usually fresh-water fish, with barbels beside the mouth like a cat's whiskers.

cathartic (ką-thàr′tik) *a.* (*Med.*) purgative; cleansing the bowels;—*n.* a purging medicine. —**cath′arise** *v.t.* to cleanse; to purify.—**cathar′sis** *n.* [Gk. *katharos,* pure].

Cathay (ka-thā′) *n.* an old name for China or Chinese Tartary.

cathedral (ką-thē′dräl) *n.* the principal church in a diocese, which contains the bishop's throne;—*a.* pert. to a cathedral [Gk. *kata,* down; *hedra,* a seat].

Catherine-wheel (kath′e-rin-hwēl) *n.* a circular, ornamented window with radiating divisions (also called 'rose-window'); a firework which rotates in burning [fr. *St. Catherine* of Alexandria martyred on a wheel].

cathode (kath′ōd) *n.* the negative pole of an electric cell; the conductor by which an electric current leaves an electrolyte, and passes over to the negative pole; opp. of *anode.*—**cathode rays,** negative ions or electrons [Gk. *kathodos,* descent].

catholic (kath′o-lik) *a.* universal; embracing all Christians; pert. to Roman Catholics; liberal or comprehensive in understanding and sympathies;—*n.* a member of the Church Universal, or of the R.C. Church.—**catholicism** (ką-thol′i-sizm) *n.* the faith and practice of Catholic Church, or of R.C. Church; breadth of view; liberality of opinion; catholicity.—**catholi′city** *n.* breadth of mind, esp. in religion [Gk. *katholikos,* general].

catkin (kat′kin) *n.* the spike of downy flowers of the willow, etc. [dim. of *cat*].

catmint, catnip (kat′mint, kat′nip) *n.* an aromatic plant with blue flowers, attractive to cats [*cat* and *mint*].

cattle (kat′l) *n.pl.* domestic livestock, esp. cows and bulls.—**catt′le-grid′** *n.,* parallel bars placed across a road or pit to prevent cattle from straying.—**catt′le-rust′ler** *n.* a cattle-thief [L.L. *capitale,* stock, fr. *caput,* the head].

Caucasian (kaw-kā′shąn) *a.* belonging to *Caucasia*; Indo-European, i.e. pert. to the white race as opposed to the yellow race. Also *n.* [fr. the *Caucasus,* mountains near the Black Sea].

caucus (kaw′kus) *n.* a small but powerful committee, esp. one connected with a political party [etym. unknown].

caudal (kaw′dal) *a.* pert. to a tail.—**caudate** *a.* having a tail [L. *cauda*].

caudle (kaw′dl) *n.* a warm drink for invalids [L. *calidus,* hot].

caught (kawt) *pa.p.* and *pa.t.* of **catch.**

caul (kawl) *n.* a net, etc. worn on the head; the membrane covering the head of some babies at birth [etym. unknown].

cauldron (kawl′dron) *n.* a large kettle or boiler [L. *calidus,* warm].

cauliflower (kaw′li-flou-ęr) *n.* a variety of

cabbage with a white flowering head [L. *caulis*, a stalk, and *flower*].
caulk, calk (kawk) *v.t.* to press tarred oakum into the seams between the planks of a boat to prevent leaks.—**caulk'er** *n.* [L.L. *calicare*, to stop up with lime, *calx*].
causal (kaw'-zal) *a.* relating to a cause or causes.—**causal'ity** *n.* the manner in which a cause works; the relation of cause and effect.—**causa'tion** *n.* agency by which an effect is produced.—**caus'ative** *a.* expressing a cause or reason [L. *causa*, cause].
cause (kawz) *n.* that which produces a result or effect; the origin or motive of an action; an action or lawsuit in court; principle supported by a person or party;—*v.t.* to produce; to be the occasion of; to induce.—**cause'less** *a.* without reason or motive [L. *causa*].
causerie (kō'-ze-rē) *n.* a chat; a gossipy newspaper article; an informal newspaper article on art or literature [Fr.=a talk].
causeway, causey (kawz'-wā, kaw'-ze) *n.* a raised paved road [L.L. *calciata*, trodden, fr. *calx*, a heel].
caustic (kaws'-tik) *a.* burning; (*Fig.*) biting, bitter, satirical;—*n.* a substance that corrodes and destroys animal tissue.—**caus'tically** *adv.* —**causti'city** *n.* corrosiveness; severity; bitterness [Gk. *kaustos*, burned].
cauter (kaw'-tẹr) *n.* a hot, searing iron.—**cau'terise** *v.t.* to burn or sear animal tissue in order to destroy diseased tissue, or promote healing.—**cauterisa'tion** *n.*—**cau'tery** *n.* the act of cauterising; a hot iron for searing [Gk. *kautērion*, a branding-iron].
caution (kaw'-shun) *n.* carefulness; prudence; wariness; a warning; security or guarantee; (*Colloq.*) an odd or droll person;—*v.t.* to advise to take care; to warn or admonish.—**cau'tious** *a.* wary; prudent; discreet.—**cau'tiously** *adv.*—**cau'tionary** *a.* containing a warning; given as security.—**cau'tioner** *n.* [L. *cavere*, *cautum*, to beware].
cavalcade (kav-al-kād') *n.* procession on horseback [L.L. *caballus*, a horse].
cavalier (kav-ạ-lēr') *n.* a horseman; a knight; a gallant; an attendant escort to a lady;—*a.* gay and offhand; supercilious; haughty and discourteous.—**Cavalier'** *n.* a partisan of Charles I in the Civil War.—**cavalier'ly** *adv.* [L.L. *caballus*, a horse].
cavalry (kav'-al-ri) *n.* horse-soldiery [L.L. *caballus*, a horse].
cave (kāv) *n.* a small chamber hollowed out of the earth horizontally, either by nature or by man; a den; a small group of seceders from a political party.—**cave'-man** *n.* a very masculine male of primitive ways.—**to cave in**, of ground, to fall in, to subside; (*Fig.*) to yield; to admit defeat [L. *cavus*, hollow].
caveat (kā'-vē-at) *n.* a warning; a legal notice to stop proceedings [L.=let him beware, fr. *cavere*, to beware].
cavendish (kav'-en-dish) *n.* tobacco, softened and pressed into plugs [fr. *Cavendish*, the first maker].
cavern (kav'-ẹrn) *n.* a deep, hollow place under the earth; a large dark cave.—**cav'erned** *a.* full of caverns.—**cav'ernous** *a.* hollow; deep-set [L. *caverna*].
caviare, caviar (kav-i-ȧr') *n.* a delicacy made from the roes of the sturgeon.—**caviare to the general**, too refined to be commonly appreciated [Turk.].
cavil (kav'-il) *v.i.* (with 'at') to raise frivolous objections; to find fault unreasonably.—*n.* a frivolous objection.—**cav'iller** *n.* [L. *cavilla*, raillery].
cavity (kav'-i-ti) *n.* a hole; a hollow place of any size [L. *cavus*, hollow].
cavort (kạ-vort') *v.i.* (*Colloq.*) to prance; to curvet; to frisk about [etym. uncertain].
caw (kaw) *v.i.* to cry like a crow or raven;—*n.* the sound made by the crow, rook, or raven.—**caw'ing** *n.* [imit. origin].
cayenne (kā-yen') *n.* a pungent red pepper, from the dried and ground fruit of capsicum plant [fr. *Cayenne*, in S. America].
cayman (kā'-mạn) *n.* a S. American alligator. Also **cai'man** [Sp. *caiman*].
cease (sēs) *v.t.* to put a stop to;—*v.i.* to stop; to discontinue; to give over.—**cease'less** *a.* without stopping.—**cease'lessly** *adv* [L. *cessare*, to cease].
cedar (sē'-dạr) *n.* species of coniferous, evergreen trees yielding durable, fragrant wood.—**ce'darn, ce'drine** *a.* [Gk. *kedros*].
cede (sēd) *v.t.* to yield; to surrender; to give up, esp. of territory [L. *cedere*].
cedilla (sẹ-dil'-ạ) *n.* a small sign (ҫ), used, principally in French, as a pronunciation mark. It is placed under 'c', when followed by a, o, or u, to indicate that the 's' sound is to be used [Gk. *zēta*, z].
ceil (sēl) *v.t.* to overlay with plaster or line with wood the inner side of the roof of a room [Fr. *ciel*, the sky].
ceiling (sē'-ling) *n.* the interior part of the roof of a room; the maximum height to which a particular aeroplane can ascend; (*Fig.*) the upper limit of production, wages, prices, etc. [Fr. *ciel*, the sky].
celandine (sel'-an-dīn) *n.* a wild plant bearing star-shaped yellow flowers, popularly known as swallow-wort. Also **lesser celandine**, pile-wort, a variety of ranunculus [Gk. *chelidōn*, a swallow].
celebrate (sel'-e-brāt) *v.t.* to make famous; to mark by ceremony, as an event or festival; to observe with solemn rites.—**cel'ebrated** *a.* renowned; famous.—**celebra'tion** *n.* the act of celebrating.—**cel'ebrant** *n.* one who celebrates. —**celeb'rity** (sel-eb'-ri-ti) *n.* renown; fame; a person of distinction [L. *celebrare*].
celerity (sel-er'-i-ti) *n.* rapidity of motion; speed; swiftness [L. *celer*, swift].
celery (sel'-e-ri) *n.* an edible plant cultivated for eating with salads or as a cooked vegetable [Fr. *céléri*, fr. Gk. *selinon*, parsley].
celesta (sel-es'-tạ) *n.* (*Mus.*) a small piano-like instrument [Fr.].
celestial (sel-est'-yạl) *a.* heavenly; divine; blessed;—*n.* an inhabitant of heaven; (*Colloq.*) a Chinaman.—**celest'ially** *adv.*—**the Celestial Empire**, China [L. *caelum*, heaven].
celibacy (sel'-i-bạ-si) *n.* single life; the unmarried state.—**cel'ibate** *n.* one unmarried; —*a.* unmarried [L. *caelebs*, unmarried].
cell (sel) *n.* a small room, as in a prison or monastery; a small cavity; the simplest unit in the structure of living matter; a small group of members of a political party; a division of a voltaic or galvanic battery.—**celled** (seld) *a.* furnished with, or containing, cells; contained in cells.—**cell'ular** *a.* consisting of, or containing, cells, as cellular tissue.—**cell'ulated** *a.* having a cellular structure [L. *cella*, a small room].
cellar (sel'-ạr) *n.* an underground store-room, esp. for wines, liquors.—**cell'arage** *n.* space for cellars; the charge for storage in cellars.—**cell'arer** *n.* a monk in charge of stores, wines, etc.; a spirit merchant.—**cell'aret** *n.* a dining-room cabinet for wines, liquors, etc. [L. *cellarium*, a pantry].
cello, 'cello (chel'-ō) *n.* (*Mus.*) a contraction for violoncello.—**cell'ist, 'cell'ist** *n.* a player on the violoncello.
Cellophane (sel'-ō-fān) *n.* a tough, transparent, waterproof material used as wrapping tissue, etc. [Protected Trade Name].
Celluloid (sel'-ū-loid) *n* a proprietary name for a hard compound used in the manufacture of imitation ivory, coral, amber, etc. [L. *cellula*, a little cell].
cellulose (sel'-ū-lōs) *n.* a chemical substance, one of the carbohydrates, forming the chief constituent of the walls of plant cells; a varnish made from compounds of cellulose [L. *cellula*, a little cell].
Celt, Kelt (selt, kelt) *n.* one of a race, in

cluding the Highlanders of Scotland, the Irish, Welsh, Bretons, Manx, and Cornish.—**Cel'tic, Kel'tic** *n.* the language spoken by the Celts.—*a.* pert. to the Celts [L. *Celticus*].

cement (sę-ment') *n.* a plastic mixture that can unite two bodies; mortar; a bond of union;—*v.t.* to unite by using cement; to join closely.—**cementa'tion** *n.* the act of cementing; the conversion of iron into steel [L. *caementum*, stone for building].

cemetery (sem'e-ter-i) *n.* a graveyard; a burying-ground, unattached to a church [Gk. *koimētērion*, a sleeping-room].

cenobite, coenobite (sē'nō-bīt) *n.* member of a religious order, dwelling in community, as opposed to a hermit or anchorite [Gk. *koinos*, common; *bios*, life].

cenotaph (sen'ō-taf) *n.* a monument erected to one buried elsewhere; an empty sepulchre [Gk. *kenos*, empty; *taphos*, a tomb].

censer (sen'sęr) *n.* a metal vessel in which incense is burned.—**cense** *v.t.* to perfume with incense [L. *incendere*, to burn].

censor (sen'sor) *n.* a Roman official who looked after property, taxes, and the people's morals; one appointed to examine books, plays, newspaper articles, etc., before publication, and ban them if containing anything objectionable; also, in time of war or crisis, to examine letters, etc., and erase anything calculated to convey information to the enemy; one who blames or finds fault; (*Psych.*) the conception of a mental tendency which inhibits unpleasant memories from appearing in consciousness, or even, unless in a disguised state, in dreams, etc.;—*v.t.* to blame or reprove; to subject to examination by the censor.—**censo'rial** *a.* pert. to correction of morals; pert. to a censor.—**censo'rious** *a.* apt to find fault.—**censo'riously** *adv.*—**censo'riousness** *n.*—**cen'sorship** *n.* the office of a censor; the act of censoring [L. *censere*, to estimate].

censure (sen'shūr) *n.* the act of finding fault; disapproval;—*v.t.* to reprove; to express disapproval of; to criticise adversely.—**cen'surable** *a.*—**cen'surably** *adv.*—**cen'surableness** *n.* [L. *censura*, opinion].

census (sen'sus) *n.* an official numbering of the inhabitants of a country.—**cen'sual** *a.* [L. *census*, register].

cent (sent) *n.* a hundred, as 10 per *cent*; an American coin worth the hundredth part of a dollar.—**cent'al** *n.* 100 lb. avoirdupois [L. *centum*].

centaur (sen'tawr) *n.* (*fem.* **cen'tauress**) (*Myth.*) a fabulous being, half man and half horse [Gk. *kentaurion*].

centaury (sen'taw-ri) *n.* a plant of the gentian family [Gk. *kentaurion*].

centenary (sen-ten'ąr-i, sen-tēn'ąr-i, sen'ten-ą-ri) *n.* a period of a hundred years; a century; the commemoration of a hundredth anniversary; a centennial.—**centenarian** (sen-te-nā'ri-ąn) *n.* a person a hundred years old [L. *centum*, a hundred].

centennial (sen-ten'i-ąl) *a.* pert. to a period of 100 years; happening once in a hundred years;—*n.* a hundredth anniversary [L. *centum*; *annus*, a year].

centesimal (sen-tes'i-mąl) *a.* hundredth; counted or counting by hundredths;—*n.* a hundredth part [L. *centum*].

centi- (sen'ti) *prefix* fr. L. *centum*, a hundred, combining to form derivatives.—**cen'tigrade** *a.* divided into 100 degrees, as the centigrade thermometer on which freezing-point is marked 0°, and boiling-point 100°.—**cen'tigram, cen'tigramme** *n.* in the Metric System, 100th part of a gramme.—**centimetre** (sen'ti-mē-tęr) *n.* 100th part of a metre = ·394 inch.

centipede, centiped (sen'ti-pēd, -ped) *n.* a small animal, of flat and elongated shape, with a segmented body, each segment having a pair of legs [L. *centum*, a hundred; *pes, pedis*, a foot].

cento (sen'tō) *n.* a poem formed of fragments taken from various poems or authors [L. *cento*, patchwork].

central (sen'trąl) *a.* relating to, or placed in, the centre; chief; important.—**cen'trally** *adv.*—**cen'tralise** *v.t.* to draw to a central point; to concentrate; to put under one control.—**centralisa'tion** *n.*—**cen'tralism** *n.* centralisation, esp. of government.—**central'ity** *n.* the state of being central.—**central heating**, steam or hot water heating of a building from one central furnace [L. *centralis*, fr. L. *centrum*].

centre, center (sen'tęr) *n.* the mid-point of anything; pivot; axis; a point to which things move or are drawn; a point of concentration;—*v.t.* and *i.* to place in the centre; to collect round a point; to be fixed; (*Sport*) to propel from the wing to centre.—**cen'tric(al)** *a.* placed in centre or middle.—**cen'trically** *adv.*—**centricity** (sen-tris'i-ti) *n.* the state of being centric.—**centre of gravity**, the point in a body about which it will balance [L. *centrum*].

centrifugal (sen-trif'ū-gąl) *a.* tending to move away from the centre of a revolving body [L. *centrum*, the centre; *fugere*, to flee].

centripetal (sen-trip'e-tąl) *a.* tending to move towards the centre [L. *centrum*, the centre; *petere*, to seek].

centumvir (sen-tum'vir) *n.* in ancient Rome, a judge appointed to deal with civil cases [L. *centum*, a hundred; *vir*, a man].

centuple (sen'tū-pl) *a.* hundredfold.—**centu'plicate** *v.t.* to multiply by 100 [L. *centum*, a hundred; *plicare*, to fold].

centurion (sen-tū'ri-on) *n.* an officer in command of a company of a hundred men in a Roman legion [L. *centurio*].

century (sen'tū-ri) *n.* a period of a hundred years; a set of a hundred; in cricket, a score of a hundred runs; a company of a Roman legion numbering a hundred soldiers under the command of a centurion [L. *centuria*].

cephalalgy (sef-al-al'ji) *n.* (*Med.*) headache; pain in the head.—**cephal'ic** *a.* pert. to the head;—*n.* a medicine for headaches [Gk. *kephalē*, the head].

cephalopod (sef'al-o-pod) *n.* a class of molluscs, including cuttlefish, octopus, etc., having their tentacles attached to the head.—**cephalopod'ic, cephalop'odous** *a.* [Gk. *kephalē*, the head; *pous, podis*, the foot].

ceramic (ser-am'ik) *a.* pert. to pottery.—**ceram'ics** *n.pl.* the art of moulding, modelling, and baking clay; the study of pottery as an art [Gk. *keramos*, pottery].

cere (sēr) *v.t.* to cover with wax;—*n.* the wax-like naked skin at base of bill in some birds.—**cera'ceous** (sē-rā'shus) *a.* like wax; waxy.—**ce'rate** *n.* an ointment of wax, oil, etc.—**cerecloth** (sēr'kloth) *n.* a cloth smeared with melted wax in which dead bodies used to be wrapped.—**cere'ment** *n.* a cerecloth.—**cereous** (sē'rēus) *a.* waxen; waxy; like wax [L. *cera*, wax].

cereal (sē're-ąl) *a.* pert. to edible grain;—*n.* any edible grain (wheat, barley, oats, etc.) [L. *Ceres*, Roman goddess of corn].

cerebrum (ser'e-brum) *n.* the upper and larger division of the brain.—**cerebell'um** *n.* the part of the brain behind and below the cerebrum.—**cer'ebral** *a.* pert. to the brain.—**cerebral haemorrhage**, rupture of an artery of the brain with a consequent escape of blood.—**cerebral hemispheres**, the two great divisions of the cerebrum.—**cer'ebrate** *v.i.* to have the brain in action.—**cerebra'tion** *n.*—**cerebro-spinal** (ser'e-brō-spī'nąl) *a.* pert. to both brain and spinal cord.—**cerebro-spinal fever** (*Med.*) an epidemic form of meningitis [L. *cerebrum*, the brain].

ceremony (ser'e-mo-ni) *n.* a sacred rite; formal observance; formality; usage of courtesy; prescribed rule; a public or private function.—**ceremo'nial** *a.* pert. to ceremony; formal;—*n*, an outward observance; usage followed in performing rites.—**ceremo'nially**

adv.—**ceremo'nious** *a.* full of ceremony; particular in observing forms.—**ceremo'niously** *adv.*—**ceremo'niousness** *n.*—**master of ceremonies,** at public functions, etc. one whose business it is to see that all forms, rules, and courtesies are observed [L. *caerimonia,* a rite].

cerise (ser-ēz') *n.* and *a.* of colour, light clear red; cherry-coloured [Fr.=cherry].

cerium (sē'ri-um) *n.* (*Chem.*) a very rare metal [named after the planet *Ceres*].

certain (ser'tin) *a.* sure; settled; undoubted; inevitable; some; one; regular; constant; of moderate quantity, degree, etc.—**cer'tainly** *adv.*—**cer'tainty** *n.* the quality of being certain.—**cer'titude** *n.* freedom from doubt; assurance; certainty.—**certes** (ser'tēz) *adv.* certainly; in truth [L. *certus*].

certificate (ser-tif'i-kāt) *n.* a written testimony to the truth of a fact; a testimonial or written statement of qualifications;—*v.t.* to attest by a certificate; to furnish with a certificate.—**certify** (ser'ti-fī) *v.t.* to testify to in writing; to vouch for the truth of; officially to declare insane.—**cer'tifiable** *a.* able to be vouched for; fit to be certified as insane.—**certifica'tion** *n.* the act of certifying [L. *certus,* certain; *facere,* to make].

cerulean (se-ròò'le-an) *a.* sky-blue; deep blue; azure.—**ceru'leous** *a.* sky-blue [L. *caeruleus*].

cerumen (se-ròò'men) *n.* ear-wax.—**ceru'minous** *a.* [L. *cera,* wax].

ceruse (sē'ròòs) *n.* white lead.—**ce'rusite** *n.* a carbonate of lead [L. *cerussa,* white lead].

cervical (ser'vi-kal) *a.* pert. to the neck [L. *cervix,* the neck].

cess (ses) *n.* a tax;—*v.t.* to tax.—**bad cess to you!** (*Irish*) bad luck to you! [short form of *assess*].

cessation (se-sā'shun) *n.* stoppage; discontinuance [L. *cessare,* to cease].

cesspool (ses'pòòl) *n.* a pit or hollow for the collection of filthy drainage water or sewage. Also **cess'pit** [etym. uncertain].

Cetacea (sē-tā'sē-a) *n.pl.* an order of mammals to which the whales belong.—**cetacean** (sē-tā'shan) *n.*—**ceta'ceous** *a.* [Gk. *kētos,* a whale].

Chablis (shab'lē) *n.* a white wine, made near *Chablis,* in Burgundy, France.

chad (shad) *n.* a fish of the herring kind. Also **shad** [O.E. *sceadda*].

chafe (chāf) *v.t.* to warm by rubbing; to wear away by rubbing; to irritate; to vex;—*v.i.* to be worn by rubbing or friction; to rage or fret;—*n.* friction; injury caused by rubbing.—**chaf'er** *n.* one who chafes; a dish for heating water.—**chaf'ing-dish** *n.* a vessel for cooking or keeping food warm on the table; a portable grate [Fr. *chauffer,* to warm.].

chafer (chā-fer) *n.* any of various beetles; a cockchafer [O.E. *cefer,* a beetle].

chaff (chaf) *n.* the husk of grains; straw cut small for cattle-feeding; worthless matter; refuse.—**chaff'y** *a.* [O.E. *ceaf*].

chaff (chaf) *n.* banter; jesting talk;—*v.t.* to tease; to make fun of (without spite) [form of *chafe,* to irritate].

chaffer (chaf'er) *v.i.* to buy and sell; to haggle about the price.—**chaff'erer** *n.* [M.E. *chapfare,* haggling].

chaffinch (chaf'insh) *n.* a small song-bird of the finch family.

chagrin (sha-grēn') *n.* ill-humour; vexation; mortification;—*v.t.* to vex deeply [Fr.].

chain (chān) *n.* a series of metal rings or links connected and forming a flexible cable; a fetter; a succession of things or events; a mountain range; anything that connects; a measure equal to 100 links, or 66 ft.;—*v.t.* to fasten or connect with a chain; to fetter; to restrain.—**chain'-bridge** *n.* a suspension bridge.—**chain'-drive** *n.* the transmitting of driving-power by means of chain-gear.—**chain'-gang** *n.* a number of convicts chained together.—**chain'-mail, -arm'our** *n.* a flexible metal shirt or cuirass made of rings closely linked.—**chain'-reac'tion** *n.* in nuclear physics, a self-sustaining process in which some neutrons from one splitting atom are able to split more atoms, setting free still more neutrons which carry on the reaction indefinitely [L. *catena,* a chain].

chair (chār) *n.* a movable seat with a back; a portable covered vehicle for carrying one person, e.g. a sedan; an official seat occupied by the president of a meeting, a university professor, a bishop, etc.; one of the iron blocks supporting the rails on a railway;—*v.t.* to carry in triumph.—**to take the chair,** to act as chairman of a meeting; to preside.—**chair'man** *n.* the presiding officer at a meeting; one who carries a sedan.—**chair'woman** *n.*—**chair'oplane** *n.* a roundabout with chairs, suspended by chains [Fr. *chaire,* a pulpit fr. Gk. *kathedra*].

chaise (shāz) *n.* a light, one-horse carriage; a posting-carriage.—**chaise'-longue** (lōng) *n.* a sofa [Fr. *chaise,* a chair, a seat].

chalcedony (kal-sed'ō-ni) *n.* a whitish or bluish-white variety of quartz; white agate.—**chalced'onic** *a.*—**chalcedonyx** (kal-sed'ō-niks) *n.* a variety of chalcedony or agate [fr. *Chalcedon,* a town in Asia Minor].

chalet (sha'lā) *n.* a timber-built house in Alps; a country residence like Swiss mountain cottage; a public lavatory [Fr.].

chalice (chal'is) *n.* a wine-cup; a goblet; a communion-cup [L. *calix*].

chalk (chawk) *n.* a soft, white, carbonate of lime;—*v.t.* to rub or mark with chalk.—**chalk'y** *a.* containing or like chalk.—**chalk'iness** *n.*—**French chalk,** a soft, impure variety of talc used by tailors, etc. for marking cloth; soap-stone [L. *calx,* limestone].

challenge (chal'enj) *n.* an invitation to a contest, esp. to a duel; defiance; the warning call of a sentry to an approaching person; exception taken to a juror;—*v.t.* to call upon a person to settle a dispute by fighting; to defy; to summon to answer; to call in question.—**chall'engeable** *a.* able to be challenged.—**chall'enger** *n.* [L. *calumnia.* Doublet of E. *calumny*].

chalybeate (ka-lib'ē-āt) *a.* impregnated with iron;—*n.* any water or liquor containing iron.—**chalybeate springs,** mineral waters containing iron salts (as at Harrogate) and having medicinal value [Gk. *chalups,* steel].

Cham (kam) *n.* formerly, the sovereign prince of Tartary; an autocrat; a dictator.—**the Great Cham,** any literary dictator, but esp. Dr. Johnson as a critic [form of *khan*].

chamber (chām'ber) *n.* a room, esp. one used for lodging, privacy, or study; a place where an assembly meets, and the assembly itself; a cavity; the cavity at the rear end of the bore of a gun; a vessel for urine;—*v.t.* to shut up or confine, as in a chamber;—*v.i.* to occupy as a chamber; to be wanton.—**cham'bers** *n.pl.* a room or rooms where professional men, esp. barristers, conduct business; lodgings; the space between the lock-gates of a canal.—**cham'ber-maid** *n.* a woman servant who has the care of bedrooms, esp. in hotels, etc.—**cham'ber-mus'ic** *n.* music suitable for performance in a house or small hall.—**cham'ber-pot** *n.* a vessel for urine.—**Upper Chamber,** the House of Lords [L. *camera,* a room].

chamberlain (chām'ber-lin) *n.* an official at the court of a monarch having the charge of domestic and ceremonial affairs; a treasurer of public money, esp. of a city.—**cham'berlainship** *n.* [fr. *chamber*].

chameleon (ka-mēl'yun) *n.* a small lizard, which changes colour with its surroundings; (*Fig.*) an inconstant person [Gk. *chamai,* on the ground; *leōn,* a lion].

chamfer (cham'fer) *v.t.* to cut a groove in; to bevel;—*n.* a groove; a bevel.—**cham'fered** *a.* [O.Fr. *chanfraindre*].

chamois (sham'wà) *n.* a goat-like species of

mountain antelope; with the pronunciation (sha′-mi), a kind of soft leather.—popularly written **sham′my** [Ger. *Gemse*, a chamois].

champ (champ) *v.t.* and *i.* to bite, chew, or munch noisily.—**to champ at the bit** (*Fig.*) to be impatient at delay in departure.

champagne (sham-pān′) *n.* a light effervescent, white wine, made in the old province of *Champagne* in N.E. France.

champaign (sham-pān′) *n.* a stretch of flat, open country; a plain;—*a.* flat; open [L. *Campania*, a plain south of Rome].

champignon (sham′-pin-yon) *n.* a mushroom, esp. the fairy-ring mushroom [Fr.].

champion (cham′-pi-on) *n.* one who fought in single combat to defend the honour of another; a defender of any cause; one capable of defeating his competitors in any form of sport;—*a.* first-class;—*v.t.* to defend; to maintain or support.—**cham′pionship** *n.* the position of a champion; defence; advocacy [L.L. *campio*, a fighter in the arena].

chance (chàns) *n.* an unforeseen occurrence; accident; risk; likelihood; opportunity; possibility;—*a.* accidental;—*v.t.* to venture upon; to risk;—*v.i.* to happen.—**chan′cy** *a.* lucky; uncertain.—**main chance,** money-making [O.Fr. *cheance*, fall of dice].

chancel (chan′-sel) *n.* the east part of a church, where the altar is placed, orig. shut off by a screen of lattice-work from the nave [L. *cancelli*, lattice-work].

chancellor (chan′-sel-or) *n.* the title of various high officials in the state, and in the law; the head of a university.—**chan′cellorship** *n.* the office of chancellor.—**chan′cellory, -ery** *n.* the premises of a chancellor.—**Chancellor of the Exchequer,** the British minister of finance [Fr. *chancelier*, orig. keeper of a barrier].

chancery (chan′-sẹr-i) *n.* formerly, the chief English court of justice next to Parliament; now a division of the High Court of Justice; an office for public records.—**in Chancery** (*Law*) under the superintendence of the Lord Chancellor [orig. *chancellory*].

chancre (shang′-kẹr) *n.* a venereal ulcer.—**chan′crous** *a.* ulcerous [Fr.].

chandelier (shan-de-lēr′) *n.* a branched framework for holding lights, esp. one hanging from the ceiling; orig. for holding candles [L. *candela*, a candle].

chandler (chand′-lẹr) *n.* orig. a candle-maker; now a dealer in candles, soap, oil, etc.; a dealer in goods for specific purposes.—**chand′lery** [L. *candela*, a candle].

change (chānj) *v.t.* to alter or make different; to put one thing for another; to shift; to quit one state for another; to exchange, as pence for a shilling; to convert;—*v.i.* to become different; to change one's clothes;—*n.* the act of changing; alteration; that which makes for variety; money of small denomination given in exchange for money of larger; balance of money returned after payment; fresh clothing; an exchange.—**change′able** *a.* variable; fickle; unsteady.—**change′ful** *a.* changeable; fickle.—**change′fully** *adv.*—**change′fulness** *n.*—**change′less** *a.* unchanging; constant.—**change′ling** *n.* a child left in place of another taken by the fairies.—**change′-house** *n.* an inn [L. *cambire*, to barter].

channel (chan′-el) *n.* a watercourse; the deeper part of a river, harbour, etc.; a strait; a groove or furrow; means of communication;—*v.t.* to form a channel; to groove or furrow [L. *canalis*].

chant (chànt) *v.t.* and *i.* to sing; to celebrate in song; to intone; to deal fraudulently in horses;—*n.* a song; melody; sacred words recited in a singing manner.—**chant′er** *n.* (*fem.* **chant′ress**) one who chants; the tube with finger-holes, in a bagpipe.—**chant′ry** *n.* an endowed chapel where masses for the dead are sung.—**chan′ty** (shan′-ti) *n.* a sailor's song [L. *cantare*, to sing].

chanticleer (chant-i-klēr′) *n.* a cock [O.Fr. *chante-cler*, sing-clear].

chaos (kā′-os) *n.* empty, infinite space; complete confusion; state of the universe before the creation.—**chaotic** (kā-ot′-ik) *a.* [Gk.].

chap (chap) *v.t.* to cleave or open longitudinally; to split; to crack;—*v.i.* to crack or open in long slits; to fissure;—*n.* a chink; a crack in the skin, esp. in the hands, caused by exposure to cold [related to *chip, chop*].

chap, chop (chap, chop) *n.* (usually *pl.*) the jaw of an animal; the jaw of a vice; the entrance of a channel [etym. uncertain].

chap (chap) *n.* (*Colloq.*) a fellow.—**chap′man** *n.* a pedlar; a hawker.—**chap′book** *n.* a book or pamphlet, hawked by chapmen [O.E. *ceap*, a bargain].

chapel (chap′-el) *n.* a private church; a subordinate place of worship, as one attached to a garrison, school, prison, etc.; a division of a church with its own altar; in England, a Dissenters' or Non-conformists' place of worship; in Scotland and Ireland, a Roman Catholic church; an association of journeymen printers [L.L. *cappella*, a cloak, orig. where the sacred cloak (or *cappella*) of St. Martin was deposited].

chaperon (shap′-e-rōn) *n.* a kind of hood; a lady who escorts an unmarried lady in public as a protector;—*v.t.* to escort as chaperon.—**chap′eronage** *n.* [Fr.=a hood].

chaplain (chap′-lin) *n.* a clergyman attached to a ship of war, army, public institution, or family.—**chap′laincy** *n.* [Fr. *chapelain*].

chaplet (chap′-let) *n.* a garland or wreath for the head; a string of beads; a division of the rosary [O.Fr. *chapelet*].

chaps (chaps) *n.pl.* overalls worn by a cowboy [fr. Sp. *chaparejos*].

chapter (chap′-tẹr) *n.* a division of a book or treatise; a bishop's council in a diocese; an organised assembly of a society, fraternity, or military order;—*v.t.* to divide into chapters [L. *caput*, the head].

char (chàr) *n.* a species of trout, found mostly in deep lake-waters [Celt.].

char (chàr) *v.t.* to reduce to charcoal; to burn to a black cinder;—*pr.p.* **char′ring**.—*pa.p.* and *pa.t.* **charred**.—**char′coal** *n.* the residue of partially burnt animal or vegetable matter, esp. wood.—**char′coal-burn′er** *n.* one who makes charcoal [etym. uncertain].

char (chàr) *n.* (*Army Slang*) tea [Hind.].

char, chare (chàr, chār) *n.* a job; work done by the day;—*v.i.* to work by the day; to do small jobs.—**char′woman** *n.* a woman who does cleaning by the day (*Colloq.* **a char**) [O.E. *cerr*].

char-a-banc (shar′-ạ-bang) *n.* a long, open coach with transverse seats.—**char′a, char′i** *n.* popular contraction for a char-a-banc [Fr.=a carriage with benches].

character (kar′-ak-tẹr) *n.* a mark, letter, figure, sign, stamp; any distinctive mark; an essential feature; nature; the total of qualities making up an individuality; a statement of the qualities of a person who has been in one's service; a testimonial; a person noted for eccentricity; a personage in a play or novel.—*v.t.* to characterise; to portray; to represent.—**char′acterise** *v.t.* to depict the peculiar qualities of; to distinguish; to give character to.—**characteris′tic** *a.* serving to mark the character of; peculiar; distinctive;—*n.* that which distinguishes a person or thing from another;—**characteris′tically** *adv.*—**characterisa′tion** *n.* the act of characterising; literary or dramatic portrayal of character (Gk. *charaktēr*, an engraved mark].

charade (shạr-ràd′) *n.* a sort of puzzle-game, consisting of the interpretation (usually dramatic) of a word [Fr.].

charge (chàrj) *n.* a load or burden; price or cost; care or trust; an earnest exhortation, as of a judge or bishop; accusation or allegation;

a clergyman's parish or the people of that parish; the amount of powder, etc., that a gun is fitted to hold; an impetuous onset or attack, or the signal for it; custody; electrical contents of accumulator or battery;—*v.t.* to lay a task, command, trust upon; to ask as payment; to accuse; to load, as a gun;—*v.i.* to make an onset.—**charge'able** *a.* that may be laid upon or charged.—**charg'er** *n.* a large, flat dish; a war-horse. [L.L. *carricare*, to load a cart].

chargé d'affaires (shàr-zhā'da-fer') *n.* a minor diplomatic emissary; a deputy ambassador [Fr.=charged with business].

chariot (char'i-ot) *n.* in ancient times, a two-wheeled car used in warfare; a four-wheeled state carriage.—**charioteer'** *n.* [Fr. dim. of *char*, a car, cart].

charity (char'i-ti) *n.* (*Bib.*) love and goodwill to men; liberality to the poor; leniency in judging others; any act of kindness; alms; a charitable cause or institution.—**char'itable** *a.* pert. to charity; liberal to the poor; generous-minded.—**char'itably** *adv.* [L. *caritas*, affection].

charivari (shàr-i-vàr'i) *n.* a mock serenade, with tin-pans, horns, etc.; in general, an uproar; in journals, a satirical medley [Fr.].

charlatan (shàr'la-tan) *n.* a quack medicine vendor; a mountebank or imposter. [It. *ciarlare*, to prate, chatter].

Charleston (charlz'ton) *n.* a strenuous dance. [fr. *Charleston*, in U.S.A.].

charlock (chàr'lok) *n.* a plant of the mustard family [O.E. *cerlic*].

charlotte (shàr'lot) *n.* (*Cookery*) a kind of pudding made by lining a mould with bread or cake, and filling it with fruit [Fr.].

charm (chàrm) *n.* a magic spell; anything supposed to possess magic power; a talisman; attractiveness.—*v.t.* to subjugate by magic; to attract irresistibly;—*v.i.* to please greatly; to be fascinating.—**charm'ing** *a.* attractive; alluring; delightful.—**charm'ingly** *adv.* [Fr. *charme*, fr. L. *carmen*, a song].

charnel (chàr'nel) *a.* containing dead bodies. —**char'nel-house** *n.* a place where the bodies or bones of the dead are deposited; a sepulchre [L. *caro, carnis*, flesh].

chart (chàrt) *n.* a map of part of the sea, showing currents, depths, islands, coasts, etc.; a diagram giving information in tabular form; a graph;—*v.t.* to represent on a chart; to map; to delineate.—**chart'less** *a.*—**chartaceous** (kàr-tā'shus) *a.* (*Bot.*) papery [L. *charta*, a paper].

charter (chàr'ter) *n.* a formal document confirming privileges, titles, or rights; an act of incorporation; a patent; the hiring of a vessel;—*v.t.* to establish by charter; to grant privileges to; to hire, as a ship.—**char'tered** *a.* [L. *charta*, a paper].

chartreuse (shàr-trez') *n.* a liqueur, manufactured by the monks of La Grande *Chartreuse*, Grenoble, France.

chary (chàr'i) *a.* careful; sparing.—**char'ily** *adv.* [O.E. *cearig*, full of care].

chase (chās) *v.t.* to pursue; to run after; to hunt; to drive away;—*v.i.* to hasten; to hurry;—*n.* pursuit; hunting of enemy, game, etc.; what is pursued or hunted; land maintained as a game preserve.—**chas'er** *n.*—**a wild-goose chase**, the pursuit of something unattainable [L. *captare*, to seize].

chase (chās) *v.t.* to enchase; to engrave metal; [abbrev. of *enchase*].

chase (chās) *n.* (*Print.*) an iron frame to hold type when set up; a wide groove [L. *capsa*, a box. Doublet of *case*].

chasm (kazm) *n.* a deep opening in the earth; a cleft [Gk. *chasma*].

chassé (sha'sā) *n.* in dancing, a rapid gliding step to the right or left [Fr.].

chassis (sha'sē) *n.* the under-carriage of a motor-car, including the engine; the frame-work of an aeroplane or gun [Fr. *chassis*, a frame].

chaste (chāst) *a.* pure; virtuous; undefiled; pure and simple in taste and style.—**chaste'ly** *adv.*—**chaste'ness** *n.*—**chas'tity** *n.* purity; virginity [L. *castus*, pure].

chasten (chā'sn) *v.t.* to correct by punishment; to purify from errors and faults; (*Fig*). to subdue [L. *castigare*, to punish].

chastise (shas'tīz') *v.t.* to inflict pain in order to reform; to punish.—**chastisement** (chas'tiz-ment) *n.* punishment; correction [L. *castigare*, to punish].

chasuble (chaz'ū-bl) *n.* a sleeveless vestment worn over the alb by the priest during Mass [L.L. *casula*, a mantle].

chat (chat) *v.i.* to talk idly or familiarly; to rid oneself of lice;—*n.* light, familiar talk; a louse;—*pr.p.* **chatt'ing**;—*pa.p.* and *pa.t.* **chatt'ed.**—**chatt'er** *v.i.* to talk idly or rapidly; to rattle together, of the teeth.—**chatt'erer** *n.* one who chatters.—**chatt'iness** *n.*—**chatt'y** *a.* talkative; gossipy; infested with body lice [imit. origin].

chat (chat) *n.* a bird belonging to a sub-family of the thrushes [imit. origin].

chateau (shà-tō') *n.* a castle; a country-seat, esp. in France; a mansion;—*pl.* **chateaux** (shà-tōz').—**chatelain** (sha'te-lang) *n.* a castellan; the owner or tenant of a castle.—**chatelaine** (sha'te-len) *n.* a female castellan; a chain fastened to a lady's girdle, with keys, seals, etc. attached [O.Fr. *chastel*. Doublet of *castle*].

chattel (chat'l) *n.*, usually in *pl.* **chattels**, any kind of property, except freehold.—**goods and chattels**, goods, possessions, and property [O.Fr. *chatel*. Doublet of *cattle*].

chatter See **chat.**

chauffeur (shō-fer', shō'fer) *n.* (*fem.* **chauffeuse'**) the paid driver of a private motor-car [Fr.=a stoker].

chauvinism (shō'vi-nizm) *n.* absurdly exaggerated patriotism; jingoism.—**chau'vinist** *n.*—**chauvinist'ic** *a.* [fr. Nicolas *Chauvin*, devoted follower of Napoleon].

chaw (chaw) *n.* a chew or quid of tobacco; a piece suitable for chewing;—*v.t.* to chew; to champ (of horses) [corrupt. of *jaw*].

cheap (chēp) *a.* low in price; of low cost, as compared with the value, or the usual cost; dealing in low-priced articles; contemptible, inferior, vulgar.—**cheap'ly** *adv.*—**cheap'ness** *n.* —**cheap'en** *v.t.* to bring down the price; to lessen the value; to render less estimable. **cheap'-jack,** or **-john** *n.* a travelling hawker, selling inferior goods [O.E. *ceap*, a bargain].

cheat (chēt) *v.t.* to deceive; to defraud; to trick;—*v.i.* to practise trickery;—*n.* a fraud; an imposture; one who cheats; an impostor. —**cheat'er** *n.* [short for *escheat*].

check (chek) *n.* a stop; a restraint; an interruption in progress; an obstacle, obstruction; control or supervision, or one employed to carry out such; a mark placed against items in a list; a cheque, or order to a bank to pay money; a term in chess to indicate that opponent's king must be moved or guarded; a criss-cross pattern in cloth, etc.—*v.t.* to restrain; to hinder; to chide or reprove; to verify; to put a mark against, in a list; in chess, to put in check;—*v.i.* to come to a sudden stop; to pause.—**checkers** *n.pl.* the game of draughts.—**check'-key** *n.* a latch-key. —**check'mate** *n.* the final movement in chess, when the king can be neither moved nor protected; complete defeat.—**luggage check,** a ticket given to a passenger depositing luggage [fr. Pers. *shah*, king].

checker (chek'er) *v.t.* to variegate with cross lines; to diversify;—*v.i.* to produce a checkered effect, esp. of alternate light and shade; —*n.* a square; a pattern like a chess-board; a piece in the game of checkers [Fr. *échiquier*].

Cheddar (ched'ar) *n.* a kind of cheese [fr. *Cheddar*, in Somerset].

chee-chee (chē´-chē´) *n.* a half-caste or Eurasian [Hind. *chhi-chhi*, fie!].

cheek (chēk) *n.* the fleshy wall or side of the mouth; each side of the face below the eyes; insolence or impudence; the side-post of a door, window, etc;—*v.t.* (*Slang*) to speak saucily to.—**cheek'y** *a.* pert; insolent [O.E. *ceace*, the cheek, jaw].

cheep (chēp) *v.i.* to chirp, as a small bird;—*n.* a small shrill sound [imit. origin].

cheer (chēr) *n.* spirits; disposition; state of mind; gaiety; expression of approval, or encouragement, by shouting; rich food; a welcome;—*v.t.* to render cheerful; to comfort; to hearten or inspirit; to salute with cheers;—*v.i.* to shout hurrah.—**cheer'er** *n.*—**cheer'ful** *a.* having good spirits.—**cheer'fully** *adv.*—**cheer'fulness** *n.*—**cheer'ily** *adv.* with cheerfulness.—**cheer'iness** *n.*—**cheer'io!** *interj.* an informal salutation at parting.—**cheer'less** *a.* gloomy; comfortless.—**cheer'lessness** *n.*—**cheer'y** *a.* in good spirits; promoting cheerfulness. [O.Fr. *chiere*, countenance; L.L. *cara*, the face].

cheese (chēz) *n.* a curd of milk, separated from the whey, and pressed into a solid mass; the ball used in skittles.—**cheese´cloth** *n.* a thin loosely woven cotton cloth, for wrapping cheese in.—**cheese´mong'er** *n.* a cheese merchant.—**cheese'-par'ing** *a.* parsimonious; scrimping.—**cheese it** (*Slang*) stop it! [O.E. *cese, cyse*, curdled milk].

cheetah (chē´-tạ) *n.* the hunting leopard of India [Hind.].

chef (shef) *n.* a head-cook.—**chef-d'oeuvre** (shā-dẹvr') *n.* a masterpiece, esp. in art or literature [Fr.].

cheiro- See **chiro-**.

cheiromancy See **chiromancy**.

chemical (kem´-i-kạl) *a.* pert. to, or made by, chemistry;—*n.* a substance used in chemistry, or produced by chemical processes.—**chem´ically** *adv.* according to chemical principles [fr. *Alchemy*].

chemise (shem-ēz') *n.* a woman's shirt.—**chemisette** (shem-ē-zet') *n.* a kind of bodice [Fr. *chemise*, a shirt].

chemist (kem´-ist) *n.* a person versed in chemistry; one permitted by law to sell medicines, drugs and poisons; a druggist; an apothecary.—**chem'istry** *n.* the study of the various substances which compose the universe, their combinations, and the processes by which they act one upon another. [shortened form of *alchemist*].

chemotherapeutics (kem´-ō-ther-a-pū´-tiks) *n.* (*Med.*) the use of chemical compounds in the treatment of disease.—**chemother'apy** *n.* treatment by this means [E. *chemical*; Gk. *therapeuein*, to heal].

chemurgy (kem´-ẹr-ji) *n.* applied chemistry directed to developing agricultural produce.

chenille (she-nēl') *n.* a soft plush-like cord of silk, wool, worsted, etc. used for ornamental trimmings, fringes, etc.; a soft, velvety fabric used for hangings, curtains, covers, etc. [Fr. *chenille*, a caterpillar].

cheque, check (chek) *n.* a specially printed form for use as a money order on a banker.—**cheque´book** *n.* a book of such forms [form of *check*].

chequer, chequered See **checker**.

cherish (cher´-ish) *v.t.* to hold dear; to treat tenderly; to foster [L. *carus*, dear].

Cherokee (cher-o-kē') *n.* one of a tribe of American Indians.

cheroot (sher-ȯȯt') *b.* a kind of cigar, open at both ends [Hind.].

cherry (cher´-i) *n.* the bright red fruit of a tree akin to the plum; a cherry-tree;—*a.* pert. to a cherry; red.—**cherr'y-brand'y** *n.* a liqueur made by steeping cherries in brandy [Gk. *kerasos*].

cherub (cher´-ub) *n.* a winged creature with a human face; an angel; a celestial spirit; a beautiful child;—*pl.* **cherubim** (cher´-ȯȯ-bim) or **cherubs** (cher´-ubz).—**cherubic** (cher-ȯȯ´-bik) *a.* [Heb. *krub*, pl. *krubim*].

chess (ches) *n.* a game of Eastern origin played by two persons on a board containing sixty-four squares, with two differently coloured sets of pieces or 'men'—**chess'man** *n.* a piece used in the game [Pers. *shah*, a king].

chest (chest) *n.* a large box; a coffer; a trunk; trunk of human body; part enclosed by ribs and breast-bone;—*v.t.* to place in a chest.—**chest'note** *n.* in singing, a very low note—**chest of drawers**, a piece of furniture fitted with drawers [O.E. *cest*].

chesterfield (ches´-ter-fēld) *n.* a long overcoat; a heavily padded sofa [after Earl of *Chesterfield*].

chestnut (ches´-nut) *n.* the fruit, seed, or nut of a forest tree belonging to the genus Castanea; the tree itself, or its timber; a reddish-brown colour; a horse of this colour; (*Colloq.*) a stale joke or story;—*a.* reddish-brown [L. *castanea.*].

cheval (shẹ-val') *n.* a horse; a support or frame.—**cheval´-glass** *n.* a large mirror within a supporting frame.—**chevalier** (shev-ạ-lēr') *n.* orig. a horseman; a cavalier; a knight [Fr. *cheval*, a horse].

cheval-de-frise (shẹ-val´-dẹ-frēz) *n.* a beam fitted with long spikes, used as a defence, esp. against cavalry;—*pl.* **chevaux'** (shẹ-vō') **de frise** [Fr.=*Friesland horses*, because first used in Friesland].

Cheviot (chēv´-i-ot) n. a famous breed of sheep reared on the *Cheviot* Hills; cloth made from their wool.

chevron (shev´-ron) *n.* a rafter; (*Her.*) the representation on a shield of two bands meeting rafter-like; (*Mil.*) a V-shaped band of braid or lace worn on the sleeve to designate rank [Fr. *chevron*, a rafter].

chew (chȯȯ) *v.t.* to bite and crush with the teeth; to masticate; to ruminate; to champ;—*n.* action of chewing; a quid of tobacco.—**chew'ing-gum** *n.* a sweetmeat (usually flavoured with mint) prepared from *chicle*, the gum of a Mexican rubber-tree.—**to chew the cud**, to chew a second time food already swallowed; to meditate [O.E. *ceowan*].

Chianti (kē-an´-ti) *n.* an Italian red or white wine [fr. *Chianti* hills in Italy].

chiaroscuro (kyȧ-ros-kȯȯ´-rō) *n.* the reproduction in art of the effects of light and shade in nature [It.=bright dark].

chic (shēk) *n.* style and elegance; effectiveness;—*a.* stylish; modish [Fr.].

chicane (shi-kān') *n.* trick or artifice; sharp practice, esp. in legal proceedings; (*Cards*) a bridge hand with no trumps in it;—*v.i.* to use shifts and trickery.—**chica'nery** *n.* trickery; sophistry; quibbling.—**chica'ner** *n.* [Fr.].

chick, chicken (chik, chikẹn) *n.* the young of fowls, esp. of hen; a young child.—**chick'-abiddy** *n.* a term of endearment to a child.—**chick'en-heart'ed** *a.* timid.— **chick'en-pox** *n.* a mild, contagious, eruptive disease.—**chick'ling** *n.* a small chicken.—**chick'weed** *n.* weed with small white blossoms used for feeding cage-birds.—**Mother Carey's chicken**, the stormy petrel [O.E. *cicen*].

chicle (chik´-l) *n.* a gum-like, milky juice obtained from several Central American trees; a chewing-gum prepared from this substance [Sp. Amer.].

chicory (chik´-o-ri) *n.* a plant whose taproot when roasted and ground is used to mix with coffee. Also called **suc'cory** [Fr. *chicorée*].

chide (chīd) *v.t.* to scold; to rebuke;—*v.i.* to find fault;—*pr.p.* **chid'ing**.—*pa.p.* **chid, chid'den**.—*pa.t.* **chid** [O.E. *cidan*].

chief (chēf) *a.* foremost in importance; principal; main; at the head; most influential;—*n.* a head or leader; a principal person or thing.—**chief'ly** *adv.* principally; for the most part.—**chief'tain** *n.* (*fem.* **chief'tainess**) the head of a clan; a commander.—**chief'ship** *n.*

chief'taincy, chief'tainship *n.* government over a clan [Fr. *chef.* fr. L. *caput,* the head].
chiff-chaff (chif′chaf) *n.* a small singing-bird of the Warbler family [imit. origin].
chiffon (shif′on) *n.* a thin, soft, gauzy material.—**chiffonier** (shif-on-ēr′) *n.* an ornamental cabinet, with drawers or shelves [Fr. *chiffon,* a rag].
chignon (shē′nyōng) *n.* a rolled-up pad or bun of hair at the back of a woman's head or on the nape of the neck [Fr.].
chilblain (chil′blān) *n.* a blain, or inflammatory swelling caused by cold and bad circulation [fr. *chill* and *blain*].
child (chīld) *n.* a very young person of either sex; offspring; descendant;—*pl.* **chil'dren,** offspring, descendants.—**child'birth** *n.* the act of bearing a child; labour.—**child'bed** *n.* childbirth.—**child'hood** *n.* the state of being a child; the time during which one is a child.—**child'ish** *a.* pert. to a child; silly; trifling.—**child'ishly** *adv.*—**child'ishness** *n.*—**child'less** *a.* without children.—**child'lessness** *n.*—**child'like** *a.* like a child; innocent; trustful; dutiful [O.E. *cild*].
chiliad (kil′i-ad) *n.* a thousand; a period of a thousand years [Gk. *chilioi,* a thousand].
chill (chil) *a.* cold; tending to cause shivering; cool in manner or feeling; discouraging;—*n.* a feeling of coldness, attended with shivering; illness caused by cold; discouragement;—*v.t.* to cool; to cause to shiver; to benumb; to dispirit; to keep meat cold;—*v.i.* to grow cold.—**chill'y,** cold; creating cold; depressing; ungenial.—**chill'iness** *n.* [O.E. *cele, ciele,* coldness].
chilli, chili (chil′i) *n.* the red pepper, or fruit of the capsicum, is called Cayenne pepper when dried and ground [Mex.].
chime (chīm) *n.* the musical sound of bells; a set of bells tuned to the musical scale (generally used in the plural);—*v.t.* and *i.* to sound harmoniously; to be in harmony; to agree with [M.E. *chimbe,* orig.=*cymbal*].
chimera, chimaera (ki-mē′rạ) *n.* a fabulous, fire-breathing monster; a creature of the imagination.—**chimer'ic(al)** *a.* [Gk. *chimaira,* orig. a she-goat].
chimney (chim′ni) *n.* the passage through which the smoke of a fireplace, etc., is carried off, a funnel; a deep, narrow cleft in a rock.—**chim'ney-cor'ner** *n.* the corner of the fireplace; the fireside.—**chim'ney-piece** *n.* a mantelpiece.—**chim'ney-pot** *n.* a pipe placed at the top of a chimney to create greater draught; short for **chimney-pot-hat,** a top hat.—**chim'ney-stack** *n.* a group of chimneys.—**chim'ney-stalk** *n.* a very tall chimney, often of a factory.—**chim'ney-sweep** *n.* one who removes the soot from chimneys [Gk. *kaminos,* a furnace].
chimpanzee (chim′pan-zē′) *n.* a large African anthropoid ape [W. Africa].
chin (chin) *n.* the part of the face below the mouth [O.E. *cin*].
China (chī′nạ) *n.* a vast country in E. Asia.—**Chinaman** *n.* a native of China.—**Chinese** (chī-nēz′) *n.* a native, the natives, or the language of China;—*a.* belonging to China.—**Chinee** (*Colloq.*) a Chinese; a Chinaman.—**chi'-na-clay** *n.* the finer kinds of pottery and porcelain clay, called kaolin.—**chi'naware** *n.* a species of fine earthenware; porcelain.—**Chi'nese-lan'tern** *n.* a collapsible lantern of coloured paper.—**Chi'nese-white** *n.* a pigment composed of white oxide of zinc.
chinchilla (chin-chil′ạ) *n.* a small animal, with very fine, soft fur; the fur itself; a breed of rabbit whose fur is used as an imitation of the chinchilla [Sp.].
chine (chīn) *n.* the backbone or spine of an animal; a piece of the backbone, with the adjoining flesh, cut for cooking; a deep ravine; a mountain ridge [Fr. *échine,* the spine].
chink (chingk) *n.* a small cleft rent, or fissure; a gap or crack; *-v.t.* to open;—*v.i.* to crack [O.E. *cinu,* a fissure].
chink (chingk) *n.* the sound of a piece of metal when struck; the ring of coin;—*v.i.* to jingle; to ring;—*v.t.* to sound by rattling, as coins, etc. [imit. origin].
Chinook (chin-ōōk′) *n.* a tribe of N.W. American Indians; a warm, dry wind from the Pacific blowing along the slope of the Rocky Mountains [Amer. Ind.].
chintz (chintz) *n.* a calico cloth, printed in different colours [Hind. *chint*].
chip (chip) *v.t.* to chop off into small pieces; to break little pieces from; to shape by cutting off pieces;—*v.i.* to break or fly off in small pieces;—*pr.p.* **chip'ping;**—*pa.p.* and *pa.t.* **chipped;**—*n.* a piece of wood, etc. separated from a larger body by an axe, etc.; a fragment; a counter, instead of money, used in gambling, esp. at poker.—**chips** *n.pl.* fried slices of potato; (*Naut.*) a ship's carpenter.—**chip'-shot** *n.* (*Golf*) a short, lofted shot on to the green.—**a chip off the old block,** one who closely resembles his father, esp. in character [fr. E. *chop*].
chipmunk (chip′mungk) *n.* the American burrowing ground-squirrel or striped gopher. Also **chip'muck** [Native].
chippendale (chip′pen-dāl) *n.* a style of furniture introduced by an 18th cent. cabinet-maker, Thomas *Chippendale.*
chiro- (kī′ro) *prefix* fr. Gk. *cheir,* the hand, combining to form derivatives.
chiromancy (kī′rō-man-si) *n.* divination by inspection of the hand; palmistry. Also **chei'romancy** [Gk. *cheir,* the hand; *manteia,* divination].
chiropodist (kī-rop′ō-dist) *n.* one skilled in the treatment of diseases of the hands and feet.—**chirop'ody** *n.* [Gk. *cheir,* the hand; *pous, podos,* the foot].
chiropractic (kī-rō-prak′tik) *n.* a method of healing which relies upon the removal of nerve interference by manual adjustment of the spine.—**chiroprac'tor** *n.* [Gk. *cheir,* the hand; *prassein,* to do].
chirp, chirrup (chẹrp, chir′up) *n.* a short, sharp note, as of a bird or cricket;—*v.i.* to make such a sound; to twitter; to talk gaily.—**chirp'er** *n.*—**chirp'ingly** *adv.* gaily.—**chirp'y** *a.* lively; cheerful [imit. origin].
chirurgeon (kī-rur′jun) *n.* an obsolete form of **surgeon.** Similarly **chirur'gery** and **chirur'gical** have been replaced by **surgery** and **surgical** [Gk. *cheir,* the hand; *ergon,* work].
chisel (chiz′ẹl) *n.* a tool sharpened to a cutting edge at the end, used in carpentry, sculpture, etc.;—*v.t.* to cut or carve with this tool; to cheat;—*pr.p.* **chis'elling;**—*pa.p* and *pa.t.* **chis'elled** [O.Fr. *cisel*].
chit (chit) *n.* a pert child [O.E. *cith,* a shoot].
chit (chit) *n.* an informal note; a voucher; a permit or pass. Also **chit'ty** [Hind. *chitthi*].
chit-chat (chit′chat) *n.* prattle; trivial talk; gossip [imit. origin].
chitin (kī′tin) *n.* a white, horny substance, forming the outer covering of insects, crustacea, etc. *a.* [Gk. *chiton,* a tunic].
chitter (chit′ẹr) *v.i.* to chirp; to shiver with cold [form of *chatter*].
chitterlings (chit′er-lings) *n.pl.* the smaller intestines of swine, etc., used as food [etym. unknown].
chivalry (shiv′ạl-ri) *n.* the system of knighthood in medieval times; a body of knights; the qualities of a knight, viz. dignity, courtesy, bravery, generosity, gallantry.—**chival'ric, chiv'alrous** *a.* pert. to chivalry;—**chiv'alrously** *adv.* [Fr. *chevalerie,* fr. *cheval,* a horse].
chive (chīv) *n.* a small herb of the onion kind [L. *cepa,* an onion].
chivvy, chivy (chiv′i) *v.t.* to chase; harass; worry; tease [fr. a hunting-cry].
chlor-, chloro- (klōr-, klō′rō) combining forms fr. Gk. *chloros,* green.

chlorine (klō´rēn) *n.* a heavy gas of yellowish-green colour used in disinfecting, bleaching, and poison-gas warfare.—**chlo'ral** *n.* a sleep-producing drug.—**chlo'rate** *n.* a salt of chloric acid.—**chlo'ric** *a.* pert. to chlorine.—**chlo'ride** *n.* a compound of chlorine with another element.—**chlo'rinate** *v.t.* disinfect or bleach, with chlorine.—**chlorina'tion** *n.*—**chlo'rite** *n.* a mineral of a green colour, soft and friable.—**chlo'roform** *n.* a colourless, volatile liquid used as an anaesthetic;—*v.t.* to make insensible by using chloroform [Gk. *chloros*, pale-green].

chlorodyne (klōr´ō-dīn) *n.* a proprietary medicine used as a narcotic and anodyne [Gk. *chloros*, pale-green; *odunē*, pain].

chlorophyll (klō´rō-fil) *n.* (*Bot.*) the green colouring matter of plants [Gk. *chloros*, pale-green; *phullon*, a leaf].

chock (chok) *n.* a wedge to steady a cask lying on its side;—*v.t.* to make fast, with a block or wedge.—**chock'full, choke'full, chock'-a-block** *a.* packed full; jammed together [form of *choke*].

chocolate (chok´ō-lāt) *n.* a paste made from the powdered seeds of the cacao plant, mixed with sugar, etc.; a beverage made by pouring boiling water or milk over this;—*a.* dark-brown [Mex. Sp.].

choice (chois) *n.* the act of choosing; the power or opportunity of choosing; selection; the thing chosen; alternative;—*a.* worthy of being chosen; rare [Fr. *choix*, fr. *choisir*, to choose].

choir (kwīr) *n.* a company of singers, esp. belonging to a church; that part of the church set apart for them; the chancel.—**choir'-screen** *n.* a screen dividing the chancel from the nave [L. *chorus*].

choke (chōk) *v.t.* to stop the breath as by compression of the windpipe; to stifle or smother;—*v.i.* to have the wind-pipe stopped; to be suffocated.—**chok'er** *n.* one who chokes; (*Colloq.*) a high collar or cravat [O.E. *aceocian*].

choke (chōk) *n.* the act of choking; an obstructing piece in mechanism.—**choke'-tube** *n.* in motoring, a tube fitted inside a carburettor to contract the opening and so increase velocity of gas [O.E. *aceocian*].

choky (chōk´i) *n.* (*Slang*) prison; jail [Hind.].

choler (kol´ẹr) *n.* bile; anger; wrath.—**chol'eric** *a.* passionate; easily angered.—**cho'lera** *n.* deadly, epidemic, bilious disease, marked by purgings, vomitings and griping pains.—**cholera'ic** *a.* pert. to cholera [Fr. *colère*, anger, fr. Gk. *cholē*, bile].

cholic (kol´ik) *a.* pert. to, or obtained from, bile [Gk. *cholē*, bile].

choose (chòòz) *v.t.* to pick out; to select; to take one thing in preference to another;—*v.i.* to decide; to think fit.—*pa.p.* **cho'sen**; *pa.t.* **chose**.—**choo'sey** *a.* (*Slang*) fastidious, difficult to please [O.E. *ceosan*].

chop (chop) *n.* See **chap**.

chop (chop) *v.t.* to barter; to exchange;—*v.i.* to shift suddenly, as wind.—**to chop and change**, to be inconstant.—**to chop logic**, to dispute with a display of logical argument [Dut. *koopen*, to buy].

chop (chop) *v.t.* to cut into pieces; to mince, by striking repeatedly with a sharp instrument; to sever by blows;—*v.i.* to make a quick stroke or repeated strokes with a sharp instrument, as an axe;—*n.* the act of chopping; a piece chopped off; a thick slice of meat attached to a rib or other bone; a cutlet.—*pr.p.* **chop'ping**.—*pa.p.* and *pa.t.* **chopped**.—**chop'per** *n.* one who chops; a large heavy knife; cleaver.—**chop'py** *a.* full of fissures; of the sea, having short, broken waves.—**chop'-stick** *n.* one of two small sticks of wood, ivory, etc., used by the Chinese in taking food [etym. uncertain].

choral (kō´rạl) *a.* pert. or belonging to a choir or chorus.—**cho'rally** *adv.*—**cho'ric** *a.* pert. to a chorus, esp. Greek dramatic chorus.—**chorist** (kō´rist), **chorister** (kor´ist-ẹr) *n.* a member of a choir [Gk. *choros*, a band of dancers and singers].

chorale (kō´rȧl') *n.* a simple, dignified melody sung to religious words [Gk. *choros*].

chord (kord) *n.* the string of a musical instrument; (*Mus.*) a series of tones having a harmonic relation to each other, and sounded simultaneously; (*Geom.*) a straight line between two points in the circumference of a circle [Gk. *chordē*, a string].

chore (chōr) *n.* any odd job, or occasional piece of house-work [O.E. *cerr*, work].

chorea (ko-rē´ạ) *n.* (*Med.*) uncontrollable spasms of limbs, body and facial muscles; St. Vitus's dance.—**chore'ic** *a.* [Gk. *choreia*, a dancing].

choreograph (ko´rē-o-graf) *n.* a designer of ballet. Also **choreog'rapher**.—**choreograph'ic** *a.* —**choreog'raphy** *n.* [Gk. *choros*, dance; *graphein*, to write].

chorography (kō-rog´rạ-fi) *n.* the art of making a map, or writing a description, of a region or country.—**chorol'ogy** *n.* the study of the geographical distribution of plants and animals [Gk. *chora*, land; *graphein*, to write; *logos*, discourse].

choroid (kō´roid) *n.* a membrane of the eye between the sclerotic and the retina [Gk. *chorion*, a membrane].

chortle (chor´tl) *v.i.* to chuckle gleefully.—**chort'ling** *n.* [invented by Lewis Carroll from *chuckle* and *snort*].

chorus (kō´rus) *n.* orig. a band of singers and dancers; a combination of voices singing together; what is sung or spoken by the chorus; in a Greek play, certain performers who witness the action, and at intervals express their feelings regarding it; the refrain;—*v.t.* to join in the refrain; to call out or sing together.—**cho'ric** *a.* pert. to a chorus [Gk. *choros*, a band of dancers and singers].

chose (chōz) *pa.t.* of **choose**.—**chosen** (chō´zn) *pa.p.* of the same verb.—**the Chosen People**, the Jews.

chough (chuf) *n.* a genus of birds of the crow family [fr. its cry].

chowder (chou´dẹr) *n.* a stew made of fish, pork, onions, etc. [Fr. *chaudière*, a pot].

chrism (krizm) *n.* holy oil, a mixture of olive oil and balm or spices, for the anointing ceremonies in confirmation, extreme unction, baptism, etc.—**chris'mal** *a.*—**chris'matory** *a.* of, or pert. to, chrism or unction;—*n.* a vessel to hold holy oil.—**chris'om** *n.* a baptismal robe [Gk. *chriein*, to anoint].

Christ (krīst) *n.* The Anointed—a name given to the Saviour, and synonymous with the Hebrew Messiah.—**Christ'hood** *n.* the condition of being the Christ.—**Christ'liness** *n.* —**Christ'like, Christ'ly** *a.* resembling Christ [Gk. = anointed].

christen (kris´n) *v.t.* to baptise in the name of Christ; to give a name to.—**Chris'tendom** *n.* all Christian countries; the whole body of Christians.—**chris'tening** *n.* baptism [Gk. *Christos*, anointed].

Christian (krist´yạn) *n.* a follower or disciple of Christ; a professed adherent of the Church of Christ;—*a.* pert. to Christ or his religion.—**chris'tianise** *v.t.* to make Christian; to convert to Christianity.—**Christian'ity** *n.* the religion of the followers of Christ.—**Chris'tianlike, Chris'tianly** *a.* in a Christian manner.—**Christian era**, the era counting from the birth of Christ.—**Christian name**, the name given at baptism; individual name, as opposed to surname or family name.—**Christian Science**, a religious doctrine of faith-healing founded in America by Mrs. Mary Eddy [Gk. *Christos*, anointed].

Christmas (kris´mạs) the annual festival in celebration of the birth of Christ, observed on Dec. 25; Christmas-day;—*a.* belonging to Christmas or its festivities.—**Christ'mas-box** *n.* a box for Christmas presents; a Christmas gift.—**Christ'mas-card** *n.* a card, sent to friends at Christmas as a token of remembrance.—**Christmas carol,** a religious hymn of joy in praise of Christ's Nativity.—**Christ'mas-eve** *n.* the evening of December 24.—**Christ'mas-rose** *n.* the Black Hellebore [E. *Christ* and *Mass*].

Christology (kris-tol'ō-ji) *n.* that branch of theology which treats of the person and character of Christ.—**christolo'gical** *a.* [Gk. *Christos*, Christ; *logos*, a discourse].

Christophany (kris-tof'ạ-ni) *n.* the appearance of Christ to men after his resurrection [Gk. *Christos*, Christ; *phainein*, to appear].

chroma-, chromo- (krō'mạ-, krō'mō-), combining forms fr. Gk. *chroma*, colour.

chromatic (krō-mat'ik) *a.* pert. to colour; (*Mus.*) proceeding by semitones.—**chromat'ics** *n.* the science of colours; (*Mus.*) chromatic notes.—**chromat'ically** *adv.* [Gk. *chroma*, colour].

chrome, chromium (krōm, krō'mi-um) *n.* a metal, very resistant to corrosion, used generally for plating other metals.—**chro'mic** *a.* pert. to, or obtained from, chrome or chromium.—**chro'mate** *n.* a salt of chromic acid.—**chro'mite** *n.* a mineral, the chief source of chromium.—**chrome colour,** a yellow prepared from a chromium salt [Gk. *chroma*, colour].

chromosome (krō'mo-sōm) *n.* (*Biol.*) one of the gene-carrying bodies in the tissue of a cell, regarded as the transmitter of hereditary factors from parent to child [Gk. *chroma*, colour; *soma*, a body].

chronic (kron'ik) *a.* continuing for a long time; of disease, deep-seated and lasting; confirmed; inveterate; (*Slang*) bad; terrible.—**chron'ically** *adv.* [Gk. *chronos*, time].

chronicle (kron'i-kl) *n.* a register of events in order of time; a history or accounts;—*v.t.* to record in order of time.—**chron'icler** *n.* [Gk. *chronika*, annals, fr. *chronos*, time].

chrono- (kron'o) a combining form fr. Gk. *chronos*, time.—**chron'ograph** *n.* an instrument for measuring and recording, time very exactly.—**chronol'ogy** *n.* the science that treats of historical dates and arranges them in order; a table of events and dates.—**chronol'oger, chronol'ogist** *n.* one who records historical events, etc.—**chronolog'ical** *a.* arranged in order of time.—**chronolog'ically** *adv.*—**chronom'eter** *n.* a very accurate watch or time-keeper.—**chronomet'ric, chronomet'rical** *a.*—**chronom'etry** *n.* the process of measuring time by instruments [*graphein*, to write; *logos*, discourse].

chrysalis (kris'ạ-lis) *n.* the golden-coloured form of an insect, shut up in a shell, in the stage before it becomes a butterfly;—*pl.* **chrysalides** (kris-al'i-dēz).—**chrys'alid** *n.* a chrysalis [Gk. *chrusos*, gold].

chrysanthemum (kris-an'the-mum) *n.* a large, mop-headed, garden flower [Gk. *chrusos*, gold; *anthemon*, a flower].

chryso- (kris'o) a combining form fr. Gk. *chrusos*, gold.—**chrysocracy** (kris-ok'rạ-si) *n.* the rule of wealth.—**chrys'olite** *n.* a yellowish-green precious stone.—**chrysoprase** (kris'ō-used as a gem [Gk. *krate in*, to rule; *lithos*,a stone; *prason*, a leek].

chub (chub) *n.* a fresh-water fish of the carp family, small and fat.—**chub'by** *a.* round and plump.—**chub'biness** *n.* [M.E. *chubbe*].

Chubb (chub) *n.* lock patented by *Chubb*, a London locksmith. [Protected Trade Name].

chuck (chuk) *v.i.* to cluck, as a hen calling her chickens; to tap under the chin;—*n.* the call of a hen; a term of endearment [imit. origin].

chuck (chuk) *n.* a pebble [etym. uncertain].

chuck (chuk) *v.t.* (*Colloq.*) to throw; to toss; to pitch; to stop;—*n.* the act of tossing.—**chuck it!** (*Slang*) stop! leave me in peace.—**chuck'er-out** *n.* one employed to eject obstreperous people [etym. uncertain].

chuck (chuk) *n.* in machinery, part of a lathe for holding an object while it is being operated on [etym. uncertain].

chuckle (chuk'l) *v.i.* to laugh in a suppressed manner;—*n.* a short, quiet laugh; the call of a hen [imit. origin].

chuckle (chuk'l) *a.* clumsy.—**chuck'le-head** *n.* a dolt, a lout [E. *chock*, a log].

chug (chug) *n.* a pull or tug; an explosive sound made by a car exhaust or a railway engine;—*v.i.* to pull or tug; to make an explosive sound as above [imit. origin].

chukker, chukka (chuk'er, -ạ) *n.* one of the periods into which a game of polo is divided [Hind.].

chum (chum) *n.* an intimate friend; a pal; a room-mate;—*v.i.* to be friendly (with); to share a room with.—*pr.p.* **chum'ming.**—*pa.p.* and *pa.t.* **chummed.**—**chum'my** *a.* friendly; sociable [etym. unknown].

chump (chump) *n.* a lump of wood; the thick end of a loin of mutton; (*Slang*) the head; a blockhead [origin uncertain].

chunk (chungk) *n.* a short, thick piece of wood, etc.—**chunk'y** *a.* [etym. uncertain].

church (church) *n.* building for Christian worship; collective body of Christians; a denomination or sect of the Christian religion; the clergy; the church service;—*v.t.* to perform a thanksgiving service over a couple in church for the first time after marriage, over judges, magistrates, etc., on their first official attendance at church.—**Church Army,** an organisation like the Salvation Army, connected with the Church of England.—**church'man** *n.* an ecclesiastic; a member of the Established Church.—**churchwar'den** *n.* an officer entrusted with the interests of the church or parish; a long clay-pipe.—**church'yard** *n.* the ground adjoining a church, generally used as a burial ground [O.E. *circe*, fr. Gk. *kuriakon*, belonging to the Lord].

churl (churl) *n.* a countryman; a surly clown.—**churl'ish** *a.*—**churl'ishly** *adv.*—**churl'ishness** *n.* [O.E. *ceorl*, a man].

churn (churn) *n.* a vessel in which cream is violently stirred to produce butter; a large milk-can;—*v.t.* to agitate cream so as to produce butter; to stir up violently;—*v.i.* to produce butter [O.E. *cyrin*].

chute (shòòt) *n.* a rapid descent in a river; a rapid; a sloping contrivance for transferring coal, rubbish, etc. to a lower level [Fr. *chute*, a fall].

chutney, chutnee (chut'ne) *n.* an E. Indian condiment, generally made with mangoes, peppers and spices [Hind. *chatni*].

chyle (kīl) *n.* the milky fluid into which food is transformed before being absorbed into the blood.—**chyl'ous** *a.* [Gk. *chulos*, juice].

chyme (kīm) *n.* the pulp into which the stomach transforms food.—**chym'ous** *a.* pert. to, or consisting of, chyme [Gk. *chumos*, juice].

cibol (sib'ol) *n.* a small, delicate variety of onion [Fr. *ciboule*; L. *cepa*, an onion].

cicada, cicala (si-kà'dạ, si-kà'lạ) *n.* an insect, the male of which emits a shrill, chirping sound [L. *cicada*, a cricket].

cicatrice, cicatrix (sik'ạ-tris, sik-ā'triks) *n.* a scar left after a healed wound;—*pl.* **cicatri'ces.**—**cicatrise** (sik'ạ-trīz) *v.t.* to heal and induce the formation of skin, as in wounded or ulcerated flesh [L. *cicatrix*, a scar].

cicerone (sis-e-rō'ne, chē-chā-rō'nā) *n.* one who shows strangers over a place; e.g. a cathedral, etc.; a guide [It. fr. L. *Cicero*].

cider, cyder (sī'dẹr) *n.* a drink made from the fermented juice of apples [Heb. *shakar*, to be intoxicated].

cigar (si-gar') *n.* tobacco-leaf made up in a roll for smoking.—**cigarette'** *n.* finely cut tobacco rolled in thin paper [Sp. *cigarillo*].

cilia (sil′i-ą) *n.pl.* the eyelashes; (*Anat.*) hair-like, vibratile processes.—**cil'iary, cil'iate, cil'iated, cilif'erous, cil'iform** *a.*

cinch (sinch) *n.* a saddle-girth; (*Slang*) a certainty; a card game;—*v.t.* to fasten a cinch round; to tighten (girth) [L. *cingula*, a girth].

cinchona (sin-kō′ną) *n.* a genus of trees yielding Peruvian bark, from which quinine is extracted; the bark itself.—**cinchonaceous** (sin-kō-nā′shus) *a.* [Sp. fr. Countess of *Chinchon*, who was cured by it in 1638].

cincture (singk′tūr) *n.* a belt; a girdle; a zone;—*v.t.* to encircle.—**cinc'tured** *a.* girdled [L. *cinctura*, a girdle].

cinder (sin′dẹr) *n.* the remains of burned coal; any partially burned combustible substance [O.E. *sinder*].

cinema (sin′e-mą) *n.* a hall or theatre where moving pictures are screened; a picture house.—**cinemat'ograph** *n.* an instrument by means of which a series of photographs can be projected so as to produce to the eye the movements of the original scene;—*v.t.* to film with a cine-camera.—**cinematograph'ic** *a.*—**Cin'emascope** *n.* Trade Name for the showing of moving pictures on a specially wide screen.—**cinematog'raphy** *n.* the art of filming.—**cin'e-cam'era** *n.* a camera for taking successive pictures of scenes involving movement.—**cin'e-projec'tor** *n.* a projector used in the showing of such pictures [Gk. *kinema*, movement; *graphein*, to write].

cineraria (sin-ẹ-rā′ri-ą) *n.* a genus of plants.

cinerary (sin′e-rą-ri) *a.* pert. to ashes; made to hold ashes.—**cinera'tion** *n.* a reducing to ashes; incineration [L. *cinerarius*, ashy].

Cingalese (sing′gą-lēz) *a.* and *n.* (pert. to) a native or language of Ceylon.

cinnabar (sin′ą-bȧr) *n.* red sulphide of mercury used as a pigment; vermilion;—*a.* vermilion coloured [Gk. *kinnabari*, vermilion].

cinnamon (sin′ą-mon) *n.* the inner bark of a laurel tree of Ceylon; an aromatic substance obtained from the bark;—*n.* and *a.* a light-brown colour.—**cinnam'ic, cinnamon'ic** *a.* [Heb. *qinnamon*].

cinque (singk) *n.* the representation, by five spots, of the figure 5 upon dice or cards.—**cinque'foil** *n.* the five-bladed clover.—**Cinque ports,** formerly Hastings, Romney, Hythe, Dover, Sandwich [L. *quinque*, five].

Cinquecento (chēn-kwā-chen′tō) *n.* the 16th cent.—the Renaissance period [It. *cinquecento*=500, but here a contraction for 1500, *mille*=1000 being understood].

cipher, cypher (sī′fẹr) *n.* the arithmetical symbol 0; any figure; a person of no account; a secret writing; a code; the key to a code;—*v.i.* to write in cipher; to work at arithmetic [Fr. *chiffre*, a figure].

circa (sir′ka) *prep.* about; around; approximately;—(*abbrev.*) **circ.** [L. *circa, circiter*].

Circassian (sẹr-kash′yąn) *a.* pert. to *Circassia*, a district in S.E. Russia;—*n.* a native of Circassia.—**Circassian circle,** a dance popular at the beginning of the 20th cent.

circle (sẹr′kl) *n.* a plane figure bounded by a single curved line called its circumference, every point of which is equally distant from a point within called the centre; the curved line that bounds such a figure; a circumference; a round body; a sphere; an orb; a ring; the company associated with a person; a society group; club or group, esp. literary; a never-ending series;—*v.t.* to move or revolve round; to encompass, as by a circle; to surround;—*v.i.* to move in a circle.—**dress circle,** first gallery in a theatre (formerly reserved for those in evening dress) [L. *circulus*].

circuit (sẹr′kit) *n.* the act of moving round; the space enclosed within a fixed limit; area; (*Law*) the round made by judges, holding assizes; the district thus visited; the path of an electric current.—**circuiteer** (sẹr-ki-tēr′) one who moves in a circuit; a judge.—**circuitous** (sẹr-kū′i-tus) *a.* round about.—**circu'itously** *adv.* [L. *circuitus*, a going round].

circular (sẹr′kū-lạr) *a.* in the form of a circle; round; moving in a circle; roundabout; addressed to a circle of people;—*n.* a notice sent out in quantities.—**cir'cularly** *adv.*—**circular'ity** *n.*—**cir'cularise** *v.t.* to send circulars to [L. *circularis*].

circulate (sẹr′kū-lāt) *v.t.* to cause to pass round as in a circle; to spread abroad;—*v.i.* to move round and return to the same point; to be spread abroad.—**circula'tion** *n.* the act of moving round; the flow of blood from, and back to, the heart; the extent of sale of a newspaper, etc.; the money circulating in a country; currency.—**cir'culative, cir'culatory** *a.* circulating.—**cir'culator** *n.*—**circulating library,** a library from which books are lent out to the public, or to subscribers [L. *circulare*].

circum- (sẹr′kum) *prefix* fr. Latin meaning *round, about*, combining to form many derivatives as in—**circumam'bient** *a.* surrounding; enclosing.—**circumam'biency** *n.* environment.—**circumam'bulate** *v.t.* and *i.* to walk round or about [L. *ambire*, to go round; *ambulare*, to walk].

circumcise (sẹr′kum-sīz) *v.t.* to cut off the foreskin.—**circumcision** (sẹr-kum-sizh′un) *n.* [L. *circum*; *caedere*, to cut].

circumference (sẹr-kum′fer-ens) *n.* the line that bounds a circle; the distance round; area.—**circumferen'tial** *a.* [L. *circum*; *ferre*, to carry].

circumflex (sẹr′kum-fleks) *n.* an accent mark (ʌ) placed over a French vowel to denote length, contraction, etc.; in Greek (⌒) [L. *circum*; *flectere*, to bend].

circumfluent (sẹr-kum′flôô-ent) *a.* flowing round.—**circum'fluence** *n.* [L. *circum*; *fluere*, to flow].

circumjacent (sẹr-kum-jā′sent) *a.* bordering on every side [L. *circum*; *jacere*, to lie].

circumlocution (sẹr-kum-lō-kū′shun) *n.* a roundabout manner of speaking.—**circumloc'utory** *a.* [L. *circum*; *loqui, locutus*, to speak].

circumnavigate (sẹr-kum-nav′i-gāt) *v.t.* to sail round.—**circumnav'igable** *a.* capable of being sailed round.—**circumnaviga'tion** *n.*—**circumnav'igator** *n.* one who sails round, esp. the world [L. *circum*; *navigare*, to sail].

circumscribe (sẹr-kum-skrīb′) *v.t.* to draw a circle round; to enclose within limits; to confine; to define.—**circumscription** (sẹr-kum-skrip′shun) *n.* limitation.—**circumscrip'tive** *a.* confined or limited in space [L. *circum*; *scribere*, to write].

circumspect (sẹr-kum-spekt) *a.* watchful on all sides; prudent; discreet.—**cir'cumspectly** *adv.*—**circumspec'tion** *n.* caution; prudence; discretion; tact.—**circumspec'tive** *a.* cautious [L. *circum*; *spicere*, to look].

circumstance (sẹr′kum-stans) *n.* a particular fact, event, or case; anything attending on, relative to, or affecting, a fact or event; accident; incident; particular;—*v.t.* to place in a particular situation.—**cir'cumstances** *n.pl.* worldly estate; condition as to pecuniary resources; situation; position; details.—**circumstantial** (sẹr-kum-stan′shạl) *a.* accidental; not essential; full of details; minute.—**circumstan'tially** *adv.*—**circumstantial'ity** *n.* minuteness of detail.—**circumstan'tiate** *v.t.* to detail exactly.—**circumstantial evidence,** evidence inferred from circumstances [L. *circum*; *stare*, to stand].

circumvent (sẹr-kum-vent′) *v.t.* to get around by stratagem; to outwit; to cheat.—**circumven'tion** *n.*—**circumven'tive** *a.* [L. *circum*; *venire*, to come].

circus (sẹr′kus) *n.* a circular enclosure for games, feats of horsemanship, acrobatic performances, etc.; also the performance itself; a ring or arena; a circular area at the intersection of streets [L. *circus*].

cirrhosis (si-rō′sis) *n.* (*Med.*) hardening and

PAINTING
19th Century

Degas: The Ballet Lesson

Manet: The Fife-player

Sisley: The Harbour at Marly

Renoir: The Swing

Whistler: Nocturne in blue and gold

PAINTING · 20th Century

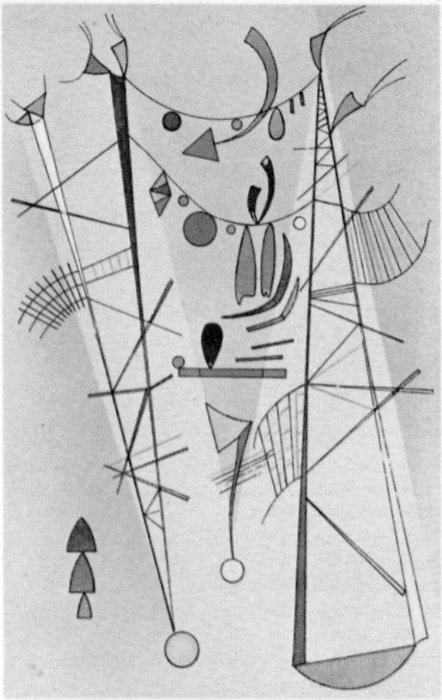

Kandinsky: abstract painting

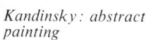

Modigliani: Girl in Blue

Picasso: Madame Z

Rouault: Clown

Dali: The Burning Giraffe

tawny-coloured enlargement of the liver.—**cirrhot'ic** *a.* [Gk. *kirrhos*, tawny].

cirrus (sir´us) *n.* a tendril; a curled filament; a lofty, fleecy cloud;—*pl.* **cirri** (sir´ī) [L. *cirrus*, a curl of hair].

cis- (sis) *pref.* fr. L. meaning 'on this side.'—**cisalp'ine** *a.* on this (the Roman) side of the Alps.—**cismon'tane** *a.* on this side of the mountains.

cist (sist) *n.* an oblong stone tomb, covered with stone slabs [Gk. *kistē*, a box].

Cistercian (sis-tẹr´shạn) *n.* a member of an order of monks, a branch of the Benedictines, founded in 1098 at Citeaux near Dijon, France. [L.L. *Cistercium*].

cistern (sis´tẹrn) *n.* a large tank for holding water; a reservoir [L. *cisterna*].

citadel (sit´ạ-del) *n.* a fortress or castle in or near a city [It. *cittadella*].

cite (sīt) *v.t.* to summon; to quote; to name; to bring forward as proof.—**cit'al** *n.* a summons.—**cita'tion** *n.* an official notice to appear; the act of quoting; the passage or words quoted.—**cita'tor** *n.* the one who cites.—**cit'atory** *a.* [L. *citare*].

cithara (sith´ạ-ra) *n.* the ancient Greek lyre.—**cith'ern, cit'tern** *n.* a kind of flat-backed guitar [Gk. *kithara*].

citizen (sit´i-zn) *n.* an inhabitant of a city; a freeman; a townsman; a member of a state;—*a.* having the character of a citizen.—**cit'izeness** *n.* a female citizen.—**cit'izenship** *n.* the state of being a citizen; the rights and duties of a citizen [O.Fr. *citeain*].

citron (sit´ron) *n.* the acidulous fruit of the citron-tree, resembling a lemon; the tree itself.—**cit'rate** *n.* a salt of citric acid.—**cit'rene** *n.* a substance found in oil of lemon.—**cit'ric** *a.* extracted from the citron, lemon, etc.—**cit'rus** *n.* a citron-tree.—**citrus fruits,** citrons, lemons, limes, oranges, etc. [L. *citrus*, a citron-tree].

cittern See **cithara.**

city (sit´i) *n.* a large town; a corporate town; the business or shopping centre of a town; a town that is, or has been, the seat of a bishop;—*a.* pert. to a city [L. *civitas*, a city].

cive See **chive.**

civet (siv´et) *n.* a perfume, with a strong musk-like smell.—**civ'et-cat** *n.* the animal, from which this perfume is obtained [Ar. *zabad*].

civic (siv´ik) *a.* pert. to a city or a citizen.—**civ'ics** *n.pl.* the study of good citizenship, municipal or national [L. *civis*, a citizen].

civil (siv´il) *a.* pert. to city, state, or citizen; lay, as opposed to military, etc.; polite.—**civ'illy** *adv.*—**civilian** (si-vil´yạn) *n.* orig. one versed in Civil Law; one whose employment is non-military;—*a.* pert. to civilian life (e.g. civilian dress).—**civil'ity** *n.* courtesy; politeness;—*pl.* acts of politeness.—**civ'ism** *n.* good citizenship.—**Civil Defence** (*World War* 2) a national civilian organisation, administered locally, to deal with air raids, etc.—**civil engineer,** one who plans railways, canals, factories, etc.—**Civil Service,** the collective name for the non-military servants of the Crown.—**civil war,** war between citizens of the same country [L. *civilis*, fr. *civis*, a citizen].

civilise (siv´il-īz) *v.t.* to reclaim from a savage state; to refine; to enlighten.—**civilisa'tion** *n.* the act of civilising, or state of being civilised [L. *civilis*].

civvy (siv´i) *n.* and *a.* (*Army Slang*) a civilian.—**civ'vies** *n.pl.* civilian clothes; mufti.—**Civvy Street,** civil life [fr. *civilian*].

clachan (klaH´ạn) *n.* a hamlet; a very small village [Gael. *clach*, a stone].

clack (klak) *v.i.* to make a sudden, sharp noise, as by striking; to talk rapidly and continually; to chatter;—*n.* a sharp, repeated, rattling sound; continual talk [imit. origin].

clad (klad) *pa.p.* and *pa.t.* of **clothe;**—*a.* clothed.

claim (klām) *v.t.* to demand as a right, or as due; to call for; to need;—*n.* the demand of a right or supposed right; a title; the thing claimed.—**claim'ant** *n.* one who claims.—**claim'-jump'er** *n.* one who seizes a piece of land marked out by a settler or miner [L. *clamare*, to shout].

clairaudience (klār-awd´i-ens) *n.* the power of hearing things not normally present to the senses [Fr. *clair*, clear; *audience*, hearing].

clairschach See **clarsach.**

clairvoyance (klār-voi´ạns) *n.* the power of seeing things not normally perceptible to the senses; second sight.—**clairvoy'ant** *n.* one who claims the power of clairvoyance. Also *a.* [Fr. *clair*, clear; *voir*, to see].

clam (klam) *n.* an edible bivalve shell-fish having the faculty of closing its shell like a vice [O.E. *clam*, a fetter].

clam (klam) *v.t.* to clog with sticky matter;—*v.i.* to be moist or sticky.—**clam'my** *a.* sticky; moist and adhesive; cold and damp.—**clam'miness** *n.* [O.E. *claeman*, to anoint].

clamant (klam´ant) *a.* crying insistently; calling loudly; demanding notice; urgent.—**clam'ancy** *n.* [L. *clamare*, to cry out].

clamber (klam´bẹr) *v.i.* to climb with difficulty, holding on with the hands [cf. Ger. *klammern*, to cling to].

clamour (klam´ur) *n.* loud shouting; tumult; outcry; uproar;—*v.i.* to shout loudly; to utter loud complaints or demands.—**clam'orous** *a.* vociferous; turbulent [L. *clamare*, to cry out].

clamp (klamp) *n.* any appliance with parts brought together by a screw for holding anything; a brace;—*v.t.* to render firm by a clamp [Dut. *klamp*].

clan (klan) *n.* a tribe bearing the same surname, united under a chieftain; one set or clique of persons having a common interest.—**clan'nish** *a.* disposed to associate only with members of the same sect or clique.—**clan'nishly** *adv.*—**clan'nishness** *n.* [Gael. *clann*, children].

clandestine (klan´des-tin) *a.* hidden; secret, and contrary to law, morals, etc.—**clan'destinely** *adv.*—**clan'destineness** *n.* [L. *clandestinus*, fr. *clam*, secretly].

clang (klang) *v.t.* to strike with a ringing, metallic sound;—*v.i.* to give forth a ringing, metallic sound;—*n.* a sharp, ringing sound.—**clang'ing** *n.* a clang [L. *clangere*].

clangour (klang´gur, klang´ur) *n.* a loud, harsh, ringing sound.—**clang'orous** *a.*—**clang'orously** *adv.* [L. *clangere*].

clank (klangk) *n.* a brief, ringing sound;—*v.t.* and *i.* to produce a sharp, ringing sound [imit. origin].

clap (klap) *v.t.* to bring together with a clap; to strike the hands together in approval; to slap;—*v.i.* to strike the hands together in applause;—*n.* a sudden, sharp noise caused by impact; applause; a slap or pat;—*pr.p.* **clap'ping.**—*pa.p.* and *pa.t.* **clapped.**—**clap'per** *n.* one who claps; the tongue of a bell.—**clap'board** *n.* thin board used to cover wooden houses.—**clap'-trap** *n.* in speech-making, tricks to win applause [M.E. *clap*].

claque (klak) *n.* a collection of persons hired to applaud in a theatre.—**claqueur** (kla´kẹr) *n.* [Fr. *claquer*, to clap].

clarendon (klar´en-don) *n.* (*Print.*) a narrow, heavy-faced or fat type, of various sizes [fr. the *Clarendon* Press, Oxford].

claret (klar´et) *n.* any red Bordeaux wine;—*a.* a purplish-red.—**clar'et-cup** *n.* drink composed of claret, lemon, ice and flavourings [Fr. *clairet*, fr. *clair*, clear].

clarify (klar´i-fī) *v.t.* to make clear or pure; to explain or clear up; to remove possibility of error;—*v.i.* to become clear.—**clarifica'tion** *n.*—**clar'ity** *n.* clearness; lucidity of mind [L. *clarus*, clear; *facere*, to make].

clarion (klar´i-on) *n.* trumpet with shrill

piercing note; its sound.—**clar'inet, clar'ionet** *n.* a wood wind-instrument.—**clarinet'tist** *n.* [Fr. *clairon*].

clarkia (klar'ki-a) *n.* a garden annual plant, having flowers of various colours [fr. an American explorer, J. *Clark*].

clarsach (klår'sąH) *n.* the old Celtic harp with wire strings [Gael. *clairseach*, a harp].

clash (klash) *v.t.* to strike noisily together;—*v.i.* to dash noisily together; to collide; to conflict; to disagree [imit. origin].

clasp (klasp, klåsp) *v.t.* to shut or fasten together with a catch or hook; to embrace; to grasp; to surround and cling to;—*n.* a catch or hook for fastening; a close embrace; a grasping of the hand; (*Mil.*) a bar on a medal-ribbon.—**clasp'-knife** *n.* a knife whose blade folds into handle [M.E. *clapse*, fr. *clyppan*, to embrace].

class (klas) *n.* an order or division or grouping of persons or things, possessing the same characteristics or status; a group of pupils or students taught together; a grouping of plants or animals; rank or standing in society.—*v.t.* to arrange in classes; to rank together;—*v.i.* to rank.—**class'able, class'ible** *a.*—**class'y** *a.* (*Colloq.*) high-class.—**class war,** hostility between classes of society [L. *classis*].

classic (klas'ik) *n.* a work, writer of recognised worth; an ancient Latin or Greek writer or book.—*a.* of model excellence in literature or art; conforming to standards of Greek and Roman art.—**class'ics** *n.pl.* ancient Latin or Greek literature.—**class'ical** *a.*—**class'ically** *adv.*—**classical'ity, class'icalness** *n.* the quality of being classical.—**classicism** (klas'i-sizm) *n.* classic principles in art and literature; classic style; a classical idiom.—**class'icist** *n.* [L. *classicus*, of the first rank].

classify (klas'i-fī) *v.t.* to arrange in classes; to put into a class.—**classifi'able** *a.*—**classifica'tion** *n.* the act of classifying [L. *classis*, a class; *facere*, to make].

clatter (klat'ẽr) *v.t.* to strike and so make a rattling noise;—*v.i.* to make rattling sounds; to prattle; to talk rapidly and idly;—*n.* a repeated rattling noise; noisy and idle talk [fr. *clack*].

clause (klawz) *n.* (*Gram.*) a sentence; a subordinate part of a sentence; (*Law*) an article or distinct portion of a document, contract, etc.; a paragraph; a subdivision [L. *claudere*, *clausum*, to shut].

claustral (klaws'trąl) *a.* pert. to a cloister; cloister-like; secluded.—**claustra'tion** *n.* the state of being confined in a cloister [L. *claustrum*, a bar or bolt].

claustrophobia (klaws-trō-fō'bi-ą) *n.* (*Med.*) a morbid dread of confined spaces [L. *claustrum*, bolt; Gk. *phobia*, fear].

clave (klāv) *pa.t.* of **cleave.**

clavichord (kla'vi-kord) *n.* a medieval musical instrument like a spinet [L. *clavis*, a key; *chorda*, a string].

clavicle (klav'i-kl) *n.* the collar-bone.—**clavi'cular** *a.* [L. *clavicula*, dim. fr. *clavis*. a key].

clavier (kla'vẽr) *n.* (*Mus.*) a stringed musical instrument with a keyboard [L. *clavis*, a key].

claw (klaw) *n.* a sharp, hooked nail, as of a beast or bird; the foot of an animal armed with hooked nails; anything like this;—*v.t.* to pull, tear, or scratch with claws or nails; to grasp.—**claw'-hamm'er** *n.* a hammer with one end of the head divided claw-like; (*Colloq.*) a dress-coat; a coat with swallow-tails [O.E. *clawu*].

clay (klā) *n.* soft earth, consisting of alumina and silica, with water; earth in general; the human body; a corpse; a tobacco-pipe, made of baked clay;—*v.t.* to purify and whiten with clay, as sugar.—**clayey** (klā'i) *a.* consisting of clay; like clay [O.E. *claeg*].

claymore (klā'mōr) *n.* a large, two-handed sword, formerly used by the Scottish Highlanders; a basket-hilted broadsword [Gael. *claidheamh*, a sword; *mor*, great].

clean (klēn) *a.* free from dirt, stain, or any defilement; pure; guiltless;—*v.t.* to free from dirt; to purify;—*adv.* so as to leave no dirt; quite; entirely.—**clean'er** *n.* one who, or that which, cleans.—**cleanliness** (klen'li-nes) *n.* freedom from dirt; purity.—**cleanly** (klen'li) *a.* habitually clean in person and habits; pure.—**cleanly** (klēn'li) *adv.* in a clean manner; neatly.—**cleanness** (klēn-nes) *n.*—**clean'-cut** *a.* well-shaped; definite.—**to make a clean breast of,** to make full confession; to reveal everything.—**to make a clean sweep** (*Fig.*) to get rid of completely [O.E. *claene*].

cleanse (klenz) *v.t.* to make clean; to make pure; to purify; to wash away; to purge.—**cleans'er** *n.* the one who, or that which, cleanses [E. *clean*].

clear (klēr) *a.* bright; free from cloud; undimmed; pure; free from obstruction; plain; distinct; manifest; without defect or drawback; transparent;—*adv.* clearly; wholly;—*v.t.* to make bright or clear; to make evident; to free from accusation; to acquit; to pass over or through; to cleanse; to empty; to make as profit; to free by payment of dues; to settle a debt; to free from difficulty, obstruction, suspicion, etc.;—*v.i.* to become clear, bright, transparent, free; (*Naut.*) to leave a port.—**clear'age** *n.* clearance.—**clear'ance** *n.* the act of clearing; a certificate that a ship has been cleared at the custom-house; in machinery, distance by which one part is clear of another.—**clear'ing** *n.* a tract of land cleared of wood for cultivation.—**clear'ly** *adv.*—**clear'ness** *n.*—**clear'-cut** *a.* sharply defined.—**clear'-eyed, clear'-see'ing, clear'-sight'ed** *a.* having acuteness of sight or intellect.—**clear'-head'ed** *a.* sagacious.—**clear'ing-sta'tion** *n.* (*War*) a place from which the wounded are removed.—**to clear off,** to depart.—**to clear out,** to remove encumbrances; (*Colloq.*) to depart without further ado [L. *clarus*, clear].

clearstory. See **clerestory.**

cleat (klēt) *n.* a wedge; (*Naut.*) a piece of wood or iron with two projecting ends, round which ropes are belayed or fastened; a porcelain insulator [O.E. *cleat*].

cleave (klēv) *v.t.* to split asunder; to cut in two;—*v.i.* to fall apart; to split; to open; to crack asunder;—*pa.p.* **clov'en** or **cleft.**—*pa.t.* **clove** or **cleft.**—**cleav'age** *n.* of rocks, the quality of splitting naturally; (*Fig.*) separation due to a difference of opinions, etc.; a rupture.—**cleav'er** *n.* one who, or that which, cleaves; a butcher's chopper [O.E. *cleofan*].

cleave (klēv) *v.i.* to adhere closely; to stick; to agree; to be faithful to;—*pa.p.* **cleaved.**—**cleaved** or **clave** [O.E. *clifian*].

cleek (klēk) *n.* an iron hook; a golf-club with an iron head and straight face [form of *clutch*].

clef (klef) *n.* (*Mus.*) a sign used to indicate the pitch [Fr., fr. L. *clavis*, a key].

cleft (kleft) *pa.p.* and *pa.t.* of the verb **cleave;**—*n.* a fissure or split; a chasm; a chink [O.E. *cleofan*].

cleg (kleg) *n.* the horse-fly; the gad-fly [O.N. *cleggi*].

clematis (klem'ą-tis) *n.* a climbing-plant; also called Traveller's Joy, and Virgin's Bower [Gk. *klēmatis*, fr. *klēma*, a twig].

clemency (klem'en-si) *n.* leniency; mildness; gentleness; mercy.—**clem'ent** *a.* mild; compassionate [L. *clemens*].

clench, clinch (klensh, klinsh) *v.t.* to grasp firmly; to close together tightly (the hands, the teeth); to confirm (a bargain);—*n.* a firm closing; decisive proof; a firm grip.—**clench'er** *n.* an unanswerable argument [O.E. *clencean*].

clerestory (klēr'stō-ri) *n.* the upper part of the central nave of churches, which rises clear of the other buildings and has its own row of windows. Also **clear'story** [fr. *clear* and *story*].

clergy (klẹr'-ji) *n.* the body of men ordained for the services of the Christian Church; the clerical order.—**cler'gyman** *n.* one of the clergy; a minister [Fr. *clergé*].

cleric (kler'-ik) *n.* a clerk or clergyman.—*a.* clerical.—**cler'ical** *a.* belonging to the clergy; pert. to a clerk or copyist [L. *clericus*].

clerihew (kler'-i-hū) *n.* a nonsensical verse of two couplets, in which is epitomised satirically the life of some notable person [invented by E. *Clerihew* Bentley].

clerk (klȧrk, klẹrk) *n.* one who is employed to do correspondence, keep accounts, etc. in an office; a clergyman; a scholar; (*U.S.*) a shop assistant;—*v.i.* to act as a clerk or secretary.—**clerk'ess** *n.* a woman-clerk or secretary.—**clerk'ly** *a.* scholar-like [O.E. *clerc*, a priest].

clever (klev'-ẹr) *a.* able; skilful; ingenious; intelligent.—**clev'erly** *adv.*—**clev'erness** *n.* intelligence [origin uncertain].

clew, clue (klòò) *n.* a ball of thread or cord; (*Myth.*) a ball of thread used as a guide through a maze; hence, anything that serves to guide one in an involved affair or helps to solve a mystery; (*Naut.*) the lower corner of a sail [O.E. *cliwen*].

cliché (klē'shā) *n.* an electrotype or stereotype plate; a photographic negative; a stereotyped or hackneyed phrase [Fr.].

click (klik) *n.* a slight, short sound, as of a latch in a door;—*v.i.* to make such a sound; (*Slang*) to be successful, esp. in striking up an acquaintance with one of the opposite sex [imit. origin].

client (klī'-ent) *n.* one who employs another (esp. a lawyer) professionally as his agent; a customer; in ancient times a dependent.—**clientele** (klī'-en-tel, klē-ong-tel') *n.* clients or customers collectively.—**cli'entship** *n.* [L. *cliens*, a follower].

cliff (klif) *n.* a high rock-face; the sheer side of a mountain.—**clift** *n.* a cleft or break in a cliff [O.E. *clif*].

climacteric (klī-mak'-te-rik) *n.* a period in human life in which a change takes place in the constitution; the menopause; any critical period;—*a.* pert. to a climacteric; critical.—**climacter'ical** *a.* climacteric [Gk. *klimaktēr*, rung of a ladder].

climate (klī'-māt) *n.* the general atmospherical conditions (temperature, moisture, etc.) of a country or region.—**climat'ic** *a.*—**climat'ical** *a.* climatic [Gk. *klima, klimatos*, slope].

climax (klī'-maks) *n.* an arrangement of words, phrases, etc. such that they rise in rhetorical force and impressiveness; acme; the point of greatest excitement or tension in a play, story, etc.—**climac'tic** *a.* pert. to a climax [Gk.=a ladder].

climb (klīm) *v.t.* and *i.* to go up, ascend (as a hill, tree, etc.); to grow upward as a plant by tendrils; to rise in the social scale; to slope upward;—*n.* a going up; an ascent.—**climb'er** *n.* [O.E. *climban*].

clime (klīm) *n.* a region or country; (*Poet.*) climate [Gk. *klima*, fr. *klinein*, to slope].

clinch (klinsh) *v.t.* and *i.* to grapple or struggle at close quarters in wrestling or boxing; to fasten with a rivet; (*Fig.*) to settle or conclude, as an agreement;—*n.* a close holding in wrestling or boxing; a rivet [fr. *clench*].

clincher-built See **clinker-built.**

cling (kling) *v.i.* to adhere or stick close to; to be attached firmly to;—*pa.p.* and *pa.t.* **clung** [O.E. *clingan*].

clinic, clinique (klin'-ik, klin-ēk') *n.* the teaching of medical subjects at the bedside; an institution where patients attend for treatment, and which is also a teaching centre.—**clin'ical** *a.* [Gk. *klinē*, a bed].

clink (klingk) *n.* a slight, sharp, tinkling sound, [imit. origin].

clink (klingk) *n.* (*Slang*) prison.

clinker (kling'-kẹr) *n.* a mass of slag and cinders from iron furnaces; a kind of brick [*Dut.*].

clinker (kling'-ker) *n.* a type of soft nail used for boots of climbers [fr. *clinch*].

clinker-built (kling'-kẹr-bilt) *a.* (*Naut.*) denoting ships whose hulls are built with planks or metal plates overlapping the one below (opp. of *carvel-built*) [fr. *clinch*].

clinophile (klī'-no-fil) *n.* a lover of bed [Gk. *kline*, a couch; *philein*, to love].

clip (klip) *v.t.* to clutch tightly;—*n.* any device for grasping or holding a thing firmly [O.E. *clyppan*, to embrace].

clip (klip) *v.t.* to cut with scissors or shears; to prune or cut short; to shear sheep; to pare the edge of a coin; to shorten or slur words;—*v.i.* to move quickly;—*n.* act of clipping; a season's shearing of wool; a rapid pace; (*Colloq.*) a sharp blow.—*pr.p.* **clip'ping.**—*pa.p.* and *pa.t.* **clipped.**—**clip'per** *n.* one who clips; a fast sailing-vessel, with a long sharp bow; fast, long distance airliner.—**clip'pers** *n.* a two-bladed instrument for cutting hair, shearing sheep, etc.—**clip'pie** *n.* (*Colloq.*) conductress of bus or tram [origin uncertain].—**clipping** *n.* item cut from newspaper.

clique (klēk) *n.* a narrow circle of persons with common interests; a coterie.—**cliqu'ish** *a.*—**cliqu'ishness** *n.* [Fr.].

cloaca (klō-ā'-kạ) *n.* a sewer; a privy; a sink of impurity; the excrementary cavity in birds, reptiles, etc.—**cloa'cal** *a.* [L.].

cloak (klōk) *n.* a long, loose, outer garment; something that conceals; a pretext;—*v.t.* to cover with a cloak; to hide; to mask or dissemble.—**cloak'room** *n.* a room where coats, hats, etc. may be temporarily left; a lavatory [O.Fr. *cloque*, a bell-shaped cloak].

cloche (klosh) *n.* glass covering used for intensive cultivation of vegetables, etc.; a close-fitting bell-shaped hat worn by women [Fr.=a bell].

clock (klok) *n.* a device which measures the time.—**clock'-wise** *adv.* in the direction of the hands of a clock; circling to the right.—**an'ti-clock'wise,** *adv.* circling to the left.—**clock'work** *n.* the movements or machinery of a clock; regular movement as of clock;—*a.* mechanically regular.—**o'clock,** by the clock.—**to clock in, to clock out,** in a factory, office, etc., to register the time of arrival and departure [Fr. *cloche*, a bell].

clock (klok) *n.* an ornament worked on a stocking on each side of the ankle.

clod (klod) *n.* a lump of earth, clay, or turf; the sod; the earth; a dull, stupid fellow;—*v.t.* to pelt with clods.—**clod'hopper** *n.* a rustic; a boor [O.E. fr. *clot*].

clog (klog) *n.* a strong, clumsy shoe with a thick wooden sole; a block of wood attached to an animal's leg to prevent it from straying; an impediment; an obstruction;—*v.t.* to hinder; to encumber; to choke up;—*v.i.* to become choked, encumbered; to adhere [M.E. *clogge*, a block of wood].

cloister (klois'-tẹr) *n.* covered arcade running along one or more walls of the inner court of a monastery or college; a monastery or nunnery; a secluded spot;—*v.t.* to confine in a cloister or within walls.—**clois'teral, clois'tral** *a.* [L. *claustrum*, a bar or bolt].

close (klōz) *v.t.* to shut; to stop up; to finish; to conclude; to complete (a wireless circuit);—*v.i.* to come together; to unite; to end.—**clos'ing** *a.* ending;—*n.* the act of shutting; the end; the conclusion.—**closure** (klōz'-ūr) *n.* the act of shutting; a closing; the close of a debate.—**closed shop,** in industry a workshop, factory, etc. in which all employees have to be members of a trade union [L. *claudere*, to shut].

close (klōs) *a.* shut up; confined; tight; stifling; unventilated; near at hand; secret;

niggardly; familiar; intimate; compact; crowded; searching;—*adv.* in a close manner or state; nearly; tightly;—*n.* an enclosed place; the precinct of a cathedral; a blind alley; a narrow passage leading from a street; a small field or paddock; a courtyard; (*Mus.*) a cadence.—**close'ly** *adv.*—**close'ness** *n.* —**close'-breed'ing** *n.* breeding between animals of the same stock that are nearly related.— **close by,** very little distant.—**close call,** a very narrow escape.—**close'-commun'ion** *n.* among Baptists, communion in the Lord's Supper with Baptists only.—**close'-corpora'tion** *n.* one that fills up its own vacancies.—**close'-fist'ed** or **close'-hand'ed** *a.* miserly; niggardly; penurious.—**close'-hauled** *a.* (*Naut.*) kept as near as possible to the point from which the wind blows.—**close'-quart'ers** *n.pl.* strong barriers formerly erected on board ship for defence against boarders; hence, **to come to close quarters,** to come into direct conflict, esp. with an enemy.—**close'-sea'son or, close'-time** *n.* a season of the year during which it is illegal to catch or kill certain kinds of game or fish (generally the breeding-season).—**a close shave,** a very narrow escape.—**close'-stool** *n.* a box with a close-fitting lid to hold a chamber-pot.—**close'-up** *n.* a close view of anything.—**(to sail) close to the wind,** to keep as near against the wind as it is possible to sail; to court disaster, esp. financially [L. *claudere*, to shut].

closet (kloꞌzet) *n.* a small private room; a lavatory; a water-closet;—*v.t.* to take into a private room for consultation [L. *claudere*, to shut].

clot (klot) *n.* a mass or lump, esp. of a soft, slimy character; (*Med.*) a coagulated mass of blood;—*v.t.* to form into clots;—*v.i.* to coagulate.—*pr.p.* **clot'ting.**—*pa.p.* and *pa.t.* **clot'ted** [O.E. *clod*].

cloth (kloth) *n.* any woven fabric, esp. of wool or hair; the dress of a profession, e.g. the clerical; a cover for a table; a duster.— *pl.* **cloths** (kloths).—**the Cloth** (*Fig.*) clergymen.—**American cloth,** a special kind of impregnated cloth, resembling thin linoleum, used for covering chairs, etc. [O.E. *clath*].

clothe (klōTH) *v.t.* to put garments on; to cover as with a garment; to furnish with raiment; (*Fig.*) to surround with; to wrap up in.—*pr.p.* **cloth'ing.**—*pa.p.* and *pa.t.* **clothed** or **clad.**—**clothes** (klōths) *n.pl.* garments; wearing apparel; short for bedclothes, i.e. sheets, blankets, etc.—**clothier** (klōTHꞌyẽr) *n.* one who makes, or sells, clothes; a tailor; an outfitter.—**cloth'ing** *n.* garments in general; dress; wearing-apparel; raiment.—**clothes'-horse** *n.* a frame for hanging clothes on to dry indoors.—**clothes'-peg** or **-pin** *n.* a forked wooden peg for fastening clothes on a line to dry [O.E. *clath*].

cloud (kloud) *n.* a body of visible vapour floating in the atmosphere; a mass of smoke, flying dust, etc.; that which has a dark, threatening aspect; a state of obscurity or impending trouble; a great multitude;—*v.t.* to overspread with clouds; to darken; to sadden; to defame;—*v.i.* to grow cloudy; to be blurred.—**cloud'y** *a.* darkened with clouds; overcast; hazy; dim; blurred; indistinct; gloomy.—**cloud'ily** *adv.*—**cloud'iness** *n.*—**cloud'-burst** *n.* a violent downpour of rain; a deluge. —**cloud'-drift** *n.* irregular drifting clouds.— **cloud'land** *n.* the region of the clouds; (*Fig.*) dreamland.—**in the clouds** (*Fig.*) unreal; absent-minded; dreamy.—**to be under a cloud,** to be under suspicion; to be in temporary disgrace [O.E. *clud*].

clout (klout) *n.* a piece of cloth used for a patch; a rag; a piece of old cloth used for cleaning, scouring, etc.; the centre of the butt at which archers shoot; a slap or blow; a short nail with a large head (used for studding boots);—*v.t.* to patch; to join in a clumsy manner; to strike with the open hand [O.E. *clut*].

clove (klōv) *n.* the flower-bud of the clove-tree, used as a spice; also yields oil.—**clove'-gillyflower** (jilꞌi-flou-er) *n.*—**clove'-pink** *n.* a pink whose scent is like cloves [Fr. *clou*, a nail, fr. L. *clavus*, shape of the clove-bud].

clove (klōv) *pa.t.* of **cleave.**

clove-hitch (klōvꞌhich) *n.* (*Naut.*) a hitch used to secure a rope round a spar.

cloven (klōvꞌn) *pa.p.* of **cleave.** Also *a.* split; divided into two parts.—**clov'en-foot'ed (-hoofed)** *a.* having the foot (hoof) divided into two parts, e.g. the ox.—**to show the cloven hoof,** to give an indication of a devilish trait in one's character [fr. *cleave*].

clover (klōꞌvẽr) *n.* a common field plant of the trefoil family, used for fodder.—**to be in clover,** to live in luxury [O.E. *clafre*].

clown (kloun) *n.* a peasant or rustic; an ill-bred man; a boor; the fool or buffoon in a play or circus;—*v.i.* to play the fool; to behave like a fool.—**clown'ish** *a.* like a clown; loutish; awkward.—**clown'ishly** *adv.*—**clown'ishness** *n.* [etym. uncertain].

cloy (kloi) *v.t.* to induce a sensation of loathing by overmuch of anything, esp. of sweetness, sentimentality, or flattery; to satiate, glut, or surfeit.—**cloy'ing** *a.* satiating; disgusting [Fr. *clouer*, to nail].

club (klub) *n.* a heavy stick, thickening towards one end, used as a weapon; a cudgel; a stick used in the game of golf; an association of people united in pursuance of a common interest; the premises in which such an association meets;—*v.t.* to beat with a club; to gather into a club;—*v.i.* to form a club; to unite for a common end; to pay shares in a common expense.—*pr.p.* **club'bing.**—*pa.p.* and *pa.t.* **clubbed.**—**club'-foot** *n.* a congenitally deformed or crooked foot; talipes.—**club'-law** *n.* rule by violence.—**club'-root** *n.* a fungus disease of plants, attacking the roots of members of the Brassica family (turnips, cabbages, etc.) [O.N. *klubba*].

cluck (kluk) *n.* the call of a hen to her chickens [imit. origin].

clue (klòò) *n.* See **clew.**

clumber (klumꞌbẽr) *n.* a kind of spaniel [fr. *Clumber*, Nottinghamshire].

clump (klump) *n.* a shapeless mass of any substance; a cluster of trees or shrubs; a heavy extra sole on a shoe; a tramping sound;—*v.t.* to put in a clump or group;— *v.i.* to tramp heavily [Dut. *klomp*].

clumsy (klumꞌzi) *a.* ill-made; awkward; ungainly.—**clum'sily** *adv.*—**clum'siness** *n.* [M.E. *clumsen*, to benumb].

clung (klung) *pa.p.* and *pa.t.* of **cling.**

cluster (klusꞌtẽr) *n.* a bunch; a number of things growing together, as grapes; a collection;—*v.t.* to collect into a bunch;— *v.i.* to grow, or be, in clusters [O.E. *clyster*].

clutch (kluch) *v.t.* and *i.* to seize or grip with the hand; to grasp;—*n.* a grasp; a tight grip; a set of eggs hatched at one time; a brood of chicks.—**clutch'es** *n.pl.* the claws; the hands; (*Fig.*) power (esp. ruthless); the coupling of two working parts, used in motor vehicles to connect or disconnect engine and transmission gear [O.E. *clyccan*].

clutter (klutꞌẽr) *n.* crowded confusion; disorder; noise;—*v.t.* to crowd together in disorder; to make untidy [origin uncertain].

Clydesdale (klīdzꞌdāl) *n.* one of a breed of heavy draught-horses [fr. River *Clyde*].

clyster (klisꞌtẽr) *n.* an injection of liquid into the bowels to wash them out.—**clys'terise** *v.t.* [Gk. *kluzein*, to wash out].

co- (kō) *prefix* meaning together, joint, etc. [fr. L. *cum*, with].

coach (kōch) *n.* a large four-wheeled travelling carriage; a tutor who prepares students for examination; a trainer in athletics;— *v.i.* to travel in a coach;—*v.t.* to tutor or train. —**coach'-box** *n.* the driver's seat on a coach.—

coach'-horse *n.* a horse trained to draw a coach.—**coach'man** *n.* the driver of a coach or carriage [Fr. *coche,* a coach].

coact (kō-akt') *v.t.* to compel.—**coac'tion** *n.* compulsion [L. *cogere, coactum,* to compel].

coadjutant (kō-ad-jóó-tant) *a.* assisting;—*n.* an assistant.—**coadjutor** (jóó-tur) *n.* an assistant; an associate and destined successor. —**coadju'trix** *n.* a female helper [L. *co-,* together; *adjuvare,* to help].

coagulate (kō-ag-ū-lāt) *v.t.* to cause to curdle or congeal; to solidify;—*v.i.* to curdle; to clot.—**coag'ulant** *n.* a substance that causes coagulation.—**coagula'tion** *n.*—**coag'-ulative** *a.* causing coagulation [L. *co-,* together; *agere,* to drive].

coal (kōl) *n.* a black substance used for fuel, composed of mineralised vegetable matter; a piece of this substance;—*v.t.* to supply with coal;—*v.i.* to take in coal.—**coal'-bed** *n.* a seam or stratum of coal.—**coal'-bunk'er** *n.* a recess for storing coal.—**coal'-field** *n.* a district where coal abounds.—**coal'-gas** *n.* gas produced from the distillation of coal.—**coal'-mine, coal'-pit** *n.* the excavation from which coal is dug.—**coal'-tar** *n.* a thick, sticky substance, produced during the distilling of coal.—**coal'-slack** *n.* coal dust.—**coal'ing-sta'-tion** *n.* a port at which ships call to lay in a store of coal.—**coal'y** *a.* like coal.—**to haul over the coals,** to take to task [O.E. *col.*].

coalesce (kō-a-les') *v.t.* to grow together; to unite into one body or mass; to fuse.—**coales'cent** *a.* coalescing.—**coales'cence** *n.* [L. *co-,* together; *alescere,* to grow up].

coalite (kōl-īt) *n.* a fuel made from coal-dust [fr. *coal*].

coalition (kō-ạ-lish-un) *n.* a union or combination of persons, parties, or states into one body; a league.—**coali'tionist** *n.* one who supports or joins a coalition [L. *co-,* together; *alescere,* to grow up].

coarse (kōrs) *a.* rough, rude; not refined; without grace or elegance; ill-mannered; vulgar; inferior.—**coarse'ly** *adv.*—**coars'en** *v.t.* and *i.* to make or become coarse.—**coarse'ness** *n.* the state of being coarse.—**coars'ish** *a.* somewhat coarse [M.E. *cors;* Fr. *gros*].

coast (kōst) *n.* country bordering the sea; the sea-shore; the country near the shore;—*v.t.* and *i.* to sail near or along the coast; to run downhill in a motor-car with engine-power shut off, or on a bicycle without pedalling; to free-wheel; to toboggan.—**coast'al** *a.* pert. to the coast.—**coast'er** *n.* a vessel trading between towns along the coast.—**coast'guard** *n.* a service organised orig. to prevent smuggling; since 1925, largely a life-saving service; a member of this service.—**coast'line** *n.* the outline of a coast.—**coast'wards** *adv.* toward the coast.—**coast'wise** *adv.* along the coast [L. *costa,* a rib, a side].

coat (kōt) *n.* an outer garment; a jacket; an overcoat; the fur or skin of an animal; a covering; a layer spread over another, as paint;—*v.t.* to cover with a coat; to clothe.—**coatee** (kō-tē') *n.* a short close-fitting coat for women.—**coat'ing** *n.* any covering; a layer; cloth for making coats.—**coat of arms,** armorial bearings; heraldic arms.—**coat of mail,** a soldier's jacket, quilted with small plates or rings of iron.—**turncoat,** one who forsakes his party, or principles; a renegade [Fr. *cotte,* an overall].

coax (kōks) *v.t.* to win over by fond pleading or flattery.—**coax'ingly** *adv.* [etym. uncertain].

co-axial (kō-ak-si-ạl) *a.* having a common axis [fr. *axis*].

cob (kob) *n.* a head of maize; a corn-cob; a lump or ball of anything; a short-legged sturdy horse; a male swan.—**cob'-nut** *n.* a large hazel-nut.—**cob'-stone** *n.* a rounded stone.—**cob'-wall** *n.* [etym. uncertain].

cobalt (kō-bawlt) *n.* a chemical metallic element classified with iron and nickel, and used as an ingredient of many alloys.—**co'balt-blue** *n.* a pigment of alumina and cobalt;—*a.* a dark-blue colour.—**cobalt'ic** *a.* [Ger. *Kobalt*].

cobalt bomb *n.* a type of atomic bomb equal in power to the hydrogen bomb and with more lethal and lasting effects.

cobble (kob-l) *v.t.* to mend or patch coarsely; to mend boots or shoes.—**cobb'ler** *n.* a mender of shoes; a boot-repairer; a clumsy workman [etym. unknown].

cobble (kob-l) *n.* a stone rounded by the action of water;—*v.t.* to pave with cobbles.—**cobb'le-stone** *n.* a rounded stone used in the paving of roads [etym. uncertain].

coble, cobble (kob-l) *n.* a small flat-bottomed fishing-boat [Celt.].

cobra (kō-brạ, kob-rạ) *n.* the venomous 'hooded' snake of Africa and India.—**cob'ric** *a.* [L. *colubra,* a snake].

cobweb (kob-web) *n.* a spider's web; anything flimsy, transparent, and fragile; a trap or entanglement [O.E. *coppe,* a spider].

coca (kō-kạ) *n.* a Peruvian plant or its dried leaf, which is a nerve stimulant.—**cocaine** (ko-kān') *n.* a drug made from coca leaves, used as a local anaesthetic [Native].

coccus (kok-us) *n.* one of the divisions of a schizocarp (a lobed fruit with a one-seeded cell); a genus of hemipterous insects; in bacteria, a spherical cell.—*pl.* **cocci** (kok-sī) [Gk. *kokkos,* a grain or seed].

coccyx (kok-siks) *n.* the triangular bone ending spinal column.—*pl.* **coccyges** (kok-si-jēz).—**coccy'geal** *a.* [Gk. *kokkux,* cuckoo, coccyx being shaped like its bill].

cochineal (koch-i-nēl) *n.* a scarlet dye-stuff, made from the dried bodies of insects [L. *coccineus,* scarlet].

cochlea (kok-lē-a] *n.* a spiral passage of the inner ear [Gk. *kochlias,* a snail from the shape of its shell].

cock (kok) *n.* the male of birds, esp. of the domestic fowl; a weather-cock; a tap to regulate the flow of fluids; the hammer of a firearm; the cocked position of a hammer (of a firearm); a chief or leader;—*v.t.* to draw back the hammer of a gun; to set up, set erect, set at an angle, as a hat;—*v.i.* to swagger.—**cock'-crow** *n.* early morning.—**cock'erel** *n.* a young cock; a swaggering youth.—**cock'-eyed** *a.* squinting.—**cocks'comb** *n.* the comb of a cock; a dandy.—**cock'sure** *a* quite sure.—**cock'tail** *n.* a horse not of pure breed; a drink concocted of spirits, bitters, sugar, etc. used as an appetiser.—**cock'y** *a.* vain and confident; full of self-assurance.—**cock'ily** *adv.*—**cock'iness** *n.*—**cock'-a-hoop** *a.* exultant.—**cock'-a-leek'ie** *n.* a soup made of boiled fowl and leeks.—**cocked hat,** a brimless hat with a point in front and behind.—**a cock-and-bull story,** a preposterous story [O.E. *coc*].

cock (kok) *n.* a pile of hay [O.E. *coc*].

cockade (ko-kād') *n.* a knot of ribbons, a rosette or badge, often worn on the hat [Fr. *cocarde,* fr. *coq,* a cock, from likeness to a cock's comb].

Cockaigne (kok-ān') *n.* an imaginary country of luxury and indulgence; also London or cockneydom [Fr. *cocagne,* origin uncertain].

cockatoo (kok-ạ-tóó') *n.* a kind of parrot with a crested head [Malay].

cockatrice (kok-ạ-tris) *n.* a fabulous animal represented as a cock with a dragon's tail; a fabulous serpent imagined to possess the powers of the basilisk, whose glance deals death [O.Fr. *cocatrice*].

cockchafer [kok-chā-fẹr) *n.* a large winged beetle [O.E. *ceafor*].

cocker (kok-ẹr) *n.* a cocker spaniel, a small variety of spaniel, used for retrieving game.

cocker (kok-ẹr) *v.t.* to pamper; to indulge [O.Fr. *coqueliner,* to dandle].

cockle (kok-l) *n.* a weed that grows among corn; the corn-rose [O.E. *coccel*].

cockle (kok-l) *n.* a bivalve shell-fish, with a

thick ribbed shell.—**cock'le-shell** *n.* the shell of a cockle; a shallow boat.—**to warm the cockles of the heart,** to cheer and hearten [Fr. *coquille*].
cockle (kok'l) *v.t.* to cause to pucker; to wrinkle [orig. uncertain].
Cockney (kok'ni) *n.* a native of London, esp. one born within sound of Bow Bells.—**cock'neydom** *n.* the home of cockneys.—**cock'neyfied** *a.* like a cockney [etym. uncertain].
cockpit (kok'pit) *n.* the pit or ring in which game-cocks fought, hence any arena of frequent strife; in aircraft, a compartment in the fuselage for the pilot and controls [*cock* and *pit*].
cockroach (kok'rōch) *n.* a black or brown beetle infesting houses [Sp. *cucaracha*].
cockswain (kok'swān, kok'sn) *n.* a petty officer in charge of a boat; a steersman of a boat. Also **cox'swain.**—Abbrev. **cox** [fr. *cock* (-boat) and *swain*].
coco, cocoa (kō'kō) *n.* a palm tree producing the coco-nut.—**co'conut, co'coanut,** the fruit of the coco palm [Sp. and Port. *coco,* a bug-bear, applied to the three 'faces' marked on the nut].
cocoa (kō'kō) *n.* a powder made from the kernels of the cacao or chocolate plant; a beverage from this [corrupt. fr. *cacao*].
cocoon (ko-kòòn') *n.* the silky envelope which the silkworm and other larvae spin for themselves before passing into the pupa stage [O.Fr. *coque,* a shell].
cod, codfish (kod, kod'fish) *n.* a large fish from northern seas, much used as food.—**cod'ling** *n.* a young cod [etym. uncertain].
cod (kod) *n.* a husk or seed-pod; a pillow-slip; a pouch [O.E. *codd,* a bag].
coda (kō'da) *n.* (*Mus.*) a short passage added at the end of a composition to round it off [It. fr. L. *cauda,* a tail].
coddle (kod'l) *v.t.* to parboil; to roast; to pamper or spoil [etym. uncertain].
code (kōd) *n.* an orderly collection of laws; a system of words, or symbols, or numbers adopted for secrecy or economy; a cipher;—*v.t.* to put into the form of a code.—**codify** (kō'di-fī) *v.t.* to collect laws, etc. into a digest [L. *codex,* a book].
codex (kō'deks) *n.* an ancient manuscript of a book, esp. of the Bible; a collection of prescriptions, esp. the French pharmacopoeia.—*pl.* **co'dices** [L. *codex,* a book].
codger (koj'ẹr) *n.* (*Colloq.*) an eccentric old man; a miser [etym. uncertain].
codicil (kod'i-sil) *n.* a supplement or appendix to a will [L. *codicillus,* dim, of *codex,* a book].
codling (kod'ling) *n.* a kind of cooking-apple. Also **cod'lin** [etym. uncertain].
codling (kod'ling) *n.* a young cod.
co-education (kō-ed-ū-kā'shun) *n.* the education of boys and girls together in mixed classes.—**co-educa'tional** *a.*
coefficient (kō-e-fish'ent) *a.* co-operating; combining;—*n.* that which unites with something else to produce a result; (*Math*). a number or other factor placed before another as a multiplier; (*Phys.*) a constant number or factor measuring some specified property of a substance.—**coeffi'ciency** *n.*
coenobite (sen'ō-bīt) *n.* See **cenobite.**
coequal (kō-ē'kwạl) *a.* equal; of the same rank or power as another;—*n.* a person having equality with another.
coerce (kō-ẹrs') *v.t.* to compel by force; to constrain; to restrain.—**coer'cible** *a.*—**coer'cive** *a.* having power to compel.—**coer'cively** *adv.*—**coercion** (kō-er'shun) *n.* coercing; state of being coerced; compulsory force; restraint [L. *coercere*].
coeval (kō-ē'vạl) *a.* of same age;—*n.* contemporary [L. *co-,* together; *aevum,* age].
co-exist (kō-eg-zist') *v.i.* to exist at the same time or together.—**co-exist'ent** *a.*
co-extend (kō-eks-tend') *v.t.* to extend equally with.—**co-exten'sive** *a.*
coffee (kof'e) *n.* an evergreen shrub, valuable for its berries; the seeds of the berries, esp. when ground and roasted; a drink from this.—**cof'fee-bean** *n.* the seed of the berry.—**cof'fee-house** *n.* a house where coffee and other refreshments are supplied [Ar. *qahwah*].
coffer (kof'ẹr) *n.* a chest for holding valuables; a large money-box; a canal-lock;—*v.t.* to put in a coffer; to hoard (money, etc.)—**coff'er-dam** *n.* in engineering, a watertight, box-like, iron structure, used in the construction of the underwater foundations of bridges, quay-walls, etc. [Fr. *coffre,* a box].
coffin (kof'in) *n.* a box or casket in which the dead are enclosed before burial or cremation;—*v.t.* to place in a coffin [Gk. *kophinos,* a basket].
cog (kog) *n.* one of a series of teeth on a wheel; a support to the roof of a mine;—*v.t.* to fit a wheel with cogs.—*pr.p.* **cog'ging.**—*pa.p.* and *pa.t.* **cogged.**—**cog'-wheel** *n.* a wheel fitted with teeth [M.E. *cogge*].
cogent (kō'jent) *a.* having great force; powerful; convincing.—**co'gently** *adv.*—**co'gence, co'gency** *n.* urgency; force; convincing power [L. *cogere,* to force].
coggle (kog'-l) *n.* a small boat; a pebble; a cobble [fr. *cobble.*]
cogitate (koj'i-tāt) *v.i.* to reflect deeply; to meditate.—**cog'itable** *a.*—**cogita'tion** *n.* contemplation; meditation; deep reflection.—**cog'itative** *a.* contemplative [L. *cogitare*].
cognac (kon'yak) *n.* a French brandy, so called from the town of *Cognac* in S.W. France; brandy in general.
cognate (kog'nāt) *a.* allied by blood or birth; of the same stock; from the same origin, formation, etc.;—*n.* a relative by birth; anything of the same origin, kind, nature, or effect [L. *cognatus,* born together].
cognisance (kog'ni-zạns, kon'i-zạns) *n.* knowledge.—**cog'nisant** *a.* having cognisance or knowledge of; competent to take judicial notice [L. *cognoscere,* to know].
cognise (kog'nīz) *v.t.* to have knowledge of; to be aware of.—**cog'nisable** *a.*—**cog'nisably** *adv.* [L. *cognoscere,* to know].
cognition (kog-ni'shun) *n.* apprehension; awareness; state of being able to perceive objects or to remember ideas.—**cog'nitive** *a.* [L. *cogniscere,* to know].
cognomen (kog-nō'men) *n.* a surname; a nickname [L. *nomen,* a name].
cognoscente (ko-nyo-shen'te, ko-no-shen'te) *n.* one who professes critical knowledge of literature, art, music etc.—*pl.* **cognoscen'ti** [It. fr. L. *cognoscere,* to know].
cohabit (kō-hab'it) *v.i.* to live together as husband and wife (usually of unmarried persons).—**cohabita'tion** *n.*
cohere (kō-hēr') *v.i.* to stick together; to be connected; to follow regularly in natural order; to be consistent; to coalesce; to adhere.—**cohe'rence, cohe'rency** *n.*—**cohe'rent** *a.* sticking together; connected; consistent.—**cohe'rently** *adv.*—**cohe'sible** *a.* capable of cohesion.—**cohe'sion** *n.* the act of sticking together.—**cohe'sive** *a.* having the power of cohering.—**cohe'siveness, cohe'sibility** *n.* [L. *cohaerere,,* to stick together].
cohort (kō'hort) *n.* a division of a Roman legion, from 300 to 600 soldiers; a company of persons [L. *cohors*].
coif (koif) *n.* a head-dress in the form of a close-fitting cap, formerly worn by serjeants-at-law, and still worn by nuns.—**coiffeur** (kwạ-fẹr') (*fem.* **coiffeuse'**) *n.* a hairdresser.—**coiffure** (kwạ-fòòr') *n.* a head-dress; a style of dressing the hair [Fr. *coiffe*].
coign (koin) *n.* a corner; a corner-stone; a wedge [same as *coin,* fr. L. *cuneus,* a wedge].
coil (koil) *v.t.* to wind in rings, as a rope; to twist into a spiral shape;—*v.i.* to take up a

spiral shape;—*n.* the spiral of rings into which anything is wound; one of the rings of the spiral [L. *colligere*, to gather].
coil (koil) *n.* turmoil; tumult; fuss.—**mortal coil**, the worries of life [etym. uncertain].
coin (koin) *n.* a wedge or corner-stone; a piece of stamped metal issued by government authority to be used as money; money.—*v.t.* to make into money; to mint; to invent or fabricate, as a word or phrase.—**coin'age** *n.* the act of coining; money coined; currency.—**coin'er** *n.* one who makes coins, esp. counterfeit coins; an inventor [L. *cuneus*, a wedge].
coincide (kō-in-sīd') *v.i.* to correspond in detail; to happen at the same time; to agree (in opinion).—**coincidence** (kō-in'sid-ens) *n.* correspondence in nature, circumstances, etc. —**coin'cident, coincident'al** *a.* occupying the same space; agreeing; simultaneous.—**coin'cidently** *adv.* [L. *co-*, together; *incidere*, to happen].
coir (koir) *n.* the fibre from the husk of the coconut, used for cordage, matting, etc. [Malay, *kayar*, cord].
coition (kō-i'shun) *n.* sexual intercourse; copulation [L. *co-*, together; *ire*, *itum*, to go].
coke (kōk) *n.* coal half burnt, and used as fuel;—*v.t.* to turn into coke [origin uncertain].
col (kol) *n.* a high pass or depression between two mountain peaks [L. *collum*, the neck].
colander (kul'ạn-dẹr) *n.* a vessel with a perforated bottom, used for straining in cookery; a sieve. Also **cull'ender** [L. *colare*, to strain].
cold (kōld) *a.* wanting in heat; chill; deficient in the emotions; spiritless;—*n.* absence of warmth; chilliness; cold weather; a disorder of the nose, throat and chest, often caused by cold, and characterised by running at the nose, hoarseness and coughing; catarrh. —**cold'ly** *adv.*—**cold'ish** *a.* somewhat cold.—**cold'ness** *n.*—**cold'-blood'ed** *a.* having cold blood, like fish; susceptible to cold; callous or heartless.—**cold war**, campaign carried on by means of economic pressure, press, radio, etc.—**to cold-shoulder**, to rebuff; to be unfriendly to [O.E. *ceald*].
cole (kōl) *n.* a name for plants of the cabbage family.—**cole'wort** *n.* the common cabbage [L. *caulis*, a stalk, esp. a cabbage stalk].
Coleoptera (kol-e-op'tẹr-ạ) *n.pl.* the order of insects, such as beetles, whose outer wings form a horny sheath or covering for the true wings [Gk. *koleos*, a sheath; *pteron*, a wing].
colic (kol'ik) *n.* severe paroxysmal pain in the abdomen [Gk. *kolon*, the lower intestine].
collaborate (ko-lab'ō-rāt) *v.i.* to work or labour together; to act jointly, esp. in works of literature, art, science.—**collabora'tion** *n.* joint labour; (*World War* 2) willing co-operation with the enemy given by an inhabitant of an occupied country.—**collab'orator** *n.* [L. *co-*; *laborare*, to work].
collapse (kol-aps') *v.i.* to fall in together; to break down; to fail suddenly; to lose strength; to give way under physical or mental strain; to become discouraged;—*v.t.* to cause to collapse (as of a lung);—*n.* a falling in or down; a sudden and complete failure; a break-down.—**collaps'able, collaps'ible** *a.* [L. *collabi*, *collapsus*, to fall to pieces].
collar (kol'ạr) *n.* something worn round the neck; the part of a garment that fits round the neck; part of the insignia of orders of knighthood, worn as a decoration round the neck; a ring; a band;—*v.t.* to seize by the collar; hence, to arrest; to capture; to grab; to put a collar on.—**coll'ar-beam** *n.* a piece of timber connecting two opposite rafters to act as a support.—**coll'ar-bone** *n.* the bone from the shoulder to the breast-bone; the clavicle [L. *collum*, the neck].
collate (ko-lāt') *v.t.* to compare critically; to arrange in order, as the sheets of a book for binding; to appoint to a benefice.—**colla'tion** *n.* the act of collating; a lunch or repast.—**colla'tive** *a.*—**colla'tor** *n.* [L. *conferre*, *collatum*, to bring together].
collateral (kol-at'e-rạl) *a.* side by side; running parallel; subordinately connected; descended from the same ancestor but through a different line; additional (of a security);—*n.* a collateral relative; a kinsman; additional security.—**collat'erally** *adv.*—**collat'eralness** [L. *con*; *latus*, the side].
colleague (kol'ēg) *n.* an associate or companion in an office or employment [L. *collega*, an associate].
collect (ko-lekt') *v.t.* to bring together; to gather; to assemble; to muster; to deduce; —*v.i.* to be assembled; to come together.—**collect** (kol'ekt) *n.* a very short prayer, consisting of one sentence, and containing only one petition.—**collect'able, collect'ible** *a.* —**collect'ed** *a.* not disconcerted; cool; self-possessed.—**collect'edly** *adv.*—**collect'edness** *n.* —**collec'tion** *n.* the act of collecting; a contribution or sum of money gathered at a meeting for a religious, charitable, etc. object; assemblage.—**collec'tive** *a.* formed by gathering; gathered into a mass, sum, or body; expressing a collection or aggregate.—**collect'ively** *adv.*—**collect'ivism** *n.* a term embracing all systems based on the Socialistic doctrine of the state, municipal, co-operative, etc. control of the economic life of the country.—**collect'ivist** *n.*—**collect'or** *n.* one who collects; an officer appointed to receive taxes, customs duties, tolls, etc.; to regain self-possession [L. *colligere*, *collectum*, to gather together].
colleen (kol'ēn) *n.* a girl [Ir. *cailin*].
college (kol'ej) *n.* an institution for higher education; the buildings, etc. of such an institution; an association of professional men, e.g. of physicians; an assembly, as of electors or cardinals.—**colle'gial** *a.* pert. to a college.—**collegian** (ko-lē'ji-ạn) *n.* a member of a college; a student.—**colle'giate** *a.* pert. to, or instituted like, a college; corporate [L. *collegium*, a society].
collet (kol'et) *n.* a collar; a neckband; the rim in which the stone of a ring is set [Fr. fr. L. *collum*, the neck].
collide (ko-līd') *v.i.* to strike or dash together; to clash; to come into conflict.—**collision** *n.* (ko-lizh'un) *n.* the act of striking together; a violent impact; a clashing; encounter; conflict [L. *collidere*, to dash together].
collie (kol'i) *n.* a breed of sheep-dog [etym. uncertain].
collier (kol'yẹr) *n.* a coal-miner; a ship whose usual cargo is coal.—**coll'iery** *n.* a coal-mine [fr. *coal*].
collinear (kol-in'ẹ-ạr) *a.* in the same straight line; aligned [L. *collineare*].
collingual (kol-ing'gwạl) *a.* speaking the same language [L. *lingua*, the tongue].
collocate (kol'ō-kāt) *v.t.* to set or place together; to arrange.—**colloca'tion** *n.* [L. *collocare*, to place together].
collodion (ko-lō'di-on) *n.* a solution of gun-cotton in ether, used in preparing photographic plates and in surgery [Gk. *kolla*, glue; *eidos*, form].
collogue (ko-lōg') *v.i.* to confer secretly; to conspire [L. *colloqui*, to speak together].
colloid (kol'oid) *a.* like glue; gelatinous;—*n.* a glue-like, non-crystalline substance, not soluble in water and unable to pass through animal membranes.—**colloid'al** *a.* like a colloid [Gk. *kolla*, glue; *eidos*, form].
collop (kol'op) *n.* a small slice or piece of meat [etym. unknown].
colloquy (kol'ō-kwi) *n.* conversation; dialogue; discussion; a conference, esp. political; a debate.—**collo'quial** *a.* pert. to, or used in, ordinary conversation.—**collo'quially** *adv.*—**collo'quialism** *n.* an expression used in ordinary conversation, but not regarded as slang [L. *colloqui*, to speak together].

collotype (kol´-ō-tīp) *n.* a process for producing illustrations by the use of a gelatinous plate [Gk. *kolla*, glue, and *type*].

collusion (ko-lū´-zhun) *n.* a secret agreement between two or more persons for a fraudulent purpose, usually in connection with legal proceedings.—**collu'sive** *a.* [L. *colludere, collusum*, to play together].

colon (kō´-lon) *n.* a punctuation mark (:), separating parts of a sentence that are almost independent and complete in themselves; (*Anat.*) that part of the large intestine extending from the caecum to the rectum.—**colon'ic** *a.* [Gk. *kolon*, a limb or member].

colonel (kur´-nel) *n.* the officer commanding a regiment or battalion.—**colon'elcy, colon'elship** *n.* the rank or quality of colonel [L. *columna*, a column. The pronunciation is due to a Sp. form *coronel*, once also used].

colonnade (kol-o-nād') *n.* a series of columns arranged symmetrically [L. *columna*, a column].

colony (kol´-on-i) *n.* a body of people who settle in a new country but remain subject to the parent state; the country thus occupied.—**colo'nial** *a.* pert. to a colony;—*n.* a colonist.—**col'onise** *v.t.* to plant or establish a colony in.—*v.i.* to settle.—**col'onist** *n.*—**colonisa'tion** *n.* [L. *colonia*].

colophon (kol´-ō-fon) *n.* individual device or inscription used by publishers and printers on the title-pages of books, etc. [Gk. *colophon*, the finish].

colophony (ko-lof´-u-ni) *n.* the dark-coloured resin obtained from turpentine.—**coloph'onite** *n.* a variety of garnet [place name *Colophon*, Asia Minor].

Colorado beetle (kol-o-rá´-dō bē-tl) *n.* a kind of beetle very injurious to the potato [fr. *Colorado*, U.S.A.].

coloration (kul-u-rā´-shun) *n.* colouring; arrangement or disposition of colours in art. Also **coloura'tion** [L. *color*, colour].

coloratura (kol-or-a-tū´-ra) *n.* (*Mus.*) ornamental runs and trills in vocal music [It.].

colossus (ko-los´-us) *n.* a gigantic statue, esp. that of Apollo at Rhodes; hence (*Fig.*) any person of great stature or enormous strength.—**coloss'al** *a.* of enormous size; gigantic [Gk. *kolossos*].

colour (kul´-ur) *n.* any hue or tint as distinguished from white; paint; complexion; a flush; false show; pretext; show of reason; kind or species; vividness in writing; in music, variety of timbre;—*v.t.* to paint or tinge with colour;—*v.i.* to blush.—**colours** *n.pl.* a flag or standard; a coloured badge, device, rosette, etc. used as a distinguishing mark.—**col'ourable** *a.* capable of being coloured; specious; plausible.—**col'ourably** *adv.*—**col'ourful** *a.* having plenty of colour.—**col'ouring** *n.* pigment; the manner of using or arranging colours; disguise; specious appearance.—**col'ourist** *n.* an artist to whom colouring is of supreme importance.—**col'our-blind** *a.* unable to distinguish between colours.—**col'our-ser'geant** *n.* (*Mil.*) formerly, the sergeant who guarded the regimental colours carried by the **colour-company** of the battalion.—**to join the colours,** to enlist in the army.—**to nail one's colours to the mast,** to commit oneself irrevocably to a particular plan of action.—**fast colours,** those that do not fade in the sun, or wash out in water.—**coloured man,** one with Negro blood; one who is not a white.—**colour bar** or **line,** discrimination in social status between white and coloured races.—**off colour,** indisposed [L. *color*, colour].

colporteur (kol-pōr-tẹr') *n.* one who carries around for sale Bibles, religious books, tracts, etc.; a book-peddler.—**col'portage** *n.* [Fr. *colporteur*, a hawker].

colt (kōlt) *n.* a young horse, esp. a male; an inexperienced youth.—**colt'ish** *a.* [O.E.].

Colt (kōlt) *n.* a repeating rifle; also a revolver invented by Samuel *Colt.* U.S.A.

colter See **coulter.**

coltsfoot (kōlts´-foot) *n.* a wild plant, with heart-shaped leaves and yellow flowers.

columbarium (kol-um-bā´-ri-um) *n.* the niche in a building wherein are placed the urns containing the ashes of the dead.—**col'umbary** *n.* a dove-cot; a pigeon-house [L. *columba*, a dove].

Columbia (kol-um´-bi-ạ) *n.* a literary name for America [fr. *Columbus*, discoverer of America].

columbine (kol´-um-bīn) *a.* of, or like, a dove; dove-coloured;—*n.* in pantomime, Harlequin's mistress; (*Bot.*) a small bell-shaped flower, with five spurred petals [L. *columba*, a dove].

columbium (kol-um´-bi-um) *n.* a metallic element, niobium.—**colum'bite** *n.* the native ore of columbium; niobite [fr. *Columbia*, U.S.A.].

column (kol´-um) *n.* a round pillar; a support; a body of troops drawn up in deep files; a division of a page; a perpendicular line of figures.—**columnar** (ko-lum´-nạr) *a.* formed in columns; having the form of columns.—**colum'nated, col'umned** *a.* furnished with, or supported on, columns.—**col'umnist** *n.* a writer who contributes column to a newspaper.—**fifth column,** a term first used in the Spanish Civil War (1936-39) to describe the column of secret agents who 'supported' the four columns of General Franco's army; (*World War* 2) enemy adherents who, by insidious propaganda among the civil population, endeavoured to lower morale or encouraged sabotage [L. *columna*].

colza (kol´-zạ) *n.* a plant related to the cabbage [Dut. *koolzaad*, cabbage-seed].

coma (kō´-mạ) *n.* (*Med.*) a deep sleep or stupor generally resulting from injury to the brain, alcoholic or narcotic poisoning; (*Fig.*) lethargy; drowsiness.—**com'atose** *a.* lethargic; drowsy [Gk. *koma*].

comb (kōm) *n.* a toothed instrument for separating, cleansing, adjusting, or fastening hair, dressing wool, etc.; also a decoration for a lady's hair; a cock's crest; the crest of a wave; the cell structure in which bees store their honey;—*v.t.* to separate, cleanse, dress, etc. with a comb;—*v.i.* to roll over or break with a white foam (said of waves).—**comb'er** *n.* one who, or that which, combs; a long, curling wave; a kind of fish, the sea-perch.—**comb'ing** *n.*—**comb'ings** *n.pl.* hair, wool, etc. removed by combing [O.E. *camb*].

combat (kum´-bat, kom´-bat) *v.t.* to fight against; to oppose by force; to contend with;—*v.i.* to struggle; to contend;—*n.* a fight; a struggle; a contest.—*pr.p.* **com'bating.**—*pa.p* and *pa.t.* **com'bated.**—**com'batant** *a.* contending; disposed to contend;—*n.* one engaged in a fight or combat.—**com'bative** *a.* disposed to combat; quarrelsome [Fr. *combattre*, to fight].

combe (kōōm) *n.* a deep valley; a hollow among hills [O.E.].

combine (kom-bīn') *v.t.* to join together; to unite; to connect;—*v.i.* to form a union; to co-operate; (*Chem.*) to unite and form a new compound.—**combine** (kom´-bīn) *n.* an association formed to control trade; a trust; a syndicate.—**com'bine-har'vester** *n.* an agricultural machine that reaps, threshes and bags the grain in one operation.—**combi'nable** *a.* capable of combining.—**com'binative, combi'natory** *a.* tending to combine.—**combination** (kom-bi-nā´-shun) *n.* union or connection; association of persons; alliance; chemical union.—**combina'tions** *n.pl.* an undergarment combining vest and drawers.—**combined operations** (*World War* 2) operations in which combined military, naval, and air forces were used [L.L. *combinare*, to put two-and-two together].

combustion (kom-bust′-yun) *n.* the act of fire on inflammable substances; the act of burning; chemical action accompanied by heat and light.—**combust′ible** *a.* liable to take fire; inflammable;—*n.* a substance that burns readily [L. *comburere*, to burn up].

come (kum) *v.i.* to approach; to arrive; to arrive at some state or condition; to move towards; to reach; to happen (to); to originate (from); to occur; to turn out to be; to appear.—*pr.p.* **com′ing**.—*pa.p.* **come**.—*pa.t.* **came**.—**a come′-back**, *n.* a return to a former activity.—**a come′-down**, *n.* a set-back; a descent in social status.—**to come by**, to pass; to obtain possession of.—**to come in for**, to obtain.—**to come of age**, to reach one's twenty-first birthday.—**to come to**, to recover consciousness; (*Naut.*) to anchor [O.E. *cuman*].

comedy (kom′-e-di) *n.* a stage play dealing with the lighter side of life, ending happily, or treating its subject humorously.—**comedian** (ko-mē′-di-ạn) *n.* an actor in comedy; a music-hall entertainer whose songs or stories are light and humorous; (*Colloq.*) a funny person; a comic.—**comedienne** (kom-ē-di-en′) *n. fem.* [Gk. *komoidia*, fr. *komos*, revel; *odē*, song].

comely (kum′-li) *a.* good-looking; graceful.—**come′liness** *n.* [O.E. *cyme*, fair].

comestible (ko-mes′-ti-bl) *a.* fit for eating.—**comes′tibles** *n.pl.* edible foodstuffs; eatables [L. *comedere*, to eat up].

comet (kom′-et) *n.* a heavenly body consisting of a diffuse, nebulous head, a nucleus, and a tail [Gk. *komētēs*, long-haired].

comfit (kum′-fit) *n.* a dry sweetmeat; a fruit, or fruit kernel, preserved with sugar and dried [L. *conficere*, to prepare].

comfort (kum′-fort) *v.t.* to allay grief or trouble; to console, cheer, gladden;—*n.* solace or consolation; ease of body or mind, or whatever causes it.—**com′forts** *n.pl.* appurtenances or circumstances which give greater ease to life.—**com′fortable** *a.* promoting or enjoying comfort.—**com′fortably** *adv.*—**com′forter** *n.* one who comforts; a knitted woollen scarf; a rubber teat for comforting a baby.—**com′fortless** *a.* lacking comfort.—**Job's comforter**, one who, in seeking to comfort, achieves the opposite [L. *confortare*, to strengthen].

comfrey, comfry (kum′-fri) *n.* a plant of the borage family [L. *confervere*, to boil together, to heal (of broken limbs)].

comic (kom′-ik) *a.* pert. to comedy; mirth-provoking; funny;—*n.* that which induces amusement or laughter; (*Colloq.*) a comedian; (*Colloq.*) a comic paper.—**com′ical** *a.* droll; ludicrous.—**com′ically** *adv.*—**comical′ity** *n.* the quality of being comical [Gk. *komos*, revel].

Cominform (kom′-in-form) *n.* *Com*munist *Inform*ation Bureau, established in Belgrade, 1947.

Comintern (kom′-in-tern) *n.* *Com*munist *Intern*ational, the international association of Communist parties.

comity (kom′-i-ti) *n.* courtesy; civility; suavity of manners [L. *comitas*].

comma (kom′-ạ) *n.* a punctuation mark (,), used to mark the shortest pauses in the division of a sentence.—**inverted commas**, quotation marks (' ', or " ") [Gk. fr. *koptein*, to cut].

command (ko-mȧnd′) *v.t.* to order or demand with authority; to govern or control; to have at one's disposal; to overlook or have a view over;—*v.i.* to be at the head;—*n.* an order; the body of troops under an officer; a district or region under a commander; a word of command; disposal; mastery or facility.—**command′ing** *a.* fitted to control; impressive or imperious.—**commandant** *n.* officer in charge of a military station or a body of troops.—**commandeer** (kom-an-dēr′) *v.t.* to seize for military purposes; to take forcible possession of.—**commander** (ko-mȧn′-dẹr) *n.* a leader; a commanding officer; in the navy, an officer ranking between a lieutenant and a captain.—**command′ment** *n.* a command; precept.—**commander-in-chief**, the officer in supreme command of the forces of a state [L. *commendare*, to entrust].

commando (ko-mȧn′-dō) *n.* (*Mil.*) a selected body of men, who undergo a special training to fit them for particularly dangerous enterprises against the enemy; a member of this body; orig. in S. Africa, a military force [Sp.].

commemorate (ko-mem′-o-rāt) *v.t.* to call, to remembrance; to celebrate the memory of someone or something by a solemn act of devotion.—**commemora′tion** *n.*—**commem′orative, commem′oratory** *a.* [L. *commemorare*].

commence (ko-mens′) *v.t.* to begin, to start, to originate;—*v.i.* to originate; to take rise; to begin.—**commence′ment** *n.* beginning [Fr. *commencer*].

commend (ko-mend′) *v.t.* to praise; to speak favourably of; to present as worthy; to entrust to.—**commend′able** *a.*—**commend′ably** *adv.*— **commend′ableness** *n.*—**commenda′tion** *n.* the act of commending; praise; approval.—**commend′atory** *a.* serving to commend [L. *commendare*, to entrust].

commensal (ko-men′-sạl) *n.* an animal or plant that lives as a tenant, but not a parasite, of another; one who eats at the same table as another; a messmate.—**commen′salism** *n.* [L. *con-*; *mensa*, a table].

commensurate (ko-men′-sū-rāt) *a.* equal in extent; proportionate; adequate.—**commen′surately** *adv.*—**commen′surateness** *n.*—**commensura′tion** *n.*—**commen′surable** *a.* having a common measure; suitably proportioned.—**commen′surably** *adv.*—**commensurabil′ity** *n.* [L. *con-*; *mensura*, a measure].

comment (ko-ment′, kom′-ent) *v.t.* and *i.* to make remarks, notes, criticisms;—**comm′ent** *n.* a note; a collection of notes; an explanation; a critical remark; an observation.—**commentary** (kom′-en-tạr-i) *n.* an exposition of a book; an historical narrative.—**running commentary** (*Wireless*) the description of an event while in actual progress, broadcast by an eye-witness.—**comm′entate** *v.t.* to annotate; to interpret the meaning of.—**comm′entator** *n.* an annotator; an expositor; one who speaks a commentary, either on events for broadcasting, or with a film [L. *comminisci*, *commentus*, to contrive].

commerce (kom′-ẹrs) *n.* buying and selling; trade or intercourse between individuals; social or personal intercourse.—**commercial** (ko-mer′-shạl) *a.* pert. to commerce; mercantile; (*Radio*) broadcast programme paid for by an advertiser.—**commercial traveller**, a travelling agent for a wholesale business firm.—**commer′cialism** *n.* business principles, methods, or viewpoint.—**commer′cially** *adv.* [L. *con-*; *merx*, merchandise].

comminate (kom′-in-āt) *v.t.* to threaten with divine wrath.—**commina′tion** *n.*—**comm′inative** *a.*—**comm′inatory** *a.* threatening [L. *comminatio*, strong threatening].

commingle (ko-ming′-gl) *v.t.* and *i.* to mingle together.

comminute (kom′-i-nūt) *v.t.* to reduce to minute particles; to pulverise.—**comminu′tion** *n.* [L. *comminuere*, to break into pieces].

commiserate (ko-miz′-e-rāt) *v.t.* and *i.* to have compassion for; to condole with; to pity; to sympathise.—**commisera′tion** *n.* [L. *commiserari*, to bewail with].

commissar (kom′-i-sȧr) *n.* one of the heads of a Soviet government department or commissariat [L. *committere*, to entrust].

commissariat (kom-i-sā′-ri-at) *n.* the army department which supplies food, stores, equipment, transport [L. *committere*, to entrust].

commissary (kom′-i-sạr-i) *n.* one to whom a duty is assigned; a deputy; a commissioner;

(*Mil.*) one who supervises the supply of food and stores to the army.—**commissa'rial** *a.*—**comm'issaryship** *n.* [L. *committere*, to entrust].

commission (ko-mish'un) *n.* the act of committing; something entrusted to be done; payment by a percentage for doing something; a legal warrant to execute some office, trust, or duty; the power under such warrant; the document that contains it; the thing to be done as agent for another; (*Mil., Naval, etc.*) a warrant of appointment, by the head of a state, to the rank of officer in the state's army, navy, etc.;—*v.t.* to give power to; to authorise; to give an order for; to appoint to the rank of officer.—**commis'sioner** *n.* one holding a commission to act; a member of a body of enquiry.—**royal commission,** a body appointed by royal warrant to conduct an impartial inquiry into any matter of public interest [L. *committere*, to entrust].

commissionaire (ko-mish-un-ār') *n.* uniformed messenger in large offices, theatres, hotels, etc.; a door-keeper [Fr.].

commit (ko-mit') *v.t.* to entrust; to give in charge; to perform; to be guilty of; to pledge or bind; to send for trial or confinement;—*pr.p.* **commit'ting**.—*pa.p.* and *pa.t.* **commit'ted,** —**commit'tal, commit'ment** *n.*—**to commit oneself,** to compromise or entangle oneself [L. *committere*].

committee (ko-mit'i) *n.* a number of persons appointed to attend to any particular business by a legislative body, court, society, etc. [L. *committere*, to entrust].

commix (ko-miks') *v.t.* and *i.* to mix or blend.—**commix'ture** *n.* the act of mixing, or state of being mixed; the mixture [fr. *mixture*].

commode (ko-mōd') *n.* a chest of drawers; a small piece of furniture containing a chamber-pot [L. *commodus*, suitable].

commodious (ko-mō'di-us) *a.* convenient; roomy; spacious.—**commo'diously** *adv.*—**commo'diousness** *n.*—**commod'ity** *n.* any useful thing; an article of trade.—**commod'ities** *n.pl.* goods [L. *commodus*, suitable].

commodore (kom'o-dōr) *n.* (*Naval*) the rank given to a captain whilst temporarily in command of a squadron; the senior captain (or the leading ship) of a convoy of merchantmen (etym. uncertain].

common (kom'un) *a.* shared by or belonging to all, or to several; public; general; ordinary; usual; frequent; vulgar; inferior; of little value; of low social status;—*n.* a tract of land belonging to a community for public use; unenclosed land not belonging to a private owner.—**comm'ons** *n.pl.* ordinary people; the lower House of Parliament, called the **House of Commons;** members elected to the lower House of Parliament; rations; food provided daily.—**comm'onalty** *n.* the general body of the people without reference to rank, position, etc.—**comm'oner** *n.* one of the common people, i.e. not a member of the nobility.—**comm'only** *adv.* in a common manner; usually; jointly; meanly.—**comm'onness** *n.*—**comm'onplace** *a.* common; ordinary; trite; hackneyed.—*n.* a common topic; a trite remark.—**comm'on-place-book** *n.* book which records things to be remembered; a note-book.—**comm'on-sense** *n.* sound and practical understanding; well-balanced judgment.—**common law,** law based on usage and custom, and confirmed by judicial decision; the unwritten law as distinguished from statute law.—**the common good,** the welfare of the community as a whole.—**to be on short commons,** to have a scanty allowance of food [L. *communis*].

commonweal (kom'un-wēl) *n.* the public welfare; the common good.—**comm'onwealth** (welth) *n.* the whole body of people.—**Comm'onwealth** *n.* since 1947 the comprehensive term for a number of independent territories linked with Gr. Britain including the Dominions and some former colonies [*common* and *weal*].

commotion (ko-mō'shun) *n.* violent motion; agitation; tumult; public disorder [L. *con-*; *movere, motum*, to move].

commune (ko-mūn') *v.i.* to converse together intimately; to have spiritual intercourse (with); (*Eccl.*) to receive the communion.—**communion** (kom-ūn'yun) *n.* the act of communing; the celebration of the Lord's Supper [L. *communis*, common].

commune (kom'ūn) *n.* people having common rights; a small administrative district (esp. in France) governed by a mayor.—**comm'unal** *a.* pert. to a commune or community; for common use.—**comm'unalise** *v.t.* to make over for common use. —**comm'unalism** *n.* a system by which small local governments have large powers.—**comm'unism** *n.* the theory of a social system in which everything is held in common, private property being abolished.—**comm'unist** *n.*—**communis'tic** *a.* [L. *communis*, common].

communicate (ko-mū'ni-kāt) *v.t.* to impart information; to reveal; to convey.—*v.i.* to have connection with; to have dealings, intercourse, correspondence, with; to partake of the Lord's Supper.—**commu'nicable** *a.*—**commu'nicably** *adv.*—**communica'tion** *n.* the act of making known; intercourse by speech, correspondence, messages, etc.; information; means of passing from one place to another; a connecting passage.—**commun'icant** *n.* one who imparts information; one who receives communion.—**commun'icative** *a.* ready to converse, or to impart information; talkative.—**commu'nicatory** *a.* imparting information [L. *communicare*].

communiqué (kom-ū'ni-kā) *n.* an official announcement [Fr.].

community (ko-mū'ni-ti) *n.* people having common interests; the public, or people in general; common possession or enjoyment [L. *communis*, common].

commute (ko-mūt') *v.t.* to exchange; to substitute; to mitigate a sentence, by changing the penalty to a lighter one; (*U.S.*) to use a season-ticket for travelling daily to one's work in town.—**commut'able** *a.* exchangeable.—**commutabil'ity** *n.*—**commuta'tion** *n.*—**comm'utator** *n.* (*Elect.*) a device for reversing the direction of an electric current [L. *con-*; *mutare*, to change].

compact (kom'pakt') *a.* firm; solid; closely packed; condensed; terse;—*v.t.* to press closely together; to make firm; (*Shak.*) to confirm.—**compact'ly** *adv.*—**compact'ness** *n.*—**compact'ed** *a.* firmly united [L. *con-*; *pangere, pactum*, to fix].

compact (kom-pakt) *n.* an agreement or contract; a mutual bargain; a league or covenant;—**com'pact** *n.* a case to hold face-powder; a pocket vanity-case [L. *con-*; *pacisci, pactus*, to make an agreement].

companion (kom-pan'yun) *n.* one who is in another's company, habitually or for the moment; comrade; an associate or partner; member of an order of knighthood.—**compan'ionable** *a.* fitted to be a companion; sociable.—**compan'ionably** *adv.*—**companionabil'ity, compan'ionableness** *n.* the quality of being a good companion.—**compan'ionship** *n.* fellowship; association; state of being a companion [L. *companium*, fellowship, fr. *con-*, *panis*, bread].

companion (kom-pan'yun) *n.* (*Naut.*) a skylight on upper deck, to let light into cabin below.—**companion-ladder,** one between cabin and quarter-deck.—**companion-way,** cabin staircase [O.Fr. *compagne*].

company (kum'pa-ni) *n.* a gathering of persons; an assembly; a group; an association of persons in trade; a social circle; visitors; a division of a regiment commanded by a captain [L. *con-*; *panis*, bread].

compare (kom-pār′) *v.t.* to notice or point out the likeness and differences of two or more things; to liken or contrast; (*Gram.*) to state the comparative and superlative of an adjective or adverb;—*v.i.* to be like; to compete with.—**comparable** (kom′pạr-ạ-bl) *a.* capable of being compared; of equal regard or value.—**com′parably** *adv.*—**comparative** (kom-par′ạ-tiv) *a.* estimated by comparison; not absolute; relative; partial (*Gram.*) expressing 'more'.—**compar′atively** *adv.*—**compar′ison** *n.* the act of comparing [L. *comparare*, to match].

compartment (kom-pȧrt′mẹnt) *n.* a part divided off; a section; a division of a railway carriage [L. *compartiri*, to divide].

compass (kum′pạs) *n.* an instrument for showing the north, and so, directions; (*Mus.*) the range of a voice in the musical scale; circuit; a circumference; measurement round; space; area; scope; reach;—*v.t.* to go round; to surround; to contrive; to attain; to accomplish.—**com′passes** *n.pl.* a mathematical instrument for describing circles, measuring, etc.—**to box the compass**, to name in their order the 32 points of the mariner's compass.—**to fetch a compass**, to make a detour [L. *con-*; *passus*, a step].

compassion (kom-pash′un) *n.* sympathy with the distress or suffering of another; pity.—**compas′sionate** *a.* full of sympathy; showing pity; merciful.—*v.t.* to pity.—**compas′sionately** *adv.*—**compas′sionateness** *n.* [L. *con-*; *pati*, *passus*, to suffer].

compatible (kom-pat′i-bl) *a.* consistent; agreeing with; capable of harmonious union.—**compat′ibly** *adv.*—**compatibil′ity** *n.* [L. *con-*; *pati*, to suffer].

compatriot (kom-pā′tri-ot, kom-pat′ri-ot) *n.* one of the same country; a fellow-countryman [L. *con-*; and *patriot*].

compeer (kom-pēr′) *n.* an equal; a companion; an associate [L. *con-*; *par*, equal].

compel (kom-pel′) *v.t.* to force; to oblige; to bring about by force;—*pr.p.* **compel′ling.** —*pa.p.* and *pa.t.* **compelled′.**—**compel′lable** *a.* [L. *compellere*, to drive together].

compendium (kom-pend′i-um) *n.* an abridgement or summary; an abstract. Also **com′pend.**—*pl.* **compend′iums**, or **compend′ia.**—**compend′ious** *a.* abridged.—**compend′iously** *adv.* —**compend′iousness** *n.* [L.=what is weighed together].

compensate (kom′pen-sāt) *v.t.* to recompense suitably; to reward; to pay;—*v.i.* to make amends; to make up for.—**compensa′tion** *n.* recompense; payment for some loss, injury, etc.—**compensa′tive, compensa′tory** *a.* compensating; making up for [L. *compensare*, to weigh together].

compere (kom′per) *n.* (*fem.* **commere**) one who explains or introduces a variety or other performance [Fr.].

compete (kom-pēt′) *v.i.* to strive against others to win something; to vie with; to contend; to rival.—**competition** (kom-pe-tish′un) *n.* the act of competing.—**compet′itive** *a.* pert. to or by competition.—**compet′itively** *adv.*—**compet′itor** *n.* one who competes; a rival.—**compet′itory** *a.* [L. *competere*, to seek with].

competent (kom′pe-tẹnt) *a.* able; skilful; properly qualified; proper; due; legitimate; suitable; sufficient.—**com′petently** *adv.*—**com′petence, com′petency** *n.* the state of being fit or capable; sufficiency, esp. of means of subsistence [L. *competere*, to seek together].

compile (kom-pīl′) *v.t.* to put together literary materials from the works of others; to collect or amass.—**compil′er** *n.*—**compila′tion** *n.* [L. *compilare*, to plunder].

complacent (kom-plā′sent) *a.* self-satisfied; pleased or gratified.—**compla′cently** *adv.*—**compla′cence, compla′cency** *n.* self-satisfaction [L. *complacere*, to please greatly].

complain (kom-plān′) *v.i.* to express distress, grief, dissatisfaction; to lament; to grumble; to be ailing.—**complain′ant** *n.* a complainer; (*Law*) a plaintiff; one who brings an action against another.—**complaint′** *n.* the expression of distress, dissatisfaction, etc.; a malady or ailment [L. *con-*; *plangere*, to bewail].

complaisant (kom-plā′zant) *a.* desirous to please; affable; obliging; gracious.—**complai′santly** *adv.*—**complai′sance** *n.* act of pleasing; civility; courtesy; affability [L. *complacere*, to please greatly].

complement (kom′ple-ment) *n.* that which supplies a deficiency; something making up a whole; the full quantity or number;—**complement′** *v.t.* to supplement; to supply a deficiency.—**complement′al, complement′ary** *a.* completing [L. *complere*, to fill up].

complete (kom-plēt′) *a.* entire; finished; perfect, with no part lacking;—*v.t.* to bring to a state of entirety; to perfect; to fulfil; to accomplish.—**complete′ly** *adv.*—**complete′ness** *n.*—**completion** (kom-plē′shun) *n.* the act of completing; fulfilment; achievement [L. *complere*, to fill up].

complex (kom′pleks) *a.* consisting of two or more parts; not simple; involved or intricate;—*n.* a complicated whole; (*Psych.*) a group of repressed emotional ideas responsible for abnormal mental condition.—**complex′ly** *adv.*—**complex′ness, complex′ity** *n.* the state of being complex; intricacy; complication [L. *complectere*, to interweave].

complexion (kom-plek′shun) *n.* colour of the skin, esp. of the face; aspect or appearance; quality or texture; character or disposition [L. *complexio*].

compliance (kom-plī′ạns) *n.* submission; a yielding; acquiescence; consent;—**compli′ant** *a.* yielding; obedient; civil.—**compli′antly** *adv.*—**compli′able** *a.* inclined to comply [fr. *comply*].

complicate (kom′pli-kāt) *v.t.* to fold or twist together; to entangle; to embarrass; to make intricate.—**com′plicated** *a.* tangled; involved.—**complica′tion** *n.* the state of being complicated [L. *con-*; *plicare*, to fold].

complicity (kom-plis′i-ti) *n.* the state of being an accomplice, of having a share in the guilt [Fr. *complice*, an accomplice].

compliment (kom′pli-mẹnt) *n.* an expression of regard or admiration; flattering speech; a formal greeting (usually *pl.*).—**compliment** (kom-pli-ment′) *v.t.* to gratify by expression of approbation; to congratulate; to express respect for.—**compliment′ary** *a.* expressing praise, admiration, civility [L. *complere*, to fill up].

compline (kom′plin) *n.* the seventh and last church service of the day. Also **com′plin** [L. *complere*, to fill up].

comply (kom-plī′) *v.i.* to yield to; to agree; to consent; to conform; to adapt oneself to.—**compli′er** *n.* [L. *complere*, to fill up].

compo (kom′po) *n.* a mixture composed of whiting, glue, etc., for plaster- and stucco-work [fr. *compo*sition].

component (kom-pō′nẹnt) *a.* constituting; composing; making up; helping to form a compound;—*n.* a part helping to make a whole [L. *componere*, to put together].

comport (kom-pōrt′) *v.t.* to behave; to conduct oneself;—*v.i.* to agree; to accord; to suit [L. *comportare*, to carry together].

compose (kom-pōz′) *v.t.* to form by uniting parts; to arrange; to put in order; to write; to invent; to adjust; to calm; to soothe; to set up the types in proper order for printing; —*v.i.* to practise composition.—**composed′** *a.* sedate; quiet; calm.—**compos′edly** *adv.*—**compos′edness** *n.*—**compos′er** *n.* one who composes; an author, esp. a musical author.—**composite** (kom′poz-it) *a.* made up of distinct parts or elements.—**composition** (kom-pō-zish′un) *n.* the act of composing; the thing formed by composing; in schools, a pupil's essay; a literary, musical, artistic, etc. work.—

compositor (kom-poz′i-tor) *n.* one who sets up type for printing; a type-setter.—**composure** (kom-pō′zhūr) *n.* calmness; tranquillity [Fr. *composer*].

compost (kom′post) *n.* a fertilising mixture; a composition for plaster-work, etc. [L. *componere*, to put together].

compote (kom′pōt) *n.* fruit stewed or preserved in syrup [Fr.].

compound (kom-pound′) *v.t.* to put together, as elements or parts, to form a whole; to combine; to mix; to compromise; to condone; to make a settlement of debt by partial payment.—**to compound a felony** (*Law*) to refrain, for some consideration, from prosecuting [L. *componere*, to put together].

compound (kom′pound) *a.* composed of elements, ingredients, or parts; not simple; mixed; composite;—*n.* a mixture; a joining; a substance to which something has been added; a word, etc. made up of parts; (*Chem.*) a substance composed of two or more elements, which are always present in the same fixed proportions.—**compound fracture**, a fracture of a bone where a portion pierces the skin, making a surface wound.—**compound interest**, is interest paid on capital plus accumulated interest [L. *componere*, to put together].

compound (kom′pound) *n.* in the East, an enclosure about a house; in S. Africa, an enclosed area in which native labourers reside [Malay, *kampong*, an enclosure].

comprehend (kom-prē-hend′) *v.t.* to understand; to grasp with the mind; to take in; to include; to comprise; to contain.—**comprehensible** (kom-prē-hen′si-bl) *a.* understandable; conceivable.—**comprehen′sibly** *adv.* **comprehensibil′ity, comprehen′sibleness** *n.*—**comprehen′sion** *n.* the act of comprehending; the capacity of the mind to perceive and understand.—**comprehen′sive** *a.* including much within narrow limits; extensive; large; capacious; inclusive.—**comprehen′sively** *adv.*—**comprehen′siveness** *n.* [L. *comprehendere*, to grasp].

compress (kom-pres′) *v.t.* to press together; to reduce the volume by pressure; to condense.—**compres′sible** *a.*—**compressibil′ity** *n.*—**compression** (kom-presh′un) *n.* the act or effect of compressing.—**compres′sive** *a.* tending to compress.—**compres′sor** *n.* [L. *compressus*. pressed together].

compress (kom′pres) *n.* (*Med.*) a pad to make pressure on a wound; a wet pad to reduce inflammation.

comprise (kom-prīz′) *v.t.* to include; to comprehend or embrace; to consist of.—**compris′able** *a.*—**compris′al** *n.* the act of comprising [Fr. *comprendre*, to include].

compromise (kom′prō-mīz) *n.* a settling of matters by mutual adjustment, each side making some concessions; a middle course;—*v.t.* and *i.* to settle by making mutual concessions; to commit oneself; to expose to the risk of scandal or disgrace [L. *con-*; *promittere*. to promise].

Comptometer (kom(p)-tom′e-tẽr) *n.* a calculating-machine [Protected Trade Name].

comptroller (kon-trō′lẽr) *n.* a form of 'controller,' only used now as a title of an auditor in Government departments [L. *contra*; *rotulus*, a roll].

compulsion (kom-pul′shun) *n.* the act or effect of compelling; force; constraint; violence; (*Pysch.*) an irresistible impulse.—**compul′sive** *a.* exercising compulsion.—**compul′sory** *a.* compelling; constraining; obligatory; enforced.—**compul′sorily** *adv.* [L. *compulsus*, driven together].

compunction (kom-pungk′shun) *n.* remorse of conscience; pity; scruple.—**compunc′tious** *a.* conscience-stricken; regretful; remorseful [L. *con-*; *pungere*, to prick].

compute (kom-pūt′) *v.t.* to count; to calculate; to estimate.—**comput′able** *a.*—**computa′tion** *n.* calculation; reckoning; estimate [L. *con*; *putare*, to reckon].

comrade (kum′rād) *n.* a close friend or companion; a mate; an associate.—**com′radeship** *n.* close friendship; fellowship; affectionate association [Sp. *camarada*, a room-mate; L. *camera*, a room].

con (kon) *v.t.* to study; to pore over; to learn by heart [O.E. *cunnan*, to know].

con (kon) *v.t.* and *i.* to superintend the steering of a vessel [L. *conducere*, to guide].

con (kon) *adv.* (*abbrev.* of **contra**), against, e.g. in the phrase **pro and con**, for and against;—**the pro and con** *n.* Also *pl.* **the pros and cons**—the advantages and disadvantages [L.].

con- (kon) *prefix* fr. L. *cum*, with, together.

conation (kō-nā′shun) *n.* (*Psych.*) the power or agency which impels to effort of any kind [L. *conari*, *conatus*, to endeavour].

concatenate (kon-kat′e-nāt) *v.t.* to link together; to unite in a series.—**concatena′tion** *n.* a series of things depending on each other; a connected chain, as of circumstances [L. *con-*; *catena*, a chain].

concave (kon′kāv) *a.* hollow and curved inwards, as the inner surface of a vault.—**concavity** (kon-kav′i-ti) *n.* hollowness [L. *con-*; *cavus*, hollow].

conceal (kon-sēl′) *v.t.* to hide or secrete; to mask or disguise; to withhold from knowledge.—**conceal′ment** *n.* [L. *con-*; *celare*, to hide].

concede (kon-sēd′) *v.t.* to yield; to admit to be true; to grant; to surrender;—*v.i.* to admit [L.*concedere*, to yield].

conceit (kon-sēt′) *n.* over-estimation of self; vanity; opinion; fanciful thought;—*v.t.* and *i.* (*Arch.*) to conceive.—**conceit′ed** *a.* vain; pleased with oneself; egotistical.—**conceit′edly** *adv.* [fr. *conceive*].

conceive (kon-sēv′) *v.t.* to form an idea in the mind; to think; to imagine; to understand; to realise;—*v.i.* to become pregnant; to have a notion.—**conceiv′able** *a.* that may be believed, imagined, or understood.—**conceiv′ably** *adv.* [L. *con-*; *capere*, to take, seize].

concentrate (kon-sen′trāt, kon′sen-trāt) *v.t.* to bring to a common centre; to reduce to small space; to increase in strength; to condense;—*v.i.* to come together; to devote all attention.—**concentra′tion** *n.* the act of concentrating; condensation; increased strength; the fixation of the mind on something.—**concentration camp**, a place of detention.—**concen′trative** *a.* tending to concentrate [L. *con-*; *centrum*, the centre].

concentre (kon-sen′tẽr) *v.t.* and *i.* to bring to a common centre; to meet in a common centre.—**concen′tric, concen′trical** *a.* having the same centre.

concept (kon′sept) *n.* an abstract notion; a mental impression of an object.—**conception** (kon-sep′shun) *n.* the act of conceiving; the thing conceived; a mental picture; an idea; a notion; (*Med.*) the beginning of pregnancy.—**concep′tive** *a.* pert. to conception; capable of conceiving.—**concep′tual** *a.* pert. to conception or to a concept [L. *concipere*, to conceive].

concern (kon-sẽrn′) *v.t.* to relate or belong to; to be of importance to; to be the business of; to make uneasy;—*n.* that which relates or belongs to one; interest in, or care for, any person or thing; worry; a business establishment.—**concerned′** *a.* connected with; interested; worried; anxious; troubled; involved.—**concern′ing** *prep.* regarding; with respect to.—**concern′ment** *n.* a thing in which one is concerned [L. *con-*; *cernere*, to distinguish].

concert (kon-sẽrt′) *v.t.* to plan together; to arrange; to design.—**concert′ed** *a.* mutually planned; (*Mus.*) arranged in parts.—**concert** (kon′sẽrt) *n.* agreement in a plan; harmony; a musical entertainment.—**concertina** (kon-sẽr-tē′nạ) *n.* a small musical wind instrument with hexagonal ends, fitted with bellows and keyboards.—**concerto** (kon-cher′tō) *n.* a musical composition arranged for a solo instrument with orchestral accompaniment [Fr. *concerter*].

concession (kon-sesh′un) *n.* the act of conceding; a special privilege; a grant; an admission.—**concessionaire** (kon-sesh-un-ār′) *n.* one who holds a concession.—**conces′sionary** *a.* [L. *con-*; *cedere*, to yield].

conch (kongk) *n.* a sea-shell; the spiral shell used as a trumpet by the Tritons [L. *concha*, a shell].

conchology (kong-kol′o-ji) *n.* the scientific study of shells and shell-fish.—**conchol′ogist** *n.* [Gk. *konchē*, a shell; *logos*, discourse].

conciliate (kon-sil′i-āt) *v.t.* to win over to goodwill; to appease; to make peace; to pacify.—**concilia′tion** *n.*—**concil′iative** *a.* conciliatory.—**concil′iatory** *a.* tending to pacify [L. *conciliare*, to bring together].

concise (kon-sīs′) *a.* brief; shortened; condensed; comprehensive.—**concise′ly** *adv.* in few words; tersely.—**concise′ness** *n.* the quality of being concise; brevity.—**concis′ion** *n.* conciseness; mutilation [L. *concisus*, fr. *caedere*, to cut].

conclave (kon′klāv) *n.* a private meeting of cardinals for the election of a pope; where they meet; any secret meeting [L. *conclave*, a room; fr. *clavis*, a key].

conclude (kon-klood′) *v.t.* to bring to an end; to close; to finish; to complete; to make a final judgment of; to infer;—*v.i.* to come to an end [L. *concludere*].

conclusion kon-kloo′shun) *n.* the end; the last part of anything; the final judgment; inference; result from experiment.—**conclu′sive** *a.* final; decisive; convincing [L. *concludere*, to end].

concoct (kon-kokt′) *v.t.* (*Arch.*) to digest in the mind; to make a mixture; to make up, esp. a story.—**concoc′tion** *n.* the act of concocting; the thing concocted [L. *concoctus*, cooked].

concomitant (kon-kom′i-tant) *a.* accompanying; attending; going along with;—*n.* an accompanying circumstance.—**concom′itance, concom′itancy** *n.* the state of being concomitant; co-existence [L. *concomitari*, to go with as companion].

concord (kong′kord, kon′kord) *n.* agreement; union between persons, as in opinions, etc.; harmony; unison; consonance;—*v.i.* to agree.—**concord′ance** *n.* agreement; an index to the words of a book (esp. of the Bible) with references to the places of their occurrence.—**concord′ant** *a.* agreeing; harmonious [L. *con-*; *cor, cordis*, the heart].

concordat (kon-kor′dat) *n.* an agreement between the pope and a sovereign or government on religious questions; a pact; a treaty [L. *con-*; *cor, cordis*, the heart].

concourse (kon′kōrs) *n.* a gathering together; an assembly; a meeting; a crowd.

concrescence (kon-kres′ens) *n.* a growing together [L. *con-*; *crescere*, to grow].

concrete (kon′krēt) *a.* made of concrete; consisting of matter, facts, etc.; solid; not abstract; specific;—*n.* a mixture of sand, cement, etc., used in building; anything real or specific, as opposed to abstract or general; *v.t.* to form into a solid mass;—*v.i.* to unite into a mass; to harden.—**concretely** (kon-krēt′li) *adv.*—**concrete′ness** *n.*—**concre′tion** *n.* the state of being concrete; a mass formed of parts pressed together. [L. *concrescere*, to grow together].

concubine (kong′kū-bīn) *n.* a woman who lives with a man without being his lawful wife.—**concubinage** (kon-kū′bi-nāj) *n.* the living together of a man and a woman not legally married [L. *con-*; *cubare*, to lie].

concupiscence (kon-kū′pis-ens) *n.* violent sexual desire; lust.—**concu′piscent, concu′piscible** *a.* lustful [L. *con-*; *cupere*, to desire].

concur (kon-kur′) *v.i.* to agree; to express agreement; to meet in the same point; to coincide.—*pr.p.* **concur′ring**—*pa.p.* and *pa.t.* **concurred′**.—**concur′rence** *n.* a meeting or coming together; agreement.—**concur′rent** *a.* acting in conjunction; agreeing in the same act; taking place at the same time; accompanying;—*n.* a joint or contributory cause.—**concur′rently** *adv.* [L. *concurrere*, to run together].

concuss (kon-kus′) *v.t.* to agitate; to disturb; to force by threats to do something [L. *concutere, concussum*, to agitate].

concussion (kon-kush′un) *n.* act of shaking by sudden striking; shock; (*Med.*) a violent disturbance of the brain caused by a blow or fall, and producing unconsciousness [L. *concussio*, a shaking together].

condemn (kon-dem′) *v.t.* to blame; to censure; to pronounce guilty; to sentence; to reprove; to declare unfit for use.—**condemna′tion** *n.* act of condemning.—**condem′natory** *a.* expressing censure [L. *condemnare*].

condense (kon-dens′) *v.t.* to make more dense, close, or compact; to make more solid; to concentrate; to change a vapour into liquid; to pack into few words;—*v.i.* to become more dense or compact; to pass from vapour to liquid.—**condensa′tion** *n.* the act of condensing; the state of being condensed; conciseness; in psycho-analysis, the symbolisation of two or more ideas by one symbol.—**condensed′** *a.* compressed; concise; (of milk) evaporated and preserved in tins.—**condens′er** *n.* one who, or that which, condenses; an apparatus for changing vapour into liquid during distillation [L. *condensare*, fr. *densus*, dense].

condescend (kon-de-send′) *v.i.* to come down from one's position, rank, or dignity; to stoop; to deign; to be gracious or affable to inferiors; to patronise.—**condescend′ing** *a.*—**condescen′sion** *n.* the act of condescending [L. *condescendere*, to come down].

condign (kon-dīn′) *a.* deserved; well-merited; adequate; sufficient.—**condign′ly** *adv.*—**condign′ness** *n.* [L. *dignus*, worthy].

condiment (kon′di-ment) *n.* a relish; seasoning for food [L. *condire*, to pickle].

condition (kon-dish′un) *n.* a thing on which a statement, happening, or existing depends; state or circumstances of anything; position as to worldly circumstances; rank; disposition; a pre-requisite; a stipulation;—*v.t.* to stipulate; to impose conditions on; to render fit and in good health;—*v.i.* to make terms.—**condi′tional** *a.* depending on conditions; not absolute.—**condi′tionally** *adv.*—**condi′tioned** *a.*—**conditioned reflex**, in psychology, an automatic response induced by repeated applications of the same stimulus [L. *conditio*].

condole (kon-dōl′) *v.i.* to grieve with; to offer sympathy.—**condol′ence, condole′ment** *n.* an expression of grief for the sorrow of another [L. *condolere*, to suffer with].

condominium (kon-dō-min′i-um) *n.* joint rule of a state by two or more states [L. *con-*, and *dominium*, dominion].

condone (kon-dōn′) *v.t.* to pardon; to forgive; to overlook.—**condonation** (kon-dō-nā′shun) *n.* [L. *condonare*, to remit].

condor (kon′dor) *n.* a large species of vulture, native to S. America [Peruv.].

conduce (kon-dūs′) *v,i.* to lead to some end or result; to help; to promote.—**conduc′ive** *a.* having a tendency to promote, help, or forward; inducing.—**conduc′iveness** *n.* [L. *conducere*, to bring together, to lead].

conduct (kon′dukt) *n.* the act of guiding; guidance; management; behaviour.—**conduct′** *v.t.* to guide; to lead; to direct; to manage; to behave.—**conduc′tance** *n.* (*Elect.*) the property of a body for conducting electricity.—**conduc′tible** *a.* able to conduct; able to be conducted.—**conduc′tion** *n.* the act of conducting; the transmission or flow of heat from one body to another.—**conduc′tive** *a.* able to transmit heat, electricity, etc.—

conductiv'ity *n.* the quality of being conductive.—**conduc'tor** *n.* a guide; the controller of a choir or orchestra; one in charge of a bus, tram, etc. who collects fares; a substance capable of transmitting heat, electricity, etc. —**conduc'tress** *n. fem.* [L. *conducere*, to lead].

conduit (kon′, kun′dit) *n.* a pipe or channel for conveying water [Fr. fr. *conduire*, to lead].

cone (kōn) *n.* a solid body tapering to a point from a circular base; anything of this shape; the fruit of the pine, fir, etc.—**conic, conical** (kon′ik,-ạl) *a.* having the form of, or pert. to, a cone.—**con'ically** *adv.*—**con'ics** *n.* (*Geom.*) the branch dealing with conic sections.—**con'iform** *a.* cone-shaped [Gk. *kōnos*].

coney *n.* See **cony.**

confab (kon′fab) *n.* (*Colloq.*) a chat.

confabulate (kon-fab′ū-lāt) *v.i.* to talk familiarly together; to chat.—**confabula'tion** *n.* [L. *confabulari*].

confection (kon-fek′shun) *n.* the act of compounding different substances into one compound; a sweetmeat; ready-made millinery, dresses, etc.—**confec'tionary** *a.*—**confec'tioner** *n.* one who makes or sells confections.—**confec'tionery** *n.* sweetmeats; a shop where sweetmeats are sold [L. *conficere*, to make up].

confederate (kon-fed′ẹr-āt) *a.* united in a league; bound by treaty; allied;—*n.* an ally; an accomplice;—*v.t.* and *i.* to unite in a league.—**confed'eracy** *n.* a union; an alliance.—**confedera'tion** *n.* the act of forming a confederacy; an alliance [L. *con-*; *foedus*, a league].

confer (kon-fer′) *v.t.* to bestow upon; to grant; to award;—*v.i.* to consult together; to take advice; to discuss.—*pr.p.* **confer'ring**.—*pa.p.* and *pa.t.* **conferred'**.—**con'ference** *n.* a meeting for discussion of problems, etc. and interchange of views; a consultation. [L. *conferre*, to bring together].

confess (kon-fes′) *v.t.* to admit; to own; to acknowledge; to grant; (of a priest) to hear the sins of;—*v.i.* to acknowledge; to declare one's sins orally to a priest.—**confes'sedly** *adv.* admittedly.—**confession** (kon-fesh′un) *n.* admission; avowal of sins; declaring one's sins to priest.—**confes'sional** *n.* the stall where a priest sits to hear confessions;—*a.* pert. to confession.—**confess'or** *n.* a priest who hears confessions.—**confession of faith,** a statement of the religious beliefs of a sect [L. *confiteri*, *confessus*, to acknowledge].

confetti (kon-fet′i) *n.pl.* small discs of coloured paper, for throwing at weddings, carnivals, etc. [It.].

confide (kon-fīd′) *v.t.* to hand over to the charge of; to entrust to; to tell a secret to; —*v.i.* to put faith in; to rely on.—**confidant'** *n.* (*fem.* **confidante'**) a person to whom one can tell one's private affairs [L. *con-*; *fidere*, to trust].

confidence (kon′fi-dens) *n.* that in which faith is put; belief; trust; feeling of security; self-reliance; presumption; intimacy; a secret. —**con'fident** *a.* trustful; having assurance; bold.—**con'fidently** *adv.*—**confidential** (kon-fi-den′shạl) *a.* enjoying, or treated with, confidence; private; secret.—**confiden'tially** *adv.* [L. *con-*; *fidere*, to trust].

configuration (kon-fig-ū-rā′shun) *n.* outward shape, form, or figure; grouping; outline; aspect [L. *con-*; *figurare*, to fashion].

confine (kon-fīn′) *v.t.* to keep within bounds; to limit; to enclose; to imprison;—*v.i.* to have a common boundary;—**con'fine** *n.* usually in *pl.* **con'fines,** boundary; limit.—**confine'ment** *n.* imprisonment; restraint; detention; child-birth [L. *confinis*, having a common frontier].

confirm (kon-fẹrm′) *v.t.* to make strong; to settle; to make valid by formal assent; to ratify; to make certain; to verify.—**confirma'tion** *n.* the act of making strong, valid, certain, etc.; proof; in certain churches, a rite administered by a bishop to *confirm* baptised persons in the vows made for them at baptism.—**confirm'ative** *a.* tending to confirm or establish.—**confirm'atory** *a.* serving to confirm.—**confirmed'** *a.* [L. *confirmare*].

confiscate (kon′fis-kāt) *v.t.* to seize by authority; to take possession of without compensation;—*a.* forfeited.—**confisca'tion** *n.* —**con'fiscator** *n.*—**confis'catory** *a.* [L. *confiscare*].

conflagration (kon-flạ-grā′shun) *n.* a destructive fire [L. *con-*; *flagrare*, to blaze].

conflict (kon-flikt′) *v.i.* to dash together; to clash; to be at odds with; to be inconsistent with; to differ.—**con'flict** *n.* a violent clashing; a trial of strength; strong disagreement.—**conflic'ting** *a.* differing; contradictory [L. *confligere*, *conflictum*, to strike against].

confluence (kon′floo̊-ens) *n.* a flowing together; the meeting of two or more rivers, streams, etc.—**con'fluent** *a.*—**con'flux** *n.* a flowing together; a large assemblage; a crowd [L. *confluere*, to flow together].

conform (con-form′) *v.t.* to make like; to bring into agreement; to adapt to rule, pattern, custom, etc.;—*v.i.* to comply; to agree;—*a.* in accord.—**conform'able** *a.* corresponding in form; similar; submissive.—**conform'ably** *adv.* —**conforma'tion** *n.* the manner in which a body is formed or shaped; structure.—**conform'ist** *n.* one who complies with the doctrine and discipline of the Established Church of England.—**conform'ity** *n.* ([L. *conformare*, to give the same shape].

confound (kon-found′) *v.t.* to mix up; to bring to confusion; to bewilder; to defeat.—**confound'ed** *a.* confused; baffled; perplexed [L. *confundere*, to pour together].

confraternity (kon-frạ-tẹr′ni-ti) *n.* a brotherhood [L. *con-*; *frater* a brother].

confront (kon-frunt′) *v.t.* to face boldly; to oppose; to bring face to face; to compare.—**confronta'tion** *n.* [Fr. *confronter*, fr. *front*, the brow].

Confucius (kon-fū′shus) *n.* Chinese philosopher K'ung fu-tszc 550-479 B.C.—**Confu'cian** *a.* pert. to him or to his philosophy.

confuse (kon-fūz′) *v.t.* to mix up; to jumble together; to muddle; to perplex; hence, to mistake one thing for another.—**confused'** *a.* mixed up; perplexed.—**confus'edly** *adv.*—**confu'sion** *n.* the state of being confused [L. *confundere*, to pour together].

confute (kon-fūt) *v.t.* to prove to be wrong; to disprove.—**confut'able** *a.* [L. *confutare*].

conga (kong′-gȧ) *n.* a ballroom dance with music based on W. Indian rhythms.

congé, congee (kōng′zhā, kon′ji) *n.* leave to depart; an act signifying departure [Fr.].

congeal (kon-gēl′) *v.t.* and *i.* to freeze, as a fluid; to stiffen; to solidify; to curdle; to coagulate;—*v.i.* to become stiff or solidified, from cold.—**congeal'able** *a.*—**congeal'ment** *n.* a thing congealed; a clot.—**congela'tion** *n.* [L. *con-*; *gelare*, to freeze].

congener (kon′je-nẹr, kon-jē′nẹr) *n.* a person or thing of the same nature or genus as another [L. *genus*, a kind].

congenial (kon-jēn′yạl) *a.* allied in disposition and tastes; kindred; agreeable; suited or adapted; sympathetic.—**congen'ially** *adv.*—**congenial'ity** *n.* [L. *con-*; *genius*, spirit].

congenital (kon-jen′i-tạl) *a.* existing at the time of birth [L. *con-*; *genitus*, born].

conger (kong′gẹr) *n.* a large species of sea-eel. Also **con'ger-eel** [Gk. *gongros*].

congeries (kon-jē′ri-ēz) *n.* a gathering of bodies into one mass; an agglomeration; a heap [L. fr. *congerere*, to bring together].

congest (kon-jest′) *v.t.* to collect into a mass; to produce a hampering accumulation; to overcrowd.—**congest'ed** *a.* overcrowded.—**conges'tion** *n.* overcrowding [L. *con-*; *gerere*, *gestum*, to bring, to carry].

conglomerate (kon-glom′e-rāt) *a.* gathered

into a mass; concentrated;—*v.t.* to bring together into a united mass;—*n.* (*Geol.*) rock composed of fragments of rock cemented together; pudding-stone.—**conglomera'tion** *n.* a mixed collection; a mixture [L. *con-*; *glomus*, a mass].

conglutinate (kon-glòó'ti-nāt) *v.t.* to glue together; to cause to adhere together;—*v.i.* to grow together [L. *con-*; *gluten*, glue].

congratulate (kon-grat'ū-lāt) *v.t.* to wish joy to; to compliment; to felicitate.—**congratulation** (kon-grat-ū-lā'shun) *n.* an expression of pleasure at the good fortune of someone; felicitation.—**congrat'ulant, congrat'ulatory** *a.* expressing good wishes or pleasure [L. *congratulari*].

congregate (kong'gre-gāt) *v.t.* to gather into a crowd or assembly;—*v.i.* to meet together, in a large body.—**congregation** (kong-gre-gā'shun) *n.* the act of assembling; an assemblage; a gathering of persons for worship in a church.—**congrega'tional** *a.*—**Congrega'tionalism** *n.* a system of church government that gives independence to each local church [L. *con-*; *grex*, a flock].

congress (kong'gres) *n.* a meeting together of persons; a formal assembly, e.g. of envoys or representatives of governments.—**Con'gress** *n.* the legislative body of the United States of America.—**congressional** (kon-gresh'un-al) *a.* [L. *congredi*, *congressus*, to meet].

congruent (kong'gròó-ent) *a.* suitable; agreeing together; corresponding.—**cong'ruence, cong'ruency** *n.* suitableness.—**congruity** (kong-gròó-i-ti) *n.* fitness; harmony; conformity.—**cong'ruous** *a.* accordant; suitable [L. *congruere*, to run together].

Coniferae (kō-nif'e-rē) *n.pl.* an order of trees, including the fir, pine, and cedar, bearing a cone-shaped fruit.—**conif'erous** *a.* belonging to the Coniferae; bearing cones [L. *conus*, a cone; *ferre*, to bear].

conjecture (kon-jek'tūr) *n.* a guess; an opinion founded on insufficient proof; surmise; inference;—*v.t.* to guess; to surmise; to infer on insufficient grounds.—**conjec'turable** *a.*—**conjec'tural** *a.* based on conjecture; guessed at.—**conjec'turally** *adv.* [L. *con-*; *jacere*, to throw].

conjoin (kon-join') *v.t.* to join together.—**conjoint'** *a.* united; concerted; associated.

conjugal (kon'jòó-gal) *a.* pert. to marriage; connubial; matrimonial.—**con'jugally** *adv.*—**conjugality** (kon-jòó-gal'i-ti) *n.* the married state [L. *conjux*, *conjugis*, a spouse].

conjugate (kon'jòó-gāt) *v.t.* (*Gram*). to recite or write all the different parts of a verb.—**conjuga'tion** *n.* the act of uniting; (*Gram.*) a class of verbs inflected in the same manner; (*Biol.*) the fusion of cells or individuals for reproduction [L. *con-*; *jugum*, a yoke].

conjunct (kon-jungkt') *a.* joined together; united; associated.—**conjunct'ly** *adv.*—**conjunc'tion** *n.* union; concurrence of events; (*Gram.*) a word used to join clauses.—**conjunc'tive** *a.* closely connected; serving to connect [L. *con-*; *jungere*, to join].

conjunctiva (kon-jungk-tī'va) *n.* the mucous membrane lining the eyelid.—**conjunctivitis** (kon-jungk-ti-vī'tis) *n.* inflammation of the conjunctiva [L. *con-*; *jungere*, to join].

conjure (kon-jòór') *v.t.* to call on by a sacred name; solemnly to implore.—**conjure** (kun'jer) *v.i.* to practise magic; to practise the arts of a conjurer; (*Fig.*) to imagine.—**conjura'tion** *n.* the act of calling upon or summoning by a sacred name.—**con'jurer, con'juror** *n.* a magician; a juggler.—**conjur'or** *n.* one bound by oath with others.—**con'jury** *n.* the tricks of a conjurer; magic; jugglery [L. *con-*; *jurare*, to swear].

connate (kon'āt) *a.* existing from birth; innate [L. *con-*; *natus*, born].

connect (ko-nekt') *v.t.* to fasten together; to associate; to relate; to attach; to join;—*v.i.* to unite; to have a close relation.—**connec'ted** *a.* joined; coherent.—**connec'tedly** *adv.*—**connec'tion, connex'ion** *n.* the act of uniting, or state of being united; that which connects; a kinsman.—**connec'tive** *a.* binding;—*n.* a connecting word.—**well connected,** of good family [L. *con-*; *nectere*, to bind]

connive (ko-nīv') *v.i.* to wink at; to pretend not to see; to co-operate secretly (with 'at').—**connivance** (ko-nī'vans) *n.* consent in wrong-doing [L. *connivere*, to shut the eyes].

connoisseur (kon-i-sėr', sūr') *n.* a competent judge, esp. in fine arts; an expert [Fr. *connaître*, to know].

connote (ko-nōt') *v.t.* to mean; to imply; to signify; to have a meaning in addition to the primary meaning.—**con'notate** *v.t.* to connote.—**connota'tion** *n.* the sum of the qualities forming the significance of a term.—**con'notative** *a.* [L. *con-*; *notare*, to mark].

connubial (ko-nū'bi-al) *a.* pert. to marriage.—**connubial'ity** *n.* [L. *con-*; *nubere*, to marry].

conoid (kō'noid) *n.* any object shaped like a cone [Gk. *konos*, a cone; *eidos*, form].

conquer (kong'kėr) *v.t.* to reduce by force, as of arms; to overcome; to subjugate or subdue; to vanquish; to surmount;—*v.i.* to be victorious; to prevail.—**con'querable** *a.*—**con'queror** *n.* one who conquers.—**conquest** (kong'kwest) *n.* the act of conquering or gaining by force; that which is conquered [L. *con-*; *quaerere*, to seek].

conquistador (kon-k(w)is'ta-dor) *n.* a conqueror, applied to the Spanish conquerors of Mexico and Peru in the 16th cent. [Sp.].

consanguineous (kon-sang-gwin'ē-us) *a.* of the same blood; related by birth.—**consanguin'ity** *n.* [L. *con-*; *sanguis*, blood].

conscience (kon'shens) *n.* the faculty by which we know right from wrong.—**conscientious** (kon-shi-en'shus) *a.* governed by dictates of conscience.—**conscien'tiously** *adv.*—**conscien'tiousness** *n.*—**conscionable** (kon'shun-a-bl) *a.* governed by conscience.—**con'science-stric'ken** *a.* seized with scruples.—**conscientious objector,** a man who refuses to serve in the armed forces, on moral or religious grounds [L. *conscire*, to be well aware].

conscious (kon'shus) *a.* having inward knowledge (of); aware (of); having the use of one's faculties.—**con'sciously** *adv.*—**con'sciousness** *n.* the state of being mentally awake to one's surroundings [L. *conscire*, to be aware].

conscribe (kon-skrīb') *v.t.* to conscript [L. *con-*; *scribere*, to write].

conscript (kon-skript') *v.t.* to enrol compulsorily for state service in the armed forces.—**con'script** *n.* one compelled to serve as a soldier, sailor, or airman, etc.—**conscrip'tion** *n.* [L. *con-*; *scribere*, to write].

consecrate (kon'se-krāt) *v.t.* to declare to be sacred; to set apart for sacred uses; to dedicate.—**consecra'tion** *n.* [L. *con-*; *sacrare*, to hallow].

consecutive (kon-sek'ū-tiv) *a.* following one another in unbroken order; successive; resulting; (*Gram.*) expressing consequence.—**consec'utively** *adv.*—**consec'utiveness** *n.*—**consecu'tion** *n.* a chain of reasoning; a succession [L. *con-*; *sequi*, to follow].

consensus (kon-sen'sus) *n.* a general agreement; unanimity [L. *con-*; *sentire*, to feel].

consent (kon-sent') *n.* oneness of mind; agreement; assent; permission;—*v.i.* to agree.—**consentaneous** (kon-sen-tā'nē-us) *a.* agreeing; suitable; consistent.—**consentient** (kon-sen'shi-ent) *a.* united in opinion; agreeing in mind.—**consen'tience** *n.* the state of being consentient [L. *con-*; *sentire*, to feel].

consequent (kon'se-kwent) *a.* following as a result;—*n.* effect.—**con'sequently** *adv.* therefore; as a result; by logical sequence.—**con'sequence** *n.* that which naturally follows; result; importance; value. -**consequential** (kon-se-kwen'shal) *a.* [L. *con-*; *sequi*, to follow].

conservatoire (kon-sẹr-vạ-twȧr′) *n.* a school for the teaching of music [Fr.].

conserve (kon-sẹrv′) *v.t.* to keep safe; to preserve; to maintain;—*n.* anything conserved; fruit, etc. prepared with sugar.—**conser′vancy** *n.* the official safe-guarding of trees, rivers, ports, etc.—**conserva′tion** *n.* preservation; safe-guarding; protection.—**conser′vative** *a.* tending to conserve; disposed to maintain existing institutions; hostile to changes;—*n.* one opposed to hasty changes or innovations.—**Conservative Party,** the traditional right-wing party in the House of Commons.—**conser′vatory** *a.* preservative;—*n.* a green-house for exotic or tender plants [L. *con-*; *servare,* to keep].

consider (kon-sid′ẹr) *v.t.* to reflect upon carefully; to examine carefully; to be of opinion; to regard as;—*v.i.* to deliberate seriously.—**consid′erable** *a.* worthy of attention; moderately large.—**consid′erably** *adv.*—**consid′erate** *a.* thoughtful for others; circumspect.—**consid′erately** *adv.*—**consid′erateness** *n.*—**considera′tion** *n.* the act of considering; deliberation; fee or recompense.—**consid′ered** *a.* carefully thought out.—**consid′ering** *prep.* in view of; taking into account [L. *considerare*].

consign (kon-sīn′) *v.t.* to give, transfer, or deliver in a formal manner; to entrust (goods) to a carrier for transport by rail, ship, etc.;—*v.i.* to agree.—**consignee** (con-sī-nē) *n.* the person to whom goods are consigned.—**consigner** (kon-sī′nẹr), **consign′or** *n.* the person who consigns goods.—**consign′ment** *n.* act of consigning; thing consigned [L. *consignare,* to seal].

consist (kon-sist′) *v.i.* to be composed of; to be in a fixed or permanent state; to subsist; to exist; to be compatible with.—**consistence, consistency** (kon-sis′tens, -ten-si) *n.* a condition of being fixed in a union; a degree of firmness or density; a combination; agreement or harmony.—**consis′tent** *a.* fixed; firm; solid as opposed to fluid; congruous; compatible [L. *con-*; *sistere,* to stand].

consistory (kon′sis-tori, kon-sis′tor-i) *a.* pert. to an ecclesiastical court with civil and criminal jurisdiction extending to clergy and laity;—*n.* any solemn assembly or council [L. *consistorium,* a council].

console (kon-sōl′) *v.t.* to comfort in distress; to solace; to encourage.—**consol′able** *a.* able to be consoled.—**consola′tion** *n.* the act of comforting; that which comforts; solace; encouragement.—**consol′atory** *a.* [L. *consolari*].

console (kon′sōl) *n.* (*Archit.*) a projection, resembling a bracket, used to give support to a moulding, frieze, etc.—**organ console,** unit comprising keyboards, stops, etc [Fr.].

consolidate (kon-sol′i-dāt) *v.t.* and *i.* to make solid; to make firm; to combine into a connected whole; to strengthen;—*a.* compact; united.—**consolida′tion** *n.* the act of making or becoming compact and firm [L. *con-*; *solidus,* solid].

Consols (kon-solz′, kon′solz) *n.pl.* British Government stock [fr. *consol*idated funds].

consonant (kon′son-ạnt) *a.* agreeing with; harmonising with; in accord;—*n.* a sound making a syllable only if with a vowel; a non-vowel.—**consonant′al** *a.* pert. to a consonant.—**con′sonantly** *adv.*—**con′sonance, con′sonancy** *n.* the quality of being consonant [L. *consonare,* to sound with].

consort [kon′sort) *n.* a companion or partner; a wife or husband.—**consort′** *v.t.* to join;—*v.i.* to keep company; to associate; to agree [L. *consors,* fr. *sors,* fate].

consortium (kon-sor′ti-um) *n.* an agreement between several countries for mutual assistance and joint action [L.]

conspectus (kon-spek′tus) *n.* a general sketch or outline of a subject; a synopsis; an epitome [L. fr. *conspicere,* to look at].

conspicuous (kon-spik′ū-us) *a.* easy to be seen; very noticeable.—**conspic′uously** *adv.*—**conspic′uousness, conspicu′ity** *n.* [L. *conspicere,* to catch sight of].

conspire (kon-spīr′) *v.i.* to unite for an evil purpose; to plot together.—**conspiracy** (kon-spir′ạ-si) *n.* a combination of persons for an evil purpose.—**conspir′ator** *n.* (*fem.* **conspir′atress**).—**conspirato′rial** *a.* [L. *conspirare,* lit. to breathe together].

constable (kun′stạ-bl, kon′stạ-bl) *n.* a high officer in State establishments of the Middle Ages; a policeman.—**con′stableship** *n.* the office of a constable.—**constabulary** (kun-stab′ū-lạr-i) *a.* pert. to constables;—*n.* a police force [L.L. *comes stabuli,* count of the stable, marshal].

constant (kon′stant) *a.* fixed; steadfast; invariable; permanent;—*n.* that which is not subject to change.—**con′stantly** *adv.*—**con′stancy** *n.* steadfastness; resolution; fidelity [L. *constare,* to stand firm].

constellation (kon-ste-lā′shun) *n.* a group of fixed stars; an assemblage of notable persons or things [L. *con-*; *stella,* a star].

consternation (kon-stẹr-nā′shun) *n.* amazement or terror that throws the mind into confusion.—**con′sternate** *v.t.* to fill with alarm or dismay [L. *con-*; *sternere,* to strew].

constipate (kon′sti-pāt) *v.t.* to clog; to make costive.—**constipa′tion** *n.* insufficient and irregular evacuation of the bowels; costiveness [L. *con-*; *stipare,* to pack].

constitute (kon′sti-tūt) *v.t.* to appoint to an office or function; to establish; to set up; to form; to compose.—**constitu′tion** *n.* the act of constituting; the natural state of body or mind; composition; the system or body of laws under which a state exists.—**constitu′tional** *a.* pert. to the constitution; due to a person's physical or mental composition;—*n.* a walk for the benefit of health.—**constitu′tionally** *adv.*—**constitu′tionalist** *n.* one who upholds constitutional government.—**constitutive** (kon′sti-tū-tiv) *a.* having powers to enact or establish.—**constit′uent** *a.* serving to compose or make up; component; —*n.* an elector; a component part; an element.—**constit′uency** *n.* a parliamentary district [L. *constituere,* to place together].

constrain (kon-strān′) *v.t.* to force or compel; to confine; to compress; to restrain; to limit. —**constraint′** *n.* compelling force; restraining force; unnaturalness or embarrassment of manner [L. *con-*; *stringere,* to press].

constrict (kon-strikt′) *v.t.* to draw together; to cramp; to cause to shrink or contract; to squeeze.—**constric′tion** *n.*—**constrict′ive** *a.* tending to constrict.—**constrict′or** *n.* that which constricts; the boa-constrictor [L. *con-*; *stringere,* to bind].

constringe (kon-strinj′) *v.t.* and *i.* same as **constrict.**—**constrin′gent** *a.*—**constrin′gency** *n.* [L. *con-*; *stringere,* to bind].

construct (kon-strukt′) *v.t.* to build; to fabricate; to devise or invent; to compile.—**construc′tion** *n.* the act of building; erection; structure; interpretation or meaning.— **construct′ive** *a.* [L. *construere,* to build].

construe (kon-strȯȯ′, kon′strȯȯ) *v.t.* to explain the structure of a sentence and the connection of the words in it; to translate; to interpret; to put a construction upon; to deduce [L. *construere,* to build].

consubstantiate (kon-sub-stan′shi-āt) *v.t.* and *i.* to unite in one substance or nature.—**consubstan′tial** *a.*—**consubstantia′tion** *n.* (*Theol.*) the doctrine of the substantial union of Christ's body and blood with the elements of the sacrament [L. *consubstantialis,* of like nature].

consuetude (kon′swē-tūd) *n.* custom; usage; habit [L. *consuetudo,* custom].

consul (kon′sul) *n.* an officer appointed by a government to represent it in a foreign country.—**con′sular** *a.*—**con′sulate** *n.* the official residence of a consul [L.].

consult (kon-sult′) *v.t.* to ask advice of; to

seek the opinion of; to look to for information; to refer to;—*v.i.* to deliberate; of a doctor, to hold himself ready for consultation.—**consult′ant** *n.* one who consults; a specialist physician who is consulted in difficult cases.—**consulta′tion** *n.* the act of consulting; a council or conference.—**consult′ative** *a.* having the privilege of consulting but not of voting; advisory [L. *consulere*].

consume (kon-sūm′) *v.t.* to waste; to destroy; to use up; to eat or drink up;—*v.i.* to waste away.—**consum′able** *a.*—**consum′er** *n.* [L. *consumere*, to use up].

consummate (kon′sum-āt) *v.t.* to complete; to finish; to perfect; (*Law*) to complete marriage by sexual intercourse.—**consumm′ate** *a.* complete; perfect [L. *consummare*].

consumpt (kon-sumt′) *n.* what is consumed. —**consump′tion** *n.* the act of consuming; the amount consumed; (*Med.*) a wasting disease of the lungs; pulmonary tuberculosis; phthisis.—**consump′tive** *a.* destructive; wasteful; wasting; affected with, or inclined to, pulmonary tuberculosis;—*n.* (*Med.*) a person suffering from consumption [L. *consumere, consumptum*, to use up].

contact (kon′takt) *n.* a touching; close union; meeting;—*v.t.* to get in touch with a person.—**contactual** (kon-tak′tū-al) *a.* implying contact. —**contact lens**, an invisible eye-glass fitting exactly over the eyeball or cornea [L. *tangere, tactum*, to touch].

contagion (kon-tā′jun) *n.* the transmission of a disease from one person to another by direct contact; that which tends to transmit disease; physical or moral pestilence.—**conta′gious** *a.* communicable by contact [L. *contagio*, fr. *tangere*, to touch].

contain (kon-tān′) *v.t.* to hold; to have room for; to comprise; to include; to restrain.—**contain′er** *n.* one who, or that which, contains; a vessel; a holder [L. *con-*; *tenere*, to hold].

contaminate (kon-tam′i-nāt) *v.t.* to soil; to taint; to corrupt; to infect.—**contam′inable** *a.* —**contamina′tion** *n.* pollution; taint; (*War*) the result of coming into contact with liquid gases or radioactive particles [L. *contamen*, contagion].

contango (kon-tang′gō) *n.* sum paid by a speculator or 'bull' who has bought shares in order to delay transfer [fr. *continue*].

contemn (kon-tem′) *v.t.* to despise; to scorn.—**contem′ner** *n.* [L. *contemnere*].

contemplate (kon′tem-plāt, kon-tem′plāt) *v.t.* to look at with attention; to meditate on; to have in view; to intend;—*v.i.* to think studiously; to reflect.—**contempla′tion** *n.* the act of contemplating.—**contem′plative** *a.* studious; thoughtful.—**contem′platively** *adv.* [L. *contemplari*].

contemporaneous (kon-tem-po-rā′ne-us) *a.* having or happening at the same time.—**contempora′neously** *adv.* at the same time.—**contemporane′ity** *n.* the state of being contemporary.—**contem′porary** *a.* living or happening at the same time; contemporaneous; present-day;—*n.* one who lives at the same time as another; a person approximately of one's own age [L. *con-*; *tempus, temporis*, time].

contempt (kon-temt′) *n.* scorn; shame; disgrace; disregard; disobedience of the rules and orders of a court of justice.—**contempt′ible** *a.* worthy of contempt; despicable.—**contempt′ibly** *adv.* despicably; meanly.—**contempt′uous** *a.* expressing contempt or disdain; scornful.—**contempt′uously** *adv.* [L. *contemnere, contemptum*, to despise].

contend (kon-tend′) *v.i.* to fight or struggle with; to strive for; to endeavour; to dispute; to assert strongly [L. *con-*; *tendere*, to stretch].

content (kon-tent′) *a.* satisfied; pleased; willing;—*v.t.* to satisfy the mind of; to please; to appease ;—*n.* satisfaction; freedom from anxiety.—**content′edly** *adv.*—**content′edness** *n.*—**content′ment** *n.* satisfaction; pleasure; ease of mind [L. *contentus*].

content (kon′tent) *n.* that which is contained; extent or area; volume.—**con′tents** *n.pl.* an index of the topics treated in a book [L. *continere, contentum*, to contain].

contention (kon-ten′shun) *n.* strife; debate; subject matter of argument or discussion.—**conten′tious** *a.* quarrelsome [L. *con-*; *tendere, tentum*, to stretch].

conterminous (kon-ter′min-us) *a.* having the same boundary; bordering; touching. Also **conter′minable, conter′minal.**

contest (kon-test′) *v.t.* to strive for; to question or resist, as a claim; to dispute; to oppose;—*v.i.* to contend or vie (with).—**contest** (kon′test) *n.* struggle; conflict; competition; dispute; strife.—**contest′able** *a.*—**contest′ant** *n.* a disputant; a competitor [L. *contestari*, to call a witness].

context (kon′tekst) *n.* that which comes immediately before or after a passage or word quoted, and therefore helps to explain it; the setting of a text.—**context′ual** *a.* pert. to the context.—**context′ually** *adv.*—**context′ure** *n.* the weaving of parts into one body; structure; style of composition in writing [L. *con-*; *texere*, to weave].

contiguity (kon-ti-gū′i-ti) *n.* the state of being contiguous; nearness.—**contiguous** (kon-tig′ū-us) *a.* touching; near; adjacent; neighbouring [L. *contiguus*, neighbouring].

continent (kon′tin-ent) *n.* one of the larger divisions of unbroken land, esp. the mainland of Europe.—**continent′al** *a.* pert. to a continent [L. *con-*; *tenere*, to hold].

continent (kon′tin-ent) *a.* exercising self-restraint in the indulgence of desires; chaste; temperate; moderate.—**con′tinence, con′tinency** *n.* [L. *con-*; *tenere*, to hold].

contingent (kon-tin′jent) *a.* liable to happen, but not sure to do so; possible; conditional;—*n.* contingency; a quota, esp. of troops.—**contin′gently** *adv.*—**contin′gence, contin′gency** *n.* [L. *contingere*, to happen].

continue (kon-tin′ū) *v.t.* to prolong or extend in duration; to go on with; to persist in; to resume;—*v.i.* to remain in a state or place; to persevere; to last.—**contin′ual** *a.* lasting; without interruption; often repeated; unceasing.—**contin′ually** *adv.*—**contin′uance** *n.* a remaining in existence; duration; uninterrupted succession.—**contin′uant** *a.*—**contin′uate** *a.* uninterrupted.—**continua′tion** *n.* the act of continuing.—**continuity** (kon-tin-ū′i-ti) *n.* the state of being continuous; uninterrupted succession; close union.—**contin′uous** *a.* united without break; uninterrupted; constant.—**contin′uously** *adv.*—**contin′uum** *n.* anything in which a continuing characteristic persists amid variations [L. *continuare*].

contort (kon-tort′) *v.t.* to twist violently; to writhe; to bend out of shape.—**contor′tion** *n.* a twisting; writhing.—**contor′tionist** *n.* an acrobat who bends his body into extraordinary and unnatural postures.—**contor′tive** *a.* [L. *con-*; *torquere, tortum*, to twist].

contour (kon′tōōr, kon-tōōr′) *n.* a bounding line; outline;—*v.t.* to draw the contour of.—**con′tour-line** *n.* a line on a map connecting points of the same elevation [L. *con-*; *tornare*, to round off].

contra- (kon′tra) Latin *prefix* meaning against, contrary, in opposition to, used to form many compounds.

contraband (kon′tra-band) *a.* prohibited by law or treaty;—*n.* goods, the exportation or importation of which is forbidden; smuggled goods.—**contraband of war**, goods not to be supplied by a neutral to a belligerent [L. *contra*; L.L. *bandum*, a ban].

contrabass (kon′tra-bās) *n.* (*Mus.*) the double-bass. Also **contrabas′so.**

contraception (kon-tra-sep′shun) *n.* the prevention by artificial means of conception; birth control.—**contracept′ive** *a.* and *n.* a drug or appliance for preventing conception [L. *contra*; and *conception*].

contract (kon-trakt') *v.t.* to draw together; to shorten; to reduce to a less volume; to incur or bring on;—*v.i.* to become smaller; to become shorter; to agree upon; to become involved in.—**contract** (kon'-trakt) *n.* a bargain; an agreement.—**contract'ed** *a.* drawn together; narrow; mean.—**contract'ible** *a.* capable of being contracted.—**contractile** (kon-trak'-tīl) *a.* tending to contract; producing contraction.—**contractil'ity** *n.* the inherent quality or force by which bodies shrink or contract.—**contrac'tion** *n.* the act of contracting; the shortening of a word by the omission of a letter or syllable.—**contract'or** *n.* one who undertakes to execute work for a fixed sum; a builder working to a contract.—**contract'ual** *a.* implying, or connected with, a contract.—**contract bridge** (*Cards*) a development of auction bridge [L. *contractus*, drawn together].

contradict (kon-tra-dikt') *v.t.* to speak against; to assert the contrary of; to deny.—**contradic'tion** *n.* denial; incompatibility; discrepancy of statements.—**contradic'tious** *a.* inclined to contradict.—**contradict'ive** *a.* containing contradiction.—**contradict'ory** *a.* implying a denial; diametrically opposed; inconsistent [L. *contradicere*, to speak against].

contradistinction (kon-tra-dis-tingk'-shun) direct contrast.—**contradistinct'ive** *a.*—**contradistin'guish** *v.t.* to note the difference between two things by contrasting their different qualities.

contralto (kon-tral'-tō) *n.* the lowest of the three varieties of female voices; a singer of that voice [It. *contra*; *alto*].

contraption (kon-trap'-shun) *n.* (*Colloq.*) a device; a gadget [perh. fr. *contrivance*].

contrapuntal (kon-tra-pun'-tal) *a.* pert. to counterpoint [See **counterpoint**].

contrary (kon'-tra-ri) *a.* opposed; opposing; different; adverse;—*n.* something the exact opposite of.—**contrariety** (kon-tra-rī'-e-ti) *n.* something contrary.—**con'trarily** *adv.*—**contrarious** (kon-trā'-ri-us) *a.* showing contrariety; repugnant; perverse.—**contrariwise** (kon'-tra-ri-wīz) *adv.* on the contrary [L. *contrarius*, fr. *contra*, against].

contrast (kon-trast') *v.t.* to bring out differences; to set in opposition for the purpose of comparing;—*v.i.* to be or stand in opposition.—**contrast** (kon'-trast) *n.* a striking difference; a comparison of objects, qualities, etc. to show their relative excellence [L. *contra*; *stare*, to stand].

contravene (kon-tra-vēn') *v.t.* to oppose; to break or infringe, as a law.—**contraven'tion** *n.* infringement of a law or treaty; transgression of a law [L. *contravenire*, to come against].

contribute (kon-trib'-ūt) *v.t.* to give or pay to a common fund; to help to a common result; to write for a newspaper, magazine, etc.;—*v.i.* to lend assistance.—**contrib'utable** *a.* liable to contribution.—**contrib'utary** *a.* paying tribute to the same sovereign lord; contributing aid; auxiliary.—**contribution** (kon-tri-bū'-shun) *n.* that which is contributed.—**contrib'utive** *a.* tending to contribute; lending aid or influence; helping.—**contrib'utor** *n.* one who contributes.—**contrib'utory** *a.* contributing to the same purpose; of a pension scheme, based on the principle of regular payment to the fund, as opposed to free [L. *contribuere*].

contrite (kon'-trīt) *a.* humbly penitent; full of remorse.—**con'tritely** *adv.*—**con'triteness** *n.*—**contrition** (kon-trish'-un) *n.* remorse [L. *con-*; *terere*, to grind].

contrive (kon-trīv') *v.t.* and *i.* to plan; to effect or bring about; to invent.—**contriv'ance** *n.* the act of planning; the thing contrived; artifice or device; mechanical invention [L. *con-*; O.Fr. *trover*, to find].

control (kon-trōl) *v.t.* to have under command; to regulate; to check; to restrain; to direct;—*n.* authority or power; government; restraint; in spiritualism, the spirit supposed to control the medium; the control system of levers, switches, etc. in aircraft and motor vehicles.—*pr.p.* **control'ling**.—*pa.p.* and *pa.t.* **controlled'**.—**control'lable** *a.*—**control'ler** *n.* one who controls.—**control'lership** *n.*—**control'ment** *n.* control.—**control experiment**, one made for the sake of comparison [L. *contra*, against; *rotulus*, a roll].

controvert (kon'-trō-vert) *v.t.* to oppose or dispute by argument; to deny or refute.—**controvert'ible** *a.*—**controvert'ibly** *adv.*—**controversy** (kon'-trō-ver-si) *n.* disputation; argument, esp. by published writings; debate.—**controversial** (kon-trō-vėr'-shal) *a.* consisting of controversy; leading to controversy; likely to provoke argument.—**controver'sially** *adv.*—**controver'sialist** *n.* [L. *contra*; *vertere*, to turn].

contumacy (kon'-tū-ma-si) *n.* contempt of orders or authority; stubborn disobedience.—**contumacious** (kon-tū-mā'-shus) *a.* rebellious.—**contuma'ciously** *adv.*—**contuma'ciousenss** *n.* [L. *contumacia*].

contumely (kon-tūm'-li) *n.* insult; affront; indignity; disdainful insolence; reproach.—**contumelious** (kon-tū-mē'-li-us) *a.* insolent; haughtily disdainful.—**contume'liously** *adv.*—**contume'liousness** *n.* [L. *contumelia*].

contuse (kon-tūz') *v.t.* to bruise or injure by beating, without breaking the skin.—**contu'sion** *n.* a bruise [L. *con-*; *tundere*, *tusum*, to beat].

conundrum (kon-un'-drum) *n.* a riddle; anything that puzzles [etym. unknown].

convalesce (kon-va-les') *v.i.* to recover from illness.—**convales'cent** *a.* recovering health;—*n.* one recovering from sickness.—**convales'cence** *n.* [L. *convalescere*].

convection (kon-vek'-shun) *n.* the act or process of transmission, esp. of heat by means of currents in liquids or gases [L. *con-*; *vehere*, *vectum*, to carry].

convene (kon-vēn') *v.t.* to call together;—*v.i.* to come together or assemble.—**conven'er** *n.* the chairman of a committee.—**conven'able** *a.* [L. *con-*; *venire*, to come].

convenient (kon-vēn'-yent) *a.* fit; suitable; affording saving of trouble; handy or easy of access.—**conven'iently** *adv.*—**conven'ience** *n.* that which is convenient; any appliance which makes for comfort; a lavatory.—**conven'iency** *n.* [L. *con-*; *venire*, to come].

convent (kon'-vent) *n.* a community, esp. of nuns, devoted to a religious life; a nunnery [L. *con-*; *venire*, to come].

conventicle (kon-ven'-ti-kl) *n.* a gathering, esp. for worship; the clandestine meeting of the Covenanters [L. *con-*; *venire*, to come].

convention (kon-ven'-shun) *n.* the act of coming together; a formal assembly of representatives; a provisional treaty; accepted usage, custom, or rule.—**conven'tional** *a.* formed by agreement or compact; sanctioned by usage; customary.—**conven'tionally** *adv.*—**conven'tionalism** *n.* that which is established by usage.—**conventional'ity** *n.* adherence to social usages and formalities [L. *con-*; *venire*, to come].

converge (kon-vėrj') *v.i.* to tend to one point; to tend to meet; to approach.—**conver'gent** *a.* tending to one point.—**conver'gence, conver'gency** *n.* a coming together [L. *con-*; *vergere*, to incline].

conversazione (kon-vėr-sat-si-ō'-nā) *n.* a meeting for conversation or discussion [It.].

converse (kon-vėrs') *v.i.* to talk with.—**convers'able** *a.* disposed to talk; affable; sociable.—**convers'ably** *adv.*—**convers'ance, convers'ancy** *n.* the state of being acquainted with.—**convers'ant** *a.* familiar or acquainted with by use or study.—**conversa'tion** *n.* talk.—**conversa'tional** *a.*—**conversa'tion(al)ist** *n.* one who excels in conversation.—**convers'ative** *a.* inclined to talk [L. *conversari*, to dwell with].

converse (kon′vers) *a.* opposite; turned round; reversed in order or relation.—*n.* the opposite; the contrary.—**con′versely** *adv.* [L. *conversus*, turned about].

convert (kon-vert′) *v.t.* to apply to another purpose; to change; to cause to adopt a religion, an opinion, etc.; in Rugby football, to complete (a try) by kicking a goal;—*v.i.* to be turned or changed.—**convert** (kon′vert) *n.* a converted person; one who has turned from sin to holiness.—**conver′sion** *n.* a change from one state to another.—**convert′er** *n.* one who, or that which, converts; (*Elect.*) a machine for changing alternating current into direct current, or altering the pressure of direct current; an iron retort used in the Bessemer method of making steel.—**convert′ible** *a.* capable of change; transformable; transmutable.—**convert′ibly** *adv.*—**con′vertite** *n.* a convert [L. *convertere*, to turn about].

convex (kon′veks, kon-veks′) *a.* curving outwards; the opposite of *concave*; bulging.—**convex′ity, convex′ness** *n.* [L. *convexus*, arched].

convey (kon-vā′) *v.t.* to carry; to transport; to transfer; to make over by deed; to impart; to communicate; to steal;—*v.i.* to steal.—**convey′able** *a.*—**convey′ance** *n.* the act of conveying; a means of transit; a vehicle; the transference of property; the legal document by which property, titles, etc., are transferred.—**convey′ancer** *n.* one skilled in the legal forms of transferring property.—**convey′ancing** *n.*—**convey′er, convey′or** *n.* [L. *con-*; *via*, a way].

convict (kon-vikt′) *v.t.* to prove guilty; to pronounce guilty.—**con′vict** *n.* a person undergoing penal servitude.—**convic′tion** *n.* the act of convicting; a verdict of guilty; the state of being convinced; a firm belief [L. *convincere, convictum*, to prove guilty].

convince (kon-vins′) *v.t.* to bring to a belief; to persuade by argument; to satisfy by proof.—**convin′cible** *a.*—**convin′cing** *a.* capable of compelling belief.—**convin′cingly** *adv.* [L. *convincere*, to prove].

convivial (kon-viv′i-al) *a.* festive; jovial; social; mirthful; merry.—**conviv′ially** *adv.*—**convivial′ity** *n.* [L. *convivium*, a feast].

convoke (kon-vōk′) *v.t.* to call together; to convene; to assemble. Also **convocate** (kon′vō-kāt).—**convoca′tion** *n.* the act of calling together; an assembly [L. *convocare*, to call together].

convolve (kon-volv′) *v.t.* and *i.* to roll or wind together; to twist; to coil.—**convolute** (kon′vō-lūt), **convolu′ted** *a.* rolled together; involved; spiral.—**convolution** (kon-vō-lū′shun) *n.* the act of rolling together; the state of being coiled [L. *convolvere*, to roll together].

Convolvulus (kon-vol′vū-lus) *n.* (*Bot.*) a genus of climbing plants, including the bindweed [L. *convolvere*, to roll round].

convoy (kon-voi′) *v.t.* to accompany or escort for protection, by land, sea, or air.—**convoy** (kon′voi) *n.* the act of convoying; escort; escorting protection [L. *con-*; *via*, a way].

convulse (kon-vuls′) *v.t.* to shake violently; to affect with violent and irregular spasms; to cause violent disturbance.—**convul′sion** *n.* any violent agitation;—*pl.* (*Med.*) violent and involuntary contractions of the muscles; spasms; fits of laughter.—**convul′sive** *a.* characterised by convulsion; spasmodic; jerky [L. *con-*; *vellere, vulsum*, to pluck].

cony, coney (kō′ni) *n.* rabbit [O.Fr. *conil*].

coo (kòò) *v.i.* to make a low, melodious sound like the note of a dove; to act in a loving manner [imit.].

cook (kòòk) *v.t.* to prepare food by boiling, roasting, baking, etc.; to concoct; to tamper with; to falsify;—*v.i.* to prepare food; to undergo cooking;—*n.* one whose occupation is to cook food.—**cook′ery** *n.* the art or process of cooking.—**cook′er** *n.* a stove for cooking [O.E. *coc*].

cookie, cooky (kòòk′i) *n.* a small plain bun; (*U.S.*) a biscuit [Dut. *kock*, cake].

cool (kòòl) *a.* slightly cold; self-possessed; dispassionate; chilly or frigid in manner; impudent;—*n.* a moderate state of cold;—*v.t.* to cause to cool; to moderate or calm;—*v.i.* to become cool; to lose one's ardour or affection.—**cool′er** *n.* a vessel in which liquors, butter, milk, etc. are cooled; (*Slang*) a prison-cell for solitary confinement.—**cool′ish** *a.* fairly cool.—**cool′ly** *adv.*—**cool′ness** *n.*—**cool′-head′ed,** *a.* calm; self-possessed.—**coolth** *n.* coolness [O.E. *col*].

coolie (kòò′li) *n.* an Asiatic labourer. Also **coo′ly** [prob. *Kuli*, name of tribe].

coomb (kòòm) *n.* See **combe**.

coon (kòòn) *n.* a raccoon; (*Slang*) a Negro [abbrev. of *raccoon*].

coop (kòòp) *n.* a basket placed over sitting fowls; a fowl-run;—*v.t.* to put in a coop (coop up); to confine [M.E. *cupe*, a basket].

cooper (kòòp′er) *n.* a maker of casks or barrels.—**coop′erage** *n.* a cooper's work or workshop [L. *cupa*, a cask].

co-operate (kō-op′e-rāt) *v.i.* to act jointly with others; to unite for a common effort.—**co-operation** (kō-op-e-rā′shun) *n.* joint action; a union of persons for the same end.—**co-operative** [kō-op′e-rā-tiv) *a.* working jointly for the same end.—**co-op′erator** *n.*—**co-operative store,** the shop of a co-operative society, where members make their purchases and share the profits [L. *co-*; *operari*, to work].

co-opt (kō-opt′) *v.t.* to choose or elect into a body or committee by the votes of its own members.—**co-op′tion, co-opta′tion** *n.* [L. *co-*; *optare*, to choose].

co-ordinate (kō-or′di-nāt) *a.* equal in degree, rank, importance, etc.;—*v.t.* to make equal in degree, etc.; to bring into order as parts of a whole; to adjust;—*n.* a person or thing of the same rank, importance, etc. as another.—**co-or′dinately** *adv.* in the same order.—**co-or′dinateness** *n.* the state of being co-ordinate.—**co-ordina′tion** *n.*—**co-or′dinative** *a.* tending to co-ordinate [L. *co-*; *ordo*, rank, order].

coot (kòòt) *n.* a small black water-fowl of the rail family [M.E. *cote*].

cop (kop) *n.* the top; a tuft [O.E. *cop*, a head].

cop (kop) *v.t.* (*Slang*) to catch or arrest;—*n.* (*Slang*) capture or arrest.—**cop′per** *n.* (*Slang*) a policeman, (*Abbrev.*) **cop**.

copal (kō′pal) *n.* a resin used in making varnishes [Mex. *copalli*, resin].

copartner (kō-pàrt′ner) *n.* a joint partner; a sharer; an associate.—**copart′nership**. *n.*

cope (kōp) *n.* a covering; a cap or hood; a long, sleeveless vestment worn by ecclesiastics during divine service;—*v.t.* to dress with a cope.—**coping** (kōp′ing) *n.* the highest course of masonry in a wall.—**cope′-stone, cop′ing-stone** *n.* the stone that crowns a wall [form of *cape*].

cope (kōp) *v.t.* to match oneself against;—*v.i.* to contend, esp. on equal terms or with success; to deal successfully (with) [L. *colaphus*, a blow with the fist].

cope (kōp) *v.t.* to exchange or barter [Dut. *koopen*, to trade].

copeck (kō′pek) *n.* a Russian copper coin of small value. Also **ko′peck** [Russ. *kopeika*].

Copernican (kō-per′ni-kan) *a.* pert. to *Copernicus* (1473-1543), the founder of modern astronomy, or to the solar system bearing his name.

copier (kop′i-er) *n.* See **copy**.

copious (kō′pi-us) *a.* abundant; plentiful; of style, not concise.—**co′piously** *adv.*—**co′piousness** *n.* [L. *copia*, plenty].

copper (kop′er) *n.* a red-coloured metal; bronze money; a bronze coin (1p or ½p); a large vessel for boiling clothes;—*a.* copper-coloured; made of copper;—*v.t.* to cover with copper.—**copp′ery** *a.* made of copper; like copper.—**copp'er-cap'tain** *n.* a sham or bogus captain.—**copp'er-head** *n.* a poisonous N. American snake.—**copp'er-plate** *n.* a plate of copper for engraving or etching; a print from such a plate; copybook writing; first-class handwriting.—**copp'ersmith** *n.* one who works in copper; one who manufactures or repairs copper utensils [L. *Cyprium aes*, bronze from the island of Cyprus].

copperas (kop'e-ras) *n.* (*Chem.*) sulphate of iron; green vitriol [Fr. *couperose*].

coppice, copse (kop'is, kops) *n.* a wood of small trees grown for periodical cutting. Also **copse'-wood** *n.* [O.Fr. *coper*, to cut].

copra (kop'rą) *n.* the dried kernel of the coco-nut palm from which coconut-oil is obtained [Malay].

coprolite (kop'rō-līt) *n.* fossilised dung of animals [Gk. *kopros*, dung; *lithos*, a stone].

copse (kops) *n.* See **coppice**.

Copt (kopt) *n.* a native Egyptian descended from the ancient Egyptians; an Egyptian Christian.—**Cop'tic** *a.*—*n.* the language.

copula (kop'ū-lą) *n.* a connecting link; a tie; a bond; (*Gram.*) the word uniting the subject and predicate.—**cop'ulate** *v.i.* to unite sexually; to have sexual intercourse. —**copula'tion** *n.*—**cop'ulative** *a.* pert. to copulation; serving to unite [L.=a bond].

copy (kop'i) *n.* an imitation of an original; a writing like another writing; an exact reproduction; a transcript; a single specimen, of a book; a piece of writing for a learner; anything to be imitated; the manuscript, etc. placed in the compositor's hands; the basic matter for a journalistic article;—*v.t.* to write, print, or engrave in imitation of an original; to imitate.—**cop'ier** *n.* one who copies; an imitator.—**cop'y-book** *n.* a book in which copies are written for learners to imitate.—**cop'yhold** *n.* (*Law*) a form of land-tenure with *copy* of the manor court-roll as title.—**cop'y-wri'ter** *n.* a writer of advertisements.—**cop'ying-pen'cil** *n.* an indelible pencil. —**cop'yright** *n.* the legal exclusive right which an author has to print, publish, and sell his own works, during a certain period of time; —*a.* protected by the law of copyright [L. *copia*, abundance].

coquet, coquette (ko-ket') *v.i.* to attempt to attract the notice, admiration, or love of; to flirt with.—*pr.p.* **coquet'ting**.—*pa.p.* and *pa.t.* **coquet'ted**.—**coquetry** (ko'ket-ri) *n.* affectation of amorous advances; trifling in love; airy graces, ogling, etc. to attract admirers. —**coquette'** *n.* a flirt.—**coquet'tish** *a.* [Fr. *coquet*, dim. of *coq*, a cock].

coracle (kor'ą-kl) *n.* a boat used by ancient Britons, consisting of a wicker frame covered with hide, oilskin, etc. [Celt.].

coral (kor'ąl) *n.* a hard limy substance growing on the bottom of tropical seas, and composed of the skeletons of zoophytes; the commonest variety is reddish-pink; a toy or ornament made of coral;—*a.* coral-coloured; made of coral.—**corallif'erous** *a.* containing coral.—**cor'alline** *a.* coral-red; consisting of coral;—*n.* a light-red colour; a pinkish sea-weed [Gk. *korallion*].

cor anglais (kor-ong'lā) *n.* (*Mus.*) instrument of the oboe family, also called 'English horn' [Fr.=English horn].

corb (korb) *n.* Same as **corf**.

corbel (kor'bel) *n.* a stone or timber projection from a wall to act as a support for something superimposed.—**cor'belling** *n.* a series of corbels [L. *corvus*, a raven].

corbie (kor'bi) *n.* (*Scot.*) the raven or crow [L. *corvus*, a crow].

cord (kord) *n.* a thick string or a thin rope of several strands; anything like a cord (e.g. spinal cord, vocal cord);—*v.t.* to bind with a cord or rope.—**cord'age** *n.* an assemblage of ropes and cords, esp. the rigging of a ship.—**cord'ed** *a.* bound with cords [Gk. *chordē*].

cordelier (kor-de-lēr') *n.* a Franciscan friar (from his girdle of knotted cord) [Fr.].

cordial (kord'yąl) *a.* of, or proceeding from, the heart; expressing warmth of heart; sincere;—*n.* anything that comforts or strengthens; a refreshing drink or medicine. —**cor'dially** *adv.*—**cordial'ity** *n.* [L. *cor, cordis*, the heart].

cordillera (kor-dil-yā'rą) *n.* a chain of mountains [Sp. *cordilla*, a little cord].

cordite (kord'īt) *n.* a smokeless explosive [fr. *cord*].

cordon (kor'don) *n.* a line of military posts enclosing an area to prevent passage; hence, a circle of persons round any place or thing to prevent access [Fr.].

cordon (kor'don) *n.* a tasselled cord or ribbon worn as a badge of honour.—**cordon bleu**, formerly, a blue ribbon worn in France by the Knights of the Holy Ghost; hence one outstanding in merit [Fr.].

corduroy (kor'dū-roi) *n.* a thick cotton fabric, corded or ribbed on the surface.—**cord'uroys** *n. pl.* trousers made of this fabric [Fr. *corde du roi*, king's cord].

cordwain, cordovan (kord'wān, kor'dō-vąn) *n.* Spanish leather; goatskin tanned and dressed.—**cord'wainer** *n.* a worker in leather [fr. *Cordoba*, in Spain].

core (kōr) *n.* the heart or inner part of, esp. of fruit;—*v.t.* to take out the core [L. *cor*, the heart].

co-respondent (kō-re-spon'dent) *n.* in a divorce suit the man or woman charged along with the respondent as guilty of adultery.

corf (korf) *n.* a submerged basket-cage for keeping lobsters, etc. alive till needed [Dut. *korf*, basket].

corgi, corgy (kor'gi) *n.* a Welsh breed of dog [W.].

coriaceous (ko-ri-ā'shus) *a.* resembling, or consisting of, leather [L. *corium*, leather].

Corinthian (kō-rin'thi-ąn) *a.* pert. to *Corinth*, a city in Greece; (*Archit.*) denoting an order of Greek architecture, of a very ornate style; licentious;—*n.* a citizen of Corinth; a man about town.

cork (kork) *n.* the outer bark of the cork-tree; a stopper for a bottle, cask, etc. cut out of cork;—*a.* made of cork;—*v.t.* to stop up with a cork; to stop up generally; to give wine, beer, etc. a corky taste.—**cork'er** *n.* (*Slang*) anything first-class.—**cork'screw** *n.* a tool for drawing corks from bottles;—*a.* shaped like a corkscrew; with a spiral twist.— **cork'y** *a.* consisting of, or resembling, cork; tasting like cork [L. *cortex*, bark].

corm (korm) *n.* an underground stem resembling a bulb, but more solid [Gk. *kormos*, the lopped trunk of a tree].

cormorant (kor'mō-rant) *n.* a voracious sea-bird, allied to the gannet and pelican; a gluttonous person [Fr. *cormoran*].

corn (korn) *n.* a single seed of oats, wheat, rye, barley, maize, etc.; an inclusive term for grain of all kinds; the plants that produce corn; (*U.S.*) maize; (*Scot.*) oats;—*v.t.* to preserve meat by salting.—**corn'cake** *n.* a cake made from maize.—**corn'chand'ler** *n.* a dealer in corn.—**corn'cob** *n.* the head or seed-pod in which are encased the grains of the maize-plant.—**corn'crake** *n.* the landrail, a migratory bird which nests in cornfields.— **corn'flour** *n.* a foodstuff consisting of the finely ground starch granules of Indian corn (maize).—**corn-flow'er** *n.* an annual weed growing in cornfields and bearing blue flowers.—**corn'loft** *n.* a granary.—**corn'popp'y** *n.* the common red poppy.—**corn'rent,** *n.* rent paid in corn instead of money.—**corn'y** *a.* (*Slang*) out of date [O.E. *corn*].

corn (korn) *n.* a horny growth of the skin, usually on toes and feet.—**corneous** (kor'nē-us) *a.* horn-like; horny. —**cor'ny** *a.* pert. to a corn [L. *cornu*, a horn].

cornea (kor'nē-ą) *n.* the transparent membrane which forms part of the outer coat of the eye-ball [L. *corneus*, horny].

cornel (kor'nel) *n.* the cornelian cherry or dogwood. Also **corne'lian-tree** [L. *cornus*, cornel].

cornelian (kor-nēl'yạn) *n.* a precious stone of a light-red or flesh colour, a variety of chalcedony. Also **carnel'ian** [L. *cornu*, horn].

corner (kor'nẹr) *n.* the point where two lines meet; the part of a room where two sides meet; an angle; a nook; an embarrassing position; (*Football, Hockey*) a free kick (from a corner of the field);—*v.t.* to drive into a corner; to put into a position of difficulty, leaving no escape; to establish a monopoly.—**corn'er-boy** *n.* one who hangs about street-corners; a street loafer.—**corn'er-stone** *n.* the stone which lies at the corner of two walls, and unites them; hence, a principal stone.—**corn'er-wise** *adv.* diagonally; with the corner in front. -**to corner the market,** to control the price of a stock or commodity by means of a monopoly [L. *cornu*, a horn].

cornet (kor'net) *n.* a kind of trumpet with valves; formerly the lowest rank of commissioned cavalry officer in the British army, now second-lieutenant; a small cone-shaped holder for ice-cream.—**cor'netcy** *n.* rank of a cornet.—**cor'netist** *n.* a cornet-player [L. *cornu*, a horn].

cornice (kor'nis) *n.* (*Archit.*) the upper part of an entablature; a moulded projection which crowns the capital or column; an ornamental moulding round the top of the walls of a room [Fr. *corniche*, a ledge].

cornicle (kor'ni-kl) *n.* a little horn or horn-like process.—**cornic'ulate** *a.* horned; having horn-like processes [L. *cornu*, a horn].

corniferous (kor-nif'e-rus) *a.* (*Geol.*) containing hornstone.—**corni'gerous** *a.* having horns [L. *cornu*, a horn].

Cornish (kor'nish) *a.* pert. to *Cornwall*, a county in S.W. England;—*n.* the ancient language of Cornwall.

cornucopia (kor-nū-kō'pi-ạ) *n.* the horn of plenty, an emblem of abundance, the horn being filled with fruit and flowers [L. *cornu*, a horn; *copia*, plenty].

corolla (ko-rol'ạ) *n.* the inner covering of a flower within the calyx, and composed of petals [L. dim. of *corona*, crown].

corollary (kor-ol'ạ-ri) *n.* an inference from a preceding statement; a deduction; a consequence [L. *corolla*, a garland].

corona (ko-rō'nạ) *n.* the flat projecting part of a cornice; a top or crown; a halo around a heavenly body; a make of cigar (Trade Name).—**coronal** (kor'o-nạl) *a.* pert. to a corona;—*n.* a crown; a wreath.—**cor'onary** *a.* resembling a crown or circlet; (*Anat.*) encircling, as of a vessel or nerve.—**coronary thrombosis** (*Med.*) a disease of the heart.—**cor'onate** *v.t.* to crown.—**corona'tion** *n.* the crowning of a sovereign.—**cor'onet** *n.* a small crown worn by the nobility [L. *corona*, a crown].

coronach (kor'o-naH) *n.* a dirge; a lament [Gael.].

coroner (kor'o-nẹr) *n.* a legal officer appointed to hold an inquest on cases of death. Also (*Dial.*) **crown'er** [L. *corona*, a crown].

corporal (kor'po-rạl) *n.* non-commissioned officer of a company or troop, next below a sergeant; he wears two stripes on his sleeve [L. *caput*, the head].

corporal (kor'po-rạl) *a.* belonging or relating to the body; bodily; material, not spiritual;—*n.* a linen cloth with which the elements of the Eucharist are covered; a communion cloth.—**cor'porally** *adv.*—**corporality** (kor-pō-ral'i-ti) *n.* the state of having a body; bodily substance.—**corporate** (kor'po-rāt) *a.* united legally in a body, and acting as an individual.—**corporately** *adv.*—**cor'porateness** *n.*—**corporation** (kor-pō-rā'shun) *n.* a united body; a legal, municipal, mercantile, or professional association; (*Colloq.*) a protuberant stomach.—**cor'porative** *a.*—**corporeal** (kor-pō'rē-ạl) *a.* pert. to the body; having a body; bodily; physical.—**corpo'really** *adv.*—**corporal punishment,** punishment inflicted on the body [L. *corpus*, body].

corps (kōr) *n.* a division of an army forming a unit; any organised body of persons.—*pl.* **corps** (kōrz) [Fr. fr. L. *corpus*, a body].

corpse (korps) *n.* a dead body, esp. of a human being [L. *corpus*, the body].

corpulence (kor'pū-lens) *n.* excessive fatness; fleshiness; stoutness.—**cor'pulency** *n.* corpulence.—**cor'pulent** *a.* [L. *corpus*, the body].

corpus (kor'pus) *n.* a body; the main substance of anything [L.=a body].

corpuscle (kor'pus-l, kor-pus'l) *n.* a little body; a minute particle; (*Anat.*) an organic cell, either moving freely, as in the blood, or intimately connected with others, as bone-corpuscles.—**corpuscular** (kor-pus'kū-lạr) *a.* [L. *corpusculum*, dim. of *corpus*, a body].

corral (ko-râl') *n.* an enclosure for cattle, or for defence;—*v.t.* to drive into a corral [Sp. fr. *corro*, a circle].

correct (ko-rekt') *a.* right; free from faults; accurate;—*v.t.* to make right; to bring to the standard of truth; to punish; to counteract.—**correct'ly** *adv.*—**correc'tion** *n.* amendment; a change to remedy a fault; punishment.—**correc'tional** *a.*—**correct'ive** *a.* having the power to correct;—*n.* that which corrects or counteracts.—**correct'ness** *n.*— **correct'or** *n.* [L. *corrigere*, to make right].

correlate (kor'e-lāt) *v.i.* to be mutually related, as father and son;—*v.t.* to place in reciprocal relation;—*n.* a correlative; either of two things or words necessarily implying the other.—**correla'tion** *n.* reciprocal relation.—**correl'ative** *a.* reciprocally related;—*n.* one who, or that which, is correspondingly related to another person or thing.—**correl'atively** *adv.*—**correlativ'ity** *n.*

correspond (kor-e-spond') *v.i.* to exchange letters; to answer or agree with in some respect; to be congruous.—**correspond'ence** *n.* exchange of letters; the letters themselves; mutual adaptation of one thing to another; suitability.—**correspond'ent** *a.* suitable; conformable; congruous;—*n.* one with whom intercourse is maintained by exchange of letters.

corridor (kor'i-dor) *n.* a gallery or passage in a building; a side-passage in a railway-train [L. *currere*, to run].

corrie (kor'ī) *n.* (*Scot.*) a deep hollow in a mountain-side [Gael. *coire*, a cauldron].

corrigendum (kor-i-jen'dum) *n.* something to be corrected, esp. a misprint in a book;—*pl.* **corrigen'da** [L.=to be corrected].

corrigent (kor'i-jent) *a.* correcting;—*n.* (*Med.*) a corrective.—**corrigible** *a.* capable of being corrected [L. *corrigere*. to correct].

corrival (ko-rī'vạl) *n.* a fellow rival.

corroborate (ko-rob'ō-rāt) *v.t.* to add strength to; to confirm; to support a statement, etc.—**corrob'orant** *a.* giving strength.—**corrobora'tion** *n*,—**corrob'orative** *a.* confirming; strengthening [L. *con-*; *robur, roboris*, strength].

corrode (ko-rōd') *v.t.* to eat away by degrees (by chemical action, disease, etc.); to rust.—**corrod'ent** *a.* corrosive;—*n.* a substance which eats away.—**corrod'ible, corros'ible** *a.* capable of being corroded.—**corro'sion** *n.*—**corros'ive** *a.* having the power of corroding; fretting or vexing;—*n.* any corrosive substance [L. *con-*; *rodere*, to gnaw].

corrugate (kor'ū-gāt) *v.t.* to form into wrinkles or folds.—**corruga'tion** *n.* the act of wrinkling; a wrinkle.—**corrugated iron,** sheet-iron, corrugated to increase its rigidity [L. *con-*; *ruga*, a wrinkle].

corrupt (ko-rupt') *v.t.* and *i.* to make rotten; to rot; to defile; to contaminate; to make evil; to bribe;—*a.* putrid; depraved; tainted with vice or sin; influenced by bribery; spoilt, by mistakes, or altered for the worse (of words, literary passages, etc.).—**corrup'ter** *n.* —**corrupt'ible** *a.* capable of being corrupted.—**corrup'tion** *n.* the act of corrupting or the state of being corrupt.—**corrup'tive** *a.* having the quality of corrupting.—**corrupt'ly** *adv.*—**corrupt'ness** *n.* [L. *corrumpere, corruptum*].

corsage (kor′-sāj) *n.* the bodice of a lady's dress [L. *corpus*, the body].

corsair (kor′-sār) *n.* a Moorish sea-marauder; a pirate; a pirate's vessel [Fr. *corsaire*].

corset (kor′-set) *n.* a woman's undergarment, fitting close to the body to give support to the figure; a pair of stays [L. *corpus*, the body].

corselet, corselette (kors′-let) *n.* a corset.—**cors'let, corse'let** *n.* a piece of armour to cover the trunk of the body; a cuirass, orig. made of leather [Fr. *corselet*, double dim. of O.Fr. *cors*, the body].

cortège (kor-tezh′) *n.* a train of attendants or procession; a funeral procession [Fr.].

Cortes (kor′-tes) *n.pl.* the legislative assembly of Spain and of Portugal [Sp. *corte*, a court].

cortex (kor′-teks) *n.* bark; sheath or skin of a plant; (*Anat.*) the outer covering of an organ, esp. the outer layer of grey matter of the brain;—*pl.* **cortices** (kor′-ti-sēz).—**cor'tical** *a.*—**cor'ticate, cor'ticated** *a.* covered with bark or a bark-like covering [L. *cortex*, the bark of a tree].

cortisone (kor′-ti-zōn) *n.* (*Med.*) a substance produced in the adrenal glands and used in the cure of rheumatism [fr. *cortex*].

corundum (ko-run′-dum) *n.* a native, crystalline form of alumina, or aluminium oxide. It is the hardest mineral except the diamond [Hind. *kurand*].

coruscate (kor′-us-kāt) *v.i.* to flash; to sparkle, to glitter; to gleam.—**corusca'tion** *n.* [L. *coruscare*, to glitter, vibrate].

corvée (kor′-vā) *n.* in former times, an obligation on serfs to render services to overlords; forced labour; a hard task [Fr.].

corvette (kor-vet′) *n.* orig. a fast full-rigged warship (small frigate) of not more than 20 guns; a small warship fitted with anti-submarine devices [Fr.].

corvine (kor′-vīn] *a.* pert. to the crow [L. *corvus*, a crow].

Corybant (kor′-i-bant) *n.* (*Myth.*) a priest of the goddess Cybele, whose worship was conducted with wild orgies and frenzied dances.—**coryban'tic** *a.* frenzied and delirious.

coryza (kō-rī′-zạ) *n.* (*Med.*) a cold in the head [Gk.].

cos (kos) *n.* a very crisp variety of lettuce with long leaves, orig. grown in *Cos*, an island in the Aegean sea.

cosecant (kō-sē′-kant) *n.* (*Trig.*) the secant of the complement of an angle.—(*Abbrev.*) **co'sec** [L. *co-*; *secare*, to cut].

cosh (kosh) *n.* (*Slang*) a bludgeon;—*v.t.* to fell with bludgeon [etym. unknown].

cosher (kosh′-ẹr) *v.t.* to feed with dainties; to coddle; to pamper [etym. unknown].

co-signatory (kō-sig′-nạ-tor-i) *a.* signing jointly;—*n.* a joint signer of a document.

cosily (kō′-zi-li) *adv.* See **cosy**.

cosine (kō′-sin) *n.* (*Trig.*) the sine of the complement of an angle.—(*Abbrev.*) **cos**.

cosmetic (koz-met′-ik) *a.* making for beauty, esp. of the skin;—*n.* any substance helping to improve or enhance the appearance [Gk. *kosmeein*, to arrange, adorn].

cosmic (koz′-mik) *a.* See **cosmos**.

cosmo- (koz′-mō) a combining form from Gk. *kosmos*, the universe.

cosmogony (koz-mog′-ō-ni) *n.* a theory of the creation of the universe and its inhabitants.—**cosmog'onist** *n.* [Gk. *kosmos*, the universe; *gignesthai*, to be born].

cosmography (koz-mog′-rạ-fi) *n.* the science of the constitution of the universe; a description of the world.—**cosmog'rapher** *n.* [Gk. *kosmos*, the universe; *graphein*, to write].

cosmology (kos-mol′-o-ji) *n.* the science of the laws which control the universe.—**cosmolog'ical** *a.*—**cosmol'ogist** *n.* [Gk. *kosmos*, the universe; *logos*, discourse].

cosmopolitan (koz-mo-pol′-i-tạn) *a.* relating to all parts of the world; free from national prejudice;—*n.* a cosmopolitan person; a citizen of the world.—also **cosmop'olite** *n.* [Gk. *kosmos*, the universe; *politēs*, a citizen].

cosmos (koz′-mos) *n.* the ordered universe; order (as opposed to 'chaos').—**cos'mic, cos'mical** *a.* pert. to the universe, or to the earth as a part of the universe; orderly.—**cos'mically** *adv.*—**cosmic rays**, radiations of great penetrating power, coming to the earth from outer space [Gk. *kosmos*, order].

Cossack (kos′-ak) *n.* one of a tribe, skilled in horsemanship, inhabiting the southern steppes of Russia [Turk. *quzzaq*, an adventurer].

cosset (kos′-et) *n.* a pet lamb; a pet;—*v.t.* to pamper [etym. uncertain].

cost (kost) *v.t.* to entail the payment, loss, or sacrifice of; to occasion; to bear; to suffer;—*n.* price; the amount paid, or to be paid, for anything; expenditure of time, labour, etc.; suffering undergone for any end.—**costs** *n.pl.* (*Law*) the expenses of a lawsuit.—**cost'ing** *n.* the system of calculating cost of production.—**cost'liness** *n.* great cost or expense; expensiveness.—**cost'ly** *a.* very dear; expensive.—**cost price**, the wholesale, as opposed to the retail, price [L. *constare*, fr. *stare*, to stand].

costal (kos′-tạl) *a.* pert. to the ribs or to the side of the body.—**cos'tate, cos'tated** *a.* ribbed [L. *costa*, a rib].

costard (kos′-tạrd) *n.* a large kind of ribbed apple; (*Arch.*) the head [origin uncertain].

costermonger (kos′-tẹr-mung-gẹr) *n.* originally a **cos'tardmonger**, i.e. a seller of apples; then an itinerant seller of fruit, vegetables, fish, etc.—(*Abbrev.*) **cos'ter**.

costive (kos′-tiv) *a.* having sluggish motion of the bowels; constipated.—**cos'tiveness** *n.* [L. *con-*; *stipare*, to press together].

costume (kos′-tūm, kos-tūm′) *n.* dress peculiar or appropriate, as to a country, period, office, or character; a woman's dress or gown.—**costumier** (kos-tūm′-i-ẹr) *n.* one who makes or deals in costumes [It. *costume*, custom, fashion].

cosy (kō′-zi) *a.* snug; comfortable;—*n.* a covering to keep a teapot hot (*tea-cosy*).—**co'sily** *adv.* [etym. uncertain].

cot (kot) *n.* a cottage [O.E. *cot*].

cot (kot) *n.* a small bed or crib, esp. for a child; a finger-stall; (*Naut.*) a swinging bed on board ship [Hind. *khat*].

co-tangent (kō-tan′-jent) *n.* (*Trig.*) the tangent of the complement of an angle.—(*Abbrev.*) **cot**.

cote (kōt) *n.* a shelter or enclosure for animals or birds; a sheep-fold [O.E. *cote*].

co-temporary (kō-tem′-po-rạ-ri) *n.* a contemporary. Also *a.*

coterie (kō′-tẹ-rē) *n.* a set or circle of persons usually with common interests [Fr.].

cotillon, cotillion (kō-tē′-yōng, kō-til′-yun) *n.* a lively dance, of French origin, for eight persons [Fr. *cotillon*, a petticoat].

Cotoneaster (kot-ō-ni-as′-tẹr) *n.* a genus of shrubs of the order Rosaceae bearing red berries [L. *cotonea*, a quince].

cottage (kot′-āj) *n.* a small dwelling house, esp. in the country.—**cott'ager** *n.* one who inhabits a cottage [O.E. *cot*].

cottar, cotter (kot′-ạr, -ẹr) *n.* in Scotland, a farm-worker who occupies rent-free a cottage [O.E. *cot*].

cotter (kot′-ẹr) *n.* a pin or wedge used for tightening or fastening, esp. parts of a machine; a split-pin [etym. unknown].

cotton (kot′-n) *n.* a soft, downy substance, resembling fine wool, got from the pods of the cotton-plant; cloth made of cotton; thread made of this fabric;—*a.* made of cotton;—*v.i.* to become friendly; to take to.

—**cott'on-gin** *n.* a machine for separating the seeds from cotton.—**cott'on-grass** *n.* a perennial sedge-like plant bearing cottony tufts.—**cott'on-tail** *n.* a wild American rabbit.—**cott'on-waste** *n.* waste or refuse from the manufacture of cotton, used instead of rags by engineers, etc. for wiping machinery.—**cott'on wool** *n.* hairs of the cotton plant, cleaned and prepared in masses, forming a fleecy wool, valuable in surgery, etc. [Ar. *qutun*].

cotyledon (kot-i-lē'don) *n.* (*Bot.*) one of the seed-lobes or primary leaves of the embryo plant.—**cotyle'donous** *a.*—**cot'yloid** *a.* cup-shaped [Gk. *kotulēdōn*, a cup-shaped cavity].

couch (kouch) *v.t.* to cause to lie down, esp. on a bed; to phrase; to express; to lower a lance, spear, etc. for action;—*v.i.* to lie down; to crouch;—*n.* a sofa; a piece of furniture for reclining on by day.—**couchant** (kouch'ant) *a.* lying down [Fr. *coucher*, fr. L. *collocare*, to place together].

couch-grass (kouch'gràs) *n.* (*Bot.*) the popular name for *Triticum repens*, a troublesome creeping weed [*quitch*-grass].

Couéism (kòò'ā-izm) *n.* a system of curing illness by auto-suggestion [fr. Emile *Coué*, a French chemist, 1857-1926].

cougar (kòò'gar) *n.* the puma or American panther [Native (S. Amer.)].

cough (kof) *n.* a noisy, violent, explosive effort to expel irritating matter from the lungs;—*v.i.* to make such an effort;—*v.t.* to expel from the lungs by a cough [M.E. *coughen*].

could (kood) *pa.t.* of the verb **can**.

couloir (kòòl'war) *n.* a dredging machine; a deep gorge in a mountain side, often filled with snow [Fr.].

coulomb (kòò-lom') *n.* the practical unit of quantity in measuring electricity; the quantity transferred by a current of one ampere in one second [Charles de *Coulomb*, a French physicist].

coulter (kōl'tẹr, kòòl'tẹr) *n.* the sharp blade of iron placed at the front end of a plough to act as a cutter [O.E. *culter*].

council (koun'sil) *n.* an assembly summoned for consultation or advice; a municipal body; the deliberation carried on in such an assembly.—**coun'cillor** *n.* a member of a council [L. *concilium*].

counsel (koun'sel) *n.* advice; opinion; deliberation together; one who gives advice, esp. legal; a barrister; an advocate;—*v.t.* to advise; admonish; recommend.—*pr.p.* **coun'selling.**—*pa.p.* and *pa.t.* **coun'selled.**—**coun'sellor** *n.* one who counsels; an adviser.—**coun'sellorship** *n.* the office of a counsellor [L. *consulere*, to consult].

count (kount) *n.* (*fem.* **coun'tess**) a title of foreign nobility equal to that of an earl in Britain [L. *comes, comitis*, companion].

count (kount) *v.t.* to number; to reckon; to sum up; to consider or esteem; to include; to recite the numerals in regular succession; —*v.i.* to depend or rely (with 'on');—*n.* the act of reckoning; the number ascertained by counting; (*Law*) a charge in an indictment.—**count'able** *a.*—**count'less** *a.* not capable of being counted; innumerable.—**count'er** *n.* one who counts; a token or disc of metal, wood, etc. used in reckoning; a table in a bank on which money is counted out.—**count'er-jump'er** *n.* a shop assistant.—**count'ing-house** *n.* the room in business houses set apart for the keeping of accounts [L. *computare*].

countenance (koun'te-nans) *n.* the face; the features; aspect; look; appearance; favour; encouragement; support;—*v.t.* to favour; to support; to encourage; to approve.—**to keep one's countenance,** to preserve one's composure [L. *continentia*, manner of holding oneself].

counter (koun'tẹr) *a.* contrary; opposite; opposed; adverse; reciprocal;—*adv.* in opposition; the opposite way;—*n.* that which is opposite; a return blow or parry;—*v.t.* and *i.* to parry; to oppose; to hinder; to do any act which opposes another; to make a counter-move.—**coun'ter-attack'** *n.* an attack launched to recapture a position recently lost to the enemy.—**coun'ter-attrac'tion** *n.* rival attraction.—**coun'ter-claim** *n.* (*Law*) a claim set up by the defendant in a suit to counter that of the plaintiff.—**coun'ter-clock-wise** *adv.* revolving in a direction opposite to the movement of the hands of a clock.—**coun'ter-espi'onage** *n.* spying directed against the enemy's system of espionage.—**coun'ter-irr'itant** *n.* a substance, the application of which, by inducing superficial irritation, relieves a more deep-seated irritation.—**coun'ter-shaft** *n.* a branch from the main shaft of a machine.—**coun'ter-ten'or** *n.* a high tenor; a man's voice singing alto.—**counter word,** a popular word which, through excessive use, has lost most of its meaning and can be fitted into a great variety of contexts [L. *contra*, against].

counteract (koun-tẹr-akt') *v.t.* to act in opposition to; to hinder; to defeat.

counterbalance (koun'tẹr-bal-ans) *v.t.* to act against with equal power or effect; to neutralise.—**counterbal'ance** *n.* equal opposing weight, power, or agency; a weight balancing or neutralising another.

countercharge (koun'tẹr-chàrj) *n.* a charge brought in opposition to another.

countercheck (koun-tẹr-chek') *v.t.* to check by an opposing check; to reprimand.

counterfeit (koun'tẹr-fēt) *v.t.* to copy without authority; to imitate with intent to deceive; to forge; to feign;—*a.* sham; forged; false;—*n.* an imitation; a forgery; an impostor.—**coun'terfeiter** *n.*

counterfoil (koun'tẹr-foil) *n.* that part of a cheque, receipt, etc. retained by the issuer for record purposes.

countermand (koun-tẹr-mand') *v.t.* to cancel an order;—*n.* a contrary order [L. *contra*; *mandare*, to command].

countermarch (koun'tẹr-march) *v.i.* to march back;—*n.* a marching back.

countermine (koun'tẹr-mīn) *n.* (*Mil.*) an underground gallery constructed to meet and surprise the mining operations of the enemy; any scheme to frustrate the designs of an opponent.

counterpane (koun'tẹr-pān) *n.* a coverlet for a bed; a stitched quilt [L. *culcita puncta*, a stitched quilt].

counterpart (koun'tẹr-pàrt) *n.* a duplicate; something complementary or correlative of another.

counterplot (koun-tẹr-plot') *v.t.* to oppose one plot by another.—**coun'terplot** *n.*

counterpoint (koun'tẹr-point) *n.* (*Mus.*) the art of combining melodies; the addition of a subsidiary melody to another so as to form a perfect melody.

counterpoise (koun'tẹr-poiz) *v.t.* to act against with equal weight or power;—*n.* a weight sufficient to balance another.

countersign (koun-tẹr-sīn') *v.t.* to sign a document already signed by another; to ratify; to attest authenticity.—**coun'tersign** *n.* a password, a military watchword.

country (kun'tri) *n.* a region; a district; a tract of land; the territory of a nation; the nation itself; land of birth, residence, etc.; rural districts as opposed to town;—*a.* rural; rustic; pert. to territory distant from a city.—**countrified** (kun'tri-fīd) *a.* rural in manner or appearance.—**coun'trify** *v.t.* to make rural.—**coun'try-dance** *n.* a dance in which the couples face each other, or line up in two long rows, facing each other.—**coun'tryman,** *n.* one who lives in the country; a rustic; one born in the same country; a compatriot.—**coun'try-seat** *n.* a country mansion.—**coun'try-side** *n.* any rural district.—**to go to the country** (*Politics*) to decide to have a general election [L.L. *contrata*].

county (koun′ti) *n.* originally the lands of a count or earl; a shire; a division of a country or state for administrative purposes; the inhabitants of a county.—**county council**, the elected representatives of the ratepayers of a county with vested powers of control and administration.—**county town**, the chief town or capital of a county [Fr. *comté*, fr. *comte*, a count].

coup (kòò) *n.* lit. a stroke or blow; then, a successful stroke or move [Fr.].

coup (koup) *v.t.* (*Scot.*) to overturn; to empty out;—*n.* a rubbish-heap; a dump.

coup d'état (kòò-dā-ta′) *n.* lit. a stroke of state; a sudden and revolutionary change of government achieved by force [Fr.].

coupé (kòò-pā′) *n.* a two-seater motor-car with enclosed body [Fr. *couper*, to cut].

couple (kup′l) *n.* two things of the same kind taken together; two; a pair; a brace; husband and wife; a leash for two hounds; that which joins two things together;—*v.t.* to join together; to marry;—*v.i.* to copulate. —**coup′let** *n.* a pair of lines of verse, esp. if rhyming and of equal length.—**coup′ling** *n.* a connection; that which couples, esp. the chain joining one railway-carriage, railway-wagon, etc. to another [L. *copula*, a bond].

coupon (kòò′pon) *n.* an interest certificate attached to a bond; a dividend warrant; a negotiable ticket or voucher; a pass or ticket; during war-time, a ticket entitling the holder to a specified amount of some rationed article; (*Betting*) a printed form on which to mark the forecasts of the results of football matches, dog-races, etc. [Fr. *couper*, to cut off].

courage (kur′āj) *n.* bravery; fearlessness; daring; boldness.—**courageous** (ku-rā′jus) *a.* full of courage.—**coura′geously** *adv.*—**coura′geousness** *n.*—**Dutch courage**, courage that is not genuine, but consequent on drinking [O.Fr. *corage*, fr. L. *cor*, the heart].

courier (kòò′ri-ẹr) *n.* a runner or messenger; a state messenger; a tourist guide who accompanies travellers [L. *currere*, to run].

course (kōrs) *n.* the act of passing from one point to another; progress or movement, both in space and in time; the ground traversed; way or direction; line of conduct; the track or ground on which a race is run; career; a series (of lessons, lectures, etc.); each of the successive divisions of a meal; a continuous line of masonry at one level in a building;—*v.t.* to hunt; to pursue; to chase;—*v.i.* to run swiftly; to gallop.—**cours′er** *n.* one who courses or hunts; a swift horse.—**cours′ing** *n.* hunting hares with greyhounds [L. *cursus*, running].

court (kōrt) *n.* an uncovered area enclosed by buildings, or by buildings and railings; a yard; the residence of a sovereign; the retinue of a sovereign; the homage or attention paid to a sovereign; a legal tribunal; the judge or judges, as distinguished from the counsel; the hall where justice is administered; (*Sport*) a space, usually rectangular, laid out for certain sports, as tennis, etc.—**courteous** (kurt′yus) *a.* polite; well-bred; of courtlike manners.—**court′eously** *adv.*—**court′eousness** *n.*—**courtier** (kōrt′yẹr) one who frequents the courts of princes; one with the manners of a frequenter of courts.—**court′ly** *a.* elegant; flattering; with the manners of a courtier.—**court′liness** *n.*—**court′-card** *n.* corrupt. of **coat′-card**; a playing-card with a coated figure, i.e. the king, queen, or knave.—**court′-mar′tial** *n.* a court of military or naval officers for the trial of persons in the army or navy;—*pl.* **courts′-mar′tial**.—**court′-plas′ter** *n.* sticking-plaster made of silk (orig. used as ornamental patches on the face by ladies of the court). [L. *cohors*, an enclosure].

court (kōrt) *v.t.* to seek the favour of; to try to gain the affections of; to seek in marriage; —*v.i.* to woo; to play the lover.—**court′ship** *n.* [L. *cohors*, an enclosure].

courtesan (kōr′te-zan) *n.* a court mistress; a prostitute [It. *cortigiana*].

courtesy (kur′tẹ-si) *n.* politeness of manners; urbanity [O.Fr. *cortoisie*].

cousin (kuz′n) *n.* formerly any kinsman; now, the son or daughter of an uncle or aunt.—**cous′in-ger′man** *n.* a first cousin or full cousin [Fr. fr. L. *consobrinus*].

cove (kōv) *n.* a small inlet or creek; a small bay;—*v.t.* to arch over [O.E. *cofa*, a chamber].

cove (kōv) *n.* (*Slang*) a person; a man; a fellow [Gipsy word].

coven (kuv′en) *n.* a meeting of witches [L. *convenire*, to come together].

covenant (kuv′e-nạnt) *n.* a mutual and solemn agreement; a contract; a compact; a written agreement;—*v.t.* to agree to by a covenant;—*v.i.* to enter into an agreement. —**cov′enanter** *n.* one who makes a covenant or agreement.—**Covenan′ters** *n.pl.* (*Scot.*) the name given to the body of strict Presbyterians, who held out against the breach of the Solemn League and Covenant, in particular to those persecuted in 1662 and later [L. *con-*; *venire*, to come].

Coventry (kov′en-tri) *n.* (*Geog.*) a city and market town of Warwickshire, England.—**to send to Coventry**, to boycott socially.

cover (kuv′ẹr) *v.t.* to be over the whole top of; to overspread; to enclose; to include; to protect; to put hat on; to point a revolver, gun, etc. at; to wager an equal sum of money; to copulate with (of a stallion with mare);—*n.* anything that covers; a lid; a wrapper; an envelope; a binding; a cloak; disguise; concealment; shelter; defence.—**cov′ering** *n.* anything that covers.—**cov′erlet** *n.* a bed-cover.—**cov′ert** *a.* covered over; concealed; sheltered; secret; veiled;—*n.* a thicket; a place sheltering game.—**cov′ertly** *adv.* secretly; in private.—**coverture** (kuv′ẹr-tūre) *n.* covering; shelter; defence; (*Law*) the condition of a married woman, legally considered as being under the protection of her husband.—**cov′ert-coat′ing** *n.* a twilled fabric, usually waterproof, for making covert-coats or light-weight overcoats.—**cov′er-point** *n.* (*Cricket*) the player who stands to the right of 'point' in order to cover or support him; the position in the field [Fr. *couvrir*, to cover].

covet (kuv′et) *v.t.* to long to possess, esp. what belongs to another; to desire unreasonably or unlawfully;—*v.i.* to have strong desire.—**cov′etable** *a.* that may be coveted.—**cov′etous** *a.* very desirous; excessively eager; avaricious for gain.—**cov′etously** *adv.*—**cov′etousness** *n.* [L. *cupiditas*, desire].

covey (kuv′i) *n.* a brood of partridges or quail; (*Fig.*) a company; a set [Fr. *couveé*, fr. *couver*, to brood].

cow (kou) *n.* the female ox; the female elephant, whale, etc.—**cow′ish** *a.* like a cow. —**cow′-boy** *n.* a boy who herds cows; (*U.S.*) on the western plains, a herdsman employed on a ranch to look after cattle.—**cow′-catch′er** *n.* (*U.S.*) a frame in front of a locomotive for removing obstructions, esp. strayed cattle, from the rails.—**cow′-grass** *n.* a species of clover.—**cow′-heel** *n.* an ox-foot boiled to a gelatinous consistency.—**cow′herd** *n.* one who herds cows.—**cow′hide** *n.* the hide of a cow; leather made from the hide of a cow. —**cow′-lick** *n.* a tuft of hair on the forehead, naturally turned back.—**cow′-pars′ley**, **cow′-pars′nip** *n.* umbelliferous plants bearing white or pink flowers and used as fodder.—**cow′-punch′er** *n.* a cowboy [O.E. *cu*].

cow (kou) *v.t.* to frighten into submission; to overawe [O.N. *kuga*, to oppress].

coward (kou′ạrd) *n.* one given to fear; one who lacks courage.—**cow′ard**, **cow′ardly** *a.* lacking in courage; afraid; mean.—**cowardice** (kou′ạr-dis) *n.* want of courage; fear.—

cow'ardliness *n.*—**cow'ardly** *adv.* in a cowardly manner; basely; meanly [Fr. *couard,* fr. L. *cauda,* a tail].
cower (kou'ẹr) *v.i.* to crouch down through fear, shame, cold [etym. uncertain].
cowl (koul) *n.* a monk's hooded cloak; the hood itself; a hooded top for a chimney; (*Motoring*) the bonnet.—**cowled** (kould) *a.* wearing a cowl; hooded.—**cow'ling** *n.* (*Aviation*) the metal cover which encloses the engine of an aero-motor [L. *cucullus,* the hood of a cloak].
cowry, cowrie [kou'ri) *n.* a small shell, used as an ornament, or as native money in parts of India and Africa [Hind. *kauri*].
cowslip (kou'slip) *n.* a common British meadow flower [O.E. *cu-slyppe,* cow dung].
coxcomb (koks'kōm) *n.* orig. a strip of red cloth notched like the comb of a cock, which jesters wore on their caps; one given to showing off; a fool; a fop.
coxswain (kok'sn), **cox** (koks) *n.* the steersman of a boat; (*Naval*) a petty officer in charge of a boat.—**to cox** *v.t.* and *i.* to act as coxswain [fr. *cock*-boat and *swain*].
coy (koi) *a.* shy; bashful; modest; pretending to be shy.—**coy'ly** *adv.*—**coy'ness** *n.* [Fr. *coi,* fr. L. *quietus*].
coyote (koi-ōt', -ō'te) *n.* the American prairie wolf [Mex.].
coz (kuz) *n.* short for 'cousin,' formerly used to address any near relative.
cozen (kuz'n) *v.t.* to flatter in order to cheat; to defraud.—**coz'enage** *n.* the art of cozening [Fr. *cousiner,* to play the part of *cousin,* in order to sponge on people].
crab (krab) *n.* an eatable crustacean with ten legs, of which the front pair are armed with strong pincers, noted for its sidelong and backward walk.—**crab'-louse** *n.* a kind of body-louse.—**crabsidle** (krab'sī-dl) *v.i.* to move sideways like a crab.—**to catch a crab,** to miss a stroke in rowing, and fall backwards [O.E. *crabba*].
crab (krab) *n.* a wild apple of sour taste; the tree; one of sour temper;—*a.* sour. Also **crab'-app'le** [etym. uncertain].
crabbed (krab'ed) *a.* harsh; rough; austere; perverse; bad-tempered; of writing, hard to read.—**crabb'edly** *adv.*—**crabb'edness** *n.* the state of being crabbed [etym. uncertain].
crack (krak) *v.t.* to break with a sharp noise, either wholly or partially; to split or break; to produce a sudden sharp sound; to snap; —*v.i.* to break partially; to burst open in chinks; to give forth a sudden, sharp sound; —*n.* a partial break; fissure; a sharp noise; a flaw; a break in the voice; a mental flaw;—*a.* superior; special; smart; expert.—**crack'er** *n.* one who cracks, that which cracks; a boaster; a small zig-zag firework; a paper cylinder which explodes when pulled asunder; a thin crisp biscuit.—**crack'-brained** *a.* crazy.—**cracks'man** *n.* a burglar.—**to crack a crib** (*Slang*) to burgle [O.E. *cracian*].
crackle (krak'l) *v.i.* to produce slight but repeated cracking sounds;—*n.* a noise composed of frequent, slight cracking sounds.—**crack'ling** *n.* a succession of small sharp reports; rind of roasted pork.—**crack'ly** *a.* crisp [O.E. *cracian,* to crack].
cracknel (krak'nel) *n.* a dry, brittle kind of biscuit [O.E. *cracian,* to crack].
cradle (krā'dl) *n.* a cot for infants that can be rocked; infancy; the place of origin of anyone or anything; a framework used as a support; —*v.t.* to place or rock in a cradle; to tend or train in infancy; to support on a cradle (as a vessel) [O.E. *cradol*].
craft (krâft) *n.* skill or dexterity; a skilled trade; cunning, artifice, or guile; a vessel; vessels collectively.—**craft'y** *a.* (*Arch.*) skilful or dexterous; cunning; artful.—**craft'ily** *adv.* —**crafts'man** *n.* one engaged in a craft or trade.—**crafts'manship** *n.* [O.E. *craeft*].
crag (krag) *n.* a steep, rugged rock or peak. —**cragged** (krag'ed) *a.*—**crag'gy** *a.* full of crags; rough; rugged.—**crag'gedness** *n.*—**crag'giness** *n.*—**crags'man** *n.* one who is expert in scaling cliffs or crags [W. *craig,* a rock].
crake (krāk) *n.* the corn-crake; its cry;—*v.i.* to cry like a corn-crake [imit.].
cram (kram) *v.t.* and *i.* to stuff; to pack tightly; to prepare a person hastily for an examination;—*n.* cramming; a crush or crowd of people; (*Slang*) a lie.—**cram'-full** *a.* packed to capacity [O.E. *crammian*].
cramp (kramp) *n.* a painful contraction of muscles of the body; that which restrains; a clamp for holding masonry, timbers, etc. together;—*v.t.* to affect with cramp; to restrict or hamper; to hold with a cramp;—*a.* narrow; cramped; restricted.—**cramp'-i'ron** *n.* a piece of iron bent over at both ends and used to hold masonry or timber together [O.Fr. *crampe*].
cran (kran) *n.* in Scotland, a measure of a catch of herrings, holding roughly 750 fish; hence, a basket, esp. for fish or fruit [Gael. *crann*].
cranberry (kran'ber-i) *n.* a red, sour, berry [prob. orig. *crane-berry*].
crane (krān) *n.* a tall wading-bird with long legs, neck, and bill; a machine for lifting and lowering heavy weights;—*v.t.* to stretch out the neck to look at something.—**crane'-fly** *n.* a genus of long-legged insects, commonly called 'daddy-long-legs.'—**crane's'-bill** *n.* the geranium [O.E. *cran*].
cranium (krā'ni-um) *n.* the skull.—*pl.* **cra'nia.** —**cra'nial** *a.* pert. to the skull.—**craniol'ogy** *n.* the study of skulls.—**craniolog'ical** *a.*—**craniol'ogist** *n.* a student of craniology [Gk. *kranion,* the skull].
crank (krangk) *n.* a bend; a handle attached to a shaft for turning it; the bent portion of an axis, used to change horizontal or vertical into rotatory motion, etc.; a fanciful twist or whimsy in speech; a faddist; an eccentric or crotchety person;—*v.t.* to provide with a crank; to shape like a crank; to operate by a crank;—*v.i.* to turn the crank, as in starting a motor-car engine (usually with 'up').—**crank'le** *v.i.* to bend or twist;—*n.* a bend or twist.—**crank'y** *a.* shaky or in bad condition, of machinery; (*Fig.*) irritable or crotchety; bad-tempered.—**crank'iness** *n.* [O.E. *cranc*].
cranny (kran'i) *n.* an open crack; a small opening; a crevice; a chink.—**crannied** (kran'id) *a.* [Fr. *cran,* a notch].
crape (krāp) *n.* a semi-transparent silk fabric of light weight, unglossed and finely crimped, often dyed black and used as a mourning material [L. *crispus,* curled].
crapulence (krap'ū-lens) *n.* sickness resulting from intoxication.—**crap'ulent, crap'ulous** *a.* [L. *crapula,* intoxication].
crash (krash) *n.* a violent fall or impact accompanied by loud noise; a burst of mixed, loud sound, e.g. of thunder, breaking crockery, etc.; bankruptcy; a sudden collapse or downfall;—*v.i.* to make a crash; to fall, come with, strike with, a crash; to collapse;—*v.t.* to break into pieces.—**crash'-hel'met** *n.* a padded helmet worn by aviators and racing motorists [imit. of the sound].
crash (krash) *n.* a coarse linen cloth, for towels, etc. [etym. uncertain].
crasis (krā'sis) *n.* (*Gram.*) union of two vowels into one long vowel or diphthong [Gk.].
crass (kras) *a.* thick; gross; dense; obtuse; stupid.—**crass'itude** *n.*—**crass'ly** *adv.*—**crass'ness** *n.* [L. *crassus,* coarse].
cratch (krach) *n.* a hay-manger or crib [Fr. *crèche,* a manger].
crate (krāt) *n.* a wicker-work hamper, or open-work packing-case [L. *cratis,* a hurdle].
crater (krā'tẹr) *n.* the cup-shaped mouth of a volcano; the cavity resulting from the

explosion of a large shell, bomb, mine, etc. [Gk. *kratēr*, a mixing-bowl].
cravat (kra-vat′) *n.* a man's neck-cloth; a necktie. [Fr. *cravate*, Croatian (scarf)].
crave (krāv) *v.t.* and *i.* to have a very strong desire for; to long for; to ask with earnestness, submission, or humility; to beg.—**cra′ver** *n.*—**cra′ving** *n.* a longing; an inordinate desire [O.E. *crafian*, to crave].
craven (krāv′n) *a.* cowardly; abject; spiritless; chicken-hearted;—*n.* a spiritless fellow; a coward [O.Fr. *cravanter*, to overthrow].
craw (kraw) *n.* crop or first stomach of fowls; stomach of any animal [M.E. *crawe*].
crawl (krawl) *v.i.* to move along the ground on the belly or on the hands and knees; to move very slowly; to move abjectly; to swim with the crawl-stroke;—*n.* a crawling motion [O.N. *krafla*, to claw].
crayfish, **crawfish** (krā′, kraw′fish) *n.* a fresh-water crustacean, resembling the lobster but smaller [Fr. *écrevisse*].
crayon (krā′on) *n.* a stick, or pencil-shaped piece, of coloured chalk; a drawing made with crayons;—*v.t.* to draw with crayons [Fr. *crayon*, a pencil; *craie*, chalk].
craze (krāz) *n.* a strong, habitual desire or passion; a general mania; an individual mania; a very common fashion;—*v.t.* to make crazy.—**crazed** *a.* weak in mind.—**craz′iness** *n.*—**craz′y** *a.* insane; extremely foolish; madly eager (for); rickety; falling to pieces; full of cracks.—**craz′ily** *adv.* [Fr. *écraser*, to break].
creak (krēk) *n.* a harsh, grating sound;—*v.i.* to make a sharp, harsh, grating sound.—**creak′y** *a.* [imit. sound].
cream (krēm) *n.* the fatty substance that rises to the surface of milk; the best part of anything; anything resembling cream;—*v.t.* to take off the cream; to add cream to;—*v.i.* to become covered with cream; to froth.—**cream′y** *a.* full of cream; resembling cream.—**cream′ery** *n.* a butter and cheese factory; a centre to which milk is sent for distribution.—**cream′iness** *n.*—**cream′-laid** *a.* of laid paper, smooth, glossy, and cream-coloured.—**cream of tartar**, acid potassium tartrate, a component of baking-powder [Gk. *chrisma*, unguent].
crease (krēs) *n.* a line or mark made by folding anything; (*Cricket*) the area within which the batsman stands and the bowler bowls;—*v.t.* to make a crease or mark on;—*v.i.* to become creased [etym. uncertain].
create (krē-āt′) *v.t.* to bring into existence out of nothing; to originate; to make; (*Slang*) to cause a commotion.—**creation** (krē-ā′shun) *n.* the act of creating, esp. of bringing the world into being; the world; anything created; any original production of the human mind.—**crea′tive** *a.* capable of creation; original.—**crea′tor** *n.* (*fem.* **crea′trix crea′tress**) one who creates; a maker.—**Creator** *n.* the Supreme Being.—**creature** (krē′tūr) *n.* anything created; any living being [L. *creare*].
crèche (kresh) *n.* a public nursery for young children [Fr.=a cradle].
credence (krē′dens) *n.* trust; belief; (*Eccles.*) a small table by the altar, holding the bread and wine before consecration.—**credentials** (krē-den′shals) *n.pl.* testimonials showing that a person is entitled to belief or credit.—**credible** (kred′i-bl) *a.* worthy of belief, trustworthy; likely.—**cred′ibly** *adv.*—**credibil′ity** *n.* [L. *credere*, to believe].
credit (kred′it) *n.* belief; trust; trustworthiness; honour or reputation; anything that procures esteem or honour; the amount at a person's disposal in a bank; in commerce, the general system of borrowing and lending based on good faith and confidence; (*U.S. Radio*) advertisement broadcast in the interval of a commercial programme.—*v.t.* to believe; to put trust in.—**cred′itable** *a.* reliable; meriting credit.—**cred′itably** *adv.*—**cred′itableness** *n.*—**cred′itor** *n.* one to whom money is due [L. *credere*, to believe].
Credo (krē′dō) *n.* the Creed; a musical setting of the Creed [L. *credo*, I believe].
credulous (kred′ū-lus) *a.* too prone to believe; easily imposed on.—**cred′ulously** *adv.*—**cred′ulousness** *n.*—**credulity** (kre-dū′li-ti) *n.* gullibility [L. *credulus*, believing].
creed (krēd) *n.* a system of religious faith; any statement of principles [L. *credere*, to believe].
creek (krēk) *n.* a small inlet; a branch or small tributary of a river [O.N. *kriki*].
creel (krēl) *n.* an osier basket; an angler's basket [Celt.].
creep (krēp) *v.i.* to move along with the body close to the ground, like a worm or reptile; to spread, like certain plants, by clinging to supports.—**creep′er** *n.* esp. a creeping plant; a genus of small birds.—**creep′y** *a.* causing a creeping sensation on the skin [O.E. *creopan*].
creese (krēs) *n.* a Malay dagger, or short sword. Also **kris** [Malay].
cremate (kre-māt′) *v.t.* to burn; to consume by burning, esp. the dead; to reduce to ashes.—**cremation** (kre-mā′shun) *n.* the act of cremating the dead.—**crema′tor** *n.*—**cremato′rium** *n.* an establishment for the cremation of bodies.—**cre′matory** *a.* [L. *cremare*, to burn].
Cremona (kre-mō′na) *n.* a fine kind of violin [made at *Cremona*, in Italy].
crenate (krē′nāt) *a.* with the edge notched; indented.—**crena′ted** *a.* crenate.—**crena′tion**, **cren′ature** *n.* [L. *crena*, a notch].
crenelle, crenel (kre-nel′) *n.* one of the indentations or embrasures in a battlement; a battlement.—**crenellated** (kren′el-lā-ted) *a.* [L. *crena*, notch].
Creole (krē′ōl) *n.* a native of Spanish America or the W. Indies, of European parentage; (*U.S.*) a white person descended from the French or Spanish settlers of Louisiana; a native of mixed parentage [Fr. fr. Sp. *criollo*].
creosote (krē′ō-sōt) *n.* an oily liquid obtained from the distillation of coal tar, extensively used to preserve wood from decay [Gk. *kreas*, flesh; *sōtēr*, preserver].
crêpe (krep) *n.* a fine, coloured silk crape material, also called **crêpe de chine** (shēn).—**crêpe rubber**, a kind of rough-surfaced rubber used for the soles of shoes, etc. [Fr.].
crepitate (krep′i-tāt) *v.i.* to burst with a sharp, abrupt sound, rapidly repeated.—**crep′itant** *a.* crackling.—**crepita′tion** *n.* (*Med.*) the grating sound heard when two ends of a broken bone rub together; a similar sound heard on auscultation of the lungs in pneumonia, etc. [L. *crepitare*, to crackle].
crept (krept) *pa.p.* and *pa.t.* of **creep**.
crepuscular (kre-pus′kū-lar) *a.* pert. to twilight; dim [L. *crepusculum*, twilight].
crescendo (kre-shen′dō) *n.* (*Mus.*) a gradual increase in loudness;—*adv.* with increase in loudness. (*Abbrev.*) **cresc.** [It.].
crescent (kres′ent) *a.* like the young moon in shape; increasing;—*n.* the moon in her first quarter; the Mohammedan faith; a semicircular street of buildings [L. *crescere*, to grow].
cress (kres) *n.* the name of various salad vegetables [O.E. *cerse*, *cresse*].
cresset (kres′et) *n.* an iron basket or cage-like container, filled with inflammable burning material [O.Fr. *craisse*, grease].
crest (krest) *n.* the comb or tuft on a bird's head; the plume or top, of a helmet; the top of a mountain, ridge, etc.; the highest part of a wave; a badge above the shield of a coat of arms;—*v.t.* to reach the top of.—**crest′fallen** *a.* cast down by defeat or failure; dispirited; dejected [L. *crista*].
cretaceous (krē-tā′shus) *a.* composed of chalk; chalky [L. *creta*, chalk].
cretinism (kret′in-izm) *n.* a disease common in Alpine villages, characterised by

abnormal and arrested physical and mental development, caused by congenital deficient thyroid secretion; a form of idiocy.—**cret'in** *n.* one suffering from cretinism.—**cret'inous** *a.* [Swiss *crestin*, a Christian].

cretonne (kret-on') *n.* a strong, unglazed printed cotton cloth [*Creton*, in France].

crevasse (kre-vas') *n.* a deep open chasm in a glacier; a fissure; a cleft [Fr.].

crevice (krev'is) *n.* a cleft; a rent; a narrow fissure; a crack [Fr. *crever*, to break, burst].

crew (kròò) *n.* a ship's or boat's company [earlier *crue*, *accrue*, a reinforcement].

crewel (kròò'el) *n.* a kind of fine worsted yarn, used in embroidery and fancy work. —**crew'ellery** *n.* [etym. uncertain].

crib (krib) *n.* a barred rack for fodder; a manger; a stall for cattle; a child's cot with barred sides; a hut or small dwelling; a key or translation (used by schoolboys or students); a plagiarism; (*Slang*) a situation; a job;—*v.t.* to shut or confine in a narrow place; at examinations, to copy unfairly [O.E. *cribb*, an ox-stall].

cribbage (krib'āj) *n.* (*Cards*) a game played by two or four players.

crick (krik) *n.* a spasm or cramp, esp. of the neck or back [etym. uncertain].

cricket (krik'et) *n.* a small, brown, chirping insect, belonging to the family of grass hoppers, locusts, etc. [Fr. *criquer*, to creak].

cricket (krik'et) *n.* an open-air game played with bats, ball, and wickets by teams of eleven a side [etym. uncertain].

crier (krī'er) *n.* one who cries; a public official who makes proclamations [fr. *cry*].

crime (krīm) *n.* a violation of the law (usually of a serious nature); an offence.—**criminal** (krim-i-nal) *a.* guilty of, or pert. to, crime; wicked;—*n.* one guilty of a crime.—**criminal'ity** *n.* guiltiness.—**crim'inally** *adv.*—**crim'inate** *v.t.* to charge with a crime.—**crimina'tion** *n.*—**crim'inative, crim'inatory** *a.* accusing.—**criminol'ogist** *n.*—**criminol'ogy** *n.* that branch of sociology which deals with the study of the physical and mental characteristics of criminals and the investigation of the causes of crime [L. *crimen*, a charge].

crimp (krimp) *v.t.* to form into tiny parallel pleats; to wrinkle; to decoy or press into military or naval service;—*n.* an agent who procures men for service as soldiers or sailors;—*a.* brittle; crisp; easily crumbled [O.E. *crimpan*, to curl].

crimson (krim'zn) *a.* of a rich deep red colour;—*n.* the colour itself [O.Sp. *cremesin*, fr. Arab. *qirmiz*, the cochineal insect].

cringe (krinj) *v.t.* to shrink; to cower; to behave obsequiously [M.E. *crengen*].

crinkle (kring'kl) *v.t.* to wrinkle; to make a series of bends, windings, or twists in a line or surface [O.E. *crincan*].

crinoline (krin'ō-līn, -lin, -lēn) *n.* a structure, used by women in the middle of the 19th cent. for expanding their skirts; a hoop skirt [L. *crinis*, hair; *linum*, flax].

cripple (krip'l) *n.* a person without the use of a limb or limbs; a lame person; -*a.* lame; —*v.t.* to lame [O.E. *crypel*].

crisis (krī'sis) *n.* the decisive moment; the turning-point, esp. in an illness; emergency; a time of difficulty or danger; *pl.* **crises** (krī'sēz) [Gk. *krisis*, decision].

crisp (krisp) *a.* brittle; breaking with a short snap; of hair, curly or wavy;—*v.t.* to make crisp;—*n.* a thin slice of potato fried hard.—**crisp'ly** *adv.*—**crisp'ness** *n.* [L. *crispus*, curled].

criss-cross (kris'kros) *a.* crossing; arranged in crossing lines;—*adv.* crossing one another in different directions; contrarily;—*v.t.* and *i.* to intersect; to mark or be marked with cross lines;—*n.* a cross-shaped mark.—**criss'-cross-row** *n.* (*Arch.*) the alphabet [corrupt. of *Christ's-cross*].

criterion (krī-tē'ri-on) *n.* a standard of judging; a rule or test by which opinions may be judged.—*pl.* **crite'ria** [Gk.].

critic (krit'ik) *n.* one who expresses a reasoned judgment on any matter, esp. on art or literature; one whose profession it is to write reviews; one given to expressing adverse judgment or finding fault.—**crit'ical** *a.* pert. to criticism or critics; captious or fault-finding; pert. to a crisis; important; crucial; decisive.—**crit'ically** *adv.*—**crit'icism** *n.* the art of making a reasoned judgment, a critical appreciation.—**crit'icise** *v.t.* and *i.* to pass judgment; to censure.—**criticis'able** *a.*—**critique** (kri-tēk') *n.* criticism; review [Gk. *krinein*, to judge].

croak (krōk) *v.t.* and *i.* to make a low, hoarse noise in the throat; (*Slang*) to die;—*n.* the hoarse, harsh sound made by a frog or a crow.—**croak'y** *a.* hoarse [imit].

crochet (krō'shā) *n.* a kind of netting or lace consisting of loops;—*v.t.* and *i.* to work in crochet [Fr. *crochet*, a small hook].

crock (krok) *n.* an earthenware pot or pitcher; a piece of broken earthenware; a broken-down person, or one crippled by ill-health.—**crock'ery** *n.* vessels and dishes of all kinds, generally made of earthenware [Gael. *crog*. a pitcher].

crocodile (krok'ō-dīl) *n.* a large, amphibious reptile of the lizard kind; school-children walking in a long double file.—**crocodil'ian** *a.* —**crocodile tears,** hypocritical tears; sham grief [Gk. *krokodilos*, a lizard].

crocus (krō'kus) *n.* a bulbous plant of the iris kind, with white, yellow, or purple flowers; saffron [Gk. *krokos*, crocus, saffron].

croft (kroft) *n.* a small area of cultivable land attached to a dwelling; a small farm.—**croft'er** *n.* one who works a croft [O.E.].

cromlech (krom'lek) *n.* a circle of upright stones, sometimes enclosing dolmens, each two or three being topped by a large, flat stone [W. *crom*, curved: *llech*, a stone].

crone (krōn) *n.* a wizened old woman [etym. uncertain].

crony (krō'ni) *n.* an intimate friend; a chum [earlier *chrony*, a contemporary, fr. Gk. *chromos*, time].

crook (krook) *n.* a hooked staff; any hook, bend, or sharp turn; a shepherd's or a bishop's staff; a thief; a swindler;—*v.t.* to bend into a crook; to curve; to pervert;—*v.i.* to be bent or curved.—**crook'ed** *a.* bent; twisted; (*Fig.*) not straightforward.—**crook'edly** *adv.*—**crook'edness** *n.*—**by hook or by crook,** by some means or other; by fair means or foul [O.N. *krokr*].

croon (kròòn) *v.t.* and *i.* to sing or hum softly; to sing in a monotonous undertone.—**croon'er** *n.*—**croon'ing** *n.* [imit.].

crop (krop) *n.* a year's produce of cultivation of any plant or plants, in a farm, field, country, etc.; a harvest; the best ore; a pouch in a bird's gullet; the craw; a hunting-whip; a closely-cut head of hair;—*v.t.* to reap the produce of a field.—*pr.p.* **crop'ping**.—*pa.p.* and *pa.t.* **cropped**.—**crop'-eared** *a.* with clipped ears; with hair short to show the ears.—**crop'per** *n.* one who, or that which, crops; (*Colloq.*) a heavy fall.—**to crop up,** to appear unexpectedly [O.E. *cropp*, the head of a plant, ear of corn, etc.].

croquet (krō'kā) *n.* an outdoor game played with balls, mallets and hoops [etym. uncertain].

croquette (krō-ket') *n.* (*Cookery*) a ball of finely minced meat, fish, etc. seasoned and fried; a rissole [Fr. *croquer*, to mince].

crosier, crozier (krō'zhyer) *n.* the pastoral staff of a bishop [O.Fr. *crosse*, a crook].

cross (kros) *n.* a stake used for crucifixion, consisting of two pieces of timber placed upon one another in the shape † or ×; in particular, **the Cross,** the one on which Christ was crucified; a model or picture of this; anything in the shape of a cross; (*Fig.*) (the Cross being the symbol of suffering) affliction; tribulation; a misfortune;—*v.t.* to mark with a cross; to make the sign of the cross.—**cross'let** *n.* a small cross.—**cross'-stitch** *n.* in embroidery, a stitch, in the form of a cross.—**cross'wise** *adv.* in the form of a cross.—**Celtic cross,** a cross having a circle at the point of intersection of the two arms.—**fiery cross** (*Scot.*) a cross passed from place to place as an alarm signal or call to arms.—**George Cross** (*World War* 2) a decoration awarded for deeds of conspicuous bravery by British civilians.—**Greek cross** (+) a vertical cross with beams of equal length.—**Latin Cross** (†) a vertical cross with a horizontal crossbeam two-thirds up.—**Maltese cross** a kind of ornamental Greek cross, formed by the points of four arrow-heads meeting at the centre.—**Saltire cross,** in heraldry, a cross in the shape of an ×, or St. Andrew's cross.—**Southern cross,** a constellation in the Antarctic.—**Victoria Cross,** a naval, military, and air force decoration, the highest award for conspicuous bravery in the presence of an enemy.—**St. Andrew's Cross,** a cross in the shape of an ×; the cross of Scotland (white diagonal arms on a blue ground).—**Cross of St. George,** a Greek cross, with arms of equal length, adopted as the Cross of England (red arms on a white ground).—**Cross of St. Patrick,** a saltire cross adopted as the cross of Ireland (red diagonal arms on a white ground) [L. *crux*, a cross].

cross (kros) *a.* transverse; intersecting; interchanged; contrary, adverse; out of temper; dishonest;—*n.* an intermixture of breeds or stocks, esp. in cattle-breeding;—*v.t.* to place so as to intersect; to pass from one side to the other of; to pass over; to thwart; to oppose; to clash; to modify the breed of animals, plants, etc. by intermixture;—*v.i.* to intersect; to move or pass from one side to the other;—*adv.* across.—**cross'ing** *n.* the act of passing across; an intersection, esp. of roads, rails, etc.; a place of crossing; a part of the street that pedestrians are expected to use for passing from one side to the other; the intermixture of breeds.—**cross'ly** *adv.* in an ill-tempered manner.—**cross'ness** *n.* the state of being cross; ill-humour; peevishness.—**cross'-ac'tion** *n.* (*Law*) an action brought by a defendant against a plaintiff on points pert. to the same case.—**cross'-bones** *n.pl.* two thigh bones crossed and surmounted by a skull, used as symbol of death, a sign of deadly danger, or the flag of a pirate ship.—**cross'-breed** *n.* a breed produced from parents of different breeds; a hybrid.—**cross'-breed'ing** *n.*—**cross'-bred** *a.*—**cross'-coun'try** *a.* across fields, avoiding roads.—**cross'-cut** *v.t.* to cut across;—*n.* a short road between two points or places.—**cross'-examina'tion** *n.* the examination of a witness by counsel on the other side; **cross'-eyed** *a.* squinting.—**cross'-fertilisa'tion** *n.* the fertilisation of one plant by the pollen of another.—**cross'-fire** *n.* (*Mil.*) intersecting lines of fire produced by having guns, rifles, machine-guns, etc. pointed inwards towards the target from two or more positions.—**cross'-grained** *a.* of wood, having the grain running across, or irregularly; of a person, ill-natured.—**cross'-hatch'ing** *n.* in drawing, etching, etc. the art of shading by parallel intersecting lines.—**cross-jack** (kroj'-ek) *n.* (*Naut.*) the sail carried on the lower yard on the mizzen-mast.—**cross'-legged** *a.* having the legs crossed.—**cross'-pur'pose** *n.* a contradictory purpose.—**cross'-ques'tion** *v.t.* to question a person, e.g. a witness, in order to verify statements already made.—**cross'-ref'erence** *n.* in a book, e.g. a dictionary, the directing of the reader to another part for related information.—**cross'-roads,** *n.* the point of intersection of two roads, esp. if one is a main road.—**cross'-row** *n.* the alphabet [See **criss'-cross**].—**cross'-sec'tion** *n.* a transversal cutting of a concrete object in order to expose the inner layers; the surface so exposed.—**a cross-section of the population,** a group of people sufficiently large to be representative of all classes.—**cross'-trees** *n.pl.* (*Naut.*) pieces of timber or iron fixed across the top of a lower mast in order to support the mast above.—**cross-word (puzz'le)** *n.* a form of puzzle in which a chequered square has to be filled in with words to which clues are given [L. *crux*, a cross].

crossbill (kros'-bil) *n.* a bird of the Finch family, whose mandibles cross.

crossbow (kros'-bō) *n.* a medieval weapon in the form of a strongly made bow attached to a grooved, musket-like stock and propelling an arrow or bolt; an arbalest.

crosse (kros) *n.* the long-handled racquet used in the game of lacrosse [Fr.].

crotch (kroch) *n.* a fork or bifurcation; the angle where the legs branch off from the human body.—**crotched** *a.* [etym. uncertain].

crotchet (kroch'-et) *n.* a small hook; a bracket in printing; a whim or fancy; (*Mus.*) a note equal in duration to half a minim.—**crotch'ety** *a.* full of whims, or fads [Fr. *crochet*, dim. of *croc*. a hook].

croton (krō'-ton) *n.* a genus of strong-scented tropical shrubs.—**cro'ton-oil** *n.* a strongly purgative oil obtained from a species of croton [Gk. *kroton*, a tick, which the croton-seeds resemble].

crouch (krouch) *v.i.* to huddle down close to the ground; to stoop low; to cringe or fawn servilely [prob. Fr. *croc*, a hook, crook].

croup (krōōp) *n.* the rump or hind-quarters of a horse; hence, the place or seat behind the saddle [Fr. *croupe*].

croup (krōōp) *n.* (*Med.*) acute inflammation of the wind-pipe, accompanied by a hoarse ringing cough and difficulty in breathing.—**croup'y** *a.* [O.E. *kropan*, to cry].

croupier (krōō'-pi-ẹr) *n.* one who assists the chairman at a public banquet; an official who sits at a gaming table to observe the cards and collect stakes [Fr.].

crow (krō) *n.* a large bird, usually wholly black, of the genus Corvus; the cry of the cock; the name of a tribe of American Indians; a crowbar;—*v.i.* to give the shrill cry of the cock; to utter a sound of pleasure.—**crow'bar** *n.* (bar with a beak) a bar of iron bent at one end, used as a lever.—**crow's'-foot** *n.* a wrinkle about the outer corners of the eyes in old age.—**crow's'-nest** *n.* a box or perch for the look-out man near the top of the mast of a whaler [O.E. *crawan*].

crowberry (krō'-ber'-i) *n.* a heath-like shrub, bearing a black berry; the cranberry.

crowd (kroud) *v.t.* to press or drive together; to fill or occupy by crushing together;—*v.i.* to be numerous; to gather in numbers;—*n.* a number of things or persons collected into a close body; a dense multitude or throng; (*Colloq.*) a set or clique [O.E. *crudan*].

crowfoot (krō'-fōōt) *n.* (*Bot.*) the Ranunculus or buttercup; (*Naut.*) a number of small cords roved through a long block, and used to suspend an awning; a caltrop.

crown (kroun) *n.* the diadem or state head-dress worn by a sovereign; the sovereign; royalty; anything resembling a crown; something achieved or consummated; the topmost part of the head; the upper part of a hat; the summit; formerly, a five-shilling piece;—*v.t.* to invest with a crown or with royal dignity; to bestow upon as a mark of honour; to top or surmount; to complete.—**crown'-col'ony** *n.* one directly administered by the home government.—**crown'-glass** *n.* the finest sort of window-glass.—**crown'-impe'rial** *n.* a plant of the lily family, with a cluster of bell-shaped flowers.—**crown'-lands** *n.pl.* lands belonging to the sovereign.—**crown'-law'yer** *n.* one employed by the crown in criminal prosecution.—**crown'-off'ice** *n.* an administrative department of the central office of the Supreme Court of Judicature, having cognisance of criminal cases.—**crown'-pa'per** *n.* paper 15×20 inches, which was formerly water-marked with a crown.—**crown'-prince** *n.* the heir apparent to the throne.—**crown'-saw** *n.* a hollow cylinder with teeth on the edge.—**crown'-wheel** *n.* a wheel with cogs at right angles to its plane.—**crown'-liv'ing** *n.* an ecclesiastical living which the crown has the right to bestow.—**crown and anchor**, a gambling game [L. *corona*, a crown].

crowner (kroun'ẹr) *n.* (*Arch.*) a coroner.

crozier (krō'zhẹr) *n.* See **crosier**.

crucial (króósh'yạl) *a.* decisive; critical; (*Anat.*) cross-shaped [L. *crux*, a cross].

crucible (króó'si-bl) *n.* an earthenware melting-pot, capable of withstanding great heat, used for melting metals, etc.; (*Fig.*) a severe test [L.L. *crucibulum*].

Cruciferae (króó-sif'e-rē) *n.pl.* (*Bot.*) a family of plants whose flower has four petals in the shape of a cross.—**crucif'erous** *a.* [L. *crux*, a cross; *ferre*, to bear].

crucify (króó'si-fī) *v.t.* to put to death by nailing to a cross; to torture; to mortify.—**cru'cifer** *n.* the cross-bearer.—**cru'cifix** *n.* an image of Christ on the Cross.—**crucifixion** (króó-si-fik'shun) *n.* death by nailing to a cross; Christ's death upon the cross; intense suffering or affliction.—**cru'ciform** *a.* cross-shaped [L. *crux*, a cross; *figere*, to fix].

crude (króód) *a.* in the natural or raw state; unripe; rough; unfinished.—**crude'ly** *adv.*—**crude'ness** *n.*—**crud'ity** *n.* roughness, rawness [L. *crudus*, raw].

cruel (króó'el) *a.* delighting in, or callous to, others' pain; merciless; hard-hearted; inhuman.—**cru'elly** *adv.*—**cru'elty** *n.* the quality of being cruel [L. *crudelis*].

cruet (króó'et) *n.* a small stoppered bottle for holding vinegar, oil, condiments, etc.; a stand for holding such bottles, mustard-pots, pepper-pots, etc. [O.Fr. *cruie*, a pot].

cruise (króóz) *v.i.* to sail about without precise destination; in motoring and aviation, to go at a normal operating speed;—*n.* an organised pleasure-sail.—**cruis'er** *n.* (*Naval*) a fast warship of medium displacement and fighting power.—**cruis'er-weight** *n.* (*Boxing*) light heavy-weight, between 11 st. 6 lb. and 12 st. 7 lb. [L. *crux*, a cross].

crumb (krum) *n.* a small particle; a bit, esp. of bread; the soft part of bread;—*v.t.* to reduce to crumbs; to cover with crumbs.—**crumb'y, crum'my** *a.* [O.E. *cruma*].

crumble (krum'bl) *v.t.* to break into crumbs or fragments;—*v.i.* to fall into crumbs.—**crum'bly** *a.* [O.E. *cruma*].

crumpet (krum'pet) *n.* a flat, soft pancake [origin uncertain].

crumple (krum'pl) *v.t.* to wrinkle; to crease; to rumple;—*v.i.* to become wrinkled or creased; to shrink irregularly.

crunch (krunsh) *n.* the sound made by chewing crisp food, treading on gravel, hard snow, etc.;—*v.t.* and *i.* to chew, tread, etc. with this sound [imit. origin].

crupper (krup'ẹr) *n.* a strap of leather buckled to a saddle, and passing under a horse's tail; the rump or croup of a horse;—*v.t.* to fit with a crupper [Fr. *croupière*].

crusade (króó-sād') *n.* a medieval Christian war to recover the Holy Land from the Saracens; a campaign against any evil or vice;—*v.i.* to join in a crusade.—**crusad'er** *n.* (*World War* 2) a make of tank [Fr. *croisade*, fr. L. *crux*, a cross].

cruse (króós, króóz) *n.* a small earthen pot for holding water, oil, etc. [O.N. *krus*].

crush (krush) *v.t.* to press between two hard bodies so as to break, bruise, or crumple; to break into fragments; to squeeze out by pressure; to defeat utterly;—*v.i.* to be broken or compressed by weight or force;—*n.* violent pressure; a closely packed crowd of people.—**crush'-hat** *n.* a collapsible hat; an opera-hat.—**to have a crush on** (*Slang*) to be in love with [O.Fr. *cruissir*].

crust (krust) *n.* the hard outer coat or covering of anything; the outer part of baked bread; pastry, etc. forming the covering of a pie; a deposit from wine collected on the interior of bottles;—*v.t.* to cover with a crust;—*v.i.* to gather into a crust; to form a crust.—**crustat'ed** *a.* covered with a crust; incrusted.—**crusta'tion** *n.*—**crust'ily** *adv.* in a crusty manner; peevishly; morosely.—**crust'iness** *n.*—**crust'y** *a.* having a crust; like a crust; hard; peevish; surly; short-tempered [L. *crusta*].

Crustacea (krus-tā'shi-ạ) *n.pl.* (*Zool.*) a class of mainly aquatic animals including lobsters, crabs, shrimps, prawns, etc.—**crusta'cean** *a.* and *n.* pert. to, or one of, the crustacea.—**crusta'ceous** *a.* having a hard shell [L. *crusta*, a rind].

crutch (kruch) *n.* a staff with a cross-piece to go under the armpit for the use of cripples; a support;—*v.t.* to support; to aid [O.E. *cryce*].

crux (kruks) *n.* a perplexing problem; a knotty point; the real issue [L. *crux*, a cross].

cry (krī) *v.t.* to call out; to shout; to proclaim or advertise by crier;—*v.i.* to call loudly; to exclaim vehemently; to weep;—*n.* a loud utterance, esp. the sound of a child or animal; a prayer; the shedding of tears; the sound of a pack of hounds on the scent, hence the pack itself.—*pa.p.* and *pa.t.* **cried** (krīd);—*pl.* **cries**.—**cri'er** *n.* one who cries; a public announcer.—**cry'ing** *a.* calling for notice or attention.—**a far cry**, a great distance.—**to cry off**, to withdraw from an agreement.—**to cry wolf**, to give a false alarm [L. *quiritare*, to wail].

cryolite (krī'ō-līt) *n.* a mineral, resembling ice in appearance, used in making aluminium [Gk. *kruos*, frost; *lithos*, stone].

crypt (kript) *n.* a cell or chapel under a church, or underground, used for burial.—**cryp'tic(al)** *a.* hidden; secret; mysterious.—**cryp'tically** *adv.* [Gk. *kruptein*, to conceal].

crypto- (krip'tō) a prefix fr. Gk. *kruptos*, hidden, secret, combining to form many compounds.

crypto (krip'tō) *n.* person who secretly owes allegiance to a political creed or party.

cryptogam (krip'tō-gam) *n.* (*Bot.*) a plant that has no apparent or true flower, as a fern, moss, etc. [Gk. *kruptos*; *gamos*, marriage].

cryptogram (krip'tō-gram) *n.* a writing in secret characters.—Also **cryp'tograph** *n.*—**cryptol'ogy** *n.* a secret language.—**cryptonym** (krip'ton-im) *n.* a secret name [Gk. *kruptos*, hidden; *graphein*, to write].

crystal (kris'tạl) *n.* a transparent, colourless quartz; an ornament made from it; a ball cut from it for crystal-gazing; a superior sort of glass; a table article made from such glass with ornamental cutting; (*Chem.*) a mineral body which has assumed a regular geometrical form;—*a.* consisting of, or like, crystal; clear; transparent.—**crys'talline** *a.* resembling crystal; transparent; pellucid.—**crys'tallise** *v.t.* to cause to form crystals; (*Fig.*) to cause to assume a definite shape;—*v.i.* to be formed into crystals; (*Fig.*) to become definite in shape.—**crystallis'able** *a.*—**crystallisa'tion** *n.*—**crystallog'raphy** *n.* the science that deals with the origin and structure of crystals.—**crys'talloid** *a.* crystal-like;—*n.* (*Chem.*) a crystalline substance which diffuses readily through animal membrane [Gk. *krustallos*, fr. *kruos*, frost].

cub (kub) *n.* the young of the bear, fox, wolf, etc.; an awkward, ill-mannered youth;—*v.i.* to bring forth young (of animals).—**cub'bing** *n.* hunting fox-cubs.—**Wolf Cub**, a junior Boy Scout [etym. unknown].

cubage (kū´bāj) *n.* the cubic content of a solid [fr. *cube*].
cubby-hole (kub´i-hōl) *n.* a small secret place for storing things, or for hiding in [dial. E. *cub*, a pen or shed].
cube (kūb) *n.* (*Geom.*) a solid body with six equal square sides; (*Math.*) the product of a number multiplied twice by itself, as 4×4×4=64, the cube of 4, or 4 to the third power;—*v.t.* to raise to the third power.—**cu'bic(al)** *a.* having the form of a cube; of three dimensions, e.g. **cubic foot.**—**cu'boid** *a.* resembling a cube in shape.—**cube'-root** *n.* the number which gives the stated number if raised to the third power, or cubed, e.g. 4 is the cube-root of 64.—**cubic content,** volume [Gk. *kubos*].
cubicle (kū´bi-kl) *n.* one of the small sleeping compartments into which a dormitory is divided [L. *cubiculum*, a bedroom].
cubism (kū´bizm) *n.* (*Art*) a phase of modern art based on a three-dimensional principle, seeing all sides and all implications of an object at the same time.—**cu'bist** *n.* [fr. *cube*].
cubit (kū´bit) *n.* a measure of length, about 18 inches, orig. the length of the forearm, from the elbow to the tip of the middle finger.—**cu'bital** *a.* [L. *cubitum*, the elbow].
cucking-stool (kuk´ing-stōōl) *n.* a stool used as a punishment-seat in which scolds and others were placed out of doors, to be exposed to public derision [Icel. *kuka*, to go to stool].
cuckold (kuk´ōld) *n.* a man whose wife is unfaithful to him;—*v.t.* to make a cuckold of; to be unfaithful to a husband.—**cuck'oldry** *n.* adultery [O.Fr. *cucu*, a cuckoo].
cuckoo (koo´kōō) *n.* a migratory bird named from its call and remarkable for laying its eggs in other birds' nests; the call of the bird; a fool.—**cuck'oo-flow'er** *n.* lady's smock.—**cuck'oo-pint** *n.* a plant, the wild arum, popularly known as wake-robin or lords-and-ladies.—**cuck'oo-spit** *n.* a frothy secretion deposited on the leaves of plants by certain insects [imit. origin].
cucumber (kū´kum-bẹr) *n.* an edible plant of the gourd family and its fruit, used as a salad and for pickling [L. *cucumis*].
cud (kud) *n.* food brought up by ruminating animals, from their first stomach, and chewed a second time.—**to chew the cud** (*Fig.*) to meditate [O.E. *cudu*].
cuddle (kud´l) *v.t.* to caress; to hug; to fondle;—*v.i.* to lie close or snug; to nestle;—*n.* a close embrace [etym. uncertain].
cuddy (kud´i) *n.* (*Naut.*) a small cabin in the fore-part of a half-decked boat; a cabin under poop of a ship [Dut. *kajuit*].
cuddy (kud´i) *n.* a donkey; a stupid fellow [perh. fr. *Cuthbert*].
cudgel (kud´jel) *n.* a short thick stick;—*v.t.* to beat with a cudgel.—*pr.p.* **cud'gelling;** —*pa.p.* and *pa.t.* **cud'gelled** [O.E. *cycgel*].
cue (kū) *n.* the long tapering stick used by a billiard player; a pigtail.—**cue'ist** *n.* a billiard player [L. *cauda*, a tail; Fr. *queue*].
cue (kū) *n.* the last words of an actor's speech as a signal to the next actor to speak; a hint [earlier 'q.,' standing for L. *quando*, when (i.e. to come on)].
cuff (kuf) *n.* a blow with the open hand;—*v.t.* to strike with the open hand [etym. uncertain].
cuff (kuf) *n.* the ending of a sleeve; the wrist-band of a sleeve [M.E. *cuffe*].
cuirass (kwi-ras') *n.* metal or leather armour, consisting of a breastplate and backplate [Fr. *cuir*, leather].
cuisine (kwē-zēn') *n.* literally a kitchen; a style of cooking [Fr. fr. *cuire*, to cook].
cuisse, cuish (kwis, kwish) *n.* protective armour for the thighs [Fr. *cuisse*, the thigh].
cul-de-sac (kool´dẹ-sak') *n.* a street or lane open only at one end; a blind alley [Fr. *cul*, bottom; *sac*, a bag].
culinary (kū´lin-ạr-i) *a.* pert. to the kitchen or cookery [L. *culina*, a kitchen].
cull (kul) *v.t.* to select, or pick out; to gather [Fr. *cueillir*, to gather].
cullender See **colander.**
culm (kulm) *n.* the stalk or stem of corn and grasses.—**culmif'erous** *a.* bearing culms [L. *culmus*, a stalk; *ferre*, to bear].
culm (kulm) *n.* coal-dust; also, stone-coal [origin uncertain].
culminate (kul´mi-nāt) *v.i.* to reach the highest point (with 'in'); to reach a climax.—**culmina'tion** *n.* the attainment of the highest point; climax [L. *culmen*, summit].
culpable (kul´pạ-bl) *a.* deserving blame or censure; criminal.—**cul'pably** *adv.*—**culpabil'ity, cul'pableness** *n.* the state of being culpable; guilt; blame [L. *culpa*, fault].
culprit (kul´prit) *n.* one accused of a crime; a criminal; an offender [L. *culpa*, a fault].
cult (kult) *n.* a system of religious belief, esp. the rites and ceremonies attendant on such belief [L. *cultus*, worship].
cultivate (kul´ti-vāt) *v.t.* to prepare for the raising of crops; to till; to produce by tillage, labour, or care; to civilise.—**cul'tivable** *a.*—**cultiva'tion** *n.* the practice of cultivating.—**cul'tivator** *n.* [L. *colere, cultum*, to till].
culture (kul´tūr) *n.* tillage or cultivation; mental training and development; refinement; civilisation; the propagation of bacteria and other micro-organisms in artificial media;—*v.t.* to cultivate.—**cul'tural** *a.* pert. to culture.—**cul'tured** *a.* educated and refined [L. *colere*, to cultivate].
culverin (kul´vẹr-in) *n.* an early type of cannon [O.Fr.=snake-like, fr. *couleuvre*, an adder].
culvert (kul´vẹrt) *n.* an arched drain or conduit for the passage of water under a road, railway, or canal [Fr. *couler*, to flow].
cumber (kum´bẹr) *v.t.* to burden or hinder with a useless load; to lumber.—**cum'bersome** *a.* burdensome; clumsy and unmanageable.—**cum'brous** *a.* bulky; heavy and unwieldy [O.Fr. *combrer*, to hinder].
cumin (kum´in) *n.* an Egyptian plant, whose aromatic seeds yield oil and are used medicinally. Also **cum'min** [Gk. *kuminon*].
cummerbund (kum´ẹr-bund) *n.* a broad sash worn as a waistband [Pers. *kamarband*, a loin band].
cumulate (kūm´ū-lāt) *v.t.* to heap together; —*a.* heaped up.—**cumula'tion** *n.*—**cum'ulative** *a.* becoming greater by successive additions; gaining force or effect by additions.—**cum'ulatively** *adv.* [L. *cumulus*, a heap].
cumulus (kū´mū-lus) *n.* a heap; a piled-up cloud mass with rounded outlines, often seen in summer [L. *cumulus*, a heap].
cunctator (kungk-tā´tor) *n.* one who delays. —**cunc'tative** *a.* delaying [L. *cunctari*, to delay].
cuneal, cuneate (kū´nē-ạl, -āt) *a.* wedge-shaped [L. *cuneus*, a wedge].
cuneiform, cuniform (kū-nē´i-form, kū´ni-form) *a.* wedge-shaped [L. *cuneus*, a wedge].
cunning (kun´ing) *a.* wily; sly; artful;—*n.* craft or skill; guile; deceit.—**cunn'ingly** *adv.* [O.E. *cunnan*, to know].
cup (kup) *n.* a small, round drinking-vessel of porcelain; also applied to other vessels for containing liquids, large or small and of various shapes; the contents of a cup; anything resembling a tea-cup in shape; an ornamental vessel given as a prize for sport, etc.;—*v.t.* to let blood by means of a cupping-glass; to hold, as in a cup; to form into a cup-shape.—**cup'ful** *n.* the quantity that a cup holds.—**cupboard** (kub´urd) *n.* a small closet with shelves for cups, plates, etc.—**cup'-tie** *n.* in association football, a game determining or contributing to the determination of the winners of a cup.—**lov'ing-cup** *n.* a large cup with several handles which is

passed round a banquet-table and is drunk from by each guest in turn.—**cupboard-love,** a pretended affection, assumed in the hope of gain.—**in one's cups,** drunk [L. *cupa*, a tub].

cupidity (kū-pid′i-ti) *n.* an eager desire for possession; greed of gain [L. *cupidus*, desirous].

cupola (kū′pō-la) *n.* a spherical vault on the top of a building; a dome [It. *cupola*, fr. L. *cupa*, a tub].

cupreous (kū′prē-us) *a.* of, pert. to, or containing copper.—**cu′pric** *a.* (*Chem.*) containing copper (with a valency of one).—**cu′prous** *a.* (*Chem.*) containing copper (with a valency of two).—**cuprif′erous** *a.* bearing or producing copper [L. *cuprum*, copper].

cupro-nickel (kū′prō-nik-el) *n.* an alloy of copper and nickel [L. *cuprum*, copper].

cur (kur) *n.* a dog of mixed breed; a mongrel; (*Fig.*) a surly, ill-bred, or cowardly fellow.—**cur′rish** *a.* like a cur; quarrelsome; churlish [O.N. *kurra*, to grumble].

curaçao (kū′ra-sō, kòò-ra-sō′) *n.* a liqueur the flavouring principle of which is bitter orange peel.—Also **curaço** [first made on the island of *Curaçao*, one of the Dut. W. Indies].

curare, curari (kòò-rá′ri) *n.* an extract from a plant *Strychnos toxifera*, used as a poison for arrow-tips by S. American Indians; used medicinally in cases of tetanus. —**curarine** (kòò-rá′rin) *n.* an alkaloid extracted from curare [Native].

curate (kū′rāt) *n.* one who has the cure of souls; an assistant to a vicar or rector.—**cu′racy, cu′rateship** *n.* [L. *cura*, care].

curator (kū-rā′tor) *n.* a superintendent, as of a museum, library, etc.; a trustee; a guardian.—**cura′torship** *n.* [L. fr. *curare*, to care].

curb (kurb) *n.* a chain or strap attached to the bit of a bridle and passing under the horse's lower jaw to give powerful control with the reins; any check or means of restraint; a stone edging to a pavement or sidewalk; a hearth fender;—*v.t.* to apply a curb to (a horse); to restrain; to confine.—**curb′-stone** *n.* a stone placed against earth or stonework to prevent its giving way [Fr. *courber*, fr. L. *curvare*, to bend].

curd (kurd) *n.* the cheesy part of milk; coagulated milk; the coagulated part of any liquid.—**curd′le** *v.t.* and *i.* to turn into curd; to coagulate [O.E. *crudan*, to press].

cure (kūr) *v.t.* to heal; to restore to health; to remedy; to preserve fish, skins, etc. by salting, drying, etc.;—*n.* the act of healing; that which heals; a remedy.—**cure of souls,** the care of a parish or congregation by a clergyman.—**cu′rable** *a.* capable of being cured.—**cu′rative** *a.* tending to cure.—**cure′-all** *n.* a remedy for all ills; a panacea [L. *curare*, fr. *cura*, care].

curfew (kur′fū) *n.* in former times, the ringing of a bell at nightfall as a signal to put out fires and extinguish lights; the time after which persons may not be out of doors [Fr. *couvre-feu*=cover fire].

curie (kū′rē) *n.* (*Chem.*) the standard unit of emanation from one gram of radium.—**curium** (kū′ri-um) *n.* a radioactive, inert, gaseous element discovered during atom bomb research [fr. M. and Mme. *Curie*, discoverers of radium].

curio (kū′ri-ō) *n.* a rare or curious object, of the kind sought for by collectors; a curiosity [abbrev. of *curiosity*].

curious (kū′ri-us) *a.* eager to know; inquisitive; puzzling; strange; minutely accurate.—**cu′riously** *adv.*—**curios′ity** *n.* eagerness to know; inquisitiveness; a strange or rare object; a novelty [L. *curiosus*, inquisitive, careful].

curl (kurl) *v.t.* to twist into ringlets; to coil; to bend into spiral or curved shape;—*v.i.* to take a spiral or curved shape or path; to turn into ringlets; to ripple; to play at the game of curling;—*n.* a ringlet of hair; anything of a similar shape;—**curl′y** *a.* having curls; tending to curl; full of ripples. —**curl′icue** *n.* a lock of hair twisted in a quaint way.—**curl′iness** *n.* the state of being curly.—**curl′ing** *n.* a game like bowls played on ice with large, rounded stones.—**curl′ing-i′rons, curl′ing-tongs,** *n.* an instrument for curling the hair.—**curl′ing-pin** or **curl′er** *n.* a strong pin used as a fastener to retain a curl or wave in position [M.E. *crul*, curly].

curlew (kurlū) *n.* a long-billed wading bird [Fr. *courlieu*, imit. of its cry].

curmudgeon (kur-muj′un) *n.* a grasping ill-natured fellow; a miser; a churl.—**curmud′-geonly** *a.* churlish [origin unknown].

currant (kur′ant) *n.* the fruit of various plants allied to the gooseberry; small dried grapes which came orig. from *Corinth*.

current (kur′ent) *a.* running; flowing; fluent; in circulation or general use;—*n.* a running; a flowing; a body of water or air in motion; the flow of a river, etc.; tendency; drift; transmission of electricity through a conductor.—**curr′ently** *adv.* in a current manner; commonly.—**curr′ency** *n.* the time during which anything is current; money in use or circulation [L *currere*, to run].

curricle (kur i-kl) *n.* a two-wheeled open carriage, drawn by two horses [L. *curriculum*, a race-course].

curriculum (ku-rik′ū-lum) *n.* a specified course of study at a school, college, university, etc.;—*pl.* **curric′ula** [L. *curriculum*, a running, a race-course].

curry (kur′i) *n.* (*Cookery*) a highly-flavoured and pungent condiment much used in the East;—*v.t.* to cook or season with curry-powder [Tamil].

curry (kur′i) *v.t.* to dress leather; to comb, rub down, and clean a horse; to beat or thrash.—**curr′ier** *n.* one who dresses tanned leather.—**to curry favour** (corr. of *favel*, a horse), to try to win favour by flattery [O.Fr. *correer*, to prepare].

curse (kurs) *v.t.* to utter a wish of evil against; to invoke evil upon; to swear at; to torment; —*v.i.* to utter blasphemous words; to swear; —*n.* the invocation of evil or injury upon a person; profane words or oaths.—**cursed** (kurs′ed, kurst) *a.* hateful; abominable.—**cur′sedly** *adv.*—**cur′sedness** *n.*—**curst** *a.* (*Arch.*) crabbed; shrewish [O.E. *cursian*].

cursive (kur′siv) *a.* written with a running hand, i.e. with all the letters joined; flowing; rapid.—**cur′sively** *adv.*—**cur′sory** *a.* characterised by haste; careless; superficial; fleeting.—**cur′sorily** *adv.*—**cur′soriness** *n.* [L. *currere*, to run].

curt (kurt) *a.* short; concise to the point of rudeness; abrupt; terse.—**curt′ly** *adv.*—**curt′-ness** *n.* [L. *curtus*, shortened].

curtail (kur-tāl′) *v.t.* to cut short; to abridge; to diminish.—**curtail′ment** *n.* decrease [L. *curtus*, shortened].

curtain (kur′tin) *n.* a hanging drapery at windows, round beds, or at doors; a screen in front of stage of a theatre; a stretch of rampart between two bastions.—*v.t.* to enclose or furnish with curtains.—**cur′tain-lec′ture** *n.* a lecture given by a wife to her husband in bed.—**cur′tain-rais′er** *n.* a short play preceding the main piece in a theatre.—**iron curtain** (*Fig.*) any hindrance to prevent outsiders from obtaining information about conditions in a country [L.L. *cortina*].

curtate (kur′tāt) *a.* shortened or reduced [L. *curtare*, to shorten].

curtsy, curtsey (kurt′si) *n.* a gesture of civility or respect made by women or girls;—*v.i.* to make a curtsey [form of *courtesy*].

curve (kurv) *n.* a bending without angles; that which is bent; an arch;—*a.* bent;—*v.t.* and *i.* to bend.—**cur′vate** *a.* curved.—**cur′vature** *n.* the curve or amount of bending

of a line.—**curvilin'ear** *a.* having, or bound by, curved lines [L. *curvus*, crooked].
curvet (kur'-vet, kur-vet') *n.* a prancing of a horse;—*v.i.* to prance [L. *curvus*, crooked].
cushat (kush'-at) *n.* the ring-dove or wood-pigeon [O.E. *cusceote*].
cushion (koosh'-un) *n.* a bag or case filled with soft stuffing or air, to support or ease the body; any stuffed or padded surface used as a rest or protector;—*v.t.* to seat on a cushion; to provide or protect with a cushion [Fr. *coussin*, a cushion, fr. L. *coxa*, the hip].
cushy (kŏŏsh'-i) *a.* (*Slang*) soft; comfortable [Urdu, fr. Pers. *khush*, pleasant].
cusp (kusp) *n.* a point or horn of a crescent, as of the moon; a prominence on a molar tooth; the point at which the two branches of a curve have a common tangent.—**cus'pid** *n.* a canine tooth.—**cus'pidal** *n.* ending in a point.—**cus'pidate, cus'pidated** *a.* having a sharp point, as canine teeth [L. *cuspis*, a point].
cuspidor(e) (kus'-pi-dor) *n.* a spittoon [Port.].
cuss (kus) *n.* (*Slang*) a fellow, as in the phrase 'a queer cuss'; a curse.—**cuss'ed** *a.* corrupt. of cursed [fr. *curse*].
custard (kus'-tạrd) *n.* a sweet dish made with milk and eggs.—**cus'tard-app'le** *n.* edible fruit of various species of W. Indian shrubs [M.E. *crustade*, a pie with a crust].
custody (kus'-to-di) *n.* a keeping or guarding; safe-keeping; guardianship; imprisonment.—**custodial** (kus-tō'-di-ạl) *a.*—**custo'dian, custo'-dier** *n.* a keeper; a caretaker [L. *custodia*, fr. *custos*, a keeper].
custom (kus'-tum) *n.* fashion; usage; habit; business patronage; toll, tax, or tribute;—**cus'toms** *n.pl.* duties levied on imports.—**cus'tomable** *a.* common; customary; liable to duty.— **cus'tomary** *a.* according to custom; established by common usage; usual; habitual.—**cus'tomarily** *adv.*—**cus'tomer** *n.* one who enters a shop to buy [O.Fr. *coustume* fr. L. *consuetudo*].
cut (kut) *v.t.* to sever, penetrate, or wound with an edged instrument; to divide; to separate; to intersect; to cross; to mow; to hew; to carve; to trim; to shape; to reduce; to abridge; intentionally to ignore a person; (*Tennis, Golf, etc.*) to hit the ball obliquely in order to impart spin to it;—*v.i.* (*Slang*) to run rapidly.—*pr.p.* **cutt'ing**.—*pa.p.* and *pa.t.* **cut**.—*n.* an act of cutting; opening made with an edged instrument; a gash; a wound; a piece cut off, as e.g. a joint of meat; a notch; the intentional avoidance of a person; a reduction, esp. in salary or wages.—**cut'ter** *n.* he who, or that which, cuts; in tailoring, the one who cuts the cloth; a warship's rowing and sailing boat.—**cut'ting** *n.* an incision; an excavation (for a road, canal, etc.) through high ground; a clipping from a newspaper; a small branch, slip, etc. cut from a plant, bush, etc. for propagation by planting or grafting;—*a.* sarcastic.—**cut'-purse** *n.* a thief: a pickpocket.—**cut'-throat** *n.* a murderer; an assassin;—*a.* merciless.—**to cut a caper,** to frisk about; to gambol.—**to cut a dash,** to make a display of elegance, esp. in dress.—**to cut dead,** intentionally to ignore the presence of a person.—**to cut one's losses,** to abandon any further attempt, by speculation, to make good one's losses.—**to cut and run,** to depart suddenly in order to avoid capture or detection; to decamp.—**to cut up,** to cut in pieces; to carve; to criticise severely.—**to be cut up** (*Fig.*) to be deeply affected; to be downcast [etym. uncertain].
cutaneous (kū-tā'-nē-us) *a.* belonging to, or affecting, the skin [L. *cutis*, the skin].
cute (kūt) *a.* clever; sharp; shrewd; (*Colloq.*) attractive [short for *acute*].
cutis (kū'-tis) *n.* the true skin, lying below the outer skin layer.—**cuticle** (kū'-ti-kl) *n.* the outer skin or epidermis.—**cutic'ular** *a.* [L. *cutis*, skin].
cutlass (kut'-las) *n.* a short, broad-bladed, curving sword used in the navy [O.Fr. *coutel*, a knife fr. L. *culter*, a ploughshare].
cutler (kut'-lẹr) *n.* one who makes, repairs, or deals in knives and cutting implements.—**cut'lery** *n.* business of a cutler; cutlers' wares [Fr. *coutelier*; *couteau*, a knife].
cutlet (kut'-let) *n.* a piece of meat or chop from the rib-bones, for broiling or frying [Fr. *cotelette*, fr. *côte*, a rib].
cuttle, cuttle-fish (kut'-l, -fish) *n.* a sea mollusc with long tentacles, which evades pursuit by ejecting an inky fluid.—**cutt'le-bone** *n.* [O.E. *cudele*].
cyanogen (sī-an'-o-jen) *n.* (*Chem.*) a colourless, poisonous gas, compounded of nitrogen and carbon.—**cyan'ic** *a.* pert. to or containing cyanogen; blue [Gk. *kuanos*, blue, and root *gen*].
cybernetics (sī-bẹr-net'-iks) *n.* the study of the self-organising machine or mechanical brain [Gk. *kubornasis*, a pilot].
cyclamen (sik'-la-men) *n.* a bulbous plant of the Primrose family [Gk. *kuklaminos*].
cycle (sī'-kl) *n.* a regularly recurring succession of events or phenomena, or the period of time occupied by such a succession; a body of myths or legends, relating to some period, person, or event; a series of songs dealing with various phases of the same subject, and meant to be sung one after the other; a bicycle or tricycle;—*v.i.* to pass through a cycle of changes; to ride a bicycle or tricycle.—**cy'clic(al)** *a.* pert. to or moving in cycles.—**cy'clist** *n.* one who rides a bicycle or tricycle.—**cy'cloid** *n.* (*Geom.*) a curve traced by a point in a circle when the circle revolves along a straight line [Gk. *kuklos*, a circle].
cyclone (sī'-klōn) *n.* a violent storm characterised by strong winds rotating about a centre of low barometric pressure.—**cyclon'ic** [Gk. *kuklos*, a circle].
cyclopaedia (sī-klō-pē'-di-ạ) *n.* see **encyclopaedia.**
cyclorama (sī-klō-rá'-mạ) *n.* circular panorama [Gk. *kuklos*, a circle; *orama*, a view].
cyclostyle (sī'-klō-stīl) *n.* an apparatus for multiplying copies of letters, etc;—*v.t.* to reproduce thus [Gk. *kuklos*, a circle; L. *stilus*, a pen].
cyclotron (sī'-klō-tron) *n.* a radio oscillator developed to disintegrate atoms, in order to study their internal structure [Gk. *kuklos*, a circle].
cyder See **cider.**
cygnet (sig'-net) *n.* a young swan [Fr. *cygne*, a swan].
cylinder (sil'-in-dẹr) *n.* a roller-like body with straight sides, the ends being equal, parallel circles; any object of similar shape.—**cylin'dric, cylin'drical** *a.* having the form of a cylinder.—**cylin'driform** *a.* shaped like a cylinder [Gk. *kulindros*, a roller].
cymbal (sim'-bạl) *n.* one of a pair of saucer-shaped pieces of brass, used as a musical instrument of percussion [Gk. *kumbalon*].
Cymry (sim'-ri, kim'-ri) *n.pl.* the Celtic name of the Welsh people.—**Cym'ric** *a.* pert. to the Welsh;—*n.* the Welsh language [W. *Cymru*, Wales].
cynic (sin'-ik) *n.* one of a set of Greek philosophers who regarded virtue as the supreme good and despised all comfort or refinement; one who believes man's conduct is based on self-interest; a misanthrope; a surly, morose man.—**cyn'ic(al)** *a.* morose; snarling; sneering.—**cyn'ically** *adv.*—**cyn'icalness** *n.*—**cynicism** (sin'-i-sizm) *n.* principles of a cynic; disbelief in goodness; misanthropy [Gk. *kunikos*, dog-like, fr. *kuon*, a dog].
cynosure (sī'-nō-, sin'-ō-shŏŏr) *n.* (*Astron.*) the constellation of the Lesser Bear, containing the Pole-star; hence, something to which all eyes are turned; a guiding star [Gk. *kuon*, a dog; *oura*, a tail].
cypher See **cipher.**
cypress (sī'-pres) *n.* a coniferous tree formerly

ARTS in ANTIQUITY · 1

Bust of Nefertiti

Egyptian mural from Nefertari's tomb

Egyptian mural—depicting musicians

ARTS in ANTIQUITY · 2

Palace of Minos

Statue of a Minoan goddess

Wall painting at Knossos

Palace ruins in Mycene

regarded as a symbol of mourning [L. *cupressus*].
cypress (sī´pres) *n.* a gauze-like fabric. Also **cy'prus** [fr. the island of *Cyprus*].
Cyprian (sip´ri-an) *a.* belonging to *Cyprus.*—**Cy'priot** *a.* belonging to Cyprus;—*n.* a native of Cyprus.
cyst (sist) *n.* (*Med.*) a bladder or membranous sac containing liquid secretion or morbid matter; a tumour.—**cys'tic** *a.* pert. to cysts [Gk. *kustis*, a bladder].
cytology (sī-tol´o-ji) *n.* (*Biol.*) the study of plant and animal cells as individual units rather than as components of tissues.—**cytoblast** (sī´tō-blast) *n.* a cell-nucleus [Gk. *kutos*, a cavity].
Czar (zår) *n.* a title used by various Slavonic rulers, esp. by the Emperors of Russia.—**Czarina** (zå-rē´na) *n.* the wife of a Czar. (Other forms are **Tsar, Tzar, Tsari'na, Tzari'na**, etc.) [fr. L. *Caesar*].
Czech (chek) *n.* a member of the Slavonic race of people inhabiting the western region of Czechoslovakia; the language spoken by them;—*a.* pert. to the people or their language.—**Czechoslovak** (chek-o-slō´vak, chel-o-slō-vak'), **Czechoslovak'ian** *a.* pert. to the country, the people, or the language of Czechoslovakia;—*n.* a native of the country; the language.

D

dab (dab) *n.* one skilled in anything; an adept [etym. unknown].
dab (dab) *n.* a small flat fish of the flounder variety [etym. unknown].
dab (dab) *v.t.* to touch gently and intermittently, as with some soft or moist substance.—*pr.p.* **dabb'ing**;—*pa.p.* **dabb'ed**;—*n.* a gentle blow with a soft substance; a small lump of anything soft, as butter [M.E. *dabban*, to strike.]
dabble (dab´l) *v.t.* to wet by little dips; to moisten;—*v.i.* to play in water; to pursue a subject superficially [M.E. *dabban*, to strike].
dabchick (dab´chik) *n.* a small grebe or water-fowl [E. *dap*, var. of *dip*].
dace (dās) *n.* a small fresh water river fish of the carp variety which darts about swiftly. Also **dart, dare** [O.Fr. *dars*, dart].
dachshund (daks´hoont) *n.* dog with long body, short legs, and drooping ears [Ger. *Dachs*, a badger; *Hund*, a dog].
dacoit, dacoyt (da-koit') *n.* one of a gang of robbers in India and Burma.—**dacoit'age, dacoit'y** *n.* brigandage [Hind. *dakait*, a robber].
dactyl (dak´til) *n.* a metrical foot in poetry, consisting of one accented syllable followed by two unaccented syllables (— ◡◡).—**dactyl'ic** *a.* pert. to or consisting of a dactyl—also **dactyl'ar.**—**dactyl'ioglyph** *n.* an engraver of finger-rings; the engraver's name on a ring.—**dactyliog'raphy** *n.* the art of engraving precious stones or rings. -**dactyl'ogram** *n.* a finger-print.—**dactylog'raphy** *n.* the science of finger-prints.—**dactylol'ogy** *n.* the finger-language of the deaf and dumb [Gk. *daktulos*, a finger].
dad, dada, daddy (dad, da´da, dad´i) *n.* father, a word used by little children [W. *tad*, a father].
dad (dad) *v.t.* to beat against something.—*n.* a lump; a blow [etym. unknown].
dadaism (då´da-izm) *n.* a school of art and literature which aims at suppressing all relations between thought and expression.—**da'daist** *n.*
daddle (dad´l) *v.i.* to totter; to walk with unsteady steps like a small child or an old man [etym. unknown].
daddy-long-legs (dad´i-long´legs) *n.* a flying insect with long body, legs, antennae, and gossamer wings; the crane-fly [fr. *dad*].
dado (dā´dō) *n.* (*Archit.*) the part of a pedestal between the base and cornice; the lower part or wide skirting of the walls of a room painted differently from the rest of a room [It. *dado*, a pedestal].
daemon (dē´mon) *n.* an inspiring influence; a divinity; genius.—**daemon'ic** *a.* more than human; supernatural [Gk. *daimon*, spirit].
daffodil (daf´ō-dil) *n.* a spring plant of the genus Narcissus; the yellow colour of the daffodil [Gk. *asphodelos*, a lily flower].
daft (daft) *a.* (*Scot.*) insane; stupid; foolish; giddy.—**daft'ness** *n.* [M.E. *daft*, mild].
dagger (dag´er) *n.* a short, two-edged sword used in close combat; a dirk; a stiletto; a mark of reference in typography (†) or (‡) [M.E. *daggen*, to slit].
daggle (dag´l) *v.t.* to trail through mud; to befoul; to bedraggle [Scand. *dagg*, dew].
dago (dā´gō) *n.* term of contempt for Spaniard, Portugese, or Italian; in U.S. people of dusky colour [Sp. *Diego*, James].
dagoba (dag´o-ba, da-gō´ba) *n.* in eastern countries, esp. Ceylon, a circular, dome-shaped temple, containing relics of Buddha or Buddhist saint [Singh. *dagaba*].
daguerrotype (da-ger´ō-tīp) *n.* in photography, an early method of taking pictures by sunlight, on plates of glass or silvered copper.—**daguerrotyp'ic** *a.* [fr. Louis *Daguerre* of Paris, the 19th cent. inventor].
Dahlia (dāl´ya) *n.* a genus of plants with large, brightly coloured flowers [fr. *Dahl*, a Swedish botanist].
Dail Eireann (doil´ār´an) *n.* the lower house of Parliament in Irish Free State (Eire) [Ir. =assembly of Ireland].
daily (dā´li) *a.* or *adv.* happening each day;—*n.* a newspaper published each day; a charwoman or non-resident servant [O.E. *daeg*, day].
dainty (dān´ti) *a.* pleasing to the taste; elegant; refined; pretty and slender; scrupulous;—*n.* a delicacy.—**dain'tily** *adv.*—**dain'tiness** *n.* [L. *dignus*, worthy].
dairy (dā´ri) *n.* the place where milk and cream are kept cool, butter is churned, and cheese is made; the shop where milk and its products are sold.—**dai'rying** *n.* the business of conducting a dairy.—**dai'rymaid, dai'ryman** *n.*—**dai'ry-farm** *n.* [Icel. *deigja*, a dairymaid].
dais (dā´is) *n.* the raised platform at upper end of a room, esp. of dining-hall [O.Fr. *deis*, fr. L.L. *discus*, a table].
daisy (dā´zi) *n.* a common wild flower growing chiefly in grass, having petals white or red, and a yellow centre; (*Slang*) a person or thing unusually pleasing.—**dai'sied** *a.*—**dai'sy-chain** *n.* chain of daisies made by inserting one stem through another.—**dai'sy-cut'ter** *n.* (*Slang*) a cricket ball that barely clears the grass (or daisies) [O.E. *daeg*, a day; *eage*, an eye].
dakoit See **dacoit.**
dale (dāl) *n.* a low place between hills; a valley or vale; a glen.—**dales'man** *n.* one living in a dale, esp. used in N. England in Lake District [O.E. *dael*, a valley].
dallop (dal´op) *n.* a lump of anything. Also **doll'op** [etym. uncertain].
dally (dal´i) *v.i.* to waste time; to act in a futile manner; to fondle or interchange caresses.—*pr.p.* **dall'ying.**—*pa.p.* **dall'ied.**—**dall'iance** *n.* the act of trifling and wasting time; love-making [M.E. *dalien*, to play].
Dalmatian (dal-mā´shun) *n.* a breed of large white dog with black or liver-coloured spots [fr. *Dalmatia*].
dalmatic (dal-ma´tik) *n.* a loose, wide-sleeved liturgical vestment worn by R.C. deacons at Mass; worn also by bishops and by the King at Coronation; orig. made of *Dalmatian* wool.
dam (dam) *n.* a female parent—used of animals [form of *dame*].

dam (dam) *n.* a barrier of earth, stones, etc. to obstruct the flow of water; the water confined by a dam;—*v.t.* to confine water by a dam.—**dam'-bus'ter**, type of huge aerial bomb [M.E. *dam*, an obstruction].

damage (dam'āj) *n.* any injury or harm to person, property, or reputation;—*v.t.* to harm; to hurt.—**dam'ages** *n.pl.* legal compensation paid to injured party.—**dam'ageable** *a.* [L. *damnum*, loss].

damask (dam'ask) *n.* a figured silk or linen fabric, orig. made at Damascus; steel ornamented with wavy pattern; a rose-pink colour, like that of damask rose;—*a.* woven with figured pattern like damask.—**damaskeen'** **damascene** (da'mas-ēn) *v.t.* to ornament, esp. iron and steel, by inlaying with another metal, or by etched lines resembling watered silk.—**dam'ask-plum** *n.* a damson.—**damask rose**, a pink rose brought orig. from Damascus, and from which the perfume, attar of roses, was distilled [fr. *Damascus*, in Syria].

damboard (dam'bōrd), **dambrod** (dam'brod) *n.* (*Scot.*) a draughtboard [Fr. *dame*, lady, piece at draughts].

dame (dām) *n.* a noble lady; the mistress of a household; (*Colloq.*) a managing woman.—**Dame** *n.* title of the wife of a knight or baronet; title of an honour awarded to women members of the Order of the British Empire (*Abbrev.*) **D.B.E.**—**dame school**, a school for young children run by a woman [Fr. *dame*, a lady].

damn (dam) *v.t.* to consign to everlasting punishment; to give over to death; (*Colloq.*) to condemn irritably (used as interjection); to destroy the reputation of;—*n.* an oath; a curse; (*Colloq.*) a trifle.—**dam'nable** *a.*—**dam'nably** *adv.*—**damna'tion** *n.* punishment in a future state.—**dam'natory** *a.* containing a sentence of condemnation.—**damned** *a.* odious; horrible [L. *damnare*, to condemn].

damozel (dam'o-zel) *n.* archaic and poetic var. of *damsel*. Also **dam'osel** [O.Fr. *damoisele*, a maiden].

damp (damp) *n.* moist air; humidity; fog; vapour; noxious gases in coal mines, wells, etc. (as fire-damp, choke-damp);—*a.* slightly moist;—*v.t.* to moisten slightly; to retard combustion (to *damp* down a fire).—**damp'en** *v.t.* to moisten; (*Fig.*) to depress.—**damp'er** *n.* one who or that which damps; a contrivance in flue of a kitchen range to regulate draught; a device to minimise vibration.—**damp'ish** *a.* rather moist.—**damp'ness** *n.* the state of being moist; humidity.—**damp'-proof** *a.* impervious to damp [Ger. *Dampf*, steam].

damsel (dam'sel) *n.* a young unmarried woman [M.E. *damizel*, Fr. *demoiselle*, a maiden].

damson (dam'zon) *n.* a small black plum used for jam or jelly (orig. a Damascus plum) [O.Fr. *damascene*, of Damascus].

dan (dan) *n.* a small buoy used as a mark in deep-sea fishing [etym. uncertain].

dance (dâns) *v.t.* and *v.i.* to move with measured steps; to move rhythmically; to caper;—*n.* a lively and rhythmical movement with certain steps and gestures; a social gathering for the purpose of dancing.—**danc'er** *n.* one who dances.—**danseuse'** *n.* a female dancer, esp. in ballet.—**to dance upon nothing**, to be hanged.—**to lead someone a dance**, to lead someone in vain pursuit.—**St. Vitus's dance** (*Med.*) nervous disorder accompanied by twitching of muscles; chorea.—**danc'ing-der'vish**, *n.* one of fanatical Mohammedan priests who practised wild, ritual dances.—**danc'ing-girl** *n.* professional dancer [Fr. *danser* to dance].

dandelion (dan-de-lī'on) *n.* a plant with large yellow flowers, and tooth-edged leaves [Fr. *dent de lion*, lion-toothed].

dander (dan'dẹr) *v.i.* to walk idly or in a leisurely way; to saunter;—*n.* an easy, aimless walk [corrupt. of *dandle*].

dander (dan'dẹr) *n.* anger; passion; temper [fr. *dandriff*].

Dandie Dinmont (dan'di-din-mont) *n.* a breed of small terrier, orig. from Teviotdale in Scotland; named after a character in Scott's *Guy Mannering*.

dandle (dan'dl) *v.t.* to move up and down in affectionate play, as an infant; to pet; to caress [It. *dondolare*, to swing].

dandriff, dandruff (dan'drif, -druf) *n.* a disease affecting the scalp and producing scurf or small scales of skin under the hair [etym. poss. W. *ton*, skin; *drwg*, bad].

dandy (dan'di) *n.* one who affects special finery in dress; a fop;—*a.* (*Colloq.*) fine; first-rate.—**dan'dify** *v.t.* to make like a dandy.—**dan'dified** *a.* foppish.—**dandi'acal** *a.* dandified.—**dan'dy-horse** *n.* a velocipede [etym. poss. Scots corrupt. of St. Andrew].

Dane (dān) *n.* a native of Denmark; a breed of dog, large and smooth coated, usually *great Dane*.—**danegeld** (dān'geld) *n.* a tax imposed by Ethelred in 10th cent. to buy off the Danes, or to subsidise a military force to prevent their landing.—**Da'nish** *a.* pert. to Denmark or the Danes;—*n.* the language of the Danes [O.E. *Dene*, a Dane].

danger (dān'jẹr) *n.* exposure to injury or evil; peril; hazard; insecurity; jeopardy.—**dan'gerous** *a.* attended with danger; involving risk.—**dan'gerously** *adv.*—**dan'gerousness** *n.* [M.E. *danger*, power].

dangle (dang'l) *v.t.* to swing loosely or carelessly; (*Fig.*) to use as a bait;—*v.i.* to hang loosely [Scand. *dangle*, to swing].

dank (dangk) *a.* unpleasantly damp or moist.—**dank'ness** *n.* [Scand. *danka*, moist].

dansant (dong'song) *n.* dancing.—**thé dansant** (tā'dong'song) *n.* afternoon tea with dancing.—**danseuse'** *n.* [See **dance**]. [Fr.].

dap (dap) *v.i.* to drop or let fall bait gently into the water; (of a ball) to bounce.—*pr.p.* **dap'ping**; *pa.p.* **dapped** [var. of *dip*].

daphne (daph'ne) *n.* a shrub of the laurel family, producing poisonous berries [Gk. *daphne*, laurel].

dapper (dap'ẹr) *a.* little and active; neat; trim; smart [Dut. *dapper*, brave].

dapple (dap'l) *n.* a spot;—*a.* spotted, applied to horses and deer.—**dapp'led** *a.* spotted, esp. of chequered pattern made by sunlight through trees [etym. unknown].

dare (dār) *v.i.* to have courage for; to venture (to); to be audacious enough;—*v.t.* to defy; to challenge; to terrify.—**dar'ing** *n.* audacity; a bold action;—*a.* bold; courageous; audacious.—**dar'ingly** *adv.*—**dare'-dev'il** *n.* a foolhardy, reckless fellow.—**I dare say**, I presume [M.E. *durran*, to dare].

darg (darg) *n.* (*Scot.*) a day's work [*day-work*].

dark (dȧrk) *a.* lacking light; black; sombre; evil; unenlightened;—*n.* absence of light; gloom; obscurity; evil.—**dark'en** *v.t.* to obstruct light; to render dim; to cloud; (*Fig.*) to sully;—*v.i.* to grow dark.—**dark'ish** *a.* rather dark.—**dark'le** *v.i.* to grow dark; to lie hid.—**dark'ling** *adv.* in the dark.—**dark'ly** *adv.*—**dark'ness** *n.*—**dark'y, dar'key** *n.* a negro.—**dark'-horse** *n.* a dark-coloured horse; (*Fig.*) a person of unknown capabilities, usually a last minute entrant or candidate.—**to darken a door**, to enter a door [O.E. *deorc*, dark].

darling (dȧr'ling) *n.* a beloved or lovable one;—*a.* cherished [dim. of O.E. *deore*, dear].

darn (dȧrn) *v.t.* to mend; to repair a hole by weaving threads at right angles to one another to imitate the original material;—*n.* the place darned.—**darn'ing-need'le** *n.* [prob. O.E. *dernan*, to hide].

dart (dȧrt) *n.* a pointed weapon thrown by hand; anything which pierces or wounds; a small seam or intake in garment to make it fit more closely; a sharp, forward movement.—*v.t.* to send forward quickly; to throw suddenly;—*v.i.* to run forward swiftly; to move like a dart.—**darts** *n.pl.* a popular game using darts and dartboard [M.E. *dart*, a javelin].

Darwinian (dår-win′i-ạn) *a.* pert. to Charles *Darwin* or to his Theory of Evolution;—*n.* one who accepts the theories of Darwin.

dash (dash) *v.t.* to throw violently; to cast down; to shatter;—*v.i.* to rush forward or move violently; to strike violently against;—*n.* a violent clashing of two bodies; a rapid movement; a mark of punctuation (—) to denote parenthesis; a small amount, as a *dash of soda*; a mild oath; a showy display.—**dash′-board** *n.* orig. a screen to protect occupants of a carriage from mud-splashes; in motor-vehicles, aircraft, etc. the panel in front of driver or pilot, containing gauges, indicators, etc.—**dash′ing** *a.* daring; spirited; showy.—**dash′y** *a.* showy [M.E. *daschen*, to strike down].

dastard (das′tard) *n.* a mean or cowardly fellow;—*a.* cowardly.—**das′tardly** *a.* despicably brutal.—**das′tardliness** *n.* [M.E. *dastard*, a stupid or mean person].

data (dā′ta) *n.pl.* (sing. **datum**) things known and from which inferences may be deduced [L. *data*, things given].

date (dāt) *n.* period or time of an event; epoch; duration; (*Slang*) appointment or engagement;—*v.t.* to note or fix the time of; to refer to as a starting-point.—*v.i.* to reckon back to a given time (foll. by *from* or *back* to).—**date′-line** *n.* approximately the 180° parallel of longitude on each side of which the date of the day differs [L. *datum*, a thing given].

date (dāt) *n.* the stone fruit of the Eastern date-palm, long-shaped, sweet and sticky.—**date′-palm** *n.* tree bearing date-fruit [Gk. *daktulos*].

dative (dā′tiv) *n.* the case of a noun which is the indirect object of a verb, or which is preceded by certain prepositions [L. *dare*, to give].

datum (dā′tum) *n.* a fact given;—*pl.* **da′ta** [L. *dare*, to give].

daub (dawb) *v.t.* to smear with mud or plaster; to paint crudely;—*n.* a crude painting; a smudge.—**daub′er** *n.* one who daubs; an inking pad used by etchers.—**daub′ing** *n.* a daub; rough cast for exterior of houses.—**daub′ster** *n.* a second-rate artist [O.Fr. *dauber*, to plaster].

daughter (daw′tẹr) *n.* a female child;—*a.* like a daughter; branch, as in *daughter-church*.—**daugh′ter-in-law** *n.* the wife of one's son [O.E. *dohtor*].

daunt (dawnt, dånt) *v.t.* to subdue the courage of; to reduce to passivity; to dismay; to dishearten; to disconcert.—**daunt′less** *a.* fearless; intrepid [O.Fr. fr. L. *domare*, to tame].

Dauphin (daw′fin) *n.* (*fem.* **Dau′phiness**) the French Crown prince; the title came to an end in 1830 [O.Fr. *daulphin*].

davenport (dav′en-pōrt) *n.* a kind of small writing desk; (*U.S.*) a settee [fr. the name of the maker].

Davis apparatus (dā-vis ap-ạ-rā′tus) *n.* an oxygen apparatus whereby a person trapped in a submarine is enabled to escape [name of inventor].

davits (da′vits) *n.* uprights, curved at top, projecting from ships' sides and fitted with tackle for lowering life-boats over side of ship [Fr. *davier*, forceps].

Davy Jones (dā′vi-jōnz) *n.* a sailor's name for the Devil.—**Davy Jones's locker**, the sea, as sailor's grave [etym unknown].

Davy-lamp (dā′vi-lamp) *n.* a safety lamp for miners; called after inventor, Sir Humphrey *Davy*.

daw (daw) *n.* a bird of the crow family; a jackdaw.—**daw′ish** *a.* like a daw [imit.].

dawdle (daw′dl) *v.i.* to loiter; to move very slowly [prob. conn. with *dandle*].

dawn (dawn) *v.i.* to grow towards daylight; to begin to be visible; (*Fig.*) to come to the mind;—*n.* daybreak; morning half-light; beginning [O.E. *daeg*, a day].

day (dā) *n.* the period from sunrise to sunset; the period of the sun's revolution on its axis; 24 hrs.; time of life; epoch.—**day′-bed** *n.* a divan.—**day′-book** *n.* a book kept by commercial firms for daily transactions.—**day′-boy** or **-girl** *n.* a pupil who is not a boarder at school.—**day′break** *n.* dawn.—**day′-dream** *n.* a reverie;—*v.i.* to indulge in reveries.—**day′-la′bourer** *n.* one who is paid for labour by the day.—**day′-light** *n.* natural light of the sun as oppos. to artificial light.—**to see daylight**, to comprehend a difficult point.—**day′-nur′sery** *n.* a creche.—**day′-school** *n.* school attended in daytime by pupils who live at home, as oppos. to *boarding*-school, or *night*-school.—**days′man** *n.* an umpire.—**day′spring** *n.* dawn.—**day′star** *n.* morning star.—**day′taller** *n.* a day-worker.—**day′time** *n.* time between sunrise and sunset.—**days of grace**, extra days, legally three days, allowed after specified date for paying an account.—**astronomical day**, from noon to noon.—**civil day**, from midnight to midnight.—**Judg(e)ment Day**, the end of the world.—**lunar** or **sidereal day**, day measured by the moon [O.E. *daeg*, a day].

daze (dāz) *v.t.* to confuse; to stupefy; to bewilder; to stun;—*n.* the state of being bewildered; stupefaction.—**dazz′le** *v.t.* to daze with sudden light; to make temporarily blind; to confuse mentally;—*n.* brilliancy.—**dazz′ling** *a.* [M.E. *dāsen*, to stupefy].

deacon (dē′kon) *n.* an assistant to a regular minister; one who superintends Church property and funds, and is concerned with business side of a Presbyterian Church; (*Scot.*) the chairman of an incorporated trade.—**dea′coness** *n.*—**dea′conhood** *n.* the office of deacon.—**dea′conry** *n.* the body of deacons.—**dea′conship** *n.* office of deacon [Gk. *diākonos*, a servant].

dead (ded) *a.* without life;—*adv.* wholly;—*n.* the most death-like time.—**dead′en** *v.t.* to impair in vigour, force, or feeling; to benumb.—**dead′ness** *n.*—**dead′-beat** *a.* without oscillation, applied to measuring instruments in which the pointer at once comes to rest; absolutely exhausted.—**dead′-end** *n.* a street with only one entrance.—**dead′-eye** *n.* a round, flat, wooden block with three holes to receive lanyard, used for tightening or extending shrouds of ship.—**dead′-heat** *n.* a race where two or more competitors reach the winning post at exactly the same time.—**dead language**, a language no longer spoken.—**dead′-lett′er** *n.* an obsolete law; an undelivered or unclaimed letter.—**dead′-lev′el** *a.* perfectly level.—**dead′-line** *n.* (*U.S.*) a painted line in a prison yard beyond which prisoners must not pass; last available date.—**dead′liness** *n.*—**dead′-load** *n.* the force acting on a structure because of gravitation; the weight of a commercial vehicle unloaded.—**dead′lock** *n.* a state of affairs which renders further progress impossible; an impasse.—**dead′-loss** *n.* a loss for which no compensation is payable.—**dead′ly** *a.* causing death; virulent; lethal;—*adv.* completely.—**deadly nightshade**, a poisonous plant, the belladonna.—**Dead March**, a funeral march.—**dead′-men** *n.pl.* (*Slang*) empty bottles.—**dead′-nett′le**, *n.* non-stinging plant resembling a nettle.—**dead′-pan** (*Slang*) *n.* an immobile face.—**dead′-reck′oning** *n.* (*Naut.*) the steering of a vessel by compass and not by the stars.—**dead′-wall** *n.* a blank wall.—**dead′-wat′er** *n.* stagnant water; the eddy-water closing in behind a ship.—**dead′-weight** *n.* a heavy burden.—**Dead Sea fruit**, fruit, pleasing to the eye, but crumbling to dust when touched; (*Fig.*) anything specious [O.E. *dead*, dead].

deaf (def) *a.* lacking partially or wholly the

sense of hearing; heedless; unwilling to listen.—**deaf'en** *v.t.* to make deaf; to render the walls of a house impervious to sound.—**deaf'ening** *a.* very loud; thunderous, as applause;—*n.* material used to make rooms sound-proof.—**deaf'ly** *adv.*—**deaf'-mute** *n.* one who is deaf and dumb.—**deaf'-mu'tism** *n.*—**deaf'ness** *n.* the state of being deaf [O.E. *deaf*, deaf].

deal (dēl) *v.t.* to divide; to dole out; to distribute, as in card games;—*v.i.* to traffic; to act; to give one's custom to; to behave towards;—*n.* a part or portion; distribution of playing cards; a business transaction; a bargain.—**deal'er** *n.*—**deal'ing** *n.* buying and selling; traffic; treatment;—*pl.* intercourse or relations with others.—**a raw deal,** iniquitously unfair treatment.—**a square deal,** fair treatment [O.E. *daelan*, to divide].

deal (dēl) *n.* plank of fir tree; pine or fir tree timber;—*a.* made of deal [O.E. *thille*, flooring]

dean (dēn) *n.* a dignitary in cathedral or collegiate churches; (in universities) the head of a faculty; a fellow of a college with disciplinary authority over undergraduates (Oxford); chairman of a guild.—**Dean of Guild,** a municipal official in Scotland with power to authorise within an area the building of new houses, and alteration of old houses.—**dean'ery** *n.* office or residence of a dean [O.Fr. *deien*, fr. L. *decanus*, an official with authority over ten monks].

dear (dēr) *a.* precious; much loved; highly esteemed or valued; costly; expensive; scarce;—*interj.* expressing sorrow, pity or wonder, as in *'Oh, dear!'*—**dear'ly** *adv.*—**dearth** (derth) *n.* deficiency; scarcity; want; famine [O.E. *deore*, precious].

death (deth) *n.* extinction of life; manner of dying; state of being dead; decease; dissolution; (*Fig.*) termination.—**death'-ag'ony** *n.* the final struggle just before death.—**death'-bed** *n.* the bed on which a person dies.—**death'-blow** *n.* a fatal stroke; (*Fig.*) overthrow.—**death'-du'ties** *n.pl.* duties payable to the State on property left at death.—**death'less** *a.* immortal.—**death'lessness** *n.*—**death'like** *a.* resembling death.—**death'ly** *adv.*—*a.* like death.—**death'-mask** *n.* a plaster-cast of a person's face taken immediately after death.—**death'-rate** *n.* the mortality rate per thousand of the population at a given time.—**death'-ratt'le** *n.* the noise in the throat sometimes made by a dying person immediately before death.—**death's'-head** *n.* the skull of a human skeleton.—**death's-head moth,** a species of moth with markings resembling skull and cross-bones.—**death'-throes** *n.pl.* last struggle before death.—**death'-warr'ant** *n.* an official document authorising execution of a criminal.—**death'-watch** *n.* a vigil; a beetle which makes a ticking sound [O.E. *death*, death].

debacle, débâcle (dā-bak'l) *n.* the sudden breaking up of ice in a river; (*Fig.*) a rout; collapse; a reverse; a disaster [Fr.].

debar (de-bȧr') *v.t.* to cut off from entrance; to hinder; to prohibit; to exclude; to preclude;—*pr.p.* **debar'ring.**—*pa.p.* **debarred'.**—**debar'ment** *n.* [L. *de*; and *bar*].

debark (de-bȧrk') *v.t.* and *v.i.* to disembark, oppos. of *embark*.—**debarka'tion, debark'ment** *n.* [Fr. *débarquer*, to disembark].

debase (de-bās') *v.t.* to reduce to a lower state; to disgrace; to degrade; to adulterate.—**debas'ing** *a.* corrupting, esp. in moral sense.

debate (de-bāt') *n.* controversy; wrangle; argument; dispute; discussion of a subject in Parliament;—*v.t.* to discuss; to dispute; to contend; to argue in detail;—*v.i.* to take part in a discussion; to reflect.—*pr.p.* **debat'ing.**—*pa.p.* **debat'ed.**—**debat'able** *a.* open to debate; questionable.—**debat'er** *n.* [L. *de*, from; *batuere*, to strike or beat].

debauch (de-bawch') *v.t.* to corrupt; to vitiate; to make depraved; to seduce; to pervert;—*n.* excess in eating and drinking; orgy; licentious indulgence; dissipation.—**debauched'** *a.* dissipated.—**debauch'ee** *n.* a dissipated person.—**debauch'ery** *n.* moral corruption; intemperate indulgence.—**debauch'ment** *n.* [O.Fr. *debaucher*, to entice].

debenture (de-ben'tūr) *n.* a certificate acknowledging a debt and guaranteeing repayment of loan with interest; [L. *debentur mihi*, first words of certificate meaning 'these sums are owing to me.']

debilitate (de-bil'i-tāt) *v.t.* to weaken; to make infirm; to prostrate; to enervate.—**debilita'tion, debil'ity** *n.* enervation; languour [L. *debilitare*, to weaken].

debit (deb'it) *n.* an item entered on debtor side of an account (oppos. of *credit*);—*v.t.* to charge with debt [L. *debere*, *debitum*, to owe].

debonair (deb'ō-ner) *a.* bearing oneself cheerfully and well; of good air or mien; spruce [Fr. *de bon air*, of amiable disposition].

debouch (de-bòòsh', de-bouch') *v.i.* to march from narrow valley into the open; (of rivers) to flow out from confined area into opener spaces.—**debouch'ure** *n.* the mouth of a river [Fr. *déboucher*, to pour out].

débris (dā'brē, deb'rē) *n.* fragments (taken collectively) of demolished buildings; rubble; ruins [Fr. *briser*, to break].

debt (det) *n.* something owed to another; a liability; an obligation.—**debt'ee** *n.* a creditor.—**debt'or** *n.* one who owes a debt; in bookkeeping (abbrev. **Dr.**) the debit side of an account.—**bad debt,** one which is unlikely to be repaid [L. *debere*, *debitum*, to owe].

debunk (dé-bungk') *v.t.* (*Slang*) to remove false sentiment from; to strip of humbug.

début, debut (dā-bòò') *n.* a first appearance in public, socially or as an artiste.—**debutant'** *n.* (*fem.* **debutante'**) one, esp. a girl, making her first appearance in society, or being presented at Court; abbrev. **deb.** [Fr. *début*, a first stroke, aim, or goal].

deca- (dek'a) *prefix* fr. Gk. *deka*, ten, found in many scientific and technical terms.

decade (dek'ād) *n.* a group of ten things; a period of ten years [Gk. *deka*, ten].

decadence (dek'a-dens or de-kā'dens) **dec'adency** *n.* deterioration; degeneration; decay; a falling off in moral or aesthetic standards.—**dec'adent** *n.* a writer or artist whose work expresses ideas and ideals of lowered moral value;—*a.* deteriorating; decaying [L. *decadentia*, a falling away].

decagon (dek'a-gon) *n.* a plane figure of ten sides and ten angles [Gk. *gonia*, an angle].

decagram(me) (dek'a-gram) *n.* in the metric system, a weight of 10 grams, i.e. 0.353 oz. [Gk. *deka*, ten; *gramma*, a weight].

decahedron (dek-a-hē'dron) *n.* a solid figure or body having ten sides.—**decahe'dral** *a.* [Gk. *deka*, ten; *hedra*, face of a solid].

decalcify (dē-kal'si-fī) *v.t.* to deprive bones (esp. teeth) of lime.

decalitre (dek'a-lē-tr) *n.* a measure of capacity equal to 10 litres—about 2¼ imperial gallons [Gk. *deka*, ten; Fr. *litre*].

Decalogue (dek'a-log) *n.* the Ten Commandments [Gk. *deka*, ten; *logos*, a word or discourse].

decametre (dek'a-mē-tr) *n.* in the metric system a measure of ten metres, or 32.8 ft. [Gk. *deka*, ten; *metron*, measure].

decamp (dē-kamp') *v.i.* to move away from a camping ground; to move off suddenly or secretly [Fr. *décamper*, to break camp].

decanal (dek'a-nal) *a.* pert. to a deanery or a dean [L. *decanus*, a dean].

decant (dē-kant') *v.t.* to pour off liquid without disturbing sediment, esp. used of wines.—**decant'er** *n.* a slender necked glass bottle into which wine is decanted [L. *de*, from; *canthus*, rim of a cup].

decapitate (dē-kap'i-tāt) *v.t.* to cut off the head; to behead; to decollate.—**decapita'tion** *n.* [L. *de*, from; *caput*, head].

decapod (dek′a-pod) *n.* a shellfish of the crab family having five pairs of legs; a cephalopod with ten legs (or arms) on the thorax; a ten-footed crustacean;—*a.* having ten legs.—**deca′podal, deca′podous** *a.* [Gk. *deka,* ten; *pous,* a foot].
decarbonise (dē-kâr′bō-nīz) *v.t.* to deprive of carbon or carbonic acid; to remove a deposit of carbon, as from a motor cylinder. Also **decar′bonate, decar′burise.—decarbonisa′tion, decarburisa′tion** *n.*
decastyle (dek′a-stīl) *n.* a colonnade with ten pillars [Gk. *deka,* ten; *stulos,* a column].
decasyllabic (dek-a-si-lab′ik) *a.* having ten syllables.—**decasy′llable** *n.* [Gk. *deka,* ten; *sun,* with; *lambanein,* to take].
decathlon (de-kath′lon) *n.* a group of ten different contests at Olympic games [Gk. *deka,* ten; *athlon,* a contest].
decay (dē-kā′) *v.i.* to rot away; to become decomposed; to waste away; to wither.—*v.t.* to impair;—*n.* gradual wasting or corruption; deterioration; consumption.—**decayed′** *a.* rotting.—**decayed′ness** *n.* [L. *de,* down; *cadere,* to fall].
decease (dē-sēs′) *n.* death;—*v.i.* to die.—**deceased′** *a.* dead;—*n.* a dead person [L. *decessus,* a departure].
deceit (dē-sēt′) *n.* fraud; duplicity; wile.—**deceit′ful** *a.* crafty; fraudulent; illusory.—**deceit′fulness** *n.*—**deceive′** *v.t.* to delude; to cheat.—**deceiv′able** *a.*—**deceiv′ableness** *n.*—**deceiv′ably** *adv.*—**deceiv′er** *n.* [L. *decipere, deceptum,* to beguile].
decelerate (dē-sel′ęr-āt) *v.t.* and *v.i.* to reduce speed [L. *de,* from; *celer,* swift].
December (dē-sem′bęr) *n.* orig. the tenth month of the Roman calendar; the twelfth month of the year [L.*decem,* ten].
decennial (dē-sen′i-ąl) *a.* lasting for ten years or happening every ten years.—**decenn′ary** *n.*—**decenn′iad** *n.*—**decenn′ially** *adv.* —**decenn′ium** *n.* a period of ten years [L. *decem,* ten; *annus,* a year].
decent (dē′sent) *a.* fitting or becoming; not immodest; suitable; comely; sufficient; (of persons) kindly; (*Colloq.*) pleasant.—**de′cency** *n.* the state or quality of being decent.—**de′cently** *adv.*—**de′centness** *n.* [L. *decere,* to be fitting].
decentralise (dē-sen′trąl-īz) *v.t.* to remove from the centre or point of concentration and distribute among smaller areas; esp. to enlarge powers of local government at expense of central authority.
deception (dē-sep′shun) *n.* the act of deceiving; fraud; illusion.—**decept′ible** *a.*—**deceptibil′ity** *n.*—**decep′tive** *a.* causing a false impression. —**decep′tively** *adv.* [L. *deceptus,* deceived].
decibel (des′i-bel) *n.* one transmission unit; one tenth of a bel.; the smallest variation in sound that the human ear can detect [L. *decem,* ten; *bel,* a coined word].
decide (dē-sīd′) *v.t.* to determine the result of; to make up one's mind about; to settle an issue;—*v.t.* to give a decision; to come to a conclusion.—**decid′ed** *a.* clear; not ambiguous; determined.—**decid′edly** *adv.*—**decision** (dē-sizh′un) *n.* the act of settling; determination; settlement; judgment.—**decis′ive** *a.* conclusive; resolute.—**decis′ively** *adv.*—**decis′iveness** *n.* [L. *decidere,* to cut off].
deciduous (de-sid′ū-us) *a.* (of trees) shedding leaves in autumn, oppos. of coniferous or evergreen; not lasting; liable to fall; (used also of a deer's horns) [L. *decidere,* to fall down].
decigram, decigramme (des′i-gram) *n.* the tenth part of a gram (metric system) [L. *decem,* ten; Fr. *gramme*].
decimal (des′i-mąl) *a.* pert. to tens; numbered or proceeding by tens;—*n.* a fraction with its denominator (unexpressed) 10, or some power of 10.—**decimalisa′tion** *n.*—**dec′imalise** *v.t.* to reduce to the decimal system.—**decimal fraction,** a fraction the (unexpressed) denominator of which is 10 or a power of 10 [L. *decimus,* tenth].
decimate (des′i-māt) *v.t.* to kill (as in Ancient Rome) every tenth man, chosen by lot, as punishment; to reduce the numbers of, very considerably;—**decima′tion** *n.* [L. *decimus,* tenth].
decimetre (des-i-mē′tr) *n.* one tenth of a metre [L. *decem,* ten; Fr. *mètre*].
decipher (dē-sī′fęr) *v.t.* to read a cipher; to make out what is illegible, unintelligible, or written in strange symbols.
decision See under **decide.**
deck (dek) *v.t.* to adorn; to cover; to dress up; to cover with a deck (of a ship); -*n.* a covering; the horizontal platform extending from one side of ship to the other; a pack of cards, or part of pack remaining after dealing.—**deck′-chair** *n.* a light-weight, collapsible, and easily portable chair, made partly of canvas.—**deck′-hand** *n.* a person employed on deck of ship.—**deck′-house** *n.* a small shelter on deck.—**deck′ing** *n.* adornment.—**hurr′icane-deck,** *n.* a half-deck.—**main′-deck** *n.* deck below the upper deck.—**quart′er-deck** *n.* part of the deck abaft the main mast.—**to sweep the deck,** to win every game.—**doub′le-deck′er** *n.* a vehicle, as tram, bus, or ferry, with upper and lower passenger-decks [Dut. *dekkan,* to cover].
deckle (dek′l) *n.* the gauge on a paper-making machine.—**deck′le-edge** *n.* the rough feathery edge of hand-made paper.—**deck′le-edged** *a.* [Ger. *Deckel,* cover].
declaim (dē-klām′) *v.t.* to recite in a rhetorical manner;—*v.i.* to make a formal speech.—**declama′tion** *n.* a set speech; a rhetorical and dramatic address.—**declam′atory** *a.* pert. to a declamation; ostentatiously rhetorical [L. *declamare,* to shout out].
declare (dē-klār′) *v.t.* to proclaim; to make clear; to state publicly; to state in the presence of a witness;—*v.i.* to make a declaration; to express a favourable attitude towards; (*Cricket*) to announce innings closed; (*at Customs*) to admit possession of dutiable goods.—**declar′able** *a.*—**declara′tion** *n.* the act of declaring; a solemn statement. —**declar′atory** *a.* making clear or manifest; explanatory [L. *declarare,* to make clear].
declension (dē-klen′shun) *n.* the act of falling away; (*Fig.*) deterioration; (*Gram.*) the inflection of nouns, pronouns, adjectives; a class of nouns, etc. so inflected.—**declen′sional** *a.* [L. *declinare,* to fall away].
decline (dē-klīn′) *v.t.* to bend downward; to refuse; to avoid; (*Gram.*) to give inflections of a word in oblique cases;—*v.i.* to slope; to hang down; to fall in value or quantity; to pine away; to languish;—*n.* a falling off; wasting disease.—**declin′able** *a.* able to be inflected.—**declina′tion** *n.* a sloping away [L. *declinare,* to fall away].
declivity (de-kliv′i-ti) *n.* a downward slope; a gradual descent.—**decliv′itous, decli′vous** *a.* [L. *declivis,* sloping down].
declutch (dē-kluch′) *v.t.* to disengage the clutch which connects engine and wheels of a motor car.
decoct (dē-kokt′) *v.t.* to prepare by boiling; to extract essence by boiling down.—**decoc′tible, decoc′tive** *a.*—**decoc′tion** *n.* the extract or essence procured by boiling; act or process of decocting [L. *decoquere,* to boil down].
decode (dē-kōd′) *v.t.* to translate a message in code into ordinary language.
décolletage (dā-kol′tàzh) *n.* the line of a woman's low cut evening dress; the neck and shoulders of a person wearing such a dress.—**décolleté** *a.* low-necked [Fr.].
decolour (dē-kul′ur) *v.t.* to deprive of colour; to bleach.
decompose (dē-kom-pōz) *v.t.* to break up into elements; to separate the constituent parts of; to analyse;—*v.i.* to decay;

become rotten.—**decomposi'tion** *n.* act of decomposing; decay; putrefaction.

decompound (dē-kom-pound') *v.t.* to compound again;—*a.* compounded a second time. —**decompound'able** *a.*

decontaminate (dē-kon-tam'in-āt) *v.t.* to cleanse from, esp. from effects of poison-gas. —**decontamina'tion** *n.*

decontrol (dē-kon-trōl') *v.t.* to release from government or state control.

décor (dā-kor') *n.* the decoration, or setting of a theatre, stage, or room [Fr.].

decorate (dek'o-rāt) *v.t.* to beautify; to embellish; to honour a person by giving a medal or badge of honour.—**dec'orated** *a.*;—**decora'tion** *n.* an ornament; a badge of honour; insignia.—**dec'orative** *a.* ornamental.—**dec'orativeness** *n.*—**dec'orator** *n.* one who papers and paints houses, shops, etc. [L. *decus*, an ornament].

decorous (de-kō'rus or dek'o-rus) *a.* becoming seemly; decent; staid.—**decor'ously** *adv.*—**decor'ousness** *n.*—**deco'rum** *n.* decency; behaviour in keeping with social conventions [L. *decus*, an ornament].

decorticate (dē-kor'ti-kāt) *v.t.* to deprive of the bark, husk, or peel.—**decortica'tion** *n.*

decoy (dē-koi') *v.t.* to lead into a snare; (*Fig.*) to allure; to entice by specially tempting means ;—*n.* a device for leading wild birds into a snare; an enticement [Dut. *kooi*, a cage].

decrease (dē-krēs') *v.t.* to lessen; to make smaller; to reduce gradually;—*v.i.* to become less; to wane; to abate;—*n.* gradual diminution; a lessening.—**decreas'ingly** *adv.* [L. *de*, from; *crescere*, to grow].

decree (dē-krē') *n.* an order made by a competent authority; an edict; decision in a law court; an established law; (*Theol.*) divine purpose.—*v.t.* to determine judicially; to order;—*v.i.* to decide authoritatively.—**decre'tal** *a.* pert. to a decree;—*n.* an order given by a high authority, esp. the Pope;—**decre'tive** *a.*—**decree nisi**, a decree which becomes absolute after fixed period, unless cause to the contrary be proved (as in Divorce cases) [L. *decretum*, decreed].

decrement (dek're-ment) *n.* the act or state of decreasing; the quantity lost by decrease [L. *decrementum*, a decrease].

decrepit (dē-krep'it) *a.* worn out or enfeebled by old age; infirm; broken down; (of things) ramshackle.—**decrep'itude, decrep'itness** *n.* [L. *decrepitus*, noiseless, very old].

decrepitate (dē-krep'i-tāt) *v.t.* to roast to crackling point (salts, etc.);—*v.i.* to crackle because of extreme heat.—**decrepita'tion** *n.* (L. *de*, from; *crepitare*, to crackle].

decrescent (dē-kres'ent) *a.* becoming gradually less; waning.

decretal See **decree.**

decry (dē-krī') *v.t.* to cry down; to bring into disrepute; to abuse.—**decri'al** *n.* act of decrying [L. *de*, from; Fr. *crier*, to cry].

decumbent (de-kum'bent) *a.* bending or lying down; recumbent [L. *decumbere*, to lie down].

decuple (dek'ū-pl) *a.* tenfold [L. *decuplus*, tenfold].

decurrent (dē-kur'ent) *a.* running or extending downward.

decussate (de-kus'āt, dek'us-āt) *v.t.* to intersect at an acute angle, as an X.—**decuss'ated, decuss'ate** *a.* crossed; intersected [L. *decussare*, to divide in form of an X].

dedicate (ded'i-kāt) *v.t.* to set apart and consecrate to a holy purpose; to give oneself wholly to a worthy purpose; to inscribe a book to someone as mark of appreciation or admiration.—**ded'icated** *a.* devoted.—**dedica'tion** *n.* —**ded'icatory** *a.* containing a dedication; complimentary [L. *dedicare*, to announce].

deduce (dē-dūs') *v.t.* to draw from; to reach a conclusion by deductive reasoning; to infer; to trace down.—**deduce'ment** *n.* that which is inferred.—**deduc'ible** *a.* inferred.—**deduct'** *v.t.* to remove; to subtract.—**deduct'ible** *a.*—**deduc'tion** *n.* the act or process of deducting; the amount subtracted; the inference or conclusion arrived at.—**deduct'ive** *a.* capable of being deduced.—**deduct'ively** *adv.* [L. *deducere*, to lead down].

dee (dē) *n.* a hollow cylinder used in the cyclotron, in which a spiral beam of protons is continuously accelerated thus increasing their energy [See **cyclotron**].

deed (dēd) *n.* that which is done; an act; exploit; achievement; a legal document or contract.—**deed'-poll** *n.* (*Law*) a deed executed by one party, the document itself having its edge *polled* or cut straight, not indented, as in *indenture*. [O.E. *daed*; *don*, to do].

deem (dēm) *v.t.* to believe on consideration; to judge.—**deem'ster** *n.* one who judges; one of two chief judges of the Isle of Man. Also **demp'ster** [O.E. *dēman*, to judge].

deep (dēp) *a.* extending far below the surface; having considerable breadth; low in situation; dark; intense; abstruse; low in pitch; sagacious;—*adv.* to a great depth;—*n.* that which is deep; the sea.—**deep'en** *v.t.* to make deep;—*v.i.* to become deeper.—**deep'most** *a.* deepest. —**deep'ness** *n.* depth.—**deep'-root'ed** *a.* firmly established.—**deep'-seat'ed** *a.* (of disease) not superficial.—**depth** *n.* the quality of being deep [O.E. *deop*, deep].

deer (dēr) *n.* any of the ruminant quadrupeds, such as stag, roebuck, fallow deer, etc.—**deer'hound** *n.* a dog for hunting deer; a stag-hound. —**deer'skin** *n.* the hide, or leather made from hide of a deer.—**deer'-stalk'er** *n.*—**deer'-stalk'ing** *n.* hunting deer by stealing on them unawares. —**deerstalker cap**, one with peaks in front and behind. [O.E. *dēor*, an animal].

deface (dē-fās') *v.t.* to destroy or mar the external appearance of; to disfigure.— **deface'able** *a.*—**deface'ment** *n.* the act or result of defacing; the thing which defaces; a blemish [Fr. *défacer*, to mar].

defalcate (dē-fal'kāt) *v.t.* to deduct a part of, esp. money, by misappropriation; to embezzle.—**defalca'tion** *n.*—**def'alcator** *n.* [L. *de*, from; *falx*, a sickle].

defame (dē-fām') *v.t.* to harm or destroy the good name or reputation of; to slander.—**defama'tion** *n.* act of defaming.—**defam'atory** *a.* tending to defame or slander [L. *diffamare*, to spread an evil report].

default (dē-fawlt') *n.* fault; neglect; defect; failure to appear in a law-court when summoned; failure to account for money held in trust.—**default'er** *n.*—**Judgment by default** (*Law*) decision given in favour of plaintiff when defendant fails to appear [O.Fr. *defaillir*, to fail].

defeasance (dē-fēz'ans) *n.* defeat; a rendering null and void.—**defeas'ible** *a.* capable of being annulled [O.Fr. *desfaire*, to undo].

defeat (de-fēt) *v.t.* to overcome; to subdue; to conquer;—*n.* act of defeating; overthrow; conquest.—**defeat'ism** *n.* the attitude of mind of those who accept their country's defeat as inevitable.—**defeat'ist** *n.*—*a.* pert. to defeatism [O.Fr. *desfait*, undone].

defecate (def'e-kāt) *v.t.* to clear or strain impurities from, as lees, dregs, etc.;—*v.i.* to void excrement from the bowels.—**defeca'tion** *n.* [L. *de*, from; *faex*, dregs].

defect (dē-fekt') *n.* a want; an imperfection; absence of something necessary for completeness.—**defec'tion** *n.* a failure in duty; the act of abandoning allegiance to a cause.—**defect'ive** *a.* incomplete; imperfect; faulty; (*Gram.*) not having all the parts to make the complete conjugation of a verb.—**defect'ively** *adv.*—**defect'iveness** *n.*—**mental defective**, one who is sub-normal in intelligence [L. *deficere*, to fail].

defence (dē-fens') *n.* the act of defending; that which shields or protects; vindication justification; (*Law*) a plea or reply to a charge —**defence'less** *a.* open to attack.—**defence'lessly**

adv.—**defence'lessness** *n.*—**Civil Defence,** an organisation in World War 2, including such services as police, A.R.P. wardens, N.F.S., etc. [L. *defendere,* to protect].
defend (dē-fend') *v.t.* to protect; to ward off attack; to maintain; to justify; to vindicate; (*Law*) to state the case of an accused person (by counsel).—**defend'able** *a.*—**defend'ant** *n.* one who defends; the accused in a criminal case; the one prosecuted in a civil case.—**defend'er** *n.*—**defens'ible** *a.*—**defensibil'ity** *n.*—**defens'ive** *a.* serving to defend; resisting attack; —*n.* the position of defending against attack. **defens'ively** adv. [L. *defendere,* to protect].
defer (dē-fer') *v.i.* to submit; to yield or bow to the opinion of another;—*v.t.* to bring or lay before.—**def'erence** *n.* the act of deferring. **deferen'tial** *a.* showing deference.—**deferen'tially** *adv.* [L. *deferre,* to bring before].
defer (dē-fer') *v.t.* to put off; to postpone;—*v.i.* to delay.—*pr.p.* **defer'ring;** *pa.p.* **deferred'.** —**defer'able, defer'rable** *a.*—**defer'ment** *n.* delay; postponement [L. *deferre,* to postpone].
defiance (dē-fī'ans) *n.* the act of defying; a challenge to combat; contempt; opposition. —**defi'ant** *a.* aggressively hostile; insolent.—**defi'antly** *adv.*—**defi'antness** *n.* [Fr. *défier,* to challenge].
deficient (dē-fish'ent) *a.* wanting; failing; lacking a full supply; incomplete.— **defic'iency, defic'ience** *n.* shortcoming, shortage; defect.—**defic'iently** *adv.*—**deficit** (def'i-sit) *n.* shortage or deficiency of revenue; excess of expenditure over income.—**deficiency disease,** disease such as scurvy, caused by lack of certain vitamins in the diet.—**mentally deficient,** sub-normal in intelligence [L. *deficere,* to be wanting].
defile (dē'fīl) *n.* a narrow pass in which troops can march only in single or narrow files;—*v.i.* (dē-fīl') to march off file by file [Fr. *défiler,* to thread].
defile (dē-fīl') *v.t.* to make unclean; to soil; to dirty; to desecrate.—**defile'ment** *n.* the act of defiling [L. *de*,; O.E. *fylan,* to pollute].
define (dē-fīn') *v.t.* to determine the boundaries of; to state the exact meaning of; to circumscribe; to designate; to specify.—**defin'able** *a.*—**definite** (def'i-nit) *a.* fixed or defined; exact; precise; unambiguous; clear; specific; restricted.—**def'initely** *adv.*—**def'initeness** *n.*—**defini'tion** *n.* description of a thing by its properties; explanation of the exact meaning of a word or term; distinctness.—**defin'itive** *a.* limiting; determining; final; positive [L. *de,* down; *finis,* end].
deflagrate (def'la-grāt) *v.t.* to burn rapidly with flames;—*v.i.* to blaze up.—**deflagra'tion** *n.* [L. *de,* down; *flagrare,* to flame].
deflate (dē-flāt') *v.t.* to empty of air or gas (as in tyre, balloon, etc.); to reduce inflated currency.—**defla'tion** *n.* [L. *de,* down; *flare,* to blow].
deflect (dē-flekt') *v.t.* to turn aside; to divert from the right direction;—*v.i.* to swerve; to deviate.—**deflect'ed** *a.*—**deflec'tion, deflex'ion** *n.*—**deflect'or** *n.* that which causes deflection [L. *de,* from; *flectere,* to bend].
deflorate (dē-flō'rāt) *a.* (*Bot.*) past the flowering stage.—**deflora'tion** *n.* [L. *de,* away; *flos,* a flower].
deflour, deflower (dē-flour') *v.t.* to deprive of flowers; to ravish.—**deflow'erer** *n.* [O.Fr. *defleurer,* to strip of flowers].
defoliation (dē-fō-li-ā'shun) *n.* the shedding of leaves.—**defol'iate** *v.t.* to deprive of leaves. —**defol'iate, defol'iated** *a.*
deforce (dē-fōrs') *v.t.* to keep from lawful possession; (*Scots Law*) to resist a bailiff [O.Fr. *deforcier*].
deforest (dē-for'est) *v.t.* to deprive of forests. —**deforesta'tion** *n.*
deform (dē-form') *v.t.* to mar or alter the form of; to make misshapen; to disfigure.—**deformed'** *a.*—**deforma'tion** *n.*—**deform'ity** *n.* the state of being disfigured; a malformation.
defraud (dē-frawd') *v.t.* to deprive of, by fraud; cheat.
defray (dē-frā') *v.t.* to bear the cost of; to provide the money for, as in to *defray the expenses.*—**defray'al, defray'ment** *n.* [O.Fr. *desfrayer,* to pay the cost].
defrock (dē-frok') *v.t.* to unfrock, as of a priest deprived of ecclesiastical status.
deft (deft) *a.* dexterous; adroit; handy.—**deft'ly** *adv.*—**deft'ness** *n.* skill; dexterity [O.E. *gedaeftan,* to make smooth].
defunct (dē-fungkt') *a.* dead; deceased; (of things) obsolete;—*n.* a dead person [L. *defunctus,* finished].
defy (dē-fī') *v.t.* to challenge; to dare; to set authority at naught.—*pr.p.* **defy'ing;** *pa.p.* **defied'** [L. *dis,* away; *fidere,* to trust].
de-gauss (dē-gous') *v.t.* (*World War* 2) to neutralise a ship's magnetism to prevent it detonating magnetic mines [L. *de,* from; *Gauss,* a German physicist].
degenerate (dē-jen'er-āt) *v.i.* to decline from a noble to a lower state of development; to become worse physically and morally;—*n.* a person of low moral standards;—*a.* having become less than one's kind.—**degen'eracy** *n.*—**degen'erately** *adv.*—**degen'erateness** *n.*—**degenera'tion** *n.* process of degenerating.—**degen'erative** *a.* tending to make degenerate [L. *degener,* unlike one's race].
deglutinate (dē-glòò'ti-nāt) *v.t.* to separate by dissolving glue [L. *de,* from; *gluten,* glue].
deglutition (dē-glòò-tish'un) *n.* the act or power of swallowing [L. *de,* down; *glutire,* to swallow].
degrade (dē-grād') *v.t.* to reduce in status; to lower the moral reputation of; to disgrace. —**degradation** (deg-ra-dā'shun) *n.* the act of degrading; the state or process of becoming degraded; degeneration; abasement [L. *de,* down; *gradus,* a step].
degree (dē-grē') *n.* a step upward or downward; station or status; extent, as in *degree of proficiency;* rank to which one is admitted by a university; the 360th part of a revolution; a measured space on a thermometer, protractor, etc.; (*Gram.*) modification of adjectives and adverbs by adding of suffix —*er* (comparative), and—*est* (superlative) to indicate intensifying of meaning.—**third degree** (*U.S.*) a long, searching cross-examination by police of a suspect [L. *de,* down; *gradus,* a step].
degression (dē-gresh'un) *n.* a going down; a lowering of rate of taxation on certain wage-levels [L. *degredi,* to go down].
degust (dē-gust') *v.t., v.i.* to taste; to relish; to sample. Also **degust'ate.**—**degusta'tion** *n.* [L. *de,* from; *gustare,* to taste].
dehiscent (dē-his'ent) *a.* (of seeds) bursting open, gaping.—**dehisce'** *v.i.* to gape;—**dehis'cence** *n.* [L. *dehiscere,* to gape].
dehumanise (dē-hūm'an-īz) *v.t.* to deprive of human qualities, or of tenderness of feeling [L. *de,* from; *humanus,* human].
dehydrate (dē-hī'drāt) *v.t.* to remove water from;—*v.i.* to lose water.—**dehydra'tion** *n.* the process of reducing bulk and weight of food by removing water from products (e.g. dried eggs, milk, potatoes, etc.) [L. *de,* from; Gk. *hudor,* water].
de-ice (dē-īs') *v.t.* to free from ice (as wings of aircraft).
deicide (dē'i-sīd) *n.* the killing of a god; one who kills a god; the act of putting Jesus Christ to death [L. *deus,* god; *caedere,* to kill].
deify (dē'i-fī) *v.t.* to make a god of; to exalt to the rank of divinity; to worship.—**deif'ic, -al** *a.* making godlike.—**deifica'tion** *n.*—**de'iform** *a.* of godlike form [L. *deus,* a god; *facere,* to make].
deign (dān) *v.i.* to condescend; to stoop;—*v.t.* to condescend to do; to grant [L. *dignari,* to deem worthy].
deism (dē'izm) *n.* belief, on purely rational

grounds, in the existence of God without accepting the revelation implied in religious dogma.—**de'ist** *n.*—**deis'tic, -al** *a.*—**de'ity** *n.* God, the Supreme Being; a pagan god or goddess [L. *deus*, god].

deject (dē-jekt') *v.t.* to cast down; to dishearten; to depress; to dispirit.—**deject'ed** *a.* downcast; moody; in low spirits.—**deject'edly** *adv.*—**deject'edness** *n.*—**dejec'tion,** lowness of spirits; (*Med.*) evacuation of the bowels [L. *de*, down; *jacere*, to throw].

dekko (dek'ō) *n.* (*Mil. Slang*) a look; a hurried glimpse [Hind. *dekhna*, look].

delaine (dę-lān') *n.* a light weight dress fabric orig. of wool (now wool mixed with cotton) [Fr. *de laine*, of wool].

delate (dē-lāt') *v.t.* to publish; to accuse; to bring information against a person [L. *delatus*, denounced].

delay (dē-lā') *v.t.* to put off; to postpone; to stop temporarily;—*v.i.* to linger; to dawdle; to procrastinate;—*n.* a stoppage; tardiness.—**delay'er** *n.* [O.Fr. *delaier*, to prolong].

delectable (de-lek'tą-bl) *a.* highly pleasing; delightful; enjoyable.—**delect'ableness** *n.*—**delect'ably** *adv.*—**delecta'tion** *n.* pleasure; delight [L. *delectare*, to delight].

delegate (del'e-gāt) *v.t.* to entrust authority to a deputy.—*n.* a deputy; a representative of a society at a conference.—**delega'tion** *n.* act of delegating; body of delegates.—**del'egacy** *n.* [L. *de*, from; *legare*, to send].

delete (dē-lēt') *v.t.* to erase; to strike out (word or passage).—**delen'da** *n.pl.* things to be blotted out.—**dele'tion** *n.* [L. *delere*, to blot out].

deleterious (del-e-tē'ri-us) *a.* capable of harming or destroying health; pernicious.—**delete'riously** *adv.*—**delete'riousness** *n.* [Gk. *dēleisthai*, to harm].

delf (delf) *n.* glazed earthenware, orig. made at *Delft* in Holland. Also **delft, delft'-ware.**

deliberate (dē-lib'e-rāt) *v.t.* to weigh in the mind; to discuss.—*v.i.* to consider carefully; to take counsel; to hesitate;—*a.* carefully considered; slow.—**delib'erately** *adv.*—**delib'erateness** *n.*—**delibera'tion** *n.* the act of carefully considering; coolness and slowness of action or speech.—**delib'erative** *a.* showing deliberation [L. *deliberare*, to ponder].

delicate (del-i-kāt) *a.* dainty; frail; slender; exquisitely wrought; nicely adjusted; highly sensitive or perceptive.—**del'icacy** *n.* fineness of shape, colour, texture, or feeling; something which pleases the palate; a dainty; tact.—**del'icately** *adv.*—**del'icateness** *n.*—**del'icates** *n.pl.* dainties [L. *delicatus*, delightful].

delicatessen (del-i-ką-tes'en) *n.pl.* table delicacies, esp. cold cooked meats, hors d'oeuvres, etc.; a shop selling these [Ger.].

delicious (dē-lish'us) *a.* exquisite; charming (to senses or mind); delightful.—**deli'ciously** *adv.* [L. *deliciae*, delight].

delight (dē-līt') *v.t.* to give great pleasure to; to charm;—*v.i.* to take delight;—*n.* the source of pleasure; great satisfaction; joy.—**delight'ful** *a.* affording delight; charming.—**delight'fully** *adv.* [L. *delectare*, to delight].

delimit (dē-lim'it) *v.t.* to fix the limit or boundaries of.—**delimita'tion** *n.*

delineate (dē-lin'ē-āt) *v.t.* to draw an outline; to sketch; to portray; (*Fig.*) to describe clearly in words.—**delinea'tion** *n.* the act of delineating; a portrayal in line or words; a sketch.—**delin'eator** *n.* [L. *de*, from; *linea*, a line].

delinquent (dē-lin'kwent) *n.* one who fails in duty; an offender or criminal, esp. of a young person;—*a.* failing in duty.—**delin'quency** [L. *de*, from; *linquere*, to leave].

deliquesce (del-i-kwes') *v.i.* to liquefy by absorbing moisture from the air.—**deliques'cence** *n.*—**deliques'cent** *a.* liquefying in air [L. *deliquescere*, to melt away].

delirious (de-lir'i-us) *a.* wandering in the mind; light-headed; raving; incoherent.—**delira'tion** *n.* madness.—**delir'iously** *adv.*—**delir'iousness** *n.*—**delir'ium** *n.* a fever of the brain caused by grave physical illness or nervous shock; strong excitement.—**delirium tremens** (*abbrev.* D.T.) violent delirium resulting from excessive alcoholism [L. *delirus*, crazy].

delitescence (del-i-tes'ens) *n.* state of being concealed.—**delites'cent** *a.* lurking; lying hid [L. *delitescere*, to lie hid].

deliver (dē-liv'ęr) *v.t.* to liberate (from danger, captivity, restraint); to save from sin; to distribute or hand over; to pronounce (as a speech); to execute (as an attack); to give birth to a child (used passively).—**deliv'erable** *a.*—**deliv'erance** *n.* liberation; state of being delivered; the formal statement of an opinion.—**deliv'erer** *n.*—**deliv'ery** *n.* the act of delivering; the style of utterance of a public speech or sermon; (*Cricket*) the manner of bowling the ball; (*Med.*) the act of giving birth [L. *de*, from; *liberare*, to set free].

dell (del) *n.* a small, deep valley; a hollow [M.E. *delle*, a dell].

Delphian, Delphic (del'fi-ąn, del'fik) *a.* pert. to the town of *Delphi* in Ancient Greece, or to the oracle of Apollo in that town; oracular.

Delphinium (del-fin'i-um) *n.* a genus of annual, biennial, and perennial herbaceous flowering plants [Gk. *delphinion*, larkspur].

delta (del'tą) *n.* the fourth letter of the Greek alphabet, its form as a capital being Δ (small letter = δ); (*Geog.*) a triangular-shaped tract of alluvium at the mouth of a large river (as Nile, Ganges) through which the distributaries of the river reach the sea.—**delta rays,** rays from radio-active metals much less powerful and penetrating than the *alpha* rays [Gk.].

delude (dē-lūd') *v.t.* to lead into error; to mislead; to beguile; to deceive.—**delud'able** *a.*—**delud'er** *n.*—**delu'sion** *n.* the act of deluding; that which deludes; a mistaken belief; (*Med.*) a hallucination.—**delu'sive** *a.* tendency to deceive or mislead.—**delu'sory** *a.* tending to delude [L. *de*; *ludere*, to play].

deluge (del'ūj) *n.* a great flow of water; torrential rain; a flood, esp. Biblical flood in time of Noah;—*v.t.* to flood; to inundate; to drench [L. *diluvium*, a washing away].

de luxe (dę lŏŏks') *a.* sumptuous; of superlative quality [Fr.].

delve (delv) *v.t.* and *v.i.* to dig with a spade; to burrow [O.E. *delfan*, to dig].

demagnetisation (dē-mag-net-ī-zā'shun) *n.* the act or process of demagnetising.—**demag'netise** *v.t.*

demagogue (dem'ą-gog) *n.* a leader of the masses; a political agitator who sways people by appealing to the emotions more than to reason.—**demagogic, -al** (dem-a-goj'(gog')-ik-ąl) *a.*—**demagogy** (dem'a-goj(g)-i) *n.* the beliefs and actions of a demagogue.—Also **dem'agoguery** [Gk. *dēmos*, the people; *agein*, to lead].

demand (dę-mand') *v.t.* to ask authoritatively or peremptorily; to question; to require;—*n.* the act of demanding; urgent claim; earnest inquiry; (*Econ.*) the requirement of purchaser or consumer, oppos. of *supply*.—**demand'ant** *n.* (*fem.* **demand'ress**) one who demands [L. *demandare*, to entrust].

demarcation, demarkation (dē-mår-kā-shun) *n.* the act of marking a line or boundary; a boundary.—**demarcate'** *v.t.* [Fr.].

demean (dē-mēn') *v.t.* to conduct or comport oneself; to behave.—**demean'our** *n.* behaviour; manner of conducting oneself [O.Fr. *demener*, to conduct].

demean (dē-mēn') *v.t.* to make mean; to debase; to degrade (used reflexively).

demented (dē-men'ted) *a.* insane; crazy; suffering from dementia.—**dement'** *v.t.* to drive mad.—**dementia** (dē-men'shi-ą) *n.* incipient loss of reason; insanity marked by complete mental deterioration.—**dementia**

praecox, insanity in adolescence [L. *de,* from; *mens,* the mind].
démenti (dā-mongʹtē) *n.* diplomatic term for an official denial of a rumour [Fr.].
demerara (demʹer-ȧr-a) *n.* a kind of brown sugar, orig. from *Demerara* in Br. Guiana.
demerit (dē-merʹit) *n.* a fault; a bad feature; a vice [L. *de,* from; *merere,* to deserve].
demesne, demain (dḛ-mēnʹ, dḛ-mānʹ) *n.* a manor-house and the estate adjacent to it; private ownership of land.—Also **domainʹ.** —**demesnʹial** *a.* [Fr.].
demi- (demʹi) *prefix* signifying *half* [L. *dimidium,* half; Fr. *demi*].
demi-god (demʹi-god) *n.* (*fem.* **demʹi-godʹdess**) a classical hero, half human, half divine.
demijohn (demʹi-jon) *n.* a glass bottle with large body, slender neck and enclosed in wicker-work [etym. doubtful; prob. fr. Fr. *dame-Jeanne*].
demi-monde (dḛm-ē-mōngdʹ, demʹi-mond) *n.* a class of women of doubtful reputation; prostitutes.—**demʹi-monʹdaine** *n.* a woman of this class [Fr. *demi,* half; *monde,* world].
demirep (demʹi-rep) *n.* a woman of doubtful reputation [Fr. *demi,* half; abbrev. of *reputation*].
demise (dē-mīzʹ) *n.* transmission by will to a successor; the conveyance of property; death;—*v.t.* to bequeath; to transmit to a successor [L. *demittere,* to send down].
demi-semiquaver (demʹi-semʹi-kwāʹvḛr) *n.* (*Mus.*) a note equal in time to half a semiquaver, or to one fourth of a quaver; the printed symbol of this note.
demit (dē-mitʹ) *v.t.* to dismiss; to resign; to abdicate voluntarily.—**demisʹsion** *n.* a lowering; degradation; resignation (of an office) [L. *de,* down; *mittere,* to send].
demi-tasse (dḛ-mē-tasʹ) *n.* a small-sized cup; a coffee cup, esp. for black coffee [Fr.].
demobilise (dē-mobʹi-līz) *v.t.* to dismiss (troops); to disband.—**demobilisaʹtion** *n.*—(*Abbrev.*) **demobʹ.**
democracy (dē-mokʹrạ-si) *n.* a form of government for the people by the will of the majority of the people (based on conception of the equality of man); a state having this form of government.—**democrat** (demʹō-krat) *n.* one who adheres to democracy; (*U.S.*) member of Democratic party (opp. of Republican party).—**democratʹic, democratʹical** *a.*—**democratʹically** *adv.* [Gk. *dēmos,* the people; *kratein,* to rule].
demography (dē-mogʹrạ-fi) *n.* the branch of science which deals with statistics of births, deaths and health of community [Gk. *dēmos,* people; *graphein,* to write].
demolish (dē-molʹish) *v.t.* to destroy; to pull down (of a building); to ruin; (*Colloq.*) to consume.—**demolʹisher** *n.*—**demoliʹtion** *n.* the act or process of pulling down; destruction [L. *de,* down; *moles,* a heap].
demon (dēʹmon) *n.* a spirit (esp. evil); a devil; sometimes like *daemon,* a friendly spirit.—**demoʹniac** *a.* pert. to a demon; possessed of an evil spirit; devilish—also **demoʹniacal;**—*n.* a human being possessed of an evil spirit.—**demonolʹatry** *n.* the worship of evil spirits.—**demonolʹater** *n.*—**demonolʹogy** *n.* the study of the characteristics of evil spirits [Gk. *daimon,* a spirit].
demonetisation (dē-mon-e-tī-zāʹshun) *n.* the act of demonetising.—**demonʹetise** *v.t.* to diminish or deprive of monetary value [L. *de,* down; *moneta,* money].
demonstrate (demʹon-strāt, de-monʹstrāt) *v.t.* to prove by pointing out; to exhibit; to explain by specimens or experiment.—**demonʹstrable** *a.* capable of being demonstrated.—**demonʹstrably** *adv.*—**demonstraʹtion** *n.* the act of making clear, esp. by practical exposition; proof beyond doubt; a display of emotion.—**demonʹstrative** *a.* proving by evidence; exhibiting with clearness; inclined to show one's feelings openly; (*Gram.*) of an adjective or pronoun which points out, as *this* or *that.*—**demʹonstrator** *n.* [L. *demonstrare,* to show].
demoralise (dē-morʹạl-īz) *v.t.* to injure the morals of; to corrupt; to weaken the courage or morale of; to throw into confusion.
demote (dē-mōtʹ) *v.t.* to reduce in rank.—**demotʹion** *n.* [by analogy with *promote*].
dempster (demʹstḛr) *n.* in the Isle of Man and the Channel Isles, a judge. Also **demʹster, deemʹster** [E. = doomster].
demulcent (dē-mulʹsent) *a.* softening; soothing [L. *demulcere,* to stroke down].
demur [dē-murʹ) *v.i.* to hesitate because of doubt, difficulty, or scruples; to object.—*pr.p.* **demurʹring;** *pa.p.* **demurredʹ;**—*n.* hesitation; pause; statement of objections.—**demurʹrable** *a.*—**demurʹrage** *n.* undue detention of a ship; compensation paid by freighters for such detention.—**demurʹrer** *n.* one who demurs; (*Law*) a plea that a case has insufficient evidence to justify its being pursued further [L. *de; morari,* to delay].
demure (dē-mūrʹ) *a.* grave; staid; shy; seemingly modest.—**demureʹly** *adv.*—**demureʹness** *n.* [O.Fr. *de murs,* of good manners].
demy (de-mīʹ) *n.* a size of printing paper 22½ inches by 17½ inches; a scholar at Magdalen College, Oxford [Fr. *demi;* L. *dimidium,* half].
den (den) *n.* a cave or hollow place; lair or cage of a wild beast; disreputable haunt; (*Colloq.*) a private sanctum, study or workshop [O.E. *denn,* a cave].
denarius (de-nāʹri-us) *n.* a Roman silver coin worth about 9d.; the 'penny' of the N.T.—**deʹnary** *a.* containing ten [L.].
denationalise (dē-nashʹun-ạl-īz) *v.t.* to deprive of national rights, character, or status; to change from state control to private control.—**denationalisaʹtion** *n.*
denature (dē-nāʹtūr) *v.t.* to make unfit for eating or drinking by adulteration.—**denaʹturant** *n.* that which changes the nature of a thing.—**denaturaʹtion** *n.*
dendri-, dendro- (denʹdri, denʹdrō) *pref.* from Gk. *dendron,* a tree as in **dendriform** (denʹdri-form) *a.* having the shape or appearance of a tree.—**dendritʹic, dendritʹical** *a.* tree-like; arborescent.—**denʹdroid, denʹdroidal** *a.* having the shape of a tree.—**dendrolʹogy** *n.* the natural history of trees.
dene (dēn) *n.* a den or small valley [M.E. *denu,* a valley].
denegation (den-e-gāʹshun) *n.* a denial; a refusal [L. *de; negare,* to deny].
denial (dē-nīʹạl) *n.* the act of denying; a flat contradiction; a refusal.—**deniʹable** *a.* [L. *de; negare,* to deny].
denigration (den-i-grāʹshun) *n.* a blackening of; (*Fig.*) defamation of a person's character.—**denʹigrate** *v.t.* [L. *de; nigrare,* to blacken].
denim (denʹim) *n.* a stout cotton twill cloth for making overalls, etc. orig. manufactured at *Nimes,* France [Fr. serge *de Nimes*].
denizen (denʹi-zn) *n.* a dweller (human being or animal); a citizen; a naturalised alien with rights of a citizen;—*v.t.* to make a denizen of.—**denʹizenship** *n.* [L. *de intus,* from within].
denominate (dē-nomʹi-nāt) *v.t.* to give a name to; to designate; to style.—**denomʹinable** *a.*—**denominaʹtion** *n.* the act of naming; a title; a class of people; a religious sect; (*Arith.*) unit of measure (money, length, etc.). **denominaʹtional** *a.*—**denomʹinative** *a.* conferring or having a distinctive name ; (*Gram.*) a verb made from a noun or adjective.—**denomʹinatively** *adv.*—**denomʹinator** *n.* the one who, or that which, designates a class; the divisor; the number below the line in a vulgar fraction [L. *de; nominare,* to name].
denote (dē-nōtʹ) *v.t.* to signify or imply; to express by a sign; to mean; to be the symbol of; (*Logic*) to indicate the objects to which

a term refers.—**deno'table** *a.*—**denota'tion** *n.* [L. *denotare*, to mark).
dénouement (dā-nòò'-mong) *n.* the unravelling of the complication of a dramatic plot; the issue or outcome of a situation; [Fr. fr. L. *de*, from; *nodare*, to tie with knots].
denounce (dē-nouns') *v.t.* to inform against; to accuse in public; to threaten; to repudiate, as a treaty.—**denounce'ment** *n.*—**denounc'er** *n.* [L. *de*; *nuntiare*, to announce].
dense (dens) *a.* compact; thick; crowded; (of vegetation) impenetrable, luxuriant; (*Fig.*) stupid.—**dense'ly** *adv.*—**dense'ness** *n.*—**den'sity** *n.* the quality of being dense; (*Chem.*) the mass per unit volume of a substance [L. *densus*, thick].
dent (dent) *n.* a small depression made (by a blow) in a surface;—*v.t.* to mark by a blow or pressure [O.E. *dynt*, a stroke].
dental (den'-tạl) *a.* pert. to the teeth or to dentistry;—*n.* and *a.* a consonant sound (e.g. *d* or *t*) made by tip of tongue behind the upper front teeth.—**den'tate, den'tated** *a.* toothed; sharply notched (e.g. leaf).—**den'tiform** *a* having the shape of a tooth.—**den'tifrice** *n.* trade name for powder, paste, or liquid used to clean and whiten teeth.—**den'tist** *n.* a medically trained specialist in the care of the teeth (also *dental surgeon*).—**den'tistry** *n.*—**denti'tion** *n.* cutting of teeth.—**den'toid** *a.* tooth-like.—**den'ture** *n.* set or part set of teeth, esp. artificial teeth [L. *dens*, a tooth].
denticle (den'-ti-kl) *n.* a small tooth or projection.—**dentic'ular, dentic'ulate, dentic'ulated** *a.* having notches or sharp projections [L. *dens*, tooth].
denude (dē-nūd') *v.t.* to lay bare; to strip; to deprive of a quality.—**denuda'tion** *n.* [L. *denudare*, to make bare].
denunciate (dē-nun'-si-āt) *v.t.* Same as **denounce**—**denuncia'tion** *n.*—**denun'ciator** *n.* one who denounces.—**denun'ciatory** *a.* [L. *de*; *nuntiare*, to announce].
deny (dē-nī') *v.t.* to declare to be untrue; to gainsay; to refuse a request; to disavow; to disown; to withhold; (*reflex.*) to abstain from.—*pr.p.* **deny'ing.**—*pa.p.* **denied'** [L. *de*; *negare*, to deny].
deodar (dē-ō-dar') *n.* a large Himalayan cedar tree [Sans. *deva dara*, divine tree].
deodate (dē'-ō-dāt) *n.* a gift from God [L. *deus*, God; *dare*, to give].
deodorise (dē-ō'-dor-īz) *v.t.* to deprive of odour.—**deo'dorant, deodoris'er** *n.* something, which destroys a fetid smell; a disinfectant [L. *de*, from; *odor*, smell].
deoxidate, deoxidise (dē-oks'-i-dāt, -dīz) *v.t.* to remove oxygen from; to reduce from the state of an oxide.—**deoxida'tion, deoxidisa'tion** *n.* the process of deoxidising.
depart (dē-pȧrt') *v.i.* to go away; to quit; to leave; to die; to abandon; to deviate (as from a policy);—*v.t.* to leave (e.g. *to depart this life*).—**depart'ed** *n.* (*sing.* and *plur.*) the dead.—**depart'ment** *n.* a self-contained section of a business or administration; a special branch of the arts or science; an administrative district of a country, as in France.—**department'al** *a.* pert. to a department; affecting only a section of a business, etc.—**depart'ure** *n.* the act of going away; removal; death; divergence from rule [L. *de*, from; *partiri*, to part].
depasture (dē-pas'-tūr) *v.t.* and *v.i.* to put cattle to graze on; to eat up grass, etc.
depauperate (dē-paw'-pẹr-āt) *v.t.* to make poor; to impoverish.—**depau'perise** *v.t.* to free from pauperism.
depend (dē-pend') *v.i.* to hang; to be sustained by; to rely on; to be contingent on; (*Law*) to be awaiting final judgment.—**depen'dable** *a.* trustworthy.—**depen'dably** *adv.*—**depen'dant** *n.* one who is supported, esp. financially by another; a retainer; a subordinate.—**depen'dent** *a.* hanging down; relying on for support or favour; varying according to; (spellings -ant, -ent are interchangeable in noun and adjective, but *-ant* is more common in noun, and *-ent* in adjective).—**depen'dence** (less common—*ance*) *n.* the state of depending, relying on.—**depen'dency** *n.* the state of being dependent on; esp. used of territory or colony subordinate to and controlled by mother-country.—**depen'dently, depen'dantly** *adv.* [L. *dependere*, to hang down].
depict (dē-pikt') *v.t.* to portray; to paint carefully; to present a visual image of; to describe in words.—**depic'tive** *a.* [L. *de*; *pingere*, *pictum*, to paint].
depilate (dep'-i-lāt) *v.t.* to remove hair from;—*a.* hairless.—**depila'tion** *n.*—**depil'atory** *n.* agent for removing superfluous hair from body;—*a.* having the property of removing hair [L. *de*, from; *pilus*, a hair].
deplenish (dē-plen'-ish) *v.t.* to empty [L. *de*, from; *plenus*, full].
deplete (dē-plēt') *v.t.* to empty; to diminish; to exhaust; to reduce in numbers.—**deple'tive, deple'tory** *a.* [L. *de*, from; *plere*, to fill].
deplore (dē-plōr') *v.t.* to weep over; to suffer remorse for; to lament; to regret; to deprecate; to express disapproval of.—**deplor'able** *a.*—**deplor'ably** *adv.* [L. *de*; *plorare*, to weep].
deploy (dē-ploi') *v.t.* to spread out; to extend troops in line; to diminish in depth (of troops).—*v.i.* to extend from column into line.—**deploy'ment** *n.* [Fr. *déployer*, to spread out].
deplume (dē-plòòm') *v.t.* to pluck the feathers from.—**depluma'tion** *n.*
depolarise (dē-pō'-lạ-rīz) *v.t.* to deprive of polarity [Gk. *polos*, pivot].
depone (dē-pōn') *v.i.* (esp. *Scots Law*) to give evidence under oath, in a law court; to depose.—**depo'nent** *n.* one who gives evidence in a court under oath; one whose disposition or written testimony is accepted as evidence in a trial; a deponent verb;—*a.* (*Gram.*) applied to a verb in Latin or Greek active in meaning, but passive in form [L. *de*, down; *ponere*, to lay].
depopulate (dē-pop'-ū-lāt) *v.t.* to reduce the number of inhabitants of an area by eviction or death;—*v.i.* to become depleted in population.—**depopula'tion** *n.*
deport (dē-pōrt') *v.t.* to carry away; to expel; to banish into exile (of undesirable aliens); (reflex.) to behave; to bear oneself.—**deporta'tion** *n.* the compulsory removal of people from one country to another; in 18th cent. transportation of convicts abroad (e.g. Australia).—**deport'ment** *n.* carriage or bearing or posture of a person [L. *de*, from; *portare*, to carry].
depose (dē-pōz') *v.t.* to remove from a throne; to oust from a high position; to degrade; (*Law*) to state upon oath.—**depos'able** *a.*—**depos'al** *n.*—**deposi'tion** *n.* removal of someone from a high position; (*Law*) act of deponing; a written declaration (signed before a magistrate) by a witness who must later appear to testify in court [L. *de*, down; *ponere*, to place].
deposit (dē-poz'-it) *v.t.* to lay down; to entrust; to let fall (as a sediment); to lodge (in a bank); to store;—*n.* that which is deposited or laid down; sediment falling to the bottom of a fluid; money placed in safe-keeping of a bank (usually with interest); a security; a pledge.—**depos'itary** *n.* one with whom anything is left in trust.—**depos'itor** *n.*—**depos'itory** *n.* a place where things are deposited; a storehouse, esp. for furniture [L. *de*, down; *ponere*, to place].
depot (dep'-ō, dē'-pō) *n.* a depository; a storehouse; (*Mil.*) regimental headquarters; training centre for recruits; (*U.S.*) a railway station [Fr. *dépôt*].
deprave (dē-prāv') *v.t.* to make bad or worse; to corrupt; to vitiate; to pervert.—**deprava'tion** *n.* the act of corrupting; moral perversion; degeneration.—**deprav'ed** *a.* immoral;

vicious.—**deprav'edly** *adv.* [L. *de*; *pravus*, vicious].

deprecate (dep'-re-kāt) *v.t.* to seek to avert by prayer; to express disapproval of.—**dep'recable** *a.*—**dep'recative, dep'recatory** *a.*—**dep'recator** *n.* [L. *de*, from; *precari*, to pray].

depreciate (dē-prē'-shi-āt) *v.t.* to lower in value; (*Fig.*) to disparage; to underrate;—*v.i.* to lose quality; to diminish in market value.—**deprecia'tion** *n.* decline in value.—**depre'ciative, depre'ciatory** *a.*—**depre'ciator** *n.* [L. *de*, down; *pretium*, price].

depredate (dep'-re-dāt) *v.t.* to plunder; to lay waste.—**depreda'tion** *n.* the act of laying waste; pillaging; theft.—**dep'redator** *n.* [L. *de*, from; *praeda*, plunder].

depress (dē-pres') *v.t.* to press down; to lower; to diminish the vigour of; to deject or cast a gloom over.—**depressed'** *a.* pressed down; unfortunate; dejected; languid.—**depress'ible** *a.*—**depres'sion** *n.* a hollow; a dip; a sinking; (*Fig.*) dejection; despondency; a slump (in trade); in meteorology, a cyclone, an area of low barometric pressure.—**depress'or** *n.* [L. *depressus*, pressed down].

deprive (dē-prīv') *v.t.* to take away; to dispossess; to debar a person from; to divest a clergyman of ecclesiastical office.—**depriva'tion** *n.* the act of depriving; the state of being deprived or dispossessed.—**depriv'able** *a.*—**depriv'ative** *a.*—**depriv'er** *n.* [L. *de*, from; *privare*, to deprive].

depth (depth) *n.* deepness; distance measured downwards from surface; breadth, as of a hem, shelf, etc.; profundity or penetration, as of mind.—**depth'-charge** *n.* a large canister type of bomb fired over the side of a ship, and detonating at a predetermined depth by an automatic timing device [O.E. *deop*, deep].

depurate (dep'-ū-rāt) *v.t.* to free from impurities, to purify [L. *de*; *purus*, pure].

depute (dē-pūt') *v.t.* to send with commission to act for another; to delegate duties to another.—**depute** (dep'-ūt) *a.* in Scotland, appointed deputy (as in Depute-Fiscal).—**deputa'tion** *n.* the act of deputing; persons authorised to transact business for others.—**dep'utise** *v.i.* to act as substitute or deputy for others.—**deputy** *n.* (dep'-ū-ti) one who is appointed to act for another [L. *deputare*, to esteem, to allot].

derail (dē-rāl') *v.t.* to cause to run off the rails.—**derail'ment** *n.* the state of being derailed.

derange (dē-rānj') *v.t.* to put out of order or place; to upset; to make insane.—**deranged'** *a.* mentally unstable; insane.—**derange'ment** *n.* [Fr. *déranger*, to disturb].

derate (dē-rāt') *v.t.* to relieve from the burden of local rates.

Derby (dar'-bi) *n.* a famous horse race called after the founder, the 12th Earl of Derby (1780); (*U.S.*) a bowler hat (pron. der'-bi); a strong kind of boot or shoe.—**Derbyshire neck**, goitre (common in Derbyshire).

derelict (der'-e-likt) *a.* forsaken; abandoned and disclaimed by owner, esp. used of ships; —*n.* a ship abandoned by captain and crew. —**derelic'tion** *n.* act of abandoning; failure in duty [L. *de*, from; *relinquere*, to leave].

deride (dē-rīd') *v.t.* to ridicule; to mock; to laugh at with scorn; to belittle.—**derid'er** *n.* —**derid'ingly** *adv.*—**derision** (dē-rizh'-un) *n.* mockery; ridicule; ironical contempt.—**deri'sive** *a.* mocking; ridiculing.—**deri'sively** *adv.*—**deri'siveness** *n.*—**deris'ory** *a.* derisive; mocking [L. *de*, down; *ridere*, to laugh].

derive (dē-rīv') *v.t.* to obtain or draw from a source; to trace the etymology (of a word); to trace the descent or origin (of a person); —*v.i.* to have as an origin; to proceed (foll. by *from*).—**deriv'able** *a.*—**der'ivate** *a.* derived; —*n.* a derivative.—**derivation** (der-i-vā'-shun) *n.* act of deriving or process of being derived; tracing of a word back to its roots; etymology.—**deriv'ative** *n.* that which is derived or traceable back to something else; a word derived from another;—*a.* obtained by derivation; secondary.—**deriv'atively** *adv.* [L. *de*, down; *rivus*, a stream].

derm (derm) *n.* the true skin below epidermis. Also **der'ma, der'mis.**—**der'mal** *a.* pert. to the skin.—**dermat'ic** *a.* consisting of skin.—**dermati'tis** *n.* inflammation of the skin by localised irritation.—**dermatol'ogy** *n.* branch of medical science concerned with the skin and skin diseases.—**dermatol'ogist** *n.* skin specialist [Gk. *derma*, a skin].

derogate (der'-ō-gāt) *v.t.* to remove or detract from; to discredit; to disparage;—*v.i.* to lessen (as reputation).—**deroga'tion** *n.* —**derog'atory** *a.* tending to impair the value of; detracting; (foll. by *to*).—**derog'atorily** *adv.* [L. *de*, from; *rogare*, to ask].

derrick (der'-ik) *n.* an apparatus like a crane for hoisting heavy weights [fr. *Derrick*, a Tyburn hangman of 17th cent.].

derring-do (der-ing-dòò) *n.* an act of reckless daring (M.E. *duryng do*].

derringer (der'-in-jer) *n.* a short-barrelled pistol with a large bore [U.S. inventor].

dervish, dervis (der'-vish, der'-vis) *n.* a member of one of the mendicant orders among the Mohammedans [Pers. *darvish*, a poor man].

descant (des'-kant) *n.* a variation harmonising with and sung or played as accompaniment to plain-song; a discourse or expatiation on a theme;—*v.i.* to discourse fully; to compose a variation on an air.—**descant'er** *n.* [L. *dis*, apart; *cantus*, song].

descend (dē-send') *v.t.* to go down into; to traverse downwards; to flow down;—*v.i.* to sink; to lower oneself or stoop to something; to fall (upon an enemy).—**descend'ant** *n.* one descended from an ancestor; offspring.—**descend'ent** *a.* descending.—**descend'ible** (or **-able**) *a.* capable of being passed down, as to an heir.—**descend'ing** *a.* and *pr.p.*—**descen'sion** *n.* descent; degradation.—**descen'sive** *a.* tending downwards. **-descent'** *n.* act of coming down; a slope or declivity; inheritance [L. *de*, down; *scandere*, to climb].

describe (dē-skrīb') *v.t.* to represent the features of; to portray in speech or writing.—**describ'able** *a.*—**descrip'tion** *n.* act of describing; a representation, in words, of the qualities of a person or thing; a class or order of things; sort; kind.—**descrip'tive** *a.* containing description.—**descrip'tively** *adv.*—**descrip'tiveness** *n.* [L. *de*, down; *scribere*, to write].

descry (dē-skrī) *v.t.* to discover by the eye; to perceive from a distance; to make out.—**descri'er** *n.* [L. *de*, down; *scribere*, to write].

desecrate (des'-e-krāt) *v.t.* to violate the sanctity of; to profane.—**des'ecrater, -or** *n.*—**desecra'tion** *n.* [L. *de*, away; *sacer*, holy].

desert (dē-zert') *n.* that which is deserved; reward (for merit); punishment (for demerit) [L. *deservire*, to serve zealously].

desert (dez'-ert) *n.* a waste region where little or no vegetation is found; esp. wide, sandy tracts in region N. and S. of lat. 23½°;—*a.* uncultivated; solitary [L. *deserere*, to abandon].

desert (dē-zert') *v.t.* to abandon; to leave; to fail;—*v.i.* to quit without permission the Army, Navy, or Air Force.—**desert'ed** *a.* abandoned. **-desert'er** *n.*—**deser'tion** *n.* the act of deserting; state of being abandoned [L. *deserere*, to abandon].

deserve (dē-zerv') *v.t.* to earn by service; to merit; to be entitled to; to warrant;—*v.i.* to be worthy of reward.—**deserv'edly** *adv.* justly. —**deserv'ing** *a.* worthy; meritorious [L. *deservire*, to serve zealously].

deshabille (des'a-bēl') *n.* partial undress; careless toilet for indoors [Fr.].

desiccate (de-sik'-āt, des'-i-kāt) *v.t.* to extract all moisture from; to dry up; to dehydrate;—*v.i.* to become dry.—**des'iccant** *a.* drying;—*n.* (*Chem.*) substance capable of absorbing moisture.—**desicca'tion** *n.* the process of extracting moisture from something; the state of being dehydrated.—**des'iccator** *n.* (*Chem.*) an apparatus used in dehydration [L. *desiccare*, to dry up].

desiderate (dē-sid'e-rāt) *v.t.* to feel the want of; to yearn to acquire something that is lacking.—**desid'erative** *a.* expressing desire.—**desidera'tion** *n.* act of desiderating.—**desidera'tum** *n.* that which is earnestly desired; an admitted need;—*pl.* **desidera'ta** [L. *desiderare*, to want].

design (dē-zīn') *v.t.* to draw the outline of; to plan;—*v.i.* to purpose;—*n.* a sketch in outline (esp. in architecture); a pattern (as in wallpaper, printed cloth, etc.); scheme or plan; purpose.—**design'able** *a.*—**designate** (des'ig-nāt) *v.t.* to mark out and make known; to nominate (as in *Moderator-Designate*).—**designa'tion** *n.* distinctive name or title.—**designa'tive** *a.*—**design'edly** *adv.* intentionally (opp. of *accidentally*).—**design'er** *n.* one who designs or makes plans or patterns; a schemer or plotter.—**design'ful** *a.*—**design'ing** *a.* artful; crafty; selfishly interested [L. *de*, down; *signare*, to mark].

desire (dē-zīr') *v.t.* to yearn for the possession of; to request; to entreat;—*n.* anything desired; a longing; object of longing; lust.—**desir'able** *a.* worth possessing.—**desir'ably** *adv.* —**desir'ableness, desirabil'ity** *n.* the state or quality of being desired.—**desir'ous** *a.* full of desire; covetous.—**desir'ously** *adv.* with earnest longing [O.Fr. *desirer*, to want].

desist (dē-zist') *v.t.* to cease; to discontinue; to forbear; to abstain.—**desist'ance, -ence** *n.* [L. *de*, from *sistere*, to stand].

desk (desk) *n.* a table (or table with moveable sloping flap), for reading or writing; a lectern [L.L. *desca*, a table].

desolate (des'o-lāt) *v.t.* to devastate; to depopulate; to make lonely or forlorn;—*a.* waste; deserted; unfrequented; dismal.—**des'olately** *adv.*—**des'olateness** *n.* the state of being desolate.—**des'olater** *n.*—**desola'tion** *n.* the act of laying waste; loneliness; misery.—**des'olatory** *a.* [L. *desolare*, to forsake].

despair (de-spār') *v.i.* to be without hope; to lose heart; to have no expectation of improvement;—*n.* despondency; hopelessness.— **despair'ing** *a.* full of despair.—**despair'ingly** *adv.* [L. *desparare*].

despatch, dispatch (des-, dis-pach') *v.t.* to send away, esp. in haste; to execute promptly (as an order); to dispose of; to kill;—*n.* something which is despatched; speed; promptitude; official message or document sent by special messenger; the sending out of mails.—**despatch'es** *n.pl.* official papers or military reports.—**despatch-rider,** a soldier, orig. mounted on horesback, now on motorcycle, who carries despatches.—**mentioned in despatches,** commended for bravery in action [Fr. *dépêcher*, to expedite].

desperado (des-pęr-a'dō) *n.* a desperate fellow; an unscrupulous ruffian;—*pl.* **despera'do(e)s** [L. *desperatus*, hopeless].

desperate (des'pęr-āt) *a.* beyond hope; critically serious; heedless of danger; furious; frantic; in dire straits.—**des'perately** *adv.*—**des'perateness** *n.*—**despera'tion** *n.* state of being desperate [L. *desperare*, to despair].

despicable (des'pik-ą-bl) *a.* contemptible; mean; vile; deserving to be despised.— **des'picably** *adv.* vilely.—**des'picableness** *n.*— **despicabil'ity** *n.* [L. *despicere*, to despise].

despight (dē-spīt') an old spelling of **despite**.

despise (dē-spīz') *v.t.* to look down upon; to hold in contempt; to disdain; to scorn.—**despis'able** *a.* contemptible.—**despis'al** *n.* contempt. [L. *despicere*, to look down on].

despite (dē-spīt') *n.* malice; contemptuous defiance; scorn; spite;—*prep.* in spite of; notwithstanding.—**despite'ful** *a.*—**despite'fully** *adv.* [L. *despicere*, to look down on].

despoil (dē-spoil') *v.t.* to take away by force; to deprive; to rob; to strip.—**despoil'er** *n.* a plunderer.—**despoil'ment, despolia'tion** *n.* [L. *de*, from; *spolium*, spoil].

despond (dē-spond) *v.i.* to be cast down in spirit.—**despond'ence, despond'ency** *n.* dejection of mind; depression.— **despond'ent** *a.* depressed.—**despond'ently** *adv.*—**despond'ingly** *adv.* [L. *de*, from; *spondere*, to promise].

despot (des'pot) *n.* one who rules with absolute power; a tyrant; one who enforces his will on others.—**despot'ic** *a.*—**despot'ically** *adv.*—**des'potism** *n.* the absolute power of one man unlimited by constitution [Gk. *despotēs*, a master].

desquamate (des'kwą-māt) *v.i.* to scale off (of skin); to peel (as in scarlet fever).—**desquama'tion** *n.* [L. *desquamatus*, scaled off].

dessert (de-zert') *n.* a course, usually fruit or sweets, served at end of a dinner [O.Fr. *desservir*, to clear the table].

destine (des'tin) *v.t.* to determine the future condition of; to fore-ordain; to doom; to decree.—**destina'tion** *n.* the purpose for which anything is destined; the place to which one is travelling.—**des'tiny** *n.* state appointed; fore-ordained lot; fate; (*Fig.*) Providence [L. *destinare*, to establish].

destitute (des'ti-tūt) *a.* in want; needy; deprived of means of sustenance;—*v.t.* to forsake.—**destitu'tion** *n.* state of abject poverty [L. *de*, from; *statuere*, to place].

destroy (dē-stroi') *v.t.* to pull down; to turn to rubble; to put an end to ; to annihilate.—*pa. p.* **destroyed'.**—**destroy'able** *a.*—**destroy'er** *n.* a type of fast warship armed with guns and torpedoes [L. *destruere*].

destruction (dē-struk'shun) *n.* the act of destroying; state of being destroyed; ruin; death.—**destruc'tible** *a.* capable of being destroyed.—**destruc'tibleness, destructibil'ity** *n.* —**destruc'tive** *a.* causing destruction; fatal.—**destruc'tively** *adv.*—**destruc'tor** *n.* a furnace for burning up town or household refuse [L. *destruere*, to destroy].

desuetude (des'wē-tūd) *n.* discontinuance of a custom or practice [L. *desuetudo*].

desultory (des'ul-tor-i) *a.* leaping from one thing to another; unmethodical; aimless; rambling.—**des'ultorily** *adv.*—**des'ultoriness** *n.* [L. *desultor*, a circus rider].

detach (dē-tach') *v.t.* to separate; to disunite; to withdraw; to detail for special service (as troops).—**detach'able** *a.*—**detached'** *a.* standing alone (e.g. of a house); impersonal; disinterested; unprejudiced.—**detach'edly** *adv.*—**detach'edness, detach'ment** *n.* process or state of being detached; that which is detached (as troops) [Fr. *détacher*, to unfasten].

detail (dē-tāl') *v.t.* to relate minutely; to record every item; to appoint for a special duty (e.g. troops).—**detail** (dē'tāl or dē-tāl') *n.* a minute part; item; particular fact.—**detailed'** *a.* giving every particular fact [Fr. *tailler*, to cut].

detain (dē-tān') *v.t.* to keep back or from; to prevent someone proceeding; to maintain possession of; (*Law*) to keep in custody.—**detain'er** *n.* one who detains; (*Law*) illegal detention of another's possessions; a writ to keep in custody.—**detain'ment** *n.*—**deten'tion** *n.* act of detaining; state of being detained [L. *detinere*, to keep back].

detect (dē-tekt') *v.t.* to uncover; to discover; to expose; to bring to light (esp. a crime); to perceive.—**detect'able, detect'ible** *a.*—**detect'er, detect'or** *n.* one who or that which detects. —**detec'tion** *n.* the discovery of something hidden; the state of being detected.—**detect'ive** *a.* employed in detecting;—*n.* a member of the police force, not in uniform, who apprehends criminals and investigates cases [L. *detegere*, to uncover].

détente (dā-tongt') *n.* a term used in diplomatic circles, for a lessening of tension in international affairs [Fr.].

deter (dē-tẹr′) *v.t.* to frighten from; to discourage; to prevent; to hinder.—*pr.p.* **deter′ring**; *pa.p.* **deterred′**.—**deter′ment** *n.* hindrance.—**deter′rent** *a.* having the power to deter;—*n.* that which deters.—**deter′rence** *n.* act of deterring [L. *deterrere*, to frighten off].

deterge (dē-tẹrj′) *v.t.* to cleanse (wound); to wipe off; to purge.—**deter′gence, deter′gency** *n.* —**deter′gent** *a.* cleansing (by rubbing or wiping);—*n.* cleansing, purifying substance [L. *detergere*, to wipe off].

deteriorate (dē-tē′ri-o-rāt) *v.t.* to make worse; to cause to depreciate;—*v.i.* to become worse; to degenerate.—**deteriora′tion** *n.* [L. *deterior*, worse].

determine (dē-tẹr′min) *v.t.* to fix the limits of; to define; to regulate the form, scope, or character of; to influence; to ascertain with precision;—*v.i.* to make a decision or resolution; (*Law*) to terminate.—**deter′minable** *a.*—**deter′minant** *a.* serving to determine, fix, or limit;—*n.* that which determines or causes determination.—**deter′minate** *a.* having fixed limits; decisive; established.—**deter′minately** *adv.*—**determina′tion** *n.* the act or process of determining fixed purpose; resolution; adherence to a definite line of action.—**deter′mined** *a.* resolute; unwavering; firm; purposeful.—**deter′minedly** *adv.*—**deter′minism** *n.* the doctrine that man is not a free agent, and that his actions and mental activity are governed by causes or motives outwith his own will [L. *determinare*, to limit].

detersion (dē′tẹr′shun) *n.* the act of cleansing.—**deter′sive** *a.* having cleansing properties;—*n.* that which cleanses; a detergent [L. *detergere*, to wipe off].

detest (dē-test′) *v.t.* to dislike intensely; to hate; to abhor; to abominate.—**detest′able** *a.* abhorrent; hateful.—**detest′ableness, detest′abil′ity** *n.*—**detesta′tion** *n.* [L. *detestari*, to execrate].

dethrone (dē-thrōn′) *v.t.* to remove from a throne; to depose.—**dethrone′ment** *n.*

detonate (det′o-nāt) *v.t.* to cause to explode; —*v.i.* to explode with a loud report.—**detona′tion** *n.* a sudden and violent explosion.—**detona′tor** *n.* a detonating substance; percussion cap or fulminating powder used to fire a charge of explosive in guns, bombs, mines, etc.; a fog-signal [L. *detonare*, to thunder].

detour (dē-tȯȯr′) *n.* a roundabout way, a circuitous route; a digression [Fr. *détour*].

detract (dē-trakt′) *v.t.* to take away a part from; to defame;—*v.i.* (with from) to diminish.—**detract′er, detract′or** *n.* (*fem.* **detract′ress**).—**detract′ingly** *adv.*—**detrac′tion** *n.* disparagement; depreciation; slander [L. *detrahere*, to draw away].

detrain (dē-trān′) *v.i.* to leave a railway train.

detriment (det′ri-ment) *n.* injury; harm; loss; mischief.—**detriment′al** *a.* injurious.—**detriment′ally** *adv.* [L. *detrimentum*, a rubbing off].

detritus (de-trī′tus) *n.* powdery substance accumulated by rubbing down a solid.—**detri′tion** *n.* a wearing away by friction [L. *detritus*, rubbed away].

detruncate (dē-trung′kāt) *v.t.* to lop off from the trunk; to shorten.—**detrunca′tion** *n.*

detumescence (dē-tū-mes′ens) *n.* the subsiding of a swelling [L. *detumescere*, to cease swelling].

deuce (dūs) *n.* a card or die with two spots; (*Tennis*) score of 40 all, after which one side must gain two successive points to win the game [L. *duo*, two].

deuce (dūs) *n.* the devil (in mild imprecations); bad luck.—**deuced′** *a.* (*Slang*) devilish; confounded [prob. *deus*, a god].

deuterium (dū-tēr′i-um) *n.* See **diplogen.**

deuterogamy (dū-tẹr-og′ą-mi) *n.* a second marriage after the death of the first spouse [Gk. *deuteros*, second: *gamos*, marriage].

deuteron (dū′tẹr-on) *n.* the nucleus of *deuterium*, the heavy isotope of hydrogen which occurs in ordinary hydrogen 1 in 5000; used in making the atomic bomb [Gk. *deuteros*, second].

Deuteronomy (dū-tẹr-on′o-mi) *n.* the fifth book of the Pentateuch containing the second exposition of the Mosaic Law [Gk. *deuteros*, second; *nomos*, law].

devaluate (dē-val′ū-āt) *v.t.* to reduce the value of (esp. the currency). Also **deval′ue, deval′orise.**—**devalua′tion** *n.* [L. *de*, down; *valere*, to be worth].

devastate (dev′as-tāt) *v.t.* to lay waste; to plunder.—**devasta′tion** *n.* act of laying waste; the state of being devastated; destruction; havoc [L. *devastare*, to lay waste].

develop (de-vel′op) *v.t.* to unroll; to unfold gradually; to increase the resources of; (*Photog.*) to produce image on photographic plate or film by chemical application;—*v.i.* to evolve by natural processes; to expand; to open out; to assume definite character.—**devel′oper** *n.* one who or that which develops; (*Photog.*) a chemical for producing image on plate or film.—**devel′opment** *n.* a gradual unfolding or growth; expansion; evolution; unravelling of a plot; the result of previous causes [Fr. *développer*, to grow gradually].

deviate (dē′vi-āt) *v.i.* to diverge; to turn away from the direct line; to swerve; to err; —*v.t.* to cause to swerve.—**devia′tion** *n.* a turning aside from the right way; divergence; error [L. *de*, from; *via*, a way].

device (dē-vīs′) *n.* that which is planned out or designed; contrivance; stratagem; (*Her.*) emblem on a shield [M.E. *devisen*, to contrive].

devil (dev′l) *v.t.* (*Cookery*) to season with mustard and broil;—*v.i.* to do the drudgery esp. legal or literary [O.E. *deofol*].

devil (dev′l) *n.* the spirit of evil; in Scripture, tempter; Satan; fiend; any very wicked person; (*Colloq.*) a fellow.—**dev′ildom** *n.* power or realm of devils.—**dev′iless, dev′ilet** *n.*—**dev′ilish** *a.* wholly evil; pert. to the devil; (*Colloq.*) excessive.—**dev′ilishly** *adv.*—**dev′ilkin** *n.*—**dev′il-may-care** *a.* reckless; happy-go-lucky.—**dev′ilment** *n.* mischief; prank.—**dev′ilry** *n.* devilish conduct; collection of devils.—**devil's advocate**, one appointed by papal court to oppose a proposed canonisation; (*Colloq.*) anyone who depreciates another's good qualities; one who maintains an argument with which he really disagrees.—**devil's coach-horse**, name for cocktail beetle, very dark in colour and swift in movement.—**Attorney's devil**, the junior Counsel to the Treasury.—**printer's devil**, a printer's youngest apprentice or message boy.—**Tasmanian devil**, a carnivorous marsupial, the dasyure.—**give the devil his due**, give even the worst person credit for something well done [O.E. *deofol*, the devil; fr. Gk. *diabolos*, slanderer].

devious (dē′vi-us) *a.* not direct; roundabout; circuitous; intricate; erring; not straightforward.—**de′viously**.—**de′viousness** *n.* [L. *de*, from; *via*, a way].

deviscerate (dē-vis′er-āt) *v.t.* to disembowel. —**deviscera′tion** *n.* [L. *de*, from; *viscera*, bowels].

devise (dē-vīz′) *v.t.* to invent; to contrive; to scheme; to plan; (*Law*) to leave as a legacy;—*v.i.* to consider;—*n.* (*Law*) the act of bequeathing real estate by will; clause in will to this effect.—**devis′able** *a.*—**devis′al,** *n.* —**devis′er** *n.* one who schemes or contrives.—**devis′or** *n.* one who bequeaths by will [M.E. *devisen*, to divide].

devitalise (dē-vī′tą-līz) *v.t.* to deprive of life or vitality.—**devitalisa′tion** *n.*

devoid (dē-void′) *a.* empty; free from; without [L. *de*, from; *viduus*, deprived].

devoir (dẹv-wȧr′) *n.* duty; service owed; act of civility [Fr. *devoir*, duty].

devolute (de-vol-ūt′) *v.t.* to delegate work to others.—**devolu′tion** *n.* delegation of State powers to subsidiary or local bodies; decentralisation; gradual retrogression (oppos. of evolution) [L. *devolutus*, rolled down]. [See **devolve**].

devolve (dē-volv') *v.t.* to roll down; to transmit; to transfer; to delegate;—*v.i.* (foll. by *upon*) to fall to the lot of; to cause to be performed by; (*Law*) to pass, by inheritance, from one to another.—**devolve'ment** *n.* [L. *devolvere*, to roll down].

devonport (dev'on-pōrt) *n.* a small writing desk.—Also **dav'enport**.

devote (dē-vōt') *v.t.* to vow; to dedicate; to consecrate; to give oneself wholly to; to doom.—**devo'ted** *a.* zealous; strongly attached to or engrossed by; doomed.—**devot'edly** *adv.* —**devot'edness** *n.*—**devotee'** *n.* one who is superstitiously devoted to a cause; a votary; a zealous supporter.—**devo'tion** *n.*—**devo'tions** *n.pl.* prayers.—**devo'tional** *a.* pert. to devotions; religious [L. *devovere*, to dedicate by vow].

devour (dē-vour') *v.t.* to swallow ravenously; to consume completely and wantonly; to destroy; (*Fig.*) to read avidly.—**devour'ment** *n.* [L. *devorare*, to swallow up].

devout (dē-vout') *a.* pious; passionately religious; solemn; intense.—**devout'ly** *adv.*—**devout'ness** *n.* [L. *devovere*, to vow].

dew (dū) *n.* moisture in the atmosphere or in the soil itself, condensed on exposed surfaces, esp. at night;—*v.t.* to moisten; to bedew; to condense.—**dew'-claw,** *n.* rudimentary inner toe of a dog's hind foot.—**dew'-drop** *n.* a minute speck of dew.—**dew'fall** *n.* the falling of dew, or the time when it falls.—**dew'iness** *n.*—**dew'y** *a.* like dew; moist with dew; refreshing.—**mountain dew** (*Colloq.*) whisky, esp. illicitly distilled [O.E. *deaw*, dew].

dewlap (dū'lap) *n.* the hanging fold of skin under the throat of oxen, dogs, etc. [O.E. *deaw*, dew; *laeppa*, a loose hanging piece].

dexter (deks'tẹr) *a.* pert. to the right hand; on the right hand side; (*Her.*) of that side of shield on wearer's right hand (and spectator's left hand), opp. of *sinister*.—**dexter'ity** *n.* right-handedness; manual skill; mental adroitness; cleverness; deftness; quickness.—**dex'terous, dex'trous** *a.* right-handed; deft.—**dex'terously** *adv.*—**dex'terousness** *n.*—**dex'tral** *a.* right as opposed to left.—**dextral'ity** *n.* right-handedness.—**dex'trally** *adv.* [L. *dexter*, on the right hand].

dextrine, dextrin (deks'trin) *n.* a soluble matter into which the interior substance of starch globules is converted by acids or diastase, so called because it has the property of turning the plane of polarisation to the right; used for stiffening fabrics, sizing paper, thickening inks, and as gum for postage-stamps.—**dex'tro-glu'cose** *n.* grape sugar.—**dex'trose** *n.* name given to glucose or grape sugar found in honey, grapes, etc.; [L. *dexter*, on the right].

dey (dā) *n.* a Turkish official title given to the governors of Algiers (before the French conquest) [Turk. *dai* 'uncle on the mother's side'].

dhobi (dō'bi) *n.* Hindu word for a laundryman.—**dho'bey-day** *n.* (*Sailor's Slang*) wash-day [Hind.].

dhow (dou) *n.* an Arab coasting vessel [etym. unknown].

diabetes (dī-ạ-bē'tēz) *n.* a disease marked by excessive flow of sugar-urine due to failure of pancreas to produce insulin [Gk. *diabetes*, fr. *dia*, through; *bainein*, to go].

diablerie, diablery (dē-ab'ler-ē) *n.* sorcery; black magic; witchery [Fr. *diable*, devil].

diabolic, diabolical (dī-ạ-bol'ik, -i-kạl) *a.* devilish; fiendish; pert. to the devil.—**diabol'ically** *adv.* [Gk. *diabolos*, the devil].

diabolo (dī-a'bol-ō) *n.* a game in which a wooden reel is whirled, tossed and caught on a string attached at each end to sticks, held in hands of the player [Gk. *dia*, through; *bolē*, a throw].

diaconal (dī-ak'o-nạl) *a.* pert. to a deacon.

diadem (dī'ạ-dem) *n.* a fillet or head band worn as the symbol of royal power; a head-dress or crown significant of royalty; (*Fig.*) sovereignty.—**di'ademed** *a.* wearing a crown [Gk. *diadēma*, fr. *diadein*, to bind round].

diaeresis, dieresis (dī-ēr'e-sis) *n.* a mark (¨) placed over the second of two consecutive vowels to indicate that each is to be pronounced separately, as in *coöperate*.—*pl.* **diaer'eses, dier'eses** [Gk. *diairesis*, division into two parts].

diaglyph (dī'ạ-glif) *n.* a sculptured or engraved production with the figures sunk below the general surface; an intaglio [Gk. *dia*, through; *gluphein*, to carve].

diagnosis (dī-ag-nō'sis) *n.* a scientific discrimination of any kind; (*Med.*) the identification of a disease from its signs and symptoms;—*pl.* **diagno'ses**.—**di'agnose** *v.t.* (*Med.*) to ascertain from signs and symptoms the nature of a disease; to identify the root-cause of any social or other problem.—**diagnos'tic** *a.* distinguishing; symptomatic;—*n.* a symptom distinguishing one disease from another; a clue.—**diagnosti'cian** *n.* [Gk. *dia*, through; *gnosis*, an inquiry].

diagonal (dī-ag'o-nạl) *n.* (*Geom.*) a straight line joining two opposite angles in a rectilineal figure; (*Print.*) the stroke (/) dividing shillings and pence;—*a.* from corner to corner; oblique.—**diag'onally** *adv.* [Gk. *dia*, through; *gonia*, a corner].

diagram (dī'ạ-gram) *n.* a figure drawn to demonstrate a theorem; a drawing or plan in outline to illustrate a statement.—**diagrammat'ically** *adv.*—**di'agraph** *n.* instrument for facilitating perspective drawing, esp. used for enlargement of maps [Gk. *dia*, through; *graphein*; to write].

dial (dī'ạl) *n.* an instrument for showing the time of day from the sun's shadow; the face of a sundial, clock, watch, etc.; any plate or face on which a pointer moves, as on a weighing machine; (*Slang.*) human face;—*v.t.* to measure on a dial; to call a number on automatic telephone;—*pr.p.* **di'alling**.—*pa.p.* **di'alled**.

dialect (dī-ạ-lekt) *n.* a group variation of language; a mode of speech peculiar to a district or social group; vernacular [Gk. *dialektos*, manner of speech].

dialectic, -al (dī-ạ-lek'tik, -ạl) *a.* pert. to dialectics;—*n.* (usually *pl.*) the art of discussion, disputation, or debate; the science of reasoning.—**dialec'tically** *adv.*—**dialecti'cian** *n.* one skilled in debate [Gk. *dialektikē*, the art of debate].

diallage (dī'ạl-āj) *n.* one of the group of minerals known as pyroxenes, laminated in structure, green or bronze in colour, its broken crystals having a sub-metallic lustre; a variety of augite, closely resembling bronzite.—**diallag'ic, dial'lagoid** *a.* [Gk. *diallagē*, change].

dialogue (dī'ạ-log) *n.* a conversation between two (or more) persons.—**dialog'ic, dialogist'ic** *a.* pert. to dialogue.—**dial'ogise** *v.i.* to speak in dialogue.—**dial'ogist** *n.* [Gk. *dialogos*, a conversation].

dialysis (dī-al'i-sis) *n.* a diaeresis; (*Chem.*) separation of colloid (non-crystalline) from crystalline substances in solution, by filtration through a porous membrane, such as parchment;—*pl.* **dial'yses**.—**dialy'tic** *a.* [Gk. *dia*, through; *luein*, to loosen].

diamagnetic (dī-ạ-mag-net'ik) *a.* a term applied to certain substances (e.g. bismuth) which, when under the influence of a magnetising force, tend to take up a position at right angles to that force [Gk. *dia*, through; *magnētis*, magnet].

diamantine (dī-ạ-man'tin) *a.* like diamonds; adamantine [Fr. *diamant*, diamond].

diameter (dī-am'e-tẹr) *n.* (*Geom.*) a straight line passing through the centre of a circle or other curvi-linear figure, and terminated by the circumference; transverse measurement; unit of magnifying power of a lens.—**diam'etrical, diamet'ric, -al** *a.* pert. to the diameter; directly opposite; contrary.—**diam'etral** *adv.* [Gk. *dia*, through; *metron*, a measure].

diamond (dī′a-mond) *n.* one of the crystalline forms of carbon and the hardest substance known; a popular gem-stone; a four-sided figure with two acute and two obtuse angles; a rhombus; one of the four suits of playing-cards; one of the smallest types of English printing (4½ point);—*a.* resembling, set with, consisting of, shaped like diamonds.—**di'amond-field** *n.* area where diamonds are found.—**diamond wedding,** the sixtieth anniversary of a marriage.—**diamond cut diamond,** used of two people well-matched in cunning.—**black diamonds** (*Colloq.*) coal.—**rough diamond,** (*Colloq.*) a worthy but uncultured person [Fr. *diamant*, diamond].

dianoetic (dī-ą-no-et′ik) *a.* intellectual; capable of thinking [Gk. *dia*, through; *noein*, to think].

Dianthus (dī-an′thus) *n.* (*Bot.*) a genus of plants to which genus belong carnations, pinks, and sweet-william [Gk. *dis*, twice; *anthos*, flower].

diapason (dī-ą-pā′zon) *n.* in Greek music, the octave or interval which includes all the tones of the diatonic scale; a concord in which all notes are an octave apart; correct pitch; harmony; a passage of swelling, mingled sound; the entire compass of a voice or instrument; the two foundation stops of an organ (*open* and *stopped diapason*) [Gk. *dia pason*=through all (the notes)].

diaper (dī′ą-pęr) *n.* an unbleached linen or cotton cloth with diamond pattern used for table linen and towels; a baby's napkin; (*Archit.*) a geometric pattern (usually diamond shaped, sometimes floral) in low relief on a flat surface;—*v.t.* to ornament with a diaper pattern [O.Fr. *diaspre*].

diaphanous (dī-af′ą-nus) *a.* having the power to transmit light (e.g. glass); transparent; translucent; pellucid. [Also **diaphan'ic.** —**diaph'anously** *adv.* [Gk. *dia*, through; *phainein*, to show].

diaphoretic (dī-ą-fo-ret′ik) *n.* (*Med.*) a medicine which induces perspiration;—*a.* promoting perspiration [Gk. *dia*, through; *phorein*, to carry].

diaphragm (dī′ą-fram) *n.* (*Anat.*) a dividing membrane; a dome-shaped muscular partition between chest and abdomen, important in respiratory motion; the midriff; vibrating disc in telephone or microphone; a disc with a circular hole used in telescope or camera to cut off part of a ray of light.—**diaphragmat'ic, diaphrag'mal** *a.* [Gk. *diaphragma*, a barrier].

diarchy (dī′ār-ki) *n.* a system of government in which power is held jointly by two persons, states, or legislative bodies [Gk. *dis*, twice; *archein*, to rule].

diarrhoea, diarrhea (dī-ą-rē′ą) *n.* an excessive and frequent looseness of the bowels.—**diarrhoe'al, diarrhoe'ic, diarrhoet'ic** *a.* [Gk. *dia*, through; *rhein*, to flow].

diary (dī′ą-ri) *n.* a daily record of events; a journal; a book in which a personal record of thoughts, action, etc. is kept.—**di'arist** *n.* [L. *dies*, a day].

diaspore (dī′ą-spōr) *n.* a group of minerals including diasporite, which is a colourless aluminium hydroxide found in bauxite [Gk. *diaspeirein*, to scatter].

diastase (dī′as-tās) *n.* an enzyme found in animal saliva and generated during germination of seeds (e.g. barley in process of malting) and capable of converting starch into sugar [Gk. *diastasis*, separation].

diastole (dī-as′to-lē) *n.* (*Med.*) a rhythmical dilatation of the heart and arteries alternating with *systole* (contraction); the lengthening of a syllable usually short, before a pause [Gk. =a putting apart].

diastyle (dī′ą-stīl) *a.* (*Archit.*) the term applied to a colonnade in which columns are grouped usually in pairs [Gk. *dia*, through; *stulos*, a column].

diathermal (dī-ą-thęrm′ąl) *a.* permeable by heat.—**diather'manous, diather'mous, diather'mic** *a.* having the property of transmitting radiant heat.—**diather'mancy** *n.*—**diather'my** *n.* a form of high frequency electrical treatment for generating heat in body tissues, used to treat cases of chronic inflammation [Gk. *dia*, through; *thermē*, heat].

diatom (dī′ą-tom) *n.* one of an order of microscopic unicellular marine or vegetable organisms.—**diatom earth,** popularly 'infusorial earth' (fossil diatoms) used in manufacture of paint, fire-proof cement, explosives etc.—**diatoma'ceous** *a.*—**diat'omite** *n.* diatom earth [Gk. *dia*, through; *tomē*, a cutting].

diatomic (dī-ą-tom′ik) *a.* (*Chem.*) consisting of two atoms.

diatonic (dī-ą-ton′ik) *a.* (*Mus.*) pert. to major or minor scales; proceeding by the tones, intervals, and harmonies of the natural scale.—**diaton'ically** *adv.* [Gk. *dia*, through; *tonos*, tone].

diatribe (dī′ą-trīb) *n.* a continued disputation; a vituperative harangue; a wordy denunciation.—**di'atribist** *n.* [Gk. *diatribē*, a means of passing the time].

dib (dib) *n.* a knuckle bone.—**dibs** *n.pl.* a children's game played orig. with small bones or stones; (*Slang*) money [etym. doubtful].

dibble (dib′l) *n.* a pointed instrument used in gardening for making holes. Also **dibb'er** —*v.t.* to plant with a dibble;—*v.i.* to make holes.—**dibb'ler** *n.* [form of *dab*].

dice (dīs) *n.pl.* small cubes on each of the six faces of which are spots representing numbers 1-6; used from Egyptian times in games of chance (*pl.* form of *die*);—*v.t.* to cut into small squares;—*v.i.* to play with dice.—**dic'er** *n.* a gambler [O.Fr. *dez*, fr. L. *datus*, given, thrown].

dicephalous (dī-sef′ą-lus) *a.* having two heads on one body [Gk. *dis*, twice; *kephalē*, the head].

dichotomy (dī-kot′om-i) *n.* a cutting in two; (*Logic*) division of ideas into two classes positive and negative.—**dichot'omise** *v.t.* and *v.i.*—**dichot'omous** *a.* [Gk. *dicha*, apart. *temnein*, to cut].

dichromism (dī-krō′mizm) *n.* (*Opt.*) (of colour-blind vision) an ability to distinguish only two or three primary colours [Gk. *dis*, twice; *chroma*, colour].

dickens (dik′enz) *n.* a mild expletive as in 'What the dickens'; the devil; the deuce [prob. fr. *Dickon*=Richard (16th cent.)].

Dickensian (dik-en′si-ąn) *a.* pert. to the works or style of Charles Dickens.

dicker (dik′ęr) *v.t.* and *v.i.* to barter; to haggle; to quibble;—*n.* a bargain; a deal [L. *decuria*, a group of ten (espec. hides)].

dickey, dicky (dik′i) *n.* the driver's seat in a carriage; seat for servants at back of old-fashioned horse-carriage; extra seat at back of two-seater motor car; (*Slang*) a false shirt front;—*a.* (*Colloq.*) weak, as a *dickey* heart.—**dick'y-bird** *n.* child's name for small bird [etym. doubtful].

dicotyledon (dī-kot-i-lē′don) *n.* (*Bot.*) a plant with two cotyledons, or seed-leaves.—**dicotyle'donous** *a.* [Gk. *dis*, twice; *kotulē*, cup].

dicta See **dictum.**

Dictaphone (dik′tą-fōn) *n.* a machine into which letters, etc. can be dictated, the wax receiving cylinder afterwards being transferred to a transcribing dictaphone which re-dictates to the typist [Protected Name].

dictate (dik-tāt′) *v.t.* to read aloud a passage for another to transcribe; to give orders;

—*v.i.* to speak with authority; to prescribe; to deliver commands.—**dictate** (dik′tāt) *n.* an order; command; direction that must be obeyed (usually *pl.*).—**dicta′tion** *n.* art or practice of dictating; that which is read aloud for another to write down, esp. as a spelling test for children.—**dicta′tor** *n.* (*fem.* **dicta′tress, dicta′trix**) one who holds absolute power.—**dictator′ial** *a.* pert. to or like a dictator; tending to force one's opinions on another.—**dictator′ially** *adv.*—**dicta′torship** *n.* [L. *dicere*, to say].

diction (dik′shun) *n.* choice of words in speaking and writing; verbal style; phraseology [L. *dicere*, to say].

dictionary (dik′shun-a-ri) *n.* a book containing, alphabetically arranged, the words of a language, their meanings and etymology; a lexicon [L. *dicere*, to say].

Dictograph (dik′tō-graf) *n.* sound-recording telephonic instrument used for inter-communication between rooms [Protected Trade Name].

dictum (dik′tum) *n.* a positive assertion; an authoritative statement or opinion; an apothegm; a maxim;—*pl.* **dic′ta** [L.=a thing said].

did (did) *pa.t.* of verb **do** [O.E. *dyde*].

didactic (di-dak′tik) *a.* designed to instruct, esp. morally; containing precepts or doctrines; (of people) opinionative.—**didac′tically** *adv.*—**didac′tics** *n.* the science of teaching [Gk. *didaskein*, to teach].

didactyl (dī-dak′til) *a.* having only two fingers or two toes [Gk. *dis*, twice; *daktulos*, a finger].

diddle (did′l) *v.t.* (*Colloq.*) to cheat; to swindle;—*v.i.* to toddle; to dandle [etym. uncertain].

Didelphia (dī-del′fi-a) *n.pl.* one of the three classes of mammalia having pouches to carry their young; the marsupials [Gk. *dis*, twice; *delphus*, a womb].

didymium (dī-dim′i-um) *n.* a rare metal consisting of two elements, neodymium and praseodymium [Gk. *didumos*, twin].

didymous (did′i-mus) *a.* twin [Gk. *didumos*].

die (dī) *n.* a small cube of wood, bone, or ivory used in games of chance, each face marked with numbers from one to six;—*pl.* **dice** (dīs).—**the die is cast**, one's fate is irrevocably settled [O.Fr. *det*, fr. L. *datus*, given, thrown].

die (dī) *v.i.* to cease to live; to become extinct or extinguished; to wither; to decline.—*pr.p.* **dy′ing**.—*pa.p.* **died**—**dy′ing** *a.* pert. to a person at the point of death; fading; languishing;—*n.* death.—**to die for** (*Colloq.*) to want desperately.—**to die hard**, to resist stubbornly; to be long in dying.—**to die in the last ditch**, to fight desperately to the last.—**a die-hard**, one who refuses to accept innovations, and clings stubbornly and conservatively to what is familiar [M.E. *deyan*, to die].

die (dī) *n.* an engraved metal block used for stamping a design as on a coin; the cubical part of a pedestal; a steel block used for cutting screws;—*pl.* **dies**.—**die′-cas′ting** *n.* method of making castings in permanent moulds.—**die′-sink′er** *n.* an engraver of dies.—**die′-sink′ing** *n.* [L. *dare*, to give].

dielectric (dī-e-lek′trik) *a.* non-conducting; insulating;—*n.* Faraday's name for a substance through or across which electric induction takes place; insulator; non-conductor [Gk. *dia*, through; *elektron*, amber].

Diesel engine (dē′zl en′jin) *n.* an internal combustion engine using heavy oil (e.g. petroleum) as fuel [fr. R. *Diesel* (d. 1913), the inventor].

diesis (dī′e-sis) *n.* (*Print.*) a mark of reference, the double dagger (‡);—*pl.* **di′eses** [Gk. *diesis*, a quarter tone].

diet (dī′et) *n.* a system of food; what one habitually eats and drinks; food specially prescribed by a doctor; a regulated allowance of provisions;—*v.t.* to prescribe a special course of foods;—*v.i.* (*Colloq.*) to slim.—**dietar′ian** *n.* one who follows a prescribed diet.—**di′etary** *n.* special course of feeding; daily allowance of food;—*a.* pert. to diet.—**dietet′ic** *a.* pert. to diet.—**dietet′ics** *n.* the science and study of food values, and their effect on health.—**dieti′cian, dieti′tian** *n.* [L. *diaeta*, a mode of living].

diet (dī′et) *n.* a legislative assembly in certain countries of Europe (e.g. *Denmark*) sitting from day to day; an international conference; (*Scots Law*) a sitting of a law court [L. *dies*, a day].

differ (dif′er) *v.i.* to be unlike; to have distinctive characteristics; to disagree (foll. by *from* or *with*); to be at variance; to fall out (foll. by *with*).—*pr.p.* **diff′ering**.—*pa.p.* **diff′ered**.—**diff′erence** *n.* unlikeness; dissimilarity; distinguishing characteristic; disagreement; contention; the amount by which one thing exceeds another in weight or number.—**diff′erent** *a.* unlike; distinct; various diverse; not the same (used with *from*).—**differen′tia** *n.* (*Logic*) the essential quality or characteristic distinguishing any one species from another in a genus (e.g. rational power in *man*);—*pl.* **differen′tiae**.—**differen′tial** *a.* characteristic; special; discriminating; (*Math.*) pert. to infinitely small quantitative differences; proceeding by increments infinitely small.—**differen′tially** *adv.*—**differen′tiate** *v.t.* to make different; to distinguish; to classify as different;—*v.i.* to acquire different characteristics.—**differentia′tion** *n.*—**diff′erently** *adv.*—**differential calculus** (*Math.*) a method of calculating the relative rate of change for continuously varying quantities.—**differential equation** (*Math.*) an equation containing differentials.—**differential gear**, a mechanism by which two sets of wheels are made to rotate at different speeds, as wheels of a car, to facilitate rounding of corners, etc. [L. *dis-*, apart; *ferre*, to bear].

difficult (dif′i-kult) *a.* hard to do or understand; not easy; laborious; awkward; (of persons) exacting; hard to please; not amenable.—**diff′icultly** *adv.*—**diff′iculty** *n.* laboriousness; an obstacle; objection; demur; that which is not easy to do or understand.—**diff′iculties** *n.pl.* financial embarrassment [L. *dis-*, not; *facilis*, easy].

diffident (dif′i-dent) *a.* wanting confidence; not self-assertive; modest; timid; shy.—**diff′idence** *n.* lack of confidence; modesty.—**diff′idently** *adv.* [L. *dis-*, not; *fidere*, to trust].

diffract (di-frakt′) *v.t.* to break or separate into parts, esp. of rays of light and sound waves.—**diffrac′tion** *n.* name given to the effect produced by the slight bending or deflection of a ray of light, by the curvature of an electro-magnetic wave around the edge of an obstacle; the phenomenon caused by light passing through a narrow slit [L. *dis*, apart; *frangere*, to break].

diffuse (dif-ūz′) *v.t.* to pour out in every direction; to spread; to scatter; to cause gases to mix by diffusion;—*v.i.* to mix; to spread, as a liquid.—**diffuse** (dif-ūs′) *a.* widely spread; prolix; rambling; wordy.—**diffusely** (di-fūs′li) *adv.* widely; in a prolix or wordy style.—**diffuse′ness** *n.* quality of being diffuse.—**diffus′ible** *a.* capable of being diffused.—**diffu′sion** *n.* act or process of scattering abroad; (*Chem.*) term applied to the intermixture of two gases or fluids without chemical combination.—**diffus′ive** *a.* spreading; expanding; prolix.—**diffus′ively** *adv.*—**diffus′iveness** *n.*—**diffused lighting**, a form of lighting in which hard brilliance is toned down by diffused transmission [L. *dis*, away; *fundere*, to pour].

dig (dig) *v.t.* to break and turn up earth, as with a spade; to excavate; to delve; (*Colloq.*) to poke or nudge someone;—*v.i.* to till the soil; to use a spade, trowel, etc.—*pr.p.* **dig'ging.**—*pa.p.* **dug.**—*n.* a thrust; poke; jibe or taunt.—**dig'ger** *n.* one who digs; an excavator; a machine which digs; (*Austral.*) a gold miner; a soldier.—**dig'gings** *n.pl.* areas where mining is carried on (esp. gold); (*Slang*) lodgings, usually *abbrev.* to **digs** [prob. O.Fr. *diguer*, to hollow out].

digamma (dī-gam'a) *n.* a letter of the primitive Greek alphabet with the sound of the English 'w' [so called from its shape (F) which was a double gamma (τ)].

digest (di-jest') *v.t.* to convert, as food in the stomach, into a substance which can be readily absorbed into the blood; to assimilate in the mind; to classify; to think over;—*v.i.* to undergo digestion.—**digest** (dī'jest) *n.* a concise summary; esp. *the Digest*, an abridged version of the Roman laws compiled by order of Emperor Justinian; a magazine containing condensed version of well-chosen articles already published elsewhere.—**diges'ter** *n.*—**diges'tible** *a.* capable of being digested; easily assimilated.—**digestibil'ity** *n.*—**diges'tion** *n.* the act of digesting.—**diges'tive** *a.* promoting, or pert. to, digestion;—*n.* any medicine that aids digestion [L. *digerere*, to arrange].

dight (dīt) *v.t.* to dress; to array;—*a.* decked; adorned [O.E. *dihtan*, to arrange].

digit (dij'it) *n.* a finger; a finger's breadth, or three-quarters of an inch; (*Arith.*) integer under 10, so-called from counting on the fingers; (*Astron.*) the twelfth part of the diameter of the sun or moon. -**dig'ital** *a.* pert. to the fingers;—*n.* one of the keys of piano or organ.—**digita'lia, dig'italin, dig'italine** *n.* the drug obtained from leaves of digitalis. —**digita'lis** *n.* a genus of hardy plants including the foxglove; a strong drug obtained from foxglove, and used medicinally as sedative, narcotic and as cardiac stimulant.—**digitar'ia** *n.* finger-grass.—**dig'itate, dig'itated** *a.* having separate fingers and toes.—**digita'tion** *n.*—**dig'itiform** *a.* arranged like fingers.—**dig'itigrade** *n.* an animal which walks on its toes (e.g. dog);—*a.* walking on the toes [L. *digitus*, a finger or toe].

diglot (dī'glot) *a.* speaking two languages [Gk. *dis*, twice; *glotta*, tongue].

dignify (dig'ni-fī) *v.t.* to invest with dignity or honour; to exalt; to elevate; to ennoble;—*pr.p.* **dig'nifying.**—*pa.p.* **dig'nified.**—**dig'nified** *a.* having nobility of bearing [L. *dignus*, worthy; *facere*, to make].

dignity (dig'ni-ti) *n.* state of being dignified in mind, character, or bearing; loftiness; high office or rank.—**dig'nitary** *n.* one who holds a position of exalted rank, esp. ecclesiastical [L. *dignus*, worthy].

digram (dī'gram) *n.* a combination of two letters having the sound of *one* of these two letters as *pn* in *pneumonia* [Gk. *dis*, twice; *gramma*, a letter].

digraph (dī'graf) *n.* two vowels or two consonants combined to express one sound as *ea* in head, *sh* in shop [Gk. *dis*, twice; *graphein*, to write].

digress (dī-gres', di-gres') *v.i.* to turn aside; to stray; to wander from the main theme, topic, or argument; to be diffuse.—**digres'sion** *n.* the act of digressing.—**digres'sional, digress'ive** *a.* [L. *dis-*, aside; *gradus*, a step].

dihedral (dī-hē'dral) *a.* having two plane faces.—**dihe'dron** *n.* a figure with two plane surfaces [Gk. *dis*, twice; *hedra*, base].

dijudicate (dī-jòò'di-kāt) *v.t.* and *v.i.* to judge, to decide between two.—**dijudica'tion** *n.* [L. *di-*, asunder; *judicare*, to judge].

dike, dyke (dīk) *n.* a ditch; a channel for running water; an artificial embankment to prevent inundation of low lying ground, as in Holland; (*Scot.*) a stone wall without mortar; (*Geol.*) igneous rock, once molten, which has filled up fissures of stratified rocks [O.E. *dic*, a ditch].

dilapidate (di-lap'i-dāt) *v.t.* (*Lit.*) to pull stone from stone; to suffer to fall into ruin; to despoil;—*v.i.* to be in a condition of disrepair.—**dilapida'ted** *a.* in ruins; decayed; tumbled down; (of persons) shabby; unkempt. —**dilapida'tion** *n.* state of being dilapidated; decay, esp. of Church property under the incumbent.—**dilap'idator** *n.* [L. *di-*, asunder; *lapis*, a stone].

dilate (di-lāt') *v.t.* to swell out; to expand in all directions; to distend;—*v.i.* to widen; (*Fig.*) to expatiate; to descant; to speak at length.—**dilat'able** *a.* capable of dilation; elastic.—**dila'tancy, dilata'tion, dila'tion** *n.* expansion; a spreading or extending in all directions.—**dila'tant** *a.*—**dilat'or, dilat'er** *n.* [L. *di-*, apart; *latus*, borne].

dilatory (dil'a-tor-i) *a.* tardy; inclined to procrastination; loitering.—**dil'atorily** *adv.*—**dil'atoriness** *n.* tardiness; procrastination [L. *dilatus*, postponed].

dilemma (di-lem'a, dī-lem'a) *n.* choice between alternatives equally undesirable; a predicament; (*Logic*) an argument which presents an antagonist with alternatives equally conclusive against him, whichever he chooses.—**on the horns of a dilemma,** confronted with a perplexity [Gk. *dis*, twice; *lēmma*, an assumption].

dilettante (dil-e-tan'te) *n.* a lover of the fine arts, esp. in a superficial way; a dabbler; —*pl.* **dilettan'ti.**—**dilettan'tish** *a.*—**dilettan'tism, dilettan'teism** *n.* [It.].

Dilfor (dil'for) *n.* (*Mil.*) a scheme for bringing sick soldiers home by special transport or sending out relatives to visit them [fr. *D*angerously *Il*l *For*ces Scheme].

diligent (dil'i-jent) *a.* steady and constant in application; industrious; assiduous.—**dil'igence** *n.* willing and painstaking effort; a type of stage-coach (18th cent.); a modern Continental motor-coach.—**dil'igently** *adv.* [L. *diligere*, to choose].

dill (dil) *n.* a perennial yellow-flowered herb the aromatic seeds of which are used in medicines, and the leaves in flavouring for sauces, etc.—**dill'-wat'er,** *n.* prepared from dill seeds and given often to babies to prevent wind [O.E. *dile*].

dilly-dally (dil'i-dal'i) *v.i.* (*Colloq.*) to loiter; to delay [reduplication of *dally*].

dilute (di-lūt', dī-lūt') *v.t.* to make thinner or more liquid by admixture; to reduce the strength of by addition of something, esp. water; (*Fig.*) to weaken the force of;—*v.i.* to become thin;—*a.* reduced in strength; attenuated; thinned down.—**dil'uent** *a.* diluting; making weaker;—*n.* that which thins or weakens the strength, colour, etc. of something, such as turpentine for thinning down paint.—**dil'utee** *n.* an unskilled worker; one directed into industry by Ministry of Labour (as in World War 2).—**dilute'ness** *n.* —**dilu'tion** *n.* act or process of diluting; state of being diluted [L. *diluere*, dissolve].

diluvium (di-lū'vi-um) *n.* a surface deposit of sand, gravel, etc. caused by action of sea or by overflowing of rivers.—**dilu'vial, dilu'vian** *a.* pert. to or produced by a flood, esp. the deluge in Noah's time [L. *diluvium*, flood].

dim (dim) *a.* not bright or distinct; faint; partially obscure; shadowy; (*Fig.*) dull of apprehension; vague;—*v.t.* to cloud; to cause to grow dim;—*v.i.* to become dull or indistinct.—*pr.p.* **dim'ming.**—*pa.p.* **dimmed.** —**dim'ly** *adv.*—**dim'mer** *n.* in motoring, a device to diminish power of headlights.—**dim'ness** *n.* state of being dim [O.E. *dim*].

dime (dīm) *n.* an American silver coin equal to 10 cents [L. *decima*, a tenth].

dimension (dī-, di-men'shun) *n.* a measurement of extent in a single direction (length breadth, height, or thickness); usually *pl.* measurement in three directions (e.g. of a room); extent; capacity; (*Fig.*) importance.—

dimen'sional *a.* capable of being measured; pert. to a dimension [L. *dimensio*, a measuring].
dimeter (dim'e-tẹr) *a.* having two metrical feet;—*n.* a verse with two measures or accents [Gk. *dis*, twice; *metron*, a measure].
diminish (di-min-ish) *v.t.* to cause to grow less; to weaken; to reduce; to impair; (*Mus.*) to lower a note by a semi-tone;—*v.i.* to become smaller.—**dimin'ished** *a.* lessened; lowered; (*Mus.*) lowered by a semi-tone [L. *diminuere*, to break in small pieces].
diminuendo (dim-in-ū-en'dō) *n.* (*Mus.*) a gradual decrease in volume of sound and marked >, the opposite of *crescendo*;—*adv.* in a gradually diminishing manner [It.].
diminution (dim-in-ū'shun) *n.* act or process of diminishing; state of being reduced in size, quality, or amount; degradation; (*Law*) an error or omission in a law plea.—**dimin'utive** *a.* of small size; minute; miniature; (*Gram.*) applied to a suffix expressing smallness, e.g. *-let*, *-ock*;—*n.* a word formed from another by addition of such a suffix, as *hamlet*, *hillock*.—**dimin'utively** *adv.*—**dimin'utiveness** *n.* [L. *diminuere*, to break in small pieces].
dimissory (dim'is-or-i) *a.* sending away; dismissing to another authority; granting official leave to depart [L. *di-*, away; *mittere*, to send].
dimity (dim'i-ti) *n.* a stout white cotton cloth ribbed or figured [prob. Gk. *dimitos*, of double thread].
dimorphic (dī-mor'fik) *a.* existing in two forms; (*Chem.*) capable of crystallising in two forms under different degrees of temperature.—**dimor'phism** *n.* the state or condition of having two different forms.—**dimor'phous** *a.* [Gk. *dis*, twice; *morphē*, shape].
dimple (dim'pl) *n.* a slight natural depression or hollow on cheek, chin, arm, etc.; a slight indentation in any surface;—*v.t.* to mark with dimples;—*v.i.* to become dimpled [prob. dimin. of *dip*].
din (din) *n.* a loud, continuous noise; racket; clamour;—*v.t.* to strike, stun with noise; to harass with insistent repetition [O.E. *dyn*, noise].
dine (dīn) *v.t.* to entertain to dinner; to give facilities or accommodation for dining;—*v.i.* to take dinner.—**din'er** *n.* one who dines; a compartment on a railway train for serving meals to passengers. Also **din'ing-car.**—**dinette** (dīn-et') *n.* a preliminary dinner; a luncheon; (*U.S.*) an alcove in a dining-room.—**dinner** (din'ẹr) *n.* the principal meal of the day.—**dinner-jacket,** a black coat (without tails) worn as informal evening dress.—**dinn'er-time** *n.* the hour at which dinner is taken [Fr. *dîner*, to dine].
ding (ding) *v.t.* to drive; to beat; to dash with violence.—**ding'-dong** *n.* the sound of bells continuously rung;—*a.* monotonous; strenuously contested as in *ding-dong struggle* [Scand.].
dinghy, dingy, dingey (ding'gi) *n.* a small boat used in the E. Indies; a rowing-boat, such as is attached to a yacht [Hind. *dengi*, a boat].
dingle (ding'gl) *n.* small wooded valley [prob. M.E. *dengel*, a hollow].
dingle-dangle (ding'gl-dang'gl) *adv.* swinging to and fro [duplication of *dangle*].
dingo (ding'gō) *n.* a member of the dog-family found only in Australia [Native].
dingy (din'ji) *a.* soiled; sullied; of a darkish colour.—**din'giness** *n.* [prob. conn. with *dung*].
dinkum (dingk'um) *a.* (*Austral.*) honest; trustworthy; dependable [etym. unknown].
dinosaur (dī'nō-sawr) *n.* a gigantic extinct four-footed reptile of the Mesozoic age [Gk. *deinos*, terrible; *sauros*, a lizard].
dinotherium (dī-no-thē'ri-um) *n.* a gigantic extinct mammal of elephant kind [Gk. *deinos*, terrible; *thērion*, a wild beast].
dint (dint) *n.* a blow; a stroke; a mark or depression made by a blow; force or energy exerted;—*v.t.* to make a mark or dent by a blow.—**by dint of,** by means of [O.E. *dynt*, a blow].
diocese (dī'ō-sēs) *n.* the district in which a bishop exercises ecclesiastical jurisdiction.—**diocesan** (dī-os'es-ạn or dī'o-sē-zạn) *a.* pert. to a diocese;—*n.* a bishop or holder of a diocese [Gk. *dioikēsis*, administration].
dioecious, diecious (dī-ē'shus) *a.* unisexual; (*Bot.*) having the stamens (male) and pistils (female) borne by separate plants of the same species; (*Zool.*) having the male and female reproductive organs separate [Gk. *dis*, twice; *oikos*, a dwelling].
diopter, dioptre (dī-op'tẹr) *n.* the unit for measuring power of a lens [Gk. *dioptron*, instrument for measuring angles].
dioptrics (dī-op'triks) *n.* that part of the science of optics which treats of the laws of refraction of light passing through different media [Gk. *dioptron*, instrument for measuring angles].
diorama (dī-ō-rȧ'mạ) *n.* a painting viewed through an opening in the wall of a darkened room, varied effects of reality being realised by skilful manipulation of lights [Gk. *dia*, through; *horama*, a sight].
dioxide (dī-ok'sīd) *n.* a substance the molecules of which comprise one part metal, two parts oxygen [Gk. *dis*, twice; *oxus*, acid].
dip (dip) *v.t.* to immerse momentarily in a liquid; to dye; to lower and raise again, as a flag; to wash as a sheep; to baptise by immersion; to lower headlights of a car;—*v.i.* to sink below a certain level; to glance cursorily at; (*Geol.*) to incline downwards.—*pr.p.* **dip'ping.**—*pa.p.* **dipped.**—*n.* a liquid into which something is dipped; immersion; (*Geol.*) inclination downward of rock-strata; a candle made by dipping wick in melted tallow; (*Colloq.*) a bathe.—**dip'per** *n.* something used for dipping; an anti-dazzle device for motor-car headlamps; a semi-aquatic diving bird, the water-ouzel, resembling a thrush; (*Colloq.*) the Great Bear.—**dip'ping-need'le** *n.* a magnetic needle indicating on a graduated circle, the magnetic dip.—**dip'-stick** *n.* a rod for calculating depth of oil in a tank.—**dip'py** *a.* (*Slang*) crazy [O.E. *dyppan*, to plunge].
dipetalous (dī-pet'ạ-lus) *a.* having two petals [Gk. *dis*, twice; *petalon*, a leaf].
diphtheria (dif-thēr'i-ạ) *n.* epidemic disease affecting mainly throat and air passages.—**diphthe'rial, diphther'ic, diphtherit'ic,** *a.*
diphthong (dif'thong) *n.* a union of two vowel sounds pronounced as one, as in p*oi*se, m*ou*th.—**diphthong'al** *a.*—**diphthong'ally** *adv.*—**diph'thongise** *v.t.* to develop a diphthong from a single vowel.—**diphthongisa'tion** *n.* [Gk. *dis*, twice; *phthongos*, sound].
diphyllous (dī-fil'us) *a.* (*Bot.*) having two leaves [Gk. *dis*, twice; *phullon*, a leaf].
diplex (dī'pleks) *a.* (*Radio*) pert. to the reception or transmission of two messages simultaneously.
diplocardiac (dip'lō-kar'di-ak) *a.* (*Biol.*) having, as some birds, a double or divided heart [Gk. *diplous*, double; *kardia*, the heart].
diplogen (dip'lō-jen) *n.* a form of hydrogen twice as heavy as the normal gas. (*U.S.*) called *deuterium* [Gk. *diplous*, double].
diploma (di-plō'mạ) *n.* a document or certificate conferring some honour, privilege, or degree, as that granted to graduates of a university;—*v.t.* to furnish with a diploma.—**dip'lomate** *n.* one who holds a diploma [Gk. *diploma*, a folded letter].
diplomacy (di-plō'mạ-si) *n.* the art of conducting international negotiations; political dexterity; tact in dealing with people.—**dip'lomat, diplo'matist** *n.* one skilled in the art of handling difficult international or

personal relations; one engaged in administering international law.—**diplomat'ic, -al** *a.* pert. to diplomacy.—**diplomat'ically** *adv.*—**diplomat'ic** *n.* an envoy at a foreign court.—**diplomat'ics** *n.pl.* the science of deciphering old manuscripts, charters, etc., of determining their authenticity, age, and historical value; palaeography.—**diplomatic corps,** the body of accredited foreign diplomatists resident in any capital [Gk. *diploma,* a folded letter].

diplopia, diplopy (dip-lō'pi-a, dip'lō-pi) *n.* (*Med.*) double vision [Gk. *diplous,* double; *ops,* the eye].

dipolar (dī-pō'lar) *a.* having two poles, as a magnet.—**dipo'larise** *v.t.* to magnetise.

dipole (dī'pōl) *n.* (*Radio*) a special type of aerial, used at short wave-lengths for distinguishing waves of different electromotive force.

dipper (dip'er) *n.* See **dip.**

dipsomania (dip-sō-mā'ni-a) *n.* an uncontrollable craving for alcoholic stimulants; confirmed drunkenness.—**dipsoman'iac** *n.* one who suffers from dipsomania.—**dipsoman'iacal** *a.*—**dipsop'athy** *n.* treatment to curtail a patient's consumption of drink.—**dipso'sis** *n.* morbid thirst [Gk. *dipsa,* thirst; *mania,* madness].

Diptera (dip'ter-a) *n.* an order of insects, including common house-fly, gnat, mosquito, which have only two wings.—**dip'teral** *a.*—**dip'teran** *n.* a dipterous insect.—**dip'teros** *n.* a double-winged temple.—**dip'terous** *a.* of the order *Diptera* [Gk. *dis,* twice; *pteron,* a wing].

diptych (dip'tik) *n.* an ancient writing tablet hinged in the middle and folding together like a book; a pair of carvings or pictures similarly hinged [Gk. *diptuchos,* folded double].

dire (dīr) *a.* dreadful; horrible; calamitous; disastrous. Also **dire'ful.**—**dire'ly, dire'fully** *adv.*—**dire'fulness** *n.* [L. *dirus,* terrible].

direct (di-rect', dī'rect) *a.* straight; straightforward; immediate; in line of descent; sincere; unambiguous;—*v.t.* to aim at; to guide; to point out the way; to manage (a business); to prescribe a course or line of procedure; to write the name and address on a missive, etc.;—*v.i.* to give direction; to act as a guide;—*adv.* in a straight line.—**direc'tion** *n.* act of directing; instruction; guidance; management; order; superscription; prescription; address (on a letter); line taken by a moving body.—**direc'tional, direct'ing, direct'ive** *a.* tending to guide or to advise.—**direct'ive** *n.* general orders from a supreme authority outlining procedure to be taken in directing a new plan or policy.—**direct'ly** *adv.* in a straight line; straightway; immediately after;—*conj.* (*Colloq.*) as soon as.—**direct'ness** *n.* the quality of being direct, frank, or unimpeded by extraneous details.—**direct'or** *n.* (*fem.* **direct'ress, direct'rix**) one who directs, esp. the producer of a film; a member of a board of managers in a large commercial firm, hospital, etc.; a counsellor; a father confessor; that which regulates a machine; in gunnery, an optical instrument for calculating line of firing.—**direct'orate** *n.* a board of directors.—**direct'orship** *n.* the office or period of office of a director.—**director'ial** *a.*—**direct'ory** *a.* containing directions; guiding;—*n.* a book containing the alphabetically arranged names and addresses of the residents of a town or district; a collection of rules for the conduct of worship.—**direct current** (*abbrev.* D.C.) (*Elect.*) a current flowing in one direction (contrasting with *alternating current* (A.C.)).—**direct heating,** a system of heating by radiation (as by coal, gas, or electric fire).—**direct speech** (*Gram.*) spoken words which, written down, are within inverted commas.—**direct tax,** a tax levied directly on taxpayer, as income tax.—**direction finder** (*Radio*) an aerial which determines direction of incoming wireless signals (*abbrev.* D/F) [L. *dirigere, directum,* to make straight].

dirge (derj) *n.* a funeral chant; a lament.—**dirge'ful** *a.* funereal [fr. L. *dirige* (lead thou), the opening word of Latin burial anthem].

dirigible (dir'i-ji-bl) *a.* capable of being directed or steered;—*n.* a navigable airship elongated in shape and propelled by engine-driven propellers.—**dir'igent** *a.* directing [L. *dirigere,* to direct].

dirk (derk) *n.* a short dagger orig. carried by Scottish clansmen;—*v.t.* to stab with a dirk [etym. doubtful].

dirndl (dirn'dl) *n.* a type of skirt gathered into a broad belt at the waist in the style of Central European peasant costumes [Ger. *Dirne,* a girl].

dirt (dert) *n.* any filthy substance, as mud, dust, excrement; loose soil; rubbish; squalor; (*Fig.*) obscenity;—*v.t.* to make foul; to besmirch.—**dirt'-cheap** *a.* (*Colloq.*) uncommonly cheap.—**dirt'ily** *adv.* in a dirty manner; meanly.—**dirt'iness** *n.*—**dirt'-track** *n.* a track for motor-cycle racing; a speedway.—**dirt'y** *a.* foul; unclean; muddy; base; (of weather) stormy; rainy.—*v.t.* to befoul [M.E. *drit,* excrement].

dis- *pref.* implying *separation,* as in *dis*miss; *negation,* as in *dis*band; *deprivation,* as in *dis*animate; *thoroughness,* as in *dis*annul.

disable (dis-ā'bl) *v.t.* to make incapable or physically unfit; to disqualify.—**disable'ment** *n.* disability.—**disabil'ity** *n.* the state of being disabled.

disabuse (dis-a-būz') *v.t.* to free from misapprehension or error; to undeceive.

disadvantage (dis-ad-van'tāj) *n.* want of advantage; a drawback; a hindrance; a handicap; detriment; hurt.—**disadvanta'geous** *a.* attended with disadvantage.—**disadvanta'geously** *adv.*

disaffect (dis-a-fekt') *v.t.* to alienate the affection of; to estrange; to fill with discontent.—**disaffect'ed** *a.* discontented; disloyal (esp. to government).—**disaffect'edly** *adv.*—**disaffect'edness, disaffec'tion** *n.* the state of being disaffected; disloyalty.

disaffirm (dis-a-ferm') *v.t.* to annul; to invalidate; to reverse a decision.—**disaffirm'ance, disaffirma'tion** *n.*

disaggregate (dis-ag'reg-āt) *v.t.* to separate into component parts; to analyse.

disagree (dis'a-grē) *v.i.* to be at variance; to differ in opinion; to be incompatible; to be detrimental to health (of food, climate, etc.).—**disagree'able** *a.* not agreeable; unpleasant; repellent.—**disagree'ableness, disagreeabil'ity** *n.*—**disagree'ably** *adv.*—**disagree'ment** *n.* difference of opinion; discord; discrepancy; unsuitableness.

disallow (dis-a-lou') *v.t.* to refuse to allow, permit, authorise, or sanction; to reject as illegal.—**disallow'able** *a.*—**disallow'ance** *n.*

disanimate (dis-an'i-māt) *v.t.* to deprive of spirit or courage.

disannul (dis-a-nul') *v.t.* to cancel or annul completely.

disappear (dis-a-pēr') *v.i.* to vanish; to become invisible; to cease to exist.—**disappear'ance** *n.* state of being invisible; act of disappearing.

disappoint (dis-a-point') *v.t.* to fail to realise the hopes of; to frustrate; to baffle; to foil.—**disappoint'ed** *a.* frustrated; baffled; cheated.—**disappoint'ing** *a.* causing disappointment.—**disappoint'ment** *n.* state of being disappointed; the frustration of one's hopes; miscarriage which disappoints.

disapprobation (dis-ap-rō-bā'shun) *n.* act of disapproving; censure; mental condemnation of what is considered wrong.

disapprove (dis-a-prōōv') *v.t.* to form an unfavourable judgment of; to censure; to refuse to sanction; to dislike;—*v.i.* (foll. by *of*).—**disapprov'al** *n.*—**disapprov'ingly** *adv.*

disarm (dis-àrm') *v.t.* to deprive of arms; to

render unable to attack; (*Fig.*) to conciliate; to allay;—*v.i.* to lay down arms, esp. national armaments.—**disarm'ament** *n.* the act of reducing, in peace-time, the output of military and naval weapons as a prevention of war; the state of being disarmed.

disarrange (dis-a̤-rānj') *v.t.* to disturb the order or arrangement of; to disorganise; to throw into confusion.—**disarrange'ment** *n.*

disarray (dis-a̤-rā') *v.t.* to break the array of; to throw into disorder; to undress;—*n.* disorder; confusion; state of undress.

disassociate (dis-a̤-sō'shi-āt) *v.t.* to disunite; to dissociate.

disaster (diz-as'te̤r) *n.* an adverse happening; mishap; sudden misfortune; catastrophe.—**disas'trous** *a.* unlucky; inauspicious.—**disas'trously** *adv.*—**disas'trousness** *n.* [L. *dis*; *astrum*, a star].

disavow (dis-a̤-vou') *v.t.* to refuse to acknowledge; to repudiate.—**disavow'al, disavow'ment** *n.*

disband (dis-band') *v.t.* to disperse (troops); to break up an organisation; to dismiss;—*v.i.* to break up; to disperse.—**disband'ment** *n.*

disbar (dis-bȧr') *v.t.* (*Law*) to expel a barrister from the bar, by order of the lawyers of the Inns of Court.—*pa.p.* **disbarr'ing**.—*pa.p.* **disbarred'**.—**disbar'ment** *n.*

disbelieve (dis-be-lēv') *v.t.* to maintain to be untrue; to refuse to believe;—*v.i.* to place no reliance or belief (foll. by *on* or *in*).—**dis'belief** *n.*—**disbeliev'er** *n.*

disbowel (dis-bou'el) *v.t.* to disembowel.

disbosom (dis-booz'um) *v.t.* to reveal.

disbud (dis-bud') *v.t.* to remove superfluous buds from, in order to strengthen remaining buds.—*pr.p.* **disbud'ding**.—*pa.p.* **disbud'ded**.

disburse (dis-burs') *v.t.* to pay out money; to expend.—**disburse'ment** *n.* expenditure.—**disburse'ments** *n.pl.* expenses.—**disburs'er** *n.* [L. *dis*, apart; Fr. *bourse*, purse].

disc, disk (disk) *n.* a flat, circular plate or surface; the face of sun or moon.—**disc'al** *a.* pert. to or resembling a disc.—**disc'-jock'ey** *n.* (*U.S. Colloq.*) announcer of a radio programme of recorded music [Gk. *diskos*, a round plate].

discard (dis-kȧrd') *v.t.* and *v.i.* to throw away cards as useless in the game; to put aside; to cast off;—*n.* the act of discarding; the card thrown out as useless.

discarnate (dis-kȧr'nāt) *a.* bereft of flesh; having no physical body.

discern (di-se̤rn') *v.t.* to distinguish clearly esp. by the sight; to perceive by the mind; to behold as separate.—**discern'er** *n.*—**discern'ible** *a.* capable of being discerned.—**discern'ibly** *adv.*—**discern'ing** *a.* discriminating; judging with insight.—**discern'ment** *n.* power or faculty of judging [L. *dis*, apart; *cernere*, to sift].

discharge (dis-chȧrj') *v.t.* to free from a load or weight; to unload a cargo; to fire off the charge with which gun is loaded; to emit, as smoke; to perform, as a duty; to pay, as an account or a debt; to demobilise, as soldiers, etc.; to dismiss, as for failure in service or duty;—*n.* act of discharging; cessation of military or naval service; performance; matter which exudes, as from an abscess; that which is discharged; the rate of flow of a liquid or waste matter through a pipe [Fr. *décharger*, to unload.]

disciple (di-sī'pl) *n.* one who receives instruction from another; one who adheres to a particular school of philosophy, religious thought, or art; a follower, esp. one of the twelve apostles of Christ.—**disci'pleship** *n.* [L. *discipulus*, a pupil].

discipline (dis'i-plin) *n.* instruction; training of the mind, or body, or the moral faculties; subjection to authority; self-control;—*v.t.* to train; to improve behaviour by judicious penal methods.—**dis'ciplinable, dis'ciplinal** *a.*—**disciplina'rian** *n.* one who enforces rigid discipline; a martinet.—**dis'ciplinary** *a.* pert. to discipline.—**dis'cipliner** *n.* [L. *disciplina*, training].

disclaim (dis-klām') *v.t.* to renounce claim to, or responsibility for; to disown; to repudiate;—*v.i.* to give up all claim (foll. by *in*).—**disclaim'ant** *n.*—**disclaim'er** *n.* denial; disavowal; repudiation.

disclose (dis-klōz') *v.t.* to unclose; to reveal; to divulge; to bring to light.—**disclo'ser** *n.*—**disclo'sure** *n.* act of disclosing or state of being disclosed; revelation.

discolour (dis-kul'ur) *v.t.* to spoil the colour of; to stain;—*v.i.* to become discoloured or stained.—**discolo(u)ra'tion, discol'ourment** *n.*—**discol'oured** *a.* stained.

discomfit (dis-kum'fit) *v.t.* to defeat; to disconcert; to foil; to baffle.—**discom'fiture** *n.* [O.Fr. *desconfit*, defeated].

discomfort (dis-kum'fort) *n.* want of comfort; uneasiness; pain;—*v.t.* to impair the comfort of; to make uneasy.

discommode (dis-ko-mōd') *v.t.* to put to inconvenience; to incommode; to disturb.

discompose (dis-kom-pōz') *v.t.* to upset the self-possession of; to disturb; to disarrange.—**discompo'sure** *n.* state of being discomposed; agitation.

disconcert (dis-kon-se̤rt') *v.t.* to discompose; to embarrass; to break up the harmony of; to frustrate.—**discon'cert** *n.* state of disagreement.

disconnect (dis-kon-ekt') *v.t.* to separate; to sever; to disjoint.—**disconnect'ed** *a.* separated.—**disconnex'ion, disconnec'tion** *n.*

disconsolate (dis-kon'sō-lāt) *a.* destitute of comfort or consolation; forlorn; utterly dejected.—**discon'solately** *adv.*—**discon'solateness, disconsola'tion** *n.*

discontent (dis-kon-tent') *a.* not content; dissatisfied;—*n.* want of contentment; dissatisfaction; state of being aggrieved;—*v.t.* to cause to be ill-pleased; to dissatisfy.—**discontent'ed** *a.*—**discontent'edly** *adv.*—**discontent'edness, discontent'ment** *n.*

discontinue (dis-kon-tin'ū) *v.t.* to interrupt; to break off; to stop;—*v.i.* to cease; to become intermittent.—**discontin'uance, discontinua'tion** *n.* interruption; cessation.—**discontinu'ity** *n.* want of continuity.—**discontin'uous** *a.* intermittent; occurring at intervals.

discord (dis'kord) *n.* want of concord or agreement; lack of harmony; strife; (*Mus.*) a combination of inharmonious sounds.—**discord** (dis-kord') *v.i.* to disagree; to be out of tune.—**discord'ance, discor'dancy** *n.* lack of spiritual (or musical) harmony.—**discor'dant** *a.* out of harmony; jarring; dissonant.—**discor'dantly** *adv.* [L. *discordia*, variance].

discount (dis-kount') *v.t.* to pay in advance (a bill of exchange not yet due); to deduct a sum or rate per cent from an account for prompt payment; to depreciate;—*v.i.* to lend money with discount.—**discount** (dis'kount) *n.* a sum of money refunded on prompt payment of a bill; the allowance made on the retail price by a wholesaler to a retailer [O.Fr. *descompter*, to count off].

discountenance (dis-koun'ten-a̤ns) *v.t.* to refuse to countenance or give approval to.

discourage (dis-kur'āj) *v.t.* to deprive of courage; to dishearten; to deter.—**discour'agement** *n.* act of discouraging; state of being discouraged; dissuasion; dejection.—**discour'aging** *a.* disheartening.

discourse (dis'kōrs) *n.* a formal speech; a sermon; a dissertation; reasoning from premises; conversation.—**discourse** (dis-kōrs') *v.t.* to utter;—*v.i.* to lecture; to converse; to hold forth (foll. usually by *upon*) [L. *discursus*, running to and fro].

discourteous (dis-kur'tyus) *a.* lacking in courtesy; ill-bred; rude.—**discourt'eously** *adv.*—**discourt'eousness, discourt'esy** *n.*

discover (dis-kuv′ėr) *v.t.* to expose to view; to find out (esp. something hitherto unknown); to bring to light.—**discov′erable** *a.*—**discov′erer** *n.*—**discov′ery** *n.* the act of finding out; that which is discovered [Fr. *découvrir*, to reveal].

discredit (dis-kred′it) *v.t.* to refuse credit to; to bring into disrepute; to disgrace; to disbelieve;—*n.* loss of credit or of reputation; doubt.—**discred′itable** *a.* disgraceful; damaging; injurious to reputation.

discreet (dis-krēt′) *a.* prudent; circumspect; judicious; cautious (in action or speech).—**discreet′ly** *adv.*—**discreet′ness** *n.* discretion [L. *discretus*, separated, prudent].

discrepancy (dis-krep′ạn-si, dis′krep-ạn-si) *n.* inconsistency; variance; difference.—**discrep′ant** *a.* not tallying; inconsistent; discordant; contrary [L. *discrepare*, to jar].

discrete (dis-krēt′) *a.* separate; distinct; disjunctive; unrelated.—**discrete′ly** *adv.*—**discrete′ness** *n.* [L. *discretus*, separated].

discretion (dis-kresh′un) *n.* the quality of being discreet; prudence; discernment; liberty to act according to one's judgment.—**discre′tional, discre′tionary** *a.*—**discre′tionally, discre′tionarily** *adv.* [L. *discretus*, separated, prudent].

discriminate (dis-krim′i-nāt) *v.t.* to detect as different; to distinguish; to select.—*v.i.* to make a distinction in.—**discrim′inately** *adv.*—**discrim′inating** *a.* able to observe subtle differences; distinctive.—**discrim′inatingly** *adv.*—**discrimina′tion** *n.* faculty of drawing nice distinctions; perception.—**discrim′inative** *a.* marking a difference; characteristic [L. *discriminare*, to divide].

discrown (dis-kroun′) *v.t.* to deprive of a crown.

discursive (dis-kur′siv) *a.* passing from one topic to another; rambling; digressive; arguing from premises to conclusion.—**discur′sively** *adv.*—**discur′siveness** *n.*—**discur′sory** *a.* discursive [L. *discursus*, a running to and fro].

discus (dis′kus) *n.* a quoit of stone or metal, used in athletic contests [Gk. *diskos*, quoit]

discuss (dis-kus′) *v.t.* to examine critically; to exchange ideas on; (*Colloq.*) to consume, as wine.—**discuss′able** (or **-ible**) *a.*—**discuss′ion** *n.* debate; act of exchanging opinions [L. *discutere*, to agitate].

disdain (dis-dān′) *v.t.* to look down upon, as unworthy or despicable; to scorn;—*n.* scorn; arrogance; contempt.—**disdain′ful** *a.*—**disdain′fully** *adv.*—**disdain′fulness** *n.* (O.Fr. *desdeigner*, to scorn].

disease (di-zēz′) *n.* absence of ease; an unhealthy condition of mind or body; malady; distemper.—**diseased′** *a.* having the health impaired [O.Fr. *desaise*, discomfort].

disembark (dis-em-bårk′) *v.t.* to put on shore; to land passengers, goods, etc.;—*v.i.* to land.—**disembarka′tion, disembark′ment** *n.*

disembarrass (dis-em-bår′as) *v.t.* to free from embarrassment.—**disembarr′assment** *n.*

disembody (dis-em-bod′i) *v.t.* to free from the body or flesh; to discharge from a military organisation.—**disembod′iment** *n.*

disembosom (dis-em-bo͝oz′um) *v.t.* to unburden oneself of a secret; to disclose.

disembowel (dis-em-bou′el) *v.t.* to take out the bowels; to gut; to eviscerate.

disenchant (dis-en-chant′) *v.t.* to free from enchantment or glamour; to disillusion; to undeceive.—**disenchant′ment** *n.*

disencumber (dis-en-kum′bėr) *v.t.* to free from encumbrance.—**disencum′brance** *n.*

disendow (dis-en-dou′) *v.t.* to deprive of endowments (esp. of a church).—**disendowed′** *a.*—**disendow′ment** *n.*

disenfranchise (dis-en-fran′chīz) *v.t.* to disfranchise; to deprive of the right to vote.—**disenfran′chisement** *n.*

disengage (dis-en-gāj′) *v.t.* to unfasten; to separate from an attachment; to release.—**disengaged′** *a.* vacant; available (for interview); at leisure.—**disengage′ment** *n.*

disentail (dis-en-tāl′) *v.t.* to break the entail of (an estate);—*n.* the act of disentailing.

disentangle (dis-en-tang′gl) *v.t.* to unravel; to untwist; to put in order what is entangled.—**disentang′lement** *n.*

disentitle (dis-en-tī′tl) *v.t.* to deprive of title or claim.

disentwine (dis-en-twīn′) *v.t.* to untwine.

disestablish (dis-es-tab′lish) *v.t.* to deprive of established position; to deprive (the Church) of State aid and recognition.—**disestab′lishment** *n.*

disesteem (dis-es-tēm′) *v.t.* to disapprove; to dislike;—*n.* disfavour; disregard.

diseur (dēz-ėr) *n.* (*fem.* **diseuse** (dēz-ėz′), an entertainer; one who recites [Fr. fr. *dire*, to say].

disfavour (dis-fā′vur) *n.* disesteem; disapproval; dislike; state of being out of favour;—*v.t.* to regard unfavourably.

disfigure (dis-fig′ur) *v.t.* to mar the appearance of; to deface; to deform.—**disfig′urement** *n.* a defect; a blemish.

disfranchise (dis-fran′chīz) *v.t.* to deprive of the rights of a citizen, esp. that of voting at elections.—**disfran′chisement** *n.*

disfrock (dis-frok′) *v.t.* to unfrock; to deprive of the right to wear clerical garb.

disgorge (dis-gorj′) *v.t.* to eject from the throat; to pour out (as a river into the sea); to hand over.—**disgorge′ment** *n.*

disgrace (dis-grās′) *n.* dishonour; discredit; shameful conduct;—*v.t.* to bring dishonour to; to degrade.—**disgrace′ful** *a.* shameful; infamous; discreditable.—**disgrace′fully** *adv.*

disgruntled (dis-grun′tld) *a.* vexed; sulky; disappointed; aggrieved.

disguise (dis-gīz′) *v.t.* to change the outward appearance of; to misrepresent;—*n.* dress, manner, voice, etc. assumed to hide a person's real identity.—**disguis′edly** *adv.* [O.Fr. *desguiser*, to change costume].

disgust (dis-gust′) *n.* loathing; nausea; aversion; repugnance;—*v.t.* to provoke disgust in.—**disgust′edly** *adv.*—**disgust′ful** *a.*—**disgust′ing** *a.* revolting; repugnant.—**disgust′ingly** *adv.* [L. *dis*; *gustus*, taste].

dish (dish) *n.* a plate or shallow concave vessel for serving food; the food in such a vessel; any concave object, like a dish;—*v.t.* to put in a dish; (*Colloq.*) to frustrate; to outwit.—**dish′-cloth, dish′-clout** *n.* a cloth for washing or drying dishes.—**dish′-wat′er** *n.* water in which dishes have been washed.—**to dish up**, to serve food ready for table [O.E. *disc*, a plate].

dishabille (dis-a-bēl′) *n.* Same as **deshabille.**

disharmony (dis-har′mo-ni) *n.* lack of harmony; discord.

dishearten (dis-hår′tn) *v.t.* to deprive of courage, confidence, or hope; to depress; to make despondent.

dishevel (di-shev′el) *v.t.* to ruffle the hair; to cause the hair or clothes to be untidy or unkempt;—*v.i.* to spread in disorder.—*pr.p.* **dishev′elling**.—*pa.p.* and *a.* **dishev′elled.**—**dishev′elment** *n.* [L. *dis*, in different directions; *capillus*, the hair].

dishonest (dis-on′est) *a.* lacking in honesty; fraudulent; inclined to cheat; unprincipled.—**dishon′estly** *adv.*—**dishon′esty** *n.*

dishonour (dis-on′ur) *n.* loss of honour; disgrace; shame; indignity;—*v.t.* to disgrace; to seduce; to refuse payment of (as a cheque).—**dishon′ourable** *a.* shameful; void of integrity; discreditable.—**dishon′ourableness** *n.*—**dishon′ourably** *adv.*

disillusion (dis-i-lo͞o′zhun) *v.t.* to free from illusion; to make the truth apparent;—*n.* state of being disillusioned.—**disillu′sionment** *n.* disenchantment.—**disillu′sive** *a.*

disincline (dis-in-klīn′) *v.t.* to make unwilling; to excite dislike or aversion.—

disinclina'tion *n.* unwillingness; reluctance; dislike.—**disinclined'** *a.*
disincorporate (dis-in-kor'-po-rāt) *v.t.* to deprive of corporate powers.
disinfect (dis-in-fekt') *v.t.* to free from infection; to destroy disease germs.—**disinfec'tant** *n.* a germicide.—**disinfec'tion** *n.*—**disinfec'tor** *n.*
disinfestation (dis-in-fes-tā'-shun) *n.* the destruction of insects (e.g. lice).
disingenuous (dis-in-jen'-ū-us) *a.* not ingenuous; actuated by ulterior motives; insincere.—**disingen'uously** *adv.*—**disingen'uousness** *n.*
disinherit (dis-in-her'-it) *v.t.* to deprive of rights and privileges of an heir.—**disinheri'tance** *n.*
disintegrate (dis-in'-te-grāt) *v.t.* to separate into component parts; to break up;—*v.i.* to crumble to pieces; to be resolved into elements.—**disin'tegrable, disin'tegrative** *a.* capable of being broken up.—**disintegra'tion** *n.* a gradual breaking up; in building, the slow crumbling away of stone.
disinter (dis-in-ter') *v.t.* to disentomb; to exhume; (*Fig.*) to unearth.
disinterested (dis-in'-ter-es-ted) *a.* free from self-interest; unprejudiced.
disjoin (dis-join') *v.t.* to sever; to disunite.—**disjoint'** *v.t.* to separate at the joints; to put out of joint; to make incoherent;—*v.i.* to fall to pieces.—**disjoint'ed** *a.* unconnected; (of speech) rambling; incoherent; illogical.—**disjoint'edly** *adv.*—**disjoint'edness** *n.*
disjunct (dis-jungkt') *a.* disjoined.—**disjunc'tion** *n.* disunion; severance; disconnection; (*Logic*) a statement of alternative possibilities.—**disjunct'ive** *a.*—**disjunct'ively** *adv.* [L. *dis*; *jungere, junctum*, to join].
disk See **disc.**
dislike (dis-līk') *v.t.* to have an aversion to; to disapprove of;—*n.* distaste; antipathy.
dislocate (dis-lō-kāt') *v.t.* to put out of place or out of joint; to upset the normal working of.—**disloca'tedly** *adv.*—**disloca'tion** *n.* (*Med.*) the displacement of a bone.
dislodge (dis-loj') *v.t.* to remove from a position of rest, hiding, or defence;—*v.i.* to depart.—**dislodg(e)'ment** *n.*
disloyal (dis-loi'-al) *a.* failing in duty or allegiance to the Crown; faithless; treacherous.—**disloy'ally** *adv.*—**disloy'alty** *n.*
dismal (diz'-mal) *a.* gloomy; dreary; depressing; bleak.—**dis'mally** *adv.*—**dis'malness, dismal'ity** *n.* [L. *dies mali*, ill-omened days].
disman (dis-man') *v.t.* to deprive (a district) of its men; to take away the human character from.
dismantle (dis-man'-tl) *v.t.* to strip of furnishings; to remove apparatus, equipment from; to destroy the defences of (a fortified town) [O.Fr. *desmanteler*, to strip].
dismay (dis-mā') *v.t.* to alarm; to deprive of courage; to fill with apprehension; to appal;—*n.* consternation; loss of courage [L. *dis*, neg.; O.H. Ger. *magan*, to be strong].
dismember (dis-mem'-ber) *v.t.* to tear limb from limb; to mutilate; to disjoint.—**dismem'berment** *n.* the taking to pieces.
dismiss (dis-mis') *v.t.* to send away; to disperse; to allow to go; to discharge from employment; to banish (from the mind).—**dismiss'al, dismis'sion** *n.* discharge; release.
dismount (dis-mount') *v.i.* to alight from a horse, bicycle, etc.;—*v.t.* to bring down from a place of elevation.
disobey (dis-ō-bā') *v.t.* to disregard orders or instructions; to refuse to do what is commanded.—**disobe'dient** *a.* refusing to obey.—**disobe'diently** *adv.*—**disobe'dience** *n.*
disoblige (dis-ō-blīj') *v.t.* to offend by an act of incivility; to refuse to grant a request to.—**disoblig'ing** *a.* ungracious; unwilling to accede to another's wishes.
disorder (dis-or'-der) *n.* want of order; muddle; confusion; discomposure; ailment of body or mind;—*v.t.* to throw out of order; to upset.—**disor'dered** *a.* out of order; deranged.—**disor'derly** *a.* confused; irregular; lawless; unruly.
disorganise (dis-or'-gan-īz) *v.t.* to upset the organic structure or regular system of; to subvert; to throw into disorder.—**disorgan'ic** *a.*—**disorganisa'tion** *n.* confusion.
disown (dis-ōn') *v.t.* to repudiate ownership of; to disclaim; to renounce.
disparage (dis-par'-āj) *v.t.* to decry; to belittle; to lower in rank or reputation; to depreciate.—**dispar'agement** *n.* unjust comparison; act of undervaluing.—**dispar'agingly** *adv.* [O.Fr. *desparagier*, to marry unequally].
disparate (dis'-par-āt) *a.* essentially different; unequal; dissimilar; incongruous.—**dis'parateness** *n.* [L. *dis*, neg.; *par*, equal].
disparity (dis-par'-i-ti) *n.* inequality in form, character, or degree; incongruity.
dispassion (dis-pash'-un) *n.* lack of feeling; serenity.—**dispas'sionate** *a.* free from passion; impartial; cool; unruffled.
dispatch See **despatch.**
dispel (dis-pel') *v.t.* to drive away; to scatter; to cause to disappear.—*pr.p.* **dispel'ling.**—*pa.p.* **dispelled'** [L. *dis*, apart; *pellere*, to drive].
dispense (dis-pens') *v.t.* to divide out in parts; to administer, as laws; to make up medicines;—*v.i.* to excuse from; to grant a dispensation from a duty or obligation.—**dispens'able** *a.* that may be dispensed with or dispensed; (*Eccles. Law*) pardonable.—**dispens'ary** *n.* a place where medicines are made up.—**dispensa'tion** *n.* the act of distributing; the mode of God's dispensing mercies (e.g. *Mosaic, Christian*); a licence to do what is normally prohibited.—**dispens'ative, dispensa'tory** *a.* granting dispensation.—**dispen'ser** *n.* one who dispenses, distributes, or administers; one who is qualified to make up medical prescriptions.—**to dispense with,** to do without [L. *dispensare*, to distribute by weight].
disperse (dis-pers') *v.t.* to scatter here and there; to spread; to distribute; to place at intervals (as troops);—*v.i.* to separate; to vanish; to be dispelled.—**dispers'al** *n.*—**dispers'edly** *adv.*—**dispers'edness** *n.*—**disper'sion** *n.* the act of dispersing; the state of being dispersed; (*Med.*) the reduction of an inflamed part; (*Opt.*) the separation of light into its constituent rays by refraction through a prism.—**disper'sive** *a.* tending to disperse [L. *di-*, asunder; *spargere, sparsum*, to scatter].
dispirit (dis-pir'-it) *v.t.* to deject; to depress; to cast down; to discourage.—**dispir'ited** *a.* spiritless; downcast; dejected.
displace (dis-plās') *v.t.* to put out of position; to oust from situation or office.—**displace'able** *a.*—**Displaced Persons,** name applied after World War 2 to people who, as the victims of war conditions were rendered homeless (*abbrev.* **D.P.**).—**displace'ment** *n.* the act of putting out of place or removing from office; the weight of water, measured in tons, displaced by a floating ship.
displant (dis-plant') *v.t.* to root up a plant; (*Fig.*) to strip a country of its inhabitants.
display (dis-plā') *v.t.* to unfold; to exhibit; to set out conspicuously;—*n.* exhibition; parade; ostentation; exaggerated expression of feeling [L. *displicare*, to unfold].
displease (dis-plēs') *v.t.* and *v.i.* to offend; to cause dissatisfaction to; to cause to be angry; to annoy.—**displeasure** (dis-plezh'-ūr) *n.* slight anger or irritation; dislike.
dispone (dis-pōn') *v.t.* (*Scots Law*) to make over (property) to another in a legal form [L. *disponere*, to dispose].
disport (dis-pōrt') *v.i.* and *reflex.* to play; to amuse oneself; to gambol; to frolic [O.Fr. (*se*) *desporter*, to amuse oneself].
dispose (dis-pōs') *v.t.* to distribute; to arrange; to regulate; to adjust; to bestow for an object or purpose; to induce a tendency or

inclination;—*v.i.* to settle; to determine.—**dispos'able** *a.* liable, free, to be disposed of or employed.—**dispos'al** *n.* the act of disposing or disposing of; control; regulation; management; transference (of property by a will).—**dispos'ed** *a.* inclined; minded; arranged.—**dispos'edly** *adv.*—**disposi'tion** *n.* the act of disposing; arrangement; guidance; temperament; (*Scots Law*) conveyance of property.—**to dispose of,** to get rid of; to refute (an argument); to finish (a task) [L. *dis,* apart; *ponere,* to place].

dispossess (dis-po-zes') *v.t.* to put out of possession; to deprive of property; to eject.—**dispossess'ion** *n.*—**dispossess'or** *n.*

dispraise (dis-prāz') *v.t.* to reproach; to dishonour; to disparage;—*n.* blame; censure; disparagement.

disprize (dis-prīz') *v.t.* to put a low value on; to underrate.

disproof (dis-pròòf') *n.* the act of disproving; refutation; a proving to be erroneous.

disproportion (dis-prō-pōr'shun) *n.* want of proportion, symmetry, proper quantity, or adequacy; inequality; disparity;—*v.t.* to make unsuitable; to mismatch.—**dispropor'tionable** *a.* disproportional; unequal.—**dispropor'tional, dispropor'tionate** *a.* out of proportion.—**dispropor'tioned** *a.*

disprove (dis-pròòv') *v.t.* to prove to be false; to refute; to prove the opposite of.

dispute (dis-pūt') *v.t.* to consider for and against; to debate; to question the validity of; to oppose by argument or by force;—*v.i.* to argue; to discuss; to contend;—*n.* an argument; a debate; an altercation; wrangling.—**dis'putable** *a.* liable to be called in question; open to argument.—**dis'putably** *adv.*—**disputabil'ity** *n.* the quality of being disputable.—**dis'putant, disput'er** *n.* one who takes part in a dispute; a controversialist.—**disputa'tion** *n.* a controversy in words; an academic discussion or argument.—**disputa'tious, disputa'tive** *a.* inclined to dispute; captious; argumentative [L. *dis,* apart; *putare,* to think].

disqualify (dis-kwol'-i-fī) *v.t.* to make unfit for some special purpose; to incapacitate; to make ineligible; to deprive of legal power or right.—**disqualifica'tion** *n.*

disquiet (dis-kwī'-et) *v.t.* to render uneasy in mind; to disturb; to make restless;—*n.* apprehensiveness; uneasiness; anxiety.—**disqui'etment, disqui'etude** *n.* uneasiness; anxiety; agitation; want of tranquillity.

disquisition (dis-kwi-zish'-un) *n.* a formal enquiry into a subject by argument or discussion; a systematic treatise; research.—**disquisi'tional, disquisi'tionary, disquis'itory, disquis'itive** *a.* [L. *disquirere,* to investigate].

disregard (dis-re-gàrd') *v.t.* to take no notice of; to ignore;—*n.* indifference; lack of attention.—**disregard'ful** *a.*—**disregard'fully** *adv.*

disrelish (dis-rel'-ish) *v.t.* to dislike the taste of; to have an aversion to;—*n.* distaste; dislike.—**disrel'ishing** *a.* offensive.

disrepair (dis-re-pār') *n.* state of being out of repair; delapidation.

disrepute (dis-re-pūt') *n.* discredit; disfavour; state of being unpopular.—**disrep'utable** *a.* disgraceful; degraded; discreditable in character.—**disrep'utableness** *n.*

disrespect (dis-re-spekt') *n.* want of respect or deference; disesteem; rudeness.—**disrespect'able** *a.* not respectable.—**disrespect'ful** *a.* uncivil; lacking in deference; inconsiderate.—**disrespect'fully** *adv.*

disrobe (dis-rōb') *v.t.* to undress; to discard official dress.

disroot (dis-ròòt') *v.t.* to tear up by the roots; to undermine; to remove completely.

disrupt (dis-rupt') *v.t.* to break or burst asunder; to create a schism (as in a Party).—**disrup'tion** *n.* the act or process of disrupting; rent; breach; schism.—**disrup'tive** *a.* causing or accompanied by disruption.—**disrup'ture** *n.* a bursting asunder. [L. *dis,* apart; *rumpere,* to break].

dissatisfy (dis-sat'-is-fī) *v.t.* to fail to satisfy; to make discontented.—**dissatisfac'tion** *n.* the state of being dissatisfied.

dissect (dis-sekt') *v.t.* to cut up; to divide a plant or a dead body of man or animal for minute examination of its parts; to anatomise; (*Fig.*) to criticise in detail.—**dissec'tion** *n.* the act or science of dissecting; the separation of the tissues of the body for critical examination; the part dissected.—**dissect'or** *n.* [L. *dis.* apart; *secare,* cut].

dissemble (dis-sem'-bl) *v.t.* to hide under a false semblance; to disguise; to conceal; to mask;—*v.i.* to give an erroneous impression; to assume a false appearance; to be hypocritical; to deceive.—**dissem'bler** *n.*—**dissem'bling** *a.* feigned; deceiving [L. *dissimulare,* to conceal a fact].

disseminate (dis-sem'-i-nāt) *v.t.* to sow, as seed; to scatter abroad; (*Fig.*) to broadcast; to propagate; to circulate.—**dissemina'tion** *n.* scattering; circulation.—**dissem'inative** *a.*—**dissem'inator** *n.* [L. *dis,* asunder; *seminare,* to sow].

dissent (dis-sent') *v.i.* to differ in opinion; to disagree; to hold views differing from those of the established church;—*n.* disagreement; difference of opinion; nonconformity.—**dissen'sion** *n.* open disagreement; quarrelling; discord.—**dissent'er** *n.* one who dissents.—**dissen'tient** *n.* one who differs in opinion.—*a.* disagreeing [L. *dis.* apart, *sentire,* to feel].

dissertate (dis'-er-tāt) *v.i.* to discourse.—**disserta'tion** *n.* a formal treatise or discourse, esp. a written thesis for a University prize or degree.—**disserta'tional, disserta'tive** *a.*—**dis'sertator** *n.* [L. *disserere,* to discuss].

disserve (dis-serv') *v.t.* to serve badly another's interests.—**disser'vice** *n.* injury; harm; a bad turn.

dissever (dis-sev'-er) *v.t.* to cut in two; to separate; to disunite.—**dissev'erance, dissevera'tion, dissev'erment** *n.* separation.

dissident (dis'-i-dent) *a.* dissentient; disagreeing;—*n.* a dissenter; a non-conformist.—**diss'idence** *n.* dissent [L. *dissidere,* to disagree].

dissimilar (dis-sim'-i-lar) *a.* unlike; not similar in quality, appearance, etc.; heterogeneous.—**dissimilar'ity, dissimil'itude** *n.* unlikeness; difference.—**dissim'ilarly** *adv.*

dissimulate (dis-sim'-ū-lāt) *v.t.* to dissemble; to feign;—*v.i.* to conceal one's true feelings; to be hypocritical.—**dissimula'tion** *n.* the act of pretending [L. *dissimulare*].

dissipate (dis'-i-pāt) *v.t.* to scatter; to squander; to dispel;—*v.i.* to disappear; to waste away; (*Colloq.*) to lead a dissolute life.—**diss'ipated** *a.* dissolute; debauched.—**dissipa'tion** *n.* act of dissipating; reckless intemperance.—**diss'ipative** *a.* [L. *dissipare,* to scatter].

dissociate (dis-sō'-shi-āt) *v.t.* to separate; to disunite; (*reflex.*) to disclaim connexion with.—**dissociabil'ity** *n.*—**disso'ciable** *a.* capable of being dissociated; incongruous.—**disso'cial** *a.* anti-social.—**dissocia'tion** *n.* the act of dissociating or state of being dissociated; separation; (*Psych.*) term used to describe disunion of the mind, or split personality.—**disso'ciative** *a.* [L. *dis,* asunder; *sociare,* to unite].

dissoluble (dis'-ol-ū-bl, di-sol'-ū-bl) *a.* capable of being dissolved, liquefied, melted, or decomposed.—**dissolubil'ity** *n.*

dissolute (dis'-o-lūt) *a.* lax in morals; dissipated.—**diss'olutely** *adv.*—**diss'oluteness** *n.*—**dissolu'tion** *n.* act of dissolving or passing into solution; disintegration, esp. of body at death; dismissal of an assembly; termination (of marriage, partnership, etc.). [L. *dis,* asunder; *solvere,* to loosen].

dissolve (di-zolv') *v.t.* to break up, esp. a solid by the action of a liquid; to terminate (as a Parliament); to annul (as a marriage);—*v.i.* to melt; to waste away; to fade out; to be dismissed.—**dissolvabil'ity, dissolv'ableness** *n.*

—**dissolv'able** *a.* capable of being turned into a liquid, or melted.—**dissolv'ent** *a.* having the power of dissolving substances [L. *dis,* asunder; *solvere,* to loosen].

dissonant (dis′o-nant) *a.* discordant; harsh; unharmonious; (*Fig.*) incompatible.—**diss′onance** *n.* Also **diss'onancy** [L. *dissonare,* to fail to harmonise].

dissuade (di-swād′) *v.t.* to persuade not to; to advise against.—**dissua'der** *n.*—**dissua'sion** *n.* act of dissuading.—**dissua'sive** *a.* tending to dissuade [L. *dis,* apart; *suadere,* to advise].

dissyllable (dis-sil′a-bl) *n.* a word of two syllables [Gk. *dis,* twice; *sullabē,* a syllable].

dissymmetry (dis-sim′e-tri) *n.* want of symmetry

distaff (dis′taf) *n.* a cleft stick for holding the fibre (wool, flax, etc.) from which thread is made in the process of hand-spinning.—**the distaff side,** the maternal side; the female line [O.E. *distaef,* the staff holding flax for spinning].

distance (dis′tans) *n.* the space between two objects; the interval between two events; remoteness; aloofness; reserve;—*v.t.* to place at a distance; to outstrip; to surpass.—**dis′tant** *a.* far off; remote in time, place, or blood-relationship; aloof; reserved; faint.—**dis'tantly** *adv.* [L. *distantia,* remoteness].

distaste (dis-tāst′) *n.* dislike, esp. of food; disgust; repugnance; aversion.—**distaste'ful** *a.* unpleasant; repellent; nauseous.

distemper (dis-tem′per) *n.* a method of painting (also called *tempera*) with pigments, in powder form, mixed with any glutinous substance soluble in water; paint of this kind; size-colouring used for indoor house decoration and for theatre scenery;—*v.t.* to paint in distemper. Also **destem'per** [O.Fr. *destremper,* to moisten with water].

distemper (dis-tem′per) *n.* a disordered state of mind or body; disease, esp. a highly infectious inflammatory disease in young dogs; bad temper [L. *dis,* apart; *temperare,* to control].

distend (dis-tend′) *v.t.* to stretch out; to swell; to inflate.—*v.i.* to become swollen or puffed out.—**disten'sible** *a.* capable of being distended.—**disten'sion, disten'tion** *n.* act of distending; state of being distended; inflation [L. *dis,* apart; *tendere,* to stretch].

distich (dis′tik) *n.* a couplet or group of two lines of verse, complete in themselves [Gk. *dis,* twice; *stichos,* a verse].

distil (dis-til′) *v.t.* to cause to fall in drops; to cause to trickle; to vaporise and recondense a liquid; (*Fig.*) to extract the essential quality of (as wisdom);—*v.i.* to trickle; to ooze; to use a still.—*pr.p.* **distil'ling**.—*pa.p.* **distilled′**.—**dis'tillate** *n.* the essence produced by distilling.—**distilla'tion** *n.* act of distilling.—**distil'latory** *a.* used in distilling.—**distil'ler** *n.*—**distil'lery** *n.* a place where distilling is carried on, esp. of alcohol [L. *de,* down; *stillare,* to drip].

distinct (dis-tingkt′) *a.* of marked difference; separate; clear; well-defined; obvious; precise.—**distinc'tion** *n.* separation; that which indicates individuality; eminence; repute; mark of honour bestowed for meritorious conduct or service.—**distinct'ive** *a.* marking distinction or difference.—**distinct'ively** *adv.*—**distinct'iveness** *n.*—**distinct'ness** *n.* clarity; precision [L. *distinctus,* separate].

distinguish (dis-ting′gwish) *v.t.* to observe the difference between; to keep apart; to give individuality to; to separate by a mark of honour; to discern;—*v.i.* to make distinctions.—**disting'uishably** *adv.*—**disting'uished** *a.* eminent; dignified.—**disting'uishing** *a.* peculiar; characteristic [L. *distinguere,* to separate].

distort (dis-tort′) *v.t.* to twist out of shape; to misrepresent; to pervert; to falsify.—**distort′ed** *a.* altered; perverted.—**distort'edly** *adv.*—**distor'tion** *n.* a twisting awry; misrepresentation; (*Radio*) any deviation from the original wave-form of speech or sound during transmission [L. *dis,* asunder; *torquere, tortum,* to twist].

distract (dis-trakt′) *v.t.* to draw away (the mind); to divert; to bewilder; to unbalance mentally.—**distract'ed** *a.* deranged; frantic.—**distract'edly** *adv.*—**distract'edness** *n.* state of being distracted; madness.—**distrac'tion** *n.* the act of distracting or the state of being distracted.—**distract'ive** *a.* causing distraction. —**distraught** (dis-trawt′) *a.* perplexed; bewildered; frantic [L. *distractus,* drawn aside].

distrain (dis-trān′) *v.t.* to seize goods, esp. to enforce payment of debt.—**distrain'ment, distraint′** *n.* seizure of goods.—**distrain'or, -′er** *n.* [L. *dis,* asunder; *stringere,* to draw tight].

distrait (dēs′trā) *a.* absent-minded [Fr.].

distress (dis-tres′) *n.* extreme pain, mental or physical; misfortune; extreme poverty;—*v.t.* to cause pain or anguish to; to harass; (*Law*) to distrain.—**distress'ful** *a.* causing suffering.—**distress'fully** *adv.*—**distressed area,** a part of the country where unemployment is rife [L. *distringere,* to pull asunder].

distribute (dis-trib′ūt) *v.t.* to divide among several; to allot or hand out; to spread out; to classify.—**distrib'utable** *a.* capable of being distributed.—**distrib'utary** *n.* a smaller river which branches off from a main river to reach the sea through a delta;—*a.* spreading out; distributing.—**distribu'tion** *n.* act of distributing; separation.—**distrib'utive** *a.* involving distribution.—**distrib'utor(-er)** *n.* one who or that which distributes [L. *dis,* asunder; *tribuere,* to allot].

district (dis′trikt) *n.* a defined tract of land; an administrative division of a country; a region;—*a.* local; regional, as in *District Council*;—*v.t.* to divide into specified areas [L. *distringere,* tighten].

distrust (dis-trust′) *v.t.* to have no faith in; to suspect; to doubt;—*n.* want of trust; doubt; suspicion; lack of confidence.—**distrust'ful** *a.* suspicious.—**distrust'fully** *adv.*

disturb (dis-turb′) *v.t.* to upset the normal condition of; to disquiet; to agitate; to ruffle. —**disturb'ance** *n.* uproar; confusion, esp. a breach of the peace; derangement [L. *dis,* asunder; *turbare,* to agitate].

disulphate (dī-sul′fāt) *n.* (*Chem.*) a sulphate containing one atom of hydrogen replaceable by a base.—**disul'phide** *n.* a sulphide containing two atoms of sulphur to the molecule.—**disulphu'ric** *a.* containing two sulphuric acid radicals [Gk. *dis,* twice; and *sulphur*].

disunion (dis-ūn′yun) *n.* separation; discord; dissension.—**disunite′** *v.t.* to cause separation; to cause a breach between.—**disu'nity** *n.* state of being disunited.

disuse (dis-ūs′) *n.* cessation of a practice or custom.—**disuse** (dis-ūz′) *v.t.* to cease to use. —**disu'sage** *n.* the gradual cessation of use or custom.

disyllable See **dissyllable**.

ditch (dich) *n.* a trench dug esp. for drainage or defence (orig. the mound of earth dug out to form a trench, hence *ditch* is a doublet of *dike*);—*v.t.* to cut a ditch in; to drain by a ditch; (*Colloq.*) to drive into a ditch;—*v.i.* to make or mend ditches; to make a forced 'landing' on the sea [O.E. *dic,* a dike or ditch].

dither (diTH′er) *n.* (*Colloq.*) a state of nervous agitation or confusion;—*v.i.* to shake; to be confused [etym. uncertain].

dithyramb (dith′i-ram) *n.* an ancient Greek choric hymn sung in honour of *Dionysus* (Bacchus), the god of wine; an ode, lofty and vehement in character.—**dithyram'bic** *a.* wild; boisterous [Gk. *dithurambos,* a hymn in honour of Bacchus].

dittany (dit′a-ni) *n.* a small perennial herbaceous plant, the leaves of which yield a fragrant oil formerly much used medicinally [fr. Mt. *Dikte,* in Crete].

ditto (dit′ō) *n.* (contracted usually to **do,**

that which has been said; the same;—*adv.* as aforesaid [L. *dictus*, said].

ditty (dit'i) *n.* a song; a short poem to be sung [L. *dictare*, to dictate or compose].

ditty-bag (dit'i-bag) *n.* a small bag used by soldiers and sailors for holding needles, thread, etc.—**ditt'y-box** *n.* a box for the same purpose [etym. unknown].

diuretic (dī-ū-ret'ik) *a.* exciting the discharge of urine;—*n.* a medicine which tends to increase the flow of urine.—**diures'is** *n.* excessive urinary excretion [Gk. *dia*, through; *ourein*, to make water].

diurnal (dī-ur'nal) *a.* belonging to the day (opp. of *nocturnal*); during a day; daily; lasting one day;—*n.* a day-book; a book containing the canonical hours of the R.C. breviary.—**diur'nally** *adv.* [L. *dies*, a day].

diuturnal (dī-ū-tur'nal) *a.* lasting long [L. *diuturnus*, lasting long].

diva (dē'va) *n.* a popular female singer; a prima donna [L. *diva*, fem. of *divus*, divine].

divagate (dī'va-gāt) *v.i.* to wander; to stray; to ramble; (*Fig.*) to digress.—**divaga'tion** *n.* [L. *divagari*, to wander].

divalent (div'a-lent or dī-vā'lent) *a.* (*Chem.*) capable of combining with two radicals; bivalent [Gk. *dis*, twice; L. *valere*, to be strong].

divan (di-van') *n.* a Turkish council of state; a council-room; a low, cushioned seat; a smoking-room; a collection of Persian poems [Pers. *diwan*, a long seat].

divaricate (dī-var'i-kāt) *v.t.* (*Bot.*) to divide into two branches;—*v.i.* to fork; to diverge; —*a.* branching; spreading; divergent.— —**divarica'tion** *n.* [L. *dis*, asunder; *varicare*, to spread the legs].

dive (dīv) *v.i.* to plunge into water head first; to remain under water, as a diver; to penetrate deeply into; to plunge the hand into; —*n.* a plunge head-first; (*Slang*) a cheap, usually basement, restaurant of ill-repute.— **div'er** *n.* one who dives.—**dive'bomb'er** *n.* a bomber-aircraft which dives low over its target.—**div'ing-bell** *n.* an apparatus originally bell-shaped, by which deep-sea divers can work under water.—**diving dress**, a water-proof suit with weighted boots and air-supplied, water-tight helmet worn by divers [O.E. *dufan*, to plunge].

diverge (di-verj)' *v.i.* to divide; to turn in different directions; to deviate from a course; to vary; to differ.—**diverge'ment, diver'gence, diver'gency** *n.* deviation from a common centre.—**diver'gent** *a.* branching off; deviating. —**diver'gently** *adv.* [L. *dis*, asunder; *vergere*, to incline].

divers (dī'vẹrz) *a.* several; sundry; various.— **diverse'** *a.* (modern var. of *divers*) of different kinds; dissimilar.—**diverse'ly** *adv.*—**diver'sity** *n.* state of being unlike; variety [L. *diversus*, different].

diversify (dī-ver'si-fī) *v.t.* to make diverse or various; to give variety to; to break the monotony of.—*pr.p.* **diver'sifying.**—*pa.p.* **diver'sified.**—**diversifica'tion** *n.* the act of diversifying; the state of being diversified; variegation [L. *diversus*, varied; *facere*, to make].

divert (dī-vert') *v.t.* to turn aside; to alter the direction of; to draw off; to amuse or entertain.—**diver'sion** *n.* the act of diverting; that which diverts.—**divert'ing** *a.* entertaining.— **divert'isement, divertissement** (dē-ver-tēs'mong) *n.* a short ballet or interlude between the acts of a play [L. *dis*, aside; *vertere*, to turn].

Dives (dī'vēs) *n.* the rich man in the parable of Lazarus [Luke 16]; any very wealthy person [L. *dives*, rich].

divest (di-vest') *v.t.* to strip, as of clothes, equipment, etc.; to dispossess; (*Reflex.*) to undress.—**divest'iture, divest'ment** *n.* [L. *dis*; *vestire*, to clothe].

divide (di-vīd') *v.t.* to separate into parts; to share; to keep apart; to antagonise; (*Math.*) to find how many times one number is contained in another;— *v.i.* to be separated; to part; in Parliament, to vote for or against a motion;—*n.* act of dividing; (*U.S.*) a watershed.—**divid'ers** *n.pl.* compasses for measuring or dividing lines, not for drawing areas.— **the Great Divide**, death [L. *dividere*, to distribute].

dividend (div'i-dend) *n.* (*Arith.*) the sum to be divided by the divisor to obtain the quotient; interest payable on loans, invested money, etc.; the share of profits payable to members of a co-operative society. [L. *dividere*, to share out].

divine (di-vīn') *a.* belonging to or having the nature of God, or a god; devoted to the worship of God; holy; sacred; heavenly; superhuman;—*n.* a priest; a clergyman; a theologian;—*v.t.* and *v.i.* to forecast by supernatural means; to practise divination.— **divina'tion** *n.* the art or act of foretelling the future by non-rational methods; intuitive prevision; augury.—**divina'tor, divin'er** *n.* (*fem.* **divin'eress**) one who divines, esp. a dowser, one who professes to locate underground water by the aid of a divining rod.—**divine'ly** *adv.*—**divine'ness** *n.*—**divining rod**, a forked twig, usually of hazel, used by professional dowsers to locate underground water.—**divin'ity** *n.* state of being divine; God; a pagan deity; the study of theology [L. *divinus*, divine].

division (di-vizh'un) *n.* the act of dividing; part of a whole; a section; a partition; difference in opinion; (*Mil.*) an army unit of 20,000 men, the normal command of a *Major-General.*—**divisibil'ity** *n.*—**divis'ible** *a.* capable of being divided.—**divi'sional, divi'sionary** *a.* pert. to or belonging to a division; indicating a separation.—**divisor** (di-vī'zor) *n.* (*Math.*) the number by which another is divided [L. *divisus*, divided].

divorce (di-vōrs') *n.* the legal dissolution of a marriage contract; separation;—*v.t.* to obtain legal dissolution of a marriage; to separate; to sever; to disunite.—**divorcee'** *n.* a divorced person.—**divorce'ment** *n.* the act of dissolving the marriage bond [L. *divortium*].

divot (div'ot) *n.* (*Scot.*) a piece of turf; sod; (*Golf*) a piece of turf cut out accidentally by golfer [etym. unknown].

divulge (di-vulj') *v.t.* to make known or public; to disclose; to communicate to others.— **divul'gate** *v.t.* to publish.—**divulga'tion, divulge'ment, divul'gence** *n.* [L. *dis*, asunder; *vulgus*, the common people].

dixie (diks'i) *n.* (*Colloq.*) a camp cooking-pot of large capacity [etym. unknown].

dizen (dī'zn, or diz'n) *v.t.* to dress showily; to deck [O.E. *dise*, bunch of flax on a distaff].

dizzy (diz'i) *a.* giddy; light-headed; causing giddiness; bewildered;—*v.t.* to make dizzy; to perplex.—**dizz'ily** *adv.*—**dizzi'ness** *n.* giddiness; vertigo [O.E. *dysig*, foolish].

djinn, djinnee See **Jinnee.**

do (dō) *n.* (*Mus.*) first of the syllables used in sol-faing; the first tone of the major diatonic scale. Also **doh.**

do (dȯȯ) *v.t.* to perform; to execute; to affect; to finish; to prepare; to suit; to confer; to offer; to swindle;—*v.i.* to act; to be; as *auxil.* verb, used to give emphasis to princ. verb as in *I do think you should go*; to avoid repetition of another verb, and in negative, emphatic and interrogative sentences.—*pr.p.* **do'ing.**—*pa.t.* **did.**—*pa.p.* **done.**—*n.* a feat; (*Colloq.*) a swindle; a special entertainment or party.—**to do away with,** to destroy.—**do'er** *n.* an agent.—**to do for,** to suit; to overwhelm; to kill; (*Colloq.*) to work for someone as a charwoman.—**to do in,** to murder.—**do'ings** *n.pl.* things done; conduct; activities; (*Slang*) a substitute word for another, as in *pass me the doings.*—**done'out** *a.* exhausted.—**to do with,** to make use of; to need; to tolerate; to suit (in health) [O.E. *don*, to do].

Dobbin (dob'in) *n.* name for patient, quiet workhorse [nickname for *Robin*].

dobchick Same as **dabchick.**
docent (dō′sent) *n.* a tutor in a university below professorial rank; curator of a museum [L. *docere*, to teach].
doch-an-doris (doH′an-dor′is) *n.* a parting cup; a stirrup-cup. Also **doch′an -dor′ach, deuch′an-dor′is** [Gael. *deoch an doruis*, drink of the door].
docile (dō′sīl or dos′il) *a.* easily instructed or managed; tractable; amenable to discipline.—**docile′ly** *adv.*—**docil′ity** *n.* quality of being docile [L. *docere*, to teach].
dock (dok) *n.* a common tap-rooted weed of genus *Rumex* [O.E. *docce*].
dock (dok) *v.t.* to cut short; to curtail; to clip (as an animal's tail);—*n.* the part of tail left after clipping [M.E. *dok*, a tail].
dock (dok) *n.* an artificial enclosure near a harbour or river where ships are berthed, loaded, etc.; enclosed space in a law court where accused stands; the platform in a station where a train is due to arrive or depart.—**dock′age** *n.* space available in docks for ships; charge made for use of docks.—**dock′er** *n.* one who works at the docks, esp. loading and unloading cargoes.—**dock′yard,** *n.* a yard or magazine near a harbour esp. for naval equipment and repairs.—**dry′dock, grav′ing-dock,** *n.* a dock from which water can be pumped out.— **floating dock,** a mobile repairing dock which floats on pontoons, and is fitted with a contrivance for pumping out the water [O.Dut. *dokke*].
docket (dok′et) *n.* a summary of a written document; a memorandum; a bill or label affixed to goods giving instructions for delivery; (*Law*) a précis of a legal judgment; a list of cases for trial;—*v.t.* to summarise; to mark the contents of papers on the back or outside sheet. Also **doc′quet** [prob. dim. of *dock*, to curtail].
doctor (dok′tor) *n.* one who holds the highest degree granted by any faculty of a university; a medical practitioner; —*v.t.* to treat medically; to adulterate; to falsify; to repair temporarily;—*v.i.* to practise medicine; to take physic.—**doc′torate** *n.* the degree or status of a university doctor.—**doc′torship** *n.*—**docto′rial** *a.* pert. to a doctor [L.=a teacher, fr. *docere*, to teach].
doctrine (dok′trin) *n.* instruction; that which is taught; principle of belief; creed; any special truth.—**doc′trinal** or **doctri′nal** *a.* pert. to doctrine, esp. Christian Church.—**doc′trinally** *adv.*—**doctrinaire** (dok-tri-nār′) *n.* a political theorist who tends to urge the application of a doctrine beyond all practical considerations;—*a.* obstinate in urging impracticable doctrines.—**doctrina′rian** *n.* a doctrinaire [Fr. fr. L. *doctrina*, teaching].
document (dok′ū-ment) *n.* an official paper containing information, giving instructions, or establishing facts;—*v.t.* to furnish with written evidence of.—**documen′tal, documen′tary** *a.* pert. to, derived from, or in the form of, a document.—**documenta′tion** *n.* the use of documentary evidence; the furnishing of such evidence in book-form.—**doc′umented** *a.* furnished with documentary evidence.—**documentary film,** film which uses characters, objects and scenes of real life [L.*documentum*, example].
dod (dod) *v.t.* to lop off.—**dodd′ered** *a.* (of trees) lopped off [M.E. *dodden*, to lop].
dodder (dod′ẹr) *v.t.* or *v.i.* to totter or tremble, as with age; to ramble in speech.—**dodd′ering** *a.* trembling.—**dodd′ery** *a.* [prob. dialect word, *dod*, to clip off].
dodecagon (dō-dek′ạ-gon) *n.* a plane figure with twelve sides and containing twelve equal angles.—**dodecag′onal** *a.* [Gk. *dodeka*, twelve; *gonia*, an angle].
dodecahedral (dō-dek-ạ-hē′drạl) *a.* pert. to a dodecahedron.—**dodecahe′dron** *n.* a solid bounded by twelve equal pentagons [Gk. *dodeka*, twelve; *hedra*, a seat].
dodge (doj) *v.t.* to evade or escape by a sudden turning; to baffle;—*v.i.* to twist aside (physically or morally); to play fast and loose; to avoid an issue by quibbling;—*n.* a trick; an artifice; (*Colloq.*) an ingenious device.—**dod′ger** *n.* [etym. unknown].
dodo (dō′dō) *n.* an extinct flightless bird, found originally in Mauritius and Madagascar —*pl.* **do′do(e)s** [Port. *doudo*, silly].
doe (dō) *n.* the female of the fallow deer; also female of antelope, rabbit, hare, goat, rat, mouse, ferret.—**doe′skin** *n.* the skin of a doe; a fine close-woven cloth [O.E. *da*, a doe].
does (duz) 3rd pers. sing. pr. ind. of verb **do.**
doff (dof) *v.t.* to do or take off, esp. the hat; to rid oneself of [contr. of *do off*].
dog (dog) *n.* a common, carnivorous quadruped of the same genus as the wolf, mainly domesticated; a worthless fellow; (*Colloq.*) a young man-about-town; one of the two constellations of stars (*Canis Major*, *Canis Minor*); a metal hook for holding logs of wood or supporting fire-irons; a spike for fastening rails to sleepers on railway track;—*a.* male, as in *dog-wolf*;—*v.t.* to follow closely, as a dog does; to keep at the heels of; to pursue relentlessly; to importune.—*pr.p.* **dog′ging.**—*pa.p.* **dogged.**—**dog′-bis′cuit** *n.* a special hard biscuit of meal and meat scraps, for dogs.—**dog′-bri′er** *n.* a dog-rose.—**dog′-cart** *n.* a high, usually two-wheeled carriage with two seats back-to-back, and a box underneath for carrying sporting dogs.—**dog′col′lar** *n.* a leather strap with name plate fastened round a dog's neck; (*Colloq.*) the collar worn by clergymen.—**dog′dais′y** *n.* the ox-eye daisy.—**dog′days** *n.pl.* the hottest period of the northern summer, generally considered from July 3rd-August 11th, when the dog-star, Sirius, rises and sets with the sun.—**dog′eared** *a.* (of a book) having the corners of the pages turned down.—**dog′ged** *a.* stubborn; persistent.—**dog′gedly** *adv.*—**dog′gedness** *n.*—**dog′fan′cier** *n.* one who breeds dogs, esp. for sale.—**dog′fish,** *n.* a species of fish of the shark order, found in British waters, and sold as rock salmon.—**dog′gish** *a.* like a dog; surly.—**dog′go** *adv.* (*Slang*) hidden, as in *to lie doggo*.—**dog′gy** *a.* pert. to dogs; fond of dogs; (*U.S.*) fashionable.—**dog′ken′nel** *n.* a small hut for dogs.—**dog Latin,** incorrect barbarous Latin .—**dog′lead** *n.* a leather strap or chain attached to a dog's collar, for leading or fastening dog.—**dog′li′cence** *n.* a licence payable by owners of dogs over 6 months old. —**dog′like** *a.* faithful.—**dog′rose** *n.* a wild-rose. —**dog's nose** (*Colloq.*) a drink made of gin and beer.—**dog′-star** *n.* alternative name for Sirius, the principal star in the constellation *Canis Major*, and the brightest star in the heavens.—**dog′-tired,** *a.* dead-beat; completely exhausted.—**dog′-tooth,** *n.* a canine tooth; the eye-tooth (of a human being); (*Archit.*) a characteristic Norman and Early English moulding, consisting of a series of ornamental pyramid-like projections.—**dog′-vi′olet** *n.* the scentless, wild violet.—**dog′-watch** *n.* one of the two-hour watches on board ship from 4-6 or 6-8 p.m.—**dog′-wood** *n.* one of the several varieties of cornel.—**a dog in the manger,** a spoil-sport; one who refuses to let another enjoy what he himself has no use for.—**the dogs** (*Colloq.*) greyhound-racing.—**a hot-dog** (*U.S.*) a sandwich made with hot sausage inside a roll.—**to give a dog a bad name, and hang it,** when a person's reputation has been lost, nothing he does, however creditable, will gain public approval.—**to go to the dogs,** to be ruined.—**to let sleeping dogs lie,** not to stir up trouble unnecessarily [O.E. *docga*, a dog].
doge (dōj) *n.* the title of the chief magistrates in the ancient republics of Venice and Genoa [It. *doge*, doublet of *duce*, a leader].
doggerel (dog′ẹr-ẹl) *n.* irregular, unpoetical burlesque verse;—*a.* halting; unrhythmic; meaningless [etym. unknown].

dogma (dog′mạ) *n.* a philosophical tenet; a theological doctrine authoritatively asserted; a principle or belief.—**dogmat′ic, -al,** *a.* pert. to a dogma; opinionative; bigoted; authoritative.—**dogmat′ically** *adv.*—**dogmat′ics** *n.* the science of systematised Christian doctrines; the study of systematic theology.—**dog′matise** *v.i.* to formulate a dogma; to express an opinion positively or arrogantly.—**dog′matiser** *n.*—**dog′matism** *n.* positive assertion; laying down the law.—**dog′matist** *n.* [Gk. *dogma*, an opinion].

doh (dō) *n.* first note in sol-fa notation. Also **do.**

doily (doi′li) *n.* a small table mat placed under dishes; a small, round, linen or paper mat put on plate holding cakes, etc. Also **doy′ley** [fr. *Doily*, a haberdasher].

dolce (dol′chā) *a.* (*Mus.*) sweet; soft.—**dolcemen′te** *adv.* sweetly and softly [It. *dolce*, sweet].

doldrums (dol′drums) *n.pl.* a belt of calms at the Equator; (*Colloq.*) a state of depression; the dumps [etym. doubtful—prob. connected with *dull*].

dole (dōl) *v.t.* to distribute in small portions; —*n.* something given or paid out; a share; alms; (*Colloq.*) weekly payment to unemployed workmen under National Insurance Act; a small portion [O.E. *dal*, a part].

dole (dōl) *n.* pain; sorrow; affliction.—**dole′ful** *a.* grievous; melancholic; dismal.—**dole′fully** *adv.*—**dole′fulness** *n.*—**dole′some** *a.* dismal; doleful [O.Fr. *doel*, mourning].

doll (dol) *n.* a puppet; a toy-baby as a child's plaything; (*Colloq.*) a pretty, rather brainless girl.—**doll′dom, doll′ship** *n.*—**to doll up** (*Colloq.*) to dress up smartly [prob. fr. *Dolly*, abbrev. of Dorothy].

dollar (dol′ạr) *n.* a silver coin, the monetary unit of U.S.A. and Canada [Ger. *Taler*, short for *Joachimstaler*, the coin being first made at the silver mines of *Joachimstal*, Bohemia].

dollop (dol′op) *n.* a lump, esp. a shapeless lump of food [prob. Scand. *dolp*, a lump].

dolly (dol′i) *n.* a wooden shaft attached to a disc with projecting arms, used in mining, pile-driving, etc.; a wooden stick for stirring clothes in a wash-tub; a mobile platform for cameras, etc. in a film-studio;—*v.i.* to wash (clothes) in a tub; to beat (red-hot metal) with a hammer; to pulverise ore with a dolly; to obtain or yield by this method.—**doll′ied** *a.*—**doll′y-shop** *n.* a marine store or pawnshop.—**doll′y-tub** *n.* a wash-tub; a large tub used in mining for final washing of ores.—**doll′y-wag′on** *n.* a wagon used for removing dirt from a mine [prob. fr. *Dolly*].

dolly (dol′i) *n.* dim. of *doll.*—*a.* childish.

dolman (dol′man) *n.* a long, loose Turkish garment; Hussar's coat worn like a cape; similar garment worn by women in Victorian days [Turk. *dolaman*, a cloak].

dolmen (dol′men) *n.* a prehistoric megalithic sepulchre formed by a large unhewn stone resting on two or more unhewn uprights [Breton, *tol*, table; *men*, stone].

dolomite (dol′o-mīt) *n.* a natural double carbonate of magnesium and calcium.—**the Dolomites,** mountains of this rock in the Tyrol [fr. *Dolomieu*, the French geologist].

dolour (dō′lur) *n.* pain; distress; anguish.—**dolori′fic** *a.* expressing sorrow.—**doloro′so** *adv.* (*Mus.*) in a mournful manner.—**dol′orous** *a.* full of grief.—**dol′orously** *adv.*—**dol′ourousness** *n.* [L. *dolere*, to grieve].

dolphin (dol′fin) *n.* a sea mammal of the whale kind, closely resembling the porpoise, and in length about seven feet; popular name for the *dorado*; a mooring buoy [Gk. *delphis*, a dolphin].

dolt (dōlt) *n.* a heavy, stupid fellow; a blockhead.—**dolt′ish** *a.* dull; slow-witted.—**dolt′ishly** *adv.* [M.E. *dold*, dulled].

Dom (dom) *n.* a title given to certain R.C. dignitaries [L. *dominus*, lord].

domain (do-mān′) *n.* that which one has dominion over; landed property; estate, esp. that round a mansion house; (*Fig.*) the scope or sphere of any branch of human knowledge.—**domain′al, doma′nial** *a.* [Fr. *domaine*, fr. L. *dominus*, a lord].

dome (dōm) *n.* a hemispherical vault reared above the roof of a building; a large cupola.—**domed′, dom′ical** *a.* possessing a dome [L. *domus*, a house].

Domesday, Doomsday-book. See **doom.**

domestic (do-mes′tik) *a.* pert. to a house or home; devoted to home and household affairs; tame (of animals); not foreign (of a country's policy);—*n.* a household servant. —**domes′tics** *n.pl.* plain cotton cloths, grey or checked.—**domes′tically** *adv.*—**domes′ticate** *v.t.* to make fond of domestic life; to tame or accustom animals to live among men.—**domestic′ity** *n.* life in a household.—**domestic science,** science of home-management, etc. [L. *domus*, a house].

domicile (dom′i-sīl) *n.* an abode; a dwelling-house; (*Law*) a person's permanent residence;—*v.t.* to establish in a fixed residence. —**domicil′iary** *a.* pert. to a domicile [L. *domicilium*, a dwelling].

dominant (dom′i-nạnt) *a.* ruling; prevailing; (*Mus.*) having harmonic importance;—*n.* (*Mus.*) the fifth note of the diatonic scale.—**dom′inance** *n.* authority; ascendancy.—**dom′inancy** *n.*—**dom′inantly** *adv.*—**dom′inate** *v.t.* and *v.i.* to rule; to influence strongly; to sway; to tower over.—**domina′tion** *n.* government; absolute authority.—**domina′tive** *a.* ruling.—**domina′tor** *n.*—**domineer′** *v.i.* to rule with arbitrary sway; to be overbearing.—**domineer′ing** *a.* arrogant.—**domin′ion** *n.* lordship; sovereignty; predominance; territory under one government; a self-governing British colony esp. the official designation of Canada and New Zealand.—**Dominion status,** the political status of a co-equal member of the British Commonwealth of Nations [L. *dominari*, to be master].

dominical (do-min′i-kạl) *a.* belonging to our Lord or the Lord's Day [L. *dominicus*, belonging to a lord].

Dominican (do-min′i-kạn) *a.* belonging to *St. Dominic*, or to the order of preaching friars, founded by him (called also the *Black Friars*);—*n.* a member of St. Dominic's order.

domino (dom′in-ō) *n.* orig. a cape worn by a teacher; a hooded cloak worn by monks, priests, etc.; a long cloak of black silk with a hood, worn at masquerades; the person wearing such a cloak; a mask; one of the 28 oblong pieces marked each with a certain number of spots, used in the game of *dominoes* [L. *dominus*, a master].

dominus (dom′i-nus) *n.* a title given to clergymen, teachers, etc.—**dom′inie** *n.* (*Scot.*) a schoolmaster; (*U.S.*) a clergyman [L. *dominus*, a master].

Don (don) *n.* (*fem.* **Doña** (don′yạ); **Don′na** (Italian spelling) *n.* a Spanish title, the equivalent of the English *Sir* (formerly applied only to noblemen); a Spaniard.—**don,** *n.* a Fellow or tutor of Oxford or Cambridge University; a master at Winchester; (*Colloq.*) an adept [Sp. fr. L. *dominus*, a master].

don (don) *v.t.* to put on; to assume.—*pr.p.* **don′ning.**—*pa.p.* **donned** [short fr. *do on*].

donation (do-nā′shun) *n.* act of giving; a gift, esp. money given to charity.—**donate′** *v.t.* to present a gift.—**don′ative** *n.* an official gift; a gratuity; a benefice bestowed by a patron without reference to the bishop;—*a.* of the nature of a donative.—**do′nor** *n.* one who gives a donation; a benefactor.—**blood′-do′nor** *n.* one who voluntarily gives a blood-transfusion [L. *donare*, to give].

done (dun) *pa.p.* of the verb **do.—done!** agreed.
donjon (dun′jun) *n.* a massive central tower in ancient castles; a keep [alternative spelling of *dungeon*].
donkey (dong′ki) *n.* an ass; (*Colloq.*) a foolish person.—**don′key-en′gine** *n.* a small auxiliary type of steam engine for working a crane or pumping water into boilers of a steam-ship [etym. doubtful, prob. a double dim. of *dun*].
don't (dōnt) (*Colloq.*) contr. of **do not.**
doodle (dòò′dl) *n.* a trifler; a simple fellow; —*v.i.* to scribble aimlessly; (*Scot.*) to drone, as a bagpipe [prob. form of *dawdle*].
doodlebug (dòò′dl-bug) *n.* (*World War* 2) a utility motor-truck used in the Army; a nickname given to the V1 bomb.
dook (dòòk) *n.* (*Scot.*) a plug of wood driven into a wall to hold a nail, etc.
doom (dòòm) *n.* judgment; legal decree; ruin; fate; evil destiny;—*v.t.* to pass sentence on; to condemn; to destine.—**doomed** *a.* under sentence.—**doom′ful** *a.*—**dooms′day** *n.* the Day of Judgment.—**Doomsday or Domesday Book**, the census compiled by order of William the Conqueror, containing an assessment of population, property, stock, etc. of England, for purposes of taxation [O.E. *dom*, a judgment].
door (dōr) *n.* the wooden or metal structure, hinged or sliding, giving access to house, room, passage, or cupboard; the frame by which an entrance is closed; (*Fig.*) a means of approach.—**door′-bell,** *n.* a bell on outside of door but ringing inside.—**door′-check** *n.* a device which prevents a door from slamming.—**door′-nail,** *n.* large-headed nail with which doors used to be studded.—**dead as a door-nail** (*Colloq.*) quite dead.—**door′-plate** *n.* a metal plate on outside of door with name of occupant.—**door′-post,** *n.* the jamb.—**door′-step** *n.* the step outside a door.—**door′-way** *n.* the entrance to a house, room, etc.—**to darken one's door,** to enter one's house.—**to show a person the door,** to evict someone [O.E. *duru*, a door].
dop (dop) *n.* in diamond cutting, the cup in which a diamond is fixed for polishing; a basin; a shell-husk used by natives as a drinking cup [Dut.].
dope (dōp) *n.* any thick liquid, or semi-liquid lubricant; a varnish; a preparation for coating the fabric surfaces of aircraft; (*Colloq.*) alcohol motor fuel; a drug (orig. given to a horse before a race); any narcotic; (*Slang*) inside information (esp. about racehorses);—*v.t.* to apply dope or varnish to; to administer dope to; (*Fig.*) to hoodwink.—**dop′y** *a.* stupefied with drugs; slow-witted [Dut. *doop*, a dipping].
doppelgänger (dop′pl-geng′er) *n.* the apparition of a living person, portending death; a ghost [Ger. (*lit.*) *double-walker*].
doquet (dok′et) *n.* See **docket.**
dor (dor) *n.* a common species of British beetle. Also called **dor′-beet′le, dor′-fly.**—**dor′-gawk,** *n.* nightjar or goat-sucker [O.E. *dora*, a humble-bee].
dorado (do-rà′dō) *n.* a Southern constellation; a species of coloured fish which, like the dolphin, changes its colours when dying [Sp. fr. *dorar*, to gild].
Dorcas (dor′kas) *n.* (Bib.) the name of the woman, in Acts 9, who made garments for the poor.—**Dorcas Society,** society of charitable women who sew and knit garments for the poor.
doree, dory (dō′rē, dō′ri) *n.* a yellow, edible fish caught in British waters. Also **John Dory** [Fr. *dorée*, gilded].
Dorian (dor′i-an) *a.* pert. to *Doris*, in ancient Greece, or to its inhabitants.—**Dor′ic,** *a.* pert. to Doris, the Dorians, or the simple style of architecture of the Dorians; (of dialect) unpolished;—*n.* a mode of Greek music the Doric dialect characterised by broad vowel sounds; any provincial dialect (e.g. Scottish).
Dorking (dor′king) *n.* a domestic fowl [fr. *Dorking*, in Surrey].
dormant (dor′mant) *a.* sleeping; hibernating; quiescent; not in action; unclaimed (as a title);—*n.* (*Archit.*) a joist.—**dor′mancy** *n.* state of being quiescent.—**dor′mer-win′dow** *n.* a small vertical window projecting from a roof slope.—**dor′mitory,** *n.* a large common sleeping apartment.—**dor′mouse** *n.* a small, hibernating rodent [L. *dormire*, to sleep].
dormy, dormie (dor′mi) *n.* (*Golf*) the term applied in a match to one player who is leading by as many holes as still remain to be played [etym. unknown].
dorp (dorp) *n.* in S. Africa, a village [Dut. *dorp*, cf. O.E. *thorp*, a village].
dorsal (dor′sal) *a.* pert. to, near, or belonging to, the back [L. *dorsum*, the back].
dory (dō′ri) *n.* See **doree.**
dory (dō′ri) *n.* a flat-bottomed fishing-boat used in Newfoundland waters [etym. doubtful].
dose (dōs) *n.* the prescribed quantity of medicine to be taken at one time; a portion; anything disagreeable that must be taken or done; the amount of radiation energy, measured in röntgens, absorbed by a person;—*v.t.* to administer or order in doses; (*Colloq.*) to adulterate.—**dos′age** *n.* the practice of dosing; the amount of a dose.—**dosim′eter** *n.* an instrument for measuring minute doses accurately; (*Atomic Warfare*) a small instrument for recording the total dose of radioactivity accumulated up to the moment.—**dose-rate meter** (*Atomic Warfare*) instrument for measuring the rate per hour at which the radiation dose is being received around the heavily contaminated central zone [Gk. *dosis*, a giving].
doss (dos) *n.* (*Slang*) a bed;—*v.i.* to go to bed.—**doss′-house,** *n.* a cheap lodging house [etym. uncertain].
dossier (dos′i-ā) *n.* a set of documents [Fr. *dossier*, a collection of documents].
dost (dust) 2nd pers. sing. pres. ind. of **do.**
dot (dot) *n.* a small point or spot made with a pen, pencil, or sharp instrument; a speck; (*Mus.*) a point placed after a note or rest to lengthen the sound or pause by one-half;—*v.t.* to mark with dots; to diversify as with small objects;—*v.i.* to make dots.—*pr.p.* **dot′ting.**—*pa.p.* **dot′ted.**—**dot′ty** *a.* marked with or consisting of dots; (*Colloq.*) weak in mind; crazy.—**dot and dash,** in Morse code, the short and long symbols [O.E. *dott*, a speck].
dot (dot) *n.* a marriage portion; a dowry. —**do′tal** *a.* pert. to a dowry [Fr. *dot*, a dowry].
dote (dōt) *v.i.* to be in one's dotage; to be foolishly sentimental; to be over-fond of—formerly spelt *doat.*—**dot′age** *n.* childishness of old people; senility; excessive fondness.—**dot′ard** *n.* one whose intellect is impaired by old age [O.Dut. *doten*, to be silly].
doth (duth) 3rd. pers. sing. pres. indic. of **do.**
dotterel, dottrel (dot′e-rel, dot′rel) *n.* a bird of the plover family, supposed to be very stupid and easily trapped; (*Fig.*) a stupid person; a dupe [fr. *dote*].
double (dub′l) *a.* denoting two things of the same kind; existing in pairs; twice as much (quantity); twice as good (quality); serving for two; acting two parts; deceitful; ambiguous;—*adv.* twice; two-fold;—*v.t.* to multiply by two; to make twice as great; to fold in two;—*v.i.* to increase to twice as much; to return upon one's track; to run (after marching);—*n.* twice as much; that which is doubled over; a fold; a duplicate; an actor's substitute or understudy; (*Tennis*) a game with two a-side; two faults in succession; a running pace, twice as quick as marching.—**doub′le-barr′elled** *a.* having two

barrels, as a gun; (*Colloq.*) having a double name joined by a hyphen.—**doub'le-bass** *n.* the largest and lowest pitched of the stringed instruments, played with a bow.—**doub'le-breast'ed** *a.* (of a coat) able to fasten over on either side.—**doub'le-cross** *v.t.* (*Slang*) to cheat a swindler.—**doub'le-deal'ing** *n.* duplicity.—**doub'le-deck'er** *n.* a ship, tramcar, or omnibus with two decks.—**doub'le-Dutch** *n.* jargon.—**doub'le-dyed** *a.* twice immersed in dye; thoroughly infamous.—**doub'le-edged,** *a.* having two edges; (*Fig.*) cutting both ways; effective for and against.—**double entendre** (dòòbl'-ong-tong'-dr) a word or phrase with two meanings, one of which is more or less improper.—**doub'le-en'try** *n.* in book-keeping, a system by which every entry is made both on debit and credit side of an account.—**doub'le-faced** *a.* hypocritical.—**doub'leness** *n.*—**doub'le-quick** *n.* and *a.* the fastest marching pace next to a run.—**doub'ler** *n.*—**double stop,** playing on two strings of the violin at one time.—**doub'let** *n.* one of a pair; a close-fitting garment for the upper part of body as worn by Elizabethan men; one of two words derived orig. from the same root but varying in spelling and meaning.—**doub'le-time** *n.* a very quick marching-pace.—**doub'le-tongued** *a.* deceitful; spiteful.—**doub'ly** *adv.* twice as much [L. *duo*, two].

doubloon (dub-lòòn') *n.* a Spanish or Portuguese coin (now obsolete) double the value of a pistole [Sp. *doblón*].

doubt (dout) *v.t.* to disbelieve; to hold questionable;—*v.i.* to be in a state of uncertainty (esp. in religious matters); to hesitate; to be apprehensive; to suspect;—*n.* uncertainty of mind; misgiving; distrust of others.—**doubt'able** *a.*—**doubt'er** *n.*—**doubt'ful** *a.* dubious; uncertain in opinion; ambiguous; equivocal; suspicious; disreputable; obscure.—**doubt'fully** *adv.*—**doubt'fulness** *n.*—**doubt'ing** *a.* undecided; hesitant; fearful.—**doubt'ingly** *adv.*—**doubt'less** *adv.* without doubt; probably.—**doubt'lessly** *adv.* [L. *dubitare*, to be uncertain].

douce (dòòs) *a.* (*Scot.*) sedate; sober.—**douceur** (dòò'-sẹr) *n.* a gift; a gratuity; a bribe [Fr. fem. of *doux*, sweet].

douche (dòòsh) *n.* a jet of water directed upon or into the body; an apparatus for douching [It. *doccia*, a water-pipe].

dough (dō) *n.* a mass of flour moistened and kneaded, afterwards to be baked; (*U.S. Slang*) money.—**dough'boy** *n.* a suet dumpling; (*U.S.*) an infantryman of the U.S. army.—**dough'-nuts** *n.* sweetened dough in shape of balls or rings, fried in fat and finally dipped in sugar.—**dough'y** *a.* [O.E. *dah*].

doughty (dou'-ti) *a.* brave; valiant.—**dought'ily** *adv.* [O.E. *dyhtig*, valiant].

dour (dòòr) *a.* (*Scot.*) obstinate; forbidding in manner.—**dour'ly** *adv.* [L. *durus*, hard].

douse, dowse (dous) *v.t.* to dip or plunge into water; (*Naut.*) to lower a sail; to put out a light [etym. doubtful].

dout (dout) *v.t.* to put out or extinguish.—**dout'er** *n.* [fr. *do out*].

dove (duv) *n.* a pigeon; a term of endearment; a symbol of peace or of the Holy Ghost.—**dove'-col'oured** *a.* soft pinkish grey.—**dove'-cot(e)** *n.* nesting box for pigeons, usually on top of a pole.—**dove'tail** *n.* a joint made by fitting one piece toothed with wedgelike projections (tenons) (shaped like a dove's tail) into cavities of corresponding shape (mortises) in another piece of timber;—*v.t.* to join together by this method; (*Fig.*) to link together [O.E. *dufe-doppa*, cf. Ger. *Taube*].

dowager (dou'-ạ-jẹr) *n.* (*Law*) widow with a jointure; title given to widow to distinguish her from wife of her husband's heir [O.Fr. *douage*, a dower].

dowdy (dou'-di) *a.* unfashionably dressed; untidy; lacking style;—*n.* a dowdy woman.—**dow'dily** *adv.*—**dow'diness** *n.* [etym. uncertain; prob. M.E. *doude*, a slut].

dowel (dou'-el) *n.* a wooden or iron pin for joining two adjacent boards or stones [cf. Ger. *Dobel*, a plug].

dower (dou'-ẹr) *n.* widow's share of her husband's property; portion a woman brings in marriage; gift; talent.—**dow'ered** *a.* possessing a dower; talented.—**dow'er-house** *n.* house occupied by widow of person of rank.—**dow'erless** *a.*—**dow'ry** *n.* a dower; a woman's marriage-portion; any endowment [L. *dotare*, to endow].

dowlas (dou'-lạs) *n.* a coarse calico cloth [*Doualas*, in Brittany].

down (doun) *n.* the fine, soft feathers of birds.—**down'y** *a.* resembling or covered with down [Scand. *dunn*].

down (doun) *n.* a hillock of sand by the sea (same as *dune*); treeless land [O.E. *dun*, a hill].

down (doun) *prep.* along a descent; towards a lower place, situation, etc.; towards the mouth of a river; in the same direction as, as in *down* wind; passing from the past to less remote times, as *down* the ages;—*adv.* in a downward direction; on the ground; to the bottom; below the horizon;—*a.* descending; outward bound (as from London);—*v.t.* to knock down; to baffle; to dispirit—used also as an *interjection* with verb get, kneel, etc. understood;—*n.* a grudge against; a reversal of fortune (as in the *ups and downs* of life).—**down'cast** *a.* depressed; (of eyes) lowered;—*n.* (in mining) a shaft for ventilation.—**down'come** *n.* a fall in prestige.—**down'fall** *n.* ruin; a heavy fall of rain, snow.—**down'fallen** *a.* ruined.—**down'-heart'ed** *a.* despondent.—**down'hill** *a.* sloping,—*adv.* on a slope.—**down'pour** *n.* a heavy fall of water, esp. rain.—**down'right** *adv.* straight down; in plain terms;—*a.* straightforward; blunt; unqualified.—**down'-set'ting** *n.* a snub.—**down'stairs** *adv.* in or to a lower floor of a house;—*a.* pert. to the ground floor;—*n.* the ground floor.—**down'-stream** *adv.* with the current.—**down'trodden** *a.* trampled underfoot; oppressed.—**down'ward** *a.* descending from a head or source; descending from a higher to a lower level;—*adv.* in a descending course; from a source.—**down'wards** *adv.*—**down town,** towards the centre of the town [O.E. *of dune*, from the hill].

dowse (douz) *v.t.* and *v.i.* to find subterranean water-supply by means of a divining rod.—**dows'er** *n.* [etym. unknown].

doxology (doks-ol'-o-ji) *n.* a short hymn of praise and honour to God. -**doxolog'ical** *a.* [Gk. *doxa*, glory; *legein*, to speak].

doxy (dok'-si) *n.* a sweetheart; a mistress [prob. dialect word].

doyen (dwa'-yen) *n.* a dean; a senior member of an academy, diplomatic corps, etc. [Fr. fr. L. *decanus*, the chief of ten].

doyley See **doily.**

doze (dōz) *v.i.* to sleep lightly; to be half asleep;—*n.* a nap [Scand. *dose*].

dozen (duz'-n) *n.* a collection or set of twelve things of the same kind;—*a.* twelve.—**baker's dozen, devil's dozen,** thirteen [Fr. *douzaine*, twelve].

drab (dràb) *n.* a thick woollen cloth; a dingy brownish-grey colour;—*a.* (*Fig.*) dull; monotonous [Fr. *drap*, cloth].

drab (dràb) *n.* a slut; a slattern; a prostitute [Celt. *drabog*, a slut].

drabble (drab'-l) *v.t.* to bedraggle; to befoul with mud [prob. conn. with *drab*, a slut].

drachm (dram) See **dram.**

drachma (drak'-mạ) *n.* a Greek coin; an ancient Greek weight [Gk. *drachmē*, a handful].

Draco (drā'-kō) *n.* a famous Athenian lawgiver of the 7th cent., responsible for a code of laws of extreme severity.—**Dracon'ic, Dracon'ian** *a.* harsh; rigorous.

draff (draf) *n.* dregs; refuse from malt after brewing; pig-swill [M.E. *draf,* dregs].

draft (draft) *n.* the act of drawing; that which is drawn; men detached from a force for special work; an order directing payment of money by a bank; a sketch or rough copy; depth of water necessary to float a ship.—**drafts** *n.pl.* (usually **draughts**) a game played on checkered board;—*v.t.* to draw the outline of; to compose and write; to draw from a military force, etc.—**draft′-horse** *n.* a horse used for drawing heavy loads [var. spelling of *draught*].

drag (drag) *v.t.* to draw with main force; to trail slowly; to pull violently; to trawl with a drag or net; to harrow (the fields);—*v.i.* to move heavily or slowly; to pass tediously. —*pr.p.* **drag′ging**.—*pa.p.* **dragged**.—*n.* a net or hook to bring up submerged things; a heavy harrow; a four-in-hand; a device acting as a brake on a wheel; a sledge.—**dragg′er** *n.*—**drag′-chain** *n.* the chain which connects an engine and tender.—**drag′-hunt** *n.* a hunt with no fox, but an artificial scent instead.—**drag′-net** *n.* a fishing-net for dragging along sea-floor; a net for catching birds [O.E. *dragan,* to draw].

dragée (dra-zhā′, dra-jē′) *n.* a chocolate drop [Fr.].

draggle (drag′l) *v.t.* and *v.i.* to make or become wet and dirty by trailing on the ground.—**dragg′led** *a.* dirty; soiled.—**dragg′le-tail** *n.* a slut [etym. uncertain].

dragoman (drag′o-man) *n.* an interpreter or guide in the East.—*pl.* **drag′omans** [Arab. *targuman,* an interpreter].

dragon (drag′on) *n.* a fabulous winged reptile represented as breathing out fire and smoke; the constellation *Draco*; a giant lizard of Malay; (*Fig.*) an over-vigilant chaperon.—**drag′onet** *n.* a little dragon; a fish of the *Pegasus* genus.—**drag′on-fish** *n.* the dragonet.—**drag′on-fly** *n.* an insect of brilliant colouring, with long slender body and two pairs of large, transparent wings.—**dragon's blood,** a carmine, resinous exudation from the scaly fruits of an E. Indian palm, used for colouring varnishes and lacquers; also obtained from the *Dracaena* or dragon-tree of the Canaries.—**dragon's teeth** (*Fig.*) things which breed strife [Gk. *drakon,* a large serpent].

dragoon (dra-gōōn′) *n.* orig. a mounted infantryman armed with a 'dragon,' or musket; a cavalryman; (*Fig.*) a harsh disciplinarian;—*v.t.* to enforce harsh disciplinary measures [Fr. *dragon,* a fire-spitting carbine].

drain (drān) *v.t.* to filter; to draw off by degrees; to make dry; to swallow down; to exhaust; to impoverish;—*v.i.* to flow off or drip away gradually;—*n.* a watercourse; a sewer or ditch; a gradual exhaustion of means, health, etc.—**drain′able** *a.*—**drain′age** *n.* act of draining; system of carrying away surplus water from an area by rivers, canals, etc.; the water or sewage thus carried away. —**drain′er** *n.* a kitchen utensil like a rack, on which plates, etc. are placed to dry; a colander or sieve.—**drain′-pipe** *n.* a pipe for draining away surplus water or liquid sewage from a building [O.E. *dragan,* to draw].

drake (drāk) *n.* the male of the duck [etym doubtful].

dram (dram) *n.* (contr. of *drachm*) a unit of weight; (*avoirdupois*) $\frac{1}{16}$ of an ounce; (*apothecary*) $\frac{1}{8}$ of an ounce; (*liquid*) $\frac{1}{8}$ of an ounce or 60 minims; a small drink of alcoholic liquor [Gk. *drachmē,* a weight; orig. a handful].

drama (drá′ma) *n.* a composition to be acted on the stage; a series of real emotional events.—**dramat′ic** *a.* pert. to the drama; striking; tense.—**dramat′ically** *adv.*—**dramatisa′tion** *n.*—**dram′atise** *v.t.* to adapt a novel, etc. for acting.—**dram′atist** *n.* a writer of plays.—**dram′aturge, dram′aturgy** *n.* the art of writing or producing plays.—**dramatis personae,** (list of) characters of a drama [Gk. *draein,* to do].

drank (drangk) *pa.t.* of **drink**.

drape (drāp) *v.t.* to hang something loosely in folds; to adorn with drapery.—**drap′er** *n.* (*fem.* **drap′eress**) formerly a maker, now a retail dealer in cloth and articles made from cloth.—**drap′eried** *a.* draped.—**drap′ery** *n.* cloth stuffs in general; hangings; the shop, or department of a shop, where cloth is sold [Fr. *drap,* cloth].

drastic (dras′tik) *a.* very powerful; harsh; thorough [Gk. *drastikos,* active].

drat (drat) *interj.* a mild expletive meaning *confound* [corrupt. of *God rot*].

draught (draft) *n.* the act of drawing; the quantity of a liquid drawn or quaffed off; a dose of medicine; the depth of water necessary to float a ship; the catch (of fish) contained in a drag-net; a sketch; a detachment; a current of air.—**draughts** *n.pl.* a game played by two people with twelve black and twelve white counters on a chess or checkered board;—*a.* drawn from a barrel, as beer;—*v.t.* (more commonly **draft**) to draw out.—**draught′-horse** *n.* a strong trace-horse capable of drawing heavy loads.—**draught′iness** *n.*—**draught′(s)man** *n.* one of the counters used in the game of draughts; (*U.S.*) checker.—**draughts′man, drafts′man** *n.* one who draws out plans of buildings, ships, planes, etc.; one who drafts Parliamentary bills, etc.—**draughts′manship** *n.*—**draught′y** *a.* full of air-currents [O.E. *dragan,* to draw].

Dravidian (dra-vid′i-an) *n.* one of the non-Aryan stock of S. India; the language of these races [fr. *Dravida,* an ancient province of S. India].

draw (draw) *v.t.* to pull along; to haul towards oneself; to entice; to extract (as a tooth); to elicit an opinion from another; to deduce; to receive (as money, salary, etc.); to inhale; to sketch; to describe; to cast lots; to bring game, such as fox, out of hiding; to take out the entrails;—*v.i.* to pull; to attract; to move towards; to be equal in a match; to sketch; to cast lots; to become stronger by infusion; to have a free passage of air (as a chimney).—*pr.p.* **draw′ing**.—*pa.t.* **drew**.—*pa.p.* **drawn**.—*n.* the act of drawing; a lottery; a game ending with same score for both sides; an attraction.—**draw′able** *a.*—**draw′back** *n.* a disadvantage.—**draw′bridge** *n.* a bridge that can be raised or let down at will, orig. a bridge across a moat.—**draw′er** *n.* one who or that which draws; one who draws a cheque; a lidless, sliding box in a table, chest, etc.—**draw′ers** *n.pl.* close fitting undergarment for lower limbs.—**draw′ing** *n.* the art of pulling or attracting; the art of representing objects by line or colour on paper, canvas, etc.—**draw′ings** *n.pl.* the gross takings of a shop.—**draw′ing-pin** *n.* a flat headed pin for fixing paper on drawing-board.—**draw′ing-room** *n.* orig. a withdrawing room; a room in which guests are entertained, esp. after dinner.—**draw′ing-ta′ble** *n.* a table which can be extended by additional leaves.—**drawn** *a.* (of a game) equal scoring for both sides.—**draw′-net** *n.* Same as **drag′-net**.—**to draw a blank,** to be unlucky in a lottery.—**to draw the line,** to stop.—**at daggers drawn,** openly hostile.—**drawn and quartered,** disembowelled and cut in quarters [O.E. *dragan,* to draw].

drawl (drawl) *v.i.* to speak with slow and lengthened tone;—*v.t.* to utter (words) in this way;—*n.* a manner of speech, slow and drawn out [Scand. *dralla,* to loiter].

dray (drā) *n.* a low cart for heavy goods.—**dray′-horse** *n.* a horse for pulling a dray.—**dray′-man** *n.* [O.E. *dragan,* to draw].

dread (dred) *n.* overwhelming apprehension; awe; terror;—*a.* dreadful; awful;—*v.t.* to regard with fear;—*v.i.* to have fear of the future.—**dread′ed** *a.* feared.—**dread′ful** *a.* orig.

full of dread; terrifying; terrible.—**dread′fully** *adv.*—**dread′fulness** *n.*—**dread′nought** *n.* one who fears nothing; a thick woollen overcoat cloth; a large-sized battleship mounting heavy guns of one calibre [O.E. *ondraeden*, to fear].

dream (drēm) *n.* a series of images or thoughts in the mind of a person asleep; an idle fancy; a vision; an aspiration;—*v.i.* to imagine things during sleep; to have yearnings;—*v.t.* to see in a dream.—*pa.t.* and *p.p.* **dreamed** or **dreamt** (dremt).—**dream′er** *n.* one who dreams.—**dream′ily** *adv.*—**dream′iness** *n.* —**dream′land** *n.* an imaginary land seen in dreams.—**dream′less** *a.*—**dream′like** *a.* visionary; shadowy; unreal.—**dream′y** *a.* given to dreams; abstracted [O.E. *dream*, joy].

drear, dreary (drēr, ′-i) *a.* dismal; gloomy; bleak.—**drear′ily** *adv.*—**drear′iness** *n.* cheerlessness [O.E. *dreorig*, mournful].

dredge (drej) *v.t.* to sprinkle.—**dredg′er, dredg′ing-box** *n.* a flour-can with perforated lid [O.Fr. *dragie*, a sweetmeat].

dredge (drej) *n.* a machine like a large scoop for taking up mud from a river-bed, harbour, etc.; a drag-net for oysters or zoological specimens. Also **dredg′er, dredg′ing-machine′**—**dredg′er** *n.* a boat fitted with a dredge;—*v.t.* to scoop up or deepen with a dredge [conn. with *drag*].

dree (drē) *v.t.* to endure; to bear the penalty of, esp. in **dree one's weird,** endure one's fate [O.E. *dreogan*, to suffer].

dregs (dregz) *n.pl.* sediment in a liquid that falls to the bottom; lees; grounds; (*Fig.*) the most worthless class [Scand. *dreggjar*, dregs].

drench (drensh) *v.t.* to wet thoroughly; to soak; to administer medicine to an animal [O.E. *drencan*, to give to drink].

dress (dres) *v.t.* to arrange in order; to put clothes on; to provide with clothes; to adorn; to treat (a sore);—*v.i.* to come into line; to put on one's clothes;—*n.* clothes; a frock; adornment.—**dress′-cir′cle** *n.* the lowest gallery in a theatre, orig. for people in evening-dress.—**dress′-coat** *n.* a swallow-tailed coat for evening-dress.—**dress′er** *n.* one who dresses; a surgeon's assistant; a kitchen side-board.—**dress′ing** *n.* clothes; an application of a sterile substance (gauze or lint, etc.) to a wound; manure; substance used to stiffen fabrics; a sauce or stuffing used to add piquancy to a dish (as salad-dressing). —**dress′ing-down** *n.* (*Colloq.*) a scolding or thrashing.—**dress′ing-gown** or **-jack′et** *n.* a loose gown or jacket worn while dressing.—**dress′ing-ta′ble** *n.* a table with mirror used while dressing.—**dress′maker** *n.* a person who makes women's dresses, etc.—**dress′making** *n.* —**dress′y** *a.* fond of dress; fashionable [O.Fr. *dresser*, to prepare].

drew (dróó) *pa.t.* of **draw.**

drey (drā) *n.* a squirrel's nest [etym. doubtful].

dribble (drib′l) *v.i.* to trickle down, esp. of saliva of babies and idiots; to drop quickly; —*v.t.* to cause to fall in drops; (*Football*) to kick the ball forward by short kicks.—**drib** *v.t.* to dribble.—**drib′let** *n.* a small drop [dim. of *drip*].

dried (drīd) *pa.t.* and *pa.p.* of verb **dry.**

drift (drift) *n.* the state or process of being driven; that which is driven; the accumulation of substance driven by the wind, as snow; a slow surface current in the sea caused usually by the prevailing wind; deviation or tendency;—*v.t.* to drive into heaps; to cause to float in a certain direction; —*v.i.* to be floated along; to be piled in heaps; (*Fig.*) to follow unconsciously some trend in policy, thought or behaviour.—**drift′age** *n.* that which has drifted, as snow, seaweed, etc.; deviation of a ship from its course.—**drift′-anch′or** *n.* an anchor for keeping a ship's head to the wind during a storm.—**drift′er** *n.* a small fishing vessel using drift nets.—**drift′ing** *n.*—**drift′-net** *n.* a large fishing net allowed to drift with the tide, used in sea fishing.—**drift′-wood** *n.* wood cast on shore by tide [O.E. *drifan*, to drive].

drill (dril) *v.t.* to pierce; to bore a hole through; to sow, as seeds, in a row; to train in military tactics; to instruct thoroughly (in mental or physical exercises);—*n.* revolving tool for boring holes in metal, stone, etc.; an implement for making holes for seed; a row of seeds or root crops; physical exercise or military training; instruction.—**drill′ing** *n.* the process of making drills; the process of tunnelling in mines [prob. Dut. *drillen*, to bore].

drink (dringk) *v.t.* to swallow, as a liquid; to empty, as a glass; to breathe in, as air; —*v.i.* to swallow a liquid; to consume intoxicating liquor, esp. in excess.—*pr.p.* **drink′ing.**—*pa.p.* **drunk.**—*n.* liquid for drinking; intoxicating liquor.—**drink′able** *a.* fit for drinking.—**drink′er** *n.* a tippler.—**drink′ing-bout** *n.* prolonged period of excessive drinking.—**to drink in,** to absorb rain; (*Fig.*) to absorb through the senses [O.E. *drincan*, to drink].

drip (drip) *v.t.* to let fall, drop by drop;—*v.i.* to ooze; to trickle.—*pr.p.* **drip′ping.**—*pa.p.* **dripped.**—*n.* a falling in drops; the sound made by water dripping; the projecting edge of a roof.—**drip′ping** *a.* thoroughly wet;—*n.* that which falls in drops, esp. fat, from meat while roasting.—**drip′-stone** *n.* a projecting moulding over doors, windows, etc. to deflect rain water [O.E. *dryppan*, to fall in drops].

drive (drīv) *v.t.* to urge on; to keep in motion; to guide the course of; to cause (a machine) to work; to strike in, as a nail; to compel; to hurry; to conclude, as a bargain; to hit a ball with force, as in golf, tennis; to chase game towards sportsmen;—*v.i.* to be forced along; to ride in a vehicle.—*pr.p.* **driv′ing.**—*pa.t.* **drove.**—*pa.p.* **driv′en.**—*n.* an excursion in a carriage, motor, etc.; a private carriage-road or avenue; driving game towards sportsmen; the capacity for getting things done.—**driv′er** *n.* one who or that which drives; a golf-club for hitting ball from the tee; a drover (of cattle).—**to drive at,** to hint at [O.E. *drifan*, to drive].

drivel (driv′l) *v.i.* to dribble like a child; to talk nonsense; to be weak or foolish.—*n.* nonsense.—**driv′eller** *n.* [O.E. *dreflian*, to slobber; conn. with *dribble*].

drizzle (driz′l) *v.t.* and *v.i.* to rain gently;—*n.* fine rain [O.E. *dreosan*, to fall].

drogue (drōg) *n.* the buoy at end of a harpoon line to check the progress of a running whale; (*Aero.*) a conical canvas sleeve trailed behind an aircraft as target; wind-direction indicator [etym. doubtful; prob. conn. with *drag*].

droit (drwȧ or droit) *n.* legal right; a fiscal duty [Fr. *droit*, right].

droll (drōl) *a.* laughable; funny; queer;—*n.* a buffoon; a jester; an odd character.—**droll′ery** *n.* [Fr. *drôle*, an amusing rascal].

dromedary (drum′e-dar-i) *n.* a breed of one-humped Arabian camel [Gk. *dromas*, running].

drone (drōn) *n.* the male of the honey-bee; (*Fig.*) an idler who lives on the work of others, like a drone-bee; a deep, humming sound; the largest pipe of the bagpipes; its sound;—*v.t.* and *v.i.* to hum; to speak or sing in a monotonous voice [O.E. *dran*, a drone].

drool (dróól) *v.i.* to slaver; to drivel; to speak foolishly [See **drivel**].

droop (dróóp) *v.i.* to hang down; to grow weak; to pine; to sag; to wilt (as flowers);—*v.t.* to lower [Scand. *drupa*, to sink].

drop (drop) *n.* a globular particle of fluid that falls or is allowed to fall; a minute quantity of fluid in medical dose; anything hanging like a drop, or resembling a drop in size (as a jewel in a pendant, ear-ring, etc.); a fall; the trap-door of a gallows;—*v.t.* to let fall drop by drop; to let fall; to dismiss or break off (as an acquaintance); to set down from a vehicle; to write a letter or pass a remark, in a casual manner; (of animals) to give birth to prematurely;—*v.i.* to fall in drops; to fall down suddenly; to sink to a lower level (as prices); to come to an end.—*pr.p.* **drop'ping**.—*pa.t.* and *pa.p.* **dropped**.—**drop'-cur'tain** *n.* a painted curtain lowered in front of theatre stage between scenes in a play.—**drop'-kick** *n.* (*Rugby*) a kick effected by letting the ball fall from the hands to the ground to be kicked immediately on the rebound.—**drop'let** *n.* a tiny drop of liquid.—**drop'per** *n.* a small glass tube from which liquid is measured out in drops.—**drop'pings** *n.pl.* dung, esp. the excrement of sheep.—**drop'-scene** *n.* a drop-curtain on theatre stage.—**to drop a brick**, (*Slang*) to make a tactless remark.—**to drop in**, to make an informal visit.—**a drop in the bucket**, a very small contribution [O.E. *dropa*, a drop].

dropsy (drop'si) *n.* a morbid collection of fluid in any part of body.—**drop'sical** *a.* [Gk. *hudrops*, fr. *hudor*, water].

drosky, droshky (dros'ki, drosh'ki) *n.* a low four-wheeled open carriage used in Russia; a cab [Russ. *droshki*].

drosophila (dros-of'i-lạ) *n.* one of a genus of flies including the fruit-fly [Gk. *drosos*, dew; *philos*, fond of].

dross (dros) *n.* the scum of metals thrown off in smelting; small coal of inferior quality; slag; refuse; (*Fig.*) anything of little or no value [O.E. *dros*, dregs].

drought, drouth (drout, drouth) *n.* dryness; want or absence of rain over a prolonged period; thirst.—**drought'iness, drouth'iness** *n.*—**drought'y, drouth'y** *a.* very dry; thirsty [O.E. *drugath*, dryness].

drove (drōv) *n.* a herd or flock, esp. on the move.—**drov'er** *n.* one who drives cattle or sheep, esp. to market [O.E. *drifan*, to drive].

drown (droun) *v.t.* to suffocate by submerging in water; to deluge; to render inaudible; to overpower;—*v.i.* to be suffocated in water [O.E. *druncnian*, to be drunk, to get drowned].

drowse (drouz) *v.t.* to make sleepy; to make stupid;—*v.i.* to doze; be heavy with sleep;—*n.* a half-sleep; a doze.—**drows'y** *a.* heavy with sleep.—**drows'ily** *adv.*—**drows'iness** *n.* [O.E. *drusian*, to be sluggish].

drub (drub) *v.t.* to beat; to cudgel;—*v.i.* to stamp.—**drub'bing** *n.* a thrashing [etym. doubtful; prob. Scand. *drabba*, to hit].

drudge (druj) *v.i.* to toil hard; to labour at menial tasks;—*n.* one who is made to do menial work; a slave.—**drudg'ery** *n.* hard, monotonous, or servile toil.—**drudg'ingly** *adv.* [O.E. *dreogan*, to perform].

drug (drug) *n.* any substance used in the composition of a medicine; a narcotic; (*Fig.*) a commodity unsaleable because of over-production;—*v.t.* to mix with drugs; to administer a drug to someone; to dose to excess;—*v.i.* to take drugs habitually and in excess.—*pr.p.* **drug'ging**.—*pa.p.* **drugged**.—**drug'-fiend** *n.* a drug addict.—**drug'gist** *n.* dealer in drugs; a pharmaceutical chemist [etym. uncertain].

drugget (drug'et) *n.* a coarse, felted woollen cloth [prob. O.Fr. *droguet*, dim. of *drogue*, trash].

Druid (drȯȯ'id) *n.* a priest of the ancient Celtic peoples of Britain, Gaul, etc. who worshipped the oak-tree.—**druid'ical** *a.*—**Dru'idism** *n.* [Celt.].

drum (drum) *n.* (*Mus.*) a percussion instrument comprising a hollow, parchment-covered cylinder beaten with a drumstick; anything drum-shaped; (*Anat.*) the middle portion of ear;—*v.t.* to play on a drum; to teach by constant repetition;—*v.i.* to beat on drum; to beat rhythmically.—*pr.p.* **drum'ming**.—*pa.p.* **drummed**.—**drum'ble** *v.t.* to make a drumming sound.—**drum-head service**, an open-air church parade held in camp.—**drum'-maj'or** *n.* the chief drummer in a regiment.—**drum'mer** *n.* one who plays a drum; (*U.S.*) a commercial traveller.—**drum'-stick** *n.* a padded stick for beating a drum; lower part of leg of cooked fowl [prob. imit. word].

drunk (drungk) *pa.p.* of **drink**;—*a.* overcome by strong drink; intoxicated;—*n.* a drunk person.—**drunk'ard** *n.* one who habitually drinks to excess.—**drunk'en** *a.* given to excessive drinking.—**drunk'enness** *n.* [O.E. *drincan*, to drink].

drupe (drȯȯp) *n.* a fleshy fruit, such as plum, cherry, or peach, with a stone or kernel containing the seed.—**drupa'ceous** *a.* [L. *drupa*, an over-ripe olive].

dry (drī) *a.* free from moisture, rain, or mist; sear; not giving milk, as a cow; thirsty; unsweetened, as wines; uninteresting; sarcastic; plain, as facts; (*U.S.*) of a district subject to Prohibition Laws;—*v.t.* to free from moisture or wetness; to drain;—*v.i.* to grow dry; to evaporate; (*Fig.*) to become void of ideas.—*pr.p.* **dry'ing**.—*pa.p.* **dried**.—**dri'er** *n.* one who or that which dries; a substance which helps paint to dry quickly; an electrical machine for drying the hair.—**dry'-bat'tery** *n.* a battery composed of *dry cells* sealed in a container to prevent leakage.—**to dry clean**, to clean garments with petrol, etc.—**dry'-fly** *n.* an artificial fly (in dry-fly fishing) played over surface of water.—**dry'-goods** *n.pl.* drapery goods.—**dry'ly, dri'ly** *adv.*—**dry measure**, a measure of bulk, used for grain, etc.—**dry'ness** *n.*—**dry'point** *n.* copper-plate engraving without acid and using a sharp needle; an engraving thus made; the needle used.—**dry'-rot** *n.* a decay of timber caused by fungoid disease.—**dry'salt** *v.t.* to preserve meat by salting and drying.—**dry'salter** *n.* orig. a dealer in salted meats, pickles, etc.; a dealer in drugs, paints, dyes, and chemicals generally.—**dry'saltery** *n.* the shop, or its contents, kept by a drysalter.—**dry'-shod** *a.* with dry feet; without wetting one's feet.—**dry'-stone** *a.* built of stone without mortar, as dykes in Scotland [O.E. *dryge*, *dry*].

dryad (drī'ad) *n.* in Greek mythology a spirit of the trees; a wood-nymph [Gk. *drus*, an oak tree].

dual (dū'ạl) *a.* consisting of two; twofold; (*Gram.*) of noun, etc. denoting two persons or things;—*n.* (*Gram.*) the dual number.—**du'ad** *n.* pair of things regarded as one.—**du'alism** *n.* a two-fold division; the belief that two separate elements co-exist in the universe, namely spirit and matter; the belief in the existence of good and evil as separate entities.—**du'alist** *n.*—**dual'ity** *n.* state of being double or having a double nature [L. *duo*, two].

dub (dub) *v.t.* to knight; to give a nickname to; to make smooth; to dress a fly for fishing; (*Film*) to provide a film with a sound track not in the original language.—*pr.p.* **dub'bing**.—*pa.p.* **dubbed**.—**dub'bin**, or **dub'bing** *n.* an oily composition for softening leather.—**dub'ber** *n.* [M.E. *dubben*, to adorn].

dubious (dū'bi-us) *a.* doubtful; liable to turn out well or ill; (of a character) shady.—**du'biously** *adv.*—**du'biousness** *n.*—**dubi'ety** *n.* hesitancy; uncertainty.—**du'bitable** *a.* doubtful.—**du'bitancy, dubita'tion** *n.* the act of doubting; uncertainty [L. *dubius*, doubtful].

ducal (dūk'ạl) *a.* pert. to a duke.—**du'cally** *adv.* in a ducal manner.—**ducat** (duk'at) *n.* a coin, first struck in Duchy of Apulia in 12th cent., and formerly used in several European countries.—**duce** (dȯȯ'chā) *n.* leader, esp. '*Il Duce*,' title used by Mussolini.—**duch'ess** *n.* the wife or widow of a duke

THE CAT FAMILY

Siamese

Persian

Puma

Tabby

Leopard

Tiger

Lion and Lioness

Ocelot

DOGS

Borzoi

Dobermann

Irish Setter

Poodles

Pug

Chow

Fox Terrier

Collie

Dachshund

a woman who holds a duchy in her own right.—**duch'y** *n.* dominions of a duke [L. *dux*, a leader].
duchess (duchˊes) *n.* See **ducal.**
duchesse (duchˊes or dôô-shes') *n.* a kind of satin.—**duchesse lace,** Brussels pillow-lace. —**duchesse set,** embroidered or lace mats for a dressing-table [Fr. *duchesse*, duchess].
duck (duk) *n.* a coarse cloth or light canvas used for small sails and for men's tropical clothing.—**ducks** *n.pl.* trousers made of this [Dut. *doeck*, linen cloth].
duck (duk) *n.* any broad-beaked, web-footed, short-legged water bird; female duck as distinct from male *drake*; (*Colloq.*) a darling; a sudden dip; a sudden lowering of head; (*Cricket*) no score; (*World War* 2) an amphibious lorry;—*v.t.* to dip suddenly in water; to bend (head) suddenly; to cringe;—*v.i.* to plunge into water; to dodge.—**duck'-bill** *n.* an Australian burrowing, egg-laying mammal, with webbed-feet and duck-like beak. Also called **duck-billed platypus.**—**duck'board** *n.* planking to cross swampy areas.—**duck'ing-stool** *n.* a stool or chair fastened to a pole, used formerly to punish women, by ducking them in water.—**duck'ling** *n.* a young duck.—**duck's-egg** (*Cricket*) failure to score any runs. —**duck'-weed** *n.* minute, floating, green plants growing on all standing waters.—**to make (play) ducks and drakes of (with),** to squander foolishly.—**a lame duck,** a defaulter on the Stock Exchange; a disabled person [O.E. *ducan*, to dive].
duct (dukt) *n.* a canal or tube for conveying fluids, esp. in animal bodies, plants, etc.—**ductless glands** (*Anat.*) endocrine glands which discharge their secretions directly into the blood (e.g. thyroid, pituitary, pancreas) [L. *ducere*, to lead].
ductile (dukˊtil) *a.* (of metals) capable of being drawn out in fine threads; (*Fig.*) tractable; easily influenced.—**ductil'ity** *n.* [L. *ducere*, to lead].
dud (dud) *n.* anything defective;—*a.* worthless; defective; futile [etym. doubtful].
dude (dūd, dôôd) *n.* (*U.S. Slang*) a fop; a brainless dandy.
dudgeon (dujˊun) *n.* the haft of a dagger [etym. unknown].
dudgeon (dujˊun) *n.* anger; resentment, as in phrase *in high dudgeon* [etym. doubtful].
duds (duds) *n.pl.* (*Colloq*). old shabby clothes [prob. Scand. *dutha*, to wrap up].
due (dū) *a.* owing; fitting to be paid or done to another; adequate; appointed to arrive (as a train); attributable;—*adv.* exactly; duly; directly;—*n.* that which is owed in money or service; right; tribute; tax.—**du'ly** *adv.* properly; at the right time [O.Fr. *deu*, fr. L. *debere*, to owe].
duel (dūˊel) *n.* a combat between two persons, generally an affair of honour; any two-sided contest;—*v.i.* to fight a duel.—*pr.p.* **du'elling.** —*pa.p.* **du'elled.**—**du'ellist** *n.* [It. fr. L.*duellum*, a fight between two].
duenna (dū-enˊą) *n.* a chaperon [Sp. doublet of *donna*].
duet (dū-et') *n.* a musical composition for two performers, vocal or instrumental.—**duet'tist** *n.* [It. *duetto*, fr. L. *duo*, two].
duff (duf) *n.* dough; a suet pudding boiled in a cloth [dial. form of *dough*].
duff (duf) *v.t.* to make old things look like new; to fake; (*Golf*) to make a bad stroke [etym. doubtful, prob. Scand. *dowf*, stupid].
duffel, duffle (dufˊl) *n.* a coarse woollen cloth with a thick nap; camping kit [fr. *Duffel* in Belgium].
dug (dug) *n.* a teat, esp. of an animal [Scand. *daegge*, to suckle].
dug (dug) *pa.t.* and *pa.p.* of **dig.**—**dugˊout** *n.* a canoe hollowed out of a tree trunk; a hole in the ground roughly roofed over to protect in trench warfare [fr. *dig*].
dugong (dūˊgong) *n.* a plant-eating aquatic mammal, the sea-cow [Malay *duyong*].
duke (dūk) *n.* (*fem.* **duch'ess**) the highest order of nobility in the British peerage; (on the Continent) a sovereign prince.—**duke'dom** *n.* the status or possessions of a duke [O.Fr. *duc.* fr. L. *dux*, a leader].
Dukhobors (dôôˊkō-borz) *n.pl.* a communistic, pacifist, religious sect founded in Russia in 18th cent., and later driven by persecution to Canada. Also **Du'khobortsi** (Russ, *dukh*, spirit; *bortsy*, wrestlers].
dulcet (dulˊset) *a.* sweet to the taste or to the ear [L. *dulcis*, sweet].
dulcimer (dulˊsi-mer) *n.* a medieval stringed instrument, prototype of the pianoforte; an old Jewish musical instrument probably like a small harp [L. *dulcis*, sweet; Gk. *melos*, a song].
dulcitone (dulˊsi-tōn) *n.* a keyboard instrument in which tuning forks are struck [L. *dulcis*, sweet; *tonus*, tone].
dull (dul) *a.* stupid; slow of hearing or seeing; tedious; uninspired; sleepy; dim or cloudy; obtuse; blunt; heavy;—*v.t.* to stupefy; to blunt; to mitigate;—*v.i.* to become dull. **dull'ard** *n.* a slow-witted person.—**dull'ness, dul'ness** *n.* [O.E. *dol*, dull-witted].
dulse (duls) *n.* an edible reddish-brown seaweed [Gael. *duileasg*].
duly See **due.**
Duma (dôômˊą) *n.* the Russian Parliament created in 1905 and lasting till 1917 [Russ. *douma*, a municipal body].
dumb (dum) *a.* lacking permanently the power of speech; mute; temporarily silent; mimed; inarticulate; (*U.S.*) stupid; unresponsive;—*v.t.* to silence.—**dumb'-bell** *n.* two heavy iron balls connected by a bar for a handle, used in gymnastic exercises; (*U.S. Slang*) a nitwit.—**dumb'ly** *adv.* mutely; in silence.—**dumb'ness** *n.*—**dumbˊshow** *n.* expresive gesture without words; a short play in mime.—**dumb'-wait'er** *n.* a dinner-wagon or trolley.—**dum(b)found'** *v.t.* to strike dumb; to nonplus; to amaze. Also **dum(b)found'er.**—**dum'my** *a.* dumb; sham;—*n.* a dumb person; a lay figure, as a tailor's dummy; a baby's rubber comforter; a sham package in a shop window; (*Cards*) the exposed hand in bridge or whist [O.E. *dumb*, mute].
dum-dum (dumˊdum) *n.* a soft-nosed bullet [fr. *Dum-Dum* in Bengal].
dump (dump) *v.t.* to throw down heavily; to deposit; to unload; to export surplus goods at a low price;—*n.* a thud; refuse or scrap heap; a temporary store for munitions, etc.—**dump'ling** *n.* a ball of dough boiled in water, stock, etc.; a suet pudding, boiled or steamed, usually containing fruit.—**dump'y** *a.* short; thick; squat;—*n.* a hassock used as a seat; a pouffe. Also **dump'ty.** -**dump'iness** *n.* [etym. uncertain].
dun (dun) *a.* a greyish-brown colour; dark;—*n.* this colour; a horse of this colour [O.E. *dunn*, dark brown].
dun (dun) *v.t.* to importune for payment of a debt.—*pr.p.* **dun'ning.**—*pa.p.* **dunned** [allied to *din*].
dunce (duns) *n.* one who is slow at learning; a dullard; a backward child [fr. *Duns Scotus* (13th cent.), a churchman opposed to the Renaissance ideas].
dunderhead (dunˊder-hed) *n.* a stupid person; a dunce. Also **dun'derpate.**—**dun'der-head'ed** *a.* [etym. unknown].
dundreary (dun-drērˊi) *a.* beardless but having side-whiskers.
dune (dūn) *n.* a low hill of sand on the seacoast [O.Dut. *duna*, a hill].
dung (dung) *n.* the excrement of animals; manure;—*v.t.* to treat with manure;—*v.i.* to drop excrement.—**dung'hill** *n.* a mound of dung; (*Fig.*) any mean condition; a vile abode [O.E. *dung*, muck].
dungaree (dungˊgą-rē) *n.* a coarse hard

wearing Indian calico.—**dung'arees** *n.pl.* trousers or overalls of this material [Hind.].

dungeon (dun′jun) *n.* orig. the principal tower or 'keep' of a castle; a damp subterranean prison-cell;—*v.t.* to confine in a dungeon [Fr. *donjon*, fr. L. *dominus*, a master].

dunk (dungk) *v.t.* to dip bread into tea, coffee, soup, etc. [Ger. *Tunker*, a dipper].

dunlin (dun′lin) *n.* a red-backed sandpiper [dial. *dun*, dark brown; dim. *ling*].

duo (dū′ō) *n.* a duet; a pair of stage artistes.

duodecennial (dū-o-de-sen′i-ạl) *a.* occurring every twelve years [L. *duodecim*, twelve; *annus*, a year].

duodecimo (dū-o-des′i-mō) *n.* formed of sheets folded into twelve leaves (*abbrev.* 12 mo.); a 12 mo. book.—**duodec'imal** *a.* proceeding by twelves;—*n.* a twelfth part.—**duodec′imals** *n.pl.* a method of computation by denominations of 12 instead of 10.—**duodec′imally** *adv.* [L. *duodecim*, twelve].

duodenary (dū-o-den′ạ-ri) *a.* relating to twelves [L. *duodeni*, twelve each].

duodenum (dū-o-dē′num) *n.* upper part of intestines so called as it is about 12 finger-breadths long;—*pl.* **duode'na**.—**duode'nal** *a.* pert. to duodenum [L. *duodeni*, twelve each].

duologue (dū′ō-log) *n.* a speech for two persons; a dialogue [Gk. *duo*, two; *logos*, a discourse].

dupe (dūp) *n.* one who is easily cheated or gulled;—*v.t.* to cheat; to mislead.—**dup'ery** *n.* the art of cheating others [etym. unknown].

duplex (dū′pleks) *a.* twofold; double.—**du'ple** *a.* double.—**du'plicate** *a.* double; exactly resembling something else;—*n.* an exact copy; a transcript;—*v.t.* to double; to make a copy of.—**duplica'tion** *n.*—**du'plicative** *a.*—**du'plicator** *n.* a machine for making copies of a document from a written or typewritten stencil; a cyclostyle. (*Zool.*) a folded membrane.—**duplic'ity** *n.* doubleness; double dealing; deceitfulness [L. *duplex*, double].

durable (dū′rạ-bl) *a.* lasting; able to resist wear and tear; not perishable; abiding.—**dur'ableness**, **durabil'ity** *n.*—**dur'ably** *adv.*—**dur'ance** *n.* continuation; confinement.—**dura'tion** *n.* durability; continuance in time; period anything lasts [L. *durare*, to last].

duralumin (du-rạ-lū′min) *n.* *Trade name* for a light, strong alloy of aluminium [from L. *durus*, hard, and *aluminium*].

durbar (dur′bȧr) *n.* an audience chamber; a state levee or reception of native princes in India; the officials at a native court [Hind. *darbar*, a ruler's court].

duress (dū-res') *n.* hardship; imprisonment; constraint [O.Fr. *duresce*, hardship].

during (dū′ring) *prep.* in the time of; in course of [*pr.p.* of obsolete *dure*].

durra (do͝o′rạ) *n.* a kind of millet much cultivated in Asia and S. Europe; Indian millet. Also **dour'a** [Ar. *durah*].

durst (durst) *pa.t.* of **dare**.

dusk (dusk) *a.* tending to darkness; darkish;—*n.* twilight; gloaming.—**dusk'y** *a.* partially dark; dim; dark-skinned [O.E. *dosc*, dark-coloured].

dust (dust) *n.* very fine particles of matter deposited on the ground or suspended in the air; minute particles of gold in a river bed; powder; the ashes of the dead; the grave.—*v.t.* to remove dust from; to sprinkle with powder.—**dust′bin** *n.* a bucket for holding dust, rubbish, etc.—**dust'cart** *n.* a cart for removing rubbish, etc.—**dust′coat** *n.* an overall; a light travelling coat.—**dust′cov'er** *n.* a book-jacket.—**dust'er** *n.* one who dusts; a cloth for dusting; (*Naut. slang*) a flag, as the **Red Duster**, i.e. the Red Ensign; a tin with perforated lid for sprinkling flour, sugar, etc.—**dust'ily** *adv.*—**dust'iness** *n.*—**dust'ing** *n.* the act or process of removing dust from furniture, etc.; a sprinkling; (*Slang*) a thrashing or stormy experience.—**dust'man** *n.* a scavenger; (*Colloq.*) sleep.—**dust'y** *a.* covered with dust; powdery.—**dust'y-mill'er** *n.* the plant, auricula.—**to lick the dust**, to grovel.—**not so dusty** (*Colloq.*) not bad or badly; fairly agreeable [O.E. *dust*, dust].

Dutch (duch) *a.* pert. to Holland, to its inhabitants, or to their language;—*n.* the language of Holland;—*pl.* the people of Holland.—**Dutch'man** *n.* (*fem.* **Dutch'woman**) a native of Holland.—**Dutch auction**, where prices start at a high figure and are gradually lowered to meet the bidder.—**Dutch courage**, a false courage inspired by intoxicants; bravado.—**Dutch treat**, an entertainment for which each person pays his own share.—**to talk like a Dutch uncle**, to rebuke a person with kindness [M. Dut. *dutsch*, pert. to the Netherlands].

duty (dū′ty) *n.* that which is due; that which is demanded by law, morality, social conscience, etc.; military service; one's proper employment; a period of work set down for each person on a roster; customs or excise dues.—**du'teous** *a.* dutiful; obedient.—**du′teously** *adv.*—**du'tiable** *a.* subject to customs duties. Also **du'tied**.—**du'tiful** *a.* attentive to duty; submissive; proceeding from a sense of duty.—**du'tifully** *adv.*—**du'tifulness** *n.*—**du'ty-free** *a.* exempt from Customs duty [O.Fr. *dueté*, what is owed].

duumvir (dū-um′vir) *n.* one of two Roman magistrates holding office jointly.—**duum′viral** *a.*—**duum'virate** *n.* a council of two [L. *duo*, two; *vir*, a man].

dux (duks) *n.* a leader; the head or top pupil of a class or school [L. *dux*, a leader].

dwarf (dwawrf) *n.* an animal, plant, or man abnormally small in size; a mannikin;—*v.t.* to hinder the growth of; to make diminutive by comparison.—**dwarf'ish**, **dwarf** *a.* undersized [O.E. *dweorg*].

dwell (dwel) *v.i.* to abide; to be domiciled; to deal with in detail, as in a speech.—**dwell'er** *n.*—**dwell'ing** *n.* habitation; abode [O.E. *dwellan*, to tarry].

dwindle (dwin′dl) *v.i.* to grow less; to shrink; to waste away;—*v.t.* to lessen;—*n.* a decline; a pining away.—**dwine** (dwīn) *v.i.* to pine away [O.E. *dwinan*, to fade].

Dyak (dī′ak) *n.* one of the aboriginal people of Borneo, chiefly known as head-hunters. Also **Day'ak** [Malay *dyak*, savage].

dyarchy (dī′ark-i) *n.* See **diarchy**.

dye (dī) *v.t.* to give a new colour to; to stain;—*v.i.* to undergo change of colour.—*pr.p.* **dye'ing**.—*pa.p.* **dyed**.—*n.* a colouring matter.—**dy'er** *n.* one who is employed in dyeing.—**dye′stuff** *n.* substance used for dyeing [O.E. *deagian*, to dye].

dying (dī′ing) *pr.p.* of **die**.

dyke (dīk) *n.* See **dike**.

dynamic (dī- (or di-) nam′ik) *a.* pert. to force in motion; pert. to dynamics; (*Med.*) functional; (*Fig.*) possessing energy and forcefulness (of character). Also **dynam'ical**.—**dynam′ics** *n.* branch of mechanics which deals with *force in motion*.—**dy'namism** *n.* a school of scientific thought which explains phenomena of universe as resulting from action of natural forces.—**dy'namist** *n.*—**dy'namite** *n.* a powerful high explosive, with great disruptive force;—*v.t.* to blow up with dynamite.—**dyn'amitard**, **dyn'amiter** *n.* one who uses dynamite, esp. for criminal purposes.—**dyn'amo** *n.* a generator for transforming mechanical energy into electrical energy (short for *dynamo-electric machine*);—*pl.* **dyn'amos**.—**dynam'ograph** *n.* the recording registered on a dynamometer.—**dynamom'eter** *n.* an instrument for measuring force [Gk. *dunamis*, power].

dynasty (din′as-ti, dī′nas-ti) *n.* a line of kings of the same family.—**dy'nast** *n.* a ruler.—**dynas'tic** *a.* [Gk. *dunastēs*, a lord].

dyne (dīn') *n.* a centimetre-gramme-second unit of force, or system [Gk. *dunamis*, force].

dysentery (dis′en-ter-i) *n.* inflammation of

the mucous membrane of the large intestine, accompanied by excessive discharge of the bowels, pain and fever.—**dysenter'ic, -al** *a.* [Gk. *dus-* ill; *entera*, the entrails].
dyslogistic (dis-lō-jis'-tik) *a.* opprobrious; conveying censure.—**dys'logy** *n.* blame; censure [Gk. *dus-* ill; *logos*, a discourse].
dyspathy (dis'-pą-thi) *n.* dislike; aversion—[Gk. *dus-* bad; *pathos*, feeling].
dyspepsia (dis-pep'-si-ą) *n.* indigestion. Also **dyspep'sy.**—**dyspep'tic** *a.* suffering from indigestion; morbid.—*n.* one who suffers from dyspepsia.—**dyspep'tically** *adv.* [Gk. *dus-*, bad; *peptein*, to digest].
dyspnoea (disp-nē'-ą) *n.* (*Med.*) difficulty in breathing [Gk. *dus-* hard; *pnoē*, breathing].
dysprosium (dis-prōz'-i-um) *n.* one of the rare earths, and the most magnetic metal known.—chem. symbol Dy [Gk. *dusprositos*, hard to get at].
dysteleology (dis-tel-ē-ol'-o-ji) *n.* doctrine of absence of purpose in nature.—**dysteleolog'ical** *a.*—**dysteleol'ogist** *n.* [Gk. *dus-* ill; *telos*, end; *logos*, discourse].
dysuria (dis-ū'-ri-ą) *n.* (*Med.*) difficulty or pain in passing urine. Also **dys'ury.**—**dysur'ic** *a.* [Gk. *dus-* bad; *ouron*, urine].

E

E.N.I.A.C. (*abbrev.*) Also *n.* (en'-i-ak) Electronic Numerical Integrator and Computor, a machine for solving mathematical problems.
each (ēch) *a.* and *pron.* denoting every one of a number, separately considered.—Abbrev. **ea.** [O.E. *aelc.*].
eager (ē'-gẹr) *a.* inflamed by desire; ardent; longing; yearning; greedy; impatient; earnest; anxious; keen.—**ea'gerly** *adv.*—**ea'gerness** *n.* [Fr. *aigre*, sour, keen].
eager See **eagre.**
eagle (ē'-gl) *n.* large bird of prey; a gold 10 dollar piece of the U.S.; a military standard in the form of the bird; (*Golf*) a hole played in two under par—**ea'gle-eyed** *a.* sharp-sighted.—**ea'gle-owl** *n.* the great horned owl of Europe.—**ea'glet** *n.* a young eagle.
eagre, eager (ē'-gẹr) *n.* a tidal bore, a single high wave which rushes up funnel-shaped estuaries [Icel. *aegir*, ocean].
ean (ēn) *v.t.* or *v.i.* to bring forth young.—**ean'ling** *n.* a young lamb; a yearling [O.E. *eanian*, to bring forth].
ear (ēr) *n.* the fruiting spike or head of corn;—*v.i.* to form ears, as corn [O.E. *ear*].
ear (ēr) *v.t.* to plough [O.E. *erian*].
ear (ēr) *n.* the organ of hearing, esp. external part of it; sensitiveness to musical sounds; attention; ear-shaped projection.—**ear'ache** *n.* acute pain in ear.—**ear'-drop** *n.* an ornamental pendant for the ear.—**ear'-drum** *n.* the middle ear or tympanum.—**eared** *a.* having ears.—**ear'-hole** *n.* aperture of external ear.—**ear'ing** *n.* a rope for fastening the upper corner of a square sail to the yard.—**ear'-lobe** *n.* the lobe of the ear; an ear-lappet in fowls.—**ear'mark** *v.t.* to mark the ears of sheep with the owner's mark; to reserve for a particular purpose.—**ear'phone** *n.* a head-phone for receiving wireless broadcasts, etc.—**ear'-ring** *n.* a ring worn suspended from lobe of ear.—**ear'shot** *n.* distance at which sounds can be heard.—**ear'-split'ting** *a.* exceedingly loud and piercing.—**ear'-trum'pet** *n.* an instrument for improving the hearing.—**ear'wax** *n.* cerumen, a waxy secretion of glands of ear.—**ear'wig** *n.* an insect with a body terminating in a pair of horny forceps.—**to have someone's ear,** to be assured of the right of approach to someone [O.E. *eare*].
earl (ẹrl) *n.* a nobleman ranking between a marquis and a viscount.—**earl'dom** *n.* territory or dignity of an earl.—**earl'-mar'shal** *n.* an officer of state in England, head of the College of Heralds [O.E. *eorl*].
early (ẹr'-li) *a.* appearing soon; in the beginning of the day; in the near future;—*adv.* in good season; betimes.—**ear'lier, ear'liest.**—**ear'liness** *n.* [O.E. *aerlice*].
earn (ẹrn) *v.t.* to gain money by labour; to merit by service; to get.—**earn'ings** *n.pl.* wages; savings [O.E. *earnian*].
earnest (ẹr'-nest) *a.* eager to obtain; zealous; strenuous;—*n.* a pledge; sum paid as binding an engagement.—**ear'nestly** *adv.*—**ear'nestness** *n.* [O.E. *eornest*, zeal].
earth (ẹrth) *n.* the planet on which we live; the soil, mould, dry land, on the surface of the earth; mineral; the world; the globe; a fox's hole; leakage of electric current to the earth; a wire which connects a wireless set or electrical apparatus with the earth, thus keeping it at zero potential.—**earths** *n.pl.* term in chemistry for certain metallic oxides;—*v.t.* to hide in the earth; to provide a path to the earth for electrical currents; to run to earth;—*v.i.* to burrow; take refuge in the ground.—**earth'-bound** *a.* fixed firmly in the earth; worldly; sordid.—**earth'-clos'et** *n.* privy in which earth is applied to the excreta as a deodorant.—**earth'en** *a.* made of earth, clay and the like.—**earth'enware** *n.* crockery and wares made of earth or clay, and baked or burnt with fire.—**earth'-fall** *n.* a landslide.—**earth'-house** *n.* underground dwelling in Scotland in pre-historic era.—**earth'iness** *n.*—**earth lead,** the wire connecting a wireless receiver with the earth, thus completing the electrical circuit.—**earth'ling** *n.* a dweller on the earth.—**earth'ly** *a.* belonging to the earth; terrestrial; worldly.—**earth'-nut** *n.* name of certain plants whose tubers are edible.—**earth'-pill'ar** *n.* a column of earth capped by a single boulder of limestone or sandstone found in the moraines of Switzerland.—**earth'quake** *n.* disturbance of the earth's surface due to contraction of a section of the crust of the earth.—**earth'-trem'or** *n.* a slight vibration of the surface of the earth.—**earth'ward** *adv.* toward the earth.—**earth'-work** *n.* mounds of earth for defence or to form embankments for railways and canals.—**earth'worm** *n.* the common worm; a despicable, mean person.—**earth'y** *a.* like or pertaining to earth; gross [O.E. *eorthe*].
ease (ēz) *n.* leisure; quiet; freedom from anxiety, bodily effort, or pain; facility; natural grace of manner;—*v.t.* to free from pain, disquiet, or oppression.—**ease'ful** *a.* restful; comfortable; quiet.—**eas'ily** *adv.*—**eas'iness** *n.*—**eas'ing** *n.* the act of alleviating or slackening; easement; relief; assistance.—**eas'y** *a.* at ease; free from pain, care, anxiety, or constraint; quiet; not difficult or burdensome; graceful; moderate; comfortable.—**stand at ease!** military term to relax after 'attention'.—**eas'y-chair** *n.* an arm-chair [Fr. *aise*].
easel (ē'-zl) *n.* a wooden frame to support pictures, etc. [Ger. *Esel*, an ass].
easement (ēz'-ment) *n.* (*Law*) a right over the land of another, e.g. right of way, right to divert water, etc. [O.Fr. *aisement*].
east (ēst) *n.* one of the four cardinal points; the part of the horizon where the sun rises; regions towards that;—*a.* on, in, or near the east;—*adv.* from or to the east.—**east'ern** *a.* toward the east; oriental.—**east'erly** *a.* from or toward the east.—*adv.* to or on the east.—**east'ernmost, east'most** *a.* furthest to the east.—**east'ing** *n.* distance eastward from a given meridian.—**east'ward** *adv.* or *a.* toward the east.—**east'wards** *adv.*—**Far East,** China, Japan, etc.—**Middle East,** Iran, Iraq, etc.—**Near East,** Turkey, Syria, Palestine, etc. [O.E. *east*].
Easter (ēs'-tẹr) *n.* a festival commemorating Christ's resurrection, falling on the Sunday after Good Friday [O.E. *Eastre*, spring festival of goddess of dawn].

easy See under **ease**.
eat (ēt) *v.t.* to chew and swallow, as food; to consume gradually; to destroy; gnaw; corrode; wear away;—*v.i.* to take food; to be eatable.—*pa.t.* **ate** (āt or et).—*pa.p.* **eat'en.** —**eat'able** *a.* or *n.* anything that may be eaten. —**eat'ing-house** *n.* a place where food is sold ready cooked; a cheap restaurant.—**eats** *n.pl,* (*U.S. slang*) food ready for consumption [O.E. *etan*].
eau (ō) *n.* French word for water;—*pl.* **eaux.** —**eau de Cologne,** a perfume obtained by distillation.—**eau-de-vie** (ō-dẹ-vē') *n.* brandy [Fr.].
eaves (ēvz) *n.pl.* the lower edges of a sloping roof overhanging the walls of a building.—**eaves'drop** *v.i.* to listen furtively to a conversation.—**eaves'drop'per** *n.* [O.E. *efes,* an edge].
ebb (eb) *n.* the reflux of tide-water to the sea; a decline; growing less; diminution;—*v.i.* to flow back; to sink; to decline.—**ebb'-tide** *n.* the ebbing or retiring tide [O.E. *ebba*].
E-boat (ē'-bōt) *n.* a small fast motor vessel, equipped with light guns and torpedoes, used by the Germans in World War 2.
ebon (eb'-on) *a.* black as ebony;—*n.* ebony.—**eb'ony,** a valuable cabinet wood, the heart-wood of which is jet-black and takes a fine polish.—**eb'onite** *n.* hard rubber or form of a vulcanite [L. *ebenus*].
ebriety (ē-brī'-et-i) *n.* drunkenness; intoxication.—**e'briated** *a.* [L. *ebrius,* drunk].
ebullient (ē-bul'-yent) *a.* boiling over; overflowing; exuberant; enthusiastic.—**ebull'ience** *n.*—**ebulli'tion** *n.* act of boiling; outburst of feeling; agitation [L. *bullire,* to boil].
ecaudate (ē-kaw'-dāt) *a.* tailless [L. *ex*; *cauda,* a tail].
eccentric (ek-sen'-trik) *a.* departing from the centre; not placed, or not having the axis placed, centrally; not circular (in orbit); irregular; odd; of a whimsical temperament; —*n.* a circular piece of metal mounted out of its centre upon a shaft; a modification of the crank contrived to change the rotary movement of a shaft into an up and down or reciprocating motion; a whimsical person; one who defies the social conventions.—**eccen'trically** *adv.*—**eccentric'ity** *n.* the distance of a focus from the centre of an ellipse; the deviation of two or more circles from a common centre; departure from normal way of conducting oneself [Gk. *ek,* from; *kentron,* centre].
ecclesia (e-klē'-zi-ạ) *n.* the general assembly of the freemen of Athens in classical times; a church; a religious assembly.—**ecclesias'tic** *n.* a person in orders; a clergyman; a priest; —*a.* belonging to the church.—**ecclesias'tical** *a.*—**ecclesias'ticism** *n.* adherence to ecclesiastical principles.—**ecclesiol'ogy** *n.* the science and study of church architecture and decoration.—**ecclesiol'ogist** *n.* [Gk. *ekklēsiastikos* fr. *ekklēsia,* church].
echelon (esh'-e-long) *n.* an arrangement of troops in parallel lines, each a little to left or right of another; (*Flying*) formation of aeroplanes in which each plane flies slightly above and to the right or left of the one in front. [Fr. *échelle,* a ladder].
echidna (e-kid'-nạ) *n.* the porcupine ant-eater of Australia [Gk.].
echinus (e-kī'-nus) *n.* a hedge-hog; a sea-urchin; a moulding having the form of eggs carved on it [Gk. *echinos,* a hedgehog].
echo (ek'-ō) *n.* repetition of sound produced by sound waves reflected from an object denser than the aerial medium; close imitation of another's remarks or ideas; reverberation; repetition; answer.—*pl.* **ech'oes.**—*v.t.* to send back the sound of; to repeat with approval; to imitate closely;—*v.i.* to resound; to be repeated.—**ech'oism** *n.* forming words to imitate natural sounds.—**ech'oist** *n.* one who merely repeats the sentiments of others.—**echola'lia** *n.* repeating a question, word for word [Gk.].
éclair (ā-klār') *n.* a long narrow, sweet cake, filled with cream, and having a chocolate or coffee glazing [Fr.].
éclat (ā-klȧ') *n.* splendour; approbation of success; renown; acclamation; show; brilliancy; lustre; applause [Fr.].
eclectic (ek-lek'-tik) *a.* selecting at will;—*n.* a thinker who selects and reconciles principles, opinions, belonging to different schools of thought [Gk. *eklegein,* to pick out].
eclipse (e-klips') *n.* an interception of the light of one heavenly body by another; temporary effacement;—*v.t.* to obscure or hide [Gk. *ek,* out; *leipein,* to leave].
ecliptic (e-klip'-tik) *n.* the great circle on the celestial sphere which lies in the plane of the sun's apparent orbit round the Earth [Gk. *ek,* out; *leipein,* to leave].
eclogue (ek'-log) *n.* a short poem of a pastoral nature [Gk. *eklogē,* a selection].
ecology (ē-kol'-o-ji) *n.* study of relations between animals and plants and their environment.—Also **oecol'ogy** [Gk. *oikos,* a house; *logos,* discourse].
economy (ē-kon'-o-mi) *n.* management of a household and its affairs; wise expenditure of money; careful use of materials; harmonious organisation.—**econom'ic(al)** *a.*—**econom'ically** *adv.*—**econom'ics** *n.pl.*—**political economy,** the science which deals with the rules governing the production, distribution and consumption of the world's resources and the management of State income and expenditure in terms of money.—**econ'omise** *v.i.* to expend with care and prudence;—*v.t.* to use with frugality.—**econ'omist** *n.* a student of economics; an economiser [Gk. *oikos,* a house; *nomos,* law].
écru (ā-kròò') *a.* a pale, yellow-brown shade, the colour of unbleached linen [Fr. *écru,* unbleached].
ecstasy (ek'-stạ-si) *n.* abnormal mental excitement when the mind is ruled by one idea, object, or emotion; a sense of uplift and joyfulness and increased well-being; excessive joy.—Also **ex'tasy.**—**ec'stasise** *v.t.* or *v.i.* to throw or go into a state of ecstasy.—**ecstat'ic** *a.* to be in a state of enthusiastic frenzy or rapture; overjoyed.—**ecstat'ically** *adv.* [Gk. *ekstasis*].
ectasis (ek'-tạ-sis) *a.* lengthening of a vowel or syllable [Gk.].
ecto-, ect-, a prefix used in the construction of compound terms, implying *outside, without* [Gk. *ektos*].
ectoplasm (ek'-to-plasm) *n.* (*Zool.*) exterior protoplasm of a cell; in spiritualism, an ethereal substance in which psychic phenomena may manifest themselves.—**ectoplas'mic** *a.* [Gk. *ektos,* outside; *plasma,* anything formed].
ecumenic, ecumenical (ek-ū-men'-ik, -i-kạl) *a.* universal; representative, or accepted as representative, of the Church, universal or catholic; general; catholic. Also **oecumen'ic, -al** [Gk. *oikoumenē,* the inhabited world].
eczema (ek'-ze-mạ) *n.* (*Med.*) a non-contagious disease of the epidermis, characterised by redness, itchiness and inflammatory eruption of the skin [Gk. *ekzema*].
edacious (ē-dā'-shus) *a.* greedy; ravenous.—**edac'ity** *n.* [L. *edax,* gluttonous].
Edda (ed'-ạ) *n.* a name of two great collections of Icelandic literature based on Norse mythology [Ice.=great-grandmother (of poetry)].
eddy (ed'-i) *n.* a current of air, smoke, or water, swirling back contrary to the main current; a vortex; a small whirlpool; a whirlwind;—*v.i.* to move in a circle.—*pr.p.* **edd'ying** —*pa.p.* **edd'ied** [O.E. *ed*=back].
edelweiss (ā'-dl-vīs) *n.* a small white flowering plant found in the Swiss Alps [Ger. *edel,* noble; *weiss,* white].
edema (ē-dē'-mạ) *n.* See **oedema.**

Eden (ē′den) *n.* the garden where Adam and Eve lived; a place of delight; a paradise [Heb. *eden*, delight].

Edentata (ed-en-tā′ta) *n.* mammals characterised by absence of front teeth or possessing very rudimentary ones, e.g. the sloth, ant-eater, etc.—**eden′tal** *a.*—**eden′tate** *a.* without front teeth; lacking teeth;—*n.* an animal, wanting front teeth and canines [L. *e*, out of; *dens*, tooth].

edge (ej) *n.* the thin cutting side of the blade of an instrument; the part adjacent to the line of division; brink; rim; keenness;—*v.t.* to put an edge on; to sharpen; to fringe; to move almost imperceptibly;—*v.i.* to move sideways.—**edged** *a.* sharp; bordered.—**edge′less** *a.*—**edge′(d)-tool** *n.* a cutting tool with a sharp edge.—**edge′ways, edge′wise** *adv.* in the direction of the edge; sideways.—**edg′ing** *n.* border or fringe; narrow lace.—**edg′y** *a.* having an edge; angular; irritable.—**to be on edge**, to be irritable [O.E. *ecg*].

edible (ed′i-bl) *a.* fit for eating;—*n.* an eatable.—**edibil′ity** *n.*—**ed′ibleness** *n.* the quality of being edible (L. *edere*, to eat)].

edict (ē′dikt) *n.* a law or decree; order proclaimed by a government or king; statute; ordinance [L. *e*; *dicere*, to say].

edify (ed′i-fī) *v.t.* to build up, esp. in character or faith; to instruct in moral and religious knowledge.—*pa.t.* and *pa.p.* **ed′ified.**—**edifica′tion** *n.* improvement of the mind or morals.—**ed′ifice** *n.* a fine building.—**ed′ifier** *n.* one who edifies.—**ed′ifying** *a.* instructive; morally improving [L. *aedificare*, to build].

edit (ed′it) *v.t.* to prepare for publication; to compile; to conduct a newspaper or periodical; to revise and alter or omit.—**edi′tion** *n.* the form in which a book is published; the number of copies of a book, newspaper, etc. printed at one time; an issue; copy or prototype; a replica.—**ed′itor** *n.* (*fem.* **ed′itress**) one who edits; one who conducts a newspaper or periodical.—**edito′rial** *n.* a leading article in a newspaper;—*a.* pert. to or written by an editor [L. *edere*, to give out].

educate (ed′ū-kāt) *v.t.* to bring up, as a child; to cultivate and dicipline, as the mind.—**ed′ucable** *a.* able to absorb education.—**educabil′ity** *n.*—**educa′tion** *n.* process of educating; upbringing; instruction; training.—**educa′tional** *a.* pert. to education.—**educa′tionally** *adv.*—**educa′tionist, educa′tionalist** *n.* one versed in the theory or practice of education.—**ed′ucative** *a.* tending to educate.—**educa′tor** *n.* one who educates [L. *e*, out; *ducere*, to lead].

educe (ē-dūs′) *v.t.* to draw or bring out that which is latent; to elicit; to extract; to evoke; to develop; to deduce.—**educ′ible** *a.*—**e′duct** *n.* that which is educed.—**educ′tion** *n.* the process of educing; the exhaustion of gases or steam from an engine; the exhaust [L. *educere*, to lead out].

Edwardian (ed-wawr′di-an) *a.* pert. to the reign of Edward VII (1901-1910).

eel (ēl) *n.* a group of fishes of the order Apodes, with elongated bodies and no ventral fins [O.E. *ael*].

e'en, e'er (ēn, er) *contr.* for *even, ever*.

eerie, eery (ē′ri) *a.* weird; superstitiously timid; frightening; nervous and frightened.—**ee′rily** *adv.*—**ee′riness** *n.* [O.E. *earg*, timid].

efface (e-fās′) *v.t.* to erase or scratch out; to rub out; wear away; obliterate; expunge; delete; destroy.—**efface′able** *a.*—**efface′ment** *n.* the act of effacing [Fr. *effacer*].

effect (e-fekt′) *n.* that which is produced by an agent or cause; result of agency or causation; consequence; impression left on the mind; reality;—*v.t.* to produce, as a cause or agent; to bring about; to accomplish; to achieve.—**effects′** *n.pl.* property; goods and chattels.—**effec′ter, effec′tor** *n.* one who produces an effect.—**effec′tible** *a.* can be effected; practicable.—**effec′tive** *a.* in a condition to produce desired result; efficient; powerful.—**effec′tively** *adv.*—**effec′tiveness** *n.*—**effec′tual** *a.* producing the intended result; efficacious; successful.—**effectual′ity** *n.*—**effec′tually** *adv.*—**effec′tuate** *v.t.* to bring to pass; to achieve; to accomplish; to effect.—**to give effect to,** to carry out; to accomplish.—**in effect,** really; for practical purposes.—**to take effect,** to become operative [L. *efficere*, to bring about].

effeminate (e-fem′i-nāt) *n.* an effeminate person;—*a.* unmanly; womanish; voluptuous; feeble; weak.—**effem′inacy** *n.* display, on the part of a man, of characteristics usually associated with women only.—**effem′inately** *adv.*—**effem′inateness** *n.*

effendi (e-fen′di) *n.* title of Turkish state officials, scholars, persons of rank, etc. [Turk. fr. Mod. Gk. *aphthentēs*, ruler].

efferent (ef′e-rent) *a.* conveying outward, or away from the centre [L. *ex*, out; *ferre*, to carry].

effervesce (ef-er-ves′) *v.i.* to bubble, to seethe, as a liquid giving off gas; to boil over—hence, to be in a state of excitement; to froth up.—**efferves′cence** *n.*—**efferves′cent** *a.* seething or bubbling [L. *effervescere*].

effete (e-fēt′) *a.* no longer capable of bearing young; barren; sterile; unfruitful; worn-out; spent [L. *effetus*, exhausted by breeding].

efficacious (ef-i-kā′shus) *a.* productive of effects; producing the desired effect.—**effica′ciously** *adv.* in an effective manner.—**effica′ciousness, efficac′ity, eff′icacy** *n.* power to produce effects [L. *efficere*, to effect].

efficient (e-fish′ent) *a.* causing effects; producing results; actively operative; capable; able; effective.—**effi′ciency** *n.* power to produce the result required; competency; **effi′ciently** *adv.* [L. *efficere*, to effect].

effigy (ef′i-ji) *n.* an image or representation of a person; a likeness in bas-relief, etc. on coins and medals; likeness; statue; figure.—*pl.* **eff′igies** (L. *effigies*, fr. *fingere*, to form].

effloresce (ef-lo-res′) *v.i.* to burst into bloom; to blossom; (*Chem.*) to lose water of crystallisation on exposure to air, so that crystals fall into powder.—**efflores′cence, efflores′cency** *n.* production of flowers; the time of flowering; redness of skin as in measles; formation of a floury powder on the surface of crystals.—**efflores′cent** *a.* [L. *efflorescere*].

effluent (ef′lòò-ent) *a.* flowing out;—*n.* a stream which flows out from another river or lake; liquid sewage in the course of purification.—**ef′fluence** *n.* a flowing out; issue; emanation.

effluvium (e-flòò′vi-um) *n.* an odour or exhalatioh with a disagreeable smell arising from putrefying matter.—*pl.* **efflu′via.**—**efflu′vial** *a.* [L. fr. *effluere*].

efflux (e′fluks) *n.* the act of flowing out; that which flows out in a stream.—**efflux′ion** *n.* an outflow; an emanation.

effort (ef′ort) *n.* putting forth an exertion of strength or power, bodily or mental; attempt; endeavour; trial essay.—**eff′ortless** *a.* without an effort [L. *ex*, out; *fortis*, strong].

effrontery (e-frun′ter-i) *n.* brazen impudence; excessive assurance; audacity [Fr. *effronté*= without brow (for blushing)].

effulge (e-fulj′) *v.i.* to shine brightly; to become famous.—**efful′gence,** *n.* great brightness, splendour, or lustre.—**efful′gent** *a.* diffusing a flood of light; splendid [L. *ex*, out; *fulgere*, to shine].

effuse (e-fūz′) *v.t.* to pour out or forth; to shed (blood);—*n.* effusion; shedding;—*a.* profuse; not compact; extravagant.—**effu′sion** *n.* act of pouring out; that which is poured out; facile piece of writing.—**effu′sive** *a.* pouring out profusely; gushing.—**effu′sively** *adv.*—**effu′siveness** *n.* [L. *ex*, out; *fundere*, *fusum*, to pour].

eft (eft) *n.* the newt or small lizard, common in ponds and ditches [See **newt**] [O.E. *efete*].

egad (e-gad′) *interj.* a mild imprecation=by God.
egal (ē′gal) *a.* equal.—**egal′ity** *n.* equality.—**egalita′rian** *n.* and *a.* believing in the principle of equality [Fr. *égalité*].
egest (e-jest′) *v.t.* to excrete; to void; to discharge [L. *e*, out; *gerere*, to carry].
egg (eg) *v.t.* to urge on; to encourage one to take action [O.N. *eggja*, fr. *egg*, edge].
egg (eg) *n.* an oval body laid by birds and a few animals in which the embryo continues development apart from parent body; matured female germ cell or ovum; a zygote; anything egg-shaped; (*Slang*) a bomb.—**egg′-cell** *n.* the ovum, as distinct from any other cells associated with it.—**egg′-cup** *n.* a cup shaped to hold egg.—**egg′-flip** *n.* a hot drink compounded of ale, with beaten eggs, sugar and spice to flavour it.—**egg′-glass** *n.* a small sand-glass for regulating boiling of eggs.—**egg′-nog** *n.* similar to egg-flip.—**egg′-shell** *n.* the calcareous outside cover of an egg.—**egg′-spoon** *n.* a small spoon used in eating boiled eggs [O.N. *egg*].
egis See **aegis.**
eglantine (eg′lan-tīn) *n.* the sweet brier; the honeysuckle [Fr. *églantine*].
ego (ē′gō, eg′ō) *n.* I; the whole person; self; the personal identity.—**e′gocentric** *a.* self-centred; egoistic.—**e′gocentricism, e′gocentricity** *n.*—**e′goism** *n.* systematic selfishness; theory that bases morality on self-interest.—**e′goist** *n.*—**egoist′ic, egoist′ical** *a.*—**e′gomania,** *n.* abnormal self-esteem.—**e′gotise** *v.* to talk or write incessantly of oneself.—**e′gotism** *n.*—**e′gotist** *n.*—**egotist′ic, -al** *a.*—**egotist′ically** *adv.* [L. *ego*, I].
egregious (e-grē′jus) *a.* remarkable; prominent; distinguished; notable.—**egre′giously** *adv.* [L. *e*, out; *grex*, a flock].
egress (ē′gres) *n.* act of leaving an enclosed place; exit; the right of departure.—**egres′sion** *n.* [L. *egressus*].
egret (ē′gret) *n.* several species of heron, including the great white heron; the aigrette [Fr. *aigrette*].
Egyptian (ē-jip′shạn) *a.* pert. to Egypt;—*n.* a native of Egypt; a gipsy.—**egyptol′ogy** *n.* study of Egyptian history, antiquities and inscriptions.—**egyptol′ogist** *n.*
eider (ī′dẹr) *n.* **the eider duck,** a species of sea-ducks yielding the commercially valuable eiderdown.—**ei′der-down** *n.* the breast-down with which the female eider-duck lines its nest, used for stuffing quilts and cushions; a quilt stuffed with this down [O.N. *aethr*].
eidograph (ī′do-graf) *n.* a form of pantograph for mechanically copying a drawing to scale [Gk. *eidos*, form; *graphein*, to write].
eight (āt) *n.* and *a.* one more than seven, written as 8 or VIII.—**eight′een** *n.* and *a.* eight more than ten, written 18 or XVIII.—**eight′eenth** *n.* and *a.* the eighth after the tenth, written 18th.—**eight′fold** *a.* eight times any quantity.—**eighth** *n.* and *a.* the first after the seventh;—*n.* one of eight equal parts of a whole, written 8th; an eighth part of an inch; (*Mus.*) the interval of an octave; the eighth note of the diatonic scale.—**eight′ieth** *a.* ordinal corresponding to eighty, coming after the seventy-ninth; written 80th;—*n.* one of eighty equal parts of a whole, written $\frac{1}{80}$.—**eight′y** *n.* and *a.* eight times ten; four-score.—**eight′-day** *n.* a clock which functions without winding for eight days.—**eight′some** *n.* a Scottish reel for eight dancers.—**figure of eight,** movement following the form of 8, at skating.—**piece of eight,** old Spanish silver coin.—**one over the eight,** (*Colloq.*) intoxicated [O.E. *eahta*].
eikon See **icon.**
eisteddfod (ī-steth′vod) *n.* an annual assembly of Welsh bards and musicians [W. *eistedd*, to sit].
either (ī′, ē′THẹr) *a.* or *pron.* one or the other; one of two; each;—*adv.* or *conj.* bringing in the first of alternatives or strengthening an added negation [O.E. *aegther*].
ejaculate (ē-jak′ū-lāt) *v.t.* to utter suddenly and briefly; to eject;—*v.i.* to utter ejaculations.—**ejac′ulation** *n.* a short, sudden exclamation; a sudden emission.—**ejac′ulatory** *a.* [L. *e*, out; *jacere*, to throw].
eject (ē-jekt′) *v.t.* to throw out; to cast forth; to turn out; to dispossess of a house or estate.—**eject′a** *n.* bodily excretions; waste matter.—**ejec′tion** *n.* the act of casting out.—**eject′ment** *n.* expulsion; dispossession; (*Law*) the forcible removal of a defaulting tenant by legal process from land or house.—**ejec′tor** *n.* [L. *e*, out; *jacere*, to throw].
eke (ēk) *v.t.* to add to or augment; to lengthen.—**to eke out,** to supplement; to prolong [O.E. *ecan*].
eke (ēk) *adv.* also; in addition to [O.E. *eac*, also].
elaborate (e-lab′o-rāt) *v.t.* to put much work and skill on; to work out in detail; to take pains with;—*a.* worked out in details; highly finished; complicated.—**elab′orately** *adv.*—**elab′orateness, elabora′tion** *n.* act of elaborating; progressive improvement [L. *e*, out; *labor*, labour].
élan (ā-long′) *n.* dash; impetuosity [Fr.].
eland (ē′land) *n.* the largest of the antelopes, found in Africa [Dut.].
elapse (e-laps′) *v.i.* of time, to pass silently by; to slip away.—**elap′sion** *n.* lapse [L. *e*; *labi*, *lapsus*, slide].
elastic (e-las′tik) *a.* possessing the property of recovering the original form, when a distorting or constraining force has been removed; not inflexible; resilient; springy; not strict, morally;—*n.* a fabric whose threads are interwoven with strands of rubber.—**elastic′ity** *n.* [Gk. *elaunein*, to drive].
elate (e-lāt′) *a.* in high spirits;—*v.t.* to raise or exalt the spirit of; to puff up; make proud; to elevate (as with success).—**elat′edly** *adv.*—**ela′tion** *n.* pride; exultation due to success [L. *elatus*, lifted up].
elbow (el′bō) *n.* the joint between the arm and forearm; right angle bend for joining two pipes; any sharp bend or turn;—*v.t.* and *v.i.* to push with the elbows; to jostle.—**el′bow-grease** *n.* (*Colloq.*) hard work, as in rubbing vigorously.—**el′-bow′room** *n.* ample room for free movement [O.E. *elnboga*].
eld (eld) *n.* old age; senility; old times.—**el′der** *a.* older; senior; prior;—*n.* one who is older; a senior; a senator; an office-bearer in the Presbyterian Church.—**eld′erliness** *n.*—**eld′erly** *a.* somewhat old; up in years.—**eld′est** *a.* the oldest of a family [O.E. *eldo*].
elder (el′dẹr) *n.* a widely distributed deciduous shrub which has masses of white clustered flowers, and yields berries used for making elderberry or elder wine. In Scotland, called the bourtree [O.E. *ellern*].
El Dorado, Eldorado (el-dō-rȧ′dō) *n.* a fabulous region abounding in gold and precious stones; any place where wealth is easily attainable; a rich gold-mine [Sp.=the gilded one].
elect (e-lekt′) *v.t.* to choose; to choose by vote; to appoint to office; to select;—*v.i.* to determine on any course of action;—*a.* chosen; selected from a number; (after a noun), appointed but not yet in office;—*n.* those predestined to eternal life.—**elec′tion** *n.* the act of electing or choosing; public voting for office.—**electioneer′** *v.i.* to canvass for votes.—**elec′tive** *a.* appointed by; dependent on choice.—**elect′ively** *adv.*—**elect′or** *n.* one with right to vote at election; title of German princes who enjoyed the privilege of disposing of the imperial crown of the Holy Roman Empire;—*fem.* **elect′ress.**—**elect′oral, electro′rial** *a.* pertaining to electors or to elections. **elec′torate** *n.* the whole body of electors [L. *eligere*].

electric (e-lek′trik) *a.* pertaining to, charged with, worked by, producing electricity;—*n.* a non-conductor of electricity, e.g. amber, glass, which when rubbed, accumulates electricity.—**electric arc,** an incandescent vapour occurring between two points of a gap in an electric circuit.—**electric battery,** an apparatus for generating electricity by chemical action.—**electric blue,** a bright middle-blue colour.—**electric chair,** used in U.S.A. for electrocuting criminals.—**electric circuit,** the path followed by electricity.—**electric current,** flow of electricity.—**electric eel,** a fresh water fish of the S. American llanos which is capable of inflicting powerful shocks.—**electric unit,** of pressure = *volt*; of current = *ampere*; of power = *watt*; of resistance = *ohm* [Gk. *ēlektron*, amber].

electrical (e-lek′tri-kal) *a.* pertaining to electricity.—**elec′trically** *adv.*

electrician (e-lek-trish′an) *n.* one who studies the science of electricity; a mechanic who makes or repairs electrical apparatus or attends to electrical installations.

electricity (e-lek-tris′i-ti) *n.* active condition of the molecules of a body or of the ether round it, produced by friction, magnetism, etc.; the force which shows itself in lightning; the study of this.

electrify (e-lek′tri-fī) *v.t.* to charge with electricity; to instal an electric system of light, power, etc.; to thrill, startle, excite by an unexpected statement or action;—*pa.t.* and *pa.p.* **elec′trified.**

electrise, electrize [e-lek′trīz) *v.t.* to electrify.—**electrisa′tion** *n.* electrification.

electro (e-lek′tro) *n.* printer's abbrev. for electrotype.—**elec′tro-,** *prefix,* used in the construction of compound words referring to some phase of electricity.

electro-analysis (e-lek′tro an-al′is-is) *n.* the quantitative separation of metals by electrolysis.

electro-biology (e-lek′tro′bī-ol′o-ji) *n.* the study of the electric currents developed in living organisms.

electro-cardiogram (e-lek′tro-car′di-o-gram) *n.* a photographic tracing of the electrical variations taking place during the contraction of the muscle of the heart.—**elec′tro-car′diograph** *n.* an apparatus to produce such photographic records.

electro-chemistry (e-lek′tro-kem′is-tri) *n.* the branch of science which deals with the chemical effects in a compound, brought about by electricity or galvanism.

electrocute (e-lek′tro-kūt) *v.t.* to cause death by electric shock.—**electrocu′tion** *n.*

electrode (e-lek′trōd) *n.* a metallic conductor of an open electric circuit in contact with some other kind of conductor such as an electrolyte, a gas, etc.; the wire used in electric arc welding; the plate of a vacuum tube, X-ray bulb, or wireless valve [Gk. *ēlektron*, amber; *hodos*, way].

electro-deposit (e-lek′tro-de-pos′it) *v.t.* to deposit a coating of a metal on another metal by the action of an electric current upon certain metallic solutions.

electro-dynamics (e-lek′tro-di-nam′iks) *n.* branch of the science of electricity which treats of the laws of electricity in motion or of electric currents and their effects.

electro-kinetics (e-lek′tro-ki-net′iks) *n.* Same as **electro-dynamics.**

electrolier (e-lek′tro-lē′ẹr) *n.* an ornamental pendant or stand fitted to carry several electric lamps.

electrology (e-lek-trol′o-ji) *n.* the science of applied electricity; the treatment of diseases by electric currents or radiations.

electrolysis (e-lek-trol′is-is) *n.* the resolution of dissolved or fused chemical compounds into elements by passing a current of electricity through them.—**elec′trolyse** *v.t.* to subject to electrolysis.—**elec′trolyte** *n.* the liquid which carries the electric current between two electrodes [Gk. *ēlektron*, amber; *luein*, to loosen].

electro-magnet (e-lek′tro-mag′net) *n.* a mass of soft iron temporarily magnetised by being placed within a coil of insulated copper wire through which a current of electricity is passing.—**elec′tro-magnet′ic** *a.*—**elec′tro-mag′netism** *n.* branch of electrical science which treats of the development of magnetism by electricity.

electro-metallurgy (e-lek′tro-met′al-ur-ji) *n.* the process by which metals and alloys are produced on a commercial scale by means of electricity, involving use of electrolysis or the electric furnace.

electrometer (e-lek-trom′et-ẹr) *n.* an electrical instrument for measuring quantity of electricity.

electro-motion (e-lek′tro-mo′shun) *n.* the flow of an electric current in a voltaic circuit.—**elec′tro-mot′ive** *a.* producing motion by means of electricity.—**electro-motive force,** the difference in electrical potential between any two points in a circuit; the pressure or voltage of an electrical current.

electron (e-lek′tron) *n.* the lightest known particle, a constituent of all atoms around whose nuclei they revolve in orbits.—**electron′ics** *n.* the branch of physics which deals with the behaviour of free electrons.—**electron microscope,** an instrument of immense magnifying power in which controlled rays of electrons are used instead of light rays.

electro-negative (e-lek′tro-neg′a-tiv) *a.* carrying a negative charge of electricity; having the tendency to form negative ions.

electropathy (e-lek-trop′a-thi) *n.* treatment of disease by means of electricity. Also **electrother′apy.**—**electrotherapeu′tics** *n.*

electro-physiology (e-lek′tro-fiz-i-ol′o-ji) *n.* the branch of science dealing with electrical phenomena of living organisms produced through physiological causes.

electro-plate (e-lek′tro-plāt) *v.t.* to cover a metal with a coating of silver, by means of electrolysis;—*n.* an article so covered.

electro-polar (e-lek′tro-pō′lar) *a.* term applied to a conductor positively electrified at one end and negatively at the other.

electro-positive (e-lek′tro-poz′i-tiv) *a.* carrying a positive charge of electricity; having the tendency to form positive ions.

electro-statics (e-lek′tro-stat′iks) *n.* the branch of electrical science which treats of the behaviour of electricity in equilibrium or at rest.

electrothermy (e-lek′tro-ther′mi) *n.* the study of heat developed by electricity.

electrotype (e-lek′tro-tīp) *n.* a facsimile printing plate of type or illustrations.

electrum (e-lek′trum) *n.* amber; an alloy of gold and silver; nickel-silver or German silver; an alloy of copper, nickel and zinc.

eleemosynary (el-ē-mos′i-na-ri) *a.* by way of charity; given in charity [Gk. *eleēmosunē*, alms].

elegant (el′e-gant) *a.* graceful; tasteful; refined; polished; comely.—**el′egantly** *adv.*—**el′egance** *n.* grace; beauty; propriety; gentility; delicate taste [L. *elegans*].

elegy (el′e-ji) *n.* a song of mourning after loss; a funeral song.—**elegi′ac** *a.* pertaining to elegy; written in elegiacs;—**elegi′acs** *n.pl.* elegiac verse or couplets, each made up of a hexameter and a pentameter.—**el′egiacal** *a.*—**ele′giast, el′egist** *n.* a writer of elegies [Gk. *elegos*, a lament].

elektron (e-lek′tron) *n.* a magnesium alloy of unusual lightness [Gk.=amber].

element (el′e-ment) *n.* the first principle or rule; a component part; ingredient; constituent; essential point; the habitation most suited to a particular animal; (*Chem.*) a substance which cannot be separated into two or more substances; the resistance wire of an electric heater.—**el'ements** *n.pl.* the bread and wine used in the Lord's Supper; fire, air, water and earth, supposed to be foundation of all things; the physical forces of nature which determine the state of the weather.—**element'al** *a.* of the powers of nature; not compounded; basic; fundamental; tremendous.—**element'ary** *a.* pertaining to the elements or first principles of anything; rudimentary; simple.—**element'als** *n.pl.* a general name given by occultists to salamanders (fire), undines (water), sylphs (air) and gnomes (earth), spirits of their respective element [L. *elementum*].

elemi (el′em-i) *n.* a fragrant gum resin.—**el'emin** *n.* a colourless oil distilled from elemi [Ar.].

elephant (el′e-fąnt) *n.* a sub-order of ungulates (hoofed mammals) of which there are two living species, the Indian and the African; the largest four-footed animal, having a long flexible trunk, two ivory tusks and exceedingly thick skin; a size of drawing paper measuring 28 by 23 in.; (*U.S.*) a large folio, measuring 14 in. by 23 in.; a moulding machine with a spindle.—**elephant'ine** *a.* huge; unwieldy; ungainly.—**elephant'oid** *a.* like an elephant.—**a white elephant,** a gift which only embarrasses the recipient [Gk. *elephas*].

elephantiasis (el-e-fan-tī′ą-sis) *n.* a tropical disease in which there is gross enlargement of the lower limbs and scrotum [Gk. *elephas,* an elephant].

elevate (el′e-vāt) *v.t.* to lift up; to raise to a higher rank or station; to elate; to exhilarate; to make louder or raise the pitch of (the voice); to augment.—**el'evated** *a.* raised; promoted; dignified; exhilarated; (*Colloq.*) tipsy; intoxicated.—**eleva'tion** *n.* the act of elevating or the state of being raised; elevated place, a hill, a height; (*Archit.*) geometrical projection, drawn to scale, of the vertical face of any part of a building or object.—**el'evator** *n.* the person or thing which lifts up; a lift or hoist; in U.S. a huge silo where grain is stored; the rudder-like movable control surfaces hinged to the edge of the tail-plane of an aeroplane, used for raising or lowering the nose of the machine.—**el'evatory** *a.* tending or having power to elevate [L. *levis,* light].

eleven (e-lev′n) *n.* and *a.* one more than ten, written as 11 or XI; a full team at cricket, association football, or hockey.—**elev'enth** *a.* the ordinal number corresponding to eleven, the next after the tenth;—*n.* one of 11 equal parts of a whole [O.E. *endlufan*].

elf (elf) *n.* a supernatural, diminutive being of folk-lore with mischievous traits; a hobgoblin; a dwarf;—*pl.* **elves**.—*v.t.* to entangle the hair.—**el'fin** *n.* a little elf; a child;—*a.* dainty, like an elf.—**elf'ish, elv'an, elv'ish** *a.* elf-like; roguish [O.E. *aelf*].

elicit (e-lis′it) *v.t.* to draw out; to extract; to bring to light facts by questioning or reasoning; to deduce [L. *elicere*].

elide (e-līd′) *v.t.* to cut off or suppress a final vowel or syllable.—**eli'sion** *n.* the suppression of a vowel or syllable [L. *elidere,* to strike out].

eligible (el′i-ji-bl) *a.* legally qualified; fit and worthy to be chosen; desirable; suitable; preferable.—**el'igibleness, eligibil'ity** *n.* [L. *eligere,* to choose].

eliminate (ē-lim′i-nāt) *v.t.* to remove; get rid of; set aside; separate; leave out of consideration; excrete; expel; obliterate.—**elim'inable** *a.* capable of being eliminated.—**elimina'tion** *n.*—**elim'inator** *n.* [L. *eliminare,* to put out of doors].

eliquation (e-li-kwā′shun) *n.* the process of separating a mixture of fusible substances by heating at a temperature just sufficient to melt the component with the lowest melting-point, the others remaining unaffected [L. *eliquare,* to clarify].

elision See **elide**.

élite (ā-lēt′) *n.* a choice or select body; the pick or best part of society [Fr.].

elixir (e-liks′ẹr) *n.* a sovereign remedy; the essence, vainly sought by the alchemists, which would have the power to transmute base metals into gold.—**elixir vitae,** the elixir of life, a cordial believed to bestow perpetual youth [Ar. *al-iksir*].

Elizabethan (e-liz-ą-bē′thąn) *a.* pert. to Queen Elizabeth or her times;—*n.* a writer or distinguished person of her reign.

elk (elk) *n.* the largest member of the deer family, found in the N. of Europe and in America where it is more commonly called the moose [O.E. *eolh*].

ell (el) *n.* a measure of length in cloth, formerly taken from the forearm but now $1\frac{1}{4}$ yds. [O.E. *eln*].

ellipse (e-lips′) *n.* a regular oval, formed by the line traced out by a point moving so that the sum of its distance from two fixed points always remains the same; the plane section across a cone not taken at right angles to the axis.—**ellip'soid** *n.* a closed solid figure of which every plane section is an ellipse.—**ellip'tic(al)** *a.* oval; pertaining to an ellipse [See **ellipsis**]. [Gk. *elleipsis,* a defect].

ellipsis (e-lip′sis) *n.* in English syntax a term denoting the omission of a word or words from a sentence whereby the complete meaning is obtained by inference.—**ellip'tic(al)** *a.* [Gk.].

elm (elm) *n.* a genus of trees, including the common elm and the wych elm [O.E.].

Elmo's fire (el′mōz fīr) *n.* a form of ball lightning where a luminous ball of fire is seen at night on a spar or yard of a ship [after St. *Elmo,* patron of sailors].

elocution (el-o-kū′shun) *n.* art of effective public speaking from the point of view of enunciation, voice-production, delivery.—**elocu'tionary** *a.*—**elocu'tionist** *n.* a teacher of elocution; one who specialises in verse-speaking [L. *e,* out; *loqui,* to speak].

elogium (ē-lō′ji-um) **eloge** (ā-lōzh′) **elogy** (el′o-ji) *n.* a discourse in panegyric of some illustrious person deceased; a funeral oration.—**el'ogist** *n.* [L.=an inscription on a tomb].

elongate (ē′long-gāt) *v.t.* to make longer; to lengthen; to prolongate; to extend; to draw out; to stretch out;—*a.* (*Bot.*) tapering.—**elonga'tion** *n.* the act of stretching out; the part extended [L. *e*; *longus,* long].

elope (e-lōp′) *v.i.* to run away clandestinely, especially of a woman who abandons home ties to run away with a lover; to abscond, bolt unexpectedly [O.Fr. *alouper*).

eloquence (el′ō-kwens) *n.* the art or power of expressing thought in fluent, impressive and graceful language; oratory; rhetoric; fluency.—**el'oquent** *a.*—**el'oquently** *adv.* [L. *e,* out; *loqui,* to speak].

else (els) *adv.* besides; other; otherwise; instead.—**else'where** *adv.* in or to some other place [O.E. *elles*].

elucidate (e-lū′si-dāt) *v.t.* to make clear or manifest; to throw light upon; to explain; illustrate.—**elucida'tion** *n.* act of throwing light upon or explaining.—**elu'cidative, elu'cidatory** *a.*—**elu'cidator** *n.* [L. *e*; *lux,* light; *dare,* to give].

elucubration See **lucubration**.

elude (e-lūd′) *v.t.* to keep out of sight; to escape by stratagem, artifice or dexterity; to evade; to avoid; to disappoint; to frustrate; to baffle.—**elu'sion** *n.* act of eluding; evasion.—**elu'sive** *a.* evasive; difficult to catch; deceptive.—**elu'sory** *a.* evasive [L. *e,* out; *ludere,* to play].

elvan See **elf.**
elver (elʹvẹr) *n.* the young of the eel, about 2 in. long [fr. *eel* and *fare*].
elves, elvish. See **elf.**
Elysium (e-lizhʹi-um) *n.* (*Myth.*) according to the Greeks, the abode of the shades of the virtuous dead in the nether world where the inhabitants lived a life of passive blessedness.—**Elys'ian** *a.*
em- (em) *pref.* in or with; or adding a transitive or casual force in the composition of verbs.
em (em) *n.* (*Print.*) Typographical unit of width, known as a pica or 12 pt. em (approx. 1/6th of an in.) used for measuring the length of a line of type.
emaciate (e-māʹshi-āt) *v.t.* to make lean; to reduce one to flesh and bones;—*v.i.* to waste away with loss of strength; to become extremely thin;—*a.* in a very lean condition. —**ema'ciated** *a.*—**emacia'tion** *n.* [L. *emaciare*, fr. *macies*, leanness].
emanate (emʹạ-nāt) *v.i.* to issue from; to originate; to proceed from; to arise (of intangible things).—**em'anant** *a.* flowing from.—**emana'tion** *n.* a flowing out from; that which issues from a source; radioactive, chemically inert gas given off by radium, thorium and actinium; an ancient doctrine of Eastern origin which derives all existences as emanations from the Supreme Essence, God, but in varying degrees of imperfection.—**em'anatist** *n.*—**em'anative, em'anatory** *a.* [L. *emanare*, to flow out].
emancipate (e-manʹsi-pāt) *v.t.* to set free from slavery or servitude; to set free from any restraint or restriction.—**emancipa'tion** *n.* the state of being set free.—**emancipa'tion** *n.* an advocate of the emancipation of slaves.—**eman'cipator** *n.* [L. *emancipare*].
emasculate (e-masʹkū-lāt) *v.t.* to castrate; to deprive of masculine qualities; to render effeminate.—**emascula'tion** *n.*—**emas'culatory** *a.* [L. *e*; *masculus*, masculine].
embalm (em-bȧm') *v.t.* to preserve a corpse from decay by means of antiseptic agents, balm, aromatic oils and spices; to perfume; to cherish tenderly some memory of.—**embalm'er** *n.*—**embalm'ing, embalm'ment** *n.* [Fr. *embaumer*].
embank (em-bangk') *v.t.* to enclose or defend with a bank, mound, or earthwork. —**embank'ment** *n.* the act of embanking; an earthwork built in low-lying ground, designed to carry a road or railway; a raised mound or dyke to prevent flooding.
embargo (em-bȧrʹgō) *n.* in international law, an order by which a government prevents a foreign ship from leaving port; an order forbidding the despatch of a certain class of goods, usually munitions, to another country; a general prohibition.—*pl.* **embar'goes.**—*v.t.* to lay an embargo upon [Sp. *embargar*, to impede].
embark (em-bȧrk') *v.t.* to put on board a ship; to enter on some business or enterprise;—*v.i.* to go on board a ship.—**embarka'tion** *n.* [Fr. *embarquer*].
embarrass (em-barʹạs) *v.t.* to disconcert; to perplex; to abash; to impede; to involve one in difficulties, esp. regarding money matters.—**embarr'assed** *a.*—**embarr'assing** *a.* disconcerting.—**embarr'assment** *n.* state of perplexity; confusion; financial difficulties [Fr. *embarrasser*].
embassy (emʹbạ-si) *n.* the person sent abroad as an ambassador along with his staff; one entrusted with a message to a foreign state; the residence of an ambassador [O.Fr. *ambasée*].
embattle (em-batʹl) *v.t.* to furnish with battlements.—**embatt'lement** *n.*
embattle (em-batʹl) *v.t.* to draw up in order of battle.—**embatt'led** *a.*
embay (em-bā') *v.t.* to enclose in a bay or inlet; to landlock.—**embay'ment** *n.* a bay.
embed (em-bed') *v.t.* to lay as in a bed; to bed in soil. Also **imbed'.**
embellish (em-belʹish) *v.t.* to make beautiful or elegant with ornaments; to add fanciful details to a report or story.—**embell'isher,** *n.*—**embell'ishingly,** *adv.*—**embell'ishment** *n.* act of embellishing or adorning; adornment; decorative ornamentation [Fr. *embellir*, to beautify].
ember (emʹbẹr) *n.* a live piece of coal or wood;—*pl.* red-hot ashes [O.E. *aemerge*].
Ember Days (emʹbẹr dāz) *n.pl.* four annually recurring periods of three days each for fasting and praying.—**Em'ber-week,** *n.* a week in which ember-days fall [O.E. *ymbryne*, revolution, period].
embezzle (em-bezʹl) *v.t.* to misappropriate fraudulently; to peculate; to purloin.—**embezz'lement** *n.*—**embezz'ler** *n.* [O.Fr. *enbesiler*, to damage, steal].
embitter (em-bitʹẹr) *v.t.* to make bitter.—**embitt'ered** *a.* exasperated; soured.
emblazon (em-blāʹzon) *v.t.* to adorn with heraldic figures; to deck in blazing colours. —**emblaze'** *v.t.* to illuminate.—**embla'zonment** *n.*—**embla'zonry** *n.* art of emblazoning; heraldic devices on a shield.
emblem (emʹblem) *n.* an object, or a representation of an object, symbolising and suggesting to the mind something different from itself; sign; badge; symbol; device;—*v.t.* to symbolise.—**em'blemise** *v.t.* to represent by means of an emblem.—**emblemat'ic, -al** *a.* pert. to an emblem.—**emblemat'ically** *adv.* [Gk. *emblema*, a thing put in].
embody, imbody (em-, im-bodʹi) *v.t.* to form into a body; to incorporate; to give concrete expression to; to represent, be an expression of.—*pa.t.* and *pa.p.* **embod'ied.**—**embod'iment** *n.* act of embodying; bodily representation.
embolden (em-bōldʹn) *v.t.* to give boldness or courage to; to encourage; to animate.
embolism (emʹbo-lizm) *n.* the insertion of days between other days to adjust the reckoning of time; (*Med.*) the result of the presence in the blood-stream of a solid foreign substance, as a clot.—**embolis'mal** *a.* [Gk. *embolē*, an insertion].
embonpoint (ong-bōng-pwang') *n.* plumpness; stoutness;—*a.* stout; well-fed [Fr.].
embosom, imbosom (em-, im-bòózʹum) *v.t.* to clasp or receive into the bosom; to enclose; to shelter; to foster.
emboss (em-bos') *v.t.* to raise or form a design above the surrounding surface, by pressure of a die on metal, leather, cardboard or similar substances.—**embossed'** *a.* —**emboss'ment** *n.* a boss or protuberance [O.Fr. *bosc*].
embouchure (ong-bòò-shòòr') *n.* the mouth of a river, gun, etc.; the mouthpiece of a wind instrument; different positions of the lip, etc. in playing wind instruments [Fr. *en*, in; *bouche*, mouth].
embowel (em-bouʹẹl) *v.t.* to disembowel; to eviscerate; to remove the bowels.
embower (em-bouʹẹr) *v.t.* to lodge, or set in a bower; to surround (with flowers).
embrace (em-brās) *v.t.* to clasp in the arms; to press to the bosom; to avail oneself of; to accept;—*n.* a clasping in the arms; a hug [Fr. *embrasser*, fr. *bras*, arm].
embrangle, imbrangle (em-, im-brangʹgl) *v.t.* to entangle; to confuse; to perplex.—**embran'glement** *n.* [fr. *embr*oil and ent*angle*].
embrasure (em-brāʹzhur) *n.* the splay or bevel of a door or window where the sides slant on the inside; the indents or crenelles of a battlement; opening in a parapet of a fort to allow cannon-fire [Fr.]
embrocate (emʹbrō-kāt) *v.t.* to moisten and rub with lotion, etc.—**embroca'tion** *n.* act of embrocating; a lotion for rubbing on body [Gk. *embrochē*, lotion].
embroglio See **imbroglio.**

embroider (em-broiʹdẹr) *v.t.* to ornament fabrics with threads of silk, linen, etc. to form a design; to embellish, exaggerate a story.—**embroid'erer** *n.*—**embroid'ery** *n.* ornamental needlework [O.Fr. *broder*].

embroil (em-broil') *v.t.* to involve in a quarrel or strife; to perplex; to entangle; to confound.—**embroil'ment** *n.* [Fr. *embrouiller*, to entangle].

embrute (em-bròòt') *v.t.* to degrade; to reduce to the level of a brute animal.

embryo (emʹbri-ō) **embryon** (emʹbri-on) *n.* foetus during first months of gestation before quickening; a plant in rudimentary stage of development within seed; initial or rudimentary stage of anything;—*pl.* **em'bryos.**—*a.* rudimentary; in the early stage.—**embryolog'ic, -al** *a.* pert. to embryology.—**embryol'ogist** *n.*—**embryol'ogy** *n.* science which deals with growth and structure of living organisms during progressive stages of development of embryo.—**embryon'ic** *a.* rudimentary; at an early stage of development [Gk. *embruon*].

embus (em-bus') *v.t.* and *i.* to put into, to mount, a bus, esp. of troops.

emend (e-mend') *v.t.* to remove faults or blemishes from; to amend, esp. of correcting a literary text; to alter for the better.—**em'endate** *v.t.*—**emenda'tion,** *n.* correction of errors or blemishes.—**em'endator** *n.*—**emen'datory** *a.* [Doublet of *amend*].

emerald (emʹẹr-ạld) *n.* precious stone of beryl species, transparent and bright-green in colour.—**emerald green,** a rich, green, but very poisonous pigment, consisting of chromic oxide.—**Emerald Isle,** Ireland [Fr. *émeraude*].

emerge (e-mẹrj') *v.i.* to rise out of a fluid; to come forth; to come into view; to come to notice.—**emer'gence** *n.* coming into view; an outgrowth from a plant.—**emer'gency** *n.* state of pressing necessity; difficult situation; urgent need.—**emer'gent** *a.* emerging; rising into view [L. *e*, out; *mergere*, to plunge].

emeritus (ē-merʹi-tus) *n.* and *a.* one who has honourably resigned a public position of trust or responsibility to go into retirement [L.=a veteran, fr. *e*, out; *merere*, to earn].

emersion (e-mẹrʹshun) *n.* emerging; reappearance of heavenly body after eclipse or occultation [L. *e*, out; *mergere*, to plunge].

emery (emʹẹr-i) *n.* a naturally occurring mixture of corundum (impure aluminium oxide) and iron oxide, exceedingly hard and used as an abrasive for polishing;—*v.t.* to rub with emery.—**emery paper,** stiff paper coated with emery-powder for polishing [Gk. *smuris*].

emesis (emʹe-sis) *n.* act of vomiting [Gk.].

emetic (e-metʹik) *a.* inducing vomiting;—*n.* any agent which causes vomiting [Gk. *emetikos*, provoking sickness].

emiction (e-mikʹshun) *n.* passing urine.—**emict'ory** *a.* promoting the flow of urine [L. *e*, out; *mingere*, to urinate].

emigrate (emʹi-grāt) *v.i.* to leave one's country to settle in another.—**em'igrant** *a.* pert. to emigration;—*n.* one who emigrates.—**emigra'tion** *n.*—**émigré** (āʹmē-grā) *n.* an emigrant, especially a member of the French aristocracy, who sought refuge and exile in a foreign country during the Revolution [L. *e*, out; *migrare*, to remove].

eminent (emʹi-nent) *a.* exalted in rank, office, or public estimation.—**em'inence** *n.* elevation; rising ground; height; rank; official dignity; fame; title of honour enjoyed by cardinals.—**em'inently** *adv.* [L. *eminere*, to stand out].

emir (e-mēr' or emʹēr) *n.* a title bestowed on chieftains in Moslem countries.—**em'irate** *n.* the office of an emir [Ar. *amir*. Doublet of *ameer*].

emissary (emʹi-sạr-i) *n.* agent charged with a secret mission; one sent on a mission [L. *e*, out; *mittere, missum*, to send].

emit (e-mit') *v.t.* to send forth; to utter (a declaration).—*pr.p.* **emit'ting.**—*pa.p.* **emit'ted.**—**emis'sion** *n.* the act of emitting; that which is emitted.—**emis'sive** *a.* emitting; emitted; radiating [L. *e*, out; *mittere*, to send].

emmet (emʹet) *n.* an ant [M.E. *emete*, an ant].

emmew, immew (e-, i-mū') *v.t.* to confine; to coop up.

emolliate (e-molʹi-āt) *v.t.* to soften; to render effeminate [L. *emollire*, to soften].

emollient (e-molʹi-ent *a.* softening; relaxing; assuaging; rendering supple;—*n.* outward application of poultices, fomentations, etc. to an inflamed part of body [L. *mollis*, soft].

emolument (e-molʹū-ment) *n.* profit arising from office or employment; gain; pay; salary; wages; fee [L. *moliri*, to toil].

emotion (e-mōʹshun) *n.* a pleasurable or painful condition of the mind which may accompany our sensations, memories or judgments; the faculty of feeling; a state of excited feeling or agitation.—**emo'tional** *a.* easily excited or upset; appealing to the emotions.—**emo'tionalism** *n.* tendency to emotional excitement.—**emo'tionally** *adv.*—**emo'tionless** *a.*—**emo'tive** *a.* causing emotion [L. *emotio*, fr. *emovere*, to stir].

empale See **impale.**

empanel, impanel (em-, im-panʹel) *v.t.* to place a name on a panel or list; to enter the names of a jury on a panel; to form a jury by roll-call.

empathy (emʹpạ-thi) *n.* that emotional effect of imagination which impels a person to assume the identity of another and experience the latter's reactions [Gk. *en*, in; *pathos*, feeling].

empennage (ong-pen-azh') *n.* the tail unit of an aeroplane [Fr. fr. L. *penna*, a feather].

emperor (emʹper-or) *n.* the title assumed by the ruler of an empire [L. *imperare*, to command].

emphasis (emʹfạ-sis) *n.* stress of utterance or force of voice given to words or syllables in order to draw attention to them; vigour of speech; intensity of expression; accent.—*pl.* **em'phases.**—**em'phasise** *v.t.* to utter with emphasis; to draw attention to the importance of.—**emphat'ic, emphat'ical** *a.* [Gk.].

empire (emʹpīr) *n.* imperial power; dominion; a country with its satellite states under the rule of an emperor or some other supreme control [L. *imperium*, command].

empiric, empirical (em-pirʹik, -ạl) *a.* based on the results of experiment, observation, or experience, and not from mathematical or scientific reasoning; having reference to actual facts; experimental.—**empir'ic** *n.* a quack doctor; one who depends for his knowledge entirely on experience.—**empir'ically** *adv.*—**empir'icism** *n.* the philosophical doctrine that assumes that all our knowledge and mental possessions are a product of purely sensuous experience; the formulation of scientific laws by the process of observation and experiment; quackery.—**empir'icist** *n.* [Gk. *en*, in; *peira*, trial].

emplacement (em-plāsʹment) *n.* the place or site of a building; a fortified platform, pit, or shelter for gun, machine-gun, or trench-mortar; placing in position.

emplane (em-plān') *v.t.* or *v.i.* to put into, or to enter, an aeroplane.

employ (em-ploi') *v.t.* to give occupation to; to make use of; to hire or engage; to busy; to engross; to exercise; to occupy.—**employ'able** *a.* fit for employment; capable of being employed.—**employee'** *n.* one who is employed at a wage or salary.—**employ'er** *n.*—**employ'ment** *n.* the act of employing or using; the state of being employed [Fr. *employer*].

empoison (em-poi′zn) *v.t.* to administer poison; to make bitter (of the mind).
emporium (em-pō′ri-um) *n.* a place of extensive commerce or trade; a mart; market; a big shop; a commercial city;—*pl.* **empo′ria** [Gk. *emporos*, trader].
empoverish See **impoverish.**
empower (em-pou′ẹr) *v.t.* to give legal or moral power or authority to; to authorise.
empress (em′pres) *n.* the wife of an emperor; a female who exercises similar supreme power to that of an emperor.
emption (emp′shun) *n.* act of buying or purchasing [L. *emere, emptum*, to buy].
empty (emp′ti) *a.* containing nothing; wanting force or meaning; void; vacant; unoccupied; destitute; hollow; unreal; senseless; inane; hungry;—*v.t.* to make empty; to pour out; to drain;—*v.i.* to become empty; to discharge;—*pa.t.* and *pa.p.* **emp′tied.**—*n.* empty container.—*pl.* **emp′ties.** —**emp′tiness** *n.* state of being empty [O.E. *aemtig*].
empurple (em-pur′pl) *v.t.* to dye or tinge with purple.
empyema (em-pī-ē′mạ) *n.* (*Med.*) a collection of pus in body cavity, esp. in pleura [Gk. *en*; *puon*, pus].
empyesis (em-pī-ē′sis) *n.* (*Med.*) suppuration [Gk.].
empyreal (em-pir′ē-ạl) *a.* of pure fire or light; pert. to highest and purest regions of heaven.—**empyr′ean** *a.* empyreal;—*n.* highest heaven, or region of pure elemental fire [Gk. *en*, in; *pur*, fire].
emu, emeu (ē′mū) *n.* a large flightless bird, native of Australia [Port.].
emulate (em′ū-lāt) *v.t.* to strive to equal or excel in qualities or actions; to vie with; to rival; to compete with; to imitate.—**emula′tion** *n.* act of attempting to equal or excel.—**em′ulative** *a.* imitating with the idea of excelling another.—**em′ulator** *n.*—**em′ulous** *a.* anxious to emulate or outdo another [L. *aemulari*, to rival].
emulsion (e-mul′shun) *n.* a liquid mixture in which a fatty or oily substance, such as cod-liver oil, is suspended in a finely divided state in water and by aid of a mucilaginous medium forms a smooth milky white fluid; the coating of silver salts on a photographic film or plate.—**emul′sic** *a.*—**emulsifica′tion** *n.* the process of making an emulsion.—**emul′sify** *v.t.*—**emul′sive** *a.* yielding a milk-like substance [L. *e*, out; *mulgere*, to milk].
en (en) *n.* a printer's unit of measurement equal to half an em [See **em**].
en- (en) *prefix* in; with;—or adding transitive or casual force in verb composition.
enable (en-ā′bl) *v.t.* to make able; to authorise; to empower; to fit; to qualify.
enact (en-akt′) *v.t.* to make into a law; to act the part of.—**enact′ing** *a.*—**enact′ive** *a.*—**enact′ment** *n.* the passing of a bill into law; a decree; a law.
enamel (en-am′el) *n.* a vitreous compound fused into surface of metal, pottery, or glass for utility and ornament; the hard, glossy surface of tooth; paint with glossy finish;—*v.t.* to coat or paint with enamel;—*pr.p.* **enam′elling.**—*pa.t.* and *pa.p.* **enam′elled** [Fr. *émail*, enamel].
enamour (en-am′ur) *v.t.* to inflame with love; to captivate; to charm; to fascinate.
enate (ē′nāt) *a.* growing out; related on the mother's side [L. *e*, out; *natus*, born].
encage (en-kāj′) *v.t.* to shut up in a cage.
encamp (en-kamp′) *v.t.* to form into a camp; —*v.i.* to settle in or pitch a camp; to settle down temporarily.—**encamp′ment** *n.* the place where troops or other individuals have pitched a camp; the act of encamping.
encarpus (en-kar′pus) *n.* a festoon of flowers or fruit on a capital or frieze [Gk. *en*, in; *karpos*, fruit].
encase, incase (en-, in-kās′); *v.t.* to enclose in a case or linings.—**encase′ment** *n.*
encaustic (en-kaws′tik) *a.* pertaining to the fixing of colours by burning;—*n.* an ancient style of decorative art, consisting in painting on heated wax [Gk. *en*, in; *kaustikos*, burnt].
encave (en-kāv′) *v.t.* to hide, as in a cave.
enceinte (ong-sangt′) *a.* pregnant; with child;—*n.* the precincts within the walls of a fort [Fr.].
encephalon (en-sef′ạl-on) *n.* the brain.—**encephal′ic** *a.* cerebral; relating to the brain.—**enceph′alogram** *n.* an instrument for measuring and recording the electrical processes of the brain [Gk. *en*, in; *kephalē*, the head].
enchain (en-chān′) *v.t.* to fasten with a chain; to link together; to hold fast.—**enchain′ment** *n.*
enchant (en-chant′) *v.t.* to charm by sorcery; to hold, as by a spell.—**enchant′ed** *a.* delighted; held by a spell.—**enchant′er** *n.* (*fem.* **enchant′ress**) one who enchants; a sorcerer.—**enchant′ingly** *adv.*—**enchant′ment** *n.* act of enchanting; incantation; magic; delight; fascination; rapture [Fr. *enchanter*].
enchase (en-chās′) *v.t.* to set within a border; to adorn with chased work; to set with jewels.—**enchased′** *a.*
encincture (en-singk′tūr) *v.t.* to surround with a girdle or garland.
encircle (en-sẹrk′l) *v.t.* to enclose in a circle; to surround; to gird in; to embrace; to circumscribe.—**encir′clement** *n.*
enclave (en-klāv′) *n.* a country, e.g. Switzerland, or an outlying province of a country, entirely surrounded by territories of another power; anything entirely enclosed into something else [L. *in*; *clavis*, a key].
enclitic (en-klit′ik) *n.* a word or particle united, for pronunciation, to another word so as to seem a part of it, e.g. *thee* in *prithee* [Gk. *en*, in; *klinein*, to lean].
encloister (en-klois′tẹr) *v.t.* to shut up in a cloister; to immure.
enclose, inclose (en-, in-klōz′) *v.t.* to shut in; to surround; to envelope; to wrap up; to fence in common ground.—**enclos′ure** *n.* the act of enclosing; ground fenced in; part of a sports ground for spectators.
encomium (en-kō′mi-um) *n.* high commendation; formal praise.—*pl.* **enco′miums.**—**enco′miast** *n.* panegyrist.—**encomias′tic(al)** *a.* —**encomias′tically** *adv.* [Gk.].
encompass (en-kum′pas) *v.t.* to describe a circle round; to encircle.—**encom′passment** *n.* investment; state of being encircled.
encore (ong-kōr′) *interj.* again! once more! —*n.* a recall awarded by an audience to a performer, artiste, etc.; the item repeated;—*v.t.* to applaud with encore [Fr.=again].
encounter (en-kount′ẹr) *v.t.* to meet face to face; to meet unexpectedly; to meet in a hostile manner; to contend against; to confront;—*n.* an unexpected meeting; a fight or combat [Fr. *encontrer*].
encourage (en-kur′āj) *v.t.* to give courage to; to inspire with hope; to embolden.—**encour′agement** *n.* that which gives courage; act of encouraging.—**encour′aging** *a.* inspiring with hope of ultimate success.—**encour′agingly** *adv.* [Fr. *encourager*].
encroach (en-krōch′) *v.i.* to invade the rights or possessions of another; to intrude on other's property.—**encroach′er** *n.*—**encroach′ingly** *adv.*—**encroach′ment** *n.* [Fr. *accrocher*, to hook on].
encrust, encrustation See **incrust.**
encumber (en-kum′bẹr) *v.t.* to load; to impede the movements of; to burden; to saddle with debts.—**encum′brance** *n.* a burden; a legal claim on an estate [Fr. *encombrer*].
encyclical (en-sīk′lik-ạl) *a.* intended to circulate among many people and in many places; —*n.* an encyclical letter, a letter addressed by the Pope to the bishops of the R.C.

Church.—Also **encyc'lic** [Gk. *en*, in; *kuklos*, a circle].

encyclopaedia, encyclopedia (en-sī-klō-pé'-di-ạ) *n.* works which give detailed account, in alphabetical order, of whole field of human knowledge, or of some particular section in it.—**encyclopae'dian** *a.* embracing all forms of knowledge.—**encyclopae'dic** *a.* having universal knowledge; full of information.—**encyclopae'dist** *n.* a compiler of an encyclopaedia, esp. French thinkers of 18th cent. who contributed to classic French 'Encyclopédie' [Gk. *enkuklios paideia*, all round education].

encyst (en-sist') *v.t.* or *v.i.* to enclose or become enclosed in a sac or cyst.

end (end) *n.* the extreme point of a line; the last part in general; termination; conclusion; ending; limit; extremity; final condition; issue; consequence; result; object; purpose; aim; death; a fragment;—*v.t.* to bring to an end or conclusion; to destroy; to put to death;—*v.i.* to come to the ultimate point; to finish; to be finished; to cease.—**end'ed** *a.* brought to an end; having ends.—**end'ing** *n.* termination; conclusion; the terminating syllable or letter of a word; suffix.—**end'less** *a.* without end; everlasting; incessant; fruitless; vain.—**end'lessly** *adv.*—**end'lessness** *n.*—**end'long** *a.* lengthwise; continuously; on end.—**end'most** *a.* at the very end; farthest.—**end'pa'per** *n.* stout paper used in the binding of books to cover the inner sides of the covers and to provide fly leaves.—**end'ways, end'wise** *adv.* with the end forward; erect; upright.—**end for end,** reversed; with the ends brought close together.—**at a loose end,** bored.—**at one's wits' end,** perplexed; unable to proceed.—**come to the end of one's tether,** to be unable to make further progress.—**to make both ends meet,** to keep out of debt; to balance income and expenditure [O.E. *ende*].

endanger (en-dān'jẹr) *v.t.* to place in jeopardy; to expose to loss or injury.—**endan'germent** *n.* danger; risk; peril; hazard.

endear (en-dēr') *v.t.* to render dear or more beloved.—**endeared'** *a.* beloved.—**endear'ing** *a.*—**endear'ingly** *adv.*—**endear'ment** *n.* the state of being, or act of, endearing; tender affection; loving word; a caress.

endeavour (en-dev'ur) *v.i.* to exert all strength for accomplishment of object; to attempt; to try; to strive; to essay; to aim;—*n.* attempt; trial; effort; struggle; essay.—**endeav'ourer** *n.* [Fr. *devoir*, duty].

endemic, endemical (en-dem'ik, -al), **endemial** (en-dē'mi-ạl) *a.* terms applied to constantly recurring diseases confined to certain peoples or localities and which arise from strictly local causes.—**endem'ic** *n.* a disease peculiar to one district or people, in contrast with *epidemic*.—**endem'ically** *adv.* [Gk. *en*, in; *dēmos*, a people].

endiron See **andiron.**

endive (en'div) *n.* an annual plant of the family *Compositae*, resembling chicory, used for salads after blanching [Fr.].

endo- (en'dō) a prefix, indicating *within*, used in the construction of compound terms [Gk. *endon*].

endocarditis (en-dō-kȧr-dī'tis) *n.* (*Med.*) inflammation of the lining membrane of the heart [Gk. *endon*, within; *kardia*, heart].

endocardium (en-dō-kȧr'dium) *n.* the lining membrane of the heart.—**endocar'diac** *a.*—**endocar'dial** *a.*

endocrine (en'dō-krīn) *a.* (*Zool.*) describing the tissues and organs giving rise to an internal secretion.—**endocrine glands,** ductless glands manufacturing secretions or hormones which are passed directly into the blood stream.—**endocrinol'ogy** *n.* study of internal secretions of ductless glands [Gk. *endon*, within; *krinein*, to separate].

endogamy (en-dog'ạm-i) *n.* the custom of compulsory marriage within the limits of a tribe or clan or between members of the same race.—**endog'amous** *a.* [Gk. *endon*, within; *gamos*, marriage].

endoparasite (en-dō-par'ạ-sīt) *n.* a parasite living inside the body of its host.

endophagy (en-do'faj-i) *n.* amongst cannibals, the practice of eating one's own kinsfolk after death as a mark of respect [Gk. *endon*, within; *phagein*, to eat].

endoplasm (en'dō-plazm) *n.* inner portion of cytoplasm of a cell [Gk. *endon*, within; *plasma* a formation].

endorse, indorse (en-, in-dors',) *v.t.* to write (esp. to sign one's name) on back of, as cheque; to back (a bill, etc.); to sanction; to confirm; to vouch for; to ratify; to enter, on back of a licence, convictions for infringements; to load or burden.—**endors'able** *a.*—**endorsee'** *n.* the person to whom a bill of exchange, etc. is assigned by endorsement.—**endorse'ment** *n.* act of endorsing.—**endors'er** *n.* [Fr. *endosser*, fr. *dos*, back; L. *dorsum*].

endoscope (en'dō-skōp) *n.* (*Med.*) an instrument for inspecting the cavities of internal parts of the body [Gk. *endon*, within; *skopein*, to see].

endoskeleton (en-dō-skel'e-ton) *n.* (*Biol.*) the internal hard supporting structures, as bones, of the body.—**endoskel'etal** *a.*

endosmosis (en-dos-mō'sis) *n.* (*Chem.*) the passage of a less dense fluid inwards through an organic semi-permeable membrane which separates it from a denser solution [Gk. *endon*, within; *osmos*, pushing].

endosperm (en'dō-spẹrm) *n.* (*Bot.*) the nutritive starchy tissue which surrounds the embryo in many seeds.—**endosper'mic** *a.* [Gk. *endon*, within; *sperma*, seed].

endow (en-dou') *v.t.* to give a dowry or marriage-portion to; to dower; to settle, by deed or will, a permanent income on; to enrich or furnish.—**endow'er** *n.*—**endow'ment** *n.* the act of settling a fund or permanent provision for an institution or individual; grant; bequest; natural capacity [O.Fr. *endouer*].

endure (en-dūr') *v.t.* to remain firm under; to bear with patience; to put up with; to sustain; to suffer; tc tolerate;—*v.i.* to continue; to last.—**endur'able** *a.* can be endured, borne, or suffered.—**endur'ableness** *n.*—**endur'ably** *adv.*—**endur'ance** *n.* power of enduring; act of bearing pain or distress; continuance; patience; fortitude; stamina.—**endur'er** *n.*—**endur'ing** *a.* and *n.*—**endur'ingly** *adv.*—**endur'ingness** *n.* durability; permanence [L. *indurare*; fr. *durus*, hard].

enema (en'e-ma, e-nē'ma) *n.* a liquid solution injected into intestine through rectum, a clyster [Gk. fr. *en*, in; *hienai*, to send].

enemy (en'em-i) *n.* one actuated by hostile feelings; an armed foe; opposing army;—*a.* of an enemy; due to an enemy [Fr. *ennemi*, fr. L. *inimicus*].

energumen (en-ẹr-gū'men) *n.* one possessed by an evil spirit; a demoniac [Gk. *energoumenos*, wrought upon].

energy (en'ẹr-ji) *n.* vigour; force; activity; (*Mech.*) the power of doing mechanical work; (*Phys.*) the equivalent of mass.—**energet'ic(al)** *a.* exerting force; vigorous; active; forcible.—**energet'ically** *adv.*—**ener'gic** *a.* exhibiting energy.—**en'ergise** *v.t.* to give energy to;—*v.i.* to act energetically [Gk. *energeia*, activity].

enervate (en'ẹr-vāt) *v.t.* to deprive of nerve, strength, or courage;—*a.* spiritless.—**en'ervating, ener'vative,** *a.*—**enerva'tion** *n.* lack of spirit or courage [L. *enervare*, to deprive of sinew].

enfeeble (en-fē'bl) *v.t.* to render feeble; to deprive of strength; to weaken; to debilitate; to enervate.—**enfee'blement** *n.*

enfeoff (en-fef') *v.t.* to give a fief to; (*Law*) to bestow or convey the fee-simple of an estate.—**enfeoff'ment** *n.*

enfilade (en-fi-lād') *n.* a line or straight passage; narrow line, as of troops in marching; fire from artillery or small arms which sweeps a line from end to end;—*v.t.* to direct enfilading fire [Fr. *enfiler*, to string on a thread].

enfold See **infold**.

enforce (en-fōrs') *v.t.* to give strength to; to put in force; to impress on mind; to compel; to impose (action) upon; to urge on; to execute.—**enforce'able** *a.*—**enforc'edly** *adv.* under threat or compulsoin.—**enforce'ment** *n.* [O.Fr. *enforcer*, to strengthen].

enfranchise (en-fran'chīz) *v.t.* to set free from slavery; to extend political rights to; to grant the privilege of voting in parliamentary elections.—**enfran'chisement** *n.*

engage (en-gāj') *v.t.* to bind by contract, pledge, or promise; to hire; to order; to employ; to undertake; to occupy; to busy; to attract; to bring into conflict; to interlock;—*v.i.* to begin to fight; to employ oneself (in); to promise.—**engaged'** *a.*—**engage'ment** *n.* act of engaging; state of being engaged; obligation by contract or agreement; pledge; betrothal; occupation; affair of business or pleasure; battle; encounter.—**engag'ing** *a.* attractive; pleasing; winsome; winning [Fr. *engager*, fr. *gage*, pledge].

engender (en-jen'der) *v.t.* to beget; to cause to exist; to sow the seeds of; to breed; to occasion or cause (strife) [Fr. *engendrer*].

engine (en'jin) *n.* any mechanical contrivance for producing and conveying motive power; a machine; a locomotive; an instrument of war; agency; means;—*a.* pert. to engines;—*v.t.* to fix or furnish with engines; to contrive.—**engineer'** *n.* one who constructs, designs, or is in charge of engines, military works, or works of public utility (roads, docks, etc.);—*v.t.* to direct or design work as a skilled engineer; to contrive; to bring about; to arrange.—**engineer'ing** *n.* the art of constructing and using machines or engines; the profession of an engineer.—**en'gine-dri'ver** *n.* one who drives an engine, esp. a locomotive.—**civil engineer**, the business of constructing railways, bridges, etc. [Fr. *engin*, fr. L. *ingenium*, skill].

English (ing'glish) *a.* belonging to England or its inhabitants;—*n.* the people or the language of England;—*v.t.* to render into English a foreign language; to anglicise.—**Eng'lander** *n.* an Englishman.—**Eng'lisher, Eng'lishman** *n.* a native of England.—**Eng'lishry** *n.* the quality or state of being an Englishman; in Ireland, people of English descent.—**English horn** (*Mus.*) the cor anglais, similar to the oboe but larger.—**Old English**, language to about 1150 A.D.—**Middle English**, 1150-1500.—**Modern English**, from 1500.—**Basic English**, a skeleton form of the English language of less than a thousand words [O.E. *Englisc*, fr. *Engle*, Angle].

engorge (en-gorj') *v.t.* to swallow greedily and in large quantities;—*v.i.* to feed with voracity; to devour.—**engorge'ment** *n.* [Fr. *engorger*, fr. *gorge*, the throat].

engraft, ingraft (en-, in-graft') *v.t.* to graft on; to plant deeply; to incorporate; to add to.—**engrafta'tion** *n.*—**engraft'ment** *n.*

engrain See **ingrain**.

engram (en'gram) *n.* the trace in the brain of any experience; the mental record which forms the basis of memory [Gk. *en*, in; *gramma*, written sign].

engrave (en-grāv') *v.t.* to draw on a metal plate a design or picture by means of an incised line or on wood by leaving a raised surface; to imprint; to make a deep impression;—*v.i.* to practise the art of engraving.—**engrav'er** *n.*—**engrav'ing** *n.* the art of cutting designs, etc. on wood, metal, or stone; an impression on art paper taken from an engraved block or plate; a print [See **grave**].

engross (en-grōs') *v.t.* to occupy wholly; to absorb; to increase in bulk; to enlarge; to copy in a large fair hand or in legal form; to buy wholesale with a view to cornering the market; to monopolise.—**engross'er** *n.*—**engross'ing** *n.* the cornering of some commodity in order to raise the price; forestalling.—**engross'ment** *n.* the act of engrossing; that which has been engrossed [Fr. *en gros*, in a large hand].

engulf, ingulf (en-, in-gulf') *v.t.* to swallow up or absorb as in a gulf; to overwhelm; to encompass wholly.—**engulf'ment** *n.*

enhance (en-hans') *v.t.* to heighten; to intensify; to increase in value or worth; to add to the effect.—**enhance'ment** *n.* [Fr. *hausser*, to raise].

enharmonic, enharmonical (en-har-mon'ik, -al) *a.* (*Mus.*) applied to intervals smaller than a semi-tone; pert. to one of the three ancient Greek scales. the others being diatonic and chromatic.—**enharmon'ically** *adv.* [Gk. *en*, in; *harmonia*, harmony].

enhearten (en-hárt'n) *v.t.* to inspire with courage; to embolden; to cheer up.

enigma (en-ig'ma) *n.* an obscure question or saying difficult of explanation; anything or anybody puzzling; a riddle.—**enigmat'ic(al)** *a.* obscure and ambiguous.—**enigmat'ically** *adv.* [Gk. *ainigma*].

enjamb(e)ment (en-jamb'ment) *n.* in verse, continuation of a sentence from one line into the next [Fr. *en*, in; *jambe*, leg].

enjoin (en-join') *v.t.* to direct with authority; to command; to order; to impose; to prescribe; (*Law*) to prohibit by judicial order; to put an injunction on.—**enjoin'ment** *n.* [Fr. *enjoindre*].

enjoy (en-joi') *v.t.* to delight in; to take pleasure in; to have the use or benefit of.—**enjoy'able** *a.* affording pleasure.—**enjoy'ably** *adv.*—**enjoy'ment** *n.* condition of enjoying; cause of joy or gratification [Fr. *joie*].

enkindle (en-kin'dl) *v.t.* to set on fire; to inflame; to excite; to rouse.

enlace (en-lās') to encircle; to surround; to entwine; to enfold; to embrace.

enlarge [en-lárj') *v.t.* and *v.i.* to make or become larger; to increase; to be diffuse in speaking or writing; to set free.—**enlarged'** *a.*—**enlar'gedly** *adv.*—**enlar'gedness** *n.*—**enlarge'ment** *n.* act of enlarging; state of being enlarged; increase; expansion; a photograph which has been enlarged.

enlighten (en-līt'en) *v.t.* to shed light on; to give information to; to instruct; to make clear; to free from superstition, etc.—**enlight'enment** *n.* act of enlightening; state of being enlightened; intellectual revival in Europe during 18th cent. amongst philosophers.

enlist (en-list') *v.t.* to enter on a list; to enrol; to secure support of;—*v.i.* to engage in public service, as soldiers; to enter heartily into a cause.—**enlist'ment** *n.*

enliven (en-līv'n) *v.t.* to give life, action, or motion to; to quicken; to excite; to make gay; to amuse.—**enliv'ener** *n.*

enmesh, emmesh, immesh (en-, em-, im-mesh') *v.t.* to catch in a mesh or net; to entangle; to trap.—**enmesh'ment** *n.*

enmity (en'mi-ti) *n.* the quality of being an enemy; hostile or unfriendly disposition; hatred; rancour; hostility [Fr. *inimitié*].

ennea (en'ē-a) a Greek prefix, signifying nine, used in the construction of compound terms.

ennead (en'ē-ad) *n.* a grouping of nine persons or things [Gk. *ennea*].

enneatic, enneatical (en-ē-at'ik, -al) *a.* occurring once in every nine of anything, e.g. once in nine days.

ennoble (en-nō'bl) *v.t.* to make noble; to raise to the peerage; to raise; to exalt; to elevate; to dignify.—**enno'blement** *n.*

ennui (ong'nwē) *n.* boredom; a feeling of intense weariness; listlessness due to satiety or lack of interest.—**ennuyé** (ong-nwē'yā) *a.* bored; in a state of ennui [Fr.].

enormous (e-nor'mus) *a.* huge; vast; excessive; prodigious; immense; colossal; gross; atrocious.—**enor'mity** *n.* quality of being enormous; a gross offence; great wickedness; atrocity.—**enor'mously** *adv.*—**enor'mousness** *n.* [L. *enormis*, abnormal].

enough (e-nuf') *a.* as much or as many as need be; sufficient; adequate.—*n.* a sufficiency; as much as satisfies conditions;—*adv.* sufficiently; fully [O.E. *genog*].

enounce (e-nouns') *v.t.* to state; to declare; to enunciate; to pronounce; to proclaim.—**enounce'ment** *n.* [L. *enuntiare*, to declare].

enow (e-nou') another form of **enough**.

enplane (en-plān') *v.t.* and *v.i.* to put or go into an aeroplane.

enquire, enquiry See **inquire, inquiry.**

enrage (en-rāj') *v.t.* to fill with rage; to provoke to frenzy or madness; to anger immoderately.—**enraged'** *a.* angry; furious.

enrapture (en-rap'chūr) *v.t.* to transport with pleasure; to delight excessively; to charm.—**enrap'tured, enrapt'** *a.* delighted beyond measure; enchanted; entranced.

enravish (en-rav'ish) *v.t.* to transport with delight; to enrapture.

enrich (en-rich') *v.t.* to make rich; to add to; to adorn; to enhance; to embellish; to fertilise.—**enrich'ment** *n.*

enrobe (en-rōb') *v.t.* to robe; to dress; to clothe; to invest.—**enrobe'ment** *n.*

enrol, enroll (en-rōl') *v.t.* to enter a name in a roll or register; to engage; to enlist; to record.—*pr.p.* **enroll'ing.**—*pa.t.* and *pa.p.* **enrolled'**—**enrol'ment** *n.* the act of enrolling; a register; a record [Fr. *enrôler*].

ens (ens) *n.* (*Philos.*) the state of being, without qualifications;—*pl.* **en'tia** [L.L.—being].

Ensa (en'sa) *n.* organisation during World War II for entertaining forces and war-workers [fr. initials of *E*ntertainments *N*ational *S*ervice *A*ssociation].

ensample (en-såm'pl) *n.* an example; pattern [O.Fr.].

ensanguine (en-sang'gwin) *v.t.* to smear with blood; to make of a crimson colour.

ensconce (en-skons') *v.t.* to shelter, as with a sconce or fort; to protect; to hide securely; to screen [L. *in*; *condere*, to hide].

ensemble (ong-som'bl) *n.* all the parts taken together; general effect; a combined effort by all performers; (*Mus.*) concerted playing by a number of musicians [Fr.=together].

enshrine (en-shrīn') *v.t.* to enclose in a shrine; to consecrate; to treasure with affection.—**enshrine'ment** *n.*

enshroud (en-shroud') *v.t.* to cover with a shroud; to hide from view.

ensiform (en'si-form) *a.* sword-shaped [L. *ensis*, sword; *forma*, a shape].

ensign (en'sīn, -in) *n.* a badge of rank or insignia of office; the colours of a regiment; the national flag displayed on board ship (*white*—Navy, coastguard, Royal Yacht Squadron;—*blue*—R.N. Reserve, Civil Service vessels;—*red*—British Merchant Navy); a commissioned officer who was entrusted with the safe-keeping of a regiment's ensign (rank abolished in 1871). -**ensign bearer**, an ensign.—**en'signcy, en'signship** *n.* rank of an ensign [Fr. *enseigne.*]

ensilage (en'sil-āj) *n.* a process of storing crops such as hay, etc. while green, to serve as winter food for cattle; fodder so stored [Fr.].

enslave (en-slāv') *v.t.* to reduce to slavery or bondage.—**enslaved'** *a.*—**enslave'ment** *n.*

ensnare, insnare (en-, in-snār',) *v.t.* to catch in a snare; to entrap; to entangle.

ensue (en-sū') *v.i.* to follow; to happen after; to be the consequence of;—*v.t.* (*Bib.*) to strive for.—**ensu'ing** *a.* [Fr. *ensuivre*, fr. L. *insequi*, to follow up].

ensure (en-shŏŏr') *v.t.* to make sure; safe, or certain; to bring about; to insure.

entablature (en-tab'la-tūr) *n.* in classic architecture, ornamental, horizontal portion of building resting upon supporting columns and consisting of architrave, frieze and cornice; an erection for machinery, mounted on pillars.—Also **entab'lement** (Fr. fr. L. *tabula*, board].

entail (en-tāl') *n.* law restricting inheritance of land to a particular heir or class of heirs;—*v.t.* to settle land on persons in succession, none of whom can then dispose of it; to involve as a result; to bring about or cause.—**entail'ment** *n.* [Fr. *entailler*, to cut into].

entangle (en-tang'gl) *v.t.* to twist or interweave so as not to be easily separated; to ravel; to knot; to perplex; to ensnare.—**entang'lement** *n.* confusion; perplexity; barbed wire fence.

entente (ong-tongt') *n.* cordial agreement or understanding between nations, not formulated as an alliance [Fr.].

enter (en'tẹr) *v.i.* to go or come into; to pass within; to pierce; to penetrate; to invade; to join (a society, etc.); to put down one's name; to share in.—**en'terclose** *n.* a passage or corridor between two rooms.—**to enter on, upon,** to begin; to take possession of [Fr. *entrer*].

enter- (en'ter) *Gk. prefix* used in the construction of compound words relating to the intestine.—**en'tera** *n.pl.* (*Med.*) the intestines.—**en'teral** *a.* by way of the intestine.—**enter'ic** *a.* of or pertaining to the intestine;—*n.* typhoid fever, an acute infectious disease affecting the small intestine; paratyphoid fevers A and B.—**enteri'tis** *n.* inflammation of the intestines [Gk. *enteron*, intestine].

enterprise (en'tẹr-prīz) *n.* that which is undertaken or attempted; force of character in launching out; daring spirit; a bold attempt; venture; energy;—*v.t.* to undertake.—**en'terprising** *a.* adventurous; go-ahead; energetic.—**en'terprisingly** *adv.* [Fr.].

entertain (en-tẹr-tān') *v.t.* to receive a guest; to show hospitality to; to lodge; to amuse; to divert; to consider favourably; to cherish; to hold in the mind.—**entertain'er** *n.*—**entertain'ing** *a.* amusing; diverting.—**entertain'ment** *n.* hospitality; amusement; public performance [Fr. *entretenir*].

entheasm (en'thē-azm) *n.* divine inspiration; religious ardour; ecstasy.—**entheast'ic** *a.*—**en'theate** *a.* divinely inspired [Gk. *entheos*, inspired, fr. *theos*, a god].

enthral, enthrall, inthral (en-, in-thrawl') *v.t.* to reduce to a state of slavery or bondage; to enslave; to thrill; to captivate; to hold spellbound;—*pr.p.* **enthrall'ing.**—*pa.t.* and *pa.p.* **enthralled'.**—**enthral'dom** *n.* state of being enthralled.—**enthral'ment** *n.* the act of enthralling; state of being enthralled; bondage; slavery.

enthrone (en-thrōn') *v.t.* to place on a throne; to raise to sovereignty; to install, as a bishop; to exalt.—**enthrone'ment** *n.*

enthusiasm (en-thū'zi-azm) *n.* passionate zeal for a person or object; religious fervour; intense ardour; fanaticism; keen interest.—**enthu'siast** *n.* one who is carried away by enthusiasm; devotee; zealot; visionary.—**enthusias'tic(al)** *a.*—**enthusias'tically** *adv.*— **enthuse'** *v.i.* (*Colloq.*) to become enthusiastic over [Gk. *enthousiasmos*, inspiration].

entice (en-tīs') *v.t.* to draw on by exciting hope or desire; to lead astray.—**entice'able** *a.* possible to be enticed or led astray.—**entice'ment** *n.* act of enticing; that which incites to evil; allurement; blandishment; inducement.—**entic'ing** *a.*—**entic'ingly** *adv.* [O.Fr. *enticier*, to provoke].

entire (en-tīr') *a.* complete in all parts; whole; unimpaired; chief; unmingled; not castrated;—*n.* a kind of ale; porter; stout.—**entire'ly** *adv.*—**entire'ness, entire'ty** *n.* completeness [Fr. *entier*, fr. L. *integer*].

entitle (en-tī'tl) *v.t.* to give a title to; to name; to qualify; to fit for; to give claim to; [O.Fr. *entiteler*].

entity (en'ti-ti) *n.* a real being; reality; existence; a material substance (L.L. *entitas*, fr. *esse*, to be].

entomb (en-tōōm′) *v.t.* to deposit in a tomb; to inter; to bury.—**entomb′ment** *n.*
entomic, entomical (en-tom′ik, -al) *a.* relating to insects [Gk. *entomon*, insect].
entomology (en-to-mol′o-ji) *n.* scientific study, classification and collection of insects. —**entomolog′ical** *a.*—**entomolog′ically** *adv.*—**entomol′ogise** *v.t.* to pursue the study of insects.—**entomol′ogist** *n.* [Gk. *entomon*, insect; *logos*, a discourse].
entoparasite (en-to-par′a-sīt) *n.* a parasite living inside the body of an animal [Gk. *entos*, within; *parasitos*].
entourage (ong-tōō-rázh′) *n.* surroundings; one's habitual associates; retinue [Fr.].
en-tout-cas (ong-tōō′ka) *n.* a small-sized umbrella which can be used as a sunshade; all-weather tennis-court [Fr.=in any case].
entozoon (en-to-zō′on) *n.* an invertebrate animal which lives as a parasite inside the body of another higher animal, e.g. the tapeworm.—*pl.* **entozo′a** [Gk. *entos*, within; *zōon*, an animal].
entr'acte (ong-trakt′) *n.* the interval or musical interlude between two acts of a play [Fr.].
entrail (en-trāl′) *v.t.* to interlace; to twist; to entwine [O.Fr. *entreillier*].
entrails (en′trālz) *n.pl.* the bowels; the intestines; the guts; the internal parts of anything [Fr. *entrailles*].
entrain (en-trān′) *v.t.* to enter or put into a railway train.
entrance (en′trans) *n.* the act of entering; right of access; a door, gateway, or passage to enter by; the beginning.—**en′trant** *a.* entering;—*n.* one who enters; a competitor.
entrance (en-trans′) *v.t.* to put into a trance; to ravish with delight and wonder.—**entrance′ment** *n.*—**entranc′ing** *a.*
entrap (en-trap′) *v.t.* to catch, as in a trap; to ensnare; to entangle.—**entrap′ment** *n.*
entreat (en-trēt′) *v.t.* to ask earnestly; to treat with;—*v.i.* to pray.—**entreat′y** *n.* act of entreating; supplication; prayer [O.Fr. *entraiter*].
entrechat (ong′tr-sha) *n.* one of a series of long graceful bounds which a ballet dancer makes [Fr. *chat*, a cat].
entrée (ong′trā) *n.* right of access; a dish served between main courses; a formal entry [Fr.].
entrench, intrench (en-, in-trensh′) *v.t.* to dig a trench; to surround, fortify with a trench;—*v.i.* to encroach.—**entrench′ment** *n.* a ditch or trench with the earth excavated from it piled up in front to form a parapet for defence; moat; rampart; infringement.
entrepot (ong′tr-pō) *n.* a bonded-warehouse; store; mart; emporium; a port where merchandise can be temporarily received for dispatch elsewhere [Fr.].
entrepreneur (ong′tr-pre-ner) *n.* a contractor; an organiser of business, trade, or entertainment [Fr. *entreprendre*, to undertake].
entresol (en′ter-sol, ong′tr-sol) *n.* a floor or suite of rooms between two main stories (usually the ground floor and the first floor) of a building.—Also **mezz′anine** [Fr. *entre*, between; *sol*, the ground].
entropy (en′trop-i) *n.* (*Phys.*) the general tendency in natural processes for a certain quantity of energy to be dissipated and become unavailable for utility purposes [Gk. *tropē*, a turn].
entrust, intrust (en-, in-trust′) *v.t.* to deliver in trust; to confide to the care of.
entry (en′tri) *n.* the act of entering; a narrow passage into a court-yard; an item noted down in a ledger, catalogue, or notebook [Fr. *entrer*].
entwine, intwine (en-, in-twīn′) *v.t.* to twist together; to plait; to embrace; to encircle.
entwist (en-twist′) *v.t.* to twist round.
enumerate (e-nū′mer-āt) *v.t.* to count, one by one; to name individually; to give in detail.—**enu′meration** *n.* the act of counting singly; a detailed account; a recapitulation. —**enu′merator** *n.* [L. *enumerare*, to number off].
enunciate (e-nun′si-āt, e-nun′shi-āt) *v.t.* to state clearly; to proclaim formally; to announce officially; to pronounce each syllable distinctly.—**enun′ciable** *a.*—**enuncia′tion** *n.* the act of enunciating; articulation or manner of pronunciation; a declaration or announcement.—**enun′ciator** *n.* [L. *e*, out; *nuntiare*, to announce].
enure See **inure.**
enuresis (en-ū-rē′sis) *n.* (*Med.*) inability to control the discharge of urine; bed-wetting [Gk. *en*, in; *ourēsis*, making water].
envelop (en-vel′up) *v.t.* to cover by folding or wrapping; to surround; to hide or conceal.—**envelope** (en′vel-ōp) *n.* a cover or wrapper, esp. the cover of a letter.—**envel′opment** *n.* the act of enveloping; a wrapping [Fr. *envelopper*].
envenom (en-ven′um) *v.t.* to impregnate with venom; to poison; to enrage; to exasperate; to embitter.
enviable, envious See **envy.**
environ (en-vī′run) *v.t.* to surround; to encompass; to encircle; to envelop; to hem in; to invest.—**envi′ronment** *n.* that which environs; external conditions which determine modifications in the development of organic life.—**envi′rons** *n.pl.* adjacent districts; neighbourhood; suburbs [Fr.=about].
envisage (en-viz′āj) *v.t.* to look in the face of; to face; to imagine; to conjure up a mental picture of; to visualise [Fr. *envisager*].
envoy (en′voi) *n.* one dispatched upon an errand or mission; a diplomatic agent of a country below the rank of ambassador; messenger; courier [Fr. *envoyer*, to send].
envoy, envoi (en′voi) *n.* an author's postscript, esp. in an additional stanza of a poem [Fr.].
envy (en′vi) *v.t.* to grudge another person's good fortune; to feel jealous of;—*pr.p.* **en′vying**;—*pa.p.* **en′vied**.—*n.* pain or vexation excited by the sight of another's superiority or success; jealousy.—**en′viable** *a.* able to be envied; desirable.—**en′viably** *adv.*—**en′vious** *a.* full of envy.—**en′viously** *adv.* [Fr. *envie*].
enwrap, inwrap (en-, in-rap′) *v.t.* to wrap up; to envelop; to engross.
enwreathe, inwreathe (en-, in-rēTH′) *v.t.* to encircle, as with a wreath.
enzyme, enzym (en′zim) *n.* a complex organic substance which in solution produces fermentation and chemical change in other substances apparently without undergoing any change itself; a form of catalyst; digestive ferment.—**enzymot′ic** *a.* [Gk. *en*, in; *zumē*, leaven].
eocene (ē′ō-sēn) *a.* (*Geol.*) a term applied to the geological strata laid down at the beginning of the Tertiary Period [Gk. *eos*, dawn; *kainos*, recent].
Eolian, Eolic See **Aeolian, Aeolic.**
eolith (ē′ō-lith) *n.* the oldest known flint implement fashioned by pre-historic men [Gk. *eos*, dawn; *lithos*, stone].
eon See **aeon.**
éonism (ā′o-nizm) *n.* (*Psych.*) impulse in some men to attire themselves as women and imitate their ways [Chevalier d'*Eon*, 1728-1810].
epacme (e-pak′mā) *n.* the period in the life of an individual or nation when its powers are fast maturing [Gk.].
epact (ē′pakt) *n.* the excess of a solar over a lunar month or year in number of days; the moon's age in days on Jan. 1 of any particular year, used for fixing the days of Easter and other movable feasts of the church [Gk. *epagein*, to intercalate].
eparch (ep′ārk) *n.* governor of a province in Byzantium and in ancient and modern

Greece; bishop in the Russian Orthodox Church [Gk. *epi*, upon; *archein*, to rule].

epaulet, epaulette (ep′ol-et) *n.* an ornamental shoulder-piece or badge of rank [Fr. *épaule*, shoulder].

épée (ā′pā) *n.* a duelling sword with a sharp point but no cutting edge; a foil in fencing; a hit on the body, scoring one point [Fr.].

epergne (e-pern′) *n.* an ornamental stand for a large dish for centre of table [Fr.].

epexegesis (ep-eks-e-jē′sis) *n.* a further explanation of a previous statement.—**epexeget′ic, epexeget′ical** *a.* [Gk. *epi*, further; and *exegesis*].

ephedrine (ef′e-drīn) *n.* an alkaloid drug, derived from plants of the genus *Ephedra* [Gk. *ephedra*].

ephemera (ef-em′er-a) *n.* pamphlets and cuttings of temporary interest and value; a genus of insects, better known as day-flies or may-flies, the larva existence of which lasts from two or three years but as adults live only for one day;—*pl.* **ephem′erae**.—**ephem′eral** *a.* lasting only for a very short period of time; transitory; fleeting; evanescent; momentary.—**ephemeral′ity** *n.* a transient glory.—**ephem′erous** *a.* short-lived; ephemeral [Gk. *epi*, for; *hēmera*, a day].

ephemeris (ef-em′er-is) *n.* (*Astron.*) a table or calendar giving for successive days the positions of heavenly bodies;—*pl.* **ephemerides** (ef-e-mer′i-dēz) such predictions of the chief stars as published in the Nautical Almanac, etc.—**ephem′erist** *n.* one who predicts the future movements of the stars [Gk. *epi*, for; *hēmera*, a day].

ephod (ef′od) *n.* a richly and emblematically embroidered sacred vestment worn by the high-priest of the Jews (Ex. 25) [Heb.].

epi- (ep′i) Gk. *prefix* meaning upon, at, in addition to, etc., used in the construction of compound terms.

epic (ep′ik) *n.* a long narrative poem in the grand style, usually dealing with the adventures of great soldiers or heroes whose deeds are part of the history of a nation;—*a.* in the grand style; lofty in conception; memorable; heroic [Gk. *epos*, a word].

epicardium (ep-i-kar′di-um) *n.* (*Med.*) the serous membrane of the pericardium, the sac which envelops the heart.—**epicar′dial** *a.* [Gk. *epi*, upon; *kardia*, the heart].

epicene (ep′i-sēn) *a.* common to both sexes; (*Gram.*) of common gender, of nouns with but one form for both genders, e.g. sheep;—*n.* a person having characteristics of both sexes; a hermaphrodite.

epicentre (ep′i-sen-ter) *n.* the point on the upper crust of the earth below which an earthquake has originated.

epicritic (ep-i-krit′ik) *a.* pert. to fine sensitivity, e.g. to the slightest sensation of heat or touch.

Epicurus (ep′i-kūr-us) *n.* a Greek philosopher (342-270 B.C.), the founder of the Epicurean school.—**ep′icure** *n.* one who applies himself to gross sensualism, esp. the delights of the table; a voluptuary; sensualist; gourmand; Sybarite.—**epicure′an** *a.* pert. to Epicurus or his system of philosophy; voluptuous;—*n.* a follower of Epicurus; a sensualist.—**epicure′anism** *n.* the doctrine that the chief end of man was physical and mental happiness.

epicycle (ep′i-sī-kl) *n.* a circle whose centre moves round in the circumference of a greater circle [Gk. *epi*, upon; *kuklos*, a wheel].

epideictic, epideictical (ep-i-dīk′tik, -al) *a.* ostentatious; showing off; pretentious.

epidemic, epidemical (ep-i-dem′ik, -al) *a.* common to, or affecting, a whole people or community; prevalent; general; prevailing for a time.—**epidem′ic** *n.* the appearance of infectious disease attacking whole communities within a certain area and within a certain period (cf. *endemic*).—**epidem′ically** *adv.* [Gk. *epi*, among; *dēmos*, the people].

epidermis (ep-i-der′mis) *n.* (*Anat.*) the outer protective layer of skin, otherwise the scarf skin, which covers the dermis or true skin underneath; (*Bot.*) a sheath, usually one cell in thickness, which forms a layer over surface of leaves.—**epider′matoid, epider′mic, epider′mal, epider′midal** *a.* [Gk. *epi*, upon; *derma*, the skin].

epidiascope (ep-i-dī′a-skōp) *n.* an optical lantern for projecting lantern slides, pictures, or images of opaque objects in their natural colours on to a screen directly (cf. *episcope*) [Gk. *epi*, upon; *dia*, through; *skopein*, to view].

epigamic (ep-i-gam′ik) *a.* attractive to the opposite sex [Gk. *epi*, upon; *gamos*, marriage].

epiglottis (ep-i-glot′is) *n.* a covering of elastic, cartilaginous tissue, which closes the opening leading into the larynx during the act of swallowing.—**epiglott′ic** *a.* [Gk. *epi*, upon; *glotta*, the tongue].

epigram (ep′i-gram) *n.* a neat, witty, pointed, or sarcastic utterance; originally an epitaph couched in verse form, and developed by the Latin epigrammatists into a short poem designed to display their wit.—**epigrammat′ic, epigrammat′ical** *a.*—**epigrammat′ically** *adv.*—**epigram′matise** *v.t.* to compose an epigram on.—**epigram′matist** *n.* [Gk. *epi*, on; *gramma*, a writing].

epigraph (ep′i-graf) *n.* an inscription, esp. on a building; a quotation from an author; an appropriate motto or popular saying placed at the beginning of a book or chapter [Gk. *epi*, upon; *graphein*, to write].

epilation (ē-pil-ā′shun) *n.* ridding the skin of superfluous hair.—**epil′atory** *n.* a preparation for procuring epilation.—Also **depil′atory** [L. e, out; *pilus*, a hair].

epilepsy (ep′i-lep-si) *n.* a violent, chronic, nervous affection, characterised by sudden convulsions and unconsciousness, followed by temporary stoppage of breath and rigidity of the body.—**epilep′tic** *n.* one subject to epilepsy [Gk. *epilēpsis*, seizure].

epilogue (ep′i-log) *n.* a short speech or poem recited at the end of a play; conclusion of a literary work [Gk. *epi*, upon; *logos*, speech].

Epiphany (e-pif′an-i) *n.* a Church festival held on the twelfth day after Christmas (Jan. 6) to commemorate the manifestation of Christ to the Magi, the Wise Men of the East; the manifestation of a god [Gk. *epi*, to; *phainein*, to show].

epiphenomenon (ep-i-fen-om′en-on) *n.* an attendant circumstance; a symptom; a by-product [Gk. *epi*, in addition to].

epiphyte (ep′i-fīt) *n.* a plant which grows on but does not draw nourishment from another plant [Gk. *epi*, upon; *phuton*, a plant].

epipolism (e-pip′o-lizm) *n.* the radiation by a substance of light of longer wavelength than the exciting light it has absorbed; fluorescence [Gk. *epipole*, a surface].

episcenium (ep-i-sēn′i-um) *n.* one of the upper tiers of columns flanking the rear of the stage of an ancient Greek theatre [Gk. *epi*, upon; *skēnē*, a stage].

episcopacy (e-pis′ko-pas-i) *n.* the government of the church by bishops; the office of a bishop; prelacy; the body of bishops.—**epis′copal** *a.* belonging to or vested in bishops; governed by bishops.—**episcopa′lian** *a.* of an episcopal system or church;—*n.* a member or adherent of an episcopal church.—**episcopa′lianism** *n.* the system of church government by bishops.—**epis′copally** *adv.*—**epis′copate** *n.* a bishopric; the office or order of bishop [Gk. *episkopos*, overseer].

episcope (ep′i-skōp) *n.* an optical lantern which projects pictures or an image of an opaque object, greatly enlarged, on a screen (cf. *epidiascope*) [Gk. *epi*, upon; *skopein*, to view].

episode (epʹi-sōd) *n.* an incident; an incidental narrative or series of events; a digression, only remotely relevant to the plot of a play or novel; (*Mus.*) an intermediate passage between various parts of a fugue.—**ep'isodal, episo'dial, episod'ic, episod'ical** *a.*—**episod'ically** *adv.* [Gk. *epeisodion*, the part of a play between choral songs].

epistle (e-pisʹl) *n.* a letter, usually of the less spontaneous type, written for effect or for instruction, as the epistles of St. Paul, St. Peter, etc. in the New Testament.—**epis'tler, epis'toler** *n.* one who communicates in writing.—**epis'tolary** *a.* pert. to epistles or letters; transacted by letter [Gk. *epistolē*].

epitaph (epʹi-taf) *n.* an inscription placed on a tombstone or cenotaph in commemoration of the dead [Gk. *epi*, upon; *taphos*, tomb].

epitasis (e-pitʹa̧-sis) *n.* the main action in a Greek play leading up to the denouement; (*Logic*) the consequent term of a proposition [Gk. *epi*, upon; *tasis*, a stretching].

epithalamium (ep-i-tha̧-lāʹmi-um) *n.* a nuptial song.—**epithala'mial, epithalam'ic** *a.* [Gk. *epi*, upon; *thalamos*, bridal chamber].

epithelium (ep-i-thēʹli-um) *n.* cellular tissue covering cutaneous, mucous, and serous surfaces.—**epithe'lial** *a.*—**epithelio'matous** *a.* [Gk. *epi*, upon; *thēlē*, a nipple].

epithet (epʹi-thet) *n.* phrase or word used adjectivally to express some quality or attribute of its object; a designation; title; appellation.—**epithet'ic, -al** *a.* [Gk. *epithetos*, added].

epitome (e-pitʹo-mē) *n.* a brief summary; an abridgement of a book; abstract; synopsis; digest.—**epit'omise** *v.t.* to make a short abstract of; to summarise; to condense.—**epit'omiser, epit'omist** *n.* [Gk. fr. *epitemnein*, to cut into].

epizoon, epizoan (ep-i-zōʹon, -a̧n) *n.* an animal or fish which infests the skin or tissues of another, either as a parasite or for the mutual benefit of both;—*pl.* **epizo'a** [Gk. *epi*, upon; *zōon*, an animal].

epoch (epʹok, ēʹpok) *n.* a fixed point or duration of time from which succeeding years are reckoned, as being specially marked by notable events; era; date; period; age.—**e'pochal** *a.* [Gk. *epochē*, a stop].

epode (epʹōd) *n.* after-song, an essential feature of the chorus in Greek drama, being sung after the strophe and antistrophe.—**epod'ic** *a.* [Gk. *epi*, after; *odē*, a song].

epopee, epopoeia (epʹo-pē, ep-o-pēʹya̧) *n.* an epic or heroic poem; the material on which an epic poem is based [Gk. *epos*, a word; *poiein*, to make].

epos (epʹos) *n.* Same as **epopee**.

Epsom (epʹsum) *n.* a town in Surrey, the name of which is associated with the 'Derby,' the 'Oaks' and other notable horse-races.—**Ep'som-salts** *n.* popular name of a saline purgative, magnesium sulphate heptahydrate.

epuration (ep-ū-rāʹshun) *n.* the act of purifying [L. *e*, out; *purus*, clean].

equable (ekʹwa̧-bl, ēʹkwa̧-bl) *a.* uniform in action or intensity; not variable; of unruffled temperament.—**equabil'ity, e'quableness** *n.*—**e'quably** *adv.* [L. *aequabilis*].

equal (ēʹkwa̧l) *a.* having the same magnitude, dimensions, value, degree, or the like; identical; capable; equable; fair or just; tantamount (to); not lop-sided;—*n.* a person of the same rank, age, etc.;—*v.t.* to be or make equal; to become equal to;—*pr.p.* **e'qualling**.—*pa.p.* **e'qualled**.—**equalisa'tion** *n.*—**e'qualise** *v.t.* to make or become equal.—**equalitar'ian** *n.* one who holds that all men are equal in status.—**equal'ity** *n.* the state of being equal.—**e'qually** *adv.*—**e'qualness** *n.* [L. *aequus*, equal].

equanimity (ē-kwa̧-nimʹi-ti) *n.* evenness of mind or temper; composure; calmness.—**equan'imous** *a.*—**equan'imously** *adv.* [L. *aequus*, even; *animus*, mind].

equate (ē-kwāt') *v.t.* to make equal; to state or assume the equality of; to reduce to an average; to bring to a common standard of comparison.—**equa'tion** *n.* the act of making equal; allowance for any inaccuracies; (*Math.*) an expression of the equality of two like algebraic magnitudes or functions by using the sign of equality (=).—**equa'tional** *a.*—**equa'tionally** *adv.* [L. *aequus*, equal].

equator (ē-kwāʹtor) *n.* a great circle supposed to be drawn round the earth 90° from each pole and dividing the globe into the N. & S. hemispheres; (*Astron.*) the celestial equator, another name for the equinoctial.—**equato'rial** *a.* of or pertaining to the equator;—*n.* an astronomical telescope, so mounted that it automatically follows the diurnal course taken by the heavenly body under observation.—**equato'rially** *adv.* [L. *aequus*, equal].

equerry (ekʹwe-ri) *n.* an officer whose duty it is to accompany the sovereign or royal prince when riding in state [Fr. *écurie*, stable].

equestrian (e-kwesʹtri-a̧n) *a.* pertaining to horses or horsemanship; mounted on a horse;—*n.* (*fem.* **eques'trienne**) a rider or circus-performer on a horse.—**eques'trianism** *n.* [L. *equus*, a horse].

equi- (ēʹkwi) *prefix* fr. L. *aequus*, equal, used in the construction of compound words.

equiangular (ē-kwi-angʹgū-la̧r) *a.* having equal angles.

equibalance (ē-kwi-ba̧lʹa̧ns) *n.* equal weight; equilibrium;—*v.t.* to counterbalance; to counterpoise.—**equibal'anced** *a.*

equidistance (ē-kwi-disʹta̧ns) *n.* an equal distance from some point.—**equidis'tant** *a.*

equilateral (ē-kwi-latʹȩ-ra̧l) *a.* having all the sides equal.

equilibrate (ē-kwi-liʹbrāt) *v.t.* to balance exactly; to equipoise.—**equili'brant** *n.* (*Phys.*) the single force which will balance any system of forces or produce equilibrium when used in conjunction with these forces.—**equilibra'tion** *n.*—**equilib'rator** *n.* in aviation the stabilising fin which controls the balance of an aeroplane [L. *aequus*, equal; *libra*, a balance].

equilibrium (ē-kwi-libʹri-um) *n.* (*Mech.*) the state of rest of a body produced by action and reaction, of a system of forces; equipoise; a state of balance.—**equilib'rial** *a.* pert. to equilibrium.—**equilib'rist** *n.* a rope-walker; an acrobat.—**equilib'rity** *n.* the state of being equally balanced; equilibrium [L. *aequus*, equal; *libra*, a balance].

equimultiple (ē-kwi-mulʹti-pl) *n.* a number multiplied by the same number as another, so that the products bear the same ratio as the original numbers.

equine, equinal (eʹkwīn, -a̧l) *a.* pert. to a horse;—*n.* a horse [L. *equus*, a horse].

equinoctial (ē-kwi-nokʹsha̧l) *a.* pert. to the equinoxes;—*n.* (*Astron.*) a great circle in the heavens corresponding to the plane of the equator when extended (cf. **equinox**).

equinox (ēʹkwi-noks) *n.* the time at which the sun crosses the equator, approx. March 21 and Sept. 22, and day and night are equal;—*pl.* points at which sun crosses equator [L. *aequus*, equal; *nox*, night].

equip (e-kwip') *v.t.* to fit out; to supply with all requisites for service; to furnish; to provide; to arm; to array; to dress;—*pr.p.* **equip'ping**.—*pa.p.* **equipped'**.—**e'quipage** *n.* furniture, especially the furniture and supplies of a vessel or army; a carriage, horses and attendants; accoutrements.—**equip'ment** *n.* act of equipping; the state of being equipped; outfit, especially a soldier's; apparatus [Fr. *équiper*].

equipment See **equip**.

equipoise (ēʹkwi-poiz) *n.* the state of equality

of weight or force; even balance; equilibrium; something used as a counterpoise;—*v.t.* to counterbalance.
equiponderate (ē-kwi-pon´dẹr-āt) *v.i.* to be equal in weight to; to balance;—*a.* of equal weight.—**equipon'derance** *n.*—**equipon'derant** *a.* [L. *aequus*, equal; *pondus, ponderis*, weight].
equitable (ek´wit-ạ-bl) *a.* giving, or disposed to give, each his due; just.—**eq'uitableness** *n.*—**eq'uitably** *adv.* fairly; justly [L. *aequus*, equal].
equitation (ek-wi-tā´shun) *n.* skill in horsemanship; a ride on horseback [Fr. fr. L. *equus*, a horse].
equity (ek´wi-ti) *n.* a body of legal principles which slowly developed in England to remedy injustices due to a too rigorous application of the letter of the law being administered until 1873 in the Chancery Division of the courts but now merged with common law; fairness; equal adjustment or distribution; giving to each his due according to the sense of natural right.—**E'quity** *n.* trade union for actors and actresses [L. *aequitas*].
equivalent (ē-kwiv´ạ-lent) *a.* equal in value, power, import, etc.; commensurate; tantamount; synonymous; (*Chem.*) of equal valency;—*n.* something of equal value, etc.; a word of equal meaning.—**equiv'alence** *n.* identical value; state or condition of being equivalent.—**equiv'alency** *n.* the power in elements of combining with or displacing one another in certain definite proportions [L. *aequus*, equal; *valere*, to be worth].
equivocal (ē-kwiv´ō-kạl) *a.* of double or doubtful meaning; questionable; ambiguous; doubtful; dubious.—**equiv'ocally** *adv.*—**equiv'ocalness** *n.*—**equiv'ocate** *v.i.* to use words of doubtful signification to mislead; to quibble; to prevaricate.—**equivoca'tion** *n.*—**equiv'ocator** *n.* [L. *aequus*, equal; *vox, vocis*, a voice].
era (ē´ra) *n.* a fixed point of time from which a series of years is reckoned; epoch; time; age; a memorable date or period [L. *aera*, counters, used in computation].
eradicate (ē-rad´i-kāt) *v.t.* to pull up by the roots; to extirpate; to exterminate; to destroy.—**erad'icable** *a.*—**eradica'tion** *n.* act of eradicating; state of being eradicated; extirpation [L. *e*, out; *radix*, a root].
erase (e-rāz´) *v.t.* to rub or scrape out; to efface; to obliterate; to expunge; to cancel.—**era'sable** *a.*—**erased'** *a.*—**era'ser** *n.* one who or that which erases.—**era'sion, erase'ment** *n.* the act of erasing; that which is erased; traces left by erasing.—**era'sure** *n.* erasion [L. *e*, out; *radere, rasum*, to scrape].
erbium (ẹr´bi-um) *n.* a metallic element belonging to the rare earth group. Symbol *Er*, atomic weight 167.64, atomic number 68 [fr. (Ytt)*erby*, in Sweden].
ere (ār) *adv.* before; sooner;—*prep.* before; —*conj.* sooner than [O.E. *aer*].
erect (e-rekt´) *v.t.* to set upright; to raise, as a building, etc.; to elevate; to construct; —*a.* upright; pointing upwards.—**erec'tion** *n.* the act of erecting; anything erected; elevation; building.—**erect'or** *n.* [L. *erectus*, set upright].
eremite (er´e-mīt) *n.* a religious zealot who lives apart from his fellows; a hermit.—**ere'mic** *a.* inhabiting deserts [Gk. *erēmos*, desolate].
erg (ẹrg) *n.* the absolute unit of measurement of work and energy in the metric system; the work done by a force which produces a velocity of a centimetre per second in a mass of one gram—10 mil. ergs equal one joule, the unit used in practice.—**ergatoc'racy** *n.* government by workers [Gk. *ergon*, work].
ergo (ẹr´gō) *adv.* therefore; consequently.—**er'gotism** *n.* a logical inference [L.].
ergosterol (ẹr-gos´tẹr-ol) *n.* a sterol obtained from oil of ergot of rye, yeast and moulds which when irradiated with the mercury vapour lamp yields a product rich in vitamin D with antirachitic properties [Gk. *stereos*, solid].
ergot (ẹr´got) *n.* product of a diseased condition of grasses, esp. rye.—**er'gotism** *n.* a chronic poisoning due to consumption of ergot-infected rye bread [Fr.=bird's spur].
Erica (e-rī´ka, er´i-ka) *n.* a genus of evergreen shrubs or bushes, popularly known as heath [Gk. *ereikē*, heath].
Erin (er´in) *n.* Ireland.
erk (ẹrk) *n.* (*Slang*) an aircraftman in the R.A.F.
ermine (ẹr´min) *n.* a member of weasel family, stoat, with a slender body, about a foot long, and short legs; the white winter coat of the stoat, highly prized as a fur; the robe of a judge in England and so used as a synonym for *judge* [O.Fr.].
erne (ẹrn) *n.* the white-tailed sea-eagle [O.E. *earn*].
erode (e-rōd´) *v.t.* to eat into; to wear away; to corrode.—**ero'dent** *n.* a caustic drug.—**erose'** *a.* appearing as if gnawed or worn irregularly.—**ero'sion** *n.* act or operation of eating away; corrosion; denudation.—**ero'sive** *a.* [L. *erodere*].
Eros (ē´ros, er´os) *n.* (*Myth.*) the Greek god of love.—**erot'ic** *a.* pertaining to love; amatory;—*n.* a love poem;—**erot'ics** *n.pl.* science and art of love.—**erot'ica** *n.* literature dealing with sexual love.—**erot'icism, er'otism** *n.* in psycho-analysis,, love in all its manifestations [Gk. *eros*, love].
erotic etc. See **Eros**.
err (ẹr) *v.i.* to commit a mistake; to be mistaken; to deviate; to go astray; to offend; to sin; to misjudge.—**errat'ic(al)** *a.* roving; wandering; eccentric; changeable; uncertain; capricious; not dependable.—**errat'ic** *n.* a wanderer; a boulder transported by a glacier or other natural force.—**errat'ically** *adv.*—**erra'tum** *n.* an error in writing or printing, noted for correction;—*pl.* **erra'ta** [L. *errare*, to wander].
errand (er´and) *n.* commission; message [O.E. *aerende*, a message].
errant (er´ant) *a.* wandering; roving; wild; abandoned; vile;—*n.* a knight-errant.—**err'antly** *adv.*—**err'antry** *n.* a state of wandering about, esp. of a knight-errant in search of adventures [L. *errare*, to wander].
erratic, erratum etc. See **err**.
error (er´or) *n.* a deviation from right or truth; a mistake; blunder; sin.—**erro'neous** *a.* wrong; incorrect; inaccurate; false.—**erro'neously** *adv.*—**erro'neousness** *n.* falsity [L. *errare*, to wander].
ersatz (er-zats´) *a.* substituted for articles in everyday use; artificial; makeshift [Ger.].
Erse (ẹrs) *n.* a corruption of 'Irish'; the name once given to Gaelic dialect of West Highlands of Scotland but now appropriated to the Celtic form as spoken in Eire.
erst (ẹrst) *adv.* formerly; of old; at first; till now; hitherto.—**erst'while** *adv.* formerly [O.E. *ærest*].
erubescent (er-ū-bes´ẹnt) *a.* reddish; rubicund; blushing.—**erubes'cence, erubes'cency** *n.* [L. *erubescere*, to redden].
eruct, eructate (ē-rukt´, -tāt) *v.t.* to belch.—**eructa'tion** *n.* belching [L. *e*, out; *ructare*, to belch].
erudite (er´ū-dīt) *a.* learned; deeply read; scholarly.—**er'uditely** *adv.*—**erudi'tion** *n.* learning; scholarship [L. *eruditus*].
erupt (ē-rupt´) *v.i.* to throw out; to break through; to break out in eruptions.—**erup'tion** *n.* act of bursting forth; a sudden sally; outburst of lava, ashes, gas, etc. from the crater of a volcano; a rash on the skin. —**erup'tive** *a.* breaking forth or out [L. *e*, out; *rumpere*, to burst].
erysipelas (er-i-sip´e-lạs) *n.* contagious disease causing acute inflammation of the skin, generally in the face. Also known as 'St.

Anthony's Fire' and 'Rose.' [Gk. fr. *eruthros*, red; *pella*, skin].

erythr-, erythro- *prefix* used in the construction of compound words [Gk. *eruthros*, red].

escalade (es-ka-lād') *n.* mounting the walls of a fortress by means of ladders;—*v.t.* to scale [Fr. fr. L. *scala*, a ladder].

escalator (es'ka-lā-tur) *n.* continuous, moving stairway [L. *scala*, a ladder].

escape (es-kāp') *v.t.* to flee; to evade; to elude; to pass unnoticed;—*v.i.* to hasten away; to avoid capture; to become free from danger;—*n.* flight from danger; evasion; leakage (of gas, etc.); an outlet for purposes of safety; a garden-plant growing wild and thriving; a conscious effort to forget mental troubles by taking up some other powerful interest.—**escap'able** *a.*—**escapade'** *n.* a wild prank or exploit.—**escape'ment** *n.* the act or means of escaping; the contrivance in a time-piece which connects the wheelwork with the pendulum, allowing a tooth to escape at each vibration.—**escap'ism** *n.* morbid desire to escape from the realities of life by concentrating on some other interest.—**escap'ist** *n.* [Fr. *échapper*].

escarp (es-kárp') *v.t.* to cut into a steep slope;—*n.* the steep, sloping bank under a rampart; a sloping bank generally.—**escarp'ment** *n.* in geology, the steep face of a cliff with the other side gradually sloping; an escarp [Fr. *escarper*].

eschalot (esh-a-lot') *n.* See **shallot.**

eschatology (es-ka-tol'o-ji) *n.* the department of dogmatic theology which treats of the so-called last things, such as death, the millenium, the return of Christ, the resurrection and the end of the world [Gk. *eschatos*, last; *logos*, discourse].

escheat (es-chēt') *n.* the legal process, now abolished, whereby tenure of land used to revert to the King in case of freehold property and to the lord of the manor in copyhold on the tenant's death without heirs; an estate so lapsing;—*v.t.* to forfeit; to confiscate;—*v.i.* to revert to the crown or lord of the manor [O.Fr. *escheoir*, to fall due].

eschew (es-chóó') *v.t.* to shun; to avoid; to abstain from [O.Fr. *eschuer*].

escort (es'kort) *n.* an armed guard for a traveller, etc.; a person or persons accompanying another on a journey for protection or as an act of courtesy.—**escort'** *v.t.* to accompany; to convoy; to conduct [Fr. *escorte*].

escribe (ē-skrīb') *v.t.* to draw a circle so that it touches one side of a triangle and the other two sides produced [L. *e*, out; *scribere*, to write].

escritoire (es-krē-twár') *n.* a writing-desk provided with drawers [O.Fr. *escriptoire*].

escudo (es-kóó'dō) *n.* the unit of Portuguese coinage; a coin current in the various S. American states [Sp.].

Esculapian (es-kū-lā'pi-an) *a.* pertaining to the art of healing [*Aesculapius*, in classic mythology, the god of medicine].

esculent (es'kū-lent) *a.* suitable as a food for man; edible; eatable.—*n.* something which is eatable [L. *esculentus*].

escutcheon (es-kuch'un) *n.* in heraldry, a shield bearing armorial bearings; a family shield; that part of a vessel's stern on which her name is inscribed; an ornamental plate or shield placed round a keyhole opening.—**escutch'eoned** *a.*—**a blot on the escutcheon**, a stain on the good name of the family [L. *scutum*, a shield].

Eskimo, Esquimau (es'ki-mō) *n.* and *a.* one of an aboriginal people of Mongolian-Indian stock, thinly scattered along the northern seaboard of America and Asia and in many of the Arctic islands;—*pl.* **Es'kimos, Es'quimaux** [etym. doubtful].

esophagus (ē-sof'a-gus) *n.* the gullet [See **oesophagus**].

esoteric [es-ō-ter'ik) *a.* arising from within; term applied to doctrines intended only for the inner circle of initiates; secret; mysterious [Gk. *esoterikos*, fr. *eso*, within].

espalier (es-pal'yer) *n.* lattice work or wired frame on which plants, especially fruit trees, are trained to grow [Fr. fr. It. *spalla*, a shoulder].

esparto (es-pár'tō) *n.* a coarse grass native to N. Africa and Spain, extensively used in paper manufacture [Sp.].

especial (es-pesh'al) *a.* distinguished; preeminent; more than ordinary.—**espec'ially** *adv.* [O.Fr. *especiel*, fr. L. *species*].

Esperanto (es-pe-ran'tō) *n.* a universal auxiliary language [coined word fr. L. *sperare*, to hope].

espial (es-pī'al) *n.* See **espy.**

espionage (es'pi-on-āj or -ázh) *n.* the practice of employing secret agents; spying [Fr. *espion*, a spy].

esplanade (es-pla-nād) *n.* the level space separating a citadel from the town; the glacis or sloping parapet leading from a fortress; a promenade, esp. along the seafront of a town [Fr.].

espouse (es-pouz') *v.t.* to marry; to betroth; to support, attach oneself to (a cause, etc.)—**espous'al** *n.* act of espousing; betrothing; adoption; support.—**espous'als** *n.pl.* promise of marriage; nuptials.—**espous'er** *n.* [O.Fr. *espouser*].

esprit (es-prē') *n.* spirit; wit; liveliness; animation.—**esprit de corps** (es-prēd'kor), loyalty and attachment to the body or corps of which one is a member [Fr.].

espy (es-pī') *v.t.* to catch sight of; to see at a distance; to discern; to perceive;—*v.i.* to look narrowly.—**espi'al** *n.* spying; observation; a spy [Fr. *espier*, to spy out].

-esque (esk) *Suffix* in the manner or style of.

Esquimau See **Eskimo.**

esquire (es-kwīr') *n.* originally, a squire or shield-bearer, one of two attendants on a knight; now a courtesy title [O.Fr. *escuyer*, fr. L. *scutarius*, a shield-bearer].

essay (es'ā) *n.* a trial; an attempt; a literary composition, shorter than a treatise.—**essay'** *v.t.* to try; to make experiment or trial of; to attempt; to endeavour.—**es'sayist** *n.* a writer of essays [Fr. *essayer*, to try].

essence (es'ens) *n.* the very being or power of a thing; the formal cause of being; peculiar nature or quality; a being; essential part; a concentration of the active ingredients of a substance in a smaller mass; (*Med.*) a solution of essential oils in rectified alcohol; a perfume.—**essen'tial** *a.* belonging to the essence; necessary to the existence of a thing; inherent;—*n.* something indispensable; a chief point; a leading principle.—**essential'ity** *n.* the quality of being essential; an essential part.—**essen'tially** *adv.*—**essen'tialness** *n.* [Fr. from L. *esse*, to be].

establish (es-tab'lish) *v.t.* to make stable or firm; to set up; to found; to enact or decree by authority; to confirm; to prove; to verify; to substantiate; to set up and endow a state church by law.—**estab'lished** *a.* fixed; settled; on the permanent staff; supported by the State.—**estab'lisher** *n.*—**estab'lishment** *n.* act of establishing; that which is established; an institution; settlement; full number of a regiment; place of business, residence, etc.; the church established by the State.—**establishmentar'ian** *a.* and *n.* supporting church establishment [L. *stabilire*, fr. *stare*, to stand].

estancia (es-tan'thi-a) *n.* a mansion; in Spanish America, a landed estate or ranch.—**estanciero** (es-tan-thē-ā'rō) *n.* the owner of a ranch in S. America [Sp.].

estate (es-tāt') *n.* condition of life; rank; position; quality; property, real or personal;

the total assets and liabilities of a bankrupt; total assets of a deceased person at the time of death; social or political group and class.—**estate duties,** taxes levied on property on death of the owner.—**Estates of the Realm,** Lords Spiritual, Lords Temporal, and Commons.—**the Three Estates,** in France, nobles, clergy and middle class.—**the Fourth Estate,** a satirical term for the press.—**real estate,** property in land [O.Fr. *estat*].

esteem (es-tēm') *v.t.* to regard with respect or affection; to set a value on; to rate highly; to estimate; to consider; to deem; —*n.* high regard; favourable opinion [L. *aestimare,* to estimate].

ester (es'-tẹr) *n.* (*Chem.*) a salt formed by interaction between ethers or alcohols and an acid [Ger.].

esthetic See **aesthetic.**

estimable (es'-tim-ạbl) *a.* able to be estimated or esteemed; worthy of regard.—**es'timably** *adv.* [L. *aestimare*].

estimate (es'-ti-māt) *v.t.* to judge and form an opinion of the value of; to compute; to calculate; to offer to complete certain work at a stated cost;—*n.* appraisement; conjecture; the computed cost of anything; valuation.—**es'timator** *n.* one who calculates the costs of material, labour, etc. for doing a certain piece of work.—**the estimates,** official statement presented to parliament of the probable expenses of the various government departments [L. *aestimare*].

estivation, aestivation (es-ti-vā'-shun) *n.* a state of torpor, affecting some insects, during the dry summer months.—**es'tival** *a.* pertaining to or continuing throughout the summer; aestival.—**es'tivate** *v.i.* (cf. *hibernate*) [L. *aestas,* summer].

Estonian, Esthonian (es-t(h)ō'-ni-ạn) *a.* pert. to *Est(h)onia,* a country on the Baltic. —**Esths** *n.pl.* the Finnish-Ugrian race.

estop (es-top') *v.t.* to hinder; to bar; to stop; (*Law*) to impede; to bar by one's own act [Fr. *étouper,* to stop up].

estrange (es-trānj') *v.t.* to alienate, as the affections; to make unfriendly; to divert from its original use, purpose, or possessor.—**estranged'** *a.*—**estrange'ment** *n.* [O.Fr. *estrangier,* to make strange].

estrich, estridge (es'-trich, -trij) *n.* the ostrich; the fine down of the ostrich, lying immediately beneath the feathers [fr. *ostrich*].

estuary (es'-tū-ạr-i) *n.* a narrow arm of the sea at the mouth of a river, up which the tides penetrate twice daily.—**es'tuarine** *a.* pert. to an estuary [L. *aestus,* tide].

esurient (es-ū'-ri-ent) *a.* hungry; voracious; gluttonous [L. *esuriens,* being hungry].

et cetera (et-set'-er-ạ) phrase meaning "and the others"; and so on; (*abbrev.*) **etc., &c.**— **etcet'eras** *n.pl.* small extras [L.].

etch (ech) *v.t.* to make an engraving by eating away the surface of a metal plate with acid;—*v.i.* to practise this art.—**etch'er** *n.* one who etches.—**etch'ing** *n.* the act or art of etching; the printed impression taken from an etched plate [Ger. *ätzen,* to eat into].

eternal (ē-tẹr'-nạl) *a.* without beginning or end in relation to time; everlasting; timeless; ceaseless; immortal; imperishable; (*Colloq.*) always recurring.—**eter'nalise, eter'nise** *v.t.* to make eternal or immortal; to perpetuate.—**eter'nally** *adv.*—**eter'nity** *n.* the infinity of time; the future state after death. —**the eternities,** inescapable truth [L. *aeternus*].

etesian (ē-tē'-zi-ạn) *a.* recurring at regular intervals; periodical [Gk. *etēsios,* annual].

ethane (ē'-thān) *n.* a colourless, odourless, inflammable gas [fr. *ether*].

ether (ē'-thẹr) *n.* the hypothetical non-material, imponderable medium supposed by physicists to permeate the whole of space and to transmit the waves of light, radiant heat and electro-magnetic radiation; the higher regions beyond the earth.—**ethe'real** *a.* pertaining to the ether; empyreal; celestial; airy; heavenly.—**etherealisa'tion** *n.*—**ethe'realise** *v.t.* to render ethereal or spiritual.—**ethereal'ity** *n.* the quality or state of being ethereal.— **ethe'really** *adv.* [Gk. *aithēr,* the upper air].

ether (ē'-thẹr) *n.* a volatile liquid, prepared by the action of sulphuric acid on alcohol, used as a solvent and as an anaesthetic.

ethic, ethical (eth'-ik, -ạl) *a.* relating to morals or moral principles.—**eth'ically** *adv.*— **eth'ics** *n.pl.* philosophy which treats of human character and conduct, of distinction between right and wrong, and moral duty and obligations to the community.—**eth'icist** *n.* a writer on ethical subjects.—**ethic dative,** the emotional dative, in which a pronoun is used to refer to the speaker, e.g. Heat *me* these irons hot [Gk. *ethos,* character].

Ethiopia (ē-thi-ōp'-i-ạ) *n.* in ancient times the territory inhabited by black or dark-coloured people; Abyssinia.—**Ethiop'ian** *n.* a native of Ethiopia; a blackamoor;—*a.* pertaining to Ethiopia [Gk. *aithein,* to burn; *ops,* the countenance].

ethnic, ethnical (eth'-nik, -ạl) *a.* pert. to races or peoples; ethnological.—**eth'nic** *n.* a heathen; a pagan.—**eth'nicism** *n.* paganism. —**ethnog'raphy** *n.* detailed study of the physical characteristics and social customs of racial groups. -**ethnog'rapher** *n.*—**ethnograph'ic** *a.*—**ethnol'ogy** *n.* the science which traces the origin and distribution of races, their peculiarities and differences.—**ethnolog'ical** *a.*—**ethnol'ogist** *n.* [Gk. *ethnos,* a people].

ethology (ē-thol'-o-ji) *n.* the systematic study of human nature, intellect, and character.—**e'thos** *n.* the character, customs and habits which distinguish a people or community from others [Gk. *ethos,* custom].

ethyl (e'-thil) *n.* (*Chem.*) the monovalent radical C_2H_5 with numerous compounds, e.g. **ethyl-acetate,** used as a stimulant; **ethyl-chloride,** anaesthetic used by dentists to 'freeze' the tissues of the gums [fr. *ether,* and Gk. *hulē,* material].

etiolate (ē'-ti-o-lāt) *v.t.* to render pale or unhealthy by denying light and fresh air; to blanch (celery, etc.);—*v.i.* to become pale by being deprived of light, etc.— **etiola'tion** *n.* [Fr. *étioler,* to become pale].

etiology See **aetiology.**

etiquette (et'-i-ket) *n.* the conventional code of good manners which governs behaviour in society and in professional and business life; formal ceremonies prescribed by authority; decorum [Fr.].

Etonian (ē-tōn'-i-ạn) *n.* one educated at Eton College.—**Eton collar,** white starched collar worn outside the jacket.—**Eton crop,** style of women's hairdressing with hair cut very short in boyish fashion.—**Eton jacket,** a boy's black dress coat, very short and tailless.

Etrurian (e-troor'-i-ạn) *a.* of Etruria, the ancient Roman name of part of N.W. Italy. —**Etrus'can** *n.* a native of ancient Etruria;— *a.* pert. to Etruria, its language, people and especially art and architecture.

étude (ā-tòód') *n.* (*Mus.*) a study; a short musical composition [Fr.].

etymology (et-i-mol'-o-ji) *n.* the investigation of the origins and meanings of words and word-forms.—**etymolog'ical** *a.*—**etymolog'ically** *adv.*—**etymol'ogist** *n.* one versed in etymology [Gk. *etumon,* true meaning; *logos,* a discourse].

eu- (ū) *prefix* used in the construction of compound words [Gk.=well].

eucaine (ū-kān') *n.* a synthetic drug, resembling cocaine, used as a local anaesthetic [Gk. *eu,* well; (*co*)*caine*].

eucalypt (ū'-kạ-lipt) *n.* any member of the genus Eucalyptus.—**eucalyp'tus** *n.* the gum tree of Australasia with tough and durable wood.—**eucalyp'tol** *n.* eucalyptus oil, a colourless, aromatic, oily liquid distilled from the leaves of the eucalyptus [Gk. *eu*, well; *kaluptos*, covered].

Eucharist (ū-ka-rist) *n.* the offering of praise and thanksgiving in the Christian Church; the Holy Communion; partaking of the consecrated elements at the sacrament of the Lord's Supper.—**eucharis'tic, eucharis'tical** *a.* [Gk. *eucharistia*, thanksgiving].

euchre (ū'ker) *n.* a game of cards for two to four players [origin unknown].

Euclidean (ū-klid'e-an) *a.* pert. to Euclid of Alexandria who founded a school of mathematics about 300 B.C.; geometric; three-dimensional.

eucrasy (ū'kra-si) *n.* (*Med.*) a well-balanced, healthy state of mind and body [Gk. *eu*, well; *krasis*, mixture].

eudemonism, eudaemonism (ū-dē'mon-izm) *n.* the doctrine that the attainment of personal happiness, power and honour is the chief end and good of man.—**eudem'onist** *n.* [Gk. *eu*, well; *daimon*, a spirit].

eugenic (ū-jen'ik) *a.* pertaining to eugenics; relating to, or tending towards, the production of fine offspring.—**eugen'ics** *n.pl.* the scientific application of the findings of the study of heredity to human beings with the object of perpetuating those inherent and hereditary qualities which aid in the development of the human race.—**eu'genist** *n.* [Gk. *eu*, well; *genes*, producing].

eugenic (ū-jen'ik) *a.* pertaining to or obtained from cloves.—**eugenic acid, eu'genol** *n.* an aromatic acid, obtained by shaking oil of cloves with alcoholic potash—used as a cure for toothache.—**eu'genin** *n.* clove camphor [Prince *Eugène* of Savoy, a patron of botany].

euhemerism (ū-hē'me-rizm) *n.* the view which interprets religious mythology on a historic basis [from the founder, *Euhemerus*, 4th cent. B.C. Sicilian philosopher].

eulogy, eulogium (ū'lo-ji, ū-lō'ji-um) *n.* a speech or writing in praise.—**eulog'ic, -al** *a.* commendatory; laudatory.—**eu'logise** *v.t.* to speak in flattering terms.—**eu'logist** *n.*—**eulogist'ic** *a.* commendatory; laudatory; encomiastic; panegyrical.—**eulogist'ically** *adv.* [Gk. *eulogia*, praise].

Eumenides (ū-men'i-dēz) *n.pl.* the Erinyes or the Furies, the three avenging deities, who punished men for their crimes [Gk.= *well-wishing*, a name given to the Furies from a dread of the consequences of calling them by their true name].

eunuch (ū'nuk) *n.* a human male from whom the testes have been removed; a castrated male, especially in the Near East, in charge of the women of the harem [Gk. *eunē*, a bed; *echein*, to keep].

eupepsy, eupepsia (ū-pep'si, -a) *n.* healthy normal digestion—opposed to *dyspepsia*.—**eupep'tic** *a.* having a good digestion; being easy of digestion.—**eupeptic'ity** *n.* [Gk. *eu*, well; *peptein*, to digest].

euphemism (ū'fem-izm) *n.* a figure of speech where a less disagreeable word or phrase is substituted for a more accurate but more offensive one.—**eu'phemise** *v.t.* or *v.i.* to soften down an expression.—**euphemist'ic** *a.* [Gk. *euphēmizein*, to use words of good omen].

euphonium (ū-fō'ni-um) *n.* a modern brass instrument of the saxhorn type [Gk. *eu*, well; *phonē*, a sound].

euphony (ū'fo-ni) *n.* pleasantness or smoothness of sound; assonance; assimilation of the sounds of syllables to facilitate pronunciation and to please the ear.—**euphon'ic, eupho'nious** *a.*—**eupho'niously** *adv.* [Gk. *eu*, well; *phōnē*, sound].

euphoria, euphory (ū-fōr'i-a, ū'for-i) *n.* a sense of health and well-being which may, however, be misleading; state of irrational happiness.—**euphor'ic** *a.* [Gk.].

euphrasy (ū'fra-zi) *n.* (*Bot.*) the plant eye-bright [Gk. *euphrasia*, delight].

Euphrosyne (ū-fros'i-nē) *n.* the Joyous One, one of the Three Graces; personification of exuberant joy [Gk.=joy].

euphuism (ū'fū-izm) *n.* an affected, elaborate, bombastic prose style of language, so called from *Euphues*, a work by John Lyly (1553-1606), in that style; a stilted expression.—**eu'phuist** *n.*—**euphuist'ic** *a.*

Eurasian (ūr-ā'zi-an) *n.* offspring of mixed European and Asiatic parentage;—*a.* pert. to Europe and Asia considered as one land-mass or continent [fr. *Europe* and *Asia*].

eurhythmics (ū-rith'miks) *n.pl.* an art of rhythmical free movement to music [Gk. *eu*, well; *rhuthmos*, rhythm].

Europe (ū'rōp) *n.* the continent which extends from the Atlantic Ocean to the Ural Mountains which divide it from Asia.—**Europe'an** *a.* belonging to Europe;—*n.* a native or inhabitant of Europe.

europium (ū-rō'pi-um) *n.* a chemical metallic element belonging to the rare earth group [fr. *Europe*].

Eustachian (ū-stā'ki-an) *a.* derived from Bartolommeo *Eustachio* (c. 1500-1574), an Italian anatomist.—**Eustachian catheter,** an instrument of silver used to pass into Eustachian tube when blocked.—**Eustachian tube,** open duct extending from throat near tonsils to middle ear.

eutaxy (ū'tak-si) *n.* good or established order [Gk. *eu*, well; *taxis*, order].

eutectic (ū-tek'tik) *a.* easily melted or fused;—*n.* in metallurgy, a particular mixture or alloy of metals in which the components are so proportioned that they all solidify, forming a finely divided aggregate, on cooling after melting, at one and the same temperature, so behaving like a pure compound [Gk. *eu*, well; *tēktos*, molten].

Euterpe (ū-ter'pē) *n.* one of the muses who presided over music.—**euter'pean** *a.* relating to music [Gk. *eu*, well; *terpein*, to please].

euthanasia (ū-than-ā'zi-a) *n.* an easy, gentle, painless death. -Also **euthan'asy** [Gk. *eu*, well; *thanatos*, death].

eutrophy (ū'trō-fi) *n.* (*Path.*) a healthy condition of the organs of nutrition.—**eutroph'ic** *n.* substance assisting nutrition [Gk. *eu*, well; *trophē*, nourishment].

evacuate (e-vak'ū-āt) *v.t.* to make empty; to withdraw from; to excrete; to discharge; to quit.—**evac'uant** *n.* a purgative.—**evacua'tion** *n.* the act of evacuating, emptying out, withdrawing from; system by which non-combatants, in time of war, are sent to safe areas; (*Med.*) the discharge of faecal matter from the rectum.—**evac'uative** *a.*—**evac'uator** *n.*—**evac'uee** *n.* a person, esp. of school age, temporarily removed from dangerous area in time of war [L. *e*, out; *vacuus*, empty].

evade (e-vād') *v.t.* to avoid by dexterity, artifice, or stratagem; to elude; to escape; to avoid; to shun; to frustrate; to baffle.—**evad'ible** *a.* [L. *e*, out; *vadere*, to go].

evaluate (e-val'ū-āt) *v.t.* to appraise or determine the value of.—**evalua'tion** *n.* estimation of worth; a quantitative comparison of values [Fr. *évaluer*].

evanesce (ev-a-nes') *v.i.* to vanish; to fade or melt away.—**evanes'cence** *n.*—**evanes'cent** *a.* vanishing; fleeting; transitory; transient; passing.—**evanes'cently** *adv.* [L. *evanescere*, to vanish].

evangel (e-van'jel) *n.* good tidings; the Gospel; one of the first four books of the New Testament.—**evangel'ic, evangel'ical** *a.* consonant with the Gospel; applied to those forms of Christianity which regard the atonement of Christ as the ground and central principle of the Christian faith; orthodox.—**evangel'ical** *n.* one who holds the views of the evangelical school.—**evangel'ically** *adv.*—**evangel'icalness, evangel'icism, evangel'icalism, evan'gelism** *n.* a religious movement to spread actively the tenets of the evangelical school.—**evangelisa'tion** *n.* the preaching of the Gospel; conversion.—**evan'gelise** *v.t.* and *v.i.* to convert, by preaching the Gospel.—**evan'gelist** *n.*—**evangelist'ic** *a.* [Gk. *eu*, well; *angelia*, tidings].

evaporate (e-vap'-or-āt) *v.t.* and *v.i.* to pass off in vapour, as a fluid; to disperse; to disappear; to vaporise.—**evap'orable, evap'orative** *a.* tending to evaporate.—**evapora'tion** *n.* [L. *e*, out; *vapor*, vapour].

evasion (e-vā'-zhun) *n.* the act of evading or eluding; subterfuge to escape the force of an accusation, interrogation, or argument; excuse; dodge.—**evas'ible** *a.* may be evaded.—**eva'sive** *a.* tending to evade; marked by evasion; not straightforward.—**eva'sively** *adv.*—**evas'iveness** *n.* [See **evade**).

eve (ēv) *n.* evening; the evening before some particular day; the period immediately preceding an event or important occasion.—**ev'en** *n.* evening (poetical).—**ev'en-song** *n.* evening prayer in the Anglican church.—**ev'en-tide** *n.* evening [O.E. *aefen*].

even (ēv'-n) *a.* level; equal in surface; uniform in rate of motion or mode of action; flat; smooth; uniform in quality; equal in amount; balanced; horizontal; equable; calm; unruffled; impartial; exactly divisible by two;—*v.t.* to make even; to smooth; to equalise;—*adv.* likewise; just; simply; so much as.—**ev'en-hand'ed** *a.* fair, impartial (of justice)-just.—**ev'enly** *adv.*—**ev'enness** *n.*—**ev'en-tem'; pered** *a.* not irascible.—**of even date,** to-day's date [O.E. *efen*].

evening (ēv'-ning) *n.* the close of day; the decline or end of life.—**evening dress,** formal dress worn at evening functions [O.E. *aefnung*].

event (e-vent') *n.* that which happens; a notable occurrence; affair; end; issue; result; effect; item at a sports meeting.—**event'ful** *a.* full of exciting events; momentous.—**event'ual** *a.* happening as a consequence; resulting in the end; ultimate.—**eventual'ity** *n.* contingency; force of circumstances.—**event'ually** *adv.*—**even'tuate** *v.i.* to happen [L. *evenire*, to come out].

ever (ev'-er) *adv.* at any time; at all times; perpetually; constantly; unceasingly.—**ev'erglade** *n.* a low, swampy, grassy tract, esp. *pl.* large marshes in Florida.—**ev'ergreen** *a.* always green;—*n.* non-deciduous tree or shrub which remains green throughout the year.—**evermore'** *adv.* unceasingly; eternally.—**ever and anon,** occasionally; every now and then [O.E. *aefre*].

everlasting (ev-er-last'-ing) *a.* enduring for ever; eternal;—*n.* eternity; a flower which does not lose shape or colour for an indefinite time; the immortelle.—**everlast'ingly** *adv.*

evert (ē-vert') *v.t.* to turn inside out.—**ever'sible** *a.* capable of being turned inside out.—**ever'sion** *n.* [L. *e*, out; *vertere*, to turn].

every (ev'-ri) *a.* each of all; all possible.—**ev'erybody** *n.* every person.—**ev'eryday** *a.* usual; ordinary; common-place; daily.—**ev'erything** *n.* all things; all.—**ev'eryway** *adv.* in every way or respect.—**ev'erywhere** *adv.* in every place; universally.—**every other,** every second; alternately [O.E. *aefre*, *ylc*, ever each].

Everyman (ev'-ri-man) *n.* the title of a morality play of the 15th cent.; the man in the street.

evict (e-vikt') *v.t.* to dispossess by a judicial process; to expel; to eject; to turn out.—**evic'tion** *n.* ejectment.—**evic'tor** *n.* [L. *evincere*, to conquer, to recover property by law].

evident (ev'-i-dent) *a.* visible; clear to the vision; obvious.—**ev'idence** *n.* that which makes evident; information in a law case; a witness; sign; indication; ground for belief; testimony; proof; attestation; corroboration;—*v.t.* to render evident; to prove; to evince.—**eviden'tial, eviden'tiary** *a.* furnishing evidence; proving conclusively.—**ev'idently** *adv.* apparently; plainly.—**to turn King's (Queen's) evidence,** to give evidence, on the part of one accused, against an accomplice [L. *e*, out; *videre*, to see].

evil (ē'-vl) *a.* having bad natural qualities; bad; ill; harmful; hurtful; disagreeable; vicious; corrupt; wicked; calamitous; unfortunate;—*n.* harm; misfortune; wickedness; depravity; sinfulness; wrong; injury;—*adv.* in an evil manner; unjustly.—**ev'il-eye** *n.* the power of bewitching others by the glance of the eyes.—**e'vil-fa'voured** *a.* ugly of appearance.—**e'villy** *adv.*—**e'vilness** *n.* depravity [O.E. *yfel*].

evince (e-vins') *v.t.* to prove beyond any reasonable doubt; to show clearly; to make evident.—**evin'cible** *a.*—**evinc'ibly** *adv.*—**evin'cive** *a.* tending to prove [L. *evincere*, to prove].

eviscerate (e-vis'-er-āt) *v.t.* to disembowel; to gut; to take out the entrails or viscera.—**eviscera'tion** *n.* [L. *e*, out; *viscera*, bowels].

evoke (ē-vōk') *v.t.* to call up; to summon forth; to draw out; to bring to pass.—**ev'ocate** *v.t.* to evoke; to call up a materialisation from the spirit world.—**evoca'tion** *n.* [L. *evocare*, to call out].

evolution (ev-ol-ū'-shun, ē-vo-lū'-shun) *n.* gradual unrolling or unfolding; the development of organisation; change; evolving; the scientific theory according to which the higher forms of life have gradually developed from simple and rudimentary forms; Darwinism; epigenesis; a manoeuvre to change position, order, and direction carried out by a body of troops.—**evolu'tional, evolu'tionary** *a.*—**evolu'tionism** *n.*—**evolu'tionist** *n.* a biologist who accepts the scientific theory of evolution [L. *evolvere*, *evolutum*, to roll out].

evolve (ē-volv') *v.t.* to unroll; to throw out; to disclose; to develop; to unfold;—*v.i.* to develop, esp. by natural process; to open out [L. *evolvere*, to roll out].

ewe (ū) *n.* a female sheep.—**ewe'-lamb** *n.* a female lamb; one's most cherished possession (cf. 2 Sam. 12) [O.E. *eowu*].

ewer (ū'-er) *n.* a large water-jug with a wide spout [O.Fr. *euwier*, fr. *eau*, water].

ex- (eks) *prefix* fr. L. *ex*, out of, used in the construction of compound terms, signifying *out of, from, former* (as ex-M.P.).

exacerbate (eks- egz-as'-er-bāt) *v.t.* to render more bitter; to increase the violence of; to exasperate; to irritate; to aggravate; to heighten.—**exacerba'tion, exacerbes'cence** *n.* [L. *ex*, out of; *acerbus*, bitter].

exact (egz-akt') *a.* accurate; correct; precise; careful;—*v.t.* to demand in full; to extort; to enforce; to insist upon.—**exact'ing** *a.* making severe demands on; demanding extreme care or accuracy.—**exac'tion** *n.* authoritative demand; unjust demand.—**exact'itude** *n.* extreme accuracy; correctness; exactness.—**exact'ly** *adv.* precisely; just so!—**exact'ness** *n.*—**exact'or, exact'er** *n.* (*fem.* **exact'ress**) one who exacts [L. *ex*, out; *agere*, *actum*, to drive].

exaggerate (egz-aj'-er-āt) *v.t.* to represent as greater than truth or justice will warrant; to magnify in the telling, describing, etc.—**exaggerat'edly** *adv.*—**exaggera'tion** *n.* a statement going beyond the facts.—**exagg'erative** *a.*—**exagg'erator** *n.*—**exagg'eratory** *a.* [L. *exaggerare*, to heap up].

exalt (egz-awlt') *v.t.* to raise high; to elevate, as in rank; to lift up; to elate with joy.—**exalta'tion** *n.* elevation in rank; a highly dignified state or position; elation.—**exalt'ed** *a.* [L. *ex*, out; *altus*, high].

examine (egz-am'-in) *v.t.* to inquire into and determine; to try and assay by the appropriate tests; to inspect; to scrutinise; to explore; to investigate; to overhaul; to interrogate.—**exam'** *n.* (*Colloq.*) examination.—**exam'en** *n.* investigation; disquisition; scrutiny.—**exam'inate, exam'inee** *n.* one who undergoes an examination test.—**examina'tion** *n.* the act of examining; interrogation; a scholastic test of knowledge, written or oral; judicial inquiry.—**exam'iner** *n.* [L. *examinare*, to weigh accurately].

example (egz-am'-pl) *n.* a pattern or copy; a thing illustrating a general rule; a specimen; sample [L. *exemplum*, a sample].

exanimate (egz-an'-i-māt) *a.* lifeless; dead; spiritless; disheartened.

exasperate (egz-as'-pẹr-āt) *v.t.* to irritate in a high degree; to rouse angry feelings; to provoke beyond endurance.—**exas'perating** *a.* extremely trying; provoking.—**exaspera'tion** *n.* state of one who is exasperated; state of anger and rage.—**exas'perator** *n.* one who exasperates [L. *ex*, out; *asper*, rough].

excandescence (eks-kan-des'-ẹns) *n.* a white or glowing heat.—**excandes'cent** *a.* [L. *ex*, out; *candescere*, to begin to glow].

excavate (eks'-kạ-vāt) *v.t.* to hollow out; to form a cavity or hole in; to dig out.—**excava'tion** *n.* the removal of earth from a site.—**ex'cavator** *n.* [L. *ex*, out; *cavus*, hollow].

exceed (ek-sēd') *v.t.* to pass or go beyond the limit of; to be greater than; to surpass; to excel.—**exceed'ing** *a.* surpassing; excessive. —**exceed'ingly** *adv.* very; to a very high degree [L. *ex*, out; *cedere*, to go].

excel (ek-sel') *v.t.* to surpass, especially in good qualities; to be better than; to exceed; to outstrip; to outdo;—*v.i.* to be very good; to be pre-eminent;—*pr.p.* **excel'ling**.—*pa.t.* and *pa.p.* **excelled'**.—**ex'cellence** *n.* the state or quality of being excellent; a title of honour.—**ex'cellency** *n.* complimentary title borne by viceroys, ambassadors, etc.—**ex'cellent** *a.* surpassing others in anything; worthy; choice; superior; valuable; distinguished.—**ex'cellently** *adv.* [L. *excellere*, to rise above].

except (ek-sept') *v.t.* to leave out; to take out; to exclude; to reject;—*v.i.* to take exception to; to object;—*prep.* with exclusion of; leaving out; excepting; all but; save;—*conj.* unless.—**except'ing** *prep.* with exception of; excluding.—**excep'tion** *n.* an excepting; that which is not included in a rule; objection.—**excep'tionable** *a.* objectionable.—**excep'tionably** *adv.*—**excep'tional** *a.* outstanding; superior.—**excep'tionally** *adv.* [L. *exceptus*, taken out].

excerpt (ek-sẹrpt') *v.t.* to extract, to quote (a passage from a book, etc.); to select.—**ex'cerpt** *n.* a passage, quoted or culled from a book, speech, etc. [L. *excerpere*, to pluck out].

excess (ek-ses') *n.* that which surpasses or goes beyond a definite limit; increase; superabundance; surplus; remainder; extravagance; intemperance.—**exces'sive** *a.* more than enough; superfluous; extravagant.—**exces'sively** *adv.* [See **exceed**].

exchange (eks-chānj') *v.t.* to give or take in return for; to change; to barter;—*n.* the act of giving or taking one thing in return for another; the method of settling debts between two countries; organised gathering or association of merchants or brokers for transaction of business; the building where such transactions take place; bourse; the method of finding the equivalent of a given sum in the money of another country; an office for interconnecting the various lines of telephone subscribers.—**exchange'able** *a.*

Exchequer (eks-chek'-ẹr) *n.* a court of law, once confined to the care of revenues, now a division of the High Court of Justice; the public treasury [O.Fr. *eschequier*, a chess-board (royal revenue accounts were originally kept by means of counters on a table marked out in chequered squares)].

excise (ek-sīz') *n.* a tax or duty upon certain articles of home production and consumption; also includes all licences with the exception of those for motor vehicles. Also called **Inland Revenue**; the department of the civil service which collects these revenues;—*v.t.* to impose an excise duty on.—**excis'able** *a.* liable to excise duty [Dut. *accijns*, excise].

excise (ek-sīz') *v.t.* to cut out; to cut off.—**excision** (ek-sizh'-un) *n.* act of cutting out or off; the surgical removal of any internal organ of the body; extirpation [L. *ex*, out; *caedere*, to cut].

excite (ek-sīt') *v.t.* to rouse; to call into action; to stir up; to set in motion; to move to strong emotion; to stimulate.—**excitabil'ity** *n.*—**excit'able** *a.* capable of being easily excited; sensitive; passionate; hasty; hot-tempered; violent.—**excitant** (ek'-si-tant) *n.* an agent which increases immediately the functional activity of the body or of some particular organs; a stimulant.—**excita'tion** *n.* the act of exciting; the excitement produced; the action of a stimulant on an organ of the body or of a plant.—**exci'tative** *a.*—**exci'tatory** *a.* tending to excite.—**excit'ed** *a.* agitated; moved by strong emotions.—**excit'edly** *adv.*—**excite'ment** *n.* abnormal activity; agitation; perturbation; commotion.—**excit'ing** *a.* rousing to action; thrilling.—**excit'ingly** *adv.* [L. *excitare*].

exclaim (eks-klām') *v.i.* and *v.t.* to utter loudly and vehemently; to vociferate; to declare suddenly;—*n.* clamour; outcry.—**exclamation** (eks-klạ-mā'-shun) *n.* loud remark or cry, expressing joy, surprise, etc.; vehement utterance.—**exclamation mark,** the mark (!) used to suggest sudden emotion.—**exclam'atory** *a.* of the nature of an exclamation [L. *ex*, out; *clamare*, to call].

exclude (eks-klòòd') *v.t.* to thrust out; to shut out; to debar from; to eject.—**exclu'sion** *n.* the act of excluding or debarring.—**exclu'sive** *a.* excluding; debarring; limited to a special favoured few.—**exclu'sively** *adv.*—**exclu'siveness** *n.* [L. *ex*, out; *claudere*, to shut].

excogitate (eks-koj'-i-tāt) *v.t.* to find out by thinking; to think out.—**excogita'tion** *n.* [L. *ex*, out; *cogitare*, to think].

excommunicate (eks-kom-ūn'-i-kāt) *v.t.* to expel from the communion of the Church by an ecclesiastical sentence; to deprive of spiritual privileges [L. *excommunicare*, to expel from a community].

excoriate (eks-kō'-ri-āt) *v.t.* to strip, wear, or rub the skin off; to flay.—**excoria'tion** *n.* [L. *ex*, out; *corium*, the skin].

excrement (eks'-kre-ment) *n.* matter excreted; faeces; ordure; dung.—**excrement'al** *a.* —**excrementi'tious** *a.* resembling faeces [L. *excrementum*].

excrement (eks'-kre-ment) *n.* that which grows on a living body, as hair, nails, feathers, etc.; a natural excrescence [L. *ex*, out; *crescere*, to grow].

excrescence (eks-kres'-ẹns) *n.* an abnormal protuberance which grows out of anything; an unnatural outgrowth of tissue, as a wart or tumour.—**excres'cent** *a.* growing out morbidly or unnaturally; superfluous [L. *ex*, out; *crescere*, to grow].

excrete (eks-krēt') *v.t.* to eject waste matter from the body; to expel.—**excre'ta** *n.pl.* the normal discharges from the animal body as urine, faeces and sweat.—**excre'tion** *n.* that which is excreted; the act of excreting.—**excre'tive** *a.*—**excre'tory** *a.* excretive [L. *excernere*, to sift out].

excruciate (eks-kròò'-shi-āt) *v.t.* to inflict the severest pain on; to torture, in body or mind.—**excru'ciating** *a.* [L. *ex*, out; *cruciare*, to torture].

exculpate (eks-kul'-pāt) *v.t.* to clear from a charge or imputation of fault or guilt.—**exculpa'tion** *n.* vindication.—**excul'patory** *a.* [L. *ex*, out; *culpa*, fault].

excursion (eks-kur'-shun) *n.* a setting out for some place of interest; a trip for pleasure or health reasons.—**excurse'** *v.i.* to go on an excursion; to digress.—**excur'sionist** *n.* one who makes a journey for pleasure.—**excur'sive** *a.* prone to wander; rambling; digressive; diffusive.—**excur'sus** *n.* a dissertation appended to a book and containing a fuller exposition of some relevant point [L. *ex*, out; *currere*, to run].

excuse (eks-kūz') *v.t.* to free from fault or blame; to free from obligation or duty; to pardon; to justify; to exempt; to let off.—**excuse** (eks-kūs') *n.* a plea offered in extenuation of a fault; an apology.—**excus'able** *a.* [L. *ex*, out; *causa*, a cause, accusation].

execrate (eks'-e-krāt) *v.t.* to feel or express hatred for; to curse; to abominate; to loathe; to detest utterly.—**ex'ecrable** *a.* deserving to be execrated.—**ex'ecrably** *adv.*—**execra'tion** *n.* act of execrating; the object execrated; a curse; imprecation [L. *exsecrari*, to curse].

execute (eks'-e-kūt) *v.t.* to carry out a task to the end; to accomplish; to give effect to; to perform, esp. music; to complete; to enforce a judgment of a court of law; to sign a deed; to put to death by sentence of a court.—**exec'utable** *a.* can be carried out.—**exec'utant** *n.* a performer, esp. of music.—**ex'ecuter** *n.* one who executes; an executioner.—**execu'tion** *n.* the act of executing or performing; death penalty inflicted by law; performance; accomplishment; mode of performance; workmanship; capital punishment.—**execu'tioner** *n.* one who executes; a hangman.—**exec'utive** *a.* capable of executing or performing; administrative;—*n.* a body appointed to administer the affairs of a corporation, a company, or a club; a high official of such a body; under the parliamentary system, members chosen from the legislature to carry into effect the laws of the country.—**exec'utively** *adv.*—**exec'utor** *n.* (*fem.* **exec'utrix, exec'utress**) one who executes or performs; a person appointed under a will to fulfil its terms and administer the estate.—**executo'rial** *a.* [L. *exsequi*, to follow out].

exegesis (eks-e-jē'-sis) *n.* literary commentary; branch of theology dealing with interpretation and elucidation of Holy Scriptures.—**ex'egete, exege'tist** *n.* one versed in interpreting the text of the Scriptures.—**exeget'ic, exeget'ical** *a.* [Gk. fr. *ex*, out; *hēgeesthai*, to lead].

exemplar (egz-em'-plar) *n.* a person or thing to be imitated; an original or pattern; model; a short story with a moral.—**exem'plarily** *adv.* in a manner to be imitated; by way of warning or example.—**exem'plariness** *n.*—**exem'plary** *a.* serving as a pattern or model; commendable [L. *exemplum*, sample].

exemplify (egz-em'-pli-fī) *v.t.* to show by example; to illustrate; to make an attested copy of.—*pr.p.* **exem'plifying**.—*pa.p.* **exem'plified**.—**exemplifica'tion** *n.* [L. *exemplum*, an example; *facere*, to make].

exempt (egz-emt') *v.t.* to free from; to grant immunity from;—*a.* not included; not liable for some duty; privileged; freed from; released from; not affected by.—**exemp'tible** *a.* able to be exempted.—**exemp'tion** *n.* act of exempting; state of being exempt; immunity; privilege; freedom; dispensation [L. *exemptum* taken out].

exequies (eks'-e-kwiz) *n.pl.* funeral rites; obsequies; funeral procession.—**exe'quial** *a.* funereal [L. *exequiae*, funeral procession].

exercise (eks'-ẹr-sīz) *n.* the act of exercising; use (of limbs, faculty, etc.); use of limbs for health; practice for the sake of training; —*pl.* military drill; family devotions;—*v.t.* to put in motion; to use or employ; to exert; to apply; to busy; to engage; to practise; —*v.i.* to take exercise [L. *exercere*, to keep at work].

exert (egz-ẹrt') *v.t.* to put forth, as strength, force, or ability; to exercise; to employ; to strain; to strive; to labour.—**exer'tion** *n.* act of exerting; effort; attempt.—**exer'tive** *a.* [L. *exserere*, to put forth].

exeunt (eks'-ē-unt) *a.* stage direction [L.=they go out]. (See **exit**).

exfoliate (eks-fō'-li-āt) *v.t.* to free the surface of splinters or small scales;—*v.i.* to fall away in flakes, layers, or scales.—**exfolia'tion** *n.* [L. *ex*, off; *folium*, a leaf].

exhale (eks-hāl') *v.t.* to breathe out; to give off as vapour or odour; to discharge; to evaporate;—*v.i.* to rise or be given off as vapour.—**exhal'able** *a.*—**exhal'ant** *a.* having the property of exhalation.—**exhala'tion** *n.* the act or process of exhaling; that which is exhaled; effluvium; mist; damp vapour [L. *ex*, out; *halare*, to breathe].

exhaust (egz-awst') *v.t.* to draw out or drain off completely; to empty; to weaken; to tire; to use up; to squander; to discuss thoroughly; —*n.* conduit through which steam, waste gases and the like, after performing work, pass from the cylinders to the outer air; the steam or burnt gases themselves.—**exhaust'ed** *a.* tired out; fatigued; emptied; drawn out; consumed.—**exhaust'ible** *a.* capable of being exhausted.—**exhaust'ion** *n.* act of exhausting or consuming; state of being completely deprived of strength or vitality.—**exhaust'ive** *a.* tending to exhaust; comprehensive; thorough.—**exhaust'ively** *adv.* [L. *ex*, out; *haurire*, *haustum*, to draw].

exhibit (egz-ib'-it) *v.t.* to hold forth or to expose to view; to present; to show; to display; to manifest; to express;—*n.* anything displayed at an exhibition.—**exhib'iter, exhib'itor** *n.* one who sends articles to an exhibition for display.—**exhibi'tion** *n.* the act of exhibiting; show; display; a public show (of works of art, etc.); a benefaction or endowment for the maintenance of scholars in English Universities; bursary; scholarship.—**exhibi'tioner** *n.* one who holds a university exhibition. —**exhibi'tionism** *n.* a tendency to show off before people.—**exhibi'tionist** *n.*—**exhib'itory** *a.* exhibiting; displaying; declaratory [L. *exhibere*, to hold forth].

exhilarate (egz-il'-ạ-rāt) *v.t.* to make cheerful; to animate.—**exhil'arant** *a.* exhilarating; exciting joy, mirth, or pleasure;—*n.* anything which exhilarates.—**exhil'arating** *a.* enlivening; cheering.—**exhilara'tion** *n.* state of being enlivened or cheerful; animation; gladness [L. *exhilarare*, fr. *hilaris*, happy].

exhort (egz-ort') *v.t.* to incite by words of advice; to advise strongly; to admonish earnestly; to urge.—**exhorta'tion** *n.* the act of exhorting; urgent advice or counsel; religious discourse.—**exhort'ative, exhort'atory** *a.* tending to exhort [L. *ex*; *hortari*, to encourage].

exhume (eks-hūm') *v.t.* to dig up, as from a grave; to unearth; to disinter.—**exhuma'tion** *n.*—**exhum'er** *n.* [L. *ex*, out; *humus*, the ground].

exigent (eks'-i-jẹnt) *a.* calling for immediate action or aid; pressing; urgent; critical.—**ex'igence, ex'igency** *n.* urgent want; emergency; immediate difficulty.—**ex'igible** *a.* capable of being exacted or demanded.—**exigu'ity, exig'uousness** *n.* smallness; slenderness.—**exig'uous** *a.* small; slender; scanty [L. *exigere*, to force out].

exile (eks'-īl, egz'-īl) *n.* separation or enforced banishment from one's native country; a banished person; one living away from his native country;—*v.t.* to banish or expel from one's native country [L. *exsilium*, banishment].

exility (eks-il'-i-ti) *n.* thinness; tenuity; fineness; smallness [L. *exilis*, slender].

exist (egz-ist') *v.t.* to be; to have a being, whether material or spiritual; to continue in being; to live; to subsist; to continue.—**exist'ence** *n.* the condition of objectivity; being; state of being actual; entity; life; reality.—**exist'ent** *a.* still existing; current living; extant.—**existen'tial** *a.* consisting in existence; ontological.—**existen'tialism** *n.* (*Philos.*) a school which describes, analyses and classifies the experiences of an individual mind considered as *existences*.—**existibil'ity** *n.* [L. *existere*, to come forth].

exit (eks'-it) *n.* a departure; a way out of a place; stage direction to indicate when an actor is to leave the stage;—*pl.* **ex'eunt**;—*v.i.* to make an exit [L.=he goes out].

exo- (eks'-ō) *prefix* fr. Gk. *exo*, outside, without, used in the construction of compound words.

exode (ek'-sōd) *n.* the concluding part of a Greek drama, all that followed the last choral ode [Gk. *ex*, out; *hodos*, a way].

exodus (eks'-o-dus) *n.* a departure, esp. of a crowd.—**Ex'odus** *n.* (*Bib.*) the second book of the Old Testament recording the departure of the children of Israel from Egypt [Gk. *exodos*, way out].

exogamy (eks-og'-ạ-mi) *n.* a custom compelling a man to marry outside his tribe, clan, or totem.—**exog'amous** *a.* practising exogamy [Gk. *exo*, outside; *gamos*, marriage].

exonerate (eg-zon'-ẹr-āt) *v.t.* to declare free from blame or responsibility; to relieve of a charge or obligation.—**exonera'tion** *n.*—**exon'erator** *n.*—**exon'erative** *a.* tending to exonerate [L. *exonerare*, to unburden].

exophthalmia, exophthalmos (eks-of-thal'-mi-ạ, -mos) *n.* protrusion of the eyeballs.—**exophthalmic goitre** (*Med.*) Graves' Disease, enlargement of the thyroid gland accompanied by protrusion of the eyeballs [Gk. *exo*; *ophthalmos*, the eye].

exorable (eks'-or-ạ-bl) *a.* capable of being moved by entreaty [L. *exorare*, to persuade by entreaty].

exorbitant (egz-or'-bi-tạnt) *a.* very excessive; extravagant; departing from an orbit or from the usual course.—**exor'bitance, exor'bitancy** *n.* enormity; extravagance.—**exor'bitantly** *adv.* [L. *ex*, out; *orbis*, a circle].

exorcise (eks'-or-sīz, eks-or'-sīz) *v.t.* to cast out (evil spirits) by invocation; to free a person of evil spirits.—**ex'orcism** *n.* the conjuration by God or Christ or some holy name, of some evil-possessing spirit to come out of a person.—**ex'orcist** *n.* [Gk. *exorkizein*].

exordium (egz-or'-di-um) *n.* the beginning of anything, especially the introductory part of a discourse or treatise.—**exor'dial** *a.* [L. fr. *ex*, out; *ordiri*, to begin].

exoskeleton (ek-sō-skel'-e-tun) *n.* (*Zool.*) external hard supporting structure such as scales, nails, feathers in vertebrates and carapace, sclerites in invertebrates—**exoskel'etal** *a.* [Gk. *exo*, outside].

exosmose, exosmosis (eks'-os-mōz, -is) *n.* (*Chem.*) the outward passage of a gas or fluid through a semi-permeable membrane [Gk. *ex*, out; *osmos*, pushing].

exoteric, exoterical (eks-o-ter'-ik, -ạl) *a.* capable of being understood by, or suited for, the many; not secret; the opposite to *esoteric* [Gk. *exoterikos*, external].

exotic (egz-ot'-ik) *a.* introduced from a foreign country; not indigenous; foreign;—*n.* a plant, a custom, etc. of foreign origin.—**exot'icism** *n.* [Gk. *exotikos*].

expand (eks-pand') *v.t.* to spread out; to enlarge; to increase in volume or bulk; to extend; to dilate; to widen; to stretch; to distend; to swell; to develop.—**expanse'** *n.* a wide extent of surface; open country; arch of the sky.—**expansibil'ity** *n.*—**expans'ible, expans'ile** *a.* capable of being expanded.—**expans'ibly** *adv.*—**expan'sion** *n.* act of expanding; condition of being expanded; increase in one or more of the dimensions of a body; spreading; distension; enlargement.—**expans'ive** *a.* widely extended; effusive; communicative; diffusive.—**expans'ively** *adv.*—**expans'iveness, expansiv'ity** *n.* [L. *ex*, out; *pandere*, to stretch].

expatiate (eks-pā'-shi-āt) *v.i.* to speak or write at great length (on); to move at large; to dilate; to ramble.—**expatia'tion** *n.*—**expa'tiative, expa'tiatory** *a.* [L. *exspatiari*, to walk about].

expatriate (eks-pā'-tri-āt, eks-pa'-tri-āt) *v.t.* to banish from one's native land; to exile;—*n.* one who has been forcibly removed from his home country, esp. in time of war.—**expatria'tion** *n.* [L. *ex*, out; *patria*, fatherland].

expect (eks-pekt') *v.t.* to wait for; to look forward to; to look on as likely to happen; to look for as one's due; to await; to hope; to anticipate.—**expect'ance, expect'ancy** *n.* the act or state of expecting; that which is expected.—**expect'ant** *a.* waiting; hopeful; looking for; agog;—*n.* one who is waiting for something to turn up to his advantage.—**expect'antly** *adv.*—**expecta'tion** *n.* act or state of looking forward to an event.—**expecta'tions** *n.pl.* prospects in life; probable gain [L. *exspectare*, to look out for].

expectorate (eks-pek'-to-rāt) *v.t.* or *v.i.* to spit; to cough up.—**expec'torant** *a.* aiding expectoration;—*n.* a drug or agent which promotes expectoration.—**expectora'tion** *n.* the act of expectorating; sputum; spittle [L. *ex*. out; *pectus*, breast].

expedient (eks-pē'-di-ẹnt) *a.* suitable; fitting; advisable; politic; desirable; convenient; useful;—*n.* suitable means to accomplish an end; means devised or employed in an exigency; shift; contrivance.—**expe'diency** *n.* fitness; advisability; self-interest.—**expe'diently** *adv.* quickly; suitably [L. *expedire*, to be fitting].

expedite (eks'-pe-dīt) *v.t.* to free from hindrance or obstacle; to hurry forward;—*a.* free from hindrance; easy; quick; unencumbered.—**ex'peditely** *adv.*—**expedi'tion** *n.* efficient promptness; speed; despatch of an army or fleet; exploring party.—**expedi'tionary** *a.*—**expedi'tious** *a.* prompt; speedy [L. *ex*, out; *pes, pedis*, a foot].

expel (eks-pel') *v.t.* to drive or force out; to cast out; to eject; to exclude; to discharge;—*pr.p.* **expel'ling**.—*pa.t.* and *pa.p.* **expelled'** [L. *ex*, out; *pellere*, to drive].

expend (eks-pend') *v.t.* to lay out; to consume by use; to spend; to disburse; to use up; to employ; to exhaust; to dissipate; to waste.—**expend'able** *a.* that may be expended or consumed.—**expend'iture** *n.* act of expending; that which is expended; expense; cost.—**expense'** *n.* big outlay; cost; expenditure.—**expens'ive** *a.* costly; dear [L. *expendere*, to weigh out].

experience (eks-pē'-ri-ẹns) *n.* practical knowledge gained by trial or practice; personal proof or trial; continuous practice; evidence; an unusual event in one's life;—*v.t.* to know by personal trial or practice; to undergo; to feel; to endure; to encounter.—**expe'rienced** *a.* skilled; expert; wise; capable; thoroughly conversant with.—**experien'tial** *a.* relating to or having experience; empirical [L. *experiri*, to test].

experiment (eks-per'-i-ment) *n.* the action of trying anything; putting to the proof or test; practical test; a trial to find out what happens;—*v.i.* to make an experiment.—**experiment'al** *a.* founded on or known by experiment; pertaining to experiment.—**experiment'alist** *n.*—**experiment'ally** *adv.*—**experimenta'tion** *n.*—**experiment'ative** *a.*—**experimen'ter, exper'imentist** *n.* one who makes experiments [L. *experiri*, to try].

expert (eks-pẹrt') *a.* taught by use, practice, or experience; having a facility from practice; adroit; dexterous; skilful.—**ex'pert** *n.* an authority; a specialist.—**expert'ly** *adv.*—**expert'ness, expert'ise** *n.* [L. *expertus*, having tried].

expiate (eks'-pi-āt) *v.t.* to make satisfaction or reparation for; to atone for; to make amends for; to pay the penalty for.—

ex'piable *a.* able to be atoned for.—**expia'tion** *n.* [L. *expiare*, to make amends for].
expire (eks-pīr') *v.t.* to breathe out; to emit; to exhale;—*v.i.* to die; to die away; to come to an end; to become invalid or void.—**expi'rant** *n.* one who is dying.—**expira'tion** *n.* the exhalation of air from the lungs; death; end of a limited period of time; close; termination.—**expi'ratory** *a.* pertaining to expiration or exhalation of air from the lungs.—**expi'ring** *a.*—**expi'ry** *n.* end; termination; conclusion [L. *ex*, out; *spirare*, to breathe].
explain (eks-plān') *v.t.* to make plain, manifest, or intelligible; to account for; to elucidate; to define.—**explain'able** *a.*—**explana'tion** *n.* act or method of explaining, expounding, or interpreting; the meaning of or reason given for anything.—**explan'ative, explan'atory** *a.* serving to explain [L. *explanare*, to make smooth].
expletive (eks'ple-tiv, eks-plē'tiv) *a.* serving only to fill out a sentence, etc.; added for ornamentation only;—*n.* a word inserted to fill up or to add force to a phrase; an exclamation; an oath [L. *expletivus*, filling out].
explicate (eks'pli-kāt) *v.t.* to unfold the meaning of; to explain; to interpret; to elucidate.—**ex'plicable** *a.* able to be explained.—**explica'tion** *n.* explanation; elucidation; exposition.—**ex'plicative, ex'plicatory** *a.* serving to explain or elucidate [L. *ex*, out; *plicare*, to fold].
explicit (eks-plis'it) *a.* stated in detail; stated, not merely implied; unambiguous; clear; plain; unequivocal.—**explic'itly** *adv.* definitely.—**explic'itness** *n.* [L. *explicitus*].
explode (eks-plōd') *v.t.* to cause to blow up; to discredit; to refute; to expose (a theory, etc.); *v.i.* to burst with a loud report; to become furious with rage; to burst into unrestrained laughter.—**explo'ded** *a.* rejected; debunked.—**explo'sion** *n.* the act of exploding; sudden release of gases, accompanied by noise and violence; a manifestation of rage.—**explo'sive** *a.* liable to explode;—*n.* a chemical compound or mixture intended to explode [L. *ex*, out; *plaudere*, to clap with the hands].
exploit (eks-ploit') *n.* a brilliant feat; a heroic deed; remarkable action, often in a bad sense;—*v.t.* to make the most of; to utilise for personal gain; to boost.—**exploit'able** *a.*—**exploit'age, exploita'tion** *n.* developing and making full use of industrial plant and materials; overworking or sweating workers for financial gain.—**exploi'ter** *n.* [Fr.].
explore (eks-plōr') *v.t.* to search through with the view of making discovery; to leave the beaten tracks; to investigate; to examine.—**explora'tion** *n.*—**explor'atory** *a.*—**explor'er** *n.* [L. *explorare*, to search out].
explosive See **explode**.
exponent (eks-pō'nent) *n.* one who expounds, demonstrates, or explains; an executant; in algebra, index number or quantity, written to the right of and above another to show how often the latter is to be multiplied by itself, e.g. $a^3=a\times a\times a$—**exponen'tial** *a.* pertaining to exponents.—**exponential function**, a quantity with a variable exponent [L. *ex*, out; *ponere*, to place].
export (eks-pōrt') *v.t.* to send goods or produce out of a country.—**ex'port** *n.* act of exporting; that which is exported.—**export'able** *a.*—**exporta'tion** *n.*—**export'er** *n.* [L. *ex*, out; *portare*, to carry].
expose (eks-pōz') *v.t.* to lay open; to leave unprotected; to put up for sale; to submit a photographic plate or film to the light.—**exposé** (eks-pō-zā') *n.* explanatory statement; an exposure or disclosure of discreditable facts.—**exposi'tion** *n.* act of exhibiting or expounding; exhibition; display; illustration; explanation.—**expos'itor** *n.*—**expos'itory** *a.* serving to explain; explanatory; exegetical.—**expo'sure** *n.* the act of exposing, laying bare, or disclosing shady or doubtful transactions; the state of being laid bare; aspect of a building relative to the cardinal points of the compass [L. *ex*, out; *ponere*, to place].
ex post facto (eks pōst fak'tō) *a.* (*Law*) by reason of an act committed afterwards; retrospective; retroactive [L.].
expostulate (eks-post'ū-lāt) *v.i.* to remonstrate with; to reason in a kindly manner with a person in opposition to his conduct.—**expostula'tion** *n.* remonstrance.—**expost'ulative, expost'ulatory** *a.* [L. *expostulare*, to demand urgently].
expound (eks-pound') *v.t.* to explain; to set forth; to clear of obscurity; to interpret; to make plain [L. *ex*, out; *ponere*, to place].
express (eks-pres') *v.t.* to press or squeeze out; to make known one's opinions or feelings; to put into words; to represent by pictorial art; to declare; to denote; to designate; to send by express;—*a.* definitely stated; closely resembling; specially designed; explicit; clear; plain; categorical; speedy;—*adv.* plainly; post-haste; by express messenger or train; specially; on purpose;—*n.* a messenger sent on a special errand; a fast train making few stops en route; a message.—**express'ible** *a.*—**expres'sion** *n.* act of expressing; lively or vivid representation of meaning, sentiment, or feeling; the reflection of character or mood in the countenance; utterance; declaration; phrase; term; remark; aspect; look; (*Math.*) a quantity denoted by algebraic symbols.—**expres'sionism** *n.* an anti-realistic art theory that all art depends on the expression of the artist's creative self, significant characteristics being exaggerated and non-essentials suppressed, without reference to accepted rules.—**expres'sionist** *n.*—**expres'sionless** *a.*—**expres'sive** *a.* serving to express, utter, or represent; full of expression.—**expres'sively** *adv.*—**expres'siveness** *n.*—**express'ly** *adv.* plainly; explicitly; specially [L. *expressus*, squeezed out, clearly stated].
exprobrate (eks'pro-brāt) *v.t.* to condemn [L. *ex*, out; *probrum*, a disgraceful act].
expropriate (eks-prō'pri-āt) *v.t.* to dispossess; to take out of the owner's hands; to deprive of one's property.—**expropria'tion** *n.* [L. *ex*, out; *proprius*, one's own].
expulsion (eks-pul'shun) *n.* the act of expelling or casting out; ejection; banishment.—**expul'sive** *a.* [L. *expulsus*, driven out].
expunge (eks-punj') *v.t.* to strike out, as with a pen; to erase; to obliterate; to cancel [L. *ex*, out; *pungere*, to prick].
expurgate (eks'pur-gāt, eks-pur'gāt) *v.t.* to remove objectionable parts (from a book, etc.); to cleanse; to purify; to purge.—**expurga'tion** *n.*—**expur'gator** *n.*—**expurgato'rial, expur'gatory** *a.* serving to purify or cleanse [L. *ex*, out; *purgare*, to purge].
exquisite (eks'kwi-zit) *a.* of extreme beauty or delicacy; of surpassing excellence; extreme, as pleasure or pain;—*n.* one who is over-nice in dress; a fop.—**ex'quisitely** *adv.* [L. *exquisitus*, sought out].
exscind (ek-sind') *v.t.* to cut off; to destroy; to remove from fellowship [L. *ex*, off; *scindere*, to cut].
ex-service (eks'ser-vis) *a.* of or pertaining to one who has served in H.M. Forces, especially during the periods of the World Wars.—**ex-ser'viceman, ex-ser'vicewoman** *n.*
exsiccate (ek'si-kāt, ek-sik'āt) *v.t.* to dry up; to evaporate.—**exsicca'tion** *n.* [L. *ex*, out; *siccus*, dry].
extant (eks-tant', eks'tant) *a.* still existing; standing out or above the surface [L. *ex*, out; *stare*, to stand].
extasy, extatic See **ecstasy, ecstatic**.
extempore (eks-tem'po-re) *a.* or *adv.* without previous study or meditation; offhand; on the spur of the moment.—**extem'poral, extempora'neous, extem'porary** *a.* impromptu.—

extem'poriness, extemporisa'tion *n.* act of speaking extempore.—**extem'porise** *v.i.* to speak extempore; to create music on the inspiration of the moment [L. *ex*, out of; *tempus, temporis*, time].
extend (eks-tend') *v.t.* to prolong in a single direction, as a line; to stretch out; to prolong in duration; to accord; to offer; to expand; to enlarge;—*v.i.* to be continued in length or breadth; to stretch.—**extend'ible, extens'ible, extens'ile** *a.* capable of being stretched, expanded, or enlarged.—**extensibil'ity** *n.*—**exten'sion** *n.* the act of extending; the state of being extended; further period of time.—**exten'sional** *a.*—**extens'ive** *a.* having wide extent; large; comprehensive; spacious.—**extens'ively** *adv.*—**extens'iveness** *n.*—**exten'sor** *n.* a muscle which straightens or extends a limb.—**extent'** *n.* space or degree to which a thing is extended; size; scope; a space; area; degree; volume; length; expanse [L. *extendere*, to stretch out].
extenuate (eks-ten'ū-āt) *v.t.* to draw out, as a line; to make thin, lean, or slender; to palliate, as a crime; to mitigate; to make less blameworthy.—**exten'uating** *a.* palliating; mitigating.—**extenua'tion** *n.* plea for mitigating a sentence or decision in favour of a prisoner or accused person; palliation.—**exten'uative, exten'uatory** *a.* [L. *ex*, out; *tenuare*, to make thin].
exterior (eks-tē'ri-or) *a.* outer; outward; external; coming from without;—*n.* the outside; outer surface; outward appearance.
exterminate (eks-tẹr'mi-nāt) *v.t.* to root out; to destroy utterly.—**extermina'tion** *n.* complete destruction or extirpation.—**exter'minative, exter'minatory** *a.*—**exter'minator** *n.* [L. *ex*, out; *terminus*, boundary].
external (eks-tẹr'nạl) *a.* not inherent or essential; outward; exterior; superficial; extrinsic; apparent;—**exter'nals** *n.pl.* outward appearances; outward rites or ceremonies; non-essentials.—**exter'nally** *adv.*—**exter'nat** *n.* a day school [L. *externus*, outside].
extersion (eks-tẹr'shun) *n.* wiping or rubbing out [L. *ex*, out; *tergere*, to wipe].
extinct (eks-tingkt') *a.* extinguished; put out; no longer existing or extant; dead.—**extinc'tion** *n.* act of extinguishing; state of being extinguished; destruction [L. *extinctus*, quenched].
extinguish (eks-ting'gwish) *v.t.* to put out; to put an end to; to quench; to destroy; to obscure by superior splendour.—**exting'uishable** *a.*—**exting'uisher** *n.* [L. *extinguere*, to quench].
extirpate (eks'tẹr-pāt) *v.t.* to pull or pluck up by the roots; to destroy utterly.—**extirp'able** *a.*—**extirpa'tion** *n.*—**ex'tirpator** *n.* [L. *exstirpare* fr. *stirps*, stem].
extol (eks-tōl') *v.t.* to praise highly.—*pr.p.* **extoll'ing.**—*pa.t.* and *pa.p.* **extolled'** [L. *extollere*, to lift up].
extort (eks-tort') *v.t.* to obtain by force or threats; to wring out; to exact.—**extors'ive** *a.* serving or tending to extort.—**extor'tion** *n.* act of extorting; illegal compulsion; unjust exaction.—**extor'tionary, extor'tionate** *a.* practising or implying extortion.—**extor'tioner, extor'tionist** *n.* [L. *ex*, out; *torquere*, to wrench].
extra- (eks'tra) *prefix* fr. L. meaning *beyond, on the other side of, on the outside of*; used in many compound words denoting *beyond, without, more than, further than*, or generally, *excess*.—**ex'tra** *a.* extraordinary; additional; —*adv.* unusually; especially;—*n.* something extra; over and above the usual charges; additional item; special edition of a newspaper; a run scored in cricket not directly due to either batsman; a person employed casually by film producers to play a minor role in a production.—**ex'tra-curric'ular** *a.* pert. to the studies or activities which are not included in the curriculum.—**ex'tra-judi'cia** *a.* out of the proper court or the ordinary legal procedure.—**ex'tra-mu'ral** *a.* beyond the walls; pert. to instruction outside a university.—**extra-sensory** (eks-tra-sen'sor-i) *a.* beyond the senses.—**extra-sensory perception**, (*abbrev. E.S.P.*) an awareness of events not presented to the physical senses, part of the data of physical research.—**ex'tra-territo'rial** *a.* outside the limits of a country or its jurisdiction [L.].
extract (eks-trakt') *v.t.* to take out, esp. by force; to obtain against a person's will; to get by pressure, distillation, etc.; to copy out; to quote; to elicit; (*Math.*) to calculate.—**ex'tract** *n.* matter obtained by distillation; concentrated drug, solution, syrup, etc.; a passage reproduced from a book, speech, etc.—**extract'able, extract'ible** *a.*—able to be extracted.—**extrac'tion** *n.* act of extracting; that which is extracted; chemical operation of removing one or more substances from others by means of a solvent; process used in obtaining a metal from its ores; parentage; ancestry; lineage; descent; arithmetical process of finding the root of a number.—**extract'ive** *a.*—**extract'or** *n.* [L. *ex*, out; *trahere, tractum*, to draw].
extradite (eks'trạ-dīt) *v.t.* to deliver up a fugitive to a foreign nation in conformity with the terms of an extradition treaty [L. *ex*, out of; *tradere*, to deliver up].
extraneous (eks-trān'ne-us) *a.* not naturally belonging to or dependent on a thing; not essential; foreign.—**extran'eously** *adv.* [L. *extraneus*].
extraordinary (eks-trạ-or'di-nạr-i, or eks-tror'-) *a.* beyond or out of the common order or method; exceeding the common degree or measure; out of the usual course; employed on a special errand or duty.—**extraor'dinarily** *adv.*—**extraor'dinariness** *n.* [L. *extra*, beyond; *ordo, ordinis*, order].
extravagant (eks-trav'a-gạnt) *a.* wandering beyond bounds; profuse in expense; excessive; prodigal; wasteful; unrestrained.—**extrav'agance** *n.* excess; prodigality; profusion. —**extrav'agate** *v.i.* to wander beyond proper limits [L. *extra*, beyond; *vagari*, to wander].
extravaganza (eks-trav-a-gan'za) *n.* an extravagant, farcical, or fantastic composition, literary or musical [It.].
extravasate (eks-trav'ạ-sāt) *v.t.* to let out of the proper vessels, as blood;—*a.* let out of its proper vessel [L. *extra*, beyond; *vas*, a vessel].
extravert See **extrovert.**
extreme (eks-trēm') *a.* at the utmost point, edge, or border; outermost; of a high or highest degree; severe; excessive; last; most urgent;—*n.* the utmost point or degree; a thing at one end or the other; the first and last of a series; great necessity.—**extreme'ly** *adv.*—**extre'mism** *n.* holding extreme views or doctrines.—**extre'mist** *n.*—**extrem'ity** *n.* the most distant point or side, as of a place or country; end; greatest difficulty.—**extrem'ities** *n.pl.* hands and feet; arms and legs; utmost distress or peril; extreme measures [L. *extremus*].
extricate (eks'tri-kāt) *v.t.* to free from difficulties or perplexities.—**ex'tricable** *a.*—**extrica'tion** *n.* act of extricating or setting free; disentanglement [L. *extricare*].
extrinsic, extrinsical (eks-trin'sik, -ạl) *a.* developing or having its origin from outside the body; not essential; not inherent [L. *extrinsecus*, on the outside].
extrovert (eks-trō-vẹrt') *n.* in psychology, a person whose emotions express themselves readily in external actions and events, as opposed to an *introvert.*—**extrover'sion** *n.* [L. *extra*, outside of; *vertere*, to turn].
extrude (eks-trŏŏd') *v.t.* to thrust out; to press out; to expel.—**extru'sion** *n.* act of extruding; expulsion; ejection.—**extru'sive, extru'sory** *a.* [L. *ex*, out; *trudere*, to thrust].
exuberant (eks-ū'bẹr-ạnt) *a.* over fruitful;

over abundant; prolific; luxurious; excessive; effusive; vivacious; very happy.—**exu'berance, exu'berancy** *n.* state of being exuberant.—**exu'berantly** *adv.* [L. *ex*; *uber*, fertile].

exude (eks-ūd') *v.t.* to discharge through the pores, as sweat; to discharge sap by incision, as a tree;—*v.i.* to ooze out; to escape slowly, as a liquid.—**exuda'tion** *n.* [L. *ex*, out; *sudare*, to sweat].

exult (egz-ult') *v.i.* to rejoice exceedingly; to leap for joy; to triumph; to gloat unduly.—**exult'ance, exult'ancy** *n.* exultation.—**exult'ant** *a.* exulting; triumphant.—**exulta'tion** *n.* triumph [L. *exultare*, to leap for joy].

exuviae (eks-ū'vi-ē) *n.pl.* (*Zool.*) cast off skin, teeth, shells, etc. of animals.—**exu'vial** *a.*—**exu'viate** *v.i.* to cast off, as skin, to moult [L. *exuere*, to strip off].

eyas (ī'as) *n.* a young unfledged hawk [*an eyas*, corruption of *a nyas*, fr. Fr. *niais*, orig. unfledged, fr. L. *nidus*, a nest].

eye (ī) *n.* the organ of sight or vision; the power of seeing; sight; perforation; eyelet; bud; shoot; view; observation; judgment; keen sense of value; vigilance; anything resembling an eye; a small staple or ring to receive a door hook; an aperture for observing; a horizontal opening on the top of a dome;—*v.t.* to observe closely or fixedly; to look at; to view;—*pr.p.* **ey'ing** or **eye'ing**.—*pa.t.* and *pa.p.* **eyed** (īd).—**eye'ball** *n.* the globe of the eye.—**eye'-bath** *n.* a small vessel used for douching the eyes.—**eye'-bright** *n.* euphrasy, a plant used as an eye-lotion.—**eye'brow** *n.* the arch of hairs above eye to catch perspiration from brow.—**eyed** *a.* having eyes; spotted as if with eyes.—**eye'glass** *n.* a glass to assist the sight; a monocle; the eyepiece of an optical instrument.—*pl.* spectacles.—**eye'hole** *n.* a peep-hole.—**eye'lash** *n.* one of the hairs which edge the eyelid.—**eye'less** *a.* without eyes; blind.—**eye'let** *n.* a small eye or hole for a lace or cord, as in garments, sails, etc.;—*v.i.* to make eyeholes.—**eye'lid** *n.* folds of skin which may be drawn at will over the eye. **eye'-o'pener** *n.* surprising news; revealing statement.—**eye'piece** *n.* lens in an optical instrument by means of which the observer views the image of the object formed in the focus of the other lenses.—**eye'-ser'vice** *n.* service performed only while being supervised; adoration.—**eye'shot** *n.* within the range of vision; a glance.—**eye'-sight** *n.* power of vision; view; observation.—**eye'sore** *n.* an object offensive to the eye.—**eye'-strain** *n.* fatigue of the eyes due to faulty muscle-balance of the two eyes.—**eye'-tooth** *n.* either of the two canine teeth of the upper jaw—**eye'wash** *n.* humbug; pretence; deception.—**eye'-wa'ter** *n.* eye-lotion; tears.—**eye'-wit'ness** *n.* one who gives testimony as to what he actually saw.—**the green eye**, jealousy.—**to see eye to eye**, to agree; to think alike [O.E. *eage*].

eyot (āt) *n.* small island esp. in middle of a river or lake [O.E. *ygeth*, *igath*].

eyre (ār) *n.* (*Law*) a journey or circuit; a court of itinerant justices.—**Justices in eyre**, itinerant judges who travelled in circuit [O.Fr. *eire*, journey; fr. L. *iter*].

eyrie, eyry See **aerie.**

F

Fabian (fā-bi-ạn) *a.* cautious or deliberately dilatory from policy; pert. to the Fabian Society;—*n.* a member of the *Fabian Society*, founded in 1884 to promote the gradual spread of Socialism by peaceful methods [fr. Q. *Fabius Maximus*, surnamed *Cunctator*, the delayer].

fable (fā'bl) *n.* a short tale or prolonged personification, often with animal characters, intended to convey a moral truth; a myth; a fiction; a falsehood;—*v.t.* and *v.i.* to feign; to romance.—**fa'bled** *a.* mythical; legendary.—**fab'ular** *a.*—**fab'ulise** *v.i.* to compose fables.—**fab'ulist** *n.*—**fab'ulous** *a.* feigned or fabled; amazing; exaggerated; immense [L. *fabula*, a story].

fabric (fab'rik) *n.* structure; framework; maintenance of a building; woven material; outer covering of an aircraft; texture.—**fab'ricate** *v.t.* to frame; to construct mechanically; to build according to standard specifications; to assemble from standardised components; to fake; to concoct.—**fabrica'tion** *n.*—**fab'ricator** *n.* [L. *fabrica*, a workshop].

facade (fa-såd') *n.* the front view or elevation of a building [Fr. fr. It. *facciata*, the front of a building].

face (fās) *n.* the front of the head including forehead, eyes, nose, mouth, cheeks and chin; the outer appearance; cast of countenance; the outer or upper surface of anything; the dial of a clock, etc.; (*Fig.*) audacity; effrontery;—*v.t.* to confront; to stand opposite to; to admit the existence of (as facts); to oppose with courage; to put a layer of different material on to, or to trim an outer surface;—*v.i.* to turn;—**face'-card** *n.* a court playing-card, as King, Queen.—**face'-cloth** *n.* a cloth laid over face of a corpse; a square of Turkish towelling for washing the face.—**face'-lift'ing** *n.* an operation performed to remove wrinkles from the face.—**face'-piece** *n.* the front part of a respirator.—**fac'er** *n.* a severe blow on the face; (*Fig.*) a sudden, difficult problem.—**face'-val'ue** *n.* apparent worth.—**fac'ial** *a.* pert. to the face;—*n.* (*Colloq.*) a beauty treatment for the face.—**facies** (fā'shi-ēz) *n.* the general appearance of anything.—**fac'ing** *n.* a covering in front for ornament or defence; the collar, cuffs, etc. of a uniform.—**to face the music**, to stand for trial; to meet an emergency boldly.—**to lose face**, to be humiliated.—**to save one's face**, to avoid being humiliated [L. *facies*, a face].

facet (fas'et) *n.* a small surface, as of a crystal or precious stone.—**fac'eted** *a.* having facets [Fr. *facette*, dim. of *face*].

facetious (fạ-sē-shus) *a.* witty; jocular.—**facetiae** (fạ-sē'shi-ē) *n.pl.* witty or humorous writings or sayings.—**face'tiously** *adv.*—**face'tiousness** *n.* [L. *facetus*, elegant].

facia, fascia (fash'i-ạ) *n.* the name-plate above a shop, etc. [L. *fascia*, a band].

facile (fas'il) *a.* easy; fluent; easily approached or influenced; courteous; glib.—**fac'ilely** *adv.*—**fac'ileness** *n.*—**facil'itate** *v.t.* to make easy; to expedite.—**facilita'tion** *n.*—**facil'ity** *n.* ease; deftness; aptitude; easiness of access [L. *facilis*, easy].

facsimile (fak-sim'i-li) *n.* an exact copy;—*a.* identical;—*v.t.* to make a facsimile.—**facsim'ilist** *n.*—**in facsimile**, accurately [L. *fac*, make (imper.); *simile*, like].

fact (fakt) *n.* anything done; anything actually true; that which has happened.—**fac'tual** *a.* pert. to facts; actual.—**mat'ter-of-fact** *a.* prosaic; unimaginative [L. *factum*, thing done].

faction (fak'shun) *n.* a group of people working together, esp. for subversive purposes; dissension; party clique.—**fac'tious** *a.* seditious.—**fac'tiously** *adv.*—**fac'tiousness** *n.* [Fr. fr. L. *factio*, a doing].

factitious (fak-tish'us) *a.* made or imitated by art, oppos. of *natural*; unreal; conventional [L. *factitare*, to do frequently].

factor (fak'tor) *n.* an agent; one who transacts business for another on commission; (*Scot.*) a steward of an estate; (*Math.*) one of numbers which, multiplied together, give a given number; a contributory element or determining cause;—*v.t.* (*Scot.*) to manage (an estate).—**fac'torage** *n.* a factor's commission.—**facto'rial** *a.* pert. to a factor.—

fac'torise *v.t.* (*Math.*) to find the factors of a given number.—**fac'torship** *n.*—**fac'tory** *n.* a building where things are manufactured; a trading settlement [L. *facere*, to do].

factotum (fak-tṓ-tum) *n.* one who manages all kinds of work for an employer [L. *fac*, do (imper,); *totum*, all].

faculty (fá-kul-ti) *n.* ability or power to act; mental aptitude; talent; natural physical function; a university department; the members of a profession, esp. medical; authorisation.—**faculta'tive** *a.* optional [L. *facultas*, power].

fad (fad) *n.* a pet whim; a fancy or notion.—**fad'dish** *a.*—**fad'dy** *a.*—**fad'dist** *n.* one given to fads [etym. unknown].

fade (fād) *v.i.* to lose freshness, brightness, or strength gradually; to disappear slowly.—**fade'less** *a.* not liable to fade; fast (of dye) [O.Fr. *fade*, dull].

faeces, feces (fḗ-sēz) *n.pl.* dregs; the solid waste matter from the bowels.—**faecal** (fḗ-kal) *a.* [L. *faeces*, grounds].

faerie, faery (fā́-ri) *n.* fairyland;—*a.* pert. to fairyland; fairy-like [var. of *fairy*].

fag (fag) *n.* toil; fatigue; at public schools, a lower form boy who does menial offices for a senior; a tedious task; (*Slang*) a cigarette;—*v.t.* to exhaust; to employ as a fag;—*v.i.* to become worn out; to be a fag.—**fag'-end** *n.* the tail end of anything; a remnant [etym. doubtful].

faggot, fagot (fág-ot) *n.* a bundle of sticks for fuel; a bundle of steel rods cut for welding; a contemptuous name for an old woman; one who gets a vote by sham property qualification; a savoury pork rissole;—*v.t.* to tie together; to gather haphazardly; to embroider with a faggot stitch.—**fagg'oting, fag'oting** *n.* a kind of embroidery [Fr. *fagot*, a bundle of sticks].

Fahrenheit (fár-en-hīt) *n.* the term applied to a type of thermometer graduated so that freezing point of water is fixed at 32°, and boiling point at 212°. [German physicist, *Fahrenheit* (1686-1736)].

faience (fā-yongs) *n.* a glazed and painted earthenware orig. made at *Faenza* in Italy.

fail (fāl) *v.i.* to be lacking; to diminish; to deteriorate; to miss; to be unsuccessful in; to go bankrupt;—*v.t.* to disappoint or desert; to omit; (*Colloq.*) to refuse to pass a candidate under examination.—*pr.p.* **fail'ing**.—*pa.p.* **failed**.—**fail'ing** *n.* a fault; a weakness; a short-coming;—*prep.* in default of.—**fail'ure** *n.* bankruptcy; lack of success [O.Fr. *faillir*, to deceive].

fain (fān) *a.* glad; inclined to; forced;—*adv.* gladly.—**fain'ness** *n.* [O.E. *faegen*, joyful].

faint (fānt) *a.* lacking strength; indistinct; giddy; unenterprising;—*v.i.* to become weak; to grow discouraged; to swoon;—*n.* a swoon.—**faint'-heart** *n.* and *a.*—**faint'-heart'ed** *a.* cowardly; timorous.—**faint'ly** *adv.* indistinctly [O.Fr. *feint*, *pa.p.* of *feindre*, to feign].

fair (fār) *a.* clear; free from fault or stain; light-coloured; blond; beautiful; not cloudy; hopeful; just; plausible; middling;—*adv.* in a fair or courteous manner; according to what is just.—**fair'-cop'y** *n.* a rewritten, corrected copy.—**fair game**, open to banter.—**fair'ish** *a.* rather fair.—**fair'ly** *adv.* justly; tolerably; wholly.—**fair'ness** *n.*—**fair'-play** *n.* straightforward justice.—**fair'-spo'ken** *n.* polite; plausible.—**fair'-way** *n.* a navigable channel on a river; (*Golf*) the stretch of ground between the tee and the green, which is free from rough grass.—**fair and square**, honest; honestly [O.E. *faeger*, pleasant]

fair (fār) *n.* periodical market held in certain places, for selling produce of a district; usually an occasion for holidays and entertainments as circus, shows, etc.—**fair'ing** *n.* a gift purchased at a fair [O.Fr. *feire*, L. *feria*, a holiday].

fairy (fā́r-i) *n.* an imaginary creature in the form of a diminutive human being, supposed to meddle, for good or for ill, with the affairs of men;—*a.* fairy-like; dainty.—**fair'yland** *n.* land of the fairies; wonderland.—**fair'y-tale** *n.* a story about fairies and magic; (*Colloq.*) improbable tale [O.Fr. *faerie*, enchantment].

faith (fāth) *n.* belief, esp. in a revealed religion; trust or reliance; a system of religious doctrines believed in; honesty; pledged word.—**faith'ful** *a.* loyal; reliable; honourable; exact.—**faith'fully** *adv.*—**faith'fulness** *n.*—**faith'-heal'ing** *n.* the belief in the efficacy of prayer to heal disease.—**faith'less** *a.* without faith; disloyal [O.Fr. *fei*, faith].

fake (fāk) *v.t.* to conceal the defects of, by artifice; to copy, as an antique, and pass it off as genuine;—*n.* a fraud; a dodge; a deception; a forgery; a faker.—**fak'er** *n.* [prob. Dut. *feague*, to touch up].

fakir (fa-kēr', fā́-ker) *n.* a member of a sect of religious mendicants in India [Ar. *faqir*, a poor man].

Falangists (fal-anj́-ists) *n.pl.* Spanish military Fascists, who co-operated with Franco during Spanish Civil War (1936-39).

falcate (fál-kāt) *a.* (*Bot.* and *Zool.*) sickle-shaped; crescent [L. *falx*. a sickle].

falchion (fawĺ-shun) *n.* sword slightly curved on one edge [L. *falx*, a sickle].

falcon (faw-kn, fál-kon) *n.* a sub-family of birds of prey, allied to the hawk, with strong curved beak and long sickle-shaped claws; one of these birds, trained to hunt game; a kind of light cannon.—**fal'coner** *n.* one who breeds and trains falcons or hawks for hunting wild-fowl.—**fal'conry** *n.* the sport of flying hawks in pursuit of game [O.Fr. *faucon*, a falcon].

falderal (fal-der-al') *n.* the refrain to a song; anything trifling; a gew-gaw. Also **folderol'**, **falderol'** [etym. doubtful].

faldstool (fawld́-stóól) *n.* a portable, folding stool; a camp stool; stool before which kings kneel at their coronation; a litany-desk [O.H. Ger. *faldstuol*, a folding stool].

fall (fawl) *v.i.* to descend from a higher to a lower position; to drop; to collapse; to abate; to decline in value; to become degraded; to happen; to be captured.—*pr.p.* **fall'ing**.—*pa.t.* **fell**.—*pa.p.* **fall'en**;—*n.* the act of falling; a drop; capitulation; the amount (of rain, snow, etc.) deposited in a specified time; a cascade; a cadence; a wrestling bout; a moral lapse, esp. that of Adam and Eve; a lace jabot; dimunition in value, amount, or volume; loose end of a tackle; (*U.S.*) the autumn.—**fall'en** *a.* prostrate; degraded; of loose morals.—**fall'ing-sick'ness** *n.* epilepsy.—**fall'ing-star** *n.* a meteor.—**to fall away**, to desert; to degenerate; to lose flesh.—**to fall back on**, to have recourse to.—**to fall behind**, to be outdistanced; to be in arrears.—**to fall for** (*Colloq.*) to be attracted or taken in by.—**to fall in** (*Mil.*) to form ranks; to join; to give way.—**to fall in with**, to meet casually; to agree to (a plan).—**to fall off**, to decrease; to deteriorate.—**to fall out**, to quarrel; to happen; (*Mil.*) to leave the ranks [O.E. *feallan*, to fall].

fallacy (fál-a-si) *n.* deceptive appearance; a delusion; an apparently forcible argument which is really illogical; sophistry.—**falla'cious** *a.* misleading; illogical.—**falla'ciously** *adv.* [L. *fallax*, deceitful].

fallal (fál-al) *n.* a piece of ribbon; any trifling and gaudy ornament or trinket.

fallible (fál-i-bl) *a.* liable to error; not reliable.—**fallibil'ity** *n.* the quality of being fallible.—**fall'ibly** *adv.* [L. *fallere*, to fail].

fallow (fál-ō) *a.* left untilled for a season; (*Fig.*) untrained (of the mind);—*n.* land which has lain untilled and unsown for a year or more;—*v.t.* to plough without sowing [etym. doubtful, prob. O.E. *fealh*, a harrow].

fallow (fal′ō) *a.* a pale reddish-yellow colour. —**fall′ow-deer** *n.* a species of deer smaller than the red deer [O.E. *fealwes,* of a brown colour].

false (fawls) *a.* untrue; inaccurate; non-essential; dishonest; deceptive; artificial; forged.—**false′face** *n.* a mask.—**false′hood** *n.* an untruth; a lie.—**false′ly** *adv.*—**false′ness** *n.* —**falsifi′able** *a.* capable of being falsified.—**falsifica′tion** *n.*—**fal′sifier** *n.* one who falsifies.—**fal′sify** *v.t.* to distort the truth; to forge; to tamper with; to prove to be untrue.—**fal′sity** *n.* an untrue statement; deception [L. *falsus,* mistaken].

falsetto (fawl-set′ō) *n.* forced high notes of a male voice [It. dim. of *falso,* false].

Falstaffian (fawl-staf′i-ạn) *a.* like Shakespeare's *Falstaff,* corpulent, convivial, boasting and robustly comic.

falter (fawl-tẹr) *v.i.* to stumble; to hesitate; to lack resolution; to stammer [etym. uncertain; poss. Scand. *faltra,* to be embarrassed].

fame (fām) *n.* public report or rumour, esp. good repute.—**famed** *a.* celebrated.—**fa′mous** *a.* celebrated; noted; eminent; excellent.—**fa′mously** *adv.* [L. *fama,* a report].

familiar (fa-mil′yạr) *a.* intimate; domestic; informal; free; unconstrained; well-known; current; conversant with;—*n.* a close acquaintance; an attendant spirit or demon. —**famil′iarise** *v.t.* to make familiar; (*Reflex.*) to get to know thoroughly (foll. by *with*).—**famil′iarism** *n.* a colloquialism.—**familiar′ity** *n.* intimacy; forwardness.—**famil′iarly** *adv.* [L. *familiaris,* pert. to a household].

family (fam′i-li) *n.* parents, children and servants as making a household; the children of the same parents; descendants of one common ancestor; (*Biol.*) group of individuals within an order or sub-division of an order; a group of languages derived from a common parent tongue.—**family tree,** a diagram representing, step by step, the genealogy of a family.—**family way,** pregnancy [L. *familia*].

famine (fam′in) *n.* large-scale scarcity of food; extreme shortage; starvation.—**fam′ish** *v.t.* to starve;—*v.i.* to feel acute hunger [L. *fames,* hunger].

fan (fan) *n.* an instrument to produce currents of air or assist ventilation; a decorative folding object, made of paper, silk, etc. used to cool face; a winnowing-implement; a small sail on a windmill to keep large sails to the wind;—*v.t.* to cool with a fan; to ventilate; to winnow; to cause to flame (as a fire); to excite; to spread out like a fan.—*pr.p.* **fan′ning**.—*pa.p.* **fanned**.—**fan′light** *n.* a window, usually semi-circular, over a doorway.—**fan′ner** *n.* a machine with revolving vanes used as a ventilator, winnowing-machine, etc.—**fan′-tail** *n.* a variety of domestic pigeon; a wedge of shortbread; a type of gas-burner.—**fan′-tailed** *a.*—**fan′-tra′cery** *n.* (*Archit.*) a type of fan-shaped roof vaulting [O.E. *fann,* a winnowing-fan].

fan (fan) *n.* (*Slang*) a devoted admirer; wildly enthusiastic follower [abbrev. of *fanatic*].

fanatic (fạ-nat′ik) *n.* a person inspired with excessive and bigoted enthusiasm, esp. a religious zealot; devotee;—*a.* over-enthusiastic; immoderately zealous.—**fanat′ical** *a.*—**fanat′ically** *adv.*—**fanat′icism** *n.* violent enthusiasm [L. *fanum,* a temple].

fancy (fan′si) *n.* the faculty of creating within the mind images of outward things; an image thus conceived; a whim; a notion; partiality;—*a.* pleasing to the taste; guided by whim; elaborate; fantastic;—*v.t.* to imagine; to have a liking for; to desire; to breed (as dogs);—*pr.p.* **fan′cying**.—*pa.p.* **fan′cied**.—**fan′cier** *n.* one who has a specialised knowledge, esp. of the breeding of animals. —**fan′ciful** *a.* capricious; unreal; fantastic.—**fan′cifully** *adv.*—**fan′cifulness** *n.*—**fan′cy-ball** *n.* a ball at which the dancers wear fancy-dress.—**fan′cy-dress** *n.* dress made according to wearer's fancy, to represent some character.—**fan′cy-free** *a.* heart-free.—**fancy man** (*Slang*) a sweetheart.—**the fancy,** sporting characters generally, esp. pugilists [contr. fr. *fantasy*].

fandango (fan-dang′gō) *n.* a Spanish dance for two persons; a ball [Sp.].

fane (fān) *n.* a temple [L. *fanum,* a temple].

fanfare (fan′fār) *n.* a flourish of trumpets. Also **fanfarade′**.—**fan′faron** *n.* a swaggerer.—**fanfaronade′** *n.* fanfare; boasting; brag;—*v.i.* to bluster [Fr. prob. imit.].

fang (fang) *n.* the canine tooth of a carnivorous animal; the long perforated tooth of a poisonous serpent.—**fanged** *a.* [O.E. *fang,* a seizing].

fangled (fang′gld) *a.* orig. meant fashionable, now exists only in the epithet *new-fangled,* new fashioned, hence unfamiliar.

fan-tan (fan′tan) *n.* a Chinese gambling game in which players guess the number of counters hidden under a bowl [Chin.].

fantasy (fan′tạ-si) *n.* fancy; mental image; caprice; hallucination. Also **phan′tasy**.—**fantasia** (fan-tā′zi-a) *n.* (*Mus.*) a composition not conforming to the usual rules of music.—**fan′tasied** *a.* fanciful.—**fan′tasm** *n.* same as **phantasm**.—**fantas′tic, -al** *a.* fanciful; wild; irregular; capricious.—**fantas′tically** *adv.* [Gk. *phantasia,* appearance].

far (får) *a.* distant; remote; more distant of two;—*adv.* to a great extent or distance; to a great height; considerably; very much; —*n.* a distant place, as in *he came from far.*—**farther** (får′THẹr) *a.* (*comp.* of **far**) more remote; tending to a greater distance;—*adv.* at, or to, a greater distance; moreover; in addition (variant of **further**).—**far′thest** *a.* (superlative of **far**) most remote in space or time;—*adv.* to greatest distance.—**far away,** distant; abstracted in mind.—**Far East,** that part of Asia including India, China, Japan.—**far′-fetched** *a.* far-brought; (*Fig.*) incredible; strained.—**far gone,** in the last stages of disease, drunkenness, etc.—**far′most** *adv.* most distant.—**far′-off** *a.* distant.—**far′-see′ing,** or **-sight′ed** *a.* seeing to a great distance; (*Fig.*) taking a long view; prudent.—**far and away,** very considerably [O.E. *feor,* far].

farad (far′ad) *n.* the unit of electrostatic capacity—the capacity of a condenser which requires one coulomb to raise its potential by one volt.—**far′aday,** *n.* the quantity of electricity required to liberate 1 gram-equivalent of an ion.—**farada′ic, farad′ic** *a.* pert. to the scientist, *Michel Faraday* (1791-1867); pert. to induced electrical currents.

farce (fårs) *n.* orig. a dramatic interlude; a style of comedy marked by boisterous humour and extravagant gesture; absurd or empty show; a pretence; stuffing for fowls, meat, fish, etc.; forcemeat;—*v.t.* to cram; to fill with stuffing.—**farceur** (får-sẹr′) *n.* a joker; a wag.—**far′cical** *a.* pert. to a farce; absurdly ludicrous; sham.—**far′cically** *adv.* [O.Fr. *farce,* stuffing].

fardel (får′del) *n.* a little pack; a burden; anything cumbersome [O.Fr. *fardel,* dim. of *farde,* a burden].

fare (fār) *v.i.* to go; to travel; to succeed; to be in any state, bad or good; to be entertained at table;—*n.* the sum paid by a passenger on a vehicle; a passenger; food and drink at table.—**farewell′** *interj.* (*Lit.*) may it go well with you; good-bye;—*n.* a parting wish for someone's welfare; the act of taking leave;—*a.* parting; last.—**farewell to,** no more of [O.E. *faran,* to go].

farina (fa-rī′na, fa-rē′na) *n.* ground corn; meal; the flour of any species of corn or root; starch; (*Bot.*) pollen.—**farina′ceous** *a.* [L. *farina,* ground corn].

farm (farm) *n.* a tract of owned or rented land set apart for cultivation or as a preserve; the buildings on this land;—*v.t.* to lease or let out land for agricultural purposes; to collect (taxes, etc.) on condition of receiving a percentage of what is yielded;—*v.i.* and *t.* to till; to cultivate.—**farm'er** *n.* (*fem.* **farm'eress**) one who cultivates leased ground; one who collects taxes, etc. for a certain rate per cent.—**farm'-house** *n.* a dwelling-house attached to a farm.—**farm'ing** *n.* the occupation of cultivating the soil.—**farm'stead** *n.* a farm with all the outbuildings attached to it.—**farm'-yard** *n.* enclosure surrounded by farm buildings [M.E. *ferme*, payment].

faro (fār'ō) *n.* a gambling game of cards [fr. *Pharaoh*, represented on one of the cards].

farouche (fà-ròosh') *a.* sullen; shy and awkward in manner [Fr. fr. L. *ferox*, fierce].

farrago (far-ā'gō, far-a'gō) *n.* a medley; a miscellaneous collection.—**farra'ginous** *a.* jumbled; confusedly mixed [L. *farrago*, mixed fodder].

farrier (far'i-ẹr) *n.* one who shoes horses; a veterinary surgeon.—**farr'iery** *n.* [L. *ferrum*, iron].

farrow (far'ō) *n.* a litter of pigs;—*v.t.* to give birth to (pigs);—*v.i.* to bring forth pigs [O.E. *fearh*, a pig].

farther (får'THẹr) *a.* more far; more remote; —*adv.* to a greater distance.—**far'thermost** *a.* most remote; farthest.

farthing (får'THing) *n.* formerly the fourth of a penny [O.E. *feorthing*, a fourth part].

farthingale (får'THing-gāl) *n.* a hoop petticoat for distending women's dress; a kind of crinoline [Sp. *verdugado*, hooped].

fasces (fas'ēz) *n.pl.* a bundle of rods with an axe, carried by Roman magistrates as a symbol of their authority; sometimes used to flog criminals [L. *fasces*, bundles].

fascia (fash'i-a) *n.* a band, fillet, or bandage; (*Archit.*) a strip of flat stone between two mouldings; the instrument board of a motor car; the flat band of metal above a shop front with owner's name, etc. [L. *fascia*, a band].

fascicle (fas'i-kl) *n.* (*Bot.*) a close cluster of leaves or flowers as in the sweet-william; a small bundle of tissues of nerve-fibres; a serial division of a book.—**fascic'ular, fascic'ulate, fascic'ulated, fas'cicled** *a.* [L. *fasciculus*, a small bundle].

fascinate (fas'i-nāt) *v.t.* to deprive of the power of movement, by a look; to bewitch; to enchant.—**fas'cinating** *a.*—**fascina'tion** *n.* the act of fascinating; enchantment; irresistible attraction; state of being bewitched.—**fas'cinator** *n.* [L. *fascinare*, to bewitch].

fascine (fa-sēn') *n.* a brushwood faggot used by military for filling ditches, trenches, etc. [L. *fascina*, a faggot].

Fascism (fash'izm) *n.* the Italian Nationalist movement organised in 1919 by Benito Mussolini on military lines, its policy being anti-parliamentary and anti-communistic, with an economic system based on State-controlled capitalism.—**Fasc'ist** *n.* [It. *fascio*, a bundle].

fash (fash) *v.t.* (*Scot.*) to vex; to annoy; to trouble;—*v.i.* to be anxious;—*n.* trouble; care [O.Fr. *fascher*, to trouble].

fashion (fash'un) *n.* the style in which a thing is made or done; pattern; the mode or cut, esp. of a dress; custom; appearance; —*v.t.* to form; to contrive; to shape.—**fash'ionable** *a.* made according to prevailing mode at a certain period; stylish; conforming to the standards of genteel society.—**fash'ionably** *adv.* [O.Fr. *facon*, a manner].

fast (fåst) *v.i.* to abstain from food; to go hungry; to deny oneself certain foods as a form of religious discipline;—*n.* abstinence from food; a day of fasting [O.E. *faestan*, to fast].

fast (fåst) *a.* securely fixed; firm; tight shut; profound; immovable; permanent, as a dye; stable; in advance of the correct time, as a clock; loyal, as friends; rapid; dissipated, as *a fast life*;—*adv.* firmly; soundly; securely; dissipatedly; rapidly; near.—**fast'ness** *n.* security; a stronghold.—**fast by,** close by.—**to play fast and loose with,** to be unreliable [O.E. *faest*, firm].

fasten (fås'n) *v.t.* to fix firmly; to hold together;—*v.i.* to fix itself; to catch (of a lock).—**fas'tener** *n.* a contrivance for fixing things firmly together; a clip.—**fas'tening** *n.* that by which anything fastens, as a lock, bolt, nut, screw [O.E. *faest*, firm].

fastidious (fas-tid'i-us) *a.* difficult to please; discriminating.—**fastid'iously** *adv.*—**fastid'iousness** *n.* [L. *fastidium*, loathing].

fat (fat) *a.* fleshy; plump; corpulent; oily; yielding a rich supply; productive; profitable;—*n.* an oily substance found in various parts of animal bodies; solid animal or vegetable oil; the best or richest part of anything;—*v.t.* to make fat;—*v.i.* to grow fat.—*pr.p.* **fat'ting**.—*pa.p.* **fat'ted**.—**fat'-head** *n.* a stupid person.—**fat'-head'ed** *a.*—**fat'ling** *n.* a young animal fattened for slaughter.—**fat'ly** *adv.* grossly; clumsily.—**fat'ness** *n.* the quality or state of being fat; corpulence; fertility.—**fat'ted** *a.* fattened.—**fat'ten** *v.t.* to make fat; to make fertile;—*v.i.* to grow fat.—**fat'tener** *n.*—**fat'tiness** *n.*—**fat'tish** *a.* rather fat.—**fat'ty** *a.* resembling or containing fat; oleaginous; greasy.—**to kill the fatted calf,** to celebrate someone's return (from Prodigal Son parable) [O.E. *faet*, fat].

fat (fat) *n.* a large tub, cistern, or vessel for holding liquids [var. of *vat*].

fate (fāt) *n.* an inevitable and irresistible power supposedly controlling human destiny; appointed lot; death; doom.—**the Fates,** the three goddesses supposed to preside over the course of human life.—**fat'al** *a.* appointed by fate; mortal; calamitous; deadly.—**fat'alism** *n.* the doctrine that all events are pre-determined and unavoidable.—**fat'alist** *n.*—**fatalist'ic** *a.* —**fatal'ity** *n.* the state of being fatal; inevitable necessity; accident causing death.—**fat'ed** *a.* destined; pre-ordained; doomed.—**fate'ful** *a.* momentous; irrevocable.—**fate'fully** *adv.*—**fate'fulness** *n.* [L. *fatum*].

father (fà'THẹr) *n.* a male parent; a male ancestor more remote than a parent; a title of respect paid to one of seniority or rank, esp. to Church dignitaries as *the Holy Father* (the Pope); a Roman Catholic priest; the first person of the Trinity; oldest member of a community; a producer, author or contriver;—*v.t.* to make oneself the father of; to adopt; to assume or admit responsibility for.—**fa'therhood** *n.* the state of being a father; paternity.—**fa'ther-in-law** *n.* (*pl.* **fa'thers-in-law**) the father of one's wife or husband.—**fa'therland** *n.* the land of one's fathers.—**fa'therless** *a.* without a father living.—**fa'therliness** *n.*—**fa'therly** *a.* and *adv.* like a father in affection and care; paternal; benevolent.—**fa'thership** *n.* [O.E. *faeder*, a father].

fathom (faTH'om) *n.* a nautical measure of depth, 6 ft.; a timber measure, 6 ft. by 6 ft. by 6 ft.;—*v.t.* to ascertain the depth of; to sound; (*Fig.*) to get to the bottom of; to understand.—**fath'omable** *n.*—**fath'omless** *a.* incapable of being fathomed; unplumbed. —**fath'omlessly** *adv.*—**fathom-line,** a line marked in fathoms, used for taking soundings [O.E. *faethm*, the outstretched arms].

fatigue (fạ-tēg') *n.* weariness from bodily or mental exertion; toil; non-military routine work of soldiers;—*v.t.* to weary by toil; to exhaust the strength of; to tire out.—*pr.p.* **fatigu'ing**.—*pa.p.* **fatigued'** [Fr. *fatiguer*, to weary].

fatuous (fat'ū-us) *a.* feeble in mind; weak; silly; inane; idiotic.—**fatu'ity** *n.* weakness of mind; imbecility; inanity; foolishness.—**fat'uousness** *n.* [L. *fatuus*, silly].

faucet (faw′set) *n.* a fixture for drawing liquor from a cask; a tap [O.Fr. *fausset*].

faugh (faw) *interj.* an exclamation of contempt or disgust [imit.].

fault (fawlt) *n.* a failing; blunder; mistake; defect; flaw; responsibility for error; (*Geol.*) a dislocation of rock-strata; in hunting, the loss of the scent-trail; (*Elect.*) a defect in electrical apparatus.—**fault'ed** *a.* (*Geol.*) broken by one or more faults.—**fault'ily** *adv.*—**fault'iness** *n.*—**fault'less** *a.* without flaws; perfect.—**fault'lessly** *adv.*—**fault'lessness** *n.* perfection.—**fault'y** *a.* imperfect; culpable; wrong [O.Fr. *faute*, error].

fauna (fawn′a) *n.* a collective term for the animals of any given geographical region or geological epoch;—*pl.* **faun'ae** (fawn′ē), **faunas** (fawn′az).—**faun** *n.* Roman deity supposed to protect shepherds [L. *Fauna*, sister of *Faunus*, a god of agriculture].

fauteuil (fō-tẹ′yẹ, fō′til) *n.* an armchair; a stall in the theatre or cinema [Fr. fr. L. *faldistolium*, a faldstool].

faveolate (fav-ē′ō-lāt) *a.* pitted; cellular; resembling a honeycomb. Also **favose** [L. *faveolus*, a little honeycomb].

favour (fā′vor) *n.* kind regard; good-will; a gracious act; partiality; token of generosity or esteem; a rosette or ornament worn at a wedding or as a badge of membership of a club or political party;—*v.t.* to regard with kindness; to show unfair bias towards; to tend to promote; to resemble in feature.—**fa'vourable** *a.* friendly; propitious; advantageous; suitable; satisfactory.—**fa'vourableness** *n.*—**fa'vourably** *adv.*—**fa'voured** *a.* fortunate; lucky; featured, as in *ill-favoured*.—**fa'vourite** *n.* a person or thing regarded with special favour; a person unduly praised; (of a race horse) the likely winner;—*a.* regarded with particular affection; most esteemed.—**fa'vouritism** *n.* undue partiality [L. *favor*, partiality].

fawn (fawn) *n.* a young deer; a fallow deer; its colour;—*a.* delicate greyish-brown;—*v.i.* to give birth to a fawn [O.Fr. *faon*, fr. L. *foetus*, offspring].

fawn (fawn) *v.i.* to flatter unctuously; to cringe; to grovel; to curry favour.—**fawn'er** *n.*—**fawn'ing** *n.* servile flattery;—*a.* overdemonstrative; cringing.—**fawn'ingly** *adv.*—**fawn'ingness** *n.* [M.E. *faunen*, to rejoice].

fay (fā) *n.* a fairy; an elf [O.Fr. *fae*].

fealty (fē′ạl-ti) *n.* fidelity to one's lord; obligations binding a vassal to his lord [O.Fr. *fealte*, fidelity].

fear (fēr) *n.* a painful emotion aroused by a sense of impending danger; alarm; dread; solicitude; anxiety; reverence towards God; —*v.t.* to regard with dread or apprehension; to anticipate (as a disaster); to hold in awe; —*v.i.* to be afraid; to be anxious.—**fear'ful** *a.* afraid; apprehensive; dreadful.—**fear'fully** *adv.*—**fear'fulness** *n.*—**fear'less** *a.* without fear; intrepid; dauntless.—**fear'lessly** *adv.*—**fear'lessness** *n.* courage; intrepidity.—**fear'some** *a.* causing fear; terrifying [O.E. *faer*, danger].

feasible (fēz′i-bl) *a.* capable of being done; possible.—**feas'ibleness**, **feasibil'ity** *n.*—**feas'ibly** *adv.* [Fr. *faisible*, that can be done].

feast (fēst) *n.* a festival; a day of joyful or solemn commemoration; a banquet;—*v.t.* to feed sumptuously; to regale;—*v.i.* to eat sumptuously; to be highly gratified or delighted.—**feast'-day** *n.* a festival; a religious commemoration, as the *Feast* of *Pentecost*.—**feast'er** *n.* [L. *festum*, a holiday].

feat (fēt) *n.* an exploit or action of extraordinary strength, courage, skill, or endurance [Fr. *fait*, fr. L. *factum*, a deed].

feather (feTH′ẹr) *n.* one of the epidermal growths forming the body-covering of a bird; a plume; the feathered end of an arrow; —*v.t.* to cover with feathers; to supply with feathers, as a cap or arrow.—**feath'er-bed** *n.* a mattress stuffed with feathers; *v.t.* (*Colloq.*) to pamper.—**feath'er-board'ing** *n.* boarding where the edge of one board overlaps a part of one below.—**feath'er-brained**, **feath'er-head'ed**, **feath'er-pat'ed** *a.* silly; frivolous; inane.—**feath'erlet** *n.* a small feather.—**feath'er-stitch** *n.* an embroidery stitch resembling a feather.—**feather-weight**, the lightest weight that may be carried by a race-horse; a boxer weighing not more than 9 st.; any very light person or thing.—**feath'ery** *a.* pert. to, covered with, or resembling feathers.—**to feather one's nest**, to accumulate wealth for oneself.—**a feather in one's cap**, an honour or distinction.—**to show the white feather**, to be a coward [O.E. *fether*, feather].

feature (fēt′ūr) *n.* form, appearance of the body, esp. any part of the face; distinctive characteristic;—*pl.* the face;—*v.t.* to portray; to outline; in cinema, to present as leading actor or actress in a film.—**feat'ureless** *a.* void of striking features.—**feature film**, film forming the main part of a cinema programme [O.Fr. *faiture*, something made].

febricule (feb′ri-kūl) *n.* a slight fever.—**febric'ity** *n.* feverishness.—**febrif'ic** *a.* causing fever.—**febrifuge** (feb′ri-fūj) *n.* a drug taken to allay fever; an antipyretic.—**febrif'ugal** *a.* —**febrile** (fē′bril, feb′ril) *a.* feverish; accompanied by fever.—**febril'ity** *n.* [L. *febris*, fever].

February (feb′ròò-ạ-ri) *n.* the second month of the year [L. *Februarius*, fr. *Februa*, the Roman festival of purification].

feces See **faeces**.

fecund (fē′kund) *a.* prolific; fruitful; fertile. —**fecundate** (fē-kun′dāt, fek′un-dāt) *v.t.* to make fruitful; to impregnate.—**fecunda'tion** *n.* —**fecund'ity** *n.* the quality or power of reproduction; fertility; productiveness; richness of invention [L. *fecundus*, fruitful].

fed (fed) *pa.t.* and *pa.p.* of the verb **feed**.—**fed'-up** *a.* (*Slang*) bored; dissatisfied.

federal (fed′ẹ-rạl) *a.* pert. to a league or treaty, esp. between states; of an association of states which, autonomous in home affairs, combine for matters of wider national and international policy; pert. to the Northern States of America in the Civil War.—**fed'eracy** *n.*—**fed'eralise** *v.t.* to form a union under a federal government.—**fed'eralism** *n.*—**fed'eralist** *n.* a supporter of such a union.—**fed'erate** *v.t.* to unite states into a federation. —*a.* united; allied.—**federa'tion** *n.* a federal union.—**fed'erative** *a.* [L. *foedus*, a compact].

fee (fē) *n.* orig. land held from a lord on condition of certain feudal services; fief; homage; remuneration for professional services; payment for special privilege;—*v.t.* to pay a fee to; to hire.—**fee-simple**, unrestricted ownership or inheritance [O.E. *feoh*, cattle or property].

feeble (fē′bl) *a.* weak; deficient in strength; frail; faint; futile; imbecile.—**fee'ble-mind'ed** *a.* mentally subnormal; irresolute.—**fee'bleness** *n.*—**fee'bly** *adv.* [Fr. *faible*, weak].

feed (fēd) *v.t.* to give food to; to supply with nourishment; to supply with material (as a machine);—*v.i.* to eat; to graze.—*pr.p.* **feed'ing**.—*pa.p.* and *pa.t.* **fed**.—*n.* that which is consumed, esp. by animals; the milk in a baby's bottle; the material supplied to a machine or the channel by which it is fed. —**feed'er** *n.* one who feeds; a device for supplying a machine with material; a channel taking water to a reservoir; a branch railway-line connected with a main line; a baby's feeding-bottle; a baby's bib.—**feed'ing** *n.* act of eating; that which is consumed; grazing.—**feed'ing-bot'tle** *n.* a specially shaped bottle for supplying liquid food to babies [O.E. *fedan*, to feed].

feel (fēl) *v.t.* to perceive by the touch; to handle; to be sensitive to; to experience

Tea factory in Ceylon

FOOD and DRINK · 1

Cornfields in Ukraine

Modern breadmaking

Japanese fisherwomen

FOOD and DRINK · 2

Italian vineyard

Cheesemaking

Rice-planting in Trinidad

emotionally; to have an intuitive awareness of;—*v.i.* to know by the touch; to be conscious of being; to give rise to a definite sensation; to be moved emotionally.—*pr.p.* **feel'ing**.—*pa.p.* **felt**.—*n.* the sensation of touch; the quality of anything touched.—**feel'er** *n.* (*Zool.*) one of the tactile organs (antennae, tentacles, etc.) of certain insects and animals; a tentative remark, proposal, etc. to sound the opinions or attitude of others.—**feel'ing** *n.* sense of touch; awareness by touch; intuition; sensibility; sympathy.—**feel'ings** *n.pl.* emotions;—*a.* kindly; responsive; possessing great sensibility.—**feel'ingly** *adv.* [O.E. *felan*, to feel].

feet (fēt) *n.pl.* of foot.

feign (fān) *v.t.* to invent; to pretend; to counterfeit.—**feigned** *a.* pretended; dissembled.—**feign'edly** *adv.*—**feign'edness** *n.*—**feign'ing** *n.* pretence; invention.—**feint** *n.* an assumed appearance; a semblance; a misleading move in boxing, military operations, etc.—*v.i.* to make a deceptive move [Fr. *feindre*, to feign].

feldspar (feld'spàr) *n.* a constituent of granite and other igneous rocks; a crystalline mineral comprising silicates of aluminium with varying proportions of potash, lime, or soda. Also (but incorrectly) **fel'spar, feld'spath**.—**feld'spathic, feld'spathose** *a.* [Ger. *Feld*, field; *Spath*, a spar].

felicity (fe-lis'i-ti) *n.* happiness; bliss; contentment.—**felic'itate** *v.t.* to express joy or pleasure to; to congratulate.—**felicita'tion** *n.* congratulation; the act of expressing good wishes.—**felic'itous** *a.* happy; prosperous; aptly expressed.—**felic'itously** *adv.*—**felic'itousness** *n.* [L. *felix*, happy].

feline (fē'līn) *a.* pert. to cats; cat-like; (*Fig.*) treacherous [L. *feles*, a cat].

fell (fel) *a.* cruel; ruthless; inhuman; bloody; keen; spirited [O.Fr. *fel*, cruel].

fell (fel) *n.* an animal's skin or hide [O.E. *fel*, a skin].

fell (fel) *pa.t.* of the verb **fall**.

fell (fel) *v.t.* to cause to fall; to cut down; to hurl to the ground.—**fell'er** *n.* [O.E. *fellan*, to cause to fall].

fell (fel) *n.* a tract of high moorland, as in the Lake District [Scand. *fiall*, rock].

fellah (fel'a) *n.* (*pl.* **fell'ahs, fell'ahin**) an Egyptian peasant or land-worker [Ar. *fellah*, a ploughman].

fellow (fel'ō) *n.* orig. one who laid down money in a common enterprise; a partner; an associate; an equal; a person; a worthless or boorish person; a member of the governing body of a college at Oxford, Cambridge, or Dublin; member of a literary or scientific society.—**fell'ow-be'ing** *n.* any member of the human race.—**fell'ow-coun'tryman** *n.* one of the same nationality.—**fell'ow-crea'ture** *n.* one of the same race or kind.—**fell'ow-feel'ing** *n.* a feeling common to different people; sympathetic understanding.—**fell'ow-trav'eller** *n.* after World War 2, one who sympathises with the Communist Party, but does not belong to it.—**fell'ow-ship** *n.* the state of being an associate; social intercourse; companionship; a foundation for the maintenance of a resident university graduate; the status of a Fellow of a College or Society [M.E. *felawe*, a partner].

felo de se (fē'lō-dē-sē) *n.* a self-murderer; a suicide [L.L. lit. 'a murderer of himself'].

felon (fel'on) *n.* one who has committed felony; (*Med.*) inflammation of top joint of the finger; a whitlow;—*a.* fierce; traitorous.—**felo'nious** *a.* wicked.—**felo'niously** *adv.*—**felo'niousness** *n.*—**fel'ony** *n.* (*Law*) orig. a crime punishable by forfeiture of all land, property, etc.; a crime more serious than a *misdemeanour* (as murder, manslaughter, rape, arson, etc.) [O.Fr. *felon*, a traitor].

felspar See **feldspar**.

felt (felt) *pa.t.* and *pa.p.* of **feel**.

felt (felt) *n.* a closely matted fabric of wool, hair, etc. not made by weaving, but by pressure of heavy steam-heated rollers;—*v.t.* to make into felt; to cover with felt;—*v.i.* to become matted like felt.—**felt'ing** *n.* the art or process of making felt; the felt itself [O.E. *felt*, something compact].

felucca (fe-luk'a) *n.* a small but fast coasting vessel used in the Mediterranean [It. *feluca*, fr. Ar. *fulk*, a ship].

female (fē'māl) *n.* one of the sex that bears young; (*Bot.*) a plant which produces fruit;—*a.* pert. to the child-bearing sex; feminine.—**femine'ity** *n.* the quality of being a woman.—**fem'inine** *a.* pert. to or associated with women; womanly; tender; (of males) effeminate.—**fem'ininely** *adv.*—**fem'inineness, feminin'ity** *n.* the nature of the female sex; womanliness.—**fem'inism** *n.* the doctrine that maintains the equality of the sexes; advocacy of women's rights.—**fem'inist** *n.* [L. *femina*, a woman].

femur (fē'mur) *n.* the thigh-bone—**fem'oral** *a.* [L. *femur*, the thigh].

fen (fen) *n.* low-lying marshy land; a bog.—**fen'nish, fen'ny** *a.* boggy; swampy.—**fen'berry** *n.* the cranberry.—**fen'fire** *n.* the will o' the wisp. [O.E. *fenn*, a bog].

fence (fens) *n.* a means of defence; a wall or hedge for enclosing; the art of fencing; a receiver of stolen goods;—*v.t.* to enclose with a fence; to fend off danger from; to guard;—*v.i.* to make a fence; to practise the art of sword-play; (*Fig.*) to evade a direct answer to an opponent's challenge; to equivocate.—**fenc'er** *n.* one who is skilled in fencing; (*Fig.*) a clever debater.—**fenc'ing** *n.* the art or practise of self-defence with the sword; the act of enclosing by a fence; the materials of which a fence is made [abbrev. of *defence*].

fend (fend) *v.t.* to keep off; to ward off; to defend;—*v.i.* to resist; to parry; (*Scot.*) to provide for; to support.—**fend'er** *n.* that which acts as a protection; kerb to prevent coals falling beyond hearth; a device, usually a bundle of rope, to break the impact of a ship drawing alongside a wharf or other vessel [abbrev. of *defend*].

fenestra (fe-nes'tra) *n.* a window; a hole; an opening. Also **fene'ster**.—**fenes'tral** *n.* in building, a window-opening covered with material other than glass;—*a.* pert. to a window; perforated.—**fenes'trate, fenestra'ted** *a.* (*Bot.*) having transparent spots.—**fenestra'tion** *n.* the state of being perforated; arrangement of windows in a building [L. *fenestra*, a window].

Fenian (fē'ni-ạn) *n.* a member of a revolutionary association of Irishmen, founded in the middle 19th cent. for the overthrow of English domination in Ireland.—**Fe'nianism** *n.* [O.Ir. *fene*, a dweller in Ireland].

fennel (fen'el) *n.* a perennial umbelliferous plant with yellow flowers [O.E. *finul*, fr. L. *faenum*, hay].

feod, feodal, feodary Same as **feud, feudal, feudary** [See **feud**].

feoff (fēf) *n.* to invest with a fee or landed property; to enfeoff [O.Fr. *feoffé*, endowed].

ferae (fē'rē) *n.pl.* wild animals.—**fe'ral** *a.* wild; not domesticated; run wild (of plants); uncultivated (of people); savage.—**fe'rine** *a.* pert. to wild animals; savage [L. *ferus*, wild].

ferial (fē'ri-ạl) *a.* pert. to a day on which no special observance is ordained by the ecclesiastical authorities; oppos. of *Fast* day or *Feast* day [L. *feriae*, holidays].

ferly (fer'li) *n.* a marvel; a wonder;—*a.* fearful [O.E. *faerlic*, sudden].

ferment (fẹr'ment) *n.* a substance which causes fermentation, as yeast; fermentation; (*Fig.*) tumult; agitation; commotion.—**ferment'** *v.t.* to induce fermentation in; to arouse a commotion;—*v.i.* to undergo fermentation; to work (of wine); to cure (of tobacco); (*Fig.*) to become excited; to be in a state of agitation.—**fermentabil'ity** *n.*—**ferment'able** *a.*—**fermenta'tion** *n.* the decomposition of organic substances produced by the action of a living organism, or of certain chemical agents.—**ferment'ative** *a.* producing fermentation; caused by fermentation [L. *fermentum*, leaven].

fern (fern) *n.* plant belonging to the class, *Filices*, and characterised by fibrous roots, and leaves called fronds.—**fern'ticle** *n.* a freckle.—**fern'y** *a.* [O.E. *fearn*, fern].

ferocity (fe-ros'i-ti) *n.* cruelty; savage fierceness of disposition; barbarity.—**fero'cious** *a.* fierce; violent; wild.—**fero'ciously** *adv.*—**fero'ciousness** *n.* [L. *ferox*, wild].

ferrara (fe-rá'ra) *n.* a broadsword of superior temper, said to have been made in Venetia by *Andrea Ferrara.*

ferreous (fer'e-us) *a.* pert. to, like, containing, made of iron [L. *ferrum*, iron].

ferret (fer'et) *n*, a small, partially domesticated variety of polecat used for driving out rabbits and rats from their holes;—*v.t.* to hunt out with ferrets; (*Fig.*) to search out by simple examination.—*pr.p.* **ferr'eting.**—*pa.p.* **ferr'eted** [O.Fr. *furet*, a ferret].

ferric (fer'ik) *a.* pert. to or extracted from iron; applied to compounds of trivalent iron. —**ferric acid**, an acid containing iron and oxygen.—**ferrif'erous** *a.* yielding iron.—**ferruginous** *a.* containing iron; of the colour of iron-rust.—**ferru'go** *n.* a plant disease caused by fungus [L. *ferrum*, iron].

ferro- (fer'ō) *prefix* fr. L. *ferrum*, containing or made of iron, occurring in compound words—**ferr'o-con'crete** *n.* reinforced concrete; concrete with inner skeleton of iron or steel. —**ferr'omagnet'ic** *a.* reacting like iron in a magnetic field; used of iron, nickel, cobalt which are more magnetic than other metals. —**ferr'otype** *n.* a positive photograph in which the sensitive film is laid on a sheet of enamelled iron or tin.—**ferr'ous** *a.* pert. to iron; (*Chem.*) applied to compounds in which iron exists in its lower valency.

ferrule (fer'il, fer'ōōl) *n.* a metal tip or ring on a cane, etc. to prevent splitting.—Also **ferr'el** [O.Fr. *virelle*, a bracelet].

ferry (fer'i) *v.t.* to transport over stretch of water by boat or aircraft.—*pr.p.* **ferr'ying.**—*pa.p.* **ferr'ied.**—*n.* a place where one is conveyed across a river, etc. by boat; the ferry-boat; the right of transporting passengers and goods by this means.—**ferr'iage** *n.* transport by ferry; the fare paid for such transport [O.E. *faran*, to go].

fertile (fer'tīl, fer'til) *a.* producing or bearing abundantly; prolific; fruitful; (*Fig.*) inventive.—**fer'tilely** *adv.*—**fer'tileness, fertilisa'tion, fertiliza'tion** *n.* the act of fertilising; enrichment of soil, by natural or artificial means; (*Biol.*) union of the female and male cells.—**fer'tilise, fer'tilize** *v.t.* to make fruitful; (*Biol.*) to fecundate; (*Bot.*) to pollinate.—**fertilis'er, fertiliz'er** *n.* one who, or that which, fertilises; material (e.g. manure, nitrates) to enrich soil.—**fertil'ity** *n.* [L. *fertilis*, fruitful].

ferule (fer'ōōl) *n.* a rod or ruler used for punishing children [L. *ferula*, a rod].

fervent (fer'vent) *a.* glowing; ardent; zealous; enthusiastic.—**fer'vency** *n.* ardour; intensity of devotion.—**fer'vently** *adv.*—**fer'vid** *a.* burning; vehement; intense.—**fervid'ity** *n.*—**fer'vidly** *adv.*—**fer'vidness** *n.* zeal; enthusiasm.—**fer'vour** *n.* heat; ardour; passion [L. *fervere*, to boil].

fescue, festue (fes'kū, -tū) *n.* orig. a straw; a teacher's small pointer used to point out letters to children learning to read; a kind of tough grass [M.E. *festu*, a bit of straw].

fesse, fess (fes) *n.* (*Her.*) a horizontal band across the middle of an escutcheon [L. *fascia*, a band].

festal (fes'tal) *a.* pert. to a feast or festival; joyous; gay.—**fest'ally** *adv.* [O.Fr. *feste*, a feast].

fester (fes'ter) *v.t.* to cause to putrefy;—*v.i.* to become inflamed; to suppurate; (*Fig.*) to become embittered;—*n.* an ulcer; suppuration; putrefaction [O.Fr. *festre*, an ulcer].

festive (fes'tiv) *a.* festal; joyous; convivial.—**fes'tival** *n.* a feast or celebration; an annual competition or periodic gathering of musical or dramatic societies.—**fes'tively** *adv.*—**festiv'ity** *n.* merriment; merrymaking; festival [L. *festivus*, festive].

festoon (fes-tōōn') *n.* a garland hanging in a curve;—*v.t.* to adorn with garlands [Fr. fr. L.L. *festo*, a garland].

fetch (fech) *v.t.* to go for and bring; to summon; to bring or yield (a price);—*v.i.* to turn; —*n.* the act of bringing; a trick or artifice.—**fetch'ing** *a.* attractive; alluring [O.E. *feccan*, to bring].

fetch (fech) *n.* an apparition; a person's double. —**fetch'-can'dle**, or **-light** *n.* a mysterious light supposed to portend death [etym. doubtful].

fête (fet or fāt) *n.* a festival; a holiday;—*v.t.* to honour with celebrations.—**fet'ed** *a.* honoured [L. *festum*, a feast].

fetid (fē-tid) *a.* having a strong offensive smell.—Also **foetid** [L. *fetidus*, stinking].

fetish, fetich, fetiche (fē'tish, fet'ish) *n.* an object or image superstitiously invested with divine or demoniac power, and, as such, reverenced devoutly; anything regarded with exaggerated reverence.—**fet'ishism, fet'ichism** *n.* fetish worship; superstitious belief in charms.—**fetishist'ic, fetichist'ic** *a.* [Port. *feitiço*, magic].

fetlock (fet'lok) *n.* the tuft of hair behind the pastern joint in a horse's leg; the part where this tuft grows [etym. doubtful)].

fetter (fet'er) *n.* a chain or shackle for the feet (usually pl.); an impediment or restriction;—*v.t.* to shackle; to restrain [O.E. *fetor*, fr. *fet*, the feet].

fettle (fet'l) *n.* readiness or fitness for work; —*v.t.* to put in order; to arrange;—*v.i.* to potter about [O.E. *fetel*, a girdle].

fetus, foetus (fē'tus) *n.* the young of vertebrate animals between the embryonic and independent states.—**fe'tal, foe'tal** *a.*—**feta'tion, foeta'tion** *n.* pregnancy.—**fe'ticide, foe'ticide** *n.* destroying of the fetus; abortion [L. *fetus*, a bringing forth].

feu (fū) (*Scots law*) tenure of land on payment of annual rent instead of military service; perpetual possession at a stipulated payment (of feu-duty);—*v.t.* to grant or let in feu.—**feu'ar** *n.* one who pays feu-duty on a property [Scots form of *feud*].

feud (fūd) *n.* a lasting, hereditary strife between families or clans; deadly hatred [M.E. *fede*, enmity].

feud (fūd) *n.* an estate or land held on condition of service; a fief.—**feud'al** *a.* pert. to feuds or to feudalism.—**feud'alism** *n.* a system which prevailed in Europe in the Middle Ages, by which vassals held land from the King and the tenants-in-chief in return for military service.—Also **feudal system.**—**feud'ary, feud'atory** *a.* holding land by feudal tenure; —*n.* a vassal holding land in fee [L. L. *feudum*, a fief].

feuilleton (fe'ye-tōng) *n.* a literary article printed on the lower part of a newspaper page [Fr. *feuille*, a leaf].

fever (fē'ver) *n.* bodily disease marked by unusual rise of temperature and usually a quickening of pulse; violent mental or emotional excitement; frenzy;—*v.t.* to put into a fever.—*v.i.* to become fevered.—**fe'vered** *a.* affected with fever; frenzied.—**fe'ver-few** *n.* a wild perennial plant akin to the camomile, possessing medicinal properties as a febrifuge.—**fe'ver-heat** *n.* abnormal temperature caused by fever; feverish excitement.—**fe'verish** *a.* slightly fevered; agitated.—**fe'verishly** *adv.* [O.E. *fefor*, fever].

few (fū) *a.* not many;—*n.* and *pron*, a small number.—**few'ness** *n.* [O.E. *feawe*, few].

fey (fā) *a.* doomed; fated to die, esp. having

an abnormal gaiety of spirit, supposed to portend death [O.E. *faege*, doomed].
fez (fez) *n.* a red, brimless felt hat with tassel, worn in Egypt, Turkey, etc.;—*pl.* **fezz'es** [prob. fr. *Fez* in Morocco].
fiacre (fē-â'kr) *n.* a hackney coach [fr. *Hotel St. Fiacre* (Paris) where such coaches were first for hire].
fiancé (fē-ong'sā) *n.* (*fem.* **fiancée**) a betrothed man [Fr. *fiancer*, to betroth].
fiasco (fē-às'kō) *n.* a failure in a musical performance; any failure [It. *fiasco*, a bottle].
fiat (fī'at) *n.* a formal command; an authoritative order [L. *fiat*, let it be done].
fib (fib) *n.* a falsehood; a mild lie;—*v.i.* to tell a petty lie [prob. an abbrev. of *fable*].
fibre (fī'bęr) *n.* one of the bundles of thread-like tissue constituting muscles, etc.; any thread-like substance, animal, mineral, or vegetable, used for weaving fabric; (*Fig.*) character, as in *moral fibre*.—**fi'bred** *a.*—**fi'breless** *a.* having no fibres; (*Fig.*) lacking strength.—**fi'briform** *a.* resembling fibre in structure.—**fi'bril** *n.* a very small fibre.—**fi'brillose** *a.* (*Bot.*) covered with fibres.— **fi'brillous** *a.* composed of small fibres.—**fi'brin, fi'brine** *n.* a proteid substance found in newly-shed blood, giving rise to the process of clotting.—**fibr'oid** *a.* of a fibrous nature;—*n.* a fibrous tumour.—**fibrosi'tis** *n.* a rheumatic condition caused by inflammation of fibrous tissues.—**fi'brous** *a.* composed of fibres.—**fi'brousness** *n.* [L. *fibra*, a fibre].
fibula (fib'ū-lą) *n.* a buckle; (*Med.*) the slender outer bone of the leg between knee and ankle. **fib'ular** *a.* [L. *fibula*, a clasp].
fichu (fē'shòò) *n.* a triangular cape worn over the shoulders and tying in front; a ruffle of lace, etc. worn at the neck [Fr.].
fickle (fik'l) *a.* inconstant; capricious; unreliable.—**fick'leness** *n.* [O.E. *ficol*, cunning].
fictile (fik'tīl) *a.* capable of being moulded; plastic; used of all objects shaped in clay by a potter [L. *fictilis*].
fiction (fik'shun) *n.* a story dealing with imaginary characters and situations; something invented, or imagined.—**fic'tional** *a.*—**ficti'tious** *a.* imaginary; feigned; false; (*Law*) assumed as true.—**ficti'tiously** *adv.* [L. *fictus*, invented].
fiddle (fid'l) *n.* a stringed musical instrument; a violin; wooden framework fixed round dining-tables on board a ship to prevent dishes falling off in stormy weather;—*v.t.* and *v.i.* to play on a fiddle; to potter with things; (*Slang*) to act or treat unscrupulously.—**fidd'le-bow** *n.* the bow strung with horsehair used in playing a violin.—**fidd'le-de-dee** *n.* nonsense.—**fidd'le-fadd'le** *v.i.* to trifle; to dawdle;—*a.* petty;—*n.* triviality;—*interj.* rubbish!—**fidd'le-stick** *n.* bow for playing on strings of a violin.—**fidd'le-sticks** (*interj.*) nonsense.—**fidd'ling** *a.* trifling; futile.—**to play second fiddle**, to take a subordinate position [O.E. *fithele*, a fiddle].
fidelity (fi-del'i-ti) *n.* faithfulness; loyalty; devotion to duty; adherence to marriage vows; accuracy [L. *fidelis*, faithful].
fidget (fij'et) *v.i.* to move restlessly; to be inattentive;—*pr.p.* **fidg'eting.**—*pa.p.* **fidg'eted.** —*n.* uneasiness.—**fidg'ets** *n.pl.* nervous restlessness.—**fidg'ety** *a.* restless; nervous; fussy; over-particular [Dim. of *fidge*, to twitch; conn. with Scand. *fike*].
fiduciary (fi-dū'shi-ą-ri) *a.* holding or held in trust; confident; firm; unwavering; (of paper currency) depending for its value on public confidence;—*n.* a trustee.—**fidu'cial** *a.* having faith or confidence; having the nature of a trust [L. *fiducia*, confidence].
fief (fēf) *n.* an estate held on condition of military service [Fr. fr. L.L. *feudum*].
field (fēld) *n.* cleared land; a division of farm land; open country; scene of a battle; the battle itself; any wide expanse; area of observation; locality of operations, as in surveying; sphere of influence within which magnetic, electrostatic, or gravitational forces are perceptible; the surface of an escutcheon; the background of a flag, coin, etc. on which a design is drawn; the people following a hunt; (*Cricket*) the side which is not batting; a collective term for all the competitors in an athletic contest or all the horses in a race; an area rich in some natural product (e.g. coal-field, oil-field);—*v.t.* (*Cricket*) to stop the ball and return it to the bowler;—*v.i.* to act as fielder at cricket.—**field'-artill'ery** *n.* light guns for active operations.—**field'-batt'ery** *n.* battery of field-guns.—**field'-book** *n.* book used for notes by land surveyor or naturalist.—**field'-day** *n.* a day for practising military manoeuvres; a review; a gala day.—**field'-dress'ing** *n.* small first-aid pack containing two bandages.—**fielder'** *n.* one who fields at cricket, base-ball, etc.—**field'-fare** *n.* a species of migratory thrush.—**field'-glass** *n.* a binocular telescope.—**field'-gun** *n.* a small cannon on a carriage.—**field'-mar'shal** *n.* the highest rank in the British, French, or German army.—**field'-mouse** *n.* a small variety of mouse living in the fields.—**field'-offi'cer** *n.* a commissioned officer in rank between a captain and a general.—**field'-piece** *n.* a field-gun.—**field'-sports** *n.pl.* out-of-door sports such as hunting, racing, etc.—**field'-work** *n.* outdoor work of a surveyor, engineer, farmer, etc.—**field'-works** *n.pl.* temporary earthworks thrown up for defence. [O.E. *feld*, a field].
fiend (fēnd) *n.* a demon; the devil; a malicious foe; (*Colloq.*) one who is crazy about something, as, *a fresh-air fiend*.—**fiend'ish** *a.* [O.E. *feond*, an enemy].
fierce (fērs) *a.* ferocious; violent; savage; intense.—**fierce'ly** *adv.*—**fierce'ness** *n.* ferocity; rage [O.Fr. *fers*, bold].
fiery (fīr'i) *a.* flaming; (*Fig.*) ardent; fierce; vehement; irritable.—**fier'ily** *adv.*—**fier'iness** *n.*—**fiery cross**, a cross, charred and dipped in blood, sent through the Highlands of Scotland to broadcast among the clans news of impending war. [fr. *fire*].
fife (fīf) *n.* a small type of flute.—**fif'er** *n.* one who plays the fife [O.Fr. *fifre*, a fife].
fifteen (fif'tēn) *a.* and *n.* five and ten; a team of fifteen players, esp. a Rugby fifteen.—**fifteenth'** *a.* the fifth after the tenth; making one of fifteen equal parts.—**The Fifteen**, the Jacobite Rebellion of 1715 [O.E. *fif*, five; *tene*, ten].
fifth (fifth) *a.* next after the fourth;—*n.* one of five equal parts of a whole.—**fifth column**, a term originating from the Spanish Civil War (1936-39) when General Franco's forces advancing on Madrid in four columns were actively assisted within the town by a 'fifth column' of partisans; in World War 2, any organisation within a country deliberately assisting the enemy by acts of sabotage, etc. —**fifth'-col'umnist** *n.*—**fifth'ly** *adv.*
fifty (fif'ti) *a.* and *n.* five times ten.—**fif'tieth** *a.* next in a series of forty-nine others; making one of fifty equal parts of a whole;—*n.* a fiftieth part.—**to go fifty-fifty** (*Colloq.*) share and share alike [O.E. *fiftig*, fifty].
fig (fig) *n.* a small bag-shaped Mediterranean fruit; the tree bearing this fruit; (*Colloq.*) something insignificant [Fr. *figue*, a fig].
figwort (fig'wort) *n.* any plant of the genus *Scrophulariae* including the snap-dragon [fr. *fig*, an old word for piles].
fight (fīt) *v.t.* to wage war against; to contend against in single combat or in battle; to oppose as in an argument;—*v.i.* to take part in single combat or battle; to resist.—*pr.p.* **fight'ing.**—*pa.p.* **fought** (fawt).—*n.* a combat; a battle; a struggle; pugnacity.—**fight'er** *n.* one who fights; (*Aero.*) an aircraft designed for fighting and used for escorting bombers on a raid.—**fight'ing** *a.* able to, or inclined to, fight; pert. to a fight [O.E. *feohtan*, to fight].

figment (fig′-ment) *n.* an invention, fiction, or fabrication [L. *figmentum*, an image].

figure (fig′-ur) *n.* outward form of anything; the form of a person; a diagram, drawing, etc.; a design; an appearance; steps in a dance; the sign of a numeral, as 1, 2, 3; price; —*v.t.* to form into a shape; to cover with patterns; to note by numeral characters; to calculate; to symbolise; to image in the mind;—*v.i.* to make a figure.—**figured′** *a.* esp. adorned with patterns, as *figured muslin.*—**fig′urative** *a.* representing by a figure; not literal; abounding in figures of speech.—**fig′uratively** *adv.*—**fig′urativeness** *n.* —**fig′urehead** *n.* ornamental figure under the bowsprit of a ship.—**fig′urine** *n.* a statuette or figure-group usually in clay or metal.—**fig′ure-dance**, dance containing many difficult figures [L. *figura*, fr. *fingere*, to form].

filament (fil′-ą-ment) *n.* a slender thread; a fibre; (*Bot.*) the stalk of a stamen; (*Elect.*) a fine wire, usually of tungsten, which glows to incandescence by the passage of an electric current.—**filament′ary, filament′ose, filament′oid** *a.* like a filament.—**filament′ous** *a.* thread-like [L. *filum*, thread].

filbert (fil′-bert) *n.* the nut of the cultivated hazel; the hazel-tree [prob. fr. *St. Philibert* whose day is Aug. 22nd].

filch (filch) *v.t.* to steal; to pilfer.—**filch′er** *n.* a thief.—**filch′ingly** *adv.* [etym. unknown].

file (fīl) *n.* an orderly line, as of soldiers one behind the other; a wire, thread, or portfolio for keeping papers in order; the papers or cards thus kept;—*v.t.* to set in order on a file; to put papers amongst others in a public record office; to submit to a court;—*v.i.* to march in a file, esp. *to file in*, or *out.*—**Indian** or **single file**, a single line of men marching one behind the other.—**rank and file**, non-commissioned soldiers; the general mass of people as distinct from well-known figures [L. *filum*, a thread].

file (fīl) *n.* a steel instrument for abrading or smoothing rough surfaces, or cutting through metal; (*Slang*) an artful dodger;—*v.t.* to cut or abrade with a file; (*Fig.*) to improve.—*pr.p.* **fi′ling.**—*pa.p.* **filed.**—**fi′ling** *n.* a particle of metal rubbed off by a file; the action of abrading stone or cutting metal [O.E. *feol*, a file].

filial (fil′-yąl) *a.* pert. to or befitting a son or daughter.—**fil′ially** *adv.*—**filia′tion** *n.* being a child; affiliation [L. *filius*, a son].

filibeg See **fillibeg**.

filibuster (fil′-i-bus-tęr) *n.* a lawless adventurer; a pirate; a buccaneer; (*U.S.*) one who deliberately obstructs legislation;—*v.i.* to act as a filibuster [Fr. *flibustier*, a freebooter].

filicide (fil′-i-sīd) *n.* murder of one's child [L. *filius*, a son; *caedere*, to kill].

filiform (fil′-i-form) *a.* thread-like; capillary [L. *filum*, a thread].

filigree (fil′-i-grē) *n.* ornamental open-work of gold or silver wire; anything highly ornamental but fragile.—**fil′igreed** *a.* [L. *filum*, thread; *granum*, grain].

Filipino (fil-i-pēn′-ō) *n.* (*fem.* **Filipin′a**) a native of the Philippine Islands.

fill (fil) *v.t.* to make full; to replenish; to occupy as a position; to supply as a vacant office; to pervade; to stop (a tooth);—*v.i.* to become full;—*n.* a full supply; as much as satisfies, or fills up a space.—**fill′er** *n.* one who, or that which, fills; a funnel-shaped vessel for filling bottles;—**fill′ing** *n.* that which fills up a space, as gold, etc. used by dentists for stopping a tooth; the woof in weaving; a savoury or sweet mixture put into sandwiches, cakes, etc.;—*a.* satisfying; ample.—**filling station**, a roadside depot for supplying petrol, oil etc., to motorists [O.E. *fyllan*, to make full].

fillet (fil′-et) *n.* a narrow band, esp. round the head; piece of meat cut from the thigh; a piece of meat boned and rolled; fish after bones are removed;—*v.t.* to bind with a fillet; to bone (meat or fish, etc.);—*pr.p.* **fill′eting.**—*pa.p.* **fill′eted** [Fr. *filet*, a thread].

fillibeg (fil′-i-beg) *n.* a kilt worn by Scottish Highlanders.—Also **fil′ibeg, phil′ibeg** [Gael. *feileadh*, a kilt; *beag*, little).

fillip (fil′-ip) *v.t.* to strike with the nail of the finger, first placed against the ball of the thumb then released with a sudden jerk; to incite; to spur on.—*pr.p.* **fill′iping.**—*pa.p.* **fill′iped.**—*n.* a jerk of the finger; an incentive: a stimulus [form of *flip*].

filly (fil′-i) *n.* a young mare; a lively or wanton young woman [dim. of *foal*].

film (film) *n.* a thin coating or membrane; a delicate filament; dimness over the eyes; (*Photog.*) a roll of flexible, sensitised material used for photography, esp. cinematography; pictures taken on this roll;—*pl.* (*Colloq.*) a cinema show;—*v.t.* to cover with a film; to take a moving picture of; to reproduce on a film.—**film′iness** *n.* the quality of being filmy. —**filmogen′ic** *a.* having features which photograph well.—**film′y** *a.* composed of or covered with film; membranous; gaudy [O.E. *filmen*, membrane].

filose (fī′-lōs) *a.* having a thread-like ending [L. *filum*, thread].

filter (fil′-tęr) *n.* a device for separating liquids from solids, or for straining impurities from liquids; any porous material such as filter-paper, charcoal, etc.; a percolator; (*Photog.*) a piece of coloured glass placed in front of the lens, passing certain rays only;—*v.t.* to purify by passing through a filter; to filtrate;—*v.i.* to pass through a filter; to percolate; to join, as at road junction, another line of traffic.—**fil′trate** *v.t.* to purify; to filter;—*n.* the clear liquid which has been strained through a filter.—**filtra′tion** *n.*—**fil′ter-bed** *n.* a layer of sand or gravel at bottom of a reservoir for purifying the water.—**fil′ter-pa′per** *n.* porous cellulose paper used as a filter, esp. in chemistry [O.Fr. *filtre*, a strainer].

filth (filth) *n.* foul matter; dirt; pollution; (*Fig.*) immorality; obscenity.—**filth′ily** *adv.*— **filth′iness** *n.*—**filth′y** *a.* unclean; foul; corrupt [O.E. *fylth*, foulness].

fimbria (fim′-bri-ą) *n.* (*Zool.*) a fringe or fringe-like structure.—**fim′briate, fim′briated** *a.* fringed [L. *fimbria*, thread].

fin (fin) *n.* a paddle-like organ of fishes and other aquatic forms serving to balance and propel; (*Aero.*) a vertical surface, fixed usually on the tail of an aircraft to aid lateral and directional stability.—**fin′ny** *a.* having fins; containing fish [O.E. *finn*, a fin].

final (fī′-nąl) *a.* pert. to the end; last; decisive; conclusive; ultimate;—*n.* the last stage of anything;—*pl.* the last examination or contest in a series.—**fi′nalist** *n.* a competitor who reaches the finals of a contest.—**final′ity** *n.* the state of being complete; conclusiveness.— **fi′nalise** *v.t.* to give a final form to.—**fi′nally** *adv.* [L. *finis*, the end].

finale (fi-nà′-lā) *n.* the end; (*Mus.*) the last movement of a musical composition; final scene of an opera [It. *finale*, the end].

finance (fi-nans′ or fī′-nans) *n.* the science of controlling public revenue and expenditure; the management of money affairs;—*pl.* the income of a state or person; resources; funds; —*v.t.* to provide funds for; to subsidise; to supply capital for.—*pr.p.* **finan′cing.**—*pa.p.* **finan′ced.**—**finan′cial** *a.* pert. to finance; fiscal. —**finan′cially** *adv.*—**finan′cier** (*U.S.* fin-an-sēr′) *n.* an officer who administers the public revenue; one who deals in large-scale money transactions [Fr. fr. L.L. *finare*, to pay a fine].

finch (finch) *n.* the name applied to various species of small, seed-eating birds including the *chaffinch, bullfinch* [O.E. *finc*, finch].

find (fīnd) *v.t.* to come to by searching; to meet with; to discover; to perceive; to experience; to supply (as funds); (*Law*) to give a verdict;—*v.i.* (*Law*) to come to a decision.— *pr.p.* **find′ing.**—*pa.p.* **found.**—*n.* a discovery esp. of unexpected value.—**find'er** *n.*—**find'ing** *n.* the act of one who finds; a legal decision arrived at by a jury after deliberation.—**all found,** with everything provided [O.E. *findan*, to find)].

findon-haddock (fin'-in-had'-ok) *n.* smoked haddock, esp. those cured at Findon, Scotland.—Also **fin'nan-had'dock.**

fine (fīn) *a.* thin; slender; minute; delicate; noble; beautiful; polished; excellent; showy; striking; refined (as *fine gold*); keen; appealing aesthetically (as the *Fine Arts*); perceptive;—*v.t.* to make fine; to refine or purify;—*v.i.* to become fine, pure, or slender;—*adv.*—**fine'-drawn** *a.* invisibly mended (of cloth); delicately thin (of wire); subtly conceived (of an argument);—**fine'ly** *adv.*—**fine'ness** *n.* the state of being fine; the amount of gold in an alloy.—**fin'er** *n.* refiner.—**fin'ery** *n.* ornament; gay clothes; a furnace for making bar-iron.—**fine'-spoken,** *a.* using fine phrases.—**fine'-spun,** *a.* drawn out to a gossamer thread; (*Fig.*) subtle; ingenious.—**finesse'** *n.* subtlety of contrivance to gain a point; stratagem; (*Whist, Bridge, etc.*) the attempt to take a trick with a low card while holding a higher card;—*v.i.* and *v.t.* to use artifice; to try to take a trick by finesse [Fr. *fin*, exact].

fine (fīn) *n.* orig. a feudal due; a sum of money imposed as a penalty for an offence; conclusion, as in phrase *in fine*;—*v.t.* to impose a fine on [L.L. *finis*, a payment].

finesse See **fine.**

finger (fing'-gẹr) *n.* a digit; any one of the extremities of the hand, excluding thumb; the width of a finger;—*v.t.* to touch with fingers; to handle; to perform with fingers; to accept (as a bribe); to purloin; to meddle with;—*v.i.* to use the fingers.—**fing'er-al'phabet** *n.* the finger-language of the deaf and dumb.—**fing'er-board** *n.* that part of a violin etc. on which fingers are placed; the keyboard of a piano.—**fing'er-bowl** *n.* a small bowl of water to cleanse fingers at dinner.—**fing'ering** *n.* the act of touching or handling lightly with fingers; the manner of manipulating the fingers in piano-playing.—**fing'er-nail** *n.* nail at finger end.—**fing'er-plate** *n.* an ornamental plate fixed above handle of a door to prevent soiling with finger-marks.—**fing'er-post** *n.* a sign-post, as at a cross-roads.—**fing'er-print** *n.* an impression of the markings on the ball of the finger serving as means of identification, esp. of criminals.—**fing'er-stall** *n.* a protective covering for an injured finger [O.E. *finger*, a finger].

fingering (fing'-gẹr-ing) *n.* fine wool for knitting stockings, etc. [prob. Fr. *fin grain*, fine grain].

finial (fin'-i-ạl) *a.* (*Archit.*) ornamental flower or foliage at the apex of a gable, pinnacle, etc. [L. *finire*, to finish].

finical (fin'-i-kạl) *a.* affectedly fine; over-fastidious; foppish.—**fin'ically** *adv.*—**fin'icking, fin'icky, fin'ikin** *a.* over-particular about trivialities [prob. fr. *fine*].

fining (fīn'-ing) *n.* the process of refining [Fr. *fin*, exact].

finis (fī'-nis) *n.* an end; conclusion [L.].

finish (fin'-ish) *v.t.* to bring to an end; to terminate; to destroy; to complete;—*v.i.* to conclude;—*n.* that which finishes, or perfects; last stage; the final coat of paint, etc. —**fin'ished** *a.* terminated; perfect; polished; (*Colloq.*) exhausted.—**fin'isher** *n.* one who or that which finishes or gives the final touches; (*Colloq.*) a decisive blow [Fr. *finir*, to finish].

finite (fī'-nīt) *a.* limited in quantity, degree, or capacity; bounded; (*Gram.*) used of a *predicate* verb (limited by number and person), oppos. of *infinitive* of verb.—**fi'nitely** *adv.*—**fin'iteness, fin'itude** *n.* [L. *finire*, to finish].

Finn (fin) *n.* a native of Finland.—**Fin'nic, Fin'nish** *a.*—**Fin'lander** *n.* a Finn.

finnan-haddock See **findon-haddock.**

fiord, fjord (fyord) *n.* a long narrow inlet of the sea, with very steep sides [Scand. *fjord*].

fir (fẹr) *n.* cone-bearing, evergreen tree, yielding valuable timber.—**fir'-cone** *n.* fruit of the fir. [O.E. *furh-* (*wudu*), fir-(wood)].

fire (fīr) *n.* heat and light caused by combustion; burning; conflagration; ignited fuel; flame; discharge of fire-arms; ardour; spiritual or mental energy; impassioned eloquence;—*v.t.* to set on fire; to kindle; to supply with fuel; to discharge (firearms, etc.); to inflame; to incite; (*Colloq.*) to dismiss;—*v.i.* to be ignited; to be stimulated; to discharge firearms.—**fire'-alarm'** *n.* an alarm giving warning of an outbreak of fire.—**fire'-arm** *n.* a weapon which discharges by fire exploding gunpowder.—**fire'-ball** *n.* a meteor; (*Mil.*) a grenade; a ball filled with combustibles.—**fire'-bomb** *n.* an incendiary bomb.—**fire'-box** *n.* the fire chamber of a locomotive.—**fire'-brand** *n.* a piece of flaming wood; a torch; (*Fig.*) one who incites others to strife.—**fire'-brick** *n.* a brick capable of withstanding great heat, used in furnaces, grates, etc.—**fire'-brigade'** *n.* men specially trained to deal with fire.—**fire'-buck'et** *n.* a bucket containing water for fire-emergency.—**fire'-bug** *n.* (*U.S.*) an incendiary; one guilty of arson.—**fire'-clay** *n.* a variety of clay, chiefly pure silicate of alumina, capable of withstanding very high temperatures and used for fire-bricks, furnace-linings, etc.—**fire'-cur'tain** *n.* fireproof curtain in a theatre.—**fire'-damp** *n.* marsh-gas generated in coal-mines, which, mixed with air, explodes violently in contact with a naked light.—**fire'-dog** *n.* (Same as **andirons**).—**fire'-drill** *n.* training, as in a school, in rapid dispersal in event of fire.—**fire'-eat'er** *n.* a juggler who pretends to eat fire; a bully.—**fire'-en'gine** *n.* a hydraulic or forcing pump for throwing water to extinguish a fire; the vehicle carrying firemen and equipment to scene of fire.—**fire'-escape'** *n.* a machine used to rescue people from the upper flats of a burning building; an outside iron stair used as emergency exit from burning building.—**fire'-fly** *n.* a type of beetle which is phosphorescent (e.g. glow-worm).—**fire'-guard** *n.* a protective grating, fixed or movable, in front of fire.—**fire'-hose** *n.* a large hose carried on fire-engine or trailer for extinguishing conflagration.—**fire'-insu'rance** *n.* insurance against loss of property by fire.—**fire'-i'rons** *n.pl.* poker, tongs, shovel, etc.; a companion set.—**fire'man** *n.* a member of a fire-brigade; a man who tends a furnace; a stoker.—**fire'-place** *n.* hearth or grate.—**fire'-plug** (*abbrev.* **F.P.**) *n.* a plug for drawing water by hose from a main to extinguish a fire; a hydrant.—**fire'proof** *a.* proof against fire; non-inflammable.—**fire'-proof'ing** *n.* rendering anything (e.g. walls, theatre curtain, etc.) fireproof; materials used.—**fir'er** *n.* an incendiary.—**fire'-rais'ing** *n.* arson.—**fire'-screen** *n.* a movable screen to intercept the direct rays of a fire; a fireguard; an ornamental screen used in summer time to cover the grate.—**fire'side** *n.* the hearth; (*Fig.*) home life.—**fire'-step** *n.* a platform on which a soldier stands to fire over trench parapet.—**fire'-stone** *n.* a kind of fireproof sandstone used in making of glass furnaces.—**fire'-war'den** *n.* (*U.S.*) forest fire-fighter; member of fire-fighting squad during enemy air-attacks.—**fire'-watch'er** *n.* a fire-spotter; one trained to be on call in event of air-raids (*World War* 2).—**fire'-wat'er** *n.* term used by Red Indians for whisky, brandy, etc.—**fire'-wood** *n.* wood for fuel; kindling.—**fire'work** *n.* a preparation containing gunpowder, sulphur, etc. for making spectacular explosions in the air, esp. at night displays or celebrations;—*pl.* pyrotechnics; (*Fig.*) a brilliant display of wit, or eloquence.—**fir'ing** *n.* the act of lighting a fire, stoking a furnace, or discharging a gun; fuel; baking of bread, etc. in an oven.—**fir'ing-line** *n.* the area of a battle zone within firing range of the enemy.—**firing party** or **squad,** soldiers detailed to fire the final salute at a military funeral, or to shoot a soldier condemned to death by court-martial.—**baptism of fire,** first time in battle; a first appearance on public platform.—**cross'-fire** *n.* fire from different directions.—**run'ning-fire** *n.* rapid succession of shots; (*Fig.*) running commentary or succession of questions, etc. [O.E. *fyr*, a fire].

firkin (fer'kin) *n.* a measure equal to the fourth part of a barrel; 9 imperial gallons; 56 lb. of butter; a small cask [O.Dut. *vierde*, four; and dim. suffix *kin*].

firm (ferm) *a.* fixed; solid; compact; rigid; steady; unwavering; stern; inflexible.—**firm'ly** *adv.*—**firm'ness** *n.* [L. *firmus*, steadfast].

firm (ferm) *n.* the name, title, or style under which a company transacts business [It. *firma*, a signature].

firmament (fer'ma-ment) *n.* the region of the air; the expanse of the sky; the heavens [L. *firmamentum*, a support, the sky].

first (ferst) *a.* preceding all others in a series or in kind; foremost (in place); earliest (in time); most eminent; most excellent; highest; chief;—*adv.* before anything else in time, place, degree, or preference;—*n.* beginning; a first-class honours degree at a university.—**first'-aid** *n.* preliminary treatment given to injured person before the arrival of a doctor.—**first'-begott'en, -born** *n.* the eldest child;—*a.* born first; eldest.—**first'-class** *a.* first-rate; of highest worth; of superior accommodation;—*adv.* in the first-class (of a train, boat, etc.);—*n.* the highest honours in an examination.—**first'-floor** *n.* the storey immediately above ground-floor; (*U.S.*) ground floor.—**first'-foot** *n.* (*Scot.*) the first visitor to cross threshold on New-Year's Day.—**first'-fruits** *n.pl.* earliest gathered fruits, orig. dedicated to God; (*Fig.*) earliest results or profits.—**first'-hand** *a.* obtained direct from the source.—**first'-house** *n.* the first of two performances given in one evening at a theatre.—**first'ling** *n.* the first-born of animals; the first product.—**first'ly** *adv.*—**first'-rate** *a.* pre-eminent in quality, size, etc.; of highest excellence [O.E. *fyrst*, first].

firth (ferth) *n.* (*Scot.*) a long narrow inlet of the sea or estuary of a river [O.N. *fird*].

fisc (fisk) *n.* the State treasury; public revenue.—**fisc'al** *a.* pert. to the public treasury or revenue;—*n.* a treasurer; (*Scot.*) one who prosecutes for the Crown in minor criminal cases; a Procurator-fiscal [Fr. fr. L. *fiscus*, a purse].

fish (fish) *n.* a cold-blooded, aquatic vertebrate animal, with limbs represented by fins, and breathing through its gills; the flesh of fish;—*pl.* **fish, fish'es.**—*v.t.* to catch by fishing;—*v.i.* to follow the occupation of a fisherman, for business or pleasure; (*Colloq.*) to extract information, etc. by indirect, subtle questions (foll. by *for*).—**fish'-car'ver** *n.* a broad flat fish-slice for serving fish at table.—**fish'-creel** *n.* an angler's basket.—**fish'-cu'rer** *n.* one engaged in the salting and smoking of fish.—**fish'er** *n.* one who fishes.—**fish'erman** *n.* one whose employment is to catch fish; one who fishes for pleasure; an angler.—**fish'ery** *n.* the business of fishing; a fishing-ground; the legal right to fish in a certain area.—**fish'-glue** *n.* isinglass; adhesive made from fish-bones.—**fish'-guan'o, fish'-manure'** *n.* fertiliser made from fish.—**fish'-hook** *n.* a barbed hook for catching fish by line.—**fish'ily** *adv.*—**fish'iness** *n.*—**fish'ing** *n.* the act of fishing; the legal right to fish in certain waters; a particular stretch of water reserved for anglers.—**fish'ing-boat** *n.* a boat used for fishing.—**fish'ing-net** *n.* a net used by trawlers for catching fish.—**fish'ing-rod** *n.* a long supple rod with line attached, used by anglers.—**fish'ing-tack'le** *n.* an angler's gear comprising, rod, lines, hooks, etc.—**fish'-ladd'er, fish'-way** *n.* a series of steps enabling salmon to ascend a water-fall.—**fish'-market** *n.* a place where fish is sold in bulk, usually by auction.—**fish'-meal** *n.* dried fish ground into meal.—**fish'mong'er** *n.* a retail dealer in fish.—**fish'-slice** *n.* a fish-carver.—**fish'-tail** *a.* shaped like the tail of a fish.—**fish'wife** *n.* a woman selling fish in the streets.—**fish'y** *a.* abounding in fish; pert. to fish (of smell); expressionless; glazed (of eye); dubious (of a story).—**bottom-fish,** fish which feed on the bottom of relatively shallow water [O.E. *fisc*, fish].

fish (fish) *n.* a strip of wood fixed longitudinally to strengthen a mast, or clamp two pieces together;—*v.t.* to splice; to join together.—**fish'-plate, -joint** *n.* a metal clamp used to join lengths of train rails together [Fr. *fiche*, a pin or peg].

fissile (fis'il) *a.* capable of being split or cleft in the direction of the grain [L. *findere*, *fissum*, to cleave].

fission (fish'un) *n.* the process of splitting or breaking up into two parts; (*Biol.*) cell-cleavage; in nuclear physics, the splitting of an atomic nucleus into two approx. equal fragments and a number of neutrons, with the liberation of a large amount of energy;—*v.t.* and *i.* to split into two parts.—**fiss'-ionable** *a.* [L. *findere, fissum*, to cleave].

fissiparous (fis-ip'a-rus) *a.* (*Biol.*) reproducing by fission or cell-cleavage [L. *fissus*, cleft; *parere*, to bring forth].

fissure (fish'ūr) *n.* a cleft, crack, or slit [L. *findere, fissum*, to cleave].

fist (fist) *n.* the hand clenched with fingers doubled into the palm; (*Colloq.*) handwriting.—**fist'ic** *a.* pugilistic.—**fist'icuff** *n.* a blow with the fist;—**fisti'cuffs** *n.pl.* boxing; a brawl.—**fist'y** *a.* [O.E. *fyst*, the fist].

fistula (fis'tū-la) *n.* a narrow duct; an old name for a water-pipe; (*Med.*) an infected channel in the body leading from an internal abscess to the surface.—**fis'tular, fis'tulose** *a.* (*Bot.*) hollowed like a pipe [L. *fistula*, a pipe].

fit (fit) *a.* adapted to an end or purpose; suitable; qualified; proper; vigorous (of bodily health);—*v.t.* to make suitable; to qualify; to adapt; to adjust; to fashion to the appropriate size;—*v.i.* to be proper or becoming.—*pr.p.* **fit'ting.**—*pa.p.* **fit'ted.**—**fit'ly** *adv.*—**fit'ment** *n.* equipment;—**fit'ments** *n.pl.* furnishings.—**fit'ness** *n.* the state of being fit; appropriateness; sound bodily health.—**fit'ter** *n.* one who or that which makes fit; a tailor or dressmaker who fits clothes on a person; a mechanic who assembles separate parts of a machine.—**fit'ting** *a.* appropriate; suitable;—*n.* anything used in fitting up; that part of the electric lighting installation which holds the bulb, shade, etc.; -**fit'tings** *n.pl.* fixtures; equipment.—**fit'tingly** *adv.*—**to fit in,** to insert neatly; to dovetail; to adapt oneself to one's company.—**to fit on,** to try on a new garment for fitting;—*n.* a fitting.—**to fit out,** to equip with stores;—*n.* equipment.—**to fit up,** to furnish with the necessary gadgets or equipment [etym. uncertain].

fit (fit) *n.* a sudden and violent attack of a disorder; a paroxysm; a seizure; a spasmodic attack (as of sneezing); a momentary impulse.—**fit'ful** *a.* spasmodic; intermittent.—**fit'fully** *adv.* [O.E. *fitt*, a struggle].

fit (fit) *n.* a song, or division of a poem; a canto [M.E. *fitte*, a stanza].

fitchew (fich'ōō) *n.* a polecat; its fur. Also **fitch'et** [O.Dut. *fisse*, a polecat].

five (fīv) *n.* four and one;—*a.* one more than four.—**fives** *n.pl.* a game of handball played against a wall.—**five'fold** *a.* five times repeated; quintuple.—**fiv'er** *n.* (*Slang*) a five-pound note; (*U.S.*) a five-dollar bill.—**the five senses**, sight, hearing, taste, touch and smell.—**five'-a-side** *n.* a football match with five players in each team [O.E. *fif*].

fix (fiks) *v.t.* to make firm; to establish; to secure; to make permanent, as a photograph; to make fast, as a dye; to immobilise; to determine; to implant; to gaze at; (*U.S.*) to put in order;—*v.i.* to settle permanently; to become hard;—*n.* (*Colloq.*) dilemma; predicament; determination of the position of a ship or aeroplane by observations or radio signals.—**fixa'tion** *n.* the act of fixing; the state of being fixed; steadiness; in psycho-analysis, an emotional arrest of part of the psycho-sexual development.—**fix'ative** *n.* a fixing agent or chemical which preserves specimens in a life-like condition;—*a.* capable of fixing colours or structure of specimens.—**fix'ature** *n.* gummy preparation for fixing the hair.—**fixed** *a.* settled; motionless; not apt to evaporate; steady.—**fix'edly** *adv.*—**fix'edness** *n.*—**fix'er** *n.* one who, or that which, fixes.—**fixid'ity, fix'ity** *n.* fixedness; immobility.—**fix'ings** *n.pl.* apparatus; trimmings.—**fix'ture** *n.* that which is fixed or attached; anything of an accessory nature annexed to house or lands; a sporting event, such as a football match, fixed for a certain date [L. *fixus*, fixed].

fizz (fiz) *v.i.* to make a hissing sound; to splutter; to effervesce;—*n.* a hissing sound; any effervescent liquid, esp. champagne or lemonade; (*Slang*) bustle.—**fiz'zle** *v.i.* to fizz or splutter.—**fizzle out**, to go out like a damp squib; (*Fig.*) to come to an ignominious end.—**fiz'zy** *a.* [imit. word].

fjord See **fiord**.

flabbergast (flab'er-gȧst) *v.t.* to overcome with amazement; to confound; to disconcert [prob. conn. with *flabby*].

flabby (flab'i) *a.* soft; yielding to the touch; drooping; (*Fig.*) weak; lacking in moral fibre.—**flab'bily** *adv.*—**flab'biness** *n.* [fr. *flap*].

flabellate (fla-bel'āt) *a.* fan-shaped.—Also **flabell'iform** [L. *flabellum*, a fan].

flaccid (flak'sid) *a.* soft; flabby; spineless; lax.—**flac'cidly** *adv.*—**flac'cidness, flac'cidity** *n.* [L. *flaccidus*, flabby].

flacket (flak'et) *n.* a bottle; a flask.

flag (flag) *v.i.* to hang loosely; to grow spiritless or dejected; to become languid; to lose vigour.—*pr.p.* **flag'ging**.—*pa.p.* **flagged** [etym. doubtful].

flag (flag) *n.* a flat, oblong paving-stone; a type of sandstone which splits easily into large slabs.—Also **flag'stone**;—*v.t.* to pave with flag-stones [Ice. *flaga*, a slab].

flag (flag) *n.* (*Bot.*) a popular name of certain British species of plants, belonging to the genus *Iris*, with long sword-shaped leaves.—**flag'gy** *a.* abounding in flags [etym. doubtful].

flag (flag) *n.* an ensign or colours; a standard; a banner as a mark of distinction, rank, or nationality; the bushy tail of a setter dog;—*v.t.* to decorate with flags or bunting; to convey a message by flag-signals.—**flag'-cap'tain** *n.* captain of admiral's flag-ship.—**flag'-day** *n.* a day on which miniature flags are given in return for donation to some charity-fund.—**flag'-lieuten'ant** *n.* an officer in a flag-ship.—**flag'-of'ficer** *n.* the commander of a squadron.—**flag'-ship** *n.* the ship flying the admiral's flag.—**flag'-staff** *n.* the pole on which a flag is flown.—**flag'-wag'ging** *n.* signalling; (*Colloq.*) undue rejoicing.—**white flag**, the symbol of truce or surrender.—**yellow flag**, a flag indicating that a ship is in quarantine.—**to dip the flag**, to lower, then hoist, flag as a mark of respect.—**to fly a flag half-mast**, to hoist flag half-way as token of mourning.—**to strike one's flag**, to surrender [etym. doubtful, prob. Scand.].

flagellate (flaj'e-lāt) *v.t.* to whip; to scourge; to flog;—*a.* (*Bot.*) having a long thread-like appendage, like a lash.—**flagel'lantism, flagella'tion** *n.*—**flagel'lant** or **flag'ellant** *n.* an ascetic who voluntarily scourges himself as punishment for sin [L. *flagellare*, to scourge].

flageolet (flaj'ō-let) *n.* a small non-reed wind instrument with mouthpiece and six holes [dim. of O.Fr. *flageol*, a pipe].

flagitious (fla-jish'us) *a.* shamefully criminal; guilty of heinous crimes; atrocious [L. *flagitiosus*, disgraceful].

flagon (flag'on) *n.* a narrow-necked vessel for holding liquids, usually with handle and spout [Fr. *flacon*, a flask].

flagrant (flā'grant) *a.* glaring; notorious; scandalous.—**fla'grance, fla'grancy** *n.* notoriety; enormity; heinousness.—**fla'grantly** *adv.* [L. *flagrare*, to burn].

flail (flāl) *n.* an implement for threshing grain by hand, consisting of a stout stick attached to a handle so that it swings freely [L. *flagellum*, a whip].

flair (flār) *n.* instinctive discernment; a keen scent [Fr. *flairer*, to scent out].

flak (flak) *n.* anti-aircraft fire (*World War* 2) [Ger. (*abbrev.*) *Flugabwehrkanone*, anti-aircraft gun].

flake (flāk) *n.* a film; a scale-like particle; a carnation with two-coloured striped petals;—*v.t.* to form into flakes; to cover with flakes;—*v.i.* to scale.—**flak'y** *a.* consisting of flakes [Scand. *flaki*, flake].

flam (flam) *n.* a freak; a whim; a sham; humbug [prob. fr. *flamfew*, a trifle (prov.)].

flambeau (flam'bō) *n.* a flaming torch; an ornamental candlestick;—*pl.* **flam'beaux** [Fr. fr. L. *flamma*, a flame].

flamboyant (flam-boi'ant) *a.* (*Archit.*) characterised by flame-like tracery and florid ornamentation of windows, panels, etc.; wavy; florid.—**flamboy'ance, flamboy'ancy** *n.* [Fr. *flamboyer*, to flame].

flame (flām) *n.* a mass of burning vapour or gas; a blaze of light; fire in general; (*Fig.*) ardour; vehemence of mind or imagination; (*Colloq.*) a sweetheart;—*v.i.* to blaze; to blush; to become violently excited, fervent, or angry.—**flame'-col'oured** *a.* of the colour of a flame; bright red or yellow.—**flame'-projec'tor** or **-throw'er** *n.* a short range trench weapon throwing ignited fuel into the enemy's lines.—**flam'ing** *a.* blazing; gaudy; fervent.—**flam'ingly** *adv.*—**flaming onion**, an anti-aircraft projectile, resembling a string of onions.—**flammabil'ity** *n.*—**flammif'erous** *a.* flame-bearing.—**flam'y** *a.* [L. *flamma*, a flame].

flamingo (fla-ming'gō) *n.* tropical wading bird with long neck and legs, and deep pink plumage;—*pl.* **flaming'o(e)s** [L. *flamma*, a flame].

flan (flan) *n.* a pastry shell or case filled, after baking, with savoury or fruit filling [O.Fr. *flaon*, a flat cake].

flaneur (flȧ-ner') *n.* a lounger; an idler; one who saunters along a street.—**flan'erie** *n.* idling [Fr. *flaner*, to idle].

flange (flanj) *n.* a projecting edge, as of a railway-carriage wheel to keep it on the rails, or of castings to fasten them together;—*v.t.* to furnish with a flange [O.Fr. *flanche*, fr. *flanc*, a side].

flank (flangk) *n.* the fleshy part of side of animal between ribs and hip; the right or left side of an army; part of a bastion; the side of a building;—*v.t.* to stand at the side of; to protect the flank of an army, etc.; to border;—*v.i.* to be posted on the side or flank [O.Fr. *flanc*, the side].

flannel (flan'el) *n.* a soft-textured, loosely woven woollen cloth.—**flann'els** *n.pl.* clothes made of this, esp. sports garments;—*a.* made of flannel;—*v.t.* to cover or rub with flannel.—**flannelette'** *n.* a cotton material imitating flannel [W. *gwlanen*, fr. *gwlan*, wool].

flap (flap) *n.* a stroke; the motion or noise of anything broad and hanging loose; a piece of flexible material attached on one side only and usually covering an opening, as of envelope; anything hinged and hanging loose; (*Colloq.*) a state of excitement.—*v.t.* to strike with something broad and flexible, such as a duster; to move rapidly up and down;—*v.i.* to flutter; to fall like a flap; to move, as wings.—*pr.p.* **flap'ping.**—*pa.p.* **flapped.**—**flap'doodle** *n.* (*Colloq.*) food of fools; humbug; sheer nonsense.—**flap'jack** *n.* a kind of broad, flat pancake; an apple-puff; a biscuit made of rolled oats, usually circular; a powder compact.—**flap'per** *n.* one who or that which flaps; (*Slang*) the hand; (*Colloq.*) an adolescent girl; a flighty, young woman [imit. word].

flare (flār) *v.i.* to burn with a glaring, unsteady or fitful flame; to exhibit showy colours;—*n.* an unsteady, blazing light; a brilliant, often coloured, light used as a signal; a spreading or curving out, as the hull of a ship, or aircraft, or hem of a skirt.—**flared** *a.* (of a skirt) cut on the cross of the material, hence, spreading or fluting out.—**flare'-path** *n.* a line of lights along the runway of an aerodrome.—**flar'ing** *a.* blazing; garish; (*Fig.*) furious.—**flar'ingly** *adv.* [Scand. *flara,* to blaze].

flash (flash) *n.* a sudden brief burst of light; an instant or moment; a fleeting emotional outburst; thieves' language; rush of water; a badge, as on soldier's uniform;—*a.* showy; tawdry; meretricious; pert. to thieves or card-sharpers;—*v.i.* to blaze suddenly and die out; to give out a bright but fitful gleam; to shine out, as a stroke of wit or sudden idea; to pass swiftly;—*v.t.* to cause to flash; to transmit instantaneously, as news by radio, telephone, etc.—**flash'-back** *n.* (*Cinema*) momentary reproduction on screen of earlier episode in film-story.—**flash'-bulb** *n.* (*Photog.*) an electric bulb giving brilliant flash for night picture.—**flash burn,** injury caused by the radiation of heat following the explosion of an atomic bomb.—**flash'ily** *adv.*—**flash'iness** *n.*—**flash'light** *n.* a light which flashes intermittently, as in a lighthouse; an electric torch; a brilliant momentary light produced by igniting magnesium powder and used by photographers, esp. indoors.—**flash'-point** *n.* the lowest temperature at which the vapour of volatile oils ignite when a small flame is applied.—**flash'y** *a.* showy; tawdry; cheap.—**a flash in the pan,** an abortive attempt; a sensational but momentary success (fr. the old flint-lock musket, which might or might not go off when fired) [etym. doubtful].

flask (flask) *n.* a narrow-necked, usually flat, bottle easily carried in the pocket; a wicker-covered bottle; a powder-horn.—**flask'et** *n.* a small flask; a long, shallow basket with handles used formerly for serving viands [It. *fiasco,* a bottle or flask].

flat (flat) *a.* level; even; tasteless; monotonous; dull; without point or spirit; uniform; downright; (*Mus.*) below the true pitch (opp. of *sharp*);—*n.* a level surface; low-lying, sometimes flooded, tract of land; a shoal; (part of) storey of house; (*Mus.*) a note, a semitone below the natural; the symbol ♭ for this; a black key of a piano; a piece of canvas mounted on a frame used as stage scenery.—*adv.* prone; abruptly. (*Mus.*) in a manner below true pitch.—**flat'-fin'ish** *n.* a matt-surface in paintwork.—**flat'-fish** *n.* a type of fish with compressed, flattened bodies, e.g. flounder, plaice, sole, etc.—**flat'-foot'ed** *a.* having fallen arches in the feet.—**flat'i'ron** *n.* an iron for smoothing linen, etc.—**flat'let** *n.* a small flat.—**flat'ly** *adv.* peremptorily.—**flat'ness** *n.*—**flat out,** of a motor car, etc. at full speed, i.e. with accelerator pressed down flat.—**flat'-race** *n.* a race over open ground.—**flat rate,** uniform rate.—**flat'-spin** *n.* (*Aero.*) a spiral dive where aircraft rotates in a plane more horizontal than vertical; a skid.—**flat'ten** *v.t.* to make flat; to lower the true musical pitch of; (*Fig.*) to dismay; to depress.—**flat'-ware** *n.* utensils such as plates, saucers, etc. [Scand. *flatr,* flat].

flatter (flat'er) *v.t.* to praise unduly and insincerely; to pay fulsome compliments to; to depict as being an improvement on the original.—**flatt'erer** *n.* one who praises; a sycophant.—**flatt'ering** *a.* over-complimentary; ingratiating.—**flatt'eringly** *adv.*—**flatt'ery** *n.* the act of flattering; undue praise; adulation [O.Fr. *flater,* to smooth].

flatulent (flat'ū-lent) *a.* pert. to or affected with wind or gas in stomach and intestines; (*Fig.*) empty; vapid.—**flat'ulence, flat'ulency** *n.* distension of stomach or intestines by excessive accumulation of wind or gas.—**flat'ulently** *adv.*—**flat'us** *n.* a puff of wind; air or gas in stomach, etc. [L. *flare,* to blow].

flaunt (flawnt) *v.t.* to display ostentatiously or impudently;—*v.i.* to wave or move in the wind; to parade showily;—*n.* a vulgar display [etym. doubtful, prob. Scand. *flanta,* to gad about].

flautist (flaw'tist) *n.* a flute-player [L.L. *flauta,* a flute].

flavour (flā'vur) *n.* relish; savour; quality affecting taste or smell; (*Fig.*) distinctive quality affecting senses.—*v.t.* to season; (*Fig.*) to give zest to.—**fla'vorous** *a.*—**fla'vouring** *n.* substance to add flavour to a dish, e.g. spice, essence [O.Fr. *flaur,* smell].

flaw (flaw) *n.* a crack; a defect; a weak point as in an argument;—*v.t.* to break; to crack; (*Law*) to make invalid.—**flaw'less** *a.* perfect [Scand. *flaga,* a slab].

flaw (flaw) *n.* a sudden gust of wind; a squall [Dut. *vlaag,* a gust of wind].

flax (flaks) *n.* the fibres of an annual purple-flowered plant, *Linum,* used for making linen; the plant itself.—**flax'en** *a.* pert. to or resembling flax; loose or flowing; of the colour of unbleached flax, hence yellowish or golden (esp. of hair) [O.E. *flaex,* flax].

flay (flā) *v.t.* to skin; (*Fig.*) to criticise bitterly [O.E. *flean,* to strike].

flea (flē) *n.* a small, wingless, very agile insect with irritating bite.—**flea'-bane** *n.* a plant with strong smell, said to drive away fleas.—**flea'-bite** *n.* the reddish spot caused by bite of a flea; (*Fig.*) a trifle.—**flea'-bitten** *a.* bitten by a flea; (*Fig.*) mean; worthless [O.E. *fleah,* a flea].

flèche (flesh) *n.* (*Archit.*) a slender spire rising from the intersection of nave and transept in Gothic churches [Fr. *flèche,* an arrow].

fleck (flek) *n.* a spot; a streak;—*v.t.* to spot; to dapple [Scand. *flekka,* to spot].

flection See **flexion.**

fled (fled) *pa.t.* and *pa.p.* of **flee.**

fledge (flej) *v.t.* to supply with feathers for flight, as an arrow; to rear a young bird;—*v.i.* to acquire feathers; to become able to fly (of birds).—**fledge'ling** *n.* a young bird just fledged; (*Fig.*) a young untried person [O.E. *flycge,* feathered].

flee (flē) *v.i.* to fly or retreat from danger;—*v.t.* to shun; to hasten from;—*pr.p.* **flee'ing.**—*pa.p.* **fled** [O.E. *fleon,* to fly].

fleece (flēs) *n.* the coat of wool covering a sheep or shorn from it; anything resembling wool;—*v.t.* to shear wool (from sheep); (*Fig.*) to rob; to swindle.—**fleec'y** *a.* woolly; resembling wool in appearance or softness [O.E. *fleos,* fleece].

fleer (flēr) *v.t.* to mock; to flout;—*v.i.* to sneer;—*n.* sneering; a contemptuous look.—**fleer'ingly** *adv.* [Scand. *flira,* to titter].

fleet (flēt) *n.* a group of ships; a force of naval vessels under one command; (*Fig.*) a number of motor-vehicles, etc. organised as a unit [O.E. *fleot,* a ship].

fleet (flēt) *n.* a creek, inlet, or small stream, as in place-name *Northfleet* [O.E. *fleot*, an inlet].

fleet (flēt) *a.* swift; nimble.—**fleet'ing** *a.* transient; ephemeral; passing.—**fleet'ingly** *adv.*—**fleet'ness** *n*, swiftness.—**fleet'-footed** *a.* swift of foot [prob. Ice. *fliotr*, swift].

fleet (flēt) *v.i.* to pass swiftly; to glide by; —*v.t.* to make to pass quickly; to while away [O.E. *fleotan*, to swim].

Fleming (flem'ing) *n.* a native of Flanders. —**Flem'ish** *a.* pert. to Flanders or to the people of Flanders;—*n.* the inhabitants of Flanders; the language of Flanders [Dut. *Vlaamsch*].

flense, flench (flens, flensh) *v.t.* to cut up the blubber of, as a whale [Dan. *flense*].

flesh (flesh) *n.* the body tissue; the muscles, fat, etc. covering the bones of an animal; the meat of animals or birds; animal nature; the body as distinct from the soul; mankind; kindred; sensuality; the pulpy part of fruit;—*v.t.* to incite to hunt, as a hound, by feeding it on flesh; to glut; to thrust into flesh, as a sword; to remove flesh from the under side of hides preparatory to tanning process.—**flesh'-col'our** *n.* the pale pink colour of the human skin (of white races).—**flesh'-eat'er** *n.* a carnivore.—**fleshed** *a.* having flesh; plump.—**flesh'er** *n.* (*Scot.*) a butcher.—**flesh'iness** *n.* state of being fleshy; plumpness.—**flesh'ings** *n.pl.* flesh-coloured tights worn by dancers, acrobats, etc.—**flesh'less** *a.* without flesh.—**flesh'liness** *n.*—**flesh'ling** *n.* one who has sensual appetite.—**flesh'ly** *a.* corporeal; corpulent; gross; sensual.—**flesh'-pot** *n.* a vessel in which meat is cooked; (*Fig.*) luxurious living.—**flesh'-tint** *n.* the colour used by artists in painting the human flesh.—**flesh'-wound** *n.* a body injury which affects only the flesh.—**flesh'y** *a.* pert. to flesh; corpulent; gross; (*Bot.*) thick and soft.—**proud flesh** (*Med.*) a growth of granular tissue over a wound.—**in the flesh**, alive [O.E. *flaesc*, flesh].

fletch (flech) *v.t.* to feather (as an arrow).—**fletch'er** *n.* a maker of arrows [Fr. *flèche*, an arrow].

fleur-de-lis (flẹr-dẹ-lē') *n.* the flower of the lily; the royal insignia of France [Fr. *fleur-de-lis*, flower of the lily].

flew (flòò) *pa.t.* of verb **fly**.

flex (fleks) *v.t.* and *v.i.* to bend (as the joints of the body); (*Geol.*) to fold (as rock strata);—*n.* (*Elect.*) flexible insulated wire or cable.—**flexibil'ity** *n.* quality of being pliable; (*Fig.*) adaptability; versatility.—**flex'ible** *a.* capable of being bent; pliant.—**flex'ibly** *adv.*—**flex'ile** *a.* bendable.—**flex'ion, flec'tion** *n.* a bend; a fold; an inflection.—**flex'or** *n.* a muscle which by contracting allows a joint to bend (opp. of *extensor*).—**flex'uose, flex'uous** *a.* bending; tortuous.—**flex'ure** *n.* act of bending, esp. under pressure; (*Geol.*) a curving or fold of rock strata [L. *flexus*, bent].

flibbertigibbet (flib'ẹr-ti-jib'et) *n.* a gossip; a flighty person [invented word].

flick (flik) *v.t.* to strike lightly, as with whip; —*n.* light, smart stroke [prob. imit. word].

flicker (flik'ẹr) *v.i.* to flutter; to waver; to quiver; to burn unsteadily.—*n.* act of wavering; quivering (as of leaves, flames, etc.).—**the flicks** (*Slang*) a cinema programme [O.E. *flicorian*, to flutter].

flight (flīt) *n.* the act or power of flying; the distance covered in flying; a journey by aeroplane; a formation of planes forming a unit of command in R.A.F.; a flock of birds; a soaring, as of the imagination; a discharge of arrows; a volley; a series of steps between successive landings.—**flight'-deck,** *n.* the deck of an air-craft carrier for planes to land or take off.—**flight'-lieuten'ant** *n.* rank in R.A.F. equivalent to army captain.—**in the first flight**, of the best quality.—**flight'y** *a.* capricious; giddy; volatile [O.E. *flyht*, flight].

flight (flīt) *n.* the act of fleeing; retreat.—**to put to flight**, to rout [O.E. *fleon*, to flee].

flim-flam (flim'flam) *n.* a trick; nonsense [invented word].

flimsy (flim'zi) *a.* thin; fragile; unsubstantial; paltry;—*n.* thin, transfer-paper; (*Slang*) reporter's paper; a banknote.—**flim'sily** *adv.*—**flim'siness** [prob. imit.].

flinch (flinsh) *v.i.* to shrink from pain; to wince; to fail.—**flinch'ing** *n.* the act of flinching [O.Fr. *flenchir*, to turn aside].

fling (fling) *v.t.* to throw from the hand; to hurl; to send out; to plunge;—*v.i.* to flounce; to throw oneself violently.—*pr.p.* **fling'ing.**—*pa.p.* **flung.**—*n.* a cast or throw; a sneer; a gibe; abandonment to pleasure; lively dance, as *Highland fling.*—**fling'er** *n.* [Scand. *flanga*, to move violently].

flint (flint) *n.* a hard brownish-grey variety of quartz, which readily produces fire when struck with steel; anything hard; a prehistoric stone weapon;—*a.* made of flint.—**flint'-glass** *n.* a kind of glass orig. made from the silica extracted from flint; name given to glass with good lustre.—**flint'-knap'ping** *n.* the process of breaking flints for road-making.—**flint'-lock** *n.* a gun-lock with a flint fixed on the hammer for firing the priming.—**flint'y** *a.* made of, or resembling, flint; (*Fig.*) hard-hearted; cruel [O.E. *flint*].

flip (flip) *n.* a hot drink composed of beer and spirits sweetened; a drink of hot milk, eggs, sugar and spirits [prob. fr. verb *flip*].

flip (flip) *v.t.* to flick; to toss by striking fingertip with thumb; to fillip; to jerk.—*pr.p.* **flip'ping.**—*pa.p.* **flipped.**—*n.* a flick; a snap; (*Colloq.*) a short trip, or pleasure flight, in an aeroplane.—**flip'per** *n.* the limb of an animal which facilitates swimming; (*Slang*) the human hand [var. of *flap*].

flippant (flip'ạnt) *a.* pert; voluble; lacking seriousness; shallow.—**flipp'ancy** *n.* undue levity; frivolousness; pertness.—**flipp'antly** *adv.* [etym. doubtful].

flirt (flẹrt) *v.t.* to jerk, as a bird's tail; to move playfully to and fro, as a fan;—*v.t.* to move about briskly; to play the coquette; to dally;—*n.* a jerk; a philanderer; a flighty girl.—**flirta'tion** *n.* the act of flirting.—**flirta'tious** *a.* [etym. doubtful].

flit (flit) *v.i.* to fly away; to dart along; to move quietly and unobtrusively; (*Scot.*) to remove from one house to another.—*pr.p.* **flit'ting.**—*pa.p.* **flit'ted** [Scand. *flytja*, to cause to float].

flitch (flich) *n.* the side of a hog, salted and cured; a steak of halibut; a plank of wood [O.E. *flicce*, a flitch of bacon].

flite, flyte (flīt) *v.i.* to wrangle; to quarrel; (*Scot.*) to scold [O.E. *flitan*].

flitter (flit'ẹr) *v.i.* to flutter.—**flitt'ermouse** *n.* a bat.—Also **flick'ermouse, flind'ermouse** [var. of *flutter*].

flivver (fliv'ẹr) *n.* (*U.S. Slang*) a cheap motor-car; (*Naval Slang*) a small destroyer [invented word].

float (flōt) *v.i.* to rest or drift on the surface of a liquid; to be buoyed up; to be suspended in air; (*Fig.*) to wander aimlessly;—*v.t.* to cause to stay on the surface of a liquid; to cover a surface with water; to set going, as a business company; to put into circulation;—*n.* anything which is buoyant; a raft; cork or quill on a fishing line, or net; a hollow floating ball of metal indicating depth of liquid in tank or cistern; a plasterer's trowel; a very low, flat lorry; (*Aero.*) a streamlined attachment to a sea-plane enabling it to float; theatre footlights.—**float'able** *a.* capable of being floated.—**float'age** *n.* the floating capacity of anything; anything afloat; flotsam.—**floata'tion** *n.* See **flotation.**—**float'er** *n.* one who or that which floats.—**float'ing** *a.* buoyant on surface of the water or in air; movable; fluctuating; in circulation; unfunded.—**floating anchor,** a sea anchor.—

floating capital, money or goods as distinct from *fixed capital*.—**floating debt**, that part of the National Debt which fluctuates according to circumstances.—**floating dock**, a floating graving-dock.—**float'ingly** *adv*.—**floating population**, shifting population.—**floating ribs**, lower ribs not connected to breast-bone [O.E. *flotian*, to float].

floccus (flok'us) *n*. a long tuft of wool or hair;—*pl*. **flocci** (flok'sī).—**floc'cular, floc'culate, floc'culent, floc'culose, floc'culous** *a*. woolly; having tufts; flaky [L. *floccus*, a lock of wool].

flock (flok) *n*. a small tuft of wool; refuse of wool in cloth-making, used for stuffing cushions, etc.; small wool fibres used in making flock-paper [L. *floccus*, a lock of wool].

flock (flok) *n*. a collection of animals (esp. sheep and goats) or birds; a crowd of people; a Christian congregation;—*v.i.* to come together in crowds [O.E. *flocc*, a band].

floe (flo) *n*. an extensive field of ice floating in the sea [Scand. *flo*, a layer].

flog (flog) *v.t.* to beat or strike, as with a rod or whip; to thrash; (*Slang*) to sell;—*v.i.* to flap in the wind (as *sails*).—*pr.p.* **flog'ging**.—*pa.p.* **flog'ged** [prob. school slang fr. L. *flagellare*, to whip].

flood (flud) *n*. an overflow of water; an inundation; a deluge; the flowing in of the tide; (*Lit.* and *Fig.*) a torrent.—*v.t.* to overflow; to drench; (*Fig.*) to overwhelm;—*v.i.* to spill over; to rise (as the tide).—*pr.p.* **flood'ing**.—*pa.p.* **flood'ed**.—**flood'-gate** *n*. a gate to stop or to let out flood-water; a sluice.—**flood'-light'ing** *n*. the artificial lighting of building exterior by lamps fitted with special reflectors.—**flood'-tide** *n*. the rising tide; (*Fig.*) peak of prosperity [O.E. *flod*, a stream].

floor (flōr) *n*. the horizontal surface of a room; a storey; any level area; bottom (of sea); part of a public hall on lower level than the platform; minimum level, esp. of prices.—*v.t.* to cover with a floor; to strike down; (*Fig.*) to perplex; to stump (in argument).—**floor'age** *n*. floor space.—**floor'-cloth** *n*. a heavy canvas material treated with oil-paint, and damp-proof, used for covering floors.—**floor'er** *n*. a knock-out blow; a baffling examination question or situation.—**floor'ing** *n*. materials for floors.—**floor'-show** *n*. a show presented on the floor among the patrons.—**floor'-walk'er** *n*. (*U.S.*) shop-walker.—**first'-floor** *n*. the storey immediately above the ground-floor; (*U.S.*) the ground-floor [O.E. *flor*, the floor].

flop (flop) *v.t.* to flap; to set down heavily.—*v.i.* to drop down suddenly or clumsily.—*pr.p.* **flop'ping**.—*pa.p.* **flopped**.—*n*. a fall, as of a soft, outspread body; (*Slang*) a fiasco.—**flop'py** *a*. slack; (of a hat brim) wide and soft [var. of *flap*].

flora (flō'rạ) *n*. the plants native to a certain geographical region or geological period; a classified list of such plants.—**flor'al** *a*. pert. to the goddess Flora, or to flowers.—**flor'ally** *adv*.—**flor'eate** *v.t.* to become adorned with flowers.—**flor'eated, flor'iated** *a*.—**flor'et** *n*. a single flower in a cluster of flowers; a small compact flower-head.—**flor'ist** *n*. a grower or seller of flowers [L. *Flora*, the goddess of flowers].

Florence (flor'ens) *n*. a gold coin of Edward III's time; a kind of wine from Florence in Italy.—**Flor'entine** *n*.—*a*. pert. to Florence [fr. Italian city of *Florence*].

florescence (flō-res'ens) *n*. a bursting into flower.—**flores'cent** *a*. [L. *florescere*, to burst into flower].

floriculture (flo'ri-kul'tūr) *n*. the cultivation of flowering plants.—**floricul'tural** *a*.—**floricul'turist** *n*. [L. *flos*, a flower; *cultura*, culture].

florid (flor'id) *a*. orig. flowery; bright in colour; over-elaborate; (of writing) euphuistic; ornate; (of complexion) highly coloured; (*Archit.*) flamboyant.—**flor'idly** *adv*.—**flor'idness** *n*. [L. *floridus*, flowery].

floriferous (flō-rif'ẹ-rus) *a*. producing flowers [L. *flos*, a flower; *ferre*, to bear].

floriform (flō'ri-form) *a*. having the shape of a flower [L. *flos*, a flower; *forma*, shape].

florin (flor'in) *n*. orig. a Florentine gold coin of 11th cent.; formerly a British silver two-shilling piece; in Holland, a guilder worth 1s. 8d. [It. *fiorino*, a little flower].

floruit (flō'ròò-it) *n*. the period of a person's life or fame [L. *floruit*, he flourished].

floss (flos) *n*. untwisted threads of very fine silk; the outer fibres of a silk-worm's cocoon.—**floss'-silk** *n*. very soft silk thread spun but not twisted, used in embroidery.—**floss'y** *a*. [It. *floscio*, soft].

flota (flō'ta) *n*. a commercial fleet [O.E. *flotian*, to float].

flotation (flō-tā'shun) *n*. the act of floating; science of floating bodies; (*Fig.*) act of launching, esp. a limited liability company. Also **floata'tion** [O.E. *flotian*, to float].

flotilla (flō-til'a) *n*. a fleet of small vessels; esp. of destroyers [Sp. *flotilla*, a little fleet].

flotsam (flot'sạm) *n*. goods lost by shipwreck and found floating on the sea [O.Fr. *flotaison*, a floating].

flounce (flouns) *v.i.* to turn abruptly; to flounder about;—*n*. a sudden, jerky movement [Scand. *flunsa*, to plunge].

flounce (flouns) *n*. a plaited border or frill on hem of a dress;—*v.t.* to trim with a flounce.—**flounc'ing** *n*. material used for flounces [M.E. *frounce*, a plait].

flounder (floun'dẹr) *n*. a small, edible flatfish, allied to the plaice [Scand. *flundra*, a flounder].

flounder (floun'dẹr) *v.i.* to struggle helplessly, as in marshy ground; to tumble about; (*Fig.*) to stumble hesitatingly, as in a speech [origin unknown].

flour (flour) *n*. the finely-ground meal of wheat, etc.; any finely powdered substance;—*v.t.* to turn into flour; to sprinkle with flour.—**flour'y** *a*. [Fr. *fleur de farine*, the flower (i.e. the best) of meal].

flourish (flur'ish) *v.t.* to decorate with flowery ornament or with florid diction; to brandish;—*v.i.* to grow luxuriantly; to prosper; to execute ostentatiously a passage of music;—*n*. ornament; a fanciful stroke of the pen; rhetorical display; (*Mus.*) florid improvisation either as prelude or addition to a composition; a fanfare; brandishing (of a weapon); (*Prov.*) fruit-tree blossom.—**flour'ishing** *a*. thriving; vigorous [M.E. *florisshen*, to blossom].

flout (flout) *v.t.* to mock; to disregard with contempt;—*v.i.* to jeer;—*n*. an expression of contempt; a gibe; an insult [prob. fr. M.E. *flouten*, to play the flute].

flow (flō) *v.i.* to run, as a liquid; to rise, as the tide; to circulate, as the blood; to issue forth; to glide along; to proceed from; to fall in waves, as the hair;—*v.t.* to overflow;—*n*. a stream; a current; the rise of the tide; any easy expression of thought, diction, etc.; copiousness; output.—**flow'ing** *a*. moving; running; fluent; curving gracefully, as lines; falling in folds, as drapery.—**flow'ingly** *adv*. [O.E. *flowan*, to flow].

flower (flou'ẹr) *n*. (*Bot.*) the reproductive organ in plants containing one or more of the separate members, petals, stamens, carpels, sepals; a blossom; the choicest part of anything; the finest type; a figure of speech; an ornament in shape of a flower.—**flow'ers** *n.pl.* a substance in the form of a powder, as *flowers of sulphur*;—*v.t.* to adorn with flowers or flower-like shapes;—*v.i.* to produce flowers; to bloom; to come to prime condition.—**flow'ered** *a*. decorated with a flower-pattern, as fabric.—**flow'eret** *n*. a small flower; a floret.—**flow'ering** *a*. having flowers.—**flow'er-pot** *n.* a pot, usually of red unglazed earthenware, in which plants can be grown.—**flow'ery** *a.* abounding in, or decorated with, flowers; (of style) highly ornate; euphuistic.—**the Flowery Kingdom,** China [L. *flos*, a flower].

flown (flōn) *pa.p.* of **fly.**

'flu (flóó) *n.* (*Colloq.*) influenza.

fluctuate (fluk'tū-āt) *v.i.* to move up and down, as a wave; to be unstable; to be irresolute;—*v.t.* to cause to waver.—**fluc'tuant** *a.*—**fluctua'tion** *n.* a rising and falling; vacillation [L. *fluctus*, a wave].

flue (flóó) *n.* a kind of fishing-net fixed or dragged [Dut. *flouw*, a fishing-net].

flue (flóó) *n.* a small shaft or duct in a chimney; a pipe for conveying air through a boiler; the opening in the pipe of an organ [etym. uncertain].

fluent (flóó'ent) *a.* flowing; ready in the use of words; (of lines) gracefully curved.—**flu'ency** *n.* the quality of being fluent; copiousness of speech; volubility.—**flu'ently** *adv.* [L. *fluere*, to flow].

fluff (fluf) *n.* light, floating down; downy growth of hair on skin;—*v.t.* to give a fluffy surface to;—*v.i.* to become downy; (*Slang*) to make errors in the speaking of a stage part.—**fluff'y** *a.* [prob. var. of *flue*].

flugelman Same as **fugleman.**

fluid (flóó'id) *n.* a substance which flows (liquid, gas, etc.); a non-solid;—*a.* capable of flowing; liquid; gaseous.—**fluid'ify** *v.t.* to make fluid.—**flu'idism, fluid'ity, flu'idness** *n.* the state or quality of being a non-solid; (*Fig.*) the state of being alterable.—**flu'idly** *adv.* [L. *fluidus*, flowing].

fluke (flóók) *n.* the flounder; a parasitic worm of the order *Trematoda*, affecting sheep, goats, etc. [O.E. *floc*, a flat-fish].

fluke (flóók) *n.* the flattened barb at the extremity of either arm of an anchor [O.E. *floc*, a flat-fish].

fluke (flóók) *n.* (*Colloq.*) any lucky chance.—**fluk'y** *a.* lucky [etym. unknown].

flummery (flum'er-i) *n.* a light, rather sour jelly, made from the husks of oats; (*Fig.*) mere flattery; insipid nonsense [etym. doubtful, prob. W. *llymru*, sour oatmeal].

flummox (flum'oks) *v.t.* (*Slang*) to disconcert; to confound. Also **flum'mux.**

flung (flung) *pa.t.* and *pa.p.* of **fling.**

flunkey (flung'ki) *n.* a liveried manservant; a footman; (*Fig.*) a toady; a cringing, obsequious person.—**flun'keydom** *n.* flunkeys collectively.—**flun'keyism** *n.* [Fr. *flanquer*, to run at the side of].

fluor (flóó'or) *n.* a mineral, fluoride of calcium, usually called *fluorspar*, and found in abundance in Derbyshire. Also called *Blue John*.—**fluoresce'** *v.i.* to exhibit fluorescence; to emit radiation.—**fluores'cence** *n.* the property of some transparent bodies which emit surface reflections of light different in colour from the mass of the material.—**fluores'cent** *a.*—**flu'oride** *n.* a compound of fluorine with another element.—**flu'orine** *n.* a gaseous very active element, pale yellowish-green in colour, found in fluorspar and cryolite.—**flu'orite** *n.* fluorspar.—**flu'orous** *a.* derived from fluor.—**fluorescent lighting,** a form of artificial diffused lighting, giving the effect of permanent daylight by means of the ultra-violet rays of a mercury vapour arc acting on a tube coated with a fluorescent powder [L. *fluere*, to flow].

flurry (flur'i) *n.* a sudden, brief gust of wind; bustle; commotion;—*v.t.* to agitate; to fluster;—*pr.p.* **flurr'ying.**—*pa.p.* **flurr'ied** [etym. doubtful].

flush (flush) *v.i.* to become suffused with blood; to turn red in the face; to blush;—*v.t.* to cause to blush or turn red; to animate with high spirits; to cleanse with a rush of water;—*n.* a flow of water; a rush of blood to the face; a mill-stream; freshness;—*a.* and *adv.* well supplied with, as in *flush of money*; lavish [origin. uncertain].

flush (flush) *v.t.* to cause to start, as a hunter, a bird;—*v.i.* to fly up quickly and suddenly from concealment;—*n.* the act of starting up; a flock of birds flying up suddenly [M.E. *fluschen*, to fly up].

flush (flush) *n.* a run of cards of the same suit [L. *fluxus*, a flowing].

flush (flush) *v.t.* to level up;—*a.* being in the same plane. [etym. doubtful].

fluster (flus'tẹr) *v.t.* to make hot and agitated; to flurry;—*v.i.* to be confused and flurried;—*n.* confusion; nervous agitation; muddle.—**flus'tered** *a.* [Scand. *flaustr*, hurry].

flute (flóót) *n.* a musical tubular wind-instrument, with finger-holes, and blow-hole at side near upper end; a stop in the pipe-organ; (*Archit.*) a vertical groove in the shaft of a column; a similar groove as in a lady's ruffle;—*v.i.* to play the flute; to sing or recite in flute-like tones;—*v.t.* to play (tune) on the flute; to make flutes or grooves in.—**flut'ed** *a.* ornamented with grooves, channels, etc.—**flut'er** *n.* one who plays the flute.—**flut'ing** *n.* action of playing a flute; the ornamental vertical grooving on a pillar, on glass, or in a lady's ruffle.—**flut'ist** *n.* one who plays a flute. Also **flaut'ist.**—**flut'y** *a.* flute-like in tone [L.L. *flauta*].

flutter (flut'ẹr) *v.t.* to cause to flap; to throw into confusion; to move quickly;—*v.i.* to flap the wings; to move with quick vibrations; (of heart) to palpitate;—*n.* quick and irregular motion; nervous hurry; confusion; (*Colloq.*) a mild gamble [O.E. *flotorian*, to float about].

fluvial (flóó'vi-ạl) *a.* pert. to, or found in, a river.—**fluviat'ic, flu'viatile** *a.* (*Bot. Geol.*) pert. to, or found in, rivers. [L. *fluvius*, a river].

fluvio- flóó'vi-o) *prefix* as in **fluviomarine'** *a.* capable of living in rivers or sea, as salmon.

flux (fluks) *n.* the act of flowing; fluidity; (*Phys.*) the rate of flow; (*Med.*) morbid discharge of body-fluid, esp. blood; dysentery; excrement; (*Chem.*) a substance added to another to promote fusibility; continuous process of change;—*v.t.* to fuse; to purge;—*v.i.* to flow.—**fluxil'ity, flux'ion** *n.* a flowing; abnormal discharge of fluid catarrh; fusion [L. *fluere*, to flow].

fly (flī) *v.t.* to cause to fly; to direct the flight of; to flee from;—*v.i.* to move through the air, as a bird or an aircraft; to become airborne; to travel by aeroplane; to move rapidly; to flee;—*pr.p.* **fly'ing.**—*pa.t.* **flew** (flóó).—*pa.p.* **flown.**—*n.* a winged insect, esp. of the order *Diptera*; a house-fly; a fish-hook in imitation of a fly; a flap on a garment covering a row of buttons.—**flies** *n.pl.* the space above a theatre stage where scenery is moved;—*a.* (*Slang*) wide-awake; nimble-witted.—**fly'blow** *n.* the larva of a fly.—**fly'blown** *a.* tainted with fly-blow; maggoty; (*Fig.*) tarnished; shop-soiled.—**fly'boat** *n.* a long narrow boat, used esp. on Dutch canals.—**fly'by-night** *n.* a gadabout; a cheat; a cab (*abbrev.* fly);—*a.* flighty; unreliable.—**fly'er, fli'er** *n.*—**fly'fish'ing** *n.* catching fish by artificial flies on hook.—**fly'ing** *n.* moving through the air; air navigation;—*a.* capable of flight; streaming; swift.—**fly'ing-boat** *n.* a seaplane.—**fly'ing-bomb** *n.* (*World War* 2) the buzz-bomb, a self-propelled bomb.—**fly'ing-but'tress** (*Archit.*) an arched prop attached only at one point to the mass of masonry whose outward thrust it is designed to counteract.—**fly'ing-col'umn** *n.* a body of soldiers equipped for rapid movement and independent of main base.—**Flying Dutchman,** the black spectral ship supposed to appear as warning to sea-captains, causing them to change their course.—**fly'ing-fish** *n.* fish which can leap from the water and fly through the air even against a strong head-wind.—**Flying Fortress** (*U.S.*) four-engined aircraft used for long-range bombing.—**fly'ing-fox** *n.* tropical fruit-eating bat with fox-like face, found in Malaya, India and E. Indies.—**fly'ing-machine'** *n.* a general term for a heavier-than-air, power-engined craft.—**fly'ing-pig** *n.* (*Slang*) a projectile fired by a trench mortar.—**fly'ing-sau'cer** *n.* name given to a saucer-like object reputedly seen flying at tremendous speeds and high altitudes.—**flying squad,** special mobile unit of police force equipped with motor cars, cycles, etc.—**flying squirrel,** squirrel-like rodent with expanding fold of skin between front and hind legs.—**flying visit,** a hasty, unexpected visit.—**fly'leaf** *n.* the blank page at the beginning or end of a book.—**fly'man** *n.* the driver of a fly (carriage); a scene-shifter in the theatre.—**fly'net** *n.* a net to protect against flies.—**fly'-pa'per** *n.* a paper smeared with sticky substance to trap flies.—**fly'rail** *n.* a hinged flap attached to a table for supporting adjustable leaf.—**fly'rod** *n.* a flexible fishing-rod used for fly-fishing.—**fly'wheel** *n.* a heavy-rimmed wheel attached to the crank-shaft of an engine to regulate its speed or accumulate power.—**fly'whisk** *n.* a device for killing flies.—**to fly off at a tangent,** to digress from the topic under discussion.—**to fly off at the handle,** to become wildly excited.—**to fly a kite,** to obtain money by accommodation bills; to obtain an indication beforehand of the real state of affairs [O.E. *fleogan*, to fly].

foal (fōl) *n.* the young of a mare or she-ass; a colt or a filly;—*v.t.* and *v.i.* to bring forth a foal [O.E. *fola*, a young animal].

foam (fōm) *n.* froth; spume; the bubbles of air on surface of effervescent liquid;—*v.i.* to froth; to bubble; to gather foam; (*Fig.*) to throw out with rage or violence.—**foam'ing** *a.*—**foam'ingly** *adv.*—**foam'rub'ber** *n.* latex made into a soft, elastic and porous substance, resembling a sponge, used chiefly in upholstery.—**foam'y** *a.* frothy [O.E. *fam*, foam].

fob (fob) *n.* a small pocket in the waistband for holding a watch.—**a fob chain,** a chain with seals, etc. dangling from the fob [Dial. H. Ger. *fuppe*, a pocket].

fob (fob) *v.t.* to cheat; to impose on;—*n.* a swindler.—*pr.p.* **fob'bing.**—*pa.p* **fobbed.**—**to fob off,** to impose on someone by deliberate trickery [prob. conn. with *fop*].

fo'c's'le See **forecastle.**

focus (fō'kus) *n.* the point at which rays of light meet after reflection or refraction; (*Geom.*) one of two points connected linearly to any point on a curve; any point of concentration;—*pl.* **fo'cuses, foci** (fō'sī);—*v.t.* to bring to a focus; to adjust; to concentrate;—*v.i.* to converge.—*pr.p.* **fo'cus(s)ing.**—*pa.p.* **fo'cus(s)ed.**—**fo'cal** *a.* pert. to a focus.—**fo'calise** *v.t.* to bring into focus; to cause to converge; to concentrate.—**focalisa'tion** *n.*—**in focus,** clearly outlined; well defined.—**out of focus,** distorted [L. *focus*, a fireplace].

fodder (fod'ẹr) *n.* food for cattle;—*v.t.* to supply with fodder [O.E. *fodor*, food].

foe (fō) *n.* an enemy; an adversary; a hostile army.—**foe'man** *n.* an enemy in war;—*pl.* **foe'men** [O.E. *fah*, hostile].

foetus See **fetus.**

fog (fog) *n.* growth of coarse grass after hay has been cut; (*Scot.*) moss; aftermath;—**fog'gage** *n.* fog; (*Scots law*) the right to graze cattle on fog [etym. unknown].

fog (fog) *n.* thick mist; watery vapour in the lower atmosphere; a cloud of dust or smoke obscuring visibility; (*Fig.*) mental confusion;—*v.t.* to shroud in fog; to perplex the mind;—*v.i.* to become cloudy or obscured.—**fog'bank** *n.* a mass of fog over the sea.—**fog'bound** *a.* hindered by fog from reaching destination, as a ship, train, etc.—**fog'gily** *adv.*—**fog'giness** *n.*—**fog'gy** *a.*—**fog'horn** *n.* a loud siren used during fog.—**fog'sig'nal** *n.* a small detonator placed on railway track during fog, the explosion caused by passing train acting as a signal to the driver.—**fog'smoke** *n.* fog [etym. uncertain].

fogy, fogey (fō'gi) *n.* a dull, old fellow; an elderly person whose ideas are behind the times [etym. unknown].

foible (foi'bl) *n.* a weakness of character; a failing [O.Fr. *foible*, weak].

foil (foil) *v.t.* to frustrate; to baffle; to put off the scent; to defeat.—*pr.p.* **foil'ing.**—*pa.p.* **foiled.**—*n.* track of a hunted animal; frustration; defeat; a blunt sword, with button on point, for fencing practice [O.Fr. *fuler*, to trample on].

foil (foil) *n.* a thin leaf of metal, as *tinfoil*; a thin leaf of metal placed under gems to increase their brilliancy or colour; a thin coating of quicksilver amalgam on the back of a mirror; (*Archit.*) a leaf-like ornament in windows, niches, etc. (*trefoil, quatrefoil, cinquefoil*, etc.); (*Fig.*) anything serving to set off something else [L. *folium*, a leaf].

foison (foi'zn) *n.* a rich harvest; abundance [O.Fr. *foison*, abundance].

foist (foist) *v.t.* to palm off; to insert surreptitiously or unwarrantably.—**foist'er** *n.* [prob. Dut. *vuisten*, to take in the hand].

fold (fold) *n.* a doubling over of a flexible material; a plait; a coil (of rope); a crease or a line made by folding; (*Geol.*) a dip in rock strata caused originally by pressure;—*v.t.* to double over; to enclose within folds or layers; to embrace;—*v.i.* to be plaited or doubled.—**fold'er** *n.* the one who or that which folds; a paper-folding instrument; a file for holding papers, etc. [O.E. *fealdan*, to fold].

fold (fōld) *n.* an enclosure for sheep; a pen; a flock of sheep; (*Fig.*) the Church; a congregation;—*v.t.* to confine in a fold or pen [O.E. *fald*, a stall].

fold (fold) *suffix*=times, and added to the cardinal numbers, as *twofold, fivefold.*

folderol See **falderal.**

foliage (fō'li-āj) *n.* leaves of a plant in general; leafage.—**fo'liaged** *a.* having leaves.—**fo'liate** *v.t.* to hammer (metal) into laminae or foil; (*Archit.*) to ornament with leaf-design; to number the leaves (not pages) of a book;—*a.* resembling a leaf.—**fo'liated** *a.*—**folia'tion** *n.* [L. *folium*, a leaf].

folio (fō'li-ō) *n.* a sheet of paper once folded; a book of such folded sheets; the two opposite pages of a ledger used for one account and numbered the same; (*Print*) page number in a book;—*a.* pert. to or formed of sheets folded so as to make two leaves;—*v.t.* to number the pages of a book on one side only [L. *folium*, a leaf].

foliole (fō'li-ōl) *n.* (*Bot.*) a leaflet; the separate part of a compound leaf.—**fo'liolate** *a.* [L. *folium*, a leaf].

folk (fōk) *n.* people in general, or as a specified class; a race.—**folks** *n.pl.* (*Colloq.*) one's own family and near relations.—**folk'dance** *n.* a traditional country-dance.—**folk'lore** *n.* popular superstitions or legends; the study of traditional beliefs.—**folk'lo'rist** *n.*—**folk'mote, folk'moot** *n.* an assembly of the people held in each shire in Anglo-Saxon times.—**folk'song** *n.* a traditional melody or ballad handed down from one generation to another, its origin being obscure.—**folk'sto'ry,** or **-tale,** *n.* a popular myth [O.E. *folc*, the people].

follicle (fol'ik-l) *n.* (*Bot.*) a one-celled seed vessel; (*Zool.*) a small sac; (*Anat.*) a gland, as in *hair-follicle.*—**follic'ular** *a.* pert. to a follicle [L. *folliculus*, a little bag].

follow (fol'ō) *v.t.* to go after; to move behind; to succeed (in a post); to adhere to (a belief); to practise (as a trade or profession); to comprehend; to watch carefully; to keep in touch with;—*v.i.* to come after; to pursue; to occur as a consequence;—*n.* the act of following.—**foll'ower** *n.* one who comes after; a disciple; a supporter; (*Colloq.*) a servant girl's sweetheart.—**foll'owing** *n.* supporters, adherents; vocation;—*a.* coming next after; (of a wind) favourable.—**to follow on,** to come after an interval has elapsed; (*Cricket*) to have a second innings when opponents are leading by a certain number of runs.—**to follow out,** to carry through a matter according to plan. —**to follow up,** to continue an action to get the maximum result; to make the most of an advantage [O.E. *folgian*, to accompany].

folly (fol'-i) *n.* want of sense; weakness of mind; a foolish action; a useless and needlessly extravagant structure [O.Fr. *fol*, a fool].

foment (fo-ment') *v.t.* to bathe with warm water to relieve pain; (*Fig.*) to encourage or instigate.—**fomenta'tion** *n.* the action of applying warm lotions; the warm lotion applied; encouragement.—**foment'er** *n.* [L. *fomentum*, a poultice].

fond (fond) *a.* orig. foolish; doting; very affectionate.—**fond of,** much attached to; addicted to.—**fond'le** *v.t.* to caress; to stroke tenderly.—**fond'ly** *adv.*—**fond'ness** *n.* [M.E. *fonned*, infatuated].

fondant (fon'-dạnt) *n.* a kind of sweetmeat which melts easily in the mouth [Fr. *fondre*, to melt].

font (font) *n.* a stone basin for holding baptismal water; a receptacle for holy water [L. *fons*, a fountain].

food (fòòd) *n.* matter which one feeds on; solid nourishment as contrasted with liquids; that which, absorbed by any organism, promotes growth; (*Fig.*) mental or spiritual nourishment.—**Food Office,** war time local centre for the issue of ration cards, emergency and priority cards, etc. under the Government's rationing scheme.—**food'-stuff** *n.* edible commodity with nourishment value [O.E. *foda*, food].

fool (fòòl) *n.* orig. an imbecile; one who behaves stupidly; one devoid of common sense; a simpleton; a clown; a dupe;—*v.t.* to make a fool of; to impose on; to hoax.—*v.i.* to behave like a fool; to trifle.—**fool'ery** *n.* silly behaviour; foolish act.—**fool'-hard'ily** *adv.*—**fool'-hard'iness** *n.*—**fool'-hard'y** *a.* recklessly daring; venturesome.—**fool'ish** *a.* weak in intellect; ill-considered; stupid.—**fool'ishly** *adv.*—**fool'ishness** *n.*—**fool'ing** *n.* foolery.—**fool'proof** *a.* (of machines) so devised that mishandling cannot cause damage to machine or personnel; so contrived that all misunderstanding is avoided.—**fools'cap** *n.* a folio writing paper about 16½ by 13½ ins. originally with water-mark comprising jester's cap and bells.—**a fool's errand,** a fruitless errand.—**fool's paradise,** a state of illusory happiness [L. *follis*, a windbag].

fool (fòòl) *n.* a dessert consisting of a purée of fruit mixed with cream or custard [perh. Fr. *fouler*, to crush (grapes)].

foot (foot) *n.* the extreme end of the lower limbs, below the ankle; a base or support, like a foot; the end of a bed, couch, etc. where the feet would normally lie; foot-soldiers; a measure of length = 12 inches; a unit in prosody, a combination of syllables measured according to quantity or stress-accent; the margin at the lower edge of a printed page;—*pl.* **feet.**—*v.t.* to traverse by walking; to add (an account); to pay (a bill); to put a new foot on;—*v.i.* to dance; to walk. —*pr.p.* **foot'ing.** -*pa.p.* **foot'ed.**—**foot** *n.* dregs; sediment.—*pl.* **foots.**—**foot'age** *n.* (*Cinema*) the length of a sound-film measured in feet.—**foot'ball,** *n.* ball used in games such as Rugby, Soccer; play with this ball.—**foot'baller** *n.*—**foot'boy** *n.* a young servant in livery.—**foot'-brake** *n.* the brake of a motor operated by foot. —**foot'-breadth** *n.* the width of a foot.—**foot'-bridge** *n.* a narrow bridge for foot-passengers. —**foot'ed** *a.* having feet or a foot (usually in compounds as *two-footed, sure-footed*).—**foot'-fall** *n.* a step; sound of a step.—**foot'gear** *n.* boots and shoes; stockings, socks.—**foot'hill** *n.* minor hill at base of higher range (usually *pl.*).—**foot'hold** *n.* a support for the foot; space to stand on.—**foot'ing** *n.* ground to stand on; status (in society)—**foot'lights** *n.pl.* a row of screened lights along the front of the stage; (*Fig.*) the theatre; the profession of acting.—**foot'-loose** *a.* free to do as one likes; untrammelled.—**foot'man** *n.* a liveried man-servant; an infantryman; a trivet.—**foot'mark** *n.* a footprint.—**foot'note** *n.* a note of reference or explanation at foot of a page.—**foot'pace** *n.* walking pace; dais.—**foot'pad** *n.* a robber who frequents highways and byways on foot.—**foot'-pas'senger** *n.* a pedestrian.—**foot'path** *n.* a narrow path for pedestrians only.—**foot'plate** *n.* the platform used by driver and fireman of a locomotive.—**foot'-pound** *n.* a unit of work being the energy required to lift 1 lb. vertically to the height of 1 ft. against gravity.—**foot'print** *n.* the impression made by a foot.—**foot'race** *n.* a race run on foot.—**foot'rot** *n.* an inflammatory disease affecting feet of sheep. —**foot'-rule** *n.* a ruler or measure one foot long. **foot'-scra'per** *n.* an iron-barred device for cleaning muddy boots before entering a house.—**foot'slog** *v.i.* (*Slang*) to tramp.—**foot'slogger** *n.* a walker; a foot-soldier. -**foot'-sol'dier** *n.* an infantryman.—**foot'sore** *a.* having tender, aching feet through over-walking.—**foot'step** *n.* tread; sound of this; print of a foot.—**foot'stool** *n.* a low stool for resting feet on.—**foot'-warm'er** *n.* a vessel, containing hot water, for keeping the feet warm.—**foot'way** *n.* a path for pedestrians.—**foot'wear** *n.* boots, shoes, etc. collectively.—**foot and mouth disease,** a highly contagious disease of sheep, swine, and esp. horned cattle.—**to put down one's foot,** to refuse firmly.—**to put one's foot in it,** to say something embarrassing.—**to fall on one's feet,** to be very lucky [O.E. *fot*, foot].

footle (fòò'-tl) *v.i.* (*Colloq.*) to bungle; to be incompetent [etym. unknown].

foozle (fòòz'-l) *v.t.* (*Colloq.*) to bungle (esp. a stroke at golf) [etym. uncertain].

fop (fop) *n.* a conceited, effeminate man; a dandy.—**fop'pery** *n.* affectation in dress; folly. —**fop'pish** *a.* vain.—**fop'pishly** *adv.*—**fop'pishness** *n.* [M.E. *foppe*, a fool].

for (for) *prep.* in place of; instead of; because of; during; as being; considering; in return for; on behalf of; in spite of; in respect of;—*conj.* because.—**as for,** regarding [O.E. *for*, for].

for- (for) *prefix.*—survives in a few words of O.E. origin, with various meanings;—utterly, as in *for*lorn; prohibition, as in *for*bid; neglect, as in *for*sake; away, as in *for*get.

forage (for'-ij) *n.* food for horses and cattle; the search for this, esp. by soldiers;—*v.t.* to supply with provender; to plunder;—*v.i.* to rove in search of food; (*Fig.*) to rummage.—**forage cap,** a soldier's undress cap [O.Fr. *fourage*, forage].

foramen (fo-rā'-men) *n.* a small aperture, esp. in a bone;—*pl.* **foram'ina.**—**foram'inate(d), foram'inous** *a.* perforated; porous [L. *foramen*, a hole].

forasmuch as (for-az-much') *conj.* seeing that; because that; since.

foray (for'-ā) *n.* an incursion into hostile territory to get plunder;—*v.t.* to pillage.—**for'ayer** *n.* [etym. obscure].

forbade (for-bad') *pa.t.* of **forbid.**

forbear (for-bār') *v.t.* to abstain from; to avoid; to bear with;—*v.i.* to refrain from; to control one's feelings.—*pa.t.* **forbore'.**—*pa.p.* **forborne'.**—**forbear'ance** *n.* restraint; leniency; patience.—**forbear'ing** *a.* long-suffering [O.E. *forberan*, to suffer, endure].

forbear (for'-bār) *n.* an ancestor.

forbid (for-bid') *v.t.* to prohibit; to order to desist; to exclude.—*pa.t.* **forbade** (for-bad') or **forbad'.**—*pa.p.* **forbid'den.**—**forbid'den** *a.* prohibited; illegal.—**forbid'ding** *a.* repellent; menacing; sinister.—**forbid'dingly** *adv.* [O.E. *forbeodan*, to prohibit].

force (fōrs) *n.* strength; energy; efficacy; coercion; precise meaning; operation; body of soldiers, police, etc.; (*Mech.*) that which produces a change in a body's state of rest or motion; (*Law*) unlawful violence to person or property.—**Forc'es** *n.pl.* Army, Navy and Air Force;—*v.t.* to compel (physically or morally); to strain; to ravish; to wring; (*Hort.*) to cause plants to bloom, or ripen before normal time.—**force'able** *a.*—**forced** *a.* achieved by great effort, or under compulsion; lacking spontaneity, as *forced laugh.*—**forc'edness** *n.*—**force'ful** *a.* full of energy; vigorous. —**force'fully** *adv.*—**force'less** *a.* weak; inert.—**forc'er** *n.* the one who, or that which, forces; the plunger of a force-pump.—**forc'ible** *a.* having force; compelling; cogent; effective.—**forc'ibly** *adv.*—**forc'ibleness** *n.*—**forc'ing** *n.* the action of using force or applying pressure; the art of ripening plants, fruits, etc. before their season.—**forc'ing-bed** *n.* a glass-covered bed for hastening the growth of plants.—**forc'ing-house** *n.* a hot-house.—**to come into force,** to become valid.—**to force the pace,** to hasten more than is necessary.—**forced landing** (*Aero.*) a landing necessitated by mishap [O.E. *force,* strength].

force (fōrs) *n.* a waterfall.—Also **foss** [Scand. *forsa,* to gush].

force (fōrs) *v.t.* to stuff (as a fowl, etc.).—**force'meat** *n.* minced, well-seasoned meat, used as stuffing etc. [Fr. *farce,* stuffing].

forceps (for'seps) *n.* a surgical instrument like tongs used by surgeons, dentists, etc. during operations.—**for'cipate(d), forcip'ulate** *a.* having the form of forceps [L. fr. *formus,* hot; *capere,* to hold].

ford (fōrd) *n.* a shallow part of a stream etc. where a crossing can be made on foot;—*v.t.* to cross by wading.—**ford'able** *a.* able to be forded [O.E. *faran,* to go].

fordo (for-dóó') *v.t.* to undo; to ruin; to exhaust [O.E. *fordon,* to destroy].

fore (fōr) *a.* in front; forward; prior;—*adv.* in front, as opp. to *aft;*—*interj.* (*Golf*) a warning cry to person in the way [O.E. *fore,* before].

fore- (fōr) *prefix* meaning in front or beforehand.

forearm (fōr'árm) *n.* the part of the arm between the elbow and the wrist.

forearm (fōr-arm') *v.t.* to take defensive precautions.

forebear (fōr'bār) *n.* (*Scot.*) var. of **for'bear.**

forebode (fōr-bōd') *v.t.* to predict (esp. something unpleasant); to prognosticate; to presage.—**forebode'ment** *n.*—**forebod'ing** *n.* an intuitive sense of impending evil or danger.—**forebod'ingly** *adv.*

forecast (fōr'kast) *n.* a prediction; (*Meteor.*) a general inference as to the probable weather during the following 24 hours;—*v.t.* and *v.i.* to conjecture beforehand the probable outcome (of an event, plan, etc.); to predict.

forecastle, fo'c'sle (fōk'sl) *n.* (*Naut.*) the upper deck forward of the foremast; forepart under deck, forming crew's quarters.

foreclose (fōr-klōz') *v.t.* (*Law*) to prevent; to exclude; to deprive of the right to redeem a mortgage.—**foreclos'ure** *n.*

forecourt (fōr'kōrt) *n.* the outer, or front court of a building or group of buildings.

foredate (fōr-dāt') *v.t.* to date beforehand; to antedate.

foredoom (fōr-dóóm') *v.t.* to judge in advance; to predestine to failure etc.

forefather (fōr'fá-thẹr) *n.* an ancestor.

forefinger (fōr'fing-gẹr) *n.* the finger next to the thumb; the index finger.

forefoot (fōr'foot) *n.* one of the front feet of a quadruped.

forefront (fōr'frunt) *n.* the foremost place; the centre of interest.

forego (fōr-gō') *v.t.* to precede.—**fore'going** *a.* preceding; just mentioned.—**fore'gone** *a.* predetermined, as in a *foregone conclusion.*

forego Same as **forgo.**

foreground (fōr'ground) *n.* the part of the ground nearest the spectator; the part of a picture which seems nearest the observer.

forehand (fōr'hand) *n.* the part of a horse in front of the rider;—*a.* done beforehand; (*Tennis*) used of a stroke played *forward* on the right or natural side, as opp. to *backhand.* —**forehand'ed** *a.*

forehead (for'ed, fōr'hed) *n.* the upper part of the face above the eyes; the brow.

foreign (for'in) *a.* situated outside a place or country; alien; irrelevant; introduced from outside.—**for'eigner** *n.* a native of another country; an alien.—**for'eignness** *n.* [O.Fr. *forain,* fr. L. *foris,* outside].

foreknow (fōr-nō') *v.t.* to know or sense beforehand.—**foreknowl'edge** *n.*

foreland (fōr'land) *n.* a promontory; a cape; shore area round a port, as oppos. to the *hinterland.*

foreleg (fōr'leg) *n.* a front leg of an animal.

forelock (fōr'lok) *n.* a lock of hair on the forehead.—**to take time by the forelock,** to seize a chance; to anticipate an issue.

foreman (fōr-mạn) *n.* the principal member and spokesman of a jury; the overseer of a group of workmen.

foremast (fōr'mást) *n.* the mast in the forepart of a vessel, nearest the bow.

forementioned (fōr-men'shund) *a.* previously mentioned in a speech or writing.

foremost (fōr'mōst) *a.* first in place or time; first in dignity or rank.—**head foremost,** head first; headlong.

forenamed (fōr'nāmd) *a.* already mentioned.

forenoon (fōr'nóón) *n.* the part of the day before noon; morning.

forensic (fo-ren'sik) *a.* pert. to the law-courts. —**foren'sically** *adv.*—**forensic medicine,** medical jurisprudence [L. *forensis,* pert. to the forum].

foreordain (fōr-or-dān') *v.t.* to predetermine; to decree beforehand.

forepart (fōr'párt) *n.* the part before the rest; the beginning; the bow of a ship.

forerun (fōr-run') *v.t.* to run before; to herald. —**forerun'ner** *n.* a messenger sent on in advance; a harbinger; a precursor.

foresaid (fōr'sed) *a.* mentioned before.

foresail (fōr'sāl or fō'sl) *n.* the lowest square sail on the foremast.

foresee (fōr-sē') *v.t.* to see beforehand; to infer.—**fore'sight** *n.* wise fore-thought; prudence; (*Mil.*) front sight on gun.

foreshadow (fōr-shad'ō) *v.t.* to shadow or typify beforehand; to suggest in advance.

foreshore (fōr'shōr) *n.* the part of the shore between the level of high tide and low tide.

foreshorten (fōr-short'n) *v.t.* to represent (in art) according to perspective; to depict to the eye, as seen obliquely.

foreshow (fōr-shō') *v.t.* to prognosticate; to foretell. Also **foreshew'.**

foresight (fōr'sīt) *n.* See **foresee.**

foreskin (fōr'skin) *n.* the skin covering the glans penis; prepuce.

forest (for'est) *n.* orig. land set apart for hunting; a tract of wooded, uncultivated land; any area preserved for game-hunting, as *deer-forest;*—*a.* sylvan;—*v.t.* to cover with trees.—**for'ester** *n.* one who has forest land, game, etc. under supervision; a forest-dweller.—**for'estry** *n.* the science of growing timber [L. *foris,* outside].

forestall (fōr-stawl') *v.t.* orig. to buy up a stock of goods before they reach the market, so as to resell at maximum price; to get in ahead of someone else.

forestay (fōr'stā) *n.* (*Naut.*) a rope reaching from the foremast head to the bowsprit end, to support the mast.

foretaste (fōr'tāst) *n.* a taste beforehand; anticipation;—*v.t.* to taste before full possession.

foretell (fōr-tel′) *v.t.* to predict; to prophesy.—*pr.p.* **foretell′ing.**—*pa.p.* **foretold′.**
forethink (fōr-thingk′) *v.t.* to realise intuitively; to anticipate.—**fore′thought** *n.* anticipation; provident care; foresight.
foretoken (fōr′tō-kn) *n.* a token or sign received beforehand; a prophetic sign;—*v.t.* to indicate beforehand.
foretop (fōr′top) *n.* (*Naut.*) platform at the head of the foremast; the hair on the forepart of the head.—**fore′topgall′ant** *a.* pert. to the mast above the **fore′top′mast.**—**fore′top′mast** *n.* the mast above the foremast.
forever (for-ev′ẹr) *adv.* always; eternally;—*n.* eternity.—**forev′ermore** *adv.*
forewarn (fōr-wawrn′) *v.t.* to warn or caution in advance.
forewoman (fōr′wŏŏm-ạn) *n.* a woman overseer in a factory, shop, etc.
foreword (fōr′wurd) *n.* a preface; an introductory note to a book.
forfeit (for′fit) *v.t.* to be deprived of, as a punishment;—*n.* that which is forfeited; a fine or penalty.—**for′feitable** *a.*—**for′feiture** *n.* the act of forfeiting; the state of being deprived of something as a punishment; the thing confiscated [O.Fr. *forfaire*, to transgress].
forfend (for-fend′) *v.t.* to ward off; to avert.
forgather, foregather (for-gaTH′ẹr) *v.i.* (*Scot.*) to meet with friends; to come together socially.
forgave (for-gāv) *pa.t.* of verb **forgive.**
forge (forj) *v.t.* a furnace with blast for heating iron red hot so that it can be hammered into shape; a smithy; (*Fig.*) a place where anything is fashioned or planned;—*v.t.* to fashion into shape by heating and hammering; to fabricate; to counterfeit;—*v.i.* to work with metals; to commit forgery.—**forg′er** *n.* one guilty of fraudulent act, esp. of copying another's signature to obtain money.—**forg′ery** *n.* the act of falsifying a document, or illegally using another's signature; that which is forged [L. *fabrica*, a workshop].
forge (forj) *v.i.* to move forward steadily.—usually **to forge ahead.**
forget (for-get′) *v.t.* to lose remembrance of; to neglect inadvertently; to disregard.—*pr.p.* **forgett′ing.**—*pa.t.* **forgot′.**—*pa.p.* **forgot′** or **forgott′en.**—**forget′able, forgett′able** *a.*—**forget′ful** *a.* apt to forget; heedless; oblivious.—**forget′fully** *adv.*—**forget′fulness** *n.*—**forget′-me-not** *n.* a well-known plant with small blue flowers, symbolic of friendship [O.E. *forgietan*, to forget].
forgive (for-giv′) *v.t.* to pardon; to cease to bear resentment against; to cancel (as a debt);—*v.i.* to exercise clemency; to grant pardon.—*pa.t.* **forgave′.**—*pa.p.* **forgiv′en.**—**forgiv′able** *a.* pardonable.—**forgive′ness** *n.*—**forgiv′ing** *a.* ready to pardon [O.E. *forgiefan*, to give up].
forgo (for-gō′) *v.t.* to renounce; to abstain from possession or enjoyment.
fork (fork) *n.* an implement with two or more prongs at the end; a table utensil of metal, silver, etc. with usually three or four prongs; anything shaped like a fork; a pronged instrument which when struck gives forth a fixed musical note (tuning-fork); the bifurcation of a road, etc.;—*pl.* the parts into which anything divides, as a road, river, etc.;—*v.i.* to diverge into two;—*v.t.* to pitch with a fork, as hay; to lift with a fork (as food); to form as a fork.—**forked, fork′y** *a.* shaped like a fork; cleft. [O.E. *forca*, a fork].
forlorn (for-lorn′) *a.* utterly lost; deserted; forsaken; wretched.—**forlorn′ly** *adv.*—**forlorn′ness** *n.* [O.E. *forleosan*, to lose].
form (form) *n.* shape or appearance; configuration; the human body; state of health; model; style; method of arrangement of details; etiquette; a long bench; a class of school-children; an official document or questionnaire with details to be filled in by applicant; the place where a hare sleeps;—*v.t.* to give shape to; to construct; to devise; to be an element of; to conceive; to build up (as a sentence);—*v.i.* to assume position; to develop.—**form′al** *a.* according to form; regular; methodical; conventional; punctilious; ceremonious.—**formalisa′tion** *n.*—**form′alise** *v.t.* and *v.i.* to give form to; to make formal.—**form′alism** *n.* the quality of being formal; undue insistence on conventional forms, esp. in religion or the arts.—**form′alist** *n.*—**formal′ity** *n.* quality of being conventional or pedantically precise; propriety.—**form′ally** *adv.*—**forma′tion** *n.* the act of forming; structure; an arrangement of troops, aircraft, etc.—**form′ative** *a.* giving form; plastic moulding; conducing to growth.—**form′less** *a.* shapeless; amorphous.—**good form,** correct etiquette [L. *forma*, shape].
-form (form) *suff.* in the shape of, as *cruciform* in the shape of a cross.
formaldehyde (form-al′de-hīd) *n.* a colourless, pungent gas, soluble in water, used in making disinfectants, and in the manufacture of plastics.
formalin (for′mạ-lin) *n.* *Trade name* for a 40% solution in water of formaldehyde gas, used as a disinfectant, deodoriser, and preservative.
format (for′ma, -mat) *n.* the general get-up of a book, its size, shape, style of binding, quality of paper, etc. [L. *forma*, a shape].
former (for′mẹr) *a.* preceding in time; long past; first mentioned.—**for′merly** *adv.*
formic (for′mik) *a.* pertaining to ants.—**form′icary** *n.* an anthill.—**form′icate** *v.i.* to crawl like an ant;—*a.* ant-like.—**formica′tion** *n.* (*Med.*) a morbid sensation of tingling, as if ants were crawling over the skin.—**formic acid,** fatty acid orig. obtained from ants [L. *formica*, an ant].
formidable (for′mi-dạ-bl) *a.* exciting fear or apprehension; overwhelming; terrible.—**for′midabil′ity, for′midableness** *n.*—**for′midably** *adv.* [L. *formidare*, to fear].
formula (form′ū-la) *n.* a prescribed form; a conventional phrase; a confession of faith; (*Math.*) a general rule or principle expressed in algebraic symbols; (*Chem.*) the series of symbols denoting the component parts of a substance; (*Med.*) a prescription;—*pl.* **form′ulas, formulae** (form′ū-lē).—**form′ular, formularisa′tion, formula′tion** *n.*—**form′ulary** *n.* a book containing formulas, or prescribed ritual;— *a.* prescribed.—**form′ulate, form′ulise** *v.t.* to reduce to a formula; to express in definite form [L. dim. of *forma*, a shape].
fornicate (for′ni-kāt) *v.i.* to indulge in unlawful sexual intercourse.—**fornica′tion** *n.* sexual intercourse between unmarried persons.—**for′nicator** *n.* (*fem.* **for′nicatress**) [L. *fornix*, an arch; a brothel].
forsake (for-sāk′) *v.t.* to abandon; to leave or give up entirely.—*pr.p.* **forsak′ing.**—*pa.t.* **forsook′.**—*pa.p.* **forsak′en.**—**forsak′en** *a.* deserted [O.E. *forsacan*, to relinquish].
forsooth (for-sŏŏth′) *adv.* in truth; indeed.
forswear (for-swār′) *v.t.* to renounce on oath; to abjure;—*v.i.* to swear falsely; to commit perjury.—*pa.t.* **forswore′.**—*pa.p.* **forsworn′** [O.E. *forswerian*, to renounce].
forsythia (for-sīth′i-a) *n.* a spring-flowering shrub with bright yellow blossoms [fr. 18th cent. gardener William *Forsyth*].
fort (fōrt) *n.* a stronghold; a small fortress; an isolated trading station, or outpost.—**fortalice** (for′ta-lis) *n.* a small fort or outwork [L. *fortis*, strong)].
forte (fōrt) *n.* a strong point; that in which one excels [Fr. *fort*, strong].
forte (for′te) *a.* and *adv.* (*Mus.*) loud; loudly;—*n.* a loud passage.—**fortis′simo** *adv.* very loudly [It. fr. L. *fortis*, strong].
forth (fōrth) *adv.* forwards, in place or time; out from concealment; into view; away.—**forth′coming** *a.* ready to come forth or appear; available.—**forth′right** *a.* straightforward;

frank.—*n.* a straight path.—**forth'with** *adv.* immediately [O.E. *fore*, before].
fortify (for´ti-fī) *v.t.* to strengthen, as by forts, batteries, etc.; to invigorate; to corroborate. —*pr.p.* **for'tifying.**—*pa.p.* **for'tified.**—**fortifica´tion** *n.* the art or act of strengthening by building defence works; the defence works built; a fortress [L. *fortis*, strong; *facere*, to make].
fortitude (for´ti-tūd) *n.* power to endure pain or confront danger; resolute endurance; stoicism [L. *fortitudo*, courage].
fortnight (fort´nīt) *n.* the space of fourteen days; two weeks.—**fort'nightly** *a.* and *adv.* at intervals of a fortnight [contr. of O.E. *feowertyne niht*, fourteen nights].
fortress (for´tres) *n.* a fortified place; a stronghold [O.Fr. *forteresse*, a stronghold].
fortuitous (for-tū´i-tus) *a.* happening by chance; accidental; casual.—**fortu'itously** *adv.* —**fortu'itousness, fortu'ity** *n.* [L. *fortuitus*, casual].
fortune (for´tūn) *n.* chance; that which befalls one; good luck or ill luck; possessions, esp. money or property.—**for'tunate** *a.* lucky; prosperous; propitious; successful.—**for'tunately** *adv.*—**for'tunateness** *n.*—**for'tunetell'er** *n.* one who reveals the future by palmistry, crystal-gazing, etc. [L. *fortuna*, chance].
forty (for´ti) *a.* and *n.* four times ten; a symbol expressing this, as 40, xl.—**for'tieth** *a.* constituting one of forty equal parts;—*n.* a fortieth part.—**forty winks,** a short nap in the day-time.—**Forties,** part of North Sea touching south-west of Norway W. to a line just E. of N.E. coast of Scotland [O.E. *feowertig*, forty].
forum (fō´rum) *n.* the market-place of ancient Rome where legal as well as commercial business was conducted; the law-courts, as distinct from Parliament; tribunal [L. *forum*, the market-place].
forward (for´wa̤rd) *adv.* towards a place in front; onwards in time; in a progressive or conspicuous way;—*a.* near or at the forepart, as in a ship; early in season; progressive; (*Colloq.*) cheeky;—*n.* (football, hockey, etc.) a. player in the front line;—*v.t.* to promote; to redirect (letter, parcel) to new address; to send out or dispatch.—**for'wardness** *n.* the state of being advanced; precocity; presumption.—**for'wards** *adv.* forward; straight before [O.E. *fore*, before; *weard*, in the direction of].
fosse (fos) *n.* a ditch; moat, or trench (dry or filled with water) [L. *fossa*, a ditch].
fossick (fos´ik) *v.i.* (*Austral.*) to dig out crevices with pick and knife; to work over in the hope of finding gold; (*Fig.*) to rummage about for pickings [prob. dialect word, *fussick*, to rummage].
fossil (fos´il) *n.* any portion of an animal or vegetable organism or imprint of such, which has undergone a process of petrifaction and lies embedded in the rock strata; (*Fig.*) an antiquated person or thing;—*a.* pert. to or resembling a fossil.—**fossilif'erous** *a.* bearing or containing fossils.—**fossil'ify, foss'ilise** *v.t.* to turn into a fossil; to petrify;—*v.i.* to become converted into a fossil [L. *fodere*, *fossum*, to dig].
foster (fos´te̤r) *v.t.* to nourish; to rear; (*Fig.*) to promote; to cherish.—**fos'ter-broth'er** *n.* a male child fostered with another child of different parents.—**fos'ter-child** *n.* a child reared by one who is not the parent.—**fos'ter-daugh'ter, fos'ter-son** *n.* a child brought up as a daughter or son, but not so by birth. —**fos'ter-fath'er, fos'ter-moth'er, fos'ter-pa'rent** *n.* [O.E. *fostrian*, to nourish].
fought (fot) *pa.t.* and *pa.p.* of verb **fight.**
foul (foul) *a.* filthy; containing offensive or putrescent matter; obscene; defaced; stormy (of weather); contrary (of wind); full of weeds; entangled (of ropes); unfair;—*n.* the breaking of a rule (in sports);—*v.t.* to make foul; to obstruct deliberately; to clog or jam;—*v.i.* to become foul, clogged, or jammed; to come into collision.—*pr.p.* **foul'ing.**—*pa.p.* **fouled.**—**foul'ly** *adv.*—**foul'-mouthed** *a.* using language scurrilous, obscene, or profane.—**foul'-play,** cheating; (*Law*) criminal violence; murder [O.E. *ful*, filthy].
foulard (fóól´ard) *n.* a light-weight silk or silk-like cotton fabric [Fr.].
found (found) *pa.t.* and *pa.p.* of verb **find.** —**found'ling** *n.* a small child who has been found abandoned.
found (found) *v.t.* to lay the basis or foundation of; to establish; to endow;—*v.i.* to rely; to depend.—**founda'tion** *n.* the act of founding; the base or substructure of a building; groundwork; underlying principle; an endowment; an endowed institution.—**founda'tioner** *n.* one who benefits by the funds of an endowed college or school; a bursar.—**founda'tion-stone** *n.* one of the stones used in the foundations of a building, esp. one laid with public ceremony.—**found'er** *n.* (*fem.* **found'ress**) one who establishes, originates, or endows [Fr. *fonder*, to establish].
found (found) *v.t.* to melt (metal, or materials for glassmaking) and pour into a mould; to cast.—**found'er** *n.*—**found'ing** *n.* metal-casting.—**found'ry, found'ery** *n.* works for casting metals; the process of metal-casting [Fr. *fondre*, to melt].
founder (foun´de̤r) *v.t.* to cause inflammation in the feet (of a horse) so as to lame; to cause to sink (as a ship);—*v.i.* to collapse; to fill with water and sink; to stick in boggy ground; to stumble and become lame [O.Fr. *fondrer*, to fall in].
fountain (foun´tān) *n.* a natural spring; an artificial jet of water.—**fount** *n.* a spring of water; a source.—**fount'ain-head** *n.* source of a stream; (*Fig.*) the origin [L. *fons*, a spring].
four (fōr) *a.* one more than three; twice two;—*n.* the sum of four units; the symbol representing this sum—4, IV.—**four'flush'er** *n.* (*U.S. Slang*) one who bluffs.—**four'fold** *a.* quadruple; folded or multiplied four times.—**four'-in-hand** *n.* a team of four horses drawing a carriage; the carriage itself.—**four'penny** *n.* an obsolete British silver coin worth fourpence.—**four'-post'er** *n.* a bed with a canopy supported on four posts.—**four'some** *n.* (*Golf*) a game for four persons.—**four'-square** *a.* having four equal sides and angles.—**four'-stroke** *a.* of an internal combustion engine firing once to every four strokes of the piston.—**four'teen** *n.* the sum of four and ten; the symbol representing this—14, XIV.;—*a.* four and ten.—**four'teenth** *a.* making one of fourteen equal parts.—**fourth** *a.* next after third;—*n.* one of four equal parts.—**fourth'ly** *adv.*—**four'-wheel'er** *n.* a carriage or cab with four wheels.—**to go on all fours,** to go on one's hands and knees (or feet) [O.E. *feower*, four].
fovea (fō´ve-a̤) *n.* (*Anat. Bot. Zool.*) a small depression.—**fo'veal, fo'veate** *a.* pitted; covered with small depressions [L.].
fowl (foul) *n.* a bird; a barn-door cock or hen; the flesh of a fowl;—*pl.* **fowls, fowl.**—*v.i.* to catch or kill wild fowl.—**fowl'er** *n.* one who traps wild fowl.—**fowl'ing-piece** *n.* a light shot-gun for shooting wild fowl [O.E. *fugol*, a bird].
fox (foks) *n.* (*fem.* **vix'en**) an animal of the canine family, genus *Vulpes*, reddish-brown in colour, with large, bushy tail and erect ears; (*Fig.*) a wily person;—*v.t.* to make sour, in fermenting; to mislead; to spy on.—**fox'-brush** *n.* the bushy tail of a fox.—**fox'-chase,** *n.* a fox-hunt.—**fox'-earth** *n.* a fox's burrow.—**fox'glove** *n.* a tall plant with white or purple-pink bell-shaped flowers and leaves which yield digitalis used medicinally as heart stimulant.—**fox'-hole** *n.*

(*Mil.*) a small trench; a dug-out for one or more men.—**fox'-hound** *n.* a fleet hound used for hunting foxes.—**fox'-hunt** *n.* the pursuit of a fox by huntsmen and hounds.—**fox'-hunt'er** *n.*—**fox'iness** *n.* the quality of being foxy; decay (in timber); discoloration (in paper); the state of being sour (of beer).—**fox'-ter'rier** *n.* a popular breed of dog trained for unearthing foxes, or 'ratting.'—**fox'-trot** *n.* a dance with syncopated rhythm.—**fox'y** *a.* pert. to foxes; cunning; reddish-brown in colour [O.E. *fox*, a fox].

foyer (fwȧ'yā) *n.* a large room in a theatre opening on to vestibule or staircase, for audience's use during intervals [Fr.].

foyson Same as **foison**.

fracas (fra-kȧ') *n.* a noisy quarrel; a disturbance; a brawl [Fr.].

fraction (frak'shun) *n.* a small portion; a fragment; (*Eccl.*) the breaking of bread in the sacrifice of the Eucharist; (*Arith.*) a division of a unit.—**decimal fraction,** a fraction expressed decimally.—**vulgar fraction,** a fraction expressed with numerator above, and denominator below the line.—**frac'tional** *a.*—**frac'tious** *a.* quarrelsome; peevish.—**frac'tiously** *adv.*—**frac'tiousness** *n.*—**frac'ture** *n.* the act of breaking; a breach or rupture; the breaking of a bone;—*v.t.* to break; to crack;—*v.i.* to become broken.—**compound fracture,** a fracture of a bone, the jagged edge of which protrudes through the skin.—**greenstick fracture,** a type of fracture common in children, in which the bone splits and bends like a twig.—**simple fracture,** a fracture where the bone is broken, but surrounding tissues and skin are undamaged [L. *frangere, fractum*, to break].

fragile (fraj'il or -īl) *a.* easily broken; frail; brittle.—**fragil'ity** *n.* [L. *fragilis*, breakable].

fragment (frag'ment) *n.* a portion broken off; an imperfect part; an unfinished portion, as of a literary composition.—**fragment'al** *a.* (*Geol.*) composed of fragments of different rocks.—**frag'mentary** *a.* broken [L. *fragmentum*, fr. *frangere*, to break].

fragrant (frā'grant) *a.* sweet smelling.—**fra'grance, fra'grancy** *n.* the quality of being sweet-scented; perfume; pleasant odour.—**fra'grantly** *adv.* [L. *fragrare*, to smell].

frail (frāl) *a.* fragile; easily destroyed; infirm; morally weak.—**frail'ly** *adv.*—**frail'ness, frail'ty** *n.* the quality of being weak [O.Fr. *fraile*, weak].

fraise (frāz) *n.* (*Fort.*) a defence comprising pointed stakes [Fr.].

frame (frām) *v.t.* to construct; to contrive; to provide with a frame; to put together, as a sentence; to articulate; (*U.S.*) to bring a false charge against;—*v.i.* to take shape;—*n.* anything made of parts fitted together; the skeleton of anything; a structure; the case or border round a picture; a mood of the mind; a glazed structure in which plants are protected from frost; a structure upon which anything is stretched.—**frame'-up** *n.* (*U.S. Slang*) a conspiracy; a faked charge.—**frame'work** *n.* the fabric which supports anything; an outline.—**fram'ing** *n.* [O.E. *framian*, to be helpful].

franc (frangk) *n.* a silver coin (100 centimes), the monetary unit of France, Belgium and Switzerland [O.Fr. *franc*].

franchise (fran'chiz, or -chīz) *n.* a privilege conferred by a king or government; the right to vote in Parliamentary elections;—*v.t.* to make free; to enfranchise [O.Fr. *franc*, free].

Franciscan (fran-sis'kạn) *n.* one of the order of friars founded by Francis of Assisi; one of the Grey Friars;—*a.* pert. to this order.

Franco (frangk'ō) *prefix*, Frank; French, in combinations such as *Franco-Prussian, Franco-Scottish*.—**Franc'ophile** *n.* one who admires France and all things French.—**Franc'ophobe** *n.* one who hates things French.

frangible (fran'ji-bl) *a.* breakable; fragile.—**frangibil'ity** *n.* [L. *frangere*, to break].

frangipane (fran'ji-pān) *n.* a pastry cake made with cream, almonds and sugar; a perfume. Also **frangipan'i** [fr. *Marquis Frangipani*].

frank (frangk) *a.* open; candid; unreserved;—*v.t.* to exempt from charge, esp. postage;—*n.* a signature on outside of a letter authorising its free delivery (orig. a privilege granted to M.P's.).—**frank'ly** *adv.* candidly.—**frank'ness** *n.* openness; honesty; candour [Fr. *franc*, free].

Frank (frangk) *n.* a member of one of the Germanic tribes from Franconia which migrated westwards, settled in Gaul in the 5th cent. and later gave France its name.—**Frank'ish** *a.* pert. to the Franks.

Frankenstein (frangk'en-stīn) *n.* any creation which brings disaster or torment to its author, from the character in Mary Shelley's romance of that name.

frankincense (frangk'in-sens) *n.* a dry, perfumed resin, burned as incense [Fr. *franc*, pure; *encens*, incense].

franklin (frangk'lin) *n.* formerly a freeholder, holding his estate free from feudal obligations; a country squire [M.E. *frankleyn*, fr. *franc*, free].

frantic (fran'tik) *a.* mad; frenzied; raving.—**fran'tically** *adv.* [O.Fr. *frenetique*, mad].

fraternal (fra-ter'nạl) *a.* pert. to a brother or brethren; brotherly.—**frater'nally** *adv.*—**fraternisa'tion** *n.*—**frat'ernise** *v.i.* to associate with others in a friendly way.—**frat'erniser** *n.*—**frater'nity** *n.* brotherhood; a group of men associated for a common purpose; a religious brotherhood; a guild [L. *frater*, a brother].

fratricide (frat'ri-sīd) *n.* the crime of killing a brother; one who commits this crime.—**fratricid'al** *a.* [L. *frater*, a brother; *caedere*, to kill].

frau (frou) *n.* a German married woman or widow; corresponding to *Mrs.* in English.—**fraulein** (froi'līn) *n.* an unmarried woman; *Miss* in English [Ger.].

fraud (frawd) *n.* deception deliberately practised; trickery; (*Colloq.*) a cheat; imposture.—**fraud'ulence, fraud'ulency** *n.* trickery, deceitfulness.—**fraud'ulent** *a.* pert. to or practising fraud; dishonest.—**fraud'ulently** *adv.* [L. *fraus*, a fraud].

fraught (frawt) *a.* freighted; laden; filled; stored [prob. Scand.].

fray (frā) *n.* an affray; a brawl; a contest [contr. of *affray*].

fray (frā) *v.t.* to wear through by friction; to ravel the edge (of cloth); (*Fig.*) to irritate, as the nerves, or temper;—*v.i.* to become frayed [Fr. *frayer*, to rub].

frazzle (fraz'l) *v.t.* (*U.S.*) to fray; to exhaust;—*n.* exhaustion [etym. unknown].

freak (frēk) *n.* a sudden whim; a prank; capricious conduct; something or someone abnormal.—**freak'ish** *a.*—**freak'ishly** *adv.*—**freak'ishness** *n.* [prob. O.E. *frec*, bold, rash].

freak (frēk) *v.t.* to spot or streak or dapple;—*n.* a streak [prob. from *freckle*].

freckle (frek'l) *n.* a small brownish spot on the skin caused by sunburn; any small spot;—*v.t.* to colour with freckles;—*v.i.* to become covered with freckles.—**freck'ly, freck'led** *a.* [M.E. *frakin*, a freckle].

free (frē) *a.* having political liberty; unrestricted; loose; independent; open; liberal; spontaneous; irregular; licentious; exempt from impositions, duties, or fees (as trade, education);—*adv.* without hindrance; gratis;—*v.t.* to set at liberty; to emancipate; to clear; to disentangle.—*pr.p.* **free'ing**.—*pa.p.* **freed**.—**free'-a'gency** *n.* the state of acting freely without constraint of will.—**free'-a'gent** *n.*—**free'booter** *n.* one who wanders about for plunder; a pillager.—**freed'man** *n.* one who has been freed from slavery.—**freed'om** *n.* liberty; franchise; immunity; indecorous familiarity; facility of address.—**free'-fight** *n.* (*Colloq.*) a melee.—**free hand,** drawn in easy, sweeping lines.—**free'-hand'ed** *a.* generous; liberal.—**free'hearted** *a.* generous-minded.—**free'hold** *n.* the tenure of property in fee-simple, or fee-tail, or for life;—*a.* held by freehold.—**free'holder** *n.*—**free kick** (*Football*) a kick allowed as compensation for opponents' breach of the rules.—**free'lance** *n.* orig. a mercenary soldier who sold his services to any country, esp. used of a journalist, not attached to a particular newspaper staff.—**free'-love** *n.* doctrine that sexual relations should be unhampered by marriage, etc.—**free'ly** *adv.*—**free'man** *n.* a man who is not a slave; one who enjoys the full privileges of a corporate body.—**freemar'tin** *n.* an imperfectly developed calf having parts of the organs of each sex.—**freema'son** *n.* orig. a member of an organisation of skilled masons; now, a member of a secret association for mutual assistance and social enjoyment.—**freemason'ic** *a.*—**freemas'onry** *n.* the system practised by Freemasons.—**free'-mind'ed** *a.* openminded; unworried.—**free'ness** *n.*—**free port,** a port open to traders and free from all restrictions, customs, duties, etc.—**free'spok'en** *a.* accustomed to speak without reserve.—**free'stone** *n.* a building-stone composed of sand and grit, easily quarried, cut, and carved without splitting into layers.—**free-think'er** *n.* one who professes to be independent of all orthodox religious authority; a rationalist.—**free'-think'ing, free'-thought** *n.*—**free'-tongued** *a.* free-spoken.—**free trade,** the policy of unrestricted international trade.—**free'-trad'er** *n.*—**free'-verse** *n.* a form of verse unrestricted in length of line, metre, stanza-form, and generally without rhyme.—**free'-will** *n.* the power of the human will to choose without restraint;—*a.* voluntary.—**Free Church,** a church not connected with the State [O.E. *freo,* free].

freesia (frē'zi-ạ) *n.* a bulbous plant with pale yellow flowers [fr. *Fries,* a Swedish botanist].

freeze (frēz) *v.t.* to harden into ice; to congeal; to preserve by refrigeration; to paralyse with cold or terror; to render credits unrealisable; —*v.i.* to become hardened into ice; to become congealed or stiff with cold.—*pr.p.* **freez'ing**.—*pa.t.* **froze**.—*pa.p.* **froz'en**.—*n.* frost. —**freez'able** *a.*—**freez'ing-point** *n.* the temperature at which a liquid turns solid, esp. that at which water freezes, marked 32° F. or 0° C. —**freez'ingly** *adv.*—**to freeze out** (*Colloq.*) to get rid of; to ignore [O.E. *freosan,* to freeze].

freight (frāt) *n.* the cargo of a ship; a load; charge for conveyance of goods;—*v.t.* to load a ship, etc.—**freight'age** *n.* charge for transport of goods; freight.—**freight'er** *n.* one who freights a ship, etc.; a cargo-boat [late form of *fraught*].

French (frensh) *a.* pert. to France or its inhabitants;—*n.* the inhabitants or the language of France.—**French bean,** the kidney bean; scarlet runner.—**French cake,** iced cake.—**French chalk,** hydrated magnesium silicate used as a dry lubricant; a variety of talc.—**French'-horn** *n.* a musical wind-instrument with mellow note like a hunting-horn.—**French'man** (*fem.* **French'woman**) *n.* a native of France.—**French'-pol'ish** *n.* a polish for wood made of shellac dissolved in methylated spirit;—*v.t.* to apply this polish to wood-surface.—**French window,** one functioning as door and window.—**to take French leave,** to go away without permission or warning.

frenzy (fren'zi) *n.* violent agitation of the mind; madness;—*v.t.* to render frantic.—**fren'zied, fren'zical** *a.*—**frenet'ic** (also **phrenet'ic**) *a.* mad; frenzied [Gk. *phrenitis,* inflammation of the brain].

freon (frē'on) *n.* gas used in refrigeration-plant, and for air-conditioning [fr. *freeze*].

frequent (frē'kwent) *a.* happening at short intervals; constantly recurring; repeated; abundant.—**frequent** (frē-kwent') *v.t.* to visit often.—**fre'quency** *n.* the state of occurring repeatedly; periodicity; (*Phys.*) number of vibrations per second of a recurring phenomenon.—**frequenta'tion** *n.* the practice of visiting repeatedly.—**frequent'ative** *a.* (*Gram.*) denoting the repetition of an action;—*n.* (*Gram.*) a word, usually a verb, expressing frequency or intensity of an action.—**frequent'er** *n.*—**fre'quently** *adv.*—**fre'quentness** *n.* [L. *frequens*].

fresco (fres'kō) *n.* a method of mural decoration on walls of fresh, still damp, plaster;—*v.t.* to paint in fresco [It. *fresco,* fresh].

fresh (fresh) *a.* vigorous; unimpaired; newly cut; not stale; brisk; original; unsalted; (*U.S. Slang*) impudent;—*n.* a stream of fresh water; a freshet.—**fresh'en** *v.t.* to make fresh;—*v.i.* to grow fresh; to become vigorous.—**fresh'ener** *n.*—**fresh'es** *n.* the partly fresh, partly salt, water at the mouths of rivers.—**fresh'et** *n.* an inundation caused by rains or melting snows; a fresh-water stream.—**fresh'man** *n.* a first-year University student. Also **fresh'er**.—**fresh'ness** *n.*—**fresh'-wat'er** *a.* pert. to or living in water which is not salt; accustomed to sail on fresh water only [M.E. *fresch,* fresh].

fret (fret) *v.t.* to wear away by friction; to eat away; to ruffle; to irritate;—*v.i.* to wear away; to be corroded; to be vexed or peevish.—*pr.p.* **fret'ting**.—*pa.p.* **fret'ted**.—*n.* vexation; irritation; the ruffled surface of water.—**fret'ful** *a.* querulous.—**fret'fully** *adv.*—**fret'fulness** *n.* [O.E. *fretan,* to devour].

fret (fret) *n.* ornamental work, consisting usually of strips, interlaced at right angles; perforated wood-carving.—**fret'-saw** *n.* a small saw used in fretwork.—**fret'ted, fret'ty** *a.* ornamented with frets.—**fret'work** *n.* decorative, perforated work on wood or metal done by a fretsaw [O.Fr. *frete,* interlaced work].

fret (fret) *n.* a small piece of wood or wire fixed on the finger-board, as of a guitar, under the strings [prob. O.Fr. *frete,* ferrule].

Freudian (froi'di-ạn) *a.* pert. to *Sigmund Freud,* (1856-1939) the Austrian psychopathist, or to his theories.

friable (frī'ạ-bl) *a.* easily crumbled or reduced to powder.—**fri'ableness, friabil'ity** *n.* [L. *friabilis,* crumbling].

friar (frī'ạr) *n.* a member of one of the four Orders of mendicant monks, the Franciscans (Grey Friars), Dominicans (Black Friars), Carmelites (White Friars), and Augustinians. —**friar's balsam,** tincture of benzoin used to heal wounds.—**friar's lantern,** the will o' the wisp.—**fri'ary** *n.* a monastery [L. *frater,* a brother].

fribble (frib'l) *a.* frivolous; trifling;—*n.* a frivolous person;—*v.i.* to fritter away time [prob. onomatopoeic].

fricassee (frik-a-sē) *n.* a dish of minced fowl, rabbit, etc. stewed with rich gravy sauce;—*v.t.* to make a fricassee [Fr.].

friction (frik'shun) *n.* the act of rubbing one thing against another; (*Phys.*) the resistance which a body encounters in moving across the surface of another with which it is in contact; (*Med.*) massage; unpleasantness.—**fric'ative** *a.* produced by friction, as consonants sounded by friction of breath forced through a narrow passage.—**fric'tional** *a.* caused by friction.—**fric'tionally** *adv.* [L. *fricare,* to rub].

Friday (frī'dā) *n.* the sixth day of the week [O.E. *Frig,* wife of Odin; *daeg,* a day].

fried (frīd) *pa.t.* and *pa.p.* of verb **fry**.

friend (frend) *n.* one attached to another by esteem and affection; an intimate associate; a supporter.—**Friend** *n.* a member of the Quakers.—**friend'less** *a.* without friends.—**friend'lily** *adv.*—**friend'liness** *n.* friend'ly feeling.—**friend'ly** *a.* having the dis position of a friend; kind; propitious.—**friend'ship** *n.* attachment to a friend, founded on mutual esteem.—**Friendly Society,** a voluntary organisation for the mutual benefit of members in sickness, old age, unemployment, etc.—**Society of Friends,** the Quaker sect [O.E. *freond*, a friend].

Friesian (frē'zhan) *n.* an inhabitant of Friesland; the language of the Friesians; a type of cattle orig. bred in Friesland, noted as milkers.—Also **Fri'sian.**

frieze (frēz) *n.* a heavy woollen cloth with nap on one side [Fr. *frise*, a curl].

frieze (frēz) *n.* (*Archit.*) the part of an entablature between the architrave and cornice; in house decoration the upper part of the wall, below the cornice [Fr. *frise*, a fringe].

frigate (frig'āt) *n.* a fast 2-decked sailing ship of war of the 18th and 19th centuries; in modern times a large sloop designed for escort and anti-submarine duties.—**frigate bird,** a tropical sea-bird of prey, allied to the gannet [It. *fregata*, a frigate].

fright (frīt) *n.* sudden and violent fear; extreme terror; alarm; (*Colloq.*) an ugly or grotesque person or object;—*v.t.* to make afraid.—**fright'en** *v.t.* to terrify; to scare.—**fright'ened** *a.* timid.—**fright'ful** *a.* terrible; calamitous; shocking.—**fright'fully** *adv.* terribly; (*Colloq.*) very.—**fright'fulness** *n.*—**fright'some** *a.* frightful [O.E. *fyrhto*, fear].

frigid (frij'id) *a.* very cold (esp. of climate); unfeeling; passionless; stiff.—**frigid'ity** *n.* coldness.—**frig'idly** *adv.*—**frig'idness** *n.*—**frigorif'ic** *a.* causing cold [L. *frigidus*, cold].

frill (fril) *n.* a plaited or gathered edging of linen, etc.; a similar edging of paper round a pie-dish, ham-knuckle, etc.; a ruffle; (*Fig.*) excessive ornament (as in style);—*v.t.* to ornament with a frill;—*v.i.* to become crinkled like a frill.—**frill'ies** *n.pl.* (*Colloq.*) women's undergarments [etym. doubtful].

fringe (frinj) *n.* loose threads as ornamental edging of cloth; border; hair cut across and partially covering forehead; the outside edge of anything;—*v.t.* to adorn with fringe; to border [O.Fr. *fringe*, a border].

frippery (frip'ẹr-i) *n.* orig. cast-off clothes; tawdry finery; useless matter; trumpery [Fr. *fripperie*, old clothes].

frisk (frisk) *v.i.* to leap; to gambol; to skip;—*n.* a frolic.—**frisk'ily** *adv.* playfully.—**frisk'iness** *n.*—**frisk'y** *a.* lively; frolicsome; gay [O.Fr. *frisque*, lively].

frisking (fris'king) *n.* (*U.S. Slang*) searching a person, usually for concealed weapons; (*Atomic Warfare*) the passing of the probe of a Contamination Meter over a person, to test for the presence or absence of radioactive contamination [fr. *frisk*].

frit (frit) *n.* the partial calcination, before complete fusion, of the materials used in the making of glass;—*v.t.* to make into glass [It. *fritta*, fried].

frith (frith) *n.* Var. of **firth.**

fritter (frit'ẹr) *n.* a slice of fruit or meat dipped in batter and fried [O.Fr. *friture*, something fried].

fritter (frit'ẹr) *v.t.* to waste (time, energy, etc.) in a futile way.—**fritt'erer** *n.* [prob. conn. with L. *frangere*, to break].

frivol (friv'ol) *v.t.* and *v.i.* to squander, esp. time or energy; to fritter away.—**frivol'ity** *n.* the act or habit of idly wasting time; lack of seriousness.—**friv'olous** *a.* trifling; silly; superficial.—**friv'olously** *adv.*—**friv'olousness** *n.* [L. *frivolus*, paltry].

frizz, friz (friz) *v.t.* to curl; to crisp; to form into little burs, as nap of cloth;—*n.* a row of small curls.—**frizz'le** *v.t.* to curl; in cooking, to crisp by frying;—*n.* curled hair [O.Fr. *friser*, to curl].

fro (frō) *adv.* from; away; back, as in *to and fro*.

frock (frok) *n.* a woman's dress; a monk's long, wide sleeved garment; a child's outer garment.—**frock'-coat** *n.* a double-breasted, full skirted black coat worn by men [O.Fr. *froc*, a monk's frock].

Froebelism (frẹ-bel-izm) *n.* a kindergarten system formulated by *Friedrich Froebel*, who emphasised the free expression of the child's creative instincts.

frog (frog) *n.* an amphibious, tailless animal, (developed from a tadpole); a V-shaped horny pad on the sole of a horse's foot; a V-shaped section of train or tram lines, where two sets of rails cross; ornamental braiding on uniform, or ornamental fastening of loop and button;—*v.t.* to ornament with frogs.—**frog'-march** *n.* a method of carrying a troublesome prisoner, face downwards, each limb being held.—**frog'-men** *n.* (*World War* 2) the nickname given to the underwater swimming men.—**Frogs** or **Frog'gies** *n.pl.* nickname given to Frenchmen [O.E. *frogga*, a frog].

frolic (frol'ik) *n.* a wild prank; a merry-making; gaiety;—*a.* full of pranks; merry;—*v.i.* to play wild pranks; to gambol.—*pr.p.* **frol'icking.**—*pa.p.* **frol'icked.**—**frol'icsome** *a.* sportive [Dut. *vroolijk*, merry].

from (from) *prep.* away; forth; out of; on account of; at a distance [O.E. *fram*, from].

frond (frond) *n.* (*Bot.*) an organ of certain flowerless plants, such as ferns, in which leaf and stem are combined and bear reproductive cells [L. *frons*, a leaf].

front (frunt) *n.* the forehead; the human countenance; the forepart; (*Mil.*) firing line; battle-zone; the promenade at a sea-side resort; stiffened breast of man's shirt; (*Fig.*) forwardness.—*a.* pert. to, or at the front of, anything;—*adv.* to the front;—*v.t.* and *v.i.* to have the face or front towards any point.—**front'age** *n.* the front part of general exposure of a building; land abutting on street, river, or sea.—**front'al** *a.* pert. to the forehead or foremost part; (*Mil.*) direct, as an attack, without flanking movement;—*n.* ornament worn on forehead; an ornamental cloth for altar front.—**front'let** *n.* a band worn across the forehead.—**to put a bold front on,** to face up boldly.—**front-page news,** news of vital importance [L. *frons*, the forehead].

frontier (frun'tēr) *n.* border of a country; an outpost;—*a.* bordering; pioneering.—**fron'tiersman** *n.* one who settles on a frontier [Fr. *frontier*, the border].

frontispiece (frun'tis-pēs) *n.* orig. the main face of a building; an engraving or decorated page fronting the title-page of a book [L. *frons*, the front; *specere*, to see].

frost (frost) *n.* condition when water turns to ice, i.e. when temperature falls below 32° F.; severe cold; frozen dew; (*Fig.*) a failure; a disappointment;—*v.t.* to cover with hoar-frost; to nip (as plants); to sharpen, as a horse's shoe, to prevent slipping.—**frost'bite** *n.* freezing of the skin and tissues due to exposure to extreme cold.—**frost'-bit'ten** *a.*—**frost'ed** *a.* covered with frost or anything resembling it; (*Fig.*) not genial.—**frost'ily** *adv.*—**frost'iness** *n.*—**frost'y** *a.* accompanied with frost; chilly; white; grey-haired; frigid (in manner or feeling) [O.E. *forst*, fr. *freosan*, to freeze].

froth (froth) *n.* spume; foam; (*Fig.*) an empty show of eloquence;—*v.t.* to cause to froth;—*v.i.* to bubble; (*Fig.*) to speak superficially.—**froth'iness** *n.*—**froth'y** *a.* light; foamy [Scand. *frotha*, froth].

frounce (frouns) *v.t.* to curl; to plait into folds; to wrinkle [O.Fr. *fronce*, a plait].

froward (frō'ard) *a.* perverse; refractory.—**fro'wardly** *adv.*—**fro'wardness** *n.* perversity; obstinacy [O.E. *fra*, away, and *ward*].

frown (froun) *v.i.* to wrinkle the brow; to scowl;—*v.t.* to rebuke by a stern look;—*n.* a wrinkling of the brow to express disapproval [O.Fr. *froignier*, to look sullen].

frowst (froust) *n.* a stuffy atmosphere;—*v.i.* to lounge about.—**frowst'y** *a.* airless; ill-ventilated; musty [etym. doubtful].

frowsy (frou'zi) *a.* musty; unkempt; slovenly [etym. uncertain].

frozen (frōz'n) *pa.p.* of the verb **freeze**.

fructify (fruk'ti-fī) *v.t.* to make fruitful; to fertilise;—*v.i.* to bear fruit; (*Fig.*) to succeed; to materialise.—**fructes'cence** *n.* the period when fruit matures.—**fructif'erous** *a.* fruit-bearing.—**fructifica'tion** *n.* act or process of bearing fruit; (*Bot.*) any spore-bearing structure.—**fruc'tose** *n.* fruit-sugar; levulose [L. *fructus*, fruit].

frugal (fròò'gal) *a.* sparing; thrifty; economical; careful.—**frugal'ity** *n.* economy; thrift. —**fru'gally** *adv.*—**fru'galness** *n.* [L. *frugalis*, thrifty].

frugiferous (fròò-jif'er-us) *a.* fruit-bearing. —**frugiv'orous** *a.* (*Zool.*) feeding on fruit [L. *frux*, fruit; *ferre*, to bear; *vorare*, to devour].

fruit (fròòt) *n.* the produce of the earth used for man's needs; the edible produce or seed of a plant; offspring; the consequence or outcome;—*v.i.* to produce fruit.—**fruit'age** *n.* fruit collectively.—**fruitar'ian** *n.* one who lives almost wholly on fruit.—**fruit'er** *n.* fruit bearing tree; fruit-carrying ship.—**fruit'erer** *n.* (*fem.* **fruit'eress**) one who sells fruit.—**fruit'ful** *a.* producing fruit; abundant.—**fruit'fully** *adv.*—**fruit'fulness** *n.* productivity.—**fruit'ing** *n.* the process of bearing fruit.—**fruit'less** *a.* having no fruit; (*Fig.*) profitless; vain; empty.—**fruit'lessly** *adv.*—**fruitlessness** *n.* —**fruit'let** *n.* a druplet.—**fruit'-su'gar** *n.* glucose; fructose.—**fruit'y** *a.* resembling fruit; mellow; (*Colloq.*) rather coarse (of humour) [O.Fr. *fruit*, fruit].

fruition (fròò-ish'un) *n.* fulfilment of hopes and desires; enjoyment from possession.—**fruit'ive** *a.* [L. *fruitio*, enjoyment].

frumentation (fròò-men-tā'shun) *n.* a distribution of grain to the starving people of Ancient Rome.—**fru'menty** *n.* wheat boiled in milk, sweetened and spiced. Also **fro'menty** [L. *frumentum*, corn].

frump (frump) *n.* a dowdy, old-fashioned woman [etym. doubtful].

frustrate (frus'trāt) *v.t.* to bring to nothing; to balk; to thwart; to circumvent.—**frustra'tion** *n.* disappointment; defeat.—**frustra'tive** *a.* [L. *frustrari*, to deceive].

frustum (frus'tum) *n.* (*Geom.*) the remaining part of a solid figure when the top has been cut off by a plane parallel to the base.—*pl.* **frus'ta** [L. *frustum*, a piece].

frutescent (fròò-tes'ent) *a.* becoming shrubby. —**fru'ticose**, **fru'ticous**, **frutic'ulose** *a.* bushy; shrub-like [L. *frutex*, a shrub].

fry (frī) *v.t.* to dress and roast with fat in a pan over the fire;—*v.i.* to be cooked in a frying-pan; to sizzle.—*pr.p.* **fry'ing**.—*pa.p.* **fried**.—*n.* a dish of anything fried.—**fry'er**, **fri'er** *n.* [O.Fr. *frire*, to roast].

fry (frī) *n.* young fish just spawned; young children [M.E. *fri*, offspring].

fuchsia (fū'shi-a) *n.* a genus of flowering plants, with drooping flowers of red and purple, or pink and white [fr. *Fuchs*, a 16th cent. German botanist].

fuddle (fud'l) *v.t.* to make confused by drink;—*v.i.* to tipple [etym. doubtful].

fudge (fuj) *interj.* stuff; nonsense;—*v.t.* to fake [etym. doubtful].

fudge (fuj) *n.* a sweetmeat of the consistency of soft tablet; space reserved in a newspaper for last minute news (in last sense also **fudge'-box**) [etym. doubtful].

fuel (fū'el) *n.* anything combustible to feed a fire, as wood, coal;—*v.t.* to provide with fuel, as a ship [O.Fr. *fouaille*, fr. L. *focus*, a hearth].

fug (fug) *n.* (*Colloq.*) stuffy atmosphere of an ill-ventilated room [etym. unknown].

fugacious (fū-gā'shus) *a.* fleeting; ephemeral; elusive.—**fuga'ciousness**, **fugac'ity** *n.* [L. *fugax*, fleeing].

fugitive (fū'ji-tiv) *a.* escaping; fleeing; fleeting; occasional;—*n.* a refugee; one who flees from justice.—**fug'itively** *adv.*—**fug'itiveness** *n.* [L. *fugere*, to flee].

fugleman (fū'gl-man) *n.* a soldier who stands in front of drilling-squad as a model or leader; spokesman. Also **flu'gelman** [Ger. *Flugelmann*, a leader of a file].

fugue (fūg) *n.* (*Mus.*) a musical composition for voices and or instruments based on chief and subsidiary themes; (*Psychiatry*) form of amnesia.—**fug'al** *a.* [L. *fuga*, flight].

fulcrum (ful'krum) *n.* (*Mech.*) the pivot of a lever; (*Fig.*) means used to achieve a purpose or stimulate others.—*pl.* **ful'crums**, **ful'cra** [L. *fulcrum*, a bed-post].

fulfil (fool-fil') *v.t.* to carry into effect; to execute; to discharge; to satisfy (as hopes).—*pr.p.* **fulfil'ling**.—*pa.p.* **fulfilled'**.—**fulfil'ler** *n.*—**fulfil'ment** *n.* accomplishment; execution [O.E. *full*, full; *fyllan*, to fill].

fulgent (ful'jent) *a.* shining; dazzling; flaming.—**ful'gency** *n.*—**ful'gently** *adv.* [L. *fulgere*, to shine].

fulgurate (ful'gū-rāt) *v.i.* to flash like lightning [L. *fulgur*, lightning].

fuliginous (fū-lij'in-us) *a.* sooty; dusky.—**fuliginos'ity** *n.* [L. *fuligo*, soot].

full (fool) *a.* filled to capacity; replete; crowded; complete; plump; final; abundant; showing the whole surface (as the moon); ample (of dress-material); (*Colloq.*) drunk; clear and resonant (of sounds);—*n.* the utmost extent; highest degree.—*adv.* quite; completely; exactly; very.—**full'-blood'ed** *a.* of pure race; vigorous.—**full'-blown** *a.* fully developed, as a flower.—**full'-bott'omed** *a.* fully spread at the extremity, as a wig.—**full'-dress** *n.* dress worn on ceremonial occasions;—*a.* formal.—**full-length**, showing whole of person's figure, as a portrait; straight out.—**full moon**, the moon with its whole disc visible.—**full'ness** **ful'ness** *n.* copiousness; completeness; satiety; corpulence; deep emotion.—**full'-stop** *n.* a period (in punctuation).—**full'y** *adv.* completely [O.E. *full*, full].

full (fool) *v.t.* to cleanse, shrink and thicken cloth in a mill;—*v.i.* to become thick or felted.—**full'er** *n.* one who fulls cloth.—**fuller's earth**, a clay used by fullers to absorb grease from newly woven cloth [O.E. *fullian*, to whiten cloth].

fulmar (fòòl'mar) *n.* sea-bird, species of petrel [prob. Scand. *full*, foul; *mar*, gull].

fulminate (ful'min-āt) *v.t.* to cause to explode; to detonate; (*Fig.*) to denounce vehemently;—*v.i.* to flash; to explode; to thunder forth official censure;—*n.* a compound of fulminic acid exploding by percussion, friction, or heat, as *fulminate of mercury*.—**ful'minant** *a.* fulminating;—*n.* an explosive.—**fulmina'tion** *n.* the act of fulminating; an explosion; a biting denunciation. —**ful'minatory**, **fulmin'eous**, **ful'minous** *a.*—**fulmin'ic** *a.* explosive [L. *fulmen*, lightning].

fulsome (fòòl'sum) *a.* excessive; cloying; nauseating; insincere, as in *fulsome flattery*.—**ful'somely** *adv.*—**ful'someness** *n.* [O.E. *full*].

fulvous (ful'vus) *a.* tawny; dull yellow. Also **ful'vid** [L. *fulvus*, tawny].

fumarole (fūm'a-rōl) *n.* a small fissure in volcano, from which gas and steam escape [Fr. *fumerole*, a smoke-hole].

fumble (fum'bl) *v.i.* to grope blindly or awkwardly;—*v.t.* to handle clumsily [Scand. *fumla*, to grope].

fume (fūm) *n.* pungent vapour from combustion or exhalation; (*Fig.*) excitement; rage;—*v.i.* to smoke; to be in a rage;—*v.t.* to subject to fumes to darken colours, as oak.—**fum'atory** *n.* a smoke-chamber.—**fum'ous**, **fum'ose**, **fum'y** *a.* producing smoke or fumes [L. *fumus*, smoke].

fumigate (fūm'i-gāt) *v.t.* to expose to

poisonous gas or smoke, esp. for the purpose of destroying germs; to perfume or deodorise.—**fum'igator** *n.* apparatus or substance used in fumigation [L. *fumigare*, to smoke].

fun (fun) *n.* merriment; hilarity; sport.—**fun'nily** *adv.*—**fun'niness, fun'niment, fun'ning** *n.* joking; drollery.—**fun'ny** *a.* full of fun; comical; droll; odd; difficult to explain [M.E. *fonnen*, to be silly].

funambulate (fū-nam'bū-lāt) *v.i.* to balance and walk on a tight-rope.—**funam'bulator, funam'bulist** *n.* [L. *funis*, a rope; *ambulare*, to walk].

function (fungk'shun) *n.* performance; the special work done by an organ or structure; office; ceremony; (*Math.*) a quantity the value of which varies with that of another quantity; a social entertainment;—*v.i.* to operate; to fulfil a set task.—**func'tional** *a.* having a special purpose; pert. to a duty or office.—**func'tionally** *adv.*—**func'tionary** *n.* an official;—*a.* functional [L. *fungi, functus*, to perform].

fund (fund) *n.* permanent stock or capital; an invested sum, the income of which is used for a set purpose; a store; ample supply;—*pl.* the stock of the National Debt; public securities;—*v.t.* to establish a fund for the payment of interest.—**fund'ed** *a.* denoting that part of the national debt for which certain sums are appropriated for payment of the interest; invested in public funds.—**sinking fund**, fund established for the reduction of the National Debt [L. *fundus*, the bottom].

fundament (fun'da-ment) *n.* the lower part or seat of the body.—**fundament'al** *a.* pert. to the foundations; basic; essential;—*n.* a primary principle; origin; (*Mus.*) the bottom note of a chord.—**fundament'alism** *n.* belief in literal truth of the Bible.—**fundament'alist** *n.*—**fundament'ally** *adv.* [L. *fundamentum*, the foundation].

funeral (fū'ne-ral) *n.* the ceremony of burying or cremating the dead; obsequies;—*a.* pert. to or used at burial.—**fu'nerary, funer'eal** *a.* [L. *funus*, burial rites].

fungus (fung'gus) *n.* the lowest division of cellular cryptogamic plants ranging from microscopic moulds to mushrooms, toadstools, puff-balls, etc.; (*Path.*) a spongy, morbid growth; proud-flesh;—*pl.* **fungi** (fun'jī), **funguses** (fung'gus-ez).—**fung'al. fung'aceous** *a.* like a fungus.—**fun'gic** (-j-), **fun'giform** (-j-) *a.* mushroom-shaped.—**fun'gicide** *n.* any preparation which destroys bacteria, moulds or fungoid growths.—**fung'oid, fung'ous** *a.* resembling a fungus; excrescent [L. *fungus*, a mushroom].

funicle (fū'ni-kl) *n.* a ligature; a fibre; (*Bot.*) the stalk of a seed.—**funic'ular** *a.*—**funicular railway**, a cable railway [L. *funiculus*, dim. of *funis*, a cord].

funk (fungk) *n.* (*Colloq.*) abject terror; panic; one who shrinks in terror;—*v.i.* and *v.t.* to be terrified of or by.—**funk'y** *a.*—**funk'-hole** *n.* a dug-out; a job through which military service is avoided [etym. unknown].

funnel (fun'el) *n.* an inverted hollow metal cone with tube, used for filling vessels with narrow inlet; the smoke-stack of a steam-ship or railway engine.—**fun'nelled** *a.* [L. *fundere*, to pour].

fur (fur) *n.* the short, fine, soft hair of certain animals; animal pelts used for coats, necklets, etc.; game (rabbits, hares, etc.) as opposed to *feathered* game; coating on the tongue; deposit on inside of kettles, etc.—*v.t.* to line, face, or cover with fur; to coat with morbid matter.—*pr.p.* **fur'ring**.—*pa.p.* **furred**.—**fur'rier** *n.* a dealer in furs.—**fur'riery** *n.* the fur-trade; furs collectively.—**fur'ry** *a.* [M.E. *forre*, fur].

furbelow (fur'be-lō) *n.* a plaited trimming on a lady's dress; an ornamental border.—**fur'belowed** *a.* [Sp. *falbala*, a flounce].

furbish (fur'bish) *v.t.* to polish; to burnish; to renovate [O.Fr. *fourbir*, to polish].

furcate (fur'kāt) *a.* forked; branched like a fork;—*v.i.* to branch out [L. *furca*, a fork].

furfur (fur'fur) *n.* scurf; dandruff.—**furfura'ceous, fur'furous** *a.* scurfy; (*Bot.*) covered with bran-like scales [L. *furfur*, bran].

furious (fū'ri-us) *a.* raging; incensed; violent; savage.—**fu'riously** *adv.*—**fu'riousness** *n.* [L. *furiosus*, raging].

furl (furl) *v.t.* to roll, as a sail [contr. of O.Fr. *fardel*, a bundle].

furlong (fur'long) *n.* eighth of mile; 220 yards [O.E. *furh*, a furrow; *lang*, long].

furlough (fur'lō) *n.* leave of absence;—*v.t.* to grant leave of absence [Dut. *verlof*, permission].

furmenty, furmity See **frumenty.**

furnace (fur'nās) *n.* an enclosed structure for the generating of heat required for smelting ores, warming houses, etc.; (*Fig.*) a time or place of severe trial or affliction [L. *fornus*, an oven].

furnish (fur'nish) *v.t.* to supply; to equip; to fit out;—*v.i.* to supply a room or house with furniture.—**fur'nisher** *n.*—**fur'nishings** *n.pl.* fittings, of a house, esp. furniture, curtains, carpets, etc. [Fr. *fournir*, to provide].

furniture (fur'ni-tūr) *n.* equipment; outfit; movables; that which is put into a house for use or ornament [Fr. *fournir*, to provide].

furor (fū'ror) *n.* wild excitement; enthusiasm [L. *furor*, rage].

furore (fŏŏ-rōr'ā) *n.* an enthusiastic outburst; acclaim; craze [It. *furore*, rage].

furrow (fur'ō) *n.* a trench made by a plough; channel; groove; deep wrinkle;—*v.t.* to plough; to mark with wrinkles.—**furr'owy** *a.* [O.E. *furh*, a furrow].

further (fur'THẹr) *a.* more remote; additional;—*adv.* to a greater distance; moreover.—**fur'thermore** *adv.* moreover; besides;—**fur'thermost** *a.* most remote.—**fur'thest** *adv.* and *a.* most remote (**far'ther, far'thest** are preferred as comp. and superl. of *far*) [O.E. *furthor*, comp. of *forth*, forwards].

further (fur'THẹr) *v.t.* to help forward; to promote.—**fur'therance** *n.* the act of furthering [O.E. *fyrthian*, to promote].

furtive (fur'tiv) *a.* done stealthily; covert; sly.—**fur'tively** *adv.* [L. *fur*, a thief].

fury (fū'ri) *n.* rage; passion; frenzy; (*Myth.*) a goddess of revenge; an avenging spirit; a virago [L. *furia*, rage].

furze (furz) *n.* a spiny, yellow-flowered evergreen plant, also called *gorse*, and *whin*.—**furz'y, furz'en** *a.* [etym. doubtful].

fuscous (fus'kus) *a.* of a dark greyish-brown colour [L. *fuscus*, dark].

fuse (fūz) *v.t.* to melt (as metal) by heat; to amalgamate;—*v.i.* to become liquid;—*n.* a tube filled with combustible matter, used in blasting or discharge of bombs, etc.; a soft wire used as a safety device in electric lighting and heating systems.—**fusibil'ity** *n.*—**fu'sible** *a.* capable of being melted or liquefied.—**fu'sion** *n.* the act or process of melting; the state of being melted or blended; coalition [L. *fundere, fusum*, to melt].

fusee (fū-zē') *n.* the spindle-shaped wheel in a clock or watch, round which the chain is wound; a match used by smokers to light a pipe in a wind. Also **fuzee'** [Fr. *fusée*, a spindleful].

fuselage (fū'ze-lij or fū-zẹ-làzh') *n.* the spindle-shaped body of an aircraft [O.Fr. *fusel*, a spindle].

fusel-oil (fū'zel-oil) *n.* a poisonous colourless oily spirit used in manufacture of lacquers and as fuel. Also called *potato-oil* [Ger. *Fusel*, bad spirit].

fusil (fū'zil) *n.* a light flint-lock musket.—**fusilier'** *n.* orig. a soldier armed with a fusil; infantryman, esp. belonging to a few regiments.—**fu'sillade** *n.* the simultaneous dis-

charge of firearms;—*v.t.* to shoot down [O.Fr. *fuisil*, a flint-musket].
fuss (fus) *n.* bustle; unnecessary ado; needless activity;—*v.i.* to become nervously agitated;—*v.t.* to worry another with excessive attentions.—**fuss′ily** *adv.*—**fuss′iness** *n.*—**fuss′y** *a.* [prob. imit. word].
fust (fust) *n.* the shaft of a column; a strong, musty smell (orig. of a cask);—*v.i.* to have a rank smell [O.Fr. *fust*, a staff or cask].
fustian (fust′yạn) *n.* a coarse cotton twilled fabric, including corduroy, moleskin, velveteen; (*Fig.*) bombast; empty boasting;—*a.* bombastic; pretentious [M.E. *fustyane*, fr. *Fustat* (Egypt) where the cloth was first made].
fustigation (fus-ti-gā′shun) *n.* a thrashing with a stick.—**fus′tigate** *v.t.* to cudgel [L. *fustigare*, to cudgel].
futile (fū′tīl, fū′til) *a.* ineffectual, unavailing, useless.—**fu′tilely** *adv.*—**futil′ity** *n.* uselessness; fruitlessness [L. *futilis*, worthless].
futtock (fut′uk) *n.* one of the timbers in the frame or rib of a ship [etym. doubtful].
future (fūt′ūr) *a.* about to happen; that is to come hereafter;—*n.* time to come; (*Gram.*) tense denoting time to come.—**fut′urism** *n.* a modern aesthetic movement marked by complete departure from tradition.—**fut′urist** *n.*—**futurist′ic** *a.*—**futur′ity** *n.* time to come [L. *futurus*, about to be].
fuze Same as **fuse.**
fuzz (fuz) *n.* fine, light particles; fluff;—*v.i.* to fly off in minute particles.—**fuzz′-ball** *n.* a puff-ball.—**fuzz′iness** *n.*—**fuzz′y** *a.*
fylfot (fil′fot) *n.* the swastika, 卐. Also called *gammadion* [prob. *fill-foot*, design for lower part of stained glass window].

G

G-man (jē′man) *n.* (*U.S. Colloq.*) an armed officer of the Federal Bureau of Investigation, a Government man.
gab (gab) *n.* (*Colloq.*) trifling talk; chatter;—*v.i.* to chatter; to talk idly.—**gab′by** *a.* talkative.—**the gift of the gab**, a talent for talking [imit. origin].
gabardine (gab′ạr-dēn) *n.* See **gaberdine.**
gabble (gab′l) *v.i.* to talk noisily or without meaning;—*n.* loud or rapid meaningless talk.—**gabb′ler** *n.* [imit. origin. fr. *gab*].
gaberdine (gab′ẹr-dēn) *n.* cloth of cotton or silk, with wool lining; material for raincoats; a loose upper garment worn by Jews. Also **gab′ardine** [etym. uncertain].
gabion (gā′bi-on) *n.* a hollow wicker cylinder filled with earth, formerly used in constructing parapets and shelters.—**ga′bionnade** *n.* a defensive work so formed [Fr. fr. L. *cavea*, a cage].
gable (gā′bl) *n.* the end of a house, esp. the vertical triangular ends of a building from the eaves to the top [O.N. *gafl*].
gaby (gā′bi) *n.* a silly person; a simpleton [O.N. *gapa*, to gape].
gad (gad) *v.i.* to go about idly; to rove; to straggle; to ramble.—*pr.p.* **gad′ding.**—*pa.p.* and *pa.t.* **gad′ded.** -**gad′about** *v.i.* to wander idly;—*n.* a pleasure-seeker, esp. a woman who neglects her work [O.E. *gaedeling*, a comrade].
gadfly (gad′flī) *n.* a cattle-biting fly; (*Fig.*) a tormentor [fr. *gad*, a goad].
gadget (gaj′et) *n.* (*Colloq.*) a general term for any small mechanical contrivance or device [etym. uncertain].
Gadhelic (gạ-del′ik) *a.* belonging to the branch of the Celtic race that includes the Irish of Eire, the Scottish Gaels, and the Manx of the Isle of Man [Gael. *Gaidhealach*].
gadolinium (gad-ō-lin′i-um) *n.* a metallic chemical element, one of the rare-earth metals [fr. *Gadolin*, a Swedish chemist].
Gael (gāl) *n.* a Scottish Highlander of Celtic origin.—**Gael′ic** *a.*—*n.* the language of the Gaels [Gael. *Gaidheal*].
gaff (gaf) *n.* a barbed fishing spear; a stick with an iron hook for landing fish; (*Naut.*) a spar for the top of a fore-and-aft sail;—*v.t.* to seize (a fish) with a gaff;—*v.i.* to use the gaff [Fr. *gaffe*].
gaff (gaf) *n.* (*Slang*) nonsense; silly talk.—**to blow the gaff** (*Slang*) to be an informer; to reveal a secret [etym. uncertain].
gaffe (gaf) *n.* an indiscretion; an injudicious act or remark [Fr.].
gaffer (gaf′ẹr) *n.* an old man, esp. a countryman; a foreman in a factory, etc. [contr. of *grandfather*].
gag (gag) *n.* something thrust into or over the mouth to prevent speech;—*v.t.* to apply a gag to; to silence by force [imit. of the victim's noises].
gag (gag) *n.* words inserted by an actor which are not in his part; (*Slang*) a joke [etym. uncertain].
gage [gāj) *n.* a pledge or pawn; a glove, gauntlet, cast down as challenge; a challenge;—*v.t.* to give as security; to pledge [O.Fr. *guage*].
gage (gāj) *n.* a kind of plum; a greengage [fr. Sir William *Gage*].
gage (gāj) *v.t.* See **gauge.**
gaggle (gag′l) *v.i.* to cackle like goose;—*n.* a flock of geese [imit.].
gaiety (gā′e-ti) *n.* mirth; merriment; glee; jollity.—**gai′ly** *adv.* merrily [Fr. *gai*].
gain (gān) *v.t.* to attain to, or reach; to get by effort; to get profit; to earn; to win;—*v.i.* to have advantage or profit; to increase; to improve; to make an advance;—*n.* profit; advantage; increase; resources acquired.—**gain′ings** *n.pl.* winnings.—**gain′er** *n.*—**gain′ful** *a.* profitable; lucrative.—**gain′fully** *adv.*—**gain′fulness** *n.* [Fr. *gagner*, to earn].
gainsay (gān′sā, gān-sā′) *v.t.* to contradict; to deny; to dispute.—*pa.p.* and *pa.t.* **gain′said** [O.E. prefix *gean*, against, and *say*].
gait (gāt) *n.* manner of walking or running; pace; way [var. of *gate*].
gaiter (gā′tẹr) *n.* covering for ankle, fitting upon upper of shoe [Fr. *guêtre*].
gal (gal) *n.* (*Slang*) a girl.
gala (ga′lạ, gā′lạ) *n.* a show or festivity.—**ga′la-day**, *n.* a holiday with rejoicing [It. *gala*, finery].
galactic (gạ-lak′tik) *a.* of, or pert. to, milk; lactic; pert. to the Galaxy or Milky Way [Gk. *gala*, *galaktos*, milk].
galantine (gal′ạn-tīn) *n.* a dish made of meat or game boiled till tender, then set in a jelly and served cold [Fr.].
galanty-show (gal-an′ti-shō) *n.* shadow pantomime [perh. fr. It. *galante*].
Galaxy (gal′ạk-si) *n.* a band of stars encircling the heavens; the Milky Way.—**gal′axy** *n.* a brilliant assembly of persons or things [Gk. *gala*, milk].
gale (gāl) *n.* a wind between a stiff breeze and a hurricane [etym. uncertain].
gale (gāl) *n.* a shrub found in marshes and wet heaths, giving off a pleasant fragrance; bog-myrtle; sweet gale [O.E. *gagel*].
galena (gạ-lē′nạ) *n.* sulphide of lead, the principal ore from which lead is extracted [L. *galena*, lead ore].
gall (gawl) *n.* bile secreted in the liver; anything bitter; (*Fig.*) bitterness; rancour; spite; (*U.S. Slang*) effrontery; impudence.—**gall′-bladd′er** *n.* a small sac on the under side of the liver, in which the bile is stored.—**gall′-stone** *n.* a concretion formed in the gall-bladder [O.E. *gealla*].
gall (gawl) *n.* excrescence, produced by an insect, in a plant, e.g. the oak-apple.—**gall′-ap′ple, gall′-nut** *n.* oak-apple; a gall used in dyeing.—**gall acid**, used in making ink [L. *galla*, an oak-apple].
gall (gawl) *v.t.* to fret and wear away by

rubbing; to vex, irritate, or harass;—*n.* a skin-wound caused by rubbing.—**gall'ing** *a.* irritating [O.E. *gealla*].

gallant (gal′ant) *a.* splendid or magnificent; noble in bearing or spirit; brave; chivalrous; courteous to women; amorous (ga-lant′);—*n.* a brave, high-spirited man; a courtly or fashionable man; a lover or paramour.—**gall'antly** *adv.*—**gall'antry** *n.* splendour of appearance; bravery; chivalry; polite attentions to ladies [Fr. *galant*].

galleon (gal′e-on) *n.* a large, clumsy sailing-ship built up high at bow and stern [Sp. *galeón*].

gallery (gal′er-i) *n.* a long corridor, hall, or room; a room or series of rooms in which works of art are exhibited; the uppermost tier of seats, esp. in theatre; audience or spectators; a passage in a mine; a tunnel [Fr. *galerie*].

galley (gal′i) *n.* a low, one-decked vessel, navigated both with oars and sails; the captain's boat on a warship; the kitchen of a ship; (*Print.*) an oblong tray on which type is placed when set up.—**gall'ey-proof** *n.* (*Print.*) a proof taken from the galley on a long strip of paper, before it is made up in pages.—**gall'ey-slave** *n.* one who was condemned for some criminal offence to row in the galleys [L.L. *galea*].

galliard (gal′yard) *n.* a lively young fellow; a lively dance [Fr. *gaillard*].

Gallic (gal′ik) *a.* pert. to ancient Gaul, or France; French.—**gall'icise** *v.t.* to make French in opinions, manners, idiom, etc.; to Frenchify [L. *Gallia*, Gaul].

galligaskins (gal-i-gas′kinz) *n.pl.* loose breeches; leather guards worn on the legs [corrupt. of O.Fr. *garguesque*, Greekish].

gallimaufry (gal-i-maw′fri) *n.* a hash of various meats; any ridiculous medley or hotch-potch [O.Fr. *galimafree*, a stew].

gallinaceous (gal-i-nā′shus) *a.* belonging to the order of birds which includes domestic fowls, pheasants, etc. [L. *gallina*, a hen].

gallipot (gal′i-pot) *n.* a small, glazed earthenware pot, for holding ointment, or medicines [fr. *galley*, and *pot*].

gallium (gal′i-um) *n.* a soft grey metal of extreme fusibility [L. *gallus*, a cock; suggesting *Lecoq* de Boisbaudran, the discoverer of it].

gallivant (gal-i-vant′) *v.i.* to gad about, pleasure-seeking, esp. with those of the opposite sex [perh. connected with *gallant*].

gallon (gal′on) *n.* a measure of capacity both for liquid and dry commodities, containing four quarts [O.Fr. *jalon*].

gallop (gal′op) *n.* fastest gait of horse, when it lifts forefeet together, and hind feet together; a ride at a gallop;—*v.i.* to ride at a gallop; to go at full speed;—*v.t.* to cause to gallop.—**gall'oping** *a.* speedy; swift.—**galloping consumption**, acute and rapid form of tuberculosis [Fr. *galoper*].

Galloway (gal′ō-wā) *n.* a small variety of horse, first bred in *Galloway*, Scotland; a breed of black hornless cattle [place name].

gallowglas (gal′ō-glas) *n.* a soldier or armed retainer of an Irish chieftain [Ir.].

gallows (gal′ōz) *n.* a frame from which criminals are hanged; any similar structure;—**gall'ows** *n.pl.* (*Scot.*) a pair of braces.—**gall'ows-tree** *n.* gallows [O.E. *galga*].

galoot (ga-lòòt′) *n.* (*Colloq.*) an uncouth or awkward fellow [origin uncertain].

galop (gal′op, ga-lop′) *n.* a lively dance; the music for such a dance [Fr.].

galore (ga-lōr′) *adv.* abundantly; in plenty;—*n.* abundance [Gael. *gu leor*, enough].

galosh, golosh (ga-losh′, go-losh′) *n.* a rubber overshoe [Fr. *galoche*].

galumph (ga-lumf′) *v.i.* to prance triumphantly, but heavily and awkwardly [word coined by Lewis Carroll].

galvanism (gal′va-nizm) *n.* the branch of science which treats of the production of electricity by chemical action.—**galvan'ic** *a.*—**gal'vanise** *v.t.* to apply galvanic action to; to stimulate by an electric current; (*Fig.*) to stimulate by words or deeds.—**galvanisa'tion** *n.*—**gal'vanising** *n.* coating with zinc (by galvanic action).—**galvanom'eter** *n.* an instrument for detecting and measuring the strength and direction of electric currents; a current-detector.—**galvan'oscope** *n.* an instrument for detecting the existence and direction of an electric current.—**galvanic battery**, an apparatus for generating electricity by chemical action on a series of zinc or copper plates.—**galvanised iron**, iron coated with zinc as preventative against rust [It. fr. name of the Italian inventor, Luigi *Galvani*, 1737-98].

gamba (gam′ba) *n.* (*Mus.*) an organ stop; short for *viol da gamba*, an old form of the violoncello [It. *gamba*, the leg].

gambit (gam′bit) *n.* in chess, opening move involving sacrifice of pawn [It. *gambetto*, wrestler's trip, fr. *gamba*, leg].

gamble (gam′bl) *v.i.* to play for money; to risk esp. by financial speculation;—*v.t.* to lose or squander in speculative ventures;—*n.* a risky undertaking; a reckless speculation [O.E. *gamen*, a game].

gamboge (gam-bōj′, -bòòj′) *n.* a gum-resin of a reddish-yellow colour used as a pigment [fr. *Cambodia*, in Annam, its source].

gambol (gam′bol) *v.i.* to leap about playfully; to skip and dance about.—*pr.p.* **gam'bolling**.—*pa.t.* and *pa.p.* **gam'bolled**.—*n.* a dancing or skipping about; a frolic [Fr. *gambade*].

game (gām) *n.* any sport; a pastime; a contest for amusement; a trial of strength, skill, or chance; an exercise or play for stakes; victory in a game; jest; frolic; mockery; hence, an object of ridicule; animals and birds protected by law and hunted by sportsmen;—*a.* pert. to animals hunted as game; brave; plucky;—*v.i.* to gamble.—**games** *n.pl.* athletic contests, e.g. Olympic games, Highland games, etc.—**game'ly** *adv.*—**game'ness** *n.*—**game'ster** *n.* a gambler.—**gam'ing** *a.* playing cards, dice, etc. for money; gambling.—**gam'y** *a.* having the flavour of dead game which has been kept uncooked for a long time.—**game'-bird** *n.* a bird which, by the Game Laws, is protected from indiscriminate shooting.—**game'-cock** *n.* breed of cock trained for cock-fighting.—**game'keeper** *n.* a man employed to breed game, prevent poaching, etc.—**game preserve**, land stocked with game preserved for hunting or shooting.—**big game**, all large animals hunted for sport, e.g. elephants, tigers, etc.—**fair game** (*Fig.*) a person considered easy subject for jest.—**to play the game**, to act in a sportsmanlike way [O.E. *gamen*].

game (gām) *a.* (*Colloq.*) of an arm or leg, crippled; crooked [O.Fr. *gambi*, bent].

gamete (gam-ēt′) *n.* a protoplasmic body, ovum, or sperm, which unites with another of opposite sex for conception.—**gam'etal** *a.* [Gk. *gamos*, marriage].

gamin (gam′in) *n.* a street-urchin, neglected and left to run wild; a city-arab [Fr.].

gamma (gam′a) *n.* the third letter of the Greek alphabet.—**gamma rays**, electro-magnetic radiations, of great penetrative powers, given off by certain radioactive substances, e.g. radium.

gammer (gam′er) *n.* an old woman [contr. for *grandmother*].

gammon (gam′on) *n.* the thigh of a pig, pickled and smoked [Fr. *jambon*, ham].

gammon (gam′on) *n.* a hoax; humbug;—*v.t.* to humbug [O.E. *gamen*, a game].

gammy (gam′i) *a.* (*Colloq.*) crippled; disabled [O.Fr. *gambi*, bent].

gamp (gamp) *n.* (*Colloq.*) a large, dilapidated-looking umbrella; any umbrella [fr. Mrs. *Gamp*, in Dickens's *Martin Chuzzlewit*].

gamut (gam′ut) *n.* the whole series of musical notes; a scale; the compass of a voice; the entire range [Med. L. *gamma*, and *ut*, names of notes].

gander (gan′dẹr) *n.* a male goose; a simpleton [O.E. *gandra*].

gang (gang) *n.* people banded together for some purpose, usually bad; body of labourers working together.—**ganger** (gang′ẹr) *n.* the foreman of a squad of workmen.—**gang′ster** *n.* hooligan; hardened criminal [O.E. *gangan*, to go].

gangling (gang′gling) *a.* lanky and loosely knit in build [O.E. *gangan*, to go].

ganglion (gang′gli-on) *n.* a mass of nerve tissue, which receives and sends out nerve fibres; a globular, hard tumour, situated on a tendon.—*pl.* **gang′lions, gang′lia.**—**gang′liale** *a.* furnished with ganglia.—**ganglion′ic** *a.* pert. to a ganglion [Gk. *ganglion*, an encysted tumour].

gangrel (gang′rel) *n.* a vagrant [O.E. *gangan*, to go, walk].

gangrene (gang′grēn) *n.* the first stage of mortification or death of tissue in the body;—*v.t.* and *v.i.* to affect with, or be affected with, gangrene.—**gang′renous** *a.* mortified; putrefying [Gk. *gangraina*].

gangway (gang′wā) *n.* a movable plank bridge thrown across the gap between a ship and the shore; a passage between rows of seats;—*interj.* make way, please! [O.E. *gangweg*].

gannet (gan′et) *n.* the solan goose, a sea-fowl of the pelican tribe [O.E. *ganot*].

gantlet (gȧnt′-let) *n.* a military or naval punishment of former times, in which the offender was made to run between files of men who struck him as he passed.—**to run the gantlet** (erroneously, **gauntlet**), to undergo this ordeal; to face any unpleasant ordeal.—Also **gant′lope** [Scand.].

gantry, gauntry (gan′tri, gawn′tri) *n.* a structure to support a crane, railway-signals, etc. [etym. uncertain].

gaol (jāl) *n.* confinement; a prison; a jail.—**gaol′er** *n.* [form of *jail*].

gap (gap) *n.* an opening; a breach; a mountain pass [O.N.=chasm].

gape (gāp) *v.i.* to open wide, esp. the mouth; to stare with open mouth; to yawn.—*n.* the act of gaping.—**the gapes**, a fit of yawning; a disease of poultry and other birds, characterised by gaping [O.N. *gapa*].

gar (gȧr) *n.* a fish of the pike family.—**gar′fish** *n.* the sea-pike [O.E. *gar*, a dart, spear].

garage (gar′ij, gar′azh) *n.* a covered enclosure for motor vehicles; a fuel and repair station for motor vehicles;—*v.t.* to place in a garage [Fr. *gare*, a station].

garb (gȧrb) *n.* clothing; mode or style of dress;—*v.t.* to dress [O.Fr. *garbe*, dress].

garbage (gȧr′bij) *n.* offal; kitchen refuse; anything worthless [etym. uncertain].

garble (gȧr′bl) *v.t.* to pick out such parts of as may serve a purpose; to pervert or mutilate, as a story, a quotation, an account, etc. [Ar. *ghirbal*, a sieve].

garboard (gȧr′bōrd) *n.* Also **garboard strake**, the first plank or plate fastened on the keel of a ship [Dut. *gaarboord*].

garden (gȧr′dn) *n.* ground for cultivation of flowers, vegetables, etc. generally attached to a house; pleasure grounds;—*v.i.* to cultivate, or work in, a garden.—**gar′dener** *n.*—**gar′dening** *n.* the act of tending a garden.—**market gardener**, one who raises fruit, vegetables, etc. for sale.—**common or garden** (*Colloq.*) quite ordinary [Fr. *jardin*].

Gardenia (gȧr-dē′ni-ạ) *n.* a genus of tropical trees and shrubs with sweet-scented, beautiful flowers [named after Alexander *Garden*, American botanist].

garefowl (gār′-foul) *n.* the great auk. Also **gair′fowl** [O.N. *geir-fugl*].

gargantuan (gȧr-gan′tū-an) *a.* immense, enormous, esp. of appetite [fr. *Gargantua*, hero of Rabelais' book of the same name].

gargle (gar′gl) to rinse (mouth or throat), preventing water from going down throat by expulsion of air from lungs;—*v.i.* to make a sound of gargling; to use a gargle;—*n.* a throat wash [O.Fr. *gargouille*, throat].

gargoyle, gargoil (gȧr′goil) *n.* a projecting spout, often in the form of a grotesque carving, found on old buildings and intended to carry off the water from the gutters [O.Fr. *gargouille*, the throat].

garish (gār′-ish) *a.* gaudy; showy; glaring; dazzling; exciting attention.—**gar′ishly** *adv.*—**gar′ishness** *n.* [M.E. *gauren*, to stare].

garland (gȧr′-land) *n.* a wreath of flowers, branches, feathers, etc.; an anthology or book of literary extracts;—*v.t.* to ornament with a garland [O.Fr. *garlande*].

garlic (gar′-lik) *n.* a plant having a bulbous root, a strong smell like onion, and a pungent taste [O.E. *garleac*].

garment (gȧr′-ment) *n.* any article of clothing [Fr. *garnement*, equipment].

garner (gȧr′-nẹr) *n.* a granary;—*v.t.* to store in a granary; to gather up [Fr. *grenier*, fr. L. *granarium*].

garnet (gȧr′-net) *n.* a semi-precious stone, usually of a dark-red colour and resembling a ruby; a dark-red colour [Fr. *grenat*].

garnish (gȧr′-nish) *v.t.* to adorn; to embellish; to ornament; (*Cookery*) to make food attractive or appetising by putting something decorative on the serving-dish;—*n.* ornament; decoration; something put on a serving dish as an embellishment.—**gar′nishment** *n.* ornament; decoration.—**gar′niture** *n.* that which garnishes [Fr. *garnir*, to furnish].

garotte (ga-rot′) *n.* See **garrotte.**

garret (gar′-et) *n.* upper floor of a house immediately under roof; an attic.—**garreteer′** *n.* one who lives in a garret; a poor author [O.Fr. *garite*, a place of safety].

garrison (gar′-i-sn) *n.* a body of troops stationed in a fort, town, etc.; the fort or town itself;—*v.t.* to occupy with a garrison [O.Fr. *garison*, fr. *garir*, to protect].

garrotte (ga-rot′) *n.* a Spanish mode of execution by strangling, with an iron collar affixed to a post and tightened by a screw; apparatus for this punishment;—*v.t.* to execute by strangulation; to seize by the throat, in order to throttle and rob.—*pr.p.* **garrott′ing**.—*pa.p.* and *pa.t.* **garrott′ed.**—**garrott′er** *n.* [Sp. *garrote*, a cudgel].

garrulous (gar′-ū-lus) *a.* talkative; loquacious.—**garr′ulously** *adv.*—**garr′ulousness** *n.*—**garrul′ity** *n.* [L. *garrire*, to chatter].

garter (gȧr′-tẹr) *n.* a string or band worn near the knee to keep a stocking up; the badge of the highest order of knighthood in Great Britain;—*v.t.* to bind with a garter [O.Fr. *gartier*, fr. *garet*, the bend of the knee].

garth (gȧrth) *n.* a paddock; a yard; a croft; a garden; a dam or weir for catching fish [O.N. *garthr*, a court].

gas (gas) *n.* an elastic fluid such as air, esp. one not liquid or solid at ordinary temperatures; such fluid, esp. coal-gas, used for heating or lighting; an anaesthetic used by dentists ('laughing gas'); (*Slang*) empty talk; (*U.S. Colloq.*) petrol, abbrev. of gasolene, or gasoline.—*pl.* **gas′es.**—*v.t.* to poison with gas;—*v.i.* (*Slang*) to talk emptily; to talk unceasingly.—*pr.p.* **gas′sing.**—*pa.p.* and *pa.t.* **gassed.**—**gaseity** (ga-sē′-i-ti) *n.* the state of being gaseous.—**gaseous** (gā′-shus) *a.* like, or in the form of, gas.—**ga′seousness** *n.*—**gasifica′tion** *n.*—**gas′ify** *v.t.* to convert into gas, as by the action of heat, or by chemical processes.—**gas′sy** *a.* full of gas.—**gas′-bag** *n.* a large bag for holding gas; (*Slang*) a very talkative person.—**gas'-brack'et** *n.* a device fixed to wall, to which is connected the pipe carrying gas for lighting purposes.—**gas'-burn'er** *n.* a piece of metal, with a small nozzle or jet, fitted to the end of a gaspipe to spread the flame.—**gas'-cook'er** *n.* a gas cooking-stove.—**gas'-en'gine** *n.* an engine operated by gas.—**gas'-hold'er** *n.* at gasworks, a huge container for storing gas (popularly, but erroneously, called a **gasom'eter**).—**gas'-jar** *n.* (*Chem.*) a large glass-jar for collecting a gas during an experiment.—**gas'-jet** *n.* the spread of flame from a gas-burner; the burner itself.—**gas'-mains** *n.* a network of pipes leading from the gas-holder.—**gas'-mant'le** *n.* a small sack of gauze, chemically treated with metallic salts and fitted to a gas-burner. It gives a brilliant incandescent light when heated by burning gas.—**gas'-me'ter** *n.* a sort of metal box used to measure the amount of gas consumed.—**gas'-range** *n.* a large type of gas cooking-stove.—**gas'-retort'** *n.* a large chamber or oven in which coal is heated to produce gas.—**gas'-stove** *n.* a heating or cooking appliance in which gas is burned.—**gas'-tar** *n.* coal-tar.—**gas'-trap** *n.* a bend in a drain-pipe, filled with water, to prevent the escape of foul gases.—**gas'-works** *n.* factory where gas is made [Word coined by Dutch chemist, Van Helmont, 1577-1644].

gas (gas) *n.* (*World Wars* 1 *and* 2) any chemical substance—solid, liquid, or gas—used to cause poisonous or irritant effects on the human body.—**gassed** *a.* incapacitated by a war gas.—**gas'-mask** *n.* the popular name for any type of Respirator designed to protect the eyes, nose, mouth and lungs against gas.

gasalier, gaselier (gas-e-lēr') *n.* a metal frame hanging from the ceiling, with brackets for gas-jets [imit. of *chandelier*].

Gascon (gas'kon) *n.* a native of *Gascony*, in S.W. France; a boaster.—**gasconade** (gas-ko-nād') *n.* boasting talk; bravado;—*v.i.* to boast; to brag; to bluster [fr. *Gascony*].

gash (gash) *v.t.* to make a long, deep cut in;—*n.* a deep cut [O.Fr. *garser*, to scarify].

gasket (gas'ket) *n.* (*Naut.*) a flat, plaited cord, used to furl the sail or tie it to the yard; a washer between parts such as the cylinder head and cylinder block [Fr. *garcette*].

gaskins (gas'kinz) *n.pl.* wide, loose hose [fr. *galligaskins*].

gasolene, gasoline (gas'ō-lēn) *n.* the American name for petrol.

gasometer (gas-om'e-tẹr) *n.* a chemical instrument for holding, testing, or mixing gases [E. *gas*; Gk. *metron*, a measure].

gasp (gasp) *v.i.* to struggle for breath with open mouth; to pant;—*v.t.* to utter with gasps;—*n.* the act of gasping; a painful catching of the breath.—**gas'per** *n.* (*Colloq.*) a cheap cigarette [O.N. *geispa*, to yawn].

gasteropod (gas'te-rō-pod) *n.* a class of molluscs, e.g. snails and whelks, having a fleshy, ventral disc, which takes the place of feet.—**gasterop'odous** *a.* [Gk. *gastēr*, the belly; *pous, podos*, the foot].

gastric (gas'trik) *a.* pert. to the stomach.—**gastritis** (gas-trī'tis) *n.* inflammation of the stomach.—**gas'tro-enteri'tis** *n.* inflammation of the stomach and intestines [Gk. *gastēr*, the belly].

gastrology (gas-trol'o-ji) *n.* the science of cookery [Gr. *gastēr*, belly; *logos*, discourse].

gastronomy (gas-tron'o-mi) *n.* the art of good eating; epicurism.—**gas'tronome, gastron'omer** *n.* one fond of good living.—Also **gastron'omist**—**gastronom'ic, gastronom'ical** *a.* [Gk. *gastēr*, the belly; *nomos*, a law].

gat (gat) *n.* (*Slang*) a pistol or revolver; abbrev. of **gat'ling-gun**.

gate (gāt) *n.* an opening into an enclosure, through a fence, wall, etc.; a mountain pass or defile; an entrance; a device for stopping passage of water through a dam or lock; the number of people paying to watch a game; also the money taken;—*v.t.* at some universities, to punish an undergraduate by confinement to the grounds; to furnish with a gate.—**gate'-crash** *v.i.* to attend a social function uninvited.—**gate'-house** *n.* the building above or beside the entrance-gate to a city, university, etc.—**gate'way** *n.* a passage through a fence or wall; an entrance.—**gate'-post** *n.* the post on which a gate is hung [O.E. *geat*, a way].

gateau (gȧ'tō) *n.* a cake [Fr.].

gather (gaTH'ẹr) *v.t.* to bring together; to collect; to pick; in sewing, to draw into puckers; to infer or deduce; to harvest;—*v.i.* to come together; to congregate; to increase; to swell up and become full of pus (of a sore or boil);—*n.* a pucker, plait, or fold in cloth.—**gath'ering** *n.* an assemblage; a crowd; an abscess [O.E. *gaderian*, fr. *gador*, together].

Gatling-gun (gat'ling-gun) *n.* machine-gun invented by R. J. *Gatling*.

gauche (gōsh) *a.* awkward; clumsy; shy and uncouth in manner.—**gaucherie** (gō'shẹ-rē) *n.* clumsiness [Fr.].

gaucho (gou'chō) *n.* a native of the S. American pampas, of Spanish descent, famous for horsemanship [Sp.].

gaud (gawd) *n.* a piece of worthless finery; a trinket; a flashy ornament.—**gaud'y** *a.* showy but tawdry; vulgarly gay; pretentious [L. *gaudium*, joy].

gauge (gāj) *v.t.* to ascertain the capacity of; to measure the ability of; to estimate.—*n.* an instrument for determining dimensions or capacity; a standard of measure; test; criterion; the distance between the rails of a railway.—**gaug'er** *n.* one who gauges, esp. an exciseman who measures the contents of casks [O.Fr. *gauge*].

Gaul (gawl) *n.* an old name for France; a Frenchman [L. *Gallia*].

Gauleiter (gou'li-tẹr) *n.* the governor of a district under the German National Socialist Party [Ger. *Gau*, a district; *Leiter*, a leader].

gaunt (gawnt) *a.* lean and haggard; pinched and grim; desolate; barren.—**gaunt'ly** *adv.*—**gaunt'ness** *n.* [etym. uncertain].

gauntlet (gawnt'let) *n.* a glove with metal plates on the back, worn formerly as armour; a glove with a long cuff.—**to run the gauntlet**, see **gantlet**.—**to throw down, to take up, the gauntlet**, to give, accept, a challenge [Fr. *gant*, a glove].

gauss (gous) *n.* (*Elect.*) the unit of density of a magnetic field [fr. Karl F. *Gauss*, a German scientist, 1777-1855].

gauze (gawz) *n.* a thin, transparent fabric of silk, linen, wire, etc.—**gauz'iness** *n.*—**gauz'y** *a.* [Fr. *gaze*].

gave (gāv) *pa.t.* of **give**.

gavel (gav'el) *n.* a mallet; a small wooden hammer used by a chairman or auctioneer [etym. uncertain].

gavel (gav'el) *n.* a small heap of wheat, rye, etc. not tied up;—*v.t.* to bind into sheaves [O.Fr. *gavelle*].

gavelkind (gav'el-kind) *n.* an old Saxon system of land tenure, under which lands were equally divided among sons on the death of the tenant [O.E. *gafol*, a tax].

gavotte (gạ-vot') *n.* an old dance after the style of the minuet but not so stately; the music for it [Fr. *gavotte*].

gawk (gawk) *n.* an awkward person; a simpleton; a booby;—*v.i.* to stare stupidly.—**gawk'y** *a.* foolish and awkward; clumsy; bashful and stupid [etym. uncertain].

gay (gā) *a.* lively; merry; light-hearted; showy; dissipated.—**gay'ly, gai'ly** *adv.*—**gay'ety, gai'ety** *n.* joyousness [Fr. *gai*].

gaze (gāz) *v.i.* to look fixedly; to fix the eyes in a steady or earnest look; to stare;—*n.* a fixed, earnest look; a long, intent look.—**gaz'er** *n.* one who gazes.—**gaze'-hound** *n.* a hound that hunts by sight, not by scent.—**gaz'ing-stock** *n.* a person gazed at in curiosity or contempt.—**at gaze,** in a gazing attitude [etym. uncertain].

gazebo (gạ-zē´-bō) *n.* an outlook turret on a roof or wall; a summer-house commanding a wide view; a belvedere [etym. unknown].

gazelle (gạ-zel') *n.* a small, swift, graceful antelope [Ar. *ghazal*].

gazette (gạ-zet') *n.* a newspaper; an official newspaper (the *London Gazette*) for announcements of government appointments, military promotions, legal notices, bankruptcies, etc.;—*v.t.* to publish in the official gazette.—*pr.p.* **gazett'ing**.—*pa.p.* and *pa.t.* **gazett'ed**.—**gazetteer** (gaz-e-tēr') *n.* formerly a writer for a gazette; now, a geographical dictionary [It. *gazetta*].

gean (gēn) *n.* the wild cherry [Fr. *guigne*].

gear (gēr) *n.* apparatus; equipment; tackle; a set of tools; harness; rigging; clothing; goods; utensils; a set of toothed wheels working together, esp. by engaging cogs, to transmit power or to change timing;—*v.t.* to provide with gear; to put in gear;—*v.i.* to be in gear.—**gear'ing** *n.* the series of toothed wheels for transmitting power, changing speed, etc.—**gear'-wheel** *n.* a wheel having teeth or cogs [M.E. *gere*].

gecko (gek´-ō) *n.* a small, nocturnal wall-lizard [Malay, *gekoq*, imit. of its cry].

gee (jē) *interj.* a command to a draught animal to turn to off-side;—*n.* horse; also (*Colloq.*) **gee'-gee**.—**gee'-up** *interj.* command esp. to horse, to go faster [origin uncertain].

geese (gēs) *n.* plural of **goose**.

geezer (gē´-zẹr) *n.* (*Slang*) an old fellow; a queer old chap [corrupt. of *guiser*].

Geiger counter (gī´-ger) *n.* a hypersensitive instrument for detecting radio-activity, cosmic radiation, etc. [H. *Geiger*, Ger. physicist].

geisha (gā´-shạ) *n.* a Japanese dancing girl.

gel (jel) *n.* (*Chem.*) a colloidal solution which has set into a jelly.—**gel'able** *a.* able to be congealed.—**gela'tion** *n.* a solidifying by means of cold [L. *gelare*, to freeze].

gelatine, gelatin (jel´-ạ-tēn, -tin) *n.* a glutinous substance got by boiling parts of animals (e.g. calves' feet). It is soluble in hot water and sets into a tremulous jelly.—**gelatinous** (je-lat´-i-nus) *a.* of the nature or consistency of gelatine; like jelly.—**gelat'inate, gelat'inise** *v.t.* to convert into gelatine.—**gelatina'tion** *n.* [It. *gelata*, jelly].

geld (geld) *n.* a payment, tax, tribute, or fine [O.E.=payment].

geld (gelt) *n.* in S. Africa, money [Dut.].

geld (geld) *v.t.* to emasculate; to castrate; to deprive (of).—**geld'ing** *n.* a castrated animal, esp. a horse [O.N. *geldr*, barren].

gelder-rose See **guelder-rose**.

gelid (jel´-id) *a.* cold as ice.—**gel'idly** *adv.*—**gel'idness, gelid'ity** *n.* [L. *gelidus*, fr. *gelu*, frost].

gelignite (jel´-ig-nīt) *n.* a gelatinised explosive used for blasting in mines [*gelatine*, and L. *ignis*, fire].

gem (jem) *n.* a precious stone of any kind; a jewel; anything of great value;—*v.t.* to adorn with gems.—**gemmeous** (jem´-e-us) *a.* pert. to, or resembling, gems; bespangled; bright [L. *gemma*].

geminate (jem´-i-nāt) *a.* doubled; existing in pairs.—**gemina'tion** *n.* [L. *geminare*, to double].

Gemini (jem´-i-nī) *n.pl.* the third sign of the Zodiac which the sun enters about May 21st; (*Astron.*) a constellation containing the two bright stars Castor and Pollux, twin heroes of Greek legend [L. *geminus*, twin-born].

gemma (jem´-ạ) *n.* (*Bot.*) a bud; (*Zool.*) a bud-like outgrowth which becomes a separate individual.—*pl.* **gem'mae**.—**gem'mate** *a.* having buds;—*v.i.* to propagate by buds, as coral.—**gemma'tion** *n.* budding; the arrangement of buds on the stalk; (*Zool.*) reproduction by gemmae.—**gemmip'arous** *a.* producing buds or gems; (*Zool.*) propagating by buds [L. *gemma*, a bud].

gen (jen) *n.* (*Army Slang*) information [abbrev. of *genuine*].

gendarme (zhong-dårm') *n.* an armed military policeman in France.—**gendarmerie** (zhong-dårm´-rē) *n.* the corps of armed police [Fr. fr. *gens d'armes*, men-at-arms].

gender (jen´-dẹr) *n.* sex, male or female; (*Gram.*) the classification of nouns according to sex (actual or attributed) [L. *genus*, *generis*, a kind].

gene (jēn) *n.* the hereditary factor which is transmitted by each parent to offspring and which determines hereditary characteristics [Gk. *genos*, origin].

genealogy (jen-e-al´-o-ji) *n.* a record of the descent of a person or family from an ancestor; the pedigree of a person or family; lineage.—**geneal'ogist** *n.* one who traces the descent of persons or families.—**genealog'ical** *a.* [Gk. *genea*, birth; *logos*, discourse].

genera (jen´-ẹ-rạ) *n.* See **genus**.

general (jen´-e-rạl) *a.* relating to a genus or kind; pert. to a whole class or order; not precise, particular, or detailed; usual, ordinary, or prevalent; embracing the whole, not local or partial;—*n.* that which embraces or comprehends the whole or the greater part; an officer in the British Army ranking immediately below a field-marshal.—**gen'erally** *adv.* as a whole; for the most part; commonly; extensively.—**general'ity** *n.* indefiniteness; vagueness; a vague statement; the main body.—**gen'eral-ship** *n.* military skill in a commander; leadership.—**generalis'simo** *n.* the chief commander of an army.—**in general,** in most respects.—**general election,** one in which every constituency chooses a representative.—**general practitioner,** a doctor whose work embraces all types of cases [L. *generalis*].

generalise (jen´-ẹr-ạl-īz) *v.t.* to reduce to general laws; to make universal in application;—*v.i.* to draw general conclusions from particular instances; to speak vaguely.—**generalisa'tion** *n.* act of generalising; a general conclusion from particular instances [fr. *general*].

generate (jen´-ẹ-rāt) *v.t.* to bring into being; to produce; to originate by chemical process; (*Math.*) to trace out.—**genera'tion** *n.* a bringing into being; the act of begetting; the act of producing; that which is generated; a step in a pedigree; all persons born about the same time; the average time in which children are ready to replace their parents (about 30 years); family; genealogy.—**generative** (jen´-ẹ-rā-tiv) *a.* having the power of generating or producing; prolific.—**gen'erator** *n.* one who, or that which, generates; a begetter; an apparatus for producing steam, etc.; a machine for converting mechanical into electrical energy [L. *generare*, to procreate].

generic (je-ner´-ik) *a.* pert. to a genus; of a general nature.—**gener'ically** *adv.*

generous (jen´-ẹ-rus) *a.* noble; noble-minded; liberal, free in giving; abundant; copious; of wine, rich.—**gen'erously** *adv.*—**generos'ity** *n.* magnanimity; nobleness of heart and feeling; liberality in giving. Also **gen'erousness** *n.* [L. *generosus*, of noble birth].

genesis (jen´-e-sis) *n.* origin; creation; mode of formation; production; birth.—*pl.* **geneses** (jen´-e-sēs).—**Gen'esis** *n.* (*Bib.*) the first book of the Old Testament [Gk.].

genet (jen´-et) *n.* See **jennet**.

genetic (je-net´-ik) *a.* pert. to origin, creation, or reproduction.—**genet'ics** *n.* the scientific study of the heredity of individuals, esp. of inherited characteristics.—**genet'icist** *n.* [Gk. *gignesthai*, to be born].

Genevan (je-nē´-vạn) *a.* pert. to *Geneva*, in Switzerland.—**Geneva Conventions,** internat-ional agreements, signed at Geneva in 1864,

1868, 1906 and 1949, to lessen sufferings of the wounded in war by providing for the neutrality of hospitals, ambulances, etc.

genial (jēn′yal) *a.* kindly; sympathetic; cordial; sociable; of a climate, mild and conducive to growth.—**geniality** (jē-ni-al′i-ti) *n.* the quality of being genial; sociability; friendliness; sympathetic cheerfulness.—**gen′ially** *adv.* [L. *genialis*].

genie (jē′ni) *n.* a sprite; a goblin; a jinnee.—*pl.* **genii** (jē′ni-ī) [corrupt, of Arab. *jinnee*, confused with *genius*].

genital (jen′i-tal) *a.* pert. to generation, or to the organs of generation.—**gen′itals** *n.pl.* the external sexual organs. Also **genitalia** (jen-i-tā′li-a) [L. *genitalis*, fr. *gignere*, to beget].

genitive (jen′i-tiv) *a.* pert. to, or indicating, source, origin, possession, etc.—*n.* (*Gram.*) the case used to indicate source, origin, possession and the like [L. *genitivus*].

genius (jē′ni-us, jēn′yus) *n.* one's mental endowment or individual talent; the animating spirit of a people, generation or locality; uncommon intellectual powers; a person endowed with the highest mental gifts.—*pl.* **geniuses** (jēn′yus-ez).—**genius** (jē′ni-us) *n.* a tutelary deity supposed by the ancients to preside over a man's life and fortune.—*pl.* **genii** (jē′ni-ī) [L.].

genocide (jen′ō-sīd) *n.* (*U.S.*) race suicide; race murder.—**gen′ocidal** *a.* [Gk. *genos*, race; L. *caedere*, to kill].

Genoese (jen-ō-ēz′) *a.* relating or belonging to *Genoa.*—Also **Genovese′**.

genre (zhong′r) *n.* a kind; sort; style.—**genre painting**, painting which portrays scenes in everyday life [Fr.=style, kind].

gens (jenz) *n.* any community of persons in a primitive state.—*pl.* **gen′tes** [L.].

gent (jent) *n.* (*Colloq.*) a gentleman; a would-be gentleman [abbrev. fr. *gentleman*].

genteel (jen-tēl′) *a.* possessing the qualities belonging to high birth and breeding; well-bred; stylish; pretentiously or affectedly refined.—**genteel′y** *adv.*—**genteel′ness** *n.*—**gentility** (jen-til′i-ti) *n.* [Fr. *gentil*].

gentian (jen′shan) *n.* the common name of Gentiana, plants whose root is used medicinally as a tonic, stomachic, and febrifuge; its flower is usually of a deep, bright blue [L. *gentiana*].

Gentile (jen′tīl) *n.* one who is not a Jew;—*a.* belonging to the nations at large, as distinguished from the Jews [L. *gens*, a nation].

gentle (jen′tl) *a.* kind and amiable; mild and refined in manner; quiet and sensitive of disposition; meek; moderate; gradual; (*Arch.*) of good family;—*n.* (*Arch.*) one of good birth; the larva of the blue-bottle;—*v.t.* to make gentle; to tame; to make docile.—**gent′ly** *adv.*—**gen′tlefolk** *n.pl.* persons of good breeding and family.—**gen′tleness** *n.*—**gen′try** (jen′tri) *n.* people of birth and good breeding; the class of people between the nobility and the middle class [L. *gentilis*].

gentleman (jen′tl-man) *n.* a man of good breeding and refined manners; a man of good family; a polite term for a man.—*pl.* **gen′tlemen.**—**gen′tlemanly** *a.*—**gen′tlemanlike** *a.* well-behaved; courteous.—**gen′tlewoman** *n.* (*Arch.*) a woman of good family or of good breeding; a woman who waits upon the person of one of high rank.—**gentleman's gentleman**, a valet.—**gentleman's agreement**, one binding in honour but not legally [L. *gentilis*].

genuflect (jen′ū-flekt) *v.i.* to bend the knee, esp. in worship.—**genuflec′tion, genuflex′ion** *n.*—**genuflec′tor** *n.*—**genuflec′tory** *a.* [L. *genu*, the knee; *flectere*, to bend].

genuine (jen′ū-in) *a.* real; true; pure; authentic; unalloyed or unadulterated.—**gen′uinely** *adv.*—**gen′uineness** *n.* [L. *genuinus*].

genus (jē′nus) *n.* a race; a class; an order; a kind; (*Nat. Hist.*) a subdivision ranking next above species, and containing a number of species having like characteristics.—*pl.* **genera** (jen′e-ra) [L. *genus, generis*, a kind].

geo-, ge- (jē′o, jē) combining forms fr. Gk. *gē*, meaning earth, ground, soil.—**geocen′tric** *a.* (*Astron.*) having reference to the earth as centre [Gk. *kentron*, the centre].

geode (jē′ōd) *n.* in mineralogy, a rounded nodule of stone, containing a small cavity, usually lined with crystals.—**geod′ic** *a.*—**geodif′erous** *a.* [Gk. *geodēs*, earth-like].

geodesy (jē-od′e-si) *n.* the mathematical survey and measurement of the earth's surface, involving allowance for curvature.—**geodet′ic, geodet′ical** *a.* [Gk. *gē*, the earth; *daiein*, to divide].

geogony (jē-og′o-ni) *n.* the doctrine of the formation of the earth.—**geogon′ic** *a.* [Gk. *gē*, the earth; *gonē*, generation].

geography (jē-og′ra-fi) *n.* the science of the earth's form, its physical divisions into seas, rivers, mountains, plains, etc.; a book on this.—**geo′grapher** *n.* one versed in geography.—**geograph′ic, geograph′ical** *a.* pert. to geography.—**geograph′ically** *adv.* [Gk. *gē*, the earth; *graphein*, to write].

geology (jē-ol′o-ji) *n.* the science of the earth's crust, the rocks, their strata, etc.—**geolog′ical** *a.*—**geolog′ically** *adv.*—**geol′ogist** *n.* [Gk. *gē*, the earth; *logos*, discourse].

geometry (jē-om′e-tri) *n.* the mathematical study of the properties of lines, angles, surfaces, and solids; a text-book on this.—**geomet′ric(al)** *a.* pert. to geometry.—**geomet′rically** *adv.*—**geometri′cian, geom′eter** *n.* one skilled in geometry.—**geometrical progression** (*Math.*) a series of quantities in which each quantity is obtained by multiplying the preceding term by a constant factor, e.g. 2, 6, 18, 54, etc. (3 being the constant factor) [Gk. *gē*, the earth; *metron*, a measure].

geophagy (jē-of′a-ji) *n.* the art or practice of eating earth, dirt, clay, etc.—Also **geoph′agism** *n.* [Gk. *gē*, earth; *phagein*, to eat].

geopolitics (jē-o-pol′i-tiks) *n.pl.* the study of the influence of geographical situation upon the politics of a nation.—**geopolit′ical** *a.* [Gk. *gē*, the earth; *politēs*, a citizen].

George (jorj) *n.* a jewelled ornament worn by Knights of the Garter, having the figure of St. *George*, on horseback; (*R.A.F. Slang*) the automatic 'pilot'.—**Georgian** (jor′ji-an) *a.* pert. to the reigns of the six *Georges*, Kings of Great Britain; relating to *Georgia*, a republic of the Soviet Union; relating to *Georgia* in the U.S.A.

georgette (jor-jet′) *n.* a fine semi-transparent silk fabric [fr. Madame *Georgette*, a French modiste].

Georgic (jor′jik) *n.* a poem on husbandry.—**geor′gic** *a.* pert. to agriculture or rustic affairs [Gk. *gē*, the earth; *ergon*, a work].

geotropism (jē-ot′ro-pizm) *n.* (*Bot.*) the tendency of a growing plant to direct its roots downwards.—**geotrop′ic** *a.* [Gk. *gē*, the earth; *tropos*, a turning].

geranium (je-rā′ni-um) *n.* plant of order Geraniaceae having showy flowers, and seed-vessels like a crane's bill; the garden 'geranium' is of genus Pelargonium [Gk. *geranos*, a crane].

gerfalcon (jer′fawl-kon, -faw-kn) *n.* a large Arctic falcon.—Also **gyr′falcon** [O.Fr. *gerfaucon*].

geriatrics (jer-i-at′riks) *n.* science of decadence in old people or the infirm; welfare of the old [Gk. *geras*, old age].

germ (jerm) *n.* the rudimentary form of a living thing, whether animal or plant; a microscopic organism; a microbe; a bud; that from which anything springs.—**germ′icide** *n.* a substance for destroying disease-germs.—**germici′dal** *a.*—**germule** (jer′mūl) *n.* a germ, esp. small or incipient.—**germ warfare**, war waged with bacteria for weapons [L. *germen*, a bud].

german (jer´man) *a.* of the first degree (only used in *brother-german, sister-german, cousin-german*); closely allied.—**germane** (jer-mān´) *a.* appropriate; relevant; allied; akin [L. *germanus*, fully akin].

German (jer´man) *a.* belonging to *Germany*; —*n.* a native of Germany; the German language.—**German´ic** *a.* pert. to Germany; Teutonic.—**Ger´manise** *v.t.* to make German. —**German measles**, a disease like measles, but less severe [L. *Germanus*].

Germander (jer-man´der) a genus of herb-like plants having medicinal properties [Gk. *chamai*, on the ground; *drus*, a tree].

germanium (jer-mā´ni-um) *n.* a metallic element, discovered 1885.—symbol **Ge** [L. *Germanus*, German].

germinal (jer´mi-nal) *a.* pert. to a germ or seed-bud [L. *germen*, bud].

germinate (jerm´in-āt) *v.i.* to sprout; to bud; to shoot; to begin to grow;—*v.t.* to cause to grow.—**germ´inative** *a.* pert. to germination.—**germina´tion** *n.*—**germ´inant** *a.* sprouting [L. *germen*, a bud].

gerontocracy (jer-on-tok´ra-si) *n.* government by old men [Gk. *geron*, an old man; *kratos*, power].

gerontology (jer-on-tol´o-ji) *n.* (*Med.*) The branch of science that studies the decline of life, esp. of man [Gk. *geron*, an old man].

gerrymander (jer-i-man´der) *v.t.* to arrange or redistribute to private advantage electoral districts [invented word fr. Governor *Gerry* of Massachusetts and *-mander*, abbrev. of *salamander*].

gerund (jer´und) *n.* part of the Latin verb used as a verbal noun; the dative of the O.E. or modern English infinitive, used to express purpose.—**gerun´dial** *a.* of the nature of a gerund.—**gerun´dive** *n.* the future participle passive of a Latin verb expressing the action of having to be done [L. *gerere*, to do].

gest, geste (jest) *n.* (*Arch.*) an exploit or high adventure; demeanour or bearing [L. *gestum*, deed].

gestalt (gesh-talt´) *n.* pattern; a whole which is more than the sum of its parts [Ger.].

Gestapo (ges-tá´pō) *n.* the secret police of the German Nazi party [contr. of *Ge*heime *Sta*ats*po*lizei=secret state-police].

gestation (jes-tā´shun) *n.* carrying young in womb; pregnancy.—**gestatory** (jes´ta-to-ri) *a.* [L. *gestare*, to bear].

gesticulate (jes-tik´ū-lāt) *v.i.* to make violent gestures or motions, esp. with hands and arms, when speaking.—**gesticula´tion** *n.* the act of gesticulating; a gesture.—**gestic´ulatory** *a.* [L. *gestus*, gesture].

gesture (jes´tūr) *n.* a motion of the head, hands, etc. as a mode of expression; an act indicating attitude of mind; a conciliatory approach;—*v.i.* to make gestures [L. *gerere*, to do].

get (get) *v.t.* to procure; to obtain; to gain possession of; to come by; to win, by almost any means; to receive; to earn; to induce or persuade; (*Colloq.*) to understand; (*Arch.*) to beget;—*v.i.* to become; to reach or attain; to bring one's self into a condition. *-pr.p.* **get´ting**.—*pa.t.* **got**.—*pa.p.* **got**; (*Arch.*) **got´ten**. —**getaway** (get´a-wā) *n.* (*Colloq.*) escape.—**get´-up** *n.* equipment; dress; appearance [O.E. *gitan*].

gewgaw (gū´gaw) *n.* a showy trifle; a toy; a bauble [O.E. *gifu*, a gift].

geyser (gī´zer, gā´zer) *n.* a hot spring which spouts water intermittently; an apparatus for heating water rapidly by gas, electricity, etc. [O.N. *geysa*, to gush].

ghastly (gȧst´li) *a.* horrible; shocking; ghost-like; death-like. Also *adv.*—**ghast´liness** *n.* [O.E. *gaestlic*, terrible].

ghat, ghaut (gawt) *n.* a mountain pass (in India); a range of mountains (in India); a flight of stairs leading down to a bathing-place in a river (in India).—**burn´ing-ghaut** *n.* a place for the burning of the dead (Hind.].

gherkin (ger´kin) *n.* a small species of cucumber used for pickling [Dut. *agurkje*].

ghetto (get´ō) *n.* the Jewish quarter in any city [It.].

ghillie (gil´i) *n.* (*Scot.*) incorrect form of gillie.

ghost (gōst) *n.* the apparition of a dead person; a spectre; a disembodied spirit; semblance or shadow; (*Colloq.*) a person who does literary or artistic work for another, who takes the credit for it.—**ghost´ly** *a.* spiritual; pert. to apparitions.—**ghost´liness** *n.*—**ghost´-like** *a.* characteristic of a ghost.—**Holy Ghost**, the Holy Spirit; the third element in the Trinity [O.E. *gast*].

ghoul (góól) *n.* imaginary evil being in East, supposed to rob graves and feed on corpses.—**ghoul´ish** *a.* [Ar. *ghul*].

ghyll (gil) *n.* Same as **gill**.

giant (jī´ant) *n.* (*fem.* **gi´antess**) a man of extraordinary bulk and stature; a person of unusual powers, bodily or intellectual.—*a.* like a giant.—**gi´antism** *n.* (*Med.*) abnormal development [Fr. *géant*].

giaour (jour) *n.* a term applied by Turks to anyone not of their religion, esp. a Christian [Turk. *jawr*, an infidel].

gib (jib) *n.* in a machine or structure, a wedge-shaped piece of metal to hold other parts in position; the arm of a crane; a gibbet.—Also **jib** [origin uncertain].

gibber (jib´er, gib´er) *v.i.* and *t.* to speak rapidly and inarticulately; to chatter like an ape.—**gibb´erish** *n.* meaningless speech; gabble; nonsense [imit. origin].

gibbet (jib´et) *n.* a gallows; a post with an arm on which an executed criminal hung; the projecting beam of a crane, on which the pulley is fixed;—*v.t.* to hang on a gallows [O.Fr. *gibet*, a stick].

gibbon (gib´on) *n.* a tail-less, long-armed ape of S.E. Asia [Fr.].

gibbous (gib´us) *a.* protuberant; humped; convex; of the moon, with the bright part greater than a semi-circle.—**gibb´ose** *a.* gibbous [L. *gibbus*, a hump].

gibe, jibe (jīb) *v.i.* to taunt; to sneer at; to scoff at;—*n.* an expression of censure mingled with contempt; a taunt; a jeer [etym. uncertain].

giblets (jib´lets) *n. pl.* the internal eatable parts of poultry, e.g. heart, liver, gizzard, etc. [O.Fr. *gibelet*].

gibus (zhē´bus) *n.* a crush-hat; an opera-hat [fr. Fr. *Gibus*, the inventor].

giddy (gid-i´) *a.* dizzy; feeling a swimming sensation in the head; liable to cause this sensation; whirling; flighty; frivolous.—**gidd´ily** *adv.*—**gidd´iness** *n.* [O.E. *gydig*, insane].

gift (gift) *n.* a present; a thing given; a donation; natural talent; faculty; power;—*v.t.* to endow; to present with; to bestow.—**gift´ed** *a.* possessing natural talent; talented.—**gift´edness** *n.* [fr. *give*].

gig (gig) *n.* a light carriage with one pair of wheels, drawn by one horse; a ship's wherry, or light boat; a rowing-boat.—**gig´lamps** *n.pl.* (*Slang*) a pair of spectacles [etym. uncertain].

gigantic (jī-gan´tik) *a.* like a giant; of extraordinary size; huge.—**gigan´tically** *adv.*—**gigan´tism** *n.* (*Med.*) abnormal overgrowth of the body or limbs [Gk. *gigas*, a giant].

giggle (gig´l) *v.i.* to laugh in a silly way, with half-suppressed catches of the breath; to titter;—*n.* such a laugh.—**gigg´ler** *n.*—**gigg´ling** *n.* [imit. origin].

gigolo (jig´o-lō) *n.* a professional male dancing-partner [Sp.].

gigot (jig´ot) *n.* a leg of mutton or of lamb [Fr.].

Gilbertian (gil-bert′i-an) *a.* whimsical, fantastic, grotesque, topsy-turvy [fr. Sir W. S. *Gilbert* (1836-1911), playwright].
gild (gild) *v.t.* to overlay with gold-leaf or gold-dust; to cover with anything like gold; to brighten; to give a fair appearance to; to embellish [O.E. *gyldan*].
gild (gild) *n.* See **guild**.
gill (jil) *n.* a measure of capacity containing the fourth part of a pint [O.Fr. *gelle*].
gill (gil) *n.* the organ of respiration in fishes and other water animals; the flap below the beak of a bird; the flesh about the chin and jaws (usually *pl.*) [Scand.].
gill (gil) *n.* a ravine or narrow valley, with a stream running through it. Also **ghyll** [O.N. *gil*, a fissure].
gillie, gilly (gil′i) *n.* in Scotland, orig. a male attendant on a chieftain; now one who attends on sportsmen.—Also (incorrectly) **ghill′ie** [Gael. *gille*, a lad].
gillyflower (jil′i-flou-er) *n.* the clove-scented pink; other similar scented flowers [Fr. *giroflée*, fr. *girofle*, a clove].
gilt (gilt) *n.* gold, or something resembling gold, laid on the surface of a thing;—*a.* yellow like gold; gilded.—**gilt′-edged** *a.* having the edges gilded; of the best quality [O.E. *gyldan*].
gimbals (jim′balz) *n.pl.* a contrivance of rings and pivots for keeping a ship's compass, etc. always in a horizontal position [L. *gemelli*, twins].
gimcrack (jim′krak) *n.* a toy or fanciful trifle; a mechanical device;—*a.* showy but worthless [E. *jim*, neat; *crack*, a lad, a boaster].
gimlet (gim′let) *n.* a small implement with a screw point and a cross handle, for boring holes in wood;—*v.t.* to bore with a gimlet [O.Fr. *guimbelet*].
gimmer (gim′er) *n.* a two-year-old ewe [O.N. *gymbr*].
gimmick (gim′ik) *n.* originally in the U.S., any small device fitted to a gaming-machine to make it unfair; a trick-of-the-trade; any mannerism peculiar to, and associated with, a particular individual, esp. any whimsicality deliberately used by a stage artiste for effect, e.g. "raising the eyebrows" [perh. fr. *gimcrack*].
gimp (gimp) *n.* a narrow fabric or braid used as an edging for furniture or a trimming for dresses [Fr. *guimpe*].
gin (jin) *n.* a distilled spirit, flavoured with juniper berries.—**gin′sling** *n.* a mixture of gin, sugar, and water [short for *geneva*, Fr. *genièvre* fr. L. *juniperus*, juniper].
gin (jin) *n.* a snare or trap; a machine for lifting or moving heavy weights; a machine for separating the seeds from cotton;—*v.t.* to clear cotton of seeds by a gin; to catch in a snare.—*pr.p.* **gin′ning.**—*pa.p.* and *pa.t.* **ginned** [contr. of *engine*].
ginger (jin′jer) *n.* a plant of the Indies with a hot-tasting spicy root; ginger-beer; (*Slang*) spirit; a light reddish-yellow colour;—*v.t.* to put life into; to animate or inspirit (with *up*).—**gin′ger-ale** *n.* an aerated beverage.—**gin′ger-beer** *n.* an effervescing beverage made by fermenting ginger, cream of tartar, and sugar, etc.—**gin′ger-bread** *n.* a cake, flavoured with ginger.—**gin′ger-pop** *n.* weak ginger-beer.—**gin′ger-wine** *n.* a wine made by fermentation, from ginger with other ingredients.—**gin′gery** *a.* hot and spicy [L. *zingiber*].
gingerly (jin′jer-li) *adv.* cautiously; with wary steps [origin uncertain].
gingham (ging′am) *n.* a kind of cotton cloth, usually checked or striped; (*Colloq.*) an umbrella [Javanese *ginggang*, striped].
gink (gink) *n.* (*Slang*) a fellow; a chap [etym. unknown].
gin rummy (jin-rum′i) *n.* a two-handed card game (or four-handed with partners).
ginseng (jin′seng) *n.* a plant, the root highly valued as medicine among the Chinese [Chin. *jin-tsan*].
gippo (jip′ō) *n.* (*Colloq.*) an Egyptian; (*Army Slang*) melted bacon fat; stew; soup.
gipsy, gypsy (jip′si) *n.* one of a nomadic tribe of Indian origin, that came by way of Egypt in the 14th cent.—*pl.* **gip′sies.**—*a.* pert. to gipsies; unconventional [corrupt. fr. *Egyptian*].
giraffe (ji-råf′) *n.* an African animal, with spotted coat and very long neck and legs; the camelopard [Fr. fr. Ar. *zaraf*].
gird (gerd) *v.i.* to gibe; to jeer.—**gird′er** *n.*—**gird′ing** *a.* and *n.* [O.E. *gyrd*, a rod].
gird (gerd) *v.t.* to encircle with any flexible band; to put a belt round; to fasten clothes thus; to equip with, or belt on, a sword.—*pa.p.* and *pa.t.* **gird′ed** or **girt.**—*n.* a child's hoop.—**gird′er** *n.* a principal piece of timber or iron in a floor to act as a supporting beam for joists; an iron or steel beam as used in constructional engineering [O.E. *gyrdan*].
girdle (ger′dl) *n.* that which girds or encircles, esp. a band which encircles the waist; a belt;—*v.t.* to bind with a belt or sash [O.E. *gyrdel*].
girl (gerl) *n.* a female child; a young unmarried woman.—**girl′hood** *n.* the state, or time, of being a girl.—**girl′ish** *a.* like a girl.—**girl′ishly** *adv.*—**girl′ishness** *n.*—**Girl Guide,** a member of an organisation for girls on the lines of the Boy Scouts.—**Girls' Training Corps,** a youth organisation for girls over 16 (abbrev. **G.T.C.**) [M.E. *gurle*].
Girondist (ji-ron′dist) *n.* a member of a moderate Republican party during the first French Revolution (1789), so called because their leaders came from the *Gironde* district of S.W. France.—Also **Giron′din.**
girt (gert) past tense and past participle of the verb **gird;**—*v.t.* to gird; to surround.
girth (gerth) *n.* band to hold a saddle, blanket, etc. in place; a belly-band; the measurement round a thing [fr. *gird*].
gist (jist) *n.* the main point of a question; the substance or essential point of any matter [O.Fr. *gist*, it lies].
gittern (git′ern) *n.* a guitar. Also **cith′ern** [Gk. *kithara*, a kind of lyre].
give (giv) *v.t.* to bestow; to make a present of; to grant; to deliver; to impart; to assign; to yield; to supply; to make over; to cause to have; to pronounce, as an opinion, etc.; to pledge, as one's word;—*v.i.* to yield; to give away; to move.—*pr.p.* **giv′ing.**—*pa.p.* **giv′en.**—*pa.t.* **gave.**—**given** (giv′n) *a.* granted; admitted; supposed; certain; particular; addicted to; inclined to.—**giv′er** *n.*—**to give away,** to hand over; to divulge, of a secret, etc.—**to give over,** to cease from; to desist [O.E. *giefan*].
gives (jivz) *n.pl.* Same as **gyves.**
gizzard (giz′ard) *n.* a bird's strong muscular second stomach [O.Fr. *gezier*].
glacé (glá′sā) *a.* of a cake, iced; of a kind of leather, polished or glossy [Fr. *glace*, ice].
glacier (glas′i-er) glā′sher) *n.* a mass of ice, formed by accumulated snow in high cold regions, which moves very slowly down a mountain; a river of ice.—**glacial** (glā′shal) pert. to ice or its action; pert. to glaciers; icy; frozen; pert. to the ice-age; crystallised.—**gla′ciate** *v.t.* to cover with ice; to turn to ice; to polish with ice.—**glacia′tion** *n.*—**glaciol′ogy** *n.* the scientific study of the formation and action of glaciers.—**glacial period,** the Ice-Age [Fr. *glace*, ice].
glacis (glā′sis, gla-sē′) *n.* in fortifications, the outer sloping bank [Fr.].
glad (glad) *a.* pleased; happy; joyous; giving joy;—*v.t.* to make glad; to gladden; to cheer.—**glad′den** *v.t.* to make glad; to cheer; to please.—**glad′ly** *adv.* with pleasure; joyfully; cheerfully.—**glad′ness** *n.*—**glad′some** *a.* joyful; cheerful; gay.—**glad eye** (*Colloq.*) an amorous glance [O.E. *glaed*].

glade (glād) *n.* a grassy open space in a wood or forest [etym. uncertain].
gladiator (glad′i-ā-tor) *n.* literally, a swordsman; in ancient Rome, professional combatant who fought in the arena [L. *gladius*, a sword].
gladiolus (glad-i-ō′lus, glạ-dī′o-lus) *n.* a plant of the iris family, with long sword-shaped leaves; the sword-lily.—*pl.* **gladio'luses,** or **gladioli** (glad-i-ō′lī, glạ-dī′o-li) [L. *gladius*, a sword].
Gladstone (glad′ston) *n.* a leather travelling-bag which is hinged along the bottom so as to open out flat. Also **Glad'stone-bag** [fr. British statesman, W. E. *Gladstone*].
glair (glār) *n.* white of egg; size or gloss made from it; any viscous substance resembling white of egg;—*v.t.* to smear with glair.—**glair'eous, glair'y** *a.* [Fr. *glaire*].
glaive, glave (glāv) *n.* (*Arch.*) broadsword; kind of halberd [L. *gladius*, sword].
glamour (glam′ur) *n.* a charm on the eyes making them see things as fairer than they really are; witchery; deceptive or alluring charm.—**glam'orous** *a.* [corrupt. of *gramarye* or *grammar*, meaning magic].
glance (glàns) *n.* a quick look; a glimpse; a flash or sudden shoot of light; an allusion or hint; an oblique hit;—*v.t.* (*Arch.*) to send by a glance;—*v.i.* to give a swift, cursory look; to allude; to fly off in an oblique direction; to dart a sudden ray of light.—**glanc'ing** *a.*—**glanc'ingly** *adv.* obliquely [Ger. *Glanz*, lustre].
gland (gland) *n.* a cell or collection of cells secreting and abstracting certain substances from the blood and transforming them into new compounds; (*Mech.*) a sleeve on a piston rod, to keep packing tight; (*Arch.*) an acorn.—**gland'ers** *n.* a disease of mucous membrane in nostrils of horses.—**gland'erous** *a.* of nature of glanders.—**glandif'erous** *a.* bearing acorns or other nuts.—**gland'iform** *a.* shaped like an acorn.—**gland'ular, gland'ulous** *a.* containing glands; consisting of glands [L. *glans*, an acorn].
glare (glār) *n.* a strong, dazzling light; an overwhelming glitter; showiness; a fierce, hostile look or stare;—*v.i.* to shine with a strong, dazzling light; to stare in a fierce and hostile manner.—**glar'ing** *a.* brilliant; open and bold [O.E. *glaer*, amber].
glass (glàs) *n.* a hard, brittle, generally transparent substance formed by fusing silica with fixed alkalis; collectively, articles made of glass, e.g. a drinking-glass or tumbler, a looking-glass or mirror, a telescope, a weather glass or barometer; the quantity contained in a drinking glass;—*a.* made of glass;—*v.t.* to cover with glass; to glaze.—**glass'es** *n.pl.* spectacles.—**glass'y** *a.* made of glass; vitreous; like glass; dull or lifeless.—**glass'ily** *adv.*—**glass'iness** *n.*—**glass'ful** *n.* the contents of a glass.—**glass′blow'ing** *n.* the art of shaping and fashioning glass by inflating it through a tube, after heating.—**glass′blow'er** *n.*—**glass′house** *n.* a greenhouse; (*Slang*) a military prison.—**glass′pa'per** *n.* paper coated with pulverised glass for polishing.—**glass'ware** *n.* articles made of glass.—**cut glass,** glass ornamented by cutting designs into it with a wheel.—**ground glass,** glass rendered untransparent by grinding, by the use of acids, etc. [O.E. *glaes*].
Glaswegian (glas-wē′ji-ạn) *n.* a citizen of Glasgow;—*a.* belonging to Glasgow.
Glauber's salt(s) (glaw′bẹrz-sawlt(s)) *n.* sulphate of soda, used in medicine as an aperient [fr. J. *Glauber*, a German chemist of the 17th cent.].
glaucoma (glaw-kō′mạ) *n.* (*Med.*) a serious eye-disease causing tension and hardening of the eyeball [Gk.].
glaucous (glaw′kus) *a.* sea-green; covered with a fine bloom, as on a blue plum [Gk. *glaukos*, blue-gray].
glaze (glāz) *n.* the vitreous, transparent coating of pottery or porcelain; any glossy coating—*v.t.* to furnish with glass, as a window; to overlay with a thin, transparent surface, as earthenware; to make glossy.—**glaz'er** *n.* a workman who glazes pottery, cloth, or paper.—**glazier** (glā′zi-ẹr) *n.* a dealer in glass; one who sets glass in windows, etc.—**gla'zy** *a.* having a glaze [O.E. *glaes*, glass].
gleam (glēm) *n.* a faint or transient ray of light; brightness; glow;—*v.i.* to shoot or dart, as rays of light; to flash; to shine faintly or fitfully [O.E. *glaem*].
glean (glēn) *v.t.* to gather after a reaper, as grain; to collect with patient labour; to cull the fairest portion of; to pick up (information)—*v.i.* to gather what is left by reapers.—**glean'er** *n.*—**glean'ings** *n.pl.* what is collected by gleaning [O.Fr. *glener*].
glebe (glēb) *n.* soil; ground; land belonging to a parish church [L. *gleba*, a clod].
glede (glēd) *n.* the common kite, a bird of prey [O.E. *glida*].
glee (glē) *n.* mirth; merriment; joy; a musical composition for three or more voices; a part song.—**glee′man** *n.* a wandering minstrel [O.E. *gleo*, mirth].
gleet (glēt) *n.* mucus; thin watery matter running from a sore [O.Fr. *glete*, a flux].
glen (glen) *n.* a valley, usually wooded and with a stream [Gael. *gleann*].
glengarry (glen-gar′i) *n.* a Highlander's cap, boat-shaped, and with two ribbons hanging down behind [fr. *Glengarry*, Inverness-shire, Scotland].
glib (glib) *a.* smooth; fluent; plausible; flippant.—**glib'ly** *adv.*—**glib'ness** *n.* [etym. uncertain].
glide (glīd) *v.i.* to move gently or smoothly; to go stealthily or gradually; of an aeroplane, to move, or descend, with engines shut off;—*n.* a sliding movement.—**glid'er** *n.* one who, or that which, glides; an aeroplane capable of flight without motive power, by utilising air currents [O.E. *glidan*].
glim (glim) *n.* (*Colloq.*) a light or lamp; the eye [O.E. *gleomu*].
glimmer (glim′ẹr) *v.i.* to shine faintly and unsteadily; to flicker;—*n.* a faint, unsteady light; a flicker [M.E. *glimeren*].
glimpse (glimps) *n.* a momentary view; a passing flash or appearance; a weak, faint light; a faint notion;—*v.t.* to catch a glimpse of; to get a passing view of;—*v.i.* to glimmer [M.E. *glimsen*, to shine faintly].
glint (glint) *n.* glitter; a faint gleam; a flash;—*v.i.* to glitter [M.E. *glent*].
glissade (glē-sàd') *n.* the act of sliding down a slope of ice or snow; in dancing, a gliding step sideways;—*v.i.* to slide down a slope of ice [Fr. *glisser*, to slide].
glisten (glis′n) *v.i.* to glitter; to sparkle; to shine;—*n.* glitter [O.E. *glisnian*].
glister (glis-tẹr) *v.i.* to glitter; to shine [O.E. *glisnian*].
glitter (glit-ẹr) *v.i.* to shine with a bright, quivering light; to sparkle; to be showy and attractive;—*n.* a bright, sparkling light; brilliance [O.N. *glitra*].
gloaming (glō-ming) *n.* evening twilight; dusk [O.E. *glomung*].
gloat (glōt) *v.i.* to gaze with eagerness, or desire; to feast the eyes, usually with unholy joy [etym. uncertain].
globe (glōb) *n.* a round body; a sphere; a heavenly sphere, esp. the earth; a sphere with a map of the earth or the stars; anything approximately of this shape, e.g. a fish-bowl, a lamp-shade, etc.—**glob'al** *a.* taking in the whole world.—**glob'ate, glob'ated** *a.* spherical.—**glob'oid** *a.* globe-shaped.—**globose', glob'ous** *a.* round, spherical (or nearly so).—**globos'ity** *n.*—**glob'ular** *a.* globe-shaped (or nearly so).—**globular'ity** *n.*—**glob'ularly** *adv.*—**globule** (glob′ūl) *n.* a small particle of matter of a spherical form; a tiny pill.—**glob'ulous** *a.*—**globe′trot'ter** *n.*

a hasty, sight-seeing traveller or tourist [L. *globus*, a round mass].

globulin (glob´ū-lin) *n.* one of the soluble proteins of the blood [fr. *globule*].

glockenspiel (glok´en-spēl) *n.* a musical instrument consisting either of a row of bells suspended from a rod, or of a series of flat bars, which when struck with a mallet give forth a bell-like sound; a carillon [Ger. *Glocke*, a bell; *Spiel*, play].

glomerate (glom´e-rāt) *v.t.* to gather into a ball;—*a.* gathered into a cluster.—**glomera´tion** *n.* [L. *glomus*, a clew of yarn].

gloom (glòòm) *n.* thick shade; partial or almost total darkness; melancholy; sullenness; —*v.i.* to become dark or threatening; to be dejected; to look sullen.—**gloom'y** *a.* dark and dreary; melancholy.—**gloom'ily** *adv.*—**gloom´iness** *n.* [O.E. *glom*].

glory (glō´ri) *n.* renown, praise, honour; whatever brings honour; praise and adoration due to God; divine happiness; height of excellence or prosperity; splendour or brilliance; a halo; —*v.i.* to be proud; boast; to exult triumphantly.—**gloriole** (glō´ri-ōl) *n.* a glory or circle of rays.—**glo'rious** *a.* illustrious; conferring renown; splendid; noble.—**glo'riously** *adv.*—**glo'riousness** *n.*—**glo'rify** *v.t.* to exalt; to praise; esp. to extol in worship; to make eternally blessed; to shed radiance on; to magnify.—**glo'rifier** *n.*—**glorifica'tion** *n.*— **glo´ry-hole** *n.* a lumber-room; an opening in a glass furnace [L. *gloria*].

gloss (glos) *n.* lustre from a smooth surface; polish; a deceptively fine exterior;—*v.t.* to make smooth and shining; to render plausible; (with *over*) to mitigate or excuse something harsh or unpleasant.—**gloss'y** *a.* smooth and shining [O.N. *glossi*, a blaze].

gloss (glos) *n.* an explanatory note upon some word or passage in a text, written in the margin or between the lines; a glossary;— *v.t.* and *i.* to annotate [Gk. *glōssa*, the tongue].

glossal (glos´al) *a.* (*Anat.*) pert. to the tongue [Gk. *glōssa*, the tongue].

glossary (glos´a-ri) *n.* a vocabulary of obscure or technical words; vocabulary to a book.—**glossa'rial** *a.* containing explanation. —**gloss'arist** *n.* a compiler of a glossary [Gk. *glōssa*, the tongue].

glottis (glot´is) *n.* (*Anat.*) the narrow opening at the top of the larynx or windpipe, between the vocal chords.—**glott'al** *a.* [Gk. fr. *glōssa*, *glōtta*, the tongue].

glove (gluv) *n.* a cover for the hand and wrist with a sheath for each finger;—*v.t.* to cover with a glove.—**glov'er** *n.* one who makes or sells gloves [O.E. *glof*].

glow (glō) *v.i.* to shine with an intense or white heat; to be bright or red; to feel hot, as the skin; to burn; to rage;—*n.* white heat; incandescence; warmth or redness of colour; sensation of warmth.—**glow'ing** *a.* bright; warm; excited; enthusiastic.—**glow'ingly** *adv.* [O.E. *glowan*].

glower (glou´er) *v.i.* to stare sullenly;—*n.* a sullen scowl [origin unknown].

gloze (glōz) *v.i.* to talk smoothly and speciously; to comment; to explain;—*v.t.* to smooth over; to palliate; to wheedle or cajole [M.E. *glosen*].

glucose (glòò´kōs) *n.* a white crystalline sugar obtained from grapes, various fruits, and other sources; grape-sugar [Gk. *glukus*, sweet].

glue (glòò) *n.* an adhesive, gelatinous substance got by boiling skins, hoofs, etc. of animals, or fish-skins;—*v.t.* to join with glue; to cause to stick fast, as with glue.—**glu'ey** *a.*—**glu'eyness** *n.* [O.Fr. *glu*.]

glum (glum) *a.* sullen; moody; morose.— **glum'ly** *adv.* [M.E. *glommen*, to frown].

glume (glòòm) *n.* the floral covering of grain or grasses.—**glu'mal** *a.*—**glu'mous** *a.* having glumes [L. *gluma*, husk].

glut (glut) *v.t.* to swallow greedily; to feed till over-full; to supply over-abundantly;—*n.* overmuch; super-abundance; surfeit [L. *gluttire*, to swallow].

gluten (glòò´ten) *n.* the protein of wheat and other cereals [L. *gluten*].

glutinate (glòò´ti-nāt) *v.t.* to unite with glue; to cement [L. *glutinare*].

glutton (glut´n) *n.* one who eats too much; (*Fig.*) one eager for anything in excess, e.g. work, books, etc.; carnivore of weasel family, wolverine.—**glutt'onise** *v.i.* to eat to excess; to gormandise.—**glutt'onous** *a.* given to gluttony.—**glutt'onously** *adv.*—**glutt'ony** *n.* [Fr. *glouton*].

glycerine (glis´er-in, -ēn) *n.* a sweet, colourless, odourless, syrupy liquid.—Also **glyc'erin** [Gk. *glukeros*, sweet].

glycogen (glī´kō-jen) *n.* the form in which the body stores carbohydrates (starch); animal starch [Gk. *glukus*, sweet].

glycol (glī´kol) *n.* an artificial compound linking glycerine and alcohol [fr. *gly*cerine and alco*hol*].

glyph (glif) *n.* a shallow vertical channel or carved fluting [Gk. *gluphein*, to carve].

glyptic (glip´tik) *a.* pert. to carving on stone. —**glyp'tics** *n.pl.* the art of engraving on precious stones.—**glyp'tograph** *n.* an engraving on a gem or precious stone.—**glyptog'raphy** *n.* [Gk. *gluptos*, carved; *graphein*, to write].

gnar (nar) *v.i.* to growl; to snarl.—Also **gnarl, gnarr** [imit. origin].

gnarl (nàrl) *n.* a knot in wood or on the trunk of a tree.—**gnarled** (nàrld), **gnar'ly** *a.* knotty; knobby [M.E. *knurre*].

gnash (nash) *v.t.* to grind the teeth together, as in anger or pain;—*n.* a snap; a sudden bite.—**gnash'ing** *n.* [imit. origin].

gnat (nat) *n.* a kind of small mosquito [O.E. *gnat*].

gnaw (naw) *v.t.* to wear away by scraping with the teeth; to bite steadily, as a dog a bone; to fret; to corrode;—*v.i.* to use the teeth in biting; to cause steady pain.—*pa.p.* **gnawed** or **gnawn**.—*pa.t.* **gnawed**.—**gnaw'er** *n.* [O.E. *gnagan*].

gneiss (nīs) *n.* a crystalline rock, consisting of quartz, feldspar, and mica, in some cases very like granite [Ger. *Gneiss*].

gnome (nōm) *n.* super-physical being, of diminutive size, the guardian of precious metals hidden in the earth; a goblin [Gk. *gnōmē*, intelligence].

gnome (nōm) *n.* a pithy saying; a maxim.— **gno'mic, gno'mical** *a.* pithy; sententious [Gk. *gnōmē*, thought, judgment].

gnomon (nō´mon) *n.* the pin, rod, or plate which casts the shadow on a sundial; an indicator; (*Geom.*) the part of a rectangular figure which remains when a similar rectangle is taken from one corner of it.—**gnomon'ic, gnomon'ical** *a.* [Gk. *gnōmōn*, pin of a sundial].

gnosis (nō´sis) *n.* science; mystical knowledge.—**gnostic** (nost´tik) *a.* pert. to knowledge; having special knowledge; pert. to the Gnostics.—**Gnos'tics** *n.pl.* followers of a religious sect in the early Christian era who had esoteric spiritual knowledge.—**Gnos´ticism** *n.* [Gk. *gignoskein*, to know].

gnu (nòò) *n.* a kind of antelope, resembling an ox; the black wildebeest [Kaffir, *ngu*].

go (gō) *v.i.* to pass from one place or condition to another; to move along; to be in motion; to proceed; to depart; to elapse; to be kept; to put; to be able to be put; to result; to contribute to a result; to tend to; to pass away; to become; to fare.—*pr.p.* **go'ing**— *pa.p.* **gone** (gon).—*pa.t.* **went**.—*n.* a going; vigour; (*Colloq.*) an attempt; the fashion.— **go'er** *n.* one who, or that which, goes.—**go'ing** *n.* the state of the ground, e.g. on a racecourse, in cross-country running, etc.—**goings on** (*Colloq.*) usually in a bad sense, strange behaviour; questionable conduct.—**gone** *a.* lapsed; lost; beyond recovery; weak and faint.—**go´between'** *n.* an intermediary.—

go′by *n.* an intentional slight.—**go′cart** *n.* wooden framework on castors, for teaching infants to walk; a baby-carriage.—**to go halves,** to share equally with.—**to go in for,** to sit an examination; to choose as a career.—**to go off,** to depart; to explode; to disappear; to become less efficient, popular, fashionable, fresh, etc.—**to go the whole hog,** not to stop at half-measures.—**to go to pieces,** to lose one's morale completely; to break up.—**to go to the dogs** (*Slang*) to become dissolute; to become a moral wreck through dissipation.—**to go west** (*Army Slang*) to be killed; hence, of money, objects, etc., to be lost, stolen, etc. [O.E. *gan*].

goad (gōd) *n.* a sharp, pointed stick for driving cattle; anything that urges to action;—*v.t.* to drive with a goad; to urge on; to irritate. [O.E. *gad*].

goal (gōl) *n.* in a race, the starting point; also, the winning-post; in football, hockey, etc., the space marked by two upright posts and a cross-bar; the act of kicking or driving the ball between these posts; an object of effort; an end or aim [Fr. *gaule*, a pole].

goat (gōt) *n.* a long-haired, ruminant quadruped with cloven hoofs, allied to the sheep, but lighter in build and with backward-curving horns; the 10th sign of the Zodiac, Capricorn, which the sun enters on Dec. 22nd. —**goatee** (gō-tē′) *n.* a small tuft of beard on the chin.—**goat-herd** *n.* one who tends goats.—**goat′ish** *a.* rank-smelling, like a goat; wanton; lecherous.—**goat′suck′er** *n.* a nocturnal bird, (mistakenly thought to suck goats); fawn-owl, night-hawk, night-jar.—**to get one's goat** (*Colloq.*) to annoy; to irritate [O.E. *gat*].

gob (gob) *n.* a lump or mouthful; a clot of spittle; (*Colloq.*) the mouth.—**gobb′et** *n.* a mouthful; a small lump, esp. of flesh [O.Fr. *gobe*, a mouthful].

gob (gob) *n.* (*Slang*) a nickname for an American sailor.

gobble (gob′l) *v.t.* to eat hurriedly or greedily; to swallow in lumps.—**gobb′ler** *n.* a greedy eater [O.Fr. *gober*, to devour].

gobble (gob′l) *n.* the throaty, gurgling cry of the turkey-cock;—*v.i.* to make such a noise; —*v.t.* to utter with a gobbling sound.—**gobb′ler** *n.* a turkey-cock [imit.].

Gobelin (gob-lang′, gob′e-lin) *n.* rich French tapestry [fr. *Gobelin*, firm of dyers and tapestry-makers in Paris in 15th cent.].

goblet (gob′let) *n.* a drinking vessel without a handle [O.Fr. *gobelet*].

goblin (gob′lin) *n.* an evil or mischievous sprite or elf; a gnome [Gk. *kobalos*, a mischievous spirit].

God (god) *n.* the Supreme Being; Jehovah.—**god** *n.* a person of more than human powers; a divinity; an idol; any person honoured unduly; any object esteemed as the chief good; —*n.pl.* false deities; (*Colloq.*) the audience in the gallery of a theatre.—**god′dess** *n.* a female god or idol.—**god′head** *n.* divinity.—**god′ly** *a.* reverencing God; pious; devout.—**god′liness** *n.* holiness; righteousness.—**god′less** *a.* wicked; impious; acknowledging no God.—**god′send** *n.* an unexpected piece of good fortune.—**god′speed** *n.* a prosperous journey; a wish for success given at parting.—**God′fear′ing,** *a.* devoutly religious.—**god′forsak′en,** dreary; dismal [O.E. *god*, cf. Ger. *Gott*].

godchild (god′chīld) *n.* one for whom a person becomes sponsor at baptism, guaranteeing his religious education.—**god′daughter** *n.*—**god′son** *n.*—**god′father** *n.* a sponsor at baptism. **god′mother** *n.* [O.E.].

godet (god′et) *n.* a triangular piece of material let into the foot of a skirt to cause it to flare out [Fr.].

godetia (go-dé′shi-ạ) *n.* a plant much cultivated for its showy flowers [fr. *Godet*, a Swiss botanist].

godwit (god′wit) *n.* a wading-bird resembling the curlew [O.E. *god*, good; *wiht*, a creature].

goffer (gof′ẹr) *v.t.* to crimp, plait, or flute, as linen ruffles, lace, paper, etc.;—*n.* a goffering implement [O.Fr. *gauffrer*].

goggle (gog′l) *v.i.* to roll the eyes; to stare;—*n.* a rolling of the eyes;—*a.* rolling; bulging; protruding (of the eyes).—**gogg′les** *n.pl.* spectacles to protect the eyes, or to cure squinting; blinds for horses [Gael. *gog*, a nod].

goitre (goi′tẹr) *n.* a swelling on the front of the neck, being the enlargement of the thyroid gland.—**goi′trous** *a.* of the nature of goitre [L. *guttur*, the throat].

gold (gōld) *n.* a precious metal of a bright yellow colour; money; riches; a bright yellow colour;—*a.* made of gold; of colour of gold; golden.—**gold′en** *a.* made of gold; having the colour of gold; precious.—**gold′finch** *n.* a beautiful singing bird, so named from the colour of the wings.—**gold′fish** *n.* a small fish of the carp family named from its colour.—**gold′smith** *n.* one who manufactures vessels and ornaments of gold.—**gold′ylocks, gold′ilocks** *n.* a plant having tufts of yellow flowers; a ranunculus.—**gold′beat′er** *n.* one who beats gold into gold-leaf.—**gold′dig′ger** *n.* one who digs or mines gold; (*Slang*) an unscrupulous flirt, expert at obtaining money from her male friends.—**gold′dust** *n.* gold in very fine particles.—**gold′leaf** *n.* gold beaten into an extremely thin leaf or foil, used for gilding.—**gold′mine** *n.* a mine from which gold is dug.—**gold′plate** *n.* vessels or utensils made of gold (collectively).—**gold′rush** *n.* the mad scramble to reach a new gold-field.—**gold standard,** a currency system under which bank-notes are exchanged for gold at any time.—**golden age,** the most flourishing period in the history of a nation.—**golden eagle,** a large, powerful eagle, so called from the yellow-tipped feathers on its head.—**golden rod,** a plant of the aster family.—**golden rule,** the rule of doing as you would be done by.—**golden wedding,** the fiftieth anniversary of one's wedding [O.E. *gold*].

golf (golf) *n.* out-door game played with set of clubs and a ball, in which the ball is driven with the fewest possible strokes, into a succession of holes.—*v.i.* to play this game.—**golf′er** *n.*—**golf′-course** *n.* ground on which game is played.—**golf′-links** *n.pl.* sea-side 'course' [Dut. *kolf*, a club].

golliwog, gollywog (gol′i-wog) *n.* a grotesque black-faced, goggle-eyed fantastically dressed doll [etym. uncertain].

golly (gol′i) *interj.* orig. a minced oath; to express joy, sorrow, surprise, etc. [fr. *God*].

golosh (go-losh′) *n.* a rubber overshoe.—Also **galosh′** [Fr. *galoche*].

gonad (gon′ad) *n.* (*Biol.*) a germ-gland in the testis of the male or the ovary of the female [Gk. *gonos*, seed].

gondola (gon′do-lạ) *n.* a long, narrow, flat-bottomed boat, used in the canals of Venice.—**gondolier** (gon-do-lēr′) *n.* the boatman who propels the gondola [It.].

gone (gon) *pa.p.* of the verb **go.**—**gon′er** *n.* (*Slang*) one who is in a hopeless state; one beyond recovery [O.E. *gan*].

gonfalon, gonfanon (gon′fạ-lon, -non) *n.* a pennon, with three or four streamers; an ensign or standard.—**gonfalonier′** *n.* a standard bearer; the chief magistrate of certain Italian republics in the Middle Ages [O.Fr. *gonfanon*].

gong (gong) *n.* a circular metal plate which gives out a deep note when struck with a soft mallet; anything used in the same way, esp. as a call to meals; (*Army Slang*) a medal [Malay].

gonococcus (gon-o-kok′us) *n.* (*Med.*) microbe of gonorrhea.—**gonorrhea** (gon-o-rē′ạ) *n.* contagious discharge of mucus from membrane of urethra or vagina; venereal disease [Gk. *gonos*, seed; *kokkos*, a berry; *rhoia*, a flowing].

good (good) *a.* commendable; right; proper; suitable; excellent; virtuous; honest; just;

Red and Yellow Bigarreau Cherries

Sour Cherry

William pears

Cox's Orange Pippin apples

Pearmain apples

FRUITS TEMPERATE CLIMATES

Louise pears

Plums

Apricots

Mirabelles

Raspberry

Blackcurrant

Wild Strawberry

Wild tulips

Single flowering tulips

Lily flowering tulips

Parrot tulips

GARDEN FLOWERS of EUROPE

Iris

Delphinium

Zinnia

Fuchsia

kind; affectionate; safe; sound; valid; solvent; adequate; full, as weight, measure, etc.; skilful;—*n.* that which is good; welfare; well-being; profit; advantage.—*n.pl.* property; wares; commodities; merchandise; freight;—*interj.* well! right! so be it!—*comp.* of adjective, **bett'er**.—*superl.* **best**.—**good'ish** *a.* (of quality) pretty good; (of quantity) fairly plentiful.—**good'ly** *a.* handsome; pleasant; agreeable; comely; graceful; of considerable size.—**good'liness** *n.* beauty of form; grace; elegance.—**good'ness** *n.* the quality of being good;—*interj.* used for emphasis.—**good'y** *a.* sentimentally good; obtrusively or weakly virtuous;—*n.* goodwife; a sweetmeat, a bonbon, or the like;—*pl.* **good'ies**, sweetmeats, etc.—**good'-breed'ing** *n.* polite manners resulting from good upbringing and education.—**good'-broth'er** (**-sister**, etc.) in Scotland, a brother (sister, etc.) -in-law.—**good'-bye** *interj.* contraction of God be with you!; farewell!—*n.* a farewell; a farewell greeting.—**good'-day** *interj.* greeting at meeting or parting.—**good'-eve'ning** *interj.* greeting at meeting or parting in evening.—**good'-fell'owship** *n.* conviviality; jolly and sociable company.—**good'-for-nothing'** *a.* of no use or value; worthless; shiftless;—*n.* a shiftless person; an idler; a loafer.—**Good Friday**, the Friday before Easter.—**good'-hu'mour** *n.* a happy or cheerful state of mind.—**good'-hu'moured** *a.* having a cheerful spirit and demeanour.—**goodman'** *n.* the master of the house.—**good'-morn'ing** *interj.* greeting at meeting or parting in morning.—**good'-na'ture** *n.* natural kindness of disposition; good temper.—**good'-na'tured** *a.*—**good'-na'turedly** *adv.*—**good'-night** *interj.* a salutation at parting for the night.—**good sense**, sound judgment.—**good'-tem'pered** *a.* not easily irritated or annoyed.—**good turn**, a kindly action.—**goodwife'** *n.* the mistress of a household.—**good'-will** *n.* benevolence; kindly disposition; (*Commerce*) the right, on transfer or sale of a business, to the reputation, trade, and custom of that business—**goods'-train** *n.* a train of goods-waggons, as opposed to a passenger-train.—**as good as**, the same as.—**to be in someone's good graces**, to be considered worthy of their favour.—**to be to the good**, to be profitable; to show a profit [O.E. *god*].

goof (gòòf) *n.* (*Slang*) a silly person.

googly (gòò'-gli) *n.* in cricket, a ball which 'breaks' in a way opposite to that in which might be expected [etym. uncertain].

Goorkha (gòòr'-kạ) *n.* See **Gurkha**.

goose (gòòs) *n.* a web-footed bird like a duck but larger; the flesh of the bird; a simpleton; a tailor's smoothing-iron;—*pl.* **geese** (gēs).—**gosling** (goz'-ling) *n.* a young goose.—**goose'-flesh** *n.* a bristling state of the skin due to cold or fright.—**goose'-grass** *n.* the popular name for Bedstraw or Galium, a common weed found in hedges.—**goose'-quill** *n* a large wing-feather of a goose; a pen made from it.—**goose'-step** *n.* (*Mil.*) a ceremonial marching-step with legs kept stiff and lifted high at each step;—*v.i.* to use the goose-step [O.E. *gos*].

gooseberry (gòòs'-, gòòz'-bẹr-i) *n.* a thorny shrub cultivated for its fruit; the fruit itself; a chaperon to lovers.—**gooseberry fool**, (*Cookery*) a purée of stewed gooseberries sweetened and mixed with cream or custard.

gopher (gō'-fẹr) *n.* a species of wood, used in the construction of Noah's ark; probably cypress [Heb.].

gopher (gō'-fẹr) *n.* in America, the ground-squirrel; a kind of rat with pouched cheeks [Fr. *gaufre*, a honeycomb].

gore (gōr) *n.* thick or clotted blood; blood.—**gor'y** *a.* bloody [O.E. *gor*, dirt].

gore (gōr) *v.t.* to pierce with a spear, with horns, or with tusks [O.E. *gar*, a spear].

gore (gōr) *n.* a triangular piece of land; a tapering piece of material inserted in a garment or a sail, to widen it;—*v.t.* to cut into a wedge-shape; to supply with a gore [O.E. *gara*, a pointed piece of land].

gorge (gorj) *n.* throat or gullet; a narrow defile between mountains; a full meal;—*v.t.* to swallow with greediness;—*v.i.* to feed greedily and to excess [L. *gurges*, a whirlpool].

gorgeous (gor'-jus) *a.* splendid; showy; magnificent; richly coloured.—**gor'geously** *adv.* [O.Fr. *gorgias*, beautiful].

gorget (gor'-jet) *n.* a piece of armour for protecting the neck; ornament worn on the neck by officers [Fr. *gorge*, the throat].

Gorgon (gor'-gon) *n.* (*Myth.*) one of three sisters of terrifying aspect; any one, esp. a woman, who is terrifying or repellent-looking.—**gorgonesque'** *a.* repulsive [Gk. *gorgos*, grim].

Gorgonzola (gor-gon-zō'-la) *n.* a kind of ewe-milk cheese made in Italy [fr. *Gorgonzola*, an Italian town].

gorilla (go-ril'-ạ) *n.* an ape inhabiting W. Africa, of great size and strength [Afr.].

gormand (gor'-mạnd) *n.* earlier form of **gourmand**, a greedy eater; a glutton.—**gor'mandise** *v.t.* and *i.* to eat greedily.—**gor'mandiser** *n.* [Fr. *gourmand*].

gorse (gors) *n.* a prickly shrub, bearing yellow flowers; furze; whin [O.E. *gorst*].

gosh (gosh) *interj.* (*Colloq.*) a minced and very mild oath [corrupt. of *God*].

goshawk (gos'-hawk) *n.* a bird of the hawk family, formerly used for hunting wild-geese [O.E. *gos*, a goose; *hafoc*, a hawk].

goslet (goz'-let) *n.* a very small goose.—**gos'ling** *n.* a young goose [dim. of *goose*].

gospel (gos'-pẹl) *n.* glad tidings; the revelation of the Christian faith; story of Christ's life as found in first four books of New Testament; doctrine; any general system of truth; anything accepted as infallibly true;—*a.* pert. to, or in accordance with, the gospel [O.E. *god*, good; *spell*, a story].

gossamer (gos'-ạ-mẹr) *n.* a filmy substance, like cobwebs, floating in the air, or stretched on bushes or grass; any thin, gauzy material [M.E. *gossomer*].

gossip (gos'-ip) *n.* idle talk about others, esp. regardless of fact; idle talk or writing; one who talks thus; formerly, a familiar friend;—*v.i.* to talk gossip; to chat.—**goss'iper** *n.*—**goss'ipy** *a.* chatty.—**goss'ipry** *n.* [M.E. *god*, God; *sib*, related].

gossoon (go-sòòn') *n.* in Ireland, a boy [Fr. *garçon*].

got (got) *pa.p.* and *pa.t.* of **get**.

Goth (goth) *n.* a member of ancient Teutonic tribe, who invaded Roman Empire in 3rd cent., finally overran it, and founded kingdoms in Italy, France, and Spain; a barbarian; a rude, ignorant person.—**Goth'ic** *a.* pert. to Goths or their language; barbarous; pert. to pointed-arch style of architecture;—*n.* the language of Goths.—**goth'icise** *v.t.* to make Gothic or barbarous.—**Goth'icism** *n.* a Gothic idiom; conformity to Gothic style of architecture; rudeness; barbarousness [L. *Gothicus*]

Gothamite (gōt'-am-īt) *n.* one of the 'wise men of Gotham,' reputed to be extremely simple-minded; hence, a simpleton; a wiseacre.

gouache (gwȧsh) *n.* water-colour painting with opaque colours mixed with water, gum, and honey; a picture painted thus [It. *guazzo*, a wash].

Gouda (gou'-dạ) *n.* a well-known kind of Dutch cheese [fr. *Gouda*, Holland].

gouge (gouj) *n.* a chisel with a curved cutting edge, for cutting grooves or holes;—*v.t.* to cut or scoop out with a gouge; to hollow out; to force out, as the eye of a person, with the thumb or finger [Fr.].

goulash (gòò-lash') *n.* a Hungarian stew seasoned with paprika [Magyar].

gourd (gòòrd) *n.* one of a number of trailing or climbing plants, including pumpkin, cucumber, squash, etc.; large, fleshy fruit of this plant; its dried rind used as water-bottle, drinking-vessel, etc. [L. *cucurbita*, a gourd].

gourmand (gòòr´-mong, -mạnd) *n.* a greedy or ravenous eater; a gormand;—*a.* gluttonous; ravenous.—**gourmet** (gòòr´-mā, gòòr´-met) *n.* a lover of good food [Fr.].

gout (gout) *n.* a disease characterised by acute inflammation and swelling of the smaller joints, esp. of the big toe or the thumb; a disease of wheat; a drop; a splash. —**gout'iness** *n.*—**gout'y** *a.* diseased with, or subject to, gout [Fr. *goutte*, a drop].

gout (gòò) *n.* taste; relish [Fr. *gout*, taste].

govern (guv´-ẹrn) *v.t.* to rule; to direct; to guide; to control; to regulate by authority; to keep in subjection; (*Gram.*) to be followed by a case, etc.;—*v.i.* to exercise authority; to administer the laws.—**gov'ernable** *a.*—**gov'ernance** *n.* direction; control; management; behaviour; deportment.—**gov'erness** *n.* woman with authority to control and direct; a lady, usually resident in a family, in charge of children's education; a tutoress.—**gov'ernment** *n.* act of governing; exercise of authority; the system of governing in a state or community; the ruling power in a state; territory over which rule is exercised; the administrative council or body; the executive power; the ministry.—**governmen'tal** *a.*—**gov'ernor** *n.* one invested with supreme authority; a ruler; a guardian; a tutor; a director, as of a bank, private school, etc.; a regulator or mechanical device for maintaining a uniform velocity, pressure, etc.; (*Slang*) father; 'sir', often **guv'nor.**—**Gov'ernor-Gen'eral** *n.* in a Dominion, representative of the Crown; a viceroy [L. *gubernare*, to steer].

gowan (gou´-ạn) *n.* (*Scot.*) the wild daisy [Gael. *gugan*, a daisy].

gowk (gouk) *n.* simpleton [O.N. *gaukr*].

gown (goun) *n.* a loose, flowing, upper garment; outer dress of a woman; official robe of professional men and scholars, as in a university, etc.;—*v.t.* to dress in a gown; —*v.i.* to put on a gown [O.Fr. *gonne*].

graal (grāl) *n.* See **grail**.

grab (grab) *v.t.* to grasp suddenly; to snatch; to clutch; to seize.—*pr.p.* **grab'bing**.—*pa.p.* and *pa.t.* **grabbed**.—*n.* a sudden clutch; greedy proceedings; a card game [etym. uncertain].

grace (grās) *n.* charm; attractiveness; easy and refined motion, manners, etc.; accomplishment; favour; divine favour; a short prayer of thanksgiving before or after a meal; a period of delay granted as a favour; the ceremonious title used when addressing a duke, or archbishop;—*n.pl.* favour; esteem; —*v.t.* to adorn; to honour; to add grace to.—**grace'ful** *a.* displaying grace or charm in form or action; elegant; easy.—**grace'fully** *adv.*—**grace'fulness** *n.*—**grace'less** *a.* wanting in grace or excellence, esp. divine grace; hence, depraved; degenerate; corrupt.—**grace'lessness** *n.*—**gracious** (grā´-shus) *a.* favourable; kind; friendly; merciful; pleasing; acceptable; virtuous; proceeding from divine grace; pleasing.—**gra'ciously** *adv.*—**gra'ciousness** *n.*—**grace'-note** *n.* (*Mus.*) a note that is an embellishment, not essential to the melody.—**good gracious!** an exclamation of surprise.—**year of grace**, the year of the Christian era.—**the three Graces** (*Myth.*) the three goddesses Aglaia, Euphrosyne, and Thalia [L. *gratia*, favour].

gracile (gras´-il) *a.* slender; gracefully slight —**gracil'ity** *n.* [L. *gracilis*, slender].

gradation (grạ-dā´-shun) *n.* successive stages in progress; degree; a step, or series of steps; the state of being graded or arranged in ranks.—**gradate** (grạ-dāt', grā´-dāt) *v.t.* to cause to pass insensibly from one colour into another [L. *gradatio*].

grade (grād) *n.* a step or degree in rank, merit, quality, etc.; a class or category; a gradient;—*v.t.* to arrange in order, or degree, or class; to classify; to blend evenly, of colours [L. *gradus*, a step].

gradient (grād´-yent) *a.* moving by steps; rising or descending by regular degrees;—*n.* the degree of slope (up or down) of a road or railway; an incline [L. *gradiens*, going, stepping].

gradual (grad´-ū-ạl) *a.* proceeding by steps or degrees; progressive; changing insensibly; —*n.* an ancient book of hymns and prayers. —**grad'ually** *adv.* [L. *gradus*, a step].

graduate (grad´-ū-āt) *v.t.* to mark with degrees; to divide into regular steps or intervals; to grade;—*v.i.* to take a university degree;—*n.* one admitted to an academic degree.—**grad'uand** *n.* one about to receive an academic degree.—**grad'uateship** *n.*—**grad'uator** *n.* an instrument for dividing a line into regular intervals.—**gradua'tion** *n.* [L. *gradus*, a step].

gradus (gra´-dus) *n.* a dictionary of prosody (Latin and Greek) designed as an aid in writing verses [L. contr. of *gradus ad Parnassum*, a stair to Parnassus, the home of the Muses].

graft, graff (grȧft, grȧf) *v.t.* to insert a bud or small branch of a tree into another; to transplant living tissue, e.g. skin, bone, etc. from one part of the body to another;—*n.* a bud, etc. so inserted, or a piece of tissue so transplanted.—**graft'er, graf'fer** *n.* [Fr. fr. Gk. *grapheion*, a pencil].

graft (grȧft) *v.i.* to toil; to exercise political privilege; to use influence unfairly for self-advancement or profit;—*n.* manual work; self-advancement or profit by unfair means; bribery.—**graft'er** *n.* [U.S.].

grail (grāl) *n.* a cup; a dish.—**The Holy Grail**, in medieval legends, the cup or vessel used by Christ at the Last Supper [O.Fr. *graal*, or *grael*, a flat dish].

grain (grān) *n.* a kernel, esp. of corn, wheat, etc.; fruit of certain kindred plants, viz. corn, wheat, rye, barley, oats, etc. (used collectively); any small, hard particle; a small portion; the 20th part of a scruple in apothecaries' weight; the 24th part of a pennyweight troy; that arrangement of the particles of any body which determines its comparative roughness; the direction of the fibres of wood; hence, (*Fig.*) natural temperament or disposition; formerly cochineal, scarlet dye, and dye in general;—*v.t.* to paint in imitation of the grain of wood; to form into grains, as sugar, powder, etc.;—*v.i.* to form grains, or assume a granular form.—**grained** (grānd) *a.* divided into small particles or grains; dyed in grain; rough.—**grain'ing** *n.* painting in imitation of the grain of wood; a process in tanning.—**grain'y** *a.* full of grains or kernels.—**against the grain**, i.e. against the fibre of the wood; hence (*Fig.*) against a person's natural inclination [L. *granum*, seed].

graip (grāp) *n.* (*Scot.*) a fork with three or four prongs used for digging potatoes and lifting manure [var. of *grope*].

gralloch (gral´-oH) *n.* the entrails of a deer; —*v.t.* to remove the entrails from; to disembowel (a deer) [Gael. *grealach*, entrails].

gram (gram) *n.* See **gramme**.

graminaceous (gram-i-nā´-shus) *a.* like or pert. to grass.—Also, **gramineal** (grạ-min´-e-ạl) *a.*—**gramin'eous** *a.*—**graminifo'lious** *a.* bearing leaves like grass.—**graminiv'orous** *a.* grass-eating [L. *gramen*, grass].

grammalogue (gram´-a-log) *n.* in short-hand, a sign or symbol representing one word [Gk. *gramma*, a letter; *logos*, a word].

grammar (gram´-ạr) *n.* the science of language; a system of general principles for speaking and writing according to the forms and usage of a language; a text-book for teaching the elements of a language. —**gramma'rian** (grạ-mā´-ri-ạn) *n.* a philologist;

one who teaches grammar.—**grammatical** (gra-mat′i-kal) *a.* pert. to grammar; according to the rules of grammar.—**grammat′ically** *adv.* [Gk. *gramma*, a letter].

gramme (gram) *n.* unit of weight in metric system=15.432 troy grains.—Also **gram** [Fr. fr. Gk. *gramma*, small weight].

gramophone (gram′o-fōn) *n.* an instrument for reproducing sounds from vibrations engraved upon a revolving wax disc [Trade name, fr. Gk. *gramma*, a letter; *phonē*, sound. Also, inversion of *phonogram*].

grampus (gram′pus) *n.* a blowing and spouting sea-creature of the whale family [L. *crassus piscis*, a fat fish].

granary (gran′a-ri) *n.* a store-house for threshed grain; a barn [L. *granum*, grain].

grand (grand) *a.* great; high in power and dignity; illustrious; eminent; distinguished; imposing; superior; splendid; lofty; noble; sublime; dignified; majestic; chief; final; indicating family relationship of the second degree;—*n.* (*Mus.*) a grand piano; (*U.S. Slang*) a thousand dollars.—**grand′ad, grand′dad** *n.* (*Colloq.*) grandfather; an old man.—**gran′dam** *n.* a grandmother; an old lady.—**grand′child** *n.* a son's or daughter's child.—**grand′daughter** *n.* a son's or daughter's daughter.—**grandee** (gran-dē′) *n.* a Spanish or Portuguese nobleman of highest rank; a great personage.—**grandeur** (gran′dūr) *n.* nobility of action; majesty; splendour; magnificence.—**grand′father** *n.* a father's or mother's father.—**grand′father('s)-clock,** *n.* a tall, old-fashioned clock, standing on the floor.—**Grand Guignol,** a performance of plays of a melodramatic or sensational type.—**grandiloquence** (gran-dil′o-kwens) *n.* lofty words or phrases; pomposity of speech; bombast.—**grandil′oquent** *a.*—**grandiose** (gran′di-ōs) *a.* imposing; striking; bombastic.—**gran′diosely** *adv.*—**grandios′ity** *n.* an inflated or bombastic style.—**grand′ly** *adv.* in a grand manner, splendidly; sublimely.—**grand′ma, grand′mamma** *n.* grandmother.—**grand′mother** *n.* a father's or mother's mother.—**grand′mother-clock** *n.* similar to a grandfather-clock but smaller.—**grand′ness** *n.* greatness; magnificence.—**grand′pa, grand′papa** *n.* a grandfather.—**grand′parent** *n.* grandfather or grandmother.—**grand piano,** a large harp-shaped piano, with a horizontal frame.—**grand′sire** *n.* a grandfather; an ancestor.—**grand slam** (*Cards*) the winning of all the tricks at Bridge.—**grand′son** *n.* a son's or daughter's son.—**grand′stand** *n.* the principal and covered, enclosure on a racecourse, football ground, etc. [L. *grandis*, great].

grange (grānj) *n.* a farm-house with its barns, stables, etc.; a barn; a granary [Fr.=a barn, fr. L. *granum*, grain].

graniferous (gra-nif′e-rus) *a.* bearing seeds like grain.—**gran′iform** *a.* shaped like a grain.—**graniv′orous** *a.* feeding on grain; eating grain or seeds [L. *granum*, grain; *ferre*, to bear; *vorare*, to devour].

granite (gran′it) *n.* a hard igneous rock, consisting of quartz, feldspar, and mica, whitish or reddish in colour.—**granit′ic** *a.*—**gran′itoid** *a.* like granite.—**granolith′ic** *a.* made of cement formed of pounded granite [It. *granito*, grained].

granny (gran′i) *n.* a grandmother; familiar for any old woman.—**grann′y-knot** *n.* (*Naut.*) a knot, similar to the reef-knot but less secure [abbrev. of *grandmother*].

grant (grȧnt) *v.t.* to allow; to yield; to concede; to bestow; to confer; to admit as true;—*n.* a bestowing; a gift; an allowance.—**grant′er, grant′or** *n.* (*Law*) the person who transfers property [O.Fr. *graanter*, to promise].

granule (gran′ūl) *n.* a little grain; a small particle.—**gran′ular** *a.* consisting of grains or granules.—**gran′ulate** *v.t.* to form into grains; to make rough on the surface;—*v.i.* to be formed into grains.—**gran′ulated** *a.*—**granula′tion** *n.* the process of forming into grains; (*Med.*) the development of new tissue in a wound, characterised by the formation of grain-like cells.—**gran′ulous** *a.* full of granular substances [L. *granulum*, dim. of *granum*, a grain].

grape (grāp) *n.* the fruit of the vine; (*Mil.*) grape-shot.—**grap′ery** *n.* a place for the cultivation of grapes.—**grap′y** *a.* like grapes.—**grape′-fruit** *n.* a sub-tropical citrus fruit similar to the orange or lemon but larger.—**grape′-hy′acinth** *n.* (*Bot.*) a small variety of hyacinth.—**grape′-shot** *n.* (*Mil.*) formerly, a number of shot or bullets which scattered when fired from a cannon.—**grape′-su′gar** *n.* a kind of sugar, so called because found abundantly in grapes; dextrose.—**grape′-vine** *n.* the grape-bearing vine plant; a means of secret communication.—**sour grapes** (*Fig.*) things falsely despised merely because unattainable [Fr. *grappe*, a bunch of grapes].

graph (graf) *n.* a diagram or curve representing the variation in value of some phenomenon according to stated conditions;—*v.t.* to show variation by means of a diagram.—**graph′ic(al)** *a.* pert. to writing or delineating; truly descriptive; vivid; picturesque.—**graph′ically** *adv.*—**graphic arts,** drawing, engraving, and painting.—**graph′ics** *n.* the art of drawing, esp. mechanical drawing.—**graph′ite** *n.* a natural form of carbon used in the making of the 'lead' of pencils; plumbago; blacklead.—**graphol′ogy** *n.* the study of handwriting as an index of character [Gk. *graphein*, to write].

grapnel (grap′nel) *n.* an iron instrument with hooks or claws for clutching an object; a small anchor with several flukes [O.Fr. *grape*, a hook].

grapple (grap′l) *v.t.* to seize firmly; to seize with a grapnel;—*v.i.* to come to grips; to contend;—*n.* a grapnel; a grip; a contest at close quarters.—**grapp′ling-i′ron** *n.* a large grapnel for clutching the side of an enemy ship [O.Fr. *grape*, a hook].

grasp (grȧsp) *v.t.* to seize firmly; to clutch; to take possession of; to understand.—*v.i.* to endeavour to seize; to catch at;—*n.* a firm grip of the hand; the power of seizing and holding; reach of the arms; mental power or capacity.—**grasp′ing** *a.* seizing; greedy of gain; exacting; miserly [O.E. *graspen*].

grass (grȧs) *n.* herbage; pasture for cattle; reeds;—*v.t.* to cover with grass; to feed with grass; (*Sport*) to throw, or bring down, to the grass, as a bird or fish.—**grass′y** *a.* covered with grass; resembling grass; green.—**grass′iness** *n.* a grassy state.—**grass′-grown** *a.* overgrown with grass.—**grass′hopper** *n.* a jumping, chirping insect, allied to the locust family.—**grass′-land** *n.* permanent pasture-land.—**grass′-snake** *n.* a harmless variety of snake.—**grass′-wid′ow** *n.* a wife left temporarily alone through the absence of her husband on business, etc. [O.E. *gaers*].

grate (grāt) *n.* a frame of bars for holding fuel in place while burning; a framework of crossed bars.—**grat′ing** *n.* a partition of parallel or cross bars [L. *cratis*, a hurdle].

grate (grāt) *v.t.* to rub into small bits with something hard; to wear away by rubbing;—*v.i.* to rub with a harsh sound; to irritate.—**grat′er** *n.* an instrument with a rough surface for rubbing off small particles of a body [Fr. *gratter*, to scratch].

grateful (grāt′fōōl) *a.* thankful; pleasant; having a due sense of benefits.—**grate′fully** *adv.*—**grate′fulness** *n.* [L. *gratus*, pleasing].

gratify (grat′i-fī) *v.t.* to give pleasure to; to do a favour to.—**grat′ifying** *a.*—**grat′ifyingly** *adv.*—**grat′ifier** *n.* one who gratifies.—**gratifica′tion** *n.* the act of pleasing; satisfaction; delight; reward [L. *gratus*, pleasing].

gratin (gra′tin) *n.* (*Cookery*) a dish prepared with a covering of bread-crumbs.—**au gratin**

(ō gra′-tin) fish, cheese, vegetables, etc. so cooked [Fr. *gratin*, fr. *gratter*, to grate].

gratis (grā′-tis, gra′-tis) *adv.* for nothing; free; without charge [L. fr. *gratia*, a favour].

gratitude (grat′-i-tūd) *n.* good will and kindness awakened by a favour received; thankfulness [L. *gratus*, pleasing, thankful].

gratuity (grą-tū′-i-ti) *n.* a present; a gift of money for services rendered; a donation; a tip.—**gratu′itous** *a.* free; voluntary; granted without claim or merit; asserted without cause or proof.—**gratu′itously** *adv.* [L. *gratuitus*, done without profit].

gratulate (grat′-ū-lāt) *v.t.* to congratulate.—**gratula′tory** *a.* [L. *gratulari*, to wish one joy].

gravamen (grą-vā′-men) *n.* stress laid on a part; substantial ground or reason for a charge; a grievance [L. *gravis*, heavy].

grave (grāv) *n.* a hole dug for a dead body; a place of burial; (*Fig.*) death.—**grave′-clothes** *n.pl.* the dress in which the dead are buried; a winding-sheet.—**grave′stone** *n.* a memorial stone set on or near a grave; a tomb-stone.—**grave′yard** *n.* a burial-ground [O.E. *graef*].

grave (grāv) *a.* weighty; important; momentous.—**grave** (grav) *n.* the 'grave' accent in French or its sign (ˋ).—**grave′ly** *adv.*—**grave′ness** *n.* [L. *gravis*, heavy].

grave (grāv) *v.t.* to carve; to engrave.—**graven image**, an idol [O.E. *grafan*, to dig].

grave (grāv) *v.t.* to clean a ship's bottom by burning or scraping off barnacles, sea-weeds, etc. [Fr. *grève*, a beach].

gravel (grav′-ęl) *n.* small stones; coarse sand; small pebbles; (*Med.*) an aggregation of minute crystals in the urine; a disease of the kidneys and bladder due to this;—*v.t.* to cover with gravel; to puzzle.—*pr.pa.* **grav′-elling**.—*pa.p.* and *pa.t.* **grav′elled**.—**grav′elly** *a.* [O.Fr. *grave*, the beach].

gravid (grav′-id) *a.* heavy, esp. being with child; pregnant [L. *gravidus*].

gravitate (grav′-i-tāt) *v.i.* to obey the law of gravitation; to tend towards a centre of attraction; to be naturally attracted to.—**gravita′tion** *n.* the act of gravitating; the tendency of all bodies to attract each other.—**gravita′tional, gravita′tive** *a.* [L. *gravis*, heavy]

gravity (grav′-i-ti) *n.* weight; heaviness; seriousness; the force of attraction of one body for another, esp. of objects to the earth.—**specific gravity**, the relative weight of any substance as compared with the weight of an equal volume of water [L. *gravitas*, fr. *gravis*, heavy].

gravy (grā′-vi) *n.* the juices from meat in cooking.—**grav′y-boat** *n.* a dish for holding gravy [etym. uncertain].

gray, grey (grā) *a.* between black and white in colour, as ashes or lead; clouded; dismal; turning white; hoary; aged;—*n.* a gray colour; a gray horse;—*v.t.* to cause to become gray;—*v.i.* to become gray.—**gray′ish** *a.* somewhat gray.—**gray′ly** *adv.*—**gray′ness** *n.*—**gray′lag** *n.* the common gray or wild goose [O.E. *graeg*).

grayling (grā′-ling) *n.* a fish of the salmon family; the umber [fr. *gray*].

graze (grāz) *v.t.* to touch lightly in passing; to abrade the skin thus;—*n.* a light touch in passing; a grazing [etym. uncertain].

graze (grāz) *v.t.* to feed, as cattle, with grass; to feed on grass;—*v.i.* to eat grass or herbage.—**grazier** (grā′-zhęr) *n.* one who pastures cattle for the market [O.E. *grasian*].

grease (grēs) *n.* soft melted fat of animals; thick oil as a lubricant;—(grēs, grēz) *v.t.* to apply grease to; (*Slang*) to bribe.—**greas′y** *a.* like grease; oily; fat; (*Fig.*) unctuous.—**greas′ily** *adv.*—**greas′er** *n.* one who greases; a Mexican creole.—**greas′iness** *n.*—**grease′-paint** *n.* a greasy kind of make-up, used by actors [Fr. *graisse*, fr. *gras*, fat].

great (grāt) *a.* large in size or number; big; long in time or duration; admirable; eminent; uncommonly gifted; of high rank; mighty; teeming; pregnant; denoting relationship, either in the ascending or descending line; (*Slang*) splendid.—**great′ly** *adv.*—**great′-ness** *n.*—**great′coat** *n.* an overcoat, esp. military.—**great′-grand′child** *n.* the child of a grandchild.—**great′-grand′-daught′er** *n.* the daughter of a grandchild.—**great′-grand′-father** *n.* the father of a grand-parent.—**great′-great′-grand′father** *n.* the father of a great-grand-parent.—**great′-grand′-pa′rent** *n.* the father or mother of a grand-parent.—**great′-grand′son** *n.* the son of a grandchild.—**Great Bear** (or Ursa Major) a group of stars in the northern heavens, also known as The Plough, or Charles's Wain.—**Great Dane**, a large dog of Danish or German origin.—**great gross**, twelve gross.—**Great War**, World War 1 (1914-18) [O.E.].

greaves (grēvz) *n.pl.* the dregs of melted tallow [O.N.].

greaves (grēvz) *n.pl.* ancient armour to protect the legs [O.Fr. *greve*, the shin-bone].

grebe (grēb) *n.* a short-winged, tailless diving-bird [Fr. *grèbe*].

Grecian (grē′-shąn) *a.* Greek; pert. to Greece;—*n.* a native of Greece; a Greek scholar.—**Grecian nose**, one whose line is a prolongation of the line of the forehead.—**grecism** (grē′-sizm) *n.* an idiom of the Greek language; a Hellenism.—**Gre′co-Ro′man, Grae′co-Ro′man** *a.* of, or pert. to, both Greece and Rome [L. *Graecus*].

greed (grēd) *n.* an eager and selfish desire or hunger; covetousness; avarice.—**greed′y** *a.* having a keen desire for food, drink, wealth, etc.; ravenous; covetous.—**greed′ily** *adv.*—**greed′iness** *n.* [O.E. *graedig*, hungry].

Greek (grēk) *a.* pert. to Greece; Grecian;—*n.* a native of Greece; the language of Greece.—**Greek architecture**, comprises the three orders, Doric, Ionic, and Corinthian.—**Greek Church**, 'Eastern,' or 'Orthodox' Church, that section of the Church which separated from Roman church in 1054.—**Greek cross**, an upright cross with arms of equal length (the cross of St. George).—**Greek gift**, a treacherous gift.—**At the Greek calends**, i.e. never, because Greeks had no calends [L. *Graecus*].

green (grēn) *a.* of colour between blue and yellow; grass-coloured; emerald-coloured; containing its natural sap; unripe; inexperienced; easily deceived; sickly; wan.—*n.* the colour; a communal piece of grass-covered land; grass-covered backcourt of tenement building; the mown turf on which game of bowls is played; (*Golf*) the putting-green.—**greens** *n.pl.* fresh leaves or branches; wreaths; green vegetables; one of the brassica family, with curled leaves.—**green′ery** *n.* a place where green plants are cultivated; vegetation.—**green′ish** *a.* somewhat green.—**green′ness** *n.* the quality of being green; freshness.—**green′-eyed** *a.* having green eyes; (*Fig.*) jealous.—**green-eyed monster**, jealousy;—**green′finch** *n.* a common British singing-bird, yellowish-green in colour.—**green′fly** *n.* an aphis, a garden pest attacking rose-bushes, fruit-bushes, etc.—**green′gage** *n.* a small, yellowish, green-coloured plum.—**green′grocer** *n.* a retailer of fresh vegetables, fruits, etc.; a fruiterer.—**green′heart** *n.* a very hard S. American wood, much used in the making of fishing rods.—**green′horn** *n.* a raw youth; a simpleton.—**green′house** *n.* a building for the preservation or rearing of plants; a glass-house.—**green′room** *n.* the retiring-room for actors in a theatre.—**green′shank** *n.* a wading bird of the sandpiper and snipe family.—**green sickness** (*Med.*) chlorosis, a kind of anaemia which attacks adolescent girls.—**green′sward** *n.* turf [O.E. *grene*].

Greenwich (grin′-ij) *n.* (*Geog.*) borough of London, site of Royal Observatory.—**Greenwich time**, British standard time

reckoned from the passage of sun over meridian at Greenwich.
greet (grēt) *v.t.* to salute; to hail; to accost; to receive; to meet.—**greet'ing** *n.* a salutation at meeting someone; expression of good wishes [O.E. *gretan*].
greeve (grēv) *n.* (*Scot.*) a land-steward; a farm-manager.—Also **grieve** [O.N. *greifi*].
gregarious (gre-gā-ri-us) *a.* living in flocks or herds; fond of company.—**grega'riously** *adv.*—**grega'riousness** *n.* [L. *gregarius*, fr. *grex*, a flock].
Gregorian (gre-gō'-ri-an) *a.* pert. to the Popes Gregory I and Gregory XIII.—**Gregorian calendar**, the present day calendar, introduced by Pope Gregory XIII in 1582. —**Gregorian chants**, church music used in R.C. worship, based on chants introduced by Pope Gregory I in the 6th cent.
gremial (grē'-mi-al) *a.* pert. to the lap or bosom;—*n.* a bosom friend; a cloth or apron used at mass or ordinations to keep the bishop's vestments from being soiled with the oil [L. *gremium*, the lap].
gremlin (grem'-lin) *n.* (*World War* 2) a mischievous pixy haunting aircraft and inducing the pilot to make mistakes [etym. uncertain].
grenade (gre-nād') *n.* an explosive shell or bomb, thrown by hand or shot from a rifle; a glass projectile containing chemicals, used as a fire-extinguisher.—**grenadier** (gren-a-dēr') *n.* formerly, a soldier trained to throw grenades; now, in the British Army, a soldier in the Grenadier Guards [Fr. *grenade*, a pomegranate].
grew (gròò) *pa.t.* of **grow**.
grey (grā) *a.* Same as **gray**.—**Grey Friar**, a Franciscan, from the grey-coloured habit worn by the order. -**grey matter**, the grey substance forming the outer layer of the brain and controlling active thought; (*Colloq.*) brains [O.E. *graeg*].
greyhound (grā'-hound) *n.* a swift, slender dog, used in coursing and racing.—**grey'cing** *n.* (*Colloq.*) greyhound-racing [O.E. *grighund*].
grid (grid) *n.* a frame of bars; a grating; a grid-iron; a luggage-carrier at the rear of a motor-car; (*Elect.*) a lead or zinc plate in a storage battery.—**the Grid**, the name for the system of main transmission lines in the national scheme for the supply of electricity in Great Britain [O.Fr. *gredil*].
grid (grid) *n.* (*Wireless*) the electrode in a thermionic valve controlling the stream of electrons emitted by the filament, usually a spiral of wire, round but not touching the filament [O.Fr. *gredil*].
griddle (grid'-l) *n.* flat, iron plate for baking [O.Fr. *gredil*, fr. L. *cratis*, hurdle].
gridiron (grid'-ī-ern) *n.* a cooking utensil of parallel metal bars, for broiling meats, fish, etc. (*Naut.*) a framework of crossbeams supporting a ship under repair [O.Fr. *gredil*, a griddle].
grief (grēf) *n.* deep sorrow; pain; distress of mind; repenting pain; the cause of sorrow or distress [Fr. fr. L. *gravis*, heavy].
grieve (grēv) *v.t.* to cause grief; to afflict; to vex; to offend;—*v.i.* to feel grief; to be distressed; to lament.—**griev'ance** *n.* a real or imaginary ground of complaint; a cause of grief or uneasiness.—**griev'er** *n.*—**griev'ous** *a.* painful; causing sadness.—**griev'ously** *adv.*—**griev'ousness** *n.* [O.Fr. *grever*, to afflict].
grieve (grēv) *n.* Same as **greeve**.
griffin, griffon (grif'-in, -on) *n.* a fabulous beast with eagle's head and wings, and lion's body; a watchful overseer [Gk. *grups*, fr. *grupos*, hook-nosed].
griffon (grif'-on) *n.* a large mountain vulture; a breed of rough-haired or wire-haired German hunting-dog [Fr.].
grig (grig) *n.* a cricket; a sand-eel; a lively creature [etym. uncertain].
grill (gril) *v.t.* to broil on a gridiron; (*Fig.*) to torment; to subject to severe cross-examination, esp. by the police;—*n.* a cooking utensil for broiling meat, fish, etc.; the food cooked on one [Fr. *gril*, a gridiron].
grille (gril) *n.* a metal grating screening a window, doorway, etc.; an entrance gate [O.Fr. *gredil*, a griddle].
grilse (grils) *n.* a salmon which returns to the river for the first time after having spent just over one year in the sea.
grim (grim) *a.* stern; severe; of forbidding aspect; fierce; sullen; surly.—**grim'ly** *adv.*—**grim'ness** *n.* [O.E. *grimm*, fierce].
grimace (gri-mās') *n.* a distortion of the face to express contempt, dislike, etc.; a wry face;—*v.i.* to make a grimace [Fr.].
grimalkin (gri-mal'-kin) *n.* an old cat, esp. a she-cat; a spiteful old woman [fr. *gray*, and *malkin*, a dim. of moll=Mary].
grime (grīm) *n.* ingrained dirt; soot;—*v.t.* to soil deeply; to dirty; to blacken.—**grim'y** *a.* dirty [origin uncertain].
grin (grin) *v.i.* to show the teeth as in laughter, derision, or pain;—*n.* the act of grinning; a wry smile [O.E. *grennian*].
grind (grīnd) *v.t.* to crush to powder between hard surfaces; to make sharp or smooth by rubbing; to turn a crank-handle, esp. of a barrel-organ; to grate;—*v.i.* to perform the action of grinding; to work hard.—*pa.p.* and *pa.t.* **ground**.—*n.* the action of grinding; a laborious task.—**grind'er** *n.* one who, or that which, grinds; one of the double teeth, used to masticate food.—**grind'ers** *n.pl.* (*Colloq.*) the teeth.—**grind'stone** *n.* a round revolving stone for grinding [O.E. *grindan*].
gringo (gring'-gō) *n.* in Spanish-speaking parts of America, a contemptuous name for Englishman or American [Mexican Sp].
grip (grip) *n.* a firm hold; a grasp or pressure of the hand; a clutch; mastery of a subject, etc.; a handle; (*U.S.*) a suitcase or travelling-bag;—*v.t.* to grasp or hold tightly; (*Fig.*) to hold the attention of.—*pr.p.* **grip'ping**.—*pa.p.* and *pa.t.* **gripped** [O.E. *gripa*].
gripe (grīp) *v.t.* to grip; to oppress; to afflict with pains of colic;—*v.i.* to get money by hard bargaining; to suffer griping pains;—*n.* grasp; seizure; clutch; oppression; severe intestinal pain due to flatulence, etc. (chiefly used in *pl.*); (*Naut.*) a rope lashing a ship's life-boat to the davits or deck.—**gri'ping** *a.* [O.E. *gripan*].
grippe (grēp) *n.* influenza [Fr.].
grisette [grē-zet') *n.* a gay young French girl of the working-class; a coquette [Fr.].
grisly (griz'-li) *a.* grim; horrible.—**gris'liness** *n.* [O.E. *grislic*, terrible].
grist (grist) *n.* a supply of corn to be ground at one time; provision; (*Fig.*) profit; gain [O.E. *grist*].
gristle (gris'-l) *n.* a smooth, solid, elastic substance in animal bodies; cartilage.—**grist'ly** *a.* [O.E. *gristle*].
grit (grit) *n.* the coarse part of meal; particles of sand; coarse sandstone; (*Fig.*) courage; spirit; resolution;—*pl.* oats or wheat coarsely ground;—*v.t.* to grind (the teeth); to grate; —*v.i.* to give forth a sound, as of sand under the feet.—*pr.p.* **gritt'ing**.—*pa.p.* and *pa.t.* **gritt'ed**.—**gritt'y** *a.* consisting of grit; courageous [O.E. *greot*, sand].
grizzle (griz'-l) *n.* a gray colour.—**grizz'led** *a.* gray; grayish; gray-haired.—**grizz'ly** *a.* gray; —*n.* a grizzly bear [Fr. *gris*, gray].
groan (grōn) *v.i.* to make a low deep sound of grief or pain; to be overburdened;—*n.* the sound.—**groan'er** *n.*—**groan'ing** *n.* [O.E. *granian*].
groat (grōt) *n.* an old English silver coin, worth fourpence [Dut. *groot*, great, thick].
groats (grōts) *n.pl.* hulled grain, esp. oats [O.E. *greot*, a particle].
grocer (grō'-ser) *n.* a dealer in tea, coffee, spices, domestic stores, etc.—**gro'cery** *n.* his

trade.—**gro'ceries** *n.pl.* wares sold by a grocer [O.Fr. *grossier*, wholesale].
grog (grog) *n.* a mixture of spirits, esp. rum and cold water.—**grog'gy** *a.* tipsy; unsteady on one's legs; shaky [fr. 'Old *Grog*,' the nickname of Admiral Vernon who first ordered watering of sailors' rum in 1740; he wore *grogram* breeches].
grogram (grog-ram) *n.* a coarse material made of silk and mohair [O.Fr. *grosgrain*, cloth of a coarse texture].
groin (groin) *n.* the depression between the belly and the thigh; (*Archit.*) the angular curve formed by the intersection of two vaults; a structure of timber, etc. to stop shifting of sand on the sea-beach [etym. uncertain].
groom (gróóm) *n.* a servant in charge of horses; a bridegroom; an officer in a Royal Household, e.g. a groom-in-waiting;—*v.t.* to tend or curry a horse.—**grooms'man** *n.* a friend attending a bridegroom at the marriage ceremony [etym. obscure].
groove (gróóv) *n.* a channel or hollow, esp. one cut by a tool, as a guide, or to receive a ridge; a rut; (*Fig.*) a routine life;—*v.t.* to cut a groove in [Dut. *groefe*, a trench].
grope (grōp) *v.t.* to feel about; to search blindly as if in the dark [O.E. *grapian*].
grosbeak (grōs'-bēk) *n.* a bird of the Finch family [Fr. *gros*, big; *bec*, a beak].
gross (grōs) *a.* coarse; indecent; rude or rough, as work; thick; solid; rank; overfed; total, not net;—*n.* twelve dozen; mass; bulk.—**gross'ly** *adv.*—**gross'ness** *n.* [Fr. (*gros*, big)].
grot (grot) *n.* a grotto [Fr. *grotte*].
grotesque (grō-tesk') *a.* wildly formed; irregular in design or form;—*n.* a whimsical figure; a caricature.—**grotesque'ness, grotesqu'erie** *n.* [Fr. fr. It. *grotta*, a grotto].
grotto (grot'-ō) *n.* a natural, picturesque cave; an artificial structure in gardens, etc. in imitation of such a cave.—*pl.* **grot'tos**, or **grot'toes** [Fr. *grotte*; It. *grotta*].
grouch (grouch) *n.* (*Colloq.*) a complaint; a grumbler;—*v.i.* to grumble [fr. *grudge*].
ground (ground) *pa.p.* and *pa.t.* of **grind**.
ground (ground) *n.* the surface of the earth; dry land; territory; a special area of land; soil; the sea-bottom; reason; motive; basis; (*Art*) the surface or coating to work on with paint;—*v.t.* to establish; to instruct in elementary principles; to place on the ground;—*v.i.* (*Naut.*) to run ashore.—**grounds** *n.pl.* dregs; sediment; enclosed lands round a mansion-house.—**ground'less** *a.* without reason; unauthorised.—**ground'ed** *a.* (*Aviat.*) of aircraft, unable to fly because of weather conditions.—**ground'ing** *n.* the background of any design; thorough knowledge of the essentials of a subject.—**ground'ling** *n.* a fish that keeps to the bottom of a river, etc.; a spectator in the pit of a theatre; a vulgar fellow.—**grounds'man, ground'man** *n.* the caretaker of a football ground, cricket pitch, etc.—**ground'work** *n.* foundation; basis; the essential part; first principles.—**ground'-bait** *n.* bait dropped to the bottom in order to attract the fish.—**ground'-floor** *n.* floor on a level, or nearly so, with the ground.—**ground'-ice** *n.* ice formed at the bottom of a river or other water; anchor-ice.—**ground'-i'vy** *n.* a British creeping plant, with purple-blue flowers.—**ground'-nut** *n.* the pea-nut; the earth-nut.—**ground'-plan** *n.* the surface representation of a building or sections of it.—**ground'-rent** *n.* rent paid to a landlord for the privilege of building on his ground.—**ground'-swell** *n.* a broad, deep swell of the ocean felt some time after a storm has ceased [O.E. *grund*].
groundsel (ground'-sel) *n.* yellow-flowered weed, often used as food for cage-birds [O.E. *grund*, ground; *swelgan*, to swallow].
group (gróóp) *n.* a number of persons or things near together, or placed or classified together; a class; a cluster, crowd, or throng; (*Art*) two or more figures forming one artistic design;—*v.t.* to arrange into groups;—*v.i.* to fall into groups.—**group'er** *n.* (*Colloq.*) a member of the Oxford Group movement.—**group'-cap'tain** *n.* (*Mil.*) a commissioned officer in the R.A.F. equivalent to captain in the navy and colonel in the army.—**group'ing** *n.* the relative arrangement of figures or objects in drawing, painting and sculpture [Fr. *groupe*].
grouse (grous) *n.* a British game-bird [etym. uncertain].
grouse (grous) *v.i.* (*Colloq.*) to grumble; to complain;—*n.* a complaint; a grumble.—**grous'er** *n.* a grumbler [etym. uncertain].
grove (grōv) *n.* a group of trees; a small wood [O.E. *graf*].
grovel (grov'-l, gruv'-l) *v.i.* to lie face downward, from fear or humility; to crawl thus; to abase oneself.—**grov'eller** *n.*—**grov'elling** *a.* servile [O.N. *a grufa*, face downwards].
grow (grō) *v.t.* to cause to grow; to produce by cultivation; to raise;—*v.i.* to develop naturally; to increase in size, height, etc.; to become by degrees.—*pa.p.* **grown** (grōn).—*pa.t.* **grew** (gróó).—**grow'er** *n.*—**growth** (grōth) *n.* the process of growing; gradual increase of animal and vegetable bodies; (*Med.*) a morbid formation; a tumour.—**grown'-up** *n.* an adult [O.E. *growan*].
growl (groul) *v.i.* to make a low guttural sound of anger; to grumble;—*n.* such a sound.—**growl'er** *n.* one who growls; (*Slang*) a four-wheeled horse-drawn cab [imit. origin].
groyne (groin) *n.* a breakwater made of wooden piles, etc. to prevent sand shifting [form of *groin*].
grub (grub) *v.t.* to dig superficially; to root up;—*v.i.* to dig; to rummage; (*Fig.*) to plod;—*n.* the larva of a beetle; that which is dug up for food; hence (*Slang*) food.—*pr.p.* **grub'bing**.—*pa.p.* and *pa.t.* **grubbed**.—**grub'ber** *n.*—**grub'biness** *n.* the state of being grubby.—**grub'by** *a.* unclean, as if from grubbing; dirty, grimy [M.E. *grobben*, to dig].
grudge (gruj) *v.t.* to be unwilling to give or allow; to envy;—*n.* a feeling of ill-will; resentment.—**grudg'ing** *a.* reluctant; regretful.—**grudg'ingly** *adv.* [O.Fr. *groucer*].
grue (gróó) *v.i.* to shudder; to feel horror.—**grue'some** *a.* [M.E. *grue*, to shudder].
gruel (gróó'-el) *n.* a food made by boiling oatmeal in water; a kind of porridge.—**gruel'ling** *n.* subjection to extreme physical effort; a trying ordeal;—*a.* exhausting [O.E.=crushed meal].
gruff (gruf) *a.* surly; rough in manner or voice.—**gruff'ly** *adv.* [Dut. *grof*].
grumble (grum'-bl) *v.i.* to murmur with discontent; to complain; to make growling sounds;—*n.* the act of grumbling; a complaint [imit. origin].
grume (gróóm) *n.* (*Med.*) a clot of blood; a fluid of viscid consistence.—**grum'ous, grum'ose** *a.* [L. *grumus*, a little heap].
grumpy (grum'-pi) *a.* surly; irritable; gruff [imit. origin].
grunt (grunt) *v.i.* of a pig, to make its characteristic sound; to utter a sound like this;—*n.* a deep, guttural sound; a pig's sound [O.E. *grunnettan*].
Gruyère (gróó-yer') *n.* a whole-milk cheese, made at *Gruyère*, Switzerland.
gryphon (grif'-on) *n.* See **griffin**.
guano (gwá'-nō) *n*, an agricultural fertiliser in the form of the solidified excrement of sea-birds [native name *huanu*, dung].
guarantee (gar-an-tē') *n.* a promise to be responsible for the payment of a debt, or the performance of a duty, in case of the failure of another person who is primarily liable; an assurance of the truth, genuineness, permanence, etc. of something; the person who gives such promise or assurance

guaranty; security;—*v.t.* to warrant; to answer for.—**guaranty** (gar′-an-ti) *n.* a warrant or surety; ground or basis of security.—**guar′antor** *n.* [Fr. *garantir*, to protect].

guard (gȧrd) *v.t.* to protect from danger; to accompany for protection; to defend;—*v.i.* to watch by way of caution or defence; to be in a state of defence or safety;—*n.* he who, or that which, guards from danger; a sentry; soldiers protecting anything; an official in charge of a coach or train; defence; the part of a sword-hilt which protects the hand.—**Guards** *n.pl.* in the British Army, the Royal Household Troops.—**guard′ant** *a.* (*Her.*) having the face turned towards the beholder.—**guard′ed** *a.* cautious; wary.—**guard′edly** *adv.*—**guard′house** *n.* a building in which a military guard is stationed; a place for the detention of military prisoners.—**guard′ian** *n.* a keeper; a protector; (*Law*) one who has custody of a minor.—**guard′ianship** *n.* the office of a guardian.—**guard′room** *n.* guardhouse.—**guards′man** *n.* a soldier in one of the regiments of Guards.—**to mount guard** (*Mil.*) to go on sentry duty [Fr. *garde*].

guava (gwȧ′-vạ) *n.* a genus of tropical American trees and shrubs, bearing pear-shaped fruit; the fruit [Sp. *guayaba*].

gubernation (gū-bẹr-nā′-shun) *n.* government.—**gubernato′rial** [L. *gubernare*, to govern].

guddle (gud′-l) *v.t.* (*Scot.*) to catch fish with the hands [etym. uncertain].

gudgeon (guj′-un) *n.* a small fresh-water fish, allied to the carp; a person easily cheated [Fr. *goujon*].

gudgeon (guj′-un) *n.* the pivot of the axle of a wheel; the pin which fixes the piston-rod to the connecting-rod [O.Fr. *goujon*, the pin of a pulley].

guelder rose (gel′-dẹr-rōz) *n.* a species of *Viburnum*, sometimes called the 'Snowball tree.'—Also **gel′der-rose** [fr. *Guelderland*, Holland].

guerdon (gẹr′-dun) *n.* a reward; recompense [O.Fr. *gueredon*].

Guernsey (gẹrn′-zi) *n.* (*Geog.*) one of the Channel Islands; breed of dairy cattle.—**guern′sey** *n.* knitted woollen shirt.

guerilla, guerrilla (gẹr-il′-a) *n.* a member of a band of irregular troops taking part in a war independently of the principal combatants;—*a.* pert. to this kind of warfare [Sp. *guerrilla*, dim. of *guerra*, war].

guess (ges) *v.t.* and *i.* to estimate without calculation or measurement; to judge at random; to conjecture; (*U.S.*) to suppose;—*n.* a rough estimate; a random judgment.—**guess′work** *n.* result obtained by random estimate [M.E. *gessen*].

guest (gest) *n.* a visitor received or entertained at another's house; one living in a hotel, boarding-house, etc.—**guest′-house** *n.* a boarding-house [O.E. *gest*].

guffaw (guf-aw′) *n.* a burst of boisterous laughter;—*v.i.* to laugh boisterously [imit. origin].

guide (gīd) *n.* one who shows the way; an adviser; one who directs or regulates; an official accompanying tourists; a conductor; a book of instruction or information; a Girl-Guide;—*v.t.* to lead; to direct; to influence; to act as a guide to; to arrange.—**guid′ance** *n.* direction; government.—**guide′-book** *n.* a descriptive handbook for tourists, travellers, etc.—**guided missile**, powered rocket or other projectile which can be directed to the target by remote control.—**guide′-post** *n.* a road sign-post.—**guid′er** *n.* officer in Girl Guides [Fr. *guider*, to guide].

guild, gild (gild) *n.* a corporation; a society for mutual help, or with a common object; a society of merchants or tradesmen.—**guild′-hall** *n.* the hall where a guild or corporation usually assembles—hence, the town-hall.—**guild′ry** (*Scot.*) *n.* the members of a guild [O.E. *gild*, money].

guilder (gil′-dẹr) *n.* a Dutch silver coin, worth 1s. 8d.; a Dutch florin. Also **gil′der** [Dut. *gulden*, gold].

guile (gīl) *n.* craft; cunning.—**guile′ful** *a.* characterised by cunning, deceit, or treachery.—**guile′less** *a.* artless; honest; innocent; sincere [O.Fr. *guile*, deceit].

guillemot (gil′-e-mot) *n.* a sea-bird, allied to the penguins, auks, and divers [Fr.].

guillotine (gil′-ō-tēn) *n.* a machine for beheading by the descending stroke of a heavy knife; a paper-cutting machine; in Parliament, a drastic cut, imposed by government, of the time allowed for debating a Bill;—*v.t.* to use a guillotine upon [fr. Joseph *Guillotin* (1738-1814)].

guilt (gilt) *n.* the fact or state of having offended; criminality and consequent liability to punishment; culpability; crime; offence.—**guilt′y** *a.* judged to have committed a crime, offence, etc.; criminal; sinful; wicked; evil.—**guilt′ily** *adv.*—**guilt′iness** *n.* criminality.—**guilt′less** *a.* innocent [O.E. *gylt*, crime, fr. *gildan*, to pay].

guinea (gin′-i) *n.* formerly, 21 shillings; a gold coin of this value, so called because the gold was from *Guinea*, in W. Africa.—**guin′ea-fowl** *n.* a fowl allied to the pheasant.—**guin′ea-pig** *n.* (corrupt. of *Guiana*-pig) a small S. American rodent, somewhat resembling a small pig; (*Fig.*) a person used as a subject for experimental tests [fr. *Guinea*, in W. Africa].

guise (gīz) *n.* external appearance, esp. one assumed; semblance; behaviour; dress.—**guiser** (gī′-zẹr) **gui′sard** *n.* a person in disguise; a mummer [Fr. *guise*, manner].

guitar (gi-tȧr′) *n.* a six-stringed musical instrument resembling the lute.—**guitar′ist** *n.* a player of the guitar [Fr. *guitare*].

gulch (gulch) *n.* a ravine; a glutton;—*v.t.* to swallow greedily [etym. unknown].

gules (gūlz) *n.* and *a.* (*Her.*) red (represented by vertical hatching) [Fr. *gueules*, throats].

gulf (gulf) *n.* a large bay; a sea extending widely into the land; an abyss; a deep chasm; immeasurable depth; a whirlpool;—*v.t.* to swallow up [Gk. *kolpos*, the bosom].

gull (gul) *n.* a long-winged, web-footed sea-bird [Bret. *gwelan*, to weep].

gull (gul) *n.* a dupe; a fool; a trick; a fraud;—*v.t.* to deceive; to trick; to defraud.—**gull′ible** *a.* easily imposed on; credulous.—**gullibil′ity** *n.* credulity [fr. *gull*, the sea-bird which was formerly considered to be stupid].

gullet (gul′-et) *n.* the food-passage from mouth to stomach; the throat [Fr. *goulet*, dim. of *gueule*, the throat].

gully (gul′-i) *n.* a channel or ravine worn by water; a ravine; a ditch [fr. *gullet*].

gully (gul-i) *n.* (*Scot.*) a big knife; (*Cricket*) a position in the field, to the right of second-slip [etym. unknown].

gulp (gulp) *v.t.* to swallow eagerly; to swallow in large draughts;—*v.t.* to gasp; to choke;—*n.* an act of gulping; an effort to swallow; a large mouthful [imit. origin].

gum (gum) *n.* the firm flesh in which the teeth are set.—**gum′boil** *n.* an abscess in the gum [O.E. *goma*, the jaws].

gum (gum) *n.* a sticky substance issuing from certain trees; this substance prepared for stiffening and adhesive purposes; a kind of sweetmeat, a jujube; abbrev. of chewing-gum;—*v.t.* to stick with gum.—*pr.p.* **gum′ming**.—*pa.p.* and *pa.t.* **gummed**.—**gummif′erous** *a.* producing gum.—**gum′miness** *n.* the state or quality of being gummy.—**gum′mous** *a.* of the nature or quality of gum.—**gum′my** *a.* consisting of gum; viscous; adhesive; producing gum; covered with gum.—**gum′-ar′abic** *n.* gum obtained from various species of the acacia.—**gum′-boots** *n.pl.* boots made of rubberised fabric, reaching to the knees.—**gum′-elas′tic** *n.* caoutchouc; india-rubber.—**gum′-tree** *n.* in the colonies, any species of eucalyptus tree.—**up a gum-tree** (*Slang*) in a difficult position; in a fix.—**chew'ing-gum** *n.* a sticky sweetmeat for chewing, the chief ingredient being chicle [Fr. *gomme*].

gumption (gum′shun) *n.* common sense; shrewdness [etym. uncertain].

gun (gun) *n.* a weapon consisting mainly of a metal tube from which missiles are thrown by explosion; a firearm in general, cannon, rifle, pistol, etc.; (*Sport*) one of a shooting party.—*v.i.* to shoot with a gun.—**gun'nage** *n.* the total of guns carried by a warship.—**gun'ner** *n.* one who works a gun; (*Mil.*) a private in an artillery regiment; (*Navy*) a warrant officer having charge of the ordnance.—**gun'nery** *n.* the firing of guns; the science of artillery.—**gun'ning** *n.* the shooting of game.—**gun'-barr'el** *n.* the metal tube of a gun.—**gun'-boat** *n.* a small vessel of light draught fitted to carry one or more guns.—**gun'-carr'iage** *n.* a heavy framework resting on wheels, on which guns are carried.—**gun'-cott'on** *n.* an explosive made of cotton steeped in nitric and sulphuric acids.—**gun'man** *n.* (*U.S.*) an armed criminal or gangster.—**gun'-met'al** *n.* an alloy of copper and tin or zinc, formerly used for guns.—**gun'pow'der** *n.* an explosive mixture of salt-petre, sulphur, and charcoal.—**gun'-runn'er** *n.* one who smuggles fire-arms on a big scale.—**gun'shot** *n.* the range of a gun, usually of a rifle or fowling-piece.—**gun'-smith** *n.* one who makes, repairs, deals in guns.—**gun'-stock** *n.* the wood in which the barrel of a gun is fixed.—**as sure as a gun** (*Colloq.*) most certainly.—**a son of a gun** (*Colloq.*) a rascal.—**a big gun** (*Slang*) a person of great importance [M.E. *gonne*].

gunnel (gun′l) *n.* Same as **gunwale**.

gunny (gun′i) *n.* strong, coarse sacking made from jute [Hind.].

Gunter's chain (gun′tẹrz chān) *n.* the surveying-chain used in measuring land; it is 4 rods or 66 feet long, and is divided into 100 links [fr. Edmund *Gunter*, English mathematician (1581-1626)].

gunwale (gun′l) *n.* upper edge of the side of a boat or ship. Also **gun'nel** [fr. *Gunhilda*, name of medieval war-engine].

gurgitation (gur-ji-tā′shun) *n.* a surging rise and fall [L. *gurgitare*, to flood].

gurgle (gur′gl) *n.* a bubbling noise;—*v.i.* to make a gurgle; to flow in a broken, noisy current [imit. origin].

Gurkha (goor′kạ) *n.* a native race of Nepal, India, who make excellent infantrymen.—Also **Ghoor'ka, Goor'kha** [Native].

gurnard, gurnet (gur′nạrd, -net) *n.* a spiny sea-fish with an angular head [O.Fr. *gornard*, fr. *grogner*, to grunt, so called because it sends out a faint grunt.]

guru (go͝o′ro͝o) *n.* a Hindu spiritual teacher [Sans.].

gush (gush) *v.i.* to flow out suddenly and copiously; (*Fig.*) to display exaggerated and effusive affection;—*n.* a sudden copious flow; affected display of sentiment.—**gush'er** *n.* a gushing person; an oil-well with a big natural flow [etym. uncertain, perh. imit].

gusset (gus′et) *n.* a triangular piece of material inserted in a garment to strengthen or enlarge it [Fr. *gousset*, the arm-pit].

gust (gust) *n.* a sudden blast of wind; a burst of rain; an outburst of passion.—**gust'y** *a.* [O.N. *gustr*].

gust (gust) *n.* a sense of pleasure in tasting food; relish; enjoyment.—**gusta'tion** *n.* the act of tasting; the sense of taste.—**gust'ative, gust'atory** *a.* pert. to the sense of taste.—**gust'o** *n.* enjoyment in doing a thing; taste; zest [L. *gustus*, taste].

gut (gut) *n.* intestine; a material made from guts of animals, as for violin strings, etc.; catgut; a narrow passage; a strait;—*n.pl.* entrails; intestines; (*Colloq.*) courage; pluck; determination.—*v.t.* to remove the entrails from, esp. from fish; to destroy the interior of a building, etc. esp. by fire.—*pr.p.* **gutt'ing**.—*pa.p.* and *pa.t.* **gutt'ed** [O.E. *guttas*, (pl.)].

gutta percha (gut′ạ pẹr′chạ) *n.* a horny, flexible substance, the hardened juice of a Malayan tree.—**gutt'y** *a.* (*Colloq.*) made of gutta percha [Malay *getah*, gum; *percha*, the tree producing it].

gutter (gut′ẹr) *n.* a passage for water; a tube or pipe for conveying rain from the eaves of a building; a channel at the side of a road, etc. for carrying off the water;—*v.t.* to make channels in;—*v.i.* to flow in streams; of a candle, to melt away by the wax forming channels and running down in drops.—**gutt'er-press** *n.* sensational news-papers.—**gutt'er-snipe** *n.* a street-arab; a child homeless or living mainly in the streets [Fr. *gouttière*, fr. *goutte*, a drop].

guttural (gut′ur-ạl) *a.* pert. to or produced in the throat;—*n.* a guttural sound [L. *guttur*, throat].

guy (gī) *n.* (*Naut.*) a rope or chain to steady other parts of a ship's tackle; a rope or chain to secure a tent, airship, etc.—Also **guy'-rope** [O.Fr. *guier*, to guide].

guy (gī) *n.* an effigy of *Guy* Fawkes to be burnt on Nov. 5; a ridiculously dressed person; (*U.S. Slang*) a fellow;—*v.t.* to exhibit in effigy; to ridicule; to make fun of [fr. *Guy* Fawkes, died 1606].

guzzle (guz′l) *v.t.* and *i.* to eat or drink greedily.—**guzz'ler** *n.* [Fr. *gosier*, the gullet].

gybe (jīb) *v.i.* (*Naut.*) of the boom of a fore-and-aft sail, to swing over to the other side [Dut. *gijpen*].

gymkhana (jim-ká′nạ) *n.* a place for athletic games; an athletic display, esp. races [Urdu *gend-khana*, a racquet-court, *lit.* a ball-house].

gymnasium (jim-nā′zi-um) *n.* a building or part of one, equipped for physical training; in Germany, a High School, usually classical (pronounced gim-ná'zi-o͝om).—*pl.* **gymna'sia, or gymna'siums**.—**gymnast** (jim′nast) *n.* one who teaches or practises gymnastic exercises.—**gymnas'tic** *a.*—**gymnas'tics** *n.pl.* muscular and bodily exercises [Gk. *gumnasion* fr. *gumnos*, naked].

gynaecology (jin- (or gin) -ē-kol′-o-ji) *n.* (*Med.*) the science which deals with the diseases and disorders of women, particularly of the organs of generation.—**gynaecol'ogist** *n.*—Also **gynecol'ogy**, etc. [Gk. *gunē*, a woman; *logos*, discourse].

gynandrous (jin-an′drus) *a.* (*Bot.*) belonging to the *Gynandria*, a class of plants having stamens and pistil united; of doubtful sex.—Also **gynan'drian**.—**gynan'der** *n.* a gynandrous plant; a woman of masculine physique [Gk. *gunē*, a woman; *anēr*, *andros*, a man].

gynecocracy (jin-ē-kok′rạ-si) *n.* government by women. Also **gynoc'racy** [Gk. *gunē*, a woman; *kratein*, to rule].

gyneolatry (jin-ē-ol′ạ-tri) *n.* extravagant devotion to, or worship of, women [Gk. *gunē*, a woman; *latreia*, worship].

gyp (jip) *n.* a college male-servant at Cambridge University [perh. contr. of *gypsy*].

gyp (jip) *n.* (*Slang*) a scolding; punishment; severe pain.

gypsophila (jip-sof′i-lạ) *n.* the 'Chalk Plant,' a hardy herbaceous perennial, bearing small white flowers [Gk. *gupsos*, chalk, *philein*, to love].

gypsum (jip′sum) *n.* a mineral, consisting mostly of sulphate of lime, which when burned in a kiln, and ground fine, is known as 'plaster of Paris' [Gk. *gupsos*, chalk].

gypsy (jip′si) *n.* See **gipsy**.

gyrate (jī′rāt) *v.i.* to revolve round a central point; to move in a circle; to move spirally.—**gy'ratory** *a.*—**gyra'tion** *n.* the act of circling, or whirling round a fixed centre [L. *gyrare*, to move in a circle].

gyre (jīr) *n.* a circular motion; wheel.—**gy'ral** *a.* rotating [Gk. *guros*, a circle].
gyrfalcon Same as **gerfalcon**.
gyromancy (jīˊro-man-si) *n.* divination performed by drawing a circle, and walking in it till dizziness causes a fall [Gk. *guros*, a circle; *manteia*, divination].
gyroscope (jīˊro-skōp) *n.* a disc or wheel so mounted that it is able to rotate about any axis; when set rotating and left undisturbed, it will maintain the same direction in space, independently of its relation to the earth.—**gyroscop'ic** *a.* [Gk. *guros*, a circle; *skopein*, to view].
gyrostat (jīˊro-stat) *n.* an instrument for illustrating the dynamics of rotation, and distinguished from a gyroscope in being free to wander about in a horizontal plane.—**gyrostatic** (jī-ro-statˊik) *a.*—**gyrostat'ics** *n.pl.* the dynamics of rotating bodies [Gk. *guros*, a circle; *statikos*, static].
gyve (jīv) *v.t.* to shackle; to fetter;—*n.* (usually in *pl.*) shackles; fetters, esp. for the leg [M.E. *gives*].

H

ha (hȧ) *interj.* denoting surprise, joy, or grief [imit. origin].
haar (hȧr) *n.* raw sea-mist, esp. on E. coast of Scotland [perh. fr. O.N. *harr*].
habeas corpus (hāˊbe-as korˊpus) *n.* writ to governor of prison to produce prisoner, to determine legality of confinement [L. = that you have the body].
haberdasher (habˊẹr-dash-ẹr) *n.* a dealer in small articles of dress, ribbons, needles, etc.—**ha'berdashery** *n.* [etym. uncertain].
habergeon (ha-bẹrˊjun) *n.* a sleeveless coat of mail [O.Fr. *haubergeon*].
habiliment (hạ-bilˊi-ment) *n.* a garment; usually in *pl.*; dress [Fr. *habiller*, to clothe].
habilitate (hạ-bilˊi-tāt) *v.t.* to fit a person for a post; to accoutre;—*v.i.* to qualify for a post; to provide capital for a mine.—**habilita'tion** *n.* [L. *habilis*, fit].
habit (habˊit) *n.* custom; usage; tendency to repeat an action in the same way; mental condition acquired by practice; dress, esp. a *riding-habit*;—*v.t.* to dress; to clothe.—**habit'ual** *a.* formed by habit.—**habit'ually** *adv.*—**habit'uate** *v.t.* to accustom to a practice or usage; to familiarise.—**habitua'tion** *n.*—**hab'itude** *n.* customary manner of action; repetition of an act, thought, or feeling; confirmed practice.—**habitué** (hạ-bitˊū-ā) *n.* a constant visitor; a frequenter (of a place) [L. *habitus*, attire, state, fr. *habere*, to have].
habitable (habˊit-ạ-bl) *a.* fit to live in.—**habitabil'ity, hab'itableness** *n.*—**hab'itably** *adv.*—**hab'itant** *n.* an inhabitant.—**hab'itat** *n.* the natural home of an animal or plant; place of residence.—**habita'tion** *n.* the act of inhabiting; a place of abode [L. *habitare*, to dwell].
hachure (hashˊūr) *n.* shading on a map to show mountains;—*v.t.* to mark with this [Fr.].
hacienda (hȧ-thē-enˊdạ) *n.* a ranch; a farm in S. America [Sp.].
hack (hak) *v.t.* to cut irregularly; to notch; (*Football*) to kick on the shin;—*v.i.* to make an effort to raise phlegm;—*n.* a cut; a notch; a bruise; a kick on the shin; a blunt axe; a pick-axe.—**hack'-saw** *n.* a special saw for cutting metal [O.E. *haccian*].
hack (hak) *n.* a horse let out for hire; a horse for ordinary riding; a horse worn out by over-work; a drudge, esp. literary;—*a.* hackneyed; hired; mercenary; worn out by service;—*v.t.* to let out for hire; to hackney;—*v.i.* to ride on the road; to ride with an ordinary horse [short for *hackney*].
hackle (hakˊl) *n.* a comb for flax; the neck feathers of a cock; any flimsy substance unspun, e.g. raw silk; artificial fly for angling;—*v.t.* to separate, as the coarse part of flax or hemp from the fine; to tear rudely asunder.—**hack'ly** *a.* rough or broken, as if hacked [fr. *hack*].
hackney (hakˊni) *n.* a horse for riding or driving; a horse (and carriage) kept for hire;—*v.t.* to use much; to make trite or commonplace.—**hack'ney, hackneyed** (hakˊnid) *a.* let out for hire; commonplace [Fr. *haquenée*, a pacing-horse].
had (had) *pa.p.* and *pa.t.* of **have**.
haddock (hadˊuk) *n.* a fish of the cod family.—**haddie** (hadˊi) *n.* (*Scot.*) haddock [etym. uncertain].
Hades (hāˊdēz) (*Myth.*) the underworld; hell [Gk.=the unseen].
hadj, hajj (hȧj) *n.* a Mohammedan pilgrimage to Mecca.—**had'ji, haj'ji** *n.* one who has made this pilgrimage [Ar.].
haemacyte, hemacyte (hēˊma-sīt) *n.* a blood-corpuscle [Gk. *haima*, blood].
haemal, hemal (hēˊmạl) *a.* of the blood; on same side of body as the heart and great blood-vessels [Gk. *haima*, blood].
haematin, hematin (hēˊma-tin, hemˊa-tin) *n.* the constituent of haemoglobin containing iron [Gk. *haima*, blood].
haematite, hematite (heˊma-tīt, hemˊa tīt) *n.* a form of iron-ore, so called because blood-coloured [Gk. *haima*, blood].
haemoglobin, hemoglobin (hē-mo-glōˊbin) *n.* the colouring matter of the red blood-corpuscles [Gk. *haima*, blood; L. *globus*, a ball].
haemophilia (hē-mo-filˊi-ạ) *n.* (*Med.*) tendency to excessive bleeding due to a deficiency in clotting power of blood.—**haemophil'iac** *n.* a bleeder [Gk. *haima*, blood; *philein*, to love].
haemorrhage, hemorrhage (hemˊor-āj) *n.* (*Med.*) a flow of blood; a discharge of blood from the blood-vessels; bleeding.—**haemorrhag'ic** *a.* [Gk. *haima*, blood; *rhēgnunai*, to burst].
haemorrhoids, hemorrhoids (hemˊor-oidz) *n.pl.* dilated veins around anus; piles.—**haemorrhoid'al** *a.* [Gk. *haima*, blood; *rhein*, to flow].
haemostasis (hē-mo-stāˊsis) *n.* (*Med.*) the stoppage of haemorrhage.—**haemostat'ic** *n.* an agent which stops bleeding; a styptic. Also *a.* [Gk. *haima*, blood; *stasis*, a standing].
hafnium (hafˊni-um) *n.* an element, resembling zirconium [L. *Hafnia*, Copenhagen].
haft (hȧft) *n.* a handle, esp. of a knife; a hilt;—*v.t.* to set in a handle [O.E. *haeft*).
hag (hag) *n.* an ugly old woman; a witch; a sorceress.—**hagg'ish** *a.* like a hag.—**hagg'ishly** *adv.*—**hag'-rid'den** *a.* ridden by witches, as horse; troubled with nightmares [O.E. *haegtesse*, a witch].
haggard (hagˊạrd) *a.* wild-looking; lean and ghastly;—*n.* untrained hawk.—**hagg'ardly** *adv.* [O.Fr. *hagard*].
haggis (hagˊis) *n.* a Scottish dish made from a sheep's heart, lungs and liver, chopped up, with oatmeal, suet, onion, etc. and boiled in the stomach-bag [perh. fr. *hag*, to chop].
haggle (hagˊl) *v.t.* to hack; to cut roughly; to mangle;—*v.i.* to dispute terms; to be difficult in bargaining;—*n.* chaffering.—**hagg'ler** *n.* [O.N. *hoggva*, to chop].
Hagiographa (hā-ji, hag-i-ogˊrạ-fạ) *n.pl.* the last of the three Jewish divisions of the Old Testament.—**hagiog'raphal, hagiograph'ic** *a.*—**hagiog'rapher** *n.* a writer of one of the Hagiographa [Gk. *hagios*, holy; *graphein*, to write].
hagiolatry (hā-ji, hag-i-olˊạ-tri) *n.* the worship of saints.—**hagiol'ater** *n.* [Gk. *hagios*, holy; *latreia*, worship].
hagiology (hā-ji-, hag-i-olˊo-ji) *n.* a history of the lives of saints.—**hagiol'ogist** *n.*—**hagiog'raphy** *n.* the branch of literature which

treats of the lives of saints [Gk. *hagios*, holy; *logos*, discourse; *graphein*, to write].

ha-ha, haw-haw (ha-hà', haw-haw') *n.* a fence or bank sunk in a slope, not visible till one is close [Fr.].

hail (hāl) *n.* frozen rain falling in pellets;—*v.i.* to rain hail;—*v.t.* to pour down like hail.—**hail'stone,** *n.* frozen rain-drops [O.E. *hagol*].

hail (hāl) *v.t.* to greet; to salute; to call to;—*n.* a greeting; a call;—*interj.* an exclamation of respectful salutation.—**hail'-fell'ow** *n.* (often **hail-fellow well met**) an intimate companion;—*a.* on intimate terms.—**to hail from,** to come from [O.N. *heill*, healthy].

hair (hār) *n.* a filament growing from the skin of an animal; such filaments collectively, esp. covering the head; bristles; anything small or fine. **-haired** *a.* having hair.—**hair'iness** *n.*—**hair'y** *a.* covered with, made of, resembling hair.—**hairbreadth** (hār'bredth), **hair's'-breadth** *n.* the breadth of a hair; a very small distance.—*a.* very narrow.—**hair'-brush** *n.* a brush for the hair.—**hair'-cloth** *n.* cloth made wholly or partly of hair.—**hair'dresser** *n.* one who dresses or cuts hair; a barber.—**hair'-oil** *n.* oil used for dressing and setting the hair.—**hair'-pen'cil** *n.* an artist's fine brush.—**hair'-pin** *n.* a special two-legged pin for controlling hair.—**hair-pin bend,** a bend of the road in the form of a **U.**—**hair'-rais'ing** *a.* (*Fig.*) terrifying; alarming.—**hair'-shirt** *n.* a shirt made of hair-cloth, worn by penitents, ascetics, etc.—**hair'-split'ting** *n.* and *a.* minute distinctions in reasoning.—**hair'-spring** *n.* a fine spring in a watch.—**hair'-trigg'er** *n.* a secondary trigger releasing the main one by very slight pressure [O.E. *haer*].

hajj See **hadj.**

hake (hāk) *n.* a sea-fish of the cod family [etym. uncertain].

halberd, halbert (hal-berd, -bert) *n.* an ancient military weapon for cutting and thrusting; a combined spear and battle-axe.—**halberdier** (hal-ber-dēr') *n.* a soldier armed with a halberd [Fr. *hallebarde*].

halcyon (hal'si-un) *n.* the kingfisher;—*a.* pert. to the halcyon, said to lay her eggs in nests floating on the sea, which remained calm during the period of incubation; hence, calm [Gk. *alkuōn*].

hale (hāl) *a.* robust; sound; healthy, esp. in old age.—**hale'ness** *n.* [O.E. *hal*, whole].

hale (hāl) *v.t.* to haul [O.Fr. *haler*, to pull].

half (hàf) *n.pl.* **halves** (hàvz) either of two equal parts of a thing; (*Colloq.*) a half-glass of whisky; (*Golf*) a hole neither won nor lost;—*a.* forming a half;—*adv.* to the extent of half;—*v.t.* to divide into two equal parts.—**half'-and-half** *n.* a mixture of two liquids, in equal proportions.—**half'-back** *n.* (*Football*) a player, or position, behind the forwards.—**half'-baked** *a.* underdone; immature; silly.—**half'-blood** *n.* the relation between persons born of the same father or the same mother, but not of both.—**half'-blue** *n.* a badge or colours awarded at Oxford or Cambridge to a sportsman not quite of the first rank.—**half'-bound** *a.* of a book, bound with leather on back and corners only.—**half'-breed** *n.* one whose parents are of different races.—**half'-bred** *a.* of mixed breed; mongrel; hence, vulgar; unrefined; ill-mannered.—**half'-broth'er** *n.* a brother by one parent only.—**half'-caste** *n.* a half-breed, esp. one of mixed European and Asiatic parentage.—**half'-cock** *n.* the middle position of the cock of a gun when retained by the first notch.—**half'-crown** *n.* formerly, British coin worth 2s. 6d.—**half'-doz'en** *n.* six.—**half'-heart'ed** *a.* wanting in true affection; ungenerous; lukewarm.—**half'ling** *n.* a person between boyhood and manhood.—**half'-mast** *adv.* the position of a flag lowered half-way down from the staff, as a signal of distress, or as a sign of mourning.—**half'-meas'ure** *n.* inadequate means to achieve an end.—**half'-moon** *n.* the moon when half its disc appears illuminated; a semi-circle.—**half'-nel'son** *n.* a hold in wrestling.—**halfpenny** (hā'pen-i) *n.* a British bronze coin worth ½p; sometimes spelt **ha'penny.**—*pl.* **halfpence** (hā'pens).—**half'penny-worth** *n.* the amount purchasable with a ½p; (*Fig.*) a very small amount.—**half'-sov'ereign** *n.* formerly a British gold coin worth 10s.—**half'-tim'bered** *a.* built with a framework of timber filled in with bricks, plastered rubble, etc.—**half'-ti'tle** *n.* the name of a book, or subdivision of a book, occupying a full page.—**half'-tone** *n.* an illustration printed from a relief plate, showing light and shade by means of minute dots, made by photographing the subject through a closely ruled screen.—**half'-wit** *n.* an imbecile; a blockhead.—**half'-wit'ted** *a.*—**halve** (hàv) *v.t.* to divide into two equal portions; to reduce to half the previous amount [O.E. *healf*].

halibut (hal'i-but) *n.* a large, flat sea-fish, allied to the turbot and flounder [M.E. *haly*, holy; *butt*, a flat-fish].

halidom (hal'i-dom) *n.* a holy place or thing; holiness.—**by my halidom,** an old-time oath [O.E. *halig*, holy].

halitus (hal'i-tus) *n.* breath; a vapour.—**halit'uous** *a.*—**halito'sis** *n.* (*Med.*) foul or offensive breath [L. *halitus*, breath].

hall (hawl) *n.* a place of public assembly; a passage-way at the entrance of a house; the house of a landed proprietor; a court of justice; a building belonging to a collegiate institution, guild, etc.; a college in a university; a students' hostel.—**hall'-mark** *n.* the mark used (at Goldsmiths' Hall, London) to indicate the standard of tested gold and silver; *-v.t.* to stamp with this mark [O.E. *heall*].

Hallelujah, Halleluiah (hal-e-lòò'yạ) *n.* and *interj.* used in songs of praise to God [Heb. *hallelu*, praise ye; *Jah*, Jehovah].

halliard See **halyard.**

hallo, halloa (ha-lō') *interj.* an exclamation to greet a person, etc. [imit.].

halloo (ha-lòò') *n.* a hunting cry; a shout or call to draw attention;—*v.t.* to encourage with shouts, esp. dogs in hunting [imit.].

hallow (hal'ō) *v.t.* to make holy; to consecrate; to treat as sacred; to reverence;—*n.* a saint.—**Hallowe'en'** *n.* the evening before All Hallows' or All Saints' day (Oct. 31st).—**Hall'owmas** *n.* the feast of All Hallows, All Saints, or All Souls (Nov. 1st).

hallucinate (hal-ū'sin-āt) *v.t.* to produce illusion in the mind of.—**hallucina'tion** *n.* illusion; seeing something that is not present; delusion.—**hallu'cinative, hallu'cinatory** *a.* [L. *hallucinari*, to wander in mind].

halm, haulm (hawm) *n.* the stalk of any kind of grain; stalks of beans, peas, etc.; thatch made of this [O.E. *healm*, stalk].

halma (hal'mạ) *n.* game, played on chequered board [Gk. *halma*, a leap].

halo (hā'lō) *n.* a circle of light round the moon, sun, etc.; a ring of light round a saint's head in a picture.—*pl.* **ha'los, ha'loes** [Gk. *halōs*, a threshing-floor; a disc].

halogen (hal'ō-jen) *n.* (*Chem.*) one of the elements chlorine, bromine, iodine, and fluorine, all of similar characteristics, and alike in that they form a saline compound by simple combination with a metal [Gk. *hals*, salt; root *gen-*, producing].

halt (hawlt) *n.* a stoppage on a march or journey; a stopping-place;—*v.t.* to cause to stop;—*v.i.* to make a stop [Ger. *Halt*, stoppage].

halt (hawlt) *a.* lame; limping; crippled;—*v.i.* to limp; to falter;—*n.* a limp; (*Scot.*) speech impediment [O.E. *heall*].

halter (hawl'tẹr) *n.* a rope or strap with head-stall to fasten horses or cattle; a noose for hanging a person;—*v.t.* to fasten with a rope or strap [O.E. *haelftre*].

halve (hàv) *v.t.* to divide into two equal parts [See **half**].

halyard, halliard (hal′yard) *n.* (*Naut.*) a rope for hoisting or lowering yards or sails [corrupt. of *halier*, fr. *hale*=to haul].

ham (ham) *n.* the region behind the knee; the thigh of any animal, esp. a hog's thigh cured by salting and smoking; (*Slang*) a raw, inexperienced person; an amateur transmitter and receiver of wireless messages.—**ham′-string** *n.* a tendon at the back of the knee;—*v.t.* to cripple by cutting this [O.E. *hamm*].

Hamite (Ham′ite) *n.* a descendant of Ham, son of Noah; an African; a negro.

hamadryad (ham-a-drī′ad) *n.* (*Myth.*) a wood-nymph; a large poisonous Indian snake.—*pl.* **hamadry′ads, or hamadryades** (ham-a-drī′a-dēz) [Gk. *hama*, together; *drus*, a tree].

Hamburg (ham′burg) *n.* a black variety of grape; a breed of domestic fowls.—**ham′burger** *n.* minced steak cooked with onions; a breakfast sausage [fr. *Hamburg*].

hamlet (ham′let) *n.* a small village [O.E. *ham*, a dwelling].

hammer (ham′er) *n.* a tool, usually with a heavy head at the end of a handle, for beating metal, driving nails, etc; a contrivance for exploding the charge of a gun;—*v.t.* and *i.* to beat with, or as with, a hammer; (*Slang*) to punish severely.—**hamm′erhead** *n.* a rapacious kind of shark.—**hamm′erhead′ed** *a.* having a head shaped like a hammer.—**hamm′erman** *n.* a blacksmith.—**hamm′er-toe** *n.* a deformed toe which has grown bent upwards.—**to hammer out** (*Fig.*) to find a solution by full investigation of all difficulties.—**to come under the hammer,** to be sold by auction.—**hammer-and-tongs** (*Fig.*) vigorously [O.E. *hamor*].

hammock (ham′ok) *n.* a kind of hanging bed, consisting of a piece of canvas, and suspended by cords from hooks [Sp. *hamaca*].

hamper (ham′per) *n.* a large covered basket for conveying goods [O.Fr. *hanapier*, a case for *hanaps*, goblets].

hamper (ham′per) *n.* a fetter; (*Naut.*) cumbrous equipment;—*v.t.* to put a fetter on; hence, to impede; to obstruct the movements of [etym. uncertain].

hamshackle (ham′shak-l) *v.t.* to fasten the head of an animal to one of the forelegs [fr. *hamper* and *shackle*].

hamster (ham′ster) *n.* a species of rat, remarkable for having cheek-pouches for holding grain, peas, acorns, etc. [Ger.].

hamstring See **ham.**

hand (hand) *n.* the extremity of the arm beyond the wrist; a pointer on a dial, e.g. on a watch; a measure of the hand's breadth, four inches; a style of handwriting; cards dealt to a player; a manual worker; a sailor; side; quarter; direction; agency; service; aid; help;—*v.t.* to give with the hand; to deliver; to pass; to hold out.—**hand′y** *a.* convenient; close at hand; clever with the hands.—**hand′y-man** *n.* one clever with his hands.—**hand′ily** *adv.*—**hand′iness** *n.*—**hand′less** *a.* clumsy; awkward.—**hand′bag** *n.* a bag for carrying in the hand.—**hand′-barr′ow** *n.* a wheel-less barrow with handles at each end.—**hand′bill** *n.* printed sheet for circulation by hand; a pruning-hook.—**hand′book** *n.* a short treatise; a manual.—**hand′-breadth** *n.* the breadth of a hand (about four inches); a palm.—**hand′-cart** *n.* a small cart drawn or pushed by hand.—**hand′cuff** *n.* shackle around wrist connected by a chain with one on other wrist; a manacle;—*v.t.* to manacle.—**hand′fast** *n.* a firm hold; betrothal; a pledge;—*v.t.* to pledge one's word by a handshake; to betroth.—**hand′ful** *n.* as much as the hand will grasp or contain.—**hand′maid(en)** *n.* a female servant.—**hand′-out** *n.* official information handed out to Press.—**hand′rail** *n.* the top rail of a staircase.—**hand′shake** *n.* a shake of the hand.—**hand′-to-hand,** *a.* in personal encounter; at close quarters.—**hand′-to-mouth** *a.* precarious; without thought of the future.—**hand′writing** *n.* the way a person writes.—**at first hand,** direct from the original source.—**in hand,** under control; under preparation.—**off′-hand** *adv.* without preparation; without attentive consideration; immediately.—**on hand,** ready for distribution; available for disposal.—**under one's hand,** properly signed.—**with a high heavy hand,** sternly; severely.—**with a high hand,** arrogantly.—**an old hand,** a person with experience; a veteran.—**second hand,** not new; having already been used.—**to change hands,** to become the property of another.—**to gain the upper hand,** to overcome.—**to set one's hand to,** to make a start; to undertake.—**to show one's hand,** to reveal one's intentions.—**to stand one's hands** (*Colloq.*) to pay for drink to one or more persons; to treat [O.E. *hand*].

handicap (hand′i-kap) *n.* a race or contest in which competitors' chances are equalised by starts given, weights carried, etc.; a condition so imposed; (*Fig.*) a disability;—*v.t.* to impose such conditions [fr. *hand in cap*; orig. a lottery game].

handicraft (hand′i-kraft) *n.* manual occupation or skill; work performed by the hand.—**hand′icraftsman** *n.* a man employed or skilled in manual occupation.—**hand′iwork, hand′y-work** *n.* work done by the hands; a thing done by anyone in person.

handkerchief (hang′ker-chif) *n.* a small square of fabric carried in the pocket for wiping the nose, etc.; a neckerchief.

handle (hand′l) *v.t.* to touch or feel with the hand; to manage; to wield; to deal with; to deal in; to treat well or ill;—*n.* the part of a thing made to hold it by; (*Fig.*) a fact that may be taken advantage of; an opportunity; a pretext.—**hand′le-bar(s)** *n.* a device to steer a bicycle.—**hand′ler** *n.* [O.E. *handlian*].

handsel, hansel (hand′, han′sel) *n.* a gift on beginning something; a New Year gift; earnest money; the first use of anything;—*v.t.* to give a handsel to; to be the first to use [O.N. *handsal*, hand sale].

handsome (han′sum) *a.* of fine appearance; generous.—**hand′somely** *adv.*—**hand′someness** *n.* [orig.=pleasant to handle].

hang (hang) *v.t.* to suspend; to put to death by suspending from gallows; to cover with, as wallpaper, curtains, pictures, etc.; to fix on hinges, as a door; to display;—*v.i.* to be suspended; to incline; to be in suspense; to linger; to cling to.—*pa.p.* and *pa.t.* **hanged** or **hung.**—*n.* slope; inclination; the way in which a thing hangs; tendency.—**hang′-dog** *n.* a degraded fellow;—*a.* having a sneaking look.—**hang′er** *n.* that by which a thing is suspended, e.g. a *coat-hanger*; a girdle or belt by which a sword was attached; a short broad sword.—**hang′ing** *n.* death by suspension; that which is hung, as linings, curtains, etc. for a room (used chiefly in *pl.*).—*a.* punishable by death; unfixed; floating.—**hang′man** *n.* one who hangs another; a public executioner.—**hang′nail** *n.* piece of skin hanging from root of finger-nail; agnail.—**hang′over** *n.* depressing after-effects of a drinking bout.—**to hang fire,** of fire-arms, to be slow in going off; (*Fig.*) to hesitate.—**to hang in the balance,** to be in doubt or suspense.—**hang! hang it! hang it all!** mild oaths [O.E. *hangian*].

hangar (hang′er, hang′ar) *n.* a shed for aircraft [Fr.=*a* shed].

hank (hangk) *n.* a coil, esp. as a measure of yarn (of cotton=840 yards; of worsted =560 yards); (*Naut.*) a ring at the corner of a sail [O.N. *hanki*].

hanker (hang′ker) *v.i.* to long for; to crave; to linger about.—**hank′ering** *n.* an uneasy longing for; a craving [etym. uncertain].

Hanoverian (han-o-vē′ri-an) *a.* pert. to the

House of *Hanover* as a British dynasty; pert. to Hanover, Germany;—*n.* native, supporter of Hanover.

Hansard (han′sărd) *n.* the printed record of debates in British Parliament; first published in 1803 by a printer, Luke *Hansard.*

hanse (hans) *n.* a league; a commercial union in the Middle Ages.—**hanse, hanseat′ic** *a.* [O.H. Ger. *hansa,* a company].

hansom (han′sum) *n.* a light two-wheeled cab with the driver's seat at the back [fr. the inventor, Joseph A. *Hansom,* 1803-1882].

hap (hap) *n.* that which happens unexpectedly; chance;—*v.i.* to befall.—**hap′less** *a.* unlucky.—**hap′lessly** *adv.*—**hap′ly** *adv.* by chance; perhaps.—**hap′-haz′ard** *n.* chance; accident.—*a.* random; without design;—*adv.* by chance.—**hap′-haz′ardly** *adv.*—**hap′-haz′ardness** *n.*—**happ′en** *v.i.* to come by chance; to occur; to take place.—**happ′ening** *n.* occurrence; event [O.N. *happ,* luck].

happy (hap′i) *a.* lucky; fortunate; successful; prosperous; glad; content; apt; fitting.—**happ′ily** *adv.*—**happ′iness** *n.* [O.N. *happ,* luck].

hara-kiri (hă-ra-kē′rē) *n.* a method of suicide by disembowelment, practised by the Japanese. Also, but incorrectly, **hari-ka′ri** [Jap. *hara,* the belly; *kiri,* to cut].

harangue (hą-rang′) *n.* a loud, noisy, public speech;—*v.i.* to deliver a harangue;—*v.t.* to speak vehemently to.—**harang′uer** *n.* [O.H. Ger.=a ring of hearers].

harass (har′ąs, ha-ras′) *v.t.* to fatigue; to worry; to trouble; to attack repeatedly.—**har′assed** *a.*—**har′asser** *n.*—**har′assing** *a.*—**har′assment** *n.* [Fr. *harasser*].

harbinger (hăr′bin-jer) *n.* one who announces another's approach; a forerunner [M.E. *herbergeour,* one sent on to provide lodgings].

harbour (hăr-bur) *n.* shelter for ships; a port; any shelter;—*v.t.* to give shelter to; to entertain as a guest; to protect;—*v.i.* to take shelter.—**har′bourage** *n.* shelter; entertainment [M.E. *herberwe*].

hard (hărd) *a.* firm; solid; resisting pressure; difficult; harsh; unfeeling; difficult to bear; strenuous; bitter, as winter; keen, as frost; of water, not making lather well with soap; (*Slang*) of alcoholic drinks, spirituous;—*n.* a beach; abbrev. of 'hard labour,' as a punishment.—**hard′en** *v.t.* to make hard or more hard; to strengthen; to confirm in wickedness or obstinacy; to make less sympathetic;—*v.i.* to become hard.—**hard′ish** *a.* somewhat hard.—**hard′ly** *adv.* with difficulty; not quite; scarcely; severely; roughly.—**hard′ness** *n.*—**hard′ship** *n.* severe toil or suffering; ill-luck; privation; suffering.—**hard-and-fast,** strict; rigid.—**hard′-bit′ten** *a.* tough in a fight.—**hard′-boiled** *a.* boiled till hard, e.g. of an egg; (*Slang*) tough; unfeeling.—**hard by,** near; close at hand.—**hard cash,** gold and silver coins, as opposed to paper-money.—**hard′-cur′rency** *n.* dollar, or any other currency convertible into dollars.—**hard′-earned** *a.* earned by hard work; well-deserved.—**hard′-fought** *a.* strenuously contested.—**hard′-grained** *a.* firm in the grain; unattractive.—**hard′-hand′ed** *a.* having hard hands, as a labourer; (*Fig.*) severe.—**hard′-head′ed** *a.* shrewd; intelligent; practical.—**hard′-heart′ed** *a.* cruel; merciless; unsympathetic.—**hard tack,** a ship-biscuit, a large coarse unsalted biscuit.—**hard up,** very short of money; poor.—**hard′ware** *n.* a business term for articles made of iron, copper, or other metals, e.g. pots, pans, etc.—**hard′-wood** *n.* wood of a close and hard texture, as oak, ash, mahogany, maple, etc.—**to die hard,** to die after a fierce struggle.—**a die-hard** (*Fig.*) one who clings desperately to long-held opinions [O.E. *heard*].

hardy (hăr′di) *a.* robust; vigorous; bold; brave; daring; able to bear exposure.—**har′dily** *adv.*—**har′dihood** *n.* extreme boldness.—**har′diness** *n.* vigour; robustness [Fr. *hardi,* bold].

hare (hār) *n.* a rodent with long hind-legs, long ears, short tail, and divided upper lip, noted for its speed;—*v.i.* (*Colloq.*) to hasten.—**hare′bell** *n.* a plant with blue bell-shaped flowers; the bluebell of Scotland.—**hare′-brained** *a.* wild; heedless.—**hare′-lip** *n.* (*Med.*) a congenital fissure in the upper lip.—**hare′-lipped** *a.*—**hare and hounds,** a paper-chase, a cross-country race in which the 'hare' drops paper to mark trail for 'hounds' in pursuit.—**to hold with the hare and run with the hounds,** to play a double game [O.E. *hara*].

harem (hā′rem, ha-rēm′) *n.* apartments for females in a Mohammedan household; the occupants [Ar. *haram,* forbidden].

haricot (har′i-kō, -kot) *n.* a French bean; the kidney-bean; a ragout or stew of mutton or lamb and vegetables [Fr. *haricot*].

hari-kari, incorrect form of **hara-kiri.**

hark (hărk) *v.i.* to listen;—*interj.* listen! hear!—**to hark back** (*Fig.*) to return to some previous point in an argument [M.E. *herkien*; cf. E. *hearken*].

harl (hărl) *v.t.* (*Scot.*) to roughcast a wall with lime; to drag along.

Harlequin (hăr′le-kwin) *n.* in pantomime, a mute character in love with Columbine; a buffoon.—**harlequinade′** *n.* the scenes in pantomime in which Harlequin, Columbine, etc. appear [It. *arlecchino*].

harlot (hăr′lot) *n.* a prostitute.—**har′lotry** *n.* prostitution [O.Fr.=a vagabond].

harm (hărm) *n.* injury; hurt; damage; misfortune;—*v.t.* to hurt; to injure.—**harm′ful** *a.* hurtful; injurious.—**harm′fully** *adv.*—**harm′fulness** *n.*—**harm′less** *a.*—**harm′lessly** *adv.*—**harm′lessness** *n.* [O.E. *hearm*].

harmony (hăr′mo-ni) *n.* agreement; concord; friendliness; peace; a melodious sound; a combination of musical notes to make chords; the science that treats of musical sounds in their combination and progression.—**harmon′ic, harmon′ical** *a.*—**harmon′ically** *adv.*—**harmon′ica** *n.* a mouth-organ.—**harmon′icon** *n.* a mouth-organ; an orchestrion.—**harmon′ics** *n.* the science of harmony, of musical sounds.—**harmonious** (hăr-mō′ni-us) *a.* vocally or musically concordant; symmetrical; living in peace and friendship.—**harmo′niously** *adv.*—**harmo′niousness** *n.*—**har′monise** *v.t.* to bring into harmony; to cause to agree; to reconcile; (*Mus.*) to arrange into parts for the voice, or with instrumental accompaniments;—*v.i.* to be in harmony; to agree.—**har′moniser** *n.*—**har′monist** *n.* a harmoniser; a musical composer.—**harmo′nium** *n.* a small reed-organ the bellows of which are operated by foot-pressure.—**harmo′niumist** *n.*—**harmonic progression,** a series of numbers whose reciprocals are in arithmetical progression, e.g. $\frac{1}{2}$, $\frac{1}{3}$, $\frac{1}{4}$, etc. or 10, 12, 15 [Gk. *harmonia,* fr. *harmozein,* to fit together].

harness (hăr′nes) *n.* the armour of knight and his horse; equipment esp. of draught horse;—*v.t.* to dress in armour; to put harness on [Fr. *harnais*].

harp (hărp) *n.* a stringed musical instrument played by hand;—*v.i.* to play on the harp; (*Fig.*) to dwell persistently upon a particular subject.—**harp′er** *n.* a player on the harp; a minstrel.—**harp′ist** *n.* a player on the harp; a harper in an orchestra.—**harp-sichord** (harp′si-kord) *n.* an old-fashioned musical instrument, a forerunner of the piano [O.E. *hearpe*].

harpoon (hăr-pōōn′) *n.* a barbed spear with a rope attached for catching whales, etc.;—*v.t.* to strike with a harpoon.—**harpoon′er** *n.* [Fr. *harpon*].

harpy (hăr′pi) *n.* (*Myth*). ravenous monster, with head and breast of woman and wings and claws of vulture; a rapacious woman [Gk. *harpazein,* to seize].

harquebuse (har′kwē-bus) *n.* an old-fashioned hand-gun; an arquebuse [Fr.].
harridan (har′i-dạn) *n.* a haggard old woman; a shrew; a vixen [corrupt. of Fr. *haridelle*, a worn-out horse].
harrier (har′i-ẹr) *n.* a kind of small hound for hunting hares; a beagle; a falcon; a cross-country runner [fr. *hare*].
harrow (har′ō) *n.* a toothed agricultural implement to level, break clods, or cover seed when sown;—*v.t.* to draw harrow over; (*Fig.*) to distress greatly.—**harr′ower** *n.*—**harr′owing** *a.* [M.E. *harwe*].
harry (har′i) *v.t.* to ravage; to pillage; to plunder [O.E. *hergian*, to make war].
harsh (harsh) *a.* rough; unpleasing to the touch or taste; severe; unfeeling.—**harsh′ly** *adv.*—**harsh′ness** *n.* [M.E. *harsk*].
hart (hart) *n.* a male deer or stag, esp. over five years old.—**harts′horn** *n.* the horn of the hart, formerly the chief source of ammonia; a solution of ammonia.—**hart's′-tongue** *n.* a common British fern [O.E. *heort*].
hartbeest, hartebeest (hart′bēst) *n.* a large S. African antelope [Dut.].
harum-scarum (har′um-skār′um) *a.* reckless; wild;—*n.* a rash person [perh. *hare*, and *scare*].
harvest (har′vest) *n.* (season for) gathering crops; the crop itself;—*v.t.* to gather in.—**har′vester** *n.* one who harvests; a reaping-machine.—**har′vest-bug** *n.* mite, found in fruit-trees, grasses, etc. in late summer.—**har′vest-home** *n.* bringing home of harvest; a social gathering to celebrate this [O.E. *haerfest*, autumn].
has (haz) 3rd sing. pres. indic. of the verb **have**.—**has′-been** *n.* (*Colloq.*) a person long past his best.
hash (hash) *v.t.* to chop into small pieces; to mince;—*n.* that which is hashed; a dish of hashed meat and vegetables; (*Slang*) a mess [Fr. *hacher*, to chop].
hashish, hasheesh (hash′ēsh) *n.* the leaves of the Indian hemp prepared for smoking or chewing as an intoxicant [Ar.].
hasp (hasp) *n.* a clasp passing over a staple for fastening a door, etc.;—*v.t.* to fasten with a hasp [O.E. *haepse*].
hassock (has′ok) *n.* a padded cushion for kneeling on in church; a tuft of grass [O.E. *hassuc*, coarse grass].
haste (hāst) *n.* speed; quickness; hurry;—*v.i.* to hasten.—**hasten** (hā′sn) *v.t.* to urge forward; to hurry on; to accelerate;—*v.i.* to be in a hurry.—**hast′ener** *n.*—**hast′y** *a.* speedy; quick; over-eager; rash; passionate.—**hast′ily** *adv.*—**hast′iness** *n.* [O.Fr. *haste*].
hat (hat) *n.* covering for head, usually with brim; red hat of cardinal, hence, dignity of a cardinal.—**hat′ter** *n.* one who makes, or sells hats.—**hat′-trick** *n.* in cricket, the taking of three wickets with successive balls; any three successive wins.—**top hat,** a silk hat with a high crown.—**to pass round the hat,** to make a collection, esp. to pay expenses [O.E. *haet*].
hatch (hach) *v.t.* to bring forth young birds from the shell; to incubate; to plot;—*v.i.* to come forth from the shell;—*n.* the act of hatching; the brood hatched.—**hatch′er** *n.*—**hatch′ery** *n.* a place for hatching eggs, esp. of fish [M.E. *hacchen*].
hatch (hach) *n.* the lower half of a divided door; an opening in a door or wall; the boards, etc. covering a hatchway; the hatchway itself.—**hatch′way** *n.* a square opening in a ship's deck through which cargo, etc. is lowered [O.E. *haec*, a gate].
hatch (hach) *v.t.* to shade with lines [Fr. *hacher*, to chop].
hatchet (hach′et) *n.* a small axe with a short handle.—**hatch′et-faced** *a.* having a face with sharp features.—**to bury the hatchet,** to make peace [Fr. *hache*, an axe].
hatchment (hach′ment) *n.* a lozenge-shaped tablet having on it the armorial bearings of a deceased person, placed in front of the house, or on his tomb after the funeral [corrupt. of *achievement*].
hate (hāt) *v.t.* to dislike strongly; to bear malice to; to detest; *n.* strong dislike; aversion; hatred.—**hate′ful** *a.* full of hate; feeling hate; detestable; ugly.—**hate′fully** *adv.*—**hate′fulness** *n.*—**hat′er** *n.*—**hat′red** *n.* aversion; active ill-will; enmity; animosity; hate [O.E. *hatian*, to hate; *hete*, hatred].
hauberk (haw′berk) *n.* a tunic of ringed mail extending below the knees; a habergeon [O.H. Ger. *hals*, the neck; *bergan*, to protect].
haughty (haw′ti) *a.* proud.—**haugh′tily** *adv.*—**haugh′tiness** *n.* [Fr. *haut*, high, fr. L. *altus*].
haul (hawl) *v.t.* to pull with force; to drag; to steer a ship closer to the wind; to close-haul;—*v.i.* of wind, to shift, to veer;—*n.* a hauling; a catch; good profit, gain, or acquisition.—**haul′age** *n.* the act of pulling; the charge for hauling; the carrying of goods, material, etc. by road.—**haul′er** *n.* one who hauls.—**haul′ier** *n.* a carter; a mine-worker who hauls coal to the foot of the shaft.—**close′-hauled** *a.* (*Naut.*) of a ship, with the sails trimmed to keep her close to the wind [Fr. *haler*].
haulm (hawm) *n.* See **halm.**
haunch (hawnsh) *n.* the part of the body between the ribs and thighs; the hip; a leg and loin of venison, etc. [Fr. *hanche*].
haunt (hawnt) *v.t.* to frequent; of ghosts, to visit regularly;—*v.i.* to loiter about a place;—*n.* a place of frequent resort.—**haunt′ed** *a.* frequently visited by ghosts [Fr. *hanter*, to frequent].
hautboy (hō′boi) *n.* an older form of the oboe [Fr. *haut*, high; *bois*, wood].
hauteur (ō-tẹr′) *n.* haughtiness; haughty manner or spirit; arrogance [Fr.].
Havana (ha-va′nạ) *n.* a fine brand of cigar [named from *Havana*, the capital of Cuba].
have (hav) *v.t.* to hold or possess; to be possessed or affected with; to seize; to bring forth; to produce; to enjoy; to be obliged (to do); (as an auxiliary verb, forms the perfect and other tenses);—*pr.p.* **hav′ing.**—*pa.p.* and *pa.t.* **had** [O.E. *habban*].
haven (hā′vn) *n.* a bay or inlet giving shelter for ships; a harbour [O.E. *haefen*].
haver (hāv′ẹr) *v.i.* (*Scot.*) to talk nonsense.
haversack (hav′ẹr-sak) *n.* a soldier's canvas ration-bag; a similar bag for travellers [Ger. *Habersack*, an oat-sack].
havoc (hav′ok) *n.* pillage; devastation; ruin [orig. to 'cry havoc,' to give the signal for pillage; O.Fr. *havot*, plunder].
haw (haw) *n.* the red berry of the hawthorn; a hedge; an enclosed garden.—**haw′finch** *n.* a small bird of the finch family.—**haw′thorn** *n.* a thorny shrub much used for hedges [O.E. *haga*, an enclosure].
haw (haw) *n.* a hesitation in speech;—*v.i.* to speak hesitatingly; to drawl.—**haw′-haw** *v.i.* to laugh boisterously [imit.].
hawk (hawk) *n.* a bird of prey of the falcon family;—*v.t.* and *i.* to hunt birds with hawks, as in falconry.—**hawk′er** *n.* a falconer.—**hawk′ing** *n.* the sport of hunting birds with hawks; falconry [O.E. *hafoc*].
hawk (hawk) *v.i.* to clear the throat noisily; to force up phlegm [imit. origin].
hawk (hawk) *v.t.* to carry about wares for sale; to peddle.—**hawk′er** *n.* an itinerant dealer; a pedlar [Dut. *heuker*, a huckster].
hawk (hawk) *n.* a plasterer's tool for holding plaster [etym. unknown].
hawse (hawz) *n.* the part of a ship's bows with holes for cables [O.E. *heals*, the prow].
hawser (haw′zẹr) *n.* a large rope or small cable [O.Fr. *haucier*, to raise].
hay (hā) *n.* grass mown and dried for fodder.—**hay′-box** *n.* box filled with hay in which

heated food is left to finish cooking.—**hay'-cock** *n.* a conical heap of hay.—**hay'-fev'er** *n.* irritation of the mucous membrane of the nose (generally by pollen from hay grasses).—**hay'-mak'er** *n.* one who cuts and dries grass for hay.—**hay'-rick** *n.*—**hay'-stack** *n.* a large pile of hay with ridged or pointed tip.—**hay'-seed** *n.* grass seed; (*Colloq.*) a rustic; a country bumpkin [O.E. *hieg*].

hazard (haz'ard) *n.* a game played with dice; chance; a chance; risk; danger; (*Golf*) an inclusive term for all obstacles on the golf-course;—*v.t.* to expose to risk; to run the risk of.—**haz'ardous** *a.* dangerous; adventurous.—**haz'ardously** *adv.* [Fr. *hasard*].

haze (hāz) *n.* a misty appearance in the air; mental obscurity.—**haz'y** *a.*—**haz'ily** *adv.*—**haz'iness** *n.* [etym. uncertain].

haze (hāz) *v.t.* to torment or punish by the imposition of disagreeable tasks; to play tricks on [O.Fr. *haser*, to annoy].

hazel (hā'zl) *n.* a nut-bearing bush or small tree; the reddish-brown colour of the nuts;—*a.* of this colour.—**ha'zel-nut** *n.* the nut of the hazel-tree.—**ha'zelly** *a.* of reddish-brown colour [O.E. *haesel*].

he (hē) *pron.* the 3rd pers. sing. masc. pronoun.—**he'-man** *n.* (*Colloq.*) a very virile man [O.E.].

head (hed) *n.* the upper part of a man's or animal's body; the brain; intellectual capacity; upper part of anything; the top; the chief part; a chief; a leader; progress; a section of a chapter; the source of a stream; a cape or headland; a crisis; freedom to go on;—*a.* chief; principal; of wind, contrary;—*v.t.* to lead; to be at the head of; to direct; to go in front, so as to hinder; hence, to check; to hit (a ball) with the head;—*v.i.* to originate; to form a head; to make for.—**head'y** *a.* impetuous; wilful; apt to intoxicate.—**head'ily** *adv.*—**head'iness** *n.* rashness; obstinacy.—**headache** (hed'āk) *n.* a nerve-pain in the head.—**head'achy** *a.*—**head'-dress** *n.* ornamental covering for the head.—**head'er** *n.* a plunge, head foremost into water; in building, a brick laid so that its end forms part of the surface of the wall.—**head'gear** *n.* ornamental covering for the head; head-dress; a hat.—**head'-hunt'ing** *n.* raiding to procure human heads as trophies.—**head'ing** *n.* the act of providing with a head; a title.—**head'lamp** *n.* a headlight.—**head'land** *n.* a cape; a promontory.—**head'light** *n.* a strong light carried on the front of a locomotive, motor-vehicle, etc.—**head'-line** *n.* a summary of news in large print in a newspaper; a caption.—**head'long** *adv.* with the head foremost; rashly;—*a.* steep; rash; reckless.—**head'man** *n.* the chief, esp. of a tribe.—**head'-mas'ter, head'-mis'tress** *n.* the chief master or mistress of a school; the principal.—**head'most** *a.* most advanced; foremost.—**head'-on** *a.* meeting head to head; head first.—**head'-phone** *n.* a telephone-receiver to clip on head (usually in *pl.*).—**head'-piece** *n.* a helmet; the head; brain-power; ornamental engraving at beginning of book or chapter.—**head'quar'ters** *n.pl.* (*Mil.*) the residence of a commander-in-chief, general, or other important officer; a centre of operations.—**head'-race** *n.* the channel leading water to a mill-wheel.—**head'-room** *n.* the amount of space between the head and the roof.—**heads'man** *n.* an executioner.—**head'stall** *n.* the part of the bridle that fits round the head.—**head'stone** *n.* the principal stone of a building; a memorial stone placed at the head of a grave.—**head'strong** *a.* obstinate; stubborn; self-willed.—**head'way** *n.* progress made by a ship in motion; hence, progress of any kind.—**head over ears,** completely; deeply.—**to keep one's head,** to keep calm [O.E. *heafod*].

heal (hēl) *v.t.* to make whole; to restore to health; to make well;—*v.i.* to become sound.—**heal'er** *n.*—**heal'ing** *a.* tending to cure;—*n.* the act or process by which a cure is effected [O.E. *haelan*, fr. *hal*, whole].

health (helth) *n.* soundness of body; general condition of the body; a toast drunk in a person's honour.—**health'y** *a.* having, or tending to give, health; sound; vigorous; hale; wholesome.—**health'ily** *adv.*—**health'iness** *n.*—**health'ful** *a.* free from disease; healthy [O.E. *haelth*, fr. *hal*, whole].

heap (hēp) *n.* a number of things lying one on another; a pile; a mass; a great quantity;—*v.t.* to throw or lay in a heap [O.E. *heap*].

hear (hēr) *v.t.* to perceive with the ear; to listen to; to heed; (*Law*) to try (a case);—*v.i.* to perceive sound; to learn by report.—*pr.p.* **hear'ing**.—*pa.p.* and *pa.t.* **heard** (herd).—**hear'er** *n.*—**hear'ing** *n.* the act of perceiving sound; the sense by which sound is perceived; audience; earshot.—**hear'say** *n.* rumour; report; common talk.—**hear! hear!** *interj.* indicating approval of a speaker's words or opinions [O.E. *hyran*].

hearken (hàr'kn) *v.i.* to listen to [O.E. *heorcnian*].

hearse (hers) *n.* a carriage for a coffin [Fr. *herse*, a harrow].

heart (hàrt) *n.* the hollow, muscular organ which makes the blood circulate; the seat or source of life; the seat of emotions and affections; the inner part of anything; mind; soul; courage; warmth or affection; a playing-card marked with a figure of a heart.—**heart'y** *a.* cordial; friendly; vigorous; in good health; of a meal, satisfying the appetite.—**heart'ily** *adv.*—**heart'iness** *n.*—**heart'less** *a.* without a heart; unfeeling.—**heart'en** *v.t.* to encourage; to incite; to stimulate; to inspirit.—**heart'ache** *n.* sorrow; anguish; mental pang.—**heart'-blood** *n.* blood in the cavity of the heart; life; essence.—**heart'break** *n.* overpowering sorrow.—**heart'-brok'en** *a.* overwhelmed with grief.—**heart'burn** *n.* a form of dyspepsia characterised by an acrid, burning sensation in the stomach.—**heart'burning** *n.* discontent; secret enmity;—*a.* causing discontent.—**heart'-felt** *a.* deeply felt; intense; sincere.—**heart's'-ease,** the common pansy.—**heart'-sick** *a.* depressed; disgusted.—**heart'-sink'ing** *n.* despondency.—**heart'some** *a.* inspiring; exhilarating.—**heart'strings** *n.pl.* (*Fig.*) affections; emotions.—**at heart,** at bottom; inwardly.—**by heart,** by rote; by memory.—**to wear one's heart on one's sleeve,** to show one's feelings openly [O.E. *heorte*].

hearth (hàrth) *n.* the fireside; the house itself; home [O.E. *heorth*].

heat (hēt) *n.* hotness; a sensation of this; hot weather or climate; warmth of feeling; anger; excitement; sexual excitement in animals, esp. female; (*Sport*) a race to decide the persons to compete in a deciding one;—*v.t.* to make hot; to excite;—*v.i.* to become hot.—**heat'ed** *a.* (*Fig.*) of argument, etc. passionate; intense.—**heat'edly** *adv.*—**heat'er** *n.*—**heat flash,** the intense heat radiation emitted by an atomic bomb at the moment of explosion.—**heat'-u'nit** *n.* the amount of heat required to raise the temperature of one pound of water one degree.—**heat'-wave** *n.* a spell of abnormally hot weather [O.E. *haete*].

heath (hēth) *n.* waste land; moor; shrub of genus Erica.—**heath'y** *a.*—**heath'-bell** *n.* heather bell.—**heath'-cock** *n.* black grouse [O.E. *haeth*].

heathen (hē'THn) *n.* one who is not an adherent of a religious system; an infidel; a pagan; (*Colloq.*) an irreligious person;—*a.* **hea'thenish** *a.*—**hea'thenism** *n.* the religious system of a heathen people.—**hea'thendom** *n.* the parts of the world where heathenism prevails [O.E. *haethen*].

heather (heTH'er) *n.* a small plant of the genus Erica, bearing purple, and sometimes white, bell-shaped flowers; heath; ling;

a. of the colour of heather.—**heath'er-bell** *n.* the flower of the plant [fr. *heath*].

heave (hēv) *v.t.* to lift with effort; to throw (something heavy); to utter (a sigh); to pull on a rope, etc.; to haul; (*Geol.*) to displace;—*v.i.* to rise and fall in alternate motions, e.g. of heavy breathing, of waves, etc.; to try to vomit;—*n.* a heaving; an effort to lift something; a rise and fall; an attempt to vomit.— *pr.p.* **heav'ing**.—*pa.p.* and *pa.t.* **heaved** or **hove**.—**to heave to**, to bring a ship to a standstill [O.E. *hebban*].

heaven (hev'n) *n.* the sky; the upper air; the abode of God; God Himself; a place of bliss; supreme happiness.—**heav'enly** *a.* pert. to, or like, heaven; pure; divine; (*Colloq.*) excellent.—*adv.* in a heavenly manner.—**heav'enliness** *n.* —**heav'enward, heav'enwards** *adv.* toward heaven.—**in the seventh heaven**, in a state of supreme bliss [O.E. *heofon*].

Heaviside layer (hev'i-sīd lā'er) *n.* the upper part of the atmosphere, which reflects wireless waves [fr. Oliver *Heaviside*, English physicist, 1850-1925].

heavy (hev'i) *a.* weighty; striking or falling with force; large in amount, as a debt; rough, as the weather; abundant, as rain; clayey, as soil; sad; hard to bear; difficult; dull; sluggish; serious; over compact; indigestible.—**heav'ily** *adv.*—**heav'iness** *n.*—**heav'y-hand'ed** *a.* awkward; severe; oppressive.—**heavy'-head'ed** *a.* drowsy.—**heav'y-heart'ed** *a.* sad.—**heavy water** (*Chem.*) water in which the normal hydrogen content has been replaced by heavy hydrogen. —**heav'y-weight** *n.* (*Boxing*) a boxer exceeding 12 st. 7 lb. in weight [O.E. *hefig*, fr. *hebban*, to heave].

hebdomad (heb'dom-ad) *n.* a group of seven things; a week.—**hebdom'adal** *a.* weekly.—**hebdom'adally** *adv.*—**hebdom'adary** *n.* a member of a chapter whose week it is to officiate in the choir [Gk. *hebdomas*, seventh].

Hebrew (hē'broo) *n.* one of the ancient inhabitants of Palestine; an Israelite; a Jew; the language.—*fem.* **He'brewess**.—**Hebraic** (hē-brā'ik) *a.* pert. to the Hebrews, or to their language.—**Hebra'ically** *adv.* after the manner of the Hebrew language; from right to left.—**he'braist** *n.* one versed in Hebrew [Heb. *'ibri,'* one from across the river (Euphrates)].

hecatomb (hek'a-tom) *n.* any large number of victims [Gk. *hekaton*, a hundred; *bous*, an ox].

heckle (hek'l) *n.* a comb for cleaning flax;—*v.t.* to comb with a hackle; to ask awkward questions of a speaker at a public meeting [origin uncertain].

hect-, hecto- (hekt, hek'to) *prefix*, fr. Gk. *hekaton*, one hundred, combining to form derivatives used in the metric system.—**hec'togram, hec'togramme** *n.* a weight of 100 grammes=3.527 ounces.—**hectolitre, hectoliter** (hek'to-lēt-er) *n.* a unit of capacity, containing 100 litres=22.01 imperial gallons.—**hectometre** (hek'to-mē-ter), **hec'tometer** *n.* a unit of length =100 metres=109.363 yards.

hectic (hek'tik) *a.* flush; consumptive; affected with hectic fever; (*Colloq.*) exciting; wild.—**hectic fever**, a fever attendant on certain protracted wasting diseases [Gk. *hektikos*, habitual].

hectograph (hek'to-graf) *n.* an apparatus for multiplying copies of writings [Gk. *hekaton*, a hundred; *graphein*, to write].

Hector (hek'tor) *n.* the chief hero of Troy in war with Greeks.—**hec'tor** *n.* a bully; a brawler; a blusterer;—*v.t.* and *i.* to bully; to bluster.

heddle (hed'l) *n.* in weaving, one of sets of parallel, doubled threads which compose the fittings employed to guide the warp threads to the lathe or batten [Scand.].

hedge (hej) *n.* a fence of bushes; a protecting barrier;—*v.t.* to enclose with a hedge; to fence, as fields; to obstruct; to hem in;—*v.i.* to make or trim hedges; to bet on both sides so as to guard against loss; to shift; to shuffle; to skulk.—**hedg'ing** *n.*—**hedg'y** *a.*—**hedge'-bill** *n.* a special kind of hook for trimming hedges.—**hedge'hog** *n.* a small quadruped, covered on the upper part of its body with prickles or spines.—**hedge'-hopp'ing** *n.* (*World War* 2) in aviation, flying very low. —**hedge'row** *n.* a row of bushes forming a hedge.—**hedge'-sparr'ow** *n.* a small bird of sparrow family [O.E. *hecg*].

hedonism (hē'do-nizm) *n.* the doctrine that pleasure is the chief good.—**he'donist** *n.* [Gk. *hēdonē*, pleasure].

heed (hēd) *v.t.* to take notice of; to care for; to mind; to observe;—*n.* attention; notice; care; caution.—**heed'ful** *a.* watchful; cautious; wary; attentive.—**heed'fully** *adv.*—**heed'fulness** *n.*—**heed'less** *a.* inattentive; careless; thoughtless [O.E. *hedan*].

heehaw (hē'haw) *v.i.* to bray, of an ass [imit. origin].

heel (hēl) *n.* hinder part of foot, shoe, boot, or stocking; hinder part of anything; a spur; (*U.S. Slang*) an undesirable person;—*v.t.* to add a heel to, as in knitting; to touch ground, or a ball, with the heel.—**heel'-ball** *n.* a waxy composition used by shoemakers for polishing the heels and soles of boots.—**heel'-tap** *n.* small amount of liquor left in bottom of glass.—**heel of Achilles** (*Fig.*) a vulnerable part.—**down at heel**, slovenly; seedy; ill-shod [O.E. *hela*].

heel (hēl) *v.i.* of a ship, to lean to one side; to incline;—*v.t.* to cause to do this [O.E. *hieldan*, to incline].

heft (heft) *v.t.* to heave up; to lift; to try the weight by lifting.—**heft'y** *a.* vigorous; stalwart [fr. *heave*].

hegemony (hē-gem'on-i, hē'jem-on-i) *n.* leadership; predominance.—**hegemon'ic** *a.* [Gk. *hēgemōn*, a leader].

hegira, hejira (hej'i-ra) *n.* Mohammed's flight from Mecca to Medina, A.D. 622, from which is dated the Mohammedan era [Ar. *hijrah*, flight].

heifer (hef'er) *n.* a young cow that has not had a calf [O.E. *heahfore*].

height (hīt) *n.* measurement from base to top; quality of being high; a high position; a small hill; eminence.—**height'en** *v.t.* to make high or higher; to intensify [O.E. *hiehthu*].

heinous (hā'nus) *a.* extremely wicked; atrocious; odious [Fr. *haineux*, hateful].

heir (ār) *n.* (*fem.* **heir'ess**) a person legally entitled to succeed to property or rank.—**heir'-appa'rent** *n.* the person who is first in the line of succession to an estate, crown, etc.—**heir'-at-law** *n.* the legal heir.—**heir'loom** *n.* article of personal property which descends to heir along with inheritance; a thing that has been in a family for generations [L. *heres*].

hejira See **hegira**.

held (held) *pa.p.* and *pa.t.* of **hold**.

helical (hel'i-kal) *a.* pert. to a helix; spiral.—**hel'icopter** *n.* an aeroplane which can rise or descend vertically; an autogyro.—**hel'idrome** *n.* an aerodrome for helicopters [Gk. *helix*, spiral; *pteron*, a wing].

heliocentric (hē-li-ō-sen'trik) *a.* (*Astron.*) taking the sun as centre. Also **heliocen'trical** [Gk. *hēlios*, the sun; *kentron*, the centre].

heliogram (hē'li-ō-gram) *n.* a message transmitted by heliograph [Gk. *hēlios*, the sun; *gramma*, a writing].

heliograph (hē'li-ō-graf) *n.* signalling apparatus employing a mirror to reflect the sun's rays; an instrument for photographing the sun;—*v.t.* to signal by means of a heliograph.—**heliograph'ic** *a.*—**heliog'raphy** *n.* [Gk. *hēlios*, the sun; *graphein*, to write].

heliolatry (hē-li-ol'a-tri) *n.* sun-worship.—**heliol'ater** *n.* a sun-worshipper.—**heliol'atrous** *a.* [Gk. *hēlios*, the sun; *latreia*, worship].

heliometer (hē-li-om'e-ter) *n.* instrument for

measuring magnitude of sun etc. [Gk. *helios*, sun; *metron*, a measure].
helioscope (hē′li-ō-skōp) *n.* a form of telescope adapted for viewing the sun without dazzling the eyes.—**helioscop′ic** *a.* [Gk. *hēlios*, the sun; *skopein*, to look].
heliotrope (hē′li-ō-trōp) *n.* a plant with fragrant purple flowers; the colour of the flowers, or their scent; a bloodstone.—**heliot′ropism** *n.* (*Bot.*) the tendency of plants to direct their growth towards light [Gk. *hēlios*, the sun; *tropos*, a turn].
helium (hē′li-um) *n.* (*Chem.*) an inert, non-inflammable, and very light gas [Gk. *hēlios*, the sun].
helix (hē′liks) *n.* a spiral, e.g. wire in a coil, or a corkscrew; (*Zool.*) a genus including the snail; (*Anat.*) the outer rim of the ear.—*pl.* **helices** (hē′li-sēz).—**hel′ical** *a.* spiral [Gk. *helix*, a spiral].
hell (hel) *n.* the abode of the damned; the lower regions; a place or state of vice, misery, or torture.—**hell′ish** *a.* infernal.—**hell′ishly** *adv.*—**hell′ishness** *n.* [O.E. *hel*].
hellebore (hel′e-bōr) *n.* a plant formerly thought to cure madness; (*Bot.*) a genus of plants, including the Christmas rose; (*Med.*) a poisonous drug [Gk *helleboros*].
Hellene (hel′ēn) *n.* an ancient Greek; a subject of modern Greece.—*pl.* **Hell′enes**, Greeks.—**Hellen′ic** *a.* pert. to the inhabitants of Greece.—**Hell′enism** *n.* the adoption of the manners, culture, and language of the Ancient Greeks; hence, Grecian culture; a Greek idiom.—**Hell′enist** *n.* a Greek scholar.—**Hellenist′ic** *a.* [Gk. *Hellēn*].
helm (helm) *n.* (*Naut.*) a tiller or wheel for turning the rudder of a ship; (*Fig.*) control; guidance;—*v.t.* to steer; to control.—**helms′man** *n.* a steersman [O.E. *helma*].
helm (helm) *n.* (*Arch.*) a helmet.—**hel′met** *n.* a defensive covering for the head; the upper part of a retort [O.E. *helm*].
helminth (hel′minth) *n.* an intestinal worm.—**helmin′thic** *a.*—**helmin′thoid** *a.* worm-shaped.—**helminthol′ogy** *n.* the natural history of worms [Gk. *helmins*, a worm].
helot (hē′lot, hel′ot) *n.* a serf in ancient Sparta; a slave; a servile person.—**he′lotism** *n.* slavery.—**he′lotry** *n.* serfdom; slavery; bondsmen [Gk. *Heilōtēs*].
help (help) *v.t.* to aid; to assist; to support; to succour; to relieve; to prevent;—*v.i.* to lend aid; to be useful;—*n.* the act of helping; one who, or that which, helps; aid; assistance; support; a domestic servant.—**help′er** *n.*—**help′ful** *a.* helping; assisting; useful; obliging.—**help′fulness** *n.*—**help′ing** *n.* a portion of food.—**help′less** *a.* not able to take care of oneself; weak; dependent.—**help′lessly** *adv.*—**help′lessness** *n.*—**help′mate** *n.* an assistant; a partner; a wife or husband.—Also **help′meet** [O.E. *helpan*].
helter-skelter (hel-tẹr′skel′tẹr) *adv.* in disorder; in hurry and confusion.
helve (helv) *n.* the handle of a tool, esp. of an axe or hatchet [O.E. *hielfe*].
Helvetia (hel-vē′shạ) *n.* the Latin, and political, name for Switzerland.—**Helvetian** (hel-vē′shạn) *a.* pert. to Switzerland.
hem (hem) *n.* border, esp. one made by sewing;—*v.t.* to fold over and sew down; to edge.—*pr.p.* **hem′ming**.—*pa.p.* and *pa.t.* **hemmed** [O.E.].
hem (hem) *interj.* and *n.* a kind of suppressed cough, calling attention or expressing doubt;—*v.i.* to make the sound.
hema-, hemo- See **haema**.
hemi-, (hem′i) *prefix* from Greek *hēmi-*, half, combining to form derivatives.
hemisphere (hem′i-sfēr) *n.* a half sphere; half of the celestial sphere; half of the earth.—**hemispher′ic, hemispher′ical** *a.*
hemistich (hem′i-stik) *n.* half a line of verse.—**hemistich′al** *a.*
hemlock (hem′lok) *n.* a poisonous umbelliferous plant used medicinally as a sedative; the poisonous drug *conium* [O.E. *hemlic*].
hemp (hemp) *n.* a plant whose fibre is used in the manufacture of coarse cloth, ropes, cables, etc.; hashish, a narcotic drug, is prepared from Indian hemp.—**hemp′en** *a.* [O.E. *henep*].
hen (hen) *n.* the female of any bird, esp. the domestic fowl; the female of certain crustaceans, e.g. the lobster, crab, etc.—**hen′coop** *n.* a large cage for poultry.—**hen′-harr′ier** *n.* a kind of falcon, having a ruff on the head.—**hen′-part′y** *n.* (*Slang*) a social gathering of women only.—**hen′-peck** *v.t.* to domineer over a husband [O.E. *henn*].
hence (hens) *adv.* from this point; for this reason;—*interj.* go away! begone!—**hence′-forth, hencefor′ward** *adv.* from now; from this time [M.E. *hennes*].
henchman (hensh′man) *n.* a servant; a loyal supporter [M.E. *henxt-man*, a groom].
hendecagon (hen-dek′ạ-gon) *n.* a plane figure having eleven sides.—**hendecag′onal**.—**hen′decasyllable** *n.* a line of poetry having eleven syllables [Gk. *hendeka*, eleven; *gōniā*, an angle; *sullabē*, a syllable].
henna (hen′ạ) *n.* the Egyptian privet; a dye made from it [Ar. *hinna*].
hepatic (hep-at′ik) *a.* pert. to the liver; liver-coloured [Gk. *hēpar*, the liver].
hepta- (hep′ta) *prefix* from Greek *hepta*, seven, combining to form derivatives.—**hep′tad** *n.* a group of seven.—**hep′tagon** *n.* a plane figure with seven sides.—**heptag′onal** *a.*
heptameter (hep-tam′e-tẹr) *n.* a line of verse of seven feet.
heptangular (hep-tang′gū-lạr) *a.* having seven angles [Gk. *hepta*, seven; E. *angular*].
heptarchy (hep′tar-ki) *n.* government by seven persons; the country governed by them.—**hep′tarch** *n.* a ruler in a heptarchy.—**heptarch′ic** *a.* [Gk. *hepta*, seven; *archein*, to rule].
heptasyllabic (hep-tạ-sil-ab′ik) *a.* seven-syllabled [Gk. *hepta*, seven].
her (hẹr) *pron.* the objective case of the pronoun **she**;—also, the possessive case used adjectivally.—**hers** *pron.* the absolute possessive case.—**herself** *pron.* emphatic. and reflexive form of *she* and *her* [O.E. fr. *hire*, gen. and dat. of *heo*, she].
herald (her′ạld) *n.* an officer who makes royal proclamations, arranges ceremonies, keeps records of those entitled to armorial bearings, etc.; a messenger; an envoy; a forerunner.—**heral′dic** *a.*—**her′aldry,** *n.* the art or office of a herald; the science of recording genealogies and blazoning armorial bearings [O.Fr. *herault*].
herb (hẹrb) *n.* a plant with a soft stem which dies down after flowering; a plant of which parts are used for medicine, food, or scent.—**herbaceous** (hẹr-bā′shus) *a.* pert. to herbs.—**herb′age** *n.* herbs; green food for cattle.—**herb′al** *a.* pert. to herbs;—*n.* a book on herbs.—**herb′alist** *n.* writer on, dealer in, herbs.—**herbarium** (hẹr-bā′ri-um) *n.* a collection of specimens of dried herbs and plants.—*pl.* **herba′riums, herba′ria**.—**herbif′erous** *a.* bearing herbs.—**herbiv′orous** *a.* eating, or living on, herbs.—**herb′orist** *n.* a herbalist.—**herb′-Rob′ert** *n.* stinking crane's-bill, a kind of geranium [L. *herba*, grass].
Hercules [hẹr′kū-lēz) *n.* (*Myth.*) Latin name of Greek hero Heracles distinguished for his prodigious strength; hence any person of extraordinary strength and size.—**Hercule′an** *a.*
herd (hẹrd) *n.* a number of animals feeding or travelling together; a drove of cattle; a large number of people; a herdsman;—*v.i.* to go in a herd;—*v.t.* to tend (a herd); to drive together.—**herds′man** *n.* one who tends cattle [O.E. *hirde*].
here (hēr) *adv.* in this place; at or to this point (opposed to *there*).—**here′about, here′-**

abouts *adv.* about this place.—**hereaf'ter** *adv.* after this;—*n.* a future existence.—**hereby'** *adv.* not far off; by means of this; by this.—**herein'** *adv.* in this.—**hereon'** *adv.* on this; hereupon.—**hereto'** *adv.* to this.—**heretobefore'** *adv.* up to the present; formerly.—**herewith'** *adv.* with this [O.E. *her*].

heredity (he-red'i-ti) *n.* the transmission of characteristic traits and qualities from parents to offspring.—**hered'itable** *a.* heritable.—**heredit'ament** *n.* (*Law*) property that may be inherited.—**hered'itary** *a.* descending by inheritance [L. *heres*, an heir].

heresy (her'e-si) *n.* opinion contrary to orthodox opinion, teaching, or belief.—**heresiarch** (he-rē'zi-ark) *n.* the originator or leader of a heresy.—**her'etic** *n.* one holding opinions contrary to orthodox faith.—**heret'ical** *a.*—**heret'ically** *adv.* [Gk. *hairesis*, a choice, a school of thought].

heritable (her'i-ta-bl) *a.* that can be inherited; attached to the property or house, as opposed to movable.—**her'itage** *n.* that which may be or is inherited.—**her'itor** *n.* one who inherits; (*Scot.*) a proprietor or landholder in a parish [L. *heres*, an heir].

Hermaphroditos (her-maf-rō-dī'tos) *n.* (*Myth.*) the son of *Hermes* and *Aphrodite* who, became joined in one body with a nymph called Salmacis.—**hermaphrodite** (her-maf'rō-dīt) *n.* and *a.* a person or animal with the characteristics of both sexes; having normally both sexual organs.—**hermaphrodit'ic, hermaphrodit'ical** *a.*—**hermaph'rodism, hermaph'roditism** *n.*

hermetic (her-met'ik) *a.* pert. to doctrines or writings of an occult or esoteric character; pert. to alchemy or magic; magical.—**hermetic sealing,** the air-tight closing of a vessel by fusion [Gk. *Hermes*].

hermit (her'mit) *n.* a person living in seclusion, esp. from religious motives; a recluse; an anchoret.—**her'mitage** *n.* the abode of a hermit [Gk. *erēmitēs*, fr. *erēmos*, solitary].

hernia (her'ni-a) *n.* (*Med.*) the external protrusion of any internal part through the enclosing membrane (commonly called rupture) [L.].

hero (hē'rō) *n.* (*fem.* **heroine** (her'ō-in)) an illustrious warrior; one greatly regarded for his achievements or qualities; the chief man in a poem, play, or story.—*pl.* **he'roes.**—**he'roic** *a.* pert. to a hero; bold; courageous; illustrious; magnanimous; narrating the exploits of heroes, as a poem; denoting the verse or measure in such poems. Also **hero'ical.**—**hero'ically** *adv.*—**hero'ics** *n.pl.* high-flown language; bombastic talk.—**heroism** (her'ō-izm) *n.* courage; valour; bravery; gallantry [Gk. *herōs*, a demigod, a hero].

heroin (her'ō-in) *n.* (*Med.*) a drug used as a sedative [Ger. trade name].

heron, hern (her'on, hern) *n.* a long-legged wading bird.—**her'onry** *n.* a place where herons breed.—**her'onshaw, hern'shaw** *n.* a young heron [O.Fr. *hairon*; Fr. *héron*].

herpes (her'pēz) *n.* a skin disease.—**herpet'ic** *a.* [Gk. fr. *herpein*, to creep].

herpetology (her-pet-ol'o-ji) *n.* the natural history of reptiles [Gk. *herpein*, to creep].

Herr (her) *n.* lord; master; the German equivalent of Mr.—*pl.* **Herr'en.**—**Herrenvolk** (her'en-fōk) *n.* In Germany, esp. in Nazi ideology, a people of superior qualities [Ger. *Herrenvolk*, master race].

herring (her'ing) *n.* a familiar sea-fish, moving in shoals, much used as a food.—**herr'ing-bone** *n.* a zig-zag pattern.—**red herring,** herring cured and dried by a special process; (*Fig.*) subject deliberately introduced into a discussion to divert criticism from main issue [O.E. *haering*].

hers See **her.**

hesitate (hez'i-tāt) *v.i.* to feel or show indecision; to hold back; to stammer.—**hes'itant** *a.* pausing; slow to decide.—**hes'itance, hes'itancy** *n.*—**hes'itative** *a.* showing hesitation.—**hesita'tion** *n.* doubt; indecision.—**hes'itantly, hes'itatingly** *adv.* [L. *haesitare*, fr. *haerere*, to stick fast].

Hesperus (hes'per-us) *n.* the planet Venus as the evening star.—**Hesperian** (hes-pē'ri-an) *a.* western [Gk. *hesperos*, evening].

Hessian (hes'i-an) *a.* pert. to *Hesse*, in Germany;—*n.* a native of Hesse; coarse cloth made of jute.—**Hessian boots,** high boots first worn by Hessian troops.

heterodox (het'er-o-doks) *a.* contrary to accepted opinion, esp. in theology; not orthodox; heretical.—**het'erodoxy** *n.* [Gk. *heteros*, different; *doxa*, an opinion].

heterodyne (het'er-o-dīn) *n.* (*Wireless*) in reception, a method by which a wave of slightly different frequency is imposed on a transmitted wave, giving rise to a 'beat' which is audible after rectification [Gk. *heteros*, different; *dunamis*, power].

heterogeneous (het-er-o-jē'ne-us) *a.* composed of diverse elements; differing in kind; dissimilar.—**heterogene'ity, heteroge'neousness** *n.* [Gk. *heteros*, different; *genos*, kind].

heterogenesis (het-er-o-jen'e-sis) *n.* the production of offspring bearing no resemblance to the parents; (*Biol.*) spontaneous generation.—**heterogenet'ic** *a.* [Gk. *heteros*, different; *genesis*, generation].

heterosexual (het-er-o-sek'sū-al) *a.* directed towards the opposite sex [Gk. *heteros*, different; L. *sexus*].

hew (hū) *v.t.* to chop or cut with an axe or sword; to cut in pieces; to shape or form.—*pa.p.* **hewed,** or **hewn.**—*pa.t.* **hewed.**—**hew'er** *n.* [O.E. *heawan*].

hexa- (hek'sa) *prefix* from Gk. *hex*, six, combining to form derivatives, e.g. **hex'agon** *n.* a plane figure having six sides and six angles.—**hexag'onal** *a.*—**hexahe'dron** *n.* a solid figure having six faces, e.g. a cube.—**hexang'ular** *a.* having six angles [Gk. *hex*; *gōnia*, an angle; *hedra*, a base; L. *angulus*, a corner].

hexachord (hek'sa-kord) *n.* (*Mus.*) a diatonic series of six notes, with a semitone between the third and fourth [Gk. *hex*, six; *chordē*, a string].

hexad (hek'sad) *n.* a group of six numbers [Gk. *hex*, six].

hexameter (hek-sam'e-ter) *n.* a verse of six feet [Gk. *hex*, six; *metron*, a measure].

hexapod (hek'sa-pod) *n.* a six-footed animal [Gk. *hex*, six; *pous*, a foot].

hexoestrol (heks-o-es'trol) *n.* (*Chem.*) hormone, synthetically prepared, used for fattening steers.

hey (hā) *interj.* used to call attention, or to express joy, wonder, or interrogation.—**hey'day** *n.* the time of fullest strength and greatest vigour [etym. uncertain].

hiatus (hī-ā'tus) *n.* a gap in a series; an opening; a lacuna; the pronunciation without elision of two adjacent vowels in successive syllables [L. fr. *hiare*, to gape].

hibernate (hī'ber-nāt) *v.i.* to winter; to pass the winter, esp. in a torpid state.—**hiberna'tion** *n.* [L. *hibernare*, fr. *hiems*, winter].

Hibernia (hī-ber'ni-a) the Latin name for Ireland.—**Hiber'nian** *a.* pert. to Hibernia; Irish;—*n.* an Irishman.

Hibiscus (hi-bis'kus) *n.* (*Bot.*) a genus of mallows [Gk. *hibiskos*].

hiccup (hik'up) *n.* (erroneously **hicc'ough**) a spasm of the breathing organs with an abrupt cough-like sound; the sound itself;—*v.i.* to have this.—*pr.p.* **hicc'upping.**—*pa.p.* and *pa.t.* **hicc'upped** [of imit. origin].

hick (hik) *n.* (*U.S. Slang*) a rustic.

hickory (hik'or-i) *n.* a N. American tree; its tough wood [*pohickery*, native name].

hidalgo (hi-dal'gō) *n.* a Spanish nobleman [Sp. *hijo de algo*=son of something].

hide (hīd) *v.t.* to put or keep out of sight;

to keep secret;—*v.i.* to lie concealed.—*pa.p.* **hid'den, hid.**—*pa.t.* **hid.**—**hid'den** *a.* concealed; secret; unknown; mysterious.—**hid'denly** *adv.*—**hi'ding** *n.* concealment; a place of concealment [O.E. *hydan*].

hide (hīd) *n.* skin of an animal; the dressed skin of an animal; human skin;—*v.t.* to flog.—**hide'bound** *a.* of animals, having the skin too close to the flesh; (*Fig.*) bigoted; narrow-minded.—**hid'ing** *n.* a flogging [O.E. *hyd*].

hide (hīd) *n.* an old measure of land, from 60 to 100 acres. [O.E. *hid*].

hideous (hid'e-us) *a.* repulsive; revolting; horrible; frightful.—**hid'eously** *adv.*—**hid'eousness** *n.* [Fr. *hideux*].

hie (hī) *v.i.* and *refl.* to go quickly; to hurry on; to urge on [O.E. *higian*, to strive].

hiemal (hī'e-mal) *a.* pert. to winter [L. *hiems*, winter].

hierarch (hī'er-ark) *n.* one who has authority in sacred things; a chief priest.—**hi'erarchal, hierarch'ical** *a.*—**hierarch'ically** *adv.*—**hi'erarchy** *n.* authority in sacred things; government by priests; the organisation of the priesthood according to different grades; each of the three orders of angels.—**hieroc'racy** *n.* government by priests [Gk. *hieros*, holy; *archein*, to rule].

hieratic (hī-er-at'ik) *a.* consecrated to sacred uses; pert. to a cursive style of ancient Egyptian writing, used by the priests [Gk. *hieratikos*, priestly].

hiero- (hī'er-o) *prefix* from Gk. *hieros*, holy, combining to form derivatives, e.g.—**hi'erograph** *n.* a sacred inscription.—**hierol'ogy** *n.* the science or study of sacred things, esp. of the writings of the ancient Egyptians.—**hi'erophant** *n.* a priest; an instructor in religious duties and sacred mysteries.

hieroglyphic (hī-er-o-glif'ik) *n.* an emblem or symbol of sacred things;—*pl.* ancient Egyptian characters or symbols used in place of letters; picture-writing.—Also **hi'eroglyph**—**hieroglyph'ic, hieroglyph'ical** *a.* [Gk. *hieros*, holy; *gluphein*, to carve].

higgle (hig'l) *v.i.* to dispute about terms, esp. in bargaining [fr. E. *haggle*).

higgledy-piggledy (hig'l-di-pig'l-di) *adv.* and *a.* in confusion [earlier *higly-pigly*, probably =huddled together like pigs].

high (hī) *a.* elevated; tall; towering; far up; elevated in rank, etc.; chief; eminent; proud; loud; angry, as words; strongly marked, as colour; dear; costly; extreme; sharp, as tone or voice; tainted, as meat; remote from equator, as latitude;—*adv.* far up; strongly; to a great extent.—**high'ly** *adv.*—**high'ball** *n.* (*U.S. Slang*) whisky and soda.—**high'-born** *a.* of noble birth.—**high'bred** *a.* of noble breeding, thoroughbred.—**high'brow** *a.* and *n.* (*Colloq.*) intellectual, esp. in a snobbish manner.—**High Church**, that section of the Anglican Church which attaches extreme importance to ecclesiastical rites and ceremonies.—**high command** (*Mil.*) the commander-in-chief of armies and his staff.—**High Court** (*Law*) a supreme court.—**high-falu'tin', high-falu'ting** *a.* bombastic.—**high'fre'quency** *n.* (*Elect.*) any frequency of alternating current from about 12,000 cycles per sec. upwards.—**high'flown** *a.* elevated; turgid; extravagant.—**high'fly'er, high'fli'er** *n.* (*Fig.*) an ambitious person.—**high'lands** *n.pl.* a mountainous region, esp. in Scotland.—**High'lander** *n.* an inhabitant of a mountainous region, esp. highlands of Scotland.—**high'lights** *n.pl.* (*Art.*) the brightest parts of a painting; (*Fig.*) moments of crisis; persons of importance.—**high'ness** *n.* the quality of being high; a title of honour to princes and princesses.—**high'pitched** *a.* of a shrill sound.—**high'road** *n.* a main road.—**high seas**, the sea or ocean beyond the three-mile belt of coastal waters. -**high'spir'ited** *a.* ardent; bold; daring; easily irritated.—**high'strung** *a.* sensitive; in a state of tension.—**high tea**, tea served with meat, fish, etc.—**high treason**, any breach of the allegiance due from a subject to the sovereign or government of a country.—**high'wat'er** *n.* high tide; the time at which the tide reaches its highest elevation.—**high'way** *n.* a main road; a public road; an ordinary route.—**high'wayman** *n.* a robber on a public road, esp. a mounted one [O.E. *heah*].

hijacker (hī'jak-er) *n.* (*U.S. Slang*) one who robs a smuggler or a bootlegger.

hijra, hijrah. See **hegira**.

hike (hīk) *v.i.* to walk; to tramp;—*v.t.* to hoist or carry on one's back;—*n.* a journey on foot.—**hik'er** *n.* [etym. uncertain].

hilarious (hi-lā'ri-us) *a.* mirthful; joyous.—**hila'riously** *adv.*—**hilar'ity** *n.* merriment; boisterous joy [Gk. *hilaros*, cheerful].

hill (hil) *n.* a natural elevation of land; a small mountain; a mound;—*v.t.* to heap up.—**hill'y** *a.* full of hills.—**hill'iness** *n.*—**hill'ock** *n.* a small hill [O.E. *hyll*].

hilt (hilt) *n.* the handle of a sword, dagger, etc. [O.E. *hilt*].

him (him) *pron.* the objective case of the pronoun **he**.—**himself'** *pron.* emphatic and reflexive form of **he** and **him** [O.E.].

hind (hīnd) *n.* the female of the stag.

hind (hind) *n.* a farm-servant; a bailiff; a rustic; a herd [M.E. *hine*, a peasant].

hind, hinder (hind, hīnd'er) *a.* at the back; placed at the back; a combining form in such words as **hind'leg.**—**hind'most, hind'ermost** *a.* the furthest behind; the last [O.E. *hinder*].

hinder (hin'der) *v.t.* to prevent from progressing; to stop.—**hin'derer** *n.*—**hin'drance** *n.* the act of impeding progress; obstruction; obstacle [O.E. *hindrian*, to keep back].

Hindustan (hin'dòò-stan) *n.* (*Geog.*) the name applied to the country of the upper valley of the R. Ganges, India.—**Hin'di, Hindee** (hin'dē) *n.* an Indo-Germanic language spoken in N. India.—**Hin'du, Hindoo** (hin'dòò) *n.* a native of Hindustan;—**Hindusta'ni, Hindoosta'nee** *n.* chief language of Hindu India; also known as 'Urdu' [Urdu, *Hind*, India].

hinge (hin'j) *n.* a movable joint, as that on which a door, lid, etc. hangs; point on which thing depends;—*v.t.* to attach with, or as with, a hinge;—*v.i.* to turn on; to depend on [M.E. *heng*].

hinny (hin'i) *n.* offspring of stallion and she-ass [L. *hinnus*; Gk. *ginnos*, a mule].

hint (hint) *n.* a slight allusion; an indirect suggestion; an indication;—*v.t.* and *i.* to allude to indirectly [O.E. *hentan*, to seize)].

hinterland (hint'er-land) *n.* the district inland from the coast or a river [Ger.].

hip (hip) *n.* the upper part of the thigh; the haunch [O.E. *hype*].

hip (hip) *n.* the fruit of the rose, esp. of the wild-rose [O.E. *heope*].

hip, hyp (hip) *n.* despondency; melancholy.—**hipped** *a.* melancholy [corrupt. of *hypochondria*].

Hippocampus (hip-o-kam'pus) *n.* a sea-horse [Gk. *hippos*, a horse; *kampos*, a sea-monster].

Hippocrates (hip-ok'ra-tēz) *n.* a Greek physician, the 'Father of Medicine,' born about 460 B.C.—**Hippocrat'ic** *a.* pert. to him.—**hip'pocras** *n.* an old-time cordial made from wine flavoured with spices, etc.

hippodrome (hip'o-drōm) *n.* in ancient Greece and Rome, a stadium for horse and chariot races; a circus [Gk. *hippos*, a horse; *dromos*, a course].

hippogriff, hippogryph (hip'o-grif) *n.* a fabulous monster, represented as a winged horse with the head of a griffin [Gk. *hippos*, a horse; *grups*, a griffin].

hippopotamus (hip-o-pot'a-mus) *n.* the river-horse; a very large pachydermatous African quadruped frequenting rivers.—*pl.* **hippopot'amuses**, or **hippopot'ami** [Gk. *hippos*, a horse; *potamos*, a river].

hircine (hẹr′sīn) *a.* pert. to a goat; strong-smelling (like a goat) [L. *hircus*, a goat].
hire (hīr) *n.* payment for the use of a thing; wages; a hiring or being hired;—*v.t.* to pay for the use of a thing; to contract with for wages; to take or give on hire.—**hir′er** *n.*—**hire′ling** *n.* one who serves for wages (generally used in contempt). [O.E. *hyr*, wages].
hirsute (hir′sūt) *a.* hairy; shaggy; (*Bot.*) set with bristles [L. *hirsutus*, hairy].
his (hiz) *pron.* and *a.* the possessive case of the pronoun **he**, belonging to him [O.E.].
hispid (hi′spid) *a.* (*Bot.*) bristly; having rough hairs [L. *hispidus*, rough].
hiss (hiss) *v.i.* to make a sound like that of *ss* as in 'ass,' esp. to express strong dislike or disapproval [imit.].
hist (hist) *interj.* a word used to command attention or silence.
histo- (his′to) *prefix* from Gk. *histos*, a web or tissue, combining to form derivatives e.g.—**histol′ogy** *n.* the science that treats of the minute structure of the tissues of animals, plants, etc. [Gk. *genesthai*, to be born; *logos*, a discourse].
history (his′to-ri) *n.* the study of past events; a record of events in the life of a nation, state, institution, epoch, etc.; a description of animals, plants, minerals, etc. existing on the earth, called **natural history.**—**historian** (his-tō′ri-ạn) *n.* a writer of history.—**histor′ic** *a.* pert. to, or noted in, history.—**histor′ical** *a.* of, or based on, history; belonging to the past.—**histor′ically** *adv.*—**histori′city** *n.* the historical character of an event; the genuineness of it.—**historiog′rapher** *n.* a writer of history, esp. as official historian.—**historiog′raphy** *n.* [Gk. *historia*, an inquiry].
histrion (his′tri-on) *n.* a stage-player; an actor.—**histrion′ic, histrion′ical** *a.* theatrical; affected.—**histrion′ically** *adv.*—**histrion′ics** *n. pl.* theatrical representation; the dramatic art [L. *histrio*, an actor].
hit (hit) *v.t.* to strike with a blow or missile; (*Fig.*) to affect injuriously; to find;—*v.i.* to strike; to light (upon).—*pr.p.* **hit′ting.**—*pa.p.* and *pa.t.* **hit.**—*n.* a blow; a stroke; a success; a lucky chance [O.E. *hyttan*].
hitch (hich) *v.t.* to raise or move with a jerk; to fasten with a loop, etc.; to fix as by a hook; to make a rope fast;—*v.i.* to be caught or fastened;—*n.* a jerk; a fastening, loop, or knot; (*Fig.*) a difficulty.—**hitch′er** *n.*—**to hitch-hike,** to travel by begging rides from motorists, etc. [etym. uncertain].
hither (hiTH′ẹr) *adv.* to or towards this place;—*a.* situated on this side.—**hith′ermost** *a.* nearest in this direction.—**hith′erto** *adv.* up to now [O.E. *hider*].
hive (hīv) *n.* a place where bees live; (*Fig.*) an industrious company;—*v.t.* to gather or place bees in a hive;—*v.i.* to enter a hive; to take shelter together; to live in company [O.E. *hyf*].
hives (hīvz) *n.* an eruptive skin disease allied to chicken-pox [etym. uncertain].
hoar (hōr) *a.* gray with age; grayish-white.—**hoar′y** *a.* white or gray with age; venerable; of great antiquity.—**hoar′frost** *n.* white frost; frozen dew [O.E. *har*].
hoard (hōrd) *n.* a stock or store, esp. if hidden away; a treasure;—*v.t.* to store secretly;—*v.i.* to lay up a store.—**hoard′er** *n.* [O.E. *hord*, treasure].
hoarding (hōr′ding) *n.* a temporary wooden fence round a house while builders are at work; a screen on which advertisements are posted [O.Fr. *hourd*, a palisade].
hoarhound (hōr′hound) See **horehound.**
hoarse (hōrs) *a.* rough and harsh sounding; husky; having a hoarse voice.—**hoarse′ly** *adv.*—**hoarse′ness** *n.* [O.E. *has*].
hoax (hōks) *v.t.* to deceive by an amusing or mischievous story; to play a trick upon for sport;—*n.* a practical joke.—**hoax′er** *n.* [contr. fr. *hocus*].
hob (hob) *n.* the projecting nave of a wheel; the flat-topped casing of a fire-place where things are placed to be kept warm.—**hobnail** (hob′nāl) *n.* a large-headed nail for boot-soles [etym. uncertain].
hob (hob) *n.* a country lout; an elf.—**hobgob′lin** *n.* a mischievous elf; a bogey [corrupt. of *Robin* or *Robert*].
hobble (hob′l) *v.i.* to walk lamely; to limp;—*v.t.* to tie the legs together of a horse, etc.;—*n.* a limping gait; a clog; a fetter; a rope for hobbling [etym. uncertain].
hobbledehoy (hob′l-de-hoi) *n.* a clumsy youth. Also **hob′badehoy,** or **hob′bedehoy** [etym. uncertain, perh. fr. *hobble*].
hobby (hob′i) *n.* formerly a small horse; a favourite pursuit or pastime.—**hobb′y-horse** *n.* a stick with a horse's head used as a child's toy-horse; at fairs, etc. a wooden horse in merry-go-round [*Hob*, for *Robert*].
hobby (hob′i) *n.* a kind of small falcon [O.Fr. *hobé*].
hobnail See **hob.**
hobnob (hob′nob) *v.i.* to drink together; to be very friendly with [etym. uncertain].
hobo (hō′bō) *n.* a tramp [*U.S. Slang*].
hock (hok) *n.* the joint of a quadruped's hind leg between the knee and the fetlock.—Also **hough** [O.E. *hoh*, the heel].
hock (hok) *n.* a German white wine; orig. a Rhenish white wine made at *Hochheim*.
hockey (hok′i) *n.* a game played with a ball and curved sticks; a kind of shinty [perh. fr. O.Fr. *hoquet*, a crook].
hocus (hō′kus) *v.i.* to hoax; to stupefy with drugs.—**ho′cus-po′cus** *n.* a juggler; a juggler's trick; trickery [a sham L. formula used by jugglers].
hod (hod) *n.* a small trough on a staff used by builders for carrying mortar, bricks, etc. [Fr. *hotte*, a basket].
hodden (hod′n) *n.* (*Scot.*) a coarse woollen cloth [etym. uncertain].
hodge-podge (hoj′poj) *n.* See **hotch-potch.**
hodometer (ho-dom′e-tẹr) *n.* an instrument for measuring the distance travelled [Gk. *hodos*, a road; *metron*, a measure].
hoe (hō) *n.* a tool for breaking ground, scraping out weeds, etc.;—*v.t.* to break up or weed with a hoe.—*pr.p.* **hoe′ing.**—*pa.p.* and *pa.t.* **hoed** [O.Fr. *houe*].
hog (hog) *n.* a swine; a pig, esp. if reared for fattening; a greedy or dirty fellow;—*v.t.* to cut short the hair of;—*v.i.* to rise archwise in the middle.—**hog′gish** *a.* like a hog.—**hog′back, hog's′-back** *n.* a crested hill-ridge; an archwise ridge on a road, esp. on a bridge over a narrow stream.—**hog′wash** *n.* kitchen swill, etc. collected and used for feeding pigs [O.E. *hogg*].
hog, hogg (hog) *n.* a yearling sheep not yet shorn.—Also **hog′gerel, hog′get** [etym. uncertain].
Hogmanay (hog-mạ-nā′) *n.* (*Scot.*) the last day of the year [O.Fr. *aguillanneuf*].
hogshead (hogz′hed) *n.* a large cask; a liquid measure of 52½ imperial gallons [O.Dut.= *oxhead*].
hoist (hoist) *v.t.* to raise aloft, esp. of flags; to raise with tackle, etc.;—*n.* a hoisting; an elevator; a lift [Dut. *hijschen*, to hoist].
hoity-toity (hoi′ti-toi′ti) *interj.* an exclamation denoting surprise, mingled with contempt.—*a.* [O.E. *hoit*].
hold (hōld) *v.t.* to keep fast; to grasp; to support in or with the hands, etc.; to own; to occupy; to detain; to celebrate; to believe;—*v.i.* to cling; not to give way; to abide (by); to keep (to); to proceed; to be in force.—*pa.p.* and *pa.t.* **held.**—*n.* a grasp; grip; claim; binding power and influence; a prison; a fortress.—**hold′er** *n.*—**hold′ing** *n.* land, farm, etc. held of a superior; stocks held.—**hold′all** *n.* a kind of valise, or portable travelling-case, for holding clothes, etc.—**to hold up,** to support; to cause delay; to obstruct; to commit

highway robbery with threats of violence [O.E. *healdan*].

hold (hōld) *n.* the space below the deck of a ship, for cargo [earlier *hole*].

hole (hōl) *n.* a hollow; cavity; pit; den; lair; burrow; opening; a perforation; mean habitation; (*Colloq.*) awkward situation;—*v.t.* to make a hole in; to perforate;—*v.i.* to go into a hole.—**hole and corner,** secret; underhand [O.E. *hol*, a hollow)].

holiday (hol′i-dā) *n.* a day or period of rest from work; a religious festival;—*v.i.* to spend a holiday [fr. *holy day*].

holla, hollo, holloa (hol′a, hol′ō) *interj.* ho there! an exclamation to call attention;—*v.i.* to call out [Fr. *holà*=*ho*, and *là*, there].

Hollander (hol′ạn-dẹr) *n.* a native of Holland. —**holl'and** *n.* a kind of coarse linen, first manufactured in Holland.—**Holl'ands** *n.* gin made in Holland; schnapps.

hollow (hol′ō) *n.* a cavity; a hole; a depression; a valley; a channel;—*a.* having a cavity; not solid; empty;—*v.t.* to make a hollow in.—**holl'ow-eyed** *a.* with sunken eyes.—**holl'ow-toned** *a.* deep toned [O.E. *holh*].

holly (hol′i) *n.* an evergreen shrub with prickly leaves [O.E. *holegn*].

hollyhock (hol′i-hok) *n.* a tall garden plant [=*holy hock*, O.E. *hoc*, mallow].

holm (hōm) *n.* an islet, esp. in a river; flat ground by a river [O.N. *holm*].

holo- (hol′o) a combining form, fr. Gk. *holos*, whole, used in many derivatives.—**holocaust** (hol′o-kawst) *n.* a burnt offering, the whole being consumed by fire; wholesale sacrifice, destruction, or slaughter—**hol'ograph** *n.* and *a.* any writing, as a letter, deed, will, etc. wholly in the hand-writing of the signer of it.—**holograph'ic** *a.* [Gk. *kaustos*, burnt; *graphein*, to write].

holster (hōl′stẹr) *n.* a leather case for a pistol. —**hol'stered** *a.* [Dut.].

holt (hōlt) *n.* a wood; a piece of woodland; a woody hill [O.E. *holt*, a wood].

holt (hōlt) *n.* an otter's den [fr. *hold*].

holus-bolus (hōl′us-bōl′us) *adv.* at a gulp; all at once [fabricated Latin].

holy (hō′li) *a.* belonging to, or devoted to, God; morally perfect; divine; sacred.—**ho'lily** *adv.*—**ho'liness** *n.* the quality of being holy.—**ho'ly-day** *n.* (modern spelling, **hol'iday**) a religious festival.—**Holy Ghost, Holy Spirit,** the third Person of the Godhead or Trinity.—**Holy Land,** Palestine.—**ho'ly-or'ders** *n.* the office of a clergyman; the Christian ministry [O.E. *halig*].

holystone (hō′li-stōn) *n.* (*Naut.*) soft sandstone for scouring a ship's deck;—*v.t.* to scour with this [etym. uncertain].

homage (hom′āj) *n.* in feudal times, service due by a vassal to his over-lord; tribute; respect paid; reverence; deference [Fr. *hommage*, fr. *homme*, a man].

Homburg (hom′bẹrg) *n.* a type of men's soft, felt hat [fr. *Homburg*, in Germany].

home (hōm) *n.* one's fixed residence; a dwelling-place; a native place or country; an institution for the infirm, sick, poor, etc.;—*a.* pert. to, or connected with, home; not foreign; domestic;—*adv.* to or at one's home; to the point aimed at; close.—**home'less** *a.*—**home'lessness** *n.* the state of being without a home.—**home'ly** *a.* belonging to home; plain; domestic.—**home'liness** *n.*—**home′farm** *n.* farm attached to a mansion or manor-house.—**home′grown** *a.* grown in one's own country.—**home'land** *n.* one's native land.—**home′made** *a.* made at home as distinct from manufactured; plain.—**home'sick** *a.* depressed in spirits through absence from home; nostalgic. —**home′sickness** *n.*—**home'spun** *a.* spun or made at home; anything plain or homely.—**home'stead** *n.* a farmhouse with outbuildings. —**Home Guard** (*World War* 2) the British citizen army first established in 1940 and enlisted for home defence (*abbrev.* **H.G.**);—*n.* a member of this body.—**Home Office,** the department of the British Government, under the **Home Secretary,** which deals with the internal administration of the country, e.g. justice, police, etc. [O.E. *ham*].

home (hōm) *v.i.* of a pigeon, to fly home;—*v.t.* in naval warfare, to guide (another ship or aircraft) by radio to the attack of a target.—**hom'er** *n.* a homing pigeon [fr. *home*].

homeopathy (hō-me-op′ạ-thi) *n.* the treatment of disease by the administration of very small doses of drugs which would produce in a healthy person effects similar to the symptoms of the disease.—Also **homoeop'athy.**—**ho'meopath, homeop'athist** *n.*—**homeopath'ic** *a.* [Gk. *homoios*, like; *pathos*, feeling].

homicide (hom′i-sīd) *n.* manslaughter; the one who kills.—**homici'dal** *a.* [L. *homo*, a man; *caedere*, to kill].

homily (hom′i-li) *n.* a tedious discourse on a religious or moral subject; a sermon. —**hom'ilist** *n.*—**homilet'ics** *n.pl.* the art of writing homilies or sermons and of delivering them.—**homilet'ic(al)** *a.* [Gk. *homilia*, intercourse].

hominy (hom′i-ni) *n.* maize-porridge [Amer.-Ind.].

homo- (ho′mō) a combining form fr. Gk. *homos*, the same, used in derivatives.—**homocen'tric** *a.* having the same centre.

homoeopathy. See **homeopathy.**

homogeneous (ho-mo-jē′ne-us) *a.* of the same kind or nature; similar; uniform.—**homoge'neousness, homogeneity** (ho-mo-je-nē′i-ti) *n.* sameness; uniformity [Gk. *homos*, the same; *genos*, a kind].

homograph (hom′o-graf) *n.* a word having the same spelling as another, but different meaning and origin [Gk. *homos*, the same; *graphein*, to write].

homologate (ho-mol′o-gāt) *v.t.* to approve; to confirm.—**homol'ogous** *a.* having the same relative value, position, etc.—**homologa'tion** *n.* [Gk. *homos*, the same; *legein*, to say].

homonym (hom′o-nim) *n.* a word having the same pronunciation as another but a different meaning, e.g. *air* and *heir* [Gk. *homos*, the same; *onoma*, a name].

homosexuality (ho-mo-seks-ū-al′i-ti) *n.* attraction between individuals of the same sex.—**homosex'ual** *n.* a person thus perverted [Gk. *homos*, the same; and *sex*].

hone (hōn) *n.* a stone for sharpening knives, etc.—*v.t.* to sharpen on one [O.E. *han*, a stone].

honest (on′est) *a.* upright; dealing fairly; just; faithful; free from fraud; unadulterated.—**hon'estly** *adv.*—**hon'esty** *n.* upright conduct or disposition; (*Bot.*) a small flowering plant with semi-transparent, silvery pods [L. *honestus*, honourable].

honey (hun′i) *n.* the sweet, thick fluid collected by bees from flowers; anything very sweet; sweetness; (*Colloq.*) sweetheart; darling;—*a.* sweet; luscious;—*v.t.* to sweeten.—*pa.p.* and *a.* **honeyed** (hun′id).—also **hon'ied** *a.* sweet; (*Fig.*) flattering.—**hon'ey-bee** *n.* the common hive-bee.—**hon'eycomb** *n.* the structure of wax in hexagonal cells in which bees place honey, eggs, etc.; anything resembling this;—*v.t.* to fill with cells or perforations.—**hon'eycombed** *a.*—**honeydew** (hun′i-dū) *n.* a sweet sticky substance found on plants in warm weather; a kind of tobacco moistened with molasses.—**hon'eymoon** *n.* the month after marriage; the holiday taken by a newly-wed couple. Also, *v.i.*—**hon'eysuckle** *n.* a climbing plant with yellow flowers; woodbine [O.E. *hunig*].

honk (hongk) *n.* the cry of the wild goose; any sound resembling this [imit.].

honorary (on′or-ar-i) *a.* conferred for the sake of honour only; holding a position without pay or usual requirements.—**honorarium** (on-o-rā′ri-um) *n.* a sum of money granted voluntarily to a person for services rendered.

—**honorif'ic** *a.* conferring honour [L. *honorarius*].

honour (on′or) *n.* high respect; renown; glory; reputation; sense of what is right or due; a source or cause of honour; high rank or position; a title of respect given to a judge, etc.; chastity; a court-card;—*v.t.* to respect highly; to confer a mark of distinction on; to accept or pay (a bill, etc.) when due.—**hon'ours** *n.pl.* public marks of respect or distinction; distinction in examinations.—**hon'ourable** *a.* worthy of honour; upright; a title of distinction or respect.—**hon'ourably** *adv.*—**hon'ourableness** *n.*—**an affair of honour,** a duel.—**maid of honour,** a lady in the service of a queen or princess; a kind of cheese-cake [Fr. *honneur*, fr. L. *honor*].

hooch (hóóch) *n.* (*U.S. Slang*) alcoholic liquor [fr. Amer.-Ind. *hoochinoo*, spirit].

hood (hood) *n.* a covering for the head and neck, often part of a cloak or gown; an appendage to a graduate's gown designating his university and degree; the folding roof of a carriage or motor-car;—*v.t.* to cover with a hood.—**hood'wink** *v.t.* to blind by covering the eyes; to impose on; to deceive.—**hood'ed-crow,** *n.* a greyish crow (also called **hood'ie-crow**). [O.E. *hod*].

hoodlum (hood′lum) *n.* (*U.S.*) a hooligan; a street-rowdy.

hoodoo (hóó′dóó) *n.* uncanny, bad luck; a cause of such luck [same as voodoo].

hoof (hóóf) *n.* the horny casing of the foot of a horse, ox, sheep, etc.;—*pl.* **hoofs, hooves** [O.E. *hof*].

hook (hook) *n.* a bent piece of metal, etc. for catching hold, hanging up, etc.; a curved tool for cutting grain, grass, etc.; a bent piece of barbed steel for catching fish;—*v.t.* and *i.* to fasten with a hook; to catch a fish with a hook; (*Golf*) to drive a ball in a curve to the left; (*Boxing*) to deliver a blow with bent elbow.—**hook'er** *n.* (*Rugby*) the player in the scrummage, who tries to hook the ball back to his own side.—**hooks and eyes,** bent metallic clips and catches used for fastening ladies' dresses.—**hook′-up** *n.* (*U.S.*) the interconnection of broadcasting stations for relaying programmes [O.E. *hoc*].

hooka, hookah (hoo′ka̤) *n.* a tobacco-pipe in which the smoke is drawn through water and a long tube [Ar. *huqqah*, a vessel].

hooker (hook′e̤r) *n.* a small Dutch sailing ship; a fishing-smack [Dut. *hoeker*].

hookworm (hook′wurm) *n.* (*Med.*) *a* parasitic worm, infesting the intestines.

hooligan (hool′i-ga̤n) *n.* one of a gang of street roughs; a rowdy.—**hool'iganism** *n.* [the name of a person].

hoop (hóóp) *n.* a band for holding together the staves of casks, etc.; a circle of wood or metal for trundling as a toy;—*v.t.* to bind with a hoop.—**hoop'la** *n.* a game played by throwing rings at objects, which are won if encircled [O.E. *hop*].

hoop (hóóp) *v.i.* to whoop;—**hoop'er** *n.* the wild swan, so called from its cry [imit.].

hooping-cough See **whooping-cough.**

hoot (hóót) *n.* the cry of an owl; a cry of disapproval; the sound of a motor-horn;—*v.t.* to assail with hoots;—*v.i.* to cry as an owl; to cry out in disapproval.—**hoot'er** *n.* a factory siren [imit.].

hooves (hóóvz) *pl.* of **hoof.**

hop (hop) *v.i.* of persons, to spring on one foot; of animals or birds, to leap or skip on all feet at once.—*pr.p.* **hop'ping.**—*pa.p.* and *pa.t,* **hopped.**—*n.* an act or the action of hopping; (*Slang*) a dance; (*Aviation*) one stage in a flight.—**hop'per** *n.* one who hops; a device for feeding material into a mill or machine; a boat for carrying dredged mud, etc. out to sea.—**hop′o'-my-thumb** *n.* a dwarf; a pigmy [O.E. *hoppian*].

hop (hop) *n.* a climbing plant with bitter cones used to flavour beer, etc.;—*v.t.* to flavour with hops;—*v.i.* to gather hops.—**hops** *n.pl.* the cones of the hop plant.—**hop′bind (-bine)** *n.* the stalk on which hops grow [Dut.].

hope (hōp) *n.* a desire combined with a belief that the thing desired will come; thing that gives grounds for hoping; thing hoped for;—*v.t.* to desire, with belief in possibility of obtaining;—*v.i.* to feel hope.—**hope'ful** *a.* full of hope.—**hope'fully** *adv.*—**hope'fulness** *n.*—**hope'less** *a.*—**hope'lessly** *adv.*—**hope'lessness** *n.* [O.E. *hopian*].

hopscotch (hop′skoch) *n.* a child's game, played on an arrangement of squares scored on the ground [E. *hop*; *scotch*, a slight cut or score].

horal (hō′ra̤l) *a.* of or pert. to an hour; hourly.—**horary** (hō′ra̤-ri) *a.* pert. to an hour [L. *hora*, an hour].

horde (hōrd) *n.* a troop of nomads or tent-dwellers; a rabble or gang [Turk. *ordu*, a camp].

horehound (hōr′hound) *n.* a plant with bitter juice, used for coughs or as a tonic.—Also **hoar'hound.** [O.E. *harehune*].

horizon (ho-rī′zun) *n.* the boundary of the part of the earth seen from any given point; the line where earth (or sea) and sky seem to meet.—**horizontal** (hor-i-zon′ta̤l) *a.* parallel to the horizon; level.—**horizon'tally** *adv.* [Gk. *horizein*, to bound].

hormone (hor′mōn) *n.* a substance secreted by certain glands which passes into the blood and stimulates the action of various organs [Gk. *hormaein*, to set moving].

horn (horn) *n.* a hard projecting organ growing from heads of cows, deer, etc.; substance which forms this organ; tentacle of a snail; a wind instrument of music; a drinking cup; a utensil for holding gunpowder; a sounding contrivance on motors as warning; either of the extremities of the crescent moon;—*v.t.* to furnish with horns; to gore; to proclaim.—**horn'y** *a.* of, or made of, horn; hard or callous.—**horn'beam** *n.* a tree resembling a beech.—**horn'bill** *n.* a large bird with a bill surmounted by a horn-like process.—**horn'book** *n.* a primer for children, formerly covered with horn to protect it.—**horn'-owl** *n.* owl, so called from two tufts of feathers on its head. —**horn'pipe** *n.* an old musical instrument; a vigorous dance; the lively tune for such a dance.—**horn'stone** *n.* a kind of quartz resembling flint.—**horn of plenty,** or cornucopia; a representation of a horn, filled with flowers, fruit and grain [O.E.].

hornblende (horn′blend) *n.* a greenish-black, opaque mineral [Ger. *Horn* (from shape of crystals); *blenden*, to dazzle].

hornet (hor′net) *n.* a large insect of the wasp family [O.E. *hyrnet*, dim. of *horn*].

horo- (hor′o) from Gk. *hōra*, time; used as a combining form, e.g.—**horography** (ho-rog′ra̤-fi) *n.* the art of constructing watches, clocks, or other instruments for indicating the hours.—**horog'rapher** *n.*—**horologe** (hor′o-loj) *n.* an instrument of any kind for telling the time.—**horol'oger, horol'ogist** *n.*—**horol'ogy** *n.* the science of measuring time; the art of making time-pieces.—**horom'etry** *n.* the art, practice, or method of measuring time by hours, etc. [Gk. *hōra*, time; *graphein*, to describe; *legein*, to tell; *metron*, a measure].

horoscope (hor′o-skōp) *n.* a chart of the heavens which predicts the character and potential abilities of the individual.—**horoscop'ic** *a.*—**horos'copist** *n.* an astrologer.—**horos'copy** *n.* the art of prediction from a horoscope; disposition of the stars at a given moment [Gk. *hōra*, time; *skopein*, to observe].

horrent (hor′ent) *a.* (*Poet.*) standing erect, as bristles; bristling [L. *horrere*, to bristle].

horrible (hor′i-bl) *a.* tending to excite horror, fear, dread.—**horr'ibly** *adv.*—**horr'ibleness** *n.*—**horr'id** *a.* frightful; shocking; abominable.—**horr'ify** *v.t.* to strike with horror, dread, repulsion; to shock.—**horrific** (ho-rif′ik) *a.* causing horror [L. *horrere*, to bristle].

horror (hor′or) *n.* a painful emotion of fear, dread and repulsion; that which excites dread and abhorrence [L. fr. *horrere*, to bristle].

horse (hors) *n.* a large hoofed quadruped used for riding, drawing vehicles, etc.; the male of the horse species, as distinct from the female (the mare); mounted soldiers; in gymnastics, a vaulting-block; a frame for drying clothes on;—*v.t.* to provide with a horse, or horses; to carry or support on the back;—*v.i.* to mount on a horse.—**hors'y** *a.* pert. to horses; fond of, or interested in, horses.—**hors'iness** *n.*—**horse'back** *n.* the back of a horse.—**on horseback**, mounted.—**horse′box** *n.* a large kind of enclosed stall used for the transport of horses.—**horse′chest'nut** *n.* a tree with conical clusters of white or pink flowers and large nuts; the nut of the tree.—**horse′cloth** *n.* a cloth covering for a horse.—**horse′fly** *n.* a stinging fly troublesome to horses.—**horse′hair** *n.* hair from the tail or mane of a horse; haircloth.—**horse′knack'er** *n.* one who buys old horses, slaughters them, and sells the hides, etc.—**horse′laugh** *n.* a loud boisterous laugh.—**horse′leech** *n.* a large kind of leech; an insatiable person; formerly, a name for a veterinary surgeon.—**horse'man** *n.* a man on horseback; a skilled rider.—**horse'manship** *n.* the art of riding or of training horses.—**horse opera** (*Film Slang*) a thriller film with a Wild West setting.—**horse′pis'tol** *n.* an old kind of large pistol.—**horse′play** *n.* rough and boisterous play.—**horse′pow'er** *n.* (abbrev. **h.p.**), the power a horse is capable of exerting; estimated (in *Mechanics*) to be the power of lifting 33,000 lb. one foot high in one minute. —**horse′ra'dish** *n.* a cultivated plant used for sauces, salads, etc.—**horse′sense** *n.* (*Colloq.*) common sense.—**horse′shoe** *n.* a curved, narrow band of iron for nailing to the under-part of the hoof [O.E. *hors*].

hortative, hortatory (hort′a-tiv, hort′a-to-ri) *a.* tending or serving to exhort; advisory [L. *hortari*, to exhort].

horticulture (hor′ti-kul-tūr) *n.* gardening; the art of cultivating a garden.—**horticul'tural** *a.*—**horticul'turist** *n.* [L. *hortus*, garden; *colere*, to cultivate].

hosanna (hō-zan′a) *n.* a cry of praise to God; an exclamation of adoration [Gk.].

hose (hōz) *n.* stockings; socks; a covering for the legs and feet; tight-fitting breeches or pants; a flexible tube or pipe for conveying water.—*pl.* **hos'es.**—*v.t.* to water with a hose. —**hose′pipe** *n.* hose used by firemen for spraying water.—**hosier** (hōz′yer) *n.* dealer in hosiery.—**hos'iery** *n.* a collective word for knitted goods [O.E. *hosa*].

hospice (hos′pis) *n.* a traveller's house of rest kept by a religious order [L. *hospitium*, fr. *hospes*, a guest].

hospitable (hos′pit-a-bl) *a.* receiving and entertaining guests in a friendly and liberal fashion.—**hos'pitably** *adv.*—**hos'pitableness** *n.*—**hospital'ity** *n.* generous reception of strangers and guests [L. *hospes*, a guest].

hospital (hos′pit-al) *n.* an institution for the care of the sick or for education of young people.—**hospitalisa'tion** *n.* a scheme for treatment in hospital in preference to home treatment.—**hos'pitalise** *v.t.*—**hos'pitaller** *n.* one of a charitable religious order, which gave shelter to the poor and strangers [L. *hospes*, a guest].

host (hōst) *n.* one who lodges or entertains another; an innkeeper; an animal or plant which has parasites living on it.—**host'ess**, a woman who entertains guests.—**hostel** (hos′tel) *n.* residence for students; (*Arch.*) an inn. —**hos'telry** *n.* an inn.—**hos'teler, hos'teller** *n.* one living in a hostel [L. *hospes*, a host or guest].

host (hōst) *n.* a large number; a multitude; a crowd; an army.—**the heavenly host**, the angels and archangels; the stars and planets [L. *hostis*, an enemy].

Host (hōst) *n.* the bread consecrated in the Eucharist [L. *hostia*, a sacrificial victim].

hostage (hos′tāj) *n.* one handed over to the enemy as security [O.Fr. *hostage*, fr. L. *hospes*, a guest].

hostel See **host**.

hostile (hos′tīl) *a.* of, or pert. to, an enemy; unfriendly; opposed.—**hos'tilely** *adv.*—**hostil'ity** *n.* opposition;—*pl.* state or acts of warfare [L. *hostis*, an enemy].

hostler, ostler (hos′ler, os′ler) *n.* a man who attends to horses; a groom at an inn [*hostler*, orig. innkeeper, fr. O.Fr. *hostel*]

hot (hot) *a.* of high temperature; very warm; of quick temper; ardent or passionate; (of dance music) florid and intricate.—**hot'ly** *adv.*—**hot'ness** *n.*—**hot'-bed** *n.* in gardening, a glass-covered bed for bringing on plants quickly; hence (*Fig.*) any place conducive to quick growth (e.g. of scandal, vice, etc.).—**hot'-blood'ed** *a.* high-spirited; quick to anger. —**hot'-dog** *n.* (*Colloq.*) a sandwich roll with hot sausage inside.—**hotfoot'** *adv.* swiftly; in great haste.—**hot'head** *n.* an impetuous person.—**hot'house** *n.* heated house, usually of glass for rearing of plants.—**hot'-pot** *n.* a dish of meat and vegetables cooked in the oven in a closed casserole [O.E. *hat*].

hotchpotch, hotchpot (hoch′poch, hoch′pot) *n.* a dish of many ingredients; a medley or mixture [Fr. *hocher*, to shake; *pot*, a pot].

hotel (hō-tel′) *n.* a large and superior kind of inn.—**hotel'keeper** *n.* (Fr. *hotel*].

Hottentot (hot′n-tot) *n.* a member of a native race of S. Africa [Dut. imit.].

houdah (hou′da) *n.* See **howdah.**

hough See **hock.**

hound (hound) *n.* a dog used in hunting, esp. in hunting by scent; despicable man;—*v.t.* to chase with, or as with, hounds; (with 'on') to urge or incite; to pursue [O.E. *hund*].

hour (our) *n.* the twenty-fourth part of a day, or 60 minutes; the time of day; an appointed time or occasion;—*pl.* the fixed times of work or of prayers.—**hour'-glass** *n.* a sand-glass running for an hour.—**hour'-hand** *n.* the index which shows the hour on the face of a watch, clock, or chronometer.—**hour'ly** *adv.* happening every hour; frequently [L. *hora*].

houri (hòò′ri, hou′ri) *n.* a nymph of the Mohammedan paradise [Pers. *huri*].

house (hous) *n.* a dwelling-place; a legislative or other assembly; a family; a business firm; audience at theatre, etc.; dynasty; a school boarding-house.—*pl.* **houses** (houz′ez) —**house** (houz) *v.t.* to shelter; to receive; to store;—*v.i.* to dwell.—**housing** (hou′zing) *n.* the providing of houses.—**housing-scheme** (skēm) *n.* houses, built under direction of local authority.—**house'ful** *n.*—**house'less** *a.*—**house'hold** *n.* the inmates of a house; family;—*a.* domestic.—**house'holder** *n.* the tenant of a house.—**house'keeper** *n.* the woman who attends to the care of the household.—**housewife** (hous′wīf) *n.* the mistress of a family; (huz′if) a little case or bag for materials used in sewing.—**housewifery** (hous′wif-ri) *n.* the business of a housewife.—**house'-boat** *n.* a flat-bottomed barge, with a house-like superstructure.—**house'-fly** *n.* the common fly or *musca domestica.*—**house'-mar'tin** *n.* the common European swallow.—**house'-physic'ian, -sur'geon** *n.* the resident medical officer of a hospital, etc.—**house'-warm'ing** *n.* a merrymaking to celebrate entry into a new house.—**household gods**, articles in the house which are endeared by long association.—**household troops**, the Guards, whose duty it is to guard the sovereign and the metropolis.—**the House**, the Houses of Parliament [O.E. *hus*].

housel (houz′el) *n.* the Eucharist [O.E. *husel*, a sacrifice].

housing (hou′zing) *n.* a saddle-cloth.—*pl.* the trappings of a horse [Fr. *housse*].
hove (hōv) *pa.p.* and *pa.t.* of **heave.**
hovel (hov′el, huv′el) *n.* a small, mean house;—*v.t.* to put in a hovel [dim. of O.E. *hof,* a dwelling].
hover (hov′ẹr, huv′ẹr) *v.i.* to hang fluttering in the air, or on the wing; to loiter in the neighbourhood [etym. uncertain].
how (hou) *adv.* in what manner; by what means; to what degree or extent; in what condition.—**howbeit** (hou-bē′it) *conj.* (*Arch.*) nevertheless.—**however** (hou-ev′ẹr) *adv.* in whatever manner or degree; all the same.—**howsoev′er** *adv.* however [O.E. *hu*].
howdah, houdah (hou′dạ) *n.* a canopied seat on an elephant's back [Urdu, *haudah*].
howitzer (hou′it-sẹr) *n.* a form of gun, with a high trajectory [Bohemian *houfnice,* an engine for hurling stones].
howl (houl) *v.i.* to utter a prolonged, wailing cry such as that of a wolf or dog; to cry; (*Colloq.*) to laugh heartily;—*v.i.* to utter with howling;—*n.* a prolonged, wailing cry as of dog or wolf; a wail or cry.—**howl′er** *n.* one who howls; (*Colloq.*) a ridiculous blunder [imit. origin].
howlet (hou′let) *n.* owlet [O.E. *ule*].
hoy (hoi) *n.* formerly, a coasting-vessel, rigged as a sloop [Dut.].
hoyden, hoiden (hoi′dn) *n.* a rude, bold girl; a tomboy.—**hoy′denish** *a.* romping; bold; boisterous [etym. uncertain].
hub (hub) *n.* the central part, or nave, of a wheel [var. of *hob*].
hubble-bubble (hub′l-bub′l) *n.* a hookah [imit. origin].
hubbub (hub′ub) *n.* a tumult, uproar, or commotion [imit. origin].
huckaback (huk′ạ-bak) *n.* a kind of coarse linen with an uneven surface, much used for towels [L. Ger. *hukkebak*].
huckle (huk′l) *n.* the hip or haunch.—**huck′le-bone** *n.* the hip-bone; the ankle-bone [dim. of *huck*=hook].
huckleberry (huk′l-ber-i) *n.* an American shrub which bears small black or dark blue berries [O.E. *heorot-berge*].
huckster (huk′stẹr) *n.* (*fem.* **huck′stress**) a retailer of small articles; a mean, mercenary fellow;—*v.i.* to peddle [O.Dut. *hoekster*].
huddle (hud′l) *v.t.* to crowd together; to heap together confusedly;—*v.i.* to press together in fear or confusion; to cower;—*n.* a crowd; tumult.—**to go into a huddle with** (*Slang*) to meet in conference with [etym. uncertain].
hue (hū) *n.* colour; tint.—**hued** *a.* having a colour (generally in compounds) [O.E. *hiw*].
hue (hū) *n.* an outcry; now only used in **hue and cry,** a loud outcry or clamour [Fr. *huer,* to hoot].
huff (huf) *n.* a fit of petulance or anger;—*v.t.* to puff up; to bully; in the game of draughts, to remove from the board a 'man' which could have taken pieces but did not;—*v.i.* to blow; to take offence; to bluster.—**huff′y** *a.* sulky; petulant [etym. uncertain].
hug (hug) *v.t.* to clasp tightly in the arms; to embrace; to cling to;—*n.* a close embrace [etym. uncertain].
huge (hūj) *a.* very large; immense; enormous.—**huge′ly** *adv.*—**huge′ness** *n.* [O.Fr. *ahuge*].
hugger-mugger (hug′ẹr-mug′ẹr) *n.* confusion; muddle; secrecy;—*a.* disorderly; secret [etym. uncertain].
Huguenot (hū′gẹ-not, -nō) *n.* a 16th cent. French Protestant [etym. uncertain].
hulk (hulk) *n.* the body of a ship, esp. dismantled ship; anything big and unwieldy;—*pl.* old government vessels formerly used as prisons.—**hul′king, hul′ky** *a.* unwieldy; clumsy [O.E. *hulc,* ship].
hull (hul) *n.* husk of any fruit, seed, or grain; frame or body of a vessel;—*v.t.* to remove shell or husk; to pierce hull of, as of a ship [O.E. *hulu,* husk].
hullabaloo (hul′ạ-bạ-lòó) *n.* uproar; outcry [imit. origin].
hullo, hulloa (hu-lō′) *interj.* used to greet, to call attention.
hum (hum) *v.t.* to sing with the lips closed;—*v.i.* to make buzzing sound, as bee.—*n.* the noise of bees or the like; a low confused droning.—*pr.p.* **hum′ming.**—*pa.p.* and *pa.t.* **hummed.**—**hum′ming-bird** *n.* a tiny, brightly-coloured, tropical bird, whose wings make a humming sound as it flies [imit. origin].
human (hū′mạn) *a.* belonging to, or having the qualities of, man or mankind.—**hu′manly** *adv.*—**hu′manness** *n.*—**humane** (hū-mān′) *a.* having the moral qualities of a man; kind; benevolent.—**humane′ly** *adv.*—**humane′ness** *n.*—**hu′manism** *n.* a philosophic mode of thought devoted to human interests; literary culture.—**hu′manist** *n.* one who pursues the study of the humanities or classical literature.—**humanis′tic** *a.* pert. to humanity; pert. to humanism or humanists.—**hu′manise** *v.t.* to render human or humane.—**human′ity** *n.* the quality of being human; human nature; the human race; kindness or benevolence; (*Scot.*) Latin.—**humani′ties** *n.pl.* the branches of polite learning, esp. Latin and Greek.—**humanita′rian** *n,* one who holds that Christ was a mere man, and denies his divinity; a philanthropist.—**hu′mankind** *n.* the whole race of man [L. *humanus*].
humble (hum′bl) *a.* thinking lowly of oneself; mean; not proud, arrogant, or assuming; modest;—*v.t.* to bring low; to humiliate; to make meek.—**hum′bly** *adv.*—**hum′bleness** *n.* [L. *humilis,* fr. *humus,* the ground].
humble-bee (hum′bl-bē) *n.* the bumble-bee; a large bee which makes a loud humming sound [freq. of *hum*].
humbles (hum′blz) *n.pl.* the entrails of a deer. Also **um′bles,** or **mum′bles.**—**hum′ble-pie** *n.* a pie made of humbles [O.Fr.].
humbug (hum′bug) *n.* a hoax; sham; nonsense; an impostor; a kind of toffee sweet-meat;—*v.t.* to hoax; to deceive [etym. uncertain].
humdrum (hum′drum) *a.* commonplace; dull [redupl. of *hum.* imit. of monotony].
humefy (hū′me-fī) *v.t.* to moisten; to soften with water [L. *humere,* to be moist].
humeral (hū′mẹr-ạl) *a.* belonging to the shoulder.—**hu′merus** *n.* the long bone of the upper arm [L. *humerus,* the shoulder].
humid (hū′mid) *a.* damp; moist.—**hu′midly** *adv.*—**humid′ity, hu′midness,** *n.* dampness; moisture [L. *humidus,* moist].
humiliate (hū-mil′i-āt) *v.t.* to humble; to lower the dignity of.—**humil′iating** *a.* humbling—**humilia′tion** *n.* the act of humiliating or state of being humiliated; abasement.—**humil′ity** *n.* the state of being humble and free from pride [L. *humiliare,* fr. *humilis,* low].
hummock (hum′ok) *n.* a hillock; a ridge on an ice-field [dim. of *hump*].
humour (hū′, ū′mur) *n.* moisture, esp. the moisture or fluids of animal bodies; state of mind; mood; disposition; caprice; fun; quality of imagination quick to perceive the ludicrous, and expressing itself in an amusing way;—*v.t.* to indulge; to comply with mood or whim of.—**hu′moral** *a.* pert. to bodily humours.—**humoresque** (hū-mor-esk′) *n.* musical composition of fanciful character.—**hu′morist** *n.* one who shows humour in speaking or writing.—**hu′morous** *a.* full of humour.—**hu′morously** *adv.*—**hu′moursome, hu′morsome** *a.* moody; capricious [L. *humor,* moisture].
hump (hump) *n.* the protuberance or hunch formed by a crooked back; a hillock; (*Slang*) depression;—*v.t.* to bend into a hump shape; to carry on the back.—**hump′back** *n.* a person with a crooked back.—**hump-backed** (hump′bakt) *a.* [etym. uncertain].

humus (hū'mus) *n.* a brown or black constituent of the soil, composed of decayed vegetable or animal matter; mould [L. *humus*, the ground].

Hun (hun) *n.* one of a barbarian race of Mongolian origin that overran Europe in the 4th and 5th centuries; hence, a barbarian.

hunch (hunsh) *n.* a hump; (*Slang*) an intuition or presentiment;—*v.t.* to bend or arch into a hump.—**hunch'back** *n.* a humpback [etym. uncertain].

hundred (hun'dred) *n.* a cardinal number, the product of ten times ten; formerly, a division of a county in England.—*a.* ten times ten.—**hun'dredfold** *a.* a hundred times as much.—**hun'dredth** *a.* last of a hundred; —*n.* one of a hundred equal parts.—**hun'dredweight** *n.* an avoirdupois weight of 112 lb. or twentieth of a ton. Usually written *cwt.* [O.E. *hund*, hundred, with *raed*, reckoning].

hung (hung) *pa.p.* and *pa.t.* of **hang**.

hunger (hung'ger) *n.* discomfort or exhaustion caused by lack of food; a craving for food; any strong desire;—*v.i.* to feel hunger; to long for;—*v.t.* to starve.—**hung'ry** *a.* feeling hunger.—**hung'rily** *adv.*—**hung'er-strike** *n.* refusal of all food by a prisoner, as a protest [O.E. *hungor*].

hunk (hungk) *n.* a lump [Prov. E.].

hunt (hunt) *v.t.* to pursue and prey on (as animals on other animals); to pursue animals or game for food or sport; to search diligently after; to drive away; to use in hunting (as a pack of hounds);—*v.i.* to go out in pursuit of game; to search;—*n.* the act of hunting; chase; search; an association of huntsmen.—**hun'ter** *n.* (*fem.* **hun'tress**) one who hunts; a horse used in hunting; a watch that has the face protected by a metal cover.—**hun'ting-crop** *n.* a short whip used in hunting.—**hunts'man** *n.* the man in charge of the pack of hounds.—**to hunt down,** to persecute [O.E. *huntian*].

hurdle (hur'dl) *n.* a portable frame of interlaced twigs or of wooden bars, for fencing; a sledge on which criminals were drawn to gallows;—*v.t.* to enclose with hurdles; to jump over.—**hur'dle-race** *n.* a race in which the competitors jump over hurdles [O.E. *hyrdel*].

hurdy-gurdy (hur'di-gur'di) *n.* an old-fashioned musical instrument played by turning a handle; a street-organ [imit. origin].

hurl (hurl) *v.t.* to send whirling; to throw with violence;—*n.* a violent throw [etym. uncertain].

hurly-burly (hur'li-bur'li) *n.* tumult; bustle; confusion [etym. uncertain].

hurrah, hurra (hu-rà') *interj.* used as a shout of joy. Also (*Colloq.*) **hurray'** [Ger.].

hurricane (hur'i-kān) *n.* a wind of 60 m.p.h. or over; a violent storm of wind, rain, thunder.—**hur'ricane-deck** *n.* the upper deck of steamboats.—**hur'ricane-lamp** *n.* an oil-lamp, for use out of doors [Sp. *huracân*].

hurry (hur'i) *v.t.* to hasten; to impel to greater speed; to urge on;—*v.i.* to move or act with haste;—*n.* the act of pressing forward in haste; quick motion.—**hur'ried** *a.* done in haste; working at speed.—**hur'riedly** *adv.* [etym. uncertain].

hurst (hurst) *n.* wood, grove [O.E. *hyrst*].

hurt (hurt) *v.t.* to cause pain; to wound or bruise; to impair or damage; to wound feelings.—*v.i.* to give pain;—*n.* wound, injury, or bruise.—**hurt'ful** *a.*—**hurt'fully** *adv.* [Fr. *heurter*, to run against]

hurtle (hur'tl) *v.t.* to brandish; to whirl;—*v.i.* to move rapidly; to rush violently; to dash (against) [freq. of *hurt*].

husband (huz'band) *n.* a married man; formerly, a tiller of the soil, a steward, or manager;—*v.t.* to manage with economy; formerly, to till the soil.—**hus'bandman** *n.* a farmer.—**hus'bandry** *n.* farming; thrift or frugality [O.E. *husbonda*, the master of the house].

hush (hush) *interj.* or *imper.* be quiet! silence! —*n.* silence or stillness;—*v.t.* to make quiet; (with *up*) to keep secret;—*v.i.* to be silent.—**hush'aby** *interj.* go to sleep! used in lulling a child to sleep [imit.].

husk (husk) *n.* the dry, external covering of certain seeds and fruits; the chaff of grain;—*pl.* waste matter; refuse;—*v.t.* to remove the outer covering.—**hus'ky** *a.* full of husks; dry, esp. of the throat, hence, rough in tone; hoarse; raucous.—**hus'kily** *adv.* —**hus'kiness** *n.* [etym. uncertain].

husky (hus'ki) *n.* a Canadian-Indian sledge-dog; an Eskimo; the Eskimo language; a sturdy fellow;—*a.* powerful [Eskimo].

hussar (hoo-zàr') *n.* one of the light cavalry of European armies [Hung. *huszar*, a free-booter].

hussif (huz'if) *n.* a case for holding needles, thread, etc. [contr. fr. *housewife*].

hussy (huz', hus'i) *n.* an ill-behaved woman; an insolent or pert girl [contr. fr. *housewife*].

hustings (hus'tingz) *n.* the principal court of the city of London; any platform from which political campaign speeches are made [O.E. *hus*, a house; *thing*, an assembly].

hustle (hus'l) *v.t.* to push about; to jostle; —*v.i.* to hurry; to bustle;—*n.* bustle; speed. —**hus'tler** *n.* [Dut. *hutselen*, to shake up].

huswife (huz'wif, -if) *n.* See **housewife**.

hut (hut) *n.* a small house or cabin.—**hut'ment** *n.* a camp of huts [Fr. *hutte*].

hutch (huch) *n.* a chest or box; a grain-bin; a pen for rabbits; a low waggon in which coal is brought up from the mine [Fr. *huche*, a coffer].

huzza, huzzah (hoo-zà') *n.* a shout of joy or approval [Ger.].

hyacinth (hī'a-sinth) *n.* a bulbous plant, bearing spikes of clustered, bell-shaped flowers; a purplish-blue colour; a red variety of zircon.—**hyacin'thine** *a.* like hyacinth [Gk. *huakinthos*, doublet of *jacinth*].

hyaena, hyena (hī-ē'na) *n.* a carnivorous mammal of Asia and Africa, allied to the dog.—**laughing hyaena,** the spotted hyaena [Gk. *huaina*, sow-like].

hyaline (hī'a-līn) *a.* glassy; transparent; crystalline [Gk. *hualos*, glass].

hybrid (hī'brid) *n.* the offspring of two animals or plants of different species; a mongrel; a word compounded from different languages;—*a.* cross-bred [L. *hibrida*].

hydra (hī'dra) *n.* (*Myth.*) a monstrous water-serpent with many heads, slain by Hercules; (*Zool.*) a small fresh-water polyp [Gk. *hudra*, a water-snake].

Hydrangea (hī-drān'je-a) *n.* a genus of shrubs producing brightly-coloured flowers [Gk. *hudor*, water; *angeion*, a vessel].

hydrant (hī'drant) *n.* a water-pipe with a nozzle to which a hose can be attached; a water-plug [Gk. *hudor*, water].

hydrate (hī'drāt) *n.* (*Chem.*) a compound of water with another compound or an element;—*v.t.* to combine with water.—**hy'drated** *a.* combined with water.—**hydra'tion** *n.* [Gk. *hudor*, water].

hydraulic (hī-drawl'ik) *a.* pert. to hydraulics; relating to the conveyance of water; worked by water-power.—**hydraul'ics** *n.pl.* the science of water conveyance or water-power.—**hydraul'ically** *adv.* [Gk. *hudor*, water; *aulos*, a pipe].

hydro *n.* See **hydropathic**.

hydro- (hī'dro) *prefix* fr. Gk. *hudor*, water, combining to form derivatives.—**hydrocar'bon** *n.* a compound of hydrogen and carbon.—**hydroceph'alus** (hī-dro-sef'a-lus) *n.* (*Med.*) an excess of cerebro-spinal fluid in the brain; water on the brain.—**hydrocephal'ic, hydroceph'alous** *a.*—**hydrochlo'ric** *a.* containing hydrogen and chlorine.—**hydrochloric acid,** a strong acid commonly called 'spirits of salts' [Gk.

kelē, a tumour; *kephalē*, the head; *chloros*, green].

hydrodynamics (hī-dro-dī-nam′iks) *n.pl.* the branch of physics which deals with the flow of fluids, whether liquids or gases.—**hydrodynam′ic, hydrodynam′ical** *a.*—**hydrokinet′ics** *n.pl.* the branch of hydrodynamics which treats of fluids in motion [Gk. *hudor*, water; *dunamis*, power; *kinein*, to move].

hydro-electric (hī-dro-e-lek′trik) *a.* pert. to the generation of electricity by utilising water-power or steam [Gk. *hudor*, water].

hydrogen (hī′dro-jen) *n.* an inflammable, colourless, and odourless gas, the lightest of all known substances.—**hydrogenous** (hī-dro′jen-us) *a.*—**hydrogen bomb** (hī′drō-jen) *n.* atom bomb of enormous power [Gk. *hudor*, water; *gennaein*, to produce].

hydrography (hī-drog′ra-fi) *n.* the science of measuring and describing seas, lakes, and rivers [Gk. *hudor*, water; *graphein*, to write].

hydrology (hī-drol′o-ji) *n.* the science of the properties, laws, etc. of water.—**hydrolysis** (hī-drol′i-sis) *n.* a chemical process by which the oxygen or hydrogen in water combines with an element, or some element of a compound, to form a new compound.—**hydrolyt′ic** *a.* [Gk. *hudor*, water; *logos*, a discourse; *luein*, to loosen].

hydrometer (hī-drom′e-ter) *n.* a graduated instrument for finding the specific gravity, and thence the strength of liquids [Gk. *hudor*, water; *metron*, a measure].

hydropathy (hī-drop′a-thi) *n.* the treatment of diseases with water, including the use of cold or warm baths.—**hydropath′ic** *a.*—*n.* an establishment, usually at a spa, where such treatment is given; (*Colloq.*) abbrev. **hy′dro** [Gk. *hudor*, water; *pathos*, suffering].

hydrophobia (hī-dro-fō′bi-a) *n.* an acute infectious disease in man caused by the bite of a mad dog; rabies; an extreme dread of water, esp. as a supposed symptom of the disease [Gk. *hudor*, water; *phobos*, fear].

hydroplane (hī′dro-plān) *n.* a kind of flat-bottomed boat designed to skim over the surface of the water [Gk. *hudor*, water; L. *planus*, level].

hydroponics (hī-dro-pon′iks) *n.pl.* the cultivation of plants, without using soil, by feeding them on chemical solutions [Gk. *hudor*, water; *ponos*, labour].

hydrosphere (hī′dro-sfēr) *n.* the aqueous envelope of the globe [Gk. *hudor*, water; *sphaira* a sphere].

hydrostatic, hydrostatical (hī-dro-stat′ik, -i-kal) *a.* relating to hydrostatics.—**hydrostat′ics** *n.pl.* the study of fluids (liquids or gases) at rest—a branch of hydrodynamics.—**hy′drostat** *n.* a device for detecting the presence of water [Gk. *hudor*, water; *statikos*, causing to stand].

hydrous (hī′drus) *a.* containing water; containing hydrogen [Gk. *hudor*, water].

hyena (hī-ē′na) *n.* See **hyaena.**

hygiene (hī′jēn) *n.* medical science which treats of preservation of health.—**hygienic** (hī-jen′ik) *a.*—**hygien′ics** *n.* science of health [Gk. *hugiēs*, healthy].

hygro- (hī′gro) *prefix* fr. Gk. *hugros*, moist, combining to form derivatives.

hygroscope (hī′gro-skōp) *n.* an instrument which indicates variations of humidity in the atmosphere, without showing its exact amount [Gk. *hugros*, moist; *skopein*, to view].

Hymen (hī′men) *n.* (*Myth.*) the god of marriage.—**hymeneal** (hī-me-nē′al) *a.* pert. to marriage [Gk. *humēn*].

hymenopteral (hī-men-op′te-ral) *a.* belonging or pert. to an order of insects (Hymenoptera) as the bee, the wasp, etc. Also **hymenop′terous** [Gk. *humēn*, membrane; *pteron*, a wing].

hymn (him) *n.* an ode or song of praise, esp. a religious one; a sacred lyric;—*v.t.* to praise in song;—*v.i.* to sing in worship.—**hym′nal, hym′nary** *n.* a hymn-book.—**hymnol′ogy** *n.* the study or composition of hymns; hymns collectively.—**hymnol′ogist** *n.* [Gk. *humnos*, a festive song].

hyoscine (hī′ō-sēn) *n.* (*Med.*) a poisonous alkaloid used as a sedative in cases of mania and delirium [Gk. *huoskuamos*, henbane].

hyp See **hip.**

hyperbola (hī-per′bo-la) *n.* (*Geom.*) a curve formed by a section of a cone when the cutting plane makes a greater angle with the base than the side of the cone makes.—**hyperbol′ic** *a.* [Gk. *huper*, over; *bolē*, a throw].

hyperbole (hī-per′bo-lē) *n.* (*Gram.*) a figure of speech which expresses much more or much less than the truth, for the sake of effect; exaggeration.—**hyperbol′ic, hyperbol′ical** *a.*—**hyperbol′ically** *adv.*—**hyper′bolise** *v.t.* and *i.* to state with hyperbole [Gk. *huper*, beyond; *bolē*, a throw].

Hyperborean (hī-per-bo′rē-an) *n.* (*Myth.*) one of a race dwelling in the extreme north; —*a.* pert. to the extreme north [Gk. *huper*, beyond; *Boreas*, the north wind].

hypercritic (hī-per-krit′ik) *n.* one who is critical beyond measure or reason;—**hypercrit′ical** *a.* excessively critical.—**hypercrit′ically** *adv.* [Gk. *huper*, over; *kritikos*, critical].

hyperphysical (hī-per-fiz′ik-al) *a.* supernatural [Gk. *huper*, beyond; *phusis*, nature].

hypersensitive (hī-per-sen′si-tiv) *a.* abnormally sensitive.—**hypersen′sitiveness, hypersensitiv′ity** *n.* [Gk. *huper*, beyond; L. *sentire*, to feel].

hypertrophy (hī-per′tro-fi) *n.* (*Med.*) abnormal enlargement of organ or part of body.—**hypertroph′ic, hyper′trophied** *a.* [Gk. *huper*, over; *trophē*, nourishment].

hyphen (hī′fen) *n.* a mark (-) used to connect syllables or compound words.—*v.t.* to connect with a hyphen.—**hy′phenate** *v.t.* to join with a hyphen.—**hy′phenated** *a.* [Gk. *hupo*, under; *hen*, one].

hypholin (hī′fol-in) *n.* a drug similar to penicillin.

hypnosis (hip-nō′sis) *n.* the state of being hypnotised; abnormal sleep.—**hypnot′ic** *a.* tending to produce sleep; pert. to hypnotism;—*n.* a drug that induces sleep.—**hyp′notise** *v.t.* to produce a mental state resembling sleep.—**hyp′notism** *n.* an abnormal mental state resembling sleep, induced by suggestion from without, or by gazing fixedly at a bright object.—**hyp′notist** *n.* [Gk. *hupnos*, sleep].

hypochondria (hip-ō-kon′dri-a) *n.* a mental disorder, in which one is tormented by melancholy and gloomy views, especially about one's own health.—Also **hypochondriasis** (hip-ō-kon-drī′a-sis).—**hypochon′driac** *a.* affected by hypochondria;—*n.* a person affected with hypochondria [Gk. *hupo*, under; *chondros*, a cartilage].

hypocrisy (hi-pok′ri-si) *n.* simulation or pretence of goodness; feigning to be what one is not; insincerity.—**hypocrite** (hip′o-krit) *n.* one who dissembles his real nature; a pretender to virtue or piety; a deceiver.—**hypocrit′ical** *a.*—**hypocrit′ically** *adv.* [Gk. *hupokritēs*, an actor].

hypodermic (hī-po-der′mik) *a.* pert. to parts underlying the skin;—*n.* the injection of a drug beneath the skin by means of a needle and small syringe.—**hypoder′mically** *adv.* [Gk. *hupo*, under; *derma*, the skin].

hypostasis (hī-pos′ta-sis) *n.* essential nature of anything; the substance of each of the three divisions of the Godhead; (*Med.*) excess of blood in an organ;—*pl.* **hypos′tases** [Gk. *hupo*, under; *stasis*, state].

hypotenuse (hī-pot′e-nūs) *n.* (*Geom.*) the side of a right-angled triangle which is opposite the right angle [Gk. *hupoteinousa*, extending under].

hypothec (hī-poth′ek) *n.* a legal security over the effects of a debtor granted to his creditors.—**hypoth'ecary** *a.*—**hypoth'ecate** *v.t.* to give in security; to mortgage [Gk. *hupothēkē*, a pledge].

hypothesis (hī-poth'e-sis) *n. pl.*—**hypoth'eses**, a supposition used as a basis from which to draw conclusions; a theory. -**hypothet'ic, hypothet'ical** *a.*—**hypothet'ically** *adv.* [Gk. *hupothesis*, a proposal].

hyson (hī'son) *n.* a species of green tea [Chin. *hsi-ch'un*, blooming spring].

hyssop (his'op) *n.* a plant whose leaves have an aromatic smell, and a warm pungent taste [Gk. *hussōpos*].

hysteria, hysterics (his-tē'ri-a, his-ter'iks) *n.* an affection of the nervous system, characterised by excitability and lack of emotional control.—**hyster'ic, hyster'ical** *a.*—**hyster'ically** *adv.* [Gk. *hustera*, womb].

hysteron-proteron (his'te-ron-prot'e-ron) *n.* a figure of speech in which sequence of thought is inverted, i.e. by putting first the word which should follow; inversion [Gk.= the last first, fr. *husteros*, the latter; *proteros*, former].

I

I, (ī) *pron.* the pronoun of the first person singular, the word by which a speaker or writer denotes himself [O.E. *ic*; cf. Ger. *ich*; L. *ego*; Gk. *egō*].

iambus (ī-am'bus) *n.* a metrical foot of two syllables, the first short or unaccented, and the second long or accented.—*pl.* **iam'buses, iam'bi.**—**iamb'** *n.* shorter form of *iambus.*—**iam'bic** *a.* [Gk. *iambos*].

iatric, iatrical (ī-at'rik, -al) *a.* pert. to physicians, medicine [Gk. *iatros*, physician].

Iberian (ī-bē'ri-an) *a.* pert. to Iberia, viz. Spain and Portugal;—*n.* early inhabitant of ancient Iberia [L. *Iberia*, Spain].

ibex (ī'beks) *n.* generic name of a group of wild goats [L.].

ibis (ī'bis) *n.* a stork-like wading bird, allied to the spoonbills [Gk.].

Icarian (ī-kā'ri-an) *a.* adventurous in flight; rash [fr. *Icarus*, who fell into the sea on his flight from Crete, his wings having melted by the sun].

ice (īs) *n.* frozen water; concreted sugar; sweetened cream or water in frozen condition; ice-cream;—*v.t.* to cover with ice; to freeze;—*pr.p.* **ic'ing.**—**ice age** (*Geol.*) Pleistocene period, the series of glacial epochs.—**ice'-axe** *n.* implement for cutting footholds in ice in mountaineering.—**ice'-belt** *n.* the belt of ice fringing land in Arctic and Antarctic regions.—**ice'berg** *n.* a detached portion of a glacier floating in the sea.—**ice'-blink** *n.* a whitish light due to reflection from a field of ice.—**ice'-boat** *n.* a boat adapted for being pulled over ice.—**ice'-bound** *a.* surrounded by or jammed in ice.—**ice'-break'er** *n.* a vessel designed to maintain an open passage through ice-bound waters.—**ice'-cap** *n.* a glacier formed by the accumulation of snow and ice on a plateau and moving out from the centre in every direction.—**ice'-com'press** *n.* a piece of lint repeatedly wrung out of ice-water and applied to the affected part of the body.—**ice'-cream** *n.* cream or milk sweetened and congealed by freezing.—**ice'-drift** *n.* masses of floating ice.—**ice'-fall** *n.* a glacier as it flows over a precipice.—**ice'-field** *n.* a vast expanse of sea either frozen or covered with floating masses of ice.—**ice'-float, ice'-floe** *n.* a large mass of floating ice.—**ice'-hock'ey** *n.* game played by skaters on ice with a hard rubber disc (the puck).—**ice'-pack** *n.* drifting field of ice, closely packed together.—**ice'-plough** *n.* an implement for cutting grooves in ice to facilitate handling it for disposal.—**ice'-rink** *n.* a place, open or under cover, where ice-sports are played.—**ice'-sheet** *n.* an enormous glacier covering a huge area, valleys and hills alike.—**ice'-whale** *n.* the right, or Greenland, whale.—**ic'ily** *adv.* spoken coldly.—**ic'iness** *n.*—**ic'ing** *n.* a covering of sugar on cakes, etc.; formation of ice on parts of an aeroplane.—**ic'y** *a.* pert. to ice; of ice; ice-like; cold; chilling; frigid.—**to break the ice,** to overcome initial awkwardness in company [O.E. *is*; Ger. *Eis*].

Icelander (īs'lan-der) *n.* a native of Iceland.—**Iceland'ic** *a.* relating to Iceland;—*n.* language of Iceland.

Ichabod (ik'a-bod) *interj.* 'the glory is departed' (1 Kings 4), a wail of lamentation or regret [Heb.].

ichneumon (ik-nū'mun) *n.* a small carnivore of the mongoose family.—**ichneumon fly,** a hymenopterous insect which destroys the larvae of harmful insects by laying eggs in their bodies [Gk. fr. *ichneuein*, to hunt after].

ichnography (ik-nog'raf-i) *n.* a ground plan or horizontal section of a building.—**ichnograph'ic** *a.*—**ichnograph'ically** *adv.* [Gk. *ichnos*, a track; *graphein*, to write].

ichnology (ik-nol'o-ji) *n.* the classification of fossil footprints [Gk. *ichnos*, track; *logos*, a discourse].

ichor (ī'kor) *n.* (*Gk. Myth.*) the ethereal fluid which flowed in the veins of the Gods; the colourless, watery discharge from ulcers.—**i'chorous, i'chorose** *a.* [Gk. *ichor*].

ichthyic (ik'thī-ik) *a.* (*Zool.*) pertaining to, or characteristic of, fish [Gk. *ichthus*, fish].

ichthyography (ik-thi-og'ra-fi) *n.* a treatise on, or a description of, fishes [Gk. *ichthus*, fish; *graphein*, to write].

ichthyoid, ichthyoidal (ik'thi-oid, -al) *a.* resembling fish [Gk. *ichthus*, fish; *eidos*, form].

ichthyology (ik-thi-ol'o-ji) *n.* the branch of zoology which treats of the classification of fishes.—**ichthyolog'ical** *a.*—**ichthyol'ogist** *n.* [Gk. *ichthus*, fish; *logos*, discourse].

ichthyophagy (ik-thi-of'a-ji) *n.* the practice of eating fish; fish diet.—**ichthyoph'agist** *n.* a fish-eater.—**ichthyoph'agous** *a.* pert. to fish-eating [Gk. *ichthus*, fish; *phagein*, to eat].

ichthyosaurus (ik-thi-o-saw'rus) *n.* a fossil marine reptile intermediate between a saurian and a fish [Gk. *ichthus*, fish; *sauros*, lizard].

icicle (īs'i-kl) *n.* a pendent conical mass of ice, slowly built up by freezing of drops of water [O.E. *isgicel*].

icon (ī'kon) *n.* any sign which resembles the thing it represents; a representation of Christ, an angel, or a saint, found in Greek and Orthodox Eastern Churches.—**icon'ic, icon'ical** *a.* pert. to icons.—**icon'oclasm** *n.* act of breaking images; an attack on the cherished beliefs or enthusiasms of others.—**icon'oclast** *n.* a breaker of images; one who exposes or destroys shams of any kind.—**iconol'ater** *n.* an image-worshipper.—**iconol'atry** *n.* image-worship.—**icon'oscope** *n.* a form of camera used in television in conjunction with a cathode ray beam [Gk. *eikōn*, an image].

icterus (ik'te-rus) *n.* jaundice.—**icter'ic, icter'ical** *a.*—**ic'terine** *a.* yellow [Gk. *ikteros*, jaundice].

id (id) *n.* in psycho-analysis, the primary source in individuals of instinctive energy and impulses [L.=it].

idea (ī-dē'a) *n.* a mental image of any external object, abstract or concrete; a product of intellectual action; way of thinking; vague belief; plan; aim; archetype; principle at the back of one's mind.—**ide'al** *a.* existing in fancy only; satisfying desires;—*n.* an imaginary type or norm of perfection to be aimed at.—**idealisa'tion** *n.*—**ide'alise** *v.t.* to represent or look upon as ideal; to make or render ideal; to refine.—**ide'aliser** *n.* an idealist.—**ide'alism** *n.* tendency to seek the highest spiritual perfection; imaginative treatment in comparative disregard of the real; the doctrine that appearances are purely the perceptions, the ideas, of subjects, that the world is to be regarded as consisting of mind; the opposite of *materialism* in science and of *realism* in art and literature.—**ide'alist** *n.*—**idealist'ic** *a.* pert. to idealism or idealists; perfect; consummate.—**ideal'ity** *n.* ideal state or quality; capacity to form ideals of beauty and perfection; condition of being mental.—**ide'ally** *adv.*—**idea'tion** *n.* the process of forming an idea.—**idea'tional** *a.* [Gk. *idea*, fr. *idein*, to see].

identical (ī-den'-ti-kạl) *a.* the very same; not different.—**iden'tically** *adv.*—**iden'ticalness** *n.* exact sameness [L. *idem*, the same].

identify (ī-den'-ti-fī) *v.t.* to establish the identity of; to ascertain or prove to be the same; to recognise; to associate (oneself) in interest, purpose, use, etc.;—*pa.p.* **iden'tified.** —**iden'tifiable** *a.*—**identifica'tion** *n.* [L. *idem*, the same; *facere*, to make].

identity (ī-den'-ti-ti) *n.* state of having the same nature or character with; absolute sameness, as opposed to mere similarity; individuality; personal character; (*Math.*) an algebraic equation in which the two expressions are equal for all values of the letters involved [L. *idem*, the same].

ideograph (id'-e-ō-graf) *n.* a picture, symbol, diagram, etc., suggesting an idea or object without specifically naming it; a character in Chinese and kindred languages.—**id'eogram** *n.* an ideograph.—**ideograph'ic, -al** *a.*—**ideog'raphy** *n.* [Gk. *idea*, an idea; *graphein*, to write].

ideology (ī-de-ol'-o-ji) *n.* mental philosophy; science of origin of ideas; visionary theorising; abstract speculation.—**ideolog'ic, ideolog'ical** *a.* unrealistic; fanciful.—**ideol'ogist** *n.* a theorist. —**ide'ologue** *n.* an ideologist [Gk. *idea*; *logos*, discourse].

Ides (īdz) *n.pl.* in the Roman calendar, the 15th day of March, May, July, and October, and the 13th day of the other months [Fr. fr. L. *Idus*].

idiocy (id'-i-ō-si) *n.* See **idiot**.

idiograph (id'-i-ō-graf) *n.* a private mark or trade-mark.—**idiograph'ic** *a.* [Gk. *idios*, one's own; *graphein*, to write].

idiom (id'-i-um) *n.* a peculiar mode of expression; the genius or peculiar cast of a language; colloquial speech; dialect.—**idiomat'ic, idiomat'ical** *a.*—**idiomat'ically** *adv.* [Gk. *idios*, one's own].

idiosyncrasy (id-i-o-sin'-krạ-si) *n.* a peculiarity in a person; fad; peculiar view.—**idiosyncrat'ic, idiosyncrat'ical** *a.* [Gk. *idios*, peculiar; *sunkrasis*, mixing together].

idiot (id'-i-ut) *n.* one mentally deficient; a born fool.—**id'iocy, id'iotcy** *n.* state of being an idiot; extreme and permanent mental deficiency.—**idiot'ic, idiot'ical** *a.* utterly senseless or stupid.—**idiot'ically** *adv.*—**id'iotism** *n.* natural imbecility [Gk. *idiōtes*, a private person].

idle (ī'-dl) *a.* doing nothing; inactive; lazy; unused; frivolous;—*v.t.* to spend in idleness; —*v.i.* to be idle or unoccupied.—**i'dleness** *n.*— **i'dler** *n.*—**idle wheel,** or **i'dler** *n.* a wheel in a gear train which changes the direction of motion without affecting velocity ratios.— **i'dly** *adv.* [O.E. *idel*].

idol (ī'-dul) *n.* an image of a deity as an object of worship; a false god; object of excessive devotion.—**idol'ater** *n.* (*fem.* **idol'atress**) a worshipper of idols.—**idol'atrise** *v.t.* to worship as an idol.—**idol'atrous** *a.*—**idol'atrously** *adv.*— **idol'atry** *n.* worship of idols or false gods; excessive and devoted admiration.—**idolisa'tion** *n.*—**i'dolise** *v.t.* to make an idol of; to love or venerate to excess.—**idolis'er** *n.* [Gk. *eidōlon*, image].

idyl, idyll (ī'-dil, id'-il) *n.* a short pastoral poem; a picture of simple perfection and loveliness.—**idyll'ic** *a.* pert. to idylls; of a perfect setting; blissful [Gk. *eidullion*, dim. of *eidos*, a picture].

if (if) *conj.* on the condition or supposition that; whether; in case that [O.E. *gif*].

igloo (ig'-lòò) *n.* a dome-shaped house built by Eskimos; a snow-hut [Eskimo].

igneous (ig'-ne-us) *a.* resembling fire; resulting from the action of fire; fiery; burning. —**ignif'erous** *a.* bearing or producing fire [L. *ignis*, fire].

ignis-fatuus (ig'-nis-fat'-ū-us) *a.* flickering pale-bluish light, seen over damp ground, probably caused by marsh gas; the Will o' the Wisp; Jack o' Lantern [L. *ignis*, fire; *fatuus*, foolish].

ignite (ig-nīt') *v.t.* to set on fire; to kindle; —*v.i.* to catch fire; to begin to burn.—**ignit'ible** *a.*—**igni'tion** *n.* act of kindling or setting on fire [L. *ignis*, fire].

ignoble (ig-nō'-bl) *a.* of low birth or family; mean; base; vulgar; plebeian; degraded; dishonourable.—**ignobil'ity, igno'bleness** *n.*—**igno'bly** *adv.* [L. *in*, not; *nobilis*, noble].

ignominy (ig'-nō-min-i) *n.* public disgrace or dishonour; infamous conduct; opprobrium; infamy.—**ignomin'ious** *a.* disgraceful; dishonourable.—**ignomin'iously** *adv.*—**ignomin'iousness** *n.* [L. *ignominia*].

ignoramus (ig-nō-rā'-mus) *n.* an ignorant person, esp. a vain pretender to knowledge; a dunce [L. = we are ignorant].

ignorant (ig'-nō-rạnt) *a.* uninstructed; uninformed; unlearned.—**ig'norance** *n.*—**ig'norantly** *adv.* [L. *ignorare*, not to know].

ignoratio elenchi (ig-no-ra'-shi-ō e-len'-ki) *n.* (*Logic*) ignoring the point at issue by concentrating on an isolated statement of one's opponents: irrelevant conclusion (*L.*).

ignore (ig-nōr') *v.t.* to refuse to take notice of; to disregard; to leave out of account; not to recognise [L. *ignorare*, not to know].

iguana (i-gwȧ'-nạ) *n.* a family of lizards, found in the tropical New World; a monitor lizard in S. Africa [Sp.].

iguanodon (i-gwȧ'-no-don) *n.* an extinct dinosaur, of about 20 feet in length, herbivorous, somewhat lizard-like in form [*iguana*, and Gk. *odous*, *odontos*, tooth].

ilex (ī'-leks) *n.* the common holly of Europe; a genus of evergreen trees and shrubs, including the holm oak [L.].

Iliad (il'-i-ad) *n.* the great epic poem attributed to Homer, the subject of which is the siege of *Ilium* or ancient Troy.

ilk (ilk) *a.* the same.—**of that ilk**, applied when surname of a person is the same as name of his ancestral estate [O.E. *ilc*].

ill (il) *a.* bad or evil in any respect; sick; out of health; wicked; faulty; ugly; disastrous; unfavourable; harsh;—*n.* evil of any kind; misfortune; misery; pain; wickedness;—*adv.* not well; faultily; unfavourably; not rightly (*compar.* worse; *superl.* worst).—**ill'ness** *n.* disease; wickedness [O.N. *illr*].

ill- (il) *prefix*, used in the construction of compound words, implying badness in some form or other.—**ill'-advised'** *a.* badly advised. —**ill'-affect'ed** *a.* not well disposed.—**ill'-blood** *n.* ill-feeling; enmity.—**ill'-disposed'** *a.* not friendly; hostile; maliciously inclined.—**ill'-fa'ted** *a.* destined to bring misfortune.—**ill'-fa'voured** *a.* ugly; deformed; villainous.—**ill'-got, ill'-gott'en** *a.* not honestly obtained.—**ill'-hum'our** *n.* bad temper.—**ill'-na'tured** *a.* surly; cross; peevish.—**ill'-o'mened** *a.* inauspicious; attended by evil omens.—**ill'-starred** *a.* born under the influence of an unlucky star; unlucky.—**ill'-tem'pered** *a.* habitually morose or crabbed.—**ill'-timed** *a.* inopportune.—**ill'-treat** *v.t.* to treat cruelly.—**ill'-u'sage** *n.* unkind or clumsy treatment.—**ill'-will** *n.* malevolence; bad feeling; enmity [O.N. *illr.*].

illegal (i-lē'-gạl) *a.* contrary to law; unlawful. —**ille'galise** *v.t.* to render unlawful.—**illegal'ity** *n.* unlawful act.—**ille'gally** *adv.*

illegible (i-lej'-i-bl) *a.* incapable of being read or deciphered; unreadable; indistinct. —**illeg'ibleness, illegibil'ity** *n.*—**illeg'ibly** *adv.*

illegitimate (i-le-jit-i-māt) *a.* not regular; not authorised by good usage; unlawful; illicit; illegal; born out of wedlock;—*n.* a bastard.—**illegit'imacy** *n.* bastardy; illegality. —**illegit'imately** *adv.* [L. *in-*, not; *legitimate*].

illiberal (i-lib'-er-al) *a.* not liberal; not free or generous; niggardly; narrow-minded; intolerant.—**illiberal'ity** *n.*

illicit (i-lis'-it) *a.* not permitted; prohibited; unlawful; unlicensed; forbidden.—**illic'itly** *adv.*—**illic'itness** *n.*

illimitable (i-lim'-it-a-bl) *a.* incapable of being limited or bounded; immeasurable; infinite.

illinium (il-in'-i-um) *n.* a metallic element of the rare earth group, atomic weight 61, isolated in 1926 by B. S. Hopkins of *Illinois* University.—Also known as *florentium.*

illiterate (i-lit'-er-āt) *a.* ignorant of letters or books; unlettered; untaught; unable to read or write;—*n.* a person unable to read or write. —**illit'erately** *adv.*—**illit'erateness, illit'eracy** *n.* inability to read or write.

illogical (i-loj'-i-kal) *a.* not according to the rules of logic; unsound; fallacious.—**illog'ically** *adv.*—**illogical'ity, illog'icalness** *n.*

illude (i-lūd') *v.t.* to play upon by artifice; to deceive [L. *in*, upon; *ludere*, to play].

illume (i-lūm') *v.t.* to make light or bright; to illuminate [L. *in*, into; *lumen*, light].

illuminate (i-lū'-mi-nāt) *v.t.* to enlighten, literally and figuratively; to light up; to throw light upon; to embellish, as a book or manuscript with gold and colours.—**illu'minable** *a.*—**illu'minant** *a.* and *n.* a source of light. —**illumina'tion** *n.* act of giving light; that which supplies light; instruction; enlightenment; splendour; a display of lights; decoration on manuscripts and books.—**illu'minative** *a.* giving light; instructive; explanatory.—**illu'minator** *n.*—**illu'mine** *v.t.* to make luminous or bright; to enlighten; to embellish; to illume [L. *illuminare*].

illusion (i-lū'-zhun) *n.* an erroneous interpretation or unreal image presented to the bodily or mental vision; a false perception; deceptive appearance, esp. as a conjuring trick; fallacy. —**illu'sionist** *n.* a professional entertainer who produces illusions.—**illu'sive, illu'sory** *a.* deceiving by false appearances.—**illu'sively** *adv.* —**illu'siveness** *n.* See **illude.**

illustrate (il'-us-trāt, il-us'-trāt) *v.t.* to make clear or bright; to exemplify, esp. by means of figures, diagrams, etc.; to adorn with pictures.—**illustra'tion** *n.* act of making clear or bright; explanation; a pictorial representation accompanying a printed description.—**illus'trative, illus'tratory** *a.* serving to illustrate. —**illus'tratively** *adv.*—**ill'ustrator, illus'trator,** *n.* [L. *illustrare*, to light up].

illustrious (i-lus'-tri-us) *a.* bright; shining; conferring honour; possessing honour or dignity.—**illus'triousness** *n.* [L. *illustris*].

image (im'-ij) *n.* a mental picture of any object; a representation, in three dimensions, of a person or object; object set up for worship; a statue; idol; figure of speech; (*Optics*) the representation of an object formed at the focus of a lens or mirror by rays of light refracted or reflected to it from all parts of the object;—*v.t.* to form an image of; to reflect; to imagine.—**im'agery** *n.* images regarded collectively; figures of speech; imagination.—**im'agism** *n.* clear-cut presentation of a subject. —**im'agist** *n.* one of a modern poetical group who concentrates on extreme clarity by the use of precise images. [L. *imago*, an image].

imagine (im-aj'-in) *v.t.* to form in the mind an idea or image; to conceive; to conjecture; to picture; to believe; to suppose;—*v.i.* to form an image of; to picture in the mind.—**imag'inable** *a.*—**imag'inableness** *n.*—**imag'inably** *adv.*—**imag'inary** *a.* existing only in imagination or fancy; fanciful; unreal.—**imag'inative** *a.* proceeding from the imagination; gifted with the creative faculty; fanciful.—**imagina'tion** *n.* the mental faculty which apprehends and forms ideas of external objects; the poetical faculty.—**imag'inatively** *adv.*—**imag'inativeness** *n.* [L. *imago*, an image].

imago (i-mā'-gō) *n.* the final, fully developed adult stage of insect development, following the larval and pupal stages [L.].

imâm, imaum (i-mâm', i-mawm') *n.* the officer who leads the devotion and prayers in Mohammedan mosques [Ar. *imam*, a chief].

imbecile (im'-be-sēl) *a.* mentally feeble; fatuous; idiotic;—*n.* one of feeble mentality. —**imbecil'ity** *n.* [L. *imbecillus*, weak in mind or body].

imbed (im-bed') *v.t.* See **embed.**

imbibe (im-bīb') *v.t.* to drink in; to absorb; to receive into the mind;—*v.i.* to drink.—**imbib'er** *n.* [L. *in*; *bibere*, to drink].

imbitter See **embitter.**

imbody See **embody.**

imbricate (im'-bri-kāt) *v.t.* to overlap, as tiles on a roof;—*a.* bent like a gutter-tile; overlapping [L. *imbrex*, a gutter-tile].

imbroglio (im-brōl'-yō) *n.* an intricate, complicated plot; confusion [It.].

imbrue, embrue (im-, em-brôô') *v.t.* to wet; to soak; to steep; to drench, as in blood [O. Fr. *embruer*, to drink in].

imbue (im-bū') *v.t.* to tinge deeply; to cause to imbibe; to dye; to stain; to saturate; to inspire [L. *imbuere*, to wet].

imburse (im-burs') *v.t.* to supply money to [Fr. fr. L. *bursa*, a purse].

imitate (im'-i-tāt) *v.t.* to follow, as a pattern, model, or example; to copy.—**im'itable** *a.* capable or worthy of being copied.—**imita'tion** *n.* a servile reproduction of an original; a copy; mimicry.—**im'itative** *a.* inclined to imitate; not original.—**im'itatively** *adv.*—**im'itativeness** *n.*—**im'itator** *n.* [L. *imitari*].

immaculate (i-mak'-ū-lāt) *a.* without blemish; spotless; unsullied; pure; undefiled.—**immac'ulately** *adv.*—**immac'ulateness** *n.*—**Immaculate Conception,** the dogma that the Blessed Virgin Mary was conceived and born without taint of sin.

immalleable (i-mal'-e-a-bl) *a.* not capable of being wrought or beaten into shape by a hammer.

immanent (im'-a-nent) *a.* abiding in; inherent; intrinsic; innate.—**imm'anence, imm'anency** *n.* [L. *in*; *manere*, to dwell].

immaterial (im-a-tē'-ri-al) *a.* not consisting of matter; of no essential consequence; unembodied; incorporeal; unimportant.—**immate'rialise** *v.t.* to separate from matter.—**immate'rialism** *n.* doctrine that matter only exists as a process of the mind; pure idealism. —**immate'rialist** *n.*

immature (im-a-tūr') *a.* not mature or ripe; raw; unformed; undeveloped; untimely.—**immature'ness, immatur'ity** *n.*

immeasurable (i-mezh'-ūr-a-bl) *a.* incapable of being measured; illimitable; infinite; boundless.—**immeas'urably** *adv.*

immediate (i-mē'-di-āt) *a.* occurring at once; not separated by others; without delay; direct; present.—**imme'diacy** *n.* immediateness. —**imme'diately** *adv.*—**imme'diateness** *n.* [L.L. *immediatus*].

immemorial (i-me-mōr'-i-al) *a.* beyond the range of memory; of great antiquity.—**immem'orable** *a.*—**immemo'rially** *adv.*

immense (i-mens') *a.* unlimited; immeasureable; very great; vast; huge; prodigious; enormous.—**immense'ly** *adv.*—**immense'ness, immens'ity** *n.* infinity; boundlessness [L. *immensus*, unmeasured].

immerge (i-merj') *v.t.* to plunge into [L. *in*; *mergere*, to plunge].

immerse (i-mers') *v.t.* to plunge into anything, esp. a fluid; to dip; to baptise by dipping the whole body.—**immers'able, immers'ible** *a.*—**immersed'** *a.* doused; submerged; engrossed.—**immer'ser** *n.* an electric heater designed for heating water.—**immer'sion** *n.* [L. *in*; *mergere*, *mersum*, to plunge].

immigrate (im′-i-grāt) *v.i.* to migrate into a country.—**imm′igrant** *n.*—**immigra′tion** *n.* [L. *in*; *migrare*, to remove].

imminent (im′-i-nent) *a.* threatening immediately to fall or occur.—**imm′inence** *n.* the near future.—**imm′inently** *adv.* [L. *imminere*, to overhang].

immiscible (im-is′-i-bl) *a.* not capable of being mixed.—**immiscibil′ity** *n.*

immitigable (im-it′-i-ga-bl) *a.* incapable of being mitigated or appeased; relentless.

immobile (i-mob′-īl) *a.* incapable of being moved; fixed; immovable.—**immob′ilise** *v.t.* to render immobile.

immoderate (i-mod′-er-āt) *a.* exceeding just bounds; excessive.—**immod′eracy, immod′erateness** *n.* extravagance.—**immod′erately** *adv.*—**immodera′tion** *n.*

immodest (i-mod′-est) *a.* wanting in modesty or delicacy; indecent; shameless; impudent.—**immod′esty** *n.* shamelessness.

immolate (im′-ō-lāt) *v.t.* to sacrifice; to offer as a sacrifice; to kill as a religious rite.—**immola′tion** *n.*—**imm′olator** *n.* [L. *immolare*, to sprinkle a victim with sacrificial meal, fr. *mola*, meal].

immoral (i-mor′-al) *a.* uninfluenced by moral principle; contrary to the divine law; wicked.—**immoral′ity** *n.* vice; profligacy; injustice.—**immor′ally** *adv.*

immortal (i-mor′-tal) *a.* not mortal; having an eternal existence; undying; deathless;—*n.* one exempt from death or decay; a divine being.—**immor′talise** *v.t.* to make famous for all time; to save from oblivion.—**immortal′ity** *n.* perpetual life. flower [Fr.].

immortelle (i-mor-tel′) *n.* an everlasting

immovable (i-mòòv′-a-bl) *a.* incapable of being moved; firmly fixed; fast; resolute.—**immov′ableness, immovabil′ity** *n.*—**immov′ably** *adv.*

immune (i-mūn′) *a.* exempt; free from infection; protected against any particular infection;—*n.* one who is so protected.—**immunisa′tion** *n.* the process of rendering a person or animal immune.—**im′munise** *v.t.*—**immun′ity** *n.* state of being immune [L. *in-*, not; *munis*, serving].

immure (i-mūr′) *v.t.* to enclose within walls; to imprison [L. *in*; *murus*, a wall].

immutable (i-mūt′-a-bl) *a.* not susceptible to any alteration; invariable; unalterable.—**immutabil′ity, immut′ableness** *n.*

imp (imp) *n.* a little demon; a brat; a mischievous child; a shoot; a scion; a graft;—*v.t.* to graft; to adopt into a family.—**imp′ish** *a.* like an imp; mischievous [O.E. *impa*, fr. Gk. *emphutos*, grafted on].

impact (im-pakt′) *v.t.* to press or drive forcibly together.—**im′pact** *n.* impulse communicated by one moving object striking another; collision [L. *in*, into; *pingere*, *pactum*, to strike].

impair (im-pār′) *v.t.* to diminish in quantity, value, excellence, or strength; to injure; to weaken [Fr. *empirer*, to grow worse].

impale (im-pāl′) *v.t.* inclose with stakes; to put to death by fixing on an upright, sharp stake.—**impale′ment** *n.* a fenced-in place [L. *in*, into; *palus*, a stake].

impalpable (im-pal′-pa-bl) *a.* not capable of being felt or perceived by the senses, esp. by touch; exceedingly fine in texture; not readily understood or grasped.—**impalpabil′ity** *n.*—**impal′pably** *adv.*

impart (im-pārt′) *v.t.* to bestow a share or portion of; to grant; to divulge; to disclose.

impartial (im-pàr′-shal) *a.* not partial; without prejudice; not taking sides; unbiased.—**impartial′ity, impar′tialness** *n.*

impartible (im-pàrt′-i-bl) *a.* capable of being imparted, shared or communicated; not divisible (of landed property).

impassable (im-pas′-a-bl) *a.* incapable of being passed; impervious; impenetrable; pathless.—**impassabil′ity, impass′ableness** *n.*

impasse (im-pàs′, im′-pàs) *n.* deadlock; dilemma; fix [Fr.].

impassion (im-pash′-un) *v.t.* to move or affect strongly with passion.—**impass′ionable, impass′ionate, impass′ioned** *a.* stirred by strong passion or fervid emotion; ardent.

impassive (im-pas′-iv) *a.* not susceptible of pain or suffering; insensible; showing no emotion; calm.—**impass′ively** *adv.*—**impass′iveness, impassiv′ity** *n.*

impasto (im-pas′-tō) *n.* painting with thick layers of pigment on a canvas to give the effect of high relief and solidity.

impatient (im-pā′-shent) *a.* uneasy or fretful under trial or suffering; averse to waiting on events; restless.—**impa′tience** *n.* want of patience.—**impa′tiently** *adv.*

impavid (im-pav′-id) *a.* fearless; intrepid; undaunted [L. *in*, not; *pavidus*, fearing].

impeach (im-pēch′) *v.t.* to charge with a crime or misdemeanour; to call to account; to denounce; to challenge.—**impeach′able** *a.*—**impeach′er** *n.*—**impeach′ment** *n.* the trial of a minister of state or high public official, in which the Lords act as judges and the Commons as accusers [orig. to hinder, Fr. *empêcher*, to prevent].

impeccable (im-pek′-a-bl) *a.* not liable to sin or error; perfect.—**impeccabil′ity, impecc′ancy** *n.* [L. *in-*, not; *peccare*, to sin].

impecunious (im-pe-kū′-ni-us) *a.* having no money; poor; hard up.—**impecunios′ity** *n.* dire poverty [L. *in-*, not; *pecunia*, money].

impede (im-pēd′) *v.t.* to stop the progress of; to hinder; to obstruct.—**impe′dance** *n.* hindrance; (*Elect.*) opposition offered to an alternating current by resistance, inductance, or capacity, or by combined effect of all three.—**imped′ible** *a.*—**imped′iment** *n.* that which hinders; stammer.—**impediment′a** *n.pl.* baggage, esp, military; encumbrances.—**impedimen′tal, imped′itive** *a.* [L. *impedire*, to shackle].

impel (im-pel′) *v.t.* to drive or urge forward; to induce; to incite.—*pr.p.* **impel′ling**.—*pa.t.* and *pa.p.* **impelled′**.—**impel′lent** *a.* impelling;—*n.* a force which impels.—**impel′ler** *n.* [L. *in*, into; *pellere*, to drive].

impend (im-pend′) *v.i.* to hang over; to threaten; to be imminent.—**impend′ence, impend′ency** *n.*—**impend′ent** *a.* impending; threatening [L. *impendere*, to hang over].

impenetrable (im-pen′-e-tra-bl) *a.* incapable of being penetrated or pierced; obscure.—**impenetrabil′ity** *n.* quality of being impenetrable; that property of matter by which it excludes all other matter from the space it occupies.

impenitent (im-pen′-i-tent) *a.* not repenting of sin; not contrite; obdurate.

imperative (im-per′-a-tiv) *a.* expressive of command; authoritative; obligatory; absolutely necessary; peremptory.—**imper′atively** *adv.* [L. *imperare*, to command].

imperceptible (im-per-sep′-ti-bl) *a.* not discernible by the senses; minute.—**impercep′tibleness, imperceptibil′ity** *n.*—**impercep′tibly** *adv.*—**impercep′tive, impercip′ient** *a.* not having power to perceive.

imperfect (im-per′-fekt) *a.* wanting some part or parts; defective; faulty;—*n.* (*Gram.*) tense denoting an action in the past but incomplete, or continuous action in the past.—**imper′fectly** *adv.*—**imperfect′ion** *n.*

imperforate, imperforated (im-per′-fo-rāt, -ed) *a.* not perforated or pierced through.

imperial (im-pē′-ri-al) *a.* pertaining to an empire or to an emperor; royal; sovereign; majestic; denoting a standard size of paper, 22×30 in.; denoting a standard of weights and measures fixed by statute;—*n.* a tuft of hair on the lower lip.—**impe′rialism** *n.* the system of government in an empire; policy of national territorial expansion.—**impe′rialist** *n.* [L. *imperium*, command, empire].

imperil (im-per′-il) *v.t.* to bring into peril; to endanger; to hazard; to risk.
imperious (im-pē′-ri-us) *a.* commanding; domineering; dictatorial; tyrannical.—**impe′riously** *adv.*—**impe′riousness** *n.* [L. *imperiosus*, full of command, fr. *imperium*].
imperishable (im-per′-ish-ạ-bl) *a.* not liable to decay or oblivion; indestructible.—**imper′ishableness** *n.*—**imperishabil′ity** *n.*
impermanence (im-pẹr′-man-ens) *n.* want of permanence or stability.
impermeable (im-pẹr′-mē-ạ-bl) *a.* not permitting passage, as of fluid or gas, through its substance; impervious.—**impermeabil′ity** *n.* —**imper′meableness** *n.*—**imper′meably** *adv.*
impersonal (im-pẹr′-sun-ạl) *a.* having no personal reference; objective; (*Gram.*) form of verb used only in 3rd person singular with nominative *it*, e.g. *it hails*.—**imper′sonally** *adv.*
impersonate (im-pẹr′-son-āt) *v.t.* to invest with a real form, body, or character; to represent in character or form; to act a part on the stage; to imitate.—**impersona′tion** *n.*—**imper′sonator** *n.*
impertinent (im-pẹr′-ti-nent) *a.* having no bearing on the subject; irrelevant; impudent; saucy; pert.—**imper′tinence** *n.*
imperturbable (im-pẹr-tur′-bạ-bl) *a.* incapable of being disturbed or agitated; unmoved; composed.—**imperturbabil′ity** *n.*—**impertur′bably** *adv.*—**imperturba′tion** *n.*
imperviable, impervious (im-pẹr′-vi-ạ-bl, -i-us) *a.* not admitting of entrance or passage through; impenetrable; impassable; not to be moved by argument or importunity.—**imper′viableness, imperviabil′ity, imper′viousness** *n.*—**imper′viously** *adv.*
impetigo (im-pe-tī′-gō) *n.* (*Med.*) an acute inflammatory, contagious skin affection [L. fr. *impetere*, to rush upon].
impetuous (im-pet′-ū-us) *a.* rushing with force and violence; ardent; vehement; hasty. —**impet′uously** *adv.*—**impet′uousness, impetuos′ity** *n.* precipitancy; fury [L. *impetus*, attack].
impetus (im′-pe-tus) *n.* the force with which a body moves; momentum; boost [L.].
impiety (im-pī′-e-ti) *n.* See **impious**.
impinge (im-pinj′) *v.i.* (foll. by *on, upon, against*) to fall or dash against; to touch on; to infringe [L. *impingere*, to strike].
impious (im′-pi-us) *a.* not pious; proceeding from or manifesting a want of reverence for the Supreme Being.—**im′piously** *adv.*—**im′piousness, impi′ety** *n.*
implacable (im-plak′-, im-plāk′-ạ-bl) *a.* inexorable; not to be appeased; unrelenting.—**implac′ableness, implacabil′ity** *n.*
implant (im-plant′) *v.t.* to set in; to insert; to sow (seed); to plant (shoots); to instil, or settle in the mind or heart.
implead (im-plēd′) *v.t.* to sue at law.
implement (im′-ple-ment) *n.* a weapon, tool, or instrument; a utensil;—*v.t.* to fulfil an obligation or contract which has been entered into; to give effect to; to carry out.—**implemen′tal** *a.* [L. *implere*, to fill up].
implicate (im′-pli-kāt) *v.t.* to involve; to include; to entangle; to imply.—**implica′tion** *n.* the implied meaning; entanglement.—**im′plicative** *a.* tending to implicate.—**im′plicatively** *adv.*—**implic′it** *a.* implied, though not actually expressed in words; implied; without questioning.—**implic′itly** *adv.* [L. *implicare* to entangle].
implore (im-plōr′) *v.t.* to entreat earnestly; to beseech.—**implora′tion** *n.*—**implor′er** *n.*—**implor′ingly** *adv.* [L. *in*, in; *plorare*, to weep].
imply (im-plī′) *v.t.* to contain by implication; to include virtually; to involve the truth of; to signify indirectly; to insinuate; to denote. —*pr.p.* **imply′ing**.—*pa.p.* **implied′** [L. *implicare*, to entangle].
impolite (im-po-līt′) *a.* uncivil; rude; discourteous.—**impolite′ly** *adv.*—**impolite′ness** *n.*
impolitic (im-pol′-i-tik) *a.* ill-advised; ill-judged; not in the best interests of; inexpedient.—**impol′icy** *n.* injudicious line of action.—**impol′iticly** *adv.*
imponderable (im-pon′-dẹr-ạ-bl) *a.* without perceptible weight; not able to be weighed; —*n.pl.* natural phenomena such as heat; electricity, etc., which do not alter the weight of substances; the unknown factors which may influence human activities.—**impon′derableness, imponderabil′ity** *n.*
import (im-pōrt′) *v.t.* to bring in from abroad; to convey a meaning; to be of consequence to. —**im′port** *n.* that which is brought in from abroad; purport; meaning; consequence.—**impor′tance** *n.* consequence; moment; value; significance; relative rank or position.—**impor′tant** *a.* carrying or possessing weight or consequence; assuming an air of gravity.—**impor′tantly** *adv.*—**importa′tion** *n.* act of bringing from another country [L. *in*, into; *portare*, to carry].
importune (im-por-tūn′) *v.t.* to request with urgency; to pester with requests; to entreat; to solicit.—**impor′tunacy, impor′tunateness** *n.*—**impor′tunate** *a.* earnestly solicitous; clamorous in urging a claim; troublesome by begging.—**impor′tunately** *adv.* [L. *importunus*, troublesome].
impose (im-pōz′) *v.t.* to lay on; to levy; to lay, as a charge or tax; to enjoin or command; to lay on hands in ordination;—*v.i.* (with *upon*) to deceive; to take undue advantage of a person's good-nature; to overawe; to impress.—**impos′able** *a.*—**impos′ing** *a.* adapted to impress considerably; commanding; grand. —**imposi′tion** *n.* act of imposing, laying on, enjoining, inflicting, etc.; that which is imposed; a tax; a burden; deception put on others; an exercise prescribed to school pupils as a punishment [Fr. *imposer*].
impossible (im-pos′-i-bl) *a.* that which cannot be done; incapable of existing in conception or in fact; unfeasible; unattainable;—*interj.* absurd!—**impossibil′ity** *n.*
impost (im′-pōst) *n.* tax or duty [Fr. *impôt*].
imposthume, impostume (im-pos′-tūm) *n.* an abscess; an ulcer.—**impos′thumate** *v.i.* to form an abscess [Fr. fr. Gk. *apostema*, an ulcer].
impostor (im-pos′-tur) *n.* one who assumes a false character; one who deceives others; a cheat.—**impos′ture** *n.* deception [L. *imponere*, to place upon].
impotent (im′-po-tent) *a.* powerless; wanting natural strength; without sexual power (of a male).—**im′potence, im′potency** *n.*
impound (im-pound′) *v.t.* to confine cattle in a pound or pen; to restrain within limits; (*Law*) to retain documents in a civil case with a view to criminal proceedings.
impoverish (im-pov′-ẹr-ish) *v.t.* to reduce to poverty; to exhaust the strength, richness, or fertility of land.—**impov′erishment** *n.* [O. Fr. *empovrir*].
impracticable (im-prak′-tik-ạ-bl) *a.* not able to be accomplished; unfeasible.—**imprac′ticability, imprac′ticableness** *n.*—**imprac′tical** *a.* not practical.
imprecate (im′-pre-kāt) *v.t.* to invoke by prayer (evil) upon; to curse.—**impreca′tion** *n.* —**im′precatory** *a.* [L. *imprecari*, to invoke by prayer].
impregnable (im-preg′-nạ-bl) *a.* not to be stormed or taken by assault; not to be moved, impressed, or shaken.—**impregnabil′ity** *n.*—**impreg′nably** *adv.* [Fr. *imprenable*, fr. L. *in-*, not; *prehendere*, to take].
impregnate (im-preg′-nāt) *v.t.* to make pregnant; to render fertile; to fecundate; to saturate.—**impregna′tion** *n.* [L. *impregnare*].
impresario (im-pre-sà′-ri-ō) *n.* an organiser of public entertainments, esp. musical recitals and grand opera [It.].
impress (im′-press) *n.* See **imprest**.
impress (im-pres′) *v.t.* to take forcibly, persons or goods, for public service; to commandeer.

—**impress'ment** *n.* [L. *in*, in, into; *praestare*, to furnish].
impress (im-pres') *v.t.* to press in or upon; to make a mark or figure upon; to fix deeply in the mind; to stamp.—**im'press** *n.* a mark made by pressure; stamp; impression wrought on the mind.—**impressibil'ity** *n.* susceptibility. —**impress'ible** *a.* capable of being impressed. —**impress'ibly** *adv.*—**impress'ion** *n.* act of impressing; a mark or stamp made by pressure; psychological effect or influence on the mind; opinion; idea.—**impress'ionable** *a.* susceptible to external influences; emotional.—**impress'ive** *a.* making or fitted to make a deep impression on the mind.—**impress'ively** *adv.*—**impress'iveness** *n.* [L. *imprimere*, fr. *premere*, to press].
impressionism (im-presh'-un-izm) *n.* a revolutionary modern movement, originating in France, in art, literature and music, aiming at reproducing the *impression* which eye and mind gather, rather than representing actual fact.—**impress'ionist** *n.*
imprest, impress (im'-prest, im'-pres) *n.* in book-keeping, the fixed sum of money available for petty expenses [L. *praestare*, to be surety for].
imprimatur (im-prī-mā'-tur) *n.* a licence to print a book; official approval [L. = ' let it be printed '].
imprint (im-print') *v.t.* to mark by pressure; to fix indelibly, as on the mind; to print.—**im'print** *n.* name of printer or publisher on title-page or at the end of a book.
imprison (im-prizn') *v.t.* to put in prison.—**impris'onment** *n.* the act of imprisoning or state of being imprisoned.
improbable (im-prob'-a-bl) *a.* unlikely.—**improbabil'ity** *n.*—**improb'ably** *adv.*
improbity (im-prob'-i-ti) *n.* want of integrity or rectitude; dishonesty.
impromptu (im-promp'-tū) *adv.* or *a.* offhand; without previous study [Fr. fr. L. *promptus*, ready].
improper (im-prop'-er) *a.* unsuitable to the end or design; unfit; indecent; inaccurate.—**improp'erly** *adv.*—**impropri'ety** *n.* offence against rules of conduct; the use of a word in its wrong sense.
impropriate (im-prō'-pri-āt) *v.t.* to appropriate to private use; to place the profits of ecclesiastical property in the hands of a layman.—**impropria'tion** *n.*—**impro'priator** *n.* [L. *in*, into; *proprius*, one's own].
improve (im-prōōv') *v.t.* to make better; to employ to good purpose; to make progress;—*v.i.* to grow better; to become more prosperous.—**improvabil'ity, improv'ableness** *n.*—**improv'able** *a.*—**improv'ably** *adv.*—**improve'ment** *n.* the act of improving; state of being improved; progress.—**improv'ingly** *adv.*
improvident (im-prov'-i-dent) *a.* not prudent or foreseeing; neglecting to provide for the future.—**improv'idence** *n.*
improvise, improvisate (im-pro-viz', im-prov'-i-zāt) *v.t.* to extemporise; to make the best of materials at hand; to compose, speak or perform without preparation.—**improvisa'tion** *n.*—**improvis'er** *n.* [L. *in-*, not; *provisus*, foreseen].
imprudent (im-prōō'-dent), *a.* lacking in prudence or discretion; injudicious; heedless. —**impru'dence** *n.*—**impru'dently** *adv.*
impudent (im'-pū-dent) *a.* shameless; wanting modesty; brazen; bold-faced; rude.—**im'pudence** *n.*—**im'pudently** *adv.* [L. *impudens*, shameless].
impugn (im-pūn') *v.t.* to call in question; to contradict; to challenge the accuracy of a statement.—**impugn'able** *a.*—**impugn'er** *n.*—**impugn'ment** *n.* [L. *impugnare*, to assail].
impulse (im'-puls) *n.* the motion or effect produced by a sudden action or applied force; push; thrust; momentum; sudden thought; motive.—**impul'sion** *n.* impelling force; incitement.—**impuls'ive** *a.* having the power of impelling; acting momentarily without due thought.—**impuls'ively** *adv.*—**impuls'iveness** *n.* [L. *impellere, impulsum*, to urge on. Cf. *impel*].
impunity (im-pūn'-i-ti) *n.* exemption from punishment, injury, or loss [L. *impunitas*].
impure (im-pūr') *a.* not pure; mixed; adulterated; foul; unchaste.—**impure'ly** *adv.*—**impu'rity, impure'ness** *n.*
impute (im-pūt') *v.t.* to ascribe to (in a bad sense); to set to the account of; to attribute to.—**imput'able** *a.*—**imput'ableness, imputabil'ity** *n.*—**imputa'tion** *n.* act of imputing; suggestion of evil; censure.—**imput'ative** *a.* imputed.—**imput'atively** *adv.* [L. *in*; *putare*, to reckon, to think].
in (in) *prep.* within; inside of; indicating a present relation to time, space, or condition; —*adv.* inside; closely; with privilege or possession; immediately.—**in as far as**, to the extent that.—**in as much as, inasmuch as**, considering that [O.E.].
inability (in-a-bil'-i-ti) *n.* want of strength, means, or power; impotence; incapacity.
inaccessible (in-ak-ses'-i-bl) *a.* not accessible; unapproachable; unattainable.—**inaccessibil'ity** *n.*—**inaccess'ibly** *adv.*
inaccurate (in-ak'-ūr-āt) *a.* not correct; not according to truth or reality; erroneous.—**inacc'uracy** *n.*—**inacc'urately** *adv.*
inactive (in-ak'-tiv) *a.* not disposed to action or effort; idle; inert; lazy; (*Chem.*) showing no tendency to combine with other elements. —**inac'tion** *n.*—**inact'ively** *adv.*—**inactiv'ity** *n.* want of action or energy.
inadequate (in-ad'-e-kwāt) *a.* insufficient; too cramped; incapable.—**inad'equacy** *n.*—**inad'equately** *adv.*—**inad'equateness** *n.*
inadmissible (in-ad-mis'-i-bl) *a.* not allowable; improper.—**inadmiss'ibly** *adv.*
inadvertent (in-ad-vert'-ent) *a.* not turning the mind to a matter; inattentive; thoughtless; careless.—**inadvert'ence, inadvert'ency** *n.*—**inadvert'ently** *adv.*
inadvisable (in-ad-vīz'-a-bl) *a.* not advisable.
inalienable (in-āl'-yen-a-bl) *a.* incapable of being separated or transferred.
inamorato (in-am-o-rà'-tō) *n.* (*fem.* **inamora'ta**) person with whom one is in love; lover; sweetheart [It. fr. L. *in*; *amor*, love].
inane (in-ān') *a.* empty; void; foolish; silly.—**inani'tion** *n.* state of being empty; exhaustion; starvation; boredom.—**inan'ity** *n.* vacuity; silly remark [L. *inanis*].
inanimate (in-an'-i-māt) *a.* not animate; destitute of life or spirit.—**inanima'tion** *n.*—**inan'imateness** *n.*
inapplicable (in-ap'-lik-a-bl) *a.* not applicable; unsuitable; irrelevant; inappropriate.
inapposite (in-a'-poz-it) *a.* not apposite; inappropriate; inapplicable; irrelevant; not pertinent; out of place.—**inap'positely** *adv.*
inappreciable (in-a-prē'-shi-a-bl) *a.* not worth reckoning; not able to be valued.
inappropriate (in-a-prō'-pri-āt) *a.* unsuitable; unbecoming; at the wrong time.—**inappro'priately** *adv.*—**inappro'priateness** *n.*
inapt (in-apt') *a.* inappropriate; unsuitable; awkward; clumsy.—**inap'titude** *n.* unfitness; awkwardness; unreadiness.—**inapt'ly** *adv.*
inarticulate (in-ar-tik'-ūl-āt) *a.* unable to put one's ideas in words; not uttered distinctly; not jointed.—**inartic'ulately** *adv.*—**inartic'ulateness** *n.*—**inarticula'tion** *n.*
inartistic (in-ar-tis'-tik) *a.* not artistic; crude; deficient in artistic taste.
inasmuch *adv.* See in.
inattentive (in-a-tent'-iv) *a.* not fixing the mind on an object; heedless; regardless; negligent.—**inatten'tion, inattent'iveness** *n.*
inaudible (in-awd'-i-bl) *a.* not able to be heard; noiseless; silent.—**inaudibil'ity, inaud'ibleness** *n.*—**inaud'ibly** *adv.*
inaugurate (in-aw'-gūr-āt) *v.t.* to induct into an office in a formal manner; to install; to set in motion or action; to begin.—**inau'gural, inau'guratory** *a.*—**inaugura'tion** *n.* opening

ceremony.—**inau'gurator** *n.* [L. *inaugurare*, to take auguries before action].
inauspicious (in-aw-spish'-us) *a.* not auspicious; ill-omened; unlucky.—**inauspic'iously** *adv.*—**inauspic'iousness** *n.*
inboard (in'-bōrd) *a.* inside the rails round a ship's side.
inborn (in'-born) *a.* born in or with; innate; natural; inherent; congenital.
inbred (in'-bred) *a.* bred within; innate; inherent.—**in'breed** *v.t.* to mate animals of the same blood-stock; to marry within the family or tribe.—**in'breeding** *n.*
Inca (ing'-ka) *n.* an aboriginal race of Peruvian Indians; the ruling caste in ancient Peru [Sp.].
incalculable (in-kal'-kū-la-bl) *a.* countless; numberless; beyond calculation; enormous.—**incalculabil'ity, incal'culableness** *n.*
incandescent (in-kan-des'-ent) *a.* glowing with white heat and providing light.—**incandes'ence** *n.* white heat [L. *in*, in; *candescere*, to begin to glow].
incantation (in-kan-tā'-shun) *n.* a formula or charm-words used to produce magical or supernatural effect.—**incan'tatory** *a.* [L. *incantare*, to sing spells. Cf. *enchant*].
incapable (in-kāp'-a-bl) *a.* wanting size or space to hold or contain; not admitting of; not susceptible of; not capable; drunk; (*Law*) barred from.—**incapabil'ity** *n.*
incapacious (in-kap-ā'-shus) *a.* of small extent; scant.—**incapa'ciousness** *n.*
incapacitate (in-kap-as'-i-tāt) *v.t.* to render incapable.—**incapacita'tion** *n.* act of disqualifying.—**incapac'ity** *n.* want of capacity; lack of normal intellectual power; inability; incapability; legal disqualification.
incarcerate (in-kàr'-ser-āt) *v.t.* to confine in a jail or prison; to imprison.—**incar'cerator** *n.* jailer [L. *in*; *carcer*, prison].
incarnadine (in-kàr'-na-dīn) *a.* flesh-coloured; of a carnation colour; crimson;—*v.t.* to dye crimson [Fr. fr. L. *caro*, flesh].
incarnate (in-kàr'-nāt) *v.t.* to embody in flesh, esp. in human form;—*a.* embodied in flesh.—**incarna'tion** *n.* embodiment; that which embodies and typifies an abstraction [L. *in*; *caro, carnis*, flesh].
incautious (in-kaw'-shus) *a.* not cautious; careless; indiscreet; unwary; rash.—**incau'tion, incau'tiousness** *n.*—**incau'tiously** *adv.*
incendiary (in-sen'-di-ar-i) *n.* one who maliciously sets fire to property; an agitator who inflames passions; a fire bomb;—*a.* pert. to malicious burning of property; tending to inflame dissension.—**incen'diarism** *n.* arson [L. *incendere*, to set on fire].
incense (in-sens') *v.t.* to inflame to violent anger [L. *incendere*, to set on fire].
incense (in'-sens) *n.* a mixture of aromatic gums and spices which, when burnt, produces a sweet-smelling smoke, used for religious purposes; flattery; adulation.—**incense'** *v.t.* to perfume with incense [L. *incendere*, to burn].
incentive (in-sent'-iv) *a.* inciting; provoking;—*n.* motive; spur; stimulus; encouragement [L. *incentivus*, setting the tune].
inception (in-sep'-shun) *n.* beginning; start; origin.—**incep'tive** *a.*—**incep'tively** *adv.* [L. *incipere, inceptum*, to begin].
incertitude (in-ser'-ti-tūd) *n.* uncertainty.
incessant (in-ses'-ant) *a.* continuing or following without interruption; ceaseless; constant; perpetual.—**incess'ancy** *n.*—**incess'antly** *adv.* [L. *in-*, not; *cessare*, to cease].
incest (in'-sest) *n.* sexual intercourse of kindred within the forbidden degrees.—**incest'uous** *a.* [L. *in-*, not; *castus*, chaste].
inch (insh) *n.* twelfth part of a linear foot; a small degree or quantity;—*v.i.* to push forward by slow degrees; to edge forward [L. *uncia*, twelfth part of anything].
inch (insh) *n.* a small island [Gael. *innis*].
inchoate (in'-kō-āt *a.* just begun; rudimentary; incomplete; undeveloped; incipient.—**in'choately** *adv.*—**inchoa'tion** *n.* early, rudimentary state.—**incho'ative** *a.* [L. *inchoare*, to begin].
incident (in'-si-dent) *a.* falling upon, as a ray of light upon a reflecting surface; naturally attaching to; striking; liable to happen;—*n.* that which takes place; event; occurrence; episode; subordinate action.—**in'cidence** *n.* the manner of falling upon (esp. of forms of taxation); range of influence.—**incident'al** *a.* happening.—**incident'ally** *adv.*—**incident'alness** *n.* [L. *incidere*, to fall in].
incinerate (in-sin'-er-āt) *v.t.* to consume by fire; to burn to ashes.—**incinera'tion** *n.*—**incin'erator** *n.* furnace for consuming refuse [L. *incinerare*, to reduce to ashes].
incipient (in-sip'-i-ent) *a.* beginning; originating; inceptive.—**incip'ience, incip'iency** *n.* [L. *incipere*, to begin].
incise (in-sīz') *v.t.* to cut into; to carve; to engrave.—**incision** (in-sizh'-un) *n.* the act of cutting with a sharp instrument; a cut; gash.—**inci'sive** *a.* having the quality of cutting or penetrating; sharp; acute; biting; trenchant; sarcastic.—**inci'sively** *adv.*—**inci'siveness** *n.*—**inci'sor** *n.* one of the eight front cutting teeth [L. *incidere*, to cut into].
incite (in-sīt') *v.t.* to move the mind to action; to spur on.—**incit'ant** *n.* a stimulant;—*a.* exciting; stimulating.—**incitation** (in-sit-ā'-shun) *n.* act of inciting; that which incites.—**incite'ment** *n.* motive; incentive.—**incit'er** *n.* [L. *incitare*, to rouse].
incivil (in-siv'-il) *a.* rude; uncivil.—**incivil'ity** *n.* want of courtesy; rudeness; impoliteness.
inclement (in-klem'-ent) *a.* not clement; unmerciful; severe; harsh; rainy; stormy.—**inclem'ency** *n.*—**inclem'ently** *adv.*
incline (in-klīn') *v.t.* to cause to deviate from a line or direction; to give a tendency to, as to the will or affections; to bend; to turn from the vertical;—*v.i.* to deviate from the vertical; to be disposed.—**in'cline** *n.* an ascent or descent; a slope.—**inclina'tion** *n.* act of inclining; bent of the mind or will; leaning; tendency towards; favour for one thing more than another; love for; desire.—**inclined'** *a.* bent; disposed [L. *in*; *clinare*, to lean].
inclose, inclosure See **enclose.**
include (in-klòòd') *v.t.* to confine within; to comprise. —**inclu'sion** *n.* act of including; state of being included or confined.—**inclu'sive** *a.* taking in the stated limit, number, or extremes; enclosing; embracing.—**inclu'sively** *adv.* [L. *includere*, to shut in].
incog (in-kog') *adv.* Same as **incognito.**
incogitable (in-koj'-i-ta-bl) *a.* incapable of being thought of; unimaginable.
incognito (in-kog'-ni-tō) *a.* and *adv.* unknown; in a disguise; in an assumed character and under an assumed name;—*n.* (*fem.* **incog'nita**) the state of being unknown; a person who conceals his identity under a false name [L. *incognitus*, unknown].
incoherent (in-kō-hēr'-ent) *a.* not connected or clear (of speech); confused.—**incoher'ence** *n.*—**incoher'ently** *adv.*
incombustible (in-kom-bust'-i-bl) *a.* not capable of being burned, decomposed, or consumed, by fire.—**incombustibil'ity, incombust'ibleness** *n.*—**incombust'ibly** *adv.*
income (in'-kum) *n.* the gain or reward from one's labours or investments; annual receipts, of a company; rent; profit; interest.—**in'comer** *n.* a newcomer to a locality.—**in'coming** *n.* taking possession of a house, farm, etc; revenue;—*a.* accruing; ensuing.—**income tax,** tax levied on income.
incommensurable (in-kom-en'-sū-ra-bl) *a.* having no common measure or standard of comparison.—**incommensurabil'ity, incommen'surableness** *n.*—**incommen'surably** *adv.*—**incommen'surate** *a.* not admitting of a common measure; unequal; out of proportion.—**incommen'surately** *adv.*

INDUSTRY · 1

Rolling Mill

Casting

Mining: Australia

Refinery at night

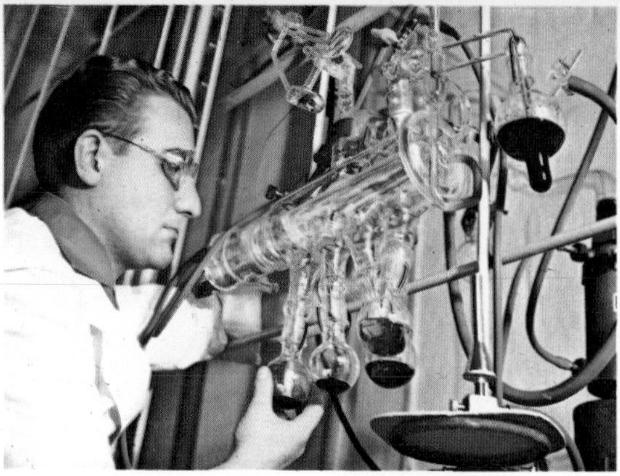

Chemical research

INDUSTRY · 2

Polymerisation plant

Polyethylene sheet manufacture

1

Removing moulds

'Throwing' a plate

incommode (in-ko-mōd′) *v.t.* to put to inconvenience; to give trouble to; to embarrass. —**incommo′dious** *a.* inconvenient; vexatious. —**incommo′diously** *adv.* [L. *in-*, not; *commodus*, convenient].

incommunicable (in-ko-mūn′i-ka-bl) *a.* incapable of being communicated or shared; inalienable, not transferable; unspeakable. —**incommunicabil′ity** *n.*—**incommun′icableness** *n.*—**incommun′icably** *adv.*—**incommun′icative** *a.* reserved; not ready to impart information.

incommunicado (in′ko-mūn-i-kà′dō) *a.* of a prisoner, deprived of communication with other people.

incomparable (in-kom′par-a-bl) *a.* not admitting any degree of comparison with another; unrivalled.—**incomparabil′ity** *n.*—**incom′parableness** *n.*—**incom′parably** *adv.*

incompatible (in-kom-pat′i-bl) *a.* incapable of existing side by side; unable to live together in harmony.—**incompatibil′ity, incompat′ibleness** *n.*—**incompat′ibly** *adv.*

incompetent (in-kom′pe-tent) *a.* not efficient in the performance of function; inadequate; incapable.—**incom′petence** *n.* incapacity.— **incom′petency** *n.*—**incom′petently** *adv.*

incomplete (in-kom-plēt′) *a.* defective; imperfect; unfinished; unaccomplished.—**incomplete′ly** *adv.*

incomprehensible (in-kom-pre-hen′si-bl) *a.* incapable of being comprehended or understood; not to be kept within bounds or limits. **incomprehensibil′ity, incomprehen′sibleness, incomprehen′sion** *n.* difficulty of understanding; quality or state of being incomprehensible.—**incomprehen′sibly** *adv.*—**incomprehen′sive** *a.* limited; not extensive.

incompressible (in-kom-pres′i-bl) *a.* cannot be compressed or reduced in bulk.

incomputable (in-kom-pūt′a-bl) *a.* cannot be computed, reckoned, or estimated.

inconceivable (in-kon-sēv′a-bl) *a.* not capable of being conceived in the mind; unthinkable. —**inconceivabil′ity, inconceiv′ableness** *n.*—**inconceiv′ably** *adv.*

inconclusive (in-kon-klōōs′iv) *a.* not decisive or conclusive; not settling a point in debate or a doubtful question.

incongruous (in-kong′grōō-us) *a.* having nothing in common; not reciprocally agreeing; (*Math.*) not co-inciding.—**incon′gruent** *a.* —**incongru′ity, incon′gruousness** *n.*

inconsequent (in-kon′se-kwent) *a.* not following from the premises; illogical; irrelevant; rambling.—**incon′sequence** *n.*—**inconsequen′tial** *a.* not to the point; illogical; of no import; trivial.—**inconsequen′tially** *adv.*

inconsiderable (in-kon-sid′er-a-bl) *a.* unworthy of consideration; unimportant.

inconsiderate (in-kon-sid′er-āt) *a.* thoughtless; careless of others' feelings; heedless; inattentive.—**inconsid′erately** *adv.*

inconsistent (in-kon-sist′ent) *a.* liable to sudden and unexpected change; changeable; not agreeing.—**inconsist′ence, inconsist′ency** *n.*

inconsolable (in-kon-sōl′a-bl) *a.* not to be comforted or consoled.

inconspicuous (in-kon-spik′ū-us) *a.* scarcely noticeable; hardly discernible.

inconstant (in-con′stant) *a.* not constant or consistent; subject to change.—**incon′stancy** *n.* fickleness.—**incon′stantly** *adv.*

incontestable (in-kon-test′a-bl) *a.* not to be disputed or contested; incontrovertible; indisputable; undeniable; indubitable; unquestionable.—**incontest′ably** *adv.*

incontinent (in-kon′ti-nent) *a.* morally incapable of restraint;—*adv.* immediately; at once; straightway.—**incon′tinence, incon′tinency** *n.*—**incon′tinently** *adv.*

incontrovertible (in-kon-tro-vert′i-bl) *a.* too clear or certain to admit of dispute; unquestionable.—**incontrovert′ibly** *adv.*

inconvenient (in-kon-vēn′yent) *a.* awkward; unsuitable.—**inconven′ience** *v.t.* to put to trouble or annoyance.—**inconven′ience, inconven′iency** *n.*—**inconven′iently** *adv.*

inconvertible (in-kon-vert′i-bl) *a.* cannot be changed or exchanged; of paper money, notes which cannot be converted into gold on demand.—**inconvertibil′ity** *n.*

inconvincible (in-kon-vin′si-bl) *a.* incapable of being convinced or assured.

inco-ordinate (in-kō-or′di-nāt) *a.* not in orderly relation with one another.

incorporate (in-kor′po-rāt) *v.t.* and *v.i.* to combine, as different ingredients, into one body or mass; to give a material form to; to constitute into a corporation; to become incorporated; to embody;—*a.* united; formed into an incorporation.—**incorpora′tion** *n.* act of incorporating; state of being incorporated; the formation or embodying of an association or society.—**incor′porative** *a.*—**incorpo′real** *a.* not possessed of a body; immaterial; unsubstantial; spiritual.—**incorporeal′ity** *n.*—**incorpor′eally** *adv.*

incorrect (in-ko-rekt′) *a.* inaccurate; not in accordance with the truth; erroneous; false. —**incorrect′ly** *adv.*—**incorrect′ness** *n.*

incorrigible (in-kor′i-ji-bl) *a.* beyond any hope of reform or improvement in conduct;— *n.* such a person.

incorrupt (in-kor-upt′) *a.* pure; undefiled; not open to bribery; not depraved.—**incorrup′tible** *a.* incapable of being corrupted; not subject to decay.

increase (in-krēs′) *v.t.* to make greater; to extend; to lengthen;—*v.i.* to become greater; to multiply by the production of young.— **in′crease** *n.* growth; produce; profit; interest; progeny; offspring; enlargement; addition.— **increas′able** *a.*—**increas′ingly** *adv.* [L. *increscere*, fr. *crescere*, to grow].

incredible (in-kred′i-bl) *a.* impossible to be believed; surpassing belief; amazing.—**incredibil′ity, -′ibleness** *n.*—**incred′ibly** *adv.*

incredulous (in-kred′ū-lus) *a.* not disposed to believe; hard of belief.—**incredu′lity** *n.* disbelief; scepticism.—**incred′ulousness** *n.*— **incred′ulously** *adv.*

increment (in′kre-ment) *n.* increase; matter added; growth; annual augmentation of a fixed amount to a salary.—**increment′al** *a.* [L. *incrementum*, fr. *increscere*, to increase].

incriminate (in-krim′i-nāt) *v.t.* to charge with a crime; to involve one in a criminal action.— **incrim′inatory** *a.* [L. *in*; *crimen*, a charge].

incrust, encrust (in-, en-krust′) *v.t.* to cover with a crust;—*v.i.* to form a hard covering or crust on the surface.—**incrusta′tion** *n.*

incubate (in′kū-bāt) *v.i.* to sit, as on eggs, for hatching; to brood; of disease germs, to pass through the stage between infection and appearance of symptoms;—*v.t.* to hatch; to ponder over.—**incuba′tion** *n.*—**in′cubative, incuba′tory** *a.*—**in′cubator** *n.* a cabinet, in which the heat is automatically regulated, used to hatch eggs [L. *in*; *cubare*, to lie].

incubus (in′kū-bus) *n.* the nightmare; any burdensome or depressing influence [L. *in*, upon; *cubare*, to lie].

inculcate (in-kul′kāt) *v.t.* (foll. by *in* or *on*) to urge forcibly and repeatedly; to impress by admonition; to implant.—**inculca′tion** *n.*— **in′culcator** *n.* [L. *inculcare*, to stamp in].

incumbent (in-kum′bent) *a.* lying or resting upon; resting on, as duty;—*n.* holder of ecclesiastical benefice.—**incum′bency** *n.* state of resting or lying upon; office or tenure of an incumbent [L. *incumbere*, to lie upon].

incunabula (in-kū-nab′ū-la) *n.pl.* term applied to books printed during the 15th cent. [L. = swaddling clothes].

incur (in-kur′) *v.t.* to become liable to; to bring upon oneself.—*pr.p.* **incurr′ing**.—*pa.t.* and *pa.p.* **incurred′** [L. *in*, into; *currere*, to run].

incurable (in-kūr′a-bl) *a.* not able to be cured; —*n.* one beyond cure.—**incur′ableness, incurabil′ity** *n.*

incurious (in-kū́-ri-us) *a.* not inquisitive or curious; indifferent.—**incu'riously** *adv.*—**incu'riousness, incurios'ity** *n.*

incursion (in-kuŕ-shun) *n.* a raid into a territory with hostile intention.—**incur'sive** *a.* [L. *in*, into; *currere*, to run].

incurve (in-kurv') *v.t.* to bend into a curve; to make crooked;—*v.i.* to bend inward.—**incur'vate** *v.t.* to bend inward or upward;—*a.* curved inward or upward.

indaba (in-dá-ba) *n.* a council meeting of natives in S. Africa [Bantu = business].

indebted (in-det́-ed) *a.* being in debt; placed under an obligation; owing; beholden; grateful.—**indebt'edness** *n.*

indecent (in-dḗ-sent) *a.* unbecoming; immodest; obscene.—**inde'cency** *n.* lack of decency.—**inde'cently** *adv.*

indecipherable (in-de-sī́-fer-ạ-bl) *a.* incapable of being deciphered; illegible.

indecision (in-de-sizh́-un) *n.* want of decision; irresoluteness; shilly-shallying.—**indeci'sive** *a.* inconclusive; doubtful; wavering.—**indeci'sively** *adv.*—**indeci'siveness** *n.*

indeclinable (in-de-klīń-ạ-bl) *a.* (*Gram.*) having no inflections or cases.

indecorous (in-de-kṓr-us, in-deḱ-o-rus) *a.* unbecoming; contrary to good manners.—**indeco'rously** *adv.*—**indeco'rousness, indeco'rum** *n.* impropriety.

indeed (in-dēd') *adv.* in reality; in truth; in fact; certainly;—used interjectionally as an expression of surprise, etc.

indefatigable (in-de-fat́-i-gạ-bl) *a.* incapable of being fatigued; unwearied; untiring.—**indefat'igableness, indefatigabil'ity** *n.*—**indefat'igably** *adv.* [L. *in-*; *defatigare*, to tire].

indefeasible (in-de-fēź-i-bl) *a.* not to be defeated; incapable of being made void; irrevocable.—**indefeasibil'ity** *n.*—**indefeas'ibly** *adv.* [O.Fr. *defaire*, to undo].

indefensible (in-de-fenś-i-bl) *a.* incapable of being maintained, vindicated, or justified; untenable; unjustifiable; unexcusable.

indefinable (in-de-fīń-ạ-bl) *a.* not able to be defined.—**indefin'ably** *adv.*

indefinite (in-deḱ-i-nit) *a.* having no known limits; (*Gram.*) not pointing out with precision the person, thing, or time to which a part of speech refers.—**indef'initely** *adv.*—**indef'initeness, indefin'itude** *n.* want of precision.—**indefinite article**, a, an.

indelible (in-deĺ-i-bl) *a.* not to be blotted out or erased; ineffaceable; ingrained.—**indelibil'ity, indel'ibleness** *n.*—**indel'ibly** *adv.* [L. *in-*, not; *delere*, to destroy, blot out].

indelicate (in-deĺ-i-kāt) *a.* offensive to good manners or to purity of mind; indecorous; unbecoming. — **indel'icacy** *n.*— **indel'icately** *adv.*

indemnify (in-dem-ni-fī) *v.t.* to reimburse; to give security against; to free one from the consequences of a technically illegal act.—*pa.t.* and *pa.p.* **indem'nified**.—**indemnifica'tion** *n.*—**indem'nitor** *n.*—**indem'nity** *n.* an agreement to render a person immune from a contingent liability; compensation [L. *indemnis*, unharmed].

indemonstrable (in-de-moń-strạ-bl) *a.* cannot be demonstrated or proved.

indent (in-dent') *v.t.* to cut into points or inequalities; to make notches or holes in; to make an order (*upon* some one *for*); to make duplicate copies of a document; to indenture; (*Print.*) to begin the first line of a paragraph farther away from the margin than the remaining lines;—*v.i.* to bargain; to wind about.—**in'dent** *n.* a cut or notch; a dent; a mark, as of a tooth; an official order for goods to be supplied.—**indenta'tion** *n.* a hollow; a depression.—**inden'ture** *n.* a contract of apprenticeship; a written agreement between two or more persons;—*v.t.* to bind by indentures [L. *in*, in; *dens*, a tooth].

independent (in-de-pend́-ent) *a.* not dependent; not subject to the control of others; unrelated; free; self-supporting; irrespective of.—**independ'ence, independ'ency** *n.*—**independ'ently** *adv.*

indescribable (in-de-skrīb́-ạ-bl) *a.* incapable of being described.

indestructible (in-de-struḱ-ti-bl) *a.* not able to be destroyed; imperishable.—**indestructibil'ity** *n.*—**indestruc'tibly** *adv.*

indeterminable (in-de-tẽŕ-min-ạ-bl) *a.* cannot be determined, classified, or fixed.—**indeter'minableness** *n.*—**indeter'minably** *adv.*—**indeter'minate** *a.* not settled or fixed in detail; indefinite.—**indeter'minately** *adv.*—**indeter'minateness, indetermina'tion** *n.* an unsettled or wavering state of the mind; vacillation.

index (iń-deks) *n.* a directing sign; that which points out, shows, indicates, or manifests, esp. a pointer or hand which directs to anything; any table for facilitating reference in a book; the forefinger or pointing finger; the ratio between the measurement of a given substance and that of a fixed standard.—*pl.* **in'dexes**.—(*Math.*) the figure or letter showing the power of a quantity; the exponent of a power.—*pl.* **in'dices**.—*v.t.* to provide with an index or table references; to place in alphabetical order in an index.—**in'dexer** *n.* one who compiles an index [L. = an indicator].

India (iń-di-ạ) *n.* a country in Asia, named from river *Indus*.—**In'diaman** *n.* a large ship engaged exclusively in the Indian trade.—**India paper**, a very thin, tough and opaque paper made of linen rags.—**in'dia-rub'ber** *n.* a form of rubber used for erasing black-lead pencil marks [Sans. *sindhu*, a river].

Indian (iń-di-an) *a.* pert. to India in Asia, to the West Indies, or to the aborigines of America;—*n.* a native of India in Asia, of the West Indies, or one of the aboriginal inhabitants of America.—**Indian club**, bottle-shaped wooden club, used in physical exercise.—**Indian corn**, maize.—**Indian file**, single file.—**Indian fire**, a composition used in firework displays, consisting of nitre, sulphur, and realgar, and burning with an intense white flame.—**Indian game**, a variety of domestic poultry valued as a meat producer.—**Indian hemp**, dried flowering tops of an annual, grown in N. India, used as narcotic and anodyne; also known as *bhang*, or *hashish*.—**Indian-ink**, ink composed of lamp-black mixed into a paste with gum.—**Indian pipe**, a flowering plant, unique in having no chlorophyll.—**Indian poke**, the white hellebore of America.—**Indian red**, an earthy pigment with a purple-russet colour, due to the presence of peroxide of iron.—**Indian summer**, in N. America, a period in autumn characterised by calms and absence of rain.—**Red Indian**, one of the aboriginal races of the New World [Sans. *sindhu*, a river].

indicate (iń-di-kāt) *v.t.* to point out; to be a sign of; to denote; to show; to signify.—**indica'tion** *n.* act of indicating; mark; token; sign.—**indic'ative** *a.* pointing out; denoting; (*Gram.*) applied to that mood of the verb which affirms or denies;—*n.* the direct mood of a verb.—**indic'atively** *adv.*—**in'dicator** *n.* one who indicates; a pointer; an instrument used to gauge and record varying conditions in mechanical operations.—**in'dicatory** *a.* [L. *indicare*, to show].

indices (iń-di-ses) *n.pl.* (*Math.*) See **index**.

indict (in-dīt') *v.t.* to charge with a crime; to accuse; to arraign; to summon for trial.—**indict'able** *a.*—**indict'ment** *n.* the act of indicting; a formal charge of crime, preferred to a court of justice [L. *in*; *dicere*, to declare].

indifferent (in-diḱ-ẽr-ent) *a.* not making a difference; having no influence or weight; of no account; uninterested; careless; neither good nor bad.—**indiff'erence** *n.* freedom from prejudice or bias; unconcern.—**indiff'erently** *adv.*

indigene (in′di-jēn) *n.* an aborigine; a native animal or plant.—**indig'enous** *a.* born or originating in a country; native.—**indig'enously** *adv.* [L. *indigena*, a native].

indigent (in′di-jent) *a.* destitute of property or means of subsistence; needy; poor.—**in′digence** *n.* [L. *indigere*, to lack].

indigest (in-di-jest′) *a.* not digested; irregular; —*n.* crude, undigested mass.—**indigest'ed** *a.* not digested; lacking order or system.—**indigestibil'ity** *n.*—**indigest'ible** *a.* incapable of being digested.—**indigest'ibly** *adv.*—**indigest'ion** *n.* inability to digest food or difficulty and discomfort in doing so; dyspepsia.—**indigest'ive** *a.* dyspeptic.

indignant (in-dig′nant) *a.* moved by a feeling of wrath, mingled with scorn or contempt; wroth; roused.—**indig'nantly** *adv.*—**indigna'tion** *n.* righteous wrath.—**indig'nity** *n.* affront; unmerited contemptuous treatment [L. *in-*, not; *dignari*, to deem worthy].

indigo (in′di-gō) *n.* a blue dye-stuff derived from many leguminous plants of the genus Indigofera, but also cheaply synthesised from naphthalene;—*a.* of a deep-blue colour [L. *indicum*, fr. *Indicus*, of India].

indirect (in-di-rekt′) *a.* not direct or straight; oblique; crooked; unfair; dishonest.—**indirec'tion** *n.* deliberate attempt to mislead; trickery.—**indirect'ly** *adv.*—**indirect'ness** *n.*

indiscernible (in-dis-ern′i-bl) *a.* not discernible; invisible; imperceptible; indistinguishable.

indiscreet (in-dis-krēt′) *a.* not discreet; imprudent; injudicious; reckless.—**indiscreet'ly** *adv.*—**indiscretion** (in-dis-kresh′un) *n.* an indiscreet act; the quality of being indiscreet; rashness; mistake.

indiscriminate (in-dis-krim′i-nāt) *a.* wanting discrimination; not making any distinction.—**indiscrim'inately** *adv.*—**indiscrim'inating, indiscrim'inative** *a.* making no distinction.—**indiscrimina'tion** *n.*

indispensable (in-dis-pen′sa-bl) *a.* absolutely necessary; not to be set aside.—**indispensabil'ity, indispens'ableness** *n.*—**indispens'ably** *adv.*

indispose (in-dis-pōz′) *v.t.* to render unfit or unsuited; to make somewhat ill; to render averse or disinclined (toward); to disorder slightly.—**indisposed'** *a.* averse; not well; ill.—**indisposi'tion** *n.*

indisputable (in-dis′pū-ta-bl) *a.* too obvious to be disputed; incontestable.

indissoluble (in-dis-ol′ū-bl) *a.* not capable of being dissolved; perpetually binding or obligatory; inviolable.—**indiss'olubleness, indissolubil'ity** *n.*—**indiss'olubly** *adv.*

indistinct (in-dis-tingkt′) *a.* not distinct or distinguishable; not clearly defined or uttered; obscure; dim.—**indistinct'ive** *a.* not capable of making distinctions; not distinctive.—**indistinct'ly** *adv.*

indistinguishable (in-dis-ting′gwish-a-bl) *a.* may not be distinguished.—**indistin'guishableness** *n.* —**indistin'guishably** *adv.*

indite (in-dīt′) *v.t.* to direct or dictate what is to be uttered or written; to compose; to write.—**indite'ment** *n.* [O. Fr. *enditer*].

indium (in′di-um) *n.* a rare metallic element, found in zinc ores [fr. its spectrum containing *indigo* lines].

individual (in-di-vid′ū-al) *a.* not divided; single; peculiar to single person or thing; distinctive; —*n.* a single being, animal, or thing.—**individualisa'tion** *n.*—**individ'ualise, individ'uate** *v.t.* to distinguish individually; to particularise.—**individ'ualism** *n.* quality of being individual; a political or economic theory which asserts the rights of the individual as against those of the community. —**individ'ualist** *n.*—**individualist'ic** *a.*—**individual'ity** *n.* separate or distinct existence; personality.—**individ'ually** *adv.* [L. *individuus*, undivided].

indivisible (in-di-viz′i-bl) *a.* not divisible; not separable into parts;—*n.* infinitely small quantity.—**indivisibil'ity, indivis'ibleness** *n.*—**indivis'ibly** *adv.*

indoctrinate (in-dok′trin-āt) *v.t.* to instruct in doctrine; to imbue with political or religious principles and dogmas.—**indoctrina'tion** *n.*

Indo-European (in′dō-ū-rō-pē′an) *a.* term applied to a family of languages spoken in Europe and Asia, including Latin, Greek, Sanskrit, Persian and the various Slavonic, Celtic, Romance and Teutonic tongues.

indolent (in′do-lent) *a.* habitually idle or lazy; indisposed to exertion or labour.—**in'dolence, in'dolency** *n.* laziness.—**in'dolently** *adv.* [L. *in-*, not; *dolere*, to feel pain].

indomitable (in-dom′it-a-bl) *a.* not to be subdued; that cannot be overcome; unconquerable; unyielding.—**indom'itably** *adv.* [L. *in-*, not; *domitare*, to tame].

Indo-English (in′dō-ing′glish) *a.* of or relating to the English people who are born or reside in India.

Indonesia (in-do-nē′zi-a) *n.* Republic of S.E. Asia (since 1945).—**Indone'sian** *a.* pert. to Indonesia;—*n.* one who is an inhabitant of Indonesia [*Indo*, and Gk. *nēsos*, an island].

indoor (in′dōr) *a.* being within doors; under cover; pert. to internal house affairs.—**in′doors** *adv.*

indorse, indorsement See **endorse.**

indubitable (in-dū′bit-a-bl) *a.* too obvious to admit of doubt; undoubted; unquestionable; quite certain.—**indu'bitably** *adv.*

induce (in-dūs′) *v.t.* to bring in; to overcome by persuasion or argument; to persuade; to produce or cause (as electricity).—**induce'ment** *n.* that which induces or persuades to action. —**induc'er** *n.*—**induc'ible** *a.* [L. *inducere*, to lead in].

induct (in-dukt′) *v.t.* to bring in or introduce; to install or put formally into possession (esp. a clergyman of a benefice or charge).—**induc'tile** *a.* of a metal not capable of being drawn out into wires or threads.—**inductil'ity** *n.*—**induc'tion** *n.* installation of a person in a benefice, charge or honourable office; an introduction to a poem or play; (*Elect.*) the transfer of a magnetic or electric state from an electrified to a non-electrified body, by proximity.—**induc'tional** *a.*—**induc'tive** *a.* leading or drawing on.—**induc'tively** *adv.*—**induc'tor** *n.* [L. *in*, into; *ducere*, to lead].

indulge (in-dulj′) *v.t.* to give freedom or scope to; to allow one his own way; to gratify;—*v.i.* (usu. followed by *in*) to give oneself to the habit or practice of.—**indul'gence** *n.* the act of indulging; favour granted; remission of the temporal penalty due for a sin.—**indul'gent** *a.* yielding; compliant; very forbearing; kind or liberal; tender.—**indul'gently** *adv.* [L. *indulgere*, to be indulgent].

indurate (in′dū-rāt) *v.t.* to make hard; to deprive of sensibility;—*v.i.* grow hard; to harden.—**indura'tion** *n.* [L. *in*, in; *durus*, hard].

industry (in′dus-tri) *n.* habitual diligence in any employment, bodily or mental; steady application to work; assiduity; a particular branch of trade or manufacture.—**indus'trial** *a.* pert. to industry or manufacture.—**indus'trialism** *n.* system of industry or manufacture on a large scale.—**indus'trially** *adv.*—**indus'trious** *a.* diligent in business or study; assiduous, active, busy.—**indus'triously** *adv.*—**indus'triousness** *n.* [L. *industria*].

indwell (in′dwel) *v.t.* and *i.* to dwell in.—**in′dwelling** *n.* residence within the heart or soul; —*a.* dwelling within; seated.

inebriate (in-ē′bri-āt) *v.t.* to make drunk; to intoxicate; to exhilarate;—*a.* intoxicated;—*n.* a habitual drunkard.—**inebria'tion, inebri'ety** *n.* drunkenness.—**ine'brious** *a.* stupidly drunk [L. *in*; *ebrius*, drunk].

inedible (in-ed′i-bl) *a.* not eatable; unfit for food.—**inedibil'ity** *n.*

ineffable (in-ef′a-bl) *a.* incapable of being expressed in words; indescribable; unutterable.

—**ineff'ableness, ineffabil'ity** *n.*—**ineff'ably** *adv.* [L. *in-*, not; *effabilis*, speakable].
ineffaceable (in-e-fas'ą-bl) *a.* incapable of being rubbed out.—**inefface'ably** *adv.*
ineffective (in-e-fek'tiv) *a.* incapable of producing any effect or the effect intended; useless; inefficient.—**ineffec'tively** *adv.*—**ineffec'tual** *a.* not producing the proper effect; vain; fruitless; futile.—**ineffectual'ity, ineffec'tualness** *n.*—**ineffec'tually** *adv.*
inefficacy (in-ef'i-ką-si) *n.* want of power to produce the proper effect.—**ineffica'cious** *a.*—**ineffica'ciously** *adv.*
inefficient (in-e-fish'ent) *a.* not fitted to perform the work; not capable; incompetent.—**ineffic'iency** *n.*—**ineffic'iently** *adv.*
inelastic (in-e-las'tik) *a.* not elastic; rigid; unyielding.—**inelastic'ity** *n.*
inelegant (in-el'e-gant) *a.* lacking in form or beauty; wanting grace or ornament.—**inel'egance, inel'egancy** *n.*—**inel'egantly** *adv.*
ineligible (in-el'i-jibl) *a.* incapable of being chosen for or elected to an office; unsuitable.—**ineligibil'ity** *n.*—**inel'igibly** *adv.*
ineluctable (in-e-luk'tą-bl) *a.* not able to be avoided; inevitable.—**ineluctabil'ity** *n.* [L. *in-*; *eluctari*, to struggle out].
inept (in-ept') *a.* not apt or fit; inexpert; unsuitable; foolish.—**inept'itude, inept'ness** *n.*—**inept'ly** *adv.* [L. *in*, not; *aptus*, fit].
inequable (in-ē', or e'kwą-bl) *a.* not equable; not uniform; unfairly distributed.
inequality (in-ē-kwol'i-ti) *n.* want of equality; disparity; dissimilarity; unevenness of surface.
inequitable (in-ek'wi-tą-bl) *a.* not fair or just; not according to equity.
ineradicable (in-e-rad'i-ką-bl) *a.* incapable of being rooted out; deep-seated.
inert (in-ẹrt') *a.* without the power of action or resistance; torpid; sluggish; slow; dull; lifeless; without active chemical properties.—**inertia** (in-ẹr'shi-ą) *n.* that property of matter by which it tends when at rest to remain so, and when in motion to continue moving in a straight line.—**inert'ly** *adv.*—**inert'ness** *n.* [L. *iners*, sluggish].
inescapable (in-es-kā'pą-bl) *a.* inevitable; incapable of escape or of being evaded.
inessential (in-es-en'shąl) *a.* not necessary; immaterial; not vital; of little consequence.
inestimable (in-es'tim-ąbl) *a.* not possible to be estimated; priceless; of untold value; incalculable; invaluable.—**ines'timably** *adv.*
inevitable (in-ev'it-ą-bl) *a.* unavoidable; certain to take place or appear.—**inev'itableness, inev'itability** *n.*—**inev'itably** *adv.* [L. *in-*; *evitare*, to avoid].
inexact (in-eg-zakt') *a.* not exact; not strictly true.—**inexact'itude, inexact'ness** *n.*
inexcusable (in-eks-kū'zą-bl) *a.* not admitting excuse or justification; unpardonable.—**inexcus'ably** *adv.*
inexhaustible (in-eg-zaws'ti-bl) *a.* incapable of being exhausted, emptied, or spent; unfailing.—**inexhaustibil'ity** *n.*—**inexhaust'ibly** *adv.*—**inexhaus'tive** *a.* not to be exhausted; unfailing; cursory.
inexorable (in-egz'or-ą-bl) *a.* not to be persuaded or moved by entreaty; unyielding.—**inex'orableness, inexorabil'ity** *n.*—**inex'orably** *adv.* [L. *in-*; *exorare*, to entreat].
inexpedient (in-eks-pē'di-ent) *a.* not advisable; impolitic; undesirable at the moment.—**inexpe'dience, inexpe'diency** *n.*
inexpensive (in-eks-pens'iv) *a.* cheap.
inexperience (in-eks-pē'ri-ens) *n.* absence or want of experience.—**inexpe'rienced** *a.* ignorant of worldly matters.
inexpert (in-eks-pẹrt') *a.* unskilled; clumsy; awkward.—**inexpert'ness** *n.*
inexpiable (in-eks'pi-ą-bl) *a.* admitting of no atonement; implacable; inexorable.
inexplicable (in-eks'pli-ką-bl) *a.* incapable of being explained; unintelligible.—**inexplicabil'ity, inex'plicableness** *n.*—**inex'plicably** *adv.*
inexplicit (in-eks-plis'it) *a.* not explicit; not clearly stated; ambiguous; equivocal.
inexpressible (in-eks-pres'i-bl) *a.* cannot be expressed; indescribable.—**inexpress'ibly** *adv.*
inexpressive (in-eks-pres'iv) *a.* not expressive; lacking emphasis; insignificant.
inextensible (in-eks-ten'si-bl) *a.* not capable of extension.—**inextensibil'ity** *n.*
inextinguishable (in-eks-ting'gwish-ą-bl) *a.* cannot be extinguished; unquenchable.
inextricable (in-eks'tri-ką-bl) *a.* not to be extricated or disentangled, as a knot or coil; incapable of being cleared up or explained.—**inex'tricably** *adv.*
infallible (in-fal'i-bl) *a.* incapable of error; certain; unerring; sure.—**infall'ibilism, infallibil'ity** *n.*—**infall'ibly** *adv.*
infamy (in'fą-mi) *n.* total loss of reputation; public disgrace; ill-fame.—**in'famous** *a.* of evil fame or reputation.—**in'famously** *adv.* [L. *in-*; *fama*, report].
infant (in'fąnt) *n.* a young babe; (*Law*) a person under 21;—*a.* pert. to infants or infancy.—**in'fancy** *n.* the early stage of life preceding childhood; (*Law*) life to the age of twenty-one; the first stage of anything.—**infant'icide** *n.* the killing of a newly-born child.—**in'fantile** *a.* pert. to infants; extremely childish.—**infant'ilism** *n.* arrested development, carrying childish characteristics into adult life.—**infantile paralysis,** an infectious disease, poliomyelitis, which leads to paralysis [L. *infans*, unable to speak].
infanta (in-fan'ta) *n.* a princess of the former Spanish or Portuguese royal families.—**infante** (in-fan'tā) *n.* a prince, other than the heir apparent, of the former [Sp.].
infantry (in'fąn-tri) *n.* foot-soldiers [It. *infanteria*].
infatuate (in-fat'ū-āt) *v.t.* to render foolish; to inspire with a foolish passion.—**infat'uated** *a.* greatly enamoured.—**infatua'tion** *n.* excessive and foolish love [L. *in*; *fatuus*, foolish].
infeasible (in-fēz'i-bl) *a.* not capable of being done or accomplished; impracticable.
infect (in-fekt') *v.t.* to affect (with disease); to make noxious; to taint; to influence the mood or emotions of people.—**infec'tion** *n.*—**infec'tious, infec'tive** *a.* causing infection; catching.—**infec'tiously** *adv.* [L. *inficere*, to dip into].
infelicity (in-fe-lis'i-ti) *n.* unhappiness; anything not appropriate.—**infelic'itous** *a.*
infer (in-fẹr') *v.t.* to draw as a conclusion; to deduce; to conclude.—*pr.p.* **infer'ring.**—*pa.t.* and *pa.p.* **inferred'.**—**infer'able** *a.*—**in'ference** *n.* deduction—**inferen'tial** *a.* deduced or deducible by inference.—**inferen'tially** *adv.* [L. *inferre* to bring in].
inferior (in-fē'ri-or) *a.* lower in rank, order, place, or excellence; of less value; poorer in quality;—*n.* a person of a lower rank or station.—**inferior'ity** *n.* a lower state of condition.—**infe'riorly** *adv.*—**inferiority complex,** in psycho-analysis, sub-conscious sense of inferiority which results in exaggerated and self-assertion [L. comp. of *inferus*, low].
infernal (in-fẹr'nal) *a.* pert. to the lower regions; hellish.—**infernal'ity** *n.*—**infer'nally** *adv.*—**infer'no** *n.* hell; any place resembling hell; furnace.—**infernal machine,** a bomb fitted with clock-work [L. *infernus*, fr. *inferus*, low].
infertile (in-fer'tīl) *a.* not fertile or productive; barren.—**infertil'ity** *n.*
infest (in-fest') *v.t.* to haunt; to swarm in such numbers as to be a source of annoyance.—**infes'ted** *a.* covered with body parasites as lice, etc.; plagued [L. *infestare*, fr. *infestus*, unsafe].
infidel (in'fi-del) *a.* unbelieving; sceptical;—*n.* one who is without religious faith; unbeliever; a non-Christian;—**infidel'ity** *n.* disbelief of Christianity; unfaithfulness to the marriage contract; treachery [L. *infidelis*, unfaithful].
infield (in'fēld) *n.* a field in close proximity to a farm-house; in cricket, the part of the ground near the wicket.—**in'fielder** *n.*

infilter (in-fil′tẹr) *v.t.* and *i.* to filter in.—**infil′trate** *v.i.* to enter gradually; to pass through enemy's lines, one by one.—**infiltra′tion** *n.*

infinite (in′fi-nit) *a.* unlimited in time or space; without end, limits, or bounds; (*Math.*) greater than any assignable quantity; numberless; immeasurable;—*n.* the boundlessness and immeasurableness of the universe; the Almighty, the Infinite Being.—**in′finitely** *adv.* exceedingly.—**in′finiteness** *n.* the state of being infinite.—**infinites′imal** *a.* infinitely small.—**infinitesimal′ity** *n.*—**infinites′imally** *adv.*—**infin′itude** *n.* boundlessness (of space and time).—**infin′ity** *n.* unlimited and endless extent. [L. *infinitus*, unbounded].

infinitive (in-fin′it-iv) *a.* unlimited; designating the mood of a verb which expresses its action without limitation of persons or numbers. [L. *infinitus*, unbounded].

infirm (in-fẹrm′) *a.* not strong; feeble; weak; sickly; irresolute.—**infirm′ary** *n.* a hospital, esp. for the weak and infirm.—**infirm′ity,** disease; failing.—**infirm′ly** *adv.* [L. *in-*; *firmus*, strong].

inflame (in-flām′) *v.t.* to set on fire; to arouse, as desire; to provoke; to be affected with inflammation.—**inflammabil′ity, inflam′mableness** *n.* the quality of being inflammable.—**inflam′mably** *adv.*—**inflamma′tion** *n.* inflaming; a morbid state of any part of the body characterised by heat, redness and pain.—**inflam′matory** *a.* ready to burst into flame at a comparatively low temperature; hot-tempered [L. *inflammare*, to set on fire].

inflate (in-flāt′) *v.t.* to swell with air or gas; to raise (price) artificially; to increase (currency) abnormally.—**inflat′ed** *a.* swollen; bloated; bombastic; pumped up.—**inflat′ingly** *adv.*—**infla′tion** *n.* swelling; increase in the amount of fiduciary (paper or token) money issued, beyond what is justified by the country's tangible resources.—**infla′tor, infla′ter** *n.* one who, or that which, inflates; a bicycle pump for tyres.—**infla′tus** *n.* a breathing into; inspiration [L. *in*; *flare*, to blow].

inflect (in-flekt′) *v.t.* to bend inwards; to modulate the voice; to modify (words) to show grammatical relationships.—**inflec′tion, inflex′ion** *n.* a bending inwards or deviation; a variation in the tone of the voice; variation in the terminations of words to express grammatical relations.—**inflect′ional, inflex′ional** *a.*—**inflective** *a.* subject to inflection.—**inflexibil′ity, inflex′ibleness** *n.*—**inflex′ible** *a.* incapable of being bent; unyielding to influence or entreaty; unbending.—**inflex′ibly** *adv.*—**inflex′ure** *n.* a bend; a curve; a fold [L. *in*, in; *flectere*, to bend].

inflict (in-flikt′) *v.t.* to lay on; to impose (a penalty, etc.); to afflict with something painful.—**inflic′tion** *n.* burden.—**inflic′tive** *a.* [L. *in*, in; *fligere*, to strike].

influence (in′flòò-ens) *n.* power over men or things; effect on the mind; (*Electrostatics*) induction of a charge by a charged conductor;—*v.t.* to act on the mind; to sway; to bias; to induce.—**influen′tial** *a.* exerting influence or power; possessing great authority.—**influen′tially** *adv.* [L. *in*, in; *fluere*, to flow].

influenza (in-flòò-en′zạ) *n.* (*Med.*) an acute, infectious epidemic catarrhal fever [It. = influence].

influx (in′fluks) *n.* act of flowing in; arrival of many strangers in a place; infusion.

infold, enfold (in-, en-fold′) *v.t.* to wrap up; to enclose; to encircle.

inform (in-form′) *v.t.* to give form to; to make known to; to tell;—*v.i.* to give information.—**inform′al** *a.* without formality, unceremonious.—**informal′ity** *n.*—**inform′ant** *n.* one who imparts news.—**informa′tion** *n.* knowledge; intelligence; news.—**infor′mative** *a.* having power to form.—**infor′matory** *a.* full of information.—**informed′** *a.* educated.—**inform′er** *n.* one who gives information about a violation of the law [L. *informare*, to give form to].

[infringement.

infraction (in-frak′shun) *n.* breach; violation;

infrangible (in-fran′ji-bl) *a.* not capable of being broken; not to be violated.—**infrangibil′ity** *n.* [L. *in-*, not; *frangere*, to break].

infra-red (in′frạ-red) *a.* the longer invisible heat rays below the red end of the visible spectrum.

infrequent (in-frē′kwent) *a.* seldom happening; rare; uncommon.—**infre′quence, infre′quency** *n.*—**infre′quently** *adv.*

infringe (in-frinj′) *v.t.* to violate; to transgress.—**infringe′ment** *n.* breach; breaking (of a law) [L. *in*; *frangere*, to break].

infuriate (in-fū′ri-āt) *v.t.* to render furious; to enrage; to madden [L. *in*; *furia*, rage].

infuscate (in-fus′kāt) *v.t.* to darken or obscure [L. *in*, in; *fuscus*, dark].

infuse (in-fūz′) *v.t.* to pour into; to instil; to inspire; to steep in order to extract soluble properties.—**infus′ible** *a.* capable of being infused; not capable of fusion.—**infusibil′ity** *n.*—**infu′sion** *n.* act of infusing, instilling, or inspiring; aqueous solution containing the soluble parts of a vegetable substance or the active principle of a drug, made by pouring boiling water over it, cooling and straining [L. *in*, in; *fundere, fusum*, to pour].

Infusoria (in-fū-sō′ri-ạ) *n.pl.* microscopic organisms, a division of the Protozoa, found in contaminated water and other fluids.—**infuso′rial, infuso′rian** *n.* and *a.*—**infu′sory** *a.* [L. *infusus*, soaked].

ingathering (in′gaTH-ẹr-ing) *n.* harvesting the fruits of the earth; harvest.

ingenious (in-jēn′yus) *a.* skilled in inventing or thinking out new ideas; curious or clever in design; skilfully contrived.—**inge′niously** *adv.*—**inge′niousness, ingenu′ity** *n.* [L. *ingenium*, natural ability].

ingénue (ang-zhā-nòò′) *n.* an artless, naïve, girl; an actress who plays such a part [Fr.].

ingenuous (in-jen′ū-us) *a.* of honourable extraction; frank, artless, innocent.—**ingen′uously** *adv.*—**ingen′uousness** *n.* [L. *ingenuus* free-born, frank].

ingle (ing′gl) *n.* a fire or fireplace [Gael. *aingeal*, a fire].

inglorious (in-glō′ri-us) *a.* without glory or honour; ignominious; disgraceful; shameful.—**inglo′riously** *adv.*—**inglo′riousness** *n.*

ingoing (in′gō-ing) *a.* pert. to a new tenant on taking possession;—*n.* the act of going in; an entrance. Also known as a *reveal*.

ingot (in′got) *n.* a metal casting, esp. of unwrought silver or gold [O.E. *in*; *geotan*, to pour].

ingraft See **engraft.**

ingrain, engrain (in-, en-grān′) *v.t.* to dye deeply, so as to penetrate the grain of wood or yarn; to fix firmly in the mind.—**ingrain′** *a.* dyed, before manufacture, into articles.—**ingrained′** *a.* deeply rooted.

ingrate (in′grāt) *a.* ungrateful;—*n.* an ungrateful person.—**ingrat′itude** *n.* want of gratitude; unthankfulness.

ingratiate (in-grā′shi-āt) *v.t.* to work oneself into favour with another [L. *in*; *gratia*, favour].

ingredient (in-grēd′yent) *n.* a component part of any mixture; one part or element of a compound [L. *ingredi*, to go in].

ingress (in′gres) *n.* entrance; power, right, or means of entrance [L. *ingredi, ingressum*, to go in].

ingrowing (in′grō-ing) *a.* growing inwards, esp. of a toe-nail.—**in′growth** *n.*—**in′grown** *a.*

ingurgitate (in-gur′ji-tāt) *v.t.* to swallow up greedily or hastily; to engulf.—**ingurgita′tion** *n.* [L. *in*, in; *gurges*, a whirlpool].

inhabit (in-hab′it) *v.t.* to live or dwell in; to occupy.—**inhab′itable** *a.* possible to be dwelt in.—**inhab′itant** *n.* one who inhabits; a residenter;—*a.* resident.—**inhabita′tion** *n.* the act of inhabiting; a dwelling-place.—**inhab′iter** *n.* [L. *in*, in; *habitare*, to dwell].

inhale (in-hāl') *v.t.* to breathe in, as air, tobacco smoke, etc.; to draw in the breath.—**inhal'ant** *n.* a volatile medicinal remedy to be inhaled.—**inhal'ant, inha'lent** *a.*—**inhala'tion** *n.* act of drawing air into the lungs [L. *in*, in; *halare*, to breathe].
inharmonic (in-hâr-mon'ik) *a.* not in harmony; discordant.—**inharmon'ical** *a.*—**inharmo'nious** *a.* discordant; unmusical; quarrelsome; incompatible.
inhere (in-hēr') *v.i.* (usu. followed by *in*) to exist in; to belong naturally to; to be a quality of; to be vested in, as legal rights.—**inher'ence, inher'ency** *n.*—**inher'ent** *a.* existing in something so as to be inseparable.—**inher'ently** *adv.* [L. *in*, in; *haerere*, to stick].
inherit (in-her'it) *v.t.* to receive by descent, or by will; to fall heir to; to derive (traits, etc.) from parents;—*v.i.* to succeed as heir.—**inher'itable** *a.* heritable.—**inher'itance** *n.* what is inherited.—**inher'itor** *n.* (*fem.* **inher'itress, inher'itrix**) [L. *in*, in; *heres*, an heir].
inhesion (in-hē-zhun) *n.* Same as **inherence.**
inhibit (in-hib'it) *v.t.* to hold back; to forbid; to restrain.—**inhibi'tion** *n.* a subconscious repressed emotion which controls or colours a person's attitude or behaviour.—**inhib'itory** *a.* prohibiting; forbidding; restraining [L. *inhibere*, to hold in].
inhibitor (in-hib'it-or) *n.* an organic solution used in car radiators and engines to obviate overheating due to scale and rust deposits.
inhospitable (in-hos'pi-tạ-bl) *a.* averse to showing kindness to strangers or guests; discourteous.—**inhos'pitableness, inhospital'ity** *n.*—**inhos'pitably** *adv.* [L. *hospes*, a guest].
inhuman (in-hū'man) *a.* not human or humane; without feeling or pity.—**inhumane'** *a.* cruel.—**inhuman'ity** *n.*
inhume (in-hūm') *v.t.* to put into the ground; to bury.—**inhuma'tion** *n.* [L. *humus*, ground].
inimical (in-im'i-kạl) *a.* like an enemy; unfriendly.—**inim'ically** *adv.* [L. *inimicus*, an enemy].
inimitable (in-im'i-tạ-bl) *a.* defying imitation; incomparable.—**inim'itably** *adv.*
iniquity (in-ik'wi-ti) *n.* gross injustice; want of moral principle; wickedness; a crime.—**iniq'uitous** *a.*—**iniq'uitously** *adv.* [L. *iniquitas* fr. *in-*, not; *aequus*, fair, even].
initial (i-nish'ạl) *a.* occurring at the beginning; commencing; early;—*v.t.* to put one's initials to, in the way of acknowledgment.—*pr.p.* **init'ialling.**—*pa.t.* and *pa.p.* **init'ialled.**—*n.* the first letter of a word, esp. a name.—**init'iate,** *v.t.* to begin; to start (a movement, etc.); to instruct in the rudiments of;—*n.* one who is initiated.—**initia'tion** *n.* the act of introducing to or instructing in the rudiments.—**init'iative** *a.* serving to initiate;—*n.* the first step; the quality of being able to set things going for the first time.—**init'iator** *n.*—**init'iatory** *a.* introductory [L. *initialis*, fr. *initium*, a beginning].
inject (in-jekt') *v.t.* to throw in; to force in; to introduce (a fluid) under the skin by means of a hollow needle.—**injec'tion** *n.* the act of injecting or throwing into; medicament so injected.—**injec'tor** *n.* [L. *injicere*, fr. *jacere*, to throw].
injudicious (in-jòò-dish'us) *a.* ill-advised; imprudent; lacking in judgment.—**injudic'ial** *a.* not according to the forms of law.—**injudic'iously** *adv.*—**injudic'iousness** *n.*
injunction (in-jungk'shun) *n.* an order or command; an exhortation; a precept [L. *in*, in; *jungere*, *junctum*, to join].
injure (in'jòòr) *v.t.* to do wrong, injury, damage, or injustice to; to lessen the value of.—**inju'rious** *a.* causing injury or damage.—**inju'riously** *adv.*—**in'jury** *n.* wrong; damage; harm [L. *injuria*, fr. *jus*, law].
injustice (in-jus'tis) *n.* an unjust act; want of justice; unkindness; wrong; injury.
ink (ingk) *n.* a fluid, black or coloured, used for writing, printing and sketching;—*v.t.* to cover or smear with ink.—**ink'bottle, ink'horn, ink'pot, ink'well** *n.* types of containers for holding ink.—**ink'iness** *n.*—**ink'y** *a.* resembling ink [O.Fr. *enque* = Fr. *encre*].
inkle (ing'kl) *v.t.* to hint at; to disclose.—**ink'ling** *n.* a hint or whisper; slight knowledge [etym. doubtful].
inland (in'land) *a.* remote from the sea; interior; carried on within a country;—*n.* the interior part of a country.—**in'lander** *n.* one who lives inland.—**inland revenue,** national income derived from taxation, excluding excise.
in-laws (in-lawz') *n.pl.* (*Colloq.*) one's relations by marriage.
inlay (in-lā') *v.t.* to ornament, by cutting out part of a surface and inserting pieces of pearl, ivory, wood, etc., to form a pattern.—*pa.p.* **inlaid'.**—*n.* inlaid pattern.
inlet (in'let) *n.* an entrance; a small bay or creek; an insertion.
inly (in'li) *adv.* internally; inwardly; secretly [O.E. *inlice*.]
inmate (in'māt) *n.* a dweller in a house or institution; a fellow-lodger; an inhabitant.
inmost See **inner.**
inn (in) *n.* a house which provides lodging accommodation for travellers; a hotel.—**inn'keeper** *n.* one who keeps an inn.—**Inns of Court,** the four voluntary societies which possess the exclusive right to call candidates to the English Bar [O.E.].
innate (i-nāt') *a.* inborn; native; natural; inherent; congenital.—**innate'ly** *adv.*—**innate'ness** *n.* [L. *innatus*].
inner (in'ẹr) *a.* farther in; interior; internal;—*n.* the part of a target next to the bull's-eye or centre.—**in'most, inn'ermost,** *a.* farthest in. [O.E. *innera*, comp. fr. *inne*, within].
innervate (in-ẹrv'āt). Also **innerve'.**—*v.t.* to give nervous strength to; to stimulate [L. *in*; *nervus*, sinew].
inning (in'ing) *n.* the ingathering of grain.—**inn'ings** *n.pl.* in games, a side's turn of batting [O.E. *inn*, in, within].
innocent (in'o-sent) *a.* free from guilt; blameless; harmless; sinless; simple;—*n.* an innocent person, esp. a child; a guileless, unsuspecting person.—**inn'ocence, inn'ocency** *n.* harmlessness; freedom from guilt.—**inn'ocently** *adv.* [L. *in-*, not; *nocere*, to harm].
innocuous (in-ok'ū-us) *a.* producing no ill effects; harmless.—**innoc'uously** *adv.*—**innoc'uousness** [L. *in-*, not; *nocere*, to harm].
innovate (in'o-vāt) *v.t.* to make changes by introducing something new.—**innova'tion** *n.* a new idea [L. *innovare*, fr. *novus*, new].
innoxious (in-ok'shus) *a.* innocuous; free from mischievous qualities; harmless in effects [L. *innoxius*].
innuendo (in-ū-en'dō) *n.* an allusive remark (usually deprecatory); an indirect hint;—*pl.* **innuen'does** [L. = by nodding to, fr. *nuere*, to nod].
innumerable (i-nū'mẹr-ạ-bl) *a.* not able to be numbered; countless; very numerous.—**innumerabil'ity** *n.*—**innu'merableness** *n.*
innutrition (i-nū-trish'un) *n.* want of nutrition.—**innutrit'ious** *a.*
inobservant (in-ob-zer'vant) *a.* not observant; heedless.—**inobser'vance** *n.* failure to observe (the law, church-going, etc.).
inobtrusive See **unobtrusive.**
inoculate (in-ok'ū-lāt) *v.t.* to insert, as the bud of a plant, in another plant for propagation; (*Med.*) to introduce into the body pathogenic bacteria (e.g. typhoid inoculation) or living virus (e.g. smallpox vaccination) by means of a hypodermic syringe; to imbue strongly with opinions.—**inocula'tion** *n.* [L. *inoculare*, fr. *oculus*, eye, bud].
inodorous (in-ō'do-rus) *a.* without smell.
inoffensive (in-o-fen'siv) *a.* giving no offence; quiet and harmless.—**inoffen'sively** *adv.*—**inoffen'siveness** *n.*
inofficial (in-o-fish'ạl) *a.* not done in the usual formal manner.

inoperable (in-op′ẹr-ạbl) *a.* (*Surgery*) not in a condition for operating on.—**inop′erative** *a.* not operating or in working order.

inopportune (in-op′or-tūn) *a.* unseasonable in time; not convenient; untimely.—**inopportune′ly** *adv.*—**inopportun′ity** *n.*

inordinate (in-or′di-nāt) *a.* not limited to the usual bounds.—**inor′dinateness** *n.*—**inor′dinately** *adv.* excessively.

inorganic, inorganical (in-or-gan′ik, -i-kạl) *a.* devoid of an organised structure; not derived from animal or vegetable life.—**inorgan′ically** *adv.*

inosculate (in-os′kū-lāt) *v.t.* and *v.i.* to join by the mouth of one vessel fitting into the mouth of another.

in-patient (in′pā-shent) *n.* a patient who is lodged and fed while receiving medical attention in a hospital.

input (in′pȯȯt) *n.* (*Elect.*) the power supplied to battery, condenser, etc.; a contribution.

inquest (in′kwest) *n.* act of inquiring; investigation; a judicial inquiry presided over by a coroner, with or without a jury, into the cause of a person's death.

inquietude (in-kwī′e-tūd) *n.* uneasiness either of body or of mind; restlessness.

inquire, enquire (in-, en-kwīr′) *v.i.* to ask questions; to make investigation; to seek information;—*v.t.* to ask about.—**inquir′er, enquir′er** *n.*—**inquir′ing** *a.* given to inquiring; prying.—**inquir′ingly** *adv.*—**inquir′y, enquir′y** *n.* investigation; a question [L. *inquirere*, fr. *quaerere*, to seek].

inquisition (in-kwi-zish′un) *n.* a strict investigation; official inquiry; an ecclesiastical tribunal, ' the Holy Office,' established by the R.C. Church in the Middle Ages for the trial and punishment of heretics.—**inquisit′ional** *a.*—**inquis′itive** *a.* apt to ask questions; prying; curious to know.—**inquis′itively** *adv.*—**inquis′itiveness** *n.*—**inquis′itor** *n.* one whose official duty it is to make inquiries; a member of the Court of Inquisition.—**inquisito′rial** *a.*—**inquisito′rially** *adv.* [L. *inquisitio*, fr. *inquirere*, to search out].

in re (in-rā) *prep.* in the matter of; concerning (often abbreviated to **re**) [L.].

inroad (in′rōd) *n.* a sudden incursion into enemy territory; a sudden invasion; raid.

insalubrious (in-sạ-lū′bri-us) *a.* unhealthy; unwholesome.—**insalu′brity** *n.*

insane (in-sān′) *a.* unsound in mind; mentally diseased; lunatic.—**insane′ly** *adv.*—**insane′ness, insan′ity** *n.* lunacy; madness.

insanitary (in-san′i-tạr-i) *a.* unhealthy; unwholesome.—**insanita′tion** *n.* lack of the usual sanitary arrangements.

insatiable (in-sā′shạ-bl) *a.* incapable of being satisfied; voracious; rapacious.—**insa′tiableness, insatiabil′ity** *n.*—**insa′tiably** *adv.*

insatiate (in-sā′shi-āt) *a.* not to be satisfied.—**insa′tiately** *adv.*—**insati′ety** (in-sạ-tī′et-i) *n.*

inscribe (in-skrīb′) *v.t.* to write upon; to engrave; to address or dedicate; to draw a geometrical figure inside another so as to touch but not intersect.—**inscrib′able** *a.*—**inscrib′er** *n.*—**inscrip′tion** *n.* a writing upon; words inscribed on a monument, coin, etc.; dedication of a book, etc.; a title.—**inscrip′tional, inscrip′tive** *a.* [L. *in*; *scribere*, to write].

inscrutable (in-skrȯȯ′tạ-bl) *a.* incapable of being searched into and understood by inquiry or study; mysterious.—**inscrutabil′ity, inscrut′ableness** *n.*—**inscrut′ably** *adv.* [L. *in-*, not; *scrutari*, to search].

insect (in′sekt) *n.* one of a class of invertebrate animals called the Hexapoda, having, in its mature state, the body divided into three distinct parts, the head, the thorax and the abdomen, and provided with three pairs of jointed legs;—*a.* pert. to insects; small; insignificant.—**Insect′a** *n.* the insect or hexapod (six-legged) class of arthropods.—**insec′ticide** *n.* the act of killing insect pests by spraying, dusting, or gas-poisoning; chemical preparation for the destruction of noxious insects.—**insectiv′orous** *a.* living on insects. [L. *in*, in; *secare*, to cut].

insecure (in-se-kūr′) *a.* not securely fixed; dangerous to life or limb; unsafe; unguarded; liable to loss.—**insecur′ity** *n.*

inseminate (in-sem′i-nāt) *v.t.* to sow; to impregnate.—**insemina′tion** *n.* the approach of the spermatozoon to the ovum; conception. [L. *in*, into; *semen*, seed].

insensate (in-sen′sāt) *a.* destitute of sense; without power of feeling; stupid; silly.—**insen′sately** *adv.*—**insen′sateness** *n.*

insensible (in-sen′si-bl) *a.* without bodily sensation; not perceived by the senses; unconscious; callous; imperceptible.—**insensibil′ity, insen′sibleness** *n.*—**insen′sibly** *adv.*

insensitive (in-sen′si-tiv) *a.* not sensitive; callous.—**insensitiv′ity, insen′sitiveness** *n.*

insentient (in-sen′shi-ent) *a.* not having perception; inanimate.

inseparable (in-sep′ạ-rạ-bl) *a.* not divisible or separable; always in close association;—*n.pl.* persons or things that are seldom seen apart.—**insep′arably** *adv.*

insert (in-sẹrt′) *v.t.* to put in; to place among; to introduce.—**in′sert** *n.* anything inserted.—**inser′tion** *n.* the act of inserting; that which is inserted [L. *in*, in; *serere*, to join].

Insessores (in-se-sō′rēz) *n.pl.* an order of birds whose feet are formed for perching on branches, etc.—**insesso′rial** *a.* [L. *in*, on; *sedere*, *sessum*, to sit].

inset (in′set) *n.* something set in; an insertion.—**inset′** *v.t.* to set in; to insert.

inshore (in′shōr) *a.* near to the shore;—*adv.* in towards the shore.

inside (in′sīd) *prep.* or *adv.* within the sides of; in the interior;—*a.* internal; interior;—*n.* the part within; stomach;—*pl.* inward parts; guts.

insidious (in-sid′i-us) *a.* lying in wait; advancing imperceptibly.—**insid′iously** *adv.*—**insid′iousness** *n.* [L. *insidiosus*, fr. *insidere*, to lie in wait].

insight (in′sīt) *n.* view of the interior of anything; mental penetration; clear understanding; power of discernment.

insignia (in-sig′ni-ạ) *n.pl.* symbols of authority, dignity, or office; badges; emblems (L. fr. *signum*, sign].

insignificant (in-sig-nif′i-kant) *a.* signifying very little; having little importance, use, or value; trifling.—**insignif′icance, insignif′icancy** *n.*—**insignif′icantly** *adv.*

insincere (in-sin-sēr′) *a.* not sincere; dissembling; hypocritical; not to be trusted.—**insincere′ly** *adv.*—**insincer′ity** *n.* hypocrisy.

insinuate (in-sin′ū-āt) *v.t.* to introduce gently and adroitly; to suggest by remote allusion; to work oneself into favour;—*v.i.* to ingratiate oneself.—**insin′uating** *a.*—**insin′uatingly** *adv.*—**insinua′tion** *n.* act of gaining favour by artful means; hint; suggestion.—**insin′uative** *a.*—**insin′uator** *n.*—**insin′uatory** *a.* [L. *insinuare*, to introduce tortuously].

insipid (in-sip′id) *a.* destitute of taste; deficient in spirit, life, or animation.—**insip′idly** *adv.*—**insip′idness, insipid′ity** *n.* want of taste [L. *insipidus*, fr. *sapidus*, tasty].

insist (in-sist′) *v.i.* to dwell upon as a matter of special moment; to be urgent or pressing; (foll. by *on* or *upon*) to hold firmly to.—**insist′ence** *n.* persistent demand or refusal to give way.—**insist′ency** *n.* pertinacity.—**insist′ent** *a.* [L. *insistere*, fr. *sistere*, to stand].

insobriety (in-sō-brī′et-i) *n.* drunkenness.

insociable (in-sō′shạ-bl) *a.* not sociable.

insolate (in′so-lāt) *v.t.* to expose to the rays of the sun.—**insola′tion** *n.* [L. *insolare*, fr. *sol* the sun].

insole (in′sōl) *n.* the inner sole of a boot or shoe.

insolent (in′so-lent) *a.* proud and haughty; overbearing.—**in′solence** *n.* contemptuous rudeness or arrogance.—**in′solently** *adv.* [L *in-*, not; *solere*, to be accustomed].

insoluble (in-sol′ū-bl) *a.* incapable of being

dissolved; inexplicable; not to be explained. —**insolubil'ity, insol'ubleness** *n.*—**insol'vable** *a.*

insolvent (in-solv´-ent) *a.* not able to pay one's debts; bankrupt;—*n.* one who is bankrupt.—**insolv'ency** *n.*

insomnia (in-som´-ni-a) *n.* chronic sleeplessness from any cause [L.].

insomuch (in-sō-much') *adv.* so that; to such a degree; in such wise that.

insouciance (ang-sóó´-sē-ongs, in-sóó'-si-ans) *n.* carelessness of feeling or manner; an air of indifference.—**insou'ciant** *a.* careless; heedless; indifferent [Fr.].

inspan (in-span') *v.t.* to yoke (oxen) to a vehicle.

inspect (in-spekt') *v.t.* to view narrowly and critically; to examine officially as troops, arms, kits, or goods offered for sale, etc.—**inspect'ingly** *adv.*—**inspec'tion** *n.* careful survey; official examination.—**inspec'tional, inspec'tive** *a.*—**inspec'tor** *n.* official examiner; a police officer ranking higher than a sergeant; person appointed to inspect state-aided schools; a superintendent.—**inspec'torate** *n.* a district under an inspector; a body of inspectors generally, esp. of school-inspectors.—**inspecto'rial** *a.*—**inspec'tress** *n.* female inspector [L. *inspicere*, to look into].

inspire (in-spīr') *v.t.* to breathe into; to infuse thought or feeling into; to affect as with a supernatural influence; to arouse;—*v.i.* to draw air into the lungs; to inhale.—**inspir'able** *a.* able to be breathed.—**inspira'tion** *n.* act of drawing in the breath; communication of ideas from a supernatural source; a bright idea.—**inspira'tional** *a.*—**inspir'atory** *a.* tending to inspire; encouraging.—**inspired'** *a.* inhaled; actuated by Divine influence [L. *in*; *spirare*, to breathe].

inspirit (in-spir´-it) *v.t.* to give new life to; to invigorate.

inspissate (in-spis´-āt) *v.t.* to thicken, as fluids and plant juices, by evaporation of moisture [L. *in*; *spissare*, to thicken].

instability (in-sta-bil´-i-ti) *n.* want of stability or firmness.

install, instal (in-stawl') *v.t.* to place in position; to have something put in; to induct, with ceremony, a person to an office of dignity. —**installa'tion** *n.* complete equipment of a building for heating, lighting, etc.; generally, placing in position for use.—**instal'ment** *n.* act of installing; a periodical payment of the part-cost of something; a portion.

instance (in´-stans) *n.* urgency; case in point; example; illustration; time; occasion; occurrence;—*v.t.* to mention as an example; to cite. —**in'stant** *a.* urgent; pressing; immediate; belonging to the current month (usu. abbreviated to inst.);—*n.* a particular point of time; moment.—**instantane'ity** *n.*—**instantan´eous** *a.* done in an instant; happening in a moment.—**instantan'eously** *adv.*—**instantan'eousness** *n.*—**instant'er** *adv.* immediately; at once. —**in'stantly** *adv.* at once [L. *in*; *stare*, to stand].

instead (in-sted') *adv.* in the stead, place, or room; in one's stead; as an alternative or substitute [*stead*].

instep (in´-step) *n.* the arched upper part of the human foot, near the ankle, which gives spring to the step; that part of a shoe, etc., which covers the instep; the hind-leg of a horse from the ham to the pastern joint.

instigate (in´-sti-gāt) *v.t.* to goad or urge forward; to incite; to bring about.—**instiga'tion** *n.* act of inciting; prompting; impulse, esp. to evil.—**in'stigator** *n.* [L. *instigare*, to incite].

instil (in-stil') (also **instill**) *v.t.* to put in by drops; to infuse slowly; to introduce by degrees (into the mind).—*pr.p.* **instil'ling.**—*pa.t.* and *pa.p.* **instilled'.**—**instilla'tion** or **instila'tion, instil'ment** or **instill'ment** *n.* the act of instilling [L. *in*; *stillare*, to drip].

instinct (in´-stingkt) *n.* in animals, a complex and almost unvarying mode of behaviour which guides them in the unreflecting spontaneous performance of acts useful for the preservation of the individual or the species; (in *neurology*) compound reflex action; (in *psychology*) an innate train of reflexes; inborn impulse or propensity; unconscious skill; intuition.—**in'stinct** *a.* charged; full; urged from within; animated.—**instinc'tive, instinc'tual** *a.* prompted by instinct; natural; spontaneous; involuntary.—**instinc'tively, instinct'ly** *adv.*—**instinctiv'ity** *n.* [L. *instinctus*, fr. *instinguere*, to urge].

institute (in´-sti-tūt) *v.t.* to establish; to found; to appoint; to set going; to originate; to lay down as a law;—*n.* a society or organisation established for promoting some public object; rule, law or principle.—**in'stitutes** *n.pl.* a book of precepts, principles or rules; a text-book on legal principles.—**institu'tion** *n.* the act of instituting or establishing; an established law, custom, or public occasion; an institute; (*sociol.*) an organised pattern of group behaviour established and generally accepted as a fundamental part of a culture, such as slavery.—**institu'tional** *a.* pert. to, or of the nature of, institutions.—**institu'tionally** *adv.*—**institu'tive** *a.* tending or intended to instigate or establish; endowed with the power to ordain; set up by authority, instituted.—**institu'tively** *adv.*—**institu'tor, institu'ter** *n.* one who instigates organises or sets in operation, a founder [L. *instituere*, to set up].

instroke (in´-strōk) *n.* an inward stroke, esp. in a steam or other engine.

instruct (in-strukt') *v.t.* to teach; to inform; to prepare someone for (e.g., an examination); to order or command; to give directions to.—**instruct'ible** *a.* able to be instructed.—**instruc´tion** *n.* the act of instructing or teaching; tuition; education; order; mandate.—**instruc´tional** *a.* pert. or relating to instruction.—**instruc'tive** *a.* fitted to instruct; containing edifying matter; conveying knowledge or information.—**instruc'tively** *adv.*—**instruc'tiveness** *n.*—**instruc'tor** *n.* (*fem.* **instruc'tress**).

instrument (in´-stroo-ment) *n.* a tool or implement esp. for scientific purposes; a person or thing made use of; a means of producing musical sounds; (*Law*) a formal or written document.—**instrument'al** *a.* serving as an instrument or means; helpful; pert. to musical, surgical, or other instruments; music performed with or composed for a musical instrument or instruments; (*Gram.*) in some inflected languages, denoting a case, having as chief function the indication of means or agency.—**instrument'alist** *n.* one skilled in playing upon a musical instrument.—**instrumental'ity** *n.* the quality of being instrumental, of serving some purpose; agency or means; good offices.—**instrument'ally** *adv.* by the use of an instrument or agency; indirectly; with musical instruments.—**instrumenta'tion** *n.* the art of writing and arranging musical compositions for the individual instruments of a band or orchestra; orchestration; the art or manner of playing upon musical instruments.—**instrument board** or **panel,** the panel directly in front of the operator of a car, motor-boat or aeroplane, which carries petrol, oil, speed, and other indicators [L. *instrumentum*, fr. *instruere*, to build].

insubordinate (in-sub-or´-di-nāt) *a.* disobedient; unruly; rebellious; mutinous.—**insubordina'tion** *n.* unruliness.

insufferable (in-suf´-er-a-bl) *a.* not able to be endured; intolerable.—**insuff'erably** *adv.*

insufficient (in-su-fish´-ent) *a.* not enough; deficient. —**insuffic'iency** *n.*

insular (in´-sū-lar) *a.* pert. to or like an island; surrounded by water; narrow-minded or prejudiced.—**in'sularism, insular'ity** *n.*—**in'sularly** *adv.* [L. *insula*, an island].

insulate (in´-sū-lāt) *v.t.* to make into an island; to keep rigidly apart from contact with other people; to bar the passage of electricity, heat, sound, light, damp, or vibration by the use of non-conducting materials.—**insula'tion** *n.* separation; isolation; (*Elect.*) prevention of leakage of a charge or a current of electricity;

any material which insulates; a contrivance used to insulate a conductor from earth [L. *insula*, an island].
insulin (inʹsū-lin) *n.* a hormone secreted in the pancreas which induces the combustion of the dextrose (sugar) content of the blood; an organic drug for the treatment of diabetes [L. *insula*, island; suggested by the medical term, islets of Langerhans, groups of cells in the pancreas].
insult (in-sult') *v.t.* to treat with insolence or contempt by words or action; to abuse; to affront.—**in'sult** *n.* gross abuse offered to another [L. *insultare*, to leap upon].
insuperable (in-sūʹper-a-bl) *a.* not able to be got over or surmounted; invincible.—**insuperabil'ity,** *n.* **insu'perably** *adv.*
insupportable (in-su-pōrʹta-bl) *a.* incapable of being borne or endured.—**insupport'ableness** *n.*—**insupport'ably** *adv.*
insure (in-shòòr') *v.t.* to make sure or certain; to make safe (against); to ensure; to secure the payment of a sum in event of loss, death, etc., by a contract and payment of sums called premiums.—**insur'able** *a.*—**insur'ance** *n.* contract between two parties whereby the insurer agrees to indemnify the insured upon the occurrence of a stipulated contingency [L. *in*; *securus*, secure].
insurgent (in-surʹjent) *a.* rising in opposition to lawful authority; rebellious;—*n.* one in revolt; a rebel. —**insur'gency** *n.* incipient stage of revolt.—Also **insurg'ence.**
insurmountable (in-sur-mounʹta-bl) *a.* not able to be surmounted or overcome.—**insurmountabil'ity** *n.*—**insurmount'ably** *adv.*
insurrection (in-su-rekʹshun) *n.* a rising against civil or political authority.—**insurrecʹtional, insurrec'tionary** *a.*—**insurrec'tionist** *n.* an insurgent [L. *insurgere*, to rise upon].
insusceptible (in-su-sepʹti-bl) *a.* not susceptible; not to be moved, affected, or impressed; proof against (disease, etc.).
intact (in-takt') *a.* untouched; uninjured; undisturbed [L. *in-*, not; *tangere*, *tactum*, to touch].
intaglio (in-talʹyō) *n.* a hollowed out design worked upon a semi-precious stone so that when applied to a soft material an impression in relief is produced; printing process done by incised plates to give a rich effect.—**intagl'iated** *a.* [It. fr. *tagliare*, to cut].
intake (inʹtāk) *n.* that which is taken in; inlet of a tube or cylinder; part where a stocking is narrowed by knitting two stitches together; point where water is diverted from a stream into a lade.
intangible (in-tanʹji-bl) *a.* not perceptible to the touch; impalpable.—**intan'gibleness, intangibil'ity** *n.*—**intan'gibly** *adv.*
integer (inʹte-jer) *n.* the whole of anything; whole number (as opposed to a fraction or a mixed number).—**in'tegral** *a.* denoting a whole number or quantity; constituting an essential part of a whole;—*n.* a whole number; (*Math.*) a sum of differentials.—**in'tegrally** *adv.* —**in'tegrate** *v.t.* to make entire; to give the sum or total; esp. in educational literature, to denote development of personality by the conscious attempt to weld into a harmonious whole its diverse aspects and abilities.—**integra'tion** *n.* act of making a whole out of parts.—**in'tegrator** *n.*—**integ'rity** *n.* the state of being entire; wholeness; probity; honesty; uprightness [L. *integer*, entire].
integument (in-tegʹū-ment) *n.* the outer protective layer of tissue which covers a plant or animal; the skin.—**integument'ary** *a.* [L. *integumentum*, fr. *integere*, to cover].
intellect (inʹte-lekt) *n.* the faculty of reasoning and thinking; mental power; mind; understanding;—*pl.* the senses.—**intellec'tive** *a.* pert. to intellect as distinguished from senses.—**intellect'ual** *a.* of high mental capacity; having the power of understanding;—*n.* one well endowed with intellect.—**intellect'ualism** *n.* the doctrine that knowledge is derived from pure reason; over-emphasis on the value of the rational faculties.—**intellectual'ity** *n.* intellectual power; intelligence.—**intellect'ually** *adv.* [L. *intelligere*, to understand].
intelligent (in-telʹi-jent) *a.* having or showing good intellect; quick at understanding.—**intell'igence** *n.* inborn quickness of understanding and adaptability to relatively new situations; information.—**intell'igently** *adv.*—**intelligent'sia** *n.* the intellectual or cultured classes.—**intell'igible** *a.* that can be readily understood; rational.—**intell'igibleness, intelligibil'ity** *n.*—**intell'igibly** *adv.*—**intelligence quotient** (abbrev. I.Q.) the numerical rating of general intelligence by use of psychological tests, the mental age, as ascertained by these tests, being divided by the actual age and multiplied by 100 [L. *intelligere*, to understand].
intemperate (in-temʹpẹr-āt) *a.* immoderate; indulging to excess any appetite or passion; addicted to an excessive use of spirituous liquors.—**intem'perance** *n.* excess of any kind; habitual over-indulgence in spirituous liquors. —**intem'perately** *adv.*—**intem'perateness** *n.* [L. *intemperatus*].
intend (in-tend') *v.t.* and *v.i.* to design; to purpose; to mean; to have in mind.—**intendʹant** *n.* one who has the charge of some public business.—**intend'ancy** *n.* the office of an intendant.—**intend'ed** *a.* and *n.* (*Colloq.*) betrothed [L. *intendere*, to bend the mind on].
intense (in-tens') *a.* to an extreme degree; very strong or acute; emotional.—**intense'ly** *adv.*—**intense'ness, inten'sity** *n.* severity; ardour; earnestness; the strength of an electric current.—**intensifica'tion** *n.*—**inten'sify** *v.t.* to render more intense; to increase or augment; —*v.i.* to become more intense.—*pa.t.* and *pa.p.* **intens'ified.**—**inten'sive** *a.* giving emphasis; unrelaxed; increasing in force.—**inten'sively** *adv.* [L. *intendere*, *intensum*, to stretch].
intent (in-tent') *a.* having the mind bent on an object; eager in pursuit of; firmly resolved; preoccupied; absorbed;—*n.* intention; aim; purpose; view; object.—**inten'tion** *n.* design; aim; purpose.—**inten'tional, inten'tioned** *a.* done purposely.—**inten'tionally** *adv.*—**intent'ly** *adv.* closely; attentively; zealously.—**intent'ness** *n.* [L. *intendere*, to turn the mind to].
inter- (inʹtẹr) *prefix* fr. L. *inter*, between, among, with, amid.
inter (in-tẹr') *v.t.* to bury.—*pr.p.* **inter'ring.**—*pa.t.* and *pa.p.* **interred'.**—**inter'ment** *n.* burial [Fr. *enterrer*, fr. L. *in*; *terra*, earth].
interact (inʹtẹr-akt) *n.* a short performance between the acts;—*v.i.* to act mutually on each other.—**interac'tion** *n.*
interbreed (in-tẹr-brēd') *v.t.* to hybridise different species of plants or animals by cross-fertilisation.—**interbreed'ing** *n.*
intercalate (in-tẹrʹka-lāt) *v.t.* to insert in or between, as an extra day in the calendar or a verse in poetry; to interpolate.—**inter'calary, inter'calar** *a.* [L. *inter*, between; *calare*, to call].
intercede (in-tẹr-sēd') *v.i.* to go between; to act as peace-maker; to plead in favour of one; to mediate.—**interced'er** *n.*—**intercess'ion** *n.* the act of interceding.—**intercess'or** *n.* a mediator; a pleader.—**intercesso'rial, intercess'ory** *a.* [L. *inter*, between; *cedere*, to go].
intercept (in-tẹr-sept') *v.t.* to stop or obstruct the passage of another; to seize in transit; (*Math.*) to cut off a part of a line at two points; —*n.* the part of a line between any two points.—**intercep'ter, intercep'tor** *n.*—**interceptʹtion** *n.*—**intercep'tive** *a.* [L. *inter*, between; *capere*, *captum*, to seize].
intercession, intercessor See **intercede.**
interchange (in-tẹr-chānj') *v.t.* to exchange; to reciprocate;—*v.i.* to succeed alternately; to exchange places;—*n.* a mutual exchange. —**interchange'able** *a.* identical.—**interchangeabil'ity, interchange'ableness** *n.*

intercommune (in-tẹr-kom-ūn′) *v.t.* to denounce for communing with rebels;—*v.i.* to have association with.—**in′tercom** *n.* internal telephonic system, generally of aircraft.—**intercommun′icate** *v.t.* to exchange conversation or messages.

interconnect (in-tẹr-ko-nekt′) *v.t.* and *v.i.* to connect mutually and intimately.

intercostal (in-tẹr-kos′tạl) a. (*Anat.*) situated between the ribs [L. *inter*, between; *costa*, a rib].

intercourse (in′tẹr-kōrs) *n.* communication; conversation; exchange of goods; correspondence by letter; coition [O.Fr. *entrecours*, fr. L. *inter*, between; *currere*, to run].

intercurrent (in-tẹr-kur′ent) *a.* running between or among; occurring during the course of another (disease); intervening.

interdepend (in-tẹr-de-pend′) *v.i.* to depend mutually.—**interdepen′dence** *n.*—**interdepen′dent** *a.*—**interdepen′dently** *adv.*

interdict (in-tẹr-dikt′) *v.t.* to forbid; to prohibit; to restrain; to debar from communion with a church; to lay under an interdict.—**in′terdict** *n.* prohibition; (*Scots law*) an injunction; an order to restrain any act or proceedings; a papal ordinance by which certain persons are debarred from participating in Sacraments, Church offices or ecclesiastical burial.—**interdic′tion** *n.*—**interdic′tive, interdic′tory** *a.* prohibitory [L. *interdicere*, to prohibit].

interest (in′tẹr-est) *v.t.* to engage and keep the attention of; to arouse the curiosity of; to cause to feel interest; to concern;—*n.* special attention; regard to personal profit or advantage; curiosity; the profit per cent derived from money lent.—**in′terested** *a.* having a share in; feeling an interest in; partial.—**in′terestedly** *adv.*—**in′terestedness** *n.*—**in′teresting** *a.* appealing to or exciting one's interest or curiosity.—**in′terestingly** *adv.*—**compound interest,** interest on the principal and also on the added interest as it falls due.—**simple interest,** interest only on the principal during the time of loan. [L. *interesse*, to be of concern to].

interfere (in-tẹr-fēr′) *v.i.* to enter into or take part in the concerns of others; to meddle; to intervene.—**interfer′ence** *n.* meddling with other people's business; uncalled for intervention; (*Radio*) anything generally which prevents the proper reception of wireless waves.—**interfer′er** *n.*—**interfer′ingly** *adv.* [L. *inter*, between; *ferire*, to strike].

interim (in′tẹr-im) *n.* the time between; the meantime;—*a.* for the time being; temporary; provisional [L.].

interior (in-tē′ri-or) *a.* inner; internal; inland, away from coast or frontiers;—*n.* the inside part or portion; the inland part of a country.—**inter′iorly** *adv.* [L. compar. of *interus*, fr. L. *intra*, within].

interject (in-tẹr-jekt′) *v.t.* to throw between; to insert; to exclaim abruptly.—**interjec′tion** *n.* act of throwing between; a word which expresses strong emotion or passion when suddenly uttered.—**interjec′tional, interjec′tionary, interject′ural** *a.*—**interjec′tionally** *adv.* [L. *inter*, between; *jacere, jactum*, to throw].

interlace (in-tẹr-lās′) *v.t.* to lace together; to entwine; to unite; to interweave.

interlard (in-tẹr-lard′) *v.t.* to mix together, as fat with lean; to diversify by mixture (of technical words, etc.).

interlink (in-tẹr-link′) *v.t.* to connect by uniting links.

interlock (in-tẹr-lok′) *v.t.* to unite by locking together; to fasten together so that one part cannot move without the other;—*v.i.* to be locked or jammed together.

interlocution (in-tẹr-lo-kū′shun) *n.* a dialogue; a conference; speaking in turn.—**interloc′utor** *n.* one who speaks in his turn; (*Scots law*) the written document containing the judgment or determination of the court.—**interloc′utory** *a.* [L. *interloqui*, to speak between].

interlope (in-tẹr-lōp′) *v.i.* to traffic without a proper licence; to intrude into other people's affairs.—**interlo′per** *n.* [L. *inter*, between; Dut. *loopen*, to run].

interlude (in′tẹr-lūd) *n.* a dramatic or musical performance given between parts of an independent play; an interval; an incident during a pause in the proceedings [L. *inter*, between; *ludus*, play].

interlunar, interlunary (in-tẹr-lōō′nạr, -nạ-ri) *a.* of the time between the old and the new moon when it is invisible.

intermarry (in-tẹr-mar′i) *v.i.* to connect families or races by a marriage between two of their members.—**intermarr′iage** *n.*

intermeddle (in-tẹr-med′l) *v.i.* to interfere, without call, in others' concerns.

intermediate (in-tẹr-mē′di-āt) *a.* lying or being between two extremes; in a middle position; intervening;—*n.* anything in between; an examination preceding the final one.—**interme′diacy** *n.* state of being intermediate; mediation.—**interme′dial** *a.* intermediate.—**interme′diary** *a.* acting between; interposed; intermediate;—*n.* one who acts as a go-between or mediator.—**interme′diately** *adv.*—**interme′dium** *n.* intervening person or instrument. [L. *inter*, between; *medius*, middle].

interment (in-tẹr′ment) *n.* burial [fr. *inter*].

intermezzo (in-tẹr-med′zō) *n.* a light dramatic entertainment between the acts of a tragedy, grand opera, etc.; an interlude; (*Mus.*) a short movement connecting more important ones in a symphony, sonata, opera, etc. [It. = in between].

interminable (in-tẹr′min-ạ-bl) *a.* endless; never ending; unlimited; extending to boredom.—**inter′minableness** *n.*—**inter′minably** *adv.*

intermingle (in-tẹr-ming′gl) *v.t.* to mingle or mix together.

intermit (in-tẹr-mit′) *v.t.* to give up or forbear for a time; to interrupt;—*v.i.* to cease for a time.—**intermiss′ion** *n.* cessation for a time; an intervening period of time; suspension; interval.—**intermiss′ive** *a.* coming after temporary cessations.—**intermit′tence, intermit′tency** *n.*—**intermit′tent** *a.* occurring at intervals, ceasing at intervals; coming and going.—**intermit′tently** *adv.* [L. *inter*, between; *mittere′ missum*, to send].

intermix (in-tẹr-miks′) *v.t.* and *v.i.* to mix together.—**intermix′ture** *n.*

intern (in-tẹrn′) *v.t.* to confine (in a place), esp. aliens or suspects in time of war;—*n.* a resident pupil; a resident doctor in a hospital; a boarder. Also **interne′**.—**internee′** *n.* one who is confined to a certain place.—**intern′ment** *n.* [L. *internus*, internal].

internal (in-tẹr′nạl) *a.* interior; inner; inward; domestic, as opposed to foreign.—**inter′nally** *adv.*—**internal combustion,** the process occurring by exploding in one or more piston-fitted cylinders a mixture of air and fuel, as petrol gas [L. *internus*, inward].

international (in-tẹr-nash′un-ạl) *a.* pert. to the relations between nations;—*n.* a game or match between teams representing their respective countries; a player who participates in such a contest; an organisation of socialists, founded in 1864 to further the interests of the working-classes in all countries.—**Internationale** *n.* party-song of the communists.—**interna′tionalism** *n.* a political theory which aims at breaking down the artificial barriers which separate nations.—**interna′tionalist** *n.*—**interna′tionally** *adv.*

internecine (in-tẹr-nē′sīn) *a.* mutually destructive; deadly; pert. to civil war [L. *inter*; *necare*, to kill].

internee See **intern.**

internuncio (in-tẹr-nun′shi-ō) *n.* the pope's representative at republics and small courts.—**internun′cial** *a.* [L. *internuntius*, a messenger].

interpellate (in-tẹr′pel-āt) *v.t.* to interrupt a

speaker in a legislative assembly by demanding an explanation (esp. in the French Chamber).—**interpella'tion** *n.*—**inter'pellator** *n.* [L. *inter*; *pellere*, to drive].
interpenetrate (in-tẹr-pen´e-trāt) *v.t.* to grow through one another; to penetrate thoroughly. —**interpenetra'tion** *n.*
interplanetary (in-tẹr-plan´e-tar-i) *a.* situated between the planets.
interplay (in´tẹr-plā) *n.* reciprocal action of two things; interchange of action and reaction; give and take.
interpolate (in-tẹr´po-lāt) *v.t.* to insert new (esp. misleading matter) into the text of a book or manuscript; to foist in; to interpose with some remark; (*Math.*) to infer the missing terms in a known series of numbers.—**interpola'tion** *n.*—**inter'polator** *n.* [L. *interpolare*, to furbish up].
interpose (in-tẹr-pōz') *v.t.* and *i.* to place or come between; to thrust in the way; to offer, as aid or service; to interfere.—**interpos'al** *n.* intervention.—**interpos'er** *n.*—**interposi'tion** *n.* [L. *inter*; *ponere*, to place].
interpret (in-tẹr´pret) *v.t.* to explain the meaning of; to put a construction on; to translate orally for the benefit of others.—**inter'pretable** *a.* capable of being explained.—**interpreta'tion** *n.* act of interpreting; translation; meaning; artiste's version of a dramatic part or musical composition.—**inter'pretative** *a.* explanatory. —**inter'preter** *n.* [L. *interpres*, an interpreter].
interregnum (in-tẹr-reg´num) *a.* the time a throne is vacant between the death or abdication of a king and the accession of his successor [L. *inter*; *regnum*, rule].
interrelation (in-tẹr-re-lā´shun) *n.* reciprocal or mutual relation; correlation; inter-connection.—**interrela'tionship** *n.*
interrogate (in-ter´o-gāt) *v.t.* to question; to examine by questioning, esp. officially.—**interroga'tion** *n.* close questioning; a question. —**interrogation mark**, the mark (?) placed after a question.—**interrog'ative** *a.* expressed in the form of a question;—*n.* a word used in asking questions.—**interrog'atively** *adv.*—**interr'ogator** *n.*—**interrog'atory** *a.* asking questions;—*n.* a written question to be answered in writing and on oath [L. *inter*; *rogare*, to ask].
interrupt (in-tẹr-rupt') *v.t.* to break in upon; to stop course of; to break continuity of.—**interrup'tedly** *adv.*—**interrup'ter** *n.*—**interrup'tion** *n.* intervention; suspension; hindrance; obstruction; impediment.—**interrup'tive** *a.*
intersect (in-tẹr-sekt') *v.t.* to cut into or between; to divide into parts; to cross one another.—**intersec'tion** *n.* an intersecting; the point where lines, roads, etc., cut or cross one another.—**intersec'tional** *a.*
intersperse (in-tẹr-spẹrs') *v.t.* to scatter or place here and there, in no fixed order; to interlard; to mingle.—**intersper'sion** *n.* [L. *inter*, among; *spargere*, *sparsum*, to scatter].
interstellar (in-tẹr-stel´ạr) *a.* passing between, or situated among, the stars. Also **interstell'ary.**
interstice (in-tẹr´stis) *n.* a small gap or chink in the body of an object or between two things; a crevice; interval.—**intersti'tial** *a.* [L. *interstitium*].
interstratification (in-tẹr-strat-i-fi-kā´shun) *n.* the state of lying between other strata.—**interstrat'ified** *a.*
intertangle (in-tẹr-tang´gl) *v.t.* to tangle together; to intertwist.—**intertang'lement** *n.*
intertribal (in-tẹr-trī´bạl) *a.* existing or taking place between tribes.
intertwine (in-tẹr-twīn) *v.t.* to twine or twist together.
interval (in´tẹr-vạl) *n.* time or distance between; a pause; a break; (*Mus.*) difference in pitch between any two tones [L. *intervallum*, fr. *inter*; *vallum*, a wall].
intervene (in-tẹr-vēn') *v.i.* to come or be between; to happen in the meantime; to interfere; to interrupt; to interpose.—**interven'er** *n.*—**interven'ient** *a.*—**interven'tion** *n.* act of coming between; interposition.—**interven´tionist** *n.* or *a.* [L. *inter*; *venire*, to come].
interview (in´tẹr-vū) *n.* a meeting for conference; a formal meeting; a meeting of a journalist and a person whose views he wishes to publish;—*v.t.* to have an interview with.—**interview'er** *n.* [Fr. *entrevue*].
interweave (in-tẹr-wēv') *v.t.* to weave together; to interlace; to connect closely.—*pa.t.* **interwove'**.—*pa.p.* **interwo'ven**.
intestate (in-tes´tāt) *a.* not having made a valid will; not disposed of by will;—*n.* a person who dies intestate.—**intest'acy** *n.* disposal of the property of a person who has died without leaving a valid will [L. *in-*, not; *testari*, to make a will].
intestine (in-tes´tin) *a.* internal; domestic; within a country; civil (of war, etc.);—*n.pl.* the canal or tube which forms the lower part of the digestive tract; the bowels; the entrails. —**intes'tinal** *a.* [L. *intestinus*].
intimate (in´ti-māt) *a.* innermost; familiar; closely-related; close;—*n.* an intimate friend; —*v.t.* to make known; to give notice of; to hint; to imply.—**in'timacy** *n.* the state of being intimate; sexual relations.—**in'timately** *adv.*— **intima'tion** *n.* an announcement [L. *intimus*, inmost].
intimidate (in-tim´i-dāt) *v.t.* to force or deter by threats; to inspire with fear; to frighten into action; to cow.—**intimida'tion** *n.*—**intim'idator** *n.* [L. *in*; *timidus*, fearful].
into (in´to͝o) *prep.* expresses motion to a point within, or a change from one state to another.
intoed (in-tōd') *a.* having the toes turned inwards.
intolerable (in-tol´e-rạ-bl) *a.* insufferable; unbearable; insupportable.—**intol'erableness** *n.*— **intol'erably** *adv.*—**intol'erance** *n.* state of being intolerant; want of forbearance; bigotry to the point of persecution.—**intol'erant** *a.*— **intol'erantly** *adv.*—**intolera'tion** *n.* intolerance.
intone (in-tōn') *v.t.* to utter or recite with a long drawn out musical note or tone; to chant; *v.i.* to modulate the voice; to give forth a deep protracted sound.—**in'tonate** *v.t.* to intone.— **intona'tion** *n.* the expressive modulation of the voice; accent; the opening phrase of a plainsong melody.
intoxicate (in-tok´si-kāt) *v.t.* to make drunk; to excite beyond self-control; rouse to madness.—**intox'icating** *a.* producing intoxication; heady.—**intox'icant** *n.* an intoxicating liquor. —**intoxica'tion** *n.* [Gk. *toxikon*, poison].
intra- (in´trạ) *prefix* fr. L. *intra*, within, inside of, used in the construction of many compound terms.—**in'tra-cell'ular** *a.* within a cell. —**in'tra-mus'cular** *a.* inside a muscle.—**in'tra-ve'nous** *a.* within a vein.
intractable (in-trak´tạ-bl) *a.* not to be managed or governed; unmanageable; stubborn; refractory.—**intractabil'ity, intract'ableness** *n.*—**intract'ably** *adv.*
intrados (in-trā´dos) *n.* the inner part of the curve of an arch or vault [L. *intra*, within; *dorsum*, the back].
intramural (in-tra-mū'-rạl) *a.* within the walls.
intranquillity (in-tran-kwil´i-ti) *n.* unquietness; inquietude.—**intran'quil** *a.*
intransigent (in-tran´si-jent) *a.* refusing in any way to compromise or to make a settlement (esp. in political matters); irreconcilable;—*n.* one who adopts this attitude.— **intran'sigentism** *n.* uncompromising disagreement with political opponents.—**intran´sigentist** *n.* [Fr. *intransigeant*].
intransitive (in-tran´si-tiv) *a.* not passing over; (*Gram.*) denoting such verbs as express an action or state which is limited to the agent, or which does not pass over to, or operate upon, an object.
intrant (in´trạnt) *n.* one who enters upon some public duty; one who matriculates at a college [L. *intrare*, to enter].
intra-territorial (in´tra-tẹr-i-tō´ri-ạl) *a.* within the bounds of a territory.

intrench See **entrench.**
intrenchant (in-trensh′ant) *a.* incapable of being cut or divided; invulnerable.
intrepid (in-trep′id) *a.* free from fear or trepidation.—**intrepid′ity** *n.* undaunted courage.—**intrep′idly** *adv.* [L. *in-*, not; *trepidus*, alarmed].
intricate (in′tri-kāt) *a.* involved; entangled; complicated; perplexed; obscure; difficult.—**in′tricacy, in′tricateness** *n.*—**in′tricately** *adv.* [L. *intricare*, to entangle].
intrigue (in-trēg′) *n.* a plot to effect some purpose by secret artifices; illicit love;—*v.i.* to form an intrigue; to scheme; to plot; to carry on illicit love;—*v.t.* to fascinate; to arouse interest in; to puzzle.—*pr.p.* **intrig′uing.**—**in′trigant, in′triguant, intrig′uer** *n.* one who intrigues.—**intrig′uing** *a.* given to intrigues; fascinating; arousing interest.—**intrig′uingly** *adv.* [Fr. fr. L. *intricare*, to entangle].
intrinsic, intrinsical (in-trin′sik, -si-kal) *a.* from within; having internal value; inherent; real; natural; genuine; essential.—**intrinsical′ity** *n.*—**intrin′sically** *adv.* [L. *intrinsecus*, inwardly].
intro- (in′trō) *prefix*, a variation of **intra**, *inwards*, used in the construction of compound terms.
introduce (in-trō-dūs′) *v.t.* to lead or bring in; to bring forward; to insert; to make known formally (one person to another); to import; to begin.—**introduc′tion** *n.* act of introducing or bringing into notice; the act of making persons formally acquainted with one another; the preliminary section of a speech or discourse; prologue; the preface to a book; an elementary treatise on some branch of knowledge.—**introduc′tory, introduc′tive** *a.* serving to introduce; prefatory; preliminary; initiating.—**introduc′tively, introduc′torily** *adv.* [L. *introducere*, to lead in].
introit (in-trō′it) *n.* a short psalm, anthem or hymn appropriate to the opening of the communion service in Anglican churches; in R.C. Church, the anthem sung at the beginning of Mass as the priest proceeds up to the altar [L. *intro*; *ire*, to go].
intromit (in-trō-mit′) *v.t.* to send in; to let in; to admit; to put in; to insert;—*v.i.* to meddle with the affairs of another.—**intromiss′ion** *n.* the act of sending in or allowing in; (*Scots law*) the act of assuming possession or management of the property of another. [L. *intro*, within; *mittere*, to send].
introspect (in-trō-spekt′) *v.t.* to look within; to inspect;—*v.i.* to pre-occupy oneself with one's own thoughts, emotions and feelings.—**introspec′tion** *n.* close (often morbid) examination of one's thoughts and feelings; generally, the act of looking into or within.—**introspec′tive** *a.*—**introspec′tively** *adv.* [L. *intro*, within; *specere*, to look].
introvert (in-trō-vert′) *v.t.* to turn inward;—*n.* in psycho-analysis, a self-centred, introspective individual. Cf. *extrovert.*—**introver′sion** *n.*—**introver′sive, introver′tive** *a.* [L. *intro*, within; *vertere*, to turn].
intrude (in-trōōd′) *v.i.* to thrust oneself in; to enter unwelcome or uninvited into company; to trespass; —*v.t.* to force in.—**intrud′er** *n.*—**intru′sion** *n.* act of entering, without invitation, to the annoyance of others.—**intru′sive** *a.*—**intru′sively** *adv.*—**intru′siveness** *n.* [L. *in*; *trudere*, to thrust].
intrust See **entrust.**
intuition (in-tū-ish′un) *n.* immediate and instinctive perception of a truth; direct understanding without reasoning.—**in′tuit** *v.t.* and *v.i.* to know intuitively.—**intuit′ional** *a.*—**intuit′ionalism, intuit′ionism** *n.* the doctrine that the perception of good and evil is by intuition.—**intuit′ionalist** *n.*—**intu′itive** *a.* having instinctively immediate knowledge or perception of something.—**intu′itively** *adv.* [L. *intueri*, to look upon].
intumesce (in-tū-mes′) *v.i.* to swell; to enlarge or expand, owing to heat.—**intumes′cence** *n.* enlargement; swelling.
intwine See **entwine.**
inundate (in′un-dāt, in-un′dāt) *v.t.* to overflow; to flood; to deluge; to overwhelm by sheer force of numbers; to fill more than is necessary.—**inunda′tion** *n.* [L. *inundare*, to flood, fr. *unda*, a wave].
inure (in-ūr′) *v.t.* to accustom (to); to habituate by use; to harden (the body) by toil, etc.—**inure′ment** *n.* [*in*, into and obs. *ure*, to work, fr. Fr. *œuvre*, work].
inutility (in-ū-til′i-ti) *n.* quality or state of being useless.—**inu′tile** *a.* useless.
invade (in-vād′) *v.t.* to enter with hostile intentions; to attack; to violate; to encroach upon.—**invad′er** *n.*—**inva′sion** *n.*—**inva′sive** *a.* [L. *invadere*, to go in].
invalid (in-val′id) *a.* not valid; void; null; no longer in current use; of no legal force; weak.—**inval′idate** *v.t.* to render invalid.—**invalida′tion** *n.*—**invalid′ity, inval′idness** *n.*
invalid (in′va-lid, or -lēd) *n.* a person enfeebled by sickness or injury;—*a.* ill; sickly; weak;—*v.t.* and *v.i.* to make invalid; to send away as an invalid.—**invalid chair**, a bath chair.
invaluable (in-val′ū-a-bl) *a.* incapable of being valued; priceless; of very great value.
Invar (in′var) *n.* a hard iron-nickel alloy which has a very small thermal expansion [Protected Trade Name, fr. E. *invar*(iable)].
invariable (in-vā′ri-a-bl) *a.* not displaying change; always uniform; (*Math.*) constant.—**inva′riableness, invariabil′ity** *n.*—**inva′riably** *adv.*—**inva′riant** *n.* a constant quantity.
invasion (in-vā′zhun) *n.* See **invade.**
invective (in-vek′tiv) *n.* violent outburst of censure; abuse; vituperation; sarcasm; satire;—*a.* abusive; satirical [L. *invectio*, fr. *invehere*, to bring against].
inveigh (in-vā′) *v.i.* to exclaim or rail against; to denounce; to declaim against.—**inveigh′er** *n.* [L. *invehere*, to bring against].
inveigle (in-vē′gl) *v.t.* to entice by deception or flattery; to allure; to ensnare; to mislead into something evil; to seduce.—**invei′glement** *n.*—**invei′gler** *n.* [Fr. *aveugler*, to blind].
invent (in-vent′) *v.t.* to devise something new or an improvement; to contrive; to originate; to think out something untrue.—**inven′tion** *n.* act of producing something new; an original mechanical contrivance; a deceit, fiction, or forgery.—**inven′tive** *a.* able to invent; of an ingenious turn of mind; resourceful.—**inven′tively** *adv.*—**inven′tor** *n.*—(*fem.* **inven′tress**) one who invents [L. *invenire*, to come upon, to discover].
inventory (in′ven-tor-i) *n.* a detailed list of articles comprising the effects of a house, etc., required for probate or insurance purposes; a catalogue of movables;—*v.t.* to make a list or schedule of [L. *inventarium*, a list of things found].
Inverness (in-ver-nes′) *n.* a kind of sleeveless cloak with a cape hanging loosely over the shoulders [*Inverness*, in Scotland].
inverse (in-vers′) *a.* inverted; opposite in order or relation.—**inverse′ly** *adv.*—**inver′sion** *n.* the act of inverting; the state of being inverted; change of order or time; (*Gram.*) a change of the natural arrangement of words.—**inver′sive** *a.* [L. *in*; *vertere, versum*, to turn].
invert (in-vert′) *v.t.* to turn over; to put upside own; to place in a contrary order.—**inver′tedly** *adv.*—**inverted commas**, quotation marks ' ' or " " [L. *in*; *vertere*, to turn].
invertebrate (in-ver′te-brāt) *a.* not having a vertebral column or backbone; spineless; weak-willed;—*n.* animal, such as an insect, snail, worm, etc., with no spinal column.
invest (in-vest′) *v.t.* to clothe, as with office or authority; to dress; to lay siege to; to lay out capital with a view to profit;—*v.i.* to make a purchase or an investment.—**inves′titure** *n.* ceremony of installing, with insignia, any one in office.—**invest′ment** *n.* the act of

investing; the capital invested to produce interest or profit; blockade.—**inves'tor** *n.* [L. *investire,* to clothe].

investigate (in-ves'-ti-gāt) *v.t.* to inquire into; to examine thoroughly.—**invest'igable** *a.*—**investiga'tion** *n.* thorough enquiry in order to bring out the facts.—**inves'tigative** *a.*—**inves'tigator** *n.*—**inves'tigatory** *a.* [L. *vestigare,* to track].

inveterate (in-vet'-ẹr-āt) *a.* firmly established by long continuance; obstinate; deep-rooted. —**invet'erately** *adv.*—**invet'eracy, invet'erateness** *n.* [L. *inveterare,* to grow old].

invidious (in-vid'-i-us) *a.* likely to provoke envy, ill-will or hatred; offensive.—**invid'iously** *adv.*—**invid'iousness** *n.* [L. *invidia,* envy].

invigilate (in-vij'-i-lāt) *v.i.* to supervise candidates at an examination.—**invigila'tion** *n.*—**invig'ilator** *n.* [L. *in,* on; *vigilare,* to watch].

invigorate (in-vig'-or-āt) *v.t.* to give vigour to; to animate with life and energy; to strengthen. —**invigora'tion** *n.* [L. *in; vigor,* force].

invincible (in-vin'-si-bl) *a.* unconquerable; indomitable; impregnable; insuperable.—**invin'cibleness, invincibil'ity** *n.*—**invin'cibly** [L. *in-,* not; *vincere,* to conquer].

inviolable (in-vī'-ol-ạ-bl) *a.* not to be profaned; not to be broken; sacred; holy.—**inviolabil'ity, invi'olableness** *n.*—**invi'olably** *adv.*—**invi'olate** *a.* unprofaned; uninjured.—**invi'olately** *adv.*—**invi'olateness** *n.* [L. *in-,* not; *violare,* to violate].

invisible (in-viz'-i-bl) *a.* incapable of being seen; unseen; indiscernible.—**invisibil'ity, invis'ibleness** *n.*—**invis'ibly** *adv.*

invite (in-vīt') *v.t.* to ask by invitation; to attract.—**invita'tion** *n.* act of inviting; the spoken or written form with which an invitation is extended.—**invit'er** *n.*—**invit'ing** *a.* alluring, attractive.—**invit'ingly** *adv.* [L. *invitare*].

invocate (in'-vō-kāt) *v.t.* to invoke; to call on in supplication.—**invoca'tion** *n.* act of addressing in prayer; a petition for divine help and guidance.—**invoc'atory** *a.* [See **invoke.**]

invoice (in'-vois) *n.* a detailed list of goods, with prices, sold or consigned to a purchaser; —*v.t.* to make such a list. [pl. of obs. *invoy,* fr. Fr. *envoi,* a sending].

invoke (in-vōk') *v.t.* to address (esp. the Deity) earnestly or solemnly in prayer; to beg for protection or assistance; to implore; to summon [L. *in; vocare,* to call].

involuntary (in-vol'-un-tạ-ri] *a.* outside the control of the will; not proceeding from choice; unintentional; instinctive.—**invol'untarily** *adv.*—**invol'untariness** *n.*

involute (in'-vo-lūt) *a.* rolled inwardly or spirally;—*n.* the locus of the far end of a perfectly flexible thread unwound from a circle and kept constantly taut.—**involu'tion** *n.* that in which anything is involved; the process of raising a quantity to any power assigned; entanglement; complication. [See **involve.**]

involve (in-volv') *v.t.* to envelop; to wrap up; to include; to comprise; to embrace; to implicate (a person); to complicate (a thing); to entail; to include; to twine; to interlace; to overwhelm; to multiply a number any number of times by itself.—**involve'ment** *n.* [L. *in; volvere, volutum,* to roll].

invulnerable (in-vul'-nẹ-rạ-bl) *a.* incapable of being wounded or injured.—**invulnerabil'ity, invul'nerableness** *n.*—**invul'nerably** *adv.*

inward (in'-wạrd) *a.* placed within; towards the inside; interior; internal; seated in the mind or soul;—*n.* that which is within.—esp. in *pl.,* the viscera;—*adv.* toward the inside; into the mind. Also **in'wards;**—**in'wardly** *adv.* in the parts within; secretly; in the mind or soul [O.E. *inneweard*].

inweave, enweave (in-wēv', en-) *v.t.* to weave into; to interweave; to intertwine.

inwrap See **enwrap.**

inwrought (in-rawt') *a.* wrought in, on, or among other things; ornamented with figures; inherent.

iodine (ī'-o-dīn) *n.* a non-metallic chemical element belonging to the halogen group.—**iodif'erous** *a.* yielding iodine.—**i'odise,** to treat substances with compounds of iodine, e.g. common salt.—**iod'oform** *n.* a powdered crystalline compound of iodine [Gk. *ioeidēs,* violet-like, from the colour of its fumes].

ion (ī'-on) *n.* electrically charged atom or radical which has gained, or lost, one or more electrons and which facilitates the transport of electricity through an electrolyte or the gas in a gas-discharge tube.—**ion'ic** *a.* pert. to ions.—**ionisa'tion** *n.* splitting up of a liquid during electrolysis or of a gas during a glow discharge, into ions.—**i'onise** *v.t.*—**ion'osphere** *n.* part of the Kennelly-Heaviside layer of ionised molecules in the upper atmosphere which reflects radio-waves back to earth [Gk. *ion,* pr.p. of *ienai,* to go].

Ionian (ī-ō'-ni-ạn) *a.* relating to Ionia, a district in Asia Minor, bordering the Aegean Sea, or to the **Ionians,** the inhabitants thereof in early times;—*n.* a native of Ionia.—**Ion'ic** *a.* pert. to the dialect, music, or philosophy of Ionia, esp. denoting the second of the Grecian orders of architecture, characterised by the fluted moulding of the shaft and the volute in the form of a ram's horn, of the capital; Ionian.—**Ionic dialect,** one of the three main branches of the ancient Greek language (Ionic, Doric, Aeolic).

ionosphere (ī-on'-o-sfēr) *n.* See **ion.**

iota (ī-ō'-ta) *n.* a very small quantity or degree; a jot [Gk. the name of the smallest letter of the Greek alphabet = I. i.].

ipecacuanha (ip-e-kak-ū-â'-nạ) *n.* a Brazilian plant; drug prepared from the root of this plant, used as an expectorant and an emetic [Native].

ir (ir) *prefix* for *in*—not, before ' r.'

Irak, Iraq (i-rak') *n.* Mesopotamia.—**Irak'i, Iraq'i** *n.* a native of Irak.

Iran (i-ran') *n.* native name of Persia.—**Irani** (i-rân'-i), *a.*—**Iran'ian** *a.* relating or pert. to Iran;—*n.* a Persian.—**Iran'ic** *a.*

irascible (ī-ras'-i-bl) *a.* easily provoked; hot-tempered; choleric.—**irascibil'ity** *n.*—**iras'cibly** *adv.* [L. *irasci,* to be angry].

irate (ī-rāt') *a.* angry; incensed; enraged [L. *iratus,* fr. *irasci,* to be angry].

ire (īr) *n.* anger; wrath; choler.—**ire'ful** *a.* full of ire, incensed; resentful; furious.—**ire'fully** *adv.*—**ire'fulness** *n.* [L. *ira,* anger].

Irene (ī-rē'-nē) *n.* in Greek mythology, the goddess of peace.—**iren'ic, (al)** *a.* promoting peace; pacific [Gk. *eirene,* peace].

irid-, irido- (ī'-rid, ī'-rid-o), *prefix* fr. Gk. *iris,* rainbow, used in the construction of compound terms, pertaining to the iris of the eye or to the genus of plants, as—**irides'cence** *n.* rainbow-like display of colours, due to interference of light, seen on floating oil, mother-of-pearl, etc.—**irides'cent** *a.*

iridium (ī-rid'-i-um) *n.* a silvery metallic chemical element belonging to the platinum group. -**iridos'mine** *n.* an alloy of iridium and osmium [Gk. *iris,* rainbow].

iris (ī'-ris) *n.* the rainbow; an appearance resembling the rainbow; the thin contractile, coloured membrane between the cornea and the lens of the eye, perforated in the centre by an opening called the pupil; a genus of flowering plants of the natural order *Iridaceae,* popularly known as flags;—*pl.* **i'rises** [Gk. *iris,* rainbow].

Irish (ī-rish) *a.* pert. to Ireland;—*n.* the early language spoken in Ireland—now known as *Erse.*—**I'rishism** *n.* a mode of speaking, phrase, or idiom of Ireland.—**I'rishman, I'rish-woman** *n.*—**Irish bull,** a ludicrous example of mixed metaphors.—**Irish Free State,** a self-governing state set up in 1922 in Southern Ireland, later (Dec. 1937) known as *Eire.*—**Irish moss,** carrageen, a form of edible seaweed.

irk (ẹrk) *v.t.* to weary; to give pain to; to trouble; to distress (used impersonally as, it irks me).—**irk'some** *a.* wearisome; tiresome; tedious; annoying.—**irk'somely** *adv.* [M.E. *irken*].

iron (ī′ėrn) *n.* the most common and useful of the metallic elements; an instrument or utensil made of iron; an instrument used, when heated, to press and smooth cloth; in golf, an iron-headed club.—**i'rons** *n.pl.* fetters; manacles; leg-supports;—*a.* made of iron; resembling some aspect of iron; robust; inflexible; unyielding;—*v.t.* to smooth with a heated flat iron; to furnish or arm with iron; to fetter. —**i'ronclad** *a.* covered or protected with sheets of iron;—*n.* a vessel prepared for naval warfare by having the parts above water plated with iron.—**i'roner** *n.* one who irons; a laundry-maid.—**i'ron-found'er** *n.* one who makes or founds iron-castings.—**i'ron-foun'dry** *n.* a place where iron and its alloys are re-melted and used for castings.—**i'ron-gray** *a.* of a dark colour.—**i'ron-horse** *n.* a locomotive.—**i'ron-lung** *n.* an apparatus which maintains artificial respiration continuously and regularly, used in the treatment of infantile paralysis.—**i'ronmaster** *n.* proprietor of ironworks.—**i'ronmonger** *n.* a dealer in hardware, much of which is of iron.—**i'ronmongery** *n.* (shop for retailing) hard-ware.—**i'ron-ore** *n.* a rock containing iron-rich compounds from which commercial iron is obtained.—**i'ron-ra'tion** *n.* a ration of highly concentrated food for use in emergency.—**I'ronside** *n.* a trooper who fought under Cromwell.—**i'ronsmith** *n.* a worker in iron.—**i'ronstone** *n.* any ore of iron mixed with clay, etc.; jewellery made from haematite to imitate black pearls.—**i'ronware** *n.* articles made of iron.—**i'ronwork** *n.* parts of a structure made of iron; anything of iron; —*pl.* a furnace where iron is smelted; a forge; a rolling-mill or foundry.—**i'rony** *a.* made of or resembling iron.—**cast′i'ron** *n.* or **pig iron,** the iron obtained by smelting iron ore with charcoal, coke, or raw coal in a blast furnace. —**corrugated iron,** plate of galvanised iron, corrugated to give it stiffness, used for temporary roofing, fencing, etc.—**galvanised iron,** sheet iron coated with zinc to minimise the effects of rusting.—**Iron age,** period following Bronze age, when iron was substituted for bronze in the making of tools, weapons, and ornaments.—**Iron Curtain,** the ban placed by the U.S.S.R. on free exchange of information, news, etc., between Eastern and Western Europe.—**to have too many irons in the fire,** to attempt to do too many things at the same time [O.E. *iren*].

irony (ī′ro-ni) *n.* covert ridicule which exposes the faults or follies of others by an assumed ignorance, accompanied by an implied conscious superiority, of what is the true state of affairs; a mode of speech in which the meaning is the opposite of that actually expressed; sarcasm; satire.—**iron'ic, iron'ical** *a.* —**iron'ically** *adv.* [Gk. *eirōneia,* dissimulation in speech].

irradiate (i-rā′di-āt) *v.t.* to shine upon, throw light upon; to illuminate;—*v.i.* to emit rays; to give forth light;—*a.* illumined with beams of light.—**irra'diance, irra'diancy** *n.* effulgence; emission of rays of light; splendour.—**irra′diant** *a.*—**irradia'tion** *n.* exposure to X-rays, ultra-violet rays, solar rays, etc.; illumination; brightness; enlightenment.—**irra'diative** *a.*—**irra'diator** *n.*

irrational (i-rash′un-ąl) *a.* incompatible with or contrary to reason;—*n.* (*Math.*) a surd.—**irrational'ity** *n.*—**irra'tionally** *adv.*

irreceptive (i-re-sep′tiv) *a.* not open to receive new ideas or impressions.

irreclaimable (i-re-klā′mą-bl) *a.* incapable of being reclaimed; beyond reformation; incorrigible.—**irreclaim'ably** *adv.*

irreconcilable (i-rek-on-sīl′ą-bl) *a.* incapable of being reconciled; inconsistent.—**irreconcil'ableness, irreconcilabil'ity** *n.*—**irreconcil'ably** *adv.*

irrecoverable (i-re-kuv′ėr-ą-bl) *a.* cannot be recovered; irreparable; irretrievable.—**irrecov'erableness** *n.*—**irrecov'erably** *adv.*

irredeemable (i-re-dēm′ą-bl) *a.* not redeemable; incorrigible; hopelessly lost; (of paper currency) not carrying the right of being convertible into cash.—**irredeem'ableness, irredeemabil'ity** *n.*—**irredeem'ably** *adv.*

irredentism (i-re-den′tizm) *n.* a political movement advocating the absorption by a country of neighbouring territory where, it is claimed, its nationals predominate.

irreducible (i-re-dūs′i-bl) *a.* that which cannot be reduced or lessened.—**irreduc'ibleness, irreducibil'ity** *n.*—**irredu'cibly** *adv.*

irreflection (i-re-flek′shun) *n.* want or absence of reflection; thoughtlessness.

irrefragable (i-ref′rą-gą-bl) *a.* incapable of being refuted; unanswerable; undeniable.—**irrefragabil'ity, irref'ragableness** *n.*—**irref'ragably** *adv.* [L. *in-,* not; *refragari,* to gainsay].

irrefutable (i-re-fū′tą-bl) *a.* that cannot be refuted.—**irrefutabil'ity** *n.*—**irrefu'tably** *adv.*

irregular (i-reg′ū-lar) *a.* not regular; not according to rule; deviating from the moral standard; (*Gram.*) not inflected according to normal rules;—*n.* a member of an armed force outwith government control.—**irregular'ity** *n.* —**irreg'ularly** *adv.*

irrelative (i-rel′ą-tiv) *a.* not relative; without mutual relations; unconnected; absolute.—**irrel'atively** *adv.*

irrelevant (i-rel′e-vąnt) *a.* not logically pertinent or to the point.—**irrel'evancy** *n.*—**irrel'evantly** *adv.*

irreligion (i-re-lij′un) *n.* state of indifference or opposition to religious beliefs.—**irrelig'ious** *a.* —**irrelig'iously** *adv.* profanely; impiously.—**irrelig'iousness** *n.* ungodliness.

irremediable (i-re-mēd′i-ą-bl) *a.* not to be remedied or redressed.—**irremed'iableness** *n.* —**irremed'iably** *adv.*

irremissible (i-re-mis′i-bl) *a.* that cannot be passed by or forgiven; unpardonable.

irremovable (i-re-mòò′vą-bl) *a.* fixed; cannot be shifted; steadfast.—**irremovabil'ity, irremov'ableness** *n.*—**irremov'ably** *adv.*

irreparable (i-rep′ar-ą-bl) *a.* that cannot be repaired or rectified.—**irreparabil'ity, irrep′arableness** *n.*—**irrep'arably** *adv.*

irreplaceable (i-re-plā′są-bl) *a.* that cannot be replaced; indispensable; unique.

irreproachable (i-re-prō′chą-bl) *a.* free from blame; upright; faultless.—**irreproach'ableness** *n.*—**irreproach'ably** *adv.*

irresistible (i-re-zis′ti-bl) *a.* incapable of being resisted; too strong, fascinating, charming, etc., to be resisted.—**irresist'ibleness, irresistibil′ity** *n.*—**irresist'ibly** *adv.*

irresolute (i-rez′ol-ūt) *a.* infirm or inconstant in purpose; vacillating; unsettled; undetermined; wavering.—**irres'olutely** *adv.*—**irres'oluteness, irresolu'tion** *n.*

irrespective (i-re-spek′tiv) *a.* and *adv.* without taking account (of); without regard to; apart from.—**irrespec'tively** *adv.*

irresponsible (i-re-spon′si-bl) *a.* not liable to answer (for consequences); carefree; without a due sense of responsibility.—**irresponsibil'ity** *n.*—**irrespons'ibly** *adv.*

irresponsive (i-re-spon′siv) *a.* not responsive (to); unanswering; taciturn; showing no enthusiasm.—**irrespons'iveness** *n.*

irretrievable (i-re-trē′vą-bl) *a.* incapable of recovery or repair.—**irretrievabil'ity, irretriev′ableness** *n.*—**irretriev'ably** *adv.*

irreverent (i-rev′e-rent) *a.* not reverent; not entertaining or manifesting due regard for the Supreme Being; disrespectful.—**irrev'erence** *n.* —**irrev'erently** *adv.*

irreversible (i-re-vėr′si-bl) *a.* that cannot be reversed, turned back, recalled, or annulled. —**irrevers'ibly** *adv.*

irrevocable (i-rev′ō-ką-bl) *a.* incapable of being recalled or revoked.—**irrevocabil'ity, irrev'ocableness** *n.*—**irrev'ocably** *adv.*

irrigate (ir′i-gāt) *v.t.* to water (by artificial channels); to wet or moisten.—**irr′igable, irr′igative** *a.* capable of being irrigated.—**irriga′tion** *n.* the artificial application of water to the land for the purpose of increasing its fertility.—**irriga′tor** *n.* [L. *irrigare*, fr. *rigare*, to moisten].

irritate (ir′i-tāt) *v.t.* to excite to anger; to annoy; to excite heat and redness in the skin by friction.—**irritabil′ity** *n.*—**irr′itable** *a.* easily provoked or annoyed; fretful; able to be acted upon by stimuli.—**irr′itableness** *n.*—**irr′itably** *adv.*—**irr′itant** *a.* irritating;—*n.* that which irritates or causes irritation.—**irrita′tion** *n.* exasperation; anger; the act of exciting heat, redness, or action in the skin or flesh by external stimulus.—**irr′itative** *a.* tending to irritate [L. *irritare*].

irruption (i-rup′shun) *n.* a sudden invasion; a violent incursion into a place; a breaking or bursting in; an inroad.—**irrup′tive** *a.* rushing in or upon with violence.—**irrup′tively** *adv.* [L. *irruptio*, fr. *rumpere*, to break].

is (iz) *v.* the third pers, sing. pres. indic. of the verb **to be** [O.E.].

Ishmaelite (ish′ma-līt) *n.* social outcast; descendant of Ishmael (*Bib.*) [Heb. (*whom*) *God hears*].

isinglass (ī′zing-glás) *n.* a glutinous whitish substance, prepared from the swimming-bladder of various species of fish, esp. the sturgeon, and used in manufacture of jellies and confections [corrupt. fr. Dut. *huizenblas*, sturgeon-bladder].

Islam, Islamism (iz′lam, -izm) *n.* the religion of Mohammed, and also the whole body of those who profess it throughout the world.—**Islam′ic, Islamit′ic** *a.* [Ar. = obedience to God].

island (ī′land) *n.* a piece of land surrounded by water; anything resembling this, e.g. a street-refuge.—**is′lander** *n.* an inhabitant of an island [earlier *iland*, O.E. *iegland*].

isle (īl) *n.* an island.—**isles′man** *n.* an islander, esp. a dweller on one of the Scottish groups of islands.—**islet** (ī′let) *n.* a tiny island [O. Fr. *isle*, L. *insula*].

ism (izm) *n.* a jocular reference to any distinctive doctrine, theory, or practice [English suffix, *-ism*].

iso- (ī′so) *prefix* fr. Gk. *isos*, equal, used in the construction of compound terms.

isobar (ī′sō-bar) *n.* a line on a map joining up all those points where the mean height of the barometer is the same;—*pl.* species of atoms having the same mass numbers but different atomic numbers, i.e. different elements.—**isobar′ic** *a.* consisting of isobars.—**isobaromet′ric** *a.* showing equal barometric pressure (Gk. *isos*, equal; *baros*, weight].

isochromatic (ī-sō-krō-mat′ik) *a.* having the same colour [Gk. *isos*, equal; *chrōma*, colour].

isochronal, isochronous (ī-sok′ro-nal, -nus) *a.* (*Phys.*) having the same frequency; uniform in time; performed in equal times [Gk. *isos*, equal; *chronos*, time].

isocryme (ī′sō-krīm) *n.* a line on a map joining up all those points having the same mean winter temperature [Gk. *isos*, equal; *krumos*, cold].

isodynamic (ī-sō-dī-nam′ik) *a.* having equal force or power.

isogon (ī′sō-gon) *n.* a plane figure having equal angles [Gk. *isos*, equal; *gonia*, angle].

isohel (ī′sō-hel) *n.* a line on a map connecting places having the same recorded amount of sunshine [Gk. *isos*, equal; *helios*, the sun].

isohyet (ī-sō-hī′et) *n.* a line drawn on a map joining places which have the same annual mean rainfall.—**isohy′etal** *a.* [Gk. *isos*, equal; *huetos*, rain].

isolate (ī′so-lāt) *v.t.* to place in a detached position; to place apart or alone; to insulate; to separate or segregate (a group of organisms); to disconnect.—**isola′tion** *n.* state of being isolated.—**isolation hospital**, a hospital for infectious diseases.—**isola′tionist** *n.* in U.S.A. one who advocates non-participation in world-politics [It. *isolato*, detached, fr. L. *insula*, an island].

isometric (ī-sō-met′rik) *a.* of equal measurement.

isomorphism (ī-sō-morf′izm) *n.* similarity of structure, esp. between the crystals of different chemical substances.—**isomor′phic** *a.* —**isomor′phous** *a.* [Gk. *isos*, equal; *morphē*, shape].

isopod (ī′sō-pod) *n.* crustacean of order *Isopoda*, with usually seven pairs of equal legs [Gk. *isos*, equal; *pous*, *podos*, foot].

Isoptera (ī-sop′ter-a) *n.* an order of insects, including the termites or white ants, with four wings exactly alike.—**isop′terous,** *a.* [Gk. *isos*, equal; *pteron*, a wing].

isosceles (ī-sos′e-lēz) *a.* having two sides which are equal (said of a triangle) [Gk. *isos*, equal; *skelos*, a leg].

isothere (ī′sō-thēr) *n.* an imaginary line on a map connecting places with the same mean summer temperature.—**isoth′eral** *a.* [Gk. *isos*, equal; *theros*, summer].

isotherm (ī′sō-therm) *n.* an imaginary line over the earth's surface, passing through points having the same mean annual temperature.—**isother′mal** *a.* having equal heat [Gk. *isos*, equal; *thermē*, heat].

isotopes (ī-sō-tōps) *n.pl.* (*Physics*) of most of the elements, atoms with nuclei of slightly different weights, as, in particular, uranium with isotopes of weight 238 and 235 [Gk. *isos*, equal; *topos*, place].

Israel (iz′ra-el) *n.* since 1948, the name of the Jewish State in Palestine; (*Bib.*) the Jewish people—**Israeli** (iz-rāl′ī) *n.* an inhabitant of Israel.—**Is′raelite** *n.* (*Bib.*) a descendant of Israel or Jacob; a Jew.—**Israelit′ic, Israelit′ish,** *a.* Jewish, Hebrew [Heb. *Israel*, a soldier of God].

issue (ish′ū) *n.* act of passing or flowing out; the act of sending out; the whole number sent out at one time; a topic of discussion or controversy; a morbid discharge from the body; egress; outlet; edition; consequence; end; result; progeny; off-spring; (*Law*) the specific point in a suit between two parties requiring to be determined;—*v.t.* to send out (a book, etc.); to put into circulation, as notes; to proclaim or set forth with authority; to supply with equipment, etc.;—*v.i.* to pass or flow out; to come out; to proceed; to be born or spring from. —**iss′ueless** *a.* without issue; childless.—**iss′uer** *n.* one who issues.—**at issue** (point) to be debated or settled.—**to join issue,** to take opposite views on a point in debate [O.Fr. *issir*, to go out, fr. L. *exire*].

isthmus (isth′mus, is′mus) *n.* a narrow neck of land connecting two larger portions.—**isth′mian** *a.* [Gk. *isthmos*].

it (it) *pron.* the neuter pronoun of the third person;—*n.* (*Colloq.*) sexual attractiveness; sex appeal; perfection [O.E. *hit*].

Italian (i-tal′yan) *a.* pert. to Italy, its inhabitants or their language;—*n.* a native of Italy; the language spoken in Italy; satinised cotton cloth.—**ital′ianate** *v.t.* to render in Italian; to make Italian.—**ital′ianise** *v.i.* to make Italian.—**ital′icism** *n.* a word, phrase, or idiom peculiar to the Italians.—**Italian warehouseman,** a dealer in exotic food products, peculiar to Italy [L. *Italia*].

italics (i-tal′iks) *n.pl.* a printing type of Italian origin, having the type sloping from the right downwards, *as the letters in which these words are printed.*—**italicisa′tion** *n.*—**ital′icise** *v.t.* to print thus.

itch (ich) *n.* an irritation in the skin; scabies; an irrepressible desire;—*v.i.* to feel uneasiness or irritation in the skin; to be inordinately anxious or desirous to; to be hankering after. —**itch′iness** *n.*—**itch′y** *a.*—**an itching palm,** a grasping disposition; greed of gain [O.E. *giccan*, to itch].

item (ī′tem) *adv.* also; likewise (used in enumerating);—*n.* any of a list of things; an entry in an account or list; a detail.—**i′temize** *v.t.* (*U.S.*) to give particulars [L.].
iterate (it′ẹ-rāt) *v.t.* to repeat; to do again; to re-iterate.—**itera′tion, it′erance** *n.* a repeating; repetition.—**it′erative, it′erant** *a.* repeating [L. *iterare*, fr. *iterum*, again].
itinerant (ī-tin-e-rạnt) *a.* travelling from place to place; travelling on circuit; of no settled abode; wandering;—*n.* one who goes from place to place; a wanderer; a roamer.—**itin′eracy, itin′erancy** *n.* the habit or act of wandering about the country.—**itin′erantly** *adv.* —**itin′erary** *n.* a record of travel; a route, line of travel; a guide-book for travellers.—**itin′erate** *v.i.* to travel up and down a country. —**itinera′tion** *n.* [L. *iter, itineris*, a journey].
its (its) the possessive case of *pron.* it.—**itself′** *pron.* the neuter reciprocal pronoun applied to things; the reflexive form of it.
ivory (ī′vor-i) *n.* the hard, white, opaque, dentrine constituting tusks of elephant, walrus, etc.—*n.pl.* the teeth;—*a.* made of or like ivory.—**i′vorine** *n.* an imitation of ivory. —**ivory black, bone′black** *n.* a fine pigment, obtained originally by calcining, in a closed vessel, ivory dust and chips.—**i′vory-nut** *n.* the seed of the **ivory palm,** which provides a substitute for animal-ivory and is known as **vegetable ivory** or corozo nut.—**black ivory,** negro slaves [Fr. *ivoire*, fr. L. *ebur*, ivory].
ivy (ī′vi) *n.* a climbing ever-green plant, common in Europe;—*pl.* **i′vies.**—**i′vied** *a.* covered with ivy [O.E. *ifig*].

J

jab (jab) *v.t.* to poke sharply; to stab;—*n.* a sharp poke, stab, or thrust [prob. imit.].
jabber (jab′ẹr) *v.i.* to chatter; to speak quickly and indistinctly.—*v.t.* to utter indistinctly;—*n.* rapid, incoherent talk.—**jabb′erer** *n.*—**jabb′eringly** *adv.* [prob. imit.].
jabot (zhȧ′bō) *n.* a frill or fall of lace on a woman's dress; orig. a ruffle on a man's shirt-front [Fr. etym. doubtful].
jacaranda (jak-a-ran′dạ) *n.* a tropical American tree yielding hard, fragrant timber, known as rose-wood [Braz.].
jacinth (ja′sinth) *n.* (*Geol.*) *a* reddish-orange variety of transparent zircon, used as a gem; the hyacinth [contr. of L. *hyacinthus*, a precious stone].
Jack (jak) *n.* a popular nickname and diminutive of *John*; a fellow; a labourer, as *steeple-jack*; a sailor; the knave in a pack of cards; a device to facilitate removal of boots, as a *boot-jack*; a mechanical device for turning a roasting-spit; a portable machine for raising heavy weights, esp. for raising a motor vehicle to change a tyre; (*Bowls*) white ball used as a mark to be aimed at; a flag or ensign; the male of certain animals, as a *Jack-hare*; a deep red-coloured rose; a young pike.—**jack** *v.t.* to raise with a jack. Also **jack′-up**—**jack′-a-dan′dy** *n.* a fop.—**jack′-boot** *n.* a long boot reaching above the knee formerly worn by cavalry.—**jack′-fool** *n.* an unmitigated ass.—**jack′-in-a-box′** *n.* a tropical tree the fruit of which rattles when touched.—**jack′-in-off′ice** *n.* an official who presumes on his position.—**jack′-in-the-box′** *n.* a child's toy comprising a small figure which springs out of a box when the lid is lifted.—**jack′knife** *n.* a strong clasp knife.—**jack o' lantern,** the will o' the wisp; a lantern made from hollowed-out turnip.—**jack′-of-all′-trades** *n.* one who can turn his hand to anything.—**jack′-pot** *n.* a pool, in poker, which cannot be opened except by player holding two jacks or better; any vessel containing hidden treasure.—**jack′-rabb′it** *n.* an American hare with very long ears.—**jack′saw** *n.* the goosander, a bird with sharp, saw-toothed beak.—**jack′-snipe** *n.* a small species of snipe.—**Jack Sprat,** a diminutive fellow.—**jack-tar,** a sailor.—**cheap jack,** a hawker or pedlar.—**Union Jack,** the national flag of Gt. Britain.—**yel′low-jack** *n.* yellow fever [fr. *John*, infl. by Fr. *Jacques*].
jack (jak) *n.* a coat of mail; a jerkin worn over armour;—**black jack,** a leather bottle [prob. Fr. *jaque*, a coat of mail].
jack (jak) *n.* an E. Indian tree with fruit like bread-fruit tree. Also **jak** [Port. *jaca*].
jackal (jak′awl) *n.* a bushy-tailed carnivorous animal of Persia and India, allied to the dog; (*Fig.*) a servile creature; a tool (from the old erroneous idea that the jackal was used as a scout in a lion-hunt) [Pers. *shaghal*].
jackanapes (jak′ạ-nāps) *n.* orig. a monkey; an impertinent fellow; a pert child.
jackaroo (jak′ạ-ròò) *n.* (*Austral. slang*) an English newcomer gaining experience in the Australian back-blocks; a novice [fr. *Jack* and *Kangaroo*].
jackass (jak′as) *n.* a male ass; a stupid fellow; a blockhead.—**laughing jackass,** the giant king-fisher of Australia [*Jack*, the male; and *ass*].
jackdaw (jak′daw) *n.* a British bird of the crow family [fr. *Jack*; *daw*].
jacket (jak′et) *n.* a short, sleeved coat; outer covering or skin (as of potatoes); an outer casing for a boiler to keep in heat; a loose dust-cover for a book;—*v.t.* to cover with a jacket; (*Slang*) to thrash [O.Fr. *jaquet*, dim. of *jaque*, a coat of mail].
Jacobean (jak-ō-bē′ạn) *a.* pert. to reign of James I; used mainly of architecture, indoor decoration, and furniture (dark oak) of Stuart period;—*n.* person of this period [L. *Jacobus*, James].
Jacobin (jak′ō-bin) *n.* a French Dominican friar, so called from monastery of *St. Jacques*, Paris; a member of society of French Revolutionists in 1789 with headquarters in the old Jacobin monastery; demagogue; variety of hooded pigeon—*a.* (also **Jacobin′ic**), extreme; turbulent; revolutionary [Fr. fr. L. *Jacobus*, James].
Jacobite (jak′ō-bīt) *n.*| adherent of James II or of his descendants, the Old and Young Pretender:—*a.* pert. to followers of James II and Stuart supporters.—**Jac′obitism** *n.* [L. *Jacob's*, James].
Jacob's ladder (jā′kobz-lad′ẹr) *n.* a plant with blue and white flowẹrs, and leaves with ladder-like arrangement; (*Naut.*)a rope ladder with wooden rungs [Heb. *ya'aqob*, Jacob].
jaconet (jak′o-net) *n.* a thin, smooth-finished muslin fabric; a thin waterproofed muslin, used in poulticing [Hind. *Jagannathi*, a town in Bengal].
jaculation (jak-ū-lā′shun) *n.* the act of throwing, as a dart.—**jac′ulate** *v.t.* to throw [L. *jaculari*, to throw, as a dart].
jade (jād) *n.* an over-worked, worn-out horse; a mean woman; a saucy wench;—*v.t.* to tire; to harass.—*pr.p.* **jad′ing.**—*pa.p.* **jad′ed.**—**jad′ed** *a.* tired; weary; off-colour [Scand, *jalda*, a mare].
jade (jād) *n.* a very hard, compact silicate of lime and magnesia, of various colours, carved for ornaments.—**jade′ite** *n.* silicate of sodium and aluminium, green in colour, found in Burma [Span. (*piedra de*) *ijada*, a stone for curing a pain in the side].
Jaffa (jaf′a) *a.* pert. to Jaffa; used of oranges exported from *Jaffa*, in Palestine.
jag (jag) *n.* a notch; a ragged protuberance; (*Bot.*) cleft or division;—*v.t.* to notch; to stab. —*pr.p.* **jag′ging.**—*pa.p.* **jagged.**—**jag′ged, jag′gy** *a.* notched; rough-edged; sharp.—**jag′gedness** *n.* [etym. doubtful].
jaguar (jag′wȧr) *n.* a large spotted yellowish beast of prey, resembling a leopard, found in S. and Central America [Braz.].
jail (jāl) *n.* a prison. Also **gaol.**—**jail′bird, gaol′bird** *n.* a prisoner; a criminal.—**jail′er, jail′or, gaol′er,** *n.* one who has charge of prisoners in

the cells.—**jail´fe'ver, ga'ol´fever** *n.* typhus [O.Fr. *gaole,* a prison].

jalap (jal´ap) *n.* a drug used as a purgative esp. in dropsy [fr. *Xalapa,* in Mexico].

jalopy (ja-lop´i) *n.* (*U.S. slang*) an old motor-car.

jalousie (zhal-òò-zē') *n.* a Venetian wooden-slatted window-blind.—**jalousied'** *a.* [Fr. *jalousie,* suspicion].

jam (jam) *n.* preserve made from fruit, boiled with sugar; (*Slang*) something easily obtained. —**jam'my** *a.* [etym. doubtful].

jam (jam) *v.t.* to squeeze tight; to wedge in; to block up; to stall (a machine);—*v.i.* to cease to function because of obstruction.—*pr.p.* **jam'ming.**—*pa.p.* **jammed.**—*n.* a crush; a hold-up (as of traffic); (*Colloq.*) a tight corner. —**jam'ming** *n.* (*Radio*) the effect of interference as when signals of similar wave length collide and the resulting sounds are unintelligible [prob. var. of *champ*].

Jamaica pepper (ja-mā´ka pep´ẹr) *n.* allspice.

jamb (jam) *n.* the side-piece of a door, fire-place, etc. [Fr. *jambe,* a leg].

jambok (jam´bok) *n.* a long piece of hide used as a whip;—*v.t.* to strike with such a whip.—Also **Sjambok** [S. Afr.].

jamboree (jam-bō-rē') *n.* an international rally of Boy Scouts; a friendly gathering; (*Euchre*) a hand containing five highest cards making a total of 16 [etym. unknown].

jampan (jam´pan) *n.* a chair on four bamboo poles carried by four bearers.—**jampanee'** *n.* its bearer [E. Ind.].

jane (jān) *n.* a hard-wearing cotton twill fabric; jean [O.Fr. *Janne*].

jangle (jang´gl) *v.t.* to ring with a discordant sound;—*v.i.* to sound out of tune; to wrangle; —*n.* a discordant sound; a dispute.—**jang'ling** *n.* [imit. O.Fr. *jangler*].

janitor (jan´i-tor) *n.* (*fem.* **jan'itrix, jan'itress**) a door-keeper; a porter [L. *janitor*].

Janizary (jan´i-zạr-i) *n.* a soldier of the Turkish infantry, orig. the bodyguard of the Sultan—suppressed in 1826. Also **Jan'issary, Janiza'rian** *a.* [Turk. *yenitsheri,* the new soldiers].

Jansenist (jan´sen-ist) *n.* a follower of *Cornelius Jansen,* R.C. bishop of Ypres whose doctrines concerning grace and freewill closely resembled those of Calvin.

janty See **jaunty.**

January (jan´ū-ar-i) *n.* the first month, dedicated by Romans to *Janus,* the god with two faces.—**jan'us-faced** *a.* untrustworthy [L. *Janus,* a Roman deity].

Japan (ja-pan') *n.* a N.E. Asiatic insular empire.—**Jap** *n. abbrev.* of Japanese; a native of Japan;—*a.* pert. to Japan.—**Japanese'** *n.* a native of Japan;—*a.* pert. to Japan, the people or language.—**japan'** *v.t.* to make black and glossy; to lacquer with black varnish.—*pr.p.* **japan'ning.**—*pa.p.* **japanned';**—*n.* the black lacquer used in japanning; work japanned [Jap.].

jape (jāp) *v.t.* to deride.—*n.* a jest [O.Fr. *japer,* to jest].

japonica (jap-on´ik-a) *n.* a garden shrub, the Japanese quince; the camellia [abbrev. of *Pyrus japonica*].

jar (jȧr) *n.* vessel narrower at top than at base, with or without handles [Fr. *jarre*].

jar (jȧr) *v.i.* to give forth a discordant sound; to vibrate discordantly; to be inconsistent with; to annoy;—*v.t.* to cause to vibrate by sudden impact; to shake physically or mentally.—*pr.p.* **jar'ring.**—*pa.p.* **jarred.**—*n.* a harsh, grating sound; angry strife; perturbation.—**jar'ringly** *adv.* [prob. imit.].

jargon (jar´gon) *n.* confused speech; gibberish; slang; the technical phraseology of experts [etym. doubtful].

jargonelle (jȧr´go-nel) *n.* a variety of pear which ripens early [Ar. *zargun,* golden].

jarrah (jȧr´a) *n.* a mahogany gum-tree of S.W. Australia [Austral.].

jasmine (jas´min) *n.* a climbing plant with fragrant white or yellow flowers.—Also **jess´amine** [Pers. *yasmin,* jasmine].

jaspé (jas´pā) *n.* a cotton cloth of shaded effect used for bedcovers, curtains, etc.

jasper (jas´pẹr) *n.* a precious stone; an impure opaque form of silica [Gk. *iaspis,* chalcedony].

jato (jā´tō) *n.* kind of rocket to assist the take-off of heavily loaded aircraft [*J*et *A*ssisted *T*ake *O*ff].

jaundice (jȧn´dis, jawn´dis) *n.* a disease, characterised by yellowness of skin and eyes; —*v.t.* to affect with jaundice.—**jaun'diced** *a.* affected with jaundice; (*Fig.*) jealous; prejudiced [Fr. *jaune,* yellow].

jaunt (jȧnt, jawnt), *v.i.* to make an excursion; —*n.* an outing; a ramble.—**jaunt'ing** *a.* rambling.—**jaunting car,** a vehicle used in Ireland, two wheeled, and with side seats back to back [etym. doubtful].

jaunty (jȧnt´i, jawnt´i) *a.* sprightly; airy; care-free.—**jaunt'ily** *adv.*—**jaunt'iness** *n.*—Also **jant'y, jant'ily, jant'iness** [Fr. *gentil,* genteel].

javelin (jav´lin) *n.* a light hand-thrown spear, about five and a half feet long [Fr.].

jaw (jaw) *n.* one of the two bones forming framework of mouth and containing the teeth; the mouth; part of any device which grips or crushes object held by it, as a vice; (*Slang*) loquacity;—*pl.* narrow entrance to a gorge.—*v.t.* to scold.—**jaw´bone** *n.* bone of the mouth in which teeth are set.—**jawed** *a.* having jaws; indicating facial appearance, as *lantern-jawed* [etym. uncertain].

jay (jā) *n.* a chattering, perching bird with gay plumage; (*Fig.*) a foolish person.—**jay´walk'er** *n.* (*U. S. colloq.*) a careless or absent-minded pedestrian who disregards all traffic regulations [etym. doubtful].

jazz (jaz) *n.* syncopated, noisy music, derived from negro spirituals, and played as accompaniment to dancing;—*a.* discordant; raucous; garish.—*v.t.* and *v.i.* to dance to jazz music.—**jaz'zy** *a.* [Negro word].

jealous (jel´us) *a.* solicitous; zealously careful; envious; suspicious; apprehensively watchful. —**jeal'ously** *adv.*—**jeal'ousness, jeal'ousy** *n.* vigilance; envy; apprehension of rivalry [O. Fr. fr. Gk. *zelos,* emulation].

jean (jān, jēn) *n.* a strong, twilled, cotton cloth;—*n.pl.* (*U. S.*) overalls; (*Colloq.*) trousers [prob. fr. L. *Genua,* Genoa].

jeep (jēp) *n.* American light motor utility truck designed for general purposes in *World War* 2 [G.P., of general purposes].

jeer (jēr) *v.i.* to mock; to deride;—*v.t.* to treat scoffingly;—*n.* a gibe; a railing remark.—**jeer'ingly** *adv.* [etym. doubtful].

Jehovah (je-hō´vạ) *n.* (*Bib.*) Hebrew name of the supreme God [Heb. *Yahweh*].

Jehu (jē´hū) *n.* (*Bib.*) King of Israel in 9th cent. B.C., noted for his furious driving.—**je'hu,** *n.* a daring driver; a coachman [Heb.].

jejune (je-jòòn') *a.* empty; barren; uninteresting; dry.—**jejune'ly** *adv.*—**jejune'ness** *n.* [L. *jejunus,* hungry].

jelly (jel´i) *n.* any gelatinous substance; the juice of fruit boiled with sugar.—**jell** *v.i.* to stiffen.—**jell'ied** *a.* thick and stiff, like jelly.—**jell'ify** *v.t.* to make into a jelly;—*v.i.* to become set like a jelly.—**jell'y-fish** *n.* popular name given to the medusa stage of certain marine animals with bell-shaped bodies, a large central mouth and tentacles [Fr. *gelée,* frost].

jemmy (jem´i) *n.* a small crowbar, as used by burglars [var. of *James*].

jennet (jen´et) *n.* a small Spanish horse.—Also **ge(n)n'et** [Sp. *jinete,* a light horseman].

jenny (jen´i) *n.* a travelling crane; a spinning machine; (*Cinema*) portable electric dynamo; a female ass; a female bird, the wren (usually *jenny-wren*) [dim. of *Jane*].

jeopardy (jep´ard-i) *n.* danger; risk.—**jeop'ard, jeop'ardise,** *v.t.* to endanger; to imperil.—**jeop'ardous** *a.* perilous.—**jeop'ardously** *adv.* [Fr. *jeu parti,* a divided game].

jerboa (jer-bō´ą) *n.* a small leaping rodent found in N. Africa and N. America [Ar.].
Jeremiah (jer-e-mī´ą) *n.* (*Bib.*) a Hebrew prophet and author of the Book of Lamentations; any doleful prophet.—**jeremi'ad** *n.* a tale of grief or complaint.
jerk (jerk) *v.t.* to throw with a quick motion; to twitch; to give a sudden pull, twist, or push;—*n.* a short, sudden thrust, or push; a spasmodic twitching.—**jerk'er** *n.*—**jerk'ily** *adv.*—**jerk'iness** *n.*—**jerk'y** *a.* fitful; spasmodic; lacking rhythm.—**physical jerks** (*Colloq.*) gymnastics [imit. word].
jerk (jerk) *v.t.* to cure (meat) by cutting in long slices and drying in the sun.—**jerked** *a.* [Peruv. *charqui*, dried beef].
jerkin (jer´kin) *n.* a close-fitting jacket or waistcoat [prob. Dut. *jurk*, a frock].
jeroboam (jer-o-bō´ąm) *n.* a large bowl; a huge bottle, in capacity eight times the ordinary size [1 Kings. 11].
Jerry (jer´i) *n.* (*Slang*) a German soldier.
jerry-builder (jer´i-bil´der) *n.* one who builds flimsy houses of second-rate material [prob. fr. *Jerry* abbrev. of *Jeremiah*].
Jersey (jer´zi) *n.* the largest of the Channel Islands; a cow of Jersey breed;—*a.* pert. to Jersey.—**jer'sey** *n.* a close-fitting, knitted, woollen jacket, vest, or pullover [fr. *Jersey*].
jess (jes) *n.* a strap of leather or silk tied round the legs of a hawk;—*v.t.* to put jesses on [O.Fr. *ges*, a throw].
jessamine See **jasmine**.
jest (jest) *n.* a joke; a quip; an object of ridicule;—*v.i.* to joke.—**jest'er** *n.* one who jests; a professional fool, originally attached to the court or lord's manor.—**jest'ful** *a.* given to jesting.—**jest'ingly** *adv.* [M.E. *jeste*, an exploit].
Jesuit (jez´ū-it) *n.* one of a religious order founded by Ignatius Loyola in 1543 under the title of The Society of Jesus; (commonly) a crafty person; a prevaricator.—**Jesuit'ic, -al,** *a.* pert, to, or resembling, a Jesuit; crafty.—**Jes'uitism, Jesuitoc'racy** *n.* government by Jesuits [fr. *Jesus*].
jet (jet) *n.* a variety of very hard, black lignite, capable of a brilliant polish and much used for ornaments;—*a.* made of, or having the glossy blackness of jet.—**jet´black** *a.* black like jet.—**jet'tiness** *n.*—**jet'ty** *a.* black as jet [O.Fr. *jel*].
jet (jet) *n.* a sudden rush, as of water or flame, from a pipe; the spout or nozzle emitting water, gas, etc.;—*v.t.* to spout forth;—*v.i.* to strut.—**jet propulsion,** propulsion of a machine by the force of a jet of fluid expelled backwards from the machine [Fr. *jeter.* to throw].
jetsam (jet´sąm) *n.* goods thrown overboard to lighten a ship in distress; goods washed ashore from a wrecked ship.—**jet'tison** *n.* jetsam;—*v.t.* to throw overboard, as cargo; (*Fig.*) to abandon, as a scheme [O.Fr. *jetée*, thrown out].
jetty (jet´i) *n.* a mole built to protect a harbour; a landing-pier [O.Fr. *jetée*, thrown out].
Jew (jōō) *n.* a person of Jewish religion or descent; term sometimes applied to one who drives a hard bargain. **Jew'ess** *n.* a Jewish girl or woman.—**Jew'ish** *a.* **Jew'ishness** *n.*—**Jew'ry** *n.* Judea; the Jewish people; Jewish quarter.—**Jew's harp**, a small, lyre-shaped musical instrument held between the lips, sounded by means of a steel tongue struck with the finger [Heb. *Yehudah*, Judah].
jewel (jōō´el) *n.* a precious stone; an ornament set with gem(s); a highly valued person or thing;—*v.t.* to adorn with jewels; to fit (as a watch) with a jewel for pivot-bearings.—*pr.p.* **jew'elling.**—*pa.p.* **jew'elled.**—**jew'eller** *n.* one who deals in jewels.—**jew'ellery, jew'elry** *n.* jewels collectively [O.Fr. *joel*, jewel].
Jezebel (jez´e-bel) *n.* a wicked, wanton woman [*Jezebel*, wife of Ahab].
jib (jib) *n.* (*Naut.*) a triangular stay-sail extended from the outer end of the jib-boom to the fore topmast-head; the projecting beam of a crane or derrick;—*v.t.* to swing (the sail) from one side of ship to the other;—*v.i.* to swing round (of the sail) as the course of the ship is changed.—**jib´boom** *n.* a spar run out from the extremity of the bowsprit [var. of *gybe*].
jib (jib) *v.i.* (of a horse) to stand still and refuse to go on; to move restively; (*Fig.*) (of a person) to refuse obstinately to go on with a task.—**to jib at,** to be reluctant to do something.—**jib'ber** *n.* [etym. doubtful].
jibe (jīb) *n.* a taunt; sneering comment.—*v.i.* to sneer.—*pr.p.* **jib'ing.**—*pa.p.* **jibed.**—Also **gibe.**
jiffy (jif´i) *n.* (*Colloq.*) a moment; an instant [etym. unknown].
jig (jig) *n.* a lively dance; music for this; a trick; a tool or fixture used to guide cutting tools in the making of duplicate parts;—*v.t.* to jerk up and down;—*v.i.* to dance; to bob up and down.—*pr.p.* **jig'ging.**—*pa.p.* **jigged.**—**jig´jog** *n.* jerky motion.—**jig´saw** *n.* a machine fret-saw.—**jig-saw puzzle,** a picture on cardboard cut into irregular pieces for putting together again [etym. uncertain].
jigamaree (jig´ą-mar-ē) *n.* word used to denote the name of something momentarily forgotten. Also **jiggumbob.**
jigger (jig´er) *n.* one who or that which jigs; any mechanical device which operates with jerky movement esp. an apparatus for washing and separating ores by shaking in sieves under water; an iron-headed golf club for approach-shots; a rest for a billiard cue; (*Naut.*) a tackle consisting of a double and single block and the fall; a template for moulding an earthenware vessel on a potter's wheel; (*Radio*) oscillation transformer coupling aerial circuit of a transformer to the source of oscillation; (*Print.*) a weight used by compositors to mark the place in the copy; (*Colloq.*) any gadget; (*Slang*) a drink;—*v.t.* to shake up and down.—**jig'ger-mast** *n.* the after-mast of a four-masted schooner [etym. uncertain].
jigger (jig´er) *n.* (*U. S.* and *S. Afr.*) a flea, the female of which burrows under the human flesh to lay its eggs, attacking especially the feet [var. of *chigoe*].
jiggery-pokery (jig´er-i-pōk´er-i) *n.* (*Colloq.*) underhand scheming.
jihad (jē-hȧd') *n.* a holy war to the death proclaimed by Mohammedans against the foes of Islam; (*Fig.*) a campaign launched against any doctrine. Also **jehad'** [Ar.].
jilt (jilt) *n.* one, esp. a woman, who capriciously disappoints a lover;—*v.t.* to deceive or disappoint in love; to break an engagement to marry [prob. fr. *jillet*, dim, of Jill].
Jim Crow (jim-krō) *n.* (*U. S.*) contemptuous name for a negro; (*Colloq.*) an enemy-aircraft spotter [*Jim* and *crow*].
jim-crow (jim´krō) *n.* a special machine-tool for straightening or bending iron bars, rails, etc. [etym. uncertain].
jimmy Same as **jemmy.**
jingle (jing´gl) *v.t.* to cause to give a sharp, tinkling sound;—*v.i.* to tinkle; to give this effect in poetry; *n.* a tinkling sound, as of bells; correspondence of sounds, rhymes, etc., in verse to catch the ear; a light, covered two-wheeled cart [imit.].
jingo (jing´gō) *n.* a mild oath, as in *By Jingo*; one who expresses vehement patriotism (from the popular song of the late 1870's, ' We don't want to fight, but *by Jingo* if we do . . .').—**jing'o, jing'oish** *a.*—**jing'oism** *n.* the political, chauvinistic principles of jingoes [etym. doubtful].
jinn (jin) *n.pl.* (*sing.* **jin'nee**) spirits of Mohammedan mythology, supposedly able to assume the forms of men and animals. Also **Djinn, Ginn** [Ar. *jinni*].
jinrikisha (jin-rik´i-shą) *n.* a small, two-

wheeled hooded carriage pulled by one or more men, commonly used in Japan (*abbrev.* **rick'shaw**) [Jap. *jin*, a man; *riki*, power; *sha*, a carriage].

jinx (jingks) *n.* (*U. S.*) a person or thing of ill-omen [etym. uncertain].

jitters (jit'ẹrz) *n.pl.* (*Slang*) a state of nervous agitation.—**jit'terbug** *n.* (*U. S.*) a jazz-dancer; a person who panics easily.—**jit'tery** *a.* [prob. imit.].

jiu-jitsu See **ju-jutsu.**

jive (jīv) *n.* and *v.i.* exuberant variation on modern swing-time dance steps.

job (job) *n.* a piece of work; labour undertaken at a stated price or paid for by the hour; (*Colloq.*) habitual employment or profession; —*pl.* lengths of defective cotton fabrics, sold usually by weight;—*a.* lumped together (of miscellaneous articles).—*v.i.* to do odd jobs; to act as a broker; to use influence unscrupulously;—*v.t.* to hire out for a specified time (as a horse); to deal unscrupulously in business.—*pr.p.* **job'bing**.—*pa.p.* **jobbed.**—**job'ber** *n.* a middleman, particularly in the Stock Exchange; one who transacts public business to his own advantage; one who does odd jobs; one who hires out horses by the day or hour. —**job'bery** *n.* underhand means to gain private profit at the expense of public money; fraudulent dealings.—**job'bing** *a.* not regularly employed;—*n.* odd jobs.—**jobbing work,** the printing of handbills, circulars, etc. [etym. unknown].

job (job) *n.* a stab with a pointed instrument;—*v.t.* to prod [var. of *jab*].

Job (jōb) *n.* (*Bib.*) a Hebrew patriarch of the Old Testament regarded as a monument of patience; any person accepting continued disaster with infinite patience.—**a Job's comforter,** one who aggravates the distress of another while pretending to console him.

Jock (jok) *n.* (*Army slang*) a Highland or Scottish soldier.

jockey (jok'i) *n.* a professional rider in horse-races; a dealer in horses; one who cheats in business;—*v.t.* to jostle against, in riding; to manoeuvre for one's own advantage; to trick; —*v.i.* to cheat.—**jock'eyism, jock'eyship** *n.* [dim. of *Jock*].

jocose (jō-kōs') *a.* given to jesting; waggish.—**jocose'ly** *adv.*—**jocose'ness, jocos'ity** *n.* the quality or state of being jocose [L. *jocus*, a jest].

jocular (jok'ū-lạr) *a.* given to jesting; merry. —**jocular'ity** *n.*—**joc'ularly** *adv.* [L. *jocus*, a joke].

jocund (jok'und) *a.* merry; gay; genial.—**jocund'ity, jocund'ness** *n.*—**joc'undly** *adv.* [L. *jucundus*, gay].

jodhpurs (jod'pŏŏrz) *n.pl.* long riding breeches, close-fitting from knee to ankle [fr. *Jodhpur*, a native Indian State].

joey (jō'i) *n.* (*Austral.*) a young kangaroo; a day labourer;—*v.t.* to mock; to chaff; to abuse [native Austral, *joe*].

jog (jog) *v.t.* to push with the elbow or hand; to nudge; to stimulate (as the memory);—*v.i.* to move on at a slow pace; to plod on.—*pr.p.* **jog'ging.**—*pa.p.* **jogged;**—*n.* a nudge; push to awaken attention; a reminder.—**jog'trot,** slow trot [etym. doubtful].

joggle (jog'l) *v.t.* to shake slightly; to join by notches to prevent sliding apart.—*v.i.* to shake; to totter.—*pr.p.* **jog'gling.**—*pa.p.* **jog'gled;**—*n.* a jolt; a joint of two bodies so constructed by means of notches, that sliding apart is prevented; a metal pin joining two pieces of stone [dim. of **jog**].

John (jon) *n.* a proper name; a familiar appellation.—**John Barleycorn,** whisky—**John Bull,** an honest, blunt fellow; the typical Englishman. —**John Doe,** fictitious plaintiff in a law-case. —**John Dory,** an edible sea-fish.—**John'ny** *n.* a dandy [L. *Johannes*, John].

Johnsonian (jon-sō'ni-ạn) *a.* pert. to *Dr. Samuel Johnson* (1709-84), or to his literary style.—**John'sonese** *n.* literary style of Dr. Johnson; imitation of this ponderous style.

join (join) *v.t.* to bring together; to fasten; to unite; to act in concert with; to become a member of; to return to (as one's ship);—*v.i.* to meet; to unite in marriage, partnership, league, etc.; to be in contact.—*n.* a junction; a fastening.—**joind'er** *n.* (*Law*) a union.—**join'er** *n.* a workman who does the wood-work of buildings.—**join'ery** *n* the trade of a joiner —**to join battle,** to begin fighting.—**to join issue,** to take different sides on a point in debate [Fr. *joindre*, to join].

joint (joint) *n.* the place where two things are joined; the articulation of two or more bones in the body; the hinge of leather, etc., joining back and sides of a book; (*Bot.*) the point where a leaf joins the stem; a cut of meat with bone prepared by butcher for the table; (*U.S. slang*) a low class public-house;—*v.t.* to unite; to provide with joints; to cut up, as meat; to fill the spaces between bricks with mortar;—*v.i.* to fit like joints;—*a.* jointed; held in common.—**joint'ed** *a.* having joints.—**joint'ing** *n.* the process of filling in brick-work, woodwork, etc., e.g. with mortar.—**joint'ly** *adv.* together; co-operatively.—**joint-stock company,** a mercantile, banking, or co-operative association with capital made up of transferable shares.—**joint'ure** *n.* property settled on a woman at marriage to be hers on the decease of her husband.—**joint'uress, joint'ress** *n.* a woman who has a jointure.—**out of joint,** dislocated; (*Fig.*) disordered [Fr. *joindre*, to join].

joist (joist) *n.* a beam to which the boards of a floor or the laths of a ceiling are nailed [O.Fr. *giste*, fr. *gésir*, to lie].

joke (jōk) *n.* something said or done to provoke laughter; a witticism; a prank;—*v.t.* to make merry with; to banter;—*v.i.* to make sport; to be merry.—**jok'er** *n.* one who makes jokes or plays pranks; (*Slang*) a fellow; (*Cards*) an extra card in the pack, used in some games, such as poker.—**jok'ingly** *adv.* [L. *jocus*, a joke].

jolly (jol'i) *a.* jovial; handsome; plump; (*Slang*) slightly intoxicated;—*v.t.* (*U. S.*) to wheedle; to cajole;—*n.* (*Slang*) a Marine;—*adv.* very; exceptionally.—**jollifica'tion** *n.* a celebration; a noisy party.—**joll'iness, joll'ity** *n.* mirth; boisterous fun [O.Fr. *joli*, gay].

jollyboat (jol'i-bōt) *n.* a ship's small-boat [prob. Dut. *jolle*, a boat].

jolt (jōlt) *v.t.* to shake with a sudden jerk;—*v.i.* to shake, as a vehicle on rough ground;—*n.* a sudden jerk [etym. unknown].

Jonah (jō'na) *n.* (*Bib.*) a Hebrew prophet; (*Colloq.*) a person who brings bad luck, especially on board a ship.

Jonathan (jon'ạ-thạn) *n.* a variety of eating apple.

jonquil (jon'kwil) *n.* a variety of narcissus, with small yellow flowers and rush-like leaves [Fr. fr. L. *juncus*, a rush].

jordan (jor'dạn) *n.* a pilgrim's bottle containing water from the River Jordan.

jorum (jō'rum) *n.* a large drinking-vessel; a large quantity of liquid. Also **jo'ram** [etym. unknown].

joss (jos) *n.* a Chinese idol.—**joss'house** *n.* a Chinese temple.—**joss'stick** *n.* a small stick of incense burned in a Chinese temple [corrupt. of Port. *deos*, a god].

jostle (jos'l) *v.t.* to push against, esp. with the elbow;—*v.i.* to push;—*n.* a pushing against [fr. *joust*].

jot (jot) *n.* an iota; something negligible;—*v.t.* to scribble down; to make a memorandum of. —*pr.p.* **jot'ting.**—*pa.p.* **jot'ted.**—**jot'ter** *n.* one who jots down; a notebook.—**not to care one jot or tittle,** not to care at all [Gk. *iota*, the letter i].

jougs (jŏŏgz) *n.* an iron ring, in which a criminal was held fast by the neck; a form of pillory in Scotland [Fr. *joug*, a yoke].

joule (jŏŏl, joul) *n.* (*Elect.*) a unit of work; the

energy expended in 1 sec. by 1 ampere flowing through a resistance of 1 ohm [fr. *J. P. Joule*, English physicist, 1818-89].

journal (jur′-nal) *n.* a diary; a book recording daily transactions of a business firm; a daily newspaper; a periodical.—**journalese′** *n.* a term of contempt for the second-rate literary style of journalists.—**jour′nalise** *v.i.* to write for a journal; to keep a daily record of events.—**jour′nalism** *n.*—**jour′nalist** *n.* one who writes professionally for a newspaper or periodical.—**journalist′ic** *a.* [Fr. fr. L. *diurnalis*, daily].

journey (jur′-ni) *n.* travel from one place to another; distance covered in a specified time;—*v.i.* to travel.—*pr.p.* **jour′neying**.—*pa.p.* **jour′neyed**.—**jour′neyman** *n.* orig. one hired to work by the day; a skilled mechanic or artisan who has completed his apprenticeship [O.Fr. *jornée*, a day].

joust (jòòst) *n.* a mock encounter on horseback; a tournament;—*v.i.* to tilt [O.Fr. *juster*, to approach].

Jove (jōv) *n.* Jupiter.—**jo′vial** *a.* orig. born under the influence of the planet Jupiter; gay; convivial.—**jovial′ity**, **jo′vialness** *n.*—**jo′vially** *adv.* [L. *jovialis*, of Jupiter].

jowl (joul) *n.* the jawbone; the cheek; the dewlap, of cattle [O.E. *ceafl*, a jaw].

joy (joi) *n.* gladness; exhilaration of spirits;—*v.i.* to rejoice; to exult;—*v.t.* to gladden.—*pr.p.* **joy′ing**.—*pa.p.* **joyed**.—**joy′ance** *n.* gaiety.—**joy′ful** *a.*—**joy′fully** *adv.*—**joy′fulness** *n.*—**joy′less** *a.* dismal.—**joy′lessly** *adv.*—**joy′lessness** *n.*—**joy′ous** *a.* full of joy.—**joy′ously** *adv.*—**joy′ousness** *n.*—**joy′-ride** *n.* (*Slang*) a pleasure ride, or stolen ride.—**joy′-stick** *n.* (*Colloq.*) the control column of an aircraft [O.Fr. *joie*, joy].

jubilant (jòò′-bi-lạnt) *a.* exulting; uttering songs of triumph.—**ju′bilantly** *adv.*—**ju′bilate** *v.i.* to rejoice; to exult.—**jubilate** (jòò-bi-lā′-tē) *n.* the hundredth psalm as a canticle in the Anglican church service; triumphant outcry.—**jubila′tion** *n.* rejoicing; exultation [L. *jubilare*, to shout for joy].

jubilee (jòò′-bi-lē) *n.* a Jewish festival of emancipation celebrated every fiftieth year; (*R.C.Ch.*) a year of indulgence granted orig. at fixed intervals, now at any time; the fiftieth anniversary of any outstanding event; a festival or time of rejoicing.—**silver jubilee**, the twenty-fifth anniversary.—**diamond jubilee**, the sixtieth anniversary [Heb. *yobel*, a ram, or ram's horn trumpet].

Judaism (jòò′-dā-izm) *n.* the religious doctrines and rites of the Jewish people.—**Juda′ic**, **-al** *a.* pert. to the Jews.—**Juda′ically** *adv.*—**Ju′daise** *v.t.* to convert to the Jewish faith;—*v.i.* to practise Judaism.—**Ju′daist** *n.* one who adheres to Judaism [L. *Judacus*, a Jew].

Judas (jòò′-dạs) *n.* (*Bib.*) the disciple of Christ who betrayed him; a traitor.—**ju′das** *n.* a peep-hole in a door.—**Ju′das-col′oured** *a.* (of hair) red.—**Ju′das-kiss** *n.* a treacherous act disguised as kindness.

judge (juj) *n.* one who judges; an officer authorised by the Crown to hear and determine civil or criminal cases, and to administer justice; an arbitrator;—*pl.* a book of the Old Testament;—*v.t.* to decide; to hear and try a case in a court of law; to give a final opinion or decision (as in a performance); to criticise;—*v.i.* to act as a judge; to form an opinion; to come to a conclusion.—**judge′ship** *n.* the office of a judge.—**judg(e)′ment** *n.* the act of judging; a legal decision arrived at by a judge in a court of law; discernment; a special infliction of suffering or death; an opinion.—**Judg(e)ment Day**, the day on which God will pronounce the final judgment on mankind.—**judg(e)′ment-seat** *n.* a judge's bench, a tribunal [L. *judex*, a judge].

judicature (jòòd′-i-kā-tūr) *n.* the power of dispensing justice; judges collectively; a court of justice; a judge's period of office.—**ju′dicable** *a.* capable of being tried or judged.—**ju′dicative** *a.* having the power to judge.—**ju′dicatory** *a.* dispensing justice.—**judic′ial** *a.* pert. to a court of justice or to a judge; impartial.—**judic′ially** *adv.*—**judic′iary** *n.* the judges of the Crown collectively;—*a.* pert. to the courts of law; passing judgment or sentence.—**judic′ious** *a.* wise; prudent; showing discrimination.—**judic′iously** *adv.*—**judic′iousness** *n.* [L. *judicare*, to judge].

judo (jòò′-dō) *n.* a form of ju-jitsu [Jap.].

jug (jug) *n.* a vessel of earthenware, glass, etc., with handle and spout;—*v.t.* to stew (rabbit or hare) in a jug or covered vessel.—*pr.p.* **jug′ging**.—*pa.p.* **jugged** [etym. uncertain].

jug (jug) *v.i.* to utter the sound, *jug* (of nightingale) [imit.].

Juggernaut (jug′-ẹr-nawt) *n.* the chief idol among the Hindus, beneath whose pyramidal carriage devotees were believed to sacrifice themselves; any fanatical idea for which people are prepared to sacrifice their lives; any irresistible, tyrannical force which crushes all that obstructs its path [Hind. *Jagannath*, the lord of the universe].

juggle (jug′-l) *v.i.* to deceive by artifice; to perform conjuring tricks;—*v.t.* to defraud;—*n.* a trick by sleight of hand; an imposture; verbal trickery.—**jugg′ler** *n.* a conjurer; a twister; a cheat.—**jugg′lery** *n.* [O.Fr. *jogler*, to jest].

jugular (jug′-ū-lạr) *a.* pert. to the neck or throat;—*n.* one of the large veins of the neck [L. *jugulum*, the throat].

juice (jòòs) *n.* sap; the liquid constituent of fruits or vegetables; any secretion of an animal body; (*Slang*) petrol or electricity used in a motor-car, aeroplane, etc.—**juic′iness** *n.*—**juic′y** *a.* full of juice [L. *jus*. broth].

ju-ju (jòò′-jòò) *n.* a W. African fetish, as an idol, to which sacrifices are made; a taboo effected by this [Afr].

jujube (jòò′-jòòb) *n.* a shrub, native of Syria, with small, edible fruit; a lozenge made of gelatine, fruit-juice, sugar, etc. [Fr. fr. Gk. *zizuphon*, an Eastern tree].

ju-jutsu (jòò-jut′-sòò) *n.* a form of wrestling, originating in Japan.—also **ju-jit′su** [Jap.].

juke-box (jòòk′-boks) *n.* (*Colloq.*) a phonograph which plays a tune when a coin is inserted. Also **jook′-box** [etym. uncertain].

julep (jòò′-lep) *n.* a sweet drink, esp. one in which medicine is taken. Also **ju′lap** [Pers. *gul*, rose; *ab*, water].

Julian (jòòl′-yạn) *a.* pert. to Julius Caesar.—**Julian Calendar**, the calendar as adjusted by Julius Caesar in 46 B.C. in which the year was made to consist of 365 days, 6 hours, instead of 365 days.

julienne (jòò-li-en′) *n.* a clear soup containing vegetables finely shredded [Fr.].

Juliet cap (jòò′-li-et kap) *n.* a small round cap of beads [fr. *Juliet*, the Shakespearian heroine].

July (jòò-lī′) *n.* the seventh month of the year [fr. L. *mensis Julius*, the month named after Julius Caesar].

jumble (jum′-bl) *v.t.* to mix in a confused mass;—*v.i.* to be in a muddle;—*n.* a miscellaneous collection; a chaotic muddle.—**jum′ble-sale** *n.* a sale of second-hand goods for a charity-fund [prob. from *jump* and *tumble*].

jumble (jum′-bl) *n.* a thin, sweet, sticky cake [etym. unknown].

jumbo (jum′-bō) *n.* a huge person, animal, or thing, esp. the famous elephant in the 1880's.

jump (jump) *v.t.* to spring over; to skip (as page of a book); to risk; to steal;—*v.i.* to lift feet from ground and alight again; to spring; to twitch; to coincide.—*pr.p.* **jump′ing**.—*pa.p.* **jumped**;—*n.* the act of jumping; a leap; a bound; a sudden, nervous start;—*pl.* (*Colloq.*) nervousness.—**jump′iness** *n.* nervous twitching.—**jump′y** *a.*—**jump′ing-bean** *n.* the seed of a Mexican plant containing larva which make it appear to jump.—**jump′ing-jack** *n.* a toy figure, the limbs of which twitch when a string is pulled.—**count′er-jump′er** *n.* a shopman, esp. in a drapery store [prob. imit.].

jumper (jump´ẹr) *n.* a loose canvas tunic worn by sailors; a knitted jersey [prob. fr. Fr. *jupe*, a petticoat].
junction (jungk´shun) *n.* the act of joining; the place or point of joining; a connection.—**junc'ture** *n.* a joint; an exigency; a particular moment in the trend of affairs [L. *jungere*, to join].
June (jòòn) *n.* the sixth month of the year [L. *Junius*, the month of Juno].
jungle (jung´gl) *n.* land covered with forest trees, tangled undergrowth, esp. the dense forests of equatorial latitudes.—**jung'le-fev'er** *n.* a severe form of malaria.—**jung'le-fowl** *n.* the supposed parent of the common domestic fowl [Hind. *jungal*, forest].
junior (jòòn´yur) *a.* younger, esp. of a son with the same name as his father; of lower status;—*n.* a young person; the younger of two; a minor; one in a subordinate position. [L. compar. of *juvenis*, young].
juniper (jòò´ni-pẹr) *n.* a genus of evergreen coniferous shrub, with dark blue berries used in flavouring gin [L. *juniperus*].
junk (jungk) *n.* a flat-bottomed Chinese vessel [Port. *junco*, a boat].
junk (jungk) *n.* pieces of old cordage used for oakum; useless, discarded articles; (*Naut.*) hard, dry salted meat;—*v.t.* to turn into junk; to cut into lumps.—**junk´deal'er, junk'man** *n.* one who buys and sells junk [L. *juncus*, a rush].
Junker (yòòng´kẹr) *n.* a young German noble; a member of that reactionary political party in Prussia which stood for the landed interests of the aristocracy.—**Junk'erism** *n.* [Ger. *Junker*, a young noble].
junket (jung´ket) *n.* orig. a cream cheese served on a rush-mat; a dish of curds usually fruit-flavoured, and served with cream; merry-making;—*v.i.* to feast; to picnic;—*v.t.* to entertain.—*pr.p.* **jun'keting.**—*pa.p.*—**jun'keted.**—**jun'keting** *n.* merrymaking; picnicking [L. *juncus*, a rush].
junta (jun´ta) *n.* a council of state in Spain or Italy [Sp. *junta*, a committee].
junto (jun´tō) *n.* a group of conspirators; a cabal [Sp. *junta*, a committee].
Jupiter (jòò´pi-tẹr) *n.* in Roman mythology, the supreme god and ruler of heaven, equivalent to the Greek Zeus. Also **Jove**; the largest and brightest of the outer planets.—**Jupiter Pluvius**, the god of rain [L. fr. *Jovis pater*, father Jove].
Jurassic (jòò-ras´ik) *a.* (*Geol.*) of the middle system of Mesazoic rocks as found in the Jura mountains; oölitic [fr. *Jura*].
juridical (jòò-rid´ik-ạl) *a.* pert. to a judge, or the administration of justice.—**jurid'ically** *adv.* [L. *juridicus*, judicial].
jurisdiction (jòò-ris-dik´shun) *n.* the administration of justice; legal authority; the limit or extent within which this authority may be exercised.—**jurisdic'tional, jurisdic'tive** *a.* [L. *jus*, law; *dicere*, to say].
jurisprudence (jòò-ris-pròò´dens) *n.* the science of law; the study of the fundamental principles underlying any legal system.—**medical jurisprudence**, forensic medicine, study of medicine as it concerns criminal law [L. *jus*, law; *prudentia*, knowledge].
jurist (jòò´rist) *n.* one versed in the law, esp. in Roman or civil law [L. *jus*, law].
jury (jòò´ri) *n.* a body of citizens (12 in England, 15 in Scotland (except in civil cases)) selected and sworn to give a verdict from the evidence produced in court; a committee chosen to decide the winners in a competition.—**ju'ror** *n.* one who serves on a jury. Also **ju'ryman, ju'rywoman** [O.Fr. *jurée*, an oath].
jurymast (jòò´ri-mạst) *n.* a temporary mast erected in a ship to replace one broken or carried away in a storm.—**jur'y-strut** *n.* (*Aero.*) a strut giving temporary support to a structure [L. *adjutare*, to aid].
jussive (jus´iv) *a.* (*Gram.*) expressing a command;—*n.* a grammatical form expressing a command [L. *jubere*, to command].
just (just) *n.* Same as **joust.**
just (just) *a.* straight; exact; complete; equitable; true; founded on fact; proper; well-deserved;—*adv.* exactly; nicely, closely; scarcely.—**just'ly** *adv.* in a just manner; deservedly; uprightly.—**just'ness** *n.* equity; fairness [L. *justus*, upright].
justice (jus´tis) *n.* the quality of being just; equity; merited reward or punishment; the administration of the law; a judge; a magistrate.—**jus'ticeship** *n.* the office of a judge.—**justic'iar** *n.* the chief judicial officer under the Norman and Plantagenet kings.—**justic'iary** *n.* a judge; a Lord Chief-Justice;—*a.* pert. to the administration of the law.—**Justice of the Peace** (J.P.), a county or borough magistrate, commissioned to keep the peace in local areas [L. *justitia*, justice].
justify (jus´ti-fī) *v.t.* to prove the justice of; to vindicate; to excuse; to adjust.—*pr.p.* **just'ifying.**—*pa.p.* **just'ified.**—**justifi'able** *a.* defensible; excusable.—**justifi'ableness** *n.*—**justifi´ably** *adv.*—**justifica'tion** *n.* vindication; (*Theol.*) absolution.—**jus'tificative, jus'tificatory** *a.* having the power to justify.—**jus'tifier** *n.* [L. *justificare*, to justify].
justle Same as **jostle.**
jut (jut) *v.i.* to project.—*pr.p.* **jut'ting.**—*pa.p.* **jut'ted** [a form of *jet*].
jute (jòòt) *n.* fibre of an Indian plant used in manufacture of carpets, cordage, sandbags, etc. [Bengali fr. Sans, *juta*, a tress of hair].
Jutes (jòòts) *n.pl.* a Teutonic tribe (prob. fr. Jutland orig.) which invaded Britain in 5th and 6th cents. [O.E. *Iote*].
juvenescent (jòò-ven-es´ent) *a.* becoming young.—**juvenesc'ence** *n.* [L. *juvenis*, young].
juvenile (jòò´ven-īl) *a.* young; youthful; puerile;—*n.* a young person; a book written for children.—**ju'venileness, juvenil'ity** *n.*—**juvenil'ia** *n.pl.* works of author produced in childhood and early youth [L. *juvenilis*, youthful].
juxtapose (juks-ta-pōs') *v.t.* to place side by side.—**juxtaposi'tion** *n.* the act of placing side by side; contiguity [L. *juxta*, near; *ponere*, to place].

K

kabala See **cabbala.**
Kaffir, Kafir (kaf´ẹr) *n.* a warlike race, a branch of the Bantu group of natives, living in the eastern part of S. Africa.—**kaffir corn,** a variety of sorghum, akin to Indian millet grown in India and S. Africa.—**Kaff'irs** *n.pl.* Stock Exchange term for S. African mine shares [Ar. = *an unbeliever*].
kaftan See **caftan.**
kaiak See **kayak.**
kail, kale (kāl) *n.* colewort; a hardy member of the cabbage family with curled leaves; broth made of cabbage or kale in Scotland.—**kail´yard** *n.* a kitchen garden.—**Kailyard School,** name given to a group of writers, including Barrie and Crockett, who dealt with humble life in rural Scotland [O.E. *cawel*, fr. L. *caulis*, a stalk].
kainite (kī´nīt) *n.* a mineral consisting of a hydrated compound of the chlorides and sulphates of magnesium and potassium, used as manure [Gk. *kainos*, new].
kainozoic See **cainozoic.**
Kaiser (kī´zẹr, kā´zẹr) *n.* the name derived from the Latin *Caesar*, given to the emperors of the Old Holy Roman Empire, and of the rulers of the German Empire.—**kai'sership** *n.* [Ger.].
kakistocracy (kak-is-tok´rạ-si) *n.* government by the worst people in the state; cf.*aristocracy* [Gk. *kakistos*, worst; *kratos*, rule].
kale See **kail.**

kaleidoscope (ka-lī´do-skōp) *n.* an optical instrument, varying patterns being displayed on rotation.—**kaleidoscop'ic** *a.* ever-changing in beauty and form; variegated [Gk. *kalos*, beautiful; *eidos*, form; *skopein*, to view].
kalends See **calends.**
kali (kā´li) *n.* the prickly salt-wort, from whose ashes caustic potash was formerly obtained for use in glass manufacture.—**ka-lium** *n.* potassium.
kalif See **caliph.**
kaligenous See under **kali.**
kalinite (kā´lin-īt) *n.* hydrous sulphate of potassium and aluminium, a product of volcanoes [Ar. *qali*, potash].
kalium See **kali.**
kames (kāmz] *n.pl.* an eskar, a high narrow ridge of gravel and sand, esp. in Scotland.
kampong (kam-pong') *n.* an enclosed space or compound; a small village [Malay].
kamsin See **khamsin.**
kanaka (ka-nak´a) *n.* a native of any South Sea island; a native labourer brought from the Pacific Islands to work on the sugar plantations of Queensland, Australia [Hawaiian = *a man*].
kangaroo (kang-ga-rōō') *n.* a ruminating marsupial found in Australia, having short, weak fore-limbs with stout tail and progressing by flying bounds.—**kangaroo´grass** *n.* a valuable fodder grass of Australia and S. Africa.
Kantian (kan´shi-an, kan´ti-an) *a.* pert. to the German philosopher, Immanuel Kant, or his school of philosophy.
Kanuck, Canuck (ka-nuk') *n.* a Canadian; a French Canadian [Amer.-Ind.].
kaolin (kā´o-lin) *n.* China clay; fine porcelain clay chiefly produced from feldspar in China, U.S.A. and Cornwall by weathering.—**kaolin poultice,** an antiseptic substitute for a linseed poultice [Chin. *kaoling*, high hill, mountain where first found].
kapok (ka-pok') *n.* a silky white vegetable fibre developed in the fruit pods of the white silk cotton-tree, used for stuffing pillows, life-belts, etc.; vegetable down; W. Indian evergreen tree [Malay].
kaput (kap-ōōt') *n.* (*Slang*) finished; no good; all over; done for [Ger.]. [Burmah.
Karens (kār´enz) *n.pl.* a native hill race of
karma (kár´ma) *n.* the law of Action and Reaction, of cause and effect or ethical causation, which affirms that good or evil actions on one life determine one's condition in lives to follow [Sans = *action*].
karob, carob (kar´ob) *n.* the locust, an evergreen Mediterranean tree; its pods provide a succulent edible pulp; the seed of the tree; carat [Fr. *caroube*].
karroo, karoo (ka-rōō') *n.* in S. Africa, one of the series of semi-barren terraces separating successive ridges of hills [Hottentot *karusa*, hard]. [Australia [Aborig.].
karri, kari (kar´i) *n.* a species of eucalyptus in
kartel See **cartel.**
kashgar (kash´gar) *n.* a fine white silky wool, used in carpet manufacture [*Kashgar*, town in Chinese Turkestan].
katabolism (ka-tab´o-lizm) *n.* (*Biol.*) the disruptive metabolism which results in the oxidation or other decomposition of protoplasm within the living organism to form less complex chemical compounds with concomitant liberation of energy—the opposite of *anabolism* [Gk. *kata*, down; *bolē*, a throw].
katagenesis (kat-a-jen´e-sis) *n.* (*Zool.*) retrogressive evolution [Gk. *kata*, down; *genesis*, origin].
katathermometer (kat-a-ther-mom´e-ter) *n.* a combination of the wet and dry bulb thermometer, designed to give an indication of the total effect of temperature, humidity, evaporation, wind, etc., on ventilation conditions.
kathode See **cathode.**
kation, cation (kat´i-on) *n.* an electro-positive ion which, in electrolysis, travels towards the kathode; a neutral atom which in consequence of losing an electron, has a positive charge [Gk. *kata*, down; *ienai*, to go].
katydid (kā´ti-did) *n.* a green insect of the grasshopper family [Imit.].
kauri, kauri-pine (kou´ri-pīn) *n.* a coniferous tree of New Zealand giving valuable timber. —**kau'ri-gum** *n.* a resinous gum dug up on the sites of ancient kauri forests [Maori].
kava (ká´va) *n.* a narcotic beverage derived from a Polynesian shrub of the pepper family. —Also **a'va** [Hawaiian].
kayak (kī´yak) *n.* the Eskimo seal-skin canoe, long, narrow and covered over.
kayles (kālz) *n.pl.* an old form of the game of ninepins [Dut. *kegel*, a pin].
keblah (keb´lá) *n.* See **kiblah.**
keck (kek) *v.i.* to retch, as if about to vomit [imit. of the sound].
keckle (kek´l) *v.t.* to protect a cable or hawser from damage by fraying, by wrapping old rope, etc., round the length likely to be affected [etym. doubtful].
kedge (kej) *n.* a small anchor used to keep a ship steady or for warping;—*v.t.* to warp, as a ship; to move a ship by means of small anchors and hawsers [Fr.].
kedgeree, kedjeree (kej´e-rē) *n.* an Indian dish of rice boiled with onions, eggs, pulse and butter; in European cookery, a breakfast dish of cold fish, boiled rice and eggs [Hind. *khichri*].
keek (kēk) *v.i.* and *n.* (*Scot.*) peep; glance [M.E. *kyken*, to peep].
keel (kēl) *n.* the length-wise beam of a ship on which the frames of the ship rest; hence, a ship; a low flat-bottomed barge used for coaling ships; a broad, flat vessel used for cooling liquids;—*v.i.* to plough with a keel; to navigate; to turn up the keel.—**keel'age** *n.* dues for ships at rest in a port or harbour.—**keel'haul** *v.t.* to haul under the keel of a ship by ropes attached to the yard-arms on each side; a form of punishment in the British navy during the 17th and 18th cents.; to rebuke a subordinate severely.—**keel'son** *n.* a large vertical girder formed of plates and angles bolted to the top of a ship's keel to bind the floor timbers to the keel and to help stiffen the ship. Also **kel'son.**—**to keel over,** to capsize [O.E. *ceol*, a ship].
keelson See **keel.**
keen (kēn) *a.* having a fine cutting edge; sharp; penetrating; piercing (of wind); eager; intense (of frost); acrimonious; caustic (tongue); shrewd; discerning.—**keen'ly** *adv.*—**keen'ness** *n* [O.E. *cene*].
keen (kēn) *n.* in Ireland, a lamentation or dirge for the dead; a coronach;—*v.i.* to wail over the dead before burial [Ir. *caoine*].
keep (kēp) *v.t.* to retain possession of; to detain; to observe; to carry out; to have the care of; to maintain; to cause to continue; to reserve; to manage; to commemorate;—*v.i.* to remain (in good condition); to continue;—*pa.p.* **kept.**—*n.* care; guardianship; maintenance; food or fodder; the chief tower or dungeon (donjon) of a castle; a stronghold.—**keep'er** *n.* one who keeps or guards; an attendant: a gamekeeper; a finger-ring to prevent another from slipping off.—**keep'ing** *n.* care; custody; support; harmony.—**keep'sake** *n.* anything given to recall the memory of the giver.—**to keep at arm's length,** to keep well away from.—**to keep company with,** to associate with.—**to keep in touch with,** to correspond with.—**to keep in with,** to remain on friendly terms out of self-interest.—**to keep one's hand in,** to maintain one's skill by occasional practice.—**to keep open house,** to be very hospitable to strangers.—**to keep the peace,** to be law-abiding.—**to keep up,** to maintain (appearances, spirits, etc.); to support.—**for keeps** (*Slang*) permanently [O.E. *cepan*].
keg (keg) *n.* a small cask or barrel [O.N. *kaggi*, cask].

kell (kell) *n.* a caul; a chrysalis; a film over the eye; a hair-net; a skull-cap [O.E. *kelle*, a caul].
kelp [kelp] *n.* the calcined ash of certain sea-weeds, used as a source of iodine; a general name for large sea-weeds [etym. unknown].
kelpie, kelpy (kel′pi) *n.* in Scots mythology, a water-spirit, usually in the form of a fear-some horse [etym. doubtful].
kelson *n.* See **keelson**, under **keel**.
Kelt, Keltic Same as **Celt, Celtic**.
kelt (kelt) *n.* a salmon which has just spawned; a spent fish [etym. doubtful].
kemp (kemp) *n.* the coarse rough hairs in wool [etym. doubtful].
ken (ken) *v.t.* to know; to recognise; to descry; —*n.* view; range of sight or knowledge [O.E. *cennan*, to know].
Kendal-green (ken′dal-grēn) *n.* a green cloth made for foresters [*Kendal*, town in Westmorland].
kennel (ken′el) *n.* a house or shelter for dogs; a pack of dogs; the hole of a fox or other animal; a small hovel of a house;—*v.t.* to confine in a kennel;—*v.i.* to live in a kennel.—*pr.p.* **kenn′elling.**—*pa.p.* **kenn′elled.**—**kenn′elmaid, kenn′elman** *n.* an attendant on dogs [Fr. *chenil*, fr. L. *canis*, a dog].
kennel (ken′el) *n.* a street gutter or channel [O.Fr. *canel*, a channel].
Kennelly Heaviside layer (ken-el′i-hev′i-sīd) *n.* a region of ionised atoms about 60-70 miles above the earth's surface, which is transparent to short wireless waves but deflects long wireless waves [fr. *Dr. A. E. Kennelly*, and *Oliver Heaviside* the discoverers].
kenotron (ken-o′tron) *n.* (*Radio*) a high-voltage double-electrode valve used for rectifying.
kenspeckle (ken′spek-l) *a.* conspicuous; well-known in a certain locality [fr. *ken*].
Kentish (ken′tish) *a.* of, or pert. to, the county of Kent.
kentledge (kent′lej) *n.* the loose balance weights of a crane; pigs of iron or lead placed on top of a monolith to cause it to sink into the ground; similar pigs placed in a ship's hold for permanent ballast [etym. doubtful].
kephalic See **cephalic.**
kepi (kā′pē) *n.* a light military cap, flat-topped with a straight peak [Fr.].
kept (kept) *pa.t.* and *pa.p.* of **keep.**
keramics Same as **ceramics.**
kerasine (ker′a-sin) *a.* horny; resembling horn [Gk. *keras*, a horn].
kerat-, kerato-, (ker′at-o) *prefix*, fr. Gk. *keras*, a horn, used in the formation of compound terms,—**keratal′gia** *n.* (*Med.*) pain affecting the cornea.—**ker′atin** *n.* an essential constituent of horny tissue, as horns, claws, nails, feathers, etc.; a nitrogenous compound containing sulphur.—**kerato′sis** *n.* (*Med.*) a skin disease characterised by abnormal thickening of the epidermis.
kerb (kerb) *n.* the edge of the pavement; the curb.—**kerb′stone** *n.* [var. of *curb*].
kerchief (ker′chif) *n.* a square of fine linen used by women to cover the head; any cloth used in dress, esp. on the head or round the neck.—**ker′chiefed** *a.* [Fr. *couvre-chef*, cover-head].
kermes (ker′mēz) *n.* a red and scarlet dye-stuff made from the dried bodies of the females of the homopterous insects, *Coccus illicis* [Ar. *kermes*, a little worm].
kermess, kermis (ker′mes) *n.* a church-festival or fair in the Low Countries; originally a dedication service at the opening of a new church [Dut. *kerk*, church; *mis*, mass].
kern [kern] *n.* See **quern.**
kern (kern) *n.* a light-armed footsoldier of Ireland or the Scottish Highlands; a boor.—**kern′ish** *a.* [Gael, *ceatharnach*, soldier].
kern (kern) *n.* in Scotland, the last sheaf of the harvest; a harvest-home. Also **kirn**;—*v.i.* to harden, as corn in ripening; to granulate [var. of *corn*].
kernel (ker′nel) *n.* the inner portion, the seed, of the stony endocarp of a drupe; the edible part of a nut; a little grain or corn; central or essential part; the nucleus [O.E. *cyrnel*, dim. of *corn*].
kerosene (ker′o-sēn) *n.* American term for paraffin oil, obtained in the fractional distillation of crude petroleum or from coal and shale [Gk. *kēros*, wax].
kersey (ker′zi) *n.* coarse woollen cloth, usually ribbed [etym. uncertain].
kerseymere (ker′zi-mēr) *n.* a fine light woollen twill cloth with an oil finish;—*pl.* trousers of this cloth [corrupt. of *cashmere*].
kerseynette (ker′zi-net) *n.* a thin woollen stuff [corrupt. of *cassinette*].
kestrel (kes′trel) *n.* a numerous genus of small falcons; a British bird of prey [Fr. *crécerelle*].
ketch (kech) *n.* a small two-masted coasting vessel [etym. doubtful].
ketchup, catchup, catsup (kech′up) *n.* a sauce made from mushrooms, tomatoes or walnuts [Malay *kechap*].
kettle (ket′l) *n.* a metal vessel, with spout and handle, used for heating and boiling water or other liquids.—**kett′ledrum** *n.* a musical percussion instrument made of a hemispherical copper shell covered with vellum.—**kett′le-drum′mer** *n.*—**kett′le-fur′nace** *n.* an open-top vessel used for melting metals with low melting points, e.g., lead, solder.—**a pretty kettle of fish**, an awkward affair [O.N. *ketill*].
key (kē) *n.* a low-lying island or reef near the coast, used esp. of Spain's former possessions off the coast of Florida.—Also **cay** [Sp. *cayo*, a reef].
key (kē) *n.* old spelling or quay.
key (kē) *n.* an instrument which shuts or opens a lock; an instrument by which anything is screwed and turned, as a *watch-key, bed-key*, etc.; a spanner; the highest central stone of an arch; a lever in a musical instrument, depressed by the fingers in playing; a lever on a type-writer for actuating the mechanism; in engineering, a hand tool for valve-control; a switch adapted for making and breaking easily contact in an electric circuit; a wedge to secure firmly a rail in the chair on railway lines; in carpentry, a small piece of hardwood inserted in joints to prevent sliding, or across grain of wood to prevent curvature; any rough surface or a space between laths or wire-meshing to secure adhesion of plaster; the winged husk containing the seed of the ash, maple, etc.; (*Mus.*) a set of related notes; solution or explanation; a translation of a foreign book, esp. the classics, or solutions to questions set.—*a.* critical; of vital importance.—**key′board** *n.* the whole range of keys on a keyed instrument; a manual.—**key′hole** *n.* a hole in a door or lock for receiving a key.—**key-industry**, an industry on which vital interests of the country or other industries depend.—**key′ing** *n.* the roughing of the surface of new plaster to secure adhesion for the next coat; the operation of starting or stopping a high-frequency current.—**key′man** *n.* an indispensable employee.—**key′mon′ey** *n.* a gratuitous sum of money demanded from a new tenant as a condition of granting a lease.—**key′note** *n.* the first tone of the scale in which a passage is written.—**key′ring** *n.* a ring for keeping a number of keys together.—**key′sig′nature** *n.* (*Mus.*) the essential sharps and flats placed at the beginning of a piece after the clef to indicate the key.—**key′stone** *n.* the wedge-shaped central voussoir at the crown of an arch; the boss of a dome.—**all keyed up**, agog with excitement and expectation.—**House of Keys**, the lower house of the Tynwald, the legislature of the Isle of Man [O.E. *caeg*].
khaki (kà′kē) *a.* dust-coloured or buff;—*n.* a cloth of this colour, used for the uniforms of soldiers.—Also **khar′ki** [Urdu = *dusty*].
khalifa, khalifat See **caliph, caliphate.**
khamsin (kam′sin) *n.* a hot, dry, south wind

accompanied by sand, similar to a sirocco, which blows over Egypt, especially in March to May [Ar.].

khan (kȧn) *n.* a title of respect in various Mohammedan countries of C. Asia and N. India; among Mongol races, a king, prince, or chief.—**khan'ate** *n.* the dominion of a khan [Pers. = a lord or prince].

khedive (ke-dēv') *n.* the title of the ruler of Egypt, from 1867 to 1914, roughly equivalent to 'Viceroy' [Fr. fr. Pers. = prince].

kiang (ki'ang) *n.* the wild ass of the barren Tibetan plateau. Also **ky'ang** [Tibetan *kyang*].

kia ora (kē'a, ōr'a) *interj.* a Maori salutation, 'Your health.'

kibble (kib'l) *n.* a large riveted steel bucket [used in mining [Ger. *Kubel*].

kibble (kib'l) *v.t.* to bruise or grind closely.—**kib'bler** *n.* a machine for cutting beans, etc., for cattle-feed [Prov. E.].

kibbutz (kē-bȯȯts') *n.* a Jewish communal settlement in Israel.—*pl.* **Kibbutzim** (kē-bȯȯts-ēm') [Heb.].

kibe (kīb) *n.* an ulcerated chilblain; a chap in the skin [W. *cibwst*, fr. *cib*, cup; *gwst*, a disease].

kiblah, keblah (kib'lạ, keb'lạ) *n.* the point towards which Mohammedans turn their faces in prayer [Ar. *qiblah*].

kibosh (kī'bosh, ki-bosh') *n.* Portland cement when blown on to sculptured work in order to give a chiaroscuro effect; (*Colloq.*) nonsense; rubbish.—**to put the kibosh on**, to silence; to defeat; to get rid of [etym. unknown].

kick [kik] *v.t.* to strike or hit with the foot;—*v.i.* to strike out with the foot; to show opposition; to resist; to recoil violently (of a rifle, etc.);—*n.* a blow with the foot; the recoil of a gun; (*Slang*) stimulation; thrill.—**kick'er** *n.* a horse liable to kick out.—**kick'ing-plate** *n.* a metal plate fixed to the horizontal bottom rail of a door to prevent damage by kicking.—**kick'-off** *n.* the commencement of a game of football.—**kick'-up** *n.* a disturbance; a shindy.—**to kick over the traces**, to throw off all restraint; to rebel openly.—**to kick the bucket** (*Slang*) to die.—**drop'-kick** *n.* in rugby, a kick made as the ball, just dropped from the hand, rebounds from the ground.—**free'-kick** *n.* in association football, the privilege granted to a football player to kick the ball once without interference from the opposing side.—**place'-kick** *n.* in rugby, the kick allowed to the side which has scored a try, the ball being carefully 'placed' [M.E. *kiken*, of unknown origin].

kicker (kik'ẹr) *n.* an agricultural machine for turning over swathes of mown grass; a tedder [fr. *kick*].

kickshaw (kik'shaw) *n.* a toy or trifle; something fantastic or uncommon, or with no particular name; a fanciful dressed dish [fr. Fr. *quelque chose*, something].

kid (kid) *n.* a young goat; leather made from the skin of a goat; (*Slang*) a child;—*pl.* gloves of smooth kid leather;—*a.* made of kid leather [O.N. *kith*].

kid (kid) *v.t.* and *i.* (*Slang*) to hoax; to pretend;—*n.* a pretence.—**kid'der** *n.* a practical joker [etym. doubtful].

Kidderminster (kid'ẹr-min-stẹr) *n.* a carpet with fine and elaborate designs. Also known as 'Scotch carpet' or 'ingrain carpet' [*Kidderminster*, town where such carpets were woven].

kidnap (kid'nap) *v.t.* to carry off, abduct, or secrete forcibly a person (esp. a child).—**kid'napper** *n.*—**kid'napping** *n.* [E. *kid*, a child; *nap*, to nab].

kidney (kid'ni) *n.* one of two glandular organs in the lumbar region of the abdominal cavity which excrete urine; nature; kind; temperament.—**kidney bean**, the kidney-shaped seed of any bean plant; the haricot or French bean [origin uncertain].

kief (kēf) *n.* dried hemp leaves, used as tobacco [in Morocco [Native].

kie-kie (kī-kī, kē'kē) *n.* the native name of a New Zealand climbing shrub, bearing large quantities of berries [Maori].

kieselguhr (kē'zl-gūr) *n.* a fine earth, nearly pure silica, consisting of the skeletons of minute algae called diatoms, used for polishing and as an absorbent for nitro-glycerine, the product being called dynamite [Ger. *Kiesel*, gravel; *Guhr*, sediment].

Kikuyu (ki-koo'ū) *n.* a native tribe of Kenya.

kilderkin (kil'dẹr-kin) *n.* a small barrel; a liquid measure containing eighteen imperial gallons or two firkins [O.Dut. *kindeken*, a small barrel].

kilerg (kil'erg) *n.* (*Physics*) a thousand ergs.

kill (kil) *v.t.* to deprive of life; to slay; to put to death; to destroy; to neutralise; to weaken or dilute; to render inactive; to pass (time);—*n.* the act or time of killing; the animal killed in a field-sport.—**kill'er** *n.* one who kills; a butcher or slaughterman; a club for killing fish.—**kill'er-whale** *n.* the grampus, a smaller variety of whale, with immense jaws and capable of swallowing seals, porpoises, etc., whole.—**kill'ing** *a.* depriving of life; very exhausting; fascinating; exceedingly funny.—**kill'ingly** *adv.*—**kill'-joy** *n.* one who depresses others or objects to innocent amusements (etym. obscure].

killock (kil'ok) *n.* a small anchor; the fluke of an anchor.—Also **kill'ick**.

Kilmarnock (kil-mar'nok) *n.* a flat, round tam-o'-shanter [town in Ayrshire, Scotland].

kiln (kil, kiln) *n.* a large oven, brick-built, generating great heat, in which various materials are dried, calcined, or hardened (clay, lime, malt, hops, etc.).—**kiln'-dry** *v.t.* to dry in a kiln [L. *culina*, an oven].

kilo- (kil'o) *prefix* fr. Gk. *chilioi*, one thousand, in the metric system denoting a thousand.—**kil'ocycle** *n.* the unit for measuring vibrations, esp. the frequency of electric oscillations and wireless waves, 1000 complete cycles or oscillations per second.—**kil'ogramme, kil'ogram** *n.* 1000 grammes, equal to 2·2046 lbs. avoirdupois.—**kil'olitre, kil'oliter** *n.* 1000 litres, equivalent to 35·31472 cubic feet and to 220·0967 imperial gallons.—**kil'ometre, kil'ometer** *n.* 1000 metres, 3280·899 English feet or nearly ⅝ of a mile.—**kil'owatt** *n.* an electric unit of power equal to 1000 watts.—**kil'owatt-hour**, *n.* one kilowatt expended for one hour, commonly called 'Board of Trade unit,' or simply 'unit.'

kilt (kilt) *n.* a short skirt usually of tartan cloth, deeply pleated, reaching from waist to knees;—*v.t.* to tuck up or pleat vertically in the fashion of Highland kilt.—**kilt'ie** *n.* (*Colloq.*) a soldier in Highland regiment [Dan. *kilte*, to tuck up].

kimbo (kim'bō) *a.* crooked; bent; arched; akimbo [var. of *akimbo*].

kimono (ki-mō'nō) *n.* a dark-striped overgarment with short wide sleeves, worn in Japan by both men and women; a dressing-gown in imitation of this style [Jap.].

kin (kin) *n.* family relations; relationship; consanguinity; affinity;—*a.* of the same nature or kind; kindred; akin.—**next of kin**, the person or persons closest in relationship to a deceased person [O.E. *cynn*].

-kin (kin) noun suffix, used as a diminutive, e.g. *lambkin*, a little lamb.

kinaesthesis (kin-ēs-thē'sis) *n.* muscle sense; the perception of muscular effort.—**kinaesthet'ic** *a.* [Gk. *kinein*, to move; *aisthesis*, perception].

kind (kīnd) *n.* genus; sort; variety; class; particular nature;—*a.* having a sympathetic nature; considerate; good; benevolent; obliging.—**kind'-heart'ed** *a.*—**kind'-heart'edness** *n.*—**kind'liness** *n.* benevolence.—**kind'ly** *a.* and *adv.*—**kind'ness** *n.* kind feeling or action.—**kind of** (*Colloq.*) somewhat; to a certain extent.—**in kind**, payment in goods, instead of money [O.E. *gecynde*, nature].

kindergarten (kin'dẹr-gȧr'tn) *n.* a school for young children where they are taught by the organising of their natural tendency to play;

the method initiated by Froebel [Ger. = children's garden].
kinderspiel (kin′der-spēl) *n.* a children's operetta [Ger. *Kind*, child; *spielen*, to play].
kindle (kin′dl) *v.t.* to set on fire; to light; to excite (the passions); to inflame; to enrage;—*v.i.* to catch fire; to be excited; to grow warm or animated.—**kin′dling** *n.* the act of starting a fire; the material for starting a fire [O.N. *kynda*].
kindred (kin′dred) *n.* relation by birth; affinity; relatives by blood or marriage;—*a.* related; cognate; of like nature; congenial; similar [M.E. *kinrede*].
kine (kīn) *n.pl.* a plural form of **cows**.
kinema (kin′e-ma) *n.* an early variant of *cinema* [Gk. *kinēma*, movement].
kinematic, kinematical (kin-e-mat′ik, -i-kal) *a.* relating to pure motion.—**kinemat′ics** *n.pl.* the branch of mechanics dealing with problems of motion as such [Gk. *kinēma*, movement].
kinetic, kinetical (ki-net′ik, -i-kal) *a.* relating to motion; imparting or growing out of motion.—**kinetic energy**, mechanical energy of a body by virtue of its motion.—**kinet′ics** *n.* the science which treats of changes in movements of matter produced by forces [Gk. *kinein*, to move].
king (king) *n.* (*fem.* **queen**) supreme ruler of a country; a sovereign; a monarch; one who is distinguished above all others of his compeers; a playing-card in each suit with a picture of a king; the chief piece in the game of chess; in draughts, a man which is crowned.—**King′at-Arms, King′-of-Arms** *n.* one of the three principal officers, under the Earl Marshal, of the College of Arms, with jurisdiction over heraldry and armoury—in Scotland, *Lyon King-of-Arms*; in Ireland, *Ulster King-of-Arms*.—**king′cob′ra** *n.* a larger and rarer snake than the common cobra; hamadryad.—**king′crab** *n.* a marine creature, of the order *Arachnida*, found on the east coast of the U.S.A.—**king′craft** *n.* the art of ruling as a king (usually in a bad sense).—**king′cup** *n.* the marsh-marigold, a common species of buttercup.—**king′dom** *n.* quality and attributes of a king; the country subject to a king; realm; sphere; domain; one of the three great divisions (animal, vegetable, and mineral) of Natural History.—**king′fisher** *n.* a native bird of the Old World, with brilliant plumage.—**king′hood** *n.* kingship; kingliness.—**king′let** *n.* a petty king; the golden-crested or golden-crowned wren.—**king′like, king′ly** *a.* royal; becoming a king.—**king′pen′guin** *n.* a species of penguin distinguished by having a coat of greyish-blue which covers the back, the head covered with black plumage.—**king′pin** *n.* the metal rod upon which the steering stub axle of a motor-car is pivoted; the swivel-pin; (*Fig.*) an important person.—**King's Bench**, one of the three divisions of the English High Court of Justice, hearing mainly common law actions.—**King's Counsel**, an honorary distinction conferred on eminent barristers giving them precedence in courts and the right to wear a silk gown (hence, *to take silk*).—**King's evidence**, the evidence in a court-of-law tendered by an accomplice, on behalf of the prosecution, against a prisoner.——**king′ship** *n.* the state or office of a king.—**King's Proctor**, the Treasury solicitor who may intervene to stop decrees *nisi* in divorce being made absolute.—**King's Regulations**, the official regulations for the organisation of the British Army or Navy [O.E. *cyning*].
kink (kingk) *n.* a short twist, accidentally formed, in a rope, wire, chain, etc.; a mental twist; a crotchet; a whim;—*v.i.* and *v.t.* to twist spontaneously; to form a kink (in) (origin uncertain].
kinsfolk (kinz′fōk) *n.* blood relations; kin; members of the same family.—**kin′ship** *n.* state or condition of being related by birth.—**kins′man, kins′wo′man** *n.* a person of the same kin or race with another [*kin*].
kiosk (ki-osk′) *n.* an open pavilion or summer-house, supported by pillars; an erection, resembling a sentry-box, for the sale of periodicals, sweets, tobacco, etc.; a band-stand [Turk. *kioshk*].
kip (kip) *n.* the untanned hide of young cattle intermediate between calves and cows.—**kip′skin** *n.* such, after tanning [etym. uncertain].
kip (kip) *n.* a unit of force equivalent to 1000 lbs.
kip (kip) *n.* (*Slang*) a house of ill-fame; a doss-house; lodging. Also **kip′shop**;—*v.i.* to go to bed.
kipper (kip′er) *n.* a herring, split, then smoked; a male salmon when spent after spawning season;—*v.t.* to cure fish by salting, smoking, or drying [origin uncertain].
kirk (kerk) *n.* (*Scot.*) a church building; the congregation or denomination; the (Established) Church of Scotland.—**kirk′sess′ion** *n.* the lowest ecclesiastical court in Scotland, composed of the ministers and elders of a parish.
kirtle (ker′tl) *n.* a kind of short gown or jacket; an outer petticoat; a bundle of flax, weighing 100 lbs.—**kir′tled** *a.* [O.E. *cyrtel*].
kismet (kis′met) *n.* fate or destiny [Ar. =fate).
kiss (kis) *v.t.* and *v.i.* to touch with the lips, in affection or reverence; to touch gently;—*n.* a salute by touching with lips.—**kiss′able** *a.*—**kiss′curl** *n.* a small lock of hair at temples.—**kiss′er** *n.* one who kisses; (*Slang*) the mouth.—**kiss′me-quick** *n.* a small bonnet; a side-curl; a pansy.—**to kiss hands**, to kiss the hand of sovereign on accepting office.—**to kiss the book**, to kiss the New Testament after taking a legal oath.—**to kiss the gunner's daughter** (*Naut.*) to be flogged while tied to the breech of a gun.—**to kiss the rod**, to accept punishment submissively [O.E. *cyssan*).
kistvaen (kist′vā-en) *n.* (*Archaeol.*) a burial-chamber made of flat stones, top and sides, and covered with earth [O.E. *cist*, chest; W. *maen*, a stone].
kit (kit) *n.* a soldier's outfit, excluding his uniform; a set of tools or implements; personal effects; a wooden tub.—**kit′bag** *n.*—**kit′box** *n.* a box for holding small tools [etym. uncertain].
kit (kit) *n.* a contr. of *kitten*.—**kit′cat** *n.* tip-cat, a game played with a shaped piece of wood.—**kit′ty** *n.* the pool in card games; (*Bowls*) the jack.
kit (kit) *n.* a small fiddle, used by itinerant dancing-masters [etym. unknown].
Kitcat (kit′kat) *n.* a club, founded in 1703; a half-portrait, 36 by 28 ins. the size adopted by Kneller for portraits of members of the club [fr. *Christopher Cat*, the proprietor of the premises where the club met].
kitchen (kich′en) *n.* a room in which food is prepared and cooked; anything savoury eaten along with bread.—**kitchenette′** *n.* a small room combining offices of kitchen, pantry and scullery.—**kit′chen-gar′den** *n.* a garden for raising vegetables for the table.—**kitch′en-maid, kitch′en-wench** *n.*—**kitchen midden**, a shell-heap or refuse-heap of pre-historic origin, of interest to archaeologists.—**kitch′en-range** *n.* a long grate with apparatus for cooking, all heated by a central fire [O.E. *cycene*, fr. L. *coquina*, a kitchen].
kite (kīt) *n.* bird of prey of Falcon family; a sheet of paper, silk, etc., stretched over a light frame and flown by means of a cord attached and held from ground.—**kite′fly′ing** *n.* a non-committal effort to discover how the public at large will react to some proposal.—**box′kite** *n.* a light framework, partly covered with cloth, to carry meteorological instruments to high altitudes [O.E. *cyta*].
kith (kith) *n.* in phrase **kith and kin**, friends and acquaintances, as well as blood-relations [O.E. *cuththu*].

kitten (kit′n) *n.* a young cat;—*v.i.* to bring forth young cats.—**kitt′enish** *a.* like a kitten; playful.—**kitt′y** *n.* a pet name for a cat [dim. of *cat*].

kittiwake (kit′i-wāk) *n.* a species of gull with long grey wings and white head and neck [imit. fr. its cry].

kittle (kit′l) *v.t.* to tickle;—*a.* difficult to manage; ticklish; hazardous; intractable.—**kitt′ly** *a.* easily tickled. -**kittle cattle,** persons difficult to handle [Scand. *kittelen*].

kitty (kit′i) *n.* See **kit** or **kitten.**

kiwi (kē′wē) *n.* a New Zealand flightless bird; the apteryx; (*Slang*) a non-flying member of the R.A.F. [imit. fr. its cry].

klang (klang) *n.* the sound of metal striking metal; a complex musical tone, consisting of a fundamental with its harmonics [Ger.].

Klaxon (klak′son) *n.* electric horn on motor-cars [Protected Trade Name].

kleptomania (klep-tō-mā′ni-a̤) *n.* an uncontrollable morbid impulse to steal or secrete things.—**kleptoma′niac** *n.* [Gk. *kleptein,* to steal; *mania,* madness].

klick See **click.**

klieg eyes (klēg-īz) *n.pl.* eye-strain due to the excessive brilliancy of incandescent flood-lighting lamps.—**klieg′light** *n.* a powerful incandescent lamp used in film studios for flood-lighting [proper name].

klipspringer [klip′spring-e̤r) *n.* a small antelope inhabiting inaccessible rocks in Cape Colony [Afrikaans =cliff-climber].

klondyking (klon′dī-king) *n.* the icing of fish in bulk, esp. herrings, for the continental market.

kloof (klo̊o̊f) *n.* a ravine; a gulley; a mountain cleft [Afrikaans].

knack (nak) *n.* inborn dexterity; adroitness; mannerism; habit; a toy or plaything.—**knack′er** *n.* a maker of toys;—*pl.* castanets; clappers.—**knack′iness** *n.* skill.—**knack′y** *a.* handy; clever; cunning [etym. uncertain].

knacker (nak′e̤r) *n.* one who deals in and disposes of old, worn-out, or diseased horses.—**knack′ery** *n.* a slaughter-house for worn-out horses [etym. uncertain].

knag (nag) *n.* a knot in wood; a peg; a branch of a deer's horn.—**knagg′y** *a.* knotty; rugged [M.E. *knagge,* a knot in wood].

knap (nap) *v.t.* to snap; to split flints for walling;—*pr.p.* **knap′ping.**—*pa.t.* and *pa.p.* **knapped.**—**knap′per** *n.* one who breaks stones. —**knap′ping-hamm′er** *n.* [Dut. *knappen,* to crack].

knapsack (nap′sak) *n.* a leather bag for food and clothing, borne on the back; a rucksack [Dut. *knapzak*].

knapweed (nap′wēd) *n.* a name applied to many plants of the genus *Centaurea* [fr. E. *knap* a knob].

knar (när) *n.* a knot in a tree or in timber.—**knarred** *a.* knotty; gnarled.—**knaur** (nawr) *n.* a swollen outgrowth from the stem or root of trees [Dut. *knorf.* knot].

knave (nāv) *n.* a dishonest person; a rascal; a boy; a servant; a playing-card with the representation of a servant or soldier.—**knav′ery** *n.* roguery; trickery; sharp practice. —**knav′ish** *a.* fraudulent; villainous; mischievous; roguish.—**knav′ishly** *adv.* [O.E. *cnafa,* a boy. Cf. Ger. *Knabe,* a boy].

knead (nēd) *v.t.* to work up flour into dough; to work or shape anything by pressure; to blend together; to massage.—**knead′er** *n.* [O.E. *cnedan*].

knee (nē) *n.* the joint formed by the articulation of the femur and the tibia, the two principal bones of the leg; a vertical convex curve in a hand-rail; anything of wood or metal bent like a knee;—*v.t.* to touch with the knees. —**knee′-breech′es** *n.pl.* breeches reaching and fastened just below the knee-joints, as in court-dress.—**knee′cap** *n.* the patella,a flattened bone in front of knee-joint; a covering to protect the knees, esp. of horses. —**knee′-pad** *n.* pad made of thick material to protect the knee.—**knee′-reflex′** *n.* the involuntary jerk given by the leg in response to a tap on the knee-cap.—**knee′-tim′ber** *n.* naturally bent timber suited for shipbuilding, etc. [O.E. *cneow*].

kneel (nēl) *v.i.* to bend the knee; to fall on the knees; to rest on the knees in prayer.—*pa.t.* and *pa.p.* **kneeled** or **knelt.**—**kneel′ing** *n.* (fr. *knee*].

knell (nel) *n.* the stroke of a bell rung at a funeral or death; a death-signal; a portent of doom;—*v.i.* to toll;—*v.t.* to summon by tolling bell [I.E. *cnyll*].

knew (nū) *pa.t.* of **know.**

knickerbockers (nik′e̤r-bok′ers) *n.pl.* loose breeches gathered in at the knees.—**knick′ers** *n.pl.* woman's undergarments; drawers; knickerbockers [fr. Diedrich *Knickerbocker,* the pseudonym of Washington Irving.]

knick-knack (nik′nak) *n.* a trifle, toy, or trinket.—**knick′knack′ery** *n.* knick-knacks collectively [reduplication of *knack*].

knife (nīf) *n.*—*pl.* **knives** (nīvz) a cutting instrument;—*v.t.* to stab with a knife.—**knife′board** *n.* a board covered with leather for cleaning knives.—**knife′edge** *n.* the wedge-shaped piece of steel with a keen edge serving as the fulcrum of a balance.—**to get one's knife into** (*Colloq.*) to have a spite against [O.E. *cnif*].

knight (nīt) *n.* orig. in feudal times, a young man admitted to the privilege of bearing arms; a person of a rank below baronet, giving the right to prefix *Sir* to his name; a champion; a minor piece in chess bearing a horse's head;—*v.t.* to dub or create a knight.—**knight′-err′ant** *n.* a knight who wandered about in search of adventures.—**knight′-err′antry** *n.*—**knight′hood** *n.* the dignity or order of knights. —**knight′liness** *n.*—**knight′ly** *a.* and *adv.*—**knight bachelor,** one who has been knighted but not admitted to any particular Order [O.E. *cniht,* youth].

knit (nit) *v.t.* to form into a knot; to tie; to form by the interlooping of yarn or thread in a series of connected knots by means of needles or pins; to cause to grow together, as a fractured bone; to contract (the brows); to unite closely;—*v.i.* to be united closely.—*pr.p.* **knit′ting.**—*pa.t.* and *pa.p.* **knit′ted.**—**knit′ter** *n.*—**knit′ting** *n.* the work of a knitter; the net-work formed by knitting.—**knit′ting-need′le** *n.* a long needle for knitting threads into stockings, etc.—**knit′wear** *n.* knitted garments [O.E. *cnyttan*].

knives (nīvz) *pl.* of **knife.**

knob (nob) *n.* a rounded lump; a hard protuberance or swelling; a boss or stud; small round handle of a door, etc.—**knobbed** *a.* set with or containing knobs.—**knob′biness** *n.*—**knob′bing** *n.* first rough dressing of stones from a quarry with a hammer.—**knob′by** *a.* full of knobs; lumpy.—**knob′kerrie** *n.* in S. Africa, a stick with a large knob on the end, used by the Kaffirs as a weapon.—**knob′-stick** *n.* an older term for black-leg, a workman who refused to go on strike [M.E. *knop*].

knock (nok) *v.t.* and *v.i.* to strike or beat with something hard or heavy; to strike against; to rap; to make a periodic noise, due to a faulty bearing in a reciprocating engine or to pinking in a petrol-engine; in N. America, to disparage, to criticise adversely;—*n.* a stroke with something heavy; a rap on a door; a blow; a turn at some game or sport.—**knock′abouts** *n.pl.* acrobats who combine skill and fun on the stage.—**knock′er** *n.* one who knocks; an ornamental metal attachment on a door. —**knock′er-up** *n.* a person who wakens workmen for a fee.—**knock′-kneed** *a.* having the knees bent inward.—**knock′-out** *n.* (*Slang*) surprising news; a blow in a boxing-match which knocks out an adversary [O.E. *cnocian*].

knoll (nōl) *n.* a small rounded hill; the top of a hill; a hillock; a mound [O.E. *cnoll*].

knoll Same as **knell.**

knop (nop) *n.* a knob; a tufted top; a bud; a round bunch of flowers [O.E. *cnoep*].
knot (not) *n.* a complication of threads, cords, or ropes, formed by tying or entangling; in cordage, a method of fastening a rope to an object or to another rope; an epaulet; ribbon folded in different ways to provide a *breast-knot*, a *shoulder-knot*, etc.; a cockade; a bond of union; a small group (of people); a difficulty; a hard lump, esp. of wood where a branch has sprung from the stem; (*Bot.*) a node in a grass stem; (*Naut.*) a measure of speed of ships, equal to one nautical mile (6,080 ft.) per hour; —*v.t.* to form a knot in; to entangle;—*v.i.* to form knots; to knit knots for a fringe.—*pr.p.* **knot'ting.**—*pa.t.* and *pa.p.* **knot'ted.**—**knot'grass** *n.* a weed found everywhere, a prostrate annual herb, with white or pink flowers and numerous stem-joints or knots on the creeping ground-stem.—**knot'tiness** *n.*—**knot'ting** *n.* the process of covering knots in wood-work before initial coat of paint.—**knot'ty** *a.* full of knots; rugged; difficult; puzzling; intricate (O.E. *cnotta*].
knout (nout) *n.* a whip consisting of leather, and sometimes wire, thongs, formerly used in Russia [Russ. *knut*, a whip].
know (nō) *v.t.* to be aware of; to have information about; to be acquainted with; to recognise; to have experience; to understand; to have sexual intercourse with;—*v.i.* to have information or understanding.—*pa.t.* **knew** (nū).—*pa.p.* **known.**—**know'all** *n.* a conceited person who thinks he knows everything.—**know'ing** *a.* professing to know; sly; cute; cunning; clever.—**know'ingly** *adv.*—**to know the ropes,** to know from experience what to do [O.E. *cnawan*].
knowledge (nol'ej) *n.* direct perception; understanding; acquaintance with; practical skill; information; learning; sexual intercourse.—**knowl'edgeable** *a.* well informed [E. *know*].
knuckle (nuk'l) *n.* the joint of a finger; the knee-joint of a calf or pig;—*v.t.* to strike with the knuckles;—*v.i.* to bend the fingers.—**knuck'le-bones** *n.* a game, dibs.—**knuck'le-duster** *n.* an iron or brass shield of rings fitting across the knuckles, used to deliver murderous blows.—**to knuckle down or under,** to yield or submit [M.E. *knokel*].
knur, knurr (nur) *n.* a knot. See **knar;** a wooden ball, used in the game of **knur and spell,** or trap-ball, the ball being projected into the air and hit with a trip-stick or bat [O.Dut. *knorre*].
knurl (nęrl) *n.* See **nurl.**
knut (nut) *n.* (*Slang*) a dandy; a fop.
koa (kō'a) *n.* Hawaiian acacia [Native].
koala (kō-ā'la) *n.* a small marsupial of arboreal habit, known in Australia as the Native Bear [Aborig.].
kobalt (kō'balt) See **cobalt.**
kobold (kō'bold) *n.* an ugly dwarfish gnome in German folklore [Ger.].
Koh-i-noor (kō'i-nōr) *n.* a famous diamond weighing 102 carats, now one of the British Crown Jewels; a superb specimen of anything [Pers. = mountain of light].
kohl (kōl) *n.* powdered antimony or lead sulphide used in the East for darkening eyebrows and eyelashes [Ar.].
kohl-rabi (kōl'rà-bi) *n.* a variety of cabbage with an edible turnip-shaped stem [Ger.].
kola (kō'la) *n.* an African tree whose seeds or nuts contain a large quantity of caffeine and are used as a stimulant by the natives; an aerated water [Native].
kolinsky (ko-lin'ski) *n.* Siberian polecat or mink; its fur [*Kola Peninsula*].
kolkhos (kōlk'hos) *n.* collective farm in Soviet Russia [Russ.].
Komintern (kom-in-tęrn') *n.* See **Comintern.**
koodoo (kòò'dòò) *n.* the striped antelope of Africa.—Also **ku'du** [S. Afr.].
kookaburra (kook'a-bur'a) *n.* the laughing jackass; the great king-fisher [Austral.].
kop, kopje (kop', kop'i) *n.* a small flattened hill in S. Africa [Dut. *kop*, a top].
Koran (kō-ràn', kō'ran) *n.* sacred book of Islam, containing revelations received by Mohammed from Angel Gabriel. Also **Alkoran', Quran'**[Ar. *quran*, reading].
kosher (kō'shęr) *a.* (of food) pure, clean, esp. meat, made ceremonially clean according to Jewish ordinances. Also *cosher* [Heb. *kasher*, proper].
kosmos See **cosmos.**
kotow, kowtow (kō-, kou-tou') *v.i.* to perform the Chinese ceremony of prostration by touching the ground with the forehead; to abase oneself; to fawn on someone;—*n.* the ceremony of kotowing; an obsequious act [Chin.].
koumiss, kumiss (kòò'mis) *n.* a fermented milk drink prepared as invalid food; an intoxicating beverage from mare's milk [Tartar *kumiz*].
kowtow See **kotow.**
kraal (kràl) *n.* a Hottentot or Kaffir village consisting of a group of huts encircled by a stockade; the community of such a village [Dut. fr. Port. *curral*, a cattle-pen].
Kraken (krà'ken) *n.* a huge fabulous sea-monster [Scand.].
krasis (krā'sis) *n.* mixture of wine and water used for the Eucharist [Gk.].
kreese Same as **creese.**
Kremlin (krem'lin) *n.* the fortified area or citadel of a Russian town or city, esp. the citadel of Moscow, the seat of Soviet government [Russ. *kreml*].
kreosote Same as **creosote.**
kreutzer (kroit'zęr) *n.* an old German coin; a modern Austrian coin comparable to farthing (100 kr. = 1 gulden) [Ger. *Kreuz*, a cross, such being stamped on coin].
Krilium (kril'i-um) *n.* a substance which, it is claimed, will improve the structure of barren and exhausted soils. [Protected Trade Name]. [Also **creese** [Malay].
kris (kris) *n.* Malay sword with a wavy blade.
Krishna (krish'nà) *n.* in Hinduism the last incarnation of Vishnu; the 2nd aspect of the Trimurti.—**Shri'Krish'na** *n.* the child god [Sans.].
krone (krōn'e) *n*, a silver coin of Denmark and Norway;—*pl.* **kro'ner.**—Also an old silver coin of Austria, once worth about 10d.; in Germany, the former ten mark gold piece.—*pl.* **kro'nen.**
Kroo (kròò) *a.* a W. African negro race living on the coast of Liberia known as **Kroo'boys.** Also **Krou, Kru** [Native, *kru*].
krypton (krip'ton) *n.* a non-metallic chemical element belonging to the group of rare-gases, present in the proportion of about one part in twenty millions in the atmosphere. Discovered by Sir. W. Ramsay [Gk. *kruptein*, to conceal].
kshatriya (kshat'ri-ya) *n.pl.* the military caste of the Hindus, ranking second, after the Brahmins [Sans.].
kudos (kū'dos) *n.* (*Colloq.*) fame; glory; credit [Gk.].
kudu Same as **koodoo.**
kuh-horn (kòò'horn) *n.* a curved horn used by Swiss herdsmen when tending herds [Ger. *Kuh*, a cow].
Ku Klux Klan (kū'kluks-klan) *n.* a lawless American secret society of hooded men, founded c. 1865, to oppose granting of privileges to the freed negroes [Gk. *kuklos*, a circle].
kukri (kook'ri) *n.* a short curved knife with a broad blade, used by Gurkhas [Hind.].
kulak (kòò'lăk) *n.* a prosperous small-holder in Russia who resisted the efforts of the Soviet to nationalise agriculture [Russ. = a fist, a forestaller].
kultur (kòòl-tòòr') *n.* German conception of the benefits of civilisation to be imposed on all others [Ger. = civilisation].

kumiss Same as **koumiss.**
kümmel (kim′el) *n.* a liqueur flavoured with cumin and caraway seeds [Ger. = caraway seed].
kumquat (kum′kwot) *n.* a shrub, native to China and Japan, producing a small orange-like fruit [Chinese = golden orange].
Kuomintang (kwō′min-táng) *n.* political party in China, founded by Sun Yat Sen (1866-1925) [Chin.].
Kurd (kòòrd) *n.* a member of a war-like nomadic race inhabiting Kurdistan, a region on the Turkish-Persian border.
Kursaal (kòòr′sál) *n.* public room for use of visitors to German spas [Ger. = cure hall].
kvass (kvas) *n.* Russian beer made from fermented rye [Russ.].
kyang See **kiang.**
kybosh See **kibosh.**
kyle (kīl) *n.* W. Scotland name for a narrow channel [Gael. *caol*, a strait].
kyllosis (kil-ō′sis) *n.* (*Med.*) club-foot [Gk.].
kyloe (kī′lō) *n.* one of a breed of small long-horned cattle in the Scottish Hebrides and Highlands [etym. unknown].
kyphosis (kī-fō′sis) *n.* humpback, angular deformity of the spine [Gk.].
kyrie (kir′i-ē) *n.* the words and music of the **Kyrie Eleison** (kī′ri-ē el-ē′i-son, kir′i-ē el-ī′son) 'Lord, have mercy on us' the part of the service in the R.C. Church which follows the introit in the Mass; the response in the Anglican communion service after each of the Ten Commandments [Gk.].

L

la (lá) *n.* (*Mus.*) syllable for sixth tone of scale in tonic sol-fa notation.
laager (lá′gẹr) *n.* (*S. Afr.*) an encampment within a circle of waggons; (*Mil.*) a parking place for army transport vehicles; any temporary camping-place;—*v.t.* to arrange in form of a laager [Cape Dut. *lager*, a camp].
labarum (lab′ạ-rum) *n.* orig. a military standard of the non-Christian Roman Empire; the imperial standard of Constantine the Great, bearing on it the letters XP (Christ) which became the symbol of the later Christianised Roman Empire [L.].
label (lā′bẹl) *n.* paper, card, etc., affixed to anything, denoting its contents, nature, ownership, destination, etc.; (*Fig.*) a classifying phrase or word applied to persons, etc.; (*Law*) a written appendix to a will; (*Her.*) fillet with pendants; (*Archit.*) a dripstone;—*v.t.* to affix a label to; to identify by a label.—*pr.p.* **la′belling.**—*pa.p.* **la′belled** [O.Fr. *label*, a strip].
labellum (lạ-bel′um) *n.* the posterior petal of a flower of the orchid type (L. *labellum*, a small lip].
labial (lā′bi-ạl) *a.* pert. to the lips; formed by the lips, as certain speech sounds such as *p*, *b*, *w*, *o*.—*n.* a sound formed by the lips.—**la′biate,-d** *n.* (*Bot.*) with calyx or corolla formed in two parts, resembling lips [L. *labium*, lip].
labiodental (lā′bi-ō-den′tạl) *a.* pert. to the lips and teeth;—*n.* a sound made with the lips and teeth.—**la′bium** *n.* a lip or lip-like structure.—*pl.* **la′bia** [L. *labium*, a lip].
laboratory (lab′or-ạ-tor-i) *n.* a place used for experiments or research in science, pharmacy, etc., or for manufacture of chemicals in industry (*Colloq.* abbrev. **lab.**) [L. *laborare*, to work].
labour (lā′bor) *n.* exertion of body or mind; toil; work demanding patience and endurance; manual workers collectively or politically; (*Med.*) the pains of childbirth;—*pl.* heroic achievements;—*v.i.* to work strenuously; to take pains; to move with difficulty; (*Med.*) to suffer the pains of childbirth; (*Naut.*) to pitch and roll.—**labo′rious** *a.* toilsome; industrious.—**labo′riously** *adv.*—**labo′riousness** *n.*—**la′boured** *a.* constrained and forced, as of literary style.—**la′bourer** *n.* a worker, esp. one who does manual work.—**Labour Exchange,** a bureau set up in local areas by the Government, to direct available labour into the appropriate channels.—**Labour Party,** a political party at home and abroad which champions the interests of the working classes.—**labour of love,** work undertaken voluntarily without thought of reward [L. *labor*, work].
Labrador dog (lab′rạ-dor dog) *n.* a dog of the Newfoundland breed [fr. *Labrador*].
labret (lá′bret) *n.* an ornament inserted into a hole pierced in the lip, worn by some primitive tribes.—**lab′ral** *a.*—**la′brose** *a.* having thick lips.—**la′brum** *n.* a lip-like structure.—*pl.* **la′bra** [L. *labrum*, a lip].
laburnum (lạ-bur′num) *n.* a small, hardy deciduous tree, with hanging racemes of beautiful yellow flowers.—**labur′nin** *n.* an alkaloid found in its unripe seeds [L.].
labyrinth (lab′i-rinth) *n.* a system of intricate winding passages; a maze; (*Med.*) the intricate passages of the internal ear.—**labyrinth′al, labyrinth′ian, labyrinth′ine** *a.* [Gk. *laburinthos*, a maze].
lac, lakh (lak) *n.* one hundred thousand, as a *lac of rupees* [Hind. *lakh*, 100,000].
lac (lak) *n.* a deep-red resinous substance, the excretion of an insect, found specially on the banyan tree, and used as a dye.—**laccic** (lak′sik) *a.* pert. to or produced from lac.—**lac′cine** *n.* a colouring matter obtained from shellac.—**lac′lake** *n.* a scarlet dye-stuff.—**seed′lac** *n.* the resinous substance cleared from twigs, etc.—**shell′lac, shel′lac** *n.* the resin melted and cleared of impurities [Hind. *lakh*, 100,000].
lace (lās) *n.* a string or cord used for fastening dress, shoes, etc.; a net-like fabric of linen, cotton, silk, with ornamental design interwoven by hand or machine; a tissue of silver or gold threads used as trimming;—*v.t.* to fasten with a lace; to ornament with lace; to mix, as coffee, with a dash of brandy;—*v.i.* to be fastened with a lace.—**lac′ing** *n.* a fastening formed by a lace threaded through eye-holes; in binding, the cords by which the leaves are fastened to the back-binding of the book; (*Colloq.*) a thrashing [O.Fr. *las*, a noose].
Lacedaemonian (las′e-dē-mō′ni-ạn) *a.* pert. to *Lacedaemon* or Sparta; Spartan.
lacerate (las′ẹr-āt) *v.t.* to tear; to rend; to injure; to afflict sorely.—**lac′erable** *a.* capable of being lacerated.—**lac′erate(d)** *a.* torn; mangled.—**lacera′tion** *n.*—**lac′erative** *a.* having the power to tear or injure [L. *lacerare*, to tear].
lachrymal (lak′ri-mạl) *a.* pert. to or producing tears, as *lachrymal* duct, the tear-duct.—*n.* one of the bones of the face close to tear-duct; a small vessel, in ancient graves, supposed to contain tears of the bereaved.—**lach′rymary, lach′rymatory** *a.* containing tears; causing tears to flow, as *lachrymatory gases*;—*n.* a lachrymal vase.—**lach′rymose, lac′rymose** *a.* tearful; morose.—**lach′rymosely** *adv.* [L. *lacrima*, a tear].
lack (lak) *v.t.* and *v.i.* to be destitute of; to want;—*n.* deficiency; shortage; need; want.—**lack′lus′tre** *a.* dim; wanting in brightness;—*n.* dimness [M.Dut. *lak*, deficiency].
lack-a-day (lak′ạ-dā) *interj.* exclamation of sorrow, regret, or dismay.—**lackadai′sical** *a.* affectedly pensive or languid.—**lackadai′sically** *adv.* [abbrev. of *Alack-a-day*].
lackey (lak′i) *n.* a liveried manservant; a footman;—*v.t.* or *v.i.* to attend or serve as a lackey. Also **lacq′uey** [O.Fr. *laquais*].
Laconian (lạ-kō′ni-ạn) *a.* pert. to Laconia or Sparta;—*n.* an inhabitant of Sparta.
laconic (lạ-kon′ik) *a.* pert. to the *Lacones*, or Spartans; (of style) brief; concise; expressing maximum meaning in the minimum of words;

Also **lacon'ical.**—**lacon'ically** *adv.*—**lac'onism, lacon'icism** *n.* a brief, pithy style of speech; terse, sententious saying.

lacquer, lacker (lak'ẹr) *n.* a varnish consisting of a solution of shellac in alcohol;—*v.t.* to cover with a film of lacquer; to varnish [Fr. *lacre*, a kind of sealing-wax].

lacrosse (la-kros') *n.* an outdoor ball-game introduced into England from Canada, played with a *crosse* or stick which has a net at the end [Fr. *la crosse*, the crook].

lacteal (lak-te-ạl) *a.* pert. to milk; milky; resembling chyle;—*n.* an absorbent vessel conveying chyle from the intestines to the thoracic duct.—**lac'tate** *n.* (*Chem.*) a salt of lactic acid, and a base.—**lacta'tion** *n.* the act of giving or secreting milk; the period during which a mother suckles her child.—**lac'teous** *a.* resembling milk.—**lactesc'ence** *n.* the process of turning milky.—**lactesc'ent** *a.* producing milk or white juice.—**lac'tic** *a.* pert. to milk; procured from milk or whey, as *lactic acid.*—**lactif'erous** *a.* bearing or conveying milk; producing a thick, milky juice, as a plant.—**lac'tose** *n.* milk-sugar; lactine [L. *lacteus*, milky].

lacuna (la-kū'nạ) *n.* a hollow; a hiatus; an omission.—*pl.* **lacu'nae** [L. *lacuna*, a pit].

lacustral (la-kus'trạl) *a.* pert. to lakes or swamps. Also **lacus'trian, lacus'trine** [L. *lacus*, a lake].

lad (lad) *n.* (*fem.* **lass**) a young man; a boy; (*Colloq.*) a reckless man.—**lad'die** *n.* a young boy [M.E. *ladde*, a serving-man].

ladanum (lad'ạ-num) *n.* a fragrant resin from leaves of a Mediterranean shrub. Also **lab'danum** [Gk. *ladanon*].

ladder (lad'ẹr) *n.* a frame of wood, steel, ropes, etc., consisting of two sides connected by rungs for climbing up; anything resembling a ladder, as a *stocking-ladder*, a vertical break caused by a defective stitch in the woven fabric;—*v.t.* to cause a ladder in a stocking;—*v.i.* to develop a ladder in a stocking [O.E. *hlaeder*, a ladder].

lade (lād) *v.t.* to load, esp. a ship or waggon; to draw (fluid) by means of a ladle.—*pa.t.* **lad'ed.**—*pa.p.* **lad'en.**—*n.* (*Scot.*) watercourse; a mill-race.—**lad'ing** *n.* the act of loading; freight [O.E. *hladan*, to load].

ladle (lā'dl) *n.* a long-handled spoon for drawing off liquid;—*v.t.* to draw off with a ladle [O.E. *hladan*, to lade].

ladrone (lạ-drōn') *n.* a robber; a pirate; a rogue [Sp. fr. L. *latro*, a robber].

lady (lā'di) *n.* orig. a woman having authority over a household or estate; a woman of social distinction, position or independent means; a well-bred woman; a wife.—*pl.* **la'dies.**—**La'dy** *n.* the title given to the wife of any nobleman ranking below a duke; the title of the daughter of a duke, marquis, or earl; the courtesy title of the wife of a knight or baronet.—**la'dybird** *n.* a small beetle usually yellow or red in colour, feeding on plant lice. Also **la'dybug, la'dy-cow.**—**La'dy-day** *n.* 25th March, the Feast of the Annunciation of the Virgin Mary.—**la'dy-fern** *n.* a common British fern with elegant lacy fronds.—**la'dyhood** *n.* the condition of being a lady.—**la'dy-in-wait'ing** *n.* a lady in Court circles appointed to attend on a Queen or Princess.—**la'dyish** *a.* affecting the airs of a lady.—**la'dy-kill'er** *n.* a man who imagines he has a fascination for women.—**la'dy-like** *a.* like a lady in manner and bearing; gracious; fastidious; (of a man) effeminate.—**la'dy-love** *n.* a sweetheart.—**la'dyship** *n.* the title of a lady.—**la'dy's-maid** *n.* the personal servant of a lady.—**lady's man,** a man who seems to prefer lady's company to that of men [O.E. *hlaefdige*, a kneader of bread].

laevo-rotation (lē'vō-rō-tā'shun) *n.* counter-clockwise or left-hand rotation.—**lae'vo-rota'tory** *a.*—**lae'vulose** *n.* fruit-sugar found in honey and certain fruits, so called because it turns the plane of polarised light to the left [L. *laevus*, left].

lag (lag) *v.t.* to bind round, as pipes, cistern, etc., with non-conducting material to prevent loss of heat;—*n.* a boiler-cover; a barrel-stave; piece of lagging material [Scand. *lög*, a barrel-edge].

lag (lag) *a.* slow; tardy;—*n.* he who or that which falls behind; the fag-end; time-lapse; retardation;—*v.i.* to move slowly; to fall behind.—*pr.p.* **lag'ging.**—*pa.p.* **lagged.**—**lag'gard** *n.* a slowcoach; a listless person.—**lag'ger** *n.* a laggard.—**lag'ging** *a.* loitering.—**lag'gingly** *adv.* [Celt.].

lag (lag) *n.* (*Colloq.*) a convict; a ticket-of-leave man [etym. unknown].

lager See **laager.**

lager-beer (lȧ'gẹr-bēr) *n.* a light German beer [Ger. *Lager*, a store; *Bier*, beer].

lagoon (la-gôôn') *n.* a marsh, shallow pond, or lake, esp. one into which the sea flows: a lake in a coral atoll [It. *laguna*].

laic (lā'ik) *a.* lay; secular;—*n.* a layman.—**la'ically** *adv.*—**la'icise** *v.t.* to secularise; to render lay or laic [Gk. *laos*, the people].

laid (lād) *pa.t.* and *pa.p.* of the verb **lay**;—*a.* put down; (of paper) having a slightly ribbed surface showing the marks of the close parallel wires on which pulp was laid.—**laid up,** indisposed; (*Naut.*) dismantled; temporarily out of service, for repairs [fr. verb *lay*].

lain (lān) *pa.p.* of verb **lie.**

lair (lār) *n.* a den or bed of a wild animal; (*Scot.*) the ground for a grave in a cemetery [O.E. *leger*, a bed].

laird (lārd) *n.* (*Scot.*) a landed proprietor; a landlord [Scots form of *lord*].

laissez-faire (les'ā-fer') *n.* a policy of non-interference. Also **lais'ser-faire'** [Fr. *laissez-faire*, 'let do.'].

laity (lā'i-ti) *n.* the people, as distinct from the clergy (See **lay**].

lake (lāk) *n.* a large sheet of water within land.—**lake'dwell'ing** *n.* a prehistoric dwelling built on piles some distance from lake-shore.—**lake'let** *n.* a small lake.—**la'ky** *a.* pert. to lakes.—**Lake District,** the region in N.W. England noted for the picturesque beauty of its many lakes and hills [O.E. *lac*, a lake].

lake (lāk) *n.* a deep-red colouring matter consisting of aluminous earth and cochineal or other red substance [Fr. *laque*]. [See **lac.**]

lakh Same as **lac.** (100,000).

Lallans (lal'anz) *n.* a modern literary form of broad Scots incorporating words from various dialects [Broad Scots = lowlands].

lam (lam) *v.t.* (*Slang*) to beat; to flog [Scand. *lama*, to beat].

lama (lȧ'mạ) *n.* a Buddhist priest in Tibet.—**La'maism** *n.* that form of Buddhist religion practised in Tibet, Mongolia, etc.—**la'masery** *n.* a Tibetan monastery.—**Da'lai-La'ma** *n.* or **Grand Lama,** the chief of the lamas [Tib. *blama*, a spiritual teacher].

lamb (lam) *n.* the young of a sheep; the flesh of lamb as food; a young and innocent person;—*v.i.* to bring forth lambs.—**lamb'kin, lamb'ling** *n.* a little lamb.—**lamb'like** *a.* gentle.—**lamb'skin** *n.* dressed skin of lamb with wool on, for rugs, slippers, etc. [O.E. *lamb*, a lamb].

lambent (lam'bent) *a.* playing on the surface; gleaming; flickering.—**lam'bency** *n.* [L. *lambere*, to lick].

lame (lām) *a.* crippled in a limb; hobbling; (*Fig.*) unsatisfactory, as an excuse; imperfect;—*v.t.* to cripple.—**lame'duck** *n.* defaulter; bankrupt; temporarily disabled ship.—**lame'ly** *adv.*—**lame'ness** *n.*—**lam'ish** *a.* rather lame [O.E. *lama*].

lamé (la'mā) *n.* a textile containing metal threads giving a gold or silver effect [Fr.].

lamella (lạ-mel'ạ) *n.* a thin plate-like structure or scale.—*pl.* **lamell'ae.**—**lam'ellar, lam'ellate** *a.* composed of thin plates or scales.—**Lamellibranchia'ta** *n.* a class of molluscs or shell-fish which are bilaterally symmetrical bivalves, such as oysters, mussels [L. *lamella*, a thin plate].

lament (lạ-ment′) *v.i.* to utter cries of sorrow; to bemoan; to mourn for;—*v.t.* to deplore;—*n.* a heartfelt expression of sorrow; an elegy or dirge.—**lam′entable** *a.* grievous; sad; mean.—**lam′entably** *adv.*—**lamenta′tion** *n.* the act of lamenting; audible expression of grief.—**Book of Lamentations** (*Bib.*) one of the poetical books of the Old Testament, embodying the lamentations of Jeremiah.—**lament′ed** *a.* mourned.—**lament′ing** *a.* grieving.—**lament′ingly** *adv.* [L. *lamentari*, to wail].

lamina (lam′i-nạ) *n.* a thin plate or scale lying over another; (*Bot.*) the blade of a leaf.—*pl.* **lam′inae.**—**lam′inable, lam′inar, lam′inary** *a.* consisting of, or resembling, thin plates.—**Lamina′ria** *n.* genus of seaweed with large leathery fronds.—**lam′inate** *v.t.* to cause to split into thin plates;—*v.i.* to split into layers.—**lam′inate, -d** *a.* formed of thin plates; stratified.—**lamina′tion** *n.* an arrangement in thin layers.—**laminif′erous** *a.* consisting of laminae [L. *lamina*, a thin plate].

Lammas (lam′ạs) *n.* the feast of first-fruits, or ' the loaf-mass ' festival of Aug. 1st [O.E. *hlaf*, a loaf; *maesse*, a feast].

lamp (lamp) *n.* a vessel containing combustible oil to be burned by a wick, or inflammable gas from a jet; any light-giving contrivance.—**lampad′omancy** *n.* divination by the flame of a burning torch.—**lamp′black** *n.* a fine soot formed by the smoke of a burning lamp; the soot formed by the condensation of smoke from burning resinous substances; the pigment from this soot.—**lamp′burn′er** *n.* the part of a lamp holding the wick.—**lamp′chim′ney** or **-glass** *n.* the glass funnel of an oil-lamp.—**to smell of the lamp,** to show traces of great labour and study, said of literary work [Gk. *lampas*, a torch].

lampas (lam′pas) *n.* a patterned material of silk and wool used in upholstery [Fr.].

lampoon (lam-pòòn′) *n.* a bitter personal satire, usually in verse; abusive or scurrilous publication;—*v.t.* to abuse in written satire; to libel.—**lampoon′er** *n.*—**lampoon′ery** *n.* [O.Fr. *lampon*, a drinking song].

lamprey (lam′pri) *n.* an eel-like fish with a round, sucking mouth by which it attaches itself to rocks and stones [L. *lambere*, to lick; *petra*, a rock].

lanary (lā′nạ-ri) *n.* a store-place for wool.—**la′nate, -d** *a.* woolly; (*Bot.*) covered with fine hairs resembling wool [L. *lana*, wool].

Lancastrian (lang-kas′tri-ạn) *a.* pert. to the royal house or dukes of Lancaster.

lance (làns) *n.* a former war-weapon consisting of a spear-head on a long wooden shaft; the soldier armed with a lance; —*v.t.* to pierce with a lance; to open with a lancet.—**lance′cor′poral** *n.* a private soldier with the temporary rank of a corporal.—**lan′ceolate** *a.* (*Bot.*) having the shape of a lance-head; tapering at both ends. Also **lan′ceolar.**—**lan′cer** *n.* a cavalry soldier armed with a lance;—*pl.* a square dance, like quadrilles.—**lan′cet** *n.* a small two-edged surgical knife.—**lan′cet-arch** *n.* narrow, pointed arch.—**lan′cet-win′dow** *n.* a type of window, tall and pointed, common in early Ecclesiastical Architecture, occurring usually in groups of three.—**lan′ciform** *a.* shaped like a lance.—**a free lance,** one who acts on his own initiative; a journalist not attached to the staff of any particular newspaper [O.Fr. *lance*, a light spear].

lancinate (lan′si-nāt) *v.t.* to tear; to lacerate [L. *lancinare*, to tear].

land (land) *n.* earth; the solid matter of surface of globe; any area of the earth; ground; soil; the inhabitants of a country; real estate;—*v.t.* to set on shore;—*v.i.* to go on shore; to disembark; (*Aero.*) to bring an aircraft to rest on land or water;—**land agent,** a person employed by an estate-owner to collect rents, let farms, etc.—**land′ar′my** *n.* one of the Women's Services recruited in both World Wars to work on the land.—**land′breeze** *n.* an off-shore current of air.—**land′crab** *n.* a crab, which lives on land but breeds in the sea.—**land′ed** *a.* pert. to, or possessing, real estate; (*Slang*) left in the lurch or in an awkward situation.—**land′fall** *n.* sighting of land by a ship at sea.—**land′girl** *n.* a member of the Women's Land Army.—**land′hold′er** *n.* a proprietor of land.—**land′ing** *n.* the act of coming to land; disembarkation; the level part of a staircase between two flights of steps; the part of a quayside where passengers land.—**land′ing-gear,** *n.* the wheeled under-carriage of an aeroplane on which it rests when landing or taking off.—**land′ing-net** *n.* a net used by anglers for landing a fish already caught by rod.—**land′ing-place** *n.* point of disembarkation on a quayside.—**land′ing-stage** *n.* a small quayside or (sometimes) floating pier at which passengers and cargo are landed from sea-going vessels.—**land′lady** *n.* the owner of estate or property who leases land to tenants; one who lets rooms in a house, with or without service; the proprietrix of an inn.—**land′less** *a.* without land or property.—**land′lock** *v.t.* to enclose by land.—**land′lord** *n.* the lord of a manor; the owner of houses rented to tenants; the proprietor of an inn, etc.—**land′lub′ber** *n.* a landsman (term used by sailors); one who knows little or nothing about boats.—**land′mark** *n.* a mark to indicate a boundary; any outstanding or elevated object indicating general direction or distinguishing a particular locality.—**land′mine** *n.* military high-explosive bomb with great destructive power.—**land′owner** *n.* one who owns land.—**land′rail** *n.* a corn-crake, a British bird, wintering in Africa, with a raucous cry frequently heard in corn-fields.—**land′scape** *n.* that portion of land which the eye can comprehend in a single view; a pictorial representation of an actual or imagined inland scene; a prospect.—**landscape gardener,** one who is employed professionally to lay out gardens according to a specified plan.—**land′scapist** *n.* a painter of landscape.—**land′slide** *n.* a fall of rock from a hillside or cliff; (*Fig.*) a sudden overwhelming change of public opinion.—**land′slip** *n.* a landslide.—**lands′man** *n.* a non-seafaring person.—**land′stew′ard** *n.* one who manages a large estate.—**land′survey′or** *n.* one who measures land and draws plans or maps.—**land′tax** *n.* a tax on land or property built on the land.—**land′wait′er** *n.* a Customs official who superintends unloading of goods from a vessel.—**land′ward** *a.* situated near the land; lying toward the land away from sea.—**land′wind** *n.* an off-shore wind.—**landed interest,** the combined interests of a landowning community [O.E. *land*, land].

landau (lan′daw) *n.* a carriage, the top of which may be opened and thrown back.—**landaulet′, landaulette′** *n.* a small type of landau; a motor-car with folding hood [fr. *Landau* (in Germany)].

Lande (longd) *n.* a sandy heather-grown tract along S.W. coast of France, now planted with pine-tree forests. Also **landes** [Fr.].

landgrave (land′grāv) *n.* a German nobleman, corresponding in rank to an earl in England, and a count in France.—**land′gravine** *n.* the wife of a landgrave.—**landgra′viate** *n.* the estates of a landgrave [Ger. *Land*, land; *Graf*, a count].

lane (lān) *n.* a narrow track between hedges or across fields; a narrow street or road; (*Fig.*) a specified route followed by ocean-going vessels [O.E. *lane*, an alley].

language (lang′gwāj) *n.* speech; tongue; expression of ideas by words or written symbols; mode of speech peculiar to a nation.—**lang′uaged** *a.*—**dead language,** a language not spoken now, as opposed to *living language* [Fr. *langue*, language].

Langue d'oc (long′dok) *n.* name for the Romance languages of S. France.—**Langue′doc**

n. a province of S. France in Middle Ages; French wines from the district.—**Langue d'oui** (long-dwē) or **Langue d'oil**, Romance language of France other than that of S. France [Fr. *langue*, a tongue; *oc*, yes; *oui*, yes].

languid (lang-gwid) *a.* feeble; listless; flagging from exhaustion.—**lang'uidly** *adv.*—**lang'uidness** *n.*—**lang'uish** *v.i.* to become languid: to droop with weariness; to become wistful.—**lang'uishing** *a.* drooping; sentimental.—**lang'uishingly** *adv.*—**lang'uishment** *n.* tenderness of look.—**lang'uor** *n.* lassitude; sentimental softness.—**lang'uorous** *a.* languid [L. *languere* to be weary].

langur (lang-gôôr) *n.* a long-tailed Indian monkey esp. the sacred *Hanuman* of the Hindus [Hind.].

laniard (lan-yard) Same as **lanyard.**

laniferous (lan-if-er-us) *a.* bearing wool; fleecy. Also **lanig'erous** (L. *lana*, wool; *ferre, gerere*, to bear].

lank (langk) *a.* drooping; weak and thin; long and straight, as hair.—**lank'y** *a.* slender.—**lank'ly** *adv.*—**lank'ness, lank'iness** *n.* [O.E. *hlanc*, lean].

lanolin, lanoline (lan-ō-lin) *n.* an oily substance obtained from wool [L. *lana*, wool; *oleum*, oil].

lantern (lant-ern) *n.* something portable or fixed, enclosing a light and protecting it from wind, rain, etc.; a little dome over a roof to give light; a square turret placed over the junction of the cross in a cathedral, with windows in each side of it; the light chamber of a lighthouse.—**lant'horn** *n.* obsolete form of *lantern*, the sides of which were often made from horn.—**lant'ern-jaws** *n.* hollow cheeks.—**Chinese lantern**, a coloured, collapsible paper-lantern.—**dark lantern**, a lantern with sliding shutter to obscure the light.—**magic lantern**, an instrument by means of which magnified images of small objects or pictures are thrown on a screen in a dark room [Fr. *lanterne*, a lamp].

lanthanum (lan-than-um) *n.* a white, malleable metallic element, one of the rare earths, allied to cerium (symbol **La**) [Gk. *lanthanein*, to lie hidden].

lanyard, laniard (lan-yard) *n.* a short rope or line for fastening; a cord, with knife attached, worn round the neck [Fr. *lanière*, a rope].

Laodicean (lā-o-di-sē-an) *a.* like the Christians of *Laodicea*; lukewarm in religion (Rev. 3) [fr. *Laodicea*].

lap (lap) *n.* the loose part of a garment; that part of the clothing between waist and knees of a person who is sitting; the part of the body thus covered; an overlying part of any substance or fixture; a course or circuit, as in bicycle-racing, etc.;—*v.t.* to lay over or on;—*v.i.* to be spread or laid on or over; to be turned over or on; to be made even.—**lap'dog** *n.* a small pet dog fondled in the lap.—**lapel'** *n.* that part of a coat or dress which laps over the facing. (*Obs.*) **lappel', lapelle'.**—**lapelled'** *a.*—**lap'ful** *n.* that which fills a lap.—**lap'pet** *n.* a part of a garment which hangs loose; a fold of flesh.—**lap'peted** *a.*—**lap-stone** *n.* a stone held in the lap, on which shoemakers hammer leather [O.E. *laeppa*, loosely].

lap (lap) *v.t.* to wrap or twist round; to enfold; to involve [M.E. *wlappen*, a form of *wrappen*].

lap (lap) *v.i.* to take up food or drink by licking; to make a sound like an animal lapping its food;—*v.t.* to lick up; to wash or flow against.—*pr.p.* **lap'ping.**—*pa.p.* **lapped** [O.E. *lapian*, to drink].

lapidary (lap-i-dar-i) *a.* pert. to stones or to the art of cutting stones; pert. to inscriptions and monuments;—*n.* one who is skilled in the cutting, polishing and engraving of precious stones; a dealer in precious stones; a treatise on precious stones. Also **lapida'rian, lap'idarist, lap'idist.**—**lapides'cence** *n.* the process of turning into stone.—**lapides'cent** *a.* petrifying.—**lapidifica'tion** *n.*—**lapid'ify** *v.t.* to turn into stone;—*v.i.* to become petrified.—*pr.p.* **lapidifying.**—*pa.p.* **lapid'ified.**—**lapil'lus** *n.* a small rounded fragment of lava ejected from a volcano in eruption.—*pl.* **lapil'li.**—**lapil'liform** *a.* shaped like a small stone.—**lap'is-lazu'li** *n.* an opaque mineral, sapphire-blue in colour, much used in jewellery, ornaments, mosaics, etc. [L. *lapis*, a stone].

Lapp (lap) *n.* a native of Lapland. Also **Lap-lander.**—**Lap'landish, Lapp'ish** *a.*

lapse (laps) *v.i.* to slip or fall; to fail to maintain a standard of conduct; to pass from one proprietor to another because of negligence; to pass slowly or by degrees;—*n.* a slip or fall; a gliding; a passing of time; an error of omission; failure to do one's duty; (*Law*) termination of legal possession through negligence.—**lapsed** *a.* no longer valid or operative; apostate [L. *lapsus*, a fall].

lapwing (lap-wing) *n.* a crested bird of the plover family, commonly called peewit (from its cry) [O.E. *hleapewince* fr. *hleapan*, to run; *wince*, that which turns].

Lar (lår) *n.* one of the household deities of the Romans.—*pl.* **Lares** (lå-rēz) [L.].

larboard [lar-bōrd) *n.* an obsolete nautical term for the left-hand side of a ship looking towards the bow. Now called *port.*—*a.* pert. to left side of ship [etym. doubtful].

larceny (lår-sen-i) *n.* theft.—**lar'cenist** *n.* one guilty of larceny; a thief.—**lar'cenous** *a.* thieving; pilfering [O.Fr. *larrecin*, theft].

larch (lårch) *n.* a genus of cone-bearing deciduous tree [L. *larix*].

lard (lård) *n.* the clarified fat of swine;—*v.t.* to smear with fat; to stuff, as meat or fowl, with bacon or pork; (*Fig.*) to embellish, as to *lard one's speech with metaphors.*—**larda'ceous** *a.* fatty.—**lard'y** *a.* [L. *lardum*, the fat of bacon]

larder (lård-er) *n.* a pantry where meat and food stuffs are kept; supply of provisions [O.Fr. *lardier*, a bacon-tub].

large (lårj) *a.* of great size; spacious; extensive; liberal; numerous; extravagant;—*adv.* in a large way.—**large-heart'ed** *a.* generous; liberal.—**large'ly** *adv.*—**large'ness** *n.* bigness; magnanimity.—**larg'ish** *a.* fairly big.—**at large**, free; escaped from prison [L. *largus*, abundant].

largess (lår-jes) *n.* a gift; a donation. Also **lar'gesse** [L. *largiri*, to give freely].

larghetto (lår-get-ō) *a.* (*Mus.*) rather slow; less slow than *largo.*—**lar'go** *a.* and *adv.* slow [It. *largo*, slow].

lariat (lar-i-at) *n.* a lasso; a rope or thong of leather, with a noose for catching wild horses, etc. [Sp. *la reata*, the rope].

lark (lårk) *n.* a frolic; a prank;—*v.i.* to play practical jokes [O.E. *lac*, play].

lark (lårk) *n.* a small, singing-bird;—*v.i.* to catch larks.—**lark'spur** *n.* the delphinium [M.E. *laverock*, a lark].

larrikin, larakin (lar-i-kin) *n.* (*Austral.*) a rough; a disorderly person;—*a.* rowdy.—**lar'rikinism** *n.* [conn. with *lark*].

larrup (lar-up) *v.t.* (*Colloq.*) to thrash [Dut. *larpen*, to beat].

larva (lår-va) *n.* an insect in the caterpillar, grub, or maggot stage.—*pl.* **lar'vae.**—**lar'val** *a.* [L. *larva*, a ghost].

larynx (lar-ingks) *n.* the upper part of the trachea or windpipe; a cartilaginous cavity containing the vocal cords.—*pl.* **lar'ynges** (-in-jēs), **lar'ynxes.**—**laryn'geal, laryn'gean** *a.* pert. to the larynx.—**laryngi'tis** *n.* inflammation of the larynx.—**laryng'oscope** *n.* a special mirror for examining the larynx [Gk. *larunx*, the throat].

lascar (las-kar) *n.* a native East-Indian sailor employed on European vessels [Pers. *lashkar*, an army].

lascivious (la-siv-i-us) *a.* loose; lustful; wanton.—**lasciv'iously** *adv.*—**lasciv'iousness** *n.* [L. *lascivus*, wanton].

lash (lash) *n.* the thong of a whip; a cord; a stroke with a whip; a satirical or sarcastic reproof; an eyelash;—*v.t.* to strike with a lash;

to dash against, as waves; to bind with a rope; to scourge with bitter criticism;—*v.i.* to ply the whip.—**lash'ing** *n.* the act of whipping; the ropes fastening anything securely;—*pl.* an abundance [etym. doubtful].

lass (las) *n.* a young woman; a girl; a sweetheart.—**lass'ie** *n.* a little girl [prob. Scand.].

lassitude (las'i-tūd) *n.* exhaustion of body or mind; languor [L. *lassus*, faint].

lasso (las-ōō') *n.* a long rope with a noose, used for catching wild horses; a lariat.—*pl.* **lasso(e)s'** —*v.t.* to catch with the lasso [Sp. fr. L. *laqueus*, a noose].

last (låst) *a.* following all the rest; most unlikely; final; supreme;—*adv.* finally; immediately before in time; in conclusion;—*n.* final appearance.—**the Last Day**, the Day of Judgment.—**the Last Supper**, the memorial supper celebrated by Jesus on the eve of his betrayal.—**at last**, finally [contr. of *latest*].

last (låst) *n.* a mould of the human foot in wood on which shoes are made or repaired;—*v.t.* to fit with a last.—**to stick to one's last**, to attend diligently to one's business (O.E. *last*, a trace or track].

last (låst) *n.* a weight estimated at 4000 lbs. but varying according to different commodities.—**last'age** *n.* the freight of a vessel [O.E. *hlaest*, a load].

last (låst) *v.i.* to continue in time; to endure; to remain unimpaired in strength or quality; to suffice.—**last'ing** *a.* durable; permanent [O.E. *laestan*, to continue on a track].

latakia (lat-ạ-kē'a) *n.* a superior quality of Turkish tobacco from *Latakia* in Syria.

latch (lach) *n.* a small piece of iron or wood used to fasten a door; a catch;—*v.t.* to fasten with a latch.—**latch'et** *n.* the thong or lace fastening a shoe.—**latch'key** *n.* a key used for raising the latch of a door; a pass-key [O.E. *laeccan*, to catch].

late (lāt) *a.* behindhand; coming after; delayed; earlier than the present time; occurring at the close of a period of time; no longer in office; deceased;—*adv.* after the usual time; not long ago; lately; far into the night, day, week, etc. —**late'ly** *adv.*—**late'ness** *n.* tardiness.—**lat'er** *a.* (comp. of *late*) subsequent; posterior.—**lat'est** *a.* (superl. of *late*) longest after the usual time; most recent or up-to-date, as news.—**latter** (lat'ẹr) *a.* (var. of *later*) later or more recent; the second of two just mentioned; modern.—**latt'erly** *adv.*—**lat'ish** *a.* somewhat late.—**of late**, recently [O.E. *laet*, slow].

lateen (la-tēn') *a.* applied to a triangular sail common in the Mediterranean [Fr. fr. L. *Latinus*, Latin].

latent (lā'tent) *a.* not visible or apparent; dormant; hid; concealed.—**la'tence, la'tency** *n.* —**la'tently** *adv.*—**latent heat**, heat which is absorbed in changing a body from solid to liquid, or liquid to gas, without increasing its temperature [L. *latere*, to lie hid].

lateral (lat'ẹ-rạl) *a.* relating to the side [L. *latus*, *lateris*, side].

Lateran (lat'e-rạn) *n.* the Pope's cathedral Church in Rome, built on the site of the palace of *Plautius Lateranus* (executed A.D. 66);—*a.* pert. to this Church.

latex (lā'teks) *n.* the milky sap of trees, plants; the milky juice of the rubber tree [L. *latex*, a liquid].

lath (låth) *n.* a thin, narrow slip of wood to support plaster, slates, etc.—*pl.* **laths** (låthz); —*v.t.* to line with laths.—**lath'en** *a.* [O.E. *laettu*, a thin strip].

lathe (lāTH) *n.* a machine-tool for turning articles of wood, metal, etc. [Scand.].

lather (låTH'ẹr) *n.* foam or froth made with soap and water; froth from sweat;—*v.t.* to spread over with lather;—*v.i.* to form a lather O.E. *leathor*, lather].

latifoliate (lat-i-fō'li-āt) *a.* broad-leaved [L. *latus*, broad; *folium*, a leaf].

Latin (lat'in) *a.* pert. to *Latium*, a part of ancient Italy with Rome as its chief centre, or to its inhabitants; written or spoken in the language of the Latins; pert. to the Roman Catholic Church (as distinct from the Greek Church); —*n.* an inhabitant of ancient Latium; the language of ancient Latium; a member of one of the modern Latin races descended linguistically from the ancient Latins.—**Lat'ian** *a.*—**Lat'iner** *n.* one who knows Latin.—**Lat'inise** *v.t.* to give a Latin form to; to translate into Latin;—*v.i.* to use Latin words.—**Lat'inism** *n.* a Latin idiom.—**Lat'inist** *n.* a Latin scholar or expert.—**Latin'ity** *n.* the Latin language and its idiom.—**Latin Church**, the Roman Catholic Church using Latin as its official language.—**Latin languages**, those languages derived mainly from Latin as French, Italian, Spanish, Rumanian, as opposed to Teutonic derived languages as English, Danish, Norwegian, etc.—**Latin Quarter**, part of Paris where University and Art students live and work.—**Classical Latin**, the language of the great Roman writers of the period (80 B.C.-A.D. 200) —**Dog Latin**, vulgar Latin.

latitude (lat'i-tūd) *n.* distance, measured in degrees, north or south of the Equator; any region defined according to latitude; the angular distance of a heavenly body from the ecliptic; (*Fig.*) breadth of signification; deviation from a standard, esp. religious or ethical; scope; range.—**latitud'inal** *a.* pert. to latitude. —**latitudina'rian** *a.* broad; liberal, esp. in religious principles;—*n.* one who departs from, or is indifferent to, strictly orthodox religious principles.—**latitudina'rianism** *n.*—**latitu'dinous** *a.* having latitude [L. *latitudo*, breadth].

latrine (la-trēn') *n.* a water-closet, esp. in barracks, hospitals, etc. [L. *latrina*, bath].

latten (lat'en) *n.* a metallic alloy of copper and zinc, with appearance of brass, used for church ornaments; sheet tin; iron-plate covered with tin.—**gold latten**, very thin sheet gold [Ger. *Latte*, a thin plate].

latter See **late**.

lattice (lat'is) *n.* a net-like framework of wood, metal, etc., formed by strips, laths, or bars crossing each other diagonally; a leaded window thus formed;—*v.t.* to furnish with a lattice.—**latt'ice-work** *n.* a trellis [Fr. *latte*, a lath].

Latvian (lat'-vi-ạn) *a.* pert. to the Baltic state of Latvia; Lettish.

laud (lawd) *v.t.* to praise in words or singing; to extol;—*n.* a eulogy; praise;—*pl.* in R.C. services, the prayers immediately after matins.—**laudabil'ity** *n.* praiseworthiness.—**laud'able** *a.* commendable.—**laud'ableness** *n.*—**laud'ably** *adv.*—**lauda'tion** *n.* praise; eulogy; the act of praising highly.—**laud'atory** *a.* expressing praise [L. *laudare*, to praise].

laudanum (law'dạ-num) *n.* a preparation of opium in spirit of wine; tincture of opium [same word as *ladanum*, transferred to a different drug].

laugh (låf) *v.i.* to express mirth spontaneously; to make an involuntary explosive sound of amusement; to be merry or gay;—*n.* mirth peculiar to human species; laughter.—**laugh'able** *a.* droll; ludicrous; comical.—**laugh'ableness** *n.*—**laugh'ably** *adv.*—**laugh'er** *n.*—**laugh'ing** *a.* happy; merry.—**laugh'ing-gas** *n.* nitrous oxide gas used as anaesthetic in dental operations.—**laugh'ing-hyae'na** *n.* the spotted hyaena with a peculiar cry like a human laugh.—**laugh'ing-jack'ass** *n.* the great kingfisher of Australia.—**laugh'ingly** *adv.*—**laugh'ing-stock** *n.* object of ridicule.—**laugh'ter** *n.* merriment; audible expression of amusement. —**to laugh in (or up) one's sleeve**, to laugh inwardly [O.E. *hlihan*, to laugh].

launch, lanch (lawnsh, lånsh) *v.t.* to throw as a lance; to let fly; to cause to slide into the water for the first time, as a ship; to initiate, as an attack; to start a new activity;—*v.i.* to go into the water; to push out to sea; to go forth; to expatiate, as in talk; to em

Meissen shell dish

Delft plate

DECORATIVE CHINA and PORCELAIN

Nymphenburg figurine

20th century vases

Sèvres ewer and basin

GLASS

1st to 2nd century glass

4th century glass

16th century glass

Enamelled glass 1616

Ruby glass 1700

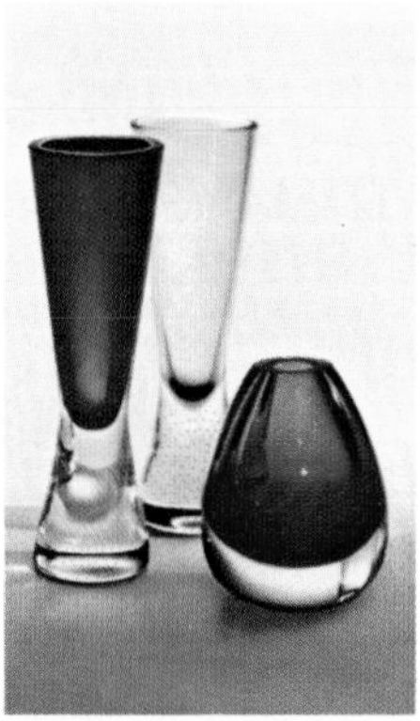

1960

Stained glass mid 12th century

bark upon;—*n.* the sliding of a ship into the water for the first time [M.E. *lanchen*, to drop].

launch (lawnsh, lȧnsh) *n.* the largest size of boat carried on a warship or other vessel; a boat driven by steam, petrol, or electricity; a pinnace [Sp. *lancha*, a pinnace].

laundry (lawn′dri, lȧn′dri) *n.* a place where clothes are washed, dried and ironed; the process of washing clothes, etc.; clothes thus washed, etc.—**laun′der** *v.t.* to wash linen;—*n.* (*Mining*) a long hollow trough for conveying powdered ore from the box where it is bruised. —**laun′derer** *n.*—**laun′dress** *n.* a woman who washes, irons, dresses, linen, etc. [L. *lavandus*, to be washed].

laurel (lor′el) *n.* evergreen shrug, much used formerly to make wreaths symbolical of honour;—*pl.* (*Fig.*) honours;—*a.* consisting of laurel.—**lau′reate** *a.* crowned with laurel;—*n.* esp. in *Poet-Laureate*, a poet attached to the Royal Household;—*v.t.* to crown with a laurel wreath; to confer a University degree on, esp. for outstanding literary merit. —**lau′reate-ship** *n.*—**lau′relled** *a.* [L.*laurus*, a bay-tree].

lava (lȧ′va) *n.* the molten rock, ejected by volcano, hardening as it cools [It. fr. L. *lavare*, to wash].

lavabo (la-vā′bō) *n.* ceremonial washing of a celebrant's hands after the offertory and before the eucharist, esp. in R.C. service; the towel or basin used in this ceremony; a wash-bowl in a monastery.

lave (lāv) *v.t.* to wash; to bathe; —*v.i.* to bathe; to wash oneself.—**lav′atory** *n.* a place for washing; a privy [L. *lavare*, to wash].

lavender (lav′en-der) *n.* an aromatic plant of mint family, yielding an essential oil; pale-lilac colour of lavender-flowers;—*a.*—*v.t.* to sprinkle or perfume with lavender.—**lav′ender-wat′er** *n.* a refreshing liquid perfume made of spirits of wine and lavender-oil [Fr. *lavande*, fr. L. *lavare*, to wash].

laverock (lav′, lāv′er-ok) *n.* a lark [M.E. *laverock*, a lark].

lavish (lav′ish) *a.* prodigal; over-generous; extravagant; ample;—*v.t.* to expend or bestow extravagantly; to squander.—**lav′ishly** *adv.*—**lav′ishment** *n.*—**lav′ishness** *n.* [O.E. *lafian*, to pour out].

law (law) *n.* a rule established by authority; a body of rules the practice of which is authorised by a community or state; legal science; established usage; a rule, principle, or maxim of science, art, etc.; the legal profession; legal procedure; (*Theol.*) the Jewish or Mosaic code, as distinct from the Gospel.—**law′abid′ing** *a.* well-behaved; conforming to the law.—**law′court** *n.* a court in which law-cases are heard and judged.—**law′ful** *a.* allowed by law; legitimate.—**law′fully** *adv.*—**law′fulness** *n.*—**law′giver** *n.* a legislator.—**law′less** *a.* not conforming to the law; violent.—**law′lessly** *adv.*—**law′lessness** *n.*—**Law′Lord** *n.* a peer in the House of Lords who holds, or has held high judicial office, and is qualified to be a member of the highest Court of Appeal in England; (*Scot.*) a judge of the Court of Session.—**law′mong′er** *n.* a second-rate lawyer. —**law′off′icer** *n.* a legal adviser of the Government.—**law′suit** *n.* a process in law for recovery of a supposed right.—**law′term** *n.* a word or phrase peculiar to legal documents, etc.; a period in the year when the law-courts sit.—**law′yer** *n.* a practitioner of law; a solicitor.—**common law**, body of laws established more by custom than by definite legislation.—**written law**, statute law, codified and written down, as distinct from *Common law* [O.E. *lagu*, a thing laid down].

lawn (lawn] *n.* an open space between woods; a stretch of closely-cut, carefully-tended grass.—**lawn′mow′er** *n.* a machine for cutting grass.—**lawn′tenn′is** *n.* an outdoor game played on a court of grass, gravel, etc., by two or four persons with racquets and balls [O.Fr *launde*, a plain].

lawn (lawn) *n.* a fine linen or cambric;—*a.* made of lawn [fr. *Laon*, a town in France].

lax (laks) *a.* slack; flabby; loose, esp. in moral sense; unrestrained; not constipated.—**lax′ative** *a.* having purgative effect;—*n.* an aperient.—**lax′ity**, **lax′ness** *n.* slackness; looseness of moral standards; want of exactness.—**lax′ly** *adv.* [L. *laxus*, loose].

lay (lā) *v.t.* to place or put down; to apply; to beat down, as corn; to cause to subside; to exorcise, as an evil spirit; to spread on a surface; to wager; to produce; to prepare; to station, as an ambush; to form, as a plot; to sight or aim a gun; to set out dishes, etc. (on a table); to charge, as with a responsibility;—*v.i.* to produce eggs.—*pr.p.* **lay′ing**.—*pa.p.* **laid**.—*n.* a situation; disposition; (*Slang*) field of operations; a line of business; the twist in a strand of rope.—**lay′er** *n.* one who, or that which lays, as a bricklayer, hen, etc.; a thickness or coating laid down; a stratum of rock or vegetation; the shoot of a plant partly covered with earth, thus laid to encourage propagation.—**lay′ering** *n.* the artificial propagation of plants by layers.—**lay′off** *n.* a slack time in industry.—**lay′out** *n.* that which is laid out; the design or plan, as of a garden. —**to lay about one**, to hit out vigorously in all directions.—**to lay down the law**, to assert dogmatically.—**to lay in**, to gather together, as a store of provisions.—**to lay it on** (*Colloq.*) to exaggerate; to charge exorbitantly.—**to lay off**, to discard; to steer (a ship) away from land.—**to lay oneself out to**, to take great trouble over. —**to lay oneself open to**, to expose oneself to (as attack, criticism).—**to be laid up**, to be confined to bed by illness; (of a ship, motor, etc.) to be temporarily out of service.—**to lay waste**, to devastate; to pillage [O.E. *lecgan*, to lay].

lay (lā) *n.* a song; a narrative poem such as was recited by minstrels [O.Fr. *lai*, a song].

lay (lā) *a.* pert. to the laity, as distinct from the clergy; unprofessional.—**la′icise** *v.t.* to deprive of clerical character.—**la′ity** *n.*—**lay′broth′er** *n.* a servant in a monastery.—**lay′fig′ure** *n.* a jointed figure used by artists in imitation of the human form; a person of rather negative character.—**lay′man** *n.* one of the laity, or people; one who is not an expert in a branch of knowledge.—**lay′read′er** *n.* one who is not a clergyman, but is authorised to read the Scripture lessons during a Church service.—**lay′sis′ter** *n.* a woman who serves the nuns in a convent [Gk. *laos*, the people].

layette (lā-yet′) *n.* a complete outfit for a new-born baby [Fr.].

lazar (laz′ar) *n.* a person afflicted with a loathsome disease, like *Lazarus*, the beggar [fr. *Lazarus*, the beggar, Luke 16].

laze (lāz) *v.i.* (*Colloq.*) to be lazy; to lounge—*n.* a lazy time [fr. *lazy*].

lazy (lā′zi) *a.* disinclined to exertion; slothful; —*v.i.* to be lazy.—**la′zily** *adv.*—**la′ziness** *n.*—**la′zy-bed**, *n.* a seed-bed for potatoes.—**la′zy-bones**, *n.* a lazy fellow; an idler [O.Fr. *lasche*, weak].

lea (lē) *n.* a meadow; land left untilled; pasturage [O.E. *leah*, a field].

leach (lēch) *v.t.* to wash by causing water to pass through; (*Bot.*) to remove salts from soil by percolation;—*v.i.* to pass through by percolation;—*n.* a vessel used for leaching. Also **letch**.—**leach′y** *a.* [O.E. *leccan*, to moisten].

lead (led) *n.* a well-known malleable bluish-grey metal, ductile and heavy, used for roofing, pipes, etc.; a plummet for sounding ocean depths; a thin strip of type metal to separate lines of print; graphite for pencils;—*pl.* sheets of lead for roof coverings;—*a.* made of, or containing lead.—**lead′ed** *a.* fitted with lead; set in lead, as panes of glass.—**lead′en** *a.* made of lead; heavy; dull.—**lead′en-heart′ed** *a.* callous; depressed.—**lead′pen′cil** *n.* a pencil containing black lead.—**lead′poi′soning** *n.* a form of poisoning called plumbism caused by lead being absorbed into the blood and tissues. —**swinging the lead** (*Slang*) trying to evade a job [O.E. *lead*, lead].

lead (lēd) *v.t.* to show the way; to guide; to direct; to persuade; to precede; (*Cards*) to play the first card of a round;—*v.i.* to go in front and show the way; to outstrip; to conduct; to tend to;—*n.* precedence; guidance; direction; priority; principal part in a play or film; an electric wire or cable; the first card played in a card-game; a dog's chain or leash. —**lead′er** *n.* a guide; a conductor; a commander; the leading editorial in a newspaper; the foremost horse in a team; (*Mus.*) a performer who leads an orchestra or choir; (*Print.*) a series of dots (. . .) to guide the eye across the page. —**leaderette′** *n.* a brief editorial. —**lead′ership** *n.* the state or function of a leader.—**lead′ing** *n.* direction; the act of guiding.—**lead′ing-art′icle** *n.* a leader or editorial in a newspaper.—**lead′ing-lad′y, -man** *n.* the actress (or actor) playing the principal rôle.—**lead′ing-ques′tion** *n.* (*Law*) a question so phrased as to suggest the answer expected.—**lead′ing-strings** *n.pl.* strap or cord used to support a young child learning to walk; (*Fig.*) a state of undue dependence.—**to lead astray,** to tempt from virtue [O.E. *laedan*, to lead].

leaf (lēf) *n.* a thin deciduous shoot from the stem or branch of a plant; anything resembling a leaf in shape or thinness; part of a book containing two pages; side of a double door or a shutter; one of the sections of a telescope table; a hinged flap; a very thinly beaten plate, as of gold.—*pl.* **leaves.**—*v.i.* to shoot out leaves.—*pr.p.* **leaf′ing.**—*pa.p.* **leafed.** —**leaf′age** *n.* leaves collectively; foliage.—**leaf′iness** *n.*—**leaf′less** *a.* devoid of leaves.—**leaf′let** *n.* a tiny leaf; a printed sheet advertisement, notice of meeting, etc.—**leaf′-met′al** *n.* metal, such as gold or silver, beaten thinner than foil, and used for decoration.—**leaf′-mould** *n.* leaves decayed and reduced to mould, used as manure.—**leaf′y** *a.* full of leaves.—**to turn over a new leaf,** to reform [O.E. *leaf*, leaf].

league (lēg) *n.* an old nautical measure equal to three geographical miles [O.Fr. *legue*, fr. (L.L.) *leuca*, a Gallic mile of 1500 paces].

league (lēg) *n.* a compact made between nations or individuals for mutual aid and the promoting of common interests; an association, as of football clubs, for match games to be played during a season;—*v.i.* to combine in an association [Fr. *ligue*, a conspiracy].

leaguer (lēg-ẹr) *n.* a military camp, esp, a siege camp [Dut. *leger*, a camp].

leak (lēk) *n.* a crack, crevice, fissure, or hole in a vessel; the oozing of liquid from such; (*Elect.*) an escape of electrical current from a faulty conductor;—*v.i.* to let fluid into, or out of, a defective vessel.—**leak′age** *n.* an oozing, or quantity of liquid which passes through a defect in a vessel; (*Fig.*) the giving away of secrets, news, etc., through unauthorised channels.—**leak′iness** *n.*—**leak′y** *a.* having leaks.—**spring a leak,** to develop a crack or flaw [Scand. *leka*, a drip].

leal (lēl) *a.* faithful; loyal; true.—**Land o′ the Leal** (*Scot.*) heaven [var. of *loyal*].

lean (lēn) *v.t.* to incline; to cause to rest against; —*v.i.* to deviate from the perpendicular; to incline.—*pa.t.* and *pa.p.* **leaned or leant** (lent). —*n.* a slope; a rest against.—**lean′ing** *n.* inclination (of body or mind).—**lean′-to** *n.* a shed or penthouse built against the wall or side of a house [O.E. *hlaenan*, to cause to incline].

lean (lēn) *a.* thin; wanting in flesh or fat; (*Fig.*) empty; impoverished;—*n.* that part of meat consisting of flesh without fat.—**lean′ly** *adv.*—**lean′ness** *n.* [O.E. *hlaene*, thin].

leap (lēp) *v.i.* to spring; to jump up or forward; to vault;—*v.t.* to pass over by leaping.—*pr.p.* **leap′ing.**—*pa.t.* **leaped** or **leapt** (lept).—*pa.p.* **leaped, leapt.**—*n.* jumping up or forward; (*Fig.*) a sudden rise (as of book-sales).—**leap′-frog** *n.* a game, in which one stoops down, and another vaults over his head.—**leap′-year** *n.* a year of 366 days [O.E. *hleapan*, to leap].

learn (lẹrn) *v.t.* to acquire knowledge; to get to know; to gain skill by practice;—*v.i.* to gain knowledge; to take example from.—*pa.t.* and *pa.p.* **learned** (lẹrnd) or **learnt.**—**learned** (lẹrn′-ed) *a.* having knowledge; erudite.—**learn′edly** *adv.*—**learn′edness** *n.*—**learn′er** *n.*—**learn′ing** *n.* that which is learned; letters; science; literature; erudition [O.E. *leornian*, to learn].

lease (lēs) *n.* a contract renting lands, houses, farms, etc., for a specified time; time covered by lease; any tenure;—*v.t.* to grant possession of lands, etc., to another for a rent; to let for a specified period of time.—*pr.p.* **leas′ing.**—*pa.p.* **leased.**—**leas′able** *a.*—**lease′hold** *a.* held on lease.—**lease′holder** *n.*—**Lease′-Lend** *n.* the pooling of material resources of Allied Nations in the struggle against Germany and Japan. Also **Lend′-Lease.** [O.Fr. *laissier*, to transmit].

leash (lēsh) *n.* a line by which a hawk or dog is held; a set of three hounds, or hares or foxes held in leash;—*v.t.* to hold by a leash; to bind [O.Fr. *lesse*, a thong].

leasing (lēz′-ing) *n.* lying; prevarication [O.E. *leasian*, to tell a lie].

least (lēst) *a.* (superl. of **little**) smallest; faintest; most minute;—*adv.* in the smallest degree;—*n.* the smallest amount.—**least′ways, least′wise** *adv.* at least; however.—**at least,** at any rate [O.E. *laest*, smallest].

leat (lēt) *n.* a channel conveying water to a mill [O.E. *gelaet*, a junction of ways].

leather (leTH′-ẹr) *n.* the skin of an animal dressed and prepared for use; anything made of leather;—*pl.* riding-breeches;—*v.t.* to apply leather to; (*Colloq.*) to thrash with a strap.—**leath′er-bound** *a.* (of a book) bound in calf, morocco, or other leather.—**leath′ering** *n.* a thrashing.—**leath′er-jack′et** *n.* a crane-fly grub; (*Austral.*) a type of eucalyptus tree; a fish; a kind of pancake.—**leath′ern** *a.* made of leather. —**leath′er-neck** *n.* (*Sailor's slang*) a soldier.—**leath′ery** *a.* like leather; tough.—**patent leather,** leather with shiny, varnished surface [O.E. *lether*, leather].

leave (lēv) *n.* liberty granted; formal good-bye; furlough; permission to be temporarily absent from duty.—**to take one's leave of,** bid farewell to.—**French leave,** absence without permission [O.E. *leaf*, permission].

leave (lēv) *v.t.* to quit; to forsake; to omit to remove; to suffer to remain unaltered; to bequeath; to permit; to entrust; to refer;—*v.i.* to cease; to desist; to depart from; to withdraw.—*pr.p.* **leav′ing.**—*pa.p.* **left.**—**leav′ings** *n.pl.* things left; relics; refuse [O.E. *laefan*, to bequeath].

leaven (lev′-n) *n.* a substance due to fermentation which causes bread dough to rise; (*Fig.*) anything which causes a general change in the mass;—*v.t.* to raise with leaven; to create a spiritual change [L. *levare*, to raise].

lecher (lech′-ẹr) *n.* a man given to lewdness; a fornicator;—*v.i.* to practise lewdness.—**lech′erous** *a.* lascivious; lustful.—**lech′erously** *adv.*—**lech′erousness, lech′ery** *n.* [O.Fr. *lechier* to lick].

lectern (lek′-tẹrn) *n.* a reading-desk in a church, [L.L. *lectrum*, a reading-desk].

lection (lek′-shun) *n.* a variation in copies of a manuscript; a portion of Scripture read during a Church service.—**lec′tionary** *n.* a book containing portions of the Scripture to be read on particular days.—**lec′tor** *n.* a reader; a minor ecclesiastic in the early church.—**lec′tress** *n.* a female reader [L. *legere*, *lectum*, to read].

lecture (lek′-tūr) *n.* a discourse on any subject; a formal reproof;—*v.t.* to instruct by discourses; to reprove;—*v.i.* to deliver a formal discourse.—**lec′turer** *n.* one who lectures; an assistant to a professor in a University de-

partment.—**lec'tureship** *n.* [L. *legere, lectum,* to read].
led (led) *pa.t.* and *pa.p.* of verb **lead.**
ledge (lej) *n.* a layer; a projection, as from a wall or cliff; a shelf; a ridge of rock near the surface of the sea [M.E. *legge,* a bar].
ledger (lej'ẹr) *n.* a book in which a business firm enters all debit and credit items in summary form; a cash book; a flat stone lying horizontally as on a grave; one of the pieces of timber used in a scaffolding;—*a.* stationary (only in compound words).—**led'ger-line** *n.* a line with hook and sinker to keep it stationary; (*Mus.*) an additional line above or below stave for note outwith the normal range. Also **leg'er** [prob. M.E. *leggan,* to lie].
lee (lē) *n.* a place protected from the wind; shelter;—*a.* pert. to the part or side farthest from the wind.—**lee'board** *n.* a plank lowered on the side of a flat-bottomed boat to diminish its drifting to leeward.—**lee'gage** *n.* the sheltered side.—**lee'shore** *n.* the shore on the lee-side of a vessel.—**lee'side** *n.* the side of a vessel opposite to the direction from which the wind is blowing.—**leeward,** (lē'wạrd, lòò'wạrd) *a.* pert. to, or in, the direction towards which the wind is blowing.—**lee'way** *n.* the side movement of a vessel to the leeward of her course; loss of progress [O.E. *hleo,* a shelter].
leech (lēch) *n.* a blood-sucking worm used for blood-letting; (*Archaic*) physician;—*v.t.* to bleed by application of leeches [O.E. *laece,* one who heals].
leek (lēk) *n.* a biennial bulbous plant allied to the onion; also, the national emblem of Wales [O.E. *leac,* leek].
leer (lēr) *n.* a sly or furtive look expressive of malignity, lasciviousness, or triumph;—*v.i.* to look with a leer.—**leer'ingly** *adv.*—**leer'y** *a.* suspicious [O.E. *hleor,* cheek].
lees (lēz) *n.pl.* the sediment which settles at the bottom of a wine-cask; dregs [Fr. *lie*].
leet (lēt) *n.* (*Scot.*) a selected list of candidates for a post or office.—**short leet,** a final list [Scand. *leiti,* a share].
left (left) *a.* on the side of the body which is westward when one is facing north. Also **left'hand.**—*n.* the side opposite to the right; in legislative assemblies, the left side of the Speaker's chair where the Opposition members sit, hence an extreme or radical party;—*adv.* to or on the left.—**left'hand** *n.* the left side;—*a.* situated on the left side; executed with the left hand.—**left'hand'ed** *a.* using the left hand more easily than the right; awkward.—**left'hand'edness** *n.*—**left'ish** *a.* having political views which tend towards the left.—**left'ward** *adv.* towards the left.—**left'wing** *n.* a political group with extremist views [M.E. *lift,* weak].
left (left) *pa.t.* and *pa.p.* of the verb **leave.**
leg (leg) *n.* the limb of an animal used in supporting the body and in walking, esp. that part of the limb between the knee and the foot; any support, as leg of a table; one of the two divisions of a forked object, as compasses; part of a garment covering the leg; (*Cricket*) field to left of, and behind, batsman; (*Naut.*) a ship's course covered on one tack;—*v.i.* (*Colloq.*) to walk briskly; to run away.—*pr.p.* **leg'ging.**—*pa.t.* and *pa.p.* **legged.**—**legged** *a.* having legs, as *three-legged stool.*—**leg'ging** *n.* a gaiter to cover the legs.—**leg'guard** *n.* (*Cricket*) padded covering to protect legs, worn by batsman, etc.—**leg'gy** *a.* having disproportionately long legs, as a very young animal.—**leg'less** *a.* without legs.—**leg'of-mut'ton** *a.* shaped like a leg of mutton, as of a sleeve; triangular, as a sail.—**leg'pull** *n.* (*Slang*) a practical joke.—**to be on its last legs,** almost worn out.—**to find one's legs** (or **feet**), to become used to, or settled down, in a new environment [Scand. *leggr,* a leg].
legacy (leg'ạ-si) *n.* a bequest; a gift of personal property by will.—**leg'atary** *n.* a legatee.—**legatee'** *n.* one who receives a legacy [L. *legare,* to bequeath].
legal (lē'gạl) *a.* pert. to, or according to, the law; defined by law; statutory; binding; constitutional.—**legalisa'tion** *n.*—**le'galise** *v.t.* to make lawful; to sanction.—**legal'ity** *n.* conformity to law.—**le'gally** *adv.*—**legal tender,** the form of money, coin, or notes, which may be lawfully used in paying a debt [L. *lex, legis,* a law].
legate (leg'āt) *n.* Pope's highest diplomatic envoy; an ambassador.—**leg'ateship** *n.*—**leg'atine** *a.* pert. to a legate.—**lega'tion** *n.* an embassy; the official residence of a diplomatic minister at a foreign court [L. *legatus,* an envoy].
legato (le-gȧ'tō) *adv.* (*Mus.*) in a smooth, gliding manner [L. *ligare,* to tie].
legend (lej'end) *n.* orig. a chronicle of the lives of the saints; any marvellous story of ancient times; an inscription on a coin, medal, etc.—**leg'endary** *n.* book of, relater of, legends;—*a.* comprising legends; fabulous; strange.—**leg'endry** *n.* legends collectively [L. *legendus,* to be read].
leger (lej'ẹr) *a.* small; light.—**legerdemain** (lej-ẹr-de-mān') *n.* a sleight of hand [Fr. *léger de main,* light of hand].
leger-line (lej'ẹr-līn) *n.* See **ledger.**
Leghorn (leg'horn) *n.* a plaited straw, from Leghorn in Italy; a hat made of this straw; a breed of domestic fowl.
legible (lej'i-bl) *a.* capable of being read.—**leg'ibly** *adv.*—**leg'ibleness, legibil'ity** *n.* [L.*legere,* to read].
legion (lē'jun) *n.* in ancient Rome, a body of infantry of from three to six thousand; a military force; a great number.—**le'gionary** *a.* relating to, or consisting of, a legion or legions; containing a great number;—*n.* a soldier of a legion [L. *legio, legionis*].
legislate (lej'is-lāt) *v.i.* to make or enact laws.—**legisla'tion** *n.* act of legislating; laws made.—**leg'islative** *a.* having power to make laws; constitutional.—**leg'islatively** *adv.*—**leg'islator** *n.* (*fem.* **leg'islatress**) one who enacts laws.—**leg'islature** *n.* the body empowered to make and repeal laws. [L. *lex,* a law; *ferre, latum,* to carry].
legitimate (le-jit'i-māt) *a.* lawful; in accordance with the law; born in lawful wedlock; justifiable; reasonable; genuine;—*v.t.* to make lawful; to render legitimate (as a child born out of wedlock); to legalise.—**legit'imacy** *n.* the state of being legitimate.—**legit'imately** *adv.*—**legit'imateness** *n.*—**legitima'tion** *n.* the act of investing with the rights and privileges of lawful birth.—**legit'imise** *v.t.* to legitimate.—**legit'imism** *n.*—**legit'imist** *n.* one who upholds hereditary monarchical government and divine right [L. *legitimus,* lawful].
legume (leg'ūm) *n.* a seed-pod with two valves and having the seeds attached at one suture, as the pea; a plant bearing seed-pods. Also **legu'men.**—*pl.* **legu'mens, legu'mina.**—**legu'minous** *a.* pert. to pulse; bearing legumes as seed vessels [Fr. *légume,* a vegetable].
leisure (lezh'òòr, lē'zhur) *n.* freedom from occupation; spare time;—*a.* unoccupied.—**lei'surable** *a.*—**lei'sured** *a.* free from business duties.—**lei'surely** *a.* unhurried; slow;—*adv.* slowly [O.Fr. *leisir,* to be lawful].
leitmotiv (līt'mō-tēf) *n.* (*Mus.*) a theme associated with a person or idea, constantly recurring in a composition [Ger. *leit,* leading; Fr. *motif,* motive].
leman (lē'mạn, lem'ạn) *n.* a sweetheart; a paramour [O.E. *leof,* loved; *mann,* a man].
lemma (lem'ạ) *n.* (*Math.*) a subsidiary proposition; (*Logic*) a premise taken for granted; a theme; a heading, headline, or head word of the pages of a dictionary [Gk. *lēmma,* something taken for granted].
lemming, leming (lem'ing) *n.* a short-tailed rodent of the vole family found in N. Europe [Scand. *lemende*].

lemon (lem′on) *n.* an oval-shaped fruit with rind pale yellow in colour and containing very acid pulp and juice; the tree which provides this fruit;—*a.* of the colour of lemon rind.—**lemonade′** *n.* a cooling drink made of lemon juice, sugar, and water (still or aerated).—**lem′on-squash** *n.* a beverage made of lemon juice and soda water.—**salts of lemon,** binoxalate of potash [Fr. *limon,* the lemon fruit].

lemon sole (lem′on sōl) *n.* a flat fish, allied to the sole proper [Fr. *limande,* a dab].

lemur (lē′mur) *n.* one of a family of nocturnal monkey-like mammals found in Madagascar [L. *lemur,* a ghost].

lend (lend) *v.t.* to grant the temporary use of, to give in general; to let out money at interest; to permit the use of; to afford; to serve for;—*v.i.* to make a loan.—*pr.p.* **lend′ing.**—*pa.p.* **lent.**—**lend′er** *n.* [O.E. *laen,* a loan].

Lend-Lease See **lease.**

length (length) *n.* the measurement of anything from end to end; extension; duration of time; extent; intervening distance, as in a race; the quantity of a syllable or vowel in prosody.—**length′en** *v.t.* to extend in length; to protract;—*v.i.* to grow longer.—**length′ily** *adv.*—**length′iness** *n.*—**length′wise** *a.* in the direction of the length.—**length′y** *a.*—**to keep at arm's length,** to discourage friendly overtures [O.E. *lang,* long].

lenient (lē′ni-ent) *a.* softening; clement; acting without severity;—*n.* (*Med.*) an emollient.—**le′nience, le′niency** *n.* the quality of being lenient; clemency.—**le′niently** *adv.*—**len′itive** *n.* a medicine which eases pain;—*a.* soothing; emollient.—**len′ity** *n.* mildness; mercy [L. *lenis,* soft].

lens (lenz) *n.* (*Optics*) a piece of glass or other transparent substance ground with one or both sides curved so as to refract rays of light, and thereby modify vision; the crystalline biconvex tissue between the cornea and retina of the eye; a magnifying glass;—*pl.* **lens′es** [L. *lens,* a lentil].

Lent (lent) *n.* a fast of 40 days from Ash Wednesday until Easter Day, commemorating the fast of our Saviour in the wilderness.—**lent′en** *a.* pert. to Lent; meagre [O.E. *lencten,* spring].

lenticular (len-tik′ū-la̤r) *a.* shaped like a lens or lentil; resembling a double-convex lens. Also **len′tiform.**—**len′toid** *a.* lens-shaped [L. *lenticula,* a small lentil].

lentil (len′til) *n.* a Mediterranean plant allied to the bean, cultivated for fodder and for its seeds [L. *lens,* a lentil].

lentisk (len′tisk) *n.* the mastic-tree [L. *lentiscus*].

lento (len′tō) *adv.* (*Mus.*) slowly [It.].

l'envoi (len-voi′ or long′vwȧ) *n.* a kind of postscript to a poem; a short, final stanza [O.Fr. *l'envoi,* the sending].

Leo (lē′ō) *n.* the lion, the fifth sign of the Zodiac which the sun enters about July 22nd.—**le′onine** *a.* of or like a lion [L. *leo,* a lion].

leopard (lep′a̤rd) *n.* a large carnivorous member of the cat family, of a yellow or fawn colour with black spots [Gk. *leōn,* lion; *pardos,* pard].

leper (lep′e̤r) *n.* a person afflicted with leprosy; (*Fig.*) an outcast.—**lep′rosy** *n.* a chronic contagious disease affecting skin, tissues and nerves.—**lep′rous** *a.* [Gk. *lepros,* scaly].

Lepidoptera (lep-i-dop′te-ra̤) *n.pl.* an order of insects having four wings covered with gossamer scales, as moths, butterflies, etc.—**lepidop′teral, lepidop′terous** *a.* [Gk. *lepis,* a scale; *pteron,* a wing].

leprechaun (lep′re-Hawn) *n.* a sprite; a brownie commonly referred to in Irish folk-stories [Ir.].

leprosy (lep′ro-si) *n.* See **leper.**

Lesbian (lez′bi-a̤n) *a.* pert. to the island of *Lesbos* (Mytilene) in the Aegean Sea, or to the ancient school of lyric poets there; amatory;—*n.* a woman who is sexually attracted to another woman.

lese-majesty (lēz′-maj′-es-ti) *n.* (*Law*) a crime committed against the sovereign, or sovereign power of a state; high treason [Fr. fr. L. *laesa majestas,* injured majesty].

lesion (lē′zhun) *n.* (*Med.*) any morbid change in the structure or functioning of the living tissues of the body; injury; (*Law*) loss or injury [L. *laedere, laesum,* to hurt].

less (les) *a.* smaller in size; not equal to in number; lower; inferior;—*adv.* in a smaller or lower degree;—*n.* a smaller portion; the inferior.—**less′en** *v.t.* to make less; to diminish;—*v.i.* to contract; to decrease.—**less′er** *a.* smaller; inferior [O.E. *laes,* less].

lessee (les-ē′) *n.* one to whom a lease is granted [fr. *lease*].

lesson (les′n) *n.* a reading; a piece of instruction; something to be learned by pupils; a Scripture passage read aloud as part of Church service; instruction gained by experience; reproof;—*v.t.* to teach [Fr. fr. L. *legere,* to read].

lest (lest) *conj.* for fear that [O.E.].

let (let) *v.t.* to allow; to give permission; to cause to do (foll. by *infin.* without *to*); to grant the temporary use of, for hire.—*pr.p.* **let′ting.**—*pa.t.* and *pa.p.* **let.**—**to let alone,** to refrain from interfering.—**to let blood,** to relieve blood pressure by cutting a vein.—**to let down,** to lower; (*Colloq.*) to fail in a promise to a person.—**to let go,** to release; to allow to pass without comment.—**let′-off** *n.* exculpation [O.E. *laeten,* to permit]. [*lettan,* to delay].

let (let) *v.t.* to hinder;—*n.* a hindrance [O.E.

lethal (lē′tha̤l) *a.* deadly; mortal.—**lethif′erous** *a.* deadly [L. *letum,* death].

lethargy (leth′a̤r-ji) *n.* unnaturally heavy drowsiness; overpowering lassitude; inertia.—**lethar′gic, lethar′gical** *a.* drowsy; apathetic.—**lethar′gically** *adv.* [Gk. *lēthargōs,* forgetful].

Lethe (lē′thē) *n.* a river of the underworld said to make those who drank of its waters forget their former existence; oblivion.—**Lethe′an** *a.* pert. to Lethe; oblivious [Gk. *lēthē,* a forgetting].

letter (let′e̤r) *n.* a mark or symbol used to represent an articulate, elementary sound; a written or printed communication; an epistle; the literal statement; printing-type;—*pl.* learning; erudition;—*v.t.* to impress or form letters on; to print in special lettering; to stamp a title on book cover, etc.—**lett′er-book** *n.* a book in which copies of business letters are kept for reference.—**lett′er-box** *n.* a box for receiving letters, as on inside of house-door; a pillar-box.—**lett′er-card** *n.* paper, gummed at edges which may be folded and sealed, without use of envelope.—**lett′er-case** *n.* a pocket-book.—**lett′ered** *a.* literate; educated; versed in literature, science, etc.; inscribed with lettering.—**lett′erer** *n.*—**lett′er-file** *n.* a device for holding letters for reference.—**lett′er-head** *n.* printed heading on business stationery.—**lett′ering** *n.* the act of impressing letters; the letters impressed.—**lett′er-press** *n.* a machine for making copies of letters.—**lett′erpress** *n.* printed matter as distinct from illustrations, diagrams, etc.; print.—**letter of credit,** a letter authorising money to be paid by a bank to the bearer.—**letters patent,** a document under seal of the State, granting some property privilege or authority, or conferring the exclusive right to use an invention or design [L. *littera,* a letter].

Lettic (let′ik) *a.* pert. to the Letts or to their language;—*n.* the language of the Letts. Also **Lett′ish.**—**Letts** *n.pl.* the inhabitants of Lithuania and Latvia.

lettuce (let′us) *n.* a common garden plant, with tender, green leaves used in salads [L. *lactuca,* lettuce].

leucocyte [lū′ko-sīt) *n.* one of the white corpuscles of the blood, destroying bacteria [Gk. *leukos,* white; *kutos,* a cell].

leucosis (lū-kō'sis) *n.* a disease characterised by undue pallor of the skin.—**leu'cous** *a.* white [Gk. *leukos*, white].
Levant (le-vant') *n.* lit. region where sun rises; Eastern Mediterranean countries;—*a.* eastern. —**Levant'er** *n.* wind blowing from E. Spain towards Levant.—**Levant'ine** *a.* pert. to Levant;—*n.* a native of the Levant; a kind of silk [L. *levare*, to raise].
levant (le-vant') *v.i.* to abscond; to decamp.—**levant'er** *n.* [L. *levare*, to raise].
levator (le-vā'tor) *n.* a muscle in the body which raises any part, as the eyelid, lips, etc. [L. *levare*, to raise].
levee (lev'ā, lev'ē) *n.* a Royal reception; orig. a reception held by Royal personage on rising from bed [Fr. *lever*, to rise].
levee (lev'e, le-vē') *n.* (*U. S.*) a river embankment, as in Mississippi Valley; a quay [Fr. *levée*, raised].
level (lev'el) *n.* a line or plane which is everywhere parallel to the horizon; a state of equality; an instrument for finding or drawing a true horizontal line;—*a.* not having one part higher than another; even; horizontal; equal in rank or degree; impartial;—*v.t.* to make horizontal; to reduce to the same height with something else; to raze; to make equal in rank, etc.; to point a gun or arrow to the mark.—*pr.p.* **lev'elling.**—*pa.t.* and *pa.p.* **lev'elled.**—**lev'el-cross'ing** *n.* point at which a road crosses a railway at the same level.—**lev'el-head'ed** *a.* balanced; prudent.—**lev'eller** *n.* one who believes in making all men equal.—**lev'elling** *n.* the act of making a surface even with another; the process of ascertaining the difference of elevation between two points, by the use of a *levelling instrument.*—**to be on the level,** to be honest in one's dealings with another [L. *libella*, a water-level].
lever (lē'ver) *n.* a bar used to exert pressure or sustain a weight at one point of its length by receiving a force or power at a second, and turning at a third on a fixed point called a fulcrum; a crowbar for prising open;—*v.t.* to raise up; to prise open.—**le'verage** *n.* the action of a lever; mechanical advantage gained by use of the lever [L. *levare*, to raise].
leveret (lev'er-et) *n.* a hare in its first year [O.Fr. *levret*, a young hare].
leviathan (le-vi'a-than) *n.* a huge aquatic animal; a whale; a sea-monster; anything of colossal size [Heb. *livyathan*, a sea-monster].
levin (lev'n) *n.* lightning [Scand. *lygna*, lightning].
levitation (lev-i-tā'shun) *n.* the act of making buoyant or light; the phenomenon of heavy bodies being made to float in air by spiritual agencies.—**lev'itate** *v.t.* [L. *levis*, light].
Levite (lē'vīt) *n.* one of the tribe of Levi; lesser priest in ancient Jewish synagogue; Jew.—**Levit'ic, -al** *a.*—**Levit'icus** *n.* (*Bib.*) third book of Old Testament [fr. *Levi*].
levity (lev'i-ti) *n.* lightness; buoyancy; want of seriousness [L. *levis*, light].
levulose (lev'ū-lōs) *n.* See **laevulose.**
levy (lev'i) *v.t.* to raise by assessment, as taxes; to enlist or collect, as troops; to impose, as a fine;—*v.i.* to raise funds by a levy.—*pr.p.* **lev'ying.**—*pa.p.* **lev'ied.**—*n.* collection of assessment by authority or compulsion, for public services; the money or troops thus collected [L. *levare*, to raise].
lew (lū) *a.* tepid [O.E. *hleow*, warm].
lewd (lūd or lòòd) *a.* base; indecent; given to unlawful indulgence.—**lewd'ly** *adv.*—**lewd'ness** *n.* [O.E. *laewede*, lay].
lewis (lū'is) *n.* an iron clamp dove-tailed into a stone block to raise it; the son of a free-mason [etym. unknown].
Lewis gun (lòò'is-gun) *n.* a light automatic machine gun with circular magazine [*Lewis*, the American inventor].
lewisite (lòò'i-sīt) *n.* a colourless or brown persistent blister gas, for use in chemical warfare [fr. W. L. *Lewis*, American chemist].
lexicon (lek'si-kon) *n.* a dictionary, esp. of Greek, or Hebrew; a word-building game played with pack of cards.—**lex'ical** *a.* pert. to a lexicon.—**lexicog'rapher** *n.* one who compiles a dictionary.—**lexicograph'ic, -al** *a.*—**lexicog'raphist, lexicol'ogist** *n.* an expert in lexicology. —**lexicog'raphy** *n.* the art or process of compiling a dictionary.—**lexicol'ogy** *n.* the science which deals with the exact significance and use of vocabulary [Gk. *lexis*, speech; *graphein*, to write; *logos*, a discourse].
Leyden jar (lī'den jàr) *n.* a jar, coated inside and out with tinfoil, used to accumulate electricity [fr. *Leyden*, in Holland].
liable (lī'a-bl) *a.* obliged in law or equity; subject; answerable; responsible.—**liabil'ity** *n.* the state of being liable; responsibility; obligation; tendency;—*pl.* debts [Fr. *lier*, to bind].
liaison (lē-ā'zōng) *n.* a union; connection; illicit intimacy between a man and a woman; (*Mil.*) contact maintained between one unit or command and another; the sounding, as in French, of the final consonant of a word before the initial vowel or mute *h* of the next word [Fr. fr. L. *ligare*, to bind].
liana (li-an'a) *n.* a climbing tropical plant of S. America and India [Fr. *liane*].
liar (lī'ar) *n.* one who tells lies [fr. *lie*].
lias (lī'as) *n.* a blue argillaceous limestone.—**lias'sic** *a.* [Fr. *liais*, a limestone].
libation (lī-bā'shun) *n.* the ceremonial pouring of wine in honour of some deity; the liquid itself; (*Colloq.*) a drink; a drinking-bout [L. *libare*, to pour a little from].
libel (lī'bel) *n.* a defamatory writing or public statement; (*Law*) a written statement by the plaintiff of his allegations in a law case; (*Colloq.*) a statement injurious to a person's character;—*v.t.* to defame by a writing, picture, etc.; to proceed against, by filing a libel.—*pr.p.* **li'belling.**—*pa.t.* and *pa.p.* **li'belled.** —**li'beller** *n.* —**li'bellous** *a.* defamatory; containing a libel.—**li'bellously** *adv.* [L. *libellus*, a little book].
liberal (lib'e-ral) *a.* fitting for a gentleman; open-minded; generous; catholic; unbiased; (in politics) favouring democratic ideals, and freedom of religion;—*n.* one who favours greater political and religious freedom; supporter of Whig or Liberal party.—**liberalisa'tion** *n.* the process of gaining greater freedom.—**lib'eralise** *v.t.* to cause to be freer or more enlightened.—**lib'eralism** *n.* the principles upheld by Liberal party.—**lib'eralist** *n.*—**liberal'ity** *n.* generosity; munificence; catholicity of mind.—**lib'erally** *adv.*—**lib'erate** *v.t.* to set free. —**lib'eration** *n.* the act of setting free; the state of being free from bondage.—**lib'erator** *n.* one who sets others free, esp. from tyranny.—**Liberal Party,** one of the political parties of Gt. Britain evolved in 1830 from the Whigs [L. *liberalis*, befitting a freeman].
liberty (lib'er-ti) *n.* freedom from bondage or restraint; power to act according to one's natural rights as an individual; privilege; freedom of act or speech unduly taken in social intercourse;—*pl.* rights, privileges, etc., conferred by grant or prescription.—**liberta'rian** *n.* one who upholds the doctrine of free-will.—**liberta'rianism** *n.*—**liber'tinage** *n.* the debauchery of a libertine.—**lib'ertine** *n.* one who leads a dissolute life;—*a.* dissolute; debauched. —**liberty man,** a sailor on furlough.—**Liberty ship,** an American ship, built specially for the duration of *World War* 2 [L. *libertas*, liberty].
libido (li-bē'dō) *n.* in psychology, the emotional craving behind all human impulse; esp. used by Freud to denote the sex-urge.—**libid'inous** *a.* lewd; obscene; lustful.—**libid'inously** *adv.* [L. *libido*, desire].
Libra (lī'bra) *n.* the balance, the 7th sign of the Zodiac [L. *libra*, a balance].
library (lī'bra-ri) *n.* a collection of books; the room or building which contains it.—**libra'rian**

n. the keeper of a library.—**libra'rianship** *n.* [L. *liber*, a book].
librate (lī′brāt) *v.t.* to poise; to balance;—*v.i.* to be poised; to oscillate.—**libra'tion** *n.* balancing; a quivering motion.—**li'bratory** *a.* [L. *libra*, a balance].
libretto (li-bret′ō) *n.* the words of an opera or oratorio.—**librett'ist** *n.* the writer of librettos [It. = a little book].
Libyan (lib′i-an) *a.* pert. to *Libya* in N. Africa or to the language of the district.
lice (līs) *pl.* of **louse.**
licence, (lī′sens) *n.* authority granted to do any act; a legal permit authorising a person's right to marry, to preach, to practise medicine, to sell tobacco, liquor, etc., to keep a dog, to possess a motor, wireless set, etc.; excess of liberty.—**li'cense, li'cence** *v.t.* to permit by grant of authority; to authorise to act in a particular manner.—**li'censable** *a.*—**li'censed** *a.* privileged; holding a licence.—**licensee'** *n.* one who is given a licence.—**li'censer** *n.* one legally entitled to grant a licence.—**licen'tiate** *n.* one who has a licence to practise a profession.—**licen'tious** *a.* using excessive licence; dissolute.—**licen'tiously** *adv.*—**licen'tiousness** *n.* [L. *licentia*, freedom].
lichen (lī-ken, lich′en) *n.* one of an order of cellular, flowerless plants usually of scaly, expanded, frond-like forms growing on rocks, tree-trunks, etc.; (*Med.*) a skin eruption accompanied by itch and inflammation [L. fr. Gk. *leichēn*, moss].
lichgate (lich′gāt) *n.* a roofed gateway or arch at entrance to churchyard where the coffin may be left to await the clergyman's arrival. Also **lych'gate.**—**lich′house** *n.* a mortuary [O.E. *lic*, a corpse].
licit (lis′it) *a.* lawful; allowable.—**lic'itly** *adv.* [L. *licitus*, lawful].
lick (lik) *v.t.* to pass or draw the tongue over; to lap; to take in by the tongue; to touch lightly (as flames); (*Colloq.*) to thrash; to be superior over;—*n.* the act of licking; (*Scot.*) a small portion; (*Colloq.*) an attempt;—*pl.* a beating.—**lick'er** *n.*—**lick'ing** *n.* a lapping with tongue; a flogging; a beating (in a competition).—**lick′spittle** *n.* an abject flatterer; a parasite [O.E. *liccian*, to lick].
lickerish (lik′er-ish) *a.* dainty; nice in the choice of food; greedy; lecherous. Also **liq'uorish** [M.E. *likerous*, dainty].
licorice, liquorice (lik′o-ris) *n.* a Mediterranean plant, the root of which contains a sweet juice; the brittle, black substance extracted from the roots of this plant, and used medicinally, esp. as a laxative [Gk. *glukus*, sweet; *rhiza*, a root].
lictor (lik′tor) *n.* an officer who attended a Roman magistrate, bearing the fasces [L. fr. *ligare*, to bind].
lid (lid) *n.* a cover of a vessel or box; the covering of the eye [O.E. *hlid*, a cover].
lido (lē′dō) *n.* a pleasure resort; a public swimming pool [It. fr. L. *litus*, a shore].
lie (lī) *v.i.* to utter untruth; to misrepresent; to deceive; to make false statement.—*pr.p.* **ly'ing.**—*pa.t.* and *pa.p.* **lied.**—*n.* a deliberate falsehood.—**li'ar** *n.* one who utters a falsehood.—**ly'ing** *a.* addicted to telling lies.—**a white lie,** an untruth uttered without evil intent [O.E. *leogan*, to lie].
lie (lī) *v.i.* to be recumbent; to be in a horizontal position or nearly so; to be situated; to lean; to be at rest; to press upon; (*Law*) to be admissible.—*pr.p.* **ly'ing.**—*pa.t.* **lay.**—*pa.p.* **lain.**—*n.* manner of lying; relative position; direction.—**lie′abed'** *n.* one who is not an early riser.—**to lie doggo,** to remain in hiding.—**to lie in,** to be in childbed.—**to lie in wait,** to be in ambush; to lie in concealment.—**to lie low,** to keep in background.—**to lie off** (*Naut.*) to anchor some distance off shore [O.E. *licgan*, to lie].
lieder (lē′der) *n.pl.* German lyrics set to music.—*sing.* **lied** [Ger. *Lied*, a song].
lief (lēf) *adv.* gladly; willingly; freely [O.E. *leof*, loved].
liege (lēj) *a.* bound by feudal tenure; (of a lord) entitled to receive homage; sovereign;—*n.* a vassal; a feudal lord to whom allegiance is owed.—*pl.* citizens generally [O.Fr. *liege*, an overlord].
lien (lī′en, lēn) *n.* (*Law*) a legal charge upon real or personal property for the satisfaction of some debt or duty [Fr. fr. L. *ligare*, to bind].
lieu (lū) *n.* place; room; stead, as in phrase '*in lieu of*' [Fr.].
lieutenant (lef-ten′ant) *n.* a deputy; an officer who takes the place of a superior in his absence; rank below a captain (*Army*) or below a commander (*Navy*).—**lieuten'ant-col'onel** *n.* the rank below a colonel.—**lieuten′ant-command'er** *n.* in the British Navy, the rank intermediate between that of lieutenant and commander corresponding to that of major (*Army*) and squadron-leader (*R.A.F.*).—**lieuten'ant-gen'eral** *n.* military rank intermediate between that of major-general and general.—**lieuten'ant-gov'ernor** *n.* State official ruling a province in a British dominion (e.g. Canada, etc.) under a governor-general.—**Lord′Lieuten'ant** *n.* the King's deputy in Ireland (till 1922); the governor of a county [Fr. *lieu*, place; *tenant*, holding].
life (līf) *n.* existence; vitality; condition of plants, animals, etc., in which they exercise functional powers; the span between birth and death; mode of living; narrative of a person's history.—*pl.* **lives,** men; persons.—**life′and-death'** *a.* desperate.—**life′assur'ance** or **insur'ance** *n.* insurance on a person's life.—**life′belt** *n.* a belt either inflated, or made buoyant with cork, for keeping person afloat in case of shipwreck.—**life′boat** *n.* a special type of boat, designed for stability in stormy seas, for saving of human lives.—**life'guard** *n.* a military bodyguard.—**Life Guards,** a regiment of household cavalry.—**life′his'tory** *n.* the cycle of life of a person, organism, etc.—**life′in'terest** *n.* interest in an estate or business which continues during one's life, but which cannot be bequeathed by will.—**life′jack'et** *n.* a life-belt.—**life'less** *a.* inanimate; dead; inert.—**life'lessly** *adv.*—**life'lessness** *n.*—**life′like** *a.* like a living creature; resembling closely.—**life′line** *n.* a line attached to a life-buoy or lifeboat; a line fired by rocket from the shore to a ship in distress; the line round the base of the thumb supposed by palmists to reveal a person's life history; (*Fig.*) that which keeps a nation alive.—**life′long** *a.* lasting a lifetime.—**life′preser'ver** *n.* any apparatus (as life-belt, -buoy, -line) for preserving or rescuing life; a loaded cane for self-defence.—**lif'er** *n.* (*Colloq.*) a criminal who has received a life-sentence.—**life′rent** *n.* a rent which one is legally entitled to receive during one's lifetime.—**life′size** *a.* resembling in proportions the living model.—**life'time** *n.* the duration of person's life.—**life′work** *n.* any task, usually creative, demanding a lifetime's work [O.E. *lif*, life].
lift (lift) *v.t.* to raise; to take up and remove; to elevate socially; to exalt spiritually; (*Colloq.*) to arrest; to steal; to take passengers on a bus, etc.;—*v.i.* to rise; to be dispersed;—*n.* the act of lifting; assistance; the helping of a person on his way by offering conveyance in one's car; an elevator; a rise in the ground; (*Aero.*) an air force acting at right angles on aircraft's wing, thereby lifting it [Scand. *lypta*, to raise].
ligament (lig′a-ment) *n.* anything which binds one thing to another; (*Anat.*) strong fibrous tissue bands connecting the bones of the body; a bond.—**ligament'al, ligament'ary, ligament'ous** *a.*—**li'gate** *v.t.* to bind; to bandage.—**liga'tion** *n.* the act of binding; the state of being bound with a ligature.—**lig'ature** *n.* anything which binds; a bandage; (*Mus.*) a line connecting two notes; (*Print.*) type consisting of two or more letters joined [L. *ligare*, to bind].

light (līt) *v.i.* to come to by chance; to alight; to settle.—*pr.p.* **light'ing.**—*pa.p.* **light'ed,** or **lit** [O.E. *lihtan,* to dismount].

light (līt) *a.* having little weight; not heavy; easy; active; nimble; loose or sandy, as soil; moderate, as wind; spongy, as cake; not heavily armed, as a cruiser; unsettled; volatile; trifling; wanton; worthless; easily disturbed, as sleep.—**light'en** *v.t.* to make less heavy; to jettison; to enliven;—*v.i.* to become less heavy or gloomy.—**light, light'ly** *adv.*—**light'er** *n.* a barge used in loading and unloading ships anchored out from the quay.—**light'erage** *n.* the price paid for loading and unloading ships.—**light'erman** *n.*—**light'-fing'ered,** *a.* dexterous.—**light-fingered gentry,** thieves.—**light'-foot'ed** *a.* agile—**light'-hand'ed** *a.* delicate of touch; empty-handed.—**light'-head'ed** *a.* delirious; inclined to faint.—**light'-heart'ed** *a.* carefree; gay.—**light'-in'fantry** *n.* a body of armed men trained for rapid movements.—**light'-mind'ed** *a.* frivolous.—**lights** *n.pl.* the lungs of a slaughtered animal.—**light'some** *a.* lively; cheerful.—**light'-weight** *a.* (of a boxer) weighing less than 9 st. 9 lbs.—**light'ness** *n.* quality of being light [O.E. *leoht,* light].

light (līt) *n.* that form of radiant energy which stimulates visual perception; anything which has luminosity; day; the illuminated part of a scene or picture; point of view; aspect; spiritual enlightenment; key-word of an acrostic; any glazed opening admitting light into a building;—*a.* bright; not dark; whitish; pale (of colour);—*v.t.* to give light or fire to;—*v.i.* to begin to burn; (*Fig.*) to express joy (as in the face).—*pr.p.* **light'ing.**—*pa.t.* and *pa.p.* **light'ed** or **lit.**—**light'en** *v.t.* to illuminate.—**light'er** *n.* a mechanical device for producing a flame, as a cigarette-lighter; one who lights street lamps, etc.—**light'house** *n.* a tower-like structure built at danger points on sea-coast and provided with very powerful light to serve as warning to ships.—**light'ing** *n.* illumination; the arrangement of lights in a private or public building to procure artistic effect.—**light'ish** *a.* rather light or pale in colour.—**light'ness** *n.*—**light'ship** *n.* a floating lighthouse.—**light'-year** *n.* (*Astron.*) the distance in a year (calculated at 6 million million miles) light travels—**to see the light,** to be born; to comprehend.—**foot'lights,** *n.pl.* the row of electric lamps along the edge of the stage in a theatre.—**Northern Lights,** aurora borealis.—**lit up** (*U.S. slang*) drunk [O.E. *leoht,* light].

lightning (līt'-ning) *n.* a flash produced by an electrical discharge between two clouds, or between cloud and ground.—**light'ning-rod** *n.* a rod serving, by a connected wire called a **light'ning-conduct'or** *n.,* to carry electric current into the earth or water, thereby preventing building from being struck by lightning [M.E. *lihtnen,* to flash].

ligneous (lig'-ne-us) *a.* woody; resembling wood.—**lig'nify** *v.t.* to convert into wood.—**lig'nin, lig'nine** *n.* an organic substance formed in the woody tissues of plants.—**lig'nite** *n.* coal of recent origin still showing ligneous texture; brown coal.—**lig'num-vit'ae** *n.* an evergreen tree of tropical America and Australia with wood of extreme hardness [L. *lignum,* wood].

ligule (lig'-ūl) *n.* (*Bot.*) a strap-shaped petal at base of a composite flower; the membrane at the top of the sheath beneath a blade of grass. Also **lig'ula.**—**lig'ular** *a.*—**lig'ulate** *a.* strap-shaped [L. *ligula,* a little tongue].

ligure (lig'-ūr) *n.* a precious stone [fr. *Liguria,* a district of Italy].

like (līk) *a.* equal; similar;—*n.* an equal; a person or thing resembling another; an exact resemblance;—*adv.* (*Archaic*) in the same manner; to an equal degree;—*conj.* (*Vulgar*) as; as if.—**like'lihood** *n.* probability.—**like'ly** *a.* probable; credible; of excellent qualities;—*adv.* probably.—**lik'en** *v.t.* to represent as similar; to compare.—**like'ness** *n.* resemblance; an image, picture, or statue.—**like'wise** *adv.* in like manner; also moreover [O.E. *gelic,* similar].

like (līk) *v.t.* to be pleased with or attracted by; to enjoy; to approve;—*v.i.* to be pleased;—*n.* a liking, as in phrase, '*likes and dislikes.*'—**lik(e)'able** *a.* pleasant; congenial; attractive.—**lik(e)'ableness** *n.*—**like'ly** *a.* pleasing.—**lik'ing** *n.* predilection; fondness; taste [O.E. *lician,* to please].

lilac (lī'-lak) *n.* a shrub, with delicately perfumed flower-clusters, purple, pale mauve, or white in colour; a pale mauve colour;—*a.* of lilac colour [Pers. *lilak,* the indigo flower].

Lilliputian (lil-i-pū'-shan) *n.* an inhabitant of *Lilliput* described by Dean Swift in his *Gulliver's Travels*; a person of diminutive size;—*a.* diminutive; dwarfed.

lilt (lilt) *n.* a light or lively tune;—*v.t.* and *v.i.* to sing [etym. doubtful].

lily (lil'-i) *n.* a bulbous plant, with fragrant and sometimes showy flowers;—*a.* resembling a lily.—**lila'ceous** *a.* pert. to lilies; lily-like.—**lil'ied** *a.* adorned with lilies.—**lil'y-liv'ered** *a.* cowardly.—**lil'y-white** *a.* pure white; unsullied.—**lil'y-of-the-vall'ey** *n.* a plant of the genus *Convallaria,* having broad leaves and sprays of strongly perfumed bell-shaped white flowers [O.E. *lilie,* a lily].

limb (lim) *n.* an extremity of the human body, as an arm or leg; a branch of a tree;—*v.t.* to give limbs to; to dismember [O.E. *lim,* a limb].

limb (lim) *n.* an edge or border; (*Astron.*) the rim of a heavenly body; (*Bot.*) the expanded part of a petal [L. *limbus,* a hem].

limbec (lim'-bek) *n.* Var. of **alembic.**

limber (lim'-bẹr) *n.* the detachable front part of a gun-carriage;—*v.t.* to attach to a gun-carriage [Fr. *limonière,* a cart with shafts].

limber (lim'-bẹr) *a.* easily bent; pliant; supple.—**to limber up,** to perform a few gymnastic exercises [etym. doubtful].

limbo (lim-bō) *n.* a region intermediate between heaven and hell in which the souls of unbaptised children etc., are confined after death; a region of forgotten things; neglect; oblivion; (*Slang*) a gaol. Also **lim'bus** [L. *limbus,* the edge].

lime (līm) *n.* the linden-tree which furnishes a white wood used for kitchen furniture, etc.:—*a.* pert. to the linden-tree [corrupt. of O.E. *lind,* the linden-tree].

lime (līm) *n.* a tree which produces a small sour kind of lemon; the fruit of this tree.—**lime'-juice** *n.* the juice of the lime, used at sea as a specific against scurvy [Fr. fr. Span. *lima*].

lime (līm) *n.* viscous substance; bird-lime; oxide of calcium; white, caustic substance from limestone, shells, marble, etc., by heat;—*v.t.* to smear with lime; to ensnare; to cement; to manure with lime.—**lime'-kiln** *n.* a furnace in which limestone is heated to produce lime.—**lime'light** *n.* a powerful light, as on a stage, produced by projecting an oxy-hydrogen flame on a ball of lime.—**lime'stone** *n.* a rock consisting chiefly of carbonate of lime.—**lim'ous** *a.* slimy.—**lim'y** *a.* covered with or impregnated with lime; sticky; resembling lime [O.E. *lim,* cement].

limen (lī'-men) *n.* the threshold of consciousness.—**li'minal** *a.* [L. *limen,* threshold].

limerick (lim'-er-ik) *n.* a five-lined nonsense verse [said to be from a song introducing the place-name *Limerick*].

limey, limy (lī-mi) *n.* (*U.S. slang*) a British person, esp. a sailor.

limit (lim'-it) *n.* boundary; edge; utmost extent; (*Slang*) an outrageous or intolerable person or thing;—*v.t.* to confine within certain bounds; to curb; to restrict the signification of.—**lim'itable** *a.* that may be bounded or restricted.—**lim'itary** *a.* placed at the boundary, as a guard; restricted.—**limita'tion** *n.* the act of restricting; the state of being limited or confined; qualification.—**limita'tive, lim'ited** *a.* circumscribed; narrow.—**lim'itedly** *adv.*—**lim'itedness** *n.*—**lim'itless** *a.* boundless; immeasurable; infinite.—**limited liability,** said of a joint stock company in which liability of the shareholder is in proportion to the amount of his stock [L. *limes,* a boundary].

limn (lim) *v.t.* to draw or paint; to illuminate a manuscript.—**lim'ner** *n.* painter; one who decorates books with pictures [M.E. *limnen,* to decorate].

limousine (lim'öö-zēn) *a.* pert. to a type of closed motor-car with roof over the driver's head;—*n.* a closed car [fr. *Limousin,* a French province].

limp (limp) *v.i.* to walk lamely; to halt;—*n.* lameness [O.E. *lemp-healt,* lame].

limp (limp) *a.* wanting in stiffness, as covers of a book; flaccid; flexible; (*Fig.*) lethargic; exhausted [Scand. *limpa,* weakness].

limpet (lim'pet) *n.* a small, univalve conical shaped shell-fish which clings firmly to rocks.—**lim'pet-mine** *n.* (*World War* 2) a small suction mine attached by hand to the hull of a ship [O.E. *lempedu,* a lamprey].

limpid (lim'pid) *a.* clear; translucent; crystal.—**limpid'ity, limp'idness** *n.*—**limp'idly** *adv.* [L. *limpidus,* clear].

lin, linn (lin) *n.* a waterfall; a pool [Gael.].

linament (lin'a-ment) *n.* lint; a tent for a wound (L. *linamentum*].

linchpin (linsh'pin) *n.* a pin used to prevent a carriage-wheel from sliding off the axle-tree [O.E. *lynis,* axle-tree; and *pin*].

Lincoln green (lingk'un-grēn) *n.* bright green fabric made at Lincoln [fr. *Lincoln*].

linctus (lingk'tus) *n.* a soothing, syrupy cough mixture; a medicine to be sucked up.—Also **linc'ture** [L. *lingere, linctum,* to lick].

linden (lin'den) *n.* the lime-tree [O.E. *lind,* the lime-tree].

line (līn) *n.* a linen thread or string; a slender cord; a thread-like mark; an extended stroke; (*Math.*) that which has one dimension, length, but no breadth or thickness; a curve connecting points which have a common significance (as the Equator, isotherms, isobars, contours, etc.); a boundary; a row or continued series; progeny; a verse; (*Colloq.*) a short letter; a course of conduct, thought, or policy; a trend; a department; a trade, business or profession; a system of buses, trains, or passenger aircraft under one management; a railway track; a formation of naval vessels; the regular infantry of an army; a unit of measurement, $\frac{1}{12}$ of an inch; harmony; graceful cut (as of a costume, dress); (*U.S.*) advice or guidance;—*pl.* a certificate of Church membership, marriage, etc.; a punishment exercise; parts of a play memorised by an actor or actress; military fieldworks;—*v.t.* to mark out with lines; to form in a line; to border.—**lin'age** *n.* amount of lines on a page; payment according to the number of lines.—**lin'eage** *n.* descendants in a line from common progenitor; pedigree.—**lin'eal** *a.* composed of lines; pert. to, or in the direction of, a line; directly descended from a common ancestor.—**lineal'ity** *n.*—**lin'eally** *adv.*—**lin'eament** *n.* feature; form; characteristic; outline of a body or figure.—**lin'ear** *a.* pert. to, or consisting of, a line; drawn in lines.—**lin'early** *adv.*—**lin'eate(d)** *a.* marked by lines.—**linea'tion** *n.* the act of marking with lines; the lines marked or engraved.—**lined** *a.* marked with lines; ruled.—**line'engrav'ing** *n.* the process of engraving lines on a copper-plate.—**line'fish** *n.* fish caught by line, not by nets.—**li'ner** *n.* a steamship or passenger aircraft belonging to a regular transport line.—**lines'man** *n.* an infantryman; a railway employee who examines and repairs railway lines; an official (at football or tennis match) who determines whether ball has crossed the outside line or not.—**line'-up** *n.* a marshalling of forces, or resources.—**the line,** the Equator.—**to shoot a line** (*World War 2 slang*) to boast, usually of one's personal exploits [L. *linea,* a string of flax].

line (līn) *v.t.* to cover on the inside, as a garment, pan, etc.—**lin'ing** *n.* the material used to line a garment, etc.; contents [M.E. *linen,* to cover].

linen (lin'en) *n.* thread or cloth made from flax; underclothing; napery;—*a.* made of flax or linen [O.E. *lin,* flax].

ling (ling) *n.* a soft-finned *elongated* fish of the cod family [O.E. *lang,* long].

ling (ling) *n.* the common heather.—**ling'y** *a.* [Scand. *lyng,* heather].

linger (ling'gẹr) *v.i.* to delay; to dally; to loiter.—**ling'erer** *n.*—**ling'ering** *a.* protracted [O.E. *lengan,* to protract].

lingerie (lang'zhẹ-rē) *n.* orig. linen goods; women's underclothing [Fr. *linge,* linen].

lingo (ling'gō) *n.* language; (*Colloq.*) jargon [corrupt. of L. *lingua,* language].

lingual (ling'gwạl) *a.* pert. to the tongue;—*n.* a sound or letter made by the tongue, as *d, l, n.*—**ling'ually** *adv.*—**ling'uiform** *a.* shaped like a tongue.—**ling'uist** *n.* fluent speaker of several languages.—**linguist'ic** *a.*—**linguist'ically** *adv.*—**linguist'ics** *n.* comparative philology.—**ling'ulate, ling'ular** *a.* (*Bot.*) shaped like a tongue [L. *lingua,* a tongue].

liniment (lin'i-ment) *n.* a lotion or soft ointment [L. *linere,* to besmear].

link (lingk) *n.* a single ring of a chain; anything doubled and closed like a link; a connection; the $\frac{1}{100}$ part of a chain (7.92 inches).—*v.t.* to connect by a link; (*Fig.*) to combine for a common purpose;—*v.i.* to be coupled.—**link'age** *n.* a system of connections.—**missing link,** a connection without which a chain of argument is incomplete; (*Zool.*) that form of animal life the scientific knowledge of which is required to complete the chain of evolution of man from the ape (O.E. *hlence,* a ring].

link (lingk) *n.* a torch of tar and tow.—**link'boy** or **-man** *n.* one who carried a link and guided people (etym. unknown].

link (lingk) *n.* a bend of a river.—**links** *n.pl.* flat ground near the sea, often laid out as a golf-course [O.E. *hlinc,* a ridge].

linn See lin.

Linnæan, Linnean (lin-ē'ạn) *a.* pert. to *Linnaeus* or *Linné,* the Swedish botanist (1707-1778).—**Linnaean system** (*Bot.*) an artificial or sexual system of botanical classification, formulated by *Linnaeus.*

linnet (lin'et) *n.* a small British song-bird of the finch family, so called from its feeding on flax-seed [O.Fr. *linette,* fr. L. *linum,* flax].

linocut (lī'nō-kut) *n.* design cut in relief on linoleum; print from it [L. *linum,* flax].

linoleum (lin-ō'le-um) *n.* floorcloth of hessian impregnated with a cement of linseed oil, cork, etc. [L. *linum,* flax; *oleum,* oil].

linotype (līn'o-tīp) *n.* a type-setting machine in which the matter is cast in solid lines of type [L. *linea,* line, and *type*].

linseed (lin'sēd) *n.* flax-seed.—**linseed cake,** compressed mass of husks of linseed, after oil has been pressed out, much used for cattle feeding.—**linseed oil,** the oil pressed out of linseed [O.E. *linsaed,* flax-seed].

linsey (lin'si) *n.* a dress material of wool and linen.—**lin'sey-wool'sey** *a.* made of wool and linen mixed; (*Fig.*) mean; shoddy; vile;—*n.* inferior stuff [O.Fr. *linsel,* and *wool*].

lint (lint) *n.* a linen material with one side teased or scraped to a soft, woolly surface, used for dressing wounds [L. *linteum,* a linen cloth].

lintel (lin'tel) *n.* a horizontal beam or stone over a doorway [L.L. *lintellus,* fr. L. *limes,* a border].

lion (lī'un) *n.* (*fem.* **li'oness**) the largest of the cat tribe, tawny-coloured, with powerful, tufted tail, the male having a shaggy mane; (*Fig.*) a person of fierce courage; a celebrity; (*Astron.*) a sign of the Zodiac (Leo).—**li'on-heart** *a.* courageous. Also **li'on-heart'ed** *a.*

—**li'onise** *v.t.* to treat as an object of curiosity or as a celebrity.—**the lion's share,** the biggest portion.—**to twist the lion's tail,** to say something derogatory of Great Britain [L. *leo,* a lion].

lip (lip) *n.* one of the two fleshy, outer edges of the mouth; the edge of anything; brim; (*Slang*) impertinent talk;—*pl.* the organs of speech as represented by the lips;—*v.t.* to touch with the lips; to speak.—*n.* hypocritical praise.—**lipped** *a.* having a brim.—**lip'read'ing** *n.* the art of ' hearing ' by reading the motions of a speaker's lips; this system as taught to the deaf.—**lip'ser'vice** *n.* superficial devotion to a person or cause.—**lip'stick,** a rouge-salve, in the form of a small stick, used by women to redden the lips [O.E. *lippa,* a lip].

liquate (lik'wāt) *v.t.* to melt; to separate or purify solids or gases by liquefying.—**liqua'tion** *n.* [L. *liquare,* to be fluid].

liquefy (lik'we-fī) *v.t.* to transform to a liquid; to melt;—*v.i.* to become liquid.—*pa.t.* and *pa.p.* **liq'uefied.**—**liquefa'cient** *a.*—**liquefac'tion** *n.* the act of liquefying; the state of being liquefied.—**liquefi'able** *a.*—**liq'uefier** *n.*—**liques'cency** *n.*—**liques'cent** *a.* melting [L. *liquefacere,* to melt].

liqueur (li- or lē-kẹr') *n.* a preparation of distilled spirits, flavoured with fruits or aromatic substances [Fr.].

liquid (lik'wid) *a.* fluid; in a state intermediate between a solid and a gas; flowing smoothly; (of sounds) pleasing to the ear;—*n.* a substance intermediate between a solid and a gas which assumes the shape of the vessel which contains it; the name popularly applied to a consonant which has a smooth flowing sound (*l, m, n, r*).—**liq'uidate** *v.t.* to make clear; to settle a debt; to wind up the affairs of a bankrupt company; to adjust; to destroy;—*v.i.* (of business) to be wound up.—**liquida'tion** *n.*—**liquida'tor** *n.* [L. *liquidus,* fluid].

liquor (lik'ur) *n.* any liquid or fluid, esp. alcoholic or spirituous fluid; a decoction. [Fr. fr. L. *liquere,* to be fluid].

liquorice (lik'o-ris) See **licorice.**

lira (lē'rạ) *n.* an Italian silver coin, originally worth about tenpence [It.].

lisle (līl) *n.* a fine hard twisted cotton thread (formerly made at *Lille,* France).

lisp (lisp) *v.i.* to speak imperfectly, esp. to substitute the sound *th* for *s*;—*v.t.* to pronounce with a lisp;—*n.* the habit of lisping.—**lisp'ing** *n.* [O.E. *wlisp,* stammering].

lissom (lis'um) *a.* supple; flexible; lithe.—**liss'omness** *n.* [fr. *lithesome*].

list (list) *n.* the outer edge or selvedge of woven cloth; a row or stripe; a roll; a catalogue; an inventory; a register; a boundary line enclosing a field of combat, esp. in *pl.* **lists**; the field thus enclosed;—*v.t.* to sew together strips of cloth; to enter in a catalogue or inventory;—*v.i.* to enlist; to engage in a public service by enrolling one's name [O.E. *liste,* a border].

list (list) *v.i.* to lean or incline; to please; to desire; (*Naut.*) to heel over;—*v.t.* to cause to heel over;—*n.* an inclination to one side [O.E. *lystan,* to desire].

listen (lis'n) *v.i.* to attend closely; to yield to advice. —**list** *v.t.* and *v.i.* to listen (poetical).—**list'ener** *n.* one who listens; (*Radio*) one who uses receiver to hear broadcasts.—**to listen in,** to hear broadcasts [O.E. *hlyst,* hearing].

listless (list'les) *a.* indifferent; languid; apathetic.—**list'lessly** *adv.*—**list'lessness** *n.* [O.E. *lust,* pleasure].

lit (lit) *pa.t.* and *pa.p.* of verb **light.**

litany (lit'ạn-i) *n.* an earnest prayer of supplication used in public worship [Gk. *litaneia,* supplication].

literal (lit'e-rạl) *a.* according to the letter; real; not figurative; word for word, as a translation.—**lit'eralness** *n.*—**lit'erally** *adv.* [L. *litera,* a letter].

literary (lit'ẹr-ar-i) *a.* pert. to letters or literature; versed in literature.—**lit'eracy** *n.* state of being literate, opp. of *illiteracy.*—**lit'erate** *a.* versed in learning and science; educated;—*n.* one who is able to read and write.—**litera'ti** *n.pl.* men of letters; educated people.—**litera'tim** *adv.* letter by letter [L. *litera,* a letter].

litharge (lith'ȧrj) *n.* monoxide of lead [Gk. *lithos,* a stone; *arguros,* silver].

lithe (līth) *a.* capable of being easily bent; supple; pliant.—**lithe'ly** *adv.*—**lithe'ness** *n.*—**lithe'some** *a.* [O.E. *lithe,* gentle].

lithia (lith'i-ạ) *n.* oxide of lithium.—**lith'ium** *n.* one of the alkaline metals, silvery white in colour, symbol **Li,** found in a few rare minerals [Gk. *lithos,* a stone].

lithogenous (li-thoj'e-nus) *a.* rock-producing, as certain corals [Gk. *lithos,* a stone; *genesthai,* to be born].

lithoglyph (lith'ō-glif) *n.* an engraving on a precious stone [Gk. *lithos,* a stone; *gluphein,* to carve].

lithograph (lith'ō-graf) *v.t.* to trace on stone, zinc, or aluminium, and transfer to paper by special printing process;—*n.* a print from stone, etc.—**lithog'rapher** *n.*—**lithograph'ic, -al** *a.*—**lithograph'ically** *adv.*—**lithog'raphy** *n.* the art of tracing designs on stone or other medium, and taking impressions of these designs [Gk. *lithos,* a stone; *graphein,* to write].

lithoid, -al (lith'oid, -ạl) *a.* resembling a stone [Gk. *lithos,* a stone].

lithology (lith-ol'o-ji) *n.* the science which treats of the characteristics and classification of rocks.—**litholog'ic, litholog'ical** *a.*—**lithol'ogist** *n.* [Gk. *lithos,* a stone; *logos,* a discourse].

lithotint (lith'ō-tint) *n.* the lithographic production of a tinted picture; the picture itself [Gk. *lithos,* a stone; and *tint*].

lithotome (lith'ō-tōm) *n.* a stone resembling an artificially cut gem; (*Surg.*) an instrument for performing a lithotomy.—**lithotom'ic** *a.*—**lithot'omist** *n.*—**lithot'omy** *n.* (*Surg.*) the operation by which stones are removed from the bladder [Gk. *lithos,* a stone; *tomē,* a cutting].

lithotype (lith'ō-tīp) *n.* a stereotype plate; a print from this plate.—**lith'otypy** *n.* [Gk. *lithos,* a stone; *tupos,* type].

Lithuanian (lith-ū-ān'i-ạn) *n.* a native of Lithuania; the language.

litigate (lit'i-gāt) *v.t.* to contest in law;—*v.i.* to carry on a lawsuit.—**lit'igable** *a.*—**lit'igant** *n.* a person engaged in a law-suit;—*a.* engaged in a lawsuit.—**litiga'tion** *n.* judicial proceedings.—**lit'igator** *n.* one who litigates.—**litigios'ity** *n.*—**litig'ious** *a.* given to engaging in lawsuits; disputatious [L. *litigare,* to dispute].

litmus (lit'mus) *n.* a bluish purple vegetable dye (obtained from lichens) which turns *red* with an acid, and *blue* with an alkali.—**litmus paper,** absorbent paper impregnated with litmus, used to test solutions [prob. fr. Dut. *lakmoes,* a blue dye].

litotes (lī'tō-tēz) *n.* a figure of speech which expresses a strong affirmative by using the negative of its contrary, as in phrase, *no mean city* [Gk. *litos,* simple].

litre (lē'tr) *n.* a unit of volume in the metric system, equal to 61·027 cubic inches, or 1·76 English pints [Gk. *litra,* a pound].

litter (lit'ẹr) *n.* a heap of straw as bedding for animals; a vehicle containing bed carried on men's shoulders; a stretcher; odds and ends left lying about; state of disorder; a family of young pigs, puppies, etc., brought forth at the one birth;—*v.t.* to bring forth young; to scatter indiscriminately about; to make untidy with odds and ends [Fr. *litière,* a bed].

little (lit'l) *a.* small in size, extent, or quantity; brief; slight; mean;—*n.* a small quantity or space;—*adv.* in a small quantity or degree (*comp.* **less**; *superl.* **least**).—**Litt'le-Eng'lander** *n.* at end of 19th cent., one opposed to Imperialism [O.E. *lytel,* small].

littoral (lit′or-al) *a.* pert. to the sea-shore, esp. to that part between high and low water marks [L. *litoralis*, pertaining to the sea-shore].
liturgy (lit′ur-ji) *n.* the established ritual for public worship in a church, esp. the Mass.—**liturge′** *n.* a leader in public worship.—**litur′gic, -al** *a.*—**litur′gically** *adv.*—**litur′gics** *n.* the study of church worship and its ritual [Gk. *leitourgia*, a public service].
live (liv) *v.i.* to have life; to subsist; to be conscious; to dwell; to enjoy life; to keep oneself (as on one's income);—*v.t.* to spend; to pass.—*pr.p.* **liv′ing.**—*pa.p.* **lived.**—**liv′able** *a.* habitable.—**liv′er** *n.*—**to live in,** to reside at one's place of business [O.E. *lifian*, to live].
live (līv) *a.* having life; quick; active; vital; unexploded, as a mine; burning, as coal; full of zest; dynamic.—**lived** (livd) *a.* used in compounds as *long-lived, short-lived.*—**live′cir′cuit** *n.* a circuit through which an electric current is passing.—**live′fence** *n.* a hedge.—**li′ven** *v.t.* to enliven.—**live′rail** *n.* a conductor-rail in an electrified railway or underground system.—**live′stock** *n.* the general term for horses, cattle, pigs, etc., on a farm.—**live′wire** *n.* a wire carrying an electric current; (*Fig.*) an able, energetic and go-ahead person [O.E. *lif*, life].
livelihood (līv′li-hood) *n.* a means of living; sustenance [O.E. *lif*, life; *lad*, a way].
livelong (liv′long) *a.* lasting throughout the whole day [orig. fr. O.E. *leof*, dear].
lively (līv′li) *a.* animated; active; gay; exciting; light;—*adv.* briskly;—**live′lily** *adv.*—**live′liness** *n.* [O.E. *liflic*, life-like].
liver (liv′er) *n.* (*Anat.*) glandular organ in body secreting bile; the flesh of this organ in animals or fowls used as food.—**liv′er-fluke** *n.* a trematoid worm.—**liv′erish** *a.* off-colour because of a disordered liver.—**liv′erwort** *n.* a moss-like plant with liver-shaped leaves.—**lil′y-liv′ered** *a.* cowardly [O.E. *lifer*, liver].
livery (liv′er-i) *n.* orig. the special dress or food *delivered* by a lord to his household retinue; a dress peculiar to a certain group, as members of a medieval guild or trade; any characteristic uniform of an employee, as of a chauffeur; a supply of food given out at stated intervals to horses, etc.; the body of liverymen in London; garb or general appearance.—**liv′eried** *a.* clothed in a livery.—**liv′ery-com′pany** *n.* one of London's city companies, orig. a trade guild.—**liv′eryman** *n.* one who wears a livery; a freeman of the city of London.—**liv′ery-sta′ble** *n.* a stable where horses and vehicles are kept for hire [O.Fr. *livrée*, an allowance].
livid (liv′id) *a.* black and blue; discoloured, as flesh, by bruising.—**livid′ity, liv′idness** *n.* [L. *lividus*, bluish].
living (liv′ing) *a.* having life; active; flowing (of water); resembling closely; contemporary;—*n.* livelihood; maintenance; mode of life; ecclesiastical benefice.—**living language,** a language still in use.—**living rock,** rock in its natural place and state.—**liv′ing-room** *n.* a sitting-room [O.E. *lif*, life].
livre (lē′vr) *n.* an old French silver coin equivalent to 20 sous or 9½d. [Fr. fr. L. *libra*, a pound].
lizard (liz′ard) *n.* an order of four-footed, scale-clad reptiles [L. *lacerta*].
llama (là′ma) *n.* a S. American two-toed ruminant, allied to the camel [Peruv.].
llano (là′nō or lyà′nō) *n.* one of the vast grassy plains of the Orinoco valley in S. America, and of Texas, in U. S.A.—*pl.* **lla′nos** [Sp. *llano*, a plain].
lo (lō) *interj.* look! behold! [O.E. *lā*, (imit.)].
loach (lōch) a small river-fish [Fr. *loche*].
load (lōd) *n.* a burden; the amount normally carried at one time; any heavy weight; a cargo; 40 cubic feet of unhewn timber; (*Elect.*) amount of electrical energy drawn from a source; (*Fig.*) burden of anxiety;—*pl.* (*Colloq.*) plenty; heaps;—*v.t.* to burden; to put on, for conveyance; to freight; to overweight; to overwhelm (with gifts, adulation, etc.); to charge (a gun); to adulterate (as wine); to weight with lead (as a cane); to insert a spool into (as a camera);—*v.i.* to take on a load or cargo; to charge a firearm; to become loaded.—**load′ed** *a.* weighted; (*Slang*) drunk.—**load′ing** *n.* the act of loading; a freight; any substance, as size, which gives body to a fabric.—**load′line** *n.* a line painted on the side of a vessel to indicate maximum immersion when loaded (*Plimsoll mark*).—**load′shed′ding** *n.* (*Electricity*) discarding part of the load.—**load′stone** *n.* See **lode′stone** [O.E. *lad*].
loaf (lōf) *n.* shaped portion of dough baked in the oven; a lump of sugar shaped like a cube, or a conical mass of sugar;—*pl.* **loaves.**—**meat′loaf** *n.* meat shape cooked in a loaf-tin [O.E. *hlaf*, a loaf].
loaf (lōf) *v.i.* to spend (time) idly; to lounge.—**loaf′er** *n.* [etym. uncertain].
loam (lōm) *n.* a rich, fertile soil of clay, sand, oxide of iron, and carbonate of lime; a mixture of clay, sand, and chopped straw used in brick-making [O.E. *lam*, clay].
loan (lōn) *n.* the act of lending; that which is lent, esp. money for interest;—*v.t.* (chiefly *U. S.* usage) to lend.—**loan′ee, loan′er** *n.*—**loan′off′ice** *n.* a pawnbroker's office; a money-lender's premises [O.N. *lan*, loan].
loath, loth (lōth) *a.* unwilling; reluctant; disinclined.—**loath′ness** *n.* [O.E. *lath*, hateful].
loathe (lōTH) *v.t.* to detest; to abominate; to be nauseated by —**loath′ing** *n.* disgust; repulsion.—**loath′ly** *adv.*—**loath′some** *a.* detestable; repugnant.—**loath′somely** *adv.*—**loath′someness** *n.* [O.E. *lath*, hateful].
lob (lob) *n.* a dull, clumsy fellow; anything thick and heavy; (*Cricket*) a slow underhand ball; (*Tennis*) a ball rising high in air over opponent's head;—*v.t.* to let fall heavily; to bowl underhand; to hit (tennis ball, shuttlecock) high into the air;—*v.i.* to deliver a lob; to walk clumsily.—*pr.p.* **lob′bing.**—*pa.p.* **lobbed.**—**lobs′pound** *n.* a prison.—**lob′worm** *n.* a large earthworm used as bait [Scand. *lobbe*, a lump of fat].
lobby (lob′i) *n.* a narrow passage, or hall, forming the entrance to a public building or private dwelling; a waiting-room; hall of House of Commons where M.P.'s may meet their constituents.—**division lobby,** corridor in House of Commons to which members retire to vote on a division.—**lobb′ying** *n.* the frequenting of the lobby to collect Parliamentary news, or to influence voting [L.L. *lobia*, a portico].
lobe (lōb) *n.* a rounded division of an organ; the lower, fleshy, rounded part of human ear; a division of the lung; (*Bot.*) rounded division of a leaf.—**lob′ar** *a.*—**lob′ate, lobed, lob′ose** *a.* consisting of lobes.—*pl.* **lob′uli** [Gk. *lobos*, the lobe of the ear].
Lobelia (lob-ē′li-a) *n.* a genus of herbaceous plants (including the blue dwarf variety) [fr. *Lobel*, botanist to James I].
lobster (lob′ster) *n.* an edible, marine, long-tailed crustacean, with pincer-claws.—**lobster pot,** wicker basket in which lobsters are trapped [corrupt. of L. *locusta*, a lobster].
local (lō′kal) *a.* pert. to a particular place; confined to a definite spot, district, or part of the body; circumscribed;—*n.* some person or thing belonging to a district; a suburban train.—**lo′cal, lo′cale** *n.* the scene of an occurrence; the scene of a film-shot.—**localisa′tion** *n.* the act of localising.—**lo′calise** *v.t.* to assign to a definite place; to decentralise; to cordon off.—**local′ity** *n.* position of a thing; site; neighbourhood.—**lo′cally** *adv.*—**locate′** *v.t.* to set in a particular place; to find the exact position of.—**loca′tion** *n.* act of locating; situation; geographical position; the out-of-doors site of a film production.—**loc′ative** *a.* pert. to a location.—*n.* (*Gram.*) the case form denoting the 'place where.'—**local anaesthetic,** an anaesthetic injected to produce insensibility in one

part of the body only.—**local government,** administration by local bodies of county or town affairs.—**local time,** time calculated from the sun.—**the local** (*Colloq.*) a public-house; the village inn [L. *locus*, a place].

loch (loH) *n.* a lake, esp. in Scotland; an arm of the sea (as Loch Fyne).—**loch'an** *n.* a small loch [Gael.].

lock (lok) *n.* a strand or tress of hair;—*pl.* hair of the head [O.E. *locc*, a tress].

lock (lok) *n.* a device for fastening a door, box, case, etc.; a mechanism on a gun released by trigger; an appliance to check the revolution of a wheel; an accidental stoppage of any mechanism; an enclosure in a canal with gate at each end for allowing vessels to pass from one level to another; the grappling hold, in wrestling; a traffic jam;—*v.t.* to fasten with a lock and key; to furnish with locks, as a canal; to hold tightly;—*v.i.* to become fast; to jam.—**lock'er** *n.* a drawer or small cupboard where valuables may be kept.—**lock'et** *n.* a small case, containing portrait, lock of hair, and worn on a chain.—**lock'fast** *a.* securely fastened.—**lock'gate** *n.* a sluice-gate on a canal.—**lock'jaw** *n.* a spasmodic contraction of the muscles of the jaw; tetanus.—**lock'nut** *n.* a second nut screwed on top of the first nut to prevent loosening.—**lock'out** *n.* a refusal by an employer to admit employees into his works, until a trade dispute has been amicably settled.—**lock'smith** *n.* one who makes and repairs locks.—**lock'stitch** *n.* a stitch by which two threads are locked together.—**lock'up** *n.* a prison [O.E. *loc*, a fastening].

locomotion (lō-kō-mō'shun) *n.* the act or process of moving from place to place.—**locomo'tive** *a.* capable of moving from one place to another;—*n.* an engine which moves by its own power, as a railway engine.—**locomotiv'ity** *n.*—**locomo'tor** *n.* person or thing with power to move;—*a.* pert. to locomotion.—**locomo'tory** *a.* [L. *locus*, a place; *movere, motum*, to move].

locus (lō'kus) *n.* the exact position of anything; (*Math.*) the path traced out by a point moving in accordance with some mathematical law;—*pl.* **loci** (lō'sī).—**locus classicus,** the most authoritative passage illustrating a certain subject [L. *locus*, a place].

locust (lō'kust) *n.* a winged insect, allied to the grasshopper and found in N. Africa and Asia.—**lo'cust-tree,** *n.* the false acacia; the carob [L. *locusta*].

locution (lo-kū'shun) *n.* speech; mode or style of speaking [L. *loqui*, to speak].

lode (lōd) *n.* a metallic vein; a water-course; an open drain.—**lode'star, load'star** *n.* a star by which one steers, esp, the Pole-star.—**lode'stone, load'stone** *n.* a metal which attracts other metals [O.E. *lad*, a course].

lodge (loj) *n.* a small country-house; a cottage at the entrance to an estate; a porter's room in a college; a branch of a society, as of Freemasons, or the building where such a society meets;—*v.i.* to dwell in temporarily; to reside; to become embedded in;—*v.t.* to deposit for preservation; to infix; to lay flat; to harbour; to put (as money) in a bank; to allege, as an accusation.—*pr.p.* **lodg'ing.**—*pa.p.* **lodged.**—**lodg(e)'ment** *n.* lodgings; accumulation of something deposited; (*Mil.*) occupation of a position by a besieging party.—**lodg'er** *n.* one who occupies rooms at weekly rent.—**lodg'ing(s)** *n.* room(s) let temporarily at weekly rent [O.Fr. *loge*, an apartment].

loft (loft) *n.* an upper room; an attic in space between top story and roof; the gallery in a church, as the *organ-loft*;—*v.t.* (*Golf*) to strike a ball high.—**loft'ily** *adv.*—**loft'iness** *n.*—**loft'y** *a.* elevated; towering; haughty [Scand. *lopt*, air].

log (log) *n.* a roughly hewn piece of timber; an apparatus to measure the speed of a ship; the tabulated record of a ship's speed; a log-book;—*a.* made of logs;—*v.t.* to fell and trim trees; to clear woodland; to keep a record of; to fine.—*pr.p.* **log'ging.**—*pa.p.* **logged.**—**log'book** *n.* a daily record of events on a ship's voyage.—**log'cab'in** *n.* a hut made of lopped tree trunks.—**log'ger** *n.* a lumberjack.—**log'ging** *n.* lumbering.—**log'line** *n.* a line marked off in knots and fastened to a log for estimating ship's speed.—**log'roll'ing** *n.* the act of clearing logs, esp. from a neighbour's land, hence mutual help esp. in politics.—**to heave the log,** to keep a record of a ship's course by means of a log[M.E. *logge*, a log].

loganberry (lō'gan-ber-i) *n.* a shrub, a cross between raspberry and blackberry [hybridised by Judge *Logan*, 1881].

logarithm (log'ạ-rithm) *n.* the index of the power to which a fixed number or base must be raised to produce the number; a method of reducing arithmetical calculations to a minimum by substituting addition and subtraction for multiplication and division.—**logarith'metic(al), logarith'mic(al)** *a.*—**logarith'mically** *adv.* [Gk. *logos*, ratio; *arithmos*, a number].

loggerhead (log'ẹr-hed) *n.* a blockhead; a dunce; a kind of turtle.—**at loggerheads,** quarrelling; at cross-purposes [fr. *log* and *head*].

loggia (lōj'a or loj'ya) *n.* a kind of open, elevated gallery with pillars, common in Italian buildings.—*pl.* **loggie** (lōj'ā).—**loggias** (lōj'yas) [Cf. **lodge**].

logic (loj'ik) *n.* the science of reasoning; the science of pure and formal thought; (*Colloq.*) commonsense.—**log'ical** *a.* pert. to formal thought; skilled in logic; deducible.—**logical'ity, log'icalness** *n.*—**log'ically** *adv.*—**logic'ian** *n.* one skilled in logic.—**to chop logic,** to argue pedantically [Gk. *logos*, speech].

logistic, -al (loj-is'tik, -ạl) *a.* expert in calculating.—**logis'tics** *n.pl.* (used as *sing.*) the art of calculating; (*Mil.*) branch of military science which deals with the moving of and providing for troops [Gk. *logizesthai*, to compute].

logogram (log'ō-gram) *n.* a symbol representing a whole word or phrase, as £ = pound; a puzzle based on an anagram [Gk. *logos*, a word; *gramma*, a letter].

logographer (lo-gog'rạ-fẹr) *n.* a speech-writer in ancient Greek times.—**logog'raphy** *n.* a method of printing in which words cast in a single type are used instead of single letters [Gk. *logos*, a word; *graphein*, to write].

loin (loin) *n.* part of animal or man above hips and on either side of spinal column; ribs of a sheep;—*pl.* lower part of back.—**loin'cloth** *n.* a strip of cloth worn round the loins [L. *lumbus*, loin].

loiter (loi'tẹr) *v.i.* to linger; to be slow in moving; to spend time idly.—**loi'terer** *n.*—**loi'teringly** *adv.* [Dut. *leuteren*, to delay].

loll (lol) *v.i.* to lounge about lazily; to hang out, as the tongue;—*v.t.* to thrust out, as the tongue [Scand. *lolla*, to be lazy].

Lollard (lol'ạrd) *n.* one of the followers of John Wycliffe in England in 14th and 15th cents.—**Loll'ardism** *n.* the doctrines preached by John Wycliffe. Also **Loll'ardry** [Dut. *lollen*, to mumble].

lolly (lol'i) *n.* a lump.—**lolly'pop, loll'ipop** *n.* a sweetmeat; a lump of fruit-flavoured toffee on a stick (etym. doubtful].

Londoner (lun'dun-ẹr) *n.* a native or citizen of London.—**Lon'don-clay** *n.* a blue clay found in London and Hampshire basin.—**London pride** (*Bot.*) a kind of saxifrage; (also *None-so-pretty*).

lone (lōn) *a.* solitary; standing by itself.—**lone'liness, lone'ness** *n.*—**lone'ly** *a.* alone; unfrequented.—**lone'some** *a.* solitary.—**lone'somely** *adv.*—**lone'someness** *n.* [abbrev. fr. *alone*].

long (long) *a.* extended in distance or time; drawn out in a line; protracted; slow in coming; continued at great length;—*adv.* to a great extent; at a point of duration far distant;—*v.i.* to be filled with a yearning; to desire.—**long'ago'** *adv.* in the remote past.

long′boat *n.* the largest boat carried by a sailing ship.—**long′bow** *n.* a bow drawn by hand—so called to distinguish it from the *Cross*-bow.—**long′drawn** *a.* protracted.—**longeron** (lon′jer-on) *n.* (*Aero.*) a main longitudinal strength member of a fuselage or nacelle.—**longevity** (long-jev′i-ti) *n.* uncommonly prolonged duration of life.—**longe′val, longe′vous** *a.* long-lived.—**long′hand** *n.* ordinary handwriting (opp. *shorthand*).—**long′head′ed** *a.* farseeing; prudent.—**long′hund′red** *n.* a hundred and twenty.—**long′ing** *n.* a yearning; a craving.—**long′ingly** *adv.*—**long′ish** *a.* rather long.—**longitude** (lon′ji-tūd) *n.* angular distance east or west of a given meridian, measured in degrees; (*Astron.*) angular distance from vernal equinox on the ecliptic.—**longitud′inal** *a.* pert. to length or longitude; lengthwise;—*n.* a girder running lengthwise in a ship or airship.—**longitud′inally** *adv.*—**long′mea′sure** *n.* linear measure.—**long′range** *a.* having the power to fire a great distance, as a gun; able to fly or sail great distances without refuelling, as aircraft, submarine, etc.—**long′shanks** *n.* a long-legged plover.—**long′shore** *a.* existing or employed on the shore.—**long′shoreman** *n.* a dock-labourer; one employed *along* the shore. **long′sight′edness** *n.* (*Med.*) hypermetropia, an abnormal eye condition whereby the rays of light are focused *beyond* and not *on* the retina.—**long′some** *a.* wearisome.—**long′spun** *a.* tedious.—**long′stand′ing** *a.* having existed for some time.—**long′suff′ering** *a.* patiently enduring.—**long′ueur** *n.* tediousness.—**long′wind′ed** *a.* able to run a great distance without becoming short of breath; tedious; loquacious.—**long′wise, long′ways** *a.* lengthwise.—**before long**, soon [O.E. *lang*, long].

loo (lòò) *n.* a card-game;—*v.t.* to win in a game of loo [abbrev. fr. *lanterloo*].

loofa, loofah (lòò′fa) *n.* the fibrous interior of a plant of the gourd type, used as a flesh-brush [Ar. *lufah*].

look (lòòk) *v.i.* to turn one's eyes upon; to seem to be; to consider; to suggest; to face, as a dwelling;—*v.t.* to express by a look;—*n.* the act of directing one's gaze upon; facial expression generally; aspect; view;—**look′er** *n.* one who looks.—**look′er-on** *n.* a spectator.—**look′ing** *n.* a search.—**look′ing-glass** *n.* a mirror.—**look′out** *n.* vigilance; a place from which a careful watch is kept; person stationed to keep watch.—**to look after**, to tend.—**look up to**, to admire.—**to have a look-in**, to be successful.—**to look in**, in television, to receive pictures by television. [O.E. *locian*, to look].

loom (lòòm) *n.* a machine for weaving cloth from thread by interlacing threads called the *woof* through threads called the *warp*; part of the shaft of an oar inside the rowlock [O.E. *geloma*, a tool].

loom (lòòm) *v.i.* to emerge indistinctly and larger than the real dimensions; to appear over the horizon; to menace; (*Fig.*) to assume great importance [etym. doubtful].

loom (lòòm) *n.* a kind of guillemot; a puffin; the ember-goose. Also **loon** [Scand. *lomr*, a sea-bird].

loon (lòòn) *n.* a rogue; a rascal; (*Scot.*) a lad [Dut. *loen*, a stupid fellow].

loony (lòòn′i) *a.* (*Colloq.*) a crazy person [fr. *lunatic*].

loop (lòòp) *n.* a doubling of string or rope, through which another string may run; ornamental fastening; (*Aero.*) an aerial manoeuvre in which plane describes a complete circle;—*v.t.* to fasten by a loop.—**looped** *a.* coiled, as a rope; folded double; knotted.—**loop′line** *n.* a branch railway which leaves and later rejoins main-line [prob. Ir. *lub*, a bend].

loop (lòòp) *n.* a narrow slit or opening in the walls of a fortification; (*Fig.*) a way out of a difficult situation. Also **loop′hole, loop′holed** *a.* [prob. cogn. M. Dut. *lupen*, to peer].

loose (lòòs) *v.t.* to free from constraint; to untie; to disconnect; to relax; to discharge; to absolve;—*v.i.* to set sail;—*a.* free; slack; unsewed; unbound; flowing; diffuse; incoherent; careless; inaccurate; lax; inclined to diarrhoea.—**loose′box** *n.* a stable where horse is free to move about.—**loose′coup′ling** *n.* (*Elect.*) inductive coupling in which the mutual inductance is small compared with the self inductance.—**loose′ly** *adv.*—**loos′en** *v.t.* to make loose; to unscrew, as a lid;—*v.i.* to become loose; to become relaxed.—**loos′ener** *n.* (*Med.*) a medicine which loosens the bowels.—**loose′ness** *n.*—**loose′tongued** *a.* prating; indiscreet.—**to be at a loose end**, to have nothing particular to do.—**to break loose**, to escape from confinement [O.E. *leas*, loose].

loosestrife (lòòs′strīf) *n.* kinds of herbaceous plants with purple or yellow flowers [Gk. *lusimacheia*, fr. proper name *Lusimachos*, fr. *luein*, loose; *machē*, battle].

loot (lòòt) *n.* plunder; the act of plundering;—*v.t.* and *v.i.* to plunder; to appropriate illegally as contents of a bombed house [Sans. *lut*, booty].

lop (lop) *v.t.* to cut off, esp. top of anything; to cut away superfluous parts.—*n.* twigs cut off from tree; act of lopping.—**lop′per** *n.*—**lop′ping** *n.* [Dut. *lubben*, to cut].

lop (lop) *v.i.* to hang down loosely.—**lop′eared** *a.* having drooping ears.—**lop′sid′ed** *a.* heavier on one side than the other; askew [prob. imit.].

lope (lōp) *v.i.* to run with a long, leisurely gait (as a mule);—*n.* an easy gait, like a canter [O.N. *hlaupa*, to leap].

loquacious (lō-kwā′shus) *a.* talkative; babbling; garrulous.—**loqua′ciously** *adv.*—**loqua′ciousness, loquac′ity** *n.* talkativeness [L. *loquax*, talkative].

loquat (lō′kwat) *n.* a low-growing Japanese plum-tree; the fruit itself [Chinese].

loran (lō′ran) *n.* (*Flying*) a navigational device which locates the position of an aeroplane [A corruption of long + range + navigation].

lorcha (lor′cha) *n.* a light, Chinese sailing-vessel, of European build, rigged as a junk [prob. Malay].

lord (lord) *n.* a master; a ruler; a king; a husband; a proprietor of a manor; any peer of the realm; courtesy title of the son of a duke or marquis, and the eldest son of an earl; the holder of certain high government offices, as Chancellor, or of judicial importance, as Chief Justice, and of municipal offices as Mayor, Provost, etc.; a form of address accorded to bishops, esp. if members of the House of Lords; the Supreme Being; Jehovah; God; Christ;—*v.i.* to play the lord; to domineer.—**lord′liness** *n.*—**lord′ling** *n.* a petty or unimportant lord.—**lord′ly** *a.* pert. to, or like, a lord; imperious; proud; magnificent.—**lord′ship** *n.* the state of being a lord; authority; estate owned by a lord; (with *his, your*) a formal mode of address in speaking to a *lord, bishop, provost*, etc.—**lords and ladies**, a popular name for the wild arum lily.—**Lord's Day**, Sunday.—**Lord's Supper**, the sacrament of communion.—**Lord Chancellor**, the president of the House of Lords, and Keeper of the Great Seal.—**Lord-Lieutenant**, the head of the magistrates of a county.—**House of Lords**, the upper house in the two-house British Parliament [O.E. *hlaford*, the keeper of the bread].

lore (lōr) *n.* learning; erudition; traditional knowledge [O.E. *lar*, lore].

lorgnette (lorn-yet′) *n.* a pair of eye-glasses attached to a long handle; an opera-glass [Fr. *lorgner*, to stare at].

lorica (lo-rī′ka) *n.* a cuirass; (*Zool.*) a protective covering of bony plates, scales, etc., like a cuirass.—**lor′icate** *v.t.* to clothe in mail; to cover with a coating or crust, as a chemical vessel for resisting fire;—*a.* (*Zool.*) having protective covering of bony plates, as crocodiles [L. *lorica*, a breastplate].

loriner (lor′i-ner) *n.* a maker of bridles, bits

and stirrups. Also **lor'imer** [O.Fr. *lorain*, a harness strap].

lorn (lorn) *a.* lost; forsaken; desolate [O.E. *loren, pa.p.* of *leosan*, to lose].

lorry (lor'i) *n.* a waggon for transporting heavy loads [etym. doubtful].

lose (lòòz) *v.t.* to be deprived of; to mislay; to forfeit; to fail to win; to miss; to waste, as time; to destroy;—*v.i.* to fail; to suffer loss; to become bewildered.—*pr.p.* **los'ing.**—*pa.t.* and *pa.p.* **lost.**—**los'able** *a.*—**los'er** *n.* one who or that which loses.—**los'ing** *a.* producing loss. —**loss** *n.* the act of losing; defeat; diminution; bereavement; harm; waste by escape or leakage; number of casualties suffered in war.—**lost** *a.* mislaid; bewildered; bereft; squandered; damned.—**at a loss,** uncertain [O.E. *leosan*, to lose].

lot (lot) *n.* what happens by chance; destiny; object used to determine something by chance; the choice thus determined; a separate part; a large number, esp. of articles at an auction sale; (*Cinema*) the area covered by film studio and its subsidiary buildings;—*v.t.* to allot; to separate into lots.—**lot'tery** *n.* a scheme by which prizes are given to people, not on merit, but by drawing lots.—**a job-lot,** a miscellaneous collection of articles, sold as one item, as at an auction sale [O.E. *hlot*, a share].

loth (lōth) *a.* Same as **loath.**

Lothario (lō-thar'i-ō) *n.* libertine, rake [fr. *Lothario*, in Rowe's *The Fair Penitent*].

lotion (lō'shun) *n.* a fluid with healing, antiseptic properties esp. for skin affections [L. *lavare, lotum*, to wash].

lotto (lot'ō) *n.* a game of chance [fr. *lot*].

lotus (lō'tus) *n.* the Egyptian water-lily; a genus of plants including the British bird's-foot trefoil; a N. African shrub, the fruit of which was reputed, in Greek legend, to induce in those who consumed it an overpowering lethargy. Also **lote, lo'tos.**—**Lotopha'gi, Lo'tus-eat'ers** *n.pl.* (*Fig.*) one who gives up an active life for one of slothful ease [Gk. *lōtos*].

loud (loud) *a.* making a great sound; noisy; flashy; obtrusive; vulgar.—**loud, loud'ly** *adv.*—**loud'ness** *n.*—**loud'speak'er** *n.* (*Radio*) kind of telephone receiver rendering received signals audible at a distance [O.E. *hlud*, loud].

lough (loH) *n.* a lake or arm of the sea.—the Irish form of **loch** [Anglo-Ir.].

louis (lòò'i) *n.* an obsolete French gold coin worth 20 francs. Also **louis d'or.**—**louis quatorze, quinze, seize,** applied to architecture, furniture, style of interior decoration characteristic of the reigns of the French Kings Louis XIV, XV, XVI [Fr.].

lounge (lounj) *v.i.* to recline at ease; to loll; to spend time idly;—*n.* the act of lounging; a room in which people may relax; a kind of sofa.—**loung'er** *n.*—**lounge'suit** *n.* a man's jacket-suit for day-time wear [etym. doubtful].

lour, lower (lour) *v.i.* to frown; to look gloomy, or threatening, as the sky;—*n.* a scowl; sullenness.—**low'ering** *a.*—**low'eringly** *adv.* [M.E. *louren*, to frown].

louse (lous) *n.* a small wingless parasitic insect infesting hair and skin of human beings; a sucking parasite found on mammals.—*pl.* **lice.**—**lous'ily** *adv.*—**lous'iness** *n.*—**lous'y** *a.* infested with lice; (*Slang*) mean; despicable [O.E. *lus*, a louse].

lout (lout) *n.* a clumsy fellow; a bumpkin;—*v.i.* to bend.—**lout'ish** *a.* awkward; clownish. —**lout'ishly** *adv.* [etym. uncertain].

louvre (lòò'vr) *n.* an opening in the roof of ancient buildings for the escape of smoke or for ventilation; a slot for ventilation in a motor-car.—**lou'vre-win'dow** *n.* a window partially closed by outward sloping boards [O.Fr. *louvert* for *l'ouvert*, the open space].

love (luv) *n.* affection; strong liking; goodwill; benevolence; charity; devoted attachment to one of the opposite sex; passion; the object of affection; the personification of love, *Cupid*; (*Tennis*) no score;—*v.t.* to show affection for; to be delighted with; to admire passionately; —*v.i.* to be in love; to delight.—**lov'able** *a.* worthy of affection; engaging.—**lov'ableness** *n.* —**love'affair'** *n.* passionate attachment between two members of the opposite sex.—**love'ap'ple** *n.* the tomato.—**love'bird** *n.* a small parrot with bright-coloured plumage.—**love'charm** *n.* a philtre.—**love'child** *n.* an illegitimate child. —**love'feast** *n.* a religious festival among the early Christians during which collections were made for the poor.—**love'in-a-mist** *n.* fennel.—**love'in-i'dleness** *n.* the pansy.—**love'knot** *n.* a bow of ribbon tied in a special way, as a token of love.—**love'less** *a.* lacking love; not founded on love.—**love'lett'er** *n.* a letter written to a sweetheart.—**love'lies-bleed'ing** *n.* a garden-flower with reddish-purple spike-flowers.—**love'lily** *adv.*—**love'liness** *n.*—**love'lock** *n.* a curl worn on the forehead or over the temple.—**love'lorn** *a.* forsaken.—**love'ly** *a.* very beautiful; —**love'mak'ing** *n.* courtship.—**love'match** *n.* a marriage founded on true love.—**love'phil'tre** or **-pot'ion** *n.* a drink supposed to induce the emotion of love towards a chosen person.—**lov'er** *n.* one who loves, esp. one of the opposite sex; an admirer, as of the arts.—**lov'erlike** *a.*—**lov'erly** *adv.* like a lover.—**love'sick** *a.* pining because of love.—**love'some** *a.* lovely.—**love'song** *n.* lyric inspired by love.—**love'sto'ry** *n.* a novel or short story with love as its theme.—**love'tok'en** *n.* an object, as a ring, given as a symbol of love.—**lov'ing** *a.* affectionate; loyal—**lov'ing-cup** *n.* large drinking-vessel with two handles, passed round at a banquet.—**lov'ingly** *adv.*—**lov'ingness** *n.* [O.E. *lufu*, love].

low (lō) *a.* not high; lying near the ground; depressed below the adjacent surface; near the horizon; shallow; not loud, as a voice; moderate, as prices; detected; lewd; weak; cold, as a temperature; humble; (of dress) décolleté;—*adv.* not high; in a low voice; cheaply.—**low'brow** *n.* non-intellectual person. —**Low Church,** the evangelical sect of the English Church as opp. to *High Church.*—**Low Countries,** the Netherlands.—**low'down** *a.* mean; underhand;—*n.* (*U.S.*) full information.—**low'er** *v.t.* to cause to descend; to take down; to humble; to diminish resistance; to make cheap; to reduce pitch;—*a.* (*compar.* of *low*) less exalted.—**low'ermost** *a.* lowest.—**Low German,** the language of the inhabitants of N. Germany.—**low'land** *n.* country which is relatively flat in comparison with surrounding hilly district.—**low'lander** *n.* an inhabitant of flat land, esp, in Scotland.—**low'life** *n.* life of peasant or humble classes.—**low'liness** *n.*—**low'ly** *a.* humble; meek.—**low'press'ure,** having only a small expansive force (less than 50 lbs. to the square inch) said of steam and steam engines.—**low relief,** bas-relief, a form of architectural decoration.—**low'spir'ited** *a.* dejected [O.N. *lagr*, low].

low (lō) *v.i.* to bellow as an ox or cow;—*n.* the noise made [O.E. *hlowan*, to low].

loyal (loi'al) *a.* faithful to the lawful government, the sovereign, a cause, or a friend.—**loy'alist** *n.* a faithful follower of a cause.—**loy'ally** *adv.*—**loy'alty** *n.* fidelity [Fr. fr. L. *lex*, a law].

lozenge (loz'enj) *n.* a figure with two acute and two obtuse angles; small (medicated) sweetmeat orig. lozenge-shaped [etym. doubtful].

lubber (lub'er) *n.* a heavy, clumsy fellow. Also, **lubb'ard.**—**lubb'erly** *a.*—**lubb'erliness** *n.*

lubricate (lòò'bri-kāt) *v.t.* to make smooth or slippery; to smear with oil, grease, etc., to reduce friction; (*Fig.*) to bribe.—**lub'ric, -al** *a.* —**lub'ricant** *n.* any oily substance used to reduce friction;—*a.* having the property of reducing friction.—**lubrica'tion** *n.*—**lub'ricative** *a.*—**lub'ricator** *n.*—**lubric'ity** *n.* slipperiness; lewdness [L. *lubricare*, to make slippery].

luce (lóós) *n.* a fresh-water fish, the pike when full grown [O.Fr. *lus*, a pike].
lucent (lóó'sent) *a.* shining; bright.—**lu'cency** *n.*—**lucer'nal** *a.* pert. to a lamp [L. *lucere*, to shine].
lucerne (lóó'sẹrn) *n.* alfalfa; a plant much used for animal fodder [etym. doubtful].
lucid (lóó'sid) *a.* shining; clear; easily understood, as of style; normally sane.—**lucid'ity, lu'cidness** *n.* the state of being clear or intelligible.—**lu'cidly** *adv.* [L. *lux*, light].
Lucifer (lóó'si-fẹr) *n.* the planet Venus, when appearing as the morning star; Satan.—**lu'cifer** *n.* a match easily ignited by friction [L. *lucifer*, light-bearing].
luck (luk) *n.* accidental fortune, good or bad; fate; chance.—**luck'ily** *adv.*—**luck'iness** *n.*—**luck'less** *n.* unfortunate.—**luck'lessly** *adv.*—**luck'lessness** *n.*—**luck'y** *a.* fortunate; fortuitous.—**luck'y-bag** *n.* a receptacle containing assorted articles which one chooses from, by dipping into the bag. Also **lucky dip** [Dut. *luk*, fate].
lucre (lóó'kẹr) *n.* material gain; profit, esp. ill-gotten; advantage.—**lu'crative** *a.* profitable.—**lu'cratively** *adv.*—**filthy lucre** (*Slang*) money [L. *lucrum*, gain].
lucubrate (lóó'kū-brāt) *v.i.* to study by lamp or candlelight, or at night.—**lucubra'tion** *n.* nocturnal study; the product of such study.—**lu'cubrator** *n.*—**lu'cubratory** *a.* [L. *lucubrare*, to work by candlelight].
luculent (lóó'kū-lent) *a.* clear; self-evident.—**lu'culently** *adv.* (L. *lux*, light].
Luddite (lud'īt) *n.* one of the secret organisations of rioters in England (1811-16). From *Ned Ludd*, who smashed two stocking-frames in a house in Nottingham.
ludicrous (lóó'di-krus) *a.* provoking laughter; ridiculous; droll.—**lu'dicrously** *adv.*—**lu'dicrousness** *n.* [L. *ludus*, sport].
ludo (lóó'dō) *n.* children's game played with counters and dice [L. *ludere*, to play].
luff (luf) *v.i.* to turn the head of a ship towards the wind; to sail nearer the wind;—*n.* the windward side of a ship [M.E. *lof*, a paddle].
luffa (luff'a) *n.* See **loofa.**
Luftlag (lóóft'lag) *n.* prisoner-of-war camp in Germany for R.A.F. personnel [Ger. *Luft*, air; *Lager*, camp].
Luftwaffe (lóóft'vȧ-fẹ) *n.* the German Air Force [Ger. *Luft*, the air; *Waffe*, a weapon].
lug (lug) *v.t.* to pull with force; to tug; to haul; to drag.—*pr.p.* **lug'ging.**—*pa.t.* and *pa.p.* **lugged.**—**lug'gage** *n.* a traveller's trunks, baggage, etc.—**lug'ger** *n.* a small vessel with lugsails.—**lug'sail** *n.* a square sail bent upon a yard which hangs obliquely to the mast. [Scand. *lugga*, to pull the hair].
lug (lug) *n.* (*Scot.*) the ear; anything resembling an ear [Scand. *lugga*, a forelock].
lugubrious (lóó-gū'bri-us) *a.* mournful; woeful; dismal.—**lugu'briously** *adv.*—**lugu'briousness** *n.* [L. *lugere*, to mourn].
lukewarm (lóók'wawrm) *a.* moderately warm; tepid. Also **luke.**—**luke'warmly** *adv.*—**luke'warmness** *n.* [M.E. *leuk*, tepid; *warm*].
lull (lul) *v.t.* to soothe to sleep; to quieten;—*v.i.* to become quiet gradually;—*n.* a period of quiet in storm or noise.—**lull'aby** *n.* a song sung to a child to soothe it to sleep [Scand. *lulla*, to sing to sleep].
lum (lum) *n.* a ventilating chimney in a mine; (*Scot.*) a chimney [Scot.]
lumbago (lum-bā'gō) *n.* a painful rheumatic affection of the lumbar muscles.—**lumbag'inous, lum'bar, lum'bal** *a.* pert. to the lower part of the back [L. *lumbus*, the loin].
lumber (lum'bẹr) *n.* anything useless and cumbersome; odds and ends hoarded; timber cut and split for market;—*v.t.* to heap in disorder.—**lum'berer** *n.* feller of timber. Also **lum'berjack, lum'berman.**—**lum'bering** *n.* [fr. *Lombard*, a pawnbroker's shop].
lumber (lum'bẹr) *v.i.* to move heavily.—**lum'berer** *n.*—**lum'bering** *a.* [Scand. *lomra*, to resound].
luminary (lóóm'in-ạr-i) *n.* any body which gives light, esp. one of the heavenly bodies; (*Fig.*) a person of outstanding qualities.—**lu'minant** *a.* giving out light.—**lumina'tion** *n.*—**lumines'cence** *n.* the quality of being luminescent; phospherescence.—**lumines'cent** *a.*—**lumenif'erous** *a.* yielding light.—**lu'minous** *a.* shining; brilliant; glowing; (*Fig.*) lucid; comprehensible.—**lu'minously** *adv.*—**lu'minousness, luminos'ity** *n.* [L. *lumen*, a light].
lump (lump) *n.* a small mass of matter of indefinite shape; a swelling; the gross; (*Colloq.*) a stupid, clumsy person;—*v.t.* to throw into a mass; to take in the gross.—**lump'y** *a.* full of lumps; uneven.—**in the lump,** taken as an aggregate [Scand. *lump*, a block].
lunar (lóó'nạr) *a.* pert. to the moon; measured by revolutions of the moon. Also **lu'nary.**—**lu'nacy** *n.* madness, formerly supposed to be influenced by changes of moon.—**lu'natic** *a.* insane;—*n.* a mad person.—**luna'tion** *n.* the period from one new moon to the next.—**lunar month,** period of the moon's revolution, about 29½ days.—**lunar year,** period of twelve synodic lunar months (354⅓ days [L. *luna*, the moon].
lunch (lunsh) *n.* a light meal taken between breakfast and dinner. Also **lunch'eon.**—*v.i.* to take lunch.—**lunch'er** *n.* [dial. *lunsh*, a lump].
lune (lóón) *n.* anything in the shape of a half-moon.—**lunette'** *n.* a crescent-shaped opening in a vault to let in light; a watch-glass with flattened centre; a detached bastion [L. *luna*, the moon].
lung (lung) *n.* one of the two main organs of respiration in a breathing animal.—**lunged** *a.* [O.E. *lungen*, lungs].
lunge (lunj) *n.* in fencing, a sudden thrust;—*v.i.* to thrust [Fr. *allonger*, to stretch].
lupin, lupine (lóó'pin) *n.* a genus of leguminous plants, some cultivated for their spikes of flowers, others for cattle-fodder and manure [L. *lupinus*, pert. to a wolf].
lupine (lóó'pīn) *a.* like a wolf; ravenous [L. *lupinus*, pert. to a wolf].
lupus (lóó'pus) *n.* a spreading tubercular condition affecting the skin [L. *lupus*, a wolf].
lurch (lurch) *n.* a sudden roll of a ship to one side; a staggering movement;—*v.i.* to stagger.—**lurch'er** *n.* a kind of hunting-dog; a sneak-thief [etym. doubtful].
lurch (lurch) *n.* a critical move in the game of cribbage.—**to leave in the lurch,** to desert in a moment of need [Fr. *lourche*, a game].
lure (lūr) *n.* a decoy used by the falconer to recall the hawk; an artificial bait;—*v.t.* to entice; to decoy [Fr. *leurre*, a bait].
lurid (lū'rid) *a.* ghastly pale; extravagantly coloured; (*Fig.*) startling.—**lu'ridly** *adv.* [L. *luridus*, pale yellow].
lurk (lurk) *v.i.* to lie hid; to lie in wait.—**lurk'er** *n.* [Scand. *lurka*, to go slowly].
luscious (lush'us) *a.* excessively sweet; cloying.—**lusc'iously** *adv.*—**lusc'iousness** *n.* [etym. doubtful].
lush (lush) *a.* fresh; juicy [*luscious*].
lust (lust) *n.* longing desire; sexual appetite; craving;—*v.i.* to desire passionately; to have sexual appetites.—**lust'ful** *a.* having inordinate carnal desires; sensual.—**lust'fully** *adv.*—**lust'fulness** *n.*—**lust'iness** *n.*—**lust'ily** *adv.*—**lust'y** *a.* vigorous; robust [O.E. *lust*, pleasure].
lustre, lustrum (lus'tẹr, lus'trum) *n.* a period of five years.—**lus'tral** *a.* pert. to, or used in, purification.—**lustra'tion** *n.* the act of purifying; the sacrifice or ceremony by which cities, fields, armies, or people were purified [L. *lustrare*, to purify].
lustre (lus'tẹr) *n.* clearness; glitter; gloss; (*Fig.*) renown; chandelier with drops or pendants of cut glass; a cotton dress fabric with glossy, silky surface; a pottery glaze.—

lus'trous *a.* gleaming; bright.—**lus'trously** *adv.* [L. *lustrare*, to make bright].
lustrine (lus'trin) *n.* a glossy silk fabric. Also **lus'tring, lute'string** [Fr. *lustrine*].
lute (lōōt) *n.* a stringed instrument like a guitar.—**lut'anist, lut'er, lut'ist** *n.* a lute-player. —**lute'string** *n.* [O.Fr. *lut*].
lute (lōōt) *n.* a cement-like composition for making joints air-tight; a rubber ring for sealing glass jars; a bricklayer's tool for levelling and scraping off surplus mortar;—*v.t.* to seal or coat with lute.—**luta'tion** *n.* [L. *lutum*, mud].
lutecium (lōō-tē'si-um) *n.* a metallic element (symbol **Lu**), one of the rare earths group [fr. *Lutetia*, the Roman name of Paris].
lutein (lōō'te-in) *n.* the yellow colouring matter found in egg-yolk [L. *luteus*, yellow].
Lutheran (lōō'thẹr-ạn) *a.* pert. to *Luther*, the German reformer, or to his doctrines;—*n.* a follower of Martin Luther.—**Lu'theranism, Lu'therism, Lu'therist** *n.*
luthern (lōō'thẹrn) *n.* a dormer-window [etym. uncertain].
luxate (luks'āt) *v.t.* to put out of joint; to dislocate.—**luxa'tion** *n.* [L. *luxare*, to dislocate].
luxury (luk'sū-ri) *n.* indulgence in the pleasures which wealth can procure; that which is not a necessity of life.—**luxu'riance, luxu'riancy, luxuri'ety** *n.*—**luxu'riant** *a.* in great abundance; dense or prolific, as vegetation.—**luxu'riantly** *adv.*—**luxu'riate** *v.i.* to grow luxuriantly; to live luxuriously.—**luxu'rious** *a.* self-indulgent in appetite, etc.; sumptuous; enervating by indulgence.—**luxu'riously** *adv.*—**luxu'riousness** *n.* [L. *luxus*, excess].
lycanthrope (lī'kạn-thrōp) *n.* a werewolf. Also **lycan'thropist.**—**lycan'thropy** *n.* insanity, in which a person imagines himself to be a wolf.—**lycanthrop'ic, lycan'thropous** *a.* [Gk. *lukos*, a wolf; *anthrōpos*, a man].
Lyceum (lī-sē'um) *n.* orig. a gymnasium in Athens where Aristotle taught his pupils; a lecture-hall; a meeting-place for literary societies [Gk. *Lukeion*].
lych-gate See **lich-gate.**
lyddite (lid'īt) *n.* picric acid; a powerful explosive used in shells [fr. *Lydd* in Kent, where it was first made].
Lydian (lid'i-ạn) *a.* pert. to *Lydia* in Asia Minor, or to its inhabitants; voluptuous or sensuous.
lye (lī) *n.* alkaline solution of wood ashes and water; used in soap-making [O.E. *leah*].
lying (lī'ing) *a.* recumbent.—**ly'ing-in** *n.* the confinement of a pregnant woman [fr. *lie*].
lying (lī'ing) *a.* untruthful;—*n.* habit of being untruthful.—**ly'ingly** *adv.* [fr. *lie*].
lyme (līm) *n.* a dog's leash.—**lyme'hound** *n.* a bloodhound [L. *ligare*, to bind].
lymph (limf) *n.* an alkaline fluid, watery in appearance, contained in the tissues and organs of the body; a vaccine.—**lymphat'ic** *a.* pert. to lymph; sluggish.—**lymphat'ics** *n.pl.* small vessels in the body containing lymph.—**lymph'oid** *a.* like, composed of, lymph [L. *lympha*, water].
lynch (linsh) *v.t.* to inflict, esp. capital punishment without recourse to customary forms of law [fr. *Charles Lynch*, a Virginian planter (18th cent.)].
lynx (lingks) *n.* an animal of the cat tribe with abnormally keen sight.—**lynx'-eyed** *a.* keen-sighted; vigilant [Gk. *lunx*].
lyre (līr) *n.* a stringed, musical instrument in use among ancient Greeks, esp. to accompany minstrels.—**ly'rate** *a.* shaped like a lyre.—**lyre'-bird** *n.* an Australian bird with tail feathers which curve upward in the shape of a lyre.—**lyr'ic** *n.* orig. a poem sung to music; a short, subjective poem expressing emotions of poet.—**lyr'ic, -al** *a.* pert. to the lyre; suitable to be sung to a musical accompaniment; used of poetry expressing emotion.—**lyr'icism** *n.* lyrical quality of a poem; emotional expression.—**lyr'ist** *n.* [Gk. *lura*, a lyre].

M

ma'am (mȧm) *n.* contr. of **madam.**
macabre (ma-kȧ'br) *a.* gruesome; ghastly; grim; like the Dance of Death. Also **macaberesque'** [O.Fr. *macabre*].
macaco (mạ-ka'kō) *n.* a species of ring-tailed lemur of Madagascar; a Brazilian monkey [Port. *macaco*, a monkey].
macadam (ma-kad'am) *n.* a road-surface material of crushed stones.—**macad'amise** *v.t.* [fr. J. L. *MacAdam*, the inventor (d. 1836)].
macaque (ma-kak') *n.* a genus of monkeys, belonging to S. Asia [Port. *macaco*, a monkey].
macaroni (mak-a-rō'ni) *n.* a paste of wheat flour made in long slender tubes; a young fop of the 18th cent.—**macaron'ic** *n.* a medley;—*a.* affected; esp. applied to burlesque verse in modern words with Latinised endings [It.].
macaroon (mak'ạ-rōōn) *n.* a small cake made of white of egg, ground almonds, sugar and flavouring [Fr. *macaron*].
Macassar-oil (mạ-kas'ar-oil) *n.* a perfumed hair oil from *Macassar* in Celebes.
macaw (mạ-kaw') *n.* a long-tailed S. American parrot [Brazil. *macao*].
mace (mās) *n.* a heavy club of metal; a staff carried as an emblem of authority; a billiard cue.—**mace'-bear'er** *n.* an official who carries the mace. Also **mac'er** [O.Fr. *mace*, a mallet].
mace (mās) *n.* a spice made from nutmeg [etym. unknown].
macerate (mas'ẹr-āt] *v.t.* to soften by soaking; (*Fig.*) to mortify the flesh.—**macera'tion** *n.* [L. *macerare*, to steep].
Mach (number) (mȧH) *n.* ratio of the air speed of an aircraft to the velocity of sound [named after Ernst *Mach*, Austrian physicist and philosopher, 1838-1916].
machete (mȧ-chā'tā) *n.* a heavy knife or cleaver used to cut down sugar-canes, and as a weapon, esp. in Cuba [Sp.].
Machiavellian (mak-i-ạ-vel'yan) *a.* pert. to Machiavelli; unscrupulous; crafty;—*n.* one who practises the perfidious political doctrine of Machiavelli; an unprincipled ruthless ruler. —**Machiavell'ianism** *n.* [fr. *Machiavelli*, the Florentine statesman (1469-1527)].
machicoulis (mȧ-shē-kōō-lē') *n.* in fortification, a loop-holed, projecting parapet, etc.—**machic'olate** *v.t.* to form with machicolations. —**machicola'tion** *n.* an opening, for pouring molten lead or hurling missiles on assailants; the act of hurling down missiles [Fr. *mâche*, mash; *coulis*, a flowing].
machinate (mak'in-āt) *v.t.* to contrive, usually with evil or ulterior motive;—*v.i.* to conspire. —**machina'tion** *n.* the act of contriving or plotting, esp. with evil intent; an intrigue.—**machina'tor** *n.* one who plots [L. *machinari*, to plot].
machine (mạ-shēn') *n.* any contrivance for the conversion and direction of motion; an engine; a vehicle; a person who acts like an automaton; a political organisation controlled for a specific purpose; a contrivance in the ancient Greek theatre to indicate to the audience a change of scene, hence the phrase *deus ex machina*;—*v.t.* to apply machinery to, esp. to sew with a machine or to print with a printing-machine.—**machine'-gun** *n.* an automatic small-arms weapon capable of continuous firing.—**machin'ery** *n.* machines collectively; the parts of a machine; any combination of means to an end.—**machine'-room** *n.* the room where printing by machine is done.—**machine'-tool** *n.* a tool for cutting, shaping and turning operated by machinery.—**machin'ist** *n.* one who makes machinery; one who works at a machine [L. *machina*, a machine].
mackerel (mak'e-rel) *n.* an edible sea-fish with blue and black stripes above and silver colour below [O.Fr. *mackerel*].

mackintosh (mak′-in-tosh) *n.* a waterproof coat [fr. *Charles MacIntosh*, the inventor.

macramé (ma-kra′-mā) *n.* fringe made of knotted thread [etym. doubtful].

macrobiotic (mak-rō-bī-ot′-ik) *a.* long-lived. —**macrobio′sis** *n.* long life. —**macro′biote** *n.* long-lived person. —**macrobio′tics** *n.* study of longevity [Gk. *makros*, long; *bios*, life].

macrocosm (mak′-rō-kozm) *n.* the great universe; (*Occult.*) God manifesting through the solar system. —**macrocos′mic** *a.* [Gk. *makros*, long; *cosmos*, the world].

macron (mak′-ron) *n.* short line put over vowel to show it is long in quantity or quality, ē—opp. of *breve*, which marks short vowel, ĕ [Gk. *makros*, long].

macroscopic (mak-rō-skop′-ik) *a.* visible to the naked eye; opp. of *microscopic*. —**macroscop′ically** *adv.* [Gk. *makros*, long; *skopein*, to see].

mactation (mak-tā′-shun) *n.* the act of killing a victim to offer as a sacrifice [L. *mactare*, to sacrifice].

macula (mak′-ū-lạ) *n.* a spot. —*pl.* **mac′ulae**. —**mac′ulate** *v.t.* to spot. —**macula′tion** *n.* the act of spotting; a spot. —**macula solaris**, a freckle. —**mac′ulose** *a.* spotted [L. *macula*].

mad (mad) *a.* (*comp.* **mad′der**; *superl.* **mad′dest**) deranged in mind; insane; crazy; frenzied; angry; infatuated; irrational, as a scheme. —**mad′cap** *n.* a rash person; a tomboy;—*a.* uncontrolled. —**mad′den** *v.t.* to enrage; to drive mad; to annoy;—*v.i.* to behave as a madman. —**mad′ding** *a.* distracted. —**mad′dingly, mad′ly** *adv.* —**mad′house** *n.* an asylum; a home for patients suffering from mental disorders. —**mad′man** *n.* a lunatic. —**mad′ness** *n.* insanity [O.E. *gemaed*, foolish].

madam (mad′ạm) *n.* a formal mode of address in speaking to a married or elderly woman; (*Colloq.*) an arrogant woman. —*pl.* **mad′ams**. —**madame** (ma-dam′) *n.* French form of Mrs. or Madam. —*pl.* **mesdames** (mā-dam′) [O.Fr. *ma dame*, my lady].

madder (mad′ẹr) *n.* a climbing plant yielding a natural red dye. —**mad′der-lake** *n.* red pigment [O.E. *maedere*, madder].

made (mād) *pa.t.* and *pa.p.* of **make**.

Madeira (mạ-dē′ra) *n.* a rich amber-coloured wine from *Madeira*. —**Madeira cake**, a kind of sponge cake, plain, without fruit [Port. fr. L. *materia*, timber].

Mademoiselle (mad-mwạ-zel′) *n.* French mode of addressing unmarried lady; governess. —*pl.* **Mesdemoiselles′** [Fr.].

Madonna (ma-don′-a) *n.* the Virgin Mary; a statue of the Virgin [It. *mia*, my; *donna*, a lady].

madrepore (mad′-rẹ-pōr) *n.* white perforate coral [It. *madre*, a mother; L. *porus*, a pore].

madrigal (mad′-ri-gạl) *n.* a short, love poem; an unaccompanied part-song, usually syncopated in rhythm, popular in 16th and 17th cents. [etym. doubtful].

maelstrom (māl′-strom) *n.* a famous whirlpool near the Lofoten Islands off the coast of Norway; any whirlpool; (*Fig.*) menacing state of affairs [Dut. = a whirlpool].

maenad (mē′-nad) *n.* a priestess of Dionysus (Bacchus); a frenzied woman [Gk. *mainas*].

maestoso (mȧ-es-tō′-sō) *a.* and *adv.* (*Mus.*) with dignity; majestic or majestically [It.].

maestro (mȧ-es′-trō) *n.* a master, esp. an eminent composer, conductor, or teacher of music. —*pl.* **maes′tri** [It.].

Mae West (mā-ouest) *n.* (*R.A.F. slang*) an inflated life-jacket [fr. *Mae West*, film star].

maffick (maf′-ik) *v.i.* to exult riotously, as on the occasion of a victory [fr. *Mafeking*, the relief of which was wildly celebrated in London in 1900].

mafia (mȧ′-fi-ạ) *n.* a Sicilian secret society; (*Fig.*) a predilection for having recourse to private justice. Also **maf′fia** [Sicilian].

magazine (mag-ạ-zēn′) *n.* a military storehouse; part of a ship where ammunition is stored; compartment in a rifle holding the cartridges; a periodical containing miscellaneous articles [Fr. *magasin*, a warehouse].

magdalene (mag′-da-lēn) *n.* a reformed prostitute; a home for such women. Also **mag′dalen** [fr. *Mary Magdalene*].

mage (māj) *n.* a magician; a wizard [Gk. *magos*, a magician].

magenta (mạ-jen′-tạ) *n.* a purplish dye-stuff from coal-tar [discovery, in year of battle of *Magenta*, 1859].

maggot (mag′-ot) *n.* a grub; larva of a house-fly; (*Fig.*) a whim. —**magg′oty** *a.* full of maggots [M.E. *maddok*, a flesh worm].

Magi (mā′-jī) *n.pl.* a class of priests among the ancient Persians; in the N.T. the Wise Men who came to visit the infant Jesus. —**Mag′ian** *a.* pert. to the Magi;—*n.* one of the Magi. [Gk. *magos*, a magician].

magic (maj′-ik) *n.* the feigned art of influencing nature or future events by occult means; sorcery; charm. —**mag′ic(al)** *a.* —**mag′ically** *adv.* —**magic′ian** *n.* one skilled in magic; a sorcerer; a conjurer. —**magic lantern**, early form of projector using slides. —**black magic**, magic by aid of evil spirits [Gk. *magikos*].

magilp (ma-gilp′) *n.* a mixture of mastic varnish and linseed oil, used with oil-paints. —Also **magilph′**, **megilp′** [prob. fr. a proper name].

magisterial (maj-is-tē′-ri-ạl) *a.* pert. to or conducted by a magistrate; authoritative; judicial; overbearing. —**magiste′rially** *adv.* [L. *magister*, a master].

magistrate (maj′-is-trāt) *n.* a person vested with public judicial authority; a justice of the peace. —**mag′istracy** *n.* the official position of a magistrate; the body of magistrates [L. *magistratus*, a high official].

Magna Carta (mag′-na kȧr′-ta) *n.* Great Charter of English public and private liberties signed by King John 1215 [L.].

magnalium (mag-nạl′-i-um) *n.* a light, easily worked alloy of aluminium and magnesium [fr. *magnesium* and *aluminium*].

magnanimity (mag-nạ-nim′-i-ti) *n.* greatness of mind; generosity of heart which exalts men above all that is base or mean. —**magnan′imous** *a.* —**magnan′imously** *adv.* [L. *magnus*, great; *animus*, the mind].

magnate (mag′-nāt) *n.* an eminent person, esp. a wealthy business man [L. *magnus*, great].

magnesium (mag-nē′-shi-um) *n.* the silvery-white metallic base of magnesia, burning with an intensely brilliant white light and used for fireworks, flash-light photography, etc. —**magne′sia** *n.* magnesium oxide, a white, alkaline substance. —**magnesian sulphate**, Epsom salts [Gk. *Magnesia* (lithos), magnesian stone].

magnet (mag′-net) *n.* the lodestone; a bar of iron having property of attracting iron, etc., and, when suspended, of pointing N. and S.; (*Fig.*) a person or thing with powers of attraction. —**magnet′ic, -al** *a.* pert. to a magnet; attractive. —**magnet′ically** *adv.* —**magnetic′ian, mag′netist** *n.* an expert in magnetism. —**magnetis′able** *a.* —**magnetisa′tion** *n.* —**mag′netise** *v.t.* to give magnetic properties to; to attract; —*v.i.* to become magnetic. —**mag′netism** *n.* the natural cause of magnetic force; the science of the phenomena of magnetic force; attraction. —**animal magnetism**, mesmerism. —**magne′to** *n.* a magneto-electric machine, esp. used to generate ignition spark in internal combustion engine. —**magnetic field**, the sphere of influence of magnetic forces. —**magnetic mine**, a submarine mine detonated by the displacement of a magnetic needle, caused by approach of a ship (its effect counteracted in *World War* 2 by *degaussing*). —**magnetic needle**, a small magnetised pivoted steel bar of a mariner's compass which always points North. —**magnetic north**, the north as indicated by the pivoted bar of the mariner's compass. —**magnetic poles**, two nearly opposite points

on the earth's surface where the dip of the needle is 90° [Gk. *magnētis* (lithos), a magnet].
magnify (mag′-ni-fī) *v.t.* to make greater; to cause to appear greater; to extol; to exaggerate.—*pa.p.* **mag′nified.**—**magnif′ic, -al,** *a.* grand; splendid.—**magnif′ically** *adv.*—**Magnif′icat** *n.* the song of the Virgin Mary (*Luke* 1,) beginning 'My soul doth magnify the Lord.'—**magnifica′tion** *n.* the act of magnifying.—**magnif′icative, magnif′icent** *a.* splendid; brilliant; ostentatious.—**magnif′icence** *n.*—**magnif′icently** *adv.*—**magnif′ico** *n.* a Venetian grandee.—**mag′nifier** *n.* one who or the instrument which magnifies [L. *magnus*, great; *facere*, to make].
magniloquent (mag-nil′-o-kwent *a.* speaking pompously; bombastic.—**magnil′oquence** *n.*—**magnil′oquently** *adv.* [L. *magnus*, great; *loqui*, to speak].
magnitude (mag′-ni-tūd) *n.* greatness; size; importance [L. *magnitudo*, greatness].
magnolia (mag-nō′-li-a) *n.* a species of N. American and Asiatic tree bearing large perfumed flowers [fr. *Magnol*, a French botanist, 1638-1715].
magnum (mag′-num) *n.* a wine-bottle holding two quarts [L. *magnus*, great].
magpie (mag′-pī) *n.* a bird of the crow family, with a harsh chattering cry; an idle chatterer; (a hit on) the outermost ring but one, of a target [contr. of *Margaret* and *pie* fr. L. *pica*, a magpie].
Magyar (mag′-yâr) *n.* dominant people of Hungary, descended from nomadic Turkish stock; the native language of Hungary.
Maharajah (ma-ha-rá′-ją) *n.* (*fem.* **Maharan′i** or **Maharan′ee**) the title of an Indian prince [Sans. *maha*, great; *raja*, a prince].
Mahatma (ma-hat′-mą) *n.* a man of saintly life with supernatural powers derived from purity of soul [Sans. *mahatma*, high-souled].
Mahdi (má′-dē) *n.* the leader and prophet of the Mohammedans whose coming is expected just prior to the end of the world; the name adopted by several Mohammedan leaders of the past [Ar. *mahdi*, the guided one].
mah-jong (má-jong′) *n.* old Chinese game for four played with small blocks [Chin.].
mahogany (mą-hog′-ąn-i) *n.* a tree of tropical America, the hard, reddish wood of which is used for furniture; the red-brown colour of mahogany [W. Ind.].
Mahomedan, Mahometan See **Mohammedan.**
mahout (mą-hout′ or mą-hòòt′) *n.* an elephant-driver or keeper [Hind.].
Mahratta (mą-rat′-a) *n.* one of a warlike race of Hindus in W. and C. India.
maid (mād) *n.* an unmarried woman; a virgin; a female domestic servant.—**maid of all work,** a general domestic servant.—**old maid,** an elderly spinster; a game of cards.—**maid′en,** *n.* a maid;—*a.* pert. to a maid; unmarried; fresh; pure; unused; first.—**maid′enhair** *n.* a kind of fern with very delicate fronds.—**maid′enhood, maid′enhead** *n.* virginity; purity; the hymen.—**maid′enliness** *n.*—**maid′enly** *a.* maiden-like.—**maiden name,** surname of a woman before marriage.—**maiden over** (*Cricket*) one in which no runs are scored.—**maiden speech,** a member's first speech esp. in Parliament.—**maiden voyage,** first ocean voyage of new ship [O.E. *maegden*, a maid].
mail (māl) *n.* defensive armour composed of steel rings or plates; armour in general;—*v.t.* to clothe in armour.—**mailed fist,** physical force [O.Fr. *maille*, mail].
mail (māl) *n.* a bag for carrying letters, etc., or its contents; the post; the person or means of conveyance for transit of letters, parcels, etc.;—*v.t.* to post; to send by mail.—**mail′bag** *n.* the sack in which letters are put for transit.—**mail′-boat, -cart, -coach, -plane, -train** *n.* means of conveyance of letters, etc., by sea, air and land [O.Fr. *male*, a trunk or mail].
maim (mām) *v.t.* to deprive of the use of a limb; to disable; to disfigure;—*n.* an injury.—**maimed′ness** *n.* (O.Fr. *mahaing*, a bruise).
main (mān) *a.* principal; first in size, importance, etc.; essential; sheer;—*n.* the chief part; strength, as in *might and main*; a wide expanse of land or ocean; the principal pipe in water, gas, or electricity system.—**main′brace** *n.* the brace of the main-yard.—**to splice the main-brace,** to hand out a double ration of rum.—**main′-chance** *n.* self-interest.—**main′door** *n.* a front door giving access to ground-floor house.—**main′land** *n.* a continent as distinct from islands.—**main′ly** *adv.*—**main′mast** *n.* the principal mast of a ship.—**main′road** *n.* a highway, esp. between two towns.—**main′sail** *n.* the principal sail on the main-mast.—**main′stay** *n.* the rope from the maintop to the deck; (*Fig.*) the chief support [O.E. *maegen*, main].
main (mān) *n.* a hand in gambling-game; a cock-fight [Fr. *main*, the hand].
maintain (mān-tān′) *v.t.* and *v.i.* to hold or keep in any state; to sustain; to preserve; to defend, as an argument; to affirm.—**maintain′able** *a.*—**maintain′er** *n.*—**main′tenance** *n.* the act of maintaining; means of support [Fr. *maintenir* to hold].
maison(n)ette (mā-zon-et′) *n.* a small compact house [Fr.].
maize (māz) *n.* Indian corn, a cereal next in importance to rice [W. Ind.].
majesty (maj′-es-ti) *n.* grandeur; exalted dignity; royal state; the title of a sovereign; the symbolic representation of the Deity enthroned.—**majest′ic, -al** *a.* possessing majesty; splendid [L. *majestas*, dignity].
majolica (ma-jol′-i-ką) *n.* a decorative, enamelled pottery [fr. *Majorca*].
major (mā′-jer) *a.* greater in number, quality, quantity, or extent; (*Mus.*) greater by a semitone;—*n.* a person who has reached the age of 21; an officer in the army ranking below a lieutenant-colonel.—**majorat** (ma-zho-rá′) *n.* primogeniture.—**ma′jor-dom′o** *n.* a steward; (*Colloq.*) an organiser.—**ma′jor-gen′eral** *n.* an army officer in rank below a lieutenant-general.—**major′ity** *n.* the greater number; full legal age (21) [L. *major*, greater].
make (māk) *v.t.* to cause to be or do; to create; to constitute; to compel; to appoint; to secure; to arrive at; to reckon; to perform;—*v.i.* to tend; to contribute.—*pa.t.* and *pa.p.* **made.**—*n.* structure; texture; form; style; brand.—**make′-believe′** *n.* pretence;—*v.i.* to pretend.—**mak′er** *n.* one who makes; a poet.—**Mak′er** *n.* God.—**make′shift** *n.* a temporary expedient.—**make′-up** *n.* arrangement or layout of a printed page, magazine, etc.; facial cosmetics; general characteristics.—**make′weight** *n.* something added to scale to make up weight.—**to make bold,** to dare to.—**to make good,** to justify one's efforts.—**to make headway,** to progress.—**to make up to,** to make friendly advances.—**on the make,** striving for pecuniary gain [O.E. *macian*, to make].
Malacca (ma-lak′-ą) *n.* a district in Malaya.—**Malacca cane,** light walking-stick made of a kind of Malayan palm-cane.
malachite (mal′-ą-kīt) *n.* a green carbonate of copper, used for inlaid work [Gk. *malachē*, mallow].
maladjustment (mal-ad-just′-ment) *n.* faulty adjustment; inability to adjust oneself to one's environment.
maladministration (mal-ad-min-is-trā′-shun) *n.* faulty administration, esp. of public affairs.
maladroit (mal-ą-droit′) *a.* clumsy; awkward. **maladroit′ly** *adv.*—**maladroit′ness** *n.*
malady (mal′-ą-di) *n.* a disease; ailment.—**mal de mer,** sea-sickness (Fr. *malade*, sick].
Malaga (mal′-ą-gą) *n.* a white wine from *Malaga*, in Spain; a sweet green grape.
Malagasy (mal-ą-gas′-i) *n.* a native of, or the language of, Madagascar;—*a.* pert. to Madagascar, its inhabitants, or language.
malaise (mal′-āz) *n.* a feeling of bodily discomfort; squeamishness [Fr.].
malapert (mal′-ą-pert) *a.* saucy; forward.

malapert'ly *adv.*—**malapert'ness** *n.* [O.Fr. *mal apert*, impudent].
malaprop(ism) (mal'ạ-prop-(izm)) *n.* the ludicrous misuse of a word, so called from *Mrs. Malaprop*, a character in Sheridan's play, *The Rivals*.—**malaprop'ian** *a.*—**malapropos** (mal-ap-rō-pō' *adv.* unseasonably; unsuitably; out of place [Fr. *mal à propos*, ill-suited].
malaria (mạ-lā'ri-ạ) *n.* fever caused by the bite of mosquito; the unhealthy air arising from swamps, orig. regarded as the source of fevers.—**mala'rian, mala'rial, mala'rious** *a.* [It. *mal'aria*, bad air].
Malay (mạ-lā') *n.* a native of the Malay Peninsula;—*a.* pert. to Malaya. Also **Malay'an.**
malcontent (mal'kon-tent) *a.* discontented; rebellious.—**malcontent'ed** *a.*—**malcontent'edly adv.**—**malcontent'edness** *n.*—**malcontent'ly** *adv.*
male (māl) *a.* pert. to the sex which begets young; masculine; (*Bot.*) having stamens;—*n.* a male animal [L. *masculus*, male].
malediction (mal-e-dik'shun) *n.* evil-speaking; a curse; an imprecation.—**maledict'ory** *a.* reviling; expressing a curse [L. *male*, badly; *dicere*, to speak].
malefactor (mal'e-fak-tor) *n.* an evil-doer; a criminal [L. *male*, badly; *facere*, to do].
malevolent (mal-ev'o-lent) *a.* evilly-disposed; vindictive. Also **malev'olous.**—**malev'olence** *n.* ill-will; malignity.—**malev'olently** *adv.* [L. *male*, badly; *velle*, to wish].
malformation (mal-for-mā'shun) *n.* irregular formation.—**malformed'** *a.* deformed; abnormally shaped.
malgre Same as **maugre.**
malic (mā'lik) *a.* derived from the apple [L. *malum*, apple].
malice (mal'is) *n.* ill-will; spite; disposition to injure others; (*Law*) criminal intention.—**malic'ious** *a.* spiteful; showing malice.—**malic'iously** *adv.*—**malic'iousness** *n.*—**with malice aforethought** (*Law*) with deliberate criminal intention [L. *malitia*, ill-will].
malign (mạ-līn) *a.* having an evil disposition towards others; spiteful; pernicious; sinister; —*v.t.* to traduce; to vilify.—**malig'nancy** *n.* (of disease) virulence. Also **malig'nance.**—**malig'nant** *a.* being evilly disposed; unpropitious; (of disease) virulent; likely to prove fatal.—**malig'nantly** *adv.*—**maligner** (ma-līn'ẹr) *n.*—**malig'nity** *n.* extreme malevolence; spite.—**malign'ly** *adv.* [L. *malignus*, ill-disposed].
malinger (mạ-ling'gẹr) *v.i.* to feign illness in order to avoid duty.—**maling'erer** *n.* a shirker [Fr. *malingre*, ailing].
mall (mel or mal) *n.* a level, shaded walk, esp. *the Mall* in St. James's Park in London—orig. an alley for the game of *pall-mall*; this game; the mallet used in playing it (var. of *maul*) [L. *malleus*, a hammer].
mallard (mal'ạrd) *n.* a wild drake or duck [etym. doubtful].
malleable (mal'e-ạ-bl) *a.* capable of being hammered or extended by beating; (*Fig.*) amenable; tractable.—**mall'eableness, malleabil'ity** *n.*—**mall'eate** *v.t.* to hammer; to draw into a plate or leaf by beating.—**mallea'tion** *n.* [L. *malleus*, a hammer].
mallemuck (mal'e-muk) *n.* the fulmar or petrel [Dut. *mal*. foolish; *mok*, a gull].
mallet (mal'et) *n.* a small wooden hammer; a long-handled wooden hammer used in the game of croquet, polo, etc. [Fr. *maillet*, a small hammer].
mallow (mal'ō) *n.* any plant of the genus *Malva*, with downy leaves, and having emollient properties [L. *malva*, mallow].
Malmsey (mȧm'ze) *n.* a sweet wine [fr. *Malvasia*, in Greece].
malnutrition (mal-nū-tri'shun) *n.* the state of being undernourished; semi-starvation.
malodorous (mal-ō'dor-us) *a.* having an offensive odour.—**malo'dour** *n.*
malpractice (mal-prak'tis) *n.* evil practice; professional impropriety or negligence.
malt (mawlt) *n.* barley or other grain steeped in water till it germinates, then dried in a kiln for use in brewing;—*v.t.* to make into malt;—*v.i.* to become malt.—**malt'ex'tract** *n.* a medicinal body-building food made from malt.—**malt'ing** *n.*—**malt liquor,** a liquor made from malt by fermentation and not by distillation, as beer, stout, ale, or porter.—**malt'ose** *n.* a sugar produced by the action of malt on starch.—**malt'ster, malt'man** *n.* one employed in a malt-house [O.E. *mealt*, malt].
Maltese (mawl'tēz) *n.* a native of *Malta*; the dialect of Malta;—*a.* pert. to Malta or to its people.—**Maltese cross,** a cross, with the four arms equal in length and forked at the ends.
Malthusian (mal-thūz'i-ạn) *a.* pert. to the theories of *Thomas Malthus*;—*n.* one who advocates deliberate limitation of population when it threatens to outgrow the food supplies available to maintain it [fr. *Malthus*, an English economist (1766-1834)].
maltreat (mal-trēt') *v.t.* to ill-treat; to abuse; to handle roughly.—**maltreat'ment** *n.*
malversation (mal-vẹr-sā'shun) *n.* corruption in office; fraudulent handling of public funds [L. *male*, ill; *versari*, to be engaged in].
Malvoisie (mal'vwȧ-zē) Same as **Malmsey.**
mamba (mȧm'bạ) *n.* a poisonous black snake, found in S. Africa [Kaffir].
mamma (mam'ȧ) *n.* milk-secreting gland in females.—*pl.* **mam'mae.**—**mam'mary** *a.* [L. *mamma*, the breast).
Mammalia (mam-ā'li-ạ) *n.pl.* (*Zool.*) the class of mammals or animals which suckle their young.—**mam'mal** *n.* one of the *Mammalia*.—**mamma'lian** *a.*—**mammal'ogy** *n.* the scientific study of mammals [L. *mamma*, the breast].
mammon (mam'on) *n.* the god of riches; wealth personified and worshipped.—**mam'monism** *n.* devotion to wealth [Syrian *mamon*, wealth].
mammoth (mam'uth) *n.* an extinct species of elephant of huge size;—*a.* colossal [Russ. *mammantu*].
man (man) *n.* a human being; an adult male; a manly person; a male servant; a husband; the human race; in feudal times, a vassal; a piece used in such games as chess, draughts, etc.—*pl.* **men.**—*v.t.* to furnish with men; to fortify.—*pr.p.* **man'ning.**—*pa.t.* and *pa.p.* **manned.**—**man'at-arms** *n.* soldier; a feudal knight.—**man-eater,** a cannibal; a tiger.—**man'ful** *a.* vigorous; sturdy.—**man'fully** *adv.*—**man'fulness** *n.*—**man'han'dle** *v.t.* (*Naut.*) to handle a boat without mechanical aid; to treat roughly.—**man'hole** *n.* an opening large enough to admit a man leading to a drain, sewer, etc.—**man'hood** *n.* the state of being a man; courage.—**man'hour** *n.* work performed by one man in one hour.—**man'kind** *n.* human beings; male sex.—**man'liness** *n.*—**man'ly** *a.* bold; resolute; dignified; not effeminate.—**man'made** *a.* fashioned by man.—**man'nish** *a.* like a man; masculine.—**man'nishly** *adv.*—**man'nishness** *n.*—**man-of-war,** a naval vessel; orig. a soldier.—**man-of-war bird,** a frigate bird. —**man'pow'er** *n.* a unit of power equal to one-eighth of a horse-power; the total number of people in industry, the armed forces, etc.—**man'servant** *n.* a male servant, as a butler, etc. —**man'slaughter** *n.* culpable homicide without malice aforethought.—**man in the street,** average man [O.E. *mann*].
manacle [man'ạ-kl) *n.* a handcuff;—*v.t.* to fetter with handcuffs [O.Fr. *manicle*].
manage (man'āj) *v.t.* to direct; to control by hand; to carry on; to cope with;—*v.i.* to direct affairs; to succeed.—**manageabil'ity** *n.* quality of being manageable.—**man'ageable** *a.* capable of being managed.—**man'ageableness** *n.*—**man'agement** *n.* the act of managing; administration; body of directors controlling a business.—**man'ager** *n.* (*fem.* **man'ageress**) one who manages: one in charge of a business, etc. —**manage'rial** *a.*—**man'aging** *a.* interfering; meddlesome [L. *manus*, the hand].
manatee (man'a-tē) *n.* a grotesque land-

mammal living in the sea, and found off the coast of W. Africa; a sea-cow [Sp.].

Manchester (man′ches-tẹr) *a.* pert to town of Manchester, in Lancashire.—**Manchester School,** political economists headed by Cobden and Bright who advocated free-trade and *laissez-faire.*—**Man′chesterism** *n.*

Manchu, Manchoo (man′chòò) *n.* one of the original inhabitants of Manchuria, who invaded China in the 17th cent. and ruled China till the establishment of the Chinese Republic in 1911.—*a.* pert. to Manchuria, or to its inhabitants [Chin.].

manciple (man′si-pl) *n.* a steward; a caterer, esp. for a college or the Inns of Court [L. *manceps,* a purchaser].

mandarin (man′dạ-rin) *n.* a European name for a Chinese provincial governor; (*Fig.*) any high government official; the language used in Chinese official circles; a small orange. Also **man′darine** [Port. *mandarim*].

mandate (man′dāt) *n.* an official order; a precept; a rescript of the Pope; a commission to act as representative of a body of people, esp. one granted by the United Nations to a State to administer another not sufficiently advanced for self-government.—**man′datary, man′datory** *n.* one to whom a mandate is given by a **man′dator.**—**man′dated** *a.* committed to a mandate, as *mandated territories.*—**man′datory** *a.* containing a mandate; directory [L. *mandatum,* an order].

mandible (man′di-bl) *n.* a jaw; in vertebrates, the lower jaw; in birds, the upper or lower beak.—**mandib′ular** *a.* pert. to the jaw [L. *mandibula*].

mandolin, mandoline (man′dō-lin) *n.* a musical instrument like a guitar [dim. of It. *mandola,* a lute].

mandrake (man′drāk) *n.* a narcotic plant the root of which was once thought to resemble the human form and to shriek when pulled.—**mandrag′ore** *n.* mandrake [M.E. *mandragge*].

mandrel (man′drel) *n.* a shaft on which objects may be fixed for turning, milling, etc.; the spindle of a lathe. Also **man′dril** [etym. doubtful].

mandrill (man′dril) *n.* a large W. African baboon [Fr.].

mane (mān) *n.* long hair on the neck of an animal [O.E. *manu,* neck].

manège (man-ezh′) *n.* the art of horsemanship; a riding-school [Fr.].

manes (mā′nēz) *n.* the shades of the dead; the deities of the underworld [L.].

manganese (mang′gạ-nēz) *n.* a greyish, hard, brittle metal which oxidises rapidly in humid atmosphere; symbol **Mn.**—**mangane′sian, mangane′sic, mangan′ic, mang′anous** *a.* [O.Fr. *manganese,* fr. *magnesia*].

mange (mānj) *n.* a parasitic disease affecting the skin of animals, and causing hair to fall out.—**man′giness** *n.*—**man′gy** *a.* infected with mange (O.Fr. *manjue,* itch].

mangel-wurzel (mang′gl-wur′zl) *n.* a large kind of beet grown for cattle-fodder [Ger. *Mangold,* a beet; *Wurzel,* a root].

manger (mānj′ẹr) *n.* a trough for holding fodder for cattle [Fr. *manger,* to eat].

mangle (mang′gl) *n.* a rolling press for smoothing linen;—*v.t.* to smooth with a mangle.—**man′gler** *n.* [Dut. *mangel*].

mangle (mang′gl) *v.t.* to hack; to mutilate; (*Fig.*) to spoil the beauty of, as a passage of poetry by faulty reading.—**man′gler** *n.* [prob. O.Fr. *mahaigner,* to maim].

mango (mang′gō) *n.* an E. Indian evergreen tree, the unripe fruit of which is used in making chutney;—*pl.* **mang′o(e)s** [Malay, *mangga,* fruit of the mango-tree].

mangold See **mangel-wurzel.**

mangrove (man′grōv) *n.* a tree of the E. and W. Indies, the bark of which is used in tanning [Malay, *manggi-manggi*].

Manhattan (man-hat′n) *n.* a cocktail, orig. American, containing whisky, vermouth, gin, bitters [Amer.].

mania (mā′ni-ạ) *n.* madness, esp. of a violently excited type; extravagant enthusiasm amounting to an obsession.—**ma′niac** *n.* a madman;—*a.* raving; frenzied.—**mani′acal** *a.* [Gk. *mania,* madness].

manicure (man′i-kūr) *n.* the care of the hands and nails; one who gives this treatment;—*v.t.* to file, and polish the nails.—**man′icurist** *n.* [L. *manus,* the hand; *cura,* care].

manifest (man′i-fest) *a.* clearly visible; apparent to the mind or senses;—*v.t.* to make clear; to reveal; —*n.* a detailed list of a ship's cargo for the scrutiny of the Customs-officers.—**manifest′able, manifest′ible** *a.* capable of being clearly revealed.—**manifesta′tion** *n.* the act of revealing; the state of being revealed; display; disclosure.—**man′ifestly** *adv.* obviously.—**man′ifestness** *n.*—**manifest′o** *n.* a public declaration of the principles or policy of a leader or party;—*pl.* **manifest′oes** [L. *manifestus,* clear].

manifold (man′i-fōld) *a.* various in kind or quality; multifarious; numerous;—*v.t.* to take many copies of, as letters, documents, etc., by a machine, such as a duplicator;—*n.* a sheet of thin paper used in duplicating; (*Mech.*) a pipe fitted with several lateral outlets, as in internal combustion engine.—**man′ifoldly** *adv.* [fr. *many* and *fold*].

man(n)ikin (man′i-kin) *n.* a little man; a dwarf; a model of the human body for use of anatomy students. Also **man′akin** [Dut. *mannekin,* a double dim. of **man**].

manilla (mạ-nil′ạ) *n.* a cheroot made in *Manila,* capital of the Philippine Islands. Also **manil′a.**—**manil(l)a hemp,** a fibre used for making ropes, twine, sails, etc.—**manil(l)a paper,** a stout buff-coloured wrapping paper.

maniple (man′i-pl) *n.* part of a Roman legion containing 60-120 men; a scarf worn on the left arm by celebrant at mass.—**manip′ular** *a.* [L. *manipulus,* a handful].

manipulate (mạ-nip′ū-lāt) *v.t.* to operate with the hands; to manage (a person) in a skilful, esp. unscrupulous way; to falsify;—*v.i.* to use the hands.—**manipula′tion** *n.*—**manip′ular, manip′ulative, manip′ulatory** *a.* pert. to manipulation.—**manip′ulator** *n.* [L. *manipulus,* a handful].

Manito (man′i-tō) *n.* spirit or god, among Amer. Indians. Also **Man′itou** [Algonquin].

manna (man′ạ) *n.* the food supplied miraculously to the Israelites in the wilderness; a sweetish juice of the ash, used as a laxative; (*Fig.*) spiritual nourishment [Heb. *man,* a gift].

mannequin (man′i-kin) *n.* one employed to parade new fashions in clothes; a clay figure for a similar purpose. Also **man′equin** [Fr. *mannequin,* a puppet].

manner (man′ẹr) *n.* way of doing anything; custom; style; a person's habitual bearing;—*pl.* social behaviour; customs.—**mann′ered** *a.* having manners, esp. in compounds *well-mannered, ill-mannered;* affected.—**mann′erism** *n.* a personal peculiarity of bearing, speech, or style of artistic expression; affectation.—**mann′erliness** *n.* politeness; decorum.—**mann′erly** *a.* having good manners; courteous; civil; respectful;—*adv.* civilly; respectfully.—**to the manner born,** having natural talent for special work or position (Fr. *manière,* manner].

manoeuvre (mạ-nòò′vẹr, or mạ-nū′vẹr) *n.* the strategic movement of armed forces; (*Fig.*) skilful management;—*pl.* peace-time exercises of army, navy, or airforce;—*v.t.* to direct skilfully;—*v.i.* to perform, manoeuvres.—**manoeuv′rer** *n.* [Fr.].

manor (man′or) *n.* the land belonging to a lord; a unit of land in feudal times over which the owner had full jurisdiction.—**man′or-house** *n.* the mansion on such an estate.—**mano′rial** *a.* pert. to a manor [O.Fr. *manoir,* a dwelling].

mansard-roof (man′sạrd ròòf) *n.* roof in which lower slope is nearly vertical and upper much inclined [fr. *François Mansard,* a French architect (d. 1666)].

manse (mans) *n.* Scottish Presbyterian

minister's residence [L.L. *mansa*, a dwelling].
mansion (man′shun) *n.* a large house; a manor-house.—**man'sion-house** *n.* a large residence.—**Mansion House**, the official residence of the Lord Mayor of London [L. *manere*, to remain].
mantel (man′tl) *n.* the shelf above a fireplace.—**man'telpiece** *n.* the framework round a fireplace [form of *mantle*].
mantilla (man-til′a) *n.* a veil covering head and shoulders, worn by Spanish women; a short cape [dim. of Sp. *mante*, a cloak].
mantis (man′tis) *n.* a genus of insects including stick-insects, and leaf-insects.—known in SouthAfrica as the Hottentot God. [Gk. *mantis*, a prophet].
mantissa (man-tis′a) *n.* the decimal part of a logarithm [L. *mantissa*, a makeweight].
mantle (man′tl) *n.* a loose outer garment; a cloak;(*Fig.*) covering; the finely-meshed fixture on a gas-jet, producing incandescent light;—*v.t.* to cover; to hide;—*v.i.* to rise and spread; to suffuse; to flush.—**mant'let** *n.* a small cloak. Also **mant'elet** [L. *mantellum*, a cloak].
mantua (man′tū-a) *n.* a woman's gown.—**man'tua-mak'er** *n.* a dressmaker, esp. in 18th cent. [Fr. *manteau*, a cloak—prob. popularly associated with *Mantua* in Italy].
manual (man′ū-al) *a.* pert. to or made by the hand;—*n.* a handbook or small text-book; a service-book of R.C. Church; a key-board of a pipe-organ; (*Collog.*) woodwork.—**man'ually** *adv.*—**manual alphabet**, finger-alphabet used by deaf and dumb.—**manual exercise**, drilling of soldiers in hand-operated weapons [L. *manus*, the hand].
manufacture (man-ū-fakt′ūr) *n.* making goods either by hand or by machine (esp. mass-production of goods); anything produced from raw materials; —*v.t.* to make from raw materials, to fabricate;—*v.i.* to be engaged in manufacture.—**manufact'ory** *n.* a place where goods are made from raw materials; a factory.—**manufact'ural** *a.*—**manufact'urer** *n.* [L. *manus*, the hand; *facere*, to make].
manumit (man-ū-mit′) *v.t.* to give freedom to a slave; to emancipate.—**manumiss'ion** *n.* [L. *manumittere*, to send from one's hand].
manumotive (man′ū-mō-tiv) *a.* propelled by hand.—**man'umotor** *n.* a vehicle propelled by hand [L. *manus*, the hand; and *motive*].
manure (ma-nūr′) *v.t.* to enrich soil with fertiliser;—*n.* any fertilising substance applied to soil to enrich it.—**manur'er** *n.* [contr. of Fr. *manoeuvrer*, to work with the hands].
manuscript (man′ū-skript) *a.* written by hand;—*n.* a book, etc., written by hand; an author's script for perusal by publisher (*abbrev.* **MS**; *pl.* **MSS**) [L. *manus*, hand; *scribere*, *scriptum*, to write].
Manx (mangks) *a*, pert. to the Isle of Man or its inhabitants;—*n.* the Gadhelic language of the Isle of Man.—**Manx cat**, a tailless breed of cat [O.N. *manskr*].
many (men′i) *a.* comprising a great number (*comp.* **more**; *superl.* **most**);—*n.* a number of people or things.—**man'ysided** *a.* (of persons) all-round; talented [O.E. *manig*, many].
Maori (mou′ri) *n.* an aborigine of New Zealand; the language of the aborigines;—*a.*pert. to the Maori [Native].
map (map) *n.* a representation, esp. on a plane surface, of the features of the earth, or of part of it; a chart of the heavens; a plan or delineation:—*v.t.* to draw a map of; to fill in details in a blank map;—*pr.p.* **map'ping**.—*pa.t.* and *pa.p.* **mapped**.—**to map out**, to plan in detail, as an itinerary [L. *mappa*, a napkin].
maple (mā′pl) *n.* a deciduous tree of the sycamore kind, valuable for its timber and the sap from which sugar is extracted [O.E. *mapultreow*, the maple tree].
maquis (mȧ′kē) *n.* in Corsica, brushwood-covered heath; scrub; bush.—**the Maquis** *n.pl.* (*World War* 2) members of French Resistance.
mar (mȧr) *v.t.* to injure; to impair; to disfigure.—*pr.p.* **mar'ring**.—*pa.p.* **marred** [O.E. *merran*, to hinder].
marabout (mar′a-bòò) *n.* a kind of stork; the feathers of this bird used as trimming for hats, etc.; a feather boa or necklet; a kind of silk [prob. Ar.].
marabout (mar′a-bòòt) *n.* a Mohammedan hermit; a shrine [Ar.].
maraschino (mar-as-kē′nō) *n.* a sweet liqueur distilled from cherries grown in Dalmatia [It. *amarasca*, a sour cherry].
Marathi (ma-rȧ′thi) *n.* the language of the *Mahrattas* [Native].
marathon (ma′ra-thon) *n.* a long-distance race (approx. 26 miles); so called from the distance run by the messenger who brought to Athens the news of the Greek victory over the Persians (at *Marathon*) in 490 B.C.
maraud (ma-rawd′) *v.i.* to rove in quest of plunder; to foray; to loot [O.Fr. *marauder*, to play the rogue].
marble (mȧr′bl) *n.* hard limestone which takes on a brilliant polish and is used for ornaments, statuary, etc.; a little ball of marble, glass, etc., used in games;—*a.* made of marble; cold; insensible;—*v.t.* to colour like streaked marble.—**mar'bled** *a.* veined like marble, as paper, pottery, etc.—**mar'bly** *a.* like marble.—**the Elgin Marbles**, the sculptured marble portions of the Parthenon brought to London by Lord Elgin in 1811; now in the British Museum [Gk. *marmairein*, to sparkle].
marcasite (mȧr′ka-sīt) *n.* white iron pyrite (used now in jewellery because of its brilliance).—**marcasit'ic** *a.* [Fr.].
marcel (mȧr-sel′) *n.* an artificial hair wave.—**marcelled'** *a.* [fr. *Marcel*, the inventor].
March (mȧrch) *n.* third month of year, named after *Mars*, Roman god of war.
march (mȧrch) *n.* a border; a frontier of a territory, esp. of Scotland and Wales—used esp. in *pl.* **march'es**.—*v.i.* to border [O.E. *mearc*, mark].
march (mȧrch) *v.i.* to move in order, as soldiers; to proceed at a steady pace; to go to war;—*v.t.* to cause to move in military array;—*n.* distance marched; a musical composition to accompany a march; (*Fig.*) steady advance, as the *march of time*.—**march'er** *n.* one who marches.—**dead′march** *n.* a funeral march [Fr. *marcher*, to walk].
marchioness (mȧr′shon-es) *n.* the wife of a marquis; lady, holding in her own right, the rank of marquis [L.L. *marchionissa*, fem. of *marchio*, ruler of the march].
marchpane (mȧrch′pān) *n.* a paste made of ground almonds, sugar, white of egg, etc., and used for small cakes, etc. Also **marzipan'** [etym. doubtful].
marconigram (mȧr-kōn′i-gram) *n.* a message by wireless telegraphy [fr. *Marconi*, the inventor].
mare (mār) *n.* the female of the horse.—**mare's nest**, a discovery of exaggerated importance; a hoax.—**mare's tail**, a marsh plant of the genus Hippuris.—**shanks's mare**, one's own legs, as a means of locomotion [O.E. *mere*, fem. of *mearh*, a horse].
margarin (mȧr′gar-in) *n.* a pearly wax-like substance obtained from animal fat; a fatty extract of certain vegetable oils.—**margarine** (mȧr′gar-ēn, mȧr′jer-ēn) *n.* a butter substitute made principally from vegetable oils.—(*Colloq. abbrev.*) **marg.** (marj) [Gk. *margaron*, a pearl].
marge (mȧrj) *n.* a margin; a shore.—**mar'gin** *n.* a border; a blank space at top, bottom and sides, of a written or printed page; allowance made for contingencies.—**mar'ginal** *a.* pert. to a margin; entered in the margin.—**margina'lia** *n.pl.* notes jotted in the margin.—**mar'ginally** *adv.*—**mar'ginate, -d** *a.* having a margin or margins [L. *margo*, the edge].
margrave (mȧr′grāv) *n.* (*fem.*) **margravine** (mar′gra vēn) *n.* orig. a lord of the marches:

a German title of nobility [Ger. *Markgraf*, a border-count].

marguerite (mår′ge-rēt) *n.* a large ox-eye daisy [L. *margarita*, a pearl].

Marian, Marist (mā′ri-ạn, mār′ist) *a.* pert. to the Virgin Mary.

marigold (mar′i-gōld) *n.* name applied to a plant bearing yellow or orange flowers [prob. fr. Virgin *Mary* and *gold*].

marijuana (mår-i-hwan′a) *n.* a type of hemp dried and used as tobacco, having a strong narcotic effect [Sp.].

marimba (mạ-rim′ba) *n.* a jazz-band instrument resembling the xylophone [Afr.].

marine (mạ-rēn′) *a.* pert. to the sea; found in, or near, the sea; pert. to shipping or overseas trade;—*n.* a soldier serving on board a warship; the naval force of a country.—**mar′iner** *n.* a sailor or seaman [L. *mare*, the sea].

Mariolatry (mā-ri-ol′ạ-tri) *n.* the worship of the Virgin Mary.—**Mariol′ater** *n.* [L. *Maria*, Mary; *latreia*, worship].

marionette (mar-i-o-net′) *n.* a puppet worked by strings [Fr. dim. of *Marion*].

marish (mar′ish) *a.* marshy;—*n.* a marsh [O.Fr. *mareis*, a marsh].

Marist (mār′ist) *n.* a member of a R.C. teaching fraternity, the Society of Mary.

marital (mar′i-tạl) *a.* pert. to a husband or to marriage [L. *maritus*, a husband].

maritime (mar′i-tīm) *a.* pert. to the sea; bordering on the sea; living near the sea; having overseas trade or naval power [L. *maritimus*, fr. *mare*, the sea].

marjoram (mår′jō-ram) *n.* an aromatic plant of the mint family used in cookery [etym. doubtful].

mark (mårk) *n.* a visible sign; a cross; a character made by one who cannot write; a stamp; a proof; a target; a point; an attainable standard; a numerical assessment of proficiency, as in an examination; a flaw or disfigurement; a peculiarity or distinguishing feature; (*Running*) starting post; indication of position, depth, etc., as *Plimsoll mark*; (formerly) a district;—*v.t.* to make a sign upon; to stamp or engrave; to notice; to assess, as an examination paper;—*v.i.* to observe particularly.—**marked** *a.* outstanding; notorious.—**mark′edly** *adv.* noticeably.—**mark′er** *n.* one who marks the score at billiards, bridge, etc.; a bridge scoring-card; a counter; an ornamental strip of leather, ribbon, paper, etc., used to mark a place in a book.—**mark′ing-ink** *n.* indelible ink for marking initials on linen, etc.—**marks′man** *n.* one who is expert at hitting a target.—**marks′manship** *n.* shooting skill.—**to mark time**, to move the feet up and down without moving forward; (*Fig.*) to remain at a standstill, as in one's work.—**a soft mark** (*Colloq.*) a credulous person, a dupe.—**beside the mark**, irrelevant.—**trade mark**, a special symbol marked on commodities to indicate the maker [O.E. *meare*, a boundary].

mark (mårk) *n.* a former unit of weight (8 oz.) for silver and gold; a medieval English coin worth 13s. 4d.; a Finnish markka; a silver German coin worth a shilling; paper-money of this value in modern Germany.—**merk** (merk) an old Scots silver coin worth 13s. 4d. [O.E. *marc*].

market (mår′ket) *n.* a public meeting place for the purchase and sale of commodities; a trading-centre; demand; country or geographical area regarded as a buyer of goods; price or value at a stated time;—*v.i.* to buy or sell;—*v.t.* to produce for sale in a market.—**mar′ketable** *a.* suitable for selling.—**mar′ketably** *adv.*—**mark′et-gar′den** *n.* a fruit and vegetable garden the produce of which is sold in the market.—**mark′et-place** *n.* the open space in which markets are held.—**mark′et-price** *n.* the current price of a commodity [L. *mercatus*, trade].

marl (mårl) *n.* a fine-grain clay, often used as manure; a soil containing carbonate of lime, used in brick-making;—*v.t.* to manure with marl.—**mar′ly** *a.* [O.Fr. *marle*, marl].

Marlag (mar′lag) *n.* (*World War* 2) a prisoner-of-war camp in Germany fo naval personnel [Ger. contr. of *Marine*, the navy; *Lager*, a camp].

marline (mår′lin) *n.* a small rope used to secure a splicing.—**mar′line-spike** *n.* a pointed tool used to separate strands of a rope in splicing [Dut. *marren*, to bind; *lijn*, a line].

marmalade (mår′mạ-lād) *n.* a preserve made of the pulp and peel of oranges, lemons, grapefruit, etc. (orig. made from quinces) [Port. *marmelo*, a quince].

marmoraceous (mår-mo-rā′shus) *a.* pert. to or resembling marble.—**mar′morate(d)** *a.* coloured like marble; encased in marble.—**marmora′tion** *n.*—**marmor′eal, marmo′rean** *a.* pert. to, or like, marble [L. *marmor*, marble].

marmoset (mår′mo-zet) *n.* a small, monkey of S. America [Fr. *marmouset*, a small grotesque figure (on fountains)].

marmot (mår′mot) *n.* a rabbit-like rodent inhabiting esp. upper slopes of Alps and Pyrenees [Fr. *marmot*, a mountain-rat].

marocain (mår′rō-kān) *n.* a dress material of silk, rayon, etc., with surface resembling morocco leather [fr. *Morocco*].

maroon (mạ-rôôn′) *n.* orig. a fugitive negro slave hiding in the mountainous regions of the W. Indies; a marooned person;—*v.t.* to put ashore on a desolate island; to isolate, cut off, by any means, in any place;—*v.i.* to loiter [Sp. (*ci*)*marron*, a runaway slave].

maroon (mạ-rôôn′) *a.* brownish-crimson;—*n.* a kind of firework with a loud report [Fr. *marron*, a chestnut].

marque (mårk) *n.* a licence granted to a private vessel to plunder enemy shipping and to use captured vessels against enemy.—usually **letters of marque** [Fr. fr. Prov. *marcar*, to seize as a pledge].

marquee (mår-kē′) *n.* a large field-tent; an awning outside a public building [orig. *marquees*, for Fr. *marquise*, the tent of a marquis].

marquetry (mår′ket-ri) *n.* decorative, inlaid wood; the process of inlaying wood with designs of coloured wood, etc. Also **mar′queterie** [Fr. *marqueter*, to variegate].

marquis (mår′kwis) *n.* in Britain, a noble ranking next below a duke. Also **mar′quess** (*fem.* **mar′chioness**).—**mar′quisate, -quessate** *n.* the rank or dignity of a marquis.—**marquise** (mår-kēz′) *n.* in France, the wife of a marquis; a type of gemmed ring [O.Fr. *marchis*, ruler of the marches].

marriage See **marry.**

marrow (mar′ō) *n.* the soft substance in the cavities of bones; (*Fig.*) the essence or pith of anything.—**marr′ow-bone** *n.* a bone containing marrow;—*pl.* the knees.—**marr′owfat** *n.* a rich variety of green pea.—**marr′owy** *a.*—**vegetable marrow**, a kind of edible gourd [O.E. *mearg*, marrow].

marry (mar′i) *v.t.* to unite, take, or give in wedlock;—*v.i.* to enter into matrimony.—*pr.p.* **marr′ying.**—*pa.t.* and *pa.p.* **marr′ied.**—**marriage** (mar′ij) *n.* the legal union of husband and wife; the ceremony, civil or religious, by which two people of opposite sex become husband and wife.—**marr′iageable** *a.* of an age to be married.—**marr′iageableness** *n.*—**marriage lines**, official certificate of marriage [L. *maritare*, to marry].

Mars (mårz) *n.* the Roman god of war; the planet second nearest Earth.—**Mar′tian** *n.* an inhabitant of the planet Mars [L.].

Marsala (mår-så′la) *n.* a sweet, light wine from *Marsala*, in Sicily.

Marseillaise (mår-sā-yez′ or mår-se-lāz′) *n.* the French national anthem.

marsh (mårsh) *n.* a tract of low, swampy land; a bog; a fen;—*a.* pert. to swampy areas.—**marsh′-fe′ver** *n.* malaria.—**marsh′-gas** *n.* fire damp.—**marsh′-mall′ow** *n.* a red flowered plant growing in marshes; a sweetmeat made from the root of this, or from gelatine.—**marsh'y** *a.* boggy; swampy [O.E. *merisc,* full of meres].

marshal (mär'shal) *n.* orig. a master of the horse; a master of ceremonies; a herald; the highest military rank, as in French army, in British army (Field-Marshal), in R.A.F. (Air-Marshal); (*U. S.*) a civil officer of a district with powers of a sheriff;—*v.t.* to dispose in order, as troops; (*Fig.*) to arrange, as ideas.—*pr.p.* **mar'shalling.**—*pa.t.* and *pa.p.* **mar'shalled.** —**marshalling yard,** a railway depot for goods-trains [O.Fr. *mareschal,* a horse servant].

Marshall Aid (mar'shal-ād) *n.* economic assistance given to Europe by the U.S.A. in accordance with the plan put forward by Gen. G. *Marshall* in 1947.

marsupial (mär-sū'pi-al) *a.* having an external pouch, to carry the young;—*n.* a marsupial or pouched animal, such as the kangaroo [L. *marsupium,* a pouch].

mart (märt) *n.* a market [contr. of *market*].

martello (mär-tel'ō) *n.* a small fortified tower erected during the period of threatened invasion by Napoleon's army (1804) [fr. Cape *Martello,* in Corsica].

marten (mär'ten) *n.* a kind of weasel, valued for its fur [O.Fr. *martre*].

martial (mär'shal) *a.* pert. to war or to the Services; warlike; military.—**Mar'tial** *a.* pert. to Mars, the god or planet.—**mar'tialism** *n.*—**mar'tially** *adv.*—**martial law,** law enforced by military authorities in times of danger and superseding the Civil law during such an emergency [L. *Mars,* the god of war].

martin [mär'tin) *n.* a kind of swallow. Also **mar'tinet** [fr. *Martin*].

martinet (mar'ti-net) *n.* a strict disciplinarian [fr. Fr. officer, *Martinet,* in army of Louis XIV].

martingale (mär'tin-gāl) *n.* a strap fastened to a horse's girth to keep its head down; (*Naut.*) a stay for a jib-boom. Also **mar'tingal** [etym. doubtful].

martini (mär-tē'nē) *n.* a cocktail of vermouth, gin and bitters [etym. doubtful].

Martinmas (mär'tin-mas) *n.* the feast of *St. Martin,* Nov. 11.

martyr (mär'tėr) *n.* one who suffers punishment or the sacrifice of his life for adherence to principles or beliefs;—*v.t.* to put to death for refusal to abandon principles; (*Fig.*) a constant sufferer.—**mar'tyrdom** *n.* the suffering and sacrifice of a martyr.—**martyrol'ogy** *n.* a history of martyrs [L. Gk. *martus,* a witness].

marvel (mär'vel) *n.* anything wonderful;—*v.i.* to wonder exceedingly.—*pr.p.* **mar'velling.** —*pa.t.* and *pa.p.* **mar'velled.**—**mar'vellous** *a.* wonderful; astonishing.—**mar'vellously** *adv.*—**mar'vellousness** *n.* [O.Fr. *merveille,* a wonder].

Marxism (marks'izm) *n.* the doctrines expounded by *Karl Marx* (1818-83), which had a profound influence on Socialists and Communists of Europe in later part of 19th cent. —**Marx'ian, Marx'ist** *a.*—**Marxist** *n.*

marybud (mā'ri-bud) *n.* the flower of a marigold [fr. *Mary* and *bud*].

marzipan (mär'zi-pan) *n.* Same as **march'pane.**

mascara (mas-ka'ra) *n.* a cosmetic preparation for darkening eyebrows and lashes.—Also **masca'ro** [fr. *mask*].

mascot (mas'kot) *n.* a person or thing reputed to bring good luck [etym. doubtful].

masculine (mas'kū-lin) *a.* male; strong; virile; (of a woman) mannish; (*Gram.*) of male gender. —**mas'culineness, masculin'ity** *n.* [L. *masculus,* male].

mash (mash) *v.t.* to beat to a pulp or soft mass; to mix malt with hot water;—*n.* a thick mixture of malt and hot water for brewing; a mixture of bran meal, boiled turnips, etc. given to horses and cattle; (*Colloq.*) mashed potatoes [O.E. *masc,* mash].

mash (mash) *v.t.* (*Slang*) to pay court to; to flirt.—**mash'er** *n.* a fop; a lady-killer [etym. doubtful].

mashie (mash'i) *n.* a golf-club with short iron head used for lofting ball. Also **mash'y** [prob. corrupt. of Fr. *massue,* a club].

mask (mask) *n.* a covering for the face; a plastic impression of a human face, as a *death-mask*; a respirator of rubber, mica, etc., to be worn as protection against poison-gas; a false face, as worn by children at Hallowe'en; a disguise; a fox's head; a masque or allegorical play incorporating dances popular in the 17th cent.; a masquerade; (*Fig.*) a pretext;—*v.t.* to hide, as with a mask;—*v.i.* to assume a disguise.—**masked ball,** a ball at which dancers wear masks [prob. Sp. *mascara,* a mask].

masochism (mas'o-kizm) *n.* a form of sex gratification by endurance of physical or mental pain.—**mas'ochist** *n.* [fr. *von Sascher-Masoch,* an Austrian novelist].

mason (mā'sn) *n.* a builder in stone; a freemason.—**mason'ic** *a.* pert. to freemasonry.—**ma'sonry** *n.* the work of a mason; stonework; freemasonry [Fr. *macon,* a mason].

masque See **mask.**

masquerade (mask-ėr-ād') *n.* an assembly of masked persons; disguise;—*v.i.* to take part in a masquerade; to disguise oneself as [Fr. *mascarade*].

mass (mas) *n.* the quantity of matter in a body; a shapeless lump; magnitude; crowd; chief portion;—*v.t.* to collect in a mass; —*v.i.* to assemble in large numbers.—**mass'ive** *a.* forming a mass; bulky; grandly moulded; weighty.—**mass'ively** *adv,*—**mass'iveness, mass'iness** *n.*—**mass'-meet'ing** *n.* a large public meeting or demonstration.—**mass'-produc'tion** *n.* cheap production in great quantities of commodity.—**mass'y** *a.* massive.—**the masses,** the common people [L. *massa,* a lump].

mass (mas) *n.* the communion service in the R.C. Church; the music to accompany high mass.—**high mass,** mass celebrated with music, incense, and elaborate ritual.—**low mass,** a simple celebration of mass without music [O.E. *maesse,* fr. L. *missa,* mass].

massacre (mas'a-kėr) *n.* general, ruthless slaughter; carnage;—*v.t.* to slaughter indiscriminately [O.Fr. *maçacre,* slaughter].

massage (ma-säzh') *n.* a curative treatment of physical disorders by kneading, rubbing, etc., carried out by specialists;—*v.t.* to treat by massage.—**mass'agist, masseur'** *n.* (*fem.* **masseuse'**) a male specialist in massage [Fr. fr. Gk. *massein,* to knead].

massif (ma-sēf') *n.* a distinctive, compact group of mountains [Fr.].

mast (mäst) *n.* upright pole supporting rigging, sails, etc., of a ship; upright post supporting wireless aerial, etc. ;—*v.t.* to furnish with mast or masts.—**mast'ed** *a.*—**mast'head** *n.* top portion of a ship's mast.—**to sail or serve before the mast,** to sail as an ordinary seaman [O.E. *maest,* the stem of a tree].

mast (mäst) *n.* fruit of oak, beech, esp. as food for swine [O.E. *maest,* fodder].

master (mäs'ter) *n.* one who directs and controls; an employer of labour; a proprietor; a ship-captain; a teacher; a graduate in Arts, or Science, of a University (*abbrevs.* M.A., M.Sc.); courtesy title given the sons of a family, esp. by servants; an expert; a famous artist, esp. an *old master*; one who organises and leads a fox-hunt, as *master of foxhounds*;—*a.* chief, dominant, pre-eminent;—*v.t.* to become the master of; to become expert at; to overcome.—**mas'ter-at-arms** *n.* a police officer on board a warship.—**mas'terful** *a.* compelling; domineering.—**mas'terfully** *adv.*—**mas'terfulness** *n.*—**mas'terhand** *n.* an expert.—**mas'ter-key** *n.* a key which opens several locks.—**mas'terly** *a.* highly competent; supremely proficient;—*adv.* with the skill of an expert.—**mas'ter-mar'iner** *n.* the captain of a merchant or fishing vessel.—**mas'ter-mind** *n.* a first-class mind; chief controlling power behind a scheme.—**mas'terpiece** *n.* a brilliantly executed work of art.—**mas'ter-stroke** *n.* a masterly action, esp. in diplomatic service, war-strategy, etc.—**mas'ter-switch** *n.* an electric switch which must be turned on before other switches will function.—**mas'tery** *n.* supremacy; superiority; consummate skill; victory.—**to be one's own master**, to be independent [L. *magister*, a master].

mastic, mastich (mas'tik) *n.* a tree, native to S. Europe, yielding a valuable pale-yellow resin used in the manufacture of fine quality varnish; the resin from this tree [Gk. *mastichē*, mastic].

masticate (mas'ti-kāt) *v.t.* to chew; to break up food with the teeth.—**mas'ticable** *a.* capable of being chewed.—**mastica'tion** *n.* the process of chewing.—**mastica'tor** *n.* a mincing machine.—**mas'ticatory** *a.* [L. *masticare*, to chew].

mastiff (mas'tif) *n.* a powerful breed of dog [O.Fr. *mastin* confused with *mestif*, mongrel].

mastitis (mas-tī'tis) *n.* (*Med.*) inflammation of the breast [Gk. *mastos*, the breast].

mastodon (mas'to-don) *n.* an extinct mammal resembling an elephant, with nipple shaped prominences on the molar teeth.—**masto-don'tic** *a.* [Gk. *mastos*, the breast; *odous*, the tooth].

mastoid (mas'toid) *a.* pert. to or like the female breast; nipple-shaped;—*n.* the prominence on the temporal bone behind the human ear [Gk. *mastos*, the breast].

masturbate (mas'tur-bāt) *v.i.* to practise sexual self-abuse.—**masturba'tion** *n.*—**mas'turbator** *n.* [L. *masturbari*].

mat (mat) *n.* a coarse fabric of twine, rope, rushes, or coconut fibre for wiping the feet on; a rug; a heat-resisting covering of cork, plastic, etc., for protecting surface of a table; a tangled mass of hair;—*v.t.* to lay or cover with mats; —*v.i.* to become a tangled mass.—*pr.p.* **mat'ting**.—*pa.t.* and *pa.p.* **mat'ted** [L. *matta*, a mat].

mat, matt (mat) *a.* having a dull finish; not shiny [Fr. *mate*].

matador, matadore (mat'a-dor) *n.* the man who kills the bull in a Spanish bullfight [Sp. fr. L. *mactare*, to kill].

match (mach) *n.* a splint of wood or taper tipped with some substance capable of ignition by friction with a rough surface; a piece of rope for firing a gun; a fuse.—**match'lock** *n.* a musket fired by a match.—**match'wood** *n.* small wood splinters used for making matches [Fr. *mèche*, a wick].

match (mach) *n.* a person or thing equal to or resembling another; a sporting contest; a marriage; a mate;—*v.i.* to correspond in quality, quantity, colour, etc. ;—*v.t.* to compete with; to unite in marriage; to be the same as, in colour, size, etc.—**match'less** *a.* having no match; peerless; unique.—**match'ma'ker** *n.* one who schemes to bring about a marriage [O.E. *gemaecca*, a mate].

mate (māt) *n.* a companion; a fellow-worker; a spouse; one of a pair (of animals, etc.); second-in-command on a merchant ship; an assistant;—*v.t.* to match; to marry;—*v.i.* to pair.—**ma'ty** *a.* (*Slang*) friendly [O.Dut. *maet*, a companion].

mate (māt) *v.t.* to checkmate (chess);—*n.* checkmate [abbrev. of *checkmate*].

mate, maté (mà'tā) *n.* an evergreen tree of Brazil and Paraguay, the leaves of which are dried and used as tea [Native *mati*, the vessel for infusing tea].

mater (mā'tẹr) *n.* a mother; one of the two membranes covering the brain and spinal cord, and distinguished as the *dura mater*, and the *pia mater* [L. *mater*, a mother].

material (ma-tē'ri-ạl) *a.* consisting of matter; corporeal; (of persons) not spiritually minded; essential; appreciable; worthy of consideration;—*n.* the substance out of which something is fashioned; fabric; the accumulated data out of which a writer creates a work of literary, historical, or scientific value; materials collectively.—**materialisa'tion** *n.*—**mate'rialise** *v.t.* to render material; to give bodily form to;—*v.i.* to become fact.—**mate'rialism** *n.* the theory that matter, and matter only, exists in the universe; an attitude to life which ignores all spiritual values.—**materialist'ic, -al** *a.* pert. to materialism.—**materialist'ically** *adv.*—**mate'rially** *adv.* appreciably [L. *materia*, matter].

materia medica (mat-tē'ri-ạ med'i-kạ) *n.* (*Med.*) the substances used in the making of medicines, drugs, etc.; the science relating to medicines and their curative properties [L. = medical material].

maternal (ma-tẹr'nạl) *a.* pert. to a mother; motherly; related on the mother's side.—**mater'nally** *adv.*—**mater'nity** *n.* motherhood; childbirth [L. *mater*, a mother].

mathematics (math-e-mat'iks) *n.* the science of quantity and space, including arithmetic, algebra, trigonometry, geometry.—**mathemat'ic,-al** *a.* pert. to mathematics; accurate.—**mathemat'ically** *adv.*—**mathemati'cian** *n.* [Gk. *mathēma*, learning].

matin (mat'in) *n.* a morning song;—*pl.* morning service in Anglican church; one of the canonical hours sung at midnight or daybreak. Also **mat'tins**.—**mat'inal** *a.*—**matinée** (mat'ē-nā) *n.* an afternoon performance in theatre or cinema [Fr. *matin*, morning].

matriarch (mā'tri-ȧrk) *n.* a woman in a position analagous to that of a patriarch.—**matriar'chal** *a.*—**matriar'chalism** *n.*—**ma'triarchy** *n.* government exercised by a mother [L. *mater*, a mother; Gk. *archein*, to rule].

matrices (mat'ri-sēz) *n.pl.* of **matrix**.

matricide (mat'ri-sīd) *n.* the murder of a mother; one who kills his own mother [L. *mater*, a mother; *caedere*, to kill].

matriculate (ma-trik'ū-lāt) *v.t.* to admit to membership, esp. of a college;—*v.i.* to enter, by matriculation.—**matricula'tion** *n.* [L. *matricula*, a register].

matrimony (mat'ri-mo-ni) *n.* marriage; wedlock.—**matrimo'nial** *a.*—**matrimo'nially** *adv.* [L. *matrimonium*].

matrix (mā'triks or mat'riks) *n.* the womb; the cavity where anything is formed; a mould, esp. for casting printer's type; rock where minerals are embedded.—*pl.* **mat'rices, mat'rixes** [L. *matrix*, the womb].

matron [mā'tron) *n.* a married woman; a woman in charge of the nursing and domestic staff of a hospital, etc.—**ma'tron-like, ma'tronly** *adv.* like a matron; mature; staid [L. *matrona*, a married lady].

matt (mat) *a.* Same as **mat**.

matter (mat'ẹr) *n.* that which occupies space and is the object of the senses; substance; cause of a difficulty; subject of a book, speech, sermon, etc.; occasion; moment; an indefinite amount; (*Med.*) pus; —*v.i.* to be of importance; to signify; (*Med.*) to discharge pus.—*pr.p.* **matt'ering**.—*pa.p.* **matt'ered**.—**matt'er-of-fact** *a.* prosaic; unimaginative [L. *materia*, matter].

matting (mat'ing) *n.* mat-work; coarse material of straw, rushes, coconut fibre, etc., used as floor-covering [fr. *mat*].

mattins Same as **matins** (*pl.* of **matin**).

mattock (mat'ok) *n.* a kind of pick-axe with only one end pointed, used for loosening soil [O.E. *mattuc*].

mattress (mat'res) *n.* a case of canvas ticking, etc., quilted and stuffed with hair, wool, kapok, or feathers, for a bed [O.E. fr. Ar. *matrah*, a place where anything is thrown].

maturate (mat'ū-rāt) *v.t.* to mature; (*Med.*) to promote suppuration in;—*v.i.* to ripen.—**matura'tion** *n.* [L. *maturus*, ripe].

mature (mạ-tūr') *a.* ripe; fully developed; (*Med.*) come to suppuration; resulting from adult experience; due for payment, as a bill; —*v.t.* to ripen; to perfect;—*v.i.* to become ripe; to become due, as a bill.—**matur'able** *a.*—**mature'ly** *adv.*—**mature'ness** *n.* ripeness; the state or quality of being fully developed.—**matur'ity** *n.* ripeness, complete development [L. *maturus*, ripe].

matutinal (mat-ū-tī′-nạl) *a.* morning; early. Also **mat′utine** [L. *matutinus*, of the early morning].
maudlin (mawd′-lin) *a.* over-sentimental; tearful; fuddled [contr. of O.Fr. *Maudeleine*, Mary Magdalen, painted as weeping].
maugre (maw′-gẹr) *prep.* in spite of [Fr. *malgré*, in spite of].
maul (mawl) *n.* a heavy wooden hammer;—*v.t.* to beat; to maltreat; to mishandle [L. *malleus*, a hammer].
Mau Mau (mou′-mou′) *n.* a secret, terrorist society of the Kikuyu tribe in Kenya.
maunder (mawn′-dẹr) *v.i.* to mutter; to drivel; to talk or to wander aimlessly [O.Fr. *mendier*, to beg.]
maundy (mawn′-di) *n.* religious ceremony of washing feet of poor and distributing alms, in commemoration of Christ's washing of disciples' feet [L. *mandare*, to command].
Mauser (mou′-zẹr) *n.* a type of repeating magazine rifle [fr. name of inventor].
mausoleum (maw-sō-lē′-um) *n.* a magnificent tomb.—**mausole′an** *a.* [orig. the tomb of *Mausolus*, King of Caria, 350 B.C.].
mauve (mawv or mōv) *n.* a reddish-purple aniline dye;—*a.* having this soft, purple colour [Fr. fr. *L. malva*, the mallow].
mavis (mā′-vis) *n.* the song-thrush; the throstle [etym. doubtful].
maw (maw) *n.* the stomach of the lower animals; in birds, the craw [O.E. *maga*, maw].
mawkish (mawk′-ish) *a.* loathsome; sickly sweet; maudlin.—**mawk** *n.* maggot.—**mawk′ishly** *adv.* [M.E. *mathek*, a maggot].
maxillar, maxillary (mak-sil′-ạr, -i) *a.* pert. to the upper jaw-bone or jaw;—*n.* the jawbone.—**maxill′a** *n.* the upper jaw;—*pl.* **maxill′ae** [L. *maxilla*, a jaw-bone].
maxim (mak′-sim) *n.* an accepted principle; an axiom; a proverb or precept [L. *maximus*, superl. of *magnus*, great].
Maxim gun (mak′-sim-gun) *n.* a machine-gun invented 1884 [fr. Sir Hiram *Maxim*].
maximum (mak′-si-mum) *a.* greatest;—*n.* the greatest number, quantity or degree; the highest point; peak.—*pl.* **max′ima.**—opp. *minimum.*—**max′imal** *a.* of the greatest value [L. superl. of *magnus*, great].
may (mā) *v.i.* expressing possibility, permission, uncertainty, hope.—*pa.t.* **might** (mīt).—**may′be** *adv.* perhaps; possibly [O.E. *maeg*, may].
May (mā) *n.* the fifth month of the year; (*Fig.*) youthful prime; hawthorn (which blossoms in May);—*v.i.* to celebrate May Day; to gather hawthorn blossom.—**May′-beet′le** *n.* the cockchafer.—**May′-bloom** *n.* hawthorn blossom.—**May′-day** *n.* the first day in May.—**May′fair** *n.* a fashionable district in London.—**May′-fly** *n.* an ephemeral insect; an artificial fly for fishing.—**May′ing** *n.* the observance of May-day festival.—**May′-lil′y** *n.* the lily of the valley.—**may′pole** *n.* a pole with streamers, around which people danced at the May-day sports [L. *Maius*, the month of May].
mayhem (mā′-hem) *n.* (*Law*) the offence of maiming by violence [O.Fr. *mahaigne*, injury].
mayonnaise (mā′-on-āz′) *n.* a sauce or dressing of egg-yolk, vinegar, oil, pepper, salt, mustard, for salads, etc.; dish, e.g. lobster, salmon, dressed with this [Fr.].
mayor (mā′-or) *n.* (*fem.* **may′oress**) the chief magistrate of a city or borough.—**may′oral** *a.*—**may′oralty, may′orship** *n.* the office of a mayor [Fr. *maire*, mayor].
maze (māz) *n.* a network of intricate paths; a labyrinth; (*Fig.*) confused condition; mental perplexity;—*v.t.* to bewilder.—**ma′zy** *a.*—**ma′zily** *adv.*—**ma′ziness** *n.* [M.E. *masen*, to confuse].
mazourka, mazurka (mạ-zŏŏr′-kạ) *n.* a Polish dance; the music for this [Pol.].
me (mē) *pron.* the objective case of first pers. pronoun, '*I*.'
me (mē) *n.* the third note in tonic sol-fa.
mead (mēd) *n.* a fermented drink made of honey, yeast and water [O.E. *meodu*].
mead (mēd) *n.* a meadow [O.E. *maed*].
meadow (med′-ō) *n.* a low, level tract of grassland pasture ground.—**meadow-sweet,** or **-wort,** fragrant plant with creamy, feathery flowers.—**mead′owy** *a.* [O.E. *mawan*, to mow].
meagre (mē′-gẹr) *a.* having little flesh; gaunt; scanty; barren.—**mea′grely** *adv.*—**mea′greness** *n.* [Fr. *maigre*, thin].
meal (mēl) *n.* the food taken at one time; a repast [O.E. *mael*, time].
meal (mēl) *n.* pulse or grain ground less finely than flour.—**meal′iness** *n.*—**meal′worm** *n.* an insect found in meal stores.—**meal′y** *a.* like meal; hoary; powdery.—**meal′y-mouthed** *a.* honey-tongued; apt to mince words [O.E. *melo*, meal].
mealie (mēl′-i) *n.* (*S. Afr.*) an ear of maize;—in *pl.* maize [S. Afr. *milje*, millet].
mean (mēn) *a.* humble in rank or birth; ignoble; sordid; lacking dignity; stingy; (*Colloq.*) disobliging; selfish.—**mean′ly** *adv.*—**mean′ness** *n.* small-mindedness; sordidness; want of dignity [O.E. *gemaene*, common].
mean (mēn) *a.* in a middle position; average; intervening;—*n.* the middlepoint of quantity, rate, position, or degree;—*pl.* resources; revenue; wealth; agency.—**mean time,** the interval between two given times.—**mean′time, mean′while** *adv.* in the intervening time.—**means test,** an inquiry into means to determine claim to pension or benefit.—**golden mean,** course midway between two extremes; happy medium [L. *medius*, the middle].
mean (mēn) *v.t.* to have in view; to intend; to signify;—*v.i.* to form in the mind; to be disposed; to have a meaning.—*pr.p.* **mean′ing.**—*pa.t.* and *pa.p.* **meant** (ment).—**mean′ing** *n.* that which is meant; sense; signification;—*a.* expressive [O.E. *maenan*, to signify].
meander (mē-an′-dẹr) *v.i.* to flow with a winding course; to saunter aimlessly;—*n.* a circuitous path; the winding course of a river (usually used in *pl.*).—**mean′dering** *a.* winding [Gk. *Maiandros*, a winding river of Asia Minor].
measles (mē′-zlz) *n.* (*Med.*) a highly contagious disease, characterised by rash of bright red spots all over body; a disease affecting cattle and pigs and caused by bladderworms.—**meas′led, meas′ly** *a.* having measles; (*Fig.*) wretched; shoddy; skimpy.—**German measles,** a disease resembling measles but less severe [Dut. *mazelen*, measles].
measure (mezh′-ūr) *n.* dimension reckoned by some standard; an instrument for measuring; a vessel of predetermined capacity; a stately dance; metre: division of the time in music; a course of action; an act of Parliament; means to an end; (*Mus.*) tempo; the notes between two bars in staff notation;—*pl.* (*Geol.*) layers of rock; strata;—*v.t.* to ascertain the quantity or dimensions of; to assess; to distribute by measure;—*v.i.* to have an ascertained value or extent; to compare favourably with.—**meas′urable** *a.* capable of being measured; moderate.—**meas′urableness** *n.*—**meas′urably** *adv.*—**meas′ured** *a.* of specified measure; uniform; (of words) calculated.—**meas′ureless** *a.* boundless; infinite.—**meas′urement** *n.* dimension, quantity, etc., ascertained by measuring with fixed unit. —**meas′urer** *n.* [L. *mensura*, a measure].
meat (mēt) *n.* flesh used as food; food of any kind.—**meat′iness** *n.*—**meat′y** *a.* full of meat; (*Fig.*) pithy; compact with ideas [O.E. *mete*, food].
Mecca (mek′-a) *n.* the reputed birthplace of Mahomet, visited annually by thousands of pilgrims.—**mecca** *n.* (*Fig.*) the focal point for people drawn together by some common interest.
mechanic, -al (me-kan′-ik, -ạl) *a.* pert. to machines, mechanism, or mechanics; produced by machinery; automatic; acting with

out thought or design; base.—**mechan'ic** *n.* one who works with machines or instruments; skilled workman.—**mechan'ically** *adv.*—**mechanic'ian** *n.* a machine-maker or repairer.—**mechan'ics** *n.* that branch of applied mathematics which deals with force and motion; the science of machines.—**mechanisa'tion** *n.* (*Mil.*) the change from animal to mechanical power in transport.—**mech'anise** *v.t.* to make mechanical.—**mech'anised** *a.*—**mech'anism** *n.* the construction of a machine; machinery, esp. its parts collectively; (*Fig.*) technique; the philosophical doctrine, dominant in the 19th cent. that all phenomena of life admit of physico-chemical proof.—**mech'anist** *n.*—**mechanist'ic** *a.* [Gk. *mēchanē*, a contrivance].

Mechlin (meH′lin) *n.* and *a.* a kind of lace, made in *Mechlin* (Malines) in Belgium.

medal (med′ạl) *n.* a piece of metal, struck like a coin, as a memento or reward;—*v.t.* to decorate with a medal.—**medall'ic** *a.* pert. to medals.—**medall'ion** *n.* a large medal; a metal disc, usually round, with portrait in bas-relief; an ornament containing miniature or hair.—**med'allist, med'alist** *n.* a maker or student of medals; one who has been awarded a medal [Fr. *médaille*, a metal disc].

meddle (med′l) *v.i.* to interfere officiously; to tamper with.—**medd'ler** *n.*—**medd'lesome** *a.* interfering.—**medd'lesomeness** *n.* [L. *miscere*, to mix].

Medes (mēdz) *n.pl.* the inhabitants of Media on S.W. of Caspian Sea, the country annexed to Persia by Cyrus about 550 B.C.—**the laws of the Medes and Persians,** that which cannot be changed [fr. *Media*].

media See **medium.**

mediaevel See **medieval.**

medial (mē′di-ạl) *a.* in, or passing through, the middle; pert. to a mean or average.—**me'dian** *a.* situated in the middle;—*n.* (*Geom.*) a line drawn from vertex of a triangle to the middle point of the opposite side [L. *medius*, the middle].

mediate (mē′di-āt) *a.* being between two extremes; intervening; depending on an intermediary; not direct;—*v.i.* to interpose between contending parties to effect a reconciliation;—*v.t.* to effect by mediation.—**me'diacy** *n.*—**me'diately** *adv.*—**me'diateness** *n.*—**media'tion** *n.* the act of mediating; the steps taken to effect a reconciliation.—**me'diatise** *v.t.* to annex a principality or small state, still leaving to the ruler his title.—**me'diator** *n.* (*fem.* **me'diatress, me'diatrix**) *n.* one who mediates.—**mediato'rial** *a.*—**me'diatory** *a.* [L. *medius*, the middle].

medic (mē′dik) *n.* a leguminous plant with leaves like clover, used as fodder. Also **medick** [Gk. *mēdikē* (*poa*), 'Median' grass].

medical (med′i-kạl) *a.* pert. to medicine or the art of healing; medicinal.—**med'icable** *a.* capable of being cured.—**med'ically** *adv.*—**med'icament** *n.* any healing remedy.—**med'icate** *v.t.* to treat with medicine; to impregnate with anything medicinal.—**med'icated** *a.*—**medica'tion** *n.*—**med'icative** *a.* tending to heal [L. *medicus*, a physician].

medicine (med′i-sin or med′sin) *n.* any substance used in the treatment of disease; the science of healing and prevention of disease; magic; (*Fig.*) salutary lesson;—*v.t.* to administer medicine to.—**medic'inal** *a.* pert. to medicine; remedial.—**medic'inally** *adv.*—**medicine man,** a magician with supposed powers of healing; a witch-doctor.—**med'ico** *n.* (*Colloq.*) a doctor or medical-student [L. *medicus*, a physician].

medieval, mediaeval (med-i-ē′vạl) *a.* pert to or characteristic of the Middle Ages.—**medi(a)e'valist** *n.* one who makes a special study of the Middle Ages [L. *medius*, middle; *aevum*, an age].

mediocre (mē′di-ō-kẹr) *a.* middling; neither good nor bad; second-rate.—**medioc'rity** *n.* a middle state [L. *mediocris*].

meditate (med′i-tāt) *v.t.* to consider thoughtfully; to intend;—*v.i.* to ponder, esp. on religious matters.—**med'itated** *a.* planned.—**medita'tion** *n.* the act of meditating; deep thought.—**med'itative** *a.* given to reflection.—**med'itatively** *adv.*—**med'itativeness** *n.* [L. *meditari*, to consider].

mediterranean (med-i-tẹr-rā′ne-ạn) *a.* (of land) far from the sea; (of water) encircled by land.—**Mediterra'nean** *a.* pert. to the almost land-locked water between S. Europe and N. Africa, so called because it was regarded as being in the *middle* of the Old World.—**Mediterranean climate,** a climate of warm, wet winters, and hot dry summers [L. *medius*, the middle; *terra*, the earth].

medium (mē′di-um) *n.* that which is in the middle; a mean; an agency; in spiritualism, an intermediary professing to give messages from the spirit world (*pl.* **me'diums**); in bacteriology, a substance used for cultivation of bacteria;—*pl.* **me'dia, me'diums.**—*a.* middle; average; middling [L. *medius*, the middle].

medlar (med′lạr) *n.* a tree with fruit like a small apple [O.Fr. *mesler*, a medlar-tree].

medley (med′li) *n.* a miscellaneous collection of things; a miscellany [O.Fr. *medler*, to mix].

Médoc (mā-dok′) *n.* a red wine from *Médoc*, Gironde, France.

medulla (me-dul′a) *n.* marrow in a bone; inner tissue of a gland; pith of hair or plants. —**medull'ar, -y** *a.* comprising or resembling marrow, pith, etc.—**med'ullate(d)** *a.* having pith.—**med'ullose** *a.* like pith [L. *medulla*, marrow].

Medusa (me-dū′zạ) *n.* (*Myth.*) one of the three Gorgons, whose viper-wreathed head, cut off by Perseus, had the power to turn the beholder into stone.—**medu'sa** *n.* a kind of jellyfish, with tentacles like Medusa's hair.—*pl.* **medu'sae** [Gk. *Medousa*].

meed (mēd) *n.* reward; recompense [O.E. *med*, a reward].

meek (mēk) *a.* submissive; humble; gentle.—**meek'ly** *adv.*—**meek'ness** *n.* humility; the quality of being meek [O.E. *meoc*, meek].

meerschaum (mēr′shawm) *n.* a fine, white clay of silicate of magnesium used for the bowl of tobacco-pipes; a pipe of this [Ger. *Meer*, the sea; *Schaum*, foam].

meet (mēt) *a.* fit; suitable.—**meet'ly** *adv.*—**meet'ness** *n.* [O.E. (*ge*)*maete*, suitable].

meet (mēt) *v.t.* to encounter; to join; to find; to satisfy; to pay, as a debt; to await arrival, as of a train;—*v.i.* to converge at a specified point; to combine; to assemble in company. —*pa.t.* and *pa.p.* **met.**—*n.* an assembly of people, as at a fox-hunt.—**meet'ing** *n.* a coming together, as of roads, rivers; encounter; people gathered together for worship, entertainment, discussion, sport, etc.—**Meeting House,** the Quakers' place of worship [O.E. *metan*, to meet].

megacycle (meg′ạ-sī-kl) *n.* (*Elect.*) one million cycles [Gk. *megas*, great; *kuklos*, a circle].

megalith (meg′ạ-lith) *n.* a huge stone.—**megalith'ic** *a.* pert. to huge ancient stone monuments or stone-circles [Gk. *megas*, great; *lithos*, a stone].

megalomania (meg-ạ-lō-mā′ni-ạ) *n.* a form of insanity in which the patient has grandiose ideas of his own importance; lust for power. —**megaloma'niac** *n.* [Gk. *megas*, great; *mania*, madness].

megaphone (meg′ạ-fōn) *n.* a large speaking-trumpet used as amplifier to make human voice audible at a great distance [Gk. *megas*, great; *phōnē*, a sound].

megilp See **magilp.**

megohm (meg′ōm) *n.* (*Elect.*) one million ohms [Gk. *megas*, great; and *ohm*].

megrim (mē′grim) *n.* a pain affecting one side of the head; migraine.—*pl.* depression [Gk. *hemi-*, half; *kranion*, the skull].

meiosis (mī-ō′sis) *n.* (*Rhet.*) litotes, understatement; (*Biol.*) the reduction of chromosomes in a reproductive cell. [Gk. *meiosis*, lessening].

mekometer (mek-om′-e-tėr) *n.* a range-finder. (*Mil.*)

melancholy (mel′an-kol-i) *n.* depression of spirits; morbidity;—*a.* gloomy; depressed; grievous.—**melanchol′ia** *n.* morbid state of depression; abnormal introspectiveness bordering on insanity.—**melanchol′ic, melanchol′ious** *a.* depressed; caused by melancholy [Gk. *melas*, black; *cholē*, bile].

Melanesian (mel-an-ēz′i-an) *a.* pert. to *Melanesia*, an island-group, 1000 miles N.E. of Australia; dark-skinned;—*n.* a native or the language of Melanesia [Gk. *melas*, black; *nēsos*, island].

mélange (mā-longzh′) *n.* a mixture; a medley [Fr. *mêler*, to mix].

melanin (mel′an-in) *n.* a black pigment found in the eye, hair and skin.—**melan′ic** *a.* black.—**mel′anism** *n.* an excess of colouring matter in the skin [Gk. *melas*, black].

Melba toast (mel′ba tōst′) *n.* a very thin slice of toasted bread.

mêlée (mel′ā) *n.* a confused, hand-to-hand fight [Fr. *mêler*, to mix].

meliorate (mē′lyo-rāt) *v.t.* to improve;—*v.i.* to become better.—**meliora′tion** *n.*—**meliora′tor** *n.*—**me′liorism** *n.* the doctrine that the world is capable of improvement [L. *melior*, better].

melliferous (mel-if′ėr-us) *a.* producing honey.—**mellif′ic** *a.* honey-making.—**mellif′luence** *n.* a flowing sweetly or smoothly.—**mellif′luent, mellif′luous** *a.*—**mellif′luently, mellif′luously** *adv.*—**mellig′enous** *a.* producing honey [L. *mel*, honey; *ferre*, to bear].

mellow (mel′ō) *a.* soft and ripe; well-matured; genial; jovial; resonant, as a voice; (*Slang*) somewhat intoxicated;—*v.t.* to soften; to ripen;—*v.i.* to become soft or ripe; to become maturely wise.—**mell′owly** *adv.*—**mell′owness** *n.* [O.E. *mearu*, soft].

melodeon (mel-ō′di-un) *n.* a small hand reed organ or harmonium; a kind of accordion [Gk. *meloidia*, a song].

melodrama (mel-o-drȧm′a) *n.* a dramatic entertainment, sensational and crudely emotional; a play of romantic sentiment and situation.—**melodramat′ic** *a.* [Gk. *melos*, a song; *drama*, a play].

melody (mel′ō-di) *n.* a rhythmical succession of single sounds forming an agreeable musical air; a tune.—**melod′ic** *a.* pert. to a form of *minor* scale.—**melo′dious** *a.* tuneful; pleasing to the ear.—**melo′diously** *adv.*—**melo′diousness** *n.*—**mel′odist** *n.* a musical composer or singer [Gk. *melōidia*, a song].

melon (mel′on) *n.* a kind of gourd with a sweet, juicy pulp, and a centre full of seeds [Gk. *mēlon*, an apple].

melt (melt) *v.t.* to reduce to a liquid state; to dissolve; to soften; (*Fig.*) to make tender;—*v.i.* to become liquid or molten; to blend; to vanish; (*Fig.*) to become tender.—*pa.p.* **melt′ed** or **mol′ten.**—**melt′ing** *n.* the act of making liquid or molten;—*a.* softening; languishing, as looks; tender.—**melt′ingly** *adv.* [O.E. *meltan*, to melt].

member (mem′bėr) *n.* a limb, esp. of an animal body; a constituent part of a complex whole; one of a society, group, parliament, etc.—**mem′bered** *a.* having limbs.—**mem′bership** *n.* the state of being a member, or one of a society; members collectively [L. *membrum*, a limb].

membrane (mem′brān) *n.* (*Anat.*) a thin, flexible tissue forming or lining an organ of the body; a sheet of parchment.—**membran′eous, mem′branous, membrana′ceous** *a.* pert. to, or resembling, a membrane [L. *membrana*, parchment].

memento (mem-en′tō) *n.* anything which serves as a reminder of a person or event; a souvenir;—*pl.* **memen′tos** or **memen′toes** [L. imper. of *meminisse*, to remember].

memoir (mem′wȧr or mem′oir) *n.* a short, biographical sketch; a scientific record of personal investigations on a set subject;—*pl.* reminiscences.—**mem′oirist** *n.* [L. *memoria*, memory].

memory (mem′o-ri) *n.* the faculty of retaining and recalling knowledge; recollection; remembrance.—**memorabil′ia** *n.pl.* things worthy of note.—**mem′orable** *a.* noteworthy; remarkable.—**mem′orably** *adv.*—**memoran′dum** *n.* a note or reminder; (*Law*) a summary of a transaction; in diplomacy, an outline of the state of a question;—*pl.* **memoran′dums,** or **memoran′da.**—**memo′rial** *a.* serving as a reminder; contained in the memory;—*n.* anything intended to commemorate a person or an event; a written statement of facts in the form of a petition presented to an official governing body; a record of historical events.—**memo′rialist** *n.*—**mem′orise** *v.t.* to commit to memory [L. *memoria*, memory].

memsahib (mem′sȧ-hib) *n.* mode of address used by Indians to a European married woman [*ma'am*; Hind. *sahib*].

men (men) *n.pl.* of **man.**

menace (men′as) *n.* a threat or threatening; potential danger;—*v.t.* to threaten.—**men′acing** *a.* impending; threatening.—**men′acingly** *adv.* [L. *minari*, to threaten].

ménage (mā-nȧzh′) *n.* a household; housewifery; a club through which purchases can be made on the instalment system [Fr. fr. L. *mansio*, a dwelling].

menagerie (men-aj′ėr-i) *n.* a collection of caged wild animals for exhibition [Fr. *ménage* a household].

mend (mend) *v.t.* to repair; to set right; to improve;—*v.i.* to improve; to convalesce; to quicken, as one's steps;—*n.* a mended place.—**mend′er** *n.*—**mend′ing** *n.* the act of repairing [fr. *amend*].

mendacious (men-dā′shus) *a.* given to telling lies; untruthful.—**menda′ciously** *adv.*—**mendac′ity** *n.* prevarication; a tendency to lying [L. *mendax*, lying].

Mendelism (men′del-izm) *n.* the theory of heredity formulated by Gregor Johann *Mendel* (1822-84).—**Mendel′ian** *a.*

mendicant (men′di-kant) *a.* begging; living as a beggar;—*n.* a beggar.—**mend′icancy, mendic′ity** *n.* begging; poverty; the practice of living by alms [L. *mendicare*, to beg].

menhir (men′hēr) *n.* a tall, massive monumental stone, erected in prehistoric times; a monolith [Breton, *men*, stone; *hir*, high].

menial (mē′ni-al) *a.* pert. to a domestic servant or service; servile; mean;—*n.* a servant; a person of mean character.—**men′ially** *adv.* [O.Fr. *mesnee*, a household].

meninx (mē′ningks) *n.* one of the three membranes enveloping the brain;—*pl.* **meninges** (men-in′jēz).—**meningi′tis** *n.* (*Med.*) inflammation of the membranes of the brain [Gk. *mēninx*, a membrane].

meniscus (mē-nis′kus) *n.* a lens convex on one side and concave on the other; the curved surface of a liquid in a vessel; (*Math.*) a crescent.—**menis′cal, menis′cate** *a.*—**menis′ciform** *a.* crescent-shaped [Gk. *mēniskos*, a crescent].

menopause (men′ō-pawz) *n.* the change of life in a woman [Gk. *mēn*, a month; *pausis*, cessation].

mensal (men′sal) *a.* monthly [L. *mensis*].

menses (men′sēz) *n.pl.* the monthly discharge from the uterus of the female.—**men′strua** *n.pl.* the menses.—**men′strual** *a.* monthly; pert. to the menses.—**men′struate** *v.i.* to discharge the menses.—**menstrua′tion** *n.* the act or process of menstruating.—**men′struous** *a.* [*pl.* of L. *mensis*, a month].

Menshevik (men′she-vik) *n.* a member of the Russian moderate Socialist party overthrown by Bolsheviks under Lenin [Russ. *menshevik*, belonging to a minority].

menstruum (men′strŏŏ-um) *n.* a solvent.

pl. **men'strua, men'struums** [L. *menstrua*, the menses].
mensurable (mens'ū-ra-bl) *a.* capable of being measured.—**mensurabil'ity** *n.*—**mens'ural** *a.* pert. to measure.—**mensura'tion** *n.* the act, process, or art of measuring.—**mensura'tive** [L. *mensura*, measure].
mental (men'tal) *a.* pert to, or of, the mind; performed in the mind; (*Colloq.*) mentally-defective.—**mental'ity** *n.* intellectual power; mental attitude.—**men'tally** *adv.*—**mental deficiency**, subnormal intelligence [L. *mens*, the mind].
menthol (men'thol) *n.* a camphor obtained from oil of peppermint and used to alleviate neuralgia.—**menthola'ted** *a.* sprinkled or flavoured with menthol [L. *mentha*, mint].
mention (men'shun) *n.* a brief notice; a casual comment;—*v.t.* to notice; to name.—**men'tionable** *a.* fit to be remarked on [L. *mentio*].
mentor (men'tor) *n.* an experienced and prudent adviser.—**mentor'ial** *a.* [Gk. *Mentōr*, the adviser of Telemachus].
menu (men'ū) *n.* a bill of fare; the food served [Fr. *menu*, a list].
Mephistopheles (mef-is-tof'el-ēz) *n.* (*Myth.*) the devil.—**Mephistophe'lean, Mephistophele'an** *a.* sinister; cynical [etym. doubtful].
mephitis (me-fī'tis) *n.* noxious exhalation, esp. from the ground or from decaying matter. —**mephit'ic** *a.* [L.].
mercantile (mer'kan-tīl) *a.* pert. to commerce. —**mer'cantilism** *n.* the mercantile system.—**mer'cantilist** *n.*—**mercantile marine**, ships and men engaged in commerce.—**mercantile system**, the economic theory that money alone is wealth and that a nation's exports should far exceed its imports [L. *mercari*, to traffic].
mercenary (mer'se-nar-i) *a.* working merely for money gain; hired; sordid;—*n.* a hired soldier.—**mer'cenarily** *adv.*—**mer'cenariness** *n.* [L. *merces*, wages].
mercer (mer'ser) *n.* a dealer in textiles or small wares.—**mer'cery** *n.* [L. *merx*, goods].
mercerise (mer'ser-īz) *v.t.* to treat cotton fabrics with caustic lye to impart a silky finish.—**merceris'ed** *a.* [fr. John *Mercer*, who discovered the process 1850].
merchant (mer'chant) *n.* one who engages in trade; wholesaler;—*a.* pert. to trade or merchandise.—**mer'chandise** *n.* commodities bought and sold in home or foreign markets. —**mer'chantman** *n.* a ship carrying goods.—**merchant navy**, the ships and men of the mercantile marine [L. *mercari*, to traffic].
Mercian (mersh'i-an) *a.* pert. to the old Anglian kingdom of *Mercia*.
Mercury (mer'kū-ri) *n.* the Roman equivalent of the Greek god, *Hermes*, the messenger of the gods, and patron of merchants and travellers; the planet of the solar system nearest to the sun.—**mer'cury** *n.* a metallic chemical element, silvery white in colour, with very low melting point (also called *quicksilver*) and used in barometers, thermometers, etc.; a messenger.—**mercu'rial** *a.* pert. to, or consisting of, mercury; sprightly; agile; erratic.—**mercu'rialise** *v.t.* (*Med.*) to affect with mercury; to expose to the vapour of mercury.—**mercu'rially** *adv.*—**mercu'ric** *a.* (*Chem.*) pert. to compounds of bi-valent mercury. —**mer'curous** *a.* (*Chem.*) pert. to compounds of univalent mercury [L. *Mercurius*, prob. fr. *merx*, goods].
mercy (mer'si) *n.* forbearance; clemency; leniency shown to one guilty of a crime or misdemeanour; compassion.—**mer'ciful** *a.* full of mercy; compassionate.—**mer'cifully** *adv.*—**mer'cifulness** *n.*—**mer'ciless** *a.* void of pity; callous; cruel.—**mer'cilessly** *adv.*—**mer'cilessness** *n.* callousness.—**Sisters of Mercy**, nuns who attend the sick and needy [L. *merces*, reward].
mere (mēr) *n.* a pool or lake. Also **meer** [O.E. *mere*, a stretch of water].
mere (mēr) *a.* nothing but; simple; orig. pure, as in *mere English.*—**mere'ly** *adv.* purely; simply; solely [L. *merus*, undiluted].
mere (mēr) *n.* a boundary; a boundary stone [O.E. *gemaere*, a boundary].
meretricious (mer-e-trish'us) *a.* pert. to a harlot; (*Fig.*) tawdry; specious; cheap (as of style).—**meretric'iously** *adv.*—**meretric'iousness** *n.* [L. *meretrix*, a harlot].
merganser (mer-gan'ser) *n.* a diving fish-eating bird like a duck [L. *mergus*, a diving-bird; *anser*, a goose].
merge (merj) *v.t.* to cause to be swallowed up; to plunge or sink;—*v.i.* to lose identity by being absorbed in something else; to be swallowed up or lost.—**mer'ger** *n.* a combine of commercial or industrial firms [L. *mergere*, to dip].
meridian (me-rid'i-an) *n.* an imaginary great circle passing through the poles at right angles to the equator; (*Astron.*) a circle passing through the poles of the heavens and the zenith of the observer; the highest attitude of sun or star; midday;—*a.* pert. to midday; supreme.—**merid'ional** *a.* pert. to the meridian; southerly.—**meridional'ity** *n.*—**merid'ionally** *adv.* —**meridian sun**, the sun at its highest [L. *meridianus*, pert. to noon].
meringue (me-rang') *n.* a mixture of sugar and white of egg, whipped till stiff, and baked in a cool oven; a small cake of this, filled with whipped cream [Fr.].
merino (me-rē'nō) *n.* a breed of sheep with very fine, thick fleece, orig. from Spain; a dress fabric of this wool;—*a.* pert. to the merino sheep or its wool [Sp. *merino*, an inspector of sheep-walks].
merit (mer'it) *n.* quality of deserving reward; excellence; worth;—*pl.* the rights and wrongs, as of a law case;—*v.t.* to earn; to deserve.—**merito'rious** *a.* deserving reward.—**merito'riously** *adv.*—**merito'riousness** *n.*—**Order of Merit** (abbrev. O.M.) awarded for outstanding achievement [L. *meritum*, desert].
merk (merk) *n.* an old Scots silver coin worth 13s. 4d. [*mark*].
merle (merl) *n.* a blackbird [L. *merula*].
merlin (mer'lin) *n.* a species of falcon [O.Fr. *esmerillon*, a falcon].
merlon (mer'lon) *n.* part of a parapet which lies between two embrasures [Fr. fr. L. *murus*, a wall].
mermaid (mer'mād) *n.* an imaginary sea-creature with the upper body and head of a woman, and the tail of a fish.—**mer'man** *n.* the male equivalent of a mermaid [O.E. *mere*, a lake; and *maid*].
merry (mer'i) *a.* gay; hilarious; lively; (*Colloq.*) slightly intoxicated.—**merr'ily** *adv.*—**merr'iment, merr'iness** *n.* gaiety with noise and laughter; hilarity.—**merr'y-go-round** *n.* a revolving machine with horses, cars, etc.—**merr'y-ma'king** *n.* festivity.—**merr'y-thought** *n.* the forked bone of a fowl's breast, the wish-bone [O.E. *myrge*, pleasant].
mersion (mer'shun) *n.* immersion.
mesentery (mes'en-ter-i) *n.* a fold of abdominal tissue keeping the intestines in place. —**mesenter'ic** *a.* [Gk. *mesos*, middle; *enteron*, intestine].
mesh (mesh) *n.* the space between the threads of a net;—*pl.* network; (*Fig.*) toils;—*v.t.* to net; to ensnare;—*v.i.* to become interlocked, as gears of a machine [O.E. *max*, net].
mesmerism (mez'mer-izm) *n.* exercising an influence over will and actions of another; animal magnetism; hypnotism.—**mesmer'ic, -al** *a.* of or pert. to mesmerism.—**mesmerisa'tion** *n.*—**mes'merise** *v.t.* to hypnotise.—**mes'meriser, mes'merist** *n.* [fr. Anton *Mesmer*, a German physician, 1733-1815].
mesne (mēn) *a.* middle; (*Law*) intermediate.—**mesne lord**, a feudal lord who had granted a third person part of land held from a superior [O.Fr. *mesne*, middle].
mesolithic (mes-ō-lith'ic) *a.* of period between Palaeolithic and Neolithic ages [Gk. *mesos*, middle; *lithos*, a stone].

meson (mēz′on, mes′on) *n.* a particle equal in charge to, but having greater mass than, an electron or positron, and less mass than a neutron or proton [Gk. *meson*, neut. of *mesos*, middle].

Mesopotamia (mes-ō-pō-tā′mi-ạ) *n.* the land between Euphrates and Tigris; now Iraq; (*Colloq.* abbrev. **Mes'pot**) [Gk. *mesos*, middle; *potamos*, a river].

Mesozoic (mes-ō-zō′ik) *a.* pert. to the second geological period, including the Triassic, Jurassic, and Cretaceous systems (Gk. *mesos*, middle; *zōē*, life].

mess (mes) *n.* unpleasant mixture; disorder; a muddle;—*v.t.* to dirty; to muddle.—**mess'y** *a.* dirty; untidy; chaotic [form of *mash*].

mess (mes) *n.* a dish of food served at one time; soft, pulpy food; a number of people who eat together, esp. in army, navy, etc., as *officers' mess*;—*v.t.* to supply with a mess; —*v.i.* to eat in company.—**mess′tin** *n.* a soldier's cooking-vessel [O.Fr. *mes*, a dish].

message (mes′āj) *n.* a communication, verbal or written, sent by one person to another; an errand; an inspired utterance;—*v.t.* to transmit by signalling.—**mess'enger** *n.* one who delivers a verbal or written communication; one employed to deliver goods from a shop [L. *mittere*, to send].

Messiah (me-sī′a) *n.* the promised Saviour of the Jews; the Christ. Also **Messi'as.**—**Messi'ah' ship** *n.*—**Messian'ic** *a.* [Heb. *mashiah*, anointed].

messuage (mes′wāj) *n.* (*Law*) a dwelling-house with lands and outbuildings attached [O.Fr. *mesuage*, a holding of land].

mestizo (mes-tē′zō) *n.* a half-caste, esp. the offspring of a Spaniard and an American Indian [Sp. fr. L. *miscere*, to mix].

met (met) *pa.t.* and *pa.p.* of the verb **meet.**

metabolism (me-tab′ol-izm) *n.* the name given to the chemical changes continually going on in the cells of living matter.—**metabol'ic** *a.*—**metab'olise** *v.t.* [Gk. *metabolē*, change].

metacarpus (met-ạ-kȧr′pus) *n.* the hand between the wrist and the fingers; the bones of this part of the hand.—**metacar'pal** *a.* [Gk. *meta*, after; *karpos*, the wrist].

metage (mēt′āj) *n.* official weighing of coal; the price paid for this [fr. *mete*].

metal (met′ạl) *n.* a mineral substance, opaque, fusible and malleable, capable of conducting heat and electricity; molten glass; stones used in macadamising roads; (*Fig.*) courage; mettle;—*pl.* railroad track;—*v.t.* to cover with metal; to lay or repair roads with metal. —**met'alled** *a.* covered with metal, as a road.—**metal'lic** *a.* pert. to, like, or consisting of, metal. —**metal'lically** *adv.*—**met'allise** *v.t.* to make metallic; to vulcanise, as rubber.—**met'allist** *n.* a metal-worker; one who advocates metal and not paper currency.—**met'alloid** *n.* an element which has both metallic and non-metallic properties, as arsenic;—*a.* pert. to or having the property of metal. Also **metalloid'al.**—**metallic oxide,** a compound of metal and oxygen.—**base metals,** copper, lead, zinc, tin as distinct from precious metals, gold and silver [Gk. *metallon*, a mine].

metallurgy (met′al-ur-ji) *n.* the art of working metals or of obtaining metals from ores.—**metallur'gic** *a.*—**met'allurgist** *n.* [Gk. *metallon*, a metal; *ergon*, a work].

metamorphosis (met-ạ-mor′fō-sis) *n.* a change of form or structure; evolution;—*pl.* **metamor'phoses.**—**metamor'phic** *a.* subject to change of form, as rocks by heat or pressure. —**metamor'phism** *n.* the state of being metamorphic.—**metamor'phose** *v.t.* to transform in form or nature [Gk. *meta*, over; *morphē*, shape].

metaphor (met′ạ-for] *n.* a figure of speech which makes an *implied* comparison between things which are not *literally* alike, e.g. 'Much have I travelled in the realms of gold.' —**metaphor'ic, -al** *a.*—**metaphor'ically** *adv.*—**metaphor'icalness** *n.*—**met'aphorist** *n.*—**mixed metaphor,** a combination of metaphors drawn from different sources, e.g. 'he drew off the mask and showed the cloven hoof' [Gk. *metapherein*, to transfer].

metaphrase (met′ạ-frāz) *n.* literal, word for word translation from foreign language (opp. of *paraphrase*); a repartee;—*v.t.* to translate literally.—**met'aphrast** *n.* one who makes a literal translation.—**metaphras'tic** *a.* literal [Gk. *meta*, over; *phrasis*, a saying].

metaphysics (met-ạ-fiz′iks) *n. sing.* the science which investigates first causes of all existence and knowledge; ontology.—**metaphys'ical** *a.*—**metaphys'ically** *adv.*—**metaphysic'ian** *n.* [Gk. *meta*, after; *phusis*, nature].

metatarsus (met-ạ-tȧr′sus) *n.* the front part of the foot.—**metatar'sal** *a.* [Gk. *meta*, beyond; *tarsos*, the flat of the foot].

metathesis (me-tath′es-is) *n.* the transposition of a letter or letters in a word, as in *curl*, orig. *crul*.—**metathet'ic** *a.* [Gk. *meta*, over; *thesis*, a placing].

metatome (met′ạ-tōm) *n.* (*Archit.*) the space between two dentils [Gk. *meta*, among; *tomē*, a cutting].

metazoon (met-a-zō′on) *n.* a multi-cellular animal;—*pl.* **metazo'a, metazo'an.** ′**metazo'ic** *a.* [Gk. *meta*, after; *zōon*, an animal].

mete (mēt) *v.t.* to measure.—**mete out,** to distribute; to allot, as punishment.—**mete'wand, mete'yard** *n.* a measuring stick; (*Fig.*) criterion [O.E. *metan*, to measure].

metempsychosis (me-tem-sī-kō′sis) *n.* the transmigration of the soul, after death, into another body.—*pl.* **metempsycho'ses** [Gk. *meta*, expressing 'change'; *en*, in; *psuchē*, the soul].

meteor (mē′te-or) *n.* any rapidly passing, luminous body seen in the atmosphere; a shooting star; (*Fig.*) a dazzling but transiently famous person.—**meteor'ic** *a.* pert. to a meteor; influenced by atmospheric conditions; (*Fig.*) dazzling; flashing.—**me'teorite** *n.* a meteoric stone.—**me'teorograph** *n.* an instrument by which variations in several meteorological elements are recorded in combination.—**meteorog'raphy** *n.*—**me'teoroid** *n.* a body in space which becomes a meteor on passing through the atmosphere of the earth.—**me'teorolite** *n.* a meteorite.—**meteorolog'ical** *a.*—**meteorol'ogist** *n.*—**meteorol'ogy** *n.* the science which treats of atmospheric phenomena, esp. in relation to weather forecasts [Gk. *meteōros*, lofty].

meter (mē′tẹr) *n.* var. spelling of **metre.**

meter (mē′tẹr) *n.* one who, or that which, measures; an instrument for recording the consumption of gas, electricity, water, etc. [Gk. *metron*, a measure].

methane (meth′ān) *n.* an inflammable, hydrocarbon gas.—**meth'anol** *n.* methyl or wood alcohol [fr. *methyl*].

method (meth′od) *n.* manner of proceeding esp. in scientific research; orderliness; classification system; technique.—**method'ic, -al** *a.* arranged systematically; orderly.—**method′ically** *adv.* [Gk. *meta*, after; *hodos*, a way].

Methodism (meth′od-izm) *n.* the doctrines and teaching of the Methodists.—**Meth'odist** *n.* a member of nonconformist sect founded in 18th cent. by Charles and John Wesley [fr. *method*].

methyl (meth′il) *n.* the chemical basis of wood-spirit.—**meth'ylate** *v.t.* to mix alcohol with methyl to make it undrinkable and exempt from duty.—**methylated spirits,** alcohol mixed with 10 per cent wood spirit and coloured with violet dye, used for industrial purposes, esp. as a liquid fuel for spirit lamps, etc. [Gk. *methu*, wine; *hulē*, wood].

meticulous (me-tik′ū-lus) *a.* orig. afraid to make a mistake; hence, over-scrupulous as to detail; over-exact.—**metic'ulously** *adv.*—**metic′ulousness** *n.* [L. *metus*, fear].

métier (māt′yā) *n.* one's profession or vocation; the occupation for which one has a special aptitude [Fr.].

Metonic (me-ton'-ik) *a.* (*Astron.*) pert. to *Meton,* an Athenian astronomer.—**Metonic cycle**, a period of 19 years at the end of which the phases of the moon appear on the same days as at the beginning of the cycle [fr. *Meton,* c. 430].

metonymy (me-ton'-i-mi) *n.* (*Rhet.*) a figure of speech in which the name of one thing is put for another associated with it, as 'the pen is mightier than the sword.'—**metonym'ic, -al** *a.* —**metonym'ically** *adv.* [Gk. *meta,* expressing change; *onoma,* a name].

metre (mē'-tẹr) *n.* unit of length in the metric system, 39·37 Eng. inches.—**met'ric** *a.*—**metric system**, a decimal system based on the French metre [Gk. *metron,* a measure].

metre, meter (mē'-tẹr) *n.* in poetry, the rhythmical group arrangement of syllables (long and short, accented and unaccented), these groups in English prosody being termed *feet*; verse; stanza-form.—**met'rical** *a.* pert. to metre or to measurement.—**met'rically** *adv.*—**metrol'ogy** *n.* the science of weights and measures.—**met'ronome** *n.* (*Mus.*) an instrument like an inverted pendulum for beating out the time in music [Gk. *metron,* a measure].

metropolis (me-trop'-o-lis) *n.* the capital town of a country; the principal ecclesiastical city. —*pl.* **metrop'olises**.—**metropol'itan** *a.* pert. to a metropolis; pert. to the see of a metropolitan bishop;—*n.* a bishop with jurisdiction over other bishops of the see [Gk. *mētēr,* a mother; *polis,* a city].

mettle (met'-l) *n.* spirit; courage.—**mett'lesome** *a.* high-spirited; ardent.—**to be on one's mettle,** to be roused to do one's best [fr. *metal*].

mew (mū) *n.* a sea-gull [O.E. *maew,* a gull].

mew (mū) *v.t.* to shed or cast; to confine, as in a cage;—*v.i.* to moult;—*n.* a cage for hawks, esp. at moulting season;—*pl.* stables, orig. the place where the king's falcons were kept [O.Fr. *muer,* to moult].

mew (mū) *n.* the cry of a cat, sea-gull, etc.; —*v.i.* to cry as a cat [imit.].

Mexican (meks'-i-kạn) *n.* a native or inhabitant of *Mexico*;—*a.* pert. to Mexico or to the people of Mexico.

mezzanine (mez'-a-nīn) *n.* (*Archit.*) a low storey between two higher ones; a window in such; in a theatre, the floor below the stage [It. *mezzo,* middle].

mezzo (med'-zō) *a.* middle.—**mez'zo-sopran'o** *n.* a type of voice between soprano and contralto. —**mez'zotint** *n.* a method of copper-plate engraving in which a roughened surface is scraped heavily or lightly according to degrees of light and shade required. Also **mezzotint'o** [It. *mezzo,* half].

miaow (mi-ou') *n.* the cry of a cat;—*v.i.* to mew [imit.].

miasma (mī-az'-mạ) *n.* infectious or noxious exhalations from decomposing matter. Also **mi'asm**.—*pl.* **mias'mata, mi'asms**.—**mias'mal, miasmat'ic, mias'matous** *a.* [Gk. *miasma,* a stain].

mica (mī'-ka) *n.* a group of mineral silicates of aluminium and potassium, sodium, etc., capable of cleavage into very thin, flexible, and often transparent laminae.—**mica'ceous** *a.* [L. *mica,* a crumb].

mice (mīs) *pl.* of **mouse**.

Michael (mī'-kl) *n.* an archangel and leader of the heavenly host.—**Michaelmas** (mik'-l-mas) *n.* the feast of St. Michael, Sept 29th.—**Michaelmas daisy**, a common garden flower of the aster family.

microbe (mī'-krōb) *n.* a minute organism; a bacterium. or disease-germ.—**micro'bial, micro'bian, micro'bic** *a.*—**micro'bicide** *n.* any substance which kills microbes.—**microbiol'ogy** *n.* the science of microbes.—**microbiolog'ical** *a.* [Gk. *mikros,* small; *bios,* life].

microcephalous (mī-krō-sef'-ạ-lus) *a.* (*Med.*) having a very small head [Gk. *mikros,* small; *kēphalà,* the head].

micrococcus (mī-krō-kok'-us) *n.* a spherical shaped organism or bacterium [Gk. *mikros,* small; *kokkos,* a berry].

microcosm (mī'-krō-kozm) *n.* man, regarded as the epitome of the universe or macrocosm; a community symbolical of humanity as a whole; miniature representation.—**microcos'mic, -al** *a.* [Gk. *mikros,* small; *kosmos,* the universe].

microfilm (mī'-krō-film) *n.* standard film used in micro-copying of books, etc. [Gk. *mikros,* small; and *film*].

micrograph (mī'-krō-graf) *n.* an instrument for producing microscopic engraving; a microphotograph.—**microg'rapher** *n.*—**micrograph'ic** *a.*—**microg'raphy** *n.* the study of microscopic objects; the art of writing or engraving on a minute scale [Gk. *mikros,* small; *graphein,* to write].

micrology (mī-krol'-o-ji) *n.* the science which deals with microscopic objects; (*Fig.*) overscrupulous attention to small details [Gk. *mikros,* small; *logos,* a discourse].

micrometer (mī-krom'-e-tẹr) *n.* an instrument for measuring very small distances or angles. —**micromet'ric, -al** *a.*[Gk. *mikros,* small; *metron,* a measure].

micron (mī'-kron) *n.* the millionth part of a metre.—**micronise** (mī'-krō-nīz) *v.t.* to pulverise into very small particles [Gk. *mikros,* small].

micro-organism (mī'-krō-or'-gan-izm) *n.* a microscopic organism; a microbe; a germ [Gk. *mikros,* small; *organon,* an instrument].

microphone (mī'-krō-fōn) *n.* an instrument for turning sound waves into electrical waves so enabling them to be transmitted as wireless waves; mouthpiece for broadcasting (*Colloq.* abbrev. **mike**); an instrument for making faint sounds louder.—**microphon'ic** *a.* [Gk. *mikros,* small; *phōne,* a sound].

microphotography (mī'-krō-fō-tog'-rạ-fi) *n.* the art of producing minute photographs which can be examined only by means of a microscope.—**microphotog'raph** *n.* [Gk. *mikros,* small; *phos,* light; *graphein,* to write].

microscope (mī'-krō-skōp) *n.* an optical instrument for magnifying minute objects.—**microscop'ic, -al** *a.* pert. to a microscope; visible only by the aid of a microscope; very minute.—**microscop'ically** *adv.*—**micros'copy** *n.* [Gk. *mikros,* small; *skopein,* to see].

microzoa (mī-krō-zō'-ạ) *n.pl.* microscopic animals.—**microzo'an** *a.* [Gk. *mikros,* small; *zōon,* an animal; *zumē,* leaven].

micturition (mik-tū-rish'-un) *n.* (*Med.*) the passing of urine; the morbid desire to pass urine frequently.—**mic'turate** *v.i.* [L. *micturire,* to pass urine].

mid (mid) *a.* situated between extremes; middle, as in *mid-air, mid-Atlantic.*—**mid'day** *n.* and *a.* noon; pert. to noon.—**mid'land** *a.* in the middle of a land area;—*n.* the central part of a country.—**Mid'lands** *n.pl.* the central counties of England.—**mid'most** *a.* middle.—**mid'night** *n.* twelve o'clock at night.—**mid'-off, mid'-on** *n.* (*Cricket*) the fielder standing on the *off* (or *on*) side of the batsman, not far from the bowler.—**mid'-ship** *a.* in the middle part of a ship.—**mid'shipman** *n.* a junior naval officer below a sub-lieutenant (orig. quartered *amidships*).—**mid'shipmite** *n.* (*Colloq.*) midshipman. —**mid'ships** *adv.* amidships.—**mid'summer** *n.* the middle of summer; the period of the summer solstice, June 21.—**mid'way** *adv.* halfway.—**mid'winter** *n.* middle of the winter; period of the winter solstice, 22nd Dec. [O.E. *mid,* middle].

mid (mid) *prep.* amidst (in poetry).

midden (mid'-n) *n.* a heap of ashes, dung, or refuse [Scand. *modding,* a dung-heap].

middle (mid'-l) *a.* equidistant from the extremes; intermediate;—*n.* middle point.—**midd'le-aged** *a.* pert. to the period of life between 40 and 60.—**midd'leman** *n.* an agent acting between producer and consumer (or retailer).—**midd'lemost** *a.* nearest the middle. —**midd'le-watch** *n.* (*Naut.*) the period between midnight and 4 a.m.—**midd'le-weight** *n.* (*Boxing*) a boxer of a weight between 10 st. 7 lbs. and 11 st. 6 lbs.—**midd'ling** *a.* of medium size, quality;—*adv.* moderately.—**Middle Ages**, the period of European history from the Fall of the Roman Empire (about A.D. 476) to the Fall of Constantinople (1453).—**middle class**, that section of the community between the aristocracy and the working classes; the bourgeoisie.—**Middle East**, that part of the world between the *Near East* and the *Far East*, including Egypt, Syria, Palestine, Arabia, Iraq and Iran.—**Middle English**, the English language as written and spoken between 1150-1500 (approx.) [O.E. *middel*, middle].

middy (mid'i) *n.* (*Colloq.*) a midshipman.

midge (mij) *n.* a gnat; a very small person.—**midg'et** *n.* a dwarf; a miniature photograph.—**midget submarine** (*World War* 2) a very small-sized submarine, manned by one or two men [O.E. *mycge*, a gnat].

midinette (mē-dē-net') *n.* a Parisian shop-girl [Fr. *midi*, noon; hence name for those girls who throng the street at lunch hour].

midriff (mid'rif) *n.* the diaphragm [O.E. *mid*, middle; *hrif*, the belly].

midst (midst) *n.* the middle;—*prep.* amidst [M.E.].

midwife (mid'wīf) *n.* a woman who assists another at childbirth.—*pl.* **mid'wives.**—**midwifery** (mid'wif-ri) *n.* the practice of obstetrics [O.E. *mid*, with; *wif*, a woman].

mien (mēn) *n.* demeanour; bearing; general appearance [etym. doubtful].

might (mīt) *pa.t.* of verb **may.**

might (mīt) *n.* power; strength; energy.—**might'iness** *n.* the state of being powerful; greatness.—**might'y** *a.* having great strength or power; exalted [O.E. *meaht*, might].

mignonette (min'yo-net) *n.* a sweet-scented, greenish-gray flowered plant [dim. of Fr. *mignon*, a darling].

migraine (mē-grān') *n.* Same as **megrim.**

migrate (mī'grāt) *v.i.* to remove one's residence from one place to another; (of birds) to fly to another place or country in search of warmer climate or better feeding grounds.—**mi'grant** *n.* a migratory bird;—*a.* accustomed to migrate.—**migra'tion** *n.* the act of migrating; a mass removal.—**mi'gratory** *a.* [L. *migrare*, to go].

Mikado (mi-kà'dō) *n.* the Emperor of Japan [Jap. *mi*, august; *kado*, the door].

mike (mīk) *n.* (*Colloq. abbrev.*) a microphone.

mike (mīk) *v.i.* (*Slang*) to shirk hard work; to malinger [O.Fr. *muchier*, to skulk].

mil (mil) *n.* $\frac{1}{1000}$ in.; £ $\frac{1}{1000}$; unit of measurement in calculating the diameter of wire [L. *mille*, a thousand].

milch (milch) *a.* giving milk [M.E. *milch*, milk].

mild (mīld) *a.* gentle; kind; placid; calm, or temperate, as weather.—**mild'ly** *adv.*—**mild'ness** [O.E. *milde*, gentle].

mildew (mil'dū) *n.* whitish coating of minute fungi on plants; a mould on paper, cloth, leather caused by dampness;—*v.t.* and *v.i.* to taint or be tainted with mildew.—**mil'dewy** *a.* [O.E. *mele*, honey; *deaw*, dew].

mile (mīl) *n.* a measure of length equal to 1760 yds. (orig. a Roman measure of 1000 paces, about 1620 yds.).—**geographical or nautical mile**, one minute of a great circle of the earth equal to 6080 ft.—**mile'age** *n.* distance in miles; rate of travel calculated in miles; (*U. S.*) travelling expenses calculated on the number of miles travelled.—**mil'er** *n.* a man or horse trained to run a mile-race.—**mile'stone** *n.* a stone on the roadside marking distance in miles; (*Fig.*) a stage or crisis in one's life [O.E. *mil*, fr. L. *mille passus*, a 1000 paces].

miliary (mil'yar-i) *a.* like millet-seeds.—**miliary fever** (*Med.*) a fever, accompanied by a rash resembling millet-seeds [L. *milium*, millet].

militant (mil'i-tant) *a.* fighting; serving as a soldier.—**mil'itancy** *n.* the state of being war like; fighting spirit.—**mil'itantly** *adv.*—**militarism** *n.* excessive emphasis on the military power of a country—opp. of *pacifism.*—**mil'itarist** *n.* one who upholds the doctrine of militarism; a student of military science and strategy.—**mil'itary** *a.* pert. to soldiers, arms, or war; warlike;—*n.* the army; a body of soldiers.—**military police**, soldiers performing duties of police in the army.—**mil'itate** *v.i.* to stand opposed to; to have an adverse effect on (foll. by *against*) [L. *miles*, a soldier].

militia (mi-lish'a) *n.* a citizen army, liable to be called out in an emergency; branch of British military forces known as Territorial Force after 1907;—**milit'iaman** *n.* [L. *miles*, a soldier].

milk (milk) *n.* a white fluid secreted by female mammals for nourishment of their young; the juice of certain plants;—*v.t.* to draw milk from; (*Colloq.*) to fleece or exploit a person;—*v.i.* to give milk.—**milk and water** *a.* insipid.—**milk'bar** *n.* a counter where milk drinks, milk shakes, etc., are sold.—**milk'en** *a.* like milk.—**milk'er** *n.* one who milks a cow; a milking-machine; a cow which yields milk.—**milk fever**, a fever sometimes contracted after childbirth.—**milk'ily** *adv.*—**milk'iness** *n.*—**milk'ing** *n.* the quality of milk yielded at one time; the drawing of milk from a cow.—**milk'like** *a.*—**milk'maid** *n.* a dairymaid or woman who milks cows.—**milk'man** *n.* a man who milks cows; a man who distributes milk, esp. from house to house.—**milk shake**, a drink made of fruit juices and milk mixed in special shaker.—**milk'sop** *n.* a weak, effeminate man.—**milk'tooth** *n.* one of the first, temporary teeth lost in childhood.—**milk'weed** *n.* kinds of wild plants with milky sap.—**milk'wood** *n.* kind of tropical trees yielding latex.—**milk'y** *a.* like, full of, or yielding milk.—**Milky Way**, the Galaxy, an irregular, luminous belt in the heavens, proceeding from the light of innumerable stars.—**condensed milk**, milk with sugar added and evaporated to the consistency of syrup.—**evaporated milk**, unsweetened condensed milk [O.E. *meolc*, milk].

mill (mil) *n.* a building equipped with machinery to grind corn, etc.; an apparatus worked by hand, electricity, etc., for grinding, as *coffee-mill*; a factory or the machinery used in manufacture, as *cotton-mill, paper-mill*; (*Slang*) a boxing match.—*v.t.* to grind; to cut fine grooves on the edges of, as of coins; to full (cloth); to dress or purify (ore); (*Slang*) to beat with the fists;—*v.i.* to go round in circles, as cattle, or crowds of people.—**mill'board** *n.* stout pasteboard used in book-binding.—**mill'dam** *n.* a dam built to conserve water supply for turning a mill-wheel.—**milled** *a.* having the edges raised and grooved, as coins; fulled, as cloth; rolled into sheets, as metal.—**mill'ing** *n.* grinding in a mill; fulling cloth, or grooving the raised edges of a coin, or pressing crude rubber under heavy rollers;—*a.* (*Slang*) confused; without direction, as *milling crowds on cup-tie day.*—**mill'pond** *n.* pond supplying water for mill-wheel.—**mill'race** *n.* the swiftly moving current of water which turns mill-wheel.—**mill'stone** *n.* one of the pair of round, flat stones used in grinding grain.—**millstone grit**, a coarse grained sandstone used in cutlery industry for sharpening knives, etc.—**mill'wheel** *n.* a water wheel for driving a mill.—**mill'wright** *n.* one who sets up machinery in a mill [O.E. *myln*, to grind].

millennium (mil-en'i-um) *n.* a thousand years; esp. the period of a thousand years when Christ will reign on earth (*Rev.* 20); a future time or perfect peace on earth.—**millenna'rian** *a.* lasting a thousand years; pert. to the millennium;—*n.* one who believes in the millennium.—**mill'ennary** *a.* comprising a thousand;—*n.* a period of a thousand years.—**millenn'ial** *a.* pert. to the millennium [L. *mille*, a thousand; *annus*, a year].

milleped, millipede (mil′e-ped, -i-pēd) *n.* an insect with many legs, as a wood-louse [L. *mille*, thousand; *pes*, a foot].

miller (mil′ẹr) *n.* one who grinds corn.—**miller's thumb**, a small river-fish; the bull-head [O.E. *myln*, to grind].

millesimal (mil-es′i-mạl) *a.* thousandth; consisting of a thousand parts;—*n.* a thousandth part [L. *mille*, a thousand].

millet (mil′et) *n.* a cereal grass bearing seeds of great nutritive value [Fr.].

milli- (mil′i) *prefix* one thousandth of.—**mill′igram, mill′igramme** *n.* one thousandth of a gram, ·0154 of a grain.—**mill′ilitre** *n.* one thousandth of a litre, ·061 cub. in.—**mill′imetre, mill′imeter** *n.* one thousandth of a metre, ·0394 in. [L. *mille*, a thousand].

milliard (mil′yard) *n.* a thousand millions; (*U.S.*) a billion [Fr.].

milliner (mil′in-ẹr) *n.* orig. a seller of *Milan* wares; one who makes or sells ladies' hats.—**mill′inery** *n.* [fr. *Milan*].

million (mil′yun) *n.* a thousand thousands (1,000,000); a very large number.—**millionaire′** *n.* (*fem.* **millionair′ess**) one whose wealth amounts to a million (or more) pounds, francs, dollars.—**mill′ionary** *a.*—**mill′ionfold** *a.*—**mill′ionth** *n.* one of a million parts;—*a.* being one of a million parts.—**the millions**, the masses [Fr.].

Mills bomb (milz′bom) *n.* a hand-grenade shaped like an egg [fr. *Mills*, the inventor].

milt (milt) *n.* the spleen; the glands or soft roe of the male fish;—*v.t.* to impregnate the female roe.—**milt′er** *n.* a male fish in the breeding season [O.E. *milte*].

mim (mim) *a.* (*Prov.*) demure; over-precise.

mime (mīm) *n.* a farce in which scenes of real life are expressed by gesture only; an actor in such a farce;—*v.i.* to act in a mime; to express by gesture only.—**mimet′ic(al)** *a.* imitative.—**mim′ic** *v.t.* to imitate; to burlesque; to ridicule by imitating another's mannerisms.—*pr.p.* **mim′icking**.—*pa.p.* **mim′icked**.—*n.* one who mimics or caricatures;—*a.* mock, as in *mimic battle*; feigned.—**mim′icry** *n.* the art or act of mimicking [Gk. *mimos*, an actor].

mimeograph (mim′ē-ō-graf, mīm′ō-graf) *n.* a form of duplicating-machine [Gk. *mimeisthai*, to imitate; *graphein*, to write].

Mimosa (mi-mō′zạ) *n.* a genus of leguminous plants, with small, fluffy yellow flowers [Gk. *mimos*, an imitator].

mina, myna, mynah (mī′na) *n.* an Indian bird allied to the starling [Hind. *maina*].

minacious (min-ā′shus) *a.* threatening.—**minac′ity** *n.* [L. *minax*, threatening].

minar (mi′när) *n.* a lighthouse; a tower.—**min′aret** *n.* a turret on a Mohammedan mosque [Ar. *manarat*, a lighthouse].

minatory (min′ạ-tor-i) *a.* threatening; menacing; minacious [L. *minari*, to threaten].

mince (mins) *v.t.* to cut or chop into very small pieces; (*Fig.*) to tone down; to extenuate;—*v.i.* to clip one's words; to speak or walk with affected elegance.—*pr.p.* **minc′ing**.—*pa.p.* **minced** (minst).—*n.* meat chopped small or put through a mincer.—**minc′er** *n.* a machine, with revolving blades, for chopping meat, nuts, etc.—**mince′meat** *n.* currants, raisins, spices, apple, suet and sugar, chopped and mixed together, used as a filling for Christmas pies.—**mince′pie** *n.* a small round pie filled with this.—**minc′ing** *a.* speaking or walking with affected elegance.—**minc′ingly** *adv.* [O.E. *minsian*, to make small].

mind (mīnd) *n.* the intellectual faculty; the understanding; memory; opinion; inclination; purpose; a person regarded as an intellectual influence;—*v.t.* to attend to; to heed; to object to; to take care of;—*v.i.* to be careful; to intend.—**mind′ed** *a.* disposed; inclined.—**mind′edness** *n.*—**mind′er** *n.* one who looks after anything.—**mind′ful** *a.* attentive; observant.—**mind′fully** *adv.*—**mind′fulness** *n.*—**mind′less** *a.* stupid; regardless.—**mind′read′er** *n.* one who can sense another's thoughts.—**absence of mind**, forgetfulness [O.E. *gemynd*, the mind].

mine (mīn) *poss. pron.* belonging to me; [O.E. *min*].

mine (mīn) *n.* a pit in the earth from which minerals are excavated; a hidden deposit of explosives to blow up a wall, vessel, etc., in war; (*Fig.*) a profitable source;—*pl.* the mining industry;—*v.i.* and *v.t.* to lay a mine under; to dig a mine or in a mine; to burrow; (*Fig.*) to undermine; to sap.—**mine′field** *n.* an area of land or stretch of the sea where mines have been laid down.—**mine′lay′er** *n.* a vessel which lays down submarine or floating mines.—**mi′ner** *n.* one who works in a mine.—**mine′sweep′er** *n.* a vessel fitted with nets for clearing a minefield [Fr. *miner*, to mine].

mineral (min′ẹr-ạl) *n.* any substance, generally inorganic, taken from the earth by mining;—*pl.* mineral waters;—*a.* pert. to minerals; containing minerals; (*Chem.*) inorganic.—**mineralisa′tion** *n.*—**min′eralise** *v.t.* to convert into minerals; to impregnate with minerals.—**min′eralist** *n.* an expert in minerals.—**mineralog′ical** *a.*—**mineralog′ically** *adv.*—**mineral′ogy** *n.* the science of minerals and their classification.—**mineral waters**, waters, naturally impregnated with mineral substance, and used medicinally; effervescent imitation of this, such as soda-water, lemonade, etc. [Fr. *miner*, to mine].

mingle (ming′gl) *v.t.* to mix; to blend; to join in;—*v.i.* to become mixed;—*n.* a jumble.—**ming′ler** *n.*—**ming′ling** *n.* blend.—**ming′lingly** *adv.* [O.E. *mengan*, to mix].

mingy (min′ji) *a.* (*Slang*) parsimonious; stingy [*mean* and *stingy*].

miniature (min′i-ạ-tūr) *n.* a small-sized painting done on ivory, vellum, etc. ; anything on a small scale;—*a.* on a small scale; minute;—*v.t.* to depict on a small scale [L. *miniare*, to paint in red lead].

minify (min′i-fī) *v.t.* to lessen; to minimise [L. *minor*, less; *facere*, to make].

minikin (min′i-kin) *n.* a pet; the smallest kind of pin;—*a.* diminutive; delicate [Dut. dim. of *minne*, love].

minim (min′im) *n.* anything very minute; (*Med.*) $\frac{1}{60}$ of a fluid drachm; a drop; (*Mus.*) a note equal to two crotchets.—**min′imal** *a.*—**min′imise** *v.t.* to reduce to the smallest proportions; to depreciate; to undervalue.—**minimisa′tion** *n.*—**min′imum** *n.* the least to which anything may be reduced.—*pl.* **min′ima** [L. *minimus*, the smallest].

minion (min′yun) *n.* a favourite; a servile flatterer; (*Print.*) a small type, now 7 point. [Fr. *mignon*, a darling].

minister (min′is-tẹr) *n.* a servant; an agent or instrument; a clergyman; one entrusted with a State department; an ambassador;—*v.i.* to act as a servant; to supply things needful.—*pr.p.* **min′istering**.—*pa.p.* **min′istered**.—**ministe′rial** *a.* executive; pert. to the work of a minister or State department.—**minister′ially** *adv.*—**min′istering** *a.* serving.—**min′istrant** *n.* one who ministers; a helper;—*a.* serving as a minister.—**ministra′tion** *n.* the act of performing a service, esp. a religious service.—**ministra′tive** *a.*—**min′istry** *n.* the act of ministering; the office or functions of a minister; the clergy or the office of a clergyman; a government department, as *Ministry of Pensions*; the Cabinet [L. *minister*, a servant].

miniver (min′i-vẹr) *n.* the fur of the Siberian (winter) ermine; the fur on judge's robes, etc. Also **min′ever, men′ever** [O.Fr. *menu*, small; *vair*, fur].

mink (mingk) *n.* a semi-aquatic animal of the weasel tribe; its very valuable brown fur [Scand.].

minnow (min′ō) *n.* a very small freshwater fish [O.E. *myne*, a small fish].

minor (mī′nor) *a.* lesser; inferior in bulk, degree, importance, etc.; subordinate; (*Mus.*) lower by a semi-tone;—*n.* a person under 21.—**minor′ity** *n.* the state of being under age, the lesser number, oppos. of *majority.*—**minor key** (*Mus.*) a key characterised by a minor third, sixth, or seventh.—**Minor Prophets,** the twelve O.T. books from Hosea to Malachi [L. *minor,* less].

Minorca (min-or´kạ) *n.* a breed of fowl [fr. *Minorca,* a Spanish island].

Minos (mī´nos) *n.* a legendary king of Crete.—**Mino'an** *a.* pert. to Crete.—**Minoan period,** the ' bronze age ' of the ancient Cretan civilisation [2500-1500 B.C.].

Minotaur (min´o-tawr) *n.* in Greek mythology a monster, half-man, half-bull [Gk. *Minos,* King of Crete; *tauros,* a bull].

minster (min-stẹr) *n.* the church of a monastery; a cathedral [O.E. *mynster,* a monastery].

minstrel (min´strẹl) *n.* a medieval bard or wandering singer who sang songs usually of his own composing, to the accompaniment of the harp; a seaside entertainer.—**min'strelsy** *n.* the art or profession of a minstrel; a group of minstrels; a collection of ballads [O.Fr. *menestrel,* a jester].

mint (mint) *n.* the place where money is coined; (*Fig.*) a source of invention or supply; —*v.t.* to make by stamping, as coins; to invent.—**mint'age** *n.* minting coins; coinage; the duty paid for minting.—**mint'er** *n.* [O.E. *mynet,* money].

mint (mint) *n.* an aromatic plant of various kinds used for medicinal and culinary purposes.—**mint julep,** an iced drink of spirits and sugar flavoured with mint [O.E. *minte,* mint].

minuend (min´ū-end) *n.* the number from which another is to be subtracted [L. *minuendus,* to be made less].

minuet (min-ū-et') *n.* a slow, stately dance; music, to which the minuet is danced. Also **minuette'** [Fr. *menuet,* fr. *menu,* small].

minus (mī´nus) *a.* less; deducted from; deficient;—*n.* the sign (—) of subtraction; an amount less than nothing.—**minus'cule** *a.* small;—*n.* a concise monastic script in use from 8th-10th cents.; a small or lower-case letter, oppos. of *majuscule* [L. *minor,* less].

minute (min-ūt') *a.* very small; slight; particular; exact.—**minute'ly** *adv.*—**minute'ness** *n.* —**minutiae** (min-ū´shi-ē) *n.pl.* minute details [L. *minuere, minutum,* to lessen].

minute (min´it) *n.* the 60th part of an hour or degree; a short draft.—*pl.* the official record of affairs transacted at a meeting;—*v.t.* to make a note of.—**min'ute-book** *n.* book containing minutes of meeting.—**min'ute-glass** *n.* a sand glass which, in running out, indicates a minute of time.—**min'ute-gun** *n.* a gun discharged every minute as a signal of distress or mourning.—**min'ute-hand** *n.* longer of two hands on clock or watch indicating minutes.—**min'utely** *adv.* occurring every minute [L. *minuere minutum,* to lessen].

minx (mingks) *n.* a pert, saucy girl [etym. doubtful].

Miocene (mī´ō-sēn) *a.* (*Geol.*) belonging to the Middle Tertiary period; less recent [Gk. *meiōn,* less; *kainos,* new].

miosis (mī-ō´sis) See **myosis, meiosis,**

miracle (mir´ạ-kl) *n.* a wonder; a supernatural happening; a prodigy.—**Miracle Play,** a popular medieval form of drama based on the lives of the Saints, or on Biblical history.—**mirac'ulous** *a.* supernatural; extraordinary.—**mirac'ulously** *adv.*—**mirac'ulousness** *n.* [L. *mirari,* to wonder].

mirage (mi-ràzh') *n.* an optical illusion caused by an image of an object below the horizon being reflected back from an upper layer of the atmosphere; (*Fig.*) a delusion [L. *mirari,* to wonder at].

mire (mīr) *n.* slimy soil; mud; (*Fig.*) defilement;—*v.t.* to plunge into or cover with mud; —*v.i.* to sink in mud.—**mi'riness** *n.*—**mi'ry** *a.* [O.N. *myrr,* marsh].

mirror (mir´or) *n.* a looking-glass; a brilliantly polished reflecting surface; (*Fig.*) a pattern; a reflection, as a *mirror of the times.*—*v.t.* to reflect.—*pr.p.* **mirr'oring.**—*pa.p.* **mirr'ored** [L. *mirare,* to look at].

mirth (mẹrth) *n.* gaiety; merriment; joyousness.—**mirth'ful** *a.* full of mirth; jovial; festive. —**mirth'fully** *adv.*—**mirth'fulness** *n.*—**mirth'less** *a.* without mirth; grim.—**mirth'lessly** *adv.* [O.E. *myrgth,* merry].

mis- (mis) *prefix.* wrong; ill.—prefixed to words of O.E. or O.Fr. origin.

misadventure (mis-ạd-ven´tūr) *n.* an unlucky adventure; a mishap.

misadvise (mis-ạd-vīz') *v.t.* to advise wrongly. —**misadvised'** *a.* ill-advised.

misalliance (mis-a-lī´ạns) *n.* an unfortunate alliance, esp. in marriage.

misanthrope (mis´ạn-thrōp) *n.* a hater of mankind; one who has no faith in his fellow men.—**misanthrop'ically** *adv.*—**misan'thropy** *n.* hatred of mankind [Gk. *misẹein,* to hate; *anthrōpos,* a man).

misapply (mis-ạ-plī') *v.t.* to apply wrongly or dishonestly.—**misapplica'tion** *n.*

misapprehend (mis-a-prē-hend') *v.t.* to apprehend wrongly; to misconceive.—**misapprehen´sion** *n.*—**misapprehen'sive** *a.*

misappropriate (mis-a-prō´pri-āt) *v.t.* to use wrongly, esp. to embezzle money.—**misappropria'tion** *n.*

misbecome (mis-be-kum') *v.t.* to suit ill.—**misbecom'ing** *a.* unseemly; indecorous.

misbegotten (mis-be-got´n) *a.* unlawfully conceived; illegitimate.

misbehave (mis-be-hāv') *v.i.* to behave badly, improperly or dishonestly.—**misbehav'iour** *n.*

misbelieve (mis-be-lēv') *v.t.* to believe wrongly.—**misbelief'** *n.* belief in false ideas.

miscalculate (mis-kal´kū-lāt) *v.t.* to calculate wrongly.—**miscalcula'tion** *n.*

miscall (mis-kawl') *v.t.* to call by a wrong name; to abuse.

miscarriage (mis-kar´ij) *n.* failure; premature birth.—**miscarr'y** *v.i.* to fail to fulfil the intended effect; to give birth prematurely.

miscast (mis-kạst') *v.t.* and *v.i.* to reckon wrongly; to allot unsuitably, as parts in a play;—*a.* wrongly allotted.

miscegenation (mis-i-jen-ā´shun) *n.* a mixture of races, esp. whites and negroes [L. *miscere,* to mix; *genus,* a race].

miscellaneous (mis-el-ān´i-us) *a.* mixed; heterogeneous.—**miscellan'eously** *adv.*—**miscellan'eousness** *n.*—**miscell'anist** *n.* a writer of miscellanies.—**miscell'any** *n.* a medley, esp. a collection of writings on various subjects.—**miscellan'ea** *n.pl.* odds and ends [L. *miscellaneus,* fr. *miscere,* to mix].

mischance (mis-chȧns') *n.* a mishap; ill-luck; disaster;—*v.i.* to happen disastrously.

mischief (mis´chif) *n.* ill; damage; the cause of injustice; trouble.—**mis'chief-mak'er** *n.* one who stirs up trouble.—**mis'chievous** *a.* tending to stir up trouble; hurtful; thoughtless.—**mis'chievously** *adv.*—**mis'chievousness** *n.* [O.Fr. *meschever,* to come to grief].

miscible (mis´i-bl) *a.* capable of being mixed to form a homogeneous substance.—**miscibil´ity** *n.* [L. *miscere,* to mix].

misconceive (mis-kon-sēv') *v.t.* to misapprehend; to mistake.—**misconcep'tion** *n.*

misconduct (mis-kon´dukt) *n.* bad management; dishonest conduct; adultery.—**misconduct'** *v.t.* to mismanage.

misconstrue (mis-kon-stròò') *v.t.* to interpret wrongly; to mistranslate, as a passage of Latin.—**misconstruc'tion** *n.*

miscount (mis-kount') *v.t.* to count wrongly; to miscalculate;—*n.* a wrong counting.

miscreant (mis´kre-ạnt) *n.* an infidel; a vile, unprincipled wretch [O.Fr. *mescreant,* unbeliever].

miscue (mis-kū) *n.* (*Billiards*) a stroke spoiled by the cue slipping;—*v.t.* to make a miscue.—*pr.p.* **miscu'ing.**—*pa.p.* **miscued'.**

misdate (mis-dāt') *v.t.* to put a wrong date on;—*n.* a wrong date.

In the Colombian Andes

MOUNTAINS and HIGHLANDS of the WORLD · 1

In the Pyrenees

Mount Shasta, California

The Rand in SW Africa

Mount Ararat

MOUNTAINS and HIGHLANDS of the WORLD · 2

In the Appalachians

In the Alps

Mount Olympus

misdeed (mis-dēd′) *n.* an evil deed, a crime.
misdemeanour (mis-dẹ-mēn′ur) *n.* dishonest conduct; (*Law*) a crime less than felony.—**misdemean′** *v.i.* to misbehave.
misdirect (mis-di-rekt′) *v.t.* to direct or advise wrongly.—**misdirec′tion** *n.*
miser (mī′zẹr) *n.* one who hoards money and lives in wretched surroundings.—**mi′serly** *a.* avaricious; niggardly.—**mi′serliness** *n.* [L. = wretched].
miserable (miz′ẹr-ạ-bl) *a.* unhappy; causing misery; worthless; shoddy.—**mis′erableness** *n.*—**mis′erably** *adv.* [L. *miser*, wretched].
misère (mi-zār′) *n.* (*Cards*) one of the calls in solo-whist by which the player must take no tricks [Fr.].
miserere (miz-e-rā′re) *n.* Psalm 51, which in the Vulgate, begins 'Miserere mei, Domine'; a musical setting for this psalm; a cry for mercy [L. = take pity].
misericorde (miz-er-i-kord′) *n.* mercy; a small dagger used by medieval knights for giving the final, fatal blow to a wounded foe [L. *misericordia*, compassion].
misery (miz′ẹ-ri) *n.* great unhappiness; extreme pain of body or mind; calamity [L. *miser*, wretched].
misfeasance (mis-fē′zạns) *n.* (*Law*) a wrong done; a misuse of lawful authority [O.Fr. *mesfaire*, to do wrong].
misfire (mis-fīr′) *n.* (of internal combustion engine, gun, etc.) failure to start or go off;—*v.i.* to fail to start or fire.
misfit (mis-fit′) *n.* a bad fit;—*v.t.* to make of the wrong size;—*v.i.* to fit badly.
misfortune (mis-for′tūn) *n.* ill-luck; a calamity.
misgive (mis-giv′) *v.t.* to fill with doubt; to cause to hesitate;—*v.i.* to fail.—**misgiv′ing** *n.* distrust; suspicion.
misgovern (mis-guv′ẹrn) *v.t.* to govern badly.—**misgov′ernment** *n.*
misguide (mis-gīd′) *v.t.* to lead astray; to advise wrongly.—**misguid′ance** *n.* [bungle.
mishandle (mis-han′dl) *v.t.* to maltreat; to
mishap (mis-hap′) *n.* ill-chance; accident.
mishit (mis-hit′) *n.* a faulty stroke, as at tennis, etc.;—*v.t.* to hit wrongly, as a ball.
misinform (mis-in-form′) *v.t.* to give wrong information to.—**misinform′ant, misinform′er** *n.*—**misinforma′tion** *n.* wrong information.
misinterpret (mis-in-tẹr′pret) *v.t.* to interpret or explain wrongly.—**misinterpreta′tion** *n.* misconception.—**misinter′preter** *n.*
misjudge (mis-juj′) *v.t* to judge wrongly; to miscalculate.—**misjudg(e)′ment** *n.*
mislay (mis-lā′) *v.t.* to lay down something in a place which cannot later be recollected.
mislead (mis-lēd′) *v.t.* to lead astray; to delude.—*pa.p.* **misled′**.—**mislead′ing** *a.*
mismanage (mis-man′āj) *v.t.* to manage incompetently.—**misman′agement** *n.*
misname (mis-nām′) *v.t.* to call by the wrong name.
misnomer (mis-nōm′ẹr) *n.* a wrong name; incorrect designation [O.Fr. *mesnommer*, to name wrongly].
misogamy (mis-og′am-i) *n.* hatred of marriage.—**misog′amist** *n.* [Gk. *miseein*, to hate; *gamos*, marriage].
misogyny (mis-oj′i-ni, or mis-og′i-ni) *n.* hatred of women.—**misog′ynist** *n.* a woman-hater.—**misogynist′ical, misog′ynous** *a.* [Gk. *miseein*, to hate; *gunē*, a woman].
misplace (mis-plās′) *v.t.* to place wrongly; to mislay; to bestow, as one's trust, on an unworthy person or object.
misprint (mis-print′) *v.t.* to make an error in printing;—*n.* an error in printing.
mispronounce (mis-pro-nouns′) *v.t.* to pronounce wrongly.—**mispronuncia′tion** *n.*
misquote (mis-kwōt′) *v.t.* to quote wrongly.—**misquota′tion** *n.* an inaccurate quotation.
misreckon (mis-rek′n) *v.t.* to estimate or reckon wrongly.—**misreck′oning** *n.*
misrelate (mis-re-lāt) *v.t.* to relate incorrectly.—**misrela′tion** *n.*
misrepresent (mis-rep-re-zent′) *v.t.* to represent falsely; to report facts inaccurately.—**misrepresenta′tion** *n.*
misrule (mis-ròòl′) *n.* disorder; misgovernment.—**Lord or Abbot of Misrule,** one who formerly presided over the revels.
Miss (mis) *n.* title of unmarried women; girl.—*pl.* **Miss′es** [contr. of *mistress*].
miss (mis) *v.t.* to fail to hit, reach, find, catch, notice: to be without; to feel the want of; to omit;—*v.i.* to fail to hit; to fall short of one's objective; (*Motoring*) to misfire;—*n.* failure to hit, reach, find, etc.; escape, as in *a lucky miss*.—**miss′ing** *a.* lost; absent; wanting.—**to miss the boat** (*Slang*) to fail to seize an opportunity [O.E. *missan*, to fail].
missal (mis′ạl) *n.* a book containing the R.C. service of the mass for a year [L. *missa*, mass].
missel (mis′l) *n.* the largest of the European thrushes, supposed to be partial to *mistletoe* berries. Also **mis′tle, miss′el-bird, miss′el-thrush** [O.E. *mistel*, mistletoe].
misshape (mis-shāp′) *v.t.* to shape badly; to deform;—*n.* deformity.—**misshap′en** *a.*
missile (mis′il or -īl) *n.* that which is thrown or shot with intent to damage;—*a.* capable of being thrown or shot [L. *mittere, missum*, to send].
mission (mish′un) *n.* the act of sending; the duty on which one is sent; a group of people sent to a foreign country to preach religion; a special field of missionary enterprise at home or abroad; a delegation sent to a foreign country to discuss matters of political or economic importance; vocation.—**miss′ionary** *a.* pert. to missions or missionaries;—*n.* one sent to preach religion, esp. in a foreign country; one who does social service among the poor.—**miss′ioner** *n.* one who conducts a district evangelical campaign [L. *mittere, missum*, to send].
missive (mis′iv) *n.* that which is sent, as a letter;—*a.* intended to be sent, or thrown [L. *mittere, missum*, to send].
misspell (mis-spel′) *v.t.* to spell wrongly.—**misspell′ing** *n.* an error in spelling.
misspend (mis-spend′) *v.t.* to spend foolishly; to squander.—*pa.t.* and *pa.p.* **misspent′**.
mist (mist) *n.* visible vapour in the lower atmosphere; droplets of rain; (*Fig.*) anything which makes comprehension difficult;—*v.t.* or *v.i.* to dim or be dimmed, as by a mist.—**mist′y** *a.* dim; obscured by a mist.—**mist′ily** *adv.*—**mist′iness** *n.* [O.E. *mist*, darkness].
mistake (mis-tāk′) *v.t.* to misunderstand; to take one person for another;—*v.i.* to err;—*n.* an error in opinion, judgment, conduct, etc.—*pa.t.* **mistook′**.—*pa.p.* **mistak′en**.—**mistak′able** *a.*—**mistak′en** *a.* guilty of error; misconceived; erroneous.—**mistak′enly** *adv.* [M.E. *mistaken*, to take wrongly].
mister (mis-tẹr) *n.* sir; title of courtesy to a man (*abbrev.* **Mr.**) [form of *master*].
misterm (mis-term′) *v.t.* to name wrongly.
mistime (mis-tīm′) *v.t.* to time wrongly.—**mistimed′** *a.* inopportune.
mistle Same as **missel.**
mistletoe (mis′l-tō, or miz′l-tō) *n.* a parasitic, evergreen plant with white berries growing in the forks of the stems [O.E. *mistel*, mistletoe; *tan*, a twig].
mistral (mis′tral) *n.* a cold, often violent, N.W. wind which blows over S. France [Fr. *mistral*, a master (wind)].
mistress (mis′tres) *n.* (*fem.* of **master**) a woman in authority, as employer, teacher; a woman-expert; a kept woman; a courtesy title given to married women (*abbrev.* **Mrs.** (mis′ez) [O.Fr. *maistresse*, fem. of *maistre* master].
mistrial (mis-trī′ạl) *n.* a trial made invalid by an error in the legal proceedings.
mistrust (mis-trust′) *n.* want of confidence;—*v.t.* to suspect; to lack faith in.—**mistrust′ful** *a.* suspicious.—**mistrust′fulness** *n.*
misunderstand (mis-un-dẹr-stand′) *v.t.* to interpret wrongly; to form a wrong judge-

ment.—**misunderstand′ing** *n.* a misconception; a slight quarrel.

misuse (mis-ūz′) *v.t.* to use improperly; to maltreat.—**misuse** (mis-ūs′) *n.* improper use. —**misu′sage** *n.* abuse.

mite (mīt) *n.* a very small coin, as the *widow's mite*; a half-farthing; any very small thing or person; a kind of arachnid, as *cheese-mite* [O. Dut. *mijt*, a small coin].

mitigate (mit′-i-gāt) *v.t.* to assuage; to relieve; to alleviate; to temper.—**mit′igable** *a.* capable of being lessened.—**mitiga′tion** *n.* alleviation; abatement.—**mit′igative, mit′igatory** *a.*—**mit′igator** *n.* [L. *mitigare*, to lessen].

mitrailleuse (mē-tra-yez′) *n.* breech-loading machine-gun with as many as 25 barrels.—**mitrailleur′** *n.* [Fr. *mitraille*, grape-shot].

mitre (mī′-ter) *n.* a bishop's headdress, a tall cap rising to a peak back and front, and elaborately embroidered; in carpentry, a joint made by two pieces of wood fitting in to each other at an angle of 45°; in sewing, a gusset;—*v.t.* to confer a mitre on; to join at an angle of 45°.—**mi′tral, mit′riform** *a.* shaped like a mitre; (*Bot.*) conical.—**mi′tre-block, -board,** or **-box** *n.* a piece of wood acting as a guide in sawing a *mitre-joint*.—**mi′tred** *a.* wearing a mitre; cut like a mitre; joined with a gusset [Gk. *mitra*, a belt].

mitten (mit′-n) *n.* a kind of glove with thumb, but palm and fingers all in one; a knitted covering for wrist and hand, but leaving fingers and thumb exposed. Also **mitt** [etym. unknown].

mix (miks) *v.t.* to unite into a mass; to blend; to cause people to be sociable;—*v.i.* to become mingled; to associate;—*n.* a mess; confusion. —**mix′able, mix′ible** *a.*—**mixed** *a.* mingled; blended; chaotic; of both sexes, as *mixed bathing*.—**mix′edly** *adv.*—**mix′er** *n.* one who or that which mixes; (*Colloq.*) one who is sociable, as a *good mixer*. —**mix′ture** *n.* the act of mixing; that which is mixed, esp. a liquid compound of drugs; (*Chem.*) a combination of substances which retain their individual properties, as contrasted with a *compound*.—**mix′-up** *n.* (*Colloq.*)confusion.—**mixed marriage,** a marriage between two people of different religions [L. *miscere*, to mix].

mizzen, mizen (miz′-n) *n.* the aftermost of the fore-and-aft sails of a vessel.—**mizz′en-mast** *n.* the mast bearing the mizzen [Fr. *misaine*, a fore-sail].

mizzle (miz′-l) *v.impers.* to rain in small drops; [—*n.* drizzle [fr. *misty*].

mnemonic, -al (ne-mon′-ik, -al) *a.* assisting the memory.—**mnemon′ics** *n.pl.* the art of assisting the memory; artificial aids to memory [Gk. *mnēmōn*, mindful].

moa (mō′-a) *n.* an extinct New Zealand flightless bird of very large size [Maori].

moan (mōn) *n.* a low cry of grief or pain;—*v.i.* to utter a low, wailing cry;—*v.t.* to lament [O.E. *maenan*, to lament].

moat (mōt) *n.* a deep trench round a castle, etc., usually filled with water (orig. a rampart of earth) [O.Fr. *mote*, a trench].

mob (mob) *n.* a disorderly crowd of people; a rabble; the populace; (*Slang*) a gang of pickpockets;—*v.t.* to attack in a disorderly crowd; to jostle.—*pr.p.* **mob′bing.**—*pa.p.* **mobbed.**—**mob′-law** *n.* lynch law.—**moboc′racy** *n.* the rule of the mob.—**mob′ocrat** *n.* a dictator.—**mobocrat′ic** *a.* [L. *mobile vulgus*, the fickle masses].

mob (mob) *n.* a mob-cap; a frilled cap, tied under the chin, worn by women in the 18th cent. [Dut. *mop*, a coif].

mobile (mō′-bīl) *a.* easily moved; changing; vacillating; (of troops) mechanised; capable of moving rapidly from one place to another;—*n.* an artistic arrangement of wires, etc., easily set in motion.—**mobilisa′tion** *n.* the wartime act of calling up men and women for active service.—**mo′bilise** *v.t.* to prepare for active service; to gather together available resources.—**mobil′ity** *n.* the state of being mobile [L. *mobilis*, movable].

moccasin (mok′-a-sin) *a.* shoe of deerskin or other soft leather worn by N. American Indians, trappers, etc.; a bedroom slipper of similar shape. Also **moc′cassin** [N. Amer. Ind. name].

Mocha (mō′-ka) *n.* a fine quality of coffee orig. from *Mocha* in Yemen.

mock (mok) *v.t.* to laugh at; to ridicule; to make a fool of; to defy; to tantalise; to feign;—*n.* ridicule; derision; jibe;—*a.* counterfeit; substitute.—**mock′er** *n.*—**mock′ery, mock′ing** *n.* the act of mocking; derision; travesty; false show.—**mock′-hero′ic** *a.* burlesquing the serious or heroic style.—**mock′ing** *n.* mockery;—*a.* scornful; derisive.—**mocking bird,** a N. American bird which imitates the songs of other birds.—**mock orange,** the syringa.—**mock turtle,** a soup made of calf's head, flavoured with curry powder, to imitate turtle soup [Fr. *moquer*, to mock].

mod (mod) *n.* a musical festival to encourage the study and practice of national songs, poetry, etc., esp. Gaelic songs, etc. [Gael.].

mode (mōd) *n.* manner, form, or method; custom; prevailing fashion; (*Mus.*) one of the two classes of keys (major or minor); also, one of the forms of scale or octave in ancient and medieval music, as Lydian, Dorian, etc.; (*Gram.*) the *mood* of the verb.—**mo′dal** *a.* relating to mode or form.—**modal′ity** *n.*—**mo′dish** *a.* fashionable.—**mo′dishly** *adv.*—**mo′dishness** *n.*—**modiste** (mōd-ēst′) *n.* a dress-maker or milliner selling the latest models [L. *modus*, manner].

model (mod′-el) *n.* an exact, three-dimensional representation of an object, in miniature; a pattern or standard to copy; one who poses for an artist; a mannequin;—*a.* serving as a model or criterion;—*v.t.* to make in model; to copy from a pattern or standard of conduct; to shape, as clay, wax, etc.;—*v.i.* to practise modelling.—*pr.p.* **mod′elling.**—*pa.p.* **mod′elled.** —**mod′eller** *n.* one who makes models.—**mod′elling** *n.* the art of working in plastic materials or of making models; shaping [O.Fr. *modelle*, a pattern].

moderate (mod′-er-āt) *a.* restrained; temperate; average; not extreme;—*v.t.* to restrain; to control; to decrease the intensity or pressure of;—*v.i.* to become less violent or intense; to act as moderator;—*n.* a person of moderate opinions in politics, religion, etc.—**mod′erately** *adv.*—**mod′erateness** *n.*—**modera′tion** *n.* the act of moderating; freedom from excess.—**Modera′tions** *n.pl.* (*abbrev.* **Mods.**) at Oxford University, the first public examination for the B.A. degree.—**mod′eratism** *n.* non-extremist views in politics, religion, etc.—**mod′erator** *n.* (*fem.* **mod′eratrix**) one who acts as arbitrator; the president of an assembly, as the *Moderator* of the General Assembly of the Church of Scotland [L. *moderari*, to limit].

modern (mod′-ern) *a.* pert. to present or recent time; up-to-date; new-fangled;—*n.* a person living in modern times; one who is up-to-date in outlook and ideas.—**modernisa′tion** *n.*—**mod′ernise** *v.t.* to bring up-to-date.—**modernis′er** *n.*—**mod′ernist** *n.* one who upholds modern ideas.—**mod′ernly** *adv.*—**mod′ernness, moder′nity** *n.* the state or quality of being modern [L. *modernus*, fr. *modo*, just now].

modest (mod′-est) *a.* unassuming; restrained; decent; retiring in manner; not excessive, as *modest means*.—**mod′estly** *adv.*—**mod′esty** *n.* the quality of being modest; absence of arrogance [L. *modestus*, moderate].

modicum (mod′-i-kum) *n.* a small quantity [L. *modicus*, moderate].

modify (mod′-i-fī) *v.t.* to moderate; to alter the form or intensity of; (*Philol.*) to change the sound of a vowel by the influence of a following vowel, as by mutation; (*Gram.*) to qualify the meaning of, as of a verb by an adverb.—**modifi′able** *a.*—**modifica′tion** *n.* the act of modifying; the state of being modified; a change of form, manner, or intensity; (*Philol.*)

change due to *mutation* or *umlaut*, the symbol of this change, as in ä, ö.—**mod'ificative, mod'ificatory** *a.* qualifying.—**mod'ifier** *n.* [L. *modificare*, to moderate].

modulate (mod'ū-lāt) *v.t.* to regulate, esp. the pitch of the voice; to adapt; (*Mus.*) to change the key of;—*v.i.* (*Mus.*) to pass from one key to another.—**mod'ular** *a.* pert. to mode, modulation, or module.—**modula'tion** *n.* the act of modulating; the changing of the pitch of the voice; (*Mus.*) transposition into a new key; (*Elect.*) the variation of the amplitude or frequency of continuous waves, usually by a lower frequency.—**mod'ulator** *n.* one who, or that which modulates; (*Mus.*) a chart of the modulation in the tonic sol-fa system.—**mod'ule** *n.* a unit of measurement; (*Archit.*) the radius of a shaft at its base, for standardising other proportions of a building.—**mod'ulus** *n.* (*Math.*) a constant number, coefficient, or quantity which measures a force, function, or effect.—*pl.* **moduli** (mod'ū-lī) [L. *modulari*, to measure].

Mogul (mō'gul) *n.* a Mongol, esp. one of the followers of Baber, the conqueror of India in the 15th cent.;—*a.* pert to the Mogul Empire.

mohair (mō'hār) *n.* the silky hair of the Angora goat; fabric made from this or similar hair [Ar. *mukhayyar*, hair-cloth].

Mohammedan (mo-ham'ed-ạn) *a.* pert. to Mohammed or to Mohammedanism;—*n.* a follower of Mohammed; a Moslem. Also **Mahom'etan, Mahom'edan.**—**Moham'medanism** *n.* the religion of Mohammed and his followers; Islam [fr. *Mohammed*, Arabian prophet.]

Mohave (mō-hȧ'vā) *n.* a tribe of American Indians. Also **Moja've** [Native].

Mohawk (mō'hawk) *n.* the name of a N. American Indian tribe [Native].

Mohican (mō-hē'kạn) *n.* a N. American Indian tribe of Algonkin stock [Native].

moidore (moi'dōr) *n.* an obsolete Portuguese coin worth about 27s. [Port. *moeda d'ouro*, coin of gold].

moiety (moi'e-ti) *n.* half; a small share [Fr. *moitié*, half].

moil (moil) *v.t.* to moisten; to dirty;—*v.i.* to drudge [M.E. *moillen*, to wet].

moire (mwȧr) *n.* watered silk fabric.—**moiré** (mwȧ'rā) *a.* watered; cloudy in appearance [var. of *mohair*].

moist (moist) *a.* damp; humid; rather wet.—**moist'en** *v.t.* to make moist; to damp slightly.—**moist'ness, moist'ure** *n.* that which causes dampness; condensed vapour.—**moist'ureless** *a.* dry [O.Fr. *moiste*, fresh].

molar (mō'lạr) *a.* grinding or able to grind, as back teeth;—*n.* a back double-tooth for grinding [L. *molere*, to grind].

molasses (mo-las'ez) *n. sing.* a dark-coloured syrup obtained from sugar in the process of manufacture; treacle [L. *mellaceus*, honey-like].

mold Same as **mould.**

mole (mōl) *n.* a slightly raised, dark brown spot on the skin [O.E. *mal*, a spot].

mole (mōl) *n.* a small burrowing insectivorous animal, with velvety, bluish-grey fur, very small eyes, and paws like miniature hands;—*v.t.* to burrow.—**mole'hill** *n.* a little mound of earth thrown up by a mole when burrowing.—**mole'skin** *n.* the fur of a mole; a kind of fustian, with soft surface like the skin of a mole [M.E. *molle*, a mole].

mole (mōl) *n.* a breakwater; a pier built to form a harbour [L. *moles*, a mass].

molecule (mol'e-kūl) *n.* the smallest portion of a substance which can retain independently the characteristics of that substance.—**molec'ular** *a.*—**molecular weight,** the weight of a molecule of a substance in relation to the weight of a hydrogen atom [dim. fr. L. *moles*, a mass].

molest (mō-lest') *v.t.* to trouble; to accost with sinister intention.—**molesta'tion** *n.* [L. *molestus*, troublesome].

mollify (mol'i-fī) *v.t.* to appease; to placate; to soften.—*pr.p.* **moll'ifying.**—*pa.p.* **moll'ified.**—**moll'ifiable** *a.*—**mollifica'tion** *n.* the act of mollifying.—**moll'ifier** *n.* [L. *mollificare*, to make soft].

mollusc, mollusk (mol'usk) *n.* an invertebrate animal with soft, pulpy body and usually a hard outer shell, as the oyster, snail, etc.—*pl.* **moll'uscs** or **mollus'ca.**—**mollus'can** *a.* pert. to molluscs;—*n.* a mollusc.—**mollus'coid, -cous** *a.* like a mollusc [L. *mollusca*, a soft nut].

molly (mol'i) *n.* an effeminate person.—**moll'ycoddle** *n.* a milksop;—*v.t.* or *v.i.* to coddle or be coddled [dim. of *Mary*].

molten (mōlt'n) *a.* melted; of metals, liquefied by intense heat.—**molt'enly** *adv.* [old *pa.p.* of *melt*].

molybdenum (mol-ib-dẹ'num) *n.* a rare metal, used for alloying special steels. Also **molyb'dena** [Gk. *molubdos*, lead].

moment (mō'ment) *n.* a minute space of time; interval; importance; the measure of a force by its effect in causing rotation.—**mo'mentarily** *adv.*—**mo'mentariness** *n.*—**mo'mentary** *a.* very brief.—**mo'mently** *adv.*—**moment'ous** *a.* of great importance.—**moment'ously** *adv.*—**moment'ousness** *n.*—**moment'um** *n.* the impetus in a body; the product of the mass of a body multiplied by its velocity; (*Fig.*) increasing force; impetus.—*pl.* **momen'ta** [L. *momentum*, movement].

monachism (mon'ak-izm) *n.* monasticism.—**mon'ac(h)al,** *a.* pert. to monks or a monastery; hermit-like [L. *monachus*, a monk].

Monad (mon'ad) *n.* the one Self that gives life and consciousness to the form; ray from one universal Absolute Principle; the ultimate atom;—*a.* pert. to monads.—**monad'ic, -al** *a.* pert. to monads.—**monad'iform** *a.*—**mon'adism, monadol'ogy** *n.* the theory of monads [Gk. *monos*, alone].

monarch (mon'ark) *n.* the supreme ruler of a state; (*Fig.*) a superior;—*a.* supreme.—**monarch'al** *a.* pert. to a monarch; sovereign.—**monarch'ial, monarch'ic, -al** *a.* pert. to a monarch or a monarchy.—**monarch'ically** *adv.*—**mon'archise** *v.t.* to govern, as a king; to convert to monarchical government.—**mon'archism** *n.* the principles of monarchy; devotion to a royalist cause.—**mon'archist** *n.* advocate of monarchy; a royalist.—**mon'archy** *n.* government of a state by a single ruler such as king, queen, or emperor; a kingdom or empire [Gk. *monos*, alone; *archein*, to rule].

monastery (mon'ạs-ter-i) *n.* a settlement of monks.—**monaste'rial, monas'tic, -al** *a.* pert. to monasteries, monks or nuns.—**monas'tic** *n.* a monk.—**monas'tically** *adv.*—**monasticism** (mon-as'ti-sizm) *n.* the monastic way of life [Gk. *monasterion*, a monastery].

Monday (mun'dā) *n.* the second day of the week [O.E. *mona*, the moon].

monetary (mun'e-tạ-ri) *a.* concerning money or the coinage; consisting of money [L. *moneta*, a mint].

money (mun'i) *n.* any form of token, as coin, banknote, used as medium of exchange, and stamped by state authority; paper currency; wealth.—*pl.* (*Law*) **mon'eys.**—**mon'ey-bill** *n.* a bill brought before Parliament concerning the national exchequer.—**mon'eyed** *a.* wealthy.—**mon'ey-grub'ber** *n.* a miser.—**mon'ey-lend'er** *n.* one who lends out money and charges interest on the sum lent.—**mon'ey-mak'ing** *a.* profitable.—**money order,** an order for money, issued at one post-office and payable at another.—**mon'ey-spin'ner** or **-spid'er** *n.* a small red spider supposed to bring good luck [L. *moneta*, a mint].

monger (mung'gẹr) *n.* a trader; a dealer, usually in compound words, as *fishmonger, ironmonger* [O.E. *mangere*, a merchant].

Mongol (mong'gol) *n.* a native of Mongolia;—*a.* pert. to Mongolia, or its inhabitants. Also **Mongol'ian.**—**mong'oloid** *a.* resembling the Mongols.

mongoose (mon′gŏŏs) *n.* a small animal like a weasel, the ichneumon of India, notable as a snake-killer.—*pl.* **mong′ooses.** Also **mong′oose** [Tamil].

mongrel (mung′grẹl) *n.* an animal, usually a dog, of mixed breed;—*a.* impure; hybrid [O.E. *mang*, a mixture].

monism (mon′izm) *n.* the philosophical doctrine which seeks to explain varied phenomena by a single principle.—**mon′ist** *n.*—**monist′ic, -al** *a.* [Gk. *monos*, single].

monition (mon-ish′un) *n.* cautionary advice; admonition; notice; (*Law*) a summons.—**mon′itive** *a.* expressing caution or warning.—**mon′itor** *n.* (*fem.* **mon′itress, mon′itrix**) one who cautions; an instructor; a school prefect; (*Naut.*) a shallow-draught, heavily armed warship for coastal service; (*World War* 2) a B.B.C. official who heard and noted foreign broadcasts, esp. from Axis countries.—**mon′itor** *v.t.* to listen-in to foreign broadcasts to spot deviations from correct wave-lengths; to hear and note details of foreign broadcasts.—**monito′rial** *a.*—**monito′rially** *adv.*—**mon′itory** *a.* warning [L. *monere, monitum*, to warn].

monk (mungk) *n.* orig. a hermit; a member of a religious community living in monastery.—**monk′hood** *n.* the state of being a monk.—**monk′ish** *a.* pert. to a monk; monastic.—**monks′hood** *n.* a herbaceous poisonous plant, the aconite [Gk. *monachos*, a monk].

monkey (mung′ki) *n.* a long-tailed mammal of the order of Primates, exclusive of man and the lemurs, but resembling man in organisation; mischievous child; the weighted head of a pile driver; a hammer for driving home bolts; (*Slang*) £500.—*pl.* **monk′eys.**—*v.i.* to imitate a monkey; to meddle with, as to *monkey around with machine parts.*—**monk′ey-jack′et** *n.* a short, tight jacket worn by sailors.—**monk′ey-nut** *n.* a pea-nut.—**monk′ey-puzz′le** *n.* the Chile pine.—**monk′ey-rail** *n.* (*Naut.*) a smaller rail above quarter-rail.—**monk′ey-trick** *n.* prank.—**monk′ey-wrench** *n.* wrench with movable jaw [etym. uncertain].

mono- (mon′o) *prefix.* meaning sole, single. [Gk. *monos*, alone, single].

monobloc (mon′ō-blok) *n.* the cylinders of the internal combustion engine in one casting [Gk. *monos*, single; and *block*].

monocarpous (mon-ō-kȧrp′us) *a.* bearing fruit only once, and dying after fructification, as wheat.—**mon′ocarp** *n.*—**monocarp′ic** *a.* [Gk. *monos*, single; *karpos*, fruit].

monochord (mon′ō-kord) *n.* a one-stringed instrument; a one-stringed device for measuring musical intervals.

monochrome (mon′ō-krōm) *n.* a painting in different tones of the same colour.—**monochromat′ic, monochro′ic** *a.* of one colour only.—**monochro′matism** *n.* colour-blindness [Gk. *monos*, single; *chrōma*, colour].

monocle (mon′o-kl) *n.* a single eye-glass [Gk. *monos*, single; L. *oculus*, the eye].

monocotyledon (mon-ō-kot-i-lē′don) *n.* a plant with only one cotyledon or seed lobe.—**monocotyle′donous** *a.* [Gk. *monos*, single; *kotulē*, a cup].

monocracy (mon-ok′rạ-si) *n.* government by a single person.—**mon′ocrat** *n.* [Gk. *monos*, single; *kratein*, to rule].

monody (mon′ō-di) *n.* an elegy expressive of the mourning of a single person; a song for one person.—**monod′ic, -al** *a.*—**mon′odist** *n.* one who writes monodies [Gk. *monos*, single; *ōdē*, song].

monogamy (mon-og′ạ-mi) *n.* the state of being married to one person at a time.—**monog′amist** *n.*—**monog′amous** *a.* [Gk. *monos*, single; *gamos*, marriage].

monogenesis (mon-ō-jen′e-sis) *n.* the descent of an organism from a single cell.—**monogenet′ic** *a.*—**monog′enism** *n.* the theory of the descent of all human beings from an original single pair. Also **monog′eny** [Gk. *monos*, single; *gignesthai*, to be born].

monogram (mon′ō-gram) *n.* two or more letters, as initials of a person's name, interwoven.—**monogrammat′ic** *a.* [Gk. *monos*, alone; *gramma*, a letter].

monograph (mon′ō-graf) *n.* a specialised treatise on a single subject or branch of a subject;—*v.t.* to write a monograph on.—**monog′rapher, monog′raphist** *n.*—**monograph′ic, -al,** *a.* pert. to a monograph [Gk. *monos*, single; *graphein*, to write].

monogynous (mon-oj′in-us) *a.* (*Bot.*) having single pistil; (*Zool.*) mating with a single female. Also **monogyn′ian.**—**monog′yny** *n.* the custom of having only one female mate [Gk. *monos*, single; *gunē*, a female].

monolith (mon′o-lith) *n.* a monument or column fashioned from a single block of stone.—**monolith′al, monolith′ic** *a.* [Gk. *monos*, alone; *lithos*, a stone].

monologue (mon′ō-log) *n.* a dramatic scene in which an actor soliloquises; a dramatic poem for a solo performer [Gk. *monos*, single; *logos*, a speech].

monomania (mon-ō-mā′ni-ạ) *n.* a form of mental derangement in which sufferer is irrational on one subject only, or is obsessed by one idea.—**monoma′niac** *n.*—**monoma′niacal** *a.* [Gk. *monos*, single; *mania*, madness].

Monomark (mon′ō-mark) *n.* a registered combination of letters and (or) numbers serving to identify the property or products of the allottee [Protected Trade Mark].

monomial (mon-ō-mi-ạl) *a.* (*Math.*) comprising a single term or expression;—*n.* an algebraic expression containing a single term [Gk. *monos*, single; *onoma*, a name].

mononym (mon′ō-nim) *n.* a name comprising a single term.—**mononym′ic** *a.* [Gk. *monos*, single; *onoma*, a name].

monophobia (mon-ō-fō′bi-ạ) *n.* (*Path.*) a morbid fear of being alone [Gk. *monos*, single; *phobos*, fear].

monoplane (mon′ō-plān) *n.* an aircraft with only one set of planes.

monopoly (mon-op′o-li) *n.* the sole right to trade in certain commodities; exclusive possession or control; Protected Trade Name for game played with dice and counters.—**monop′olise** *v.t.* to have a monopoly; to take the lead, to exclusion of others.—**monop′oliser, monop′olist** *n.* one who has a monopoly.—**monopolis′tic** *a.* [Gk. *monos*, single; *pōlein*, to sell].

monosyllable (mon-ō-sil′ạ-bl) *n.* a word of one syllable.—**monosyllab′ic** *a.* having one syllable; speaking in words of one syllable.—**monosyl′labism** *n.*

monotheism (mon′ō-thē-izm) *n.* the doctrine which admits of one God only.—**mon′otheist** *n.*—**monotheis′tic** *a.*

monotint (mon′ō-tint) *n.* a sketch or painting in one tint.

monotone (mon′ō-tōn) *n.* a single, unvaried tone or sound; a series of sounds of uniform pitch; sameness of any kind;—*v.t.* and *v.i.* to intone; to chant.—**monoton′ic, monot′onous** *a.* uttered or recited in one tone; dull; unvaried.—**monot′onously** *adv.*—**monot′ony** *n.* tedious uniformity of tone; lack of variety or variation; sameness [Gk. *monos*, single; *tonos*, a tone].

Monotype (mon′ō-tīp) *n.* (*Biol.*) a single example of a species; (*Print.*) a two-part machine for setting and casting type in individual letters, as distinct from *linotype.*—**monotyp′ic** *a.* [Gk. *monos*, single; and *type*] [Protected Trade Mark].

monovalent (mon′ō-val-ent) *a.* (*Chem.*) having a valency of one; univalent.—**mon′ovalence, mon′ovalency** *n.*

monoxide (mo-nok′sīd) *n.* oxide containing one oxygen atom in a molecule.

Monroeism (mon-rō′izm) *n.* the doctrine of the non-intervention by European Powers in the political affairs of the American continents, as enunciated by President Monroe of U.S.A. in 1823. Also called *The Monroe Doctrine.*

Monseigneur (mōng-sen′yẹr) *n.* my lord; a

title (*abbrev.* **Mgr.**) given in France to princes, bishops, etc.—*pl.* **Messeigneurs** (mā-sen-yer′)—**Monsignor** (mon-sin-yōr′) (*abbrev.* **Mgr.** or **Monsig.**,) an Italian title given to prelates.—Also **monsigno′re.**—*pl.* **monsigno′ri** [L. *meus*, my; *senior*, older].

monsoon (mon-sōōn′) *n.* a seasonal wind of S. Asia which blows *on-shore* from the S.W. in summer, and *off-shore* from the N.E. in winter; the very heavy rainfall season as in summer, esp. in India.—**monsoon′al** *a.* [prob. Ar. *mausin*, a season].

monster (mon′stẹr) *n.* a creature of unnatural shape; a prodigy; a freak; a person of abnormal callousness, cruelty, or wickedness;—*a.* huge.—**monstros′ity** *n.* an unnatural production; an abnormal creature; a freak.—**mon′strous** *a.* abnormal; enormous; horrible; shocking.—**monstrously** *adv.* [L. *monstrum*, a marvel].

monstrance (mon′strạns) *n.* a shrine in which the consecrated host is shown in R.C. services [L. *monstrare*, to show].

montage (mon′tāj, -tȧzh) *n.* (*Cinema*) the final assembling together of various shots of a film into one well-arranged series of consecutive pictures [Fr. *monter*, to mount].

montane (mon′tān) *a.* pert. to or inhabiting mountainous country. Also **montan′ic** [L. *montanus*, mountainous].

montbretia (mont-brē′shi-ạ) *n.* a bulb plant with brilliant orange flowers [fr. *de Montbret*, French botanist].

Montessori System (mon-te-sō′ri-sis′tem) *n.* educational system evolved by Dr. Maria *Montessori* (b. 1869) its purpose being to give free scope to child's individuality and creative powers.—**Montesso′rian** *a.*

month (munth) *n.* one of the twelve divisions of the year—a *calendar* month of 31, 30 or 28 (29) days; the period of the complete revolution of the moon—a *lunar* month, about 29 days; a period of 28 days, or four complete weeks.—**month′ly** *a.* lasting, performed in, a month;—*n.* a publication as a magazine, produced once each month;—*pl.* the menses;—*adv.* once a month [O.E. *monath*, a month].

monument (mon′ū-ment) *n.* any structure, as a tombstone, building tablet, erected to the memory of person, or event; an ancient record; any achievement of lasting value.—**monument′al** *a.* like, or worthy of a monument; massive; colossal.—**monument′ally** *adv.* [L. *monumentum*, fr. *monere*, to remind].

moo (mōō) *v.i.* to make the noise of a cow; to low;—*n.* the lowing of a cow [imit.].

mooch, mouch (mōōch) *v.t.* and *v.i.* (*Colloq.*) to loiter; to slouch; to sponge from another [O.Fr. *muchier*, to hang about].

mood (mōōd) *n.* mode; (*Gram.*) the inflection of a verb expressing its function, as *indicative, imperative, subjunctive, infinitive*; (*Logic*) a form of syllogism; (*Mus.*) mode; the arrangement of intervals in the scale, as *major, minor* [var. of *mode*].

mood (mōōd) *n.* disposition; frame of mind; temper.—**mood′ily** *adv.*—**mood′iness** *n.* the state of being moody; temporary depression of spirits; captiousness.—**mood′y** *a.* peevish; sulky; depressed; angry [O.E. *mod*, mind].

moon (mōōn) *n.* the satellite which revolves round the earth in the period of a lunar month; any secondary planet; a month; anything crescent-shaped or shining like the moon;—*v.i.* to gaze or wander about aimlessly.—**moon′beam** *n.* a ray of moonlight.—**moon′calf** *n.* a monster; a dolt.—**moon′faced** *a.* having a round, expressionless face.—**moon′light** *n.* light of the moon;—*a.* lit by the moon; occurring during moonlight.—**moon′lit** *a.* illumined by moon.—**moon′raker** *n.* a crazy person.—**moon′shine** *n.* light of the moon; empty show; smuggled liquor.—**moon′stone** *n.* an almost pellucid form of felspar.—**moon′struck** *a.* lunatic.—**moon′y** *a.* silly.—**to shoot the moon**, to disappear over-night [O.E. *mona*, the moon].

Moor (mōōr) *n.* a native of the Barbary States; one of the Moslem conquerors of Southern Spain in the 8th cent.—**Moor′ish** *a.* [L. *Maurus*, an inhabitant of *Mauretania*].

moor (mōōr) *n.* stretch of heath with peaty soil.—**moor′cock, moor′fowl** *n.* red grouse.—**moor′hen** *n.* female moor-cock; water-hen.—**moor′ish, moor′y** *a.*—**moor′land** *n.* a heath [O.E. *mor*, marshland].

moor (mōōr) *v.t.* to secure by cables and anchors, as a vessel.—**moor′age** *n.* place where vessel or airship is moored; charge for mooring.—**moor′ing** *n.* the act of securing a ship, etc., by cables and anchors; the place where a ship is moored [prob. Dut. *marren*, to tie].

moose (mōōs) *n.* largest species of deer; N. American elk [Native].

moot (mōōt) *v.t.* to suggest for debate; to discuss;—*a.* debatable;—*n.* in olden times, a council.—**moot′able** *a.* capable of being debated.—**moot′case, moot′point** *n.* a debatable case, or point [O.E. *gemot*, an assembly].

mop (mop) *n.* a bunch of soft cotton yarn or rags attached to handle for washing or polishing; a bushy head of hair;—*v.t.* to wipe or polish with a mop; to wipe perspiration from.—*pr.p.* **mop′ping.**—*pa.p.* **mopped** [L. *mappa*, a napkin].

mope (mōp) *v.i.* to be dull or depressed; to sulk.—**mop′ing** *a.* listless.—**mop′ishly** *adv.* dispiritedly.—**mop′ish** *a.* dull.—**mop′ishly** *adv.*—**mop′ishness** *n.* [Dut. *moppen*, to sulk].

moppet (mop′et) *n.* a cloth-doll; a child.—**mop′sy** *n.* untidy woman [fr. *mop*].

moped (mōped) *n.* a pedal cycle fitted with an auxiliary motor (fr. **mo**tor and **ped**al).

moquette (mō-ket′) *n.* a carpet material of velvety pile.—**uncut moquette,** a dull surfaced fabric used for upholstery [Fr.].

moraine (mō-rān′) *n.* rock debris which accumulates along the sides or at the end of a glacier [Fr.].

moral (mor′ạl) *a.* pert. to the conduct or duties of man; ethical; virtuous; chaste; discriminating between right and wrong; didactic; verified by reason or probability;—*n.* the underlying meaning implied in a fable, allegory, etc.—*pl.* ethics; conduct, esp. concerning sex-relations; habits.—**moralisa′tion** *n.*—**mor′alise** *v.t.* to explain in a moral sense; to draw a moral from;—*v.i.* to reflect on ethical values of.—**mor′aliser** *n.*—**mor′alist** *n.* one who moralises; one who studies or teaches ethics; one who accepts ethics instead of religion as an adequate guide to good living.—**moralist′ic** *a.*—**moral′ity** *n.* the practice of moral duties; virtue; ethics; the right or wrong of a thing; an early form of pre-Shakespearian drama, in which the characters were the virtues and vices of men personified.—**mor′ally** *adv.* in a moral manner; practically.—**moral philosophy,** the science of right living and the just conduct of affairs; ethics.—**moral victory,** a defeat, which in a deeper sense, is a victory (L. *mos*, *moris*, a custom].

morale (mo-rȧl′) *n.* the disposition or mental state which causes a man or body of people to face an emergency with spirit, fortitude and unflagging zeal [Fr.].

morass (mo-ras′) *n.* a bog; marshy ground; a fen.—**morass′y** *a.* [Dut. *moeras*, a marsh].

moratorium (mor-ạ-tō′ri-um) *n.* an act authorising the suspension of payments or reparations by a bank or debtor state, for a given period of time; the period of suspension of payments [L. *mora*, delay].

moray (mō′rā) *n.* a sharp-toothed marine eel. Also **ma′ray, mu′ray, mur′ry** [Gk. *muraina*].

morbid (mor′bid) *a.* diseased; unhealthy; (of the mind) excessively introspective.—**morbid′ity** *n.* the state of being morbid.—**mor′bidly** *adv.*—**mor′bidness** *n.*—**morbif′ic** *a.* causing unhealthiness of body or mind [L. *morbus*, disease].

mordant (mor′dant) *n.* any substance, metallic or vegetable, which fixes dyes; a corrosive acid used in copper-plate engraving;—*a.* biting; corrosive; (*Fig.*) scathing; sarcastic.—**morda'cious** *a.* acrid; (*Fig.*) sarcastic.—**morda'ciously** *adv.*—**mordac'ity** *n.* the quality of being mordacious.—**mor'dantly** *adv.* [L. *mordere*, to bite].

more (mōr) *a.* greater in amount, degree, quality, etc.; in greater number; additional—*adv.* in a greater quantity, extent, etc.; besides; —*n.* something additional.—*superl.* most [O.E. *mara*, greater].

morel, moril (mo-rel', -ril') *n.* an edible mushroom [Fr. *morille*].

morel (mo-rel') *n.* the common and deadly nightshade [O.Fr. *morel*, black].

morello (mo-rel'-ō) *n.* a variety of dark red cherry used esp. in manufacture of cherry-brandy. Also **morel', mor'el** [It. *morello*, dark-skinned].

moreover (mōr-ō-vẹr) *adv.* besides; also; further [fr. *more*].

Moresque (mō-resk') *a.* Moorish; Arabesque —*n.* Moorish decoration [Fr. fr. *Moor*].

morganatic (mor-gạn-at'-ik) *a.* applied to a marriage between a man of high, esp. royal rank, and a woman of lower station, the issue having no claim to his rank or property.—**morganat'ically** *adv.* [Ger. *Morgengabe*, a morning-gift].

morgue (morg) *n.* a mortuary where bodies of people killed in street accidents, etc., are taken to await identification [Fr.].

moribund (mor'-i-bund) *a.* at the point of death [L. *moribundus*, dying].

morion, morrion (mō'-ri-on) *n.* a light helmet without visor or beaver [Fr.].

Morisco (mo-ris'-kō) *n.* the Moorish language; one of the Moors who remained in S. Spain after 1492, and became Christian; a Moorish dance;—*a.* Moorish [Sp.].

Mormon (mor'-mon) *n.* a member of 'The Church of Jesus Christ of Latter-day Saints' founded by Joseph Smith in 1830 in Utah, U.S.A. and professing theocracy and, formerly, polygamy; (*Fig.*) a polygamist;—*a.* pert. to this sect.—**Mor'monism** *n.* [fr. the fictitious Book of *Mormon*].

morn (morn) *n.* the early part of the day [O.E. *morgen*, morning].

morning (mor'-ning) *n.* the first part of the day between dawn and midday; (*Fig.*) the first part of anything;—*a.* pert. to or happening in the early part of the day.—**mor'ning-coat** *n.* a tail-coat with cutaway front.—**morn'ing-room** *n.* a room used esp. in the morning, for breakfast, etc.—**morning watch** (*Naut.*) 4-8 a.m. [M.E. *morwening*, the coming of the day].

morocco (mo-rok'-ō) *n.* orig. a fine goat-skin leather; any skin grained in imitation of goat-skin [fr. *Morocco*].

moron (mōr'-on) *n.* an adult with the mental development of a 7 yr. old child [Gk. *moros*, stupid].

morose (mō-rōs') *a.* sullen; gloomy; soured in nature.—**morose'ly** *adv.*—**morose'ness** *n.* [L. *morosus*, fretful].

Morpheus (mor'-fi-us) *n.* in Greek mythology, the god of dreams, the son of Night and Sleep. —**Mor'phean, Morphet'ic** *a.*

morphia (mor'-fi-ạ) *n.* an alkaloid of opium; a drug used to induce sleep and to deaden pain. Also **mor'phine** [fr. *Morpheus*].

morphic (mor'-fik) *a.* pert. to shape or form.— —**morphogen'esis** *n.* the production of an organ or organism; evolution of form.—**morphog'eny** *n.* morphology.—**morphog'raphy** *n.* the description of the structure of an organism.—**morpholog'ic, -al** *a.*—**morphol'ogist** *n.*—**morphol'ogy** *n.* the science of the structure and shape of organisms.—**morphon'omy** *n.* the laws governing the science of morphology [Gk. *morphē*, a shape].

morris, morrice (mor'-is) *n.* a dance popular in medieval England, representing characters such as Robin Hood, Maid Marian, etc.; orig. an imitation of a Moorish dance [var. of *Moorish*].

morris (mor'-is) *n.* a popular medieval outdoor game of draughts.—**nine men's morris,** this game played with nine stones. Also **mer'ils** [etym. uncertain].

morrow (mor'-ō) *n.* next day; (*Poet.*) morning [O.E. *morgen*, the morning].

Morse (mors) *n.* a system of telegraphic signalling in which the alphabet is represented by various combinations of dots and dashes, as devised by the American inventor S. F. B. *Morse* (1791-1872).

morsel (mor'-sẹl) *n.* a mouthful; a small piece [O.Fr. dim fr. L. *morsus*, a bite].

mort (mort) *n.* a note sounded on a hunting horn denoting death of the animal pursued [Fr. *mort*, death].

mortal (mor'-tạl) *a.* subject to death; fatal; meriting damnation, as sin; implacable, as a foe;—*n.* a human being;—*adv.* (*Colloq.*) very. —**mortal'ity** *n.* death; death-rate; the human race.—**mor'tally** *adv.* fatally; sorely [L. *mortalis*, fr. *mors*, death].

mortar (mor-tạr) *n.* a thick bowl of porcelain, glass, etc., in which substances are pounded with a pestle; a mill for pulverising ores; (*Mil.*) a wide-mouthed piece of ordnance for short-distance firing of heavy shells; a cement made of lime, sand and water, used in building;—*v.t.* to pound in a mortar; to cement, as bricks, with mortar.—**mor'tar-board** *n.* a square board used when mixing mortar; an academic cap [L. *mortarium*, a mortar].

mortgage (mor'-gāj) *n.* (*Law*) a conveyance of property in security of a loan; the deed effecting this;—*v.t.* to pledge as security.—**mortgagee'** *n.* one who gives a mortgage.—**mort'gager, mort'gagor** *n.* one who receives a mortgage from a mortgagee [O.Fr. *mort*, dead; *gage*, a pledge].

mortician (mor-tish'-ạn) *n.* (*U.S.*) an undertaker [L. *mors*, death].

mortify (mor'-ti-fī) *v.t.* to discipline the flesh; to humiliate; to vex;—*v.i.* (*Med.*) to become gangrenous.—*pa.t.* and *pa.p.* **mor'tified.**—**mortifica'tion** *n.* the act of mortifying or the state of being mortified; the death of one part of a living body; humiliation; (*Scots law*) a charitable bequest; (*Med.*) gangrene [L. *mors*, death; *facere*, to make].

mortise (mor'-tis) *n.* a hole in a piece of wood to receive the projection or tenon of another piece, made to fit it. Also **mor'tice.**—*v.t.* to cut or make a mortise in; to join with a mortice.—*pr.p.* **mor'tising.**—*pa.p.* **mor'tised** [etym. unknown].

mortmain (mort'-mān) *n.* an inalienable bequest; the holding of land by a corporation or, as formerly, by a monastery, which cannot be transferred to new ownership [O.Fr. *mortmain*, dead hand].

mortuary (mor'-tū-ạr-i) *n.* a place for the temporary reception of dead bodies;—*a.* pert. to burial [L. *mortus*, dead].

mosaic (mō-zā'-ik) *a.* pert. to or made of mosaic;—*n.* inlaid work of coloured glass or marble; the flooring or pattern made of this; (*Fig.*) a patchwork.—**mosa'ically** *adv.* [Gk. *mousa*, a muse].

Mosaic (mō-zā'-ik) *a.* (*Bib.*) pert. to *Moses*, or to the laws and writings attributed to him.

moschatel (mos'-kạ-tel) *n.* a plant with light green flowers and a musk-perfume [L. *muscus*, musk].

Moselle (mō-zel') *n.* a light wine from the Moselle district [Fr.].

Moslem (moz'-lem) *n.* a Mohammedan;—*a.* pert. to the Mohammedans or their religion. Also **Mus'lim.**—**Mos'lemism** *n.* [Ar. *salama*, submit to God].

mosque (mosk) *n.* a Mohammedan temple [Ar. *masjid*, temple].

mosquito (mos-kē'-tō) *n.* gnat-like insect.—*pl.* **mosqui'to(e)s.**—**mosquito curtain, net,** a net-covering to ward off mosquitoes [L. *musca*, a fly].

moss (mos) *n.* a small, thickly growing, cryptogamous plant which thrives on moist surfaces; lichen; a bog; a peat moor.—**moss′ag′ate** *n.* an agate with moss-like markings.—**moss′grown** *a.* closely covered with moss.—**moss′iness** *n.*—**moss′land** *n.* peat bog.—**moss′rose** *n.* a species of rose with moss-like growth on the calyx.—**moss′troop′er** *n.* a marauder of the Scottish Borders in the 16th and 17th cents.—**moss′y** *a.* covered with moss [O.E. *mos*, bog-land].

most (mōst) *a.* (superl. of **more**) the greatest number or quantity; greatest;—*adv.* in the greatest degree.—**most′ly** *adv.* for the most part [O.E. *maest*, most].

mot (mō) *n.* pithy, witty, saying [Fr. = word].

mote (mōt) *n.* a small particle; a speck of dust; (*Fig.*) a very small defect.—**mot′ed, mot′ey** *a.* [O.E. *mot*, a particle].

motet (mō-tet′) *n.* a musical composition for (unaccompanied) voices, to words from Scripture [Fr. dim. of *mot*, a word].

moth (moth) *n.* a nocturnal winged insect; larva of this insect which feeds on cloth, esp. woollens.—**moth′balls** *n.pl.* camphor balls to ward off moths from clothes.—**moth′eat′en** *a.* eaten into holes by moth larva; (*Fig.*) decrepit [O.E. *moththe*, a moth].

mother (muTH′ẹr) *n.* a female parent; mode of address to elderly woman; the head of a convent; the origin of anything;—*a.* natural; native; original;—*v.t.* to adopt as a son or daughter; to cherish, as a mother her child.—**mother-coun′try** *n.* native land.—**moth′ercraft** *n.* the art of being a good mother; training in the duties and tasks of a mother.—**moth′erhood** *n.* the state of being a mother.—**moth′ering** *n.* motherly care; the old custom of visiting one's parents on the fourth Sunday in Lent (*Mothering Sunday*).—**moth′er-in-law** *n.* the mother of one's wife or husband.—**moth′erliness** *n.*—**moth′erly** *a.* pert. to a mother; kindly.—**moth′er-of-pearl** *n.* the iridescent lining of several kinds of shells.—**Mother Superior,** the head of a convent.—**moth′er-tongue** *n.* one's native language.—**Queen Mother,** the mother of the reigning sovereign [O.E. *modor*, a mother].

motif (mō-tēf′) *n.* the dominant theme in a literary or musical composition [Fr.].

motile (mō′tīl) *a.* (*Zool.*; *Bot.*) capable of movement [L. *movere, motum*, to move].

motion (mō′shun) *n.* the act of moving; movement; impulse; a proposal made in an assembly; (*Med.*) an evacuation of the bowels;—*v.t.* to guide by gesture;—*v.i.* to make a significant movement.—**mo′tionless** *a.* still; immobile.—**mo′tion-pic′ture** *n.* a cinema film [L. *movere, motum*, to move].

motive (mō′tiv) *n.* that which incites to action; inner impulse; dominant theme; motif;—*a.* causing movement or motion;—*v.t.* to impel; to motivate.—**mo′tivate** *v.t.* to incite.—**motiva′tion** *n.*—**mo′tiveless** *a.* without purpose or direction.—**motiv′ity** *n.* capacity to produce motion [L. *movere, motum*, to move].

motley (mot′li) *a.* parti-coloured; diversified;—*n.* a jester's dress [etym. uncertain].

motor (mō′tor) *n.* that which imparts motion; a machine which imparts motive power, esp. the internal combustion engine; a motor-car;—*a.* causing motion; (*Anat.*) producing muscular activity, as *motor-nerves*;—*v.t.* and *v.i.* to travel by, or convey in, a motor-driven vehicle.—**mo′tor-bi′cycle, mo′tor-cy′cle** *n.* a cycle driven by a motor.—**mo′tor-boat** *n.* a boat with petrol-driven engine.—**mo′tor-bus** *n.* a public transport vehicle with internal combustion engine.—**mo′torise** *v.t.* to mechanise (the transport of) the army.—**mo′torist** *n.* one who drives or travels in a motor car.—**motor spirit,** petrol, etc., used to drive motor-engine [L. *motor*, a mover].

mottle (mot′l) *v.t.* to mark with spots of different colours; to dapple.—**mott′led** *a.* variegated, as *mottled* soap [prob. fr. *motley*].

motto (mot′ō) *n.* a short appropriate sentence or phrase added to armorial bearings; a maxim or aphorism; quotation prefixed to a book, or chapter of a book.—*pl.* **mott′oes.**—**mott′oed** *a.* [L. *muttum*, a murmur].

mouch Same as **mooch.**

moue (mòò) *n.* a pout [Fr.].

moujik (mòò′zhik) *n.* a Russian peasant [Russ. *muzhik*].

mould (mōld) *n.* the hollow shape in which anything is cast or set; a templet; (*Fig.*) character;—*v.t.* to shape in a mould; to fashion; (*Fig.*) to influence.—**mould′er** *n.* one who moulds or makes moulds, as *ironmoulder*.—**mould′ing** *n.* anything moulded, esp. relief ornamentation on cornices, etc.; art or process of making moulds [L. *modulus*, a small measure].

mould (mōld) *n.* fine, soft soil; the upper layer of the earth; the grave;—*v.t.* to cover with mould.—**mould′er** *v.i.* to decay; to crumble away; to turn to dust.—**mould′warp** *n.* the mole which throws up little heaps of earth [O.E. *molde*, the earth].

mould (mōld) *n.* a minute bluish-coloured fungus which grows on such things as leather, cheese, bread, esp. if exposed to damp; mildew.—**mould′iness** *n.*—**mould′y** *a.* covered with or affected by mould; musty; (*Fig.*) antiquated [etym. uncertain].

moult (mōlt) *v.t.* and *i.* to cast or shed feathers, as of birds;—*n.* the act of casting feathers [L. *mutare*, to change].

mound (mound) *n.* an artificial elevation of the earth; a knoll; an earthwork for defensive purposes;—*v.t.* to fortify with a mound [O.E. *mund*, a defence].

mount (mount) *n.* a mountain or hill (*abbrev.* **Mt.**); that on which anything is mounted for exhibition; a horse for riding;—*v.t.* to raise up; to ascend; to get on a horse; to frame (a picture); to set (gem-stones); to put on a slide for microscope examination; to stage a play with appropriate costumes, scenery, etc.; to raise guns into position;—*v.i.* to rise up; to get up; to increase.—**mount′ed** *a.* raised; (of a picture) having a cardboard edging or backing.—**mount′ing-block** *n.* block used to facilitate mounting of a horse.—**to mount guard,** to be on sentry-duty; to keep watch over [L. *mons*, a mountain].

mountain (mount′ān or -in) *n.* a high hill;—*a.* pert. to a mountain; growing or living on a mountain.—**mount′ain-ash** *n.* the rowan-tree.—**mount′ain-dew** *n.* Scotch whisky.—**mountaineer′** *n.* one who lives on a mountain; one who climbs high mountains.—**mountaineer′ing** *n.* the practice or sport of climbing mountains.—**mount′ain-lime′stone** *n.* limestone layers between Old Red Sandstone and coal seams.—**mount′ainous** *a.* very steep; full of mountains; colossal.—**mount′ain-rail′way** *n.* a railway operating on cogged central rail for ascent of very steep gradients [L. *mons*, a mountain].

mountebank (moun′te-bangk) *n.* a quack doctor; a charlatan [It. *montambanco*, mount on bench or platform].

mounty (moun′ti) *n.* a member of the Canadian N.W. Mounted Police.

mourn (mōrn) *v.t.* to grieve over; to lament;—*v.i.* to express grief; to wear mourning.—**mourn′er** *n.* one who mourns; one who attends a funeral—**mourn′ful** *a.* sad; dismal.—**mourn′fully** *adv.*—**mourn′fulness** *n.*—**mourn′ing** *n.* the act of grieving; lamentation; wearing of black as a sign of grief; the period during which such clothes are worn.—**mourn′ingly** *adv.* [O.E. *murnan*, to grieve].

mouse (mous) *n.* a small rodent found in fields, or in houses; a lead weight on the cords of sash-windows.—*pl.* **mice.**—**mouse** (mouz) *v.t.* and *v.i.* to catch mice; to search for patiently or slyly; to prowl.—**mouse′col′our** *a.* dark greyish-brown.—**mous′er** *n.* a cat which catches mice.—**mouse′trap** *n.* a small trap with wire-spring for catching mice.—**mous′y** *a.* resembling a mouse, esp. in colour; smelling of

mice; (*Fig.*) timid; nondescript [O.E. *mus*, a mouse].
mousse (mōōs) *n.* a dessert of frozen whipped cream, eggs, sugar and flavouring [Fr. *mousse*, froth].
moustache (mus-tash') *n.* hair on upper lip.—**moustache'-cup** *n.* cup partly covered on top, to keep moustache dry.—**moustached', moustach'ioed** *a.* [Fr. fr. Gk. *mustax*, upper lip].
mouth (mouth) *n.* an opening between lips of men and animals through which food is taken; lips, as a feature; the cavity behind the lips containing teeth, tongue, palate, and vocal organs; an opening as of a bottle, cave, etc.; the estuary of a river; a wry face.—*pl.* **mouths** (mouTHz).—**mouth'ful** *n.* as much as the mouth conveniently holds; a small amount.—*pl.* **mouth'fuls.**—**mouth'-or'gan** *n.* harmonica; Jew's harp; pan-pipes.—**mouth'piece** *n.* the part of a musical instrument, tobacco-pipe, cigarette-holder, etc., held in mouth; (*Fig.*) a spokesman; a newspaper (as expressing public opinion) [O.E. *muth*, the mouth].
mouth (mouTH) *v.t.* to utter with overloud voice; to speak with exaggerated movement of lips and jaws; to rant.—**mouthed** *a.* having a mouth [O.E. *muth*, the mouth].
move (mōōv) *v.t.* to set in motion; to stir emotions of; to prevail on; to incite; to propose for consideration;—*v.i.* to change one's position, posture, residence, etc.; to march; to make a proposal or recommendation;—*n.* the act of moving; a change of residence; a movement, as in game of draughts.—**mov'able, move'able** *n.* an article of furniture;—*pl.* (*Law*) the furnishings of a house which are not permanent fixtures; —*a.* able to be moved, or changed in time; shifting.—**movable feast,** a church festival, the date of which varies annually.—**mov'ableness** *n.*—**mov'ably** *adv.*—**move'ment** *n.* the act of moving; deportment; the part of a machine which moves; organised activity of a society; a division of a complex musical composition.—**mov'er** *n.* one who moves; one who tables a motion; an originator.—**mov'ies** *n.pl.* (*Colloq.*) cinema films or cinema theatre.—**mov'ing** *a.* causing to change place; in motion; affecting the emotions; pathetic.—**moving picture** (*abbrev.* **movie**) the cinematograph.—**moving staircase,** an escalator [L. *movere*, to move].
mow (mō) *v.t.* to cut with a scythe; to cut down in great numbers, as enemy.—*pr.p.* **mow'ing.**—*pa.t.* **mowed.**—*pa.p.* **mown.**—**mow'er** *n.* one who mows; a machine for cutting crops [O.E. *mawan*, to mow].
mow (mō) *n.* a heap of hay or corn, esp. in a barn;—*v.t.* to put in a mow.—*pr.p.* **mow'ing.**—*pa.t.* and *pa.p.* **mowed** [O.E. *muga*, a heap].
mow (mō, mou) *n.* a grimace; a moue;—*v.t.* to make a wry face.—**mops and mows,** gestures and grimaces [Fr. *moue*, a grimace].
much (much) *a.* (*comp.* **more;** *superl.* **most**) great in quantity or amount; abundant;—*n.* a great quantity;—*adv.* to a great degree or extent; almost.—**much'ness** *n.* the state of being much.—**much'ly** *adv.* (*Colloq.*) much.—**much of a muchness,** more or less the same [M.E. *muchel*, much].
mucic (mū'-sik) *a.* pert. to, or derived from, gums; viscous [L. *mucus*, slime from the nose].
mucid (mū'-sid) *a.* mouldy; musty. Also **mu'cidous.**—**mu'cidness, mu'cor** *n.* [L. *mucidus*, mouldy].
mucilage (mū'-si-lāj) *n.* a gummy substance extracted from plants and animals; a solution of gum in water.—**mucilag'inous** *a.* pert. to mucilage; slimy; viscous [L. *mucere*, to be musty].
muck (muk) *n.* moist dung; anything vile or filthy;—*v.t.* to manure; to make filthy; (*Slang*) to make untidy.—**muck'iness** *n.*—**muck'y** *a.* filthy [O.N. *myki*, dung].
mucus (mū'-kus) *n.* a viscid fluid secreted by the mucous glands.—**mu'coid** *a.* like mucus.—**mu'cous** *a.* like, secreting mucus.—**mucous membrane,** membrane which secretes mucus [L. *mucus*, slime from nose].
mud (mud) *n.* soft, moist earth; (*Fig.*) aspersions, as in *to throw mud at a person's memory*; —*v.t.* to bury in mud; to foul; to stir up the dregs in a liquid;—*v.i.* to be submerged in mud.—**mud'-bath** *n.* a bath of mud impregnated with mineral salts in treatment of rheumatism.—**mud'dily** *adv.*—**mud'diness** *n.*—**mud'dy** *a.* consisting of mire or mud; miry; cloudy, as liquid; (*Fig.*) stupid;—*v.t.* to soil with mud.—*pr.p.* **mud'dying.**—*pa.t.* and *pa.p.* **mud'died.**—**mud'dy-head'ed** *a.* stupid.—**mud'-flat** *n.* a stretch of mud below high-water mark.—**mud'-guard** *n.* a screen to protect from mud-splashes, as on wheels of a motor-vehicle, bicycle, etc.—**mud'-lark** *n.* one who cleans out sewers; one who fishes up odds and ends from mud of tidal rivers; a street urchin.—**mud'-pack** *n.* a treatment with impregnated mud which has a beneficial effect on the skin [O.L. Ger. *mudde*, mud].
muddle (mud'-l) *v.t.* to make muddy; to confuse; to bewilder; to deal incompetently with.—*v.i.* to be confused;—*n.* confusion; jumble; —**mudd'lehead** *n.* one who is confused in mind.—**mudd'leheaded** *a.* [fr. *mud*].
muezzin (mōō-ez'-in) *n.* an official in a Mohammedan mosque who from a minaret summons worshippers to prayer. Also **muedd'in** [Ar.].
muff (muf) *n.* a warm covering for both hands, usually made of fur, shaped like a cylinder open at both ends [prob. fr. Dut. *mof*, mitten].
muff (muf) *n.* an awkward person, esp. at sports;—*v.t.* to bungle, esp. at cricket, golf etc. [etym. uncertain].
muffin (muf'-in) *n.* a round, flat scone or cake of yeast dough, eaten toasted and buttered [etym. uncertain].
muffle (muf'-l) *v.t.* to wrap up for warmth or to hide something; to deaden (sound of);—*n.* something used to deaden sound; a boxing-glove.—**muff'led** *a.* smothered (of sound); wrapped up.—**muff'ler** *n.* a scarf; a silencer, as in a motor-car [O.Fr. *moufle*, a thick glove].
mufti (muf'-ti) *n.* a Mohammedan priest; civilian dress worn by soldiers, etc., when off duty [Ar.].
mug (mug) *n.* a straight-sided earthenware or metal cup with or without a handle; a tankard; the contents of this; (*Slang*) the face [etym. unknown].
mug (mug) *n.* (*Slang*) a dupe; a greenhorn [etym. unknown].
mug (mug) *v.i.* (*Slang*) to study very hard [etym. unknown].
muggins (mug'-inz) *n.* a simpleton; a game of dominoes or cards [etym. uncertain].
muggy (mug'-i) *a.* warm and humid, as weather; close; enervating. Also **mug'gish** [O.N. *mugga*, a mist].
mugwump (mug'-wump) *n.* Indian chief; (*U.S.*) one who holds non-party political views; a self-important person [N. Amer. Ind. *mugquomp*, big chief].
Muhammedan See **Mohammedan.**
mulatto (mū-lat'-ō) *n.* (*fem.* **mulatt'ress**) offspring of white person and negro.—*pl.* **mulatt'oes** [Port. *mulato*, of mixed breed].
mulberry (mul'-ber-i) *n.* a deciduous tree on the leaves of which the silkworm feeds; the fruit of this tree; a purplish-brown colour [L. *morum*, a mulberry].
Mulberry harbour (mul'-ber-ri-hár'-bur) *n.* (*World War* 2) portable pre-fabricated harbour, by means of which invasion of Europe was made possible on D-day.
mulch (mulsh) *n.* a protective covering of straw, manure, etc., for roots of young plants; —*v.t.* to treat with mulch. Also **mulsh** [M.E. *molsh*, soft].
mulct (mulkt) *n.* a fine imposed as a penalty; —*v.t.* to impose a fine on; to deprive of [L. *mulcta*, a fine].
mule (mūl) *n.* the hybrid offspring of a male ass and a mare; any hybrid animal; machine

used in cotton-spinning; a heelless bedroom-slipper; (*Fig.*) an obstinate person.—**muleteer'** *n.* a mule-driver.—**mul'ish** *a.* obstinate; pig-headed.—**mul'ishly** *adv.*—**mul'ishness** *n.* [O.E. *mul,* a he-ass].
mull (mul) *v.t.* to heat, sweeten and spice (wine, ale, etc.).—**mulled** *a.*—**mull'er** *n.* [etym. unknown].
mull (mul) *n.* a muddle;—*v.t.* to bungle; to mismanage [etym. unknown].
mull (mul) *n.* (*Scot.*) a headland or promontory [O.N. *muli,* a snout].
mull (mul) *v.t.* and *v.i.* (*U. S.*) to muse upon; to cogitate [etym. uncertain].
mullet (mul'et) *n.* an edible sea-fish [L. *mullus,* the red mullet].
mulligatawny (mul-i-gạ-taw'ni) *n.* a rich soup flavoured with curry, and thickened with rice [Tamil].
mullion (mul'yun) *n.* a dividing upright between the lights of windows, panels, etc. —**mull'ion, munn'ion** *v.t.* to divide by mullions.—**mull'ioned** *a.* [L. *mancus,* maimed].
multi- (mul'ti) *prefix,* fr. L. *multus,* many. Also **mult-**, before a vowel as in *multangular.*
multicolour (mul'ti-kul-ur) *a.* having many colours. Also **mul'ti-coloured.**
multifarious (mul-ti-fā'ri-us) *a.* manifold; made up of many parts.—**multifa'riously** *adv.* —**multifa'riousness** *n.* diversity [L. *multus,* many; *fari,* to speak].
multiform (mul'ti-form) *a.* having many forms.—**multifor'mity** *n.*—**multifor'mous** *a.*
multilateral (mul-ti-lat'ẹr-ạl) *a.* having many sides.—**multilateral school,** an omnibus school having a diversity of courses, as academic, commercial, technical, etc. [L. *multus,* many; *latus,* a side].
multilineal (mul-ti-lin'e-ạl) *a.* having many lines. Also **multilin'ear.**
multi-millionaire (mul'ti-mil'yun-ār) *n.* a person who is worth several million pounds.
multinomial (mul-ti-nō'mi-ạl) *a.* (*Math.*) expressed by more than two terms; polynomial;—*n.* a quantity of three or more terms connected by the sign plus or minus.
multipartite (mul-ti-par'tīt) *a.* having many parts.
multiped (mul'ti-ped) *n.* and *a.* (animal) with many feet. Also **mul'tipede.**
multiple (mul'ti-pl) *a.* manifold; of many; parts; repeated many times;—*n.* (*Math.*) a quantity containing another an exact number of times.—**mul'tiple-fiss'ion** *n.* repeated division.—**multiple shop,** or **store,** a retail business with branches in different parts of town or country [L. *multiplex,* manifold].
multiply (mul'ti-plī) *v.t.* to increase in number; to add a number to itself a given number of times;—*v.i.* to increase; to grow in number.—*pr.p.* **multiply'ing.**—*pa.t.* and *pa.p.* **mul'tiplied.** —**mul'tiplex** *a.* multiple; (of telegraph) capable of transmitting numerous messages over the same wire.—**mul'tipliable, mul'tiplicable** *a.* capable of being multiplied.—**multiplicand'** *n.* the number to be multiplied.—**multiplica'tion** *n.* the act of multiplying; a rule or operation by which any given number may be added to itself any specified number of times (the symbol used = ×).—**mul'tiplicative** *a.*—**mult'iplicator** *n.* a multiplier.—**multiplic'ity** *n.* the state of being multiplied; great number.—**mul'tiplier** *n.* a number by which another, the *multiplicand,* is multiplied [L. *multus,* many; *plicare,* to fold].
multi-ply (mul'ti-plī) *n.* plywood of more than three layers.
multisyllable (mul-ti-sil'ạ-bl) *n.* a word of many syllables.
multitude (mul'ti-tūd) *n.* a great number; numerousness; a crowd; an assemblage.—**multitud'inous** *a.* made up of a very great number [L. *multitudo*].
multivalent (mul-tiv'ạ-lent) *a.* (*Chem.*) having more than one valency.—**multiv'alence, multival'ency** *n.*
multivalve (mul'ti-valv) *a.* having many valves; (*Radio*) consisting of many thermionic valves;—*n.* a mollusc with a shell of many valves.—**multival'vular** *a.*
multure (mul'tūr) *n.* a grinding of corn; a toll paid in kind to a miller for corn ground [L. *molere,* to grind].
mum (mum) *a.* silent;—*n.* silence;—*interj.* be quiet.—**mum's the word,** keep it a secret [imit.].
mumble (mum'bl) *v.t.* to utter indistinctly; to chew, as with toothless gums;—*v.i.* to speak indistinctly;—*n.* an indistinct utterance.—**mum'bler** *n.* [fr. *mum*].
Mumbo-jumbo (mum-bō jum'bō) *n.* an idol worshipped by certain African negroes; anything credulously or superstitiously worshipped (etym. unknown].
mumm, mum (mum) *v.t.* to perform in dumb show; to act in a mask.—**mumm'er** *n.* one who acts in dumb show, esp. in ceremonies connected with Christmas; a buffoon.—**mumm'ery** *n.* performance in dumb show; exaggerated ceremony.—**mumm'ing** *n.* [Dut. *mommen,* to mask].
mummy [mum'i) *n.* a dead body preserved by embalming.—*pa.p.* **mumm'ified.**—**mummification** *n.*—**mumm'ify** *v.t.* to embalm and dry as a mummy;—*v.i.* to become dried up like a mummy.—**mumm'y-wheat** *n.* a species of Egyptian wheat [Pers. *mum,* wax].
mump (mump) *v.t.* and *v.i.* to mumble; to be sullen; to play the hypocrite.—**mump'er** *n.* one who mumps; a whining beggar.—**mump'ing, mump'ish** *a.* sulky; dour; begging.—**mump'ingly, mump'ishly** *adv.*—**mump'ishness** *n.*—**mumps** *n.* a highly infectious disease causing painful swelling of the face and neck-glands (form of *mum*).
munch (munsh) *v.t.* and *v.i.* to chew noisily.—**munch'er** *n.* [M.E. imit.].
mundane (mun'dān) *a.* pert. to this world.—**mun'danely** *adv.*—**mundan'ity** *n.* [L. *mundus,* the world].
munerary (mū'nẹ-rā-ri) *a.* of the nature of a gift [L. *munus,* a gift].
mungoose Same as **mongoose.**
municipal (mū-nis'i-pạl) *a.* pert to a corporation or city.—**municipal'ity** *n.* a town or district with its own corporation or council administering local self-government; in France, a division of the country.—**munic'ipally** *adv.* [L. *municipium,* a free town].
munificence (mū-nif'i-sens) *n.* liberality; generosity.—**munif'icent** *a.* very generous.—**munif'icently** *adv.* [L. *munus,* a gift; *facere,* to make].
muniment (mū'ni-ment) *n.* a stronghold;—*pl.* title deeds; charter.—**mu'niment-room** *n.* a fire-proof room for the storing of valuable charters, legal documents, etc. [L. *munire,* to fortify].
munition (mū-nish'un) *v.t.* to equip with the weapons of war;—*n.* (usually *pl.*) military stores; weapons of war, as guns, tanks, shells, etc. [L. *munitus,* fortified].
munnion Same as **mullion.**
murder (mur'dẹr) *n.* homicide with premeditated and malicious intent;—*v.t.* to commit a murder; to kill; to mar by incompetence. —**mur'derer** *n.* (*fem.* **mur'deress**) one guilty of murder.—**mur'derous** *a.* pert. to murder; bloody; homicidal.—**mur'derously** *adv.* [O.E. *morthor,* murder].
muriate (mū'ri-āt) *n.* commercial name for chloride;—*v.t.* to put into brine.—**muriate of soda,** common salt.—**muria'tic** *a.* pert. to or obtained from sea-salt.—**muriatic acid,** hydrochloric acid [L. *muria,* brine].
murk (murk) *a.* dark;—*n.* misty darkness; gloom.—**murk'y** *a.* dark; misty.—**murk'ily** *adv.* **murk'iness** *n.* [O.E. *mirce,* dark].
murmur (mur'mur) *n.* a low, unbroken sound, as of wind, water, etc.; a complaint expressed in subdued tones; softly uttered speech;—*v.i.* to make a low sound; to speak in subdued

tones; to complain; to grumble.—*pr.p.* **mur′muring.**—*pa.p.* **mur′mured.**—**mur′murer** *n.*—**mur′murous** *a.* pert. to a murmur; making subdued sounds; grumbling [L. *murmur*, a low sound].

murrain (mur′in) *n.* a disease affecting cattle, esp. foot-and-mouth disease [O.Fr. *morine*, a carcase].

murther, murtherer. Same as **murder, murderer.**

muscadel (mus′ka-del) *n.* a musk-flavoured grape; a wine made from this grape; a raisin; a fragrant pear. Also **mus′cat, mus′catel, mus′cadine** [It. *moscato*, musk-flavoured].

muscle (mus′l) *n.* a band of contractile fibrous tissue which produces movement in an animal body; strength.—**mus′cled** *a.* having muscle; muscular.—**mus′cular** *a.* pert. to muscle; brawny; strong.—**muscular′ity** *n.*—**mus′cularly** *adv.*—**to muscle in** (*Amer. slang*) to break in by force [L. *musculus*, a muscle].

muscoid (mus′koid) *a.* (*Bot.*) like moss;—*n.* a moss-like plant.—**muscol′ogy** *n.* the study of mosses [L. *muscus*, moss].

Muscovite (mus′kō-vīt) *n.* a native or inhabitant of Moscow or of Russia.—**mus′covite** *n.* white mica. (Also **muscovy glass.**)—*a.* pert. to Moscow or to Russia.

Muscovy duck (mus′ko-vi duk) *n.* a musk-duck of C. and S. America, so called because it has a faint musky smell.

Muse (mūz) *n.* in Greek mythology, one of the nine daughters of Zeus and Mnemosyne, who each presided over one of the liberal arts.—**muse** *n.* inspiration.—**the muse,** poetry [Gk. *Mousa*].

muse (mūz) *v.i.* to think over dreamily; to ponder; to consider meditatively;—*n.* reverie; contemplation.—**muse′ful** *a.*—**mus′er** *n.*—**mus′ingly** *adv.* reflectively [O.Fr. *muser*, to loiter].

musette (mū-zet′) *n.* a small bagpipe; a melody for this instrument; a reed stop on an organ; a country dance (O.Fr. *musette*, a small bagpipe].

museum (mū-zē′um) *n.* a permanent collection of works of art, antiques, objects of natural history, the sciences, etc., and all material expressions of the history of man; the building housing such a collection [Gk. *Mouseion*, a temple of the Muses].

mush (mush) *n.* a pulp; (*Amer.*) porridge of maize meal; (*Slang*) sentimentality.—**mush′y** *a.* [form of *mash*].

mush (mush) *v.t.* (*Amer. slang*) to journey on foot with dogs over snowy wastes.

mushroom (mush′rōōm) *n.* an edible fungus of very quick growth; (*Fig.*) an upstart;—*a.* of rapid growth, as *mushroom town*; shaped like a mushroom [prob. fr. Fr. *mousse*, moss].

music (mū′zik) *n.* the art of combining sounds or sequences of notes into harmonious patterns pleasing to the ear and satisfying to the emotions; melody; musical composition or score.—**mu′sical** *a.* pert. to music; set to music; appreciative of music; trained or skilled in the art of music.—**mu′sically** *adv.*—**mu′sicalness** *n.*—**mu′sical-box** *n.* a clockwork box which when wound up plays a tune.—**musical comedy,** a form of light entertainment in which songs, dialogue, dancing, humour are combined with a not too serious plot.—**mu′sicale** *n.* (*Amer.*) a private party with music.—**mu′sic-case, -fol′io, -hold′er** *n.* a case, etc., for carrying sheet music.—**mu′sic-hall** *n.* a theatre where light variety programmes are performed.—**musi′cian** *n.* a composer or skilled performer of musical compositions.—**musicol′ogy** *n.* the scientific study of music [Gk. *mousikos*, pert. to the Muses].

musk (musk) *n.* a fragrant substance obtained from a gland of the musk-deer; the perfume of this; any plant with a musky perfume.—**musk′-cat** *n.* civet.—**musk′-deer** *n.* a small, hornless deer of C. Asia with gland secreting commercial musk. Also **Mus′covy-duck.**—**musk′ily** *adv.*—**musk′iness** *n.*—**musk′-mallow** *n.* a variety of the mallow plant with faint musky smell.—**musk′-mel′on** *n.* common melon.—**musk′-or′chis** *n.* the orchid.—**musk′-ox** *n.* a sheep-like ox with brown, long-haired shaggy coat, inhabiting Canadian Arctic.—**musk′-rat** *n.* a large N. American water-rat with musk-gland, valued for its fur; the musquash.—**musk′-rose** *n.* a climbing rose with white blossoms faintly perfumed with musk.—**musk′-tree, -wood** *n.* trees with musky smell, growing mainly in W. Indies and Australia.—**musk′y** *a.* having the smell of musk [L. *muscus*, musk].

musket (mus′ket) *n.* (formerly) a hand gun or matchlock.—**mus′keteer** *n.* a soldier armed with a musket, esp. a member of the French king's bodyguard during 17th cent.—**mus′ketry** *n.* muskets collectively; troops armed with muskets; musket-practice [O.Fr. *mousquet*, a sparrow-hawk].

Muslim (mus′lim) *n.* Same as **Moslem.**

muslin (muz′lin) *n.* a thin cotton cloth of open weave, white or coloured;—*a.* made of muslin [fr. *Mosul*, in Iraq].

musquash (mus′kwosh) *n.* the musk-rat, or its fur [Amer. Ind.].

muss (mus) *v.t.* to disorganise; to make chaotic.—**muss′y** *a.* [etym. uncertain].

mussel (mus′l) *n.* a class of marine bi-valve shell-fish. Also **musc′le.**—**mus′culite** *n.* a fossilised mussel [L. *musculus*, mussel].

Mussulman (mus′ul-man) *n.* a Mohammedan; a Moslem.—*pl.* **Muss′ulmans** [Ar.].

must (must) *v.i.* to be obliged, by physical or moral necessity [O.E. *moste*, pret. of verb, *mot*, may].

must (must) *n.* wine newly pressed from grapes but not fermented [L. *mustus*, new].

must (must) *n.* mouldiness [prob. fr. *musty*].

mustache Same as **moustache.**

mustang (mus′tang) *n.* a wild horse of the American prairies; a bronco [Sp. *mestengo*, belonging to graziers].

mustard (mus′terd) *n.* a plant with yellow flowers and pungent seeds; a yellow powder, made from the seeds, used as a condiment.—**mustard gas,** dichlorodiethyl sulphide, an oily liquid, irritant war-gas causing blistering.—**mus′tard-plas′ter** *n.* a poultice made with mustard.—**wild mustard,** charlock.—**to be as keen as mustard,** to be full of zest [O.Fr. *moustarde*, mustard].

muster (mus′ter) *v.t.* to assemble, as troops for a parade; to gather together, as one's resources;—*v.i.* to be assembled together;—*n.* an assembling of troops, etc.—**to pass muster,** to be up to standard [O.Fr. *mostre*, show].

musty (mus′ti) *a.* mouldy; stale; sour.—**must′ily** *adv.*—**must′iness** *n.* fustiness; mouldiness [L. *mustum*, new wine].

mutable (mū′ta-bl) *a.* subject to change; inconstant.—**mutabil′ity, mu′tableness** *n.* the state or quality of being mutable.—**mu′tably** *adv.*—**mutate′** *v.t.* to change, as a vowel by the influence of another in a subsequent syllable.—**muta′tion** *n.* change; in phonology, the process of 'umlaut' or vowel change; (*Biol.*) a complete divergence from racial type which may ultimately give rise to a new species.—**mu′tative, mu′tatory** *a.* [L. *mutare*, to change].

mute (mūt) *a.* dumb; silent; unexpressed in words; not sounded, as '*l*' of *calm*;—*n.* a person who is dumb; a professional mourner at a funeral; a 'stopped' consonant, such as b, d, p, t;—*v.t.* to muffle the sound of.—**mute′ly** *adv.*—**mute′ness** *n.* [L. *mutus*, dumb].

mutilate (mū′til-āt) *v.t.* to maim; to cut off; to impair by removing an essential part.—**mutila′tion** *n.*—**mu′tilator** *n.* [L. *mutilus*, maimed].

mutiny (mū′ti-ni) *n.* insurrection against lawful authority, esp. military or naval;—*v.i.* to rise in mutiny.—*pr.p.* **mu′tinying.**—*pa.p.* **mu′tinied.**—**mu′tineer** *n.*—**mu′tinous** *a.* rebellious; seditious [Fr. *mutin*, mutinous].

mutt (mut) *n.* (*Amer. slang*) a fool.

mutter (mut′ėr) *v.t.* to speak indistinctly or in a low voice; to grumble.—**mutt′erer** *n.*—**mutt′ering** *n.* [prob. imitative].
mutton (mut′n) *n.* the flesh of sheep; a sheep. —**mutt′on-chop** *n.* rib of mutton for boiling or grilling.—**mutton-chop whiskers,** side-whiskers shaped like a mutton-chop.—**mutton-head,** a stupid person.—**to return to our muttons,** to return to subject under discussion [Fr. *mouton,* a sheep].
mutual (mū′tū-ạl) *a.* reciprocally acting or related; interchanged; done by each to the other; (*incorrectly*) common to several, as in Dickens's *Our Mutual Friend.*—**mutual′ity** *n.* the quality of being reciprocal.—**mu′tually** *adv.* [L. *mutuus,* borrowed].
muzhik (mo͝o-zhik′) *n.* a Russian peasant; a fur cape. Also **mujik′** [Russ.].
muzzle (muz′l) *v.t.* the snout; the mouth and nose of an animal; a cage-like fastening for the mouth to prevent biting; the open end of a gun;—*v.t.* to put a muzzle on; to gag; to enforce silence.—**muzz′le-load′er** *n.* a gun loaded at the muzzle, opp. of *breech-loader* [L. *musus,* a snout].
muzzy (muzz′i) *a.* dazed; bewildered; tipsy.—**muzz′iness** *n.* [etym. uncertain].
my (mī) *poss. a.* belonging to me (contr. of *mine;* O.E. *min,* of me].
mycetes (mī-sē′tēz) *n.pl.* fungi.—**mycetol′ogy** *n.* Same as **mycol′ogy.**—**mycol′ogist** *n.*—**mycology** (mī-kol′o-ji) *n.* the science of fungi. —**mycoph′agy** *n.* the eating of fungi [Gk. *mukēs,* a mushroom].
myelin (mī′e-lin) *n.* (*Zool.*) the fatty substance forming the sheath of nerve fibres.—**myeli′tis** *n.* inflammation of the spinal cord.—**myelomeningi′tis** *n.* spinal meningitis [Gk. *muelos,* marrow].
myna(h) (mī′nạ) *n.* an Indian starling. Also **mi′na** [Hind.].
mynheer (mīn-hār′) *n.* (*S. Afr.*) a term of respect used to a superior or to a clergyman; a gentleman [Dut.].
myoid (mī′oid) *a.* pert. to muscles.—**myocardi′tis** *n.* (*Med.*) inflammation of the heart muscle [Gk. *mus,* a muscle].
myopia (mī-ō′pi-ạ) *n.* short-sightedness.—**my′ope** *n.* a short-sighted person.—**myop′ic** *a.* [Gk. *muein,* to close; *ōps,* the eye].
myositis (mī-ō-sī′tis) *n.* inflammation of a muscle [Gk. *mus,* a muscle].
myosotis (mī-ō-sō′tis) *n.* a genus of herbs of the borage family, including the forget-me-not [Gk. = mouse-ear].
myriad (mir′i-ạd) *n.* an immense number;—*a.* countless [Gk. *murias,* ten thousand].
myriapod (mir′i-ạ-pod) *n.* (*Zool.*) an animal with great number of legs, as centipedes, millipedes [Gk. *murias,* ten thousand; *pous,* a foot].
myrmecology (mir-mẹ-kol′o-ji) *n.* the scientific study of ants and ant-life [Gk. *murmēx,* an ant].
Myrmidon (mėr′mi-don) *n.* in Greek mythology one of the 'ant-men' supposed to have been created from ants; follower of Achilles in Trojan war noted for cruelty.—**myr′midon** *n.* a brutal fighter; one who carries out orders with ruthlessness [Gk. *Murmidones,* the ant-men].
myrrh (mėr) *n.* a transparent yellow-brown aromatic gum resin used formerly as incense, now used in antiseptics.—**myr′rhic, myr′rhy** *a.* [Gk. *murrha,* myrrh].
myrtle (mėr′tl) *n.* an evergreen plant with fragrant white flowers and glossy leaves [O.Fr. *myrtille,* the myrtle-berry].
myself (mī-self′) *pron.* I or me, used emphatically, or reflexively.
mystery (mis′tėr-i) *n.* anything strange and inexplicable; a puzzle; a religious truth beyond human understanding; secrecy; a medieval drama based on Scripture;—*pl.* rites known to and practised by initiated only.—**myster′ious** *a* strange; occult; incomprehensible. —**myste′riously** *adv.*—**myste′riousness** *n.* [Gk. *mustēria,* secret religious rites].
mystic (mis′tik) *a.* pert. to a mystery or to secret religious rites; symbolical of spiritual truth; strange;—*n.* one who believes in mysticism; one who seeks to have direct contact with the Divine by way of spiritual ecstasy and contemplation.—**mys′tical** *a.*—**mys′tically** *adv.*—**mys′ticism** *n.* the doctrine of the mystics; study of spiritual experience; obscurity of doctrine.—**mystifica′tion** *n.* **mys′tify** *v.t.* to perplex; to puzzle.—*pr.p.* **mys′tifying.**—*pa.p.* **mys′tified** [Gk. *mustikos,* pert. to one initiated in the mysteries].
myth (mith) *n.* a fable; a legend embodying primitive faith in the supernatural; an invented story; an imaginary person or thing. —**myth′ic, -al** *a.* pert. to myths; fabulous; non-existent.—**myth′ically** *adv.*—**mytholog′ic, -al** *a.* pert. to mythology; legendary.—**mytholog′ically** *adv.*—**mythol′ogiser** *n.*—**mythol′ogist** *n.* one who has studied myths of various countries; a writer of fables.—**mythol′ogy** *n.* a collection of myths; the science of myths; a treatise on myths [Gk. *muthos,* a story].
myxoedema (mik-se-dē′mạ) *n.*(*Med.*)a disease caused by deficiency of secretion from thyroid gland [Gk. *muxa,* mucus; *oidēma,* swelling].
myxomatosis (mik-sō-ma-tō-sis) *n.* a contagious and deadly disease affecting rabbits [Gk. *muxa,* mucus].

N

Naafi (naf′i) *n.* the official organisation which provides canteens and shopping facilities for men and women in the services [*N*avy, *A*rmy, and *A*ir *F*orce *I*nstitutes].
nab (nab) *v.t.* (*Slang*) to catch hold of; to seize suddenly [Dan. *nappe,* to catch].
nabob (nā′bob) *n.* a Mohammedan chief in India; an Anglo-Indian who had returned home after acquiring great wealth in India; any man of great wealth. Also **na′wab,** the more correct form [Hind. *nawwab*].
nacelle (na-sel′) *n.* a small boat; the part fixed to the wing of an aeroplane serving to enclose engine, crew, passengers, and goods [Fr. fr. L. *navicella,* a little ship].
nacre (nā′kėr) *n.* mother-of-pearl.—**na′creous** *a.* like mother-of-pearl [Fr. fr. Sp. *nacar*].
nadir (nā′dir) *n.* point of the heavens directly opposite the zenith; the lowest or most depressed stage [Ar. *nazir,* opposite].
naevus (nē′vus) *n.* a congenital birth-mark formed by a cluster of small dilated blood-vessels. Also **neave** (nēv) [L.].
nag (nag) *n.* a small horse; any horse [etym. uncertain].
nag (nag) *v.t.* and *v.i.* to worry by constant fault-finding; to scold pertinaciously.—*pr.p.* **nag′ging.**—*pa.t.* and *pa.p.* **nagged.**—**nag′ger** *n.* [Sw. *nagga,* to peck].
naiad (nā′ad, or nī′ad] *n.* in Greek mythology, a nymph of the fresh-water fountain and streams.—*pl.* **nai′ades** [Gk. *naias*].
naïf See **naïve.**
nail (nāl) *n.* the horny shield covering the ends of the fingers or toes; a claw; a strip of pointed metal provided with a head, for fastening wood, etc.; a British cloth measure, 2 inches;—*v.t.* to fasten with a nail; to fix or secure; to confirm or pin down; to catch out or expose; to seize hold of.—**nail′brush** *n.* a small brush for cleaning the finger-nails.—**nail′er** *n.* one who makes nails.—**nail′ery** *n.* a factory where nails are made.—**nail′rod** *n.* a long strip of sheet-iron from which nails are furnished; a coarse dark tobacco, made up in thin rolls or plugs.—**on the nail,** immediately, esp. of payment [O.E. *naegel*].
naïve (nạ-ēv′, nāv) *a.* having native or unaffected simplicity; childishly frank; artless. Also **naïf.**—**naïve′ly** *adv.*—**naïveté** (nȧ-ēv-tā′

n. childlike ingenuousness; simple unaffectedness. Also **naïv'ety** [Fr.].

naked (nā´ked) *a.* having no clothes; exposed; bare; nude; uncovered; unarmed; unprovided for; manifest; evident; undisguised; simple; sheer.—**na'kedly** *adv.*—**na'kedness** *n.*—**naked eye**, the eye, unassisted by glasses [O.E. *nacod*].

namby-pamby (nam´bi-pam´bi) *a.* insipid; lacking strength of character; weakly sentimental [from *Ambrose Philips*, a poet who wrote childishly affected verse].

name (nām) *n.* the term by which any person or thing is known; appellation; designation; title; fame; reputation; credit; repute; family; —*v.t.* to give a name to; to call or mention by name; to nominate; to specify; to christen; to proceed to suspend a recalcitrant member of parliament in the House of Commons by first formally mentioning him by name.—**name'less** *a.* without a name; dishonoured; obscure; unspeakable.—**name'lessly** *adv.*—**name'ly** *adv.* by name; that is to say.—**name'sake** *n.* a person who bears the same name as another [O.E. *nama*].

nancy (nan´si) *n.* an effeminate youth; a homosexual.—**nan'cy-pret'ty** *n.* (*Bot.*) a corruption of *none-so-pretty*, the saxifrage also known as *London Pride*.

nankeen (nan-kēn') *n.* a calico fabric dyed buff by a tanning solution [*Nanking*, in China, where first woven].

nanny (nan´i) *n.* a child's nurse.—**nan'ny-goat** [*n.* a she-goat.

nap (nap) *n.* a short sleep; a doze;—*v.i.* to indulge in a short sleep; to be unprepared [O.E. *knappian*].

nap (nap) *n.* fine hairy surface of cloth; the pile of velvet; the fine natural fur of a silk hat, etc.;—*v.t.* to raise a nap on cloth by teasing [Dut. *nop*].

nap (nap) *n.* a card game [invented in the time of *Napoleon* III].

nap (nap) *v.t.* of racing tipsters, to advise a client to bet on a certain horse as a sure winner of a race.

napalm (nā´pȧm) *n.* jellied petrol, used in air-raids and having a devastating burning effect.

nape (nāp) *n.* the back part of the neck [O.E. *hnaepp*, bowl].

napery (nā´pe̤r-i) *n.* household linen, esp. for the table [O.Fr. *naperie*].

naphtha (naf´tha̤, nap´tha̤) *n.* a clear, volatile, inflammable liquid distilled from petroleum, wood, etc.; a thin, pure rock oil.—**naph'thalene** *n.* a white, solid crystalline hydrocarbon distilled from coal-tar and familiar in the form of moth-balls.—**naphthal'ic** *a.* [Gk.].

napkin (nap´kin) *n.* a cloth used for wiping the hands or lips at table; a serviette to protect the clothes at table [Fr. *nappe*, cloth].

napoleon (na-pō´lē-on) *n.* a French gold coin of the First and Second French empires, then worth 20 francs (15/10½); the game of nap.—**Napoleon'ic**, *a.* pert. to Napoleon I or III.

napoo (na-pȯȯ') *a.* (*Slang*) no good; no more; finished; gone; dead [fr. Fr. *il n'y en a plus*, there is no more].

nappy (nap´i) *n.* a baby's napkin [dim.].

Narcissus (na̤r-sis´us) *n.* a numerous genus of bulbous plants belonging to the order Amaryllidaceae, including the daffodil, the jonquil and the narcissus [Gk. *Narkissos*].

Narcissus (na̤r-sis´us) *n.* in Greek mythology, a youth doomed to fall in love with his own image until he pined away and died, his corpse being changed into the flower which bears his name.—**narciss'ism** *n.* in psycho-analysis, an abnormal love and admiration for oneself.—**narciss'ist** *n.* [Gk.].

narcotic (nar-kot´ik) *a.* producing stupor or inducing sleep;—*n.* a substance which induces sleep, and in large doses, insensibility and stupor.—**narco'sis** *n.* a state of unconsciousness or stupor with complete deadening of sensibility to pain, produced by the use of narcotics [Gk. *narkōtikos*, benumbed].

nard (nȧrd) *n.* the spikenard, a plant which yields an odorous unguent; an aromatic ointment.—**nard'ine** *a.* [Pers.].

narghile (nȧr´gi-le) *n.* a hookah or tobacco-pipe in which the smoke is drawn through perfumed water [Pers. *nargileh*].

nark (nark) *n.* (*Slang*) a police decoy or spy; an informer [Romany, *nak*, nose].

narrate (na̤-rāt', nar´āt) *v.t.* to relate; to tell (story) in detail; to give an account of; to describe.—**narra'tion** *n.* act of relating; an account.—**narr'ative** *n.* a tale; a detailed account of events;—*a.* pert. to, containing, narration.—**narr'atively** *adv.*—**narra'tor** *n.* one who narrates; on radio, one who supplies the connecting links between the various episodes of a dramatic broadcast [L. *narrare*].

narrow (nar´ō) *a.* of little breadth; not wide or broad; limited; niggardly; bigoted; illiberal; accurate;—*v.t.* to make narrow;—*v.i.* to become narrow;—*n.pl.* straits.—**narrow gauge**, of railway lines less than 4 ft. 8½ in. apart.—**narr'owly** *adv.*—**narr'ow-min'ded** *a.* bigoted; illiberal; prejudiced [O.E. *nearu*].

narwhal (nȧr´whal) *n.* a cetaceous mammal, closely related to the white whale, with one large protruding tusk. Also **nar'wal** [Dan. *narhval*].

nasal (nā´za̤l) *a.* pert. to the nose; modified by the nose, as the sound of *m*;—*n.* a nasal sound or letter, such as *m* or *n*.—**na'salise** *v.i.* to render (a sound) nasally.—**nasal'ity** *n.* the quality of being nasal.—**na'sally** *adv.* through the nose.—**nasal organ**, the nose [L. *nasus*, the nose].

nascent (nas´e̤nt) *a.* at the moment of being born; just beginning to exist [L. *nasci*, to be born].

nasturtium (nas-tur´shi-um) *n.* (*Bot.*) a genus of plants of the Cruciferae family including water-cress; a common trailing garden plant of the genus Tropaeolum [L. = twisting the nose].

nasty (nȧs´ti) *a.* very dirty; filthy; foul; impure; disgusting; offensive; repulsive; unpropitious (of the weather, etc.); ill-natured; indecent.—**nas'tily** *adv.*—**nas'tiness** *n.* [etym. uncertain].

natal (nā´ta̤l) *a.* pert. to one's place of birth or date of birth; native.—**natali'tial** *a.* pert. to a birthday.—**natal'ity** *n.* birth-rate.—**natal day**, birthday [L. *natus*, born].

natant (nā´ta̤nt) *a.* (*Bot.*) floating on the surface.—**nata'tion** *n.* swimming.—**natato'res** *n.pl.* aquatic birds with webbed feet adapted for swimming.—**natato'rial** *a.* natatory.—**natato'rium** *n.* a swimming-pool, or -school.—**na'tatory** *a.* used or adapted for swimming [L. *natare*, to swim].

natheless (nȧ´the-les) *adv.* nevertheless [=not by that less].

nation (nā´shun) *n.* a people inhabiting a country under the same government; an aggregation of persons of the same origin and language; a race of people;—*pl.* the Gentiles [L. *natio*, a tribe].

national (nash´un-a̤l) *a.* belonging to or pertaining to a nation; public; general;—*n.* member of a nation.—**nationalisa'tion** *n.*—**nat'ionalise** *v.t.* to make national; to acquire and manage by the State; to make a nation of.—**nat'ionalism** *n.*—**nat'ionalist** *n.* one who advocates a policy of national independence.—**national'ity** *n.* the quality of being a nation or belonging to a nation; one's nation; patriotism.—**nat'ionally** *adv.*—**national anthem**, a hymn or song expressive of patriotism, praise, or thanksgiving, commonly sung by people of a nation at public gatherings.—**national debt**, the debt due from a nation to individual creditors.—**national health insurance**, compulsory insurance against illness.—**national registration**, a system adopted during the First and Second World Wars under which all inhabitants of Britain had to register for various purposes.—**National Socialist Party**, the German [Fascist Party (Nazis) under Adolf Hitler (1922-1945).—**National Trust**, a society founded in 1895 for preserving places of historic interest, or natural beauty [fr. *nation*]

native (nā´tiv) *a.* pert. to one's birth; belonging by birth; innate; indigenous; natural; of metals, occurring in a natural state;—*n.* a person born in a place;—*pl.* oysters reared in an artificial bed.—**na'tively** *adv.*—**nativ'ity** *n.* the time or circumstances of birth; in astrology, the position of the stars at a person's birth.—**The Nativity**, the birth of Christ [L. *nativus*, inborn].

natron (nā´trun) *n.* a naturally-occurring mineral form of sodium-carbonate [Gk. *nitron*].

natter (nat´ẹr) *v.t.* and *v.i.* (*Prov.*) to nag; to find fault [O.N. *knetta*, to grumble].

natterjack (nat´ẹr-jak) *n.* a British species of toad which walks and runs instead of leaping [O.E. *attor*, poison].

natty (nat´i) *a.* neat; trim; tidy; spruce; deft.—**natt'ily** *adv.* [etym. unknown].

natural (nat´ū-rạl) *a.* in accordance with, belonging to, or derived from, nature; inborn; unconstrained; normal; in a state of nature; unaffected; unassuming; true to life; illegitimate; (*Mus.*) not modified by a flat or sharp;—*n.* an idiot; (*Mus.*) a character (♮) to remove the effect of an accidental sharp or flat which has preceded it.—**naturalisa'tion** *n.*—**nat'uralise** *v.t.* to give to an alien the rights of a native subject; to adopt a foreign word etc., as native; to accustom, as to a climate.—**nat'uralism**, *n.* natural condition or quality; the system of those who deny supernatural agency, divine revelation, miracles, prophecies, etc.; theory of acting which holds that sincere acting must be a reproduction of emotion actually experienced.—**nat'uralist** *n.* one versed or interested in natural history.—**naturalis'tic** *a.* in accordance with nature.—**naturalis'tically** *adv.*—**nat'urally** *adv.*—**nat'uralness** *n.*—**natural gas**, an inflammable product, usually methane, occurring in association with mineral oil deposits.—**natural history**, the science which deals with the earth's crust and its productions, but applied more especially to biology or zoology.—**natural philosophy**, the science of nature and of the physical properties of bodies; physics.—**natural religion**, religion which is derived from nature and reason without resource to supernatural revelation.—**natural science**, the science of nature as distinguished from mental and moral science and mathematics.—**natural selection**, the survival of individuals, in the wild state, which possess advantageous variations [*nature*].

nature (nā´tūr) *n.* the world, the universe, known and unknown; the power underlying all phenomena in the material world; the innate or essential qualities of a thing; the environment of man; the sum total of inheritance; natural disposition; innate character; of a material, the average excellence of its qualities when unaffected by deteriorating influences; sort; kind; vital functions of organs of the body; state of nakedness.—**na'tured** *a.* in compounds, **good-**, **bad-na'tured** *a.* showing one's innate disposition.—**nature knowledge**, **nature study**, a school subject to increase the powers of observation by examining natural objects [L. *natura*].

naught (nawt) *n.* nothing; no-whit; figure 0; zero;—*adv.* in no degree;—*a.* worthless.—**naught'y** *a.* wayward; not behaving well; mischievous; bad.—**naught'ily** *adv.*—**naught'iness** *n.* [O.E. *nawiht*, no whit].

nausea (naw´si-a, naw´s(h)e-ạ) *n.* any sickness of the stomach, accompanied with a propensity to vomit; a feeling of sickness or disgust; sea-sickness.—**nau'seate** *v.i.* to feel nausea; to become squeamish;—*v.t.* to loathe; to fill with loathing or disgust.—**nau'seous** *a.* loathsome; disgusting; producing nausea.—**nau'seously** *adv.*—**nau'seousness** *n.* [Gk. = sea-sickness, fr. *naus*, a ship].

nautch (nawch) *n.* a dance of India, performed by **nautch girls** [Hind. *nach*, a dance].

nautical (naw´ti-kạl) *a.* pert. to ships, seamen, or to navigation.—**nau'tically** *adv.*—**nautical mile**, 6,046 to 6,108 ft. (Admiralty measured mile is 6,080 ft.) [Gk. *nautēs*, a sailor].

nautilus (naw´ti-lus) *n.* a genus of cephalopod molluscs with many-chambered spiral shells.—*pl.* **nau'tiluses** or **nau'tili**.—**nau'tiloid** *a.* [Gk. *nautilos*, a sailor].

naval (nā´vạl) *a.* pert. to ships, esp. warships; belonging to or serving with the navy; nautical; marine; maritime [L. *navis*, a ship].

nave (nāv) *n.* the central piece or hub from which the spokes of a wheel radiate; the boss of a wheel [O.E. *nafu*].

nave (nāv) *n.* the middle or body, of a church, extending from the choir or chancel to the main entrance, so called because of its resemblance in shape to an inverted ship [L. *navis*, a ship].

navel (nā´vl) *n.* the umbilicus, place of attachment of the umbilical cord to the body of the embryo, marked by a rounded depression in the centre of the lower part of the abdomen [O.E. *nafela*].

navicert (nav´i-sẹrt) *n.* during the Second World War, a certificate granted by a British Consul abroad to the effect that no contraband was included in a ship's cargo [coined from *navi*gation *cert*ificate].

navicular (nạ-vik´ū-lạr) *a.* shaped like a boat or canoe; relating to small ships or boats [L. *navicularis*, fr. *navis*, a ship].

navigate (nav´i-gāt) *v.t.* to steer or manage a ship when sailing; to sail upon or through;—*v.i.* to sail.—**nav'igable** *a.* may be sailed over or upon; sea-worthy; steerable (of balloons).—**navigabil'ity**, **nav'igableness** *n.*—**nav'igably** *adv.*—**naviga'tion** *n.* the science of directing course of seagoing vessel and of ascertaining its position at any given time; the control and direction of aircraft in flight; shipping; voyage; artificial water-way or canal.—**nav'igator** *n.* [L. *navigare*, to sail].

navvy (nav´i) *n.* a labourer on the construction of roads, railways, canals, etc.—**steam´nav'vy** *n.* a mechanical excavator [fr. *navigator*].

navy (nā´vi) *n.* a fleet; the warships of a country with their crews and organisation.—**na'vy-blue** *n.* and *a.* dark-blue, the colour of the naval uniform worn by British navymen [L. *navis*, a ship].

nawab See **nabob**.

nay (nā) *adv.* no; not only this, but;—*n.* denial; refusal [O.N. *nei*, never].

naye paise (neē pessā) *n.* a unit of Indian currency, adopted in 1957 on the introduction of decimal coinage.

Nazarene (naz´ạ-rēn) *n.* a native of *Nazareth*; term used by Jews and Mohammedans for a Christian; name given to Jesus Christ;—*pl.* an early Christian sect.

Nazarite (naz´ạ-rīt) *n.* a person among the ancient Jews who vowed to abstain from wine and from cutting the hair [Heb. *nazar*, to abstain]. [doublet of 'ness' [O.E. *naes*].

naze (nāz) *n.* a promontory; a headland; a

Nazi (nȧt´zi) *n.* and *a.* a member of the National Socialist Party of Germany (1922-1945).—**Naz'ism**, **Naz'iism** *n.* [Ger. *nazional*, national].

Neanderthal (nē-ȧn´dẹr-tȧl) *a.* denoting a man of the earliest long-headed race in Europe which became extinct at least 50,000 years ago.—**nean'derthaloid** *a.* resembling the prehistoric skull found in 1857 in a cave in the *Neanderthal*, a valley between Dusseldorf and Elberfeld.

neap (nēp) *a.* low;—*n.* neap-tide.—**neaped** *a.* of a ship aground until the first spring tide.—**neap'tide** *n.* the tide whose rise and fall is least marked, occurring 7½ days after the time of new moon and full moon [O.E. *nep*.].

Neapolitan (nē-a-pol'i-tan) *a.* and *n.* pert. to Naples or its inhabitants [Gk. *Neapolis*, fr. *neos*, new; *polis*, a city].
near (nēr) *adv.* at or to a short distance;—*prep.* close to;—*a.* close; closely related; stingy;—*v.t.* and *v.i.* to approach.—**near'by** *a.* in close proximity; adjacent.—**Near East,** part of Asia nearest Europe, from Asia Minor to Persia.—**near'hand** *a.* close at hand;—*adv.* nearly.—**near'ly** *adv.* closely; intimately; almost.—**near'ness** *n.*—**near'side** *n.* of horses, vehicles, etc., the left side; the side nearest the pavement.—**near'sight'ed** *a.* myopic; short-sighted.—**near'sight'edness** *n.* [O.E. *near*, nigher].
neat (nēt) *n.* the ox or cow, as distinguished from other domestic animals; cattle.—**neat'herd** *n.* [O.E. *neat*, cattle].
neat (nēt) *a.* clean; unsoiled; pure; spruce; trim; well-fitting; undiluted; clever; in good taste; handy; dexterous; precise; exact; net.—**neat'ly** *adv.*—**neat'ness** *n.* [Fr. *net*, clean, pure].
neb (neb) *n.* the bill or beak of a bird; the nose [O.E. *nebb* the face].
nebula (neb'ū-la) *n.* a little cloud; a slight greyish speck on the cornea of the eye; a celestial phenomenon consisting of vastly diffused gas or of tenuous material throughout which fine dust in an incandescent state is distributed.—*pl.* **neb'ulae.**—**neb'ular** *a.*—**nebulos'ity** *n.* cloudiness; vagueness.—**neb'ulous** *a.* cloudy, hazy, indistinct; vague; formless; pert. to nebula.—**neb'ulousness** *n.* [L. = mist].
necessary (nes'e-sar-i) *a.* needful; requisite; indispensable; that must be done;—*n.* a needful thing; essential need.—**nec'essarily** *adv.*—**nec'essariness** *n.*—**necessa'rian** *n.* a determinist [L. *necessarius*].
necessity (ne-ses'i-ti) *n.* pressing need; indispensability; compulsion; needfulness; urgency; poverty; a requisite; an essential.—**necessita'rian** *n.* one who holds that the will is not free but determined by inherited tendency and environment.—**necessita'rianism** *n.*—**necess'itate** *v.t.* to make necessary or indispensable; to force; to oblige.—**necess'itous** *a.* poor; needy; destitute [L. *necessitas*].
neck (nek) *n.* the part of the body joining the head to the trunk; the narrower part of a bottle, etc.; a narrow piece of anything between wider parts;—*v.t.* (*Slang*) to hug; to cuddle.—**neck'erchief** *n.* a band of cloth or kerchief worn round the neck and folded, tie-form, in front.—**neck'lace** *n.* a string of beads or precious stones worn round neck.—**neck'let** *n.* neck ornament; small collar, usually of fur.—**neck'tie** *n.* a tie for the neck.—**neck and crop,** completely [O.E. *hnecca*, nape of neck].
necro- (nek'ro) *prefix*, fr. Gk. *nekros*, a dead body, used in the construction of compound terms, signifying death in some form.—**necrol'ogy** *n.* a register of deaths; a collection of obituary notices.—**nec'romancy** *n.* the art of predicting future events by conjuring up the spirits of the dead; black magic; enchantment.—**nec'romancer** *n.* a sorcerer; a wizard.—**necroman'tic** *a.* pert. to magic.—**necrop'olis** *n.* a cemetery.—**nec'ropsy, necros'copy** *n.* a post-mortem; autopsy.—**necro'sis** *n.* gangrene, mortification; canker.—**necrot'ic** *a.*
nectar (nek'tar) *n.* the fabled drink of the gods, with the power of conferring immortality; any delicious beverage; honey-like secretion of the nectary gland of flowers.—**necta'real, necta'rean, necta'reous, nec'tarous** *a.* sweet as nectar; resembling nectar; delicious.—**nec'tared** *a.* flavoured with nectar; very sweet.—**nec'tarine** *a.* sweet as nectar;—*n.* a smooth-skinned variety of peach.—**nec'tary** *n.* the honey-gland at the base of petals and usually between the stamens to further cross-fertilisation by insects [Gk. *nektar*].
need (nēd) *n.* a constitutional or acquired craving or want, appeased by recurrent satisfactions; want; necessity; requirement; poverty; destitution; extremity; urgency;—*v.t.* to be in want of; to require;—*v.i.* to be under a necessity.—**need'ful** *a.* needy; necessary; requisite.—**the needful,** amount of ready-cash required for some specific object.—**need'fully** *adv.*—**need'fulness** *n.*—**need'ily** *adv.*—**need'iness** *n.* temporary lack of money.—**need'less** *a.* unnecessary; not needed.—**need'lessly** *adv.*—**need'lessness** *n.*—**need'y** *a.* in need; indigent [O.E. *nied*].
needle (nēd'l) *n.* a short pointed instrument with an eye, for passing thread through cloth, etc.; a knitting-pin; anything like a needle, as the magnet of a compass, a hypodermic syringe, an etcher's burin, an obelisk, a sharp-pointed rock, leaf of the pine, etc.; the reproducing needle of a gramophone;—*a.* to denote a keenly contested and evenly-matched game, boxing-match, etc.—**need'le-case** *n.* a case for holding needles and sewing accessories.—**needle machine,** an embroidery machine.—**need'lepoint** *n.* a hand-made lace, made with a needle and a single thread.—**need'lewoman** *n.* a sempstress.—**need'lework** *n.* sewing; embroidery.—**need'ly** *a.* thorny [O.E. *naedl*].
ne'er (nār) *adv.* poetical form of *never*.—**ne'er'do-well** *a.* and *n.* good-for-nothing; worthless; scapegrace.
nefarious (ne-fā'ri-us) *a.* wicked in the extreme; iniquitous; monstrous.—**nefa'riously** *adv.*—**nefa'riousness** *n.* [L. *nefarius*].
negate (ne-gāt') *v.t.* to deny; to prove the contrary.—**nega'tion** *n.* the act of denying; negative statement; disavowal; contradiction [L. *negare*, to deny].
negative (neg'a-tiv) *a.* expressing denial, prohibition, or refusal; lacking positive qualities; not positive; stopping or withholding; (*Elect.*) at a lower electric potential; (*Algebra*) minus;—*n.* a proposition in which something is denied; a negative word; a photographic plate in which lights and shades are reversed;—*v.t* to refuse to sanction; to reject.—**neg'atively** *adv.*—**neg'ativeness** *n.*—**negative electricity,** developed in resinous bodies, such as amber, by rubbing with flannel.—**negative pole,** a pole which is at a lower potential relatively to the other, the positive pole; that by which electricity enters a cell or generator, but leaves a battery (denoted by the minus sign); of a magnet, that which points to the south.—**negative quantity** (*Math.*) quantity preceded by the minus sign [L. *negare*, to deny].
negatron (neg'a-tron) *n.* the negative electron; (*Radio*) a type of thermionic valve for obtaining negative resistance [*nega*(tive), (elec)*tron*].
neglect (ne-glekt') *v.t.* to disregard; to take no care of; to fail to do; to omit through carelessness; to slight;—*n.* omission; disregard; careless treatment; slight.—**neglect'edness** *n.*—**neglect'er** *n.*—**neglect'ful** *a.* careless; inclined to be heedless.—**neglect'fully** *adv.* [L. *negligere*, to neglect].
négligé (nā'glē-zhā) *n.* an easy-fitting unceremonious attire;—*a.* carelessly or untidily dressed.—**neg'ligee** *n.* a loose gown; morning wear; a long coral necklace [Fr.].
negligence (neg'li-jens) *n.* want of due care; carelessness; habitual neglect.—**neg'ligent** *a.* to neglect; careless; inattentive; untidy.—**neg'ligently** *adv.*—**neg'ligible** *a.* hardly worth noticing; may be neglected [L. *neglegere*, to neglect].
negotiate (ne-gō'shi-āt) *v.t.* to settle by bargaining; to arrange; to transfer (a bill, etc.); to surmount;—*v.i.* to discuss with a view to finding terms of agreement; to bargain.—**nego'tiable** *a.* capable of being negotiated; transferable; able to be surmounted.—**negotiabil'ity** *n.*—**negotia'tion** *n.*—**nego'tiant, nego'tiator** *n.* (*fem.* **nego'tiatrix**) one who negotiates.—**negotia'tory** *a.* [L. *negotiari*, fr. *negotium* business].
Negrito (ne-grē'tō) *n.* a dwarfish Negro-like race of the Philippines; any Negro tribe of small stature. Also **Negrill'o** [Sp.].
Negro (nē'grō) *n.* member of one main ethno-

logical groups of human race, with dark skin, fuzzy hair, broad nose and protruding lips;—*a.* pert. to Negroes.—**Ne'gress** *n.* Negro woman. —**ne'grohead** *n.* tobacco soaked in molasses, made in the form of a twist and put up in rolls.—**Ne'groid** *a.* resembling the Negroes; of a Negro type. [Sp. fr. L. *niger*, black].

Negus (nē'gus) *n.* the sovereign or ruler of Abyssinia (= king].

negus (nē'gus) *n.* a drink compounded of (port)wine, hot-water, spice and sugar [after inventor, Col. *Negus*, 18th cent.].

neigh (nā) *v.i.* to whinny, like horse;—*n.* cry of horse [O.E. *hnaegan*].

neighbour (nā'bur) *n.* a person who lives, works, near another;—*a.* neighbouring;—*v.t.* to adjoin; to be near.—**neigh'bourhood** *n.* state of being near to each other; adjoining district and its people; proximity; vicinity.—**neigh'bouring** *a.* close by.—**neigh'bourly** *a.* becoming a neighbour; friendly; sociable; genial; helpful.—**neigh'bourliness** *n.* [O.E. *neahgebur*].

neither (nē'THer, nī'THer) *a.* and *pron.* not the one or the other;—*adv.* not on the one hand; not either;—*conj.* nor yet [O.E. *nahwaether*, not whether].

nematode, nematoid (nem'a-tōd, -toid) *a.* thread-like.—**Nematoi'dea** *n.pl.* round-worms, thread-worms [Gk. *nēma*, thread; *eidos*, form].

nemesia (nem-ē'si-a) *n.* a hardy garden plant, belonging to the order Scrophulariaceae [L. *nemus*, a grove].

Nemesis (nem'e-sis) *n.* (*Myth.*) the Greek goddess of vengeance; inevitable retributive justice [Gk. *nemein*, to distribute, deal out].

nenuphar (nen'ū-far) *n.* the great white water-lily [Pers.].

neo- (nē'ō) *prefix* used in the construction of compound terms, signifying *new, recent* [Gk. *neos*].

neodymium (nē-ō-dim'i-um) *n.* a metallic element belonging to the group of rare-earth metals [Gk. *neos*, new; and *didymium* (a once supposed element)].

neolite (nē'ō-līt) *n.* a dark-green mineral, silicate of aluminium and magnesium, found in basalt [Gk. *neos*, new; *lithos*, a stone].

neolithic (nē-ō-lith'ik) *a.* (*Geol.*) pert. to the New Stone Age.

neology (nē-ol'o-ji) *n.* the introduction of new words into a language; new doctrines, esp. rationalistic, in theology.—**neolo'gian, neol'ogist** *n.* one who coins new words or holds novel doctrines in religion.—**neolog'ic, neolog'ical** *a.*—**neol'ogise** *v.i.* to coin new words.—**neol'ogism** *n.* a newly-coined word or phrase [Gk. *neos*, new; *logos*, word].

neon (nē'on) *n.* a non-metallic chemical element belonging to the group of the rare gases, occurring in minute traces in the air.—**neon-lamp, -sign,** or **-tube,** one containing neon gas and glowing with a characteristic reddish-orange light [Gk. *neos*, new].

neophobia (nē-ō-fō'bi-a) *n.* a dread of the unknown [Gk. *neos*, new; *phobos*, fear].

neophyte (nē'ō-fīt) *n.* one newly admitted to a religious order or initiated into the practice of secret rites; a novice or tyro; a proselyte or convert to the R.C. Church [Gk. *neos*, new; *phutos*, grown].

neoytterbium (nē'ō-i-ter'bi-um) *n.* a rare-earth metal [Gk. *neos*, new; and *ytterbium*].

neozoic (nē-ō-zō'ik) *a.* (*Geol.*) denoting rock-formations of recent period, succeeding the mesozoic [Gk. *neos*, new; *zōē*, life].

nepenthe, nepenthes (nē-pen'thē, -thēz) *n.* in Greek mythology, a drug mentioned in the *Odyssey* with power of banishing grief; any narcotic drug to relieve pain; genus of Asiatic plants, including pitcher plant [Gk. *nē-*, not; *penthos*, grief].

nephew (nev'ū, nef'ū) *n.* a brother's or sister's son; originally, a grandson, e.g. in Judges 12 [Fr. *neveu*, fr. L. *nepos*, a nephew or grandchild].

nephoscope (nef'ō-skōp) *n.* a meteorological instrument used to determine the wind velocity and direction immediately overhead by observing cloud movements [Gk. *nephos*, cloud; *skopein*, to view].

nephr-, nephro- (nef'rō) *prefix* used in the construction of compound terms, from Greek *nephros*, a kidney.—**nephral'gia, nephral'gy** *n.* pain in the kidney.—**neph'ric** *a.* pert. to the kidneys.—**nephrit'ic(al)** *a.* pert. to (diseases of) the kidneys—**nephri'tis** *n.* Bright's disease, non-infective inflammation of the kidney.

nepotism (nep'o-tizm) *n.* undue favouritism in awarding public appointments to one's relations [L. *nepos*, a nephew].

Neptune (nep'tūn) *n.* (*Myth.*) the Roman god of the sea; second most remote planet of solar system [L.].

neptunium (nep-tūn'i-um) *n.* a radio-active element found when uranium is bombarded with neutrons and used in the atom bomb [fr. *Neptune*].

nereid (nē'rē-id) *n.* in Greek mythology, a nymph of the sea, one of the daughters of *Nereus*; (*Zool.*) a sea-centipede; a sea-worm.

nerve (nerv) *n.* one of the bundles of fibres which convey impulses either from brain (motor nerves) to muscles, etc., producing motion, or to brain (sensory nerves) from skin, eyes, nose, etc., producing sensation; mid-rib or vein of a leaf; sinew; tendon; fortitude; courage; cool assurance; impudence.—*pl.* irritability; unusual sensitiveness to fear, annoyance, etc.;—*v.t.* to give courage or strength to.—**nerved** *a.*—**nerve'less** *a.* lacking in strength or will; incapable of effort. **nerve'lessness** *n.*—**ner'vine** *a.* acting on the nerves;—*n.* a nerve-tonic.—**ner'vy** *a.* nervous; timid; fidgety [L. *nervus*, sinew].

nervous (nerv'us) *a.* of the nerves; vigorous; easily stimulated; timid.—**nerv'ously** *adv.*—**nerv'ousness** *n.*—**nervous debility,** a lowering of activity and force of nervous system [L. *nervus*, a sinew].

nescience (nēsh'yens, nesh'ens) *n.* the condition of complete ignorance; want of knowledge; agnosticism, the theory that certain forms of reality, as the soul, are beyond our knowledge.—**nesc'ient** *a.* ignorant; agnostic [L. *nescire*, not to know].

ness (nes) *n.* a promontory; a headland; a cape [O.E. *naess*].

nest (nest) *n.* the place in which a bird lays and hatches its eggs; an egg-laying animal's breeding-place; any snug retreat; a set of boxes, tables, etc., which fit into one another;—*v.t.* to form a nest for;—*v.i.* to occupy or build a nest.—**nest'ling** *n.* a bird too young to leave the nest.—**nest'-egg** *n.* an egg left in a nest to induce a bird to lay; a small sum of money put aside for some later, useful purpose [O.E.].

nestle (nes'l) *v.t.* to settle comfortably and close to one another; to lie snugly, as in a nest; (of a house) to be situated in a sheltered spot [O.E. *nestlian*].

net (net) *n.* an open-work fabric of meshes of cord, etc.; sections of this used to catch fish, protect fruit, etc.; lace formed by netting; a snare.—*a.* made of netting; reticulate; caught in a net;—*v.t.* to cover with, or catch in, a net; to veil;—*v.i.* to make net or network.—*pr.p.* **net'ting.**—*pa.t.* and *pa.p.* **net'ted.**—**net'ted** *a.*—**net'ting** *n.* the act or process of forming network; net-like fabric; snaring by means of a net.—**net'ball** *n.* a game, the object of which is to propel a football with the hand into a netted ring.—**net'fish** *n.* any fish caught in a net.—**net'work** *n.* anything made like, or resembling, a net; (*Broadcasting*) a centralised service organisation producing programmes carried by long-distance telephone wires to affiliated stations for broadcasting [O.E. *nett*.]

net, nett (net) *a.* left after all deductions; free from deduction;—*v.t.* to gain or produce as clear profit;—*pr.p.* **net'ting.**—*pa.p.* **net'ted.**

net price, cash price without discount [Fr. = clean].
nether (neTH′ėr) *a.* lower; low-lying; lying below; belonging to the lower regions.—**neth′ermost** *a.* lowest.—**neth′erward(s)** *adv.* in a downward direction [O.E. *neothera*].
Netherlands (neTH′ėr-landz) *n.pl.* the Kingdom of the Netherlands, Holland.—**Neth′erlander** *n.* a Dutchman; an inhabitant of Holland [E. = lower lands].
nettle (net′l) *n.* a common weed covered with fine stinging hairs which contain an acrid and caustic fluid;—*v.t.* to irritate; to provoke; to make angry; to rouse to action.—**net′tle-rash** *n.* an irritating eruption in the skin causing a sensation like the stinging of nettles.—**net′tle-wort** *n.* any kind of nettle [O.E. *netele*].
neur-, neuro- (nūr-, nū′rō) *prefix* used in the formation of compound terms, from Greek, *neuron*, a nerve.
neural (nū′ral) *a.* pert. to the nerves or nervous system [Gk. *neuron*, a nerve].
neuralgia (nū-ral′ji-a) *n.* a spasmodic or continuous pain occurring along the course of one or more distinct nerves.—**neural′gic** *a.* [Gk. *neuron*, a nerve; *algos*, pain].
neurasthenia (nū-ras-thē′ni-a) *n.* a condition of nervous debility characterised by lack of energy, restlessness, headache and insomnia.—**neurasthen′ic** *a.* [Gk. *neuron*, a nerve; *astheneia*, weakness].
neuration (nū-rā′shun) *n.* See **nervation.**
neuraxis (nūr-ak′sis) *n.* the cerebro-spinal axis, or central nervous system, including the brain and spinal cord.
neuritis (nū-rī′tis) *n.* an inflammatory condition of a nerve [Gk. *neuron*, a nerve].
neurology (nū-rol′o-ji) *n.* the study of the structure, function and diseases of the nervous system.—**neurolog′ical** *a.*—**neurol′ogist** *n.* [Gk. *neuron*, a nerve; *logos*, discourse].
neuron (nū′ron) *n.* a nerve cell and all its processes [Gk. = nerve].
neuropath (nū′rō-path) *n.* a person suffering from a nervous disorder; a neuropathist.—**neuropath′ic, neuropath′ical** *a.* pert. to nervous diseases.—**neuropath′ically** *adv.*—**neurop′athist** *n.* a nerve specialist.—**neuropathol′ogy** *n.* the pathology of the nervous system.—**neurop′athy** *n.* an abnormal or diseased condition of the nervous system [Gk. *neuron*, nerve; *pathos*, suffering].
Neuroptera (nū-rop′tėr-a) *n.* an order of nerve-winged insects (including dragonflies, May-flies) with four similar reticulated wings.—**neurop′teral, neurop′terous** *a.* [Gk. *neuron*, nerve; *pteron*, a wing].
neurosis (nū-rō′sis) *n.* a class of functional disorders of the nervous system, not attributable to organic disease.—**neurot′ic** *a.* pert. to the nerves;—*n.* a highly-strung person of morbid mentality [Gk. *neuron*, a nerve].
neuter (nū′tėr) *a.* neither masculine nor feminine; (*Bot.*) possessing neither stamens nor carpels;—*n.* the neuter gender; an imperfectly developed female, as the worker-bee; one who is neutral [L. = neither].
neutral (nū′tral) *a.* taking neither side in a war, dispute, etc.; indifferent; without bias; grey; intermediate (shade of colour); neither acid nor alkaline; asexual;—*n.* nation, person, not taking sides in a dispute; the position in a gear-mechanism when no power is transmitted.—**neu′tralise** *v.t.* to render neutral; to make ineffective; to counter-balance.—**neu′traliser** *n.*—**neutral′ity** *n.* non-intervention by a state or third-party in a dispute; the state of being neutral.—**neu′trally** *adv.* [L. *neuter*, neither].
neutrodyne (nū′trō-dīn) *a.* (*Radio*) a form of valve-control to prevent interference and to gain clearness of sound [L. *neuter*, neither; Gk. *dunamis*, power].
neutron (nū′tron) *n.* one of the minute particles composing the nucleus of an atom, and having approx. the same mass as a proton (*q.v.*) but being electrically neutral [L. *neuter*, neither].
never (nev′ėr) *adv.* at no time; not ever; in no degree; (*Colloq.*) surely not.—**nev′ermore** *adv.* at no future time.—**nevertheless′** *conj.* none the less; for all that; in spite of that; notwithstanding [O.E. *naefre*].
new (nū) *a.* not existing before; lately discovered or invented; not ancient;—*adv.* (usually **new-**), recently; fresh.—**new′ly** *adv.*—**new′ish** *a.* somewhat new.—**new′ness** *n.*—**new′born** *a.* recently born; born anew.—**new′com′er** *n.* one who has just settled down in a strange place or taken up a new post.—**new′fang′led** *a.* lately devised; novel (in a depreciatory sense).—**new′fash′ioned** *a.* just come into fashion; the latest in style.—**new′style** *n.* a chronological term to denote dates reckoned by the Gregorian calendar.—**New Deal**, a campaign initiated in 1933 by President Franklin Roosevelt in U.S.A. involving a complete overhaul of American economic life, the development of the national resources, and the safeguarding of living conditions for labour.—**New Englander**, a native or resident of any of the six N.E. states of the U.S.A.—**New Learning**, the Renaissance.—**new moon**, the period when the first faint crescent of the moon becomes visible.—**New Red Sandstone** (*Geol.*) lower division of Triassic series of rocks.—**New Testament**, later of the two main divisions of Bible.—**New World**, N. and S. America [O.E. *niwe*].
newel (nū′el) *n.* the post supporting the balustrade to a flight of stairs; the central, upright post to which the inner ends of the steps of a circular or spiral staircase are attached [L. *nodus*, a knot].
Newfoundland (nū′fund-land) *a.* a large, handsome dog with thick curly hair.
news (nūz) *n.sing.* report of recent happenings; fresh information; tidings; intelligence.—**news′agent** *n.* a shop-keeper who sells and distributes newspapers.—**news′bull′etin** *n.* the latest news, esp. as disseminated by wireless-broadcasters.—**news letter**, a small printed sheet issued at irregular intervals during the 17th cent. giving the news and gossip of the coffee-houses; a modern revival claiming to give exclusive news.—**news′monger** *n.* busybody; gossip.—**news′paper** *n.* a journal, daily or weekly, giving latest news.—**news′print** *n.* cheap paper for newspapers.—**news′reel** *n.* a cinematograph film depicting items of news and topical features.—**news′ven′dor, news′ven′der** *n.* one who sells newspapers, esp. on the streets.—**new′sy** *a.* gossipy; full of news.
newt (nūt) *n.* a long-tailed amphibian animal; the water-lizard; an eft [*a newt* for *an ewt*, fr. O.E. *efeta*, an eft].
Newtonian (nū-tō′ni-an) *a.* pert. to Sir Isaac *Newton* (*d.* 1727).
next (nekst) *a.* nearest; immediately following in place or time;—*adv.* nearest or immediately after; on the first future occasion;—*prep.* nearest to.—**next′ly** *adv.* in the next place.—**next′-of-kin,** *n.* nearest blood-relative [O.E. *niehst*, superl. of *neah*, nigh].
nexus (nek′sus) *n.* a tie, connection, or bond [L. *nectere*, to bind].
nib (nib) *n.* something small and pointed; beak of a bird; point of a pen;—*pl.* crushed cocoa-beans.—**nibbed** *a.* having a nib [form of *neb*].
nibble (nib′l) *v.t.* to bite a little at a time; to gnaw;—*v.i.* to catch at (as a fish); to dally with; to find fault;—*n.* a tiny bite [frequent. of *nip*].
niblick (nib′lik) *n.* a golf-club with an iron-head, well laid back, designed for lofting [etym. doubtful].
nice (nīs) *a.* hard to please; exact; difficult to decide; discriminating; delicate; dainty; (*Colloq.*) agreeable; attractive; handsome; kind.—**nice′ly** *adv.*—**nice′ness** *n.*—**nic′ety** *n.* precision; minute distinction or detail; delicacy; exactness [O.Fr. *nice*, foolish].
Nicene (nī′sēn) *a.* pert. to town of Nicaea

Asia Minor, at which was drawn up **Nicene Creed,** a statement of Christian belief as opposed to Arianism (A.D. 325).

niche (nich) *n.* a recess in a wall for a statue, bust, etc.; one's ordained position in life or public estimation;—*v.t.* to place in a niche.—**niched** *a.* [Fr. fr. It. *nicchia*].

Nichrome (ni´krōm) *n.* a nickel-chromium alloy with a high ohmic resistance value, used in the manufacture of resistance wire, etc. [Protected Trade Name].

Nick (nik) *n.* the devil; as in the phrase **Old Nick** [perhaps fr. *Nicholas*].

nick (nik) *v.t.* to make a notch in; to indent; to catch in time;—*n.* a notch; a slit; a score; the opportune moment as *in the nick of time* [etym. uncertain].

nickel (nik´el) *n.* a silver white metallic element, malleable and ductile, and much used in alloys and plating; in U.S.A. a five cent piece of nickel;—*v.t.* to plate with nickel.—*pr.p.* **nick'elling.**—*pa.p.* **nick'elled.**—**nick'el-plat'ing** *n.* plating of metals with nickel to provide a bright surface and to keep down rust.—**nick'el-sil'ver** *n.* an alloy of copper, nickel and zinc; German silver [Sw. abbrev. fr. Ger. *Kupfernickel,* copper nickel (ore)].

nicker (nik´er) *v.i.* to neigh; to snigger;—*n.* a neigh; a giggle [corrupt. of *snigger*].

nicknack See **knick-knack.**

nickname (nik´nām) *n.* a name given in contempt, derision, or familiarity to some person, nation, or object [orig. *an eke name,* an added name, fr. *eke,* to increase].

nicotine (nik´o-tēn) *n.* an alkaloid present in the tobacco plant; colourless and highly poisonous when pure, it is used in the manufacture of insecticides for fruit trees [Jean *Nicot* (1530-1600), who introduced the plant into Europe].

nictate (nik´tāt) *v.i.* to wink. Also **nic'titate.**—**nictita'tion** *n.* rapid and involuntary blinking of eyelids [L. *nictare,* to wink].

nidification (nid-i-fi-kā´shun) *n.* the act of building a nest.—**nid'ify** *v.i.* to build a nest.—**ni'dus** *n.* a nest; (*Med.*) a nucleus of infection [L. *nidus,* a nest; *facere,* to make].

nidor (nī´dor) *n.* the pungent odour of cooked food.—**ni'dorous** *a.* [L. *nidor,* smell].

nidus See **nidification.**

niece (nēs) *n.* the daughter of a brother or sister [Fr. *nièce,* fr. L. *neptis*].

nifty (nif´ti) *a.* (*Colloq.*) neat; tidy; smart.

niggard (nig´ard) *n.* a very miserly person;—*a.* stingy. Also **nigg'ardly.**—**nigg'ardliness** *n.* meanness [etym. uncertain].

nigger (nig´er) *n.* a Negro—in derision or contempt; a person of black colour.—**nigg'er-brown** *a.* dark-brown [Fr. *nègre*].

niggle (nig´l) *v.i.* to trifle away one's time; to be too particular about details; to complain about trivial matters.—**nigg'ler** *n.*—**nigg'ling, nigg'ly** *a.* and *n.* [etym. uncertain].

nigh (nī) *a.* near; closely applied;—*adv.* almost; near;—*prep.* near to [O.E. *neah*].

night (nīt) *n.* the time of darkness from sunset to sunrise; end of daylight; intellectual or spiritual darkness; ignorance; death.—**night'ly** *a.* happening or done every night; of the night;—*adv.* every night; by night.—**night´bird** *n.* a nocturnal bird such as the owl; a bad character who prowls about by night; one who habitually keeps late hours.—**night'cap** *n.* a cap worn in bed; a glass of spirits taken at bed-time.—**night´churr** *n.* the night-jar, so called from its sound.—**night´club** *n.* establishment for dancing and entertainment remaining open until early morning.—**night´dress, night´gown** *n.* a loose gown worn in bed.—**night'fall** *n.* the close of day.—**night´fire** *n.* the will o' the wisp.—**night´hawk** *n.* the British night-jar.—**night´jar** *n.* the goat-sucker, a nocturnal migrant bird found in S. England.—**night´light** *n.* a small stubby candle or electric bulb of low wattage kept burning all night. **night'long** *a.* persisting all night.—**night'mare** *n.* a terrifying feeling of oppression or suffocation arising during sleep; an incubus.—**night´school** *n.* a school for the continuation of studies after working hours.—**night'shade** *n.* plants of potato family, some with very poisonous berries.—**night´shift** *n.* employees who work regularly during night; duration of this work.—**night´shirt** *n.* a loose shirt used for sleeping in.—**night´time** *n.* period of night; first hours of darkness.—**night'ward** *a.* towards night-time.—**night´watch** *n.* a guard or watch at night; duty of night-watching.—**night´watch'man** *n.* [O.E. *niht*].

nightingale (nīt´ing-gāl) *n.* a bird of the thrush family, the male being renowned for its beautiful song at night [O.E. *niht,* night; *galan,* to sing].

nihil, nil (nī´hil, nil) *n.* nothing; zero.—**ni'hilism** *n.* the rejection of all religious and moral principles as the only means of obtaining social progress; the denial of all reality in phenomena; in 19th cent. the opposition in Russia to all constituted authority or government.—**ni'hilist** *n.*—**nihilist'ic** *a.* [L.].

nimble (nim´bl) *a.* light and quick in motion.—**nim'ble-fing'ered** *a.* dexterous; given to pilfering.—**nim'bleness** *n.*—**nim'ble-wit'ted** *a.* quick-witted.—**nim'bly** *adv.* [O.E. *niman,* to take].

nimbus (nim´bus) *n.* a rain-cloud; in representation of saints, angels, etc., the circle of light surrounding the head; a halo; an aureole.—*pl.* **nim'bi** [L. = cloud].

niminy-piminy (nim´i-ni-pim´i-ni) *a.* prim; precise; priggish; affectedly nice in manners and speech [imit.].

nincompoop (nin´kom-pôôp) *n.* a feeble character; a foolish-minded person; a simpleton; a ninny [origin uncertain].

nine (nīn) *a.* and *n.* one more than eight.—**nine´fold** *a.* nine times repeated.—**nine'teen** *a.* and *n.* nine and ten.—**nine'teenth** *a.* and *n.*—**nine'tieth** *a.* the tenth after the eightieth.—**nine'ty** *a.* and *n.*—**ninth** *a.* the first after the eighth;—*n.*—**ninth'ly** *adv.*—**nine´pins** *n.* a game in which nine erect wooden pegs are to be knocked down by a ball; skittles.—**the Nine,** the Muses [O.E. *nigon*].

ninny (nin´i) *n.* a fool; a dolt; a simpleton [It. *ninno,* a child].

ninon (nē-nōng) *n.* a glossy light-weight dress fabric of silk [Fr. proper name].

nip (nip) *v.t.* to pinch sharply; to detach by pinching; to check growth (as by frost); to smart.—*pr.p.* **nip'ping.**—*pa.t.* and *pa.p.* **nipped.**—*n.* a pinch; sharp touch of frost; a sip; a small measure of spirits.—**nip´cheese** *n.* a skin-flint.—**nip'per** *n.* a fore-tooth of a horse; a satirist; a young boy; a thief; the great claw or chela (as of a crab);—*pl.* small pincers.—**nip'piness** *n.* agility; touch of frost.—**nip'pingly** *adv.*—**nip'py** *a.* agile; nimble; sharp in taste; parsimonious; curt; smarting [etym. uncertain, cf. Dut. *nijpen*].

nipple (nip´l) *n.* the protuberance in the centre of a woman's breast by which milk is obtained during breast-feeding; the outlet of the mammary glands; a teat; a small metal projection pierced so that oil or grease may be forced into a bearing surface by means of a grease-gun [etym. uncertain. Cf. *nib*].

Nippon (nip´on) *n.* the Empire of Japan [Jap. = rising of the sun].

Nirvana (nir-vâ´na) *n.* in Buddhism, that state of blissful repose or absolute existence reached by one in whom all craving for existence is extinguished [Sans.].

nisi (nī´sī) *conj.* unless.—**decree nisi** (*Law*) a decree to take effect after a certain period of time has elapsed unless some valid objection arises [L.].

Nissen hut (nis´en hut) *n.* a trade-name for a semi-circular portable hut, readily bolted together from sections of corrugated iron, for temporary use [*Nissen* Buildings, Ltd.].

nit (nit) *n.* the egg of an insect-parasite, esp. of a head-louse [O.E. *hnitu*].

nitid (nit'id) *a.* shining; lustrous; gay [L. *nitidus*].

nitre (nī'tẹr) *n.* potassium nitrate; saltpetre, a white crystalline solid used in the manufacture of gun-powder, acids, etc.—**ni'trate** *n.* a salt of nitric acid.—**ni'trated** *a.* combined with nitric acid.—**nitra'tion** *n.* the conversion of nitrites into nitrates by the action of bacteria; the introduction of a nitro-group (NO_2) into an organic substance.—**ni'tric** *a.* pert. to nitre.—**nitric acid**, a powerful, corrosive acid, prepared from nitre and sulphuric acid; aqua fortis.—**ni'tride** *n.* a compound of a metal with nitrogen.—**ni'trify** *v.t.* to treat a metal with nitric acid.—**ni'trite** *n.* a salt of nitrous acid.—**nitrous oxide**, laughing gas, used as an anaesthetic in dentistry [Gk. *nitron*].

nitro- (nī'trō) *prefix* used in the formation of compound terms, signifying formed by, or containing, *nitre.*—**ni'tro-glyc'erine** *n.* a powerful oily liquid explosive.

nitrogen (nī'trō-jen) *n.* a non-metallic gaseous chemical element, colourless, odourless and tasteless, forming nearly four-fifths of the atmosphere.—**nitrog'enous** *a.*

nitwit (nit'wit) *n.* (*Colloq.*) a blockhead; a fool.—**nitwit'ted** *a.* stupid; irresponsible [Dut. *niets*, nothing; O.E. *witan*, to know].

nival (nī'vạl) *a.* covered with snow; snowy [L. *nix, nivis*, snow].

nix (niks) *n.* a water-sprite or elf which lures men to their death; a kelpie.—*pl.* **nix'ies.** Also **nix'ie** [Ger.].

nix (niks) *n.* (*Slang*) nothing [Dut. *niets*].

Nizam (nī-zam') *n.* the ruler of Hyderabad, India; a viceroy or administrator of justice in the Mogul Empire of India; a soldier in the Turkish army [Hind.].

no (nō) *a.* not any;—*adv.* expresses a negative reply to a question or request; not at all;—*n.* a refusal; a denial; a negative vote.—**noes** *n.pl.* term used in parliamentary proceedings, *the noes have it.*—**no'-ball** *n.* in cricket, a ball not properly bowled.—**no man's land**, waste land; the terrain between the trenches of opposing forces [O.E. *na*].

nob (nob) *n.* (*Colloq.*) one of high social standing [contr. of *nobleman*].

nob (nob) *n.* (*Slang*) the head [fr. *knob*].

nobble (nob'l) *v.t.* to grab; to steal; to lame deliberately a horse entered for a race; to stun [frequentative of *nab*].

Nobel Prize (nō-bel' prīz) *n.* one of a series of five prizes awarded annually to persons who have distinguished themselves in physics, chemistry, medicine, literature, or the promotion of peace [Alfred *Nobel*, Swedish inventor (1833-96)].

nobelium (no-bēl'i-um) *n.* the elemental 102, synthesised in 1957 at the *Nobel* Institute of Physics, Stockholm, by the fusion of the heavy isotype of carbon (carbon 103) with an atom of curium.

nobility (nō-bil'i-ti) *n.* the class holding special rank, usually hereditary, in a state; the quality of being noble; grandeur; loftiness and sincerity of mind or character [L. *nobilis*, noble].

noble (nō'bl) *a.* distinguished by deeds, character, rank, or birth; of lofty character; titled;—*n.* a nobleman; a peer; an old English gold coin, worth 6s. 8d. nominally.—**no'bleman** *n.* (*fem.* **no'blewoman**).—**no'bleness** *n.*—**no'bly** *adv.*—**the noble art**, boxing [L. *nobilis*].

nobody (nō'bod-i) *n.* no one; a person of no importance.—*pl.* **no'bodies.**

nocent (nō'sent) *a.* injurious; hurtful; mischievous [L. *nocere*, to hurt].

nock (nok) *n.* notch, esp. of bow or arrow; upper end of fore-and-aft sail [*notch*].

nocturn (nok'turn) *n.* a service held during the night.—**noc'turne** *n.* a night-piece, a painting of a night-scene; a musical composition of a gentle and simple character.—**noctur'nal** *a.* pertaining to night; happening or active by night;—*n.* a primitive instrument for determining latitude at night.—**noctur'nally** *adv.* [L. *nocturnus*, of the night].

nocuous (nok'ū-us) *a.* hurtful; noxious.—**noc'uously** *adv.* [L. *nocere*, to hurt].

nod (nod) *v.t.* and *v.i.* to incline the head forward by a quick motion, signifying assent or from drowsiness; to droop the head; to be sleepy; to sway; to bow by way of recognition.—*pr.p.* **nod'ding.**—*pa.t.* and *pa.p.* **nod'ded.**—*n.* an act of nodding.—**nod'der** *n.* [etym. uncertain].

nodal See **node.**

noddle (nod'l) *n.* a jocular expression for the head;—*v.i.* to nod repeatedly.

noddy (nod'i) *n.* a simpleton; a fool; a sea-bird, one of the terns, said to be particularly stupid [fr. *nod*].

node (nōd) *n.* a knot or knob; (*Geom.*) a point at which a curve crosses itself to form a loop; (*Elect.*) a point in a circuit carrying alternating currents at which the amplitude of current or voltage is a minimum; (*Astron.*) one of two points at which the orbit of a planet intersects the plane of the ecliptic; (*Phys.*) a point of permanent rest in a vibrating body; (*Med.*) a small protuberance or hard swelling; a constriction; (*Bot.*) the part of a stem to which a leaf is attached; an articulation.—**nod'al, nod'ical** *a.* pert. to nodes.—**nodat'ed** *a.* knotted.—**noda'tion** *n.* the act of making knots.—**nodif'erous** *a.* (*Bot.*) having nodes.—**nod'ose** *a.* full of knots.—**nod'ular** *a.* like a nodule.—**nod'ulated** *a.* having nodules.—**nod'ule** *n.* a small node or swelling [L. *nodus*, a knot].

Noël (nō'el) *n.* Christmas; a carol. Also **Now'el** [Fr. fr. L. *natalis*, birthday].

nog (nog) *n.* a wooden peg; a cog [Scand.].

nog (nog) *n.* a small pot or mug; a kind of strong ale.—**nog'gin** *n.* a nog; a small mug [Ir. *noigin*].

nohow (nō'hou) *adv.* in no way; not at all; by no means; out of sorts.

noise (noiz) *n.* sudden or harsh sound; glamour, din; loud outcry; gossip or talk;—*v.t.* to spread by rumour;—*v.i.* to sound loud.—**noise'less** *a.* making no noise; silent.—**noise'lessly** *adv.*—**noise'lessness** *n.*—**nois'y** *a.* making much noise; clamorous; turbulent.—**nois'ily** *adv.*—**nois'iness** *n.* [Fr.].

noisome (noi'sum) *a.* injurious to health; noxious; unwholesome; offensive; disgusting; evil-smelling.—**noi'somely** *adv.*—**noi'someness** *n.* [obs. *noy*, for *annoy*].

noll (nol) *n.* the crown of the head [O.E. knoll].

nomad (nō'mad) *a.* roaming from pasture to pasture;—*n.* a wanderer; a member of a wandering tribe.—**nomad'ic** *a.* pert. to nomads; pastoral; having no fixed dwelling place.—**nomad'ically** *adv.*—**nom'adism** *n.* [Gk. *nomas*, pasturing].

nomenclator (nō'men-klā-tor) *n.* one who gives names to things.—**no'menclatory, no'menclatural** *a.*—**no'menclature** *n.* a system of naming; the vocabulary of a science, etc. [L. *nomen*, a name; *calare*, to call].

nomial (nō'mi-ạl) *n.* (*Alg.*) a single term [L. *nomen*, a name].

nominal (nom'in-ạl) *a.* pert. to a name; existing only in name; ostensible; titular; formal.—**nom'inalism** *n.* the doctrine that the universal, or general, has no objective existence or validity, being merely a name expressing the qualities of various objects resembling one another in certain respects.—**nom'inalist** *n.* one who holds these views, the opposite of a *realist.*—**nominalist'ic** *a.*—**nom'inally** *adv.* in name only; not really [L. *nominalis*, fr. *nomen*, a name].

nominate (nom'i-nāt) *v.t.* to name; to put forward the name of, as a candidate; to propose; to designate.—**nomina'tion** *n.* act of naming or nominating; power or privilege of nominating.—**nom'inative** *a.* (*Gram.*) denoting the subject;—*n.* a noun or pronoun which is the subject of a verb.—**nom'inator** *n.* one who nominates.—**nominee'** *n.* one named or proposed for office; a person on whose life an annuity or lease depends [L. *nominare*, to name].

nom(o)- *prefix* from Greek *nomos*, a law, used in the formation of compound words.—**nomis'tic** *a.* pert. to laws founded on the teachings of sacred writings.—**nomol'ogy** *n.* the science which investigates the laws of legislation and government; the science of the conformity of human actions to rules of conduct prescribed by law [Gk. *nomos*, law].

non- (non) *prefix* from L. *non* = not, used in the formation of compound terms signifying absence or omission.—**non'com'batant** *n.* a member of the armed forces whose duties do not entail an active part in military operations, e.g. chaplain, surgeon, etc.; an unarmed civilian.—**non'commis'sioned** *a.* of ranks between a private and second-lieutenant, not being appointed by royal warrant;—(*abbrev.*) **non'com.**—**non'commit'tal** *a.* deliberately avoiding any direct statement as to one's opinions or course of future action.—**non'commu'nicant** *n.* one who is not a member of a church or is lax in attendance at holy communion.—**non'conduc'tor** *n.* a substance which will not conduct electricity, heat, or sound; insulator; dielectric.—**non'content'** *n.* a peer in the House of Lords who votes for the negative.—**non'ferr'ous** *a.* of an alloy or metal containing no, or only the merest trace of, iron.—**non'interven'tion** *n.* not intervening or interfering in the affairs or policies of another, esp, in international affairs.—**non'stop** *a.* not stopping at intermediate stations, etc.; continuous.

nonage (non'āj) *n.* legal infancy; minority (under 21 years of age); a period of immaturity [L. *non*, not; and *age*].

nonagenarian (non-ạ-je-nā'ri-ạn) *n.* one who is ninety years old or upwards;—*a.* relating to ninety [L. *nonaginta*, ninety].

nonagon (non'a-gon) *n.* a nine-sided plane figure [L. *nonus*, ninth; Gk. *gōnia*, an angle].

nonce (nons) *n.* **for the nonce,** for the occasion only; for the present [earlier *the*(*n*) *-anes*, the once].

nonchalance (non'shạ-lạns) *n.* unconcern; coolness; indifference; carelessness.—**non'chalant** *a.*—**non'chalantly** *adv.* [Fr. *non*, not; *chaleur*, heat].

nonconformist (non-kon-for'mist) *n.* a dissenter; a protestant who refuses to comply with the usages and rites of the Church of England.—**nonconfor'ming** *a.*—**nonconfor'mity** *n.* [L. *non*, not].

nondescript (non'de-skript) *a.* not hitherto described; novel; odd; indeterminate; abnormal;—*n.* [L. *non*, not; *descriptus*, described].

none (nun) *a.* and *pron.* no one; not anything.—**none'such, non'such** *n.* a person or thing without a rival or equal; a variety of apple, greenish-brown in colour; a species of trefoil or lucerne.—**none'so-prett'y** *n.* a common English garden-plant, *Saxifraga umbrosa*, also known as London Pride or Nancy Pretty.—**none the less,** nevertheless; all the same [O.E. *nan*].

none (nōn) *n.* one of the canonical hours of the R.C. Breviary, the *ninth* hour after sunrise at the equinox, viz. 3 p.m., or the appropriate mass celebrated at this time [L. *nonus*, ninth].

nonentity (non-en'ti-ti) *n.* negation of being; a thing not existing; non-existence; a person of no importance; a mere nobody [L. *non*, not; *ens, entis*, a being].

Nones (nōnz) *n.pl.* in the Roman calendar, the ninth day before the Ides, falling in March, May, July and October on the 7th of the month, in other months on the 5th [L. *nonus*, ninth].

nonjuror (non-jòò'ror) *n.* one who refused to swear allegiance to William and Mary, 1688; a Jacobite.—**nonjur'ing** *a.*

nonpareil (non-pạ-rel') *n.* a person or thing without an equal; a nonesuch; a pattern of book edge marbling; a printing type, between ruby and emerald, counting 6 points;—*a.* unrivalled; peerless; matchless [Fr. *non*, not; *pareil*, equal].

nonplus (non'plus) *n.* perplexity; puzzle; embarrassment; inability to say or do more; quandary;—*v.t.* to confound or bewilder completely; to bring to a standstill [L. *non*, not; *plus*, more].

nonsense (non'sens) *n.* lack of sense; language without meaning; absurdity; trifling; silly conduct.—**nonsen'sical** *a.*—**nonsen'sically** *adv.* [L. *non*, not].

nonsuch See **none.**

noodle (nòò'dl) *n.* a simpleton; a blockhead [conn. with *noddy*].

noodle (nòò'dl) *n.* a strip of dough, made of flour and eggs, baked and served in soups [etym. uncertain].

nook (nook) *n.* a corner; a recess; a secluded retreat [etym. uncertain].

noon (nòòn) *n.* midday; twelve o'clock by day; the exact instant when, at any given place, the sun crosses the meridian.—**noon'day, noon'tide** *n.* and *a.* midday [L. *nona* (*hora*), ninth hour, hour of mass, later changed from 3 p.m. to midday].

noose (nòòs) *n.* a running loop with a slip knot which binds the closer the more it is drawn; snare; tight knot;—*v.t.* to tie, catch in noose [L. *nodus*, knot].

nor (nor) a particle introducing the second clause of a negative proposition; and not [M.E. *nother*].

Nordic (nor'dik) *a.* of or pert. to peoples of Germanic stock; long-headed, very tall, blue-eyed and blond [Ger. *nord*, north].

norm (norm) *n.* a rule or authoritative standard; a unit for comparison; a standard type or pattern; a model; a class-average test score.—**nor'ma** *n.* a rule, pattern, or standard; a pattern or templet; a mason's square for testing.—**nor'mal** *a.* conforming to type or natural law; perpendicular;—*n.* a perpendicular to a line, surface, or tangent at point of contact.—**normalcy** (nor'mal-si) *n.* (esp. *U.S.*) normality (an ill-formed word).—**normalisa'tion, normal'ity** *n.*—**nor'mally** *adv.*—**nor'mative** *a.* setting up a norm; regulative.—**normal school,** formerly, a training-college for teachers [L. *norma*, a rule].

Norman (nor'mạn) *n.* a native of Normandy;—*a.* pert. to Normandy or the Normans.—**Norman architecture,** a style of medieval architecture characterised by rounded arch and massive simplicity.—**Norman French,** language spoken by Normans at time of Conquest [O.Fr. *Normant*, fr. Scand. = Northmen].

Norse (nors) *a.* pert. to Scandinavia, its language, or its people;—*n.* the old Scandinavian language [Scand. *norsk*, north].

north (north) *n.* the region or cardinal point opposite to the midday sun; the part of the world, of a country, etc., towards this point;—*adv.* towards or in the north;—*a.* to, from, or in the north.—**nor'therly** *a.* towards the north; of winds, coming from the north.—**nor'thern** *a.* pert. to the north; in or of the north.—**nor'therner** *n.* an inhabitant of the northern parts of a country.—**nor'thernly** *adv.* in a northern direction.—**nor'thernmost** *a.* situated at the most northerly point.—**north'ward, north'wardly** *a.* situated towards the north;—*adv.* in a northerly direction.—**north'wards** *adv.*—**north'east (-west)** *n.* the point between the north and the east (west);—*a.* pert. to, or from, the north-east (-west).—**north'east'er (-west'er)** *n.* a wind from the north-east (-west).—**north'east'erly (-west'erly)** *a.* towards or coming from the north-east (-west).—**north'east'ern (-west'ern)** *a.* belonging to the north-east (-west).—**north'east'ward (-west'ward)** *a.* towards the north-east (-west).—**northern lights,** aurora borealis.—**nor'thing** *n.* motion or distance northward; difference of latitude as a ship sails in a northerly direction; in surveying, a north latitude.—**North Pole**, northern extremity of earth's axis.—**north′star** *n.* polar star, the only star which does not change its apparent position [O.E.].

Norwegian (nor-wē′ji-ạn) *a.* pert. to Norway; —*n.* a native or language of Norway.

nose (nōz) *n.* the organ for breathing and smelling; power of smelling; any projection resembling a nose, as prow of a ship; (*Slang*) an informer;—*v.t.* to detect by smell; to oppose to the face; to speak through nose;—*v.i.* to smell; to pry officiously.—**nose′bag** *n.* a bag containing provender fastened to a horse's head.—**nose′dive** *n.* in aviation, a sudden steep plunge directly towards an objective, usually from a great height;—*v.i.* to perform this evolution.—**nose′gay** *n.* a bunch of sweet-smelling flowers; a bouquet.—**nos′ing** *n.* the moulded projecting edge of the tread of a step; beading round the edge of a board [O.E. *nosu*].

noso- (nos′ō) *prefix* fr. Greek, *nosos*, disease, used in formation of compound words.—**nosol′ogy** *n.* branch of medicine treating generally of diseases; systematic classification of phases of disease.—**nosolog′ical** *a.*—**nosol′ogist** *n.*

nostalgia (nos-tal′ji-ạ) *n.* home-sickness; a phase of melancholia due to the unsatisfied desire to return home.—**nostal′gic** *a.* [Gk. *nostos*, return; *algos*, pain].

nostril (nos′tril) *n.* one of the external openings of the nose;—*pl.* the anterior nares [O.E. *nosu*, nose; *thyrel*, opening].

nostrum (nos′trum) *n.* a quack, secret remedy; a patent medicine of doubtful efficacy; a pet scheme, pushed by some political visionary [L. = our (unfailing remedy, etc.)].

not (not) *adv.* a word expressing denial, negation, or refusal [*nought*].

notable (nō′tạ-bl) *a.* worthy of notice; remarkable;—*n.* a person of distinction.—**notabil′ia** *n.pl.* things worth noting; famous remarks.—**notabil′ity** *n.* an eminent person.—**not′ableness** *n.*—**not′ably** *adv.* [L. *nota*, note].

notary (nō′tạ-ri) *n.* a *notary-public*, a person, usually a solicitor, authorised to record statements, to certify deeds, to take affidavits, etc., on oath [L. *notarius*, a secretary].

notation (nō-tā′shun) *n.* the art of representing the pitch and time of musical sounds by signs; any system of figures, signs and symbols which conveys information [L. *nota*, a mark].

notch (noch) *n.* a V-shaped cut or indentation; nick; a groove formed in a piece of timber to receive another piece; a run scored at cricket; *v.t.* to make notches in; to indent; to secure by a notch; to score (a run) [etym. uncertain].

note (nōt) *n.* a mark; a brief comment; a memorandum; a short letter; a diplomatic paper; a written or printed promise of payment; a character to indicate a musical tone; notice; distinction; fame; regard;—*v.t.* to observe; to set down in writing; to attend to; to heed.—**note′book** *n.* a book for jotting down notes, memoranda, etc.—**not′ed** *a.* well-known by reputation or report; eminent; celebrated; distinguished; notorious.—**not′edly** *adv.*—**not′edness** *n.*—**note′pa′per** *n.* a small size of writing paper.—**note′worthy** *a.* worthy of notice; remarkable.—**note of hand**, a promissory note, a written promise to pay a sum by a stipulated time [L. *notare*, to mark].

nothing (nuth′ing) *n.* not anything of account, value, note, or the like; non-existence; nonentity; nought; zero; trifle; bagatelle;—*adv.* in no degree; not at all.—**noth′ingness** *n.* [fr. *no thing*].

notice (nō′tis) *n.* act of noting; remarking, or observing; observation; cognisance; regard; note; heed; consideration; respect; news; a review; formal intimation;—*v.t.* to observe; to remark upon; to treat with regard.—**no′ticeable** *a.* capable or worthy of observation; conspicuous; attracting attention; appreciable.—**no′ticeably** *adv.*—**to give notice**, to warn beforehand.—**to receive one's notice**, to be informed that one's services are about to be terminated [L. *notus*, known].

notify (nō′ti-fī) *v.t.* to make known; to report; to give notice of or to; to announce; to inform; to apprise.—*pa.p.* **no′tified**.—**no′tifiable** *a.* must, by law, be reported to the appropriate authorities.—**notifica′tion** *n.* official notice or announcement [L. *notus*, known; *facere*, to make].

notion (nō′shun) *n.* mental apprehension of whatever may be known or imagined; idea; conception; opinion; belief; sentiment; fancy; inclination [L. *notio*].

notoriety (nō-tō-rī′et-i) *n.* the state of being generally known, esp. in a disreputable way; public exposure; discreditable publicity.—**noto′rious** *a.* known by all and sundry (usually in a bad sense); infamous.—**noto′riously** *adv.*—**noto′riousness** *n.* a notoriety [L. *notus*, known].

notwithstanding (not-with-stand′ing) *adv.* nevertheless; however; yet;—*prep.* in spite of; despite;—*conj.* although.

nougat (nòò′gȧ) *n.* a sweetmeat of almonds, pistachio-nuts, or other nuts, in a sugar and honey paste [Fr.].

nought (nawt) *n.* nothing; zero;—*adv.* in no degree; not at all. Also **naught**.

noumenon (nou′me-non) *n.* a term used by Kant for the object of pure thought free from all elements of sense—the opposite to *phenomenon*.—*pl.* **nou′mena**.—**nou′menal** *a.* [Gk. = a thing perceived].

noun (noun) *n.* (*Gram.*) a word used as a name of a person, quality, or thing; a substantive [L. *nomen*, a name].

nourish (nur′ish) *v.t.* to supply with food; to feed and cause to grow; to nurture; to cherish; to tend; to encourage; to educate.—**nour′ishable** *a.*—**nour′ishing** *a.* nutritious.—**nour′ishment** *n.* food; nutriment; the act or state of nourishing [Fr. *nourrir*, fr. L. *nutrire*, to feed].

nous (nous, or nòòs) *n.* mind; reason; common-sense; gumption; intelligence [Gk.].

nova (nō′va) *n.* a new star, one which appears suddenly with a brightness which soon declines until no longer visible.—*pl.* **no′vae** [L. = new].

novel (nov′ẹl) *a.* of recent origin or introduction; new; recent; unusual;—*n.* a fictitious prose tale dealing with the adventures or feelings of imaginary persons so as to portray, by the description of action and thought, the varieties of human life and character.—**novelette′** *n.* a shorter form of novel, usually with a strong love-interest.—**nov′elist** *n.* a writer of novels.—**nov′elty** *n.* newness; something new or unusual [L. *novus*, new].

November (nō-vem′bẹr) *n.* the eleventh month of the year [L. *novem*, nine, as the old Roman year began in March].

novenary (nov′en-ạ-ri) *a.* pertaining to the number nine.—**noven′dial** *a.* happening every ninth day.—**noven′nial** *a.* happening every ninth year [L. *novem*, nine].

novice (nov′is) *n.* a candidate for admission to a religious order; one new to anything; an inexperienced person; a beginner or tyro (esp. at games).—**novi′ciate**, **novi′tiate** *n.* the state or time of being a novice; a novice [L. *novus*, new].

Novocaine (nō′vō-kān) *n.* a proprietary non-irritant drug which has replaced cocaine as a local anaesthetic [L. *novus*, new; and *cocaine*].

now (nou) *adv.* at the present time;—*conj.* this being the case;—*n.* the present time.—**now′adays** *adv.* in these days.—**now! now!** a form of admonition.—**now and then**, occasionally [O.E. *nu*].

Nowel See **Noël**.

nowhere (nō′hwār) *adv.* not in any place; (*Colloq.*) not in the reckoning; far behind.—**no′wise** *adv.* not in any manner or degree.

noxa (nok′sạ) *n.pl.* (*Zool.*) stimuli which warn the organism of danger, by causing pain.—

nox'al *a.*—**nox'ious** *a.* hurtful; pernicious; unwholesome.—**nox'iously** *adv.*—**nox'iousness** *n.* [L. *noxa*, injury].
nozzle (noz'l) *n.* the nose; the snout; a projecting spout or vent; the outlet end of a pipe, hose, etc. [dim. of *nose*].
nuance (nòò-ans') *n.* a shade or subtle variation in colour, tone of voice, etc.; (*Mus.*) a delicate gradation of tone and expression in performance on an instrument [Fr. = a shade].
nub (nub) *n.* a knob; lump; protuberance; point; gist.
nubile (nū'bil) *a.* of marriageable age.—**nubil'ity** *n.* [L. *nubere*, to marry].
nuciform (nūs'i-form) *a.* nut-shaped.—**nuci'ferous** *a.* bearing nuts.—**nuciv'orous** *a.* pert. to a nut-eating animal [L. *nux*, a nut].
nucleus (nū'klē-us) *n.* a central mass which increases by successive accretions; the starting point of some project or idea; (*Astron.*) the dark centre of a sun-spot; the denser core or head of a comet; (*Biol.*) the inner essential part of a living cell; (*Physics*) the core of the atom, where nearly all the mass is concentrated, composed of protons and neutrons.—*pl.* **nu'clei.**—**nuclear** *a.*—**nuclear energy,** a more exact term for atomic energy; energy freed or absorbed during reactions taking place in atomic nuclei.—**nuclear fission,** a process of disintegration which breaks up into chemically different atoms.—**nu'cleate** *v.t.* to gather into or round a nucleus.—**nu'cleated** *a.* possessing a nucleus.—**nu'cleole, nucleo'lus** *n.* a minute body of condensed chromatin inside a nucleus which divides during mitosis [L. = kernel].
nude (nūd) *a.* bare; naked; undraped; uncovered;—*n.* a picture or piece of sculpture in the nude.—**nude'ly** *adv.*—**nu'dity, nude'ness** *n.* nakedness.—**nu'dism** *n.* cult emphasising practice of nudity for health.—**nu'dist** *n.* [L. *nudus*, naked].
nudge (nuj) *v.t.* to touch slightly with the elbow in order to attract attention;—*n.* a gentle push [etym. uncertain].
nugae (nū'gē) *n.pl.* trifles; things of little value.—**nu'gatory** *a.* trifling; futile; vain; ineffectual; of no force [L.].
nugget (nug'et) *n.* rough lump or mass, esp. of native gold [etym. uncertain].
nuisance (nū'sạns) *n.* something harmful, offensive, or annoying; a troublesome person; a pest; an inconvenience [Fr. *nuisant*, harming; fr. L. *nocere*, to harm].
null (nul) *a.* of no legal validity; void; invalid; non-existent; of no importance;—*n.* something of no force, or value;—*v.t.* to annul; to render void.—**null'ify** *v.t.* to make null; to render useless; to invalidate;—*pa.p.* **null'ified.**—**nullifica'tion** *n.* act of nullifying;—**null'ifier** *n.*—**null'ity** *n.* state of being null and void; suit to contest validity of marriage [L. *nullus*, none].
nullah (nul'ạ) *n.* a water-course liable to dry up; the dry bed of a torrent [Ind.].
numb (num) *a.* devoid or deprived of sensation or motion; torpid; insensible; insensitive; chilled; benumbed;—*v.t.* to benumb; to deaden; to paralyse.—**numb'ness** *n.* [O.E. *numen*, taken].
number (num'bẹr) *n.* a word used to indicate how great any quantity is when compared with the unit quantity, one; a sum or aggregate of quantities; a collection of things; an assembly; a single issue of a publication; a song; a piece of music; (*Gram.*) classification of words as to singular or plural;—*pl.* metrical feet or verses; poetry; rhythm;—*v.t.* to give a number to; to count; to reckon; to estimate; to tell;—*v.i.* to amount to.—**Num'bers** *n.pl.* (*Bib.*) fourth book of Pentateuch.—**num'berer** *n.*—**num'berless** *a.* innumerable.—**numerabil'ity,** **nu'merableness** *n.*—**nu'merable** *a.* may be numbered or counted [Fr. *nombre*, fr. L. *numerus*].
numeral (nū'mẹr-ạl) *a.* designating a number;—*n.* a sign or word denoting a number.—**nu'merable** *a.* able to be counted.—**nu'merably** *adv.*—**nu'merally** *adv.* according to number.—**nu'merary** *a.* belonging to, or an integral part of, a certain number, as opposed to *supernumerary*.—**nu'merate** *v.t.* to count; to read figures according to their notation.—**numera'tion** *n.*—**nu'merator** *n.* top part of a fraction, figure showing how many of the fractional units are taken.—**numer'ic(al)** *a.* of, or in respect of, numbers.—**numer'ically** *adv.*—**nu'merous** *a.* many.—**nu'merously** *adv.*—**nu'merousness** *n.* [L. *numerus*, a number].
numismatic (nū-mis-mat'ik) *a.* pert. to coins or medals;—*n.pl.* scientific study of coins and medals, esp. as an aid to study of archaeology.—**numis'matist** *n.*—**numismatog'raphy, numismatol'ogy** *n.* science of coins and medals in relation to archaeology and history.—**numismatol'ogist** *n.* [L. *numisma*, current coin].
numskull (num'skul) *n.* dolt; dunce; a stupid person; a blockhead [*numb, skull*].
nun (nun) *n.* a female member of a religious order, vowed to celibacy, and dedicated to active or contemplative life; white-hooded, fancy pigeon.—**nun'nery** *n.* convent of nuns [L.L. *nonna*].
nuncio (nun'shi-ō) *n.* messenger; ambassador representing Pope at foreign court.—**nun'ciature** *n.* office of nuncio [It fr. L. *nuntius*, a messenger].
nuncupate (nung'kū-pāt) *v.t.* and *v.i.* to vow publicly; to dedicate; to declare orally, as a will.—**nuncupa'tion** *n.*—**nun'cupative** *a.* pert. to vowing, dedicating; nominal—**nun'cupator** *n.*—**nun'cupatory** *a.* oral; verbal [L. *nuncupare*, to name].
nuptial (nup'shạl) *a.* pert. to or constituting ceremony of marriage;—*pl.* wedding ceremony; marriage [L. *nuptiae*, wedding].
nurl, knurl (nurl) *v.t.* to roughen edge of a circular object; to mill; to indent.—**nur'ling** *n.* indentations on edge of coin or of some types of set screws [etym. uncertain].
nurse (nurs) *n.* a person trained for the care of the sick or injured; a woman tending another's child;—*v.t.* to tend, as a nurse; to suckle; to foster; to husband; to harbour (a grievance); to keep in touch with (a parliamentary constituency); to manage skilfully (the early stages of some project).—**nurse'maid, nurs'ery-maid** *n.* a girl in charge of young children.—**nurs'er** *n.*—**nurs'ery** *n.* a room set aside for children; a place for the rearing of plants.—**nurs'eryman** *n.* one who raises plants for sale.—**nursery rhymes,** jingling rhymes written to amuse young children.—**nursery school,** a kindergarten, for children of 2-5 years of age.—**nurs'ling** *n.* an infant; anything which is carefully tended at inception.—**wet'-nurse** *n.* woman who suckles infant of another [Fr. *nourrice*, fr. L. *nutrix*, a nurse].
nurture (nur'tūr) *n.* nurturing; education; rearing; breeding; nourishment; (*Biol.*) the various environmental forces, which combined, act on an organism and further its existence;—*v.t.* to nourish; to cherish; to tend; to train; to rear; to bring up.—**nurt'urer** *n.* [Fr. *nourriture*, nourishment].
nut (nut) *n.* a fruit consisting of a hard shell enclosing a kernel; a hollow metal collar, the internal surface of which carries a groove or thread into which the thread of a screw fits; (*Slang*) the head; (*U.S.*) blockhead;—*n.pl.* a form of kitchen-coal, in small lumps free from coal-dust;—*v.i.* to gather nuts;—*pr.p.* **nut'ting.**—*pa.t.* and *pa.p.* **nut'ted.**—**nut'-brown** *a.* of the colour of a nut.—**nut butter,** a butter substitute made from nut-oil.—**nut'cracker** *n.* an instrument for cracking nuts; bird of crow family.—**nut'hatch, nut'jobber, nut'pecker** *n.* a climbing bird, allied to titmice.—**nut'shell** *n.* the hard shell enclosing the kernel of a nut.—**nut'ter** *n.* one who gathers nuts.—**nut'tiness** *n.* taste of nuts.—**nut'ting** *n.*—**nut'ty** *a.* abounding in

nuts; having a nut-flavour; (*Slang*) silly; imbecile.—**nut′-wrench** *n.* an instrument for screwing or unscrewing nuts.—**a hard nut to crack**, a difficult problem to solve; a person difficult to deal with [O.E. *hnutu*).

nutant (nū′-tant) *a.* (*Bot.*) hanging with the apex of the flower downwards; nodding.—**nuta′tion** *n.* nodding; (*Astron.*) slight periodic wobbling of direction of Earth's axis [L. *nutare*, to nod].

nutmeg (nut′-meg) *n.* an aromatic flavouring spice obtained from the fruit of a tree of the E. and W. Indies [E. *nut*; O.Fr. *mugue*, musk].

nutrient (nū′-tri-ent) *a.* nourishing;—*n.* something nutritious.—**nu′triment** *n.* that which nourishes; food; sustenance.—**nutri′tion** *n.* the act of nourishing.—**nutri′tional, nutri′tious, nu′tritive, nu′tritory** *a.* nourishing; promoting growth [L. *nutrire*, to nourish].

nux vomica (nuks vom′-ik-a) *n.* the dried ripe seed of an E. Indian plant, from which strychnine and brucine are obtained [L. *nux*, not; *vomere*, to vomit].

nuzzle (nuz′-l) *v.t.* and *v.i.* to rub with the nose; to nestle; to cherish; to burrow or press with the nose [*nose*].

nyctalopia (nik-ta-lō′-pi-a) *n.* recurrent night-blindness [Gk. *nux*, night; *alaos*, blind; *ōps*, eye].

nylon (nī′-lon) *n.* an artificial silk fabric the yarn of which is produced synthetically [fr. *N*(ew) *Y*(ork), *Lon*(don)].

nymph (nimf) *n.* a tutelary goddess inhabiting a mountain, grove, fountain, river, etc.; a girl distinguished by her grace and charm.—**nymph′al, nymphe′an, nymph′ic, nymph′ical** *a.* —**nymph′-like** *a.*—**nymphoma′nia** *n.* a morbid and uncontrollable sexual desire in women.—**nymphoma′niac** *n.* [Gk. *numphē*, a bride].

nymph, nympha (nimf, -a) *n.* the pupa or chrysalis of an insect [Gk. *numphē*, a nymph].

nystagmus (nis-tag′-mus) *n.* eye-disease with involuntary twitching oscillation of eyes [Gk. *nustazein*, to nod].

O

O, oh (ō) *interj.* an exclamation of address, surprise, sorrow, wonder, entreaty [O.E. *ea*].

oaf (ōf) *n.* a changeling; dolt; lout; awkward fellow.—*pl.* **oafs** or **oaves**.—**oaf′ish** *a.* loutish; awkward [O.N. *alfr*, an elf].

oak (ōk) *n.* a familiar forest-tree yielding a hard, durable timber.—**oak′en** *a.* made of oak.—**oak′ling** *n.* a young oak.—**oak′-app′le** *n.* a gall or swelling on oak-leaves caused by the gall-fly [O.E. *ac*].

oakum (ōk′-um) *n.* loose fibre got by untwisting and picking old tarry ropes, etc., used for caulking seams of ships [O.E. *acumba*, tow].

oar (ōr) *n.* a wooden lever with a broad blade worked by the hands to propel a boat; an oarsman;—*v.t.* and *v.i.* to row.—**oared** *a.* having oars.—**oars′man** *n.* a rower.—**oars′manship** *n.* the art of rowing.—**to put in one's oar** (*Slang*) to meddle; to interfere [O.E. *ar*].

oasis (ō-ā′-sis) *n.* a fertile spot in the desert.—*pl.* **oases** (ō-ā′-sēz) [Gk.].

oast (ōst) *n.* a kiln for drying hops or malt.—**oast′-house** *n.* [O.E. *ast*].

oat (ōt) *n.* but usually in *pl.* **oats**, the grain of a common cereal plant, used as food; the plant; (*Poet.*) a shepherd's musical pipe; a pastoral song.—**oat′en** *a.* made of oat-straw or oatmeal.—**oat′cake** *n.* a thin cake of oatmeal. —**oat′meal** *n.* meal made from oats.—**to sow one's wild oats**, to indulge in youthful follies before settling down [O.E. *ate*].

oath (ōth) *n.* confirmation of the truth by naming something sacred, esp. God; a blasphemous use of the name of God; any imprecation.—*pl.* **oaths** (ōTHz) [O.E. *ath*].

obbligato ob-li-gà′-tō) *n.* (*Mus.*) a part in a musical composition for a particular instrument, of such importance that it is indispensable to the proper rendering of the piece; —also *a.* Also **obliga′to** [It.].

obdurate (ob′-dū-rāt) *a.* hard-hearted; stubborn; unyielding.—**ob′durately** *adv.*—**ob′duracy** *n.* hard-heartedness; stubbornness [L. *obduratus*, hardened].

obedient (ō-bē′-di-ent) *a.* subject to authority; willing to obey.—**obe′diently** *adv.*—**obe′dience** *n.* submission to authority; doing what one is told [L. *obedire*].

obeisance (ō-bā′-sans) *n.* a bow, curtsy or gesture of deference [Fr. *obéissance*, obedience].

obelisk (ob′-e-lisk) *n.* a tall, four-sided, tapering pillar, ending in a small pyramid; in printing, a reference mark (†) also called 'dagger'; a sign (– or ÷). Also called **ob′elus**, *pl.* **ob′eli** [Gk. *obeliskos*].

obese (ō-bēs′) *a.* fat; fleshy.—**obese′ness, obes′ity** *n.* excessive fatness [L. *obesus*].

obey (ō-bā′) *v.i.* to do as ordered; to be obedient; to submit to authority;—*v.t.* to comply with the orders of; to yield submission to; to be ruled by [L. *obedire*].

obfuscate (ob-fus′-kāt) *v.t.* to darken; to confuse or bewilder.—**obfusca′tion** *n.* obscurity; confusion [L. *obfuscare*, to darken].

obit (ō′-bit) *n.* (*Slang*) abbrev. of **obituary**; résumé of life of public figure at his death.—**obit′uary** *a.* pert. or relating to death of person; —*n.* an account or biographical sketch of a deceased person [L. *obitus*, approach, fr. *obire*, to go to meet].

object (ob′-jekt) *n.* anything presented to the mind or the senses; a material thing; an end or aim; (*Gram.*) a noun, pronoun, or clause governed by, and dependent on, a transitive verb or a preposition.—**ob′jectless** *a.* having no aim or purpose.—**ob′ject-glass** *n.* a lens in a telescope, etc., nearest to the object viewed [L. *objectus*, thrown in the way].

object (ob-jekt′) *v.t.* to offer in opposition; to put forward as reason against;—*v.i.* to make verbal opposition; to protest against; to feel dislike or reluctance.—**objection** (ob-jek′-shun) *n.* act of objecting; adverse reason; difficulty or drawback; argument against.—**objec′tionable** *a.* justly liable to objection; disagreeable. —**objec′tionably** *adv.*—**objec′tor** *n.* [L. *ob*, in the way of; *jacere*, to throw].

objective (ob-jek′-tiv) *a.* pert. to the object; relating to that which is external to the mind; opp. of 'subjective'; (*Gram.*) denoting the case of the object;—*n.* the point aimed at in a military attack; (*Gram.*) the case of the object.—**objec′tively** *adv.*—**objectiv′ity** *n.* the quality of being objective [Fr. *objectif*].

objurgate (ob′-jur-gāt, ob-jur′-gāt) *v.t.* to reprove; to blame; to chide.—**objurga′tion** *n.*—**objur′gatory** *a.* [L. *objurgare*, to blame].

oblate (ob-lāt′) *a.* (*Geom.*) flattened at the poles (said of a spheroid, like the earth); orange-shaped.—**oblate′ness** *n.* [L. *oblatus*, brought forward].

oblate (ob′-lāt) *n.* a person dedicated to religious work, esp. the monastic service.—**obla′tion** *n.* something offered to God, or a god; a gift to the church for pious uses [L. *oblatus*, brought forward, offered].

obligate (ob′-li-gāt) *v.t.* to bind, esp. by legal contract; to put under obligation.—**obliga′tion** *n.* the binding power of a promise or contract; indebtedness for a favour of kindness; a favour; a duty; a legal bond.—**oblig′atory** *a.* binding legally or morally; compulsory.—**oblig′atorily** *adv.* [L. *obligare*, fr. *ligare*, to bind].

oblige (ō-blīj′) *v.t.* to constrain by physical, moral, or legal force; to lay under an obligation; to do a favour to; to compel;—*v.i.* to contribute to the entertainment.—**obliged′** *a.* grateful; indebted.—**oblige′ment** *n.* a favour.—**oblig′ing** *a.* helpful; courteous.—**oblig′ingly** *adv.* —**oblig′ingness** *n.* [L. *obligare*, fr. *ligare*, to bind].

oblique (ob-lēk′) *a.* slanting; inclined; indirect; obscure; not straightforward; underhand.—**obliqu'ely** *adv.*—**oblique'ness, obliquity** (ob-likʹwi-ti) *n.* slant or inclination; deviation from moral uprightness; dishonesty.—**oblique angle**, an acute or obtuse angle, as opposed to a right angle [L. *obliquus*].

obliterate (ob-litʹe-rāt) *v.t.* to blot out; to efface or destroy.—**oblitera'tion** *n.* the act of blotting out; destruction; extinction.—**oblit'erative** *a.* [L. *obliterare*, fr. *litera*, a letter].

oblivion (ob-livʹi-un) *n.* a forgetting, or being forgotten; forgetfulness; a general amnesty.—**obliv'ious** *a.* forgetful; causing to forget; heedless.—**obliv'iously** *adv.*—**obliv'iousness** *n.* [L. *oblivisci*, to forget].

oblong (obʹlong) *a.* longer than broad;—*n.* (*Geom.*) a rectangular figure with adjacent sides unequal [L. *oblongus*].

obloquy (obʹlo-kwi) *n.* abusive speech; disgrace [L. *obloquium*, a speaking against].

obnoxious (ob-nokʹshus) *a.* offensive; objectionable.—**obnox'iously** *adv.*—**obnox'iousness** *n.* [L. *obnoxius*, exposed to harm].

oboe (ōʹboi, ōʹbō) *n.* (*Mus.*) a wood-wind instrument like the clarionet, but of thinner tone; a hautboy; an organ reed-stop.—**o'boist** *n.* [Fr. *hautbois*].

obscene (ob-sēn') *a.* offensive to modesty; indecent; filthy; disgusting.—**obscene'ly** *adv.*—**obscene'ness** *n.*—**obscenity** (ob-senʹi-ti) *n.* lewdness; indecency [L. *obscenus*].

obscure (ob-skūr') *a.* dark; hidden; unknown; humble; abstruse;—*v.t.* to dim; to conceal; to make less intelligible; to make doubtful.—**obscure'ly** *adv.*—**obscure'ness** *n.* the quality of being obscure.—**obscu'rant, obscu'rantist** *n.* one who opposes the spread of enlightenment amongst the people.—**obscu'rantism** *n.*—**obscura'tion** *n.* the act of obscuring; the state of being obscured.—**obscure'ment** *n.* obscuration.—**obscu'rity** *n.* absence of light; a state of retirement, or of being unknown; indistinctness; lack of clear expression; dubiety of meaning; humility [L. *obscurus*].

obsecrate (obʹse-krāt) *v.t.* to beseech; to entreat [L. *obsecrare*, fr. *sacer*. sacred].

obsequies (obʹse-kwiz) *n.pl.* funeral rites; a funeral.—**obse'quial** *a.* [L.L. *obsequiae*].

obsequious (ob-sēʹkwi-us) *a.* servile; fawning.—**obse'quiously** *adv.*—**obse'quiousness** *n.* [L. *obsequi*, to gratify].

observe (ob-zerv') *v.t.* to watch; to note systematically; to perform or keep religiously; to remark;—*v.i.* to take notice; to make a remark; to comment.—**observ'able** *a.*—**observʹably** *adv.*—**observ'ableness** *n.*—**observ'ance** *n.* the act of observing; a paying attention; the keeping of a law, custom, religious rite; a religious rite; a rule or practice.—**observ'ant** *a.* quick to notice; alert; carefully attentive; obedient to.—**observ'antly** *adv.*—**observa'tion** *n.* the action or habit of observing; the result of watching, examining, and noting; attentive watchfulness; a comment; a remark.—**observa'tional** *a.*—**observa'tionally** *adv.*—**observʹatory** *n.* a building for the observation and study of astronomical, meteorological, etc., phenomena.—**observ'er** *n.* one who observes; an attentive spectator; member of crew of aircraft who makes aerial observations [L. *observare*, fr. *servare*, to guard].

obsess (ob-ses') *v.t.* to haunt; to fill the mind completely; to preoccupy.—**obsession** (ob-seshʹun) *n.* complete domination of the mind by one idea; a fixed idea [L. *obsidere, obsessum*, to besiege].

obsidian (ob-sidʹi-an) *n.* vitreous lava or glassy volcanic rock [after *Obsidius*, or *Obsius*, the discoverer].

obsolete (obʹsol-ēt) *a.* no longer in use; out of date.—**ob'soletely** *adv.*—**ob'soleteness** *n.*—**obsolesc'ent** *a.* becoming obsolete; going out of use.—**obsolesc'ence** *n.* [L. *obsolescere*, to grow out of use].

obstacle (obʹsta-kl) *n.* anything that stands in the way; an obstruction; a hindrance [L. *ob*, in the way of; *stare*, to stand].

obstetrics (ob-stetʹriks) *n.* (*Med.*) the science dealing with the care of pregnant women; midwifery.—**obstet'ric, obstet'rical** *a.*—**obstetricʹian** *n.* a specialist in midwifery [L. *obstetrix*, a midwife].

obstinate (obʹsti-nāt) *a.* stubborn; not easily moved by argument; unyielding.—**ob'stinately** *adv.*—**ob'stinateness** *n.*—**ob'stinacy** *n.* unreasonable firmness; stubbornness; resolution; persistency [L. *obstinatus*].

obstreperous (ob-strepʹe-rus) *a.* noisy; clamorous; vociferous; turbulent.—**obstrepʹerously** *adv.*—**obstrep'erousness** *n.* [L. *ob*, against; *strepere*, to make a noise].

obstruct (ob-strukt') *v.t.* to block up; to impede; to hinder the passage of; to retard; to oppose; to block out.—**obstruc'ter, obstruc'tor** *n.*—**obstruc'tion** *n.* the act of obstructing; that which obstructs or hinders.—**obstruc'tive** *a.* hindering; tending to put obstacles in the way of.—**obstruc'tively** *adv.* [L. *ob*, against; *struere*, to build up].

obtain (ob-tān') *v.t.* to gain; to acquire; to secure; to procure by effort;—*v.i.* to be customary or prevalent; to hold good.—**obtain'able** *a.* procurable.—**obtain'ment** *n.* acquirement. Also **obten'tion** [L. *obtinere*].

obtrude (ob-tròòd') *v.t.* to thrust forward unsolicited; to urge unduly;—*v.i.* to intrude.—**obtru'der** *n.*—**obtru'sion** *n.* the act of obtruding.—**obtru'sive** *a.* tending to thrust itself upon the attention unduly.—**obtru'sively** *adv.* [L. *ob*; *trudere*, to thrust].

obtuse (ob-tūs') *a.* blunt; dull of perception; stupid; (*Geom.*) greater than a right angle, but less than 180°.—**obtuse'ly** *adv.*—**obtuse'ness** *n.* [L. *obtundere, obtusum*, to blunt].

obverse (obʹvers) *a.* having the base narrower than the apex; being a counterpart; facing the observer; of a coin, bearing the head;—*n.* face of a coin, medal, etc. (opp. of 'reverse'); the front or principal aspect; a counterpart.—**obverse'ly** *adv.* [L. *ob*, toward; *vertere, versum*, to turn].

obviate (obʹvi-āt) *v.t.* to intercept and remove (as difficulties); to make unnecessary; to avoid [L. *ob*; *viare*, to go].

obvious (obʹvi-us) *a.* what meets us on the way; hence, easily seen or understood; evident; apparent.—**ob'viously** *adv.*—**ob'viousness** *n.* [L. *obvius*, in the way].

ocarina (ok-a-rēʹna) *n.* a small musical wind-instrument made of terra cotta [It. *oca*, a goose, from its shape].

occasion (o-kāʹzhun) *n.* opportunity; a juncture favourable for something; reason or justification; a time of important occurrence;—*pl.* affairs or business; also formerly, needs;—*v.t.* to cause; to bring about.—**occa'sional** *a.* occurring now and then; incidental; meant for a special occasion.—**occa'sionally** *adv.* from time to time [L. *occasio*, fr. *cadere*, to fall].

occident (okʹsi-dent) *n.* part of the horizon where the sun sets; the west.—**occiden'tal** *a.* western;—*n.* native of western country [L. *occidere*, to go down].

occiput (okʹsi-put) *n.* the back part of the head.—**occip'ital** *a.* pert. to the occiput [L. *ob*, over against; *caput*, the head].

occlude (o-klòòd') *v.t.* to shut in or out; (*Chem.*) to absorb gas.—**occlu'sion** *n.*—**occluʹsive** *a.* serving to shut in or out [L. *ob*; *claudere, clausum*, to shut].

occult (ok-ult') *a.* hidden from view; secret; mysterious; magical; supernatural;—*v.t.* to conceal; to hide from view; to eclipse.—**occult'ly** *adv.*—**occulta'tion** *n.* the eclipse of a heavenly body by another.—**occult'ism** *n.* the doctrine or study of the supernatural, magical, etc.—**occult'ness** *n.* mystery; secretness [L. *occulere*, to hide].

occupy (okʹū-pī) *v.t.* to take possession of; to inhabit; to fill; to employ;—*pa.p.* and *pa.t.* **occ'upied.**—**occ'upancy** *n.* the act of having or holding possession; the period during which one is an occupant; tenure.—**occ'upant** *n.* one who occupies or is in possession.—**occupa'tion** *n.* occupancy; possession; temporary possession of enemy country by the victor; employment; trade; calling; business; profession.—**occupa'tional** *a.*—**occ'upier** *n.* the person in possession; an occupant; a tenant [L. *occupare*, to take possession of].

occur (o-kur') *v.i.* to come to the mind; to happen; to be met with.—*pr.p.* **occur'ring.**—*pa.p.* and *pa.t.* **occurred'.**—**occur'rence** *n.* a happening; an event; an incident [L. *occurrere*, to run against].

ocean (ō'shạn) *n.* great body of water surrounding land of globe; one of the large divisions of this (Arctic, Antarctic, Atlantic, Indian, Pacific); the sea;—*a.* pert. to the great sea.—**oceanic** (ō-shi-an-ik, ō-si-an'ik) *a.* pert. to, found, or formed in the ocean.—**oceanog'raphy** *n.* the scientific description of ocean phenomena.—**oceanog'rapher** *n.*—**oceanograph'ic, oceanograph'ical** *a.*—**oceanol'ogy** *n.* branch of science which relates to the ocean [Gk. *ōkeanos*, a stream encircling the world].

ocelot (ō'se-lot) *n.* a S. Amer. quadruped of the leopard family [Mex. *ocelotl*].

ochre (ō'kẹr) *n.* various natural earths used as yellow, brown, or red pigments.—**o'chr(e)ous, o'chry** *a.* [Gk. *ōchra*, yellow ochre].

oct-, octa-, octo- (okt, ok'ta, ok'to) *prefix* fr. Gk. *oktō*, eight, combining to form derivatives. —**oc'tagon** *n.* a plane figure with 8 sides and 8 angles.—**octag'onal** *a.*—**octahe'dron** *n.* a solid figure with 8 plane faces.—**octahe'dral** *a.*—**oc'tane** *n.* (*Chem.*) a hydrocarbon of the paraffin series, obtained from petroleum and used as a motor-spirit, esp for aeroplanes.—**octang'ular** *a.* having 8 angles.—**oc'tant** *n.* the eighth part of a circle; an instrument for measuring angles, having an arc of 45° [Gk. *gōnia*, an angle; *hedra*, a base; *stulos*, a pillar.

octave (ok'tāv) *n.* the week following the celebration of a principal Church festival; the day falling a week after a festival; a stanza of 8 lines; (*Mus.*) an interval of 8 diatonic notes comprising a complete scale; a note 8 tones above or below another note; a group of 8 [L. *octavus*, eighth].

octavo (ok-tā'vō) *n.* the size of a sheet of paper that has been folded three times, thus making 8 leaves (average size = 6″ × 9½″); hence, a book having 8 leaves to the sheet—(*abbrev.*) **8vo** [L. *octavus*, eighth].

octennial (ok-ten'i-ạl) *a.* happening every eighth year; lasting for 8 years [L. *octo*, eight; *annus*, a year].

octet (ok-tet') *n.* (*Mus.*) a group of 8 musicians or singers; a composition for such a group; a group of 8 lines, esp. the first 8 lines of a sonnet [L. *octo*, eight].

October (ok-tō'bẹr) *n.* tenth month [*eighth* month of ancient Roman year].

octogenarian (ok-tō-jẹ-nā'ri-ạn) *a.* and *n.* (one) between 80 and 90 years of age [L. *octogenarius*, of eighty].

octopus (ok'to-pus) *n.* a mollusc with 8 arms or tentacles covered with suckers [Gk. *oktō*, eight; *pous*, a foot].

ocular (ok'ū-lạr) *a.* pert. to the eye, or to sight; visual;—*n.* the eye-piece of an optical instrument.—**oc'ulist** *n.* a specialist in the defects and diseases of the eye; an eye-surgeon [L. *oculus*, the eye].

od (ōd, od) *n.* formerly, mysterious natural force which manifested itself in phenomena of mesmerism, magnetism, etc.—**o'dic** *a.*—**o'dism** *n.* belief in this force [coined word].

odalisque (ō'dạ-lisk) *n.* a female slave or concubine in a Turkish harem. Also **o'dalisk** [Fr. fr. Turk.].

odd (od) *a.* not even; not divisible by two; left over after a round number has been taken; extra; surplus; casual or outside the reckoning; occasional; out-of-the-way; queer or eccentric; strange.—**odd'ity** *n.* quality of being odd; peculiarity; queer person or thing.—**odd'ly** *adv.* in an odd manner.—**odd'ment** *n.* something left over; part of a broken set; a remnant; a trifle.—**odd'ness** *n.* the state of being odd.—**odds** *n.pl.* the difference in favour of one as against another; inequality; advantage or superiority; the ratio by which one person's bet exceeds another's; likelihood or probability.—**Oddfellow**, a member of a friendly society resembling freemasons [O.N. *odda-* (*tala*), odd- (number)].

ode (ōd) *n.* orig. a poem intended to be sung; now, a lyric poem of exalted tone [Gk. *ōdē*, a song].

odium (ō'di-um) *n.* hatred; the state of being hated; general abhorrence incurred by a person or action; stigma.—**o'dious** *a.* hateful; offensive; exciting repugnance.—**o'diously** *adv.* —**o'diousness** *n.* [L. = hatred].

odont- (ō-dont) *prefix* from the Gk. *odous*, *odontos*, a tooth.—**odontalgia** (ō-don-tal'ji-ạ) *n.* toothache.—**odontol'ogy** *n.* the science of the teeth [Gk. *algos*, pain; *logos*, discourse].

odour (ō'dur) *n.* smell; fragrance; perfume; repute or estimation.—**odoriferous** (ō-do-rif'ẹ-rus) *a.* sweet-scented; (*Colloq.*) having a strong or unpleasant smell.—**odorif'erously** *adv.*—**odorif'erousness** *n.*—**o'dourless** *a.*—**o'dorous** *a.* fragrant; scented.—**o'dorously** *adv.*—**o'dorousness** *n* [L. *odor*].

Odysseus (o-dis'ūs, o-dis'ē-us) *n.* (*Myth.*) (L. Ulysses) hero of Homer's **Odyssey** (od'i-si) *n.* a Greek epic poem glorifying the adventures and wanderings of Odysseus; hence, any long, adventurous journey.

oecumenic, oecumenical (ek-ū-men'ik, -i-kạl) *a.* relating to the whole Christian world or church; universal; world-wide [Gk. *gē oikoumenē*, the inhabited earth].

oedema (ē-dēm'a) *n.* dropsical swelling—**oedematous** *a.* [Gk.]

Oedipus (ē-di-pus) *n.* (*Myth.*) a king of Thebes who unwittingly slew his father and married Jocasta his mother.—**Oedipus complex,** in psycho-analysis, a complex involving a preponderating love by a person for the parent of opposite sex.

Oerlikon (ẹr'li-kon) *n.* rapid-firing, anti-aircraft gun of Swiss origin [Oerliken, near Zurich].

oesophagus (ē-sof'ạ-gus) *n.* (*Anat.*) the canal by which food passes to stomach; the gullet. —**osophag'eal** *a.* [Gk. *oisophagos*].

of (ov, uv) *prep.* belonging to; from; proceeding from; relating to; concerning [O.E.].

off (of) *adv.* away; in general, denotes removal or separation, also completion, as in *to finish off*;—*prep.* not on; away from;—*a.* distant; on the farther side; in traffic directions, farthest from the pavement; discontinued; free;—*interj.* begone! depart!—**off'ing** *n.* the more distant part of the sea visible to an observer.—**off'-chance** *n.* a slight chance.—**off colour,** out of condition; indisposed.—**off-hand'** *a.* without preparation; free and easy; curt;—*adv.* without hesitation; impromptu.—**off'-li'cence** *n.* permission to sell alcoholic liquors for consumption off the premises only. —**off'set** *n.* a shoot or side-branch; a sum set off against another as an equivalent; compensation; (*Print.*) the smudging of a clean sheet; a process in lithography;—*v.t.* to counterbalance or compensate.—**off'shoot** *n.* that which shoots off or separates from a main branch or channel; a descendant.—**off-side'** *a.* (*Football, etc.*) of a player, being in such a position that he may not, under penalty, touch the ball himself nor interfere with an opponent or with play.—**off'spring** *n.* children; progeny; issue.—**off and on,** intermittently [form of *of*].

offal (of'ạl) *n.* waste meat; entrails of animals; anything thrown away as worthless; refuse [fr. *off* and *fall*].

offence (o-fens') *n.* transgression; sin; crime; insult; wrong; resentment: displeasure; a cause of displeasure.—**offens'ive** *a.* causing or giving offence; used in attack; insulting; unpleasant;—*n.* attack; onset; aggressive action.—**offens'ively** *adv.*—**offens'iveness** *n.* [L. *offendere*, to strike against].

offend (o-fend') *v.t.* to displease; to make angry; to wound the feelings of;—*v.i.* to do wrong; to sin or transgress.—**offend'er** *n.* [L. *offendere*, to strike against].

offer (of'ėr) *v.t.* to present for acceptance or refusal; to tender; to bid, as a price; to propose; to attempt; to express readiness to do;—*v.i.* to present itself or to occur;—*n.* a presentation; a price bid; to tender; a proposal, esp. of marriage.—**off'ering** *n.* that which is offered.—**off'erer** *n.* [L. *offerre*].

offertory (of'ėr-tor-i) *n.* a part of the mass during which the elements are offered up; the collection of money during the church service [L. *offertorium*].

office (of'is) *n.* a duty; a service; a function; an official position; a form of worship; a religious service; a place for doing business.—**off'ices** *n.pl.* parts of, or attached to, a house in which domestic work is done, e.g. kitchens, stables, etc.; outhouses; an act of kindness; help.—**off'icer** *n.* a person who holds an official position; one who holds commissioned rank in the navy, army, air-force, etc.—**off'ice-bear'er** *n.* one who holds office, esp. in a society, club, etc. [L. *officium*, duty].

official (of-ish'ạl) *a.* pert. to an office; vouched for by one holding office; authorised;—*n.* one holding an office, esp. in a public body.—**offic'ially** *adv.*—**offic'ialdom** *n.* officials collectively; their work, usually in contemptuous sense [L. *officium*, a duty).

officiate (o-fish'i-āt) *v.i.* to perform the duties of an officer; to perform a divine service [L. *officium*, duty].

officious (o-fish'us) *a.* given to exaggerate the duties of an office; importunate in offering service; meddlesome.—**offic'iously** *adv.*—**offic'iousness** *n.* [L. *officium*, a duty].

often (of'n) *adv.* frequently; many times.—**oft, oft'entimes, oft'times,** *adv.* archaic forms of 'often' [O.E. *oft*].

ogee (ō'jē) *n.* (*Archit.*) a moulding forming an S-shape;—also *a.*—**ogee'd** (ō-jēd') *a.* [Fr. *ogive*].

ogive (ō'jīv) *n.* (*Archit.*) a pointed arch or [window.—**ogi'val** *a.* [Fr.].

ogle (ō'gl) *v.i.* to make eyes;—*v.t.* to make eyes at; to cast amorous glances at;—*n.* an amorous glance.—**o'gler** *n.* [L.Ger. *oegeln*, fr. *oegen*, to eye].

Ogpu (og'pôô) *n.* secret police of Soviet-Russia [fr. initials of *Obedinennoe Gossudarstvennoe Politicheskoe Upravleniye*, U.S.S.R. Political State Administration].

ogre (ō-gėr) *n.* (*fem.* **o'gress**) a fabulous man-eating giant.—**o'greish, o'grish** *a.* [Fr.].

oh (ō) *interj.* an exclamation of surprise, sorrow, pain, etc.—Also **oho'!**

ohm (ōm) *n.* the standard unit of electrical resistance.—**ohm'meter** *n.* an instrument for measuring electrical current and resistance [fr. Georg S. *Ohm* (1787-1854)].

oil (oil) *n.* one of several kinds of light viscous liquids, obtained from various plants, animal substances, and minerals, used as lubricants, illuminants, fuel, medicines, etc.;—*v.t.* to apply oil to;—*v.i.* to take oil aboard as fuel.—**oil'er** *n.* one who, or that which, oils; an oil-can.—**oil'y** *a.* consisting of, or resembling, oil; greasy; fawning; subservient.—**oil'ily** *adv.*—**oil'iness** *n.*—**oils** *n.pl.* (*Paint.*) short for 'oil-colours.'—**oil'cake** *n.* a cake of compressed linseed, used as cattle-food.—**oil'can** *n.* a can, fitted with a protruding tube, for oiling machinery.—**oil'cloth** *n.* coarse canvas cloth coated with oil, to make a kind of linoleum.—**oil'col'ours** *n.pl.* (*Paint.*) colours made by grinding pigments in oil.—**oil'en'gine** *n.* an internal-combustion engine using vaporised oil as an explosive mixture.—**oil'field** *n.* a region rich in mineral oil.—**oil'paint'ing** *n.* one done in oil-colours.—**oil'skin** *n.* cloth made waterproof with oil;—*pl.* overcoat of this material.—**oil'well** *n.* boring made in district yielding petroleum [L. *oleum*].

ointment (oint'ment) *n.* that which anoints; an unguent; a soft, fatty substance, as a preparation for healing or beautifying the skin [O.Fr. *oignement*].

okapi (o-kà'pē) *n.* an African animal of the giraffe family [Native].

okay (ō-kā') *a.* and *adv.* abbrev. to **O.K.**, an expression signifying approval.

old (ōld) *a.* advanced in age; having lived or existed long; belonging to an earlier period; not new or fresh; stale; out of date.—**old'en** *a.* old; ancient; pert. to the past.—**old'ish** *a.* somewhat old.—**old'ness** *n.*—**old'fash'ioned** *a.* out of date; not modern.—**old gold,** a dull, lustreless, gold colour.—**Old Harry,** the devil; Satan.—**old maid,** an elderly spinster; (*Cards*) a round game.—**old man's beard,** a kind of moss; wild clematis.—**old master,** an old painting by a famous artist, esp. of 15th and 16th cents.—**Old Nick,** the devil.—**old school,** the school at which one was educated;—*a.* old-fashioned.—**old style,** the Julian calendar method (before 1752) of reckoning time, the year consisting of 365 days, 6 hours.—**Old Testament,** the first division of Bible.—**Old World,** the Eastern hemisphere [O.E. *eald*].

oleaginous (ō-lē-aj'i-nus) *a.* oily; greasy; (*Fig.*) fawning; unctuous [L. *oleum*, oil].

oleander (ō-lē-an'dėr) *n.* a beautiful, evergreen shrub with red and white flowers; the evergreen rose-bay [Fr.].

oleaster (ō-lē-as'tėr) *n.* the wild olive [L. fr. *olea*, an olive].

olefine (o'lif-ēn) *n.* any hydrocarbon of the ethylene series (L. *oleum*, oil).

oleo- (ō'lē-ō) *prefix* fr. L. *oleum*, oil.—**o'leograph** *n.* a lithograph in oil colours [Gk. *graphein*, to write;].

olfaction (ol-fak'shun) *n.* smelling; sense of smell.—**olfac'tory** *a.* pert. to smelling [L. *olere*, to smell; *facere*, to make].

oligarchy (ol'i-gàr-ki) *n.* government in which supreme power rests with a few; those who constitute the ruling few.—**ol'igarch** *n.* a member of an oligarchy.—**oligarchal** (ol-i-gàr'kạl) *a.* Also **oligar'chic(al)** [Gk. *oligos*, few; *archein*, to rule].

oligocene (ol'i-gō-sēn) *a.* (*Geol.*) pert. to a geological period between the eocene and miocene [Gk. *oligos*, little; *kainos*, recent].

olio (ō'li-ō) *n.* a highly-spiced stew of meat and vegetables; (*Fig.*) a medley [Sp. *olla*, fr. L. *olla*, a pot].

olive (ol'iv) *n.* an evergreen tree, long cultivated in the Mediterranean countries for its fruit; its oval, oil-yielding fruit; a colour, of a greyish, ashy green;—*a.* of the colour of an unripe olive, or of the foliage.—**olivaceous** (o-liv-ā'shus) *a.* olive-green.—**ol'ive-branch** *n.* an emblem or offer of peace.—**ol'ive-oil** *n.* oil expressed from olives [L. *oliva*].

olivil (ol'i-vil) *n.* a starch-like substance obtained from the gum of the olive-tree.

Olympia (ō-lim'pi-ạ) (*Class. Hist.*) a plain in ancient Greece, the scene of the Olympic Games.—**Olymp'iad** *n.* the name given to period of four years between each celebration of Olympic Games.—**Olym'pic** *a.* pert. to Olympia, or to the games.—**Olym'pics** *n.pl.* the Olympic Games.

Olympian (ō-lim'pi-ạn) *a.* (*Myth.*) pert. to Mount *Olympus* in Thessaly, the abode of the twelve principal Greek gods; hence, heavenly, noble, majestic;—*n.* a dweller in Olympus.

ombre (om'bėr) *n.* an old card game for three players [Sp. *hombre*].

omega (ō'me-ga) *n.* the last letter of the Greek alphabet; hence, the end.—**the alpha and omega,** the beginning and the end [Gk.].

omelette, omelet (om'ẹ-let) *n.* (*Cookery*) a dish of eggs beaten up with water or milk and seasonings and cooked in a frying-pan [Fr.].

omen (ō′men) *n.* a sign of some future event; a foreboding;—*v.t.* to fore-shadow by means of signs; to augur; to predict [L.].
ominous (om′i-nus) *a.* foreboding evil; threatening; inauspicious.—**om'inously** *adv.*—**om'inousness** *n.* [L. *ominosus*, fr. *omen*].
omit (ō-mit′) *v.t.* to leave out; to neglect; to fail to perform.—*pr.p.* **omit'ting.**—*pa.p.* and *pa.t.* **omit'ted.**—**omission** (ō-mish′un) *n.* the act of omitting; neglect; failure to do; that which is omitted or left undone.—**omiss'ible** *a.* that may be omitted.—**omiss'ive** *a.* omitting to send [L. *omittere*].
omni- (om′ni) *prefix* fr. L. *omnis*, all, used in derivatives.
omnibus (om′ni-bus) *n.* a large, four-wheeled, horse-drawn, public vehicle; later, a motor-bus.—(*abbrev.*) **bus**;—*a.* used in the sense of 'several in one,' e.g. **omnibus volume**, a book containing reprints of several works originally published separately; an anthology [L. *omnibus* = for all].
omnifarious (om′ni-fā′ri-us) *a.* consisting of all varieties [L.].
omnipotent (om-nip′o-tent) *a.* all-powerful, esp. of God; almighty.—**omnip'otently** *adv.*—**omnip'otence** *n.* unlimited power.
omnipresent (om-ni-prez′ent) *a.* present in all places at the same time.—**omnipres'ence** *n.* [L. *omnis*, all; and *present*].
omniscience (om-nish′i-ens) *n.* infinite knowledge.—**omnisc'ient** *a.* all-knowing.
omnium (om′ni-um) *n.* on the Stock Exchange, the value of the aggregate stocks in a funded loan.
omnivorous (om-niv′ō-rus) *a.* all-devouring; eating every kind of food.—**omniv'orously** *adv.* [L. *omnis*, all; *vorare*, to devour].
on (on) *prep.* above and touching; in addition to; following from; referring to; at; near; towards, etc.;—*adv.* so as to be on; forwards; continuously [O.E.].
once (wuns) *adv.* at one time; on one occasion; formerly; ever;—*n.* one time.—**at once**, immediately [fr. *one*].
oncoming (on′kum-ing) *a.* approaching;—*n.* approach [fr. *on* and *coming*].
oncost (on′kost) *n.* the total charges borne by any commercial or industrial concern, exclusive of salaries and wages [fr. *on* and *cost*].
one (wun) *a.* the lowest cardinal number; single; undivided; only; without others; identical;—*n.* the number or figure 1; unity; a single specimen;—*pron.* a particular but not stated person; any person.—**one'ness** *n.* unity; uniformity; singleness.—**one'self** *pron.* one's own self or person.—**one′horse** *a.* drawn by one horse; (*Colloq.*) of no importance; insignificant; paltry.—**one-sid'ed** *a.* esp. of a contest, game, etc., limited to one side; considering one side only; partial; unfair.—**one′way** *a.* denoting a system of traffic circulation in one direction only [O.E. *an*].
onerous (on′er-us) *a.* burdensome; oppressive.—**on'erously** *adv.*—**on'erousness** *n.* [L. *onus*, *oneris*, a burden].
ongoing (on′gō-ing) *n.* a going on; advance; procedure.—**on'goings** *n.pl.* behaviour.
onion (un′yun) *n.* an edible, bulbous plant with pungent odour.—**on'iony** *a.*—**flaming onions** (*World War* 2) an anti-aircraft rocket shell [L. *unio*].
onlooker (on′lòòker) *n.* a spectator; an observer [fr. *on* and *look*].
only (ōn′li) *a.* being the one specimen; single; sole;—*adv.* solely; singly; merely; exclusively;—*conj.* but then; except that; with this reservation [O.E. *anlic*, one like].
onomatopoeia (on-ō-mat-ō-pē′ya) *n.* the formation of a word by using sounds that resemble or suggest the object or action to be named, e.g. *hiss*, *ping-pong*.—**onomatopoe'ic**, **onomatopoet'ic** *a.* [Gk. *onoma*, a name; *poiein*, to make].
onset (on′set) *n.* a violent attack; an assault [fr. *on* and *set*].
onshore (on′shōr) *a.* towards the land, esp. of a wind [fr. *on* and *shore*].
onslaught (on′slawt) *n.* an attack; an onset; an assault [Dut. *aanslag*].
onto (on′tòò) *prep.* upon; on the top; to; on to.
ontology *n.* the science that treats of reality of being; metaphysics.—**ontolog'ical** *a.*—**ontol′ogist** *n.* [Gk. *ōn*, *ontos*, being; *logos*, discourse].
onus (ō′nus) *n.* burden; responsibility [L.].
onward (on′ward) *a.* and *adv.* advancing; going on; forward.—**on'wards** *adv.* in a forward direction; ahead [E. *on*; O.E. *weard*, in the direction of].
onyx (on′iks) *n.* a variety of quartz, in variously coloured layers, used for making cameos [Gk. *onux*, a finger-nail].
oodles (òò′dlz) *n.pl.* (*Slang*) superabundance, esp. of money [etym. uncertain].
oolite (ō′o-līt) *n.* granular limestone, its grains resembling eggs of roe of fish.—**oolit'ic** *a.* [Gk. *ōion*, egg; *lithos*, stone].
oology (ō-ol′o-ji) *n.* the study of birds' eggs [Gk. *ōion*, an egg; *logos*, discourse].
ooze (òòz) *n.* soft mud or slime; a gentle flow; a kind of deposit on the bottom of the sea;—*v.i.* to flow gently; to leak or percolate;—*v.t.* to exude or give out slowly.—**ooz'y** *a.* slimy; muddy; miry [M.E. *wose*, fr. O.E. *wase*, mud].
opacity (ō-pas′i-ti) *n.* See **opaque.**
opal (ō′pal) *n.* a mineral much used as a gem owing to its beautiful and varying hues of green, yellow and red.—**opalescent** (ō-pal-es′ent) *a.* of changing iridescent colour, like an opal.—**opalesc'ence** *n.*—**opaline** (ō′pal-īn) *a.* like opal;—*n.* semi-transparent white glass [L. *opalus*].
opaque (ō-pāk′) *a.* not transparent; impenetrable to sight; not lucid; dull-witted.—**opaqu'ely** *adv.*—**opaqu'eness** *n.*—**opa'city** *n.* opaqueness; the quality of not transmitting light; obscurity [L. *opacus*].
ope (ōp) *v.t.* and *i.* (*Poet.*) to open.
open (ō′pn) *a.* not shut or blocked up; allowing passage in or out; not covered (with trees); not fenced; without restrictions; available; exposed; frank and sincere;—*n.* clear, unobstructed space;—*v.t.* to set open; to uncover; to give access to; to begin; to cut or break into;—*v.i.* to become open; to begin; (*Theatre*) to have a first performance.—**o'pener** *n.* one who or that which opens.—**o'pening** *a.* first in order; initial;—*n.* a hole or gap; an open or cleared space; an opportunity; a beginning.—**o'penly** *adv.* publicly; frankly.—**o'penness** *n.*—**o'pencast** *a.* (*Mining*) excavated from the surface, instead of from underground.—**o'pen-hand'ed** *a.* generous; liberal.—**o'pen-heart'ed** *a.* frank.—**o'pen-mind'ed** *a.* free from prejudices [O.E.].
opera (op′e-ra) *n.* a musical drama; the theatre where opera is performed.—**operat'ic** *a.* pert. to opera.—**operett'a** *n.* a short light opera.—**grand opera**, opera in which no spoken dialogue is permitted.—**opera bouffe** (bòòf) a farcical play set to music.—**op'era-glass** (or **glass'es**) *n.* a small binocular used in theatres.—**op'era-hat** *n.* a man's collapsible tall hat [It. fr. L. *opera*, work].
operate (op′e-rāt) *v.t.* to cause to function; to effect;—*v.i.* to work; to produce an effect; to exert power; to perform an act of surgery; to deal in stocks and shares, esp. speculatively.—**opera'tion** *n.* the act of operating; a method or mode of action; treatment involving surgical skill; movement of an army or fleet (usu. in *pl.*).—**opera'tional** *a.* pertaining to operations.—**op'erative** *a.* having the power of acting; exerting force; producing the desired effect; efficacious;—*n.* artisan or workman; factory-hand.—**op'erator** *n.* [L. *operari*, to work].
operculum (ō-per′kū-lum) *n.* a lid or cover, in plants; a lid-like structure in molluscs; the gill-cover of fish.—**oper'cular**, **oper'culate** *a.* [L. fr. *operire*, to cover].
operose (op′ē-rōs) *a.* laborious; tedious.—**op'erosely** *adv.*—**op'eroseness** *n.* [L. *opus*, work].

ophi(o)- (of′i(o)) *prefix* fr. Gk. *ophis*, a snake.—**ophid′ian** (ō-fid′i-ạn) *n.* a snake;—*a.* pert. to the ophidia or snakes; snake-like.

ophthalmia (of-thal′mi-ạ) *n.* (*Med.*) inflammation of the eye.—**ophthal′mic** *a.* of the eye.—**ophthal′mist, ophthalmol′ogist** *n.* one skilled in the study of the eye.—**ophthal′moscope** *n.* an instrument for viewing the interior of the eye [Gk. *ophthalmos*, the eye; *logos*, discourse; *skopein*, to view].

opiate (ō′pi-āt) *n.* any preparation of opium; a narcotic;—*a.* containing opium; inducing sleep.—**opiat′ic** *a.* [fr. *opium*].

opine (ō-pīn′) *v.t.* and *i.* to think or suppose; to hold or express an opinion [L. *opinari*].

opinion (ō-pin′yun) *n.* judgment or belief; estimation; formal statement by an expert.—**opin′ionated** *a.* dogmatic.—**opin′ionative** *a.* stubborn.—**opin′ionatively** *adv.*—**opin′ionativeness** *n.* [L. *opinio*].

opium (ō′pi-um) *n.* the narcotic juice of a kind of poppy used to induce sleep or allay pain [Gk. *opion*, poppy-juice].

opopanax *n.* a gum-resin used in perfume-making, and formerly in medicine [Gk. *opos*, juice].

opossum (ō-pos′um) *n.* a small American marsupial animal. Also **pos′sum** [N. Amer. Ind.].

oppidan (op′i-dạn) *n.* a town-dweller; at Eton, a scholar who lodges in town [L. *oppidum*, a town].

opponent (o-pō′nent) *a.* opposite; opposing; antagonistic;—*n.* one who opposes [L. *opponere*, to place against].

opportune (op-or-tūn′) *a.* well-timed; convenient.—**opportun′ely** *adv.*—**opportune′ness** *n.*—**opportun′ism** *n.* the policy of doing what is expedient at the time regardless of principle.—**opportun′ist** *n.*—**opportun′ity** *n.* a fit or convenient time; a good chance [L. *opportunus*].

oppose (o-pōz′) *v.t.* to set against; to resist; to compete with.—**oppos′able** *a.*—**oppos′er** *n.* [L. *opponere*, to place against].

opposite (op′o-zit) *a.* contrary facing; situated in front; adverse; contrary; diametrically different;—*n.* the contrary;—*prep.* and *adv.* in front of; on the other side.—**opp′ositely** *adv.* facing each other.—**opp′ositeness** *n.*—**opposition** (op-o-zish′un) *n.* the state of being opposite; resistance; contradiction; an obstacle; a party opposed to that in power [L. *opponere, oppositum*, to place against].

oppress (o-pres′) *v.t.* to govern with tyranny; to treat severely; to lie heavy on.—**oppression** (o-presh′un) *n.* harshness; severity; tyranny; dejection.—**oppres′sive** *a.* unreasonably burdensome; hard to bear.—**oppress′ively** *adv.*—**oppress′iveness** *n.*—**oppress′or** *n.* [L. *opprimere, oppressum*, to press down].

opprobrium (o-prō′bri-um) *n.* reproach; disgrace; infamy.—**oppro′brious** *a.* reproachful and contemptuous; shameful.—**opprobriously** *adv.*—**oppro′briousness** *n.* [L.].

oppugn (o-pūn′) *v.t.* to fight against; to oppose.—**oppugn′er** *n.*—**oppug′nant** (o-pug′nạnt) *a.* opposing.—**oppug′nancy** *n.* opposition [L. *oppugnare*, to fight against].

opt (opt) *v.i.* to make a choice; to exercise an option; to choose.—**optative** (op-tā′tiv, op′tạ-tiv) *a.* expressing wish or desire;—*n.* (*Gram.*) a mood of the verb expressing wish.—**op′tatively** *adv.* [L. *optare*, to wish].

optic (op′tic) *a.* pert. to the eye or to sight; pert. to optics;—*n.* (*Colloq.*) the eye.—**op′tics** *n.* the science which deals with light and its relation to sight.—**op′tical** *a.* pert. to vision; visual.—**op′tically** *adv.*—**optician** (op-tish′ạn) *n.* one skilled in optics; a maker of, or dealer in, optical instruments, esp. spectacles [Gk. *optikos*].

optimism (op′ti-mizm) *n.* belief that everything is ordered for the best; disposition to look on bright side.—**op′timist** *n.* believer in optimism; one who takes hopeful view.—**optimis′tical** *a.*—**optimis′tically** *adv.* [L. *optimus*, best].

option (op′shun) *n.* the power or right of choosing; choice.—**op′tional** *a.* left to one's free choice.—**op′tionally** *adv.* [L. *optare*, to choose].

opulent (op′ū-lent) *a.* wealthy; abundantly rich.—**op′ulently** *adv.*—**op′ulence, op′ulency** *n.* wealth; riches [L. *opulentus*].

opus (ō′pus) *n.* a work; a musical composition;—*pl.* **opera** (op′ẹ-rạ).—**magnum opus**, a writer's most important work [L. *opusculum* dim. of *opus*, work].

or (or) *conj.* introducing an alternative; if not; (*Arch.*) before [M.E. *other*].

oracle (or′ạ-kl) *n.* medium by which divine utterances were transmitted, often a priest or priestess; shrine where ancient Greeks consulted deity; response given, often obscure; a person of outstanding wisdom.—**orac′ular** *a.* of nature of oracle; authoritative; ambiguous; forecasting the future.—**orac′ularly** *adv.* [L. *oraculum*].

oral (ō′rạl) *a.* spoken; not written; using speech; pert. to the mouth.—**o′rally** *adv.* [L. *os, oris*, the mouth].

orange (or′ạnj) *n.* a juicy, gold-coloured fruit; tree bearing it; reddish yellow colour like an orange;—*a.* reddish yellow in colour.—**orangeade** (or-ạnj-ād′) *n.* drink of orange juice, sugar, and water.—**or′angery** *n.* a plantation or nursery of orange-trees [Arab. *naranj*].

orang-outang, orang-utan (ō-rang′ōō-tang′, ō′rang-ōō′tan) *n.* a large man-like ape [Malayan = man of the woods].

orate (ō-rāt′) *v.i.* to talk loftily; to harangue.—**oration** (ō-rā′shun) *n.* a formal and dignified public discourse.—**or′ator** *n.* one who delivers an oration; one distinguished for gift of public speaking.—**orator′ical** *a.* pert. to orator(y); rhetorical.—**orator′ically** *adv.*—**oratorio** (or-ạ-tō′ri-ō) *n.* a sort of sacred musical drama.—**or′atory** *n.* the art or exercise of speaking in public; rhetorical skill; eloquence; a chapel or small room for private devotions [L. *orare*, to speak].

orb (orb) *n.* a circle; a sphere or globe; a heavenly body; the globe surmounted by a cross, which forms part of the regalia; (*Poet.*) the eye.—**or′bit** *n.* (*Astron.*) path traced by one heavenly body in its revolution round another; (*Fig.*) range of influence or action; the eye-socket.—**or′bital** *a.* [L. *orbis*, a circle].

Orcadian (or-kā′di-ạn) *a.* of, or pert. to, the Orkney Islands;—*n.* a native of these islands [L. *Orcades*].

orchard (or′chạrd) *n.* a garden or enclosure containing fruit-trees [O.E. *ortgeard*].

orchestra (or′kes-trạ) *n.* the space in a theatre occupied by a band of musicians; a band of performers on various musical instruments.—**orches′tral** *a.*—**or′chestrate** *v.t.* to arrange music for performance by an orchestra.—**orchestra′tion** *n.* [Gk. *orcheisthai*, to dance].

orchid, orchis (or′kid, or′kis) *n.* a genus of plants with fantastically-shaped flowers of varied and brilliant colours.—**orchidaceous** (or-ki-dā′shus) *a.* pert. to the orchid [Gk. *orchis*, a testicle].

ordain (or-dān′) *v.t.* to decree; to enact; to destine; to appoint; to admit to the Christian ministry; to confer holy orders upon.—**ordain′ment** *n.* (rare).—**ordina′tion** *n.* the act of ordaining or decreeing; admission to the Christian ministry [L. *ordo*, order].

ordeal (or′dē-ạl, or′dēl) *n.* an ancient method of trial by requiring the accused to undergo a dangerous physical test; a trying experience; a test of endurance [O.E. *ordal*, a judicial test].

order (or′dẹr) *n.* rank; class; group; regular arrangement; sequence; succession; method; regulation; a command or direction; mode of procedure; an instruction; a monastic society; one of the five styles of architecture (Doric, Ionic, Corinthian, Tuscan, and Composite); a sub-division of a class of plants or animals, made up of genera; an honour conferred for distinguished civil or military services; in trade, detailed instructions, by a customer, of goods to be supplied;—*v.t.* to arrange; to command; to require; to regulate; to systematise; to give an order for.—**or′derly** *a.* methodical; tidy; well-regulated; peaceable; (*Mil.*) esp. of a junior officer, on duty to supervise daily routine;—*n.* a soldier following an officer to carry orders; in a military hospital, a soldier-attendant;—*adv.* in right order.—**or′derliness** *n.*—**holy orders,** generally, ordination to the Christian ministry.—**to take orders,** to accept instructions; (*Church*) to be ordained.—**by order,** by command.—**in order to,** for the purpose of [L. *ordo*, order].

ordinal (or′di-nạl) *a.* and *n.* showing order or position in a series, e.g. *first*, *second*, etc.; a church service-book for use at ordinations [L. *ordo*, order].

ordinance (or′din-ạns) *n.* an established rule, religious rite, or ceremony; a decree [O. Fr. *ordenance*].

ordinary (or′di-nạ-ri) *a.* usual; regular; habitual; normal, commonplace; plain;—*n.* ecclesiastical judge; a bishop in his diocese; a church-service book; meal supplied at a fixed time and place.—**or′dinarily** *adv.* [L. *ordo*, order].

ordination See **ordain.**

ordnance (ord′nạns) *n.* collective term for heavy mounted guns; military stores.—**ordnance survey,** the Government department which prepares official maps of the British Isles [var. of *ordinance*].

ordure (or′dūr) *n.* dung; filth; (*Fig.*) obscenity [O.Fr. *ord.* vile].

ore (ōr) *n.* a native mineral from which metal is extracted [O.E. *ora*].

organ (or′gạn) *n.* a musical instrument of pipes worked by bellows and played by keys; a member of an animal or plant exercising a special function; a medium of information.—**organ′ic** *a.* pert. to or affecting bodily organs; having either animal or vegetable life; derived from living organisms; systematic; organised.—**organ′ically** *adv.*—**or′ganism** *n.* an organised body or system; a living body.—**or′ganist** *n.* a player on the organ.—**or′gan-grinder** *n.* a player on a barrel-organ.—**or′gan-loft** *n.* gallery for an organ.—**or′gan-screen** *n.* a decorated screen on which organ is placed.—**or′gan-stop** *n.* a series of pipes of uniform tone or quality; one of a series of knobs for manipulating and controlling them.—**organic chemistry,** the branch of chemistry dealing with the compounds of carbon [Gk. *organon*, an instrument].

organdie (or′gạn-di) *n.* a muslin of great transparency and lightness [Fr. *organdi*].

organise (or′gạ-nīz) *v.t.* to furnish with organs; to give a definite structure; to prepare for transaction of business; to get up, arrange, or put into working order; to unite in a society.—**organis′able** *a.*—**organisa′tion** *n.* act of organising; the manner in which the branches of a service, etc., are arranged; individuals systematically united for some work; a society.—**or′ganiser** *n.* [Gk. *organon*, an instrument].

orgasm (or′gazm) *n.* immoderate action or excitement, esp. sexual.—**orgas′tic** *a.* [Gk. *orgaein*, to be lustful].

orgy (or′ji) *n.* a drunken or licentious revel; a debauch.—*pl.* **orgies** (or′jiz).—**orgias′tic** *a.* of the nature of orgies [Gk. *orgia* (pl.) Bacchic rites].

oriel (ō′ri-ẹl) *n.* a projecting window; the recess in a room formed by such a window [O.Fr. *oriol*, a porch].

orient (ō′ri-ẹnt) *a.* rising, as the sun; eastern; lustrous (applied to pearls);—*n.* the east; Eastern countries;—*v.t.* to place so as to face the east; to determine the position of, with respect to the east; to take one's bearings.—**orien′tal** *a.* eastern; pert. to, coming from, of, the east;—*n.* an Asiatic.—**o′rientate** *v.t.* and *i.* to orient; to bring into clearly understood relations.—**orienta′tion** *n.* the act of turning to, or determining, the east; sense of direction; determining one's position [L. *oriens*, rising, fr. *oriri*, to rise].

orifice (or′i-fis) *n.* a mouth or opening; perforation; vent [L. *orificium*, fr. *os*, the mouth; *facere*, to make].

origin (or′i-jin) *n.* beginning; starting-point; a source; parentage; birth; nationality.—**original** (or-ij′in-ạl) *a.* earliest; first; primitive; new, not copied or derived; thinking or acting for oneself;—*n.* origin; model; a pattern.—**orig′inally** *adv.*—**original′ity** *n.* the quality of being original; initiative.—**orig′inate** *v.t.* to bring into being; to initiate;—*v.i.* to begin; to arise.—**orig′inative** *a.*—**origina′tion** *n.*—**orig′inator** *n.* [L. *origo*, fr. *oriri*, to rise].

oriole (ō′ri-ōl) *n.* a brightly-coloured bird of the thrush family, esp. the 'golden oriole' [O.Fr. *oriol*, fr. L. *aurum*, gold].

orison (or′i-zon) *n.* a prayer or supplication [O.Fr. fr. L. *orare*, to pray].

orlop (or′lop) *n.* the lowest deck in a ship [Dut. *overloop*].

ormolu (or′mo-lòò) *n.* an alloy of copper, zinc and tin, resembling gold; gilded bronze; a preparation of gold-leaf used for gilding furniture; an article made of, or decorated with, this substance [Fr. *or*, gold; *moulu*, ground, fr. *moudre*, to grind].

ornament (or′nạ-ment) *n.* decoration; any object to adorn or decorate;—*v.t.* to adorn; to beautify; to embellish.—**ornament′al** *a.* serving to decorate.—**ornament′ally** *adv.*—**ornamenta′tion** *n.* decoration.—**ornate′** *a.* richly decorated.—**ornate′ly** *adv.*—**ornate′ness** *n.* [L. *ornamentum*].

ornitho- (or′ni-tho) *prefix* fr. Gk. *ornis*, *ornithos*, a bird, used in derivatives.—**ornithol′ogy** *n.* the scientific study of birds.—**ornitholog′ical** *a.*—**ornithol′ogist** *n.*—**ornithorhynchus** (or-ni-tho-ring′kus) *n.* the Australian duck-billed platypus, an aquatic, furred mammal whose young are hatched from eggs [Gk. *logos*, discourse; *rhunchos*, the beak].

orography, orology (or-og′rạ-fi, or-ol′o-ji) *n.* the branch of physical geography dealing with mountains, their description, etc.—**orograph′ical, orolo′gical** *a.* [Gk. *oros*, a mountain; *graphein*, to write; *logos*, discourse].

orotund (ō′rō-tund) *a.* of voice or speech, full, clear, and musical; of style, pompous [L. *os*, *oris*, the mouth; *rotundus*, round].

orphan (or′fạn) *n.* and *a.* a child bereft of one or both parents;—*v.t.* to make an orphan.—**or′phanage** *n.* a home or institution for orphans.—**or′phanhood, or′phanism** *n.* [Gk. *orphanos*, bereaved].

orpiment (or′pi-ment) *n.* a yellow mineral of the arsenic group, used as a dye [L. *aurum*, gold; *pigmentum*, a pigment].

orrery (or′ẹ-ri) *n.* a mechanical model of the solar system, showing the revolutions of the planets, etc. [fr. the Earl of *Orrery*, for whom one was made in 1715].

orris (or′is) *n.* a kind of iris.—**orr′is-root** *n.* the dried root, used as a powder in perfumery and medicine [form of *iris*].

orthodox (or′tho-doks) *a.* having the correct faith; sound in opinions or doctrine; conventional.—**or′thodoxly** *adv.*—**or′thodoxy** *n.* soundness of faith, esp. in religion. Also **or′thodoxness** [Gk. *orthos*, right; *doxa*, opinion].

orthography (or-thog′rạ-fi) *n.* correct spelling.—**orthog′rapher** *n.*—**orthograph′ic, orthograph′ical** *a.*—**orthograph′ically** *adv.* [Gk. *orthos*, correct; *graphein*, to write].

orthopaedia (or-thō-pē′di-ạ) *n.* treatment and cure of bodily deformities, esp. in children. Also **orthop(a)e′dy.**—**orthopae′dic** *a.*—**orthopae′dics** *n.* surgery dealing with correction and cure of deformities.—**orthopae′dist** *n.* [Gk. *orthos*, straight; *pais*, *paidos*, a child].

ortolan (or′tol-ạn) *n.* a small bird, the garden-bunting [L. *hortus*, a garden].

Oscar (os´kar) *n.* In the U.S. a gold-plated statuette, awarded by Motion Picture Academy to the director, actor, script-writer, etc., for the year's best performance.
oscillate (os´i-lāt) *v.i.* to swing to and fro; to vibrate; to vary between extremes; (*Wireless*) to set up wave motion in a receiving set.—**oscilla'tion** *n.* a pendulum-like motion; variation between extremes; (*Wireless*) a form of interference.—**os'cillator** *n.*—**os'cillatory** *a.* swinging to and fro; vibrating [L. *oscillare*, to swing].
osculate (os´kū-lāt) *v.t.* and *i.* to kiss; (*Math.*) to touch, as curves; of species, having characteristics in common.—**os'culant** *a.*—**oscula'tion** *n.* kissing; contact.—**os'culatory** *a.* pert. to kissing, or to the touching of curves [L. *osculum*, a kiss].
osier (ō-zi-er) *n.* a species of willow, used in basket-making; a willow-branch;—*a.* made of, or like, osiers [Fr.].
osmium (ōs´mi-um) *n.* (*Chem.*) a hard, bluish-white metal, of the rare earth group [fr. Gk. *osmē*, a smell (osmium oxide has a disagreeable smell)].
osmosis (os-mō´sis) *n.* (*Chem.*) the tendency of fluid substances, if separated by a porous membrane, to filter through it and become equally diffused. Also **os'mose.**—**osmot'ic** *a.* [Gk. *ōsmos*, fr. *ōthein*, to push].
osprey (os´prā) *n.* the fish-hawk or sea-eagle; erroneously applied to an egret-plume used in millinery [corrupt. of *ossifrage*, the sea-eagle].
oss- (os) *prefix* fr. L. *os*, *ossis*, bone, used in many derivatives.—**osseous** (os´ē-us) *a.* pert. to or resembling bone; bony.—**oss'icle** *n.* a small bone, esp. of the middle ear.—**ossif'erous** *a.* containing, or yielding, bones.—**ossifica'tion** *n.* hardening into bone.—**oss'ify** *v.t.* to harden into bone;—*v.i.* to become bone, of cartilage, etc.—**ossuary** (os´ū-ar-i) *n.* a memorial place, esp. near a battlefield, for holding the bones of the dead; a charnel-house.
ossifrage (os'i-frāj) *n.* the sea-eagle [L. *ossifraga*, the bone-breaker].
osteal (os´te-al) *a.* (*Med.*) pert. to, or like, bone.—**ostei'tis** *n.* inflammation of the bone [Gk. *osteon*, bone].
ostensible (os-ten´si-bl) *a.* professed; used as a blind; plausible; apparent.—**osten'sibly** *adv.*—**ostensibil'ity** *n.* [L. *ostendere*, to show].
ostentation (os-ten-tā´shun) *n.* vainglorious display; showing off.—**ostenta'tious** *a.* fond of display; characterised by display.—**ostenta´tiously** *adv.*—**ostenta'tiousness** *n.* [L. *ostendere*, to show].
osteo- (os´te-o) *prefix* fr. Gk. *osteon*, bone, used in derivatives mainly medical.—**os'teo-arthritis** (ar-thrī´tis) *n.* chronic inflammation of a joint.—**os'teoid** *a.* resembling bone.—**osteol'ogy** *n.* that branch of anatomy dealing with bones, their structure, etc.—**osteol'ogist** *n.* [Gk. *arthron*, a joint.
osteopathy (os-te-o´path-i) *n.* a system of healing, based on the belief that the human body can effect its own cure with the aid of manipulative treatment of the spinal column, joints, etc.; manipulative surgery.—**os'teopath** *n.* a practitioner of this system.—**osteopath'ic** *a.* [Gk. *osteon*, bone; *pathos*, feeling].
ostler (os´ler) *n.* a stableman at an inn; a groom. Same as **host'ler** [E. *hostel*].
ostracise (os´tra-sīz) *v.t.* to exclude from society; to exile; to boycott.—**os'tracism** *n.* exclusion from society; social boycotting [Gk. *ostrakon*, a potsherd used in voting].
ostrich (os´trich) *n.* a large flightless bird, native of Africa [Gk. *strouthos*].
other (uTH´er) *a.* and *pron.* not this; not the same; different; opposite; additional;—*adv.* otherwise.—**oth'erwise** *adv.* differently; in another way;—*conj.* else; if not.—**otherwhere** *adv.* elsewhere.—**every other**, every second (one); each alternate.—**oth'er-world'ly** *a.* thinking of the future life; spiritual [O.E. *other*].
otitis (ō-tī´tis) *n.* (*Med.*) inflammation of the ear [Gk. *ous*, *ōtos*, the ear].
otiose (ō´shi-ōs) *a.* at ease; at leisure; not required; superfluous; futile (L. *otium*, ease].
ottava rima (o-tà-va-rē´ma) *n.* a stanza of eight lines, the first six rhyming alternately, the last two forming a couplet, thus a b a b a b c c [It. *ottava*, octave].
otter (ot´er) *n.* an aquatic, fish-eating animal of the weasel family; a kind of fishing tackle; (*War*) an apparatus attached to the bow of a ship to clear away mines; a paravane [O.E. *otor*].
otto (ot´ō) *n.* See **attar.**
Ottoman (ot´o-man) *a.* pert. to the Turks;—*n.* a Turk; a kind of cushioned settee or divan without back or arms [fr. Turkish Sultan *Othman*, or *Osman*].
oubliette (ōō-blē-et') *n.* an underground dungeon, esp. one entered only through a trapdoor [Fr. *oublier*, to forget].
ouch (ouch) *n.* a setting for a precious stone; an ornament [O.Fr. *nouche*].
ought (awt) *auxil. v.* to be bound by moral obligation or duty [O.E. *ahte*, owed].
ought (awt) *n.* a form of 'nought'; nothing.
ouija (wē´ja, -ya) *n.* board with letters, used at seances to answer questions [coined fr. Fr. *oui*, yes; Ger. *ja*, yes].
ounce (ouns) *n.* a unit of weight, abbrev. **oz.**; in avoirdupois weight = $\frac{1}{16}$ of a pound; in troy weight = $\frac{1}{12}$ of a pound [L. *uncia*, a twelfth part].
ounce (ouns) *n.* a carnivorous animal resembling the leopard [O.Fr. *once*].
our (our) *a.* belonging to us.—**ours** *poss. pron.* used in place of *our* with a noun.—**ourself'** *pron.* myself (in regal or formal style).—**ourselves'** *pron. pl.* we, i.e. not others [O.E. *ure*].
ousel (ōō´zl) *n.* See **ouzel.**
oust (oust) *v.t.* to put out; to expel; to dispossess, esp. by unfair means [O.Fr. *oster*; Fr. *ôter*, to remove].
out (out) *adv.* on, at, or to, the outside; from within; from among; away; not in the usual or right place; not at home; in bloom; disclosed; exhausted; destitute; in error; at a loss; on strike; unemployed;—*a.* outlying; remote;—*prep.* outside; out of;—*interj.* away! begone!—*v.t.* to put out; to knock out;—**out'er** *a.* being on the outside; away from the inside;—*n.* on a target, ring farthest from the centre; a shot recorded there.—**out'ermost, out'most** *a.* on extreme outside [O.E. *ut*].
outbalance (out-bal´ans) *v.t.* to exceed in weight; to be heavier than.
outbid (out-bid') *v.t.* to bid more than; to offer a higher price.—*pr.p.* **outbid'ding.**—*pa.p.* **outbid'** or **outbid'den.**—*pa.t.* **outbade'.**
outboard (out´bōrd) *a.* projecting beyond and outside the hull of a ship, e.g. of a ladder; also, of a detachable motor-engine fixed to the stern of a small-boat.
outbreak (out´brāk) *n.* a sudden breaking out; a burst, esp. of anger; the beginning, esp. of an epidemic of disease, of war, etc.
outbuilding (out´bild-ing) *n.* an outhouse; a building detached from the main building.
outburst (out´burst) *n.* a bursting out, esp. of anger, laughter, cheering, etc.
outcast (out´cast) *a.* cast out as useless;—*n.* one rejected by society.—**out'caste** *n.* in India, one not belonging to one of the four hereditary classes of society.
outclass (out-klas') *v.t.* to exceed in skill or quality; to surpass.
outcome (out´kum) *n.* issue; result.
outcrop (out´krop) *n.* the coming out of a stratum of rock, coal, etc., to the surface of the ground.—**outcrop coal**, surface-coal.
outcry (out´krī) *n.* a loud cry; a cry of distress, complaint, disapproval, etc.
outdistance (out-dis´tans) *v.t.* to surpass in speed; to get ahead of.
outdo (out-dōō') *v.t.* to excel; surpass.

outdoor (out′dōr) *a.* out of doors; in the open air.—**out′doors** *adv.* outside.
outfield (out′fēld) *n.* the field or fields farthest from the farm-buildings; (*Cricket*) the outer part of a cricket-ground.
outfit (out′fit) *n.* a supply of things, esp. clothes, tools, etc., required for any purpose; equipment; kit; (*Slang*) a company of people; a crowd;—*v.t.* to supply with equipment, etc. —**out′fitter** *n.* one who supplies clothes, equipment, etc.
outflank (out-flangk′) *v.t.* (*Mil.*) to succeed in getting beyond the flank of the enemy.
outgo (out-gō′) *v.t.* to go beyond;—*n.* (out′gō) expenditure; outlay.—**out′going** *n.* going out; expenditure;—*a.* departing.
outgrow (out-grō′) *v.t.* to surpass in growth; to become too large or old for; to grow out of. —**out′growth** *n.* what grows out of anything; an offshoot.
outhouse (out′hous) *n.* a building, esp. a small erection, outside a main house.
outing (out′ing) *n.* a going out; an excursion; a trip; an airing.
outlandish (out′land′ish) *a.* remote; isolated; foreign; barbarous; not according to custom; queer; fantastic.
outlaw (out′law) *n.* one placed beyond the protection of the law; a bandit;—*v.t.* to declare to be an outlaw.—**out′lawry** *n.* the legal process of putting a person beyond the protection of the law.
outlay (out′lā) *n.* expenditure; expenses.
outlet (out′let) *n.* a passage or way out; an exit; a vent; an opening.
outline (out′līn) *n.* the lines that bound a figure; a boundary; a sketch without details; a rough draft; a general plan;—*v.t.* to draw in outline; to sketch; to give a general plan of; to summarise.
outlive (out-liv′) *v.t.* to live longer than.
outlook (out′look) *n.* a looking out; a prospect; a person's point of view; prospects.
outlying (out′lī-ing) *a.* lying at a distance; remote; isolated; detached.
outmoded (out-mō′dẹd) *a.* driven out of fashion; out of fashion.
outnumber (out-num′bẹr) *v.t.* to exceed in number.
out-patient (out′pā′shent) *n.* a patient who comes to a hospital, infirmary, etc., for treatment but is non-resident.
outpost (out′pōst) *n.* (*Mil.*) a small detachment posted on guard some distance from the main body; a picket.
outpour (out-pōr′) *v.t.* to pour out; to flow over.—**out′pour, out′pouring** *n.* an overflow; (*Fig.*) an abundance of emotion.
output (out′po͝ot) *n.* production; the amount of goods produced in a given time.
outrage (out′rāj) *n.* excessive violence; violation of others' rights; gross insult or indignity; —*v.t.* to do grievous wrong or violence to; to insult grossly; to shock.—**outrageous** (out-rā′jus) *a.* violent; atrocious.—**outra′geously** *adv.*—**outra′geousness** *n.*
outrance (o͝o-trongs′) *n.* the farthest limit; excess.—**à outrance,** to the bitter end; (the incorrect form *a l'outrance* used in English).—**outré** (o͝o′trā) *a.* beyond customary limits; exaggerated; extravagantly odd [Fr. *outre*, beyond].
outride (out-rīd′) *v.t.* to ride faster than; to ride farther than; (*Naut.*) of a ship, to live through a storm.—*pa.p.* **outrid′den.**—*pa.t.* **outrode′.**—**out′rider** *n.* a servant on horseback who rides beside a carriage.
outrigger (out′rig-ẹr) *n.* (*Naut.*) a projecting spar for extending sails, ropes, etc.; a frame on the side of a rowing-boat with a rowlock at the outer edge; projecting framework, with a float attached to it, to prevent a canoe from upsetting [earlier *outligger*; Dut. *uitlegger*, outlyer].
outrun (out-run′) *v.t.* to exceed in speed; to run farther than; to run faster than; to leave behind.
outset (out′set) *n.* a setting out; commencement; beginning; start.
outside (out-sīd′) *n.* the outer surface; the exterior; the farthest limit;—*a.* pert. to the outer part; exterior; external; outdoor;—*adv.* not inside; out of doors; in the open air;—*prep.* on the outer part of; beyond.—**outsi′der** *n.* one not belonging to a particular party, set, circle, etc.; a horse considered to have no chance of winning a particular race.
outsize (out′sīz) *a.* and *n.* larger than the normal size, esp. of garments.
outskirt (out′skẹrt) *n.* generally in *pl.* **out′skirts,** the outer skirt; the border; the suburbs of a town.
outspan (out-span′) *v.t.* to unyoke; to unharness.
outspoken (out-spō′kn) *a.* not afraid to speak aloud one's opinions; bold of speech.
outstanding (out-stand′ing) *a.* standing out; prominent; conspicuous; of debts, unpaid; of work, etc., still to be done.
outstrip (out-strip′) *v.t.* to surpass in speed; to outrun; to leave behind.
outvote (out-vōt′) *v.t.* to defeat by a greater number of votes.
outward (out′wạrd) *a.* pert. to the outside; external; exterior;—*adv.* towards the outside. —**out′wards** *adv.* outward; towards the outside. —**out′wardly** *adv.* externally.
outweigh (out-wā′) *v.t.* to exceed in weight, value, influence, etc.
outwit (out-wit′) *v.t.* to defeat by cunning, stratagem, etc.; to get the better of.
outwork (out′wurk) *n.* part of fortress outside principal wall or main line of defence.
ouzel (o͝o′zl) *n.* a bird of the thrush family. Also **ou′sel** [O.E. *osle*].
ova (ō′va) *n.pl.* eggs; the female germ-cells.—**o′vary** *n.* one of two reproductive organs in female animal in which the ova are formed and developed; (*Bot.*) the part of the pistil containing the seed.—*pl.* **o′varies.**—**ovarial, ova′rian** (ō-vā′ri-ạl, -ạn) *a.* pert. to the ovary [L. *ovum*, an egg].
oval (ō′vạl) *a.* egg-shaped; elliptical;—*n.* an oval figure or thing.—**o′vally** *adv.* [L. *ovum*, an egg].
ovation (ō-vā′shun) *n.* an enthusiastic burst of applause; a triumphant reception [L. *ovatio*, a lesser form of triumph].
oven (uv′n) *n.* an iron box or enclosed chamber in a stove, range, etc., for baking or heating [O.E. *ofēn*].
over (ō′vẹr) *prep.* above; on; upon; more than; in excess of; across; from side to side of; throughout; etc.;—*adv.* above; above and beyond; going beyond; in excess; too much; past; finished; across;—*a.* upper; outer; covering;—*n.* (*Cricket*) the number of balls delivered from each wicket alternately.—**o′verall** *a.* inclusive [O.E. *ofer*].
overact (ō-vẹr-akt′) *v.t.* and *i.* to play a part (in a play) in an exaggerated manner.
overall (ō′vẹr-awl) *n.* a loose garment worn over the ordinary clothing as a protection against dirt, etc. Also *n.pl.*
overarm (ō′vẹr-årm) *a.* and *adv.* in swimming, cricket, etc., with the hand and arm raised above the shoulder.
overawe (ō-vẹr-aw′) *v.t.* to restrain by fear.
overbalance (ō-vẹr-bal′ạns) *v.t.* to exceed in weight, value, etc.;—*v.i.* to lose one's balance; to fall over.
overbear (ō-vẹr-bār′) *v.t.* to bear down; to repress; to overpower.—**overbear′ing** *a.* domineering; imperious; dogmatical.
overboard (ō′vẹr-bōrd) *adv.* over the side of a ship; out of a ship into the water.
overcast (ō-vẹr-kast′) *v.t.* to cast over; to cloud; to darken; to stitch over roughly.—**o′vercast** *a.* cloudy; dull.
overcharge (ō-vẹr-chårj′) *v.t.* and *i.* to load too heavily; to charge at too high a price.
overcoat (ō′vẹr-kōt) *n.* an outdoor garment for men worn over ordinary dress; a greatcoat; a top-coat.

overcome (ō-vẹr-kum′) *v.t.* and *i.* to conquer; to overpower; to get the better of.
overdo (ō-vẹr-dòò′) *v.t.* to do too much; to fatigue; to exaggerate; to cook too much.—**overdone′** *a.* exaggerated; over-acted; fatigued; overcooked.—*pa.t.* **overdid′**.
overdose (ō-vẹr-dōz′) *v.t.* to give an excessive dose;—*n.* too great a dose.
overdraw (ō-vẹr-draw′) *v.t.* and *i.* to exaggerate; to draw money in excess of one's credit.—**o′verdraft** *n.* act of overdrawing; amount drawn from bank in excess of credit.
overdress (ō-vẹr-dres′) *v.t.* and *i.* to dress too showily for good taste.
overdue (ō-vẹr-dū′) *a.* unpaid at right time; not having arrived at right time.
overestimate (ō-vẹr-es′ti-māt) *v.t.* to estimate too highly.
overflow (ō-vẹr-flō′) *v.t.* to flow over; to flood; to fill too full;—*v.i.* to flow over the edge, bank, etc.; to abound.—**o′verflow** *n.* what flows over; flood; excess; superabundance; surplus; pipe for surplus water.
overgrow (ō-vẹr-grō′) *v.t.* to grow beyond; to cover with growth;—*v.i.* to grow beyond normal size.—**overgrown** (ō-vẹr-grōn′) *a.* covered with grass, weeds, etc.—**o′vergrowth** *n.*
overhand (ō′vẹr-hand) *a.* and *adv.* (*Cricket, Swimming, etc.*) with the hand raised above the level of the shoulder.
overhang (ō-vẹr-hang′) *v.t.* and *i.* to hang over; to jut over; (*Fig.*) to threaten.
overhaul (ō-vẹr-hawl′) *v.t.* to examine thoroughly and set in order; to overtake in pursuit.—**o′verhaul** *n.* a thorough examination, esp, for repairs; repair.
overhead (ō-vẹr-hed) *a.* and *adv.* over the head; above; aloft; in the sky.—**overhead charges, costs,** the permanent expenses of running a business, over and above cost of manufacturing and of raw materials.
overhear (ō-vẹr-hēr′) *v.t.* to hear by accident.—*pa.p.* and *pa.t.* **overheard′**.
overjoy (ō-vẹr-joi′) *v.t.* to fill with great joy; to make excessively glad.
overland (ō′vẹr-land) *a.* and *adv.* wholly by land, esp. of a journey.
overlap (ō-vẹr-lap′) *v.t.* and *i.* to lap over; to rest upon and extend beyond.
overlay (ō-vẹr-lā′) *v.t.* to spread over; to cover completely; to span.
overleaf (ō′vẹr-lēf) *adv.* on the other side of a leaf of a book; on the next page.
overlie (ō-vẹr-lī′) *v.t.* to lie on the top of; to smother a baby by lying on it in bed.
overload (ō-vẹr-lōd′) *v.t.* to place too heavy a load on.—**o′verload** *n.* an excessive load.
overlook (ō-vẹr-look′) *v.t.* to look over; to inspect; to superintend; to fail to notice by carelessness; to excuse; to pardon.
overlord (ō′vẹr-lord) *n.* one who is lord over another; a feudal superior.
overmantel (ō′vẹr-man-tl) *n.* a piece of furniture, with mirror and shelves, fixed over the mantelpiece.
overmuch (ō-vẹr-much′) *a.* and *adv.* too [much.
overnight (ō-vẹr-nīt) *adv,* through and during the night; on the previous evening.
overpower (ō-vẹr-pou′ẹr) *v.t.* to conquer by superior strength; to subdue; to crush.
overrate (ō-vẹr-rāt′) *v.t.* to put too high a value on; to assess too highly.
overreach (ō-vẹr-rēch′) *v.t.* to reach beyond; to cheat.
override (ō-vẹr-rīd′) *v.t.* to ride over; to ride too much; to set aside; to cancel.—*pa.p.* **overrid′den.**—*pa.t.* **overrode′**.
overrule (ō-vẹr-ròòl′) *v.t.* to rule against or over; to set aside by superior authority.
overrun (ō-vẹr-run′) *v.t.* to run over; to grow over, e.g. as weeds; to take possession by spreading over, e.g. as an invading army.
oversea, overseas (ō′vẹr-sē, -sēz) *a.* and *adv.* from or to a country or place over the sea; foreign; abroad.
oversee (ō-vẹr-sē′) *v.t.* to inspect; to superintend; to supervise.—**overse′er** (sē′ẹr) *n.* an inspector; a superintendent; a supervisor; a manager.
overshadow (ō-vẹr-shad′ō) *v.t.* to cast a shadow over; (*Fig.*) to outshine (a person).
overshoe (ō′vẹr-shòò) *n.* a shoe made of india-rubber, felt, etc., worn over the ordinary shoe; a galosh.
overshoot (ō-vẹr-shòòt′) *v.t.* to shoot beyond or over; to send too far; to go too far; to exceed.—*pa.p.* and *pa.t.* **overshot′**.
oversight (ō′vẹr-sīt) *n.* failure to notice; unintentional neglect; management.
overstate (ō-vẹr-stāt′) *v.t.* to exaggerate.—**overstate′ment** *n.* exaggeration.
overstrain (ō-vẹr-strān′) *v.t.* and *i.* to strain too much; to stretch too far; (*Fig.*) to work too hard;—*n.* overwork.—**overstrained′** *a.* strained too far; (*Fig.*) exaggerated.
overstrung (ō-vẹr-strung′) *a.* too highly strung; in a state of nervous tension; of a piano, having some of the longer strings crossing others obliquely, in order to save space.
overt (ō′vẹrt) *a.* open to view; public.—**o′vertly** *adv.* [Fr. *ouvert,* open].
overtake (ō-vẹr-tāk′) *v.t.* to come up with; to catch; to take by surprise.
overthrow (ō-vẹr-thrō′) *v.t.* to throw over or down; to upset; to defeat.—**o′verthrow** *n.* the act of throwing over; defeat; ruin; fall; (*Cricket*) a ball which has been returned to, but not stopped by, a fielder near the wicket.
overtime (ō′vẹr-tīm) *n.* time at work beyond the regular hours; the extra wages paid for such work.
overture (ō′vẹr-tūr) *n.* an opening of negotiations; a proposal; an offer; (*Mus.*) an orchestral introduction to an opera, etc. [Fr. *ouvrir,* to open].
overturn (ō-vẹr-tẹrn′) *v.t.* and *i.* to throw down or over; to upset; to turn over; to capsize; to subvert.—**o′verturn** *n.*
overweening (ō-vẹr-wē′ning) *a.* thinking too much of oneself; vain; arrogant [O.E. *ofer-wenian,* to become insolent].
overweight (ō′vẹr-wāt) *n.* excess weight; extra weight beyond the just weight.
overwhelm (ō-vẹr-hwelm′) *v.t.* to crush; to submerge; to overpower.—**overwhelm′ing** *a.* decisive; irresistible.—**overwhelm′ingly** *adv.* [M.E. *whelmen,* to overturn].
overwork (ō-vẹr-wurk′) *v.t.* and *i.* to work too hard.—**o′verwork** *n.*—**overwrought** (ō-vẹr-rawt′) *a.* tired out; highly excited.
ovi- (ō′vi) *prefix* fr. L. *ovum,* an egg, used in derivatives.—**o′viduct** *n.* a passage for the egg, from the ovary.—**ovif′erous** *a.* egg-bearing.—**o′viform** *a.* egg-shaped.—**ovip′arous** *a.* producing eggs.
ovine (ō′vīn) *a.* pert. to sheep; like a sheep [L. *ovis,* a sheep].
ovo- (ō-vo) *prefix* fr. L. *ovum,* an egg, used in derivatives.—**o′void** *a.* egg-shaped; oval.
ovum (ō′vum) *n.* the female egg-cell; also, the embryo after fertilisation by the male sperm; an egg.—*pl.* **o′va** [L. *ovum,* an egg].
owe (ō) *v.t.* to be bound to repay; to be indebted for.—**owing** (ō′ing) *a.* requiring to be paid [O.E. *agan*].
owl (oul) *n.* a night bird of prey; (*Fig.*) a dull, stupid-looking person.—**owl′et** *n.* a young owl; a small owl.—**owl′ish** *a.* owl-like in appearance [O.E. *ule*].
own (ōn) *a.* is used to emphasise possession, e.g. my *own* money;—*v.t.* to possess; to acknowledge; to admit;—*v.i.* to confess.—**own′er** *n.* the rightful possessor.—**own′ership** *n.* right of possession [O.E. *agen* (*a.*); *agnian* (*v.*)].
ox (oks) *n.* a large cloven-footed and usually horned farm animal; a male cow.—*pl.* **ox′en.**—**ox′eye** *n.* one of several kinds of flowering plants [O.E. *oxa*].
oxalic acid *n.* a poisonous acid found as an acid salt in wood-sorrel.—**ox′alate** *n.* a salt of oxalic acid [Gk. *oxus,* sharp, bitter].

oxide (ok′sīd) *n.* a compound of oxygen and one other element.—**ox′idise** *v.t.* and *i.* to combine with oxygen to form an oxide; of metals, to rust, to become rusty.—**oxidisa′tion** *n.* [Gk. *oxus*, acid].
oxlip (oks′lip) *n.* species of primrose; greater cowslip [O.E. *oxa*, an ox; *slyppe*, dung].
oxy- (oks′i) *prefix* fr. Gk. *oxus* sharp, used in derivatives.—**ox′y-acetylene** (a-set′i-lēn) *a.* denoting a very hot blowpipe flame, produced by a mixture of oxygen and acetylene, and used in welding steel and other metallurgical processes.
oxygen (oks′i-jen) *n.* a colourless, odourless, and tasteless gas, forming about ⅕ by volume of the atmosphere, and essential to life, combustion, etc.—**ox′ygenate, ox′ygenise** *v.t.* to combine or treat with oxygen.—**oxygena′tion** *n.*—**oxygenous** (ok-sij′e-nus) *a.* pert. to, or obtained from, oxygen [Gk. *oxus*, acid; *gignesthai*, to be born].
oxymoron (ok-si-mō′ron) *n.* a figure of speech in which two words or phrases of opposite meaning are set together for emphasis or effect, e.g. 'falsely true' [Gk. *oxus*, sharp; *mōros*, dull, stupid].
oyster (ois′tẹr) *n.* an edible, bivalve shellfish. **oys′ter-catch′er** *n.* a wading-bird of the plover family; the sea-pie [Gk. *ostreon*].
ozone (ō′zōn) *n.* a condensed and very active form of oxygen with a peculiar, pungent odour; popularly, invigorating sea-side air.—**ozon′ic** *a.* [Gk. *ozein*, to smell.]

P

pabulum (pab′ū-lum) *n.* food; nourishment (for body and mind).—**pab′ular** *a.* [L.].
pace (pās) *n.* a step; the length of a step in walking (about 30 inches); gait; rate of movement;—*v.t.* to measure by steps; to set the speed for;—*v.i.* to walk in a slow, measured fashion.—**paced** *a.* having a certain gait.—**pac′er** *n.* one who sets the pace for another [L. *passus*, a step].
pacha (pạ-shaw′) *n.* See **pasha.**
pachy- (pak′i) *prefix* from Gk. *pachus*, thick. —**pach′yderm** *n.* a thick-skinned, non-ruminant quadruped, e.g. the elephant.—**pachyder′matous** *a.* thick-skinned; insensitive.
pacify (pas′i-fī) *v.t.* to appease; to tranquillise. —**pacif′icism, pac′ifism** *n.* a doctrine which advocates abolition of war; anti-militarism.—**pacif′icist, pac′ifist** *n.*—**pacif′ic** *a.* peaceful; calm or tranquil; peaceable, not warlike.—**pacifica′tion** *n.*—**pacif′icatory** *a.* tending to make peace; conciliatory.—**pac′ifier** *n.* [L. *pacificus*, peace-making, fr. *pax*, peace].
pack (pak) *n.* bundle for carrying, esp. on back; a lot or set; a band (of animals); a set of playing-cards; (*Rugby*) the forwards; mass of floating ice; treatment of a fevered patient by enveloping in moist wrapping; army rucksack. —*v.t.* to arrange closely in a bundle, box or bag; to stow away within; to fill, press together; to carry; to load; (with *off*) to dismiss summarily;—*v.i.* to collect in packs, bales, or bundles.—**pack′age** *n.* a bundle or parcel; a charge for packing goods.—**pack′er** *n.* one who packs.—**pack′et** *n.* a small package; a packet-boat or mail-boat; (*Slang*) a large sum of money.—**pack′et-boat** *n.* a ship that sails regularly for the conveyance of mail and passengers.—**pack′horse** *n.* a horse for carrying burdens, in panniers or in packs.—**pack′ing** *n.* any material used to pack, fill up, or make close.—**pack′ing-case** *n.* a box in which to pack goods.—**pack′man** *n.* a pedlar.—**pack′sadd′le** *n.* a saddle for supporting loads on animal's back [Fr. *paquet*].
pact (pakt) *n.* an agreement; a compact [L. *pactum*, a thing covenanted].
pad (pad) *n.* anything stuffed with soft material, to fill out or protect; a cushion; a shin-guard (in games); sheets of paper fastened together in a block; the foot or sole of certain animals;—*v.t.* to furnish with a pad; to stuff; to expand.—*pr.p.* **padd′ing.**—*pa.p.* and *pa.t.* **padd′ed.**—**padd′ing** *n.* the material used in stuffing; unnecessary matter inserted in a book or speech, etc., to expand it [etym. uncertain].
pad (pad) *n.* an easy-paced horse, or padnag; a path or road; a footpad or highway-robber; —*v.i.* to trudge along; to travel on foot [Dut. *pad*, a path].
paddle (pad′l) *n.* a short oar with a broad blade at one or each end; a blade or float of a paddle-wheel; a flipper;—*v.t.* and *i.* to propel by paddles [etym. uncertain].
paddle (pad′l) *v.i.* to walk with bare feet in shallow water; to dabble [etym. uncertain].
paddock (pad′ok) *n.* a small grass field or enclosure; on a race-course, the enclosure where horses are saddled before race [earlier *parrock*, fr. O.E. *pearroc*, a park].
paddock (pad′ok) *n.* a toad; a frog [O.E. *pade*, a toad].
paddy (pad′i) *n.* rice in the husk; rice in general [Malay *padi*].
padlock (pad′lok) *n.* a detachable lock with a hinged hoop to go through a staple or ring;—*v.t.* to fasten with a padlock [etym. uncertain].
padnag (pad′nag) *n.* an easy-paced horse [*pad* and *nag*].
padre (pȧ′drā) *n.* title given to priest; chaplain with H.M. Forces [It. and Sp. = father, fr. L. *pater*].
paean (pē′ạn) *n.* orig. a joyful song in honour of Apollo; hence, any shout, song, or hymn of triumph [Gk. *Paian*, the physician of the Gods, epithet of Apollo].
paediatrics (pē-di-at′riks) *n.* (*Med.*) the branch dealing with the diseases and disorders of children. Also **pediat′rics.**—**paediatri′cian** *n.* [Gk. *pais, paidos*, a child; *iatrikos*, healing].
pagan (pā′gạn) *n.* a heathen; one who worships false gods; an idolater;—*a.* heathenish; idolatrous.—**pa′ganish** *a.*—**pa′ganise** *v.t.* to render pagan.—**pa′ganism** *n.* [L. *paganus*, a peasant].
page (pāj) *n.* one side of a leaf of a book or manuscript;—*v.t.* to number the pages of.—**paginal** (pa′jin-ạl) *a.*—**paginate** (pa′jin-āt) *v.t.* to page a book; to number the pages consecutively.—**pagina′tion** *n.* [Fr. *page*, fr. L. *pagina*, a leaf].
page (pāj) *n.* formerly, a boy in service of a person of rank; a uniformed boy-attendant esp. in a hotel;—*v.t.* to summon by sending a page to call [Fr. *page*].
pageant (paj′ẹnt, pā′jẹnt) *n.* a show of persons in costume in procession, dramatic scenes, etc. usually illustrating history; a spectacle.—**page′antry** *n.* a brilliant display; pomp [L.L. *pagina*, a stage].
pagoda (pạ-gō′dạ) *n.* a temple or sacred tower in India, Burma, etc. [Port. *pagode*].
paid (pād) *pa.p.* and *pa.t.* of the verb **pay.**
pail (pāl) *n.* a round, open vessel of wood, tin, etc., for carrying liquids; a bucket [etym. uncertain].
paillasse (pal′i-as, pal-yas′). See **pal′liasse.**
pain (pān) *n.* bodily or mental suffering; distress; ache; penalty or punishment;—*pl.* trouble; exertion;—*v.t.* to inflict bodily or mental suffering upon.—**pain′ful** *a.* full of pain; causing pain; difficult; distressing.—**pain′fully** *adv.*—**pain′fulness** *n.*—**pain′less** *a.*—**pain′lessly** *adv.*—**pain′lessness** *n.*—**pains′taking** *a.* carefully laborious [L. *poena*, punishment].
paint (pānt) *n.* colouring matter for putting on surface with brush, etc.;—*v.t.* to cover or besmear with paint; to make a picture of with paint; to adorn with, or as with, paint;—*v.i.* to practise the art of painting.—**pain′ter** *n.* one who paints.—**pain′ting** *n.* laying on colours; the art of representing natural objects in colours; a picture in paint.—**Painted Lady,** an

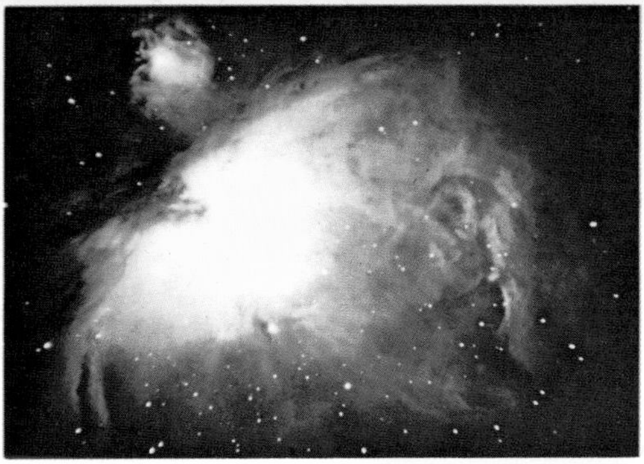

Orion nebula

THE DISTANT UNIVERSE · NEBULAE

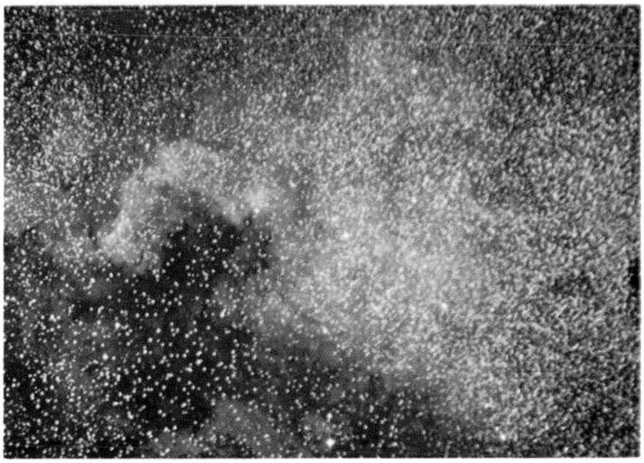

North American Nebula in Cygnus

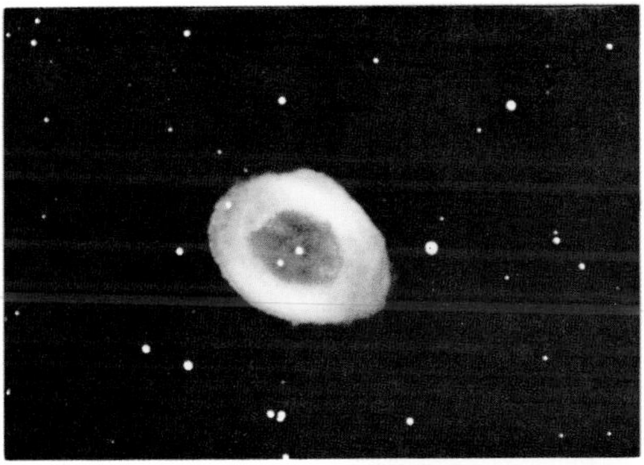

Ring Nebula in Lyra

Andromeda Nebula

Loch Tay, Scotland

LAKES and INLAND SEAS of the WORLD

Königsee, Bavaria

Sea of Galilee

Lake Titicaca

orange-red butterfly with black and white spots [L. *pingere*, to paint].

painter (pān′tẹr) *n.* a rope at the bow of a boat, used to fasten it to any other object [L. *panthera*, a fowler's net].

pair (pār) *n.* two things of a kind; a single article composed of two similar pieces, e.g. a pair of scissors; a courting, engaged, or married couple; a mated couple of animals or birds;—*v.t.* to unite in couples;—*v.i.* to be joined in couples; to mate [L. *par*, equal].

pal (pal) *n.* (*Colloq.*) a mate or partner; a close friend; an accomplice [Gipsy].

palace (pal′is) *n.* the house in which an emperor, king, bishop, or other great personage, resides; any magnificent house.—**palatial** (pạ-lā′shạl) *a.* [L. *palatium*].

paladin (pal′ạ-din) *n.* a knight-errant; one of the twelve peers of Charlemagne [L. *palatinus*, an officer of the palace].

palae-, pale-, palaeo-, paleo- (pal′ē(-o)) *prefix* from Gk. *palaios*, ancient.—**palaeography** (pal-ē-og′rạ-fi) *n.* ancient writings; art of deciphering ancient writings.—**palaeograph′ic** *a.* —**palaeog′rapher** *n.*—**palaeolith** (pal′ē-ō-lith) *n.* an unpolished stone implement of the earlier stone age.—**palaeolith′ic** *a.*—**palaeology** (pal-ē-ol′o-ji) *n.* study of antiquities; archaeology.—**palaeol′ogist** *n.*—**palaeontology** (pal-ē-on-tol′o-ji) *n.* the study of fossils.—**palaeontol′ogist** *n.*—**paleontolog′ical** *a.*—**palaeozoic** (pal-ē-ō-zō′ik) *a.* denoting the lowest fossiliferous strata and the earliest forms of life.

palanquin (pal-an-kēn′) *n.* a light, covered litter suspended from poles and borne on the shoulders of men—used in India and the East. Also **palankeen′** [Hind. = a bed].

palate (pal′ạt) *n.* the roof of the mouth; sense of taste; relish.—**pal′atable** *a.* agreeable to the taste; savoury.—**pal′atably** *adv.*—**pal′atal** *a.* pert. to palate; of a sound, produced by placing tongue against palate [L. *palatum*].

palatine (pal′ạ-tīn) *a.* pert. to a palace; having royal privileges;—*n.* one who possesses royal privileges; a count palatine.—**palat′inate** *n.* the office or dignity of a palatine; the territory under his jurisdiction [L. *Mons Palatinus*, the Palatine hill].

palaver (pạ-lȧ′vẹr) *n.* idle talk; empty conversation [Port. *palavra*, a word].

pale (pāl) *a.* faint in colour; not ruddy or fresh; whitish; dim; wan;—*v.t.* to make pale;—*v.i.* to grow white; to become pale.—**pale′ly** *adv.*—**pale′ness** *n.* lack of colour; wanness.—**pal′ish** *a.* somewhat pale.—**pale ale**, a light-coloured beer.—**pale′face** *n.* name given to a white person by Red Indians [Fr. *pâle*, fr. L. *pallidus*, pale].

pale (pāl) *n.* a pointed wooden stake; a narrow board used for making a fence; a boundary;—*v.t.* to enclose with stakes; to encompass.—**pal′ing** *n.* a fence formed of wooden stakes; fencing [L. *palus*, a stake].

palette (pal′et) *n.* a thin oval board; board on which a painter mixes his colours.—**pal′ette-knife** *n.* a thin-bladed knife for mixing colours [L. *pala*, a spade].

palfrey (pawl′, pal′fri) *n.* a small saddle-horse, esp. for a lady [O. Fr. *palefrei*, fr. L. *paraveredus*, an extra post-horse].

Pali (pȧ′lē) *n.* the sacred language of the Buddhists [Sans. *pali*, canon].

palimpsest (pal′imp-sest) *n.* a parchment-manuscript that has been written upon twice, the first writing having been erased [Gk. *palin*, again; *psēstos*, rubbed].

palindrome (pal′in-drōm) *n.* a word or sentence that is the same when read backward or forward, e.g. *level* [Gk. *palin*, back; *dromos*, running].

palisade (pal-is-ād′) *n.* fence of pales or stakes driven into ground;—*v.t.* to enclose with such fence [L. *palus*, stake].

pall (pawl) *n.* a large, usually black cloth laid over the coffin at a funeral; an ecclesiastical mantle; (*Fig.*) a covering [L. *pallium*, a cloak].

pall (pawl) *v.t.* to make tedious or insipid;—*v.i.* to become tedious or insipid [prob. shortened fr. *appal*].

palladian (pạ-lā′di-ạn) *a.* denoting a classical style of architecture [fr. Andria *Palladio*, a 16th cent. Italian architect].

palladium (pa-lā′di-um) *n.* a rare metal of the platinum group [fr. Gk. *Pallas*].

Palladium (pạ-lā′di-um) *n.* a safeguard.

pallet (pal′et) *n.* a small, rude bed; a straw mattress [Fr. *paille*, straw].

pallet (pal′et) *n.* a palette; a tool with a flat wooden blade used by potters and other workers [form of *palette*].

palliasse (pal′i-as, pal-yas′) *n.* hard under-mattress of straw. Also **paillasse** [Fr. *paille*, straw, fr. L. *palea*, chaff].

palliate (pal′i-āt) *v.t.* to lessen or abate without curing; to excuse or extenuate.—**pallia′tion** *n.*—**palliative** (pal′i-ā-tiv) *a.* serving to extenuate, to mitigate.—*n.* that which excuses, mitigates, alleviates [L. *palliatus*, dressed in a cloak].

pallid (pal′id) *a.* deficient in colour; pale; wan. —**pall′idly** *adv.*—**pall′idness** *n.*—**pall′or** *n.* paleness [L. *pallidus*, pale].

pall-mall (pel-mel′) *n.* an old game in which a wooden ball was driven with a mallet through an iron arch; the alley in which the game was played [It. *palla*, a ball; *maglio*, a mallet].

palm (pȧm) *n.* the inner, slightly concave surface of hand, between wrist and fingers; lineal measure, reckoned as 3 or 4 inches; flat, expanding end of any arm-like projection, esp. blade of oar; that part of ski on which it runs; —*v.t.* to conceal in the palm; to impose by fraud (with 'off').—**palmar** (pal′mẹr) *a.* pert. to the palm.—**pal′mate** *a.* having shape of hand; (*Zool.*) web-footed.—**palmist** (pȧ′, or pal′mist) *n.* one who claims to tell fortunes by the palm of the hand.—**palmistry** (pȧ′ or pal′mis-tri) *n.* telling fortunes by the lines on the hand [L. *palma*, the palm].

palm (pȧm) *n.* a branchless, tropical tree having at its summit a tuft of large leaves shaped like the palm of the hand; a branch or leaf of this tree used as a symbol of victory; prize of honour.—**palmer** (pȧ′mẹr) *n.* in the Middle Ages, one who visited the Holy Land, and bore a branch of palm in token thereof; an itinerant monk.—**palmet′to** *n.* a species of palm tree.—**palmif′erous** *a.* producing palm trees.—**palm′y** *a.* bearing palms; (*Fig.*) prosperous; flourishing.—**palm′-butt′er** *n.* palm-oil.—**palm′-oil** *n.* an oil or fat obtained from fruit of species of palms, and used to make soap, candles, etc.; (*Slang*) bribe or tip.—**Palm Sunday**, Sunday before Easter [L. *palma*, a palm].

palmyra (pal-mī′ra) *n.* a tall E. Indian palm [Port. *palmeira*].

palomino (pal-o-minō) *n.* a cream-coloured horse of Arabian stock. Its mane and tail are usually lighter coloured. [Sp.]

palpable (pal′pạ-bl) *a.* that may be touched or felt; certain; obvious.—**pal′pably** *adv.*—**pal′pableness** *n.*—**pal′pate** *v.t.* to examine with the hand.—**palpa′tion** *n.* examination by touch [L. *palpare*, to feel].

palpitate (pal′pi-tāt) *v.i.* to beat rapidly, as heart; to throb; to pulsate.—**palpita′tion** *n.* [L. *palpitare*, fr. *palpare*, to feel].

palsy (pawl′zi) *n.* paralysis; a loss of power of movement or of feeling;—*v.t.* to paralyse.—**pal′sied** *a.* [fr. *paralysis*].

palter (pawl′tẹr) *v.i.* to trifle with; to deal evasively; to use trickery; to dodge.—**pal′terer** *n.*—**pal′try** *a.* mean; worthless.—**pal′triness** *n.* [etym. uncertain].

paludal (pal′ū-dạl, pa-lū′dạl) *a.* pert to a marsh; malarial [L. *palus*, *paludis*, a marsh].

pampas (pam′pạz) *n.pl.* vast grassy, treeless plains in S. America [Sp. *pampa*, fr. Peruv. *bamba*, a plain].

pamper (pam′pẹr) *v.t.* to gratify unduly; to

over-indulge; to coddle.—**pam'perer** *n.* [perh. Low Ger. *pampen*, to cram].

pamphlet (pam´flet) *n.* a thin, paper-covered, unbound book; a short treatise or essay on a current topic.—**pamphleteer** (pam-fle-tēr') *n.* a writer of pamphlets [O.Fr. *Pamphilet*, the title of a medieval poem (taken as the type of a small book)].

pan (pan) *n.* a broad, shallow metal vessel for household use; anything resembling this; of an old type of gun, part of the flint-lock that held the priming; abbrev. of brain-pan, the upper part of the skull:—*v.t.* and *i.* to wash gold-bearing soil in a pan in order to separate earth and gold; to move a cinema-camera, while it is taking a picture horizontally (fr. *panorama*) [O.E. *panne*].

pan- (pan) *prefix* fr. Gk. *pas*, *pantos*, all, used in such words as—**pan-Amer'ican** *a.* pert. to movement of the 21 American republics to foster collaboration between N. and S. America.

panacea (pan-a-sē´a) *n.* a cure for all diseases; a universal remedy [Gk. *panakeia*, a universal remedy].

panache (pan-ash') *n.* plume of feathers used as head-dress; a swaggering manner [Fr.].

panama (pan-a-må') *n.* a hat made of fine, pliant strawlike material [made in S. America, but not in *Panama*].

pancake (pan´kāk) *n.* a thin cake of batter fried in a pan;—*v.i.* to land an aeroplane almost vertically and in a level position.

panchromatic (pan-krō-mat´ik) *a.* (*Phot.*) pert. to plates or films which, although reproduction is in monochrome, give to all colours their proper values [Gk. *pan*, all; *chrōma*, colour].

pancreas (pan´krē-as) *n.* (*Anat.*) digestive gland behind stomach; in animals, the sweetbread.—**pancreat'ic** *a.* [Gk. *pan*, all; *kreas*, flesh].

panda (pan-da) *n.* a raccoon-like animal found in S. and E. borders of Tibet; the bear-cat [Native word].

pandect (pan´dekt) *n.* usually a treatise that contains the whole of any science;—*pl.* any code of laws [Gk. *pandektēs*, all receiving, comprehensive].

pandemic (pan-dem´ik) *a.* of a disease, universal; widely distributed; affecting a nation [Gk. *pan*, all; *dēmos*, people].

pandemonium (pan-de-mō´ni-um) *n.* the abode of evil spirits; any disorderly, noisy place or gathering; a riotous uproar [Gk. *pan*, all; *daimōn*, a demon].

pander (pan´der) *n.* (*fem.* **pan'deress**) a go-between in base love intrigues; one who ministers to the evil desires and passions of others;—*v.i.* to act as a pander; to help to satisfy any unworthy desires [fr. *Pandarus*, in the story of Troilus and Cressida].

pane (pān) *n.* a sheet of glass in a window; a square in a pattern.—**paned** (pānd) *a.* [Fr. *pan*, a flat section].

panegyric (pan-e-jir´ik) *n.* a speech of praise; a eulogium.—**panegyr'ical** *a.*—**pan'egyrist** *n.* one who writes or pronounces a eulogy.—**pane´gyrise** *v.t.* to praise highly [Gk. *pan*, all; *agora*, an assembly].

panel (pan´el) *n.* a rectangular piece of cloth, parchment, or wood; a sunk portion of a door; a list of jurors; a jury; list of medical practitioners registered to serve patients insured under National Health Service Act.—*v.t.* to divide into, or decorate with, panels.—**pan'elling** *n.* panelled work [O.Fr. = a small panel].

pang (pang) *n.* a sudden pain, physical or mental; a throe [etym. doubtful].

panic (pan´ik) *n.* sudden terror, often unreasoning; infectious fear;—*a.* extreme and illogical (of fear);—*v.i.* to be seized with sudden, uncontrollable fright.—*pa.t.* **pan'icked**.—**pan'icky** *a.* affected by panic.—**pan'ic-mong'er** *n.* one who tries to create panic.—**pan'ic-strick'en** *a.* seized with paralysing fear [Gk. = fear excited by *Pan*].

panjandrum (pan-jan´drum) *n.* a burlesque title for an imaginary potentate; a pompous person [invented word].

pannier (pan´yer) *n.* one of a pair of baskets carried on each side of a pack-animal; a puffing-out round hips of a lady's skirt; framework to achieve this [L. *panarium*, a bread-basket].

pannikin (pan´i-kin) *n.* a small tin mug [fr. *pan*].

panoply (pan´o-pli) *n.* a complete suit of armour; anything that covers or envelops completely.—**pan'oplied** *a.* fully armed [Gk. *pan*, all; *hopla*, arms].

panorama (pan-o-rá´ma) *n.* a complete view in every direction; a picture exhibited by being unrolled and made to pass continuously before the spectator.—**panoram'ic** *a.* [Gk. *pan*, all; *horama*, a view].

pansy (pan´zi) *n.* a cultivated species of violet. Also called Heart's-ease or Love-in-Idleness; (*Slang*) an effeminate man [Fr. *pensée*, thought].

pant (pant) *v.i.* to breathe quickly and in a laboured manner; to gasp for breath; to yearn (with ' for ' or ' after ');—*v.t.* to utter gaspingly;—*n.* a gasp [O.Fr.].

pantaloon (pan-ta-lòòn') *n.* an elderly, ridiculous character in Italian comedy of former times;—*pl.* tight trousers [It. *pantalone*, buffoon, who was always represented with long tight trousers].

pantechnicon (pan-tek´ni-kon) *n.* storage place for furniture; large van for transporting furniture [Gk. *pan*, all; *technē*, art].

pantheism (pan´thē-izm) *n.* the doctrine that identifies God with the universe, everything being considered as part of or a manifestation of Him.—**pan'theist** *n.*—**pantheis'tic(al)** *a.*—**pantheol'ogy** *n.* a system which embraces all religions and all gods [Gk. *pan*, all; *theos*, god].

Pantheon (pan´thē-on) *n.* a circular temple in Rome; a building in Paris, where the illustrious dead of France are buried; a temple dedicated to all the gods [Gk. *pan*, all; *theos*, a god].

panther (pan´ther) *n.* (*fem.* **pan'theress**) a variety of leopard [Gk. *panthēr*].

pantile (pan´tīl) *n.* a roofing tile curved like the letter S [*pan* and *tile*].

panto- (pan´tō) *prefix* fr. Gk. *pas*, *pantos*, all, used in derivatives.—**pan'tograph** *n.* an instrument for copying drawings, maps, etc., on an enlarged, a reduced, or the same scale [Gk. *graphein*, to write].

pantomime (pan´tō-mīm) *n.* a dramatic entertainment in dumb show; a Christmas-time dramatic and spectacular entertainment usually founded on a fairy tale;—*v.t.* and *i.* to act or express by gestures only.—**pantomim'ic** *a.*—**pan'tomimist** *n.* [Gk. *pas*, *pantos*, all; *mimos*, mimic].

pantry (pan´tri) *n.* a small room for storing food or kitchen utensils [L. *panis*, bread].

pants (pants) *n.pl.* (*Colloq.*) trousers; short trousers of a light fabric; men's long tight drawers [abbrev. of *pantaloons*].

panzer (pant´ser) *a.* (*World War* 2) armoured, esp. in **panzer division**, a mechanised division of the German army [Ger. *Panzer*, armour].

pap (pap) *n.* soft food for infants, etc., e.g. bread soaked in milk [fr. baby language].

pap (pap) *n.* a nipple; a teat; a woman's breast; a small round hill resembling a nipple in shape [M.E. *pappe*].

papacy (pā-pa-si) *n.* the office and dignity of the Pope; Popes collectively.—**papal** (pā´pal) *a.* [It. *papa*, father].

papaverous (pa-pav´er-us) *a.* pert. to or resembling the poppy. Also **papavera'ceous** *a.* [L. *papaver*, the poppy].

papaw (pa-paw') *n.* a palm-like S. American tree.

paper (pā´per) *n.* a material made by pressing pulp of rags, straw, wood, etc., into thin flat sheets; a sheet of paper written or printed on; a newspaper; an article or essay; a document; paper-hangings for covering walls; a set of examination questions;—*n.pl.* document(s) establishing one's identity; ship's official documents;—*a.* consisting of paper;—*v.t.* to cover with paper.—**pa'pery** *a.* resembling paper.—**pa'per-chase** *n.* a cross-country race in which runners going ahead lay a trail of torn-up pieces of paper.—**pa'per-clip** *n.* an appliance for holding together sheets of paper, etc.—**pa'per-hang'er** *n.* a tradesman, usually a painter, who hangs paper on walls.—**pa'per-knife** *n.* a knife with a blunt blade for opening envelopes, etc.—**pa'per-mon'ey** *n.* official pieces of paper issued by a government or bank for circulation instead of gold, silver, etc., coins; bank-notes.—**pa'per-weight** *n.* small, heavy object to prevent loose sheets of paper from being displaced [Gk. *papuros,* a Nile rush fr. which paper was made].

papier-mâché (pap'yā-mȧ'shā) *n.* paper pulp, mixed with glue, etc., shaped or moulded into articles, e.g. trays, fancy boxes, etc. [Fr. *papier,* paper; *mâché,* chewed].

papilionaceous (pą-pil-yo-nā'shus) *a.* like a butterfly [L. *papilio,* a butterfly].

papilla (pą-pil'a) *n.* a small nipple-shaped protuberance in a part of the body, e.g. on surface of tongue [L. *papilla,* the nipple].

papist (pā'pist) *n.* a supporter of the papal system; a Roman Catholic.—**papist'ic(al)** *a.* pert. to the doctrines, etc., of the Church of Rome; Popish.—**pa'pistry** *n.* Popery [Fr. *papiste,* fr. *pape,* the Pope].

papoose (pą-po͝os') *n.* a N. American Indian baby.

pappus (pap'us) *n.* down, as on the seeds of the thistle, dandelion, etc.—**pappose** (pap-ōs') *a.* downy [Gk. *pappos,* down].

papula, papule (pap'ū-lą, -ūl) *n.* a pimple on the skin [L.].

papyrus (pą-pī'rus) *n.* a species of reed, the pith of which was used by the ancients for making paper; a manuscript on papyrus.—*pl.* **papy'ri** [Gk. *papuros,* an Egyptian rush].

par (pȧr) *n.* equality of value or circumstances; face value (of stocks and shares); (*Golf*) the number of strokes for hole or course in perfect play [L. *par,* equal].

parable (par'ą-bl) *n.* fable or allegory with a moral.—**parabol'ical** *a.*—**parabol'ically** *adv.* [Gk. *parabolē,* a comparison].

parabola (pą-ra'bo-la) *n.* (*Geom.*) a conic section made by a plane parallel to side of cone.—**parabol'ic(al)** *a.*—**para'boloid** *n.* solid formed when parabola is revolved round its axis [Gk. *para,* beside; *bolē,* a throw].

parachute (par'ą-sho͝ot) *n.* a collapsible umbrella-like device used to retard the descent of a falling body.—**par'achutist** *n.*—**par'achute-troops** *n.pl.* See **paratroops** [Fr. *parer,* to make ready; *chute,* a fall].

paraclete (par'a-klēt) *n.* (*Bib.*) the name given to the Holy Ghost; one called to aid or support; an advocate [Gk. *paraklētos,* called to help].

parade (pą-rād') *n.* display; show; a public walk or procession; a muster of troops for drill or inspection; the ground on which such a muster takes place;—*v.t.* to make a display or spectacle of; to marshal in military order;—*v.i.* to march in military array; to march in procession with display [L. *parare,* to prepare].

paradigm (par'ą-dim) *n.* an example; a model; (*Gram.*) a word, esp. a noun, verb, etc., given as an example of grammatical inflexions.—**paradigmat'ic** *a.*—**paradigmat'ically** *adv.* [Gk. *paradeigma,* a model].

paradise (par'ą-dīs) *n.* the garden of Eden; Heaven; a state of bliss.—**paradisaic** (par-a-di-sā'ik), **paradisa'ical** *a.* pert. to or like paradise [Gk. *paradeisos,* a pleasure-ground].

paradox (par'a-doks) *n.* a statement seemingly absurd or self-contradictory, but really founded on truth.—**paradox'ical** *a.*—**paradox'ically** *adv.* [Gk. *para,* against; *doxa,* an opinion].

paraffin (par'ą-fin) *n.* a white wax-like substance obtained from shale, coal-tar, wood, etc.; oil from the same source used as an illuminant or lubricant [L. *parum,* little; *affinis,* related].

paragon (par'a-gon) *n.* a pattern of excellence; a person or thing of the highest excellence [It. *paragone*].

paragraph (par'ą-graf) *n.* a distinct part of a writing; a section or sub-division of a passage, indicated by the sign ¶, or begun on a new line;—*v.t.* to arrange in paragraphs.—**paragraph'ic** *a.* [Gk. *paragraphos,* a marginal stroke].

parakeet (par'ą-kēt) *n.* a small long-tailed parrot. Also **par'rakeet, par'oquet** [Fr. *perroquet,* a parrot].

paraldehyde (par-al'de-hīd) *n.* a powerful narcotic [Gk. *para* and *aldehyde*].

parallel (par'ą-lel) *a.* continuously at equal distance; precisely corresponding; similar;—*n.* a line equidistant from another at all points; a thing exactly like another; a comparison; a line of latitude;—*v.t.* to make parallel; to represent as similar; to compare.—*pr.p.* **par'alleling** or **par'allelling**.—*pa.p.* and *pa.t.* **par'alleled** or **par'allelled**.—**par'allelism** *n.* the state of being parallel; comparison, resemblance.—**parallel bars,** horizontal bars for gymnastic exercises [Gk. *parallēlos,* beside one another].

parallelogram (par-ą-lel'ō-gram) *n.* a four-sided plane figure with both pairs of opposite sides parallel [Gk. *parallēlos,* beside one another; *gramma,* a line].

paralysis (pą-ral'i-sis) *n.* (*Med.*) loss of power of movement or sensation.—**paralyse** (par'ą-līz) *v.t.* to affect with paralysis; to make useless; to cripple.—**paralyt'ic** *a.* pert. to, affected with, paralysis;—*n.* one affected with paralysis.—**infantile paralysis,** inflammation of grey matter in spinal cord, usually in children; poliomyelitis [Gk. *para,* beside; *luein,* to loosen; doublet of *palsy*].

paramount (par'ą-mount) *a.* superior; of highest importance; chief.—**par'amountcy** *n.* the quality of being paramount.—**par'amountly** *adv.* [Fr. *par amont,* upwards].

paramour (par'ą-mo͝or) *n.* a partner in an illicit love intrigue; a mistress [Fr. *par amour,* through love].

paranoia, paranoea (par-ą-noi'ą, -nē'ą) *n.* (*Med.*) a form of chronic insanity, often characterised by delusions of grandeur, persecution, etc.—**paranoi'ac** *a.* and *n.* [Gk. *para,* beside; *noein,* to think].

parapet (par'ą-pet) *n.* a low wall or railing at the edge of a bridge, quay, balcony, etc.; a breastwork to protect soldiers, esp. a mound along the front of a trench [It. *parare,* to ward off; *petto,* the breast].

paraphernalia (par-ą-fẹr-nā'li-ą) *n.pl.* personal belongings; furnishings or accessories; (*Law*) goods of wife beyond dowry [Gk. *para,* beyond; *phernē,* a dower].

paraphrase (par'ą-frāz) *n.* a re-statement of a passage; a free translation into the same or another language; an interpretation; a versified passage of Scripture;—*v.t.* to express in other words; to interpret freely.—**par'aphrast** *n.* one who paraphrases.—**paraphras'tic** *a.*—**paraphras'tically** *adv.* [Gk. *para; phrazein,* to speak].

parasite (par'ą-sīt) *n.* formerly, one who habitually ate at the table of another, repaying with flattery; a hanger-on; a toady; a plant or animal that lives on another.—**parasit'ic** *a.*—**parasit'ically** *adv.*—**parasitol'ogy** *n.* the study of parasites, esp. as causes of disease.—**parasitolog'ical** *a.*—**parasitol'ogist** *n.* [Gk. *parasitos;* fr. *para,* beside; *sitos,* food].

parasol (par'ą-sol) *n.* a small, light umbrella used to protect from the sun's rays [It. *parare,* to ward off; *sole,* the sun].

paratroops (par′ạ-tro͝ops) *n.pl.* (*World War* 2) troops organised to descend by parachute with their equipment from aeroplanes and gliders.—**par′atrooper** *n.*

paravane (par′ạ-vān) *n.* (*Naval War*) a contrivance like an under-water kite towed from a ship's bows, used to sweep aside and cut the moorings of submerged mines [Gk. *para*, beside; and *vane*].

parboil (pȧr′boil) *v.t.* to boil partially; (*Fig.*) to overheat [L. *per*, thoroughly, confused with 'part'; *boil*].

parcel (pȧr′sẹl) *n.* (*Arch.*) a part or portion; a bundle or package (wrapped in paper); a number of things forming a group or lot; a piece of land;—*v.t.* to divide into portions; to distribute; to wrap up.—*pr.p.* **par′celling**.—*pa.p.* and *p.t.* **par′celled** [Fr. *parcelle*, a little part].

parch (pȧrch) *v.t.* to scorch; to shrivel with heat; to dry to an extreme degree;—*v.i.* to be scorched [M.E. *parchen*].

parchment (pȧrch′mẹnt) *n.* the skin of a sheep or goat, etc., prepared for writing on; a document written on this [fr. *Pergamum* in Asia Minor, where first used].

pard (pȧrd) *n.* the leopard or panther; (*Poet.*) any spotted animal [Gk. *pardos*].

pardon (pȧr′don) *v.t.* to forgive; to free from punishment; to excuse;—*n.* forgiveness; remission of a penalty.—**par′donable** *a.* excusable.—**par′donably** *adv.*—**par′donableness** *n.*—**par′doner** *n.* one who pardons; formerly, one who sold pardons or papal indulgences [Fr. *pardonner*].

pare (pār) *v.t.* to cut or shave off; to remove the outer skin; to peel.—**par′er** *n.*—**par′ing** *n.* the action of paring; that which is pared off [Fr. *parer*, to make ready].

paregoric (par-e-gor′ik) *a.* soothing; assuaging pain;—*n.* a soothing medicine [Gk. *parēgorikos*, comforting].

parent (pār-ẹnt) *n.* a father or mother; one who, or that which, brings forth or produces.—**par′entage** *n.* descent from parents; birth; extraction.—**parental** (pạ-rent′ạl) *a.* pert. to, or becoming, parents; tender; affectionate.—**parent′ally** *adv.* [L. *parere*, to bring forth].

parenthesis (pạ-ren′the-sis) *n.* a word or sentence inserted in a passage independently of the grammatical sequence and usually marked off by brackets, dashes, or commas;—**paren′theses** (-sēz) *n.pl.* round brackets ( ), used for this.—**parenthet′ic, parenthet′ical** *a.* expressed as a parenthesis; interposed.—**parenthet′ically** *adv.* [Gk. *para*, beside; *en*, in; *thesis*, a placing].

parhelion (par-hē′li-on) *n.* a mock sun.—*pl.* **parhe′lia** [Gk. *para*, beside; *hēlios*, the sun].

pariah (par′, pār′i-ạ) *n.* in S. India, one deprived of all religious or social rights; a member of the lowest or no caste; an outcast from society; a yellow, ownerless dog in India [Tamil, *paraiyar*, a drummer].

parietal (pạ-rī′e-tạl) *a.* pert. to a wall; pert. to the wall of the body or its cavities [L. *paries* a wall].

parish (par′ish) *n.* a sub-division of a county; orig. an ecclesiastical district; a district under a priest or clergyman;—*a.* pert. to a parish.—**parishioner** (pạ-rish′on-ẹr) *n.* an inhabitant of a parish; a member of a parish church [Gk. *para*, beside; *oikos*, a dwelling].

parity (par′i-ti) *n.* equality; analogy; close correspondence [L. *par*, *paris*, equal].

park (pȧrk) *n.* a large enclosed piece of ground, usually with grass and trees, attached to a country house; similar ground in towns, for public use and recreation; a sports' ground; a place set aside for storing motor-cars, etc.;—*v.t.* to enclose in a park; to leave in a park, e.g. a motor-car [O.E. *pearroc*; Fr. *parc*].

parka (pȧr′kạ) *n.* an Eskimo outer garment of undressed skin [Aleutian].

parlance (pȧr′lạns) *n.* a way of speaking; a form of speech.—**parley** (pȧr′li) *n.* a meeting between leaders of opposing forces to discuss terms;—*v.i.* to hold a discussion about terms [Fr. *parler*, to speak].

parliament (pȧr′lạ-mẹnt) *n.* the supreme legislature of the United Kingdom, composed of the House of Lords and House of Commons; any similar foreign assembly.—**parliament′ary** *a.* pert. to, enacted by, or according to, the established rules of parliament; of language, admissible in parliamentary debate, hence, decorous and non-abusive.—**parliamenta′rian** *n.* a skilled debater in parliament [Fr. *parlement*, fr. *parler*, to speak].

parlour (pȧr′lur) *n.* a family sitting-room; a private room in an inn; orig. a room for private conversation [Fr. *parloir*, fr. *parler*, to speak].

parlous (pȧr′lus) *a.* hard to escape from; perilous; critical [fr. *perilous*].

Parnassus (pȧr-nas′us) *n.* a mountain in ancient Greece, sacred to Apollo and the Muses; (*Fig.*) poetry; an anthology of poetry.—**Parnass′ian** *a.* pert. to, or inhabiting, Parnassus;—*n.* one of a school of later 19th cent. French poets, who were reactionaries to the Romantic school.

parochial (pạ-rō′ki-ạl) *a.* pert. to a parish; provincial; narrow-minded; petty.—**paro′chially** *adv.*—**paro′chialism** *n.* [L. *parochia*, a parish, fr. Gk. *paroikein*, to dwell near].

parody (par′o-di) *n.* an imitation of a poem, song, etc., where the style is the same but the theme ludicrously different; a feeble imitation;—*v.t.* to write a parody of; to burlesque in verse.—**par′odist** *n.* [Gk. *para*, beside (i.e. imitating); *ōdē*, a song].

parole (pạ-rōl′) *n.* word of honour, esp. a promise given by a prisoner of war not to attempt to escape [Fr. *parole*, a word].

paronomasia (par-ō-nō-mā′zi-ạ) *n.* a play on words; a pun.—**par′onym** *n.* a word similar in sound to another but different in spelling and meaning, e.g. *fair* and *fare*.—**paron′ymous** *a.* [Gk. *para*, beside; *onoma*, a name].

parotid (pạ-rot′id) *a.* near the ear;—*n.* a large salivary gland, in front of and below the ear [Gk. *para*, beside; *ous*, *ōtos*, the ear].

paroxysm (par′ok-sizm) *n.* sudden, violent attack of pain, rage, laughter; fit; convulsion [Gk. *para*, beyond; *oxus*, sharp].

parquet (pȧr′ket) *n.* flooring of wooden blocks instead of boards;—*v.t.* to lay such a floor.—**parquetry** (pȧr′ke-tri) *n.* [Fr. *parquet*, flooring].

parr (pȧr) *n.* a young salmon [etym. uncertain].

parrakeet (par′a-kēt) *n.* Same as **parakeet**.

parricide (par′i-sīd) *n.* one who murders his father, a parent, a near relative, or a person who is venerated; the crime itself [L. *pater*, a father; *caedere*, to kill].

parrot (par′ot) *n.* tropical bird with bright plumage and short hooked beak; one who repeats words, actions, ideas, etc. of another [Fr. *perroquet*, a parrot].

parry (par′i) *v.t.* to ward off; to turn aside; to avoid; to evade [L. *parare*, to prepare].

parse (pȧrz) *v.t.* to classify a word or analyse a sentence in terms of grammar.—**par′sing** *n.* [fr. school question in L. *quae pars orationis?* What part of speech?].

Parsee, Parsi (pȧr′sē) *n.* a follower of the disciples of Zoroaster, or their descendants in Persia and India; a fire-worshipper.—**Par′seeism** *n.* [Pers. *Parsi*, a Persian].

parsimony (pȧr′si-mon-i) *n.* stinginess; undue economy; excessive thrift.—**parsimo′nious** (pȧr-so-mō′ni-us) *a.* stingy; excessively frugal; niggardly.—**parsimo′niously** *adv.*—**parsimo′niousness** *n.* [L. *parcere*, to spare].

parsley (pȧrs′li) *n.* a garden herb, used as a flavouring or garnish in cookery.—**cow parsley**, wild chervil [Gk. *petroselinon*, rock parsley].

parsnip (pȧrs′nip) *n.* a root-vegetable, carrot-like in shape [L. fr. *pastinare*, to dig up].

parson (pȧr′sn) *n.* a clergyman; the incumbent of a parish.—**par′sonage** *n.* the residence of a parson.—**parson's nose**, the rump of a fowl [*person*].

part (part) *n.* a portion, fragment, or section of a whole; a share or lot; a division; an actor's role; duty; interest; a melody in a harmonic piece;—*pl.* accomplishments or talents; region;—*v.t.* to divide; to separate; to share;—*v.i.* to separate; to take leave; to part with or give up; (*Slang*) to pay out money.—**part'ing** *n.* the act of separating; leave-taking; division; dividing-line;—*a.* given on taking leave.—**part'ly** *adv.* in part; in some measure or degree.—**part'ible** *a.* divisible.—**partibil'ity** *n.* susceptibility of division or partition [L. *pars*, a part].

partake (pår-tāk') *v.t.* and *i.* to have or take a share in; to take food or drink.—*pa.p.* **partak'en**.—*pa.t.* **partook'**.—**parta'ker** *n.* [fr. *part* and *take*].

parterre (pår-ter') *n.* an ornamental arrangement of flower-beds; the pit of a theatre [Fr. *par terre*, on the earth].

parthenogenesis (pår-the-nō-jen'e-sis) *n.* reproduction without sexual union [Gk. *parthenos*, virgin; *genesis*, birth].

Parthia (pår'thi-a) *n.* (*Geog.*) an ancient country corresponding to N. Iran.—**a Parthian shot**, originally, a deadly arrow shot while the Parthian soldier was pretending to retreat; a parting shot.

partial (pår'shal) *a.* affecting only a part; not total; inclined to favour unreasonably.—**par'tially** *adv.*—**partial'ity** *n.* quality of being partial; favouritism; fondness for [L. *pars*, part].

participate (pår-tis'i-pāt) *v.t.* and *i.* to share in; to partake (foll. by 'in').—**partic'ipant** *n.* a partaker;—*a.* sharing.—**partic'ipator** *n.*—**participation** (pår-tis-i-pā'shun) *n.* [L. *pars*, part; *capere*, to take].

participle (pår'ti-si-pl) *n.* (*Gram.*) an adjective formed by inflection from a verb.—**particip'ial** *a.* [L. *particeps*, sharing].

particle (pår'ti-kl) *n.* a minute portion of matter; the least possible amount; an atom; (*Gram.*) a part of speech which is uninflected and of subordinate importance [L. *particula*, a little part].

parti-coloured (pår'ti-kul-urd) *a.* partly of one colour, partly of another; variegated. Also **par'ty-col'oured**.

particular (pår-tik'ū-lar) *a.* relating to a single person or thing, not general; considered apart from others; minute in details; nice or fastidious in taste;—*n.* a single point or circumstance; a detail or item.—**partic'ularly** *adv.* especially; in a high degree; with great attention.—**particular'ity** *n.* quality or state of being particular; individual characteristic.—**partic'ularise** *v.t.* and *i.* to mention one by one; to give in detail; to specify.—**particularisa'tion** *n.* [L. *particularis*].

partisan (pår'ti-zan) *n.* adherent, often prejudiced, of a party or cause; a member of irregular troops engaged in risky enterprises;—*a.* adhering to a faction.—**par'tisanship** *n.* adherence to a party [Fr.].

partisan, partizan (par'ti-zan) *n.* a long-handled pike [O.Fr. *pertuisane*].

partition (pår-tish'un) *n.* division or separation; any of the parts into which a thing is divided; that which divides or separates, as a wall, etc.;—*v.t.* to divide into shares; to divide by walls.—**par'titive** *n.* a word expressing partition; a distributive;—*a.* denoting a part.—**par'titively** *adv.* [L. *partitio*].

partner (pårt'ner) *n.* a partaker; a sharer; an associate, esp. in business; a husband or wife; one who dances with another; in golf, tennis, etc., one who plays with another;—*v.t.* in games, to play with another against opponents.—**part'nership** *n.* the state of being a partner; the association of two or more persons for business [L. *pars*, a part].

partridge (pår'trij) *n.* a small game-bird of the grouse family [Gk. *perdix*].

parturient (pår-tū'ri-ent) *a.* bringing forth or about to bring forth young; prolific.—**parturi'tion** *n.* the act of bringing forth young [L. *parturire*, to be in labour].

party (pår'ti) *n.* a number of persons united in opinion; a political group; a social assembly; a participator; an accessory; a litigant;—*a.* pert. to a party or faction.—**par'ty-col'oured** *a.* parti-coloured [O.Fr. *partir*, to divide].

parvenu (pår've-nū) *n.* an upstart; a self-made person; one who has risen socially, esp. by the influence of money [Fr. fr. *parvenir*, to arrive at].

Pasch (pask) *n.* the Jewish festival of the Passover; Easter.—**Pas'chal** *a.* [Heb. *pasach*, to pass over].

pasha (på'sha, pa-sha') *n.* a Turkish official of high rank [Turk.].

pasquin (pas'kwin) *n.* a writer of lampoons or satires; a lampoon or satire;—*v.t.* and *i.* to lampoon.—**pas'quinade** *n.* a lampoon [fr. It. *Pasquino*, a cobbler in whose yard a mutilated Roman statue was dug up, on which political lampoons were afterwards written or posted].

pass (pås) *v.t.* to go by, beyond, through etc.; to spend; to exceed; to approve; to disregard; to circulate; to send through; to move;—*v.i.* to go; to elapse; to undergo examination successfully; to happen; to die; to circulate.—*pa.p.* **passed, past**.—*pa.t.* **passed**.—*n.* a passage or way, esp. a narrow and difficult one; a passport; a permit; condition; success in an examination, test, etc.; in football, hockey, etc., the passing of the ball from one player to another.—**pass'able** *a.* that may be passed or crossed; fairly good; admissible; current.—**pass'ably** *adv.*—**pass'book** *n.* a small book issued by a bank in which are entered a customer's deposits and withdrawals.—**pass'key** *n.* a latch-key; a master-key.—**pass'port** *n.* an official document, issued by a State Department, granting permission to travel abroad.—**pass'word** *n.* (*Mil.*) a selected word given to sentries, soldiers, etc. used to distinguish friend from enemy.—**to pass the buck** (*Slang*) to shift responsibility to another [L. *passus*, a step].

passage (pas'āj) *n.* the act, time, or right of passing; movement from one place to another; a journey; a voyage; fare for a voyage; entrance or exit; a corridor; part of a book, etc.; the passing of a law; an encounter; an incident.—**passage of arms**, a feat of arms.—**bird of passage**, a migratory bird [Fr. fr. L. *passus*, a step, a pace].

passé (på-sā') *a.* past one's best; faded; rather out of date; antiquated [Fr.].

passenger (pas'en-jer) *n.* a traveller, esp. by some conveyance; (*Colloq.*) one of a team who does not pull his full weight;—*a.* adapted for carrying passengers [O.Fr. *passager*].

passe-partout (pås-pår-tòó') *n.* something that enables one to pass anywhere, e.g. a master-key; a method of framing photographs or small pictures with the use of gummed tape [Fr.].

Passeriformes (pas'er-i-for-mēz) *n.* the largest order of birds, including all perching and song birds.—**passerine** (pas'er-in) *a.* pert. to this order;—*n.* a bird of this order [L. *passer*, a sparrow].

passion (pash'un) *n.* the story of Christ's suffering and last agony; intense emotion, as of grief, rage, love; eager desire.—**pass'ionate** *a.* easily moved to anger; moved by strong emotions; vehement.—**pass'ionately** *adv.*—**pass'ionateness** *n.*—**pass'ionless** *a.*—**pass'ion-flow'er** *n.* a plant of the genus Passiflora, with large purple flowers and edible fruit.—**pass'ion-play** *n.* a theatrical representation of Christ's passion.—**pass'ion-week** *n.* the week immediately preceding Easter [L. *passio*, fr. *pati*, to suffer].

passive (pas'iv) *a.* suffering; submissive; acted upon, not acting;—*n.* (*Gram.*) (or passive voice) the form of the verb which expresses that the subject is acted upon.—**pass'ively** *adv.* —**pass'iveness** *n.*—**passiv'ity** *n.* state of being passive; inertia [L. *pati, passus,* to suffer].

Passover (pȧs´ō-vęr) *n.* a feast of the Jews to commemorate the time when God, smiting the first-born of the Egyptians, passed over the houses of the Israelites [*pass* and *over*].

past (pȧst) *a.* pert. to former time; gone by; elapsed; ended;—*n.* former state; bygone times; one's earlier life;—*prep.* beyond; after; exceeding; beyond the scope of;—*adv.* by; beyond.—**past master,** a former master of a guild, freemasons, etc.; one adept or proficient [fr. *pass*].

paste (pāst) *n.* a soft composition, as of flour and water; dough prepared for pies, etc.; any soft plastic mixture or adhesive; pounded meat or fish; a fine glass for making artificial gems;—*v.t.* to fasten with paste; (*Slang*) to thrash.—**pasty** (pās´ti, pas´ti) *n.* a pie enclosed in paste and baked without a dish;—*a.* (pās´ti) like paste.—**pas'try** (pās´tri) *n.* the crust of pies and tarts; articles of food made of paste or dough.—**pas'try-cook** *n.* one who makes and sells pastry.—**pasteboard** (pāst´bōrd) *n.* a stiff, thick paper;—*a.* made of pasteboard; flimsy or unsubstantial [O.Fr.].

pastel (pas´tel) *n.* a coloured crayon; a drawing made with such crayons.—**pastel shades,** delicate and subdued colours, esp. in fabrics [Fr. fr. L. *pastillus,* a little loaf].

pastern (pas´tęrn) *n.* part of horse's leg between fetlock and hoof [O.Fr. *pasturon,* shackle of horse at pasture].

Pasteur (pas-tęr') *n.* a French chemist, famous for his researches in hydrophobia, and suggestion of inoculation as a cure for many diseases.—**pasteurisa'tion** *n.* the sterilisation of milk, etc. by heating to 140° F. or over and then cooling.—**pas'teurise** *v.t.*

pastiche, pasticcio (pas-tēsh', pas-tēch´ō) *n.* a medley made up from various sources; a picture or literary composition in the style of a recognised author or artist [It.].

pastille, pastil (pas-tēl', pas´til) *n.* an aromatic substance burned for cleansing or scenting a room; a small lozenge, aromatic or medicated [Fr. fr. L. *pastillus,* a little loaf].

pastime (pȧs´tīm) *n.* that which amuses and makes time pass agreeably; recreation; diversion [fr. *pass* and *time*].

pastor (pȧs´tor) *n.* a minister of the gospel.—**pas'toral** *a.* pert. to shepherds or rural life; relating to the cure of souls, or the office of a pastor;—*n.* a poem describing rural life; an idyll.—**pas'torally** *adv.*—**pas'torate** *n.* the office or jurisdiction of a spiritual pastor. —**pas'torship** *n.* the office or rank of a pastor [L. *pastor,* a herdsman].

pasture (pȧs´tūr) *n.* grass for food of cattle; ground on which cattle graze;—*v.t.* to feed on grass;—*v.i.* to graze.—**past'urable** *a.* —**past'urage** *n.* pasture-land; the business of grazing cattle [L. *pascere,* to feed].

pasty (pās´ti, pas´ti) *n.* See **paste.**

pat (pat) *n.* a light, quick blow, esp. with hand or fingers; a small lump, esp. of butter;—*v.t.* to strike gently.—*pr.p.* **pat'ting.**—*pa.p.* and *pa.t.* **pat'ted** [imit. origin].

pat (pat) *a.* ready; apt; at right moment;—*adv.* opportunely; without hesitation.—**pat'ness** *n.* [fr. *pat,* a light blow].

patch (pach) *n.* a piece of material used to mend a hole, rent, etc.; spot on surface of anything; small spot of black silk formerly worn on cheek by ladies;—*v.t.* to mend with a patch; to repair clumsily.—**patch'y** *a.* full of patches; unequal.—**patch'work** *n.* work made by sewing together pieces of cloth of different material and colour [O.Fr. *pieche,* a piece].

pate (pāt) *n.* the top of the head; the head [etym. uncertain].

pâté (pȧ-tā') *n.* paste; patty; pie.—**pâté de foie gras** (pȧt-ā' dę fwȧ-grȧ) a kind of meat paste made of fat goose-liver [Fr. *pâté,* paste, pie; *foie,* liver; *gras,* fat].

patella (pą-tel´ą) *n.* the knee-cap [L. = small pan].

paten (pat´ęn) *n.* a thin metal plate; the plate on which the consecrated bread in the eucharist is placed [L. *patina,* a plate].

patent (pā´tent, pat´ent) *a.* open; evident; open to public perusal, as *letters patent;* protected by a patent;—*n.* short for *letters patent,* an official document granting a right, privilege, or title of nobility; such a document securing the exclusive right to invention; invention itself.—**patent** (pā´tent) *v.t.* to secure or protect by a patent.—**pa'tently** *adv.* openly; evidently.—**patentee** (pā-ten-tē', pat-en-tē') *n.* one who has secured a patent.—**patent leather,** leather with a varnished or lacquered surface [L. *patens,* open].

pater (pā´tęr) *n.* (*Colloq.*) father.—**paterfamilias** (pā´tęr- or pat´ęr-fą-mil´i-as) *n.* the head of a family [L. *pater,* a father; *familia,* a household].

paternal (pą-tęr´nąl) *a.* pert. to a father; fatherly; hereditary.—**pater'nally** *adv.*—**pater´nity** *n.* the relation of a father to his offspring; authorship [L. *pater,* a father].

paternoster (pat-ęr-nos´tęr) *n.* the Lord's Prayer [L. *pater,* father; *noster,* our].

path (path) *n.* a way, course, or track; course of action, conduct, or procedure.—**path'finder** *n.* a pioneer; (*World War* 2) an R.A.F. pilot selected to find the best direction from which to approach enemy target.—**path'way** *n.* a narrow footway [O.E. *paeth*].

pathetic (pą-thet´ik) *a.* affecting or moving the tender emotions; causing pity; touching. Also **pathet'ical.**—**pathet'ically** *adv.*

patho- (pa´tho) *prefix* fr. Gk. *pathos,* suffering, feeling, used in derivatives.—**pathogen'esis, pathog'eny** *n.* the origin and development of disease.—**pathogenet'ic, pathogen'ic** *a.* causing disease.—**pathol'ogy** *n.* the science and study of diseases, their causes, nature, cures, etc.—**patholog'ic, patholog'ical** *a.*—**patholog'ically** *adv.* **pathol'ogist** *n.* [Gk. *genesis,* birth; *logos,* discourse].

pathos (pā´thos) *n.* the power of exciting tender emotions; deep feeling [Gk. fr. *paschein,* to suffer].

patient (pā´shęnt) *a.* bearing trials without murmuring; not easily made angry; calm; not hasty;—*n.* a person under medical treatment.—**pa'tiently** *adv.*—**pa'tience** *n.* the quality of enduring with calmness; a card-game for one player [L. *pati,* to suffer].

patina (pą-tē´ną, pat´i-na) *n.* a film formed on antique bronze from exposure; the gloss on antique, well cared-for furniture; (*Colloq.*) surface [L. *patina,* a dish].

patio (pȧt´i-ō) *n.* the inner court of a Spanish house, open to the sky [Sp.].

patois (pat´wȧ) *n.* a dialect; illiterate or provincial form of speech; jargon [Fr.].

patriarch (pā´tri-ȧrk) *n.* the father and ruler of a family, esp. in Biblical history; the highest dignitary in the Eastern church; a venerable old man.—**patriarch'al** *a.*—**pat'riarchate** *n.* dignity or jurisdiction of a patriarch.—**pat'riarchy** *n.* government by the head or father of a tribe [Gk. *pater,* father; *archein,* to rule].

patrician (pą-trish´ąn) *a.* pert. to the senators of ancient Rome and their descendants; of high birth; noble or aristocratic;—*n.* a person of high birth [L. *patricius,* fr. *pater,* father, senator].

patricide (pat´ri-sīd) *n.* See **parricide.**

patrimony (pat´ri-mo-ni) *n.* a right or estate inherited from one's father or ancestors; heritage; a church estate or revenue.—**patrimo'nial** *a.*—**patrimo'nially** *adv.* [L. *patrimonium* fr. *pater,* father].

patriot (pā´tri-ot, pat´ri-ot) *n.* one who loves his country and upholds its interests.—**patriot'ic** *a.* filled with patriotism.—**patriot'ically** *adv.*—**pa'triotism** *n.* love for, and loyalty to, one's country [L. *patria,* fatherland].

patristic (pa̤-tris′-tik) *a.* pert. to the fathers of the Christian church [L. *pater, patris*, father].

patrol (pa̤-trōl′) *v.t.* and *i.* to go or walk round a camp, garrison, etc. in order to protect it.—*pr.p.* **patrol′ling.**—*pa.p.* and *pa.t.* **patrolled′.**—*n.* a going of the rounds by a guard; the man or men who go the rounds [O.Fr. *patrouiller*].

patron (pā′-trun) *n.* (*fem.* **pa′troness**) a man under whose protection another has placed himself; a guardian saint; one who has the right of appointment to a church living or benefice; a regular customer.—**pa′tronage** *n.* countenance, support, or encouragement given to a person or cause; condescending manner; in trade, regular custom.—**patronise** (pat′-ro-nīz) *v.t.* to act as a patron to; to assume the air of a superior towards; to frequent, as a customer.—**pat′ronising** *a.*—**pat′ronisingly** *adv.*—**patron saint,** a saint who is regarded as the special protector of a person, country, city, trade, etc. [L. *patronus*, fr. *pater*, father].

patronymic (pat-ro-nim′-ik) *n.* a name derived from parent or ancestor; a surname [Gk. *patōr*, father; *onoma*, a name].

patten (pat′-en) *n.* a wooden sole with an iron ring, for raising the feet above mud; a clog; (*Archit.*) the base of a column [Fr. *patin*].

patter (pat′-e̤r) *v.i.* to make a quick succession of small taps or sounds, like those of rain falling [frequentative of *pat*].

patter (pat′-e̤r) *v.t.* to speak rapidly and indistinctly; to mutter;—*v.i.* to talk glibly or mechanically; to say prayers;—*n.* chatter; prattle; lingo of a profession or class; jargon [fr. *paternoster*].

pattern (pat′-e̤rn) *n.* a model, example, or guide that is to be copied, or is worthy of imitation;—*a.* model; ideal;—*v.t.* to design from a pattern; to imitate.—**pat′ternmaker** *n.* a worker in a foundry employed to make patterns for moulds [M.E. *patron*, a model].

patty (pat′-i) *n.* a little pie [Fr. *pâté*].

paucity (paw′-si-ti) *n.* fewness; scarcity; smallness of quantity [L. *paucus*, few].

paunch (pawnsh, pânsh) *n.* the belly [L. *pantex*].

pauper (paw′-pe̤r) *n.* (*fem.* **pau′peress**) a very poor person, esp. one supported by the public.—**pau′perise** *v.t.* to reduce to pauperism [L. = poor].

pause (pawz) *n.* a temporary stop or rest; cessation; hesitation; a break in speaking, reading, or writing; in music, a sign (⌣) or (⌒) to indicate the prolongation of a note or rest;—*v.i.* to make a short stop; to cease for a time [Gk. *pausis*].

pavan, pavane (pa̤-van′) *n.* old-time stately dance, or its music [Fr. *pavane*].

pave (pāv) *v.t.* to form a level surface with stone, brick, etc.; to make smooth and even; (*Fig.*) to prepare.—**pave′ment** *n.* a paved floor; a paved road or footpath; in towns, a sidewalk for pedestrians; (*U.S.*) the traffic way [L. *pavire*, to ram down].

pavid (pav′-id) *a.* timid; shy [L. *pavidus*].

pavilion (pa̤-vil′-yun) *n.* orig. a tent; hence, anything like a tent, e.g. a garden summer-house; a club-house on a playing-field, etc. [Fr. fr. L. *papilio*, a butterfly, a tent].

paw (paw) *n.* the foot of an animal having claws; (*Slang*) the hand;—*v.t.* and *i.* to scrape with the forefoot; (*Colloq.*) to stroke or fondle with hands [O.Fr. *poe*].

pawky (pawk′-i) *a.* (*Scot.*) sly; artful; cunning; ironical [etym. uncertain].

pawn (pawn) *n.* something deposited as security for money borrowed; a pledge; the state of being pledged;—*v.t.* to deposit as security for a loan; to pledge.—**pawn′broker** *n.* one who lends money on something deposited with him.—**pawn′shop** *n.* the place of business of a pawnbroker [O.Fr. *pan*, fr. L. *pannus*, cloth].

pawn (pawn) *n.* a piece of the lowest rank in the game of chess; (*Fig.*) a person who is a mere tool in the hands of another [L.L. *pedo*, a foot-soldier].

pax (paks) *n.* the kiss of peace;—*interj.* (*Colloq.*) a truce! leave me alone! [L. *pax*, peace].

pay (pā) *v.t.* to discharge one's obligations to; to give money, etc., for goods received or services rendered;—*v.i.* to recompense; to be remunerative; to be worth the trouble.—*pa.p.* and *pa.t.* **paid** (pād).—*n.* reward; compensation; wages; salary.—**pay′able** *a.* justly due; profitable.—**payee** (pā-ē′) *n.* one to whom money is paid.—**pay′er** *n.* one who pays.—**pay′ment** *n.* the act of paying; discharge of a debt; recompense; punishment.—**paying guest,** boarder or lodger [L. *pacare*, to appease].

pay (pā) *v.t.* (*Naut.*) to cover with pitch; to caulk the seams of a ship [L. *picare*, to pitch].

pea (pē) *n.* the fruit, growing in pods, of a leguminous plant; the plant itself.—*pl.* **peas.** Also **pease** (pēz) peas collectively.—**pea′nut** *n.* the earth-nut; the monkey-nut.—**pea′soup** *n.* soup made of dried peas, esp. yellow split peas.—**pea′soup′er** *n.* (*Colloq.*) a thick yellow fog, esp. in London.—**sweet pea,** a climbing garden annual, bearing sweet-scented flowers [Gk. *pisos*].

peace (pēs) *n.* calm; repose; freedom from disturbance, war, or hostilities.—**peace′able** *a.* in a state of peace; disposed to peace; not quarrelsome.—**peace′ably** *adv.*—**peace′ableness** *n.*—**peace′ful** *a.* free from war, tumult, or commotion; mild; undisturbed.—**peace′fully** *adv.*—**peace′fulness** *n.*—**peace′maker** *n.* one who makes peace [L. *pax, pacis*].

peach (pēch) *n.* a juicy stone-fruit with whitish flesh, and a velvety skin; the tree which bears this fruit; a soft pale orange-pink colour.—**peach′y** *a.* like, or characteristic of, a peach.—**peach Melba,** ice-cream with peaches [Fr. *pêche*].

peach (pēch) *v.i.* (*Slang*) to inform against; to tell tales [*abbrev.* fr. *impeach*].

peacock (pē′-kok) *n.* (*fem.* **pea′hen**) *a.* bird remarkable for the beauty of its plumage, and for its large tail; a person vain of his appearance.—**pea′fowl** *n.* the peacock or peahen.—**peacock blue,** lustrous greenish-blue [L. *pavo*, a peacock; and *cock*].

pea-jacket (pē′-jak-et) *n.* a thick woollen jacket worn by seamen [Dut. *pij*, a coat of coarse, woollen material; and *jacket*].

peak (pēk) *v.i.* to waste or pine away.—**peak′y** *a.* thin, sickly [etym. unknown].

peak (pēk) *n.* the sharp top of a hill; the pointed end of anything; the projecting part of a cap-brim; the maximum point of a curve or record.—**peaked** *a.* pointed; projecting [Fr. *pic*; conn. with *pike*].

peal (pēl) *n.* a loud sound, or succession of loud sounds, as of thunder, bells, laughter, etc.; a set of bells attuned to each other;—*v.t.* and *i.* to sound loudly; to celebrate [*abbrev.* fr. *appeal*].

pear (pār) *n.* a sweet, juicy fruit of oval shape; tree on which it grows [L. *pirum*].

pearl (pe̤rl) *n.* a hard, smooth, lustrous substance, found in several molluscs, particularly pearl oyster, and used as a gem; something very precious; a small size of printing type, between ruby and diamond; colour of a pearl, a creamy grey;—*a.* made of pearls; pert. to pearls;—*v.t.* to adorn with pearls; to take a round form like pearls.—**pear′ly** *a.* of the colour of pearls; like pearls; abounding in pearls; clear; pure.—**pear′liness** *n.*—**moth′er-of-pearl** *n.* the inside surface or lining of pearl-oyster and other shells.—**pear′lies** *n.pl.* costermongers' dress covered with pearl buttons [Fr. *perle*].

peasant (pez′-a̤nt) *n.* a rural labourer; a rustic;—*a.* rural.—**peas′antry** *n.* peasants collectively [Fr. *paysan*].

pease (pēz) *n.pl.* peas collectively [Gk. *pisos*].

peat (pēt) *n.* a brown, fibrous turf, formed of decayed vegetable matter, which is used as fuel.—**peat'y** *a.* like peat, in texture or colour. —**peat'-bog, peat'-moss** *n.* marshland of which the foundation is peat.—**peat'-hag** *n.* a pool in peaty ground [etym. uncertain].

peavey (pē'-vi) *n.* a lumberman's cant-hook [fr. *Peavey*, the inventor].

pebble (peb'-l) *n.* a small, roundish stone; transparent and colourless rock-crystal used for spectacle lenses.—**pebb'led, pebb'ly** *a.* full of pebbles [O.E. *papol*].

peccable (pek'-ą-bl) *a.* liable to sin.—**peccabil'ity** *n.* liability to sin.—**pecc'ant** *a.* sinful; offensive; causing trouble; (*Med.*) morbid.—**pecc'ancy** *n.* [L. *peccare*, to sin].

peccadillo (pek-ą-dil'-ō) *n.* a trifling offence; a slight mistake; an indiscreet action.—*pl.* **peccadil'los**, or **peccadil'loes** [Sp. *pecadillo*, fr. *pecado*, a sin; L. *peccare*, to sin].

peck (pek) *n.* a measure of capacity for dry goods = 2 gallons, or the fourth part of a bushel; a great deal [O.Fr. *pek*].

peck (pek) *v.t.* and *i.* to strike with the beak; to pick up with the beak; to dab; to eat little quantities at a time;—*n.* (*Colloq.*) a kiss.—**peck'er** *n.* that which pecks; (*Slang*) spirits; courage.—**peck'ish** *a.* (*Colloq.*) somewhat hungry [form of *pick*].

pectoral (pek'-tor-ął) *a.* pert. to the breast or chest [L. *pectus*, the breast].

peculate (pek'-ū-lāt) *v.t.* and *i.* to embezzle; to steal. —**pecula'tion** *n.* embezzlement.—**pec'ulator** *n.* [L. *peculari*].

peculiar (pe-kūl'-yąr) *a.* one's own; belonging solely to; appropriate; particular; singular; strange.—**pecul'iarly** *adv.*—**peculiar'ity** (pe-kū-li-ar'-i-ti) *n.* something that belongs to only one person, thing, class, people; a distinguishing feature; characteristic [L. *peculium*, private property, fr. *pecus*, cattle].

pecuniary (pe-kū'-ni-ą-ri) *a.* pert. to, or consisting of, money.—**pecu'niarily** *adv.* [L. *pecunia*, money, fr. *pecus*, cattle].

pedagogue (ped'-ą-gog) *n.* a schoolmaster; a pedantic teacher.—**pedagogic** (ped-ą-goj'-ik), **pedagog'ical** *a.*—**pedagogy** (ped'-ą-goj-i), **pedagog'ics** *n.* science of teaching [Gk. *pais*, a boy; *agogos*, leading].

pedal (ped'-ął) *a.* pert. to the foot;—*n.* a mechanical contrivance to transmit power by using foot as a lever, e.g. on bicycle, sewing-machine.—*v.t.* and *i.* to use the pedals of an organ, piano, etc.; to propel a bicycle by pedalling.—*pr.p.* **ped'al(l)ing.**—*pa.p.* and *pa.t.* **ped'al(l)ed** [L. *pes*, *pedis*, the foot].

pedant (ped'-ąnt) *n.* one who insists unnecessarily on petty details of book-learning, grammatical rules, etc.; one who shows off his learning.—**pedant'ic(al)** *a.*—**pedant'ically** *adv.*—**ped'antry** *n.* [perh. conn. with *pedagogue*].

peddle (ped'-l) *v.i.* to travel from place to place selling small articles;—*v.t.* to sell or hawk goods thus.—**ped'lar** *n.* one who peddles goods; a door-to-door hawker. Also **ped'(d)ler** [O.E. *ped*, a basket].

pedestal (ped'-es-tąl) *n.* anything that serves as a support or foundation; the base of a column, statue, etc. [Fr. *piédestal*].

pedestrian (pe-des'-tri-ąn) *a.* going on, performed on, foot; of walking; commonplace; —*n.* a walker; one who journeys on foot [L. *pedester*, fr. *pes*, a foot].

pediatrics (ped-i-at'-riks) *n.* See **paediatrics.**

pedicel (ped'-i-sel) *n.* a small, short footstalk of a leaf, flower, or fruit; (*Anat.* and *Zool.*) a narrow stalk-like part by which a larger part is attached [L. *pediculus*, dim. of *pes*, *pedis*, the foot].

pediculus (pe-dik'-ū-lus) *n.* the body louse.—**pedic'ular, pedic'ulous** *a.* lousy [L. *pediculus*, a louse].

pedicure (ped'-i-kūr) *n.* treatment of the feet; a chiropodist [L. *pes*, *pedis*, the foot; *cura*, care].

pedigree (ped'-i-grē) *n.* a line of ancestors; genealogy;—*a.* having a line of ancestors [M.E. *pedegru* fr. Fr. *pied de grue*, crane's-foot, (the shape of a genealogical tree)].

pediment (ped'-i-męnt) *n.* (*Archit.*) the triangular ornamental facing of a portico, door, or window, etc.—**pedimen'tal** *a.* [earlier *periment*, perh. fr. *pyramid*].

pedlar (ped'-ląr) *n.* See **peddle.**

pedometer (pe-dom'-ę-tęr) *n.* an instrument which measures the distance walked by recording the number of steps [L. *pes*, *pedis*, the foot; Gk. *metron*, a measure].

peduncle (pe-dung'-kl) *n.* a flower-stalk; (*Zool.*) a stalk or stalk-like process in an animal body. —**pedun'cular** *a.* [dim. of L. *pes*, *pedis*, a foot].

peek (pēk) *v.i.* to peep; to peer; to look slyly through half-closed eyes;—*n.* a sly glance [etym. uncertain].

peel (pēl) *v.t.* to strip off the skin, bark, or rind; to free from a covering;—*v.i.* to come off, as the skin or rind;—*n.* the outside skin of a fruit; rind or bark [L. *pilare*, to deprive of hair].

peel (pēl) *n.* an old square fortified tower [L. *palus*, a stake].

peel (pēl) *n.* wooden shovel used by bakers; the blade of an oar [L. *pala*, a spade].

peeler (pē'-lęr) *n.* a policeman.—**Peel'ite** *n.* a free-trader and adherent of Sir Robert Peel (1788-1850), a British statesman.

peep (pēp) *v.i.* to look through a crevice; to look furtively or slyly; to emerge slowly;—*n.* a furtive or sly glance.—**peep'-show** *n.* a small exhibit, viewed through an aperture containing a magnifying glass [etym. uncertain].

peep (pēp) *v.i.* to cry, as a chick [imit.].

peer (pēr) *n.* (*fem.* **peer'ess**) an equal in any respect; a nobleman; a member of the House of Lords; an associate.—**peer'age** *n.* the rank of a peer; the body of peers.—**peer'less** *a.* having no equal.—**peer'lessly** *adv.*—**peer'lessness** *n.* [L. *par*, equal].

peer (pēr) *v.i.* to look closely and intently; to peep; to appear [etym. doubtful].

peevish (pē'-vish) *a.* fretful; irritable; hard to please; childish.—**peev'ishly** *adv.*—**peev'ishness** *n.*—**peeve** *v.t.* to annoy; to irritate [etym. uncertain].

peewit (pē'-wit) *n.* See **pewit.**

peg (peg) *n.* a wooden nail or pin; an excuse; a drink, esp. brandy or whisky, with soda; a step or degree;—*v.t.* to fix or mark with a peg;—*v.i.* to persevere [etym. uncertain].

Pekin, Peking (pē-kin'(g)) *n.* (*Geog.*) capital of China; a kind of silk stuff.—**Pekin(g)ese'** *n.* a native of Pekin; a breed of Chinese lap-dog.—*abbrev.* **peke.**

pekoe (pē'-kō, pek'-ō) *n.* a black tea of superior quality [Chin. *pek*, white; *ho*, down (i.e. with 'down' on the leaves)].

pelagian (pe-lā'-ji-ąn) *a.* pert. to the deep sea; —*n.* an animal living in the deep sea.—**pelagic** (pe-laj'-ik) *a.* pert. to, or done on, the open sea [Gk. *pelagos*, the sea].

pelargonium (pel-ar-gō'-ni-um) *n.* the flowering plant popularly called the geranium [Gk. *pelargos*, a stork].

pêle-mêle (pel-mel') *adv.* See **pell-mell.**

pelf (pelf) *n.* (*Slang*) money [O.Fr. *pelfre*, stolen property].

pelican (pel'-i-kąn) *n.* a large water-fowl, remarkable for its enormous pouch beneath its bill [Gk. *pelekan*].

pelisse (pe-lēs') *n.* formerly, a robe of silk or other material, worn by ladies; a fur-lined coat; a hussar's jacket [L. *pellis*, skin].

pellet (pel'-et) *n.* a little ball; a pill; small shot [Fr. *pelote*, a ball].

pell-mell (pel-mel') *adv.* in utter confusion; helter-skelter. Also **pêle-mêle** [Fr. *mêler*, to mix; *pêle*, being a rhyme with *mêle*].

pellucid (pe-lū'-sid) *a.* perfectly clear; translucent.—**pellu'cidly** *adv.*—**pellu'cidness** *n.* [L. *per*, very; *lucidus*, clear].

pelmet (pel'-met) *n.* a canopy, or valance, at the top of a window, esp. to conceal curtain rods [etym. uncertain].

pelt (pelt) *n.* raw hide; undressed skin of fur-bearing animal [L. *pellis*, skin].
pelt (pelt) *v.t.* to strike with missiles;—*v.i.* of rain, etc. to fall heavily; to throw missiles; to run fast [etym. uncertain].
pelvis (pel´vis) *n.* (*Anat.*) the bony basin-shaped cavity at the base of the human trunk. —**pel'vic** *a.* [L. = a basin].
pemmican (pem´i-kạn) *n.* beef or venison, dried, pounded, and compressed into cakes, formerly eaten by N. American Indians [Amer.-Ind., *pimekan*].
pen (pen) *n.* an instrument for writing with ink; a large wing-feather (a quill) used for writing;—*v.t.* to write; to compose and set down.—*pr.p.* **pen'ning**.—*pa.p.* and *pa.t.* **penned**. —**penknife** (pen´nīf) *n.* a pocket-knife, formerly used for splitting and preparing a quill for writing.—**pen'man** *n.* one who writes a good hand; an author.—**pen'manship** *n.*—**pen'name** *n.* an assumed name of author.—**pen´push'er** *n.* (*Colloq.*) a clerk [L. *penna*, a feather].
pen (pen) *n.* a female swan, the male being the 'cob' [etym. uncertain].
pen (pen) *n.* a small enclosure, as for sheep; a coop.—*v.t.* to confine in a pen; to shut in. [O.E. *penn*].
penal (pē´nạl) *a.* pert. to, prescribing, incurring, inflicting, punishment.—**pe'nalise** *v.t.* to make penal; to impose a penalty upon; to handicap.—**pe'nally** *adv.*—**penalty** (pen´ạl-ti) *n.* punishment for a crime or offence; in games, a handicap imposed for infringement of rule, etc. [L. *poena*, punishment].
penance (pen´ạns) *n.* suffering submitted to in penitence; act of atonement [L. *penitentia*].
Penates (pen-ā´tēz) *n.pl.* the household gods of ancient Rome [L.].
pence (pens) *n.pl.* See **penny**
penchant (pong´shong) *n.* a strong mental inclination [Fr. *pencher*, to lean].
pencil (pen´sil) *n.* an artist's fine brush; a crayon or stick of black lead enclosed in wood, used for writing or drawing; (*Math.*) a system of rays which converge to, or diverge from, a point;—*v.t.* to draw, write with pencil.—**pen'cilled** *a.* marked, as with pencil; having pencils of rays.—**pen'cilling** *n.* the work of a pencil or a fine brush; fine markings [L. *penicillum*, a little tail].
pendant (pen´dạnt) *n.* a hanging ornament, esp. a locket or earring; a lamp or chandelier hanging from the ceiling; an addition or appendix; a complement or parallel.—**pen'dent** *a.* suspended; hanging; projecting.—**pen'dently** *adv.*—**pen'ding** *a.* awaiting settlement; in suspense; undecided;—*prep.* during; until [L. *pendere*, to hang].
pendulous (pen´dū-lus) *a.* hanging loosely; swinging.—**pen'dulously** *adv.*—**pen'dulousness** *n.* —**pen'dulum** *n.* a body suspended from a fixed point, and swinging freely; the swinging rod with weighted end which regulates movements of a clock, etc. [L. *pendulus*, hanging].
penetrate (pen´e-trāt) *v.t.* to enter into; to pierce; to pervade or spread through; to touch with feeling; to arrive at the meaning of;—*v.i.* to make a way to, or through.—**pene'trating** *a.*—**pen'etrable** *a.* capable of being entered or pierced; susceptible.—**pen'etrably** *adv.*—**penetrabil'ity** *n.*—**penetra'tion** *n.* act or power of penetrating; insight; acuteness.—**pen'etrative** *a.* piercing; discerning [L. *penetrare*].
penguin (pen´gwin) *n.* a flightless sea-bird inhabiting the S. temperate and Antarctic regions [W. *pen*, head; *gwyn*, white].
penicillin (pen-i-sil´in) *n.* the extract from the fungus penicillium, used to prevent the growth of certain disease bacteria [L. *penicillum*, a painter's brush].
peninsula (pe-nin´sū-lạ) *n.* a portion of land nearly surrounded by water, and connected with the mainland by an isthmus [L. *paene*, almost; *insula*, an island].
penis (pē´nis) *n.* the male organ of generation. —**pe'nial** *a.* [L.].
penitent (pen´i-tẹnt) *a.* deeply affected by sense of guilt; contrite; repentant;—*n.* one who repents of sin.—**pen'itently** *adv.*—**pen'itence** *n.* sorrow for having sinned; repentance.—**penitential** (pen-i-ten´shạl) *a.* pert. to or expressing penitence;—*n.* among R.C.s, a book containing rules of penance.—**peniten'tially** *adv.* —**penitentiary** (pen-i-ten´shạ-ri) *a.* relating to penance;—*n.* an office, or officer, of papal court, who prescribes penance; house of correction; (*U.S.*) gaol [L. *paenitere*, to repent].
pennant (pen´ạnt) *n.* a very long, narrow flag tapering to a point. Also **penn'on** [Fr. *pennon*, fr. L. *penna*, a feather].
pennate (pen´āt) *a.* winged; feathered. Also **penn'ated**.—**penn'iform** *a.* feather-shaped [L. *penna*, a feather].
pennon (pen´on) *n.* a narrow piece of bunting, esp. on a lance, etc.; a streamer; a pinion or wing of a bird.—**penn'oned** *a.* [Fr. *pennon*, fr. L. *penna*, a feather].
penny (pen´i) *n.* originally a silver coin, then a copper one; now made of bronze and value the 100th part of a pound, (formerly the twelfth part of a shilling); small sum.—*pl.* **pennies** (pen´iz) denoting the number of coins, and **pence** (pens) the amount of pennies in value.—**penn'iless** *a.* without money—**pennyweight** (pen´i-wāt) *n.* a troy weight of 24 grains (*abbrev.* **dwt.**).—**penn'yworth** *n.* as much as is given for a penny; a small quantity—**penny farthing** (*Colloq.*) an early form of bicycle with one very large wheel and one small one [O.E. *penig*).
pennyroyal (pen´i-roi-ạl) *n.* a perennial aromatic herb of the mint family [corrupt. of O.Fr. *puliol*, thyme; and *royal*].
pensile (pen´sīl) *a.* hanging; suspended; pendulous [L. *pensilis*].
pension (pen´shun) *n.* an annual grant of money for past services; an annuity paid to retired officers, soldiers, etc.;—*v.t.* to grant a pension to.—**pen'sionable** *a.* entitled, or entitling, to a pension.—**pen'sioner** *n.* one who receives a pension [L. *pensio*, payment].
pension (pong´sē-ōng) *n.* a boarding-house.—**en pension terms**, inclusive charges for board and lodging [Fr. = a boarding-house].
pensive (pen´siv) *a.* thoughtful; deep in thought; musing; reflecting; somewhat melancholy.—**pen'sively** *adv.*—**pen'siveness** *n.* [Fr. *pensif*, fr. *penser*, to think].
pent (pent) *a.* closely confined; shut up [fr. *pen* = an enclosure].
penta- (pen´ta) *prefix* fr. Gk. *pente*, five, used in derivatives.—**pen'tagon** *n.* (*Geom.*) a plane figure having five angles and five sides.—**pentag'onal** *a.*—**pen'tagram** *n.* a five-pointed star, formerly a magic symbol.—**pentam'eter** *n.* verse of five feet.
pentane (pen´tān) *n.* a paraffin hydrocarbon, a very inflammable liquid [Gk. *pente*, five].
Pentateuch (pen´tạ-tūk) *n.* the first five books of the Old Testament [Gk. *pente*, five; *teuchos*, a book].
Pentecost (pen´te-kost) *n.* a Jewish festival, celebrated on the 50th day after the Passover; a Christian festival (Whitsunday) commemorating the descent of the Holy Ghost on the Apostles.—**Pentecost'al** *a.* [Gk. *pentēkostos*, fiftieth].
penthouse (pent´hous) *n.* an outhouse attached to a main building, its roof sloping down from the wall.—**pent'roof** *n.* roof with a slope on one side only [Fr. *appentis*, fr. L. *pendere*, to hang].
Pentothal (pen´tō-thal) *n.* a drug which when injected acts on the brain, resulting in a free confession by the patient of his true feelings and desires; sometimes called the 'truth' drug [Registered Trade Name].
penult (pē-nult', pe´nult) *n.* the last syllable but one of a word.—**penultimate** (pe-nult´im-āt) *a.* next before the last;—*n.* the last syllable but one; the last member but one of a series [L. *paene*, almost; *ultimus*, last].
penumbra (pen-um´brȧ) *n.* in an eclipse, the partially shadowed region which surrounds

the perfect or full shadow; half-shadow [L. *paene*, almost; *umbra*, shade].

penury (pen'ū-ri) *n.* extreme poverty; want or indigence; scarcity.—**penurious** (pe-nū'ri-us) *a.* miserly; poor; scanty.—**penu'riously** *adv.*—**penu'riousness** *n.* [L. *penuria*].

peon (pē'on) *n.* in Mexico, a day-labourer or serf; in India, a native constable, foot-soldier, or messenger [Sp.].

peony (pē'o-ni) *n.* plant having beautiful, showy flowers [Gk. *paiōnia*, healing, fr. *Paiōn*, the physician of the gods].

people (pē'pl) *n.* the body of persons that compose a community, tribe, nation, or race; the populace as distinct from rulers;—*pl.* inhabitants; —*v.t.* to populate [L. *populus*].

pep (pep) *n.* (*Slang*) vigour; energy; go.

pepper (pep'ẹr) *n.* a pungent, spicy condiment obtained from an E. Indian plant;—*v.t.* to sprinkle with pepper; to pelt with missiles.—**pepp'ery** *a.* having the qualities of pepper; pungent; (*Fig.*) irritable.—**pepp'eriness** *n.*—**pepp'ercorn** *n.* the berry or fruit of the pepper-plant; something of insignificant value.—**pepp'ermint** *n.* a pungent plant which yields a volatile oil; the essence got from this oil; a lozenge flavoured with this essence [Gk. *peperi*].

pepsin, pepsine (pep'sin) *n.* a ferment formed in gastric juice of man and animals, and serving as an aid to digestion.—**pep'tic** *a.* pert. to pepsin and to digestion;—*n.pl.* medicines that promote digestion.—**peptone** (pep'tōn) *n.* one of the soluble compounds due to the action of pepsin, etc. on proteins.—**pep'tonise** *v.t.* to convert food into peptones [Gk. *pepsis*, digestion].

peradventure (per-ad-ven'tūr) *adv.* by chance; perhaps; possibly;—*n.* doubt; question [O.Fr. *par aventure*].

perambulate (pẹr-am'bū-lāt) *v.t.* to walk through or over; formerly to survey the boundaries of;—*v.i.* to walk about; to stroll.—**perambula'tion** *n.*—**peram'bulator** *n.* one who perambulates; a small carriage for a child.—**peram'bulatory** *a.* [L. *per*; *ambulare*, to walk].

perceive (pẹr-sēv') *v.t.* to obtain knowledge of through the senses; to see, hear, or feel; to understand; to discern.—**perceiv'able** *a.*—**perceiv'ably** *adv.*—**perceiv'er** *n.*—**perceptible** (pẹr-sep'ti-bl) *a.* capable of being perceived; discernible.—**percep'tibly** *adv.*—**percep'tibility** *n.*—**perception** (pẹr-sep'shun) *n.* the faculty of perceiving; intuitive judgment.—**percep'tive** *a.* having perception; used in perception.—**perceptiv'ity** *n.* power of perception.—**percep'tual** *a.* involving perception [L. *percipere*].

percentage (pẹr-sen'tāj) *n.* proportion or rate per hundred.—**per centum** (*abbrev.* **per cent**) by, in, or for, each hundred [L. *per*, through; *centum*, a hundred].

perch (pẹrch) *n.* an edible fresh-water fish [Gk. *perkē*].

perch (pẹrch) *n.* roosting bar for birds; high place; lineal measure (also 'pole' or 'rod') = 5½ yards; a measure of area = 30¼ square yards;—*v.t.* to place on a perch;—*v.i.* to alight or settle on a perch; to roost [L. *pertica*, a pole].

perchance (pẹr-chȧns') *adv.* perhaps; by chance [L. *per*, through; and *chance*].

percipient (pẹr-sip'i-ẹnt) *a.* having the faculty of perception; perceiving;—*n.* one who has the power of perceiving.—**percip'ience, percip'iency** *n.* [L. *percipere*, to perceive].

percolate (pẹr'kō-lāt) *v.t.* and *i.* to pass slowly through small openings, as a liquid; to filter.—**percola'tion** *n.*—**per'colator** *n.* a filtering machine; a coffee-pot fitted with a filter [L. *per*, through; *colare*, to strain].

percuss (pẹr-kus') *v.t.* to strike sharply.—**percus'sion** *n.* a collision; an impact; a vibratory shock; (*Med.*) tapping the body to determine condition of internal organ.—**percus'sive** *a.* [L. *percutere*, *percussum*, to strike].

perdition (pẹr-dish'un) *n.* utter loss; ruin; damnation [L. *perdere*, to lose].

peregrinate (per'e-gri-nāt) *v.i.* to travel from place to place; to journey.—**peregrina'tion** *n.* a wandering about.—**peregrina'tor** *n.*—**per'egrine** *n.* a kind of hawk or falcon [L. *peregrinus*, foreign].

peremptory (per'emp-tō-ri) *a.* authoritative; dictatorial; non-debatable; decisive; absolute.—**per'emptorily** *adv.*—**per'emptoriness** *n.* [L. *perimere*, *peremptum*, to destroy].

perennial (pẹ-ren'i-ạl) *a.* lasting through the year; lasting; everlasting; lasting more than two years;—*n.* a plant lasting for such a time.—**perenn'ially** *adv.* [L. *per*, through; *annus*, a year].

perfect (pẹr'fekt) *a.* complete; finished; faultless; correct; excellent; of the highest quality; (*Gram.*) a tense denoting completed action;—**perfect'** or **per'fect** *v.t.* to finish or complete; to make perfect; to improve; to make skilful.—**per'fectly** *adv.*—**perfect'ible** *a.* capable of becoming perfect.—**perfectibil'ity** *n.*—**perfec'tion** *n.* state of being perfect.—**perfec'tionist** *n.* one who believes that moral perfection is attainable, or that he has attained it. [L. *perfectus*, done thoroughly].

perfervid (pẹr-fer'vid) *a.* very fervid; very eager [L. *perfervidus*].

perfidy (pẹr'fi-di) *n.* treachery; breach of faith; violation of trust.—**perfid'ious** *a.* treacherous.—**perfid'iously** *adv.*—**perfid'iousness** *n.* [L. *perfidia*, faithlessness].

perforate (pẹr'fō-rāt) *v.t.* to bore through; to pierce; to make a series of holes in.—**perfora'tion** *n.* act of perforating; a hole, or series of holes [L. *per*, through; *forare*, to bore].

perforce (pẹr-fōrs') *adv.* by force; of necessity [L. *per*; and *force*].

perform (pẹr-form') *v.t.* to bring to completion; to accomplish; to fulfil; to represent on the stage;—*v.i.* to do; to play, as on a musical instrument.—**perform'ing** *a.* trained to act a part or do tricks.—**perform'er** *n.*—**perform'ance** *n.* act of performing; execution or carrying out; the thing done [L. *per*, thoroughly; Fr. *fournir*, to furnish or complete].

perfume (pẹr'fūm) *n.* a sweet scent or fragrance; a substance which emits an agreeable scent.—**perfume'** *v.t.* to fill or imbue with an agreeable odour; to scent.—**perfum'er** *n.* a maker or seller of perfumes.—**perfum'ery** *n.* perfumes in general; the art of making perfumes [L. *per*, through; *fumare*, to smoke].

perfunctory (pẹr-fungk'tō-ri) *a.* done as a duty, carelessly and without interest; indifferent; superficial.—**perfunc'torily** *adv.*—**perfunc'toriness** *n.* [L. *perfungi*, to perform.

pergola (pẹr'gō-la) *n.* an arbour or covered walk formed of growing plants trained over trellis-work; an elevated balcony [It.].

perhaps (pẹr-haps') *adv.* it may be; possibly; perchance [L. *per*, through; E. *hap*, chance].

pericardium (per-i-kar'di-um) *n.* (*Anat.*) the double membranous sac which encloses the heart.—**pericar'diac, pericar'dial** *a.* [Gk. *peri*, round; *kardia*, the heart].

pericarp (per'i-kȧrp) *n.* (*Bot.*) that which encloses the seed of a plant.—**pericar'pial** *a.* [Gk. *peri*, round; *karpos*, fruit].

perigee (per'i-jē) *n.* that point in the moon's orbit nearest to the earth.—opp. to *apogee* [Gk. *peri*, round; *gē*, the earth].

perihelion (per-i-hē'li-on) *n.* that point in the orbit of a planet or comet nearest to the sun [Gk. *peri*, round; *hēlios*, the sun].

peril (per'il) *n.* danger; hazard; exposure to injury or loss;—*v.t.* to expose to danger; to risk.—**per'ilous** *a.* full of peril.—**per'ilously** *adv.*—**per'ilousness** *n.* [L. *periculum*, danger].

perimeter (pẹ-rim'e-tẹr) *n.* (*Geom.*) the outer boundary of a plane figure; the sum of all its sides; circumference.—**perimet'rical** *a.* [Gk. *peri*, around; *metron*, a measure].

period (pē'ri-od) *n.* a particular portion of

time; the time in which a heavenly body makes a revolution; a series of years; a cycle; conclusion; a punctuation mark (.), at the end of a sentence;—*pl.* menstruation;—*a.* of furniture, dress, a play, etc., belonging to a particular period in history.—**period'ic** *a.* recurring at regular intervals.—**period'ical** *a.* periodic; pert. to a periodical;—*n.* a publication, esp. a magazine issued at regular intervals.—**period'ically** *adv.*—**periodicity** (pē-ri-o-dis'it-i) *n.* the tendency to recur at regular intervals [Gk. *peri*, around; *hodos*, a way].

peripatetic (per-i-pa-tet'ik) *a.* walking about; pert. to the philosophy of Aristotle, from his habit of teaching his disciples while walking about;—*n.* a disciple of the philosophy of Aristotle; one whose business, etc. obliges him to do a lot of walking about.—**peripatet'icism** *n.* [Gk. *peri*, around, about; *patein*, to walk].

periphery (pe-rif'e-ri) *n.* the length round a circular surface; circumference; perimeter; the outside.—**periph'eral** *a.* [Gk. *peri*, around, *pherein*, to bear].

periphrasis (pe-rif'ra-sis) *n.* a roundabout way of speaking or writing; circumlocution.—*pl.* **periph'rases**.—**periphras'tic** *a.* circumlocutory.—**periphras'tically** *adv.* [Gk. *peri*, around; *phrasis*, speaking].

periscope (per'i-skōp) *n.* an optical instrument (used in trench warfare, submarines, etc.) which enables an observer to view surrounding objects from a lower level [Gk. *peri*, around; *skopein*, to see].

perish (per'ish) *v.t.* and *i.* to die; to waste away; to decay; to be destroyed.—**per'ishable** *a.* liable to perish, decay, etc., e.g. fish, fruit, etc. [L. *perire*; *per*, completely; *ire*, to go].

peristyle (per'i-stīl) *n.* a row of columns round courts, or square; court or square itself [Gk. *peri*, around; *stulos*, a pillar].

peritoneum (per-i-to-nē'um) *n.* membrane which lines abdominal cavity, and surrounds intestines, etc.—**peritoni'tis** *n.* inflammation of peritoneum [Gk. *peritonaion*, fr. *peri*, around; *teinein*, to stretch].

periwig (per'i-wig) *n.* a wig; a peruke.—**per'i-wigged** *a.* [Fr. *perruque*, a wig].

periwinkle (per'i-wing-kl) *n.* an edible shell-fish known as a 'winkle' [O.E. *pinewincle*, a whelk].

periwinkle (per'i-wing-kl) *n.* a trailing shrub with blue flowers [L. *pervinca*].

perjure (per'jur) *v.t.* to violate one's oath (used reflex.); to forswear oneself.—**per'jured** *a.* guilty of perjury.—**per'jury** *n.* false testimony; the crime of violating one's oath.—**per'jurer** *n.*—**perjur'ious**, **per'jurous** *a.* guilty of perjury [L. *per*; *jurare* to swear].

perk (perk) *a.* pert; smart;—*v.t.* to make spruce or trim;—*v.i.* to become brisk and lively again (with 'up').—*perk'y a.* jaunty; pert; trim [Celt].

permanent (per'ma-nent) *a.* remaining unaltered; lasting.—**per'manently** *adv.*—**per'manence**, **per'manency** *n.* quality of being permanent; continuance in the same state; one who, that which, is permanent.—**permanent way**, railway lines [L. *per*, through; *manere*, to remain].

permanganate (per-mang'gan-āt) *n.* a salt of an acid of manganese, esp. the potash salt, which, dissolved in water, forms a useful disinfectant and antiseptic.

permeate (per'mē-āt) *v.t.* to penetrate and pass through the texture of; to diffuse itself through; to saturate.—**per'meable** *a.* admitting of passage of fluids.—**per'meably** *adv.*—**permeability** (per-mē-a-bil'i-ti) *n.*—**permea'tion** *n.*—**permeative** (per'mē-ā-tiv) *a.* capable of permeating [L. *per*, through; *meare*, to pass].

permit (per-mit') *v.t.* to allow; to give leave or liberty to;—*v.i.* to give leave.—**permit** (per'mit) *n.* written permission.—*pr.p.* **permitt'ing**.—*pa.p.* and *pa.t.* **permitt'ed**.—**permiss'ion** *n.* authorisation; leave or licence granted.—**permiss'ible** *a.* which may be permitted; allowable.—**permiss'ibly** *adv.*—**permiss'ive** *a.* granting liberty; allowing.—**permiss'ively** *adv.* [L. *permittere*].

permute (per-mūt') *v.t.* to change the order of.—**permut'able** *a.* capable of being permuted or exchanged.—**permut'ably** *adv.*—**permut'ableness**, **permutabil'ity** *n.*—**permuta'tion** *n.* (*Math.*) the arrangement of a number of quantities in every possible order [L. *per*, thoroughly; *mutare*, to change].

pernicious (per-nish'us) *a.* having the quality of destroying or injuring; wicked or mischievous.—**perni'ciously** *adv.*—**perni'ciousness** *n.* [L. *per*, thoroughly; *nex*, death by violence].

pernickety (per-nik'e-ti) *a.* (*Colloq.*) unduly fastidious about trifles [Scot.].

peroration (per-o-rā'shun) *n.* the concluding part of an oration.—**per'orate** *v.i.* to make a peroration; (*Colloq.*) to deliver a speech [L. *perorare*, to speak to the end].

peroxide (per-ok'sīd) *n.* (*Chem.*) oxide containing more oxygen than the normal oxide of an element;—*v.t.* (*Colloq.*) to bleach the hair with peroxide of hydrogen.—**peroxide of hydrogen**, a thick, syrupy liquid used in solution as a bleach and as an antiseptic.

perpend (per-pend') *v.t.* and *i.* (*Arch.*) to weigh in the mind; to ponder [L. *per*, thoroughly; *pendere*, to weigh].

perpendicular (per-pen-dik'ū-lar) *a.* exactly upright or vertical; at right angles to the plane of the horizon; at right angles to a given line or surface;—*n.* a line at right angles to the plane of the horizon; a line at right angles to any line or plane; the latest of the styles of English Gothic architecture, marked by stiff, straight lines.—**perpendic'ularly** *adv.* [L. *perpendiculum*, a plumb-line].

perpetrate (per'pe-trāt) *v.t.* to commit (something bad, esp. a crime); to be guilty of.—**perpetra'tion** *n.*—**per'petrator** *n.* [L. *perpetrare*, to accomplish].

perpetual (per-pet'ū-al) *a.* continuing indefinitely; everlasting.—**perpet'ually** *adv.*—**perpet'uate** *v.t.* to make perpetual; not to allow to be forgotten.—**perpetua'tion** *n.*—**perpetuity** (per-pe-tū'i-ti) *n.* the state or quality of being perpetual [L. *perpetualis*].

perplex (per-pleks') *v.t.* to make intricate, or difficult; to puzzle; to bewilder.—**perplex'ed** *a.* puzzled; bewildered.—**perplex'ing** *a.* puzzling.—**perplex'ity** *n.* bewilderment; embarrassment; a confused state of mind [L. *per*, thoroughly; *plectere*, to weave].

perquisite (per'kwiz-it) *n.* a casual payment in addition to salary, etc.; a gratuity; a tip; a thing that after serving its purpose is customarily taken possession of by a servant, etc.—**perquisi'tion** *n.* a careful search; close investigation [L. *perquisitum*, a thing eagerly sought].

perry (per'i) *n.* a fermented drink made from the juice of pears [L. *pirum*, a pear].

persecute (per'se-kūt) *v.t.* to oppress unjustly for the holding of an opinion; to subject to persistent ill-treatment; to harass; to worry.—**persecu'tion** *n.*—**per'secutor** *n.* [L. *persequi*, to pursue].

persevere (per-se-vēr') *v.i.* to persist; to maintain an effort; not to give in.—**perseve'ring** *a.*—**perseve'ringly** *adv.*—**perseve'rance** *n.* persistence [L. *per*, thoroughly; *severus*, strict].

Persian (per'zi'an) *a.* pert. to *Persia* (now Iran) its people, or the language;—*n.* a native, or the language, of Persia.—**Persian cat**, a breed of cat with long, silky fur.

persiflage (per'si-flàzh) *n.* idle banter; frivolous talk; light mockery [Fr. fr. L. *per*, through; *sibilare*, to hiss].

persimmon (per-sim'on) *n.* an American tree, the date-plum [Amer.-Ind.].

persist (per-sist') *v.i.* to continue firmly in a state or action in spite of obstacles or objections.—**persis'tent** *a.* persisting; steady; persevering; lasting.—**persis'tently** *adv.*—**per-**

sis'tence, persis'tency *a.* perseverance; continuous effort; obstinacy; tenacity [L. *persistere*, fr. *sistere*, to stand].

person (pẹr'sun) *n.* a human being; an individual; the body of a human being; a character in a play; (*Gram.*) one of the three classes of personal pronouns (first, second, or third) showing the relation of the subject to a verb, as speaking, spoken to, or spoken of.—**per'sonable** *a.* attractive in appearance.—**per'sonage** *n.* a person, esp. of rank or social position.—**per'sonal** *a.* pert. to, peculiar to, or done by, a person; pert. to bodily appearance; directed against a person; (*Gram.*) denoting the pronouns, I, thou, he, she, it, we, you, and they.—**per'sonally** *adv.* in person; individually.—**personal'ity** *n.* individuality; distinctive personal qualities.—**personal'ities** *n.pl.* offensive remarks made to, or about, a person.—**personalty** (pẹr'sun-ạl-ti) *n.* (*Law*) personal effects; movable possessions.—**per'sonate** *v.t.* to assume character of; to pretend to be.—**persona'tor** *n.*—**in person,** by one's self [L. *persona*].

personnel (pẹr-sun-el') *n.* the persons employed in a public service, business, office, etc.; staff [Fr. fr. L. *persona*, a person].

personify (pẹr-son'i-fī) *v.t.* to endow inanimate objects or abstract ideas with human attributes; to be an outstanding example of.—*pr.p.* **person'ifying.**—*pa.p.* and *pa.t.* **person'ified.**—**personifica'tion** *n.* [L. *persona*, a person; *facere*, to make].

perspective (pẹr-spek'tiv) *n.* the art of drawing objects on a plane surface to give impression of looking at the objects themselves; the relative distance of objects to the eye, indicated by the convergence of their receding lines; (*Fig.*) a right proportion [L. *per*, through; *specere*, to look].

Perspex (pẹr'speks) *n.* a thermo-plastic, transparent substance used as a substitute for glass [Protected Trade Name].

perspicacious (pẹr-spi-kā'shus) *a.* quick-sighted; of acute discernment; of keen understanding.—**perspica'ciously** *adv.*—**perspicacity** (pẹr-spi-kas'i-ti) *n.* quick mental insight or discernment.—**perspicuous** (pẹr-spik'ū-us) *a.* clear to the understanding; lucid; plain; obvious.—**perspic'uously** *adv.*—**perspic'uousness** *n.*—**perspicuity** (pẹr-spi-kū'i-ti) *n.* clearness [L. *perspicax*, keen of sight].

perspire (per-spīr') *v.t.* to emit through the pores of the skin;—*v.i.* to evacuate the moisture of the body through the pores of the skin; to sweat.—**perspira'tion** *n.* the process of perspiring; the moisture emitted [L. *per*, through; *spirare*, to breathe].

persuade (pẹr-swād') *v.t.* to influence by argument, entreaty, etc.; to induce; to win over.—**persuasive** (pẹr-swā'siv) *a.* having the power of persuading; winning.—**persua'sively** *adv.*—**persua'siveness** *n.*—**persuasion** (pẹr-swā'zhun) *n.* the act of persuading; the quality of persuading; settled opinion or conviction; belief; sect.—**persua'sible** *a.* open to persuasion [L. *per*, thoroughly; *suadere*, to advise].

pert (pẹrt) *a.* lively; bold; forward; saucy.—**pert'ly** *adv.*—**pert'ness** *n.* [O.Fr. *apert*].

pertain (pẹr-tān') *v.i.* to belong; to concern [L. *pertinere*, to belong].

pertinacious (per-ti-nā'shus) *a.* adhering to an opinion, etc. with obstinacy; persevering; resolute; unyielding.—**pertina'ciously** *adv.*—**pertina'ciousness** *n.*—**pertinacity** (pẹr-ti-nas'i-ti) *n.* [L. *pertinax*, tenacious].

pertinent (pẹr'ti-nent) *a.* related to the subject or matter in hand; to the point.—**per'tinently** *adv.*—**per'tinence, per'tinency** *n.* [L. *pertinere*, to belong].

perturb (pẹr-turb') *v.t.* to disturb; to trouble greatly.—**perturbation** (pẹr-tur-bā'shun) *n.* mental uneasiness or disquiet; disorder or confusion [L. *per*, thoroughly; *turbare*, to disturb].

Peru (pẹr-ôô') *n.* (*Geog.*) a republic in the west coast of S. America.—**Peru'vian** *n.* a native of Peru;—*a.* pert. to Peru.

peruke (pe-rôôk', per-ūk', pẹr'ūk) *n.* a wig; a periwig [Fr. *perruque*].

peruse (pẹ-rôôz', per-ūz') *v.t.* to read through; to examine minutely.—**peru'sal** *n.* the act of perusing [*per*, thoroughly; and *use*].

pervade (pẹr-vād') *v.t.* to spread through the whole of; to be diffused through all parts of.—**pervasion** (pẹr-vā'zhun) *n.*—**perva'sive** (pẹr-vā'siv) *a.* having power to pervade [L. *per*, through; *vadere*, to go].

perverse (pẹr-vẹrs') *a.* obstinately or unreasonably wrong; refusing to do the right, or to admit error; self-willed.—**perverse'ness, perver'sity** *n.* [L. *per*, thoroughly; *vertere*, to turn].

perversion (pẹr-ver'shun) *n.* a turning from the true purpose, use, or meaning; corruption; unnatural manifestation of sexual desire.—**perver'sive** *a.* tending to pervert [L. *per*, thoroughly; *vertere*, to turn].

pervert (pẹr-vẹrt') *v.t.* to turn from its proper purpose; to misinterpret; to lead astray; to corrupt.—**pervert** (pẹr'vert) *n.* one who has deviated from the normal, esp. from right to wrong [L. *per*, thoroughly; *vertere*, to turn].

pervious (pẹr'vi-us) *a.* giving passage to; penetrable; permeable.—**per'viousness** *n.* [L. *per*, through; *via*, a way].

pessimism (pes'i-mizm) *n.* the doctrine that the world is fundamentally evil; the tendency to look on the dark side of things (opp. of *optimism*); melancholy.—**pess'imist** *n.*—**pessimis'tic** *a.*—**pessimis'tically** *adv.* [L. *pessimus*, worst].

pest (pest) *n.* (*Arch.*) a plague or pestilence; a troublesome or harmful thing or person; (*Colloq.*) nuisance.—**pest'house** *n.* formerly, a hospital for cases of plague, etc.—**pestif'erous** *a.* pestilential; carrying disease [L. *pestis*, a plague].

pester (pes'tẹr) *v.t.* to trouble or vex persistently; to annoy [O.Fr. *empestrer*, fr. L.L. *pastorium*, a foot-shackle].

pesticide (pes'ti-sīd) *n.* a pest killer.

pestilence (pes'ti-lens) *n.* any infectious or contagious, deadly disease.—**pes'tilent** *a.* producing disease; noxious; harmful to morals.—**pestilential** (pes-ti-len'shạl) *a.* pert. to, or producing, pestilence; destructive; wicked [L. *pestis*, plague].

pestle (pes'tl, pes-l) *n.* an instrument for pounding substances in a mortar [L. *pistillum*, fr. *pinsere*, to pound].

pet (pet) *n.* an animal or person kept or regarded with affection; a favourite; a darling;—*a.* favourite;—*v.t.* to make a pet of; to treat with indulgence.—*pr.p.* **pet'ting.**—*pa.p.* and *pa.t.* **pet'ted** [etym. uncertain].

pet (pet) *n.* a sudden fit of ill-temper; peevishness [etym. uncertain].

petal (pet'ạl) *n.* a coloured flower-leaf.—**pet'aled, pet'alled** *a.* having petals.—**pet'aline** *a.* pert. to, resembling, attached to, a petal [Gk. *petalon*, a thin plate].

petard (pet-ȧrd') *n.* formerly, a kind of small bomb; a kind of firework; a paper cracker.—**hoist with his own petard,** beaten with his own weapons [Fr. *pétard*, fr. *péter*, to explode].

peter out (pē'tẹr-out) *v.i.* (*Mining*) of a vein, seam, etc., to become exhausted; to give out, e.g. of engine [etym. uncertain].

petersham (pē'tẹr-shạm) *n.* heavy overcoat, also breeches, formerly fashionable; cloth used to make such garments; thick corded-silk ribbon [fr. Viscount *Petersham*].

petiole (pet'i-ōl) *n.* (*Bot.*) the leaf-stalk of a plant [L. *petiolus*, a little foot].

petit (pẹ-tē') French adjective meaning small; little.—*fem.* **petite** (pẹ-tēt') of a woman, small, dainty, and trim of figure.—**petit point** (pwang) a small, slanting stitch used in embroidery and tapestry; a tent stitch.

petition (pe-tish'un) *n.* an earnest request or prayer, esp. one presented to a sovereign or parliament;—*v.t.* and *i.* to present a petition to; to entreat.—**petit'ionary** *a.*—**petit'ioner** *n.* [L. *petere*, to ask].

petrel (pet´rel) *n.* a small, long-winged sea-bird [fr. St. *Peter*, who walked on the waters].

petrify (pet´ri-fī) *v.t.* to turn into stone; to make hard like stone; (*Fig.*) to make motionless with fear;—*v.i.* to become like stone.—*pr.p.* **pet'rifying**.—*pa.p.* and *pa.t.* **pet'rified**.—*n.*—**petrifac'tive** *a.* [L. and Gk. *petra*, rock, stone; *facere*, to make].

petro- (pet´ro) *prefix* fr. L. and Gk. *petra*, rock, stone, used in derivatives.—**petrogeny** (pet-roj´e-ni) *n.* the science of the origin of rocks.—**petrog'raphy** *n.* the science of describing and classifying rocks.—**petrograph'ic(al)** *a.*—**petrol'ogy** *n.* a branch of geology dealing with the composition, structure, and classification of rocks, their origin and sequence of formation.—**petrolog'ic(al)** *a.*—**petrous** (pe´trus) *a.* pert. to, or like, rock; rocky; hard [Gk. *genesis*, origin; *graphein*, to write; *logos*, discourse].

petroleum (pe-trō´le-um) *n.* rock-oil, a mineral oil drawn from the earth by means of wells.—**pet'rol** *n.* refined petroleum; motor-spirit; (*U.S.*) gasoline.—**petrol'ic** *a.* [L. *petra*, rock; *oleum*, oil].

petticoat (pet´i-kōt) *n.* a woman's underskirt; (*Colloq.*) a woman;—*a.* feminine [orig. *petty coat*, a small coat].

pettifogger (pet´i-fog-er) *n.* a low class lawyer; one given to mean dealing in small matters.—**pett'ifog** *v.i.*—**pett'ifoggery** *n.* low trickery; wrangling over trifles.—**pett'ifogging** *a.* underhand; paltry [etym. uncertain].

pettish (pet´ish) *a.* cross; petulant; easily annoyed.—**pett'ishly** *adv.*—**pett'ishness** *n.* petulance; sulkiness [fr. *pet*, a fit of temper].

petty (pet´i) *a.* small; unimportant; trivial; small-minded; of lower rank.—**pett'ily** *adv.*—**pett'iness** *n.*—**petty cash**, small items of expenditure, esp. in an office.—**petty officer**, a non-commissioned officer in the Navy [Fr. *petit*, small].

petulant (pet´ū-lant) *a.* given to small fits of temper; inclined to complain; irritable.—**pet'ulantly** *adv.*—**pet'ulance**, **pet'ulancy** *n.* peevishness; crossness; fretfulness [L. *petulans*, wanton].

petunia (pē-tū´ni-a) *n.* a common garden plant with showy flowers, white, purple, or violet; purplish red [Braz. *petun*, tobacco].

pew (pū) *n.* a long, fixed bench in a church [O.Fr. *puie*, a platform].

pewee (pē´wē) *n.* a small American bird, the flycatcher [imit. of its note].

pewit (pē´wit) *n.* the lapwing. Also **pee'wit** [imit. of its cry].

pewter (pū´ter) *n.* an alloy of tin and lead or some other metal, esp. copper; ware made of this;—*a.* made of pewter [O.Fr. *peutre*].

Phaethon (fā´e-thon) *n.* (*Myth.*) the son of Helios, god of the Sun, who received permission to drive the chariot of the sun for one day.—**phaeton** (fā´ton) *n.* a light, four-wheeled, open carriage.

phalange (fal´anj) *n.* (*Anat.*) a small bone of a toe or finger.—Also **phal'anx** [fr. *phalanx*].

phalanger (fa-lan´jer) *n.* genus of furry marsupial, some winged; flying squirrel [Gk. *phalangion*, a spider's web].

phalanx (fal´angks, fā´langks) *n.* in ancient Greece, a company of soldiers in close array; hence, any compact body of people.—*pl.* **phal'anxes** [Gk.].

phallus (fal´us) *n.* the penis.—*pl.* **phall'i**.—**phall'ic** *a.* [Gk. *phallos*].

phantasm (fan´tazm) *n.* an imaginary vision; a phantom; a spectre; an illusion.—**phantas'mal**, **phantas'mic** *a.*—**phantasmagoria** (fan-taz-ma-gō´ri-a) *n.* an exhibition of optical illusions; hence, a crowd of dim or unreal figures.—**phantasmagor'ic** *a.*—**phan'tasy** *n.* See **fantasy**.—**phan'tom** (fan´tom) *n.* an apparition; a spectre; a ghost;—*a.* spectral [Gk. *phainein*, to show].

Pharaoh (fā´rō) *n.* 'The Great House,' a title of the kings of ancient Egypt.

Pharisee (far´i-sē) *n.* (*Bib.*) one of a Jewish sect noted for their strict observance of the forms of the Law.—**Pharisaic** (far-i-sā´ik), **Pharisa'ical** *a.*—**Pharisa'ically** *adv.*—**Pharisa'ism**, **Pharisee'ism** *n.* [Heb. *parash*, to separate].

pharmaceutical (fȧr-ma-sū´tik-al) *a.* pert. to pharmacy.—**pharmaceu'tics** *n.pl.* the science of pharmacy.—**pharmaceu'tist** *n.* [Gk. *pharmakon*, a drug].

pharmacy (fȧr´ma-si) *n.* the science of preparing, compounding, and dispensing drugs and medicines; a chemist's shop; a drug-store.—**phar'macist** *n.* one skilled in pharmacy.—**pharmacol'ogy** *n.* the study of drugs and their action.—**pharmacol'ogist** *n.* one skilled in pharmacy.—**pharmacopoeia** (fȧr-ma-kō-pē´ya) *n.* a standard and authoritative book containing a list of medicinal drugs with information on their preparation and dosage [Gk. *pharmakon*, a drug].

Pharos (fā´ros) *n.* island of ancient Egypt with the first lighthouse.—**phare**, **pha'ros** *n.* a lighthouse; a beacon.

pharynx (far´ingks) *n.* the cone-shaped cavity at back of mouth, opening into the gullet.—*pl.* **phar'ynges**.—**pharyngeal** (far-in´jē-al, far-in-jē´al) *a.* Also **pharyn'gal**.—**pharyngitis** (far-in-jī´tis) *n.* (*Med.*) inflammation of pharynx.—**pharyn'goscope** *n.* instrument for examining throat [Gk. *pharunx*, the pharynx].

phase (fāz) *n.* (*Astron.*) an aspect of moon or a planet; a stage in development; an aspect of a subject or question.—**pha'sic** *a.* [Gk. *phasis*, an appearance].

pheasant (fez´ant) *n.* a game-bird with brilliant plumage [Gk. *Phasis*, a river in Colchis, whence the bird first came].

phenacetin (fe-nas´e-tin) *n.* a carbolic derivative of coal tar used as a drug to relieve pain and reduce temperatures [Gk. *phainein*, to shine; *acetum*, vinegar].

phenomenon (fe-nom´e-non) *n.* anything appearing or observed, esp. if having scientific interest; a remarkable person or thing; (*Philos.*) sense appearance as opposed to real existence.—*pl.* **phenom'ena**.—**phenom'enal** *a.* pert. to a phenomenon; remarkable; extraordinary.—**phenom'enally** *adv.* [Gk. *phainomenon*, a thing appearing].

phew (fū) *interj.* expressing disgust, impatience, relief, etc.

phial (fī´al) *n.* a small glass bottle; a vial [Gk. *phialē*, a flat vessel].

philabeg, philibeg (fil´a(i)-beg) *n.* kilt worn by Highlanders of Scotland. Also **fil(l)ibeg** [Gael. *feileadh*, a kilt; *beag*, small].

philander (fi-lan´der) *v.i.* to flirt; to amuse oneself with love-making.—**philan'derer** *n.* [Gk. *philos*, loving; *anēr*, a man].

philanthropy (fi-lan´thro-pi) *n.* love of mankind; benevolence towards one's fellow-men.—**philanthropic** (fil-an-throp´ik), **philanthrop'ical** *a.*—**philanthrop'ically** *adv.*—**philan'thropist** *n.* one who loves and seeks to do good to his fellow-men. Also **phil'anthrope** [Gk. *philos*, loving; *anthrōpos*, man].

philately (fi-lat´e-li) *n.* stamp-collecting.—**philat'elic** *a.*—**philat'elist** *n.* [Gk. *philos*, loving; *atelēs*, franked].

philharmonic (fil-har-mon´ik) *a.* loving harmony or music; musical [Gk. *philos*, loving; *harmonia*, harmony].

Philippic (fil-ip´ik) *n.* orig. one of Demosthenes's three great orations against Philip of Macedon; now, any violent invective, spoken or written.

Philistine (fil´is-tīn, -tin) *n.* (*Bib.*) one of the ancient inhabitants of the coastal plains of Palestine, continually at war with the Israelites; a person with no love of music, painting, etc.; an uncultured person.

philology (fi-lol´o-ji) *n.* scientific study of origin, development, etc. of languages.—**philolog'ical** *a.*—**philologian** (fi-lol-ō´ji-an) **philol'**

ogist *n.* student of philology [Gk. *philos*, loving; *logos*, word, speech].
Philomel (fil'ō-mel) (*Poet.*) a nightingale.
philosophy (fi-los'o-fi) *n.* lit. 'love of wisdom'; originally, any branch of investigation of natural phenomena; now, the study of beliefs regarding God, existence, conduct, etc. and of man's relation with the universe; a calmness of mind; resignation.—**philos'opher** *n.* a student of philosophy.—**philosophic** (fil-o-sof'ik) **philosoph'ical** *a.* pert. to philosophy; wise; calm.—**philosoph'ically** *adv.*—**philos'ophise** *v.i.* to reason like a philosopher; to theorise; to moralise.—**philos'ophism** *n.* a pretended system of philosophy; sophism.—**moral philosophy**, the study of ethics.—**natural philosophy**, a branch of scientific study, physics.—**philosopher's stone**, a substance sought for by alchemists of old, supposed to transform base metals into gold [Gk. *philos*, loving; *sophia*, wisdom].
philtre, philter (fil'tẹr) *n.* a love potion; a drink supposed to excite love [Gk. *philtron*, fr. *philos*, loving).
phlebitis (fle-bī'tis) *n.* (*Med.*) inflammation of a vein.—**phlebit'ic** *a.*—**phlebot'omy** *n.* (*Surg.*) blood-letting [Gk. *phleps*, a vein].
phlegm (flem) *n.* a secretion of thick, slimy mucous substance discharged from throat by expectoration; calmness; sang-froid; sluggishness.—**phlegmatic** (fleg-mat'ik) *a.* cool and collected; unemotional.—**phlegmat'ically** *adv.* [Gk. *phlegma*].
phlogiston (flo-jis'ton) *n.* an element, the 'principle of fire,' once supposed to exist in all combustible bodies, and to be the cause of inflammability.—**phlogis'tic** *a.* [Gk. *phlogistos*, inflammable].
Phlox (floks) *n.* a genus of garden plants [Gk. = a flame].
phobia (fō'bi-ạ) *n.* a morbid dread of anything; used esp. as a suffix, e.g. claustro*phobia*, hydro*phobia*, etc. [Gk. *phobos*, fear].
Phoenix, Phenix (fē'niks) *n.* (*Myth.*) a fabulous Arabian bird, said to have lived for 500 years; it then burned itself but rose again from its ashes; hence, symbol of immortality; a paragon [Gk. *phoinix*].
phone (fōn) *n.*, *v.t.* and *i.* (*Colloq.*) *abbrev.* of **tel'ephone** [Gk. *phōnē*, sound].
phone (fōn) *n.* a sound made in speaking.—**phon'ic** *a.* pert. to sound, esp. to speech sounds; phonetic.—**phon'ics** *n.pl.* used as *sing.* phonetics; acoustics [Gk. *phōnē*].
phonetic (fō-net'ik) *a.* pert. to the voice; pert. to, or representing, vocal sounds. Also **phonet'ical** *a.*—**phonet'ically** *adv.*—**phonet'ics** *n.* the branch of the study of language which deals with speech sounds, and their symbols.—**phoneti'cian** *n.* a student of phonetics.—**phonet'icise** *v.t.* to represent phonetically.—**phonetic spelling**, a simplified system of spelling in which same letter or symbol is always used for same sound, e.g. cat = kat [Gk. *phōnē*, sound].
phoney, phony (fō'ni) *a.* (*Slang.*) sham; counterfeit [U.S. slang; origin uncertain].
phono- (fō'nō) *prefix* fr. Gk. *phōnē*, sound, used in many derivatives.—**pho'nogram** *n.* a character or symbol, esp. in shorthand, used to represent a speech sound; a phonograph record.—**pho'nograph** *n.* an early type of gramophone.—**phonog'raphy** *n.* the recording or reproducing of sound with a phonograph; a system of shorthand.—**phonol'ogy** *n.* study of speech sounds; phonetics.—**phonolog'ic(al)** *a.* —**phonol'ogist** *n.*
phosgene (fos'jēn) *n.* carbon oxychloride, a poison-gas [Gk. *phōs*, light; *genesis*, origin].
phosphate (fos'fāt) *n.* a salt of phosphoric acid.—**phosphat'ic** *a.*—**phosphate of lime**, commercially, bone-ash.—**phos'phide** *n.* a compound of phosphorus with another element, e.g. copper.—**phos'phite** *n.* a salt of phosphorous acid [fr. *phosphorus*].
phosphorus (fos'for-us) *n.* a non-metallic element, a yellowish wax-like substance giving out a pale light in the dark.—**phos'phorous** *a.* pert. to phosphorus.—**phosphorescence** (fos-for-es'ens) *n.* the giving out of light without heat, as phosphorus, the glow-worm, decaying fish, etc.—**phosphoresc'ent** *a.*—**phosphor'ic** *a.* pert. to, or obtained from, phosphorus; phosphorous.—**phos'phureted** *a.* combined with phosphorus [Gk. *phōs*, light; *phoros*, bearing].
photo (fō'tō) *n.* (*Colloq.*) *abbrev.* of photograph; —*v.t.* to photograph.
photo- (fō'tō) *prefix* fr. Gk. *phōs*, *phōtos*, light, used in derivatives.—**photo-chemistry** (fō-tō-kem'is-tri) *n.* the branch of chemistry which treats of the chemical action of light.—**pho'to-electric'ity** *n.* electricity produced by the action of light on a metallic surface.—**pho'to-elec'tron** *n.* an electron liberated from a metallic surface by the action of a beam of light.—**photofinish**, in racing, a photo taken at the finish to show correct placing of contestants.—**photogen'ic** *a.* producing light; photographic; of a person, having features, etc. that photograph well.
photography (fō-tog'rạ-fi) *n.* the art of producing pictures by the chemical action of light on a sensitive plate or film.—**pho'tograph** *n.* a picture so made;—*v.t.* to take a photograph of.—**photog'rapher** *n.*—**photograph'ic, photograph'ical** *a.* pert. to, resembling, or produced by, photography.—**photograph'ically** *adv.*—**photogravure** (fō-tō-grạ-vūr) *n.* a method of producing prints from a photograph etched on a metal plate;—*v.t.* to reproduce thus;—*n.* a print so made.—**photolithography** (fō-tō-li-thog'rạ-fi) *n.* a method of preparing a photograph for transfer to stone from which prints can be produced [Gk. *phōs*, light; *graphein*, to write; Fr. *gravure*, an engraving; Gk. *lithos*, a stone].
photology (fō-tol'o-ji) *n.* the science of light. —**photom'eter** *n.* an instrument for measuring the intensity of light [Gk. *phōs*, light; *logos*, discourse; *metron*, a measure].
photon (fō'ton) *n.* the unit of measurement of light-intensity [Gk. *phōs*, *phōtos*, light].
Photostat (fō'tō-stat) *n.* a photographic apparatus for making copies of documents, etc. direct on paper;—*v.t.* to copy thus.—**photostat'ic** *a.* [Protected Trade Name].
photosynthesis (fō-tō-sin'the-sis) *n.* the process by which a plant, under the influence of sunlight, can build up, in its chlorophyll-containing cells, carbohydrates from the carbon dioxide of the atmosphere and from the hydrogen of the water in the soil [Gk. *phōs*, *phōtos*, light; *sun*, together; *thesis*, a placing].
phototelegraphy (fō-tō-tel-eg'rạ-fi) *n.* the transmission by telegraph of photographs, illustrations, etc. [*photo* and *telegraphy*].
phrase (frāz) *n.* a small group of words forming part of a sentence; a short pithy expression; a characteristic mode of expression; (*Mus.*) a short, distinct part of a longer passage;—*v.t.* to express suitably in words.—**phraseogram** (frā'ze-ō-gram) *n.* in shorthand, a symbol used to represent a phrase.—**phraseol'ogy** *n.* a mode of expression; the choice of words used in speaking or writing [Gk. *phrazein*, to speak].
phren (fren) *n.* the mind; (*Med.*) the diaphragm.—**phrenesis** (fren-ē'sis) *n.* delirium.—**phrenet'ic** *a.* having the mind disordered; frenzied; frantic [Gk. *phrēn*, the diaphragm, the mind].
phrenology (fre-nol'o-ji) *n.* character reading from the shape of the head.—**phrenolog'ic(al)** *a.*—**phrenolog'ically** *adv.*—**phrenol'ogist** *n.* [Gk. *phrēn*, mind; *logos*, discourse].
phthisis (thī'sis) *n.* (*Med.*) a wasting away of the lungs; consumption.—**phthisic** (thī'sik), **phthisical** (thiz'ik-ạl) *a.* [Gk. fr. *phthiein*, to waste away].
phut (fut) *n.* the sound of a bladder collapsing. —**to go phut** (*Colloq.*) to collapse; to break down [Hind. *phatna*, to burst].

phylactery (fil-ak′tẹ-ri) *n.* a charm or amulet; strips of vellum, inscribed with certain verses of the Law, enclosed in a small leather case and worn on the forehead or left arm by male Jews during morning prayer [Gk. *phulassein,* to guard].

phylogeny (fī-loj′e-ni) *n.* (*Bot.*) the evolution of an animal or plant type.—**phylum** (fī′lum) *n.* (*Bot.*) one of the primary divisions of the animal or plant kingdoms.—*pl.* **phy'la** [Gk. *phulon,* a race; *genesis,* origin].

physic (fiz′ik) *n.* (*Arch.*) the art of healing; a drug; medicine in general;—*v.t.* to give a dose of physic to.—*pr.p.* **phys'icking.**—*pa.p.* and *pa.t.* **phys'icked.**—**physician** (fi-zish′ạn) *n.* one skilled in the art of healing; a medical doctor [Gk. *phusis,* nature].

physical (fiz′ik-ạl) *a.* pert. to physics; pert. to nature; bodily, as opposed to mental or moral; material.—**phys'ically** *adv.* [Gk. *phusis,* nature].

physics (fiz′iks) *n.* sciences (excluding chemistry and biology) which deal with natural phenomena, e.g. motion, force, light, sound, electricity, etc. Also called ' Natural Philosophy.'—**physicist** (fiz′i-sist) *n.* [Gk. *phusis,* nature].

physiognomy (fiz-i-og′no-mi, fiz-i-on′o-mi) *n.* art of judging character from contours of face; face itself; expression of the face.—**physiognom'ic, physiognom'ical** *a.*—**physiog'nomist** *n.* [Gk. *phusis,* nature; *gnōmōn,* a judge].

physiography (fiz-i-og′rạ-fi) *n.* the study and description of natural phenomena; physical geography.—**physiog'rapher** *n.* [Gk. *phusis,* nature; *graphein,* to write].

physiology (fiz-i-ol′o-ji) *n.* science which deals with functions and life processes of plants, animals, and human beings.—**physiolog'ical** *a.* —**physiol'ogist** *n.* [Gk. *phusis,* nature; *logos,* discourse].

physiotherapy (fiz-i-ō-ther′ạ-pi) *n.* the application of massage, manipulation, light, heat, electricity, etc., for treatment of certain disabilities [Gk. *phusis,* nature; *therapeuein,* to cure].

physique (fi-zēk′) *n.* bodily structure and development [Fr. fr. Gk. *phusis,* nature].

phyto- (fī′tō) *prefix* fr. Gk. *phuton,* a plant.—**phytogenesis** (fī-tō-jen′ẹ-sis), **phytogeny** (fī-toj′e-ni) *n.* the evolution of plants.

pi (pī) *n.* the Greek letter π, esp. as a mathematical symbol for the ratio of the circumference of a circle to its diameter, approx. $3\frac{1}{7}$, or 3.14159.

pianissimo *adv.* very softly [It.].

piano (pē-à′nō) *adv.* (*Mus.*) softly.—**pianis′simo** *adv.* very softly [It.].

piano (pē-à′nō) *n. abbrev.* of **pianoforte** (pē-à-nō-for′tā) *n.* a musical instrument having wires of graduated tension, struck by hammers moved by notes on a keyboard.—**Piano'la** *n.* (Protected Trade Name) a mechanically played piano.—**pianist** (pē′ạ-nist, pē-an′ist) *n.* one who plays the piano [It. *piano e forte* = soft and strong].

piastre (pi-as′tẹr) *n.* a monetary unit of several Eastern countries, including Turkey, Egypt (approx. value = $2\frac{1}{2}$d.). Also **pias'ter** [It. *piastra*].

piazza (pē-at′sạ, pē-az′ạ) *n.* a large open square, surrounded by buildings or colonnades; a public square [It.].

pibroch (pē′broH) *n.* a selection of music for the Scottish bagpipes [Gael. *piob,* a pipe].

pica (pī′kạ) *n.* (*Print.*) a size of type, having 6 lines to the inch [L. *pica,* a magpie, fr. the contrast between the black print and white paper].

picador (pik-ạ-dor′) *n.* a mounted bullfighter armed with a lance to prod the bull [Sp. *pica,* a pike].

picaroon (pik′ạ-ròòn) *n.* an adventurer; a pirate.—**picaresque** (pik-a-resk′) *a.* of a novel, dealing with the lives and adventures of rogues [Sp. *picaro,* a rogue].

piccalilli (pik-ạ-lil′i) *n.* a pickle of vegetables [etym. uncertain].

piccaninny (pik′ạ-nin-i) *n.* a small child; a Negro baby [Sp. *pequeño,* small].

piccolo (pik′o-lō) *n.* (*Mus.*) a small flute, sounding an octave higher than the ordinary flute [It.].

pick (pik) *v.t.* to peck at, like birds with their bills; to pierce with a pointed instrument; to open with a pointed instrument, as a lock; to pluck, or cull, as flowers, etc.; to raise or lift (with 'up'); to choose or select; to rob; to pluck the strings of a musical instrument; (*Colloq.*) to eat;—*v.i.* to eat daintily or without appetite; (*Colloq.*) to nag; to find fault with (with 'on');—*n.* a sharp-pointed tool, used for breaking up earth, etc.; the act of choosing; choice; the right of selection; the choicest or best of anything.—**pick'axe** *n.* an instrument for digging, with a straight or curved metal head having a point at one end and a transverse blade at the other.—**pick'ing** *n.* the act of one who picks; stealing;—*pl.* gleanings; perquisites, often obtained by slightly underhand methods.—**pick'pocket** *n.* one who steals from pockets.—**pick′-me-up** *n.* a drink that acts as a stimulant or restorative [Scand.].

pick-a-back (pik′a-bak) *adv.* on the shoulders or back [etym. uncertain].

pickerel (pik′ẹ-rel) *n.* a young pike; a kind of pike [dim. fr. *pike*].

picket (pik′et) *n.* a sharpened stake (used in fortifications, etc.); a peg or pale; a guard posted in front of an army; a party sent out by trade unions to dissuade men from working during a strike;—*v.t.* to fence with pickets; to post, as a guard; to beset with pickets [Fr. *piquet,* fr. *pic,* a pike].

pickle (pik′l) *n.* brine or vinegar in which fish, meat, or vegetables are preserved; any food preserved in brine or vinegar; a difficult situation;—*v.t.* to preserve with salt or vinegar.—**pick'led** *a.* (*Slang*) drunk.—**pick'les** *n.pl.* vegetables in vinegar and spices [etym. uncertain].

picnic (pik′nik) *n.* pleasure excursion with meal out of doors; agreeable situation;—*v.i.* to go on a picnic.—*pr.p.* **pic'nicking.**—*pa.p.* and *pa.t.* **pic'nicked** [Fr. *pique-nique,* etym. uncertain].

picot (pē′kō) *n.* a small projecting loop of thread forming part of an ornamental edging to ribbon, lace, etc. [Fr.].

picotee (pik-o-tē′) *n.* a variety of carnation [Fr. *picoté,* marked with points].

picric (pik′rik) *a.* pert. to **picric acid,** a poisonous, crystalline substance used in solution as a dressing for burns, etc. [Gk. *pikros,* bitter].

Pict (pikt) *n.* one of an ancient race, formerly inhabiting E. Scotland.—**Pic'tish** *a.* [Perh. fr. L. *pictus,* painted].

pictograph (pik′to-graf) *n.* a picture representing an idea; writing in pictorial symbols [L. *pingere, pictum,* to paint; Gk. *graphein,* to write].

pictorial (pik-tō′ri-ạl) *a.* pert. to pictures; expressed by pictures; illustrated.—**picto'rially** *adv.* [L. *pictor,* a painter, fr. *pingere,* to paint]

picture (pik′tūr) *n.* a representation of objects or scenes on paper, canvas, etc., by drawing, painting, photography, etc.; a mental image; a likeness or copy; an illustration; picturesque object; a graphic or vivid description in words; —*v.t.* to draw or paint an image or representation of; to describe graphically; to recall vividly.—**picturesque** (pik-tū-resk′) *a.* making pleasing picture; vivid in description.—**picturesque'ly** *adv.*—**picturesque'ness** *n.*—**pic'ture-gall'ery** *n.* a hall containing a collection of pictures for exhibition.—**pic'ture-house, pic'ture-pal'ace,** *n.* a cinema [L. *pingere, pictum,* to paint].

piddle (pid′l) *v.i.* (*Arch.*) to trifle;—**pidd'ling** *a.* trifling [etym. uncertain].

pidgin (pij′in) *n.* Chinese corruption of English word *business.*—**pidgin** or **pigeon English,** a jargon used in China between foreigners and natives.

pie (pī) *n.* (*Cookery*) a dish of meat or fruit covered with paste and baked; (*Print.*) a confused mass of type [etym. uncertain].

pie (pī) *n.* a magpie; a kind of woodpecker.—**piebald** (pī'bawld) *a.* irregularly marked; streaked with any two colours.—**pied** *a.* piebald; variegated [L. *pica*, a magpie; *bald* = *balled*, streaked].

piece (pēs) *n.* a part of anything; a bit; a portion; a single object; a separate example; a coin; a counter in chess, draughts, etc.; a literary work; a musical composition; a gun; a plot of land;—*v.t.* to mend; to put together.—**piece'goods** *n.pl.* textile fabrics, e.g. shirtings, long-cloths, etc. sold by recognised lengths of the material.—**piece'meal** *adv.* little by little; gradually.—**piece'work** *n.* work paid for by the amount done, and not by the hour, day, etc.—**piece of eight**, an old Spanish dollar = eight reals [Fr. *pièce*].

pier (pēr) *n.* a piece of solid, upright masonry, as a support or pillar for an arch, bridge, or beam; a structure built out over the water as a landing-stage.—**pier'glass** *n.* a tall mirror, esp. a wall-mirror between two windows [Fr. *pierre*, stone, fr. L. *petra*].

pierce (pērs) *v.t.* to thrust into, esp. with a pointed instrument; to make a hole in; to penetrate;—*v.i.* to enter; to penetrate.—**pierc'ing** *a.* penetrating; sharp; keen.—**pierc'ingly** *adv.* [Fr. *percer*].

pierrot (pē'er-ō) *n.* (*fem.* **pierrette'**) a French pantomime character; a member of a troupe of seaside entertainers [Fr. dim. of *Pierre*, Peter].

piety (pī'e-ti) *n.* the quality of being pious; devotion to religion; affectionate respect for one's parents.—**pi'etist** *n.* an ultra-pious person; a sanctimonious person.—**pietist'ic** *a.*—**pi'etism** *n.* [L. *pietas*, fr. *pius*, pious].

piffle (pif'l) *n.* (*Colloq.*) rubbish; twaddle.—**piff'ling** *a.* worthless [etym. uncertain].

pig (pig) *n.* a hoofed domestic animal, reared for its flesh; oblong mass of smelted metal, as pig-iron;—*v.i.* to bring forth pigs.—**pigg'ish** *a.* pert. to, or like, pigs; dirty; greedy; stubborn.—**pigg'ery** *n.* a place where swine are kept.—**pig'tail** *n.* the tail of a pig; a queue or plait of hair hanging from the back of the head; a roll of twisted tobacco.—**pig'eyed** *a.* having small, sly eyes.—**pig'head'ed** *a.* obstinate; stupidly perverse.—**pig'iron, -lead**, iron, lead, cast in rough oblong bars.—**pig'nut** *n.* the earth-nut.—**pig'skin** *n.* strong leather made from the pig's skin, and used for saddles, etc.—**pig'sticking** *n.* hunting wild boar with a spear, popular in India.—**pig'sty** *n.* a covered enclosure for keeping pigs in; a dirty house or room [M.E. *pigge*].

pigeon (pij'un) *n.* any bird of the dove family, both wild and domesticated; a simpleton or dupe.—**pig'eon-Eng'lish** *n.* See **pidgin-English**.—**pig'eon-heart'ed** *a.* timid.—**pig'eon-hole** *n.* a little division in a desk or case, for holding papers, etc.;—*v.t.* to place in the pigeon-hole of a desk, etc.; to shelve for future reference; to classify.—**pig'eon-liv'ered** *a.* meek; cowardly.—**pig'eon-toed** *a.* having turned-in toes [Fr. fr. L. *pipio, pipionis*, a young piping bird].

pigment (pig'ment) *n.* paint; colouring matter; colouring matter in animal tissues and cells.—**pigmenta'tion** *n.* (*Med.*) the deposit of colouring matter, esp. when excessive [L. *pigmentum*].

pigmy (pig'mi) *n.* See **pygmy**.

pike (pīk) *n.* a sharp point; an old weapon consisting of a long, wooden shaft with a flat-pointed steel head; a voracious freshwater fish; a turnpike or toll-bar.—**pike'staff** *n.* a staff with a sharp metal spike [O.E. *pic*, a point].

pilaster (pi-las'ter) *n.* a square column, usually set in a wall [It. *pilastro*, fr. L. *pila*, a pillar].

pilchard (pil'chard) *n.* a sea-fish resembling the herring, but smaller [etym. uncertain].

pile (pīl) *n.* a mass or collection of things; a heap; a large building or mass of buildings; an electric battery, consisting of superimposed metal plates; (*Colloq.*) a large fortune;—*v.t.* to throw into a pile or heap; to accumulate (up) [L. *pila*, a pillar].

pile (pīl) *n.* in atomic energy research, the nuclear energy furnace, made by accumulation of uranium and graphite. When the pile becomes greater than a certain critical size, it becomes intensely radio-active, radiating neutrons and gamma rays.

pile (pīl) *n.* a beam driven vertically into the ground to support a building, a bridge, etc.;—*v.t.* to drive piles into; to support with piles.—**pile'dri'ver** *n.* an engine for driving in piles [O.E. *pil*, a dart].

pile (pīl) *n.* fur or hair; nap of a fabric, esp. if thick and close-set, as in velvet [L. *pilus*, a hair].

piles (pīlz) *n.pl.* a disease of the rectum; haemorrhoids [L. *pila*, a ball].

pilfer (pil'fer) *v.t.* and *i.* to steal in small quantities [O.Fr. *pelfrer*].

pilgrim (pil'grim) *n.* a traveller, esp. one who journeys to visit a holy place.—**pil'grimage** *n.* journey to a holy place; the journey of life [O.Fr. *pelegrin*, fr. L. *peregrinus*, a stranger].

pill (pil) *n.* a small ball of medicine, to be swallowed whole; anything disagreeable that has to be endured; (*Slang*) any ball.—**pill'box** *n.* (*Mil.*) a small, concrete fort [L. *pilula*, dim. fr. *pila*, a ball].

pillage (pil'āj) *n.* the act of plundering; plunder or spoil, esp. in war;—*v.t.* to plunder [Fr. *piller*, fr. L. *pilare*, to plunder].

pillar (pil'ar) *n.* a slender upright structure of stone, iron, etc.; a column; a support.—**pill'ared** *a.*—**pill'ar-box** *n.* a hollow iron pillar in which letters can be posted [L. *pila*, a column].

pillion (pil'yun) *n.* a cushioned-pad put behind the saddle on a horse or motor-cycle as a seat for a second person [Gael. *pillean*, a pack-saddle].

pillory (pil'o-ri) *n.* an old instrument used to punish offenders, consisting of a frame with holes for head and hands in which the person was confined and exposed to pelting and ridicule;—*v.t.* to punish by putting into a pillory; to expose to ridicule and abuse.—*pr.p.* **pill'orying**.—*pa.p.* and *pa.t.* **pill'oried** [Fr. *pilori*].

pillow (pil'ō) *n.* a cushion for the head, esp. for a person in bed;—*v.t.* to place on a pillow.—**pill'ow-case, pill'ow-slip** *n.* a removable covering for a pillow [O.E. *pyle*].

pilose (pī'lōs) *a.* hairy; covered with hair. Also **pi'lous**.—**pilos'ity** *n.* [L. *pilus*, hair].

pilot (pī'lot) *n.* a person qualified to take charge of a ship entering or leaving a harbour, or where knowledge of local waters is needed; one qualified to operate an aircraft; a steersman; a guide;—*v.t.* to direct the course of; to guide through dangers or difficulties.—**pi'lot-cloth** *n.* a heavy, blue, woollen cloth for overcoats.—**pi'lot-en'gine** *n.* a locomotive sent on ahead to clear the way for a train.—**pi'lot-fish** *n.* a tropical fish, said to guide sharks to their prey.—**pilot light**, a small jet of gas kept burning in order to light a cooker, geyser, etc.—**pilot officer** (*R.A.F.*) an officer of equivalent rank to a second lieutenant in the Army or act. sub-lieut. R.N. [Fr. *pilote*].

Pilsener (pil'se-ner) *n.* a kind of lager beer [fr. *Pilsen*, Czechoslovakia].

pimento (pi-men'tō) *n.* allspice, a spice prepared from the Jamaica pepper-tree [Sp. fr. L. *pigmentum*, spice].

pimp (pimp) *n.* a procurer; a pander;—*v.i.* to pander [Fr. *pimper*, to dress up].

pimpernel (pim'per-nel) *n.* an annual plant of the primrose family [Fr. fr. L. *bipennis*, two-winged].

pimple (pim'pl) *n.* a small, red, pustular spot

on the skin.—**pim'pled, pim'ply** *a.* having pimples [etym. uncertain].

pin (pin) *n.* a short, thin piece of stiff wire with a point and head for fastening soft materials together; a wooden or metal peg or rivet; (*Golf*) a thin metal or wooden stick (with a flag) to mark the position of the hole; a trifle; —*pl.* (*Slang*) the legs;—*v.t.* to fasten with pins; to seize and hold fast.—*pr.p.* **pin'ning.**—*pa.p.* and *pa.t.* **pinned.**—**pin'cushion** *n.* a small pad in which pins are stuck.—**pin'-mon'ey** *n.* originally, a sum of money settled on a wife for her private expenses; hence, a wife's dress allowance.—**pin'point** *v.t.* (*R.A.F.*) to locate (a target) with great accuracy.—**pin'prick** *n.* a prick with a pin; (*Fig.*) a petty annoyance or irritation.—**pin'-ta'ble** *n.* a game in which balls are to be shot into various holes round obstacles originally formed by pins.—**pin-up girl** (*Colloq.*) one whose photograph is pinned up on the wall; hence, any good-looking girl [O.E. *pinn*, a peg].

pinafore (pin'ạ-fōr) *n.* an apron for a child or young girl [E. *pin* and *afore*].

pince-nez (pangs'nā) *n.* a pair of eyeglasses fixed to the nose by a spring-clip [Fr. *pincer*, to pinch; *nez*, the nose].

pincers (pin'sẹrz) *n.pl.* a tool for gripping, composed of two limbs crossed and pivoted; nippers; pliers; the claw of a lobster, crab, etc.—**pincer-movement** (*Mil.*) a two-fold attack converging on the enemy's position [Fr. *pincer*, to pinch].

pinch (pinsh) *v.t.* to nip or squeeze, e.g. between the thumb and finger; to stint; to make thin, e.g. by hunger; (*Slang*) to steal; (*Slang*) to arrest;—*v.i.* to press hard; to be miserly;—*n.* as much as can be taken up between the thumb and finger; a nip; an emergency.—**pinched** *a.* (*Fig.*) thin and hungry-looking [Fr. *pincer*].

pinchbeck (pinsh'bek) *n.* a zinc and copper alloy; cheap jewellery;—*a.* counterfeit; sham; flashy; tawdry [invented, by C. *Pinchbeck*, a London watchmaker].

Pindar (pin'dar) *n.* great lyric poet of ancient Greece (522-442 B.C.).—**Pindar'ic** *a.* pert. to the poet or his poetry;—*n.* an imitation of one of his odes.

pine (pīn) *n.* a coniferous tree with evergreen, needle-like leaves; wood of this tree; a pineapple.—**pi'ney, pi'ny** *a.* abounding with pines.—**pine'-app'le** *n.* tropical plant and its fruit resembling a pine-cone; the ananas.—**pine'cone** *n.* fruit of the pine.—**pine'-need'le** *n.* the leaf of the pine-tree [L. *pinus*].

pine (pīn) *v.i.* to waste away from grief, anxiety, want, etc.; to languish; to wither; to desire eagerly [O.E. *pinian*, fr. *pin*, pain].

pinfold (pin'fōld) *n.* an enclosure in which stray cattle are confined; a pound [for *pind-fold* = pound-fold].

ping (ping) *n.* the sound that a bullet makes going through the air.—**ping'pong** *n.* table-tennis [imit.].

pinion (pin'yun) *n.* the outermost joint of a bird's wing; (*Poet.*) wing; feather; a small wheel with teeth working into the teeth of a larger wheel;—*v.t.* to cut off the pinion; to restrain by binding arms to body; to shackle [O.Fr. *pignon*].

pink (pingk) *n.* a clove-scented garden-flower of various colours; a light crimson colour; that which is supremely excellent; the scarlet colour of a fox-hunter's coat;—*a.* of a pale crimson colour [etym. uncertain].

pink (pingk) *v.t.* to pierce with small holes; to pierce with a sword, etc.; to ornament the edge with scallops, etc. [M.E. *pinken*, to prick].

pink (pingk) *n.* a boat with a very narrow stern.—**pink'-sterned** *a.* [Dut.].

pink (pingk) *v.i.* of a motor-engine, to make a metallic, knocking sound [imit.].

pinna (pin'ạ) *n.* a feather; the fin of a fish.—**pinn'ate, pinn'ated** *a.* feather-shaped; having wings or fins [L. *pinna*, for *penna*, a feather].

pinnace (pin'ạs) *n.* a warship's boat, usually with eight oars; a light sailing-vessel [Fr. *pinasse*, prob. fr. L. *pinus*, pine].

pinnacle (pin'ạ-kl) *n.* a slender turret elevated above the main building; a rocky mountain peak; a summit; (*Fig.*) the climax [L. *pinna*, a feather, a battlement].

pint (pīnt) *n.* a liquid measure equal to 4 gills or ½ quart [Fr. *pinte*].

pintle (pin'tl) *n.* pivot-pin; bolt on which rudder turns [dim. of *pin*].

pinto (pin'tō) *n.* a piebald horse [Sp.].

pioneer (pī-o-nēr') *n.* (*Mil.*) one of an advance body clearing or repairing a road for troops; an explorer; one who originates anything or prepares the way for others;—*v.i.* to open a way or originate [Fr. *pionnier*, fr. *pion*, a foot-soldier].

pious (pī'us) *a.* having reverence and love for God; marked by pretended or mistaken devotion; (*Arch.*) showing respect towards parents, etc.—**pi'ously** *adv.* [L. *pius*].

pip (pip) *n.* the seed of an apple, orange, etc. —**pip'less** *a.* [*abbrev.* fr. *pippin*].

pip (pip) *n.* a disease in the mouth of fowls.—**to have the pip,** to be depressed, or irritable [L.L. *pipita*, fr. *pituita*, phlegm, rheum].

pip (pip) *n.* the star on an officer's shoulder; each spot on a domino, playing-card, dice, etc.; (*Radio*) each of the six shrill notes broadcast as a time signal.

pip (pip) *v.t.* (*Colloq.*) to wound; to fail, esp. in an examination.

pipe (pīp) *n.* a tubular instrument of music; any long tube; a tube of clay, wood, etc. with a bowl for smoking; a bird's note; a wine-measure, usually containing 126 gallons; a pipeful of tobacco; a funnel; a pipe-like vein of ore;—*pl.* bagpipes;—*v.t.* to perform on a pipe; to utter in a shrill tone; to convey by means of pipes; to ornament with a piping or fancy edging;—*v.i.* to play on a pipe, esp. the bagpipes; to whistle.—**piped** (pīpt) *a.* furnished with a pipe; tubular; conveyed by pipes.—**pi'ping** *a.* giving forth a shrill sound;—*n.* the act of playing on a pipe; a system of pipes (for gas, water, etc.); a kind of cord trimming for ladies' dresses; ornamentation made on cakes by forcing icing through a small nozzle.—**pi'per** *n.*—**pipe'-clay** *n.* a fine, whitish clay used in the manufacture of tobacco-pipes;—*v.t.* to whiten with pipe-clay.—**pipe'line** *n.* a long line of piping for conveying water from reservoir to towns, oil from wells to sea-ports, etc.—**pipe'-ma'jor** *n.* (*Mil.*) the non-commissioned officer in command of a pipe-band [O.E. *pipe*, fr. L. *pipa*].

pipette (pi-pet') *n.* a thin, glass tube used for withdrawing small quantities of a liquid from a vessel [Fr. dim. of *pipe*].

pipit (pip'it) *n.* a small bird, resembling the lark [imit.].

pipkin (pip'kin) *n.* a small earthenware jar or pan [etym. uncertain].

pippin (pip'in) *n.* one of several kinds of apple [O.Fr. *pepin*, a seed].

piquant (pē'kạnt) *a.* agreeably pungent to the taste; (*Fig.*) arousing curiosity.—**pi'quantly** *adv.*—**piquancy** (pē'kạn-si) *n.* pungency [Fr. *piquer*, to prick].

pique (pēk) *v.t.* to irritate; to hurt the pride of; to displease; to stimulate; to pride oneself. —*pr.p.* **piq'uing.**—*pa.p.* and *pa.t.* **piqued** (pēkt);—*n.* annoyance from a slight; vexation [Fr. *piquer*, to prick].

pique (pēk) *n.* (*Cards*) in the game of piquet, the scoring of 30 points before opponents have scored at all;—*v.t.* and *i.* to make this score [Fr.].

piqué (pē'kā) *n.* a stiff, ribbed cotton fabric [Fr.].

piquet (pi-ket') *n.* a card game for 2, 3, or 4 players, with 32 cards [Fr.].

pirate (pī'rāt) *n.* a sea-robber; a vessel manned by sea-robbers; a publisher, etc. who infringes copyright;—*v.t.* and *i.* to act as a pirate; to plunder; to publish or reproduce regardless of copyright.—**pirat'ical** *a.*—**pirat'ically** *adv.*—**pi'racy** *n.* [Gk. *peirates*, fr. *peiraein*, to attempt].

pirouette (pir-òò-et') *n.* a spinning round on one toe;—*v.i.* to do this [Fr.].

piscatology (pis-ka-tol'-o-ji) *n.* the study of fishes.—**piscator** (pis-kā'-tor) *n.* an angler; a fisherman.—**piscato'rial, pis'catory** *a.* pert. to fishes or fishing.—**pis'ciform** *a.* fish-shaped.—**pisciv'orous** *a.* fish-eating [L. *piscis*, a fish].

Pisces (pi'-sēz) *n.pl.* (*Astron.*) the Fishes, the twelfth sign of the zodiac, which the sun enters on Feb. 20 [L. *piscis*, a fish].

piscina (pis-ī'-na) *n.* a stone basin near the altar; a tank for fish.—**pisci'nal** *a.* [L. *piscis*, a fish].

piscine (pis'-īn) *a.* pert. to fishes;—*n.* a bathing-pool [L. *piscis*, a fish].

piss (pis) *v.i.* to make water;—*n.* urine [Fr. *pisser*].

pistachio (pis-ta'(tā')-shi-ō) *n.* the nut of an Asiatic tree, whose kernel is used for flavouring [Sp. fr. Gk. *pistakion*].

pistil (pis'-til) *n.* the seed-bearing organ of a flower, consisting of the stigma, style, and ovary.—**pis'tillate** *a.* having a pistil but no stamen [L. *pistillum*, a pestle].

pistol (pis'-tl) *n.* a small hand-gun;—*v.t.* to shoot with a pistol [Fr. *pistolet*, fr. *Pistoia* Italy].

pistole (pis-tōl') *n.* an obsolete gold coin, originally Spanish, worth 16s. to 18s. [Fr.].

piston (pis'-tun) *n.* a closely fitting metal disc moving to and fro in a hollow cylinder, e.g. as in a steam-engine, motor-car, etc.—**pis'ton-rod** *n.* a rod which connects the piston with another part of the machinery [It. *pistone*, fr. L. *pinsere*, *pistum*, to pound].

pit (pit) *n.* a deep hole in the ground, esp. one from which coal etc. is dug or quarried; the abyss of hell; an area for cock-fighting, etc.; in the theatre, the cheaper priced seats behind the orchestra stalls; in motor-racing, the base where cars are re-filled, etc.; a small indentation in the skin left by the pustule of certain diseases, e.g. smallpox;—*v.t.* to mark with little hollows, as by pustules; to place in a pit; to put forward as an antagonist in a contest.—**pitt'ed** *a.* marked with small hollows.—**pit'fall** *n.* a pit lightly covered, intended to entrap animals; (*Fig.*) any hidden danger [O.E. *pytt*, fr. L. *puteus*, a well].

pitapat (pit'-a-pat) *adv.* in a flutter; with palpitation;—*n.* a light, quick step [reduplication of *pat*].

pitch (pich) *n.* a thick, black, sticky substance obtained by boiling down tar;—*v.t.* to cover over, smear with pitch.—**pitch'iness** *n.*—**pitch'black, pitch'-dark** *a.* very dark.—**pitch'blende** *n.* natural ore consisting mainly of uranium oxide, a source of radium.—**pitch'-pine** *n.* a pine abounding in resinous matter [L. *pix*].

pitch (pich) *v.t.* to throw, toss, fling; to set up (a tent, camp, wickets, etc.); to set the key-note of;—*v.i.* to alight; to fix one's choice on (with 'on'); to plunge or fall forward; to slope down; of a ship, to plunge.—*n.* the act of tossing or casting or, in golf, lofting the ball; a throw or cast; degree of elevation or depth; the highest point; the plunging motion of a vessel lengthwise; degree of acuteness of musical note; (*Cricket*) the ground between wickets; station for a street vendor or beggar; the distance between consecutive threads of a screw, or between successive teeth of a gear.—**pitched** (picht) *a.* sloping; fully arranged for and deliberately entered upon, as a *pitched battle*.—**pitch'er** *n.*—**pitch'fork** *n.* a fork for tossing hay, etc.; a tuning-fork;—*v.t.* to lift with a pitchfork; (*Fig.*) to thrust suddenly into.—**pitch and toss**, a gambling game, played by tossing coins [form of *pick*].

pitcher (pich'-er) *n.* a jug; a vessel usually with a handle and a lip or spout [L.L. *picarium*, a goblet].

pith (pith) *n.* the soft, spongy substance in the centre of plant stems; the essential substance; force or vigour; importance.—**pith'y** *a.* consisting of pith; terse and forceful; energetic.—**pith'ily** *adv.*—**pith'iness** *n.*—**pith'less** *a.* [O.E. *pitha*].

pittance (pit'-ans) *n.* orig. an allowance of food or drink; a very small or insufficient portion or allowance [Fr. *pitance*, allowance of food in a monastery].

pituitary (pi-tū'-i-tari) *a.* secreting mucus.—**pituitary gland**, a ductless gland at base of the brain, secreting an endocrine influencing growth [L. *pituita*, mucus].

pity (pit'-i) *n.* sympathy or sorrow for others' suffering; a cause of grief or regret;—*v.t.* to feel grief or sympathy for.—*pa.t.* and *pa.p.* **pit'ied.**—**pit'ying** *a.* expressing pity.—**pit'yingly** *adv.*—**pit'iable** *a.* deserving pity.—**pit'iably** *adv.*—**pit'iful** *a.* full of pity; tender; woeful; exciting pity.—**pit'ifully** *adv.*—**pit'ifulness** *n.*—**pit'iless** *a.* feeling no pity; hard-hearted.—**pit'ilessly** *adv.*—**pit'ilessness** *n.*—**piteous** (pit'-e-us) *a.* fitted to excite pity; sad or sorrowful; wretched.—**pit'eously** *adv.*—**pit'eousness** *n.* [L. *pietas*, piety].

pivot (piv'-ut) *n.* a pin or shaft on which a wheel or other body turns; that on which important results depend;—*v.i.* to turn as on a pivot [Fr.].

pixy, pixie (pik'-si) *n.* a fairy or elf.—**pix'y-hood** *n.* a woman's peaked bonnet.—**pix'ilated** *a.* amusingly eccentric [Scand.].

pizzicato (pit-si-kà'-tō) *a.* (*Mus.*) a direction for stringed instruments denoting that the strings be plucked with the fingers [It.].

placable (plak'-a-bl, plā'-ka-bl) *a.* readily appeased or pacified; willing to forgive.—**placabil'ity, plac'ableness** *n.*—**placate** (pla-kāt') *v.t.* to appease, conciliate.—**plac'atory** *a.* conciliatory [L. *placare*, to appease].

placard (plak'-ard) *n.* a written or printed paper posted in a public place.—**placard** (pla-kard') *v.t.* to post placards [Fr.].

place (plās) *n.* orig. an open space in a town; a particular part of space; a spot; a locality; a building; rank; position; priority of position; stead; duty; office or employment; (*Sport*) a position among the first three competitors to finish;—*v.t.* to put in a particular spot; to find a position for; to appoint; to fix; to put; to identify.—**placed** *pa.p.* of the verb;—*a.* in a race, etc., to be first, second, or third at the finish.—**place'-kick** *n.* (*Rugby*) one made by kicking the ball after it has been placed on the ground for the purpose.—**to give place**, to make room for [L. *platea*, a broad street; fr. Gk. *platus*, broad].

placenta (pla-sen'-ta) *n.* (*Med.*) the soft, spongy substance (expelled from the womb after birth) through which the mother's blood nourishes the foetus; the after-birth; (*Bot.*) the part of the plant to which the seeds are attached.—**placen'tal** *a.* [L. = a flat cake].

placid (plas'-id) *a.* calm; peaceful.—**plac'idly** *adv.*—**placid'ity** *n.* mildness; sweetness of disposition; serenity [L. *placidus*, fr. *placere*, to please].

placket (plak'-et) *n.* a slit at the top of a woman's skirt [Fr. *plaquet*].

plagiarise (plā'-ji-ar-īz) *v.t.* to steal the words, ideas, etc. of another and use them as one's own.—**pla'giarism** *n.* the act of plagiarising; literary theft.—**pla'giarist** *n.*—**pla'giary** *n.* plagiarism; plagiarist [L. *plagiarius*, a kidnapper].

plague (plāg) *n.* a deadly, epidemic, and infectious disease; a pestilence; (*Colloq.*) a nuisance;—*v.t.* to vex;—to trouble or annoy.—*pr.p.* **plag'uing.**—*pa.p.* and *pa.t.* **plagued.**—**plaguey** (plā'-gi) *a.* [L. *plaga*, a blow].

plaice (plās) *n.* a flat-fish allied to the flounder [Gk. *platus*, flat].

plaid (plād, plad) *n.* a long, woollen garment, usually with a tartan pattern, worn as a wrap by Scottish Highlanders;—*a.* marked with chequered stripes [Gael. *plaide*].

plain (plān) *a.* level; flat; even; evident; clear; unobstructed; not intricate; simple; ordinary; without decoration; not beautiful;—*adv.* clearly;—*n.* a tract of level country.—**plain'ly** *adv.*—**plain'ness** *n.*—**plain-sail'ing** *n.* an unobstructed course of action.—**plain-song** *n.* the traditional recitative-like music of the chants of the R.C. church, sung in unison [L. *planus*, smooth].

plaint (plānt) *n.* (*Poet.*) a mournful song; a lamentation; (*Law*) a statement in writing of the complaint, accusation, etc.—**plain'tiff** *n.* the one who sues in a court of law; the prosecutor.—**plain'tive** *a.* expressing grief; sad; mournful.—**plain'tively** *adv.* [L. *plangere, planctum*, to lament].

plait (plat, plāt) *n.* a fold; a braid of hair, straw, etc.;—*v.t.* to interweave strands of hair, straw, etc. Also **pleat** [L. *plicatus*, folded].

plan (plan) *n.* a drawing representing a thing's horizontal section; a diagram; a map; a project; a design; a scheme;—*v.t.* to make a plan of; to arrange beforehand.—*pr.p.* **plan-ning**.—*pa.p.* and *pa.t.* **planned** [L. *planus*, flat].

planchette (plan-shet') *n.* a board, mounted on castors and a pencil point, believed to transmit spiritualistic messages under light finger-pressure [Fr.].

plane (plān) *n.* a carpenter's tool for smoothing wood;—*v.t.* to make smooth with a plane. —**pla'ner** *n.* [L. *planus*, level].

plane (plān) *n.* one of several kinds of trees, e.g. the sycamore [Gk. *platanos*, fr. *platus*, broad].

plane (plān) *n.* a flat, level surface; (*Geom.*) a surface such that, if any two points on it be joined by a straight line, that line will lie wholly on the surface;—*a.* perfectly level; pert. to, or lying in, a plane.—**plane geometry**, branch of geometry which deals with plane, not solid, figures [L. *planus*. level].

plane (plān) *n. abbrev.* of 'aeroplane'; the wing of an aeroplane or glider;—*v.i.* to glide in an aeroplane [Fr. *planer*, to hover].

planet (plan-et) *n.* a celestial body revolving round the sun (e.g. Venus, Mars, etc.) as distinct from the fixed stars.—**planetarium** (plan-e-tā-ri-um) *n.* a working model of the planetary system.—**plan'etary** *a.* pert. to planets; of the nature of a planet; erratic; wandering; (*Astrol.*) under the influence of a planet.—**plan'etoid** *n.* a minor planet [Gk. *planētēs*, wanderer].

plangent (plan-jent) *a.* of sound, vibrating; thrilling; resounding.—**plang-ency** (plan-jen-si) *n.* [L. *plangere*, to beat the breast].

planish (plan-ish) *v.t.* to make smooth or flat by light hammering; to flatten between rollers.—**plan'isher** *n.* [L. *planus*, level].

plank (plangk) *n.* a thick, heavy board; an article of policy in a political programme;—*v.t.* to lay with planks.—**plank'ing** *n.* planks collectively [L. *planca*].

plankton (plangk-tun) *n.* the minute animal and vegetable organisms floating in the ocean [Gk. *planktos*, wandering].

plant (plånt) *n.* a living organism belonging to the vegetable kingdom, generally excluding trees and shrubs; a slip or cutting; machinery, tools, etc., used in an industrial undertaking; (*Slang*) a swindle, hoax, trick;—*v.t.* to set in ground for growth;—*v.i.* to sow seeds, or set shoots, in the ground.—**plantation** (plan-tā-shun) *n.* area planted with trees; (*U.S.*) large estate; a colony.—**plan'ter** *n.* one who plants; the owner of a plantation [O.E.].

plantain (plan-tān) *n.* a common roadside weed with broad leaves and a spike of close-set, greenish flowers [L. *plantago*].

plantain (plan-tān) *n.* a tropical tree of the same genus as the banana; the fruit of the tree [Sp. *plantano*].

plaque (plak) *n.* a thin, flat, ornamental tablet hung on a wall or inserted into a wall or furniture [Fr.].

plash (plash) *n.* a puddle; a splashing sound;—*v.i.* to dabble in water.—**plash'y** *a.* [Dut. *plassen*, to splash].

plasm (plazm) *n.* (*Biol.*) the living matter of a cell; protoplasm.—**plasma** (plaz-ma) *n.* (*Med.*) protoplasm; the fluid part of the blood, as opposed to the corpuscles.—**plasmat'ic, plas-mic** *a.* [Gk. *plasma*, fr. *plassein*, to form or mould].

plaster (plås-ter) *n.* a composition of lime, water, and sand, for coating walls; gypsum, for making ornaments, mouldings, etc.; (*Med.*) an adhesive, curative application; (*Surg.*) a composition used to hold a limb, etc. rigid;—*v.t.* to cover with a plaster, as a wound: to smooth over or conceal.—**plas'terer** *n.* [Gk. *plassein*, to mould].

plastic (plas-tik) *a.* capable of moulding or of being moulded; pliable; capable of change;—*n.* a substance capable of being moulded.—**plas'tics** *n.pl.* the art of moulding; a group of synthetic products derived from casein, cellulose, etc. moulded into any form.—**plasticity** (plas-tis-i-ti) *n.* quality of being plastic.—**plastic art**, the art of representing figures in sculpture or by modelling in clay.—**plastic surgery**, the art of restoring lost or damaged parts of the body by grafting on sound tissue [Gk. *plassein*, to mould].

Plasticine (plas-ti-sēn) *n.* a modelling material easy to manipulate. used for teaching children [Protected Trade Name].

plastron (plas-tron) *n.* a breast-plate; part of a garment covering the breast [Fr.].

plat (plat) Same as **plait**.

plate (plāt) *n.* a shallow, round dish from which food is eaten; a plateful; a flat, thin sheet of metal, glass, etc.; utensils of gold or silver; short for 'dental plate,' a thin sheet of vulcanite, or metal, to hold artificial teeth; (*Photog.*) short for 'photographic plate';—*v.t* to cover with a thin coating of gold, silver, or other metal; to protect with steel plates, e.g. as a ship.—**pla'ter** *n.* a shipyard worker who fixes steel plates on a ship.—**plate-arm'our** *n.* very heavy, protective armour for warships. —**plate-glass** *n.* thick glass, rolled in sheets and used for windows, mirrors, etc.—**plate-lay'er** *n.* a railroad worker who lays down or repairs rails.—**photographic plate or film**, a thin sheet of glass or celluloid coated with sensitive emulsion [Gk. *platus*, broad].

plateau (pla-tō') *n.* a tract of level, high ground.—*pl.* **plateaus, plateaux** (pla-tōz') [Fr. fr. Gk. *platus*, broad, flat].

platen, (plat-en) *n.* (*Print.*) the plate which presses the paper against the type; the roller of a typewriter [O.Fr. *platine*, a flat piece].

platform (plat-form) *n.* a wooden structure raised above the level of the floor, as a stand for speakers; a landing-stage at a railway-station; (*Mil.*) a stage on which a gun is mounted; (*Fig.*) policy of a political party [Fr. *plate-forme* = flat form].

platinum (plat-in-um) *n.* a hard, silvery-white, malleable metal.—**platin'ic, plat'inous** *a.* —**plat'inoid** *n.* a metal found associated with platinum, e.g. iridium; an alloy of copper, zinc, nickel, and tungsten [Sp. *platina*, fr. *plata*, silver].

platitude (plat-i-tūd) *n.* a commonplace remark; dullness of writing or speaking.—**platitu'dinous** *a.* [Fr. fr. Gk. *platus*, flat].

Plato (plā-tō) *n.* a famous Greek philosopher (427-347 B.C.).—**Platonic** (pla-ton-ik), **Platon-ical** *a.* pert. to Plato or to his philosophy.—**Pla'tonism** *n.* the doctrines of Plato.—**Pla'tonist** *n.*—**Platonic love,** spiritual affection between man and woman without sexual desire.

platoon (pla-tòòn') *n.* (*Mil.*) a small body of soldiers employed as a unit [Fr. *peloton*, a knot, a ball].

platter (plat-er) *n.* a large, shallow plate or dish [Fr. *plat*, a dish].

platypus (plat-i-pus) *n.* a small, aquatic, furred animal of Australia, which has a bill like a duck, burrows, lays eggs, but suckles its young; the duckbill [Gk. *platus*, flat; *pous*, a foot].

plaudit (plaw′-dit) *n.* enthusiastic applause.—**plaud′itory** *a.* applauding; commending [L. *plaudere*, to clap the hands].

plausible (plaw′-zi-bl) *a.* having the appearance of being true; apparently right; fair-spoken.—**plaus′ibly** *adv.*—**plausibil′ity** [L. *plaudere*, to praise].

play (plā) *v.t.* and *i.* to move with light or irregular motion; to frolic; to flutter; to amuse oneself; to take part in a game; to gamble; to act a part on the stage; to perform on a musical instrument; to operate; to trifle with; to delude;—*n.* a brisk or free movement; activity; action; amusement; fun; frolic; sport; gambling; a dramatic piece or performance.—**play′er** *n.* one who plays; an actor; a performer on a musical instrument; a gambler.—**play′able** *a.* able to be played.—**play′ful** *a.* fond of play or fun; lively.—**play′fully** *adv.*—**play′bill** *n.* a bill or poster to advertise a play.—**play′boy** *n.* an habitual pleasure-seeker.—**play′fellow** *n.* a companion in play; a chum.—**play′ground** *n.* an open space or courtyard for recreation.—**play′house** *n.* a theatre.—**play′mate** *n.* playfellow.—**play′pen** *n.* a portable wooden enclosure for small children to play in.—**play′thing** *n.* a toy.—**playwright** (plā′-rīt) *n.* a writer of plays; a dramatist.—**play′ing-card** *n.* one of a set of cards, usually 52 in number, used in card-games [O.E. *plegan*, to play].

plea (plē) *n.* (*Law*) the defendant's answer to the plaintiff's declaration; an excuse; entreaty [Fr. *plaider*, to plead].

pleach (plēch) *v.t.* to bend and intertwine the branches of [L. *plectere*, to weave].

plead (plēd) *v.t.* to allege in proof or vindication; to offer in excuse; (*Law*) to argue at the bar;—*v.i.* to carry on a lawsuit; to present an answer to the declaration of a plaintiff; to urge reasons in support of or against; to beg or implore.—*pa.p.* and *pa.t.* **plead′ed.** Also (*Colloq.*) **pled.**—**plead′er** *n.*—**plead′ing** *a.* entreating;—*n.* the art of conducting a cause as an advocate; entreaty; supplication;—*n.pl.* written statements of plaintiff and defendant in support of their claims.—**plead′ingly** *adv.* [Fr. *plaider*].

pleasance (plez′ans) *n.* a pleasure-garden [L. *placere*, to please].

please (plēz) *v.t.* to excite agreeable sensations or emotions in; to gratify; to delight; to satisfy;—*v.i.* to like or think fit; to choose; to give pleasure; used as *abbrev.* of 'if you please,' in a polite request.—**pleasant** (plez′ant) *a.* fitted to please; cheerful; lively; merry; agreeable.—**pleas′antly** *adv.*—**pleas′antness** *n.*—**pleasantry** (plez′ant-ri) *n.* playfulness in conversation; a joke; a humorous act;—*pl.* **pleas′antries.**—**pleasing** (plē′zing) *a.* agreeable; gratifying.—**plea′singly** *adv.*—**plea′singness** *n.*—**pleasure** (plezh′ur) *n.* agreeable sensation or emotion; gratification of the senses or mind; amusement, diversion, or self-indulgence; choice; a source of gratification.—**pleas′urable** *a.*—**pleas′urably** *adv.* [L. *placere*, to please].

pleat (plēt) *n.* a flattened fold; a crease;—*v.t.* to crease [var. of *plait*].

plebs (plebz) *n.* in ancient Rome the common people.—**plebeian** (ple-bē′an) *a.* pert. or belonging to the common people; vulgar; popular; uncultured;—*n.* a member of the lower classes [L. *plebs*].

plebiscite (pleb′i-sīt, pleb′i-sit) *n.* a vote of the whole community or nation [L. *plebiscitum*, a decree of the plebs].

plectrum (plek′-trum) *n.* a small instrument used for plucking the strings of a lyre or other like instruments of music [Gk. *plēktron*, fr. *plēssein*, to strike].

pledge (plej) *n.* something deposited as a security; a sign or token of anything; a drinking to the health of; a solemn promise;—*v.t.* to deposit in pawn; to leave as security; to engage for, by promise or declaration; to drink the health of [O.Fr. *plege*].

Pleistocene (plīs′-tō-sēn) *n.* (*Geol.*) deposits of the last glacial period, following the Tertiary.—*a.* pert. to this period [Gk. *pleistos*, most; *kainos*, new].

plenary (plē′na-ri) *a.* full, entire, complete; unqualified; (of an assembly) fully attended.—**ple′narily** *adv.*—**ple′nariness** *n.*—**plenipotentiary** (plen-i-pō-ten′sha-ri) *n.* an ambassador with full powers;—*a.* possessing full powers.—**plenish** (plen′ish) *v.t.* to furnish; to provide with the necessary stock or implements.—**plenitude** (plen′i-tūd) *n.* fulness; repletion; abundance [L. *plenus*, full; *potens*, potent].

plenty (plen′ti) *n.* a full supply; abundance; quite enough; sufficiency.—**plenteous** (plen′tē-us) *a.* copious; abundant; ample; rich.—**plen′teously** *adv.*—**plen′teousness** *n.*—**plen′tiful** *a.* abundant; ample.—**plen′tifully** *adv.*—**plen′tifulness** *n.* [L. *plenus*, full].

plenum (plē′num) *n.* space as considered to be full of matter (opposed to *vacuum*); a condition of fulness [L. *plenus*, full].

plethora (pleth′o-ra) *n.* an excess of red corpuscles in the blood; superabundance.—**plethor′ic** *a.* [Gk. *plethōra*, fulness].

pleura (ploo′-ra) *n.* (*Med.*) the membrane lining the chest and covering the lungs.—*pl.* **pleu′rae.**—**pleu′ral** *a.*—**pleu′risy** *n.* (*Med.*) inflammation of the pleura.—**pleurit′ic** *a.* pert. to, or causing, pleurisy [Gk. *pleura*, the side].

plexus (pleks′us) *n.* a network, esp. of nerves, blood-vessels, fibres, etc.—**plex′al** *a.* [L. = a twining].

pliable (plī′a-bl) *a.* easily bent; easily influenced. Also **pliant** (plī′ant).—**pli′ably, pli′antly** *adv.*—**pliabil′ity, pli′ancy** *n.* [L. *plicare*, to fold].

plica (plī′ka) *n.* a fold.—**pli′cate, pli′cated** *a.* (*Bot.*) folded; pleated [L. *plicare*, to fold].

pliers (plī′erz) *n.pl.* small pincers with a flat grip.

plight (plīt) *n.* a state or condition of a distressing kind; predicament [L. *plicare*, to fold; O.E. *plit*, a fold or plait].

plight (plīt) *n.* solemn promise; pledge;—*v.t.* to pledge, as one's word of honour; to betroth [O.E. *pliht*, risk].

Plimsoll line (plim′sol-līn) *n.* a circle with a horizontal line through the centre as a mark on merchant-vessels to indicate the maximum draught permitted when loaded [Samuel *Plimsoll*, (1824-1898)].

plimsolls (plim′sols) *n.pl.* rubber-soled shoes with canvas uppers [etym. uncertain].

plinth (plinth) *n.* a square slab, forming the base of a column; the projecting band running along the foot of a wall [Gk. *plinthos*, a brick].

Pliocene (plī′o-sēn) *n.* (*Geol.*) the deposits belonging to the latest Tertiary period;—*a.* pert. to this period [Gk. *pleion*, more; *kainos*, recent].

plod (plod) *v.t.* to tread with a heavy step;—*v.i* to walk or work laboriously; to toil or drudge.—**plod′der** *n.*—**plod′ding** *a.* [imit.].

plot (plot) *n.* a small patch of ground; a plan of a field, farm, etc. drawn to scale;—*v.t.* to draw a graph of.—*pr.p.* **plott′ing.**—*pa.p.* and *pa.t.* **plott′ed** [O.E.].

plot (plot) *n.* the plan of a play, romance, novel, etc.; a complicated scheme, plan, or stratagem; conspiracy;—*v.t.* to plan or devise;—*v.i.* to conspire [Fr. *complot*].

plough (plou) *n.* an implement with a heavy cutting blade for turning up the soil;—*v.t.* to turn up with the plough; to furrow; to advance laboriously; to reject a candidate in an examination;—*v.i.* to till the soil with a plough.—**plough′share** *n.* the heavy iron blade of a plough which cuts into the ground.—**the Plough** (*Astron.*) the seven stars constituting the Great Bear, so-called because of the shape [O.E. *ploh*].

plover (pluv′ėr) *n.* one of various kinds of wading-birds [L. *pluvia*, rain].

ploy (ploi) *n.* (*Colloq.*) occupation; prank.

pluck (pluk) *v.t.* to pull off; to pick, as flowers; to strip off feathers, as a fowl; to snatch, or pull with sudden force;—*n.* a pull or twitch; the act of plucking; courage or spirit.—**pluck'y** *a.* brave; spirited.—**pluck'ily** *adv.*—**pluck'iness** *n.* [O.E. *pluccian*].

plug (plug) *n.* anything used to stop a hole; a bung or stopper; a cake of compressed tobacco; (*Elect.*) a device for easy connecting and disconnecting of a circuit; *abbrev.* for sparking-plug;—*v.t.* to stop with a plug; to insert a plug in; to shoot; (*Slang*) to advertise a song or tune by having it played constantly;—*v.i.* (*Colloq.*) to keep doggedly at work (with 'at').—*pr.p.* **plugg'ing**.—*pa.p.* and *pa.t.* **plugged** [Dut.].

plum (plum) *n.* a round or oval stone-fruit; the tree that bears it; a particularly good appointment or position; a dark purplish colour.—**plum′cake, plum′pudd'ing** *n.* a cake or pudding containing raisins, currants, etc.—**plum′duff** *n.* (*Colloq.*) a suet pudding made of flour and raisins [O.E. *plume*, fr. L. *prunum*].

plumage (plòò′māj) *n.* a bird's feathers, collectively [Fr. fr. L. *pluma*, a feather].

plumb (plum) *n.* a plummet; a weight of lead attached to a line, and used to determine perpendicularity; the perpendicular position;—*a.* perpendicular;—*adv.* perpendicularly; (*U.S.*, *Colloq.*) utterly, absolutely;—*v.t.* to adjust by a plumb-line; to sound or take the depth of water with a plummet.—**plumber** (plum′ėr) *n.* artisan who attends to water and sewage system of building.—**plum'bic** *a.* (*Chem.*) like lead.—**plumbing** (plum′ing) *n.* the art of working in lead; the trade of a plumber; the system of water and sewage pipes in a building.—**plumb′line** *n.* a weighted string for testing the perpendicular.—**plumb′bob** *n.* the weight at the end of this line [L. *plumbum*, lead].

plumbago (plum-bā′gō) *n.* black lead; graphite [L. *plumbum*, lead].

plume (plòòm) *n.* a feather or tuft of feathers; a crest on a helmet; a token of honour;—*v.t.* to furnish with plumes; to strip of feathers; to clean feathers of bird; (*Fig.*) to boast of [L. *pluma*, a feather].

plummet (plum′et) *n.* a plumb-line; a sounding-line [L. *plumbum*, lead].

plump (plump) *a.* of rounded form; moderately fat.—**plump'ness** *n.* [Dut. *plomp*, blunt].

plump (plump) *v.i.* to fall or sit down heavily and suddenly; to vote for one candidate;—*v.t.* to drop or throw abruptly;—*a.* direct; abrupt; downright;—*adv.* heavily; abruptly; bluntly;—*n.* (*Colloq.*) a sudden fall, esp. of rain [perh. imit. origin].

plumule (plòò′mūl) *n.* a small, downy feather; a first feather [L. *pluma*, a feather].

plunder (plun′dėr) *v.t.* to rob systematically; to take by force;—*n.* the act of robbing by force; property so obtained.—**plun'derer** *n.* [Ger. *plündern*].

plunge (plunj) *v.t.* to thrust forcibly into; to immerse suddenly in a liquid;—*v.i.* to throw oneself headlong into; (*Colloq.*) to gamble recklessly;—*n.* the act of plunging; a dive; a sudden rush.—**plun'ger** *n.* one who plunges; a solid, cylindrical rod used as a piston in pumps [Fr. *plonger*, fr. L. *plumbum*, lead].

pluperfect (plòò′pėr-fekt) *a.* (*Gram.*) of a tense, expressing action completed before another action in the past [L. *plus quam perfectum*, more than perfect].

plural (plòò′ral) *a.* more than one; (*Gram.*) denoting more than one person or thing;—*n.* (*Gram.*) a word in its plural form.—**plu'rally** *adv.*—**plu'ralism** *n.* the holding of more than one appointment, benefice, etc. simultaneously; (*Philos.*) doctrine that existence has more than one ultimate principle.—**plu'ralist** *n.*—**pluralis'tic** *a.*—**plural'ity** *n.* large number; holding of two or more offices, etc. simultaneously; a majority of votes [L. *plus*, more].

plus (plus) *n.* symbol of addition (+); positive quantity; extra quantity;—*a.* to be added; (*Math.*, *Elect.*, *etc.*) positive;—*prep.* with the addition of.—**plus-fours'** *n.pl.* wide knickerbockers worn by golfers [L. *plus*, more].

plush (plush) *n.* a fabric with a long, velvet-like nap [Fr. *peluche*, fr. L. *pilus*, hair].

Pluto (plòò′tō) *n.* (*Myth.*) god of the Lower World; (*World War* 2) code name (fr. the initial letters of *P*ipe *L*ine *u*nder *t*he *O*cean.) for the oil pipeline system from England to France.—**Pluton'ian** *a.* pert. to Pluto or infernal regions; subterranean; dark.—**Pluton'ic** *a.* Plutonian.—**Plutonic rocks** (*Geol.*) name given to igneous rocks formed by action of intense subterranean heat.—**pluton'ium** *n.* a metal of high atomic weight made by bombarding atoms of uranium with neutrons.

plutocracy (plòò-tok′ra-si) *n.* government by the rich; the wealthy class.—**plu'tocrat** *n.* a wealthy person.—**plutocrat'ic** *a.* [Gk. *ploutos*; wealth; *kratein*, to rule].

pluvial (plòò′vi-al) *a.* pert. to rain; rainy; caused by the action of rain.—**plu'vious** *a.* pluvial [L. *pluvia*, rain]

ply (plī) *v.t.* to wield; to work at steadily; to use or practise with diligence; to urge;—*v.i.* to work steadily; of a boat, motor vehicle, etc. to run regularly for hire between fixed places.—*pr.p.* **ply'ing**.—*pa.p.* and *pa.t.* **plied** [fr. *apply*].

ply (plī) *n.* a fold; a plait; a bend; a twist; a strand of yarn; thickness.—*pl.* **plies**.—**ply'wood** *n.* board made of two or more thin layers of wood cemented together [Fr. *plier*, to fold, fr. L. *plicare*].

pneumatic (nū-mat′ik) *a.* pert. to air or gas; inflated with wind or air; operated by compressed air.—**pneumat'ics** *n.pl.* the branch of physics dealing with the mechanical properties of gases [Gk. *pneuma*, breath].

pneumatology (nū-ma-tol′o-ji) *n.* the science of the functions of the mind; the doctrine of spiritual existences; pneumatics [Gk. *pneuma*, spirit; *logos*, a discourse].

pneumonia (nū-mō′ni-a) *n.* acute inflammation of a lung.—**pneumon'ic** *a.* pert. to lungs [Gk. *pneuma*, breath].

poach (pōch) *v.t.* to cook eggs, by breaking them into a pan of boiling water [Fr. *pocher*].

poach (pōch) *v.t.* and *i.* to take game or fish from another's property without permission or by illegal methods.—**poach'er** *n.*—**poach'ing** *n.* [Fr. *poche*, a pocket].

pock (pok) *n.* pustule on skin, as in smallpox.—**pock'mark** *n.* pit left in skin by pock [O.E. *poc*, a pustule].

pocket (pok′et) *n.* a small pouch or bag inserted into a garment; a socket, cavity, or hollow; (*Mil.*) isolated area held by the enemy;—*v.t.* to put in the pocket; to take surreptitiously, esp. money; to accept without resentment, as an insult.—**pock'et-batt'leship** *n.* a heavily armoured, high-powered, German battleship, of not more than 10,000 tons.—**pock'et-book** *n.* a small book or case for holding money or papers.—**pock'et-mon'ey** *n.* money for small, personal expenses, e.g. allowance to child.—**in pocket**, having funds [Fr. *pochette*, dim, of *poche*, pouch].

pod (pod) *n.* a seed-vessel of a plant, esp. a legume, as peas, beans, etc.;—*v.i.* to produce pods; to remove the pods from peas or beans [etym. uncertain].

podge (poj) *n.* a short, fat person.—**podg'y** *a.* short and fat; thick [etym. uncertain].

poem (pō′em) *n.* a composition in verse; any composition written in elevated and imaginative language; opp. to 'prose.'—**po'esy** *n.* the art of composing poems; metrical composition.—**po'et** *n.* (*fem.* **po'etess**) the author of a poem; one skilled in making poetry.—**poet'ic(al)** *a.* pert. to poetry; expressed in poetry; possessing the imaginative beauties of poetry.—**poet'ically** *adv.*—**poet'ics** *n.* principles of art of poetry; criticism of poetry.—**poetry** (pō'et-ri) *n.* language of imagination expressed in verse; metrical composition.—**poetaster** (pō'et-as-tẹr) *n.* a would-be poet; a petty rhymster.—**poet'icise, po'etise** *v.t.* and *i.* to treat poetically; to write poetry.—**poetic justice**, ideal justice, in which crime is punished and virtue rewarded.—**poetic licence**, latitude in grammar or facts, allowed to poets.—**poet laureate**, official court poet [Gk. *poiēma*, fr. *poiein*, to make].

poignant (poi'nạnt) *a.* acutely painful; stinging; sharp; pungent.—**poig'nantly** *adv.*—**poig'nancy** *n.* [L. *pungere*, to prick].

poind (pind, poind) *v.t.* (*Scots Law*) to seize a debtor's goods [O.E. *pund*, an enclosure].

point (point) *n.* sharp or tapering end of anything; dot or mark; dot in decimal system; punctuation mark; full stop; (*Geom.*) that which has position but no magnitude; item or detail; gist of argument; striking or effective part of a speech, story, etc.; moment of time; purpose; physical quality in animals, esp. for judging purposes; (*Geog.*) headland; movable rail changing a train to other rails; one of the 32 direction marks of a compass; unit of scoring in certain games; (*Print.*) unit of measurement of size of type (72 points = 1 inch); a fine lace made with a needle; (*Cricket*) position of fieldsman to the immediate right of batsman;—*v.t.* to sharpen; to give value, force, etc. to words, etc.; to aim or direct; to fill up joints with mortar; to punctuate;—*v.i.* to show direction or position by extending a finger, stick, etc.; of a dog, to indicate the position of game by standing facing it.—**point'ed** *a.* having a sharp point; sharp; direct; telling; of a remark, etc., aimed at a particular person; (*Archit.*) pert. to the style having pointed arches, i.e. Gothic.—**point'edly** *adv.*—**point'edness** *n.*—**point'less** *a.* having no point; unsharpened; blunt; irrelevant; insipid.—**point'er** *n.* one who, or that which, points; an index; a rod, stick for pointing on blackboard; an indicator; a breed of dog trained to stop and point at game.—**point'ing** *n.* punctuation; filling the crevices of walls with mortar.—**point'-blank** *a.* aimed horizontally;—*adv.* at short range; hence (*Fig.*) directly; plainly.—**point'-to-point'** *n.* (*Racing*) steeplechase horse-race, esp. for hunters, for 3 or 4 miles (formerly from one point to another across country) [L. *punctum*, fr. *pungere*, to prick].

poise (poiz) *v.t.* to place or hold in a balanced or steady position;—*v.i.* to be so held; to hover; to balance;—*n.* equilibrium; carriage of the head, body, etc.; (*Fig.*) self-possession [L. *pendere*, to weigh].

poison (poi'zn) *n.* any substance which kills or injures when introduced into a living organism; that which has an evil influence on health or moral purity;—*v.t.* to give poison to; to infect; to corrupt.—**poi'soner** *n.*—**poi'sonous** *a.* having a deadly or injurious quality; corrupting.—**poi'sonously** *adv.*—**poi'son-i'vy** *n.* a N. American vine which, if touched, causes a skin rash.—**poi'son-pen** *n.* writer of malicious, anonymous letters [L. *potio*, a draught].

poke (pōk) *v.t.* to push or thrust against with a pointed object, e.g. with a finger, stick, etc.; to stir; to thrust in;—*v.i.* to make thrusts; to pry;—*n.* the act of poking; a thrust or push; a woman's bonnet with a projecting brim (a poke-bonnet).—**po'ker** *n.* a metal rod for stirring the fire.—**po'ker-work** *n.* the art of burning designs on a wood-surface with a hot poker.—**po'ky** *a.* small; confined; shabby [M.E. *poken*].

poke (pōk) *n.* a sack; a small bag [Fr. *poche*, a pocket].

poker (pō'kẹr) *n.* a card-game in which the players bet on the value of their hands.—**po'ker-faced** *a.* having a face which expresses no emotion [etym. uncertain].

Polack (pōl'ak) *n.* a Pole;—*a.* Polish.

polar (pō'lạr) *a.* pert. to, or situated near, the North or South Poles; pert. to the magnetic poles (points on the earth's surface where a magnetic needle dips vertically); pert. to either pole of a magnet; magnetic; directly opposed; having polarity.—**polar'ity** *n.* the state of being polar; the condition of having opposite poles; the power of being attracted to one pole, and repelled from the other.—**polar bear**, a large, white bear, found in the Arctic regions.—**polar circles**, the parallels of latitude encircling the earth 23° 28′ from the North and South Poles [Gk. *polos*, a pivot].

polarise (pō'lạ-rīz) *v.t.* to give polarity to; (*Elect.*) to reduce the electromotive force (E.M.F.) of a primary cell by the accumulation of certain electrolytic products on the plates; (*Chem.*) to separate the positive and negative charges on a molecule; (*Light*) to confine the vibrations of light waves to certain directions, e.g. to a plane.—**polarisa'tion** *n.* [fr. *polar*].

polder (pōl'dẹr) *n.* a bog; a morass; marshy land, esp. in the Netherlands, reclaimed from the sea and cultivated [Dut.].

pole (pōl) *n.* a long, rounded piece of wood or metal; a measure of length = 5½ yards; a measure of area = 30¼ square yards;—*v.t.* to propel with a pole.—**pole'-jump** *n.* in athletics, a jump over a high bar with the help of a long pole [L. *palus*, a stake].

pole (pōl) *n.* either of the ends of the axis of a sphere, esp. of the earth (in the latter case called the North Pole and South Pole); either of the opposite ends or terminals of a magnet, electric battery, etc.—**pole'-star** *n.* the North Star; (*Fig.*) a guide; an indicator; a lodestar [Gk. *polos*, a pivot].

Pole (pōl) *n.* a native of Poland.—**Po'lish** *a.* pert. to Poland or the Poles.

pole-axe (pōl'aks) *n.* a battle-axe with a long handle. Also **pole'-ax** [E. *poll*, the head, and *axe*].

polecat (pōl'kat) *n.* a small, carnivorous animal, resembling the weasel [O.Fr. *pole*, a hen (fr. its preying on poultry)].

polemic (po-lem'ik) *a.* controversial; disputatious;—*n.* controversy; controversialist.—**polem'ics** *n.pl.* art of controversy; controversial writings or discussions, esp. religious. Also **polem'ical** *a.*—**polem'ically** *adv.* [Gk. *polemos*, war].

police (po-lēs') *n.* the civil force which maintains public order; the internal government of a country or city;—*v.t.* to control with police; to keep in order.—**police'con'stable, police'man, police'off'icer** *n.* (*fem.* **police'wo'man**) member of a police force.—**police'court** *n.* a court for the trial of minor offences.—**police'mag'istrate** *n.* one who presides over a police-court.—**police'off'ice, police'sta'tion** *n.* the headquarters of the police, and temporary prison for petty offenders [Gk. *polis*, a city].

policy (pol'i-si) *n.* a course of action adopted, esp. in state affairs; prudent procedure [Gk. *polis*, a city].

policy (pol'i-si) *n.* a document containing a contract of insurance [Gk. *apodeixis*, proof].

policy (pol'i-si) *n.* (*Scot.*) often in *pl.* **pol'icies**, the grounds of a gentleman's country-house [Gk. *polis*, a city, state].

poliomyelitis (pol-i-ō-mī-e-lī'tis) *n.* (*Med.*) inflammation of the grey matter of the spinal cord.—*abbrev.* **polio** [Gk. *polios*, grey; *muelos*, marrow].

polish (pol'ish) *v.t.* to make smooth and glossy; to make polite and cultured;—*v.i.* to become polished;—*n.* the act of polishing; a smooth, glassy surface; a substance used in polishing; (*Fig.*) refinement; elegance of manners.—**pol'isher** *n.* [Fr. *polir*, fr. L. *polire*].

Polish (pō'lish) *n.* See **Pole**.

polite (po-līt') *a.* elegant in manners, well bred; courteous; obliging.—**polite'ly** *adv.* **polite'ness** *n.* [L. *politus*, polished].

politic (pol′i-tik) *a.* prudent; wise; shrewd; cunning; advisable.—**pol′itics** *n.pl.* the art of government; political affairs, life, or principles. —**pol′iticly** *adv.*—**polit′ical** *a.* pert. to the state or its affairs; pert. to politics.—**polit′ically** *adv.* —**politician** (pol-i-tish′an) *n.* one versed in the science of government; a member of a political party.—**pol′ity** *n.* civil government; the form or constitution of government.—**political economy**, the science dealing with the nature, production, distribution, and consumption of wealth [Fr. *politique*, fr. Gk. *polis*, a city].

polka (pōl′ka) *n.* a lively dance of Bohemian origin; music for it [fr. *Polish*].

poll (pōl) *n.* (top of) the head; a register of persons; a list of persons entitled to vote; (the place) of voting; number of votes recorded;—*v.t.* to cut off the top of, e.g. tree; to cut short horns of cattle; to canvass; to receive (votes); to cast a vote;—*v.i.* to vote.—**poll′-tax** *n.* a tax on each person.—**poll′ing-booth** *n.* a voting-place at an election [Low Ger. *polle*, the head].

pollard (pol′ard) *n.* a tree on which a close head of young branches has been made by polling; a hornless animal of a normally horned variety. See **poll**.

pollen (pol′en) *n.* the fertilising dust of a flower.—**poll′inate** *v.t.* to fertilise a flower by conveying pollen to the pistil [L. = fine flour].

pollute (po-lūt′) *v.t.* to make foul or unclean; to defile; to profane; to desecrate.—**pollu′tion** *n.* defilement [L. *polluere*].

polo (pō′lō) *n.* a game like hockey played on ponies; short for **wa′ter-po′lo**, a ball game played by swimmers.

polonaise (pol-on-āz′) *n.* a slow stately dance, of Polish origin; the music for it [Fr. = Polish].

polonium (po-lō′ni-um) *n.* a metallic, chemical element, having radio-active properties [fr. *Poland*].

polony (po-lō′ni) *n.* a kind of partly-cooked pork sausage [fr. *Bologna*, Italy, where first made].

poltergeist (pol′ter-gīst) *n.* a mysterious spirit believed to create noise and disturbance [Ger. *Polter*, uproar; *Geist*, a ghost].

poltroon (pol-trōōn′) *n.* a coward.—**poltroon′ery** *n.* cowardice; lack of spirit [Fr. *poltron*, fr. It. *poltro*, lazy].

poly- (pol′i) *prefix* fr. Gk. *polus*, many, much, used in derivatives.—**polyan′dry** *n.* a custom esp. in Tibet, by which a wife is shared between several husbands.—**polyan′drous** *a.* (*Bot.*) having more than 20 stamens.—**polyan′thus** *n.* (*Bot.*) a kind of garden primula. —**pol′ychrome** *n.* a picture, statue, etc. in several colours.—**polychromat′ic, polychro′mic, pol′ychromous** *a.* many-coloured.

polygamy (pol-ig′a-mi) *n.* the practice of having more than one wife at the same time. —**polyg′amous** *a.*—**polyg′amist** *n.* [Gk. *polus*, many; *gamos*, marriage].

polyglot (pol′i-glot) *a.* pert. to, or speaking, several languages;—*n.* a person who speaks several languages; a book, esp. the Bible, in which the text is printed side by side in different languages [Gk. *polus*, many; *glōtta*, the tongue].

polygon (pol′i-gon) *n.* a plane figure with more than four sides or angles.—**polyg′onal** *a.* [Gk. *polus*, many; *gōnia*, an angle].

polygyny (pol-ij′i-ni) *n.* practice of polygamy by a man [Gk. *polus*, many; *gunē*, a woman].

polyhedron (pol-i-hē′dron) *n.* (*Geom.*) a solid figure with many faces, usually more than six [Gk. *polus*, many; *hedra*, a base].

polymorphous (pol-i-mor′fus) *a.* assuming many forms. Also **polymor′phic**.—**polymor′phism** *n.* [Gk. *polus*, many; *morphē*, form].

Polynesia (pol-i-nē′zi-a) *n.* (*Geog.*) the group of islands in the S. Pacific, east of Australia.—**Polyne′sian** *a.* [Gk. *polus*, many; *nēsos*, an island].

polynomial (pol-i-nō′mi-al) *n.* (*Alg.*) a quantity having many terms [Gk. *polus*, many; L. *nomen*, a name].

polyp, polype (pol′ip) *n.* a small, marine animal with tube-like tentacles, e.g. the sea-anemone; a polypus.—**pol′ypus, pol′yp** *n.* (*Med.*) a small tumour in the mucous membrane of the nose, etc.—**pol′ypous** *a.* [Gk. *polus*, many; *pous*, a foot].

polyphonic (pol-i-fon′ik) *a.* pert. to polyphony.—**polyphony** (pol-if′on-i) *n.* (*Mus.*) a kind of composition in which melodic strains are simultaneously developed without being subordinate to each other [Gk. *polus*, many; *phonē*, a voice].

polysyllable (pol-i-sil′a-bl) *n.* a word of three or more syllables.—**polysyllab′ic** *a.* [Gk. *polus*, many, and *syllable*].

polytechnic (pol-i-tek′nik) *a.* pert. to many arts and sciences;—*n.* a school or college of applied arts and sciences [Gk. *polus*, many; *technē*, art].

polytheism (pol′i-thē-izm) *n.* belief in the existence of many gods, or in more than one. —**pol′ytheist** *n.*—**polytheist′ic** *a.* [Gk. *polus*, many; *theos*, a god].

pom (pom) *n.* *abbrev.* for **pomeranian dog.**

pomade (po-mad′) *n.* scented ointment for the hair. Also **poma′tum** [Fr. *pommade*].

pomander (pō-man′der) *n.* a perfumed ball, box, or bag [O.Fr. *pomme d'ambre* = apple of amber].

pome (pōm) *n.* any fruit having a fleshy body, core, etc. like the apple, pear, pomegranate, etc.—**pomicul′ture** *n.* fruit-growing [L. *pomum*, an apple].

pomegranate (pom′gra-nāt) *n.* a large fruit containing many seeds in a red pulp [L. *pomum*, an apple; *granatum*, having many seeds].

pomeranian (pom-er-ā′ni-an) *n.* a small breed of dog with bushy tail, sharp pointed muzzle, prick ears and long silky hair.—*Abbrev.* **pom** [fr. *Pomerania*, in Germany].

pommel (pum′el) *n.* the knob of a sword hilt; the front part of a saddle;—*v.t.* to strike repeatedly; to beat with the fists.—*pr.p.* **pomm′elling**.—*pa.p.* and *pa.t.* **pomm′elled** [O. Fr. *pomel*, a little apple].

pomp (pomp) *n.* splendid display or ceremony; magnificence.—**pomp′ous** *n.* showy with grandeur; of a person, self-important; of language, inflated.—**pomp′ously** *adv.*—**pomp′ousness** *n.*—**pompos′ity** *n.* vain-glory [Gk. *pompē*, a solemn procession].

pom-pom (pom′pom) *n.* (*Nav.*) a multi-barrelled automatic quick-firing gun [imit.].

pompon (pom′pon) *n.* the ball of coloured wool worn in front of the shako, etc.; small, compact chrysanthemum [Fr.].

pond (pond) *n.* a pool of standing water, either naturally or more often artificially enclosed [same as *pound*].

ponder (pon′der) *v.t.* to weigh in the mind; to consider attentively;—*v.i.* to meditate or muse; to deliberate (on).—**pon′derer** *n.*—**pon′dering** *a.* [L. *pondus*, weight].

ponderous (pon′der-us) *a.* very heavy; weighty; massive; unwieldy; dull or lacking in spirit.—**pon′derously** *adv.*—**pon′derousness** *n.* —**ponderos′ity** *n.*—**pon′derable** *a.* having appreciable weight.—**pon′derableness** *n.* [L. *ponderosus*].

poniard (pon′yard) *n.* a slender dagger;—*v.t.* to pierce with a poniard [Fr. *poignard*, fr. *poing*, the fist].

pontiff (pon′tif) *n.* the Pope; a bishop; a high priest.—**pontif′ical** *a.* belonging to a high priest; popish; pompous and dogmatic;—*n.pl.* the garb of a priest, bishop, or pope.—**pontif′ically** *adv.*—**pontif′icate** *n.* the state, dignity, or term of office of a priest, bishop, or pope.—**pon′tify** *v.i.* to act the pontiff; to speak in a bombastic manner [L. *pontifex*, a high priest].

pontoon (pon-tōōn′) *n.* a low, flat-bottomed

boat used as a support in building a temporary bridge; a bridge of boats [Fr. fr. L. *pons, pontis,* a bridge].

pontoon (pon-tóón′) *n.* a gambling card-game, vingt et un [corrupt. of Fr. *vingt et un,* twenty-one].

pony (pō′ni) *n.* a small breed of horse; (*Slang*) £25 [O.Fr. *poulenet,* fr. *poulain,* a colt].

poodle (póó′dl) *n.* one of a breed of dogs with thick, curly hair, often clipped into ornamental tufts [Ger. *Pudel*].

pooh (póó) *interj.* an exclamation of scorn or contempt.—**pooh-pooh′** *v.t.* (*Colloq.*) to express contempt for [imit.].

pool (póól) *n.* a small body of still water; a small pond; a deep place in a river [O.E. *pol*].

pool (póól) *n.* the collective stakes in various games; the place where the stakes are put; a variety of billiards; a combination of capitalists to fix prices and divide business; the common fund;—*v.t.* to put into a common fund;—*v.i.* to form a pool [Fr. *poule,* a hen].

poop (póóp) *n.* the raised deck at the stern of a ship; the stern itself;—*v.t.* to break over the poop of [L. *puppis,* the stern].

poor (póór) *a.* having little or no money; without means; needy; miserable; wretched; unfortunate; feeble; deserving of pity; unproductive; of inferior quality.—**poor′ly** *adv.* in want; inadequately; with little or no success; without spirit;—*a.* somewhat ill; out of sorts.—**poor′ness** *n.*—**poor′spir′ited** *a.* cowardly; mean.—**poor′house** *n.* an institution for lodging the poor at public expense [L. *pauper,* poor].

pop (pop) *n.* an abrupt, small explosive sound; a shot; an effervescing drink, e.g. champagne, ginger-beer, etc.; —*v.i.* to make a sharp, quick sound; to go or come unexpectedly or suddenly; to dart;—*v.t.* to put or place suddenly; (*Slang*) to pawn.—*adv.* suddenly.—*pr.p.* **pop′ping.** —*pa.p.* and *pa.t.* **popped.**—**pop′corn** *n.* Indian corn exposed to heat causing it to burst open.—**pop′gun** *n.* a child's toy gun for shooting pellets, etc. by the expansion of compressed air.—**pop′shop** *n.* (*Colloq.*) a pawnshop [imit. origin].

Pope (pōp) *n.* the Bishop of Rome and head of the R.C. Church.—**popish** (pō′pish) *a.* pert. to the Pope or the papacy.—**pope′dom** *n.* the office, dignity, or jurisdiction of the Pope.—**popery** (pō′pe-ri) *n.* the R.C. religion (a Protestant term, often used offensively).—**pope's′eye** *n.* the gland surrounded with fat in the thigh of an ox or sheep; a slice of meat from that part, esp. **pope's-eye steak,** noted for its delicacy.—**pope's′nose** *n.* the fleshy part of the tail of a cooked fowl; the parson's nose [L. *papa,* father].

popinjay (pop′in-jā) *n.* a parrot; the green woodpecker; formerly in archery, a mark like a parrot, to be shot at; a vain, conceited fellow [O.Fr. *papegai,* a parrot].

poplar (pop′lar) *n.* a tree noted for its slender tallness [L. *populus*].

poplin (pop′lin) *n.* a corded fabric of silk and worsted [etym. uncertain].

poppet (pop′et) *n.* timber to support a vessel while being launched; a darling [= puppet].

poppy (pop′i) *n.* a bright flowered plant one species of which yields opium [L. *papaver,* a poppy]. | [sense [etym. uncertain].

poppycock (pop′i-kok) *n.* (*U.S. slang*) non-

populace (pop′ū-las) *n.* the common people; the masses.—**pop′ulate** *v.t.* to people.—**popula′tion** *n.* the total number of people in a country, town, etc.—**pop′ulous** *a.* thickly inhabited [L. *populus,* the people].

popular (pop′ū-lar) *a.* pert. to the common people; liked by the people; finding general favour; easily understood.—**pop′ularly** *adv.*—**pop′ularise** *v.t.* to make popular; to make familiar, plain, easy, etc. to all.—**popularisa′tion** *n.*—**popular′ity** *n.* the state or quality of being liked by the people; public favour [L. *populus,* the people].

porcelain (pors′lan, por′se-lān) *n.* the finest kind of earthenware—white, glazed and semi-transparent; china-ware;—*a.* made of porcelain.—**porcelain clay,** kaolin [It. *porcellana,* a delicate shell-fish].

porch (pōrch) *n.* a covered entrance to a doorway; a portico [L. *porticus,* a colonnade].

porcine (por′sīn) *a.* pert. to, or like, swine; swinish [L. *porcus,* a pig].

porcupine (por′kū-pīn) *n.* a large quadruped of the rodent family, covered with spines [L. *porcus,* a pig; *spina,* a spine].

pore (pōr) *n.* a minute opening in the skin for the passage of perspiration.—**por′ous** *a.* full of pores.—**por′ousness** *n.*—**porosity** (pō-ros′i-ti) *n.* [Gk. *poros,* a passage].

pore (pōr) *v.i.* to look at with steady attention, esp. in reading or studying (with 'over'); to ponder [M.E. *pouren*].

pork (pōrk) *n.* the flesh of swine used for food.—**por′ky** *a.* like pork; fat; greasy.—**por′ker** *n.* a hog, fattened for eating.—**pork′ling** *n.* a young pig [L. *porcus,* a pig].

pornography (por-nog′ra-fi) *n.* obscene literature or pictures.—**pornog′rapher** *n.*—**pornograph′ic** *a.* [Gk. *pornē,* a harlot; *graphein,* to write].

porphyry (por′fi-ri) *n.* a rock with a dark, reddish-purple ground-mass, enclosing crystals of felspar.—**porphyrit′ic** *a.* [Gk. *porphuros,* purple].

porpoise (por′pus) *n.* a blunt-nosed cetacean mammal 5 to 8 feet long, frequenting the Northern Seas; a dolphin [L. *porcus,* a hog; *piscis,* a fish].

porridge (por′ij) *n.* a breakfast dish made by stirring oatmeal into boiling, salted, water [form of *pottage*].

porringer (por′in-jer) *n.* a small bowl-shaped dish meant for holding porridge [Fr. *potager,* a soup-basin].

port (pōrt) *n.* a harbour; a town with a harbour; a haven; a refuge [L. *portus*].

port (pōrt) *n.* city gate; gateway.—**port′hole** *n.* window in side of ship [L. *porta,* gate].

port (pōrt) *n.* the way in which a person carries himself; demeanour;—*v.t.* (*Mil.*) to carry (a rifle) slanting upwards in front of the body.—**port′ly** *a.* dignified in appearance; corpulent [L. *portare,* to carry].

port (pōrt) *n.* a strong, sweet, dark-red wine [fr. *Oporto,* in Portugal].

port (pōrt) *n.* the left side of a ship, looking towards the bow (formerly *larboard*);—*v.t.* and *i.* to turn (helm) to left side [etym. uncertain].

portable (pōrt-abl) *a.* capable of being easily carried [L. *portare,* to carry].

portage (pōr′tāj) *n.* the act of carrying or transporting goods; the charge for transport; in N. America, the carrying of goods, boats, etc. between two navigable bodies of water [L. *portare,* to carry].

portal (pōrt′al) *n.* a gate or entrance; the smaller of two gateways side by side [Fr. *portail,* fr. L. *porta,* a gate].

portcullis (pōrt-kul′is) *n.* a strong grating hung over the gateway of a castle, etc. to be lowered as an aid to defence [L. *porta,* gate; *colare,* to filter].

portend (pōr-tend′) *v.t.* to foretell; to give warning in advance; to be an omen of.—**por′tent** *n.* an omen, esp. of evil.—**portent′ous** *a.* serving to portend; ominous [L. *portendere,* to foretell].

porter (pōr′ter) *n.* (*fem.* **por′t(e)ress** a door- or gate-keeper; (*U.S.*) railway sleeping-car attendant [L. *porta,* gate].

porter (pōr′ter) *n.* one employed to carry baggage, esp. at stations or hotels; a dark-brown, bitter beer.—**por′terage** *n.* fee for hire of a porter.—**por′ter-house** *n.* (*U.S.*) a restaurant.—**porterhouse steak** *n.* a choice cut of beef next to sirloin [L. *portare,* to carry].

portfolio (pōrt-fō′li-ō) *n.* flatcase for holding loose documents, drawings, etc.; the papers themselves; office of a minister of state [L. *portare*, to carry; *folium*, a leaf].

portico (pōr′ti-kō) *n.* (*Archit.*) a row of columns in front of the entrance to a building; a colonnade; a porch with columns; a covered walk.—*pl.* **por′ticoes, por′ticos** [L. *porticus*].

portion (pōr′shun) *n.* a piece; a part; a share; a helping of food; destiny; lot; a dowry; —*v.t.* to divide into shares; to give a dowry to.—**por′tionless** *a.* [L. *portio*].

portmanteau (pōrt-man′tō) *n.* a leather travelling-bag; a suitcase [Fr. *porter*, to carry; *manteau*, a cloak].

portray (pōr-trā′) *v.t.* to represent by drawing, painting, acting, or imitating; to describe vividly in words.—**portray′al** *n.* the act of portraying; description.—**portray′er** *n.*—**portrait** (pōr′trāt) *n.* picture of a person, esp. of the face; a graphic description of a person in words.—**por′traiture** *n.* the art of portrait painting [L. *protrahere*, to draw forth].

Portuguese (pōr′tū-gēz, pōr-tū-gēz′) *a.* pert. to *Portugal*, or its inhabitants.

pose (pōz) *n.* attitude or posture of a person, natural or assumed; a mental attitude or attitudinising;—*v.t.* to place in a position for the sake of effect; to lay down or assert;—*v.i.* to assume an attitude; to affect or pretend to be of a certain character.—**poseur** (pō-zer′) *n.* (*fem.*) **poseuse** (pō-zez′) an affected, attitudinising person [Fr. *poser*, to place].

pose (pōz) *v.t.* to puzzle; to embarrass by questioning.—**po′ser** *n.* [short. fr. *oppose*].

posh (posh) *a.* (*Slang*) smart; spruce; stylish.

posit (poz′it) *v.t.* to place or set in position; to lay down as a fact or principle [L. *ponere*, *positum*, to place].

position (pō-zish′un) *n.* place or station; the manner in which anything is arranged; posture; social rank or standing; employment; state of affairs.—**posit′ional** *a.* [L. *ponere*, *positum*, to place].

positive (poz′i-tiv) *a.* formally laid down; clearly stated; absolute; dogmatic; of real value; confident; not negative; plus; (*Math.*) pert. to a quantity greater than zero; (*Gram.*) denoting the simplest value of an adjective or adverb; (*Colloq.*) utter; downright;—*n.* the positive degree of an adjective or adverb, i.e. without comparison; in photography, a print in which the lights and shadows are not reversed (as in the negative).—**pos′itively** *adv.* —**pos′itiveness** *n.*—**pos′itivism** *n.* the philosophical system which recognises only matters of fact and experience.—**pos′itivist** *n.* a believer in this doctrine.—**positive pole**, of a magnet, the north-seeking-pole.—**positive sign**, the sign (+ read *plus*) of addition [L. *ponere*, *positum*, to place].

positron (poz′i-tron) *n.* particle differing from an electron in that it has positive electrical charge; a *posi*tive elec*tron*.

posse (pos′e) *n.* a company or force, usually with legal authority; in America, men, under orders of the sheriff, maintaining law and order [L. *posse*, to be able].

possess (po-zes′) *v.t.* to own or hold as property; to have as an attribute; to seize or obtain; to enter into and influence, as an evil spirit or passions.—**possessed′** *a.* influenced, as by an evil spirit; demented.—**possession** *n.* the act of possessing; ownership; actual occupancy; the state of being possessed; the thing possessed.—**possess′ive** *a.* denoting possession; —*n.* (*Gram.*) the possessive case or pronoun. —**possess′ively** *adv.*—**possess′or** *n.* [L. *possidere*, *possessum*, to possess].

posset (pos′et) *n.* a remedy against colds, etc. made from hot milk curdled by adding wine, ale, etc. [O.Fr. *possette*].

possible (pos′i-bl) *a.* capable of being or of coming into, being; liable to happen; worthy of consideration;—*n.* the highest attainable mark or score.—**poss′ibly** *adv.*—**possibil′ity** *n.* quality of being possible; that which is possible [L. *possibilis*].

possum (pos′um) *n.* (*Colloq.*) in N. America, an opossum.—**to play possum**, to sham death; to feign illness; to pretend to be ignorant of; to deceive [fr. *opossum*].

post (pōst) *n.* a piece of timber or metal, set upright as a support; a prop or pillar;—*v.t.* to attach to a post or wall, as a notice or advertisement.—**post′er** *n.* one who posts bills; a large placard for posting up in a public place [L. *postis*].

post (pōst) *n.* a fixed place; a military station or the soldiers occupying it; an office or position of trust, service, or emolument; a trading settlement; formerly, a stage on the road for riders carrying mail; a postman; an established conveyance of letters; the mail; a size of writing-paper;—*v.t.* to station or place; to send by post; to inform; to travel with speed.—**post′age** *n.* the cost of conveyance by post.—**post′al** *a.* pert. to the post-office or mail-service.—**post′al-or′der** *n.* (*abbrev.* **P.O.**) a money order issued by one post-office authorising payment at another.—**post′man** *n.* one who collects and delivers letters.—**post′mark** *n.* a post-office mark which cancels the postage-stamp and gives place and time of posting or arrival.—**post′master** *n.* the manager of a post-office.—**post′master-gen′eral** *n.* the chief of the post-office department of a government.—**post′card** *n.* a stamped card on which a message may be sent through the post.—**post′chaise, post′coach** *n.* a four-wheeled carriage hired by those who travelled with post-horses.—**post′haste** *n.* haste or speed in travelling;—*a.* expeditious;—*adv.* with speed. —**post′horse** *n.* one of a number kept at each stage on a travelling route, for hiring out to travellers by post-chaise.—**post′off′ice** *n.* an office where letters and parcels are received for distribution; the government postal department.—**post′age-stamp** *n.* an adhesive stamp, affixed to postal packets to indicate payment [L. *ponere*, to place].

post- (pōst) *adv.* and *prefix* fr. L. *post*, after, behind, used in many compound words.—**post-date′** *v.t.* to put on a document, letter, etc., a date later than the actual one.—**post′dilu′vian** *a.* living or happening after the Flood. —**post′grad′uate** *a.* of academic study, research, etc., undertaken after taking a university degree.—**post′impres′sionism** *n.* a movement in painting, sculpture, etc. which aims at artistic self-expression, or subjective as opposed to objective representation of things.—**post′mor′tem** *a.* after death;—*n.* the dissection of a body after death; an autopsy.—**post′na′tal** *a.* after birth.—**post′o′bit** *n.* a bond to secure to a lender money on the death of an individual from whom the borrower has expectations.—**post′prim′ary** *a.* of education, beyond the elementary school stage; secondary.

poste restante (pōst-res′tant, -tongt) *n.* a department in a post-office, to which letters can be addressed to be kept till called for [Fr. *poste*, post-office; *rester*, to remain].

posterior (pos-tē′ri-or) *a.* coming after; situated behind; later; hinder;—*n.* the rump. —**poste′riorly** *adv.*—**posterior′ity** *n.* the state of being later or subsequent.—**posterity** (pos-ter′it-i) *n.* future generations; descendants [L. *posterus*, behind].

postern (pōs′tern) *n.* a back door or gate;—*a.* rear; private [L. *posterus*, behind].

posthumous (pos′tū-mus) *a.* born after the death of the father; published after the death of the author; occurring after death.—**post′humously** *adv.* [L. *postumus*, last, but confused with L. *humus*, the ground].

postil (pos′til) *n.* a marginal note, esp. in the Bible; a sermon or homily.—**pos′tillate** *v.t.* and *i.* to explain by a postil [L. *post illa* (*verba*), after those (words)].

postilion, postillion (pōs-til′yun) *n.* the rider mounted on the near horse of a team drawing a carriage [Fr. *postillon*].

postpone (pōst-pōn′) *v.t.* to put off till a

future time; to defer; to delay.—**postpone′ment** *n.* the act of postponing.—**postpon′er** *n.* [L. *post*, after; *ponere*, to place].

postprandial (pōst-pran′di-ạl) *a.* after dinner [L. *post*, after; *prandium*, repast].

postscript (pōst′skript) *n.* something added to a letter after the signature; an addition to a book.—*abbrev.* **PS.** [L. *post*, after; *scribere*, *scriptum*, to write].

postulate (pos′tū-lāt) *v.t.* to assume without proof; to lay down as self-evident; to stipulate; —*n.* a proposition assumed without proof; (*Geom.*) a claim to assume the possibility of a simple operation.—**pos′tulant** *n.* one who makes a request or petition; a candidate, esp. for admission to a religious order.—**postula′tion** *n.* —**postulatory** (pos′tū-lā-tor-i) *a.* [L. *postulare*, to demand].

posture (pos′tūr) *n.* the position of a body, figure, etc. or of its several members; attitude;—*v.i.* to assume an artificial or affected attitude.—**pos′tural** *a.* [L. *ponere*, *positum*, to place].

posy (pō′zi) *n.* a bouquet; a motto or verse sent with a bunch of flowers, or cut on a ring [= *poesy*].

pot (pot) *n.* a rounded vessel of metal, earthenware, etc., used for cooking, holding fluids, plants, etc.; the contents of a pot; (*Colloq.*) a prize or trophy; a large sum of money;—*v.t.* to plant in pots; to preserve (as jam, chutney, etc.); to shoot at; in billiards, to pocket.—*pr.p.* **pot′ting.**—*pa.p.* and *pa.t.* **pot′ted.**—**potsherd** (pot′sherd) *n.* a piece of a broken pot.—**pot′bell′ied** *a.* corpulent.—**pot′boil′er** *n.* a literary or artistic work produced solely for the sake of money.—**pot′boy** *n.* a publican's assistant.—**pot′hang′er, pot′hook** *n.* a hook on which pots were hung over open fires; a letter shaped like a pot-hook, used in learning to write.—**pot′hole** *n.* cavity formed in rock by action of stones in the eddy of a stream; a hole in the roadway.—**pot′house** *n.* a low alehouse.—**pot′luck** *n.* whatever may happen to have been provided for a meal.—**pot′man** *n.* a publican's assistant.—**pot′shot** *n.* a shot at random [O.E. *pott*].

potable (pō′tạ-bl) *a.* drinkable.—**potation** (pō-tā′shun) *n.* a drinking, or drinking-bout; a draught [L. *potare*, to drink].

potash (pot′ash) *n.* a powerful alkali obtained from wood-ashes. Also **pot′ass.**—**potass′ium** *n.* the metallic base of potash.—**potash-water**, aerated water [*pot* and *ash*].

potato (pō-tā′tō) *n.* an edible tuber widely grown for food.—*pl.* **pota′toes** [Sp. *patata*].

poteen, potheen (po-tēn′) *n.* Irish whisky, esp. if illicitly distilled [Ir. *poitin*].

potent (pō′tẹnt) *a.* having great authority or influence; powerful; mighty; procreative.—**po′tently** *adv.*—**po′tency** *n.* moral or physical power; influence; energy; efficacy.—**po′tentate** *n.* one who possesses power; a prince.—**potential** (pō-ten′shạl) *a.* latent; existing in possibility but not in actuality;—*n.* inherent capability of doing anything; (*Elect.*) the level of electric pressure.—**poten′tially** *adv.*—**potentiality** (pō-ten-shi-al′i-ti) *n.* possibility, as distinct from actuality; power of capacity.—**potential difference** (*Elect.*) the difference of pressure between two points; voltage [L. *potens*, powerful, fr. *posse*, to be able].

pother (poTH′ẹr) *n.* disturbance; fuss;—*v.t.* to harass; to worry; to puzzle;—*v.i.* to fuss [etym. uncertain].

potion (pō′shun) *n.* a dose, esp. of liquid, medicine, or poison; a draught [L. *potio*, fr. *potare*, to drink].

pot-pourri (pō-pòò-rē′) *n.* a mixture of dried rose-petals, spices, etc.; a musical or literary medley [Fr. *pot*, a pot; *pourri*, rotten].

pottage (pot′āj) *n.* soup or stew; (*Bib.*) a dish of lentils [Fr. *potage*, soup].

potter (pot′ẹr) *n.* a maker of earthenware vessels.—**pott′ery** *n.* pots, vessels, etc. made of earthenware; the place where it is made; the art of making it [fr. *pot*].

potter (pot′ẹr) *v.i.* to work or act in a feeble, unsystematic way; to loiter; to dawdle [O.E. *potian*, to poke].

pottle (pot′l) *n.* an old liquid measure of 4 pints; a pot holding this quantity; a small fruit-basket [dim. fr. *pot*].

potty (pot′i) *a.* (*Slang*) crazy; silly; trivial [etym. uncertain].

pouch (pouch) *n.* a small bag or sack; a pocket; a bag-like receptacle in which certain animals, e.g. the kangaroo, carry their young;—*v.t.* to pocket; to cause to hang like a pouch [Fr. *poche*, a pocket].

pouf, pouffe (pòòf) *n.* a large drum-shaped cushion, used as a seat [Fr.].

poult (pōlt) *n.* a young fowl.—**poultry** (pōl′tri) *n.* domestic fowls.—**poult′erer** *n.* a dealer in poultry [Fr. *poule*, a hen; *poulet*, a chicken].

poultice (pōl′tis) *n.* a hot, moist mixture of bread, mustard, linseed, etc. applied to a sore, etc.;—*v.t.* to apply a poultice to [L. *puls*, porridge].

pounce (pouns) *v.i.* to spring upon suddenly; to swoop;—*n.* a swoop or sudden descent [etym. uncertain].

pounce (pouns) *n.* a fine powder used to prevent ink from spreading on unsized paper; a powder used for dusting over perforations in order to trace a pattern;—*v.t.* to sprinkle with pounce.—**poun′cet-box** *n.* a small perfume-box with a perforated top [L. *pumex*, pumice].

pound (pound) *n.* a measure of weight (*abbrev.* **lb.**), 16 ounces avoirdupois, or 12 ounces troy; a unit of British money (*abbrev.* **£**), 100 pence.—**pound sterling**, the British standard pound of 100 pence as a gold coin or paper note.—**pound′age** *n.* a commission, allowance, or charge of so much per pound.—**pound′al** *n.* a unit of force; the force which, acting on a mass of one pound, will impart to it an acceleration of one foot per second per second [L. *pondus*, weight].

pound (pound) *v.t.* and *i.* to beat or strike; to crush to pieces or to powder; to walk, run, etc., heavily [O.E. *punian*].

pound (pound) *n.* an enclosure for animals;—*v.t.* to shut up in one [O.E. *pund*, an enclosure].

pour (pōr) *v.i.* to come out in a stream, crowd, etc.; to flow freely; to rain heavily;—*v.t.* to cause to flow, as a liquid from a vessel; to shed; to utter [etym. unknown].

pourparler (pòòr-par′lā) *n.* a preliminary and informal discussion [Fr. *parler*, to speak; *pour* = L. *pro*, before].

poussette (pòò-set′) *v.i.* to swing round in couples, with hands joined, as in a country-dance;—*n.* the movement [Fr. *pousser*, to push].

pout (pout) *v.i.* to thrust out the lips, as in displeasure, etc.; to look sullen or sulky;—*n.* the act of pouting; a protrusion of the lips.—**pout′er** *n.* one who pouts; a pigeon with the power of inflating its crop [etym. uncertain].

poverty (pov′ẹr-ti) *n.* the state of being poor; poorness; lack of means [L. *paupertas*, fr. *pauper*, poor].

powder (pou′dẹr) *n.* dust; a solid matter in fine dry particles; a medicine in this form; short for gunpowder, face-powder, etc.;—*v.t.* to reduce to powder; to pulverise; to sprinkle with powder;—*v.i.* to fall into powder; to crumble.—**pow′dery** *a.* like powder.—**pow′der-mag′azine** *n.* a place where powder is stored.—**pow′der-puff** *n.* a pad of soft material used for applying face-powder to skin [Fr. *poudre*, fr. L. *pulvis*, dust].

power (pou′ẹr) *n.* a capacity for action, physical, mental, or moral; energy; might; agency or motive force; authority; one in authority; influence or ascendancy; a nation; mechanical energy; (*Math.*) the product arising from the continued multiplication of a number by itself.—**pow′erful** *a.* having great power; intense; capable of producing great effect.

pow'erfully *adv.* —**pow'erfulness** *n.* —**pow'erless** *a.* —**pow'erlessly** *adv.* —**pow'erlessness** *n.* —**pow'er-house, pow'er-sta'tion** *n.* a building where electric power is generated [O.Fr. *poer*].

pow-wow (pou'wou) *n.* orig. a feast, dance, or conference among N. American Indians; hence, any conference [N. Amer. Ind.].

pox (poks) *n.* a disease attended with pustules on the skin, as small-pox, chicken-pox, etc.; syphilis (orig. pl. of *pock*].

practice (prak'tis) *n.* performance or execution, as opposed to theory; custom or habit; systematic exercise for instruction; training; exercise of a profession; in arithmetic, a method for abridging operations. —**prac'tise** *v.t.* to put into action; to do frequently or habitually; to exercise a profession; to exercise oneself in; to train; —*v.i.* to perform certain acts customarily; to exercise a profession. —**prac'ticable** *a.* capable of being accomplished or put into practice; capable of being used, e.g. a weapon, a road, etc. —**prac'ticably** *adv.* —**prac'ticableness** *n.* —**practicabil'ity** *n.* —**prac'tical** *a.* pert. to practice or action; capable of being turned to account; useful; virtual. —**prac'tically** *adv.* —**prac'ticalness** *n.* —**practical'ity** *n.* —**practitioner** (prak-tish'un-ẹr) *n.* one engaged in a profession, esp. law or medicine. —**general practitioner** (*abbrev.* **G.P.**) one who practises in all branches of medicine and surgery [Gk. *praktikos*, concerned with action].

pragmatic, pragmatical (prag-mat'ik,-i-kạl) *a.* pert. to state affairs; pert. to business; concerned with practical consequences; matter-of-fact; officious or meddlesome. —**pragmat'ically** *adv.* —**pragmat'icalness** *n.* —**prag'matise** *v.t.* to represent an imaginary thing as real. —**prag'matism** *n.* a philosophy based on the conception that the truth of a doctrine is to to be judged by its practical consequences. —**prag'matist** *n.* [Gk. *pragmatikos*, pert. to business].

prairie (prā'ri) *n.* a large tract of grass-land, destitute of trees. —**prai'rie-chick'en** *n.* American species of grouse. —**prai'rie-dog** *n.* a small American rodent. —**prai'rie-hen** *n.* a prairie-chicken. —**prai'rie-oy'ster** *n.* a cocktail, made by dropping a raw egg-yolk into a mixture of spirits. —**prai'rie-schoon'er** *n.* a large, covered waggon, formerly used by emigrants going from east to west America. —**prai'rie-wolf** *n.* the coyote [Fr. fr. L. *pratum*, a meadow].

praise (prās) *v.t.* to express approval or admiration; to glorify; —*n.* approval of merit; commendation. —**praise'worthy** *a.* deserving of praise. —**praise'worthiness** *n.* [O.Fr. *preiser*].

praline (prȧ'lēn) *n.* a sweetmeat made by roasting almonds in boiling sugar [Fr. fr. *Duplessis-Praslin*, who first made it].

pram (pram) *n.* (*Colloq.*) *abbrev.* of **perambulator**, a baby-carriage.

pram (prȧm) *n.* a flat-bottomed lighter or barge [Dut. *praam*].

prance (prȧns) *v.i.* to spring or bound like a high-spirited horse; to swagger; to caper, esp. of children; —*n.* a prancing movement. —**pranc'er** *n.* —**pranc'ing** *n.* the act of prancing [etym. uncertain].

prandial (pran'di-ạl) *a.* pert. to dinner [L. *prandium*, lunch].

prang (prang) *n.* (*World War 2, R.A.F. Slang*) a crash-landing; —*v.t.* and *i.* to crash [etym. unknown].

prank (prangk) *v.t.* and *i.* to adorn or rig out showily; to show off [etym. uncertain].

prank (prangk) *n.* a mischievous trick; a practical joke [etym. uncertain].

prate (prāt) *v.t.* and *i.* to talk idly; to utter foolishly; —*n.* chatter [M.E. *praten*].

prattle (prat'l) *v.i.* to utter childishly; to babble; —*n.* childish talk [fr. *prate*].

prawn (prawn) *n.* an edible crustacean of the shrimp family [etym. unknown].

praxis (prak'sis) *n.* practice; a set of examples for practice [Gk. fr. *prassein*, to do].

pray (prā) *v.t.* to ask earnestly; to entreat; to petition; —*v.i.* to make a request or confession, esp. to God; to pay one's devotions to God. —**pray'er** *n.* one who prays; the act of praying; an earnest entreaty; the words used; the thing asked for; a petition, esp. to a public body. —*n.pl.* family worship; divine service. —**pray'erful** *a.* devout [L. *precari*].

pre- (prē) *prefix* fr. L. *prae*, before, beforehand, used with many nouns and verbs.

preach (prēch) *v.i.* and *t.* to deliver a sermon; to speak publicly on a religious subject, esp. as a clergyman; to advocate. —**preach'er** *n.* —**preach'ify** *v.i.* to moralise. —**preach'ment** *n.* a sermon of exaggerated solemnity [L. *praedicare*, to proclaim].

preamble (prē-am'bl) *n.* the introductory part of a discourse, story, document, etc.; a preface [L. *praeambulus*, walking before].

pre-arrange (prē-ạ-rānj') *v.t.* to arrange beforehand. —**pre-arrange'ment** *n.*

prebend (preb'ẹnd) *n.* the stipend of a canon or member of a cathedral chapter. —**preb'endal** *a.* —**preb'endary** *n.* a clergyman in receipt of a prebend [L. *praebere*, to allow].

precarious (prẹ-kā'ri-us) *a.* depending on the will or pleasure of another; depending on circumstances; uncertain; dangerous; perilous. —**preca'riously** *adv.* —**preca'riousness** *n.* [L. *precarius*, obtained by entreaty].

precatory (prek'ạ-tor-i) *a.* expressing entreaty; supplicatory [L. *precari*, to pray].

precaution (prẹ-kaw'shun) *n.* care taken beforehand. —*v.t.* to forewarn. —**precau'tionary** *a.* characterised by precaution.

precede (prē-sēd') *v.t.* to go before in place, time, rank, or importance. —**preced'ent** *a.* preceding; going before in time; —**pre'cedent** *n.* something done, or said, that may serve as an example in similar cases. —**preced'ently** *adv.* —**precedence** (prē-sē'dẹns) *n.* the act of preceding; priority in position, rank, or time. —**prece'ding** *a.* going before in time, place, or order; antecedent; previous [L. *prae*, before; *cedere*, to go].

precentor (prē-sen'tur) *n.* one who leads the choir in a cathedral [L. *prae*, before; *cantor*, a singer].

precept (prē'sept) *n.* an instruction intended as a rule of conduct, esp. moral conduct; a maxim; a commandment or exhortation; (*Law*) a written warrant or mandate given to an administrative officer. —**precep'tive** *a.* using precepts. —**precep'tor** *n.* (*fem.* **precep'tress**) a teacher; an instructor [L. *praecipere, praeceptum*, to order].

precession (prē-sesh'un) *n.* a going before. —**preces'sional** *a.* [L. *praecedere*, to go before].

precinct (prē'singt) *n.* the enclosure within the walls of sacred or official buildings; a boundary or limit; a minor territorial division. —*pl.* ground attached to an ecclesiastical building [L. *prae*, before; *cingere*, to gird].

precious (presh'us) *a.* of great value or price; costly; highly esteemed; over-refined; fastidious; (*Colloq.*) contemptible; —*adv.* extremely. —**prec'iously** *adv.* —**prec'iousness** *n.* —**preciosity** (pres(h)-i-os'i-ti) *n.* affected refinement of language or manners [Fr. *précieux*, fr. L. *pretium*, price].

precipice (pres'i-pis) *n.* a very steep or perpendicular place, as a cliff-face. —**precip'itous** *a.* very steep. —**precip'itously** *adv.* —**precip'itousness** *n.* [L. *praeceps*, headlong, fr. *prae*, before; *caput*, the head].

precipitate (pre-sip'i-tāt) *v.t.* to throw headlong; to urge on eagerly; to hasten the occurrence of; (*Chem.*) to cause to separate and fall to the bottom, as a substance in solution; of vapour, to condense; —*v.i.* (*Chem.*) to fall to the bottom of a vessel, as a sediment; —*n.* (*Chem.*) that which is precipitated in a liquid; sediment; —*a.* headlong; rash or over-hasty. —**precip'itately** *adv.* —**precip'itable** *a.* (*Chem.*) that may be precipitated. —**precipitabil'ity** *n.* —**precip'itance, precip'itancy** *n.* headlong hurry; rash haste.—**precip'itant** *a.* falling headlong; too hasty; unexpectedly hastened; —*n.* (*Chem.*) a substance which, added to a liquid, decomposes it and precipitates a sediment.—**precip'itantly** *adv.*—**precipitation** (pre-sip-i-tā'shun) *n.* the act of precipitating; rash haste; a falling headlong; condensation of vapour.—**precip'itative** *a.* tending to precipitate.—**precip'itator** *n.* [L. *praeceps*, headlong].

précis (prā-sē') *n.* a concise statement; an abstract or summary [Fr.].

precise (pre-sīs') *a.* exact; definite; formal; prim.—**precise'ly** *adv.*—**precise'ness** *n.*—**precision** (pre-sizh'un) *n.* accuracy; definiteness;—*a.* done with, or capable of, great accuracy [Fr. *précis*, exact].

preclude (pre-klòòd') *v.t.* to shut out; to hinder; to prevent from happening.—**preclusion** (pre-klòò'zhun) *n.*—**preclu'sive** *a.* shutting out; hindering beforehand [L. *prae*, before; *claudere*, to shut].

precocious (pre-kō'shus) *a.* ripe or developed too soon; having the mental powers or bodily growth developed at an early age; premature; forward.—**preco'ciously** *adv.*—**preco'ciousness, precocity** (pre-kos'i-ti) *n.* [L. *praecox*, early ripe].

precognition (prē-kog-nish'un) *n.* previous knowledge; (*Scots Law*) examination of witnesses before a trial.

preconceive (prē-kon-sēv') *v.t.* to form an opinion or idea of beforehand.—**preconcep'tion** *n.* a prejudice.

preconcert (prē-kon-sert') *v.t.* to settle beforehand.

precursor (prē-kur'sor) *n.* a person or thing going before, to indicate the approach of someone or something; a forerunner; a harbinger.—**precur'sive, precur'sory** *a.* [L. *prae*, before; *currere*, to run].

predacious (prē-dā'shus) *a.* living on prey; predatory.—**predatory** (pred'a-tor-i) *a.* living by preying on others; plundering; pillaging [L. *praeda*, booty].

predate (prē-dāt') *v.t.* to date earlier than the true date; to antedate [*pre* and *date*].

predecessor (prē-dē-ses'ur) *n.* one who has preceded another in an office, position, etc. [L. *prae*, before; *decedere*, to withdraw].

predestine (prē-des'tin) *v.t.* to destine beforehand; to foreordain.—**predes'tinate** *v.t.* to determine beforehand; to foreordain.—**predestina'tion** *n.* (*Theol.*) the doctrine that the salvation or damnation of individuals has been foreordained by God; the determination beforehand of future events; destiny; fate.—**predestina'rian** *n.* a believer in this doctrine [*pre* and *destine*].

predetermine (prē-dē-ter'min) *v.t.* to determine beforehand.—**predeter'minate** *a.* determined beforehand.—**predetermina'tion** *n.*

predicable (pred'i-ka-bl) *a.* able to be predicated or affirmed;—*n.* anything that can be affirmed of something.—**predicabil'ity** *n.* [L. *praedicare*, to proclaim].

predicament (pre-dik'a-ment) *n.* an awkward plight; a trying situation [L. *praedicare*, to proclaim].

predicant (pred'i-kant) *a.* pert. to preaching; preaching;—*n.* one who preaches; a preaching friar, esp. a Dominican [L. *praedicare*, to proclaim].

predicate (pred'i-kāt) *v.t.* to affirm; to assert; to declare;—*n.* that which is predicated; (*Gram.*) a statement made about the subject of the sentence.—**predica'tion** *n.* assertion; affirmation.—**pred'icative** *a.* expressing predication; affirming.—**pred'icatively** *adv.* [L. *praedicare*, to proclaim].

predict (prē-dikt') *v.t.* to tell beforehand; to foretell; to prophesy.—**predic'table** *a.*—**predic'tion** *n.* the act of foretelling; prophecy.—**predic'tive** *a.* foretelling; prophetic.—**predic'tor** *n.* [L. *praedicere*, to say before].

predigest (prē-di-jest') *v.t.* to subject food to artificial digestion before eating.

predilection (prē-di-lek'shun) *n.* a prepossession of mind in favour of something; partiality [L. *prae*, before; *dilectus*, chosen].

predispose (prē-dis-pōz') *v.t.* to incline beforehand; to give a tendency or bias to; to render susceptible to.—**predisposi'tion** *n.*

predominate (prē-dom'i-nāt) *v.i.* to surpass in strength, influence, or authority; to rule; to have ascendancy; to prevail.—**predom'inance, predom'inancy** *n.* ascendancy; superiority.—**predom'inant** *a.* superior in influence, authority, etc.; having ascendancy; controlling.—**predom'inantly** *adv.* [*pre* and *dominate*].

pre-eminent (prē-em'i-nent) *a.* distinguished above others; outstanding.—**pre-em'inently** *adv.*—**pre-em'inence** *n.*

pre-emption (prē-em'shun) *n.* the act or right of purchasing before others.—**pre-empt** (prē-emt') *v.t.* to appropriate beforehand.—**pre-emp'tive** *a.* [L. *prae*, before; *emptio*, a buying].

preen (prēn) *v.t.* to trim or dress with the beak, as birds do their feathers; to plume or smarten oneself [form of *prune*].

pre-exist (prē-eg-zist') *v.i.* to exist beforehand, or before something else.—**pre-exis'tence** *n.*—**pre-exis'tent** *a.*

prefab (prē-fab') *n.* (*Colloq.*) a prefabricated house.

prefabricate (prē-fab'ri-kāt) *v.t.* to build houses and ships in standardised units in factories for rapid assembly on sites or shipyards.—**prefabrica'tion** *n.*

preface (pref'as) *n.* introductory remarks at beginning of book, or spoken before a discourse; foreword;—*v.t.* to furnish with a preface.—**prefatory** (pref'a-to-ri) *a.* introductory [L. *prae*, before; *fari*, to speak].

prefect (prē'fekt) *n.* an ancient Roman magistrate; the governor of a French civil department; a senior boy in a school, appointed to maintain discipline.—**prefecto'rial** *a.*—**pre'fectship** *n.* the office or jurisdiction of a prefect [L. *praefectus*, set before].

prefer (prē-fer') *v.t.* to like better; to choose rather; to promote to an office or dignity.—**pref'erable** *a.* worthy of preference; more desirable.—**pref'erably** *adv.*—**pref'erableness** *n.* —**pref'erence** *n.* the act of preferring one thing before another; what is preferred; choice.—**preferential** (pref-e-ren'shal) *a.* giving or receiving a preference.—**preferen'tially** *adv.* —**prefer'ment** *n.* advancement or promotion; a position of honour, esp. in Church [L. *prae*, before; *ferre*, to bear].

prefix (prē'fiks) *n.* a letter, syllable, or word put at the beginning of another word to modify its meaning, e.g. *pre*digest, *under*ground.—**prefix** (prē-fiks') *v.t.* to place at the beginning.

pregnable (preg'na-bl) *a.* able to be taken by assault or force [L. *prehendere*, to take].

pregnant (preg'nant) *a.* being with child; fruitful; full of meaning.—**preg'nantly** *adv.*—**preg'nancy** *n.* [L. *praegnans*].

prehensile (prē-hen'sil) *a.* (*Zool.*) capable of grasping [L. *prehendere*, to seize].

prehistory (prē-hist'or-i) *n.* the period before written records were kept; the study of this period.—**prehistor'ic** *a.*

prejudice (prej'ū-dis) *n.* an opinion, favourable or unfavourable (more often the latter), formed without fair examination of facts; harm; bias;—*v.t.* to bias; to influence; to injure.—**prejudicial** (prej-ū-di'shal) *a.* injurious.—**prejudi'cially** *adv.* [L. *prae*, before; *judicium*, judgment].

prelate (prel'at) *n.* a bishop, or other Church dignitary of equal or higher rank.—**prelat'ic, prelat'ical** *a.*—**prel'acy** *n.* the office or dignity of a prelate; government by prelates; episcopacy; bishops collectively.—**prel'atist** *n.* an advocate of government by prelates [L. *praelatus*, put before].

prelect (prē-lekt') *v.i.* to deliver a lecture or discourse in public.—**prelec'tion** *n.* a lecture.—**prelec'tor** *n.* a lecturer [L. *prae*, before; *legere*, *lectum*, to read].

preliminary (pre-lim'i-na-ri) *a.* introductory;

preparatory;—*n.* an introduction; a preparatory measure; (often used in *pl.*) [L. *prae*, before; *limen*, a threshold].
prelude (prel′ūd) *n.* an introductory performance or event; a musical introduction; a preliminary;—*v.t.* to serve as a prelude or forerunner to.—**prelu′sive, prelu′sory** *a.* introductory [L. *prae*, before; *ludere*, to play].
premature (pre′, prē′mạ-tūr) *a.* ripe before the natural or proper time; untimely; overhasty.—**premature′ly** *adv.*—**premature′ness, prematur′ity** *n.* early flowering or maturity.
premeditate (prē-med′i-tāt) *v.t.* to think, consider, or revolve in the mind beforehand.
premier (prē′mi-ẹr, prem′yẹr) *a.* first; chief or principal; most ancient;—*n.* the prime minister.—**prem′iership** *n.* [Fr. fr. L. *primarius*, of the first rank].
première (prẹ-myer′) *n.* a first public performance of a play [Fr. = first].
premise (pre-mīz′) *v.t.* to set forth beforehand, or as introductory to the main subject; to lay down general propositions on which the subsequent reasonings rest.—**premise** (prem′is) *n.* Also **pre′miss**, a proposition previously supposed or proved; a proposition from which an inference or conclusion is drawn; (*Logic*) either of the two propositions of a syllogism from which the conclusion is drawn.—**prem′ises** *n.pl.* a building with its adjuncts [L. *prae*, before; *mittere, missum*, to send].
premium (prē′mi-um) *n.* a recompense; a prize; a fee paid to learn a trade or profession; money paid for insurance; the amount exceeding the par value of shares or stock.—**at a premium**, above par; in great demand [L. *praemium*, reward].
premonition (prē-mo-nish′un) *n.* previous warning or information; an instinctive foreboding; presentiment.—**premon′itor** *n.* a forewarner.—**premon′itory** *a.* giving previous warning or notice.—**premon′itorily** *adv.* [L. *prae*, before; *monere*, to warn].
pre-natal (prē-nā′tạl) *a.* previous to birth.
prentice (pren′tis) *n.* an apprentice [fr. *apprentice*].
preoccupy (prē-ok′ū-pī) *v.t.* to take possession of before another; to engage the attention of.—**preoc′cupied** *a.* occupied previously; engrossed in thought; absorbed in meditation.—**preoc′cupancy** *n.* the act of taking possession of before others.—**preoccupa′tion** *n.*
preordain (prē-or-dān′) *v.t.* to ordain beforehand; to foreordain.—**preordinance** (prē-or′di-nạns) *n.* a previous decree.
prep (prep) *n.* (*School Slang*) preparation; preparatory class.
prepaid (prē-pād′) *a.* paid in advance.
prepare (pre-pār′) *v.t.* to make ready for use; to fit for a particular purpose; to provide; to fit out;—*v.i.* to make things ready; to make oneself ready.—**preparation** (prep-ạ-rā′shun) *n.* the act of making ready for use; readiness; a substance, esp. medicine or food, specially made up for use; the act of, or time for, learning home lessons (*abbrev.* **prep.**).—**prepar′ative** *a.* tending to prepare for;—*n.* anything which serves to prepare.—**prepar′atively** *adv.*—**prepar′atory** *a.* preparing the way; preliminary; introductory.—**preparedness** (pre-pār′ed-nes) *n.* [L. *prae*, before; *parare*, to make ready].
prepay (prē-pā′) *v.t.* to pay beforehand [*pre* and *pay*].
prepense (pre-pens′) *a.* premeditated; deliberate [L. *prae*, before; *pensare*, to weigh].
preponderate (pre-pon′dẹr-āt) *v.i.* to exceed in power, influence, numbers, etc.; to outweigh.—**prepon′derance** *n.* superiority of power, numbers, etc.—**prepon′derant** *a.*—**prepon′derantly** *adv.* [L. *prae*, before; *pondus, ponderis*, a weight].
preposition (prep-ō-zish′un) *n.* (*Gram.*) a word, e.g. *with, by, for*, etc., used before a noun or pronoun to show the relation to some other word in the sentence.—**preposi′tional** *a.* [L. *prae*, before; *ponere, positum*, to place].
prepossess (prē-po-zes′) *v.t.* to possess beforehand; to influence a person's mind, heart, etc. beforehand; to prejudice favourably.—**prepossess′sing** *a.* tending to win a favourable opinion; attractive.—**preposses′singly** *adv.*—**preposses′sion** *n.*
preposterous (pre-pos′tẹr-us) *a.* contrary to nature, truth, reason, or common sense; utterly absurd.—**prepos′terously** *adv.*—**prepos′terousness** *n.* [L. = before behind, fr. *prae*, before; *posterus*, after].
Pre-Raphaelitism (prē-raf′ā-el-it-izm) *n.* a revival, begun in 1848 by a group of English artists (Holman Hunt, Rossetti, Millais, etc.), of the style of Italian painting before *Raphael* (b. 1483) characterised by strict adherence to natural form and effect.—**Pre-Raph′aelite** *a.*
prerogative (prē-rog′ạ-tiv) *n.* an exclusive right or privilege by reason of rank, position, etc.—*a.* privileged [L. *prae*, before; *rogare*, to ask].
presage (pres′āj) *n.* an indication of what is going to happen; an omen.—**presage** (prē-sāj′) *v.t.* to foretell; to forebode; to have a presentiment of.—**presage′ful** *a.* warning [L. *prae*, before; *sagire*, to perceive acutely].
presbyopia (prez-bi-ō′pi-ạ) *n.* long-sightedness (occurring in old age) [Gk. *presbutēs*, an old man; *ops*, an eye].
presbyter (prez′bi-tẹr) *n.* a priest or elder in the early Christian Church; in Episcopal churches, one ordained to the second order in the ministry; a member of a presbytery.—**Presbyterian** (prez-bi-tē′ri-ạn) *n.* one belonging to Presbyterian Church;—*a.* pert. or belonging to Presbyterian Church.—**Presbyte′rianism** *n.*—**pres′bytery** *n.* a body of elders in Christian Church; a court of all pastors within a certain district, and one ruling elder from each church; space in a cathedral between altar and choir [Gk. *presbuteros*, elder, fr. *presbus*, old].
prescience (prē′shi-ẹns) *n.* knowledge of events before they take place.—**pre′scient** *a.* having foreknowledge of events [O.Fr. fr. L. *praescientia*, foreknowledge].
prescribe (pre-skrīb′) *v.t.* to lay down authoritatively for direction; to set out rules for; (*Med.*) to order or advise the use of.—**prescrib′er** *n.*—**pre′script** *n.* direction; ordinance.—**prescription** (pre-skrip′shun) *n.* the act of prescribing or directing; a doctor's direction for use of medicine.—**prescrip′tive** *a.* acquired by immemorial use [L. *praescribere*, to write before].
pre-selective (prē-sẹ-lek′tiv) *a.* in motoring, relating to a gearbox in which the change-speed lever can be moved before the change is actually desired, the change being completed by depressing the clutch pedal.—**preselec′tor** *n.* the apparatus.
present (prez′ẹnt) *a.* being in a certain place; here or at hand; now existing; (*Gram.*) pert. to time that now is;—*n.* present time; (*Gram.*) the present tense.—**pres′ence** *n.* the state of being present; nearness or proximity; the person of a superior; personality; mien or appearance; apparition.—**pres′ently** *adv.* at once; soon; by and by [L. *praesens*, being present].
present (pre-zent′) *v.t.* to introduce into the presence of; to exhibit or offer to the notice; to offer as a gift; to bestow; to aim, as a weapon;—*n.* a gift.—**present′able** *a.* fit to be presented.—**presentation** (prez-en-tā′shun) *n.* the act of presenting; the state of being presented; that which is presented.—**present′ment** *n.* the act or state of presenting; representation; the laying of a formal statement before a court or authority [L. *praesentare*, to place before].
presentiment (prē-sen′ti-ment) *n.* a previous notion or opinion; anticipation of evil; foreboding.
preserve (prē-zẹrv′) *v.t.* to keep from injury or destruction; to keep in a sound state;—*n.*

that which is preserved, as fruit, etc.; any medium used in preserving; a place for the preservation of game, fish, etc.—**preser'ver** *n.* —**preser'vable** *a.* —**preservation** (prez-ẹr-vā'-shun) *n.* the act of preserving or keeping safe; the state of being preserved; safety.—**preser'vative** *n.* that which preserves; —*a.* having the power of preserving.—**preser'vatory** *a.* tending to preserve; —*n.* that which preserves [L. *prae,* before; *servare,* to protect].

preside (prē-zīd') *v.i.* to be chairman of a meeting; to direct; to control; to superintend. —**president** (prez'-i-dent) *n.* (*fem.* **pres'identress**) the head of a society, company, association, etc.; the elected head of a republic.—**pres'idency** *n.* presidentship.—**presiden'tial** *a.* pert. to a president, his office, dignity, etc.—**pres'identship** *n.* the office, or term of office, of a president.—**presiding officer,** the official in charge of election arrangements at a polling-station [L. *prae,* before; *sedere,* to sit].

press (pres) *v.t.* to push or squeeze; to crush; to hug; to embrace closely; to drive with violence; to hurry; to urge steadily; to force; to solicit with importunity; to constrain; to smooth by pressure; —*v.i.* to exert pressure; to strive eagerly; to crowd; to throng; to hasten; —*n.* an instrument or machine for squeezing, compressing, etc.; a printing-machine; printing and publishing; newspapers collectively; a crowd; a throng; urgent demands; stress; a cupboard.—**press'ing** *a.* urgent; persistent.—**press'-a'gent** *n.* one employed to advertise and secure publicity for any person or organisation.—**press'-cutt'ing** *n.* an item cut out of a newspaper.—**press'-mark** *n.* a mark on a book to show its place in library. —**press'-room** *n.* the room in a publishing establishment where printing-presses are operated. —**to go to press,** of a newspaper, to start printing [L. *pressare,* fr. *premere,* to squeeze].

press (pres) *v.t.* to force to serve in the navy or army; to take for royal or public use; to requisition.—**press'-gang** *n.* men formerly employed to obtain recruits for navy (or army), by force [L. *praestare,* to furnish].

pressure (presh'-ūr) *n.* the act of pressing; state of being pressed; influence; authority.

pressurisation (presh-ū-rī-zā'-shun) *n.* maintenance of same pressure inside aircraft at great altitudes as at a few thousand feet.—**pressurise** (presh'-ūr-īz) *v.t.*

prestidigitation (pres-ti-dij-i-tā'-shun) *n.* conjuring; sleight of hand.—**prestidig'itator** *n.* a conjurer (conjuror); a juggler; a magician [L. *praesto,* ready; *digitus,* a finger].

prestige (pres-tēzh', pres'-tij) *n.* influence resulting from past achievement, character, reputation, etc. [Fr. = marvel].

presto (pres'-tō) *adv.* (*Mus.*) quickly [It. fr. L. *praesto,* ready].

presume (prē-zūm') *v.t.* to take for granted; to suppose to be true without proof; to venture; —*v.i.* to act in a forward manner; to take liberties.—**presum'able** *a.* probable.—**presum'ably** *adv.*—**presumption** (prē-zum'-shun) *n.* the act of, or grounds for, presuming; strong probability; that which is taken for granted; arrogance of opinion or conduct; boldness.—**presumptive** (prē-zum'-tiv) *a.* presuming; based on probability; that may be assumed as true or valid until the contrary is proved.—**presump'tively** *adv.*—**presump'tuous** *a.* forward; taking liberties.—**presump'tuously** *adv.*—**presump'tuousness** *n.* [L. *prae,* before; *sumere,* to take].

presuppose (prē-su-pōz') *v.t.* to assume or take for granted beforehand.—**presupposi'tion** *n.* [*pre* and *suppose*].

pretend (pre-tend') *v.t.* to assert falsely; to counterfeit; to make believe; —*v.i.* to lay claim (to); to make pretence; to sham.—**preten'der** *n.* one who simulates or feigns; a claimant, esp. to the throne.—**pretence'** *n.* simulation; the act of laying claim; assumption; pretext.—**preten'sion** *n.* the act of advancing a claim, esp. a false claim; a right alleged or assumed.—**pretentious** (pre-ten'-shus) *a.* given to outward show; presumptuous and arrogant.—**pre'tentiously** *adv.* —**preten'tiousness** *n.* [L. *prae,* before; *tendere,* to stretch].

preter- (prē'-tẹr) *prefix* fr. L. *praeter,* meaning beyond, above, more than, etc., used in combining forms.—**preternat'ural** *a.* beyond or different from what is natural; abnormal.

preterit, preterite (pret'-ẹr-it) *a.* (*Gram.*) past (applied to the tense that expresses past action or state); —*n.* (*Gram.*) the preterite or past definite tense [L. *praeter,* beyond; *ire, itum,* to go].

pretermit (prē-tẹr-mit') *v.t.* to pass by; to omit; to disregard.—*pr.p.* **pretermit'ting**—*pa.p.* and *pa.t.* **pretermit'ted.**—**pretermiss'ion** *n.* passing by; omission; neglect [L. *praeter,* beyond; *mittere,* to send].

pretext (prē'-tekst) *n.* ostensible reason or motive which cloaks the real reason; pretence [L. *prae,* before; *texere,* to weave].

pretty (prit'-i) *a.* of a beauty that is charming and attractive, but not striking or imposing; neat and tasteful; elegant; pleasing; fine or excellent in an ironical sense; (*Arch.*) brave; —*adv.* in some degree; moderately; fairly; rather.—**prett'ily** *adv.*—**prett'iness** *n.* [O.E. *praettig,* crafty].

prevail (pre-vāl') *v.i.* to gain the upper hand or mastery; to succeed; to be current; to be in force; to persuade or induce (with 'on' or 'upon').—**prevail'ing** *a.*—**prevalent** (prev'-ạ-lent) *a.* gaining advantage or superiority; most generally received; extensively existing; rife. —**prev'alently** *adv.*—**prev'alence** *n.* the condition of being prevalent [L. *prae,* before; *valere,* to be strong].

prevaricate (pre-var'-i-kāt) *v.i.* to evade the truth; to quibble.—**prevarica'tion** *n.* deviation from the truth.—**prevar'icator** *n.* [L. *prae,* before; *varus,* crooked].

prevent (pre-vent') *v.t.* to keep from happening; to stop.—**prevent'able** *a.*—**prevention** (pre-ven'-shun) *n.* hindering; obstruction; hindrance; preventive.—**preven'tive** *a.* tending to prevent or ward off; —*n.* that which prevents; antidote to keep off disease [L. *prae,* before; *venire, ventum,* to come].

pre-view (prē'-vū) *n.* a private showing of works of art, films, etc. before being exhibited in public [*pre* and *view*].

previous (prē'-vi-us) *a.* preceding; happening before; (*Slang*) hasty.—**pre'viously** *adv.*—**pre'viousness** *n.* [L. *prae,* before; *via,* a way].

previse (prē-vīz') *v.t.* to foresee; to forewarn. —**previ'sion** *n.* foresight; foreknowledge [L. *prae,* before; *videre, visum,* to see].

prey (prā) *n.* any animal hunted and killed for food by another animal; a victim; spoil; plunder; —*v.i.* (with 'on' or 'upon') to seize and devour; to treat as prey; to pillage; to weigh heavily [Fr. *proie,* fr. L. *praeda*].

price (prīs) *n.* the amount at which a thing is valued, bought, or sold; value; cost; reward; —*v.t.* to fix the price of; to ask the cost of.—**price'less** *a.* beyond any price.—**price'lessness** *n.* [L. *pretium,* price].

prick (prik) *n.* a sharp-pointed instrument; a dot, mark, or puncture made by a sharp point; the act of pricking; a sharp, stinging pain; hence, (*Fig.*) remorse; a spur; —*v.t.* to pierce slightly with a sharp point; to incite; to affect with sharp pain; to sting; to erect (the ears); to deck out.—**prick'er** *n.* that which pricks; a sharp-pointed instrument.—**prick'-eared** *a.* having pointed ears (prick = a goad for oxen) [O.E. *prica,* a point].

prickle (prik'-l) *n.* a small sharp point; a thorn; a spike; a bristle; —*v.t.* to prick slightly; to cover with small points; —*v.i.* to feel a tingling sensation.—**prick'ly** *a.* full of prickles; stinging; tingling.—**prick'liness** *n.*—**prick'ly-pear** *n.* a kind of cactus [O.E. *prica,* a point].

pride (prīd) *n.* the state or quality of being

proud; too high an opinion of oneself; worthy self-esteem.—**pride'ful** *a.* full of pride; arrogant; scornful.—**pride'fully** *adv.*—**to pride oneself on (upon),** to be proud of; to take credit for [O.E. *pryte*, fr. *prut*, proud].

priest (prēst) *n.* (*fem.* **priest'ess**) a clergyman; in R.C. and Episcopal churches, one of the order between deacon and bishop; in pagan times, one who officiated at the altar, or performed the rites of sacrifice.—**priest'like, priest'ly** *a.*—**priest'liness** *n.*—**priest'craft** *n.* priestly policy; the stratagems practised by priests.—**priest'hood** *n.* the office or duty of a priest; priests collectively [O.E. *preost*, fr. Gk. *presbuteros*, elder].

prig (prig) *n.* a conceited person who professes superior culture, morality, manners, etc.—**prig'gish** *a.* [etym. uncertain].

prim (prim) *a.* formal and precise; affectedly nice; prudish;—*v.t.* to shape or arrange with precision or affectation.—**prim'ly** *adv.*—**prim'ness** *n.* [O.Fr. fr. L. *primus*, first].

prima (prē'mạ) *a.* first.—**prima donna,** the principal female singer in an opera.—**prima facie** (fā'shi-ē) at first view.—**prima facie case,** a case based on sufficient evidence to go to a jury [It. *prima*, first; *donna*, a woman; L. *facies*, appearance].

primacy (prī'mạ-si) *n.* See **primate.**

primal (prī'mạl) *a.* first; original; chief.—**pri'mary** *a.* first in order of time, development, importance; preparatory; elementary;—*n.* that which stands highest in rank or importance; a large feather on the last joint of a bird's wing.—**pri'marily** *adv.* in the first place.—**pri'mariness** *n.*—**primary colours,** red, orange, yellow, green, blue, indigo and violet; also, (*Physiol.*) red, green, and a bluish violet, from a combination of which any colour may be obtained [L. *primus*, first].

primate (prī'māt) *n.* the chief dignitary in a church; an archbishop.—**primacy** (prī'mạ-si) *n.* the chief dignity in a national church; the office or dignity of an archbishop [L.L. *primas*, a chief, fr. *primus*, first].

Primates (prī-mā'tēz) *n.pl.* the highest order of mammals [L. *primus*, first].

prime (prīm) *a.* first in time; original; first in degree or importance; foremost; of highest quality; (*Math.*) that cannot be separated into factors;—*n.* the earliest stage or beginning; spring; youth; full health or strength; the best portion;—*v.t.* to prepare a firearm by charging with powder; to prepare wood with a protective coating before painting it; to fill with water, etc., as a pump, to make it start working; to instruct beforehand.—**pri'mer** *n.* one who, or that which, primes, esp. a percussion cap, etc. used to ignite the powder of cartridges, etc.; a small, elementary book used in teaching.—**prime'ly** *adv.*—**prime'ness** *n.*—**pri'ming** *n.* the powder, etc. used to fire the charge in firearms.—**prime minister,** the first minister of state.—**prime number,** a number divisible without remainder only by itself or unity [L. *primus*, first].

primeval (prī-mē'vạl) *a.* original; primitive; pert. to the first age of the world.—**prime'vally** *adv.* [L. *primus*, first; *aevum*, age].

primitive (prim'i-tiv) *a.* pert. to the beginning or origin; being the earliest of its kind; old-fashioned; plain and rude; (*Biol.*) rudimentary; undeveloped;—*n.* a primary word, not derived from another.—**prim'itively** *adv.*—**prim'itiveness** *n.* [L. *primitivus*, fr. *primus*, first].

primogeniture (prī-mō-jen'i-tūr) *n.* the state of being the first-born child; the right of the eldest son to inherit his parents' property.—**primogen'ital, primogen'itary** *a.*—**primogen'itor** *n.* the earliest ancestor [L. *primus*, first; *genitor*, a father, fr. *gignere*, to beget].

primordial (prī-mor'di-ạl) *a.* existing from the beginning; first in order; primeval [L. *primus*, first; *ordiri*, to begin].

primrose (prim'rōz) *n.* a plant bearing pale-yellow flowers in spring; this colour;—*a.* pale-yellow; gay [M.E. *primerole*, fr. L. *primus*, first].

Primula (prim'ū-lạ) *n.* a genus of plants including the primrose [L. *primus*, first].

primus (prī'mus, prē'mus) *n.* in the Scottish Episcopal Church, the presiding bishop;—*a.* first; elder or eldest [L. = first].

Primus (prī-mus, prē'mus) *n.* a kind of small cooking-stove burning vaporised oil [Protected Trade Name].

prince (prins) *n.* (*fem.* **princess'**) a ruler or chief; the son of a king or emperor; in many foreign countries, a title of nobility.—**prince'dom** *n.* the jurisdiction, rank, or estate of a prince.—**prince'let, prince'ling** *n.* a young prince; a petty prince.—**prince'ly** *a.* pert. to, or worthy of, a prince; stately; august; dignified.—**prince'liness** *n.*—**Prince Consort,** the husband of a reigning queen [L. *princeps*, a prince].

principal (prin'si-pạl) *a.* chief in importance; first in rank, character, etc.;—*n.* the chief person in authority; the most important thing; a leader; the head of certain institutes, esp. a university, college, or school; the chief actor in a crime; a chief debtor; a person for whom another is agent; a sum of money lent and yielding interest.—**prin'cipally** *adv.*—**prin'cipalship** *n.* the office or dignity of a principal.—**principal'ity** *n.* the territory or dignity of a prince; sovereignty [L. *principalis*].

principia (prin-sip'i-ạ) *n.pl.* first principles; beginnings [L. *principium*, a beginning].

principle (prin'si-pl) *n.* a fundamental truth or law; a moral rule or settled reason of action; uprightness; honesty; an element.—**prin'cipled** *a.* guided by certain rules of conduct [L. *principium*, a beginning].

prink (pringk) *v.t.* and *i.* to dress up ostentatiously;—**prink'er** *n.* [fr. *prank*].

print (print) *v.t.* to impress; to reproduce words, pictures, etc. by pressing inked types on paper, etc.; to produce in this way; to write in imitation of this; to publish;—*n.* an impression or mark left on a surface by something pressed against it; printed cotton fabric; printed lettering; an engraving; a photograph.—**print'er** *n.* one engaged in the setting of type for, and the printing of books, newspapers, etc.—**print'ing-press** *n.* a machine for reproducing on paper, etc. impressions made by inked type.—**printer's devil,** the youngest apprentice in a printing-office; a compositor's errand-boy.—**printer's pie,** a mass of jumbled types [L. *premere* to press].

prior (prī'or) *a.* previous; former; earlier; preceding in time;—*n.* (*fem.* **pri'oress**) the superior of a priory; one next in dignity to an abbot.—**priority** (prī-or'i-ti) *n.* the state of being antecedent in time; precedence; preference in regard to privilege.—**pri'ory** *n.* a religious house, the head of which was a prior or prioress [L. *prior*, former].

prise (prīz) *n.* a lever;—*v.t.* to raise as if by means of a lever [O.Fr. *prise*, a hold].

prism (prizm) *n.* (*Geom.*) a solid whose bases or ends are any similar, equal, and parallel plane figures, and whose sides are parallelograms; (*Optics*) a transparent figure of this nature, usually with triangular ends.—**prismat'ic(al)** *a.*—**prismat'ically** *adv.*—**prismoid** (priz'moid) *n.* a prism-like solid.—**prismoi'dal** *a.*—**prismatic colours,** the seven colours, red, orange, yellow, green, blue, indigo, violet, into which a ray of light is separated by a prism [Gk. *prisma*; *eidos*, form].

prison (priz'n) *n.* building, for confinement of criminals; jail; any place of confinement or restraint; —*v.t.* to imprison.—**prisoner** (priz'nẹr) *n.* one confined in prison; one captured in war [L. *prensio*, fr. *praehendere*, to seize].

pristine (pris'tīn) *a.* belonging to the earliest time; original; former [L. *pristinus*, fr. *priscus*, of old].

prithee (priTH'ē) *interj.* (*Arch.*) corrupt. of *I pray thee.*

private (prī′-vạt) *a.* not public; belonging to or concerning an individual; peculiar to oneself; personal; secluded; secret; of a soldier, not holding any rank;—*n.* a common soldier.—**pri′vately** *adv.*—**pri′vateness** *n.*—**privacy** (priv′-ạ-si, prī-vạ-si) *n.* the state of being in retirement from company; solitude; seclusion; secrecy [L. *privatus*, fr. *privus*, single].

privateer (prī-vạ-tēr′) *n.* an armed private vessel commissioned by a government to attack enemy ships.

privation (prī-vā′-shun) *n.* the state of being deprived, esp. of something required; destitution; want.—**privative** (priv′-ạ-tiv) *a.* causing privation; consisting in the absence of something; denoting negation;—*n.* that which derives its character from the absence of something.—**priv′atively** *adv.*

privet (priv′-et) *n.* an evergreen European shrub [etym. uncertain].

privilege (priv′-i-lej) *n.* a special right or advantage;—*v.t.* to grant some special favour to.—**priv′ileged** *a.* enjoying a special right or immunity [L. *privilegium*, private law, fr. *lex*, a law].

privy (priv′-i) *a.* private; confidential; secret; admitted to knowledge of a secret;—*n.* a person having an interest in a law-suit; a latrine.—**priv′ily** *adv.*—**priv′ity** *n.* private knowledge; connivance.—**privy to**, secretly informed of.—**Privy Council**, the council which advises the sovereign on matters of government [Fr. *privé*, fr. L. *privatus*, private].

prize (prīz) *n.* a reward given for success in competition; a reward given for merit; a thing striven for; a thing won by chance, e.g. in a lottery.—*v.t.* to value highly; to esteem.—**prize′-fight** *n.* a professional boxing-match.—**prize′-fight′er** *n.* [O.Fr. *pris*, fr. L. *pretium*, price].

prize (prīz) *n.* an enemy ship or property captured in naval warfare.—**prize′-court** *n.* an Admiralty court to adjudicate on prizes captured in naval warfare [Fr. *prise*, a seizing, fr. L. *praehendere*, to seize].

prize (prīz) *v.t.* Same as **prise**.

pro- (prō) *prefix* fr. L. or Gk. meaning for; instead of; on behalf of; in front of; before; forward; according to.

proa (prō′-a) *n.* a long, narrow canoe, noted for its speed [Malay].

probable (prob′-ạ-bl) *a.* likely; to be expected; having more evidence for than against.—**prob′ably** *adv.*—**probabil′ity** *n.* likelihood; anything that has appearance of truth [L. *probare*, to prove].

probate (prō′-bāt) *n.* the process by which a last will and testament is legally authenticated after the testator's death; an official copy of a will [L. *probare*, to prove].

probation (prō-bā′-shun) *n.* proving; proof; a trial or test of a person's character, conduct, ability, etc.; the testing of a candidate before admission to full membership of a body, esp. a religious sect or order; a system of releasing offenders, esp. juveniles, and placing them under supervision of **Probation Officer**.—**proba′tional** *a.*—**proba′tionary** *a.* serving to test.—**proba′tioner** *n.* a person undergoing probation.—**probative** (prō′-bạ-tiv) *a.* pert. to, serving for, or offering, trial or proof [L. *probare*, to prove].

probe (prōb) *n.* (*Med.*) instrument for examining a wound, ulcer, cavity, etc.;—*v.t.* to explore a wound, etc. with a probe; (*Fig.*) to examine thoroughly [L. *probare*, to prove].

probity (prob′-i-ti) *n.* tried integrity; rectitude; honesty [L. *probus*, good].

problem (prob′-lẹm) *n.* a matter proposed for solution; a question difficult of solution; a puzzle.—**problemat′ic(al)** *a.* questionable; uncertain; disputable; doubtful.—**problemat′ically** *adv.* [Gk. *problēma*, a thing thrown before].

proboscis (prō-bos′-is) *n.* an elephant's trunk; the snout of other animals [Gk. fr. *pro*, before; *boskein*, to feed].

proceed (prō-sēd′) *v.i.* to move onward; to advance; to renew progress; to pass from one point or topic to another; to come forth, as from a source; to carry on a series of acts; to take legal proceedings.—**proceed′ing** *n.* going forward; movement or process;—*pl.* (*Law*) the several steps of prosecuting a charge, claim, etc.; a record of business done by a society.—**proceeds** (prō′-sēdz) *n.pl.* produce; yield; sum realised by a sale.—**procedure** (prō-sēd′-ūr) *n.* act, method of proceeding [L. *procedere*, to go forward].

process (prō′-ses) *n.* continued forward movement; lapse (of time); a series of actions or measures; a method of operation; (*Anat.*) a projecting part or growth; (*Law*) procedure;—*v.t.* to subject to some process, as food or material.—**process** (prō-ces′) *v.i.* (*Colloq.*) to walk in a procession.—**procession** (prō-sesh′-un) *n.* marching forward; regular progress.—**proces′sional** *a.* pert. to a procession;—*n.* a hymn sung during a church procession.—**pro′cess-ser′ver** *n.* a sheriff's officer; a bailiff [L. *processus*, fr. *procedere*, to go forward].

proclaim (prō-klām′) *v.t.* to make known by public announcement; to publish.—**proclaim′ant, proclaim′er** *n.* one who proclaims.—**proclamation** (prok-la-mā′-shun) *n.* the act of announcing publicly; an official public announcement [L. *pro*, before; *clamare*, to cry out].

proclivity (prō-kliv′-i-ti) *n.* inclination; propensity; proneness; aptitude [L. *pro*, forward; *clivus*, a slope].

proconsul (prō-kon′-sul) *n.* a Roman official who discharged the duties of a consul, esp. as governor of a colony or province.—**procon′sular** *a.*—**procon′sulate, procon′sulship** *n.* [L.].

procrastinate (prō-kras′-ti-nāt) *v.i.* to put off till some future time.—**procrastina′tion** *n.* a putting off till a future time; dilatoriness.—**procras′tinator** *n.* [L. *procrastinare*, fr. *cras*, tomorrow].

procreate (prō′-krē-āt) *v.t.* to bring into being; to beget; to generate.—**procrea′tion** *n.* the reproduction of the species; generation.—**pro′creative** *a.* having the power to beget; productive.—**pro′creativeness** *n.*—**pro′creator** *n.* [L. *pro*, forth; *creare*, to produce].

Procrustes (prō-krus′-tēz) *n.* (*Myth.*) an ancient Greek legendary brigand who placed his captives on a bed, stretched their legs if too short for it, and amputated them if too long.—**Procrus′tean** *a.* descriptive of extreme measures to make anything conform to a standard.

proctor (prok′-tor) *n.* one who manages the affairs of another; a procurator; a university official in charge of discipline; an attorney in an ecclesiastical court.—**procto′rial** *a.*—**proc′torship** *n.*—**King's Proctor**, the Crown solicitor in divorce suits, who may intervene when collusion is alleged to have occurred [*abbrev.* of *procurator*].

procumbent (prō-kum′-bẹnt) *a.* lying face down; (*Bot.*) growing along the ground [L. *pro*, forward; *cumbere*, to lie down].

procuration (prok-ū-rā′-shun) *n.* management of another's affairs; the instrument empowering a person to transact the affairs of another; money paid to a bishop or archdeacon by incumbents, as an equivalent to that formerly due for visitations.—**proc′uracy** *n.* the office of a procurator; the management of another's affairs.—**proc′urator** *n.* one who acts for another, esp. in legal affairs.—**proc′urator-fis′cal** *n.* in Scotland, a public prosecutor [L. *pro*, for; *curare*, to see to].

procure (prō-kūr′) *v.t.* to acquire; to obtain; to get; to bring about;—*v.i.* to act as a procurer.—**procur′able** *a.* obtainable.—**procure′ment** *n.* the act of procuring or obtaining; management.—**procur′er** *n.* (*fem.* **proc′uress**) one who procures; one who supplies women for immoral purposes [L. *pro*, for; *curare*, to see to].

prod (prod) *v.t.* to poke with something

Palma, Majorca

Corsica

COASTS and HARBOURS of the WORLD

Rabat, Morocco

Narvik, Norway

Manhattan, New York

PORTS of the WORLD

Manáos on the Rio Negro, Brazil

Dubrovnik

Hamburg

pointed; to goad;—*n.* a pointed instrument for prodding.—*pr.p.* **prod'ding.**—*pa.p.* and *pa.t.* **prod'ded** [etym. uncertain].

prodigal (prod′i-gạl) *a.* wasteful; spending recklessly;—*n.* one who spends recklessly; a spendthrift.—**prod'igally** *adv.*—**prodigal'ity** *n.* reckless extravagance [L. *prodigere,* to squander].

prodigy (prod′i-ji) *n.* a portent; anything unusual and unnatural; a person or thing causing wonder; a marvel; a very gifted child; a monster.—**prodigious** (prō-dij′us) *a.* like a prodigy; marvellous; enormous; extraordinary.—**prodig'iously** *adv.*—**prodig'iousness** *n.* [L. *prodigium,* a portent or sign].

produce (prō-dūs′) *v.t.* to bring forth; to exhibit; to give birth to; to yield; to make; to cause; of a play, to present it on the stage; (*Geom.*) of a line, to extend in length.—**produce** (prod′ūs) *n.* that which is produced; product; agricultural products; crops.—**produc'er** *n.*—**produ'cible** *a.* [L. *pro,* forward; *ducere,* to lead].

product (prod′ukt) *n.* that which is produced; (*Arith.*) a number resulting from the multiplying of two or more numbers.—**produc'tion** *n.* the act of producing; the things produced.—**produc'tive** *a.* having the power to produce; creative; fertile; efficient.—**produc'tively** *adv.*—**produc'tiveness, productiv'ity** *n.* [L. *pro,* forward; *ducere,* to lead].

proem (prō′em) *n.* a preface; an introduction; a prelude.—**proem'ial** *a.* [Gr. *pro,* before; *oimos,* a path].

profane (pro-fān′) *a.* not sacred; irreverent; blasphemous; given to swearing;—*v.t.* to treat with irreverence; to put to a wrong or unworthy use; to desecrate; to pollute or defile.—**profane'ly** *adv.*—**profane'ness** *n.*—**profan'er** *n.*—**profanation** (prof-ạ-nā′shun) *n.* the act of violating sacred things.—**profanity** (pro-fan′i-ti) *n.* profaneness; irreverence; the use of oaths and bad language [L. *pro,* before; *fanum,* a temple].

profess (pro-fes′) *v.t.* to make open declaration of; to confess publicly; to affirm belief in; to pretend to knowledge or skill in.—**professed'** *a.* openly acknowledged.—**professedly** (pro-fes′ed-li) *adv.*—**profession** (pro-fesh′un) *n.* the act of professing; that which one professes; occupation or calling, esp. one requiring learning.—**profes'sional** *a.* pert. to a profession or calling; engaged in any game or sport for money, as opposed to *amateur*;—*n.* one who makes a livelihood in sport or games (*abbrev.* **pro**).—**profes'sionally** *adv.* [L. *profiteri, professus,* to acknowledge].

professor (pro-fes′ẹr) *n.* one who makes profession; a teacher in a university.—**professorial** (pro-fe-sō′ri-ạl) *a.* pert. to a professor.—**professo'rially** *adv.*—**professoriate** (pro-fe-sō′ri-āt) *n.* the office of a professor; his period of office; body of professors.—**profes'sorship** *n.* [L. *profiteri, professus,* to acknowledge].

proffer (prof′ẹr) *v.t.* to offer for acceptance;—*n.* an offer made.—**proff'erer** *n.* [L. *proferre,* to bring forward].

proficient (pro-fish′ẹnt) *a.* thoroughly versed or qualified in any art or occupation; skilled; adept;—*n.* an expert.—**profi'ciently** *adv.*—**profi'cience, profi'ciency** *n.* expertness [L. *proficere,* to be useful].

profile (prō′fīl, prō′fēl) *n.* an outline or contour; a portrait in a side view; the side-face; short biographical sketch;—*v.t.* to draw the outline of [L. *pro,* before; *filum,* thread].

profit (prof′it) *n.* advantage or benefit; the excess of returns over expenditure; pecuniary gain in any transaction or occupation;—*v.t.* to be of service to;—*v.i.* to gain advantage; to grow richer.—**prof'itable** *a.* yielding profit or gain; advantageous; helpful.—**prof'itably** *adv.*—**prof'itableness** *n.*—**profiteer** (prof-i-tēr′) *n.* one who makes excessive profits;—*v.i.* to make such profits [L. *profectus,* fr. *proficere,* to make progress].

profligate (prof′li-gāt) *a.* abandoned to vice; dissolute;—*n.* a depraved person.—**prof'ligately** *adv.*—**prof'ligateness** *n.*—**profligacy** (prof′li-gạ-si) *n.* a vicious and dissolute manner of living [L. *profligatus,* ruined].

profound (prō-found′) *a.* deep; intellectually deep; learned; deeply felt.—**profound'ly** *adv.*—**profound'ness** *n.*—**profun'dity** *n.* depth of place, knowledge, skill, feeling [L. *profundus,* deep].

profuse (prō-fūs′) *a.* giving or given generously; lavish; extravagant.—**profuse'ly** *adv.*—**profuse′ness, profusion** (prō-fū′zhun) *n.* lavishness; prodigality; great abundance [L. *pro,* forth; *fundere, fusum,* to pour].

progeny (proj′e-ni) *n.* descendants; offspring; children; race.—**progen'itive** *a.* pert. to the production of offspring.—**progenitor** (prō-jen′i-tor) *n.* (*fem.* **progen'itress, progen'itrix**) ancestor; forefather [L. *pro,* before; *gignere,* to beget].

prognosis (prog-nō′sis) *n.* a forecast; (*Med.*) foretelling the course of a disease.—*pl.* **progno'ses.**—**prognostic** (prog-nos′tik) *a.* foretelling; forecasting; predicting;—*n.* a forecast; a prediction.—**prognos'ticate** *v.t.* to foretell; to predict; to prophesy.—**prognostica'tion** *n.*—**prognos'ticator** *n.* [Gk. *pro,* before; *gnōsis,* knowledge].

programme, program (prō′gram) *n.* a plan or detailed notes of intended proceedings at a public entertainment, ceremony, etc.; a party policy at election time [Gk. *pro,* before; *gramma,* a writing].

progress (prog′res, prō′gres) *n.* a moving forward; advancement; development; a state journey.—**progress** (prō-gres′) *v.i.* to move forward; to advance; to develop; to improve.—**progression** (prō-gresh′un) *n.* the act of moving forward; onward movement; progress.—**progres'sional** *a.*—**progress'ive** *a.* moving forward gradually; advancing; improving; favouring progress or reform.—**progress'ively** *adv.*—**progress'iveness** *n.*—**progressive bridge (whist)** (*Cards*) a form of bridge (whist) in which partners change after each game.—**arithmetical progression,** a series of numbers increasing or decreasing by the same amount, e.g. 3, 6, 9, 12, 15, etc.—**geometrical progression,** a series of numbers increasing or decreasing by a common ratio, e.g. 3, 9, 27, 81, etc. [L. *progredi, progressus,* to go forward].

prohibit (prō-hib′it) *v.t.* to forbid; to prevent; to hinder; to interdict by authority.—**prohib′iter, prohib'itor** *n.*—**prohibition** (prō-hi-bish′un) *n.* the act of forbidding; interdict; the forbidding by law of manufacture, importation, sale, or purchase of alcoholic liquors.—**prohibi'tionist** *n.* one in favour of prohibition.—**prohib'itive, prohib'itory** *a.* tending to forbid, prevent, or exclude; exclusive.—**prohib'itively** *adv.* [L. *prohibere*].

project (prō-jekt′) *v.t.* to throw or cast forward; to plan; to contrive; to scheme; to throw a photographic image on a screen;—*v.i.* to jut out; to protrude.—**project** (proj′ekt) *n.* a plan; a scheme; a design.—**projectile** (prō-jek′tīl) *a.* capable of being thrown;—*n.* a heavy missile, esp. a shell, or cannon ball.—**projec'tion** *n.* the act of projecting; something that juts out; a plan; delineation; the representation on a plane of a curved surface or sphere; in psychology, mistaking for reality something which is only an image in the mind.—**projec'tive** *a.*—**projec'tor** *n.* an apparatus for throwing photographic images, esp. films, on a screen [L. *projicere, projectum,* to throw forward].

prolapse (prō′laps) *n.* (*Med.*) the falling down of a part of the body from its normal position, esp. womb or rectum. Also **prolap'sus.**—**prolapse** (prō-laps′) *v.i.* to fall down or protrude [L. *prolapsus,* fr. *prolabi,* to fall or slide forward].

prolate (prō′lāt) *a.* (*Geom.*) elongated towards the poles [L. *proferre, prolatum,* to bring forward].

prolegomena (prō-le-gom′e-nạ) *n.pl.* introductory remarks prefixed to a book or treatise.—*sing.* **prolegom′enon** [Gk. *pro*, before; *legomenos*, being said].

prolepsis (prō-lep′sis) *n.* a figure of speech by which objections are anticipated and answered; an error in chronology, consisting in antedating an event;—*pl.* **prolep′ses.**—**prolep′tic, prolep′tical** *a.*—**prolep′tically** *adv.* [Gk. *pro*, before; *lēpsis*, a taking].

proletarian (prō-le-tā′ri-ạn) *a.* pert. to the proletariat; belonging to the commonalty;—*n.* one of the proletariat.—**proletariat(e)** (prō-le-tā′ri-at) *n.* propertyless wage-earners who live by sale of their labour [L. *proles*, offspring].

proliferous (prō-lif′ẹ-rus) *a.* (*Biol.*) reproducing freely by cell division; developing anthers.—**prolif′erously** *adv.*—**prolif′erate** *v.t.* to bear;—*v.i.* to reproduce by repeated cell division.—**prolifera′tion** *n.* increase [L. *proles*, offspring; *ferre*, to bear].

prolific (prō-lif′ik) *a.* bringing forth offspring; fruitful; abundantly productive; bringing about results.—**prolif′ically** *adv.* [L. *proles*, offspring; *facere*, to make].

prolix (prō′liks) *a.* long drawn out; diffuse; verbose; wordy.—**prolix′ly** *adv.*—**prolix′ness** *n.*—**prolix′ity** *n.* verbosity [L. *prolixus*, extended].

prolocutor (prō-lok′ū-tor) *n.* the speaker or chairman of a convocation [L. *pro*; *loqui locutus*, to speak].

prologue (prō′log) *n.* the preface or introduction to a discourse, poem, book, or performance, esp. the address spoken before a dramatic performance;—*v.t.* to preface [Gk. *pro*, before; *logos*, discourse].

prolong (prō-long′) *v.t.* to lengthen out; to extend the duration of.—**prolonga′tion** *n.* the act of lengthening out; a part prolonged; extension [L. *pro*; *longus*, long].

prom (prom) *n.* (*Colloq. abbrev.*) a promenade concert; promenade at sea-side resort.

promenade (prom-e-nȧd′, -nād′) *n.* a leisurely walk, generally in a public place; a place adapted for such a walk;—*v.i.* to walk for pleasure, display, or exercise.—**promena′der** *n.*—**promenade concert,** one at which the audience may walk about during the music; (*Colloq. abbrev.*) **prom.** [Fr.].

prominent (prom′i-nẹnt) *a.* sticking out; projecting; conspicuous; distinguished.—**prom′inently** *adv.*—**prom′inence, prom′inency** *n.* the state of being prominent; projection; eminence [L. *prominere*, to jut out].

promiscuous (prō-mis′kū-us) *a.* mixed without order or distinction; confused; not limited to one particular individual or class.—**promis′cuously** *adv.*—**promis′cuousness, promiscuity** (prom-is-kū′i-ti) *n.* [L. *promiscuus*, fr. *miscere*, to mix].

promise (prom′is) *n.* an undertaking to do or not to do something; cause or grounds for hope;—*v.t.* to give one's word to do or not to do something; to give cause for expectation; to undertake; to agree to give;—*v.i.* to assure by a promise; to give grounds for hope.—**prom′iser** *n.* one who promises.—**prom′isor** *n.* (*Law*) the person by whom a promise is made.—**prom′ising** *a.* likely to turn out well or to succeed; hopeful [L. *promittere*, *promissum*, to promise].

promissory (prom′i-sor-i) *a.* contaiinng a promise.—**promissory note,** written agreement to pay sum to named person at specified date [L. *promittere*, to promise].

promontory (prom′on-tor-i) *n.* a point of high land jutting out into the sea [L. *promontorium*, fr. *mons*, a mountain].

promote (prō-mōt′) *v.t.* to move forward; to move up to a higher rank or position; to encourage the growth or development of; to organise or float a new business venture or company.—**promo′ter** *n.* a supporter; an initiator, esp. of a new business venture, etc.—**promo′tion** *n.* advancement; preferment; a higher rank, station, or position; encouragement.—**promo′tive** *a.* [L. *promovere*, *promotum*, to move forward].

prompt (promt) *a.* ready and quick to act; done at once; punctual;—*v.t.* to excite to action; to suggest; to help out (actor or speaker) by reading, suggesting next words.—**prompt′ly** *adv.*—**prompt′er** *n.* one who reminds or helps out an actor, speaker, etc.—**prompt′itude, prompt′ness** *n.* readiness; quickness of decision and action.—**prompt′side** *n.* (*abbrev.* **P.S.**) right side of stage (facing audience) [L. *promptus*, fr. *promere*, to put forth].

promulgate (prom′ul-gāt) *v.t.* to proclaim; to publish; to make known officially.—**promulga′tion** *n.* [L. *promulgare*].

prone (prōn) *a.* lying face downwards; bending forward; sloping; steep; inclined; naturally disposed.—**prone′ly** *adv.*—**prone′ness** *n.* inclination; tendency [L. *pronus*].

prong (prong) *n.* one of the pointed ends of a fork; a spike [etym. uncertain].

pronoun (prō′noun) *n.* (*Gram.*) a word used instead of a noun.—**pronom′inal** *a.*—**pronom′inally** *adv.* [*pro* and *noun*].

pronounce (prō-nouns′) *v.t.* to speak with the correct sound and accent; to speak distinctly; to utter formally or officially; to declare or affirm.—**pronounced′** *a.* strongly marked; very definite or decided.—**pronounce′able** *a.*—**pronounce′ment** *n.* a formal declaration.—**pronoun′cer** *n.*—**pronoun′cing** *a.* teaching or indicating pronunciation.—**pronunciation** (prō-nun-si-ā′shun) *n.* the act of uttering with the proper sound and accent; the mode of uttering words [L. *pronuntiare*, to proclaim].

pronto (pron′tō) *a.* and *adv.* (*Colloq.*) prompt; promptly; quick; quickly [Sp.].

proof (prōōf) *n.* something which proves; a test or trial; any process to ascertain correctness, truth, or facts; demonstration; evidence that convinces the mind and produces belief; argument; (*Arch.*) proved trustworthiness; standard strength of alcoholic spirits; (*Print.*) a trial impression from type, on which corrections may be made;—*a.* firm in resisting; impenetrable; serving as proof or designating a certain standard or quality;—*v.t.* to render proof against.—**proof′ing** *n.* the act of rendering materials impenetrable to water; a substance used in effecting this.—**proof′-read′er** *n.* one who corrects printer's proofs.—**proof′spir′it** *n.* a mixture of alcohol and water, containing not less than a standard quantity of alcohol [L. *probare*, to prove].

prop (prop) *v.t.* to support, or prevent from falling, by placing something under or against; to sustain.—*n.* that which supports; a stay [M.E. *proppe*].

propaganda (prop-ạ-gan′dạ) *n.* an association or scheme for propagating a doctrine or set of principles; the opinions or beliefs thus spread; a society in Rome charged with the management of missions.—**propagan′dise** *v.t.* and *i.* to spread propaganda.—**propagan′dist** *n.* [fr. L. *de propaganda fide*, concerning the spreading of the faith].

propagate (prop′ạ-gāt) *v.t.* to cause to multiply or reproduce by generation; to breed; to spread the knowledge of; to transmit or carry forward;—*v.i.* to have young; to breed.—**prop′agator** *n.*—**propaga′tion** *n.* [L. *propagare*, to propagate plants by slips].

propel (prō-pel′) *v.t.* to drive forward; to press onward by force; to push.—*pr.p.* **propell′ing.**—*pa.p.* **propelled′.**—**propell′er** *n.* one who, or that which, propels; a revolving shaft with blades for driving a ship or aeroplane [L. *pro*, forward; *pellere*, to drive].

propensity (prō-pen′si-ti) *n.* bent of mind; leaning or inclination; disposition; natural tendency; bias; proclivity.—**propense′** *a.* (*Arch.*) inclined; disposed.—**propense′ly** *adv.* [L. *pro*, forward; *pendere*, *pensum*, to hang].

proper (prop′ẹr) *a.* particular individual;

belonging to oneself; befitting one's nature; correct or according to usage; (*Arch.*) handsome; thorough or complete;—*adv.* (*Colloq.*) very; exceedingly.—**prop'erly** *adv.*—**proper fraction** (*Arith.*) one in which the numerator is less than the denominator [L. *proprius*, own].

property (prop'ẹr-ti) *n.* an inherent or essential quality or peculiarity; ownership; the thing owned; possessions; an estate;—*pl.* theatrical requisites, as scenery, dresses, etc. [L. *proprietas*, fr. *proprius*, own).

prophecy (prof'e-si) *n.* foretelling future events; prediction.—**prophesy** (prof'e-sī) *v.t.* to foretell; to predict;—*v.i.* to utter predictions. —*pr.p.* **proph'esying**.—*pa.p.* and *pa.t.* **proph'esied**.—**prophet** (prof'et) *n.* (*fem.* **proph'etess**) one who foretells future events; in the Bible, an inspired teacher or revealer of the Divine Will.—**prophet'ic(al)** *a.* [Gk. *prophētēs*, afore-speaker].

prophylactic (prof-i-lak'tik) *a.* (*Med.*) tending to prevent disease; preventive;—*n.* medicine or treatment tending to prevent disease.—**prophylax'is** *n.* preventive treatment of disease, e.g. by inoculation [Gk. *phulassein*, to guard].

propinquity (prō-ping'kwi-ti) *n.* nearness in time or place; nearness in blood relationship [L. *propinquitas*, fr. *prope*, near].

propitiate (prō-pish'i-āt) *v.t.* to appease; to conciliate; to gain the favour of.—**propitia'tion** *n.* appeasement; conciliation; atonement.—**propi'tiator** *n.*—**propi'tiatory** *a.* serving, or intended, to propitiate. —**propitious** (prō-pish'us) *a.* favourable; favourably inclined; kind; auspicious.—**propi'tiously** *adv.*—**propi'tiousness** *n.* [L. *propitiare*].

proportion (pro-pōr'shun) *n.* relative size, number, or degree; comparison; relation; equal or just share; relation between connected things or parts; symmetrical arrangement, distribution, or adjustment; equality of ratios; (*Arith.*) the rule of three;—*n.pl.* dimensions; —*v.t.* to arrange the proportions of; to divide into equal or just shares.—**propor'tionable** *a.* capable of being proportioned or made proportional. —**propor'tionably** *adv.*—**propor'tional** *a.* pert. to proportion; having a due proportion;—*n.* a number or quantity in an arithmetical or mathematical proportion.—**propor'tionally** *adv.*—**proportional'ity** *n.*—**propor'tionate** *a.* adjusted so as to correspond in size, amount, or degree; proportional.—**propor'tioned** *a.* having suitable dimensions or measurements.—**propor'tionment** *n.* [L. *proportio*, fr. *portio*, a share].

propose (pro-pōz') *v.t.* to offer for consideration to suggest; to nominate;—*v.i.* to form a plan; to intend; to offer oneself in marriage.—**propo'sal** *n.* the act of proposing; what is offered for consideration; an offer, esp. of marriage.—**propo'ser** *n.*—**proposi'tion** *n.* a proposal; a statement or assertion.—**proposi'tional** *a.* [L. *proponere*, to put forward].

propound (pro-pound') *v.t.* to offer for consideration; to propose; to set (a problem) [L. *pro*, forth; *ponere*, to place].

proprietor (prō-prī'ẹ'tor) *n.* (*fem.* **propri'etress**, **propri'etrix**) one who is the owner of property; an owner.—**propri'etary** *a.* pert. to an owner; made and sold by an individual or firm having the exclusive rights of manufacture and sale.—**propri'etorship** *n.* [L. *proprius*, one's own].

propriety (prō-prī'e-ti) *n.* properness; correct conduct.—**the propri'eties** *n.pl.* the manners and conventions observed in polite society [L. *proprius*, one's own].

propulsion (prō-pul'shun) *n.* the act of driving forward.—**propul'sive**, **propul'sory** *a.* tending, or having power, to propel [L. *pro*, forward; *pellere*, *pulsum*, to drive].

prorogue (prō-rōg') *v.t.* to adjourn for an indefinite time (applied to parliament);—**proroga'tion** *n.* [L. *prorogare*, to defer].

prosaic, prosaical (prō-zā'ik, -i-kạl) *a.* dull and unimaginative; commonplace.—**prosa'ically** *adv.* [L. *prosus* or *prorsus*, straightforward].

proscenium (prō-sē'ni-um) *n.* the part of the stage in front of the curtain [Gk. *pro*, before; *skēnē*, the stage].

proscribe (prō-skrīb') *v.t.* to put outside the protection of the law; to outlaw; to prohibit. —**proscrib'er** *n.*—**proscrip'tion** *n.* the act of proscribing; prohibition; denunciation.—**proscrip'tive** *a.* proscribing [L. *proscribere*, to publish].

prose (prōz) *n.* ordinary language in speech and writing; language not in verse;—*a.* pert. to prose; not poetical;—*v.i.* to write prose; to speak or write in a dull, tedious manner.—**pro'sy** *a.* dull and tedious.—**pro'sily** *adv.*—**pro'siness** *n.* [L. *prosa* (*oratio*), direct (speech)].

prosecute (pros'e-kūt) *v.t.* to follow or pursue with a view to reaching or accomplishing something; (*Law*) to proceed against judicially;—*v.i.* to carry on a legal suit. —**prosecu'tion** *n.* (*Law*) the institution and carrying on of a suit in a court of law; the party by which legal proceedings are instituted, as opposed to the *defence*.—**pros'ecutor** *n.* (*fem.* **pros'ecutrix**) one who prosecutes; a public prosecuting counsel [L. *prosequi*, to follow].

proselyte (pros'e-līt) *n.* a convert to some party or religion;—*v.t.* to convert.—**pros'elytise** *v.t.* to make converts.—**pros'elytism** *n.* [Gk. *prosēlutos*, a newcomer].

prosody (pros'o-di) *n.* the science of versification.—**prosodiacal** (pros-ō-dī'a-kạl), **prosodial** (pro-sō'di-ạl), **prosodic** (pro-sod'ik) *a.*—**pros'odist** *n.* one skilled in prosody [Gk. *pros*, to; *ōdē*, a song].

prospect (pros'pekt) *n.* that which the eye sees at one time; a wide view; anticipation; reasonable hope; promise of future good.—**prospect'** *v.t.* and *i.* to search or explore (a region), esp. for precious metals, oil, etc.—**prospec'tive** *a.* looking forward; relating to the future.—**prospec'tively** *adv.*—**prospec'tor** *n.*—**prospec'tus** *n.* a circular or pamphlet outlining the main features of a proposed commercial undertaking, a new publication, a school, hotel, etc. [L. *prospicere*, to look forward].

prosper (pros'pẹr) *v.t.* to cause to succeed;—*v.i.* to succeed; to do well.—**prosper'ity** *n.* the state of succeeding or flourishing; success.—**pros'perous** *a.* thriving; successful; doing well. —**pros'perously** *adv.* [L. *prosper*, fortunate].

prostate [pros'tāt) *n.* a small gland at the neck of the bladder in males. Also **prostate gland** [Gk. *pro*, before; *statos*, placed].

prostitute (pros'ti-tūt) *n.* a woman who hires herself for sexual intercourse; a harlot;—*v.t.* to make a prostitute of; to sell basely; to put to base, infamous, or unworthy use.—**prostitu'tion** *n.* [L. *prostituere*, to offer for sale].

prostrate (pros'trāt) *a.* lying on the ground face downwards; mentally or physically exhausted;—**prostrate'** *v.t.* to lay flat on the ground; to bow down in adoration; to overcome.—**prostra'tion** *n.* [L. *pro*, forward; *sternere*, *stratum*, to lay flat].

protagonist (prō-tag'on-ist) *n.* the principal actor in a Greek drama; a leading character [Gk. *prōtos*, first; *agōnistēs*, an actor].

protasis (prot'ạ-sis) *n.* the introductory clause of a conditional sentence, the consequent clause being the 'apodosis' [Gk. *pro*, forward; *tasis*, a stretching].

Protean (prō'tē-ạn) *a.* (*Myth.*) pert. to *Proteus*, a sea-god who changed his shape at will to avoid divulging the future.—**pro'tean** *a.* readily changing form or appearance; inconstant.

protect (prō-tekt') *v.t.* to defend; to guard; to put a tariff on imports to encourage home industry.—**protec'tion** *n.* defending from injury or harm; state of being defended; that which defends.—**protec'tionism** *n.* the doctrine of protecting industries by taxing competing imports.—protec'tive *a.* affording protection; sheltering.—protec'tively *adv.*—protec'tor *n.* one who, or that which, defends.—protec'torate *n.* (period of) office of a protector of a state; political administration of a state or territory by another country.—protec'toral, protecto'rial *a.* [L. *pro.* in front of; *tegere*, to cover].

protégé (pro-tā-zhā') *n.* (*fem.* protégée) one under the care, protection, or patronage of another (Fr. *protéger*, to protect].

protein (prō'-tē-in, prō'-tēn) *n.* a nitrogenous compound similar to white of egg, an essential constituent of all animal and vegetable organisms. Also pro'teid [Gk. *prōtos*, first].

protest (prō-test') *v.i.* to assert formally; to make a declaration against;—*v.t.* to affirm solemnly; to object to.—protest (prō'-test) *n.* a declaration of objection.—protestant (prot'-es-tant) *n.* one who holds an opposite opinion.—Prot'estant *a.* pert. or belonging to any branch of the Western Church outside the Roman communion;—*n.* a member of such a church. —Prot'estantism *n.*—protesta'tion *n.* a solemn declaration, esp. of dissent [L. *pro*, before; *testari*, to witness].

prothalamion (prō-tha-lā'-mi-on) *n.* a song written in honour of a marriage. Also prothala'mium [Gk. *pro*, before; *thalamos*, the bridal chamber].

proto- (prō'-tō) *prefix* fr. Gk. *prōtos*, first; hence, original; primitive.—pro'to-actin'ium *n.* (*Chem.*) a metallic radio-active element.—pro'to-mar'tyr *n.* the first to be sacrificed in any cause, esp. the first Christian martyr, St. Stephen.—pro'toplasm *n.* a semi-fluid substance forming the basis of the primitive tissue of animal and vegetable life; living matter.—protoplasmat'ic, protoplas'mic *a.*—prototype (prō'-tō-tīp) *n.* original or model from which anything is copied; a pattern.—pro'totypal, prototyp'ic(al) *a.*—Protozoa (prō-tō-zō'-a) *n.pl.* first or lowest division of animal kingdom, consisting of microscopic, unicellular organisms.—protozoon (prō-tō-zō'-on) *n.* a member of this division.—protozo'al, protozo'an *a.*—protozo'ic *a.* (*Geol.*) containing remains of the earliest forms of life.

protocol (prō'-to-kol) *n.* an original copy; a rough draft, esp. a draft of terms signed by negotiating parties as the basis of a formal treaty or agreement [Gk. *prōtokollon*, a fly-leaf glued on to a book].

proton (prō'-ton) *n.* in physics, the unit of positive electricity, found in the nuclei of all atoms [Gk. *prōtos*, first].

protract (prō-trakt') *v.t.* to lengthen; to draw out; to prolong; to delay; to defer; to draw to scale.—protrac'ted *a.* prolonged; long drawn out; tedious.—protrac'tion *n.*—protrac'tive *a.* prolonging; delaying.—protrac'tor *n.* a mathematical instrument for measuring angles; (*Anat.*) a muscle which draws forward or extends a limb [L. *pro*, forward; *trahere*, *tractum*, to draw].

protrude (prō-trōōd') *v.t.* and *i.* to stick out; to project; to thrust forward.—protru'sion *n.* the act of thrusting forward; the state of being protruded or thrust forward; that which protrudes.—protru'sive *a.* thrusting forward; protruding [L. *pro*, forward; *trudere*, *trusum*, to thrust].

protuberant (prō-tū'-be-rant) *a.* bulging; swelling out; prominent.—protu'berantly *adv.* —protu'berance *n.* a swelling; a prominence [L. *protuberare*, to swell].

proud (proud) *a.* having excessive conceit of oneself; haughty; arrogant; self-respecting.—proud'ly *adv.*—proud flesh, excessive granulation in tissue of healing wound [O.E. *prut*, proud].

prove (prōōv) *v.t.* to try by experiment; to ascertain as fact, by evidence; to demonstrate; to show; to endure; to suffer; to establish the validity of (a will, etc.).—*v.i.* to turn out (to be, etc.); to be found by trial; to make trial.—*pr.p.* prov'ing.—*pa.p.* and *pa.t.* proved—*pa.p.* (*Scots Law*) prov'en.—prov'able *a.* able to be proved.—prov'ably *adv.* [L. *probare*, to test].

provenance (prov'-e-nans) *n.* source or place of origin. Also prove'nience (pro-vē'-ni-ens) [L. *pro*, forth; *venire*, to come].

Provence (prō-vongs') *n.* (*Geog.*) a province of S.E. France.—Provençal (prō-vong-sal') *a.*

provender (prov'-en-der) *n.* a dry food for beasts, e.g. corn, hay, oats; fodder; hence, provisions; food [O.Fr. *provendre*].

proverb (prov'-erb) *n.* a short pithy saying to express a truth or point a moral; an adage.—Prov'erbs *n.pl.* (*Bib.*) book of Old Testament. —prover'bial *a.* pert. to or resembling a proverb; well-known.—prover'bially *adv.* [L. *proverbium*, fr. *verbum*, a word].

provide (prō-vīd') *v.t.* to get or make ready for future use; to prepare; to supply; to furnish;—*v.i.* to make preparation; to set forth as a previous condition.—provid'ed (that), provid'ing (that) *conj.* on condition that.—providence (prov'-i-dens) *n.* foresight; prudence; wise economy; frugality; God's care; an event regarded as an act of God.—Prov'idence *n.* God Himself.—prov'ident *a.* prudent; thrifty.—prov'idently *adv.*—providential (prov-i-den'-shal) *a.* effected by divine foresight; fortunate; lucky.—providen'tially *adv.*—provi'der *n.* [L. *pro*, before; *videre*, to see].

province (prov'-ins) *n.* a division of a country or empire; an administrative district; a district under the jurisdiction of an archbishop; a sphere of action; a department of knowledge; one's special duty.—the provinces *n.pl.* any part of the country outside the capital.—provincial (prō-vin'-shal) *a.* pert. to a province or the provinces; countrified; unpolished;—*n.* an inhabitant of a province or of the provinces.—provin'cially *adv.* [L. *provincia*].

provision (prō-vizh'-un) *n.* the act of providing; measures taken beforehand; store esp. of food (generally in *pl.*); a condition or proviso;—*v.t.* to supply with provisions.—provis'ional *a.* temporary; adopted for the time being.—provis'ionally *adv.* [L. *pro*, before; *videre*, *visum*, to see].

proviso (prō-vī'-zō) *n.* a condition or stipulation in a deed of contract.—*pl.* provi'sos or provi'soes.—provi'sory *a.* containing a proviso or condition; temporary [L. *proviso quod*, it being provided that].

provoke (pro-vōk') *v.t.* to excite or stimulate to action, esp. to arouse to anger or passion; to bring about or call forth.—provok'ing *a.*—provocation (prov-o-kā'-shun) *n.* the act of provoking; that which provokes.—provocative (prō-vok'-a-tiv) *a.* serving or tending to provoke.—provoc'atively *adv.*—provoc'ativeness *n.* [L. *provocare*, to call forth].

provost (prov'-ost) *n.* a person appointed to superintend or preside, as the head of certain colleges or religious communities; the chief magistrate of Scottish towns.—provost-marshal (prov-ō'-mar'-shal) *n.* an officer in charge of the military police, or of prisoners in the navy [L. *praepositus*, placed before].

prow (prou) *n.* the forepart or bow of a ship; (*Poetic*) a ship [L. *prora*].

prowess (prou'-es) *n.* bravery, esp. in war; valour; achievement [Fr. *prouesse*].

prowl (proul) *v.i.* to roam about stealthily, esp. in search of prey, etc.;—*n.* the act of prowling [M.E. *prollen*].

proximate (prok'-si-māt) *a.* next or nearest; closest; immediately following or preceding. —prox'imately *adv.*—proxim'ity *n.* being next in time, place, etc.; immediate nearness.—prox'imo *adv.* in or of the coming month [L. *proximus*, nearest].

proxy (prok'-si) *n.* an authorised agent or substitute; one deputed to act for another; a writing empowering one person to vote for another [short fr. *procuracy*].

prude (prōōd) *n.* a woman of affected, or over-sensitive, modesty or reserve.—prud'ish *a.* like

a prude.—**prud'ery** *n.* affected coyness; primness; stiffness [O.Fr. *prode,* discreet].
prudent (pròò'dent) *a.* cautious and judicious; careful; not extravagant.—**pru'dently** *adv.*—**pru'dence** *n.* the habit of acting with careful deliberation; wisdom applied to practice.—**prudential** (pròò-den'shal) *a.*—**pruden'tially** *adv.* [L. *prudens,* foreseeing].
prune (pròòn) *n.* a dried plum [Fr. fr. L. *prunum,* a plum].
prune (pròòn) *v.t.* to cut off dead parts, excessive branches, etc.; to remove anything superfluous.—**pru'ning-hook** *n.* a knife with curved blade for pruning trees, etc. [O.Fr. *proignier*].
prurient (pròò'ri-ent) *a.* given to, or springing from, unclean or lewd thoughts.—**pru'riently** *adv.*—**pru'rience, pru'riency** *n.* [L. *prurire,* to itch].
Prussia (prush'a) *n.* (*Geog.*) formerly the leading State of Germany, and the recognised home of German militarism.—**Pruss'ian** *n./a.*—**Prussian blue,** a deep-blue salt of potassium and iron, used as a pigment.—**prussic acid,** hydrocyanic acid, a violent and rapid poison.
pry (prī) *v.i.* to look curiously; to peer; to nose about.—*pr.p.* **pry'ing.**—*pa.p.* and *pa.t.* **pried** (prīd).—**pri'er, pry'er** *n.* [M.E. *prien,* to peer].
psalm (såm) *n.* a sacred song or hymn.—**the Psalms** (*Bib.*) a book of the Old Testament.—**psalmist** (såm'ist, sal'mist) *n.* a writer of psalms.—**psalmody** (så'mo-di, sal'mo-di) *n.* the art or practice of singing sacred music; psalms collectively.—**psal'modist** *n.* a singer of psalms.—**Psalter** (sawl'tęr) *n.* the Book of Psalms.—**psal'tery** *n.* an obsolete stringed instrument like the zither [Gk. *psalmos,* a twanging of strings].
pseud(o)- (sū'dō) *prefix* fr. Gk. *pseudes,* false, used in many derivatives to signify, false; pretended; sham; not real; wrongly held to be, etc.—**pseudonym** (sū'dō-nim) *n.* a fictitious name assumed, esp. by an author; a nom de plume.—**pseudon'ymous** *a.*
pshaw (shaw) *interj.* expressing contempt, impatience, etc. [imit.].
psittacosis (sit-a-kō'sis) *n.* (*Med.*) a fatal disease found in parrots and communicable to man [L. *psittacus,* a parrot].
Psyche (sī'kę) *n.* (*Myth.*) a nymph who married Cupid.—**psy'che** *n.* the soul personified; the principle of life [Gk. *psuchē,* soul, mind].
psychiatry (sik-ī'atri, sī-kī'a-tri) *n.* study and treatment of mental disorders.—**psychi'ater, psychi'atrist** *n.* a specialist in mental disorders.—**psychiat'ric(al)** *a.* [Gk. *psuchē,* mind; *iatros,* a physician].
psychic, psychical (sī'kik, -ki-kal) *a.* pert. to soul, spirit, or mind; spiritualistic.—**psy'chically** *adv.*—**psy'chic** *n.* one sensitive to spiritualistic forces; medium.—**psy'chicist** *n.* [Gk. *psuchē,* soul, mind].
psycho-analysis (sī'kō-an-al'i-sis) *n.* process of studying the unconscious mind; a method of treating mental disturbances, in which causes are traced to forgotten memories and repressions affecting the mind unconsciously removed.—**psy'cho-an'alyse** *v.t.* to treat thus.—**psy'cho-an'alyst** *n.*—**psy'cho-analy'tic(al).**
psychology (sī-kol'o-ji) *n.* the scientific study of the mind and its activities.—**psycholog'ical** *a.*—**psycholog'ically** *adv.*—**psychol'ogist** *n.* [Gk. *psuchē,* the mind; *logos,* a discourse].
psychopathology (sī-kō-pa-thol'o-ji) *n.* the science or study of mental diseases.—**psychopathy** (sī-kop'a-thi) *n.* minor mental affliction.—**psy'chopath** *n.* one so afflicted.—**psycopath'ic** *a.*
psychosis (sī-kō'sis) *n.* a general term for any disorder of the mind.—*pl.* **psycho'ses** [Gk. *psuchē,* the mind].
psychosomatic (sī-kō-som-at'ik) *a.* of mind and body as a unit; treatment of physical diseases as having a mental origin [Gk. *soma,* body].
psychotherapy (sī-kō-ther'a-pi) *n.* the treatment of disease through the mind, e.g. by hypnotism, auto-suggestion, etc.—**psychotherapeut'ic (-al)** *a.*
ptarmigan (tår'mi-gan) *n.* a bird of the grouse family whose plumage turns white in winter [Gael. *tarmachan*].
ptero- (ter'o) *prefix* fr. Gk. *pteron,* a wing.—**pterodactyl** (ter-o-dak'til) *n.* extinct flying reptile with bat-like wings [Gk. *daktulos,* a finger].
Ptolemy (tol'e-mi) *n.* the name of a dynasty of Egyptian kings, from 323 to 30 B.C.; a famous Egyptian astronomer of the 2nd cent. A.D.—**Ptolemaic** (tol-e-mā'ik) *a.* pert. to the Ptolemies, to the astronomer, or to his system.—**Ptolemaic system,** the system of astronomy which assumed the earth to be the centre of the universe, and stationary.—**Ptolema'ist** *n.*
ptomaine (tō'mān, to-mān') *n.* substance, usually poisonous, found in putrefying organic matter [Gk. *ptōma,* a corpse].
pub (pub) *n.* (*Colloq.*) a public-house.
puberty (pū'bęr-ti) *n.* the earliest age at which an individual is capable of reproduction.—**pu'beral** *a.*—**pubescence** (pū-bes'ęns) *n.* the period of sexual development; puberty.—**pubes'cent** *a.* [L. *pubertas,* fr. *pubes,* adult].
public (pub'lik) *a.* of, or pert. to, the people; not private or secret; open to general use; accessible to all; serving the people;—*n.* community or its members; a section of community.—**pub'licly** *adv.*—**pub'lican** *n.* keeper of a public-house or inn; in ancient Rome, tax-collector.—**publica'tion** *n.* making known to the public; proclamation; printing a book, etc. for sale or distribution; a book, periodical, magazine, etc.—**pub'licise** *v.t.* to make widely known; to advertise.—**pub'licist** *n.* one versed in, or who writes on, international law, or matters of political or economic interest.—**publicity** (pub-lis'i-ti) *n.* the state of being generally known; notoriety; advertisement.—**pub'lic-house** *n.* inn, or tavern for sale of alcoholic liquors for consumption on premises.—**public prosecutor,** the legal officer appointed to prosecute criminals in serious cases on behalf of the Crown.—**public school,** a large boarding-school, usually endowed, and managed by a board of governors, e.g. Eton, Harrow, etc.; an elementary or primary school, esp. in Scotland; a council-school [L. *publicus,* fr. *populus,* the people].
publish (pub'lish) *v.t.* to make generally known; to proclaim; to print and issue for sale (books, music, etc.); to put into circulation.—**pub'lisher** *n.* [L. *publicare,* fr. *populus,* the people].
puce (pūs) *a.* flea-coloured; brownish-purple;—*n.* the colour [Fr. = a flea].
Puck (puk) *n.* Robin Goodfellow, a mischievous elf in *Midsummer Night's Dream.*—**puck'ish** *a.* [O.E. *puca*].
puck (puk) *n.* a rubber quoit used instead of a ball in ice-hockey [etym. uncertain].
pucker (puk-ęr) *v.t.* and *i.* to gather into small folds or wrinkles; to wrinkle;—*n.* a wrinkle; a fold [fr. *poke,* a bag].
pudding (pòò'ding) *n.* name of various forms of cooked foods, usually in a soft mass, served as a dessert; meat cooked in a covering of flour; a kind of sausage stuffed with blood meal, suet, and other ingredients; (*Naut.*) a rope-fender.—**pudd'ing-stone** *n.* (*Geol.*) conglomerate rock made of rounded pebbles [Fr. *boudin,* black pudding].
puddle (pud'l) *n.* a small pool of dirty water; a mixture of clay and water used as rough cement;—*v.t.* to make muddy; to line embankments, etc. with puddle; to stir about molten pig-iron to remove carbon and so make it malleable;—*v.i.* to make muddy.—**pudd'ling** *n.*—**pudd'ler** *n.* [O.E. *pudd,* a ditch].
puerile (pū'ęr-īl) *a.* boyish; childish; foolish;

silly.—pu'erilely *adv.*—pueril'ity *n.* childishness; triviality [L. *puer*, a boy].
puerperal (pū-er'per-al) *a.* pert. to, or caused by, child-birth.—puerperal fever (*Med.*) a fever developing after child-birth [L. *puer*, a child; *parere*, to bear].
puff (puf) *n.* a short blast of breath or wind; its sound; a small quantity of smoke, etc.; a whiff; a light pastry; a soft pad for applying powder; exaggerated praise, esp. in a newspaper;—*v.i.* to send out smoke, etc. in puffs; to breathe hard; to pant; to swell up;—*v.t.* to send out in a puff; to blow out; to smoke hard; to cause to swell; to praise unduly.—puff'er *n.*—puff'ing *n.* the act of praising unduly.—puff'ingly *adv.*—puff'y *a.* inflated; swollen; breathing hard.—puff'iness *n.*—puff'add'er *n.* a venomous African viper which inflates its body when disturbed.—puff'ball *n.* a ball-shaped fungus.—puff'paste *n.* a short, flaky paste for making light pastry [imit. origin].
puffin (puf'in) *n.* a sea-bird of the auk family with a parrot-like beak [M.E. *pofin*].
pug (pug) *n.* a small, snub-nosed dog; monkey; a fox; a shunting-locomotive.—pug'faced *a.* monkey-faced.—pug'nose *n.* a snub nose [etym. uncertain].
pug (pug) *v.t.* to make clay plastic by grinding with water; to fill in spaces with mortar in order to deaden sound;—*n.* clay prepared for brickmaking [etym. uncertain].
pugilism (pū'ji-lizm) *n.* the art of fighting with the fists; boxing.—pu'gilist *n.* a boxer.—pugilist'ic *a.* [L. *pugil*, a boxer, fr. *pugnus*, the fist].
pugnacious (pug-nā'shus) *a.* given to fighting; quarrelsome.—pugna'ciously *adv.*—pugnacity (pug-nas'i-ti) *n.* inclination to fight; quarrelsomeness [L. *pugnare*, to fight].
puisne (pū'ne) *a.* (*Law*) junior, or lower in rank [O.Fr. fr. L. *post*, after; *natus*, born].
puissant (pū'i-sant, pwēs'ant) *a.* powerful; mighty.—pu'issantly *adv.*—pu'issance *n.* power [Fr. fr. L. *potens*, powerful].
puke (pūk) *v.i.* and *t.* to vomit [origin uncertain].
pukka (puk'a) *a.* (*Anglo-Ind.*) of full weight; real; genuine [Hind. *pakka*, ripe].
pulchritude (pul'kri-tūd) *n.* beauty; comeliness [L. *pulcher*, beautiful].
pule (pūl) *v.i.* to chirp; to cry weakly; to whimper; to whine [imit. origin].
pull (pool) *v.t.* to draw towards one; to drag; to haul; to tug at; to pluck; to gather; to row a boat;—*v.i.* to draw with force; to tug;—*n.* act of pulling; force exerted by it; a tug; strain; effort; (*Colloq.*) influence, unfair advantage; (*Print.*) a rough proof; (*Golf*) a curving shot to the left.—pull'er *n.*—pull'over *n.* jersey put on by pulling over head [O.E. *pullian*].
pullet (pool'et) *n.* a young hen [Fr. *poulet*, dim. of *poule*, a hen].
pulley (pool'i) *n.* a small wheel with a grooved rim on which runs a rope, used for hauling or lifting weights [Fr. *poulie*].
Pullman-car (pŏŏl'man-kàr) *n.* a railway car adapted for sleeping; also one having individual seats. Also Pull'man [fr. G. M. *Pullman* (1831-97), the inventor].
pulmo- (pul'mō) *prefix* from L. *pulmo*, the lung.—pulmonary (pul'mo-na-ri) *a.* pert. to or affecting the lungs pulmon'ic *a.* pert. to, or affecting, the lungs.
pulp (pulp) *n.* a soft, moist, cohering mass of animal or vegetable matter; the soft, succulent part of fruit; the material of which paper is made;—*v.t.* to reduce to pulp; to remove the pulp from.—pul'py *a.* like pulp.—pul'piness *n.* [L. *pulpa*, flesh, pith].
pulpit (pŏŏl'pit) *n.* elevated place in a church for preacher; a desk [L. *pulpitum*, a stage].
pulsate (pul'sāt, pul-sāt') *v.t.* to beat or throb, as the heart; to vibrate; to quiver.—pulsa'tion *n.* a beating or throbbing.—pul'satile *a.* pulsating; producing sounds by being struck, as a drum.—pul'sative, pul'satory *a.* capable of pulsating; throbbing [L. *pulsare*, to throb].
pulse (puls) *n.* the beating or throbbing of the heart or blood-vessels, esp. of the arteries; the place, esp. on the wrist, where this rhythmical beat is felt; any measured or regular beat.—*v.i.* to throb or pulsate [L. *pulsus*, beating.
pulse (puls) *n.* leguminous plants or their seeds, as beans, peas, etc. [L. *puls*, porridge].
pulverise (pul'ver-īz) *v.t.* to reduce to a fine powder; to smash or demolish;—*v.i.* to fall down into dust.—pulverisa'tion *n.*—pul'veriser *n.*—pulverisable (pul-ve-rī'za-bl) *a.* that may be reduced to powder [L. *pulvis*, dust].
puma (pū'ma) *n.* a large American carnivorous animal of the cat family; the cougar; the American panther [Peruv.].
pumice (pū'mis, pum'is) *n.*—Also pum'ice-stone, a light, porous variety of lava, used for cleaning, polishing, etc.—pumiceous (pū-mi'shus) *a.* [L. *pumex*].
pummel (pum'el) *n.* a pommel;—*v.t.* to pommel; to beat with the fists.
pump (pump) *n.* an appliance used for raising water, putting in or taking out air or liquid, etc.;—*v.t.* to raise with a pump, as water; to free from water by means of a pump; (*Fig.*) to extract information by artful questioning;—*v.i.* to work a pump; to raise water with a pump.—pump'room *n.* a room at a spa for patrons who drink the waters [Fr. *pompe*].
pump (pump) *n.* a low, thin-soled dancing-shoe [Dut. *pampoesje*].
pumpkin (pump'kin) *n.* a plant of the gourd family; its fruit, used as food [O.Fr. *pompon*, fr. Gk. *pepon*, ripe].
pun (pun) *n.* a play on words similar in sound but different in sense;—*v.i.* to use puns.—pun'ster *n.* one who makes puns.
punch (punsh) *n.* a drink made of spirits or wine, flavoured with lemon-juice, sugar, and spice [Hind. *panch*, five (ingredients)].
punch (punsh) *n.* a tool used for making holes or dents; a machine for perforating tickets;—*v.t.* to perforate, dent, or stamp with a punch [Fr. *poinçon*, an awl, fr. L. *pungere*, to pierce].
punch (punsh) *v.t.* to strike with the fist; to beat; to bruise; of cattle, to drive;—*n.* a blow with the fist; (*Slang*) energy [fr. *punish*].
puncheon (pun'shun) *n.* a large cask of varying capacity (72-120 gallons); a measure of this amount [Fr. *poinçon*].
punctate (pungk'tāt) *a.* having many points; having dots scattered over the surface. Also punc'tated [L. *pungere*, to pierce].
punctilio (pungk-til'i-ō) *n.* a fine point of etiquette; formality.—punctil'ious *a.* attentive to punctilio; strict in the observance of rules of conduct, etc.; scrupulously correct.—punctil'iously *adv.*—punctil'iousness *n.* [L. *punctum*, a point].
punctual (pungk'tū-al) *a.* arriving at the proper or fixed time; prompt; not late; (*Geom.*) pert. to a point.—punc'tually *adv.*—punctual'ity *n.* [L. *punctum*, a point].
punctuate (pungk'tū-āt) *v.t.* to separate into sentences, clauses, etc. by periods, commas, colons, etc.; to emphasise in some significant manner; to interrupt at intervals.—punctua'tion *n.* the act or system of separating by the use of punctuation marks (the period, comma, colon, semi-colon, etc.) [L. *punctum*, a point].
puncture (pungk'tūr) *n.* an act of pricking; a small hole made by a sharp point, esp. in a tyre; a perforation;—*v.t.* to make a hole with a sharp point [L. *pungere*, to prick].
pundit (pun'dit) *n.* a title given to a Hindu scholar; (*Colloq.*) any learned person; one who claims to be an authority [Hind. *pandit*].
pungent (pun'jent) *a.* sharply affecting the taste or smell; sharply painful; pricking; stinging; sarcastic; caustic.—pun'gently *adv.*—pun'gency *n.* [L. *pungere*, to prick].
Punic (pū'nik) *a.* fr. L. *Punicus*, Cartha-

ginian; hence pert. to the Carthaginians; faithless; treacherous; deceitful.
punish (pun′ish) *v.t.* to cause an offender to suffer for an offence; to inflict a penalty on; to chastise; to visit with bodily pain.—**pun′ishable** *a.*—**pun′ishment** *n.* penalty inflicted for a crime; chastisement; correction.—**punitive** (pū′ni-tiv) *a.* pert. to or inflicting punishment [L. *punire*, to punish].
punk (pungk) *n.* crumbly, decayed wood;—*a.* worthless [etym. uncertain].
punkah, punka (pung′kạ) *n.* in India, a large fan for cooling the air of a room [Hind. *pankha*, a fan].
punnet (pun′et) *n.* a small, shallow, chip basket for fruit [etym. unknown].
punt (punt) *n.* a flat-bottomed boat;—*v.t.* and *i.* to propel a boat by means of a pole.—**punt′er** *n.* [L. *pons, pontis*, a bridge].
punt (punt) *v.t.* and *i.* to kick a football, when dropped from the hands, before it touches the ground;—*n.* such a kick [etym. uncertain].
punt (punt) *v.i.* (*Colloq.*) to back horses.—**punt′er** *n.* [L. *punctum*, a point].
puny (pū′ni) *a.* small and feeble; petty.—**pu′niness** *n.* [O.Fr. *puisne*, fr. L. *post natus*, born after].
pup (pup) *n.* a puppy or young dog; a conceited, foppish fellow;—*v.i.* to bring forth puppies or whelps [short fr. *puppy*, fr. Fr. *poupée*, a doll or puppet].
pupa (pū′pạ) *n.* the third stage in the metamorphosis of an insect, when it is in a cocoon; a chrysalis.—*pl.* **pupae** (pū′pē).—**pu′pal** *a.*—**pu′pate** *v.i.* to become a pupa [L. *pupa*, a girl, a doll].
pupil (pū′pil) *n.* a youth or scholar of either sex; a boy or girl under the age of puberty and so under the care of a guardian or tutor; a ward; the small circular opening in the centre of the iris of the eye, through which rays of light pass to the retina.—**pu′pilage, pu′pillage** *n.* the state of being a pupil; the period of time during which one is a pupil or minor.—**pu′pilary, pu′pillary** *a.* pert. to a pupil or ward; pert. to the pupil of the eye [L. *pupillus*, an orphan boy].
puppet (pup′et) *n.* a small figure with jointed limbs manipulated by wires; a marionette; a person whose actions are completely controlled by another.—**pupp′etry** *n.* a puppet-show; trivial finery [Fr. *poupée*, a doll; L. *puppa*].
puppy (pup′i) *n.* See **pup**.
purblind (pur′blind) *a.* almost blind; dull in understanding.—**pur′blindly** *adv.*—**pur′blindness** *n.* [fr. *pure* and *blind*].
purchase (pur′chạs) *v.t.* to buy; to obtain by any outlay of labour, time, sacrifice, etc.; (*Law*) to obtain by any means other than inheritance;—*n.* acquisition of anything for a price or equivalent; a thing bought; any advantageous hold that may be secured in order to exert force.—**pur′chasable** *a.*—**pur′chaser** *n.*—**pur′chase-tax** *n.* a percentage tax added to the retail price of certain articles [Fr. *pourchasser*, to obtain by pursuit].
purdah (pur′dạ) *n.* a curtain; the Indian system of secluding women [Hind.].
pure (pūr) *a.* free from all extraneous matter; untainted; spotless; blameless; unsullied; chaste; innocent; absolute; theoretical, not applied.—**pure′ly** *adv.* entirely; solely.—**pure′ness** *n.*—**pu′rity** *n.* freedom from all extraneous matter; freedom from sin or evil; innocence; chastity [L. *purus*].
purée (póó rā′) *n.* a thick soup made from vegetables, meat, etc. boiled to a pulp and rubbed through a sieve [Fr.].
purfle (pur′fl) *n.* a border of embroidered work;—*v.t.* to edge with embroidery or piping.—**pur′fling** *n.* an inlaid ornamental border on the edges of stringed instruments [L. *pro*, before; *filum*, a thread].
purge (purj) *v.t.* to purify; to cleanse; to clear out; to clear from guilt, accusation, or the charge of a crime, etc.; to remove from an organisation, political party, army, etc. undesirable or suspect members; to cleanse the bowels by taking a cathartic medicine;—*n.* a cleansing, esp. of the bowels; a purgative.—**purgation** (pur-gā′shun) *n.* act of cleansing or purifying; act of freeing from imputation of guilt; purging.—**purgative** (pur′gạ-tiv) *a.* having the power of purging;—*n.* any medicine which will cause evacuation of bowels.—**purgatory** (pur′gạ-tor-i) *a.* tending to cleanse; purifying; expiatory;—*n.* in R.C. faith, place where souls of dead are purified by suffering; (*Fig.*) a place or state of torment.—**purgato′rial** *a.* [L. *purgare*, fr. *purus*, pure].
purify (pū′ri-fī) *v.t.* to make pure, clear, or clean; to free from impurities; to free from guilt or defilement;—*v.i.* to become pure.—*pr.p.* **pu′rifying**.—*pa.p.* and *pa.t.* **pu′rified**.—**purification** (pū-ri-fi-kā′shun) *n.* the act of removing impurities; act of cleansing, esp. from guilt or sin.—**pu′rificative** *a.*—**pu′rificator** *n.*—**pu′rificatory** *a.* tending to cleanse.—**pu′rifier** *n.* [L. *purus*, pure; *facere*, to make].
purist (pū′rist) *n.* an advocate of extreme care or precision in choice of words, etc.; a stickler for correctness, esp. of style [L. *purus*, pure].
Puritan (pū′ri-tạn) *n.* a member of the extreme Protestant party, who desired further *purification* of the Church after the Elizabethan reformation.—**pu′ritan** *n.* a person of extreme strictness in morals or religion; a bigot; a kill-joy;—*a.* pert. to Puritans or to puritan.—**puritan′ic(al)** *a.* pert. to Puritans, their doctrine and practice; over-scrupulous.—**puritan′ically** *adv.*—**pu′ritanism** *n.* doctrine and practice of Puritans; narrow-mindedness; bigotry [L. *puritas*, purity, fr. *purus*].
purl (purl) *n.* an embroidered border; a knitting-stitch that is reverse of plain stitch;—*v.t.* to ornament with purls;—*v.i.* to knit in purl. Also **pearl** [fr. *purfle*].
purl (purl) *v.i.* to flow with a burbling sound or gentle murmur [imit. origin].
purlieu (pur′lū) *n.* ground bordering on something.—**pur′lieus** *n.pl.* outlying districts; outskirts [O.Fr. *purallee*, a survey].
purloin (pur-loin′) *v.t.* to steal; to pilfer [O.Fr. *purloigner*, to put far away].
purple (pur′pl) *n.* a colour between crimson and violet obtained from a mixture of red and blue; robe of this colour, formerly reserved for royalty; hence royal dignity;—*a.* purple-coloured; dark-red;—*v.t.* to make or dye a purple colour;—*v.i.* to become purple.—**born to the purple**, of princely rank [Gk. *porphura*, shell-fish that gave Tyrian purple].
purport (pur′pōrt) *n.* meaning; apparent meaning; import; aim.—**purport** (pur-pōrt′) *v.t.* to mean; to be intended to seem [O.Fr. *porporter*, to embody].
purpose (pur′pos) *n.* object in view; aim; end; plan; intention; effect; purport;—*v.t.* to intend; to mean to.—**pur′posely** *adv.* intentionally; deliberately.—**pur′poseful** *a.* determined; resolute.—**pur′posefully** *adv.*—**pur′poseless** *a.* aimless.—**pur′poselessly** *adv.*—**pur′posive** *a.* done with a purpose.—**pur′posiveness** *n.* [O.Fr. *porpos*, fr. *porposer*, to propose].
purpura (pur′pū-ra) *n.* (*Med.*) the appearance of purple patches under the skin, caused by haemorrhage; shell-fish, yielding purplish fluid.—**pur′purate** *a.* purple-coloured.—**purpureal** (pur-pū′rē-ạl) *a.* purple.—**purpu′ric** *a.* pert. to purpura [Gk. *porphura*]. See **purple**.
purr (pur) *n.* a low, murmuring sound made by a cat when pleased;—*v.i.* to utter such a sound [imit. origin].
purse (purs) *n.* a small bag or pouch to carry money in; money offered as a prize, or collected as a present; money;—*v.t.* to wrinkle up; to pucker.—**purs′er** *n.* (*Naut.*) officer in charge of accounts, etc. on board a ship.—**purse′ful** *a.* enough to fill a purse.—**purse′**

strings *n.pl.* power to control expenditure [Fr. *bourse*, a purse, fr. Gk. *bursa*, a hide].

pursue (pur-sū′) *v.t.* to follow with the aim of overtaking; to run after; to chase; to aim at; to seek; to continue;—*v.i.* to go on; to proceed; to prosecute at law.—**pursu′er** *n.* one who pursues; (*Scots Law*) the plaintiff.—**pursu′ance** *n.* the act of pursuing.—**pursu′ant** *a.* done in consequence, or performance, of anything.—**pursuit′** (pur-sūt′) *n.* the act of pursuing; a running after; chase; attempt to catch; profession; occupation.—**pursuivant** (pur′swi-vant) *n.* an attendant; a state messenger; an officer of the College of Arms ranking below a herald [Fr. *poursuivre*, fr. L. *prosequi*, to follow].

pursy (pur′si) *a.* small and stout; short-winded [O.Fr. *polsif*, fr. L. *pulsare*, to push].

purtenance (pur′te-nans) *n.* that which pertains or belongs to; formerly, the intestines of a slaughtered animal [contr. fr. *appurtenance*].

purulent (pū′rū-lent, pur′ū-lent) *a.* pert. to, containing, or discharging pus, or matter; septic; suppurating.—**pu′rulence, pu′rulency** *n.* [L. *pus, puris*, matter].

purvey (pur-vā′) *v.t.* to furnish or provide; to supply, esp. provisions;—*v.i.* as a business, to supply provisions for others; to cater.—**purvey′ance** *n.* act of purveying; supplies; former royal prerogative of requisitioning supplies, or enforcing personal service.—**purvey′or** *n.* [L. *providere*, to provide].

purview (pur′vū)*n.* a stipulation or condition; the enacting clauses of a statute; scope; range; limits [Fr. *pourvu*, provided].

pus (pus) *n.* the yellowish-white matter produced by suppuration [L. *pus*, matter].

push (po͝osh) *v.t.* to move or try to move away by pressure; to drive or impel; to press hard; to press or urge forward; to shove; to thrust; —*v.i.* to make a thrust; to press hard in order to move;—*n.* a thrust; any pressure or force applied; emergency; enterprise; (*Mil.*) an advance or attack on a large scale; (*Colloq.*) dismissal from a post, job, etc.—**push′er** *n.*—**push′ful, push′ing** *a.* given to pushing oneself or one's claims; self-assertive.—**push′ingly** *adv.* [Fr. *pousser*, fr. L. *pellere*, to drive].

pusillanimous (pū-si-lan′i-mus) *a.* cowardly; timid; faint-hearted; mean-spirited.—**pusillan′imously** *adv.*—**pusillanim′ity** *n.* [L. *pusillus*, very small; *animus*, spirit].

puss (po͝os) *n.* a familiar name for a cat; a hare; a young girl.—**puss′y** *n.* dim. of puss; a cat.—**puss′-in-the-cor′ner** *n.* a children's game [orig. a name to call a cat].

pustule (pus′tūl) *n.* a small swelling or pimple containing pus.—**pus′tular, pus′tulous** *a.* [L. *pustula*, a blister].

put (po͝ot) *v.t.* to place; to set; to lay; to apply; to state; to propose; to urge; to throw; to cast;—*v.i.* to place.—*pr.p.* **putting** (po͝ot′ing).—*pa.p.* and *pa.t.* **put**.—*n.* a throw, esp. of a heavy weight.—**to put about** (*Naut.*) to alter a ship's course; to inconvenience; to make known. [Late O.E. *putian*].

putative (pū′ta-tiv) *a.* commonly thought; supposed; reputed.—**pu′tatively** *adv.*—**puta′tion** *n.* [L. *putare*, to think].

putrefy (pū′tre-fī) *v.t.* and *i.* to make or become rotten; to corrupt; to decompose; to rot.—*pa.p.* and *pa.t.* **pu′trefied**.—**putrefac′tion** *n.* the process of putrefying; the rotting of animal or vegetable matter; rottenness; decomposition.—**putrefac′tive** *a.* pert. to or causing putrefaction.—**putres′cence** *n.* tendency to decay; decay; rottenness.—**putres′cent** *a.*—**putrid** (pū′trid) *a.* in a state of decay; (*Colloq.*) very bad.—**putrid′ity, pu′tridness** *n.* [L. *putere*, to rot; *facere*, to make].

putsch (po͝och) *n.* a revolutionary outbreak; a rising; a coup d'état [Ger.].

putt (put) *v.t.* and *i.* (*Golf*) to hit a ball on the putting-green in the direction of the hole; (*Scot.*) to throw (a weight or iron ball) from the shoulder;—*n.* the stroke so made in golf; the throw of the weight.—**putt′er** *n.* one who putts; a short golf-club [var. of *put*].

puttee (put′ē) *n.* a strip of cloth wrapped spirally from ankle to knee, to act as a legging. Also **put′tie** [Hind. *patti*, a bandage].

putty (put′i) *n.* a kind of paste or cement, of whiting and linseed-oil; a polishing powder of calcined tin, used by jewellers; a mixture of fine lime (without sand) and water, used by plasterers;—*v.t.* to fix, fill up, etc. with putty.—**putt′ier** *n.* [Fr. *potée*, the contents of a pot].

puzzle (puz′l) *n.* a bewildering or perplexing question; a problem, etc. requiring clever thinking to solve it; a conundrum;—*v.t.* to perplex; to bewilder; (with 'out') to solve after hard thinking; (with 'over') to think hard over;—*v.i.* to be bewildered.—**puzz′ler** *n.*—**puzz′ling** *a.* bewildering; perplexing [fr. M.E. *opposal*, a question, interrogation].

pyaemia, pyemia (pī-ē′mi-a) *n.* (*Med.*) blood-poisoning characterised by formation of abscesses [Gk. *puon*, pus; *haima*, blood].

pyedog (pī′dog) *n.* stray mongrel; pariah dog. Also **pie′dog** [Hind. *pahi*, outsider].

Pygmy, Pigmy (pig′mi) *n.* one of a race of dwarf Negroes of C. Africa.—*pl.* **Pyg′mies, Pig′mies**.—**pyg′my, pig′my** *n.* a very small person or thing; a dwarf;—*a.* diminutive [Gk. *pugmē*, a measure of length from elbow to knuckles].

pyjamas (pi-, pī-ja′maz) *n.pl.* loose trousers, worn by Mohammedans; a sleeping-suit. Also **paja′mas** [Pers. *paejamah*, a leg garment].

pylon (pī′lon) *n.* the gateway of an ancient Egyptian temple; a large metal tower, to support power-transmission cables [Gk. *pulōn*, a gateway].

pyorrhoea (pī-o-rē′a) *n.* (*Med.*) a discharge of pus; a dental disease characterised by the discharge of pus from the gums. Also **pyorrhe′a** [Gk. *puon*, pus; *rhoia*, a flowing].

pyramid (pir′a-mid) *n.* a solid figure on a triangular, square, or polygonal base, and with sloping sides meeting at an apex; a structure of this shape, esp. the ancient Egyptian (usually with a square base);—*n.pl.* (*Billiards*) a game played with balls arranged in the form of a solid triangle.—**pyram′idal** *a.* pert. to, or having the form of, a pyramid.—**pyram′idally** *adv.* [Gk. *puramis*].

pyre (pīr) *n.* a pile of wood for burning a dead body; a funeral pile [Gk. *pur*, fire].

Pyrethrum (pir-eth′rum) *n.* (*Bot.*) a genus of herbaceous perennial plants, including the fever-few [Gk. *pur*, fire].

pyretic (pī-ret′ik) *a.* (*Med.*) pert. to, producing, or relieving, fever; feverish.—**pyrex′ia** *n.* fever [Gk. *puretos*, fever, fr. *pur*, fire].

pyrite (pī′rīt) *n.* a yellow mineral formed of sulphur and iron; iron pyrites.—**pyrites** (pir-ī′tēz, pī′rīts) *n.pl.* a name for many compounds of metals with sulphur or arsenic, esp. iron pyrites, or copper pyrites.—**pyrit′ic, pyritif′erous, pyr′itous** *a.* pert. to, or yielding, pyrites [Gk. *pur*, fire].

pyro- (pī′rō) *prefix* fr. Gk. *pur*, fire, used in many derivatives.—**py′ro-electric′ity** *n.* the property possessed by some crystals, e.g. tourmaline, of becoming electrically polar when they are heated.

pyrography (pī-rog′ra-fi) *n.* the art of producing a design on wood by burning it in with a heated metal point; pokerwork [Gk. *pur*, fire; *graphein*, to write].

pyrolatry (pī-rol′a-tri) *n.* fire-worship [Gk. *pur*, fire; *latreia*, worship].

pyromania (pī-rō-mā′ni-a) *n.* a mania for setting things on fire.—**pyroma′niac** *n.* [Gk. *pur*, fire; and *mania*].

pyrometer (pī-rom′e-ter) *n.* an instrument for measuring high temperatures.—**pyromet′ric, pyromet′rical** *a.* [Gk. *pur*, fire; *metron*, a measure].

pyrotechnics (pī-rō-tek′niks) *n.pl.* the art of making fireworks; the art of displaying them.

Also **pyrotech'ny.**—**pyrotech'nic, pyrotech'nical** *a.* [Gk. *pur*, fire; *technē*, art].
Pyrrhus (pir'-us) *n.* (*Class. Hist.*) King of Epirus (318-272 B.C.) who defeated Romans at Asculum, 279 B.C. but lost so many men that it originated the term, **a Pyrrhic victory,** one so costly as to be almost a defeat; an empty victory.
Pythagoras (pi-tha'-gō-ras) *n.* a Greek philosopher and mathematician (582-507 B.C.).—**Pythagore'an** *a.* pert. to the philosopher or to his teaching.—*n.* a disciple of Pythagoras.
python (pī'-thon) *n.* a large, non-poisonous snake that kills its prey by crushing it; a spirit; a soothsayer.—**Py'thoness** *n.* (*Myth.*) the priestess of Apollo at Delphi; a witch [Gk. *Puthōn*, the serpent slain by Apollo near Delphi].
pyx (piks) *n.* the vessel in which the consecrated bread or Host is kept; a box at the Royal Mint, London, in which specimen coins are kept for trial and assay;—*v.t.* to test by assay.—**pyx'is** *n.* a small pyx; a casket [Gk. *puxis*, fr. *puxos*, a box-tree].

Q

Q-boat (kū'-bōt) *n.* (*World War* 1) ship disguised as cargo or fishing vessel and carrying concealed guns, employed in anti-submarine warfare [Q = Query].
quack (kwak) *v.i.* to cry like a duck; to act as a quack;—*n.* cry of duck or like sound; one who pretends to skill in an art esp. in medicine; a charlatan;—*a.* pert. to quackery.—**quack'ery** *n.*—**quack'salver** *n.* a quack doctor [imit.].
Quadragesima (kwod-ra-jes'-i-ma) *n.* (*Church*) the season of Lent, because lasting for 40 days.—**Quadrages'imal** *a.* pert. to Lent [L. *quadragesimus*, fortieth].
quadrangle (kwod'-rang-gl) *n.* in geometry, a plane figure having four equal sides and angles; a square or court surrounded by buildings (*abbrev.* **quad.**).—**quadrang'ular** *a.* [L. *quattuor*, four and *angle*].
quadrant (kwod'-rant) *n.* the fourth part of the area of a circle; an arc of 90°; an instrument for taking altitude of heavenly bodies; in gunnery, an instrument to mark the degrees of a gun's elevation; in motoring, a metal arc forming a combined rack and index for operation of control levers [L. *quadrans*, a fourth part].
quadrate (kwod'-rāt) *a.* having four equal sides and four right angles; square; divisible by four (used chiefly in anatomical names);—*n.* a square;—**quadrate'** *v.i.* to square; to agree; to suit.—**quadrat'ic** *a.* pert. to, or resembling, a square; square; (*Alg.*) involving the second but no higher power of the unknown quantity, esp. in **quadratic equation.**—**quadrature** (kwod'-ra-tūr) *n.* the act of squaring or reducing to a square; the position of one heavenly body with respect to another 90° away [L. *quadratus*, squared].
quadrennial (kwod-ren'-i-al) *a.* occurring once in four years; comprising four years.—**quadren'nially** *adv.*—**quadrenn'ium** *n.* four years [L. *quattuor*, four; *annus*, year].
quadricentennial (kwod-ri-sen-ten'-i-al) *a.* pert. to a period of four hundred years;—*n.* the four hundredth anniversary [L. *quattuor*, four; *centum*, hundred; *annus*, a year].
quadrilateral (kwod-ri-lat'-er-al) *a.* having four sides;—*n.* (*Geom.*) a plane figure having four sides [L. *quattuor*, four; *latus*, side].
quadrille (ka-dril', kwo-dril') *n.* an 18th cent. game played by four persons with forty cards; a square dance; also, the music played to such a dance [Fr. through Sp. fr. L. *quadrus*, square].
quadrillion (kwo-dril'-yun) *n.* a million raised to the fourth power, represented by a unit with 24 ciphers annexed; in the French and U.S. notation, with 15 ciphers annexed [L. *quattuor*, four and *million*].
quadrinomial (kwod-ri-nō'-mi-al) *a.* (*Alg.*) consisting of four terms.
quadripartite (kwod-ri-pâr'-tīt) *a.* divided into four parts.
quadrireme (kwod'-ri-rēm) *a.* in ancient times, a galley with four benches of oars [L. *quattuor*, four; *remus*, an oar].
quadroon (kwod-rōōn') *n.* offspring of mulatto and white; one who is one-fourth Negro [Sp. *cuarterón*, fr. L. *quartus*, fourth].
quadrumane (kwod'-rōō-mān) *n.* an animal which has all four feet formed like hands.—**quadru'manous** *a.* four-handed [L. *quattuor*, four; *manus*, the hand].
quadruped (kwod'-rōō-ped) *n.* an animal having four feet;—*a.* having four feet [L. *quattuor*, four; *pes*, *pedis*, a foot].
quadruple (kwod'-rōō-pl) *a.* fourfold;—*n.* a fourfold amount; a sum four times as great as another;—*v.t.* to multiply by four;—*v.i.* to be multiplied by four.—**quad'ruplet** *n.* one of four children born at a birth; a bicycle for four.—**quadru'plicate** *v.t.* to multiply by four;—*n.* one of four things corresponding exactly;—*a.* fourfold.—**quadruplica'tion** *n.* [L. *quadruplus*, fourfold].
quaff (kwaf) *v.t.* to swallow in large draughts;—*v.i.* to drink largely [etym. uncertain].
quag (kwag) *n.* a marshy spot; a bog.—**quagg'y** *a.* spongy; boggy; like a quagmire.—**quagmire** (kwag'-mīr) *n.* soft, wet land, yielding under the feet; (*Fig.*) a difficult position [fr. *quake*].
quagga (kwag'-a) *n.* an African quadruped of the horse family, closely related to the zebra [Kaffir].
quaich, quaigh (kwāH) *n.* a shallow, bowl-shaped drinking vessel [Gael. *cuach*, a cup].
quail (kwāl) *v.i.* to lose spirit; to shrink or cower; to flinch [Fr. *cailler*, to curdle].
quail (kwāl) *n.* a game-bird allied to the partridge [Fr. *caille*].
quaint (kwānt) *a.* interestingly old-fashioned or odd; curious and fanciful; singular; whimsical.—**quaint'ly** *adv.*—**quaint'ness** *n.* [O. Fr. *cointe*, prudent].
quake (kwāk) *v.i.* to tremble or shake with fear, cold, or emotion; to quiver or vibrate;—*n.* a shaking or trembling; *abbrev.* of 'earthquake' [O.E. *cwacian*].
Quaker (kwā-ker) *n.* (*fem.* **Qua'keress**) a member of the Society of Friends, a religious sect founded in the 17th cent. by George Fox, the name being first given to them by a judge whom Fox had bade '*quake* before the Lord.'—**Qua'kerism** *n.*
qualify (kwol'-i-fī) *v.t.* to ascribe a quality to; to describe (as); to fit for active service or office; to prepare by requisite training for special duty; to furnish with the legal title to; to limit; to diminish; to reduce the strength of, as liquors;—*v.i.* to make oneself competent; to render oneself fit for.—**qual'ifier** *n.*—**qual'ifiable** *a.*—**qualifica'tion** *n.* the act of qualifying or condition of being qualified; any endowment or acquirement that fits a person for an office or employment; abatement; modification; restriction; attribution of a quality [L. *qualis*, of what kind; *facere*, to make].
quality (kwol'-i-ti) *n.* a particular property inherent in a body or substance; the essential attribute, or distinguishing feature, or characteristic of anything; character or nature; degree of excellence; excellence or superiority of character; rank or high birth.—**qual'itative** *a.* relating to quality; concerned with quality.—**qual'itatively** *adv.* [L. *qualitas*, fr. *qualis*, of what kind].
qualm (kwâm) *n.* a sudden attack of illness, faintness, nausea, distress; a scruple of conscience [Ger. *Qualm*, vapour].

quandary (kwon′dạ-ri, kwon-dā′ri) *n.* a state of perplexity; a predicament; a dilemma [etym. uncertain].
quantify (kwon′ti-fī) *v.t.* to fix or express the quantity of; to modify with respect to.—**quantifica′tion** *n.* [L. *quantus*, how much; *facere*, to make].
quantity (kwon′ti-ti) *n.* property of things ascertained by measuring; amount; bulk; a certain part; a considerable amount; number; (*Pros.*) the length or shortness of vowels, sounds, or syllables;—*pl.* abundance; profusion.—**quantitative** (kwon′ti-tā-tiv) *a.* relating to quantity.—**quantity surveyor**, a specialist estimator of the costs of erecting buildings, etc. [L. *quantus*, how much].
quantum (kwon′tum) *n.* a large quantity or amount; a specified, desired, or required amount; a sufficient amount.—**quantum theory**, in physics, the theory that energy transferences take place not continuously, but in bursts of a minimum quantity or quantum [L. *quantus*, how much].
quarantine (kwor′ạn-tēn) *n.* the period (orig. forty days) during which a ship, with infectious disease aboard, is isolated;—*v.t.* to put under quarantine [Fr. *quarantaine*, forty days].
quarrel (kwor′ẹl) *n.* rupture of friendly relations; an angry altercation; a dispute;—*v.i.* to dispute; to wrangle; to disagree.—*pr.p.* **quarr′elling.**—*pa.p.* and *pa.t.* **quarr′elled.**—**quarr′eller** *n.*—**quarr′elsome** *a.* apt to quarrel; irascible; contentious [L. *queri*, to complain].
quarrel (kwor′ẹl) *n.* a heavy square-headed arrow for a crossbow; a diamond-shaped pane of glass; a glazier's diamond [O. Fr. fr.L. *quadrus*, square].
quarry (kwor′i) *n.* an excavation whence stone is dug for building; any source from which material or (*Fig.*) information may be extracted;—*v.t.* to dig from a quarry.—*pa.p.* and *pa.t.* **quarr′ied** [L. *quadrare*, to square, hew (stones)].
quarry (kwor′i) *n.* orig. the game hunted with hawks; the object of pursuit; prey; victim [O.Fr. *cuiree*, fr. L. *corium*, skin].
quart (kwort) *n.* the fourth part of a gallon; two pints [L. *quartus*, fourth].
quarter (kwor′tẹr) *n.* fourth part; in avoirdupois weight, fourth of 1 cwt., or 28 lb.; in dry measure, 8 bushels, as of grain; one of the four cardinal points of the compass; (*Her.*) one of the four parts into which a shield is divided by quartering; one limb of a quadruped with the adjacent parts; a term in a school, etc.; part of a ship's side aft of mainmast; a region; a territory; a division of a town, or county; merciful treatment or exemption from death granted to enemy;—*pl.* assigned position; lodgings, esp. for soldiers; shelter;—*v.t.* to divide into four equal parts; to divide up a traitor's body; to furnish with shelter; (*Her.*) to bear as an appendage to the hereditary arms; of game-dogs, to traverse the ground in all directions in search of game;—*v.i.* to have temporary residence.—**quar′tering** *n.* an assignment of quarters for soldiers; (*Her.*) the partition of a shield into compartments.—**quar′terly** *a.* consisting of a fourth part; occurring every quarter of a year;—*n.* a review or magazine published four times a year;—*adv.* by quarters; once in a quarter of a year.—**quar′ter-day** *n.* one of the four days in the year, when rents fall due.—**quar′ter-deck** *n.* part of deck of a ship which extends from stern to mainmast; (*Fig.*) the officers of a naval vessel.—**quar′termaster** *n.* (*Mil.*) an officer in charge of quarters, clothing, stores, etc.; (*Naut.*) a petty officer who attends to steering, signals, stowage, etc.—**quar′termaster-ser′geant** *n.* the N.C.O. assistant to the quartermaster.—**quar′ter-ses′sions** *n.* court held quarterly by the justices of the peace.—**quar′ter-staff** *n.* a long, stout staff, formerly a weapon [L. *quartarius*, fr. *quartus*, fourth].
quartern (kwor′tẹrn) *n.* orig. quarter of peck, stone, or pint; now generally used only in **quartern-loaf**, weighing four pounds [O.Fr. *quarteron*, fr. L. *quartus*, fourth].
quartet, quartette (kwor-tet′) *n.* (*Mus.*) a composition of four parts, each performed by a single voice or instrument; set of four who perform this; a stanza of four lines; a group of four [Fr.].
quarto (kwor′tō) *a.* denoting the size of a book in which the paper is folded to give four leaves to the sheet (*abbrev.* **4to**);—*n.* a book of the size of the fourth of a sheet [L. *in quarto*, in a fourth part].
quartz (kworts) *n.* kinds of mineral, consisting of pure silica or silicon dioxide, found in massive and in hexagonal crystals [Ger. *Quarz*].
quash (kwosh) *v.t.* to crush; to quell; (*Law*) to annul, overthrow, or make void [L. *quassare*, to shake].
quasi (kwā′sī, kwȧ′sē) as if; as it were; in a certain sense or degree; seeming; apparently; it is used as adj. or adv. and as prefix to noun, adj., or adv. [L.].
quassia (kwosh′i-a) *n.* S. American tree, the wood and bark of which yield a bitter decoction used as a tonic [fr. Negro *Quassi*, who discovered its value].
quatercentenary (kwo-tẹr-sen-tē′nạ-ri, kwa′tẹr-sen′ti-nạ-ri) *n.* a 400th anniversary [L. *quater*, four times].
quatern (kwot′ern) *a.* consisting of a set of four; growing by fours.—**quaternary** (kwo-tẹr′nạ-ri) *a.* consisting of four; by fours; (*Geol.*) denoting strata more recent than the Upper Tertiary;—*n.* the number four [L. *quaterni*, four each, fr. *quattuor*, four].
quaternion (kwa-tẹr′ni-on) *n.* a set of four parts, objects, or individuals; (*Math.*) the quotient of two vectors; or of two directed right lines in space, considered as depending on four geometrical elements, and as expressible by an algebraic symbol of quadrinomial form;—*pl.* (*Math.*) the calculus of the quaternion [L. *quaterni*, four each, fr. *quattuor*, four].
quatrain (kwot′rān) *n.* (*Pros.*) a stanza of four lines, generally rhyming alternately [L. *quattuor*, four].
quaver (kwā′vẹr) *v.i.* to shake, tremble, or vibrate; to sing or play with tremulous modulations;—*v.t.* to utter or sing with quavers or trills;—*n.* a trembling, esp. of the voice; (*Mus.*) a note equal to half a crochet [etym. uncertain].
quay (kē) *n.* a landing-place used for the loading and unloading of ships; a wharf.—**quay′age** *n.* payment for use of a quay; space occupied by quays [Fr. *quai*].
quean (kwēn) *n.* an ill-behaved girl; (*Scot.*) a girl [O.E. *cwene*, a woman].
queasy (kwē′zi) *a.* affected with nausea; squeamish; fastidious.—**quea′sily** *adv.*—**quea′siness** *n.* [etym. uncertain].
queen (kwēn) *n.* the consort of a king; a woman who is the sovereign of a kingdom; the sovereign of a swarm of bees; any woman who is pre-eminent; one of the chief pieces in a game of chess.—*v.i.* to act the part of a queen (usu. 'to queen it').—**queen′ly** *a.* like, appropriate to a queen; majestic.—**queen′liness** *n.*—**queen′hood** *n.* state or position of a queen.—**queen′cake** *n.* a small, light cake.—**queen′bee** *n.* fully-developed female of a hive; a radio-controlled plane used for anti-aircraft firing practice.—**queen′con′sort** *n.* the wife of a king.—**queen′dow′ager** *n.* the widow of a king.—**queen′moth′er** *n.* a queen-dowager who is also mother of reigning monarch.—**queen′of-the-mead′ow** *n.* the flower meadow-sweet.—**queen′re′gent** *n.* a queen who reigns as regent.—**queen-reg′nant** *n.* a queen reigning in her own right.—**Queen's Bench**, one of the three divisions of the English High Court of Justice, hearing mainly common law actions.—**Queen's Counsel**, an honorary distinction con-

ferred on eminent barristers giving them precedence in courts and the right to wear a silk gown (hence, *to take silk*).—**Queen's Messenger**, a courier appointed by Foreign Office to carry despatches to its representatives in foreign capitals, the silver greyhound being the badge of office.—**Queen's Proctor**, the Treasury solicitor who may intervene to stop decrees *nisi* in divorce being made absolute.—**Queen's Regulations**, the official regulations for the organisation of the British Army or Navy [O.E. *cwen*, a woman].

Queensberry (kwēnz′ber-i) *a.* applied to the 'Rules of Boxing,' originally drawn up by the Marquess of *Queensberry* (1844-1900), a famous patron of the sport.

queer (kwēr) *a.* odd; singular; quaint; of a questionable character; open to suspicion; faint or out of sorts;—*v.t.* (*Slang*) to spoil.—**queer'ly** *adv.*—**queer'ish** *a.* somewhat queer.—**queer'ness** *n.*—**in Queer Street** (*Slang*) in trouble or difficulty, esp. financially [Ger. *quer*, athwart, crosswise].

quell (kwel) *v.t.* to subdue; to put down; to suppress forcibly [O.E. *cwellan*, to kill].

quench (kwensh) *v.t.* to extinguish; to put out, as fire or light; to cool or allay; to repress; to stifle; to slake (thirst);—*v.i.* to become cool.—**quench'able** *a.*—**quench'less** *a.*—**quench'er** *n.* that which quenches; (*Slang*) a drink [O.E. *cwencan*].

Quercus (kwẹr′kus) *n.* a genus of trees, containing the oaks.—**quercine** (kwẹr′sin) *a.* [L. *quercus*, an oak].

quern (kwẹrn) *n.* a primitive handmill for grinding grain [O.E. *cweorn*].

querulous (kwer′ū-lus) *a.* peevish; fretful; whining; discontented.—**quer'ulously** *adv.*—**quer'ulousness** *n.* [L. *queri*, to complain].

query (kwē′ri) *n.* a question; an inquiry; a mark of interrogation;—*v.t.* to inquire into; to call in question; to mark as of doubtful accuracy;—*v.i.* to express doubt [L. *quaerere* to seek or inquire].

quest (kwest) *n.* search; the act of seeking; the thing sought;—*v.i.* to search; to seek [L. *quaerere, quaestum*, to seek].

question (kwest′yun) *n.* interrogation; inquiry; that which is asked; subject of inquiry or debate; (subject of) dispute; a matter of doubt or difficulty; a problem;—*v.t.* to inquire of by asking questions; to be uncertain of; to challenge; to take objection to; to interrogate;—**quest'ionable** *a.* doubtful; suspicious.—**quest'ionably** *adv.*—**quest'ionableness** *n.*—**quest′ioner** *n.*—**quest'ion-mark** *n.* a mark of interrogation.—**out of the question**, not to be thought of.—**to beg the question**, to assume as fact something which is to be proved (L. *quaestio*, fr. *quaerere*, to seek, ask].

questionnaire (kes-ti-on-ār′) *n.* a list of questions drawn up for formal answer, and submitted in general to a series of individuals or bodies, with a view to establishing statistics. Also **ques'tionary** [Fr.].

queue (kū) *n.* the tie of a wig; a pig-tail; a file of people awaiting their turn to be attended to;—*v.t.* to dress hair in a queue;—*v.i.* to form or join a queue [Fr. fr. L. *cauda*, a tail].

quibble (kwib′l) *n.* an evasion of the point in question by a play upon words, or by stressing unimportant aspect of it; an equivocation or pretence;—*v.i.* to use quibbles; to trifle in argument.—**quibb'ler** *n.* [dim. of obs. *quib*].

quick (kwik) *a.* alive; living; smart; animated; sprightly; ready or prompt; sensitive; rapid; hasty; impatient; fresh and invigorating; pregnant;—*n.* sensitive flesh under nails; part of the tissue keenly susceptible to pain; (*Fig.*) one's tenderest susceptibilities; living plants collectively;—*adv.* also **quick'ly**, rapidly; speedily; promptly; with haste.—**quick'ness** *n.*—**quick'en** *v.t.* to make alive; to make active or sprightly; to hasten; to sharpen or stimulate;—*v.i.* to become alive; to move with greater rapidity.—**quick'ener** *n.*—**quick'ening** *n.* a making or becoming quick; first movement of foetus in womb.—**quick'lime** *n.* unslaked lime, any carbonate of lime, as chalk, limestone, oyster-shells, etc. deprived of its carbonic acid.—**quick'sand** *n.* sand, readily yielding to pressure, esp. if loose and mixed with water.—**quick'set** *n.* a living plant, esp. hawthorn, planted as a hedge;—*a.* formed, as a hedge, of living plants.—**quick'silver** *n.* mercury.—**quick′step** *n.* a march at rate of 120 paces a minute; a lively dance; a quick foxtrot [O.E. *cwic*, alive].

quid (kwid) *n.* a portion suitable for chewing, esp. of tobacco; a cud [form of *cud*].

quid (kwid) *n.* (*Slang*) a pound sterling.—*pl.* **quid** [etym. unknown].

quiddity (kwid′i-ti) *n.* a trifling nicety; a quibble; the essence of anything; a subtlety [L. *quidditas* fr. *quid*, what?].

quidnunc (kwid′nungk) *n.* a gossip; a busybody [L. = what now?].

quiesce (kwī-es′) *v.i.* to become still or silent.—**quiescent** (kwī-es′ẹnt) *a.* still; inert; motionless; at rest.—**quies'cently** *adv.*—**quies'cence, quies'cency** *n.* [L. *quiescere*, to rest].

quiet (kwī′ẹt) *a.* still; peaceful; not agitated; placid; of gentle disposition; not showy;—*n.* calm; peace; tranquillity;—*v.t.* to reduce to a state of rest; to calm; to allay or appease; to soothe;—*v.i.* to become quiet.—**qui'eten** *v.t.* and *i.* to quiet.—**qui'etly** *adv.*—**qui'etness** *n.*—**qui'etude** *n.* freedom from noise, disturbance, alarm; tranquillity; repose.—**quietus** (kwī-ē′tus) *n.* final acquittance, of debt, etc.; (*Fig.*) extinction [L. *quietus*].

quietism (kwī′et-izm) *n.* a mystic religious doctrine, based on the theory that Christian perfection is attained by the passive contemplation of God [L. *quies*, rest].

quiff (kwif) *n.* curl plastered down on a man's forehead [possibly conn. with *coif*].

quill (kwil) *n.* a large, strong, hollow feather of the goose, swan, crow, etc.; this used as a pen; a pen; a spine or prickle, as of a porcupine; a piece of small reed on which weavers wind thread; the tube of a musical instrument; an implement for striking the strings of certain instruments;—*v.t.* to plait or form into small ridges [etym. uncertain].

quilt (kwilt) *n.* bed-coverlet made of two pieces of material sewn together, filled with padding and stitched across in patterns; any thick, warm coverlet;—*v.t.* to stitch together, like a quilt, with a soft filling; to pad [L. *culcita*, a cushion].

quinary (kwī′nạ-ri) *a.* consisting of, or arranged in, fives [L. *quinque*, five].

quince (kwins) *n.* a hard, yellow, acid fruit, somewhat like an apple [Fr. *coing*; L. *cydonium*; fr. *Cydonia*, a city in Crete].

quincentenary (kwin-sen-tē′nạ-ri, kwin-sen′te-nạ-ri) *n.* a five-hundredth anniversary. Also **quingente'nary** [L. *quinque*, five; *centum*, a hundred].

quincunx (kwin′kungks) *n.* an arrangement, esp. of trees, by fives, one being placed at each corner and one in the middle of a square.—**quincun'cial** *a.* [L.].

quinine (kwi-nēn′, kwi-nīn′) *n.* a bitter alkaloid obtained from various species of cinchona bark; it is used as a tonic and febrifuge.—**quin'ic** *a.* [Peruv. *kina*, bark].

quinqu(e)- (kwin′kw(e)), *prefix* fr. L. *quinque*, five.

quinquagesima (kwin-kwạ-jes′i-mạ) *n.* a period of fifty days.—**Quinquagesima Sunday**, the Sunday before Ash Wednesday, so called because fifty days before Easter [L. *quinquagesimus*, fiftieth].

quinquennial (kwin-kwen′i-ạl) *a.* occurring once in five years, or lasting five years.—**quinquenn'ially** *adv.*—**quinquenn'iad, quinquenn'ium** *n.* a period of five years [L. *quinque*, five; *annus*, a year].

quinquereme (kwin′kwe-rēm) *n.* an ancient

galley with five tiers of rowers [L. *quinque*, five; *remus*, an oar].

quinsy (kwin′zi) *n.* a severe inflammation of the throat accompanied by fever and suppuration of the tonsils [Gk. *kunanchē*, fr. *kuōn*, a dog; *anchein*, to choke].

quintal (kwin′tạl) *n.* a weight of 100 or 112 lb.; a hundredweight; the modern French quintal is 100 kilograms, i.e. 220 lbs. [Fr. through Arab. fr. L. *centum*, a hundred].

quintessence (kwin-tes′ẹns) *n.* among the Pythagoreans, the fifth essence in natural bodies, in addition to the four elements, earth, air, fire, water; the pure essence of anything; essential part of a thing.—**quintessen′tial** *a.* [L. *quinta essentia*, fifth essence].

quintet, quintette (kwin-tet′) *n.* (*Mus.*) a composition for five voices or instruments; a company of five singers or players; a set of five [L. *quintus*, fifth].

quintillion (kwin-til′yun) *n.* a number produced by involving a million to the fifth power; a unit with 30 ciphers following; in French and American notation, a unit with 18 ciphers [fr. L. *quintus*, fifth, and after the analogy of billion].

quintuple (kwin′tū-pl) *a.* multiplied by five; fivefold;—*v.t.* to make fivefold; to multiply by five.—**quin′tuplet** *n.pl.* five children at a birth (*Colloq.* **quins**) [fr. L. *quintus*, fifth, by imit. of quadruple].

quip (kwip) *n.* a smart, sarcastic turn of phrase; a gibe; a witty saying [L. *quippe*, forsooth (ironical)].

quire (kwīr) *n.* See **choir**.

quire (kwīr) *n.* 24 sheets of writing-paper, the twentieth part of a ream; twenty-four sheets of the same size, each having a single fold [O.Fr. *quaier*, fr. L. *quattuor*, four].

quirk (kwẹrk) *n.* sudden turn or twist; artful evasion; quibble; a witty saying; knack.—**quirk′ish** *a.*—**quirk′y** *a.* [etym. uncertain].

quirt (kwẹrt) *n.* a kind of riding-whip [Sp. *cuerda*, a rope].

Quisling (kwiz′ling) *n.* Vidkun Quisling (1887-1945) Norwegian politician and head of puppet government during German occupation of Norway (1940-45).—**quis′ling** *n.* a treacherous betrayer of one's country; a collaborator with an enemy.

quit (kwit) *v.t.* to depart from; to leave; to cease from; to give up; to let go; to conduct (oneself); (*Arch.*) to requite; to satisfy a claim; (*Arch.*) to acquit;—*v.i.* to depart; to stop doing a thing;—*a.* released from obligation; free.—*pr.p.* **quitt′ing**.—*pa.p.* and *pa.t.* **quitt′ed**.—**quitt′ance** *n.* discharge from a debt of obligation; acquittance; receipt; requital.—**quitt′er** *n.* (*Colloq.*) a person easily discouraged.—**quit′rent** *n.* a rent paid by a landholder in lieu of service.—**to be quits**, to be equal with another person by repayment (of money, of good, or evil) [O.Fr. *quiter*, fr. L. *quietare*, to calm].

quitch-grass (kwich′gras) *n.* dog-grass or couch-grass [form of *quick*].

quite (kwīt) *adv.* completely; wholly; entirely; totally; to a considerable extent; positively [M.E. *quite*, free].

quiver (kwiv′ẹr) *n.* a case or sheath for holding arrows.—**quiv′erful** *n.* (*Fig.*) a numerous family [O.Fr. *cuivre*, fr. Ger.].

quiver (kwiv′ẹr) *v.i.* to shake with a tremulous motion; to tremble; to shiver;—*n.* the act of quivering; a tremor; a shiver [O.E. *cwifer*, to risk].

qui vive? (kē-vēv′) *n.* who goes there? the challenge of a French sentinel.—**to be on the qui vive**, to be on the alert [Fr. = long live who? *i.e.* on whose side are you?].

Quixote (kwiks′ot) *n.* the hero of the great romance of Miguel Cervantes (1547-1616).—**quixot′ic** *a.* like Don Quixote; ideally and extravagantly romantic.—**quixot′ically** *adv.*—**quix′otism**.—**quix′otry** *n.*

quiz (kwiz) *n.* a puzzle or riddle; a hoax or jest; one who quizzes others; an odd or eccentric person; a game in which two sides answer questions on general knowledge.—*pl.* **quiz′zes**.—*v.t.* to puzzle; to tease; to eye rudely or contemptuously; to interrogate.—**quiz′zer** *n.*—**quiz′zical** *a.*—**quiz′zing-glass** *n.* a monocle [etym. unknown].

quod (kwod) *n.* a quadrangle or court, as in a prison; hence (*Slang*), a prison.

quoif (koif) *n.* See **coif**.

quoin (koin) *n.* (*Archit.*) the external angle, esp. of a building; a corner-stone; (*Gun.*) a metallic wedge inserted under the breech of a gun to raise it; (*Print.*) a small wooden wedge used to lock the types in the galley, etc. [Fr. *coin*, a corner].

quoit (koit) *n.* a flat, iron ring to be pitched at a fixed object in play;—*pl.* game of throwing these on to a peg;—*v.i.* to play at quoits [etym. unknown].

quondam (kwon′dam) *a.* former; that was once; sometime [L. = formerly).

quorum (kwō′rum) *n.* the number of members that must be present at a meeting to make its transactions valid [L.].

quota (kwō′ta) *n.* a proportional part or share [L. *quot*, how many?].

quote (kwōt) *v.t.* to copy or repeat a passage from; to cite; to state a price for; —*n.* (*Slang*) a quotation;—*pl.* quotation marks.—**quotation** (kwō-tā′shun) *n.*—**quota′tion-marks** *n.pl.* marks used to indicate beginning and end of a quotation [Late L. *quotare*, to distinguish by numbers, fr. L. *quot*, how many?].

quoth (kwoth) *v.t.* said; spoke (used only in the 1st and 3rd persons) [O.E. *cwethan*, to say].

quotidian (kwō-tid′i-ạn) *a.* daily;—*n.* thing returning daily, esp. fever [L. *quotidie*, daily].

quotient (kwō′shẹnt) *n.* number resulting from division of one number by another [L. *quotiens*, how many times?].

R

rabbet (rab′et) *n.* a groove made so as to form, with a corresponding edge, a close joint;—*v.t.* to cut with such an edge [O.Fr. *raboter*, to plane].

rabbi (rab′i, rab′ī), **rabbin** (rab′in) *n.* a Jewish teacher of the Law.—**rabbin′ic(al)** [Heb. = my master].

rabbit (rab′it) *n.* a small, burrowing rodent mammal, like the hare, but smaller; (*Slang*) a duffer; a poor performer at sport;—*v.i.* to hunt rabbits.—**rabb′it-hutch** *n.* a box for rearing tame rabbits.—**rabb′itry, rabb′it-warr′en** *n.* the breeding-place of wild rabbits [etym. uncertain].

rabble (rab′l) *n.* a noisy, disorderly crowd; the common herd;—*v.t.* to mob; to hustle.—**rabb′lement** *n.* tumult; rabble [etym. unknown].

rabdomancy (rab′do-mạn-si) *n.* divination by rods or wands [Gk. *rhabdos*, rod; *manteia*, divination].

Rabelaisian (rab-ẹ-lā′zi-ạn) *a.* pert. to *Rabelais* (c. 1495-1553), exuberantly and coarsely humorous.

rabid (rab′id) *a.* furious; fanatical; affected with rabies.—**rab′idly** *adv.*—**rab′idness, rabid′ity** *n.* [L. *rabidus*].

rabies (rā′bēz) *n.* canine madness; hydrophobia.—**ra′bious** *a.* raging; furious [L. fr. *rabere*, to be mad].

raccoon, racoon (rạ-kòòn′) *n.* one of a genus of plantigrade carnivorous mammals of N. America, of the bear family [Algonquin].

race (rās) *n.* the descendants of a common ancestor; distinct variety of human species; a peculiar breed, as of horses, etc.; lineage; descent.—**ra′cial** *a.* pert. to race or lineage.—**rac′ially** *adv.*—**ra′cialism, race′hat′red** *n.* animosity shown to peoples of different race [It. *razza*].

race (rās) *n.* running; swift progress; rapid motion; a contest involving speed; a strong current of water esp. leading to a water-wheel which it drives; the steel rings of an anti-friction ball-bearing;—*v.t.* to cause to run rapidly;—*v.i.* to run swiftly; of an engine, pedal, etc., to move rapidly and erratically. —**ra'cer** *n.* one who races; a racehorse, yacht, car, etc., used for racing.—**race'course, race'ground** *n.* ground for horse-races.—**race'horse** *n.* a horse bred to run for a stake or prize.—**race'track** *n.* a track used for dog-racing.—**rac'ing** *n.* [O.N. *ras*, a swift course].

raceme (ra'sēm) *n.* an inflorescence in which the flowers are produced on subsidiary branches borne on the main stem, as in the fox-glove.—**racemed'** *a.* having racemes [L. *racemus*, a cluster].

rachis (rā'kis) *n.* an axial structure, such as vertebral column in animals, the stem of a plant, a quill, etc.—*pl.* **ra'chides.**—**rachit'ic** *a.* rickety.—**rachitis** (ra-kī'tis) *n.* rickets [Gk. *rhachis*, the spine].

rack (rak) *n.* an instrument for stretching; an instrument of torture by which the limbs were racked to point of dislocation; hence, torture; an open framework for displaying books, bottles, hats, baggage, etc.; a framework in which hay is placed; a straight cogged bar to gear with a toothed wheel to produce linear motion from rotary motion, or vice-versa;—*v.t.* to stretch almost to breaking point; to overstrain; to torture; to extort excessive rent; to place in a rack.—**racked** *a.* —**rack'ing** *a.* agonising (pain).—**rack'rent** *n.* an excessive rent [Dut. *rak*, fr. *rekken*, to stretch].

rack (rak) *n.* thin, driving clouds; ruin; destruction;—*v.i.* to drift, as vapour [Scand. *rak*, *rek*, wreck, drift].

racket, racquet (rak'et) *n.* bat used in tennis, etc.;—*pl.* a ball game played in a paved court with walls; a snow-shoe [Fr. *raquette*].

racket (rak'et) *n.* a confused, clattering noise; din; an occupation by which much money is made illegally;—*v.i.* to make noise or clatter. —**racketeer'** *n.* U.S. slang for one who blackmails business men; a gangster [etym. uncertain].

racoon See **raccoon.**

racquet See **racket.**

racy (rā'si) *a.* having a strong flavour; spicy; pungent.—**ra'cily** *adv.*—**ra'ciness** *n.*

radar (rā'dår) *n.* radiolocation or apparatus used in it (fr. initial letters of *ra*dio, *d*etection, *a*nd *r*anging).

raddle (rad'l), **reddle** (red'l) *n.* a form of red ochre;—*v.t.* to mark sheep with raddle; to paint with rouge.—**radd'ler** *n.* [fr. *ruddle*].

raddle (rad'l) *v.t.* to interweave; to beat;—*n.* a fence made of interwoven branches [etym. uncertain].

radial (rā'di-al) *a.* pert. to a ray, radius, or radium; branching out like spokes of a wheel [L. *radius*, a ray].

radian (rā'di-an) *n.* in plane trigonometry the unit of circular measure, the angle subtended at the centre of a circle by an arc equal in length to the radius (= 57°.3).

radiant (rā'di-ant) *a.* emitting rays; beaming; radiating;—*n.* (*Astron.*) point in sky from which a shower of meteors appears to come; (*Opt.*) luminous point from which rays of light emanate.—**ra'diance, ra'diancy** *n.* radiant intensity; brilliancy; splendour.—**ra'diantly** *adv.* [L. *radius*, a ray].

radiate (rā'di-āt) *v.i.* to branch out like the spokes of a wheel; to emit rays; to shine;—*v.t.* to emit rays, as heat, etc.—*a.* formed of rays diverging from a centre; radially symmetrical.—**radia'tion** *n.* emission and diffusion of rays from central point.—**ra'diator** *n.* any device which radiates or emits rays of heat or light; apparatus for heating rooms by means of steam or hot water; in motoring, apparatus to split up and cool circulating water in water-cooling system [L. *radius*, a ray].

radical (rad'i-kal) *a.* pert. to the root; original; basic; complete; thorough; of extreme or advanced liberal views;—*n.* a root; a primitive word; a politician who advocates thorough reforms; (*Chem.*) a basal atomic group of elements which passes unchanged through a series of reactions of the compound of which it is a part; (*Bot.*) a radicle; a rootlet; (*Math.*) a quantity expressed as the root of another.—**Rad'icalism** *n.* root and branch political reform.—**rad'ically** *adv.*—**rad'icalness** *n.* [L. *radix*, a root].

radicle (rad'i-kl) *n.* (*Med.*) the initial fibril of a nerve; (*Bot.*) the primary root of an embryo plant; any rootlet [L. *radix*, a root].

radio- (rā'di-ō) *prefix* used in formation of compound terms referring to the *radius* of the forearm.—**ra'dio-car'pal** *a.* pert. to radius and wrist.—**ra'dio-mus'cular** *a.* pert. to radius and muscles.—**ra'dio-ul'nar** *a.* pert. to radius and ulna [L. *radius*, a ray].

radio- (rā'di-ō) *prefix* used in the formation of compound terms with the meaning 'of rays,' 'of radiation,' 'of radium,' as in—**ra'dio-ac'tive** *a.* emitting invisible rays which penetrate matter.—**ra'dio-activ'ity** *n.*—**ra'dio-el'ement** *n.* metallic chemical element having radio-active properties.—**ra'diograph** *n.* an instrument for measuring and recording the intensity of the heat given off by the sun; a photograph taken by means of Röntgen rays.—**radiog'rapher** *n.* —**radiog'raphy** *n.*—**radiol'ogy** *n.* the science of radio-activity in medicine.—**radiol'ogist** *n.*—**radios'copy** *n.* examination by X-rays.—**radiother'apy, ra'diotherapeu'tics** *n.* treatment of disease by radium or X-rays [L. *radius*, a ray].

radio (rā'di-ō) *n.* wireless telephony or telegraphy; wireless; broadcasting; apparatus for reception of broadcast; a radio telegram.—**ra'diogram** *n.* a telegram transmitted by radio; a combination of radio receiver and gramophone.—**ra'dio-loca'tion** *n.* system of locating targets by reflecting radio short-wave beams from their surfaces so as to appear illuminated on a screen; also known as *radar* [L. *radius*, a ray].

radish (rad'ish) *n.* an annual herb with pungent edible root [L. *radix*, a root].

radium (rā'di-um) *n.* a metallic, radio-active element which undergoes spontaneous disintegration, giving off corpuscular and wave radiations [L. *radius*, a ray].

radius (rā'di-us) *n.* a straight line from centre of circle to circumference; the spoke of a wheel; a ray; distance from any one place; the bone on the thumb side of forearm; movable arm of a sextant.—*pl.* **rad'ii** (L. = a ray].

radix (rā'diks) *n.* a root; source; origin; a radical; (*Anat.*) the point of origin of a structure, as the root of a tooth; (*Math.*) fundamental base of system of logarithms or numbers [L. = root].

radon (rā'don) *n.* a gaseous, radio-active element, formed by the disintegration of radium, formerly known as *niton*; radium emanation.

raff (raf) *n.* a promiscuous heap; the mob; a worthless fellow.—**raf'fish** *a.*—*cf.* **riff-raff** [O. Fr. *raffer*, to snatch].

raffia (råf'i-a) *n.* the fibre from a cultivated palm used for mats, baskets, etc. Also **ra'phia** [Native].

raffle (raf'l) *n.* a lottery in which several persons subscribe towards or beyond the value of an article, the ultimate possessor being decided by lot;—*v.t.* to sell by raffle.—**raff'ler** *n.* [orig. a dicing game, Fr. *rafle*].

raft (raft) *n.* an improvised float of planks fastened together; a mass of logs chained together for easy transportation down a river;—*v.i.* to proceed by raft [O.N. *raptr*].

rafter (raft'er) *n.* a sloping beam, from the ridge to the eaves, to which the roof-covering is attached;—*v.t.* to provide with rafters [O.E. *raefter*].

rag (rag) *n.* a fragment of cloth; a remnant; a patch; (*Slang*) a newspaper;—*pl.* mean or tattered attire;—*a.* made of rags.—**rag'amuffin** *n.* a ragged, dirty and disreputable person.—**rag'man, rag'picker** *n.* one who collects rags.—**rag'tag** *n.* the rabble; riff-raff. —**rag'time** *n.* popular dance music, of Negro origin, marked by strong syncopation;—*a.* farcical.—**rag'wort** *n.* a common roadside plant with bright, yellow flowers [O.E. *ragg*].

rag (rag) *v.t.* to tease; to torment; to play practical jokes on; to nag;—*v.i.* to be noisy and riotous.—*pr.p.* **ragg'ing.**—*pa.t.* and *pa.p.* **ragged.**—*n.* a disorderly row (esp. by university students) [etym. uncertain].

rage (rāj) *n.* violent excitement; extreme anger; craze; fashion;—*v.i.* to be furious with anger; to rave; to proceed violently and without check (as a storm, battle, etc.).—**ra'ging** *a.* —**ra'gingly** *adv.* [Fr. fr. L. *rabies*, madness].

ragged (rag'ed) *a.* worn to tatters; dressed in rags; jagged; slip-shod; imperfectly performed; not rhythmical.—**ragg'edly** *adv.*—**ragg'edness** *n.*—**ragged robin,** the cuckoo-gillyflower, a crimson-flowered wild plant, with a reddish hairy stem.

raglan (rag'lạn) *n.* an overcoat with wide sleeves running up to the neck, not to the shoulders [fr. Lord *Raglan*, 1788-1855].

ragout (rạ-gòò') *n.* fragments of meat, stewed and highly seasoned; a hash [Fr.].

raid (rād) *n.* a hostile incursion depending on surprise and rapidity; surprise visit by police to suspected premises; an attack on a town by hostile aircraft;—*v.t.* to make a sudden attack upon.—**raid'er** *n.* [var. of *road*].

rail (rāl) *n.* a piece of timber or metal extending from one post to another, as of a fence or balustrade; bars of steel on which the flanged wheels of vehicles run; a track for locomotives; a railway; a horizontal bar for support; top of ship's bulwarks;—*v.t.* to enclose with rails; to send by railway.—**rail'chair** *n.* an iron piece fastened to a sleeper and holding a rail in position.—**rail'head** *n.* farthest point to which rails have been laid; (*Mil.*) a railway depot.—**rail'ing** *n.* material for rails;—*pl.* an open iron-protection or form of fence of upright iron-bars joined by horizontal bars.—**rail'road** *n.* railway.—**rail'way** *n.* a road on which steel rails are laid for wheels to run on; a system of such rails [O.Fr. *reille*, fr. L. *regula*, a rule].

rail (rāl) *n.* wading-birds including **land'-rail** or corn-crake; **wat'er-rail,** coot and moor-hen [Fr. *râle*].

rail (rāl) *v.i.* to use insolent and reproachful language; to utter abuse; to reproach.—**rail'er** *n.*—**rail'lery** *n.* good-humoured banter; chaff; ridicule; rallying [Fr. *railler*].

raiment (rā'mẹnt) *n.* clothing; dress; apparel [for *arraiment*, fr. *array*].

rain (rān) *n.* condensed moisture, falling in drops from clouds; a shower;—*v.t.* and *v.i.* to fall as rain; to pour down like rain.—**rain'bow** *n.* arch showing seven prismatic colours and formed by refraction and reflection of sun's rays in falling rain in part of sky opposite sun.—**rain'cloud** *n.* a nimbus.—**rain'coat** *n.* a light, rainproof overcoat.—**rain'fall** *n.* a fall of rain; the amount of rain, in inches, or centimetres, which falls in a particular place in a given time.—**rain'gauge** *n.* an instrument for the scientific measuring of rainfall.—**rain'iness** *n.*—**rain'less** *a.*—**rain'proof** *a.* impervious to rain.—*n.* an over-garment from shower-proof cloth.—**rain'storm** *n.*—**rain'tight** *a.* impervious to rain.—**rain'y** *a.* [O.E. *regn*].

raise (rāz) *v.t.* to cause to rise; to elevate; to promote; to build up; to collect; to produce by cultivation; to rear; to institute; to levy; to enliven; to give up (siege); to heighten (voice);—*n.* an ascent; (*Colloq.*) an increase in wages.—**rais'able** *a.*—**raised** *a.* elevated.—**rais'ing** *n.*—**to raise Cain, a dust, the devil, hell,** etc., to make a scene.—**to raise the wind,** to obtain ready-money [O.N. *reisa*].

raisin (rā'zn) *n.* a dried grape [O.Fr. *raizin* fr. L. *racemus*, a bunch of grapes].

raj (rạj) *n.* sovereignty; rule; dominion.—**ra'jah, ra'ja** *n.* king, prince, or noble of Hindu race [Hind. *raja*].

rake (rāk) *n.* a long-handled implement with a cross-bar toothed for smoothing earth, gathering leaves, etc.; an agricultural machine used in hay-making;—*v.t.* and *v.i.* to scrape with a toothed implement; to draw together, as mown hay; to sweep or search over; to ransack; to scour; to fire shot lengthwise into a ship, etc.—**a rake off** (*Colloq.*) a monetary commission, esp. if illegal [O.E. *raca*].

rake (rāk) *n.* a dissolute man of fashion; a libertine.—**rake'hell** *n.* a debauched fellow; a roué.—**ra'kish** *a.*—**ra'kishly** *adv.* [M.E. *rakel*, corrupt, of *rake-hell*].

rake (rāk) *n.* an angle of inclination; the inclination of masts from the perpendicular; the projection of the upper parts of the stem and stern beyond the keel of a ship;—*v.i.* to incline from perpendicular.—**ra'kish** *a.* having a backward inclination of the masts; stylish or speedy-looking.—**ra'kishly** *adv.* [Scand. *raka*, to reach].

rally (ral'i) *v.t.* and *v.i.* to re-assemble; to collect and restore order, as troops in confusion; to recover (strength, health); to return a ball (in tennis.)—*pr.p.* **rall'ying.**—*pa.t.* and *pa.p.* **rall'ied.**—*n.* act of rallying; assembly; outdoor demonstration; lively exchange of strokes in tennis [Fr. *rallier*].

rally (ral'i) *v.t.* to attack with raillery; to tease; —*n.* banter [Fr. *railler*].

ram (ram) *n.* male sheep; a tup; a swinging beam with a metal head for battering; a hydraulic engine; a beak projecting from bow of warship; (*Astron.*) Aries, one of the signs of zodiac;—*v.t.* to consolidate loose material with a rammer; to drive against with violence; to butt; to cram; to press down.—*pr.p.* **ram'ming.**—*pa.t.* and *pa.p.* **rammed** [O.E. *ram*].

Ramadan (ràm'ạ-dàn) *n.* the ninth month of the Mohammedan year, when Moslems may not eat between dawn and sunset. Also **Ram'adhan, Rham'azan** [Ar. = the hot month].

ramble (ram'bl) *v.i.* to walk without definite route; to talk or write incoherently;—*n.* a short stroll or walk.—**ram'bler** *n.* one who rambles; a climbing-rose.—**ram'bling** *a.* wandering [etym. uncertain].

rambustious (ram-bus'tyus) *a.* (*Slang*) boisterous; noisy. Also **rambunc'tious.**

ramify (ram'i-fī) *v.t.* and *v.i.* to branch out in various directions.—*pa.p.* **ram'ified.**—**ramifica'tion** *n.* a branch; any sub-division proceeding from a main structure [L. *ramus*, a branch; *facere*, to make].

rammer (ram'ẹr) *n.* one who, or that which, rams [fr. *ram*].

ramose, ramous (rā'mōs, -mus) *a.* branched, as a stem or root; consisting of branches [L. *ramus*, a branch].

ramp (ramp) *v.i.* to climb, as a plant; to creep up; to leap; to rear up on hind legs; to frolic; to rage;—*n.* a leap; a bound; a romp; a gradual slope; mechanical device for lifting bodily motor cars, etc. from ground [Fr. *ramper*, to climb].

ramp (ramp) *n.* a bare-faced swindle [etym. uncertain].

rampage (ram-pāj') *n.* a state of excitement or passion, as **on the rampage;**—*v.i.* to rush about, in a rage; to act violently.—**rampa'geous, rampac'ious** *a.*—**rampa'geously** *adv.*—**rampa'geousness** *n.* [fr. *ramp*].

rampant (ramp'ạnt) *a.* leaping; rearing; climbing; violent; luxuriant; rank; (*Her.*) erect on one of the hind-legs.—**ramp'ancy** *n.* [Fr. *ramper*, to climb].

rampart (ram'part) *n.* mound of earth around fortified place; that which provides security; —*v.t.* to strengthen with ramparts [Fr. *rempart*].

ramrod (ram′rod) *n.* rod used in ramming down charge of a gun; a rod for cleaning barrel of a rifle, etc. [fr. *ram.*].
ramshackle (ram′shak-l) *a.* tumble-down; rickety; beyond repair; crazy. Also **ram′shackled, ram′shackly**—*v.t.* and *v.i.* to rummage about; to ransack; to search for (formerly *ransackle*]. See **ransack.**
ramstam (ram′stam) *a.* rash; impetuous;—*adv.* headlong [*ram* and *stamp*].
ran (ran) *pa.t.* of **run.**
rana (rå′nå) *n.* (*fem.* **ra′nee**) the title of the ruling prince in some parts of India [Hind.].
ranch (ranch) *n.* prairie land in America for sheep- and cattle-rearing; a farm;—*v.i.* to keep a ranch.—**ranch′er** *n.* a man employed on ranch [Sp. Amer. *rancho*, a grazing farm].
rancid (ran′sid) *a.* having a rank smell; smelling or tasting like stale fat; tainted.—**ran′cidly** *adv.*—**ran′cidness, rancid′ity** *n.* [L. *rancidus*].
rancour (rang′kur) *n.* bitter and inveterate ill-feeling.—**ran′corous** *a.* evincing intense and bitter hatred; malignant.—**ran′corously** *adv.* [L. *rancor*].
rand (rand) *n.* border, margin; thin inner sole; strip of flesh or leather; high land above river valley, as **The Rand** in Transvaal [O.E. *rand*, a border].
random (ran′dum) *a.* done haphazardly; aimless; fortuitous;—*n.* in phrase, **at random,** haphazard [O.Fr. *randon*, headlong rush].
randy (ran′di) *a.* riotous; disorderly; lusty [fr. *rant*].
ranee, rani (rån′ē) *n.* in India, a queen or wife of a prince. See **rana.**
rang (rang) *pa.t.* of **ring.**
range (rānj) *v.t.* to set in a row; to rank; to rove over;—*v.i.* to extend; to roam; to be in line with; to pass from one point to another; to fluctuate between, as prices, etc.;—*n.* a rank; a row; a block of buildings; a long and wide kitchen stove; line of mountains; compass or register of voice or instrument; distance to a target; place for practice shooting; pasture land; a ranch.—**range′find′er** *n.* optical instrument for finding distance to given objective.—**rang′er** *n.* keeper of park or forest; Girl Guide aged 16 and upwards; dog which beats the ground for game.—**rang′ers** *n.pl.* a body of mounted troops.—**ran′gy** *a.* roaming; roomy; in Australia, hilly [Fr. *ranger*, fr. *rang*, a rank].
rani See **ranee.**
rank (rangk) *n.* row or line; soldiers standing side by side; grade in armed services; status; a class; social position; title; eminence; relative position;—*pl.* common soldiers;—*v.t.* to arrange in class, order, or division; to place in line or abreast; to take rank over;—*v.i.* to be placed in a rank or class; to possess social or official distinction.—**rank′er** *n.* commissioned officer risen from ranks.—**rank′ing** *n.* arrangement; disposition [Fr. *rang*].
rank (rangk) *a.* growing too thickly; exuberant; offensively strong of smell; rancid; gross; vile; excessive.—**rank′le** *v.i.* to be inflamed; to become more violent; to remain a sore point with.—**rank′ly** *adv.*—**rank′ness** *n.* [O.E. *ranc*, strong, proud].
ransack (ran′sak) *v.t.* to search thoroughly; to plunder [O.N. *rannsaka*].
ransom (ran′sum) *n.* a price paid for release of prisoner; immense sum of money;—*v.t.* to redeem from captivity [O.Fr. fr. L. *redemptio*, buying back].
rant (rant) *v.i.* to rave; to talk bombastically and noisily;—*n.* noisy and meaningless declamation; boisterous talk; wild gaiety.—**rant′er** *n.* [O.Dut. *ranten*, to rave].
Ranunculus (ra̤-nung′kū-lus) *n.* plants belonging to **Ranuncula′ceae,** including crowfoot, buttercup, etc.—*pl.* **Ranun′culi** [L. = a little frog, as supposed to grow where frogs abound].
rap (rap) *n.* a smart, light blow; a knock on door, etc.; a tap;—*v.t.* and *v.i.* to deliver a smart blow; to knock;—*pr.p.* **rap′ping.**—*pa.t.* and *pa.p.* **rapped** [prob. imit.].
rap (rap) *v.t.* to seize forcibly and violently; to snatch; to hurry away; to transport out of oneself [L. *rapere*, to seize].
rap (rap) *n.* an Irish coin, counterfeited and current during the reign of George I, hence the expression, **not worth a rap** [contr. of Ir. *rapparee*, a robber].
rapacious (ra̤-pā′shus) *a.* subsisting on prey; greedy; grasping.—**rapa′ciously** *adv.*—**rapa′ciousness, rapa′city** *n.* [L. *rapere*, to seize].
rape (rāp) *n.* carnal knowledge of a female against her will; the act of snatching or carrying off by force;—*v.t.* to ravish or violate [L. *rapere*, to seize].
rape (rāp) *n.* an annual of the cabbage family, the seeds of which yield vegetable oils [L. *rapum*, turnip].
raphia See **raffia.**
rapid (rap′id) *a.* very quick; fast; speedy; hurried; descending steeply.—**rap′ids** *n.pl.* part of a river where current rushes over rocks or through narrow gorge.—**rapid′ity** *n.*—**rap′idly** *adv.*—**rap′idness** *n.* [L. *rapidus*].
rapier (rā′pi-e̤r) *n.* a light, slender, pointed sword, for thrusting only [Fr. *rapière*].
rapine (rap′in) *n.* act of plundering; spoliation; pillage; plunder; depredation [L. *rapina*, fr. *rapere*, to snatch].
rapport (ra-por′) *n.* harmony; agreement.—**en rapport,** in relation to; in harmony with [Fr.].
rapprochement (ra-prosh′mong) *n.* reconciliation; restoration of friendly relations, esp. between States [Fr.].
rapscallion (rap-skal′yun) *n.* a scamp; a rascal. See **rascall′ion.**
rapt (rapt) *a.* snatched away; intent; transported; in a state of rapture.—**rap′ture** *n.* extreme joy; ecstasy; bliss; exultation.—**rap′turous** *a.* ecstatic; exulting.—**rap′turously** *adv.* [L. *rapere, raptum*, to snatch away].
Raptores (rap-tō′rēz) *n.pl.* an order of preying birds, as eagles, hawks, owls, etc.—**rapto′rial, rapto′rious** *a.* rapacious; living upon prey.
rare (rār) *a.* underdone (of meat) [O.E. *hrer*].
rare (rār) *a.* uncommon, few and far between; thin, not dense, as air; extremely valuable; of the highest excellence; singular.—**rarefac′tion** *n.* act of rarefying; decrease of quantity of a gas in fixed volume.—**rarefy** (rar′e-fī or rā′re-fī) *v.t.* to make rare or less dense;—*v.i.* to become less dense;—*pa.p.* **rar′efied.**—**rare′ly** *adv.*—**rare′ness** *n.*—**rar′ity** *n.* state of being rare; thinness; something rare or seldom seen [L. *rarus*].
rarebit (rār′bit) *n.* (*Cookery*) a Welsh rabbit; a delicacy [corrupt. of *rabbit*].
rascal (ras′ka̤l) *n.* a rogue; a scoundrel; a trickster; a scamp;—*a.* mean; low.—**ras′calism, rascal′ity** *n.* knavery; base villainy.—**rascall′ion** *n.* a low, mean wretch.—**ras′cally** *a.* [O.Fr. *rascaille*, the rabble].
rase (rāz) *v.t.* See **raze.**
rash (rash) *a.* quick; rapid; without reflection; precipitate.—**rash′ly** *adv.*—**rash′ness** *n.* [Dut. *rasch*, quick].
rash (rash) *n.* a temporary, superficial eruption of the skin [O.Fr. *rasche*, itch].
rasher (rash′e̤r) *n.* a thin slice of bacon [Fr. *arracher*, to tear up].
rasp (rasp) *v.t.* to rub or file; to scrape (skin) roughly; to speak in grating manner; to irritate;—*n.* a form of file with one side flat and the other rounded; a rough, grating sound.—**rasp′ing** *a.* emitting a harsh, grating sound; irritating.—**rasp′ingly** *adv.* [O.Fr. *rasper*].
rasp (rasp) *n.* contr. of *rasp*-berry.—**rasp′berry** *n.* a plant, cultivated for its fruit; a small drupe, the fruit of the plant; (*Slang*) derisory applause [E. *rasp*, rough, like a file].
raster (ras′te̤r) *n.* in television, rectangular illumination formed on screen of cathode ray tube by scanning rays [Fr. *raser*, to scrape].

rat (rat) *n.* large rodent; one who deserts his party; one who works at less than established wage;—*v.i.* to hunt rats; to abandon party or associates in times of difficulty.—*pr.p.* **rat'ting.** —*pa.t.* and *pa.p.* **rat'ted.**—**rat'ter** *n.* a rat-catcher; a terrier which kills rats.—**rat'tery** *n.* apostasy.—**rat'ting** *n.* [O.E. *raet*].

ratable See **rate.**

ratafia (rat-a-fē´a) *n.* a liqueur, such as curaçoa; a cordial or flavouring essence, compounded with oil of almonds or peach and cherry kernels; sweet biscuit [Fr.].

ratan See **rattan.**

rataplan (rat´a-plong') *n.* the beat of a military side-drum [Fr. imit.].

ratch (rach) *n.* a ratchet; a ratchet-wheel.—**ratch'et** *n.* a bar or piece of mechanism turning at one end upon a pivot, while the other end falls into teeth of wheel, allowing the latter to move in one direction only; a mechanical contrivance whereby, by means of a spindle rotated by a ratchet-wheel, a to-and-fro movement is converted into a circular movement, as on braces, drills, jacks, screw-drivers, etc.—**ratch'et-wheel** *n.* a circular wheel having angular teeth, into which a ratchet may drop to prevent wheel from running back [Fr. *rochet*, ratchet of a clock].

rate (rāt) *n.* established measure; degree; standard; proportion; ratio; value; price; movement, as fast or slow;—*pl.* local taxation;—*v.t.* to estimate value; to settle relative scale, rank, or position of; to levy rates from; —*v.i.* to be set in a class, as a ship; to have rank.—**rat'able, rate'able** *a.* liable to payment of local rates.—**ratabil'ity** *n.*—**rat'al** *a.* pert. to rates.—**rat'ing** *n.* assessment; (*Naut.*) an enlisted seaman; tonnage class of a racing yacht. —**rate'payer** *n.* one assessed for local rates [O.Fr. fr. L. *rata (pars)*, fixed portion].

rate (rāt) *v.t.* to take to task; to chide; to scold; to reprove [etym. uncertain].

rath (ràth) *a.* and *adv.* early; premature; betimes; speedily.—Also **rathe** (rāth).—**rath'ly** *adv.* suddenly [O.E. *hrathe*, quickly].

rather (ràTH´er) *adv.* preferably; on the other hand; somewhat [O.E. *hrathe*, quickly].

ratify (rat´i-fī) *v.t.* to confirm or sanction officially; to make valid;—*pa.p.* **rat'ified.**—**ratifica'tion** *n.* [L. *ratus*, fixed; *facere*, to make].

ratine (ra´tēn) *n.* See **ratteen.**

rating See **rate.**

ratio (rā´shi-ō) *n.* relation one quantity has to another, as expressed by number of times one can be divided by the other; proportion; rate; degree [L.].

ratiocinate (rash-i-os´i-nāt) *v.i.* to reason; to argue.—**ratiocina'tion** *n.* deductive reasoning from premises.—**ratioc'inative, ratioc'inatory** *a.* [L. *ratiocinari*, to reckon].

ration (rā´shun, ra´shun) *n.* fixed allotted portion; daily allowance of food, drink, etc., to armed forces;—*pl.* provisions;—*v.t.* to limit to fixed amount [Fr. fr. L. *ratio*].

rational (rash´on-al) *a.* sane; sensible; reasonable; equitable; fair; just; (*Math.*) a quantity expressed in finite terms or whose root is a whole number.—**rationa'le** *n.* logical basis; exposition of principles.—**rationalisa'tion** *n.* in psychology, the attempt to square one's conscience by inventing specious reasons for one's own conduct; in business, industry, commerce, the unification of control for buying, producing and distributing goods, to secure greater efficiency and profits.—**rat'ionalise** *v.t.* —**rat'ionalism** *n.* philosophy which makes reason the sole guide; system opposed to supernatural or divine revelation.—**rat'ionalist** *a.*—**rationalist'ic(al)** *a.*—**rationalist'ically** *adv.* —**rational'ity** *n.* the power or faculty of reasoning; soundness of mind.—**rat'ionally** *adv.*—**rat'ionalness** *n.* [L. *rationalis*, fr. *ratio*, reason].

ratline, ratlin, rattling (rat´lin) *n.* (*Naut.*) one of the horizontal lines of the rope-ladder for climbing the rigging.

ratsbane (ratz´bān) *n.* a poison for rats and mice, arsenious acid mixed with bran.

rattan, ratan (ra-tan') *n.* a species of palm found in India and the Malay Peninsula; a walking-stick made from a rattan-cane [Malay, *rotan*].

ratteen, ratine (ra-tēn') *n.* a kind of thick woollen stuff, quilted or twilled [Fr. *ratine*].

rattle (rat´l) *v.i.* to clatter; to speak (on), eagerly and noisily; to move along, quickly and noisily;—*v.t.* to shake briskly, causing sharp noises; to disconcert, or ruffle;—*n.* a rapid succession of clattering sounds; loud, rapid talk or talker; a toy for making a noise. —**ratt'le-brained, -head'ed, -pa'ted** *a.* empty-headed; giddy; lacking stability.—**ratt'le-snake** *n.* an American poisonous snake.—**ratt'ling** *n.* clattering;—*a.* smart; brisk; lively; first-rate;—*adv.* extremely; very [M.E. *ratelen*].

rattling See **ratline.**

ratty (rat´i) *a.* (*Slang*) irritable; angry.

raucous (raw´kus) *a.* hoarse; harsh; rough.—**rau'cously** *adv.* [L. *raucus*].

ravage (rav´āj) *v.t.* to lay waste; to despoil; to plunder; to sack;—*n.* ruin; destruction [Fr.].

rave (rāv) *v.i.* to talk in delirium or with great enthusiasm.—**ra'ver** *n.*—**ra'ving** *n.* delirium; incoherent or wild talk;—*a.* delirious; distracted.—**ra'vingly** *adv.* [O.Fr. *raver*].

ravel (rav´el) *v.t.* to entangle; to make intricate; to fray out;—*v.i.* to become twisted and involved; to fall into confusion.—*pr.p.* **rav'elling.** —*pa.t.* and *pa.p.* **rav'elled.**—*n.* complication; entanglement [Dut. *ravelen*].

ravelin (rav´lin) *n.* in fortification, the detached outwork which protected the salient of a bastion [Fr. fr. It. *rivellino*].

raven (rāv´n) *n.* crow with glossy black plumage predatory in habit;—*a.* glossy black, esp. of hair [O.E. *hraefn*].

raven, ravin (rav´n) *v.t.* and *v.i.* to obtain by violence; to devour; to prowl for prey; to be ravenous;—*n.* rapine; plunder; spoil.—**rav'ener** *n.* a plunderer.—**rav'enous, rav'ined** *a.* famished; voracious; eager for prey.—**rav'enously** *adv.* [Fr. *ravir*, fr. L. *rapere*, to seize].

ravine (ra-vēn') *n.* a deep, narrow gorge; a gully [O.Fr. fr. L. *rapere*, to carry off].

ravish (rav´ish) *v.t.* to seize and carry away by violence; to violate; to deflower; to enrapture; to charm eye or ear.—**rav'isher** *n.*—**rav'ishing** *a.* entrancing; captivating.—**rav'ishingly** *adv.* —**rav'ishment** *n.* [Fr. *ravir*, fr. L. *rapere*, to carry off].

raw (raw) *a.* not cooked; not covered with skin; bleak; chilly and damp; unpractised; not manufactured.—*n.* a sore; a gall.—**raw´boned** *a.* having little flesh; gaunt.—**raw´hide** *n.* compressed untanned leather; a riding-whip of coarse, untanned leather thongs.—**raw'ly** *adv.*—**raw'ness** *n.*—**raw deal,** unfair and undeserved treatment [O.E. *hreaw*].

ray (rā) *n.* a narrow beam of light; the path along which light and electro-magnetic waves travel in space; a heat radiation; one of a number of lines diverging from a common point or centre; a gleam or suggestion (of hope, truth, etc.);—*v.t.* and *v.i.* to radiate; to send forth rays.—**rayed** *a.* having rays [O.Fr. *raye*, fr. L. *radius*, a beam].

ray (rā) *n.* a flat-fish allied to skate, shark, and dog-fish [O.Fr. *raye*].

rayon (rā´on) *n.* a synthetic fibrous material in imitation of silk [Fr.].

raze, rase (rāz) *v.t.* to level to the ground; to destroy completely; to demolish; to wipe out; to delete; to erase; to graze (the skin) [Fr. *raser*, fr. L. *radere*, *rasum*, to scrape].

razor (rā´zur) *n.* a keen-edged cutting appliance for shaving.—**ra'zor´back** *n.* kind of hog; rorqual or fin-backed whale.—**ra'zor-bill** *n.* N. Atlantic sea-bird, of Auk family.—**ra'zor-shell** *n.* mollusc bivalve with razor-shaped shell [Fr. *rasoir*, fr. L. *radere*, *rasum*, to scrape].

razure (rāz′ūr) *n.* erasure.
razzle (raz′l) *n.* (*Slang*) a drunken spree. Also **razz'le-dazz'le**.
re-, (rē) *prefix* used in the formation of compound words, usually signifying *back* or *again* [L.].
re (rē) *prep.* in reference to; concerning.—**in re**, in the case (of) [L. *res*, thing].
reach (rēch) *v.t.* to extend; to stretch; to touch by extending hand; to attain to or arrive at; to come to; to obtain; to gain;—*v.i.* to stretch out the hand; to strain after; to be extended; to arrive;—*n.* reaching; easy distance; mental range; scope; grasp; straight stretch of water [O.E. *raecan*, to stretch out].
react (rē-akt′) *v.i.* to respond to stimulus; to exercise a reciprocal effect on each other; to resist the action of another body by an opposite effect; (*Chem.*) to cause or undergo a chemical or physical change when brought in contact with another substance or exposed to light, heat, etc.—**reac'tance** *n.* (*Elect.*)resistance in a coil to an alternating current due to capacitance or inductance in the circuit.—**reac'tion** *n.* action in opposite direction to another; the response to stimulus; revulsion of feeling.—**reac'tionary** *a.* tendency to reaction.—*n.* one opposed to progressive ideas in politics, religion, thought, etc.—**reac'tionist** *n.* a reactionary.—**reactiva'tion** *n.* the restoration of an atom or molecule to an activated state.—**reac'tive** *a.* having the power to react.
re-act (rē′akt) *v.t.* to act again; to repeat.
reactor (rē-act′or) *n.* apparatus for generating heat by nuclear fission.
read (rēd) *v.t.* to peruse and understand written or printed matter; to interpret mentally; to read and utter; to understand any indicating instrument (as a gas-meter);—*v.i.* to perform the act of reading; to find mentioned in writing or print; to surmise.—*pa.t.* and *pa.p.* **read** (red).—**read** (rēd) *n.* a reading; perusal.—**read** (red) *a.* versed in books; learned.—**read'able** (rēd) *a.* well written; informative; interesting; legible.—**read'ably** (rēd) *adv.*—**read'er** (rēd) *n.* one who reads; one whose office is to read prayers; a university lecturer; one who determines suitability for publication of manuscripts offered to publisher; corrector of printer's proofs; a reading-book.—**read'ing** (rēd) *a.* pert. to reading;—*n.* act of reading; a public recital of passages from books; interpretation of a book; formal recital of a bill or enactment.—**reading room**, room for silent reading and study [O.E. *raedan*, to make out].
readdress (rē-a̤-dres′) *v.t.* to address again.
readily, readiness See **ready.**
readjust (rē-a̤-just′) *v.t.* to adjust or put in order again.—**readjust'ment** *n.*
ready (red′i) *a.* prepared; fitted for use; handy; prompt; quick; willing; easy; familiar; apt; glib;—*adv.* in state of preparation; beforehand;—*n.* position of a fighting unit or their weapons, as *at the ready*.—**read'ily** *adv.*—**read′iness** *n.*—**read'y-made** *a.* not made to measure.—**ready money**, cash in hand.—**read'y-reck'oner** *n.* a book of tabulated calculations [O.E. *raede*].
reagent (rē-ā′je̤nt) *n.* any substance, generally in a solution, employed to bring about a characteristic reaction in chemical analysis.—**rea'gency** *n.*
real (rē′a̤l) *a.* actual; not sham; not fictitious or imaginary; not assumed; unaffected; (*Law*) heritable; denoting property not movable or personal, as lands and tenements.—**real'ity** *n.* actuality; fact; truth; (*Law*) realty.—**re'ally** *adv.* actually; indeed;—*interj.* is that so?—**re'altor** *n.* dealer in real estate.—**re'alty** *n.* immobility or fixed permanent nature of real property.—**real estate, real property**, immovable property, covering freehold lands and buildings, proprietary rights in or over lands, as mineral rights [L.L. *realis*, fr. L. *res*, a thing].
real (rē′a̤l, rā-àl′) *n.* an obsolete Spanish coin [Sp. fr. L. *regalis*, royal].
realise (re′a̤l-īz) *v.t.* to make real; to yield (profit); to convert into money; to apprehend or grasp the significance of.—**realisa'tion** *n.*—**re'alism** *n.* regarding things as they are; practical outlook on life; representation in art or letters of real life, even if sordid and repellent; (*Philos.*) doctrine that matter has a separate existence apart from conceptions of it in the mind; doctrine that general terms and ideas have objective existence and are not mere names.—**re'alist** *n.*—**realis'tic** *a.* pert. to realism; actual; factual; practical; true to life.—**realis'tically** *adv.* [Fr. *réaliser*].
reality, realtor, realty See **real** (1).
realm (relm) *n.* kingdom; province; region [O.Fr. *realme*, fr. L. *regalis*, royal].
ream (rēm) *n.* a paper measure containing from 472 to 516 sheets, usually 480 sheets (20 quires) [Ar. *rizmah*, bundle].
ream, reem (rēm) *v.t.* to enlarge or make a tapered or conical hole with a reamer.—**ream'er** *n.* a machine-tool for enlarging a hole [O.E. *rum*, room].
reap (rēp) *v.t.* to cut down ripe grain for harvesting; to harvest; to receive as fruits of one's labour.—**reap'er** *n.* a harvester; a reaping-machine [O.E. *ripan*].
reappear (rē-a̤-pēr′) *v.i.* to appear a second time.—**reappear'ance** *n.* a second appearance.
rear (rēr) *n.* back or hindmost part; part of army or fleet behind the others.—**rear'most** *a.* last of all; at the very back.—**rear′ad'miral** *n.* lowest rank of admiral.—**rear'guard** *n.* troops detailed to protect main body from rear attacks.—**rear'ward** *n.* the rearguard; the hind or latter part;—*a.* in, or to, the rear [L. *retro*, behind].
rear (rēr) *v.t.* to raise; to bring to maturity, as young; to breed, as cattle; to erect or build;—*v.i.* to rise up on the hindlegs, as a horse [O.E. *raeran*].
rearm (rē-arm′) *v.t.* to equip the fighting services with new types of weapons of offence and defence.—**rearm'ament** *n.*
rearmost See **rear.**
rearmouse See **reremouse.**
rearrange (rē-a̤-rānj′) *v.t.* to arrange anew; to set in a different order.—**rearrange'ment** *n.*
reason (rē′zn) *n.* faculty of thinking; power of understanding; intelligence; the logical premise of an argument; cause; motive; purpose; excuse;—*v.i.* to exercise rational faculty; to deduce from facts or premises; to argue with;—*v.t.* to discuss by arguments.—**rea'sonable** *a.* rational; just; fair.—**rea'sonableness** *n.*—**rea'sonably** *adv.*—**rea'soner** *n.*—**rea'soning** *n.*—**in reason**, in moderation; reasonable [Fr. *raison*, fr. L. *ratio*, reason].
reassemble (rē-a̤-sem′bl) *v.t.* and *v.i.* to assemble or bring together again.
reassure (rē-a̤-shòór′) *v.t.* to free from fear; to allay anxiety; to restore confidence, or spirit to.—**re′assure'** *v.t.* to re-insure against loss.—**reassur′ance, re'assur'ance** *n.* confirmation repeated; further insurance to cover risk accepted by insurance-broker.—**reassur'ing** *a.* comforting.
reave, reaver See **reive.**
rebate (re-bāt′) *v.t.* to blunt; to allow as discount;—*n.* deduction; discount [Fr. *rabattre*, to beat down].
rebate (rē-bāt′) *n.* a groove cut into edge of a piece of timber or placed in a surface; a recess in a wall to receive a door or window-frame, etc.
rebec, rebeck (rē′bek) *n.* a crude musical instrument, the forerunner of the viol [O.Fr. fr. Ar. *rebab*].
rebel (reb′e̤l) *n.* one who resists the lawful authority of a government; insurgent; revolter; revolutionist; one who is defiant;—*a.* rebellious.—**rebel** (re-bel′) *v.i.* to take up arms against state or government; to revolt.—*pr.p.* **rebel'ling.**—*pa.t.* and *pa.p.* **rebelled'.**—**rebell'ion**

n. organised resistance to authority; insurrection; mutiny.—**rebell'ious** *a.*—**rebell'iously** *adv.* —**rebell'iousness** *n.* [L. *rebellare,* fr. *bellum,* war]. [volume.—**rebound'** *n.* and *a.*
rebind (rē-bīnd') *v.t.* to bind anew, esp. a
rebirth (rē-bẹrth') *n.* state of being born again, spiritually; reincarnation; renaissance, as in the Rebirth of Learning.
rebore (rē-bōr') *v.t.* to smooth and enlarge the bores of the cylinders of an internal combustion engine.—**rebor'ing** *n.*
rebound (rē-bound') *v.i.* to leap back; to recoil; to bound repeatedly; to reverberate;—*v.t.* to cause to fly back;—*n.* rebounding; recoil.
rebuff (re-buf') *n.* a blunt, contemptuous refusal; a snub; a repulse;—*v.t.* to beat back; to check; to snub [It. *rebuffo,* reproof].
rebuke (re-būk') *v.t.* to censure; to reprove; to reprimand; to find fault with;—*n.* reprimand; reproof; severe talking to [O.Fr. *revuchier,* repulse].
rebus (rē'bus) *n.* an enigmatical representation of a name, word, or phrase by pictures suggesting syllables [L. = by things].
rebut (re-but') *v.t.* to butt or drive back; to refute; to repel; to disprove;—*pr.p.* **rebut'ting.** —*pa.t.* and *pa.p.* **rebut'ted.**—**rebut'table** *a.*—**rebut'tal** *n.* refutation of an argument [Fr. *revoutier,* to repulse].
recalcitrate (re-kal'si-trāt) *v.i.* to kick back; to be refractory.—**recal'citrant** *n.* one who defies authority;—*a.* refractory; wilfully disobedient. —**recal'citrance, recalcitra'tion** *n.* [L. *recalcitrare,* to kick back].
recall (rē-kawl') *v.t.* to call back; to take back (a gift, etc.); to annul or revoke; to call to mind; to remember;—*n.* act of recalling; a summons to return, often tantamount to dismissal from office; an encore.
recant (re-kant') *v.t.* to take back, words or opinions; to retract;—*v.i.* to unsay. —**recanta'tion** *n.* [L. *recantare,* fr. *re-,* back; *cantare,* to sing].
recapitulate (rē-kạ-pit'ū-lāt) *v.t.* to relate in brief the matter or substance of a previous discourse;—*v.i.* to sum up what has been previously said.—**recapitula'tion** *n.* recapitulating; a summary.—**recapit'ulative, recapit'ulatory** *a.* [L. *capitulum,* a small head].
recapture (rē-kap'tūr) *v.t.* to capture back; to regain;—*n.* act of retaking.
recast (rē-kȧst') *v.t.* to cast or mould again; to remodel; to throw back; to add up figures in a column, a second time.
recede (re-sēd') *v.i.* to move or fall back; to retreat; to withdraw; to retire; to retrograde; to ebb.—**reced'ing** *a.*
receipt (rē-sēt') *n.* the act of receiving; a written acknowledgment of money received; a place where moneys are officially received; a prescription; a recipe in cookery;—*pl.* cash-drawings;—*v.t.* to give a receipt for [L. *recipere, receptum,* to receive].
receive (re-sēv') *v.t.* to take; to accept; to get (an offer, etc.); to acquire; to welcome or entertain; to hold; to experience; to take or buy stolen goods.—**receiv'able** *a.*—**receiv'er** *n.* one who receives; receptacle, place of storage, etc.; one who is convicted of receiving goods knowing them to have been stolen; officer appointed by Bankruptcy Court to receive profits of business being wound up by that court; (*Chem.*) a vessel into which spirits are emitted from the still in distillation; a wireless receiving set; ear-piece of a telephone; a vessel for containing gases.—**receiv'ing** *n.* [O.Fr. fr. L. *recipere,* to take back].
recension (re-sen'shun) *n.* a critical revisal of a text; a revised edition [L. *recensere,* to revise].
recent (rē'sẹnt) *a.* that has lately happened; new; (*Geol.*) of the Post-Tertiary period.—**re'cently** *adv.*—**re'centness** *n.* [L. *recens*].
recept (rē'sept) *n.* a mental conception arising from repeated sensuous impressions.—**recep'tacle** *n.* a vessel—that which receives, or into which anything is received and held [L. *recipere, receptum,* to receive].
reception (rē-sep'shun) *n.* receiving; welcome; ceremonial occasion when guests are personally announced; the quality of signals received in broadcasting.—**recep'tible** *a.* receivable.—**recep'tionist** *n.* official in hotel, office, etc., who receives guests or clients.—**recep'tive** *a.* able to grasp ideas or impressions quickly.—**recep'tiveness, receptiv'ity** *n.* [L. *recipere, receptum,* to receive].
recess (rē-ses') *n.* a withdrawing or retiring; suspension of business; vacation, as of legislative body or school; a retired place; a niche or cavity in a wall; (*Zool.*) a small cleft or indentation in an organ.—**recessed'** *a.* fitted with recess.—**reces'sion** *n.* act of receding or withdrawing; a period of reduced trade or business.—**reces'sional** *a.* pert. to recession;—*n.* hymn sung as clergyman leaves chancel.—**recess'ive** *a.* receding.—**recess'iveness** *n.* [L. *recessus,* fr. *recedere,* to recede].
recharge (rē-charj') *v.t.* to charge again; to reload a gun, etc.
recherché (rẹ-sher'shā) *a.* of studied elegance; choice; exquisite; exclusive [Fr.].
recipe (res'i-pe) *n.* a prescription; a cookery receipt [L. imperative = take thou!].
recipient (re-sip'i-ẹnt) *a.* receptive;—*n.* one who receives [L. *recipere,* to receive].
reciprocal (re-sip'ro-kạl) *a.* moving backwards and forwards; alternating; mutual; complementary; (*Gram.*) reflexive;—*n.* idea or term alternating with, or corresponding to, another by contrast or opposition; quantity arising from dividing unity by any quantity;—*pl.* two numbers which multiplied give unity, e.g. $\frac{5}{8} \times \frac{8}{5} = 1$.—**recip'rocally** *adv.*—**recip'rocalness** *n.*—**recip'rocate** *v.t.* to make return for; to interchange;—*v.i.* to move backwards and forwards; to act interchangeably; to alternate.—**recip'rocating** *a.* applied to mechanism of which the parts move backwards and forwards alternately. Also **recip'rocatory.**—**reciproca'tion** *n.* mutual giving and receiving.—**recip'rocative** *a.*—**reciprocity** (res-i-pros'i-ti) *n.* action and reaction; the discharge of mutual duties or obligations; in international trade, equal facilities or advantages gained by abolition of prohibitory or protective duties, or by equalising the rates in each country [L. *reciprocus,* turning back].
recision (re-sizh'un) *n.* the act of cutting off or back [L. *recidere, recisum*].
recite (re-sīt') *v.t.* and *v.i.* to repeat aloud esp. before an audience.—**reci'tal** *n.* act of reciting; what is recited; detailed narration; a musical or dramatic performance by one person or by one composer or author.—**recita'tion** *n.* reciting; repetition of poem from memory.—**recitative'** *n.* declamation to musical accompaniment, as in opera;—*a.* in the style of recitative.—**reci'ter** *n.* [L. *recitare,* to read aloud].
reck (rek) *v.t.* and *v.i.* to take account (of); to heed; to care (for).—**reck'less** *a.* rashly negligent.—**reck'lessly** *adv.*—**reck'lessness** *n.* [O.E. *reccan,* to care for].
reckon (rek'n) *v.t.* and *v.i.* to count; to calculate; to estimate; to value; to think; to be of opinion.—**reck'oner** *n.* one who reckons; table of calculations (usu. **ready reckoner**).—**reck'oning** *n.* computing; calculation; way of thinking [O.E. *gerecenian,* to explain].
reclaim (rē-klām') *v.t.* to call back; to demand the return of; to bring into a state of productiveness, as waste land, etc.; to win back from error or sin.—**reclaim'able** *a.* able to be reclaimed or reformed.—**reclaim'ably** *adv.*—**reclama'tion** *n.*
recline (re-klīn') *v.t.* to lean back;—*v.i.* to assume a recumbent position; to repose; to rest.—**reclin'er** *n.* [L. *reclinare*].
recluse (re-klōōs') *a.* secluded from the world; solitary;—*n.* an anchorite; a hermit.—**reclu'sion** *n.* [L. *reclusus,* shut away].

recognise (rek′og-nīz) *v.t.* to know again; to identify; to acknowledge; to treat as valid; to notice; to realise; to salute.—**recognis′able** *a.* capable of being recognised.—**recognis′ably** *adv.* —**recog′nisance** *n.* acknowledgment of a person or thing; avowal; an obligation, under penalty, entered into before some court or magistrate to do, or to refrain from doing, some particular act; sum pledged as surety.—**recogni′tion** *n.* recognising; acknowledgment.—**recog′nitive, recog′nitory** *a.* [L. *recognoscere*].

recoil (re-koil′) *v.i.* to start, roll, bound, fall back; to draw back; to rebound;—*n.* return motion; a starting or falling back [Fr. *reculer*, to spring back].

recollect (rek′o-lekt) *v.t.* to recall; to remember.—**recollec′tion** *n.* recollecting; power of recalling ideas to the mind; remembrance; memory.—**recollec′tive** *a.* [L. *recolligere*, to collect again].

recommend (rek-o-mend′) *v.t.* to speak well of; to commend to one's care; to entrust; to approve; to praise.—**recommend′able** *a.* worthy of recommendation.—**recommenda′tion** *n.* recommending; a statement that one is worthy of favour or trial.—**recommend′atory** *a.*

recompense (rek′om-pens) *v.t.* to repay; to reward; to make an equivalent return for service, loss, etc.; to make up for; to punish; —*n.* repayment; requital [Fr. *récompenser*].

reconcile (rek-on-sīl′) *v.t.* to conciliate anew; to restore to friendship; to make agree; to become resigned (to); to adjust or compose. —**rec′oncilable** *a.*—**rec′oncilement, reconcilia′tion** *n.* renewal of friendship; harmonising of apparently opposed ideas, etc.; (*Bib.*) expiation; propitiation; atonement.—**reconcil′iatory** *a.* [L. *reconciliare*].

recondite (rek′on-dīt) *a.* hidden from view or mental perception; obscure; little known.—**recondite′ness** *n.* [L. *reconditus*, hidden away].

recondition (rē-kon-dish′un) *v.t.* to restore to sound condition, either person or thing; to renovate; to repair; to refit.

reconnaissance (re-kon′ā-sans) *n.* an examination or survey, by land or air, for engineering or military operations [Fr.].

reconnoitre (rek-on-noi′ter) *v.t.* to make a preliminary survey of, esp. with a view to military operations;—*v.i.* to make reconnaissance; to scout;—*n.* a preliminary survey [Fr. *reconnoître*, old spelling of *reconnaître*, to recognise].

reconsider (rē-kon-sid′er) *v.t.* to consider again; to take up for renewed discussion.

reconstitute (rē-kon′sti-tūt) *v.t.* to constitute anew; to reconstruct; to restore a dehydrated substance to original form.—**reconstit′uent** *a.*—**reconstitu′tion** *n.*

reconstruct (rē-kon-strukt′) *v.t.* to rebuild; to enact (crime) on actual spot, in course of judicial proceedings.—**reconstruc′tion** *n.*

record (re-kord′) *v.t.* to commit to writing; to make a note of; to register (a vote); to inscribe; to make a sound record;—*v.i.* to speak, sing, etc. for reproduction on a gramophone record. —**record** (rek′ord) *n.* register; authentic copy of any writing; personal history; list; catalogue; finest performance or highest amount ever known; a disc, cylinder, roll, etc. for mechanical reproduction of sound;—*pl.* public documents.—**recor′der** *n.* one who registers writings or transactions; (*Law*) the chief judicial officer of a city or borough, presiding over the Quarter Sessions; apparatus for registering data, by some form of symbol or line; instrument which transforms sounds into disc impressions; an ancient, flute-like musical instrument.—**recor′ding** *n.* the making, or reproduction of, sound by mechanical means. —**off the record,** unofficial [L. *recordari*, to remember].

recount (rē-kount′) *v.t.* to count again; to relate; to recite; to enumerate;—*n.* a second enumeration, esp. of votes at election [O.Fr. *reconter*].

recoup (rē-kòòp′) *v.t.* to recover equivalent for what has been lost or damaged; to compensate.—**recoup′ment** *n.* [Fr. *recouper*, to cut again].

recourse (re-kōrs′) *n.* application made to another in difficulty or distress; a resorting to; access [L. *recurrere*, to run back].

recover (re-kuv′er) *v.t.* to get back; to win back; to revive; to cure; to rescue; (*Law*) to obtain (damages) as compensation for loss, etc.;—*v.i.* to regain health or a former state. —**recov′erable** *a.*—**recov′ery** *n.* regaining, retaking, or obtaining possession; restoration to health; amends for a bad start in business, sport, etc. [O.Fr. *recuvrer*, fr. L. *recuperare*].

re-cover (rē-kuv′er) *v.t.* to put a fresh cover on.

recreant (rek′re-ant) *a.* cowardly; craven; false; apostate;—*n.* a craven; an apostate.—**rec′reancy** *n.* [O.Fr. *recroire*, to take back one's pledge].

recreate (rek′rē-āt) *v.t.* to give fresh life to; to restore; to reanimate; to refresh from weariness; to cheer.—**recrea′tion** *n.* recreating; any pleasurable interest; pastime; amusement. —**recrea′tional, recrea′tive** *a.* [L. *recreare*, to make again].

recriminate (re-krim′i-nāt) *v.t.* and *v.i.* to charge an accuser with a similar crime.—**recrimina′tion** *n.* a counter-charge brought by the accused against the accuser; mutual abuse and blame.—**recrim′inative, recrim′inatory** *a.* [L. *re-*, back; *crimen*, charge].

recrudesce (rē-kròò-des′) *v.i.* to break out again; to revive.—**recrudes′cence, recrudes′cency** *n.*—**recrudes′cent** *a.* [L. *recrudescere*, to become raw again].

recruit (re-kròòt′) *v.t.* to repair by fresh supplies; to renew in strength; to enlist persons for army, navy, etc.;—*v.i.* to gain health, spirits, etc.; to obtain new adherents;—*n.* a newly-enlisted soldier; a fresh adherent.—**recruit′al, recruit′ing, recruit′ment** *n.* [O.Fr. *recruter*, fr. L. *recrescere*, to grow again].

rectangle (rek′tang-gl) *n.* a four-sided figure with four right angles.—**rectang′ular** *a.* [L. *rectus*, right, straight; *angulus*, an angle].

rectify (rek′ti-fī) *v.t.* to set right; to correct; to purify; to convert an alternating current of electricity into a direct current;—*pa.t.* and *pa.p.* **rec′tified.**—**rectifi′able** *a.* able to be rectified or set right.—**rectifica′tion** *n.*—**rec′tifier** *n.* one who corrects; a device which rectifies, as a wireless valve, converting alternating current into direct; a transformer; one who refines spirits by repeated distillations [L. *rectus*, straight; *facere*, to make].

rectilineal, rectilinear (rek-ti-lin′e-al, -ar) *a.* consisting of, or bounded by, right lines; straight-lined.—**rectilin′eally** *adv.*—**rectilinear′ity** *n.* [L. *rectus*, straight; *linea*, a line].

rectitude (rek′ti-tūd) *n.* moral uprightness; honesty of purpose [L. fr. *rectus*, right].

recto (rek′tō) *n.* the right-hand page of an open book—opp. to *verso* [L. = on the right].

rector (rek′tor) *n.* clergyman of Church of England who has charge and care of a parish; incumbent of Episcopal church in Scotland or U.S.A.; the head of Exeter and Lincoln Colleges, Oxford; headmaster of certain senior secondary schools in Scotland; nominal head of a Scottish university.—**rec′toral** *a.* pert. to rector or rectory.—**recto′rial** *a.* rectoral;—*n.* in Scottish universities, a rectorial election.—**rec′torate, rec′torship** *n.* the office of rector.—**rec′tory** *n.* house of a rector [L. fr. *regere*, *rectum*, to rule].

rectum (rek′tum) *n.* lower end of the large intestine.—*pl.* **rec′ta.**—**rec′tal** *a.* pert. to the rectum [L. *rectus*, straight].

recumbent (re-kum′bent) *a.* reclining; lying on back.—**recum′bence, recum′bency** *n.*—**recum′bently** *adv.* [L. *recumbere*, to lie down].

recuperate (re-kū′per-āt) *v.i.* to win back health and strength; to convalesce; to recover. —**recupera′tion** *n.* convalescence; slow return to health.—**recu'perative, recu'peratory** *a.* [L. *recuperare*, to recover].

recur (re-kur') *v.i.* to happen again; to return periodically; —*pr.p.* **recur'ring**.—*pa.t.* and *pa.p* **recurred'**.—**recur'rence, recur'rency** *n.*—**recur'rent** *a.* returning periodically [L. *re-*, again; *currere*, to run].

recurve (re-kurv') *v.t.* to bend backwards.

recusant (rek'ū-zant) *a.* obstinate in refusal; specifically, refusing to conform to rites of Established Church;—*n.* dissenter or nonconformist who refuses to conform to authority, esp. in religious matters.—**rec'usance, rec'usancy** *n.* [L. *recusare*, to refuse].

red (red) *a.* (*comp.* **red'der**; *superl.* **red'dest**) of the colour of arterial blood, rubies, glowing fire, etc.; of colour, including shades, as scarlet, crimson, vermilion, orange-red and the like; of or connected with bloodshed, revolution, left-wing politics, etc.;—*n.* colour of blood; a socialist; communist, bolshevist; a Russian soldier; a danger signal.—**red'den** *v.t.* to make red;—*v.i.* to become red; to blush; to flush; to rust.—**red'ly** *adv.*—**red'ness** *n.* state or quality of being red; blushing; rust.—**red admiral**, British butterfly, black with a red band, and white spots on upper wings.—**red Biddy**, a mixture of red wine and methylated spirits.—**red'blood'ed** *a.* having reddish blood; manly.—**red'breast** *n.* the robin.—**red'cap** *n.* a breed of poultry with large rose-shaped comb; military policeman; goblin.—**red'coat** *n.* a British soldier, because of the bright scarlet tunic.—**red corpuscle**, a coloured blood-corpuscle, containing haemoglobin and carrying oxygen.—**Red Cross**, international emblem of organisations for relief of sick and wounded in war-time.—**red'currant** *n.* shrubby bush bearing clusters of small red berries.—**red'deer** *n.* in Britain, the common stag or hind.—**red ensign**, flag of the mercantile marine.—**red flag**, danger signal, as on a railway; national flag of Soviet Russia; international communist anthem.—**red'hack'le** *n.* a red plume, worn on headgear of the Highland regiment, the Black Watch.—**red'hand'ed** *a.* having red hands—hence, in the very act, orig. of a murderer.—**red hat**, a cardinal's hat; a staff officer.—**red'heat** *n.* temperature of a body emitting red rays, about 700°-800° C.—**red herring**, the common herring, cured by drying, smoking and salting; (*Colloq.*) any topic introduced to divert attention from main issue.—**red'hot** *a.* heated to redness; eager; enthusiastic.—**Red'Ind'ian** *n.* a copper-coloured aboriginal native of N. America.—**red'lead** *n.* an oxide of lead, minium, used as a pigment for ironwork.—**red'let'ter** *a.* applied to principal holy saints' days of Church calendar, —hence, any memorable (day).—**red light**, a danger signal on railways and at cross-roads.—**red ochre**, ruddle.—**red pepper**, chillies, such as cayenne pepper.—**red'poll, red'pole** *n.* the smallest British finch, allied to linnet.—**red polls**, hornless cattle, bred in E. Anglia.—**red'shank** *n.* a shore bird of the Plover family.—**red'shirt** *n.* a follower of Garibaldi (1807-82) in Italian wars of independence.—**red'skin** *n.* a N. American Indian.—**red'start** *n.* a resident British song-bird of thrush family.—**red tape**, slavish adherence to official regulations, fr. red tape used for tying up government documents.—**red'wing** *n.* a song-bird, resembling song-thrush.—**red'wood** *n.* any wood yielding a red dye; the sequoia tree of California, a gigantic evergreen coniferous tree.—**to paint the town red**, to indulge in a drunken orgy.—**to see red**, to become infuriated [O.E. *read*].

redact (re-dakt') *v.t.* to digest or reduce to order, literary, or scientific materials.—**redac'tion** *n.*—**redac'tor** *n.* an editor [L. *redigere*, *redactum*, to drive back].

redan (re-dan') *n.* in fortification, a fieldwork having two faces uniting, so as to form a salient angle towards the enemy [O.Fr. *redent*, a double notching].

reddition (re-dish'un) *n.* the act of returning anything.—**redd'itive** *a.* answering [L. *reddere*, to give back].

reddle (red'l) *n.* See **raddle**.

rede (rēd) *v.t.* to advise; expound (riddle, dream);—*n.* advice; counsel; resolve; a proverb.—**rede'less** *a.* with no one to advise; foolish [O.E. *read*].

redeem (re-dēm') *v.t.* to purchase back; to regain, as mortgaged property, by paying principal, interest and costs of mortgage; to take out of pawn; to ransom; to deliver from sin; to make good; to recover.—**redeem'able** *a.*—**redeem'ableness** *n.*—**redeem'er** *n.* [L. *redimere*, to buy back].

redeless See **rede**.

redemption (rē-demp'shun) *n.* redeeming or buying back; deliverance from sin; the Atonement.—**redemp'tionary** *n.* one released from bond or obligation by fulfilment of certain conditions.—**redemp'tioner** *n.* one who has redeemed himself.—**redemp'tive** *a.* redeeming.—**redemp'tory** *a.* paid as ransom; serving to redeem [L. *redimere*, *redemptum*, to buy back].

red-hot poker (red-hot pō'kẹr) *n.* the Kniphofia, ornamental plant of the lily-order, with flame-coloured flowers.

redintegrate (re-din'te-grāt) *v.t.* to make whole again; to renew.—**redintegra'tion** *n.* [L. *redintegrare*, to make whole again].

redirect (rē-di-rekt') *v.t.* to direct again; to re-address a communication.—**redirec'tion** *n.*

redistribute (rē-dis-trib'ūt) *v.t.* to deal out or apportion again.—**redistribu'tion** *n.*

redolent (red'ō-lẹnt) *a.* diffusing a strong or fragrant odour; scented; reminiscent (of).—**red'olence** *n.* [L. *redolere*, to smell strongly].

redoubt, redout (re-dout') *n.* military detached fieldwork, enclosed by earthworks and a high parapet with deep trenches behind and shelter pits; a central part within field fortifications for a final stand by the defenders [Fr. *redoute*, fr. L. *re-*, back; *ducere*, to lead].

redoubtable (re-dou'tạ-bl) *a.* dreaded; formidable; valiant.—**redoubt'ed** *a.* redoubtable [O.Fr. *redouter*, to fear].

redound (re-dound') *v.i.* to contribute or turn to; to conduce (to); to recoil; to react (upon) [L. *re-*, back; *undare*, to surge].

redraft (rē-draft') *v.t.* to draft or draw up a second time;—*n.* a second copy; a new bill of exchange which the holder of a protested bill draws on the drawer or endorses for the amount of the protested bill along with costs and charges.

redress (rē-dres') *v.t.* to make amends for; to set right; to compensate; to adjust; to dress a second time;—*n.* reparation; amendment; relief; remedy.—**redress'er** *n.*—**redress'ible** *a.* [Fr. *redresser*].

reduce (re-dūs') *v.t.* to diminish in number, length, quantity, value, price, etc.; to lower; to degrade; (*Chem.*) to remove oxygen or add hydrogen; to decrease valency number; to separate metal from its ore by heat and chemical affinities; to add electrons to an ion; (*Arith.*) to change, as numbers, from one denomination into another without altering value; to slim; to impoverish; to subdue; to capture (as a fort).—**reduced'** *a.* impoverished.—**reduc'ible** *a.* capable of being reduced.—**reduc'tion** *n.* reducing; subjugation; diminution; curtailment; (*Arith.*) changing numbers from one denomination to another, or changing form of a quantity, without altering value.—**reduc'tive** *a.* having the power of reducing.—**reduc'tively** *adv.*—**reducing agent**, a reagent for abstracting oxygen or adding hydrogen [L. *re-*, back; *ducere*, to lead].

redundant (re-dun'dạnt) *a.* superfluous; serving no useful purpose; using more words than necessary for complete meaning.—**redun'dance, redun'dancy** *n.*—**redun'dantly** *adv.* [L. *redundare*, to overflow].

re-echo (rē-ek'ō) *v.t.* to echo back; to reverberate;—*v.i.* to resound;—*n.* the repetition of an echo.

reed (rēd) *n.* a tall hollow-stemmed grass growing in water or marshes; in certain wind-instruments, a thin strip of cane or metal which vibrates and produces a musical sound; a musical instrument made of the hollow joint of some plant; a pastoral pipe; thatching straw; an arrow; pastoral poetry; a narrow strip of whale-bone;—*pl.* a moulding on the surface of the material consisting of a series of sunk beads without a quirk;—*v.t.* to thatch; to fit with a reed.—**reed'bunt'ing** *n.* the black-headed bunting, frequenting lakes and marshes.—**reed'ed** *a.* covered with reeds; moulded like reeds.—**reed'en** *a.* consisting or made of reeds.—**reed'er** *n.* a thatcher.—**reed'iness** *n.*—**reed'in'strument** *n.* (*Mus.*) a wind-instrument played by means of a reed, as the oboe, English horn, bassoon, clarinet, saxophone, etc.—**reed'pipe** *n.* organ pipe whose tone is produced by vibration of metal tongue.—**reed'stop** *n.* organ stop owing its tone to vibration of little metal tongues enclosed in metal tubes.—**reed'war'bler, reed'wren** *n.* brownish-coloured bird which frequents marshes in South of England.—**reed'y** *a.* abounding with reeds; possessing harsh and thin tone of a reed, as certain voices [O.E. *hreod*].

reedling (rēd'ling) *n.* the bearded titmouse.

reef (rēf) *n.* a portion of a square sail which can be rolled up and made fast to the yard or boom;—*v.t.* to reduce the area of sail by taking in a reef.—**reef'er** *n.* one who reefs; a midshipman; a sailor's close-fitting jacket.—**reef'knot** *n.* (*Naut.*) a square knot; one in which the ends lie parallel with the cord and will not slip [O.N. *rif*, reef, rib].

reef (rēf) *n.* a ridge of rock near the surface of the sea; a lode of auriferous rock; the outcrop of a lode or vein [O.N. *rif*].

reek (rēk) *n.* smoke; vapour; fume;—*v.i.* to emit smoke; to steam.—**reek'ing** *a.* smelling strongly.—**reek'y** *a.* smoky [O.E. *rec*].

reel (rēl) *n.* frame or bobbin on which yarn or cloth is wound; spool for thread; cylinder turning on an axis on which seamen wind the log-lines, and anglers their fishing-line; in cinematography, a flanged spool on which cinema film is wound; a portion of film, usually 1000 feet;—*v.t.* to wind upon a reel; to draw (in) by means of a reel.—**to reel off**, to enumerate or recite rapidly [O.E. *hreol*].

reel (rēl) *v.i.* to stagger; to sway from side to side; to whirl; to be dizzy [O.E. *hreol*].

reel (rēl) *n.* a sprightly dance-tune; a Scottish dance for two or more couples [Gael. *righil*].

reem Same as **ream** (2).

reeve (rēv) *v.t.* to pass line through any hole in a block, cleat, ring-bolt, etc., for the purpose of pulling a larger rope after it (Dut. *reef*, a reef].

reeve (rēv) *n.* official in early English times charged with fiscal and judicial duties, as shire-reeve (sheriff), borough-reeve; a steward [O.E. *gerefa*].

reeve (rēv) *n.* female ruff (or sandpiper).

refection (re-fek'shun) *n.* refreshment; a simple repast; a lunch.—**refec'tory** *n.* a hall in a monastery, convent, school, or college where meals are served [L. *reficere*, *refectum*, to remake].

refer (re-fer') *v.t.* to carry or send back; to transfer to another court; to appeal to; to direct to; to assign to;—*v.i.* to have reference or relation to; to offer, as testimony in evidence of character, qualification, etc.; to allude (to).—*pr.p.* **refer'ring.**—*pa.t.* and *pa.p.* **referred'.**—**ref'erable, refer'rible** *a.* may be referred or assigned to.—**referee'** *n.* an arbitrator; one named by a candidate for a post as willing to give testimony of character, etc.; an umpire; a neutral judge in various sports.—**ref'erence** *n.* appeal to the judgment of another; relation; one of whom inquiries can be made; a passage in a book to which reader is referred; a quotation; a testimonial.—**referen'dum** *n.* a popular vote for ascertaining the national will on a single definite issue.—**referen'tial** *a.* containing a reference; used for reference [L. *re-*, back; *ferre*, to carry].

refine (re-fīn') *v.t.* to purify; to reduce crude metals to a finer state; to clarify; to polish or improve; to free from coarseness, vulgarity, etc.;—*v.i.* to become pure; to improve in accuracy, excellence, or good taste.—**refined'** *a.* purified or clarified; polished; well-bred.—**refin'edly** *adv.*—**refine'ment** *n.*—**refin'ery** *n.* place where process of refining sugar, oil, metals, etc., is effected [Fr. *raffiner*].

reflect (re-flekt') *v.t.* to throw back, esp. rays of light, heat, or sound, from surfaces; to mirror;—*v.i.* to throw back light, heat, etc.; to meditate; to consider attentively.—**to reflect on,** to cast discredit on; to disparage.—**reflec'ted** *a.* cast or thrown back (as light); folded back on itself; reflexed.—**reflect'ible** *a.*—**reflect'ing** *a.* thoughtful; throwing back rays of light, etc.—**reflect'ingly** *adv.*—**reflec'tion** *n.* reflecting; return of rays of heat or light, or waves of sound, from a surface; image given back from mirror or other reflecting surface; in radio, the rebound of waves from the reflecting layers, Appleton or Heaviside-Kennelly, back to earth; meditation; contemplation.—**reflect'ive** *a.* reflecting; meditative; (*Gram.*) reflexive; reciprocal.—**reflect'ively** *adv.*—**reflect'iveness** *n.*—**reflect'or** *n.* a reflecting surface used to alter the direction of rays of light, heat, etc. [L. *reflectere*, to bend back].

reflex (rē'fleks) *a.* turned, bent, or directed backwards; introspective; reflective; reflected; (*Mech.*) produced by reaction; (*Anat.*) denoting the involuntary action of the motor nerves under a stimulus from the sensory nerves; involuntary; automatic;—*n.* reflection; a reflected image; a reflex-action;—*v.t.* to bend back; to reflect.—**reflex'ible, reflect'ible** *a.*—**reflexibil'ity** *n.*—**reflex'ive** *a.* bending or turned backwards; reflective; of certain verbs, whose subject and object are the same person or thing; of pronouns which serve as objects to reflexive verbs, as *myself*, etc.—**reflex'ively** *adv.*—**reflex'ly** *adv.*—**conditioned reflex,** reflex action due to power of association and suggestion [L. *re-*, back; *flectere*, to bend].

reflux (rē'fluks) *n.* a flowing back; ebb;—*a.* **re'fluent.**—**ref'luence, ref'luency** *n.*

reform (rē-form') *v.t.* to form again; to reconstruct; to restore; to reclaim; to amend; to improve; to eliminate (abuse, malpractice);—*v.i.* to amend one's ways; to improve;—*n.* amendment; improvement; rectification; correction.—**refor'mable** *a.*—**reforma'tion** *n.* the act of forming or shaping again; change for the better; religious movement of 16th cent. in which a large section of the church broke away from Rome.—**refor'mative** *a.* forming again; aiming at reform.—**refor'matory** *a.* tending to reform; —*n.* former name for approved school.—**reformed'** *a.* formed again or in a new fashion; amended; reclaimed.—**refor'mer** *n.* one who reforms; an advocate of political reform.—**refor'mist** *n.* a reformer.

refract (re-frakt') *v.t.* to bend sharply back; to cause to deviate from a direct course, as rays of light on passing from one medium to another.—**refrac'table** *a.*—**refrac'ted** *a.*—**refrac'ting** *a.* serving to refract; refractive.—**refrac'tion** *n.*—**refrac'tive** *a.* having power to turn from a direct course; pert. to refraction [L. *re-*, back; *frangere*, *fractum*, to break].

refractory (re-frak'to-ri) *a.* sullen or perverse in opposition or disobedience; suitable for lining furnaces because of resistance to fusion at very high temperatures; (*Med.*) resistent to treatment.—**refrac'torily** *adv.*—**refrac'toriness** *n.* [L. *re-*, back; *frangere*, to break].

refragable (ref'ra-ga-bl) *a.* capable of being refuted, resisted, or opposed.—**refragabil'ity** *n.* [L. *refragari*, to resist].

refrain (re-frān′) *v.t.* to hold back; to restrain; —*v.i.* to abstain.—**refrain′ment** *n.* [L. *refrenare*, to bridle].
refrain (re-frān′) *n.* chorus recurring at end of each verse of song; constant theme [Fr. fr. L. *refringere*, to break off].
refrangible (re-fran′ji-bl) *a.* able to be refracted.—**refrangibil′ity, refran′gibleness** *n.* [L. *re-*, back; *frangere*, to break].
refresh (re-fresh′) *v.t.* to make fresh again; to revive; to renew; to enliven; to provide with refreshment; to freshen up.—**refresh′er** *n.* one who, or that which, refreshes; an extra fee paid to legal counsel, in addition to retaining fee; (*Slang*) a refreshing drink.—**refresh′ing** *a.* invigorating; reviving.—**refresh′ment** *n.* restoration of strength; that which adds fresh vigour, as rest, drink, or food—hence, *pl.* food and drink [O.Fr. *refrescher*].
refrigerate (re-frij′ẹr-āt) *v.t.* to make cold or frozen; to preserve food, etc., by cooling;—*v.i.* to become cold.—**refrigera′tion** *n.*—**refrig′erative, refrig′eratory** *a.* cooling.—**refrig′erator** *n.* apparatus and plant for the manufacture of ice; specially constructed chamber for preserving food by mechanical production of low temperatures [L. *re-*, again; *frigus*, cold].
reft (reft) *pa.p.* of **reave.**
refuge (ref′ūj) *n.* shelter; asylum; retreat; harbour; small platform in a roadway for pedestrians; a street-island;—*v.t.* to shelter; to find shelter for;—*v.i.* to take shelter.—**refugee′** *n.* one who flees to a place of safety [L. *re-*, back; *fugere*, to flee].
refulgent (re-ful′jẹnt) *a.* shining; splendid.—**reful′gence** *n.* splendour. Also **reful′gency** [L. *re-*, again; *fulgere*, to shine].
refund (rē-fund′] *v.t.* to return in payment or compensation for; to repay.—**re′fund** *n.* repayment [L. *re-*, back; *fundere*, to pour].
refurbish (rē-fur′bish) *v.t.* to furbish up again; to retouch; to renovate; to polish up.
refuse (re-fūz′) *v.t.* to deny or reject; to decline; —*v.i.* to decline something offered; not to comply.—**refu′sal** *n.* act of refusing; the first chance of accepting or declining an offer; an option [Fr. *refuser*, fr. L. *recusare*, to decline, to refuse].
refuse (ref′ūs) *a.* rejected; worthless;—*n.* waste matter; garbage; trash [Fr. *refuser*, to refuse].
re-fuse (rē-fūz′) *v.t.* of metals, to fuse or melt again.—**refu′sion** *n.*
refute (re-fūt′) *v.t.* to overthrow by argument; to prove to be false.—**refu′table** *a.* capable of being refuted.—**refu′tably** *adv.*—**refuta′tion** *n.* [L. *refutare*, to repel].
regain (rē-gān′) *v.t.* to recover; to retrieve; to get back; to reach again.
regal (rē′gạl) *n.* a miniature portable reed-organ [Fr. *régale*].
regal (rē′gạl) *a.* pert. to a king; kingly; royal. —**regalia** (re-gā′li-a) *n.pl.* insignia of royalty, as crown, sceptres, orbs, etc.—**regal′ity** *n.* royalty; sovereignty; an ensign of royalty.—**re′gally** *adv.* [L. *regalis*, royal].
regale (re-gāl′) *v.t.* to entertain in sumptuous manner; to refresh;—*v.i.* to feast;—*n.* banquet; feast.—**regale′ment** *n.* refreshment [Fr. *régaler*].
regard (re-gȧrd′) *v.t.* to observe; to gaze; to consider; to pay respect to;—*n.* aspect; esteem; account; gaze; heed; concern;—*pl.* compliments; good wishes.—**regard′able** *a.*—**regard′ful** *a.* heedful.—**regard′fully** *adv.*—**regard′ing** *prep.* concerning—also **in, with, regard to, as regards.**—**regard′less** *a.* without regard; careless; neglectful.—**regard′lessly** *adv.* [Fr. *regarder*].
regatta (re-gat′ạ) *n.* series of races in which yachts, rowing boats, etc. participate [It. orig. a gondola race in Venice].
regency (rē′jẹn-si) *n.* See **regent.**
regenerate (rē-jen′ẹr-āt) *v.t.* and *v.i.* to give fresh life or vigour to; to reorganise; to recreate the moral nature; to cause to be born again;—*a.* born anew; changed from a natural to a spiritual state; regenerated.—**regen′eracy, regenera′tion** *n.*—**regen′erative** *a.* pert. to regeneration.—**regen′eratively** *adv.*
regent (rē′jẹnt) *a.* holding the office of regent; exercising vicarious authority;—*n.* one who governs a kingdom during the minority, absence, or disability of sovereign.—**re′gency** *n.* office and jurisdiction of a regent [L. *regere*, to rule].
regicide (rej′i-sīd) *n.* one who assassinates a king.—**regici′dal** *a.* [L. *rex, regis*, a king; *caedere*, to slay].
régime (rā-zhēm′) *n.* style of rule or management; administration; an ordered mode of dieting [Fr.].
regimen (rej′i-men) *n.* orderly government; systematic method of dieting [L. = rule, government].
regiment (rej′i-mẹnt) *n.* a body of soldiers commanded by a senior officer and consisting of companies, batteries, battalions, or squadrons, according to branch of service;—*v.t.* to form into a regiment; to systematise. **regiment′al** *a.* pert. to a regiment; (*Slang*) very authoritative;—*n.pl.* the uniform worn by troops of a regiment.—**regimenta′tion** *n.* thorough systemisation and control of lives of people without consulting them [L. *regimentum*, government].
region (rē′jun) *n.* territory of indefinite extent; district; part of body; sphere or realm (esp. of abstract speculation);—*pl.* separate parts of the universe.—**re′gional** *a.*—**re′gionally** *adv.* [L. *regio*, a district].
register (rej′is-tẹr) *n.* a written account; an official record; a list; the book in which a record is kept; an alphabetical index; an archive; a catalogue; a roll; a calendar; registrar—as in Scotland, *Lord Clerk Register*, keeper of public archives; a metal damper to close a chimney; any mechanical contrivance which registers or records; (*Mus.*) row of organ pipes with same tone colour; organ stop; compass of a voice or instrument;—*v.t.* to record; to enrol; to lodge a complaint in writing.—**reg′istrable** *a.*—**reg′istered** *a.* enrolled. —**reg′istrant** *n.* one who registers.—**reg′istrar** *n.* an official who keeps a register or record of transactions.—**registra′tion** *n.* entry or record, e.g. of births, etc.; form of insurance of postal packages; the selection of stops by an organist while playing an organ.—**reg′istry** *n.* act of registering; office for registering births, deaths and marriages; agency for supplying domestic servants, etc.—**registered post,** a method of postal delivery by which mail is insured against loss or damage in transit [O.Fr. *registre*].
regius (rē′ji-us) *a.* appointed by the crown; royal.—**regius professor,** one whose chair was founded by Henry VIII. In Scottish Universities, one who receives a crown appointment as professor [L. = royal].
regnal (reg′nạl) *a.* pert. to reign of monarch.—**reg′nancy** *n.* rule; reign; predominance.—**reg′nant** *a.* reigning; ruling by hereditary right [L. *regnare*, to reign].
regress (rē-gres′) *n.* passage back; the power of passing back; re-entry;—*v.i.* to go or fall back; to return to a former state; (*Astron.*) to move from east to west.—**regres′sion** *n.* returning; retrogression; (*Psych.*) diversion of psychic energy, owing to obstacles encountered, into channels of fantasy instead of reality.—**regress′ive** *a.* [L. *regressus*, fr. *regredi*, to go back].
regret (re-gret′) *v.t.* to grieve over; to lament; to deplore;—*pr.p.* **regret′ting.**—*pa.t.* and *pa.p.* **regret′ted.**—*n.* grief; sorrow; remorse.—**regret′ful** *a.*—**regret′fully** *adv.*—**regret′table** *a.* deserving regret; lamentable.—**regret′tably** *adv.* [Fr. *regretter*].
regular (reg′ū-lạr) *a.* conforming to, governed by rule; periodical; symmetrical; orderly; strict habitual; straight; level; natural; standing (army); (*Colloq.*) out and out; belonging to a

monastic order (opp. to *secular*); (*Mus.*) strict; —*n.* a member of any religious order who professes to follow a certain rule (*regula*) of life; a soldier belonging to a permanent, standing army.—**reg′ularise** *v.t.* to make regular.—**regularisa′tion** *n.*—**regular′ity** *n.* conformity to rule; uniformity.—**reg′ularly** *adv.* [L. *regula*, a rule].

regulate (reg′-ū-lāt) *v.t.* to adjust by rule, method, etc.; to dispose; to arrange; to rule; to control.—**regula′tion** *n.* regulating or controlling; state of being reduced to order; a bye-law; an order.—**reg′ulative** *a.* tending to regulate.—**reg′ulator** *n.* one who, or that which, regulates; a mechanical contrivance for regulating motion [L. *regula*, a rule].

regulus (reg′-ū-lus) *n.* golden-crested wren; a mass of partly purified ore; commercially pure metallic antimony [L. = a petty king].

regurgitate (re-gur′-ji-tāt) *v.t.* to throw, flow, or pour back in great quantity;—*v.i.* to be thrown or poured back.—**regurgita′tion** *n.* [L. *re-*, back; *gurges*, a gulf].

rehabilitate (rē-hạ-bil′-i-tāt) *v.t.* to restore to reputation or former position; to reinstate.—**rehabilita′tion** *n.* [L. *re-*, again; *habilitare*, to make fit].

rehash (rē-hash′) *v.t.* to mix together and use or serve up a second time;—*n.* old materials used over again.

rehearse (re-hẹrs′) *v.t.* and *v.i.* to repeat aloud; to practise (play, etc.); to recite; to recapitulate; to narrate.—**rehear′sal** *n.* trial performance of a play, opera, etc. [O.Fr. *rehercer*, to repeat (lit. rake over again)].

Reich (rīH) *n.* German Confederation of States.—**Reichs′tag** *n.* the German parliament. —**Reichswehr** (rīHs′-vār) *n.* German army and navy [Ger.].

reify (rē′-i-fī) *v.t.* to make concrete or real.—**reifica′tion** *n.* [L. *res*, a thing; *facere*, to make].

reign (rān) *n.* royal authority; the period during which a sovereign occupies throne; influence;—*v.i.* to possess sovereign power; to be predominant [O.Fr. *regne*, fr. L. *regnare*, to rule].

reimburse (rē-im-burs′) *v.t.* to refund; to pay back; to give the equivalent of.—**reimburse′ment** *n.*—**reimbur′ser** *n.* [Fr. *rembourser*, fr. *bourse*, a purse].

rein (rān) *n.* strap of bridle to govern a horse, etc.; means of controlling, curbing; restraint; —*pl.* power, or means of exercising power;—*v.t.* to govern with rein or bridle; to restrain [O.Fr. *reine*, fr. L. *retinere*, to hold back].

reincarnate (rē-in-kȧr′-nāt) *v.t.* to embody again in the flesh.—**reincarna′tion** *n.* belief in re-birth of human soul in another physical body; metempsychosis.

reindeer (rān′-dēr) *n.* deer of colder regions.—**rein′deer-moss** *n.* lichen, the winter food of reindeer [O.N. *hreinndyri*].

reinforce (rē-in-fōrs′) *v.t.* to strengthen with new force, esp. of troops or ships; to corroborate.—**reinforce′ment** *n.* reinforcing; additional troops or ships to strengthen fighting forces; steel bar incorporated in reinforced concrete.—**reinforced concrete** *n.* concrete strengthened by the inclusion in it of steel nets, rods, girders, etc. [Fr. *renforcer*].

reins (rānz) *n.pl.* kidneys; loins [L. *renes*].

reinstate (rē-in-stāt′) *v.t.* to restore to former position.—**reinstate′ment** *n.*

reissue (rē-ish′-ū) *v.t.* to issue again; to republish;—*n.* a new issue; a reprint.

reiterate (rē-it′-ẹr-āt) *v.t.* to repeat again and again.—**reit′erant** *a.* reiterating.—**reitera′tion** *n.* —**reit′erative** *n.* and *a.* (*Gram.*) a word, or part of a word, repeated so as to form a reduplicated word.

reive, reave (rēv) *v.t.* to steal; to rob.—*pa.p.* **reft.**—**reiv′er, reav′er** *n.* a robber; a freebooter [O.E. *reafian*, to rob].

reject (re-jekt′) *v.t.* to cast from one; to throw away; to refuse; to put aside; —*n.* a person or thing rejected as not up to standard.—**rejec′table** *a.*—**rejec′tion** *n.* [L. *re-*, back; *jacere*, to throw].

rejoice (re-jois′) *v.t.* to give joy to; to cheer; to gladden;—*v.i.* to exult; to triumph.—**rejoic′ing** *n.* act of expressing joy;—*pl.* public expression of joy; festivities.—**rejoic′ingly** *adv.* [Fr. *réjouir*].

rejoin (rē-join′) *v.t.* to unite again; to meet again; to enter again, as society, etc.;—*v.i.* to reply.—**rejoin′der** *n.* a curt, abrupt reply; a repartee [Fr. *rejoindre*].

rejuvenate (rē-jòò′-ven-āt) *v.t.* to make young again.—**rejuvena′tion** *n.*—**rejuvena′tor** *n.*—**rejuvenesce′** *v.i.* to grow young again.—**rejuvenes′cence** *n.*—**rejuvenes′cent** *a.*—**reju′venise** *v.t.* to rejuvenate [L. *re-*, again; *juvenis*, young].

relapse (re-laps′) *v.i.* to slide back, esp. into state of ill-health, error, evil ways;—*n.* a falling back; a sudden return of grave symptoms after convalescence [L. *relabi*, *relapsus*, to slip back].

relate (re-lāt′) *v.t.* to narrate; to recount; to tell; to establish relation between;—*v.i.* to have relation (to); to refer (to).—**relat′ed** *a.* connected by blood or marriage; allied; akin. —**rela′tion** *n.* telling; account; feeling between persons or nations; connection between things; kindred; connection by consanguinity or affinity; a relative.—**rela′tional** *a.* indicating some relation.—**rela′tionship** *n.* [L. *referre*, *relatum*, to bring back].

relative (rel′-ạ-tiv) *a.* dependent on relation to something else, not absolute; respecting; connected; related; (*Gram.*) noting a relation or reference to antecedent word or sentence;—*n.* a person connected by blood or affinity; a word relating to an antecedent word, clause, or sentence.—**rel′atively** *adv.* comparatively.—**rel′ativeness** *n.*—**relativ′ity** *n.* being relative; doctrine in philosophy that knowledge is not absolute but conditioned; in physics, the doctrine that measurement is conditioned by the choice of co-ordinate axes [fr. *relate*].

relax (re-laks′) *v.t.* to make less severe or stern; to loosen;—*v.i.* to become loosened or feeble; to unbend; to become less severe; to ease up. —**relaxa′tion** *n.* act of relaxing; recreation; mitigation; alleviation.—**relax′ing** *a.* enervating; not bracing [L. *re-*, again; *laxus*, loose].

relay (rē-lā′) *n.* supplies conveniently stored at successive stages of a route; a gang of men, a fresh set of horses, etc., ready to relieve others; a device for making or breaking a local electrical circuit; an electro-magnetic device for allowing a weak signal from a distance to control a more powerful local electrical circuit; a low-powered broadcasting station which broadcasts programmes originating in another station;—*v.t.* to pass on, as a message, broadcast, etc.—**relay race,** a race between teams of which each runner does a part of the distance [Fr. *relais*, a rest].

release (re-lēs′) *v.t.* to set free; to allow to quit; to exempt from obligation; (*Law*) to remit a claim;—*n.* liberation; exemption; discharge; acquittance; a catch for controlling mechanical parts of a machine; (*Law*) a discharge of a right or claim.—**releas′able** *a.* [O. Fr. *relaissier*].

relegate (rel′-e-gāt) *v.t.* to send away; to banish; to consign; to demote.—**relega′tion** *n.* [L. *re-*, back; *legare*, to send].

relent (re-lent′) *v.i.* to give up harsh intention; to yield.—**relent′less** *a.* showing no pity or sympathy.—**relent′lessly** *adv.*—**relent′lessness** *n.* [Fr. *ralentir*, to slacken].

relevant (rel′-e-vạnt) *a.* bearing upon the case in hand; pertinent; appropriate.—**rel′evance, rel′evancy** *n.*—**rel′evantly** *adv.* [L. *relevare*, to raise up].

reliable (re-lī′-ạ-bl) *a.* trustworthy; honest; creditable.—**reliabil′ity, reli′ableness** *n.* quality or state of being reliable.—**reli′ably** *adv.*—**reli′ance** *n.* trust; confidence; dependence.—**reli′ant** *a.* confident; trusting [fr. *rely*].

relic (rel′-ik) *n.* something surviving from the

past; part of body of a saint or martyr, preserved with religious veneration;—*pl.* a corpse; remains of the dead [L. *reliquus,* remaining].

relict (rel′ikt) *n.* widow [L. *relicta,* left behind].

relied (re-līd′) *pa. p.* and *pa.t.* of **rely.**

relief (re-lēf′) *n.* removal or alleviation of pain, distress, or other evil; help; comfort; remedy; one who relieves another at his post; prominence; a sculptured figure standing out from a plane surface.—**relief′map** *n.* a map in clay, etc. showing the elevations and depressions of a country in relief [L. *re-,* again; *levare,* to raise].

relieve (re-lēv′) *v.t.* to set off by contrast; to alleviate; to free from trial, evil, or distress; to release from a post by substitution of another; to remedy; to indemnify; to lighten (gloom, etc.).—**reliev′ing** *a.* serving to relieve. —**relieving officer,** official appointed to superintend relief of poor [L. *re-,* again; *levare,* to raise].

religion (re-lij′un) *n.* belief in supernatural power which governs universe; recognition of God as object of worship; practical piety; any system of faith and worship; reverence; holiness.—**relig′ionist, relig′ionary, relig′ioner** *n.* one who makes inordinate professions of religion. —**religio′sity** *n.* sense of, or tendency towards, religiousness.—**relig′ious** *a.* pert. to religion; pious; teaching religion; conscientious.—**relig′iously** *adv.* [L. *religio*].

relinquish (re-ling′kwish) *v.t.* to give up; to yield; to cede; to resign.—**relin′quisher** *n.*—**relin′quishment** *n.* [L. *relinquere*].

reliquary (rel′i-kwar-i) *n.* a depository or casket in which relics of saints or martyrs are preserved; a shrine [Fr. *reliquaire*].

relish (rel′ish) *v.t.* to taste with pleasure; to like immensely;—*v.i.* to have a pleasing taste; to smack (of); to savour;—*n.* savour; flavour; what is used to make food more palatable, as sauce, seasoning, etc.; appetite; zest; gusto [O.Fr. *reles,* aftertaste].

reluctant (re-luk′tant) *a.* unwilling; disinclined.—**reluct′ance** *n.*—**reluc′tancy** *n.*—**reluc′tantly** *adv.* [L. *reluctari,* to struggle against].

rely (re-lī′) *v.i.* to trust; to depend; to confide; —*pa.t.* and *pa.p.* **relied′.**—**reli′er** *n.* [L. *religare,* to bind fast].

remain (re-mān′) *v.i.* to stay; to continue or endure; to abide; to last;—*n.pl.* a corpse; unpublished literary works of deceased.—**remain′der** *n.* what remains; remnant; in real property law, an interest in an estate which only operates after the termination of a prior interest [L. *re-,* back; *manere,* to stay].

remand (re-mȧnd′) *v.t.* to send back to prison, an accused person while further inquiries are made;—*n.* such a recommittal.—**remand home,** a place of detention for young delinquents [L. *re-,* back; *mandare,* to commit].

remark (re-mȧrk′) *v.t.* to take notice of; to express in words or writing; to regard; to speak; to say; to comment;—*n.* comment; notice; heed; regard;—*v.i.* to make a remark (on).—**remark′able** *a.* extraordinary.—**remark′ableness** *n.*—**remark′ably** *adv.* [Fr. *remarquer*].

remedy (rem′e-di) *n.* a means of curing or relieving a disease, trouble, fault, etc.; legal means to recover a right, or to obtain redress; cure; antidote;—*v.t.* to restore to health; to heal; to cure; to put right.—*pa.p.* **rem′edied.**—**reme′diable** *a.* curable.—**reme′dial** *a.* affording a remedy [L. *remedium*].

remember (re-mem′bẹr) *v.t.* to retain in the memory; to recollect; to reward for services rendered; to remind;—*v.i.* to have in mind.—**remem′berable** *a.*—**remem′brance** *n.* act or power of remembering; state of being remembered; recollection; memory; token; memento; keepsake.—**remem′brancer** *n.* one who or that which reminds; an officer of City of London, who acts as parliamentary agent in connection with promotion of city bills; officer of the Exchequer [L. *re-*; *memor,* mindful].

remind (rē-mīnd′) *v.t.* to recall to memory; to cause to remember.—**remind′er** *n.* one who, or that which, reminds.

reminiscence (rem-i-nis′ẹns) *n.* state of calling to mind; a recollection; a remembrance; something recalling past events;—*pl.* autobiographical notes; memoirs.—**reminis′cent** *a.* [L. *reminisci,* to remember].

remise (rē-mīz′) *v.t.* to send back or remit, esp. in law; to resign or surrender (property, etc.) by deed;—*n.* (*Law*) a surrender [O.Fr.].

remiss (re-mis′) *a.* not energetic or exact in duty; careless in fulfilling engagements.—**remiss′ful** *a.* forgiving.—**remiss′ible** *a.* able to be pardoned.—**remis′sion** *n.* abatement; diminution; period of moderation of intensity of a fever or other disease; pardon; forgiveness of sin.—**remiss′ive** *a.* slackening; moderating. —**remiss′ly** *adv.*—**remiss′ness** *n.* slackness; neglect [L. *remissus,* slack].

remit (re-mit′) *v.t.* to send back; to refer; to transfer; to send accused for trial to a higher court; to transmit to a distance, as money bills; to return; to restore; to slacken (efforts); to decrease; to forgive; to refrain from exacting (debt, etc.);—*v.i.* to abate in force; to slacken off.—*pr.p.* **remit′ting.**—*pa.t.* and *pa.p.* **remit′ted.**—*n.* remission.—**remit′ment, remit′tal** *n.* a remit.—**remit′tance** *n.* transmitting money, bills, or the like to a distant place; the money sent.—**remit′tent** *a.* increasing and decreasing at periodic intervals [L. *remittere,* to send back].

remnant (rem′nạnt) *n.* fragment of cloth; scrap; residue; remainder [O.Fr. *remanant,* remaining].

remonstrate (re-mon′strāt) *v.t.* to make evident by strong protestations;—*v.i.* to present strong reasons against; to speak strongly against course of conduct.—**remon′strance** *n.* expostulation; formal protest.—**remon′strant** *n.* one who remonstrates;—*a.* expostulatory.—**remonstra′tion** *n.* the act of remonstrating.—**remon′strative, remon′stratory** *a.* [L. *re-,* again; *monstrare,* to point out].

remorse (re-mors′) *n.* self-reproach excited by sense of guilt; repentance.—**remorse′ful** *a.* penitent; repentant.—**remorse′fully** *adv.*—**remorse′less** *a.* relentless; pitiless [L. *remordere,* to bite again].

remote (re-mōt′) *a.* far back in time or space; not near; slight; unlikely; aloof.—**remote′ly** *adv.*—**remote′ness** *n.*—**remote control,** control of apparatus from a distance, by magnets energised by electric currents sent via wireless [L. *re-,* back; *movere, motum,* to move].

remove (re-mōōv′) *v.t.* to take or put away; to dislodge; to transfer; to withdraw; to extract; to banish; to dismiss from a post; to eject; to oust;—*v.i.* to change place or residence;—*n.* removal; change of place; a step in any scale of gradation; a move; a posting-stage for fresh horses.—**removabil′ity** *n.*—**remo′vable** *a.* not permanently fixed.—**remo′vably** *adv.*—**remo′val** *n.* removing; transferring to another house; dismissal from a post; departure; death, esp. by violence.—**removed′** *a.* denoting nearness of relationship, as **cousin once removed,** parent's cousin or child of cousin.—**remo′ver** *n.* [L. *re-,* back; *movere,* to move].

remunerate (re-mū′nẹ-rāt) *v.t.* to reward for services; to recompense; to compensate.—**remu′nerable** *a.* that may, or should be, remunerated.—**remunera′tion** *n.* reward; recompense; salary.—**remu′nerative** *a.* lucrative; well-paid [L. *re-,* again; *munerare,* to give].

ren (ren) *n.* kidney.—*pl.* **re′nes.**—**re′nal** *a.* pert. to kidneys [L. *renes*].

renaissance (re-nā′sạns) *n.* a rebirth; a period of intellectual revival, esp. of learning in fourteenth to sixteenth cents.;—*a.* pert. to renaissance. Also **renas′cence** [Fr.].

renascent (re-nas′ẹnt) *a.* springing into being again; regaining lost vigour.—**renas′cence** *n.*

See **renaissance** [L. *re-*, again; *nasci*, to be born].
rencounter, rencontre (ren-koun′-tẹr, rong-kōng′-tr) *n.* an unpremeditated encounter; a minor conflict; a clash; a duel [Fr. *rencontrer*, to meet].
rend (rend) *v.t.* to tear asunder; to pull to pieces; to split; to lacerate; to crack.—*pa.t.* and *pa.p.* **rent** [O.E. *rendan*, to cut].
render (ren′-dẹr) *v.t.* to give in return; to deliver up; to supply; to present; to make or cause to be; to translate from one language into another; to reproduce music; to portray; to extract animal fats by heating; to clarify. —**ren′derable** *a.*—**ren′derer** *n.*—**ren′dering** *n.* the act of rendering; translation; version; interpretation.—**rendi′tion** *n.* surrender, as of fugitives from justice, at the request of a foreign government; translation; version; interpretation [Fr. *rendre*].
rendezvous (ren′ *or* rong′-de-vòò) *n.* place of resort; an appointed place for meeting;—*v.i.* to assemble at a pre-arranged place [Fr. = betake yourselves].
rendition See **render**.
renegade (ren′-e-gād) *n.* one faithless to principle or party; a deserter;—*a.* apostate; false; traitorous. —**ren′egate** *n.* a renegade;—*a.* apostate; false; traitorous.—**renege′** *v.t.* and *v.i.* to deny; to desert; to turn renegade; to revoke at cards.—**rene′ger** *n.* [L. *re-*, again; *negare*, to deny].
renew (rē-nū′) *v.t.* and *v.i.* to restore; to renovate; to revive; to begin again; to recommence.—**renew′able** *a.*—**renew′al** *n.* revival; restoration; regeneration.
rennet (ren′-et) *n.* one of several sub-varieties of dessert apple [etym. uncertain].
rennet (ren′-et) *n.* any preparation from animal intestines, used for curdling milk and in preparation of cheese.—**ren′nin** *n.* a casein-digesting enzyme or ferment in gastric juice which curdles milk [M.E. *rennen*, to run, congeal].
renounce (re-nouns′) *v.t.* to disavow; to give up; to resign; to reject;—*v.i.* to fail in following suit when a card of the suit is in the player's hand.—**renounce′ment, renuncia′tion** *n.* [L. *renuntiare*, to protest against].
renovate (ren′-o-vāt) *v.t.* to render as good as new; to overhaul and repair; to renew.—**renova′tion** *n.* renewal;—*pl.* repairs and improvements. —**ren′ovator, ren′ovater** *n.* [L. *renovare*, fr. *novus*, new].
renown (re-noun′) *n.* great reputation; fame; celebrity;—*v.t.* to make renowned.—**renowned′** *a.* famous; noted; eminent [O.Fr. *renoun*, fr. *renomer*, to make famous].
rent (rent) *pa.t.* and *pa.p.* of **rend**;—*n.* an opening made by rending; a tear; a fissure; a split; a breach; a rupture; a rift.
rent (rent) *n.* a periodical payment at an agreed rate for use and enjoyment of something, esp. land, houses; rental; hiring charge; —*v.t.* to lease; to hold by lease; to hire;—*v.i.* to be leased or let for rent.—**rent′able** *a.*—**rent′al** *n.* a rent-roll; the annual amount of rent payable.—**rent′er** *n.* one who rents [Fr. *rente*, income].
renunciation (re-nun-si-ā′-shun) *n.* a surrender of claim or interest; disavowal; disowning; rejection; formal repudiation. Also **renun′ciance**.—**renun′ciative, renunciat′ory** *a.* [fr. *renounce*].
reorganise (rē-or′-gạ-nīz) *v.t.* to organise anew; to reduce again to a regular system.
rep, repp (rep), **reps** (reps) *n.* a thick corded worsted, cotton, or silk fabric [prob. fr. *rib*].
repair (re-pār′) *v.t.* to restore to a sound or good state after injury; to mend; to retrieve; to redress;—*n.* restoration; reparation; patching; mending.—**repair′able** *a.*—**repair′er** *n.* [O. Fr. *reparer*].
repair (re-pār′) *v.i.* to go; to betake oneself (to); to resort;—*n.* haunt; resort [L. *repatriare*, to return to one's country].
reparable (rep′-a-rạ-bl) *a.* that can be made good.—**rep′arably** *adv.*—**repara′tion** *n.* repairing or making amends; indemnity; redress; compensation; atonement.—**repar′ative** *a.* [O.Fr. *reparer*].
repartee (rep-ạr-tē′) *n.* apt, witty reply; gift of making such replies [Fr. *repartie*, orig. answering thrust in fencing].
repast (re-past′) *n.* a meal; victuals;—*v.t.* and *v.i.* to feed [Fr. *repas*, a meal].
repatriate (rē-pā-tri-āt, rē-pat′-ri-āt) *v.t.* to restore to one's own country; to bring back prisoners of war and refugees from abroad.—**repatria′tion** *n.*
repay (rē-pā′) *v.t.* to pay back; to make return or requital for; to compensate; to requite.—*pa.t.* and *pa.p.* **repaid′**.—**repay′able** *a.* meant or expected to be repaid.—**repay′ment** *n.*
repeal (rē-pēl′) *v.t.* to revoke, rescind, annul, as a deed, will, law, or statute; to abrogate; to cancel; to abolish;—*n.* revocation; abrogation; annulment.—**repeal′able** *a.* [O.Fr. *rapeler*, fr. *appeler*, to appeal].
repeat (re-pēt′) *v.t.* to say or do again; to reiterate; to echo; to recite a piece learnt by heart; to rehearse; to recapitulate; to recur; to regurgitate (of food); —*n.* repetition; encore; (*Mus.*) sign that a movement is to be performed twice, indicated by inclusion within dots of part to be repeated.—**repeat′able** *a.*—**repeat′ed** *a.* frequent; recurring.—**repeat′edly** *adv.*—**repeat′er** *n.* one who, or that which, repeats; fire-arm which may be discharged many times in quick succession; a watch which, at the touch of a spring, strikes the last hour and the appropriate quarter, so giving an indication of the approximate time; (*Arith.*) a decimal in which same figure(s) repeat ad infinitum.—**repeat′ing** *n.* [L. *repetere*, to try or seek again].
repel (re-pel′) *v.t.* to drive back; to repulse; to oppose; to excite revulsion in;—*v.i.* to have a negative electrical power; to cause repugnance.—*pr.p.* **repel′ling**.—*pa.t.* and *pa.p.* **repelled′**.—**repel′lence, repel′lency** *n.* state of being repellent.—**repel′lent** *a.* driving back; tending to repel;—*n.* that which repels.—**repel′ler** *n.* [L. *re-*, back; *pellere*, to drive].
repent (re-pent′) *v.t.* and *v.i.* to feel regret for a deed or omission.—**repent′ance** *n.* sorrow or regret; contrition; penitence.—**repent′ant** *a.* [Fr. *se repentir*].
repercuss (rē-pẹr-kus′) *v.t.* and *v.i.* to beat or drive back, as sound or air.—**repercus′sion** *n.* act of driving back; reverberation; rebound; recoil; echo; indirect effect or consequence.—**repercus′sive** *a.* driving back [fr. *percussion*].
repertoire (rep-ẹr-twȧr′) *n.* list of plays, operas, musical works, dramatic rôles, within sphere of operations of stock theatrical company or of an individual.—**rep′ertory** *n.* a repertoire; a place in which things are disposed in an orderly manner; a treasury; a magazine;—*a.* pert. to the stock plays of a resident company.—**repertory theatre**, a theatre with a permanent company and a repertoire of plays [Fr. fr. L. *repertorium*].
repetition (rep-e-tish′-un) *n.* act of repeating; the thing repeated; poetry or prose learnt by heart and repeated as a school exercise.—**repeti′tious** *a.* full of repetitions.—**repet′itive** *a.* involving much repetition [fr. *repeat*].
repine (rē-pīn′) *v.i.* to fret or vex oneself; to be discontented; to complain; to murmur.—**repin′er** *n.*—**repin′ing** *n.*
replace (rē-plās′) *v.t.* to put back into its place; to supply an equivalent for; to substitute for. —**replace′able** *a.*—**replace′ment** *n.* restoration; substitution.
replenish (rē-plen′-ish) *v.t.* to fill up again; to restock; to refill; to furnish; to supply.—**replen′ishment** *n.* [L. *re-*, again; *plenus*, full].
replete (re-plēt′) *a.* full; completely filled; surfeited.—**replete′ness, reple′tion** *n.* satiety; surfeit; (*Med.*) fullness of blood; plethora [L. *re-*, again; *plere*, *pletum*, to fill].

replica (rep′li-ka) *n.* exact copy of work of art by the artist of the original; facsimile.—**rep′licate** *v.t.* to fold or bend back; to make a copy of.—**replica′tion** *n.* an answer; reply; (*Law*) reply of a plaintiff to defendant's plea [L. *replicare*, to fold back].

reply (re-plī′) *v.t.* and *v.i.* to return an answer; to respond; to rejoin.—*pa.t.* and *pa.p.* **replied′**. —*n.* answer; rejoinder; response [O.Fr. *replier*, fr. L. *replicare*, to fold back].

repone (rē-pōn′) *v.t.* to replace; to restore; to reply [L. *re-*, back; *ponere*, to place].

report (re-pōrt′) *v.t.* to relate; to take down in writing; to give an account of; to name as an offender; to communicate; to narrate;—*v.i.* to make official statement; to furnish in writing an account of a speech, or the proceedings of a public assembly; to betake oneself as to superior officer;—*n.* an official statement of facts; rumour; noise; reverberation, as of gun; account of proceedings, debates, etc. of public bodies; (*Bib.*) repute; reputation.—**report′er** *n.* one who reports, esp. for newspapers.—**report′ing** *n.*—**reported speech**, not using the exact words spoken but reporting statements in the third person; indirect speech [Fr. *reporter*, fr. L. *reportare*, to bring back].

repose (re-pōz′) *v.t.* to rely on; to lean (on); to confide (in); to calm; to deposit;—*v.i.* to rest; to sleep; to recline;—*n.* sleep; relaxation.—**reposed′** *a.* calm; tranquil.—**repos′it** *v.t.* to lay up, to lodge, in a place of safety.—**repos′itory** *n.* place where valuables are deposited for safety; a shop; magazine; depot; store-house [Fr. *reposer*, fr. L. *reponere*, to place back].

repoussé (re-pōōs′ā) *a.* embossed; hammered into relief from reverse side;—*n.* a style of raised ornamentation in metal.—**repoussage** (re-pōō-sazh′) *n.* [Fr.].

repp See **rep.**

reprehend (rep-re-hend′) *v.t.* to find fault with; to blame; to rebuke.—**reprehen′sible** *a.* unworthy; blameworthy.—**reprehen′sibly** *adv.* —**reprehen′sive** *a.* containing reproof.—**reprehen′sively** *adv.*—**reprehen′sory** *a.* given in reproof [L. *reprehendere*, lit. to take hold again].

represent (rep-re-zent′) *v.t.* to exhibit the counterpart or image of; to recall by description or portrait; to pretend to be; to allege; to act or play the part of; to personate; to imitate; to deputise for; to be the member (of parliament, etc.) for.—**represent′able** *a.*—**representa′tion** *n.* describing, or showing; that which represents, as a picture; description; account; a dramatic performance; a protest; the act of representing (in parliament, etc.).—**representa′tional** *a.*—**represent′ative** *a.* typical; representing all shades of classes or of opinions; exhibiting a likeness; portraying;—*n.* an agent, deputy, delegate, or substitute; local member of parliament.—**representative government**, one in which the people are directly represented by deputies [Fr. *représenter*].

repress (re-pres′) *v.t.* to keep down or under; to put down; to reduce to subjection; to quell; to check.—**repress′er, repress′or** *n.*—**repress′ible** *a.* capable of being repressed.—**repress′ibly** *adv.* —**repres′sion** *n.* check; restraint; in psychoanalysis, process arising out of mental conflict by which unconsciously or subconsciously instincts are subdued and painful thoughts and tendencies are automatically excluded from consciousness.—**repress′ive** *a.* designed to crush or repress [L. *reprimere*, *repressum*, to repress].

reprieve (re-prēv′) *v.t.* to remit or commute a sentence; to grant temporary relief; to give a respite to;—*n.* temporary suspension of execution of sentence; rest or relief [for earlier *repry*, fr. Fr. *reprendre*, to take back].

reprimand (rep′ri-mand) *v.t.* to reprove severely; to chide.—*n.* a sharp rebuke; a severe admonition [Fr. *réprimande*, fr. *réprimer*, to repress].

reprint (rē-print′) *v.t.* to print again.—**re′print** *n.* a second or a new impression or edition of any printed work.

reprisal (re-prī′zal) *n.* an act of retaliation or retribution [Fr. *représaille*].

reproach (re-prōch′) *v.t.* to censure; to upbraid; to rebuke; to reprove; to charge (with); —*n.* reproof; rebuke; discredit; an object of scorn.—**reproach′ful** *a.* expressing censure; conveying protest and sorrow.—**reproach′fully** *adv.* [Fr. *reprocher*].

reprobate (rep′rō-bāt) *v.t.* to disapprove with signs of extreme dislike; to exclude from hopes of salvation;—*a.* disallowed; rejected; abandoned to error and apostasy; cast off by God; —*n.* profligate; hardened sinner; scoundrel.—**reproba′tion** *n.* condition of those pre-ordained to eternal perdition; condemnation; censure; rejection [L. *reprobare*, to reprove].

reproduce (rē-prō-dūs′) *v.t.* to produce over again; to produce likeness or copy of; to imitate;—*v.i.* to propagate; to generate.—**reprodu′cible** *a.*—**reproduc′tion** *n.* a repeat; a facsimile, as of a painting, photograph, etc.; wireless signals from loud-speaker of a receiving set; process of multiplication of living individuals or units whereby the species is perpetuated, either sexual or asexual.—**reproduc′tive** *a.* pert. to reproduction; yielding a return or profits; fertile.—**reproduc′tiveness, reproductiv′ity** *n.*

reproof (re-prōōf′) *n.* reprimand; rebuke; censure; admonition.—**reprove′** *v.t.* to charge with a fault; to rebuke.—**reprov′able** *a.* deserving or calling for censure.—**repro′val** *n.* reproof [O.Fr. *reprover*, fr. L. *reprobare*, to reprove].

reptile (rep′tīl) *n.* animal of class **Reptil′ia**—cold-blooded, air-breathing vertebrates which move on their bellies or by means of small, short legs; a grovelling or contemptible person; —*a.* of reptile skin; creeping; grovelling; low; mean.—**reptil′ian** *a.* belonging to reptiles [L. *reptilis*, creeping].

republic (re-pub′lik) *n.* a state, without a hereditary head, in which supremacy of the people or its elected representatives is formally acknowledged; commonwealth.—**repub′lican** *a.* pert. to republic;—*n.* one who favours a republican system of government; a democrat; one of the two great traditional political parties of the U.S.A.—**repub′licanism** *n.* [L. *res publica*, common weal].

repudiate (re-pū′di-āt) *v.t.* to cast off; to reject; to discard; to disclaim; to disown; to divorce; to refuse (payment).—**repudia′tion** *n.* rejection; disavowal.—**repu′diator** *n.* [L. *re-*, away; *pudere*, to be ashamed].

repugn (re-pūn) *v.t.* and *v.i.* to oppose; to resist; to make a stand against.—**repug′nance** *n.* state or condition of being repugnant.—**repug′nancy** *n.* a settled or habitual feeling of aversion.—**repug′nant** *a.* contrary; distasteful in a high degree; offensive; hostile; adverse; opposed to; contradictory; refractory [L. *repugnare*, to fight back].

repulse (re-puls′) *v.t.* to beat or drive back; to repel decisively; to reject; to rebuff;—*n.* state of being repulsed; act of driving off; a local defeat; check; rebuff; rejection.—**repul′ser** *n.*—**repul′sion** *n.* act of driving back; state of being repelled; feeling of aversion; repugnance.—**repul′sive** *a.* loathsome; disgusting; causing aversion.—**repul′sively** *adv.*—**repul′siveness** *n.* repulsion.—**repul′sory** *a.* repulsive [L. *repellere*, *repulsum*, to drive back].

repute (re-pūt′) *v.t.* to account or consider; to hold; to reckon;—*n.* good character; reputation; credit; esteem.—**reputa′tion** *n.* estimation in which a person is held; repute; known or reported character; general credit; good name; fame; renown.—**rep′utable** *a.* held in esteem; respectable; creditable.—**rep′utably** *adv.*—**reput′edly** *adv.* generally understood or believed [L. *reputare*, to reckon].

request (re-kwest′) *v.t.* to ask for earnestly;

to petition; to beg;—*n.* expression of desire for; petition; suit; demand; requisition.—**request'er** *n.* [O.Fr. *requeste*].

requiem (rek′wi-em) *n.* celebration of Holy Eucharist for soul of a dead person, the name derived from introit, *Requiem aeternam dona eis, Domine*, Grant them, O Lord, eternal rest; dirge; music for such a mass.

require (re-kwīr′) *v.t.* to insist upon having; to claim as by right; to make necessary; to demand; to need; to lack.—**require'ment** *n.* act of requiring; what is required; want; need; an essential condition [L. *requirere*, to seek].

requisite (rek′wi-zit) *a.* necessary; needful; indispensable; essential;—*n.* something necessary or indispensable.—**requisi'tion** *n.* a levy of necessaries, with or without payment, made on a community by a military force; formal demand made by one state to another for surrender of a fugitive from justice; a written order for materials or supplies; a formal demand;—*v.t.* to demand certain supplies or materials, esp. for troops; to request formally; to seize.—**requisi'tionist** *n.* one who makes a requisition [L. *requirere, requisitum*, to seek].

requite (re-kwīt′) *v.t.* to return an equivalent in good or evil; to repay; to reward; to retaliate on.—**requi'tal** *n.* that which requites or repays; compensation; retaliation [*re-*, and *quit*].

reredos (rēr′dos) *n.* an elaborately carved screen or wall panelling, behind a church altar [O.Fr. *rere*, rear; *dos*, the back].

reremouse (rēr′mous) *n.* a bat. Also **rear'mouse** [O.E. *hrermus*].

rescind (re-sind′) *v.t.* to annul; to cancel; to revoke; to repeal; to reverse; to abrogate.—**rescind'able** *a.*—**rescind'ment, recis'sion** *n.* act of abrogating or annulling.—**rescis'sory** *a.* having power or effect of rescinding [L. *rescindere*, to cut off].

rescript (rē′skript) *n.* in early Roman Empire, answers of emperors to questions officially put to them; a decretal epistle of the Popes; an edict or decree.

rescue (res′kū) *v.t.* to free from danger, evil, or restraint; to set at liberty; to deliver.—*pr.p.* **res'cuing.**—*n.* rescuing; deliverance.—**res'cuer** *n.* [O.Fr. *rescourre*].

research (re-serch′) *n.* diligent search or inquiry; scientific investigation and study to discover facts; scrutiny;—*a.* pert. to research;—*v.i.* to make research; to examine with care.—**research'er** *n.*

reseat (rē-sēt′) *v.t.* to provide with a new seat or set of seats; to patch (trousers, etc.).

resemble (re-zem′bl) *v.t.* to be like or similar to; to compare; to liken.—**resem'blance** *n.* likeness; similarity.—**resem'bling** *a.* [Fr. *ressembler*].

resent (re-zent′) *v.t.* to consider as an injury or affront; to take ill; to be angry at.—**resent'er** *n.*—**resent'ful** *a.* full of, or readily given to, resentment.—**resent'fully** *adv.*—**resent'ment** *n.* deep sense of affront; indignation; displeasure [L. *re-*, again; *sentire*, to feel].

reserve (re-zerv′) *v.t.* to hold back; to set apart; to keep for future use; to retain; to keep for some person;—*a.* acting as a reserve;—*n.* keeping back; what is reserved; supply of stores for future use; troops, etc., held back from line of battle to assist when necessary; body of men discharged from armed forces but liable to be recalled in an emergency; funds set aside for possible contingencies; minimum price acceptable at auction; reticence; concealment of feelings or friendliness; an area of land for a particular purpose.—**reserva'tion** *n.* reserving or keeping back; what is kept back; booking of a hotel-room, etc.; a proviso or condition; a tract of land reserved for some public use.—**reserved'** *a.* kept back; retained or booked for another; not free or frank; uncommunicative.—**reser'vedly** *adv.*—**reser'vedness** *n.*—**reser'vist,** a member of the armed forces belonging to reserves.—**reserved occupation,** one which exempts a worker from military or national service [L. *reservare*, to keep back].

reservoir (rez′er-vwår) *n.* enclosed area for storage and filtering of water; basin; cistern [Fr.].

reset (rē-set′) *v.t.* to set over again, as a page of printed matter; to furnish with a new setting or border.

reset (re-set′) *v.t.* and *v.i.* (*Scots Law*) to receive, knowingly, stolen goods; to hide and harbour a deserter or criminal.—*pr.p.* **reset'ting.**—*pa.t.* and *pa.p.* **reset'ted.**—**reset'ter** *n.* [O.Fr. *receter*, to receive].

reshuffle (rē-shuf′l) *v.t.* to rearrange (the order of cards, etc.); to cause office-bearers to exchange offices;—*n.* rearrangement.

reside (re-zīd′) *v.i.* to dwell permanently; to abide; to live; to be vested in; to be inherent in.—**res'idence** *n.* act of dwelling in a place; place where one resides; house; abode.—**res'idency** *n.* a residence, esp. official residence of a British government agent at a foreign court.—**res'ident** *a.* dwelling; residing;—*n.* one who resides in a place; formerly a British government representative, resident at capital of Indian State.—**res'identer** *n.* one who resides more or less permanently in a place.—**residen'tial** *a.* pert. to a resident or a residence; pert. to a part of a town consisting mainly of dwelling-houses.—**residen'tiary** *a.* having residence;—*n.* a resident, esp. clergyman required to reside for a certain time within precincts of cathedral [L. *residere*, fr. *sedere*, to sit].

residue (rez′i-dū) *n.* balance or remainder, esp. of debt or account.—**resid'ual** *a.* remaining after a part is taken away.—**resid'uary** *a.* pert. to residue or part remaining.—**resid'uum** *n.* what is left after any process of separation or purification; balance or remainder [L. *residuum*].

resign (re-zīn′) *v.t.* and *v.i.* to relinquish formally (office, etc.); to yield to; to give up; to submit to.—**resigna'tion** *n.* giving up, as a claim, possession, office, or place; abdication; relinquishment; patience and endurance.—**resigned'** *a.* relinquished; surrendered; acquiescent; submissive; patient.—**resigned'ly** *adv.* [L. *resignare*, to unseal].

resile (rē-zīl′) *v.i.* to start back; to draw back from a previous offer, decision, etc.; to retreat; to recoil; to rebound.—*pr.p.* **resil'ing.**—**resil'ience, resil'iency** *n.* springing back or rebounding; elasticity, esp. of mind.—**resil'ient** *a.* leaping or springing back; rebounding; elastic; buoyant; possessing power of quick recovery [L. *resilire*, to jump back].

resin (rez′in) *n.* general term for brittle, glassy, thickened juices exuded by certain plants; a resinous substance left after distillation of crude turpentine; fossilised remains, as amber, copal, kauri gum, etc.;—*v.t.* to dress or coat with resin.—**resina'ceous** *a.* resinous.—**res'inous** *a.* of, or like resin [L. *resina*].

resist (re-zist′) *v.t.* and *v.i.* to stand against; to oppose; to withstand; to strive against; to hinder.—**resis'tance** *n.* opposition; hindrance; electrical term denoting opposition offered by a circuit to passage of a current through it; power possessed by an individual to resist disease; in physics, forces tending to arrest movement;—*n.pl.* in psycho-analysis, mental forces opposed to self-knowledge.—**resis'tant** *n.* one who, or that which, resists.—**resis'tant, resis'tent** *a.* offering or making resistance.—**resis'ter** *n.*—**resistibil'ity, resis'tibleness** *n.* the quality or state of being resistible.—**resis'tible** *a.*—**resis'tibly, resis'tingly** *adv.*—**resist'less** *a.* irresistible; unable to resist.—**resist'lessly** *adv.*—**resist'lessness** *n.*—**resis'tor** *n.* a resistance coil or similar apparatus possessing resistance to electrical current.—**resistance box,** a box with a number of resistance-coils.—**resistance coil,** a coil of insulated wire whose resistance has been adjusted to a stated value.—**resistance movement,** the organised, underground movement in occupied country against invader [L. *resistere*, to oppose].

resolute (rez´o-lūt) *a.* having a decided purpose; determined;—*n.* a determined person; in mechanics, horizontal or vertical component of a resultant force.—**res'olutely** *adv.* —**res'oluteness** *n.* determination.—**resolu'tion** *n.* act, purpose, or process of resolving; intention; firmness; decision of court or vote of assembly; motion or declaration; courage; boldness [L. *resolvere, resolutum*, to unite].

resolve (re-zolv') *v.t.* to separate the component parts of; to solve and reduce to a different form; to make clear; to unravel; (*Math.*) to solve; (*Med.*) to clear of inflammation;—*v.i.* to determine; to decide; to purpose; to melt; to dissolve; to determine unanimously or by vote;—*n.* act of resolving; that which is resolved on; firm determination.—**resol'vable** *a.* capable of being solved, reduced to first principles, or decomposed.—**resolved'** *a.* determined; resolute.—**resol'vedly** *adv.*—**resolv'edness** *n.* firm determination [L. *resolvere*, to untie].

resonant (rez´o-nạnt) *a.* resounding; echoing; sonorous; ringing.—**res'onance, res'onancy** *n.* the phenomenon exhibited by vibrating systems, which are brought into oscillation by a periodic disturbance, the frequency of which is equal to that of the system [L. *re-*, again; *sonare*, to sound].

resort (re-zort') *v.i.* to betake oneself; to go; to repair; to have recourse; to apply (to); to frequent;—*n.* a frequented place; a haunt; recourse; aid.—**last resort,** the last resource [Fr. *ressortir*, to rebound, to go back].

resound (re-zound') *v.t.* to sound back; to send back sound;—*v.i.* to echo; to reverberate; to be much spoken about;—*n.* echo; return of sound.—**resound'ing** *a.*

resource (re-sōrs') *n.* that to which one resorts, or on which one depends, for supply or support; skill in improvising; expedient; shift; means; contrivance;—*pl.* pecuniary means; funds; wealth.—**resource'ful** *a.* clever in devising fresh expedients; ingenious.—**resource'fully** *adv.*—**resource'fulness** *n.* [Fr. *ressource*].

respect (re-spekt') *v.t.* to esteem; to honour; to treat or handle carefully; to pay heed to; to concern; to refer to; to relate to;—*n.* consideration; proper deference;—*pl.* expression of esteem; good wishes.—**respec'table** *a.* worthy of respect; reputable; decent; moderate; commonplace.—**respectabil'ity, respec'tableness** *n.*—**respec'tably** *adv.*—**respect'ful** *a.* deferential; reverential; polite.—**respect'fully** *adv.*—**respect´fulness** *n.*—**respec'ting** *prep.* regarding; concerning.—**respec'tive** *a.* relative; not absolute; relating to particular persons or things, each to each; particular; own; several.—**respec'tively** *adv.* as relating to each; relatively [L. *respicere, respectum*, to look back at].

resperse (rē-spẹrs') *v.t.* to sprinkle; to disperse in small quantities.—**resper'sion** *n.* act of sprinkling [L. *respersus*, sprinkled].

respire (re-spīr') *v.t.* and *v.i.* to breathe; to take rest.—**respir'able** *a.* fit to be breathed.—**respira'tion** *n.* process of breathing.—**respira´tional, respirative** (res´ or rē-spīr´) *a.* respiratory.—**res'pirator** *n.* an appliance for covering mouth and nostrils in order to purify or warm the air breathed in, or for inhalation of medicated vapours; a gas-mask.—**respiratory** (res´ or res-pi´) *a.* serving for, pert. to, respiration [L. *respirare*].

respite (res´pit, res´pīt) *n.* a temporary intermission; suspension of execution of a capital sentence; suspension of labour; stop; reprieve; —*v.t.* to grant a respite to; to reprieve; to relieve by interval of rest; to delay [O.Fr. *respit*].

resplendent (re-splen´dẹnt) *a.* shining with brilliant lustre; very bright; dazzling.—**resplen'dence, resplen'dency** *n.*—**resplen'dently** *adv.* [L. *resplendere*, to shine].

respond (re-spond') *v.i.* to answer; to reply; to correspond to; to suit; to react; to make a liturgical response.—**respon'dent** *a.* answering; giving response;—*n.* (*Law*) one who answers in certain proceedings, esp. in a chancery or divorce suit; defendant; one who refutes in a debate [L. *respondere*, to reply].

response (re-spons') *n.* answer or reply; part of liturgy said or sung by choir and congregation in answer to versicles of priest; in R.C. church, anthem after morning lessons, etc.—**responsibil'ity** *n.* state of being responsible; that for which any one is responsible; a duty; a charge; an obligation placed on a person who holds a position of trust as agent for another.—**respon'sible** *a.* accountable; trustworthy; rational.—**respon'sibly** *adv.*—**respon´sions** *n.pl.* at Oxford, the first of the three examinations leading to graduation as B.A.—**respon'sive** *a.* able, ready, or inclined, to respond; correspondent.—**respon'sively** *adv.*—**respon'siveness** *n.* the state of being responsive [L. *respondere, responsum*, to reply].

rest (rest) *n.* repose; a cessation from motion or labour; that on which anything rests or leans; a place where one may rest; a pause;—*v.t.* to lay at rest;—*v.i.* to cease from action; to repose; to stand or be fixed (on); to sleep; to be dead; to remain (with), for decision, etc.; to trust; to be undisturbed.—**rest'ful** *a.* soothing; peaceful; quiet.—**rest'fully** *adv.*—**rest'fulness** *n.*—**rest'less** *a.* continually on the move; unsettled in mind; uneasy.—**rest'lessly** *adv.*—**rest'lessness** *n.*—**to lay to rest,** to bury [O.E.].

rest (rest) *v.i.* to remain; to continue to be; to depend;—*n.* that which is left over or remains; remainder [L. *restare*, to remain].

restaurant (res´to-rong, res´tor-ant) *n.* a place where customers are provided with meals on payment; a tea-room; a café.—**restaurateur** (res-to´rạ-tẹr) *n.* proprietor of a restaurant [Fr.].

restitute (res´ti-tūt) *v.t.* to restore.—**restitu´tion** *n.* the act of restoring, esp. to the rightful owner; reparation, indemnification, compensation.—**res'titutive** *a.*—**res'titutor** *n.* [L. *restituere, restitutum*, to replace].

restive (res´tiv) *a.* impatient; fidgety; uneasy; obstinate; stubborn.—**res'tively** *adv.*—**res'tiveness** *n.* [O.Fr. *restif*, stubborn, fr. L. *restare*, to remain].

restore (re-stōr') *v.t.* to give back or return; to recover from ruin or decay; to repair; to renew; to replace; to reinstate; to heal; to revive; to cure; to recover from error or corruption, as the text of a book.—**restor'able** *a.*—**restora'tion** *n.* replacement; recovery; reconstruction; re-establishment; establishment of monarchy by return of Charles II in 1660; (*Theol.*) universal salvation.—**restor'ative** *a.* having power to renew strength, vigour, etc.;—*n.* a remedy for restoring health and vigour.—**restor'atively** *adv.* [L. *restaurare*, to repair].

restrain (re-strān') *v.t.* to hold back; to hinder; to check; to withhold; to forbear.—**restrain'able** *a.*—**restrain'edly** *adv.* with restraint.—**restrain´ment** *n.*—**restraint'** *n.* curb; repression; hindrance; imprisonment [O.Fr. *restraindre*, fr. L. *re-*, back; *stringere*, to bind].

restrict (re-strikt') *v.t.* to restrain within bounds; to limit.—**restric'ted** *a.* limited.—**restric'tedly** *adv.*—**restric'tion** *n.* act of restricting; state of being restricted; limitation, confinement; restraint.—**restric'tive** *a.* having the power to restrict.—**restric'tively** *adv.* [L. *restringere, restrictum*, to bind fast].

result (re-zult') *v.i.* to follow, as a consequence; to issue (in); to happen; to terminate;—*n.* issue; effect; decision; outcome; answer to a calculation.—**resul'tant** *a.* following as a result;—*n.* in mechanics, the single force which can be used to replace, in every respect, two or more forces [L. *resultare*, to leap back].

resume (rē-zūm') *v.t.* to renew; to recommence;

to summarise.—**résumé** (rā-zū-mā') *n.* a summing up; an abridgement; a summary; an abstract.—**resum'able** *a.*—**resump'tion** *n.* act of taking back or taking again; a fresh start. —**resump'tive** *a.* resuming [L. *re-*, again; *sumere*, to take].

resurge (re-surj')*v.i.* to rise again.—**resur'gence** *n.*—**resur'gent** *a.* rising again (from the dead). —**resurrect'** *v.t.* to restore to life; to use once more; to take from the grave.—**resurrec'tion** *n.* resuscitation of the body after death and its reunion with the soul; Christ's rising from the grave after Crucifixion; a revival.—**resurrec'tional, resurrec'tionary** *a.*—**resurrec'tionist, resurrec'tion-man** *n.* one who stealthily exhumed bodies from the grave to sell for anatomical purposes [L. *re-*, again; *surgere*, to rise].

resuscitate (re-sus'i-tāt) *v.t.* to restore to life one apparently dead; to revive; to revivify;—*v.i.* to come to life again.—**resus'citable** *a.* capable of being restored to life again.—**resus'citant** *n.* one who, or that which, resuscitates.—**resuscita'tion** *n.*—**resus'citative** *a.* tending to revive or reanimate.—**resus'citator** *n.* [L. *resuscitare*, to raise up again].

retail (rē-tāl') *v.t.* to sell in small quantities; to tell frequently.—**re'tail** *a.* denoting sale in small quantities, as opposed to wholesale;—*n.* sale in small quantities.—**retail'er** *n.*—**retail'ment** *n.* [O.Fr. *retailler*, to cut up].

retain (re-tān') *v.t.* to continue to keep in possession; to hold; to reserve; to engage services of.—**retain'able** *a.*—**retain'er** *n.* one who retains; adherent or follower; dependant; a fee paid to secure services of, esp. barrister. —**retain'ment** *n.* the act of retaining [L. *retinere*, to hold back].

retaliate (re-tal'i-āt) *v.t.* and *v.i.* to repay in kind; to return like for like; to requite; to revenge.—**retalia'tion** *n.*—**retal'iative, retal'iatory** *a.*—**retal'iator** *n.* [L. *retaliare*, fr. *talis*, like, such].

retard (re-tȧrd') *v.t.* to hinder progress; to make slow or late; to impede.—**retarda'tion** *n.* delaying; hindrance; diminishing velocity of a moving body; rate of loss of velocity; delayed mental development in children due to physical or environmental causes, not to mental defect.—**retard'ment** *n.* [L. *retardare*, fr. *tardus*, slow].

retch (rech) *v.i.* to strain at vomiting.—**retch'ing** *n.* [O.E. *hraecan*].

retention (re-ten'shun) *n.* act or power of retaining; stoppage; holding back; inability to void urine.—**reten'tive** *a.*—**reten'tively** *adv.*—**reten'tiveness** *n.* [fr. *retain*].

retiary (rē'shi-ạ-ri, rē'ti-ạ-ri) *a.* net-like; weaving a net to catch prey.—**Retiar'iae** *n.pl.* (*Zool.*) spiders [L. *rete*, a net].

reticent (ret'i-sẹnt) *a.* reserved; taciturn; uncommunicative.—**ret'icence** *n.* also **ret'icency**.—**ret'icently** *adv.* [L. *reticere*, fr. *tacere*, to be silent].

reticle (ret'i-kl) *n.* small net or net-bag.—**ret'icule** *n.* a little net-work bag; a reticle; a lady's work-bag.—**retic'ular, retic'ulary** *a.* having the form of a net; formed with interstices.—**retic'ulate** *v.t.* to cover with net-like lines; to make like a net;—*a.* Also **retic'ulated**, netted; having veins, fibres, hairs, or lines crossing like net-work, as a leaf.—**reticula'tion** *n.* [Fr. *réticule*, fr. L. *rete*, a net].

retiform (rē'ti-form) *a.* having form of a net; reticulated [L. *rete*, a net; *forma*, form].

retina (ret'i-nạ) *n.* innermost, semi-transparent, sensory layer of the eye from which sense impressions are passed to the brain.—**ret'inal** *a.* [L. *rete*, a net].

retinue (ret'i-nū) *n.* a body of hired servants or followers; a train of attendants; suite [Fr. *retenir*, to retain].

retire (re-tīr') *v.t.* to compel one to retire from office; to withdraw from circulation notes or bills;—*v.i.* to go back; to withdraw; to retreat; to give up formally one's work or office; to go to bed.—**reti'ral** *n.* act of retiring; occasion when one retires from office, etc.—**retired'** *a.* secluded; private; sequestered; withdrawn permanently from one's daily work.—**retired'ly** *adv.*—**retired'ness, retire'ment** *n.* act of retiring; state of being retired.—**retir'ing** *a.* reserved; modest; pert. to a withdrawal from work or office [Fr. *retirer*, to pull back].

retort (re-tort') *v.t.* to bend or curve back; to repay in kind; to hurl back (charge, etc.);—*v.i.* to make a smart reply;—*n.* vigorous reply or repartee; a vessel in which substances are distilled [L. *retorquere, retortum*, to twist back].

retrace (rē-trās') *v.t.* to trace back or over again; to go back the same way; to draw over a former tracing.—**retrace'able** *a.*

retract (re-trakt') *v.t.* and *v.i.* to draw back; to take back, as a statement; to go back on one's word.—**retrac'table, retrac'tible** *a.* able to be retracted.—**retracta'tion** *n.* recalling of a statement or opinion; recantation.—**retrac'tile** *a.* (*Zool.*) capable of being drawn back or inwards, as claws, etc.—**retrac'tion** *n.* the act of drawing back; disavowal; recantation; (*Surg.*) a drawing up or shortening of a part; —**retrac'tive** *a.* ready to retract.—**retrac'tively** *adv.* [L. *re-*, back; *trahere, tractum*, to draw].

retread (rē-tred') *v.t.* to tread again; to replace a worn tread on the outer cover of a rubber tyre with a new tread.

retreat (re-trēt') *n.* retiring or withdrawing; a military signal for retiring; a military call, at sunset, on a bugle; place of seclusion; period of retirement for prayer and meditation;—*v.i.* to move back; to betake oneself to a place of security; to retire before an enemy. —**retreat'ing** *a.* sloping backward, as forehead or chin [Fr. *retraite*, fr. *retraire*, to draw back].

retrench (re-trensh')*v.t.* to cut down (expense, etc.); to curtail; to diminish; to lessen;—*v.i.* to economise.—**retrench'ment** *n.* diminution of expenditure; economy; (*Fort.*) extra parapet and ditch within a rampart to prolong defence [Fr. *retrancher*, to cut off].

retribution (ret-ri-bū'shun) *n.* just or suitable return, esp. for evil deeds; requital; repayment; vengeance.—**retribute** (re-tri'būt, ret'ri-būt) *v.t.* to pay back.—**retrib'utive, retrib'utory** *a.* [L. *retributio*].

retrieve (re-trēv') *v.t.* to gain back; to recover; to remedy the evil consequences of; to re-establish (former position, fortune, etc.); to repair; (of a dog) to find and bring back shot game.—**retriev'able** *a.*—**retriev'ably** *adv.*—**retriev'al, retrieve'ment** *n.*—**retriev'er** *n.* dog trained to find and bring back game [Fr. *retrouver*, to find again].

retro- (ret'rō, rē'trō) *prefix* fr. L. *retro*, back, backward, used in the formation of compound words.

retroact (rē-trō-akt') *v.i.* to act backwards; to react; to have a retrospective effect.—**retroac'tion** *n.*—**retroac'tive** *a.* acting in regard to past events; retrospective.—**retroact'ively** *adv.* [L. *retro*, backward; *agere, actum*, to act].

retrocede (rē-trō-sēd') *v.t.* to go or move back. —**retroces'sion** *n.* the act of retroceding or going back [L. *retro*, backward; *cedere*, to go].

retrograde (ret'rō-, rē'trō-grād) *v.i.* to move backward; to deteriorate; to decline;—*a.* tending to a backward direction; deteriorating; reactionary; retrogressive.—**retrograda'tion** *n.*—**ret'rogress** *v.i.* to move backwards; to deteriorate.—**retrogres'sion** *n.* act of going backward; a decline into an inferior state of development.—**retrogress'ive** *a.* moving backward; reactionary; degenerating; assuming baser characteristics.—**retrogress'ively** *adv.* [L. *retro*, backward; *gradi*, to go].

retrorse (re-trors') *a.* bending or pointing backwards, as feathers of birds. Also **ret'roverse**.—**retrorse'ly** *adv.* [L. *retro*, backwards; *vertere, versum*, to turn].

retrospect (ret'rō-, rē'trō-spekt) *n.* a looking back; survey of past events; a review.—**retrospec'tion** *n.*—**retrospec'tive** *a.* tending to

look back; applicable to past events; of laws, rules, etc., having force as if enacted or authorised at earlier date.—**retrospec'tively** *adv.* [L. *retro*, backward; *specere*, to look].
retroussé (rẹ-tróó'sā) *a.* turned up, as the end of a nose; pug [Fr.].
retroverse (rē'trō-, ret'rō-vers) *a.* bent backwards; retrorse.—**retrover'sion** *n.*—**retrovert** (rē', ret') *v.t.* to turn back;—*n.* one who returns to his original creed or opinions [L. *retro*, backward; *vertere, versum*, to turn].
retry (rē-trī') *v.t.* to try again; to put on trial a second time.
returf (rē-turf') *v.t.* to lay down new turf.
return (re-turn') *v.t.* to bring, give, or send back; to restore; to report officially; to elect; to yield (a profit); to reciprocate;—*v.i.* to go or come back; to recur; to reply;—*n.* coming back to the same place; what is returned, as a payment; profit; an official report, esp. as to numbers; repayment; restitution.—**return'able** *a.* capable of being returned; required to be returned or delivered up.—**return'match** *n.* second game played by same opponents.—**return'tick'et** *n.* ticket for journey, there and back.—**return'ing-off'icer** *n.* officer who makes returns of writs, precepts, juries, etc.; presiding officer at election [Fr. *retourner*].
reunion (rē-ūn'yun) *n.* union formed anew after separation; a social gathering.—**reunite'** *v.t.* to unite again; to join after separation;—*v.i.* to join and cohere again.
rev (rev) *n.* (*Colloq.*) revolution of an engine;—*v.t.* and *v.i.* to run (an engine).—*pr.p.* **rev'ving.** —*pa.t.* and *pa.p.* **revved.**
reveal (re-vēl') *v.t.* to disclose; to discover by supernatural power; to show. —**reveal'able** *a.*—**reveal'er** *n.*—**reveal'ment** *n.* disclosure; revelation.—**revealed law,** divine law.—**revealed religion,** founded on revelation, whereby God supernaturally manifests himself through prophets, etc. Opposite of *natural religion* [L. *revelare*, to draw back the veil].
reveille (re-val'i, re-vāl'ye) *n.* the bugle-call or roll of drums sounded in military establishments at daybreak to rouse inmates [Fr. *réveillez* (*-vous*) wake up!].
revel (rev'ẹl) *v.i.* to make merry; to carouse; to delight (in); to luxuriate.—*pr.p.* **rev'elling.** —*pa.t.* and *pa.p.* **rev'elled.**—*n.* festivity; noisy celebration;—*pl.* entertainment, with music and dancing.—**rev'eller** *n.*—**rev'elment, rev'elry** *n.* noisy and spontaneous festivity [O.Fr. *reveler*, to make tumult].
revelation (rev-e-lā'shun) *n.* act of revealing; knowledge of God, or of divine things, imparted to man by His direct operation either on individual soul or through appointed intermediary; (*Bib.*) last book of New Testament —the Apocalypse.—**revela'tional, rev'elatory** *a.* [L. *revelare*, to draw back the veil].
revenant (rev'ẹ-nạnt) *n.* one returned from long absence or apparently from the dead; a spectre; a ghostly visitant [Fr.].
revenge (re-venj') *v.t.* to make retaliation for; to return injury for injury; to avenge;—*n.* revenging; infliction of injury in return for injury; passion for vengeance.—**revenge'ful** *a.* full of revenge; vindictive.—**revenge'fully** *adv.* —**revenge'fulness** *n.* [O.Fr. *revenger*, fr. L. *re-*, again; *vindicare*, to claim].
revenue (rev'e-nū) *n.* income derived from any source, esp. annual income of a state or institution; proceeds; receipts; profits.—**in'land-rev'enue** *n.* public money from income tax, estate or death duties, excise, licences, etc. [Fr. *revenue*, return, fr. L. *revenire*, to come back].
rever See **revers.**
reverberate (re-vẹr'bẹr-āt) *v.t.* and *v.i.* to send back, as sound; to reflect, as light or heat; to re-echo; to resound.—**reverb'erant** *a.* resounding; beating back.—**reverbera'tion** *n.*—**rever'berative** *a.* tending to reverberate.—**rever'berator** *n.*—**rever'beratory** *a.* producing reverberation [L. *reverberare*, to beat back].
revere (re-vēr') *v.t.* to regard with mingled fear, respect and affection; to reverence.—**rever'able** *a.* worthy of respect.—**rev'erence** *n.* awe mingled with respect and esteem; veneration; a bow, curtsey, or genuflection; a title applied to a clergyman;—*v.t.* to revere; to venerate.—**rev'erend** *a.* worthy of reverence; venerable; a title of respect given to clergy (abridged **Rev.**)—**rev'erent** *a.* feeling, showing, behaving with, reverence.—**reveren'tial** *a.* respectful.—**reveren'tially, rev'erently** *adv.* [O.Fr. *reverer*, fr. L. *vereri*, to feel awe].
reverie, revery (rev'ẹr-i) *n.* state of mind, akin to dreaming; rhapsody; musing [Fr. *rêverie*, fr. *rêver*, to dream].
revers (re-vār' or rē-vēr') *n.* part of garment turned back for ornamentation, as lapel. Also **rever'.**—*pl.* **revers'** [O.Fr. = reverse].
reverse (re-vẹrs') *v.t.* to change completely; to give a contrary decision; to annul; to overturn; to repeal; to revoke; to transpose; to invert;—*v.i.* to change direction; to come back;—*n.* side which appears when object is turned round; opposite or contrary; crest-side of coin or medal, as distinguished from *obverse*; check; defeat; misfortune;—*a.* turned backward; opposite; upside-down.—**rever'sal** *n.* reversing, changing, overthrowing, annulling.—**reversed'** *a.* turned in opposite direction; inverted; annulled.—**rever'sedly** *adv.*—**reversibil'ity** *n.* property of being reversible.—**rever'sible** *a.* capable of being used on both sides or in either direction.—**rever'sibly** *adv.*—**rever'sion** *n.* returning or reverting; a deferred annuity; right or hope of future possession; (*Law*) return of estate to grantor or his next-of-kin, after death of grantee or legatee; interest which reverts to a landlord after expiry of lease; (*Biol.*) a tendency to revert to long-concealed characters of previous generations; atavism; throw-back.—**rever'sional, revers'ionary** *a.* involving a reversion; returning to a person after a time or event.—**revers'ive** *a.* tending to cause reversion.—**rever'so** *n.* left-hand page of a book [L. *re-*, back; *vertere, versum*, to turn].
revert (re-vẹrt') *v.i.* to return to former state or rank; to come back to subject; to turn backwards; (*Law*) to return by reversion to donor; —*v.t.* to turn back or reverse.—**revert'ible** *a.* [L. *re-*, again; *vertere*, to turn].
revet (re-vet') *v.t.* to face a wall with masonry, sand-bags, etc.—*pr.p.* **revet'ting.**—*pa.t.* and *pa.p.* **revet'ted.**—**revet'ment** *n.* a retaining wall; facing of a trench [Fr. *revêtir*, to clothe].
review (re-vū') *v.t.* to re-examine; to revise; to consider critically (book); to inspect troops, etc.—*n.* revision; survey; inspection, esp. of massed military, air, or naval forces; a critical notice of a book, etc.; periodical devoted to critical articles, discussion of current events, etc.—**review'er** *n.* one who writes critical reviews; examiner; inspector [Fr. *revoir*, to see again].
revile (re-vīl') *v.t.* to abuse with opprobrious language; to vilify; to defame.—**revile'ment** *n.* —**revil'er** *n.* [O.Fr. *reviler*].
revise (re-vīz') *v.t.* to look over and correct; to review, alter and amend;—*n.* review; a further printer's proof to ensure all corrections have been made.—**revi'sal** *n.* review; re-examination.—**revi'sion** *n.* revisal; revised copy of book or document.—**revi'ser, revi'sor** *n.* proof-reader.—**revi'sional, revi'sionary** *a.* pert. to revision.—**revi'sory** *a.* having power to revise.—**Revised Version,** new translation of Bible in 1881 (New Testament) and 1884 (Old Testament) [L. *revisere*].
revive (re-vīv') *v.i.* to come back to life, vigour, etc.; to awaken;—*v.t.* to resuscitate; to re-animate; to renew; to recover from neglect; to refresh (memory).—**revivabil'ity** *n.* —**revi'vable** *a.* capable of being revived.—**revi'vably** *adv.*—**revi'val** *n.* reviving or being revived; renewed activity, of trade, etc.; a wave of religious enthusiasm worked up by

powerful preachers; awakening; reappearance of old, neglected play, etc.—**revi'valism** *n.* religious fervour during evangelical revival.—**revi'valist** *n.* one who promotes religious revivals.—**revi'ver** *n.* one who, or that which, revives; a stimulant.—**revivifica'tion** *n.* renewal of life and energy.—**reviv'ify** *v.t.* to reanimate; to reinvigorate;—*v.i.* to regain power of reacting chemically [L. *re-*, again; *vivere*, to live].

revoke (re-vōk') *v.t.* to annul; to repeal; to reverse (a decision);—*v.i.* at cards, to fail to follow suit; to renounce.—*n.* neglect to follow suit at cards.—**revoke'ment** *n.* revoking.—**revok'er** *n.*—**rev'ocable** *a.* able to be revoked.—**rev'ocableness, revocabil'ity** *n.*—**rev'ocably** *adv.*—**revoca'tion** *n.* repeal; reversal.—**rev'ocatory** *a.* [L. *revocare*, to recall].

revolt (re-vōlt') *v.i.* to renounce allegiance; to rise in rebellion; to feel disgust;—*v.t.* to shock; to repel;—*n.* act of revolting; rebellion; mutiny; disgust; loathing.—**revol'ter** *n.*—**revol'ting** *a.* disgusting.—**revol'tingly** *adv.* [Fr. *révolter*].

revolution (rev-o-lū'shun) *n.* motion of body round its orbit or focus; turning round on axis (but preferably, *rotation*); (*Geol.*) a period when great earth movements were taking place; time marked by a regular recurrence (as seasons); a radical change in constitution of a country after revolt.—**revolu'tionary** *a.* pert. to revolution; marked by great and violent changes;—*n.* one who participates in a revolution.—**revolu'tionise** *v.t.* to change completely [L. *revolvere, revolutum*, to turn round].

revolve (re-volv') *v.i.* to turn round on an axis; to rotate; to meditate;—*v.t.* to cause to turn; to rotate; to reflect upon.—**revol'vable** *a.*—**revolv'er** *n.* pistol with several loading chambers on a cylinder, so arranged as to be discharged in succession by the same lock [L. *revolvere*, to turn round].

revue (re-vū') *n.* theatrical entertainment, partly musical comedy, with little continuity of structure or connected plot [Fr.].

revulsion (re-vul'shun) *n.* sudden, violent change of feeling; repugnance or abhorrence; reaction; counter-irritant.—**revul'sive** *a.* tending to revulsion [L. *revellere, revulsum*, to tear away].

reward (re-wawrd') *v.t.* to give in return for; to recompense; to remunerate;—*n.* what is given in return; return for voluntary act; money offered for recovery of articles or assistance in any form.—**reward'er** *n.*—**reward'ful** *a.* [O.Fr. *rewarder* = Fr. *regarder*, to look upon].

rex (reks) *n.* a king.—**rex'ist** *n.* a Belgian Fascist; a royalist [L.].

Rexine (reks'ēn) *n.* a substitute for leather [Protected Trade Name].

Reynard (rā'nąrd, ren'ąrd) *n.* the fox in an epic of the Middle Ages; a fox. Also **Ren'ard** [Fr. *renard*; Ger. *Reinhard*].

rhabdo- (rab'dō) *prefix* used in formation of scientific compound terms, signifying *a rod* or *rod-like*.—**rhab'doid** *a.* rod-shaped.—**rhab'domancy** *n.* divination by divining-rod, usually of hazel, to trace presence of minerals or metals under-ground [Gk. *rhabdos*, a rod].

rhachis (rā'kis) *n.* the spine; rachis.—**rhachiomyelitis** (rā-ki-ō-mī-e-lī'tis) *n.* (*Med.*) inflammation of spinal cord [Gk.].

rhadamanthine, rhadamantine (rad-ą-man'thin, -tin) *a.* pert. to *Rhadamanthus*, in Greek mythology, one of the judges of the dead in the nether world; hence, judicially strict, impartial, and severe.

rhapsody (rap'so-di) *n.* collection of verses, esp. one of the books of Homer, recited by the rhapsodists—hence, any number of passages gathered together without natural connection; a wild, rambling composition or discourse; (*Mus.*) a wild, irregular composition in a free style.—**rhap'sode** *n.* a rhapsodist.—**rhapsod'ic(al)** *a.* in wild, irregular style; gushing.—**rhapsod'ically** *adv.*—**rhap'sodise** *v.t.* and *v.i.* to sing or recite, as a rhapsody; to be ecstatic over.—**rhap'sodist** *n.* one who recites or composes a rhapsody [Gk. *rhapsōdia*].

rhea (rē'a) *n.* the S. American three-toed ostrich; the nandu [Gk.].

rheic (rē'ik) *a.* pert. to rhubarb.—**rhe'in** *n.* [Gk. *rhēon*, rhubarb].

Rhenish (ren'ish) *a.* of or pert. to River Rhine;—*n.* wine from grapes grown in Rhineland [L. *Rhenus*].

rhenium (rē'ni-um) *n.* very rare metallic chemical element used for increasing electrical resistance of tungsten [L. *Rhenus*, the Rhine].

rheo- (rē'o) *prefix* used in the formation of scientific compound terms, signifying *flowing* from Gk. *rhein*, to flow.—**rheom'eter** *n.* instrument for measuring force of electric currents; galvanometer.—**rhe'ostat** *n.* instrument for controlling and varying within limits value of resistance in electrical circuit.—**rheostat'ic** *a.*—**rheostat'ics** *n.* statics of fluids.

rhesus (rē'sus) *n.* small Indian monkey, looked upon as sacred by Hindus and allowed into precincts of temples.—**rhe'sian** *a.*—**rhesus factor** (*Med.*) a peculiarity of red cells of blood of most individuals, the so-called **rhesus positive**, rendering transfusion of their blood unsuitable for rhesus negative minority of patients.

rhetoric (ret'o-rik) *n.* art of persuasive or effective speech; declamation; artificial eloquence or sophistry; exaggerated oratory.—**rhetor'ical** *a.* oratorical; declamatory; bombastic.—**rhetorical question**, statement in the form of question to which there is only one rational answer.—**rhetor'ically** *adv.*—**rhetoric'ian** *n.* a teacher of or one well versed in principles of rhetoric [Gk. *rhētorikos*, fr. *rhētōr*, a public speaker].

rheum (ròòm) *n.* thin, serous fluid secreted by mucous glands and discharged from nostrils or eyes during catarrh or a common cold; tears; spleen.—**rheumat'ic, rheumat'ical** *a.* pert. to or suffering from rheumatism.—**rheum'atism** *n.* group of diseases with symptoms of sharp pains and swelling in muscles and larger joints.—**rheum'atoid** *a.* resembling rheumatism.—**rheum'y** *a.* full of watery humour or rheum (esp. eyes); damp.—**rheumatoid arthritis**, severe chronic inflammation of joints, esp. knees and fingers [Gk. *rheuma*, flow].

rhinal (rī-nąl) *a.* pert. to the nose [Gk. *rhis, rhinos*, nose].

rhinestone (rīn'stōn) *n.* kind of rock-crystal; paste imitation of diamonds [fr. the *Rhine*].

rhinoceros (rī-nos'ę-ros) *n.* thick-skinned mammal allied to elephant, hippopotamus, tapir, etc. with strong horn (sometimes two) on nose [Gk. *rhis, rhinos*, the nose; *keras*, a horn].

rhiz-, rhizo- (rīz', rī'zo) *prefix* used in construction of compound terms, from Greek, *rhiza*, a root.—**rhi'zome** *n.* subterranean shoot, often bearing scales which are membranous, and usually giving off adventitious roots.—**rhizom'atous** *a.* of the nature of a rhizome.

rhod-, rhodo- (rōd, rō'dō) *prefix* used in the formation of compound terms, signifying rose-coloured, from Greek, *rhodon*, a rose.—**rho'dium** *n.* a metallic chemical element related to ruthenium and palladium whose salts are rosy-red; scented wood of Canary convolvulus, rose-wood.—**rhod'ocyte** *n.* red blood corpuscle.—**rhododen'dron** *n.* evergreen flowering shrub of the order Ericaceae with magnificent red or white blossoms.

rhodomontade See **rodomontade**.

rhoeadic (rē-ad'ik) *a.* pert. to, or derived from, poppies [Gk. *rhoias*, a poppy].

rhombus (rom'bus) *n.* (*Geom.*) parallelogram whose sides are all equal, but whose angles are not right angles.—**rhomb** *n.* a lozenge or diamond-shaped figure; rhombus.—**rhom'bic, rhom'biform, rhom'boid, rhomboi'dal** *a.* having shape of rhomboid.—**rhom'boid** *n.* parallelogram like rhombus, but having only opposite sides and angles equal [Gk. *rhombos*].

rhone (rōn) *n.* eaves-gutter which collects rain from roof. Also **rone.**—**rhone'pipe** *n.* pipe which drains rain-water from rhone [O.E. *rinnan*, to run].

rhubarb (ròò'bàrb) *n.* two species of cultivated plants, familiar rhubarb of kitchen-garden, and an eastern variety whose roots are used as a purgative [Gk. *rha*, rhubarb; *barbaron*, foreign].

rhumb, rumb (rum) *n.* any one of 32 cardinal points on compass-card; angle separating these, 11° 15′ [Gk. *rhombos*, a rhomb].

rhyme, rime (rīm) *n.* identity of sound in word endings of verses; verses, usually two, in rhyme with each other; a couplet; word answering in sound to another word;—*v.t.* to put into rhyme;—*v.i.* to make verses.—**rhy'mer, rhym'ster** *n.* one who makes rhymes; a minor poet; a poetaster.—**rhyme scheme,** pattern or arrangement of rhymes in stanza [O.E. *rim*, number].

rhysimeter (rī-sim'e-tẹr) *n.* instrument for measuring velocity of fluids and speed of ships [Gk. *rhusis*, flowing; *metron*, measure].

rhythm (rithm) *n.* regular or measured flow of sound, as in music and poetry, or of action, as in dancing; measured, periodic movement, as in heart pulsations; regular recurrence; symmetry.—**rhyth'mic(al)** *a.*—**rhyth'mically** *adv.* —**rhyth'mics** *n.* science of rhythm [Gk. *rhuthmos*, fr. *rhein*, to flow].

riant (rī'ạnt) *a.* laughing; merry; genial.—**ri'ancy** *n.* gaiety [Fr. *rire*, to laugh].

rib (rib) *n.* one of arched and very elastic bones springing from vertebral column; anything resembling a rib, as a bar of a fire-grate, wire support of umbrella, a curved rafter, a transverse beam for stiffening wing of aircraft, girder which strengthens side of ship, etc.—*v.t.* to furnish with ribs.—*pr.p.* **rib'bing.**—*pa.t.* and *pa.p.* **ribbed.**—**rib'bing** *n.* an arrangement of ribs.—**rib'vault'ing** *n.* narrow arch below surface of vault to support or enrich it [O.E. *ribb*].

ribald (rib'ạld) *a.* low; vulgar; indecent;—*n.* a ribald person.—**rib'aldry** *n.* vulgar, indecent language or conduct; obscenity.—**rib'aldish, rib'aldrous** *a.* [Fr. *ribaud*].

ribbon, riband, ribband (rib'un, rib'ạnd) *n.* fillet, commonly of silk or satin, as trimming or fastening for a dress; coloured piece of silk (riband) as war-medal; part of insignia of order of knighthood.—**ribb'onite** *n.* soft lead used in ribbon form to caulk joints of socketed pipes.—**ribbon development,** building along main roads without corresponding development in back-areas.—**ribb'on-worm** *n.* the tape-worm.—**Blue Ribbon,** decoration worn by members of the Order of the Garter; badge of total abstinence society [O.Fr. *riban*].

riboflavin (rī'bō-flā-vin) *n.* chemical substance present in vitamin B2 complex, with marked growth-promoting properties [L.L. *ribus*, currant; *flavus*, yellow].

rice (rīs) *n.* annual grass plant, cultivated in Asia, the principal food of one-third of world. —**rice'pa'per** *n.* very thin and delicate paper used in China and Japan for drawing and painting [Gk. *oruza*].

rich (rich) *a.* wealthy; abounding in possessions; well supplied; fertile; abounding in nutritive qualities; of food, highly seasoned or flavoured; mellow and harmonious (voice); —*n.* the wealthy classes. —**rich'es** *n.pl.* wealth; opulence; plenty.—**rich'ly** *adv.*—**rich'ness** *n.* opulence; wealth [O.E. *rice*, rich].

rick (rik) *n.* stack of grain or hay; sprain; wrench;—*v.t.* to pile up in ricks.—**rick'bar'ton** *n.* rickyard [O.E. *hreac*].

rickets (rik'ets) *n.* rachitis, infantile disease marked by defective development of bones. —**rick'etiness** *n.* being rickety; tottering state; shakiness.—**rick'ety** *a.* affected with rickets; shaky; unstable; insecure [etym. uncertain].

rickshaw (rik'shaw) *n.* Japanese *jinriksha*—a light two-wheeled, hooded vehicle on springs, drawn by one man [Jap. *jin*, man; *riki*, strength; *sha*, vehicle].

ricochet (rik'ō-shā, -shet) *n.* glancing rebound of object after striking flat surface at oblique angle;—*v.t.* and *v.i.* to rebound or glance off. —*pr.p.* **ricochet'ting.**—*pa.t.* and *pa.p.* **ricochet'ted** [Fr.].

rid (rid) *v.t.* to free; to deliver; to relieve of; to remove by violence; to disencumber.—*pr.p.* **rid'ding.**—*pa.t.* and *pa.p.* **rid.**—**rid'dance** *n.* deliverance; forcible removal.—**a good riddance,** a welcome relief [O.E. *hreddan*, to snatch away].

ridden (rid'n) *pa.p.* of **ride.**

riddle (rid'l) *n.* large sieve for sifting or screening gravel, etc.;—*v.t.* to separate, as grain from chaff, with a riddle; to pierce with holes as in a sieve; to pull (theory, etc.) to pieces. —**ridd'lings** *n.pl.* coarse material left in sieve [O.E. *hridder*].

riddle (rid'l) *n.* enigma; puzzling fact, thing, person;—*v.i.* to speak in, make, riddles.—**ridd'lemeree** *n.* stuff and nonsense [O.E. *raedelse.* fr. *raedan*, to read, to guess].

ride (rīd) *v.t.* to be mounted on horse, bicycle, etc.; to traverse or cover distance;—*v.i.* to be carried on back of an animal; to be borne along in a vehicle; to lie securely at anchor; to float lightly.—*pr.p.* **rid'ing.**—*pa.t.* **rode;**—*pa.p.* **rid'den.**—*n.* act of riding; journey, on horseback, in a vehicle, etc.; riding-track; district of excise officer.—**rid'er** *n.* one who rides; addition to a document; supplement to original motion or verdict; (*Math.*) an exercise on some book problem or theorem.—**rid'ing** *a.* used for riding on; used by a rider;—*n.* a track prepared for riding exercise.—**rid'ing-ha'bit** *n.* dress worn by ladies on horseback.—**rid'ing-light** *n.* white light on forestay of vessel at anchor.—**riding-whip,** light whip with a short lash.—**to ride over,** to tyrannise or lord over.—**to ride rough-shod,** to show no consideration for others.—**riding the marches,** ceremonial riding round boundaries of town or burgh [O.E. *ridan*].

ridge (rij) *n.* line of meeting of two sloping surfaces; long narrow hill; strip of upturned soil between furrows; highest part of roof; horizontal beam to which tops of rafters are fixed; tongue of high pressure on meteorological map;—*v.t.* to form into ridges;—*v.i.* to rise in ridges; to wrinkle.—**ridge'bone** *n.* the spine.—**ridged** *a.* having ridges on its surface. —**ridge'way** *n.* road built along the crest of a hill. —**ridg'y** *a.* rising in ridges [O.E. *hrycg*, the back].

ridicule (rid'i-kūl) *n.* mockery; sarcasm; irony; raillery; derision;—*v.t.* to deride; to satirise; to mock; to make fun of.—**rid'iculer** *n.*—**ridic'ulous** *a.* exciting ridicule; ludicrous; droll; laughable. —**ridic'ulously** *adv.* [L. *ridere*, to laugh].

Riding (rī'ding) *n.* one of three divisions of Yorkshire [fr. O.N. *thrithe*, third].

riever See **reiver.**

rife (rīf) *a.* prevailing; prevalent; abundant; plentiful.—**rife'ly** *adv.*—**rife'ness** *n.* [O.E.].

riff-raff (rif'raf) *n.* sweepings; refuse; the rabble [M.E. *rif* and *raf*].

rifle (rī'fl) *v.t.* to search and rob; to strip; to plunder.—**ri'fler** *n.*—**rifl'ing** *n.* pillaging [O.Fr. *rifler*, fr. Ice. *hrifa*, to seize].

rifle (rī'fl) *v.t.* to make spiral grooves in (gun-barrel, etc.); to groove; to channel; to whet, as a scythe;—*n.* a musket whose barrel is grooved.—**ri'fling** *n.* the arrangement of grooves in a gun-barrel or rifle-tube.—**ri'fleman** *n.* private in the Rifle Brigade; a man armed with rifle [Dan. *rifle*, to groove].

rift (rift) *n.* cleft; fissure; ford;—*v.t.* and *v.i.* to cleave; to split.—**rift valley,** a valley caused by subsidence of land between two parallel geological faults [fr. *rive*, to rend].

Jelly fish

WORLD of the SEAS and RIVERS

Tunicates: 1. Ciona intestinalis 2. Pyura papillosa 3. Dendrodoa grossulariata 4. Botrylloides rubrum 5. Distomus type 6. Polycyclus renieri 7. Clavelina lepadiformis

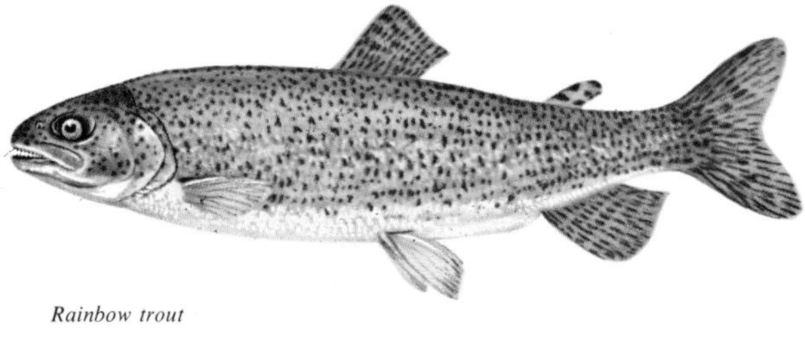

Rainbow trout

Coral reef

Starfish

WORLD of the SEA

Shells: Cypraea tigris (left), Strombus gigas (top), Pyramidell maculosa (bottom)

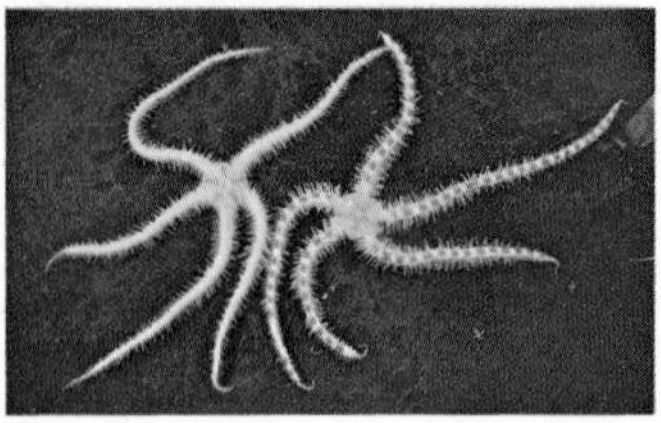

Starfish

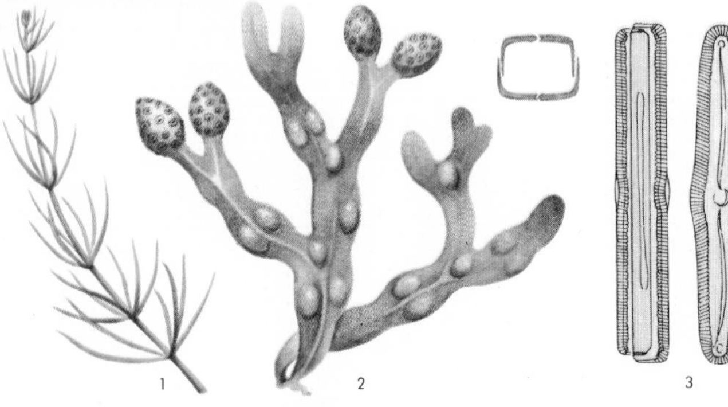

Algae: 1. Green algae 2. Bladderwrack 3. Diatom—sections

rig (rig) *v.t.* to provide (ship) with spars, ropes, etc.; to equip; to clothe.—*pr.p.* **rig'ging.**—*pa.t.* and *pa.p.* **rigged.**—*n.* manner in which masts and sails of vessel are rigged; equipment used in erecting or installing machinery, etc.; costume; style of dress; a horse and trap.—**rig'ger** *n.*—**rig'ging** *n.* system of ropes and tackle, esp. for supporting mast or controlling sails; adjustment of different components of an aircraft.—**rigging lines,** the cordage by which harness is attached to parachute.—**rig'-out** *n.* outfit;—*v.t.* to supply with complete outfit [Scand.].

rig (rig) *n.* a frolic; trick; dodge; a swindle; a wanton person;—*v.i.* to romp;—*v.t.* to raise prices by prior arrangement or by creating artificial scarcity, hence, **to rig the market** [etym. doubtful].

rig (rig) *n.* the back or top of anything; a ridge between furrows; a path.—**rig'ging** *n.* the ridge of a roof [O.E. *hrycg*, the back].

rigadoon (rig-a-dòòn') *n.* lively old French dance [Fr. *rigaudon*].

right (rīt) *a.* straight; proper; upright; in accordance with truth and duty; not left; being on same side as right hand; in politics, implying preservation of existing, established order or of restoring former institutions; (*Geom.*) applied to regular figures rising perpendicularly; correct; true;—*adv.* in a right manner; according to standard of truth and justice; very; correctly; properly; exactly; to the right hand;—*n.* that which is correct; uprightness; a just claim; legal title; that which is on right side, or opposite to left; political party inclined towards conservatism and preservation of status quo;—*v.t.* to set upright; to do justice to; to righten;—*v.i.* to recover proper or natural position; to become upright.—**right'en** *v.t.* to set right.—**right'ful** *a.* legitimate; lawful; true; honest; reasonable; fair.—**right'fully** *adv.*—**right'fulness** *n.* righteousness; justice.—**right'ly** *adv.* in accordance with justice; correctly.—**right'ness** *n.* correctness; justice.—**right'-about'** *adv.* in or to the opposite direction.—**right'-ang'led** *a.* having a **right angle,** one of ninety degrees.—**right'-hand** *a.* belonging to the right hand; pert. to most reliable assistant or man.—**right'-of-way** *n.* right of individual to pass over another's lands.—**right off** *adv.* immediately [O.E. *riht*].

righteous (rī'tyus) *a.* doing what is right; accepted of God, as free from sin; just; upright; godly.—**right'eously** *adv.* in a righteous manner.—**right'eousness** *n.* purity of heart and conduct; holiness; godliness; uprightness; honesty [O.E. *riht*, right; *wis*, wise].

rigid (rij'id) *a.* stiff; not easily bent.—**rigid'ity** *n.* resistance to change of form; stiffness; severity.—**rig'idly** *adv.*—**rig'idness** *n.* [L. *rigidus*].

rigmarole (rig'ma-rōl) *n.* a succession of meaningless, rambling statements; foolish talk;—*a.* incoherent [corrupt. of *ragman-roll*, a list of many names].

rigor (rig'or) *n.* (*Med.*) attack of cold and shivering, accompanied by rise of temperature and perspiration, followed by weakness; insensitive state of plants or animals.—**rig'orism** *n.* strictness; austerity.—**rig'orist** *n.* a person of strict principles.—**rigor mortis,** stiffening of body after death [L.].

rigour (rig'ur) *n.* being rigid; stiffness of opinion; harshness; strictness.—**rig'orous** *a.* severe; stiff; austere; strict; exact.—**rig'orously** *adv.*—**rig'orousness** *n.* [L. *rigor*, fr. *rigere*, to be stiff].

rile (rīl) *v.t.* to anger; to exasperate; to irritate [a form of *roil*].

rilievo (rē-lē-ā'vō) *n.* relief, in carving, etc. Also **relie'vo** [It.].

rill (ril) *n.* a small brook; a rivulet; a streamlet.—**rill'et** *n.* a tiny stream.—**rill'-marks** *n.pl.* the narrow furrows left on sands by the receding tide [Ger. *Rille*, a furrow].

rim (rim) *n.* margin; brim; border; metal ring forming outer edge of road-wheel and carrying the tyre;—*v.t.* to furnish with a rim;—*pr.p.* **rim'ming.**—*pa.t.* and *pa.p.* **rimmed.**—**rim'less** *a.* [O.E. *rima*].

rime Same as **rhyme.**

rime (rīm) *n.* white or hoar frost; frozen dew or vapour.—**ri'my** *a.* [O.E. *hrim*].

rimose (rī'mōs) *a.* having surface covered with fissures or cracks. Also **ri'mous** [L. *rimosus*].

rind (rīnd) *n.* the external covering or coating of trees, fruits, cheese, bacon, etc.; skin; peel; husk; bark;—*v.t.* to strip off a rind; to peel [O.E. *rinde*].

rinderpest (rin'der-pest) *n.* cattle plague; a malignant and contagious fever [Ger.].

ring (ring) *n.* small circle of gold, etc. esp. on finger; band, coil, rim; circle formed for dance or sports; round enclosure, as in circus, auction mart, etc.; area within roped square for boxing, etc.; a combination of persons to control prices within a trade;—*v.t.* to encircle; to put ring through an animal's nose; to tie horses together by passing rope through snaffles and fastening ends together.—**ring'-dove** *n.* pigeon, whose neck is surrounded by ring-shaped, white mark.—**ringed'-plo'ver** *n.* bird with black and white ring round neck.—**ring'ing** *n.*—**ring'leader** *n.* the leader of people associated together for a common object, usually in defiance of law and order.—**ring'less** *a.*—**ring'let** *n.* small ring; long curl of hair.—**ring'-mail** *n.* chain-armour.—**ring'-mas'ter** *n.* one who directs performance in circus-ring.—**ring'-ou'sel** *n.* member of thrush family, with broad white patch on throat.—**ring'-tail** *n.* additional sail set abaft and beyond spanker, in light winds; young golden-eagle.—**ring'worm** *n.* contagious disease of skin, esp. of scalp, leaving circular bare patches [O.E. *hring*].

ring (ring) *v.t.* to cause to sound, esp. by striking; to produce, by ringing;—*v.i.* to give out a clear resonant sound, as a bell; to chime; to resound; to be filled, as with praise, tidings, etc.; to continue sounding, as ears; to tingle.—*pa.t.* **rang,** *rarely* **rung.**—*pa.p.* **rung.**—*n.* a resonant note; chime (of church bells); act of ringing, to draw attention.—**to ring down,** to cause theatre curtain to be lowered; to wind up or conclude a transaction or business.—**to ring false,** to sound insincere.—**to ring changes upon,** to vary [O.E. *hringan*].

rink (ringk) *n.* broad strip, 18 to 21 feet wide, of a bowling-green; covered-in place for skating or curling; members of a side at bowls or curling; floor for roller-skating, etc. [etym. doubtful].

rinse (rins) *v.t.* to wash out, by filling with water, etc., and emptying; to wash without the use of soap [Fr. *rincer*].

riot (rī'ot) *n.* tumultuous disturbance of peace; wanton behaviour; noisy festivity; tumult; uproar; broil; profusion; luxury;—*v.i.* to make, or engage in, riot; to revel; to disturb peace.—**ri'oter** *n.*—**ri'oting** *n.*—**ri'otous** *a.* engaging in riot; unruly; rebellious.—**ri'otously** *adv.*—**ri'otousness** *n.*—**ri'otry** *n.* riotous conduct.—**to read the riot act** (*Colloq.*) to scold and threaten punishment.—**to run riot,** to behave wildly, without restraint [O.Fr. *riotte*].

rip (rip) *v.t.* to rend; to slash; to tear off or out; to slit; to saw wood along direction of grain;—*v.i.* to tear; to move quickly and freely.—*pr.p.* **rip'ping.**—*pa.t.* and *pa.p.* **ripped.**—*n.* rent; tear; dissipated person.—**rip'per** *n.*—**rip'ping** *a.* (*Colloq.*) splendid; capital.—**rip'pingly** *adv.*—**rip'-cord** *n.* cord to withdraw parachute from pack so that ascending air forces it open.—**rip'-saw** *n.* saw with large teeth for cutting timber in direction of grain [O.N. *rippa*, to scratch].

rip (rip) *n.* a stretch of broken water in sea or river [etym. doubtful].

riparian (rī-pā'ri-an) *a.* pert. to, or situated on, banks of a river [L. *ripa*, a river-bank].

ripe (rīp) *a.* ready for reaping; mature; fully developed; sound (judgment, etc.); ready (for) —*v.i.* to ripen.—**ripe'ly** *adv.*—**ri'pen** *v.t.* to hasten process of riping; to mature;—*v.i.* to grow ripe; to come to perfection.—**ripe'ness** *n.* [O.E.].

riposte (ri-post') *n.* quick return thrust in fencing; smart reply; repartee [Fr.].

ripple (rip'l) *n.* fretting or dimpling of surface of water; a little wave; subdued murmur or sound;—*v.t.* to cause ripple in;—*v.i.* to flow or form into little waves.—**ripp'le-mark** *n.* furrow left in sand by receding tide or wind. [var. of *rimple*, for O.E. *hrimpan*, to wrinkle].

rise (rīz) *v.i.* to ascend; to get up; to get out of bed; to appear above horizon; to originate; to swell; to increase in value, price, power; to adjourn; to revolt; to reach a higher rank; to revive.—*pr.p.* **ri'sing**.—*pa.t.* **rose**.—*pa.p.* **ris'en**. —*n.* act of rising; that which rises or seems to rise; increase, as of price, wages, etc.; source; elevation, as of voice.—**ri'ser** *n.* one who, or that which, rises; vertical part of a step.—**ri'sing** *n.* getting up; revolt; insurrection;—*a.* nearing; approaching; advancing. —**to take a rise out of**, to joke at someone's expense; to fool [O.E. *risan*].

risible (riz'i-bl) *a.* very prone to laugh; capable of exciting laughter; mirth-provoking.—**risibil'ity**, **ris'ibleness** *n.*—**ris'ibly** *adv.* [L. *risibilis*, fr. *ridere*, to laugh].

risk (risk) *n.* danger; peril; hazard; amount covered by insurance; person or object insured;—*v.t.* to expose to danger or possible loss.—**risk'er** *n.*—**risk'y** *a.* [Fr. *risque*].

risorgimento (rē-sor-jē-men'tō) *n.* period (1830-1870) of struggle for national unity and emancipation in Italy [It. = revival].

risorial (ri-sō'ri-al) *a.* causing laughter;risible [L. *ridere, risum*, to laugh].

risotto (ri-zot'tō) *n.* Italian dish of shredded onions, meat, and rice, cooked in fat [It.].

rissole (ris'ōl) *n.* fish or meat minced and fried with bread-crumbs and eggs [Fr.].

rite (rīt) *n.* former practice or custom, esp. religious; form; solemnity; ceremonial.—**rit'ual** *a.* pert. to rites; ceremonial;—*n.* manner of performing divine service; prescribed book of rites.—**rit'ualism** *n.* practices of school of religious thought which insists on importance of decorous ceremonial in public worship and administration of Sacraments, esp. of the High Church Anglicans.—**rit'ualist** *n.*—**ritualist'ic** *a.*—**rit'ually** *adv.* [L. *ritus*].

rival (rī'val) *n.* competitor; emulator; opponent;—*a.* having same pretensions or claims; competing;—*v.t.* to vie with; to strive to equal or excel; to emulate.—*pr.p.* **ri'valling**. —*pa.t.* and *pa.p.* **ri'valled**.—**ri'valry** *n.* keen competition; emulation [L. *rivalis*].

rive (rīv) *v.t.* to rend asunder; to split; to cleave;—*v.i.* to be split or rent asunder.—*pa.t.* **rived**.—*pa.p.* **rived**, **riv'en** [O.N. *rifa*].

river (riv'er) *n.* natural stream of water flowing in a channel; a copious flow; abundance. —**riv'erain**, **riv'erine** *a.* situated near or on river.—**riv'er-bas'in** *n.* area drained by a river and its tributaries.—**riv'er-bed** *n.* channel of a river.—**riv'er-horse** *n.* the hippopotamus.—**riv'er-side** *n.* the bank of a river [Fr. *rivière*].

rivet (riv'et) *n.* cylindrical iron or steel pin with strong flat head at one end, used for uniting two overlapping plates, etc. by hammering down the stub end;—*v.t.* to fasten with rivets; to clinch; to fasten firmly.—**riv'eter** *n.* [Fr.].

rivulet (riv'ū-let) *n.* a little river.

roach (rōch) *n.* carp-like fresh-water fish with red fins and silvery body [O.Fr. *roche*].

roach (rōch) *n.* an *abbrev.* of **cockroach**.

road (rōd) *n.* a track or way prepared for passengers, vehicles, etc.; direction; way; route; a place where vessels may ride at anchor.—**road'block** *n.* an obstruction placed across a road for defensive purposes.—**road'hog** *n.* motor-cyclist or motorist who drives to the danger of others.—**road'house** *n.* a restaurant, hotel, etc., on main-roads.—**road'man**, **roads'man** *n.* one employed in repairing roads.—**road'met'al** *n.* broken stones used in macadamising roads.—**road'roll'er** *n.* heavy roller for consolidating fresh surface of macadamised roads.—**road show**, travelling company of actors.—**road'side** *n.* strip of ground along edge of road.—**road'stead** *n.* anchorage providing part shelter for a vessel while off shore.—**road'survey'or** *n.* one who supervises construction and repair of roads.—**road'way** *n.* carriage-way of a road.—**to take to the road**, to adopt life of a tramp; to become a highwayman [O.E. *rad*, riding].

roam (rōm) *v.t.* and *v.i.* to wander; to ramble; to rove;—*n.* a ramble; a walk.—**roam'er** *n.* [etym. uncertain].

roan (rōn) *a.* having coat in which the main colour is thickly interspersed with another, esp. bay or sorrel or chestnut mixed with white or grey;—*n.* a roan horse; sumac-tanned smooth-grained sheep-skin, dyed and finished [Fr. *rouan*].

roar (rōr) *v.t.* and *v.i.* to shout; to bawl; to squall; to make loud, confused sound, as winds, waves, traffic, etc.; to laugh loudly;—*n.* sound of roaring; a loud cry.—**roar'ing** *n.* act or sound of roaring.—**roar'ingly** *adv.*—**Roaring Forties**, area of Southern Ocean between 40° and 50° S. latitude where strong W. and N.W. winds are prevalent.—**roaring trade**, brisk, profitable business [O.E. *rarian*].

roary (rō-ri) *a.* conspicuous; loud, as of colour; boisterous. Also **rory** [fr. *roar*].

roast (rōst) *v.t.* to cook by exposure to open fire or in oven; to expose to heat (as coffee, etc.); (*Slang*) to reprimand; to abuse;—*v.i.* to become over-heated;—*n.* what is roasted, as joint of meat;—*a.* roasted.—**roas'ting** *n.* [O.Fr. *rostir*].

rob (rob) *v.t.* to take by force or stealth; to plunder; to steal.—*pr.p.* **rob'bing**.—*pa.t.* and *pa.p.* **robbed**.—**rob'ber** *n.*—**rob'bery** *n.* forcibly depriving a person of money or of goods [O.Fr. *rober*].

robe (rōb) *n.* a long outer garment, esp. of flowing style; ceremonial dress denoting state, rank, or office; gown;—*v.t.* to invest with a robe; to array; to dress.—**rob'ing** *n.* [Fr.].

robin (rob'in) *n.* small, brown red-breasted bird of thrush family; the ruddock; robin-redbreast.—**rob'inet** *n.* robin; tap or cock of steam-engine [O.Fr. *Robin*, for *Robert*].

robot (rō'bot) *n.* automaton; mechanical man; machine which performs varied and highly-skilled operations as if impelled by a human brain; person of machine-like efficiency [fr. play, R.U.R. (Rossum's Universal *Robots*), by Karel Capek]. [Pol. *robotnik*, workman].

robust (rō-bust') *a.* strong; muscular; sound; vigorous.—**robust'ious** *a.* boisterous; violent.—**robust'ly** *adv.*—**robust'ness** *n.* [L. *robustus*, fr. *robur*, an oak, strength].

roc (rok) *n.* gigantic legendary bird of Arabian tales, capable of mighty feats of strength [Pers. *rukh*].

Rochelle salt (rō-shel'sawlt] *n.* tartrate of sodium and potassium, used as aperient and as an ingredient of Seidlitz powder [*La Rochelle*, a town in France].

rochet (roch'et) *n.* garment like a surplice, of white lawn, usually with tight sleeves, worn by bishops [O.Fr.].

rock (rok) *n.* large mass of stone; (*Geol.*) any natural deposit of sand, earth, or clay when in natural beds; firm foundation; defence, fortress, strength; sweetmeat in long cylindrical form.—**rock'er** *n.* rock-dove.—**rock'ery** *n.* small artificial mound of stones planted with Alpine plants.—**rock'iness** *n.*—**rock'y** *a.* rugged; resembling rocks; unfeeling. —**rock'bott'om** *a.* lowest possible;—*n.* fundamental principles.—**rock'cake** *n.* currant cake with a hard crust.—**rock'crys'tal** *n.* transparent quartz used in making certain lenses.

—**rock′dove** *n.* dove or pigeon with two black bars on wings.—**rock′gar′den** *n.* a garden laid out for growing rock-plants.—**rock′ling** *n.* one of several species of cod.—**rock′oil** *n.* petroleum.—**rock′plants** *n.pl.* plants which thrive in dry exposed places among stones and rocks. —**rock′salt** *n.* unrefined sodium chloride found in great natural deposits.—**rock′tar** *n.* petroleum.—**the Rock,** Gibraltar.—**on the rocks** (*Colloq.*) having no money or resources [Fr. *roche*].

rock (rok) *v.t.* to sway to and fro; to put to sleep by rocking; to lull; to shake;—*v.i.* to be moved, backward and forward; to reel; to totter.—**rock′er** *n.* curving piece of wood on which cradle or chair rocks; rocking-horse or -chair; pivoted lever having a rocking motion by means of which movement is conveyed from one point of machine to another.—**rock′y** *a.* disposed to rock; shaky.—**rock′ing** *n.* act or state of moving to and fro.—**rock′ing-chair** *n.* chair mounted on rockers.—**rock′ing-horse** *n.* wooden horse mounted on rockers; a hobby-horse.—**off one's rocker** (*Slang*) eccentric [O.E. *roccian*].

rocket (rok′et) *n.* cylindrical tube filled with a mixture of sulphur, nitre, and charcoal, which, on ignition, hurls the tube forward by action of liberated gases; a similar tube which draws a life-line towards ship in distress; fire-work;—*v.i.* to soar up; to increase rapidly in price, etc.—**rock′et-bomb** *n.* high-explosive bomb which is rocket-projected.—**rocket plane,** plane propelled by rockets [It. *rocchetta*, dim. of *rocca*, a distaff].

rococo (rō-kō′kō) *n.* style of architecture, overlaid with profusion of fantastic ornamentation [Fr.].

rod (rod) *n.* slender, straight, round bar, wand, stick, or switch; birch rod for punishment; cane; emblem of authority; oppression; fishing-rod; lightning conductor; English linear measure, a *pole* or *perch*, equal to 5½ yards or 16½ feet.—**rod′bacter′ium** *n.* bacillus [O.E. *rodd*].

rode (rōd) *pa. t.* of **ride.**

rodent (rō′dent) *a.* gnawing;—*n.* gnawing animal, as rabbit, rat [L. *rodere*, to gnaw].

rodeo (rō-dā′ō) *n.* round-up of cattle to be branded or marked; exhibition and contest in steer-wrestling and buck-jumping by cowboys [Sp.].

rodomont (rod′ō-mont) *n.* a braggart;—*a.* boasting; bragging.—**rodomontade′, rhodomontade′** *n.* vain boasting; bluster; rant;—*v.i.* to boast; to brag; to bluster [*Rodomonte*, the blustering opponent of Charlemagne, depicted in Ariosto's *Orlando Furioso*].

roe (rō) *n.* small, elegant deer of forests of N. Scotland; female hart.—**roe′buck** *n.* male of roe [O.E. *rah*].

roe (rō) *n.* the eggs or spawn of fish [Scand.].

roentgen (runt′gen) *n.* (*Nuclear Physics*) measuring unit of radiation dose. See also **Röntgen.**

rogation (rō-gā′shun) *n.* in ancient Rome demand, by consuls or tribunes, of a law to be passed by people; litany; supplication.—**Rogation Days,** three days preceding Ascension Day, on which special litanies are sung or recited by R.C. clergy and people in public procession, invoking a blessing on crops.—**ro′gatory** *a.* commissioned to gather information [L. *rogare*, to ask].

rogue (rōg) *n.* vagrant; sturdy beggar; vagabond; knave; wag.—**rog′uery** *n.* knavish tricks; cheating; fraud; waggery.—**rog′uish** *a.* dishonest; waggish.—**rog′uishly** *adv.*—**rog′uishness** *n.*—**rogue′el′ephant** *n.* an elephant of dangerous temper living apart from herd.—**rogues' gallery,** a collection of photographs of convicted criminals kept by police [O.Fr. *rogue*, proud].

rogue (rōg) *v.t.* and *v.i.* to remove plant from crop (potatoes, cereals, etc.) when that plant falls short of standard or is of another variety from the crop, in order to keep strain pure;—*n.* plant so removed; plant that falls short of a standard or has reverted to original type [etym. uncertain].

roist, roister (roist, rois′ter) *v.i.* to bluster; to bully; to swagger.—**rois′ter, rois′terer** *n.*—**rois′terly** *adv.* [O.Fr. *ruster*, a rough, rude fellow, fr. L. *rusticus*, rustic].

rôle (rōl) *n.* a part played by an actor in a drama—hence, any conspicuous part or task in public life [Fr.].

roll (rōl) *v.t.* to turn over and over; to move by turning on an axis; to form into a spherical body; to bind by winding; to drive forward with a swift and easy motion; to level with a roller; to beat with rapid strokes, as a drum; to utter (vowels, letter *r*) with a full, long-drawn sound;—*v.i.* to move forward by turning; to revolve upon an axis; to keep falling over and over; to sway; to reel; to rock from side to side, as ship; to wallow; of aircraft, to turn about the axis, *i.e.* a line from nose to tail, in flight;—*n.* rolling; a piece of paper, etc. rolled up; any object thus shaped; bread baked into small crisp oval or rounded shapes; official document; list; register; catalogue; continuous sound, as thunder; a full cork-screw revolution of an aeroplane about its longitudinal fore and aft axis during flight.—**roll′able** *a.*—**roll′call** *n.* calling over list of names to check absentees.—**rolled gold,** a plate of alloy with thin sheets of gold welded firmly to its surface.—**roll′er** *n.* cylinder of wood, stone, metal, etc. used in husbandry and the arts; a cylinder which distributes ink over type in printing; long, swelling wave; long, broad bandage; small, insectivorous bird which tumbles about in the air.—**roll′er-skate** *n.* skate with wheels or rollers instead of steel runner.—**roll-film** *n.* photographic film rolled on to spool.—**roll′ing** *a.* moving on wheels; turning over and over; undulating, as a plain; —*n.* (*Naut.*) heeling of ship from side to side. —**roll′ing-mill** *n.* apparatus for rolling pieces of metal into rods, bars, sheets, plates, etc.—**roll′ing-pin** *n.* cylindrical piece of wood or glass for rolling out paste or dough.—**roll′ing-plant, roll′ing-stock** *n.* locomotives, carriages, wagons, etc. of railway.—**rolling stone,** person incapable of settling down in any one place.—**roll′top** *n.* type of opening roof for car; desk with flexible sliding cover [Fr. *rouler*, fr. L. *rotula*, a little wheel].

rollick (rol′ik) *v.i.* to move about in a boisterous, careless manner;—*n.* frolicsome gaiety. —**roll′icking** *a.* jovial; care-free; high-spirited [etym. unknown].

rollock See **rowlock.**

roly-poly (rō′li-pō′li) *n.* in baking, a sheet of paste covered with jam and rolled in the form of a cylinder [redupl. of *roll*].

rom (rom) *n.* a male gipsy.—*pl.* **rom′a** [Gipsy = man, husband].

Romaic (rō-mā′ik) *n.* modern vernacular Greek language;—*a.* of modern Greece or its language [Fr. *romaïque*, fr. Mod. Gk. *Rhōmaikos*, fr. *Rhōmē*, Rome].

Roman (rō′man) *a.* pert. to Rome or Roman people; pert. to R.C. religion; in printing, upright letters as distinguished from *Italic* characters; expressed in letters, not in figures, as I., IV., i., iv., etc. (as distinguished from Arabic numerals, 1, 4, etc.);—*n.* native, citizen, resident of Rome.—**Roman′ic** *a.* pert. to Rome or its people; pert. to languages which sprang out of Latin;—*n.* Romance languages.—**ro′manise** *v.t.* to introduce many words and idioms derived from Latin; to convert to Roman Catholicism;—*v.i.* to use Latin expressions; to conform to R.C. opinions or practices. —**Ro′manism** *n.* tenets of Church of Rome.—**Ro′manist** *n.*—**Rom′ish** *a.* relating to Rome or to R.C. church.—**Rom′ist** *n.* Roman Catholic. —**Roman candle,** a firework which throws out differently coloured stars.—**Roman Catholic,** a member or adherent of section of Christian

Church which acknowledges supremacy of Pope;—*a.* pert. to Church of Rome.—**Roman Catholicism**, doctrines and tenets of R.C. church [L. *Romanus*, fr. *Roma*, Rome].

Romance (rō-mans′) *n.* vernacular languages of certain countries in southern Europe, developed from Latin and including Italian, Spanish, French, Provençal, Roumanian, Romansch, etc.;—*a.* pert. to these languages. —**romance′** *n.* narrative of knight-errantry in Middle Ages; ballad of adventures in love and war; any fictitious narrative treating of olden times; historical novel; story depending mainly on love-interest; highly-coloured falsehood; (*Mus.*) composition sentimental and expressive in character;—*v.i.* to write or tell romances; embroider one's account or description with extravagances; to lie unblushingly.—**roman′cer, roman′cist** *n.*—**romanesque′** *a.* (*Paint.*) representing subjects and scenes appropriate to romance; resembling Roman architecture;—*n.* portrayal of fabulous or fanciful subjects; style of drawing and colouring in fantastic forms, and not from life; any form of architecture derived from Roman, as Byzantine, Lombard, Saxon, etc.—**roman′tic** *a.* pert. to romance; fictitious; fanciful; sentimental; imaginative.—**roman′tically** *adv.*—**roman′ticism** *n.* the reactionary movement in literature and art against formalism and classicism; state of being romantic [O.Fr. *romans*, It. *romanza*].

Romany, Rommany (rom′ą-ni) *n.* a gipsy; the language of the gipsies. Also **Rom′ani.**—**Romany rye**, a gentleman who cultivates the society of gipsies [Gipsy *rom*, a man].

romp (romp) *v.i.* to leap and frisk about in play; to frolic;—*n.* a tom-boy; a boisterous form of play.—**romp′ers** *n.pl.* a child's overall, with leg openings [earlier, *ramp*].

rondeau (ron′dō) *n.* poem, usually of thirteen lines with only two rhymes, the opening words recurring additionally, as a burden, after eighth and thirteenth lines; (*Mus.*) rondo.—**ron′del** *n.* poem of thirteen or fourteen iambic lines, first two lines of which are repeated in middle and at close.—**ron′do** *n.* musical setting of a rondeau; sonata movement in music in which a principal theme is repeated two or three times [Fr.].

rone (rōn) *n.* See **rhone.**

Roneo (rō′ne-ō) *n.* a duplicating machine;—*v.* to duplicate letters, etc. by this means [Protected Trade Name].

Röntgen rays (runt′gen rāz) *n.pl.* X-rays.—**rönt′genise** *v.t.* to submit to action of X-rays [Wilhelm von *Röntgen* (1845-1923), German physicist].

rood (ròòd) *n.* fourth part of acre, equal to 40 square poles or 1,210 square yards; a cross or crucifix, esp. one placed in a church over entrance to choir.—**rood′arch** *n.* arch between nave and chancel of church.—**rood′loft** *n.* a small gallery over rood-screen of church.—**rood′screen** *n.* open-work screen, highly ornamented, separating choir from nave in Gothic churches [O.E. *rod*, a rod, a cross].

roof (ròòf) *n.* outside structure covering building; framework supporting this covering; stratum immediately above seam in mine; upper part of any hollow structure or object, as roof of cave, mouth, etc.; ceiling;—*v.t.* to cover with a roof; to shelter.—**roof′gar′den** *n.* miniature garden on flat roof.—**roof′tree** *n.* a common rafter or spar.—**Mansard roof**, a roof having a break in slope, lower part being steeper than upper [O.E. *hrof*].

rook (rook) *n.* in chess, one of the four pieces placed on corner squares of the board; also known as a castle [Pers. *rukh*].

rook (rook) *n.* blue-black, hoarse-voiced bird of crow family; swindler; a card-sharper;—*v.t.* to cheat; to swindle.—**rook′ery** *n.* colony of rooks and their nests; overcrowded, slum tenement.—**rook′ie** *n.* (*fem.* **rookette′**) Army slang for a recruit [O.E. *hroc*].

room (ròòm) *n.* (enough) space; apartment or chamber; scope; opportunity; occasion;—*pl.* lodgings;—*v.i.* (*U.S.*) to lodge.—**room′ful** *a.*—**room′ily** *adv.*—**room′iness** *n.* spaciousness.—**room′y** *a.* spacious; wide [O.E. *rum*].

roost (ròòst) *n.* pole on which birds rest at night; perch; collection of fowls roosting together;—*v.i.* to settle down to sleep, as birds on a perch; to perch.—**roost′er** *n.* a cock [O.E. *hrost*].

root (ròòt) *n.* part of plant which grows down into soil seeking nourishment for whole plant; plant whose root is edible, as beetroot; part of anything which grows like root, as of tooth, cancer, etc.; source; origin; vital part; basis; bottom; primitive word from which other words are derived; (*Math.*) factor of quantity which, when multiplied by itself the number of times indicated by the index number, will produce that quantity, e.g. 4 is third (or cube) root of 64 (symbol $\sqrt[3]{}$), for $4 \times 4 \times 4 = 64$;—*v.t.* to plant and fix in earth; to impress deeply in mind; to establish firmly;—*v.i.* to enter earth, as roots; to be firmly fixed or established.—**root′crop** *n.* plant grown for edible value of its roots, e.g. turnip.—**root′ed** *a.* firmly established.—**root′stock** *n.* a rhizome. —**root and branch**, entirely; completely [O.E *wyrt*].

root (ròòt) *v.t.* and *v.i.* to turn up with the snout, as swine; to extirpate; to rummage; to uncover [O.E. *wrot*, a snout].

root (ròòt) *v.i.* to cheer [*U.S. Slang*].

rope (rōp) *v.t.* stout cord of several twisted strands of fibre or metal wire; row of objects strung together, as onions, pearls, etc.;—*v.t.* to fasten with a rope; to mark off a racing track, etc., with ropes; to lasso. —**rope′cord** *n.* ornamental cord used by upholsterers.—**rope′danc′er** *n.* one who performs on a rope raised above ground.—**rope′ladd′er, rope′bridge**, etc. *n.* one made of ropes.—**ro′pery** *n.* a place where ropes are made.—**rope′yarn** *n.* thread or small lines of yarn twisted into strands for making ropes or serving rigging, etc.—**ro′piness** *n.* stringiness; stickiness.—**ro′ping** *a.* [O.E. *rap*].

Roquefort (rok-for′) *n.* a green cheese of ewe's milk [*Roquefort*, in France].

rorqual (ror′kwąl) *n.* a genus of whale, the largest of living animals [Scand. *rör*, red; *hval*, whale].

rory See **roary.**

rosacea (rō-zā′sē-ą) *n.* form of acne, marked by redness of nose and pimples [L. fr. *rosa*, a rose].

Rosaceae (rō-zā′sē-ē) *n.pl.* order of plants including dog-rose, strawberry, blackberry, cherry, hawthorn.—**rosa′ceous** *a.* rose-like; belonging to rose family.—**rosa′rium** *n.* rose-garden [L. *rosa*, rose].

rosary (rō′zą-ri) *n.* rose-garden; string of beads on which are counted Ave Marias and Paternosters [L. *rosa*, a rose].

roscid (ros′id) *a.* dewy [L. *ros*, dew].

rose (rōz) *pa.t.* of rise.

rose (rōz) *n.* typical genus (*Rosa*) of plant family Rosaceae, consisting of spiny, wing-leaved shrubs and red, yellow, or white flowers; flower of one of these shrubs; delicate shade of pink; rosette; perforated nozzle of tube or pipe, as on watering-can.—**ro′seal** *a.* resembling rose in colour or fragrance.—**ro′seate** *a.* rosy; full of roses; of rose colour; blooming; optimistic.—**rose′bay** *n.* a willow-herb with showy spikes of large pink or purple flowers.—**rose′bud** *n.* the bud of the rose; a young girl in her teens.—**rose′coloured** *a.* having colour of a rose; unwarrantably optimistic; extravagantly extolled. Also **rose′hued.**—**ro′sery** *n.* nursery for rearing rose-bushes.—**rose′wa′ter** *n.* water tinctured with roses by distillation;—*a.* having fragrance of rose-water—hence, affectedly delicate.—**rose′win′dow** *n.* circular window with a series of mullions diverging from centre.—**rose′wood** *n.* rich, dark-red hardwood from S. America, used for furniture-making.—**ros′ily** *adv.*—

ros'iness *n.*—**ros'y** *a.* like a rose; blooming; red; blushing; bright; favourable.—**under the rose,** strictly confidential; secret; *sub rosa* [L. *rosa,* a rose].

rosemary (rōzˊmạ-ri, rōzˊmā-ri) *n.* a small, fragrant evergreen shrub, emblem of fidelity [L. *ros,* dew; *marinus,* marine].

rosette (rō-zet') *n.* something fashioned to resemble a rose, as bunch of ribbon; a rose-shaped architectural ornament.—**roset'ted** *a.* [Fr. dim. of *rose*].

rosin (rozˊin) *n.* resin in solid state;—*v.t.* to rub or cover with rosin.—**ros'iny** *a.* like rosin [Fr. *résine*].

rossignol (rosˊi-nyol) *n.* the nightingale; the Canadian song-sparrow [Fr.].

roster (rosˊtẹr) *n.* a list or plan showing turns of duty; register of names [Dut. *rooster,* a corrupt. of L. *register*].

rostrum (rosˊtrum) *n.-n.pl.* **ros'trums, ros'tra,** beak or bill of bird; snout or pointed organ; beak of a ship; raised platform; pulpit.—**ros'tral** *a.* pert. to rostrum, beak, or snout.—**ros'trate, ros'trated** *a.* beaked [L. = a beak, fr. *rodere,* to gnaw].

rosy. See **rose.**

rot (rot) *v.t.* and *v.i.* to decompose naturally; to corrupt; to putrefy; to moulder away.—*pr.p.* **rot'ting.**—*pa.t.* and *pa.p.* **rot'ted.**—*n.* rotting; decomposition; decay; disease of sheep, as foot-rot; form of decay which attacks timber, usually **dryˊrot;** disease, injurious to potato; (*Slang*) nonsense [O.E. *rotian*].

rota (rōˊtạ) *n.* wheel; course; roster, list, or roll; (*Mus.*) a round; an ecclesiastical tribunal in the R.C. church which acts as court of appeal.—**ro'tal** *a.* [L. = wheel].

rotary (rōˊtạr-i) *a.* turning, as a wheel; rotatory;—*n.* type-cylinder printing-machine; international association of business men's clubs.—**Rota'rian** *n.* member of Rotary Club.—**rotary engine,** in aviation, aero-engine in which cylinder and crank-case rotate with airscrew [L. *rota,* a wheel].

rotate (rō-tāt') *v.t.* to cause to revolve;—*v.i.* to move round pivot; to go in rotation; to revolve; to spin.—**ro'tate** *a.* (*Bot.*) wheel-shaped, as a calyx.—**rota'tion** *n.* turning, as a wheel or solid body on its axis; (*Astron.*) period of rotation of planet about its imaginary axis; serial change, as *rotation of crops.*—**rota'tional** *a.*—**rota'tor** *n.*—**ro'tatory** *a.* turning on an axis, as a wheel; going in a circle; following in succession [L. *rota,* a wheel].

rote (rōt) *n.* mechanical repetition of words [O.Fr. *rote,* track].

rote (rōt) *n.* early English stringed instrument of dulcimer type [O.Fr. = a fiddle].

rotor (rōˊtor) *n.* revolving portion of dynamo, motor, or turbine.—**ro'tor-ship** *n.* ship propelled by effect of wind pressure on one or more revolving cylinders erected from the deck [short for *rotator*].

rotten (rotˊn) *a.* putrefied; decayed; carious; unsound; corrupt; (*Slang*) bad; worthless.—**rott'enly** *adv.*—**rott'enness** *n.*—**rott'en-bor'ough** *n.* town become practically non-existent, yet retaining right to return member of parliament.—**rott'er** *n.* (*Slang*) a worthless, unprincipled person [fr. *rot*].

rotund (rō-tund') *a.* round; circular; globular; spherical; plump.—**rotun'da** *n.* circular building or apartment, covered by dome.—**rotun'dity, rotund'ness** *n.* globular form; completeness [L. *rotundus,* fr. *rota,* a wheel].

rouble, ruble (ròòˊbl) *n.* Russian monetary unit and silver coin; divided into 100 copeks (kopeks) [Russ. *rubl*].

roué (ròòˊā) *n.* a libertine; a profligate; a rake [Fr. = one broken on the wheel].

rouge (ròòzh) *n.* fine red powder used by jewellers as polish-material; cosmetic for tinting cheeks;—*v.t.* and *v.i.* to tint (face) with rouge [Fr. = red].

rough (ruf) *a.* not smooth; rugged; uneven; unhewn; shapeless; uncut; unpolished; rude; harsh; boisterous; stormy; approximate; unfair; having aspirated sound of *h*;—*adv.* in rough manner;—*n.* rude, coarse fellow; crude, unfashioned state; parts of golf-course adjoining fairway and greens;—*v.t.* to make rough; to roughen; to rough-hew; to shape out in rough and ready way.—**rough'age** *n.* fibrous, unassimilated portions of food which promote intestinal movement.—**roughˊcast** *n.* method of finishing outside plaster-work by covering with mixture of lime and pebbles or gravel.—**rough diamond,** uncut diamond; a person of ability and worth, but uncouth.—**rough'en** *v.t.* to make rough;—*v.i.* to become rough.—**roughˊhew** *v.t.* to hew coarsely; to give first form to a thing.—**roughˊhouse** *n.* rag; horse-play; a disturbance indoors.—**rough'ly** *adv.*—**roughˊneck** *n.* in U.S.A., (*Colloq.*) ill-mannered fellow; a tough.—**rough'ness** *n.*—**to rough it,** to put up with hardship and discomfort [O.E. *ruh*].

roulade (ròò-làd') *n.* (*Mus.*) embellishment; trill; shake [Fr. *rouler,* to roll].

rouleau (ròò-lō') *n.* little roll; roll of coins in paper;—*pl.* **rouleaux', rouleaus'.**—**rouleaux'** *n.pl.* little rolls or chains of red corpuscles [Fr. dim. of O.Fr. *role,* a roll].

roulette (ròò-let') *n.* game of chance, played with a revolving disc and a ball [Fr. dim. of O.Fr. *roule,* wheel].

round (round) *a.* circular; spherical; globular; rotund; whole; total; not fractional or divisional, as a sum; large; plump; smooth; flowing, as style or diction; plain; fair; candid; decided, as assertion; (of vowel) pronounced with rounded lips;—*n.* circle; globe; circuit; cycle; series; a course of action performed by persons in turn; carousal; bumpers; toasts; a certain amount (of applause); walk by guard to visit posts, sentries, etc.; beat of policeman, milkman, etc.; a game (of golf); one of successive stages in knock-out competition, as cup-tie football; short bout, limited in time, between two boxers; step of a ladder; ammunition unit; circular dance; short, vocal piece, in which singers start at regular intervals after each other;—*adv.* on all sides; circularly; back to the starting point; on every side of; about;—*v.t.* to make circular, spherical, or cylindrical; to go round; to smooth; to polish;—*v.i.* to grow or become round or full in form.—**round'about** *a.* indirect; circuitous;—*n.* merry-go-round; obstacle at cross-roads to compel traffic to slow down.—**roun'del** *n.* round figure; kind of dance; rondel; small circular shield.—**roun'delay** *n.* round or country dance; an air or tune in three parts, in which the first strain is repeated in the others.—**round'er** *n.* a tool for rounding-off objects; one who habitually goes round beat;—*pl.* outdoor game with ball and stick.—**Round'head** *n.* a Puritan (so called from practice of cropping hair close); republican in time of Commonwealth.—**roundˊhouse** *n.* in merchant navy, a cabin built on after part of quarter-deck; sentry-box or guard-room.—**round'ly** *adv.* vigorously; fully; plainly; bluntly; openly.—**round'ness** *n.*—**roundˊrob'in** *n.* petition, etc. having signatures arranged in a circular form so as to give no clue to order of signing.—**roundˊshot** *n.* cannon-ball.—**rounds'man** *n.* person who delivers goods regularly on prescribed beat.—**round-table conference,** one where all participants are on equal footing.—**roundˊup,** *n.* collecting cattle into herds; throwing cordon round area by police or military for interrogating all found within;—*v.t.* to collect and bring into confined space.—**to round off,** to bring to a grand conclusion.—**to come round,** to recover consciousness [Fr. *rond*].

round (round) *v.t.* and *v.i.* to whisper.—**to round on,** to inform against; to scold [O.E. *runian,* to whisper].

roup (roup) *n.* (*Scot.*) sale of goods by auction [O.E. *hropan,* to cry].

roup (roup) *n.* a contagious disease of domestic poultry [O.E. *hropan*, to cry].

rouse (rouz) *v.t.* to wake from sleep; to excite to action; to agitate; to startle or surprise;—*v.i.* to awake from sleep or repose.—**rous'er** *n.* —**rous'ing** *a.*—**rous'ingly** *adv.*—**rous'y** *a.* noisy; rowdy [etym. unknown].

rout (rout) *n.* fashionable assembly; tumultuous crowd; rabble; defeat of army or confusion of troops in flight;—*v.t.* to defeat and throw into confusion [L. *ruptus*, broken].

rout (rout) *v.i.* to roar; to snore [O.E. *hrutan*].

rout (rout) *v.t.* to turn up with the snout; to cut grooves by scooping or gouging;—*v.i.* to poke about.

route (ròòt) *n.* course or way which is travelled or to be followed.—**en route,** on the way [Fr.].

routine (ròò-tēn') *n.* regular course of action or procedure adhered to by order or habit;—*a.* in ordinary way of business; according to rule [Fr.].

rove (rōv) *n.* a small metal ring or washer for holding a rivet in place [fr. *reeve*].

rove (rōv) *v.t.* to wander or ramble over; to plough into ridges;—*v.i.* to wander about; to ramble.—**ro'ver** *n.* wanderer; robber or pirate; Boy Scout.—**rov'ing** *n.* and *a.*—**roving commission,** a business tour without restriction as to places to be visited [Dut. *roofer*, a robber]

row (rō) *n.* persons or things in straight line; a rank; a file; a line [O.E. *raw*].

row (rō) *v.t.* to impel (a boat) with oars; to transport, by rowing;—*v.i.* to labour with oar;—*n.* spell of rowing; a trip in a rowing-boat.—**row'boat, row'ing-boat** *n.* boat impelled solely by oars.—**row'er** *n.*—**row'lock** *n.* space cut in wash-strake, just above gunwale of boat, to take weight and thrust of oars; two thole-pins for same purpose. Also **roll'ock, rull'ock** [O.E. *rowan*].

row (rou) *n.* riotous, noisy disturbance; a dispute; shindy; brawl.—**row'dy** *a.* noisy and rough;—*n.* hooligan.—**row'dyism, row'diness** *n.* [etym. uncertain].

rowan (rou-ạn) *n.* mountain-ash producing clusters of red berries. Also **roan'-tree, rod'dan,** etc. [Scand.].

rowel (rou'ẹl) *n.* wheel of a spur, furnished with sharp points [Fr. *roue*, a wheel].

royal (roi'ạl) *a.* pert. to the crown; worthy of, befitting, patronised by, a king or queen; kingly;—*n.* standard size of paper, 20 by 25 inches (for printing), 19 by 24 inches (for writing and drawing); small sail above top-gallant-sail; third shoot of stag's head; gold coin; tuft of beard on lower lip, an imperial.—**roy'alism** *n.* principles of government by king. —**roy'alist** *n.* adherent to sovereign, or one attached to kingly government.—**roy'ally** *adv.* —**roy'alty** *n.* kingship; kingly office; person of king or sovereign; members of royal family; royal prerogative; royal domain; payment to owner of land for right to work minerals, or to inventor for use of his invention, or to author depending on sales of his book.—**royal burgh** (*Scot.*) town holding a charter granted by sovereign.—**royal commission,** committee of experts appointed by the Crown to investigate matter of public interest or administration. —**royal mast,** fourth division of a mast from the deck [Fr. fr. L. *regalis*, fr. *rex*, a king].

royster, roysterer. See **roister, roisterer.**

rub (rub) *v.t.* to subject to friction; to abrade; to chafe; to remove by friction; to wipe; to scour; to touch slightly;—*v.i.* to come into contact accompanied by friction; to become frayed or worn with friction.—*pr.p.* **rub'bing.** —*pa.t.* and *pa.p.* **rubbed.**—*n.* rubbing; difficulty, impediment, drawback; a slight collision.—**rub'bing, rub'-off** *n.* impression of coin, lettering on book, etc. obtained by rubbing thin paper placed on object and rubbed with pencil or similar article.—**to rub in,** to emphasise by constant reiteration [etym. obscure].

rubber (rub'ẹr) *n.* one who or that which rubs; a masseur or masseuse.—**rubb'ing** *n.* applying friction to a surface; an impression taken of a coin, inscriptions on stone, etc. by covering with paper, tin-foil, etc. and rubbing lightly [fr. *rub*].

rubber (rub'ẹr) *n.* coagulated sap of certain tropical trees; caoutchouc; gum elastic; india-rubber for erasing pencil marks.—*pl.* over-shoes; galoshes:—*a.* made of rubber.—**rubb'erised** *a.* impregnated or mixed with rubber, as rubberised fabrics.—**rubb'er-neck** *n.* a tourist eager to see every important building, sight, or spectacle [fr. *rub*].

rubber (rub'ẹr) *n.* series of three games at various card games; a series of an odd number of games or contests at various games [fr. *rub*].

rubbish (rub'ish) *n.* waste or rejected matter; anything worthless; refuse; nonsense; absurdities.—**rubb'ish-heap** *n.* mass of rubbish. —**rubb'ishy** *a.* worthless [etym. uncertain].

rubble (rub'l) *n.* upper fragmentary, decomposed mass of stone overlying a solid stratum of rock; masonry built of rough stone, of all sizes and shapes; water-worn or rough stones used to fill up spaces between walls, etc.—**rubb'ly** *a.* of the nature of rubble [O.Fr. *robel*, dim. of *robe, robbe*, trash].

rube (ròòb) *n.* in N. America, a farmer; a rustic [*abbrev.* fr. *Reuben*].

Rubicon (ròò-bi-kon) *n.* stream in Italy, between Roman Italy and Cisalpine Gaul.—**to cross the Rubicon,** to take a decisive, irrevocable step in any adventurous undertaking, as Caesar did when, by crossing, he virtually declared war against the republic.

rubicund (ròò'bi-kund) *a.* ruddy; florid; flushed; rosy; reddish.—**rubicun'dity, rub'icundness** *n.* [L. *rubicundus*, fr. *ruber*, red].

rubidium (ròò-bid'i-um) *n.* rare silvery metallic element, one of the alkali metals [L. *rubidus*, red].

rubied (ròò'bid) *a.* ruby-coloured; florid.

ruble. See **rouble.**

rubric (ròò'brik) *n.* medieval manuscript or printed book in which initial letter was illumined in red; heading or portion of such a work, printed in red—hence, the title of a chapter, statute, etc. originally in red; an ecclesiastical injunction or rule; a matter definitely settled by authority;—*v.t.* to illumine with or print in red; to enact.—**ru'brical** *a.* coloured in red; placed in rubrics. —**ru'bricate** *v.t.* to mark in red; to formulate as a rubric.—**rubric'ian** *n.* one versed in the rubrics.—**ru'bricist** *n.* a strict adherent to rubrics; a formalist [L. *rubrica*, red earth, fr. *ruber*, red].

ruby (ròò'bi) *n.* a transparent variety of corundum, carmine red, pink, purple, or violet in colour, next to diamond in hardness and value as gem; purple-tinged red colour; carbuncle; printing type, equal to $5\frac{1}{2}$ points, smaller than nonpareil;—*a.* having the dark-red colour of a ruby.—**ru'bious** *a.* ruby-coloured.—**rock ruby,** a red garnet [L. *ruber*, red].

ruche (ròòsh) *n.* pleated trimming for dresses, sewn down the middle and not at top, as in box pleatings.—**ruch'ing** *n.* in millinery, succession of box-pleats, one on top of the other, gathered or pleated in the centre, leaving the edges free [Fr.].

ruck, ruckle (ruk, ruk'l) *v.t.* to wrinkle; to crease;—*v.i.* to be drawn into folds;—*n.* fold; crease; wrinkle [O.N. *hrukka*].

ruck (ruk) *n.* rank and file; common herd [etym. doubtful].

rucksack (ròòk'sak) *n.* pack carried on back by climbers, etc. [Ger. = 'back-pack'].

ruction (ruk'shun) *n.* disturbance; row; rumpus [perh. fr. *eruption*].

rudd (rud) *n.* British fresh-water fish allied to the roach [O.E. *rudu*, redness].

rudder (rud'ẹr) *n.* flat frame fastened vertically to stern-post of ship, which controls direction; in aeroplane, flat plane surface hinged to stern-

post of fin in tail unit and used to provide directional control and stability; anything which guides, as a bird's tail-feathers [O.E. *rothor*].
ruddle (rud′l) *n.* species of red earth; red ochre, used for marking sheep;—*v.t.* to mark (sheep) with ruddle. Also **radd'le, redd'le.**—**rudd'leman** *n.* one who digs ruddle [O.E. *rudu*, redness].
ruddoc, ruddock (rud′ok) *n.* the redbreast; a gold coin [O.E. *rudig*, reddish].
ruddy (rud′i) *a.* of a red colour; of healthy flesh colour; rosy; florid; (*Slang*) bloody; damnable.—**rudd'ier** *a.* redder.—**rudd'iest** *a.* reddest.—**rudd'ily** *adv.*—**rudd'iness** *n.* [O.E. *rudig*, reddish].
rude (rōōd) *a.* primitive; roughly made; uneducated; uncivil; rustic.—**rude'ly** *adv.*—**rude′ness** *n.* [L. *rudis*, rough].
rudiment (rōō′di-ment) *n.* beginning; germ; vestige; (*Biol.*) imperfectly developed or formed organ;—*pl.* elements, first principles, beginning (of knowledge, etc.); elementary text-book.—**rudimen'tal, rudimen'tary** *a.*—**rudimen'tarily** *adv.* [L. *rudimentum*, fr. *rudis*, rude].
rue (rōō) *v.t.* and *v.i.* to grieve for; to lament; to regret; to repent of.—*pr.p.* **rue'ing.**—*n.* sorrow; remorse.—**rue'ful** *a.* woeful; mournful; sorrowful.—**rue'fully** *adv.* [O.E. *hreowan*, to be sorry for].
rue (rōō) *n.* aromatic, bushy, evergreen shrub; any bitter infusion [L. *ruta*].
ruff (ruf) *n.* broad, circular collar, plaited, crimped, or fluted; something formed in plaits, or puckered; light-brown mottled bird, the male being ringed with ruff or frill of long, black, red-barred feathers during breeding-season; (*fem.*) **reeve**; neck fringe of long hair or feathers; breed of domestic pigeons.—**ruffed** *a.* [etym. uncertain].
ruff (ruf) *n.* trumping at cards when one cannot follow suit;—*v.t.* to trump instead of following suit [O.Fr. *roffle*].
ruffe (ruf) *n.* a small, speckled, fresh-water edible fish of the Perch family [*ruff*].
ruffian (ruf′i-an) *n.* a rough, lawless fellow; desperado;—*a.* brutal.—**ruff'ianism** *n.* conduct of a ruffian.—**ruff'ianly** *adv.* [O.Fr. fr. It. *ruffiano*].
ruffle (ruf′l) *v.t.* to make into a ruff; to draw into wrinkles, open plaits, or folds; to furnish with ruffles; to roughen surface of; to crumple; to disorder; to annoy; to put out (of temper);—*v.i.* to flutter; to jar; to be at variance; to grow rough;—*n.* a strip of plaited cloth, attached to a garment; a frill; agitation; commotion [Dut. *ruifelen*, to rumple].
rufous (rōō′fus) *a.* (*Bot.*) brownish-red; having red hair [L. *rufus*, red].
rug (rug) *n.* thick, woollen wrap; mat for floor of shaggy or thick-piled surface; a rough, shaggy dog [Scand.].
rugby (rug′bi) *n.* the handling code of football, played with teams of 15 players each [fr. *Rugby* public school].
rugged (rug′ed) *a.* rough; uneven; jagged; wrinkled; coarse; harsh; inharmonious; grating; homely; unpolished.—**rugg'edly** *adv.*—**rugg'edness** *n.* [*rug*].
rugger (rug′er) *n.* popular name for rugby.
rugose, rugous (rōō′gōs -gus) *a.* wrinkled; corrugated.—**ru'gosely** *adv.*—**rugos'ity** *n.* state of being wrinkled [L. *ruga*, a wrinkle].
ruin (rōō′in) *n.* downfall; eternal misery; remains of demolished or decayed city, fortress, castle, work or art, etc.; state of being decayed;—*v.t.* to bring to ruin; to injure; to spoil; to mar; to cause loss of fortune or livelihood to.—**ru'ins** *n.pl.* ruined buildings, etc.—**ruina'tion** *n.* subversion; overthrow; demolition; destruction; decay.—**ru'iner** *n.*—**ru'inous** *a.* fallen to ruin; decayed; dilapidated; injurious; destructive; pernicious.—**ru'inously** *adv.* [L. *ruina*, fr. *ruere*, to rush down].
rule (rōōl) *n.* act, power, or mode of directing; government; sway; control; authority; precept; prescribed law; established principle or mode of action; regulation; habitual practice; standard; test; code of conduct in a religious order; an instrument to draw straight lines; ruler; (*Print.*) thin strip of brass or type metal, type high, used to separate columns; dash or score, a mark of punctuation;—*v.t.* to govern; to control; to determine; to decide authoritatively; to mark with straight lines, using ruler;—*v.i.* to have command; to order by rule; to maintain a level, as prices in commercial market; to prevail.—**ru'ler** *n.* one who rules; governor; sovereign; instrument with straight edges for drawing lines; a rule.—**ru'ling** *a.* governing; controlling; managing; predominant;—*n.* an authoritative decision; a point of law settled by a court of law [L. *regula*, fr. *regere*, to govern].
rum (rum) *n.* spirit distilled from fermented skimmings of sugar-boilers and molasses.—**rum′runn'er** *n.* bootlegger; person illegally introducing spirituous liquors [etym. uncertain].
rum (rum) *a.* queer; odd; droll; strange.—**rumm'y** *a.* rum; queer [perh. a var. of Romany, *rom*, a gipsy].
rumb (rum) *n.* See **rhumb.**
rumba, rhumba (rōōm′ba) *n.* a dance imported from Central America [Sp.].
rumble (rum′bl) *v.i.* to make a low, vibrant, continuous sound; to reverberate;—*v.t.* to rattle; (*Slang*) to detect or see through—*n.* dull, vibrant, confused noise, as of thunder; rumour; seat for footmen at back of carriage.—**rum'bler** *n.* [imit.].
rumbustious See **rambustious.**
ruminant (rōō′mi-nant) *n.* animal which chews cud, as sheep, cow;—*a.* chewing cud.—**ru'minate** *v.t.* to chew over again; to ponder over; to muse on;—*v.i.* to chew cud; to meditate.—**rumina'tingly** *adv.*—**rumina'tion** *n.*—**ru'minative** *a.*—**ru'minator** *n.* [L. *ruminare*, to chew cud].
rummage (rum′āj) *v.t.* to search thoroughly into or through; to ransack;—*v.i.* to make a search;—*n.* careful search; disorderly heap; lumber; upheaval.—**rumm'ager** *n.* [orig. stowage of casks, O.Fr. *arrumage*].
rummy (rum′i) *n.* a simple card game for any number of players.
rumour (rōō′mur) *n.* current but unproved report; common talk; fame;—*v.t.* to put round as a rumour [L. *rumor*, noise].
rump (rump) *n.* end of backbone of animal with the parts adjacent; buttocks; hinder part; remnant of anything [Scand.].
rumple (rum′pl) *v.t.* to make uneven; to crease; to crumple;—*n.* an irregular fold or plait [O.E. *hrimpan*, to wrinkle].
rumpus (rum′pus) *n.* an uproar; a noisy disturbance; a row [etym. doubtful].
run (run) *v.i.* to move rapidly on legs; to hurry; to contend in a race; to stand as candidate for; to travel or sail regularly; to extend; to retreat; to flee; to flow; to continue in operation; to continue without falling due, as a promissory note or bill; to have legal force; to fuse; to melt; to average; to turn or rotate; to be worded;—*v.t.* to cause to run; to drive, push, or thrust; to manage; to maintain regularly, as bus-service; to operate; to evade (a blockade); to smuggle; to incur (risk).—*pr.p.* **run'ning.**—*pa.t.* **ran.**—*pa.p.* **run.**—*n.* flow; channel; course run; regular, scheduled journey; pleasure trip by car, cycle, etc.; unconstrained liberty; range of ground for grazing cattle, feeding poultry, etc.; trend; rhythm; kind or variety; vogue; point gained in cricket or baseball; a great demand; period play holds the stage; (*Mus.*) rapid scale passage, roulade.—**run'about** *n.* a light motor-car, esp. for short distance work; a gadabout.—**run'away** *n.* fugitive; horse which has bolted.—**run'ner** *n.* one taking part in a race; messenger; bookmaker's assistant; a long,

slender prostrate stem which runs along the ground; one of curved pieces on which sleigh slides; formerly, detective officer; device for facilitating movement of sliding doors, etc.; narrow strip of carpet; smuggler. —**run'ner-up** *n.* one who gains second place.—**run'ning** *a.* flowing; entered for a race, as a horse; successive (numbers); continuous (as an order, account); discharging (pus); cursive; easy in style; effortless;—*n.* moving or flowing quickly; chance of winning.—**run'ning-board** *n.* narrow, horizontal platform running along locomotive, carriage, motor-car etc., to provide step for entering or leaving.—**running commentary,** broadcast description of event by eye-witness.—**running in,** operating new machine with a light load only until all running parts move sweetly.—**running knot,** knot made so as to tighten when rope is pulled.—**run'way** *n.* prepared track on airfields for landing and taking-off.—**also ran,** an unsuccessful competitor.—**in the long run,** in the end; ultimately.—**to run amok,** to go mad.—**to run off,** to repeat from memory; to cause to flow out; to print further copies.—**to run on,** to continue talking; to dwell on.—**to run out,** to come to an end; to dismiss a batsman out of his crease at cricket.—**to run riot,** to give way to excess.—**to run to earth,** to capture after a long pursuit.—**to run to seed,** to grow too quickly to be of value; to deteriorate after a promising start [O.E. *rinnan*].

runagate (run'-a-gāt) *n.* a fugitive; a vagabond; a deserter [var. of *renegade*].

rundle (run'-dl) *n.* a rung or step of a ladder; a ring; a ball; the drum of a capstan.—**run'dled** *a.* circular [fr. *round*].

rune (rōōn) *n.* letter or character of old Teutonic and Scandinavian alphabets; magic symbol; mystery.—**run'ic** *a.* [O.N. *run,* a mystery].

rung (rung) *pa.p.* of **ring.**

rung (rung) *n.* stave of a ladder; cross-bar or spoke [O.E. *hrung,* a beam].

runnel (run'-ẹl) *n.* small brook or rivulet; a gutter [O.E. *rinnelle,* a brook].

runt (runt) *n.* small, weak specimen of any animal; mean, contemptible person; large-sized carrier-pigeon; stem of cabbage; dead stump of tree [etym. doubtful].

rupee (rōō-pē') *n.* standard Indian monetary unit, silver coin [Urdu, *rupiyah*].

rupture (rup'-tūr) *n.* breaking or bursting; state of being violently parted; breach of concord between individuals or nations; hernia; forcible bursting, breaking, or tearing of a bodily organ or structure;—*v.t.* to part by violence; to burst (as a blood-vessel) [L. *ruptura,* fr. *rumpere,* to break].

rural (rōō'-rạl) *a.* pert. to the country; pert. to farming or agriculture; rustic; pastoral.—**ru'ralise** *v.t.* to make rural;—*v.i.* to live in the country; to become rural.—**ru'ralism** *n.*—**ru'rally** *adv.* [L. *ruralis,* fr. *rus,* the country].

Ruritania (rōō-ri-tā'-ni-ạ) *n.* any fictitious country in Europe [invented by Anthony Hope].

ruse (rōōz) *n.* artifice; trick; stratagem; wile [Fr.].

rush (rush) *v.t.* to carry along violently and rapidly; to take by sudden assault; to hasten forward; to overcharge grossly; —*v.i.* to move violently or rapidly; to speed;—*n.* impetuous, forward movement; heavy current of water, air, etc.; eager demand (for an article); stampede of cattle.—**rush'er** *n.* one who acts precipitately; a slave-driver [M.E. *ruschen*].

rush (rush) *n.* name of plants of genus Juncus, found in marshy places; stem as a material for baskets, etc.; thing of little worth; taper; straw.—**rush'-bott'omed** *a.* of chair with seat made of rushes.—**rush'-can'dle, rush'-light** *n.* primitive form of light made from a peeled rush, dried and dipped in boiling fat or grease. —**rush'en** *a.* made of rushes.—**rush'y** *a.* [O.E. *rysc*].

rusk (rusk) *n.* biscuit or light, hard bread [Sp. *rosca,* roll of bread].

Russ (rus) *n.* Russian; language of Russians. —**Russ'ian** *a.* pert. to Russia;—*n.* general name for Slav races in Russia; native or inhabitant of Russia; Russian language.—**Rus'so-** *prefix* Russian.—**Russia leather,** orig. soft kind of leather dyed a deep red.—**Russian boot,** high-legged boot, worn by women in wet or cold weather.—**Russian wolf-hound,** the borzoi.

russel (rus'-ẹl) *n.* twilled woollen fabric.—**russel cord,** a rep fabric used for academic gowns, etc. [O.Fr. *roussel,* red].

russet (rus'-et) *a.* of reddish-brown colour; homespun cloth dyed this colour; dessert apple of russet colour [Fr. *roux,* red].

rust (rust) *n.* film which appears on metals on account of atmospheric corrosion, esp. oxide of iron which forms reddish coat on surface of that metal; mildew;—*v.t.* to corrode with rust; to impair by inactivity;—*v.i.* to become rusty; to dissipate one's potential powers by inaction.—**rust'ily** *adv.*—**rust'iness** *n.*—**rust'proof** *a.* not liable to rust.—**rust'y** *a.* covered with rust; rust-coloured; impaired by neglect or disuse; out of practice [O.E.].

rustic (rus'-tik) *a.* pert. to the country; rural; awkward;—*n.* inhabitant of the country; peasant.—**rus'tically** *adv.*—**rus'ticate** *v.t.* to compel to reside in country; to banish from college for a time;—*v.i.* to live in the country. —**rustica'tion** *n.*—**rustic'ity** *n.* state of being rustic; rustic manners; simplicity; artlessness [L. *rusticus,* fr. *rus,* the country].

rustle (rus'-l) *v.i.* to make soft, swishing sounds, like rubbing of silk cloth or dry leaves; to be active and on the move;—*v.t.* to steal, esp. cattle;—*n.* a soft, whispering sound.—**rus'tler** *n.* one who, or that which, rustles; bustler; cattle-thief.—**rus'tling** *n.* [imit. origin]

rut (rut) *n.* furrow made by wheel; settled habit or way of living; groove;—*v.t.* to form ruts in;—*pr.p.* **rut'ting.**—*pa.t.* and *pa.p.* **rut'ted** [Fr. *route,* a way, track, etc.].

rut (rut) *n.* time of sexual excitement and urge among animals, esp. of deer;—*v.i.* to be in heat [O.Fr. fr. L. *rugire,* to roar].

ruth (rōōth) *n.* pity; tenderness; compassion. —**ruth'ful** *a.* compassionate.—**ruth'fully** *adv.*—**ruth'less** *a.* pitiless; cruel.—**ruth'lessly** *adv.*—**ruth'lessness** *n.* [*rue*].

ruthenium (rōō-thē'-ni-um) *n.* a spongy metallic element, related to rhodium and palladium [fr. *Ruthenia*].

rye (rī) *n.* a kind of grass allied to wheat, used for bread-making and distilling of hollands; in U.S.A., potent whisky made from rye.—**rye'-grass** *n.* grass-like plant as fodder for cattle [O.E. *ryge*].

ryot (rī'-ot) *n.* peasant cultivator of soil in India [Urdu, *raiyat,* subject].

rypeck, ryepeck (rī'-peck) *n.* ironshod pole used to move punt; quart [etym. unknown].

S

Sabaism (sā'-bā-izm). Also **Sa'baeism, Sa'beism, Sa'baeanism.** See **Sabianism.**

Sabbath (sab'-ạth) *n.* seventh day of week, a day of rest enjoined upon Jews in the decalogue; Sunday; Lord's Day; intermission of pain, effort, sorrow.—**Sabbata'rian** *n.* member of certain Christian sects, e.g. Seventh-day Adventists, who observe seventh-day, Saturday, as the Sabbath; strict observer of Sabbath.—**Sabbata'rianism** *n.*—**Sabbat'ic, -al** *a.* pert. to Sabbath; rest-bringing.—**Sabbatical year,** in the Jewish ritual, every seventh, in which the lands were left untilled, etc.; a year periodically interrupting one's normal course of work, wholly devoted to further intensive study or one's special subject [Heb. *shabbath*].

sabeline (sab′e-lin) *a.* of, or pert. to the sable [O.Fr.].

Sabian (sā′bi-an) *a.* relating to religion of Saba in Arabia, or to worship of heavenly bodies;—*n.* worshipper of sun, moon and stars; adherent of Sabian religion.—**Sabianism, Sa'baism** *n.*

Sabine (sab′īn) *n.* one of an ancient tribe of Italy who became merged with the Romans;—*a.* pert. to the Sabines.

sable (sā′bl) *n.* small carnivorous mammal of weasel tribe; sable fur; (*Her.*) tincture or colour black;—*pl.* mourning garments;—*a.* black; made of sable [O.Fr.].

sabot (sab′ō) *n.* a wooden shoe worn by the peasantry of France and Belgium [Fr.].

sabotage (sá′bo-tázh) *n.* wilful damage or destruction of property perpetrated for political or economic reasons.—**sab'oteur** *n.* one who commits sabotage [Fr. *sabot*].

sabre (sā′ber) *n.* sword with broad and heavy blade, slightly curved toward the point; cavalry sword;—*v.t.* to wound or cut down with sabre.—**sa'bre-tache** (tash) *n.* leathern case suspended from sword-belt worn by cavalry and artillery officers.—**sa'bre-tooth** *n.* extinct tiger-like animal with long upper canine teeth.—**sabreur'** *n.* cavalry man [Fr.].

sac (sak) *n.* pouch-like structure or receptacle in animal or plant; cyst-like cavity [Fr. = sack].

saccharin, saccharine (sak′a-rin) *n.* a white crystalline solid substance, with an intensely sweet taste.—**sac'charine** *a.* pert. to sugar; over-sweet; cloying; sickly sentimental—**sac'charify** *v.t.* to convert into sugar.—**saccharin'ity** *n.*—**sac'charise** *v.t.* to convert into sugar.—**sac'charoid, -al** *a.* having granular texture resembling that of loaf-sugar.—**sac'charose** *n.* cane-sugar.—**sac'charous** *a.* sugary [Gk. *sakchari*, sugar].

saccule (sak′ūl) *n.* a small sac; a cyst.—**sac'cular** *a.* like a sac [dim. of L. *saccus*, a bag].

sacerdotal (sas-er-dō′tal) *a.* pert. to priests, or to the order of priests.—**sacerdo'talism** *n.* the system, spirit, or character of priesthood; priestcraft; undue exaltation of person and sacred character of priests.—**sacerdo'talist** *n.*—**sacerdo'tally** *adv.* [L. *sacerdos*, a priest].

sachem (sā′chem) *n.* a Red Indian chief; a sagamore; a political boss, esp. a Tammany leader [Amer.-Ind.].

sachet (sa′shā) *n.* a small scent-bag or perfume cushion [Fr.].

sack (sak) *n.* a large bag, usually of coarse material; contents of sack; loose garment or cloak; measure or weight, varying according to locality; (*Colloq.*) dismissal from employment;—*v.t.* to put into sacks; (*Colloq.*) to dismiss from employment.—**sack'cloth** *n.* coarse fabric of great strength used for making sacks; in Scripture, garment worn in mourning or as penance.—**sack'ful** *n.* quantity which fills sack.—**sack'ing** *n.* coarse cloth or canvas.—**sack'race** *n.* race in which legs of contestants are encased in sacks [Heb. *saq*, a coarse cloth].

sack (sak) *n.* old name for various kinds of dry wines, esp. Spanish sherry; a warmed and spiced drink of sherry, etc. [Fr. *sec*, dry].

sack (sak) *v.t.* to plunder or pillage; to lay waste;—*n.* pillage of town; devastation.—**sack'age, sack'ing** *n.* [Fr. *sac*, plunder].

sackbut (sak′but) *n.* primitive bass trumpet; in scriptural times, stringed instrument of harp family [Fr. *saquebute*].

sacrament (sak′ra-ment) *n.* one of the ceremonial observances in Christian Church enjoined by Christ esp. the Eucharist; one of additional observances of Roman and Eastern Churches, confirmation, penance, holy order, matrimony and extreme unction; Lord's Supper; solemn oath; sacred obligation; materials used in a sacrament.—**sacramen'tal** *n.* any observance, ceremony, or act of the nature of a sacrament instituted by R.C. Church;—*a.* belonging to, or of nature of, sacrament.—**sacramen'tally** *adv.*—**sacramenta'rian** *n.* one who believes in efficacy of sacraments to confer grace and salvation.—**sacramenta'rianism** *n.*—**sacramen'tary** *a.* pert. to sacrament of Lord's Supper or to sacramentarians [L. *sacer*, sacred].

sacrarium (sa-krā′ri-um) *n.* part of chancel of a Christian church containing altar or communion table [L.].

sacred (sā′kred) *a.* holy; pert. to worship of God; consecrated to God; divine; religious, as writing, history, etc.; dedicated.—**sa'credly** *adv.*—**sa'credness** *n.* [L. *sacer*, holy].

sacrifice (sak′ri-fīs, or -fīz) *v.t.* to consecrate ceremonially offering of victim by way of expiation or propitiation to deity; to surrender for sake of obtaining some other advantage; to offer up; to immolate;—*v.i.* to make offerings to God of things consumed on the altar;—*n.* anything consecrated and offered to divinity; anything given up for sake of others.—**sac'rificer** *n.*—**sacrifi'cial** *a.* relating to, performing, sacrifice.—**sacrific'ially** *adv.* [L. *sacrificium*].

sacrilege (sak′ri-lej) *n.* profanation of sacred place or thing; church robbery.—**sacrile'gious** *a.* violating sacred things; profane; desecrating.—**sacrile'giously** *adv.*—**sacrile'giousness** *n.*—**sacrile'gist** *n.* one guilty of sacrilege [L. *sacer*, sacred; *legere*, to gather].

sacrist (sā′krist) *n.* sacristan; church official in charge of books and music scrolls.—**sac'ristan** *n.* officer in church entrusted with care of sacristy or vestry and responsible for books, vestments, and sacred vessels; sexton; minor canon.—**sac'risty** *n.* vestry [L. *sacer*, sacred].

sacrosanct (sak′rō-sangkt) *a.* secure by religious fear against desecration or violence; inviolable and sacred in the highest degree.—**sacrosanc'tity** *n.* [L. *sacrosanctus*, consecrated].

sacrum (sā′krum) *n.* a composite bone, triangular in shape, at the base of the spinal column.—*pl.* **sa'cra** [L. = the sacred (bone)].

sad (sad) *a.* sorrowful; affected with grief; deplorably bad; sombre-coloured; (*Bread*) heavy or doughy;—*v.t.* to sadden;—*v.i.* to become doughy.—**sad'den** *v.t.* to make sad or sorrowful; (*Dyeing*) to tone down colours by addition of mordants;—*v.i.* to become sorrowful and downcast.—**sad'ly** *adv.*—**sad'ness** *n.* [O.E. *saed*, sated].

saddle (sad′l) *n.* rider's seat to fasten on horse, or form part of a cycle, etc.; part of a shaft; joint of mutton or venison containing part of backbone with ribs on each side; ridge of hill, col; sliding portion of machine which carries cutting-tool or other slides or rests;—*v.t.* to put a saddle upon; to burden with; to encumber.—**sadd'le-back** *n.* hill whose outline resembles a saddle; an unwholesome type of oyster; the harp-seal; the great black-backed gull.—**sadd'le-backed** *a.* having low back, with elevated head and neck (of horse).—**sadd'le-bag** *n.* one of two bags united by strap and hanging on either side of horse.—**sadd'le-bow** *n.* bow or arch in front of saddle.—**sadd'le-cloth** *n.* housing or cloth placed upon saddle.—**sadd'le-girth** *n.* band passing under belly of horse to hold saddle in place.—**sadd'le-horse** *n.* horse for riding, as distinguished from one for driving.—**sadd'ler** *n.* one who makes saddles and harness for horses.—**sadd'lery** *n.* materials for making saddles and harness; occupation of saddler; room for storing saddles.—**sadd'le-shaped** *a.*—**sadd'le-tree** *n.* frame of saddle [O.E. *sadol*].

Sadducee (sad′ū-sē) *n.* one of sect of Jews, politically opposed to Pharisees, denying resurrection, immortality of soul and existence of angels and spirits.—**Sadduce'an** *a.* pert. to Sadducees; sceptical; irreligious [Heb. fr. reputed founder, *Zadok*, or fr. *Zadokites*, race of priests].

sadism (sā′dizm, sá′dizm) *n.* insatiate love of

inflicting pain for its own sake.—**sa'dist** *n.* one who practises this; a consistently inhumane person.—**sadis'tic** *a.* [Marquis de *Sade* (1740-1814) whose writings exemplify it].

safari (sa-fà'-rē) *n.* hunting-expedition [Swahili, *safar*, a journey].

safe (sāf) *a.* free from harm; unharmed; unhurt; sound; protected; sure;—*n.* a fire-proof chest for protection of money and valuables; case with wire-gauze panels to keep meat, etc. fresh.—**safe'-con'duct** *n.* passport to pass through a dangerous zone.—**safe'-depos'it** *n.* strong-room where valuables are stored and protected.—**safe'guard** *n.* protection; precaution; convoy; escort; passport;—*v.t.* to make safe; to protect.—**safe'ly** *adv.*—**safe'ness** *n.*—**safe'ty** *n.*—**safe'ty-belt** *n.* belt to keep person afloat in water.—**safe'-ty-catch** *n.* contrivance to prevent accidental discharge of gun.—**safety curtain**, fire-resisting curtain between stage and auditorium.—**safe'ty-lamp** *n.* lamp surrounded with cylinder of wire-gauze to minimise danger of igniting 'fire-damp' in mines.—**safe'ty-ra'zor** *n.* one in which blade fits into holder with guard to ensure safety for rapid shaving.—**safe'ty-valve** *n.* automatically-acting valve fitted to boiler, to permit escape of steam when pressure reaches danger point; outlet for pent-up emotion [Fr. *sauf*, fr. L. *salvus*].

saffron (saf'-run) *n.* plant of iris family, whose orange-yellow stigmas yield yellow saffron used in medicine and as a flavouring and colouring in cookery;—*a.* deep yellow [Fr. *safran*].

sag (sag) *v.i.* to sink in middle; to hang sideways or curve downwards under pressure; to give way; to tire.—*pr.p.* **sagg'ing**.—*pa.p.* **sagged**.—*n.* a droop [M.E. *saggen*].

saga (sà'-ga, sā'-ga) *n.* collection of ancient Scandinavian myths and legends of Viking heroes; novels describing life of a family [O.N. = a tale].

sagacious (sa-gā'-shus) *a.* quick of thought; acute; shrewd.—**saga'ciously** *adv.*—**saga'ciousness, sagac'ity** *n.* penetration; shrewdness; discernment; wisdom [L. *sagax*].

sage (sāj) *n.* dwarf shrub of mint family, used for flavouring.—**sage'-green** *a.* grey mixed slightly with green [Fr. *sauge*, fr. L. *salvia*].

sage (sāj) *a.* wise; discerning; solemn;—*n.* wise man.—**sage'ly** *adv.*—**sage'ness** *n.* [Fr. fr. L. *sapere*, to be wise].

Sagitta (saj'-it-a) *n.* a constellation north of Aquila—the Arrow.—**sag'ittal, sag'ittate, -d** *a.* arrow-shaped; in direction of arrow.—**sag'ittally** *adv.*—**Saggita'rius** *n.* the Archer, 9th sign of zodiac, which sun enters about 22nd November; constellation in Milky Way [L. = arrow].

sago (sā'-gō) *n.* dry, granulated starch, prepared from pith of several palms, used as article of diet [Malay, *sagu*].

sahib (sà'-ib) *n.* (*fem.* **sa'hiba** or **mem sa'hib**) courtesy title in India for European or high-born Indian [Ar. = lord, master].

said (sed) *pa.t.* and *pa.p.* of **say**; the before-mentioned; already specified; aforesaid.

sail (sāl) *n.* sheet of canvas to catch wind for propelling ship; sailing-vessel; a journey upon the water; arm of windmill;—*v.t.* to navigate; to pass in a ship; to fly through;—*v.i.* to travel by water; to begin a voyage; to glide in stately fashion.—**sail'able** *a.* navigable.—**sail'-cloth** *n.* canvas used in making sails.—**sail'ing** *n.* art of navigating.—**sail'ing-boat** *n.* a boat propelled by sails.—**sail'less** *a.*—**sail'maker** *n.* one who makes sails; officer who repairs sails and has charge of sail-room.—**sail'or** *n.* mariner; seaman; tar.—**sail'or-hat** *n.* straw hat.—**sail'-yard** *n.* yard or spar on which sails are extended.—**full sail**, with all sails set.—**under sail**, to have sails spread.—**to sail close to the wind**, to sail with sails of ship barely full; to run great risks.—**to sail under false colours**, to act under false pretences [O.E. *segel*].

sainfoin (sān'-foin) *n.* less correctly **saint'foin** *n.* perennial, tough-rooted forage plant of leguminous family [Fr. *sain*, wholesome; *foin*, hay].

saint (sānt) *n.* outstandingly devout and virtuous person; one of the blessed in heaven; one formally canonised by R.C. Church; angel;—*v.t.* to canonise.—**saint'ed** *a.* pious; hallowed; sacred; dead.—**saint'hood** *n.*—**saint'like, saint'ly** *a.* devout; godly; pious.—**saint'liness** *n.*—**saint's day**, day on which falls celebration of particular saint.—**All-Saints' Day**, 1st November.—**St. Andrew's Day**, 30th Nov.—**St. Anthony's fire**, erysipelas.—**St. Bernard**, dog famous for guiding and rescuing travellers lost in snow.—**St. David's Day**, 1st March.—**St. Elmo's fire**, electrical appearances sometimes seen about masts of ships, steeples, etc.—**St. George's Day**, 23rd April.—**St. John's wort**, bright-yellow blossoming plant, floral symbol of superstition.—**St. Leger**, horse-race for three-year-olds.—**St. Martin's summer**, warm, damp weather at end of autumn; in U.S. 'Indian Summer.'—**St. Patrick's Day**, 17th March.—**St. Swithin's Day**, 15th July.—**St. Valentine's Day**, 14th February.—**St. Vitus's dance**, chorea.—**Latter-day Saints**, the Mormons.—**patron saint**, saint held to be a protector [Fr. fr. L. *sanctus*, consecrated].

sake (sāk) *n.* final cause; behalf; purpose; account; regard.—**for the sake of**, on behalf of [O.E. *sacu*, dispute at law].

sake (sà'-kē) *n.* national beverage of Japan, fermented from rice [Jap.].

saki (sak'-i) *n.* monkey of forests of Amazon [Native].

sal (sal) *n.* salt (much used in compound words pert. to chemistry and pharmacy).—**sal'ammo'niac** *n.* ammonium chloride, used in composition of electric batteries and in medicine as expectorant and stomachic.—**sal'-vola'tile** *n.* mixture of ammonium carbonate with oil of nutmeg, oil of lemon and alcohol, used as a stimulant, antacid, or expectorant [L.].

salaam, salam (sa-làm') *n.* salutation of ceremony or respect in the East;—*v.t.* to salute; to greet [Ar. = peace].

salacious (sa-lā'-shus) *a.* lustful; lewd; lecherous.—**sala'ciously** *adv.*—**sala'ciousness, salac'ity** *n.* [L. *salax*, fr. *salire*, to leap].

salad (sal'-ad) *n.* green uncooked vegetables or fruit dressed with salt, vinegar, oil or spices, eggs often added.—**sal'ad-cream** *n.* a prepared dressing for salads.—**salad days**, early years of youthful inexperience.—**sal'ad-oil** *n.* olive-oil [Fr. *salade*, fr. L. *sal*, salt].

salamander (sal-a-man'-der) *n.* small, tailed amphibian, allied to newt (medieval salamander was a fabulous creature believed to live and delight in fire).—**salaman'driform, salaman'drine** *a.* pert. to or shaped like a salamander; fire-resisting [Gk. *salamandra*].

salame (sa-là'-mā) *n.* Italian salted sausage.

salary (sal'-a-ri) *n.* fixed remuneration, usually monthly, for services rendered; stipend.—**sal'aried** *a* [L. *salarium*, saltmoney, soldier's pay].

sale (sāl) *n.* exchange of anything for money; demand (for article); public exposition of goods; auction; a special disposal of stock at reduced prices.—**sale'able, sal'able** *a.* capable of being sold.—**sale'ableness** *n.*—**sale'ably** *adv.*—**sale'-price** *n.* special, low price.—**sale'-room** *n.* auction-room; retail department of wholesale house.—**sales'man** *n.* shop-assistant.—**sales'manship** *n.* art of selling goods.—**sales'woman** *n.*—**sale of work**, a special sale of articles made or contributed by members of organisation to raise funds for specific object [O.E. *sala*].

salep, salop (sal'-ep, -op) *n.* nutritious powder, used for similar purposes as arrowroot [Ar. *saleb*].

Salian (sā'-li-an) *n.* one of a tribe of Franks who inhabited banks of Yssel, a tributary of lower Rhine;—*a.* pert. to this tribe.—**Salic**

Law, law which excluded females from succession to land.

salicin (sal′i-sin) *n.* a bitter white crystalline glucocide obtained from bark of willow and poplar, used as drug.—**sali′cylate** *n.* any salt of salicylic acid.—**salicy′lic** *a.* derived from willow.—**salicylic acid,** white crystalline solid obtained from willow-bark or synthetically from phenol [L. *salix,* a willow].

salient (sā′li-ent) *a.* moving by leaps; projecting outwards; springing; prominent, striking, noteworthy;—*n.* external angle formed by intersection of adjacent surfaces; projecting angle in line of fortifications, system of trenches.—**sa′liently** *adv.* [L. *salire,* to leap].

saliferous (sa-lif′er-us) *a.* bearing or producing salt [L. *sal,* salt; *ferre,* to bear].

salify (sal′i-fī) *v.t.* to form a salt by combining an acid with a base.—*pa.t.* and *pa.p.* **sal′ified.** —**salifi′able** *a.*—**salifica′tion** *n.* [L. *sal,* salt; *facere,* to make].

saline (sāl′īn, sa-līn′) *a.* of or containing salt; salty;—*n.* salt-spring; a fruit salt used as aperient.—**sali′na** *n.* salt-marsh; salt-works.—**salinif′erous** *a.* producing salt.—**salin′ity** *n.* salty quality; degree of saltness [L. *salinus*].

saliva (sa-lī′va) *n.* digestive fluid or spittle, secreted in mouth by salivary glands.—**sali′val** *a.* pert. to saliva.—**sal′ivary** *a.* pert. to, producing, saliva.—**sal′ivate** *v.t.* to produce abnormal secretion of saliva.—**saliva′tion** *n.* [L.].

sallow (sal′ō) *n.* small tree or shrub, allied to willow [O.E. *sealh*].

sallow (sal′ō) *a.* of sickly-yellow colour; of pale complexion; unhealthy looking.—**sall′owish** *a.* somewhat sallow.—**sall′owness** *n.* [O.E. *salo*].

sally (sal′i) *n.* sudden eruption; issuing of troops from place besieged to attack besiegers; sortie; witticism;—*v.i.* to issue suddenly.—*pa.t.* and *pa.p.* **sall′ied** [L. *salire,* to leap].

Sally-lunn (sal′i-lun) *n.* sweet, spongy tea-cake [Bath street-vendor in 18th cent.].

salmi, salmis (sal′mē) *n.* ragout or stew of game-birds [Fr.].

salmon (sam′un) *n.* silver-scaled fish with orange-pink flesh.—**salm′on-col′our** *n.* orange-pink.—**salm′on-fly** *n.* artificial fly for catching salmon with rod and line.—**salm′on-fry** *n.* salmon under two years old.—**Salmon′idae** *n. pl.* family of sea- and fresh-water fishes including salmon, trout, grayling and smelt.—**salm′on-trout** *n.* sea- or white-trout, fish resembling salmon in colour but smaller [L. *salmo*].

salon (sa-lōng′) *n.* spacious apartment for reception of company [Fr.].

saloon (sa-lòòn′) *n.* lofty, spacious hall; state-room; public reception-room; public dining-room; principal cabin in steamer; railway-car not divided into usual compartments; limousine with all seats enclosed.—**saloon′-bar** *n.* a well-appointed section of a public-house [Fr. *salon*].

salop See **salep.**

salsify, salsafy (sal′si-fi, sal′sa-fi) *n.* hardy, biennial, composite herb of chicory family, used in cookery. [Fr. fr. It. *sassefrica,* goat's beard].

salt (sawlt) *n.* sodium chloride or common salt, substance used for seasoning food and for preservation of meat, etc.; compound resulting from reaction between acid and a base; electrolyte which is neither acid nor base; savour; piquancy; wit; an old sailor;—*pl.* (*Chem.*) combinations of acids with alkaline or salifiable bases; (*Med.*) saline cathartics, as Epsom, Rochelle, etc.;—*a.* containing or tasting of salt; pungent; lecherous; (*Colloq.*) costly; expensive;—*v.t.* to season or sprinkle with salt; to acclimatise.—**salt′er** *n.* drysalter; sea-trout which returns to fresh water.—**sal′tern** *n.* salt-works.—**salt′ing** *n.* salt marsh.—**salt′less** *a.* without salt; tasteless; wersh.—**salt′-lick** *n.* salt for animals to lick.—**salt′-marsh** *n.* land under pasturage liable to be overflowed by sea.—**salt′ness** *n.* salt taste; state of being salt. —**salt′-pan** *n.* a steel pan, about 36 ft. by 24 ft. by 20 in. deep used for the evaporation of brine.—**salt′-spring** *n.* a brine-spring of therapeutic value.—**salt′-wat′er** *n.* water impregnated with salt; sea-water.—**salt′y** *a.* saltish. —**salt of the earth,** persons of the highest reputation or worth.—**Attic salt,** delicate, subtle wit.—**to take with a grain of salt,** to be sceptical of [O.E. *sealt*].

saltant (sal′tant) *a.* leaping; jumping; dancing. —**sal′tate** *v.i.* to leap; to jump; to skip.—**salta′tion** *n.* [L. *salire,* to leap].

saltire, saltier (sal-tīr) *n.* cross in the shape of an X, or St. Andrew's cross [O.Fr. *saultoir*].

saltpetre (sawlt′pē-ter) *n.* common name for nitre or potassium nitrate, used in manufacture of glass, nitric acid, etc. [L. *sal petrae,* salt of the rock].

salubrious (sa-lū′bri-us) *a.* wholesome; healthy.—**salu′briously** *adv.*—**salu′briousness, salu′brity** *n.* [L. *salus,* health].

saluki (sa-lòò′ki) *n.* gazelle-hound, native to Persia and Arabia [Ar.].

salutary (sal′u-ta-ri) *a.* wholesome; resulting in good; healthful; promotive of public safety; beneficial.—**sal′utarily** *adv.*—**sal′utariness** *n.* [L. *salus,* health].

salute (sa-lūt′) *v.t.* to address with expressions of kind wishes; to recognise one of superior rank by a sign; to honour by a discharge of cannon or small arms, by striking colours, etc.; to greet; to kiss;—*n.* greeting showing respect.—**saluta′tion** *n.* saluting; words uttered in welcome; opening words of a letter.—**salu′tatory** *a.* welcoming [L. *salutare,* to wish health to].

salvage (sal′vāj) See **salve.**

Salvarsan (sal′var-san) *n.* preparation of arsenic used by injection for cure of anthrax and syphilis.—**Ne′o-sal′varsan** *n.* a derivative of salvarsan, now more commonly employed [Protected Trade Name, fr. L. *salvare,* to save; E. *arsenic*].

salvation (sal-vā′shun) *n.* preservation from destruction; redemption; deliverance; safety. —**Salvation Army,** international religious organisation for revival of religion among the masses.—**salva′tionist** *n.* active member of Salvation Army [L. *salvare,* to save].

salve (salv) *v.t.* to save ship or retrieve property from danger or destruction.—**salvabil′ity** *n.*—**sal′vable** *a.* capable of being used or reconstructed in spite of damage.—**sal′vage** *n.* compensation allowed to persons who assist in saving ship or cargo, or property in general from destruction; property, so saved.—**salv′or, salv′er** *n.* [L. *salvare,* to save].

salve (salv, sàv) *n.* healing ointment applied to wounds or sores;—*v.t.* to anoint with such; to heal; to soothe (conscience) [O.E. *sealf*].

salver (sal′ver) *n.* tray, generally of silver, for presenting refreshments, letters, visiting-cards, etc. [Sp. *salva,* a tasting of food by a servant as a precaution against poisoning, fr. L. *salvare,* to save].

Salvia (sal′vi-a) *n.* large genus of aromatic herbs and shrubs including common sage [L. = sage].

salvo (sal′vō) *n.* guns fired simultaneously, or in succession as salute; sustained applause or welcome from large crowd.—*pl.* **sal′vo(e)s** [It. *salva,* a volley].

sal-volatile (sal-vol-a′til-e) *n.* See **sal.**

salvor (sal′vor) *n.* See **salve.**

samara (sam′a-ra, sa-màr′a) *n.* the dry, single-seeded, indehiscent, winged fruit of the elm, birch, sycamore, ash and maple [L. = elm-seed].

Samaritan (sa-mar′i-tan) *a.* pert to Samaria in Palestine;—*n.* native or inhabitant of Samaria; kind-hearted, charitable person (fr. parable of good Samaritan, Luke 10).

samarium (sa-mā′ri-um) *n.* hard and brittle

metallic chemical element belonging to rare-earth group.—**sam'arskite** *n.* radio-active ore containing tantalum and traces of samarium [*Samarski*, a Russian mineralogist].

samba (sam′ba) *n.* a dance of S. American origin; the music for such a dance [Sp.].

sambo (sam′bō) *n.* offspring of black person and mulatto; humorously, Negro [Sp. *zambo*, fr. L. *scambus*, bow-legged].

Sam Browne (sam broun) *n.* leather belt formerly part of British officer's service uniform [name of inventor].

same (sām) *a.* identical; not different; of like kind; unchanged; uniform; aforesaid.—**same'ly** *adv.*—**same'ness** *n.* near resemblance; uniformity [O.N. *samr*].

samite (sam′īt) *n.* rich silk material; any lustrous silk stuff [Fr. *samit*, fr. Gk. *hexamitos*, woven with six threads].

samovar (sam′o-vȧr) *n.* Russian tea-urn [Russ.].

Samoyed (sam′ō-yed) *n.* Mongolian race inhabiting N. shores of Russia and Siberia.—**Sam'oyede** *n.* breed of dog, orig. a sledge-dog.

sampan (sam′pan) *n.* a Chinese light river-vessel. Also **san'pan** [Malay fr. Chin. *san*, three; *pan*, a board].

samphire (sam′fīr) *n.* herb found on rocks and cliffs, St. Peter's wort; sea-fennel [corrupt. fr. Fr. *Saint Pierre*].

sample (sam′pl) *n.* specimen; example;—*v.t.* to take or give a sample of; to try; to test; to taste.—**samp'ler** *n.* one who makes up samples; pattern work; beginner's exercise in embroidery [M.E. *essample*; fr. L. *exemplum*, example].

Samurai (sa′mòò-rī) *n.* (*s.* and *pl.*) member of hereditary military caste in Japan from 12th to mid 19th cent. Now applied to any Japanese army officer.

sanable (san′ạ-bl) *a.* curable.—**sanabil'ity, san'ableness** *n.*—**san'ative** *a.* having power to cure or heal.—**san'ativeness** *n.*—**sanato'rium** *n.* (*pl.* **sanato'ria**) institution for open-air treatment of tuberculosis; institution for convalescent patients. Also **sanata'rium**; in N. America, **sanito'rium, sanita'rium.** See **sanitary.**—**san'atory** *a.* healing [L. *sanare*, to heal].

sanctify (sangk′ti-fī) *v.t.* to set apart as sacred or holy; to hallow; to consecrate; to purify.—*pa.t.* and *pa.p.* **sanc'tified.**—**sanctanim'ity** *n.* religious devotion; holiness of mind.—**sanctifica'tion** *n.* sanctifying or making holy.—**sanc'tified** *a.* hallowed; sanctimonious.—**sanc′tifiedly** *adv.*—**sanctimo'nious** *a.* hypocritically pious.—**sanctimon'iously** *adv.*—**sanctimo'niousness, sanc'timony** *n.* holiness; devoutness; (*Ironically*) affected piety.—**sanc'titude** *n.* saintliness; holiness.—**sanc'tity** *n.* quality of being sacred; state of being pure and devout; state of being solemnly binding on one; inviolability [L. *sanctus*, holy].

sanction (sangk′shun) *n.* solemn ratification; express permission; authorisation; approval; legal use of force to secure obedience to law; anything which serves to move a person to observe or refrain from given mode of conduct;—*v.t.* and *v.i.* to confirm; to authorise; to countenance.—**sanc'tions** *n.pl.* measures to enforce fulfilment of international treaty obligations.—**sanc'tionary** *a.* ratifying [L. *sanctus*, holy].

sanctuary (sangk′tū-ạ-ri) *n.* holy place; shrine; eastern part of choir of church; place of protection for fugitives.—**sanc'tum** *n.* sacred place; private room or study. -**sanctum sanctorum,** holy of holies in Jewish temple; exclusive private place [L. *sanctus*, holy].

sand (sand) *n.* fine, loose grains of quartz or other mineral matter formed by disintegration of rocks;—*n.pl.* sandy beach; desert region;—*v.t.* to sprinkle or cover with sand.—**sand′bag** *n.* bag filled with sand or earth, for repairing breaches in fortification, etc.—**sand′bank** *n.* shoal of sand thrown up by sea.—**sand′bar** *n.* barrier of sand facing entrance of river-estuary.—**sand′blast** *n.* jet of sand driven by a blast of air or steam, for roughening glass or enamel.—**sand′dune** *n.* ridge of loose sand.—**sand'ed** *a.* sprinkled with sand.—**sand′glass** *n.* hour-glass, instrument for measuring time by running of sand.—**sand′grass** *n.* grass whose roots bind loose sand.—**sand'iness** *n.* state of being sandy; a sandy colour.—**sand'ing** *n.* cleaning up wood by rubbing with sand-paper.—**sand′jet** *n.* See **sand′blast.**—**sand′mar'tin** *n.* small swallow.—**sand′paper** *n.* stout paper or cloth coated with glue and then sprinkled over with sand, used as an abrading agent for smoothing wood, etc.—*v.t.* to smooth with sandpaper.—**sand′piper** *n.* small wading bird of plover family.—**sand′pit** *n.* place from which sand is dug out.—**sand′run'ner** *n.* a sandpiper.—**sand′shoe** *n.* shoe with canvas uppers and rubber soles.—**sand'star** *n.* sea-animal resembling the starfish.—**sand'stone** *n.* rock employed for building and making grindstones.—**sand′storm** *n.* a storm of wind carrying dust.—**sand'y** *a.* like or covered with sand; not firm or stable; yellowish-brown [O.E.].

sandal (san′dạl) *n.* a shoe consisting of flat sole, bound to foot by straps or thongs.—**san'dalled** *a.* [Gk. *sandalon*].

sandal-wood (san′dạl-wóód) *n.* fragrant heartwood of santalum, used in East for trinket-boxes, incense and perfumery [Ar. *sandal*].

sanderling (san′der-ling) *n.* a wading-bird of the plover family; the ruddy plover.

sandwich (sand′wich) *n.* two thin pieces of bread and butter, with thin slice of meat, etc., between them (said to have been a favourite dish of Earl of *Sandwich*);—*v.t.* to make into sandwich; to form of alternating layers of different nature; to insert or squeeze in between, making a tight fit.—**sand'wich-man** *n.* man carrying two advertising boards, one slung before and one behind him.

sane (sān) *a.* of sound mind; not deranged; sensible; rational; reasonable; lucid.—**sane'ly** *adv.*—**sane'ness** *n.* [L. *sanus*, healthy].

sang (sang) *pa.t.* of sing.

sang-froid (song-frwȧ′) *n.* composure of mind; imperturbability; freedom from agitation [Fr. *sang*, blood; *froid*, cold].

sanguine (sang′gwin) *a.* deep red; florid; warm; hopeful; lively; bloodthirsty.—**san′guinarily** *adv.*—**san'guinariness** *n.*—**san'guinary** *a.* bloody; bloodthirsty; murderous.—**san′guinely** *adv.*—**san'guineness** *n.* fulness of blood; plethora; ruddiness; ardour; confidence.—**sanguin'eous** *a.* bloody; blood-red; blood-stained; containing blood.—**sanguin'ity** *n.* sanguineness; relationship by blood.—**sanguiv′orous** *a.* blood-feeding, as fleas, vampires, etc. [L. *sanguis*, blood].

Sanhedrim, Sanhedrin (san′hē-drim, -drin) *n.* supreme court of justice and legislative council of Ancient Jerusalem; any similar Jewish assembly [Heb. fr. Gk. *sun*, together; *hedra*, seat].

sanify (san′i-fī) *v.t.* to make healthy; to improve the sanitary conditions of [L. *sanus*, sound; *facere*, to make].

sanitary (san′i-tạ-ri) *a.* pert. to health; hygienic; relating to drains.—**sanitar'ian** *n.* one interested in the promotion of hygienic reforms.—**san'itarily** *adv.*—**sanita'tion** *n.* the measures taken to promote health and to prevent disease; hygiene.—**sanito'rium, sanita′rium** *n.* private hospital for treatment of special or chronic diseases; health retreat; sanatorium.—**sanitary towel,** pad or absorbent material for use during menstruation [L. *sanitas*, health].

sanity (san′i-ti) *n.* state of being sane; soundness of mind [L. *sanus*, sane].

sank (sangk) *pa.t.* of the verb **sink.**

sans (sanz) *prep.* without; lacking [Fr.].

Sanscrit See **Sanskrit.**

sansculotte (song-kū-lot′) *n.* ragged fellow;

a name given in the first French Revolution to extreme republican party, who rejected knee-breeches as badge peculiar to upper classes—hence, extreme republican, Jacobin [Fr. = without knee-breeches].

sanserif (san-ser′if) *n.* (*Typography*) type face without serifs at termination of lines, e.g. SANSERIF [Fr. *sans*, without].

Sanskrit, Sanscrit (sans′krit) *n.* classic literary language of ancient India, member of Aryan family of languages [Sans. *samskrita*, perfected, finished].

Santa Claus (san′ta klawz) *n.* traditional 'Father Christmas' of children [corrupt. of *St. Nicholas*, patron saint of children].

sap (sap) *n.* watery juice of plants, containing mineral salts, proteins and carbohydrates; simple, confiding person.—**sap′head** *n.* sap, dolt.—**sap′less** *a.*—**sap′ling** *n.* young tree; youth; young greyhound not yet entered for racing.—**sap′piness** *n.* succulence; juiciness; doltishness.—**sap′py** *a.* juicy; silly.—**sap′rot** *n.* dry rot in timber.—**sap′wood** *n.* alburnum, exterior part of wood of tree next to bark [O.E. *saep*].

sap (sap) *n.* tunnel driven under enemy positions for purpose of attack;—*v.t.* and *v.i.* to undermine; to impair insidiously; to exhaust gradually.—*pr.p.* **sap′ping.**—*pa.t.* and *pa.p.* **sapped.**—**sap′per** *n.* a member of the Royal Engineers [It. *zappa*, a spade].

sapid (sap′id) *a.* savoury; palatable; tasty.—**sapid′ity** *n.*—**sap′idless** *a.* tasteless.—**sap′idness** *n.* [L. *sapere*, to taste].

sapient (sā′pi-ent) *a.* discerning; wise; sage; shrewd; (ironically) knowing, would-be wise.—**sa′pience** *n.*—**sa′piently** *adv.* [L. *sapiens*, wise].

saponaceous (sap-o-nā′shus) *a.* resembling soap; slippery, as if soaped.—**sapon′ify** *v.t.* to convert into soap.—**sap′onin** *n.* glucoside obtained from common soapwort used as expectorant, emetic, and for foam-baths and fire-appliances, due to its frothy qualities [L. *sapo*, soap].

sapor (sā′por) *n.* taste; savour; flavour.—**saporif′ic** *a.* producing taste or flavour.—**saporos′ity** *n.* [L. = taste].

sapper. See **sap.**

Sapphic (saf′ik) *a.* pert. to Sappho, lyric poetess of Greece of 7th cent. B.C.; denoting verse in which three lines of five feet each are followed by line of two feet;—*n.* Sapphic verse.—**sapph′ism** *n.* unnatural sexual intercourse between women.

sapphire (saf′īr) *n.* pure crystallised alumina; translucent precious stone of various shades of blue; (*Her.*) tincture blue;—*a.* deep, pure blue [Gk. *sappheiros*].

saraband, sarabande (sar′a-band) *n.* slow, stately dance, introduced by Moors into Spain in 16th cent.; in England, country dance [Pers. *sarband*, a fillet].

Saracen (sar′a-sen) *n.* Arab or Mohammedan who invaded Europe and Africa; an infidel.—**Saracen′ic, Saracen′ical** *a.*—**Sar′acenism** *n.* [L. *Saracenus*].

saratoga, saratoga trunk (sar-a-tō′ga-trungk) *n.* a large travelling-trunk for ladies' dresses [*Saratoga* Springs, U.S.A.].

sarcasm (sar′kazm) *n.* taunt; scoffing gibe; veiled sneer; irony; use of such expressions.—**sarcas′tic, -al** *a.* bitterly satirical and cutting; taunting.—**sarcas′tically** *adv.* [Gk. *sarkasmos*].

sarcology (sâr-kol′o-ji) *n.* branch of anatomy which treats of soft parts of body, as distinguished from osteology.—**sarcolog′ic, -al** *a.*—**sarcol′ogist** *n.* [Gk. *sarx*, flesh; *logos*, a discourse].

sarcophagus (sâr-kof′a-gus) *n.* kind of limestone used by Greeks for coffins and believed to consume flesh of bodies deposited in it; stone coffin; monumental chest or vase of stone, erected over graves.—*pl.* **sarcoph′agi** [Gk. *sarx*, flesh; *phagein*, to eat].

sard (sârd) *n.* rare variety of cornelian [*Sardis*, ancient capital of Lydia].

sardine (sâr-dēn′) *n.* small fish of herring family, esp. pilchard, in young stage salted and preserved in olive-oil [It. *sardina*, fr. the island of Sardinia].

sardonic (sâr-don′ik) *a.* (of laugh, smile) bitter, scornful, derisive, mocking.—**sardon′ically** *adv.* [L. *sardonicus*].

sardonyx (sâr′don-iks) *n.* semi-precious stone [Gk. = Sardinian onyx].

Sargassum (sâr-gas′um) *n.* genus of seaweeds.—**sargass′o** *n.* gulf-weed.—**Sargasso Sea,** part of Atlantic which, being free from ocean currents, is covered with sea-weed [Sp. *sargazo*].

sari (sâr′ē) *n.* light cotton cloth with fancy-coloured border used as loin robe by Hindu women; long scarf of embroidered gauze or silk. Also **sar′ee** [Hind.].

sark (sârk) *n.* shirt; chemise; body garment.—**sar′king** *n.* linen for shirt-making; thin boards to afford a hold for slates or tiles on roofs [O.E. *syrce*].

sarong (sa-rong′) *n.* garment draped round waist by Malayans [Malay].

sarrasin, sarasin (sâr′a-sin) *n.* a portcullis [Fr.].

sarsaparilla (sâr-sa-pa-ril′a) *n.* several plants of genus Smilax, with roots yielding medicinal sarsaparilla, a mild diuretic. Also **sar′sa** [Sp. *zarzaparilla*].

sarsenet. See **sarcenet.**

sartorial (sâr-tō′ri-al) *a.* pert. to tailor, tailoring [L. *sartor*, a tailor].

sash (sash) *n.* silken band; belt or band, usually decorative, worn round body [Arab. *shash*].

sash (sash) *n.* frame of window which carries panes of glass [Fr. *chassis*].

saskatoon (sas-ka-tōōn′) *n.* in N. America, service tree; small edible berry, fruit of the service tree [N. Amer. Ind.].

Sassenach (sas′e-naH) *n.* name given in Scotland to Englishman [Gael. *Sasunnach*, a Saxon].

sat (sat) *pa.t.* and *pa.p.* of **sit.**

Satan (sā′tan) *n.* the devil.—**satan′ic, -al** *a.* devilish; infernal; diabolical.—**satan′ically** *adv.* [Heb. = enemy].

satchel (sach′el) *n.* small bag for books [L. *saccellus*, small sack].

sate (sat or sāt) Same as **sat,** *pa.t.* of **sit.**

sate (sāt) *v.t.* to satisfy appetite of; to glut [earlier *sade*, to make sad].

sateen (sa-tēn′) *n.* glossy cloth for linings, etc., made of cotton or woollen fabric in imitation of satin. Also **satteen′** [fr. *satin*].

satellite (sat′el-līt) *n.* one constantly in attendance upon important personage; an obsequious follower; (*Astron.*) a secondary body which revolves round planets of solar system; a moon.—**satellite** (earth) *n.* an object launched into space by man to orbit the earth for scientific purposes.—**satellite town,** small town specially developed to absorb part of population and industries of over-crowded neighbouring city.—**satellit′ic** *a.* [L. *satelles*].

sati. See **suttee.**

satiate (sā′shi-āt) *v.t.* to satisfy appetite of; to surfeit; to sate;—*a.* filled to satiety; glutted; surfeited.—**satiabil′ity** *n.*—**sa′tiable** *a.* capable of being satisfied.—**satia′tion** *n.* state of being satiated.—**satiety** (sa-tī′e-ti) *n.* state of being satiated; feeling of having had too much [L. *satiare*, fr. *satis*, enough].

satin (sat′in) *n.* soft, rich, silk fabric with smooth, lustrous surface;—*a.* made of satin;—*v.t.* to give a satin finish to.—**sat′inet** *n.* thin kind of satin; glossy cloth of cotton warp and woollen weft, to imitate satin.—**sat′in-jean** *n.* a smooth-surfaced twilled cotton fabric.—**sat′in-stitch** *n.* stitch in embroidery and wool-work in close parallel lines to produce sheeny effect.—**sat′in-wood** *n.* beautiful hard yellow wood, valued in cabinet work for veneers.—**sat′iny** *a.* [Fr. fr. It. *seta*, silk].

satire (sat′īr) *n.* literary composition holding

up to ridicule vice or folly of the times; use of irony, sarcasm, invective, or wit.—**satir'ic, -al** *a.*—**satir'ically** *adv.*—**satir'icalness** *n.*—**sat'irise** *v.t.* to make object of satire.—**sat'irist** *n.* [L. *satira*, a literary medley].

satisfy (sat'is-fī) *v.t.* to gratify fully; to pay, fulfil, supply, recompense, adequately; to convince; to content; to answer; to free from doubt;—*v.i.* to give content; to supply to the full; to make payment.—*pa.t.* and *pa.p.* **sat'isfied.**—**satisfac'tion** *n.* complete enjoyment; contentment; assurance; amends; recompense; payment.—**satisfac'torily** *adv.*—**satisfac'toriness** *n.*—**satisfac'tory** *a.* giving satisfaction; yielding content; agreeable.—**sat'isfying** *a.* affording satisfaction, esp. of food.—**sat'isfyingly** *adv.* [L. *satisfacere*].

satrap (sat'rap, sā'trap) *n.* governor of province under ancient Persian monarchy; petty, despotic governor.—**sat'rapal** *a.*—**sat'rapy** *n.* government, jurisdiction, or district of satrap [Gk. *satrapēs*].

Satsuma Japan.

satteen. See **sateen.**

saturate (sat'ū-rāt) *v.t.* to soak thoroughly; to steep; to drench; to bring concentrated fire to bear on target;—*a.* saturated; very intense (of colour).—**satura'tion** *n.* act of saturating; complete penetration; condition of being saturated; solution of a body in a solvent, until solvent can absorb no more; in magnetism, state when increase of magnetising force produces no further increase of flux-density in magnet.—**satura'tor** *n.* contrivance for saturating air of factory, etc. with water-vapour [L. *saturare*].

Saturday (sat'ur-dā) *n.* seventh day of week [O.E. *Saeterdaeg*, day of Saturn].

Saturn (sat'urn) *n.* old deity, father of Jupiter; sixth of major planets in order of distance from sun.—**Saturna'lia** *n.pl.* festival in ancient Rome in honour of Saturn; time of carnival and unrestrained license; orgy.—**saturna'lian** *a.*—**Satur'nian** *a.* pert. to epoch of Saturn; primitive; golden; distinguished for simplicity and peacefulness.—**sa'turnine** *a.* gloomy, sluggish in temperament [L. *Saturnus*, god of agriculture].

satyr (sat'ẹr) *n.* woodland deity in Greek mythology, represented with hair-clad man's body, with legs and hoofs of a goat, fond of sensual enjoyment; lecherous person.—**satyri'asis** *n.* excessive and morbid desire for sexual intercourse exhibited by men. Also **satyroma'nia.**—**satyroma'niac** *n.* a man with unrestrainable sexual desires.—**satyr'ical** *a.* pert. to satyrs [Gk. *saturos*].

sauce (saws) *n.* liquid seasoning for food to render it more palatable or to whet appetite; condiment; relish; (*Colloq.*) impudence; cheek; —*v.t.* to season with sauce; to give flavour or interest to; to be rude in speech or manner.—**sauce'boat, sauce'tureen'** *n.* dish with lip for serving sauce.—**sauce'pan** *n.* metal pot with lid and long handle used for cooking.—**sau'cy** *a.* bold; pert; cheeky.—**sau'cily** *adv.*—**sau'ciness** *n.* [Fr. fr. L. *sal*. salt].

saucer (saw'sẹr) *n.* orig. vessel for sauce; small curved plate put under cup, etc. to catch spilt liquid [Fr. *saucière*].

sauerkraut (sour'krout) *n.* German dish of shredded young white cabbage laid in layers, with salt and spice-seeds, pressed in casks and allowed to ferment [Ger.].

sault (sō) *n.* rapid in a river, esp. in Canada [Fr. fr. L. *salire*, to leap].

saunter (sawn'tẹr, sån'tẹr) *v.i.* to stroll; to loiter; linger.—*n.* leisurely walk or stroll.—**saun'terer** *n.*—**saun'tering** *n.*—**saun'teringly** *adv.* [etym. unknown].

saurian (saw'ri-ạn) *n.* lizard-like reptile, esp. ancient types as dinosaur, iguanodon, etc.;—*a.* resembling a lizard. Also **saur'oid** *a.* [Gk. *sauros*, a lizard].

sausage (saw'sāj) *n.* meat minced and seasoned and enclosed in thin membranous casing obtained from small entrails of pig or sheep; (*Colloq.*) wind sock which gives wind direction on aerodrome.—**sau'sage-roll** *n.* meat minced and seasoned, enveloped in roll of flour paste and cooked [Fr. *saucisse*].

sauté (sō'tā) *a.* fried lightly and quickly in a saucepan kept moving [Fr.].

sauterelle (sō-te-rel') *n.* mason's implement for tracing and forming angles [Fr.].

Sauterne (sō-tern') *n.* a well-known white wine, from *Sauternes*, S. W. France.

savage (sav-āj') *a.* pert. to forest; remote from human habitation; wild; uncivilised; primitive; cruel;—*n.* man in native state of primitiveness; a barbarian;—*v.t.* to tear at and worry; —*v.i.* to play the savage.—**sav'agely** *adv.*—**sav'ageness, sav'agery** *n.* ferocity; barbarism [L. *silvaticus*, fr. *silva*, a wood].

savanna, savannah (sạ-van'ạ) *n.* in tropical America extensive open plain destitute of trees and covered with grass or low vegetation [Sp. *sabana*].

savant (sav'ong, sa'vant) *n.* a man of learning [Fr. fr. *savoir*, to know].

save (sav) *v.t.* to rescue, preserve from danger, evil, etc.; to redeem; to protect; to secure; to maintain (face, etc.); to keep for future; to lay by; to hoard; to obviate need of; to spare; to except;—*v.i.* to lay by money; to economise; —*prep.* except;—*conj.* but.—**sav'able, save'able** *a.* capable of being saved; retrievable.—**sa'ver** *n.* one who, or that which, saves.—**sa'ving** *a.* frugal; thrifty; delivering from sin; implying reservation, as *saving clause*;—*prep.* excepting; with apology to;—*n.* economy;—*pl.* earnings or gains put by for future.—**sa'vingly** *adv.*—**sa'vings-bank** *n.* bank for receipt and accumulation of small savings [Fr. *sauver*, fr. L. *salvare*, to save].

saveloy (sav'ẹ-loi) *n.* highly-seasoned dried sausage, made of salted pork [earlier *cervelas*, It. *cervellata*, fr. *cervello*, brain].

saviour (sāv'yur) *n.* one who saves or delivers from destruction or danger; a deliverer or redeemer; the Redeemer, Jesus Christ [L. *salvare*, to save].

savoir-faire (sav-wȧr-fer') *n.* the knack of knowing the right thing to do at the right time; tact [Fr.].

savory (sā'vor-i) *n.* genus of aromatic plants, often grown as pot-herbs, the leaves being used in cooking as flavouring [fr. *savour*].

savour, savor (sā'vur) *n.* taste; flavour; relish; odour; smack; in Scripture, character; reputation;—*v.t.* to like; to taste or smell with pleasure; to relish;—*v.i.* to have a particular smell or taste; to resemble; to indicate.—**sa'vourily** *adv.*—**sa'vouriness** *n.*—**sa'vourless** *a.*—**sa'voury** *a.* having savour; tasty—*n.* tasty dish at beginning or end of dinner [L. *sapor*, taste].

Savoy (sạ-voi') *n.* a former duchy in S.E. France.—**savoy'** *n.* a hardy winter variety of cabbage with curly leaves, orig. from *Savoy*.—**Savoyard'** *n.* a native of Savoy.

savvy, savvey (sav'i) *v.t.* (*Slang*) to understand;—*n.* intelligence [Sp. *saber*; Fr. *savoir*, to know].

saw (saw) *pa.t.* of the verb **see.**

saw (saw) *n.* old saying; maxim; proverb; aphorism; adage (O.E. *sagu*].

saw (saw) *n.* hand or mechanical tool with thin blade, band, or circular disc with serrated edge, used for cutting;—*v.t.* and *v.i.* to cut with a saw;—*pa.t.* **sawed.**—*pa.p.* **sawed** or **sawn.**—**saw'bones** *n.* (*Slang*) surgeon.—**saw'dust** *n.* small particles of wood, etc. made by action of a saw.—**saw'er** *n.* one who saws; sawyer.—**saw'fish** *n.* genus of tropical ray-like fish whose snout is extended into long flat serrated beak.—**saw'mill** *n.* place where logs are sawn by mechanical power.—**saw'pit** *n.* pit over which timber is sawn by two men, one standing below, the other above the timber while using two-handed saw.—**saw'toothed** *a.* having serrations like a saw.—**saw'yer** *n.* one who saws timber; beetle of longhorn family with saw-like mandibles.—**circular saw**, a power-driven steel disc with teeth on its periphery, for sawing logs.—**cross-cut saw**, large two-handled saw for cutting across grain of wood.—**fret′saw** *n.* very narrow saw with fine teeth for cutting plywood.—**hack′saw** *n.* one for cutting metal.—**jig′saw, jigg′er-saw** *n.* machine fret-saw [O.E. *saga*].

Saxe (saks) *a.* pert. to or made in Saxony; of light blue shade;—*n.* light-blue shade, Saxony blue [Fr. *Saxe*, Saxony].

saxhorn (saks′horn) *n.* brass wind-instrument [Adolphe *Sax*, inventor, c. 1842].

saxifrage (sak′si-frāj) *n.* popular name of various plants, most of them true rock plants, with tufted foliage and panicles of white, yellow, or red flowers [L. *saxum*, a stone; *frangere*, to break].

Saxon (sak′sun) *n.* one of the people who formerly dwelt in N. Germany and who invaded England in the 5th and 6th cents.; a person of English race; native of Saxony; language of Saxons; —*a.* pert. to Saxons, their country, their language; Anglo-Saxon [O.E. *Seaxa*, *Seaxan*, fr. *seax*, a knife].

Saxony (sak′sun-i) *n.* very fine quality of wool; flannel [*Saxony*, where first produced].

saxophone (sak′sō-fōn) *n.* brass wind-instrument, with a reed and clarinet mouth-piece, fingered like an oboe [A. J. *Sax*, the inventor; Gk. *phōnē*, a sound].

say (sā) *v.t.* to utter with speaking voice; to state; to express; to allege; to repeat (lesson, etc.); to recite; to take as near enough.—*pa.t.* and *pa.p.* **said** (sed).—*n.* something said; what one has to say; share in a decision.—**say′er** *n.* a speaker.—**say′ing** *n.* a verbal utterance; spoken or written expression of thought; proverbial expression; adage; maxim [O.E. *secgan*].

say (sā) *n.* trial; assay; proof by trial;—*v.t.* to assay [fr. *assay*].

say (sā) *n.* thin silk; kind of serge used for linings, aprons, etc.—**sayette′** *n.* light stuff, made of pure wool, adapted for linings, etc. [Fr.].

scab (skab) *n.* crust forming over open wound or sore; contagious skin disease, resembling mange, which attacks horses, cattle and sheep; potato-disease; disease of apple and pear; blackleg; despicable person;—*v.i.* to heal over; to form a scab.—*pa.t.* and *pa.p.* **scabbed**.—*pr.p.* **scab′bing**.—**scab′bed** *a.* covered with scabs; paltry; vile; impure.—**scab′bedness, scab′biness** *n.*—**scab′bily** *adv.* vilely.—**scab′by** *a.* scabbed.—**scab′mite** *n.* the itch-mite [O.N. *skabbi*].

scabbard (skab′ard) *n.* sheath for sword or dagger;—*v.t.* [O.Fr. *escalberc*].

scabies (skā′bi-ēz) *n.* skin disease caused by parasite burrowing under skin; the itch; the scab [L.].

Scabiosa (skā-bi-ō′sa) *n.* Also **sca′bious**, a genus of annual and perennial plants of teasel family [L. *scabies*, because reputed to cure the itch].

scabious (skā′bi-us) *a.* consisting of scabs; scabby; itchy [L. *scabies*, the itch].

scabrid (skab′rid) *a.* (*Bot.*) having a rough, file-like surface.—**scab′rous** *a.* rough; (*Bot.*) having wart-like excrescences; harsh [L. *scabridus*, rough].

scad (skad) *n.* the British species of the horse-mackerel [form of *shad*].

scaffold (skaf′old) *n.* temporary erection, of timber or metal, used in erecting, altering, or repairing buildings; framework; stage; platform, esp. for execution of criminal;—*v.t.* to furnish with a scaffold; to prop up; to sustain.—**scaff′olding** *n.* scaffold [O.Fr. *eschafault*].

scalawag, scallawag See **scallywag**.

scald (skawld) *v.t.* to burn with moist heat or hot liquid; to cleanse by rinsing with boiling water; to heat milk to point approaching boiling-point;—*n.* injury by scalding [L. *ex*, out of; *calidus*, hot].

scald, skald (skawld, skald) *n.* ancient Scandinavian poet who sang or recited verses extolling deeds of heroes.—**scal′dic, skal′dic** *a.* [O.N. *skald*].

scale (skāl) *n.* dish of a balance; balance itself; machine for weighing, chiefly in *pl.*; Libra, one of signs of zodiac;—*v.t.* to weigh, as in scales; to measure; to estimate [O.N. *skal*, bowl].

scale (skāl) *n.* horny or bony plate-like outgrowth from skin of certain mammals, reptiles, and fishes; any thin layer or flake on surface;—*v.t.* to deprive of scales;—*v.i.* to come off or peel in thin layers.—**scaled** *a.* having scales.—**scale′less** *a.*—**scal′iness** *n.* being scaly.—**scal′ing** *n.* removing of scales.—**scal′y** *a.* covered with scales; resembling scales [O.Fr. *escale*, husk].

scale (skāl) *n.* ladder; series of steps or gradations; comparative rank in society; ratio between dimensions as shown on map, etc. to actual distance, or length; scope; basis for a numerical system, as *binary scale*; (*Mus.*) succession of notes arranged in order of pitch between given note and its octave; gamut;—*v.t.* to climb by a ladder; to clamber up; to mount [L. *scala*, a ladder].

scalene (ska-lēn′) *a.* uneven; (*Geom.*) having all three sides unequal;—*n.* a scalene triangle [Gk. *skalēnos*, uneven].

scall (scawl) *n.* scabbiness; scurf; leprosy;—*a.* mean; paltry; low.—**scalled, scald** *a.* scabby [O.N. *skalli*, bald head].

scallion (skal′yun) *n.* a variety of shallot [L. (*cepa*) *Ascalonia*, onion of Ascalon].

scallop, scollop (skal′op, skol′op) *n.* bivalve mollusc with ribbed, fan-shaped shell and beautiful colouring; fringed, ornamental curved edge; dish resembling scallop shell to serve oysters, etc.;—*v.t.* to cut edge of material into scallops [O.Fr. *escalope*, a shell].

scallywag (skal′i-wag) *n.* scamp; a worthless fellow; scapegrace. Also **scal′awag, scall′awag** [etym. doubtful].

scalp (skalp) *n.* covering dome of cranium consisting of skin and hair; skin and hair torn off by Indian warriors as token of victory; bare mountain top;—*v.t.* to deprive of integument of head; to criticise savagely [contr. of *scallop*].

scalp (skalp) *n.* area off coasts of Britain consisting of a flat surface formed by sandbanks overlying clay where oysters and mussels breed; a scaup [etym. doubtful].

scalpel (skalp′el) *n.* small, straight, surgical knife with convex edge [L. *scalpere*, to cut].

scamble (skam′bl) *v.i.* to sprawl; to scramble;—*v.t.* to squander.—**scam′bling** *a.* noisy; turbulent;—*n.* a hasty meal [etym. doubtful].

scamp (skamp) *n.* scoundrel; rascal; rogue;—*v.t.* to execute work carelessly; to skimp [O.Fr. *escamper*, to decamp].

scamper (skam′per) *v.i.* to run about; to run away in haste and trepidation;—*n.* a hasty, impulsive flight [fr. *scamp*].

scan (skan) *v.t.* to examine closely; to scrutinise; to measure or read (verse) by its metrical feet; (*Radar*) to traverse an area with electronic beams.—*v.i.* to be metrically correct.—*pr.p.* **scan′ning**.—*pa.t.* and *pa.p.* **scanned**.—**scan′ning** *n.* (*Television*) process of dissecting a picture to be transmitted.—**scan′sion** *n.* act or mode of scanning poetry [L. *scandere*, to climb].

scandal (skan′dal) *n.* malicious gossip; outrage; disgrace; injury to a person's character;—*v.t.* to defame; to traduce.—**scan′dal-bear′er, scan′dal-mong′er** *n.* one who delights in retailing malicious scandal and gossip.—**scan′dalise** *v.t.* to shock popular morals or sentiments; to defame; to disgrace; to vilify.—**scan′dalous** *a.* giving offence; bringing shame; libellous; disgraceful.—**scan′dalously** *adv.*—**scan′dalousness** *n.* [Gk. *skandalon*, a cause of stumbling].

scandalise (skan′da-līz) *v.t.* to reduce the area of sail on a ship [fr. *scantle*].

Scandinavia (skan-di-nā′vi-a) *n.* peninsula of

Norway and Sweden, but historically and linguistically includes Denmark and Iceland. —**Scandina′vian** *a.* pert. to Scandinavia [L. *Scandinavia* or *Scandia*].

scandium (skan′di-um) *n.* a metallic chemical element belonging to group of the rare earths. Symbol Sc. [L. *Scandia*, Scandinavia].

scansion. See **scan**.

scant (skant) *a.* barely sufficient; inadequate; —*v.t.* to put on short allowance; to supply grudgingly;—*adv.* scarcely; not quite;—*n.* scarcity.—**scant′ily** *adv.*—**scant′iness** *n.*—**scant′ly** *adv.* sparingly; scarcely; barely.—**scant′ness** *n.* scantiness; insufficiency. —**scant′y** *a.* [O. N. *skamt*, short].

scantle (skan′tl) *v.t.* to divide into small pieces; to partition.—**scant′let** *n.* fragment.—**scant′ling** *n.* little piece;—*pl.* the dimensions of all the principal items in a structure in engineering practice [Fr. *échantillon*, a sample].

scape (skāp) *n.* an escape; an escapade; a freak;—*v.t.* and *v.i.* to escape from; to avoid; to shun.—**scape′goat** *n.* in Mosaic ritual, goat upon whose head were symbolically placed sins of people; one who has to shoulder blame due to another.—**scape′grace** *n.* graceless, good-for-nothing fellow [fr. *escape*].

scaphoid (skaf′oid) *a.* boat-shaped [Gk. *skaphē*, a boat; *eidos*, form].

scapula (skap′ū-la̦) *n.* shoulder-blade.—**scap′ular** *a.* pert. to scapula;—*n.* bandage for shoulder blade; part of habit of certain religious orders in R.C. church, consisting of two bands of woollen stuff, of which one crosses the back and the other the stomach. Also **scap′ulary** [L. *scapulae*, the shoulder-blades].

scar (skȧr) *n.* permanent mark left on skin after healing of a wound, burn; a cicatrix; any blemish;—*v.t.* to mark with scar;—*v.i.* to heal with a scar [O.Fr. *escare*].

scar (skȧr) *n.* bare and broken place on side of mountain; precipitous bank or cliff. Also **scaur** [O.N. *sker*].

scarab (skar′a̦b) *n.* dung-rolling beetle, regarded by ancient Egyptians as emblematic of solar power; gem cut in shape of this beetle, as amulet [L. *scarabaeus*].

scaramouch (skar′a̦-mouch) *n.* buffoon in motley dress; personage in old Italian comedy characterised by bragging and poltroonery [*Scaramuccia*, famous Italian merry-andrew of the 17th cent.].

scarce (skārs) *a.* not plentiful; deficient; wanting; rare; infrequent; uncommon; scanty;—*adv.* hardly; scarcely.—**scarce′ly** *adv.* with difficulty; hardly; only just; not quite.—**scarce′ness, scarc′ity** *n.* being scarce; lack; deficiency [O.Fr. *escars*].

scare (skār) *v.t.* to terrify suddenly; to alarm; to drive away by frightening;—*n.* sudden alarm (esp. causeless); panic; fright.—**scare′crow** *n.* figure set up to frighten away birds from crops; a miserable-looking person in rags. —**scare′-mong′er** *n.* alarmist [O.N. *skirra*].

scarf (skȧrf) *n.* long, narrow, light article of dress worn loosely over shoulders or about neck; necktie; a muffler. —*pl.* **scarfs, scarves** [O.Fr. *escrepe*, a purse hanging from the neck].

scarf (skȧrf) *v.t.* to unite lengthways two pieces of timber by letting notched end of one into a similar end of the other, then securing them with bolt or strap.—*n.* joint for connecting timbers lengthways, the two pieces overlapping [Scand. = *skarf*, a joint].

scarify (skar′i-fī) *v.t.* to scratch or slightly cut the skin; to stir the surface soil of; to lacerate; to criticise unmercifully.—*pa.t.* and *pa.p.* **scar′ified.**—**scarifica′tion** *n.*—**scar′ifier** *n.* [L. *scarificare*].

scarlatina (skȧrla̦-tē′na̦) *n.* scarlet fever [It.].

scarlet (skȧr′let) *n.* bright red colour of many shades; cloth of scarlet colour;—*a.* of this colour;—*v.t.* to redden;—*v.i.* to blush.—**scar′let-bean** *n.* scarlet-runner.—**scar′let-fe′ver** *n.* scarlatina.—**scar′let-hat** *n.* a cardinal's hat. —**scarlet pimpernel,** small annual herb with red flowers.—**scar′let-run′ner** *n.* bean plant with twining stem and scarlet flowers [O.Fr. *escarlate*].

scarp (skȧrp) *n.* steep inside slope of ditch in fortifications;—*v.t.* to make steep.—**scarped** *a.* steeply sloping [It. *scarpa*].

scary (skār′i) *a.* producing fright or alarm; exceedingly timid [fr. *scare*].

scat (skat) *n.* a rain-squall [perh. from *scud*].

scathe, scath (skāth) *n.* harm; injury; damage; waste;—*v.t.* to injure; to damage.—**scathe′ful** *a.* hurtful; injurious.—**scathe′fulness** *n.*—**scath(e)′less** *a.* unhurt; unharmed; uninjured; undamaged.—**sca′thing** *a.* damaging; cutting; biting.—**sca′thingly** *adv.* [O.N. *skatha*].

scatology (skat-ol′o-ji) *n.* scientific study of fossilised excrement of animals; obscene literature.—**scatolog′ical** *a.* [Gk. *skōr*, *skatos*, dung].

scat-singer (skat′sing-e̦r) *n.* (*U.S.*) in a dance band, a vocal accompaniment of humorous noises [etym. doubtful].

scatter (skat′e̦r) *v.t.* to strew about; to sprinkle around; to put to rout; to disperse; —*v.i.* to take to flight; to disperse.—**scatt′er-brain** *n.* a giddy, thoughtless person.—**scatt′er-brained** *a.* —**scatt′ered** *a.* widely separated or distributed; distracted; wandering; sporadic; desultory.—**scatt′erer** *n.*—**scatt′ering** *n.* act of dispersing; effect of irregularly reflected light; (*Radio*) general re-radiation of wave-energy when a ray meets an obstacle in its path;—*a.* dispersing; sporadic; diversified.—**scatt′eringly** *adv.* [etym. uncertain].

scaup (skawp) *n.* poor, hard land; firm sandbank uncovered at low tide [fr. *scalp*].

scaup (skawp) *n.* bed of shell-fish.— **-duck** *n.* pochard, dun-bird [O.N. *skalp*].

scaur (skawr) *n.* See **scar**, a precipitous cliff.

scavenger (skav′en-je̦r) *n.* one employed in cleaning streets, removing refuse, etc.; animal which feeds on carrion;—*v.i.* to scavenge.—**scav′enge** *v.t.* to cleanse streets, etc. [orig. *scavager*, inspector of goods for sale, later, of street cleansing, fr. O.E. *sceawian*, to inspect].

scelerate (sel′e̦-rāt) *a.* wicked;—*n.* a criminal; a villain.—**scel′erous** *a.* [L. *scelus*, crime].

scena (shā′na) *n.* in grand opera, dramatic vocal solo consisting of both recitative and air.—*pl.* **scene** (shā′nā) [It.].

scenario (sen-ȧ′ri-ō′) *n.* script or written version of play to be produced by cinematograph; plot of a play.—**scenar′ist** *n.* [It.].

scene (sēn) *n.* stage of a theatre; place, time of action of novel, play, etc.; a sub-division of a play; spectacle, show, or view; episode; unseemly display of temper; minor disturbance.—**scen′ery** *n.* painted stage-scenes; natural features of landscape which please eye.—**scene′shift′er** *n.* one who manages the scenery in theatrical representation.—**scen′ic** *a.* pert. to scenery, esp. of theatre; theatrical; picturesque.—**scen′ic-rail′way** *n.* miniature railway running through artificial panoramic scenery, as on fair-ground, etc.—**scenograph′ic, -al** *a.* drawn in perspective.—**scenograph′ically** *adv.*—**scenog′raphy** *n.* [L. *scena*].

scent (sent) *v.t.* to discern or track by sense of smell; to give a perfume to; to detect; to become suspicious of;—*v.i.* to smell;—*n.* odour or perfume; fragrance; aroma; paper trail in game of hare and hounds.—**scent′ed** *a.* perfumed.—**scent′gland** *n.* a gland which secretes odoriferous matter.—**to put off the scent,** to mislead wilfully [Fr. *sentir*, to smell].

sceptic, skeptic (skep′tik) *n.* one who doubts esp. existence of God, or doctrines of Christianity; rationalist; agnostic; unbeliever; —*a.* sceptical.—**scep′sis, skep′sis** *n.* scepticism. —**scep′tical** *a.* doubtful; doubting; disbelieving; incredulous.—**scep′tically** *adv.*—**scep′ticalness** *n.* —**scep′ticise** *v.i.* to doubt everything.—**scep′ticism** *n.* doubt in absence of conclusive evidence; theory that positive truth is unattainable by human intellect; a doubt of the

existence of the supernatural or of a god; agnosticism [Gk. *skeptesthai*, to investigate].
sceptre (sep′tẹr) *n.* ornamental staff or baton, as symbol of royal power; royal mace; royal or imperial dignity.—**scep′tred** *a.* invested with a sceptre; regal [Gk. *skēptron*, a staff].
schedule (shed′ūl, in U.S.A. sked′) *n.* written or printed scroll of paper; smaller document forming part of principal document, deed, etc.; official, tabulated list; an inventory; time-table;—*v.t.* to note and enter in list [L. a small scroll].
schema (skē′ma) *n.* plan or diagram; synopsis; outline; scheme; figure of speech.—*pl.* **sche′mata.**—**schemat′ic** *a.*—**schemat′ically** *adv.*—**sche′matise** *v.t.* to a form scheme; to represent diagrammatically [Gk.].
scheme (skēm) *n.* plan; design; system; plot; machination; draft; outline; a syllabus; tabulated statement; horoscope;—*v.t.* to plan; to contrive; to frame;—*v.i.* to intrigue; to plot.—**sche′mer** *n.* intriguer.—**sche′ming** *n.* and *a.* planning; intriguing; plotting.—**sche′mist** *n.* schemer; astrologer [Gk. *schēma*, form].
scherzo (sker′tsō) *n.* (*Mus.*) composition of a lively, playful character [It. = a jest].
schilling (shil′ing) *n.* orig. a German silver coin, re-introduced into Austrian monetary system in 1925 [Ger.].
schipperke (ship′, skip′pẹr-ki) *n.* a smallish, alert, tailless dog [Dut. = ' the little skipper', originally a dog on canal boats].
schism (sizm) *n.* split of a community into factions; division of a church or religious denomination; crime of promoting this.—**schismat′ic** *a.*—*n.* one who separates from a church; dissenter.—**schismat′ical** *a.* schismatic.—**schismat′ically** *adv.* [Gk. *schisma*, a cleft].
schist (shist) *n.* any crystalline metamorphic rock which has polished structure and splits into thin irregular plates.—**schista′ceous** *a.* blue-grey; slate-coloured.—**schist′ic, schist′ous, schist′ose** *a.* having the structure of schist; resembling schist [Fr. *schiste*, fr. Gk. *schizein*, to split].
schizo- (skiz′, skīz′o) *prefix* fr. Greek, *schizein*, to cleave, used in the construction of compound terms.—**schiz′oid** *a.* exhibiting slight symptoms of schizophrenia.—**schizophren′ia** *n.* mental disorder known as 'split personality,' characterised by asocial behaviour, introversion, and loss of touch with one's environment.—**schizophren′ic** *a.*
schnapps, schnaps (shnaps) *n.* kind of Holland gin [Ger.].
scholar (skol′ạr) *n.* schoolboy or schoolgirl; student; learner; disciple; learned person; holder of scholarship.—**schol′arly** *a.* learned.—**schol′arship** *n.* learning; erudition; a grant; exhibition; bursary.—**scholas′tic** *a.* pert. to schools, scholars, or education; pert. to schools or scholars of philosophy of Middle Ages; pedantic; very subtle and abstruse; formal;—*n.* schoolman who expounded medieval philosophy; Jesuit student who has not yet taken Holy Orders.—**scholas′tically** *adv.*—**Scholas′ticism** *n.* system of philosophy during Middle Ages which attempted to harmonise doctrines of Aristotle with teachings of Church [Gk. *scholē*, a school].
scholiast (skō′li-ast) *n.* ancient commentator or annotator of classical texts.—**scholias′tic** *a.*—**scho′lium** *n.*—*pl.* **scho′lia**, marginal note or comment; grammatical or philological note [Gk. *scholiastēs*, commentator].
school (skóól) *n.* a shoal (of fish, whales, etc.) [Dut. *school*, crowd].
school (skóól) *n.* institution for teaching or giving instruction in any subject; academy; seminary; institute; gymnasium; pupils of a school; group of writers, artists, thinkers, etc. with principles or methods in common; lecture hall; branch of study; degree examination (usually in *pl.*); system; habit or practice;—*v.t.* to educate; to discipline; to instruct; to tutor.—**school′boy** *n.* boy attending school or of school age.—**school′fellow, school′mate** *n.* contemporary at school.—**school′ing** *n.* instruction in school; tuition; education.—**school inspector**, official appointed to examine schools.—**school′man** *n.* (*fem.* **school′mis′tress**) learned doctor of Middle Ages, versed in scholasticism.—**school′mast′er** *n.* master in charge of school; male teacher in school.—**school′room** *n.* a place for teaching in.—**school′teach′er** *n.* one certificated to teach.—**boarding school**, residential school for boys or girls.—**grammar school**, secondary school where emphasis is on teaching of Latin and Greek.—**preparatory school**, private school which prepares young boys for public schools in England.—**public school**, in England, endowed school whose headmaster is a member of the Headmasters' Conference; in Scotland, a state-aided school, elementary or primary [Gk. *scholē*, leisure; place for discussion].
schooner (skóó′nẹr) *n.* small, sharp-built vessel, having two masts, fore-and-aft rigged; extra large glass for holding beer; in N. America, long drink [orig. *scooner*, fr. Prov. E. *scoon*, to make flat stone skip along surface of water. O.E. *scunian*].
schottische, shottish (sho-tēsh′, shot′ish) *n.* round dance resembling polka; music in $\frac{2}{4}$ time for this dance.—**Highland schottische**, lively dance to strathspey tunes, Highland fling [Ger. = Scottish].
sciatica (sī-at′i-ka) *n.* neuralgia of sciatic nerve, with pains in region of hip.—**sciat′ic, -al** *a.* situated in, or pert. to, hip region.—**sciat′ically** *adv.* [Late L. fr. Gk. *ischion*, hip-joint].
science (sī′ẹns) *n.* systematic knowledge of natural or physical phenomena; truth ascertained by observation, experiment, and induction; ordered arrangement of facts known under classes or heads; theoretical knowledge as distinguished from practical; knowledge of principles and rules of invention, construction, mechanism, etc. as distinguished from art.—**scientif′ic, -al** *a.*—**scientif′ically** *adv.*—**sci′entism** *n.* outlook and practice of scientist.—**sci′entist** *n.* a person versed in science, esp. natural science.—**Christian Science**, religious doctrine of faith-healing, bodily diseases being due to errors of mortal mind and therefore curable by faith and prayer.—**domestic science**, study of good housekeeping.—**natural science, physical science**, science which investigates nature and properties of material bodies and natural phenomena.—**pure science**, science based on self-evident truths, as mathematics, logic, etc. [L. *scientia*, knowledge].
scimitar (sim′i-tạr) *n.* short sabre with curved, sharp-edged blade broadening from handle [Pers. *shimshir*].
scintilla (sin-til′ạ) *n.* spark; gleams; least particle; atom.—**scin′tillant** *a.* emitting sparks; sparkling.—**scin′tillate** *v.i.* to emit sparks; to sparkle; to glisten, to coruscate.—**scintilla′tion** *n.* [L. = a spark].
sciolism (sī′ō-lizm) *n.* superficial knowledge used to impress others.—**sci′olist** *n.* one possessed of superficial knowledge; charlatan.—**sciolis′tic** *a.* [L. *scire*, to know].
scion (sī′on) *n.* slip for grafting; offshoot; young member of family; a descendant; heir [Fr.].
scirocco. See **sirocco.**
sciscitation (sis-i-tā′shun) *n.* the act of inquiring; demand [L. *sciscitari*, to inquire].
scissile, scissible (sis′īl, sis′i-bl) *a.* (*Bot.*) capable of being cut, split, or divided.—**sciss′ion** *n.* act of cutting [L. *scindere, scissum*, to cut].
scissors (siz′ẹrz) *n.pl.* instrument of two sharp-edged blades pivoted together for cutting; small shears.—**sciss′or** *v.t.* to cut with scissors.—**sciss′or-bill** *n.* bird of skimmer family [Fr. *ciseaux*].
Sclav, Sclavonic, etc. See **Slav**, etc.
scler- sclero- (sklēr, sklē′ro) *prefix* fr. Gk.

sklēros, hard, used in the construction of compound terms, implying hardness or dryness—**scle'ra** *n.* strong, opaque fibrous membrane forming outer coat of eyeball.—the white of the eye.—**scler'al** *a.* hard, bony.—**scleri'tis** *n.* inflammation of sclera of eye.—**scleroder'ma, scleroder'mia** *n.* chronic skin disease characterised by hardness and rigidity.—**scleroder'matous** *a.* (*Zool.*) possessing a hard, bony, external structure for protection.—**scleroder'mic, scleroder'mous, sclerodermit'ic** *a.* pert. to scleroderma; having a hard outer skin.—**scle'roid** *a.* of hard texture.—**sclero'ma** *n.* hardening of tissues.—**sclero'sal** *a.* pert. to sclerosis.—**sclero'sis** *n.* hardening of organ as a result of excessive growth of connective tissue; induration.—**sclerot'ic** *a.* indurated; hardened; pert. to sclera;—*n.* external hard coat of eye; the sclera.—**scle'rous** *a.* hard; indurated; bony.

scobs (skobz) *n.* dross of metals; shavings; sawdust; filings.—**scobic'ular, scob'iform** *a.* resembling sawdust [L. *scobs*, sawdust].

scoff (skof) *v.t.* to treat with derision; to mock at;—*v.i.* to jeer;—*n.* expression of scorn; an object of derision.—**scoff'er** *n.*—**scoff'ingly** *adv.* [Scand.].

scoff (skof) *v.t.* (*Slang*) to eat greedily; to eat the whole of [etym. uncertain].

scold (skōld) *v.t.* and *v.i.* to find fault (with); to chide; to reprove angrily; to rebuke;—*n.* one who scolds; a nagging, brawling woman.—**scold'er** *n.*—**scold'ing** *n.* violent rating; harsh rebuke.—**scold'ingly** *adv.* [Ger. *schelten*, to brawl].

scollop Same as **scallop.**

sconce (skons) *n.* ornamental bracket fixed to wall, for carrying a light; lantern for candle; projecting partition or screen, to provide cover; protection for head, hence head itself, wits; small fort or breastwork; a bulwark; fine imposed for some misdemeanour;—*v.t.* to fortify or defend with a sconce; to impose fine as at Oxford or Cambridge [O.Fr. *esconce*, fr. L. *abscondere*, to hide].

scone (skon, skōn) *n.* (*Scot.*) a thin, flat cake baked on griddle [etym. doubtful].

scoop (skóóp) *n.* article for ladling; kind of shovel; hollow piece of wood for baling boats; lucrative speculation on Stock Exchange; publication of exclusive news in newspaper;—*v.t.* to ladle out, shovel, lift, dig or hollow out with scoop; to publish exclusive news; to gain or secure, as in *to scoop the pool* [prob. fr. Sw. *skopa*, a scoop].

scoot (skóót) *v.i.* to move off quickly; to dart away suddenly; to scamper off.—**scoot'er** *n.* a toy consisting of flat board mounted on two wheels, on which one foot rests, propelled by other foot and guided by handle attached to front wheel [fr. *shoot*].

scope (skōp) *n.* range of activity or application; space for action; room; play; outlet; opportunity; aim; length of cable paid out when ship is riding at anchor [It. *scopo*, a target].

scorbutic (skor-bū'tik) *a.* affected with, or relating to, scurvy [etym. uncertain].

scorch (skorch) *v.t.* to burn the surface of; to parch; to shrivel; to char; to singe; to wither; to blast;—*v.i.* to be burnt on surface; to dry up; to parch; to drive at excessive speed.—**scorched-earth policy**, destroying everything of value in path of hostile army.—**scorch'er** *n.* anything which scorches; a biting, sarcastic remark; one who drives furiously; hot, sultry day.—**scorch'ing** *a.* burning superficially; oppressively hot; scathing.—**scorch'ingly** *adv.* [etym. uncertain].

score (skōr) *n.* a cut, notch, line, stroke; tally-mark, reckoning, bill, account; number twenty; reason; sake; number of points, runs, goals, etc. made in a game; arrangement of different parts of a musical composition on the page so that each bar may be read in all parts simultaneously;—*v.t.* to mark with lines, scratches, furrows; to cut; to engrave; to write down in proper order; to orchestrate; to enter in account book, to record; to make (points, etc.) in game; to cross out;—*v.i.* to add a point, run, goal, etc. in a game; to make a telling remark; to achieve a success.—**scor'er** *n.* one who keeps official record of points, runs, etc. made in the course of a game; one who makes the point, run, etc. in a game.—**scor'ing** *n.*—**score'book, -card, -sheet, scor'ing-card** *n.* for recording points, etc. made in game.—**to score off**, to gain the advantage over [O.N. *skor*, notch].

scoria (skō'ri-ạ) *n.* dross or slag resulting from smelting of metal ores; rough, angular, cindery-looking material sent out by volcano.—**sco'riae** *n.pl.* frothy-looking volcanic ashes.—**sco'rify** *v.t.* to reduce to dross or slag [Gk. *skoria*, dross].

scorn (skorn) *n.* extreme disdain or contempt; object of derision;—*v.t.* to contemn; to despise; to spurn.—**scorn'ful** *a.*—**scorn'fully** *adv.* [O.Fr. *escarnir*].

Scorpio (skor'pi-ō) *n.* Scorpion, 8th sign of zodiac, which the sun enters about 23rd October; scorpion.—**scor'pion** *n.* insect allied to spiders having slender tail which ends in very acute sting; whip armed with points like scorpion's tail; (*World War* 2) tank with anti-mine flail; vindictive person with virulent tongue [L.].

scot (skot) *n.* formerly, tax, contribution, fine. Also **shot.**—**scot'free** *a.* unhurt; exempt from payment [O.N. *skot*, a tax].

Scot (skot) *n.* native of Scotland; one of the Scoti or Scots, a Celtic tribe from Ireland who settled in N. Britain in 5th cent. and ultimately gave whole country name of Scotland [O.E. *Scottas* (*pl.*), Irishmen].

Scotch (skoch) *a.* pert. to Scotland or its inhabitants; Scots (adj. form usually preferred in Scotland); Scottish;—*n.* Scots; Scots dialect; Scotch whisky.—**Scotch (Scottish) bluebell**, the harebell.—**Scotch'bonn'ets** *n.pl.* a fungus, the fairy-ring mushroom.—**Scotch broth**, broth made of pearl-barley, various vegetables and beef for seasoning.—**Scotch collie**, sheep-dog with long-haired coat and sharp muzzle.—**Scotch fir**, indigenous pine in Britain—also known as **Scotch pine**, Northern pine and Baltic fir or pine.—**Scotch kail**, broth.—**Scotch'man** *n.* a Scotsman.—**Scotch mist**, a very fine rain.—**Scotch terrier**, small short-legged, rough-coated dog; Aberdeen terrier.—**Scotch thistle**, national emblem of Scotland.

scotch (skoch) *v.t.* to support, as a wheel, by placing some object to prevent its rolling; to prevent progress being made, to kill project in its initial stages;—*n.* prop. wedge, strut, or shoulder.

scotch (skoch) *v.* to wound slightly; to maim; to hack; to abrade;—*n.* scratch; notch; mark or score [etym. uncertain].

Scotia (skō'shạ) *n.* poetical name for Scotland [*Scoti*, a Celtic tribe].

Scoticè, Scoticism See **Scotticè, Scotticism.**

Scots (skotz) *n.* dialect of English spoken in Lowland Scotland;—*a.* pert. to Scotland; Scottish.—**Scots'man, Scots'woman** *n.* native of Scotland.—**Scots Greys**, oldest dragoon regiment in British army.—**Scots Guards**, one of five regiments forming Foot Guard of Household Troops [O.E. *Scottas*].

Scotticè (skot'i-sē) *adv.* in the Scots language, dialect, or manner.—**Scott'icism** *n.* idiom, expression, or word peculiar to Scots language or people.—**Scott'icise** *v.t.* to make conform to Scots ways or speech [L. *Scotticus*, Scottish].

Scottish (skot'ish) *a.* pert. to Scotland or its people; Scots; Scotch [O.E. *Scottas*].

scoundrel (skoun'drel) *n.* rascal; villain; vagabond.—**scoun'drelism** *n.* rascality; baseness.—**scound'relly** *a.* villainous; rascally [etym. uncertain].

scour (skour) *v.t.* to clean or polish the surface of, by hard rubbing; to purge violently; to

flush out;—*v.i.* to clean by rubbing; to be purged to excess;—*n.* clearing action of swift, deep current or rush of water.—**scour′er** *n.* [O.Fr. *escurer*].
scour (skour) *v.t.* to pass rapidly along or over in search of something; to range; to rake;—*v.i.* to scamper; to rove over; to scurry along.—**scour′er** *n.* one who roams streets at night [etym. uncertain].
scourge (skurj) *n.* whip made of leather thongs; lash; punishment; a grievous affliction; pest; one who inflicts pain or devastates country;—*v.t.* to flog; to lash; to chastise; to devastate [L. *excoriare*].
scout (skout) *n.* one sent out to reconnoitre; look-out; a Boy Scout; reconnaissance aeroplane; college man-servant at Oxford;—*v.t.* to reconnoitre; to spy out.—**scout′master** *n.* adult instructor and organiser in the Boy Scouts [O.Fr. *escoute*, fr. *escouter*, to listen].
scout (skout) *n.* a high rock [O.N. *skuta*, to jut out].
scout (skout) *v.t.* to reject with contempt; to sneer at [etym. uncertain].
scow (skou) *n.* large flat-bottomed barge, with square ends; lighter for carrying deck-loads [Dut. *schouw*].
scowl (skoul) *v.i.* to wrinkle brows in displeasure; to frown gloomily or sullenly; to look sour, sullen, or annoyed;—*n.* a gloomy, angry frown [Scand.].
scrabble (skrab′l) *v.t.* to scribble; to scrawl;—*v.i.* to scratch with hands; to move on hands and knees [var. of *scrapple*, freq. of *scrape*].
scrag (skrag) *n.* anything thin, lean, gaunt, or shrivelled; raw-boned person; long, thin neck; lean end of neck of mutton;—*v.t.* to wring neck of; to hang; to execute.—**scrag′ged** *a.* rough and uneven; knobby; rugged; ill-disposed.—**scrag′gedness, scrag′giness** *n.*—**scrag′gily** *adv.*—**scrag′gly** *a.* rough and unkempt-looking.—**scrag′gy** *a.* lean; jagged [earlier *crag*].
scram (skram) *interj.* (*Slang*) clear out!
scramble (skram′bl) *v.i.* to move by crawling, climbing, etc. on all fours; to clamber; to struggle with others for;—*v.t.* to collect together hurriedly and confusedly; to cook eggs by stirring when broken, in frying-pan;—*n.* scrambling; disorderly proceeding; rough-and-tumble.—**scram′bling** *a.* climbing; snatching; straggling [etym. uncertain, cf. *scrabble*].
scran (skran) *n.* (*Slang*) scraps of food [O.N. *skran*, refuse].
scranch (skransh) *v.t.* to grind with the teeth. Also **scrunch** [imit.].
scrannel (skran′ẹl) *a.* grating; squeaking; screechy; thin; miserable [etym. uncertain].
scrap (skrap) *n.* small detached piece or fragment; material left over which can be used as raw material again; coloured picture, cut round main outline, for pasting into a scrap-book;—*pl.* odds and ends;—*v.t.* to throw out; to discard;—*pa.t.* and *pa.p.* **scrapped**.—*pr.p.* **scrap′ping**.—**scrap′heap** *n.* a rubbish heap; pile of old iron, etc.—**scrap′met′al** *n.* fragments of any metal collected for remelting.—**scrap′pily** *adv.*—**scrap′piness** *n.*—**scrap′py** *a.* consisting of scraps or odds and ends; fragmentary [O.N. *skrap*].
scrap (skrap) *n.* (*Slang*) a fight; a rough-and-tumble;—*v.i.* to fight with the fists [var. of *scrape*].
scrap (skrap) *n.* snare for birds.
scrape (skrāp) *v.t.* to abrade; to grate; to scratch; to remove by rubbing; to clean or smooth thus;—*v.i.* to produce grating noise by rubbing; to live parsimoniously; to bow awkwardly with drawing back of foot; to scratch in earth, as fowls;—*n.* act or sound of scraping; scratch; predicament; embarrassing situation.—**scrap′er** *n.* one who, or that which, scrapes; miser; fiddler; metal bar for scraping mud off soles of shoes; tool with thin blade for scraping.—**scrap′er-board** *n.* prepared card-board for artists, with a surface which may be scraped away or left to be inked [O.E. *scrapian*].
scratch (skrach) *v.t.* to score or mark a narrow surface wound with claws, nails, or anything pointed; to abrade skin; to erase; to scrape; to withdraw name of entrant for race or competition; to write in a hasty, careless manner;—*v.i.* to use claws or nails in tearing, abrading, or shallow digging; to strike out one's name from list of competitors;—*n.* slight wound, mark, or sound made by sharp instrument; mark indicating the starting point of back-marker in a handicap race; one who concedes a start in distance, time, etc. to other competitors; noise associated with the playing of a gramophone record;—*a.* taken at random, brought together in a hurry, as *a scratch team*; denoting competitor without handicap.—**scratch′er** *n.*—**scratch′y** *a.* [mixture of earlier *scrat* and *cratch*, both of Teut. origin].
scrawl (skrawl) *v.t.* to write or draw untidily; to scribble;—*v.i.* to write unskilfully and inelegantly;—*n.* hasty, careless writing; scribble; trivial composition.—**scrawl′er** *n.* [perh. fr. *scrabble*].
scrawl (skrawl) *n.* in U.S., brushwood.
scrawny (skraw′ni) *a.* lean; scraggy; raw-boned; gaunt.—**scraw′niness** *n.* (Cf. *scranny*).
scream (skrēm) *v.t.* and *v.i.* to utter a piercing cry; to shriek; to laugh immoderately;—*n.* a shrill, piercing cry; uncontrollable fit of laughter; a person who excites much laughter; laughter-provoking incident.—**scream′ing** *a.* [imit. origin].
scree (skrē) *n.* pile of débris at base of cliff or hill; a talus (etym. uncertain].
screech (skrēch) *v.i.* to utter a harsh, shrill cry; to scream;—*n.* a shrill and sudden, harsh cry.—**screech′hawk** *n.* night-jar.—**screech′owl** *n.* owl with persistent harsh call [earlier *scritch* of imit. origin].
screed (skrēd) *n.* long letter or passage; long boring speech; list of grievances, etc.; fragment or shred [O.E. *screade*, a shred].
screen (skrēn) *n.* piece of furniture to shelter from heat, light, draught, or observation; partition of stone, metal, or wood, cutting off one part of ecclesiastical building from the rest; coarse, rectangular riddle for grading coal, pulverised material, etc.; white surface on which image is projected by optical means; troops thrown out towards enemy to protect main body;—*v.t.* to provide with shelter or concealment; to protect from blame or censure; to conceal; to sift; to riddle; to film; to project film, lantern slide, etc. on a screen; to subject a person to political scrutiny.—**screen′grid** *n.* (*Radio*) third electrode in a screened grid or pentode valve.—**screened′grid** *n.* a tetrode (four electrode) valve used in high-frequency amplification.—**screen′ing** *n.* employing a metal sheath to screen a magnetic field from the outside surroundings; (*Nuclear Physics*) reduction in intensity of radiations on passing through matter.—**the screen**, the cinema.—**smoke′screen** *n.* dense smoke artificially disseminated to conceal movements [O.Fr. *escran*].
screeve (skrēv) *v.t.* to write or draw; to concoct begging letter [L. *scribere*, to write].
screw (skròò) *n.* in mechanics, a machine consisting of an inclined plane wound round a cylinder; cylinder with a spiral ridge running round it, used as holding agent or as mechanical power; turn of screw; twist to one side; a screw-propeller; tractor; skin-flint; moral pressure or compulsion; (*Slang*) wages; salary;—*v.t.* to fasten with screw; to press or stretch with screw; to work by turning; to twist round; to treat harshly; to obtain by pressure; to extort;—*v.i.* to assume a spiral motion; to move like a screw.—**screw′bolt** *n.* metal bolt with a flat head at one end and screw at other used with nut for fastening timbers, etc. together.—**screw′driv′er** *n.* tool for turning screws.—**screwed** *a.* (*Slang*) drunk; tipsy.—**screw′er** *n.*—**screw′ing** *a.* turning; exacting; stingy.—**screw′nail** *n.* small nail

with a flat, slotted head and fine thread.—**screw'-propell'er** *n.* revolving shaft carrying two or more symmetrically arranged fan-like blades or flanges to create forward thrust of a ship.—**screw'-rudd'er** *n.* screw instead of rudder for steering a ship.—**screw'-thread** *n.* spiral ridge, triangular or rectangular in section, on a screw cylinder.—**screw'-wrench** *n.* a tool for gripping the flat surfaces of screws and turning them.—**screw'y** *a.* tortuous, like the thread or motion of a screw; (*Slang*) crazy; daft [O.Fr. *escroue*].

scribble (skrib'-l) *v.t.* and *v.i.* to write carelessly; to draw meaningless lines; to write worthless stuff; to scrawl;—*n.* something scribbled.—**scribb'ler** *n.* bad or careless writer; a writer of unimportant trifles; an author.—**scribb'ling** *a.* used for scribbling;—*n.* careless writing [freq. of *scribe*, fr. L. *scribere*, to write].

scribble (skrib'-l) *v.t.* to card or tease wool [Scand. *skrubbla*, to card].

scribe (skrīb) *n.* a writer; official or public writer; clerk; copyist; secretary; an author; official copyist and expounder of Mosaic and traditional Jewish law; a scriber;—*v.t.* to incise wood, metal, etc. with a sharp point as a guide to cutting; to mark off, to trim off edge of a board so as to fit to another edge or to a surface;—*v.i.* to write.—**scri'bal** *a.* pert. to a scribe.—**scri'ber** *n.* sharp-pointed instrument used to mark off metal work (L. *scribere*, to write].

scrimmage (skrim'-āj) *n.* a confused struggle; a tussle for the ball in football; a scrum. Also **scrumm'age** (Cf. *skirmish*].

scrimp (skrimp) *v.t.* to make too short or small; to stint;—*a.* scanty.—**scrimped** *a.* stinted; pinched.—**scrimp'ly** *adv.*—**scrimp'ness** *n.*—**scrimp'y** *a.* [O.E. *scrimman*, to shrink].

scrimshank (skrim'-shangk) *v.i.* (*Slang*) to be work-shy; to dodge or shirk a duty.—**scrim'-shanker** *n.* [etym. unknown].

scrimshaw (skrim'-shaw) *v.t.* and *v.i.* to make decorative article out of odds-and-ends;—*n.* such work [etym. unknown].

scrip (skrip) *n.* small bag or wallet; satchel [O.Fr. *escrepe*].

scrip (skrip) *n.* a writing; interim certificate of holding bonds, stock, or shares [var. of *script*].

script (skript) *n.* kind of type, used in printing and typewriting, to imitate handwriting; a writing; hand-writing; producer's version of words of play, or of scenes and words of film; text of spoken part in broadcast; (*Law*) original or principal document [L. *scribere*, *scriptum*, to write].

scripture (skrip'-tūr) *n.* anything written; sacred writing; passage from Bible.—**the Scriptures**, Old and New Testaments.—**scrip'tural**, **scrip'ture** *a.* according to Scriptures; biblical [L. *scribere*, *scriptum*, to write].

scrivener (skriv'-ẹn-ẹr) *n.* one who draws up contracts or other documents; one who places money at interest on behalf of clients; public writer; notary [L. *scribere*, to write].

scrofula (skrof'-ū-lạ) *n.* constitutional weakness, due to malnutrition in early life.—**scrofulit'ic**, **scrof'ulous** *a.* [L. = a little sow].

scroll (skrōl) *n.* roll of paper or parchment; a writing formed into a roll; a list; flourish at end of signature; curved head of violin; system of architectural ornament consisting of spiral volutes; (*Her.*) motto-bearing ribbon or inscription.—**scrolled** *a.* formed like, or contained in, a scroll [O.Fr. *escrou*].

scrotum (skrō'-tum) *n.* external muscular sac which lodges testicles of the male.—**scrot'al** *a.* [L.].

scrounge (skrounj) *v.t.* and *v.i.* (*Slang*) to cadge; to pilfer, esp. public property.—**scroun'ger** *n.*—**scroun'ging** *n.*

scrub (skrub) *v.t.* to clean with a hard brush and water; to scour; to rub;—*v.i.* to be penurious; to work hard for a living;—*pa.t.* and *pa.p.* **scrubbed**.—*pr.p.* **scrub'bing**.—*n.* one who labours hard and lives meanly; stunted growth, found in semi-deserts; underwood; brushwood; worn-out brush; worthless horse.—**scrub'ber** *n.* one who, or that which, scrubs.—**scrub'bing** *n.* and *a.*—**scrub'bing-board** *n.* a corrugated board for scouring clothes.—**scrub'bing-brush** *n.* brush with extra-strong bristles.—**scrub'by** *a.* mean and small; stunted; covered with scrub; unshaved.—**scrub'-wood** *n.* a small, stunted tree [obs. Dut. *schrubben*].

scruff (skruf) *n.* the back of the neck; nape. Also **skruff** [etym. uncertain].

scruffy (skruf'-i) *a.* scurfy; unkempt [var. of *scurfy*].

scrum (skrum) *n.* (*Abbrev.*) scrummage (in rugby football).—**scrum'-half** *n.* half-back in rugby, who stands fairly close to scrummage, puts ball into scrum and attempts to retrieve it.—**scrumm'age** *n.* scrimmage; in rugby, pushing compact mass of rival forwards waiting for ball to be inserted [fr. *scrimmage*].

scrumbling. See **scumbling.**

scrumptious (skrum'-shus) *a.* (*Slang*) delicious; delightful; nice; fastidious.

scrunch (skrunsh) *v.t.* to crush with the teeth; to crunch; to crush [fr. *crunch*].

scruple (skròò'-pl) *n.* small weight equal to 20 troy gr. apothecaries' weight or 1.296 grammes (symbol, ℈); very small quantity; feeling of doubt; conscientious objection; qualm;—*v.i.* to hesitate from doubt; to have compunction.—**scru'pulous** *a.* extremely conscientious; attentive to small points.—**scru'pulously** *adv.*—**scru'pulousness**, **scrupulos'ity** *n.* [L. *scrupulus*].

scrutiny (skròò'-ti-ni) *n.* close search; critical examination; searching look or gaze; official re-examination of votes cast at an election.—**scruta'tor** *n.* one who examines closely.—**scru'tinate**, **scru'tinise** *v.t.* to examine into critically.—**scru'tiniser** *n.* one who makes a close examination.—**scru'tinisingly** *adv.* [L. *scrutari*, to examine closely].

scud (skud) *v.i.* to move quickly; to run before a gale;—*v.t.* to slap; to skelp.—*pr.p.* **scud'ding**.—*pa.t.* and *pa.p.* **scud'ded**.—*n.* act of moving quickly; ragged cloud drifting rapidly in strong wind [etym. uncertain].

scuff Same as **scruff**.

scuff (skuff) *v.t.* to graze against one in passing;—*v.i.* to shuffle along without raising the feet [Sw. *skuffa*, to push].

scuffle (skuf'-l) *v.i.* to struggle at close quarters; to fight confusedly;—*n.* confused fight, or struggle; rough and tumble.—**scuff'ler** *n.* [Sw. *skuffa*, to push].

sculduddery (skul-dud'-e-ri) *n.* (*Scot.*) obscenity; lewdness [etym. doubtful].

scull (skul) *n.* short light oar pulled with the one hand; light racing boat of a long, narrow build; cock-boat;—*v.t.* to propel boat by two sculls; to propel boat by means of oar placed over stern and worked alternately, first one way and then the other.—**scull'er** *n.* [etym. uncertain].

scullery (skul'-ẹr-i) *n.* small room off kitchen where rough work is done [O.Fr. *escuelerie*, fr. *escuele*, a dish].

scullion (skul'-yun) *n.* male underservant who performed menial work; low, mean, dirty fellow [O.Fr. *escouillon*, a dish-clout].

sculp (skulp) *v.t.* to sculpture; to carve; to engrave; to flay [L. *sculpere*, to carve].

sculpture (skulp'-tūr) *n.* art of reproducing objects in relief or in the round out of hard material by means of chisel; carved work; art of modelling in clay or other plastic material, figures or objects to be later cast in bronze or other metals; a copper-engraving;—*v.t.* to represent, by sculpture.—**sculp'tor** *n.* (*fem.* **sculp'tress**) one who carves or moulds figures.—**sculp'tural** *a.* [L. *sculpere*, *sculptum*, to carve].

scum (skum) *n.* impurities which rise to surface of liquids; foam or froth, if of dirty appearance; vile person or thing, riff-raff;—

v.t. to take scum off; to skim; *—v.i.* to throw up scum. *—pr.p.* **scum'ming.** *—pa.t.* and *pa.p.* **scummed.**—**scum'my** *a.* covered with scum; low-bred [Dan. *skum*, froth].

scumble (skum'bl) *v.t.* to apply opaque colours with little body as a wash to soften the tone of an under-coat of paint.—**scum'bling, scrum'bling** *n.* process of softening the tints of a picture by blending them with a neutral tint laid on with a nearly dry brush [freq. of *scum*].

scupper (skup'ẹr) *n.* channel alongside bulwarks of ship to drain away water from deck through scupper-holes; *—v.t.* to throw into the scupper; to endanger; to slaughter; to sink [O.Fr. *escopir*, to spit out].

scurf (skurf) *n.* dry scales or flakes formed on skin, esp. of head; dandruff; anything adhering to surface.—**scurf'iness** *n.*—**scurf'y** *a.* covered with scurf [O.E. *sceorf*].

scurrilous, scurrile, scurril (skur'i-lus, skur'il) *a.* obscenely vulgar; foul-mouthed; indecent; abusive; vile.—**scurril'ity, scur'rilousness** *n.* vulgar language; vile abuse.—**scur'rilously** *adv.* [L. *scurrilis*].

scurry, skurry (skur'i) *v.i.* to hurry along; to run hastily.—*pa.t.* and *pa.p.* **scurr'ied.**—**scurr'y, scurr'ying** *n.* [fr. *scour*].

scurvy (skur'vi) *n.* deficiency disease due to lack of vitamin C; (*Med.*) scorbutus;—*a.* afflicted with the disease; scurfy; mean; low; vile.—**scur'vily** *adv.* in a scurvy manner; meanly; vilely.—**scur'viness** *n.* [fr. *scurf*].

scut (skut) *n.* a short tail, as that of a hare [O.N. *skjota*, to jut out].

scutage (skū'tāj) *n.* in feudal law, a tax on a knight's fee or holding [L. *scutum*, a shield].

scutate (skū'tāt) *a.* (*Bot.*) shield-shaped; (*Zool.*) protected by scales or shield-like processes [L. *scutum*, a shield].

scutcheon, scutchin (skuch'un, -in) *n.* shield for armorial bearings; escutcheon; name-plate; plate to which door-knob is fixed [var. of *escutcheon*].

scutella (skū-tel'a) *n.* horny plate or scale.—**scu'tellate, -d** *a.* (*Bot.*) rounded and nearly flat, like a saucer.—**scutell'iform** *a.* scutellate.—**scu'tiform** *a.* (*Bot.*) shield-shaped [L. = a salver].

scutter (skut'ẹr) *v.i.* to run away hastily; to scurry [fr. *scuttle*].

scuttle (skut'l) *n.* broad, shallow, open basket; wide-mouthed vessel for holding coal [O.E. *scutel*].

scuttle (skut'l) *n.* hole with a cover, for light and air, cut in ship's deck or hatchway; hinged cover of glass to close a port-hole;—*v.t.* to make hole in ship, esp. to sink it.—**scutt'ler** *n.* one who scuttles; one who wrecks project [O.Fr. *escoutille*, a hatchway].

scuttle (skut'l) *v.i.* to rush away; to run hurriedly [freq. of *scud*].

scythe (siTH) *n.* mowing implement with long curved blade swung by bent handle held in both hands;—*v.t.* to cut with scythe; to mow [O.E. *sithe*].

sea (sē) *n.* mass of salt water covering greater part of earth's surface; named broad tract of this; certain large expanses of inland water, when salt; billow, or surge; swell of ocean; vast expanse; flood; large quantity.—**sea'anem'one** *n.* beautifully coloured radiate marine animal, found on rocks on sea-coast.—**sea'board** *n.* coast-line and its neighbourhood; seashore.—**sea'borne** *a.* carried on the sea or on a sea-going vessel.—**sea'breeze** *n.* one which blows from sea toward land.—**sea'cap'tain** *n.* captain of sea-going vessel; skipper.—**sea'coast** *n.* shore or border of land adjacent to sea.—**sea'dog** *n.* dog-fish; seal; pirate; old, experienced sailor.—**sea'farer** *n.* one who travels by sea; sailor.—**sea'faring** *a.*—**sea'fenn'el** *n.* samphire.—**sea'front** *n.* land adjoining sea; promenade or esplanade facing sea; part of building facing sea.—**sea'girt** *a.* encircled by the sea.—**sea'go'ing** *a.* pert. to vessels which make long voyages by sea.—**sea'green** *a.* having colour of sea-water; being of faint green colour, with a slightly bluish tinge.—**sea'gull** *n.* any gull.—**sea'horse** *n.* a small fish, allied to needle-fish and pipe-fish, with horse-like head; the hippopotamus; the walrus; fabulous animal, part horse, part fish.—**sea'legs** *n.pl.* ability to walk on ship's deck in spite of rough seas.—**sea'level** *n.* level of the sea taken at mean-tide.—**sea'li'on** *n.* lion-headed, large-eared type of seal, eared-seal.—**Sea Lord,** naval member of the Board of Admiralty.—**sea'man** *n.* deck-hand on board a mercantile ship; rating in British Navy.—**sea'manlike, sea'manly** *a.*—**sea'manship** *n.* art of managing and navigating properly ship at sea.—**sea'mew** *n.* seagull; any gull.—**sea'mile** *n.* geometrical mile, 60th part of a degree of latitude, a distance varying with the latitude, mean value being 6076.8 ft.—**sea'pink** *n.* species of thrift which grows on sandy shores.—**sea'plane** *n.* aeroplane which can take off from and alight on sea.—**sea'port** *n.* town with harbour.—**sea power,** command of the seas; nation with powerful fleet.—**sea'scape** *n.* a picture representing maritime scene or view.—**Sea'Scout** *n.* member of special branch of Boy Scouts who receive training in seamanship, etc.—**sea'ser'pent** *n.* enormous marine animal of serpentine form said to inhabit ocean.—**sea'shell** *n.* a marine shell.—**sea'shore** *n.* land adjacent to sea; (*Law*) ground between ordinary high-water mark and low-water mark.—**sea'sick** *a.* suffering from seasickness.—**sea'sickness** *n.* a disturbance of the nervous system with nausea and vomiting, produced by rolling and pitching of vessel at sea.—**sea'side** *n.* and *a.* land adjacent to the sea.—**sea'trout** *n.* salmon-trout.—**sea'wall** *n.* embankment to prevent erosion or flooding.—**sea'ward** *a.* and *adv.* towards the sea.—**sea'wa'ter** *n.* salt-water.—**sea'way** *n.* rate of progress of a vessel under way.—**sea'weed** *n.* collective name for large group of marine plants (Algae) distributed from above high-water mark to depth of about fifty fathoms.—**sea'worthy** *n.* fit for proceeding to sea; able to stand up to buffetings of waves.—**sea'worthiness** *n.*—**sea'wrack** *n.* sea-weed thrown up by the sea.—**at sea,** on the ocean; away from land; bewildered.—**half-seas over,** half-drunk, tipsy.—**high seas,** the open sea [O.E. *sae*].

seal (sēl) *n.* an aquatic carnivorous animal with flippers as limbs, of which the eared variety furnishes rich fur pelt as well as oil;—*v.i.* to hunt for seals.—**seal'er** *n.* ship, or person, engaged in seal-fishing.—**seal'ery** *n.* seal-fishing station.—**seal'skin** *n.* dressed skin or fur of eared-seal;—*a.* made of seal-skin [O.E. *seolh*].

seal (sēl) *n.* piece of metal or stone engraved with a device, cipher, or motto for impression on wax, lead, etc.; impression made by this (on letters, documents, etc.); that which closes or secures; symbol, token, or indication; arrangement for making drain-pipe joints air-tight;—*v.t.* to affix a seal to; to confirm; to ratify; to settle, as doom; to shut up; to close up joints, cracks, etc.—**sealed** *a.* having a seal affixed; enclosed; ratified.—**seal'ing-wax** *n.* wax composed of shellac or other resinous substances and turpentine tinted with colouring matter.—**seal'ring** *n.* a signet ring.—**Great Seal,** official seal of United Kingdom, used to seal treaties, writs summoning parliament, etc.—**Privy Seal,** official seal affixed to state documents of minor importance [O.Fr. *seel*, fr. L. *sigillum*, a seal].

Sealyham (sēl'i-ham) *n.* small rough-coated terrier with very short legs, a Welsh breed of dog [village in Wales].

seam (sēm) *n.* line of junction of two edges, e.g. of two pieces of cloth, or of two planks; thin layer or stratum, esp. of coal;—*v.t.* to join by sewing together; to mark with furrows or wrinkles; to scar.—**seam'less** *a.* having no seams; woven in the piece.—**seam'ster** *n.* (*fem.*

seam'stress, semp'stress) one who sews by profession.—**seam'y** *a.* showing seams; sordid [O.E. fr. *siwian*, to sew].

sean (sēn) *n.* a seine-net, used in fishing. See [**seine.**

séance (sā´ongs) *n.* session of a public body; assembly; meeting of spiritualists for consulting spirits and communicating with 'the other world' [Fr.].

sear (sēr) *v.t.* to scorch or brand with a hot iron; to dry up; to wither; to cauterise; to render callous;—*a.* dry; withered; burned; hardened.—**searing iron**, iron for cauterising flesh [O.E. *searian*].

sear (sēr) *n.* the catch in the lock of a firearm which holds it at cock or half-cock. Also **sere** [O.Fr. fr. L. *sera*, a bar].

search (sẹrch) *v.t.* to look over or through in order to find; to probe into;—*v.i.* to look for; to seek; to explore;—*n.* searching; quest; inquiry; investigation.—**searched** *a.* in art, pert. to outline, silhouette effect, accurately depicted in vigorous and characteristic way.—**search'er** *n.* one who searches; custom-house officer who searches for articles liable to duty.—**search'ing** *a.* thorough; penetrating; keen; minute; trying; severe.—**search'ingly** *adv.*—**search'ingness** *n.*—**search'light** *n.* electric arc-light which sends concentrated beam in any desired direction.—**search´warr'ant** *n.* warrant to enable police to enter premises of suspected person [Fr. *chercher*, to look for].

season (sē´zn) *n.* one of four divisions of year—spring, summer, autumn, winter; in tropical regions, the wet or dry period of year; busy holiday period; fashionable time of the year for high society; convenient time; period; time; interval; (*Colloq.*) season-ticket; seasoning;—*v.t.* to render suitable; to habituate; to give relish to; to spice; to mature;—*v.i.* to grow fit for use; to become adapted to climate; to become accustomed to.—**sea'sonable** *a.* suitable or appropriate for the season; opportune; timely; fit.—**sea'sonableness** *n.*—**sea'sonably** *adv.*—**sea'sonal** *a.* depending on, or varying with, seasons.—**sea'sonally** *adv.*—**sea'soning** *n.* flavouring.—**sea'son-tick'et** *n.* one valid for definite period.—**close season**, time when something is not lawful or permitted [L. *satio*, sowing].

seat (sēt) *n.* thing made or used for sitting on; manner of sitting (of riding, etc.); right to sit (e.g. in council, etc.); sitting part of body; part of trousers which covers buttocks; locality of disease, trouble, etc.; country-house; mansion; place from which a country is governed;—*v.t.* to place on a seat; to cause to sit down; to assign a seat to; to fit up with seats; to establish;—*v.i.* to rest; to lie down.—**seat'ed** *a.* fixed; confirmed; settled.—**seat'ing** *n.* setting on, or fitting up with, seats [O.N. *saeti*].

sebaceous (sẹ-bā´shus) *a.* made of, or pert. to, tallow or fat; secreting oily matter [L. *sebum*, tallow].

secability (sek-ạ-bil´i-ti) *n.* capability of being cut or divided [L. *secare*, to cut].

secant (sē´kạnt, sek´ạnt) *a.* cutting; incising; dividing into two parts;—*n.* any straight line which cuts another line, curve, or figure; a straight line drawn from centre of circle through one end of an arc, and terminated by a tangent drawn through other end; in trigonometry, ratio of hypotenuse to another side of a right-angled triangle is secant of angle between these two sides. [L. *secare*, to cut.]

secateurs (sek-a-tẹrz') *n.pl.* small hand pruning shears [Fr.].

secede (sẹ-sēd') *v.i.* to withdraw formally from federation, alliance, etc.—**sece'der** *n.* one who secedes; one of a party who left Established Church of Scotland in 1733.—**seces'sion** *n.* seceding from fellowship, alliance, etc.; withdrawal; departure [L. *secedere*, to go apart].

seclude (sẹ-klōōd') *v.t.* to shut up apart; to guard from or to remove from sight or resort.—**seclud'ed** *a.* living apart; retired; remote; sequestered.—**seclud'edly** *adv.*—**seclu'sion** *n.*—**seclu'sive** *a.* tending to seclude; retiring [L. *secludere*, to shut away].

second (sek´und) *a.* next to first; other; another; inferior; subordinate;—*n.* one who, or that which, follows the first; one next and inferior; one assisting esp. principal in duel or boxing-match; sixtieth part of a minute; (*Mus.*) interval contained between two notes on adjacent degrees of the staff; moment;—*n.pl.* coarse kind of flour; inferior quality, brand, etc. of commodity or article;—*v.t.* to support, esp. a motion before a meeting or council; to back; to encourage.—**second'** *v.t.* to 'lend' an official of one department to another for special duties.—**secon'ded** *a.* to be so transferred.—**Second Advent**, belief that Christ will return to earth in visible form.—**sec'ond-best** *n.* and *a.* best except one.—**second childhood**, dotage; senility.—**sec'ond-class** *a.* of an inferior order; mediocre.—**sec'ond-cous'in** *n.* child of first cousin.—**sec'onder** *n.* one who supports another.—**sec'ond-hand** *a.* not new; having been used or worn; indirect.—**sec'ond-lieuten'ant** *n.* lowest commissioned rank in British Army.—**sec'ondly** *adv.* in the second place.—**second'ment** *n.* temporary transfer of official to another department.—**second nature**, acquired habit.—**sec'ond-rate** *a.* of inferior quality, value, etc.—**sec'ond-sight** *n.* prophetic vision esp. of Scottish Highlanders.—**to play second fiddle**, to play or act subordinate part [L. *secundus*].

secondary (sek´un-dạr-i) *a.* succeeding next in order to the first; of second place, origin, rank; second-rate; inferior; unimportant; pert. to education and schools intermediate between elementary schools and university; (*Geol.*) relating to Mesozoic period;—*n.* one who occupies a subordinate place.—**secondary colour**, colour obtained by combination of primary colours, blue, red, and yellow.—**sec'ondarily** *adv.* in a secondary or subordinate manner; not primarily.—**sec'ondariness** *n.* [fr. *second*].

secret (sē´kret) *a.* kept or meant to be kept from general knowledge; concealed; unseen; private;—*n.* something kept secret or concealed; a mystery; governing principle known only to initiated.—**se'crecy** *n.* keeping or being kept secret; fidelity in keeping a secret; retirement; privacy; concealment.—**se'cretly** *adv.*—**se'cretness** *n.* secrecy.—**se'cretive** (or -krē´) *a.* uncommunicative; reticent; underhand.—**se'cretively** *adv.*—**se'cretiveness** *n.* [L. *secretus*, separated].

secretary (sek´re-tạ-ri) *n.* one employed by another or appointed by a society to deal with papers and correspondence, keep records, prepare business, etc.; confidential clerk; minister in charge of a particular department of government; escritoire; secretaire.—**secretaire'** *n.* writing-desk for deeds and papers.—**secreta'rial** *a.* pert. to duties of a secretary.—**secreta'riat, secreta'riate** *n.* administrative office or officials controlled by secretary.—**sec'retary-bird** *n.* bird of prey of S. Africa and Senegambia.—**Secretary of State**, cabinet minister in charge of certain important government departments; in U.S., equivalent of Foreign Secretary.—**sec'retaryship** *n.* office or post of a secretary [fr. *secret*].

secrete (se-krēt') *v.t.* to hide; to conceal; of gland, etc. to collect and supply particular substance in body;—*a.* separate; distinct.—**secre'ta** *n.pl.* products of secretion.—**secre'tion** *n.* substance elaborated by gland out of blood or body-fluids; process of so secreting or elaborating.—**secre'tional** *a.*—**secre'tive** *a.* promoting or causing secretion.—**secre'tor** *n.* a secreting organ or gland.—**secre'tory** *a.* secretion-forming [L. *secernere, secretum*, to set apart].

sect (sekt) *n.* body of persons separated from others in virtue of some special doctrines held in variance with parent body; religious denomination; followers of philosopher or religious leader; party; faction; cutting; scion. —**secta'rian** *a.* pert. to a sect; narrow-minded; bigoted. Also **secta'rial.**—*n.* one of a sect; a bigot; a partisan.—**secta'rianism** *n.* bigoted devotion to the interests of a sect.—**sec'tary** *n.* one of a sect; a dissenter [L. *secta*, fr. *sequi*, to follow].

sectant (sek'tant) *n.* (*Geom.*) the portion of space cut off by three planes and extending to infinity [L. *secare, sectum*, to cut].

section (sek'shun) *n.* cutting or separating by cutting; part separated from the rest; division; portion; a piece; a sub-division of subject matter of book, chapter, statute; signature; printer's reference mark (§) used for footnotes; representation of portion of building or object exposed when cut by imaginary vertical plane so as to show its construction and interior; surveyor's scaled drawing showing variations in surface level of ground along base-line; (*Geom.*) plane figure formed by cutting a solid by another plane; line formed by intersection of two surfaces; distinct part of a city, country, people, etc.; smallest military unit, four sections forming a platoon; (*Bot.* and *Zool.*) thin, translucent slice of organic or inorganic matter mounted on slide for detailed microscopic examination.—**sec'tional** *a.* pert. to, made up of sections; partial; local; (of paper) ruled in small squares. —**sec'tionalism** *n.* partial regard for limited interests of one particular class at expense of all others.—**sec'tionally** *adv.*—**sec'tionise** *v.t.* to divide out in sections [L. *secare, sectum*, to cut].

sector (sek'tur) *n.* portion of circle enclosed by two radii and the arc which they intercept; mathematical instrument graduated with sines, tangents, etc., used for finding fourth proportional in making planes, diagrams, etc.; in military affairs, a definite length of trench or front line.—**sec'toral** *a.* [L. *secare, sectum*, to cut].

secular (sek'ū-lar) *a.* worldly; temporal, as opposed to spiritual; lay; civil; profane; lasting for, occurring once in, a century or age; —*n.* layman; clergyman, not bound by vow of poverty and not belonging to religious order.—**secularisa'tion** *n.*—**sec'ularise** *v.t.* to convert from spiritual to secular use; to make worldly.—**sec'ularism** *n.* ethical doctrine which advocates a moral code independent of all religious considerations or practices.—**sec'ularist** *n.*—**secular'ity** *n.* worldliness; indifference towards future existence.—**sec'ularly** *adv.* [L. *saecularis*, fr. *saeculum*, an age, a century].

secure (se-kūr') *a.* free from care, anxiety, fear; safe; fixed; stable; in close custody; certain; confident;—*v.t.* to make safe, certain, fast; to close, or confine, effectually; to gain possession of; to obtain; to insure; to assure.—**secur'able** *a.*—**secur'ance** *n.* assurance; confirmation.—**secure'ly** *adv.*—**secure'ness** *n.* free from anxiety; feeling of security.—**secur'er** *n.*—**secur'ity** *n.* being secure; what secures; protection; assurance; anything given as bond, caution, or pledge.—**Secu'rity Coun'cil** *n.* branch of United Nations Organisation, set up in 1945, to settle international disputes and to prevent aggression.—**secur'ities** *n.pl.* general term for shares, bonds, stocks, debentures, etc. bought and sold on the Stock Exchange; documents giving to holder right to possess certain property [L. *securus*, fr. *se-*, without; *cura*, care].

sedan (se-dan') *n.* old-time closed conveyance with a chair inside for one, carried on two poles; a sedan-chair; a closed-in motor-car [orig. made at *Sedan*, France].

sedate (se-dāt') *a.* staid; not excitable, composed; calm; prim.—**sedate'ly** *adv.*—**sedate'ness** *n.* calmness; composure; primness.—**sed'ative** *a.* tending to calm; soothing;—*n.* agent, external or internal, which soothes [L. *sedare*, to calm].

sedentary (sed'en-ta-ri) *a.* sitting much; requiring sitting posture, as certain forms of employment; inactive.—**sed'entariness** *n.* [L. *sedere*, to sit].

sederunt (se-dē'runt) *n.* a single sitting of a court, or of a body of men in deliberation [L. = they sat, fr. *sedere*, to sit].

sedge (sej) *n.* rush-like plant growing in swampy grounds; any marsh-grass.—**sedge'war'bler** *n.* sedge-wren; reed-warbler.—**sedg'y** *a.* over-grown with sedge [O.E. *secg*].

sediment (sed'i-ment) *n.* matter which settles to bottom of liquid; lees; dregs.—**sedimen'tary** *a.* composed of sediment, esp. of rock laid down as deposits by water action.—**sedimenta'tion** *n.* [L. *sedere*, to settle].

sedition (se-dish'un) *n.* any act aimed at disturbing peace of realm or producing public disorder; insurrection.—**sedi'tionary** *n.* one who incites sedition.—**sedi'tious** *a.* pert. to, tending to excite sedition.—**sedi'tiously** *adv.*—**sedi'tiousness** *n.* [L. *seditio*, a going apart].

seduce (se-dūs') *v.t.* to lead astray; to draw aside from path of rectitude and duty; to induce woman to surrender chastity; to allure. —**seduce'ment** *n.* seduction.—**sedu'cer** *n.*—**sedu'cible** *a.* liable to be led astray; corruptible. —**seduc'tion** *n.* act of seducing.—**seduc'tive** *a.* —**seduc'tively** *adv.*—**seduc'tiveness** *n.* [L. *seducere*, to lead aside].

sedulous (sed'ū-lus) *a.* diligent; steady; industrious; persevering.—**sedu'lity** *n.*—**sed'ulousness** *n.*—**sed'ulously** *adv.* [L. *sedulus*].

see (sē) *n.* diocese or jurisdiction of bishop; province of archbishop.—**the Holy See,** the papal court [O.Fr. *siet*, fr. L. *sedere*, to sit].

see (sē) *v.t.* to perceive by eye; to behold; to observe; to note; to mark; to form an idea; to understand; to have interview with; to visit; to meet with;—*v.i.* to have the power of sight; to pay regard; to consider; to give heed; to understand; to apprehend.—*pa.t.* **saw.**—*pa.p.* **seen.**—**se'er** *n.* one who sees; one who foresees events, has second-sight; a prophet; a vaticinator.—**see'ing** *conj.* considering; since; —*n.* act of perceiving; sight [O.E. *seon*].

seed (sēd) *n.* embryo, fertilised ovule, which gives origin to new plant; one grain of this; such grains saved or used for sowing; that from which anything springs; origin; source; progeny; offspring; children; descendants; generation; first principle;—*v.t.* to sow with seed; to remove seeds from; to arrange draw for sports tournament, so that best players, etc. should not be drawn against each other in earlier rounds;—*v.i.* to produce seed; to shed seed.—**seed'ed** *a.* sown; matured.—**seed'ily** *adv.* in seedy manner.—**seed'iness** *n.* being seedy or off colour; shabbiness.—**seed'less** *a.*—**seed'ling** *n.* young plant, no longer depending on seed for food.—**seeds'man** *n.* one who deals in seeds.—**seed'-vess'el** *n.* case, envelope, or pericarp which contains seeds; pod.—**seed'y** *a.* abounding with seeds; run to seed; exhausted; worn out; miserable looking.—**to run to seed,** to produce flowers and seed at expense of leaves or roots; to go to waste or ruin [O.E. *saed*].

seek (sēk) *v.t.* to make search or enquiry for; to look for; to ask for; to strive after;—*v.i.* to make search.—*pa.t.* and *pa.p.* **sought.**—**seek'er** *n.* [O.E. *secan*].

seel (sēl) *n.* good fortune.—**seel'y** *a.* lucky; happy; artless; silly [O.E. *sael*].

seem (sēm) *v.i.* to appear (to be or to do); to look; to pretend; to appear to one's judgment; —*v.t.* to beseem; to suit.—**seem'ing** *a.* appearing like; apparent; ostensible; plausible; specious;—*n.* appearance; apparent likeness; judgment.—**seem'ingly** *adv.*—**seem'liness** *n.*—**seem'ly** *a.* fit; becoming;—*adv.* in a decent or proper manner [O.N. *sōma*].

seen (sēn) *pa.p.* of **see.**

seep (sēp) *v.i.* to ooze; to trickle; to drip; to leak away; to drain slowly. Also **sipe, sype.**—**seep'age** *n.* Also **sip'age** [O.E. *sipian*, to soak].

seer (sēr) *n.* one who mystically foresees events; a prophet; a prognosticator; a soothsayer.—**seer'ship** *n.* [fr. *see*].

seer-fish. See **seir-fish.**

seersucker (sēr-suk'ẹr) *n.* a light-weight linen fabric, woven in India (fr. Pers. *shir o shakkar* = milk and sugar].

seesaw (sē'saw) *n.* game in which two children sit at opposite ends of plank supported in middle and swing up and down; plank for this; to-and-fro motion; vacillation;—*a.* moving up or down; alternate; reciprocal;—*v.i.* to move upward and downward [imit.].

seethe (sēTH) *v.t.* to boil, cook, or soak in hot water;—*v.i.* to be in a state of ebullition; to be violently agitated or in confused movement;—*pa.t.* **seethed** or **sod.**—*pa.p.* **seethed** or **sodd'en** [O.E. *seothan*, to boil].

segment (seg'mẹnt) *n.* part cut off from a figure by a line; part of circle contained between chord and arc of that circle; section; portion; part;—*v.t.* and *v.i.* to separate into segments.—**segmen'tal** *a.* relating to a segment.—**seg'mentary, seg'mentate** *a.* having the form of a segment.—**segmenta'tion** *n.* act of dividing into segments; state of being divided into segments.—**segment'ed** *a.* [L. *segmentum*].

segregate (seg'rẹ-gāt) *v.t.* and *v.i.* to set or go apart from the rest; to isolate; to separate;—*a.* set apart; separate from the others.—**segrega'tion** *n.* [L. *segregare*, to remove from the flock (*grex*)].

seguidilla (seg-i-dēl'yạ) *n.* graceful, lively Spanish dance; music for it [Sp.].

Seignior (sēn'yor), **Seigneur** (sēn'yẹr) *n.* a feudal lord of a manor; title of honour or respectful address.—**seign'iorage, seign'orage** *n.* anything claimed by sovereign or feudal superior as prerogative.—**seignioral'ty** *n.* authority or domains of a seignior.—**seignio'rial, seigneu'rial, signo'rial** *a.* manorial.—**seign'iorise** *v.t.* to lord it over.—**seign'iory, seign'ory** *n.* authority of seignior; lordship or feudal domain; manorial rights; municipal council in medieval Italian republic.—**grand seignor,** Sultan of Turkey [Fr. fr. L. *senior*, elder].

seine (sān, sēn) *n.* seine-net, open bag-net for sea-fishing. Also **sean;**—*v.t.* to catch fish by dragging a seine-net through water [Fr. fr. L. *sagena*, a fishing-net].

seism (sīsm) *n.* earthquake.—**seis'mal, seis'mic** *a.* pert. to or produced by earthquake.—**seis'mogram** *n.* record of earthquake made by seismograph.—**seis'mograph** *n.* instrument which records distance and intensity of slightest earth tremors.—**seismolog'ic, -al** *a.*—**seismol'ogist** *n.* one versed in seismology.—**seismol'ogy** *n.* the study of earthquakes and their causes and effects [Gk. *seismos*, an earthquake].

seize (sēz) *v.t.* to grasp; to take hold of; to take possession of by force or legal authority; to arrest; to capture; to fasten; to comprehend;—*v.i.* of bearing parts or piston of machine, to adhere or stick tightly through excessively high temperature.—**seiz'able** *a.*—**seiz'ure** *n.* act of seizing; thing or property seized; sudden attack, as apoplectic stroke [Fr. *saisir*].

select (sẹ-lekt') *v.t.* to choose; to cull; to elect; to prefer;—*a.* of choice quality; of special excellence; chosen; picked; exclusive;—*n.* the best people.—**selec'tance** *n.* (*Radio*) selectivity.—**selec'ted** *a.*—**selec'tedly** *adv.*—**selec'tion** *n.* selecting; things selected; variety of articles for sale; book containing select pieces; (*Mus.*) medley of airs; (*Biol.*) process, according to the evolutionary theory, by which certain members of species survive and others, unfit, are gradually eliminated.—**selec'tive** *a.* having power of selection; discriminating.—**selec'tively** *adv.*—**selectiv'ity** *n.* (*Radio*) property of receiving set whereby discrimination can be made between a number of simultaneous signals or programmes on differing carrier-wave frequencies.—**selec'tor** *n.* one who, or an electric device which, selects [L. *seligere, selectum*].

Selene (se-lē-nē) *n.* (Gk. *Myth.*) goddess of moon.—**sele'niscope** *n.* instrument for taking observations of moon.—**sele'nograph** *n.* showing surface of moon.—**selenog'raphy** *n.* study of moon surface [Gk. = moon].

selenite (sel'en-īt) *n.* a colourless and translucent crystalline form of gypsum (calcium sulphate) [Gk. *selēnē*, the moon].

selenium (se-lē'ni-um) *n.* non-metallic element with remarkable property of altering its electrical resistance according to intensity of light falling on it [Gk. *selēnē*, the moon].

self (self) *n.* one's individual person; one's personal interest; ego; subject of individual consciousness; selfishness.—*pl.* **selves** (selvz).—*pron. affix* used to express emphasis or a reflexive usage;—*a.* of colour, uniform, same throughout; same; plain;—*prefix* used in innumerable compounds.—**self'-aban'donment** *n.* disregard of self.—**self'-abnega'tion** *n.* self-denial.—**self'-abuse'** *n.* masturbation; abuse of one's own powers.—**self'-assur'ance** *n.* self-confidence.—**self'-cen'tred** *a.* egoistic.—**self'-con'fidence** *n.* whole-hearted reliance on one's own powers and resources.—**self'-con'fident** *a.*—**self'-con'sciousness** *n.* an embarrassed state of mind leading to confusion due to belief that one is object of critical judgment by others present.—**self'-con'scious** *a.*—**self'-contained'** *a.* of a reserved nature; complete in itself; (of a house) having a separate entrance, detached.—**self'-control'** *n.* control over oneself, temper, emotions, and desires; self-command.—**self'-defence'** *n.* the act of defending one's person or justifying one's actions.—**self'-deni'al** *n.* refraining from gratifying one's desires or appetites; unselfishness, to the point of deprivation.—**self'-determina'tion** *n.* free-will; right of a people or nation to work out its own problems and destiny, free from interference from without.—**self'-gov'erning** *a.* autonomous; having a legislature elected by, and responsible to, those governed.—**self'-gov'ernment** *n.*—**self'-indul'gence** *n.* undue gratification of one's appetites or desires.—**self'-in'terest** *n.* exclusive regard to one's own profit or advantage; selfishness.—**sel'fish** *a.* concerned unduly over personal profit or pleasure; lacking consideration for others; mercenary; greedy.—**self'ishly** *adv.*—**self'ishness** *n.*—**self'less** *a.* having no regard to self; unselfish.—**self'-pit'y** *n.* morbid pleasure in nursing one's woes.—**self'-possessed'** *a.* calm and collected; able to control one's feelings and emotions; composed; undisturbed.—**self'-preserva'tion** *n.* instinctive impulse to avoid injury or death.—**self'-reli'ant** *a.* not depending or relying on others.—**self'-reli'ance** *n.*—**self'-respect'** *n.* a proper regard for one's own person, character, or reputation.—**self'-respect'ing** *a.*—**self'-respect'ful** *a.*—**self'-right'eous** *a.* thinking oneself faultless; esteeming oneself as better than others; priggish; pharisaical; hypocritical; sanctimonious.—**self'-sac'rifice** *n.* foregoing personal advantage or comfort for the sake of others.—**self'same** *a.* the very same; identical.—**self'-satisfac'tion** *n.* personal reassurance; (in a bad sense) smug conceit.—**self'-sat'isfied** *a.*—**self'-seek'er** *n.* one who seeks only his own profit or pleasure.—**self'-seek'ing** *a.* seeking one's own interest or happiness.—**self'-start'er** *n.* an automatic contrivance used for starting internal-combustion engine of motor-car.—**self'-styled** *a.* so-called, without any real warrant or authority; self-assumed; would-be; pretended.—**self'-suffi'cient** *a.* sufficient in itself; relying on one's own powers.—**self'-sugges'tion** *n.* a reflex mental process leading to a belief originating in the subliminal mind.—**self'-support'ing** *a.* not dependent on others for a living [O.E.].

sell (sel) *n.* seat; throne; saddle.—**sell'iform** *a.* saddle-shaped [L. *sella*, a seat].

sell (sel) *v.t.* to dispose of for an equivalent,

usually money; to deal in; to betray for money or a consideration; to delude; to trick; to have for sale; to promote sale of;—*v.i.* to fetch a price; to be in demand;—*pa.t.* and *pa.p.* **sold**.—*n.* deception; hoax; disappointment.—**sell'er** *n.* one who sells; vendor [O.E. *sellan*].

seltzer (selt´sẹr) *n.* a carbonated mineral water found at Nieder-Selters in Prussia; artificial mineral water of similar composition aerated with carbon dioxide.—**selt'zogene** *n.* a gazogene [corrupt. of *Selters*].

selvage, selvedge (sel´vāj) *n.* edge of cloth finished to prevent ravelling out; strong edging of web [for *self-edge*].

selves (selvz) *n.pl.* of **self**.

semantic (se-man´tik) *a.* pert. to meaning of words.—**seman'tics** *n.pl.* branch of linguistic research concerned with studying changes in meaning of words [Gk. *sēmainein*, to mean].

semaphore (sem´ạ-fōr) *n.* a post with movable arm or arms used for signalling; a system of signalling by human or mechanical arms [Gk. *sēma*, sign; *pherein*, to bear].

semasiology (se-mā-si-ol´o-ji) *n.* the science of the development of the meanings of words; semantics.—**semasiolog'ical** *a.* [Gk. *sēmasia*, meaning; *logos* a discourse].

semblable (sem´blạ-bl) *a.* similar; resembling; —*n.* likeness.—**sem'blance** *n.* real or seeming likeness; appearance; image; form; figure [Fr. *sembler*, to seem].

semeiography (se-mī-og´rạ-fi) *n.* study of signs and symbols.—**semeiol'ogy, semiol'ogy** *n.* (*Med.*) study of signs and symptoms of disease; symptomatology.—**semeiot'ics** *n.* science or language of signs [Gk. *sēmeion*, a mark].

semen (sē´men) *n.* whitish, viscid secretion formed by male reproductive organs, containing fertilising spermatozoa by which impregnation of female is effected [L. = seed].

semester (se-mes´tẹr) *n.* college half-year session in universities of Germany, America, etc. [Fr. *semestre*, fr. L. *sex*, six; *mensis*, a month].

semi- (sem´i), *prefix* with the meaning of half, partly, imperfectly, etc., used in the construction of compound terms, the meaning being usually obvious.—**sem'i-an'nual** *a.* half-yearly.—**sem'i-an'nular** *a.* forming a semicircle.—**sem'ibreve** *n.* (*Mus.*) standard note of measurement, a whole note—half the length of a breve and equivalent to two minims or four crotchets (symbol 𝅝).—**sem'icircle** *n.* plane figure bounded by diameter and portion of circumference of a circle which it cuts off. —**sem'icircled, semicir'cular** *a.*—**sem'icolon** *n.* punctuation mark (;) used to separate clauses of a sentence requiring a more marked separation than is indicated by a comma.—**sem'i-detached'** *a.* (of house) joined by a party-wall with another house but free on all sides. —**sem'i-fi'nal** *n.* a match, round, etc. qualifying winner to contest the final.—**semiquaver** *n.* (*Mus.*) one half of a quaver; a 16th note or rest (symbol).—**sem'itone** *n.* (*Mus.*) half a tone; one of the intervals of diatonic scale. —**sem'i-trop'ical** *a.* between tropical and temperate; sub-tropical [L. = half].

seminal (sem´i-nạl) *a.* pert. to seed of plants or semen of animals; radical; germinal; reproductive.—**sem'inate** *v.t.* to sow; to propagate; to disseminate.—**semina'tion** *n.* act of sowing or disseminating; seeding.—**seminif'erous, seminif'ic** *a.* seed-bearing [L. *semen*, seed].

seminar (sem´in-ar) *n.* group of advanced students pursuing research in a specific subject under supervision [L. *semen*, seed].

seminary (sem´in-ạr-i) *n.* place of education; academy; school or college; a training college for R.C. priesthood; breeding-ground or nursery;—*a.* trained in seminary.—**sem'inarist** *n.* R.C. priest educated in foreign seminary; student at seminary [L. *seminarium*, a seed-plot].

Seminole (sem´i-nōl) one of a nomadic tribe of American Indians, formerly living S.E. of the Mississippi (Florida, etc.).

semiography, semiology, semiotics, etc. Alternative for **semeiography**, etc.

Semite (sem´īt, sē´mīt) *n.* one of a group of races, speaking allied languages; they include Jews, Arabs and Syrians; supposed to be descendants of Shem (*see* Genesis, 10).—**Semit'ic** *a.* pert. to Semites or to language, customs, etc. of these races.

semolina (sem-ō-lē´nạ) *n.* hard grains of wheat after fine parts have passed through during milling—used in production of spaghetti, macaroni, etc. Also **sem'ola** [L. *simila*, wheatmeal].

sempiternal (sem-pi-tẹr´nạl) *a.* everlasting; never-ending; without beginning or end; eternal.—**sempiter'nity** *n.* future duration without end [L. *sempiternus*, fr. *semper*, always].

sempster (sem´stẹr) *n.* (*fem.* **semp'stress**) one who sews by profession [fr. *seamster*].

sen (sen) *n.* Japanese copper coin, in value 1-100th part of a yen or dollar [Jap.].

senate (sen´at) supreme legislative and administrative assembly in ancient Rome; ' Upper House ' in legislature, e.g. U.S. and some British Dominions; governing body in many universities.—**sen'ator** *n.* a member of a senate.—**senato'rial** *a.*—**sen'atorship** *n.* office or position of senator.—**sena'tus** *n.* governing body in certain universities [L. *senatus*, council of old men, fr. *senex*, old man].

send (send) *v.t.* to cause to go; to transmit; to forward; to despatch; to delegate; to depute; to cast; to throw; to confer;—*v.i.* to despatch messenger; to transmit message.—*pa.t.* and *pa.p.* **sent**.—**to send down**, to expel from college or university; to rusticate [O.E. *sendan*].

senectitude (se-nek´ti-tūd) *n.* old age [L. *senex*, an old man].

senescence (se-nes´ẹns) *n.* the state of growing old; decay; old age.—**senes'cent** *a.* growing old [L. *senescere*, to grow old].

seneschal (sen´e-shạl) *n.* functionary who superintended household feasts and ceremonies of feudal lord in Middle Ages; steward; majordomo [O.Fr.].

senile (sē´nīl) *a.* pert. to old age; aged; doting. —**senil'ity** *n.* degenerative physical conditions accompanying old age; old age [L. *senex*, old man].

senior (sē´nyur, sē´ni-ẹr) *a.* older; superior in rank or standing; prior;—*n.* a person older, or of higher rank, or of longer service, than another; an aged person.—**senior'ity** *n.* state of being older, or higher in rank, or longer in service; priority; superiority. Also **se'niory**.—**senior service**, the navy [L. = older].

senna (sen´a) *n.* a valuable purgative drug, obtained from the dried leaves and pods of a number of shrubs and herbs of the genus Cassia [Ar. *sana*].

sennet (sen´et) *n.* a flourish of trumpets [O.Fr. *sinet*, a sign].

sennight (sen´īt) *n.* a week. Also **se'nnight** [*seven night*].

señor (se-nyōr') *n.* Spanish form of address; sir; gentleman; equivalent to Mr.;—**seño'ra** *n.* lady; madam; Mrs.—**señori'ta** *n.* young lady; Miss.

sensation (sen-sā´shun) *n.* what we learn through senses; state of physical consciousness; effect produced on a sense-organ by external stimulus; excited feeling or state of excitement; exciting event; strong impression. —**sen'sate, sen'sated** *a.* perceived by the senses. —**sensa'tional** *a.* pert. to perception by senses; producing great excitement and surprise; melodramatic.—**sensa'tionalist** *n.*—**sensa'tionally** *adv.* [L. *sensus*, feeling].

sense (sens) *n.* any of the bodily faculties of perception or feeling; sensitiveness of any or all of these faculties; ability to perceive, mental alertness; consciousness; significance;

meaning; coherence; wisdom; good judgment; prudence.—*pl.* wits; faculties; *v.t.* to perceive; to suspect; to understand.—**sense'less** *a.* destitute of sense; insensible; unfeeling; silly; foolish; stupid; absurd.—**sense'lessly** *adv.*—**sense'lessness** *n.* [L. *sentire, sensum*, to feel].

sensible (sen'si-bl) *a.* capable of being perceived by the senses; characterised by good sense; perceptible; aware; conscious; appreciable; reasonable; judicious; wise; sensitive.—**sensibil'ity** *n.* power of experiencing sensation; faculty by which mind receives sensuous intuitions; capacity of feeling.—**sen'sibly** *adv.* [fr. *sense*].

sensitise (sen'si-tīz) *v.t.* to render sensitive; in photography, to render film, paper, etc. sensitive to the chemical action of light.—**sen'sitiser** *n.* [L. *sensus*, feeling].

sensitive (sen'si-tiv) *a.* open to, or acutely affected by, external stimuli or impressions; easily affected or altered; responsive to slight changes; reacting readily to light rays; easily upset by criticism;—*n.* one who is sensitive.—**sen'sitively** *adv.*—**sen'sitiveness** *n.* quality or state of being sensitive.—**sensitiv'ity** *n.* sensitiveness; keen sensibility; capacity to receive and respond to external stimuli [Fr. *sensitif*, fr. L. *sentire*, to feel].

sensory (sen'sory) *a.* pert. to, or serving, senses; conveying sensations, as the nerve-fibres [L. *sensus*, feeling].

sensual (sen'sū-al) *a.* depending on the senses only and not on the mind; given to pursuit of pleasures of sense, self-indulgent; carnal; voluptuous; lewd.—**sensualisa'tion** *n.*—**sen'sualise** *v.t.* to make or render sensual; to debase by gratifying carnal appetites or passions.—**sen'sualism** *n.* fleshly indulgence; luxurious living.—**sen'sualist** *n.* one given to lewd or loose mode of life; voluptuary.—**sensualist'ic** *a.*—**sensual'ity** *n.* state of being sensual; lewdness; debauchery.—**sen'sually** *adv.*—**sen'suous** *a.* stimulating, or apprehended by, sense.—**sen'suously** *adv.*—**sen'suousness** *n.* [L. *sensus*, feeling].

sent (sent) *pa.t.* and *pa.p.* of **send**.

sentence (sen'tens) *n.* combination of words, which is complete as expressing a thought; opinion; axiom; maxim; judgment passed on criminal by court or judge; decision;—*v.t.* to pass sentence upon; to condemn.—**senten'tious** *a.* abounding with axioms and maxims; short and energetic; pithy; bombastic; pompously moralising.—**senten'tiously** *adv.*—**senten'tiousness** *n.* [L. *sententia*, an opinion].

sentient (sen'shi-ent) *a.* feeling or capable of feeling; perceiving by senses; sensitive; thinking; reflecting.—**sen'tience, sen'tiency** *n.* consciousness at a sensory level.—**sen'tiently** *adv.* [L. *sentire*, to feel].

sentiment (sen'ti-ment) *n.* abstract emotion; tendency to be moved by feeling rather than by reason; verbal expression of feeling; saying; idea; opinion.—**sentimen'tal** *a.* abounding with sentiment; romantic; emotional; foolishly tender.—**sentimen'talism, sentimental'ity** *n.* affected and distorted expression of sentiment revealing a superficiality of feeling.—**sentimen'talist** *n.* one given to sentimental talk; one swayed by emotions rather than by reason.—**sentimen'tally** *adv.* [O.Fr. *sentement*, fr. L. *sentire*, to feel].

sentinel (sen'ti-nel) *n.* guard; sentry;—*a.* acting as sentinel; watching [Fr. *sentinelle*].

sentry (sen'tri) *n.* soldier on guard; sentinel; duty of sentry.—**sen'try-box** *n.* small shelter against weather used by sentry.—**sen'try-go** *n.* sentry duty [fr. *sanctuary*, a place of safety, a shelter for a watchman, a watchman].

sepal (sep'al, sē'pal) *n.* (*Bot.*) leaf-like member of outer covering, or calyx, of flower.—**sep'alous** *a.* having sepals [Fr. *sépale*].

separate (sep'a-rāt) *v.t.* to part in any manner; to divide; to disconnect; to detach; to sever; to sunder; to put apart;—*v.i.* to part; to withdraw; to become disunited;—*a.* divided; disconnected; apart; distinct; individual.—**separabil'ity** *n.*—**sep'arable** *a.* able to be separated or disconnected.—**sep'arableness** *n.*—**sep'arably** *adv.*—**sep'arately** *adv.*—**sep'arateness** *n.*—**separa'tion** *n.* act of separating; state of being separate.—**separa'tionist** *n.* one who supports policy of breaking away from a union of states or countries; a separatist.—**sep'aratism** *n.* act or policy of separating or withdrawing from any union; secession.—**sep'aratist** *n.* one who secedes from church or political union; seceder; schismatic; home-ruler [L. *separare*].

sepia (sē'pi-a) *n.* brown pigment obtained from ink-bags of cuttlefish or octopus, used as water-colour [Gk. = cuttlefish].

sepoy (sē'poi) *n.* native of India employed as soldier in British service [Hind. *sipahi*, a soldier].

sepsis (sep'sis) *n.* (*Med.*) state of having bodily tissue infected by pathogenic bacteria; putrefaction; putridity; rot.—**sep'tic** *a.* [Gk. = putrefaction].

sept (sept) *n.* clan, race, or family, proceeding from common progenitor.—**sep'tal** *a.* pert. to sept; (*Biol.*) pert. to a septum [etym. uncertain. Cf. *sect*].

septaemia. Same as **septicaemia**. See **septic.**

September (sep-tem'bẹr) *n.* ninth month of year [L. *septem*, seven, as being 7th month of Roman year].

septenary (sep'tẹ-na-ri) *a.* consisting of seven; lasting seven years; occurring once in seven years.—**septen'nial** *a.* continuing seven years; occurring once in every seven years.—**septen'nium** *n.* a period of seven years [L. *septem*, seven].

septet, septette (sep-tet') *n.* (*Mus.*) composition for seven voices or instruments [L. *septem*, seven].

septic (sep'tik) *a.* pert. to sepsis; causing or caused by blood-poisoning or putrefaction; infected; putrefying. Also **sep'tical.**—**septicae'mia, septice'mia, septae'mia** *n.* invasion of blood and other tissues by living pathogenic bacteria; blood-poisoning.—**sep'tically** *adv.*—**septicae'mic, septice'mic** *a.* pert. to septicaemia [Gk. *sēptikos*, putrefying].

septuagenarian (sep-tū-aj-e-nā'ri-an) *n.* person between seventy and eighty years of age.—**septuag'enary** *a.* consisting of seventy; seventy years old. [L. *septuaginta*, seventy].

Septuagesima (sep-tū-a-jes'i-ma) *n.* third Sunday before Lent, seventy days before Easter.—**septuages'imal** *a.* pert. to the number seventy [L. *septuagesimus*, seventieth].

Septuagint (sep'tū-a-jint) *n.* the first and only complete version in Greek of the Old Testament, made by 6 scholars from 12 tribes (approximately 70).—**Septuagin'tal** *a.* [L. *septuaginta*, seventy].

septuple (sep'tū-pl) *a.* sevenfold;—*v.t.* to multiply by seven [L. *septem*, seven].

sepulchre (sep'ul-kẹr) *n.* tomb; grave; burial vault;—*v.t.* to place in a sepulchre.—**sepul'chral** *a.* pert. to burial, the grave, or monuments erected to dead; funereal; mournful.—**sep'ulture** *n.* act of burying the dead [L. *sepulcrum*].

sequacious (se-kwā'shus) *a.* following; attendant; easily led.—**sequa'ciousness, sequac'ity** *n.* [L. *sequi*, to follow].

sequel (sē'kwel) *n.* that which follows; consequence; issue; end; continuation, complete in itself, of a novel or narrative previously published [L. *sequi*, to follow].

sequence (sē'kwens) *n.* connected series; succession; run of three or more cards of same suit in numerical order; part of scenario of film; (*Mus.*) repetition of musical figure, either melodic or harmonic, on different degrees of scale.—**se'quent** *a.* following; succeeding;—*n.* sequence.—**sequen'tial** *a.* in succession.—**sequen'tially** *adv.* [L. *sequi*, to follow].

sequester (se-kwes'tẹr) *v.t.* to put aside; to separate; to seclude; the cause to retire into obscurity; to withdraw from society; (*Law*) to put into the hands of a trustee; to sequestrate;—*v.i.* to renounce, on the part of a widow, all interest in her husband's property; —*n.* a mediator. —**seques'tered** *a.* withdrawn from public view; secluded. —**seques'trable** *a.* liable to sequestration. —**seques'trate** *v.t.* (*Law*) to sequester. —**sequestra'tion** *n.* reparation; retirement; the act of taking thing from parties contending for it, and entrusting it to a neutral party [L. *sequestrare*, to put in safe keeping].

sequin (sē'kwin) *n.* ornamental metal disc on dresses, etc.; formerly Venetian gold coin [It. *zecchino*, fr. *zecca*, mint].

Sequoia (sē-kwoi'ą) *n.* genus of gigantic coniferous evergreen trees native to California [fr. *Sequoiah*, a Cherokee Indian chief].

seraglio (se-ral'yō) *n.* harem or women's quarters in royal household; orig. palace of former Turkish sultans at Istanbul [It. *serraglio*, an enclosure, fr. L. *sera*, a bolt].

serai (se-rá'i) *n.* place for accommodation of travellers in India and Tartary; caravansary or khan.—**serail'** *n.* a seraglio; a harem [Pers. = a palace].

serang (se-rang') *n.* boatswain of a Lascar crew [Pers. *sarhang*, commander].

seraph (ser'ąf) *n.* one of an order of angels ranking highest in Jewish and Christian angelology.—**ser'aphs, ser'aphim** *n.pl.*—**seraph'ic, seraph'ical** *a.*—**seraph'ically** *adv.* [Heb.].

Serb, Serbian (sęrb, sęr'bi-ąn) *a.* pert. to Serbia;—*n.* native or inhabitant of Serbia, the chief constituent state of Jugo-Slavia.—**Serb-Croa'tian** *n.* one of the Slavonic group of languages spoken in Jugo-Slavia.

sere (sēr) *a.* dry; withered [fr. *sear*].

sere (sēr) *n.* Same as **sear**, part of a gun-lock.

serenade (ser-e-nād') *n.* musical composition intended orig. for open-air performance; music of quiet, simple, melodious character sung or played at night below person's window, esp. by lover;—*v.t.* to entertain with serenade.—**serena'der** *n.*—**serena'ta** *n.* instrumental work, between suite and symphony, orig. intended for performance in open air [It. *serenata*, fr. *sereno*, the open air].

serendipity (ser-ęn-dip'i-ti) *n.* knack of stumbling upon interesting discoveries in a casual manner [word coined by Horace Walpole to burlesque hero of fairy-tale, ' The Three Princes of Serendip '].

serene (sę-rēn') *a.* clear and calm; unclouded; fair; bright; unruffled; quiet; placid; composed; sedate;—*n.* clearness; calmness.—**serene'ly** *adv.*—**serene'ness, seren'itude, seren'ity** *n.* condition or quality of being serene [L. *serenus*, clear].

serf (sęrf) *n.* under feudalism, labourer who was attached to an estate and could be transferred with it to a new owner; a bondman; vassal; drudge.—**serf'age, serf'dom, serf'hood** *n.* [L. *servus*, a slave].

serge (sęrj) *n.* hard-wearing worsted fabric [L. *serica*, silk].

sergeant, serjeant (sár'jęnt) *n.* non-commissioned officer in army, ranking above corporal; police officer ranking between inspector and constable; in law, the name (often *Serjeant*) given, until 1875, to certain English barristers. Also **Ser'jeant-at-law**; title of certain officers of royal household; in Elizabethan times, bailiff.—**ser'geancy, ser'geantcy, ser'geantship** *n.*—**Ser'geant-at-arms** *n.* officer attendant on Speaker of House of Commons, charged with preservation of order. —**ser'geant-ma'jor** *n.* highest non-commissioned officer [Fr. *sergent*, fr. L. *serviens*, serving].

serial (sē'ri-ąl) *a.* consisting of a series; appearing in successive parts or instalments; —*n.* a periodical publication; a tale or other writing published in successive numbers of a periodical.—**se'rialise** *v.t.* to publish as a serial. —**se'rially, se'riately** *adv.* in a regular series or order.—**se'riatim** *adv.* point by point; one after another; in regular order [fr. *series*].

series (sē'rēz, sē'ri-ēz) *n. sing.* and *pl.* succession of related objects or matters; sequence; order; books, bound and printed in same style, usually on kindred subjects; (*Elect.*) end-to-end arrangement of batteries or circuits which are traversed by the same current [L.].

serif (ser'if) *n.* (*Printing*) a fine line at the end of the stems and arms of unconnected Roman type letters, as M, K, l, y, etc. Also **cer'iph, ser'iph** (etym. unknown].

serious (sē'ri-us) *a.* grave in manner or disposition; earnest; important; attended with danger; in earnest.—**se'riously** *adv.* in a serious manner; solemnly; gravely; dangerously.—**se'riousness** *n.* [L. *serius*].

seriph. See **serif.**

serjeant. See **sergeant.**

sermon (sęr'mun) *n.* discourse of religious instruction or exhortation founded on some text or passage of scripture, spoken or read from a pulpit; serious and admonitory address; —*v.t.* to tutor; to lecture; to harangue.—**sermon'ic, -al** *a.* of the nature of a sermon.—**ser'monise** *v.i.* to preach earnestly; to compose a sermon; to dogmatise.—**sermoni'ser** *n.* [L. *sermo*, a discourse].

serosity See **serous.**

serous (sē'rus) *a.* pert. to, containing, or producing serum; watery; thin.—**seros'ity** *n.* state of being serous; serous fluid; serum [L. *serum*].

serpent (sęr'pent) *n.* snake; reptile without feet; treacherous or malicious person; kind of firework; constellation in northern hemisphere; (*Mus.*) bass wooden wind instrument bent in a serpentine form;—*v.i.* to wind like a serpent; to meander;—*v.t.* to curl or wind round; to encircle;—*a.* deceitful; treacherous. —**ser'pentary** *n.* a drug reputed to cure bite of rattlesnake or of mad dog.—**ser'pentine** *a.* relating to, or like, serpent; winding; spiral; meandering; crafty; treacherous;—*n.* magnesian mineral of obscure green colour, with spotted appearance resembling serpent's skin; kind of firework;—*v.i.* to wind in and out like a serpent.—**ser'pentinely** *adv.* [L. *serpere*, to creep].

serrate, serrated (ser'āt, -ed) *a.* notched or cut like saw.—**serra'tion** *n.* formation in shape of saw.—**ser'rature** *n.* series of notches, like that of saw.—**ser'riform** *a.* toothed like a saw. —**ser'rous** *a.* like teeth of a saw; irregular [L. *serra*, a saw].

serried (ser'id) *a.* in close order; pressed shoulder to shoulder [Fr. *serrer*, to lock].

serum (sē'rum) *n.* watery secretion; whey; thin straw-coloured fluid, residue of plasma or liquid part of the blood; such fluid, used for inoculation or vaccination [L. = whey].

servant (sęr'vąnt) *n.* personal or domestic attendant; one who serves or obeys orders; menial; helper; dependant; term of respect or civility employed in official correspondence. —**civil servant**, member of the civil service; government employee [L. *servire*, to serve].

serve (sęrv) *v.t.* to work for; to be a servant to; to minister to; to wait on; to attend; to help; to distribute, as rations, stores, etc.; to promote; to advance; to forward; to satisfy; to deliver formally;—*v.i.* to work under another; to carry out duties; to be a member of a military, naval, etc. unit; to be useful, or suitable, or enough; in tennis, to resume play by striking the ball diagonally across court;—*n.* in tennis, act of serving a ball.—**serv'able** *a.* capable of being served.—**ser'ver** *n.* one who serves; a salver or small tray [L. *servire*, to serve].

service (sęr'vis) *n.* state of being a servant; work done for and benefit conferred on another; act of kindness; department of State employ; employment of persons engaged in this; military, naval, or air-force duty;

advantage; use; form of divine worship; regular supply, as water, bus, rail, etc.; (*Law*) serving of a process or summons; turn for serving ball at tennis, fives, etc.; a set of dishes, etc.;—*v.t.* to perform service for, e.g., motor cars, etc.; also **ser'ving.**—**ser'viceable** *a.* useful; helpful; convenient; in fair working order.—**serviceabil'ity, ser'viceableness** *n.* usefulness.—**ser'viceably** *adv.*—**service dress,** ordinary uniform.—**active service,** military, naval, or air-force service against an enemy.—**din'ner-, ta'ble-, tea-ser'vice,** complete set of the appropriate dishes.—**senior service,** Royal Navy.—**the Services,** Army, Navy, and Royal Air Force.—**to take service,** to engage as servant [L. *servire,* to serve].

service (sẹr´-vis) *n.* a small fruit-tree resembling the mountain ash [corrupt. of L. *sorbus*].

servient (sẹr´-vi-ẹnt) *a.* serving; subordinate [L. *servire* to serve].

serviette (sẹr-vi-et') *n.* a table-napkin [Fr.].

servile (sẹr´-vīl) *a.* pert. to or befitting a servant or slave; mean; fawning; dependent; menial.—**ser'vilely** *adv.*—**servil'ity** *n.* state of being servile; slavery; bondage; slavishness [L. *servilis,* slavish].

servitor (ser'vi-tor) *n.* male attendant; follower or adherent.—**ser'vitude** *n.* state of subjection to a master; slavery; bondage [L. *servire,* to serve].

sesame (ses´-ạ-me) *n.* annual herbaceous plant cultivated in India and Asia Minor for seeds from which oil is extracted.—**open sesame,** charm, mentioned in *Arabian Nights,* by which door of robbers' dungeon flew open; hence, specific for gaining entrance to a place; key to solving difficulty [Gk.].

sesqui- (ses´-kwi) *prefix* denoting a proportion of 3: 2.—**sesquial'teral, sesquial'terate, sesquial´terous** *a.* one and a half more.—**sesquicenten´nial** *a.* pert. to a century and a half;—*n.* the 150th anniversary.—**sesquipeda'lian** *a.* measuring a foot and a half long; applied humorously to any long cumbersome technical word or to one given to using unnecessarily long words; very tall or long.—**sesquipeda'lianism** *n.* [L. *sesqui,* one half more].

sessile (ses´-īl) *a.* attached without any sensible support; fixed and stationary [L. *sessilis,* low, fr. *sedere, sessum,* to sit].

session (sesh´-un) *n.* actual sitting of a court, council, etc. for transaction of business; term during which a court, council, and the like, meet for business; a period of time at school or college when a definite course of instruction is given; period between meeting and prorogation of parliament; in Scotland, lowest Presbyterian church court comprising minister and elders; kirk-session; meeting.—**ses'sional** *a.* pert. to session(s).—**Court of Session,** Supreme Civil Court of Scotland [L. *sessio,* fr. *sedere,* to sit].

sestet, sestette (ses´-tet) *n.* (*Mus.*) composition for six instruments or voices; last six lines of a sonnet [L. *sextus,* sixth].

set (set) *v.t.* to cause to sit; to seat; to place; to plant; to make ready; to put up; to adjust; to arrange (of hair) while wet; to fix, as precious stone in metal; to convert into curd; (of razor, etc.) to give fine edge; to extend (sail); to reduce from dislocated or fractured state, as limb; to adapt, as words to music; to compose type-matter; to grant to a tenant; to let; to place a brooding fowl on nest of eggs; to crouch or point, as dog, to game; to clench (teeth); to stake; to suit (of dress);—*v.i.* to pass below horizon; to go down; to strike root; to become fixed or rigid; to congeal or solidify; to put forth an effort; to tend; to begin.—*pr.p.* **set'ting.**—*pa.t.* and *pa.p.* **set.**—**to set at naught,** to defy; to reckon as of no account.—**to set back,** to cause to deteriorate; to impede.—**to set on foot,** to start (some project, business, plan, etc.).—**to set out,** to start on a journey; to begin; to mark out.—**to set sail,** to begin a voyage.—**to set to,** to apply oneself vigorously; to begin to fight [O.E. *settan*].

set (set) *n.* a number of things or persons associated as being similar or complementary or used together, etc.; the manner in which a thing is set, hangs, or fits, as a dress; permanent change of shape or figure in consequence of pressure or cooling; an attitude or posture; young plant, cutting, or slip for planting out; direction, tendency, drift; figure of square dance; group or clique; setting of sun; organised settings and equipment to form the ensemble of a scene for stage or film representation; (*Radio*) complete apparatus for reception (or transmission) of wireless signals and broadcasts; (*Tennis*) series of games forming unit for match-scoring purposes; (*Print.*) width of type character; a wooden or granite block or sett;—*a.* fixed; firm; prescribed; regular; established; arranged; appointed; formal; obstinate; determined; fully grown.—**set'back** *n.* check to progress; overflow.—**set'square** *n.* flat triangular drawing instrument for making or testing angles of 30°, 60°, 90°, or of 45°, 90° [O.Fr. *sette,* sect].

seta (sē´-tȧ) *n.* bristle or bristle-like structure.—**seta'ceous, setose', se'tous** *a.* bristly [L. = a bristle].

sett (set) *n.* tennis-set; small wood or stone paving block, rectangular in shape; cutting tool or chisel, used by blacksmiths; in weaving, the number of ends or threads per inch [fr. *set*].

settee (se-tē') *n.* couch or sofa [Cf. *settle*].

setter (set´-ẹr) *n.* hunting-dog of spaniel family trained to crouch or set when game is perceived [fr. *set*].

setting (set´-ing) *n.* fixing, adjusting, or putting in place; direction of stream; descending below horizon, as of sun; bezel which holds a precious stone, etc. in position; fixing a drawing in crayon, pastels, or pencil by spraying with a solution of zinc in alcohol; mounting of scene in play or film; background.—**setting lotion,** fixative to assist hair to set well [fr. *set*].

settle (set´-l) *v.t.* to put in place, order, arrangement, etc.; to fix; to establish; to make secure or quiet; to decide upon; to bring (dispute) to an end; to reconcile; to calm; to pay; to liquidate; to secure by legal deed, as a pension, annuity, etc.; to colonise;—*v.i.* to become fixed or stationary; to come to rest; to (cause to) sink to bottom; to subside; to take up permanent residence in; to dwell; to become calm; to become clear (of liquid).—**sett'led** *a.* fixed; permanent; deep-rooted; decided; quiet; methodical; adjusted by agreement.—**sett'lement** *n.* act of settling; state of being settled; ordination or installation, as a pastor; colonisation; a colony; (*Law*) transfer of real or personal property to trustees to hold for benefit of persons in succession; sum secured to a person, esp. jointure made to woman at her marriage.—**sett'ler** *n.* one who makes his home in a new country; colonist.—**sett'ling** *n.* the act of making a settlement; act of subsiding; adjusting of matters in dispute;—*pl.* sediment; dregs; lees [O.E. *setl,* a seat].

settle (set´-l) *n.* long high-backed bench; settee [O.E. *setl,* a seat].

seven (sev´-n) *a.* one more than six;—*n.* number greater by one than six.—**sev'en-a-side** *n.* abbreviated form of rugby-football, seven men making up a side or team.—**sev'en-fold** *a.* repeated seven times; increased to seven times the size;—*adv.* seven times as much or as often.—**sev'en-night, se'n'night** *n.* period of seven nights and days; week [O.E. *seofon*].

seventeen (sev´-ẹn-tēn) *a.* one more than sixteen;—*n.* sum of ten and seven.—**sev'enteenth** *a.* and *n.* the seventh after the tenth [O.E. *seofontiene*].

seventh (sev´-ẹnth) *a.* constituting one of seven equal parts;—*n.* one of seven equal parts.

seventh-day Adventists, Christian sect believing in second coming of Christ in person and observing seventh day as Sabbath.—**seventh heaven,** supreme ecstasy or beatitude.—**sev'enthly** *adv.* [fr. *seven*].

seventy (sev'n-ti) *a.* seven times ten;—*n.* sum of seven times ten.—**sev'entieth** *a.* constituting one of seventy equal parts;—*n.* one of seventy equal parts [O.E. *seofontig*].

sever (sev'ẹr) *v.t.* to part or divide by violence; to sunder; to cut or break off;—*v.i.* to divide; to make a separation.—**sev'erable** *a.*—**sev'erance** *n.* separation; partition [Fr. fr. L. *separare*].

several (sev'ẹr-ạl) *a.* more than two; some; separate; distinct; various; different;—*pron.* several persons or things.—**sev'erally** *adv.* apart from others [O.Fr. fr. L. *separare*].

severe (se-vēr') *a.* serious; rigidly methodical; painful; not flowery, as style; very searching.—**severe'ly** *adv.*—**severe'ness, sever'ity** *n.* sternness; harshness; rigour; austerity; intensity [L. *severus*].

Sèvres (sev'r) *n.* and *a.* name of a fine porcelain ware made at *Sèvres*, France.

sew (sō) *v.t.* to fasten together with needle and thread; to join with stitches;—*v.i.* to practise sewing.—**sew'er** *n.* one who sews.—**sew'ing** *n.* and *a.*—**sew'ing-machine** *n.* automatic machine adapted for all kinds of sewing operations [O.E. *seowian*].

sewage (sū'āj) *n.* drainage; organic refuse and excrement carried off by a regular system of underground pipes.—**sew'age-farm** *n.* establishment where sewage is scientifically treated to provide innocuous sludge or manure [fr. *sewer*].

sewer (sū'ẹr, sȯȯ'ẹr) *n.* underground drain or conduit to remove waste water and organic refuse.—**sew'erage** *n.* underground system of pipes and conduits to carry off surface water and organic refuse [O.Fr. *esseveur*].

sex (seks) *n.* state of being male or female; sum-total of characteristics which distinguish male and female organisms; function by which most animal and plant species are perpetuated as a result of fusion of two nuclei from separate individuals; males or females collectively.—**sex appeal,** what makes person sexually desirable or attractive.—**sex'ual** *a.* pert. to sex or sexes; pert. to genital organs.—**sexual intercourse,** coition.—**sexual'ity** *n.* state or quality of being sexual.—**sex'ually** *adv.* [L. *sexus*].

sexagenary (sek-saj'e-nạ-ri) *a.* pert. to the number sixty; proceeding by sixties.—**sexagenar'ian** *n.* person of age of sixty [L. *sexaginta*, sixty].

Sexagesima (sek-sa-jes'i-ma) *n.* second Sunday before Lent, sixty days before Easter.—**sexages'imal** *a.* pert. to number sixty [L. *sexagesimus*, sixtieth].

sexcentenary (sek-sen-tē'nạ-ri, or sek-sen'te-nạ-ri) *n.* and *a.* (of) the 600th anniversary; (of) the space of 600 years.

sexennial (seks-en'yạl) *a.* continuing for six years; happening once every six years. Also **sextenn'ial.**—**sexenn'ially, sextenn'ially** *adv.* [L. *sex*, six; *annus*, a year].

sexisyllabic (sek-si-si-lab'ik) *a.* having six syllables.—**sex'isyllable** *n.* [L. *sex*, six].

sextain (seks'tān) *n.* a stanza of six lines.

sextant (seks'tạnt) *n.* sixth part of circle; reflecting instrument consisting of graduated brass sector the sixth part of a circle, used in surveying and navigation for measuring altitudes of celestial bodies and their angular distances [L. *sextus*, sixth].

sextennial. See **sexennial.**

sextet, sextette (seks-tet') *n.* musical composition for six voices or instruments; company of six singers or instrumentalists [L. *sex*, six].

sexton (seks'tun) *n.* church lay-officer acting as caretaker and may also be grave-digger [corrupt, of *sacristan*].

sextuple (seks'tū-pl) *a.* sixfold; six times as many;—*v.t.* to multiply by six [L. *sex*, six; *plicare*, to fold].

sforzando (sfor-tsȧn'dō) *a.* (*Mus.*) forced or pressed; strongly accented. Usually *abbrev.* to **sf., sfz.,** or denoted by symbols ∧, >. [It.].

shabby (shab'i) *a.* torn or worn to rags; poorly dressed; faded; worn; mean; dishonourable.—**shabb'ily** *adv.*—**shabb'iness** *n.* [O.E. *sceabb*, scab].

shack (shak) *n.* roughly built wooden hut; shanty [etym. doubtful].

shack (shak) *v.i.* to fall, as grain at harvest; to feed on stubble or waste grain; to roam or wander about, as tramp;—*v.t.* to chase after or retrieve (ball);—*n.* grain, etc. fallen on ground [fr. *shake*].

shackle (shak'l) *n.* metal loop or staple; U-shaped steel link with a pin closing the free ends, used for joining lengths of chain-cables; (*Naut.*) a length of chain-cable, equal to 12½ fathoms;—*pl.* fetters; manacles; anything which hampers; restraints;—*v.t.* to fetter; to trammel or hamper [O.E. *sceacul*, a bond].

shad (shad) *n.* name of several species of herring family [O.E. *sceadd*].

shaddock (shad'ok) *n.* large fruit of orange family, native of Malay Peninsula; grape-fruit [fr. Capt. *Shaddock*, who first introduced it into W. Indies].

shade (shād) *n.* partial darkness, due to interception of light; place sheltered from light, heat, etc.; screen; darker part of anything; depth of colour; tint; hue; a very minute difference; shadow; ghost; spirit;—*pl.* invisible world or region of the dead; Hades; total darkness;—*v.t.* to shelter or screen, from light or a source of heat; to darken; to dim; to represent shades in a drawing; to pass almost imperceptibly from one form or colour to another.—**sha'ded** *a.*—**sha'dily** *adv.* in shady manner.—**sha'diness** *n.* quality of being shady.—**sha'ding** *n.* interception of light; tinting or lining a picture or drawing to show parts in relief.—**sha'dy** *a.* providing shade; in shade; disreputable; not respectable; doubtful; suspicious [O.E. *sceadu*].

shadow (shad'ō) *n.* patch of shade; dark figure projected by anything which intercepts rays of light; darker or less illuminated part of picture; gloom; inseparable companion; ghost; phantom; gloom; slight trace;—*v.t.* to cast a shadow over; to follow and watch closely; to outline.—**shad'ow-box'ing** *n.* boxing practice, without opponent.—**shadow cabinet,** group of leading members of political party out of office, regarded as probable members of Cabinet, if, and when, party comes into power.—**shad'ower** *n.* one who dogs the foot-steps of another.—**shad'ow-graph** *n.* representation, usually made by hands and fingers, of animals or objects produced as shadow upon sheet or wall; X-ray photograph, radiograph.—**shad'owiness** *n.* state of being shadowy or indistinct.—**shad'owing** *n.* gradation of light and colour; shading.—**shad'owy** *a.* full of shadow; serving to shade; faintly representative; unsubstantial; obscure; unreal; fanciful [O.E. *sceadu*].

shaft (shaft) *n.* straight rod, stem, or handle; shank; stem of arrow; arrow; anything long and slender, as a tall chimney, the well of an elevator, vertical passage leading down to mine or excavation, etc.; part of column between base and capital; revolving rod for transmitting power; stem of feather; pole of carriage.—**shaft'ing** *n.* system of long rods and pulleys used to transmit power to machinery [O.E. *sceaft*].

shag (shag) *n.* coarse, matted wool or hair; long and coarse nap on some types of woollen fabrics; strong mixture of tobacco leaves cut and shredded for smoking;—*a.* rough; shaggy.—**shag'gedness, shag'giness** *n.*—**shag'gy** *a.* covered with rough hair or wool; rugged; tousy; unkempt [O.E. *sceacga*, a head of hair].

shagreen (shą-grēn') *n.* untanned leather made from belly skins of sharks, rays, etc.; imitation of this leather used, after being dyed green, in manufacture of luxury articles [var. of *chagrin*].

Shah (shå) *n. abbrev.* of Shah-in-Shah (King of Kings), the title given to the monarchs of Iran, Persia [Pers.].

shake (shāk) *v.t.* to cause to move with quick vibrations; to weaken stability of; to impair resolution of; to trill, as note in music; to agitate; to convulse;—*v.i.* to tremble; to shiver; to totter.—*pa.t.* **shook.**—*pa.p.* **shak'en.** —*n.* shaking; vibration; jolt; severe shock to system as result of illness; friendly grasping of hands by two individuals; (*Mus.*) trill; (*Colloq.*) moment.—**shake'down** *n.* any temporary substitute for a bed.—**shak'en** *a.* weakened; agitated; cracked.—**shak'ily** *adv.* —**shak'iness** *n.*—**shak'y** *a.* easily moved; unsteady; weak; tottering; unreliable.—**to shake off,** to get rid of [O.E. *sceacan*].

shako (shak'ō) *n.* military peaked headdress, shaped like truncated cone and usually plumed in front [Hung. *csako*].

shale (shāl) *n.* shell or husk; pod; (*Geol.*) clay or mud become hardened and which splits into thin plates, parallel to stratification.—**shale'oil** *n.* grade of naphtha, obtained by carbonisation of oil-shales.—**sha'ly** *a.* [O.E. *scealu*, scale].

shall (shal) *v.i.* and *aux.* used to make compound tenses or moods to express futurity, obligation, command, condition or intention [O.E. *sceal*].

shallop (shal'op) *n.* a light open boat or vessel; a small fore-and-aft rigged fishing-vessel [Fr. *chaloupe*].

shallot (shą-lot') *n.* bulbous-rooted plant like onion. Also **(e)shalot'** [Fr. *échalote*].

shallow (shal'ō) *a.* having little depth of water; having little knowledge; superficial; not sincere; slight; trivial;—*n.* place where water is of little depth; shoal, flat, or sandbank.—**shall'owly** *adv.*—**shall'owness** *n.* [etym. doubtful].

shalt (shalt) *2nd pers. sing.* of **shall.**

sham (sham) *n.* any trick, fraud, or device which deludes; imposture; pretence; counterfeit; imitation;—*a.* counterfeit; false; pretended;—*v.t.* to counterfeit; to feign; to pretend;—*v.i.* to make false pretences.—*pr.p.* **sham'ming.**—*pa.t.* and *pa.p.* **shammed** [etym. uncertain].

Shaman (sham'an) *n.* a priest or medicine-man who practises Shamanism.—**Sham'anism** *n.* religious cult of native races of northern C. Asia [Hind. = idolater].

shamble (sham'bl) *v.i.* to walk unsteadily with shuffling gait [etym. uncertain].

shambles (sham'blz) *n.pl.* slaughter-house, place where animals are killed and their flesh prepared for food; hence a scene of carnage [O.E. *scamel*, a bench].

shame (shām) *n.* emotion caused by consciousness of something wrong or dishonouring in one's conduct or state; cause of disgrace; dishonour; ignominy; (*Biblical*) modesty;—*v.t.* to cause to feel shame; to disgrace; to degrade; to force by shame (into).—**shame'faced, shame'fast** *a.* bashful; modest; shy; sheepish.—**shame'facedly** *adv.*—**shame'facedness, shame'fastness** *n.* excessive shyness or bashfulness.—**shame'ful** *a.* disgraceful.—**shame'fully** *adv.*—**shame'fulness** *n.*—**shame'less** *a.* destitute of shame; brazen-faced; immodest.—**shame'lessly** *adv.*—**shame'lessness** *n*, [O.E. *sceamu*].

shammy (sham'i) *n.* leather prepared orig. from skin of chamois. Also **cham'ois, sham'oy,** buck or doe leather; wash-leather [Fr. *chamois*].

shampoo (sham-póó') *v.t.* to wash (scalp) with something forming lather in rubbing; to massage parts of body after hot bath;—*n.* act of shampooing; state of being shampooed.—**shampoo'er** *n.* [Hind. *champna*, to knead].

shamrock (sham'rok) *n.* small trefoil plant; national emblem of Ireland [Ir. *seamrog*, trefoil].

Shan (shan) *n.* and *a.* one of several tribes of Mogul origin inhabiting the frontiers of Burma, Siam and S. China.

shandygaff (shan'di-gaf) *n.* mixture of beer and ginger-beer [etym. doubtful].

shanghai (shang-hī') *n.* a long-legged fowl;—*v.t.* to drug or render unconscious by violence a man so that he may be shipped as member of a crew; to crimp.—*pa.t.* and *pa.p.* **shanghaied'** [*Shanghai*, China].

Shangri-la (shang'ri lå') *n.* escape, a peaceful, untroubled place to which one may escape [From the name of the hidden retreat in James Hilton's *Lost Horizon*].

shank (shangk) *n.* lower part of leg, from knee to ankle; shin-bone; stem of anchor, pipe, etc.; shaft of a column; long connecting part of an appliance.—**Shank's mare,** one's own legs [O.E. *sceanca*, leg].

shantung' (shan-tung') *n.* silk cloth with rough, knotted surface made from the wild silkworm [Chinese province].

shanty (shant'i) *n.* mean dwelling; temporary wooden building [Fr. *chantier*, a workshop].

shanty (shant'i) *n.* sailor's song, sung while heaving at capstan or windlass. Also **chant'y, chant'ie** [Fr. *chanter*, to sing].

shape (shāp) *v.t.* to mould or make into a particular form; to give shape to; to figure; to devise; to cut out, as a dress;—*v.i.* to assume a form or definite pattern;—*n.* form; figure; appearance; outline; pattern; jelly, etc. turned out of mould.—**shap'able, shape'able** *a.* capable of being shaped; shapely.—**shape'less** *a.* without regular shape or form; deformed; ugly.—**shape'lessness** *n.*—**shape'liness** *n.* beauty of shape or outline.—**shape'ly** *a.* well-proportioned; symmetrical [O.E. *sciep-pan*].

shard (shård) *n.* broken fragment, esp. of earthenware; hard wing-case of beetle; cow-dung [O.E. *sceard*, a fragment].

share (shār) *n.* pointed, wedge-shaped, cutting blade of plough [O.E. *scear*].

share (shār) *n.* part allotted; portion; division; lot; indivisible unit of ownership in public company entitling one to share in profits; quota;—*v.t.* to give or allot a share; to enjoy with others; to divide; to distribute; to allot; to apportion;—*v.i.* to take a share; to partake; to participate.—**share'cap'ital** *n.* money obtained from sale of shares in company in order to finance company's undertakings. —**share'holder** *n.* one who by possessing share(s) in company, etc. is entitled to share in profits.—**shar'er** *n.* [O.E. *scearu*, a cutting or division].

shark (shårk) *n.* general name applied to certain voracious marine fishes with sharp teeth in a crescentic mouth placed on under-side of the head; swindler; rapacious fellow; sharper; cheat.—**shark'skin** *n.* stiff, smooth-finished rayon fabric [etym. unknown].

sharp (shårp) *a.* having keen, cutting edge or fine point; having ready perception; quick; shrewd; acid; acrid; witty; pungent; sarcastic; harsh; painful; intense; dealing cleverly but unfairly; artful; strongly marked, esp. in outline; shrill; (*Mus.*) raised a semi-tone in pitch;—*n.* acute sound, esp. note raised semi-tone above its proper pitch; (*Mus.*) sign raising note before which it is placed a semi-tone;—*v.i.* to play the sharper; to cheat in bargaining, etc.;—*adv.* punctually.—**sharp'en** *v.t.* to give a keen edge or fine point to; to make more eager or intelligent; to make more tart or acid; (*Mus.*) to raise a semi-tone.—**sharp'ener** *n.* one who, or that which, sharpens; instrument for putting fine point on lead-pencil, etc.—**sharp'er** *n.* swindler; cheat; rogue.—**sharp'eyed** *a.* very observant.—**sharp'ly** *adv.*—**sharp'ness** *n.*—**sharp'set** *a.* ravenous; very hungry.—**sharp'shoot'er** *n.* skilled, long-range marksman.—**sharp'shoot'ing** *n.*—

sharp′-sight′ed *a.*—**sharp′-wit′ted** *a.* having acute mind [O.E. *scearp*].

shatter (shat′-ẹr) *v.t.* to break into many pieces; to smash; to crack; to disorder;—*v.i.* to fly in pieces [doublet of *scatter*].

shave (shāv) *v.t.* to pare away; to cut close, esp. hair of face or head with razor; to cut off thin slices; to miss narrowly; to graze;—*v.i.* to shave oneself;—*pa.p.* **shaved** or **sha′ven.** —*n.* act of shaving; thin slice or shaving; tool for shaving hoops, etc.; narrow escape; close miss.—**sha′ver** *n.* one who shaves; (*Slang*) a young lad.—**sha′ving** *n.* act of shaving; what is shaved off.—**close** or **near shave,** very narrow escape from danger [O.E. *sceafan*, to scrape].

Shavian (shā′-vi-ạn) *a.* in style of George Bernard *Shaw* (1856-1950), playwright, characterised by the free use of paradox, epigram, satire and mordant wit.

shaw (shaw) *n.* small wood; thicket; grove; stem of a plant with its leaves, as potato, etc. [O.E. *scaga*].

shawl (shawl) *n.* cloth used by women as loose covering for neck and shoulders;—*v.t* to wrap in a shawl [Pers. *shal*].

shawm, shalm (shawm) *n.* shepherd's pipe, ancient double-reed instrument, similar to oboe [Gk. *kalamos*, reed].

shay (shā) *n.* an obsolete one-horse carriage [var. of *chaise*].

she (shē) *pron.* this or that female; feminine pronoun of the third person; a female (used humorously as a noun); also, in compound-words, as *she-bear* [O.E. *seo*].

sheaf (shēf) *n.* bundle of stalks of wheat, rye, oats, or other grain; any similar bundle; a sheave;—*pl.* **sheaves.**—*v.t.* to make sheaves; —*v.i.* to collect and bind corn, etc. into sheaves [O.E. *sceaf*].

shear (shēr) *v.t.* to clip or cut through with shears or scissors; to clip wool (from sheep); to fleece; to cut down, as with a sickle; to reap.—*v.i.* to divide or part with a scissor-like action.—*pa.t.* **sheared, shore.**—*pa.p.* **shorn** (rarely **sheared**).—*n.* (*Engineering*) stress in a body in a state of tension due to a force acting parallel with its section; deviation; curve;—*pl.* a cutting instrument, consisting of two blades movable on a pin; large pair of scissors; a scissor-shaped erection of beams used as a crane.—**shear′-bill** *n.* scissor-bill or black-skimmer.—**shear′er** *n.*—**shear′ing** *n.* operation of clipping or cutting with shears; wool, etc. cut off with shears; deformation in which parallel planes in a body remain parallel but are relatively displaced by sliding movement in a direction parallel to themselves.—**shear′-ling** *n.* sheep only once sheared [O.E. *sceran*].

sheath (shēth) *n.* close-fitting cover, esp. for knife or sword; scabbard; thin protective covering.—**sheathe** *v.t.* to put into a sheath; to envelop; to encase.—**sheath′ing** *n.* that which sheathes; metal covering for under-water structures as a protection against sea-organisms.—**sheath′-knife** *n.* knife with a fixed blade fitting into a sheath when not in use [O.E. *scaeth*].

sheave (shēv) *n.* grooved wheel in block, rail, mast, yard, etc. on which a rope works [doublet of *shive*].

sheave (shēv) *v.t.* to bind into sheaves; to sheaf [fr. *sheaf*].

shed (shed) *n.* temporary roofed shelter used as store or workshop; outhouse [doublet of *shade*].

shed (shed) *v.t.* to cause to emanate, proceed, or flow out; to spill; to let fall; to cast off, as hair, feathers, shell; to spread; to radiate; to separate; to divide.—*pr.p.* **shed′ding.**—*pa.t.* and *pa.p.* **shed.**—*n.* division or parting, as of hair; a watershed [O.E. *sceadan*, to divide].

sheen (shēn) *n.* gloss; glitter; brightness; light reflected by a bright surface.—**sheen′y** *a.* [O.E. *sciene*, beautiful].

sheep (shēp) *n. sing.* and *pl.* ruminant mammal, valued for its flesh and its soft fleecy wool; simple, bashful person;—*pl.* pastor's church congregation.—**sheep′cot, sheep′-cote** *n.* enclosure affording shelter for sheep.—**sheep′-dip** *n.* tank containing insecticide through which sheep are passed to free them from ticks; anti-parasitic solution or sheep-wash so used.—**sheep′-dog** *n.* any breed of dog trained to tend and round up sheep.—**sheep′-farm** *n.* sheep-run. —**sheep′-fold** *n.* sheep-cote.—**sheep′-hook** *n.* a shepherd's crook.—**sheep′ish** *a.* like a sheep; bashful; shy and embarrassed; awkwardly timid and diffident.—**sheep′ishly** *adv.*—**sheep′-ishness** *n.*—**sheep′-pen** *n.* sheep-cote.—**sheep's eyes,** fond, languishing glances; leer.—**sheep′-shank** *n.* knot or hitch for temporarily shortening rope, halyard, etc.; something lank, slender, or weak.—**sheep′-shear′er** *n.* one who clips wool from sheep.—**sheep′-shear′ing** *n.*—**sheep′skin** *n.* skin of sheep; leather, parchment, or rug made from this.—**black sheep,** disreputable member of family; rogue [O.E. *sceap*].

sheer (shēr) *a.* pure; unmixed; absolute; downright; perpendicular; of linen or silk, very fine;—*adv.* quite; completely [O.E. *scir*, pure, bright].

sheer (shēr) *v.i.* to deviate from the right course; (with *off*) to move away; to swerve; to turn aside;—*n.* longitudinal, upward curvature of ship's deck towards bow or stern. —**sheer′-hulk** *n.* old vessel fitted with sheers.—**sheers** *n.* See **shears** [Dut. *scheren*].

sheet (shēt) *n.* any broad expanse; a broad piece of cloth spread on bed; broad piece of paper; newspaper; broad expanse of water, or the like; broad, thinly expanded portion of metal or other substance;—*v.t.* to cover, as with a sheet.—**sheet′-copp′er, -i′ron, -lead, -met′al,** etc. *n.* appropriate metal in broad, thin sheets.—**sheet′-glass** *n.* glass blown first in cylindrical form, then made ribbon-shaped by being continuously drawn up an annealing tower and finally, when flat, cut into sheets. —**sheet′ing** *n.* process of forming into sheets; calico or linen cloths used for bed coverings; —**sheet′-light′ning** *n.* sudden glow appearing on horizon due to reflection of forked lightning.—**sheet′-mus′ic** *n.* music printed on unbound sheets of paper [O.E. *scete*].

sheet (shēt) *n.* rope attached to lower lee corner of sail in order to extend it to wind; ship's sail;—*pl.* open space at bow or stern of undecked boat.—**sheet′-anch′or** *n.* large anchor carried in ship's waist, for emergencies; chief support [O.E. *sceata*].

Sheik, Sheikh (shāk, shēk) *n.* Arab chief; a title of respect to Moslem ecclesiasts [Ar.].

shekel (shek′-l) *n.* among ancient Hebrews, orig. weight, and later name of a gold or silver coin.—*pl.* (*Colloq.*) money; coins; cash [Heb. *sheqel*].

sheldrake (shel′-drāk) *n.* (*fem.* **shel′duck**) genus of wild duck [O.E. *sheld*, variegated; and *drake*].

shelf (shelf) *n.* board fixed horizontally on frame, or to wall, for holding things; sand-bank in sea, or ledge of rocks, rendering water shallow; reef; shoal.—*pl.* **shelves** (shelvz).—**shelf′y** *a.* [O.E. *scelf*].

shell (shel) *n.* hard, rigid, outer, protective covering of many animals, particularly molluscs; outer covering of eggs of birds; protective covering of certain seeds; hollow steel container, filled with high explosive, for discharging from mortar or gun; outer part of structure left when interior is removed; inner coffin; frail racing boat or skiff; in motoring, radiator casing; group of electrons in atom all having same principal quantum number; intermediate form at some schools; musical instrument.—**shell′back** *n.* old sailor; barnacle.—**shelled** *a.* having shell; stripped of shell; damaged by shellfire.—**shell′-egg** *n.* egg of domestic fowl.—**shell′fish** *n.* aquatic animal with external covering of shell, as oysters, lobster; crustacean; mollusc.—**shell′-jack′et** *n.*

an undress military jacket.—**shell′-proof** *a.* capable of withstanding bombs or high-explosives.—**shell′-shock** *n.* war-neurosis, disturbance of mind and nervous system due to war conditions [O.E. *sciell*].

shellac, shell-lac (she-lak′, shel′-lak) *n.* refined, melted form of seed-lac, obtained from resinous deposit secreted by insects on certain Eastern trees, used as varnish.—*v.t.* to cover with shellac [*shel(l)* and *lac*].

shelter (shel′-tẹr) *n.* place or structure giving protection; that which covers or defends; an air-raid shelter; a place of refuge; asylum;—*v.t.* to give protection to; to screen from wind or rain;—*v.i.* to take shelter.—**shel′terer** *n.* [etym. uncertain].

sheltie, shelty (shel′-ti) *n.* a Shetland pony [Ice. *Hjalti*, Shetlander].

shelve (shelv) *v.t.* to furnish with shelves; to place on a shelf; to put aside, as unfit for use; to defer indefinitely consideration of some proposal;—*v.i.* to slope gradually; to incline.—**shel′ving** *n.* act of fitting up shelves; material for shelves.—**shel′vy** *a.* full of rocks or sandbanks; sloping; shallow [fr. *shelf*].

shemozzle (she-mozl′) *n.* (*Slang*) rough-and-tumble; brawling; uproar.

shenanigan (she-nan′-i-gạn) *n.* (*Slang*) frolicking; practical joking.

shepherd (shep′-ẹrd) *n.* (*fem.* **shep′herdess**) one who tends sheep; pastor of church;—*v.t.* to tend sheep; to watch over and guide.—**shep′herd's-crook** *n.* long staff, with end curved to form large hook.—**shep′herd's-pie,** *n.* minced meat mixed with potatoes and onions baked in oven.—**shep′herd's-purse, -bag, -pouch** *n.* common British weed.—**shepherd tartan, shepherd's tartan,** kind of small black and white check pattern [O.E. *sceaphirde*].

sheppy, sheppey (shep′-i) *n.* a sheep-cote or pen [fr. *sheep*].

Sheraton (sher′-ạ-tun) *n.* style of furniture design distinguished for grace and beauty [Thomas *Sheraton* (1751-1806), the designer].

sherbet (shẹr′-bẹt) *n.* cooling drink used in East, composed of fruit juice diluted with iced-water and sweetened; in Britain, usually made effervescent [Ar. *sharbat*, a drink].

sherd. See **shard.**

sherif, shereef (shẹ-rēf′) *n.* title bestowed upon descendants of Mohammed through daughter Fatima; prince, ruler; chief magistrate of Mecca [Ar. *sharif*, noble].

sheriff (sher′-if) *n.* orig. governor of a shire, a 'shire-reeve'; in England, chief officer of Crown in every county; in Scotland, law-officer of Crown; in U.S.A., a police official with many ministerial functions.—**sher′iffalty, sher′iffdom, sher′iffship** *n.* the office or jurisdiction of sheriff [O.E. *scirgerefa*, a shire-reeve].

Sherpa (sher′-pa) *n.* one belonging to a N.E. Nepal tribe, whose male members are often employed as porters or guides on Himalayan mountaineering expeditions.

sherry (sher′-i) *n.* Spanish wine of deep amber colour [fr. *Jerez* de la Frontera, also known as *Xeres*, near Cadiz].

Shetland (shet′-land) (*Geog.*) group of islands off N. coast of Scotland.—**Shet′lander** *n.*—**Shetland pony,** 'shelty,' small breed of pony.

shew (shō). Same as **show.**

shewbred, showbread (shō′-bred) *n.* in ancient, Mosaic ritual, loaves of bread, formerly placed before the Lord on the golden table in the sanctuary and renewed every Sabbath [fr. *show*].

shibboleth (shib′-bo-leth) *n.* word by which Gileadites distinguished Ephraimite, from his inability to sound *sh* in the word, and so discovered whether he was friend or foe (*see Judges* 12); hence, party cry or watchword [Heb.].

shield (shēld) *n.* broad piece of armour carried on arm; buckler; anything which protects or defends; escutcheon or field on which are placed bearings in coats of arms; trophy in shape of a shield;—*v.t.* to protect; to defend; to screen; to ward off; to forfend [O.E. *scield*].

shieling (shē′-ling) *n.* Highland hut or small cottage, such as used by shepherds. Also **sheal′ing, sheel′ing** [O.N. *skjōl*, shelter].

shift (shift) *v.t.* to change position (of); to transfer from one place to another; to remove; to move; to change, as clothes;—*v.i.* to move; to change place,course; to change in opinion; to manage or contrive;—*n.* change; evasion; expedient; squad or relay of workmen; time of their working; woman's undergarment.—**shift′er** *n.* one employed to shift scenery, articles, etc.; trickster; adjustable spanner.—**shift′iness** *n.* trickiness of character or behaviour.—**shift′ing** *a.* changing place or position; displacing; fickle; unreliable.—**shift′less** *a.* lacking in resource or character; aimless; not to be depended upon.—**shift′lessness** *n.*—**shift′y** *a.* shuffling; not to be trusted; unreliable.—**to shift one's ground,** to veer round in argument.—**to make shift,** to manage or contrive somehow [O.E. *sciftan*, to arrange].

shillelagh, shillelah (shi-lā′-a) *n.* oak or blackthorn sapling; cudgel. Also **shillal′ah** [*Shillelagh*, Co. Wicklow].

shilling (shil′-ing) *n.* formerly British silver coin of the value of twelve pence.—**to cut off with a shilling,** to disinherit without any dubiety [O.E. *scilling*].

shilly-shally (shil′-i-shal′-i) *n.* foolish trifling; indecision; *v.i.* to hesitate or trifle; to waver.—**shill′y-shall′ier** *n.* [redupl. of *shall I*].

shily Same as **shyly.**

shimmer (shim′-ẹr) *v.i.* to shine with faint, tremulous light; to gleam; to glisten;—*n.* faint, quivering light or gleam.—**shimm′ering** *n.* [O.E. *scimian*].

shimmy (shim′-i) *n.* chemise; dance characterised by exaggerated wriggling;—*v.i.* to wobble [fr. *chemise*].

shin (shin) *n.* fore-part of leg, between ankle and knee; shank;—*v.i.* to climb (up) with aid of one's arms and legs; to swarm (up).—**shin′-bone** *n.* tibia, larger of two bones of leg [O.E. *scinu*].

shindig (shin′-dig) *n.* (*U.S. Slang*) social evening; jollification [var. of *shindy*].

shindy (shin′-di) *n.* excessive noise and tumult; uproar [Romany, *chindi*, quarrel].

shindy. Same as **shinty.**

shine (shīn) *v.i.* to give out or reflect light; to radiate; to beam; to gleam; to glisten; to glitter; to perform in brilliant fashion.—*pa.t.* and *pa.p.* **shone.**—*v.t.* to cause to shine; to polish, shoes, etc.—*pa.t.* and *pa.p.* **shined.**—*n.* brightness; gloss; (*Slang*) fuss; row; shindy.—**shi′ner** *n.*—**shi′ning** *a.* glistening; splendid.—**shi′niness** *n.*—**shi′ny** *a.* bright; glossy; unclouded [O.E. *scinan*].

shingle (shing′-gl) *n.* rounded water-worn pebbles, occurring near high-water mark of sea-beaches or on banks of rivers.—**shing′ly** *a.* [fr. *chink*].

shingle (shing′-gl) *n.* thin, wooden, rectangular slat, used as a roofing tile; style of hairdressing for women;—*v.t.* to cover with shingles or tiles, as a roof; to crop women's hair close at nape of neck [L. *scindula*].

shingles (shing′-glz) *n.pl.* (*Med.*) *Herpes Zoster*, acute inflammation of nerve ganglia in spine, accompanied by severe pain and later a vesicular eruption, usually round the waist [L. *cingulum*, a belt].

Shinto (shin′-tō) *n.* native religion of Japan, manifested by payment of religious honour to Mikado, combined with ancestor-worship.—**Shin′toism** *n.* principles of Shinto [Chin. *shin*, god; *tao*, the way].

shinty (shin′-ti) *n.* ball-game played mainly in Gaelic-speaking parts of Scotland, intermediate between hockey and Irish hurley; stick used [etym. doubtful].

ship (ship) *n.* sailing-vessel with three masts, all square-rigged; any vessel other than those propelled by oars; vessel for carriage of

FAMOUS RIVERS · 1

Mississippi at Memphis

Guadalquivir at Seville

Nile in upper Egypt

Danube

FAMOUS RIVERS · 2

Jordan

Vltava at Prague

Victoria Falls on the Zambezi

passengers and goods by sea;—*v.t.* to put on board ship for transportation; to engage for service on board a ship; to place object in position, as oar; to receive on deck force of wave;—*v.i.* to embark.—*pr.p.* **ship'ping.**—*pa.t.* and *pa.p.* **shipped.**—**ship'board** *n.* deck or side of ship.—**ship'break'er** *n.* one who breaks up obsolete ships for scrap-metal, etc.—**ship'brok'er** *n.* agent for a shipping-company; one who transacts marine-insurance deals.—**ship'builder** *n.* one who constructs ships; naval architect.—**ship'building** *n.*—**ship'chand'ler** *n.* one who deals in equipment for a ship.—**ship'chand'lery** *n.*—**ship'man** *n.* sailor.—*pl.* **ship'men.**—**ship'mas'ter** *n.* captain or commander of ship.—**ship'mate** *n.* fellow-sailor.—**ship'ment** *n.* process of shipping; that which is shipped; cargo.—**ship'mon'ey** *n.* formerly, tax leviable on port-towns to furnish navy in times of danger.—**ship'own'er** *n.*—**ship'per** *n.* one who forwards commodities by ship.—**ship'ping** *n.* collective body of ships in one place; mercantile vessels generally; tonnage.—**ship'ping-a'gent** *n.* one who arranges the shipment of goods or passengers.—**ship'rigged** *a.* rigged with square sails and spreading yards.—**ship'shape** *a.* in a seamanlike manner; hence, orderly, trim, tidy;—*adv.* properly.—**ship's log,** device for reckoning speed of vessel at sea; official day-to-day record of events on board ship.—**ship'way** *n.* sloping berth on which ships are built.—**ship'wreck** *n.* loss of ship by mischance; total destruction; ruin.—**ship'wright** *n.* carpenter actively engaged in building or repairing ships.—**ship'yard** *n.* place where ships are built or repaired.—**to ship a sea,** to have wave breaking over gunwale [O.E. *scip*].

Shir See **shirr.**

shire (shīr) *n.* territorial division, usually identical with county, but sometimes comprising smaller district; county.—**shire'town** *n.* capital town of county; county town.—**the Shires,** the midland counties of England whose names all end in **-*shire*** [O.E. *scir,* district].

shirk (sherk) *v.t.* to evade; to try to avoid (duty, etc.);—*n.* one who seeks to avoid duty.—**shirk'er** *n.* a shirk [etym. uncertain].

shirr, shir (sher) *n.* in ornamental needlework, row of puckering or gathering;—*v.t.* to gather with parallel threads run through [etym. doubtful].

shirt (shert) *n.* undergarment worn on upper part of body by men and boys; jersey worn in field games; woman's blouse;—*v.t.* to clothe, as with shirt.—**shirt'front** *n.* starched front part of a shirt; dickey or detachable front.—**boiled shirt,** shirt with starched front for evening-wear.—**to keep one's shirt on** (*Slang*) to keep cool and unruffled [O.E. *scyrte*].

shist See **schist.**

shiver (shiv'er) *v.i.* to quiver or shake from cold or fear; to tremble; to shudder; to vibrate;—*v.t.* to cause to shake in wind (applied to sails);—*n.* shaking or shuddering caused by cold, fear; a vibration.—**shiv'ery** *a.* inclined to shiver; tremulous; timid to excess [etym. uncertain].

shiver (shiv'er) *n.* small piece or splinter into which thing breaks by application of sudden violence;—*v.t.* and *v.i.* to break into many small pieces or splinters; to shatter [M.E. *scifre*].

shoal (shōl) *n.* large number of fish swimming together; a great quantity;—*v.i.* to form into shoals; to crowd together [O.E. *scolu,* company, fr. L. *schola,* a school].

shoal (shōl) *n.* a sandbank or bar; shallow water;—*a.* shallow;—*v.i.* to become shallow.—**shoal'er** *n.* coasting-vessel.—**shoal'y** *a.* full of shoals or shallows [O.E. *sceald,* shallow].

shock (shok) *n.* violent impact or concussion when bodies collide; clash; percussion; conflict; emotional disturbance produced by anything unexpected, offensive, or displeasing; sudden depression of the system due to violent injury or strong mental emotion; paralytic stroke; effect of electric discharge through body;—*v.t.* to strike against suddenly; to strike with surprise, horror, or disgust.—**shock'absorb'er** *n.* anything to lighten a blow, shock, or ordeal.—**shock'er** *n.* highly sensational tale of no literary merit.—**shock'ing** *a.* appalling; terrifying; frightful; repulsive; offensive.—**shock'ingly** *adv.*—**shock'ingness** *n.*—**shock'proof** *a.* able to withstand shocks [Fr. *choquer*].

shock (shok) *n.* disordered mass of hair;—*a.* shaggy; bushy.—**shock'head, -ed** *a.* having a thick, bushy head of hair [O.E. *scucca,* a demon].

shock (shok) *n.* group of sheaves of grain;—*v.t.* to make into shocks [Dut. *schocke*].

shod (shod) *pa.t.* and *pa.p.* of verb **shoe.**

shoddy (shod'i) *n.* inferior textile material;—*a.* made of shoddy; pert. to shoddy; inferior; of poor material; second rate [etym. unknown].

shode See **shoad.**

shoe (shòò) *n.* covering for foot, but not enclosing ankle; metal rim or curved bar nailed to horse's hoof; various protective plates or under-coverings; plate of iron or slip of wood, nailed to bottom of runner of sledge; apparatus which bears on the live rail in an electric railway in order to collect current to actuate the motor;—*v.t.* to furnish with shoes; to put shoes on.—*pr.p.* **shoe'ing.**—*pa.t.* and *pa.p.* **shod.**—**shoe'black** *n.* one who polishes shoes.—**shoe'brush** *n.* brush for polishing shoes.—**shoe'horn** *n.* curved piece of horn, metal, etc. used to help foot into shoe.—**shoe'lace** *n.* shoe-string for fastening shoe on foot.—**shoe'less** *a.*—**shoe'maker** *n.*—**sho'er** *n.* one who makes or puts on shoes.—**shoe'string** *n.* a shoe-lace [O.E. *scoh*].

shog (shog) *n.* push;—*v.t.* and *v.i.* to shake; to swing.—**shogg'le** *v.t.* and *v.i.* to shake; to wobble (W. *ysog,* a jolt].

shogun (shō'gòòn) *n.* title of hereditary commander-in-chief of Japanese army from 17th cent. until 1868.—**sho'gunal** *a.*—**sho'gunate** *n.* [Jap. *sho,* to hold; *gun,* army].

shone (shon) *pa.t.* and *pa.p.* of **shine.**

shoo (shòò) *interj.* begone! (used esp. in scaring away fowls and other animals);—*v.t.* to scare or drive away [imit.].

shook (shook) *pa.t.* of **shake.**

shoon (shòòn) *n.pl.* an older pl. of *shoe.*

shoot (shòòt) *v.t.* to discharge missile from gun, etc.; to kill or wound with such a missile; to fire; to hit; to cast (a net); to hurl; to propel quickly; to thrust out; to pass swiftly over (rapids) or through (arch of bridge); to photograph episode or sequence of motion-picture;—*v.i.* to move swiftly and suddenly; to let off a gun, etc.; to go after game with gun; to jut out; to sprout; to bud; to dart through (as severe pain); to advance; to kick towards goal-mouth.—*pa.t.* and *pa.p.* **shot.**—*n.* shooting; expedition to shoot; young branch or stem; inclined plane down which timber, coal, rubbish, etc. slide; chute; a rapid or fall in stream.—**shoot'er** *n.* one who shoots; implement for shooting; ball at cricket which rolls along ground instead of rebounding.—**shoot'ing** *n.* act of discharging fire-arms, etc.; the act of killing game.—**shoot'ing-box** *n.* small lodge for accommodation of sportsmen.—**shoot'ing-gall'ery** *n.* long room for practice with miniature rifles.—**shoot'ing-star** *n.* incandescent meteor.—**shoot'ing-stick** *n.* printer's implement for driving home little wedges of wood or quoins when locking up page in chase; walking-stick which can be converted into seat.—**to shoot a line** (*Slang*) to brag; to exaggerate [O.E. *sceotan*].

shop (shop) *n.* building where goods are made, or bought and sold; workshop;—*v.i.* to visit shops to purchase articles;—*v.t.* (*Slang*) to arrest or imprison.—*pr.p.* **shop'ping.**—*pa.t.* and *pa.p.* **shopped.**—**shop'assis'tant** *n.* one employed in retail trade.—**shop'count'er** *n.* table in shop on which transactions are completed. —**shop'keeper** *n.* one who keeps retail shop.—**shop'keeping** *n.*—**shop'lift'er** *n.* one who makes petty thefts from shop counters.—**shop'mate** *n.* fellow workman in shop or workshop.—**shop'ping** *n.* visiting shops with view to purchasing.—**shop'ping-bag, -bas'ket** *n.* receptacle for holding articles purchased.—**shop'soiled, shop'worn** *a.* soiled or tarnished by long exposure in shop.—**shop'stew'ard** *n.* trade-union representative of workers in factory, etc.—**shop'walk'er** *n.* one employed in large shop to superintend staff and to assist customers.—**to talk shop,** to talk exclusively about one's daily business or particular interests [Fr. *échoppe,* a booth].

shore (shōr) *pa.t.* of **shear.**

shore (shōr) *n.* land adjoining sea or large lake;—*v.t.* to put ashore [Dut. *schor*].

shore (shōr) *n.* strong beam set obliquely against wall of building or ship to prevent movement during structural alterations;—*v.t.* to support by post or buttress; to prop [etym. uncertain].

shorn (shorn) *pa.p.* of **shear;**—*a.* cut off; having the hair or wool cut off or sheared; deprived (of) [fr. *shear*].

short (short) *a.* having little length; not long in space; not extended in time; limited or lacking in quantity; hasty of temper; crumbling in the mouth; pronounced with less prolonged accent; brief; near; direct; concise; pithy; abrupt; destitute; crisp; dilute. —*adv.* suddenly; abruptly; without reaching the end;—*n.* short film to support feature film; short-circuit;—*pl.* short trousers reaching down to above knees.—**short'age** *n.* insufficient supply; deficiency.—**short'bread, short'-cake** *n.* rich, brittle form of sweet cake.—**short'breathed** *a.* having short breath or quick respiration.—**short'cir'cuit** *n.* passage of electric current by a shorter route than that designed for it;—*v.t.* to cause short-circuit; to by-pass. —**short'coming** *n.* failing; fault; falling short; defect.—**short'comm'ons** *n.* reduced allowance of food; scanty rations.—**short'cut** *n.* quicker but unorthodox way of reaching a place or of accomplishing a task, etc.—**short'en** *v.t.* to make shorter; to render friable, as shortbread, with butter or lard; to abridge; to lessen; to diminish; to reduce; to dress (baby) in shorter clothes;—*v.i.* to contract; to lessen.—**short'ening** *n.* lard used when baking crisp pastry or shortbread.—**short'hand** *n.* system of rapid reporting by means of signs or symbols; stenography.—**short'hand'ed** *a.* not having the full complement or staff on duty.—**short'hand-typ'ist** *n.* one who types from shorthand notes. —**short'head** *n.* in racing, distance less than the length of a horse's head.—**short'horn** *n.* a breed of domestic cattle with short horns, valued for its rich milk yield and for beef.—**short'ly** *adv.* in a brief time; soon; in a few words; curtly.—**short'ness** *n.*—**short shrift,** summary treatment.—**short'sight'ed** *a.* not able to see distinctly objects some distance away; lacking in foresight; heedless.—**short'sight'edly** *adv.*—**short'sight'(edness)** *n.*—**short'slip** *n.* in cricket, part of field, or fielder, a short distance obliquely behind wicket-keeper on off-side of batter.—**short'tem'pered** *a.* easily roused to anger.—**short time,** not working the usual full hours owing to bad trade or other causes.—**short waves** (*Radio*) electro-magnetic waves whose wavelength is, by international definition, between 10 and 50 metres.—**short'wind'ed** *a.* affected with shortness of breath; asthmatic; easily made out of breath. —**in short,** briefly.—**little short of,** almost.—**nothing short of,** really [O.E. *sceort*].

shot (shot) *pa.t.* and *pa.p.* of **shoot.**

shot (shot) *n.* in weaving, a single thread of weft;—*a.* pert. to fabrics woven with warp and weft of contrasting tints or colours, so that shade changes according to angle of light [fr. *shoot*].

shot (shot) *n.* reckoning; one's share of expenses incurred; (*Slang*) dose, esp. of drug [O.E. *scot*].

shot (shot) *n.* act of shooting; skilled marksman; one of small pellets, contained in cartridge fired from sporting rifle; heavy, solid, round missile, formerly fired from cannon; range of such missiles; charge of blasting powder; stroke in billiards, tennis, etc.; young hog; cast of fishing-nets at sea; in cinematography, continuous strip of film showing without interruption one view or action-sequence; a try or attempt;—*v.t.* to load or weight with shot.—*pr.p.* **shot'ting.**—*pa.t.* and *pa.p.* **shot'ted.**—**shot'cart'ridge** *n.* cartridge containing small shot.—**shot'fir'ing** *n.* method of blasting in mines.—**shot'gun** *n.* smooth-bore gun for shooting small game.—**big shot,** important person.—**a shot in the locker,** something kept in reserve [O.E. *sceot*].

should (shood) *v.* and *aux.* used in Future-in-the-Past tenses of verbs with pronouns I or we; auxiliary used after words expressing opinion, intention, desire, probability, obligation, etc. (Cf. *shall*).

shoulder (shōl'dẹr) *n.* ball and socket joint formed by humerus (bone of the upper arm) with scapula (shoulder-blade); upper joint of foreleg of animal; anything resembling human shoulder, as prominent part of hill;—*v.t.* to push forward with shoulders; to bear (burden, etc.); to accept (responsibility);—*v.i.* to push forward through crowd.—**shoul'der-belt** *n.* belt which passes across shoulder; baldric.—**shoul'der-blade, -bone** *n.* flat bone of shoulder; scapula.—**to give one the cold shoulder,** to ignore or treat coldly [O.E. *sculdor*].

shout (shout) *n.* loud, piercing cry; call for help;—*v.t.* and *v.i.* to utter loud and sudden cry [etym. uncertain].

shove (shuv) *v.t.* to push; to press against; to jostle;—*v.i.* to push forward; to push off from shore in a boat, using oar;—*n.* act of pushing; push [O.E. *scufan*].

shovel (shuv'l) *n.* spade with broad blade slightly hollowed; scoop;—*v.t.* to lift or move with a shovel;—*v.i.* to use shovel.—*pr.p.* **shov'elling.**—*pa.t.* and *pa.p.* **shov'elled.**—**shov'el-board, shuff'le-board, shove'board** *n.* game of shove-ha'penny; board on which game is played.—**shov'el-hat** *n.* clerical head-gear with broad brim turned up at sides and projecting over forehead.—**shov'eller** *n.* [O.E. *scofl*].

show (shō) *v.t.* to present to view; to point out; to display; to exhibit; to disclose; to divulge; to explain; to manifest; to evince; to demonstrate; to prove; to conduct; to usher; to guide;—*v.i.* to appear; to be visible; to come into sight.—*pa.p.* **shown** or **showed.**—*n.* act of showing; that which is shown; spectacle; exhibition; sight; parade; display; semblance; likeness.—**show'bill** *n.* broad sheet containing advertisement.—**show'bread** *n.* Same as **shewbread.**—**show'case** *n.* glass case for display of goods, museum exhibits, etc.—**show'down** *n.* laying down of cards, face upwards, at poker or other card games; open disclosure of truth, clarification.—**shower** (shō'ẹr) *n.* one who shows or exhibits.—**show'ily** *adv.* ostentatiously; pompously.—**show'iness** *n.*—**show'man** *n.* proprietor of a show at a fair, etc.; one employed in such a show; specious, self-advertising person.—**show'manship** *n.*—**show'place** *n.* place of local interest made especially attractive to draw tourists.—**show'room** *n.* room where goods are laid out for inspection.—**show'y** *a.* gaudy; attracting attention; loud; ostentatious; specious; plausible.—**to show a leg,** to get out of bed.—**to show off,** to make an ostentatious display.—**to show up,** to stand out prominently; to expose; to hold up to ridicule [O.E. *sceawian,* to look at].

shower (shou'ẹr) *n.* a brief fall of rain or hail; anything coming down like rain; great number;—*v.t.* to wet with rain; to give abundantly;—*v.i.* to rain; to pour down.—**show'er-bath** *n.* bath equipped with fine-spraying apparatus.—**show'eriness** *n.* state of being showery or unsettled.—**show'er-proof** *a.* impervious to rain.—**show'ery** *a.* raining intermittently [O.E. *scur*].

shrank (shrangk) *pa.t.* of **shrink**.

shrapnel (shrap'nel) *n.* shell timed to explode over, and shower bullets and splinters on, personnel; shell-splinters [invented by Gen. H. *Shrapnel*].

shred (shred) *n.* long, narrow piece cut or torn off; strip; fragment; small portion; particle; bit; rag; tatter; scrap;—*v.t.* to cut or tear to shreds; to tear into strips.—*pr.p.* **shred'ding.** —*pa.t.* and *pa.p.* **shred'ded** [O.E. *screade*].

shrew (shròò) *n.* noisy, quarrelsome woman; scold; a termagant. Also **shrew'mouse,** most diminutive of existing mammals, resembling, but unrelated to, mouse.—**shrew'ish** *a.* having manners of a shrew.—**shrew'ishly** *adv.*—**shrew'ishness** *n.* [O.E. *screawa,* shrew-mouse].

shrewd (shròòd) *a.* intelligent; discerning; sagacious; knowing; artful; cunning; subtle. —**shrewd'ly** *adv.*—**shrewd'ness** *n.* [fr. *shrew*].

shriek (shrēk) *v.t.* and *v.i.* to scream, from fright, anguish, or bad temper; to screech;—*n.* a loud, shrill cry [imit. origin].

shrieval (shrē'val) *a.* pert. to sheriff.—**shriev'alty** *n.* office of sheriff; sheriffalty.—**shrieve** *n.* sheriff;—*v.t.* to confess or hear confession; to shrive [fr. *shrive*].

shrift (shrift) *n.* confession made to a priest; absolution.—**short shrift,** summary treatment [O.E. *scrifan,* to prescribe (penance)].

shrike (shrīk) *n.* bird which preys on birds, frogs, and insects, and impales victims on thorns; butcher-bird [imit. of cry].

shrill (shril) *a.* uttering an acute sound; piercing; high-pitched; importunate;—*v.i.* to sound in a shrill tone.—**shrill'y** *adv.* piercingly [imit. origin].

shrimp (shrimp) *n.* small edible crustacean allied to prawns; small, puny, wizened person; object of contempt; dwarf;—*v.i.* to catch shrimps with net.—**shrimp'er** *n.* [etym. uncertain].

shrine (shrīn) *n.* case in which sacred relics are deposited; tomb of saint; place of worship, esp. by wayside; any sacred place [L. *scrinium,* coffer].

shrink (shringk) *v.i.* to become wrinkled by contraction; to shrivel; to contract; to dwindle; to recoil; to draw back;—*v.t.* to cause to contract.—*pa.t.* **shrank, shrunk.**—*pa.p.* **shrunk.**—**shrink'age** *n.* act or amount of shrinking.—**shrunk'en** *a.* contracted; shrivelled; narrowed in size [O.E. *scrincan*].

shrive (shrīv) *v.t.* to give absolution to; to confess (used reflexively);—*v.i.* to receive confessions [O.E. *scrifan,* to prescribe (penance)].

shrivel (shriv'l) *v.t.* and *v.i.* to cause to contract; to wither.—*pr.p.* **shriv'elling.**—*pa.t.* and *pa.p.* **shriv'elled** [etym. uncertain].

shroud (shroud) *n.* that which clothes or covers; sheet for a corpse; winding-sheet;—*pl.* strongest of the wire-rope stays which support mast athwartships;—*v.t.* to enclose in winding-sheet; to cover with shroud; to screen; to wrap up; to conceal [O.E. *scrud,* a garment].

shrove (shrōv) *n.* shrift; shriving.—*pa.t.* of the verb **shrive.**—**Shrove'tide** *n.* period immediately before Lent, ending on Shrove Tuesday [fr. *shrive*].

shrub (shrub) *n.* any hard-wooded plant of smaller and thicker growth than tree; bush; low, dwarf tree.—**shrub'bery** *a.* collection of shrubs; place where shrubs are planted.—**shrub'by** *a.* of nature of shrub; full of shrubs [O.E. *scrybb*].

shrug (shrug) *v.i.* to raise and narrow shoulders in disdain, etc.—*v.t.* to move (shoulders) thus; to contract.—*pr.p.* **shrug'ging.**—*pa.t.* and *pa.p.* **shrugged.**—*n.* drawing up of shoulders [etym. unknown].

shrunk, shrunken See **shrink.**

shuck (shuk) *n.* husk or pod; shell of nut; shock or stook;—*v.t.* to remove husk, pod, or shell from [Cf. *chuck,* to throw].

shudder (shud'er) *v.i.* to tremble violently, esp. with horror or fear; to shiver; to quake; —*n.* trembling or shaking; shiver.—**shudd'ering** *n.* and *a.* trembling; shivering [M.E. Cf. Ger. *schaudern*].

shuffle (shuf'l) *v.t.* to shove one way and the other; to throw into disorder; to mix (cards); to scrape (feet) along ground;—*v.i.* to change position of cards in pack; to practise shifts; to prevaricate; to move in a slovenly manner; to scrape floor with foot in dancing;—*n.* act of throwing into confusion by change of places; artifice or pretext; rapid, scraping movement of foot in dancing.—**shuff'le-board** *n.* a shovel-board.—**shuff'ler** *n.* [etym. uncertain].

shun (shun) *v.t.* to keep clear of; to get out of the way of; to avoid.—*pr.p.* **shun'ning.**—*pa.t.* and *pa.p.* **shunned** [O.E. *scunian*].

shunt (shunt) *v.t.* to move or turn off to one side; to move (train) from one line to another; to divert (electric current);—*v.i.* to go aside; to turn off.—*n.* act of shunting.—**shunt'er** *n.* railway employee who shunts rolling-stock.—**shunt'ing** *n.* [etym. uncertain].

shut (shut) *v.t.* to close to hinder ingress or egress; to fasten; to secure; to bar; to forbid entrance to;—*v.i.* to close itself; to become closed.—*pr.p.* **shut'ting.**—*pa.t.* and *pa.p.* **shut.** —*a.* closed; barred; made fast.—**shut'down** *n.* stoppage of work or activity.—**shut'ter** *n.* one who, or that which, shuts; movable protective screen for window; automatic device in camera which allows light from lens to act on film or plate for a predetermined period.—**to shut down,** to stop working; to close (business, etc.).—**to shut up,** to close; to fasten securely; (*Colloq.*) to stop talking [O.E. *scyttan*].

shuttle (shut'l) *n.* instrument used in weaving for shooting thread of woof between threads of warp; similar appliance in sewing-machine to form a lock stitch;—*v.t.* and *v.i.* to move backwards and forwards.—**shutt'lecock** *n.* cork with fan of feathers for use with battledore or in badminton; game itself.—**shuttle service,** transport service on a short route with only one vehicle operating between two points [O.E. *scytel,* a missile].

shy (shī) *a.* sensitively timid; reserved; coy; easily frightened; shrinking; modest; bashful; cautious;—*v.i.* to start suddenly aside.—*pa.t.* and *pa.p.* **shied.**—**shy'ly, shi'ly** *adv.*—**shy'ness** *n.* —**shy'ster** *n.* unscrupulous lawyer; a twister; welsher.—**to fight shy of,** to avoid [O.Fr. *eschif*].

shy (shī) *v.t.* to throw; to fling.—*pa.t.* and *pa.p.* **shied.**—*n.* throw; cast; trial [etym. uncertain].

Siamese (sī-am-ēz') *a.* pert. to Siam, the people, or language;—*n.* native of Siam; the language.—**Siamese twins,** male twins born in Siam whose bodies were united by a fleshy band (1811-74); name now applied to any 'joined twins'.

sib, sibbe (sib) *a.* having kinship; related by blood; kin; akin, in affinity;—*n.* a blood relation [O.E. Cf. Ger. *sippe*].

Siberian (sī-bē'ri-an) *a.* pert. to Siberia, formerly known as Asiatic Russia.

sibilance (sib'i-lans) *n.* hissing sound; quality of being sibilant. Also **sib'ilancy.**—**sib'ilant** *a.* —*n.* letter uttered with hissing of voice, as *s, x,* etc.—**sib'ilate** *v.t.* to pronounce with hissing sound [L. *sibilare,* to whistle].

Sibyl (sib'il) *n.* a name applied to certain votaresses of Apollo, endowed with visionary, prophetic power; prophetess; fortune-teller; witch.—**sib'yllic, sib'ylline** *a.* prophetic; oracular; obscure; mysterious; occult [Gk. *Sibulla*].

sic (sik) *adv.* abbreviated form of *sic in*

originali (Lat. = so it stands in the original) printed in brackets as guarantee that passage has been quoted correctly; so; thus [L.].

siccate (sik′āt) *v.t.* to dry.—**sicca′tion** *n.* act or process of drying.—**sicc′ative** *a.* drying; causing or tending to dry;—*n.* a drier [L. *siccus*, dry].

Sicilian (si-sil′yạn) *a.* pert. to island of Sicily; —*n.* native of Sicily.

sick (sik) *a.* affected with or attended by nausea; inclined to vomit; ill; ailing; disgusted; tired of; morbid;—*v.t.* to make sick; to sicken; —*v.i.* to become sick; to sicken.—**sick′bay** *n.* place set aside on main deck of ship or elsewhere for treating the sick.—**sick′ben′efit** *n.* allowance made to insured person while ill and off duty.—**sick′en** *v.t.* to make sick; to disgust;—*v.i.* to become sick; to be filled with abhorrence.—**sick′ening** *a.* causing sickness or disgust; nauseating.—**sick′eningly** *adv.*—**sick′head′ache** *n.* migraine.—**sick′leave** *n.* leave of absence from duty on account of illness.—**sick′liness** *n.* state of being sickly.—**sick′list** *n.* list of sick persons.—**sick′ly** *a.* somewhat sick; ailing; infirm; weakly.—**sick′ness** *n.* state of being sick; illness; disordered state of stomach attended by retching [O.E. *seoc*].

sickle (sik′l) *n.* reaping-hook with semicircular blade and a short handle [L. *secula*, fr. *secare*, to cut].

side (sīd) *n.* one of surfaces of object, esp. upright inner or outer surface; one of the edges of plane figure; margin; verge; border; any part viewed as opposite to another; part of body from hip to shoulder; slope, as of a hill; one of two parties, teams, or sets of opponents; body of partisans; sect or faction; line of descent traced through one parent; bias given to a ball by striking it on the side; side-spin; region; priggish conceit; affectation; —*a.* being on the side; lateral; indirect; incidental;—*v.i.* (with) to hold or embrace the opinions of another; to give support to one of two or more contending parties.—**side′arms** *n.pl.* weapons carried on side of body.—**side′board** *n.* piece of furniture designed to hold dining utensils, etc. in dining-room.—**side′car** *n.* small box- or canoe-shaped body attached to motor-cycle; Irish jaunting-car.—**side′glance** *n.* glace or furtive look to one side.—**side′is′sue** *n.* subsidiary to main argument or business.—**side′light** *n.* any source of light situated at side of room, door, etc.; lantern, showing red or green, on side of a vessel; incidental information or illustration of how other people live and conduct themselves.—**side′line** *n.* any form of profitable work which is ancillary to one's main business or profession.—**side′ling** *a.* and *adv.* sideways; aslant. —**side′long** *a.* lateral; oblique; not directly forward;—*adv.* obliquely; on the side.—**sid′er** *n.* supporter; backer; partisan.—**side′rail** *n.* additional rail fixed to side of stair-wall; third rail to act as check on pronounced railway curve.—**side-saddle**, saddle for woman on horseback, not astride, but with both feet on one side of horse.—**side′show** *n.* minor entertainment or attraction; subordinate affair.—**side′slip** *n.* involuntary skid or slide sideways; —*v.i.* to skid.—**sides′man** *n.* officer, who assists churchwarden; church usher.—**side′split′ting** *a.* exceedingly ludicrous and laughter-provoking. —**side′step** *n.* step to one side;—*v.i.* to step to one side.—**side′stroke** *n.* style of swimming where body is turned on one side.—**side′track** *v.t.* to shunt into siding; to postpone indefinitely; to shelve;—*n.* a railway siding.—**side′view** *n.* oblique view; a view on or from one side.—**side′walk** *n.* a raised foot-pavement. —**side′ward, side′wards** *adv.* towards the side. —**side′ways, side′wise** *adv.* towards or from the side; edgewise; laterally; obliquely;—*a.* lateral.—**side′whisk′ers** *n.pl.* whiskers confined to cheeks.—**sid′ing** *n.* short line of rails on which trains or wagons are shunted from main line.—**si′dle** *v.i.* to move sideways; to edge alongside;—*v.t.* to cause to move sideways.—**side by side,** close together; alongside.—**no side,** Rugby football term for call of time [O.E.].

sidereal (sī-dē′rē-ạl) *a.* relating to constellations and fixed stars; measured or determined by apparent motion of stars.—**sidereal year,** period during which earth makes revolution in its orbit with respect to a fixed star, 365 days 6 hrs. 9-10 mins. [L. *sidus*, *sideris*, a star].

siderite (sid′ẹr-īt) *n.* brown ironstone, a carbonate of iron found in shaly beds; also known as spathic ore, chalybite; meteorite consisting chiefly of nickel-iron; the lodestone [Gk. *sidēritis*, the lodestone].

sidesman, siding, sidle See **side.**

siege (sēj) *n.* investiture of town or fortified place by hostile troops in order to induce it to surrender either by starvation or by attack at suitable juncture; continuous effort to gain (affection, influence, etc.); seat; position; rank;—*v.t.* to besiege.—**state of siege,** suspension of civil law and assumption of special powers by military authorities during period of emergency [Fr. *siège*, seat, siege].

sienna (sē-en′a) *n.* natural yellow earth which provides pigment.—**burnt sienna,** pigment giving dull-brown tint.—**raw sienna,** pigment giving a reddish-brown tint [fr. *Sienna*, Italy].

sierra (sē-er′a) *n.* chain of mountains with saw-like ridge [Sp. fr. L. *serra*, a saw].

siesta (sē-es′ta) *n.* rest or sleep in afternoon esp. in hot countries; afternoon nap [Sp. = the sixth (hour) i.e. noon].

sieve (siv) *n.* utensil with wire netting for separating fine part of any pulverised substance from the coarse;—*v.t.* to put through sieve; to sift [O.E. *sife*].

siffle (sif′l) *n.* whistling, hissing sound;—*v.t* to whistle; to hiss.—**siff′leur** *n.* (*fem.* **siff′leuse**) one who has made an art of whistling [Fr. *siffler*].

sift (sift) *v.t.* to separate coarser portion from finer; to sieve; to bolt; to scrutinise; to examine closely [O.E. *sife*, a sieve].

sigh (sī) *v.i.* to make a deep, single respiration, as expression of exhaustion or sorrow;—*v.t.* to utter sighs over;—*n.* long, deep breath, expressive of sorrow, fatigue, regret, or relief [O.E. *sican*].

sight (sīt) *n.* one of the five senses; act of seeing; faculty of seeing; that which is seen; view; glimpse; anything novel or remarkable; show; exhibition; spectacle; inspection; (*Colloq.*) pitiful object; a piece of metal near breech of firearm to assist the eye in correct aiming; any guide for eye to assist direction;—*v.t.* to catch sight of; to see; to give proper elevation and direction to instrument by means of a sight;—*v.i.* to take aim by means of a sight. —**sight′less** *a.* blind; not appearing to sight; invisible.—**sight′lessly** *adv.*—**sight′lessness** *n.* blindness.—**sight′liness** *n.* comeliness.—**sight′ly** *a.* pleasing to the eye; graceful; handsome.—**sight′read′er** *n.* one who reads or interprets at sight, as music, etc.—**sight′read′ing** *n.*—**sight′see′ing** *n.* indiscriminate viewing of places or objects of interest.—**sight′se′er** *n.*—**sec′ond-sight** *n.* gift of prophetic vision.—**at sight,** immediately; without study or previous examination [O.E. *sihth*, fr. *seon*, to see].

sigil (sij′il) *n.* seal; signature; occult sign.—**sig′illary** *a.* [L. *sigillum*, a seal].

sigma (sig′ma) *n.* the Greek letter (Σ, σ, s) corresponding to letter *s*; symbol indicating, in mathematics, etc., summation; 200; millesecond or $\frac{1}{1000}$ second.—**sig′mate, sig′moid** *a.* curved like letter S. [Gk.].

sign (sīn) *n.* movement, mark, or indication to convey some meaning; token; symbol; omen; signboard; password; (*Math.*) character indicating relation of quantities, or operation to be performed, as +, ×, ÷, = etc.; (*Mus.*) any character, as flat, sharp, dot, etc.; (*Astron.*) the twelfth part of the ecliptic or zodiac;—*v.t.* to represent by sign; to affix signature to; to ratify;—*v.i.* to make a signal, sign, or gesture; to append one's signature.—**sign′board** *n.* board displayed outside or near a building, etc. advertising business carried on within.—**sign′man′ual** *n.* the signature or mark appended by one to legal instrument; specifically, royal signature.—**sign′paint′er** *n.* one who paints signs for inns, shops, etc.—**sign′post** *n.* post supporting signboard, esp. to show way at cross-roads [L. *signum*].

signal (sig′nạl) *n.* sign to give notice of some occurrence, command, or danger to persons at a distance; that which in the first place impels any action; sign; token; semaphore, esp. on railway; (*Radio*) any communication made by emission of wireless waves from a transmitter;—*v.t.* to communicate by signals;—*v.i.* to make signals.—*pr.p.* **sig′nalling**.—*pa.t.* and *pa.p.* **sig′nalled**.—*a.* eminent; remarkable; extraordinary; conspicuous.—**sig′nal-box, -cab′in** *n.* place from where railway signals are manipulated.—**sig′nalise** *v.t.* to make notable, distinguished, or remarkable; to render noteworthy.—**sig′naller** *n.* one who signals; member of Signal Corps in British Army.—**sig′nally** *adv.* eminently; remarkably.—**sig′nalman** *n.* one whose duty it is to convey or interpret information by signals; one who works railway signals [L. *signum*, a sign].

signatory (sig′nạ-tor-i) *a.* and *n.* (one) bound by signature to terms of agreement. Also **sig′natary** [L. *signare*, to sign].

signature (sig′nạ-tūr) *n.* a sign, stamp, or mark impressed; a person's name written by himself; act of writing it; letter or number printed at bottom of first page of section of book to facilitate arrangement when binding; (*Mus.*) the flats or sharps after clef which indicate key (**key signature**), followed by appropriate signs giving value of the measures contained in each bar (**time signature**).—**signature tune**, short introductory tune associated with specific dance-band, etc. [L. *signare*, to sign].

signet (sig′nẹt) *n.* seal, esp. privy seal, one of three royal seals used for authenticating documents.—**sig′net-ring** *n.* finger-ring on which is engraved monogram or initials of owner.—**Writer to the Signet**, in Scotland, solicitor corresponding to English attorney, privileged to prepare Crown writs [L. *signum*, a mark].

signify (sig′ni-fī) *v.t.* to make known by a sign; to convey notion of; to denote; to imply; to indicate; to mean;—*v.i.* to express meaning; to purport; to be of consequence.—*pa.t.* and *pa.p.* **sig′nified**.—**signif′icance** *n.* importance; force; weight; meaning; import; moment.—**signif′icant** *a.* fitted or designed to signify or make known something; important.—**signif′icantly** *adv.*—**significa′tion** *n.* act of signifying; that which is expressed by signs or words; meaning; sense.—**signif′icative** *a.*—**signif′icatory** *a.* having meaning [L. *significare*, fr. *signum*, a sign; *facere*, to make].

signor, signior (sē′nyor) *n.* Italian lord or gentleman; title of respect or address equivalent to *Mr.*—**signora** (sē-nyō′rạ) *n. fem.* of signor [It.].

Sikh (sēk, sik) *n.* one of a native religious and military community of the Punjab, India [Hind. = a disciple].

silage (sī′lāj) *n.* compressed, acid-fermented fodder, orig. packed green in a silo for preservation [fr. *ensilage*].

silence (sī′lẹns) *n.* stillness; quietness; calm; refraining from speech; muteness; dumbness; secrecy; oblivion;—*interj.* be quiet!;—*v.t.* to cause to be still; to forbid to speak; to hush; to calm; to refute; to gag; to kill.—**si′lencer** *n.* internal-combustion engine, a chamber into which the exhaust is passed, reducing or eliminating the noise.—**si′lent** *a.* free from sound or noise; indisposed to talk; unpronounced, as a vowel or consonant.—**si′lently** *adv.*—**si′lentness** *n.* [L. *silentium*].

silex (sī′leks) *n.* silica; any flinty substance as sand, quartz, flint, etc. [L. = flint].

silhouette (sil-ȯȯ-et′) *n.* portrait or picture cut from black paper or done in solid black upon a light ground; outline of object seen against the light;—*v.t.* to represent in outline; to cause to stand out in dark shadow against a light background [Fr.].

silica (sil′i-ka) *n.* silicon dioxide, main component of most rocks, occurring in nature as sand, flint, quartz, crystal, etc.—**sil′icate** *n.* salt of silicic acid.—**sil′icated** *a.* combined or coated with silica.—**silicate of soda**, water-glass.—**siliceous** (sil-ish′us) *a.* pert. to silica in a finely divided state. Also **silic′ious**.—**silicic** (sil-is′ik) *a.* derived from or containing silica.—**silic′ify** *v.t.* to convert into silica; to petrify;—*v.i.* to become siliceous.—*pa.t.* and *pa.p.* **silic′ified**.—**sil′icon** *n.* non-metallic dark-brown chemical element, chief constituent of many types of rock. Also **silicium** (si-lish′i-um).—**silico′sis** *n.* (*Med.*) chronic fibrosis of lung, caused by inhaling dust.—**silicot′ic** *a.* affected by silicosis [L. *silex*].

silicones (sil′i-kōnz) *n.pl.* new family of synthetic rubbers, made from same basic materials—petroleum, brine, ordinary sand [L. *silex*, flint].

silk (silk) *n.* fine, soft, lustrous thread obtained from cocoons made by larvae of certain moths, esp. silkworm; thread or fabric made from this; (*Colloq.*) King's Counsel;—*a.* made of silk.—**silk′en** *a.* made of, or resembling, silk; soft; smooth; silky.—**silk′hat** *n.* top hat covered with plush and ironed to produce high, silky polish.—**silk′iness** *n.* quality of being soft and smooth to the touch.—**silk′screen** *a.* and *n.* (pert. to) the reproduction of a design by means of a pattern made on a screen of nylon or silk.—**silk′worm** *n.* caterpillar of any moth which produces silk, esp. Bombyx mori.—**silk′y** *a.* made of, or pert. to, silk; silklike; smooth; glossy; soft; suave; agreeable.—**artificial silk**, rayon.—**to take silk**, to become a King's (Queen's) Counsel [O.E. *seoloc*].

sill (sil) *n.* base or foundation; horizontal member of stone, brick, or wood at the bottom of window frame, door, or opening [O.E. *syll*].

sillabub (sil′ạ-bub) *n.* milk or cream beaten up with sugar into froth; dish of sponge-cakes, fruits, and wine, covered with whipped cream; anything light or gossamer. Also **sill′ibub** [etym. uncertain].

sillibub See **sillabub**.

sillock, silloc (sil′ok) *n.* saithe or coal-fish. Also **sil′lik, sel′lok** [dim. of *sill*].

silly (sil′i) *a.* weak in intellect; foolish; senseless; stupid; indiscreet; (*Arch.*) simple; innocent; harmless;—*n.* silly person; booby;—*adv.* in a silly fashion.—**sill′ily** *adv.*—**sill′iness** *n.* foolishness.—**silly point**, in cricket, stance of fielder on off-side, in front of, and close to, batsman [O.E. *saelig*, happy, fortunate].

silo (sī′lō) *n.* large grain store or elevator; pit in which green crops are preserved for future use as fodder;—*v.t.* to preserve in a silo. Cf. **ensilage** [Sp.].

silt (silt) *n.* fine, alluvial, soil particles, between soils and clays, deposited from water; mud; slime; sediment;—*v.t.* to choke or obstruct with silt (generally with up);—*v.i.* to become filled up with silt; to ooze; to percolate [etym. uncertain].

Silurian (si-lū′ri-ạn) *a.* pert. to Silures who inhabited part of England and S. Wales; denoting group, or strata, of sedimentary rocks immediately below Old Red Sandstone; early palaeozoic; greyish-green.

silvan, sylvan (sil′vạn) *a.* pert. to woods or groves; wooded; rural.—**sil′va, syl′va** *n.* natural history of forest trees (of a country) [L. *silva*, a wood].

silver (sil′vẹr) *n.* soft, white, metallic element, very malleable and ductile; silverware; silver coins; anything resembling silver;—*a.* made of, or resembling, silver; white or grey, as hair; having a pale lustre, as moon; soft and melodious, as voice or sound; bright; silvery; —*v.t.* to coat or plate with silver; to apply amalgam of tin-foil and quicksilver to back of a mirror; to tinge with white or grey; to render smooth and bright;—*v.i.* to become gradually white, as hair.—**sil'ver-bath** *n.* solution of silver nitrate, used for sensitising plates in photography; flat dish used for this. —**silver birch**, forest tree with thin, silvery bark which peels off in long papery strips.—**sil'ver-fish** *n.* name applied to various varieties of fish, as smelt-like atherine, artificially bred gold-fish.—**sil'ver-fox** *n.* fox now specially bred in semi-captivity for its glossy, silver-tipped, black fur.—**sil'ver-gilt** *n.* silver or silver-plate with a thin coating of gold;—*a.* pert. to silver so covered.—**sil'ver-grey** *a.* of a grey or bluish-grey colour like that of silver.—**sil'veriness** *n.* state or quality of being silvery.—**sil'vering** *n.* process of coating glass with silver film; silver so used.—**sil'verise** *v.t.* to coat or cover thinly with a film of silver.—**sil'ver-leaf** *n.* silver beaten out into thin, fine leaf.—**sil'verling** *n.* small silver coin.—**silver lining**, prospect of better times to come.—**sil'vern** *a.* made of, or resembling, silver.—**silver paper**, tin-foil, a special quality of tissue-paper used for wrapping.—**sil'ver-plate** *n.* metallic articles coated with silver.—**sil'ver-pla'ted** *a.*—**sil'ver-pla'ting** *n.* deposition of silver on another metal by electrolysis.—**silver screen**, screen in cinemas; cinematography.—**sil'verside** *n.* upper part of a round of beef suitable for salting.—**sil'versmith** *n.* worker in silver.—**sil'ver-stick** *n.* field-officer of Life Guards on duty at royal palace whose insignia of office is a silver wand.—**sil'verware** *n.* articles made of silver.—**silver wedding**, 25th anniversary of marriage.—**sil'very** *a.* like silver; white; lustrous; (of sound) soft and clear [O.E. *siolfor*].

simar, simarre (si-mȧr') *n.* a woman's long dress or robe; also, a light covering; a scarf [Sp. *chamarra*, a sheepskin coat].

simia (sim'i-a) *n.* anthropoid ape; orang-utang; monkey or ape generally.—**sim'ian** *a.* Also **sim'ial** [L. = ape].

similar (sim'i-lar) *a.* like; resembling; exactly corresponding; (*Geom.*) of plane figures, differing in size but having all corresponding angles and side ratios uniform.—**similar'ity** *n.* quality or state of being similar.—**sim'ilarly** *adv.* [L. *similis*, like].

simile (sim'i-le) *n.* explicit statement of some point of resemblance observed to exist between two things which differ in other respects; similitude [L. *similis*, like].

similitude (si-mil'i-tūd) *n.* state of being similar or like; resemblance; likeness; parable [L. *similis*, like].

simmer (sim'er) *v.t.* to cause to boil gently; —*v.i.* to be just bubbling or just below boiling-point; to be in a state of suppressed anger or laughter;—*n.* gentle, gradual heating [imit. origin].

simnel (sim'nel) *n.* rich plum-cake offered as a gift at Christmas, Easter, or Mid-Lent; a simnel-cake [O.Fr. *simenel*].

simoniac (si-mō'ni-ak) *n.* one guilty of simony. —**simoni'acal** *a.*—**simoni'acally** *adv.*—**si'monist** *n.* one who practices simony [Cf. *simony*].

simony (sim'on-i, sī'mon-i) *n.* the offence of offering or accepting money or other reward for nomination or appointment to an ecclesiastical office. See *Acts* 8.

simoom (si-mōōm') *n.* hot, dry, sand-laden wind of N. Africa, Syria, Arabia. Also **simoon'** [Ar. *samm*, poison].

simper (sim'per) *v.i.* to smile in a silly, affected manner; to smirk;—*n.* smile with air of silliness or affectation.—**sim'perer** *n.* [etym. uncertain].

simple (sim'pl) *a.* single; not complex; entire; mere; plain; honest; clear; intelligible; simple-minded; (*Chem.*) elementary; (*Med.*) non-malignant;—*n.* something not compounded; ingredient; medicinal herb.—**sim'ple-heart'ed** *a.* artless; guileless; sincere.—**simple interest**, money paid on principal borrowed but not on accrued interest as in compound interest.—**sim'ple-mind'ed** *a.* ingenuous; open; frank; unsuspecting; harmless.—**sim'pleness** *n.* quality or state of being simple; artlessness; innocence; weakness of intellect; simplicity.—**sim'pleton** *n.* foolish person; person of weak intellect.—**simplic'ity** *n.* artlessness of mind; sincerity; clearness; simpleness.—**simplifica'tion** *n.* act of making simple or clear; thing simplified.—**sim'plificative** *a.* tending to simplify.—**sim'plify** *v.t.* to make or render simple, plain, or easy.—*pa.t.* and *pa.p.* **sim'plified.**—**sim'ply** *adv.* in a simple manner; plainly; unostentatiously; without affectation; absolutely; foolishly [L. *simplus*].

simulacrum (sim-ū-lā'krum) *n.* image; phantom; representation; semblance; a sham. —*pl.* **simula'cra** [L.].

simulant (sim'ū-lant) *a.* simulating; having the appearance of;—*n.* one simulating something.—**sim'ular** *a.* simulated; counterfeit; feigned;—*n.* one who pretends to be what he is not; hypocrite; a simulator.

simulate (sim'ū-lāt) *v.t.* to assume the mere appearance of, without the reality; to feign; to mimic; to counterfeit.—**simula'tion** *n.*—**sim'ulator** *n.* [*L. simulare*, to make like].

simultaneous (sim-ul-tā'nē-us) *a.* existing or occurring at same time; (*Alg.*) of set of equations satisfied by same values of the variables or unknown quantities.—**simultane'ity, simulta'neousness** *n.* quality or state of happening at same time.—**simulta'neously** *adv.* [L. *simul*].

sin (sin) *n.* transgression against divine or moral law, esp. when committed consciously; conduct or state of mind of a habitual or unrepentantsinner; moraldepravity; iniquity; wickedness; ungodliness; evil; immorality; crime; trespass;—*v.i.* to depart from path of duty prescribed by God; to violate any rule of duty; to do wrong.—*pr.p.* **sin'ning.**—*pa.t.* and *pa.p.* **sinned.**—**sin'ful** *a.* iniquitous; wicked; unholy.—**sin'fully** *adv.*—**sin'fulness** *n.* depravity; moral corruption.—**sin'ner** *n.* one who sins; morally depraved person.—**mortal sin**, serious transgression of divine law, committed with due deliberation.—**original sin**, inherent tendency to sin born within us, legacy from original sin of Adam.—**venial sin**, pardonable, or less serious, lapse into wrongdoing [O.E. *synn*].

since (sins) *adv.* from then till now; subsequently; ago;—*prep.* at some time subsequent to; after;—*conj.* from the time that; seeing that; because that; inasmuch as [earlier *sithens*, O.E. *siththan*].

sincere (sin-sēr') *a.* not assumed or merely professed; straightforward.—**sincere'ly** *adv.*—**sincere'ness, sincer'ity** *n.* state or quality of being sincere; honesty of mind or intention; truthfulness; genuineness [L. *sincerus*, pure].

sine (sīn) *n.* (*abbrev.* **sin**) (*Math.*) perpendicular drawn from one extremity of an arc to diameter drawn through other extremity; function of one of the two acute angles in a right-angle triangle, ratio of line subtending this angle to hypotenuse [L. *sinus*, a curve].

sinecure (sī'nē-kūr, sin'e-kūr) *n.* orig. an ecclesiastical benefice without cure of souls; office, position, etc. with salary but without duties.—**si'necurist** *n.* one who holds, or seeks sinecure [L. *sine cura*, without care].

sinew (sin'ū) *n.* ligament or tendon which joins muscle to bone; muscle; nerve;—*pl.* strength; source of strength or vigour.—**sin'ewed** *a.* having sinews; strong; firm, vigorous.—**sin'ewiness** *n.* quality or state of being sinewy.—**sin'ewous** *a.* sinewy.—**sin'ewy** *a.* well braced with sinews; muscular; nervous; strong [O.E. *sinu*].

sing (sing) *v.t.* to utter with musical modulations of voice; to celebrate in song; to praise in verse;—*v.i.* to utter sounds with melodious modulations of voice; to pipe, twitter, chirp, as birds; to hum, as a kettle on the boil; to reverberate.—*pa.t.* **sang** or **sung**.—*pa.p.* **sung**. —**sing'er** *n.* one who sings, esp. one who sings well; vocalist.—**sing'ing** *n.* art of singing; vocal music; a humming noise (in the ear, on a telephone circuit, etc.).—**sing'ing-gall'ery** *n.* a gallery in church for choir [O.E. *singan*].

singe (sinj) *v.t.* to burn slightly the surface of; to scorch; to char; to burn loose fluff from yarns.—*pr.p.* **singe'ing**.—*n.* superficial burn [O.E. *sencgan*, to make hiss].

Singhalese Same as **Cingalese**.

single (sing'gl) *a.* sole; alone; separate; individual; not double; unmarried; (ticket) valid for journey in one direction only; sincere; whole-hearted; straightforward; upright;—*n.* unit; (*Cricket*) one run; (*Tennis*) game confined to two opponents; ticket valid for journey in one direction only;—*v.t.* (with *out*) to select from among a number; to pick; to choose.—**sing'le-bless'edness** *n.* celibacy; state of being unmarried.—**sing'le-breast'ed** *a.* of a garment, buttoning on one side only.—**sing'le-deck'er** *n.* passenger vehicle having no roof seats.—**sing'le-en'try** *n.* in bookkeeping, entry of each transaction on one side only of an account.—**sing'le-hand'ed** *a.* and *adv.* without help; unassisted.—**sing'le-heart'ed** *a.* sincere; guileless; without duplicity.—**single'mind'ed** *a.* having but one purpose or aim; honest; upright; sincere.—**sing'leness** *n.* state of being single; honesty of purpose; freedom from deceit or guile; sincerity.—**sing'le-stick** *n.* fencing with a basket-hilted ash-stick; stick used.—**sing'ly** *adv.* one by one; by oneself; individually; alone; sincerely; single-mindedly [L. *singuli*, one at a time].

singlet (sing'glet) *n.* undervest [fr. *single*].

singleton (sing'gl-ton) *n.* (*Cards*) hand containing only one card of some suit, or the card itself [dim. of *single*].

singsong (sing'song) *n.* drawling, monotonous fashion of uttering; droning; impromptu gathering where all contribute a song or join in communal singing;—*a.* monotonous; droning [redup. of *sing*].

singular (sing'gū-lar) *a.* existing by itself; denoting one person or thing; individual; unique;—*n.* single instance; word in the singular number.—**sing'ularise** *v.t.* to make singular or unique.—**singular'ity** *n.* state of being singular; anything unusual or remarkable; strangeness of manner or appearance; oddity.—**sing'ularly** *adv.* in a singular manner; strangely; remarkably [L. *singularis*].

Sinhalese *n.* and *a.* See **Cingalese**.

Sinic (sin'ik) *a.* Chinese.—**sin'icise** *v.t.* to give a Chinese character to.—**sin'icism** *n.* mode of thought or customs peculiar to the Chinese [Gk. *Sinai*, the Chinese].

sinister (sin'is-ter) *a.* on left hand; evil-looking; unlucky (left being regarded as unlucky side); threatening; (*Her.*) side of escutcheon on left of person standing behind it.—**sin'isterly** *adv.* in a sinister manner.—**sin'istral** *a.* to the left; reversed; (*Bot.*) having whorls not turning normally [L. = on the left hand].

sink (singk) *v.t.* to cause to sink; to submerge; to lower out of sight; to dig; to excavate; to ruin; to suppress; to invest;—*v.i.* to fall; to subside; to descend; to penetrate (into); to decline in value, health, or social status; to be dying; to droop; to decay; to become submerged; to yield.—*pa.t.* **sank** or **sunk**.—*pa.p.* **sunk**.—*n.* a receptacle for washing up, with pipe for carrying away waste water; marsh or area in which river water percolates through surface and disappears; place notoriously associated with evildoing; filthy dwelling-place; cesspool.—**sink'er** *n.* weight fixed to anything to make it sink, as on net, fishing-line, etc.—**sink'ing** *n.* operation of excavating; subsidence; settling; abatement; ebb; part sunk below surrounding surface.—**sinking fund**, fund set aside at regular intervals to provide replacement of wasting asset or repayment of particular liability at a fixed future date [O.E. *sincan*].

Sinn Fein (shin fān') *n.* Irish policy and movement which aimed at independent self-government.—**Sinn Fein'er** *n.* [Ir. = we ourselves].

Sino-Japanese (sī'no-jap-a-nēz') *a.* pert. to China and Japan [Gk. *Sinai*, Chinese].

sinology (sī-nol'o-ji) *n.* that branch of knowledge which deals with the Chinese language, culture, history, religion and art.—**sinol'ogist, sin'ologue** *n.* one versed in Chinese culture and language [Gk. *Sinai*, the Chinese; *logos*, a discourse].

sinter (sin'ter) *n.* silica deposited in neighbourhood of geysers and hot springs; partial fusion under influence of heat (Ger. *sintern*, to drop].

sinuate (sin'ū-āt) *v.t.* and *v.i.* to bend in and out; to wind; to turn;—*a.* (*Bot.*) wavy; tortuous; curved on the margin, as a leaf. Also **sin'uated**.—**sinua'tion** *n.*—**sin'uose, sin'uous** *a.* bending in and out; of serpentine or undulating form; morally crooked; supple.—**sinuos'ity** *n.* quality of being sinuous.—**sin'uously** *adv.* [L. *sinus*, a fold].

sinus (sī'nus) *n.* opening; hollow; cavity; groove or passage in tissues leading to a deep-seated abscess, usually in nose or ear.—**sinusi'tis** *n.* inflammation of sinus, esp. of bones of forehead or jaws [L. *sinus*, a curve].

Sioux (sôô) *n.* member of great Siouan division of N. American aborigines; their language.—*pl.* **Sioux** (sôô, sôôz) [Fr. form of native word].

sip (sip) *v.t.* and *v.i.* to drink or imbibe in very small quantities; to taste.—*pr.p.* **sip'ping**.—*pa.t.* and *pa.p.* **sipped**.—*n.* a portion of liquid sipped with the lips; a mouthful [O.E. *sypian*, to soak].

siphon, syphon (sī'fon) *n.* a bent tube or pipe by which a liquid can be transferred by atmospheric pressure from one receptacle to another; bottle provided with internal tube and lever top, for holding and delivering aerated water; projecting tube in mantle of shell of bivalve along which currents of water can flow;—*v.t.* to draw off by means of a siphon.—**si'phonage, sy'phonage** *n.* action of a siphon [Gk. = tube].

sir (ser) *n.* a title of respect to any man of position; title of knight or baronet; formerly priest or curate; sirrah [var. of *sire*].

sirdar (ser'dår, ser-dår') *n.* in India, a native chief; a leader; a military officer [Pers. *sar*, head; *dar*, holding].

sire (sīr) *n.* father; one who stands in the relation of a father, as a king or emperor; male parent of an animal (applied esp. to horses); —*pl.* ancestors;—*v.t.* to beget (of animals) [Fr. fr. L. *senior*, elder].

siren (sī'ren) *n.* (*Myth.*) one of several nymphs said to sing with such sweetness that sailors were lured to death; mermaid; sweet singer; seductive alluring woman; form of horn which emits series of loud, piercing notes used as warning signal of approaching danger; steam-whistle or hooter; the mud-eel;—*a.* pert. to, or resembling a siren; alluring; seductive [Gk. *Seirēn*].

Sirius (sir'i-us) *n.* (*Astron.*) a fixed star of the first magnitude known as the Dog-star (Canis Major) [L.].

sirloin (ser'loin) *n.* the upper part of a loin of beef [O.Fr. *surloigne*].

sirocco (si-rok'ō) *n.* a hot, southerly, dust-laden wind from Africa, chiefly experienced in Italy, Malta and Sicily [It.].

sirop, sirup See **syrup**.

sirrah (ser'a) *n.* (*Archaic*) term formerly

applied to man to express reproach or contempt [form of *sir*].

sisal (sis′al, sī′sal) *n.* fibre plant, native to Florida and Yucatan providing **sis′al-grass** (**sis′al-hemp**) [*Sisal*, a seaport in Yucatan].

sissy (sis′i) *n.* (*Colloq.*) sister; ineffective effeminate man or boy;—*a.* effeminate.

sister (sis′tẹr) *n.* female whose parents are same as those of another person; correlative of brother; woman of the same faith; female of the same society, convent, abbey; nun;—*a.* standing in relation of sister; related; of a similar nature to, as institute, college, etc.—**sis′ter-ger′man** *n.* a full sister.—**sis′terhood** *n.* state of being a sister; society of women united in one faith or order.—**sis′ter-in-law** *n.* husband's or wife's sister; brother's wife.—*pl.* **sis′ters-in-law.**—**sis′ter′like, sis′terly** *a.* like a sister; becoming or befitting a sister; affectionate [O.N. *systir*].

Sistine (sis′tin, sis-tēn) *a.* pert. to any Pope named Sixtus.—**Sistine Chapel,** the Pope's private chapel in the Vatican at Rome, built in 1473 for Pope Sixtus VI.

sit (sit) *v.i.* to rest upon haunches, a seat, etc.; to remain; to rest; to perch, as birds; (of hen) to cover and warm eggs for hatching; to be officially engaged in transacting business, as court, council, etc.; to be in session; to be representative in Parliament for constituency; to pose for portrait; to press or weigh (upon); to be in a particular quarter, as wind; to fit (of clothes);—*v.t.* to keep good seat, upon, as on horseback; to place upon seat; to put carefully in position; to compete in (examination).—*pr.p.* **sit′ting.**—*pa.t.* and *pa.p.* **sat.**—*n.* position assumed by an object after being placed.—**sit′ter** *n.* one who sits; one who poses for artist; an easy catch, shot, or target; bird sitting on its eggs.—**sit′ting** *n.* state of resting on a seat, etc.; act of placing oneself on a seat; session; business meeting; occasion when food is served to group of people; time given up to posing for artist; clutch of eggs for incubation;—*a.* resting on haunches; perched.—**sit′ting-room** *n.* room for sitting in; parlour; reception-room; small drawing-room; waiting-room.—**sit-down strike,** form of strike in which strikers refuse to leave their place of work.—**to sit for,** to represent in parliament; to pose for an artist [O.E. *sittan*].

site (sīt) *n.* place, situation; plot of ground for, or with, building; position; place where anything is fixed;—*v.t.* to place in position; to locate [L. *situs*, a site].

sith (sith) *adv. prep.* and *conj.* since.—**sith′ence, sith′ens** [short for M.E. *sithen*].

sitology, sitiology (sī-tol′o-ji, sit-i-ol′o-ji) *n.* that department of medicine which relates to the regulation of diet; dietetics [Gk. *sitos*, food; *logos*, a discourse].

situate (sit′ū-āt) *v.t.* to give a site to; to place in a particular state or set of circumstances; to place; to locate;—*a.* located; situated;—**situa′ted** *a.* resident; located; placed with reference to other affairs, etc.; conditioned.—**situa′tion** *n.* location; place or position; seat; site; condition; job; office; post; plight; predicament [L. *situs*, a site].

six (siks) *a.* one more than five;—*n.* sum of three and three; symbol 6 or VI.—**six′er** *n.* hit scoring six at cricket.—**six′fold** *a.* six times as much or as many.—**six′footer** *n.* person six feet in height.—**six′pence** *n.* silver coin in British currency of value of six pennies.—**six′penny** *a.* worth sixpence; bought or sold for sixpence; paltry; cheap; of small value.—**six′shoot′er** *n.* a six-chambered revolver.—**six′teen** *n.* and *a.* six and ten, symbol 16 or XVI.—**six′teenth** *a.* sixth after the tenth; being one of sixteen equal parts into which anything is divided;—*n.* one of sixteen equal parts; a division of the inch, in common usage; (*Mus.*) semiquaver.—**sixth** *a.* next in order after the fifth; one of six equal parts;—*n.* (*Mus.*) an interval comprising six degrees of the staff, as A to F.—**sixth′ly** *adv.*—**six′ty** *a.* six times ten; three score;—*n.* symbol 60 or LX.—**six′tieth** *a.* next in order after the fifty-ninth; one of sixty equal parts;—*n.*—**at sixes and sevens,** in disorder and confusion [O.E. *siex*].

sizar (sī′zar) *n.* student at Cambridge or Dublin Universities charged lower fees [O.Fr. *size*, allowance of food].

size (sīz) *n.* bulk; bigness; comparative magnitude; dimensions; extent; conventional measure of dimension;—*v.t.* to arrange according to size.—**si′zable** *a.* of considerable size or bulk.—**size′stick** *n.* boot-retailer's instrument used for measuring length of foot.—**to size up,** to estimate possibilities of; to take measure of [contr. of *assize*].

size (sīz) *n.* substance of a gelatinous nature, like weak glue;—*v.t.* to treat or cover with size [Fr. *assise*, a layer (e.g. of paint, etc.)].

sizzle (siz′l) *v.i.* to make hissing or sputtering noise; to shrivel up;—*n.* hissing, sputtering noise; extreme heat.—**sizz′ling** *n.* [imit. word].

sjambok (shȧm′bok) *n.* short, heavy horse-whip, made of strip of dried, rhinoceros hide [Afrikaans].

skald See **scald.**

skate (skāt) *n.* steel blade with framework to attach it to boot, used for gliding over ice;—*v.i.* to travel over ice on skates.—**ska′ter** *n.*—**ska′ting** *n.*—**ska′ting-rink** *n.* stretch of ice (usually under cover) for skating; ice-rink.—**roll′er-skate** *n.* skate with castors in place of steel blade [Dut. *schaats*].

skate (skāt) *n.* a large, edible, flat fish of the ray family [O.N. *skata*].

skathe See **scathe.**

skean (skēn) *n.* Highland dagger or dirk; long knife. Also **skeen, skene.**—**skean′-dhu** (dōō) *n.* dirk worn in top of stocking [Gael. *sgian*, knife; *dubh*, black].

skedaddle (ske-dad′l) *v.i.* (*Colloq.*) to scamper off;—*n.* hasty, disorderly flight [etym. unknown].

skeen See **skean.**

skein (skān) *n.* small hank, of fixed length, of thread, silk, or yarn, doubled and secured by loose knot; knot of thread or yarn; a flight of wild geese or swans.—**a tangled skein,** a complicated, confused affair [O.Fr. *escaigne*].

skeleton (skel′e-ton) *n.* bony framework providing support for human or animal body; any framework, as of building, plant, etc.; general outline;—*a.* pert. to skeleton; containing mere outlines. Also **skel′etal.**—**skeleton crew, staff, etc.,** minimum number of men employed on some essential duty.—**skel′eton-key** *n.* key designed to open or pick lock by avoiding impeding wards [Gk. *skeletos*, dried up].

skellum (skel′um) *n.* a blackguard; a good-for-nothing; a rascal [Ger. *Schelm*, a rogue].

skelter (skel′tẹr) *v.i.* to rush; to hurry; to dash along. See **helter-skelter.**

skene See **skean.**

skep (skep) *n.* beehive made of straw; light basket [O.N. *skeppa*, a basket].

skepsis, skeptic See **sceptic.**

skerry (sker′i) *n.* rocky isle; reef; piece of lime in brick-earth [O.N. *sker*].

sketch (skech) *n.* first rough draught or plan of any design; outline; drawing in pen, pencil, or similar medium; descriptive essay or account, in light vein; a short, humorous one-act play;—*v.t.* to draw outline of; to make rough draught of; to plan by giving principal ideas of;—*v.i.* to draw; to make sketches.—**sketch′er** *n.*—**sketch′ily** *adv.*—**sketch′iness** *n.* lack of detail.—**sketch′y** *a.* containing outline or rough form; inadequate; incomplete [Dut. *schets*].

skew (skū) *a.* awry; oblique; askew; off the straight;—*adv.* awry; obliquely;—*n.* anything set obliquely or at an angle to some other object; a deviation;—*v.t.* to put askew; to turn aside;—*v.i.* to walk sideways; to shy; to skid.—**skew′bald** *a.* of horse, bay and white in patches.—**skewed** *a.* distorted.—**skew′-eyed** *a.*

squinting.—**skew'gee** *a.* off the straight; crooked [O.Fr. *escuer*].
skewer (skū'ẹr) *n.* pointed rod for fastening meat to a spit, or for keeping it in form while roasting (formerly used instead of pins);—*v.t.* to fasten with skewers [etym. uncertain].
ski (skē, in Norway, shē) *n.* long wooden runner strapped to foot, for running, sliding and jumping over snow;—*v.i.* to run, slide, or jump on skis.—**skier** (skē'er, shē'er) *n.* one who skis [Norw.].
skiagraph (skī'a-graf) *n.* an X-ray photograph. Also **ski'agram.**—**skiag'rapher** *n.* one who takes X-ray photographs.—**skiagraph'ic** *a.* [Gk. *skia*, a shadow; *graphein*, to write].
skid (skid) *n.* a piece of timber to protect side of vessel from injury; drag placed under wheel to check speed of vehicle descending steep gradient; inclined plane down which logs, etc. slide;—*v.i.* to slide along without revolving; to slip;—*v.t.* to slide a log down an incline; to place on skids.—**skid'way** *n.* inclined plane down which logs slide [O.N. *skidh*].
skied (skīd) *pa.t.* and *pa.p.* of **sky.**
skiff (skif) *n.* long, narrow sculling-boat, of light structure, for one rower; any light, small boat [Fr. *esquif*].
skiffle (skifl) *a.* and *n.* (descriptive of) a kind of folk-music in the playing of which a group of musicians accompany a singing guitarist and give him exaggerated rhythmic support on a variety of instruments, e.g. rattles, whistles, drums, etc.—**skiffl'er** *n.* a player of skiffle music [orig. unknown].
skill (skil) *n.* practical ability and dexterity; knowledge; understanding; expertness; aptitude.—**skil'ful** *a.* expert; skilled; adept; adroit; dexterous.—**skil'fully** *adv.*—**skil'fulness** *n.*—**skilled** *a.* having knowledge, united with dexterity [O.N. *skil*, distinction].
skillet (skil'et) *n.* small metal vessel with long handle, for heating water, stewing vegetables, etc. [O.Fr. *escuellete*].
skilly (skil'i) *n.* watery soup or gruel [etym. unknown].
skim (skim) *v.t.* to remove from surface of liquid; to glide over lightly and rapidly; to glance over print in superficial way; to graze;—*v.i.* to pass lightly over; to glide along; to hasten over superficially.—*pr.p.* **skim'ming.**—*pa.t.* and *pa.p.* **skimmed.**—*n.* thick matter which forms on surface of liquid; scum.—**skim'mer** *n.* one who, or that which, skims.—**skim'-milk** *n.* milk from which cream has been removed [O.Fr. *escumer*].
skimp (skimp) *v.t.* to stint; to do imperfectly;—*v.i.* to be mean or parsimonious; to economise in petty fashion;—*a.* scanty; spare; meagre.—**skimp'y** *a.* scant; meagre [etym. uncertain].
skin (skin) *n.* external protective covering of animal bodies; epidermis; a hide; a pelt; receptacle of skin for water or wine; exterior coat of fruits and plants; husk or bark; thick scum;—*v.t.* to strip off skin or hide of; to flay; to graze; to peel; to cheat; to swindle;—*v.i.* to peel off; to become covered with skin.—**skin'-deep** *a.* superficial.—**skin'-flint** *n.* miser; niggard.—**skin'ful** *n.* as much as the stomach can hold.—**skin'-game** *n.* wholesale cheating and swindling.—**skin'-graft'ing** *n.* transplanting healthy skin to wound to form a new skin.—**skin'ner** *n.* dealer in hides; furrier.—**skin'niness** *n.* leanness.—**skin'ny** *a.* having thick skin; of skin; very lean or thin; mean; grasping.—**skin'-tight** *a.* fitting close to skin.—**skin'-tights** *n.pl.* theatrical costume fitting close to limbs.—**to have a thick skin,** to be not at all sensitive.—**by the skin of one's teeth,** very narrowly [O.N. *skinn*].
skip (skip) *v.t.* to lean over lightly; to omit;—*v.i.* to leap lightly, esp. in frolic; to frisk; to clear repeatedly a rope swung in play under one's feet; to run away hastily; to pay hurried visits.—*pr.p.* **skip'ping.**—*pa.t.* and *pa.p.* **skipped.**—*n.* light leap, spring, or bound.—**skipped area** (*Radio*) area where signals from a transmitting station are not audible although heard much farther away owing to reflection from ionosphere.—**skip'per** *n.* one who skips.—**skip'ping** *a.* characterised by skips; flighty; giddy.—**skip'pingly** *adv.* [etym. uncertain].
skip (skip) *n.* a rectangular steel box with a hinged door, working in guides in a mine-shaft, used for hoisting ore, etc.; bucket hanging from cableway for transporting minerals, etc. Also **skep** [O.E. *scep*].
skip (skip) *n.* captain of bowling or curling team;—*v.t.* and *v.i.* to act as this.
skipper (skip'ẹr) *n.* captain of ship or team [Dut. *schipper*].
skir (skẹr) *v.t.* to scour; to ramble over;—*v.i.* to move rapidly. Also **scur** [fr. *scour*].
skirl (skẹrl) *v.i.* to scream shrilly;—*n.* shrill, high-pitched scream; music of bagpipe [var. of *shrill*].
skirmish (skẹr'mish) *n.* irregular, minor engagement between two parties of soldiers; brush; encounter;—*v.i.* to take part in skirmish.—**skir'misher** *n.* [Fr. *escarmouche*].
skirt (skẹrt) *n.* lower part of coat, gown; outer garment of a woman fitted to and hanging from waist; petticoat; edge of any part of dress; flap; border; margin; edge; rim; diaphragm of animal; midriff of beef;—*v.t.* to border; to pass or go round edge of;—*v.i.* to be on border.—**skirt'ing** *n.* material for women's skirts; border.—**skirt'ing-board** *n.* narrow, moulded board between plaster of internal wall and floor [O.N. *skyrta*].
skit (skit) *n.* satirical gibe; squib; lampoon; caricature; burlesque; stage parody.—*v.t.* to burlesque; to write a skit upon;—*v.i.* to leap aside; to shy.—**skitt'ish** *a.* frisky; frivolous; fickle; volatile; timid.—**skitt'ishly** *adv.*—**skitt'ishness** *n.* [etym. uncertain].
skittles (skit'lz) *n.pl.* nine-pins, game in which object is to overturn nine wooden skittles.—**to skittle out,** to bowl out opposing batsmen in rapid succession [form of *shuttle*].
skive (skiv) *v.t.* in shoe-making, to pare away or bevel edges of leather; to grind (diamonds) on skive;—*n.* high-speed metal lap or wheel for polishing diamonds [Ice. *skifa*, to split].
skivvy (skiv'i) *n.* (*Colloq.*) domestic servant [etym. doubtful].
skoal (skōl) *interj.* salutation, hail! in toasting [Dan. *skaal*, bowl; a toast].
skoff (skof) *n.* in S. Africa, food;—*v.t.* (*Slang*) to eat greedily; to bolt food [Dut. *schofttijd*, breakfast, meal-time].
skua (skū'a) *n.* family of Arctic or Antarctic birds, allied to the gulls [O.N. *skufr*].
skulk (skulk) *v.i.* to sneak out of the way; to lurk or keep out of sight in a furtive manner; to act sullenly;—*n.* one who skulks [etym. uncertain].
skull (skul) *n.* bony framework which encloses brain; cranium along with bones of face.—**skull'cap** *n.* metal headpiece; brimless cap fitting close to head [M.E. *skulle*].
skunk (skungk) *n.* small N. American burrowing animal, allied to weasel and otter, which defends itself by emitting evil-smelling fluid; a base, mean person [N. Amer.-Ind. *seganku*].
sky (skī) *n.* the apparent vault of heaven; heavens; firmament; weather; climate.—*pl.* **skies.**—*v.t.* to hit ball so as to rise almost perpendicularly; to hang high on wall, esp. picture.—*pa.t.* and *pa.p.* **skied.**—**sky'-blue** *n.* and *a.* azure; cerulean.—**sky'er** *n.* ball hit high into air.—**sky'ey** *a.* like the sky. Also **ski'ey.**—**sky'gaz'er** *n.* visionary.—**sky'-high** *a.* and *adv.* at a great elevation; carried away with excitement or anticipation.—**sky'lark** *n.* bird which sings as it soars;—*v.i.* to indulge in boisterous byplay.—**sky'-lark'ing** *n.* orig. playing frolicsome pranks about rigging of ship; noisy frolicking and horse-play.—**sky'light** *n.* glazed opening in roof of ceiling.—**sky'line** *n.* horizon.—**sky'-pi'lot** *n.* clergyman.—**sky'scraper** *n.* lofty

building with numerous storeys, characteristic of American architecture; triangular sky-sail. —**sky'sign** *n.* advertising sign perched high upon building against skyline; design traced in sky by trail of smoke from aeroplane.—**sky'writ'ing** *n.* writing in air for advertising or propaganda purposes by sky-sign method [O.N. *sky*, a cloud].

Skye (skī) *n.* or **Skye'terr'ier**, breed of Scotch terrier, with long hair, long body and short legs, orig. bred in Skye.

slab (slab) *n.* thickish, flat, rectangular piece of anything; concrete paving-block; thick slice of cake, etc.; outside piece of a log during sawing;—*v.t.* to cut or split in form of slabs [etym. uncertain].

slabber (slab'er) *v.i.* to slaver, slobber, dribble;—*v.t.* to cover with saliva. Also **slobb'er.**—**slabb'erer, slobb'erer** *n.* [var. of *slaver*].

slack (slak) *a.* not taut; not closely drawn together; not holding fast; remiss about one's duties; easy-going;—*n.* part of a rope which hangs loose; quiet time.—**slack, slack'en** *v.t.* to loosen; to moderate; to relax; to diminish; to abate; to slake;—*v.i.* to become slack; to lose cohesion; to relax; to dodge work; to languish; to flag.—**slack'er** *n.* one who shirks work.—**slack'ly** *adv.*—**slack'ness** *n.*—**slacks** *n.pl.* loose trousers worn by men or women.—**to slack(en) off,** to lessen one's energies; to ease off [O.E. *slaec*].

slack (slak) *n.* the finer screenings of coal which pass through a half-inch mesh; coal-dust; dross.—**slack'heap** *n.* a dump for slack [Ger. *Schlacke*, dross].

slade (slād) *n.* little dell; flat, undrained ground; open space in a wood; peat spade; sloping pathway [O.E. *slaed*].

slag (slag) *n.* fusible silicate formed during smelting of ores; scoriae of a volcano;—*v.i.* to form slag;—*v.t.* to tap out slag during smelting.—**slag'gy** *a.* pert. to, like, slag [Ger. *Schlacke*, dross].

slain (slān) *pa.p.* of the verb **slay.**

slake (slāk) *v.t.* to quench; to extinguish; to combine quicklime with water; to slacken;—*v.i.* to become mixed with water; to become extinct; to diminish.—**slaked lime,** hydrate of lime formed by mixing quicklime and water [O.E. *slacian*].

slam (slam) *v.t.* to shut violently and noisily; to bang; to hit; to dash down; to win all, or all but one, of the tricks at cards.—*pr.p.* **slam'ming.**—*pa.t.* and *pa.p.* **slammed.**—*n.* act of slamming; bang.—**slam (grand or little)** thirteen or twelve tricks taken in one deal in cards [imit. origin].

slander (slan'der) *n.* false or malicious statement about person; defamation of character by spoken word; calumny;—*v.t.* to injure by maliciously uttering false report; to defame. —**slan'derer** *n.*—**slan'derous** *a.* calumnious; infamous.—**slan'derously** *adv.*—**slan'derousness** *n.* [Fr. *esclandre*].

slang (slang) *n.* word or expression in common colloquial use but not regarded as standard English; jargon peculiar to certain sections of public, trades, etc.; argot;—*a.* pert. to slang; —*v.t.* to vituperate; to revile; to scold.—**slang'ily** *adv.*—**slang'iness** *n.*—**slang'y** *a.* of nature of, or given to use of, slang [etym. uncertain].

slant (slant) *v.t.* to turn from a direct line; to give a sloping direction to;—*v.i.* to lie obliquely; to slope; to incline;—*n.* slanting direction or position; slope; a gibe; oblique point of view or illuminating remark (on); puff of wind;—*a.* inclining; sloping; oblique. —**slan'tingly** *adv.*—**slant'ly, slant'wise** *adv.* in slanting, oblique, or indirect direction or manner; aslant [Swed. *slinta*, to slide].

slap (slap) *n.* blow with open hand or flat instrument;—*v.t.* to strike with open hand or something flat.—*pr.p.* **slap'ping.**—*pa.t.* and *pa.p.* **slapped.**—*adv.* with a sudden blow; instantly; directly.—**slap'bang** *adv.* suddenly; violently; headlong.—**slap'dash** *adv.* impetuously;—*a.* careless; slipshod.—**slap'stick** *n.* wooden wand carried by harlequin, to produce illusion of resounding smack when used in knock-about farce; boisterous knock-about farce of pantomime or music-hall.—**slap'up** *a.* (*Colloq.*) up-to-date; grand; stylish [imit. origin].

slash (slash) *v.t.* to cut by striking violently and haphazardly; to make gashes in; to slit; —*v.i.* to strike violently and at random with edged weapon;—*n.* long cut; gash; cutting stroke; large slit in garment.—**slash'er** *n.* [O.Fr. *esclachier*, to sever].

slat (slat) *n.* narrow strip of wood or stone; a lath.—*pl.* (*Slang*) ribs.—**slat'ted** *a.* covered with slats [O.Fr. *esclat*, fragment].

slate (slāt) *n.* a form of shale, composed mainly of aluminium silicate, which splits readily into thin leaves; prepared piece of such stone, esp. thin piece for roofing houses, etc.; table for writing upon; dark blue-grey colour;—*a.* made of slate; bluish-grey;—*v.t.* to cover with slates; to upbraid; to reprimand.—**slate'clay** *n.* shale.—**slate'col'oured** *a.* dark bluish-grey. Also **slate'grey.**—**slate'pen'cil** *n.* stick of soft slate or moulded slate powder, for writing on slates.—**sla'ter** *n.* one who shapes slates or covers roofs with slates; wood-louse.—**sla'ting** *n.* act of covering with slates; roof-covering thus put on; severe reprimand; harsh criticism.—**sla'ty** *a.* having nature or colour of slate [O.Fr. *esclat*, a splinter].

slatter (slat'er) *v.t.* to waste; to spill or lose carelessly;—*v.i.* to be careless of dress and dirty.—**slatt'ern** *n.* slut; sloven.—**slatt'ernliness** *n.*—**slatt'ernly** *a.* like a slattern;—*adv.* in slovenly, untidy manner.—**slatt'ery** *a.* wet; dirty [Scand. *slat*, to strike].

slaughter (slaw'ter) *n.* act of slaughtering; carnage; massacre; butchery; bloodshed; killing of animals to provide food;—*v.t.* to kill; to slay in battle; to butcher.—**slaugh'terer** *n* —**slaugh'terhouse** *n.* place where cattle are slaughtered.—**slaugh'terous** *a.* bent on slaughter; murderously-inclined; destructive.—**slaugh'terously** *adv.* [O.N. *slatr*, butcher's meat].

Slav, Sclav (slàv) *n.* a member of a group of peoples in E. and S.E. Europe, comprising Russians, Ukrainians, White Russians, Poles, Czechs, Slovaks, Serbians, Croats, Slovenes and Bulgarians;—*a.* relating to the Slavs; Slavic; Slavonic.—**Slav'ic** *a.*—**Slavon'ic, Sclavon'ic** *a.* Slavic [etym. unknown].

slave (slāv) *n.* person held legally in bondage to another; bondman; vassal; serf; drudge; one who has lost all powers of resistance to some pernicious habit or vice;—*v.i.* to work like a slave, to toil unremittingly.—**slave'dri'ver** *n.* an overseer in charge of slaves at work; exacting task-master.—**slave'mar'ket** *n.* bazaar for sale of slaves.—**sla'ver** *n.* person or ship engaged in slave traffic.—**sla'very** *n.* condition of slave compelled to perform compulsory work for another; bondage; servitude; drudgery.—**slave'ship** *n.* vessel used for transporting slaves.—**slave'trade** *n.* traffic in human beings.—**slave'tra'der** *n.*—**sla'vey** *n.* (*Slang*) domestic servant, esp. general servant.—**sla'vish** *a.* pert. to slaves; menial; drudging; servile; obsequious; cringing; fawning; base; mean.—**sla'vishly** *adv.*—**sla'vishness** *n.*—**white slavery,** traffic in women and girls for immoral purposes abroad [Fr. *esclave*, fr. *Slav*].

slaver (slăv'er) *n.* saliva running from mouth; gross flattery; sentimental nonsense;—*v.t.* to smear with saliva issuing from mouth;—*v.i.* to slobber; to talk in a weakly sentimental fashion.—**slav'erer** *n.* [O.N. *slafra*, to slaver].

slaw (slaw) *n.* sliced cabbage served cooked, or uncooked, as a salad [Dut. *sla*, salad].

slay (slā) *v.t.* to kill; to murder; to assassinate; to slaughter.—*pa.t.* **slew.**—*pa.p.* **slain.**—**slay'er** *n.* [O.E. *slean*, to smite].

sleave (slēv) *n.* knotted or entangled part of

silk or thread; floss silk; tangled silk;—*v.t.* to separate and divide as into threads [etym. uncertain].

sled, sledge (sled, slej) *n.* a carriage on runners, for conveying loads over hard snow or ice; a sleigh;—*v.t.* to convey on a sled;—*v.i.* to ride on a sled [Dut. *slede*].

sledge (slej) *n.* large, heavy hammer.—**sledge′hamm′er** *n.* heavy hammer with a long handle [O.E. *slecg*].

sleek (slēk) *a.* having a smooth surface; glossy; not rough; plausible; ingratiating;—*v.t.* to make smooth; to calm; to soothe;—*v.i.* to glide; to sweep smoothly.—*adv.* smoothly; neatly; skilfully.—**sleek′ly** *adv.*—**sleek′ness** *n.* [O.N. *slikr*, smooth].

sleep (slēp) *v.i.* to rest by suspension of exercise of powers of body and mind; to become numb (of limb); to slumber; to doze; to repose; to rest; to be dead.—*pa.t.* and *pa.p.* **slept.**—*n.* slumber; repose; rest; death.—**sleep′er** *n.* one who sleeps; berth in railway sleeping-car; one of the strong, horizontal pieces of timber which bear weight of engine-frames, shores or struts, railway lines, etc.—**sleep′ily** *adv.* in drowsy manner.—**sleep′iness** *n.*—**sleep′ing** *a.* resting in sleep; inducing sleep; adapted for sleeping;—*n.* state of resting in sleep; state of not being raised or discussed.—**sleep′ing-bag** *n.* bag of thick material, waterproofed on outside, for sleeping in the open.—**sleep′ing-car** or **carr′iage** *n.* railway-carriage with sleeping-berths.—**sleep′ing-draught** *n.* medicine used for inducing sleep; soporific; opiate.—**sleep′ing-part′ner** *n.* business associate who takes no active part in management.—**sleep′ing-sick′ness** *n.* tropical disease, especially common among the natives of C. and W. Africa; trypanosomiasis.—**sleep′less** *a.* wakeful; restless; alert; vigilant; unremitting.—**sleep′lessly** *adv.*—**sleep′lessness** *n.*—**sleep′walk′er** *n.* one who walks in his sleep or in trance; somnambulist.—**sleep′walk′ing** *n.*—**sleep′y** *a.* inclined to sleep; drowsy.—**sleep′y-sick′ness** *n.* epidemic European disease [O.E. *slaepan*].

sleet (slēt) *n.* mixture of melting snow and rain;—*v.i.* to snow or hail with rain.—**sleet′iness** *n.*—**sleet′y** *a.* [M.E. *slete*].

sleeve (slēv) *n.* part of garment which covers arm; casing surrounding shaft of engine; drogue or wind-sock used on aerodromes as wind-indicator;—*v.t.* to furnish with sleeves.—**sleeve′band** *n.* wristband or cuff.—**sleeve′link** *n.* two buttons or studs linked together and securing edges of cuff or wristband.—**sleeve valve,** sliding valve fitted between cylinder and piston of engine.—**to laugh up one's sleeve,** to be inwardly amused at someone [O.E. *sliefe*].

sleigh (slā) *n.* a sled or sledge;—*v.i.* to drive in a sleigh [Dut. *slee*].

sleight (slīt) *n.* artful trick; feat so dexterously performed that manner of performance escapes observation.—**sleight′of-hand** *n.* legerdemain; conjuring [O.N. *slaegth*].

slender (slen′dẹr) *a.* thin or narrow; weak; feeble; not strong.—**slen′derly** *adv.*—**slen′derness** *n.* [M.E. *slendre*].

slept (slept) *pa.t.* and *pa.p.* of **sleep.**

sleuth (slòòth) *n.* track of man or beast, as followed by scent; bloodhound; a relentless tracker; detective.—**sleuth′hound** *n.* bloodhound [O.N. *sloth*, a track].

slew (slòò) *pa.t.* of **slay.**

slew, slue (slòò) *v.t.* and *v.i.* to turn about for positioning purposes round a fixed point; to swing round [etym. unknown].

slice (slīs) *v.t.* and *v.i.* to cut off thin flat pieces; to strike a ball so that its line of flight diverges well to the right;—*n.* thin, flat piece cut off; broad, flat, thin knife for serving fish; spatula; share or portion; stroke at golf, etc. in which ball curls away to the right.—**sli′cer** *n.* [O.Fr. *esclice*].

slick (slik) *a.* smooth; sleek; smooth-tongued; quick in reply; smart; deft; clever;—*adv.* deftly; cleverly; simultaneously; at once;—*v.t.* to sleek; to make glossy. See **sleek.**

slicker (slik′ẹr) *n.* waterproof coat.

slid, slidden See **slide.**

slidder (slid′ẹr) *v.i.* to slip; to slide in all directions.—**slidd′ery** *a.* [O.E. *slidan*].

slide (slīd) *v.i.* to slip smoothly along; to slip, to glide, esp. over ice; to pass imperceptibly; to deteriorate morally;—*v.t.* to move something into position by pushing along the surface of another body; to thrust along; to pass imperceptibly.—*pr.p.* **sli′ding.**—*pa.t.* **slid.**—*pa.p.* **slid** or **slidd′en.**—*n.* sliding; track on ice made by sliding; sliding part of mechanism; anything which moves freely in or out; photographic plate-holder; smooth and easy passage; chute; a narrow piece of glass to carry small object to be examined under microscope; woman's hair clip; moving part of trombone or trumpet.—**sli′der** *n.* one who slides; (*Colloq.*) ice-cream between two thin wafer-biscuits.—**slide′rule, sli′ding-rule** *n.* mathematical instrument for rapid calculations.—**sli′ding-roof** *n.* roof of theatre, saloon-car, etc. designed to slide open.—**sli′ding-scale** *n.* schedule of wages, prices, duties, etc. showing the automatic variations of these according to fluctuations of other factors, as cost of living, etc.—**sli′ding-seat** *n.* seat in rowing-boat which moves with motions of rower [O.E. *slidan*].

slight (slīt) *a.* trifling; inconsiderable; not substantial; slim; slender;—*n.* contempt by ignoring another; disdain; insult;—*v.t.* to ignore; to disdain; to insult.—**slight′ing** *n.* scorn; disrespect;—*a.* disparaging.—**slight′ingly** *adv.*—**slight′ly** *adv.* to slight extent; not seriously.—**slight′ness** *n.* [O.N. *slettr*].

slily (slī′li) *adv.* slyly. See **sly.**

slim (slim) *a.* of small diameter or thickness; slender; thin; slight; unsubstantial; cunning;—*v.i.* to reduce weight by diet and exercise;—**slim′ly** *adv.* frail [Dut. = crafty].

slime (slīm) *n.* soft, sticky, moist earth or clay; greasy, viscous mud; mire; mucus; viscous secretion of snails, etc.; fawning words or actions.—**slim′ly** *adv.* in a slimy manner.—**slim′iness** *n.*—**sli′my** *a.* consisting of, or covered with slime [O.E. *slim*].

sliness Same as **slyness.**

sling (sling) *n.* pocket of leather, etc., with a string attached at each end for hurling a stone; catapult; swinging throw; strap attached to rifle; hanging bandage, for supporting an arm or hand; rope, chain, belt, etc. for hoisting weights;—*v.t.* to throw by means of sling or swinging motion of arm; to hoist or lower by means of slings; to suspend.—*pa.t.* and *pa.p.* **slung.**—**sling′er** *n.* [O.N. *slyngva*].

sling (sling) *n.* American iced drink of sweetened gin (or rum) with nutmeg; gin-sling [Ger. *schlingen*, to swallow].

slink (slingk) *v.i.* to move in a stealthy, furtive manner.—*pa.t.* and *pa.p.* **slunk** [O.E. *slincan*, to creep].

slip (slip) *v.t.* to move an object secretly or furtively into another position; to put on, or off gently; to loosen; to release (dog); to omit; to miss; to overlook; to escape (memory); to escape from; of animals, to give premature birth to;—*v.i.* to lose one's foothold; to move smoothly along surface of; to withdraw quietly; to slide; to stumble; to make a mistake; to lose one's chance; to fall into fault.—*pr.p.* **slip′ping.**—*pa.t.* and *pa.p.* **slipped.**—*n.* act of slipping; unintentional error; stumble; false step; twig for grafting separated from main stock; leash for dog; long, narrow, piece; loose garment worn under woman's blouse; pinafore; covering for a pillow; in cricket, position on the off-side, behind wicket; fieldsman in this position; revolution of wheels without movement along surface of the road; in aviation, pitch of airscrew, less distance it actually travels in one revolution; sideslip;—*pl.* short bathing drawers or pants worn by men; wings of theatre; slipway in shipbuilding yard.—**slip′-cov′er** *n.* a loose-covering for upholstered furniture.—**slip′-knot** *n.* running knot which slips along rope around which it is made, forming loop.—**slip′per** *n.* light shoe for indoor use; dancing-shoe; a drag or brake-shoe for braking wagon wheel.—**slip′perily** *adv.*—**slip′periness, slip′piness** *n.* condition of being slippery.—**slip′pery** *a.* so smooth as to cause slipping or to be difficult to hold or catch; not affording a firm footing; unstable; untrustworthy; changeable; artful; wily.—**slip′py** *a.* slippery; lively; nimble; brisk; quick.—**slip′-shod** *a.* having shoes down at heel; untidy; slovenly; inaccurate.—**slip′-stream** *n.* stream of air driven astern by air-screw of aeroplane.—**slip′way** *n.* long inclined plane down which a cradle runs from which ships are launched.—**to slip the cable,** to sail without hoisting anchor; to throw over domination of another [O.E. *slipan*].

slit (slit) *v.t.* to cut lengthwise; to cut open; to sever; to rend; to split;—*v.i.* to be slit.—*pr.p.* **slit′ting.**—*pa.t.* and *pa.p.* **slit.**—*n.* straight, narrow cut or incision; narrow opening in box.—**slit′ter** *n.* one who slits; machine for cutting material into strips.—**slit trench** *n.* narrow trench for one [O.E. *slitan*].

slither (sliTH′-er) *v.i.* to slide and bump (down a slope, etc.);—*a.* slippery;—*n.* a limestone rubble.—**slith′ery** *a.* slippery [var. of *slidder*].

sliver (slī′-ver, sliv′-er) *v.t.* to divide into long, thin strips;—*v.i.* to split; to become split off;—*n.* piece cut lengthwise [O.E. *slifan*, to split].

slobber Same as **slabber.**

sloe (slō) *n.* blackthorn; small wild plum, the fruit of blackthorn.—**sloe′-gin** *n.* liqueur from gin and sloes [O.E. *sla*].

slog (slog) *v.t.* to hit wildly and vigorously;—*v.i.* to work or study with dogged determination; to trudge along;—*pr.p.* **slog′ging.**—*pa.t.* and *pa.p.* **slogged.**—*n.* a wild swipe at ball; hard and tiring spell of work.—**slog′ger** *n.* [O.E. *slean*, to strike].

slogan (slō′-gan) *n.* war-cry of Highland clan in Scotland; distinctive phrase used by a political party; catchword for focusing public interest, etc. [Gael. *sluagh-ghairm*].

sloop (slòòp) *n.* one-masted sailing vessel; (*Old navy*) small warship rated below a frigate; (*Modern navy*) warship of about 1,000 tons displacement for escort and general duties. [Dut. *sloep*].

slop (slop) *n.* water carelessly spilled; puddle;—*pl.* semi-liquid food; water in which anything has been washed;—*v.t.* to spill; to soil by spilling over;—*v.i.* to overthrow or be spilled.—*pr.p.* **slop′ping.**—*pa.t.* and *pa.p.* **slopped.**—**slop′-ba′sin, slop′-bowl** *n.* basin or bowl for holding dregs from tea-cups.—**slop′pily** *adv.*—**slop′piness** *n.*—**slop′py** *a.* wet; muddy; weak; slovenly; untidy; mawkishly sentimental [O.E. *sloppe*].

slop (slop) *n.* a smock-frock; a night-gown;—*pl.* loose-fitting breeches; an overall; ready-made clothes [O.N. *sloppr*, a loose-fitting robe].

slop (slop) *n.* (*Slang*) policeman [a form of backslang from word *police*].

slope (slōp) *n.* upward or downward inclination; slant; side of hill; position of rifle resting on shoulder;—*v.t.* to form with slope; to place slanting;—*v.i.* to assume oblique direction; to be inclined; (*Slang*) to decamp; to make off.—**slo′ping** *a.* inclined from straight line or plane.—**slope arms!** military command to place rifle on shoulder [O.E. *slupan*, to slip away].

slosh (slosh) *n.* soft mud; (*Slang*) sentimental gush; heavy blow;—*v.t.* (*Slang*) to hit wildly and violently [fr. *slush*].

slot (slot) *n.* broad flat wooden bar or slat, used for holding together larger pieces of timber [Dut. = a lock].

slot (slot) *n.* hollow or defile between two ridges or hills; wide ditch; slit cut out for reception of object or part of machine; slit where coins are inserted into automatic machines;—*v.t.* to make a slot in.—*pr.p.* **slot′ting.**—*pa.t.* and *pa.p.* **slot′ted.**—**slot′-machine′** *n.* automatic machine worked by insertion of coin [O.Fr. *esclot*].

slote (slōt) *n.* stage trap-door. Also **slot.**

sloth (sloth) *n.* lethargy; indolence.—**sloth′ful** *a.* inactive; sluggish; lazy.—**sloth′fully** *adv.*—**sloth′fulness** *n.* [O.E. *slaewth*, fr. *slaw*, slow].

sloth (slōth, sloth) *n.* group of edentate mammals of S. America which cling mostly to branches of trees [fr. *slow*].

slotter (slot′-er) *n.* filth; dirt;—*v.t.* to defile; to foul; to pollute [fr. *slattern*].

slouch (slouch) *n.* ungraceful, stooping manner of walking or standing; shambling gait;—*v.i.* to shamble;—*v.t.* to depress; to cause to hang down loosely.—**slouch′-hat** *n.* soft hat or trilby with a broad, flexible brim.—**slouch′y** *a.* inclined to slouch [etym. uncertain].

slough (slou) *n.* bog; swamp [O.E. *sloh*].

slough (sluf) *n.* cast-off outer skin, esp. of snake; dead mass of soft tissues which separates from healthy tissues in gangrene or ulcers;—*v.t.* to cast off, or shed, as a slough;—*v.i.* to separate as dead matter which forms over sore; to drop off [etym. uncertain].

Slovak (slō-vak′) *n.* member of Slav people in northern Carpathians, closely related to Czechs; language spoken in Slovakia;—*a.* pert. to Slovaks. Also **Slovak′ian.**

sloven (sluv′-n) *n.* person careless of dress, or negligent of cleanliness; slattern; slut.—**slov′enliness** *n.*—**slov′enly** *a.*—*adv.* in slipshod manner [etym. uncertain].

slow (slō) *a.* not swift; not quick in motion; gradual; indicating time later than true time; mentally sluggish; dull; wearisome;—*adv.* slowly;—*v.t.* to render slow; to retard; to reduce speed of:—*v.i.* to slacken speed.—**slow′coach** *n.* loiterer; laggard.—**slow′ly** *adv.*—**slow′-match** *n.* fuse made so as to burn slowly, for firing mines, etc.—**slow′mo′tion** *n.* and *a.* in cinematography, motion shown in exaggeratedly slow time.—**slow′ness** *n.*—**slow′-sight′ed, slow′-witt′ed** *a.* mentally slow, dull; apathetic.—**slow in the uptake** (*Colloq.*) slow-witted [O.E. *slaw*, sluggish].

slow-worm (slō′-wurm) *n.* blind-worm or grass-snake [O.E. *slawyrm*, a 'slayworm'].

slubber (slub′-er) *v.t.* to do slovenly or carelessly; to soil; to bedaub;—*v.i.* to slabber [Dut. *slobberen*].

sludge (sluj) *n.* mud which settles at bottom of waterways, of vessel containing water, or a shaft when drilling; semi-solid, slimy matter precipitated from sewage in sedimentation tank.—**slud′gy** *a.* muddy; miry; oozy; slushy [var. of *slush*].

slue See **slew.**

slug (slug) *n.* sluggard; hindrance; one of land-snails, a common pest in gardens.—**slug′-a-bed** *n.* one rather fond of lying in bed; a sluggard.—**slug′gard** *n.* person habitually lazy, idle, and inactive; drone;—*a.* lazy; sluggish; slothful.—**slug′gish** *a.* disinclined to exert oneself; habitually indolent; slothful; slow-moving.—**slug′gishly** *adv.*—**slug′gishness** *n.* [Scand.].

slug (slug) *n.* small thick disc of metal; a piece of metal fired from gun; solid line of type cast by linotype process [etym. uncertain].

slug (slug) *v.i.* to strike heavily; to slog;—*n.* heavy blow [O.E. *slean*, to strike].

sluice (slòòs) *n.* valve or shutter for regulating flow and volume of water from reservoir; flood-gate or water-gate; artificial channel along which stream flows; rough-and-ready wash; sluicing;—*v.t.* to provide with sluices; to wash out, or pour over with water; to wash by dipping one's head in free-running stream.—**sluice′-box** *n.* trough used in gold-mining [O.Fr. *escluse*].

slum (slum) *n.* squalid house, street, or quarter of town, characterised by gross overcrowding, dilapidation, poverty, vice and dirt;—*v.i.* to visit slums.—*pr.p.* **slum'ming.**—*pa.t.* and *pa.p.* **slummed.**—**slum-clear'ance** *n.* substitution of new houses for old, dilapidated buildings [etym. unknown].
slumber (slum'ber) *v.i.* to sleep lightly; to be in a state of negligence, sloth, or inactivity;—*n.* light sleep; doze.—**slum'berer** *n.*—**slum'berous, slum'brous** *a.* inducing slumber or drowsiness; drowsy [O.E. *sluma*].
slummock (slum'ok) *v.t.* and *v.i.* to swallow hastily; to move awkwardly; to gabble [etym. unknown].
slump (slump) *n.* sudden, sharp fall in prices or volume of business done; industrial or financial depression;—*v.i.* to decline suddenly in value, volume, or esteem; to sink suddenly when crossing snow, ice, boggy ground, etc. [etym. uncertain].
slump (slump) *v.t.* to lump together in a mass or as one;—*a.* gross; total, without detailing specific items [Dut. *slomp*].
slung (slung) *pa.t.* and *pa.p.* of **sling.**
slunk (slungk) *pa.t.* and *pa.p.* of **slink.**
slur (slur) *v.t.* to pass over lightly; to bring into disrepute; to depreciate; to insult; to blur type, in printing; to pronounce indistinctly; (*Mus.*) to sing or play in a smooth, gliding style; to run one into the other, as notes.—*pr.p.* **slur'ring.**—*pa.t.* and *pa.p.* **slurred.**—*n.* slight mark or stain; stigma; reproach; implied insult; (*Mus.*) mark, thus (‿ or ⁀) connecting notes that are to be sung to same syllable, or made in one continued breath; a tie [O. Dut. *slooren,* to trail (in mud)].
slush (slush) *n.* half-melted snow mixed with mud; any greasy, pasty mass; trashy literature;—*v.t.* to sluice or flush a place with water.—**slush'y** *a.* [var. of *sludge*].
slut (slut) *n.* dirty, untidy woman; slattern.—**slut'tish** *a.* untidy and dirty.—**slut'tishly** *adv.*—**slut'tishness** *n.* [M.E. *slutte*].
sly (slī) *a.* artfully cunning; secretly mischievous.—**sly'ly, sli'ly** *adv.* in a sly manner.—**sly'ness, sli'ness** *n.* [O.N. *slaegr*].
smack (smak) *v.t.* to make a loud, quick noise (with lips) as in kissing or after tasting; to slap loudly; to strike;—*v.i.* to make sharp, quick noise with lips;—*n.* quick, sharp noise, esp. with lips; a loud kiss; a slap [imit. origin].
smack (smak) *v.i.* to have a taste or flavour; to give a suggestion (of);—*n.* a slight taste [O.E. *smaec,* taste].
smack (smak) *n.* small sailing-vessel, usually for fishing [Dut. *smak*].
small (smawl) *a.* little in size, number, degree, etc.; not large; unimportant; short; weak; slender; mean;—*n.* small or slender part, esp. of back.—**small'ish** *a.* rather small.—**small'ness** *n.*—**smalls** *n.pl.* at Oxford University, the first examination for the degree of B.A.; responsions; (*Colloq.*) small articles of clothing.—**small'-arms** *n.pl.* hand firearms, e.g. rifles, pistols, etc.—**small change,** coins of small value, e.g. pennies, sixpences, etc.—**small'-talk** *n.* gossip; light conversation [O.E. *smael*].
smallpox (smawl'poks) *n.* infectious disease, characterised by fever and an eruption developing into pustules; variola [E. *small;* O.E. *poc,* a pustule].
smarm (smarm) *v.t.* and *v.i.* to anoint; to smooth, esp. hair; (*Colloq.*) to fawn; to ingratiate.—**smar'my** *a.* unctuous; fawning [etym. uncertain, perh. fr. *smear*].
smart (smart) *n.* sharp, stinging pain; (*Fig.*) pang of grief;—*v.i.* to feel such a pain; to be punished (with 'for');—*a.* causing a sharp, stinging pain; clever; active; shrewd; trim; neat; well-dressed; fashionable.—**smart'ly** *adv.*—**smart'ness** *n.*—**smarten** (smar'tn) *v.t.* and *v.i.* to make or become smart; to make brighter [O.E. *smeortan,* to feel pain].
smash (smash) *v.t.* to break into pieces; to shatter; to hit hard; to ruin;—*v.i.* to break into pieces; to dash violently against; of a business firm, to fail;—*n.* crash; heavy blow; accident, wrecking vehicles; utter ruin; of business firm, bankruptcy.—**smash'ing** *a.* crushing; (*Slang*) excellent [fr. E. *mash,* to mix up].
smatter (smat'er) *v.i.* to talk superficially;—**smatt'ering** *n.* slight, superficial knowledge [etym. uncertain].
smear (smēr) *v.t.* to rub over with a greasy, oily, or sticky substance; to daub; to impute disgrace to;—*n.* mark made thus; stain.—**smear'iness** *n.*—**smear'y** *a.* marked with smears [O.E. *smeru,* fat].
smeddum (smed'um) *n.* fine powder; sagacity; quickness; spirit; mettle [O.E. *smedema,* fine flour].
smell (smel) *n.* sense of perceiving odours by nose; act of smelling; (unpleasant) odour; scent; perfume;—*v.t.* to perceive by nose; (*Fig.*) to suspect;—*v.i.* to use nose; to give out odour.—*pr.p.* **smell'ing.**—*pa.p.* and *pa.t.* **smelled** or **smelt.**—**smell'ing** *n.* the sense of smell.—**smell'y** *a.* having unpleasant smell.—**smell'ing-salts** *n.pl.* scented ammonium carbonate used to relieve faintness, headache, etc. [M.E. *smel*].
smelt (smelt) *n.* small, silvery fish of salmon family [O.E. *smelt*].
smelt (smelt) *v.t.* to melt or fuse ore in order to extract metal.—**smel'tery** *n.* a place for smelting ores.—**smel'ting** *n.* [Sw. *smalta,* to melt].
smew (smū) *n.* diving-bird, allied to the merganser [O.E. *smee,* smooth].
Smilax (smī'laks) *n.* genus of evergreen climbing shrubs [Gk. = bindweed].
smile (smīl) *v.i.* to express pleasure, approval, amusement, contempt, irony, etc. by curving lips; to look happy;—*v.t.* to express by smile;—*n.* act of smiling; pleasant facial expression.—**smi'ling** *a.* cheerful; gay; joyous.—**smi'lingly** *adv.* [Sw. *smila,* to smile].
smirch (smerch) *v.t.* to smear over; to dirty; to soil; to stain; to bring disgrace upon;—*n.* stain [M.E. *smeren,* to smear].
smirk (smerk) *v.i.* to smile in an affected or conceited manner;—*n.* affected or silly smile [O.E. *smercian,* to smile].
smit (smit) *v.t.* to infect; to mar;—*n.* infection; stain [O.E. *smittian,* to spot].
smite (smīt) *v.t.* to hit hard; to strike with hand, fist, weapon, etc.; to defeat; to afflict;—*v.i.* to strike.—*pa.p.* **smitten** (smit'n).—*pa.t.* **smote** (smōt).—**smi'ter** *n.* [O.E. *smitan,* to smear].
smith (smith) *n.* one who shapes metal, esp. with hammer and anvil; blacksmith.—**smith'y** *n.* smith's workshop; forge [O.E. *smith*].
smithereens (smiTH-er-ēnz') *n.pl.* (*Colloq.*) small bits. Also **smith'ers** [fr. *smite*].
smitten (smit'n) *pa.p.* of **smite.**
smock (smok) *n.* woman's undergarment; a smock-frock.—**smock'-frock** *n.* coarse linen smock, worn over clothes, by farm-labourers.—**smock'ing** *n.* gathering of dress, blouse, etc. into honeycomb pattern [O.E. *smoc*].
smog *n.* mixture of smoke and fog in atmosphere (from *smoke* and *fog*); **smog mask** *n.* worn for protection against smog.
smoke (smōk) *n.* cloudy mass of suspended particles that rises from fire or anything burning; spell of tobacco-smoking; (*Colloq.*) cigar or cigarette;—*v.t.* to consume (tobacco opium, etc.) by smoking; to expose to smoke (esp. in curing fish, etc.);—*v.i.* to inhale and expel smoke of burning tobacco; to give off smoke.—**smo'ker** *n.* one who smokes tobacco; railway-carriage, in which smoking is permitted; smoking-concert.—**smo'king** *n.*—**smo'kiness** *n.*—**smo'ky** *a.* emitting smoke; filled with smoke; having colour, taste of smoke.—**smo'kily** *adv.*—**smoke'-ball, -bomb, -shell** *n.* (*Mil.*) one emitting dense smoke to conceal

operations.—**smo'king-con'cert** *n.* social gathering, for men only, at which smoking is allowed [O.E. *smoca*].

smolt (smōlt) *n.* young salmon when it first leaves the river for the sea.

smooth (smòòTH) *a.* not rough; level; polished; gently flowing; calm; steady in motion; plausible;—*v.t.* to make smooth; to polish; to calm; to soothe; to make easy;—*adv.* in a smooth manner.—**smooth'ly** *adv.*—**smooth'ness** *n.* state of being smooth [O.E. *smoth*].

smote (smōt) *pa.p.* and *pa.t.* of **smite**.

smother (smuTH'ẹr) *v.t.* to destroy by depriving of air; to suffocate; to conceal;—*v.i.* to be suffocated; to be without air;—*n.* thick smoke or dust [O.E. *smorian*, to choke].

smoulder (smōl'dẹr) *v.i.* to burn slowly without flame; (*Fig.*) of feelings, esp. anger, resentment, etc., to exist inwardly [M.E. *smolder*, stifling smoke].

smudge (smuj) *n.* smear; stain; dirty mark; blot; smoky fire to drive off insects or protect fruit-trees from pests;—*v.t.* to smear; to make a dirty mark;—*v.i.* to become dirty or blurred.—**smud'gy** *a.* [etym. uncertain].

smug (smug) *a.* very neat and prim; self-satisfied; complacent.—**smug'ly** *adv.*—**smug'ness** *n.* [L. Ger. *smuk*, neat].

smuggle (smug'l) *v.t.* to import or export goods secretly to evade customs duties; to bring in, or take out, secretly, esp. against regulations.—**smugg'ler** *n.*—**smugg'ling** *n.* [L. Ger. *smuggeln*].

smut (smut) *n.* black particle of dirt; spot caused by this; fungoid disease of cereals, characterised by blackening of ears of oats, barley, etc.; lewd or obscene talk or writing;—*v.t.* to blacken; to smudge.—*pr.p.* **smutt'ing.**—*pa.p.* and *pa.t.* **smut'ted.**—**smut'ty** *a.* soiled with smut; obscene; lewd.—**smut'tily** *adv.*—**smut'tiness** *n.* [etym. uncertain].

smutch (smuch) *v.t.* to blacken, as with soot, etc.;—*n.* dirty spot; stain; smudge [a form of *smut*].

snack (snak) *n.* share; slight, hasty meal.—**snack'bar,-coun'ter, -room** *n.* part of restaurant for service of light, hurried meals [fr. *snatch*].

snaffle (snaf'l) *n.* horse's bridle, with mouth-bit jointed in middle but without curb;—*v.t.* to put one on a horse [Dut. *snavel*, nose of animal].

snaffle (snaf'l) *v.t.* (*Slang*) to steal; to purloin [perh. fr. *snap*].

snag (snag) *n.* stump projecting from tree-trunk; stump or tree-trunk sticking up in a river, impeding passage of boats; any obstacle, drawback, or catch;—*v.t.* to catch on a snag; to clear of snags [O.N. *snagi*, a point].

snail (snāl) *n.* slow-moving mollusc with spiral shell.—**snail'ery** *n.* place where edible snails are reared [O.E. *snaegel*].

snake (snāk) *n.* long, scaly, limbless reptile; serpent; treacherous person;—*v.t.* (*U.S. Colloq.*) to drag along, e.g. log.—**snak'y** *a.* pert. to, or resembling, snake; full of snakes.—**a snake in the grass** (*Fig.*) hidden enemy [O.E. *snaca*].

snap (snap) *v.t.* to break abruptly; to crack; to seize suddenly; to snatch; to bite; to shut with click; (*Photog.*) to take snapshot of;—*v.i.* to break short; to try to bite; to utter sharp, cross words; to make a quick, sharp sound; to sparkle.—*pr.p.* **snap'ping.**—*pa.p.* and *pa.t.* **snapped.**—*n.* act of seizing suddenly, esp. with teeth; bite; sudden breaking; quick, sharp sound; small spring catch, as of a bracelet; crisp gingerbread biscuit; short spell of frosty weather; (*Photog.*) short for snapshot; card-game;—*a.* sudden; unprepared; without warning.—**snap'per** *n.* one who snaps; kind of fresh-water turtle.—**snap'pish** *a.* apt to snap, as dog; short-tempered. **-snap'pishness** *n.*—**snap'py** *a.* snappish; lively; brisk; (*Colloq.*) smartly dressed; quick.—**snap'dragon** *n.* (*Bot.*) Antirrhinum; party game.—**snap'shot** *n.* hasty shot; photograph taken by giving instantaneous or very quick exposure [Dut. *snappen*].

snare (snār) *n.* running noose of cord or wire, used to trap animals or birds; a trap; anything by which one is deceived;—*n.pl.* (*Mus.*) catgut strings across lower head of side-drum, to produce rattling sound;—*v.t.* to catch with snare; to entangle [O.N. *snara*].

snarl (snárl) *v.i.* to growl like an angry dog; to speak in a surly manner;—*n.* growling sound; surly tone of voice.—**snar'ler** *n.* [imit. origin].

snarl (snárl) *n.* tangle or knot of hair, wool, etc.; complication;—*v.t.* and *v.i.* to entangle or become entangled [fr. *snare*].

snatch (snach) *v.t.* to seize hastily or without permission; to grasp;—*v.i.* to make quick grab or bite (at);—*n.* quick grab; small bit or fragment [M.E. *snacchen*].

sneak (snēk) *v.i.* to creep or steal away; to slink;—*v.t.* (*Slang*) to steal;—*n.* mean, cowardly fellow; tell-tale.—**sneak'er** *n.*—**sneak'ers** *n.pl.* (*U.S.*) light, soft-soled shoes.—**sneak'ing** *a.* mean; cowardly; secret.—**sneak'ingly** *adv.*—**sneak'iness, sneak'ingness** *n.* quality of being sneaky; slyness.—**sneak'y** *a.* somewhat sneaking; mean; underhand [O.E. *snican*, to creep].

snee (snē) *n.* a large knife [Ger. *schneiden*, to cut].

sneer (snēr) *v.i.* to show contempt by facial expression, as by curling lips; to smile, speak, or write scornfully;—*n.* look of contempt or ridicule; scornful utterance.—**sneer'er** *n.*—**sneer'ing** *a.*—**sneer'ingly** *adv.* [etym. uncertain].

sneeze (snēz) *v.i.* to expel air through nose with sudden convulsive spasm and noise;—*n.* a sneezing [O.E. *fneosan*].

snick (snik) *n.* small cut; notch; nick;—*v.t.* to cut; to notch; to clip; to hit cricket-ball with edge of bat [Scand. *snikka*, to cut].

snicker (snik'ẹr) *v.i.* to laugh with small, audible catches of voice; to giggle;—*n.* half-suppressed laugh [imit. origin].

sniff (snif) *v.i.* to draw in breath through nose with sharp hiss; to express disapproval, etc. by sniffing; to snuff;—*v.t.* to take up through nose; to smell;—*n.* act of sniffing; that which is sniffed.—**snif'fle** *v.i.* to sniff noisily through nose; to snuffle.—**snif'fler** *n.* one who sniffles.—**snift** *v.i.* to sniff; to snuff.—**snift'er** *v.i.* to sniff; to sniffle;—*n.* a sniff; (*Slang*) small drink, esp. of whisky [imit. origin].

snigger (snig'ẹr) *v.i.* to laugh in half-suppressed manner; to giggle;—*n.* sly, suppressed laugh; to giggle [imit. origin].

snip (snip) *v.t.* to clip off with scissors; to cut;—*n.* a single, quick stroke, as with scissors; a bit cut off; (*Slang*) in betting, certainty; (*Colloq.*) tailor.—*pr.p.* **snip'ping.**—*pa.p.* and *pa.t.* **snipped.**—**snip'per** *n.* one who snips.—**snip'pet** *n.* little bit snipped off; a fragment.—**snips** *n.pl.* strong hand-shears for cutting sheet-metal [Dut. *snippen*].

snipe (snīp) *n.* long-billed gamebird, frequenting marshy places; simpleton;—*v.i.* to shoot snipe; (*Mil.*) to shoot from cover;—*v.t.* to hit by so shooting.—*pr.p.* **snip'ing.**—*pa.p.* and *pa.t.* **sniped.**—**snip'er** *n.* [O.N. *snipa*].

snivel (sniv'l) *n.* running at the nose; sham emotion; whining, as of child.—*v.i.* to run at the nose; to show real or sham sorrow; to cry, or whine, as children.—*pr.p.* **sniv'elling.**—*pa.p.* and *pa.t.* **sniv'elled.**—**sniv'eller** *n* [O.E. *snyflan*].

snob (snob) *n.* one who judges by social rank or wealth rather than merit; one who ignores those whom he considers his social inferiors; cobbler.—**snob'bery** *n.*—**snob'bish** *a.*—**snob'bishly** *adv.*—**snob'bishness** *n.* [etym. uncertain].

snood (snòòd) *n.* ribbon formerly worn to hold back hair; fillet; fine, short line fixing a fish-hook to long line [O.E. *snod*].

snook (snòòk) *n.* vulgar gesture of contempt, made by placing thumb at point of nose and

extending fingers.—**to cock a snook,** to make this gesture [etym. uncertain].
snooker (snōō′-kẹr) *n.* game resembling pool or pyramids [etym. uncertain].
snoop (snōōp) *v.i.* (*Colloq.*) to investigate slyly; to pry into;—*n.* one who acts thus. Also **snoop′er** [perh. fr. *snook*].
snooze (snōōz) *n.* short sleep; nap;—*v.i.* to take a snooze [perh. fr. *snore*].
snore (snōr) *v.i.* to breathe heavily and noisily during sleep;—*n.* such noisy breathing.—**snor′er** *n.* [O.E. *snora,* a snore].
snort (snort) *v.i.* to force air with violence through nose, as horses; to express feeling by such a sound;—*v.t.* to express by snort;—*n.* snorting sound [imit. origin].
snot (snot) *n.* (*Vulg.*) mucus secreted in nose; mean fellow.—**snot′ty** *a.* filthy, esp. if due to snots; mean; (*Colloq.*) offended; petulant;—*n.* (*Navy Slang*) a midshipman.—**snot′tily** *adv.* [O.E. *gesnot*].
snout (snout) *n.* projecting nose of animal, esp. of pig; any projection like a snout [O.E. *snut*].
snow (snō) *n.* frozen vapour which falls in flakes; snowfall; mass of flakes on the ground; (*Slang*) narcotic drug, in powdered form;—*v.t.* to let fall or throw down like snow; to cover with snow.—**snow′y** *a.* covered with, full of snow; white.—**snow′ily** *adv.*—**snow′iness** *n.*—**snow′ball** *n.* round mass of snow pressed or rolled together; shrub bearing ball-like clusters of white flowers, guelder-rose; anything increasing like snowball, esp. mass movement where every helper brings in others;—*v.t.* to pelt with snowballs;—*v.i.* to throw snowballs.—**snow′-blind′ness** *n.* temporary blindness caused by glare of sun from snow.—**snow′-bound** *a.* shut in by heavy snowfall.—**snow′drift** *n.* mass of snow driven into a heap by wind.—**snow′drop** *n.* bulbous plant bearing white flowers in early spring.—**snow′fall** *n.* falling of snow; amount of snow falling in given time or place.—**snow′-field** *n.* wide expanse of snow-covered territory.—**snow′flake** *n.* small, thin, feathery mass of snow.—**snow′-line** *n.* line on mountain above which snow never melts.—**snow′-man** *n.* figure of man shaped out of snow.—**snow′-plough** *n.* machine for clearing snow from roads, etc.—**snow′-shoe** *n.* light, wooden framework with interwoven leather thongs for travelling over deep snow.—**snow′storm** *n.* heavy fall of snow.—**snow′white** *a.* as white as snow [O.E. *snaw*].
snub (snub) *v.t.* to check or rebuke with rudeness or indifference; to repress intentionally;—*n.* intentional slight; rebuff; check;—*a.* of nose, short, flat, and slightly turned-up [O.N. *snubba,* to rebuke].
snuff (snuf) *n.* charred part of wick of candle or lamp;—*v.t.* to nip this off; to extinguish.—**snuff′ers** *n.pl.* instrument resembling scissors, for nipping off snuff from wick [M.E. *snoffe*].
snuff (snuf) *v.t.* to draw up or through nostrils; to sniff; to smell; to inhale;—*v.i.* to draw air or snuff into nose; to take snuff;—*n.* powdered tobacco for inhaling through nose; sniff.—**snuff′er** *n.* one who snuffs.—**snuff′-mull** *n.* snuff-box [Dut. *snuffen*].
snuffle (snuf′-l) *v.i.* to breathe hard through nose, esp. when obstructed; to sniff continually; to speak through nose;—*n.* act of snuffling; a nasal twang.—**snuf′fler** *n.* one who snuffles [fr. *snuff*].
snug (snug) *a.* cosy; trim; comfortable; sheltered.—**snug′ly** *adv.*—**snug′ness** *n.* cosiness.—**snug′gery** *n.* a cosy room.—**snug′gle** *v.i.* to lie close to, for warmth or from affection; to nestle [Scand.].
so (sō) *adv.* in this manner or degree; in such manner; very; to such degree (with *as* or *that* coming after); the case being such; accordingly;—*conj.* therefore; in case that;—*interj.* well!—**so long!** (*Colloq.*) good-bye.—**so′-so** *a.* (*Colloq.*) fair; middling; tolerable;—*adv.* fairly; tolerably [O.E. *swa*].
soak (sōk) *v.t.* to steep; to wet thoroughly;—*v.i.* to lie steeped in water or other fluid; to drink to excess;—*n.* a soaking; the act of soaking; heavy rain; a hard drinker.—**soak′er** *n.* one who soaks; a habitual drinker.—**soak′ing** *a.* wetting thoroughly; drenching;—*n.* a drenching by rain [O.E. *socian*].
soap (sōp) *n.* compound of oil or fat with alkali, used in washing;—*v.t.* and *v.i.* to apply soap to.—**soap′y** *a.* pert. to soap; covered with soap; (*Fig.*) flattering; oily.—**soap′iness** *n.*—**soap′-bub′ble** *n.* iridescent bubble from soap-suds.—**soap′-op′era** *n.* (*U.S. Colloq.*) highly dramatised radio serial.—**soap′stone** *n.* soft, smooth stone, with soapy feel; steatite; talc.—**soap′-suds** *n.pl.* foamy mixture of soap and water; suds [O.E. *sape*].
soar (sōr) *v.i.* to fly high; to mount into air; (*Fig.*) to rise far above normal [L. *ex,* out of; *aura,* the air].
sob (sob) *v.i.* to catch breath, esp. in weeping; to sigh with convulsive motion.—*pr.p.* **sob′bing.**—*pa.p.* and *pa.t.* **sobbed.**—*n.* convulsive catching of breath, esp. in weeping or sighing [imit. origin].
sober (sō-bẹr) *a.* temperate; not intoxicated; exercising cool reason; subdued;—*v.t.* and *v.i.* to make or become sober.—**so′berly** *adv.*—**so′berness** *n.* state of being sober.—**sobriety** (sō-brī′-e-ti) *n.* habit of being sober; habitual temperance; moderation; seriousness; calmness [L. *sobrius*].
sobriquet (sō-brē-kā′) *n.* nickname; assumed name. Also **soubriquet** (sōō-) [Fr.].
soccer (sok′-ẹr) *n.* (*Colloq.*) association football [fr. *soc* in *association*].
sociable (sō′-shạ-bl) *a.* inclined to be friendly; fond of company.—**so′ciably** *adv.*—**so′ciableness** *n.*—**sociabil′ity** *n.* friendliness; geniality [L. *socius,* a companion].
social (sō′-shạl) *a.* pert. to society; affecting public interest; pert. to upper classes, world of fashion, etc.; living in communities, as ants; sociable; companionable; convivial;—*n.* social meeting.—**so′cially** *adv.*—**socialite** (sō′-shal-īt) *n.* member of fashionable society [L. *socius,* a companion].
socialism (sō′-shạl-izm) *n.* economic and political system, aiming at public or government ownership of means of production, etc.—**so′cialise** *v.t.* to make social; to transfer industry, etc. from private to public or government ownership.—**socialisa′tion** *n.*—**so′cialist** *a.* pert. to socialism.—**socialist′ic** *a.*—**socialist′ically** *adv.* [L. *socius,* a companion].
society (so-sī′-e-ti) *n.* people in general; community; people of culture and good breeding in any community; the upper classes; the world of fashion; fellowship; intercourse; a company; an association; a club [L. *socius,* a companion].
sociology (sō-shi-ol′-o-ji) *n.* science of origin, development, and nature of problems confronting society; social science.—**sociolog′ical** *a.*—**sociol′ogist** *n.* a student of sociology [L. *socius,* a companion; Gk. *logos,* a discourse].
sock (sok) *n.* orig. a low-heeled shoe worn by actor of comedy; half-stocking, esp. for men [L. *soccus,* a light shoe].
sock (sok) *v.t.* (*Slang*) to hit hard; to thrash.
socket (sok′-ẹt) *n.* opening or hollow into which anything is fitted; cavity of eye, tooth, etc.;—*v.t.* to provide with, or place in, socket [dim. of *sock*].
Socrates (sok′-rạ-tēz) *n.* a famous Greek philosopher (469-399 B.C.).—**Socrat′ic** *a.*—**Socrat′ically** *adv.*—**Socratic method,** teaching by series of questions and answers.
sod (sod) *n.* flat piece of earth with grass; turf [etym. uncertain].
soda (sō′-dạ) *n.* name applied to various compounds of sodium, e.g. *baking-soda, caustic soda, washing-soda.* (See **sodium**); (*Colloq.*) soda-water.—**so′da-fount′ain** *n.* case for holding soda-water; shop selling soft drinks, ices, etc.—**so′da-wa′ter** *n.* drink made by charging

water with carbonic acid gas [It. fr. L. *solidus*, firm].

sodality (sō-dal′i-ti) *n.* fraternity; a religious association, esp. of members of the R.C. Church [L. *sodalis*, a comrade].

sodden (sod′n) *a.* soaked; soft with moisture; dull and heavy; stupid [orig. *pa.p.* of **seethe**].

sodium (sō′di-um) *n.* silvery-white metallic alkaline element, the base of soda (symbol, Na. fr. L. *natrium*).—**sodium bicarbonate**, compound of sodium and carbon, used in cooking, medicine, etc.; baking-soda.—**sodium carbonate**, washing-soda.—**sodium chloride**, common household salt [fr. *soda*].

Sodom (sod′um) *n.* (*Bib.*) a city of ancient Palestine, consumed by fire, together with Gomorrah, for its wickedness.—**sod′omite** (*Vulg. abbrev.* **sod**) *n.* one guilty of sodomy.—**sod′omy** *n.* unnatural sexual intercourse, esp. between males.

sofa (sō′fa) *n.* long, padded couch, with raised back [formerly *sopha*, fr. Ar. *suffah*, a bench].

soft (soft) *a.* yielding easily to pressure; not hard; easily shaped or moulded; smooth; gentle; melodious; quiet; susceptible; over-sentimental; weak; weak in intellect; not astringent; containing no alcohol; in phonetics, esp. of consonants 'c' and 'g,' pronounced with a sibilant sound;—*adv.* softly; quietly.—*interj.* hold! stop! not so fast.—**soft′ish** *a.* somewhat soft.—**soft′ly** *adv.* quietly.—**soft′ness** *n.*—**soft′head′ed** *a.* weak in intellect.—**soft′heart′ed** *a.* kind; gentle; merciful [O.E. *softe*].

softball (soft′bawl) *n.* variant of the game of baseball [*soft* and *ball*].

soften (sof′n) *v.t.* to make soft or softer; to lighten; to mitigate; to tone down; to make less loud;—*v.i.* to become soft or softer.—**soft′ening** *n.* act, process, or result of becoming soft or softer [O.E. *softe*].

soggy (sog′i) *a.* soaked with water; sodden [Icel. *soggr*, damp].

soigné (swan′yā) *a.* well-finished; trim; neat; exquisitely groomed [Fr.].

soil (soil) *v.t.* to make dirty; to defile; to stain;—*v.i.* to become dirty; to show stains;—*n.* dirty mark [O.Fr. *soillier*, perh. fr. L. *sus*, a pig].

soil (soil) *n.* top layer of earth's surface; earth, as food for plants [L. *solum*, the ground].

soirée (swà-rā′) *n.* a social evening, a reception [Fr. = evening].

sojourn (sō′jurn, so-jurn′) *v.i.* originally, to stay for a day; to dwell for a time;—*n.* short stay [L. *sub*, under; *diurnus*, of a day].

sol (sol) *n.* (*Mus.*) the fifth note in the sol-fa notation. Also **soh.**

Sol (sol) *n.* the sun [L. = the sun].

solace (sol′as) *n.* comfort in grief; consolation;—*v.t.* to console [L. *solari*, to comfort].

solan (sō′lan) *n.* large sea-bird like a goose; a gannet. Also **so′lan-goose** [O.N. *sula*].

solar (sō′lar) *a.* pert. to, caused by, measured by sun.—**so′larise** *v.t.* and *v.i.* to expose to sun's rays.—**solarium** (sō-lar′i-um) *n.* room or balcony, esp. in hospital, etc. adapted for sun-bathing.—*pl.* **solar′ia**.—**solar plexus** (*Med.*) network of nerve tissue and fibres at back of stomach.—**solar system**, sun and nine planets revolving round it [L. *sol*, the sun].

solatium (sō-lā′shi-um) *n.* (*Law*) money compensation, awarded as a solace for wounded feelings [L. = solace].

sold (sōld) *pa.p.* and *pa.t.* of **sell.**

solder (sol′der, sōl′der, sod′er) *n.* easily melted alloy for joining metals;—*v.t.* to join or mend with solder [L. *solidare*, to make solid].

soldier (sōl′jer) *n.* man engaged in military service; private or N.C.O. as distinguished from commissioned officer.—**sol′diery** *n.* soldiers collectively; troops.—**soldier of fortune**, one willing to serve in army of any country; military adventurer [L. *solidus*, a coin = the pay of a soldier].

sole (sōl) *n.* flat of the foot; under part of boot or shoe; lower part of anything, or that on which anything rests; small flat-fish, used for food;—*v.t.* to supply with a sole [L. *solea*].

sole (sōl) *a.* being, or acting, without another; alone; only.—**sole′ly** *adv.* alone; only.—**sole′ness** *n.* [L. *solus*, alone].

solecism (sol′e-sizm) *n.* gross breach of grammar; a breach of etiquette.—**sol′ecist** *n.* one guilty of solecisms.—**solecist′ic, solecist′ical** *a.*—**solecist′ically** *adv.* [Gk. *soloikos*, speaking incorrectly].

solemn (sol′em) *a.* marked, or performed, with religious ceremony; impressive; grave; inspiring awe or dread.—**sol′emnly** *adv.*—**sol′emnness** *n.*—**sol′emnise** *v.t.* to perform with ritual ceremony or legal form; to celebrate, esp. festival.—**solemnisa′tion** *n.*—**solemnity** (sol-em′ni-ti) *n.* sacred rite or formal celebration; gravity; seriousness [L. *sollemnis*, yearly, solemn].

Solen (sō′len) *n.* genus of bivalve molluscs having a long, slender shell; razor-shell.—**so′lenoid** *n.* (*Elect.*) cylindrical coil of wire (without fixed iron core) forming electro-magnet when carrying current [Gk. *sōlēn*, a channel pipe; *eidos*, form].

sol-fa (sol-fà′) *v.i.* to sing notes of scale with syllables *sol*, *fa*, etc.;—*n.* use of these syllables in singing;—*a.* pert. to system of musical notation [It.].

solicit (so-lis′it) *v.t.* to ask with earnestness; to petition; to entreat;—*v.i.* to try to obtain, as custom, etc.; to accost.—**solic′itant** *n.* one who solicits; petitioner.—**solicita′tion** *n.* earnest request; invitation; petition.—**solic′itous** *a.* anxious; eager; earnest.—**solic′itously** *adv.*—**solic′itousness, solic′itude** *n.* being solicitous; uneasiness; anxiety; concern; carefulness [L. *sollicitare*, to stir up].

solicitor (so-lis′i-tor) *n.* one who solicits; person legally qualified to represent another in a court of law.—**Solicitor-General**, law officer of Crown, ranking below Attorney-General (in England) or below Lord Advocate (in Scotland) [L. *sollicitare*, to stir up].

solid (sol′id) *a.* not in a liquid or gaseous state; hard; compact; firm; not hollow; dependable; sound; unanimous; (*Geom.*) having length, breadth, and thickness; (*Colloq.*) whole; complete;—*n.* firm, compact body; (*Geom.*) that which has length, breadth and thickness; (*Physics*) substance which is not liquid nor gaseous.—**sol′idly** *adv.* firmly; unitedly; unanimously.—**solidar′ity** *n.* state of being solidly united in support of common interests, rights, etc.—**solid′ity** *n.* state of being solid; compactness; hardness; firmness.—**sol′idness** *n.* [L. *solidus*, firm].

solidify (so-lid′i-fī) *v.t.* to make solid or firm; to harden;—*v.i.* to become solid [L. *solidus*, firm; *facere*, to make].

solidus (sol′i-dus) *n.* oblique stroke (/) denoting English shilling.—*pl.* **sol′idi** [L.].

soliloquy (so-lil′o-kwi) *n.* talking to oneself; monologue, esp. by actor alone on stage.—**solil′oquise** *v.i.* to recite a soliloquy [L. *solus*, alone; *loqui*, to speak].

solitaire (sol-i-tār′) *n.* single gem, esp. diamond, set by itself; game for one person, played on a board with marbles; (*Cards*) game for one, patience; recluse [Fr. fr. L. *solus*, alone].

solitary (sol′i-tar-i) *a.* living alone; done or spent alone; lonely; secluded; desolate; single; sole;—*n.* one who lives in solitude; hermit; recluse.—**sol′itarily** *adv.*—**sol′itariness** *n.*—**sol′itude** *n.* being alone; loneliness; lonely place or life [L. *solus*, alone].

solo (sō′lō) *n.* musical composition played or sung by one person.—*pl.* **solos** (sō′lōz) or **soli** (sō′lē); in aviation, flight by single person; short for—**so′lo-whist** *n.* card game;—*a.* done or performed by one person; unaccompanied; alone.—**soloist** (sō′lō-ist) *n.* (*Mus.*) performer of solos [It. fr. L. *solus*, alone].

Solomon's seal, figure in form of six-pointed

star, made by interlacing of two triangles; (*Bot.*) plant like lily of the valley.

solstice (sol'stis) *n.* either of two points in sun's path at which sun is farthest N. or S. from equator; they mark mid-summer and mid-winter respectively.—**solstitial** (sol-sti'shąl) *a.* [L. *sol*, the sun; *sistere*, to cause to stand].

soluble (sol'ū-bl) *a.* capable of being dissolved in a liquid; able to be solved or explained.—**solubil'ity** *n.* [L. *solubilis*, fr. *solvere*, to loosen].

solus (sō'lus) *a.* as a stage direction, alone.—*fem.* **so'la** [L. = alone].

solution (so-lū'shun) *n.* process of finding answer to problem; answer itself; dissolving gas, liquid, or solid, esp. in liquid; mixture so obtained; commonly, a mixture of a solid in a liquid; separation; disintegration;—*v.t.* to coat with solution, as a puncture.—**sol'ute** *n.* substance dissolved in a solution [L. *solvere*, *solutum*, to loosen].

solve (solv) *v.t.* orig. to loosen or separate parts of; to work out; to find the answer to; to explain; to make clear.—**sol'vable** *a.* capable of explanation; able to be worked out.—**sol'ver** *n.* one who solves.—**sol'vent** *a.* having the power to dissolve another substance; able to pay all one's debts;—*n.* substance, able to dissolve another substance.—**sol'vency** *n.* state of being able to pay one's debts [L. *solvere*, to loosen].

somatic (sō-mat'ik) *a.* pert. to the human body; corporeal; physical. Also **somat'ical** [Gk. *sōma*, a body].

sombre (som'bẹr) *a.* dark; gloomy; melancholy.—**som'brely** *adv.*—**som'breness** *n.* darkness; gloominess.—**som'brous** *a.* (*Poet.*) sombre.—**som'brously** *adv.* [Fr. fr. L. *sub umbra*, under shade].

sombrero (som-brā'rō) *n.* broad-brimmed felt hat [Sp. *sombra*, shade].

some (sum) *a.* denoting an indefinite number, amount, or extent; amount of; one or other; a certain; particular; approximately; (*Colloq.*) remarkable;—(*pron.*) quantity; portion; particular persons not named;—*adv.* approximately.—**some'body** *n.* person not definitely known; person of importance.—**some'how** *adv.* in one way or another; by any means.—**some'one** *n.* somebody; person not named.—**some'such** *a.* denoting person or thing of the kind specified.—**some'thing** *n.* thing not clearly defined; an indefinite quantity or degree;—*adv.* in some degree.—**some'time** *adv.* at a time not definitely stated; at one time or other; at a future time;—*a.* former.—**some'times** *adv.* at times; now and then; occasionally; at intervals.—**some'what** *n.* indefinite amount or degree; more or less; something;—*adv.* to some extent; rather.—**some'where** *adv.* in an unnamed or unknown place [O.E. *sum*].

somersault (sum'ẹr-sawlt) *n.* leap in which one turns heels over head;—*v.i.* to make such a leap. Also **somerset** (sum'ẹr-set) [L. *supra*, above; *saltus*, a leap].

somite (sō'mīt) *n.* segment of body of a vertebrate or articulate animal.—**somit'ic** *a.* [Gk. *sōma*, a body].

somnambulate (som-nam'bū-lāt) *v.i.* to walk in one's sleep.—**somnambula'tion** *n.* the act of walking in one's sleep.—**somnam'bulism** *n.* habit of walking in one's sleep; sleep-walking.—**somnam'bulist** *n.* a sleep-walker.—**somnambulist'ic** *a.* [L. *somnus*, sleep; *ambulare*, to walk].

somnifacient (som-ni-fā'shẹnt) *a.* inducing sleep;—*n.* soporific.—**somnif'erous** *a.* inducing sleep.—**somnif'ic** *a.* causing sleep [L. *somnus*, sleep; *facere*, to make; *ferre*, to bring].

somnolent (som'no-lẹnt) *a.* sleepy; drowsy.—**som'nolently** *adv.* drowsily.—**som'nolence** *n.* sleepiness; drowsiness. Also **som'nolency.**—**somnoles'cent** *a.* half-asleep [L. *somnus*, sleep].

son (sun) *n.* male child; male descendant, however distant; term of affection; native of a place; disciple.—**son'-in-law** *n.* the husband of one's daughter [O.E. *sunu*].

sonant (sō'nạnt) *a.* pert. to sound; (*Phonetics*) of certain alphabetic sounds, voiced;—*n.* letter as uttered.—**so'nancy** *n.* [L. *sonare*, to sound].

sonata (so-nà'tạ) *n.* a musical composition in three or four movements.—**sonatina** (so-nạ-tē'nạ) *n.* a short sonata [It. fr. L. *sonare*, to sound].

song (song) *n.* singing; poem, or piece of poetry, esp. if set to music; piece of music to be sung; musical sounds made by birds; (*Colloq.*) a mere trifle.—**song'bird** *n.* a singing bird.—**song'ster** *n.* (*fem.* **song'stress**) one who sings a song-bird [O.E. *sang*, fr. *singan*, to sing].

sonnet (son'et) *n.* poem of fourteen lines of iambic pentameter, with a definite rhyme scheme.—**sonneteer'** *n.* a writer of sonnets [It. *sonetto*, fr. L. *sonus*, a sound].

sonorous (so-nō'rus) *a.* giving out a deep, loud sound when struck; resonant; high-sounding.—**sono'rously** *adv.*—**sonor'ity**, **sono'rousness** *n.* [L. *sonorus*, noisy].

soon (sôôn) *adv.* in a short time; shortly; without delay; early; willingly.—**as soon as**, immediately after [O.E. *sona*, at once].

soot (soot) *n.* a black powdery substance formed by burning of coal, etc.;—*v.t.* to cover with soot.—**soot'y** *a.* pert. to, or like, soot; covered with soot; black; dingy; dirty.—**soot'iness** *n.* [O.E. *sot*].

sooth (sôôth) *n.* truth; reality;—*a.* true; faithful.—**sooth'sayer** *n.* one who claims to be able to foretell future.—**sooth'saying** *n.* [O.E. *soth*, true].

soothe (sôôTH) *v.t.* to please with soft words or kind actions; to calm; to comfort; to allay, as pain.—**sooth'ing** *a.*—**sooth'ingly** *adv.* [O.E. *sothian*, to show to be true].

sop (sop) *n.* piece of bread, etc., dipped in a liquid; anything given to pacify or quieten; bribe;—*v.t.* to steep in liquid.—*pr.p.* **sop'ping.**—*pa.p.* and *pa.t.* **sopped.**—**sop'ping** *a.* soaked; wet through.—**sop'py** *a.* soaked; (*Colloq.*) ridiculously sentimental; sloppy.—**to throw a sop to Cerberus**, to placate by giving a bribe, etc. [O.E. *sopp*, fr. *supan*, to sip].

sophism (sof'izm) *n.* specious argument; clever but fallacious reasoning.—**soph'ist** *n.* orig. in ancient Greece, teacher of logic, rhetoric, philosophy; one who uses fallacious arguments or who quibbles.—**soph'istry** *n.* practice of sophists.—**sophis'tic**, **sophis'tical** *a.*—**sophis'tically** *adv.*—**sophis'ticate** *v.t.* to deceive by using sophisms; to make artificial; to falsify; to adulterate.—**sophis'ticated** *a.* wise in ways of the world; not genuine; artificial.—**sophistica'tion** *n.* [Gk. *sophisma*, fr. *sophos*, wise].

sophister (sof'is-tẹr) *n.* formerly, university student after first year.—**sophomore** (sof'ō-mōr) *n.* (*U.S.*) second-year student of university, college, or high school [Gk. *sophos*, wise].

sopor (sō'por) *n.* coma.—**soporif'ic** *a.* causing or inducing sleep;—*n.* drug, which induces deep sleep.—**soporif'erous**, **so'porose**, **so'porous** *a.* causing sleep; sleepy.—**soporif'erously** *adv.*—**soporif'erousness** *n.* [L. *sopor*, deep sleep; *facere*, to make].

soprano (sō-prà'nō) *n.* highest type of female or boy's voice; soprano singer;—*pl.* **sopra'nos**, **soprani** (sō-prà'nī) [It. fr. *sopra*, above].

sorcery (sor'sẹr-i) *n.* witchcraft; magic; enchantment.—**sor'cerer** *n.* a magician.—*fem.* **sor'ceress**, a witch [L. *sortiri*. to cast lots].

sordid (sor'did) *a.* filthy; squalid; meanly avaricious.—**sor'didly** *adv.*—**sor'didness** *n.* [L. *sordidus*, dirty].

sore (sōr) *a.* painful when touched; causing pain; tender; severe; intense; distressed; grieved; angry;—*adv.* painfully, grievously; intensely;—*n.* place where pain is felt; diseased, injured, or bruised spot on body; ulcer; boil.—**sore'ly** *adv.*—**sore'ness** *n.* [O.E. *sar*].

sorghum (sor′gum) *n.* cane-like grasses, including millet; Chinese sugar-cane; molasses [etym. uncertain].
Soroptimist (sor-op′tim-ist) *n.* member of women's Rotary club [L. *soror*, sister, and *optimist*].
sororal (so-rō′ral) *a.* pert. to sisters; sisterly. —**soror′icide** *n.* murder, or murderer, of sister. —**soror′ity** *n.* (*U.S.*) a girls' or women's society [L. *soror*, a sister].
sorosis (so-rō′sis) *n.* compound fleshy fruit, e.g. pineapple [Gk. *sōros*, heap].
sorrel (sor′el) *n.* meadow plant with sour taste [O.Fr. *surelle*].
sorrel (sor′el) *a.* reddish-brown;—*n.* (horse of) reddish-brown colour [O.Fr. *sorel*].
sorrow (sor′ō) *n.* pain of mind; grief; sadness; distress; cause of grief, etc.;—*v.i.* to feel pain of mind; to grieve. —**sorr′ower** *n.* —**sorr′owful** *a.* causing sorrow; sad; unhappy.—**sorr′owfully** *adv.*—**sorr′owfulness** *n.* [O.E. *sorh*].
sorry (sor′i) *a.* feeling regret; pained in mind; mean; shabby; wretched; worthless.—**sorr′ily** *adv.*—**sorr′iness** *n.* [O.E. *sarig*].
sort (sort) *n.* kind or class; persons or things having same qualities; quality; character; order or rank;—*v.t.* to classify; to put in order. —**sort′er** *n.* —**of a sort, of sorts,** of middling quality; not up to standard.—**out of sorts,** unwell [L. *sors*, a share, a lot].
sortie (sor′tē) *n.* sally by besieged forces to attack besiegers; flight by warplane [Fr. *sortir*, to go out].
S. O. S. (es-ō-es) *n.* international code-signal call of distress, esp, by wireless in Morse (. . . — — — . . .); any desperate appeal for help.
sot (sot) *n.* confirmed drunkard.—**sot′tish** *a.* pert. to sot; stupid through drink [Fr. *sot*, foolish].
sotto voce (sot′tō vō′chā) *adv.* under one's breath [It. *sotto*, under; *voce*, the voice].
sou (sóó) *n.* former French coin of various values; French halfpenny [Fr. fr. L. *solidus*, a coin].
soubrette (sóó-bret′) *n.* pert, coquettish maidservant in French comedy [Fr.].
soubriquet See **sobriquet.**
soufflé (sóó′flā) *n.* a delicate dish made from whites of eggs beaten to a froth, flavoured, and baked [Fr. *souffler*, to blow].
sough (suf, sou, *Scot*, sooH) *n.* low murmuring, sighing, or whistling sound, as of the wind through trees;—*v.i.* to make this sound [O.E. *swogan*, to resound].
sought (sawt) *pa.p.* and *pa.t.* of **seek.**
soul (sōl) *n.* spiritual and immortal part of human being; seat of emotion, sentiment, and aspiration; the centre of moral and intellectual powers; vigour; energy; spirit; the essence; the moving spirit; a human being.—**soul′ful** *a.* full of soul, emotion, or sentiment; expressing elevated feeling.—**soul′fully** *adv.*—**soul′less** *a.* without a soul; not inspired; prosaic [O.E. *sawol*].
sound (sound) *a.* healthy; in good condition; solid; entire; profound; free from error; reliable; solvent, as a business firm;—*adv.* soundly; completely.—**sound′ly** *adv.* thoroughly.—**sound′ness** *n.* [O.E. *gesund*, healthy].
sound (sound) *n.* long, narrow stretch of water; channel; strait [O.E. *sund*].
sound (sound) *v.t.* to find depth of water, by means of line and lead; (*Fig.*) to try to discover the opinions of;—*v.i.* to find depth of water; of a whale, to dive suddenly.—**sound′ing** *n.* measuring the depth of water, esp. with a weighted line; measurement obtained [Fr. *sonder*].
sound (sound) *n.* that which is heard; the distance to which a sound is heard; earshot; a noise; a report;—*v.t.* to cause to make a sound; to utter; to play on; to signal; to examine with stethoscope;—*v.i.* to make a noise; to be conveyed by sound; to appear; to seem.—**sound′ing** *a.* making a sound; resonant —**sound barrier** (*Aero.*) colloq. term for phenomena occurring when an aircraft reaches speed in excess of that of sound.—**sound′-track** *n.* strip on one side of cinema film which records sound vibrations and so produces dialogue.—**sound′-waves** *n.pl.* vibrations of the air producing sound.—**sound′ing-board, sound′ing-box** *n.* board or box which reinforces sound from musical instrument; canopy over pulpit for directing voice towards the congregation [L. *sonus*].
soup (sóóp) *n.* liquid food made by boiling meat or vegetables.—**to be in the soup** (*Slang*) to be in serious trouble [Fr. *soupe*, fr. *souper*, to sup].
soupçon (sóóp-sōng′) *n.* suspicion; hence, very small quantity; a taste [Fr.].
sour (sour) *a.* acid; having a sharp taste; pungent; rancid; of milk, turned; of soil, cold and wet; (*Fig.*) cross;—*v.t.* and *v.i.* to make or become sour.—**soured** *a.* embittered; aggrieved.—**sour′ly** *adv.*—**sour′ness** *n.* [O.E. *sur*].
source (sōrs) *n.* spring; fountain; origin (of stream) [L. *surgere*, to rise].
sourdough (sour′dō) *n.* batter of flour and water left till it sours or ferments, then baked; (*U.S.*) an old-timer, esp. in Alaska [*sour* and *dough*].
souse (sous) *v.t.* to steep in brine; to pickle; to plunge into a liquid; to soak;—*n.* a pickle made with salt; brine; anything steeped in it; a drenching [form of *sauce*, fr. L. *sal*, salt].
soutane (sóó-tan′) *n.* gown worn by R.C. priests; cassock [L. *subtus*, beneath].
south (south) *n.* cardinal point of compass opposite north; region lying to that side;—*a.* pert. to, or coming from, the south;—*adv.* towards the south;—*v.i.* to move towards the south.—**southerly** *a.* (suTH′er-li) *a.* pert. to south.—**south′ern** *a.* in, from, or towards, the south.—**south′erner** *n.* native of south of a country, etc.—**south′ernly** *adv.* towards the south.—**south′ernmost** (also **south′ermost, south′most**) *a.* lying farthest towards the south.—**south′ward** *a.* and *adv.* towards south;—*n.* southern direction.—**south′wardly** *a.* and *adv.* —**south′wards** *adv.*—**sou′west′er** (or **south′west′er**) *n.* a strong wind from south-west; waterproof hat [O.E. *suth*].
southernwood (suTH′ern-wood) *n.* an aromatic plant, allied to wormwood [E. *southern* and *wood*].
souvenir (sóó-ve-nēr′, sóó′ven-ēr) *n.* a keepsake; a memento [Fr. *souvenir*, to remind].
sovereign (suv′ran, sov′ran, suv′er-in, sov′er-in) *n.* ruler; formerly, British gold coin=one pound sterling = 20 shillings; —*a.* supreme in power; chief; efficacious in highest degree.—**sov′ereignty** *n.* right to exercise supreme power [O.Fr. *sovrain*, fr. L. *supra*, above].
soviet (sov′yet, sō′vi-et) *n.* council.—**Sov′iet** *n.* political body, consisting of representatives of workers and peasants, elected to local municipalities, regional councils, etc. and sending delegates to higher congresses. Also *a.* —**Soviet Union,** short for the 'Union of Socialist Soviet Republics,' i.e. Russia;—*abbrev.* **U.S.S.R.** [Russ. = a council].
sow (sou) *n.* female pig; in smelting, bar of cast iron [O.E. *sugu*].
sow (sō) *v.t.* to scatter or deposit (seed); to spread abroad; to disseminate;—*v.i.* to scatter seed.—*pa.p.* **sown** (sōn) or **sowed** (sōd).—*pa.t.* **sowed.**—**sow′er** *n.* [O.E. *sawan*].
soy (soi) *n.* sauce made from soy-bean (soya-bean).—**soy′-bean, soy′a-bean** *n.* seed of leguminous plant of Far East, yielding oil (for margarine), flour, cattle fodder, and a fertiliser [Jap, *shoyu*].
Spa (spå) *n.* inland watering-place in Belgium. —**spa** *n.* any place with mineral spring.
space (spās) *n.* expanse of universe; area; room; period of time; extent; empty place; —*v.t.* to place at intervals.—**spa′cious** (spā′shus) *a.* roomy; capacious; extensive.

spa'ciously *adv.*—**spa'ciousness** *n.* [Fr. *espace*, fr. L. *spatium*].

spade (spād) *n.* digging-tool, with flat blade and long handle;—*v.t.* to dig with spade.—**spade'work** *n.* toilsome work preliminary to main task [O.E. *spadu*].

spade (spād) *n.* (*Cards*) one of two black suits, marked by figure like a pointed spade [Sp. *espada*, a sword].

spaghetti (spa-get'ti) *n.* foodstuff resembling macaroni but thinner [It. *spago*, cord].

spake (spāk) *pa.t.* (*Arch.*) of **speak**.

Spam (spam) *n.* chopped, spiced ham [Proprietary name, fr. *sp*iced h*am*].

span (span) *pa.t.* of **spin**.

span (span) *n.* distance between thumb and little finger, when fingers are fully extended; this distance as measure = 9 in.; short distance or period of time; distance between supports of arch, roof, etc.; of aeroplane, distance from wing-tip to wing-tip; pair, of horses or oxen harnessed together;—*v.t.* to reach from one side of to the other; to extend across.—*pr.p.* **span'ning**.—*pa.p.* and *pa.t.* **spanned**.—**span'ner** *n.* one who spans; tool for tightening screw-nuts; a wrench [O.E. *spann*].

spandrel (span'drel) *n.* (*Archit.*) the space between outer curves of arch and square head over it; ornamental design in corner of postage-stamp [etym. uncertain].

spangle (spang'gl) *n.* a small piece of glittering metal, used to ornament dresses;—*v.t.* to adorn with spangles;—*v.i.* to glitter [O.E. *spang*, a buckle].

Spaniard (span'yard) *n.* native of Spain.—**Span'ish** *a.* of, or pert. to, Spain;—*n.* language of Spain.—**Spanish Main**, mainland of S. America bordering Caribbean Sea.

spaniel (span'yel) *n.* breed of dogs, with long, drooping ears; fawning person [O.Fr. *espagneul*, Spanish].

spank (spangk) *v.i.* to move with vigour or spirit.—**spank'ing** *a.* moving with quick, lively step; dashing.—**spank'er** *n.* fast-going horse, ship, etc.; (*Naut.*) fore-and-aft sail attached to the mast nearest the stern [Dan. *spanke*, to strut].

spank (spangk) *v.t.* to strike with flat of hand; to slap;—*n.* slap [imit. origin].

spar (spȧr) *v.i.* to fight with the fists, in fun or in earnest; to fight with spurs on, as in cock-fighting; to dispute, esp. in fun.—*pr.p.* **spar'ring**.—*pa.p.* and *pa.t.* **sparred** [etym. uncertain].

spar (spȧr) *n.* pole or beam, esp. as part of ship's rigging [O.N. *sparri*].

spar (spȧr) *n.* crystalline mineral which breaks into smooth layers, and has some degree of lustre [O.E. *spaerstan*, gypsum].

spare (spār) *v.t.* and *v.i.* to use frugally; to do without; to save; to omit; to leave unhurt; to give away;—*a.* frugal; scanty; scarce; parsimonious; thin; lean; additional; in reserve; not in use;—*n.* that which is held in reserve.—*pl.* **spares** or **spare'parts**, duplicate parts of a machine.—**spare'ly** *adv.*—**spare'ness** *n.* thinness; leanness.—**spar'ing** *a.* frugal; saving; scanty; merciful.—**spar'ingly** *adv.* [O.E. *sparian*].

spark (spȧrk) *n.* small glowing or burning particle; flash of light; trace or particle of anything; in internal-combustion engines, electric flash which ignites explosive mixture in cylinder; (*Colloq.*) gay, dashing young fellow;—*v.i.* to send out sparks.—*pl.* **sparks** (*Naut. Slang*) wireless operator.—**spark'ing-plug** *n.* in internal-combustion engines, device, screwed into cylinder head, for providing electric spark to ignite mixture of air and petrol vapour [O.E. *spearca*].

sparkle (spȧrk'l) *n.* small spark; a glitter; a gleam;—*v.i.* to emit small flashes of light; to gleam; to emit little bubbles; to effervesce.—**spark'ler** *n.* one who, or that which, sparkles; (*Slang*) a diamond.—**spark'ling** *a.* emitting sparks; flashing; gleaming; glittering; of wines, effervescent [O.E. *spearca*].

sparrow (spar'ō) *n.* small brown bird of finch family.—**sparr'ow-grass** *n.* asparagus.—**sparr'ow-hawk** *n.* one of the falcon family, which hunts small birds [O.E. *spearwa*].

sparse (spȧrs) *a.* thinly scattered; scanty; rare.—**sparse'ly** *adv.*—**sparse'ness** *n.* scantiness [L. *spargere*, *sparsum*, to scatter].

Sparta (spȧr'ta) *n.* ancient Greek city-state.—**Spar'tan** *n.* citizen of this town; one who faces danger, etc. without flinching;—*a.* pert. to Sparta; dauntless.

spasm (spazm) *n.* sudden, involuntary contraction of muscle(s); sudden, convulsive movement, effort, emotion, etc.; fitful effort; a paroxysm.—**spasmod'ic** *n.* medicine for relieving spasms.—**spasmod'ic(al)** *a.* pert. to spasms; convulsive; fitful.—**spasmod'ically** *adv.* by fits and starts.—**spas'tic** *a.* (*Med.*) pert. to spasms; in a rigid condition, due to spasm; applied to children suffering from cerebral palsy.—*n.* such a child.—**spas'tics** *n.pl.* (*Med.*) condition showing tendency to spasm or muscular contraction [Gk. *spasmos*, fr. *spaein*, to draw].

spat (spat) *pa.t.* of **spit**.

spat (spat) *n.* kind of cloth gaiter, reaching a little above ankle. Usually in *pl.* **spats** [*abbrev.* of *spatterdash*].

spat (spat) *n.* spawn of shell-fish or oyster;—*v.i.* to spawn, of oysters [fr. *spit*].

spate (spāt) *n.* flood in a river, esp. after heavy rain; inundation [Gael. *speid*].

spathe (spāTH) *n.* leaflike sheath enveloping flower cluster.—**spathed, spa'those, spa'thous** *a.* [Gk. *spathē*, a broad blade].

spatial (spā'shal) *a.* pert. to space.—**spa'tially** *adv.* [L. *spatium*].

spatter (spat'er) *v.t.* to cast drops of water, mud, etc. over; to splash; to speak ill of;—*v.i.* to fall in drops;—*n.* the act of spattering; a slight splash [Dut. *spatten*, to burst].

spatula (spat'ū-la) *n.* broad-bladed knife for spreading paints, ointments; (*Med.*) small instrument for holding down tongue during examination of throat.—**spat'ular, spat'ulate** *a.* shaped like spatula [Gk. *spathē*, a broad blade].

spavin (spav'in) *n.* swelling on horse's leg, causing lameness.—**spav'ined** *a.* affected with spavin [O.Fr. *esparvain*].

spawn (spawn) *n.* eggs of fish, frogs; offspring;—*v.t.* and *v.i.* of fish, frogs, to cast eggs; to produce offspring [O.Fr. *espandre*, fr. L. *expandere*, to spread out].

speak (spēk) *v.i.* to utter words; to tell; to deliver a discourse;—*v.t.* to utter; to pronounce; to express in words; to express silently or by signs; to address.—*pr.p.* **speak'ing**.—*pa.p.* **spo'ken**.—*pa.t.* **spoke** or (*Arch.*) **spake**.—**speak'er** *n.* one who speaks; orator.—**the Speaker**, president of British House of Commons and of similar legislative bodies.—**speak'ing** *n.*—*a.* having power to utter words; eloquent; (*Fig.*) lifelike, e.g. of picture.—**speak'eas'y** *n.* (*U.S.*) illicit drinking-den, esp. during Prohibition; shebeen [O.E. *sprecan*].

spear (spēr) *n.* long, pointed weapon, used in fighting, hunting, etc.; sharp-pointed instrument for catching fish; lance; pike;—*v.t.* to pierce or kill with spear.—**spear'head** *n.* iron point, barb, or prong of a spear; leader of an advance; (*Mil.*) deep penetration, on a narrow front, into an enemy position.—**spear'mint** *n.* common mint.—**spear'side** *n.* male branch of a family [O.E. *spere*].

special (spesh'al) *a.* pert. to a species or sort; particular; beyond the usual; distinct; intimate; designed for a particular person or purpose.—**spec'ially** *adv.*—**spec'ialise** *v.t.* to make special or distinct; to adapt for a particular purpose;—*v.i.* to devote oneself to a particular branch of study.—**specialisa'tion** *n.* act of specialising.—**spec'ialist** *n.* one trained and skilled in a special branch.—**specialist'ic** *a.*—**speciality** (spesh-i-al'i-ti), **specialty** (spesh'al-ti) *n.* a special characteristic of a person or thing; a special product; that in which a

person is highly skilled.—**special constable,** man sworn in to help police in emergency, esp. in wartime [L. *species*, a kind].
specie (spē′shē) *n.* coined money, esp. gold or silver, as distinct from paper money [L. *species*, a kind].
species (spē′shēz, -shiz) *n.* kind; variety; sort; class; subdivision of a more general class or genus [L. *species*, a kind].
specific (spe-sif′ik) *a.* pert. to, or characteristic of, a species; peculiar to; well defined; precise; —*n.* (*Med.*) infallible remedy.—**specif′ically** *adv.*—**specific gravity,** weight of substance expressed in relation to weight of equal volume of water [L. *species*, a kind; *facere*, to make].
specification (spes-i-fi-kā′shun) *n.* act of specifying.—**spec′ify** *v.t.* to state definitely; to give details of; to indicate precisely.—**specifi′able** *a.* [L. *species*, a kind; *facere*, to make].
specimen (spes′i-men) *n.* part of anything, or one of a number of things, used to show nature and quality of the whole; sample [L. *specere*, to look].
specious (spē′shus) *a.* having a fair appearance; superficially fair or just; apparently acceptable, esp. at first sight.—**spe′ciously** *adv.* —**specios′ity, spe′ciousness** *n.* [L. *speciosus*, fair to see, fr. *species*, kind, appearance].
speck (spek) *n.* small spot; particle; very small thing; stain;—*v.t.* to mark with specks.—**speck′le** *n.* a small speck or spot;—*v.t.* to mark with small spots.—**speck′led** *a.* spotted; variegated.—**speck′less** *a.* unstained; perfectly clean [O.E. *specca*].
spectacle (spek′ta-kl) *n.* sight; show; thing exhibited; a pageant.—**spec′tacles** *n.pl.* arrangement of lenses, to help defective or weak eyesight.—**spec′tacled** *a.* wearing spectacles.—**spectac′ular** *a.* showy; grand; making great display.—**spectac′ularly** *adv.* [L. *spectare*, to look at].
spectator (spek-tā′tor) *n.* (*fem.* **specta′tress, specta′trix**) one who looks on; an onlooker [L. *spectare*, to look at].
spectre (spek′ter) *n.* ghost; apparition.—**spec′tral** *a.* pert. to a spectre; ghostly; pert. to spectrum.—**spec′trally** *adv.*—**spec′trum** *n.* the coloured band into which a ray of light can be separated as in the rainbow [L. *spectrum*, an image].
spectro- (spek′tro) *prefix* fr. L. *spectrum*, an image, used in many derivatives.—**spec′trograph** *n.* scientific instrument for photographing spectra.—**spec′troscope** *n.* instrument for production and examination of spectra.—**spectroscop′ic, spectroscop′ical** *a.* [Gk. *graphein*, to write; *skopein*, to view].
speculate (spek′ū-lāt) *v.i.* to make theories or guesses; to meditate; to engage in risky commercial transactions.—**specula′tion** *n.* act of speculating; theorising; guess; practice of buying shares, etc. in the hope of selling at a high profit.—**spec′ulative** *a.* given to speculation.—**spec′ulatively** *adv.*—**spec′ulator** *n.*—**spec′ulatory** *a.* speculative [L. *speculari*, to observe].
speculum (spek′ū-lum) *n.* mirror; reflector of polished metals, esp. as used in reflecting-telescopes; (*Surg.*) instrument for examining interior cavity of body.—*pl.* **spec′ula** [L. fr. *specere*, to observe].
sped (sped) *pa.p.* and *pa.t.* of **speed.**
speech (spēch) *n.* power of speaking; what is spoken; faculty of expressing thoughts in words; enunciation; remarks; conversation; language; formal address; an oration.—**speech′less** *a.* without power of speech; dumb; silent.—**speech′lessly** *adv.*—**speech′lessness** *n.*—**speech′ify** *v.i.* to make speech, esp. long and tedious one.—**speech′ifier** *n.* [O.E. *spraec*].
speed (spēd) *n.* swiftness of motion; rate of progress; velocity;—*v.t.* to cause to move faster; to aid; to bid farewell to;—*v.i.* to move quickly or at speed beyond legal limit; to succeed.—*pa.p.* and *pa.t.* **sped.**—**speed′y** *a.* quick; rapid.—**speed′ily** *adv.*—**speed′-boat** *n.* very fast motor-boat.—**speedom′eter** *n.* instrument indicating speed, usually in miles per hour.—**speed′way** *n.* track for motor-cycle racing.—**speed′well** *n.* small plant of genus Veronica, bearing white, blue, or purple flowers [O.E. *sped*].
spelaean, spelean (spē-lē′an) *a.* pert. to, dwelling in, cave [Gk. *spēlaion*, cave].
spell (spel) *n.* word or words supposed to have magical power; magic formula; fascination.—**spell′bind** *v.t.* to hold as if by spell; to enchant; to fascinate.—**spell′bound** *a.* fascinated; enchanted; entranced [O.E. *spell*, a narrative].
spell (spel) *n.* a turn of work or duty, esp. to relieve another; a brief period of time [O.E. *spelian*, to act for].
spell (spel) *v.t.* to read letter by letter; to mean;—*v.i.* to form words with proper letters. —*pa.p.* and *pa.t.* **spelled** or **spelt** [O.E. *spell*, a narrative].
spencer (spen′ser) *n.* a short over-jacket [fr. Earl *Spencer*, (1782-1845)].
spend (spend) *v.t.* and *v.i.* to pay out; to disburse; to pass, as time; to employ; to waste; to exhaust.—**spent** *a.* exhausted; worn out; inefficient; of a fish, having deposited spawn. —**spen′der** *n.* one who spends.—**spend′thrift** *n.* one who spends money foolishly or extravagantly;—*a.* extravagant [O.E. *spenden*].
sperm (sperm) *n.* fertilising fluid of male animals; semen.—**sperm′-oil** *n.* oil obtained from sperm-whale.—**sperm′-whale** *n.* cachalot, large whale, valuable for its oil and for spermaceti.—**spermaceti** (sper-ma-sē′ti, sper-ma-set′i) *n.* wax-like substance obtained from head of sperm-whale, used for making candles, etc.—**spermat′ic, spermat′ical** *a.* pert. to sperm [Gk. *sperma*, seed].
spermato- (sper-mat′o) *prefix* fr. Gk. *sperma*, seed.—**sper′matoid** *a.* resembling sperm.—**spermatozoon** (sper-mat-o-zō′on) *n.* male generative cell, found in semen and capable of fertilising ovum, or female germ cell.—*pl.* **spermatozo′a.**—**spermatozo′al, spermatozo′an** *a.*
spew, spue (spū) *v.t.* and *v.i.* to eject from the stomach; to vomit [O.E. *spiwan*].
sphagnum (sfag′num) *n.* bog-moss [Gk. *sphagnos*].
sphere (sfēr) *n.* round, solid body; ball; globe; revolution; orbit; range of knowledge, influence, etc.; field of action; social status; position;—*v.t.* to put in a sphere; to encircle. —**sphe′ral** (sfē′ral) *a.* formed like a sphere.—**spheric** (sfer′ik) *a.* pert. to heavenly bodies.—**spher′ical** *a.* sphere-shaped.—**spher′ically** *adv.* —**spheric′ity** *n.* roundness.—**spheroid** (sfē′roid) *n.* body almost, but not quite, spherical, e.g. orange, earth, etc.—**spheroi′dal** *a.* having form of spheroid. Also **spheroi′dic, spheroi′dical.**—**spherule** (sfer′ūl) *n.* a small sphere.—**spher′ular, spher′ulate** *a.* [Gk. *sphaira*, a globe].
sphincter (sfingk′ter) *n.* (*Anat.*) circular muscle which contracts or expands orifice of an organ, e.g. round anus [Gk. *sphingein*, to bind tight].
sphinx (sfingks) *n.* (*Myth.*) fabulous monster, with winged body of lion and head of woman, which proposed riddles to passers-by, and strangled all unable to solve them; statue of this; (*Fig.*) one whose thoughts are difficult to guess; enigmatic person [Gk. *sphinx*, literally, the strangler].
sphygmus (sfig′mus) *n.* (*Med.*) pulse.—**sphyg′mic** *a.* [Gk. *sphugmos*, the pulse].
spice (spīs) *n.* aromatic substance, used for seasoning; spices collectively; (*Fig.*) anything that adds flavour, etc.; a trace;—*v.t.* to season with spice.—**spi′cery** *n.* spices collectively.—**spi′cey** *a.* seasoned with spices; aromatic; fragrant; dashing.—**spi′cily** *adv.* [O.Fr. *espice*].
spick (spik) *n.* spike; nail;—*a.* neat; tidy.—**spick and span,** fresh and new; neat, clean [*spick*, spike; fr. O.N. *span-nyr*, new as chip just split].
spider (spī′der) *n.* small, eight-legged insect-

like animal that spins web to catch flies, etc. —**spi'dery** *a.* like a spider; full of spiders; very thin.—**spi'der-crab** *n.* spiderlike crab, with long, thin legs.—**spi'der-mon'key** *n.* monkey with long, thin legs and tail [O.E. *spinnan,* to spin].

spied (spīd) *pa.p.* and *pa.t.* of **spy.**

spigot (spig'ut) *n.* peg for stopping hole in cask; part of a water-tap which controls flow [L. *spica,* an ear of corn].

spike (spīk) *n.* sharp-pointed piece of metal or wood; large nail; ear of corn, etc.; (*Bot.*) flower-cluster growing from central stem;—*v.t.* to supply, set, fasten, or pierce with spikes.—**spi'ky** *a.* furnished with spikes; pointed [O.N. *spik,* a nail, fr. L. *spica,* an ear of corn].

spikenard (spīk'nąrd) *n.* Indian plant like valerian; fragrant oil extracted from its roots [L. *spica nardi,* a spike of nard].

spill (spil) *v.t.* to cause to flow out; to pour out; to shed (blood); to throw off, as from horse, etc.; to upset;—*v.i.* to flow over; to be shed; to be lost or wasted;—*n.* overflow; fall or tumble, as from vehicle, horse, etc.—*pa.p.* and *pa.t.* **spilled** or **spilt.**—**spill'er** *n.*—**spill'way** *n.* channel for overflow water from dam [O.E. *spillan,* to destroy].

spill (spil) *n.* thin strip of wood or twist of paper, for lighting a fire, pipe, etc.; a peg [Dut. *speld,* a splinter].

spin (spin) *v.t.* to twist into threads; to cause to revolve rapidly; to whirl; to twirl; to draw out tediously, as a story; to prolong;—*v.i.* to make thread; to revolve rapidly; to move swiftly;—*n.* rapid whirling motion; short, quick run or drive.—*pr.p.* **spin'ning.**—*pa.p.* and *pa.t.* **spun** or (*Arch.*) **span.**—**spin'ner** *n.* one who spins.—**spin'ning-jenn'y** (jenny = gin or engine) *n.* machine for spinning several threads simultaneously.—**spin'ning-wheel** *n.* household machine in which a large wheel is turned by treadle, for spinning cotton, wool, flax, etc. into thread or yarn [O.E. *spinnan*].

spinach (spin'āj) *n.* vegetable used for food. Also **spin'age.**—**spina'ceous** *a.* [O.Fr. *espinage*].

spindle (spin'dl) *n.* long, slender rod, used in spinning, for twisting and winding the thread; measure of yarn, thread, or silk; shaft; axis; —*v.i.* to grow long and slender.—**spin'dly** *a.* long and slender [O.E. *spinel,* fr. *spinnan,* to spin].

spindrift (spin'drift) *n.* spray blown from surface of sea. Also **spoon'drift.**

spine (spīn) *n.* thorn; prickle; backbone; back of book.—**spi'nal** *a.* pert. to spine or backbone. **spine'less** *a.* having no spine; weak of character.—**spi'ny** *a.* full of spines; like a spine; thorny; prickly; perplexing.—**spi'nose** (spī'nōs), **spi'nous** *a.* full of spines; prickly.—**spinal column,** the backbone [L. *spina,* a thorn].

spinet (spin'et) *n.* musical instrument like a harpsichord [O.Fr. *espinette,* fr. L. *spina*].

spinnaker (spin'a-kęr) *n.* a large triangular sail [etym. uncertain].

spinney (spin'i) *n.* small wood; grove. Also **spin'ny** [L. *spinetum,* fr. *spina,* thorn].

spinster (spin'stęr) *n.* orig. one who spins; unmarried woman.—**spin'sterhood** *n.*—**spin'stress** *n.* woman who spins [O.E. *spinnan,* to spin].

spiracle (spī'rą-kl, spir'ą-kl) *n.* breathing-hole; blow-hole of whale.—**spirac'ular, spirac'ulate** *a.* [L. *spirare,* to breathe].

Spiraea (spī-rē'a) *n.* a genus of herbaceous plants, including meadow-sweet, bearing white or pink flowers [Gk. *speira,* a coil].

spirant (spī'rąnt) *n.* consonant pronounced with perceptible emission of breath [L. *spirare,* to breathe].

spire (spīr) *n.* winding line like threads of screw; curl; coil.—**spi'ral** *a.* winding; coiled;—*n.* spiral curve; coil; whorl;—*v.i.* to follow spiral line; to coil; to curve [Gk. *speira,* coil].

spire (spīr) *n.* blade of grass; stalk; slender shoot; anything tall and tapering to point; (tapering part of) steeple; peak;—*v.t.* to furnish with spire;—*v.i.* to rise high, like spire. —**spi'ral** *a.* like a spire.—**spi'ry** *a.* having spires; tapering [O.E. *spir,* a stalk].

spirit (spir'it) *n.* vital force; immortal part of man; soul; spectre; ghost; frame of mind; disposition; temper; eager desire; mental vigour; courage; cheerfulness; essential character; leader of cause, etc.; liquid got by distillation, esp. alcoholic;—*v.t.* to carry away mysteriously; to put energy into.—**spir'its** *n.pl.* a state of mind; mood; distilled alcoholic liquor.—**spir'ited** *a.* full of spirit and vigour; lively; animated.—**spir'itedly** *adv.*—**spir'itedness** *n.*—**spir'itism** *n.* See **spiritualism.**—**spir'itless** *a.* without spirit or life; lacking energy; listless.—**spir'itlessly** *adv.*—**spir'ituous** *a.* containing alcohol; distilled.—**spir'it-lamp** *n.* lamp in which alcohol is burned, usually methylated spirit.—**spir'it-lev'el** *n.* instrument for finding or testing horizontal line [L. *spiritus,* fr. *spirare,* to breathe].

spiritual (spir'i-tū-ąl) *a.* pert. to spirit or mind; not material; unworldly; pert. to sacred things; holy;—*n.* Negro sacred song or hymn. —**spir'itually** *adv.*—**spir'itualise** *v.t.* to make spiritual; to make pure in heart.—**spir'itualism, spir'itism** *n.* religious belief that spirits of dead can communicate with living people.—**spir'itualist** *n.*—**spir'itualistic** *a.* [L. *spiritus,* breath].

spit (spit) *n.* pointed rod put through meat for roasting; sandy point of land projecting into sea;—*v.t.* to thrust spit through; to impale [O.E. *spitu*].

spit (spit) *v.t.* to eject from mouth; to expel; —*v.i.* to eject saliva from mouth; to expectorate; to hiss, esp. of cats;—*n.* saliva; act of spitting; light fall of fine rain; an exact likeness.—*pr.p.* **spit'ting.**—*pa.p.* **spat.**—*pa.t.* **spat** (*Arch.* **spit**).—**spit'ter** *n.*—**spit'tle** *n.* saliva ejected from mouth; sputum.—**spittoon'** *n.* a vessel for spittle; cuspidor [O.E. *spittan*].

spit (spit) *n.* in digging, the depth of a spade, i.e. 8 to 12 inches [Dut.].

spite (spīt) *n.* malice; ill-will;—*v.t.* to treat maliciously; to try to injure or thwart; to vex; to annoy.—**spite'ful** *a.* full of ill-feeling; desirous of thwarting.—**spite'fully** *adv.*—**spite'fulness** *n.*—**in spite of,** in defiance of; notwithstanding [fr. *despite*].

spitfire (spit'fīr) *n.* hot-tempered person.—**Spit'fire** *n.* (*World War* 2) fighter aeroplane [*spit* and *fire*].

spits (spitz) *n.* a Pomeranian dog [Ger.].

spiv (spiv) *n.* (*Colloq.*) one who lives on his wits; social drone; work-shy person; formerly, police informer; bookmaker's runner [corruption of *spiff,* dandyish].

splash (splash) *v.t.* to spatter water, mud, etc. over; to soil thus; to print in bold headlines; —*v.i.* to dash or scatter, of liquids; to dabble in water; to fall in drops;—*n.* sound of object falling into liquid; water, mud, etc. dashed, about; spot; daub; patch of colour.—**splash'y** *a.* full of dirty water; wet and muddy.—**splash'board** *n.* mud-guard [imit. origin].

splatter (splat'ęr) *v.t.* and *v.i.* to splash continuously; to spatter [fr. *spatter*].

splay (splā) *v.t.* to slope; to slant; to spread outwards;—*a.* turned outwards; flat and broad; *n.* sloped surface of opening, as window. —**splay'foot** *n.* flat foot [fr. *display*].

spleen (splēn) *n.* ductless organ lying to left of stomach; anger; ill-humour; spite; melancholy; irritability.—**spleen'ful** *a.* showing spleen; ill-humoured [Gk. *splēn*].

splendid (splen'did) *a.* magnificent; gorgeous; (*Colloq.*) excellent.—**splen'didly** *adv.*—**splendour** (splen'dęr) *n.* brilliant lustre; gorgeousness; pomp [L. *splendere,* to shine].

splenetic (sple-net'ik) *a.* pert. to spleen; affected with spleen; morose; irritable.—**splenetic** (splen'e-tik) *n.* one suffering from disease of spleen; remedy for this.—**splen'ic** *a.* pert. to the spleen [Gk. *splēn*].

splice (splīs) *v.t.* to join, as two ends of a rope, by weaving strands together; to join, as wood, etc. by overlapping and binding; (*Colloq.*) to marry;—*n.* union of two ends of ropes, etc. by splicing.—**to splice the mainbrace** (*Naval*) to serve a tot of rum to all on board [Dut. *splissen*].

splint (splint) *n.* piece split off; rigid piece of material for holding broken limb in position; bony excrescence on inside of horse's leg;—*v.t.* to bind with splints.—**splint'er** *n.* piece of wood, metal, etc. split off;—*v.t.* and *v.i.* to break off into long, thin pieces; to shiver [Swed. *splint*].

split (split) *v.t.* to cut lengthwise; to cleave; to tear apart; to separate; to divide;—*v.i.* to break asunder; to cut lengthwise; to dash to pieces; to betray a secret;—*n.* crack; fissure; a breach in political party;—*pl.* sitting down with legs stretched apart until they are flat on floor.—*pr.p.* **split'ting.**—*pa.p.* and *pa.t.* **split.**—**split'ting** *n.* cleaving or rending;—*a.* severe; distressing.—**split infinitive,** insertion of adverb or adverbial phrase between 'to' and verb of infinitive.—**split'-new** *a.* brand-new.—**to split hairs,** to make fine distinctions [Dut. *splitten*].

splutter (splut'ẹr) *v.t.* to utter incoherently with spitting sounds;—*v.i.* to emit such sounds; to speak hastily and confusedly;—*n.* such sounds or speech; a confused noise.—**splutt'erer** *n.* [imit. origin].

Spode (spōd) *n.* highly decorated porcelain [Josiah *Spode*, pottery manufacturer of the 18th cent.].

spoil (spoil) *v.t.* to damage; to injure; to take by force; to plunder; to cause to decay; to harm character of by indulgence;—*v.i.* to go bad; to decay;—*n.* booty; prey; plunder; pillage.—*pa.p.* and *pa.t.* **spoiled** or **spoilt.**—**spoil'-sport** *n.* one who takes a delight in interfering with enjoyment of others [L. *spoliare*].

spoke (spōk) *pa.t.* of the verb **speak.**—**spoken** (spōk'n) *pa.p.*—**spokes'man** *n.* one deputed to speak for others; a representative.

spoke (spōk) *n.* one of small bars connecting hub of wheel with rim; rung of ladder; a hand-spike.—**to put a spoke in one's wheel,** to frustrate person by putting difficulties in his way.—**spoke'shave** *n.* tool for planing wood [O.E. *spaca*].

spoliate (spō'li-āt) *v.t.* to spoil; to plunder;—*v.i.* to practise plundering.—**spo'liative** *a.* tending to diminish.—**spolia'tion** *n.* the act of spoiling; robbery; destruction.—**spo'liator** *n.* pillager [L. *spoliare*].

spondee (spon'dē) *n.* in poetry, a foot of two long syllables, marked (— —).—**spondaic** (spon-dā'ik) *a.* [Gk. *spondē*, drink-offering (this metre was much used in hymns accompanying drink-offerings].

spondulicks (spon-dū'liks) *n.pl.* (*Slang*) money; funds [etym. unknown].

sponge (spunj) *n.* marine animal of cellular structure, outer coating of whose body is perforated to allow entrance of water; skeleton of this animal, used to absorb water; act of cleaning with sponge; sponge-cake; (*Colloq.*) parasite; sponger; hanger-on; (*Colloq.*) habitual drinker;—*v.t.* to wipe, cleanse, with sponge;—*v.i.* to live at expense of others.—**spong'er** *n.*—**spongy** (spunj'i) *a.* sponge-like; of open texture; full of small holes; absorbent; wet and soft, esp. of ground.—**spong'iness** *n.*—**sponge'-cake** *n.* light, sweet cake.—**to throw up the sponge,** to acknowledge defeat [Fr. *éponge*, fr. Gk. *spongia*].

sponsal (spon'sạl) *a.* relating to betrothal or marriage [L. *spondere*, to promise].

sponsor (spon'sur) *n.* one who promises for another; surety; godfather or godmother; guarantor; a patron;—*v.t.* to support; to act as guarantor or patron of; to pay for a wireless programme including advertisements of one's own goods.—**sponso'rial** *a.*—**spon'sorship** *n.* [L. *spondere, sponsum*, to promise].

spontaneous (spon-tā'ne-us) *a.* of one's own free-will; voluntary; natural; produced by some internal cause, said of physical effects, as combustion, growth, etc.—**sponta'neously** *adv.*—**spontaneity** (spon-tạ-nē'i-ti), **sponta'neousness** *n.* [L. *sponte*, of one's own free-will].

spoof (spòòf) *n.* hoax; swindle;—*v.t.* to fool; to hoax.

spook (spòòk) *n.* ghost; apparition.—**spook'ish, spook'y** *a.* pert. to ghosts [Dut.].

spool (spòòl) *n.* small cylinder for winding thread, yarn, etc.; reel; bobbin;—*v.t.* to wind on spool [O.Fr. *espole*].

spoon (spòòn) *n.* implement, with bowl at end of handle, for carrying food to the mouth, etc.; golf-club with wooden head;—*v.t.* and *v.i.* to use, lift with spoon; (*Golf*) to scoop ball high in air.—**spoon'ful** *n.* quantity spoon can hold; small quantity; (*Med.*) half an ounce.—**spoon'bill** *n.* long-legged wading bird.—**spoon'-feed** *v.t.* to feed with a spoon; (*Fig.*) to do over-much for a person, thus weakening his self-reliance.—**spoon'-fed** *a.* [O.E. *spon*].

spoonerism (spòòn'ẹr-izm) *n.* transportation of letters of spoken words, causing a humorous effect, e.g. a *half-warmed fish* for a 'half-formed wish' [fr. Dr. A. W. *Spooner* (1844-1930), noted for such slips].

spoor (spòòr) *n.* track or trail of wild animal [Dut. = a track].

sporadic (spo-rad'ik) *a.* occurring singly here and there; occasional. Also **sporad'ical.**—**sporad'ically** *adv.* [Gk. *sporadikos*, fr. *speirein*, to sow].

spore (spōr) *n.* in flowerless plants, e.g. in ferns, minute cell with reproductive powers; germ; seed.—**sporan'gium** *n.* spore-case.—*pl.* **sporan'gia.**—**sporan'gial** *a.*—**spo'roid** *a.* spore-like [Gk. *spora*, seed].

sporran (spor'ạn) *n.* large pouch worn in front of the kilt [Gael. *sporan*].

sport (spōrt) *n.* that which amuses; diversion; pastime; merriment; object of jest; mockery; outdoor game or recreation; freak of nature; (*Colloq.*) broad-minded person; good loser; one willing to take a chance;—*v.t.* to display in public; to show off;—*v.i.* to play; to take part in out-door recreation.—**sports** *n.pl.* games; athletic meetings.—**sport'ing** *a.* pert. to sport or sportsmen; willing to take a chance.—**sport'ive** *a.* pert. to sport; playful.—**sports'man, sports'woman** *n.*—**sports'manship** *n.* practice or skill of a sportsman; fair-mindedness; generosity towards opponent [fr. *disport*].

spot (spot) *n.* speck; blemish, esp. on reputation; pimple; place; locality; (*Colloq.*) small quantity of anything; a drink;—*v.t.* to cover with spots; to stain; to place billiard-ball on marked point; (*Colloq.*) to detect; to recognise;—*v.i.* to become marked.—*pr.p.* **spot'ting.**—*pa.p.* and *pa.t.* **spot'ted.**—**spot'less** *a.* without spot or stain; scrupulously clean; pure; innocent.—**spot'lessly** *adv.*—**spot'lessness** *n.*—**spot'ted, spot'ty** *a.* marked with spots or stains; irregular.—**spot'tedness, spot'tiness** *n.*—**spot'ter** *n.* one who spots.—**spot cash,** immediate payment; ready money.—**spot'-light** *n.* apparatus used to throw concentrated beam of light on performer on stage; light thrown.—**spotted dog** (*Slang*) currant dumpling; raisin pudding.—**on the spot,** immediately [O.N. *spotti*].

spouse (spouz) *n.* married person, husband or wife.—**spous'al** *a.* pert. to spouse, marriage;—*n.* marriage.—**spous'als** *n.pl.* marriage; nuptials [L. *sponsus*, promised].

spout (spout) *v.t.* to throw out, as liquid through a pipe; to utter in a pompous manner; to recite;—*v.i.* to gush out in jet; to speak volubly, esp. in public; of whale, to force up column of water when breathing through spiracle; to blow;—*n.* projecting tube, pipe, etc., for pouring liquid; a pipe or tube for leading off rain from roof; copious discharge.—**spout'er** *n.*—**up the spout** (*Slang*) in pawn; in difficulties [etym. uncertain].

sprag (sprag) *n.* piece of wood used to lock wheel of vehicle; device to prevent vehicle running backwards on hill [Dan.].
sprain (sprān) *v.t.* to wrench or twist muscles or ligaments of a joint; to overstrain;—*n.* such wrenching [etym. uncertain].
sprang (sprang) *pa.t.* of the verb **spring**.
sprat (sprat) *n.* small sea-fish, allied to herring and pilchard [O.E. *sprot*].
sprawl (sprawl) *v.i.* to sit or lie with legs outstretched or in ungainly position; to move about awkwardly; to spread out irregularly; to write carelessly and irregularly;—*n.* act of sprawling [O.E. *spreawlian*].
spray (sprā) *n.* twigs; small, graceful branch with leaves and blossoms; sprig.—**spray'ey** *a.* [etym. uncertain].
spray (sprā) *n.* fine droplets of water driven by wind from tops of waves, etc.; shower of fine droplets of any liquid, e.g. medicine, perfume, etc.; spraying-machine; atomiser;—*v.t.* to sprinkle with shower of fine drops.—**spray'er** *n.* spraying-machine [L. Ger. *Sprei*].
spread (spred) *v.t.* to stretch out; to extend; to cover surface with; to scatter; to unfold, as wings; to circulate, as news, etc.; to convey from one to another, as disease; to set and lay food on table;—*v.i.* to extend in all directions; to become spread, scattered, circulated, etc.;—*n.* extension; expanse; range; (*Colloq.*) feast.—*pa.p.* and *pa.t.* **spread**.—**spread'ing** *n.* act of extending.—**spread-ea'gle** *n.* eagle with wings stretched out;—*a.* with arms and legs stretched out; bombastic; extravagant;—*v.t.* to tie up a person, with outstretched limbs [O.E. *spraedan*].
spree (sprē) *n.* lively frolic; drinking-bout [Ir. *spre*, a spark].
sprig (sprig) *n.* small shoot or twig; ornament in form of spray; scion; youth; small, headless nail;—*v.t.* to mark, adorn, with figures of sprigs or sprays [O.E. *spraec*, a twig].
spright (sprīt) *n.* (*Arch.*) sprite; spirit.—**spright'ly** *a.* lively; airy; vivacious.—**spright'liness** *n.* [old form of *sprite*].
spring (spring) *v.i.* to leap; to jump; to shoot up, out, or forth; to appear; to recoil; to result, as from a cause; to issue, as from parent or ancestor; to appear above ground; to grow; to thrive;—*v.t.* to cause to spring up; to produce unexpectedly; to start, as game; to cause to explode, as a mine; to develop leak; to bend so as to weaken; to release, as catch of trap; (*Archit.*) to throw off arch from abutment or pier;—*n.* a leap; a bound; a jump; recoil; a contrivance of coiled or bent metal with much resilience; resilience; flow of water from earth; fountain; any source of supply; cause; origin; a crack; season of year.—*pa.p.* **sprung**.—*pa.t.* **sprang** or **sprung**.—**spring'er** *n.* one who springs; one who rouses game; breed of spaniel.—**spring'y** *a.* elastic; light in tread or gait.—**spring'iness** *n.*—**spring-bal'ance** *n.* instrument for measuring weight by compression of spiral spring.—**spring-bed** *n.* mattress of spiral springs set in wooden frame.—**spring'board** *n.* springy board used in jumping and diving.—**spring-gun** *n.* gun with wire fastened to trigger, discharged when person comes against the wire.—**spring-head** *n.* fountain-head; source of a stream.—**spring tide**, tide that happens near time of new moon and of full moon, and rises higher than ordinary tides (opp. of *neap* tide).—**spring-time** *n.* season of spring [O.E. *springan*].
springbok (spring-bok) *n.* small S. African gazelle or antelope [S. Afr. Dut.].
springe (sprinj) *n.* snare with a spring-noose;—*v.t.* to catch in a springe [fr. *spring*].
sprinkle (spring-kl) *v.t.* to scatter small drops of water, sand, etc.; to scatter on; to baptise with drops of water; to purify; to cleanse;—*v.i.* to scatter (a liquid or any fine substance);—*n.* small quantity scattered; occasional drops of rain; utensil for sprinkling.—**sprin'kled** *a.* marked by small spots.—**sprin'kler** *n.* one who sprinkles.—**sprin'kling** *n.* act of scattering; small quantity falling in drops [O.E. *sprengan*].
sprint (sprint) *v.i./n.* run at full speed.—**sprin'ter** *n.* [Cf. *spurt*].
sprit (sprit) *n.* (*Naut.*) small spar set diagonally across fore-and-aft sail to extend it [O.E. *spreot*, a pole].
sprite (sprīt) *n.* spirit; apparition; elf; a fairy; a goblin [older form = *spright*, fr. L. *spiritus*, spirit].
sprocket (sprok-et) *n.* toothlike projection on outer rim of wheel, e.g. of bicycle, for engaging links of chain [etym. uncertain].
sprout (sprout) *v.i.* to begin to grow; to put forth shoots; to spring up;—*n.* shoot; bud.—**brussels sprouts**, miniature cabbages growing on stalk [O.E. *sprutan*].
spruce (sprôôs) *a.* neat in dress; smart; dapper; trim;—*v.t.* and *v.i.* to smarten up; to dress smartly.—**spruce'ly** *adv.*—**spruce'ness** *n.* [M.E. *Spruce*, Prussia].
spruce (sprôôs) *n.* common name of some coniferous trees, esp. Spruce-fir or Norwegian Spruce; its wood; Prussian leather [M.E. *Spruce*, Prussia].
sprung (sprung) *pa.p.* and *pa.t.* of the verb **spring**; (*Colloq.*) intoxicated.
spry (sprī) *a.* nimble; agile; gay [Scand.].
spud (spud) *n.* small spade-like implement; (*Colloq.*) potato.—**spud'dy** *a.* short and fat [etym. uncertain).
spue (spū) *v.t.* and *v.i.* See **spew**.
spume (spūm) *n.* froth; foam; scum;—*v.i.* to froth; to foam.—**spu'mous** *a.* consisting of froth or scum; foamy.—**spu'my** *a.* foamy [L. *spuma*].
spun (spun) *pa.p.* and *pa.t.* of verb **spin**.
spunk (spungk) *n.* wood that readily takes fire; match; [*Fig.*) spirit.—**spunk'y** *a.* plucky [L. *spongia*, a sponge].
spur (spur) *n.* pricking instrument worn on horseman's heels, used as goad; (*Fig.*) incitement, instigation; projection on the leg of a cock; mountain projecting from range; projection;—*v.t.* to apply spurs to; to urge to action;—*v.i.* to ride hard; to press forward.—*pr.p.* **spur'ring**.—*pa.p.* and *pa.t.* also *a.* **spurred** (spurd), wearing spurs; (*Bot.*) having spur-like shoots; incited [O.E. *spora*].
spurge (spurj) *n.* plant of several species, having acrid, milky juice;—*v.t.* to discharge [L. *expurgare*, to purge].
spurious (spū-ri-us) *a.* not genuine or authentic; counterfeit; false.—**spu'riously** *adv.*—**spu'riousness** *n.* [L. *spurius*].
spurn (spurn) *v.t.* to drive away, as with foot; to reject with disdain; to scorn to accept;—*n.* disdainful rejection [O.E. *spornan*; connected with *spur*].
spurt (spurt) *v.t.* to force out suddenly in a stream; to squirt;—*v.i.* to gush out with force; to make a short, sudden, and strong effort, esp. in a race;—*n.* a sudden, strong flow from opening; short, sudden, and strong effort. Also **spirt** [O.E. *sprytlan*].
sputnik (spôôt-nēk') *n.* In Russia, a fellow traveller; a satellite; name commonly given to earth satellites first launched by Russians in 1957.
sputter (sput-er) *v.t.* to throw out with haste and noise; to utter excitedly and indistinctly;—*v.i.* to scatter drops of saliva, as in excited speech; to speak rapidly; to fly off with crackling noise, as sparks from burning wood;—*n.* act of sputtering; sound made.—**sputt'erer** *n.* [fr. *spout*].
sputum (spūtum) *n.* spittle; saliva.—*pl.* **spu'ta** [L. *spuere*, *sputum*, to spit].
spy (spī) *n.* one who enters enemy territory secretly, to gain information; secret agent; one who keeps watch on others.—*pl.* **spies**.—*v.t.* to catch sight of; to notice; to discern;—*v.i.* to act as a spy.—*pa.p.* and *pa.t.* **spied** (spīd).—**spy-glass** *n.* small telescope [Fr. *espion*, fr. L. *specere*, to look].

squab (skwob) *a.* fat and short; squat; plump; unfeathered [etym. uncertain].
squabble (skwob´l) *v.i.* to contend in debate; to wrangle; to dispute noisily;—*n.* petty, noisy quarrel; a brawl [imit. origin].
squad (skwod) *n.* (*Mil.*) small party of soldiers at drill, etc.; small party of men at work; gang [Fr. *escouade*].
squadron (skwod´run) *n.* division of a cavalry regiment comprising two 'troops'; warships grouped into a unit; Royal Air Force formation of two or more 'flights.'—**squad'ron-lead'er** *n.* (*R.A.F.*) rank equivalent to Lieut.-Commander in Navy or Major in Army [Fr. *escadron*, fr. It. *squadra*, a square].
squalid (skwol´id) *a.* mean and dirty, esp. through neglect; filthy; foul.—**squal'idly** *adv.* —**squalid'ity, squal'idness, squal'or** *n.* filth; foulness [L. *squalere*, to be stiff (with dirt)].
squall (skwawl) *v.t.* and *v.i.* to scream or cry out violently;—*n.* loud scream; sudden gust of wind.—**squall'y** *a.* [imit. origin].
squaloid (skwā´loid, skwal´oid) *a.* pert. to, like, a shark [L. *squalus*, a sea-fish].
squama (skwā´mạ) *n.* scale; scale-like part of bone; scale-like feather.—*pl.* **squamae** (skwā´mē) [L. = a scale].
squander (skwon´dẹr) *v.t.* to waste; to dissipate.—**squan'derer** *n.* spendthrift.—**squand'erma'nia** (mā´ni-ạ) *n.* a passion for reckless spending, esp. of public money [Scand.].
square (skwār) *n.* plane figure with four equal sides and four right angles; anything shaped like this; in town, open space of this shape; carpenter's instrument for testing or drawing right angles; body of soldiers drawn up in form of square; short for *barracks-square*, drill-, or parade-ground; (*Math.*) product of a number or quantity multiplied by itself; *a.* square-shaped; rectangular; rightly fitted; giving equal justice; fair; balanced, as accounts; settled, as account or bill;—*adv.* squarely; directly; —*v.t.* to make like a square; to place at right angles; (*Math.*) to multiply by itself; to balance; to settle; to put right; (*Colloq.*) to win over by bribery; (*Golf*) to draw level with opponent;—*v.i.* to agree exactly; to fit; to suit.—**square'ly** *adv.* in a square form or manner; honestly; fairly.—**square'ness** *n.*—**squa'rish** *a.* nearly square.—**square dance,** old-fashioned dance for four couples.—**square inch, foot, yard,** etc., area equal to surface of square with sides one inch, foot, yard, etc. long.—**square´leg** (*Cricket*) fielder who stands to batsman's left.—**square´rigged** *a.* (*Naut.*) having chief sails stretched along yards slung horizontally to mast by the middle.—**square root,** number or quantity which, when multiplied by itself, produces the number of which it is the square root.—**to square up,** to put things in order; to settle debts [L. *quadrare*, to square, fr. *quattuor*, four].
squash (skwosh) *v.t.* to beat or crush flat; to squeeze to pulp; (*Fig.*) to suppress;—*v.i.* to fall into a soft, flat mass;—*n.* anything soft and easily crushed; soft drink with flavour of crushed fruit; packed crowd; short for **squash rackets,** game played in a walled court with small hollow rubber ball [L. *ex*, out; *coactare*, to force].
squash (skwosh) *n.* gourdlike fruit [Amer.-Ind. *asquash*, raw, green].
squat (skwot) *v.i.* to sit on heels; to crouch, as animal; to settle on land without having title to it;—*a.* short and thick; sitting close to ground.—*pr.p.* **squat'ting.**—*pa.p.* and *pa.t.* **squat'ted.**—**squat'ter** *n.* one who squats; one who settles on land or in house, without legal right [O.Fr. *esquatir*].
squaw (skwaw) *n.* Red Indian woman, esp. wife [N. Amer.-Ind. *squa*].
squawk (skwawk) *n.* shrill, harsh cry;—*v.i.* to utter such a cry [fr. *squeak*].
squeak (skwēk) *n.* short, sharp, shrill sound; sharp, unpleasant, grating sound;—*v.i.* to utter, or make, such sound; (*Slang*) to give away secret.—**squeak'er** *n.*—**squeak'y** *a.* [imit. origin].
squeal (skwēl) *n.* long, shrill cry;—*v.i.* to utter long, shrill cry; (*Slang*) to turn informer.—**squeal'er** *n.* [imit. origin].
squeamish (skwēm´ish) *a.* easily made sick; easily shocked; over-scrupulous; fussy.—**squeam'ishly** *adv.* [O.Fr. *escoymous*].
squeegee (skwē´jē) *n.* brush or broom, with rubber edge on head, for clearing water from deck of ship, floor, pavement, etc.;—*a.* (*Colloq.*) not straight. Also **squil'gee** [fr. *squeeze*].
squeeze (skwēz) *v.t.* to press or crush; to compress; to extract by pressure; to cause to pass, esp. by force; to hug; to subject to extortion; —*v.i.* to force one's way; to press;—*n.* pressure; compression; close hug or embrace; crowd.—**squeez'ers** *n.pl.* contrivance, like a large pair of pliers [O.E. *cwisan*].
squelch (skwelch) *n.* crushing blow; suppression; sound made when withdrawing feet from sodden ground;—*v.t.* to crush down;—*v.i.* to make sound of a squelch [imit. origin].
squib (skwib) *n.* small firework; a short satire; a petty lampoon [etym. uncertain].
squid (skwid) *n.* a kind of cuttle-fish [etym. uncertain].
squilgee (skwil´jē) *n.* Same as **squeegee.**
squill (skwil) *n.* plant of lily family whose bulb has emetic properties.—**squills** *n.pl.* drug from bulb of squill, used as expectorant and diuretic [Gk. *skilla*].
squint (skwint) *a.* looking obliquely; having eyes turned in different directions; looking with suspicion;—*v.t.* to cause to squint;—*v.i.* to have eyes turned in different directions; to glance side-ways;—*n.* act, habit of squinting; (*Med.*) strabismus; hasty glance; peep.—**squint´eyed** *a.* having eyes that squint [earlier *asquint*; etym. uncertain].
squire (skwīr) *n.* formerly, knight's attendant; esquire; country gentleman; landed proprietor; lady's escort;—*v.t.* to escort (a lady) [fr. *esquire*].
squirm (skwirm) *v.i.* to move like a snake, eel, worm, etc.; to wriggle [imit. origin].
squirrel (skwir´ẹl) *n.* small graceful animal with bushy tail, living in trees and feeding on nuts; its fur [O.Fr. *escureul*, fr. Gk. *skia*, shade; *oura*, a tail].
squirt (skwẹrt) *v.t.* and *v.i.* to eject, or be ejected, in a jet; to spurt;—*n.* instrument for squirting; syringe; thin jet of liquid.—**squirt'er** *n.* [etym. uncertain].
stab (stab) *v.t.* to pierce or wound with pointed instrument; to hurt feelings of;—*v.i.* to strike with pointed weapon;—*n.* blow or wound so inflicted; sudden pain.—*pr.p.* **stab'bing.**—*pa.p.* and *pa.t.* **stabbed.**—**stab'ber** *n.* [perh. fr. Gael. *stob*, stake].
stabilise (stab´i-līz, stā´bi-līz) *v.t.* to make stable, steady, fixed, etc.; to fix exchange value of currency of a country.—**stabilisa'tion** *n.*—**stab'iliser** *n.* that which stabilises; horizontal tailplane of aircraft.—**stability** (stạ-bil´i-ti) *n.* steadiness [L. *stabilis*, fr. *stare*, to stand].
stable (stā´bl) *a.* firmly fixed, established; steady; lasting; resolute;—**sta'bly** *adv.*—**sta'bleness** *n.* stability [L. *stabilis*, fr. *stare*, to stand].
stable (stā´bl) *n.* building for horses, usually divided into stalls; racehorse-trainer's establishment;—*v.t.* to put into, or keep in, stable; —*v.i.* to be in stable [L. *stabulum*, a stall, fr. *stare*, to stand].
staccato (stak-kȧ´tō) *a.* and *adv.* (*Mus.*) direction to play notes in abrupt, disconnected fashion; short, sharp, and distinct [It. fr. L. *staccare*, to separate].
stack (stak) *n.* large heap or pile, esp. of hay, straw, or wood; number of chimneys standing together; tall chimney, esp. of factory; chimney of locomotive; funnel of steamer; a precipitous shaft of rock;—*v.t.* to heap or pile

up; to arrange pack of cards for cheating [O.N. *stakkr*, a haystack].

stadium (stā′di-um) *n.* ancient Greek measure of length equal to 606 feet 9 inches; arena of this length for foot-races; large sports-ground. —*pl.* **sta′dia** [L. fr. Gk. *stadion*].

staff (stȧf) *n. pl.* **staffs** or **staves** (stāvz) pole or stick used in walking, climbing, etc. or for support or defence; prop; comfort; stick, as emblem of office or authority; flagpole; (*Mus.*) five lines and four spaces on which music is written; (*Arch.*) stanza.—(with *pl.* **staffs**) body of persons working in office, school, etc.; (*Mil.*) body of selected officers, attached in advisory capacity to army commander;—*v.t.* to provide with staff.—**staff college**, military college where selected army officers are trained [O.E. *staef*].

stag (stag) *n.* male of red or other large deer. —**stag′hound** *n.* Scottish deer-hound, resembling, but larger than, greyhound.—**stag party** (*Slang*) party for men only [O.E. *stagga*].

stage (stāj) *n.* raised floor or platform esp. of theatre, etc.; theatrical profession; dramatic art or literature; scene of action; degree of progress; point of development; bus or tramway stopping-place; distance between two of them;—*v.t.* to put (a play) on stage.—**sta′ging** *n.* scaffolding.—**stagy** (stā′ji) *a.* theatrical; affectedly theatrical; artificial.—**sta′giness** *n.* —**stage′-coach** *n.* four-wheeled coach, running as a public passenger vehicle for journeys between towns.—**stage′-fright** *n.* extreme nervousness felt when facing audience.—**stage′-struck** *a.* smitten with love for stage as career.—**stage′-whis′per** *n.* whisper but loud enough for audience to hear.—**old stager**, person of long experience, esp. actor [O.Fr. *estage*, fr. L. *stare*, to stand].

stagger (stag′ẹr) *v.i.* to walk or stand unsteadily; to reel; to totter; to hesitate;—*v.t.* to cause to reel; to cause to hesitate; to shock; to distribute over a period; to arrange in zigzag fashion;—*n.* act of staggering; unsteady movement.—**stagg′ers** *n.pl.* disease of horses, cattle, etc.—**stagg′erer** *n.*—**stagg′ering** *a.* amazing; astounding [O.N. *stakra*, to push].

stagnate (stag′nāt) *v.i.* to cease to flow; to be motionless; to be dull.—**stag′nant** *a.* of water, not flowing; hence, foul; impure; (*Fig.*) not brisk; dull.—**stag′nantly** *adv.*—**stagna′tion** *n.* act of stagnating; dullness [L. *stagnum*, pool].

staid (stād) *a.* of sober and quiet character; steady; sedate; grave.—**staid′ly** *adv.*—**staid′ness** *n.* [for *stayed*, fr. *stay*].

stain (stān) *v.t.* and *v.i.* to discolour; to spot; to blot; to dye; to colour, as wood, glass, etc.; (*Fig.*) to mark with guilt;—*n.* discoloration; spot; dye; taint of guilt; disgrace.—**stain′less** *a.* without a stain; not liable to stain or rust, esp. of a kind of steel—**stained-glass**, glass with colours fused into it [for *distain*, fr. O.Fr. *desteindre*, fr. L. *dis*, away; *tingere*, to dye].

stair (stār) *n.* steps one above the other for connecting different levels.—**stairs** *n.pl.* flight of steps.—**stair′case** *n.* space in which flight of steps is placed. Also **stair′way** [O.E. *staeger*, fr. *stigan*, to ascend].

stake (stāk) *n.* sharpened stick or post; post to which one condemned to be burned, was tied; death by burning; money laid down as wager; interest in result of enterprise;—*pl.* money to be contended for, e.g. in horse-racing, etc.;—*v.t.* to secure or mark out with stakes; to wager; to risk; to pledge.—**at stake**, risked; in danger; involved [O.E. *staca*].

stalactite (stal′ak-tīt, stạ-lak′tīt) *n.* deposit of carbonate of lime, hanging like icicle from roof of cave.—**stalac′tic**, **stalactit′ic** *a.* [Gk. *stalaktos*, dropping].

Stalag (sta′lag) *n.* (*World War* 2) prisoner-of-war camp in Germany for n.c.o.s and men [Ger. *Standlager*, cantonment].

stalagmite (stal′ag-mīt, stạ-lag′mīt) *n.* deposit of carbonate of lime rising from floor of cave. —**stalagmit′ic(al)** [Gk. *stalagma*, that which drops].

stale (stāl) *a.* not fresh; kept too long, as bread; tasteless; musty; having lost power to please; common;—*v.t.* to make tasteless; to spoil novelty of;—*v.i.* to lose freshness.—**stale′ly** *adv.*—**stale′ness** *n.* [O.Fr. *estale*, spread out].

stale (stāl) *v.i.* of horses, to make water;—*n.* urine of horses, etc. [etym. uncertain].

stalemate (stāl′māt) *n.* (*Chess*) position, resulting in drawn game; deadlock; standstill [prob. fr. *stale* and *mate*].

stalk (stawk) *n.* stem of plant, leaf, etc.; tall chimney [O.E. *stalu*].

stalk (stawk) *v.i.* to steal up to game cautiously; to walk in stiff and stately manner;—*v.t.* to steal up to (game, etc.); to track down;—*n.* act of stealing up to game; stiff and stately gait.—**stalk′er** *n.*—**stalk′ing-horse** *n.* horse, or figure or one, behind which a sportsman takes cover when stalking game; pretence; feint; pretext [O.E. *stealcian*, to walk cautiously].

stall (stawl) *n.* compartment for animal in stable; erection for display and sale of goods; seat in cathedral or collegiate church, reserved for ecclesiastical dignitary; front seat in theatre, etc.; protective sheath for injured finger;—*v.t.* and *v.i.* to place or keep in stall; to come to a standstill; of engine of motor-car, to stop running unintentionally; of aircraft, to lose flying speed and controllability [O.E. *steall*, a standing-place, esp. for cattle].

stall (stawl) *n.* ambush; decoy;—*v.i.* (*U.S.*) to evade question in conversation or under interrogation [O.E. *stelan*, to steal].

stallion (stal′yun) *n.* an uncastrated male horse, esp. one kept for breeding.

stalwart (stawl′wạrt) *a.* sturdy; strong; brave; steadfast;—*n.* strong, muscular person; staunch supporter.—**stal′wartly** *adv.* [O.E. *staelwierthe*, serviceable].

stamen (stā′mẹn) *n.* (*Bot.*) male organ of flowering plant, pollen-bearing part.—**stamina** (stam′i-nạ) *n.* power of endurance; staying-power; vigour.—**stam′inal** *a.* pert. to stamens, or to stamina.—**staminif′erous** *a.* bearing stamens [L. = fibre, thread].

stammer (stam′ẹr) *v.i.* to speak with repetition of syllables or hesitatingly; to stutter;—*n.* halting enunciation; stutter.—**stamm′erer** *n.* —**stamm′ering** *n.* stammer; stutter [O.E. *stamerian*].

stamp (stamp) *v.i.* to put down a foot with force;—*v.t.* to set down (a foot) heavily or with force; to make a mark on; to affix postage stamp; to distinguish by a mark; to brand; to fix deeply; to coin;—*n.* act of stamping; instrument for making imprinted mark; mark imprinted; die; piece of gummed paper printed with device, as evidence of postage, etc.; character; form.—**stamp′er** *n.*—**stamp′-du′ty** *n.* tax imposed on bonds, legacies, etc. [O.E. *stempan*].

stampede (stam-pēd′) *n.* sudden, frightened rush, esp. of herd of cattle, crowd, etc.;—*v.t.* to put into a state of panic;—*v.i.* to take part in a stampede; to rush off in a general panic [Sp. *estampido*, a crash].

stance (stans) *n.* position of feet in certain games, e.g. golf, cricket, etc.; site; stand or stall in a market-place; station, esp. for buses [L. *stare*, to stand].

stanch (stȧnsh) *v.t.* to stop or check flow (of blood) [O.Fr. *estancher*, to stop a flow; *estanche*, watertight].

stanchion (stan′shun) *n.* upright support; iron bar, used as prop [O.Fr. *estance*, fr. L. *stare*, to stand].

stand (stand) *v.i.* to remain at rest in upright position; to be situated; to become or remain stationary; to stop; to endure; to adhere to principles; to have a position, order, or rank; to consist; to place oneself; to offer oneself as candidate; to adhere to; to persist; to insist; to be of certain height; (*Naut.*) to hold course or direction; to continue in force (*Colloq.*) to treat;—*v.t.* to endure; to sustain; to maintain; to resist; to withstand; to admit;—*pa.p.* and *pa.t.* **stood.**—*n.* place where one stands; place in town for motor-vehicles; structure for spectators to stand on for better view; piece of furniture on which things may be placed; stall for display of goods; resistance.—**stand′-by** *n.* something in reserve.—**stand′-in** *n.* (*Film*) actor or actress who stands in the place of principal player until scene is ready to be shot.—**stand′-off, stand′-off′ish** *a.* haughty; reserved; aloof.—**stand′-off′ishness** *n.*—**stand′point** *n.* fundamental principle; a point of view.—**to stand down,** to withdraw; to demobilise temporarily.—**to stand out,** to project; to be conspicuous [O.E. *standan*].

standard (stan′dạrd) *n.* pole with a flag; flag, esp. ensign of war; royal banner; weight, measure, model, quality, etc. to which others must conform; criterion; upright support;—*a.* serving as established rule, model, etc.; having fixed value; uniform; standing upright.—**stan′dardise** *v.t.* to make of, or bring to, uniform level of weight, measure, quality, etc.—**standardisa′tion** *n.* [O.Fr. *estendard,* a royal banner].

standing (stan′ding) *a.* established by law, custom, etc.; settled; permanent; not flowing; erect;—*n.* duration; existence; continuance; reputation.—**standing army,** force maintained in peacetime.—**standing orders,** permanent rules [O.E. *standan*].

stang (stang) *n.* pole, rod, or perch; long bar; shaft [O.E. *staeng*].

stank (stank) *pa.t.* of the verb **stink.**

stannary (stan′ạ-ri) *n.* tin-mines or tin-works in specified district;—*a.* pert. to these.—**stann′ic** *a.* pert. to tin.—**stannif′erous** *a.* containing or producing tin.—**stann′ous** *a.* containing tin [L. *stannum,* tin].

stanza (stan′zạ) *n.* group of lines or verses of poetry having definite pattern; loosely, division of poem.—**stanzaic** (stan-zā′ik) *a.* [It. *stanza,* fr. L. *stare,* to stand].

staple (stā′pl) *n.* settled mart or market; chief product of a country or district; unmanufactured material; fibre of wool, cotton, flax, etc.;—*a.* established in commerce; settled; regularly produced or made for market; principal; chief;—*v.t.* of textiles, to grade according to length and quality of fibre.—**sta′pler** *n.* dealer in staple commodities [O.Fr. *estaple,* a general market].

staple (stā′pl) *n.* U-shaped piece of metal with pointed ends to drive into wood, used with hook, as locking device for a door, etc.—**sta′pler** *n.* mechanical device for fastening papers together [O.E. *stapel,* a prop].

star (står) *n.* shining celestial body, seen as twinkling point of light; asterisk; leading actor or actress;—*v.t.* to set or adorn with stars; to cast (in play) as leading actor;—*v.i.* to shine, as star; to play principal part.—**star′let** *n.* small star.—**star′light** *n.* light from stars.—**star′lit** *a.*—**star′ry** *a.* pert. to, or like, stars; covered with stars; shining like stars.—**starr′iness** *n.*—**star′fish** *n.* marine animal allied to sea-urchin.—**star′gaz′ing** *n.* practice of observing stars; astrology.—**star′spang′led** *a.* thickly set or studded with stars.—**Star of Bethlehem** (*Bib.*) star of the Nativity; (*Bot.*) garden plant of lily family [O.E. *steorra*].

starboard (står′bōrd) *n.* right-hand side of a ship, looking forward;—*a.* pert. to, or on, this side;—*v.t.* to put (the helm) to starboard [O.E. *steorbord,* the steer side].

starch (stårch) *n.* substance forming main food element in bread, potatoes, etc. and used, mixed with water, for stiffening linen, etc.; (*Fig.*) formality; primness;—*v.t.* to stiffen with starch.—**starch′y** *a.* pert. to, containing, starch; stiff; formal; prim.—**starch′ily** *adv.*—**starch′iness** *n.* [O.E. *stearc,* rigid].

stare (stār) *v.i.* to look fixedly; to gaze;—*v.t* to abash by staring at; to be obvious to; to be visible to;—*n.* fixed, steady look.—**sta′rer** *n.*—**sta′ring** *n. a.* [O.E. *starian*].

stark (stårk) *a.* stiff; rigid; strong; downright; utter;—*adv.* completely.—**stark′ly** *adv.*—**stark′ness** *n.* stiffness [O.E. *stearc,* rigid].

starling (står′ling) *n.* bird, bluish-black and speckled [O.E. *staer,* starling].

start (stårt) *v.i.* to make sudden movement; to spring; to wince; to begin, esp. journey; to become loosened or displaced;—*v.t.* to cause to move suddenly; to set going; to begin; to alarm; to loosen; to displace;—*n.* sudden involuntary movement, spring or leap; act of setting out; beginning; in sports, advantage of lead in race.—**start′er** *n.*—**by fits and starts,** spasmodically [O.E. *sturtan*].

startle (stårt′l) *v.t.* to cause to start; to excite by sudden alarm; to give a fright to;—*v.i.* to move abruptly, esp. from fright, apprehension, etc.—**start′ling** *a.* alarming; astonishing; surprising.—**start′lingly** *adv.* [fr. *start*].

starve (stårv) *v.i.* to suffer from cold or hunger; to die of hunger; to be short of something necessary;—*v.t.* to cause to suffer or die from lack of food, warmth, etc.—**starva′tion** *n.* the suffering from lack of food, warmth, etc.—**starve′ling** *a.* hungry; lean; emaciated;—*n.* one weak from lack of food [O.E. *steorfan,* to die].

state (stāt) *n.* condition of person or thing; place or situation; temporary aspect of affairs; rank; high position; formal dignity; politically organised community; civil powers of such;—*a.* pert. to state; governmental; royal; public; ceremonial;—*v.t.* to set forth; to express in words; to specify.—**sta′ted** *a.* fixed; regular; established; settled.—**state′ly** *a.* dignified; imposing; majestic.—**state′liness** *n.*—**state′ment** *n.* act of expressing in words; what is expressed; formal account.—**state′-aid′ed** *a.* partially supported out of public funds.—**state′craft** *n.* political sagacity; statesmanship.—**state′less** *a.* without nationality.—**state′room** *n.* a private cabin in a ship.—**states′man** *n.* one skilled in art of government; able politician.—**states′man-like** *a.* possessing qualities of a statesman.—**states′manly** *a.*—**states′manship** *n.* [L. *status,* fr. *stare,* to stand].

static (stat′ik) *a.* pert. to bodies at rest, or in equilibrium; motionless;—*n.* (*Wireless*) crackling noises during reception; atmospherics.—**stat′ical** *a.* static.—**stat′ics** *n.pl.* branch of mechanics dealing with bodies at rest [Gk. *statikos,* causing to stand].

station (stā′shun) *n.* place where thing or person stands; position; situation; condition of life; rank; regular stopping-place for railway trains; local or district office for police force, fire-brigade, etc.;—*v.t.* to put in a position; to place; to set; to appoint to place of duty.—**sta′tionary** *a.* not moving; fixed; regular; stable [L. *statio,* fr. *stare,* to stand].

stationer (stā′shun-ẹr) *n.* one who deals in writing materials.—**sta′tionery** *n.* wares sold by stationer.—**Stationery Office,** Government department responsible for supply of stationery, and for publication and sale of all official reports, pamphlets, statistics, etc. [fr. *station,* first booksellers exhibiting their stocks on stalls or stations].

statistics (stạ-tis′tiks) *n.pl.* numerical data collected systematically, summarised, and tabulated; science of collecting and interpreting such information.—**statis′tic(al)** *a.*—**statis′tically** *adv.*—**statistician** (sta-tis-tish′ạn) *n.* one skilled in statistics.—**sta′tist** (sta′-tist) *n.* statistician; statesman [Gk. *statizein,* to set up].

stator (stā′tor) *n.* (*Elect.*) the stationary part of a generator [L. *stare,* to stand].

statue (stat′ū) *n.* image of person or animal, carved out of solid substance or cast in metal.—**stat′uary** *n.* art of making statues; collection of statues; one who makes statues; sculptor.—**statuesque′** (stat-ū-esk′) *a.* like a statue; immobile.—**statuette** (stat-ū-et′) *n.* small statue [L. *statua,* a standing image].

stature (stat′ūr) *n.* the height of a person or animal [L. *statura*, fr. *stare*, to stand].

status (stā′tus) *n.* position; rank; position of affairs [L. fr. *stare*, to stand].

statute (stat′ūt) *n.* law passed by legislature; Act of Parliament; permanent rules defining purposes and governing operations of corporation, institution, etc.—**stat′utable** *a.* made by statute; in accordance with statutes.—**stat′utory** *a.* enacted, defined, or authorised by statute [L. *statutum*, that which is set up].

staunch (stawnsh) *a.* firm; loyal; trustworthy.—**staunch′ly** *adv.*—**staunch′ness** *n.* [fr. *stanch*].

stave (stāv) *n.* one of curved strips of wood forming cask; rung of ladder; staff; five lines and spaces on which musical notes are written; verse or stanza;—*v.t.* to fit with staves; to break stave(s) of (cask); to knock hole in side of; to ward off; to defer.—*pa.p.* and *pa.t.* **staved** or **stove** [fr. *staff*].

staves (stāvz) *n.pl.* See **staff** and **stave**.

stay (stā) *v.t.* to restrain; to check; to stop; to support; to satisfy; to last;—*v.i.* to remain; to continue in a place; to dwell; to pause;—*n.* remaining or continuing in a place; halt; support; postponement, esp. of a legal proceeding.—**stays** *n.pl.* laced corset.—**stay′er** *n.* one who, or that which, stays or supports; in a race, person or horse having qualities of endurance.—**stay-in strike,** industrial dispute in which workers refuse to leave factory, etc. until their demands are granted [O.E. *staeg*].

stay (stā) *n.* (*Naut.*) strong rope or wire to support a mast or spar;—*v.t.* to support or incline to one side with stays; to put on the other tack;—*v.i.* to change tack; to go about [O.E. *staeg*].

stead (sted) *n.* place which another had; place; use; benefit; advantage; service; place of abode; frame of bed.—**in stead,** in place.—**in good stead,** of service.—**stead′ing** *n.* outhouses of farm [O.E. *stede*, position, place].

steadfast (sted′fast) *a.* firmly fixed; steady; constant.—**stead′fastly** *adv.*—**stead′fastness** *n.* [O.E. *stede*, place; *faest*, firm].

steady (sted′i) *a.* firm; constant; uniform; temperate; industrious; reliable;—*v.t.* to make steady; to support;—*v.i.* to become steady;—*pr.p.* **stead′ying.**—*pa.p.* and *pa.t.* **stead′ied.**—*n.* support.—**stead′ier** *a.* more steady.—**stead′iest** *a.* most steady.—**stead′ily** *adv.*—**stead′iness** *n.* [O.E. *stede*, position, place].

steak (stāk) *n.* slice of meat, esp. beef; also, slice of fish [O.N. *steik*].

steal (stēl) *v.t.* to take by theft; to get by cunning or surprise; to win gradually by skill, affection, etc.;—*v.i.* to take what is not one's own; to move silently, or secretly.—*pa.p.* **sto′len** (stō′lẹn).—*pa.t.* **stole** (stōl).—**stealth** (stelth) *n.* secret means used to accomplish anything; concealed act.—**stealthy** (stel′thi) *a.* done by stealth.—**stealth′ily** *adv.*—**stealth′iness** *n.* [O.E. *stelan*].

steam (stēm) *n.* vapour rising from boiling water; water in gaseous state; any exhalation of heated bodies;—*a.* worked by steam;—*v.t.* to apply steam to; to cook or treat with steam;—*v.i.* to give off steam; to rise in vapour; to move under power of steam.—**steam′y** *a.* pert. to, or like, steam; full of steam; misty.—**steam′iness** *n.*—**steam′er** *n.* steamship; vessel for cooking or washing by steam; road-engine, fire-escape, etc., operated by steam.—**steam′boat, steam′ship** *n.* a vessel propelled by steam.—**steam′en′gine** *n.* engine worked by steam.—**steam′roll′er** *n.* heavy roller, driven by steam, used in road-making [O.E. *steam*].

stearin (stē′ạ-rin) *n.* solid fat-like substance occurring in natural fats.—**ste′arine** *n.* hard, waxy solid used in manufacture of candles.—**ste′aric** *a.* [Gk. *stear*, suet].

steed (stēd) *n.* horse [O.E. *steda*, stallion].

steel (stēl) *n.* hard and malleable metal, made by mixing carbon in iron; tool or weapon of steel; instrument for sharpening knives;—*a.* made of steel; hard; inflexible; unfeeling;—*v.t.* to overlay, point, or edge, with steel; to harden; to make obdurate.—**steel′y** *a.* made of, or like, steel; hard; obdurate; relentless.—**steel′iness** *n.*—**steel′engrav′ing** *n.* art of engraving on steel plates; design engraved on steel plate; print from this [O.E. *style*].

steelyard (stēl′yạrd) *n.* balance with unequal arms and movable weight [etym. uncertain].

steep (stēp) *a.* having abrupt or decided slope; precipitous; difficult; (*Colloq.*) very high or exorbitant, esp. of prices;—*n.* steep place; precipice.—**steep′ly** *adv.*—**steep′en** *v.t.* and *v.i.* to make, or become, steep [O.E. *steap*].

steep (stēp) *v.t.* to soak in a liquid; to drench; to saturate;—*v.i.* to be soaked;—*n.* act or process of steeping; liquid used [O.N. *steypa*, to pour out].

steeple (stē′pl) *n.* a church tower with a spire.—**stee′plechase** *n.* a cross-country horse-race in which ditches, hedges, etc. must be jumped; a similar horse-race on a course specially set with artificial obstacles; a cross-country foot-race.—**stee′plejack** *n.* a skilled workman who climbs steeples, tall chimneys, etc. [O.E. *steap*, lofty].

steer (stēr) *n.* a young male ox; a bullock [O.E. *steor*, a bullock].

steer (stēr) *v.t.* to guide or direct the course of (a ship, motor-car, etc.) by means of a rudder, wheel, etc.;—*v.i.* to guide a ship, motor-car, etc.; to direct one's course.—**steer′age** *n.* the act of steering; the part of a ship allotted to passengers paying the lowest fare.—**steer′er, steers′man** *n.* the man who steers a ship; the helmsman of a ship.—**steer′age-way** *n.* sufficient movement of a vessel through the water to enable it to answer the helm.—**steer′ing-col′umn** *n.* a hollow, cylindrical rod on a motor-vehicle, to the top of which the steering-wheel is fixed.—**steer′ing-gear** *n.* the mechanism for steering a vessel, motor-vehicle, etc.—**steer′ing-wheel** *n.* the wheel for directing the course of a ship or for guiding a motor-vehicle [O.E. *stieran*].

stela, stele (stē′lạ, stē′lē) *n.* an ancient upright stone tablet or pillar.—*pl.* **ste′lae** [Gk. *stēlē*, to set, stand].

stellar (stel′ạr) *a.* pert. to, or like, stars; starry.—**stell′ate, stell′ated** *a.* arranged in the form of a star; star-shaped; radiating.—**stell′iform** *a.* star-shaped.—**stell′ular** *a.* like little stars [L. *stella*, a star].

stem (stem) *n.* the principal stalk of a tree or plant; any slender stalk of a plant; any slender shaft resembling a stalk; branch of family; curved or upright piece of timber or metal to which two sides of ship are joined; part of word to which inflectional endings are added;—*v.t.* to remove the stem of.—*pr.p.* **stem′ming.**—*pa.p.* and *pa.t.* **stemmed** [O.E. *stefn*].

stem (stem) *v.t.* to check; to stop; to dam up.—*pr.p.* **stem′ming.**—*pa.p.* and *pa.t.* **stemmed** [O.N. *stemma*].

stench (stensh) *n.* strong, offensive odour [O.E. *stenc*].

stencil (sten′sil) *n.* thin sheet of metal, paper, etc. pierced with pattern or letters, so that when placed on any surface and brushed over with paint, ink, etc., the design is reproduced; design so reproduced;—*v.t.* to mark or paint thus.—*pr.p.* **sten′cilling.**—*pa.p.* and *pa.t.* **sten′cilled** [etym. uncertain].

Sten gun (sten′gun) *n.* (*World War* 2) light, automatic weapon [*ST* for initials of designer; *EN* for *Enfield*, the makers].

stenography (sten-og′rạ-fi) *n.* shorthand writing.—**sten′ograph** *n.* character used in stenography; the script; stenographic machine;—*v.i.* to write in shorthand.—**stenog′rapher, stenog′raphist** *n.*—**steno′type** *n.* a machine for writing shorthand; shorthand-writer.—**stenograph′ic, stenograph′ical** *a.* [Gk. *stenos*, narrow; *graphein*, to write].

Stentor (stent′or) *n.* Greek herald in Homer's

Iliad.—**stento'rian** *a.* of voice, extremely loud or powerful; brazen-voiced.
step (step) *v.i.* to move and set down the foot; to walk, esp. short distance; to walk slowly;—*v.t.* to set or place, as foot; to measure in paces; (*Naut.*) to set up (mast);—*n.* act of stepping; complete movement of foot in walking, dancing, etc.; distance so covered; manner of walking; footprint; footfall; tread of stair; degree of progress; act; measure; grade; (*Naut.*) socket for mast;—*pl.* portable ladder.—*pr.p.* **step'ping.**—*pa.p.* and *pa.t.* **stepped.**—**step'per** *n.*—**step'ping-stone** *n.* stone for stepping on when crossing stream, etc.; (*Fig.*) aid to success [O.E. *staeppan*].
step- (step) *prefix,* showing relationship acquired by remarriage.—**step'father** *n.* second, or later, husband of one's mother. Similarly **step'mother, step'brother, step'sister.**
steppe (step) *n.* vast, treeless plain, as in Siberia [Russ. = a heath].
stercoral (ster'ko-ral) *a.* pert. to dung or excrement. Also **ster'corary.**—**stercora'ceous** *a.* [L. *stercus, stercoris,* dung].
stereo- (ster'e-ō) fr. Gk. *stereos,* solid, used in many derivatives.—**ster'eograph** *n.* double photograph of same scene, for use in stereoscope.—**stereog'raphy** *n.* the art of representing solid bodies on a plane surface.
stereoscope (ster'e-, stē'rē-ō-skōp) *n.* optical instrument in which two pictures taken at different view-points are combined into one image, with effect of depth and solidity.—**stereoscop'ic(al)** *a.*—**stereoscop'ically** *adv.*—**stereo'scopy** *n.* [Gk. *stereos,* solid; *skopein,* to view].
stereotype (ster'e-, stē'rē-ō-tīp) *n.* in printing, plate made by pouring metal into mould of plaster or papier-maché made from original type;—*a.* pert. to stereotypes;—*v.t.* to make a stereotype from; to print from stereotypes; to fix unalterably; (*Fig.*) to reduce to empty formula; to make always the same.—**ste'reotyped** *a.*—**ste'reotyper, ste'reotypist** *n.*—**stereotypog'raphy** *n.* art of printing from stereotypes [Gk. *stereos,* solid; and *type*].
sterile (ster'il, ster'īl) *a.* barren; not fertile; unable to have offspring; producing no fruit, seed, or crops; (*Med.*) entirely free from germs of all kinds.—**ster'ilise** *v.t.* to make sterile; to deprive of power of having offspring; to destroy germs, esp. by heat or antiseptics.—**sterilisa'tion** *n.*—**ster'iliser** *n.*—**steril'ity** *n.* barrenness [L. *sterilis,* barren].
sterling (ster'ling) *a.* pert. to standard value, weight, or purity; of solid worth; genuine; pure; denoting British money;—*n.* British money. [etym. uncertain—perh. fr. O.E. *steorling,* a coin with a star].
stern (stern) *a.* severe; strict; rigorous.—**stern'ly** *adv.*—**stern'ness** *n.* [O.E. *styrne*].
stern (stern) *n.* after part of ship; rump or tail of animal.—**stern'most** *a.* farthest astern [O.N. *stjorn,* steering].
sternum (ster'num) *n.* breast-bone.—*pl.* **ster'na.**—**ster'nal** *a.* [Gk. *sternon,* the chest].
sternutation (ster-nū-tā'shun) *n.* act of sneezing; sneeze.—**sternuta'tive, sternuta'tory** *a.* exciting to sneeze;—*n.* anything which causes sneezing [L. *sternutare,* to sneeze].
stertor (ster'tor) *n.* heavy, sonorous breathing.—**ster'torous** *a.* snoring; characterised by snoring sound.—**ster'torously** *adv.* [L. *stertere,* to snore].
stet (stet) *v.i.* word used by proof-readers as instruction to printer to cancel previous correction [L. = let it stand].
stethoscope (steth'o-skōp) *n.* instrument for listening to action of lungs or heart.—**stethoscop'ic** *a.* [Gk. *stēthos,* chest; *skopein,* to see].
Stetson (stet'sun) *n.* kind of soft hat, for men [fr. the same of the maker].
stevedore (stēv'e-dōr) *n.* one who loads and unloads ships [Sp. *estivador,* a wool-packer, fr. L. *stipare,* to press together].
stew (stū) *v.t.* to cook slowly in a closed vessel; to simmer;—*v.i.* to be cooked slowly; to feel uncomfortably warm; (*Slang*) to study hard;—*n.* stewed meat; a swot; (*Colloq.*) nervous anxiety [O.Fr. *estuve,* a stove].
steward (stū'ard) *n.* one who manages another's property; on ship, attendant on passengers; catering-manager of club; official who manages race-meeting, assembly, etc.—**stew'ardess** *n. fem.* female steward.—**stew'ardship** *n.* office of steward; management.—**stew'ardry** *n.* stewardship [O.E. *stigweard,* a major-domo, fr. *stig,* a house; *weard,* a ward].
stibium (stib'i-um) *n.* antimony [L.].
stich (stik) *n.* verse or line of poetry, of whatever measure or number of feet.—**stich'ic** *a.* pert. to stich.—**stichom'etry** *n.* measurement of manuscript by number of lines it contains.—**stichomet'ric, stichomet'rical** *a.* [Gk. *stichos,* row].
stick (stik) *n.* small branch cut off tree or shrub; staff; walking-stick; rod; (*Print.*) instrument in which types are arranged in words and lines; (*R.A.F.*) set of bombs dropped one after the other; (*Colloq.*) stiff or dull person [O.E. *sticca*].
stick (stik) *v.t.* to stab; to pierce; to jab; to puncture; to fasten; to cause to adhere; to fix; to thrust; (*Colloq.*) to endure;—*v.i.* to pierce; to adhere closely; to remain fixed; to stop; to halt; to hesitate; to be unable to proceed; to be puzzled, e.g. by a problem.—*pa.p.* and *pa.t.* **stuck.**—**stick'er** *n.* one who sticks; one who perseveres.—**stick'y** *a.* adhesive; viscous; glutinous; tenacious; (*Colloq.*) embarrassing; rough; painful.—**stick'iness** *n.*—**stick'ing-plas'ter** *n.* adhesive bandage for small wounds, cuts, etc.—**stuck up,** conceited [O.E. *stician,* to pierce].
stickle (stik'l) *v.i.* to hold out stubbornly.—**stick'ler** *n.* one who insists on trifles of procedure, etc. [O.E. *stihtan,* to control].
stickle (stik'l) *n.* sharp point; prickle; spine.—**stick'leback** *n.* small spiny-backed freshwater fish [O.E. *sticel,* a prickle].
stiff (stif) *a.* not easily bent; not flexible or pliant; moved with difficulty; firm; hard; thick; stubborn; formal in manner; (*Colloq.*) high in price; (*Slang*) fool; corpse.—**stiff'ly** *adv.*—**stiff'ness** *n.*—**stiff'en** *v.t.* and *v.i.* to make or become stiff or stiffer.—**stiff'ener** *n.* one who, or that which, stiffens.—**stiff'-necked** *a.* stubborn; obstinate [O.E. *stif*].
stifle (stī'fl) *v.t.* and *v.i.* to smother; to choke; to extinguish; to suppress sound of; to repress.—**sti'fling** *a.* airless; close [etym. uncertain].
stigma (stig'ma) *n.* brand; mark of disgrace; stain on character; blemish on skin; (*Bot.*) top of pistil of a flower.—*pl.* **stig'mas** or **stig'mata.**—**stigmata** (stig'ma-ta) *n.pl.* marks resembling five wounds of Christ, said to have been miraculously impressed on bodies of certain saints.—**stigmat'ic(al)** *a.* pert. to, or marked with, stigma; giving reproach or disgrace.—**stigmat'ically** *adv.*—**stig'matise** *v.t.* to mark with stigma or stigmata; to hold up to disgrace [Gk. *stigma,* a tattoo mark].
stile (stīl) *n.* arrangement of steps for climbing fence or wall; in panelling or framing, upright sidepiece [O.E. *stigel*].
stiletto (sti-let'ō) *n.* small dagger; pointed instrument used in needlework [It. fr. L. *stilus,* a pointed instrument].
still (stil) *a.* motionless; silent; quiet; peaceful; of wine, not sparkling;—*n.* stillness; (*Cinema*) enlargement of one unit of film;—*v.t.* to quiet; to silence; to calm;—*adv.* to this time; yet; even;—*conj.* yet; however.—**still'y** *a.* still; quiet; calm;—*adv.* silently; quietly.—**still'ness** *n.*—**still'-birth** *n.* state of being dead at time of birth.—**still'-born** *a.*—**still life** (*Art*) inanimate objects as subject of painting [O.E. *stille*].
still (stil) *n.* apparatus for distilling alcoholic liquors;—*v.t.* to expel spirit from liquors by heating into vapour and then cooling; to

distil; (*Poet.*) to let fall in drops [L. *stillare*, to drip].

stilt (stilt) *n.* pole with foot-rest, for walking raised from ground;—*v.i.* to walk on stilts.—**stilt'ed** *a.* (*Fig.*) formal; stiff; pretentious [Dut. *stelt*].

Stilton (stil'ton) *n.* rich cheese, orig. made at *Stilton*, in Huntingdonshire.

stimulus (stim'ū-lus) *n.* goad; incentive; stimulant; (*Bot.*) sting; prickle.—*pl.* **stim'uli.** —**stim'ulate** *v.t.* to rouse to activity; to excite; to increase vital energy of.—**stim'ulant** *a.* serving to stimulate;—*n.* that which spurs on; (*Med.*) any agent or drug which increases temporarily action of any organ of body.—**stimula'tion** *n.*—**stim'ulative** *a.* having quality of stimulating;—*n.* stimulant [L. *stimulus*, a goad].

sting (sting) *n.* pointed organ often poisonous, of certain animals, insects, or plants; thrust, wound, or pain of one; any acute physical or mental pain;—*v.t.* to thrust sting into; to cause sharp pain to; to hurt feelings; to incite to action; (*Slang*) to overcharge;—*v.i.* to use a sting.—*pa.p.* and *pa.t.* **stung.**—**sting'er** *n.*—**sting'ing** *a.* that uses a sting; causing acute pain; keen; sharp.—**sting'ingly** *adv.* [O.E. *stingan*].

stingy (stin'ji) *a.* meanly avaricious; miserly. —**stin'gily** *adv.*—**stin'giness** *n.* [fr. *sting*].

stink (stingk) *v.i.* to give out strongly offensive smell;—*pa.p.* **stunk** (stungk).—*pa.t.* **stank** (stangk) or **stunk.**—*n.* stench.—**stink'er** *n.* one who, or that which, stinks.—**stink'ing** *a.*—**stink'ingly** *adv.* [O.E. *stincan*].

stint (stint) *v.t.* to limit; to keep on short allowance; to skimp;—*v.i.* to be frugal;—*n.* limitation of supply or effort; allotted task.—**stint'ed** *a.* limited; scanty [O.E. *styntan*, to blunt].

stipe (stīp) *n.* (*Bot.*) the stalk or stem of a fungus or mushroom; the leaf-stalk of a fern [L. *stipes*, a stem].

stipend (stī'pend) *n.* money paid for a person's services; (*Scot.*) salary of clergyman.—**stipend'iary** *a.* receiving salary;—*n.* one who performs services for fixed salary [L. *stipendium*, wages].

stipple (stip'l) *v.t.* and *v.i.* to engrave, draw, or paint by using dots instead of lines;—*n.* this process.—**stipp'ler** *n.* one who stipples; brush, tool, used for stippling.—**stipp'ling** *n.* [Dut. *stip*, a point].

stipulate (stip'ū-lāt) *v.i.* to arrange; to settle definitely; to insist on in making a bargain or agreement.—**stipula'tion** *n.* act of stipulating; specified condition.—**stip'ulator** *n.* [L. *stipulari*].

stir (ster) *v.t.* to set or keep in motion; to move; to mix up ingredients, materials, etc. by circular motion of utensil; to rouse; to incite;—*v.i.* to begin to move; to be in motion; to be out to bed;—*pr.p.* **stir'ring.**—*pa.p.* and *pa.t.* **stirred.** —*n.* act of stirring; commotion.—**stir'rer** *n.*—**stir'ring** *a.* active; energetic; exciting; rousing; —*n.* act of stirring [O.E. *styrian*].

stirrup (stir'up) *n.* metal loop hung from strap, for foot of rider on horse.—**stirr'up-cup** *n.* drink given to departing rider.—**stirr'up-pump** *n.* portable, hand-operated pump [O.E. *stigrap*, mount rope].

stitch (stich) *n.* in sewing, a single pass of needle; loop or turn of thread thus made; in knitting, crocheting, etc., single turn of yarn or thread round needle or hook; (*Fig.*) bit of clothing; sharp, sudden pain in the side;—*v.t.* and *v.i.* to form stitches; to sew.—**stitch'er** *n.* —**stitch'ing** *n.* work done by sewing [O.E. *stician*, to pierce].

stithy (stith'i) *n.* anvil; forge;—*v.t.* to forge on anvil [O.N. *stethi*, anvil].

stiver (stī'ver) *n.* old Dutch coin of small value; trifle [Dut. *stuiver*].

stoat (stōt) *n.* ermine or weasel, esp. in its summer fur of reddish-brown colour [etym. unknown].

stock (stok) *n.* stump or post; stem or trunk of tree or plant; upright block of wood; piece of wood to which the barrel, lock, etc. of firearm are secured; crossbar of anchor; ancestry; family; domestic animals on farm; fund; supply of goods trader has on hand; government securities; capital of company or corporation; quantity; supply; juices of meat, etc. to form a liquid used as foundation of soup; close-fitting band of cloth worn round neck; garden plant bearing fragrant flowers; gillyflower;—*pl.* frame of timber supporting a ship while building; old instrument of punishment in form of wooden frame with holes in it, to confine hands and feet of offenders;—*v.t.* to lay in supply for future use; to store; to keep for sale;—*a.* used, or available, for constant supply; commonplace; conventional.—**stock'breed'er** *n.* one who raises cattle, horses, etc.—**stock'broker** *n.* one who buys and sells stocks or shares for others.—**stock'broking** *n.*—**stock exchange,** building in which stockbrokers meet to buy and sell stocks and shares.—**stock'-in-trade** *n.* all goods merchant, shopkeeper, etc. has on hand for supply to public.—**stock'ist** *n.* one who keeps supply of certain goods.—**stock market,** stock exchange.—**stock'still** *a.* still as stock or post; motionless.—**stock'ta'king** *n.* act of preparing inventory of goods on hand in trading establishment.—**stock'whip** *n.* heavy whip, with short handle and long lash.—**stock'yard** *n.* large yard with pens for cattle, sheep, pigs, etc., esp. for those to be slaughtered [O.E. *stocc*, a stick].

stockade (sto-kād') *n.* enclosure or pen made with posts and stakes;—*v.t.* to surround, enclose, or defend by erecting line of stakes [Sp. *estacada*, a stake].

stockfish (stok-fish) *n.* salted and dried codfish, hake, etc. [fr. *stock*].

stocking (stok'ing) *n.* woven or knitted covering for foot and leg; wind-indicator at aerodrome.—**stockinet',** **stockinette'** *n.* elastic knitted fabric [for *nether stock*, lower hose].

stocky (stok'i) *a.* short and stout; thickset.—**stock'ily** *adv.* [fr. *stock*].

stodge (stoj) *v.i.* to stuff; to cram.—**stodg'y** *a.* heavy; lumpy; indigestible; (*Fig.*) dull and uninteresting.—**stodg'iness** *n.* [etym. uncertain].

stoep (stòòp) *n.* in S. Africa, veranda in front of house [Dut.].

Stoic (stō'ik) *n.* disciple of the Greek philosopher Zeno (342-270 B.C.).—**sto'ic** *n.* one who suffers without complaint; person of great self-control; one indifferent to pleasure or pain.—**sto'ical** *a.* suffering without complaint; being indifferent to pleasure or pain.—**sto'ically** *adv.*—**sto'icism** *n.* endurance of pain, hardship, etc. without complaint [Gk. *stoa*, porch (where Zeno taught this philosophy)].

stoke (stōk) *v.t.* and *v.i.* to stir up, feed, or tend (fire).—**stok'er** *n.*—**stoke'hole** *n.* mouth of furnace; furnace-room of steamer [Dut. *stoken*, to kindle a fire].

stole (stōl) *pa.t.* of **steal**—**sto'len** *pa.p.*

stole (stōl) *n.* long, loose garment, reaching to feet; long, narrow scarf worn by bishops, priests, etc. during mass; woman's long, narrow scarf [Gk. *stolē*, a robe].

stolid (stol'id) *a.* dull or stupid; not easily excited.—**stol'idly** *adv.*—**stol'idness, stolid'ity** *n.* [L. *stolidus*].

stomach (stum'ak) *n.* chief digestive organ in any animal; appetite; desire; spirit;—*v.t.* to put up with; to endure.—**stomacher** (stum'ak-er) *n.* part of a woman's dress covering stomach, generally lower part of bodice.—**stomachic** (stum-ak'ik), **stomach'ical** *a.* pert. to stomach; aiding digestion.—**stomach'ic** *n.* (*Med.*) any medicine for aiding digestion —**stom'ach-pump** *n.* rubber tube about 18 in. long, for washing out stomach, and for feeding patients [Gk. *stomachos*, the gullet, fr. *stoma*, a mouth].

stone (stōn) *n.* hard, earthy matter of which rock is made; piece of rock; a measure of weight equal to 14 lb.; hard centre of certain fruits; gem; concretion in kidneys or bladder; calculus; testicle;—*a.* made of stone, stoneware, earthenware;—*v.t.* to pelt with stones; to remove stones from, as from fruits.—**sto'ny** *a.* like stone; full of stones; (*Fig.*) hard; pitiless.—**sto'nily** *adv.*—**sto'niness** *n.*—**Stone Age,** primitive stage of human development when man used stone for tools and weapons.—**stone'blind** *a.* entirely blind.—**stone'chat** *n.* small bird, with orange-red breast and black legs and bill; wheat-ear.—**stone'crop** *n.* creeping plant found on old walls, etc.; wall-pepper.—**stone'dead** *a.* quite dead; lifeless.—**stone'deaf** *a.* completely deaf.—**stone'ma'son** *n.* worker or builder in stone.—**stone's'throw** *n.* as far as one can throw a stone; hence, not far away. Also **stone'cast, stone's'cast, stone'shot.**—**stone'wall** *v.t.* and *v.i.* to offer stubborn resistance.—**stone'ware** *n.* hard, coarse, glazed pottery; earthenware.—**sto'ny-broke** *a.* (*Slang*) quite penniless [O.E. *stan*].

stood (stŏŏd) *pa.p.* and *pa.t.* of **stand.**

stooge (stŏŏj) *n.* (*Slang*) one who bears blame for others; actor serving as butt of another's jokes;—*v.i.* to act as stooge [etym. uncertain].

stook (stŏŏk) *n.* group of sheaves of corn, etc. set up in field;—*v.t.* to set up in stooks [M.E. *stouk*].

stool (stŏŏl) *n.* chair with no back; low backless seat for resting feet on; seat for evacuating bowels; discharge from bowels.—**stool'pi'geon** *n.* pigeon used to trap other pigeons; person used as decoy.—**to fall between two stools** (*Fig.*) to lose both of two things, opportunities, etc. [O.E. *stol*].

stoop (stŏŏp) *v.i.* to bend body; to lean forward; to have shoulders bowed forward, as from age; to bow one's head; to submit; to condescend; to swoop down, as bird of prey;—*v.t.* to cause to lean forward;—*n.* act of stooping; stooping carriage of head and shoulders [O.E. *stupian*].

stoop (stŏŏp) *n.* See **stoup.**

stop (stop) *v.t.* to fill up opening; to keep from going forward; to bring to a halt; to obstruct; to check; to impede; to hinder; to suspend; to withhold; to desist from; to bring to an end; to leave off; to punctuate;—*v.i.* to cease to go forward; to halt; to leave off.—*pr.p.* **stop'ping.**—*pa.p.* and *pa.t.* **stopped;**—*n.* act of stopping; state of being stopped; halt; halting-place; pause; delay; hindrance; any device for checking movement, e.g. peg, pin, plug, etc.; punctuation mark; (*Mus.*) any device for altering or regulating pitch, e.g. vent-hole in wind instrument; set of organ pipes; lever for putting it in action; consonant (p, t, etc.) produced by checking escape of breath from mouth by closure of lips, teeth, etc.—**stop'page** *n.* state of being stopped; act of stopping; obstruction; cessation; deduction from wages.—**stop'per** *n.* one who, or that which, stops; plug for closing mouth of bottle, etc.; (*Naut.*) short rope;—*v.t.* to close opening with stopper.—**stop'ping** *n.* material for filling up cracks, holes, etc.; in dentistry, material for filling cavity of tooth.—**stop'cock** *n.* short pipe with key for tap, for regulating flow of liquid from vessel.—**stop'gap** *n.* that which closes gap or opening; makeshift; a temporary substitute.—**stop'press** *n.* news put into a newspaper, generally in a special column, after printing has begun.—**stop'watch** *n.* special watch whose hands can be started or stopped instantly, used for exact timing of races.—**full stop,** in punctuation, period [O.E. *stoppian,* to plug].

store (stōr) *n.* great quantity; abundance; reserve supply; stock; a place for keeping goods; shop; warehouse;—*v.t.* to collect; to accumulate; to hoard; to place in a warehouse.—**sto'rage** *n.* act of placing goods in a warehouse; space occupied by them; price paid.—**store'catt'le** *n.* cattle kept for fattening [L. *instaurare,* to restore].

storey, story (stō'ri) *n.* horizontal division of building; set of rooms on one floor.—*pl.* **sto'reys, sto'ries.**—**storeyed** (stō'rid), **sto'ried** *a.* having storeys or floors [var. of *story*].

stork (stork) *n.* large wading-bird allied to heron and ibis.—**stork's'bill** *n.* plant of geranium family [O.E. *storc*].

storm (storm) *n.* violent wind or disturbance of atmosphere; tempest; gale; assault on fortified place; vehemence; commotion; outburst of emotion;—*v.t.* to take by storm; to assault;—*v.i.* to raise tempest; to rage; to fume; to scold violently.—**storm'y** *a.* tempestuous; boisterous; violent; passionate.—**storm'ily** *adv.*—**storm'iness** *n.*—**storm'bound** *a.* delayed by storms.—**storm'cone, storm'drum** *n.* large cone (drum) made of stout canvas, used as part of storm-signal.—**storm'stayed** *a.* prevented from proceeding by stormy weather.—**storm'troop'er** *n.* member of a body formed in Germany by Hitler, disbanded 1934.—**storm'troops** *n.* troops specially trained to attack strongly fortified positions.—**storm'y-pet'rel** *n.* small sea-bird, Mother Carey's Chicken [O.E. *storm*].

story (stō'ri) *n.* history or narrative of facts or events; account; tale; legend; anecdote; (*Colloq.*) falsehood; a lie.—*pl.* **sto'ries.**—**storied** (stō'rid) *a.* told in a story; having a history.—**sto'ry-tell'er** *n.* one who tells stories; novelist; romancer; (*Colloq.*) a liar [Gk. *historia*].

story (stō'ri) *n.* See **sto'rey.**

stot (stot) *n.* young bullock; steer [O.N. *stutr,* a bull].

stoup (stŏŏp) *n.* flagon; holy-water basin. Also [**stoop** [O.N. *staup*].

stout (stout) *a.* strong; robust; vigorous; bold; resolute; fat; thickset; bulky;—*n.* strong, dark-coloured beer; porter.—**stout'ly** *adv.*—**stout'ness** *n.*—**stout'heart'ed** *a.* brave; courageous; intrepid [O.Fr. *estout,* proud, fierce].

stove (stōv) *n.* apparatus with enclosed fire, for cooking, warming room, etc.; oven of blast-furnace;—*v.t.* to heat; to keep warm.—**stove'pipe** *n.* metal pipe for carrying off smoke from stove [O.E. *stofa,* a heated room].

stove (stōv) *pa.p.* and *pa.t.* of **stave.**

stow (stō) *v.t.* to fill by packing closely; to arrange compactly, as cargo in ship; to be silent about; to conceal.—**stow'age** *n.* act of packing closely; space for stowing goods; charge made for stowing goods.—**stow'away** *n.* one who hides on ship to obtain free passage [O.E. *stow,* a place].

strabismus (stra-biz'mus) *n.* (*Med.*) squint [Gk. *strabos,* squinting].

straddle (strad'l) *v.i.* to spread legs wide; to stand or walk with legs apart;—*v.t.* to bestride something; in gunnery, to drop shells beyond and short of (target);—*n.* act of straddling; distance between legs in such position;—*adv.* astride [fr. *stride*].

Stradivarius (strad-i-va'ri-us) *n.* a violin, usually of great value, made at Cremona, Italy, by Antonio *Stradivari* (1649-1737).

strafe (strāf) *v.t.* (*Mil. Slang*) to bombard heavily [Ger. *strafen,* to punish].

straggle (strag'l) *v.i.* to wander from direct course; to stray; to get dispersed; to lag behind; to stretch beyond proper limits, as branches of plant.—**stragg'ler** *n.* one who, or that which, straggles.—**stragg'ling** *a.* wandering; uneven; scattered [etym. uncertain].

straight (strāt) *a.* passing from one point to another by nearest course; without a bend; direct; honest; upright; frank; (*Slang*) of whisky, etc. undiluted;—*n.* straightness; straight part, e.g. of racing-track;—*adv.* in a direct line or manner; directly; without ambiguity; at once.—**straight'ly** *adv.*—**straight'en** *v.t.* to make straight; to put in order;—*v.i.* to become straight.—**straight'ener** *n.*—**straight'away** *adv.* straight forward; (*Colloq.*) at once.—**straightfor'ward** *a.* proceeding in a straight course; honest; frank; simple.—**straightfor'**

wardly *adv.*—straightfor'wardness *n.*—straight'ness *n.* state of being straight; narrowness; tightness [O.E. *streht*].
strain (strān) *n.* race; breed; stock; inherited quality [O.E. *streon*].
strain (strān) *v.t.* to stretch tight; to stretch to the full or to excess; to exert to the utmost; to injure by over-exertion, as muscle; to wrench; to force; to stress; to pass through sieve; to filter;—*v.i.* to make great effort; to filter;—*n.* act of straining; stretching force; violent effort; injury caused by over-exertion; wrench, esp. or muscle; sound; tune; style; manner; tone of speaking or writing.—strain'er *n.* filter; sieve [L. *stringere*, to make tight].
strait (strāt) *a.* narrow; strict; rigorous; difficult;—*n.* narrow channel of water connecting two larger areas; difficulty; financial embarrassment.—strait'ly *adv.* strictly; narrowly.—strait'en *v.t.* to make strait; to narrow; to restrict; to put into position of difficulty or distress.—strait'jack'et, -waist'coat *n.* garment for restraint of violent lunatics.—strait'laced *a.* laced tightly in stays; puritanical; austere [L. *stringere, strictum*, to draw tight].
strand (strand) *n.* edge of sea or lake; the shore;—*v.t.* to cause to run aground; to drive ashore; (*Fig.*) to leave in helpless position;—*v.i.* to run aground; to be driven ashore.—strand'ed *a.* driven on shore; left in a state of difficulty or embarrassment [O.E. *strand*].
strand (strand) *n.* single string or wire of rope; any string, e.g. of hair, pearls, etc.;—*v.t.* to make rope by twisting strands together [O.Fr. *estran*, a rope].
strange (strānj) *a.* foreign; belonging to another person or place; unaccustomed; not familiar; uncommon; odd; wonderful, extraordinary; shy; inexperienced.—strange'ly *adv.* —strange'ness *n.*—stran'ger *n.* one from another country, town, place, etc.; unknown person; newcomer; one unaccustomed (to) [O.Fr. *estrange*, fr. L. *extraneus*, outer].
strangle (strang'gl) *v.t.* to kill by squeezing throat; to choke; to stifle; to suppress.—strang'ler *n.*—strang'ulate *v.t.* to constrict so that circulation of blood is impeded; to compress; to strangle.—strangula'tion *n.* [L. *strangulare*].
strap (strap) *n.* long, narrow strip of leather, cloth, or metal; strop; strip of any material for binding together or keeping in place;—*v.t.* to fasten, bind, chastise with strap; to sharpen (a razor).—*pr.p.* strap'ping.—*pa.p.* and *pa.t.* strapped.—strap'ping *n.* act of fastening with strap; material used; punishment with strap; —*a.* tall, robust, and handsome [O.E. *strop*, fr. L. *struppus*].
strata (strā'ta, strat'a) *n.pl.* See stratum.
stratagem (strat'a-jem) *n.* artifice in war; scheme for deceiving enemy; ruse [Gk. *stratēgein*, to lead an army].
strategy (strat'e-ji) *n.* art of conducting military or naval operations; generalship.—strategic (stra-tej'ik, stra-tē'jik) *a.* pert. to, based on, strategy.—strateg'ics *n.pl.* strategy. —strateg'ical *a.*—strateg'ically *adv.*—strat'egist *n.* one skilled in strategy [Gk. *stratēgein*, to lead army].
strathspey (strath-spā') *n.* lively Scottish dance; music played for it [fr. *Strathspey*, Scotland].
stratify (strat'i-fī) *v.t.* to form or deposit in strata or layers.—*pa.p.* and *pa.t.* strat'ified.—stratifica'tion *n.* arrangement in strata or layers.—strat'iform *a.* in form of strata [L. *stratum*, a layer].
stratosphere (strā'tō-sfēr) *n.* upper part of atmosphere, six miles or more above earth [L. *stratum*, layer, and *sphere*].
stratum (strā'tum, strat'um) *n.* bed of earth, rock, coal, etc. in series of layers; any bed or layer; class in society.—*pl.* stra'ta.—stra'tus *n.* cloud form, in low, horizontal layers or bands. —*pl.* stra'ti [L. *stratum*, fr. *sternere*, to spread out].
straw (straw) *n.* stalk of corn, etc. after grain has been thrashed out; collection of such dry stalks, used for fodder, etc.; thing of very little value;—*a.* made of straw [O.E. *streaw*].
strawberry (straw'be-ri) *n.* creeping plant of genus Fragaria; its fruit, a red berry with delicious taste [O.E. *streaw*, straw; *berige*, a berry].
stray (strā) *v.i.* to wander from path; to get lost; to digress; (*Fig.*) to err;—*v.t.* to cause to stray;—*a.* wandering; strayed; lost; occasional;—*n.* stray animal; lost child [O.Fr. *estraier*].
streak (strēk) *n.* line, or long band, of different colour from the background; stripe; flash of lightning; trait; strain;—*v.t.* to mark with streaks.—streaked, streak'y *a.* having streaks; striped [O.E. *strica*, a stroke].
stream (strēm) *n.* flowing body of water, or other liquid; river, brook, etc.; current; course; trend; steady flow of air or light, or people;—*v.i.* to issue in stream; to flow or move freely; to stretch in long line; to float or wave in air;—*v.t.* to send out in a stream; to send forth rays of light. —stream'er *n.* long, narrow flag; pennant; auroral beam of light shooting up from horizon.—stream'let *n.* little stream.—stream'line *n.* line of current of air; shape of a body (e.g. motor-car, ship, etc.) calculated to offer least resistance to air or water when passing through it;—*v.t.* to design body of this shape [O.E. *stream*].
street (strēt) *n.* road in town or village, usually with houses or buildings at the side.—street'walk'er *n.* one who walks the streets; prostitute [L. *strata (via)*, a paved (way)].
strength (strength) *n.* quality of being strong; capacity for exertion; ability to endure; power or vigour; physical, mental, or moral force; potency of liquid, esp. of distilled or malted liquors; intensity; force of expression; vigour of style; support; security; force in numbers, e.g. of army.—strength'en *v.t.* to make strong or stronger; to reinforce;—*v.i.* to become or grow strong or stronger.—strength'ener *n.* [O.E. *strengthu*].
strenuous (stren'ū-us) *a.* eagerly pressing; urgent; energetic; full of, requiring effort; bold; earnest.—stren'uously *adv.*—stren'uousness *n.* [L. *strenuus*].
streptococcus (strep-tō-kok'us) *n.* (*Med.*) bacterium of chain formation, the organism responsible for serious septicaemias.—*pl.* streptococ'i (-kok'ī) [Gk. *streptos*, bent; *kokkos*, grain].
streptomycin (strep-tō-mī'sēn) *n.* (*Med.*) drug related to penicillin [Gk. *streptos*, bent; *mukēs*, fungus].
stress (stres) *n.* force; pressure; strain; emphasis; weight or importance; accent; (*Mech.*) force producing change in shape of body;—*v.t.* to lay stress on [O.Fr. *estrecier*].
stretch (strech) *v.t.* to pull out; to tighten; to reach out; to strain; to exaggerate;—*v.i.* to be drawn out; to be extended; to spread;—*n.* extension; strain; effort; utmost extent of meaning; expanse; scope; long line or surface; direction; course; unbroken period of time.—stretch'er *n.* one who, or that which, stretches; a frame or litter for carrying sick or wounded; brick or stone laid lengthwise along line of wall.—at a stretch, continuously.—to stretch a point, to make concession [O.E. *streccan*].
strew (strōō) *v.t.* to scatter over surface; to spread loosely. —*pa.p.* strewed or strewn, —*pa.t.* strewed [O.E. *streowian*].
stria (strī'a) *n.* line or small groove.—*pl.* striae (strī'ē) thread-like lines, as on surface of shells; (*Archit.*) fillets between flutes of columns.—stri'ate, stria'ted *a.* marked with striae.—stria'tion *n.* [L. *stria*, a furrow].
stricken (strik'n) *a.* struck; smitten; afflicted (with illness, etc.); worn out (by age) [fr. *strike*].
strict (strikt) *a.* stern; severe; exacting; rigid; unswerving; defined; without exception;

accurate; restricted.—**strict'ly** *adv.*—**strict'ness** *n.*—**stric'ture** *n.* severe criticism; (*Med.*)morbid contraction of any passage of body, esp. urethra [L. *stringere, strictum,* to tighten].
stride (strīd) *n.* long step, or its length;—*v.t.* to pass over with one long step;—*v.i.* to walk, with long steps.—*pa.p.* **stridden** (strid'n).—*pa.t.* **strode** [O.E. *stridan*].
strident (strī'dent) *a.* harsh in tone; grating; jarring.—**stri'dently** *adv.* [L. *stridere,* to creak].
strife (strīf) *n.* conflict; struggle for victory; contest; rivalry [O.Fr. *estrif*].
strike (strīk) *v.t.* to hit; to smite; to punish; to dash against; to collide; to sound; to cause to sound; to occur; to impress; to afflict; to stamp; to cause to light, as match; to lower, as flag or sail; to take down, as tent; to ratify; to conclude; to come upon unexpectedly, as gold; to cancel;—*v.i.* to hit; to deliver blow; to dash; to clash; to run aground; to stop work for increase of wages, etc.; to take root, of a plant;—*n.* a stoppage of work to enforce demand; (*Colloq.*) find, esp. in prospecting for gold; stroke of luck.—*pa.p.* **struck**, or **strick'en** (*obsolete*).—*pa.t.* **struck**.—**stri'ker** *n.* one who, or that which, strikes.—**stri'king** *a.* affecting with strong emotions; impressive.—**stri'kingly** *adv.* [O.E. *strican,* to move, to wipe].
string (string) *n.* cord; twine; ribbon; thick thread; cord or thread on which things are arranged, e.g. *string of pearls*; chain; succession; series; stretched cord of gut or wire for musical instrument; vegetable fibre, as *string beans*; (*Colloq.*) all race-horses from certain stable;—*pl.* stringed musical instruments collectively;—*v.t.* to furnish with strings; to put on string, as beads, pearls, etc.;—*v.i.* to stretch out into a long line; to form strings; to become fibrous.—*pa.p.* and *pa.t.* **strung**.—**stringed** (stringd) *a.* having strings, as violin, etc.—**string'y** *a.* fibrous; of person, long and thin.—**string'iness** *n.*—**string'-beans** *n.pl.* French beans [O.E. *streng*].
stringent (strin'jent) *a.* binding strongly; strict; rigid; severe.—**strin'gently** *adv.*—**strin'gency, strin'gentness** *n.* [L. *stringere,* to tighten].
strip (strip) *v.t.* to pull or tear off; to peel; to skin; to lay bare; to divest; to rob;—*v.i.* to take off one's clothes;—*n.* long, narrow piece of anything.—*pr.p.* **strip'ping**.—*pa.p.* and *pa.t.* **stripped** (stript).—**strip'ling** *n.* youth [O.S. *strypan,* to plunder].
stripe (strīp) *n.* narrow line, band, or mark; strip of material of a different colour from the rest; (*Mil.*) V-shaped strip of material worn on sleeve as badge of rank; chevron; stroke made with lash, whip, scourge, etc.; weal;—*v.t* to mark with stripes; to lash.—**striped** (strīpt) *a.* [Dut. *streep*].
strive (strīv) *v.i.* to try hard; to make an effort; to struggle; to battle; to contend.—*pa.p.* **striv'en**.—*pa.t.* **strove**.—**stri'ver** *n.* [O.Fr. *estriver*].
strode (strōd) *pa.t.* of **stride**.
stroke (strōk) *n.* blow; paralytic fit; apoplexy; any sudden seizure of illness, misfortune, etc.; sound of bell or clock; mark made by pen, pencil, brush, etc.; completed movement of club, stick, racquet, etc.; in swimming, completed movement of arm; in rowing, sweep of an oar; rower nearest stern who sets the time and pace; entire movement of piston from one end to other of cylinder; single, sudden effort, esp. if successful, in business, diplomacy, etc.; —*v.t.* to set time and pace for rowers [O.E. *stracian,* to strike].
stroke (strōk) *v.t.* to pass hand gently over; to caress; to soothe;—*n.* act of stroking [O.E. *stracian,* to strike].
stroll (strōl) *v.i.* to walk leisurely from place to place; to saunter; to ramble;—*n.* a leisurely walk.—**stroll'er** *n.* [etym. uncertain].
strong (strong) *a.* having physical force; powerful; muscular; able to resist attack; healthy; firm; solid; steadfast; well-established; violent; forcible; intense; determined; not easily broken; positive.—**strong'ly** *adv.*—**strong'-box** *n.* box for storage of valuables; safe. —**strong drink**, drink containing alcohol.—**strong'hold** *n.* fortified place.—**strong'-room** *n.* specially constructed chamber or vault, usually burglar- and fire-proof, for storage of valuables [O.E. *strang*].
strontium (stron'shum) *n.* (*Chem.*) a yellowish, reactive, metallic element (symbol **Sr.**) [first found at *Strontian,* Argyllshire, Scotland].
strop (strop) *n.* strip of leather for sharpening razor;—*v.t.* to sharpen on strop.—*pr.p.* **strop'ping**. —*pa.p.* and *pa.t.* **stropped** (stropt) [L. *struppus*].
strophe (strōf'e) *n.* in ancient Greek drama, song sung by chorus while dancing from right to left of orchestra; stanza.—**stroph'ic** *a.* [Gk. *strophē,* a turning].
strove (strōv) *pa.t.* of **strive**.
struck (struk) *pa.p.* and *pa.t.* of **strike**.
structure (struk'tūr) *n.* that which is built; building; manner of building; arrangement of parts or elements; organisation.—**struc'tural** *a.*—**struc'turally** *adv.* [L. *struere, structum,* to build].
struggle (strug'l) *v.i.* to put forth great efforts, esp. accompanied by violent twistings of body; to contend; to strive;—*n.* violent physical effort; any kind of work in face of difficulties; strife.—**strugg'ler** *n.* [etym. uncertain].
strum (strum) *v.t.* and *v.i.* to play badly and noisily on (stringed instrument).—*pr.p.* **strum'ming**.—*pa.p.* and *pa.t.* **strummed** [imit. origin].
strumpet (strum'pet) *n.* prostitute; harlot;—*a.* inconstant [etym. uncertain].
strung (strung) *pa.p.* and *pa.t.* of **string**.
strut (strut) *v.i.* to walk pompously; to walk with affected dignity;—*n.* stiff, proud and affected walk; pompous gait.—*pa.p.* **strutt'ing**. —*pa.p.* and *pa.t.* **strut'ted** [O.E. *strutian,* to stick out stiffly].
strut (strut) *n.* rigid support, usually set obliquely; support for rafter; brace;—*v.t.* to brace [etym. uncertain].
strychnine (strik'nēn, or -nin, or -nīn) *n.* highly poisonous alkaloid, used medicinally as nerve and spinal stimulant. Also **strych'nia** [Gk. *struchnos,* the nightshade].
stub (stub) *n.* stump of a tree; short, remaining part of pencil, cigarette, etc.;—*v.t.* to clear (ground) by rooting up stumps of trees; to strike toe against fixed object.—*pr.p.* **stub'bing**. —*pa.p.* and *pa.t.* **stubbed**.—**stubbed** *a.* short and blunt like stump; obtuse.—**stub'by** *a.* abounding with stubs; short and thick-set.—**stub'biness** *n.* [O.E. *stybb*].
stubble (stub'l) *n.* short ends of cornstalks left after reaping; short growth of beard.—**stubb'led** *a.* covered with stubble.—**stubb'ly** *a.* pert. to, or like, stubble; bristly [L. *stipula,* fr. *stipes,* stalk].
stubborn (stub'orn) *a.* fixed in opinion; obstinate; headstrong.—**stubb'ornly** *adv.*—**stubb'ornness** *n.* [M.E. *stoburn*].
stucco (stuk'ō) *n.* plaster of lime, sand, etc. used on walls, and in decorative work;—*v.t.* to make of stucco [It.].
stuck (stuk) *pa.p.* and *pa.t.* of **stick**.—**stuck'-up** *a.* (*Colloq.*) conceited.
stud (stud) *n.* a movable, double-headed button; ornamental button or knob; large flat-headed nail; boss;—*v.t.* to furnish with studs; to set thickly in, or scatter over.—*pr.p.* **stud'ding**.—*pa.p.* and *pa.t.* **stud'ded** [O.E. *studu,* a post].
stud (stud) *n.* collection of horses, kept for breeding or racing; place where they are kept. —**stud'-book** *n.* official book for recording pedigrees of thoroughbred animals [O.E. *stod*].
student (stū'dent) *n.* one who studies; scholar at university or other post-school institution for higher education.—**stu'dentship** *n.* scholar-

ORDERS and DECORATIONS

Maltese Cross

Ritterkreuz

O. of the Holy Sepulchre

O. of St George (Bavaria)

Verdienstorden

O. Pour le mérite (peace)

O. of the Holy Spirit

Légion d'Honneur

O. of the Garter

O.B.E.

O. of the Golden Fleece

O. Pour le mérite (military)

O. of the Cross of St John

Iron Cross

O. of Lenin

Legion of Honour

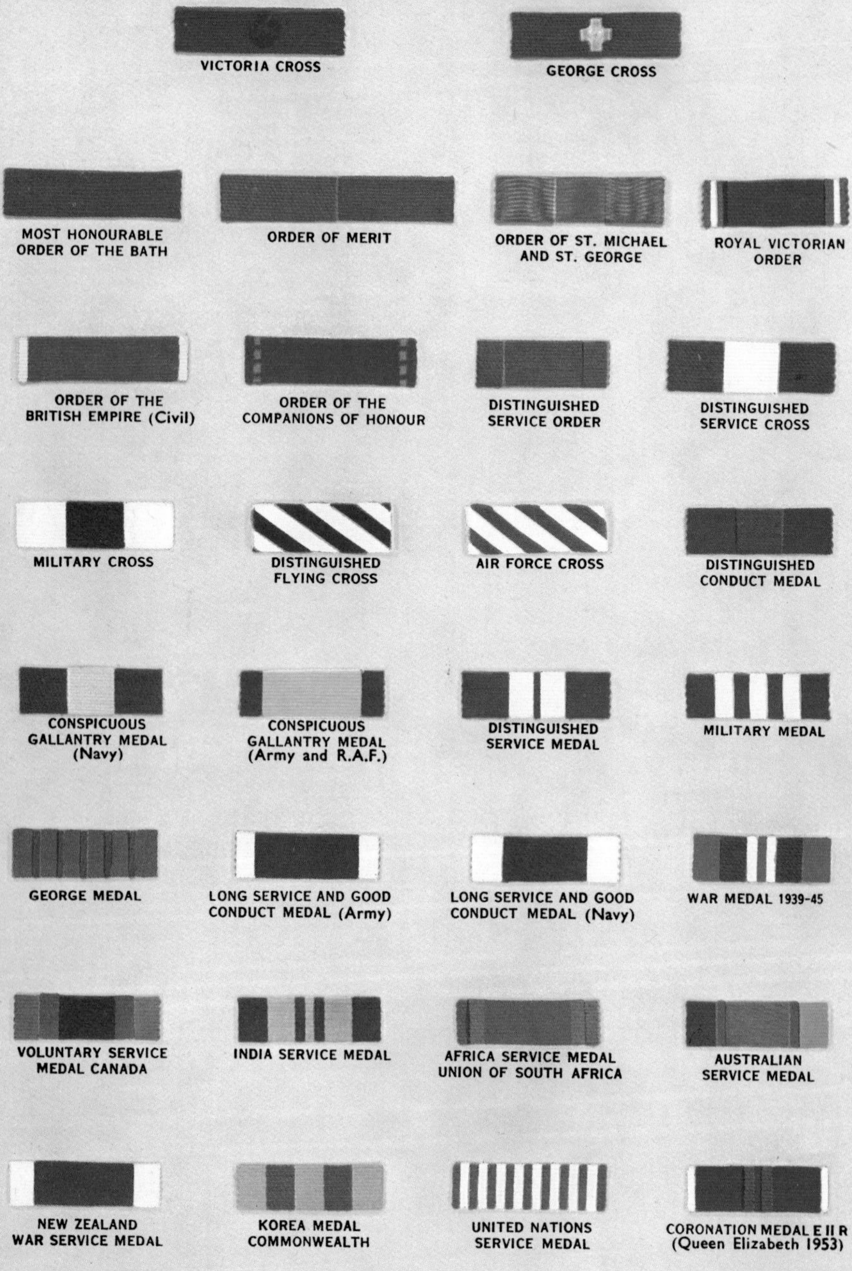

MEDAL RIBBONS

The ribbons of some Commonwealth orders of chivalry, decorations and medals. The Orders of Merit and of the Companions of Honour are never worn as ribbons alone; the Military version of the Order of the British Empire has an additional thin grey vertical stripe down the centre.

ship at university, etc. [L. *studere*, to be zealous].

studio (stū'di-ō) *n.* workroom of artist, sculptor, or professional photographer; where film plays are produced; a room equipped for broadcasting of radio and television programmes.—*pl.* **stu'dios** [It.].

studious (stū'di-us) *a.* given to, or fond of, study; thoughtful; contemplative; painstaking; careful (of); deliberate.—**stu'diously** *adv.* [L. *studium*, zeal].

study (stud'i) *n.* application of the mind to books, etc. to gain knowledge; subject of such application; branch of learning; thoughtful attention; meditation; aim; room for study; preliminary sketch by an artist;—*v.t.* to set the mind to; to examine carefully; to scrutinise; to ponder over;—*v.i.* to read books closely in order to gain knowledge.—**studied** (stud'id) *pa.p.* and *pa.t.*;—also *a.* examined closely; carefully considered and planned [L. *studium*, zeal].

stuff (stuf) *n.* essential part; textile fabric, esp. woollen; cloth not yet made into garments; goods; belongings; useless matter; worthless things, trash, esp. in *stuff and nonsense*;—*v.t.* to fill by pressing closely; to cram; in cookery, to fill, e.g. chicken with seasoning; to fill skin, e.g. of animal, bird, etc. to preserve it as specimen;—*v.i.* (*Colloq.*) to eat greedily.—**stuff'ing** *n.* material used to stuff or fill anything; (*Slang*) spirit; vim; stamina; courage [O.Fr. *estoffe*, fr. L. *stupa*, tow].

stuffy (stuf'i) *a.* badly ventilated; airless.—**stuff'iness** *n.* [Fr. *étouffer*, to choke, stifle].

stultify (stul'ti-fī) *v.t.* to make to look ridiculous; to make ineffectual; to destroy the force of.—**stultifica'tion** *n.* [L. *stultus*, foolish; *facere*, to make].

stumble (stum'bl) *v.i.* to trip in walking and nearly fall; to walk in unsteady manner; to fall into error; to speak hesitatingly;—*v.t.* to cause to trip; to mislead;—*n.* act of stumbling; wrong step; error.—**stum'blingly** *adv.*—**stum'bling-block** *n.* obstacle; hindrance [M.E. akin to *stammer*].

stump (stump) *n.* part of tree left after trunk is cut down; part of limb, tooth, etc. after main part has been removed; remnant; in cricket, one of three upright rods forming wicket;—*pl.* (*Slang*) legs;—*v.t.* to reduce to a stump; to cut off main part; in cricket, to dismiss batsman by 'breaking' wicket when he is out of his ground; (*Colloq.*) to puzzle or perplex; to tour (district) making political speeches;—*v.i.* to walk noisily or heavily.—**stump'y** *a.* full of stumps; short and thick [akin to *stub*].

stun (stun) *v.t.* to knock senseless; to daze; to stupefy; to amaze.—*pr.p.* **stun'ning**.—*pa.p.* and *pa.t.* **stunned** (stund).—**stun'ner** *n.*—**stun'ning** *a.* rendering senseless; stupefying; (*Slang*) striking; excellent [O.Fr. *estoner*].

stung (stung) *pa.p.* and *pa.t.* of **sting**.

stunk (stungk) *pa.p.* and *pa.t.* of **stink**.

stunt (stunt) *v.t.* to check the growth of; to dwarf.—**stunt'ed** *a.* underdeveloped; dwarfed [O.E. *stunt*, dull].

stunt (stunt) *n.* any spectacular feat of skill or daring, esp. if for display, or to gain publicity (U.S. slang; etym. uncertain].

stupefy (stū'pe-fī) *v.t.* to make stupid; to deprive of full consciousness; to dull the senses; to amaze.—**stupefac'tion** *n.* act of making stupid; dazed condition; utter amazement [L. *stupere*, to be amazed; *facere*, to make].

stupendous (stū-pen'dus) *a.* astonishing, esp. because of size, power, etc.; amazing.—**stupen'dously** *adv.*—**stupen'dousness** *n.* [L. *stupere*, to be amazed].

stupid (stū'pid) *a.* slow-witted; unintelligent; foolish; silly.—**stu'pidly** *adv.*—**stupid'ity, stu'pidness** *n.* [L. *stupidus*].

stupor (stū'por) *n.* complete or partial loss of consciousness; dazed state; overpowering amazement [L. *stupor*, fr. *stupere*, to be struck senseless].

sturdy (stur'di) *a.* hard; robust; vigorous; strongly built; firm.—**stur'dily** *adv.*—**stur'diness** *n.* [O.Fr. *estourdi*, stunned, amazed].

sturgeon (stur'jun) *n.* large fish, whose roe is made into caviare and air-bladder into isinglass [Fr. *esturgeon*].

stutter (stut'ẹr) *v.i.* and *v.t.* to speak with difficulty, esp. with repetition of initial consonants; to stammer;—*n.* the act or habit of stuttering.—**stutt'erer** *n.* one who stutters.—**stutt'ering** *a.* [M.E. *stoten*].

sty (stī) *n.* place to keep pigs in; hence, any filthy place [O.E. *stig*].

sty, stye (stī) *n.* small abscess on eyelid [O.E. *stigend*].

Stygian (stij'i-ạn) *a.* pert. to river *Styx* in Hades; infernal; gloomy; dismal [L. *Stygius*, fr. Gk. *stugein*, to hate].

style (stīl) *n.* pointed instrument used by the ancients for writing on waxed tablets; engraving-tool; etching-needle; manner of expressing thought in writing, speaking, acting, painting, etc.; in the arts, mode of expression or performance peculiar to individual, group, or period; in games, manner of play and bodily action; mode of dress; fashion; fine appearance; mode of address; title; mode of reckoning time; sort, kind, make, shape, etc. of anything; (*Bot.*) stem-like part of pistil of flower, supporting stigma; pin of a sun-dial;—*v.t.* to give title, official or particular, in addressing or speaking of (person); to term; to name; to call.—**sty'let** *n.* little style; poniard; stiletto; probe.—**sty'lise** *v.t.* in art, to make conform to convention.—**sty'lish** *a.* fashionable; elegant.—**sty'lishly** *adv.*—**sty'lishness** *n.*—**sty'list** *n.* writer, who is attentive to form and style; one who is master of style.—**sty'lus** *n.* style; pen [L. *stilus*].

stylograph (stī'lō-graf) *n.* fountain-pen, resembling pencil, with needle-like writing-point instead of nib.—**stylograph'ic** *a.* **stylograph'ically** *adv.* [L. *stilus*, style; Gk. *graphein*, to write].

stymie (stī'mi) *n.* (*Golf*) position on putting-green resulting from one player's ball coming to rest between hole and opponent's ball; (*Fig.*) to thwart [etym. unknown].

styptic (stip'tik) *a.* contracting; astringent; —*n.* (*Med.*) any substance used to arrest bleeding [Gk. *stuphein*, to contract].

suasion (swā'zhun) *n.* persuasion; advisory influence.—**sua'sible** *a.* able to be persuaded.—**sua'sive** *a.* having power to persuade [L. *suadere, suasum*, to advise].

suave (swāv, swȧv) *a.* pleasant; agreeable; smoothly polite; bland.—**suave'ly** *adv.*—**suav'ity** *n.* [L. *suavis*, sweet].

sub (sub) *n.* (*Colloq.*) shortened form of subaltern, sub-lieutenant, subscription, subsistence money, substitute, etc.

sub- (sub) *prefix*, meaning under, below, from below, lower, inferior, nearly, about, somewhat, slightly, moderately, used in many words, e.g.—**subacute'** *a.* moderately acute or severe [L.].

subaltern (sub'ạl-tẹrn, su-bawl'tẹrn) *n.* (*Mil.*) commissioned officer under rank of captain; first or second lieutenant;—*a.* of lower rank [L. *sub*, under; *alternus*, in turn].

subaqueous (sub-ā'kwe-us) *a.* living, lying, or formed under water.—**subaquat'ic** *a.*

subarctic (sub-ȧrk'tik) *a.* pert. to region or climate immediately next to the Arctic.

subastral (sub-as'trạl) *a.* situated under the stars; terrestrial.

subatom (sub-at'om) *n.* (*Chem.*) a component part of an atom.—**subatom'ic** *a.*

subconscious (sub-kon'shus) *a.* pert. to unconscious activities which go on in mind; partially conscious;—*n.* subconscious mind.—**subcon'sciously** *adv.*

subcutaneous (sub-kū-tā'ne-us) *a.* under the skin.—**subcutic'ular** *a.* under the cuticle.

subdivide (sub-di-vīd′) *v.t.* to divide a part, or parts of, into other parts; to divide again; —*v.i.* to be subdivided.—**subdivi′sion** *n.* act of subdividing; result of subdividing.

subduce (sub-dūs′) *v.t.* to withdraw; to take away. Also **subduct** (sub-dukt′).—**subduc′tion** *n.* [L. *subducere*, to withdraw].

subdue (sub-dū′) *v.t.* to bring under one's power; to conquer; to bring under control; to reduce force or strength of; to soften.—**subdued′** *a.* —**subdu′er** *n.*—**subdu′al** *n.* act of subduing; state of being subdued. —**subdu′able** *a.* [L. *subducere*, to withdraw].

sub-edit (sub-ed′it) *v.t.* to act under an editor; to be assistant editor; to prepare copy for.—**sub-ed′itor** *n.*

subfusc (sub′fusk) *a.* of darkish colour; sober-hued. Also **subfus′cous.**

subheading (sub-hed′ing) *n.* division of main heading.

subhuman (sub-hū′mạn) *a.* less than human.

subject (sub′jekt) *a.* under power or control of another; owing allegiance; subordinate; dependent; liable to; prone; exposed;—*n.* one under the power or control of another; one owing allegiance to a sovereign, state, government, etc.; a person, animal, etc. used as an object of experiment, treatment, operation, etc.; matter under consideration or discussion, written or spoken; topic; theme; (*Mus.*) principal theme or melody of movement; (*Gram.*) a word or words in sentence of which something is affirmed; (*Philos.*) conscious self; thinking mind.—**subject** (sub-jekt′)*v.t.* to bring under power or control of; to subdue; to cause to undergo; to submit.—**subjec′tion** *n.* act of bringing under power or control; state of being under control.—**subjec′tive** *a.* pert. to subject; existing in the mind; arising from senses; relating to, or reflecting, thoughts and feelings of person; (*Gram.*) pert. to subject of sentence.—**subjec′tively** *adv.*—**subjec′tiveness** *n.* —**subjectiv′ity** *n.* state of being subjective; theological doctrine that bases religious beliefs on subjective experience [L. *sub*, under; *jacere*, to throw].

subjoin (sub-join′) *v.t.* to append; to annex.—**subjoin′der** *n.* something added at end; subsequent remark.

subjugate (sub′jòò-gāt) *v.t.* literally, to bring under the yoke; to force to submit; to conquer.—**subjuga′tion** *n.*—**sub′jugator** *n.* [L. *sub*, and *jugum*, yoke].

subjunctive (sub-jungk′tiv) *a.* subjoined; denoting subjunctive mood;—*n.* subjunctive mood.—**subjunctive mood** (*Gram.*) mood of verb implying condition, doubt, or wish [L. *sub*; *jungere*, to join].

sublease (sub-lēs′) *n.* lease granted to another tenant by one who is himself a tenant;—*v.t.* to grant or hold a sublease.

sublet (sub-let′) *v.t.* to let to another tenant property, of which one is a tenant.

sub-lieutenant (sub-lef-ten′ạnt) *n.* a naval officer ranking above midshipman and below lieutenant.—**sub-lieuten′ancy** *n.*

sublimate (sub′lim-āt) *v.t.* (*Chem.*) to convert solid direct into vapour and then allow it to solidify again; to purify thus; in psychoanalysis, to direct repressed impulses, esp. sexual, towards new aims and activities;—*n.* (*Chem.*) substance that has been sublimated. —**sublima′tion** *n.* [L. *sublimare*, to lift up].

sublime (sub-līm′) *a.* exalted; elevated; high in place; eminent; inspiring awe, adoration, etc.; majestic; grandiose;—*n.* that which is sublime;—*v.t.* to sublimate; to purify; to exalt; to ennoble.—**sublime′ly** *adv.*—**sublime′ness, sublimity** (sub-lim′i-ti) *n.* [L. *sublimis*, high].

subliminal (sub-lim′in-ạl) *a.* in psychology, below level of consciousness; latent.

sub-machine-gun (sub-mạ-shēn′gun) *n.* (*Mil.*) light, portable machine-gun.

submarine (sub-mạ-rēn′) *a.* situated, living, or able to travel under surface of sea; —*n.* submersible boat, esp. one armed with torpedoes.

submerge (sub-mẹrj′) *v.t.* to put under water; to cover with water; to flood; (*Fig.*) to overwhelm;—*v.i.* to go under water.—**submer′gence** *n.* [L. *sub*; *mergere*, to dip].

submerse (sub-mẹrs′) *v.t.* to submerge; to put under water.—**submer′sible** *a.* able to be submersed;—*n.* submarine boat.—**submer′sion** *n.* [L. *submergere*].

submit (sub-mit′) *v.t.* to put forward for consideration; to surrender;—*v.i.* to yield oneself to another; to surrender.—*pr.p.* **submit′ting.** —*pa.p.* and *pa.t.* **submit′ted.**—**submis′sion** *n.* act of submitting; confession of inferiority or error; surrender; humility; meekness.—**submis′sive** *a.* ready to submit; obedient; docile; humble.—**submis′sively** *adv.*—**submis′siveness** *n.* docility of behaviour; resignation [L. *sub*, under; *mittere*, to put].

submultiple (sub-mul′ti-pl) *n.* number or quantity that divides into another exactly.

subnormal (sub-nor′mạl) *a.* below normal.

subordinate (sub-or′di-nāt) *a.* lower in rank, importance, power, etc.;—*n.* one of lower rank, importance, etc. than another; one under the orders of another;—*v.t.* to make or treat as subordinate; to consider of less importance; to make subject.—**subor′dinately** *adv.* —**subor′dinacy, subor′dinateness** *n.* state of being subordinate.—**subordina′tion** *n.* [L. *sub*, under; *ordinare*, to set in order].

suborn (sub-orn′) *v.t.* to induce (person) to commit perjury; to bribe to do evil.—**suborna′tion** *n.*—**suborn′er** *n.* [L. *sub*, under; *ornare*, to furnish].

subpoena (sub-pē′na) *n.* (*Law*) writ summoning person to appear in court (under penalty for non-appearance);—*v.t.* to issue such an order [L. *sub poena*, under penalty, first words of writ].

subreption (sub-rep′shun) *n.* act of obtaining advantage by concealment or misrepresentation of truth.—**subrep′tive** *a.* surreptitious [L. *sub*, under; *rapere*, to seize].

subscribe (sub-skrīb′) *v.t.* to write underneath; to sign name at end of paper or document; to give, or promise to give, (money) on behalf of cause; to contribute;—*v.i.* to promise in writing to give a sum of money to a cause; (with *to*) to pay in advance for regular supply of issues of newspaper, magazine, etc.; to agree with or support.—**subscrib′er** *n.*—**sub′script** *a.* written underneath.—**subscrip′tion** *n.* act of subscribing; name or signature of subscriber; money subscribed or gifted; fee for membership of society, club, etc.

subsequent (sub′se-kwẹnt) *a.* following or coming after in time; happening later.—**sub′sequently** *adv.*—**sub′sequence, sub′sequency** *n.* [L. *sub*; *sequi*, to follow].

subserve (sub-sẹrv′) *v.t.* to serve in small way; to help forward; to promote.—**subser′vient** *a.* serving to promote some purpose; submissive; servile.—**subser′viently** *adv.*—**subser′vience, subser′viency** *n.* state of being subservient.

subside (sub-sīd′) *v.i.* to sink or fall to the bottom; to settle; to sink to lower level; to collapse; to abate; to come to an end.—**subsi′dence, subsi′dency** *n.* act of subsiding [L. *sub*, under; *sidere*, to settle].

subsidiary (sub-sid′i-ạ-ri) *a.* pert. to subsidy; aiding; helping; supplementary; secondary; auxiliary;—*n.* one who, or that which, helps; auxiliary; accessory [L. *subsidium*, a reserve].

subsidy (sub′si-di) *n.* financial aid; government grant for various purposes, e.g. to encourage certain industries, to keep cost of living steady, etc.; formerly, grant of money to king from subjects; also, money paid by one state to another in return for help in time of war.—**sub′sidise** *v.t.* to pay subsidy to [L. *subsidium*].

subsist (sub-sist′) *v.i.* to continue to be; to exist; to live (on);—*v.t.* to support with food; to feed.—**subsist′ent** *a.* having real being; existing.—**subsist′ence** *n.* act of subsisting; things or means by which one supports life;

livelihood [L. *subsistere*, fr. *sistere*, to stand].
subsoil (sub′soil) *n.* the layer of earth lying just below the top layer.
subsonic (sub-son′ik) *a.* pert. to speeds less than that of sound; below 700-750 m.p.h.
substance (sub′stạns) *n.* essence; stuff, material, etc. of which anything is made; matter; essential matter of book, speech, discussion, etc.; real point; property.—**substantial** (sub-stan′shạl) *a.* pert. to or having substance; material; essential; really existing, i.e. not imaginary.—**substan′tially** *adv.*—**substantiate** (sub-stan′shi-āt) *v.t.* to make substantial; to give substance to; to bring evidence for; to establish truth of; to confirm.—**substantia′tion** *n.*—**sub′stantive** *a.* having independent existence; real; solid; fixed; permanent; (*Gram.*) expressing existence; pert. to noun, or used as noun;—*n.* (*Gram.*) noun.—**sub′stantively** *adv.* [L. *substare*, to stand under, to be present].
substitute (sub′sti-tūt) *v.t.* to put in place of another; to exchange.—*v.i.* to take place of another;—*n.* one who, that which, is put in place of another.—**substitu′tion** *n.*—**substitu′tional, substitu′tionary** *a.* [L. *sub*, under; *statuere*, to appoint].
substratum (sub-strā′tum) *n.* underlying stratum or layer of soil, rock, etc.; a basic element.—*pl.* **substra′ta.**
subsume (sub-sūm′) *v.t.* to include under a class as belonging to it, e.g. 'all sparrows are birds.'—**subsump′tion** *n.*
subtenant (sub-ten′ạnt) *n.* tenant who rents house, farm, etc. from one who is himself a tenant.—**subten′ancy** *n.*
subtend (sub-tend′) *v.t.* (*Geom.*) of line, to extend under or be opposite to, e.g. angle.
subterfuge (sub′tẹr-fūj) *n.* that to which a person resorts in order to escape from a difficult situation, to conceal real motives, to avoid censure, etc.; an underhand trick; evasion [L. *subter*, under; *fugere*, to flee].
subterranean (sub-te-rā′ne-ạn) *a.* being or lying under surface of earth. Also **subterra′neous, subterrene** (sub-te-rēn′), **subterres′trial** [L. *sub*, under; *terra*, the earth].
subtil, subtile (sub′til, sut′l) *a.* (archaic forms of *subtle*) finely spun; made in delicate fashion; fine; rare.—**sub′tilely** *adv.*—**sub′tilty** *n.* [L. *sub*, under; *tela*, a web].
sub-title (sub′tī-tl) *n.* additional title of book; half-title; film caption.
subtle (sut′l) *a.* delicate; acute; discerning; clever; crafty; ingenious; intricate; making fine distinctions; evasive.—**subt′ly** *adv.*—**subt′leness, subtlety** (sutl′ti) *n.* quality of being subtle; artfulness; acuteness; a fine distinction [L. *subtilis*, fine woven].
subtopia (sub-tō′pi-a) *n.* name used to designate sprawling, architectural ugliness in town- and country-planning.
subtract (sub-trakt′) *v.t.* to take away (part) from rest; to deduct one number from another to find difference.—**subtrac′tion** *n.* act or operation of subtracting.—**subtrac′tive** *a.* subtracting; pert. to subtraction.—**sub′trahend** *n.* quantity or number to be subtracted from another [L. *sub*; *trahere*, to draw].
subtropical (sub-trop′i-kạl) *a.* designating zone just outside region of the tropics.
suburb (sub′urb) *n.* residential district on outskirts of town;—*pl.* outskirts.—**suburb′an** *a.* pert. to, living in, suburb; affectedly superior; socially snobbish;—*n.* one who lives in the suburbs.—**suburb′ia** *n.* suburbs and their inhabitants [L. *sub*, under; *urbs*, city].
subvention (sub-ven′shun) *n.* act of coming to the help of; government grant; subsidy [L. *sub*, under; *venire*, to come].
subvert (sub-vert′) *v.t.* to turn upside down; to overthrow, esp. government; to destroy; to ruin utterly; to corrupt.—**subver′sion** *n.* the act of subverting; entire overthrow; complete ruin; corruption.—**subver′sive** *a.* [L. *sub*, under; *vertere*, to turn].
subway (sub′wā) *n.* underground passage; underground railway.
succeed (suk-sēd′) *v.t.* to come immediately after; to follow in order; to take place of, esp. of one who has left or died;—*v.i.* to come next in order; to become heir (to); to achieve one's aim; to prosper.—**succeed′er** *n.* successor.—**success′** *n.* act of succeeding; state of having succeeded; accomplishment; attainment; issue, result, outcome; prosperity; one who has achieved success.—**success′ful** *a.* resulting in success; brought to a favourable end; fortunate; prosperous.—**success′fully** *adv.*—**success′fulness** *n.*—**succession** (suk-sesh′un) *n.* act of following in order; sequence; series of persons or things according to some established rule; line of descendants; race; act or right of entering into possession of property, place, office, title, etc., of another, esp. of one near of kin.—**succes′sive** *a.* following in order; consecutive.—**succes′sively** *adv.*—**succes′sor** *n.* one who succeeds or takes place of another; heir to throne or title [L. *succedere*].
succinct (suk-singkt′) *a.* closely compressed; expressed in few words; terse; concise.—**succinct′ly** *adv.*—**succinct′ness** *n.* terseness; brevity [L. *succingere*, to gird up].
succour (suk′ur) *v.t.* to help esp. in great difficulty or distress; to relieve; to comfort;—*n.* aid; support [L. *succurrere*, fr. *currere*, to run].
succulent (suk′ū-lẹnt) *a.* full of juice; juicy.—**succ′ulently** *adv.*—**succ′ulence** *n.* juiciness [L. *succus*, juice].
succumb (su-kum′) *v.i.* to yield; to submit; to die [L. *sub*, under; *cumbere*, to lie down].
such (such) *a.* of like kind; of that kind; of same kind; similar; of degree, quality, etc. mentioned; certain or particular;—*pron.* used to denote a certain person or thing; these or those.—**such′like** *a.* similar;—*pron.* similar things (but not defined); this or that [O.E. *swylc*].
suck (suk) *v.t.* to draw into mouth (by using lips and tongue); to draw liquid from (by using mouth); to roll (sweet) in mouth; to drink in; to absorb; to imbibe;—*v.i.* to draw in with mouth; to drink from mother's breast;—*n.* act of drawing with the mouth; milk drawn from mother's breast.—**suck′er** *n.* one who, or that which, sucks; organ by which animal adheres by suction to any object; circular piece of leather, which, when soaked in water, is used as a toy to lift stones, etc. by suction; shoot of plant from roots or lower part of stem; (*U.S. Slang*) person easily deceived.—**suck′ing** *a.* drawing nourishment from mother's breast; young; inexperienced.—**suck′le** *v.t.* to give suck to; to feed at mother's breast.—**suck′ling** *n.* young child or animal not yet weaned [O.E. *sucan*].
sucrose (sū′krōs) *n.* white, sweet, crystalline substance; cane-sugar, beet-sugar, etc. [Fr. *sucre*, sugar].
suction (suk′shun) *n.* act of sucking or drawing in; act of drawing liquids, gases, dust, etc. into vessel by exhausting air in it; 'force' that causes one object to adhere to another when air between them is exhausted.—**sucto′rial** *a.* pert. to suction.—**suc′tion-pump** *n.* pump in which water or other liquid is raised by atmospheric pressure [L. *sugere*, *suctum*, to suck].
sudation (sū-dā′shun) *n.* sweating.—**sudatorium** (sū-dạ-tō′ri-um) *n.* room with heated air, to promote sweating.—*pl.* **sudato′ria.**—**su′datory** *a.* sweating; inducing perspiration;—*n.* hot-air bath [L. *sudare*, to sweat].
sudden (sud′n) *a.* happening without notice or warning; coming unexpectedly; done with haste; abrupt.—**sud′denly** *adv.*—**sud′denness** *n.*—**of a sudden, all of a sudden,** or **on a sudden,** suddenly; unexpectedly [Fr. *soudain*, fr. L. *subitus*, unexpected].
sudor (sū′dor) *n.* sweat.—**su′doral** *a.* pert. to sweat.—**sudorif′erous** *a.* causing or secreting

sweat.—**sudorif'ic** *a.* and *n.* (a drug for) inducing perspiration [L.].

suds (sudz) *n.pl.* boiling-water in which soap has been dissolved; froth and bubbles on it [O.E. *seothan*, to seethe].

sue (sū) *v.t.* (*Law*) to seek justice by taking legal proceedings; to prosecute;—*v.i.* to begin legal proceedings; to petition; to entreat; to woo [L. *sequi*, to follow].

suède (swād) *n.* soft, undressed kid leather, used for making gloves, shoes, etc.;—*a.* made of undressed kid [Fr. *Suède*, Sweden].

suet (sū'et, sòò'et) *n.* hard animal fat around kidneys and loins, used in cooking.—**su'ety** *a.* [L. *sebum*, fat].

suffer (suf'ęr) *v.t.* to endure; to undergo; to bear; to be affected by; to allow; to tolerate;—*v.i.* to undergo pain, punishment, etc.; to sustain a loss.—**suff'erable** *a.* able to be suffered; bearable.—**suff'erance** *n.* the state of suffering; toleration.—**on sufferance** permitted but with reluctance [L. *sub*, under; *ferre*, to bear].

suffice (su-fīs') *v.t.* to satisfy;—*v.i.* to be enough; to meet the needs of; to be satisfied.—**sufficient** (su-fish'ęnt) *a.* enough; satisfying the needs of.—**suffi'ciently** *adv.*—**suffi'ciency** *n.* [L. *sufficere*, to satisfy].

suffix (suf'iks) *n.* letter or syllable added to end of word; affix.—**suffix'** *v.t.* to add to end of.—**suff'ixal** *a.* [L. *sub*; *figere*, to fix].

sufflate (su-flāt') *v.t.* to inflate; to blow up.—**suffla'tion** *n.* [L. *sufflare*, to inflate].

suffocate (suf'ō-kāt) *v.t.* to kill by choking; to smother; to stifle;—*v.i.* to be choked, stifled, or smothered.—**suff'ocating** *a.* choking; gasping for breath.—**suff'ocatingly** *adv.*—**suffoca'tion** *n.* [L. *suffocare*, fr. L. *sub*, under; *fauces*, the throat].

suffragan (suf'rą-gąn) *a.* assisting;—*n.* assistant bishop [L. *suffragari*, to vote for].

suffrage (suf'rāj) *n.* vote; right to vote; approval.—**suffragette'** *n.* woman who agitated for women's right to parliamentary vote [L. *suffragium*, a vote].

suffuse (su-fūz') *v.t.* to pour from underneath and spread over, as fluid; to well up; to flood; to cover.—**suffu'sion** *n.* [L. *sub*, under; *fundere*, to pour].

sugar (shòòg'ąr) *n.* sweet, crystalline substance obtained from certain vegetable products, e.g. sugar-cane, sugar-beet, maple, etc.; any sweet substance like sugar; (*Fig.*) sweet words; flattery;—*v.t.* to sweeten with sugar;—*v.i.* to turn into sugar.—**sug'ary** *a.* made of, tasting of, or containing sugar; sweet; flattering.—**sug'ariness** *n.*—**sug'ar-cane,** tall grass whose sap yields sugar.—**sug'ar-loaf** *n.* a cone-shaped mass of hard, refined sugar.—**sug'ar-plum** *n.* sweetmeat formed into plum-shaped ball.—**sug'ar-refi'ner** *n.* one who refines raw sugar.—**sug'ar-refi'nery** *n.*—**sug'ar-tongs** *n.pl.* implement for lifting cube-shaped lumps of sugar [Fr. *sucre*, fr. Ar. *sukkar*].

suggest (su-jest') *v.t.* to bring forward; to propose; to hint; to insinuate.—**sugges'ter** *n.*—**sugges'tion** *n.* proposal; hint; veiled, indecent offer to woman; in psychiatry, influence exercised over subconscious mind of a person, esp. one suffering from a nervous disorder, resulting in a passive acceptance by him of impulses, beliefs, etc.—**sugges'tive** *a.* tending to call up an idea to the mind; hinting at; tending to bring to the mind indecent thoughts; improper.—**sugges'tively** *adv.*—**sugges'tiveness** *n.* [L. *suggerere*, to carry up].

suicide (sū'i-sīd) *n.* one who kills himself intentionally; act of doing this.—**suicidal** (sū-i-sī'dąl) *a.* pert. to, tending to suicide; (*Fig.*) disastrous; ruinous.—**suici'dally** *adv.* [L. *sui*, of oneself; *caedere*, to kill].

suit (sūt) *n.* act of suing; petition; request; action in court of law; courtship; series or set of things of same kind or material; set of clothes; any of four sets in pack of cards;—*v.t.* to fit; to go with; to become; to be adapted to; to meet desires of;—*v.i.* to agree; to be convenient.—**suit'able** *a.* proper; appropriate; becoming.—**suit'ably** *adv.*—**suitabil'ity, suit'ableness** *n.*—**suit'ing** *n.* suit of clothes; material suitable for making this.—**suit'or** *n.* one who sues; a wooer; a lover.—**suit'case** *n.* flat travelling-bag for holding clothes, etc. [Fr. *suivre*, to follow, fr. L. *sequi*].

suite (swēt) *n.* train of followers or attendants; retinue; a number of things used together, e.g. set of apartments, furniture; (*Mus.*) series of dances or other pieces [Fr. fr. *suivre*, to follow].

sulcus (sul'kus) *n.* groove; a furrow.—**sul'cate, sul'cated** *a.* [L. = a furrow].

sulk (sulk) *v.i.* to be silent owing to ill-humour, etc.; to be sullen;—*n.* sullen fit or mood.—**sulks** *n.pl.* sullen mood.—**sulk'y** *a.* silent and sullen; morose;—*n.* light two-wheeled carriage for one person.—**sulk'ily** *adv.*—**sulk'iness** *n.* state of being sulky; sullenness [etym. unknown].

sullen (sul'en) *a.* gloomily ill-humoured; silently obstinate; morose.—**sull'enly** *adv.*—**sull'enness** *n.* the state of being sullen [L. *solus*, alone].

sully (sul'i) *v.t.* to soil; to stain; (*Fig.*) to disgrace;—*v.i.* to be sullied [Fr. *souiller*, to soil].

sulphate (sul'fāt) *n.* salt of sulphuric acid.—**sul'phide** *n.* compound of sulphur with metal or other element.—**sul'phite** *n.* salt of sulphurous acid [L. *sulphur*].

sulphonal (sul'fō-nal) *n.* (*Chem.* and *Med.*) colourless and tasteless crystalline substance, used as anaesthetic and hypnotic.—**sulphonamide** (sul-fon'am-īd) *n.* (*Chem.*) amide of sulphonic acid.—*a.* denoting group of drugs used as internal germicides in treatment of many bacterial diseases.—**sulphon'ic** *a.* (*Chem.*) pert. to or denoting group So_2 OH.

sulphur (sul'fur) *n.* yellow, non-metallic element, burning with blue flame and giving off suffocating odour; brimstone.—**sulphurate** (sul'fū-rāt) *v.t.* to combine with sulphur; to treat with sulphur.—**sulphuret** (sul'fū-ret) *n.* a sulphide.—**sulphu'ric** *a.* pert. to, obtained from, sulphur.—**sul'phurise** *v.t.* to combine with sulphur; to sulphurate.—**sul'phurous** *a.* pert. to, like, containing sulphur; sulphureous; (*Fig.*) hellish; profane.—**sul'phury** *a.* like sulphur.—**sulphuric acid,** colourless acid, having strong corrosive action [L. *sulphur*].

sultan (sul'tąn) *n.* Mohammedan prince or ruler.—**sulta'na** *n.* wife, mother, or daughter of sultan; kind of raisin [Fr. fr. Ar. *sultan*, victorious].

sultry (sul'tri) *a.* hot, close, and oppressive; sweltering.—**sul'trily** *adv.*—**sul'triness** *n.* [form of *sweltry*, fr. *swelter*].

sum (sum) *n.* result obtained by adding together two or more things, quantities, etc.; full amount; total; aggregate; summary; quantity of money; arithmetical problem;—*v.t.* (generally with *up*) to add up; to find total amount; to make summary of main parts.—*pr.p.* **summ'ing.**—*pa.p.* and *pa.t.* **summed.**—**summa'tion** *n.* act of summing up; addition; total reckoning [L. *summa*, total amount].

summary (sum'ą-ri) *a.* expressed in few words; concise; done quickly and without formality;—*n.* abridgment or statement of chief points of longer document, speech, etc.; epitome.—**summ'arily** *adv.* in summary manner.—**summ'arise** *v.t.* to make summary of.—**summ'arist** *n.* [Fr. *sommaire*].

summer (sum'ęr) *n.* warmest of four seasons of year, season between spring and autumn; commonly, months of June, July, and August;—*pl.* 'years,' in counting age;—*a.* pert. to period of summer;—*v.i.* to pass the summer.—**summ'ery** *a.* like summer.—**summ'er-house** *n.* permanent garden-shelter or outhouse [O.E. *sumor*].

summersault, summerset *n.* See **somersault.**

summit (sum′it) *n.* highest point; top, esp. of mountain [L. *summus*, highest].
summon (sum′on) *v.t.* to demand appearance of, esp. in court of law; to cite; to send for; to gather up (energy, etc.).—**summ′oner** *n.* one who summons.—**summ′ons** *n.* (*Law*) document ordering person to appear in court; any authoritative demand;—*v.t.* to serve with summons [L. *summonere*, to hint, fr. *sub*, under, secretly; *monere*, to warn].
sump (sump) *n.* lowest part of excavation, esp. of mine, in which water collects; well in crank-case of motor vehicle for oil [Dut. *somp*].
sumpter (sump′tẹr) *n.* animal, esp. a horse for carrying burdens; pack-horse [O.Fr. *sommetier*, a pack-horse driver].
sumptuary (sump′tū-ạ-ri) *a.* pert. to, or regulating, expenditure.—**sump′tuous** *a.* costly; lavish; magnificent.—**sump′tuously** *adv.*—**sump′tuousness** *n.* [L. *sumptus*, cost].
sun (sun) *n.* luminous body round which earth and other planets revolve; its rays; any other heavenly body forming the centre of system of planets; anything resembling sun, esp. in brightness;—*v.t.* to expose to sun's rays; to warm (oneself) in sunshine; to bask.—*pr.p.* **sun′ning.**—*pa.p.* and *pa.t.* **sunned.**—**sun′ny** *a.* pert. to, like, sun; exposed to sun; warmed by sun; (*Fig.*) cheerful.—**sun′niness** *n.* state of being sunny.—**sun′bathe** *v.i.* to expose body to sun.—**sun′beam** *n.* ray of sunlight.—**sun′blind** *n.* movable shade for protecting windows from sun.—**sun′burn** *n.* darkening of skin, accompanied often by burning sensation, due to exposure to sun;—*v.t.* and *v.i.* to darken by exposure to sun.—**sun′burned, sun′burnt** *a.*—**sun′dew** *n.* bog plant secreting sticky fluid on which insects are caught.—**sun′di′al** *n.* device for showing time by shadow which a raised pin casts on plate marked with hours.—**sun′down** *n*, sunset; broad-brimmed hat.—**sun′flower** *n.* tall plant with large, round, yellow-rayed flower-heads.—**sun′light** *n.* light of sun.—**sun′lit** *a.* lighted up by sun.—**sun′rise** *n.* first appearance of sun above horizon in morning; time of its appearance; dawn; east.—**sun′set** *n.* descent of sun below horizon; time of its disappearance; west.—**sun′shade** *n.* parasol.—**sun′shine** *n.* light of sun; (*Fig.*) cheerfulness.—**sun′shiny** *a.* bright with sunshine; pleasant.—**sun′spot** *n.* dark, irregular patches seen periodically on surface of sun; freckle.—**sun′stroke** *n.* feverish and sudden prostration caused by undue exposure to very strong sunlight.—**sun′wor′ship** *n.* worship of sun as god [O.E. *sunne*].
sundae (sun′dā) *n.* ice-cream served with crushed fruit [perh. fr. *Sunday*].
Sunday (sun′dā) *n.* first day of week; Christian Sabbath;—*a.* pert. to first day of week [O.E. *sunnan*, sun; *daeg*, day].
sunder (sun′dẹr) *v.t.* to separate; to divide; to sever;—*v.i.* to come apart.—**sun′dry** *a.* separate; several; various.—**sun′dries** *n.pl.* sundry things; odd items.—**all and sundry**, all collectively and individually; everybody [O.E. *syndrian*, to separate].
sung (sung) *pa.p.* of **sing.**
sunk (sungk) *pa.p.* of **sink**; also one form of the *pa.t.*—**sunk′en** *a.*
sup (sup) *v.t.* to take in sips; to sip; to eat with spoon, as soup;—*v.i.* to have supper; to sip;—*n.* small mouthful; sip.—*pr.p.* **sup′ping.**—*pa.p.* and *pa.t.* **supped** [O.E. *supan*].
super (sū′per) *n.* supernumerary (actor); (*Colloq. abbrev.*) superintendent; (*Colloq.*) short for superfine, super-excellent, etc.; hence; first-rate [L. *super*, above].
super- (sū′per) *prefix* fr. L. *super*, above, over, beyond, etc., combining to form many words.
superable (sū′pẹr-ạbl) *a.* capable of being overcome [L. *superare*, to overcome].
superabound (sū-pẹr-ạ-bound′) *v.i.* to be exceedingly abundant.—**superabund′ant** *a.* much more than enough; excessive.—**superabund′antly** *adv.*—**superabund′ance** *n.*
superannuate (sū-pẹr-an′ū-āt) *v.t.* to pension off because of age or infirmity.—**superannua′tion** *n.* state of being superannuated; pension of superannuated person; regular contribution made by employee towards pension [L. *super*, above; *annus*, year].
superb (sū-pẹrb′) *a.* grand; splendid; magnificent; stately; elegant.—**superb′ly** *adv.*—**superb′ness** *n.* [L. *superbus*, proud].
supercargo (sū-pẹr-kar′gō) *n.* ship's officer who takes charge of cargo.
supercharge (sū-pẹr-chârj′) *v.t.* to charge or fill to excess.—**supercharg′er** *n.* in internal-combustion engine, device for forcing extra supply of petrol mixture into cylinders.
superciliary (sū-pẹr-sil′i-ạr-i) *a.* pert. to eyebrow.—**supercil′ious** *a.* lofty with pride; haughty and indifferent.—**supercil′iously** *adv.*—**supercil′iousness** *n.* [L. *supercilium*, the eyebrow].
supercool (sū′pẹr-kòòl) *v.t.* (*Chem.*) to cool (liquid) below its freezing-point without solidifying it.—**su′percooling** *n.*
super-ego (sū-pẹr-eg′ō) *n.* in psycho-analysis, that unconscious morality which directs action of censor.
supererogation (sū-pẹr-er-ō-gā′shun) *n.* doing more than duty or necessity requires.—**supererog′ative, supererog′atory** *a.* [L. *super*, above; *erogare*, to expend].
superficies (sū-pẹr-fish′i-ēz) *n.* outer surface; surface area.—**superficial** (sū-pẹr-fish′ạl) *a.* lying on surface; not deep; shallow; understanding only what is obvious; slight.—**superfi′cially** *adv.*—**superficial′ity** (fish-i-al′i-ti). Also **superfi′cialness** [L. *super*, above; *facies*, the face].
superfine (sū-pẹr-fīn) *a.* fine above others; of first class quality; very fine or subtle.
superfluous (sū-pẹr′flòò-us) *a.* more than is required or desired; useless.—**super′fluously** *adv.*—**superflu′ity** *n.* state of being superfluous; quantity beyond what is required; a superabundance.—**super′fluousness** *n.* [L. *super*, over; *fluere*, to flow].
superheat (sū-pẹr-hēt′) *v.t.* to heat (steam) above boiling-point of water, done under a pressure greater than atmospheric; to heat (liquid) above its boiling-point.
superheterodyne (sū-pẹr-het′ẹr-ō-dīn) *n.* (*Wireless*) receiving-set of great power and selectivity.—*abbrev.* **superhet′.**
superhuman (sū-pẹr-hū′mạn) *a.* more than human; divine; excessively powerful.
superimpose (sū-pẹr-im-pōz′) *v.t.* to lay upon another thing.—**superimposi′tion** *n.*
superintend (sū-pẹr-in-tend′) *v.t.* to manage; to supervise; to direct; to control;—*v.i.* to supervise.—**superinten′dence, superinten′dency** *n.*—**superinten′dent** *a.* superintending;—*n.* one who superintends; police officer above inspector.
superior (sū-pē′ri-or) *a.* upper; higher in place, position, rank, quality, etc.; surpassing others; being above, or beyond, power or influence of; too dignified to be affected by; supercilious; snobbish;—*n.* one who is above another, esp. in rank or office; head of monastery or other religious house.—**superior′ity** *n.* state or quality of being superior; advantage [L. *superior*, higher].
superlative (sū-pẹr′lạ-tiv) *a.* of or in the highest degree; surpassing all others; supreme; (*Gram.*) denoting, as form of adjective or adverb, highest degree of quality;—*n.* superlative degree of adjective or adverb.—**super′latively** *adv.* [L. *superlativus*, exaggerated, fr. *super*, above; *ferre*, *latum*, to carry].
superman (sū′pẹr-man) *n.* 'Übermensch' or overman of Nietzsche's philosophy; ideal man; one endowed with powers beyond those of the ordinary man.
supernal (sū-pẹr′nạl) *a.* pert. to things above; celestial; heavenly; exalted.
supernatural (sū-pẹr-nat′ū-rạl) *a.* beyond

powers or laws of nature; miraculous; spiritual.—**supernat'urally** *adv.*
supernumerary (sū-pẹr-nū'mẹr-ạr-i) *a.* exceeding the number required; over and above what is necessary;—*n.* person or thing in excess of what is necessary or usual; actor with no speaking part [L. *super*, above; *numerus*, a number].
superphosphate (sū-pẹr-fos'fāt) *n.* acid phosphate; mixture of calcium sulphate and calcium acid phosphate as fertiliser.
superscribe (sū-pẹr-skrīb') *v.t.* to write or engrave on outside or top of; to write name, etc. of a person on the top or cover of.—**superscrip'tion** *n.* act of superscribing; words written or engraved on top or outside of anything.
supersede (sū-pẹr-sēd') *v.t.* to set aside; to replace by another person or thing; to take the place of.—**superses'sion** *n.* [L. *super*, above; *sedere*, to sit].
supersonic (sū-pẹr-son'ik) *a.* pert. to sound-waves of too high a frequency to be audible; denoting a speed greater than that of sound, i.e. more than 750 miles per hour.
superstition (sū-pẹr-stish'un) *n.* belief in, or fear of, what is unknown, mysterious, or supernatural; religion, opinion, or practice based on belief in divination, magic, omens, etc.—**supersti'tious** *a.* pert. to, believing in, or based on, superstition.—**supersti'tiously** *adv.*—**supersti'tiousness** *n.* [L. *superstitio*, excessive fear of the gods].
superstratum (sū-pẹr-strā'tum) *n.* layer above another layer.
superstructure (sū-pẹr-struk'tūr) *n.* structure built on top of another; the part of building above foundation.—**superstruc'tive, superstruc'tural** *a.*
supertax (sū'pẹr-taks) *n.* tax on large incomes in addition to income-tax.
supervene (sū-pẹr-vēn') *v.i.* to happen in addition, or unexpectedly; to follow closely upon.—**superve'nient** *a.* happening in addition.—**superven'tion** *n.* act of supervening [L. *super*, above; *venire*, to come].
supervise (sū-pẹr-vīz') *v.t.* to oversee; to superintend; to inspect; to direct and control.—**supervision** (vizh'un) *n.* act of supervising; superintendence; inspection. Also **supervi'sal** *n.*—**supervisor** (vī'zor) *n.*—**supervi'sory** *a.* pert. to supervision [L. *super*, over; *videre, visum*, to see].
supine (sū'pīn) *a.* lying on one's back; (*Fig.*) indolent; inactive;—*n.* either of two Latin verbal forms, the first ending in *um*, the second in *u*.—**supine'ly** *adv.*—**supine'ness** *n.* [L. *supinus*, fr. *sub*, under].
supper (sup'ẹr) *n.* the last meal of the day [Fr. *souper*, to sup].
supplant (su-plant') *v.t.* to displace (person) esp. by unfair means; to take the place of.—**supplant'er** *n.* [L. *supplantare*, to trip up, fr. *planta*, the sole of the foot].
supple (sup'l) *a.* easily bent; flexible; (*Fig.*) docile; obsequious;—*v.t.* and *v.i.* to make or become supple.—**supp'ly** *adv.* in supple manner.—**supp'leness** *n.* [L. *supplex*, suppliant]
supplement (sup'le-mẹnt) *n.* something added to fill up or supply deficiency; appendix; special number of newspaper; extra charge; (*Geom.*) number of degrees which must be added to angle or arc to make 180° or two right angles.—**supplement'** *v.t.* to fill up or supply deficiency; to add to; to complete.—**supplement'al** *a.*—**supplement'ary** *a.* added to supply deficiency; additional [L. *supplementum*, fr. *supplere*, to fill up].
suppliant (sup'li-ạnt) *a.* supplicating; asking humbly and submissively; beseeching;—*n.* one who supplicates.—**supp'liantly** *adv.*—**supp'licant** *a.* supplicating;—*n.* one who supplicates; suppliant.—**supp'licate** *v.t.* and *v.i.* to ask humbly; to beg earnestly; to petition.—**supplica'tion** *n.*—**supp'licatory** *a.* [L. *supplicare*, to kneel down, fr. *plicare*, to fold].
supply (su-plī') *v.t.* to provide what is needed; to furnish; to fill the place of;—*n.* act of supplying; what is supplied; stock; store; temporary substitute who does duty for another.—**supplies'** *n.pl.* food or money; sums of money granted by parliament to meet public expenditure for current year.—**suppli'er** *n.* one who supplies [L. *supplere*, to fill up].
support (su-pōrt') *v.t.* to keep from falling; to bear weight of; to sustain; to bear or tolerate; to encourage; to furnish with means of living; to confirm; to defend;—*n.* act of sustaining; advocacy; maintenance or subsistence; one who, or that which, supports.—**suppor'ter** *n.* one who, or that which, supports; *pl.* (*Her.*) figures placed one on each side of the escutcheon [L. *sub*, under; *portare*, to carry].
suppose (su-pōz') *v.t.* to assume as true without proof; to advance or accept as a possible or probable fact, condition, etc.; to imagine.—**supposed'** *a.* imagined; accepted; put forward as authentic.—**supposedly** (su-pōz'ed-li) *adv.*—**suppos'able** *a.* [Fr. *supposer*, fr. L. *sub*, under; *ponere*, to place].
supposition (sup-o-zish'un) *n.* act of supposing; assumption; that which is supposed; belief without proof.—**supposi'tional** *a.*—**supposi'tionally** *adv.*—**supposititious** (su-poz-i-tish'us) *a.* put by trick in place belonging to another; spurious; counterfeit.—**suppositi'tiously** *adv.* [L. *sub*, under; *ponere, positum*, to place].
suppository (su-poz'i-tor-i) *n.* medicinal substance introduced into rectum or other canal of body [L. *sub*, under; *ponere, positum*, to place].
suppress (su-pres') *v.t.* to put down or subdue; to overpower and crush; to quell; to conceal.—**suppression** (su-presh'un) *n.* act of crushing or subduing; state of being suppressed.—**suppress'ive** *a.* tending to suppress.—**suppress'or** *n.* [L. *sub*, under; *premere, pressum*, to press].
suppurate (sup'ū-rāt) *v.i.* to form pus; to fester.—**sup'purative** *a.* tending to suppurate; accompanied by suppuration.—**suppura'tion** *n.* [L. *sub*, under; *pus*, matter].
supra (sū'prạ) L. *prefix*, meaning above, over, beyond.
supreme (sū-prēm') *a.* holding highest authority; highest or most excellent; greatest possible; uttermost.—**supreme'ly** *adv.*—**supreme'ness** *n.*—**supremacy** (sū-prem'ạ-si) *n.* state of being highest in power and authority; utmost excellence [L. *supremus*, superl. of *superus*, upper].
sur (sur) *prefix*, meaning over, above, upon, in addition [Fr. fr. L. *super*, over].
surcease (sur-sēs') *v.t.* (*Arch.*) to cause to cease;—*v.i.* to cease;—*n.* cessation [O.Fr. *sursis*, fr. *surseoir*, fr. L. *supersedere*, to refrain from].
surcharge (sur-chârj') *v.t.* to make additional charge; to overload or overburden.—**surcharge** (sur'chârj, sur-charj') *n.* excessive charge, load, or burden; additional words or marks superimposed on postage stamp.
surcingle (sur'sing-gl) *n.* belt, band, or girth for holding something on a horse's back [L. *super*, over; *cingulum*, a belt].
surcoat (sur'kōt) *n.* long and flowing cloak worn by knights over armour [O.Fr. *surcote*, an over-garment].
surd (surd) *a.* (*Math.*) not capable of being expressed in rational numbers; radical; involving surds; (*Phon.*) uttered with breath alone, not voice, as *f, p, k*, etc.;—*n.* (*Math.*) quantity that cannot be expressed by rational numbers, or which has no root [L. *surdus*, deaf].
sure (shŏŏr) *a.* certain; positive; admitting of no doubt; firmly established; strong or secure.—**sure'ly** *adv.* certainly; undoubtedly; securely.—**sure'ness** *n.*—**surety** (shŏŏr'ti) *n.* certainty; that which makes sure; security against loss or damage; one who makes himself responsible for obligations of another [L. *securus*, sure].
surf (surf) *n.* foam or broken water of sea breaking on shore or reefs, etc.—**surf'y** *a.*—

surf′-ri′ding *n.* sport, consisting in riding on long, narrow boards over surf [etym. uncertain].

surface (sur′-fās) *n.* external layer or outer face of anything; outside; exterior;—*a.* involving the surface only;—*v.t.* to cover with special surface; to smooth;—*v.i.* to come to the surface.—**sur′faceman** *n.* man engaged in keeping permanent way of railway in repair; miner in surface works of mine [L. *super,* over; *facies,* the face].

surfeit (sur′-fit) *v.t.* to overfeed; to fill to satiety;—*n.* excess in eating and drinking; oppression caused by such excess.—**sur′feiter** *n.* a glutton.—**sur′feiting** *n.* gluttony [Fr. *surfaire,* to overdo].

surge (surj) *n.* rolling swell of water; large wave or billow;—*v.i.* to swell; to rise high and roll, as waves.—**sur′gent, sur′gy** *a.* [L. *surgere,* to rise].

surgeon (sur′-jun) *n.* medical man qualified to perform operations; one who practises surgery.—**sur′gery** *n.* branch of medicine dealing with cure of disease or injury by manual operation; doctor's consulting-rooms.—**sur′gical** *a.* pert. to surgeons or surgery.—**sur′gically** *adv.* [Fr. *chirurgien*].

surloin (sur′-loin) *n.* the sirloin [Fr.].

surly (sur′-li) *a.* of unfriendly temper; gloomily morose; uncivil; sullen.—**sur′lily** *adv.*—**sur′liness** *n.* [etym. uncertain].

surmise (sur-mīz′) *v.t.* to imagine or infer something without proper grounds; to make a guess; to conjecture;—*n.* supposition; a guess or conjecture [O.Fr. *surmise,* accusation].

surmount (sur-mount′) *v.t.* to rise above; to overtop; to conquer or overcome.—**surmount′able** *a.* [Fr. *sur,* over; *monter,* to mount].

surname (sur′-nām) *n.* name added to baptismal or Christian name; family name [Fr. *surnom*].

surpass (sur-pas′) *v.t.* to go beyond; to excel; to outstrip.—**surpass′ing** *a.* excellent; in an eminent degree; exceeding others [Fr. *sur,* beyond; *passer,* to pass].

surplice (sur′-plis) *n.* white linen vestment worn over cassock by clergy of Anglican Church [L.L. *superpellicium,* overgarment].

surplus (sur′-plus) *n.* excess beyond what is wanted; excess of income over expenditure;—*a.* more than enough [L. *super,* over; *plus,* more].

surprise (sur-prīz′) *v.t.* to fall or come upon unawares; to capture by unexpected attack; to strike with astonishment;—*n.* act of coming upon unawares; astonishment; unexpected event, piece of news, gift, etc.—**surpris′al** *n.* act of surprising or state of being surprised.—**surpris′ing** *a.* wonderful; remarkable.—**surpris′ingly** *adv.* [Fr. *surprendre,* fr. L. *super,* over; *prehendere,* to catch].

surrealism (su-rē′-al-izm) *n.* 20th cent. phase in art and literature of expressing subconscious in images without order or coherence, as in dream.—**surre′alist** *n.*—**surrealis′tic** *a.* [Fr. *sur,* over; *realism*].

surrender (su-ren′-der) *v.t.* to yield or hand over to power of another; to resign; to yield to emotion, etc.;—*v.i.* to cease resistance; to give oneself up into power of another; to capitulate;—*n.* act of surrendering.—**surren′derer** *n.* [L. *super,* over; *reddere,* to restore].

surreption (su-rep′-shun) *n.* act of obtaining in stealthy or crafty manner [L. *surreptio,* fr. *sub,* under; *rapere,* to seize].

surreptitious (sur-ep-tish′-us) *a.* done by stealth; furtive; clandestine; underhand.—**surrepti′tiously** *adv.* [L. *surripere,* fr. *sub,* under; *rapere,* to seize].

surrey (sur′-ā) *n.* lightly-built, four-wheeled carriage [prob. fr. proper name].

surrogate (sur′-ō-gāt) *n.* deputy or delegate; deputy who acts for bishop or chancellor of diocese [L. *sub,* under; *rogare,* to ask].

surround (su-round′) *v.t.* to be on all sides of; to encircle; (*Mil.*) to cut off from communication or retreat;—*n.* that which surrounds; border or framework.—**surroun′dings** *n.pl.* things which environ; neighbourhood [O.Fr. *suronder,* fr. L. *superundare,* to overflow].

surtax (sur′-taks) *n.* additional tax;—*v.t.* to impose extra tax on.

surtout (sur-tòò′) *n.* a long, close-fitting overcoat [Fr. *sur,* over; *tout,* all].

surveillance (sur-vā′-lans, sur-vā′-yans) *n.* close watch; supervision [Fr. fr. *surveiller,* to watch over].

survey (sur-vā′) *v.t.* to look over; to view as from high place; to take broad, general view; to determine shape, extent, position, contour, etc. of tract of land.—**survey** (sur′-vā) *n.* general view, as from high place; attentive scrutiny; measured plan or chart of any tract of country.—**survey′or** *n.* one versed in the art of surveying, i.e. measuring and mapping surfaces.—**survey′orship** *n.* [L. *super,* over; *videre,* to see].

survive (sur-vīv′) *v.t.* to live longer than; to outlive or outlast;—*v.i.* to remain alive.—**survi′val** *n.* living longer than, or beyond, life of another person, thing, or event; any rite, habit, belief, etc. remaining in existence after what justified it has passed away.—**survi′vor** *n.* one who lives longer than another; one who remains alive in spite of some event which might have caused death [L. *super,* over; *vivere,* to live].

susceptible (su-sep′-ti-bl) *a.* capable of; readily impressed; sensitive; touchy; amorous.—**suscep′tibly** *adv.*—**suscep′tibleness** *n.*—**susceptibil′ity** *n.* capacity for feeling, or emotional excitement; sensitiveness;—*pl.* sensitive spots in person's nature.—**suscep′tive** *a.* receptive of emotional impressions [L. *suscipere,* to take up, receive].

suspect (sus-pekt′) *v.t.* to imagine existence or presence of; to imagine to be guilty; to conjecture; to mistrust.—**sus′pect** *n.* suspected person;—*a.* inspiring distrust [L. *suspicere,* to look at secretly].

suspend (sus-pend′) *v.t.* to cause to hang; to bring to a stop temporarily; to debar from an office or privilege; to defer or keep undecided.—**suspen′der** *n.* one who suspends; contrivance for supporting sock;—*pl.* (*U.S.*) braces.—**suspense′** *n.* state of being suspended; state of uncertainty or anxiety; indecision.—**suspen′sion** *n.* act of suspending or state of being suspended; delay or deferment; temporary withdrawal from office, function, or privilege.—**suspen′sor** *n.* something which suspends.—**suspen′sory** *a.* pert. to suspension; hanging [L. *sub,* under; *pendere,* to hang].

suspicion (sus-pish′-un) *n.* act of suspecting; imagining of something being wrong, on little evidence; doubt; mistrust; slight trace or hint.—**suspic′ious** *a.* feeling suspicion; mistrustful; arousing suspicion.—**suspic′iously** *adv.* [L. *suspicere,* to look at secretly].

suspire (sus-pīr′) *v.i.* to fetch long, deep breath [L. *suspirare,* to breathe out].

sustain (sus-tān′) *v.t.* to keep from falling or sinking; to nourish or keep alive; to endure or undergo; (*Law*) to allow the validity of.—**sustain′able** *a.*—**sustain′er** *n.*—**sustenance** (sus′-te-nans) *n.* that which sustains (life); food, nourishment.—**sustenta′tion** *n.* maintenance [L. *sustinere,* to support].

sutler (sut′-ler) *n.* formerly person who followed army and sold provisions, liquors, etc., to troops.—**sut′lery** *n.* work [Dut. *zoetelaar,* a small tradesman].

suttee (su-tē′) *n.* Hindu widow who immolates herself on funeral pyre of husband; hence (wrongly), sacrifice.—**suttee′ism** *n.* [Sans. *sati,* a faithful wife].

suture (sū′-tūr) *n.* act of sewing; sewing up of wound; material used for this; connection or seam, between bones of skull;—*v.t.* to join by stitching.—**su′tural** *a.*—**su′tured** *a.* united by sutures [L. *suere, sutum,* to sew].

suzerain (sū-ze′-rān) *n.* feudal lord; paramount

ruler.—**su'zerainty** *n.* authority or dominion of **suzerain** [Fr. *suzerain*, paramount].
svelte (svelt) *a.* supple; lithe; lissom [Fr.].
swab (swob) *n.* mop for rubbing over floors, decks, etc.; (*Surg.*) absorbent pad;—*v.t.* to clean with mop or swab.—*pr.p.* **swabb'ing.**—*pa.t.* and *pa.p.* **swabbed.**—**swabb'er** *n.* [Dut. *zwabber*, ship's drudge].
swaddle (swod′l) *v.t.* to bind tightly with, or as with, bandages.—**swadd'ling-band, -cloth** *n.* long binder formerly wrapped round infants [O.E. *swathu*, a bandage].
swag (swag) *n.* bundle; stolen goods or booty; in Australia, a tramping bushman's pack [O.N. *svagga*, to walk unsteadily].
swagger (swag′er) *v.i.* to walk with a conceited or defiant strut; to boast or brag;—*n.* defiant or conceited bearing; boastfulness;—*a.* (*Slang*) smart.—**swagg'erer** *n.*—**swagg'ering** *a.* [perh. O.N. *svagga*, to walk unsteadily].
Swahili (swa-hē′li) *n.* people of mixed Bantu and Arab stock, occupying Zanzibar and adjoining territory; their language.—**Swahi′lian** *a.* [Ar. = coast-man].
swain (swān) *n.* country lad; rustic lover; (*Colloq.*) suitor [O.N. *sveinn*, a boy, a servant].
swallow (swol′ō) *n.* small migratory, passerine, insectivorous bird.—**swall'ow-tail** *n.* forked tail; kind of butterfly [O.E. *swealwe*].
swallow (swol′ō) *v.t.* to receive into stomach through mouth and throat; to absorb; to accept without criticism or scruple;—*v.i.* to perform act of swallowing;—*n.* act of swallowing; amount taken down at one gulp.—**swall'ower** *n.* [O.E. *swelgan*].
swam (swam) *pa.t.* of **swim.**
swamp (swomp) *n.* tract of wet, spongy, low-lying ground; marsh;—*v.t.* to cause to fill with water, as boat;—*v.i.* to founder; to sink.—**swam'py** *a.* [Scand. *svamp*, a sponge].
swan (swon) *n.* large, web-footed bird of goose family, having very long, gracefully-curving neck.—**swan'nery** *n.* place where swans are bred.—**swan's′down** *n.* fine, soft feathers on swan, used for dress-trimmings, powder-puffs, etc.; thick cotton or woollen cloth with soft nap on one side.—**swan′shot** *n.* shot of a large size.—**swan′song** *n.* song which, according to myth, swan sings before dying; last work of poet, composer, etc.—**swan′up'ping, swan′hop'ping** *n.* marking swans with owner's mark; refers esp. to annual outing to mark royal swans on Thames [O.E.].
swank (swangk) *v.i.* (*Slang*) to show off; to swagger;—*n.* (*Slang*) showing off; swagger; bluff;—*a.* (*Slang*) fine; smart.—**swank'y** *a.* [etym. uncertain].
swap (swop). See **swop.**
sward (swawrd) *n.* land covered with short green grass; turf;—*v.t.* to cover with sward.—**sward'ed** *a.* [O.E. *sweard*, skin of bacon].
swarm (swawrm) *n.* large number of insects esp. in motion; cluster of honey-bees leaving hive to form colony elsewhere; great multitude or throng;—*v.i.* of bees, to emigrate in swarm; to collect in large numbers [O.E. *swearm*].
swarm (swawrm) *v.i.* to climb with arms and legs [etym. uncertain].
swart, swarth (swawrt, swawrth) *a.* (*Arch.*) of dark hue; swarthy.—**swarth'y** *a.* dark in hue; of dark complexion; sunburnt.—**swarth'ily** *adv.*—**swarth'iness** *n.* [O.E. *sweart*].
swashbuckler (swash′buckler) *n.* literally, one who strikes his shield; swaggering bully; braggart.—**swash'buckling** *a.* bragging, bullying [imit.].
swastika, svastika (swas', svas′ti-kȧ) *n.* symbol in form of Greek cross with ends of arms bent at right angles, all in same direction, thus 卐. Used as badge of Nazi party. Also called *fylfot* [Sans. *svasti*, well-being].
swat (swot) *v.t.* (*Colloq.*) to hit smartly; to kill, esp. insects [etym. uncertain].
swatch (swoch) *n.* piece of cloth, cut as a sample of quality [var. of *swath*].
swath (swawth) *n.* line of hay or grain cut by scythe or mowing-machine; whole sweep of scythe. Also **swathe** (swāth) [O.E. *swaeth*, a track].
swathe (swāTH) *v.t.* to bind with bandage; to envelop in wraps;—*n.* bandage; folded or draped band [O.E. *swathian*].
sway (swā) *v.t.* to cause to incline to one side or the other; to influence or direct;—*v.i.* to incline or be drawn to one side or the other; to swing unsteadily; to totter;—*n.* swaying or swinging movement; control [M.E. *sweyen*].
swear (swār) *v.t.* to utter, affirm or declare on oath;—*v.i.* to utter solemn declaration with appeal to God for truth of what is affirmed; (*Law*) to give evidence on oath; to use name of God or sacred things profanely; to curse.—*n.* (*Colloq.*) oath or profane word.—*pa.p.* **sworn.**—*pa.t.* **swore.**—**swear'er** *n.*—**swear'ing** *n.* the use of profane language.—**swear'word** *n.* (*Colloq.*) profane word.—**to swear by,** (*Colloq.*) to have great confidence in [O.E. *swerian*].
sweat (swet) *n.* moisture excreted from skin; perspiration; moisture exuding from any substance; state of sweating; anything that induces sweat; toil or drudgery; (*Colloq.*) state of anxiety;—*v.t.* to cause to excrete moisture from skin; to exude from skin; to employ at wrongfully low wages;—*v.i.* to excrete moisture from skin; to toil or drudge at.—**sweat'er** *n.* warm, woollen jersey or jacket.—**sweat'y** *a.* damp with sweat; causing sweat; like sweat.—**sweat'ily** *adv.*—**sweat'iness** *n.* [O.E. *swat*].
Swede (swēd) *n.* native of Sweden; kind of turnip.—**Swed'ish** *a.* pert. to Sweden;—*n.* language of Swedes.
sweep (swēp) *v.t.* to pass brush or broom over to remove loose dirt; to pass rapidly over, with brushing motion; to scan rapidly;—*v.i.* to pass with swiftness or violence; to move with dignity; to extend in a curve; to effect cleaning with a broom;—*n.* act of sweeping; reach of a stroke; curving or wide-flung gesture or movement; powerful drive forward, covering large area; long, heavy oar, used either to steer or to propel; one who sweeps chimneys; sail of windmill; (*Slang*) base person; cad; (*Colloq.*) sweepstake.—*pa.p.* and *pa.t.* **swept.**—**sweep'er** *n.* one who, or that which, sweeps.—**sweep'ing** *a.* moving swiftly; of great scope; comprehensive. — **sweep'ingly** *adv.* — **sweep′stake(s)** *n.* gambling on horse-racing, in which participators' stakes are pooled, and apportioned to drawers of winning horses [O.E. *swapan*].
sweet (swēt) *a.* tasting like sugar; having agreeable taste; fragrant; melodious; pleasing to eye; gentle; affectionate; dear or beloved; likeable;—*n.* sweetmeat; sweet dish served as dessert; darling;—*pl.* sweetmeats, confections.—**sweet'en** *v.t.* to make sweet, pleasing, or kind; to make pure and salubrious.—**sweet'ening** *n.* act of making sweet; ingredient which sweetens.—**sweet'ly** *adv.* (*Colloq.*) smoothly; without friction.—**sweet'ness** *n.*—**sweet'bread** *n.* pancreas of animal, as food.—**sweet'heart** *n.* lover or beloved person; darling.—**sweet'meat** *n.* smal confection chiefly of sugar or chocolate.—**sweet′pea** *n.* leguminous plant, bearing bright, sweet-scented flowers.—**sweet′pota'to** *n.* creeping plant, bearing sweetish, starchy tubers, used as vegetable.—**sweet′will'iam** *n.* garden-plant, bearing clusters of small pink or red flowers.—**sweet'y** *n.* (*Colloq.*) sweetmeat.—**to be sweet on,** to be in love with [O.E. *swete*].
swell (swel) *v.t.* to increase size; to dilate; to augment;—*v.i.* to grow larger; to expand; to rise in waves; to grow louder; to be filled to bursting point with some emotion.—*n.* act of swelling; increase in bulk, intensity, importance, etc.; slight rise in ground level; slow heaving and sinking of sea after storm; one of enclosed clefts in large organ; (*Mus.*) crescendo followed by diminuendo; (*Colloq.*)

a dandy;—*a.* (*Slang*) excellent.—*pr.p.* **swell′ing.**—*pa.p.* **swoll′en** or **swelled.**—*pa.t.* **swell′ed.** —**swell′ing** *n.* act of swelling; state of being swollen; prominence or protuberance; (*Med.*) enlargement [O.E. *swellan*].

swelter (swel′tẹr) *v.i.* to be oppressive, or oppressed, with heat; to perspire profusely;—*n.* heated or sweaty state.—**swel′try** *a.* [O.E. *sweltan*, to swoon or perish].

swept (swept) *pa.t.* and *pa.p.* of **sweep.**

swerve (swẹrv) *v.i.* to depart from straight line; to deviate; to wander or turn aside from duty, custom, aim, etc.;—*v.t.* to cause to bend or turn aside;—*n.* act of swerving [O.E. *sweorfan*, to rub or file].

swift (swift) *a.* quick; rapid; prompt; moving quickly.—**swift′ly** *adv.*—**swift′ness** *n.* speed [O.E. *swifan*, to move quickly].

swift (swift) *n.* long-winged, quick-flying migratory bird, resembling swallow; common newt [O.E. *swifan*, to move quickly].

swig (swig) *v.t.* and *v.i.* (*Colloq.*) to gulp down; to drink in long draughts;—*n.* long draught [O.E. *swelgan*, to swallow].

swill (swil) *v.t.* and *v.i.* to drink greedily; to rinse or flush;—*n.* act of swilling; pig-food; slops.—**swill′er** *n.*—**swill′ings** *n.pl.* hogwash [O.E. *swilian*, to wash].

swim (swim) *v.i.* to propel oneself in water by means of hands, feet, or fins, etc.; to float on surface; to move with gliding motion, resembling swimming;—*v.t.* to cross or pass over by swimming; to cause to swim;—*n.* act of swimming; spell of swimming.—*pr.p.* **swimm′ing.**—*pa.t.* **swam.**—*pa.p.* **swum** or **swam.**—**swimm′er** *n.*—**swimm′ingly** *adv.* easily, successfully, without obstacle [O.E. *swimman*]

swim (swim) *v.i.* to be dizzy or giddy;—*n.* dizziness or unconsciousness [O.E. *swima*, a swoon].

swindle (swin′dl) *v.t.* and *v.i.* to cheat or defraud; to obtain by fraud;—*n.* act of defrauding; false pretences.—**swind′ler** *n.* [Ger. *schwindeln*, to cheat].

swine (swīn) *n. sing.* and *pl.* thick-skinned domestic animal, fed for its flesh; pig; hog; person of bestial disposition or habits.—**swine′herd** *n.* one who tends swine.—**swin′ish** *a.* like swine; gross, brutal.—**swin′ishly** *adv.* [O.E. *swin*].

swing (swing) *v.i.* to move to and fro, esp. as suspended body; to sway; to vibrate; to turn on pivot; to progress with easy, swaying gait; to be executed by hanging; to wheel round;—*v.t.* to fix up so as to hang freely; to move to and fro; to cause to wheel about a point; to brandish;—*n.* act of swinging or causing to swing; extent, sweep, or power of anything that is swung; motion to and fro; seat suspended by ropes, on which one may swing. —*pa.p.* and *pa.t.* **swung.**—**swing′er** *n.*—**swing′ing** *a.* moving to and fro; moving with vigour and rhythm.—**swing′ingly** *adv.*—**swing′boat** *n.* boat-shaped carriage slung from frame, used in recreation parks.—**swing′bridge** *n.* bridge which can be pivoted round to allow vessels passage along river, canal, etc.—**to swing the lead** (*Naval and Military Slang*) to malinger [O.E. *swingan*, to swing, whirl].

swing (swing) *n.* (*Mus.*) kind of jazz music [O.E. *swingan*].

swinge (swinj) *v.t.* to beat soundly; to whip; to chastise.—**swin′geing** *a.* very large; thumping [O.E. *swengan*, to shake, dash].

swipe (swīp) *v.t.* and *v.i.* to strike with a wide, sweeping blow, as with a bat, racket, etc.;—(*Slang*) to steal by snatching;—*n.* hard stroke [O.E. *swipian*, to beat].

swirl (swẹrl) *n.* eddy of wind or water; whirling motion;—*v.i.* to form eddies;—*v.t.* to carry along with whirling motion [O.N. *svirla*, to whirl round].

swish (swish) *n.* whistling or hissing sound;—*v.i.* to move with hissing or rustling sound; —*v.t.* to flourish; to flog;—*a.* (*Slang*) smart; elegant [imit.].

Swiss (swis) *n. sing.* and *pl.* native of Switzerland; people of Switzerland;—*a.* pert. to Switzerland or the Swiss [O. Ger. *Swiz*].

switch (swich) *n.* flexible twig or rod; tufted end of animal's tail; tress of false hair; stiff-bristled brush or broom; on railway, movable rail for transferring carriages from one set of lines to another; (*Elect.*) device for making, breaking, or transferring, electric current; act of switching;—*v.t.* to strike with switch; to whisk; to sweep with stiff broom; to shift or shunt (train) to another track; (*Elect.*) to turn electric current off or on with switch; to transfer one's thoughts to another subject; to transfer.—**switch′back** *n.* zigzag method of ascending slopes, to lessen gradient; in amusements park, miniature railway with sudden and steep rises and descents;—*a.* resembling such railway.—**switch′board** *n.* set of switches at telephone exchange [Old Dut. *swick*, a whip].

swither (swiTH′ẹr) *v.i.* to hesitate; to vacillate [O.E.].

swivel (swiv′l) *n.* ring turning on pivot, forming connection between two pieces of mechanism and enabling one to rotate independently of the other;—*v.i.* to swing on pivot;—*v.t.* to cause to turn as on pivot.—*pr.p.* **swiv′elling.**—*pa.p.* and *pa.t.* **swiv′elled** [O.E. *swifan*, to move quickly].

swollen (swōln) *a.* swelled.—*pa.p.* of **swell.**

swoon (swòòn) *v.i.* to faint;—*n.* fainting fit [O.E. *swogan*, to sigh deeply].

swoop (swòòp) *v.t.* to catch up with sweeping motion (with 'up');—*v.i.* to sweep down swiftly upon prey, as hawk or eagle; to pounce;—*n.* sweeping downward flight of bird of prey; pounce [O.E. *swapan*, to rush, sweep].

swop, swap (swop) *v.t.* and *v.i.* to exchange; to barter;—*n.* exchange.—*pr.p.* **swop′ping.**—*pa.p.* and *pa.t.* **swopped** [perh. same as O.E. *swap*, to strike].

sword (sōrd, sord) *n.* weapon for cutting or thrusting, having long blade; emblem of judicial punishment or of authority and power; destruction by war; military power.—**sword′arm, -hand** *n.* right arm or hand.—**sword′fish** *n.* large fish allied to mackerel, with upper jaw elongated into sword-like process. —**sword′play** *n.* fencing.—**swords′man** *n.* one skilful with sword.—**swords′manship** *n.*—**sword′stick, -cane** *n.* cane or walking-stick containing slender sword.—**to cross swords,** to oppose in fight, controversy, argument [O.E. *sweord*].

swore (swōr) *pa.t.* of **swear.**—**sworn** *pa.p.* of the same verb.

swot (swot) *v.t.* and *v.i.* (*Slang*) to study hard or long;—*n.* one who studies hard [var. of *sweat*].

swum (swum) *pa.p.* of **swim.**

swung (swung) *pa.p.* and *pa.t.* of **swing.**

sybarite (sib′ạ-rīt) *n.* person devoted to luxury and pleasure.—**sybarit′ic, sybarit′ical** *a.* [L. *Sybaris*, Greek city].

sybo (sī′bō) *n.* small variety of onion;—*pl.* **sy′boes** [Fr. *ciboule*].

sycamore (sik′ạ-mōr) *n.* tree with broad leaves, allied to plane-tree and maple; kind of fig-tree of Egypt and Asia Minor [Gk. *sukon*, fig; *moron*, black mulberry].

sycophant (sik′ō-fạnt) *n.* orig. (it is said) informer against those who exported figs contrary to law in Athens; tale-bearer or informer; flatterer, or one who fawns on rich or famous; parasite;—*a.* servile; obsequious. —**syc′ophancy, syco′phantism** *n.*—**sycophan′tic, sycophan′tical, syc′ophantish** *a.* [Gk. *sukophantēs*, fr. *sukon*, a fig; *phainein*, to show].

syllable (sil′ạ-bl) *n.* sound uttered at single effort of voice, and constituting word, or part of word;—*v.t.* to divide into syllables; to articulate.—**syllab′ic, syllab′ical** *a.* pert. to, or consisting of, a syllable(s).—**syllab′ically** *adv.* [Gk. *sullabē*, that which is held together].

syllabub (sil′a-bub) *n.* See **sillabub.**
syllabus (sil′a-bus) *n.* compendium containing heads of discourse; outline or programme of topics treated of, as in book, course of lectures, etc. [Gk. *sun*, together; *lambanein*, to take].
syllogism (sil′ō-jizm) *n.* formal statement of argument, consisting of three parts, major premise, minor premise, and conclusion, conclusion following naturally from premises.—**syll′ogise** *v.t.* and *v.i.* to reason by means of syllogisms.—**syllogis′tic, syllogis′tical** *a.*—**syllogis′tically** *adv.* [Gk. *sullogismos*, a reckoning together].
sylph (silf) *n.* elemental spirit of the air; fairy or sprite; graceful girl.—**syl′phid** *n.* little sylph.—**sylph′like** *a.* graceful and slender [Fr. *sylphe*].
sylva, silva (sil′va) *n.* forest-trees collectively.—**syl′van** *a.* forest-like; abounding in forests; rural; rustic.—**syl′viculture** *n.* forestry; culture of trees [L. *silva*, a wood].
symbiosis (sim-bi-ō′sis) *n.* (*Biol.*) living together of different organisms for mutual benefit, as in the lichens.—**symbiot′ic** *a.*—**sym′biont** *n.* organism living in symbiosis [Gk. *sun*, together; *bios*, life].
symbol (sim′bol) *n.* something that represents something else, esp. concrete representation of moral or intellectual quality; emblem; type character or sign used to indicate relation or operation in mathematics; in chemistry, letter or letters standing for atom of element.—**symbol′ic, symbol′ical** *a.*—**symbol′ically** *adv.*—**sym′bolise** *v.t.* to stand for, or represent; to represent by a symbol or symbols.—**sym′bolism** *n.* representation by symbols; system of symbols; investing of any practice with symbolic meaning; in art and literature, tendency to represent emotions by means of symbols, and to invest ordinary objects with imaginative meanings.—**sym′bolist** *n.* one who uses symbols; adherent of symbolism in art and literature [Gk. *sumbolon*, a token].
symmetry (sim′e-tri) *n.* due proportion between several parts of object; exact correspondence of opposite sides of an object to each other; beauty of form.—**symmet′ric, symmet′rical** *a.*—**symmet′rically** *adv.*—**symmet′ricalness** *n.*—**sym′metrise** *v.t.* to make symmetrical [Gk. *sun*, together; *metron*, measure].
sympathy (sim′pa-thi) *n.* fellow-feeling, esp. feeling for another person in pain or grief; sharing of emotion, interest, desire, etc.; compassion or pity.—**sympathet′ic(al)** *a.* exhibiting or expressing sympathy; compassionate; congenial; (*Med.*) denoting nerve system in body.—**sympathet′ically***adv.*—**sym′pathise** *v.i.* to feel or express sympathy; to agree.—**sym′pathiser** *n.* [Gk. *sun*, together; *pathos*, feeling].
symphony (sim′fo-ni) *n.* harmony of sound; (*Mus.*) composition for full orchestra, consisting usually of four contrasted sections or movements.—**symphon′ic** *a.*—**sym′phonist** *n.* composer of symphonies.—**symphonic poem,** composition of symphonic scope without symphonic form [Gk. *sun*, together; *phōnē*, sound].
symposium (sim-pō′zi-um) *n.* drinking together; any convivial gathering, esp. one at which interchange or discussion of ideas takes place; series of short articles by several writers dealing with common topic.—*pl.* **sympo′sia** [Gk. *sun*, together; *posis*, a drinking.]
symptom (sim′tom) *n.* (*Med.*) perceptible change in body or its functions, which indicates disease; sign of the existence of something else.—**symptomat′ic, symptomat′ical** *a.* [Gk. *sun*, together; *ptōma*, a fall].
syn- (sin) *prefix* from Gk. *sun*, meaning with, together, at the same time; becomes *sym-*, before *p*, *b*, and *m*, and *syl-* before *l*.
synagogue (sin′a-gog) *n.* congregation of Jews met for worship; Jewish place of worship.—**synagogical** (sin-a-goj′i-kal) *a.* [Gk. *sun*, together; *agein*, to lead].
synchro-mesh (sin′krō-mesh) *a.* of system of automatic gear-changing in car.
synchronise (sin′krō-nīz) *v.i.* to agree in time; to be simultaneous;—*v.t.* to cause to occur at the same time; to run machines at exactly the same speed.—**synchronisa′tion** *n.*—**syn′chronism** *n.* concurrence of events in time; simultaneousness.—**syn′chronal** *a.* happening at same time; lasting the same time.—**syn′chronous** *a.* happening at the same time; simultaneous [Gk. *sun*, together; *chronos*, time].
synchrotron (sing′krō-tron) *n.* scientific machine, used in atom research, for accelerating electrons to very high speeds [Gk. *sun*, together; *chronos*, time].
syncopate (sin′kō-pāt) *v.t.* (*Gram.*) to contract, as a word, by taking one or more letters or syllables from middle; in music, to alter rhythm by accenting a usually unaccented note, or causing the accent to fall on a rest, or silent beat.—**syncopa′tion** *n.* [Gk. *sun*, together; *kopē*, a cutting].
syncope (sin′kō-pe) *n.* the elision of one or more letters from the middle of a word; (*Med.*) a fainting or swooning.—**syn′copal, syncop′ic** *a.* [Gk. *sun*, together; *kopē*, a cutting].
syndic (sin′dik) *n.* magistrate or government official having different duties in different countries; legal representative chosen to act as agent for corporation or company; in Cambridge Univ., member of special committee of senate.—**syn′dicate** *n.* council of syndics; body of persons associated to carry out enterprise; association of industrialists or financiers formed to carry out industrial project, or to acquire monopoly in certain goods;—*v.t.* to control by a syndicate; to publish news, etc. simultaneously in several periodicals owned by one syndicate [Gk. *sundikos*, an advocate, fr. *sun*, together; *dikē*, justice].
syndicalism (sin′di-kal-izm) *n.* movement aiming at replacing national State by federation of trade unions, and transferring control of production to unions of workers.—**syn′dicalist** *n.*—**syndicalis′tic** *a.* [Fr. *syndicalisme*, fr. *syndicat*, a trade union].
synecdoche (si-nek′do-kē) *n.* (*Rhet.*) figure of speech by which the whole is put for the part, or a part for the whole [Gk.].
synod (sin′od) *n.* church court, superior to presbysteries, but subordinate to General Assembly; convention or council.—**syn′odal, synod′ic, synod′ical** *a.*—**synod′ically** *adv.* [Gk. *sunodos*, assembly].
synonym (sin′o-nim) *n.* word which has same meaning as another.—**synon′ymous** *a.*—**synon′ymously** *adv.* [Gk. *sun*, together; *onoma*, name].
synopsis (si-nop′sis) *n.* general outlook, view; summary.—*pl.* **synop′ses** (sēz).—**synop′tic, synop′tical** *a.*—**synop′tically** *adv.* [Gk. *sun*, together; *opsis*, view].
synovia (si-nō′vi-a) *n.* fluid secreted from glands in the joints of body.—**syno′vial** *a.*—**synovi′tis** (sin-o-vī′tis) *n.* [Gk. *sun*, together; L. *ovum*, egg].
syntax (sin′taks) *n.* part of grammar that treats of construction of sentences, and correct arrangement of words therein; rules governing sentence-construction.—**syntac′tic, syntac′tical** *a.*—**syntac′tically** *adv.* [Gk. *sun*-together; *tassein*, to put in order].
synthesis (sin′the-sis) *n.* combination or putting together; combining of parts into whole (opp. to *analysis*); (*Chem.*) uniting of elements to form compound; (*Gram.*) building up of words into sentences, and of sentences into one of a more complex nature.—*pl.* **syntheses** (sin′the-sēz).—**synthet′ic, synthet′ical** *a.* pert. to, consisting in synthesis; not derived from nature; artificial; spurious.—**synthet′ically** *adv.*—**syn′thesise, syn′thetise** *v.t.* to combine by synthesis.—**syn′thesist, syn′thetist** *n.* [Gk. *sun*, together; *thesis*, a placing].
syntony (sin′ton-i) *n.* in wireless, state in

which frequencies of oscillations of transmitter and receiving-set are equal.—**synton'ic** *a.* (*Mus.*) sharp; intense; in wireless, of corresponding frequency [Gk. *sun*, together; *tonos*, a tone].

syphilis (sif'i-lis) *n.* contagious venereal disease.—**syphilit'ic** *a.* [fr. *Syphilus*, shepherd in Latin poem (1530)].

syphon (sī'fon) *n.* See **siphon.**

syren (sī'ren) *n.* See **siren.**

Syria (sir'i-a) *n.* country in S.E. Asia.—**Syr'iac** *n.* language of Syria;—*a.* pert. to Syria or to its language.—**Syr'ian** *n.* native of Syria;—*a.* pert. to Syria.

syringa (sir-ing'ga) *n.* lilac; applied to mock-orange, shrub with large white or creamy flowers [Gk. *surinx*, pipe].

syringe (sir-inj', sir'inj) *n.* tube and piston serving to draw in and then expel fluid; squirt;—*v.t.* to inject by means of syringe [Gk. *surinx*, a pipe or reed].

syrinx (sir'ingks) *n.* (*Mus.*) Pan-pipe; (*Anat.*) a duct.—*pl.* **syr'inxes, syr'inges** (gēz).—**syringeal** (si-rin'je-al) *a.* [Gk. *surinx*, a reed or pipe].

syrup, sirup (sir'up) *n.* fluid separated from sugar in process of refining.—**syr'upy** *a.* [O.Fr. *syrop*, fr. Ar. *sharab*, a beverage].

system (sis'tem) *n.* assemblage of objects arranged after some distinct method, usually logical or scientific; whole scheme of created things regarded as forming one complete whole; universe; organisation; classification; set of doctrines or principles; the body as functional unity.—**systemat'ic, systemat'ical** *a.* —**systemat'ically** *adv.*—**sys'tematise, sys'temise** *v.t.* to reduce to system; to arrange methodically.—**systematisa'tion, systemisa'tion** *n.* [Gk. *sustema*, fr. *sun*, together; *histanai*, to place].

systole (sis'to-lē) *n.* contraction of heart and arteries for expelling blood and carrying on circulation.—opp. to *diastole*; (*Gram.*) shortening of long syllable.—**systol'ic** *a.* contracting [Gk. fr. *sun*, together, *stellein*, to place].

T

tab (tab) *n.* small tag or flap; a shoe-tongue; a label; a check [fr. *tape*].

tabard (tà'bard) *n.* sleeveless tunic worn over armour by knights; tunic emblazoned with Royal arms, worn by heralds. Also **ta'berd.**

tabby (tab'i) *n.* stout kind of watered silk; striped cat, esp. female; (*Colloq.*) old maid; a malicious gossip;—*a.* striped;—*v.t.* to give watered finish to, as silk.—**tabb'y-cat** *n.* striped or brindled female cat [Ar. *attabi*, a watered silk].

taber Same as **tabour.**

tabernacle (tab'er-na-kl) *n.* movable shelter esp. for religious worship by Israelites; nonconformist meeting-place for worship; (*Fig.*) human body [L. *tabernaculum*, a small tent].

tablature (tab'la-tūr) *n.* painting on ceiling or wall; mental picture [fr. *table*].

table (tā'bl) *n.* smooth flat surface of wood, etc. supported by legs, as article of furniture for working at, or serving meals; any flat surface, esp. slab bearing inscription; food served on table; memorandum-book; systematic arrangement of figures, facts, etc. as *multiplication table*; index, scheme, or schedule; synopsis; one of the divisions of decalogue; upper, flat surface of gemstone;—*a.* pert. to or shaped like a table;—*v.t.* to form into a table or catalogue; to lay down, as money in payment of a bill; to set down in writing for subsequent consideration.—**ta'ble-land** *n.*—**ta'ble-ten'nis** *n.* game of indoor-tennis played on a table; ping-pong [L. *tabula*, a board].

tableau (tab'lō) *n.* vivid representation of scene in history, literature, art, etc. by group of persons appropriately dressed and posed.—*pl.* **tableaux** (tab'lōz).—**tableau vivant** (tab'lō-vē'vong) *n.* living picture; tableau.—*pl.* **vivants** (vē'vong) [Fr. *tableau*, a picture].

tablet (tab'let) *n.* anything flat on which to write; pad; slab of stone with inscription; a sweetmeat cut in small, flat squares [dim. of *table*].

tabloid (tab'loid) *n.* *Registered trade name* for small, compressed flat lozenge containing a drug; (*U.S.*) illustrated newspaper, giving topical and usually sensational events in compressed form.

taboo, tabu (ta-bòò') *n.* system among natives of the Pacific islands by which certain objects and persons are set aside as sacred or accursed; political, social, or religious prohibition;—*a.* prohibited; proscribed;—*v.t.* to forbid the use of; to ostracise [Polynesian *tapu*, consecrated].

tabor, tabour (tā'bur) *n.* small drum like a tambourine.—**tab'oret** *n.* small tabor.—**tab'orine** *n.* a small drum.—**tab'ouret** *n.* embroidery frame; low cushioned stool; needle-case.—**tab'ret** *n.* a small tabor [O.Fr. *tabour*, a drum].

tabular (tab'ū-lar) *a.* pert. to, or resembling, a table in shape; having a broad, flat top; arranged systematically in tables or columns. —**tab'ularise** *v.t.* to tabulate.—**tab'ularly** *adv.*—**tab'ulate** *v.t.* to reduce to tabular form [L. *tabula*, a table].

tachy(o)meter (tak-i(o)m'e-ter) *n.* surveyor's instrument for speedy measurement of distance and location of points [Gk. *tachus*, swift; *metron*, a measure].

tacit (tas'it) *a.* implied, but not expressed; silent.—**tac'itly** *adv.*—**tac'iturn** *a.* silent; reserved of speech.—**taciturn'ity** *n.* habitual silence or restraint.—**tac'iturnly** *adv.* [L. *tacitus*, silent].

tack (tak) *n.* small sharp-pointed nail; long stitch; ship's course in relation to position of her sails; (*Fig.*) course of action; reliance; land held on lease; stickiness, as of gum, varnish, etc.; (*Slang*) food;—*v.t.* to fasten with long, loose stitches; to append; to nail with;—*v.i.* to change ship's course by moving position of sails; (*Fig.*) to make change of policy.—**tack'er** *n.*—**tack'iness** *n.* stickiness.—**tack'y** *a.* sticky; viscous [O.Fr. *tache*, nail].

tackle (tak'l) *n.* mechanism of ropes and pulleys for raising heavy weights; rigging, etc. of ship; equipment or gear; (*Rugby*) move by player to grasp and stop opponent;—*v.t.* to harness; to fix by ropes and pulleys; to lay hold of; to undertake; to argue a point;—*v.i.* to perform operation of tackling.—**tack'ling** *n.* gear; rigging of a ship.—**tack'le-block** *n.* pulley [Scand. *taka*, to grasp].

tact (takt) *n.* intuitive understanding of people; awareness of right thing to do or say to avoid giving offence; (*Mus.*) emphatic stroke in beating time.—**tact'ful** *a.*—**tact'fully** *adv.*—**tact'ile** *a.* capable of being touched or felt; tangible.—**tact'less** *a.* wanting in tact.—**tact'ual** *a.* pert. to sense of touch [L. *tangere*, *tactum*, to touch].

tactics (tak'tiks) *n. sing.* science of disposing of military, naval, and air units to the best advantage; adroit management of situation. —**tac'tic, -al** *a.*—**tac'tically** *adv.*—**tactic'ian** *n.* [Gk. *taktika*, tactics].

tadpole (tad'pōl) *n.* young of frog in its first state before gills and tail are absorbed [O.E. *tad*, a toad; and *poll*].

taffeta (taf'e-ta) *n.* light-weight glossy silk of plain weave. Also **taff'ety** [Pers. *taftah*, woven].

taffrail, tafferel (taf'rāl, taf'e-rel) *n.* rail round stern of ship; upper part of ship's stern [Dut. *tafereel*, a panel].

tag (tag) *n.* metal point at end of a shoelace, etc.; tab on back of boot; tie-on label; appendage; catchword; hackneyed phrase; ragged end; refrain; game in which one player chases and tries to touch another;—*v.t.* to fit with tags; to add on; to follow behind.—*pr.p.* **tag'ging.**—*pa.t.* and *pa.p.*

tagged.—**tag'-end** *n.* tail-end.—**tag'-rag** *n.* and *a.* anything ragged; the rabble, as in phrase *tag-rag* (or *rag-tag*) *and bob-tail* [Scand. *tagg*, a spike].

Tahitian (ta-hē′-ti-ạn) *a.* pert. to island of Tahiti or its inhabitants.

Taic (tȧ′-ik) *a.* pert. to inhabitants of Indo-China or their language;—*n.* [Chin.].

tail (tāl) *n.* (*Law*) a limitation of ownership; entail;—*a.* being entailed.—**tail'age** *n.* [Fr. *taille*, cutting].

tail (tāl) *n.* flexible prolongation of animal's spine; back, lower, or inferior part of anything; reverse side of coin; queue; train of attendants; upward or downward stroke of letter, minim, crochet, etc.; (*Aero.*) group of stabilising planes or fins at rear of aeroplane; —*pl.* tail-coat;—*v.t.* to furnish with tail; to extend in line; to trail; to cut off stalk.—**tail'-board** *n.* movable board at back of cart.—**tail'-coat** *n.* man's evening-dress coat with tails.—**tailed** *a.* possessing a tail.—**tail'less** *a.* without a tail.—**tail'-light** *n.* red rear-light of vehicle.—**tail'-piece** *n.* ebony strip below bridge of violin to which strings are attached; ornamental design marking close of chapter in book.—**tail'-plane** *n.* (*Aero.*) stabilising surface at rear of aircraft [O.E. *taegl*, a tail].

tailor (tāl′-or) *n.* (*fem.* **tail'oress**) one who makes clothes;—*v.t.* and *v.i.* to make men's suits, women's costumes, etc.—**tail'oring** *n.* work of a tailor.—**tail'or-made** *a.* made by tailor; plain in style and perfectly fitting [O.Fr. *taillier*, to cut].

taint (tānt) *v.t.* to impregnate with something poisonous; to contaminate;—*v.i.* to be infected with incipient putrefaction;—*n.* tincture; corruption; (*Fig.*) moral blemish [L. *tingere, tinctum*, to dye].

take (tāk) *v.t.* to grasp; to capture; to entrap; to remove; to win; to purchase; to inhale; to choose; to assume; to suppose; to photograph;—*v.i.* to be effective; to catch; to please; to go; to direct course of; to resort to.—*pr.p.* **ta'king**.—*pa.t.* **took**.—*pa.p.* **ta'ken**. —*n.* quantity of fish caught at one time; drawings at theatre performance; one of several cinema-shots of same scene.—**take'-in** *n.* (*Slang*) fraud; hoax.—**take'-off** *n.* mimicry; caricature; (*Aero.*) moment when aircraft leaves ground.—**ta'ker** *n.*—**ta'king** *n.* act of taking or gaining possession; agitation;—*pl.* cash drawings of shop, theatre, etc.;—*a.* attractive; infectious.—**ta'kingly** *adv.*—**ta'kingness** *n.* quality of being attractive.—**to take after**, to resemble in face or character.—**to take for**, to mistake.—**to take in**, to furl (sail); to hoax.—**to take in hand**, to undertake. —**to take in vain**, to blaspheme.—**to take to**, to become addicted to; to feel liking for (person) [Scand. *taka*, to seize].

talc (talk) *n.* hydrated silica of magnesia; fine, slightly perfumed toilet-powder; soft pearly-lustred mineral with soapy feel; commercial name for *mica*.—**tal'cose** *a.* pert. to or composed of talc.—**tal'cum** *n.* powdered talc, as toilet powder [Ar. *talq*].

tale (tāl) *n.* narrative; story; what is told; false report; reckoning.—**tale'-bear'er** *n.* one who spitefully informs against another; scandalmonger.—**old wives' tale**, far-fetched story [O.E. *talu*, a reckoning].

talent (tal′-ẹnt) *n.* ancient weight and denomination of money; faculty; special or outstanding ability.—**tal'ented** *a.* gifted [Gk. *talanton*].

talisman (tal′-is-mạn) *n.* object endowed with magical power of protecting the wearer from harm; lucky charm.—**talisman'ic, -al** *a.* [Gk. *telesma*, payment].

talk (tawk) *v.t.* and *v.i.* to converse; to speak; to discuss; to persuade;—*n.* conversation; short dissertation; rumour; gossip.—**talk'ative** *a.* loquacious; chatty.—**talk'atively** *adv.*—**talk'ativeness** *n.*—**talk'er** *n.* one who talks; a gossip.—**talk'ie** *n.* (*Slang*) a sound-film.—**talk'ing** *a.* capable of speaking.—**to talk big**, to boast.—**to talk round**, to fail to reach a conclusion; to persuade.—**to talk shop**, to talk exclusively of one's daily occupation [M.E. *talken*, to speak].

tall (tawl) *a.* high in stature; lofty; (*Slang*) excessive; exaggerated.—**tall'ness** *n.* [etym. doubtful].

tallboy (tawl′-boi) *n.* high, narrow chest of drawers; additional metal chimneypot to counteract blow-down of smoke [*tall* and *boy*].

tallow (tal′-ō) *n.* animal fat melted down and used in manufacture of candles, etc.;—*v.t.* to smear with tallow.—**tall'ow-can'dle** *n.* candle made of tallow.—**tall'ow-chand'ler** *n.* one who sells tallow-candles.—**tall'owish** *a.* pasty; greasy [M.E. *talgh*, tallow].

tally (tal′-i) *n.* stick notched to indicate purchases made, and afterwards split in two, one part being kept by the seller, the other by the buyer; duplicate of business account; match; identity label;—*pl.* **tall'ies**.—*v.t.* to score with corresponding notches; to make to fit;—*v.i.* to correspond; to conform. —*pa.t.* and *pa.p.* **tall'ied**.—**tall'ier** *n.* one who keeps a tally [L. *talea*, a slip of wood].

tally-ho (tal-i-hō′) *interj.* huntsman's cry to urge on hounds [Fr. *taiaut*, hunting-cry].

Talmud (tal′-mud) *n.* standard collection of texts and commentaries on Jewish religious law.—**Tal'mudic(al)** *a.*—**Tal'mudist** *n.* student of the Talmud.—**Talmudis'tic** *a.* [Aramaic *talmud*, instruction].

talon (tal′-on) *n.* hooked claw of bird of prey.—**tal'oned** *a.* having talons [L. *talus*, the heel].

tamarind (tam′-ạ-rind) *n.* tropical tree, its bark and pods used for medicines, etc.; its hard wood used for furniture [Ar. *tamr*, date; *Hind*, India].

tamarisk (tam′-ạr-isk) *n.* evergreen shrub with pink and white flowers [L. *tamarix*, tamarisk].

tambour (tam′-bôôr) *n.* small flat drum; circular embroidery-frame; piece of embroidery worked in metal threads on tambour; palisade constructed to defend a gateway; kind of fish [Fr.=a drum].

tambourin (tong′-bôô-rang) *n.* small Provençal drum; dance; music for dance.—**tambourine'** *n.* round, shallow, single-sided drum with jingling metal discs used to accompany Spanish dances [Fr.].

tame (tām) *a.* domesticated; subdued; insipid; dull;—*v.t.* to domesticate; to discipline; to curb; to reclaim.—**tamabil'ity, tameabil'ity** *n.*—**tame'ableness** *n.*—**tame'able** *a.* capable of being domesticated.—**tame'ly** *adv.* —**tame'ness** *n.*—**tam'er** *n.* one who tames wild animals [O.E. *tam*, tame].

Tamil (tam′-l) *n.* Dravidian language spoken in S. India and Ceylon; native of S. India or Ceylon.

Tammany (tam′-ạ-ni) *n.* orig. a democratic organisation founded in 1805 in New York, its ostensible objects being charity and reform of the franchise; later wielded great and often suspect political power;—*a.*—**Tam'manyism** *n.* (*Colloq.*) unscrupulous politics [fr. the name of a Red Indian chief].

tam o' shanter (tam′-ō-shan′-tẹr) *n.* round woollen cap.—*abbrev.* **tam'my** [fr. Burns's poem *Tam o' Shanter*].

tamp (tamp) *v.t.* to ram down; to plug a shot-hole with clay during blasting operations.—**tamp'ing** *n.* [etym. doubtful].

tamper (tam′-pẹr) *v.i.* to meddle; to interfere with; to corrupt; to alter (as document, cheque) with malicious intent.—**tam'perer** *n.* [var. of *temper*].

tan (tan) *n.* bark of oak, etc. bruised to extract tannic acid for tanning leather; yellowish brown colour; sunburn;—*v.t.* to convert skins into leather by soaking in tannic acid; to make bronze-coloured; to toughen; (*Colloq.*) to thrash;—*v.i.* to become sunburned.—*pr.p.* **tan'ning**.—*pa.t.* and *pa.p.*

tanned.—tan'nage *n.* process of tanning; materials used in tanning.—**tan'nate** *n.* (*Chem.*) salt of tannic acid.—**tan'ner** *n.* one who works in tannery.—**tan'nery** *n.* place where leather is made.—**tan'nic** *a.* pert. to tannin.—**tan'nin** *n.* now called **tannic acid.—tan'ning** *n.* [etym. doubtful].

tandem (tan'dem) *adv.* one behind the other;—*n.* pair of horses so harnessed; a bicycle for two people sitting one behind other [L. *tandem*, at length].

tang (tang) *n.* a projection or prong (of a tool) which fits into the handle; a pungent smell or taste; a distinctive flavour;—*v.t.* to furnish (a tool) with a tang.—**tanged, tang'y** *a.* [Scand. *tange*, a point].

tangent (tan'jent) *n.* (*Geom.*) line which touches curve but, when produced, does not cut it;—*a.* touching but not intersecting.—**tan'gency, tan'gence** *n.* state of touching.—**tangen'tial** *a.* pert. to, or in direction of, a tangent.—**tangen'tially** *adv.* [L. *tangere*, to touch].

Tangerine (tan'je-rēn) *n.* native of Tangiers;—*a.* pert. to Tangiers.—**tan'gerine** *n.* small sweet orange named after Tangiers.

tangible (tan'ji-bl) *a.* perceptible by the touch; palpable; concrete.—**tangibil'ity, tan'gibleness** *n.* quality of being tangible.—**tan'gibly** *adv.* [L. *tangere*, to touch].

tangle (tang'gl) *n.* knot of ravelled threads, hair, etc.; edible species of seaweed, also called *tangle-wrack*; confusion;—*v.t.* to form into a confused mass; to ravel; to muddle [Scand. *thang*, seaweed].

tango (tang'gō) *n.* S. American dance of Spanish origin in two-four time [Sp.].

tank (tangk) *n.* large basin, cistern, or reservoir; immerser for photographic films; part of a railway engine, motor car etc. where water, petrol, etc. is stored; a mechanically propelled bullet-proof heavily armoured car with caterpillar wheels;—*v.t.* to store or immerse in a tank.—**tank'age** *n.* storage of water, oil, gas, etc. in a tank; cost of this; liquid capacity of tank; fertilising agent from refuse of fats.—**tank'er** *n.* oil-driven vessel designed to carry liquid cargo, e.g. petroleum, rubber-latex, etc. [L. *stagnum*, a pool].

tankard (tang'kard) *n.* large drinking-vessel, sometimes with lid, holding about a pint [O.Fr. *tancquard*, drinking-vessel].

tanner (tan'er) *n.* (*Slang*) a sixpence.

tannin See **tan.**

tansy (tan'si) *n.* perennial plant common in hedgerows, bearing small yellow flowers, and bitter aromatic leaves [perh. fr. Gk. *athanasia*, immortality].

tantalise (tan'ta-līz) *v.t.* to torment by keeping just out of reach something ardently desired; to tease; to provoke.—**tantalis'ing** *a.* provocative; teasing; irritating.—**tantalis'ingly** *adv.*—**tan'talus** *n.* locked case containing spirit decanters. See **Tantalus.**

tantalum (tan'ta-lum) *n.* (*Chem.*) rare metallic element, symbol **Ta**, used for filaments of electric lamps, chemical apparatus, and surgical instruments [fr. *Tantalus*].

Tantalus (tan'tal-us) *n.* in Greek mythology, Lydian king who was plunged in water up to his chin with fruit dangling near his lips, but water and fruit receded when he attempted to reach them.

tantamount (tan'ta-mount) *a.* equivalent in value or significance.—**tan'tity** *n.*—**tan'to** *adv.* (*Mus.*) so much [L. *tantus*, so much].

tantivy (tan-tiv'i) *adv.* speedily; swiftly;—*a.* swift;—*n.* a hunting-cry; a gallop [imit.].

tantrum (tan'trum) *n.* fit of bad temper over nothing [etym. unknown].

Taoism (tā'ō-izm) *n.* a Chinese philosophical and religious system founded on the doctrines of *Lao-tsze* (born 604 B.C.).—**Ta'oist** *n.* one who believes in Taoism.—**Taoist'ic** *a.* [Chin. *tao*, a way].

tap (tap) *v.t.* to strike lightly; to fix patch of leather on worn shoe;—*v.i.* to strike gentle blow.—*pr.p.* **tap'ping**.—*pa.p.* **tapped**.—*n.* a rap; leather patch on shoe-sole [imit].

tap (tap) *n.* hole, pipe, or screw-device with valve, through which liquid is drawn; plug or bung; liquor of particular brewing in a cask; instrument of hardened steel for cutting internal screwheads; (*Elect.*) connection made at intermediate point on circuit;—*v.t.* to pierce to let fluid flow out, as from a cask, tree, etc.; to furnish (cask) with tap; (*Surg.*) to draw off fluid from body, as from lung, abdomen, etc.; to listen-in deliberately to telephone conversation; (*Slang*) to borrow money from;—*v.i.* to act as tapster.—*pr.p.* **tap'ping**.—*pa.p.* **tapped**.—**tap'-house** *n.* inn or tavern.—**tap'per** *n.* one who taps.—**tap'-room** *n.* bar, of inn or hotel, for sale of liquor.—**tap'-root** *n.* the root of a plant which goes straight down into earth without dividing.—**tap'ster** *n.* barman.—**on tap,** of liquor, drawn from cask, not bottled; (*Fig.*) at hand [O.E. *taeppa*, a tap].

tape (tāp) *n.* narrow piece of woven material used for tying, fastening clothes, etc.; strip of this marking winning post on race-track; strip of paper used in a printing telegraph instrument; strip of paper or linen marked off in inches used for measuring; (*Slang*) liquor;—*v.t.* to tie with tape or finish with loops of tape; to measure.—**tape'-machine'** *n.* teleprinter.—**tape'-meas'ure** *n.* inch-tape.—**tape'worm** *n.* parasite found in alimentary canal of vertebrates.—**red tape,** officialdom, because red tape was used to tie up legal documents [O.E. *taeppe*, a fillet].

taper (tā'per) *n.* long wick coated thinly with wax; a small light;—*a.* narrowing gradually towards one end;—*v.i.* to narrow gradually;—*v.t.* to cause to narrow.—**ta'pering** *a.* narrowing gradually.—**ta'peringly** *adv.* [O.E. *tapor*].

tapestry (tap'es-tri) *n.* fabric covering for furniture, walls, etc. woven by needles, not in shuttles [Fr. *tapis*, carpet].

tapioca (tap-i-ō'ka) *n.* farinaceous substance in irregular grains, obtained from manioc [Braz. *tipi*, residue; *ok*, to press out].

tapir (tā'pir) *n.* ungulate mammal with pig-like body, and short, flexible proboscis—found in C. and S. America, and in Malaya [Braz.].

tapis (tap'is or tap'ē) *n.* carpeting; tapestry; formerly, cover of council table [Fr. *tapis*, carpet].

tappet (tap'et) *n.* small lever connected with the valves of a steam-engine cylinder; small cam; in internal combustion engine, short steel rod conveying to the valve-stem movement imparted by lift of cam [O.Fr. *tapper*, to rap].

tar (târ) *n.* sailor [*abbrev.* of *tarpaulin*].

tar (târ) *n.* dark-brown or black viscid liquid, a by-product in destructive distillation of wood (esp. pine), coal, etc., used for water-proofing, road-laying, and as antiseptic and preservative;—*v.t.* to smear, cover, or treat with tar.—*pr.p.* **tar'ring**.—*pa.t.* and *pa.p* **tarred**.—**tar'-macad'am** *n.* a mixture of tar and small even-sized stones for road-surfacing, from *Macadam*, inventor.—**tar'ry** *a.* pert. to, smeared with, or smelling of, tar.—**tar'ry-fing'ered** *a.* (*Fig.*) light-fingered; addicted to thieving.—**to tar and feather,** to smear with tar and roll in feathers, as punishment.—**to be tarred with the same brush or stick,** to have the same faults as another [O.E. *teru*, pitch].

tarantella (tar-an-tel'a) *n.* Italian dance with rapid, whirling movements; music for it [fr. *Taranto*, in S. Italy].

tarantula (ta-ran'tū-la) *n.* large, hairy, venomous spider of S. Europe [fr. *Taranto*].

tarboosh (târ'boosh) *n.* cap resembling a fez,

usually with dark blue tassel, worn by Moslems. Also **tar'bouche** [Ar.].

tardy (târ′di) *a.* slow; dilatory; late; backward.—**tar'dily** *adv.*—**tar'diness** *n.* [L. *tardus*].

tare (tār) *n.* vetch, used for cattle-fodder; a weed, prob. darnel, growing among corn (Matthew 13, 25) [etym. uncertain].

tare (tār) *n.* allowance made for weight of container, such as cask, crate, etc. in reckoning price of dutiable goods; weight of vehicle when empty [Ar. *tarhah*, that which is rejected].

targe (târj) *n.* small, round shield. Also **tar'get** [Scand. *targe*, a shield].

target (târ′get) *n.* mark to aim at in shooting practice, esp. flat circular board with bull's eye in centre of series of concentric circles; circular railway signal near switches; butt; object of attack [fr. *targe*].

tariff (ta′rif) *n.* list of goods (imports and exports) on which duty is payable; list of charges, as in hotel, restaurant, etc. [Ar. *ta'rif*, giving information].

tarmac (târ′mak) *n.* tar macadam.

tarn (târn) *n.* small lake among mountains [Scand.].

tarnish (târ′nish) *v.t.* to lessen lustre of; (*Fig.*) to sully, as one's reputation;—*v.i.* to become dull, dim, or sullied [Fr. *ternir*, to tarnish].

taro (tâ′rō) *n.* plant of Pacific islands, cultivated for edible leaves and root [Native].

tarpaulin (târ-paw′lin) *n.* canvas sheet treated with tar to make it waterproof; oilskin coat, hat, etc. Also **tarpaul'ing** [fr. *tar* and *pauling*, a covering].

tarpon (târ′pon) *n.* large edible fish of herring family caught in the W. Indies. Also **tar'pum** [etym. doubtful].

tarragon (tar′a-gon) *n.* perennial herb cultivated for its aromatic leaves, used in making *tarragon vinegar* [Gk. *drakon*, a dragon].

tarry (tar′i) *v.i.* to stay; to linger; to delay; to stay behind.—*pr.p.* **tar'rying**.—*pa.t.* and *pa.p.* **tar'ried** [L. *tardus*, slow].

tarsus (târ′sus) *n.* ankle.—*pl.* **tar'si**.—**tar'sal** *a.* pert. to the tarsus [Gk. *tarsos*, the sole of the foot].

tart (târt) *a.* sour to taste; acid; (*Fig.*) caustic; severe.—**tart'ish** *a.* rather sour.—**tart'ly** *adv.*—**tart'ness** *n.* [O.E. *teart*, acid].

tart (târt) *n.* fruit baked in oven with covering of paste; small pastry cake containing fruit or jam; (*Slang*) girl; prostitute.—**tart'let** *n.* small tart [O.Fr. *tarte*, a tart].

tartan (târ′tạn) *n.* woollen cloth of coloured checks, each genuine Scottish clan possessing its own pattern;—*a.* made of tartan [etym. unknown].

Tartar (târ-tạr) *n.* native of Tartary. Also **Ta'tar**.—**tar'tar** *n.* irritable, quick-tempered person.—**to catch a Tartar**, to seize on someone or something too difficult to manage [fr. *Tatar*, a Mongol tribe].

tartar (târ′tạr) *n.* crude potassium tartrate; crust deposited in wine cask during fermentation (purified, it is called **cream of tartar**; in crude form, **argol**); acid incrustation on teeth.—**tarta'reous, tar'tarous** *a.* consisting of tartar; having a crumbling surface.—**tartar'ic** *a.* pert. to, or obtained from, tartar.—**tar'trate** *n.* a salt of tartaric acid.—**tartaric acid**, organic hydroxy-acid found in many fruits; in powder form used in manufacture of cooling drinks.—**cream of tartar**, purified form of tartar used medicinally and as raising-agent in baking [Fr. *tartre*].

tashed (tasht) *a.* (*Scot.*) untidy; tawdry.

task (task) *n.* specific amount of work apportioned and imposed by another; set lesson; drudgery; uncongenial labour;—*v.t.* to impose task on; to exact.—**task'er** *n.*—**task'-force** *n.* body of soldiers sent to do specific operation.—**task'master** (*fem.* **task'mistress**) *n.* overseer.—**to take to task**, to rebuke; to call in question [L. *taxare*, to rate].

Tasmanian (tas-mā′ni-ạn) *a.* pert. to or belonging to Tasmania;—*n.* native of Tasmania.—**Tasmanian devil**, the dasyure, fierce nocturnal marsupial found only in Tasmania [fr. *Tasman*, discoverer].

Tass (tas) *n.* official news agency of the U.S.S.R. [Russ. *Telegrafnoje Agentstvo Sovjetskovo Sojuza*=Soviet Telegraphic Agency].

tass (tas) *n.* drinking-cup [Fr. *tasse*, cup].

tassel (tas′l) *n.* ornamental fringed knot of silk, wool, etc.; pendent flower of some plants.—**tass'elled** *a.* ornamented with tassel(s) [L. *taxillus*, a small die].

taste (tāst) *v.t.* to perceive or test by tongue or palate; to appraise flavour of by sipping; to experience; to participate in;—*v.i.* to try food with mouth; to eat or drink very small quantity; to have specific flavour;—*n.* act of tasting; one of five senses; flavour; predilection; aesthetic appreciation; judgment; small amount.—**taste'ful** *a.* having or showing good taste.—**taste'fully** *adv.*—**taste'fulness** *n.*—**taste'less** *a.* insipid.—**taste'lessly** *adv.*—**taste'lessness** *n.*—**tast'er** *n.* one whose palate is trained to discern subtle differences in flavour, as *tea-taster*.—**tast'ily** *adv.* with good taste.—**tast'y** *a.* having good taste; savoury [L. *taxare*, to estimate].

tat (tat) *v.i.* to make tatting.—**tat'ting** *n.* lace-like edging made from fine crochet or sewing thread [prob. Scand. *taeta*, shreds].

ta-ta (tâ-tâ′) *n.* and *interj.* (*Colloq.*) good-bye.

Tatar (tâ′tạr) *n.* Same as **Tartar**.

tatter (tat′ẹr) *n.* rag; shred of cloth or paper hanging loosely;—*v.t.* and *v.i.* to tear or hang in tatters.—**tatterdema'lion** *n.* ragged fellow.—**tatt'ered** *a.* ragged; torn in small pieces.—**tatt'ery** *a.* [Scand. *toturr*, rag].

tattle (tat′l) *v.i.* to prattle; to talk much of trivial matters; to gossip;—*n.* chatter.—**tatt'ler** *n.* a gossip [imit].

tattoo (tạ-tóó′) *n.* beat of drum or bugle as signal; sudden rapping; military pageant, usually at night;—*v.i.* to beat tattoo [Dut. *taptoe*].

tattoo (tạ-tóó′) *v.t.* to prick coloured designs, initials, etc. into skin with inedlible coloured inks;—*n.* such design.—**tattoo'er** *n.* [Tahitian *tatau*].

tau (tou) *n.* Greek letter T.—**tau'-cross**, a T-shaped cross [Gk.].

taught (tawt) *pa.t.* and *pa.p.* of verb **teach**.

taunt (tawnt) *v.t.* to reproach with severe or insulting words; to gibe at; to sneer at;—*n.* gibe; sarcastic remark.—**taunt'er** *n.*—**taunt'ing** *a.* [O.Fr. *tanter*, to provoke].

Taurus (taw′rus) *n.* Bull, 2nd sign of Zodiac, which sun enters about April 21st.—**tau'rian** *a.* pert. to a bull.—**tau'rine** *a.* bovine.—**tauro'machy** *n.* bull-fighting [Gk. *tauros*, a bull].

taut (tawt) *a.* tight; fully stretched; (of a ship) trim.—**taut'en** *v.t.* to make tight or tense.—**taut'ness** *n.* [a form of *tight*].

tautology (taw-tol′o-ji) *n.* needless repetition of same idea in different words in same sentence.—**tautolog'ic, -al** *a.*—**tautolog'ically** *adv.*—**tautol'ogism** *n.* superfluous use of words [Gk. *tauto*, the same; *logos*, a word].

tavern (tav′ẹrn) *n.* licensed house for sale of liquor; inn; hostelry.—**tav'erner** *n.* inn-keeper [L. *taberna*, booth].

taw (taw) *n.* large marble for children's, game; the line in which the marble is thrown; a game of marbles [Gk. letter T.].

tawdry (taw′dri) *a.* showy but cheap; gaudy; flashy.—**taw'drily** *adv.*—**tawd'riness** *n.* [fr. *St. Audrey*, at whose fair on Oct. 17 cheap laces and gewgaws were sold].

tawny (taw′ni) *a.* of yellow-brown colour.—**taw'niness** *n.* [O.Fr. *tanné*, tanned].

tax (taks) *n.* levy imposed by State on income, property, etc.; burden; severe test;—*v.t.* to impose tax on; to subject to severe strain; to challenge or accuse; (*Law*) to assess cost of actions in court.—**tax'able** *a.* capable of being taxed; subject to taxation.—**tax'able-**

ness, **taxabil'ity** *n.*—**tax'ably** *adv.*—**taxa'tion** *n.* act of levying taxes; assessing of bill of costs; aggregate of particular taxes.—**tax'-collect'or** *n.* official who gathers in taxes.—**tax'er** *n.*—**tax'-free** *a.* exempt from taxation.—**tax'payer** *n.* one subject to taxation [L. *taxare*, to rate].

taxi (taks'i) *n.* (*abbrev.* of **taximeter cab**) a motor-car for hire, fitted with a taximeter; any car plying for hire;—*v.i.* to travel by taxi; of aircraft, to travel on ground (or surface of water) under its own power.—*pr.p.* **tax'ying, tax'i-ing.**—*pa.p.* **tax'ied.**—**tax'i-cab** *n.* motor-car for public hire.—**tax'i-driv'er, tax'i-man** *n.*—**tax'imeter** *n.* instrument which automatically registers mileage and corresponding fare of journey by taxi.

taxidermy (taks'i-der-mi) *n.* art of preparing and preserving pelts of animals for exhibition. **tax'idermist** *n.* [Gk. *taxis*, arrangement; *derma*, the skin].

taxis (taks'is) *n.* classification; order.—**taxol'ogy** *n.* science of classification.—**taxon'omy** *n.* principles of taxology, esp. in relation to natural history [Gk. *taxis*, an arrangement].

tea (tē) *n.* dried and prepared leaf of tea-plant, native to China and Japan, and grown in India, Ceylon, etc.; infusion of dry tea in boiling water; any infusion of plant leaves, or of chopped meat; meal at which tea is drunk.—**tea'-cadd'y, -can'ister** *n.* air-tight box for holding tea.—**tea'-cake** *n.* flat, round, slightly sweet scone, usually served hot and buttered.—**tea'-cloth** *n.* ornamental cloth for tea-table or tray.—**tea'-co'sy** *n.* padded cover to keep a tea-pot hot.—**tea'-cup** *n.* small size cup used in drinking tea.—**tea'-cupful** *n.* amount contained in teacup.—**tea'-gar'den** *n.* tea-plantation; public garden where afternoon tea is served.—**tea'-gown** *n.* loose gown worn for tea.—**tea'-kett'le** *n.* smallish-sized kettle, as used for infusing tea.—**tea'-lead** *n.* thin foil for lining tea-chests.—**tea'-par'ty** *n.* social entertainment at which tea is served.—**tea'-pot** *n.* vessel with spout in which tea is infused.—**tea'-room** *n.* restaurant where tea, coffee, etc. are served.—**tea'-ser'vice** *n.*—**tea'-set** *n.* cups, saucers, plates, etc. for use at tea.—**tea'spoon** *n.* small-sized spoon used with the teacup.—**tea'spoonful** *n.*—**tea'-tast'er** *n.* one trained to test quality of tea by tasting.—**tea'-time** *n.* when tea is taken.—**tea'-tray** *n.* small tray holding tea-cups, etc. for afternoon tea.—**tea'-urn** *n.* vessel with tap near bottom rim, for serving tea to large numbers.—**black tea,** tea allowed to ferment between two processes of rolling and firing.—**green tea,** tea left exposed to air for only short time before firing.—**Russian tea,** tea served in glasses with slice of lemon and sugar.—**storm in a teacup,** quarrel over nothing [Chin.].

teach (tēch) *v.t.* to instruct; to educate; to discipline; to impart knowledge of;—*v.i.* to follow profession of a teacher.—*pa.t.* and *pa.p.* **taught** (tawt).—**teachabil'ity** *n.*—**teach'able** *a.* capable of being taught; willing to learn.—**teach'ableness** *n.*—**teach'er** *n.* one who instructs; one trained to teach in school or college [O.E. *taecan*, to teach].

teak (tēk) *n.* tree of E. Indies yielding very hard, durable timber [Malay].

teal (tēl) *n.* web-footed water-fowl like small duck [etym. doubtful].

team (tēm) *n.* two or more oxen, horses, or other beasts of burden harnessed together; group of people working together for common purpose; side of players in game, as *football team*.—**team'ster** *n.* one who drives team.—**team'wise** *adv.*—**team'work** *n.* co-operation among members of a group [O.E. *team*, offspring].

tear (tēr) *n.* small drop of fluid secreted by lachrymal gland, appearing in and flowing from eyes, under emotional stimulus; any transparent drop;—*pl.* grief; sorrow.—**tear'-drop** *n.* tear.—**tear'ful** *a.* weeping.—**tear'fully** *adv.*—**tear'fulness** *n.*—**tear'-gas** *n.* irritant poison gas causing abnormal watering of eyes and temporary blindness.—**tear'less** *a.* dry-eyed [O.E. *tear*, a tear].

tear (tār) *v.t.* to pull apart forcibly; to rend; to shatter; to lacerate;—*v.i.* to move violently; to rush; to rage.—*pr.p.* **tear'ing.**—*pa.t.* **tore.**—*pa.p.* **torn.**—*n.* rent; fissure.—**tear'er** *n.* [O.E. *teran*, to tear].

tease (tēz) *v.t.* to comb or card, as wool or flax; to raise pile of cloth; to harass; to annoy in fun; to chaff.—**teas'er** *n.* a poser; difficult question to answer.—**teas'ing** *a.* [O.E. *taesan*, to pluck].

teat (tēt) *n.* nipple of female breast; dug of animal; rubber nipple of baby's feeding-bottle [O.E. *tit*].

technic, -al (tek'nik, -al) *a.* pert. to any of the arts, esp. to useful or mechanical arts; connected with particular art or science; accurately defined; involving legal point.—**technical'ity** *n.* state of being technical; term peculiar to specific art; point of procedure.—**tech'nically** *adv.*—**tech'nicalness** *n.*—**technic'ian** *n.* expert in particular art or branch of knowledge.—**tech'nicist** *n.* technician.—**tech'nics** *n.pl.* arts in general; industrial arts.—**technique** (tek-nēk') *n.* skill acquired by thorough mastery of subject; method of handling materials of an art; executive ability.—**technolog'ic, -al** *a.* pert. to technology—**technol'ogist** *n.*—**technol'ogy** *n.* science of mechanical and industrial arts, as contrasted with fine arts; technical terminology [Gk. *technē*, art].

Technicolor (tek'ni-kul'or) *n.* trade name for colour cinematography.

techy, tetchy (tech'i) *a.* peevish; fretful.—**tech'ily** *adv.* [Fr. *tache*, a blemish].

tectonic (tek-ton'ik) *a.* pert. to building; (*Geol.*) pert. to earth's crust [Gk. *tekton*, builder].

teddy-bear (ted'i-bār) *n.* stuffed toy-bear for children [named after *Theodore* (*Teddy*) Roosevelt].

Te Deum (tē-dē'um) *n.* Latin hymn named from the opening words *Te Deum laudamus*, 'We praise thee, O God' [L.].

tedious (tē'di-us) *a.* wearisome; protracted; irksome; monotonous.—**tedios'ity, te'diousness** *n.*—**te'diously** *adv.*—**te'dium** *n.* wearisomeness; monotony. Also **tae'dium** [L. *taedium*, weariness].

tee (tē) *n.* mark aimed at in games, such as quoits, bowls; tiny cone of sand, wooden peg, etc. on which golf-ball is placed for first drive of each hole; teeing-ground which marks beginning of each hole on golf-course.—*v.t.* to place (golf-ball) on tee [etym. uncertain].

tee (tē) *n.* the letter T; anything shaped like a T;—*a.* having the form of a T.

teem (tēm) *v.t.* to produce; to bring forth;—*v.i.* to bring forth, as animal; to be prolific; to be stocked to overflowing.—**teem'ing** *a.* prolific; over-abundant [O.E. *team*, offspring].

teem (tēm) *v.t.* to pour; to empty;—*v.i.* to rain in torrents [Scand. *tomr*, empty].

teens (tēnz) *n.pl.* the years of one's age, thir*teen* to nine*teen*.—**teen'-a'ger** *n.* a young person, esp. a girl, 13-19 years of age.

teeny (tēn'i) *a.* very small [*tiny*].

teepee (té'pé) *n.* (*U.S.*) a wigwam, one of the conical tents of N. American Indians. Also **te'pee'.**

teeter (té'ter) *v.i.* (*U.S. colloq.*) to seesaw; to vacillate; to idle [fr. *titter*].

teeth See **tooth.**

teething (tēTH'ing) *n.* the process, in babyhood, of cutting the first teeth.—**teethe** *v.i.* to cut the first teeth [fr. *tooth*].

teetotal (tē-tō'tal) *a.* pert. to teetotalism; abstemious.—**teeto'taler, teeto'taller** *n.* one who abstains from intoxicating liquors.—**teeto'talism** *n.* [redupl. of initial letter of *total*].

tee-totum (tē-tō'tum) *n.* toy-top with letters

on four sides; letter T on one side indicated the top score.
tegument (teg′ū-ment) *n.* covering, esp. of living body; skin; integument.—**tegumen'tal, -tary** *a.* [L. *tegere*, to cover].
tela (tē′la) *n.* tissue.—*pl.* **te'lae**.—**te'lar** *a.* pert. to tissue or web.—**tela'rian** *a.* web-spinning; —*n.* spider.—**tel'ary** *a.* pert. to a tela; spun [L.].
telecast (tel′e-kast) *v.i.* to transmit programme by television [Gk. *tēle*, far; and *cast*].
telecommunication (tel′i-ko-mūn-i-kā′shun) *n.* communication by electric means, telegraph, telephone, etc. [Gk. *tēle*, far, and *communication*].
telecontrol (tel′e-kon-trōl) *n.* control of aircraft, etc. from distance by radio.
telegenic (tel-e-jen′ik) *a.* favourable to the medium of television.
telegram (tel′e-gram) *n.* message sent by telegraph.—**telegram'mic** *a.*
telegraph (tel′e-graf) *n.* electrical apparatus for transmitting messages by code to a distance; any signalling device for transmitting messages;—*v.i.* to send a message by telegraph; to signal.—**tele'grapher** (or te-leg′), **tel'egraphist** (or te-leg′) *n.* one who operates telegraph.—**telegraph'ic, -al** *a.*—**telegraph'ically** *adv.*—**tele'graphy** *n.* electrical transmission of messages to a distance.—**wireless telegraphy,** transmission of messages, news, etc. by means of electric waves; radio [Gk. *tēle*, far; *graphein*, to write].
telemark (tel′e-mark) *n.* a quick turn on skis [Norw.].
telemechanics (tel-e-me-kan′iks) *n.pl.* the science of mechanical control from a distance, by rays.
telemeter (te-lem′e-ter) *n.* instrument for determining distances in surveying, gun-practice, etc.
teleology (tel-e-ol′o-ji) *n.* science or doctrine of final causes.—**teleolog'ic, -al** *a.*—**teleolog′ically** *adv.* [Gk. *telos*, end; *logos*, discourse].
telepathy (te-lep′a-thi) *n.* occult communication of facts, feelings, impressions between mind and mind at a distance; thought-transference.—**telepath'ic** *a.*—**telepath'ically** *adv.*—[Gk. *tēle*, far; *pathos*, feeling].
telephone (tel′e-fōn) *n.* electrical instrument by which sound is transmitted and reproduced at a distance; .—*v.t.* and *v.i.* to communicate by telephone.—**telephon'ic** *a*.—**tel'ephonist** (or tel-ef′) *n.* telephone-operator, esp. at switchboard of exchange..—**tele'phony** *n.* art or process of operating telephone [Gk. *tēle*, far; *phōnē*, a sound].
teleprinter (tel-e-prin′ter) *n.* electrical apparatus like typewriter by which typed messages are sent and received by wire.
teleprompter (tel-e-promp′ter) *n.* in television, a device to enable the speaker to refer to his script out of sight of the cameras, thus giving viewers the impression of an unscripted talk.
telescope (tel′e-skōp) *n.* optical instrument for magnifying distant objects;—*v.t.* to slide or drive together, as parts of telescope;—*v.i.* to be impacted violently, as carriages in railway-collision.—**telescop'ic, -al** *a.* pert. to or like a telescope.—**telescop'ically** *adv.*[Gk. *tēle*, afar; *skopein*, to see].
teletype (tel′e-tīp) *n.* automatically printed telegram; the apparatus by which this is done [Gk. *tēle*, far; and *type*].
teletypewriter (tel-e-tīp′rīt-er(*n.* invention by which material typed on one typewriter is by electrical control simultaneously typed on machines at a distance.
televiewer (tel′e-vū-er) *n.* one who views a televised programme; a viewer.
television (tel-e-vizh′un) *n.* transmission of scenes, persons, etc. at a distance by means of electro-magnetic wireless waves.—**tel'evise** *v.t.* to transmit by television [Gk. *tēle*, far, and *vision*].
telford (tel′ford) *n.* type of road-surfacing consisting of layer of stones topped by smaller stones and gravel, and subjected to pressure [fr. *Telford*, inventor].
tell (tel) *v.t.* orig. to count; to recount or narrate; to divulge; to reckon; to discover;—*v.i.* to produce marked effect; to betray (as secret); to report.—*pa.t.* and *pa.p.* **told**.—**tell'er** *n.* narrator; bank-clerk who pays out money; Member of House of Commons who counts votes; enumerator.—**tell'ing** *a.* effective; impressive; striking.—**tell'ingly** *adv.*—**tell′tale** *n.* one who betrays confidence; an informer;—*a.* warning; tending to betray.—**to tell off,** to detail for special duty; (*Slang*) to scold [O.E. *tellan*, to count].
tellurium (te-lū′ri-um) *n.* (*Chem.*) bluish-white element, brittle and lustrous, resembling sulphur in its chemical properties (symbol **Te**).—**tellu'ric** *a.* pert. to, derived from, the earth or from tellurium [L. *tellus*, the earth].
temerity (te-mer′i-ti) *n.* rashness; audacity; heedless [L. *temere*, rashly].
temper (tem′per) *v.t.* to mingle in due proportion; to soften, as clay, by moistening; to bring (metal) to desired degree of hardness and elasticity by heating, cooling, and re-heating; to regulate;—*n.* due proportion; consistency required and achieved by tempering; (*Fig.*) balanced attitude of mind; composure; anger; irritation.—**tem'pered** *a.* having a certain consistency, as clay, or degree of toughness, as steel; having a certain disposition, as *good-tempered, bad-tempered.*—**tem'peredly** *adv.*—**tem'pering** *n.* [L. *temperare*, to combine in due proportion].
tempera Same as **distemper**.
temperament (tem′per-a-ment) *n.* emotional mood; natural disposition; physical, moral and mental constitution peculiar to individuals; (*Mus.*) system of adjusting tones of keyboard instrument, such as a piano, so as to adapt the scale for all keys.—**temperamen'tal** *a.* liable to moods. [L. *temperamentum*, disposition].
temperance (tem′per-ans) *n.* moderation; self-discipline, esp. of natural appetites; total abstinence from, or moderation in, consumption of intoxicationg liquors; sobriety [L. *temperantia*, moderation].
temperate (tem′per-āt) *a.* moderate; abstemious; sober; (of climate) equable; not extreme.—**tem'perately** *adv.*—**tem'perateness** *n.* —**tem'perative** *a.*—**tem'perature** *n.* degree of heat or cold of atmosphere or of a human or living body; (*Colloq.*) fevered condition.—**temperate zones,** areas of earth between Polar Circles and Tropics.—**to run a temperature,** to become fevered [L. *temperare*, to moderate].
tempest (tem′pest) *n.* wind storm of great violence; (*Fig.*) any violent commotion.—**tempes'tuous** *a.* pert. to tempest; violent.—**tempes'tuously** *adv.*—**tempes'tuousness** *n.*—[L. *tempestas*, weather, storm].
Templar (tem′plar) *n.* one of a religious order of knights founded in 12th cent. for protection of Holy Sepulchre and pilgrims visiting it; lawyer or law-student with chambers in the Temple, London [fr. *temple*].
template (tem′plāt) *n.* pattern of wood or metal cut to shape required for finished flat object [prob. fr. L. *templum*, small rafter].
temple (tem′pl) *n.* place of worship; place dedicated to pagan deity; Christian church; shrine [L. *templum*, a sacred place].
temple (tem′pl) *n.* part of forehead between outer end of eye and hair.—**tem'poral** *a.* [L. *tempora*, the temples].
tempo (tem′pō) *n.* (*Mus.*) time; degree of speed or slowness at which passage should be played or sung; the degree of movement, as in the plot of a drama [It.].
temporal (tem′por-al) *a.* pert. to time or to this life; transient; secular; political as opposed to ecclesiastical, as *temporal power* of

the Pope.—**temporal'ity** *n.* material welfare;—*pl.* material possessions, esp. ecclesiastical revenues.—**tem'porally** *adv.*—**tem'porariness** *n.* —**tem'poralty** *n.* laity.—**tem'porarily** *adv.*—only for a time.—**tem'porariness** *n.*—**tem'porary, tempora'neous** *a.* lasting only for a time; fleeting.—**temporisa'tion** *n.* —**tem'porise** *v.i.* to act so as to gain time; to hedge; to compromise.—**tem'poriser** *n.*—**tem'porising** *n.* [L. *tempus*, time].

tempt (temt) *v.t.* to attempt; to induce to do something wrong; to entice.—**tempta'tion** *n.* act of tempting; that which tempts; inducement to do evil; attraction.—**tempt'er** *n.* (*fem.* **tempt'ress**) one who tempts, esp. Satan.—**tempt'ing** *a.* attractive; seductive.—**tempt'ingly** *adv.*—**tempt'ingness** *n.* [O.Fr. *tempter*, to entice].

ten (ten) *a.* twice five; one more than nine;—*n.* the number nine and one; the figure or symbol representing this, as 10, x.—**ten'fold** *a.* ten times repeated;—*adv.* ten times as much.—**tenth** *a.* next after the ninth; being one of ten equal divisions of anything;—*n.* one of ten equal parts; tenth part of anything; tithe.—**tenth'ly** *adv.* [O.E. *ten*, ten].

tenable (ten'ą-bl) *a.* capable of being held, defended, or logically maintained.—**tenabil'ity, ten'ableness** *n.* [L. *tenere*, to hold].

tenacious (te-nā'shus) *a.* holding fast; adhesive; retentive; close-fisted; pertinacious.—**tena'ciously** *adv.*—**tena'ciousness** *n.*—**tena'city** *n.* [L. *tenax*, holding fast].

tenant (ten'ąnt) *n.* (*Law*) one who has legal possession of real estate; one who occupies property for which he pays rent;—*v.t.* to hold or occupy as tenant.—**ten'ancy** *n.* act of holding land or property as tenant; property held by tenant.—**ten'antable** *a.* fit for occupation by tenant.—**ten'antry** *n.* tenants or employees collectively on estate [L. *tenere*, to hold].

tench (tensh) *n.* fresh-water fish of carp family supposed to be very tenacious of life [L. *tenere*, to hold].

tend (tend) *v.i.* to hold a course; to have a bias or inclination.—**ten'dency** *n.* inclination; bent.—**tenden'cious, tenden'tious** *a.* (of writings) propagandist; having a biased outlook [L. *tendere*, to stretch].

tend (tend) *v.t.* to look after; to minister to.—**ten'der** *n.* one who tends; small vessel supplying larger one with stores, etc., or landing passengers; truck attached to locomotive, carrying water and fuel [contr. of *attend*].

tender (ten'dęr) *v.t.* to offer in payment or for acceptance;—*v.i.* to make offer or estimate;—*n.* an offer, esp. contract to undertake specific work, or to supply goods at fixed rate; estimate.—**legal tender,** currency recognised as legally acceptable in payment of a debt [L. *tendere*, to stretch out].

tender (ten'dęr) *a.* soft; easily impressed; delicate; expressive of gentler passions; considerate; immature; sore; not tough (of meat).—**ten'derfoot** *n.* one not yet hardened to colonial prairie life; novice; Boy Scout before he has passed third test.—**ten'derly** *adv.*—**ten'derness** *n.* [L. *tener*, delicate].

tendon (ten'don) *n.* a tough fibrous cord attaching muscle to bone.—**ten'dinous** *a.* [L. *tendere*, to stretch].

tendril (ten'dril) *n.* spiral shoot of climbing plant by which it clings to another body for support; curl, as of hair;—*a.* clinging [Fr. *tendrille*].

tenebrous (ten'e-brus) *a.* dark; obscure;Also **ten'ebrose.**—**tenebros'ity** *n.* darkness; gloom [L. *tenebrae*, darkness].

tenement (ten'e-męnt) *n.* building divided into separate flats and let to different tenants. —**tenement'al, tenement'ary** *a.* [L. *tenere*, to hold].

tenet (ten'et) *n.* any opinion, dogma, or principle which a person holds as true [L. *tenere*, to hold].

tenfold See **ten.**

tennantite (ten'ąnt-īt) *n.* a sulphide of copper and arsenic [fr. *Tennant*, a chemist].

tenner (ten'ęr) *n.* (*Colloq.*) a ten-pound note.

tennis (ten'is) *n.* an ancient game for two or four players, played in a covered court by striking a ball, orig. with the hands later with racquets, across a net; a modern version of this played outside on grass or concrete court, often called *lawn-tennis*.—**tenn'is-court** *n.* specially marked-out court where tennis is played [etym. obscure].

tenon (ten'on) *n.* end of piece of wood shaped for insertion into cavity (*mortise*) in another piece to form a join;—*v.t.* to join with tenons. —**ten'on-saw** *n.* thin back-saw used in cutting tenons [L. *tenere*, to hold].

tenor (ten'or) *n.* general drift, course, or direction, of thought; purport; (*Mus.*) highest male adult voice; one who sings tenor;—*a.* pert. to tenor voice [L. *tenere*, to hold].

tense (tens) *n.* (*Gram.*) form of verb which indicates *time* of action, as *present*, *past* or *future tense* [L. *tempus*, time].

tense (tens) *a.* stretched; strained almost to breaking point; unrelaxed; alert; (of vowel) made by tongue tensed, as ē.—**tense'ly** *adv.*—**tense'ness** *n.* state of being tense.—**tensibil'ity, tensil'ity** *n.* the quality of being tensile.—**ten'sible, ten'sile** *a.* capable of being stretched or subjected to stress, as metals; capable of being made taut, as violin strings.—**ten'sion** *n.* act of stretching; strain; a state of being nervously excited or overwrought; (of metals) *pulling* stress as opposed to *compressive* stress; (*Elect.*) voltage.—**ten'sor** *n.* body-muscle which stretches [L. *tendere*, to stretch].

tent (tent) *n.* portable canvas shelter stretched and supported by poles and firmly pegged ropes; small plug of compressed absorbent gauze, or lint, which swells when moistened, used to keep open a wound, etc.;—*v.i.* to live in tent; to pitch tent;—*v.t.* to keep open, as wound, with tent.—**tent'-bed** *n.* canopied-bed; camp-bed.—**tent'ed** *a.* covered with tents.—**tent'-peg** *n.* strong wooden or iron peg to which tent ropes are fastened [L. *tendere*, to stretch].

tentacle (ten'tąkl) *n.* long flexible appendage of head or mouth in many lower animals for exploring, touching, grasping, and sometimes moving; feeler.—**tentac'ular** *a.* [L. *tentare*, to feel].

tentative (ten'tą-tiv) *a.* experimental; trying; —*n.* something done or suggested as a feeler towards general opinion.—**ten'tatively** *adv.* [L. *tentare*, to try].

tenter (ten'tęr) *n.* overseer or foreman in factory [contr. from *attend*].

tenter (ten'tęr) *n.* machine for stretching cloth by means of hooks;—*v.t.* to stretch on hooks. —**ten'ter-hook** *n.* one of the sharp hooks by which cloth is stretched on a tenter.—**on tenterhooks,** state of anxiety [L. *tendere*, to stretch].

tenuity (te-nū'i-ti) *n.* smallness of diameter; thinness.—**ten'uate** *v.t.* to make tenuous.—**ten'uous** *a.* slender; gossamer-like; over-subtle. —**ten'uousness** *n.* [L. *tenuis*, thin].

tenure (ten'ūr) *n.* holding of office, property, etc.; condition of occupancy [L. *tenere*, to hold].

tepee (tē'pē) *n.* Indian wigwam or tent. Also **tee'pee.**

tepefy (tep'e-fī) *v.t.* to make moderately warm.—*pa.t.* and *pa.p.* **tep'efied.**—**tepefac'tion** *n.* [L. *tepere*, to be warm; *facere*, to make].

tepid (tep'id) *a.* moderately warm; luke-warm. —**tepid'ity, tep'idness** *n.* state of being luke-warm [L. *tepidus*, warm].

teratology (ter-ą-tol'o-ji) *n.* science of animal and vegetable freaks [Gk. *teras*, a monster; *logos*, discourse].

terbium (tęr'bi-um) *n.* (*Chem.*) metallic element, one of the rare earths, chemical symbol **Tb.** [fr. *Ytterby*, in Sweden].

tercel (tėr′sel) *n.* a young male falcon. Also **tier'cel** [dim. of L. *tertius*, third].

tercentenary (tėr′sen-tē′nạ-ri or tėr-sen′te-nạ-ri) *n.* the 300th anniversary of an event; —*a.* pert. to a period of 300 years [L. *ter*, thrice; *centum*, a hundred].

tercet (tėr′set) *n.* (*Mus.*) triplet; (*Pros.*) group of three lines or verses. Also **tier'cet** [L. *ter*, thrice].

terebene (ter′e-bēn) *n.* disinfectant liquid, made by treating oil of turpentine and sulphuric acid; used also for thinning down paint.—**tereb'ic** *a.* pert. to turpentine.—**ter'ebinth** *n.* turpentine-tree.—**terebinth'ine** *a.* [Gk. *terebinthos*].

teredo (te-rē′dō) *n.* ship-worm, mollusc which causes destruction to ship hulls by boring. Also **ter'edine** [Gk. *terēdōn*, woodworm].

tergiversate (tėr′ji-vėr-sāt) *v.i.* to make use of subterfuges; to be shifty or vacillating; to apostatise.—**tergiversa'tion** *n.*—**ter'giversator** *n.* one who changes sides [L. *tergum*, the back; *vertere*, to turn].

term (tėrm) *n.* boundary; limit, esp. of time; period during which law-courts are sitting; fixed day when rent is due; period during which schools, universities, etc. are open; word or expression with specific meaning; (*Math.*) member of compound quantity;—*pl.* mode of expression; stipulation; relationship, as *on friendly terms*; charge for accommodation, etc. as *hotel terms*, or for instruction given;—*v.t.* to give name to; to call.—**terminolog'ical** *a.* pert. to terminology or specific language used.—**terminolog'ically** *adv.*—**terminol'ogy** *n.* technical words; nomenclature.—**to come to terms**, to reach agreement, usually by compromise [L. *terminus*, the end].

Termagant (tėr′mạ-gạnt) *n.* imaginary god of Saracens depicted in old plays as of violent nature.—**ter'magant** *n.* quarrelsome, shrewish woman;—*a.* scolding; quarrelsome.

terminate (tėr′min-āt) *v.t.* to set limit to; to end; to conclude;—*v.i.* to come to an end; to finish.—**ter'minable** *a.* capable of being terminated; liable to cease.—**ter'minal** *n.* extremity; (*Elect.*) metal attachment such as screw, block, clamp for connecting end of circuit; end of lightning-conductor;—*a.* pert. to end; belonging to terminus; occurring in, or, at end of, a term; (*Bot.*) growing at tip.—**ter'minally** *adv.*—**termina'tion** *n.* act of terminating; finish; conclusion; ending of word.—**termina'tional** *a.*—**ter'minative** *a.* serving to terminate; definite.—**ter'minatively** *adv.*—**ter′minus** *n.* end; farthest limit; railway-station, aerodrome, etc. at end of long-distance line.—*pl.* **ter'mini, ter'minuses** [L. *terminus*, the end].

termite (tėr′mīt) *n.* insect of order of *Isoptera*, found in tropical countries erroneously called the *white ant* [L. *termes*, a wood-worm].

tern (tėrn) *n.* sea-bird allied to gull, with forked tail [Scand.].

tern (tėrn) *n.* that which consists of three;—*a.* threefold.—**ter'nal, ter'nary** *a.* consisting of three; proceeding by threes; (*Chem.*) comprising three compounds.—**ter'nate** *a.* arranged in threes; (*Bot.*) having three leaflets.—**ter′nion** *n.* group of three [L. *terni*, three each].

Terpsichore (tėrp-sik′ō-rē) *n.* (*Myth.*) Muse of choral song and dancing.—**Terpsichore'an** *a.* pert. to Terpsichore or to dancing [Gk. *Terpsichorē*, fond of dancing].

terra (ter′a) *n.* earth, as in various Latin phrases.—**terr'a-cot'ta** *n.* reddish, brick-like earthenware, porous and unglazed.—**terr'a-fir'ma** *n.* dry land.—**terr'a-incog'nita** *n.* unexplored territory.—**terra'nean** *a.* belonging to surface of earth.—**terra'neous** *a.* growing on land.—**terraqueous** (ter-ā′kwe-us) *a.* comprising both land and water, as the globe [L. *terra*, the earth].

terrace (ter′as) *n.* raised shelf of earth, natural or artificial; row of houses built on a terrace; promenade;—*v.t.* to form into terraces [L. *terra*, the earth].

terrain (ter′ān) *n.* tract of land; ground considered by tactician suitable or not for defence [L. *terra*, the earth].

terrapin (ter′ạ-pin) *n.* edible tortoise found in eastern U.S.A. [Amer.-Ind.].

terrazzo-paving (te-rat′sō-pāv-ing) *n.* kind of mosaic paving in concrete chips [It.].

terrene (te-rēn′) *a.* pert. to earth; earthy; terrestrial [L. *terra*, the earth].

terrestrial (ter-es′tri-ạl) *a.* pert. to earth; existing on earth; earthly, opp. to *celestial*;—*n.* inhabitant of earth [L. *terra*, the earth].

terrible (ter′i-bl) *a.* calculated to inspire fear or awe; frightful; dreadful; formidable; (*Colloq.*) excessive.—**terr'ibleness** *n.*—**terr'ibly** *adv.* [L. *terrere*, to frighten].

terrier (ter′i-ẹr) *n.* breed of small or medium-sized dog, originally trained for hunting foxes, badgers, etc. [M.E. *terrere*, a burrowing dog].

terrier (ter′i-ẹr) *n.* book or register containing site, and extent of private person's land [L. *terra*, the earth].

Terrier (ter′i-ẹr) *n.* (*Colloq.*) member of the Territorial Army.

terrify (ter′i-fī) *v.t.* to frighten greatly; to inspire with terror.—*pa.t.* and *pa. p.* **terr'ified.**—**terrif'ic** *a.* causing terror or alarm; (*Colloq.*) tremendous.—**terrif'ically** *adv.* [L. *terrere*, to terrify; *facere*, to make].

territory (ter′i-to-ri) *n.* large tract of land, esp. under one governmental administration; part of country which has not yet attained political independence.—**territo'rial** *a.* pert. to territory; limited to certain district;—*n.* member of *Territorial Army*, voluntary home-defence force in Britain [L. *terra*, the earth].

terror (ter′or) *n.* extreme fear; violent dread; one who or that which causes terror.—**terrorisa'tion** *n.*—**terr'orise** *v.t.* to fill with terror; to rule by intimidation.—**terr'oriser** *n.*—**terr'orism** *n.* mass-organised ruthlessness.—**terr'orist** *n.* one who rules by terror.—**terr'or-strick'en, -smit'ten, -struck** *a.* paralysed with fear; terrified [L. *terrere*, to frighten].

terse (tėrs) *a.* (of speech, writing, etc.) concise; succinct; brief; laconic; (of persons) abrupt.—**terse'ly** *adv.*—**terse'ness** *n.* [L. *terpere, tersum*, to smooth .]

tertian (tėr′shạn) *a.* (*Med.*) occurring every third day;—*n.* fever, such as malaria, with paroxysms occurring at intervals of forty-eight hours [L. *tertius*, third].

tertiary (tėr′shạr-i) *a.* of third formation or rank; (*Geol.*) pert. to era of rock formation following Mezozoic;—*n.* (*Geol.*) the tertiary era [L. *tertius*, third].

Terylene (ter′i-lēn) *n.* a synthetic textile yarn, manufactured by Imperial Chemical Industries, from a product of *ter*ephthalic acid and eth*ylene* glycol (Protected Trade Name].

terza-rima (ter′tsa-rē′ma) *n.* form of stanza-arrangement of iambic pentameter lines in groups of three, rhyming aba, bcb, cdc [It. *terza*, third; *rima*, rhyme].

tessellate (tes′e-lāt) *v.t.* to pave with tesserae; to make mosaic paving with square-cut stones.—**tess'ella, tess'era** *n.* (*pl.* **tess'ellae, tess'erae**) one of the square stones used in tessellated paving.—**tessella'tion** *n.* process of making tessellated paving [L. *tessera*, a square block].

test (test) *n.* vessel in which metals are refined; critical examination; standard; grounds for admission or exclusion; (*Chem.*) reagent; substance used to analyse compound into its several constituents; a touchstone;—*v.t.* to make critical examination of; to put to proof; (*Chem.*) to analyse nature and properties of a compound.—**test'-case** *n.* (*Law*) case tried for purpose of establishing a precedent.—**test'er** *n.*—**test'ing** *n.*—*a.* demanding endurance.—**test′-match** *n.* cricket-match between international sides, as England *v.* Australia.—**test′pa'per** *n.* examination question-paper; litmus or other impregnated paper used to test acid or alkaline content of chemical solution.—test'pi'lot *n.* experienced pilot engaged in testing flying qualities of new types of aircraft.—test'tube *n.* glass tube rounded and closed at one end, used for testing liquids. [L. *testa*, earthen pot].

test (test) *v.t.* (*Law*) to attest and date;—*v.i.* to make a will.—test'able *a.* capable of being bequeathed by will.—test'acy *n.* state of being testate.—tes'tate *a.* having left a valid will.—testa'tor *n.* (*fem.* testa'trix) one who makes a will [L. *testari*, to witness].

testa (tes'tạ) *n.* (*pl.* testae) (*Zool.*) hard outer shell of molluscs; (*Bot.*) seed-coat. Also test.—testa'cean *a.* having hard shell.—testa'ceous *a.* testacean; brick-coloured [L. *testa*, shell].

testament (tes'tạ-mẹnt) *n.* solemn declaration of one's will; one of the two great divisions of the Bible, as the *Old Testament*, or the *New Testament*.—testamen'tal, testamen'tary *a.* pert. to testament or will; bestowed by will [L. *testari*, to witness].

tester (tes'tẹr) *n.* flat canopy, esp. over a bed [O.Fr. *teste*, the head].

tester (tes'tẹr) *n.* a teston; sixpence.

testicle (tes'ti-kl) *n.* one of the two male reproductive glands.—testic'ular *a.*—testic'ulate, -d *a.* having testicles; resembling testicle in shape.—test'is *n.* a testicle.—*pl.* test'es [L. *testis*, testicle].

testify (tes'ti-fī) *v.i.* to bear witness; to affirm or declare solemnly; to give evidence upon oath.—*v.t.* to bear witness to; to manifest.—tes'tifier *n.* [L. *testis*, a witness; *facere*, to make].

testimony (tes'ti-mon-i) *n.* solemn declaration or affirmation; witness; proof of some fact; in Scripture, the two tables of the law; divine revelation as a whole.—testimo'nial *a.* containing testimony;—*n.* written declaration testifying to character and qualities of person, esp. of applicant for a post; written tribute to person's outstanding worth [L. *testimonium*, an attestation].

teston (tes'ton) *n.* tester; silver coin of Henry VIII's time, orig. worth a shilling; sixpence [O.Fr. *teste*, head].

testy (tes'ti) *a.* fretful; irascible.—test'ily *adv.* —test'iness *n.* ([O.Fr. *teste*, head].

tetanus (tet'ạ-nus) *n.* a disease in which a virus causes spasms of violent muscular contraction; lockjaw; any spasmodic muscular contraction or rigidity caused by intake of drugs.—tetan'ic *a.* [Gk. *tetanos*, stretched].

tetchy See techy.

tether (teTH'ẹr) *n.* rope or chain fastened to grazing animal to keep it from straying;—*v.t.* to confine with tether; to restrict movements of [Scand.].

tetra- (tet'rạ) *prefix* meaning *four* [Gk.].

tetractomy (te-trak'tom-i) *n.* division into four parts [Gk. *tetra-*, four; *tomē*, a cutting].

tetrad (tet'rad) *n.* the number four; group of four things [Gk. *tetras*].

tetra-ethyl lead (tet'rạ-eth'il led) *n.* colourless liquid, one of various substances used to eliminate 'knocking' in petrol-driven engines.

tetragon (tet'rạ-gon) *n.* a plane figure, having four angles.—tetrag'onal *a.*

tetragram (tet'rạ-gram) *n.* word of four letters; (*Geom.*) figure formed by four right angles.

tetrahedron (tet-rạ-hē'dron) *n.* solid figure enclosed by four triangles; triangular-based pyramid.—tetrahe'dral *a.* [Gk. *tetra-*, four; *hedra*, a base].

tetralin (tet'rạ-lin) *n.* colourless turpentine substitute [fr. *tetra-hydro-naphthalene*].

tetralogy (te-tral'o-ji) *n.* group of four dramas or operas connected by some central event or character [Gk. *tetra-*, four; *logos*, a discourse].

tetrameter (te-tram'e-tẹr) *n.* verse of four measures.

tetrapod (tet'rạ-pod) *n.* (*Zool.*) insect with four feet;—*a.* having four feet.

tetrarch (tet'rạrk) *n.* Roman governor of fourth part of a province.—tet'rarchate, tet'rarchy *n.* office of tetrarch; province ruled by tetrarch.—tet'rarchic, -al *a.* [Gk. *tetra-*, four; *archos*, ruler].

tetrastyle (tet'rạ-stīl) *a.* having four pillars.

tetrode (tet'rōd) *n.* (*Radio*) four-electrode thermionic valve [Gk. *tetra-*, four; *electrode*].

tetter (tet'ẹr) *n.* skin disease; ringworm;—*v.t.* to affect with this.—tett'erous *a.* [O.E. *teter*, ringworm].

Teuton (tū'ton) *n.* member of one of Germanic races; (*Colloq.*) a German.—Teuton'ic *a.* pert. to Teutons or their language.—Teutonic languages, those languages from which modern German, English, Scandinavian, and Dutch are derived [L. *Teutones*].

tewel (tū'ẹl) *n.* a flue [O.Fr. *tuel*, a pipe].

text (tekst) *n.* original words of author, orator, etc. as distinct from paraphrase or commentary; verse of passage of Scripture chosen as theme of sermon.—text'book *n.* manual of instruction.—tex'tual *a.* pert. to text or subject-matter; based on actual text or wording; literal.—tex'tually *adv.* [L. *texere*, to weave].

textile (teks'tīl) *a.* pert. to weaving; capable of being woven;—*n.* fabric made on loom.—texto'rial *a.* pert. to weaving [L. *texere*, to weave].

texture (teks'tur) *n.* that which is woven; manner of weaving threads in fabric; quality of surface of a woven material; disposition of several parts of anything in relation to whole; quality (as of mind). [L. *texere*].

Thailand (tī'land) *n.* Siam.

thalassic (tha-las'ik) *a.* pert. to the sea; living in the sea [Gk. *thalassa*, the sea.]

thaler (tȧ'lẹr) *n.* former German silver coin worth about 3s.

thallium (thal'i-um) *n.* (*Chem.*) rare metal (symbol Tl) bluish white and soft; so called because of brilliant green line in its spectrum [Gk. *thallos*, green shoot].

thallus (thal'us) *n.* simple plant organism which shows little or no differentiation into leaves, stem, or root as in *fungi*, *algae*, etc.—*pl.* thall'i [Gk. *thallos*, green shoot].

than (THan) *conj.* introducing adverbial clause of comparison and occurring after comparative form of an adjective or adverb [O.E. *thonne*, than].

thane (thān) *n.* in Anglo-Saxon community, member of class between freemen and nobility.—thane'dom *n.* property held by a thane [O.E. *thegn*, soldier].

thank (thangk) *v.t.* to express gratitude for favour;—*n.* expression of gratitude (usually in *pl.*).—thank'ful *a.* grateful; appreciative.—thank'fully *adv.*—thank'fulness *n.* gratitude.—thank'less *a.* ungrateful; unappreciated by others.—thank'lessly *adv.*—thank'lessness *n.* ingratitude.—thank'off'ering *n.* gift made as token of gratitude.—thanks'giving *n.* act of rendering thanks; service held as expression of thanks for Divine goodness.—Thanksgiving Day (*U.S.*) day, usually last Thursday in November, set apart for rendering thanks to God for blessings granted to nation [O.E. *thanc*, thanks].

that (THat) *demons. pron.* or *a.* (*pl.* those) pointing out a person or thing, or referring to something already mentioned; not this but the other;—*rel. pron.* who or which;—*conj.* introducing a noun cl., adjective cl., or adverbial cl. of purpose, result, degree or reason [O.E. *thaet*].

thatch (thach) *n.* straw, rushes, heather, etc. used to roof cottage, or cover stacks of grain; (*Colloq.*) hair;—*v.t.* to roof with thatch.—thatch'er *n.*—thatch'ing *n.* act or craft of roofing with thatch; materials used [O.E. *thaec*, a roof, thatch].

thaumaturgy (thaw'mạ-tur-ji) *n.* art of working miracles; conjuring.—thau'maturge *n.* miracle worker; magician; conjurer.—thaumatur'gic *a.* [Gk. *thauma*, a wonder].

thaw (thaw) *v.t.* to cause to melt by increasing temperature; to liquefy;—*v.i.* to melt, as ice, snow, etc.; to become warmer; (*Fig.*) to become genial;—*n.* melting of ice or snow O.E. *thawian*, to melt].

the (THẹ, emphatic THē) *a.* or *definite article*, placed before nouns, and used to specify general conception, or to denote particular person or thing;—*adv.* by so much; by that amount, as *the more, the merrier* [O.E.].

thearchy (thē'ȧr-ki) *n.* theocracy; government by gods [Gk. *theos*, a god; *archē*, rule].

theatre (thē'ạ-tẹr) *n.* in Ancient Greece, a large, open-air structure used for public assemblies, staging of dramas, etc.; playhouse; stage; lecture or demonstration room for anatomy studies; room in hospital where surgical operations are performed; field of military, naval, or air operations.—**theat'ric, -al** *a.*—**theat'rically** *adv.*—**theat'ricals** *n.pl.* dramatic performances, esp. by amateurs [Gk. *theatron*].

thé dansant (tā-dong'song) *n.* afternoon tea with dancing [Fr.].

thee (THē) *pron.* objective case of **thou**.

theft (theft) *n.* act of stealing; that which is stolen [O.E. *theof*, a thief].

thegn Same as **thane**.

theine (thē'in) *n.* alkaloid of tea-plant; caffeine.—**the'ic** *n.* one who drinks tea excessively [Mod.L. *thea*, tea].

their (THār) *a.* and *pron.* of them; possessive case of **they**.—**theirs** *poss. pron*, form of *their* used absolutely [Scand. *theira*, their].

theism (thē'izm) *n.* belief in existence of personal God who actively manifests Himself in world.—**the'ist** *n.*—**theis'tic, -al** *a.* [Gk. *theos*, a god].

them (THem) *pron.* objective and dative case of **they** [O.E. *thaem*].

theme (thēm) *n.* subject-matter of writing, discourse, or discussion; brief essay; (*Mus.*) groundwork melody recurring at intervals and with variations.—**the'ma** *n.* subject for discussion.—**themat'ic** *a.* pert. to.—**themat'ically** *adv.*—**theme'song** *n.* recurring melody in play, revue, or film [Gk. *thema*, something laid down].

themselves (THem-selvz') *pron. pl.* of **himself, herself, and itself.**

then (THen) *adv.* at that time (past or future); immediately afterwards; thereupon; that being so; for this reason; in consequence of;—*conj.* moreover; therefore;—*a.* existing or acting at particular time.—**now and then**, occasionally [doublet of *than*].

thence (THens) *adv.* from that place; from that time; for that reason.—**thence'forth** *adv.* from that time on.—**thencefor'ward** *adv.* thenceforth [M.E. *thennes*].

theocracy (thē-ok'rạ-si) *n.* government of State professedly in the name, and under direction, of God; government by priests.—**the'ocrat, theoc'ratist** *n.* ruler under this system.—**theocrat'ic, -al** *a.* [Gk. *theos*, a god; *kratos*, power].

theodolite (thē-od'ō-līt) *n.* instrument for measuring angles, used in surveying [etym. unknown].

theogony (thē-og'o-ni) *n.* branch of heathen theology dealing with genealogy of gods.—**theogon'ic** *a.* [Gk. *theos*, a god; *gonē*, generation].

theology (thē-ol'o-ji) *n.* science which treats of facts and phenomena of religion, and relations between God and man.—**theol'oger, theolog'ian** *n.* one learned in theology; professor of divinity.—**theolog'ic, -al** *a.* pert. to theology.—**theolog'ically** *adv.*—**theol'ogise** *v.t.* to render theological; to theorise upon theological matters.—**theologis'er** *n.*—**theol'ogist** *n.* student of, authority on, theology [Gk. *theos*, god; *logos*, discourse].

theophany (thē-of'ạ-ni) *n.* manifestation of God to men, in human form; Incarnation.—**theophan'ic** *a.* [Gk. *theos*, a god; *phainesthai*, to appear].

theorem (thē'or-ẹm) *n.* established principle; speculative truth; (*Math.*) proposition to be proved by logical reasoning; algebraical formula.—**theoremat'ic, -al** *a.* [Gk. *theorēma*, speculation].

theory (thē'o-ri) *n.* supposition put forward to explain something; speculation; exposition of general principles as distinct from practice and execution; (*Colloq.*) general idea; notion.—**theoret'ic, -al** *a.* pert. to or based on theory; speculative as opp. to *practical*.—**theoret'ics** *n.pl.* speculative side of science.—**the'orise** *v.t.* to form a theory; to speculate.—**the'oriser, the'orist** *n.* [Gk. *theoria*, speculation].

theosophy (thē-os'ō-fi) *n.* name given by the Alexandrian philosophers to ancient Wisdom-Religion in 3rd cent. A.D.; the eternal revelation of Divine Spirit which forms source of all religions, arts, and sciences of the world; knowledge of God by immediate Divine illumination.—**the'osoph, theos'opher, theos'ophist** *n.* one who believes in theosophy.—**theosoph'ic, -al** *a.* [Gk. *theos*, a god; *sophia*, wisdom].

therapeutic (ther-ạ-pū'tik) *a.* pert. to healing.—**therapeu'tically** *adv.*—**therapeu'tics** *n.* branch of medicine concerned with treatment and cure of diseases.—**therapeu'tist** *n.* [Gk. *therapeuein*, to attend (medically)].

therapy (ther'ạ-pi) *n.* remedial treatment, as *radio-therapy*, for cure of disease by radium [Gk. *therapeia*, (medical) attendance].

there (THār) *adv.* in that place; farther off—opp. to *here*; as an introductory adverb it adds little to the meaning of the sentence as '*There is someone at the door*';—*interj.* expressing surprise, alarm.—**there'about, there'abouts** *adv.* near that place, number, or quantity.—**thereaft'er** *adv.* after that time; accordingly.—**thereat'** *adv.* at that place; by means of that.—**thereby'** *adv.* by that means; in consequence.—**there'fore** *conj.* and *adv.* for that or this reason; consequently;accordingly.—**therein'** *adv.* in that, or this place, time, or thing; in that particular.—**thereinaft'er** *adv.* afterwards in same document.—**thereof'** *adv.* of that or this.—**thereon'** *adv.* on that or this.—**thereto'** *adv.* to that or this.—**there'upon** *adv.* upon that or this; consequently; immediately.—**therewith'** *adv.* with that or this; straightway.—**there'withal** *adv.* over and above; at the same time [O.E. *thaer*, there].

therm (thẹrm) *n.* term used in Britain for thermal unit (*abbrev.* B.Th.U.), amount of heat required to raise 1 lb. of water through 1°F.; (of household gas supply) measuring 100,000 British thermal units.—**ther'mae** *n.pl.* hot springs; Roman baths.—**ther'mal** *a.* pert. to heat.—**ther'mic** *a.* caused by heat.—**ther'mically** *adv.*—**thermatol'ogy** *n.* medical treatment of ailments by hot springs, etc. [Gk. *thermē*, heat].

thermion (thẹr'mi-on) *n.* positively or negatively charged particle or ion emitted from incandescent substance.—**thermion'ic** *a.* pert. to thermions.—**thermionic current** (*Radio*) flow of electrons from filament to plate of thermionic valve.—**thermion'ics** *n.* branch of science dealing with emission of electrons from substances under action of heat [Gk. *thermē*, heat; *ion*, going].

thermit (thẹr'mit) *n*, aluminium powder mixed with metal oxide, which, when ignited, emits tremendous heat, used esp. in welding and for incendiary bombs. Also **ther'mite** [Gk. *thermē*, heat].

thermochemistry (thẹr-mō-kem'is-tri) *n.* branch of science which deals with changes of heat during chemical processes.

thermodynamics (thẹr-mō-dī-nam'iks) *n.* branch of science which deals with the conversion of heat into mechanical energy.

thermoelectricity (thẹr-mō-el-ek-tris'i-ti) *n.* electricity developed by action of heat alone on two different metals.—**thermoelec'tric, -al** *a.* [Gk. *thermē*, heat; and *electricity*].

thermogenesis (thėr-mō-jen′e-sis) *n.* production of heat, esp. in human body.—**thermogenet′ic, thermogen′ic** *a.*
thermogram (thėr′mō-gram) *n.* recording on a thermograph.—**ther′mograph** *n.* instrument for automatically registering varying temperatures on a graph.
thermology (thėr-mol′o-ji) *n.* the science of heat [Gk. *thermē*, heat; *logos*, a discourse].
thermometer (thėr-mom′e-tėr) *n.* instrument for measuring temperature, usually consisting of graduated and sealed glass tube with bulb containing mercury.—**thermomet′ric, -al** *a.*—**thermomet′rically** *adv.*—**thermom′etry** *n.*—**clinical thermometer,** small glass-thermometer for measuring temperature of human body [Gk. *thermē*, heat; *metron*, measure].
thermomotor (thėr-mō-mō′tor) *n.* engine worked by heat or hot air.
thermopile (thėr′mō-pīl) *n.* a battery for measuring minute variations in temperature.
thermoscope (thėr′mō-skōp) *n.* instrument for detecting fluctuations in temperature without actual measurement.
Thermos (thėr′mos) *n.* vessel generically known as a vacuum flask; double-walled glass bottle or the like which substantially retains temperature of liquids by the device of surrounding interior vessel with a vacuum jacket [Protected Trade Name].
thermostat (thėr′mō-stat) *n.* instrument which controls temperature automatically, used in refrigerators, stoves, hot-water tanks, incubators, etc.—**thermostat′ic** *a.*—**thermostat′ically** *adv.*—**thermostat′ics** *n.* science dealing with equilibrium of heat [Gk. *thermē*, heat; and *static*].
thermotic (thėr-mot′ik) *a.* pert. to heat. Also **thermot′ical.**—**thermot′ics** *n.* the science of heat [Gk. *thermōtēs*, heat].
thesaurus (the-saw′rus) *n.* treasury of knowledge, etc.; lexicon; encyclopaedia [Gk. *thēsauros*, treasure-house].
these (THēz) *demons. a.* and *pron. pl.* of **this.**
thesis (thē′sis) *n.* what is laid down as a proposition; dissertation, esp. a University Honours degree.—*pl.* **the′ses.**—**thet′ic** *a.*—**thet′ically** *adv.* [Gk. *thesis*, placing].
Thespis (thes′pis) *n.* Athenian of 6th cent. A.D. supposed inventor of tragedy.—**Thes′pian** *a.* pert. to drama;—*n.* an actor.
theurgy (thē′ur-ji) *n.* black art; necromancy; art of working so-called miracles by supernatural agency.—**theur′gic** *a.* [Gk. *theos*, god; *ergon*, a work].
thew (thū) *n.* muscle; sinew; brawn; (*Fig.*) mental vigour.—usually used in *pl.* [O.E. *theaw*, manner, or strength].
they (THā) *pron. pers. pl.* of **he, she, it;** indefinitely, for a number of persons.
thiamin, thiamene (thī′a-mēn) *n.* Vitamin B, complex compound, deficiency of which causes beri-beri [Gk. *theion*, sulphur, and *amine*].
thick (thik) *a.* dense; foggy; muddy; not thin; abundant; packed; frequent; muffled, as *thick voice*; mentally dull; (*Slang*) intimate;—*n.* thickest part;—*adv.* thickly; to a considerable depth; fast.—**thick′en** *v.t.* to make thick;—*v.i.* to become thick.—**thick′ening** *n.* something added to liquid, as cornflour, to thicken it.—**thick′et** *n.* a shrubbery.—**thick-head′ed** *a.* dull mentally.—**thick′ly** *adv.*—**thick′ness** *n.* quality of being thick; measurement of depth between opposite surfaces; layer.—**thick′-set** *a.* closely planted; sturdily built [O.E. *thicce*, thick].
thief (thēf) *n.* (*pl.* **thieves**) one who steals the goods and property of another.—**thieve** *v.t.* to take by theft;—*v.i.* to steal.—**thiev′ery** *n.*—**thiev′ish** *a.* addicted to stealing.—**thiev′ishly** *adv.*—**thiev′ishness** *n.* [O.E. *theof*].
thigh (thī) *n.* fleshy part of leg between knee and trunk [O.E. *theoh*, thigh].
thimble (thim′bl) *n.* metal or bone cap for tip of middle finger, in sewing; anything shaped like a thimble.—**thim′bleful** *n.* the quantity contained in a thimble; very small amount of liquid [O.E. *thymel*, thumb-stall].
thin (thin) *a.* having little depth or thickness; slim; lean; emaciated; sparse; fine;—*adv.* sparsely; not closely packed;—*v.t.* to make thin; to rarefy;—*v.i.* to grow or become thin; to slim.—**thin′ly** *adv.*—**thin′ness** *n.*—**thin′ning** *n.* practice of removing some plants to give remainder a richer soil in which to mature [O.E. *thynne*, thin].
thine (THīn) *pron.* (*poss.* form of **thou**) belonging to thee; thy [O.E. *thin*, thine].
thing (thing) *n.* material or inanimate object; entity; specimen; commodity; event; action; person (in pity or contempt);—*pl.* belongings; clothes; furniture.—**thing′amy, thing′umabob, thing′umajig, thing′ummy** *n.* word used for name which has escaped one's memory [O.E. *thing*, an object].
think (thingk) *v.t.* to conceive; to surmise; to believe; to consider; to esteem;—*v.i.* to reason; to form judgment; to deliberate; to imagine; to discover; to recollect.—*pa.t.* and *pa.p.* **thought** (thawt).—**think′able** *a.* capable of being thought or considered.—**think′er** *n.* one who thinks; sage or philosopher.—**think′ing** *a.* reflective; rational [O.E. *thencan*].
third (thėrd) *a.* next after the second; forming one of three equal divisions;—*n.* one of three equal parts; (*Mus.*) interval of three diatonic degrees of the scale.—**third′-class** *a.* pert. to accommodation for passengers not travelling first or second class; inferior.—**third estate,** the commons.—**third′ing** *n.* third part of anything.—**third′ly** *adv.*—**third man** (*Cricket*) fielder standing on off-side between point and slip.—**third′-rate** *a.* of third-class quality; inferior; shoddy.—**Third Reich,** Nazi regime in Germany 1933-45.—**Third Republic,** republican government in France in 1871 [O.E. *thridda*, third].
thirst (thėrst) *n.* desire to drink; suffering endured by too long abstinence from drinking; (of soil) drought; (*Fig.*) craving;—*v.i.* to crave for something to drink; to wish for earnestly.—**thirst′er** *n.*—**thirst′ily** *adv.*—**thirst′iness** *n.*—**thirst′y** *a.* having a desire to drink; dry; parched; eager for [O.E. *thurst*, thirst].
thirteen (thėr′tēn) *a.* ten and three;—*n.* sum of ten and three; symbol representing thirteen units, as 13, XIII.—**thir′teenth** *a.* next in order after twelfth; being one of thirteen equal parts;—*n.* one of these parts [O.E. *threo*, three; *tyn*, ten].
thirty (thėr′ti) *a.* three times ten;—*n.* sum of three times ten; symbol representing this, as 30, XXX.—**thir′tieth** *a.* next in order after twenty-ninth; being one of thirty equal parts;—*n.* thirtieth part [O.E. *thritig*, thirty].
this (THis) *demons. pron.* and *a.* denoting a person or thing near at hand, just mentioned, or about to be mentioned [O.E.].
thistle (this′l) *n.* one of the numerous prickly plants of the genus *Carduus*, with yellow or purple flowers; national emblem of Scotland.—**this′tle-down** *n.* feathery down of thistle seeds.—**thist′ly** *a.* overgrown with thistles [O.E. *thistel*, a thistle].
thither (thith′ėr) *adv.* to that place; to that point, end, or result.—**thith′erward** *adv.* toward that place [O.E. *thider*].
thole (thōl) *v.t.* pin in gunwale of boat to keep oar in rowlock. Also **thole′-pin, thowel, thowl** [O.E. *thol*, a rowlock].
thole (thōl) *v.t.* and *i.* to endure [O.E. *tholian*, to suffer].
Thomism (tō′mizm) *n.* doctrines expounded in theology of *Thomas Aquinas* (1226-74).—**Tho′mist** *n.* adherent of Thomism.—*a.* pert. to Thomism.
thong (thong) *n.* narrow strap of leather used for reins, whip-lash, etc.; long narrow

strip of leather used in leather-craft [O.E. *thwang*, a thong].

thorax (thṓ-raks) *n.* part of body between neck and abdomen; chest-cavity containing heart, lungs, etc.—**thorac'ic** *a.* [Gk. *thorax*, breastplate].

thorium (thṓ-ri-um) *n.* (*Chem.*) radio-active metallic element, used in manufacture of incandescent gas-mantles—symbol **Th.** Also **thori'num** [fr. *Thor*, Norse God of Thunder].

thorn (thorn) *n.* sharp, woody shoot on stem of tree or shrub; prickle; hawthorn; (*Fig.*) anything which causes trouble or annoyance; name in O.E. for symbol= th.—**thorn'y** *a.* full of thorns; prickly; jaggy; (*Fig.*) beset with difficulties [O.E. *thorn*, a prickle].

thoron (thṓ-ron) *n.* (*Chem.*) radio-active emanation resulting from decomposition of thorium.

thorough (thuŕ-ō) *a.* passing through or to the end; complete; absolute.—*adv.* through.—**thor'oughbred** *a.* (of animals) pure bred from pedigree stock; (of people) aristocratic hence, high-spirited; mettlesome;—*n.* animal (esp. horse) of pure breed.—**thor'oughfare** *n.* passage through; unobstructed passage.—**thor'ough-go'ing** *a.* very thorough.—**thor'oughly** *adv.*—**thor'oughness** *n.*—**thor'ough-paced** *a.* absolute [form of *through*].

thorp (thorp) *n.* hamlet; village [O.E. *thorp*, village].

those (THōz) *a.* and *pron. pl.* of **that.**

thou (THou) *pron. pres., 2nd sing.* denoting the person addressed (used now only in solemn address, and by the Quakers).

though (THō) *conj.* granting; admitting; even if; notwithstanding; however [O.E. *theah*].

thought (thawt) *pa.t.* and *pa.p.* of **think.**

thought (thawt) *n.* act of thinking; that which one thinks; reflection; opinion; serious consideration.—**thought'ful** *a.* contemplative; attentive; considerate.—**thought'fully** *adv.*—**thought'fulness** *n.*—**thought'less** *a.* without thought; heedless; impulsive; inconsiderate.—**thought'lessly** *adv.*—**thought'lessness** *n.*—**thought'-read'er** *n.* one who professes to read another's thoughts.—**thought'-read'ing** *n.*—**thought'-trans'ference** *n.* telepathy [O.E. *gethoht*, thought].

thousand (thoú-zand) *a.* consisting of ten hundred; used indefinitely to express large number;—*n.* the number ten hundred; symbol representing any large number.—**thou'sandfold** *a.* multiplied by a thousand.—**thou'sandth** *a.* constituting one of thousand equal parts; next in order after nine hundred and ninety-nine;—*n.* thousandth part [O.E. *thusend*, a thousand].

thowel, thowl See **thole.**

thrall (thrawl) *n.* slave; bondsman; servitude; durance.—**thral'dom, thrall'dom** *n.* bondage [O.N. *thrael*, bondage].

thrash (thrash) *v.t.* to separate grain from chaff by use of flail or threshing-machine; to thresh; to flog. Also **thresh.**—**thrash'er** *n.*—**thrash'ing, thresh'ing** *n.* act of thrashing grain, etc.; corporal punishment; flogging.—**thrash'-ing-, thresh'ing-floor** *n.* space on which grain is thrashed.—**thrash'ing-, thresh'ing-machine'**, or **-mill** *n.* agricultural machine for thrashing grain.—**to thrash out**, to argue about from every angle [O.E. *therscan*, to beat].

thrasonical (thrā-soń-ik-al) *a.* boastful; bragging.—**thrason'ically** *adv.* [fr. *Thraso*, a braggart in Terence's *Eunuchus*].

thraw (thraw) *v.t.* (*Scot.*) to twist; to wrench.—**thrawn** *a.* twisted; obstinate; perverse [var. of *throw*].

thread (thred) *n.* very thin twist of wool, cotton, linen, silk, etc.; filament as of gold, silver; prominent spiral part of screw; (*Fig.*) consecutive train of thought;—*v.t.* to pass thread through eye of needle; to string together, as beads; to pick one's way with careful deliberation.—**thread'bare** *a.* worn away with wear; shabby; (*Fig.*) hackneyed; trite.—**thread'-worm** *n.* thread-like parasitic worm often found in intestines of children.—**thread'y** *a.* consisting of thread; resembling thread [O.E. *thrawan*, to twist].

threat (thret) *n.* declaration of determination to harm another; menace.—**threat'en** *v.t.* to menace; to declare intention to do harm to; to portend.—**threat'ener** *n.*—**threat'ening** *a.* menacing; portending something undesirable; (of clouds or sky) lowering.—**threat'eningly** *adv.*—**threat'ful** *a.* forbidding [O.E. *threatnian*, to urge].

three (thrē) *a.* two and one;—*n.* sum of two and one; symbol of this sum, 3 or iii.—**three'-cor'nered** *a.* having three corners; triangular; of an election contest, having candidates of three political parties.—**three'-fold** *a.* triple.—**three'hand'ed** *a.* (of cards. esp. Bridge) played with three players and dummy.—**three-legged race,** race run by pairs of competitors, right leg of one being tied to left leg of other.—**threepenny bit** (thrĕp', or -thriṕ-ni-bit) formerly, British coin worth three pennies.—**three'-ply** *a.* having three layers or thicknesses; having three strands twisted together, as wool.—**three'-quar'ter** *n.* (*Rugby*) one of the four backs behind half-backs.—**three'score** *a.* and *n.* sixty.—**three'some** *n.* game (as golf) played by three players; dance performed by three people.—**the three R's**, reading, writing, arithmetic [O.E. *threo*, three].

threnody (threń-o-di) *n.* song of lamentation; elegy; dirge. Also **thren'ode.**—**threnet'ic, -al, threno'dial, threnod'ic** *a.* pert. to threnody; funereal.—**thren'odist** *n.* [Gk. *thrēnos*, lament; *odē*, song].

thresh See **thrash.**

threshold (thresh́-ōld) *n.* door-sill; piece of wood or stone immediately under door [O.E. *therscan*, to thresh; *wald*, wood].

threw (thrôô) *pa.t.* of **throw.**

thrice (thrīs) *adv.* three times; repeatedly; much, as in *thrice blessed* [O.E. *thriwa*].

thrift (thrift) *n.* thriving condition; economical management; frugality; plant, the sea-pink.—**thrift'ily** *adv.*—**thrift'iness** *n.* frugality.—**thrift'less** *a.* extravagant; wasteful.—**thrift'lessly** *adv.*—**thrift'y** *a.* (*comp.* **thrift'ier;** *superl.* **thrift'iest**) economical; frugal; sparing [fr. *thrive*].

thrill (thril) *n.* emotional excitement; throb; quivering sensation running through nerves and body;—*v.t.* to pierce; to stir deeply; to arouse tingling emotional response;—*v.i.* to feel a glow of excitement, enthusiasm, etc.—**thrill'er** *n.* novel, play, or film, etc. with sensational plot.—**thrill'ing** *a.* causing a thrill; exciting.—**thrill'ingly** *adv.* [O.E. *thyrlian*, to bore a hole].

thrive (thrīv) *v.i.* to prosper; to grow abundantly; to develop healthily.—*pa.t.* **throve** and **thrived.**—*pa.p.* **thriven** (thriv́-n) **thrived.**—**thri'ving** *a.* flourishing; prosperous.—**thri'vingly** *adv.* [O.N. *thrifa*, to grasp].

throat (thrōt) *n.* forepart of neck; passage connecting back of mouth with lungs, stomach, etc.; narrow entrance.—**throat'iness** *n.* quality of having throaty or muffled voice.—**throat'y** *a.* guttural; muffled [O.E. *throte*, the throat].

throb (throb) *v.i.* to pulsate; to beat, as heart, with more than usual force.—*pr.p.* **throb'bing.**—*pa.t.* and *pa.p.* **throbbed.**—*n.* pulsation; palpitation (of heart, etc.); beat [etym. doubtful].

throe (thrō) *n.* suffering; pain;—*pl.* pains of childbirth.—**to be in the throes of,** to be struggling with a difficult task [O.E. *thrawa*, suffering].

thrombosis (throm-bṓ-sis) *n.* formation of blood clot in vein or artery during life [Gk. *thrombos*, a lump, a clot].

throne (thrōn) *n.* chair of state; royal seat;

bishop's seat in his cathedral; sovereign power and dignity;—*v.t.* to place on royal seat; to exalt.—*pr.p.* **thron'ing**.—*pa.p.* **throned** [Gk. *thronos*, a seat].

throng (throng) *n.* multitude; crowd;—*v.t.* to mass together; to press in crowds [O.E. *thringan*, to press].

throstle (thros'l) *n.* the song-thrush or mavis [O.E. *throstle*, a thrush].

throttle (throt'l) *n.* windpipe; valve controlling pressure of steam;—*v.t.* to choke by external pressure on windpipe; to shut off steam in steam-engine; (*Fig.*) to suppress; to silence;—*v.i.* to pant for breath, as if suffocated; to open or close throttle of an engine.—**to throttle down**, to slow down by closing throttle [dim. of *throat*].

through (thrōō) *prep.* from end to end of; going in at one side and out the other; by passing between; across; along; by means of; as consequence of;—*adv.* from one end or side to the other; from beginning to end.—*a.* (of railway train) passing from one main station to another without intermediate stops; unobstructed, as *through-road*.—**through and through**, completely.—**through'ly** *adv.* thoroughly.—**throughout'** *adv.* and *prep.* wholly; completely; during entire time of.—**to pull through**, to recover from serious illness [O.E. *thurh*, through].

throw (thrō) *v.t.* to fling, cast, or hurl; to propel; to send; to venture, at dice; to twist into thread, as silk; to mould clay; to unseat, as of a horseman; to shed, as snake's skin; to produce offspring, as animal; to spread carelessly;—*v.i.* to cast dice; to hurl.—*pr.p.* **throw'ing**.—*pa.t.* **threw**.—*pa.p.* **thrown**.—*n.* the act of throwing; round in wrestling-match.—**throw'-back** *n.* one who in his characteristics reverts to ancestral type.—**throw'er** *n.* one who or that which throws.—**thrown** *a.* twisted.—**to throw down the gauntlet**, to challenge.—**to throw light on**, to elucidate.—**to throw up**, to eruct hurriedly; to vomit.—**to throw up the sponge**, to admit defeat [O.E. *thrawan*, to throw].

thrum (thrum) *n.* fringe of threads left on loom after web is cut off [O.N. *thromr*, edge].

thrum (thrum) *v.t.* to strum on instrument; to play carelessly; to drum with fingers [O.N. *thruma*, rattle].

thrush (thrush) *n.* song-bird, esp. mavis or throstle [O.E. *thrysce*].

thrush (thrush) *n.* (*Med.*) inflammatory disease affecting mouth, tongue and lips, commonly found in young children; a disease affecting the feet of horses, etc. [O.E. *thyrre*, dry].

thrust (thrust) *v.t.* to push or drive with sudden force; to pierce; to obtrude;—*v.i.* to make a push; to attack with a pointed weapon; to intrude; to push way through.—*pa.t.* and *pa.p.* **thrust**.—*n.* stab; attack; assault; horizontal outward pressure as of arch against its abutments; stress acting horizontally, as in machinery; (*Geol.*) upward bulge of layer of rock due to lateral pressure.—**thrust'er** *n.*—**thrust'ful** *a.* energetic; self-assertive.—**thrust'fully** *adv.*—**thrust'fulness** *n.* [Scand. *thrysta*, to press].

thud (thud) *n.* dull sound made by blow or heavy fall;—*v.i.* to make sound of thud; [O.E. *thoden*, noise].

thug (thug) *n.* one of band of professional robbers and assassins of N. India (suppressed in 1830's) who strangled or poisoned victims; cut-throat ruffian; (*U.S.*) gangster.—**thug'gery, thug'gism** *n.* gangsterism.

Thule (thū'lē) *n.* name in ancient times for most northerly parts of Europe, esp. Orkneys, Shetlands, Iceland, etc.—**ultima Thule**, furthest north of known world [Gk. *Thoulē*].

thulium (thū'li-um) *n.* (*Chem.*) metallic element belonging to rare earths, chemical symbol **Tm**.—**thul'ite** *n.* silicate of aluminium and calcium; also called *zoisite* [fr. *Thulē*].

thumb (thum) *n.* short, thick finger of human hand; part of glove which covers this;—*v.t.* to manipulate awkwardly; to soil with thumb-marks; (*Slang*) to hold up thumb, to solicit lift in motor-car.—**thumbed** *a.* having thumbs; soiled with thumb-marks.—**thumb'-in'dex** *n.* system of indexing in which right-hand edges of leaves of notebook or ledger are indented and marked with letters of alphabet to facilitate reference.—**thumb'kin** *n.* a thumb-screw.—**thumb'-nail** *n.* nail on human thumb.—**thumb-nail sketch**, miniature; succinct description.—**thumb'stall** *n.* sheath like a glove thumb for injured thumb.—**thumb'screw** *n.* old instrument of torture by which thumb was compressed till the joint broke.—**by rule of thumb**, by rough and ready method [O.E. *thuma*, a thumb].

thump (thump) *n.* blow of fist; sudden fall of heavy body or weight; thud;—*v.t.* to beat with something heavy;—*v.i.* to strike or fall with a thud.—**thump'er** *n.*—**tub'-thump'er** *n.* (*Slang*) street-corner orator.—**thump'ing** *a.* very large; much exaggerated [imit.].

thunder (thun'der) *n.* rumbling sound which follows lightning-flash; any very loud noise;—*v.t.* to declaim or rage with loud voice;—*v.i.* to rumble with thunder; to roar.—**thun'der-bolt** *n.* flash of lightning followed by peal of thunder; (*Fig.*) anything totally unexpected and unpleasant.—**thun'der-clap** *n.* a peal of thunder.—**the thunderer**, the god Jupiter; (*Colloq.*) *The Times* newspaper.—**thun'dering** *n.* thunder; booming, as of guns.—*a.* making a loud noise; (*Colloq.*) outstanding; excessive.—**thun'derous** *a.* thundery; booming like thunder.—**thun'derously** *adv.*—**thun'der-plump** *n.* torrential rainfall accompanied by thunder.—**thun'der-storm** *n.* storm of thunder and lightning with torrential rain.—**thun'der-struck** *a.* struck by lightning; (*Fig.*) speechless with amazement.—**thun'dery** *a.* pert. to thunder; sultry.—**to steal someone's thunder**, to win applause expected by someone else [O.E. *thunian*, to rattle].

thurible (thū'ri-bl) *n.* a metal censer.—**thu'rifer** *n.* one who carries and swings a thurible [L. *thus*, *thuris*, frankincense].

Thursday (thurz'dā) *n.* fifth day of week, after *Thor*, Scandinavian god of thunder.

thus (THus) *adv.* in this or that manner; to this degree or extent; so; in this wise.—**thus'wise** *adv.* in this manner.—**thus far**, so far [O.E. *thus*, by this].

thwack (thwak) *v.t.* to beat; to flog; to belabour;—*n.* heavy blow; a hard slap [O.E. *thaccian*, to stroke].

thwart (thwawrt) *a.* lying across; transverse; athwart;—*v.t.* to hinder; to frustrate; to baulk;—*n.* seat across or athwart a rowing-boat;—*adv.* and *prep.* across.—**thwar'ting** *a.*—**thwart'ships** *adv.* across the ship [O.N. *thvert*, perverse].

thy (THī) *poss. a.* of thee; belonging to thee [contr. fr. *thine*).

thyme (tīm) *n.* small flowering-shrub cultivated for its aromatic leaves for use as flavouring in cookery [Gk. *thumon*].

thymus (thī'mus) *n.* small ductless gland in upper part of chest; corresponds to sweet-bread of calves and lambs [Gk.].

thyroid (thī'roid) *a.* having shape of shield; signifying cartilage of larynx or a gland of trachea.—**thyroid gland**, ductless gland situated in neck on either side of trachea, secreting hormone which profoundly affects physique and temperament of human beings [Gk. *thureos*, a shield; *eidos*, a form].

thyself (THī-self) *pron. reflex.* or *emphatic*, of a person, thou or thee.

tiara (tī-àr'a) *n.* lofty ornamental turban worn by ancient Persian kings and dignitaries; triple, gem-studded crown worn by Pope on ceremonial occasions; gem-studded head-dress or coronet worn by ladies [Gk. *tiara*, head-dress].

tibia (tib′i-a) *n.* shin-bone; inner and usually larger of two bones of leg, between knee and ankle.—*pl.* **tib′iae.**—**tib′ial** *a.* pert. to tibia; pert. to Roman flute, the tibia [L. *tibia*, shin-bone].
tic (tik) *n.* spasmodic twitching of muscle, esp. of face [Fr. *tic*, twitching].
tick (tik) *n.* a parasitic blood-sucking insect which infests esp. sheep, cows, etc. [M.E. *teke*].
tick (tik) *n.* cover of bed-mattress, pillow, etc. stuffed with feathers, wool, kapok, etc.—**tick′ing** *n.* specially strong cotton or linen material used for mattress covers, etc. [Gk. *thēkē*, a case].
tick (tik) *n.* (*Slang*) credit; trust;—*v.i.* to give credit [*abbrev.* of *ticket*].
tick (tik) *v.i.* to make small, recurring, clicking sound, as watch; to beat steadily; —*n.* sound made by watch ticking; (*Colloq.*) very short time.—**tick′er** *n.* anything which ticks regularly; (*Colloq.*) watch or clock; tape-machine; the heart [imit.].
tick (tik) *v.t.* to mark or dot lightly;—*n.* small mark placed after word, item, entry, etc., esp. in checking; very small piece.—**ticked** *a.* spotted.—**to tick off,** (*Colloq.*) to rebuke [M.E. *tek*, a touch].
ticket (tik′et) *n.* piece of carboard or paper entitling admission to anything, to travel by public transport, to participate in function, lottery, etc.;—*v.t.* to mark with ticket.—**tick′et-of-leave** *n.* permit to convict to be at liberty with certain restrictions, before expiry of his sentence.—**season ticket,** ticket entitling holder to attend a series of concerts, lectures, etc. or to travel daily between certain specified stations over a certain period of time [O.Fr. *etiquet*, label].
tickle (tik′l) *v.t.* to touch skin lightly so as to excite nerves and cause laughter; to titillate; to amuse;—*v.i.* to feel sensation of tickling; to itch; to be gratified.—**tick′ler** *n.*—**tick′lish** *a.* difficult to understand or solve; requiring skilful handling.—**tick′lishly** *adv.*—**tick′lishness** *n.* [freq. of *tick*, to touch lightly].
tidbit Same as **titbit.**
tiddler (tid′lẹr) *n.* (*Colloq.*) stickleback.
tiddley (tid′li) *a.* (*Slang*) intoxicated.
tiddley-winks (tid′li-wingks) *n.pl.* game in which players try to flick small counters into dice-cup [etym. uncertain].
tide (tīd) *n.* time; season, as in *eventide, Eastertide*; periodical rise and fall of ocean due to attraction of moon and sun; (*Fig.*) trend.—**to tide over,** to manage temporarily; to surmount meantime.—**ti′dal** *a.* pert. to tide. —**tidal basin,** harbour which is affected by tides.—**tidal wave,** mountainous wave as caused by earthquake, atom-bomb explosion, etc.—**tide′gate** *n.* gate which is opened to let water flow into basin at high tide, and shut to prevent water flowing out at ebb-tide.—**tide′less** *a.* having no tides.—**tide′-tab′le** *n.* table giving times, throughout year, of highwater at principal sea-ports of the country.—**tide′-wat′er** *n.* part of river estuary affected by tides.—**tide′-way** *n.* channel in which tide sets.—**ebb,** or **low, tide,** the falling level of the sea.—**flood,** or **high, tide,** the rising level of the sea.—**neap tide,** minimum tide.—**spring tide,** maximum tide [O.E. *tid*, time].
tidings (tī′dingz) *n.pl.* news; information [O.N. *tithindi*, to happen].
tidy (tī′di) *a.* neat; orderly; (*Colloq.*) comfortable; of fair size;—*n.* chair-back cover; ornamental receptacle on dressing-table, for hair-combings, etc.;—*v.t.* to put in order; to titivate.—*pa.t.* and *pa.p.* **ti′died.**—**ti′dily** *adv.*—**ti′diness** *n.* [M.E. *tidy*, timely].
tie (tī) *v.t.* to fasten by rope, string, etc.; to fashion into knot; to bind together, as rafters, by connecting piece of wood or metal; (*Fig.*) to hamper; (*Mus.*) to connect two notes with tie;—*v.i.* (*Sport*) to make equal score, etc.—*pr.p.* **ty′ing.**—*pa.t.* and *pa.p.* **tied.**—*n.* knot; necktie; fastening; connecting-link; equality of score; draw; one of series of matches in which losing teams are eliminated, till two remaining winning sides play final match; (*Mus.*) curved line connecting two notes indicating that sound is sustained for length of both notes; (*U.S.*) railway-sleeper.—**tie′-beam** *n.* horizontal timber connecting two rafters.—**ti′er** *n.* one who ties [O.E. *teah*, a rope].
tier (tēr) *n.* row or rank, esp. when two or more rows are arranged behind and above the other [Fr. *tirer*, to draw].
tierce (tērs) *n.* cask containing third of pipe or 42 wine gallons; cask containing 336 or 304 lbs.; third of canonical hours or service at 9 a.m.; in fencing, particular thrust (third position); (*Mus.*) two octaves and a third.—**tier′cet** *n.* See **tercet** [Fr. *tiers*, third].
tiff (tif) *n.* slight quarrel. Also **tift.**—*v.i.* to be in the huff [etym. uncertain].
tiffany (tif′a-ni) *n.* kind of gauze or very thin silk [Gk. *Theophania*, festival of manifestation of God].
tiffin (tif′in) *n.* (*Anglo-Ind.*) lunch.—**tiff** *v.i.* to have lunch [fr. E. *tiff*, draught].
tig (tig) *n.* children's game in which player chases another until he touches him;—*v.t.* to touch thus [form of *tag*].
tiger (tī′gẹr) *n.* (*fem.* **ti′gress**) fierce carnivorous quadruped of cat tribe, with tawny black-striped coat; (*U.S.*) jaguar; (*S. Afr.*) leopard; (of person) first-rate sportsman.—**ti′ger-cat** *n.* wild cat; ocelot or margay.—**ti′g(e)rish** *a.* like a tiger; fierce; rapacious.—**ti′ger-lil′y** *n.* tall Chinese lily with flaming orange flowers spotted with black.—**ti′ger-moth** *n.* any of the varieties of moths with dark streaked or spotted wings.—**ti′ger-shark** *n.* voracious shark of East Indian waters [Gk. *tigris*].
tight (tīt) *a.* firm; compact; compressed; not leaky; fitting close or too close to body; neat; tense; restricted for want of money; dangerous; (*Colloq.*) mean; (*Slang*) drunk; finicky;—*adv.* firmly.—**tight′en** *v.t.* to make tight or tighter; to make taut;—*v.i.* to become tight or tighter.—**tight′ener** *n.*—**tight′ly** *adv.*—**tight′ness** *n.*—**tight′rope** *n.* a strong, taut rope, or steel wire on which rope-dancers perform. —**tights** *n.pl.* close-fitting woven hose and trunks worn by acrobats, dancers, etc. [O.N. *thettr*, watertight].
tike (tīk) *n.* a dog; a cur; a boorish fellow; a Yorkshireman [O.N. *tik*, a cur].
tilde (til′dā) *n.* the mark ( ) placed over the letter *n* in Spanish, to indicate a following *y* sound, as in cañon (canyon).
tile (tīl) *n.* a thin piece of slate or baked clay, used for roofs, walls, floors, drains, etc.; (*Slang*) a silk top-hat;—*v.t.* to cover with tiles.—**ti′ler** *n.* one who makes or lays tiles; the doorkeeper at a Freemasons' lodge; a kiln for firing tiles. Also **ty′ler.**—**ti′lery** *n.* a place where tiles are made [L. *tegula*].
tilka (til′ka) *n.* the Hindu caste-mark on the forehead [Sans.].
till (til) *n.* a money-box or drawer in a shop counter; a cash-register [etym. doubtful].
till (til) *prep.* as late as; until;—*conj.* till the time when [M.E. *til*, up to].
till (til) *v.t.* to cultivate; to plough the soil, sow seeds, etc.—**till′age** *n.* the act of preparing the soil for cultivation; the cultivated land.—**till′er** *n.* [O.E. *tilian*, to till].
till (til) *n.* boulder-clay [etym. uncertain].
tiller (til′ẹr) *n.* a bar used as a lever, esp. for turning a rudder [O.Fr. *tellier*, a weaver's beam].
tilt (tilt) *v.t.* to raise one end of; to tip up; to thrust, as a lance; to forge with a tilt-hammer;—*v.i.* to charge on horseback with a lance, as in a tournament; to heel over;—*n.* a thrust, as with a lance; a medieval sport in which competitors armed with lances charged each other; a tilt-hammer; inclination forward.—**tilt′er** *n.*—**tilt′-ham′mer** *n.* a heavy

hammer used in iron works and tilted by a wheel.—**to run full tilt**, to run very rapidly [O.E. *teall*, tottering].

tilt (tilt) *n.* a tent; the canvas covering of a cart; a small canvas awning over the stern-sheets of a boat;—*v.t.* to cover with an awning [O.E. *teld*, a tent].

tilth (tilth) *n.* act of tilling; cultivated land [O.E. *tilian*, to till].

Tim (tim) *n.* the 'speaking clock' which answers the time to telephone subscribers.

timbal (tim′bal) *n.* kettledrum [Sp. *timbal*, a kettledrum].

timber (tim′bėr) *n.* trees felled and prepared as building material; trees collectively; single unit of wooden framework of house; rib of ship;—*v.t.* to furnish with timber.—**tim′bered** *a.* furnished with timber; built of timber; well-wooded.—**tim′ber-line** *n.* tree-line, above which altitude trees will not grow [O.E. *timber*, material for building a house].

timbre (tam′br, tim′bėr) *n.* special tone-quality in sound of human voice or instrument [Fr. *timbre*].

timbrel (tim′brel) *n.* kind of drum, or tambourine [O.Fr. *timbre*].

time (tīm) *n.* particular moment; period of duration; conception of past, present, and future, as sequence; epoch; system of measuring duration, as *Greenwich time*; opportunity; occasion; (*Mus.*) rhythmical arrangement of beats within measures or bars;—*pl.* period characterised by certain marked tendencies, as *Victorian times*; term indicating multiplication, as *four times four*;—*v.t.* to ascertain time taken, as by racing competitor; to select precise moment for; (*Mus.*) to measure;—*v.i.* to keep or beat time.—**time′-bomb** *n.* delayed-action bomb.—**time′-gun** *n.* gun fitted with an electrical device which causes it to fire at a given time.—**time′-hon′oured** *a.* revered because of age; venerable.—**time′-keep′er** *n.* one who keeps a record of men's hours of work; clock or watch.—**time′-lag** *n.* period of time which elapses between cause and its effect.—**time′-less** *a.* eternal; unending.—**time′lessly** *adv.*—**time′-lim′it** *n.* time permitted for completion or expiry of anything.—**time′liness** *n.*—**time′ly** *a.* in good time; opportune.—**timeous, timous** (tīm-us) *a.* (*Scots Law*) in good time.—**time′ously, tim′ously** *adv.*—**time′-piece** *n.* clock.—**tim′er** *n.* a stop-watch.—**time′-serv′er** *n.*—**time′-serv′ing** *n.* selfish opportunism.—**time′-ta′ble** *n.* tabulated list of duties; roster; booklet containing times of departure and arrival of trains, buses, steamers, etc.—**time′-work** *n.* work paid for at so much an hour, or day, opp. to *piece-work*.—**time′-worn** *a.* aged; decayed.—**tim′ing** *n.*—**Greenwich time**, British standard time as settled by passage of sun over meridian at Greenwich.—**to do time** (*Slang*) to serve sentence of imprisonment.—**to mark time**, to keep feet moving on one spot; (*Fig.*) to delay [O.E. *tima*, *time*].

timid (tim′id) *a.* wanting courage; lacking in self-confidence; shy.—**timid′ity** *n.* shyness; diffidence.—**tim′idly** *adv.*—**tim′idness** *n.*—**tim′orous** *a.* frightened; very timid.—**tim′orously** *adv.*—**tim′orousness** *n.* [L. *timidus*, faint-hearted].

timocracy (tī-mok′ra-si) *n.* government in which possession of property is necessary qualification for holders of offices [Gk. *timē*, honour; *kratos*, power].

timothy (tim′ō-thi) *n.* timothy-grass grown for hay, and valued as fodder.

timpano, tympano (tim′pa-nō) *n.* kettle-drum, esp. as part of percussion section of orchestra.—*pl.* **tim′pani, tym′pani** [Gk. *tumpanon*, a kettledrum].

tin (tin) *n.* soft, whitish-grey metal, very malleable and ductile, used for tin-plating, as constituent of alloys (e.g. pewter, bronze) and for food-containers in canning industry; tin-can; (*Slang*) money;—*a.* made of tin or plated with tin;—*v.t.* to plate with tin; to preserve, as food, in an air-tight tin-plated container.—*pr.p.* **tin′ning**.—*pa.p.* and *pa.t.* **tinned**.—**tin′foil** *n.* wafer-thin sheets of tin; so-called 'silver-paper.'—**tin′-op′ener** *n.* gadget for opening tins containing food, etc.—**tinned** *a.* preserved in a tin; plated with tin.—**tin′ner, tin′man** *n.* a tin-miner; one who makes tin-plate.—**tin′ning** *n.*—**tin′ny** *a.* like tin; making a sound like tin when struck.—**tin′-plate** *n.* sheet-iron coated with tin, to protect it from oxidation.—**tin′-pot** *a.* valueless; trivial.—**tin′smith** *n.* worker in tin or tin-plate industry.—**tin′type** *n.* (*Photog.*) ferrotype; positive on varnished tin-plate.—**tin′-ware** *n.* utensils, etc. made of tin [O.E. *tin*, tin].

Tin Pan Alley (tin′pan-a′li) (*U.S. Slang*) the world of the composers of popular music.

tincture (tingk′tūr) *n.* tinge or shade of colour; (*Fig.*) faint taste; veneer; (*Pharm.*) solution of a substance in alcohol;—*v.t.* to tinge; to imbue; (*Fig.*) to affect to a small degree [L. *tinctura*, dyeing].

tinder (tin′dėr) *n.* anything inflammable used for kindling fire from a spark [O.E. *tynder*, tinder].

tine (tīn) *n.* tooth or prong of fork; spike of harrow; branch of deer's antler.—**tined** *a.* spiked [O.E. *tind*, point].

ting (ting) *n.* sharp, metallic sound, as of bell; tinkle;—*v.t.* and *v.i.* to tinkle.—**ting′-a-ling** *adv.* tinkling repeatedly [imit.].

tinge (tinj) *v.t.* to colour slightly; to imbue; to temper.—*pr.p.* **ting(e)′ing**—*n.* a faint touch [L. *tingere*, to dye].

tingle (ting′gl) *v.i.* to feel faint thrill or pricking sensation;—*v.t.* to ring;—*n.* pricking sensation [prob. freq. of *ting*].

tinker (tingk′ėr) *n.* mender of pots, kettles, etc., esp. one who travels round countryside; rough and ready worker; (*Colloq.*) an untidy person;—*v.i.* to do the work of a tinker.—**to tinker away at**, to potter about trying to repair things [M.E. *tinker*, one who makes a sharp sound].

tinkle (tingk′l) *v.t.* to cause to make small, quick, metallic sounds; to clink;—*v.i.* to make series of quick, sharp sounds; to jingle;—*n.* small, sharp, clinking sound.—**tink′ling** *n.* [M.E. *tinken*, to chink].

tinsel (tin′sel) *n.* very thin, glittering, metallic sheets, used in strips for decorations, etc.; dress fabric with metallic threads interwoven; (*Fig.*) anything showy or flashy;—*a.* gaudy; showy and cheap;—*v.t.* to decorate with tinsel; to make gaudy.—*pr.p.* **tin′selling** *pa.t.* and *pa.p.* **tin′selled**.—**tin′selly** *a.* showy; meretricious [Fr. *étincelle*, a spark].

tint (tint) *n.* hue or dye; faint tinge; colour with admixture of white;—*v.t.* to give faint colouring to; to tinge; to stipple [L. *tinctus*, dyed].

tintinnabulation (tin-tin-ab-ū-lā′shun) *n.* tinkling sound of bells pealing.—**tintinnab′-ulant, tintinnab′ular, tintinnab′ulary, tintinnab′-ulous** *a.* [L. *tintinnare*, to jingle].

tiny (tī′ni) *a.* (*comp.* **ti′nier**; *superl.* **ti′niest**) very small; diminutive. Also **teen′y** (child's form of word) [etym. uncertain].

tip (tip) *n.* point of anything small; end;—*v.t.* to form a point on; to cover tip of.—*pr.p.* **tip′ping**.—*pa.p.* **tipped**.—**tip′toe** *adv.* on tips of toes;—*v.t.* to walk on tips of toes; to walk stealthily.—**on tiptoe**, quietly; all agog.—**tip′-staff** *n.* officer carrying metal-tipped staff; constable; staff itself.—**tip′top** *n.* highest or utmost degree;—*a.* first-rate [var. of *top*].

tip (tip) *v.t.* to touch lightly; to tap; to tilt; to cant, as liquid; to weigh down, as scales; (*Slang*) to give useful hint to, esp. about betting odds; to recompense with small gratuity;—*v.i.* to fall to one side; to give gratuity;—*n.* light stroke; private information; advice; gratuity; refuse-dump.—**tip'ping** *n.*—**tip'ster** *n.* one who sells tips regarding horse-racing, etc.—**tip'-tilt'ed** *a.* (of a nose) slightly turned up; retrousse.—**tip'-up** *a.* (of seats) tilting backwards to allow people room to pass along.—**to tip off,** to warn [M.E. *tipen,* to overthrow].

tippet (tip'et) *n.* short cape of cloth or fur [L. *tapete,* tapestry].

tipple (tip'l) *v.i.* to drink small quantities frequently; to indulge habitually in intoxicating drinks;—*v.t.* to drink excessively;—*n.* strong drink.—**tipp'ler** *n.* [Scand. *tipla,* to drink little and often].

tipsy (tip'si) *a.* intoxicated; staggering.—**tip'sily** *adv.*—**tip'siness** *n.*—**tip'sy-cake** *n.* sponge-cake soaked in sherry [fr. *tipple*].

tirade (tī-rād') *n.* long denunciatory speech; diatribe; volley of abuse [It. *tirata,* a drawing out].

tire (tīr) *v.t.* to weary or fatigue;—*v.i.* to become wearied, bored, or impatient.—**tired** *a.* wearied; bored.—**tired'ness** *n.*—**tire'less** *a.* unwearied; indefatigable.—**tire'lessly** *adv.*—**tire'some** *a.* exhausting; dull; provoking [O.E. *tiorian,* to be tired].

tire (tīr) *n.* attire; apparel; head-dress;—*v.t.* to dress.—**tir'ing-house** or **-room** *n.* part of theatre where actors dress [short for *attire*].

tire, tyre (tīr) *n.* hoop of iron placed round a wheel; solid rubber hoop round carriage-wheels; outer rubber tube of cycle or motor-car wheel [form of *attire*].

tiro (tī'rō) *n.* beginner; novice. Also (incorrectly) **ty'ro** [L. *tiro,* recruit].

tisane (tē-zan') *n.* medicinal tea; infusion of herbs. Also **ptisan'** [Fr. fr. Gk. *ptisanē,* barley gruel].

tissue (tish'ū) *n.* fine cloth interwoven with gold or silver or with figured colours; (*Biol.*) any of cellular structures which make up various organs of plant or animal body; unbroken series; web;—*a.* made of tissue;—*v.t.* to make into tissue.—**tis'sued** *a.* made of or resembling tissue.—**tis'sue-pa'per** *n.* very soft, white or coloured semi-transparent paper [Fr. *tissu,* fr. L. *texere,* to weave].

tit (tit) *n.* small bird, e.g. titmouse [O.N. *tittr,* a little bird].

tit (tit) *n.* small blow, as in phrase, **tit for tat,** blow for blow; retaliation.

tit (tit) *n.* teat [O.E. *tit,* a nipple].

Titan (tī'tan) *n.* (*fem.* **Ti'taness**) (*Gk. Myth.*) one of sons of Uranus and Ge (Heaven and Earth); person of magnificent physique or of brilliant intellectual capacity;—*a.* pert. to Titans; colossal; mighty.—**Titan'ic** *a.* pert. to Titans; epic; colossal.

titanium (tī-tā'ni-um) *n.* metallic chemical element.—**tita'nian, titan'ic, titanit'ic, titanif'erous, ti'tanous** *a.* pert. to, or containing, titanium.—**ti'tanite** *n.* compound of titanium and silicate of calcium. Also called *sphene* [fr. *titan*].

titbit (tit'bit) *n.* choice morsel. Also **tid'bit** [Scand. *tittr,* a small bird].

tithe (tīth) *n.* tenth part; orig. tenth part of produce of land and cattle allotted to upkeep of Church and clergy, later paid in form of tax; small portion;—*v.t.* to levy a tithe.—**ti'ther** *n.* tithe-gatherer [O.E. *teotha,* tenth].

Titianesque (tish-an-esk') *a.* pert. to, or in manner of, *Titian,* Italian painter.—**Tit'ian** *a.* rich auburn; from colour of hair in many portraits by Titian.

titillate (tit'il-lāt) *v.t.* to tickle, usually in sense of stimulating mind, palate, etc.—**titilla'tion** *n.* process of titillating; any pleasurable sensation.—**titilla'tive** *a.* [L. *titillare,* to tickle].

titivate (tit'i-vāt) *v.i.* and *v.t.* (*Slang*) to put finishing touches to one's general appearance [perh. fr. *tidy*].

titlark (tit'lárk) *n.* titling; pipit [fr. *tit*].

title (tī'tl) *n.* inscription put over, or under, or at beginning of, anything; designation; appellation denoting rank or pre-eminence; that which constitutes just claim or right; (*Law*) legal proof of right of possession; title-deed.—**ti'tled** *a.* having title, esp. aristocratic title.—**ti'tle-deed** *n.* document giving proof of legal ownership of property.—**ti'tle-leaf,** or **-page** *n.* page of book on which is inscribed name of book and author.—**ti'tle-role** *n.* part in play from which it takes its name [L. *titulus,* title].

titmouse (tit'mous) *n.* small bird which builds in holes of trees; tit; tomtit.—*pl.* **tit'mice** [M.E. *tit,* small; *mase,* name for several small birds].

titrate (tī'trāt) *v.t.* to determine amount of ingredient in solution by adding quantities of standard solution until required chemical reaction is observed.—**titra'tion** *n.* [Fr. *titre,* title].

titter (tit'er) *v.i.* to give smothered laugh; to giggle;—*n.* giggle; restrained laugh.—**titt'erer** *n.* [imit.].

tittle (tit'l) *n.* minute particle; whit; jot [L. *titulus,* superscription, small stroke to indicate contraction].

tittup (tit'up) *v.i.* to prance about in carefree manner [imit].

titular (tit'ū-lar) *a.* pert. to or of title; nominal; ruling in name but not in deed.—**titular'ity** *n.*—**tit'ularly** *adv.*—**tit'ulary** *a.* titular;—*n.* nominal holder of title [L. *titulus,* a title].

tmesis (tmē'sis) *n.* separation of two parts of compound word by one or more interpolated words, as 'from *what* direction *soever*' [Gk. fr. *temnein,* to cut].

to (tóó) *prep.* expressing motion towards; as far as; regarding; unto; upon; besides; compared with; as to; expressing purpose, as in gerundial infinitive; indicating dative case or indirect object; preceding infinitive mood of the verb; (*U.S.*) involved in;—*adv.* forward; into customary position; on [O.E. *to,* to].

toad (tōd) *n.* amphibian of genus *Bufo,* resembling frog, but brownish with dry warty skin, and short legs; (*Fig.*) mean, detestable person.—**toad'-in-the-hole** *n.* meat or sausages cooked in batter.—**toad'stool** *n.* fungus resembling mushroom, but poisonous.—**toad'y** *n.* obsequious flatterer; social parasite;—*v.i.* to flatter excessively; to fawn on.—*pr.p.* **toad'ying.**—*pa.t.* and *pa.p.* **toad'ied.**—**toad'yism** *n.* sycophancy [O.E. *tadige,* a toad].

toast (tōst) *v.t.* to dry or warm by exposure to fire; to crisp and brown (as bread) before fire, under grill, etc.; to drink to health of, or in honour of;—*v.i.* to drink a toast;—*n.* slice of bread crisped and browned on both sides by heat of fire, etc.; orig. piece of toasted bread soaked in wine; person in whose honour toast is drunk; lady whose popularity is acknowledged by frequent toasts in her honour.—**toast'er** *n.* one who or that which toasts; electrical table device for toasting bread.—**toast'ing-fork,** or **-iron** *n.* long-handled fork for toasting bread, etc. at open fire.—**toast'-mast'er** *n.* one who formally announces toasts at public function [L. *tostus,* roasted].

tobacco (to-bak'ō) *n.* plant of genus *Nicotiana,* dried leaves of which are used for chewing, smoking, or as snuff.—*pl.* **tobacc'os.**—**tobacc'onist** *n.* one who sells tobacco, cigarettes, matches, etc. [Sp. *tabaco*].

toboggan (to-bog'an) *n.* sledge used for coasting down snow-clad hill slopes;—*v.i.* to slide down hills on sledge. Also **tobog'an, tabog'gan, tobog'gin.**—**tobog'ganing** *n.* [Amer.-Ind.].

toby (tō'bi) *n.* small jug in shape of an old man wearing a three-cornered hat [fr. *Toby,* personal name].

toccata (tok-kà'ta) *n.* (*Mus.*) composition for organ or piano which tests player's technique and touch [It.].

Toc H (tok āch) *n.* society organised to keep alive the spirit of comradeship in the war of 1914-18. Its first meetings were held at Talbot House, Poperinghe.
tocsin (tok′sin) *n.* alarm-bell or its ringing sound [Fr.].
today, to-day (tòò-dā′) *n.* this day; present day; *adv.* on this day; at the present time [O.E. *to-daege*, today].
toddle (tod′l) *v.i.* to walk with short, hesitating steps, as child; (*Colloq.*) to stroll.—**todd′ler** *n.* child just learning to walk [prob. form of *totter*].
toddy (tod′i) *n.* fermented juice of certain E. Indian palm-trees; drink of whisky, sugar, and hot water [Hind. *tari*, juice of palm-tree].
to-do (tòò-dòò′) *n.* a commotion; a fuss [fr. *to* and *do*].
toe (tō) *n.* one of five small digits of foot; forepart of hoof; part of boot, shoe, or stocking covering toes; outer end of head of golf-club;—*v.t.* to touch or reach with toe.—**toe′-cap** *n.* additional cap of leather on the toe of boot or shoe.—**toed** *a.* having toes [O.E. *ta*, the toe].
toff (tof) *n.* (*Slang*) a dandy; a swell [etym. doubtful].
toffee, toffy (tof′i) *n.* hard sweetmeat made of sugar, butter, flavouring, etc. boiled together [etym. uncertain].
tog (tog) *n.* (*Slang*) dress.—usu. in *pl.*—*v.i.* to dress [prob. fr. L. *toga*, a robe].
toga (tō′ga) *n.* loose outer garment worn by Roman citizens.—**toga′ted, to′ged** *a.* wearing a toga [L. fr. *tegere*, to cover].
together (tòò-geTH′ẹr) *adv.* in company; in or into union; simultaneously; in same place [O.E. *to*, to; *geador*, together].
toggle (tog′l) *n.* (*Naut.*) cigar-shaped bar of wood put through eye of rope, to prevent it slipping through loop of another rope; cross-piece at free end of watch-chain;—*v.t.* to fix with toggle [etym. uncertain].
toil (toil) *v.i.* to labour; to move with difficulty;—*n.* exhausting labour; drudgery; exertion; task.—**toil′er** *n.* one who works hard.—**toil′ful, toil′some** *a.* laborious.—**toil′somely** *adv.*—**toil′someness** *n.*—**toil′worn** *a.* weary with toil; (of hands) hard and lined with toil [O.Fr. *touiller*, to entangle].
toil (toil) *n.* a net or snare; mesh.—usu. *pl.* [Fr. *toile*, cloth].
toilet (toil′et) *n.* orig. dressing-table or its cover; process of dressing; mode of dressing; a lavatory. Also **toilette** (twą-let′).—**toil′et-glass** *n.* mirror for dressing-table.—**toil′et-pa′per** *n.* thin paper for lavatory use.—**toil′et-pow′der** *n.* talcum powder [Fr. *toilette*, dim. of *toile*, cloth].
Tokay (tō-kā′) *n.* sweet aromatic wine made at *Tokay* in Hungary.
token (tō′kẹn) *n.* sign; symbol; concrete expression of esteem; card issued with stamp of certain value and exchangeable for goods, as *book-token*.—**to′ken-pay′ment** *n.* deposit paid as token of later payment of full debt [O.E. *tacen*, symbol].
told (tōld) *pa.t.* and *pa.p.* of verb **tell.**
tolerate (tol′ẹr-āt) *v.t.* to suffer to be done; to endure.—**tol′erable** *a.* endurable; supportable; passably good.—**tolerabil′ity, tol′erableness** *n.*—**tol′erably** *adv.*—**tol′erance** *n.* forbearance.—**tol′erant** *a.* forbearing; long-suffering; broad-minded.—**tol′erantly** *adv.*—**tolera′tion** *n.* act of tolerating; practice of allowing people to worship as they please; granting to minorities of political liberty. -**tolera′tor** *n.* [L. *tolerare*, to bear].
toll (tōl) *n.* tax, esp. for right to use bridge, ferry, public road, etc.; portion of grain retained by miller as payment for grinding; cross-roads where toll was formerly exacted from travellers.—*v.i.* to exact toll.—**toll′bar** *n.* formerly bar which could be swung across road to stop travellers liable to pay toll.—**toll′booth, tol′booth,** *n.* orig. temporary booth erected for payment of tolls, esp. in market-place; (*Scot.*) town gaol.—**to take toll of,** to cause great loss [O.E. *toll*, tax].
toll (tōl) *v.t.* to cause to ring slowly, as bell, esp. to signify death;—*v.i.* to peal with slow, sonorous sounds;—*n.* sound of bell tolling [M.E. *tollen*, to pull].
Tom (tom) *n.* short for *Thomas*.—**tom** *n.* used to denote male animal as *tom-cat*.—**tom′boy** *n.* hoyden; romping, mischievous girl.—**tom′fool** *n.* complete fool.—**tomfool′ery** *n.* nonsensical behaviour.—**Tom Thumb,** midget.
tomahawk (tom′ą-hawk) *n.* war-hatchet used by N. American Indians;—*v.t.* to wound or kill with tomahawk [Amer.-Ind.].
tomato (to-mà′tō) *n.* plant with red or yellow fruit much used in salads.—*pl.* **toma′toes** [Sp. *tomate*].
tomb (tòòm) *n.* a grave; underground vault; stone erected over a grave.—**tomb′stone** *n.* stone erected over grave [Gk. *tumbos*, a sepulchral mound].
tombola (tom′bō-la) *n.* kind of lottery [It. fr. *tombolare*, to tumble].
tome (tōm) *n.* a book; a large, heavy volume [Gk. *tomos*, a piece cut off].
tommy (tom′i) *n.* bread; rolls; provisions, esp. as formerly given to workmen instead of wages.—**Tommy Atkins,** British Army private.—**tomm′y-rot** *n.* (*Slang*) utter nonsense. —**tomm′y-shop** *n.* shop providing tommy under tommy-system.
tommy-gun (tom′i-gun) *n.* automatic short-barrelled, light machine-gun [fr. inventor General John *Thompson*].
tomorrow, to-morrow (tòò-mor′ō) *n.* day after today;—*adv.* on the following day [O.E. *to*, and *morgen*, morning].
tompion (tom′pi-on) *n.* stopper of gun barrel; inking-pad of lithographic printer. Also **tom′pon** [var. of *tampion*].
tomtit (tom′tit) *n.* a small bird, the titmouse [fr. *tit* as in *titmouse*].
tom-tom (tom′tom) *n.* small drum used by Indian and African natives; a gong. Also **tam′tam** [Hind.].
ton (tun) *n.* (var. of **tun**) weight consisting of 20 cwt. or 2240 lb; measure of capacity varying according to article being measured;.—*pl.* (*Colloq.*) great amount or number.—**ton′nage** *n.* cubical content (100 cub. ft.) or burden (40 cub. ft.) of ship in *tons*; duty on ships estimated per ton; shipping collectively assessed in tons. Also **tun′nage** [O.E. *tunne*, vat].
ton (tōng) *n.* fashion; latest mode.—**tonish, tony** (tō′nish, tō′ni) *a.* very fashionable [Fr.].
tone (tōn) *n.* quality or pitch of musical sound; modulation of speaking or singing voice; colour-values of picture; (*Mus.*) one of larger intervals of diatonic scale, smaller intervals being called *semitones*; [*Med.*) natural healthy functioning of bodily organs; general character, as of manners, morals, or sentiment; (*Gram.*) stress on one syllable of word;—*v.t.* to give tone or quality to; to modify colour or general effect of, as in photograph; to tune (instrument);—*v.i.* to blend (with).—**to′nal** *a.* pert. to tone.—**tonal′ity** *n.* quality of tone or pitch; system of variation of keys in musical composition; colour-scheme of picture.—**to′nally** *adv.*—**tone′-deaf** *a.* unable to distinguish musical intervals.—**toned** *a.* having tone.—**tone′-poem** *n.* descriptive orchestral composition.—**to tone down,** to modify, as loudness of sound, brilliance of colour, or intensity of feelings, etc.—**to tone in,** to cause to harmonise;—*v.i.* to blend (with).
tonga (tong′ga) *n.* a light, two-wheeled vehicle used in India [Hind.].
tong (tong) *n.* secret society in China [Chin. *t'ang*, meeting-place].
tongs (tongz) *n.pl.* implement consisting of pair of pivoted levers, for grasping, e.g. pieces of coal. [O.E. *tange*, tongs].

tongue (tung) *n.* flexible muscular organ in mouth used in tasting, swallowing, and for speech; facility of utterance; language; anything shaped like a tongue; flame; clapper of bell; narrow spit of land; slip of wood fitting into groove;—*v.t.* to modulate with tongue as notes of flute; to chide;—*v.i.* to use tongue as in playing staccato passage on flute; to chatter.—**tongued** *a.* having a tongue.—**tongue-tied** *n.* having tongue defect causing speech-impediment; (*Fig.*) speechless through shyness.—**tongue'-twist'er** *n.* number of words, usually alliterative, difficult to repeat rapidly.—**to hold one's tongue,** to be silent. [O.E. *tunge*].

tonic (ton'ik) *a.* pert. to tones or sounds; having an invigorating effect, bodily or mentally;—*n.* a medicine which tones up the system; anything invigorating; (*Mus.*) a key-note.—**ton'ically** *adv.*—**toni'city** *n.*—**tonic sol-fa,** a system of musical notation in which the sounds are represented by syllables, as *doh, ray, me, fah,* etc. [Gk. *tonos,* tension].

tonight, to-night (tòò-nīt') *n.* this night; night following this present day;—*adv.* on this night [fr. *to* and *night*].

tonite (tō'nīt) *n.* explosive made of gun-cotton and nitrate of barium [L. *tonare,* to thunder].

tonnage (tun'āj) *n.* See **ton.**

tonneau (ton'ō) *n.* back portion of body of motor-car [Fr.=a cask].

tonsil (ton'sil) *n.* one of two oval-shaped lymphoid organs on either side of pharynx.—**tonsil(l)i'tis** *n.* inflammation of the tonsils [L. *tonsillae,* tonsils].

tonsure (ton'shūr) *n.* act of shaving part of head as token of religious dedication; shaved crown of priest's head.—**ton'sor** *n.* barber.—**tonso'rial** *a.* pert. to shaving.—**ton'sured** *a.* shaven; having a tonsure [L. *tonsura,* clipping].

tontine (ton'tēn) *n.* form of joint annuity whereby sum received by subscribers increases as their number decreases, until with death of last survivor the tontine completely lapses.—**tontin'er** *n.* [fr. *Lorenzo Tonti,* 17th cent. Italian, the originator].

too (tòò) *adv.* over; in addition; more than enough; moreover [stressed form of *to*].

took (tòòk) *pa.t.* of **take.**

tool (tòòl) *n.* implement or utensil operated by hand, or by machinery; cutting or shaping part of a machine; means to an end;—*v.t.* to cut, shape, or mark with a tool, esp. to chisel stone; to indent a design on leather book-cover, etc. with pointed tool.—**tool'ing** *n.* [O.E. *tol,* a tool].

toot (tòòt) *v.t.* to cause to sound, as a motor-horn;—*n.* unmusical sound; hoot.—**toot'le** *n.* small toot;—*v.i.* to blow succession of short, sharp sounds, as on flute, horn, etc. [imit.].

tooth (tòòth) *n.* bone projection in gums of upper and lower jaws of vertebrates, used in mastication; prong as of comb, saw, rake; cog of wheel.—*pl.* **teeth.**—*v.t.* to provide with teeth; to indent; to interlock.—**tooth'ache** *n.* pain in teeth.—**tooth'brush** *n.* small brush for cleaning teeth.—**tooth'comb** *n.* small comb with teeth very close together.—**toothed** *a.* having teeth.—**tooth'ful** *n.* small glass of spirits.—**tooth'glass** *n.* small tumbler for mixing mouth-wash.—**tooth'pick** *n.* small pointed quill or stick for removing particles of food lodged between teeth.—**tooth'some** *a.* palatable; pleasant to taste.—**tooth'y** *a.* having prominent teeth; toothed.—**a sweet tooth,** fondness for sweet things to eat [O.E. *toth,* a tooth].

top (top) *n.* highest part of anything; upper side; highest rank; first in merit, as of examination-candidates; green part above ground of root vegetable; (*Naut.*) platform surrounding head of lower-mast. Also *pl.* **tops.**—*a.* highest; most eminent; excellent;—*v.t.* to cover on the top; to rise above; to cut off top of; to hit, as golf-ball, above centre; to surpass;—*v.i.* to be outstanding.—*pr.p.* **top'ping.**—*pa.t.* and *pa.p.* **topped.**—**top'boot** *n.* riding-boot with band of light-coloured leather round the top.—**top'coat** *n.* overcoat.—**top'ful** *a.* brimming over.—**top'hat** *n.* tall silk-hat.—**top'heav'y** *a.* unbalanced; having top too heavy for base.—**top'hole** *a* (*Slang*) excellent.—**top'most** *a.* supreme; highest.—**top'notch** *a.* describing persons of high ability or anything which is super-excellent.—**top'per** something placed on the top; one who excels; (*Slang*) top-hat; good sport.—**top'ping** *n.* act of lopping off top of something, as highest branches of tree; what is cut off;—*a.* (*Colloq.*) first-rate.—**top'pingly** *adv.*—**top'sail** *n.* square sail on top-mast.—**top'soil** *n.* surface layer of soil [O.E. *top,* summit].

top (top) *n.* child's toy made to spin on its pointed end, by means of a string or by whipping [etym. doubtful].

topaz (tō'paz) *n.* gem-stone, translucent and of varied colours [etym, uncertain].

tope (tōp) *v.i.* to drink hard or to excess.—**to'per** *n.* [Fr. *toper,* to clinch bargain (or 'wet' it)].

topee (tō-pē') *n.* cork or pith helmet worn by Europeans in tropical climates. Also **topi'** [Hind. *topi,* hat].

topia (tō'pi-a) *n.* mural decoration comprising landscapes, popular in Roman houses.—**to'piary** *a.* pert. to landscape gardening; cut into ornamental shapes, as trees, hedges, etc. Also **topa'rian.** -**to'piarist** *n.* [L. *topia,* ornamental gardening].

topic (top'ik) *n.* subject of essay, discourse, or conversation; branch of general subject.—**top'ical** *a.* pert. to a place; up-to-date; concerning local matters.—**top'ically** *adv.* [Gk. *topos,* a place].

topography (to-pog'ra-fi) *n.* description of a place; scientific description of physical features of region.—**topog'rapher** *n.*—**topograph'ic, -al** *a.*—**topograph'ically** *adv.* [Gk. *topos,* a place; *graphein,* to write].

topology (to-pol'o-ji) *n.* use of place-names as an aid to memory, by associating things with particular town or region [Gk. *topos,* a place; *logos,* a discourse].

topple (top'l) *v.t.* to throw down; to overturn;—*v.i.* to overbalance [freq. of *top*].

topsy-turvy (top'si-tur'vi) *adv.* upside down;—*a.* turned upside down;—*n.* disorder; chaos [prob. O.E. *top,* and *tearflian,* to roll].

toque (tōk) *n.* small, brimless hat worn by women [Fr.].

tor (tor) *n.* pointed hill [O.E. *torr,* a heap].

torch (torch) *n.* piece of wood or rope soaked in inflammable liquid, and used as portable light.—**torch'bear'er** *n.* one who carries a torch.—**electric torch,** small hand-light containing electric battery and bulb, operated by sliding switch [L. *torquere,* to twist].

tore (tōr) *pa.t.* of **tear.**

toreador (tor-e-a-dor') *n.* bull-fighter [Sp. fr. L. *taurus,* a bull].

torment (tor'ment) *n.* extreme pain of body; anguish of mind; misery; cause of anguish.—**torment'** *v.t.* to inflict pain upon; to torture; to vex; to tease.—**torment'ing** *a.* -**torment'ingly** *adv.*—**tormen'tor,** **tormen'ter** *n.* (*fem.* **tormen'tress**) [L. *tormentum,* instrument of torture].

torn (tōrn) *pa.p.* of **tear.**

tornado (tor-nā'dō) *n.* violent gust of wind; whirling progressive wind-storm causing wide-spread devastation.—*pl.* **torna'does** [Sp. *tronada,* thunder-storm].

torpedo (tor-pē'dō) *n.* cigar-shaped under-water projectile with high explosive charge; type of explosive mine; electric ray, fish which electrocutes its prey.—*pl.* **torpe'does.**—*v.t.* to attack, hit, or sink with torpedoes.—**torpe'do-boat** *n.* a small, swift naval vessel armed chiefly with torpedoes.—**torpedo-boat destroyer** (*abbrev.* **T.B.D.**) now **destroyer**, fast warship armed with guns, torpedoes and anti-submarine equipment.—**torpe'doist** *n.* expert in handling and firing torpedoes [L. *torpere*, to be numb].

torpid (tor'pid) *a.* numb; lethargic; physically or mentally inert.—**torpid'ity** *n.* inactivity; lethargy.—**tor'pidly** *adv.*—**tor'pidness** *n.*—**tor'pitude** *n.* torpidity.—**tor'por** *n.* numbness; sluggishness; mental inertia.—**torporif'ic** *a.* causing torpor [L. *torpere*, to be numb].

torque (tork) *n.* collar of gold wires twisted together, worn by ancient Britons, Gauls, etc. Also **torc**; (*Mech.*) rotating force in mechanism.—**torqued** *a.* wreathed [L. *torquere*, to twist].

torrefy (tor'e-fī) *v.t.* to scorch; to parch; to roast, as metals.—**torrefac'tion** *n.* [L. *torrere*, to burn; *facere*, to make].

torrent (tor'ent) *n.* swift-flowing stream; downpour, as of rain; (*Fig.*) rapid flow as of words;—*a.* rushing.—**torren'tial** *a.* pert. to, or resembling torrent; overwhelming.—**torren'tially** *adv.* [L. *torrens*, a boiling stream].

torrid (tor'id) *a.* parched; dried with heat; arid.—**torrid'ity**, **tor'ridness** *n.*—**torrid zone**, broad belt lying between Tropics of Cancer and Capricorn [L. *torrere*, to burn].

torsion (tor'shun) *n.* act of turning or twisting; (*Mech.*) force with which twisted wire or similar body tends to return to original position.—**tor'sional** *a.*—**torsion balance**, delicate scientific instrument for measuring minute forces by means of small bar suspended horizontally at end of very fine wire [L. *torquere*, to twist].

torso (tor'sō) *n.* trunk of human body; statue with head and limbs cut off [It.].

tort (tort) *n.* (*Law*) private injury to person or property for which damages may be claimed in court of law.—**tor'tious** *a.*—**tor'tiously** *adv.* [L. *torquere*, *tortum* to twist].

tortilla (tor-tē'lya) *n.* round, thin cake of maize, used in Mexico as bread substitute [Sp. dim. of *torta*, a tart].

tortoise (tor'tis or tor'toiz) *n.* toothless land reptile or turtle, encased in dome-shaped scaly box-like shell;—**tor'toise-shell** *n.* mottled brown outer shell of hawksbill tortoise used commercially for combs, etc.;—*a.* mottled like tortoiseshell [L. *tortus*, twisted].

tortuous (tor'tū-us) *a.* full of twists; crooked; devious; circuitous; deceitful.—**tor'tuose** *a.* wreathed; twisted.—**tortuos'ity** *n.*—**tor'tuously** *adv.*—**tor'tuousness** (L. *tortuosus*, fr. *torquere*, to twist].

torture (tor'tūr) *n.* act of deliberately inflicting extreme pain as punishment or reprisal, esp. to extort information or confession; anguish; torment;—*v.t.* to put to torture; to inflict agony on.—**tor'turer** *n.*—**tor'turing** *a.* agonising; causing torment [L. *tortura*, twisting].

Tory (tō'ri) *n.* member of Conservative party in British politics; orig. supporter of Stuarts in 17th cent.—**To'ryism** *n.* [Ir. *toruighe*, a pursuer].

tosh (tosh) *n.* (*Slang*) rubbish; nonsense.

toss (tos) *v.t.* to throw upwards with a jerk; to cause to rise and fall; to agitate violently;—*v.i.* to be tossed; to roll and tumble; to be restless;—*n.* fling; sudden fall from horseback; distance anything is tossed.—**toss'er** *n.* one who tosses.—**toss'ing** *n.*—**toss'pot** *n.* heavy drinker.—**a toss-up**, spinning of coin to decide issue; even chance.—**to toss off**, to swallow in one gulp; to execute work easily and quickly [W. *tosio*, to jerk].

tot (tot) *n.* anything small, esp. a child; small drinking-cup; a dram [Scand. *tottr*, dwarf].

tot (tot) *v.t.* to add; to count up;—*n.* column of addition [*abbrev.* of *total*].

total (tō'tal) *a.* full; complete; utter; absolute;—*n.* the whole; sum; aggregate;—*v.t.* to sum; to add;—*v.i.* to amount to.—**totalita'rian** *a.* relating to one-party dictatorial form of government.—**to'talisator**, **to'taliser**, (*Colloq.*) **the tote** *n.* automatic betting-machine at horse and dog races.—**total'ity** *n.* whole sum; entirety.—**to'tally** *adv.*—**to'talness** *n.* [L. *totus* whole].

tote (tōt) *v.t.* to carry; to bear; to transport.—**to'ter** *n.* [etym. uncertain].

totem (tō'tem) *n.* natural object, such as animal or plant, taken by primitive tribe as emblem of their mysterious, hereditary relationship with that object; image of this.—**to'tem-pole** *n.* ornamental staff with 'totem' carved on one end [Amer.-Ind.].

totter (tot'er) *v.i.* to walk with faltering steps; to sway; to shake; to reel.—**tott'erer** *n.*—**tott'ering** *a.* shaky; insecure.—**tott'eringly** *adv.*—**tott'ery** *a.* shaky; unsteady [O.E. *tealt*, unsteady].

toucan (tóó-kân', or tóó'kan) *n.* bird of Brazil with very long orange beak and black plumage [Braz.].

touch (tuch) *v.t.* to come in contact with; to finger; to reach; to attain to; to concern; to meddle with; to treat of, superficially; to move deeply; to equal in merit; to play on; (*Slang*) to borrow from;—*v.i.* to be in contact; to take effect on;—*n.* contact; sense of feeling; quality of response in handling of instrument or colour; individual style of execution; unique quality; trace or tinge; test; mild attack; (*Football*) part of field beyond touch-lines.—**touch'able** *a.* capable of being touched.—**touch'ableness** *n.*—**touch and go**, precarious situation.—**touch down** (*Rugby*) handling of ball on ground behind goal-line.—**touched** *a.* (*Slang*) crazy.—**touch'er** *n.*—**touch'ily** *adv.*—**touch'iness** *n.*—**touch'ing** *a.* emotionally moving; pathetic;—*prep.* concerning; referring to.—**touch'ingly** *adv.*—**touch'ingness** *n.*—**touch'judge** *n.* linesman at rugby match.—**touch'line** *n.* side line of rugby—or football-field.—**touch'stone** *n.* Lydian stone, variety of compact, siliceous schist, used for testing purity of gold and silver by streak impressed by it on stone; (*Fig.*) criterion; standard of judgment.—**touch'y** *a.* easily offended; hypersensitive.—**to touch at** (of ships) to call at.—**to touch on**, to refer to briefly [Fr. *toucher*, to touch].

tough (tuf) *a.* flexible but not brittle; not easily broken; firm; difficult to chew; stout-hearted; vigorous; hardy; difficult to solve; (*U.S. Slang*) vicious;—*n.* a bully; a gangster.—**toughen'** *v.t.* to make tough, or hardy;—*v.i.* to become tough.—**tough'ish** *a.* rather tough.—**tough'ly** *adv.*—**tough'ness** *n.* [O.E. *toh*, tough].

toupee (tóó-pē') *n.* tuft or artificial lock of hair to cover bald patch. Also **toup'et** [Fr. *toupet*, a tuft of hair].

tour (tóór) *n.* journey from place to place in a country; excursion; spell of duty;—*v.t.* to travel round; to visit as part of tour.—**tour'er** *n.* open motor-car. Also **tour'ing-car**.—**tour'ism** *n.*—**tour'ist** *n.* one who makes a tour; sightseer [Fr. *tour*, a turn].

tourmalin(e) (tóór'ma-lin) *n.* crystalline mineral; of various colours, and lustrous, it is used for optical instruments, and for gems [fr. Singh. *toramalli*, cornelian].

tournament (tóór'na-ment) *n.* mock-fight, common form of contest and entertainment in medieval times; any sports competition or championship.—**tour'ney** *n.* a tournament [O.Fr. *tournoiement*, a turning].

tourniquet (tóór'ni-kā, or -ket) *n.* surgical instrument for arresting haemorrhage by compression; a bandage, pad, or first aid device, tightened and periodically released by means of a small stick or pencil inserted in a knot, and used to arrest bleeding in accidental injury [Fr. fr. *tourner*, to turn].

touse (touz) *v.t.* to pull; to haul; to tear;—*v.i.* to tear about.—**tous'er** *n.*—**tous'le** *v.t.* to make untidy by pulling, as hair; to dishevel.—**tous'led** *a.* untidy.—**tous'y** *a.* shaggy; unkempt [conn. with *tussle*].

tout (tout) *v.i.* to solicit custom; to cadge for orders;—*n.* one who pesters people to be customers; hanger-on at racing-stables [O.E. *totian*, to peep out].

tow (tō) *v.t.* to drag through water by rope; to pull along with rope;—*n.* act of pulling; rope used for towing; course fibre of hemp used in rope-making.—**tow'age** *n.* act of or charge for towing.—**tow'(ing)-path** *n.* path alongside canal used by horses towing canal barge.—**to take in tow,** to pull along; (*Fig.*) to take charge of [O.E. *togian*, to pull].

toward (tō'ȧrd) **towards** (tō'ȧrdz) *prep.* in direction of; near (of time); with respect to; regarding;—*adv.* nearly; at hand [O.E. *toweard*, future].

towel (tou'ẹl) *n.* cloth for drying skin, or for domestic purposes.—**tow'elling** *n.* soft fabric for making towels.—**to throw in the towel,** to acknowledge defeat [O.H. Ger. *twahan*, to wash].

tower (tou'ẹr) *n.* lofty, round or square stone structure; citadel; fortress;—*v.i.* to be lofty or very high; to soar; to excel.—**tow'ered** *a.* having towers.—**tow'ering** *a.* lofty; (*Fig.*) violent [L. *turris*, tower].

town (toun) *n.* collection of houses etc., larger than village; inhabitants of town;—*a.* pert. to town.—**town'clerk** *n.* official in charge of administrative side of town's affairs.—**town'coun'cil** *n.* group of representatives, elected by ratepayers to manage municipal affairs.—**town'ship** *n.* district under administration of town-council; parish.—**towns'people** *n.* inhabitants of town [O.E. *tun*, an enclosure].

toxicology (tok-si-kol'o-ji) *n.* science of poisons, their effects, nature, etc.—**toxae'mia, toxe'mia, toxice'mia, toxicae'mia** *n.* blood-poisoning, caused by absorption into blood of toxins.—**toxae'mic, toxe'mic** *a.*—**tox'ic, -al** *a.* poisonous.—**tox'ically** *adv.*—**tox'icant** *a.* poisonous;—*n.* poison.—**toxicolog'ical** *a.*—**toxicol'ogist** *n.* one who studies toxicology.—**tox'in** *n.* poison usually of bacterial origin [Gk. *toxikon*, poison].

toxophilite (tok-sof'i-līt) *n.* student of, or expert in, archery.—**toxophilit'ic** *a.* [Gk. *toxon*, bow; *philos*, fond of].

toy (toi) *n.* child's plaything; bauble; trifle;—*v.i.* to dally; to trifle; [Dut. *tuig*, tool].

trace (trās) *n.* mark; footprint; vestige; minute quantity; remains; outline; barely perceptible sign;—*v.t.* to pass through; to copy or draw exactly; to follow track of; to work out step by step; to form laboriously; to walk or tread;—*v.i.* to move.—**trace'able** *a.* capable of being traced or detected; attributable.—**trace'ableness** *n.*—**trace'ably** *adv.*—**trac'er** *n.* one who traces.—**trac'er-bull'et** or **-shell** *n.* bullet or shell, path of which is indicated by trail of smoke or flame.—**tra'cery** *n.* ornamental openwork formed in head of Gothic window by the mullions diverging into arches, curves, etc.; any delicate and intricate pattern of lines.—**tra'cing** *n.* traced copy of drawing.—**tra'cing-pa'per** *n.* specially prepared, transparent paper for tracing design, etc. [L. *trahere*, to draw].

trace (trās) *n.* strap, rope, chain, by which horse pulls vehicle.—**trace'horse** *n.* draught-horse hitched on in front of horse and lorry to draw heavy loads up steep hill [Fr. fr. L. *trahere*, to draw].

trachea (trā'ke-a, trạ-kē'a) *n.* windpipe between lungs and back of throat.—*pl.* **trache'ae.**—**tra'cheal** *a.* pert. to the trachea.—**tracheo'tomy** *n.* (*Surg.*) operation by which opening is made in windpipe [Gk. *tracheia* (*artēria*), windpipe, and *trachēlos*, neck].

track (trak) *n.* mark left by something; footprint; pathway trodden out by usage; laid-out course for racing; (of railway) permanent way; (of motor-vehicles) distance between road-wheels on one axle; (of aircraft) actual direction along which aeroplane is passing over ground; wheelband of tank or tractor; (*Fig.*) evidence; trace;—*v.t.* to follow trail or traces of; to tow as boat by rope from bank;—*v.i.* (of wheels) to move so that rear wheels follow exactly on track of the front wheels; to move cinema-camera backwards, forwards, or in horizontal line while taking pictures.—**track'er** *n.* one who or that which tracks, or tows canal boat by rope.—**in one's tracks,** where one stands.—**sound'track** *n.* (*Cinema*) part of cinematograph film which records sounds accompanying it [O.Fr. *trac*, track of horse].

tract (trakt) *n.* region of indefinite extent; continuous period of time; dissertation; short treatise on practical religion.—**tractabil'ity** *n.* quality or state of being tractable.—**trac'table** *a.* docile; amenable to reason.—**trac'tableness** *n.*—**trac'tably** *adv.*—**trac'tile** *a.* capable of being drawn out; (of metals) ductile.—**tractil'ity** *n.*—**trac'tion** *n.* act of drawing solid body along a plane.—**trac'tional** *a.*—**trac'tion-en'gine** *n.* locomotive, steam-driven, for haulage.—**trac'tive** *a.* having power to haul heavy loads; pulling.—**trac'tor** *n.* traction-engine; motor-vehicle for drawing agricultural machinery [L. *trahere, tractum*, to draw].

Tractarian (trakt-ār'i-ạn) *n.* one of the writers of *Tracts of the Times*, published at Oxford in 1830's and 1840's.—**Tractar'ianism** *n.* doctrine advocating breaking away from extreme Protestant rationalism of Anglican Church, and return to ritualism and sacramental emphasis of early Catholic Church; Oxford Movement [fr. *tract*].

trade (trād) *n.* the business of buying and selling; commerce; barter; occupation, esp. in industry, shopkeeping, etc.; employees collectively in a particular trade; vocation;—*v.t.* to carry on a trade; to engage in commerce;—*v.t.* to exchange.—**trade'mark** *n.* registered name or device on maker's goods.—**trade'name** *n.* registered name given by manufacturer to proprietary article.—**trade'price** *n.* price of commodities as sold by wholesalers to retailers.—**trad'er** *n.* merchant (wholesale or retail); trading-vessel.—**trade'-show** *n.* preview of a film shown to cinema managers, press critics, etc.—**trades'man** *n.* shopkeeper; skilled workman.—**trade'un'ion, trades'un'ion** *n.* legally recognised association of workmen, clerks, etc. for purpose of securing their rights, safe-guarding wage-scales, and preventing exploitation by employers.—**trade'un'ionist** *n.* member of trade-union.—**trade'wind** *n.* one of two prevailing winds which blow steadily between the tropics and the Equator; in Northern Hemisphere it is N.E. wind, in Southern Hemisphere, S.E.—**trad'ing** *n.*—**to trade on,** to exploit [O.E. *tredan*, to tread].

tradition (trạ-dish'un) *n.* belief, custom, narrative, etc. transmitted by word of mouth from age to age; religious doctrine not recorded in writing, but preserved orally from generation to generation.—**tradi'tional, tradi'tionary** *a.* handed down from age to age [L. *tradere*, to hand over].

traduce (trạ-dūs)' *v.t.* to defame the character of; to calumniate.—**traduce'ment** *b.* calumny.—**tradu'cer** *n.* a slanderer [L. *traducere*, to lead along].

traffic (traf'ik) *n.* commerce; barter; illegal buying and selling, as *drug-traffic*; movement of people, vehicles, etc. to and fro, in streets; coming and going of ships, railway-trains, aircraft, etc.; people, vehicles, etc. collectively in any given area;—*v.i.* to carry on trade; to do business, esp. illegally;—*v.t.* to barter.—*pr.p.* **traff'icking.**—*pa.t.* and *pa.p.* **traff'icked.**—**traffica'tor** *n.* movable arrow-indicator by which motorist signals intention to turn left or right.—**traff'icker** *n.*—**traff'ic-lights** *n.pl.* indicator fitted with red, amber and green lights erected at street crossings to control traffic [Fr. *trafiquer*, to traffic].

tragedy (traj′e-di) *n.* serious and dignified dramatic composition in prose or verse with unhappy ending, principal characters being victims of circumstance, environment, or of fatal flaw in character; sad or calamitous event.—**trage′dian** *n.* actor in or writer of tragedy.—**trage′dienne** *n. fem.*—**trag′ic, -al** *a.* pert. to tragedy; distressing; calamitous.—**trag′ically** *adv.*—**tragic irony,** use in tragedy of words which convey a deeper meaning to audience than to speaker—form of *dramatic irony*.—**trag′i-com′edy** *n.* drama combining tragedy and comedy [Gk. *tragos*, goat; *aeidein*, to sing.—prob. because actors wore goat skins, or goat was prize].

trail (trāl) *v.t.* to draw along ground or through water; to drag; to follow track of; to carry rifle loosely in hand, parallel with ground; to make a track by treading the ground;—*v.i.* to dangle loosely, touching ground; to grow to great length as plant; to drag one foot wearily after other;—*n.* track followed by hunter; visible trace left by anything; scent of hunted animal; anything drawn to length; part of gun-carriage which rests on ground during firing; mode of carrying rifle at trailing position; tail of meteor.—**trail′er** *n.* vehicle towed by another; (*Cinema*) advance excerpt shown as advertisement of coming film.—**trailing edge** (*Aero.*) rear-edge of aircraft's wing [O.Fr. *trailler*, to tow a boat].

train (trān) *v.t.* orig. to entice; to draw along; to discipline; to instruct or educate; to submit person to arduous physical exercise, etc. for athletics; to teach animal to be obedient, to perform tricks, or compete in races; to cause plant to grow in certain way; to turn, as gun, in a certain direction, before firing;—*v.i.* to exercise body or mind to achieve high standard of efficiency;—*n.* retinue; procession of people; line of carriages drawn by locomotive on railway-track; trailing back-folds of lady's evening dress; string of pack-animals; sequence of events, ideas, etc.; trail of gunpowder to lead fire to explosive charge.—**train′-band** *n.* body of citizens trained for home defence, established in London in 14th cent.—**train′-bear′er** *n.* one who carries train of high official's robe, bride's dress, etc.—**trained** *a.* skilled; proficient; fully qualified.—**train′ee** *n.* one who is training to be a skilled worker, esp. in industry.—**train′er** *n.* one who supervises training of athletes, horses, dogs, etc.—**train′ing** *n.*—**train′ing-coll′ege,** *n.* for instruction in practice and theory of teaching.—**train′ing-ship** *n.* vessel for training boys in seamanship.—**to put in train,** to set things going; to make necessary preparations [O.Fr. *trahiner*, to drag].

train-oil (trān′oil) *n.* oil extracted from blubber of whales [O.Dut. *traen*, whale oil].

trait (trā or trāt) *n.* distinguishing feature, esp. in character; (rare) stroke; touch [Fr. *trait*, a feature].

traitor (trā′tor) *n.* (*fem.* **trait′ress**) one who betrays person, country, or cause.—**trait′orous** *a.* guilty of treachery; pert. to treason or to traitors.—**trait′orously** *adv.* [L. *tradere*, to hand over].

traject (tra-jekt′) *v.t.* to throw across; to cast through.—**tra′ject** *n.* ferry.—**trajec′tion** *n.* crossing; act of throwing across.—**trajec′tory** *n.* curve of projectile in its flight through space [L. *trans*, across; *jacere*, to throw].

tram (tram) *n.* tramcar; public vehicle running on rails on roadway; truck, tub, etc. running on rails;—*v.t.* to convey by tram;—*v.i.* to travel by tram.—**tram′-line** *n.* one of two rails on roadway on which tramcar runs;—*pl.* (*Colloq.*) parallel lines down sides of tennis-court.—**tram′-way** *n.* system for transport of passengers by tramcars [etym. doubtful].

trammel (tram′el) *n.* long net for catching birds or fishes; shackle for training horse to walk slowly; anything which impedes movement;—*v.t.* to impede; to hinder; to confine.—*pr.p.* **tramm′elling.**—*pa.p.* **tramm′elled** [O.Fr. *tramail*, a net].

tramp (tramp) *v.t.* to tread heavily; to walk over or through;—*v.i.* to go on a walking tour; to plod; to wander as vagrant;—*n.* homeless vagrant; a long walk; cargo-boat with no regular route.—**tramp′er** *n.* [M.E. *trampen*, to tramp].

trample (tram′pl) *v.t.* to tread heavily underfoot; (*Fig.*) to oppress; to treat with contempt;—*v.i.* to tread rapidly;—*n.* act of trampling.—**tramp′ler** *n.* [freq. of *tramp*].

trampolinist (tram-pol-in′ist) *n.* a gymnast or circus performer who uses a spring-board [It. *trampolino*, a spring-board].

trance (trans) *n.* state of complete insensibility, due to morbid nervous condition, or produced by hypnotism; condition in which human soul passes from body into another state of being; ecstasy [O.Fr. *transe*, a swoon].

tranquil (trang′kwil) *a.* calm; serene; undisturbed.—**tranquill′ity** *n.* state of being tranquil; serenity; composure (of mind).—**tran′quilness** *n.* [L. *tranquillus*].

trans- (tranz, trans) *pref.* meaning across, beyond, on the other side of [L. *trans*, across].

transact (tranz-akt′) *v.t.* to carry through; to negotiate;—*v.i.* to do (business).—**transac′tion** *n.* act of transacting business;—*pl.* records of, or lectures delivered to, a society.

transalpine (tranz-al′pīn) *a.* north of Alps (as from Rome).

transatlantic (tranz-at-lan′tik) *a.* across the [Atlantic.

transcend (tran-send′) *v.t.* to go beyond; to excel; to surpass.—**transcen′dence, transcen′dency** *n.* quality of being transcendent; (*Theol.*) supremacy of God above all human limitations.—**transcen′dent** *a.* supreme in excellence; surpassing all; beyond all human knowledge.—**transcenden′tal** *a.* abstruse; mystical; intuitive.—**transcenden′talism** *n.*—**transcenden′talist** *n.*—**transcenden′tally** *adv.* [L. *trans*, across; *scandere*, to climb].

transcontinental (tranz-kon-ti-nen′tal) *a.* crossing a continent.

transcribe (tran-skrīb) *v.t.* to copy out; to write over again; to reproduce in longhand or typescript notes taken in shorthand; (*Mus.*) to rearrange composition for another instrument or voice.—**transcrib′er** *n.*—**trans′cript** *n.* that which is transcribed; written copy.—**transcrip′tion** *n.* act of copying; transcript.

transect (tran-sekt′) *v.t.* to cut transversely.

transept (tran′sept) *n.* transverse portion of church at right angles to nave [L. *septum*, enclosure].

transfer (trans-fer′) *v.t.* to move from one place to another; to transport; to remove; to pass an impression from one surface to another, as in lithography, photography, etc.; to convey, as property, legally to another.—*pr.p.* **transfer′ring.**—*pa.t.* and *pa.p.* **transferred′.**—**trans′fer** *n.* removal from one place to another.—**transferabil′ity, transferribil′ity** *n.*—**trans′ferable, transfer′rible** *a.* capable of being transferred; valid for use by another.—**trans′ference** *n.* the act of transferring; in psycho-analysis, redirection of emotion, when under analytical examination, towards the analyst.—**thought′-trans′ference** *n.* telepathy.—**transfer′or, transfer′er** *n.* [L. *trans*, across; *ferre*, to bear].

transfigure (trans-fig′ūr) *v.t.* to change outward appearance of; to make more beautiful or radiant.—**transfigura′tion** *n.* change of form.—**The Transfiguration,** miraculous outward transformation of Christ when on the Mount with Peter, James and John (*Matt.* 17); festival on Aug. 6th commemorating this.

transfix (trans-fiks′) *v.t.* to pierce through; to impale; (*Fig.*) to astound; to stun.

transform (trans-form′) *v.t.* to change form, nature, character, or disposition of; to transmute;—*v.i.* to be changed.—**transform′able** *a.* capable of being changed.—**transforma′tion** *n.* change of outward appearance or inner nature.—**transfor′mator, transfor′mer** *n.* one who or that which transforms; an electrical device for changing voltage up or down.—**transfor′ming** *a.* [L. *transformare*, to change].

transfuse (tranz-fūz′) *v.t.* to pour, as liquid, from one receptacle into another; (*Med.*) to transfer blood from one person to vein of another in same blood-group; (*Fig.*) to imbue.—**transfu′sion** *n.* [L. *trans*, across; *fundere, fusum*, to pour].

transgress (tranz-gres′) *v.t.* to overstep a limit; to violate law or commandment;—*v.i.* to offend by violating a law; to sin.—**transgres′sion** *n.* act of violating civil or moral law; offence; crime.—**transgres′sor** *n.* [L. *transgredi, transgressus*, to step across].

tranship (tran-ship′) *v.i.* to convey or transfer from one ship to another.

transient (tran′zi-ent) *a.* fleeting; ephemeral; momentary; not permanent.—**tran′sience, tran′siency** *n.* the quality of being transient.—**tran′siently** *adv.* [L. *trans*, across; *ire*, to go].

transit (tran′zit) *n.* the act of conveying; conveyance; (*Astron.*) apparent passage of celestial body across meridian of a place, or of a smaller planet across disc of larger.—**trans′it-du′ty** *n.* charge payable on goods in cross-country transit.—**transi′tion** *n.* passage from one place to another; change from one state or condition to another; (*Mus.*) passing directly from one key to another.—**transi′tional, transi′tionary** *a.*—**transi′tionally** *adv.*—**trans′itive** *a.* having power of passing across; (*Gram.*) denoting verb the action of which passes on to direct object, as *he broke his leg.*—**trans′itively** *adv.*—**trans′itiveness** *n.*—**trans′itorily** *adv.*—**trans′itoriness** *n.* state of being transitory.—**trans′itory** *a.* continuing for a brief while only; ephemeral; transient.—**in transit,** phrase used of goods during period between leaving factory, shop, etc. and being received by retailer, purchaser, etc. [L. *transitus*, a passing across].

translate (tranz-lāt′) *v.t.* to remove from one place to another; to appoint bishop to different see; to convey to Heaven without death of physical body; to change from one medium to another; to turn from one language to another;—*v.i.* to be capable of translation.—**transla′tion** *n.*—**transla′tor** *n.* [L. *transferre, translatum*, to carry over].

transliterate (tranz-lit′e-rāt) *v.t.* to write words of language in alphabetic symbols of another.—**translitera′tion** *n.*—**translit′erator** *n.*

translucent (tranz-lòò′sent) *a.* semi-transparent; diffusing light but not revealing definite contours of object, as *frosted glass.*—**translu′cence, translu′cency** *n.*—**translu′cently** *adv.*—**translu′cid** *a.* translucent [L. *trans*, across; *lucere*, to shine].

transmigrate (tranz′mī-grāt) *v.i.* to pass from one country to another as permanent residence; (of soul) to pass at death into another body or state.—**transmigra′tion** *n.*—**trans′migrator** *n.*—**transmi′gratory** *a.*

transmit (tranz-mit′) *v.t.* to send from one person or place to another; to communicate; to hand on, as by heredity.—*pr.p.* **transmit′ting.**—*pa.t.* and *pa.p.* **transmit′ted.**—**transmissibil′ity** *n.*—**transmis′sible, transmit′tible** *a.* capable of being transmitted.—**transmis′sion** *n.* act of sending from one place or person to another; in motoring, gear by which power is transmitted from engine to live axle; (*Radio.*) radiation of ether waves by transmitting station; the relaying of a broadcast.—**transmit′tal** *n.* transmission.—**transmit′tance** *n.*—**transmit′ter** *n.* one who or that which transmits; apparatus for transmitting wireless waves through space [L. *trans*, across; *mittere*, to send].

transmogrify (tranz-mog′ri-fī) *v.t.* (*Colloq.*) to transform completely, as by magic.—**transmogrifica′tion** *n.* [coined word].

transmontane (tranz-mon-tān′) *a.* across, or beyond, the mountains.

transmute (tranz-mūt′) *v.t.* to change from one nature, species, form, or substance into another.—**transmu′table** *a.* capable of being changed in form.—**transmu′tableness** *n.*—**transmutabil′ity** *n.*—**transmu′tably** *adv.*—**transmu′tant** *a.*—**transmuta′tion** *n.* act or process of transforming; alteration, esp. biological evolution of one species into another; in alchemy, supposed change of baser metals into gold; (*Geom.*) reduction of figure or area to another having same superficial extent or solidity.—**transmu′tative** *a.*—**transmu′ter** *n.* [L. *trans*, across; *mutare*, to change].

transom (tran′sum) *n.* horizontal mullion or cross-bar in window; lintel; beam across stern-post of ship; any horizontal strut to give support [L. *transtrum*, cross-beam].

transparent (tranz-pār′ent) *a.* that may be distinctly seen through; pervious to light; clear; (*Fig.*) ingenuous; obvious.—**transpar′ence, transpar′ency** *n.*—**transpar′ently** *adv.*—**transpar′entness** *n.* [L. *trans*, across; *parere*, to appear].

transpire (tran-spīr′) *v.t.* to emit through pores of skin;—*v.i.* to exhale; (*Bot.*) to lose water by evaporation; (*Fig.*) to come out by degrees; wrongly used as a synonym for *to happen.*—**transpira′tion** *n.* [L. *trans*, across; *spirare*, to breathe].

transplant (tranz-plant′) *v.t.* to remove and plant elsewhere; (*Surg.*) to graft live tissue from one part of body to another.—**trans′plant′able** *a.*

transpontine (tranz-pon′tīn) *a.* lit. across the bridge; pert. to part of London on Surrey side of Thames; (of style) melodramatic, as supposedly characteristic of third-rate theatre shows in that district [L. *trans*, across; *pons*, a bridge].

transport (tranz-pōrt′) *v.t.* to convey from one place to another; to banish, as criminal, to penal colony; (*Fig.*) to overwhelm emotionally.—**trans′port** *n.* transportation; conveyance of people or commodities; vehicles collectively used in conveyance of passengers; a troop-ship; (*Fig.*) passion; ecstasy.—**transpor′table** *a.* capable of being conveyed.—**transporta′tion** *n.* act of transporting from place to place; banishment, for felony.—**transpor′ted** *a.* (*Fig.*) carried away with emotion [L. *trans*, across; *portare*, to carry].

transpose (tranz-pōz′) *v.t.* to change respective place or order of two things; to alter order of words; (*Mus.*) to change key of a composition.—**transpo′sable** *a.*—**transpo′sal** *n.* change of order.—**transposi′tion** *n.* act of putting one thing in the place of another; substitution; (*Mus.*) raising or lowering of key of a composition [L. *trans*, across; *ponere, positum*, to place].

trans-ship Same as **tranship.**

transubstantiate (tran-sub-stan′shi-āt) *v.t.* to change into another substance.—**transubstantia′tion** *n.* doctrine held by R.C. Church that the 'whole substance' of the bread and wine in the Eucharist is, by reason of its consecration, changed into flesh and blood of Christ, the appearance only of the bread and wine remaining the same [L. *trans*, across; *substantia*, substance].

transude (tran-sūd′) *v.i.* to pass through pores of substance; to perspire.—*pr.p.* **transud′ing** [L. *trans*, across; *sudare*, to sweat].

transuranic element (tranz-ū-rā′nik) *n.* any element with atomic number exceeding that of uranium, e.g. neptunium, plutonium, etc. [*trans*+*uranium*+*ic*].

transverse (tranz-vers′) *a.* lying in cross-wise

Amazon parrot

King parakeet

Blossom headed parakeet

Yellow backed lory

Red lory

BIRDS of TROPICAL REGIONS

Ostrich

Ibis

Hoopoe

Oroya peruviana

Pilocereus sartorianus

Victoria regia water lily

FLOWERS of TROPICAL REGIONS

Dendrobium laddigesii

Zygocactus truncatus

Cattleya dowiana

Vanda coerulea

Miltonia 'Hanover'

direction;—*adv.* cross-wise.—**transver'sal** *n.* line which cuts across, esp. parallel lines.—**transverse'ly** *adv.* [L. *trans*, across; *vertere, versum*, to turn].

trap (trap) *n.* device, mechanical or otherwise, for catching animals, vermin, etc.; snare; U-shaped bend in pipe which, by being always full of water, prevents foul air or gas from escaping; light two-wheeled carriage; (*Fig.*) stratagem; deliberate plot to catch person unawares;—*v.t.* to catch in a snare, or by stratagem.—*pr.p.* **trap'ping**.—*pa.p.* **trapped**.—**trap'-door** *n.* hinged door in floor, or leading to loft.—**trap'per** *n.* one who traps animals, esp. for their pelts [etym. uncertain].

trap (trap) *n.* one of several dark-coloured igneous rocks, so called because of resemblance in the mass, to a flight of stairs.—**trap'pean, trap'pous, trap'py** *a.* [Scand. *trappa*, a flight of stairs].

trap (trap) horse-cloth; trapping;—*pl.* one's belongings, luggage, etc.;—*v.t.* to adorn.—**trap'pings** *n.pl.* ornaments, gay coverings, esp. those on horse in olden times [Fr. *drap*, cloth].

trapan (tra̦-pan') *v.t.* to ensnare; to catch by deception.—*pr.p.* **trapan'ning**.—*pa.t.* and *pa.p.* **trapanned'**.—*n.* trick; snare. Also **trepan'** [prob. fr. *trap*, snare].

trape (trāp) *v.i.* to trail along.—**trapes** *n.* a slut; a vagrant.—**trapes, traipse** *v.i.* to walk about idly [perh. fr. *tramp*].

trapezium [tra̦-pē'zi-um) *n.* quadrilateral with only one pair of sides parallel; (*Anat.*) one of bones of wrist.—*pl.* **trape'zia, trape'ziums**.—**trapeze'** *n.* apparatus comprising horizontal cross-bar swing for gymnastics, acrobatic exhibitions, etc.—**trap'ezoid** *n.* quadrilateral with none of its sides parallel.—**trapezoid'al** *a.* [Gk. *trapezion*, a little table].

Trappist (trap'ist) *n.* member of Cistercian order of monks, founded orig. at Abbey of *La Trappe*, Orne, France, noted for austerity of its rules which include vow of perpetual silence.

trash (trash) *v.t.* to lop off, as branches, leaves, etc.;—*n.* worthless refuse; rubbish; loppings of trees, bruised sugar-canes, etc.—**trash'ery** *n.* trash.—**trash'ily** *adv.* **trash'iness** *n.*—**trash'y** *a.* worthless; cheap; shoddy [prob. Scand. *tros*, twigs for fuel].

trass (tras) *n.* volcanic earth mixed with cement to give it strength [Dut. *tras*].

trauma (traw'ma̦) *n.* (*Med.*) bodily injury caused by violence; nervous shock (psychic trauma).—*pl.* **trauma'ta**.—**traumat'ic** *a.* [Gk. *trauma*, a wound].

travail (tra'vāl) *n.* painful, arduous labour; pains of childbirth;—*v.i.* to labour with difficulty; to suffer pangs of childbirth [Fr. *travail*, labour].

trave (trāv) *n.* beam; frame in blacksmith's shop to keep horse steady during shoeing process [L. *trabs*, beam].

travel (trav'e̦l) *v.t.* to journey over; to pass;—*v.i.* to move; to journey on foot or in a vehicle; to tour, esp. abroad.—*pr.p.* **trav'elling**.—*pa.t.* and *pa.p.* **trav'elled**.—*n.* act of travelling; journey; touring, esp. abroad; in motoring, distance a component is permitted to move;—*pl.* prolonged journey, esp. abroad; book describing traveller's experiences and observations.—**trav'elled** *a.* having sojourned extensively, esp. abroad.—**trav'eller** *n.* one who travels widely; an employee of business company who travels in certain area soliciting orders for his firm. Also **commercial traveller**.—**traveller's cheque**, cheque issued by bank and payable at any branch of that bank in area visited by the traveller.—**traveller's joy**, clinging plant, species of wild clematis.—**trav'elling** *a.* mobile.—**trav'elogue** *n.* travel-lecture illustrated by lantern slides, film, etc.; geographical film [a form of *travail*].

traverse (trav'e̦rs) *a.* lying across; built crosswise; sailing in zig-zag fashion;—*n.* anything set across; a partition; (*Archit.*) barrier, movable screen, or curtain; (*Geom.*) line or plane intersecting other lines or planes; gallery across church; course cut across face of precipice;—*v.t.* to cross; to thwart; to obstruct; to survey scientifically; to rake with gun fire from end to end; to pivot laterally; to discuss, as topic, from every angle;—*v.i.* to turn, as on pivot; to walk sideways;—*adv.* athwart; crosswise.—**trav'ersable** *a.* capable of being traversed.—**trav'erser** *n.* [L. *trans*, across; *vertere, versum*, to turn].

travesty (trav'es-ti) *n.* burlesque imitation of a work; parody;—*v.t.* to make a burlesque version of; to caricature [Fr. *travestir*, to disguise].

trawl (trawl) *v.t.* to catch fish with a trawl;—*v.i.* to drag with a trawl;—*n.* trawl-net, shaped like a large bag with one end open.—**trawl'er** *n.* one who fishes with a trawl; fishing-vessel which uses a trawl-net.—**trawl'ing** *n.* [O.Fr. *trauler*, to drag].

tray (trā) *n.* flat, shallow, rimmed vessel used for carrying dishes, food, or letters; a salver [O.E. *trog*, a trough].

treachery (trech'e̦r-i) *n.* violation of allegiance or faith; treason; perfidy.—**treach'erous** *a.* disloyal; perfidious.—**treach'erously** *adv.* [O.Fr. *trechier*, to deceive].

treacle (trē'kl) *n.* thick dark-brown syrup which drains from sugar during refining; molasses.—**trea'cly** *a.* like treacle; sweet, thick and sticky [Fr. fr. Gk. *thēriake*, antidote to poisons].

tread (tred) *v.i.* to walk; to move with stately or measured step; (of fowls) to copulate; to crush or step on by mistake;—*v.t.* to step or walk on; to crush with foot; to oppress; to operate with foot, as treadle.—*pr.p.* **tread'ing**.—*pa.t.* **trod**.—*pa.p.* **trod** or **trod'den**.—*n.* act of stepping; pace; that which one steps on, as surface of horizontal step of flight of stairs; wear and tear on carpet; sole of boot or shoe; part of a rubber tyre in contact with ground.—**tread'ing** *n.*—**tread'le, tred'dle** *n.* part of machine operated by foot-pressure, as sewing-machine, harmonium, etc.; pedal;—*v.i.* to work treadle.—**tread'ler** *n.*—**tread'mill** *n.* mill worked by persons treading upon steps on periphery of a wheel, once disciplinary exercise for convicts; (*Fig.*) drudgery.—**to tread on a person's toes** or **corns**, to offend his sensibilities [O.E. *tredan*, to tread].

treason (trē'zn) *n.* disloyalty; treachery.—**trea'sonable** *a.* pert. to or involving treason.—**trea'sonableness** *n.*—**trea'sonably** *adv.*—**trea'sonous** *a.* treasonable,—**high treason**, violation by subject of allegiance to Sovereign or State [O.Fr. *traison*, betrayal].

treasure (trezh'ūr) *n.* accumulated wealth; hoard of valuables; that which has great worth;—*v.t.* to hoard; to collect; to value; to cherish, as friendship.—**treas'ure-chest** *n.* box for storing valuables.—**treas'urer** *n.* person appointed to take charge of funds of society, church, club, etc.—**treas'urer-ship** *n.*—**treas'ure-trove** *n.* any money, bullion, treasure, etc., of unknown ownership, found buried, which becomes property of Crown.—**treas'ury** *n.* place where treasure, hoarded wealth, or public funds are deposited; (*Fig.*) storehouse of facts and information; anthology.—**Treas'ury** *n.* government department which controls management of public revenues.—**treas'ury-note** *n.* currency note for £1 or 10s. [Fr. *trésor*, treasure].

treat (trēt) *v.t.* to handle; to entertain with food or drink; to pay for another's entertainment or refreshment; to behave towards; to apply a remedy to; to subject, as a substance, to chemical experiment; to consider as a topic for discussion; to discourse on;—*v.i.* to discourse; to come to terms of agreement, as between nations; to give entertainment; —*n.* entertainment given as a celebration or expression of regard; something that gives special pleasure; (*Colloq.*) one's turn to pay for another's entertainment.—**treat'er** *n.*—**treat'ing** *n.* act of standing treat.—**treat'ise** *n.* dissertation on particular theme.—**treat'ment** *n.* act or mode of treating person or subject; method of counteracting disease or of applying remedy for injury.—**treat'y** *n.* a negotiated agreement between states; a pact [L. *tractare*, to handle].

treble (treb'l) *a.* threefold; triple; (*Mus.*) playing or singing highest part;—*n.* highest of four principal parts in music; soprano part; soprano voice;—*v.t.* to multiply by three;—*v.i.* to become three times as much. —*pa.p.* **treb'led**.—**treb'ly** *adv.* [L. *triplus*].

treddle (tred'l) *n.* See **tread**.

tree (trē) perennial plant, having trunk, bole, or woody stem with branches; anything resembling cross-like form of tree; cross of Christ;—*v.t.* to chase up a tree; to corner.—**tree'less** *a.* devoid of trees; bare.—**tree'-top** *n.* uppermost branches of tree.—**boot'-tree** *n.* foot-shaped mould for preserving shape of boot (shoe).—**family tree**, genealogical table of ancestry [O.E. *treow*, tree].

trefoil (trē'foil) *n.* plant of genus *Trifolium*, with leaves comprising three leaflets; clover; (*Archit.*) ornament of three cusps in circle resembling three-leaved clover [L. *tres*, three; *folium*, leaf].

trek (trek) *v.i.* to travel by ox-wagon; to migrate, esp. a large body of people; (*Slang*) to decamp;—*n.* journey by ox-wagon; mass-migration.—**trek'ker** *n.* [Dut. *trekken*, to draw].

trellis (trel'is) *n.* light-weight lattice structure of spars for screens, doors, and as frame for climbing-plants.—**trell'ised** *a.*—**trell'is-work** *n.* lattice-work [L. *trilix*, three-ply].

tremble (trem'bl) *v.i.* to shake involuntarily from fear, cold, old age, etc.; to quiver; to quake;—*n.* involuntary shaking; quiver; tremor.—**trem'bler** *n.* one who or that which trembles; (*Elect.*) automatic device for breaking circuit; electric bell. Also **trem'bler-bell**.—**trem'bling** *n*, state or action of quivering.—**trem'blingly** *adv.*—**trem'bly** *a.* shaky;—*adv.* shakily.—**trem'ulant, trem'ulous** *a.* quivering; quaking.—**trem'ulously** *adv.*—**trem'ulousness** *n.* [L. *tremere*, to shake].

tremendous (tre-men'dus) *a.* awe-inspiring; overwhelming; formidable; momentous; (*Colloq.*) great.—**tremen'dously** *adv.*—**tremen'dousness** *n.* [L. *tremere*, to tremble].

tremolando (trem-ō-lan'dō) *adv.* (*Mus.*) tremulously.—**trem'olo** *n.* quivering of singing voice; device on pipe-organ to produce throbbing sound.—**trem'ulant** *n.* organ-device to procure tremolo effect. Also **trem'olant** [It.].

tremor (trem'or) *n.* involuntary quiver; a momentary thrill; shaking, as caused by earthquake.—**trem'orless** *a.* steady [L.].

tremulous See **tremble**.

trench (trensh) *n.* to cut or dig, as a ditch; to turn over soil by digging deeply; to fortify with ditch using earth dug out for rampart;—*v.i.* to encroach;—*n.* ditch; deep ditch or breastwork formed by earth piled up, as parapet to protect soldiers from enemy fire.—**tren'chancy** *n.* quality of being trenchant.—**tren'chant, trench'ing** *a.* sharp, as a blade; (*Fig.*) caustic; biting.—**trench'-coat** *n.* knee-length waterproof coat worn in trenches, as in *World War* 1.—**trench'er** *n.* one who digs trenches.—**trench'ing** *n.*—**trench'-mor'tar** *n.* short range mortar for hurling bombs, etc. into enemy trenches [O.Fr. *trenchier*, to cut].

trencher (tren'sher) *n.* formerly wooden plate for holding food; table; bread-board; (*Fig.*) pleasures of eating.—**tren'cher-cap** (or **tren'cher**) *n.* college or university cap, with flat, square board on top.—**a good trencherman**, one who has hearty appetite [O.Fr. *trenchoir*, platter].

trend (trend) *v.i.* to run or stretch in a certain direction;—*n.* inclination; tendency [O.E. *trendln*, to make round].

trepan (tre-pan') See **trapan**.

trepan (tre-pan') *n.* (*Surg.*) cylindrical saw for removing circular piece of bone from skull, to relieve pressure on brain;—*v.t.* to operate with trepan.—**trepana'tion, trepan'ning** *n.* [Gk. *trupanon*, borer].

trepang (tre-pang') *n.* sea-slug, dried and used by Chinese for food [Malay].

trepid (trep'id) *a.* quaking.—**trepida'tion** *n.* involuntary trembling; alarm; fluster [L. *trepidus*, trembling].

trespass (tres'pas) *v.i.* to cross unlawfully boundary line of another's property; to intrude; to encroach; to violate moral law;—*n.* **tres'passer** *n.* [L. *trans*, across; *passus*, a step].

tress (tres) *n.* lock, curl, plait, or strand of hair; ringlet;—*v.t.* to form into ringlets or plaits; to braid.—**tressed** *a.* having tresses [O.Fr. *tresse*, a lock of hair].

trestle, tressel (tres'l) *n.* movable wooden frame consisting of two pairs of braced legs fixed underneath horizontal bar, used to support planks, table, platform, etc.; similar metal or stone construction supporting a bridge [O.Fr. *trestel*, a cross-beam].

trews (trōōz) *n.pl.* trousers, esp. of tartan cloth, as worn by soldiers of some Highland regiments [Gael. *triubhas*].

tri- (trī) *prefix* meaning three, thrice, threefold [L. *tres*, Gk. *treis*, *tria*, three].

triad (trī'ad) *n.* union of three; (*Chem.*) trivalent atom; (*Mus.*) the common chord, one of three notes; poem with triple grouping, common in Celtic literature.—**triad'ic** *a.*—**triad'ist** *n.* writer of triads [Gk. *trias*, group of three].

trial (trī'al) *n.* act of trying, testing, or proving properties of anything; experimental examination; affliction; judicial examination in law-court of accused person; temptation [fr. *try*].

trialogue (trī'a-log) *n.* conversation involving three persons.

triangle (trī'ang-gl) *n.* (*Math.*) figure bounded by three lines and containing three angles; anything shaped like a triangle; set-square; (*Mus.*) small percussion instrument consisting of a bar of steel bent in shape of triangle and struck with small steel rod.—**tri'angled** *a.* —**triang'ular** *a.* having three angles; shaped like triangle.—**triangular'ity** *n.*—**triang'ularly** *adv.*—**the eternal triangle**, three persons, two of them husband and wife, and the third the lover of one of them.

triarchy (trī'ār-ki) *n.* government by three persons; a state so governed.

Trias (trī'as) *n.* (*Geol.*) system of rocks formed during geological period intermediate between Permian and Jurassic, composed of three layers or strata; new red sandstone of British Isles.—**trias'sic** *a.* [Gk. *trias*, a group of three].

triatomic (trī-a-tom'ik) *a.* consisting of three atoms; having valency of three.

tribe (trīb) *n.* family, race, or succession of generations descending from same progenitor; nation of barbarian clans each under one leader; group of plants or animals within which members reveal common characteristics; (*Colloq.*) very large family.—**trib'al** *a.* —**trib'alism** *n.* tribal feeling; clannishness.—**trib'ally** *adv.*—**tribes'man** *n.* one of a tribe [L. *tribus*, one of *three* divisions of Roman people].

tribulation (trib-ū-lā'shun) *n.* severe affliction; prolonged suffering, esp. of mind [L. *tribulum*, instrument for threshing corn].

tribune (trib'ūn) *n.* in ancient Rome, magis-

trate chosen by the people to defend their rights; champion of the masses; a raised platform or pulpit.—**tribu'nal** *n.* bench on which judge or magistrates sit; court of justice.—**trib'unary** *a.*—**trib'unate, trib'une-ship** *n.* office or functions of tribune [L. *tribus*, a tribe].
tribute (trib'ūt) *n.* pre-arranged payment made at stated times by one state to another as price of peace and protection; contribution; personal testimony to achievements or qualities of another.—**trib'utarily** *adv.*—**trib'utary** *a.* paying tribute; subordinate; contributory; (of river) flowing into main river;—*n.* state liable for tribute; stream flowing into larger river [L. *tribuere*, to assign].
trice (trīs) *n.* moment; orig. a pulley; haul—hence, **in a trice,** in an instant; orig. at one haul [O.Dut. *trisen*, to hoist].
tricennial (trī-sen'i-al) *a.* pert. to thirty years; occurring once every thirty years [L. *tricennium*, thirty years].
tricentenary (trī-sen'te-na-ri) *n.* space of three hundred years; three-hundredth anniversary. Also **tercen'tenary.**
triceps (trī'seps) *a.* three-headed;—*n.* three-headed muscle as at back of upper arm [L. *tres*, three; *caput*, the head].
tricho- (tri'ko) *pref.* fr. Gk. *thrix, trichos*, hair.
trichology (tri-kol'o-ji) *n.* expert study of hair and diseases affecting it.
trichosis (tri-kō'sis) *n.* any disease affecting the hair; (*Zool.*) hair distribution.
trichotomous (trī-kot'ō-mus) *a.* divided into three or threes. Also **trichotom'ic.**—**trichot'omously** *adv.*—**trichot'omy** *n.* division into three parts [Gk. *tricha*, in three; *tomē*, a cutting.]
trick (trik) *n.* artifice or stratagem designed to deceive; conjurer's sleight of hand; prank for mischief, or to annoy; mannerism; dexterity; cards played out in one round, and taken by player with winning card; spell at the helm of ship;—*v.t.* to deceive; to hoax; to mystify.—**trick'er** *n.* cheat.—**trick'ery** *n.* act of playing tricks; fraud.—**trick'ily** *adv.*—**trick'iness** *n.* quality of being tricky; intricacy.—**trick'ish** *a.* prone to play tricks.—**trick'ishly** *adv.*—**trick'ishness** *n.*—**trick'sey, trick'sy** *a.* ingenious; neat.—**trick'ster,** *n.* cheat; swindler.—**trick'y** *a.* full of tricks; requiring great dexterity of hand; intricate.—**a dirty trick** (*Slang*) a mean prank [O.Fr. *tricher*, to beguile].
trick (trik) *v.t.* to dress; to trim; to decorate.—**trick'ing** *n.* [etym. doubtful].
trickle (trik'l) *v.i.* to flow gently in a slow, thin stream;—*n.* thin flow of liquid; rill.—**trick'let** *n.* little rill [etym. doubtful].
tricolour (trī-kul-or) *n.* national flag of three colours, esp. French National Flag.—**tri'coloured** *a.*
tricorn (trī'korn) *a.* having three horns, or points;—*n.* three-cornered hat; cake of paste in shape of tricorn. Also **tri'corne** [L. *tricornis*, three-horned].
tricot (trē'kō) *n.* hand-knitted fabric of yarn or wool; machine-made knitwear fabric.—**tric'otine** *n.* a ribbed, fine woollen fabric, machine-made [Fr. *tricot*, knitting].
tricuspid (trī-kus'pid) *a.* having three cusps or points, as certain teeth, or a valve of the right ventricle of the heart.
tricycle (trī'si-kl) *n.* three-wheeled cycle, esp. for children's use;—*v.t.* to ride a tricycle.—**tri'cyclist** *n.* [Gk. *treis*, three; *kuklos*, a circle].
trident (trī'dent) *n.* three-pronged sceptre, symbol of Neptune; any three-pronged instrument, such as fish-spear.—**tri'dent, trident'ate, tri'dented** *a.* having three prongs [L. *tres*, three; *dens*, a tooth].
tried See **try.**
triennial (trī-en'i-al) *a.* lasting for three years; happening once every three years.—**trienn'ially** *adv.* [L. *tres*, three; *annus*, a year].
trier See **try.**
trifle (trī'fl) *n.* anything of little value or importance; paltry amount; dessert of sponge-cake and jam, soaked in sherry, covered with custard and topped with whipped cream; pewter;—*v.i.* to speak or act lightly; to be facetious; to toy.—**tri'fler** *n.*—**tri'fling** *a.*—trivial.—**tri'flingly** *adv.* [O.Fr. *trufle*, mockery].
triform (trī'form) *a.* having a triple form. Also **tri'formed.**—**triform'ity** *n.*—**triform'ous** *a.*
trifurcate (trī'fur-kāt) *a.* having three branches or forks. Also **trifurca'ted.**—**trifur'cate** *v.t.* to divide into three branches.—**trifurca'tion** *n.* [L. *tres*, three; *furca*, a fork].
trig (trig) *a.* trim; neat; compact; smart.—**trig'ly** *adv.*—**trig'ness** [O.N. *tryggr*, firm].
trig (trig) *n.* skid, for wheel; any obstacle used to prevent movement of vehicle; starting-mark in game of skittles, etc. [O.N. *tryggr*, firm].
trigamous (trig'a-mus) *a.* having three husbands or wives at same time; (*Bot.*) having male, female, and hermaphrodite flowers on same flower-head.—**trig'amy** *n.* [Gk. *treis*, three; *gamos*, marriage].
trigger (trig'er) *n.* catch of firearm which, when pulled, releases hammer of lock; device fitted on wheel for retarding speed of vehicle going down steep incline [Dut. *trekken*, to pull].
triglyph (trī'glif) *n.* triple-grooved ornament in frieze of Doric column, repeated at equal intervals.—**triglyph'ic, -al** *a.* [Gk. *treis*, three; *gluphein*, to carve].
trigonometry (trig-o-nom'et-ri) *n.* branch of mathematics which deals with relations between sides and angles of triangle.—**trigonom'eter** *n.* instrument for solving plane right-angled triangles by inspection.—**trig'onomet'ric, -al** *a.*—**trigonomet'rically** *adv.* [Gk. *trigonon*, a triangle; *metron*, a measure].
trihedral (trī-hē'dral) *a.* (*Math.*) having three sides or faces.—**trihe'dron** *n.* figure with three equal sides [Gk. *treis*, three; *hedra*, seat].
trilateral (trī-lat'er-al) *a.* having three sides; arranged by three parties, as *trilateral pact*;—*n.* a triangle.—**trilat'erally** *adv.*
trilby (tril'bi) *n.* (*Colloq.*) man's soft felt-hat [fr. *Trilby*, novel by *Du Maurier*].
trilinear (trī-lin'ē-ar) *a.* consisting of three lines [L. *tres*, three; *linea*, a line].
trilingual (trī-ling'gwal) *a.* expressed in three languages; speaking three languages.
trilith (trī'lith) *n.* ancient monument of two upright stones and a third resting across the top, as at Stonehenge.—**trilith'ic** *a.* [Gk. *treis*, three; *lithos*, a stone].
trill (tril) *v.t.* and *v.i.* to sing or play (instrument) with tremulous or vibratory quality; to pronounce, as letter 'r';—*n.* shake or vibration of voice, produced by singing, in rapid alternation, two notes, semitone apart; consonant, such as 'r' pronounced with trill [It. *trillare*, to shake].
trillion (tril'yun) *n.* million million million (British) i.e. 1 with 18 ciphers; a million million (U.S.) i.e. 1 with 12 ciphers.
trilogy (tril'o-ji) *n.* group of three plays, novels, etc. with common theme, or common central character [Gk. *treis*, three; *logos*, a speech or discourse].
trim (trim) *a.* neat; firm; compact; in good order or health;—*adv.* neatly;—*v.t.* to put in order; to dress; to decorate, as hat; to clip shorter; to supply with oil and adjust wick, as lamp; (*Naut.*) to arrange sails according to wind-direction;—*v.i.* to balance; to fluctuate between two parties, so as to appear to favour each.—*pr.p.* **trim'ming.**—*pa.t.* and *pa.p.* **trimmed.**—*n.* dress; decoration; disposition; state of bodily fitness or mental alertness; state of readiness.—**trim'ly** *adv.*—**trim'mer** *n.* one who trims; instrument for clipping; one who, for expediency, supports whichever party is in power; time-server.—**trim'ming** *n.* that which trims, edges, or decorates; (*Fig.*) affectation of style.—**trim'-**

ness *n.* neatness; compactness; readiness for use [O.E. *trymian*, to strengthen].

trimeter (trim′e-tẹr) *n.* verse containing three measures, as 'Bird thōu nēvēr wērt.'—**trim′eter, trimet′ric, -al** *a.*

trinal (trī′nạl) *a.* threefold; of three, as *trinal unity*, three in one.—**tri′nary** *a.* consisting of three parts; ternary.—**trine** *a.* threefold;—*n.* group of three; aspect of two planets distant from each other 120°, or one-third of the zodiac [L. *trinus*].

trinitrotoluene (trī-nī-trō-tol′ū-ēn) *n.* (*abbrev.* **T.N.T.**) high explosive produced by adding toluene to nitric and sulphuric acids, much used in *World Wars* 1 and 2.

Trinity (trin′i-ti) *n.* union in one Godhead of Father, Son, and Holy Ghost; any combination of three people or things as one.—**Trinita′rian** *a.* pert. to doctrine of the Trinity;—*n.* one who believes in this doctrine.—**Trinita′rianism** *n.*—**Trinity Sunday,** Sunday following Whitsunday, observed in R.C. and Anglican churches as festival of Holy Trinity [L. *trinitas*, three].

trinket (tring′ket) *n.* small ornament worn as ring, brooch, etc.; ornament of little value.—**trin′ketry** *n.* trinkets [prob. fr. M.E. *trenket*, small knife].

trinomial (trī-nō′mi-ạl) *a.* (*Bot. Zool.*) having three names as of *order, species* and *sub-species*; (*Math.*) consisting of three terms connected by sign × or —;—*n.* a trinomial quantity [L. *tres*, three; *nomen*, a name].

trio (trē′ō, or trī′o) *n.* group of three persons performing together; (*Mus.*) composition arranged for three voices, or instruments.—*pl.* **tri′os** [It. fr. L. *tres*, three].

triode (trī′ōd) *n.* (*Radio*) three-electrode thermionic valve [Gk. *treis*, three; *hodos*, a way].

triolet (trē′ or trī′ō-let) *n.* short poem of eight lines with rhyme-pattern abaaabab, lines 1, 4, 7 having identical rhymes, and lines 2 and 8, another identical rhyme [Fr. *triolet*, a little trio].

trioxide (trī-oks′īd) *n.* (*Chem.*) compound comprising three atoms of oxygen with some other element [*tri-*, and *oxide*].

trip (trip) *v.t.* to cause to stumble; to frustrate; to loose, as ship's anchor; to start up, as machine, by releasing clutch;—*v.i.* to walk or dance lightly; to stumble over an obstacle; to make a false step; (with *up*) to detect in another's statement an error of fact.—*pr.p.* **tripp′ing**.—*pa.p.* **tripped**.—*n.* quick, light step; short journey for pleasure; false step; indiscretion in speech or conduct.—**trip′-ham′mer** *n.* tilt-hammer used in forges.—**trip′per** *n.* one who trips; holiday-maker, esp. day-excursionist.—**tripp′ing** *a.* light-footed.—**tripp′ingly** *adv.* with dainty step [M.E. *trippen*, to tread on].

tripartite (trī-pȧr′tīt, or trip′ȧr-tīt) *a.* divided into three parts; having three corresponding parts; arranged or agreed to, by three parties or nations, as *tripartite pact.*—**tri′partitely** *adv.*—**triparti′tion** *n.*

tripe (trīp) *n.* large stomach of ruminating animal, esp. of sheep, or ox, prepared for food; (*Vulg.*) entrails; (*Slang*) rubbish [etym. doubtful].

triphthong (trif′thong) *n.* a syllable containing three vowels together, as in *beauty* [Gk. *treis*, three; *phthongos*, a sound].

triple (trip′l) *a.* consisting of three united; three times repeated; treble;—*v.t.* to make three times as much or as many;—*v.i.* to become trebled.—**trip′le-crown** *n.* papal tiara consisting of three crowns one on top of the other, and studded with gems.—**trip′let** *n.* three of a kind; three consecutive verses rhyming together; (*Mus.*) three notes played in the time of two; (*Colloq.*) one of three children born at a birth.—**trip′lex** *a.* threefold;—*n.* (*Mus.*) triple time.—**Triplex glass,** a *proprietary name* for splinter-proof glass made by sandwiching a layer of plastic or celluloid material between two layers of glass, used for windscreen of motor-cars, etc.—**trip′licate**; *a.* threefold; made three times as much;—*n.* third copy corresponding exactly to two others of the same kind;—*v.t.* to treble; to make three copies of.—**triplica′tion** *n.* the act or process of trebling.—**trip′ly** *adv.* [L. *triplex*, three-fold].

tripod (trī′pod) *n.* stool, vessel, etc. on three-legged support; three-legged, folding-stand for a camera, theodolite, etc.;—*a.* having three legs.—**tripod′al** *a.* [Gk. *treis*, three; *pous*, *podos*, a foot].

tripoli (trip′ō-li) *n.* mineral substance used for polishing metals, stones, etc.; originally brought from *Tripoli*. Also **trip′olite**.

tripos (trī′pos) *n.* honours degree examination at Cambridge University [fr. old custom by which graduate sat on a *tripos* or three-legged stool at graduation ceremony].

triptych (trip′tik) *n.* writing-tablet in three parts; altar-piece or picture in three panels, side panels hinged to fold back on centre one [Gk. *treis*, three; *ptux*, *ptuchos*, a fold].

trireme (trī′rēm) *n.* Greek or Roman galley or war-vessel with three banks of oars [L. *tres*, three; *remus*, an oar].

trisect (trī-sekt′) *v.t.* to divide into three equal parts, as a line or angle.—**trisec′tion** *n.* division into three equal parts.

trist (trēst) *a.* sad; gloomy.—**tristesse′** *n.* sadness.—**trist′ful** *a.* sorrowful.—**trist′fully** *adv.* [Fr. *triste*, sad].

trisulphide (trī-sul′fīd) *n.* (*Chem.*) chemical compound comprising three atoms of sulphur and another element.

trisyllable (trī- or tri-sil′ạ-bl) *n.* word of three syllables.—**trisyllab′ic, -al** *a.*—**trisyllab′ically** *adv.* [Gk. *treis*, three; *sullabē*, syllable].

trite (trīt) *a.* made stale by use; hackneyed; banal.—**trite′ly** *adv.*—**trite′ness** *n.* [L. *tritus*, rubbed away].

tritium (trish′i-um, trit′,) *n.* isotope of hydrogen of triple mass, not found in nature but produced by irradiating lithium in an uranium pile [Gk. *tritos*, third].

Triton (trī′ton) *n.* (*Gk. Myth.*) merman demi-god, son of Poseidon, god of the sea, depicted as carrying sea-shell used as trumpet to summon storms or calms.—**tri′ton** *n.* (*Zool.*) marine mollusc with spiral shell.

triturate (trit′ū-rāt) *v.t.* to rub or grind to a very fine powder.—**trit′urable** *a.* capable of being pulverised.—**tritura′tion** *n.* [L. *triturare*, to pulverise].

triumph (trī′umf) *n.* in ancient Rome, magnificent ceremonial in honour of a victorious general; victory; conquest; rejoicing; great achievement;—*v.i.* to celebrate victory with pomp and ceremony; to achieve supremacy; to prevail; to exult.—**trium′phal** *a.* pert. to triumph; expressing joy for success.—**trium′phant** *a.* rejoicing for victory; successful.—**trium′phantly** *adv.* [L. *triumphus*, a solemn procession].

triumvir (trī-um′vir) *n.* one of three men sharing governing power in ancient Rome.—*pl.* **trium′viri, trium′virs.**—**trium′viral** *a.*—**trium′virate** *n.* coalition of three men in office or authority [L. *tres*, three; *vir*, a man].

triune (trī′ūn) *a.* three in one.—**triun′ity** *n.* [L. *tres*, three; *unus*, one].

trivalent (trī′vā-lẹnt) *a.* (*Chem.*) having valency of three; capable of combining with or replacing three atoms of hydrogen.—**tri′valence** *n.*

trivet (triv′et) *n.* three-legged stool, table or support; iron tripod for standing a pot or kettle close to fire; iron bracket for hooking on to bars of a kitchen range [L. *tres*, three; *pes*, foot].

trivial (triv′i-ạl) *a.* paltry; of little consequence; everyday.—**triv′ialism** *n.*—**trivial′ity**

n. state or quality of being trivial; trifle; anything commonplace or insignificant.—**triv'ially** *adv.*—**triv'ialness** *n.* [L. *trivialis*, pert. to crossroads, hence commonplace].

troche (trō'kē, or trōk, or trōsh) *n.* medicinal lozenge [Gk. *trochos*, pill].

trochee (trō'kē) *n.* in English prosody, metrical foot of two syllables, first one accented, as *ho'ly*.—**trocha'ic** *n.* trochaic foot or verse.—**trocha'ic, -al** *a.* consisting of trochees [Gk. *trochaios*, running].

trod, trodden *pa.t., pa.p.* of **tread**.

troglodyte (trog'lō-dīt) *n.* cave-dweller; kind of ape; a hermit.—**trog'lodyte, troglody'tic, -al** *a.*—**trog'lodytism** *n.* [Gk. *troglē*, a cave; *duein*, to enter].

troika (troi'ka) *n.* Russian carriage or sledge drawn by three horses abreast [Russ.].

Trojan (trō'jạn) *a.* pert. to ancient Troy;—*n.* inhabitant of Troy.—**to work like a Trojan**, to work very hard and perseveringly (as the Trojans defending Troy).

troll (trōl) *n.* in Scandinavian mythology, orig. a giant, but later a mischievous hump-backed cave-dwelling dwarf [Scand.].

troll (trōl) *v.t.* and *v.i.* to roll; to sing in succession the parts of a round; to fish with baited line trailing behind boat; (formerly) to pass bottle round;—*n.* a round or catch.—**troll'er** *n.* one who or that which trolls.—**troll'ey, troll'y** *n.* form of truck body of which can be tilted over; light two-wheeled hand-cart; pulley to connect electric tramcar with overhead wires; low truck running on rails.—**troll'ey-bus** *n.* omnibus with overhead trolley but not running on rails.—**troll'ey-car** *n.* (*U.S.*) electric tramcar [etym. doubtful].

trollop (trol'op) *n.* a slattern; a prostitute;—*v.i.* to draggle; to be slovenly.—**troll'opy** *a.* slovenly; tawdry [prob. fr. *troll*].

trombone (trom'bōn) *n.* deep-toned brass musical instrument, its notes controlled by a sliding tube.—**trom'bonist** *n.* one who performs on trombone [It. *tromba*, a trumpet].

troop (trȯȯp) *n.* large assembly of people; body of cavalry; light-horse, or dragoons; command of this; troupe;—*pl.* soldiers collectively; an army;—*v.i.* to flock; to gather in a crowd.—**troop'-carr'ier** *n.* transport-plane for troops.—**troop'er** *n.* non-commissioned cavalryman; troop-horse; troop-ship; (*U.S.*) mounted policeman, esp. of Royal Canadian Mounted Police.—**troop'-horse** *n.* cavalry horse.—**troop'-ship** *n.* vessel for transporting soldiers.—**trooping the colours**, a ceremony held at the public mounting of garrison-guards [Fr. *troupe*].

trope (trōp) *n.* word or phrase used metaphorically.—**tro'pical** *a.* figurative.—**tro'pically** *adv.*—**tro'pist** *n.* one who uses figurative language.—**tropolog'ic, -al** *a.* containing figures of speech.—**tropol'ogy** *n.* figurative language; study of such language; a metaphorical interpretation of the Bible [Gk. *tropos*, a turn].

trophic, -al (trof'ik, -ạl) *a.* pert. to nutrition.—**tro'phi** *n.pl.* masticating organs of insect.—**trophol'ogy** *n.* the scientific study of nutrition [Gk. *trophē*, feeding].

trophy (trō'fi) *n.* orig. pile of arms taken from vanquished enemy; memorial of victory; memento; mural decoration, as stag's antlers; prize, esp. for sports, etc. [Gk. *tropaion*, a trophy].

tropic (trop'ik) *n.* one of the two circles of celestial sphere, situated 23½° N. (*Tropic of Cancer*) and 23½° S. (*Tropic of Capricorn*) of Equator, and marking the point reached by the sun at its greatest declination north and south; one of the two corresponding parallels of latitude on terrestrial globe.—*pl.* region (*torrid zone*) between tropics of Cancer and Capricorn.—**trop'ic, -al** *a.* pert. to or within tropics; (of climate) very hot.—**trop'ically** *adv.* [Gk. *tropos*, a turn].

troposphere (trop'ō-sfēr) *n.* lower layer of atmosphere below stratosphere [Gk. *tropos*, a turn; *sphaira*, sphere].

troppo (trop'pō) *adv.* (*Mus.*) too much.—**non troppo**, moderately [It.].

trot (trot) *v.i.* (of horse) to move at sharp pace; (of person) to move along fast;—*v.t.* to cause to trot.—*pr.p.* **trot'ting**.—*pa.p.* **trot'ted**.—*n.* normal pace of horse; quick walk.—**trot'ter** *n.* one who trots; horse which trots; foot of an animal; (*Colloq.*) the foot [O.Fr. *troter*].

troth (troth) *n.* truth; fidelity;—*v.t.* to plight.—**to plight one's troth**, to become engaged to be married [O.E. *treowth*, truth].

troubadour (trȯȯ'bạ-dȯȯr) *n.* one of school of Provencal poets between 11th and 13th cents., whose poems were devoted to subjects lyrical and amatory [Prov. *trobador*, poet].

trouble (trub'l) *v.t.* to stir up; to vex; to perplex; (*Colloq.*) to bother;—*v.i.* to take pains; to feel anxiety;—*n.* disturbance; agitation of mind; unrest; ailment; inconvenience.—**troub'ler** *n.*—**troub'lesome** *a.* difficult; vexatious; irksome.—**troub'lesomely** *adv.*—**troub'lesomeness** *n.*—**troub'lous** *a.* disturbed [L. *turbare*, to disturb].

trough (trof) *n.* long, open vessel for water or fodder for animals; channel; depression, as between waves; part of cyclone where atmospheric pressure is lowest [O.E. *trog*, hollow vessel of wood].

trounce (trouns) *v.t.* to punish or beat severely; to defeat completely; (*Fig.*) to castigate [Fr. *tronce*, a stump].

troupe (trȯȯp) *n.* company or troop, esp. of actors, acrobats, etc.—**troup'er** *n.* member of a theatrical troupe [Fr.].

trousers (trou'zẹrs) *n.pl.* a man's two-legged outer garment extending from waist to ankles; long, frilled drawers worn by women in 19th cent.; slacks.—**trou'sered** *a.* wearing trousers.—**trou'ser-press,** or **-stret'cher** *n.* device for keeping trousers in shape [O.Fr. *trousses*, breeches].

trousseau (trȯȯ'sō) *n.* bride's outfit of clothes, etc. [Fr.].

trout (trout) *n.* fish, resembling salmon but smaller, found in lake, river, and sea [O.E. *truht*, trout].

trow (trō) *v.i.* to believe; to suppose to be true [O.E. *treowian*, to trust].

trowel (trou'ẹl) *n.* mason's tool for spreading and dressing mortar; garden tool for scooping out earth, plants, etc.;—*v.t.* to smooth or lift with trowel [L. *trulla*, a small ladle].

trowsers Same as **trousers**.

troy-weight (troi'wāt) *n.* system of weight for precious metals and gems [fr. *Troyes*, in France; the pound weight was adopted in England in 14th cent.].

truant (trȯȯ'ạnt) *n.* one who wastes his time; pupil who absents himself from school;—*a.* wandering from duty; idle;—*v.i.* to play truant.—**tru'ancy, truant'ship** *n.* [O.Fr. *truant*, vagrant].

Trubenise (trȯȯ'ben-īz) *v.t.* to bind two layers of fabric by intermediate layer of cellulose acetate—**tru'benised** *a.*—**tru'benising** *n.* [Protected Trade Name].

truce (trȯȯs) *n.* temporary cessation of hostilities; armistice; lull [O.E. *treow*, faith].

truck (truk) *v.t.* to exchange; to barter;—*v.i.* to deal with by exchange;—*n.* exchange of commodities; (*Colloq.*) smallwares; rubbish; junk; (*U.S.*) garden produce.—**truck'age** *n.* system of barter.—**truck'er** *n.* [Fr. *troquer*, to truck].

truck (truk) *n.* small wooden wheel; open wagon for heavy transport by rail; porter's barrow for heavy luggage; (*U.S.*) a lorry.—**truck'age** *n.* transport by trucks; cost of such transport.—**truck'le** *n.* small wheel or castor; truckle-bed; (*Fig.*) to fawn on; to toady to.—**truck'le-bed** *n.* low bed on castors which may be pushed beneath another [Gk. *trochos*, a wheel].

truculent (truk′ū-lent) *a.* fierce; aggressive; ruthless.—**truc′ulence, truc′ulency** *n.*—**truc′u-lently** *adv.* [L. *trux*, fierce].
trudge (truj) *v.t.* to go on foot; to plod along; —*n.* wearisome walk [etym. doubtful].
trudgen (truj′en) *n.* fast racing-stroke in swimming. Also (incorrectly) **trud′geon** [fr. *J. Trudgen*, English swimmer].
true (trôô) *a.* conformable with fact; genuine; exact; loyal; trustworthy;—*v.t.* to adjust accurately, as machine; to straighten;—*adv.* truly; conforming to type (of plants, etc.),—**true′blue** *n.* (*Fig.*) person of unquestionable integrity and loyalty.—**true′ness** *n.*—**true′pen′ny** *n.* honest fellow.—**tru′ism** *n.* self-evident truth.—**tru′ly** *adv.* [O.E. *treowe*, true].
truffle (truf′l) *n.* tuber-shaped edible underground fungus with unique flavour [prob. L. *tuber*, swelling, truffle].
trug (trug) *n.* mason's hod; a gardener's shallow wooden basket [etym. uncertain].
truism See **true**.
trull (trul) *n.* a drab; trollop [var. of *troll*].
trump (trump) *n.* trumpet; its sound; Jew's harp.—**trump′et** *n.* wind instrument of brass, consisting of long tube bent twice on itself, ending in wide bell-shaped mouth, and having finger stops; powerful reed-stop of pipe-organ with full trumpet-like sound; ear-trumpet for the deaf;—*v.t.* to proclaim by trumpet; to bellow; (*Fig.*) to praise loudly;—*v.i.* to play on trumpet; (of elephant) to utter characteristic cry through trunk.—**trum′pet-call** *n.* summons on a trumpet; imperative call to action.—**trum′peter** *n.* one who plays on trumpet; kind of domestic pigeon; long-necked S. American bird, resembling crane.—**trum′peting** *n.*—**to blow one's own trumpet,** to praise oneself [Fr. *trompe*, trumpet].
trump (trump) *n.* one of the suit of cards, declared by cutting, dealing, or bidding, which takes any card of another suit; (*Colloq.*) good-natured fellow;—*v.t.* to play trump-card; to take a trick with trump.—**trump′card** *n.* (*Fig.*) best means to desired end [Fr. *triomphe*, triumph, game of cards].
trump (trump) *v.t.* to impose upon; to deceive.—**trum′pery** *n.* anything showy but of little value; rubbish.—**to trump up,** to concoct; to gather indiscriminately [Fr. *tromper*, to deceive].
truncate (trung′kāt) *v.t.* to cut off; to lop; to maim.—**trunc′ate, -d** *a.* appearing as if cut off at tip; blunt [L. *truncare*, to cut off].
truncheon (trun′shun) *n.* short staff; policeman's baton; a baton of office, as of Earl Marshal—*v.t.* to cudgel [O.Fr. *tronchon*, a broken shaft or trunk].
trundle (trun′dl) *n.* anything round or capable of being rolled; a small wheel or castor; low truck; small wheel, its teeth formed of cylinders or spindles, as in mill-machinery;—*v.t.* to roll on little wheels; to bowl, as child's hoop, barrel, etc.;—*v.i.* to roll.—**trun′dle-bed** *n.* a truckle-bed [O.E. *trendel*, a wheel].
trunk (trungk) *n.* stem of tree, as distinct from branches and roots; body minus head and limbs; torso; shaft of column; main part of anything; main lines of railway, bus, or telephone system; large box of metal, hide, etc., with hinged lid, for storage or as luggage;—*pl.* short, tight-fitting pants, esp. for swimming.—**trunc′al** *a.* pert. to the trunk.—**trunk′call** *n.* long-distance telephone call involving use of trunk-line.—**trunk′line** *n.* main line of railway, bus, telegraph, or telephone system.—**trunk′road** *n.* highway directly connecting important centres [L. *truncus*, maimed].
trunk (trungk) *n.* proboscis of elephant [orig. *trump*; fr. Fr. *trompe*, trumpet].
truss (trus) *n.* bundle; as hay or straw; tuft of flowers on top of a long stem; framework of beams or girders constructed to bear heavy loads; (*Med.*) appliance to keep hernia in place; (*Naut.*) iron clamp fixing lower yards to masts;—*v.t.* to bind or pack close; to support, as a roof, or bridge-span, with truss; to skewer, as fowl, before cooking.—**to truss up,** to tie very firmly [Fr. *trousse*, a bundle].
trust (trust) *n.* confidence; reliance; implicit faith; moral responsibility; property used for benefit of another; combine of business firms in which shareholders turn over stock to board of trustees;—*v.t.* to rely upon; to have implicit faith in; to credit; to entrust; to hope; to believe;—*v.i.* to be confident or to confide in;—*a.* held in trust.—**trust′deed** *n.* (*Law*) document conveying property to trustee.—**trustee′** *n.* person to whom a trust is committed.—**trustee′ship** *n.* functions of trustee.—**trust′er** *n.*—**trust′estate′** *n.* estate managed by trustees.—**trust′ful** *a.* trusting; having implicit faith.—**trust′fully** *adv.*—**trust′fulness** *n.*—**trust′ily** *adv.* faithfully; confidently. —**trust′iness** *n.* quality of being trusty.—**trust′ing** *a.* confiding.—**trust′ingly** *adv.*—**trust′worthiness** *n.*—**trust′worthy** *a.* worthy of trust; reliable; accurate.—**trust′y** *a.* (*comp.* **trust′ier** *superl.* **trust′iest**) staunch; reliable [O.N. *traust*, confidence].
truth (trôôth) *n.* honesty; conformity to fact or reality; veracity; constancy; true statement; religious tenet based on revelation.—**truth′ful** *a.* honest; reliable.—**truth′fully** *adv.*—**truth′fulness** *n.*—**truth′less** *a.* [O.E. *treowe*, true].
try (trī) *v.t.* to test; to attempt; to examine judicially; to purify or refine, as metals; to make demands upon;—*v.i.* to endeavour; to make effort.—*pa.t.* and *pa.p.* **tried.**—*n.* trial; effort; in Rugby football, point gained when player manages to place ball over back line of his opponents; (*Colloq.*) attempt.—**tried** *a.* proved; afflicted.—**tri′er** *n.* one who tries—[O.Fr. *trier*, to pick out].
tryst (trīst) *n.* appointment to meet; place appointed for meeting; fair;—*v.t.* to make appointment; (*Colloq.*) to order beforehand.—*v.i.* to agree on rendezvous.—**tryst′er** *n.* [var. of *trust*].
Tsar (tsår) *n.* same as **Czar**.
tsetse (tset′se) *n.* African fly; its bite is generally fatal to animals, causing in men *sleeping-sickness* [S. Afr.].
T-square (tē-skwār) *n.* ruler with cross-bar at one end for drawing parallel lines.
tuan (tū′an) title of respect in Malaya, equivalent of *master* [Malay.].
tub (tub) *n.* open, wooden vessel formed of staves, heading and hoops, as used for washing clothes, etc.; small cask; slow, cumbersome boat;—*v.i.* (*Colloq.*) to have a bath.—**tub′by** *a.* shaped like a tub; (of persons) squat and portly.—**tub′thump′er** *n.* (*Colloq.*) street-corner orator; a ranting preacher or politician [M.E. *tubbe*, a tub].
tuba (tū′ba) *n.* (*Mus.*) largest brass instrument of orchestra producing rich, deep tone, and consisting of coiled tube ending in wide, bell-shaped mouth; organ-stop producing similar effect.—*pl.* **tu′bae, tu′bas** [L. *tuba*, trumpet].
tube (tūb) *n.* long hollow cylinder for conveyance of liquids, gas, etc.; pipe; siphon; *abbrev.* for tube-railway where rails are laid through immense steel tubes; (*Anat.*) cylindrical-shaped organ; small tinfoil container with screw cap for holding paint, solder, glue, etc.; stem of plant; inner rubber tyre of bicycle or motor-car wheel; (*U.S.*) a valve.—**tu′bing** *n.* act or process of making tubes; length of tube, esp. rubber.—**tu′bular** *a.*, **tu′bulate, -d, tu′bulous, tu′bulose** *a.*—**tu′bule** *n.* a small tube [L. *tubus*, a tube].
tuber (tū′ber) *n.* fleshy, rounded underground stem or root, containing buds for new plant, as of *potato*, *artichoke*, etc.; (*Med.*) a swelling.—**tu′berous, tu′berose** *a.* having tubers; knobby [L. *tuber*, a swelling].
tubercle (tū′ber-kl) *n.* small swelling; nodule; (*Med.*) morbid growth, esp. on lung causing

tuberculosis.—**tu'bercled** *a.* having tubercles.—**tuber'cular, tuber'culate, -d, tuber'culose, tuber'culous** *a.* pert. to tubercles; nodular; affected with tuberculosis.—**tuber'culin** *n.* liquid extract from tubercle bacillus, used as injection in testing for, or in treatment of, tuberculosis.—**tuberculo'sis** *n.* (*Colloq. abbrev.* **T.B.**) consumption; phthisis, disease caused by infection with the tubercle bacillus.—**tuber'culum** *n.* tubercle [L. *tuberculum*, a small tuber].

tuberose (tū'be-rōs, or tūb'rōz) *n.* a bulbous plant with creamy-white, fragrant flower-spikes [L. *tuber*, a swelling].

tuck (tuk) *v.t.* to make fold(s) in cloth before stitching down; to roll up, as sleeves; to make compact; to cram; to enclose snugly in bed-clothes;—*n.* flat fold in garment to shorten it, or as ornament; (*Slang*) food, esp. sweets, cakes, etc.—**tuck'er** *n.* tucked linen or lace front worn formerly by women;—*v.t.* (*U.S. slang*) to exhaust [M.E. *tukken*, to pull].

tuck (tuk) *n.* the beat of a drum.—**tuck'et** *n.* flourish of trumpets [Fr. *toquer*, to touch].

Tudor (tū'dor) *a.* pert. to period of Tudors (1485-1603) or to style of architecture in that period.

Tuesday (tūz'dā) *n.* third day of week [O.E. *Tiwesdaeg*, day of *Tiw*, god of war].

tufa (tū'fa) *n.* variety of porous carbonate of lime deposited by springs.—**tufa'ceous** *a.* [It. fr. L. *tofus*, soft stone].

tuft (tuft) *n.* cluster; bunch of something soft, as hair, feathers, etc.; imperial (beard);—*v.t.* to adorn with, arrange in tufts.—**tuft'ed, tuft'y** *a.*—**tuft'-hunt'er** *n.* one who cultivates friendship of people of standing [etym. uncertain].

tuft (tuft) *n.* green knoll; a plantation.—**tuff'et** *n.* mound [O.E. *toft*, knoll].

tug (tug) *v.t.* to pull with effort; to haul along; to jerk forward;—*v.i.* to pull with great effort; to comb, as hair, with difficulty.—*pr.p.* **tug'ging.**—*pa.t* and *pa.p.* **tugged.**—*n.* strong pull; tussle; small steamboat used to tow larger vessel.—**tug'-boat** *n.* a small but powerful boat used for towing.—**tug'-of-war** *n.* event at sports meeetings, in which two teams pull at either end of rope, until losing team is drawn over centre-line [O.N. *toga*, to pull].

tuition (tū-ish'un) *n.* orig. guardianship; private coaching for examination; teaching.—**tui'tional, tui'tionary** *a.* [L. *tueri*, to watch].

tulip (tū'lip) *n.* bulbous plant of order Liliaceae, especially popular in Holland [Turk. *tulbend*, turban].

tulle (tòòl) *n.* fine silk net used for dresses, etc. [fr. *Tulle*, near Bordeaux in France].

tumble (tum'bl) *v.i.* to fall heavily; to trip over; to toss from side to side; to turn head over heels; to perform acrobatic tricks; to slump, as prices;—*v.t.* to overturn; to rumple, as bedclothes; to toss about, as contents of drawer; to shoot, as rabbit;—*n.* act of tumbling; toss; somersault.—**tum'ble-down** *a.* ramshackle; derelict.—**tum'bler** *n.* one who tumbles; acrobat; kind of pigeon which appears to perform somersaults when in flight; glass drinking-vessel, formerly with rounded, pointed base and easily tumbled; spring catch of a lock.—**tum'bler-switch** *n.* (*Elect.*) switch turned over to produce or shut off current, esp. in lamp circuits.—**tum'bling** *n.* act of falling or turning somersault [O.E. *tumbian*, to dance].

tumbrel (tum'brel) **tumbril** (tum'bril) *n.* covered cart used for transport of army stores; dung-cart; low open cart in which victims of French Revolutionists were conveyed to guillotine; ducking-stool for scolds [Fr. *tomber*, to fall].

tumefy (tū'me-fī) *v.t.* to cause to swell;—*v.i.* to swell; to develop into a tumour.—*pa.t.* and *pa.p.* **tu'mefied.**—**tumefac'tion** *n.* a swelling; a tumour [L. *tumere*, to swell; *facere*, to make].

tumid (tū'mid) *a.* swollen; turgid; pompous.—**tumes'cence** *n.* state of swelling; turgidity.—**tumes'cent** *a.*—**tumid'ity** *n.*—**tu'midly** *adv.*—**tu'midness** *n.* [L. *tumere*].

tumour (tū'mor) *n.* (*Med.*) morbid, parasitic over-growth of tissue, sometimes accompanied by swelling; a cancer,—**tu'morous** *a.* [L. *tumere*, to swell].

tumult (tū'mult) *n.* commotion; violent uproar; mass hysteria; storm.—**tumult'uary, tumult'uous** *a.* confused; uproarious; disturbing.—**tumult'uously** *adv.*—**tumult'uousness** *n.* [L. *tumultus*, uproar].

tumulus (tū'mū-lus) *n.* artificial burial mound, erected by primitive peoples; barrow.—*pl.* **tu'muli.**—**tu'mular, -y, tu'mulous** *a.* [L. fr. *tumere*, to swell].

tun (tun) *n.* large cask; measure of liquid, as for wine, consisting of two pipes, or four hogsheads or 252 gallons; vat in a brewery;—*v.t.* to store in casks.—**tun'nage** *n.* tax formerly levied on every tun of imported wine [O.E. *tunne*, a cask].

tuna (tòò'na) *n.* prickly pear or its fruit; Californian tunny-fish [Sp.].

tundra (tòòn'dra) *n.* cold desert; term used of zone north of Arctic Circle, where there is scanty vegetation [Russ. *tundra*, a marsh].

tune (tūn) *n.* melody; rhythmical arrangement of notes and chords in particular key; quality of being in pitch; temper of mind;—*v.t.* to adjust to proper pitch; to harmonise; to adapt or make efficient, esp. part of machine; (*Radio*) to adjust circuit to give resonance at desired frequency.—**tu'nable** *a.* capable of being tuned, as piano.—**tu'nableness** *n.*—**tu'nably** *adv.*—**tune'ful** *a.* melodious; harmonious.—**tune'fully** *adv.*—**tune'fulness** *n.*—**tune'less** *a.* without melody; discordant; silent.—**tu'ner** *n.*—**tu'ning-fork** *n.* steel two-pronged instrument giving specified note when struck.—**in tune** (*Fig.*) mentally and emotionally adjusted, as to one's company or environment.—**out of tune**, at variance with.—**to tune in** (*Radio*) to adjust wireless set to desired wavelength [O.Fr. *ton*, a tone].

tungsten (tung'sten) *n.* hard grey metallic element used in alloys, special forms of steel, and for filaments in electric lamps [Scand. *tung*, heavy; *sten*, a stone].

tunic (tū'nik) *n.* short-sleeved knee-length garment worn by women and boys in ancient Greece and Rome; short-sleeved vestment worn by deacon at mass; girl's dress for gymnastics; jacket of uniform, as worn by soldiers, policemen, etc. [L. *tunica*, under-garment of both sexes].

tunnel (tun'el) *n.* arched subterranean passage usually as track for railway-line;—*v.t.* to cut tunnel through; to excavate.—*pr.p.* **tunn'elling.**—*pa.t.* and *pa.p.* **tunn'elled.** [O.Fr. *tonne*, tun or cask].

tunny (tun'i) *n.* edible fish of mackerel family found in Mediterranean, larger variety found off east and west seaboard of U.S.A.; tuna fish [Gk. *thunnos*].

tup (tup) *n.* a ram; weighted head of pile-driver or steam-hammer;—*v.t.* (of ram) to copulate with [etym. uncertain].

turban (tur'ban) *n.* Oriental male head-dress comprising long strip of cloth swathed round head or cap; close-fitting cap or scarf-head-dress worn by women; whorls of certain shells [Turk. *tulbend*].

turbid (tur'bid) *a.* having dregs disturbed; muddy; (*Fig.*) disturbed.—**tur'bidly** *adv.*—**tur'bidness, turbid'ity** *n.* [L. *turbidus*, fr. *turbare*, to disturb].

turbine (tur'bīn) or -bin) *n.* horizontal water-wheel with curved floats on periphery; rotary engine driven by steam, hot air, or water striking on curved vanes of wheel, or drum; high speed prime mover used for generating electrical energy.—**tur'binal** *a.* coiled like a spiral.—**tur'bine-steam'er** *n.* boat driven by steam-turbine.—**tur'bo-jet'** *n.* jet propelled gas turbine.—**turbo-prop,** jet engine in which turbine is coupled to propeller [L. *turbo,* whirl].

turbot (tur´bot) *n.* large flat sea-fish, next in size to the halibut, [L. *turbo,* a top].

turbulent (tur´bū-lent) *a.* disturbed; in violent commotion; swirling; (*Fig.*) refractory.—**tur'bulence, tur'bulency** *n.* [L. *turbare,* to disturb].

Turcoman (tur´kō-man) *n.* same as **Turkoman.**

turd (turd) *n.* ball of dung [O.E. *tord*].

tureen (tu-rēn' or tū´rēn) *n.* large, deep dish with removable cover, for serving soup [Fr. *terrine,* an earthen vessel].

turf (turf) *n.* surface soil containing matted roots, grass, etc.; sward; sod; peat; a race-course.—*pl.* **turfs,** (obsolete) **turves.**—*v.t.* to cover with turf, as lawn; (*Slang*) to throw out unceremoniously.—**The Turf,** horseracing and betting [O.E. *turf,* turf].

turgent (tur´jent) *a.* swelling; puffing up like a tumour; (*Fig.*) pompous; bombastic.—**tur'gently** *adv.*—**turges'cence, turges'cency** *n.* swelling caused by congestion; (*Fig.*) empty bombast.—**tur'gid** *a.* swollen; distended abnormally; (*Fig.*) bombastic.—**turgid'ity, tur´gidness** *n.* [L. *turgere,* to swell].

Turk (turk) *n.* native of *Turkey;* Ottoman; a fierce person; a Mohammedan.—**Turkey carpet,** wool carpet with bold pattern of brilliant colours and thick pile.—**Turkey red,** brilliant red dye; cotton cloth dyed with this.—**Turk´ish** *a.* pert. to Turks or Turkey.—**Turkish bath,** steam or hot air bath after which person is rubbed down, massaged, etc.—**Turkish delight,** soft sweetmeat.—**Turkish towel,** orig. a rough surfaced towel; a towel of cotton fabric with loops uncut, giving it specially absorbent qualities.—**Turk'oman** *n.* one of the Turkish race living in C. Asia.—*pl.* **Turk´omans.**

turkey (tur´ki) *n.* large, gallinaceous bird, bred for food, esp. at Christmas.—**tur'key-trot** *n.* an eccentric rag-time dance [fr. *Turkey,* from which country the bird was supposed to come].

turmeric (tur´mer-ik) *n.* E. Indian plant; root of this powdered, and used in dyes, medicines, condiments, curry-powder, etc. [etym. doubtful].

turmoil (tur´moil) *n.* commotion; harassing; labour; upset;—*v.t.* to harass; to exhaust;—*v.i.* to be upset [etym. doubtful].

turn (turn) *v.t.* to move round; to cause to revolve; to deflect; to form on lathe; to apply; to convert; to upset or nauseate; to blunt;—*v.i.* to rotate; to hinge; to depend; to become giddy, nauseated, or upset; (of tides) to change from ebb to flow or the reverse; to become sour, as milk;—*n.* act of turning; change of direction; single revolution, as of wheel; bend; an action, as *good turn;* action done in rotation with others; short walk; a subtle quality of expression, as *turn of phrase;* single performance, as on variety-stage; crisis.—**turn'about** *n.* merry-go-round.—**turn'coat** *n.* renegade; one who betrays party or other principles.—**turn'cock** *n.* one who operates stopcock on water-main, etc.—**turn'er** *n.* one who or that which turns; one who turns things on lathe.—**turn'ing** *n.* act of turning; deflection; winding; junction of two roads or streets; process of shaping and rounding articles with lathe.—**turn'ing-point** *n.* decisive moment; crisis.—**turn'key** *n.* one in charge of prison keys; warder.—**turn´out** *n.* act of coming forth; production, as of factory; strike; striker; number of people at any gathering; carriage and horses, driver, etc.—**turn'over** *n.* total sales made by a business in certain period; rate at which employees of factory are replaced by others; tart of paste folded over a filling of jam, or fruit.—**turn'pike** *n.* gate across road at point where toll is due.—**turnpike road,** orig. a main road with toll-gate.—**turn´screw** *n.* screw-driver.—**turn'spit** *n.* one who turns a spit; a menial.—**turn´stile** *n.* revolving gate for controlling admission of people.—**turn´ta'ble** *n.* revolving circular platform for turning locomotives on to another line or in opposite direction.—**turn´up** *n.* disturbance; domestic upheaval.—**turn about,** alternately.—**to turn down,** to decline, as offer; to reject, as application.—**to turn in,** to bend inwards; to hand in; to go to bed.—**to turn upon,** to attack suddenly; to retort.—**to turn one's head,** to make one conceited; to make one giddy.—**to turn the scale,** to decide an issue.—**to turn the tables on,** to reverse conditions.—**to turn turtle,** to turn upside down.—**in turn,** in sequence.—**on the turn,** at moment of changing, as tides [O.E. *tyrnan,* to turn].

turnip (tur´nip) *n.* plant of mustard family with large globular root much cultivated for food and cattle-fodder [etym. doubtful, prob. fr. O.E. *naep,* turnip].

turpentine (tur´pen-tīn) *n.* oily liquid extracted by distillation of resin exuded by pine and other coniferous trees; (*Colloq. abbrev.*) **turps** [Gk. *terebinthos,* terebinth tree].

turpitude (tur´pi-tūd) *n.* revolting baseness; lewdness; infamy [L. *turpis,* base].

turquoise (tur´koiz or -kwoiz) *n.* bluish-green gem-stone.—**tur'quoise-green** *n.* pale jade colour [so called because first brought from Persia to Europe via *Turkey*].

turret (tur´et) *n.* small tower on building; revolving gun-tower on ship, tank, or aircraft.—**turr'eted** *a.* having turrets [O.Fr. *tourete,* a little tower].

turtle (tur´tl) *n.* marine tortoise with hard shell and limbs like paddles; **hawksbill turtle** yields tortoiseshell, **green turtle** is used for soup.—**mock´-tur'tle** *n.* soup of calf's head with curry flavouring.—**to turn turtle** (*Naut. slang*) to capsize [Sp. *tortuga,* tortoise].

turtle (tur´tl) *n.* kind of pigeon, noted for its soft cooing and its affection for its mate. Also **tur'tle-dove** [L. *turtur,* a dove].

Tuscan (tus´kan) *a.* pert. to Tuscany in Italy; (*Archit.*) denoting the simplest of the five classical styles in architecture.

tusk (tusk) *n.* the long, protruding side-tooth of certain animals such as elephant, wild boar, walrus.—**tusked** *a.*—**tusk'er** *n.* elephant with fully developed tusks.—**tusk'y** *a.* [O.E. *tusc,* tooth].

tusser (tus´er) *n.* silkworm of India; rather coarse fawn-coloured silk fibre spun by tusser; hard-wearing, uneven-textured fawn silk fabric, from this fibre. Also **tuss'ah, tuss'ar, tuss'eh, tuss'ore, tuss'ur** [Hind. *tassar,* shuttle].

tussle (tus´l) *n.* struggle; scuffle;—*v.t.* to struggle [etym. doubtful].

tussock (tus´ok) *n.* clump, tuft, or hillock of growing grass [etym. doubtful].

tussore-silk Same as **tusser-silk.**

tut (tut) *interj.* exclamation of irritation or rebuke.

tutelage (tū´te-lāj) *n.* guardianship; state or period of being under this.—**tu'telar, tu'telary** *a.* having protection over a person or place; protective [L. *tutela*].

tutor (tū´tor) *n.* (*fem.* **tu'toress**) (*Law*) one in charge of minor; private teacher; university lecturer who directs and supervises studies of undergraduates;—*v.t.* to teach; to prepare another for special examination by private coaching; to discipline; to have guardianship of.—**tuto'rial** *a.* pert. to tutor;—*n.* (*Colloq.*) extra tuition given by college tutor, usually to section of class.—**tuto'rially** *adv.*—**tu'toring** *n.*—**tu'torship** *n.*—**tu'trix** *n.* (*Law*) female guardian [L. *tutor,* a guardian)].

tutti-frutti (tóót´i fróót´i) *n.* macédoine of fruits; ice-cream sundae with fruit, nuts, etc. [It.=all fruits].

tutu (tóó´tóó) *n.* ballet dancer's skirt [Fr.].

tuxedo (tuk-sē´dō) *n.* (*U.S.*) dinner-jacket [fr. *Tuxedo Park,* country-club, near New York].

twaddle (twod´l) *n.* inane conversation; nonsensical talk;—*v.i.* to talk inanely.—**twadd'ler** *n.*—**twadd'ling** *n.* twaddle.—**twadd'ly** *a.* silly.

twain (twān) *n.* two; pair.—**in twain,** in two parts; asunder [O.E. *twegen,* two].

twang (twang) *n.* sharp, rather harsh sound made by tense string sharply plucked; nasalised speech;—*v.t.* to pluck tense string of instrument so that it emits twang; (*Colloq.*) to strum, as banjo;—*v.i.* to speak with a twang [imit.].

tweak (twēk) *v.t.* to twist and pull with sudden jerk; to nip sharply;—*n.* sharp pinch or jerk [var. of *twitch*].

tweed (twēd) *n.* woollen twilled fabric esp. for costumes, coats, suits;—*a.* of tweed [fr. mistaken reading of '*tweel*'].

tweel (twēl) *n.* (*Scot.*) a var. of **twill**; the original word for *tweed.*

'tween (twēn) *contr.* of **between.**—**'tween deck,** between upper and lower decks.

tweeny (twē´ni) *n.* (*Colloq.*) servant girl helping cook and housemaid [fr. *between*].

tweezers (twēz´ẹrz) *n. sing.* small pair of pincers, esp. for pulling out superfluous hairs [prob. fr. *tweeze,* obsolete word for surgeon's case of instruments].

twelve (twelv) *a.* one more than eleven; two and ten; dozen;—*n.* sum of ten and two; symbol representing twelve units, as 12, xii.—**twelfth** *a.* next after eleventh; constituting one of twelve equal parts;—*n.* one of twelve equal parts.—**Twelfth Day,** January 6th, twelfth day after Christmas; Feast of Epiphany.— **twelfth'ly** *adv.*—**Twelfth Night,** evening of, or evening before, Twelfth Day, when festivities and special entertainments were held.—**the Twelve,** twelve Apostles.—**twelve´month** *n.* a year [O.E. *twelf,* twelve].

twenty (twen´ti) *a.* twice ten; nineteen and one;—*n.* number next after nineteen; score; symbol representing twenty units, as 20, xx.—**twen'tieth** *a.* next after nineteenth;—*n.* one of twenty equal parts.—**twen'ty-fold** *adv.* twenty times as many [O.E. *twentig*].

twerp (twẹrp) *n.* (*Slang*) cad.

twice (twīs) *adv.* two times; doubly [O.E. *twa,* two].

twiddle (twid´l) *v.t.* to play with; to twirl idly;—*v.i.* to spin round; to trifle with.—**to twiddle one's thumbs,** to have nothing to do [etym. doubtful].

twig (twig) *n.* small shoot or branch of tree; divining-rod.—**twig'gy** *a.* covered with twigs [O.E. *twig,* branch].

twig (twig) *v.t.* and *i.* (*Colloq.*) to notice; to understand [Ir. *tuigim,* discern].

twilight (twi´līt) *n.* half-light preceding sunrise or immediately after sunset; faint, indeterminate light;—*a.* partially illuminated; obscure.—**twilight sleep,** in obstetrics, modern method of inducing state of partial insensibility in woman in confinement by use of drug, scopolamine-morphine [lit, 'between-light'; O.E. *twa,* two; *leoht,* light].

twill (twil) *n.* fabric woven with diagonal ribbing;—*v.t.* to weave with twill [O.E. *twilic,* two-threaded].

twin (twin) *n.* one of two born at birth; exact counterpart;—*a.* twofold; being one of two born at a birth; consisting of two identical parts; growing in pairs.—**twin´beds** *n.pl.* two single beds of identical size side by side.—**twin´born** *a.* born at the same birth.—**twin´broth'er, -sis'ter** *n.*—**twin´screw** *n.* a vessel with two propellers on separate shafts [O.E. *twinn,* double].

twine (twīn) *n.* cord composed of two or more strands twisted together; string; tangle;—*v,t.* to twist together, as fibres; to entwine; to encircle;—*v.i.* to wind; to coil spirally, as tendrils of plant; to follow circuitous route.—**twi'ning** *a.* winding; coiling [O.E. *twin,* double-thread].

twinge (twinj) *n.* sudden, acute spasm of pain; pang;—*v.t.* (*rare*) to tweak; to effect momentarily with sudden pain [O.E. *twengan,* to pinch].

twinkle (twing´kl) *v.i.* to blink; to sparkle; (of eyes) to light up; (of feet) to move quickly and neatly;—*n.* act of twinkling; gleam of amusement in eyes; flicker; quick movement of feet, esp. in dancing; sparkle.—**twink'ler** *n.*—**twink'ling** *n.* twinkle [O.E. *twinclian,* to sparkle].

twirl (twirl) *v.t.* to whirl round; to flourish;—*v.i.* to turn round rapidly;—*n.* a rapid, rotary motion; a flourish.—**to twirl one's thumbs,** to have nothing to do [O.E. *thwiril,* a whisk for beating milk].

twist (twist) *v.t.* to contort; to coil spirally; to wind; to encircle; to distort; to form, as cord, from several fibres wound together;—*v.i.* to become tangled or distorted; to wriggle; to be united by winding round each other; to coil; to follow a roundabout course; (*Fig.*) to cheat;—*n.* cord; string; coil; single strand of rope; small roll of tobacco; an abnormality.—**twist'ed** *a.*—**twist'er** *n.* one who, or that which, twists; swindler [O.E. *twist,* rope].

twit (twit) *v.t.* to taunt; to reproach; to tease. —*pr.p.* **twit'ting.**—*pa.t.* and *pa.p.* **twit'ted.**—*n.* taunt [O.E. *twiccian,* to pluck].

twitch (twich) *v.t.* to pull suddenly with a slight jerk; to snatch;—*v.i.* to be suddenly jerked; to contract with sudden spasm, as a muscle; to quiver;—*n.* sudden spasmodic contraction of fibre or muscle.—**twitch'ing** *n.* [O.E. *twiccian,* to pluck].

twitch-grass (twich´gras) *n.* prolific weed, couch-grass or quitch-grass.

twitter (twit´ẹr) *n.* chirping sound; slight trembling of nerves; half-suppressed laugh;—*v.i.* to make succession of small light sounds; to chirp; to talk rapidly and nervously; to titter.—**twitt'ering** *n.* act of twittering; agitation; causing incoherence [imit.].

'twixt (twikst) *prep.* contr. of **between.**

two (to̍o̍) *a.* one and one;—*n.* sum of one and one; symbol representing two units, as 2, ii; a pair.—**two´deck'er** *n.* double-decker bus; (*Colloq.*) sandwich with three layers of bread and two different fillings.—**two´edged** *a.* having two sharp edges, as a sword; (*Fig.*) ambiguous.—**two´faced** *a.* having two faces; hypocritical; double-dealing.—**two´fold** *a.* double; doubly.—**two´hand'ed** *a.* requiring two hands or two players; ambidextrous.—**twopence** (tup´ẹns) *n.* sum of two pennies.—**twopenny** (tup´ẹn-i) *a.* costing two pennies; (*Colloq.*) worthless;—*n.* kind of ale.—**twopenny halfpenny** (tup´ẹn-i hāp´ẹn-i) *a.* rubbishy; quite valueless.—**two´ply** *a.* having two strands twisted together in two layers, as wool.—**two´seat'er** *n.* small motor-car designed for two people only; tandem bicycle.—**two´sid'ed** *a.* having two surfaces or aspects; (of cloth) reversible; (*Fig.*) double-dealing.—**two´stroke** *a.* denoting an internal combustion engine making one explosion to every two piston-strokes.

Tyburn (tī´burn) *n.* historically famous place of execution in London.—**Tyburn tree,** gallows.

tycoon (tī-ko̍o̍n') *n.* the title by which the shogun or Japanese hereditary commander-in-chief was known to foreigners between 1854-1868; head of great business combine; a magnate [Jap. *taikun,* great prince].

tyke (tīk) *n.* var. of **tike.**

tymbal (tim´bạl) *n.* Same as **timbal.**

tympan (tim´pạn) *n.* ancient Irish musical instrument; [Gk. *tumpanaon,* a kettle-drum].

tympanum (tim´pạn-um) *n.* a drum (*Anat.*) cavity of the middle-ear; ear-drum; (*Archit.*) flat, triangular space between sides of pediment; similar space over door between lintel and arch.—*pl.* **tym'pana.**—**tym'panal, tympan'ic** *a.* like a drum; pert. to middle ear.—**tym'panist** *n.* one who plays drum or any percussion instrument [Gk. *tumpanon,* a kettle-drum].

Tyn(e)wald, Tin(e)wald (tin′wold) *n.* Manx Parliament, usually *Tyn(e)wald Court* [O.N. *thing-vollr*, the assembly field].

type (tīp) *n.* mark or impression of something; model; pattern; person representative of group or of certain quality; stamp on either side of a coin; (*Chem.*) compound which has basic composition of other more complex compounds; (*Biol.*) individual specimen representative of species; (*Print.*) metal block on one end of which is raised letter, etc. required for letterpress printing; such blocks collectively; style or form of printing;—*v.t.* to typify; to represent in type; to reproduce by means of typewriter; to classify;—*v.i.* to use a typewriter.—**ty′pal** *a.*—**type′cutt′er** *n.* one who engraves blocks for printing-types.—**type′found′er** *n.* one who casts type for printing.—**type′met′al** *n.* alloy of lead, antimony, and tin used for casting type.—**type′script** *n.* a typewritten document.—**type′set′ting** *n.* process or occupation of preparing type for printing.—**type′write** *v.i.* to produce by means of a typewriter.—**type′writer** *n.* machine with keyboard operated by fingers, which produces printed characters on paper; operator of such machine.—**type′writing** *n.*—**type′written** *a.*—**typic, -al** (tip′ic, -ạl) *a.* pert. to type; symbolic; true to type.—**typical′ity** *n.*—**typ′ically** *adv.*—**typ′icalness, typifica′tion** *n.*—**ty′pifier** *n.*—**typ′ify** *v.t.* to represent by image; to symbolise; to exemplify.—*pa.p.* **typ′ified.**—**typ′ing** *n.* act of typing; script typed.—**typ′ist** *n.* one who operates typewriting machine.—**typog′rapher** *n.* printer.—**typograph′ic, -al** *a.* pert. to printing.—**typog′raphy** *n.* art of printing; style or mode of printing [Gk. *tupos*, mark of a blow].

typhoid (tī′foid) *a.* resembling typhus; pert. to enteric fever;—*n.* infectious disease characterised by severe diarrhoea, profound weakness, and rash. Also called *enteric fever*.—**typhoid′al** *a.* [Gk. *tuphos*, fever; *eidos*, form].

typhoon (tī-fòòn′) *n.* cyclonic hurricane occurring in China seas.—**typhon′ic** *a.* [Ar. *tufan*].

typhus (tī′fus) *n.* highly contagious disease caused by virus conveyed by body lice and characterised by purplish rash, prostration, and abnormally high temperature.—**ty′phous** *a.* [Gk. *tuphos*, fever].

tyrant (tī′rạnt) *n.* (*fem.* **tyr′anness**) in ancient Greece, usurper; harsh, despotic ruler; any person enforcing his will on others, cruelly and arbitrarily.—**tyran′nic, -al, tyrannous** (tir′ạn-us) *a.*—**tyran′nically** *adv.*—**tyr′annously** *ad.*—**tyran′nicalness** *n.*—**tyr′annise** *v.i.* to rule tyrannically; to exert authority ruthlessly;—*v.t.* to subject to tyrannical authority.—**tyranny** (tir′ạ-ni) *n.* orig. office of a Greek tyrant; despotic government; cruelly harsh enforcement of authority (Gk. *turannos*, an unconstitutional ruler].

tyre See **tire.**

Tyrian (tir′i-ạn) *a.* pert. to ancient Phoenician seaport of *Tyre*; of deep purple colour, as dye formerly made at Tyre from gland of shell-fish.

tyro (tī′rō) *n.* See **tiro.**

Tyrolese (tir-ol-ēz′) *a.* pert. to Austrian Tyrol;—*n.* native of the Tyrol.

tythe (tīTH) *n.* Same as **tithe.**

Tzar, Tzarina Same as **Czar, Czarina.**

tzigany (tsig-á′ni) *n.* Hungarian gipsy. Also **tzigane′** [Hung. *Cigany*, a gipsy].

U

ubiquity (ū-bik′wi-ti) *n.* existing in all places at same time; omnipresence.—**ubiq′uitous, ubiq′uitary** *a.* existing or being everywhere.—**ubiq′uitously** *adv.*—**ubiq′uitousness** *n.* omnipresence [L. *ubique*, everywhere].

U-boat (ū′bōt) *n.* German submarine [Ger. *untersee*, under the sea, and *boat*].

udder (ud′ẹr) *n.* milk-gland of certain animals, as cow [O.E. *uder*, udder].

udometer (ū-dom′e-tẹr) *n.* an instrument for measuring rainfall.—**udom′etry** *n.*—**udom′ograph** *n.* self-registering rain-gauge [L. *udus*, moist; *metron*, measure].

ugh (uh) *interj.* exclamation of disgust.

ugly (ug′li) *a.* offensive to the sight; of disagreeable aspect; dangerous, of *situation*.—**ug′lify** *v.t.* to make ugly.—**ug′liness** *n.*—**ug′some** *a.* hideous [O.N. *uggr*, fear].

Uhlan (òò′lan) *n.* cavalryman armed with lance, as in certain C. European armies, esp. Prussian [Polish, *ulan*, lancer].

Uitlander (òò-it′lan-dẹr) *n.* Boer name for incomers to Transvaal in S. Africa, the majority of whom were British. [S. Afr. *uitlander*, an outlander].

ukase (ū-kās′) *n.* official Russian decree [Russ, *ukaz*, edict].

Ukrainian (ū-krān (or krīn)′i-ạn) *n.* citizen of *Ukraine*, republic in S.W. Russia;—*a.* pert. to Ukraine.

ukulele (ū-kòò-lā′li) *n.* small four-stringed instrument like guitar [Hawaiian].

ulcer (ul′sẹr) *n.* superficial sore discharging pus; (*Fig.*) source of corruption.—**ul′cerate** *v.i.* to become ulcerous; to suppurate.—**ul′cerated** *a.*—**ulcera′tion** *n.* state of discharging pus.—**ul′cered** *a.* having ulcers.—**ul′cerous** *a.* pert. to ulcer.—**ul′cerously** *adv.*—**ul′cerousness** *n.* [L. *ulcus*].

ullage (ul′āj) *n.* amount which cask lacks of being full.—**ull′ing** [O.Fr. *eullage*, the filling up of a cask].

ulna (ul′nạ) *n.* inner and larger of two bones of forearm.—*pl.* **ul′nae.**—**ul′nar** *a.* [L. *ulna*, elbow].

ulster (ul′stẹr) *n.* long loose overcoat or mackintosh usually with a hood, originally manufactured in *Ulster*.—**ul′stered** *a.*

ulterior (ul-tē′ri-or) *a.* situated on the farther side; beyond; (of motives) undisclosed; not frankly stated.—**ulte′riorly** *adv.* [L. *ulterior*, farther].

ultimate (ul′ti-māt) *a.* farthest; final; primary; conclusive.—**ul′timately** *adv.*—**ultima′tum** *n.* final proposition; final terms offered as basis of treaty.—*pl.* **ultima′tums,** or **ultima′ta.**—**ul′timo** *a.* in the month preceding current one (*abbrev.* **ult.**) [L. *ultimus*, last].

ultra (ul′trạ) *a.* beyond; extreme; in combination words with or without hyphen, as *ultra-modern* [L. *ultra*, beyond].

ultramarine (ul-trạ-mạ-rēn′) *a.* situated beyond the sea;—*n.* bright-blue pigment obtained from powdered lapis lazuli, or produced synthetically [L. *ultra*, beyond; *mare*, the sea (*lapis lazuli* formerly brought from *beyond the sea*)].

ultramontane (ul-trạ-mon′tān) *a.* being beyond the mountains, esp. the Alps; used of Italians by those on northern side of Alps, and vice versa; pert. to absolute temporal and spiritual power of Papacy or to party upholding this claim;—*n.* advocate of extreme or ultra-papal views.—**ultramon′tanism** *n.*—**ultramon′tanist** *n.*

ultra-short (ul-trạ-short′) *a.* (*Radio*) used of electro-magnetic waves of wavelength under 10 metres.

ultrasonics (ul-trạ-son′iks) *n.* the science of mechanical vibrations of frequencies greater than those normally audible to the ear [L. *ultra*, beyond; *sonus*, a sound].

ultra-violet (ul-trạ′vī-o-let) *a.* beyond limit of visibility at violet end of the spectrum.

ululant (ūl′ū-lạnt) *a.* howling; hooting.—**ul′ulate** *v.i.* to howl; to hoot.—**ulula′tion** *n.* [L. *ululare*, to howl].

umbel (um′bẹl) *n.* (*Bot.*) flower-cluster, the stalks of which rise from a common centre on main stem, forming a convexed surface above, as in carrot, parsley, etc.—**um′bellal,**

um'bellar, um'bellate, -d *a.* having umbels.—**umbellif'erous** *a.* bearing umbels.—**umbell'iform** *a.* having shape of umbel [L. *umbella*, little shade].
umber (umʹbẹr) *n.* natural earth pigment, yellowish-brown in colour when *raw*, reddish-brown when calcined or *burnt* [fr. *Umbria*, in Italy].
umbilic, -al (um-bilʹik, -ạl) *a.* pert. to umbilicus or navel.—**umbilic'ular** *a.* pert. to navel.—**umbilical cord** (*Anat.*) fibrous cord joining foetus to placenta [L. *umbilicus*, the navel].
umbles (umʹblz) *n.pl.* entrails of a deer [orig. *numbles*, fr. O.Fr. *nombles*].
umbra (umʹbrạ) *n.* shadow; (*Astron.*) complete shadow cast by earth or moon in eclipse, as opposed to *penumbra*, partial shadow in eclipse.—**um'bral** *a.* [L. *umbra*, shadow].
umbrage (umʹbrāj) *n.* shadow; (*Fig.*) feeling of resentment.—**umbra'geous** *a.* shady.—**umbra'geously** *adv.*—**to take umbrage**, to feel resentful [L. *umbra*, shadow].
umbrella (um-brelʹa) *n.* light-weight circular covering of silk or other material on framework of spokes, carried as protection against rain (or sun); overhead protective screen of fighter aircraft during combined operations.—**umbrell'a-stand** *n.* stand for holding umbrellas [It. *ombrella*, dim. of *ombra*, shade].
umbrose (umʹbrōz) *a.* shady.—**umbros'ity** *n.* [L. *umbra*, shadow].
umlaut (ŏŏmʹlout) *n.* term used to denote mutation caused by influence of vowel *i* (earlier *j*) on preceding vowel such as a, o, u; in Modern German this vowel-mutation is indicated by diaeresis over vowel, as in Führer (Fuehrer); in English it is seen in plural forms of man (*men*), mouse (*mice*), foot (*feet*). Also called **i'-muta'tion** [Ger. *um*, about; *Laut*, sound].
umpire (umʹpīr) *n.* person chosen to arbitrate in dispute; impartial person chosen to see that rules of game are properly enforced; referee [orig. *numpire*, fr. O.Fr. *nomper*, peerless].
umpteen (umpʹtēn) *a.* (*Slang*) innumerable [invented on analogy of thir*teen*, etc.].
un- *prefix* before nouns, adjectives, and adverbs adding negative force; before verbs, expressing reversal of the action, separation, etc.
unabashed (un-ạ-basht') *a.* unashamed.
unabated (un-ạ-bāʹted) *a.* not diminished; fully maintained.
unable (un-āʹbl) *a.* not able; impotent; lacking skill, strength, or training.
unabridged (unʹạ-briid) *a.* not shortened; (of text) in full.
unaccented (un-ạk-sentʹed) *a.* not accented; unstressed.—**unaccent'uated** *a.* not accented.
unacceptable (un-ạk-septʹạ-bl) *a.* not acceptable; undesirable.—**unaccept'ableness.**
unaccommodating (un-ạ-komʹō-dāt-ing) *a.* not compliant; disobliging.
unaccompanied (un-ạ-kumʹpạ-nid) *a.* not accompanied; sung or played on instrument without piano, organ, or orchestral accompaniment.
unaccountable (un-ạ-kountʹạ-bl) *a.* not accountable; inexplicable.
unaccustomed (un-ạ-kusʹtomd) *a.* not accustomed; unusual.—**unaccus'tomedness** *n.*
unadorned (un-ạ-dornd') *a.* not adorned; plain; void of ornament.
unadulterate (un-ạ-dulʹte-rāt) *a.* not adulterated; pure. Also **unadul'terated.**
unaffected (un-ạ-fektʹed) *a.* not affected; unmoved; straightforward; sincere.—**un'affect'edly** *adv.* simply; void of affectation.
unalloyed (un-ạ-loid') *a.* not alloyed; pure; (*Fig.*) complete; unqualified.
unalterable (un-awlʹtẹr-ạ-bl) *a.* not capable of alteration; fixed; permanent.—**unalterabil'ity, unal'terableness** *n.*—**unal'terably** *adv.*—**unal'tered** *a.* unchanged.
unamiable (un-āʹmi-ạ-bl) *a.* not amiable; boorish.—**unamiabil'ity, una'miableness** *n.*
unanealed, unaneled (un-ạ-nēld') *a.* not having received extreme unction.
unanimous (ū-nanʹi-mus) *a.* all of one mind; agreed to by all parties.—**unanim'ity** *n.* state of being unanimous.—**unan'imously** *adv.*—**unan'imousness** *n.* [L. *unus*, one; *animus*, mind].
unannealed (un-ạ-nēld') *a.* (of metals) not tempered; not treated by the process of heating followed by cooling or quenching.
unanswerable (un-anʹsẹr-ạ-bl) *a.* not answerable; irrefutable; conclusive.—**unanswerabil'ity, unan'swerableness** *n.*
unappetising (un-ap-e-tīzʹing) *a.* not appetising; uninviting; repulsive.
unappreciated (un-ạ-prēʹshi-ā-ted) *a.* not appreciated; not valued.—**unappre'ciative** *a.* not appreciative; lacking in gratitude.
unapproachable (un-ạ-prōchʹạ-bl) *a.* not approachable; inaccessible; (of a person) having an aloof manner.—**unapproach'ableness** *n.*—**unapproach'ably** *adv.*
unarm (un-ärm') *v.t.* to disarm; to render harmless;—*v.i.* to lay down arms.—**unarmed'** *a.* defenceless.—**unar'moured** *a.* without weapons; (of ships, etc.) not protected by armour-plating.
unashamed (un-ạ-shāmd') *a.* not ashamed; unabashed; brazen.
unasked (un-askd') *a.* not asked; unsolicited.
unassailable (un-ạ-sālʹạ-bl) *a.* not assailable; irrefutable; invincible.—**unassailed'** *a.*
unassimilated (un-ạ-simʹi-lā-ted) *a.* not assimilated.—**unassim'ilable** *a.* not capable of mixing thoroughly.—**unassim'ilating** *a.*
unassuming (un-ạ-sūmʹing) *a.* not assuming; modest; not overbearing.
unattached (un-ạ-tachd') *a.* not attached; dangling; not posted to a particular regiment; non-resident; (*Colloq.*) not married or engaged.
unattainable (un-ạ-tānʹạ-bl) *a.* beyond one's reach; not attainable.—**unattain'ably** *adv.*
unattended (un-ạ-tendʹed) *a.* not accompanied, as by a servant; not attended to; untreated.—**unattend'ing** *a.* not attending.—**unattent'ive** *a.* inattentive.
unattested (un-ạ-testʹed) *a.* not attested; unsupported by the evidence of a witness.
unattractive (un-ạ-traktʹiv) *a.* not attractive; repellent; plain; not prepossessing.—**unattract'ively** *adv.*—**unattract'iveness** *n.*
unauthorised (un-awʹthor-īzd) *a.* not authorised; unsanctioned by authority.—**unauthorita'tive** *a.*
unavailing (un-ạ-vālʹing) *a.* not availing; fruitless; having no result.—**unavailabil'ity** *n.*—**unavail'able** *a.* not procurable; not at one's disposal.—**unavail'ingly** *adv.* fruitlessly.
unavoidable (un-ạ-voidʹạ-bl) *a.* not avoidable; inevitable; inescapable; incapable of being made null and void.—**unavoid'ableness** *n.*—**unavoid'ably** *adv.*—**unavoid'ed** *a.*
unaware (un-ạ-wār') *a.* having no information.—*adv.* unawares.—**unawares'** *adv.* unexpectedly; without previous warning.
unbaked (un-bākt') *a.* not baked; (*Fig.*) immature.
unbalance (un-balʹạns) *v.t.* to upset; to unhinge.—**unbal'anced** *a.* not balanced; lacking equipoise, or mental stability; not adjusted or equal on credit and debit sides (of ledger).—**unbal'ance** *n.*
unbated (un-bātʹed) *a.* not repressed; (of sword) not blunted.
unbearable (un-bārʹạ-bl) *a.* not bearable; intolerable; (of pain) excruciating.—**unbear'ableness** *n.*—**unbear'ably** *adv.*
unbeaten (un-bēʹtn) *a.* not flogged; unconquered; unsurpassed; untrodden.
unbecoming (un-bē-kumʹing) *a.* not becoming; not suited to the wearer; (of behaviour) immodest; indecorous.—**unbecom'ingly** *adv.*—**unbecom'ingness** *n.*
unbeknown (un-bē-nōn') *a.* unknown.—**unbeknownst'** *adv.* without the knowledge of.

unbelief (un-bē-lēf') *n.* scepticism, esp. regarding divine revelation.—**unbelievabil'ity** *n.* state of being incredible.—**unbeliev'able** *a.* —**unbelieved'** *a.*—**unbeliev'er** *n.* sceptic.—**unbeliev'ing** *a.* not believing in divine revelation.—**unbeliev'ingly** *adv.*
unbelt (un-belt') *v.t.* to undo the belt of; to take off a belt, as of sword.
unbend (un-bend') *v.t.* to free from bent position; to straighten; to relax; to loose, as anchor;—*v.i.* to become relaxed; to become more friendly.—**unbend'ing** *a.* not pliable; rigid; (*Fig.*) coldly aloof; resolute.—**unbend'ingly** *adv.*—**unbent'** *a.* straight.
unbias (un-bī'ạs) *v.t.* to rid of prejudice.—**unbi'as(s)ed** *a.* unprejudiced; impartial.
unbidden (un-bid'ẹn) *a.* not invited; unpremeditated.
unbind (un-bīnd') *v.t.* to remove band or fetter from; to loosen; to remove the covers from (a book).
unbitten (un-bit'n) *a.* not bitten; (*Slang*) not enthusiastic.
unbleached (un-blēcht') *a.* not bleached; having its natural colour.
unblemished (un-blem'isht) *a.* not blemished; faultless; (of character) pure; perfect.—**unblem'ishable** *a.*
unblooded (un-blood'ed) *a.* (of animal) not thoroughbred.
unbodied (un-bod'id) *a.* freed from the body; incorporeal.
unbolt (un-bōlt') *v.t.* to withdraw a bolt from; to unfasten.—**'-ed** *a.* unfastened.
unbolted (un-bōlt'ed) *a.* (of grain) unsifted; not having bran separated by bolter; coarse.
unborn (un-born') *a.* not yet born; future, as *unborn generations*.
unbosom (un-bo͝oz'um) *v.t.* to disclose freely; to reveal one's intimate longings.
unbound (un-bound') *a.* not bound; free; without outer binding, as a book.—**unbound'ed** *a.* illimitable; abundant; irrepressible.—**-edly** *adv.*—**-edness** *n.*
unbowed (un-boud') *a.* not bowed; invincible.
unbreakable (un-brāk'ạ-bl) *a.* not breakable; non-brittle, as of plastics.
unbridle (un-brī'dl) *v.t.* to remove the bridle from, as a horse.—**unbri'dled** *a.* unrestrained; violently passionate.—**unbri'dledness** *n.*
unbroken (un-brō'kn) *a.* complete; whole; (of horse) untamed; inviolate; continuous; unsurpassed.—**-ly** *adv.*—**-edness** *n.*
unburden (un-bur'dn) *v.t.* to relieve of a burden; (*Fig.*) to relieve the mind of anxiety. —**unbur'dened** *a.*
unbusinesslike (un-biz'nes-līk) *a.* not businesslike; not methodical.
unbutton (un-but'n) *v.t.* to loose the buttons of; to unfasten; to dismantle, of steel structural framework.
uncage (un-kāj') *v.t.* to free from a cage.
uncalculated (un-kal'kū-lā-ted) *a.* not calculated; unexpected.
uncalled (un-kawld') *a.* not summoned.—**uncalled for**, superfluous; gratuitous.
uncanny (un-kan'i) *a.* weird; unearthly.—**uncann'ily** *adv.*—**uncann'iness** *n.*
uncate (ung'kāt) *a.* hooked [L. *uncus*, a hook].
uncaused (un-kawzd') *a.* not caused; without cause; self-existent.
unceasing (un-sēs'ing) *a.* not ceasing; continual; incessant.—**unceas'ingly** *adv.*
unceremonious (un-ser-e-mōn'i-us) *a.* not ceremonious; informal; abrupt.—**unceremon'iously** *adv.*—**unceremon'iousness** *n.*
uncertain (un-sẹr'ten) *a.* not certain; not positively known; unreliable; insecure.—**uncer'tainly** *adv.*—**uncer'tainness** *n.*—**uncer'tainty** *n.* state of being or that which is uncertain; lack of reassurance.
unchain (un-chān') *v.t.* to free from chains or bondage.
unchangeable (un-chān'jạ-bl) *a.* not changeable; constant; immutable.—**unchangeabil'ity, unchange'ableness** *n.*—**unchange'ably** *adv.*—**unchanged'** *a.* unaltered; static.—**unchang'ing** *a.* —**unchang'ingly** *adv.*
uncharitable (un-chȧr'i-tạ-bl) *a.* not charitable; mean; censorious.—**unchar'itableness** *n.* —**unchar'itably** *adv.*
uncharted (un-chȧr'ted) *a.* not shown on a map; unexplored.
unchristian (un-kris'tyạn) *a.* not Christian; contrary to principles of Christianity; pagan; not humanitarian.—**unchris'tianly** *adv.*
unchurch (un-church') *v.t.* to excommunicate; to deprive of name and status of a church.
uncial (un'shạl) *a.* pert. to a type of rounded script, found in ancient MSS from 4th-9th cents.;—*n.* uncial letter or manuscript.—**un'cialise** *v.t.* to form like uncials [L. *uncia*, inch; (*lit.*) letters, an inch high].
unciform (un'si-form) *a.* shaped like a hook. —**un'cinal, un'cinate** *a.* hooked; having hook-like prickles.—**Uncina'ria** *n.pl.* hook-worms [L. *uncus*, a hook].
uncircumcised (un-sir'kum-sīzd) *a.* not circumcised; Gentile; (*Fig.*) unregenerate. —**uncircumcis'ion** *n.*
uncivil (un-siv'il) *a.* not civil; rude.—**uncivilised'** *a.* barbarous.—**unciv'illy** *adv.*
uncle (ung'kl) *n.* brother of one's father or mother; any elderly man; (*Slang*) pawnbroker. —**Uncle Sam** (*Fig.*) United States of America; typical American citizen [L. *avunculus*, mother's brother].
unclean (un-klēn') *a.* not clean; filthy; ceremonially unsanctified; obscene.—**uncleanliness** *n.* (un-klen'li-nes).—**uncleanly** (un-klēn'li or -klen'li) *adv.*—**unclean'ness** *n.*
unclench (un-klensh') *v.t.* to open what is clenched.
unclothe (un-klōTH') *v.t.* to divest of clothes. —**unclothed'** *a.* naked.
uncock (un-kok') *v.t.* to let down hammer of gun without exploding charge.
uncoil (un-koil') *v.t.* to unwind the coils of.
uncomely (un-kum'li) *a.* not comely; unprepossessing; ugly; obscene.
uncomfortable (un-kum'for-tạ-bl) *a.* not comfortable; uneasy; awkward.—**uncom'fortableness** *n.*—**uncom'fortably** *adv.*—**uncom'forted** *a.* not consoled.
uncommercial (un-kom-ẹr'shạl) *a.* not commercial; not backed by profit-making motives.
uncommon (un-kom'on) *a.* not common; rare; extraordinary;—*adv.* (*Colloq.*) remarkably.—**uncomm'only** *adv.*—**uncomm'onness** *n.*
uncommunicative (un-ko-mū'ni-kā-tiv) *a.* not communicative; discreet; taciturn.—**uncommu'nicable** *a.* not capable of being shared or communicated.—**uncommu'nicableness** *n.*—**uncommu'nicated** *a.*
uncomplaining (un-kom-plā'ning) *a.* not complaining; resigned.—**uncomplain'ingly** *adv.* without complaint.
uncompleted (un-kom-plē'ted) *a.* not completed; unfinished.
uncomplimentary (un-kom-pli-men'tạ-ri) *a.* not complimentary; unflattering.
uncompromising (un-kom-prō-mī'zing) *a.* not compromising; making no concession; rigid.—**uncom'promisingly** *adv.*
unconcealed (un-kon-sēld') *a.* not concealed; openly shown; frank.
unconcern (un-kon-sẹrn') *n.* lack of concern; apathy.—**unconcerned'** *a.* not concerned; disinterested; apathetic; not involved.—**unconcer'nedly** *adv.*—**-edness** *n.*
unconditioned (un-kon-dish'und) *a.* not subject to conditions; absolute; instinctive. —**uncondi'tional** *a.* complete; absolute; without reservation.—**uncondi'tionally** *adv.*—**unconditioned reflexes**, the instinctive responses of an animal to external stimuli.
unconfirmed (un-kon-fırmd') *a.* not confirmed; not substantiated by authoritative

evidence; not having received the religious rite of confirmation.

uncongenial (un-kon-jē′ni-ạl) *a.* not congenial; temperamentally disagreeable.—**uncongenial′ity** *n.*—**uncongeʹnially** *adv.*

unconnected (un-kon-ek′ted) *a.* not connected; disjointed; incoherent; unrelated.

unconquerable (un-kong′kẹr-ạ-bl) *a.* not able to be conquered; invincible.

unconscionable (un-kon′shun-ạ-bl) *a.* beyond reason; unscrupulous; excessive.—**uncon′scionableness** *n.*—**uncon′scionably** *adv.*

unconscious (un-kon′shus) *a.* not conscious; unaware; deprived of consciousness; involuntary.—**uncon′sciously** *adv.*—**uncon′sciousness** *n.* state of being insensible.—**the unconscious,** in psycho-analysis, part of mind which appears to act without a conscious effort of will.

unconstitutional (un-kon-sti-tū′shun-ạl) *a.* not constitutional; contrary to the constitution, as of a society or state.—**unconstitutional′ity** *n.*—**unconstitu′tionally** *adv.*

unconstrained (un-kon-strānd′) *a.* not constrained; not embarrassed; voluntary.—**unconstrain′edly** *adv.*—**unconstraint′** *n.*

uncontrollable (un-kon-trōl′ạ-bl) *a.* not capable of being controlled; unmanageable; irrepressible.—**uncontroll′ableness** *n.*—**uncontroll′ably** *adv.*—**uncontrolled′** *a.* not controlled; (of prices) not restricted by government regulations.—**uncontroll′edly** *adv.*

unconventional (un-kon-ven′shun-ạl) *a.* not conventional; original; bohemian.—**unconventional′ity** *n.*—**unconven′tionally** *adv.*

unconversant (un-kon-vẹr′sạnt) *a.* not conversant (followed by *with* or *in*); unfamiliar (with).

unconverted (un-kon-vẹr′ted) *a.* not converted; unchanged in heart; heathen; not changed in opinion; (*Rugby*) of a try, not converted into a goal.—**unconver′sion** *n.*—**unconver′tible** *a.* not convertible.

unconvinced (un-kon-vinsd′) *a.* not convinced; not reassured; not persuaded.—**unconvin′cing** *a.* not convincing.

uncork (un-kork′) *v.t.* to remove the cork from.

uncouple (un-kup′l) *v.t.* to loose, as a dog from a leash; to disjoin, as railway carriages.—**uncoup′led** *a.* not mated.

uncouth (un-kȯȯth′) *a.* awkward in manner; strange; unpolished; unseemly.—**uncouth′ly** *adv.*—**uncouth′ness** *n.* [O.E. *cuth*, known].

uncovenanted (un-kuv′ẹ-nạn-ted) *a.* not agreed to, or bound by, a covenant.—**uncovenanted benefit,** National Insurance benefit not covered by contributions.

uncover (un-kuv′ẹr) *v.t.* to remove the cover of; to expose to view; to leave unprotected;—*v.i.* to take off one's hat.

unction (ungk′shun) *n.* act of anointing with oil, as in ceremony of consecration or coronation; anointing the dying, according to last rites administered by R.C. Church; (*Med.*) ointment; act of applying ointment; unguent; (*Fig.*) that which soothes; fervour of language arousing deep religious devotion in another; insincere emotion; gush.—**unctuos′ity** *n.* the quality or state of being unctuous.—**unc′tuous** *a.* oily; (*Fig.*) excessively suave.—**unc′tuously** *adv.*—**unc′tuousness** *n.*—**extreme unction,** R.C. rite of anointing the dying [L. *unguere, unctum*, to anoint].

uncular (ung′kū-lạr) *a.* pert. to an uncle.

uncultivable (un-kul′tiv-ạ-bl) *a.* not capable of being cultivated; waste.—**uncul′tivated** *a.* not cultivated; not tilled; (*Fig.*) undeveloped.—**uncul′tured** *a.* not cultured; not educated.

uncurb (un-kurb′) *v.t.* to free from a curb.—**uncurbed′** *a.* not curbed; unrestrained.

uncus (ung′kus) *n.* hook or hook-like formation; barb.—*pl.* **unci** (ung′si) [L. *uncus*, a hook].

uncut (un-kut′) *a.* not cut; having the pages untrimmed, as a book.

undamped (un-dampt′) *a.* not damped; dry (*Fig.*) not downhearted or dispirited.

undated (un′dā-ted) *a.* wavy, as a leaf. Also **un′date.**—**un′dose** *a.* having wavy depressions [L. *unda*, a wave].

undated (un-dā′ted) *a.* not bearing a date, as a letter.

undaunted (un-dawn′ted) *a.* not daunted; fearless; intrepid.—**undaun′tedly** *adv.*

undeceive (un-de-sēv′) *v.t.* to free from deception; to disillusion.—**undeceived′** *a.*

undecennial (un-dē-sen′i-ạl) *a.* pert. to, or lasting, a period of eleven years; happening every eleventh year. Also **undecenn′ary** [L. *undecim*, eleven].

undecided (un-dē-sī′ded) *a.* not settled; irresolute; vacillating.—**undeci′dable** *a.* not capable of being settled.—**undeci′dedly** *adv.*

undecipherable (un-dē-sī′fẹr-ạ-bl) *a.* impossible to decipher; illegible.

undeclared (un-dē′klārd′) *a.* not declared; (of taxable goods at customs) not admitted as being in one's possession during customs' examination.

undefended (un-dē-fen′ded) *a.* not defended; (of a law-suit, divorce case, etc.) without any defence being produced in court.

undefined (un-dē-fīnd′) *a.* not defined; vague; not made clear by definition.—**undefin′able** *a.* not capable of being defined.

undemocratic (un-dem-ō-krat′ik) *a.* not according to the principles of democracy.—**undemoc′ratise** *v.t.* to make undemocratic.

undemonstrative (un-de-mon′strạ-tiv) *a.* not demonstrative; reserved.—**undemon′stratively** *adv.*—**undemon′strativeness** *n.*

undeniable (un-de-nī′ạ-bl) *a.* not capable of being refuted or denied; certain; obvious.—**undeni′ably** *adv.* palpably; certainly.

undependable (un-dē-pen′dạ-bl) *a.* not dependable; unreliable; fickle.

under (un′dẹr) *prep.* below; beneath; subjected to; less than; liable to; included in; in the care of; during the period of; bound by;—*adv.* in a lower degree or position; less;—*a.* subordinate; lower in rank or degree.—**under age,** younger than 21 years.—**under arms,** mobilised for active service.—**under cover,** sheltered.—**under fire,** exposed to enemy assault.—**under one's breath,** in a whisper [O.E. *under*, under].

underact (un-dẹr-akt′) *v.t.* or *v.i.* to act a part in a play in a colourless, ineffective way.—**underac′tion** *n.*

underbid (un-dẹr-bid′) *v.t.* to bid a price less than the real value of an article; to sell goods more cheaply than another; to make lower bid at bridge than one's cards justify.

underbred (un-dẹr-bred′) *a.* of inferior manners; vulgar.

underbrush (un′dẹr-brush) *n.* undergrowth of shrubs and bushes.

undercarriage (un′dẹr-kar-ij) *n.* (*Aero.*) landing-gear of aircraft including wheels, skids, etc.

undercharge (un-dẹr-chårj′) *v.t.* to charge less than true price;—*n.* price below the real value.

underclay (un′dẹr-klā) *n.* a bed of clay beneath a coal seam.

underclothes (un′dẹr-klōTHz) *n. pl.* garments worn below the outer clothing, esp. next the skin; underclothing; lingerie.—**underclothed′** *a.*—**un′derclothing** *n.*

undercover (un′dẹr-kuv-ẹr) *a.* (*Colloq.*) secret; used esp. of secret service agents.

undercurrent (un′dẹr-kur-ẹnt) *n.* current under surface of main stream, sometimes flowing in a contrary direction; (*Fig.*) hidden tendency;—*a.* hidden.

undercut (un-dẹr-kut′) *v.t.* to cut away from below, as coal seam; to strike from beneath; to sell goods cheaply in order to capture a market or monopoly; (*Golf*) to loft (a ball);—*a.* produced by cutting away from below.—**un′dercut** *n.* act of cutting away from below meat on under side of sirloin; (*Boxing*) punch from underneath.

under-develop (un-dẹr-de-vel′op) *v.t.* (*Photog.*) to develop insufficiently so that the photographic print is indistinct.—**un'der-devel'oped** *a.* not developed physically; (of film) not sufficiently developed.

underdo (un-dẹr-do͝o′) *v.t.* to cook insufficiently.—**underdone′** *a.* not sufficiently cooked.

underdog (un′dẹr-dog) *n.* dog which is beaten in fight; (*Fig.*) person who fares badly in any struggle.

underdose (un-dẹr-dōs′) *v.t.* to give an insufficient dose (of medicine) to.—**un'derdose** *n.* an insufficient dose.

underestimate (un-dẹr-es′ti-māt) *v.t.* to miscalculate the value of; to rate at too low a figure;—*n.* an inadequate valuation.

under-exposed (un-dẹr-eks-pōzd′) *a.* (*Photog.*) insufficiently exposed to the light to impress details on a sensitive surface with clarity of outline.—**un'der-expos'ure** *n.*

underfeed (un-dẹr-fed′) *v.t.* to feed insufficiently; to undernourish.—**underfed′** *a.*

underfelt (un′dẹr-felt) *n.* felt laid underneath carpet to minimise wear and tear.

underfoot (un-dẹr-fo͝ot′) *adv.* beneath the feet; (*Fig.*) in subjection.

undergarment (un′dẹr-gȧr-mẹnt) *n.* a garment worn underneath the outer clothes.

undergo (un-dẹr-gō′) *v.t.* to bear; to suffer; to sustain; to participate in.—*pr.p.* **undergo'ing.** —*pa.t.* **underwent′**.—*pa.p.* **undergone′**.

undergraduate (un-dẹr-grad′ū-āt) *n.* student attending classes for degree at university;—*a.* pert. to such student or university course. —**undergrad'uateship** *n.*

underground (un′dẹr-ground) *a.* under the ground; subterranean; (*Fig.*) secret;—*n.* underground railway-system; a subway; (*Fig.*) secret organisation or resistance movement.—**underground′** *adv.* below surface of earth; (*Fig.*) secretly.

undergrowth (un′dẹr-grōth) *n.* small trees, shrubs, or plants growing beside taller trees.

underhand (un′dẹr-hand) *adv.* by secret means; fraudulently; (*Cricket*) bowled with hand and arm kept below shoulder level; (*Tennis*) served or played with racquet kept below waist-level; secretly; clandestine; slyly. —**underhan'ded** *a.* secret; short-handed, as shop staff.—**underhan'dedly** *adv.*—**underhan'dedness** *n.*

underhung (un-dẹr-hung′) *a.* projecting beyond upper jaw, as lower jaw.

underived (un-dē-rīvd′) *a.* not derived; original; natural.

underlay (un-dẹr-lā′) *v.t.* to lay underneath; to support by something put below;—*v.i.* to incline from perpendicular;—*n.* piece of paper, cardboard, etc. used by printers to raise type-plate; (*Geol.*) inclination of vein from perpendicular; floor covering of felt, cork-oak, etc. laid underneath a carpet. Also **underlie′**.

underlie (un-dẹr-lī′) *v.t.* to lie underneath; (Fig.) to be the basis of;—*n.* (*Geol.*) an underlay.—**underly'ing** *a.*

underline (un-dẹr-līn′) *v.t.* to mark with line below, for emphasis; to emphasise.—**un'derline** *n.*

underling (un′dẹr-ling) *n.* one who holds inferior position; subordinate member of a staff; a weakling.

underman (un-dẹr-man′) *v.t.* to supply, as ship, with too small a crew; to employ too small a staff, for the work on hand.—**undermanned′** *a.*

undermentioned (un′dẹr-men-shund) *a.* referred to below or later in the text.

undermine (un-dẹr-mīn′) *v.t.* to excavate for the purpose of mining, blasting, etc.; to erode; (*Fig.*) to sap, as one's energy; to weaken insidiously, as another's faith.

underneath (un-dẹr-nēth′) *adv.* and *prep.* beneath; below; in a lower place.

undernourished (un-dẹr-nur′ishd) *a.* insufficiently nourished.

underpay (un-dẹr-pā′) *v.t.* to pay inadequately for the work done; to exploit.—**underpay'ment** *n.*

under-populated (un-dẹr-pop′ū-lā-ted) *a.* not fully populated in relation to the resources of an area.

underproof (un′dẹr-pro͝of) *a.* containing less alcohol than proof-spirit.

underrate (un-dẹr-rāt′) *v.t.* to rate too low; to underestimate.—**un'derrate** *n.* price lower than the real value.

underscore (un-dẹr-skōr′) *v.t.* to underline for emphasis.

under-secretary (un′dẹr-sek′re-tạ-ri) *n.* assistant-secretary, esp. of Government department.—**Parliamentary Under-Secretary,** M.P. acting as secretary to Minister with portfolio. —**Permanent Under-Secretary,** Civil Servant who is head of State department.—**un'dersec'retaryship** *n.*

undersell (un-dẹr-sel′) *v.t.* to sell more cheaply than another.—**undersell'er** *n.*

underset (un′dẹr-set) *n.* (*Naut.*) undersurface current contrary in direction to the flow of the main stream.—**underset′** *v.t.* to support as masonry, from underneath.

undershot (un′dẹr-shot) *a.* (of mill-wheel) turned by water flowing under.

undershrub (un′dẹr-shrub) *n.* a small shrub.

undersign (un-dẹr-sīn′) *v.t.* to write one's name at the foot of or underneath; to subscribe.—**undersigned′** *a.* and *n.*

under-sized (un′dẹr-sīzd) *a.* smaller than normal size; dwarf.

underskirt (un′dẹr-skẹrt) *n.* petticoat; skirt over which drapery, as of lace, is arranged.

understand (un-dẹr-stand′) *v.t.* to comprehend; to grasp the significance of.

understate (un-dẹr-stāt′) *v.t.* to state less strongly than truth warrants; to minimise deliberately.—**un'derstatement** *n.*

understudy (un′dẹr-stud-i) *n.* actor ready to deputise for principal actor (or actress) at a moment's notice;—*v.t.* to study theatrical part for this purpose.

undertake (un-dẹr-tāk′) *v.t.* to take upon oneself as a special duty; to embark on; to agree (to do); to warrant;—*v.i.* to be under obligation to act for another; to make arrangements for burial.—*pa.t.* **undertook′**.—*pa.p.* **underta'ken.**—**underta'ker** *n.* one who undertakes; contractor; one who manages a burial.—**un'dertaking** *n.* project; guarantee.

undertone (un′dẹr-tōn) *n.* low, subdued tone of voice or colour.

undertow (un′dẹr-tō) *n.* under current or backwash of a wave after it has reached the shore; underset.

undervalue (un-dẹr-val′ū) *v.t.* to set too low a price on; to esteem lightly; to underestimate;—*n.* an underestimate.—**un'dervalua'tion** *n.*

underwear (un′dẹr-wār) *n.* underclothes.

underwent (un-dẹr-went′) *pa.t.* of **undergo′**.

underwood (un′dẹr-wo͝od) *n.* small trees growing among larger trees; coppice.

underwork (un-dẹr-wurk′) *v.t.* to work for lower wages than; to demand less work than is due; (*Fig.*) to undermine; to contrive secretly;—*v.i.* to do less work than is due; to slack.—*pa.t.* and *pa.p.* **un'derworked, un'derwrought.**—**un'derwork** *n.* inadequate labour; slacking; subordinate task.

underworld (un′dẹr-wurld) *n.* the nether regions; Hades; the antipodes; section of community which lives by vice and crime.

underwrite (un-dẹr-rīt′) *v.t.* to write under something else; to subscribe; to append one's signature to insurance policy (esp. marine insurance) whereby one guarantees to compensate for loss or damage on payment of certain premium per cent; to undertake to buy shares not bought by the public, and thereby guarantee success of issue of business capital.—*pr.p.* **underwri'ting.**—*pa.t.* **underwrote'.**—*pa.p.* **underwrit'ten.**—**un'derwriter** *n.*

underwrought (un-der-rawt') *pa.t.* and *pa.p.* of **underwork.**

undeserved (un-de-zervd') *a.* not merited; unwarranted.—**undeser'ving** *a.* not deserving; unworthy.—**undeser'vingly** *adv.*

undesirable (un-dē-zīr'a-bl) *a.* not desirable; having no appreciable virtues;—*n.* person of ill-repute.—**undesirabil'ity, undesir'ableness** *n.*—**undesir'ably** *adv.*—**undesir'ing, undesir'ous** *a.* not desirous.

undetermined (un-de-ter'mind) *a.* not determined; undecided; irresolute.—**undeter'minable** *a.* not able to be determined.—**undeter'minate** *a.* indeterminate; vague.

undeterred (un-de-terd') *a.* not deterred; unhindered; resolute.

undeveloped (un-de-vel'opt) *a.* not developed or matured; (of land) not yet exploited or explored.

undeviating (un-dē'vi-ā-ting) *a.* not deviating; resolute in pursuing a straight course; (*Fig.*) resolute of purpose.

undid (un-did') *pa.t.* of **undo'.**

undies (un'diz) *n.pl.* (*Colloq. abbrev.*) women's underwear.

undifferentiated (un-dif-e-ren'shi-ā-ted) *a.* not differentiated; homogeneous.

undigenous (un-dij'e-nus) *a.* originated or generated by water [L. *unda,* a wave; *gignere,* to produce].

undigested (un-di-jes'ted) *a.* not digested; (*Fig.*) not understood; unanalysed.—**undiges'tible** *a.* indigestible.

undiluted (un-dil-ū'ted) *a.* not diluted; not weakened by the addition of water or other liquid; of full strength.—**undilu'tion** *n.*

undine (un-dīn') *n.* water-sprite; (*Med.*) small glass flask used for irrigating eyes with lotion.—**undi'nal** *a.* [L. *unda,* a wave].

undisciplined (un-dis'i-plind) *a.* not disciplined; not controlled; not trained to obey.—**undis'ciplinable** *a.* uncontrollable.

undiscriminating (un-dis-krim'i-nā-ting) *a.* not discriminating; not critical.

undisposed (un-dis-pōzd') *a.* not disposed; disinclined; not sold off or distributed.

undisputed (un-dis-pū'ted) *a.* not disputed; unchallenged.—**undispu'table** *a.* indisputable.—**undispu'tableness** *n.*—**undispu'tedly** *adv.*

undistinguished (un-dis-ting'gwisht) *a.* not distinguished; ordinary; not famous.—**undisting'uishable** *a.* not known, the one from the other.—**undisting'uishableness** *n.*

undo (un-dòò') *v.t.* to reverse what has been done; to annul; to loose; to unfasten; to damage character of.—*pa.t.* **undid'.**—*pa.p.* **undone'.**—**undo'er** *n.*—**undo'ing** *n.* act of reversing what has been done; ruin, esp. of reputation.—**undone'** *a.* ruined.

undomesticate (un-dō-mes'ti-kāt) *v.t.* to make unfit for domestic life; to allow to revert to wild state.—**undomes'ticated** *a.* untamed; not fond of housework.

undose (un'dōs) *a.* wavy [L. *unda,* wave].

undoubted (un-dout'ed) *a.* not doubted; certain; genuine.—**undoubt'able** *a.* unquestionable.—**undoubt'ably** *adv.*—**undoubt'edly** *adv.* without doubt; certainly.—**undoubt'ful** *a.* unsuspicious.

undress (un-dres') *v.t.* to divest of clothes or covering; to remove dressing from a wound.—*v.i.* to take off (one's) clothes.—**un'dress** *n.* and *a.* informal dress; off-duty military uniform.—**undressed'** *a.*

undue (un-dū') *a.* not in accordance with what is due or proper; immoderate; not befitting the occasion.—**undue'ness** *n.*

undulate (un'dū-lāt) *v.t.* to move up and down like waves; to cause to vibrate;—*v.i.* to move up and down; to vibrate; to have wavy edge;—*a.* wavy.—**un'dulant** *a.* undulating; wavy.—**un'dulately** *adv.*—**un'dulating** *a.* wavy; having series of rounded ridges and depressions, as surface of landscape.—**un'dulatingly** *adv.*—**undula'tion** *n.* wave; fluctuating motion, as of waves; wave-like contour of stretch of land; series of wavy lines; vibratory motion.—**un'dulatory** *a.* pert. to undulation; moving like a wave; pert. to theory of light which argues that light is transmitted through ether by wave motions.—**un'dulose, un'dulous** *a.* [L. *unda,* a wave].

unduly (un-dū'li) *adv.* in an undue manner; immoderately; improperly.

undying (un-dī'ing) *a.* not dying; immortal; everlasting.—**undy'ingly** *adv.*—**undy'ingness** *n.*

unearned (un-ernd') *a.* not earned by personal labour.—**unearned income,** income derived from sources other than salary, fees, etc. on which one is liable to pay higher rate of income tax.—**unearned increment,** increased value of property, land, etc. due to circumstances other than owner's expenditure on its upkeep.

unearth (un-erth') *v.t.* to dig up; to drive as a fox, rabbit, etc. from its burrow; (*Fig*). to bring to light.—**unearth'liness** *n.* -**unearth'ly** *a.* not of this world; supernatural.

uneasy (un-ē'zi) *a.* not at ease; worried; uncomfortable.—**uneas'iness** *n,* restlessness; constraint; anxiety.—**uneas'ily** *adv.*

uneconomic (un-ek-on-om'ik) *a.* not economic; not in accordance with the principles of economics.—**uneconom'ical** *a.* not economical; wasteful; thriftless.

unedifying (un-ed'i-fī-ing) *a.* not edifying; demoralising.

unemployed (un-em-ploid') *a.* not employed; out of work.—**unemploy'able** *a.* not capable of being employed.—**unemploy'ment** *n.* state of being unemployed.—**unemployment benefit,** money received by unemployed workers according to conditions laid down by insurance acts.—**unemployment insurance,** State insurance against periods of unemployment contributed to by workers, employers, etc.

unending (un-en'ding) *a.* never-ending; infinite; incessant.—**unend'ed** *a.*—**-ingly** *adv.*

unenlightened (un-en-līt'nd) *a.* not enlightened; living in state of intellectual or spiritual darkness.

unequal (un-ē'kwal) *a.* not equal; not of the same length, weight, etc.; ill-assorted or ill-balanced.—**une'qualled** *a.* not matched; peerless.—**une'qually** *adv.*—**une'qualness** *n.*

unequivocal (un-ē-kwiv'ō-kal) *a.* not equivocal; undoubted; unambiguous; plain.—**unequiv'ocally** *adv.*

Unesco (ū-nes'kō) *n.* coined-word from initial letters of *United Nations Educational, Scientific and Cultural Organisation,* established in November, 1945.

uneven (un-ē'vn) *a.* not even; rough; not of equal length or quality; not divisible by two without remainder; odd.—**une'venly** *adv.*—**une'venness** *n.*

unexceptionable (un-ek-sep'shun-a-bl) *a.* without exception; irreproachable; perfect.—**unexcep'tional** *a.* not exceptional; usual.

unexecuted (un-eks'e-kū-ted) *a.* not executed; (of legal document) not signed by witness or witnesses.

unexpected (un-eks-pek'ted) *a.* not expected; sudden; without warning.

unextirpated (un-eks'tir-pā-ted) *a.* not extirpated; not wiped out.

unfadable (un-fā'da-bl) *a.* not liable to fade; imperishable.—**unfa'ded** *a.* not faded; fresh.—**unfa'ding** *a.* everlasting.

unfailing (un-fā'ling) *a.* not liable to fail; ever loyal; inexhaustible.—**unfail'ingly** *adv.*

unfair (un-fār') *a.* not fair; unjust; prejudiced; contrary to the rules of the game.—**unfair'ly** *adv.*—**unfair'ness** *n.*

unfaithful (un-fāth'fòòl) *a.* not faithful; disloyal; inaccurate or misleading.

unfamiliar (un-fa-mil'yar) *a.* not familiar; strange; not experienced in or acquainted with.—**unfamil'iarity** *n.*—**unfamil'iarly** *adv.*

unfashionable (un-fashʹun-ạ-bl) *a.* not fashionable; dowdy.—**unfashʹionableness** *n.*—**unfashʹionably** *adv.*—**unfashʹioned** *a.* not moulded or fashioned.
unfasten (un-fasʹn) *v.t.* to loose; to undo.—**unfastʹened** *a.* not fastened.
unfathomable (un-fathʹom-ạ-bl) *a.* not fathomable; not capable of being plumbed; (*Fig.*) inexplicable.—**unfathʹomableness** *n.*—**unfathʹomably** *adv.*—**unfathʹomed** *a.* unplumbed; bottomless; not solved.
unfeeling (un-fēlʹing) *a.* void of feeling; callous; unsympathetic.—**unfeelʹingly** *adv.*
unfeigned (un-fānd') *a.* not feigned; genuine; sincere.—**unfeignʹedly** *adv.*—**unfeignʹedness** *n.*
unfetter (un-fetʹẹr) *v.t.* to remove the fetters from; to emancipate.—**unfettʹered** *a.*
unfilial (un-filʹyạl) *a.* not becoming to a son or daughter; disrespectful.
unfinished (un-finʹisht) *a.* not finished; roughly executed; not polished.—**unfinʹish** *n.*—**unfinʹishable** *a.*
unfit (un-fit') *a.* not fit; unqualified; improper; not adapted for;—*v.t.* to disqualify.—**unfitʹly** *adv.*—**unfitʹness** *n.*—**unfitʹting** *a.* unsuitable.—**unfitʹtingly** *adv.*
unfledged (un-flejd') *a.* not yet covered with feathers; (*Fig.*) immature.
unfleshed (un-fleshd') *a.* (of sword) not yet used in fighting; not having tasted blood.—**unfleshʹly** *a.* uncorporeal.—**unfleshʹy** *a.* having no flesh.
unflinching (un-flinʹshing) *a.* not flinching; resolute.—**unflinʹchingly** *adv.*
unfold (un-fōld') *v.t.* to open the folds of; to spread out; (*Fig.*) to disclose;—*v.i.* to expand.—**unfoldʹer** *n.*—**unfoldʹing** *n.*
unforeseen (un-fōr-sēn') *a.* unexpected.—**unforeseeʹable** *a.* not capable of being foreseen; unpredictable.
unforgettable (un-for-getʹạ-bl) *a.* not forgettable; memorable.
unforgivable (un-for-givʹạ-bl) *a.* unpardonable; not excusable.—**unforgivʹing** *a.* not forgiving; relentless.—**unforgivʹingness** *n.*
unformed (un-formd') *a.* not formed; amorphous; immature.
unfortunate (un-forʹtū-nāt) *a.* not fortunate; ill-timed; unsuccessful.—*n.* prostitute.—**unforʹtunately** *adv.*—**unforʹtunateness** *n.*
unfounded (un-founʹded) *a.* not founded; baseless.
unfrequented (un-frē-kwenʹted) *a.* not frequented; seldom visited.—**unfreʹquent** *a.* not frequent; happening seldom.
unfriendly (un-frendʹli) *a.* not friendly; hostile.—**unfriendʹed** *a.* having no friends.—**unfriendʹliness** *n.*
unfrock (un-frok') *v.t.* to deprive of a frock, esp. to deprive of the status of a monk or priest.—**unfrocked'** *a.*
unfunded (un-funʹded) *a.* not funded; having no permanent funds for payment of its interest; floating.—**unfunded debt**, that portion of the international debt which represents war debts.
unfurl (un-furl') *v.t.* to loose from furled state, as a flag; to unfold; to expand;—*v.i.* to be spread out.
unfurnished (un-furʹnisht) *a.* not furnished; devoid of furniture.—**unfurʹnish** *v.t.* to remove furniture from.
ungainly (un-gānʹli) *a.* clumsy; awkward;—*adv.* in a clumsy manner.—**ungainʹliness** *n.* [M.E. *ungein*, awkward].
ungarnished (un-garʹnisht) *a.* not garnished; served without decoration.
unglaze (un-glāz') *v.t.* to remove glass from.—**unglazed'** *a.* not fitted with glass; (of pottery) having matt surface.
ungodly (un-godʹli) *a.* not godly; profane; (*Slang*) shocking.—**ungodʹlily** *adv.* in an ungodly manner.—**ungodʹliness** *n.* the state of being ungodly; wickedness.
ungovernable (un-guvʹẹr-nạ-bl) *a.* uncontrolled; incapable of restraint.—**ungovʹernableness** *n.*—**ungovʹernably** *adv.*—**ungovʹerned** *a.* not governed; unbridled.
ungracious (un-grāʹshus) *a.* lacking in courtesy; not kindly.—**ungraceʹfully** *adv.*—**ungraceʹfulness** *n.*—**ungraʹciously** *adv.*—**ungraceʹful** *a.* not graceful; gawky.
ungrammatical (un-grạ-matʹi-kạl) *a.* not grammatical; not in accordance with the rules of grammar.—**ungrammatʹically** *adv.*
ungrateful (un-grātʹfóól) *a.* not grateful; not appreciative; not repaying the labour expended.—**ungrateʹfully** *adv.*—**ungrateʹfulness** *n.* ingratitude.
ungrounded (un-grounʹded) *a.* having no foundation; false.
ungrudging (un-grujʹing) *a.* not grudging; generous.—**ungrudged'** *a.* not stinted.—**ungrudgʹingly** *adv.*
ungual (ungʹgwạl) *a.* having nails, hooves, or claws.—**ungʹulate** *a.* having hoofs.—**ungulʹigrade** *a.* walking on hoofs [L. *unguis*, a nail].
unguarded (un-garʹded) *a.* not guarded; careless; indiscreet.—**unguarʹdedly** *adv.*—**unguarʹdedness** *n.*
unguent (ungʹgwẹnt) *n.* ointment.—**ungʹuentary** *a.* pert. to unguents.—**unguenʹtous** *a.* resembling an unguent.—**ungʹuinous** *a.* oily [L. *unguere*, to anoint].
unhallowed (un-halʹōd) *n.* not hallowed; profane; wicked.—**unhallʹowing** *n.*
unhand (un-hand') *v.t.* to let go.—**unhandʹily** *adv.* awkwardly.—**unhandʹiness** *n.*—**unhandʹled** *a.* not handled.—**unhandʹy** *a.* not handy; inconvenient; lacking skill.
unhappy (un-hapʹi) *a.* not happy; miserable; out of place; tactless—**unhappʹily** *adv.*—**unhappʹiness** *n.*
unhealthy (un-helʹthi) *a.* not healthy or hygienic; habitually weak or ill; not wholesome.—**unhealthʹful** *a.*—**unhealthʹfully** *adv.*—**unhealthʹily** *adv.*—**unhealthʹiness** *n.*
unheard (un-hẹrd') *a.* not heard; not given hearing.—**unheard of,** unprecedented.
unhesitating (un-hezʹi-tā-ting) *a.* not hesitating; spontaneous; resolute.—**unhesitaʹtingly** *adv.* without hesitation.
unhinge (un-hinj') *v.t.* to take from the hinges; (*Fig.*) to cause mental instability.—**unhinged'** *a.* (of the mind) unstable; distraught.—**unhinge'ment** *n.*
unholy (un-hōʹli) *a.* not holy; profane; polluted; (*Colloq.*) frightful.—**unhoʹlily** *adv.*—**unhoʹliness** *n.* the quality of being unholy.
unhook (un-hóók') *v.t.* to loosen from a hook; to detach hooks from; to open.
unhorse (un-hors') *v.t.* to throw from a horse; to cause to fall from a horse.
unhouseled (un-houzʹld) *a.* not having received the sacrament.
unhurt (un-hurt') *a.* not hurt; uninjured.—**unhurtʹful** *a.* innocuous.
unhygienic (un-hī-jenʹik) *a.* not hygienic; insanitary; unhealthy.
uni-, (ūʹni) *pfx.* one or single [fr. L. *unus*, one].
uniaxial (ū-ni-akʹsi-ạl) *a.* having a single axis; having one direction along which ray of light can travel without bifurcation. Also **uniaxʹal.**—**uniaxʹially** *adv.*
unicellular (ū-ni-selʹū-lạr) *a.* having a single cell; monocellular.
unicorn (ūʹni-korn) *n.* fabulous composite animal with horse's body and a single horn protruding from forehead; team of three horses, with two abreast, and single one in front [L. *unus*, one; *cornu*, horn].
unideal (un-ī-dēʹạl) *a.* realistic; prosaic.—**unideʹalism** *n.*
uniform (ūʹni-form) *a.* having always same form; conforming to one pattern; regular; consistent; not varying, as temperature;—*n.* official dress, as a livery, etc.—**uʹniformed** *a.* wearing uniform.—**uniformʹity** *n.* conformity to pattern or standard.—**uʹniformly** *adv.*—**uʹniformness** *n.*
unify (ūʹni-fī) *v.t.* to make into one; to make uniform.—**uʹnifiable** *a.* capable of being made

one.—**unifica'tion** *n.* act of unifying; state of being made one; welding together of separate parts.
unilaminar (ū-ni-lam′i-nạr) *a.* having only one lamina.
unilateral (ū-ni-lat′ẹ-rạl) *a.* one-sided; binding one side only, as in party agreement.—**unilateral'ity** *n.*—**unilat'erally** *adv.*.
uniliteral (ū-ni-lit′ẹ-rạl) *a.* consisting of one letter only [L. *unus*, one; *litera*, a letter].
unilocular (ū-ni-lok′ū-lạr) *a.* (*Bot.*) having single chamber or cavity.
unimaginable (un-i-maj′i-nạ-bl) *a.* not imaginable; inconceivable.—**unimag'inableness** *n.*—**unimag'inably** *adv.*—**unimag'inative** *a.* not imaginative; dull; uninspired.—**unimag'inatively** *adv.*—**unimag'inativeness** *n.*—**unimag′ined** *a.* not imagined.
unimpaired (un-im-pārd') *a.* not impaired; not weakened; undamaged.
unimpeachable (un-im-pē′chạ-bl) *a.* not impeachable; irreproachable; blameless.—**unimpeachabil'ity, unimpeach'ableness** *n.*—**unimpeach'ably** *adv.*—**unimpeached'** *a.*
unimportant (un-im-pōr′tạnt) *a.* not important; insignificant.—**unimpor'tance** *n.*
uninflected (un-in-flek′ted) *a.* not inflected; having no inflexions, as words of language.
uninformed (un-in-formd') *a.* having no accurate information; ignorant; not expert.
uninhabitable (un-in-hab′i-tạ-bl) *a.* not inhabitable; not fit for living in.—**uninhabitabil'ity, uninhab'itableness** *n.*—**uninhab'ited** *a.* having no inhabitants; desert.
uninspired (un-in-spīrd') *a.* not inspired; prosaic.
uninsured (un-in-sūrd') *a.* not insured; not covered by insurance policy.
unintelligent (un-in-tel′i-jẹnt) *a.* not intelligent; mentally dull.—**unintell'igence** *n.*—**unintell'igently** *adv.*—**unintelligibil'ity** *n.*—**unintell'igible** *a.* not intelligible; not capable of being comprehended.—**unintell'igibleness** *n.*—**unintell'igibly** *adv.*
unintentional (un-in-ten′shun-ạl) *a.* not intentional; accidental; involuntary.—**uninten′tionally** *adv.*
uninterested (un-in′tẹr-es-ted) *a.* not interested.—**unin'teresting** *a.* not interesting; dull.—**unin'terestingly** *adv.*
uninterrupted (un-in-tẹr-up′ted) *a.* not interrupted; continuous.—**-tedly** *adv.*
uninvited (un-in-vī′ted) *a.* not invited; unasked.—**uninvi'ting** *a.* not inviting; unprepossessing.—**uninvi'tingly** *adv.*
union (ūn′yun) *n.* act of joining two or more things into one; federation; marriage; harmony; combination of administrative bodies for a common purpose; trade-union;—*pl.* fabric containing two or more kinds of fibre, one yarn usually being of less expensive kind. —**un'ioned** *a.* joined.—**un'ionist** *n.* one who supports union.—**Un'ionist** *n.* member of Conservative party in British politics; orig. one who opposed Gladstone's proposal in 1885 to give Ireland Home Rule.—**Union Jack,** national flag of United Kingdom consisting of crosses of St. George, St. Andrew, and St. Patrick [Fr. *union*, fr.L. *unus*, one].
union (ūn′yun) *n.* large pearl, the only one of its kind [L. *unio*, single pearl].
uniparous (ū-nip′ạ-rus) *a.* producing normally just one at a birth; (*Bot.*) having single stem [L. *unus*, one; *parere*, to bring forth].
unique (ū-nēk') *a.* single in kind; having no like or equal; peerless.—**unique'ly** *adv.*—**unique'ness, uniq'uity** *n.*
unisexual (ū-ni-sek′sū-ạl) *a.* of one sex only, as a plant; not hermaphrodite or bisexual.—**unisexual'ity** *n.*—**unisex'ually** *adv.*
unison (ū′ni-son) *n.* harmony; concord; (*Mus.*) identity of pitch.—**in unison,** with all voices singing the same notes or notes with interval of an octave; (*Fig.*) in agreement.
unit (ū′nit) *n.* single thing or person; group regarded as one; standard of measurement; (*Math.*) the least whole number.—**u'nitary** *a.* pert. to unit(s); whole [L. *unus*, one].
Unitarian (ū-ni-tā′ri-ạn) *n.* one who rejects doctrine of the Trinity and asserts the oneness of God.—**Unita'rianism** *n.* [L. *unus*, one].
unite (ū-nīt') *v.t.* to join; to make into one; to form a whole; to associate; to cause to adhere;—*v.i.* to be joined together; to grow together; to act as one; to harmonise.—**uni'ted** *a.* joined together; harmonious; unanimous.—**uni'tedly** *adv.*—**uni'ter** *n.*—**u'nity** *n.* state of oneness; agreement; coherence; combination of separate parts into connected whole, or of different people with common aim; (*Math.*) any quantity taken as one.—**United Nations,** name given orig. during latter part of *World War* 2 to those nations subscribing to the *United Nations Declaration* at Washington, Jan. 1, 1942 (number of nations increased later to 47).—**United Nations Organisation,** organisation of peace-loving states set up after *World War* 2 with Security Council as chief executive body.—popular *abbrev.* **UNO** (*q.v.*).—**United States,** federal union of states, as U.S.A. [L. *unus*, one].
univalve (ū′ni-valv) *a.* having only one valve;—*n.* a single-celled mollusc.—**unival′vular** *a.* having one valve only.
universe (ū′ni-vẹrs) *n.* all created things regarded as a system or whole; the world.—**univer'sal** *a.* pert. to universe; embracing all created things; world-wide; general (as opp. of *particular*); total;—*n.* universal proposition; general concept; (in motoring) universal joint.—**univer'salise** *v.t.* to make universal.—**Univer'salism** *n.* theological doctrine of the ultimate salvation of all mankihd.—**Univer′salist** *n.*—**universalist'ic** *a.*—**universal'ity** *n.*—**universal joint** (in motoring) device whereby one part of machine has perfect freedom of motion in relation to another.—**univer'sally** *adv.*—**univer'salness** *n.* [L. *unus*, one; *vertere, versum*, to turn].
university (ū-ni-vẹr′si-ti) *n.* institution for educating students in higher branches of learning, and having authority to confer degrees; members of university collectively [L. *universitas*, a corporation].
univocal (ū-niv′ō-kạl) *a.* having one meaning only; unequivocal; sure; (*Mus.*) having unison in sounds;—*n.* word with only one meaning [L. *unus*, one; *vox*, a voice].
unjust (un-just') *a.* not just; partial; biassed; dishonest.—**unjustifi'able** *a.* not justifiable.—**unjustifi'ably** *adv.*—**unjust'ly** *adv.* unfairly.—**unjust'ness** *n.*
unkempt (un-kemt') *a.* dishevelled; rough [O.E. *un-*, not; *cemban*, to comb].
unkind (un-kīnd') *a.* lacking in kindness; cruel; callous.—**unkind'liness** *n.* lack of kindliness.—**unkind'ly** *a.* not kindly; harsh;—*adv.* cruelly; in a manner contrary to nature.—**unkind'ness** *n.* lack of kindness.
unknowable (un-nō′ạ-bl) *a.* not capable of being known;—*n.* that which is beyond man's power to understand; the absolute.—**unknow′ableness** *n.*—**unknow'ably** *adv.*—**unknow'ing** *a.* ignorant.—**unknow'ingly** *adv.*—**unknown'** *a.* not known; incalcualble;—*n.* unknown quantity; unexplored regions of mind; part of globe as yet unvisited by man.
unlawful (un-law′fōōl) *a.* not lawful; contrary to the law; illicit.—**unlaw'fully** *adv.* illegally.—**unlaw'fulness** *n.*
unleash (un-lēsh) *v.t.* to free from a leash; to let go, as a dog.
unleavened (un-lev′nd) *a.* not leavened made without yeast, as *unleavened bread.*
unleisured (un-lezh′ūrd) *a.* having no leisure; busy.—**unlei'suredness** *n.*
unless (un-les') *conj.* except; if not; supposing that.
unlettered (un-let′ẹrd *a.* illiterate.
unlicensed (un-lī′senst) *a.* not licensed; having no permit to sell certain commodities, as tobacco, wine, etc.

unlike (un-līk′) *a.* not like; dissimilar;—*prep.* different from;—*adv.* in a different way from. —**unlike′lihood, unlike′ness** *n.*—**unlike′ly** *a.* improbable; unpromising;—*adv.* improbably.—**unlike′liness** *n.*

unlimited (un-limꞌi-ted′) *a.* not limited; boundless; unrestricted.—**unlim′itedly** *adv.*—**unlim′itedness** *n.*

unload (un-lōd′) *v.t.* to remove load from; to remove charge from, as gun; to sell out quickly, as stocks, shares, etc. before slump; (*Fig.*) to unburden, as one's mind;—*v.i.* to discharge cargo.—**unload′ed** *a.* not containing a charge, as gun; not containing a plate or film, as camera.

unlock (un-lok′) *v.t.* to unfasten what is locked; to open with a key.

unloose (un-lòòs′) *v.t.* to make free; to set free. —**unloos′en** *v.t.* to unloose.

unlovable (un-luv-ą-bl) *a.* not lovable; disagreeable; unattractive.—**unloved′** *a.* not loved.—**unlove′liness** *n.* lack of loveliness; uglīness.—**unlove′ly** *a.* not lovely; repellent.—**unlov′ing** *a.* not loving; cold.

unlucky (un-lukꞌi) *a.* not lucky; unfortunate; inauspicious; inopportune.—**unluck′ily** *adv.*—**unluck′iness** *n.*

unmake (un-māk′) *v.t.* to destroy what has been made; to annul; to pick out stitching of a garment before remaking.—**unmade′** *a.* not made.—**unmak′able** *a.*—**unmak′ing** *n.*

unman (un-man′) *v.t.* to deprive of manly courage; to deprive of men, as ship's crew.—**unman′like** *a.* not manlike.—**unman′liness** *n.*—**unman′ly** *a.* cowardly; effeminate.

unmanageable (un-manꞌāj-ą-bl) *a.* not manageable; difficult to control.—**unman′ageableness** *n.*—**unman′ageably** *adv.*—**unman′aged** *a.* not domesticated.

unmannerly (un-manꞌęr-li) *a.* not polite; ill-bred.—**unmann′ered** *a.* discourteous.—**unmannꞌerliness** *n.* rudeness.

unmarried (un-marꞌid) *a.* not married; single.—**unmarr′iageable** *a.* not fit to marry; under age to marry, without parents' consent.—**unmarr′iageableness** *n.*

unmeaning (un-mēnꞌing) *a.* without meaning; unintentional; insignificant.—**unmeanꞌingly** *adv.*—**unmeant** (un-ment′) *a.* not intended; accidental.

unmeasured (un-mezhꞌūrd) *a.* not measured; limitless; not stinted; over-abundant.—**unmeas′urable** *a.*—**unmeas′urableness** *n.*—**unmeas′urably** *adv.*

unmentionable (un-menꞌshun-ą-bl) *a.* not worthy of mention; not fit to be mentioned.—**unmen′tionableness** *n.*—**unmen′tionables** *n.pl.* facetious synonym for trousers.

unminded (un-mīnꞌded) *a.* not remembered. —**unmind′ful** *a.* forgetful; regardless.—**unmind′fully** *adv.*—**unmind′fulness** *n.*

unmistakable (un-mis-tāꞌką-bl) *a.* not mistakable; recognisable; well-defined.—**unmistaꞌkableness** *n.*—**unmista′kably** *adv.*

unmoor (un-mòòr′) *v.t.* (*Naut.*) to release from moorings;—*v.i.* to cast off moorings.

unmoral (un-morꞌąl) *a.* not moral; not concerned with morality or ethics.—**unmor′alising** *a.* not given to reflecting on ethical values.—**unmoral′ity** *n.*

unmounted (un-mounꞌted) *a.* not mounted; on foot; (of gem) unset; (of picture) not framed or pasted on cardboard.

unmoved (un-mòòvd′) *a.* not moved; calm; not stirred emotionally.—**unmov′able, unmoveꞌable** *a.* incapable of being moved, physically, or emotionally.—**unmov′ably** *adv.*—**unmov′edly** *adv.*—**unmov′ing** *a.*

unmusical (un-mūꞌzi-kąl) *a.* not musical; discordant; not fond of, or unskilled in, music.—**unmusical′ity** *n.*—**unmus′ically** *adv.*

unnatural (un-natꞌū-rąl) *a.* not natural; not in accordance with usual course of events; not composed; abnormal.—**unnat′uralise** *v.t.*—**unnat′uralised** *a.* not naturalised; alien.—**unnat′urally** *adv.*

unnavigable (un-navꞌi-gą-bl) *a.* not navigable.—**unnavigabil′ity** *n.*—**unnav′igated** *a.* not sailed over; uncharted.

unnecessary (un-nesꞌe-są-ri) *a.* not necessary; superfluous; needless.—**unnec′essarily** *adv.*—**unnec′essariness** *n.*

unnerve (un-nerv′) *v.t.* to cause someone to lose his nerve; to undermine the courage of.—**unnerved′** *a.* afraid; deprived of nerve.

Uno (ūꞌnō) *n.* a coined word from the initial letters of the *United Nations Organisation.* Also **U.N.O.**

unobtrusive (un-ob-tròòꞌsiv) *a.* not obtrusive; unassuming.—**unobtrus′ively** *adv.*—**unobtrus′iveness** *n.*

unoccupied (un-okꞌū-pīd) *a.* not occupied; untenanted; not engaged in work; not under control of troops.

unopposed (un-o-pōzd′) *a.* not opposed; having no rival candidate in an election.

unorthodox (un-orꞌthō-doks) *a.* not orthodox. —**unorth′odoxy** *n.* heresy.

unostentatious (un-os-ten-tāꞌshus) *a.* not ostentatious; not showy; modest.—**unostentaꞌtiously** *adv.* unobtrusively.

unpack (un-pak′) *v.t.* to remove from a pack or trunk; to open by removing packing;—*v.i.* to empty contents of.

unpaid (un-pād′) *a.* not paid; honorary; still outstanding, as a debt.

unpalatable (un-palꞌą-tą-bl) *a.* not palatable; disagreeable; unpleasant.

unparalleled (un-parꞌą-leld) *a.* having no equal; unprecedented.

unparliamentary (un-pȧr-li-menꞌtą-ri) *a.* not in accordance with Parliamentary procedure; not fit for usage in Parliament.—**unparliamentary language,** abuse.

unpeople (un-pēꞌpl) *v.t.* to depopulate.

unperturbed (un-pęr-turbd′) *a.* not perturbed unruffled.—**unpertur′bedness** *n.*

unpick (un-pik′) *v.t.* to unfasten; to undo the stitching of.—**unpicked′** *a.*

unplaced (un-plāst′) *a.* not placed; (of horses) not one of the winners in a race.—**unplace′** *v.t.* to displace.

unpleasant (un-plezꞌąnt) *a.* not pleasant; disagreeable.—**unpleas′antly** *adv.*—**unpleas′antness** *n.*—**unpleasing** (un-plēꞌzing) *a.* unattractive.—**unplea′singly** *adv.*—**unpleas′urable** *a.* not pleasurable.

unpolished (un-polꞌisht) *a.* not polished; rough; (*Fig.*) uncouth.

unpopular (un-popꞌū-ląr) *a.* not popular; out of favour.—**unpopular′ity** *n.*

unprecedented (un-pres-e-denꞌted) *a.* without precedent; having no earlier example; novel.—**unprec′edently** *adv.*

unpremeditated (un-prē-medꞌi-tā-ted) *a.* not premeditated; not previously planned; spontaneous.—**unpremed′itable** *a.*—**unpremed′itatedly** *adv.*—**unpremed′itatedness, unpremedita′tion** *n.*

unprepared (un-prē-pārd′) *a.* not prepared; done without preparation; not ready.—**unprepar′edly** *adv.*—**unprepar′edness** *n.*

unprepossessing (un-prē-pō-zesꞌing) *a.* not prepossessing; not attractive.—**unprepossessed′** *a.* impartial; not prejudiced.

unprincipled (un-prinꞌsi-pld) *a.* having no moral principles; unscrupulous.

unprintable (un-prinꞌtą-bl) *a.* not printable; too shocking to be set down in print.

unproductive (un-prō-dukꞌtiv) *a.* not productive; barren; not profitable.—**unproduc′tively** *adv.*—**unproduc′tiveness** *n.*

unprofessional (un-prō-feshꞌun-ąl) *a.* not belonging to a profession; not in accordance with professional etiquette; (*Colloq.*) unskilled.—**unprofes′sionally** *adv.*

unprofitable (un-profꞌi-tą-bl) *a.* not profitable; fruitless; disadvantageous.—**unprof′itableness** *n.*—**unprof′itably** *adv.*

unqualified (un-kwolꞌi-fīd) *a.* not qualified; not having proper qualifications; not modified; absolute.—**unqual′ifiedness** *n.*

unquestionable (un-kwes′tyun-a-bl) *a.* not questionable; certain.—**unques′tionabil′ity, unques′tionableness** *n.*—**unques′tionably** *adv.*—**unques′tioned** *a.* not questioned; not disputed.—**unques′tioning** *a.* unhesitating.

unravel (un-rav′el) *v.t.* to disentangle; to separate; to solve, as a mystery;—*v.i.* to be disentangled.—**unrav′elment** *n.*

unread (un-red′) *a.* not perused; (of persons) ignorant.—**unreadable** (un-rēd′a-bl) *a.* illegible; (of books) not attractive as reading matter; dull.—**unread′ableness** *n.*

unreal (un-rēl′) *a.* not real; insubstantial; illusive.—**unrealis′able** *a.* not realisable.—**unrealis′ableness** *n.*—**unrealised′** *a.* not realised; unfulfilled.—**unreal′ity** *n.* want of reality.—**unre′ally** *adv.*

unreasonable (un-rē′zn-a-bl) *a.* not reasonable; impulsive; immoderate; (of prices) exorbitant.—**unrea′son** *n.* want of reason.—**unrea′sonableness** *n.*—**unrea′sonably** *adv.*—**unrea′soned** *a.* not thought out logically.—**unrea′soning** *a.* irrational.

unrecognised (un-rek′og-nīzd) *a.* not recognised; denied due honour.—**unrecognis′able** *a.* not recognisable.—**-is′ably** *adv.*

unrectified (un-rek′ti-fīd) *a.* not corrected; (*Chem.*) not distilled.

unreeve (un-rēv′) *v.t.* (*Naut.*) to withdraw rope from any block, dead-eye, etc. through which it has been passed.

unrefined (un-rē-fīnd′) *a.* not refined; unpolished; not purified, as sugar.

unregenerate (un-rē-jen′e-rāt) *a.* not converted to new spiritual state.—**unregen′eracy, unregenera′tion** *n.*

unrelated (un-rē-lā′ted) *a.* not related; having no apparent connection; diverse.—**unrel′ative** *a.* not relative.

unrelenting (un-rē-len′ting) *a.* adamant; inflexible; merciless.—**unrelen′tingly** *adv.*

unreliable (un-rē-lī′a-bl) *a.* not reliable; fickle; not to be trusted.—**unreliabil′ity, unreli′ableness** *n.*

unremitting (un-rē-mit′ing) *a.* not relaxing; incessant; persistent.—**unremit′ted** *a.* not remitted.—**unremit′tedly, unremit′tingly** *adv.*—**unremit′tingness** *n.*

unrequited (un-rē-kwī′ted) *a.* not requited.—**unrequit′able** *a.* not capable of being requited or returned.—**unrequi′tedly** *adv.*

unrest (un-rest′) *n.* want of rest; disquiet; political or social agitation.—**unrest′ful** *a.*—**unrest′fulness** *n.*—**unrest′ing** *a.* not resting.—**unrest′ingly** *adv.*—**unrest′ingness** *n.*

unrestricted (un-rē-strik′ted) *a.* not restricted; decontrolled.—**unrestric′tedly** *adv.*

unrighteous (un-rī′tyus) *a.* not righteous; evil; unjust; contrary to law and equity.—**unright′eously** *adv.*—**unright′eousness** *n.*—**unright′ful** *a.*—**unright′fully** *adv.*—**-fulness** *n.*

unripe (un-rīp′) *a.* not ripe.—**unri′pened** *a.* immature.—**unripe′ness** *n.*

unrobe (un-rōb′) *v.t.* to undress;—*v.i.* to remove one's robe, esp. an academic or official robe.

Unrra (un′rà) *n.* coined word from initial letters of *United Nations Relief and Rehabilitation Administration,* temporary organisation (officially ended 31st Dec., 1946) set up to deal with immediate economic problems of liberated and post-war Europe. Also **U.N.R.R.A.**

unruffled (un-ruf′ld) *a.* not ruffled; placid.—**unruff′le** *v.i.* to become placid.

unruled (un-ròòld′) *a.* not ruled; ungoverned; (of paper) blank; unrestrained.—**unrul′iness** *n.* state of being unruly.—**unrul′y** *a.* lawless; disobedient.

unsafe (un-sāf′) *a.* not safe; risky.—**unsafe′ly** *adv.*—**unsafe′ness** *n.*—**unsafe′ty** *n.*

unsatisfactory (un-sat-is-fak′to-ri) *a.* not satisfactory.—**unsatisfac′torily** *adv.*—**unsat′isfied** *a.* not satisfied; discontented.—**unsatisfy′ing** *a.*—**unsatisfy′ingness** *n.*

unsavoury (un-sā′vor-i) *a.* not savoury; tasteless; (*Fig.*) disgusting.—**unsa′vourily** *adv.*—**unsa′vouriness** *n.*

unsay (un-sā′) *v.t.* to retract (what has been said).

unscathed (un-skāTHt′) *a.* unharmed; without injury.

unscramble (un-skram′bl) *v.t.* to decode a secret message.

unscrupulous (un-skròò′pū-lus) *a.* not scrupulous; ruthless; having no moral principles.—**unscru′pulously** *adv.*—**unscru′pulousness** *n.*

unseal (un-sēl′) *v.t.* to remove or break the seal of.—**unsealed′** *a.*

unseasonable (un-sē-zn-a-bl) *a.* not seasonable; inopportune; abnormal for the time of year, as of weather.—**unsea′sonableness** *n.*—**unsea′sonably** *adv.*—**unsea′soned** *a.* not matured; not flavoured with seasoning.

unseat (un-sēt′) *v.t.* to throw from a horse; to deprive of Parliamentary seat.

unseemliness (un-sēm′li-nes) *n.* the state or quality of being unseemly.—**unseem′ly** *a.* not seemly; indecorous; unbecoming;—*adv.* indecorously.

unseen (un-sēn′) *a.* not seen; invisible;—*n.* an unprepared passage for translation in a language examination.—**the Unseen,** the spiritual world; the life beyond.

unselfconscious (un-self-kon′shus) *a.* not self-conscious; natural.—**unselfcon′sciously** *adv.*—**unselfcon′sciousness** *n.*

unselfish (un-sel′fish) *a.* not selfish; altruistic.—**unsel′fishly** *adv.*—**unsel′fishness** *n.*

unsettle (un-set′l) *v.t.* to move or loosen from a fixed position; to disturb mind; to make restless or discontented.—**unsett′led** *a.* not settled; changeable, as weather; unpaid, as bills; not allocated; not inhabited.—**unsett′ledly** *adv.*—**unsett′ledness, unsett′lement** *n.*—**unsett′ling** *a.* disturbing.

unshackle (un-shak′l) *v.t.* to set free from shackles; to unfetter.—**unshack′led** *a.*

unship (un-ship′) *v.t.* to remove from a ship; to unload; to remove from the place where it is fitted.—**unship′ment** *n.*

unshod (un-shod′) *a.* barefoot.

unsighted (un-sī′ted) *a.* not sighted; not observed; (of gun) without sights; (of shot) aimed blindly.—**unsight′able** *a.* invisible.—**unsight′liness** *n.* ugliness.—**unsight′ly** *a.* ugly; revolting to the sight.

unskilful (un-skil′fòòl) *a.* not skilful; not expert; awkward.—**unskil′fully** *adv.*—**unskil′fulness** *n.* lack of skill or experience.—**unskilled′** *a.* untrained; requiring no apprenticeship.

unsling (un-sling′) *v.t.* (*Naut.*) to remove slings from, as from cargo; to take down something which is hanging by sling, as a rifle.—**unslung′** *a.*

unsmirched (un-smircht′) *a.* not smirched; clean; (*Fig.*) innocent.

unsociable (un-sō′sha-bl) *a.* not sociable; over-reserved in society; unfriendly.—**unsociabil′ity, unso′ciableness** *n.*—**unso′ciably** *adv.*—**unso′cial** *a.* not social.

unsolicited (un-sō-lis-i-ted) *a.* not solicited; gratuitous.—**unsolic′itous** *a.* not solicitous.

unsophisticated (un-sō-fis′ti-kā-ted) *a.* not sophisticated; ingenuous; simple; unadulterated.—**unsophis′ticatedly** *adv.*—**unsophis′ticatedness, unsophistica′tion** *n.*

unsound (un-sound′) *a.* imperfect; damaged; decayed; (of the mind) insane; not based on logical reasoning; fallacious.—**unsound′ly** *adv.*—**unsound′ness** *n.*

unspeakable (un-spēk′a-bl) *a.* beyond utterance or description (in good or bad sense); ineffable.—**unspeak′ably** *adv.*—**unspeak′ing** *a.* dumb.

unspoiled (un-spoilt′) *a.* not spoiled; unblemished; ingenuous. Also **unspoilt′.**

unsporting (un-spōr′ting) *a.* (*Colloq.*) not like sportsman; unfair.—**unsports′manlike** *a.* not in accordance with the rules of fair play; not chivalrous.

unsprung (un-sprung′) *a.* not fitted with springs, as a vehicle, chair, etc.
unstable (un-stā′-bl) *a.* not stable; fluctuating; shifting; unbalanced; unreliable; (*Chem.*) subject to change.—**unstabil′ity, unsta′bleness** *n.*
unsteady (un-sted′-i) *a.* not steady; shaky; (*Fig.*) unreliable;—*v.t.* to make unsteady.—**unstead′fast** *a.* not steadfast; wavering.—**unstead′fastly** *adv.*—**unstead′fastness** *n.*—**unstead′ily** *adv.*—**unsteadi′ness** *n.*
unstop (un-stop′) *v.t.* to open by removing a stopper, as a bottle; to clear away an obstruction.—**unstopped′** *a.* not stopped; having no cork or stopper; (of consonant) made with air-passage half open.
unstrained (un-strānd′) *a.* not strained, as through a filter; (*Fig.*) relaxed; friendly.
unstuck (un-stuk′) *a.* not glued together.—**to come unstuck** (*Colloq.*) to come to grief; to fail; to break down.
unsullied (un-sul′-id) *a.* not sullied; unblemished; not disgraced.
unsung (un-sung′) *a.* not sung; not honoured in poetry; not praised publicly.
unsupported (un-su-pōr′-ted) *a.* not supported; without backing.—**unsuppor′table** *a.* not supportable; intolerable.—**unsuppor′tably** *adv.*—**unsuppor′tableness** *n.*
unsure (un-shòòr′) *a.* not sure; unsafe.—**unsure′ly** *adv.*
unswerving (un-swer′-ving) *a.* not swerving; not deviating; resolute.—**-vingly** *adv.*
unsympathetic (un-sim-pa-thet′-ik) *a.* not sympathetic; callous.—**unsympathet′ically** *adv.*—**unsym′pathy** *n.* lack of sympathy.—**unsympathisabil′ity** *n.*—**unsympathis′able** *a.*
untamed (un-tāmd′) *a.* not tamed; wild; undisciplined.—**unta′mable** *a.* incapable of being tamed, controlled, or domesticated.
unthink (un-thingk′) *v.t.* to dismiss from one's mind; to change one's opinion.—**unthink′able** *a.* not capable of being contemplated; (*Colloq.*) highly improbable.—**unthink′ing** *a.* not thinking; heedless.—**unthinking′ly** *adv.*
untidy (un-tī′-di) *a.* not tidy; lacking orderliness.—**unti′dily** *adv.*—**unti′diness** *n.*
untie (un-tī′) *v.t.* to undo what is tied; to loosen a knot.—**untied′** *a.*
until (un-til′) *prep.* till; to; as far as; as late as;—*conj.* up to the time that; to the degree that.
untimely (un-tīm′-li) *a.* not timely; premature; inopportune.—**untime′liness** *n.*—**untime′ous** *a.* untimely.—**untime′ously** *adv.*
untiring (un-tīr′-ing) *a.* not tiring; indefatigable.—**untir′able** *a.* incapable of being tired out.—**untired′** *a.* not tired.—**untir′ingly** *adv.*
unto (un′-tòò) *prep.* to [M.E. *und to,* as far as].
untouchable (un-tuch′-a-bl) *a.* incapable of being touched; unfit to be touched; unassailable; belonging to non-caste masses of India;—*n.* non-caste Indian whose touch or even shadow is held to defile member of a higher caste.—**untouchabil′ity** *n,*—**untouched′** *a.* not touched.
untoward (un-tō′-ard) *a.* awkward; inconvenient; unlucky.
untravelled (un-trav′-eld) *a.* not having travelled; unexplored; provincially-minded.
untried (un-trīd′) *a.* not tried; not experienced; not tested; not having undergone trial by court of law.
untrue (un-tròò′) *a.* not true; false; disloyal; not conforming to a requisite standard.—**untrue′ness** *n.*—**untru′ly** *adv.* falsely.—**untruth′** *n.*—**untruth′ful** *a.* dishonest; lying.—**untruth′fully** *adv.*—**untruth′fulness** *n.*
untutored (un-tū′-tord) *a.* untaught; ignorant; raw.
unused (un-ūzd′) *a.* not used; not accustomed.—**unu′sual** *a.* not usual; uncommon; extraordinary.—**unu′sually** *adv.*—**unu′sualness** *n.*
unutterable (un-ut′-er-a-bl) *a.* unspeakable; beyond utterance; thorough-going.—**unutterabil′ity, unutt′erableness** *n.*—**unutt′erably** *adv.*—**unutt′ered** *a.* unspoken.
unvarnished (un-vàr′-nisht) *a.* not varnished; plain; straightforward.
unveil (un-vāl′) *v.t.* to remove a veil from; to perform in public the act of uncovering a newly erected statue; (*Fig.*) to disclose;—*v.i.* to become unveiled.
unwarrantable (un-wor′-an-ta-bl) *a.* not justifiable; improper.—**unwarrantabil′ity, unwarr′antableness** *n.*—**unwarr′antably** *adv.*—**unwarr′anted** *a.* unauthorised; not carrying a guarantee.—**unwarr′antedly** *adv.*
unwary (un-wā′-ri) *a.* not cautious; rash.—**unwa′rily** *adv.*—**unwa′riness** *n.*
unwashed (un-wosht′) *a.* not washed; dirty; not reached by the sea.—**the Great Unwashed** (*Colloq.*) the mob.
unwell (un-wel′) *a.* not well; indisposed.
unwept (un-wept′) *a.* not mourned or regretted.
unwholesome (un-hōl′-sum) *a.* not wholesome; unhealthy; morally decadent.—**unwhole′somely** *adv.*—**unwhole′someness** *n.*
unwieldy (un-wēl′-di) *a.* awkward to handle or move; bulky; unmanageable.—**unwiel′dily** *adv.*—**unwiel′diness** *n.*
unwilling (un-wil′-ing) *a.* not willing; reluctant; disobliging.—**unwilled′** *a.* spontaneous.—**unwill′ingly** *adv.*—**unwill′ingness** *n.*
unwind (un-wīnd′) *v.t.* to wind off; to loose what has been wound; to roll into a ball from a skein, as wool, silk, etc.;—*v.i.* to become unwound.
unwitting (un-wit′-ing) *a.* unawares; not knowing.—**unwitt′ingly** *adv.*
unwonted (un-wōn′ (or wun′) -ted) *a.* unaccustomed; unusual.—**unwon′tedly** *adv.*—**unwon′tedness** *n.*
unworldly (un-wurld′-li) *a.* not worldly; spiritual; not actuated by self-interest.—**unworld′liness** *n.*
unworthy (un-wur′-thi) *a.* not worthy; discreditable; unbecoming; not deserving praise.—**unworth′ily** *adv.*—**unworth′iness** *n.*
unwritten (un-rit′-n) *a.* not written; oral; not expressed in writing.—**unwritten law** (*Law*) custom by which a man is acquitted of the crime of killing the seducer of his wife or daughter.
unwrung (un-rung′) *a.* not wrung; not galled.—**his withers are unwrung** (*Fig.*) he is unaffected by the accusation.
unyielding (un-yēl′-ding) *a.* not yielding; stubborn; implacable; not flexible.—**unyiel′dingly** *adv.*—**unyiel′dingness** *n.*
up (up) *adv.* to a higher place; aloft; on high; on one's legs; out of bed; above horizon; in progress; in revolt; as far as; of equal merit, as in ***he is not up to his father in skill***; thoroughly; well versed in; competent.
upas (ū′-pas) *n.* tree of E. Indian islands, yielding sap of deadly poisonous properties; antiar-tree; (*Fig.*) anything of poisonous or corrupt influence [Malay, *upas,* poison].
upbraid (up-brād′) *v.t.* to reprove severely; to chide;—*v.i.* to voice a reproach.—**upbraid′ing** *n.* reproach;—*a.* reproachful [O.E. *up,* on; *bregdan,* to braid].
upbringing (up′-bring-ing) *n* the process of rearing and training a child; education.
up-country (up′-kun-tri) *adv.* inland;—*a.* away from the sea.
upheave (up-hēv′) *v.t.* to lift up, as heavy weight.—**upheav′al** *n.* raising up, as of earth's surface, by volcanic force; (*Fig.*) any revolutionary change in ideas, etc.
upheld (up-held′) *pa.t.* and *pa.p.* of **uphold.**
uphill (up′-hill) *a.* going up; laborious; difficult;—*adv.* towards higher level.
uphold (up-hōld′) *v.t.* to hold up; to sustain; to approve; to maintain, as verdict in law court.—**uphold′er** *n.*
upholsterer (up-hōl′-ster-er) *n.* one who supplies furniture, curtains, carpets, etc.

one who upholsters chairs, etc.—**uphol'ster** *v.t.* to stuff and cover furniture with tapestry, moquette, hide, etc.—**uphol'stery** *n.* craft of stuffing and covering furniture, etc.; materials used.
upkeep (up'kēp) *n.* maintenance; money required for maintenance, as of a home.
upland (up'land) *n.* high land;—*pl.* dissected plateau;—*a.* pert. to or situated in higher elevations of district.—**up'lander** *n.*
uplift (up-lift') *v.t.* to lift up; to draw money out of the bank.—**up'lift** *n.* upheaval; (*Fig.*) emotional or religious stimulus.
up-line (up'līn) *n.* railway line leading from the provinces to a main terminus.
upmost (up'mōst) *a.* uppermost.
upon (up-on') *prep.* on [O.E. *uppon*, on].
upper (up'ẹr) *a.* (comp. of **up**) higher in place, rank, or dignity; superior.—*superl.* **up'permost, up'most.**—*n.* upper part of boot or shoe.—**up'per-case** *n.* (*Print.*) case containing capital letters, reference marks, etc.—**up'per-cut** *n.* (*Boxing*) blow struck upwards inside opponent's guard;—*v.t.* to deliver such blow.—**up'per-hand** *n.* superiority; advantage over another.—**up'permost** *a.* highest.—**up'pish** *a.* arrogant; affectedly superior in manner or attitude.—**up'pishly** *adv.*—**up'pishness** *n.* [fr. *up*].
uprise (up-rīz') *v.i.* to rise up.—**upri'sing** *n.* act of rising; insurrection; revolt.
uproar (up'rōr) *n.* tumult; violent, noisy disturbance.—**uproar'ious** *a.* making a noise and tumult; rowdy.—**uproar'iously** *adv.*—**uproar'iousness** *n.* [Dut. *oproer*].
uproot (up-ròòt') *v.t.* to tear up by the roots; to eradicate.—**uproot'al** *n.*
upset (up-set') *v.t.* to turn upside down; to knock over; to defeat, as government; (*Fig.*) to disturb or distress.—**up'set** *n.* an overturn; overthrow; confusion;—*a.* fixed.—**upset price,** lowest price at which goods will be sold by auction.
upshot (up'shot) *n.* final issue; conclusion.
upside (up'sīd) *n.* the upper side.—**up'side-down'** *adv.* with the upper side underneath; inverted; in disorder.—**to be upsides with,** to be on equal terms with; to be quits.
upstairs (up-stārz') *adv.* in the upper storey.—**up'stairs** *a.* pert. to upper flat;—*n.* upper flat.
upstanding (up-stand'ing) *a.* (of a man etc.) well set-up; erect.
upstart (up'stårt) *n.* one who has suddenly risen to wealth, power, or honour; parvenu; —*a.* arrogant;—*v.i.* to rise suddenly.
upstream (up'strēm) *adv.* in direction of source (of stream).
upstroke (up'strōk) *n.* the upward line in handwriting; upward stroke.
upsurge (up-surj') *v.t.* to surge upwards.—**up surge** *n.* welling, as of emotion.
upthrust (up'thrust) *n.* upward thrust, esp. of rock strata.
uptown (up'toun) *a.* pert. to, or in upper part of, town;—*adv.*
upturn (up-turn') *v.t.* to turn up.—**up'turn** *n.* disturbance.—**up'turning** *n.*
upward (up'wạrd) *a.* directed towards a higher place;—*adv.* upwards.—**up'wards, up'wardly** *adv.* towards higher elevation or number [O.E. *upweard*, upward].
uraninite (ūr-an'in-īt) *n.* pitchblende, in which uranium was first found in 1789.
uranite (ū'rạ-nīt) *n.* an almost transparent ore of uranium.—**uranit'ic** *a.*
uranium (ū-rā'ni-um) *n.* radio-active metallic element (symbol **U**), used as an alloy in steel manufacture and a variety of it, U 235, in the production of atom bomb.—**uran'ic, u'ranous** *a.* [fr. *Uranus*, the planet].
uranography (ū-rạ-nog'rạ-fi) *n.* descriptive astronomy.—**uranom'etry** *n.* measurement of heavens; chart of heavens [Gk. *ouranos*, heaven].
urban (ur'bạn) *a.* pert. to, or living in, city or town.—**urbane'** *a.* refined; suave; courteous.—**urbane'ly** *adv.*—**urban'ity** *n.* politeness.—**urbanise'** *v.t.* to make urban; to bring town conditions and advantages to rural areas.—**Urban District,** in England and Wales, district authorised in 1894 to set up necessary councils for administration of local government [L. *urbs*].
urchin (ur'chin) *n.* hedgehog; sea-urchin; goblin; mischievous child; a child [L. *ericius*, hedgehog].
Urdu (òòr'dòò) *n.* form of Hindustani, mixture of Persian, Arabic, and Hindi [Hind. *urdu*, camp].
urea (ū'rē-ạ) *n.* white, crystalline solid, the principle organic constituent of urine [Gk. *ouron*, urine].
ureter (ū-rē'tẹr) *n.* one of two ducts of kidney conveying urine to bladder.—**ure'thra** *n.* duct by which urine passes from bladder.—*pl.* **ure'thrae.**—**ure'thral** *a.* [Gk. *ouron*, urine].
urge (urj) *v.t.* to press; to drive; to exhort; to stimulate; to solicit earnestly;—*v.i.* to press onward; to make allegations;—*n.* act of urging; incentive; irresistible impulse.—**ur'gency** *n.* quality of being urgent; compelling necessity; importunity.—**ur'gent** *a.* calling for immediate attention; clamant; importunate.—**ur'gently** *adv.*—**ur'ger** *n.* [L. *urgere*, to press].
urine (ū'rin) *n.* yellowish fluid secreted by kidneys, passed through ureters to bladder from which it is discharged through urethra. —**ure'sis** *n.* desire to pass urine frequently.—**u'ric** *a.* pert. to or produced from urine.—**u'rinal** *n.* vessel into which urine may be discharged; public lavatory.—**u'rinary** *a.* pert. to urine.—**u'rinate** *v.i.* to pass urine.—**urina'tion** *n.*—**urogen'ital** *a.* pert. to urinary and genital organs. Also **urinogen'ital, urinogen'itary** [Gk. *ouron*, urine].
urn (urn) *n.* vase-shaped vessel of pottery or metal with pedestal, and narrow neck, for ashes of dead after cremation; the grave; vessel of various forms usually fitted with tap, for liquid in bulk, as *tea-urn.*—**urn'al** *a.* [L. *urna*, urn].
urry (ur'i) *n.* darkish clay in proximity to coal bed [etym. uncertain].
ursine (ur'sin) *a.* pert. to or resembling a bear;—*n.* bear.—**ur'siform** *a.* resembling bear in shape [L. *ursus*].
us (us) *pron. pl.* the objective form of **we.**—**us'ward** *adv.* towards us.
use (ūz) *v.t.* to make use of; to employ; to consume or expend (as in material); to practise habitually; to accustom; to treat;—*v.i.* to be accustomed (only in past tense).—**use** (ūs) *n.* act of using or employing for specific purpose; utility; custom; (*Law*) profit derived from trust.—**u'sable** *a.* fit for use.—**u'sableness** *n.*—**u'sage** *n.* mode of using; treatment; long-established custom.—**u'sance** *n.* usage; usury; usual time allowed for payment of foreign bills of exchange.—**use'ful** *a.* of use; handy; profitable; serviceable; (*Colloq.*) influential—**useful load** (*Aero.*) gross weight of aircraft less tare weight.—**use'fully** *adv.*—**use'fulness** *n.*—**use'less** *a.* of no use; inefficient; futile; (*Slang*) unwell.—**use'lessly** *adv.*—**use'lessness** *n.*—**u'ser** *n.* one who uses anything.—**use and wont,** habitual and long-established practice [L. *uti*, *usus*, to use].
usher (ush'ẹr) *n.* doorkeeper, esp. in court of law; one who conducts wedding guests to seats in church; official who introduces strangers or walks before person of high rank; assistant-master in school;—*v.t.* to introduce; to inaugurate; to show into room and announce the name (of a visitor).—**usherette'** *n.* girl employed, as in cinema, to show patrons to seats.—**to usher in,** to precede [O.Fr. *ussier*, fr. L. *ostiarius*, a doorkeeper].
usquebaugh (us'kwe-baw) *n.* whisky [Gael. *uisge*, water; *beatha*, life].

usual (ū-zhū-ạl) *a.* customary; ordinary.—**u'sually** *adv.*—**u'sualness** *n.* [L. *usus*].

usufruct (ū′zū-frukt) *n.* right of using and enjoying produce, benefit, or profits of another's property provided that the property remains undamaged.—**usufruc'tuary** *a.* pert. to usufruct;—*n.* one who has the use of another's property by usufruct [L. *usus*, use; *fructus*, fruit].

usurp (ū-zurp′) *v.t.* to take possession of unlawfully or by force.—**usurpa'tion** *n.* act of usurping; violent or unlawful seizing of power [L. *usurpare*, to gain].

usury (ū′zhū-ri) *n.* orig. business of lending money with interest; charging of exorbitant interest on money lent.—**u'surer** *n.* money-lender, esp. one who charges exorbitant rates of interest.—**usu'rious** *a.*—**usu'riously** *adv.* [L. *usura*, use].

utensil (ū-ten′sil) *n.* vessel of any kind which forms part of everyday domestic equipment [L. *utensilis*, fit for use].

uterine (ū′tẹr-in) *a.* pert. to uterus or womb; born of the same mother but by a different father [L. *uterus*, womb].

utilise (ū′ti-līz) *v.t.* to make useful; to turn to profit.—**u'tilisable** *a.*—**utilisa'tion** *n.*—**u'tiliser** *n.*—**util'ity** *n.* usefulness; quality of being advantageous [L. *utilis*, useful].

utilitarian (ū-til-i-tā′ri-ạn) *a.* pert. to utility or utilitarianism; of practical use.—**Utilita'rian** *n.* one who accepts doctrines of Utilitarianism.—**Utilita'rianism** *n.* ethical doctrine, the ultimate aim and criterion of all human actions must be 'the greatest happiness for the greatest number' [L. *utilis*, useful].

utmost (ut′mōst) *a.* situated at farthest point or extremity; to highest degree;—*n.* most that can be; greatest possible effort [O.E. *ut*, out].

utopia (ū-tō′pi-ạ) *n.* any ideal, state, constitution, system, or way of life.—**uto'pian** *a.* ideally perfect but impracticable; visionary; chimerical [=nowhere; Gk. *ou*, not; *topos*, place].

utricle (ū′tri-kl) *n.* (*Bot.*) little bag or bladder, esp. of aquatic plant.—**utric'ular, utric'ulate** *a.* [L. *utriculus*, small bag).

utter (ut′ẹr) *a.* farthest out; extreme; total; unconditional.—**utt'erly** *adv.*—**utt'erness** *n.* [O.E. *utor*, outer].

utter (ut′ẹr) *v.t.* to speak; to disclose; to put into circulation.—**utt'erable** *a.* capable of being uttered or pronounced.—**utt'erableness** *n.*—**utt'erance** *n.* act of speaking; manner of delivering speech; pronunciation.—**utt'erer** *n.* [O.E. *utian*, to put out].

uttermost (ut′ẹr-mōst) *a.* farthest out; utmost;—*n.* the highest degree.

uvula (ū′vū-lạ) *n.* fleshy tag suspended from middle of lower border of soft palate.—**u'vular** *a.* [L. *uva*, grape].

uxorious (uk-sō′ri-us) *a.* foolishly or excessively fond of one's wife.—**uxo'rial** *a.* pert. to wife.—**uxo'riously** *adv.*—**uxo'riousness** *n.* [L. *uxor*].

V

vacant (vā′kạnt) *a.* empty; void; not occupied; disengaged; unintelligent.—**va'cantly** *adv.*—**va'cancy** *n.* emptiness; idleness; listlessness; want of thought; place or post, unfilled.—**vacate** (vạ-kāt′) *v.t.* to leave empty or unoccupied; to quit possession of; to make void.—**vaca'tion** *n.* act of vacating; intermission of stated employment; recess; holidays.—**vaca'tional** *a.* [L. *vacare*, to be empty].

vaccine (vak′sin, vak′sēn) *a.* pert. to, or obtained from, cows;—*n.* virus of cowpox, used in vaccination; any substance used for inoculation against disease.—**vac'cinate** *v.t.* to inoculate with cowpox, to ward off smallpox or lessen severity of its attack.—**vaccina'tion** *n.* act or practice of vaccinating [L. *vacca*, cow].

vacillate (vas′i-lāt) *v.i.* to move to and fro; to waver; to be unsteady; to fluctuate in opinion.—**vac'illant, vac'illating, vac'illatory** *a.*—**vac'illancy, vacilla'tion** *n.* [L. *vacillare*].

vacuous (vak′ū-us) *a.* empty; vacant; expressionless; unintelligent.—**vac'uousness** *n.*—**vacuity** (vạ-kū′i-ti) *n.* emptiness; empty space; lack of intelligence.—**vac'uum** *n.* space devoid of all matter; space from which air, or other gas, has been almost wholly removed, as by air-pump.—**vac'uum-clean'er** *n.* apparatus for removing dust from esp. carpets by suction.—**vac'uum-flask** *n.* double-walled flask with vacuum between walls, for keeping contents at temperature at which they were inserted [L. *vacuus*, empty].

vade-mecum (vā′de-mē′kum) *n.* small handbook or manual for ready reference; pocket-companion [L.=go with me].

vagabond (vag′a-bond) *a.* moving from place to place without settled habitation; wandering;—*n.* wanderer or vagrant, having no settled habitation; idle scamp; rascal.—**vag'abondage** *n.* state or condition of vagabond [L. *vagari*, to wander].

vagary (vạ-gā′ri) *n.* whimsical or freakish notion; unaccountable proceeding; caprice [L. *vagari*, to wander].

vagina (vạ-jī′nạ) *n.* (*Anat.*) canal which leads from uterus to external orifice; (*Bot.*) sheath as of leaf.—**vaginal** (vaj′i-nạl) *a.* [L.].

vagrant (vā′grạnt) *a.* wandering from place to place; moving without certain direction; roving;—*n.* idle wanderer; vagabond; itinerant beggar.—**va'grantly** *adv.*—**va'grancy** *n.* [L. *vagari*, to wander].

vague (vāg) *a.* uncertain; indefinite; indistinct; not clearly expressed.—**vague'ly** *adv.*—**vague'ness** *n.* [L. *vagus*, wandering].

vain (vān) *a.* useless; unavailing; fruitless; empty; worthless; unsatisfying; conceited; silly; showy.—**vain'ly** *adv.*—**vanity** (van′i-ti) *n.* idle show; empty pleasure; futility; conceit; ostentation.—**van'ity-bag** *n.* lady's small handbag fitted with powder puff, mirror, lipstick, etc. [L. *vanus*, empty].

vainglory (vān-glō′ri) *n.* excessive vanity; boastfulness.—**vainglo'rious** *a.* due to vanity; boastful; vaunting.—**vainglo'riously** *adv.*—**vainglo'riousness** *n.* [*vain* and *glory*].

valance (val′ạns) *n.* hanging drapery for a window, bed, couch, etc. esp. that for hiding the space beneath a bed. Also **val'ence** [Fr. *Valence*, in France].

vale (vāl) *n.* valley [L. *vallis*, valley].

valediction (val-e-dik′shun) *n.* farewell; a bidding farewell.—**valedic'tory** *a.* bidding farewell; suitable for leave-taking [L. *valedicere*, to say farewell].

valence, valency (vā′lens, vā′len-si) *n.* (*Chem.*) the combining power of an element or atom as compared with a hydrogen atom [L. *valere*, to be strong].

Valenciennes (val-en-sēnz′) *n.* rich lace, made orig. at *Valenciennes*, in France.

valentine (val′en-tīn) *n.* sweetheart chosen on *St. Valentine's* day; letter containing professions of love, sent to one of opposite sex on *St. Valentine's* day, Feb. 14th [L. proper name *Valentinus*].

valerian (val-ēr′i-ạn) *n.* flowering herb with strong odour; its root, used as sedative drug [O.Fr. *valeriane*].

valet (val′et, val′ā) *n.* man-servant who attends on a gentleman [Fr. *valet*, a groom. Doublet of *varlet*].

valetudinarian (val-e-tū-di-nā′ri-ạn) *a.* sickly; infirm; solicitous about one's own health;—*n.* person of sickly constitution; person disposed to live life of an invalid.—**valetudina'rianism** *n.*—**valetu'dinary** *a.* infirm; sickly [L. *valetudo*, health].

Valhalla (vạl-hal′a) *n.* (*Norse myth.*) hall of

immortality where Odin received souls of heroes slain in battle [O.N. *valr*, slain; *holl*, hall].
valiant (val′yạnt) *a.* brave; heroic; courageous; intrepid.—**val′iantly** *adv.*—**val′iantness** *n.* —**val′iance, val′iancy** *n.* valour; courage [L. *valere*, to be strong].
valid (val′id) *a.* strong; sound or well-grounded; capable of being justified; (*Law*) legally sound; executed with proper formalities.—**val′idly** *adv.*—**val′idate** *v.t.* to make valid; to ratify.—**val′idness** *n.*—**valid′ity** *n.* [L. *validus*, strong].
valise (vạ-lēs′) *n.* a small travelling-bag; a portmanteau [Fr.].
Valkyr (val′kir) *n.* (*Norse myth.*) one of Odin's nine handmaidens, whose duty it was to select those worthy to be slain in battle and to conduct them to Valhalla. Also **Valkyrie** (val-kī′ri), **Valkyria** (val-kir′ya). —**valky′rian** *a.*
valley (val′i) *n.* low ground between hills; river-basin [L. *vallis*, vale]. [work [L.].
vallum (val′um) *n.* a rampart; an earth-
valour (val′or) *n.* bravery; prowess in war; courage; intrepidity.—**val′orous** *a.* brave; fearless.—**val′orously** *adv.*—**val′orousness** *n.* [L. *valere*, to be strong].
valse (vȧls) *n.* waltz, esp. one played as concert piece [Fr.].
value (val′ū) *n.* worth; utility; importance; estimated worth or valuation; precise signification; equivalent; (*Mus.*) duration of note;—*v.t.* to estimate worth of; to hold in respect and admiration; to prize.—**val′uer** *n.*—**val′ueless** *a.*—**val′uable** *a.* precious; worth a good price; worthy;—*n.* thing of value (generally *pl.*).—**val′uableness** *n.*— **val′uate** *v.t.* to set value on; to appraise.—**valua′tion** *n.* value set upon a thing, esp. by professional valuer.—**val′uator** *n.* [L. *valere*, to be worth].
valve (valv) *n.* folding door, or one of its leaves; device for covering aperture (as in tube) so arranged as to open communication in one direction, and close it in the other; (*Anat.*) structure (as in blood-vessel) which allows flow of fluid in one direction only; (*Zool.*) either of two sections of shell of mollusc; (*Radio*) vacuum tube or bulb containing electrodes and giving very sensitive control of flow of electrical current; (*Mus.*) device in certain instruments (as horn, trumpet, etc.) for changing fundamental tone by definite interval.—**val′vular** *a.* [L. *valva*, leaf of folding door].
vamoose, vamose (va-mōōs′, va-mōs′) *v.i.* (*U.S. slang*) to depart quickly; to leave; to decamp [Sp. *vamos*, let us go].
vamp (vamp) *n.* upper leather of shoe or boot; new patch put on old article; (*Mus.*) improvised accompaniment;—*v.t.* to provide (shoe, etc.) with new upper leather; to patch; (*Mus.*) to improvise accompaniment to [Fr. *avant-pied*, front of foot].
vamp (vamp) *n.* (*Slang*) woman who allures and exploits men; adventuress;—*v.t.* and *v.i.* (*Slang*) to allure and exploit; to flirt unscrupulously [contr. of *vampire*].
vampire (vam′pīr) *n.* reanimated body of dead person who cannot rest quietly in grave, but arises from it at night and sucks blood of sleepers; (*Fig.*) one who lives by preying on others; extortioner.—**vam′pire-bat** *n.* of several species of bat of S. America which sucks blood of animals and even of persons [Fr. fr. Serbian *vampir*].
van (van) *n.* covered wagon for goods; closed carriage attached to train (for luggage, guard, etc.) [contr. of *caravan*].
van (van) *n.* leading division of army or fleet; leaders of a movement.—**van′guard** *n.* detachment of troops who march ahead of army [Fr. *avant*, before; *garde*, a guard].
van (van) *n.* fan for winnowing grain; wing;—*v.t.* to winnow; to test quality of ore by washing on shovel.—**van′ner** *n.* [L. *vannus*, a fan].
vanadium (vạ-nā′di-um) *n.* a metallic element (the hardest known) used in manufacture of hard steel [fr. *Vanadis*, Scand. goddess].
Vandal (van′dạl) *n.* one of the Germanic nations which ravaged Gaul, Spain, N. Africa and Rome about 5th cent.—**van′dal** *n.* one who wantonly damages or destroys work of art or of literature; barbarian.—**van′dalism** *n.* [L. *Vandalus*, Vandal].
vandyke (van-dīk′) *n.* one of the points forming an edge, as of lace, ribbon, etc.; broad collar with deep points of lace as worn in portraits by *Van Dyck*; painting by Van Dyck.—**Vandyke beard,** pointed beard.—**vandyke brown,** dark brown [*Van Dyck*, Flemish painter].
vane (vān) *n.* a device at the top of a spire; etc. to show the direction of the wind; a weather-cock; the blade of a propeller, of a windmill, etc.; a fin on a bomb to prevent swerving [O.E. *fana*, a banner].
vanguard (van′gȧrd) *n.* See **van** (2).
vanilla (vạ-nil′ạ) *n.* tropical American plant of orchid family; long pod of plant, used as flavouring.—**vanill′ic** *a.* [dim. fr. Sp. *vaina*, sheath].
vanish (van′ish) *v.i.* to pass away; to be lost to view; to disappear; (*Math.*) to become zero.—**van′isher** *n.*—**van′ishing** *a.* disappearing.—**van′ishingly** *adv.* [L. *evanescere*, fr. *vanus*, empty].
vanity (van′i-ti) *n.* See **vain.**
vanquish (vang′kwish) *v.t.* to conquer in battle; to defeat in any contest; to get the better of; to refute.—**van′quishable** *a.*—**van′quisher** *n.* [Fr. *vaincre*, fr. L. *vincere*].
vantage (van′tāj) *n.* better situation or opportunity; advantage; in tennis, same as 'advantage.' Used esp. in **vantage-ground, coign of vantage,** position of advantage [M.E. *avantage*, advantage].
vapid (vap′id) *a.* having lost its life and spirit; flat; inspid.—**vap′idly** *adv.*—**vap′idness** *n.*—**vapid′ity** *n.* [L. *vapidus*, stale].
vapour (vā′pur) *n.* any light, cloudy substance which impairs clearness of atmosphere, as mist, fog, smoke, etc.; anything unsubstantial;—*pl.* (*Arch.*) disease of nervous debility; depression; melancholy;—*v.i.* to pass off in vapour; (*Fig.*) to talk idly; to brag.—**va′porise** *v.t.* to convert into vapour;—*v.i.* to pass off in vapour.—**vaporisa′tion** *n.*—**va′poriser** *n.* mechanism for splitting liquid into fine particles.—**va′pourish** *a.* full of vapours; prone to depression or hysteria.—**va′pourishness** *n.*—**va′porous** *a.* like vapour; unreal; vain.—**va′porously** *adv.*—**va′pourousness** *n.*—**va′pourings** *n.pl.* inane talk.—**va′poury** *a.* full of vapours; depressed or peevish.—**va′pour-bath, vapora′rium** *n.* steam-bath or Turkish bath [L. *vapor*].
variable (vā′ri-ạ-bl) *a.* changeable; capable of being adapted; unsteady or fickle;—*n.* that which is subject to change; symbol that may have infinite number of values; indeterminate quantity; shifting wind.—**va′riably** *adv.*—**va′riableness** *n.*—**variabil′ity** *n.* (*Biol.*) tendency to vary from average characteristics of species.—**va′riant** *a.* different; diverse;—*n.* different form or reading.—**va′riance** *n.* difference that produces controversy; state of discord or disagreement. —**variation** (vā-ri-ā′shun) *n.* act of varying; alteration; modification; extent to which thing varies; (*Gram.*) change of termination; in magnetism, deviation of magnetic needle from true north; (*Mus.*) repetition of theme or melody with various embellishments and elaborations.—**at variance,** not in harmony or agreement [L. *varius*, various].
varicoloured (vā′ri-kul-urd) *a.* having various colours.
varicose (var′i-kōs) *a.* enlarged or dilated, as veins, esp. in legs [L. *varix*, a dilated vein; fr. *varus*, crooked].
variegate (vā′ri-e-gāt) *v.t.* to diversify by

patches of different colours; to streak, spot, dapple, etc.—**variega'tion** *n.* [L. *varius*, various; *agere*, to make].

variety (vạ-rī´e-ti) *n.* state of being varied; diversity; collection of different things; many-sidedness; one of class of objects within a larger class to which it is allied; subdivision of a species.—**vari'ety-show** *n.* mixed entertainment, consisting of songs, dances, short sketches, juggling, etc. [L. *varietas*, variety, fr. *varius*, various].

variorum (vā-ri-ō´rum) *a.* designating an edition of a work with notes by various commentators [L.=of various men].

various (vā´ri-us) *a.* different; diverse; manifold; separate; diversified.—**va'riously** *adv.*—**va'riousness** *n.* [L. *varius*].

varlet (vȧr´let) *n.* page or attendant; scoundrel [O.Fr. *varlet*, var. of *vaslet*, fr. L.L. *vassalus*, vassal].

varnish (vȧr´nish) *n.* clear, resinous liquid laid on work to give it gloss; glossy appearance; glaze; (*Fig.*) outward show; fair appearance glossing over questionable conduct;—*v.t.* to lay varnish on; (*Fig.*) to conceal something with fair appearance [Fr. *vernis*, varnish].

vary (vā´ri) *v.t.* to change; to make different or modify; to diversify;—*v.i.* to alter, or be altered; to be different; to be at variance; to deviate.—**va'ried** *a.* various; diverse; diversified [L. *variare*, to vary].

vas (vas) *n.* (*Anat.*) vessel or duct containing blood, etc.—**vascular** (vas´kū-lạr) *a.* (*Anat.*) pert. to vessels or ducts for conveying blood, lymph, sap, etc.—**vascular system**, all blood-vessels of the body.—**vas'culum** *n.* botanist's collecting-box.—**vasomo'tor** *a.* controlling tension of blood-vessels [L.].

vase (vȧz, (*U.S.*) vāz) *n.* vessel, anciently used for sacrificial purposes, sometimes for domestic purposes, now for flowers or merely for decoration; large sculptured vessel, used as ornament, in gardens, on gate-posts, etc. [L. *vas*, vessel].

Vaseline (vas´e-lēn) *n.* Protected Trade Name applied to brand of petroleum used in ointments, pomades, as lubricant, etc. [Ger. *Wasser*, water; Gk. *elaion*, oil].

vassal (vas´ạl) *n.* one who holds land from superior, and vows fealty and homage to him; dependant; bondman or slave.—**vass'alage** *n.* state of being a vassal [Fr. fr. Celt. *gwaz*, servant].

vast (vȧst) *a.* of great extent; very spacious; very great in numbers or quantity;—*n.* (*Poet.*) boundless space.—**vast'ly** *adv.*—**vast'ness** *n.* [L. *vastus*, very great].

vat (vat) *n.* large vessel, tub, or cistern, generally for holding liquids [O.E. *foet*, a vessel, cask].

vatic (vat´ik) *a.* prophetic; oracular. Also **vatic'inal**.—**vatic'inate** *v.t.* and *v.i.* to prophesy; to foretell [L. *vates*, a prophet].

Vatican (vat´i-kạn) *n.* palace and official residence of Pope on Vatican Hill (L. *Mons Vaticanus*), in Rome; papal authority.

vaudeville (vōd´vil, -vēl) *n.* orig. light, gay song, sung to familiar air; theatrical piece with light or satirical songs; now often applied to variety-show [fr. *Vau de Vire* in Normandy, where this type of song was first composed].

vault (vawlt) *n.* arched roof; apartment covered with vault, esp. subterranean; cellar; sky; anything resembling a vault;—*v.t.* to cover with arched roof; to form like vault.—**vaul'ted** *a.* arched [L. *volutus*, turned].

vault (vawlt) *v.i.* to spring or jump with hands resting on something; to leap or curvet, as horse;—*v.t.* to spring or jump over;—*n.* such a spring.—**vaul'ting-horse** *n.* wooden stand, used by gymnasts for vaulting over [Fr. *volte*, turn; fr. L. *volutus*].

vaunt (vawnt, vȧnt) *v.i.* to brag or boast;—*v.t.* to boast of; to make vain display of;—*n.* boast; vainglorious display [O.Fr. *vanter*; fr. L. *vanitas*, vanity].

veal (vēl) *n.* flesh of a calf killed for the table [O.Fr. *veel*, fr. L. *vitellus*, calf].

vector (vek´tor) *n.* (*Math.*) any quantity requiring direction to be stated as well as magnitude in order to define it properly, e.g. velocity; disease-carrying insect.—**vecto'rial** *a.* [L. *vehere*, *vectum*, to convey].

Veda (vā´dạ) *n.* most ancient sacred literature of Hindus.—**Ve'dic** *a.* pert. to the Vedas [Sans. *veda*, knowledge].

vedette (ve-det') *n.* mounted sentinel placed in advance of outposts to give notice of danger; (*Nav.*) fast motor-launch for reconnaissance purposes [It. *vedetta*, fr. *vedere*, to see, fr. L. *videre*].

veer (vēr) *v.t.* and *v.i.* to turn; of wind, to change direction, esp. clockwise; (*Naut.*) to change ship's course; (*Fig.*) to change one's opinion or point of view; (*Naut.*) to pay out rope [Fr. *virer*].

vegetable (vej´e-tạ-bl) *a.* belonging to plants; having nature of plants;—*n.* plant, esp. plant used as food, e.g. potato, carrot, cabbage, bean.—**vegetarian** (vej-e-tā´ri-ạn) *n.* one who abstains from animal flesh and lives on vegetables, eggs, milk, etc.;—*a.* pert. to vegetarianism; consisting of vegetables.—**vegeta'rianism** *n.*—**veg'etate** *v.i.* to grow as plant does; to lead idle, useless, unthinking life.—**vegeta'tion** *n.* process of vegetating; vegetable growth; plants in general.—**vegetable marrow**, egg-shaped gourd with tender flesh [L. *vegetabilis*, enlivening, fr. *vegetare*, to quicken].

vehement (vē´he-mẹnt) *a.* acting with great force; impetuous; vigorous; passionate.—**ve'hemently** *adv.*—**ve'hemence, ve'hemency** *n.* impetuosity; fury; violence; force [L. *vehemens*, very eager].

vehicle (vē´i-kl, vē´hi-kl) *n.* any means of conveyance (esp. on land) as carriage, cart, etc.; liquid medium in which drugs are taken, or pigments applied; any person or thing used as means or medium of expression or communication.—**vehicular** (vé-hik´ū-lạr) *a.* Also **vehic'ulatory** [L. *vehiculum*, fr. *vehere*, to carry].

veil (vāl) *n.* piece of thin, gauzy material worn by women to hide or protect face; covering; curtain; disguise;—*v.t.* to cover with veil; to conceal.—**veiled** *a.* covered; concealed; disguised.—**veil'ing** *n.* act of covering with veil; material from which veil is made.—**to take the veil**, to become a nun [L. *velum*].

vein (vān) *n.* each of the vessels or tubes which receive blood from capillaries and return it to heart; any blood-vessel; (*Biol.*) one of the small branching ribs of leaf or of insect's wing; layer of mineral intersecting a stratum of rock; streak or wave of different colour appearing in wood, marble, etc.; distinctive tendency; mood or cast of mind;—*v.t.* to mark with veins.—**vein'ing** *n.* system of veins; streaked surface.— **vein'ous, vein'y** *a.* [L. *vena*].

veld, veldt (felt, velt) *n.* in S. Africa, open grass-country [Dut. *veld*, a field].

veleta (vel-ē´ta) *n.* kind of waltz [etym. uncertain].

vellum (vel´um) *n.* fine parchment made of calf's-skin [O.Fr. *velin*, fr. L. *vitulus*, calf].

velocipede (ve-los´i-pēd) *n.* a vehicle propelled by the rider, early form of bicycle [L. *velox*, swift; *pes*, the foot].

velocity (ve-los´i-ti) *n.* rate of motion; swiftness; speed; distance traversed in unit time in a given direction [L. *velox*, swift; Gk. *metron*, a measure].

velours (vẹ-lōōr') *n.* fabric resembling velvet or plush; hat made of velours. Also **velour'** and **velure** (vel´ūr).—**veloutine'** *n.* corded fabric [Fr.=velvet].

velvet (vel´vet) *n.* soft material of silk with thick short pile on one side;—*a.* made of velvet; soft and delicate.—**vel'vety** *a.* soft as velvet.—**velveteen'** *n.* poor velvet made of cotton, or of silk and cotton mixed [L.L. *vellutum*, fr. L. *villus*, shaggy hair].

venal (vē´nal) *a.* to be obtained for money; prepared to take bribes; mercenary.—**ve'nally** *adv.*—**venal'ity** *n.* quality of being purchasable [L. *venalis*, fr. *venus*, sale].

venatic, venatical (ve-nat´ik, -i-kal) *a.* relating to hunting [L. *venari*, to hunt].

vend (vend) *v.t.* to sell; to dispose of by sale.—**ven'dible** *a.* saleable.—**ven'dibly** *adv.*—**vendibil'ity, ven'dibleness** *n.* the quality of being saleable.—**ven'dor** *n.* person who sells; seller [L. *vendere*].

vendetta (ven-det´a) *n.* blood-feud, in which it was the duty of the relative of murdered man to avenge his death by killing murderer or relative of murderer; any bitter feud [It. fr. L. *vindicta*, revenge].

veneer (ve-nēr') *n.* thin layer of valuable wood glued to surface of inferior wood; thin coating of finer substance; (*Fig.*) superficial charm or polish of manner;—*v.t.* to coat or overlay with substance giving superior surface; (*Fig.*) to disguise with superficial charm.—**veneer'ing** *n.* act of treating with veneer; thin layer used in this process [Fr. *fournir*, to furnish].

venerate (ven´e-rāt) *v.t.* to regard with respect and reverence.—**ven'erator** *n.*—**venera'tion** *n.* respect mingled with awe; worship.—**ven'erable** *a.* worthy of veneration; deserving respect by reason of age, character, etc.; sacred by reason of religious or historical associations.—**ven'erably** *adv.* [L. *venerari*, to worship].

venereal (ve-nē´re-al) *a.* pert. to sexual intercourse; arising from sexual intercourse with infected persons [L. *Venus, Veneris*, goddess of Love].

venery (ven´e-ri) *n.* (*Arch.*) hunting; sports of the chase [L. *venari*, to hunt].

Venetian (ve-nē´shan) *a.* pert. to city of Venice, Italy;—*n.* native, inhabitant of Venice.—**venetian blind,** blind made of thin, horizontal slips of wood, so hung as to overlap each other when closed.

vengeance (ven´jans) *n.* infliction of pain or loss on another in return for injury or offence.—**venge'ful** *a.* disposed to revenge; vindictive.—**venge'fully** *adv.*—**venge'fulness** *n.* [L. *vindicare*, to avenge].

venial (vē´ni-al) *a.* capable of being forgiven; excusable.—**ve'nially** *adv.*—**ve'nialness** *n.*—**venial'ity** *n.* [L. *venialis*, pardonable, fr. *venia*, forgiveness].

venison (ven´i-zn, ven´zn) *n.* flesh of the deer [Fr. *venaison*, fr. L. *venari*, to hunt].

vennel (ven´el) *n.* narrow street; lane or alley (Fr. *venelle*, small street].

venom (ven´om) *n.* poison, esp. that secreted by serpents, bees, etc.; spite; malice.—**ven'omous** *a.* poisonous; spiteful; malicious.—**ven'omously** *adv.*—**ven'omousness** *n.* [L. *venenum*, poison].

venous, venose (vē´nus, vē´nōs) *a.* pert. to veins [L. *venosus*, fr. *vena*, vein].

vent (vent) *n.* small opening; outlet; flue or funnel of fireplace; touch-hole of gun; stop of wind-instrument; utterance; emission; voice; escape; anus of certain lower animals;—*v.t.* to give opening or outlet to; to let escape; to utter or voice; to publish.—**to give vent to,** to pour forth; to suffer to escape [Fr. *fendre*, fr. L. *findere*, to cleave].

ventilate (ven´ti-lāt) *v.t.* to fan or winnow; to remove foul air from and supply with fresh air; to expose to discussion; to make public.—**ventila'tion** *n.* replacement of vitiated air by fresh air; free exposure to air; open discussion.—**ven'tilator** *n.* contrivance for keeping air fresh [L. *ventilare*, fr. *ventus*, wind].

ventral (ven´tral) *a.* belonging to belly; abdominal; opp. of *dorsal*;—*n.* one of the pair of fins on belly of fish.—**ven'tricle** *n.* (*Anat.* or *Zool.*) small belly-like cavity in certain organs, esp. one of chambers of heart from which blood is forced into arteries.—**ventric'ular** *a.* [L. *ventralis*, fr. *venter*, belly].

ventriloquism (ven-tril´o-kwizm) *n.* art of speaking in such a way that words or sounds seem to come from some source other than speaker. Also **ventril'oquy.**—**ventril'oquist** *n.*—**ventril'oquise** *v.i.* to practise ventriloquism [L. *venter*, belly; *loqui*, to speak].

venture (ven´tūr) *n.* undertaking of chance or danger; business speculation;—*v.t.* to expose to hazard; to risk;—*v.i.* to run risk; to dare; to have presumption to.—**ven'turer** *n.*—**ven'turous** *a.* daring; fearless.—**ven'turously** *adv.*—**ven'turousness** *n.*—**ven'turesome** *a.* bold; inclined to venture.—**vent'uresomely** *adv.*—**vent'uresomeness** *n.*—**at a venture,** at random [shortened form of *adventure*].

venue (ven´ū) *n.* district in which case is tried; meeting-place; the scene [L. *venire*, to come].

Venus (vē´nus) *n.* (*Myth.*) Roman goddess of Love and Beauty; brightest planet of solar system; beautiful woman [L.].

veracious (ve-rā´shus) *a.* truthful; true.—**vera'ciously** *adv.*—**veracity** (ve-ras´i-ti) *n.* quality of being truthful; truth; correctness [L. *verax, veracis*, fr. *verus*, true].

veranda, verandah (ve-ran´da) *n.* light, open portico or gallery, along side of house, with roof supported on pillars; covered balcony [Sp. *veranda*, balcony].

verb (verb) *n.* (*Gram.*) part of speech which expresses action or state of being.—**ver'bal** *a.* pert. to words; expressed in words, esp. spoken words; literal or word for word; pert. to verb; derived from verb.—**ver'bally** *adv.*—**ver'balise** *v.t.* and *v.i.* to put into words; to turn into verb.—**verbalisa'tion** *n.*—**ver'balism** *n.* something expressed orally; over-attention to use of words; empty words.—**verbatim** (ver-bā´tim) *a.* and *adv.* word for word [L. *verbum*, a word].

Verbena (ver-bē´na) *n.* genus of plants of family Verbenaceae, used in ornamental flower-beds. Also called **ver'vain** [L.].

verbiage (ver´bi-āj) *n.* excess of words; use of many more words than are necessary; wordiness, often with little sense.—**verbigera'tion** *n.* the meaningless repetition of words and phrases.—**verbose** (ver-bōs') *a.* prolix; tedious because of excess of words.—**verbose'ly** *adv.*—**verbose'ness, verbosity** (ver-bos´i-ti) *n.* [L. *verbum*, a word].

verdant (ver´dant) *a.* green or fresh; flourishing; (*Colloq.*) ignorant or unsophisticated.—**ver'dantly** *adv.*—**ver'dancy** *n.* greenness; (*Colloq.*) inexperience.—**verdure** (ver´dūr) *n.* greenness or freshness; green vegetation [O.Fr. *verd*, fr. L. *viridis*, green].

verdict (ver´dikt) *n.* decision of jury in a trial; decision or judgment [O.Fr. *verdit*, fr. L. *vere dictum*, truly said].

verdigris (ver´di-grēs) *n.* green rust on copper; basic acetate of copper, used as pigment, etc. [O.Fr. *verd de Gris*, Greek green].

verge (verj) *n.* rod of office; mace of bishop, etc.; area of jurisdiction of marshal of king's household; limit, border, or edge; brink; grass edging of flower-bed, avenue, etc.—**ver'ger** *n.* one who carries verge or emblem of authority; attendant upon bishop, etc.; beadle or pew-opener of church [L. *virga*, slender twig or rod].

verge (verj) *v.i.* to tend; to slope; to border upon [L. *vergere*, to tend towards].

verify (ver´i-fī) *v.t.* to prove to be true; to confirm truth of; to make good or fulfil.—**ver'ifier** *n.*—**ver'ifiable** *a.*—**verifiabil'ity** *n.*—**verifica'tion** *n.* act of verifying or state of being verified; confirmation.—**ver'ily** *adv.* (*Arch.*) truly; certainly [L. *verus*, true; *facere*, to make].

verisimilar (ver-i-sim´i-lar) *a.* having the appearance of truth; probable; likely.—**verisim'ilarly** *adv.*—**verisimil'itude** *n.* appear-

ance of truth; probability; likelihood [L. *verus*, true; *similis*, like].
veritable (ver´i-tạ-bl) *a.* actual; true; genuine. —**ver'itably** *adv.* [L. *veritas*, truth].
verity (ver´i-ti) *n.* quality of being true; truth; reality [L. *veritas*].
verjuice (vẹr´jòòs) *n.* sour juice of crab-apples, unripe grapes, etc. used in cooking [Fr. *verjus*, fr. L. *viridis*, green; *jus*, juice].
vermi- (vẹr´mi) *prefix.* fr. L. *vermis*, worm.—**ver'mian** *a.* worm-like; pert. to worms.—**vermicelli** (vẹr-mi-sel´i, -chel´i) *n.* paste made from same ingredients as macaroni, and formed into slender, worm-like threads.—**ver'micide** *n.* any substance that destroys worms.—**vermici'dal** *a.*—**vermic'ular** *a.* pert. to worm; like a worm in shape or movement; vermiculate.—**vermic'ulate** *a.*—*v.t.* to do inlaid work in pattern like worm-tracks.—**vermicula'tion** *n.*—**ver'miform** *a.* having shape of a worm.
vermilion (vẹr-mil´yun) *n.* cinnabar; prepared red sulphide of mercury; beautiful red colour;—*v.t.* to colour with delicate red [L. *vermiculus*, little worm].
vermin (vẹr´min) *n.* collectively noxious or mischievous little animals, birds, or insects, e.g. squirrels, rats, worms, lice, etc.; low contemptible persons.—**ver'minous** *a.* infested by vermin; caused by vermin; tending to breed vermin [L. *vermis*, worm].
vermouth, vermuth (vẹr´mòòth, -mòòt) *n.* cordial of white wine flavoured with wormwood, used as aperitif [Ger.].
vernacular (vẹr-nak´ū-lạr) *a.* belonging to country of one's birth; native (usu. applied only to language or idiom);—*n.* native idiom of place; mother tongue [L. *vernaculus*, native, fr. *verna*, home-born slave].
vernal (vẹr´nạl) *a.* belonging to, or appearing in, spring; of youth.—**ver'nally** *adv.*—**vernal equinox**, equinox occurring about March 21 [L. *ver*, spring].
vernier (vẹr´ni-ẹr) *n.* short, graduated-scale instrument, for measuring fractional parts of its spaces [fr. Pierre *Vernier*, inventor].
Veronal (ver´o-nạl) *n.* hypnotic or sedative drug [Protected Trade Name].
Veronica (vẹ-ron´i-kạ) *n.* genus of plants, including speedwell [L. *vettonica*, betony].
verruca (ve-rū´ka) *n.* wart or wart-like elevation.—**verr'ucose, verr'ucous** *a.* [L.].
versatile (vẹr´sạ-tīl) *a.* having aptitude in many subjects; liable to change; capable of moving freely in all directions.—**ver'satilely** *adv.*—**versatil'ity** *n.* [L. *versatilis*, fr. *versare*, fr. *vertere*, to turn].
verse (vẹrs) *n.* metrical line containing certain number of feet; metrical arrangement and language; short division of any composition; stanza; stave; piece of poetry.—**versed** (vẹrst) *a.* skilled; experienced (foll. by 'in'); practised—**ver'sicle** *n.* little verse.—**versify** (vẹr´si-fī) *v.t.* to turn prose into verse; to express in verse.—*v.i.* to make verses.—**ver'sifier** *n.* [L. *vertere*, *versum*, to turn].
version (vẹr´shun) *n.* translation; school exercise, generally of translation into a foreign language; account from particular point of view [L. *versio*, fr. *vertere*, to turn].
vers libre (ver-lēbr') *n.* free verse, ignoring rules of metrical composition [Fr.].
verso (vẹr´sō) *n.* left-hand page; reverse side of coin or medal [L.].
versus (vẹr´sus) *prep.* (*Law, Games*) against —*abbrev.* **v.** [L.].
vertebra (vẹr´te-brạ) *n.* one of the small bony segments of spinal column.—*pl.* **ver'tebrae.**—**ver'tebral** *a.* pert. to vertebrae or spine.—**ver'tebrate** *a.* having backbone;—*n.* vertebrate animal [L.].
vertex (vẹr´teks) *n.* highest point; summit; (*Astron.*) zenith; (*Geom.*) angular point of triangle etc.—*pl.* **vertexes, vertices** (vẹr´tek-ses, -ti-sēz).—**ver'tical** *a.* situated at vertex; directly overhead or in the zenith; upright or perpendicular;—*n.* vertical line.—**ver'tically** *adv.*—**vert'icalness** *n.*—**vertical'ity** *n.* [L. *vertex*, top].
vertigo (vẹr´ti-gō, vẹr-tī-gō) *n.* sensation of whirling or swimming of head, with loss of equilibrium; dizziness; giddiness.—**vertiginous** (vẹr-tij´i-nus) *a.* revolving; giddy; causing giddiness.—**vertig'inously** *adv.* [L. *vertigo*, whirling, fr. *vertere*, to turn].
vertu (vẹr´tòò) *n.* See **virtu.**
vervain (vẹr´vān) *n.* plant of genus *Verbena*, formerly a charm against various ills, including witchcraft [L. *verbena*].
verve (vẹrv) *n.* enthusiasm or vigour; energy; spirit [Fr.].
very (ver´i) *a.* true; real; actual; genuine; now used chiefly to emphasise word following.—*adv.* in a high degree; extremely.—**ver'ily** *adv.* truly [L. *versus*, true].
Very light (ver´i-līt) *n.* firework fired from Very pistol and used as a signal of distress [fr. inventor].
vesical (ves´i-kạl) *a.* (*Med.*) pert. to bladder.—**ves'icant** *a.* tending to raise blisters;—*n.* blistering application.—**ves'icate** *v.t.* to raise blisters on.—**vesica'tion** *n.* process of blistering.—**ves'icle** *n.* small bladder-like structure; blister; cyst.—**vesicular** (ve-sik´ū-lạr) *a.* pert. to vesicles.—**vesic'ulate, vesic'ulose, vesic'ulous** *a.* vesicular [L. *vesica*, bladder].
Vesper (ves´pẹr) *n.* the evening star, Venus; evening;—*a.* pert. to evening or vespers.—**ves'pers** *n.pl.* sixth canonical hour; evensong; evening service of R.C. Church.
vessel (ves´ẹl) *n.* utensil for holding either liquids or solids; ship, esp. large one; (*Anat.*) tube or canal in which blood and other fluids are contained; in Biblical language, one regarded as recipient of something, e.g. of divine spirit [L. *vas*, vase].
vest (vest) *n.* waistcoat; knitted or woven undergarment; vestment;—*v.t.* to clothe; to cover; to put in possession; to endow; to give right of present or future enjoyment; to furnish with authority.—**ves'ted** *a.* that cannot be transferred or taken away.—**vest'ment** *n.* ceremonial or official garment.—**ves'ture** *n.* clothing; dress; covering [L. *vestis*, garment].
Vesta (ves´tạ) *n.* (*Myth.*) Roman goddess of the hearth, whose sacred fire was kept constantly burning and guarded in her temple by **Vestal Virgins**; small planet.—**ves'ta** *n.* short match with wax shank.—**ves'tal** *a.* pert. to Vesta or her worship; vowed to chastity;—*n.* virgin, vowed to service of Vesta; nun; old maid.
vestibule (ves´ti-būl) *n.* entrance to house; porch; hall next outer door of house; [L. *vestibulum*, forecourt].
vestige (ves´tij) *n.* orig. footprint; trace or sign; track; mark of something that has been; remains; (*Anat.*) trace of some part or organ formerly present in body.—**vesti'gial** *a.* [L. *vestigium*, a footprint].
vestry (ves´tri) *n.* room attached to church for holding ecclesiastical vestments, prayer meetings, etc.; assembly of parishioners to deal with parochial affairs [L. *vestiarium*, fr. *vestis*, garment].
vet (vet) *n.* (*Colloq. abbrev.*) veterinary surgeon; —*v.t.* to examine or treat animal; (*Colloq. Fig.*) to examine or check.
vetch (vech) *n.* plant of bean family used for fodder [L. *vicia*].
veteran (vet´ẹ-rạn) *n.* person who has served a long time, esp. soldier;—*a.* long exercised in anything [L. *veteranus*, fr. *vetus*, old].
veterinary (vet´ẹ-ri-nạ-ri) *a.* pert. to healing diseases of domestic animals.—**veterinarian** (vet-ẹ-ri-nā´ri-ạn) *n.* one skilled in treating diseases of animals; now **veterinary surgeon** [L. *veterinarius*, pert. to beasts of burden].
veto (vē´tō) *n.* power or right of forbidding.—*pl.* **ve'toes.**—*v.t.* to withold assent to; to negative [L. *veto*, I forbid].

vex (veks) *v.t.* to make angry; to irritate; to grieve; to distress.—**vexa'tion** *n.*—**vexa'tious** *a.* causing vexation; distressing.—**vexa'tiously** *adv.*—**vexa'tiousness** *n.* [L. *vexare*, to harass].

via (vī'ạ, vē'ạ) *prep.* by way of [L.=way].

viable (vī'ạ-bl) *a.* born alive and sufficiently developed to be able to live; capable of living or growth.—**viabil'ity** *n.* [L. *vita*, life].

viaduct (vī'ạ-dukt) *n.* high bridge or series of arches for carrying road or railway over valley or stream [L. *via*, way; *ducere*, to lead].

vial (vī'ạl) *n.* small glass bottle; phial [Gk. *phialē*, shallow bowl].

viand (vī'ạnd) *n.* article of food; chiefly *pl.* food, victuals, provisions [L. *vivenda*, provisions, fr. *vivere*, to live].

viaticum (vī-at'i-kum) *n.* Communion or Eucharist given to dying persons; portable altar [L. *via*, a way].

vibrate (vī-brāt', vī'brāt) *v.t.* to move to and fro; to cause to quiver; to measure by vibrations or oscillations;—*v.i.* to swing or oscillate; to quiver; to thrill or throb; of sound, to produce quivering effect; to sound tremulous.—**vibra'tion** *n.*—**vibrator** (vī-brā'tor, vī' brā-tor) *n.* one who, or that which, causes vibration.—**vi'bratory** *a.* vibrating; causing vibration.—**vi'brant** *a.* vibrating; thrilling or throbbing; sonorous [L. *vibrare*, to swing or shake].

Viburnum (vī-bur'num) *n.* different kinds of shrubs of honeysuckle family, including guelder-rose [L.].

vicar (vik'ạr) *n.* clergyman of parish in whch tithes belong to chapter, college, layman, etc. who receives them, and allows out of them a salary to clergyman.—**vic'arage** *n.* residence of vicar.—**vicarial** (vī-kā'ri-ạl) *a.* pert. to, acting as, vicar.—**vic'arship** *n.*—**vicarious** (vī-kā'ri-us) *a.* delegated; substituted; done or suffered for another,—**vica'riously** *adv.*—**vica'riousness** *n.* (L. *vicarius*, deputy].

vice (vīs) *n.* depravity or immoral conduct; blemish or defect in character, etc.; failing or bad habit.—**vicious** (vish'us) *a.* depraved; wicked; not pure in style; spiteful; not well broken, as horse.—**vic'iously** *adv.*—**vic'iousness** *n.*—**vicious circle**, describes state in which remedy for evil produces second evil, which when remedied in its turn leads back to first [L. *vitium*, blemish, fault].

vice (vīs) *n.* device with two jaws that can be brought together by screw; fixed to edge of work-bench it holds anything which needs filing, etc. [Fr. *vis*, a screw].

vice- (vīs) *prefix* in words signifying persons, and denoting one who acts in place of another, or one who is second in authority, as *vice-admiral, vice-chairman, vice-chancellor*, etc. [L. *vice*, in place of].

vicegerent (vīs-jē'rẹnt) *a.* exercising delegated power;—*n.* holder of delegated authority [L. *vice*, in place of; *gerere*, to act].

viceroy (vīs'roi) *n.* governor of country or province who rules as representative of his king.

vice versa (vī'se-vẹr'sa) *adv.* the order being reversed; the other way round [L.].

vicinity (vi-sin'i-ti) *n.* neighbourhood; nearness or proximity.—**vic'inage** *n.* vicinity; neighbourhood [L. *vicinus*, near].

vicissitude (vi-sis'i-tūd) *n.* regular change or succession; alteration; change of circumstances, esp. of fortune;—*pl.* ups and downs of fortune.—**vicissitu'dinary, vicissitu'dinous** *a.* [L. *vicissitudo*, alteration].

victim (vik'tim) *n.* living being sacrificed in performance of religious ceremony; person, or thing, destroyed or sacrificed; person who suffers; dupe or prey.—**vic'timise** *v.t.* to make victim of.—**victimisa'tion** *n.* [L. *victima*].

victor (vik'tor) *n.* (*fem.* **vic'tress, vic'trix**) one who defeats enemy in battle; conqueror; winner in contest.—**vic'tory** *n.* defeat of enemy in battle, or of antagonist in contest; conquest; triumph.—**victorious** (vik-tō'ri-us) *a.* having conquered; indicating victory; triumphant; winning.—**victo'riously** *adv.*—**victo'riousness** *n.* [L. *victor*, fr. *vincere*, to conquer].

Victoria (vik-tō'ri-ạ) *n.* Queen of Gt. Britain, (1837-1901).—**victo'ria** *n.* low, light, four-wheeled carriage.—**Victoria Cross** (*abbrev.* **V.C.**), highest military decoration for valour, founded in 1856.—**Victo'rian** *n.* person living in reign of Queen Victoria;—*a.* pert. to, living in, reign of Queen Victoria; old-fashioned; easily shocked.

victual (vit'l) *v.t.* to supply with provisions;—*v.i.* to take in provisions.—**vict'uals** *n.pl.* food.—**victualler** (vit'lẹr) *n.* one who supplies provisions [L. *victualia*, fr. *vivere, victum*, to live].

vidette *n.* See **vedette**.

vie (vī) *v.i.* to strive for superiority; to contend.—*pr.p.* **vy'ing**.—*pa.p.* and *pa.t.* **vied** (vīd) [O.Fr. *envier*, to challenge].

view (vū) *n.* sight; inspection by eye or mind; power of seeing; range of sight; what is seen; pictured representation of scene; manner of looking at anything, esp. mental survey; opinion; aim or intention.—*v.t.* to see; to look at; to survey mentally; to consider.—**view'er** *n.* one who views; one who receives television programme.—**view'-halloo'** *n.* huntsman's cry on seeing fox break cover.—**view'less** *a.* (*Poet.*) invisible.—**view'-find'er** *n.* device in camera for showing limits of picture.—**on view**, open to inspection.—**in view of**, having regard to; taking into consideration [L. *videre*, to see].

vigil (vij'il) *n.* staying awake, either for religious exercises, or to keep watch; watch or watching; in church, eve of feast;—*pl.* nocturnal devotions.—**vig'ilant** *a.* wakeful; watchful; alert; circumspect.—**vig'ilantly** *adv.*—**vig'ilance** *n.* wakefulness; watchfulness [L. *vigilia*, a watch].

vignette (vēn-yet', vin-yet') *n.* orig. running ornament of leaves or tendrils; small designs in printing, used as headings or tail-pieces; any engraving, wood-cut, etc. not enclosed within border; photograph or portrait showing only head or quarter-length likeness against shaded background; (*Fig.*) short, neat description in words [Fr. dim. of *vigne*, vine].

vigour (vig'or) *n.* active strength; capacity for exertion; energy; vitality; forcefulness of style, in writing.—**vig'orous** *a.* full of physical or mental strength; powerful.—**vig'orously** *adv.*—**vig'orousness** *n.* [L. *vigor*].

viking (vik'ing, vī'king) *n.* one of the Scandinavian sea-rovers or pirates, who from the 8th to 10th cents. ravaged the north-west coasts of Europe [O.N. *vikingr*].

vilayet (vil-á'-yet) *n.* province of the Turkish Empire [Turk.].

vile (vīl) *a.* mean; worthless; base; depraved; repulsive; (*Colloq.*) shockingly bad.—**vile'ly** *adv.*—**vile'ness** *n.*—**vilify** (vil'i-fī) *v.t.* to speak ill of; to try to degrade by slander; to defame or traduce.—**vil'ifier** *n.*—**vilifica'tion** *n.* [L. *vilis*, cheap, base].

villa (vil'ạ) *n.* orig. country seat; suburban residence [L.=a farm-house].

village (vil'āj) *n.* assemblage of houses, smaller than town and larger than hamlet;—*a.* pert. to village; rustic.—**vill'ager** *n.* an inhabitant of a village [L. *villaticus*, belonging to a farm-house].

villain (vil'ạn) *n.* wicked, depraved or criminal person; rascal; (*Hist.*) feudal serf.—**vill'ainous** *a.* wicked; vile.—**vill'ainously** *adv.*—**vill'ainousness** *n.*—**vill'ainy** *n.* extreme wickedness; an act of great depravity [L.L. *villanus*, farm servant].

villanelle (vil-ạ-nel') *n.* poem of 19 lines on 2 rhymes. It consists of 5 three-lined stanzas, followed by one of four lines [Fr. fr. It. *villanella*].

villein (vil′en) *n.* tenant by villenage; serf;—*a.* pert. to villein or villenage.—**vil′lenage** *n.* tenure of lands and tenements by menial services; serfdom [fr. *villain*].
villus (vil′us) *n.* one of the small, fine, hair-like processes which cover certain membranes; one of the fine soft hairs covering certain fruits, flowers, or plants.—*pl.* **villi** (vil′ī) [L. *villus*, shaggy hair].
vim (vim) *n.* (*Colloq.*) force; energy; vigour [L. *vis*, force].
vinaigrette (vin-ā-gret′) *n.* small box, containing sponge saturated with aromatic vinegar [Fr. dim. fr. *vinaigre*, vinegar].
vincible (vin′si-bl) *a.* that may be conquered [L. *vincere*].
vinculum (ving′kū-lum) *n.* bond of union; (*Alg.*) straight, horizontal mark placed over several members of compound quantity to be treated as one quantity.—*pl.* **vin′cula** [L.=bond, fr. *vincire*, to bind].
vindicate (vin′di-kāt) *v.t.* to justify; to maintain as true and correct; to clear of suspicion, dishonour, etc.—**vin′dicable** *a.*—**vindicabil′ity** *n.*—**vindica′tion** *n.* justification; defence of statement against denial or doubt.—**vin′dicator** *n.*—**vin′dicatory** *a.* [L. *vindicare*, to claim].
vindictive (vin-dik′tiv) *a.* given to revenge; revengeful.—**vindic′tively** *adv.*—**vindic′tiveness** *n.* [L. *vindicta*, vengeance].
vine (vīn) *n.* woody, climbing plant that produces grapes; any plant which trails or climbs.—**vi′nery** *n.* greenhouse(s) for rearing vines by use of heating.—**vineyard** (vin′yąrd) *n.* plantation of grape-vines.—**vi′nic** *a.* pert. to, or obtained from, wine; alcoholic.—**vin′iculture** *n.* cultivation of vines.—**vi′nose, vi′nous** *a.* pert. to, or like, wine; due to wine [L. *vinum*, wine].
vinegar (vin′e-gąr) *n.* acid liquor obtained from malt, wine, cider, etc. by fermentation, and used as condiment or in pickling.—**vin′egary** *a.* like vinegar; sour [Fr. *vinaigre*, fr. L. *vinum*, wine; *acer*, sour].
vingt-un, vingt et un (vangt-ung′, vangt-ā-ung′) *n.* card game, in which the object is to count as near as possible to the number of 21 spots, without exceeding it; also called pontoon [Fr.=twenty-one].
vintage (vin′tāj) *n.* gathering of grapes; season's yield of grapes or wine; wine of particular year.—**vint′ner** *n.* one who deals in wine; tavern-keeper.—**vintage wine,** wine made from grapes of particularly good year [L. *vindemia*, vintage].
viol (vī′ol) *n.* medieval stringed musical instrument like violin but larger.—**bass′-vi′ol** *n.* violoncello.—**violist** (vī-ō′list) *n.* one who plays viol [Fr. *viole*].
viola (vē-ō′la) *n.* instrument larger than violin, but smaller than violoncello; alto or tenor violin.—**violist** (vī-ō′list) *n.* one who plays the viola [It.].
Viola (vī′ō-lą) *n.* (*Bot.*) genus of plants including violet and pansy [L.].
violate (vī′o-lāt) *v.t.* to infringe or break a promise; to treat with disrespect; to outrage or rape.—**viola′tion** *n.* transgression; profanation; ravishment; infringement; interruption.—**vi′olator** *n.* [L. *violare*].
violence (vī′o-lens) *n.* force; vehemence; intensity; assault or outrage.—**vi′olent** *a.* characterised by physical force, esp. improper force; forcible; furious; passionate.—**vi′olently** *adv.* [L. *violare*, fr. *vis*, force].
violet (vī′o-let) *n.* flower of genus Viola, generally of bluish-purple colour; colour produced by combining blue and red;—*a.* bluish or purple [Fr. fr. L. *viola*].
violin (vī-o-lin′, vī′o-lin) *n.* modern musical instrument of viol family, with four strings, played with bow; fiddle.—**violin′ist** *n.* [It. *violino*].
violoncello (vē-o-lon-chel′ō, vī-o-lon-sel′ō) *n.* bass violin, much larger than violin. It is held between player's knees; usually *abbrev.* to **'cello.**—**violoncell′ist** *n.* [It. dim. of *violone*, bass viol].
viper (vīpęr) *n.* various kinds of venomous snakes, esp. adder; malignant or malicious person.—**vi′perish** *a.* like a viper; malignant.—**vi′perous** *a.* venomous [L. *vipera*].
virago (vi-rā′gō) *n.* turbulent or scolding woman; manlike woman [L.].
virgin (vęr′jin) *n.* girl or woman who has not had sexual intercourse with man; maiden;—*a.* without experience of sexual intercourse; unsullied; chaste; fresh; untilled (of land).—**vir′ginal** *a.* pert. to virgin; maidenly; fresh and pure;—*n.* old musical instrument like spinet.—**virgin′ity** *n.*—**the Virgin,** mother of Christ [L. *virgo, virginis*, maiden].
Virginia (vęr-jin′i-ą) *n.* kind of tobacco, grown in Virginia, U.S.A.—**Virginia creeper,** climbing vine whose leaves turn bright red in autumn.
Virgo (vęr′gō) *n.* (*Astron.*) the Virgin, one of the signs of Zodiac [L. *virgo*, virgin].
virid (vir′id) *a.* green.—**virides′cent** *a.* turning green; greenish.—**virid′ian** *n.* bluish-green pigment.—**virid′ity, vir′idness** *n.* greenness; verdure [L. *viridis*, green].
virile (vir′il or -īl) *a.* pert. to man; masculine; strong; (of style) having vigour.—**viril′ity** *n.* being a man; manliness; power of procreation [L. *vir*, man].
virtu (vęr′too, vęr-too′) *n.* objects of art or antiquity, collectively; taste for objects of art [It. fr. L. *virtus*, excellence].
virtual (vęr′tū-ąl) *a.* being in essence or effect, though not in fact; potential.—**vir′tually** *adv.* to all intents and purposes.—**virtual′ity** *n.* [L. *virtus*, excellence].
virtue (vęr′tū) *n.* moral excellence; merit; good quality; female chastity; power or efficacy.—**vir′tuous** *a.* upright; dutiful; chaste.—**vir′tuously** *adv.*—**vir′tuousness** *n.* [L. *virtus* manly excellence].
virtuoso (vir-tū-ō′sō) *n.* one with great knowledge of fine arts; highly skilled musician, painter, etc.—*pl.* **virtuo′si, virtuo′sos.**—**virtuosity** (vir-tū-os′i-ti) *n.* great technical skill in fine arts, esp. music [It.].
virulent (vir′ū-lent) *a.* extremely poisonous; bitter in enmity; malignant; deadly—**vir′ulently** *adv*—**vir′ulence** *n* acrimony; rancour; malignity; bitterness.
virus (vī′rus) *n.* poisonous matter; substance causing infectious disease,
visa (vē′zą) *n.* official endorsement, as on passport, in proof that document has been examined and found correct [Fr. fr. L. *videre*, to see].
visage (viz′āj) *n.* face; countenance; look or appearance.—**visaged** (viz′ājd) *a.* [Fr.].
vis-a-vis (vēz-ą-vē′) *adv.* face to face;—*n.* person facing another [Fr.=face to face].
viscera (vis′e-rą) *n.pl.* internal organs lying in large cavities of body such as abdomen, e.g. intestines; entrails.—**vis′ceral** *a.*—**vis′cerate** *v.t.* to disembowel [pl. of L. *viscus*].
viscid (vis′id) *a.* glutinous; sticky; tenacious.—**viscid′ity** *n.*—**viscose** (vis′kōs) *n.* viscid solution of cellulose, drawn into fibres and used in making artificial silk.—**viscous** (vis′kus) *a.* glutinous; tenacious; clammy.—**viscos′ity** *n.* [L. *viscidus*, sticky, fr. *viscum*, bird-lime].
viscount (vī′kount) *n.* (*fem.* **vi′scountess**) a degree or title of nobility next in rank below earl [L. *vice*, in place of; *comes*, companion, count].
visé (vē′zā) *n.* (*U.S.*) Same as **visa.**
visible (viz′i-bl) *a.* that can be seen; perceptible; in view.—**vis′ibly** *adv.*—**visibil′ity** *n.* degree of clarity of atmosphere, esp. for flying [L. *visibilis*, fr. *videre*, to see].
Visigoth (viz′i-goth) *n.* branch of Goths that settled in south of France and Spain [Teut. *west*, west; *Gothi*, Goths.].
vision (vizh′un) *n.* act or faculty of seeing external objects; sight; thing seen; imaginary

sight; phantom; imaginative insight or foresight.—**vis'ionary** *a.* apt to see visions; indulging in fancy or reverie; impractical; existing only in the imagination;—*n.* one prone to see visions [L. *visio*, sight, fr. *videre*, to see].
visit (viz'it) *v.t.* to go, or come, to see; (*Bib.*) to benefit; to punish;—*v.i.* to be a guest; to keep up interchange of visits;—*n.* act of visiting or going to see; stay or sojourn; official or formal inspection.—**vis'itant** *a.* visiting. *n.* one who visits; migratory bird.—**visita'tion** *n.* act of visiting; formal or official inspection; visit of inordinate length; dispensation of divine favour or anger.—**vis'itor** *n.* one who visits.—**visito'rial, visitato'rial** *a.* pert. to official visit or visitor [L. *visitare*, fr. *videre*, to see].
visor, vizor (vīz'ẹr) *n.* front part of helmet which can be lifted to show face; peak of cap.—**vis'ored** *a.* having or wearing visor [Fr. *visière*, fr. O.Fr. *vis*, face].
vista (vis'tạ) *n.* view, esp. distant view, as through avenue of trees; mental view [It. fr. L. *videre*, to see].
visual (viz', vizh'ū-ạl) *a.* relating to sight; used in seeing; visible.—**vis'ually** *adv.* by sight; with reference to vision.—**vis'ualise** *v.t.* to make visual; to call up mental picture of.—**visualisa'tion** *n.* [L. *visualis*].
Vita-glass (vī'ta-glȧs) *n.* kind of glass which ultra-violet rays can penetrate [Protected Trade Name].
vital (vī'tạl) *a.* necessary to or containing life; very necessary.—**vi'tals** *n.pl.* essential internal organs, as lungs, heart, brain.—**vi'tally** *adv.*—**vi'talise** *v.t.* to give life to; to lend vigour to.—**vitalisa'tion** *n.*—**vital'ity** *n.* the principle of life; vital force; vigour [L. *vitalis*, belonging to life].
vitamin (vit'a-, vī'ta-min) *n.* group of chemical substances present in various foodstuffs, and indispensable to health and growth [L. *vita*, life].
vitiate (vish'i-āt) *v.t.* to make vicious, faulty, or impure; to debase; to impair; to invalidate.—**vitia'tion** *n.* [L. *vitium*, vice].
Vitis (vī'tis) *n.* genus of plants including the vine.—**vit'iculture** *n.* cultivation of vines [L. *vitis*, vine].
vitreous (vit're-us) *a.* pert. to, or resembling, glass; glassy; derived from glass.—**vit'reousness** *n.*—**vitres'cent** *a.* tending to become like glass; capable of being formed into glass.—**vitres'cence** *n.* [L. *vitrum*, glass].
vitrify (vit'ri-fī) *v.t.* to convert into glass or glassy substance;—*v.i.* to be converted into glass.—**vit'rifiable** *a.*—**vitrifac'tion, vitrifica'tion** *n.* [L. *vitrum*, glass; *facere*, to make].
vitriol (vit'ri-ol) *n.* sulphuric acid.—**vitriol'ic** *a.* pert. to, resembling, derived from, vitriol; (*Fig.*) caustic; bitter [L. *vitreolus*, of glass].
vituperate (vī-tū'pẹ-rāt) *v.t.* to abuse in words; to revile; to berate.—**vitu'perative** *a.* abusive; scolding.—**vitu'peratively** *adv.*—**vitu'perator** *n*—**vitupera'tion** *n* [L. *vituperare*, to blame].
viva (vī'vạ) *n.* (*Colloq.*) viva voce examination.
vivace (vē-vȧ'che) *adv.* (*Mus.*) in lively manner; with spirit [It.].
vivacious (vi-, vī-vā'shus) *a.* lively; sprightly; animated; having great vitality.—**viva'ciously** *adv.*—**vivacity** (vi-, vī-vas'i-ti) *n.* liveliness; sprightliness [L. *vivax*, fr. *vivere*, to live].
vivarium (vī-vā'ri-um) *n.* place for keeping or raising living animals [L.].
viva voce (vī'va vō'sē) *adv.* orally;—*a.* oral;—*n.* (*Colloq.*) oral examination.—*abbrev.* **vi'va** [L.=with the living voice].
vivid (viv'id) *a.* animated; lively; clear; evoking brilliant images; (of colour) bright; glaring.—**viv'idly** *adv.*—**viv'idness** *n.* [L. *vividus*, lively, fr. *vivere*, to live].
vivify (viv'i-fī) *v.t.* to endue with life; to animate; to make vivid.—**vivifica'tion** *n.* [L. *vivus*, living; *facere*, to make].
viviparous (vī-vip'ạ-rus) *a.* producing young in living state, instead of eggs.—**vivip'arously** *adv.*—**vivip'arousness, vivipa'rity** *n.* [L. *vivus*, living; *parere*, to give birth].
vivisection (vi-vi-sek'shun) *n.* dissection of, or experimenting on, living animals for purpose of physiological investigations [L. *vivus*, alive; *secare*, to cut].
vixen (vik'sn) *n.* she-fox; cross bad-tempered woman.—**vix'enish** *a.* like a vixen; shrewish [O.E. *fyxen*, a she-fox].
vizard (viz'ạrd) *n.* Same as **visor.**
vizier, vizir (vi-zēr') *n.* high executive officer in Turkey and other Oriental countries.—**Grand Vizier**, Turkish Prime Minister [Ar. *wazir*].
vocable (vō'kạ-bl) *n.* a word, esp. with ref. to sound rather than meaning; term; name [L. *vocabulum*, an appellation].
vocabulary (vō-kab'ū-lạ-ri) *n.* list of words, usu. arranged in alphabetical order and explained; word-book; stock of words used by language, class, or individual [L. *vocabulum* appellation].
vocal (vō'kạl) *a.* pert. to voice or speech; having voice; uttered by voice; (*Phon.*) sounded; having character of vowel.—**vo'cally** *adv.*—**vo'calise** *v.t.* to make vocal; to utter with voice, and not merely with breath;—*v.i.* to make vocal sounds, as in singing.—**vo'calist** *n.* [L. *vox*, the voice].
vocation (vō-kā'shun) *n.* divine call to religious career; profession, or occupation.—**voca'tional** *a.* [L. *vocare*, to call].
vocative (vok'ạ-tiv) *a.* relating to, used in, calling or address;—*n.* (*Gram.*) case used in addressing person [L. *vocare*, to call].
vociferate (vō-sif'ẹ-rāt) *v.t.* to utter noisily or violently; to bawl;—*v.i.* to cry with loud voice or with vehemence.—**vocifera'tion** *n.* vehement utterance; outcry.—**vocif'erator** *n.*—**vocif'erous** *a.* making loud outcry; noisy or clamorous.—**vocif'erously** *adv.* [L. *vox, vocis*, the voice; *ferre*, to carry].
vodka (vod'kạ) *n.* in Russia and Poland alcoholic liquor distilled from rye or potatoes [Russ.=little water].
vogue (vōg) *n.* prevailing fashion; mode; style; current usage [Fr.].
voice (vois) *n.* faculty of uttering audible sounds; sound produced by organs of respiration; utterance; quality of utterance; expression of feeling or opinion; vote; share in discussion; (*Gram.*) mode of inflecting verbs to show relation of subject to action, as *active, passive voice*;—*v.t.* to give expression to; to announce.—**voiced** (voist) *a.* furnished with voice or with expression; (*Phon.*) uttered with vocal tone [L. *vox*, voice].
void (void) *a.* empty; being without; destitute—*n.* an empty space;—*v.t.* to make vacant; to empty out; to make ineffectual or invalid.—**void'ness** *n.*—**void'able** *a.*—**void'ance** *n.* act of voiding; state of being void; (*Eccles.*) ejection from benefice [O.Fr. *voit*].
voile (voil, vwȧl) *n.* thin cotton, woollen, or silk material [Fr.=veil].
volant (vō'lạnt) *a.* borne through the air; nimble; capable of flying [L. *volare*, to fly].
Volapuk (vol-ȧ-pŏŏk') *n.* artificial language invented in 1879 [=world's speech].
volatile (vol'ạ-tīl) *a.* evaporating quickly; easily passing into aeriform state; (*Fig.*) spirited; lively; fickle; changeable.—**volat'ilise** *v.t.* and *v.i.* to render or become volatile; to cause to pass off in vapour.—**volat'ilisable** *a.*—**volatilisa'tion** *n.*—**volatil'ity** *n.* [L. *volatilis*, flying].
volcano (vol-kā'nō) *n.* opening in crust of earth, from which heated solid, liquid, and gaseous matters are ejected.—**volcanic** (vol-kan'ik) *a.*—**volcan'ically** *adv.* [It. fr. L. *Vulcanus*, god of fire, whose forge was supposed to be below Mt. Etna].
vole (vōl) *n.* mouse-like rodent living out of [doors Scan. *voll*, field].

volitant (vol´i-tạnt) *a.* volant; flying; having power of flight.—**volita'tion** *n.* flight; power of flying [L. *volare,* to fly].

volition (vō-lish´un) *n.* act of willing or choosing; exercise of will.—**voli'tional** *a.* pert. to volition.—**voli'tionally** *adv.* [L. *volo, velle,* to be willing].

volley (vol´i) *n.* discharge of many shots or missiles at one time; missiles so discharged; (*Fig.*) rapid utterance; (*Tennis*) return of ball before it touches ground;—*v.t.* to discharge in a volley;—*v.i.* to fly in a volley; to sound together; (*Tennis*) to return ball before it touches ground [L. *volare,* to fly].

volt (vōlt) *n.* practical unit of electromotive force, being the pressure which causes current of one ampere to flow through resistance of one ohm.—**volt'age** *n.* electromotive force reckoned in volts.—**volt'meter** *n.* instrument used for measuring electromotive force in volts [*Volta,* Italian scientist].

volt, volte (vōlt) *n.* in fencing, sudden turn or movement to avoid thrust; gait, or track, made by horse going sideways round centre; circle so made [Fr. *volte,* fr. L. *volvere,* to roll].

volte-face (volt-fas') *n.* turning round; (*Fig.*) sudden and unexpected reversal of opinion or direction [Fr.].

voluble (vol´ū-bl) *a.* having flowing and rapid utterance; fluent in speech; glib.—**vol'ubly** *adv.*—**vol'ubleness, volubil'ity** *n.* [L. *volubilis,* fr. *volvere,* to roll].

volume (vol´ūm) *n.* formerly roll or scroll; book; part of a work which is bound; bulk or compass; cubical content; power, fullness, of voice or musical tone.—**volumet'ric** *a.* pert. to measurement by volume.—**volumet'rically** *adv.*—**volu'minal** *a.* pert. to cubical content.—**volum'inous** *a.* consisting of many coils; consisting of many volumes; bulky.—**volum'inousness** *n.*—**voluminos'ity** *n.* [L. *volumen,* roll or scroll, fr. *volvere,* to roll].

voluntary (vol´un-tạr-i) *a.* proceeding from choice or free will; unconstrained; spontaneous; subject to the will;—*n.* organ solo played during, or after, church service.—**vol'untarily** *adv.*—**vol'untariness** *n.* [L. *voluntas,* will].

volunteer (vol-un-tēr') *n.* one who enters service, esp. military, of his own free will;—*a.* entering into service of one's own free will; pert. to volunteers;—*v.t.* to offer or bestow voluntarily;—*v.i.* to enter into service of one's own free will [L. *voluntas,* free will].

voluptuary (vo-lup´tū-ạ-ri) *n.* one addicted to luxurious living or sensual gratification; sensualist; epicure;—*a.* concerned with, or promoting, sensual pleasure.—**volup'tuous** *a.* —**volup'tuously** *adv.*—**volup'tuousness** *n.* [L. *voluptas,* pleasure].

volute (vo-lūt') *n.* (*Archit.*) spiral scroll used in Ionic, Corinthian, and Composite capitals; (*Zool.*) tropical spiral shell; whorl of shell.—**volut'ed** *a.*—**volu'tion** *n.* a wreath or whorl; a convolution [L. *volvere, volutum,* to roll].

vomit (vom´it) *v.t.* to eject from stomach by mouth; to spew or disgorge;—*v.i.* to eject contents of stomach by mouth;—*n.* matter ejected from stomach.—**vom'itory** *a.* provoking vomiting;—*n.* emetic; large door in a Roman amphitheatre [L. *vomere,* to throw up].

voodoo (vòò´dòò) *n.* system of magical rites prevalent among certain Negro races; one who practises such rites; evil spirit;—*a.* belonging to, or connected with, system of voodoo.—**voo'dooism** *n.* [Creole Fr. *vaudoux,* a Negro sorcerer].

voracious (vo-rā´shus) *a.* greedy in eating; eager to devour; ravenous.—**vora'ciously** *adv.* —**vora'ciousness** *n.*—**voracity** (vo-ras´i-ti) *n.* greediness of appetite; ravenousness [L. *vorax,* greedy to devour].

vortex (vor´teks) *n.* whirling motion of any fluid, forming kind of cavity in centre of circle; whirlpool; any system of society, etc. which draws in human beings irresistibly.—*pl.* **vortices, vortexes** (vor´ti-sēz, vor´tek-sez).—**vor'tical** *a.*—**vor'tically** *adv.* [L.].

vorticism (vor´ti-sizm) *n.* modern movement in painting which depicts everything as assemblage of vortices [L. *vortex,* whirlpool].

votary (vō´tạ-ri) *a.* consecrated by vow or promise;—*n.* one engaged by vow; one devoted to any service, study, etc.—**vo'taress** *n.* (*fem.*) [L. *votum,* vow].

vote (vōt) *n.* formal expression of wish, choice, or opinion, of individual, or a body of persons; expression of will by a majority; right to vote; suffrage; what is given or allowed by vote;—*v.t.* to enact, grant, or establish, by vote; to declare by general consent;—*v.i.* to express one's choice, will, or preference.—**vo'ter** *n.* [L. *votum,* vow].

votive (vō´tiv) *a.* offered or consecrated by vow; given in fulfilment of vow [L. *votivus,* promised by vow].

vouch (vouch) *v.t.* to warrant; to attest; to affirm;—*v.i.* to bear witness; to be guarantee (for).—**vouch'er** *n.* one who bears witness or attests to anything; paper or document that serves to vouch truth of accounts, or to establish facts; receipt [L. *vocare,* to call].

vouchsafe (vouch-sāf') *v.t.* to condescend to grant or do something;—*v.i.* to deign.

vow (vou) *n.* solemn promise made esp. to deity;—*v.t.* to consecrate or dedicate by solemn promise; to devote;—*v.i.* to make vow or solemn promise; (*Arch.*) to declare [L. *votum,* vow].

vowel (vou´ẹl) *n.* any vocal sound (*a, e, i, o, u*) produced with least possible friction or hindrance from any organ of speech; letter or character that represents such sound;—*a.* pert. to vowel [L. *vocalis,* fr. *vox,* voice].

voyage (voi´āj) *n.* journey esp. by sea;—*v.i.* to sail or traverse by water.—**voy'ager** *n.* one who makes voyage [Fr. fr. L. *viaticum,* travelling money, fr. *via,* way].

Vulcan (vul´kạn) *n.* (*Myth.*) Roman god of fire and of metal-working.—**vul'canise** *v.t.* to treat rubber with sulphur at high temperature to increase durability and elasticity.—**vulcanisa'tion** *n.*—**vul'canite** *n.* rubber hardened by vulcanising [L. *Vulcanus,* god of fire].

vulgar (vul´gạr) *a.* of common people; in common use; coarse or offensive; rude; boorish;—*n.* common people.—**vul'garly** *adv.* —**vulga'rian** *n.* vulgar person, esp. rich and unrefined.—**vul'garise** *v.t.* to make vulgar.—**vulgarisa'tion** *n.*—**vul'garism** *n.* vulgar expression; grossness of manners.—**vulgar'ity, vul'garness** *n.* commonness; lack of refinement in manners; coarseness of ideas or language. —**vulgar fraction,** fraction expressed by numerator and denominator [L. *vulgaris,* fr. *vulgus,* the common people].

vulnerable (vul´nẹ-rạ-bl) *a.* capable of being wounded; offering opening to criticism; assailable; in contract bridge, denoting side which has won first game in rubber and is subject to increased honours and penalties.—**vul'nerableness, vulnerabil'ity** *n.*—**vul'nerably** *adv.* [L. *vulnus,* wound].

vulpine (vul´pin, vul´pīn) *a.* pert. to fox; cunning; crafty [L. *vulpes,* fox].

vulture (vul´tūr) *n.* large, rapacious bird of prey; rapacious person.—**vul'turine, vul'turish, vul'turous** *a.* characteristic of vulture; rapacious [L. *vultur*].

vulva (vul´vạ) *n.* fissure in external organ of generation in female [L.].

vying (vī´ing) *pr.p.* of vie.

W

wad (wod) *n.* little tuft or bundle; soft mass of loose, fibrous substance, for stuffing, etc., roll of bank-notes;—*v.t.* to form into wad;

to line with wadding; to pad;—*pr.p.* **wad'ding.** —*pa.t.* and *pa.p.* **wad'ded.**—**wad'ding** *n.* soft material for wads; cotton-wool [Scand.].

waddle (wod'l) *v.i.* to walk like duck, with short swaying steps;—*n.* clumsy, slow, rocking gait [freq. of *wade*].

wade (wād) *v.i.* to walk through something which hampers movement, as water, mud, etc.; to cope with accumulation of work;—*v.t.* to cross (stream) by wading;—*n.* ford.—**wa'der** *n.* one who wades; long-legged bird, e.g. stork, heron.—**wa'ders** *n.pl.* high waterproof boots [O.E. *wadan*].

wadi, wady (wod'i) *n.* channel of stream which is flooded in rainy weather and at other seasons dry [Ar. *wadi*, ravine].

Wafd (wåfd) *n.* extremist Egyptian National party.—**Waf'dist** *n.* and *a.* [Ar.].

wafer (wā'fẹr) *n.* very thin biscuit; thin disc of unleavened bread, used in Eucharist service of R.C. Church; thin, adhesive disc for sealing letters;—*v.t.* to seal or close with wafer.—**wa'fery** *a.* [O.Fr. *waufre*].

waffle (wof'l) *n.* a thin cake of batter [Dut. *wafel*, a wafer].

waft (waft) *v.t.* to impel lightly through water or air; to beckon to;—*v.i.* to float gently;—*n.* breath or slight current of air or odour; puff; signal given by hand [O.E *wafian*, to wave].

wag (wag) *v.t.* to cause to move to and fro; —*v.i.* to shake; to swing; to vibrate.—*pr.p.* **wag'ging.**—*pa.p.* **wagged.**—*n.* swinging motion, to and fro [O.E. *wagian*].

wag (wag) *n.* droll, witty person; humorist.—**wag'gery** *n.* pleasantry; prank; jocularity.—**wag'gish** *a.* frolicsome; droll.—**wag'gishly** *adv.* —**wag'gishness** *n.* [orig. E. *wag-halter*, one who deserves hanging—jocularly].

wage (wāj) *v.t.* to pledge; to venture on; to carry on;—*n.* payment paid for labour or work done; hire; reward; pay;—*pl.* used with a *sing.* significance.—**wage'-freeze, wage'-sta'sis,** *n.* condition where wages are not allowed to rise [O.Fr. *gagier*].

wager (wā'jẹr) *n.* something staked on issue of future event or of some disputed point; bet; stake; pledge;—*v.t.* to bet; to lay wager [O.Fr. *wageure*, fr. Gothic, *wadi*, pledge].

waggle (wag'l) *v.t.* to move one way and the other; to wag;—*v.i.* to reel or move from side to side [freq. of *wag*].

wagon, waggon (wag'on) *n.* four-wheeled vehicle or truck, for carrying heavy freight; railway goods truck.—**wag'oner, wagg'oner** *n.* one who drives wagon.—**wagonette', waggonette'** *n.* four-wheeled open carriage, drawn by horses, with two lengthwise seats facing one another behind driver's crosswise seat [Dut. *wagen*].

wagon-lit (va-gōng-lē') *n.* sleeping-carriage on a train [Fr.].

wagtail (wag'tāl) *n.* bird distinguished by long tail almost constantly in motion.

waif (wāf) *n.* homeless person, esp. neglected child; stray article or animal [Icel. *veif*].

wail (wāl) *v.t.* and *v.i.* to lament (over); to express sorrow audibly; to weep; tobewail; to bemoan; to cry loudly;—*n.* loud weeping; great mourning; doleful cry.—**wail'er** *n.*—**wail'ing** *n.* sobbing.—**wail'ingly** *adv.* [O.N. *vaela*].

wain (wān) *n.* wagon, esp. in farm use.—**wain'-wright** *n.* wagon-wright [O.E. *waegen*].

wainscot (wān'skot) *n.* panelling of wood used as lining for inner walls of building, extending short way from floor to ceiling; skirting-board;—*v.t.* to line with wainscoting. —**wain'scoting, wain'scotting** *n.* wall panelling material [Low. Ger. *wagenschot*, oak-wood].

waist (wāst) *n.* part of human body immediately below ribs and above hips; middle part of anything; part of upper deck of ship which lies between quarter-deck and forecastle.—**waist'-band** *n.* part of dress or trousers which fits round waist.—**waist'coat** *n.* short garment without sleeves, worn under jacket or coat [M.E. *waste*, growth, fr. *wax*, to grow].

wait (wāt) *v.t.* to stay for; to attend;—*v.i.* to stop until arrival of some person or event; to be expecting; to serve at table; to attend (on);—*n.* act, period of waiting;—*pl.* itinerant musicians esp. at Christmas.—**wait'er** *n.* one who waits; attendant in place of public entertainment; salver or tray.—**wait'ing** *n.* and *a.*—**wait'ing-list** *n.* list of names of those wishing some article, etc. in short supply.—**wait'ing-maid, -wo'man** *n.* woman who waits on lady.—**wait'ing-room** *n.* room set aside for use of people waiting in public place.—**wait'ress** *n.* female waiter.—**to wait upon, on,** to attend to wants of someone; to call upon; to await someone's convenience [O.Fr. *waitier*, to lurk].

waive (wāv) *v.t.* to give up claim to; to forgo; (*Law*) to throw away.—**wai'ver** *n.* (*Law*) declining to accept a thing [O.N.Fr. *weyver*, to renounce].

wake (wāk) *v.t.* to rouse from sleep; to bring to life again; to waken; to excite; to kindle; to provoke; to hold watch over corpse at night;—*v.i.* to awaken; to watch; to hold night revel; to be stirred up or roused to action.—*pa.t.* and *pa.p.* **waked** or **woke.**—*pr.p.* **wa'king.**—*n.* vigil; act of sitting up overnight with corpse; a local festival or holiday.—**wake'ful** *a.* indisposed to sleep; sleepless; watchful; vigilant; wary.—**wake'fully** *adv.*—**wake'fulness** *n.*—**wa'ken** *v.t.* and *v.i.* to wake.—**wake'ner** *n.* one who or that which wakens.—**wa'king** *a.* as in *waking hours*, period when one is not asleep [O.E. *wacian*].

wake (wāk) *n.* that part of track immediately astern of ship; air-disturbance caused in rear of aeroplane in flight.—**in the wake of,** following behind; in rear of [Dut. *wak*].

wale (wāl) *n.* mark left on flesh by rod or whip; single ridge or streak produced vertically on width of knitted fabric;—*v.t.* to mark with wales.—**wa'ling** *n.* wale, piece of heavy timber fastened horizontally to tie together boards supporting sides of trench or vertical pieces of a jetty [O.E. *walu*].

walk (wawk) *v.t.* to pass through, along, upon; to cause to step slowly; to lead, drive, or ride (horse) at a slow pace; to frequent, as prostitute;—*v.i.* to go on foot; to appear as spectre; to move off; to conduct oneself;—*n.* act of walking; slowest pace of quadruped; characteristic gait or style of walking; avenue set with trees; stroll; distance walked over; sphere of life; conduct.—**walk'er** *n.* one who walks.—**walk'ie-talk'ie** *n.* portable wireless combined transmitting and receiving set.—**walk'ing-stick** *n.* stick or cane used in walking; candidate for parliament nominated by political association; insect which resembles twig.—**walk'-out** *n.* a strike.—**walk'-o'ver** *n.* in sporting contests, event with only one competitor; easy victory.—**to walk on,** to take subordinate part in play or film [O.E. *wealcan*, to roll].

wall (wawl) *n.* structure of brick, stone, etc. serving as fence, side of building, etc.; surface of one; means of defence;—*pl.* fortifications; works for defence;—*v.t.* to enclose with wall; to block up with wall.—**wall'-bars** *n.pl.* horizontal rods affixed to wall of a gymnasium for body-exercises.—**wall'-board** *n.* lining of various materials for applying to rough surface of walls.—**walled** *a.* provided with walls; fortified.—**wall'flower** *n.* garden plant, with sweet-scented flowers; lady left sitting at dance for lack of partners [L. *vallum*].

walla, wallah (wol'ạ) *n.* merchant; worker; fellow; person [Hind.].

wallaby (wol'ạ-bi) *n.* a small kangaroo.—**wall'abies** *n.pl.* (*Slang*) Australians [Austral. native name].

wallaroo (wol-ạ-rōō') *n.* large kangaroo [Austral.].

wallet (wol′-et) *n.* knapsack; pocket-book for letters, bank-notes, etc.; bag, fitted to hold tools [etym. doubtful].

wall-eye (wawl′-ī) *n.* affection of the eye due to opacity of cornea; glaucoma.—**wall′-eyed** *a.* [Scand.].

Walloon (wȧ-lōōn′) *n.* descendant of ancient Belgae, race of mixed Celtic and Roman stock, now French speaking population of Belgium; their dialect;—*a.* of, or pert. to, Walloons [O.Fr. *Wallon*, fr. L. *Gallus*, a Gaul].

wallop (wol′-op) *v.t.* to beat soundly; to flog; to whip;—*n.* stroke or blow, esp. with flat of hand; (*Colloq.*) inferior beer.—**wall′oping** *n.* a thrashing;—*a.* tremendous; big; [etym. doubtful].

wallow (wol′-ō) *v.i.* to roll about (in mud, etc.); to thrive or revel in filth or gross vice [O.E. *wealwian*, to roll round].

walnut (wawl′-nut) *n.* large tree producing rich, dark-brown wood of fine texture; fruit of tree, large nut with crinkled shell [O.E. *wealh*, foreign; *knutu*, nut].

walrus (wol′-rus) *n.* mammal closely related to seal but with down-turned tusks [Dan. *hvalros*=whale-horse].

waltz (wawlts) *n.* ballroom dance in three-four time; music for this dance; valse;—*v.i.* to dance a waltz; to skip about, from joy, etc.—**waltz′er** *n.*—**waltz′ing** *n.* [Ger. *walzer*, fr. *walzen*, to roll].

wampum (wom′-pum) *n.* strings of shells, strung like beads, used as money and for ornament by N. American Indians [Native, *wompi*, white].

wan (won) *a.* having a sickly hue; pale; bloodless; pallid; cadaverous; ashy; gloomy.—**wan′ly** *adv.*—**wan′ness** *n.* [O.E. *wann*].

wand (wond) *n.* long, slender, straight rod; rod used by conjurers or as sign of authority [O.N. *vondr*, switch].

wander (won′-dẹr) *v.t.* to roam over; to confuse purposely;—*v.i.* to ramble; to go astray; to be delirious; to err; to depart from subject.—**wan′derer** *n.*—**wan′dering** *a.* rambling; unsettled;—*n.* journeying here and there, usually in *pl.*—**wan′deringly** *adv.*—**wanderlust** (vȧn′-dẹr-lōōst) *n.* an irrepressible urge to wander or travel [O.E. *wandrian*].

wane (wān) *v.i.* to decrease; to fail;—*n.* decrease of illuminated part of moon; decline; diminution; declension; decay [O.E. *wanian*, fr. *wan*, wanting].

wangle (wang′-gl) *v.t.* to wag or dangle; to oscillate; (*Colloq.*) to obtain by deception or trickery;—*n.* (*Colloq.*) trickery; artifice; fake.

want (wont) *n.* scarcity of what is needed; poverty; feeble-mindedness;—*v.t.* to be without; to have occasion for; to lack; to need; to require; to crave;—*v.i.* to be lacking or missed.—**wan′ted** *a.* desired; required; sought after; searched for (by police).—**wan′ting** *a.* absent; feeble-minded; deficient.—*prep.* without; minus.—**wants** *n.pl.* requirements [O.N. *vant*].

wanton (won′-ton) *a.* moving or flying about loosely; playful; dissolute; unrestrained;—*n.* lewd person; vain trifler;—*v.i.* to rove and ramble without restraint; to frolic; to play; to revel; to act lasciviously; to grow luxuriantly.—**wan′tonly** *adv.*—**wan′tonness** *n.* [M.E. *wantowen*].

wapiti (wop′-i-ti) *n.* N. American stag related to red deer [Amer.-Ind.].

war (wawr) *n.* armed conflict between two (groups of) states; state of opposition or hostility; profession of arms; art of war;—*v.i.* to make war; to carry on hostilities; to contend.—*pr.p.* **war′ring**.—*pa.t.* and *pa.p.* **warred**.—**war′-cry** *n.* wild whoop or battle-cry uttered by attacking troops; slogan.—**war′-dance** *n.* wild dance, among savages, preliminary to entering battle.—**war′fare** *n.* hostilities.—**war′-god** *n.* personification of war, as Ares and Mars.—**war′-head** *n.* explosive cap on missile.—**war′-horse** *n.* charger.—**war′like** *a.* disposed for war; having martial appearance; belligerent; hostile.—**war loan**, issue of Treasury bonds made to finance war expenditure.—**war′-lord** *n.* one who instigates war.—**war′monger** *n.* one who foments war or strife.—**War Office**, ministry in charge of military affairs.—**war′-paint** *n.* special adornment of Indians when on warpath; (*Slang*) full dress or regalia.—**war′path** *n.* military foray, esp. among Red Indians on scalping expedition.—**war′ship** *n.* vessel equipped for war. Also **man′-of-war**.—**civil war**, war between citizens of same country.—**cold war**, state of international hostility short of actual warfare [O.N.Fr. *werre*, Fr. *guerre*].

warble (wawr′-bl) *v.t.* to sing in quavering manner; to trill; to carol;—*v.i.* to sound melodiously;—*n.* soft, sweet flow of melody; carol; song.—**war′bler** *n.* one that warbles; various greenish-brown birds with pleasant trilling song [O.N. Fr. *werbler*].

warble (wawr′-bl) *n.* hard tumour on back of horse.—**warble fly**, fly which lays its eggs in fetlocks of cattle [etym. doubtful].

ward (wawrd) *v.t.* to watch; to guard; to defend; to repel;—*v.i.* to be on the watch; to keep guard;—*n.* watch; guard; guardianship; pupil; minor; stronghold; cell; custody; division of city; room for patients in hospital; slot in key; defensive movement in fencing, parry.—**ward′en** *n.* formerly governor of district; head of college, institution, corporate body, etc.; manager of church; civil defence officer; keeper; guardian.—**ward′er** *n.* jailer; staff of authority.—**ward′robe** *n.* cupboard for holding clothes; wearing apparel in general.—**ward′-room** *n.* mess-room on liner or battleship for senior officers.—**ward′ship** *n.* office of guardian; state of being under guardian.—**ward in Chancery**, minor under protection of Court of Chancery [O.E. *weard*, protection].

ware (wār) *a.* cautious; wary;—*v.t.* to guard against; to beware of [O.E. *waer*, cautious].

ware (wār) *n.* article of merchandise; pottery; usually in combinations as, *earthen-ware*, *hardware*, etc.;—*pl.* goods for sale; commodities; merchandise.—**ware′house** *n.* storehouse for goods; large commercial establishment;—*v.t.* to store in warehouse [O.E. *waru*].

warily, wariness See **wary**.

warlock (wawr′-lok) *n.* wizard; one in league with evil spirits; sorcerer [O.E. *waer*, compact; *leogan*, to lie].

warm (wawrm) *a.* having heat in moderate degree; not cold; hearty; earnest; excited; passionate; affectionate;—*v.t.* to communicate moderate degree of heat to; to excite interest or zeal in;—*v.i.* to become moderately heated; to become animated.—**warm′-blood′ed** *a.* of animals with fairly high and constant body-temperature; passionate; generous.—**warm′-heart′ed** *a.* affectionate; kindly disposed; sympathetic. — **warm′ly** *adv.* — **warm′ness, warmth** *n.* slight heat; cordiality; heartiness; glowing effect of warm colours [O.E. *wearm*].

warn (wawrn) *v.t.* to make aware; to notify by authority; to caution; to admonish; to put on guard.—**war′ner** *n.*—**war′ning** *n.* advance notice of anything; admonition; caution; notice to leave premises, situation, etc.;—*a.* cautioning [O.E. *warnian*].

warp (wawrp) *v.t.* to twist permanently out of shape; to bend; to pervert; to draw vessel or heavy object along by means of cable coiled on windlass; to stretch into lengths for weaving;—*v.i.* to turn, twist, or be twisted;—*n.* distortion of unseasoned timber due to unequal shrinkage in drying; system of spun threads extended lengthwise in loom on which weft is woven; a towing-line.—**warped** *a.* twisted by unequal shrinkage; perverted; depraved.—**warp′er** *n.* one who, or that which, warps.—**warp′ing** *n.* [O.E. *weorpan*, to throw, to cast].

warrant (wor′-ạnt) *v.t.* to give power or right to do (or forbear) with assurance of safety

Havana, Cuba: seafront

WORLD CAPITALS · 1

Rome: Spanish Steps

Reykjavik, Iceland

Singapore

Wellington, New Zealand

WORLD CAPITALS · 2

Beirut, Lebanon

Istanbul, Turkey

Oslo, Norway

to guarantee to be as represented; to vouch for; to assure; to indemnify against loss;—*n.* (*Law*) instrument which warrants or justifies act otherwise not permissible or legal; instrument giving power to arrest offender; negotiable writing which authorises person to receive something; naval or military writ inferior to commission.—**warr'antable** *a.* justifiable; legitimate; fit to be hunted, as **warrantable stag**.—**warr'antableness** *n.*—**warr'anted** *a.* guaranteed.—**warr'anter, warr'antor** *n.* one who warrants; guarantor.—**warr'anty** *n.* security; guarantee.—**warrant officer**, officer in Navy and Army intermediate between non-commissioned and commissioned officer [O.Fr. *warantir*].

warren (wor'-en) *n.* enclosure for breeding rabbits and other game; overcrowded slum or rookery [O.Fr. *warenne*, Fr. *garenne*].

warrior (wawr'-i-er) *n.* soldier; fighting man; brave fighter [*war*].

wart (wawrt) *n.* small hard conical excrescence on skin; (*Bot.*) hard, glandular protuberance on plants and trees.—**wart'hog** *n.* African mammal of pig family with large warty protuberances on face.—**wart'y** *a.* like or covered with warts [O.E. *wearte*].

wary (wā'-ri) *a.* cautious; heedful; careful; prudent.—**wa'rily** *adv.*—**wa'riness** *n.* [*ware*].

was (woz) *pa.t.* of verb **to be** [O.E. *waes*].

wash (wosh) *v.t.* to cleanse by ablution; to free from dirt with water and soap; to tint lightly and thinly; to separate, as gold, by action of water;—*v.i.* to perform act of ablution; to cleanse clothes in water; to be washable;—*n.* clothes, etc. washed at one time; liquid applied to surface as lotion or coat of colour; flow of body of water; rough water left behind by vessel in motion; marsh or fen, shallow bay or inlet; blade of an oar.—**wash'able** *a.*—**wash'-board** *n.* skirting board; board with a corrugated surface for washing clothes on; board above gunwale of boat to keep waves from washing over.—**wash'-draw'ing** *n.* a drawing done by brush in one tint only.—**wash'er** *n.* one who washes; metal disc for distributing pressure from nut or head of bolt; flat ring to make a tight joint by increasing gripping action of nut.—**wash'erman, wash'erwoman** *n.*—**wash'-house, wash'-ba'sin, wash'-bowl, wash'-pot, wash'-tub** *n.* for washing purposes.—**wash'iness** *n.* state of being washy, weak, or watery.—**wash'ing** *n.* act of one who washes; ablution; clothes washed at one time;—*a.* used in, or intended for, washing.—**washing soda**, decahydrate sodium carbonate (Na_2 CO_3 $10H_2O$).—**wash'-out** *n.* cavity in road, etc. caused by action of flood-water; (*Colloq.*) failure or fiasco.—**wash'y** *a.* watery; dilute; weak; thin; insipid; sloppy.—**washed out**, exhausted; faded [O.E. *wascan*].

wasp (wosp) *n.* stinging insect like bee with yellow and black barred colouring; an ill-natured, irritable person.—**was'pish** *a.* like wasp; irritable; snappy.—**was'pishly** *adv.*—**was'pishness** *n.*—**wasp'-waist'ed** *a.* having slender waist [O.E. *waesp, waeps*].

wassail (wos'-āl) *n.* ancient salutation in drinking; roystering festivity; drinking-bout; festal song; spiced ale flavoured with apples, nutmegs, sugar, etc.;—*v.i.* to carouse; to hold wassail.—**wass'ailer** *n.* [O.E. *wes hal*, be hale='your health'].

waste (wāst) *v.t.* to expend uselessly; to use extravagantly; to squander; to lay waste; to desolate; to spoil;—*v.i.* to wear away by degrees; to corrode; to decrease; to wither;—*a.* lying unused; of no worth; desolate; unproductive;—*n.* act of wasting; that which is wasted; refuse; uncultivated country; loss; squandering.—**was'tage** *n.* loss by use, leakage, or decay.—**waste'ful** *a.* full of waste; destructive; prodigal; extravagant.—**waste'fully** *adv.*—**waste'fulness** *n.*—**waste'-pipe** *n.* discharge-pipe for used water.—**was'ter** *n.* one who or that which wastes; article spoiled in manufacture, esp. casting; (*Slang*) ne'er-do-well; wastrel.—**was'trel** *n.* waster; profligate; waif.—**to waste away**, to be in state of decline.—**to lay waste**, to devastate.—**to run to waste**, to be wasted for lack of use or attention [O.Fr. *waster*; L. *vastare*, to lay waste].

wastel (wos'-tel) *n.* superior form of white flour [O.Fr.=a cake].

watch (woch) *n.* state of being on the look-out; close observation; vigil; one who watches; watchman; sentry; city night-patrol of earlier times; portable time-keeper for pocket, wrist, or fob; one of seven divisions of working day on ship; sailors on duty at the same time; division of the night;—*v.t.* to give heed to; to keep in view; to guard; to observe closely;—*v.i.* to be vigilant; to be on watch; to keep guard; to be wakeful; to look out (for); to wait (for).—**watch'-chain** *n.* chain for securing pocket-watch.—**watch'-commit'tee** *n.* members of town council or corporation delegated to supervise policing and lighting.—**watch'er** *n.*—**watch'ful** *a.* vigilant; attentive; cautious.—**watch'fully** *adv.*—**watch'fulness** *n.*—**watch'glass** *n.* glass covering of face of watch; sand-glass used formerly on ships to measure half-hour periods.—**watch'-keep'er** *n.* officer of the watch.—**watch'man** *n.* man who guards property.—**watch-night service**, religious service held on New Year's Eve.—**watch'word** *n.* password; a slogan; rallying cry [O.E. *waecce*].

water (waw'-ter) *n.* transparent, tasteless liquid, substance of rain, rivers, etc.; body of water; river; lake; sea; saliva; tear; urine; serum; transparency of gem; lustre;—*pl.* waves;—*v.t.* to wet or soak with water; to put water into; to cause animal to drink; to irrigate; to give cloth wavy appearance;—*v.i.* to shed water; to issue as tears; to gather saliva in mouth as symptom of appetite; to take in or obtain water.—**wa'ter-bail'iff** *n.* one detailed to prevent poaching on preserved stretch of river; water-bailie; a custom-house officer.—**wa'ter-batt'ery** *n.* series of simple voltaic cells having copper and zinc plates immersed in water.—**wa'ter-boat'man** *n.* boat-fly, pond bug which swims back downwards.—**wa'ter-bus'** *n*, small river craft used as form of public transport.—**wa'ter-butt** *n.* large barrel for catching rain-water from roof.—**wa'ter-chute** *n.* artificial sloping water-way down which boats plunge for amusement or logs are conveyed from high level.—**wa'ter-clos'et** *n.* sanitary convenience flushed by water.—**wa'ter-col'our** *n.* artist's colour ground up with water or isinglass; painting in this medium.—**wa'ter-col'ourist** *n.*—**wa'tercourse** *n.* channel worn out by running water.—**wa'ter-cress** *n.* aquatic plant with succulent leaves.—**wa'tered** *a.* diluted with water; of silk fabrics upon which wavy pattern has been produced.—**wa'ter-divin'er** *n.* dowser.—**wa'terer** *n.* one who waters; can for watering with.—**wa'terfall** *n.* fall or perpendicular descent of water of river; cascade; cataract.—**wa'ter-fowl** *n.* any aquatic bird with webbed feet and coat of closely packed feathers or down.—**wa'ter-gauge** *n.* instrument for measuring height of water in boiler, etc.—**wa'ter-glass** *n.* mixture of soluble silicates of potash and soda, used in storing eggs or for preserving stone-work.—**wa'teriness** *n.* state of being watery.—**wa'tering-place** *n.* a place where water may be obtained; resort for mineral water or bathing; spa; holiday-resort.—**wa'terish** *a.* containing too much water; watery; thin.—**wa'terless** *a.*—**wa'ter-lev'el** *n.* level formed by surface of still water; levelling instrument in which water is employed.—**wa'ter-lil'y** *n.* aquatic plant with fragrant flowers and large floating leaves.—**wa'ter-line** *n.* line on hull of ship to which water reaches.—**wa'ter-logged** *a.* of ground, saturated or full of water.—**wa'ter-main** *n.*

large pipe running under streets, for conveying water.—**wa'terman** *n.* man who manages water-craft; ferryman.—**wa'ter-mark** *n.* in paper-making, faint translucent design stamped in substance of sheet of paper and serving as trade-mark.—**wa'ter-mel'on** *n.* large fruit with smooth, dark-green spotted rind and red, white, or yellow pulp.—**wa'ter-po'lo** *n.* ball game played in water.—**wa'ter-pow'er** *n.* power of water used as prime mover.—**wa'ter-proof** *a.* impervious to water;—*n.* cloth or coat rendered water-proof;—*v.t.* to make impervious to water.—**wa'ter-shed, wa'ter-part'ing** *n.* the elevated line of division in a catchment area between two separate river-systems.—**wa'ter-spout** *n.* whirlwind over water, producing vortex connecting sea and cloud, resulting in moving gyrating pillar of water.—**wa'ter-tank** *n.* cistern for holding water.—**wa'ter-tight** *a.* so fitted as to prevent water escaping or entering.—**wa'ter-tow'er** *n.* on railways, etc. raised tank to give steady supply of water at suitable pressure.—**wa'ter-tur'bine** *n.* water-wheel with curved vanes on its rim, driven by momentum of falling water.—**wa'ter-way** *n.* fairway for vessels; navigable channel; aperture of water-cock.—**wa'ter-wings** *n.pl.* small rubber floats filled with air to support learners at swimming.—**wa'ter-works** *n.pl.* reservoirs, etc. for the purification, supply and distribution of water; (*Slang*) tears.—**wa'tery** *a.* resembling water; thin or transparent, as a liquid.—**above water,** financially sound; solvent.—**heavy water,** deuterium oxide, differing from ordinary water in its density, boiling-point, and physiological actions.—**high (low) water,** highest (lowest) elevation of tide; maximum (minimum) point of success, etc.—**mineral water,** water impregnated withmineral matter and possessing specific medicinal properties; artificially aerated water.—**in hot water,** involved in trouble.—**in low water,** financially embarrassed.—**of the first water,** of finest quality.—**to hold water,** of statement, to be tenable or correct.—**to water down,** to moderate [O.E. *waeter*].

watt (wot) *n.* unit of power represented by current of one ampere produced by electromotive force of one volt (746 watts=1 horse-power) [fr. James *Watt*, 1736-1819].

wattle (wot'l) *n.* twig or flexible rod; interwoven twigs; hurdle made of such rods; fleshy excrescence, usually red, under throat of cock or turkey; one of numerous species of Australian acacia;—*v.t.* to bind with twigs; to plait.—**watt'led** *a.*—**watt'ling** *n.* interwoven twigs used for protection of escarpment [O.E. *watel*, *watul*, hurdle].

waul, wawl (wawl) *v.i.* to cry, as a cat; to caterwaul; to squall [imit.].

wave (wāv) *n.* waving movement or gesture of hand; advancing ridge or swell on surface of liquid; surge; undulation; unevenness; extended group of attacking troops or planes; rise of enthusiasm, heat, etc.; wave-like style of hair-dressing; spatial form of electrical oscillation propagated along conductor or through space;—*pl.* (*Poet.*) the sea;—*v.t.* to raise into inequalities of surface; to move to and fro; to give the shape of waves; to brandish; to beckon;—*v.i.* to wave one way and the other; to flap; to undulate; to signal.—**wave'band** *n.* range of wavelengths allotted for broadcasting, morse signals, etc.—**waved** *a.* undulating.—**wave frequency,** number of vibrations of wave per second.—**wav'ily** *adv.*—**wave'-length** *n.* distance between maximum positive points of two successive waves; velocity of wave divided by frequency of oscillations.—**wave'let** *n.* ripple.—**wave'like** *a.*—**wave'son** *n.* goods floating on sea after shipwreck.—**wa'viness** *n.*—**wa'ving** *a.* moving to and fro.—**wa'vy** *a.* undulating; full of waves [O.E. *wafian*, to brandish].

waver (wā'vẹr) *v.i.* to move to and fro; to fluctuate; to totter.—**wa'verer** *n.* hesitant, vacillating person.—**wa'vering** *n.* and *a.*—**wa'veringly** *adv.* irresolutely; vacillatingly [M.E. *waveren*, to wander about].

wawl See **waul.**

wax (waks) *n.* a fatty acid ester of a monohydric alcohol, an amorphous, yellowish, sticky substance derived from animal and vegetable substances; beeswax; sealing-wax; cerumen, waxy secretion of ear; in mining, puddled clay;—*v.t.* to smear, rub, or polish with wax.—**wax'-bill** *n.* name given to several small, seed-eating cage-birds.—**wax'-can'dle** *n.* candle made of wax.—**wax'cloth** *n.* oil-cloth for floors; waterproof table-cloth.—**wax'en** *a.* made of or resembling wax; plastic; impressionable.—**wax'er** *n.* one who, or that which, waxes.—**wax'iness** *n.* waxy appearance.—**wax'ing** *n.*—**wax'-light** *n.* wax candle or taper.—**wax'-pa'per** *n.* paper coated with wax, used for air-tight packing.—**wax'-wing** *n.* hook-billed bird of chatterer family with quills tipped with red horn-like appendages resembling sealing-wax.—**wax'work** *n.* figure modelled in wax.—*pl.* exhibition of wax figures.—**wax'y** *a.* made of or like wax [O.E. *weax*, beeswax].

wax (waks) *v.i.* to increase in size; to grow; opposite of *wane* [O.E. *weaxan*].

wax (waks) *n.* (*Slang*) fit of anger; rage.

way (wā) *n.* street; highway; passage; path; lane; route; progress; distance; method; mode; custom; usage; habit; means; plan; scheme; momentum; movement of ship through water; state or condition.—**way'-bill** *n.* list of passengers or articles carried by vehicle.—**way'farer** *n.* wanderer on foot.—**way'faring** *a.* travelling;—*n.* journeying; pilgrimage.—**way'lay** *v.t.* to lie or wait in ambush for.—*pa.t.* and *pa.p.* **way'laid.**—**waylay'er** *n.*—**way'side** *n.* border of road or path;—*a.* adjoining side of road.—**way'ward** *a.* liking one's way; forward; perverse; refractory; wilful.—**way'wardly** *adv.*—**way'wardness** *n.*—**ways and means,** methods; resources.—**by the way,** as we proceed; incidentally.—**each way** (to lay bet) for a win and a place.—**right'of-way** *n.* right, established by old custom, to use path through private property; such a path.—**under way,** of vessel when moving.—**to make way,** to step aside; to advance [O.E. *weg*].

we (wē) *pron.* plural form of **I**; another person, or others, and I [O.E.].

weak (wēk) *a.* feeble; frail; delicate; fragile; easily influenced; simple; low; faint; thin; watery; diluted; inconclusive; (*Gram.*) of verb, forming past by addition of *d* or *t*.—**weak'en** *v.t.* to make weak;—*v.i.* to become weak or less resolute.—**weak'-head'ed, weak'-mind'ed** *a.* of feeble intelligence; mentally deficient.—**weak'-kneed** *a.* irresolute.—**weak'ling** *n.* feeble person, physically or mentally.—**weak'ly** *adv.*—**weak'ness** *n.*—**weak'-end'ing** *n.* in prosody, a feminine ending, extra unaccented syllable.—**weaker sex,** women [O.N. *veikr*].

weal (wēl) *n.* streak left on flesh by blow of stick or whip; wale [fr. *wale*].

weal (wēl) *n.* prosperity; welfare.—**the common weal,** well-being and general welfare of state or community [O.E. *wela*].

weald (wēld) *n.* woodland; open country; wold.—**The Weald,** land lying between N. and S. Downs, comprising portions of Kent and Sussex [fr. *wild*].

wealth (welth) *n.* riches; affluence; opulence; abundance.—**wealth'iness** *n.* riches; opulence.—**wealth'y** *a.* [O.E. *wela*, well-being].

wean (wēn) *v.t.* to discontinue gradually breast-feeding of infant; to detach or alienate.—**wean'ling** *n.* newly-weaned infant [O.E. *wenian*, to accustom].

weapon (wep'un, wep'n) *n.* instrument to fight with [O.E. *waepen*].

wear (wār) *v.t.* to carry, clothes, decorations and the like, upon the person; to consume by use; to deteriorate by rubbing;—*v.i.* to last or hold out; to be impaired gradually by use or exposure.—*pa.t.* **wore**.—*pa.p.* **worn**. —*n.* act of wearing; impairment from use; style of dress; fashion; article worn.—**wear'able** *a.* fit to be worn.—**wear'er** *n.*—**wear'ing** *a.* intended for wearing; exhausting to mind and body.—**wear'ing-appar'el** *n.* dress in general.—**wear and tear**, loss or deterioration due to usage.—**to wear off**, to disappear slowly [O.E. *werian*].

wear (wār) *v.t.* to bring ship on the other tack by presenting stern to wind;—*v.i.* to come round on other tack—opposite to *tack* [var. of *veer*].

wear (wēr) *n.* See **weir**.

weary (wēr-i) *a.* fatigued; tired; bored; exhausted; tiresome;—*v.t.* to exhaust one's strength or patience; to make weary;—*v.i.* to become weary; to long (for).—*pa.t.* and *pa.p.* **wear'ied**.—*pr.p.* **wear'ying**.—**wear'ily** *adv.* —**wear'iness** *n.* fatigue; tedium; ennui.—**wear'isome** *a.* tedious; causing annoyance.—**wear'isomely** *adv.*—**wear'isomeness** *n.* [O.E. *werig*].

weasand (wē-zand) *n.* the windpipe; the throttle; the trachea. Also **we'sand** [O.E. *wasend*, the gullet].

weasel (wē-zl) *n.* small, long-bodied, short-legged, bloodthirsty carnivore, related to stoat and polecat [O.E. *wesle*].

weather (weTH-er) *n.* combination of all atmospheric phenomena existing at one time in any particular place;—*v.t.* to expose to the air; to season by exposure to air; to sail to windward of; to endure;—*v.i.* to decompose or disintegrate, owing to atmospheric conditions.—**weath'er-beat'en** *a.* seasoned, marked, or roughened by continual exposure to rough weather.—**weath'er-bureau** (bū-rō') *n.* meteorological office.—**weath'er-chart** *n.* synoptic chart, an outline map on which lines are plotted to indicate areas of similar atmospheric pressure along with other meteorological conditions.—**weath'ercock** *n.* pivoted vane, commonly in shape of cock, to indicate direction of wind; one who changes his mind repeatedly.—**weath'er-fore'cast** *n.* prediction of probable future weather conditions based on scientific data collected by meteorological office.—**weath'er-gauge** *n.* bearing of ship to windward of another.—**weath'er-glass** *n.* instrument to indicate changes in atmospheric pressure; barometer. —**weath'ering** *n.* sloping surface on window-sills, etc. to throw off rain-water; process of decomposing of rocks exposed to elements.—**weather report**, daily report of meteorological conditions.—**weath'erside** *n.* side which faces wind.—**weath'er-vane** *n.* weather-cock.—**to keep one's weather eye open**, to be on one's guard.—**under the weather**, rather depressed; out-of-sorts [O.E. *weder*].

weave (wēv) *v.t.* to cross the warp by the weft on loom; to interlace threads, etc.; to plait; to construct, to fabricate, as a tale;—*v.i.* to practise weaving.—*pa.t.* **wove**.—*pa.p.* **wov'en**. —*n.* style of weaving.—**weav'er** *n.* [O.E. *wefan*].

weazen (wē-zn) *a.* See **wizen**.

web (web) *n.* that which is woven; whole piece of cloth woven in loom; weaver's warp; piece of linen cloth of specific size; membrane which unites toes of water-fowls; network spun by spider; anything as plot, intrigue, cunningly woven.—**webbed** *a.* having toes united by membrane of skin.—**web'bing** *n.* strong, hemp fabric woven in narrow strips, used for chairs, etc. [O.E. *webb*].

Webley (web-li) *n.* automatic pistol [Messrs. F. *Webley* and Sons]. [a female weaver].

webster (web-ster) *n.* weaver [O.E. *webbestre*,

wed (wed) *v.t.* to take for husband or wife; to marry; to join closely;—*v.i.* to contract matrimony.—*pr.p.* **wed'ding**.—*pa.t.* and *pa.p.* **wed'ded** or **wed**.—**wed'ded** *a.* married; wholly devoted (to art, etc.)—**wed'ding** *n.* nuptial ceremony; nuptials; marriage.—**tin, silver, ruby, golden, diamond wedding**, 10th, 25th, 40th, 50th, 60th anniversary of a wedding [O.E. *weddian*].

wedge (wej) *n.* piece of wood or metal, tapering to thin edge at fore end, used for splitting, lifting heavy weights, or rendering rigid two parts of structure; anything shaped like wedge;—*v.t.* to jam; to compress; to force (in); to squeeze (in); to fasten with wedge.—**wedged** *a.* cuneiform or wedge-shaped; jammed tight.—**the thin edge of the wedge**, first step or concession, insignificant in itself, which may lead to momentous results or inordinate demands [O.E. *wecg*].

Wedgwood (wej-wòòd) *n.* and *a.* pottery ware as invented by Josiah *Wedgwood* (1730-1795), celebrated English potter.

wedlock (wed-lok) *n.* marriage; married state [O.E. *wedd*, a pledge; *lac*, a gift].

Wednesday (wednz-dā, wenz-dā) *n.* fourth day of week [O.E. *Wodnesdaeg*, day of Woden, Norse god].

wee (wē) *a.* small; tiny [M.E. *we*, *wei*, bit].

weed (wēd) *n.* plant growing where it is not desired; sorry, worthless person or animal; (*Colloq.*) cigar; tobacco;—*v.t.* to free from weeds.—**weed'-kill'er** *n.* preparation for killing weeds.—**weed'y** *a.* full of weeds; lanky and weakly.—**to weed out**, to extirpate; to eliminate [O.E. *weod*].

weed (wēd) *n.* garment; mourning garb, as of widow (usually in *pl.*) [O.E. *waed*].

week (wēk) *n.* seven successive days, usually Sunday to Sunday.—**week'day** *n.* any day of week except Sunday.—**week'-end** *n.* Friday or Saturday to Monday; holiday for this period. —**week'ly** *a.* pert. to a week; happening once a week — *n.* publication issued weekly;—*adv.* once a week.—**Holy Week, Passion Week**, week preceding Easter Sunday [O.E. *wicu*].

ween (wēn) *v.i.* (*Poet.*) to think; to fancy; to imagine; to believe [O.E. *wenan*].

weep (wēp) *v.i.* to grieve for by shedding tears; to cry; to drip; to rain;—*v.t.* to lament; to bewail.—*pa.t.* and *pa.p.* **wept**.—**weep'er** *n.* one who weeps; crape hat-band worn by men at funerals; male professional mourner; mourning sleeve, sash, or veil; a side-whisker.—**weep'ing** *a.* of trees whose branches droop, as **weep'ing will'ow**.—**weep'y** *a.* easily made weep [O E *wepan*].

weevil (wēv-il) *n.* common name given to thousands of different kinds of small beetles, all distinguished by heads lengthened out to resemble beaks—larvae attack plants and stored grain [O.E. *wifel*].

weft (weft) *n.* filling thread carried by shuttle under and over the warp in a weaving-loom [O.E. *wefta*].

weigh (wā) *v.t.* to find weight of; to be equivalent to in weight; to deliberate or consider carefully; to oppress; to raise (anchor, etc.);—*v.i.* to have weight; to be considered as important; to press hard; to bear heavily (on).—**weigh'-bridge** *n.* machine with platform for weighing both vehicle and goods.—**weigh'er** *n.*—**weigh'ing-machine'** *n.* balance or scale; a spring balance; steelyard, etc.—**weight** *n.* gravity as property of bodies; heavy mass; object of known mass for weighing; importance; power and influence;—*v.t.* to make more heavy.—**weight'ily** *adv.*—**weight'iness** *n.*—**weigh'ty** *a.* having great weight; important; momentous; forcible.—**dead'-weight** *n.* heavy burden [O.E. *wegan*].

weir, wear (wēr) *n.* dam in river; fence of stakes set in stream for taking fish [O.E. *wer*].

weird (wērd) *n.* spell or charm; fate; destiny;—*a.* skilled in witchcraft; unearthly; uncanny; supernatural.—**weird'ly** *adv.*—**weird'ness** *n.* [O.E. *wyrd*, fate].

welch, welcher See **welsh**.

welcome (wel-kum) *a.* received gladly; causing gladness; free to enjoy or use;—*n.*

kind or hearty reception; salutation;—*v.t.* to greet with kindness and pleasure.

weld (weld) *v.t.* to join pieces of heated, plastic metal by fusion without soldering materials, etc.; to unite closely;—*n.* homogeneous joint between two metals.—**wel'der** *n.* [var. of *well*, to boil up].

welfare (wel´fār) *n.* well-doing or well-being; prosperity.—**welfare centre,** clinic at which nursing-mothers can obtain advice and treatment for their infants.

welkin (wel´kin) *n.* sky; vault of heaven [O.E. *wolcen*, cloud].

well (wel) *n.* shaft or tube sunk deep in ground to obtain water or oil; spring; fountain; source; bottom of lift- or elevator-shaft; cavity or pit below ground-level; chamber for catching surplus water or oil; enclosure in hold of fishing-vessel, for preservation of fish;—*v.i.* to issue forth in volume, as water [O.E. *wella*].

well (wel) *a.* in good health; hale; fortunate; comfortable; satisfactory; proper;—*adv.* rightly; agreeably; favourably; skilfully; satisfactorily; soundly;—*interj.* exclamation of surprise, interrogation, resignation, etc.—**well'-advised'** *a.* prudent; sensible.—**well'-appoint'ed** *a.* handsomely furnished or equipped.—**well'-bal'anced** *a.* eminently sane.—**well'-be'ing** *n.* welfare.—**well'-born** *a.* of good family.—**well'-bred** *a.* courteous and refined in manners; of good stock.—**well'-fa'voured** *a.* good-looking; pleasing to the eye.—**well'-informed'** *a.* knowing inner facts; possessing wide range of general knowledge.—**well'-mean'ing** *a.* having good intentions.—**well'-nigh** *adv.* nearly; almost.—**well'-off** *a.* rich; highly favoured.—**well'-spo'ken** *a.* cultured in speech; favourably commented on.—**well'-timed** *a.* opportune.—**well'-to-do** *a.* wealthy.—**as well as,** in addition to; besides [O.E. *wel.*]

Wellington (wel´ing-ton) *n.* long-range bomber aircraft in *World War* 2.—**well'ingtons** *n.pl.* rubber boots reaching to below knee [Duke of *Wellington*].

Welsh, Welch (welsh) *a.* relating to Wales or its inhabitants;—*n.* language of Wales, one of the Celtic family of languages; people of Wales.—**Welsh'man, Welsh'woman** *n.*—**Welsh rabbit,** or **rarebit,** savoury consisting of melted cheese on toast [O.E. *waelisc*, foreign].

welsh, welch (welsh) *v.t.* and *v.i.* of bookmakers, to cheat, by absconding from a racecourse without paying out on winning bets.—**welsh'er, welch'er** *n.* [perh. fr. Ger. *welken*, to fade].

welt (welt) *n.* hem or cord round edge or border; narrow strip of leather between upper and sole of shoe; weal; (*Slang*) a sharp blow;—*v.t.* to furnish with welt; to flog; to beat soundly.—**welt'ed** *a.*—**welt'ing** *n.* [etym. uncertain].

welter (wel´tẹr) *v.i.* to roll about; to wallow in slime, blood, etc.;—*n.* confusion; turmoil.—**wel'tering** *a.* [O.E. *wealt*, unsteady].

welter (wel´tẹr) *a.* pert. to heavily-weighted race in horse-racing;—*n.* heavy-weight rider; in boxing, class where contestants weigh between 135lb. and 147lb. (in America, 145lb.); boxer of this weight

wen (wen) *n* small superficial tumour or cyst, esp. on scalp [O.E. *wenn*].

wench (wensh) *n.* girl; maid; lewd woman;—*v.i.* to associate with lewd women.—**wench'ing** *n.* fornication [O.E. *wencel*].

wend (wend) *v.t.* to direct; to betake (one's way);—*v.i.* to go [O.E. *wendan*, to turn].

went (went) *pa.t.* of **wend**; *pa.t.* of **go.**

wept (wept) *pa.t.* and *pa.p.* of **weep.**

were (wer) *pa.t.* plural, and subjunctive singular and plural, of **be** [O.E. *waeron*].

werewolf, werwolf (wēr´wŏŏlf) *n.* human being who, at will, could take form of wolf while retaining human intelligence [O.E. *wer*, a man; *wulf*, a wold].

Wesleyan (wes´li-ạn) *n.* pert. to Wesley or Wesleyanism.—**Wes'leyanism** *n.* Wesleyan Methodism, i.e. religion practised in methodical manner [John *Wesley*, (1703-1791)].

west (west) *n.* point in heavens where sun sets; one of four cardinal points of compass; region of country lying to the west;—*a.* situated in, facing, coming from the west;—*adv.* to the west.—**wes'tering** *a.* setting in the west.—**west'erly** *a.* situated in west; of wind, blowing from west;—*adv.* in west direction;—*n.* wind blowing from west.—**west'ern** *a.* situated in west; coming from west;—*n.* inhabitant of western country or district; film featuring cowboys in Western States of U.S.A.—**wes'terner** *n.* native of the west.—**wes'ternmost, west'most** *a.* farthest to west.—**west'ward** *a.* and *adv.* towards west.—**west'wards** *adv.*—**West Country,** south-west England.—**to go west** (*Slang*) to die; to disappear [O.E.].

wet (wet) *a.* containing water; full of moisture; humid; dank; damp; rainy;—*n.* water; moisture; rain; (*Slang*) drink;—*v.t.* to make wet; to moisten;—*pr.p.* **wet'ting**.—*pa.p.* **wet** or **wet'ted.**—**wet'-blan'ket** *n.* a kill-joy.—**wet'ness** *n.*—**wet'-nurse** *n.* woman who suckles child of another.—**wet'tish** *a.* humid; damp [O.E. *waet*].

wether (weTH´ẹr) *n.* castrated ram [O.E.].

whack (hwak) *v.t.* to hit, esp. with stick; to beat; (*Slang*) to share (out);—*v.i.* to strike with smart blow;—*n.* blow; thwack; share.—**whack'er** *n.* (*Slang*) extra-large specimen; preposterous lie.—**whack'ing** *a.* very large; amazing;—*n.* a drubbing [fr. *thwack*).

whale (hwāl) *n.* large fish-like mammal;—*v.i.* to hunt for whales.—**whale'-back** *n.* type of freight vessel on Great Lakes of N. America with covered-in rounded deck.—**whale'-boat** *n.* long boat with sharp bow at each end.—**whale'-bone** *n.* baleen, an elastic, flexible horny product of jaws of baleen-whale.—**whale'-oil** *n.* lubricating oil extracted from blubber of sperm whale.—**whal'er** *n.* man or ship engaged in whaling industry.—**bull'-whale** *n.* full-grown male whale [O.E. *hwael*].

whale (hwāl) *v.t.* (*Slang*) to thrash.—**whal'ing** *a.* (*U.S.*); exceedingly big.—*n.* a thrashing.

wharf (hwawrf) *n.* structure on bank of navigable waters at which vessels can be loaded or unloaded; quay.—*pl.* **wharfs, wharves.**—*v.t.* to moor at, or place on, wharf.—**wharf'age** *n.* charge for use of wharf; wharf accommodation.—**wharfinger** (hwawr´fin-jẹr) *n.* one who owns or has charge of wharf [O.E. *hwearf*].

what (hwot) *pron.* interrogative pronoun (used elliptically, in exclamation, or adjectively); relative pronoun, meaning that which (used adjectively); such . . . as; whatever;—*adv.* why? in what respect? to what degree?—**whatev'er** *pron.* anything that; all that.—**whatso'ever** *pron.* whatever [O.E. *hwaet*].

whatnot (hwot´not) *n.* piece of furniture, having shelves for books, bric-a-brac, etc. [prob. short for '*and what not*'].

wheal (hwēl) *n.* raised stripe or ridge of thickened muscle fibre on skin due to stimulation; weal [O.E. *hwele*].

wheat (hwēt) *n.* edible portion of annual corn-grass providing most important bread-food of the world.—**wheat'en** *a.* made of wheat or wholemeal. [O.E. *hwaete*].

wheatear (hwēt´ēr) *n.* small passeriform bird, with brownish-grey plumage and black wing tips [corrupt. fr. *white-arse*].

wheedle (hwē´dl) *v.t.* to cajole; to coax.—**wheed'ler** *n.* [etym. uncertain].

wheel (hwēl) *n.* circular frame or disc turning on axis; instrument formerly used for punishing criminals; rotation; cycle; steering-wheel; wheeling movement; (*U.S. slang*) dollar;—*v.t.* to convey on wheels; to furnish with wheels;—*v.i.* to turn on, or as on, axis; to change direction by pivoting about an end unit, as troops on the march; to roll forward; to revolve.—**wheel'barrow** *n.* conveyance with a single wheel and two shafts for pushing.—**wheel'er** *n.* one who wheels; maker of wheels; hindmost horse, nearest wheels of carriage; wheel-horse.—**wheel'-house** *n.* (*Naut.*) a deck-house to shelter steersman.—**wheel'ing** *n.*—**wheel'-spin** *n.* revolution of wheels without full grip of road.—**wheel'wright** *n.* one who makes and repairs wheels [O.E. *hweol*].

wheeze (hwēz) *v.i.* to breathe audibly and with difficulty;—*n.* (*Colloq.*) joke; dodge; subterfuge.—**wheez'y** *a.* [O.N. *hvaesa*, to hiss].

whelk (hwelk) *n.* spiral-shelled sea-snail, the common whelk used as bait and food [O.E. *weoloc*].

whelm (hwelm) *v.t.* to cover completely; to submerge; to engulf [etym. uncertain].

whelp (hwelp) *n.* young dog or puppy; lion-cub; a youth (contemptuously);—*v.i.* and *v.t.* to bring forth young [O.E. *hwelp*].

when (hwen) *adv.* and *conj.* at what time? at the time that; whereas; at which time.—**whence** *adv.* and *conj.* from what place; from what, or which, cause, etc.—**whencesoev'er** *adv.* and *conj.* from what place, source, or cause, soever.—**whene'er'** *adv.* and *conj* at whatever time. Also **whenev'er.**—**whensoev'er** *adv.* and *conj.* whenever [O.E. *hwaenne*].

where (hwār) *adv.* and *conj.* at what place?; in what circumstances? at or to the place in which.—**whereabout'** *adv.* and *conj.* about where; near what or which place?—*n.* place where one is. Also **where'abouts.**—**whereas'** *conj.* considering that; when in fact.—**whereat'** *adv.* and *conj.* at which; at what.—**whereby'** *adv.* and *conj.* by which; by what.—**where'fore** *adv.* for which reason? why?—*conj.* accordingly; in consequence of which;—*n.* the cause.—**wherein'** *adv.* in which; in which, or what, respect, etc.; in what.—**whereof'** *adv.* of which; of what.—**whereon'** *adv.* on which; on what.—**wheresoev'er** *adv.* in, or to, whatever place.—**whereto'** *adv.* to which; to what; to what end. Also **whereun'to.**—**whereupon'** *adv.* upon which; in consequence of which.—**where'er', wherev'er** *adv.* at whatever place.—**wherewith'** *adv.* with which; with what.—**wherewithal'** *adv.* wherewith.—**the wherewithal,** the money; the means [O.E. *hwaer*].

wherry (hwer'-i) *n.* shallow light boat, for fast sailing; half-decked vessel used in fishing.—*pl.* **wherr'ies** *n.* [etym. unknown].

whet (hwet) *v.t.* to sharpen by rubbing; to make sharp, keen, or eager; to stir up;—*n.* act of sharpening.—*pr.p.* **whet'ting.**—*pa.t.* and *pa.p.* **whet'ted.**—**whet'stone** *n.* fine-grained stone used for sharpening cutlery and tools; stimulant.—**whet'ter** *n.* [O.E. *hwettan*].

whether (hweTH'-er) *pron.* which of two;—*conj.* used to introduce the first of two or more alternative clauses, the other(s) being connected by *or* [O.E. *hwaether*].

whew (hwū) *n.* or *interj.* whistling sound, expressing astonishment, dismay, or pain.

whey (hwā) *n.* clear liquid left as residue of milk after separation of fat and casein (curd).—**whey'-face** *n.* palefaced person.—**whey'faced** *a.* [O.E. *hwaeg*].

which (hwich) *pron.* interrogative, signifying *who*, or *what one*, of a number; a relative, used of things; also used adjectively.—**whichev'er, whichsoev'er** *pron.* whether one or the other [O.E. *hwile*].

whiff (hwif) *n.* puff of air, smoke, etc.; an odour; a smoke;—*v.t.* to throw out in whiffs; to blow;—*v.i.* to emit whiffs, as of smoke [imit.].

whiffle (hwif'-l) *v.t.* to disperse, as by a puff;—*v.i.* to veer, as wind; to be fickle; to prevaricate [fr. *whiff*].

Whig (hwig) *n.* orig. in Scotland, Covenanter; later, name extended in contempt to English political party supporting Hanoverian succession but after 1832 replaced by term, 'Liberal';—*a.* pert. to Whigs.—**whig'gish** *a.*—**whig'gery, whig'gism** *n.* [contr. fr. Scots *whiggamore*].

whiggamore (hwig'-a-mōr) *n.* (*Scot.*) orig. one who brought in corn, so called because of the prevalent use of the expression 'whiggam' to urge on the horses; term then transferred to the Covenanting party; hence, a Presbyterian; a Whig.

while (hwīl) *n.* space of time;—*conj.* during time when; as long as; whereas;—*adv.* during which.—**whilom** (hwīl'-om) *adv.* formerly; one;—*a.* quondam.—**whilst** *conj.* and *n.* while.—**to while away,** to pass (time, usually idly) [O.E. *hwil*, time].

whim (hwim) *n.* passing fancy; caprice; fad.—**whim'sical** *a.* capricious; freakish; fanciful; fantastical; quaint.—**whimsical'ity** *n.* fanciful idea; whim.—**whim'sically** *adv.*—**whim'sicalness** *n.*—**whim'sy, whim'sey** *n.* whim; caprice; fancy;—*a.* [O.N. *hvima*, to have straying eyes].

whimbrel (hwim'-brel) *n.* bird, resembling, but smaller than, curlew [imit.].

whimper (hwim'-per) *v.i.* and *v.t.* to cry, or utter, with low, fretful, broken voice;—*n.* low, peevish, or whining cry.—**whim'perer** *n.*—**whim'pering** *n.*

whin (hwin) *n.* whinstone [etym. doubtful].

whin (hwin) *n.* shrub with yellow flowers; gorse; furze.—**whin'chat** *n.* small bird of Thrush family [W. *chwyn*, weeds].

whine (hwīn) *n.* drawling; plaintive wail; unmanly complaint;—*v.i.* to utter plaintive cry; to complain in unmanly way.—**whi'ner** *n.*—**whi'ning** *n.* [O.E. *hwinan*].

whinny (hwin'-i) *v.i.* to neigh;—*n.* sound made by horse [O.E. *hwinan*, to whine].

whinstone (hwin'-stōn) *n.* (*Scot.*) basaltic or hard unstratified rock; greenstone; diorite. Also **whin** [etym. doubtful].

whip (hwip) *v.t.* to strike with lash; to flog; to sew slightly; to bind ends of rope with twine; to snatch or jerk (away); to beat into froth, as cream or eggs; (*Colloq.*) to defeat decisively;—*v.i.* to start suddenly.—*pr.p.* **whip'ping.**—*pa.t.* and *pa.p.* **whipped.**—*n.* lash attached to handle for urging on or correction; coachman; M.P. appointed to ensure fullest possible attendance of members of his parliamentary party at important debates; notice demanding attendance sent to M.P.s by party-whip.—**whip'cord** *n.* worsted fabric with bold, diagonal, warp twill.—**whip'-hand** *n.* hand which holds whip; mastery, upper hand.—**whip'per-snap'per** *n.* insignificant person; impertinent young fellow.—**whip'ping** *n.* flogging.—**whip'-round** *n.* collection on behalf of colleague [M.E. *whippen*].

whippet (hwip'-et) *n.* cross-bred dog of greyhound type, for racing; fast-moving, light military tank [prob. fr. *whip*].

whip-poor-will (hwip'-pŏŏr-wil) *n.* American bird of nightjar family.

whirr (hwir) *v.i.* to dart, fly, or revolve with buzzing or whizzing noise.—*pr.p.* **whir'ring.**—*pa.t.* and *pa.p.* **whirred.**—*n.* buzzing or whizzing sound [Dan. *hvirre*, to twirl].

whirl (hwerl) *v.t.* to turn round rapidly; to cause to rotate;—*v.i.* to rotate rapidly; to spin; to gyrate;—*n.* rapid rotation; anything which whirls; bewilderment.—**whirl'igig** *n.* spinning toy; merry-go-round.—**whirl'ing** *n.* and *a.*—**whirl'pool** *n.* vortex or circular eddy of water.—**whirl'wind** *n.* forward-moving, funnel-shaped column of air revolving rapidly and spirally round low-pressure core [O.N. *hvirfila*, ring].

whisk (hwisk) *n.* rapid, sweeping motion; small bunch of feathers, hair, etc. used for brush; instrument for beating eggs, etc.—*v. t.* to sweep, or agitate, with light, rapid motion;—*v.i.* to move nimbly and speedily.—**whisk'er** *n.* one who, or that which, whisks; moustache.—*pl.* hair on man's cheeks; long, stiff hairs at side of mouth of cat or other animal.—**whis'kered** *a.* [Scand. *visk*, wisp].

whisky (hwis'-ki) *n.* distilled alcoholic liquor

made from various grains.—*pl.* **whisk'ies.** Also **whisk'ey** [*Gael. uisge beatha,* water of life].
whisper (hwis′pẹr) *v.t.* to utter in low, sibilant tone; to suggest secretly or furtively;—*v.i.* to speak in whispers, under breath; to rustle;—*n.* low, soft, sibilant remark; hint or insinuation; rumour.—**whis'perer** *n.*—**whis'pering-gall'ery** *n.* place so shaped that whisper, or other faint sound, is heard at an unusually long distance [O.E. *hwisprian*].
whist (hwist) *n.* card game for four players (two a side) [fr. *whisk*].
whistle (hwis′l) *n.* sound made by forcing breath through rounded and nearly closed lips; small musical instrument; form of hooter;—*v.i.* to make such sound;—*v.i.* and *v.t.* to render tune by whistling; to signal, by whistling.—**whist'ler** *n.* one who whistles [O.E. *hwistlian*].
whit (hwit) *n.* smallest part imaginable; jot [O.E. *wiht*].
white (hwīt) *a.* of the colour of snow; light in colour; hoary; pale; pure; clean; bright; spotless; unblemished; (*Colloq.*) honest; just; decent;—*n.* colour of pure snow; albuminous part of an egg; white part of eye-ball surrounding iris;—*v.t.* to whiten.—**white'-alloy', -met'al** *n.* tin-base alloy of lead, copper, and antimony, resembling silver.—**white'-ant** *n.* termite, insect which reduces timber to powder.—**white'bait** *n.* newly hatched young of sprat, herring, and related fishes, used as table delicacy and for bait.—**white'beam** *n.* tree with white down on underside of leaves. —**white corpuscle,** leucocyte.—**white elephant,** sacred elephant of Siam; gift entailing more bother and expense than it is worth.—**white'-feath'er** *n.* symbol of cowardice.—**white'-fish** *n.* non-oily fish, such as whiting, haddock, cod, plaice, etc.; lake-fish of carp family.—**white flag,** sign of truce or surrender. —**white'-fri'ar** *n.* mendicant monk, of Carmelite order.—**white'-heat** *n.* temperature at which substances become incandescent; state of extreme excitement or passion.—**white'-horse** *n.* white-crested wave.—**white'-lead** *n.* compound of lead carbonate and hydrated oxide of lead, used as base and pigment for paint.—**white lie,** harmless fib.—**whi'ten** *v.t.* and *v.i.* to make or turn white.—**whit'ener** *n.* —**whit'ening** *n.* whiting.—**white'ness** *n.*—**white paper,** government report on matter of public interest recently investigated —**white'-pudd'ing** *n.* kind of sausage containing oatmeal, suet, and seasoning.—**white slave,** woman or girl enticed away for purposes of prostitution. —**white'throat** *n.* small bird of warbler family. —**white'wash** *n.* mixture of whiting, water, and size, for lining walls;—*v.t.* to cover with whitewash; to clear reputation of.—**whi'tish** *a.* somewhat white [O.E. *hwit*].
whither (hwiTH′ẹr) *adv.* to which, or what, place?—**whithersoev'er** *adv.* to whatever place [O.E. *hwider*].
whiting (hwī-ting) *n.* edible sea-fish; pulverised chalk, for making putty and whitewash [fr. *white*].
whitlow (hwit′lō) *n.* suppurating and inflammatory sore affecting finger-nails; [for *whickflaw*—i.e. *quick,* sensitive part under finger-nail, *flaw,* crack].
Whitsunday (hwit′sun-dā) *n.* seventh Sunday after Easter, festival day of Church, kept in commemoration of descent of Holy Ghost.—**Whit'sun, Whit'suntide, Whit Week,** week containing Whitsunday [so called because newly baptised appeared in white garments].
whittle (hwit′l) *v.t.* and *v.i.* to cut off thin slices or shavings with knife; to pare away [O.E. *thwitan,* to cut].
whizz, whiz (hwiz) *v.i.* to make hissing sound, as arrow flying through air.—*pr.p.* **whiz'zing.**—*pa.t.* and *pa.p.* **whizzed.**—*n.* violent hissing and humming sound.—**whiz'zingly** *adv.*—**whizz'-bang** *n.* (*Slang*) high-velocity, light shell whose explosion occurs almost immediately after its flight through the air is first heard [imit.].
who (hòò) *pron.* relative or interrogative, referring to persons.—**whoev'er** *pron.* whatever person; any one, without exception.—**whom** *pron.* objective case of who.—**whom'soever** *pron.* objective of **who'soever** *pron.* any person, without exception.—**whose** *pron.* possessive case of **who** or **which.**—**whodunit** [hòò-dun′it) *n.* (*Colloq.*) a detective story [O.E. *hwa*].
whoa (wō) *interj.* stop! [var. of *ho*].
whole (hōl) *a.* entire; complete; not defective or imperfect; unimpaired; healthy; sound; —*n.* entire thing; complete system; aggregate; gross; sum; amount; totality.—**whole'-heart'ed** *a.* hearty; sincere; enthusiastic.—**whole'-hog** *n.* complete programme without any reservations.—**whole'-meal** *n.* and *a.* wheaten flour containing also part of husk of grain.—**whole'ness** *n.*—**whole'sale** *n.* sale of goods in bulk to retailers;—*a.* selling or buying in large quantities; extensive; indiscriminate.—**whole'saler** *n.*—**whole'some** *a.* tending to promote health; healthy; nourishing; beneficial.—**whole'someness** *n.*—**whol'ly** *adv.* completely; perfectly [O.E. *hal*].
whom See **who.**
whoop (hwòòp, hòòp) *n.* loud cry or yell; halloo; hoot, as of owl;—*v.i.* to utter loud, high-pitched cry; to halloo; to hoot.—**whoop'er** *n.* one who whoops; whistling swan, bird with a loud harsh note.—**whoop'ing-, hoop'ing-cough** *n.* infectious disease marked by fits of convulsive coughing, followed by characteristic loud whoop or indrawing of breath.—**to make whoopee** (*Slang*) to celebrate uproariously [O.Fr. *houper,* to shout].
whop (hwop) *v.t.* to beat severely; to thrash. —**whop'per** *n.* anything unusually large; monstrous lie.—**whop'ping** *a.* (*Slang*) very big [fr. *whip*].
whore (hōr) *n* harlot; prostitute; unchaste woman;—*v.i.* to have unlawful sexual intercourse —**whore'dom** *n* fornication; idolatry —**whore'monger** *n* fornicator; lecher; pander —**whore'son** *n.* bastard;—*a.* bastard-like; mean; scurvy [O.N. *hora,* adultress].
whorl (hworl) *n.* spiral turn of univalve shell; ring of leaves, petals, etc.—**whorled** *a.* [O.E. *hweorfan,* to turn].
whort (hwort) *n.* fruit of whortleberry; shrub itself.—**whor'tle, whor'tleberry** *n.* small shrub, with bluish-black fruit used for jelly-making; bilberry [O.E. *wyrtil,* dim. of *wyrt,* wort].
whose (hòòz) **who'soever, whom'soever** See **who.**
why (hwī) *adv.* and *conj.* for what reason? on which account? wherefore?—*interj.* expletive to show surprise, indignation, protest [O.E. *hwi*].
wick (wik) *n.* cotton cord which draws up oil or wax, as in lamp or candle, to be burned [M.E. *wicke,* fr. O.E. *weoce*].
wicked (wik′ed) *a.* addicted to vice; evil; immoral; mischievous.—**wick'edly** *adv.*—**wick'edness** *n.* [M.E. *wikke,* feeble].
wicker (wik′ẹr) *n.* small twig or osier; wicker-work; withe;—*a.* made of pliant twigs, withes, or osiers.—**wick'er-work** *n.* basket-work [Cf. O.E. *wican,* to bend].
wicket (wik′et) *n.* small door or gate, adjacent to or let into larger door; three upright stumps with bails at which bowler aims in cricket; part of pitch where stumps are.—**wick'et-keep'er** *n.* fieldsman who stands immediately behind wicket [O.Fr. *wiket*].
wide (wīd) *a.* broad; spacious; distant; comprehensive; bulging; missing the mark;—*adv.* to a distance; far; astray;—*n.* ball bowled wide of wicket out of batsman's reach.—**wide'-awake'** *a.* fully awake;—*n.* a soft, wide-brimmed felt hat.—**wide'ly** *adv.*—**wi'den** *v.t.* to make wide or wider;—*v.i.* to grow wide or wider; to expand.—**wide'ness** *n.* width.—**wide'-spread** *a.* extending on all

sides; diffused; circulating amongst numerous people.—**width** *n.* wideness; breadth [O.E. *wid*].
widgeon, wigeon (wij′on) *n.* common duck which winters in Britain [O.Fr. *vigeon*].
widow (wid′ō) *n.* woman who has lost husband by death;—*v.t.* to bereave of husband; to be a widow to.—**wid′ower** *n.* man whose wife is dead.—**wid′ow-hood** *n.*—**grass widow,** wife temporarily separated from husband [O.E. *widwe*].
width See **wide.**
wield (wēld) *v.t.* to use with full command or power; to swing; to handle; to manage; to control.—**wield′able** *a.*—**wield′er** *n.*—**wield′iness** *n.*—**wiel′dy** *a.* manageable; controllable [O.E. *gewieldan*, to govern].
wife (wīf) *n.* married woman; spouse; (*Colloq.*) woman.—*pl.* **wives.**—**wife′less** *a.* without wife; unmarried.—**wife′ly** *a.* tender, as befits a wife [O.E. *wif*].
wig (wig) *n.* artificial covering for head to imitate natural hair.—**wigged** *a.* wearing a wig [for *periwig*].
wig (wig) *v.t.* (*Colloq.*) to scold.—**wig′ging** *n.* scolding; keelhauling [etym. uncertain].
wiggle (wig′l) *v.i.* to waggle; to wriggle;—*n.* a wriggling motion [var. of *waggle*].
wight (wīt) *n.* person [O.E. *wiht*].
wight (wīt) *a.* nimble [O.N. *vigr*, warlike].
wigwag (wig′wag) *v.i.* to twist about; to signal with flags, etc. [fr. *wag*].
wigwam (wig′wam) *n.* Amer.-Ind. hut [N. Amer.-Ind. *wekouomut*, in his house].
wild (wīld) *a.* living in state of nature; not domesticated; native; desert; savage; turbulent; untidy; annoyed;—*n.* uncultivated, uninhabited region.—**wild′-cat** *n.* untamed, undomesticated cat;—*a.* reckless; financially unsound; highly speculative.—**wild′-fire** *n.* Greek fire; anything which burns rapidly; sheet-lightning; erysipelas.—**wild′-goose-chase** *n.* foolish, futile pursuit or enterprise due to ignorance.—**wild′ly** *adv.*—**wild′ness** *n.*—**to sow wild oats,** to be given to youthful excesses [O.E. *wilde*].
wildebeest (wil′dẹ-bēst) *n.* gnu [S. Afr. Dut.].
wilder (wil′dẹr) *v.t.* to cause to lose the way; to bewilder [fr. *bewilder*].
wilderness (wil′dẹr-nẹs) *n.* tract of land uncultivated and uninhabited by human beings; waste; desert; wild; state of confusion [O.E. *wildor*, wild animal].
wile (wīl) *n.* trick or stratagem practised for ensnaring or alluring; artifice; lure; ruse;—*v.t.* to entice; to allure.—**wi′liness** *n.* artfulness; guile; cunning.—**wi′ly** *a.* full of wiles; crafty; artful; sly [O.E. *wil*].
wilful (wil′fo͝ol) *a.* governed by the will without yielding to reason; obstinate; intentional.—**wil′fully** *adv.*—**wil′fulness** *n.* obstinacy; stubbornness [fr. *will*].
wiliness See **wile.**
will (wil) *n.* power of choosing what one will do; volition; determination; discretion; wish; desire; (*Law*) declaration in writing showing how property is to be disposed by after death;—*v.t.* to determine by choice; to ordain; to decree; to bequeath; to devise;—*v.i.* to exercise act of volition; to choose; to elect; to desire; to wish;—*v.* used as an auxiliary, to denote futurity dependent on subject of verb, intention, or insistence.—*pa.t.* **would.**—**will′ing** *a.* favourably inclined; minded; disposed; ready; spontaneous.—**will′ingly** *adv.* readily; gladly.—**will′ingness** *n.*—**will′-pow′er** *n.* strength of will.—**at will,** at pleasure.—**with a will,** zealously and heartily [O.E. *willan*].
will-o′-the-wisp (wil′ō-thẹ-wisp) *n.* ignis fatuus, jack-o′-lantern, flickering, pale-bluish flame seen over marshes; any person or thing that deceives by dazzling or evanescent appearances.
willow (wil′ō) *n.* name of number of trees of genus Salix, applied to all not called osiers or sallows; pliant shoot of tree; cricket-bat.—**will′ow-herb** *n.* tall, perennial plant with willow-like leaves and bunched purple flowers.—**willow pattern,** design used in decorating china-ware, blue on white ground.—**will′ow-war′bler, -wren** *n.* birds visiting Britain in summer.—**will′ow-weed** *n.* purple loose-strife; knotweed.—**will′owy** *a.* abounding in willows; pliant; supple and slender.—**weep′ing-will′ow** *n.* waterside tree with beautiful pendent twigs [O.E. *welig*].
willy-nilly (wil′i-nil′i) *a.* vacillating;—*adv.* willingly or unwillingly [*will* and *nill*].
wilt (wilt) *v.i.* to fade; to droop; to wither;—*v.t.* to depress [etym. uncertain].
Wilton (wil′tun) *n.* velvet-pile carpet [*Wilton*, town in Wiltshire].
wily See **wile.**
wimple (wim′pl) *n.* covering for neck, chin and sides of face, still retained by nuns; veil;—*v.i.* to ripple; to undulate [O.E. *wimpel*].
win (win) *v.t.* to gain by success in competition or contest; to earn; to obtain; to attract; to reach, after difficulty;—*v.i.* to be victorious;—*pr.p.* **win′ning.**—*pa.t.* and *pa.p.* **won.**—*n.* victory; success.—**win′ner** *n.*—**win′ning** *n.* act of gaining; process of obtaining coal from seam;—*pl.* sum won in game or competition;—*a.* attractive; alluring; charming.—**win′ningly** *adv.* [O.E. *winnan*, to strive].
wince (wins) *v.i.* to shrink or flinch, as from blow or pain;—*n.* act of wincing.—**win′cer** *n.* [O.Fr. *guinchir*, to shrink].
wincey, winsey (win′si) *n.* cotton flannelette.—**win′ceyette** *n.* light, plain cotton fabric, slightly raised on both sides [fr. *linsey-woolsey*].
winch (winsh) *n.* hoisting machine; a wheel-crank; a windlass. Also **wince** [O.E. *wince*, pulley].
Winchester (win′ches-tẹr) *n.* repeating rifle with under-lever action [*maker*].
wind (wind) *n.* air in motion; current of air; breeze; breath; power of respiration; flatulence; idle talk; hint or suggestion; point of compass;—*pl.* wind-instruments of orchestra;—*v.t.* to follow by scent; to run, ride, or drive till breathless; to rest (horse) that it may recover wind; to expose to wind;—*v.t.* (wīnd) to sound by blowing (horn, etc.).—*pa.p.* **wind′ed** or **wound.**—**wind′bag** *n.* leathern bag, part of bagpipe, filled with wind by mouth; (*Slang*) empty, pompous talker.—**wind′-bound** *a.* detained by adverse winds.—**wind′-cheat′er** *n.* outer garment with hood attached of light windproof fabric.—**wind′fall** *n.* anything blown down by wind, as fruit; unexpected legacy or other gain.—**wind′-flow′er** *n.* the wood-anemone.—**wind′-gauge** *n.* anemometer, instrument for measuring force of wind.—**wind′ily** *adv.*—**wind′iness** *n.*—**wind′-in′strument** *n.* musical instrument played by blowing or air-pressure.—**wind′-jamm′er** *n.* (*Colloq.*) merchant sailing ship; army-bugler.—**wind′less** *a.* calm; out of breath.—**wind′mill** *n.* mill worked by action of wind on vanes or sails.—**wind′pipe** *n.* trachea; cartilaginous pipe admitting air to lungs.—**wind′-screen, -shield** *n.* protection against wind for driver or pilot—**wind′-tunn′el** *n.* in aviation, tunnel-shaped chamber for making experiments with model aircraft in artificially created atmospheric conditions.—**wind′-up** *n.* (*Slang*) panicky apprehension.—**wind′ward** *n.* point from which wind blows;—*a.* facing the wind;—*adv.* toward the wind.—**wind′y** *a.* consisting of, exposed to wind; tempestuous; flatulent; empty; (*Slang*) frightened.—**before the wind,** with the wind driving behind.—**in the wind,** afoot; astir; in secret preparation.—**second wind,** restoration of normal breathing.—**to get wind of,** to be secretly informed of.—**to raise the wind** (*Slang*) to procure the money necessary.—**to sail close to the wind,** to risk running into trouble by one's actions or remarks [O.E.].

wind (wīnd) *v t.* to twist round; to coil; to twine; to wrap; to make ready for working by tightening spring; to meander;—*v.i.* to twine; to vary from direct course —*pa.t.* and *pa.p.* **wound.**—**wind'er** *n.* one who, or that which, winds; step, wider at one end than the other —**wind'ing** *a.* twisting or bending from direct line; sinuous; meandering; serpentine; —*n.* turning; twist.—**wind'ing-sheet** *n.* sheet in which corpse is wrapped.—**wind'-up** *n.* conclusion; closing stages.—**to wind up,** to coil up; to bring to conclusion; to arrange and adjust for final settlement the affairs of business or society about to be dissolved; to excite to high degree.—**wound'-up** *a.* highly excited [O.E. *windan*].

windlass (wind'lạs) *n.* form of winch for hoisting or hauling purposes, consisting of horizontal drum with rope or chain, and crank with handle for turning [O.N. *vindill,* winder; *ass,* pole].

window (win'dō) *n.* opening in wall to admit air and light, usually covered with glass.—**win'dow-box** *n.* box for growing plants outside window.—**win'dow-dress'ing** *n.* effective arrangement of goods in shop-window.—**win'dow-sill** *n.* flat portion of window-opening on which window rests [O.N. *vindauga,* wind-eye].

wine (wīn) *n.* fermented juice of grape; similar liquor made from other fruits;—*v.i.* to drink much wine at a sitting.—**wine'-bibb'er** *n.* one who tipples in wine; drunkard. —**wine'press** *n.* apparatus for pressing juice out of grapes [O.E. *win,* fr. L. *vinum*].

wing (wing) *n.* organ of flight; one of two feathered fore-limbs of bird; flight; main lifting surface of aeroplane; aerofoil; side portion of a building; right or left division of army or fleet; unit of Royal Air Force consisting of two or more squadrons; in football, etc. section of team to right or left of field; pressed metal mudguard on front wheel of motor-car; sidepiece;—*pl.* the side walls of a stage;—*v.t.* to furnish with wings; to enable to proceed quicker; to wound in wing, arm, or shoulder;—*v.i.* to soar on the wing.—**wing'-comman'der** *n.* Royal Air Force officer ranking below group captain and above squadron-leader and corresponding to lieut.-colonel in army.—**winged** *a.* furnished with wings; wounded in wing; swift.—**wing resistance,** drag caused by wings of aeroplane. —**wing'-span, wing'-spread** *n.* distance between tips of outstretched wings of bird or of aerofoils of aeroplane [O.N. *vaengr*].

wink (wingk) *v.t.* and *v.i.* to close and open eyelids; to blink; to convey hint by flick of eyelid; to twinkle;—*n.* act of winking; hint conveyed by winking.—**forty winks,** short nap.—**to wink at,** to connive at; to affect not to see [O.E. *wincian*].

winkle (wing'kl) *n.* See **periwinkle.**

winner, winning See **win.**

winnow (win'ō) *v.t.* to separate grain from chaff by means of wind or current of air; to fan; to separate; to sift; to sort out.—**winn'owing** *a.* and *n.* [O.E. *windwian*].

winsey See **wincey.**

winsome (win'sum) *a.* cheerful; charming; attractive.—**win'somely** *adv.*—**win'someness** *n.* [O.E. *wynsum,* fr. *wynn,* joy].

winter (win'tẹr) *n.* fourth season; (*Astron.*) in northern latitudes, period between winter solstice and vernal equinox (22nd Dec.—20th-21st March); any dismal, gloomy time; —*a.* wintry; pert. to winter;—*v.t.* to keep and feed throughout winter;—*v.i.* to pass the winter.—**win'ter-gar'den** *n.* large conservatory or glass structure with exotic plants, often used for public concerts, etc.—**win'tergreen** *n.* aromatic herb from which is obtained, oil of wintergreen, used as a medicine for rheumatism and flavouring.—**win'ter-quar'ters** *n.pl.* winter residence; place where troops settle in for winter.—**winter sports,** open-air sports amidst ice or snow.—**win'triness** *n.*—**win'try, win'tery** *a.* suitable to winter; cold; snowy [O.E.].

wipe (wīp) *v.t.* to rub lightly, so as to clean or dry; to strike off gently; to clear away; to efface;—*n.* act of wiping clean or dry; a blow.—**wi'per** *n.* one who, or that which, wipes; in motoring, automatically operated arm to keep part of wind-screen free from rain or dust.—**wi'ping** *n.* act of wiping.—**to wipe out,** to erase; to destroy utterly [O.E. *wipian*].

wire (wīr) *n.* metal drawn into form of a thread or cord; telegraphy; telegram; string of instrument;—*v.t.* to bind or stiffen with wire; to pierce with wire; to fence with wire; to install (building) with wires for electric circuit; to telegraph; to snare;—*a.* formed of wire.—**wired** *a.*—**wire'gauze** *n.* finely woven wire used in making steam-tight joints.—**wire'-haired** *a.* (of terriers) with short, wiry hair.—**wire'-nett'ing** *n.* galvanised wire woven into net form.—**wire'-pull'er** *n.* one who exercises influence behind scenes, esp. in public affairs.—**wi'rer** *n.* one who installs wire; snarer of game —**wire'-worm** *n.* larva of various click-beetles, very destructive to roots of plants.—**wi'rily** *adv.*—**wi'riness** *n.* state of being wiry; toughness of physique.—**wi'ring** *n.* system of electric wires forming circuit.—**wi'ry** *a.*—**a live wire,** wire charged with electricity; enterprising person [O.E. *wir*].

wireless (wīr'les) *n.* and *a.* term used in same sense as *radio*;—*a.* without wires; pert. to radio;—*n.* wireless telegraphy or telephone; radio-broadcasting; a radio-set;—*v.t.* and *v.i.* to transmit message by wireless telegraphy or telephony.—**wire'less-op'erator** *n.* one who receives and transmits wireless messages as a profession [fr. *wire*].

wisdom (wiz'dum) *n.* quality of being wise; knowledge and the capacity to make use of it; judgment.—**wis'dom-tooth** *n.* posterior molar tooth, cut about twentieth year [O.E.].

-wise (wīz) *adv. suffix.* in the way or manner of, arranged like, as in *clockwise, likewise, crosswise,* etc.

wise (wīz) *n.* way; manner [O.E. *wise*].

wise (wīz) *a.* enlightened; sagacious; learned; dictated by wisdom.—**wise'-crack** *n.* concise witty statement;—*v.i.* to utter one.—**wise'ly** *adv.*—**wise'ness** *n.* [O.E. *wis*].

wiseacre (wī'zā-kẹr) *n.* one who makes undue pretensions to wisdom; a foolish know-all [O. Dut. *wijssegger,* soothsayer].

wish (wish) *v.t.* to desire; to long for; to hanker after; to request;—*v.i.* to have a desire; to yearn;—*n.* expression or object of desire; longing; request.—**wish'(ing)-bone** *n.* forked bone of fowl's breast —**wish'er** *n.*—**wish'ful** *a.* eager; desirous; anxious; longing; wistful —**wish'fully** *adv.*—**wish'fulness** *n.*—**wish'ful-think'ing** *n.* state of make-believe that what one ardently desires is an accomplished fact [O.E. *wyscan*].

wish-wash (wish'wosh) *n.* thin, weak, insipid liquor.—**wish'y-wash'y** *a.* thin and weak; highly diluted [redupl. of *wash*].

wisp (wisp) *n* twisted handful, usually of hay; whisk or small broom; stray lock of hair [M.E. *wisp, wips,* Cf. **wipe**].

wist (wist) *v.t.* and *v.i.* to know [O.E. *wiste, pa.t.* of *witan,* to know].

wistaria (wis-tā'ri-ạ) *n.* hardy climbing leguminous shrub, with blue, purple, white and mauve flowers [*Wistar,* Amer. anatomist, 1761-1818].

wistful (wist'fŏŏl) *a.* pensive; sadly contemplative; earnestly longing; wishful; eager; thoughtful.—**wist'fully** *adv.*—**wist'fulness** *n.* [var. of *wishful*].

wit (wit) *n.* intellect; understanding; (one with) ingenuity in connecting amusingly incongruous ideas; humour; pleasantry;—*pl.* mental faculties;—*v.i.* to know.—**wit'less** *a.* lacking wit or understanding; silly; stupid.

—wit'lessly *adv.* in all innocence.—**wit'lessness** *n.*—**witt'icism** *n.* witty remark.—**witt'ily** *adv.*—**witt'iness** *n.*—**witt'ingly** *adv.* with foreknowledge or design; knowingly; of set purpose.—**witt'y** *a.* possessed of wit; amusing. —**at one's wits' end,** baffled; perplexed what to do.—**to wit,** namely; that is to imply [O.E. *witan*, to know].

witan (wit'an) *n.pl.* members of the witenagemot [O.E. *wita*, wise man].

witch (wich) *n.* woman who was supposed to practise sorcery; ugly old woman; hag; crone;—*v.t.* to bewitch; to enchant.—**witch'craft** *n.* black art; sorcery; necromancy. —**witch'-doc'tor** *n.* among savage tribes, medicine-man.—**witch'ery** *n.* arts of a witch; sorcery.—**witch'-hunt** *n.* esp. in U.S. search for, and subsequent trial of, political prisoners.—**witch'ing** *a.* bewitching; fascinating.—**witch'ingly** *adv.* [O.E. *wicca*].

witch, wych (wich) *n.* the **witch'-elm.**—**witch'-al'der** *n* low shrub with alder-like leaves.—**witch'-ha'zel** *n.* shrub with yellow flowers and edible seeds; astringent principle of dried bark and leaves of the tree, used, in distilled form, as astringent drug [O.E. *wice*, drooping].

Witenagemot (wit'e-na-ge-mōt) *n.* national council of England in Anglo-Saxon times [O.E. *wita*, wise man; *gemot*, meeting].

with (wiTH) *prep.* in company or possession of; in relation to; against; by means of; denoting association, cause, agency, comparison, immediate sequence, etc. [O.E.].

with (wiTH) *n.* See **withe.**

withal (wiTH-awl') *adv.* with the rest; also.

withdraw (wiTH-draw') *v.t.* to take away; to recall; to retract;—*v.i.* to go away; to retire; to retreat; to recede.—*pa.t.* **withdrew'.** —*pa.p.* **withdrawn'.**—**withdraw'al** *n.*

withe (wīTH, with) *n.* tough, flexible twig, esp. willow, reed, or osier. Also **with, wyth, with'y.** —**with'y** *a.* made of withes; flexible and tough [O.E. *withig*, willow].

wither wiTH'er) *v.t.* to cause to fade and become dry; to blight; to rebuff;—*v.i.* to fade; to decay; to languish.—**with'ering** *a.* blighting; scorching;;—*n.* process of withering.—**with'eringly** *adv.* scathingly; contemptuously [var. of *weather*].

withers (wiTH'erz) *n.pl.* ridge between horse's shoulder-blades [O.E. *wither*, resistance].

withhold (wiTH-hōld') *v.t.* to hold or keep *pa.p.* **withheld'.**

within (wiTH-in') *prep.* in the inner or interior part of; in the compass of;—*adv.* in the inner part; inwardly; at home.

without (wiTH-out') *prep.* on or at the outside of; out of; not within; beyond; out of the limits of; destitute of; exempt from; all but;—*adv.* on the outside; out of doors;—*conj.* except; unless.

withstand (wiTH-stand') *v.t.* to oppose; to stand against; to resist.—*pa.t.* and *pa.p.* **withstood'.**—**withstand'er** *n.* opponent; resister.

withy See **withe.**

witness (wit'nes) *n.* testimony; one who, or that which, furnishes evidence or proof; one who has seen or has knowledge of incident; one who attests another person's signature to document;—*v.t.* to be witness of or to;—*v.i.* to give evidence; to testify.—**wit'ness-box** *n.* enclosure where witness stands in court of law.—**wit'nesser** *n.* [O.E. *witnes*, evidence].

witticism, witty, etc. See **wit.**

wive (wīv) *v.t.* to provide with or take for a wife;—*v.i.* to take a wife [fr. *wife*].

wivern See **wyvern.**

wives (wīvz) *pl.* of **wife.**

wizard (wiz'ard) *n.* one devoted to black art; sorcerer; magician; conjurer;—*a.* with magical powers; (*Slang*) excellent; marvellous.—**wiz'ardry** *n.* [fr. *wise*].

wizen, wizened (wiz'n, wiz'nd) *a.* dried up; withered [O.E. *wisnian*, to wither].

woad (wōd) *n.* plant yielding blue dye derived from pounded leaves [O.E. *wad*].

wobble, wabble (wob'l) *v.i.* to rock from side to side; to vacillate; to be hesitant;—*n.* rocking, unequal motion.—**wobb'ler, wabb'ler** *n.*—**wobb'ly, wabb'ly** *a.* shaky; unsteady [freq. of *wap*].

woe, wo (wō) *n.* grief; heavy calamity; affliction; sorrow; misery.—**woe'begone, wo'-begone** *a.* overwhelmed with woe; sorrowful; wretched.—**woe'ful, wo'ful** *a.* sorrowful; pitiful; paltry.—**woe'fully, wo'fully** *adv.* [O.E. *wa*].

woke, woken See **wake.**

wold (wōld) *n.* wood; open tract of country; low hill [O.E. *weald, wald*, a forest].

wolf (wóólf) *n.* carnivorous wild animal, allied to dog; rapacious, cruel person; (*Slang*) lady-killer.—*pl.* **wolves** (wóólvz).—*v.t.* to devour ravenously.—**wolf'-cub** *n.* young wolf; junior member of Boy Scouts.—**wolf'-dog** *n.* animal bred from wolf and dog; large dog for hunting wolves.—**wolf'-hound** *n.* dog bred for hunting wolves.—**wol'fish, wol'vish** *a.* rapacious, like wolf; voracious; fierce and greedy.—**wol'fishly** *adv.*—**wol'fishness** *n.*—**wolf's'-bane** *n.* aconite.—**to keep the wolf from the door,** to eke out bare existence [O.E. *wulf*].

wolfram (wóólf'ram) *n.* the mineral, ferrous tungstate, the chief source of the metal tungsten. Also **wolf'ramite** [Ger.].

wolverine, wolverene (wóól-ve-rēn') *n.* a carnivorous mammal inhabiting Arctic region —the glutton or carcajou [fr. *wolf*].

woman (woom'an) *n.* adult human female; women collectively.—*pl.* **women** (wim'en).—**wom'anhood** *n.* adult stage of women; the better qualities of women.—**wom'anish** *a.* effeminate.—**wom'anishness** *n.*—**wom'ankind, wom'enkind** *n.* female sex.—**wom'anlike** *a.* like, or characteristic of, a woman.—**wom'anliness** *n.*—**wom'anly** *a.* befitting a mature woman; essentially feminine;—*adv.* in manner expected of a woman [O.E. *wifmann*].

womb (wóóm) *n.* female organ of conception and gestation; uterus; matrix [O.E. *wamb*, belly].

wombat (wom'bat) *n.* group of Australian and Tasmanian fur-bearing, burrowing marsupial animals [Austral. *womback*].

women (wim'in) *pl.* of **woman.**

won (wun) *pa.t.* and *pa.p.* of **win.**

wonder (wun'der) *n.* astonishment; surprise; amazement; admiration; prodigy; miracle;—*v.i.* to feel wonder; to marvel; to be doubtful. —**won'derer** *n.*—**won'derful** *a.* very fine; remarkable; amazing.—**won'derfully** *adv.*—**won'derfulness** *n.*—**won'dering** *a.*—**won'deringly** *adv.* in a wondering and expectant manner.—**won'derland** *n.* land of marvels; fairyland.—**won'drous** *a.* wonderful.—**won'drously** *adv.* [O.E. *wundor*].

wonky (wong'ki.) *a.* (*Slang*) shaky; wobbly; out of order [Ger. *wanken*, to stagger].

wont (wōnt) *a.* accustomed; used;—*n.* habit; custom; use;—*v.i.* to be accustomed.—**won'ted** *a.* accustomed; habitual; usual.—**won'tedness** [O.E. *gewun*, usual].

won't (wōnt) *v.i.* a contr. of **will not.**

woo (wóó) *v.t.* to make love to; to court; to endeavour to gain (sleep, etc.).—**woo'er** *n.* one who woos —**woo'ing** *n.* [O.E. *wogian*].

wood (wood) *n.* land with growing trees close together; copse; grove; forest; hard, stiffening tissue in stem and branches of tree; timber; wood-wind instrument; (*Colloq.* at game of bowls) a bowl;—*v.t.* to supply with wood;—*v.i.* to take in wood.—**wood'-al'cohol** *n.* methyl alcohol, product of dry distillation of wood, esp. beech and birch.—**wood'bine, wood'bind** *n.* wild honeysuckle; (*U.S.*) Virginia creeper.—**wood'-car'ver** *n.*—**wood'-car'ving** *n.* carving in wood for decorative purposes.—**wood'chuck** *n.* small N. American burrowing rodent.—**wood'-coal** *n.* wood-charcoal; lignite or brown coal.—**wood'cock** *n.* migrant game-bird of snipe family.—**wood'craft** *n.* arboriculture, expert knowledge of woodland conditions; skill in the chase.—**wood'cut** *n.* engraving on wood; impression from such engravings.—**wood'-cut'ter** *n.*—**wood'ed** *a.* covered with trees.—**wood'en** *a.* made of wood; clumsy; stupid.—**wood'-engra'ver** *n.*—**wood'-engra'ving** *n.* art or process of cutting design on a boxwood block so as to leave it in relief for printing; impression from such block; woodcut.—**wood'en-head** *n.* a numskull; a blockhead.—**wood'enly** *adv.* stupidly.—**wood'enness** *n.* wooden quality; stiffness; stupidity. —**wood'iness** *b.*—**wood'land** *n.* and *a.* (of) wooded country.—**wood'-louse** *n.* the slater, prolific in damp places, esp. under decaying timber.—**wood'man** *n.* forester; woodcutter; hunter.—**wood'-nymph** *n.* fabled goddess of woods, a dryad.—**wood'pecker** *n.* bird which taps and bores with bill the bark of trees in search for larvae.—**wood'-pig'eon** *n.* cushat or ring-dove.—**wood'-pulp** *n.* wood crushed and pulped for paper-making.—**woods'man** *n.* forest dweller.—**wood'-sorr'el** *n.* perennial herb of geranium order with small white flowers and acid leaves.—**wood'-spir'it** *n.* methyl alcohol —**wood'-wind** *n.* wooden musical instrument, as flute, oboe, clarinet, bassoon, etc.—**wood'work** *n.* tuition in handling wood and tools; fittings made of wood.—**wood'y** *a.* abounding with, consisting of, wood —**not out of the wood,** still in jeopardy [O.E. *wudu*, forest].

wooer See **woo.**

woof (wōōf) *n.* threads which cross warp in weaving; weft; texture [O.E. *owef*].

wool (wool) *n.* soft, curled hair of sheep, goat, etc.; yarn or cloth of this;—**wool'-gath'ering** *n.* day-dreaming.—**wool'len** *n.* cloth made of wool;—*pl.* woollen goods;—*a.* made of, pert. to, wool.—**wool'liness** *n.*—**wool'ly** *a.* of, or like wool; muddled and confused.—**wool'-pack** *n.* a pack of wool weighing 240lbs.; a cirro-cumulus cloud, a shadowless cloud resembling a fleecy woollen ball.—**wool'sack** *n.* sack or bag of wool; seat of Lord Chancellor in House of Lords, as Speaker of the House.—**wool'sey** *n.* material of cotton and wool mixed; linsey-woolsey.—**dyed in the wool,** become inherent; out-and-out [O.E. *wull*].

wop (wop) *n.* (*Slang*) term applied to an Italian [It. *guappo*, blusterer].

word (wẹrd) *n.* spoken or written sign of idea; term; vocable; oral expression; message; order; password; promise; brief remark or observation; proverb;—*pl.* speech; language, esp. contentious; wordy quarrel;—*v.t.* to express in words; to phrase;—*v.i.* to talk; to discourse.—**word'ed** *a.* phrased; expressed.—**word'ily** *adv.* verbosely; pedantically.—**wor'diness** *n.* verbosity; prolixity.—**wor'ding** *n.* precise words used; phrasing; phraseology.—**word perfect.** able to repeat correctly from memory.—**word'y** *a.* verbose; prolix; shrilly vocal.—**word for word,** literally; verbatim.—**by word of mouth,** orally [O.E. *word*].

wore (wōr) *pa.t.* of **wear.**

work (wẹrk) *n.* exertion of strength; effort directed to an end; employment; toil; manual labour; occupation; production; achievement; deed; manufacture; fabric; that which is produced by mental labour; book; embroidery; (*Phys.*) result of force overcoming resistance over definite distance; —*pl.* structures in engineering; manufacturing establishment; mechanism of a watch, etc.; fortifications;—*v.i.* to exert oneself; to labour; to act; to be effective; to have influence (on, upon);—*v.t.* to produce or form by labour; to operate; to perform; to effect; to stir and mix, as dough, etc.; to embroider.—**work'able** *a.* capable of being worked.—**work'-bag, -bas'ket, -box** *n.* receptacle for holding work-implements, esp. for needlework.—**work'-day** *n.* day when work is done; week-day.—**work'er** *n.* one who is employed; one who works conscientiously.—**work'house** *n.* formerly institute for able-bodied paupers; building in which work is done.—**work'ing** *n.* act of labouring or doing something useful; mode of operation; fermentation;—*pl.* a mine as a whole, or a part of it where work is being carried on, e.g. level, slope, etc.; *-a.* labouring; fermenting.—**working party,** group appointed in an advisory capacity, to study methods of attaining maximum efficiency in industry.—**work'man** *n.* one actually engaged in manual labour; craftsman.—**work'manlike** *a.* befitting skilled workman.—**work'manship** *n.*—**work'room** *n.* room for working in.—**work'shop** *n.* place where things are made or repaired.—**to work off,** to get rid of gradually. —**to work out,** to solve (problem); to plan in detail; to exhaust (mine, etc.).—**to work up,** to excite unduly; to study intensively [O.E. *weorc*].

world (wẹrld) *n.* earth and its inhabitants; whole system of things; universe; any planet or star; this life; general affairs of life; public society; human race; mankind; great quantity or number.—**world'liness** *n.* state of being worldly.—**wordl'ing** *n.* one who is absorbed in the affairs, interests, or pleasures of this world.—**world'ly** *a.* relating to the world; engrossed in temporal pursuits; earthly; mundane; carnal; not spiritual.—**world'ly-wise** *a.* experienced in the ways of people.—**world'-wea'ry, -wea'ried** *a.* tired of worldly affairs.—**world'wide** *a.* extending to every corner of the globe.—**man (woman) of the world,** one with much worldly experience. —**old'-world** *a.* old-fashioned; quaint.—**the New World,** N. and S. America.—**the Old World,** Europe, Africa, and Asia [O.E. *weorold*].

worm (wurm) *n.* small, limbless, invertebrate animal with soft, long, and jointed body; spiral thread; small, metal screw with endless thread to gear with toothed wheel; spiral pipe through which vapour passes in distillation; emblem of corruption, of decay, or remorse; grovelling, contemptible fellow;—*pl.* disease of digestive organs or intestines of humans and animals due to parasitic worms;—*v.t.* to work (onesefl) in insidiously; to insinuate oneself;—*v.i.* to work slowly and secretly.—**worm'cast** *n.* earth voided and thrown up by earthworm.—**worm'-drive** *n.* in motoring, system in which power is communicated to road-wheels by means of worm, through worm-wheel.—**worm'eaten** *a.* of wooden furniture, etc., full of holes gnawed by worms; old; antiquated.—**worm'-wheel** *n.* cogged wheel whose teeth engage smoothly with coarse threaded screw or worm.—**worm'y** *a.* worm-like; abounding with worms; grovelling; gloomy [O.E. *wyrm*, serpent].

wormwood (wurm'-wood) *n.* bitter plant, Artemisia, used in making absinthe, vermouth, etc.; bitterness [O.E. *wermod*].

worn (wōrn) *pa.p.* of **wear.**—**worn'-out** *a.* no longer serviceable; exhausted; tired.

worry (wur'-i) *v.t.* to torment; to vex; to plague; to tear or mangle with teeth;—*v.i.* to express undue care and anxiety;—*n.* mental disturbance due to care and anxiety; trouble; vexation.—**worr'ier** *n.*—**worr'isome** *a.* causing trouble, anxiety, or worry.—**worr'ying** *a.* vexatious; harassing; exhausting.—**worr'yingly** *adv.* [O.E. *wyrgan*, to strangle].

worse (wurs) *a.* bad, ill, evil, in a higher degree; of less value; in poorer health; more sick;—*adv.* in a manner more evil or bad.—**wor'sen** *v.t.* to make worse; to impair; —*v.i.* to grow worse; to deteriorate.—**wor'sening** *n.* [O.E. *wyrsa*].

worship (wur'-ship) *n.* dignity; honour; religious reverence and homage; adoration; title of honour and respect in addressing those of high station;—*v.t.* to adore; to pay divine honours to;—*v.i.* to perform religious

service; to attend church.—*pr.p.* **wor'shipping.** —*pa.t.* and *pa.p.* **wor'shipped.**—**wor'shipful** *a.* highly worthy of respect or reverence.—**wor'shipfully** *adv.*—**wor'shipper** *n.* [O.E. *weorth-scipe*=worth-ship].
worst (wurst) *a.* bad or evil in highest degree; of least value or worth;—*adv.* in most inferior manner or degree;—*n.* that which is most bad or evil;—*v.t.* to get the better of; to defeat [O.E. *wyrst, wyrsta*].
worsted (woorst'ed, woost'ed) *n.* yarn spun from long-fibred wools which are combed, not carded; cloth of this yarn;—*a.* made of worsted [*Worstead*, in Norfolk].
wort (wurt) *n.* plant, herb—usually appearing as the last element of a compound term, e.g. *milkwort*, etc. [O.E. *wyrt*].
wort (wort) *n.* in brewing of beer, liquid portion of mash of malted grain produced during fermenting process before hops and yeast are added; malt extract used as a medium for culture of micro-organisms [O.E. *wyrt*, a plant].
worth (wurth) *n.* quality of thing which renders it valuable or useful; relative excellence of conduct or of character; value, in terms of money; merit; excellence; virtue; usefulness; cost;—*a.* equal in value to; meriting; having wealth or estate to the value of.—**worth'ily** *adv.* in a worthy manner; commendably.—**worth'iness** *n.*—**worth'less** *a.* of no worth or value; useless; despicable; vile.—**worth'lessly** *adv.*—**worth'lessness** *n.*—**worth'y** *a.* having worth or excellence; deserving; meritorious; suitable;—*n.* man of eminent worth; local celebrity.—*pl.* **wor'thies** [E. *weorth*].
wot (wot) *v.i.* to know; to be aware [O.E. fr. *witan*, to know].
would (wood) *pa.t.* of **will.**—**would'-be** *a.* desiring or professing to be;—*n.* a pretender.
wound (wound) *pa.t.* and *pa.p.* of **wind.**
wound (wòònd) *n.* injury; cut, stab, bruise, or rent; hurt (to feelings); damage;—*v.t.* to hurt by violence; to hurt feelings of; to injure.—**wound'er** *n.* [O.E. *wund*].
wove (wōv) *pa.t.* of **weave.**—**wo'ven** *pa.p.* of **weave.**—**wove'-pa'per** *n.* paper with woven marks of a fine wire gauze.
wow (wou) *interj.* exclamation of astonishment;—*n.* (*Slang*) great success.
wrack (rak) *n.* sea-weed thrown ashore by waves; shipwreck; ruin. Also **rack** [var. of *wreck*].
wraith (rāth) *n.* apparition of person seen shortly before or after death; spectre; ghost [O.N. *vorthr*, guardian].
wrangle (rang'gl) *v.i.* to dispute angrily; to bicker; in universities, to maintain or oppose a thesis;—*n.* angry dispute; an argument.—**wrang'ler** *n.* angry disputant; at Cambridge, one placed in the first class of Part II of Mathematical Tripos.—**wrang'lership** *n.* [M.E. *wranglen*, to dispute].
wrap (rap) *v.t.* to cover by winding or folding something round; to roll, wind, or fold together; to enfold; to envelop; to muffle.—*pr.p.* **wrap'ping.**—*pa.t.* and *pa.p.* **wrapped.**—*n.* a loose garment; a covering.—**wrap'per** *n.* one who, or that which, wraps; loose dressing-gown worn by women; negligée.—**wrap'ping** *n.* wrapping material [earlier *wlap*, etym. uncertain].
wrapt (rapt) *a.* Same as **rapt,** ecstatic; transported.
wrath (ràth) *n.* violent anger; indignation; rage; fury;—*a.* very angry.—**wrath'ful** *a.* full of wrath; angry; furious; raging; indignant.—**wrath'fully** *adv.*—**wrath'fulness** *n.*—**wrath'ily** *adv.* [O.E. *wrath*, angry].
wreak (rēk) *v.t.* to inflict (vengeance, etc.); to avenge [O.E. *wrecan*, to avenge].
wreath (rēth) *n.* garland or crown of flowers, leaves, etc. entwined together; chaplet; ornamental band for head; drift of snow; wisp of smoke; defect in glass.—**wreathe** (rēTH) *v.t.* to surround; to form into a wreath; to wind round; to encircle;—*v.i.* to be interwoven or entwined [O.E. *wraeth*, a fillet].
wreck (rek) *n.* destruction of vessel; hulk of wrecked ship; remains of anything destroyed or ruined; desolation;—*v.t.* to destroy, as vessel; to bring ruin upon; to upset completely.—**wreck'age** *n.* shattered remains of wrecked vessel or cargo.—**wreck'er** *n.* one who wrecks; one who lures ships to destruction; one who plunders wrecked ship; one lawfully employed in salvaging, or recovering cargo from, wreck [O.E. *wraec*, exile].
wren (ren) *n.* tiny song-bird about 4 in. long, with reddish-brown plumage [O.E. *wrenna*].
wrench (rensh) *v.t.* to wrest, twist, or force off by violence; to wring; to sprain; to distort;—*n.* sudden, violent twist; spanner with adjustable jaws; sprain [O.E. *wrenc*, trick].
wrest (rest) *v.t.* to pull or force away by violence; to extort; to twist from its natural meaning; to distort;—*n.* violent pulling or twisting [O.E. *wraestan*].
wrestle (res'l) *v.i.* to contend by grappling and trying to throw another down; to struggle; to strive (with).—**wrest'ler** *n.*—**wrest'ling** *n.* sport in which contestants endeavour to throw each other to the ground in accordance with rules [O.E. *wraestlian*, fr. *wraestan*, to twist about].
wretch (rech) *n.* miserable creature; one sunk in vice or degradation; one profoundly unhappy.—**wretch'ed** *a.* very miserable; very poor or mean; despicable.—**wretch'edly** *adv.*—**wretch'edness** *n.* [O.E. *wraecca*, an outcast].
wrick, rick (rick) *v.t.* to sprain;—*n.* slight twist or turn [Low Ger. *wrikken*, to turn].
wriggle (rig'l) *v.i.* to move sinuously, like a worm; to keep turning in prone position from side to side; to squirm;—*v.t.* to cause to wriggle;—*n.* act of wriggling; wriggling motion.—**wrigg'ler** *n.* **wrigg'ling** *n.* [Dut. *wriggelen*, to move].
wright (rīt) *n.* one who fashions articles of wood, metal, etc., as *wheelwright*; artificer; a builder [O.E. *wyrhta*].
wring (ring) *v.t.* to twist and compress; to turn and strain with violence; to squeeze or press out; to pain; to distort; to extort;—*v.i.* to turn or twist, as with pain; to writhe in anguish.—*pa.t.* and *pa.p.* **wrung.**—**wring'er** *n.* one who wrings; machine for pressing out water from wet clothes, etc.; mangle.—**wringing wet,** absolutely soaking [O.E. *wringan*].
wrinkle (ring'kl) *n.* ridge or furrow on surface due to twisting, shrinking, or puckering; crease in skin; fold; corrugation;—*v.t.* to contract into wrinkles;—*v.i.* to shrink unevenly.—**wrink'ling** *n.*—**wrink'ly** *a.* [O.E. *wrincle*].
wrinkle (ring'kl) *n.* valuable hint; good tip [O.E. *wrenc*, trick].
wrist (rist) *n.* joint connecting the forearm and hand; the carpus.—**wrist'band** *n.* part of shirt sleeve covering wrist; elastic band to give support to injured wrist.—**wrist'let** *n.* band clasping wrist fairly tightly; bracelet; (*Slang*) handcuff [O.E.].
writ (rit) obsolete *pa.t.* and *pa.p.* of **write.**
writ (rit) *n.* that which is written; in law, mandatory precept issued by a court; order of Crown calling for election of member to represent constituency in House of Commons.—**Holy Writ,** the Scriptures [fr. *write*].
write (rīt) *v.t.* to set down or express in letters or words; to indite; to copy on paper; to compose, as book, song, etc.; to declare emphatically;—*v.i.* to form characters representing sounds or ideas; to be occupied in writing; to express ideas in words.—*pr.p.* **wri'ting.**—*pa.t.* and *pa.p.* **writ'ten.**—**wri'ter** *n.* one who writes; scribe; clerk; author; law-agent or solicitor.—**wri'ter's-cramp** *n.* neurosis

of muscles of hand.—**write'-up** *n.* (*Colloq.*) favourable press criticism.—**wri'ting** *n.* mechanical act of forming characters on paper or any other material; anything written;—*pl.* literary or musical works; official papers; legal instruments of conveyance; deeds.—**wri'ting-book** *n.* copybook for practising writing; writer.—**wri'ting-case** *n.* small case for holding writing-materials.—**writ'ten** *a.* expressed in writing.—**Writer to the Signet,** in Scotland, solicitor privileged to prepare Crown writs.—**to write off,** to cancel, as bad debts [O.E. *writan*].

writhe (rīTH) *v.t.* to twist or distort; to turn to and fro;—*v.i.* to twist or roll about (as in pain); to wriggle [O.E. *writhan*].

written (rit'n) *pa.p.* of **write.**

wrong (rong) *a.* not right; incorrect; mistaken; bad; evil; immoral; injurious; unjust; illegal; unsuitable; improper; unfit;—*n.* harm; evil; injustice; trespass; transgression; error;—*adv.* not rightly; erroneously;—*v.t.* to treat with injustice; to injure; to impute evil to unjustly.—**wrong'-do'er** *n.* one who injures another; one who breaks law; offender; sinner.—**wrong'ful** *a.* unjust; unfair; unrighteous; causing wrong.—**wrong'fully** *adv.* —**wrong'fulness** *n.*—**wrong'head'ed** *a.* obstinate; stubborn; perverse.—**wrong'ly** *adv.*—**wrong'ness** *n.*—**wrong'ous** *a.* constituting a wrong; unjust; illegal.—**wrong'ously** *adv.*—**in the wrong,** at fault; blameworthy; mistaken [O.E. *wrang*, injustice].

wrote (rōt) *pa.t.* of **write.**

wroth (roth) *a.* full of wrath; exasperated; angry; incensed; indignant [fr. *wrath*].

wrought (rawt) *pa.t.* and *pa.p.* of **work.**—**wrought'-i'ron** *n.* purest form of commercial iron, fibrous, ductile, and malleable, prepared by puddling.—**wrought'-up** *a.* excited; frenzied [O.E. *worhte*, worked].

wrung (rung) *pa.t.* and *pa.p.* of **wring.**

wry (rī) *a.* turned to one side; twisted; distorted; crooked; askew.—**wry'ly** *adv.*—**wry'neck** *n.* condition in which head leans permanently towards shoulder; bird of woodpecker family which twists and turns its neck.—**wry'-necked** *a.*—**wry'ness** *n.* crookedness [O.E. *wrigian*, to twist].

wyandotte (wī'an-dot) *n.* breed of domestic fowls [name of N. Amer. tribe].

wych-elm See **witch-elm.**

wynd (wīnd) *n.* narrow lane or alley [O.E. *windan*, to turn round].

wythe Same as **withe.**

wyvern, wivern (wī'vẹrn) *n.* (*Her.*) imaginary monster, with two clawed feet, two wings and serpent's tail [O.Fr. *wivre*, viper, fr. L. *vipera*, viper].

X

xantippe (zan-tip'e) *n.* a scold; a shrewish woman [*Xantippē*, wife of Socrates].

X-chromosome (eks'krō'mō-sōm) *n.* (*Biol.*) chromosome which determines the sex of the future organism.

xebec (zē'bek) *n.* small three-masted vessel with lateen and square sails, used formerly in the Mediterranean by the Algerine pirates [Fr. *chebec*].

xenial (zē'ni-ạl) *a.* hospitable; pert. to hospitality.—**xe'nium** *n.* parting gift to a guest [Gk. *xenos*, stranger].

xenogamy (zen-og'ạ-mi) *n.* (*Bot.*) cross-fertilisation [Gk. *xenos*, stranger; *gamos*, marriage].

xenogenesis (zen-ō-jen'ẹ-sis) *n.* generation of organism totally unlike parent.—**xenogenet'ic** *a.* [Gk. *xenos*, stranger; *genesis*, birth].

xenomania (zen-ō-mā'ni-ạ) *n.* mania for anything foreign or exotic [Gk. *xenos*, foreign; *mania*, madness].

xenon (zen'on) *n.* non-metallic element belonging to group of rare or inactive gases [Gk. *xenos*, a stranger].

xenophobia (zen-ō-fōb'i-ạ) *n.* dislike, hatred, fear of strangers or aliens [Gk. *xenos*, stranger; *phobos*, fear].

xerography (ze-rog'ra-fi) *n.* a process similar to photography, but not requiring specially sensitised paper or plates, using instead a special photo-conductive plate.

X-rays (eks'rāz) *n.pl.* Röntgen rays—electro-magnetic rays of very short wavelength, capable of penetrating matter opaque to light rays and imprinting on sensitive photographic plate picture of objects.

xylograph (zī'lō-graf) *n.* wood-engraving; impression from wood-block.—**xylog'rapher** *n.* —**xylograph'ic** *a.*—**xylog'raphy** *n.* wood-engraving; decorative painting on wood [Gk. *xulon*, wood; *graphein*, to write].

xyloid (zī'loid) *a.* of the nature of wood; woody; resembling wood; ligneous.—**xyloi'dine** *n.* explosive compound prepared by action of nitric acid on starch or woody fibres [Gk. *xulon*, wood].

xylol (zī'lol) *n.* commercial name for xylene, dimethyl benzene—hydrocarbon derived from coal-tar used medicinally and as solvent for fats [Gk. *xulon*, wood; L. *oleum*, oil].

xylonite (zī'lō-nīt) *n.* variety of celluloid, made by mixing pyroxylin and camphor under high pressure [Gk. *xulon*, wood].

xylophone (zī'lō-fōn) *n.* musical instrument consisting of blocks of resonant wood, notes being produced by striking blocks with two small hammers [Gk. *xulon*, wood; *phonē*, a voice].

xylopyrography (zī-lō-pī-rog'rạ-fi) *n.* production of designs in wood by charring with hot iron; poker-painting [Gk. *xulon*, wood; *pur*, fire; *graphein*, to write].

xyster (zis'tẹr) *n.* surgical instrument for scraping bones [Gk. fr. *xuein*, to scrape].

Y

yacht (yot) *n.* light sailing or steam vessel, for pleasure or racing;—*v.i.* to sail in a yacht. —**yacht'ing** *n.* art of sailing a yacht;—*a.* pert. to yacht.—**yachts'man** *n.*—**yachts'manship** *n.* [Dut. *jagt*].

yaffle (yaf'l) *n.* the green woodpecker. Also **yaff'il** [imit. origin].

Yahoo (yạ-hòò') *n.* in Swift's *Gulliver's Travels*, imaginary man-like animals with bestial habits; brutish person.

yak (yak) *n.* species of ox found in C. Asia, with a hump and long hair [Tibetan, *gyag*].

Yale (yāl) *a.* denoting a cylinder lock, or key to fit it, invented by American locksmith, Linus *Yale* [Protected Trade Name].

yam (yam) *n.* tuber of tropical climbing-plant; sweet potato [Port. *inhame*].

yammer (yam'ẹr) *v.i.* to whine; to wail; to talk incoherently [O.E. *geomor*, sad].

yank (yangk) *v.t.* and *v.i.* (*Slang*) to jerk; to tug; to pull quickly;—*n.* quick tug.

Yank (yangk) *n.* (*Slang*) Yankee.

Yankee (yang'kē) *n.* (in U.S.A.) citizen of New England, or of Northern States; (in Europe) an American;—*a.* American [etym. uncertain].

yaourt (ya'òòrt) *n.* drink made from fermented milk [Turk. *yoghurt*].

yap (yap) *v.i.* to yelp; (*Slang*) to chatter incessantly;—*n.* yelp.—*pr.p.* **yap'ping.**—*pa.p.* and *pa.t.* **yapped** [imit. origin].

yapp (yap) *n.* style of bookbinding in limp leather projecting beyond edges of book [fr. *Yapp*, the inventor].

yarborough (yàr'bu-ro) *n.* (*Cards*) whist or bridge hand containing no card higher than a nine [fr. an Earl of *Yarborough*, who offered odds against the possibility].

yard (yárd) *n.* standard measure of length, equal to three feet or thirty-six inches; measuring rod of this length; yard-stick; (*Naut.*) spar set crosswise to mast, for supporting a sail.—**yard'-arm** *n.* either half of a ship's yard [O.E. *gyrd*, a rod].

yard (yárd) *n.* small, enclosed piece of ground near a building; enclosure within which specific kind of work is carried on, as *brick-yard, a railway-yard*, etc.—**The Yard**, i.e. Scotland Yard, headquarters of Criminal Investigation Department of London Metropolitan Police [O.E. *geard*, enclosure].

yarn (yárn) *n.* spun thread, esp. for knitting or weaving; thread of rope; (*Colloq.*) story; anecdote; chat;—*v.i.* to tell a story.

yarrow (yar-ō) *n.* plant having strong odour and pungent taste [O.E. *gearwe*].

yashmak (yash'-mak) *n.* veil worn by Mohammedan women, covering the face from beneath the eyes down [Ar.].

yataghan (yat-ạ-gan) *n.* Turkish dagger, without a hilt and usually curved [Turk.].

yaw (yaw) *v.i.* of ship or aircraft, to fail to keep steady course;—*n.* act of yawing; temporary deviation from a straight course [O.N. *jaga*, to bend].

yawl (yawl) *n.* small, two-masted sailing-boat, with smaller mast at stern; ship's small boat [Dut. *jol*].

yawn (yawn) *v.i.* to open mouth involuntarily through sleepiness, etc.; to gape;—*n.* involuntary opening of mouth through sleepiness, etc.; a gaping.—**yawn'ing** *a.* gaping [O.E. *geonian*].

yaws (yawz) *n.* tropical, contagious disease of the skin, usually chronic; (*Med.*) framboesia [Afr. *yaw*, a rasberry].

yclept (i-klept') *a.* (*Arch.*) called [O.E.] *clipian*, to call].

ye (yē) *pron.* (*Arch.*) nominative plural of [you [O.E. *ge.*]

ye (yē) *a.* an archaic form of the definite article 'the.'

yea (yā) *interj.* [*Arch.*) yes; ay; indeed; [verily [O.E. *gea*].

yean (yēn) *v.t.* and *v.i.* to bring forth young as sheep or goat.— **yean'ling** *n.* a lamb; kid [O.E. *eanian*].

year (yēr) *n.* time taken by one revolution of earth round sun, i.e. about 365¼ days; twelve months; scholastic session in school, university, etc.;—*pl.* age; old age.—**year'ly** *a.* and *adv.* happening every year; annual.—**year'-ling** *n.* young animal, esp. horse, in second year;—*a.* being a year old.—**year'-book** *n.* reference book of facts and statistics published yearly.—**leap year**, year of 366 days, occurring every fourth year [O.E. *gear*].

yearn (yẹrn) *v.i.* to seek earnestly; to feel longing or desire; to long for.—**yearn'ing** *n.* earnest desire; longing;—*a.* desirous.—**yearn'-ingly** *adv.* [O.E. *giernan*].

yeast (yēst) *n.* froth that rises on malt liquors during fermentation; vegetable growth causing this fermentation, used, esp. in bread-baking, as fermenting agent to raise dough.—**yeast'y** *a.* frothy; fermenting; restless.—**yeast'iness** *n.* [O.E. *gist*].

yelk (yelk) *n.* Same as **yolk.**

yell (yel) *v.i.* to cry out in a loud, shrill tone; to scream; to shriek;—*n.* a loud, shrill cry.—**yell'ing** *n.* [O.E. *gellan*].

yellow (yel-ō) *n.* primary colour; colour of gold, lemons, buttercups, etc.;—*a.* of this colour; (*Colloq.*) cowardly; mean; despicable; of newspaper sensational;—*v.t.* to make yellow;—*v.i.* to become yellow.—**yellow'owish, yell'owy** *a.* somewhat yellow.—**yell'owishness** *n.*—**yell'owness** *n.*—**yell'ow-back** *n.* formerly cheap novel, usually bound in yellow paper covers.—**yell'ow-fe'ver** *n.* infectious, tropical disease, characterised by a yellow skin, vomiting, etc.—**yell'ow-hamm'er** *n.* yellow song-bird; yellow-bunting.— **yell'ow-jack** *n.* (*Colloq.*) yellow-fever; yellow flag flown by ships, etc. in quarantine [O.E. *geolu*].

yelp (yelp) *n.* sharp, shrill bark or cry;—*v.i.* to utter such a bark or cry.—**yelp'er** *n.* [O.E. *gilpan*, to boast].

yen (yen) *n.* monetary unit of Japan; gold or silver coin [Jap.].

yeoman (yō-mạn) *n.* man owning and farming his own land; freeholder; middle-class farmer; officer of royal household; member of volunteer force of cavalry, orig. recruited from country; (*Navy*) petty officer in charge of signals.—*pl.* **yeo'men.**—**yeo'manly** *a.*—**yeo'manry** *n.* yeomen collectively.—**Yeoman of the Guard**, formerly, corps of veteran soldiers, employed on ceremonial occasions and as a royal bodyguard; now warders of Tower of London.—**yeoman service**, long and faithful service; effective aid [contr. of *young man*].

yerba (yẹr-bạ) *n.* Paraguay tea; maté [Sp. fr. L. *herba*, a herb].

yes (yes) *interj.* word expressing affirmation or consent.—**yes'-man** *n.* servile and obedient supporter [O.E. *gese*].

yester (yes-tẹr) *a.* (*Arch.*) pert. to yesterday; denoting period of time just past, esp. in compounds, e.g. 'yester-eve.'—**yes'terday** *n.* day before to-day;—*adv.* on the day before to-day.—**yes'ter-year** *n.* last year [O.E. *geostran*].

yet (yet) *adv.* in addition; besides; at the same time; still; at the present time; now; hitherto; at last; even; after all;—*conj.* nevertheless; moreover; notwithstanding.—**as yet**, up to the present time [O.E. *giet*].

yew (ū) *n.* cone-bearing, evergreen tree; its fine-grained wood, formerly used for making bows for archers [O.E. *iw*].

Yiddish (yid'-ish) *n.* a mixture of Middle German and High Hebrew, spoken by Jews;—*a.* pert. to or in this language.—**Yidd'isher** *n.* Jew.— (*Slang*) **Yid** *n.* Jew [Ger. *Judisch*, Jewish].

yield (yēld) *v.t.* to produce; to give in return, esp. for labour, investment, etc.; to bring forth; to concede; to surrender;—*v.i.* to submit; to comply; to give way; to produce; to bear;—*n.* amount produced; return for labour, investment, etc.; profit; crop.—**yield'ing** *a.*—**yield'ingly** *adv.* [O.E. *gieldan* to pay].

yodel, yodle (yō'-dl) *v.t.* and *v.i.* to sing or warble, with frequent changes from the natural voice to falsetto tone;—*n.* falsetto warbling.—**yo'deller, yo'deler** *n.* one who yodels [Ger. *jodeln*].

yoga (yō'-ga) *n.* system of Hindu philosophy; strict spiritual discipline practised to gain control over forces of one's own being, to gain occult powers, but chiefly to attain union with the Deity or Universal Spirit.—**yo'gi** *n.* one who practises yoga.—**yo'gism** *n.* [Sans.=union].

yoghourt (yō'-gòòrt) *n.* drink made from fermented milk. Also **ya'ourt** [Turk. *yoghurt*].

yoicks (yoiks) *interj.* old fox-hunting cry [etym. unknown].

yoke (yōk) *n.* wooden frame-work fastened over necks of two oxen, etc, to hold them together, and to which a plough, etc. is attached; anything having shape or use of a yoke; separately cut piece of material fitting closely over shoulders; bond or tie; emblem of submission; servitude; bondage; sway; dominion; couple of animals working together;—*v.t.* to put a yoke on; to couple or join, esp. to unite in marriage; to bring into servitude; to attach draft animal to vehicle;—*v.i.* to be joined; to match with [O.E. *geoc*].

yokel (yō'-kl) *n.* rustic; ploughman [etym. uncertain].

yolk (yōk) *n.* yellow part of egg [O.E. *geolca*].

yon (yon) *a.* that; those; yonder;—*adv.* yonder.—**yon'der** *a.* that or those there;—*adv.* at a distance within view [O.E. *geon*].

yore (yōr) *n.* the past; old times [O.E. *geara*, fr. *gear*, year].

york (york) *v.t.* to bowl out cricketer with yorker.—**york'er** *n.* ball so bowled that it hits ground directly under batter's bat [prob. conn. with *Yorkshire*].

Yorkshire (york'-shẹr) *n.* county in north of England.—**Yorkshire pudding,** batter baked in roasting tin along with meat.—**Yorkshire terrier,** small, shaggy terrier, resembling Skye terrier.

you (ū) *pron.* pronoun of second person in nominative or objective case, indicating person or persons addressed; also used indefinitely meaning, one, they, people in general.—**your** (ūr) *a.* gen. case of *you,* meaning, of you, pert. to you; generally used as possess. adj. meaning, belonging to you.—**yours** *pron.* possessive of *you,* when used absolutely, without following noun.—**yourself'** *pron.* your own person or self [often used for emphasis or as a reflexive).—*pl.* **yourselves'** [O.E. *eow, eower*].

young (yung) *a.* not far advanced in growth, life, or existence; not yet old; vigorous; immature;—*n.* offspring of animals.—**young'-ish** *a.* somewhat young.—**young'ling** *n.* young person or animal.—**young'ster** *n.* young person or animal; child; lad.—**with young,** pregnant [O.E. *geong*].

younker (yung'-kẹr) *n.* youngster; youth; stripling [Dut. *jonker,* fr. *jong,* young; *heer,* sir, gentleman].

youth (yòòth) *n.* state of being young; life from childhood to manhood; lad or young man; young persons collectively.—**youth'ful** *a.* possessing youth; pert. to youth; vigorous.—**youth'fully** *adv.*—**youth'fulness** *n.*—**youth hostels,** buildings providing accommodation for young persons on walking or cycling holidays [O.E. *geoguth*].

yowl (youl) *v.i.* to howl;—*n.* cry of a dog; long, mournful cry [M.E. *yowlen*].

Yo-yo (yō'-yō) *n.* toy consisting of flat spool with string wound round it, which when released from hand spins up and down string [Protected Trade Name].

ytterbium (i-tẹr'-bi-um) *n.* element discovered in gadolinite.—**ytter'bic** *a.* [fr. *Ytterby,* in Sweden].

yttrium (it'-ri-um) *n.* rare metal found at *Ytterby,* in Sweden.—**ytt'ria** *n.* oxide of yttrium.—**ytt'rious, ytt'ric** *a.*

Yucca (yuk'-a) *n.* genus of lilaceous plants, having tall, handsome flowers [W. Ind. name].

Yugo-Slav (yòò'-gō-slàv) *a.* pert. to *Yugo-Slavia,* the country of the Serbs, Croats, and Slovenes, in the N.W. of the Balkan Peninsula;—*n.* a native of Yugo-Slavia. Also **Ju'go-Slav.** [Slav. *jug,* the south].

yule (yòòl) *n.* feast of Christmas.—**yule'tide** *n.* season of Christmas.—**yule'-log** *n.* log of wood to burn on the open hearth at Christmas time [O.E. *geol*].

Z

zamba (zam'-ba) *n.* Latin-American dance [Sp. *zamba,* bandy-legged].

zamindar Same as **zemindar.**

zany (zā'-ni) *n.* formerly, buffoon who mimicked principal clown; simpleton.—**za'nyism** *n.* [corrupt. of It. *Giovanni*].

zareba (zạ-rē'-bạ) *n.* village in Sudan, protected by stockade against enemies and wild animals. Also **zari'ba, zeri'ba** [Ar. *zaribah,* an enclosure].

zeal (zēl) *n.* intense enthusiasm for cause or person; passionate ardour.—**zealot** (zel'-ot) *n.* fanatic; enthusiast.—**zeal'otry** *n.* fanaticism.—**zealous** (zel'-us) *a.* ardent; enthusiastic; earnest.—**zeal'ously** *adv.*—**zeal'ousness** *n.* [Gk. *zēlos,* ardour].

zebec (zē'-bek) *n.* Same as **xe'bec.**

zebra (zē'-brạ) *n.* genus of African quadrupeds of horse-family, with tawny coat striped with black.—**zebra crossing,** street crossing for pedestrians, marked with black and white lines [W. Afr.].

zebroid (zē'-broid) *n.* offspring of male zebra and mare. Also **zebru'la.**—**ze'brass** *n.* offspring of male zebra and she-ass.

zebu (zē'-bū) *n.* the humped Indian ox [Fr.].

zemindar (zem'-in-dar) *n.* Indian landowner paying rent direct to the Government. Also **zam'indar.**—**zam'indary** *a.* [Pers.—a landowner].

zenana (ze-nà'-nạ) *n.* women's apartments in Hindu household, equivalent to Moslem harem [Pers. *zan,* woman].

Zend (zend) *n.* interpretation of the *Avesta,* sacred writings of Zoroastrians; Iranian language in which Zend-Avesta is written.—**Zend'-Avest'a** *n.* sacred writings and commentary thereon (Zend) of Zoroastrians [Pers. *Avistak va Zand,* text and commentary].

zenith (zen'-ith) *n.* point of heavens directly above observer's head; summit; height of success; acme; climax.—**zen'ithal** *a.* [Ar. *samt.* path].

zephyr (zef'-ir) *n.* west wind; gentle breeze; fine, soft woollen fabric [Gk. *zephuros,* west wind].

Zeppelin (zep'-e-lin) *n.* cigar-shaped long-range dirigible German airship [fr. Count *Zeppelin,* inventor].

zero (zē'-rō) *n.* nought; cipher; neutral fixed point from which graduated scale is measured, as on thermometer, barometer, etc.; (*Fig.*) lowest point.—*pl.* **zer'os.**—**zero hour,** precise moment at which military offensive, etc. is timed to begin; crucial moment [Ar. *cifr.* a cipher].

Zeta (zē'-ta) *n.* Name of experimental thermonuclear apparatus which, it is hoped, will be used for controlling the energy obtained from changing of light nuclei into heavy nuclei, and channelling it for useful purposes. (from Zero Energy Thermo'-nuclear Assembly).

zest (zest) *n.* orig. piece of orange or lemon peel; relish; fillip; stimulus; keen pleasure.—**zest'ful** *a.* [O.Fr. *zeste,* lemon peel].

zeugma (zūg'-mạ) *n.* condensed sentence in which word, such as a verb, is used with two nouns to one of which only it applies.—**zeugmat'ic** *a.* [Gk. *zeugnunai,* to yoke].

Zeus (zūs) *n.* in Greek mythology, chief deity and father of gods and men, his seat being Mt. Olympus [Gk.].

zigzag (zig'-zag) *n.* line with short sharp turns;—*a.* forming zig-zag;—*v.i.* to form, or move with, short sharp turns.—*pr.p.* **zig'zagging.**—*pa.p.* **zig'zagged.**—*adv.* [Ger. *Zacke,* sharp point].

zinc (zingk) *n.* hard, bluish-metal used in alloys, esp. brass, and because of its resistance to corrosion, for galvanising iron;—*v.t.* to coat with zinc, to galvanise.—*pr.p.* **zinck'ing** or **zinc'ing.**—*pa.t.* and *pa.p.* **zincked** or **zinced.**—**zinc alloys** (*Met.*) alloys containing percentage of zinc, as brass, etc.—**zinc'ic** *a.* pert. to zinc.—**zincif'erous, zinckif'erous** *a.* containing zinc.—**z nc'o** *n.* (*Abbrev.*) of zincograph waxed-zinc engraving plate for etching; print of this;—*v.t.* to etch zinc plate with acid.—**zincog'raph** *n.* See **zinco.**—**zincog'rapher** *n.*—**zincograph'ic** *a.*—**zinco'graphy** *n.* process of engraving on zinc by method employed for wood-cuts.—**zinc'oid** *a.* resembling zinc.—**zinc'otype** *n.* zincograph.—**zinc'ous** *a.* pert. to zinc [Ger. *Zink,* zinc].

Zingaro (zing'-gạ-rō) *n.* Italian name for gipsy.—*fem.* **Zing'ara,**—*pl.* **Zing'ari, Zing'are.**

zinnia (zin'-i-a) *n.* plant with bright-coloured flowers like an aster [fr. *Zinn,* a German botanist].

Zion (zī'-on) *n.* hill in Jerusalem; town of Jerusalem; Church of God; heaven.—**Zi'onism** *n.* movement among Jews to create Jewish National Home in Palestine.—**Zi'onist** *n.* advocate of Zionism [Heb. *tsiyon,* a hill].

zip (zip) *n.* whizzing sound, as of bullet in air; (*Slang*) energy;—*v.t.* to shut with a zipper.—**zip fastener**, device of interlocking, flexible 'teeth' opened and shut by sliding clip. Also **zip'per** *n.* [imit.].

zircon (zirʹkon) *n.* silicate of zirconium occurring in crystals and including jacinth, jargoon, hyacinth.—**zirco'nium** *n.* metal obtained from zircon, and resembling titanium [Ar. *zarqun*, vermilion].

zither (zithʹẹr) *n.* flat, stringed instrument comprising resonance box with strings. Also **zith'ern** [Ger.].

zloty (zloʹti) *n.* Polish coin valued, in normal currency, at 10d. [Pol.].

zoanthropy (zō-anʹthrō-pi) *n.* form of monomania in which man believes himself to be one of the lower animals [Gk. *zōon*, animal; *anthropos*, man].

zodiac (zōʹdi-ak) *n.* (*Astron.*) imaginary belt in heavens following path of sun, and divided into twelve equal areas containing twelve constellations, each represented by appropriate symbols, called the *signs of the zodiac*; namely Aries (*Ram*), Taurus (*Bull*), Gemini (*Twins*), Cancer (*Crab*), Leo (*Lion*), Virgo (*Virgin*), Libra (*Balance*), Scorpio (*Scorpion*), Sagittarius (*Archer*), Capricornus (*Goat*), Aquarius (*Water-bearer*),Pisces (*Fishes*) —**zodi'acal** *a.* [Gk. *zōdiakos*, fr. *zōon*, animal].

zoiatria (zō-i-atʹri-ạ) *n.* veterinary science [Gk. *zōon*, an animal; *iatreia*, healing].

zoic (zōʹik) *a.* pert. to, or having, animal life; (*Geol.*) containing fossilised animals [Gk. *zōon*, animal].

zombie, zombi (zomʹbi) *n.* orig. in Africa, deity of the python, in West Indies, corpse alleged to have been revived by black magic; the power which enters such a body. (W. African *zumbi*, fetish).

zone (zōn) *n.* girdle; climatic or vegetation belt; one of five belts into which earth is divided by latitude lines, as *frigid zone* of Arctic and Antarctic, *torrid zone* between Tropics of Cancer and Capricorn, *temperate zone* north of Tropic of Cancer and south of Tropic of Capricorn;—*v.t.* to enclose; to divide into zones; to divide country into regional areas.—**zo'nal** *a.* pert. to or divided into zones.—**zoned** *a.* having zones; distributed regionally [Gk. *zonē*, a girdle].

Zoo (zȯȯ) *n.* (*Colloq.*) Zoological Gardens.

zoo- (zōʹō) *prefix* (derived from Greek word *zōon*, animal) used in compound words, such as *zoochemistry*, *zoogeny*, etc.

zoochemistry (zō-ō-kemʹis-tri) *n.* chemistry of constituents of animal body [Gk. *zōon*, animal; and *chemistry*].

zoodynamics (zō-ō-dī-namʹiks) *n.* science of animal physiology.

zoogeny (zō-ojʹẹn-i) *n.* doctrine of origin of living creatures. Also **zoog'ony**.—**zoogen'ic** *a.* [Gk. *zōon*, animal; *genesis*, production].

zoogeography (zō-ō-jē-ogʹrạ-fi) *n.* science which treats of the regional distribution of animals in the world.—**zoogeog'rapher** *n.*—**zoogeograph'ic, -al** *a.*

zooid (zōʹoid) *a.* resembling an animal;—*n.* organism capable of relatively independent existence; a compound organism [Gk. *zōon*, an animal; *eidos*, a form].

zoolatry (zō-olʹạ-tri) *n.* animal worship.—**zool'ater** *n.*—**zool'atrous** *a.* [Gk. *zōon*, animal; *latreia*, worship].

zoolite (zōʹō-līt) *n.* fossil animal. Also **zool'ith.** —**zoolith'ic, zoolit'ic** *a.* [Gk. *zōon*, animal; *lithos*, stone].

zoology (zȯȯ-, zō-olʹo-ji) *n.* natural history of animals, part of science of biology.—**zoolog'ical** *a.*—**zoolog'ically** *adv.*—**zool'ogist** *n.* one versed in zoology.—**zoological gardens,** large park where wild animals are kept for exhibition [Gk. *zōon*, animal; *logos*, discourse].

zoom (zȯȯm) *n.*—*v.i.* (of prices) to become inflated; (of aircraft) to turn suddenly upwards at sharp angle [imit.].

zoon (zōʹon) *n*, individual animal; complete product of fertilised germ.—*pl.* **zo'a, zo'ons.**—**zo'onic** *a.* pert. to animals [Gk. *zōon*, animal].

zoonomy (zō-onʹō-mi) *n.* science which treats of animal life. Also **zoono'mia.**—**zoonom'ic** *a.*—**zoon'omist** *n.* [Gk. *zōon*, animal; *nomos*, law].

zoophagous (zō-ofʹạ-gus) *a.* feeding on animals; carnivorous. Also **zooph'agan** [Gk. *zōon*, animal; *phagein*, to eat].

zoophilist (zō-ofʹil-ist) *n.* lover of animals.—**zooph'ily** *n.* love of animals [Gk. *zōon*, animal; *philos*, fond of].

zoophyte (zōʹō-fīt) *n.* plant-like animal, such as sponge.—**zoophyt'ic, -al** *a.* pert. to zoophytes.—**zoophytol'ogy** *n.* study of zoophytes [Gk. *zōon*, animal; *phuton*, plant].

zoot suit (zootʹsoot) *n.* (*U.S.*) flashy type of man's suit, generally with padded shoulders, fitted waist, knee-length jacket and tight trousers (Orig. unknown).

Zoroastrian (zō-rō-asʹtri-ạn) *n.* follower of Zoroaster;—*a.* pert. to Zoroaster or his religion;—**zoroas'trianism** *n.* ancient Persian religious doctrine taught by Zoroaster, principal feature of which is the recognition of the dual principle of good and evil; religion of the Parsees [fr. L. corrupt. of Persian *Zarathustra*].

Zouave (zȯȯ-ȧv') *n.* soldier of French light infantry corps, orig. recruited from Algeria, its members wearing Moorish dress [fr. *Zouaoua*, tribe in Algeria].

zounds (zoundz) *interj.* of anger and surprise [corrupt. of *God's wounds*].

zuccheta (tsȯȯk-ketʹa) *n.* skull cap worn by R.C. ecclesiastics, and differing in colour according to rank of wearer. Also **zucchet'to** [It. *zucca*, a gourd].

Zulu (zȯȯʹlȯȯ) *n.* member of Bantu tribe of S. Africa;—*a.* pert. to Zulus or to Zululand [Native].

zygal (zīʹgạl) *a.* pert. to a yoke; formed like the letter H [Gk. *zugon*, a yoke].

zygon (zīʹgon) *n.* yoke; H-shaped fissure [Gk.].

zyme (zīm) *n.* ferment; leaven; disease-germ. —**zy'mic** *a.*—**zymic acid,** impure lactic acid.—**zy'mogen** *n.* any substance producing fermentation.—**zymogen'ic** *a.*—**zy'moid** *a.* resembling ferment.—**zymo'sis** *n.* fermentation. —**zymot'ic** *a.* pert. to or caused by fermentation.—**zymot'ically** *adv.*—**zymotic disease,** infectious or contagious disease caused by germs introduced into body from without [Gk. *zumē*, leaven].

FOREIGN WORDS AND PHRASES

ab (L.) from.—**ab extra**, from outside.—**ab initio**, from the beginning.—**ab intra**, from within.—**ab origine**, from the origin; from the beginning.
à bas (Fr.) down with!
à bon marché (Fr.) at a bargain; cheap.
absit (L.) lit. 'let him be absent'; hence, a permit or pass to be absent from college quarters during the night.—**absit invidia**, lit. 'let envy be absent'; all envy apart.—**absit omen**, let this not be an ill omen.
accessit (L.) he came next; he followed.
Achtung (Ger.) give heed; look out; beware; danger.
ad astra (L.) to the stars.
à deux (Fr.) for two; between two.
ad extremum (L.) to the extreme.
ad finem (L.) to the end; towards the end.
ad hoc (L.) lit. 'for this'; for a special purpose; for a particular occasion (as, an *ad hoc* committee).
ad infinitum (L.) to infinity; without end.
ad interim (L.) in the meanwhile; for the time being.
ad libitum (L.) lit. 'to what is desired'; at pleasure; at will; freely. Abbrev. **ad lib.**
ad nauseam (L.) to the point of disgust; enough to make one sick.
ad referendum (L.) for further consideration.
adsum (L.) lit. 'I am present'; at roll-call, esp. in a University class, 'Present!'
ad summum (L.) to the highest point.
ad valorem (L.) according to the value.
ad verbum (L.) lit. 'to the word'; word for word.
ad vitam aut culpam (L.) lit. 'for life or fault'; for life or till grave misdemeanour be proved.
aequo animo (L.) lit. 'with an equable mind'; with equanimity.
aetatis (L.) at the age of. Abbrev. **aet.**, or **aetat.**
affaire d'amour (Fr.) a love affair.—**affaire de coeur**, an affair of the heart.—**affaire d'honneur**, an affair of honour; a duel.
à fond (Fr.) lit. 'to the bottom'; thoroughly.
a fortiori (L.) with stronger or greater reason.
agent provocateur (Fr.) a police spy or secret service agent who professes sympathy with a suspected person in order to incite him to commit an incriminating act.
à la, à l' (Fr.) in the . . . manner, fashion, style, e.g. **à la française**, in the French manner.
à la carte (Fr.) unrestricted choice from the bill of fare or menu in a restaurant, hotel, etc.
à la mode (Fr.) in the fashion; fashionable.
alea jacta est (L.) the die is cast.
al fresco (It.) in the open air.
alma mater (L.) lit. 'a mild, gentle, benign mother,' a term used by students to designate the University, etc. at which they were educated.
à l'outrance (Fr.) to the utmost; with desperation; to the bitter end.
alter ego (L.) lit. 'another I'; one's second self; a close friend.
amor patriae (L.) love of one's native land.—**amor vincit omnia**, love conquers all things.
amour-propre (Fr.) lit. 'self-love'; exaggerated self-esteem; readiness to take offence at slights; conceit; vanity.
ancien régime (Fr.) lit. 'the old rule'; the old form of government.
anno Domini (L.) in the year of our Lord. Abbrev. A.D.
annus mirabilis (L.) a wonderful year; a year of wonders.
ante meridiem (L.) before midday. Abbrev. **a.m.**
a posteriori (L.) lit. 'from the latter'; from effect to cause; by experiment.
après moi le déluge (Fr.) lit. 'after me the deluge'; posterity is no concern of mine.
a priori (L.) lit. 'from the former'; from cause to effect.
à propos (Fr.) to the purpose; opportunely; timely.—**à propos de**, concerning.
aqua (L.) water.—**aqua vitae**, the water of life; brandy.
argumentum ad hominem lit. 'an argument to the man'; an attack on the professed principles, character, etc. of an opponent.
arrière-pensée (Fr.) lit. 'a rear thought'; dissembled thought; mental reservation; ulterior motive.
ars est celare artem (L.) true art is to conceal art.—**ars longa, vita brevis**, art is long, life is short.
auberge (Fr.) an inn; a hostel.—**aubergiste**, an innkeeper.
au contraire (Fr.) on the contrary.
au courant (Fr.) lit. 'in the stream'; aware of; acquainted with; well-informed.
audaces fortuna juvat (L.) fortune favours the bold.
au fait (Fr.) well acquainted with; having expert knowledge; well-informed.
auf Wiedersehen (Ger.) till we meet again; good-bye; farewell.
au revoir (Fr.) till we meet again; good-bye.
autres temps, autres moeurs (Fr.) other times, other customs.
aut vincere, aut mori (L.) either to conquer or to die; victory or death.
avant-coureur (Fr.) a forerunner; a precursor; a harbinger.—**avant-garde**, the vanguard.—**avant-goût**, a foretaste.
ave (L.) hail!—**ave atque vale**, hail and farewell!—**ave, imperator, morituri te salutant**, hail, emperor! those about to die salute thee.—**ave Maria**, hail Mary!
à votre santé (Fr.) lit. 'to your health'; good health!

bain-marie (Fr.) (*Cookery*) boiling water in which is placed a saucepan containing food, sauces, etc., to be kept warm; a double saucepan.
ballon d'essai (Fr.) lit. 'a trial balloon'; a statement circulated in order to test opinion; a feeler.
bas bleu (Fr.) a blue-stocking; a literary lady.
battue (Fr.) slaughter of game on a large scale.
beatae memoriae (L.) of blessed memory.
beau (Fr.) beautiful; fine.
beaux-arts (Fr.) the fine arts.
bel esprit (Fr.) a person of wit or genius; a clever person.—*pl.* **beaux esprits.**
belles-lettres (Fr.) literature; learning.
ben trovato (It.) lit. 'well found'; cleverly invented or imagined.—**ben venuto**, welcome!
berceau (Fr.) a cradle.—**berceuse**, a cradle-song; a lullaby.
bête (Fr.) a beast; a stupid creature; a simpleton.—**bête noire**, lit. 'a black beast'; a bugbear; a pet aversion.
billet-doux (Fr.) a love-letter.—*pl.* **billets-doux.**
bis (L.) twice; (*Mus.*) repeat; (Fr.) encore!—**bis dat qui cito dat** (L.) he gives twice who gives quickly.
blasé (Fr.) indifferent; bored.
Blut und Eisen (Ger.) blood and iron (the essence of the doctrine of Bismarck).
Bock (Ger.) a kind of lager beer; a glass of beer.
bombe (Fr.) (*Cookery*) a cone-shaped dessert sweet, usually an ice.
bon (Fr.) good.—**bon marché**, cheap.—**bon mot**, a witty saying.

bona fide (L.) in good faith.—**bona fides,** good faith; integrity.
bon gré, mal gré (Fr.) lit. 'willing or unwilling'; willy-nilly.
bonjour (Fr.) good-morning; good-day;—**bonsoir,** good-evening; good-night.
bonne (Fr.) a nursemaid; a general servant.
bonne bouche (Fr.) a choice morsel.
bouillabaisse (Fr.) a kind of fish stew, a speciality of the south of France.
bourse (Fr.) a purse.—**Bourse,** the Stock Exchange.
boutique (Fr.) a shop.
boutonnière (Fr.) a buttonhole; a posy for the buttonhole.
brasserie (Fr.) a brewery; a common term for a café-restaurant.
brava (It.) well done; splendid.
buon giorno (It.) good-morning; good-day.—**buona notte,** good-night.—**buona sera,** good-evening.

caballero (Sp.) a gentleman.
café (Fr.) coffee.
camarade (Fr.) a comrade.—**camaraderie,** comradeship.
camarilla (Sp.) a political clique.
campo santo (It.) lit. 'holy ground'; an Italian cemetery; a burial-ground.
canaille (Fr.) the rabble; the mob; the scum of the earth.
cantabile (It.) lit. 'fit to be sung'.
capias (L.) lit. 'take thou'; a writ for the arrest of a person.
carte [Fr.) a card; the bill of fare; the menu.—**carte blanche,** lit. 'a blank sheet of paper'; a free hand.
casus belli [L.) a plea for going to war; any act, occurrence, etc. serious enough to justify a declaration of war.
cause célèbre (Fr.) lit. 'a celebrated case'; a celebrated, and usually sensational, lawsuit.
cavaliere servente (It.) lit. 'a serving gentleman'; one who is always dancing attendance on ladies; a lady's man.
caveat actor (L.) lit. 'let the doer beware'.
cave canem (L.) beware of the dog.
cela va sans dire (Fr.) 'that goes without saying'; it's agreed; naturally.
c'est-à-dire (Fr.) 'that is to say'; namely.
certiorari (L.) lit. 'to be made more certain'; a writ ordering a case to be brought before a higher court.
cetera desunt (L.) lit. 'other things are missing'; the rest is awanting.
ceteris paribus (L.) other things being equal.
c'est magnifique, mais ce n'est pas la guerre (Fr.) it's magnificent, but it isn't war.
château (Fr.) a country-seat; a mansion-house in the country.—*pl.* **châteaux.**
chef de cuisine (Fr.) the head-cook, gen. **chef** alone.—**chef d'oeuvre,** a masterpiece; an unrivalled performance.
chemin de fer (Fr.) lit. 'road of iron'; a railway. Also the card-game of baccarat.
cherchez la femme (Fr.) lit. 'look for the woman' [implying the powerful, but secret, influence of women in many matters].
che sarà, sarà (It.) what will be, will be.
chevalier (Fr.) a knight.—**Chevalier de la Légion d'Honneur,** Knight of the Legion of Honour.
chevaux de frise (Fr.) lit. 'Friesland horses'; an old-time military defence against cavalry, consisting of a rampart of sharpened stakes.
ci-gît (Fr.) 'here lies,' as an inscription on a tombstone [fr. *ici*, here; *gésir*, to lie].
cogito ergo sum (L.) I think, therefore I am (i.e. I exist) [the essence of Descartes' philosophy].
coiffeur (Fr.) a hairdresser.
comitas inter gentes (L.) lit. 'politeness between nations'; international courtesy.
comme il faut (Fr.) 'as it should be'; correct; proper.
commune bonum (L.) a common good.
compos mentis (L.) of sound mind; sane.—**non compos mentis,** not of sound mind.
compte rendu (Fr.) lit. 'an account rendered'; a detailed report, esp. of a meeting, lecture, etc.
con (It.) with.—**con amore,** with love; with zeal; enthusiastically.—**con brio,** with spirit; lively.—**con dolore,** with grief.—**con spirito,** with spirit.
concours (Fr.) a competition.
conditio sine qua non (L.) an indispensable condition.
confer (L.) compare. Abbrev. **cf.**
confiteor (L.) I confess.
confrère (Fr.) a colleague.
congé (Fr.) dismissal; leave of absence; a short holiday.
conseil (Fr.) a council.—**conseil d'état,** a council of state; a Privy Council.
consommé (Fr.) (*Cookery*) a clear soup.
contra (L.) against, contrary to.—**contra bonos mores,** contrary to good manners or morals; a breach of good manners.
contretemps (Fr.) a mischance; a mishap; a hitch; an untoward event.
convenances (Fr.) the proprieties; conventions; common decency; decorum.
corps (Fr.) a body.—**corps de ballet,** the dancers of a ballet.
corpus (L.) the body.—**corpus delicti,** lit. 'the body of the crime'; the essence or substance of the offence.
cosi fan tutte (It.) lit. 'so do all (women)'; what else can you expect from a woman?
coup (Fr.) a stroke.—**coup d'essai,** a trial stroke; a first attempt.—**coup d'état,** lit. 'a stroke of state (policy)'; extraordinary measures taken by a government when the safety of the state is in danger; also, and now more commonly, the sudden, and often violent, overthrow of government by unconstitutional methods.—**coup de grâce,** 'a stroke of mercy'; formerly, the stroke which finished the sufferings of those broken on the wheel; the fatal blow.
couturière (Fr.) a dressmaker.
credenda (L.) things to be believed; creeds; tenets.
crème (Fr.) cream.—**crème de la crème,** 'the cream of the cream'; the very best.—**crème de menthe,** a peppermint-flavoured, green-coloured liqueur.
croûtons (Fr.) (*Cookery*) cubes of toast for serving with soup.
crimen laesae majestatis (L.) lit. the 'crime of injuring majesty,' i.e. the Sovereign; high treason; lèse-majesté.
cui bono? (L.) who gains by it? to whose advantage is it?
cum grano salis (L.) with a grain of salt; with due allowance for exaggeration, inaccuracy, etc.
custos (L.) a keeper; a guardian.

da capo (It.) (*Mus.*) repeat from the beginning. Abbrev. **D.C.**
d'accord (Fr.) agreed.
danse (Fr.) a dance.—**danseuse,** a female dancer.—**danse macabre,** lit. 'a ghastly dance'; a dance of death.
de bonne grâce (Fr.) willingly; with a good grace.
déclassé (Fr.) (*fem.* **déclassée**) one who has come down in the world.
de facto (L.) in fact; actual; actually.
défense (Fr.) prohibition; a forbidding.—**défense d'afficher,** post no bills.—**défense d'entrer,** no admittance.—**défense de fumer,** no smoking.
defensor fidei (L.) defender of the faith. Abbrev. **F.D.** or **Fid. Def.**
de gustibus non est disputandum (L.) there is no disputing about tastes.
de haut en bas (Fr.) lit. 'from top to bottom'; contemptuously; in a condescending manner.
Dei gratia (L.) by the grace of God. Abbrev. **Dei Gra.**
déjeuner (Fr.) breakfast or lunch.—**petit déjeuner,** little breakfast (coffee and rolls).
de jure (L.) in law; rightful; rightfully.
delenda est Carthago (L.) lit. 'Carthage

must be destroyed'; often used as an injunction to exterminate or to take extreme measures against. [del.
delineavit (L.) (*Art.*) (he) drew this. Abbrev.
de luxe (Fr.) luxurious; sumptuous.
de mal en pis (Fr.) from bad to worse.
démarche (Fr.) a diplomatic measure or step.
démodé (Fr.) out of fashion; antiquated.
de mortuis nil nisi bonum (L.) (speak) nothing but good of the dead.
de nouveau (Fr.) afresh.—**de novo** (L.) afresh.
Deo gratias (L.) thanks be to God.—**Deo volente**, God willing. Abbrev. **D.V.**
de profundis (L.) out of the depths (of sorrow).
de rigueur (Fr.) obligatory; indispensable; demanded by etiquette.
dernier cri (Fr.) lit. 'the latest cry'; the latest fashion; the very latest.
de trop (Fr.) superfluous; out of place; unwanted; in the way.
deus ex machina (L.) lit. 'a god out of the machine' (in the stage effects of the classical theatre); hence, a divine intervention; an artificial literary device to resolve the difficulties of a drama.
Deus vobiscum! (L.) God be with you!
Deus vult! (L.) God wills it!
dies irae (L.) the day of wrath.—**Dies Irae**, the day of judgment.
Dieu et mon droit (Fr.) God and my right (motto of the sovereigns of Great Britain).
distingué (Fr.) (*fem.* **distinguée**) distinguished-looking; of aristocratic bearing.
distrait (Fr.) (*fem.* **distraite**) absent-minded.
divertissement (Fr.) amusement; a light interlude; entertainment. [rule.
divide et impera (L.) divide (your rivals) and
Dominus noster (L.) our Lord.—**Dominus vobiscum**, the Lord be with you.
(la) donna è mobile (It.) woman is fickle.
droit (Fr.) legal right; moral right.
duce (It.) a leader.
dulce et decorum est pro patria mori (L.) it is sweet and noble to die for one's country.
dum spiro, spero (L.) so long as I breathe, I hope; while there's life there's hope.

embarras de choix (Fr.) lit. 'embarrassment of choice'; so many as to make choice difficult.—**embarras de richesse(s)**, a superfluity of good things.
en (Fr.) in; while.—**en avant**! forward! onward! —**en clair**, in clear (language), i.e. not in code. —**en déshabillé**, in undress.—**en famille**, within the family circle; by themselves.—**en fête**, making holiday.—**en masse**, in a body.—**en passant**, in passing; by the way; casually.
enfant (Fr.) a child.—**enfant gâté**, a spoiled child.—**enfant prodigue**, a prodigal son.—**enfant terrible**, a child who makes ill-timed or embarrassing remarks.
entre (Fr.) between.—**entre nous**, between ourselves; in confidence.
e pluribus unum (L.) one out of many.
errare est humanum (L.) to err is human.
Ersatz (Ger.) a substitute;—*a.* synthetic.
esse (L.) to be.—**in esse**, in existence.
esto perpetua (L.) be thou perpetual (often applied to The Church).
et alia or **alii** (L.) and others. Abbrev. **et a.**—**et alibi**, and elsewhere.
e tenebris lux (L.) light out of darkness.
et hoc genus omne (L.) and everything of this kind.
et sequens (L.) and the following. Abbrev. **et seq.**—**et sequentes**, and those that follow. Abbrev. **et seqq.**
et sic de similibus (L.) and so of everything of a like nature.
et tu, Brute! (L.) you too, Brutus! (words of Julius Caesar on realising his betrayal by his well-loved friend, Brutus).
eureka (Gk.) lit. 'I have found it' (the exclamation of Archimedes when he discovered a method of measuring the purity of the gold in King Hiero's crown); hence, an exclamation of triumph on making a discovery.
ex (L.) out of; from.—**ex animo**, sincerely; heartily.—**ex cathedra**, 'from the chair or pulpit'; authoritatively.—**ex gratia**, as a favour (not as a legal right).—**ex hypothesi**, from the assumption; hypothetically.—**ex libris**, lit. 'from the books'; from the library (of). Abbrev. **ex lib.**—**ex officio**, by virtue of one's office; officially.—**ex parte**, on one side only; one-sided; biased.—**ex post facto**, retrospective.
exempli gratia (L.) by way of example; for instance. Abbrev. **e.g.**
exeunt omnes (L.) all go out (a stage direction).
experto crede (L.) believe one who speaks from experience.
extra (L.) beyond, outside of.—**extra judicium**, out of court.—**extra muros**, beyond the walls.

facile princeps (L.) easily the first.—**facillime princeps**, by far the most distinguished.
facta non verba (L.) deeds, not words.
factum est (L.) it is done.
fait accompli (Fr.) an accomplished fact.
faites votre jeu (vos jeux), messieurs! (Fr.) put down your stakes, gentlemen! (the croupier's words at the gaming-table).
farce (Fr.) (*Cookery*) force-meat, esp. as stuffing.—**farci**, stuffed.
faubourg (Fr.) a suburb.
faute de mieux (Fr.) for want of something better.
faux pas (Fr.) lit. a 'false step'; an embarrassing remark; a tactless action.
fecit (L.) he (she) did it (used in artists' signatures).—*pl.* **fecerunt**.
felo de se (L.L.) lit. 'a felon of himself'; suicide; a suicide.
femme (Fr.) a woman; a wife.—**femme de chambre**, a chambermaid.
festa (It.) a festival; a fête.
festina lente (L.) hasten slowly.
feu (Fr.) fire;—*pl.* **feux**.—**feu de joie**, a bonfire; a salute of guns in token of joy.
fiat justitia, ruat coelum (L.) let justice be done, though the heavens fall.
fiat lux (L.) let there be light.
fide non armis (L.) by faith, not by arms.
Fidei Defensor (L.) Defender of the Faith (one of the titles of British monarchs). Abbrev. **Fid Def.**
fides et justitia (L.) fidelity and justice.
fides Punica (L.) Punic (i.e. Carthaginian) faith; treachery.
fille (Fr.) girl; daughter.—**fille de joie**, a prostitute.—**fille d'honneur**, a maid of honour.
fin de siècle (Fr.) lit. 'the end of the century' (i.e. 19th cent.); decadent.
flagrante delicto (L.) in the very act; with full evidence of guilt.
floreat! (L.) let it flourish!
foie gras (Fr.) lit. 'fat liver' (of goose) made into **pâté de foie gras**.
force majeure (Fr.) lit. 'superior force'; compelling circumstances; coercion.
fortiter in re, suaviter in modo (L.) firmly in action, pleasantly in manner.
fortuna favet fatuis (L.) Fortune favours fools.
frappé (Fr.) (*Cookery*) iced; cooled.
Frau (Ger.) a married woman; Mrs.; abbrev. Fr.—*pl.* **Frauen**.—**Fräulein**, an unmarried woman; Miss. Abbrev. Frl.—*pl.* (the same.)
frisette (Fr.) a fringe of hair.—**friseur**, lit. a 'curler'; a hairdresser.
frit (Fr.) (*fem.* **frite**) fried.
fugit irreparabile tempus (L.) time, that cannot be recalled, flies away.
furor loquendi (L.) a mania for speaking.—**furor scribendi**, a mania for writing.

galant (Fr.) gay; elegant; attentive to ladies. —**galanterie**, politeness, esp. to ladies.
garçon (Fr.) a boy; a waiter; a bachelor.

garni (Fr.) furnished (of a room, lodgings, etc.); garnished (of a dish).—**garniture**, trimmings, esp. of a dish.
gasconnade (Fr.) boasting; bragging; drawing the long bow.
Gasthaus (Ger.) an inn; a hotel.—**Gasthof**, a hotel.
gaudeamus igitur (L.) let us therefore [rejoice.
gloria (L.) glory.—**gloria in excelsis**, glory to God in the highest.—**gloria Patri**, glory be to the Father.
Glück (Ger.) happiness; fortune; luck; chance.—**glücklich**, happy; fortunate.—**Glückliches Neujahr!** a happy (prosperous) New Year.—**Glückliche Reise!** a safe journey to you! Bon voyage!
Gott (Ger.) God; a god.—*pl.* **Götter**, the gods.—**Gott mit uns**, God with us (the motto of Germany under the Kaisers).—**Götterdämmerung**, the twilight of the gods.
grâce à Dieu! (Fr.) thanks to God!
gradus (L.) a step.—**gradatim**, gradually; by degrees.—**gradus ad Parnassum**, a step or way to Parnassus (the abode of the Muses); a textbook for teaching Latin versification.
grand (Fr.) great.—**grand seigneur**, a great lord.—**grand siècle**, lit. a 'great century.'
grande (Fr.) *fem.* of **grand**, great.—**grande passion**, passionate love; infatuation.
gut (Ger.) good.—**Guten Abend!** Good evening!—**Guten Morgen!** Good morning!—**Gute Nacht!** Good night!—**Guten Tag!** Good day!

habitué (Fr.) a frequenter; habitual visitor; regular attender.
hachis (Fr.) hash; mincemeat.
hacienda (Sp.) a landed estate; a ranch.
Hausfrau (Ger.) a housewife.
haut (Fr.) high.—**hauteur**, height; haughtiness; arrogance.—**haut ton**, the fashionable world.
Heil! (Ger.) hail!
Herr (Ger.) a gentleman; Mr.; master; lord.—*pl.* **Herren**.—**Der Herr**, the Lord; God.
hic et ubique (L.) here and everywhere.
hic jacet (L.) here lies (on tombstones).
hoi polloi (Gk.) the many; the common herd; the vulgar mob.
homme propose, mais Dieu dispose (Fr.) man proposes, but God disposes.
homo sapiens (L.) man the thinker; man as a species.
honi soit qui mal y pense (O.Fr.) evil be to him who evil thinks (the motto of the Order of the Garter). *Honi* ought to be spelt *honni*.
honoris causa (L.) lit. 'for the sake of honour'; as a mark of honour; honorary.
horribile dictu (L.) horrible to relate.
hors (Fr.) outside; beyond.—**hors concours**, not competing (for a prize).—**hors de combat**, unfit to fight; disabled.—**hors d'oeuvre**, a dish of assorted appetisers served before the first course.
hôtel (Fr.) a hotel; a mansion; a public building.—**Hôtel de Ville**, the town-hall.
humanum est errare (L.) to err is human.

ibidem (L.) in the same place; in the same passage. Abbrev. **ib.** or **ibid.**
ici on parle français (Fr.) French spoken here.
idée fixe (Fr.) lit. 'a fixed idea'; an obsession; a recurring theme in music.
idem (L.) the same. Abbrev. **id.**
id est (L.) that is. Abbrev. **i.e.**
Iesus Hominum Salvator (L.) Jesus, the Saviour of Men. Abbrev. **I.H.S.**—**Iesus Nazarenus, Rex Iudaeorum**, Jesus of Nazareth, King of the Jews. Abbrev. **I.N.R.I.**
il penseroso (It.) the thoughtful man.
imperator (L.) emperor.
imperium in imperio (L.) a government existing within another government; a body existing under, but wholly independent of, a superior body.
in (L.) in.—**in absentia**, in absence.—**in articulo mortis**, at the point of death.—**in camera**, in the (judge's) room instead of in open court; in secret.—**in esse**, in being; actual.—**in excelsis**, in the highest.—**in initio**, in the beginning; at the outset.—**in loco**, in the (proper) place; on the spot.—**in loco parentis**, in the position of a parent.—**in memoriam**, in, or to, the memory (of).—**in nomine Dei**, in the name of the Lord.—**in perpetuum**, for ever and ever; in perpetuity.—**in re**, in the matter of.—**in rerum natura**, in the nature of things.—**in situ**, in its (original) position.—**in toto**, totally; wholly.—**in transitu**, progressing; on its passage; in transit (of goods).
incredibile dictu (L.) unbelievable to tell; marvellous to relate.
Index Expurgatorius (L.) a list of books whose publication is prohibited (by the R.C. Church) until certain passages have been expunged or corrected.—**Index Librorum Prohibitorum**, a list of books strictly forbidden to be read by Roman Catholics.
infra dignitatem (L.) beneath one's dignity; undignified. Abbrev. **infra dig.**
in hoc signo vinces (L.) in this sign thou shalt conquer.
instanter (L.) instantly; at once.
inter (L.) between; among.—**inter alia**, among other things.
intra muros (L.) within the walls.
in vino veritas (L.) in wine truth (comes out).
ipse dixit (L.) he himself said it;—*n.* a dogmatic assertion.—**ipsissima verba**, the very words (used); the actual words.—**ipso facto**, lit. 'in the fact itself'; by the very fact, act, or deed; automatically.

jambon (Fr.) ham.
je ne sais quoi (Fr.) lit. 'I do not know what'; an inexplicable something.
jeu (Fr.) game; play.—**jeu d'esprit**, a witticism.—**jeu de mots**, a play upon words; a pun.—**jeu de théâtre**, dumb show; gesture.
jeune (Fr.) young.—**jeune fille**, a girl.—**jeune premier**, the juvenile lead in a play.
jeunesse (Fr.) youth.—**jeunesse dorée**, gilded youth; smart young men of society.
joie de vivre (Fr.) the joy of living.
jour (Fr.) a day.—**jour de fête**, a saint's day; a festival; a holiday.
jure divino (L.) by divine law.—**jure humano**, by human law. [—**jus civile**, civil law.
jus (L.) law; right.—**jus canonicum**, canon law.
j'y suis, j'y reste! (Fr.) here I am, and here I remain!

Kamerad (Ger.) a comrade; (*World War* 1) used for 'I surrender!'
Kampf (Ger.) a fight; a struggle.
Kinder, Kirche, und Küche (Ger.) lit. 'children, church, and kitchen' (woman's proper sphere).

laborare est orare (L.) to work is to pray.
labore et honore (L.) by labour and honour.
labor omnia vincit (L.) labour conquers everything.
l'allegro (It.) the cheerful man.
lapsus (L.) a slip.—**lapsus calami**, a slip of the pen.—**lapsus linguae**, a slip of the tongue.—**lapsus memoriae**, a slip of the memory.
laudator temporis acti (L.) 'one who praises past times.'
Laus Deo! (L.) Praise be to God!
le beau monde (Fr.) the fashionable world.
legum (L.) of laws.—**Legum Baccalaureus**, Bachelor of Laws. Abbrev. **LL.B.**—**Legum Doctor**, Doctor of Laws. Abbrev. **LL.D.**
le roi le veut (Fr.) the king wills it.
l'état! c'est moi! (Fr.) the state! *I* am the state! (attributed to Louis XIV).
lex (L.) a law.—**lex non scripta**, the unwritten law; common law.—**lex scripta**, the written law; statute law.—**lex talionis**, the law of retaliation; an eye for an eye, a tooth for a tooth.
libra (L.) a pound.—*pl.* **librae**.

literati (L.) learned men; men of letters.
Litterarum Doctor (L.) Doctor of Letters (University degree). Abbrev. **Litt.D.**
littérateur (Fr.) a man of letters; a literary man.
loco citato (L.) in the place or passage quoted. Abbrev. **loc. cit.** or **l.c.**
locum tenens (L.) lit. 'holding the place'; a temporary substitute; a deputy.
loquitur (L.) speaks (a stage direction). Abbrev. **loq.**

ma foi! (Fr.) upon my faith! upon my word!
magister (L.) a master.—**Magister Artium**, Master of Arts. Abbrev. **M.A.**
magna est veritas et praevalet (L.) great is truth, and it prevails.
magnum bonum (L.) a great good; a boon. —**magnum opus**, a great work; a masterpiece.
maison (Fr.) a house.
maître (Fr.) (*fem.* **maîtresse**) a master.—**maître d'hôtel**, a butler; a head-waiter.
malade (Fr.) ill; sick.—**malade imaginaire**, an 'imaginary invalid'; a hypochondriac.
maladresse (Fr.) unskilfulness; awkwardness; want of tact.
mala fide (L.) in bad faith; falsely.—**mala fides**, bad faith.
mal à propos (Fr.) ill-timed; out of place; inopportunely.
mal de mer (Fr.) sea-sickness.—**mal du pays**, home-sickness; nostalgia.
malentendu (Fr.) a misunderstanding; misapprehension.
mañana (Sp.) to-morrow.
marché (Fr.) a market.—**marché noir**, 'black' market.
Mardi gras (Fr.) Shrove Tuesday.
mare (L.) the sea.—**Mare Nostrum**, lit. 'our sea'; the Mediterranean Sea (one of Mussolini's bombastic phrases).
mariage de convenance (Fr.) a marriage of convenience.
matelot (Fr.) a sailor.
mauvais (Fr.) bad.—**mauvais goût**, bad taste.
mauvaise (Fr.) bad, *fem.* of **mauvais**.—**mauvaise honte**, false shame; bashfulness.
mea culpa (L.) through my fault.
memento mori (L.) remember that you must die.
memorabilia (L.) memorable acts or deeds.
memoria in aeterna (L.) in eternal remembrance.
mens (L.) the mind.—**mens sana in corpore sano**, a healthy mind in a healthy body.
mésalliance (Fr.) a marriage with one of lower social standing.
meum et tuum (L.) mine and thine.
milieu (Fr.) surroundings; environment.
mirabile dictu (L.) wonderful to relate.—**mirabile visu**, wonderful to see.—**mirabilia**, wonders.
modus (L.) mode; way; method.—**modus agendi**, a way of acting.—**modus operandi**, the way of proceeding or of setting to work; a plan of working.—**modus vivendi**, lit. 'a way of living'.
mon Dieu! (Fr.) my God! my goodness!
monsieur (Fr.) a gentleman; Sir; Mr.—*pl.* **messieurs.**
more (L.) in the manner of; after the fashion of.—**more majorum**, after the manner of one's ancestors.
multum (L.) much.—**multum in parvo**, much in little; a compendium of knowledge.
mutandum (L.) something to be changed.—**mutatis mutandis**, after making the necessary changes.
mutatio elenchi (L.) a shifting of the argument.

natus (L.) born. Abbrev. **n.**
nec tamen consumebatur (L.) nor was it (i.e. the bush) consumed. See Exodus, 3 [the motto of the Church of Scotland].
nemine contra dicente (L.) no one contradicting; without opposition. Abbrev. **nem. con.**
nemo me impune lacessit (L.) no one shall attack me with impunity (motto of Scotland and of the Order of the Thistle).
ne plus ultra (L.) nothing more beyond; the utmost point; the very perfection.
nihil (L.) nothing.—**nihil ad rem**, nothing to the point.—**nihil sine labore**, nothing without work.—**nihil tetigit quod non ornavit**, he touched nothing without adorning it.
nil (L.) nothing. Abbrev. of **nihil.**—**nil desperandum**, never despair.
n'importe (Fr.) it does not matter.
nisi Dominus, frustra (L.) unless the Lord is with you, your efforts are in vain.
nisi prius (L.) unless previously (judged).
noblesse (Fr.) nobility; noble birth.—**noblesse oblige**, lit. 'noble birth compels,' i.e. nobly born must nobly do; rank carries with it certain obligations.
nolle prosequi (L.) lit. 'to be unwilling to proceed'; the abandonment of a law-suit.
nom (Fr.) a name.—**nom de guerre**, lit. a 'war-name'; a pen-name.—**nom de plume**, a pen-name.—**nom de théâtre**, a stage-name.
non (L.) not.—**non compos mentis**, not of sound mind.—**non est**, it is not; it does not exist.—**non est disputandum**, it is not to be disputed.—**non possumus**, we cannot; often used to express inability to assist, unwillingness to co-operate, etc.—**non sequitur**, it does not follow (logically); it is not a necessary deduction.
non multa, sed multum (L.) not many, but much; not quantity, but quality.
non nobis, Domine, sed tibi sit gloria (L.) not unto us, O Lord, but unto Thee be the glory (the beginning of Psalm 115).
non progredi est regredi (L.) not to progress is to go backward.
nota bene (L.) mark well; pay particular attention. Abbrev. **N.B.**
notanda (L.) things to be noted.
Notre Dame (Fr.) Our Lady (used of churches dedicated to the Virgin Mary).
nouveau (Fr.) new.—**nouveauté**, a novelty.—**nouveau riche**, lit. 'new rich'; an upstart.—*pl.* **nouveaux riches.**
nulla bona (L.) (having) no goods or assets (which can be distrained for debt).
nulli secundus (L.) second to none.

obiit (L.) he (she) died. Abbrev. **ob.**
obiter (L.) by the way; casually.—**obiter dictum**, a casual remark; a passing observation.—*pl.* **obiter dicta.**
oeuf (Fr.) an egg.—**oeuf à la coque**, a boiled egg. —**oeuf sur le plat**, a baked or fried egg.—**oeufs brouillés**, scrambled eggs.
oeuvre (Fr.) a literary or artistic work.
omnia (L.) all things.—**omnia mutantur, nos et mutamur in illis**, all things change, and we change with them.
on dit (Fr.) lit. 'one says'; a rumour; a piece of hearsay.
opera (L.) works, *pl.* of **opus.**
orare (L.) to pray.—**ora et labora**, pray and work.—**ora pro nobis**, pray for us.
orné (Fr.) (*fem.* **ornée**) adorned; ornate.
O tempora! **O mores**! (L.) O the times! O the customs! i.e. How evil they are!

pace (L.) by leave of.—**pace tua**, by your leave; with your permission.
palmam qui meruit, ferat (L.) let him who has won the palm (of victory) wear it.
panem et circenses! (L.) lit. 'bread and circuses!' i.e. (give us) food and entertainment (a demand of the populace of ancient Rome).
par (Fr.) by.—**par excellence**, pre-eminently.—**par exemple**, for example.
pari passu (L.) lit. 'with equal step'; in the same degree or proportion; likewise.
parti (Fr.) a marriage-match; a political party; a decision.—**parti pris**, lit. a 'decision (already)

taken'; a preconceived view; set purpose; prejudice; bias.
particeps criminis (L.) an accomplice in the crime.—*pl.* **participes criminis.**
pas (Fr.) a step.—**pas seul**, a solo dance.—**pas de deux**, a dance for two.—**pas de quatre**, a dance for four.—**Pas de Calais**, the Straits of Dover.
passim (L.) everywhere; all through; in many [places.
pater (L.) father.—**Pater Noster**, Our Father. —**pater patriae**, the father of his country.
pâtisserie (Fr.) pastry; confectionery; a pastry-cook's shop; a tea-room.
patres (L.) fathers.—*pl.* of **pater.**—**patres conscripti**, lit. 'the conscript fathers'; the Roman Senate.
patria (L.) one's native land.—**patrie** (Fr.) [native land.
pax (L.) peace.—**pax Dei**, the peace of God.— **pax vobiscum**, peace (be) with you.
peccavi (L.) I have sinned.
pendente lite (L.) while the law-suit is pending.
pension (Fr.) board and lodging; a boarding- [house.
per (L.) through; by.—**per annum**, by the year; yearly; annually.—**per capita**, lit. 'by the heads'; individually; each; a head.—**per contra**, on the other side, i.e. of the account, to counterbalance it; on the other hand.— **per diem**, by the day; each day; daily.—**per se**, by itself; of itself.
per ardua ad astra (L.) through difficulties to the stars (the motto of the R.A.F.).
persona (L.) a person.—*pl.* **personae.**—**persona grata**, an acceptable person.
petitio principii (L.) in logic, a begging of the question.
pièce de résistance (Fr.) the principal dish of a meal, esp. the meat-course; (*Fig.*) the principal item on the programme.
pied-à-terre (Fr.) an occasional lodging.
pis (Fr.) worse; worst.—**pis-aller**, the worst shift; the last resource; a makeshift.
place aux dames (Fr.) (make) room for the ladies; ladies first.
poilu (Fr.) (*Colloq.*) a French soldier.
polichinelle (Fr.) a clown; a buffoon; Punch; —**polichinello** (It.).
pomme (Fr.) an apple.—**pomme de terre**, lit. an 'earth-apple'; a potato.
pontifex (L.) a priest, a bishop.—**Pontifex maximus**, the highest bishop; the chief priest (one of the designations of the Pope).
poseur (Fr.) (*fem.* **poseuse**) one who poses; an affected person.
posse comitatus (L.) lit. the 'power of the county'; a force of citizens called out by the sheriff to quell a riot.
post (L.) after.—**post meridiem**, after noon. Abbrev. **p.m.**—**post mortem**, after death.— **post obitum**, after death.—**post prandium**, after dinner.
post factum nullum consilium (L.) after the deed is done, consultation is useless.
post hoc, ergo propter hoc (L.) lit. 'after this, therefore because of this'; a fallacious assumption that an event which follows another must be the result of it.
pour encourager les autres (Fr.) in order to encourage the others (often used ironically).
pour faire rire (Fr.) in order to excite laughter.
pour passer le temps (Fr.) in order to pass away the time.
pour prendre congé (Fr.) to take leave. Abbrev. **P.P.C.** (written on a visiting-card in lieu of a personal farewell).
praemonitus, praemunitus (L.) forewarned, forearmed.
préfet (Fr.) a prefect; the chief magistrate or governor of a French *département* (county).— **préfecture**, the headquarters of a *préfet.*
primo (L.) in the first place.
primus (L.) first; the first (to bear the name). —**primus inter pares**, the first among equals.
princeps (L.) first; chief.—**principia**, first principles; elements.
prix (Fr.) prize; price.
pro (L.) for.—**pro aris et focis**, for altars and firesides; for God and our homes.—**pro bono publico**, for the public good.—**pro et con**, for and against.—**pro forma**, for form's sake.— **pro tempore**, for the time being. Abbrev. **pro. tem.**
proxime accessit (L.) he (or she) came next (to the prize-winner(s)); the runner-up.—*pl.* **proxime accesserunt.**
Punica fides (L.) lit. 'Punic, i.e. Carthaginian, faith'; treachery.

qua (L.) as; in the capacity of.
quam primum (L.) as soon as possible.— **quam celerrime**, as quickly as possible.
quantum (L.) as much.—**quantum libet**, in prescriptions, as much as you please. Abbrev. **q.l.**—**quantum sufficit**, as much as is needed. Abbrev. **q.s.**
quasi (L.) as it were; in a manner.—**quasi dicat**, as if one should say. Abbrev. **q.d.**
que faire? (Fr.) what's to be done?
que voulez-vous? (Fr.) what would you?
quid pro quo (L.) lit. 'something for something'; an equivalent return.
qui s'excuse, s'accuse (Fr.) he who excuses himself, accuses himself.
qui va là? (Fr.) who goes there?—**qui vive?** lit. 'long live—who?'; who goes there? (a sentry's challenge).
quoad (L.) so far as; as regards.—**quoad hoc**, as far as this (is concerned).
quod erat demonstrandum (L.) which was to be demonstrated or proved. Abbrev. **Q.E.D.**—**quod erat faciendum**, which was to be done. Abbrev. **Q.E.F.**
quod vide (L.) which see. Abbrev. **q.v.**
quo vadis? (L.) whither goest thou?

raison d'être (Fr.) lit. 'reason for existence'; justification.
rara avis (L.) lit. 'a rare bird'; something very unusual; a prodigy.
reductio ad absurdum (L.) reducing the position to an absurdity.
régime (Fr.) form of government.—**ancien régime**, the form of government in France before the Revolution; the old order.
regina (L.) queen. Abbrev. **R.** or **Reg.**
rentes (Fr.) French government stock; income from investments.—**rentier**, one who lives on his investments; a person of independent means.
répondez, s'il vous plaît (Fr.) reply, please. Abbrev. **R.S.V.P.**
République Française (Fr.) the French Republic. Abbrev. **R.F.**
requiescat in pace (L.) may he (she) rest in peace. Abbrev. **R.I.P.**
res (L.) a thing; things.—**res angusta domi**, pecuniary difficulties.—**res angustae**, straitened circumstances.—**res judicata**, a thing already judged or settled.
resurgam (L.) I shall rise again.
revenons à nos moutons (Fr.) lit. 'let us return to our sheep'; hence, let us come back to the matter we were discussing.
rex (L.) a king. Abbrev. **R.**—**Rex et Imperator**, king and emperor.
rien ne va plus (Fr.) no more stakes accepted (the call of the croupier at the gaming-table).
roi (Fr.) king.—**le roi le veult (veut)**, lit. 'the king wills it' (the phrase indicating royal assent to an act of parliament).
roman (Fr.) a novel.—**roman policier**, a detective story.
rôti (Fr.) roast.—**rôti de boeuf, de porc, de veau**, roast beef, pork, veal.

sacré (Fr.) sacred.—**Sacré Coeur**, the Sacred Heart (a famous church in Paris).
salve! (L.) hail!
sans (Fr.) without.—**sans cérémonie** or **façon**, without ceremony or fuss.—**sans faute**, without fail.—**sans pareil**, without equal; peerless.

—**sans peur**, without fear.—**sans peur et sans reproche**, without fear and without reproach (used of the medieval knight Bayard).—**sans souci**, without care; carefree; happy-go-lucky.
sauté (Fr.) (*Cookery*) fried lightly.
sauve qui peut (Fr.) lit. ' let him save himself who can' (the phrase of flight, indicating panic, stampede, rout).
savoir-faire (Fr.) tact; common-sense; knowing the right thing to do.—**savoir-vivre**, good breeding.
Schnitzel (Ger.) (*Cookery*) a cutlet.
scripsit (L.) he (she) wrote it.
sculpsit (L.) he (she) sculptured it.
secundo (L.) second.
secundum (L.) according to.—**secundum artem**, according to art; artistically; skilfully.—**secundum usum**, according to established custom.
secundus (L.) the second (to bear the name).
semper (L.) always.—**semper fidelis**, ever faithful.—**semper idem**, always the same (man).—**semper paratus**, always ready.
senatus (L.) the (Roman) senate.—**senatus populusque Romanus**, the senate and the Roman people. Abbrev. **S.P.Q.R.**
sequens (L.) the following. Abbrev. **seq.**—*pl.* **sequentes, sequentia**. Abbrev. **seqq.**—**sequitur**, he (she, it) follows; a consequence.
sic itur ad astra (L.) this is the way to the stars; such is the way to immortality.
sic transit gloria mundi (L.) thus passes away the glory of the world.
siècle (Fr.) a century.
s'il vous plaît (Fr.) if you please.
simpliciter (L.) simply; absolutely.
sine (L.) without.—**sine die**, without a day being set; indefinitely.—**sine invidia**, without envy.—**sine prole**, without issue; childless.—**sine qua non**, an indispensable condition; an essential.
soigné (Fr.) (*fem*, **soignée**) well finished; nicely cooked; well-groomed; trim.
soli Deo gloria (L.) glory to God alone.
spero meliora (L.) I hope for better things.
splendide mendax (L.) lit. 'gloriously false,' i.e. false in a good cause.
statim (L.) immediately.
status quo (**ante bellum**) (L.) the position as it was (before the war); the pre-existing state of affairs.
sub (L.) under.—**sub judice**, under consideration.—**sub poena**, under a penalty.—**sub rosa**, lit. 'under the rose'; secretly.—**sub sigillo**, lit. 'under the seal'; confidentially.
sui generis (L.) of its own kind; peculiar; unique; the only one of its kind.
summum bonum (L.) the supreme good.
sursum corda! (L.) lift up your hearts!
suum cuique (L.) let each have his own.

tabula rasa (L.) lit. 'a smoothed tablet'; a clean sheet; a blank page.
taedium vitae (L.) weariness of life; ennui.
tant mieux (Fr.) so much the better.—**tant pis** (Fr.) so much the worse.
Te Deum laudamus (L.) we praise Thee, O God.
tempora mutantur, et nos (or **nos et**) **mutamur in illis** (L.) times are changed, and we change with them.
tempus (L.) time.—**tempus fugit**, time flies.
tertio (L.) in the third place; thirdly.—**tertius**, the third (to bear the name).
tertium quid (L.) a third something, intermediary between two opposite principles.
tête (Fr.) the head.—**tête-à-tête**, a confidential talk between two people.
timeo Danaos et dona ferentes (L.) I fear the Greeks even when bearing gifts.
totidem verbis (L.) in these very words.
toties quoties (L.) as often as.
toujours la politesse (Fr.) politeness at all times.
tour de force (Fr.) a feat of strength or skill; an outstanding effort.
tout (Fr.) all; everything.—**tout à fait**, entirely; completely.—**tout ensemble**, lit. 'all together'; the general effect.

ubique (L.) everywhere (the motto of the Royal Artillery).
ultima Thule, the utmost boundary or limit (Thule was the most remote northern land known to the Romans).
ultra vires (L.) beyond one's powers.
ut infra (L.) as below mentioned (in a book, etc.).—**ut supra**, as above mentioned.

vade in pace (L.) go in peace.—**vade mecum**, go with me; a handy reference book or indispensable pocket companion.
vale! (L.) farewell!
valet de chambre (Fr.) a gentleman's personal manservant.
veni, vidi, vici (L.) I came, I saw, I conquered.
ventre à terre (Fr.) lit. ' belly to the ground '; at full speed.
verboten (Ger.) forbidden.
verbum satis sapienti (L.) a word to the wise is enough. Abbrev. **verb. sap.**
via, veritas, vita (L.) the way, the truth, and the life.
vide (L.) see (as an instruction to the reader of a book, etc.).—**vide infra**, see below.—**vide supra**, see above.
videlicet (L.) that is to say; to wit; namely. Abbrev. **viz.**
vi et armis (L.) by force of arms.
vin (Fr.) wine.—**vin blanc**, white wine.—**vin mousseux**, sparkling wine.—**vin ordinaire**, the cheap wine in everyday use in France.—**vin rouge**, red wine.
virginibus puerisque (L.) for maidens and youths.
vita brevis, ars longa (L.) life is short, art is long.
vivat! (L.) long live!—**vivat rex (regina)** long live the king (queen).
vive! (Fr.) long live! three cheers for!
voilà (Fr.) there! behold!
vol-au-vent (Fr.) (*Cookery*) a case of light, flaky pastry with a savoury filling.
vox populi (L.) the voice of the people; public opinion.—**vox populi, vox Dei**, the voice of the people is the voice of God.

Zeitgeist (Ger.) the spirit or tendency of the age.

CUSTOMARY ABBREVIATIONS

A argon; adult (motion picture certificate).
A.A. anti-aircraft; Automobile Association.
A.A.A. Amateur Athletic Association; Agricultural Adjustment Agency (*U.S.*).
A.A.C.C.A. Associate of the Association of Certified and Corporate Accountants.
A. & S. H. Argyll and Sutherland Highlanders.
A.B. able seaman; Assistance Board; Bachelor of Arts [L. *Artium Baccalaureus*].
A.B.A. Amateur Boxing Association.
abbr., abbrev. abbreviation.
abs. re. the defender being absent [L. *absente reo*.
A.C. Aircraftman; Alternating Current; Athletic Club.
a/c account.
A.C.A. Associate of the Institute of Chartered Accountants.
A.C.C. Army Catering Corps.
acct. account; accountant.
A.C.F. Army Cadet Force; Air Cadet Force.
A.C.G.B. Arts Council of Great Britain.
A.C.G.B.I. Automobile Club of Great Britain and Ireland.
A.C.I. Army Council Instruction.

A.C.I.I. Associate of the Chartered Insurance Institute.
A.C.I.S. Associate of the Chartered Institute of Secretaries.
A.C.M. Air Chief-Marshal.
A.C.T.H. Adreno-corticotropic hormone.
A.C.U. Auto-Cycle Union.
A.D. in the year of our Lord [L. *anno Domini*].
a.d. after date.
ad. advertisement.
A.D.C. aide-de camp; Amateur Dramatic Club.
add. addendum.
ad fin. at, or to, the end [L. *ad finem*].
A.D.G. Assistant Director-General.
ad infin. to infinity; for ever [L. *ad infinitum*].
ad init. at, or to, the beginning [L. *ad initium*].
ad int. in the meantime [L. *ad interim*].
ad lib. at pleasure; at will; as much as desired [L. *ad libitum*].
ad loc. at the place [L. *ad locum*].
adv. adverb; against [L. *adversus*].
ad val. according to the value [L. *ad valorem*].
advert. advertisment.
advt. advertisement.
A.E.C. Agricultural Executive Committee; Army Educational Corps.
A.E.F. Allied Expeditionary Force.
A.E.R.E. Atomic Energy Research Establishment.
aet., aetat. aged (so many years) [L. *aetatis*].
A.E.U. Amalgamated Engineering Union.
A.F.A. Amateur Football Association; Associate of the Faculty of Actuaries.
A.F.A. S. Associate of the Faculty of Architects and Surveyors.
A.F.C. Air Force Cross.
A.F.L. American Federation of Labour.
A.F.M. Air Force Medal.
A.F.O. Admiralty Fleet Order.
A.F.S. Associate of the Faculty of Secretaries; Auxiliary Fire Service.
Ag silver [L. *argentum*].
A.I. Artificial Insemination.
A.I.C. Army Intelligence Corps; Associate of the Institute of Chemistry.
A.I.C.E., A.Inst. C.E. Associate of the Institution of Civil Engineers.
A.I.D. Artificial Insemination by Donor.
A.I.L. Associate of the Institute of Linguists.
A.I.Mech.E. Associate of the Institution of Mechanical Engineers.
A.I.Min.E. Associate of the Institution of Mining Engineers.
A.I.S.A. Associate of Incorporated Secretaries' Association.
A.L.A. Associate of the Library Association; American Library Association.
alt. alternate; altitude; alto.
A.M. Air Ministry; Hail Mary! [L. *AveMaria*]. Master of Arts [L. *Artium Magister*].
a.m. before noon [L. *ante meridiem*].
A.M.C. Association of Municipal Corporations.
A.M.I.C.E. Associate Member of the Institution of Civil Engineers.
A.M.I.Chem.E. Associate Member of the Institution of Chemical Engineers.
A.M.I.E.E. Associate Member of the Institution of Electrical Engineers.
A.M.I.M.E. Associate Member of the Institution of Mechanical Engineers.
A.M.I.Min.E. Associate Member of the Institution of Mining Engineers.
A.M.I.R.E. Associate Member of the Institution of Radio Engineers.
A.M.I.Struct.E. Associate Member of the Institution of Structural Engineers.
A.M.S. Army Medical Service.
anon. anonymous.
A.N.Z.A.C. Australian and New Zealand Army Corps (Dardanelles, 1915).
A.O. Army Order.
A.O.C. Air Officer Commanding.
A.O.D. Ancient Order of Druids; Army Ordnance Department.
A.O.F. Ancient Order of Foresters.
A.O.H. Ancient Order of Hibernians.
A.O.S. Ancient Order of Shepherds.
A.P. Associated Press.
ap. in the works of (an author) [L. *apud*].
appro. approbation; approval.
approx. approximate(ly).
A.P.S. Associate of the Pharmaceutical Society.
A.R.A. Associate of the Royal Academy.
A.R.A.D. Associate of the Royal Academy of Dancing.
A.R.Ae.S. Associate of the Royal Aeronautical Society.
A.R.A.M. Associate of the Royal Academy of Music.
arch. archaic; architecture.
archit. architecture.
A.R.C.M. Associate of the Royal College of Music.
A.R.C.O. Associate of the Royal College of Organists.
A.R.C.S. Associate of the Royal College of Science.
A.R.I.B.A. Associate of the Royal Institute of British Architects.
A.R.P. Air Raid Precautions.
A.R.S.A. Associate of the Royal Scottish Academy; Associate of the Royal Society of Arts.
A.R.S.W. Associate of the Royal Scottish Society for Painters in Water Colours.
A.R.W.S. Associate of the Royal Society of Painters in Water Colours.
A.S. Anglo-Saxon.
A.S.A. Amateur Swimming Association.
A.S.A.A. Associate of the Society of Incorporated Accountants and Auditors.
A.S.E. Amalgamated Society of Engineers.
A.S.L.E.F. Associated Society of Locomotive Engineers and Firemen.
A.S.R.S. Amalgamated Society of Railway Servants.
Assoc. Associate; Association.
Asst. Assistant.
astr., astron. astronomer; astronomy.
A.S.W.W. Amalgamated Society of Wood Workers.
A.T.A. Air Transport Auxiliary.
A.T.C. Air Training Corps.
A.T.S. Auxiliary Territorial Service, now the W.R.A.C. (*q.v.*).
A.U. (*Physics*) Angström unit.
A.V. Authorised Version (of the Bible).
A.V.C. Army Veterinary Corps.
avdp., avoir. avoirdupois.
Ave. Avenue.
A.V.M. Air Vice-Marshal.

B

B. British; black (on lead-pencils).
b. born; book; bowled (by); brother.
B.A. Bachelor of Arts [*Baccalaureus Artium*]; British Academy; British Association.
B.Agr., B.Agric. Bachelor of Agriculture.
B. & F.B.S. British and Foreign Bible Society.
B.A.O.R. (*World War* 2) British Army of the Rhine.
Bart., Bt. Baronet.
Bart's St. Bartholomew's Hospital.
B.B. Boys' Brigade.
B.B.C. British Broadcasting Corporation.
B.C. before Christ; British Columbia; British Council; Board of Control; battery commander; bomber command.
B.Ch. Bachelor of Surgery [L. *Baccalaureus Chirurgiae*].
B.Ch.D. Bachelor of Dental Surgery.
B.C.L. Bachelor of Civil Law.
B.Comm. Bachelor of Commerce.
B.D. Bachelor of Divinity.
Bde. Brigade.
B.D.S. Bachelor of Dental Surgery; bomb-disposal squad.

B.D.S.T. British Double Summer Time.
B.E.A. British Electricity Authority; British European Airways; British East Africa; British Engineers' Association.
B.E.A.C. British European Airways Corporation.
B.Ed. Bachelor of Education.
B.E.F. British Expeditionary Force.
B.E.M. British Empire Medal.
B.Eng. Bachelor of Engineering.
B. ès L. Bachelier ès Lettres (Fr. = Bachelor of Letters).
B. ès Sc. Bachelier ès Sciences (Fr. = Bachelor of Science).
b.f. brought forward; (*Slang*) bloody fool.
B.F.B.S. British and Foreign Bible Society.
B.F.I. British Film Institute.
b.h.p. brake horse-power.
Bib. Bible; biblical.
B.I.F. British Industries Fair.
B.I.M. British Institute of Management.
B.L. Bachelor of Law; Bachelor of Letters; British Legion; breech-loading.
b.l., B/L. bill of lading.
bl. barrel; bale.
B.L.A. British Liberation Army.
B.L.E.S.M.A. British Limbless Ex-Service Men's Association.
B.Litt. Bachelor of Letters (Literature) [L. *Baccalaureus Literarum*].
B.M. Bachelor of Medicine; British Museum; Brigade-Major; of blessed memory [L. *Beatae Memoriae*]; bench mark.
B.M.A. British Medical Association.
B.M.J. British Medical Journal.
B.Mus. Bachelor of Music.
bn. battalion.
B.O. (*Colloq.*) body odour.
B.O.A.C. British Overseas Airways Corporation.
B. of H. Board of Health; Band of Hope.
B. of T. Board of Trade.
bot. botany; botanical; bought.
B.P. British Pharmacopoeia; British Public.
b.p. birthplace; bill of parcels; bills payable; boiling-point; below proof.
B.Q. may he (she) rest well [L. *bene quiescat*].
Br. brother.
B.R. British Railways.
br. bombardier; bridge; brig; bugler.
B.R.C.S. British Red Cross Society.
Brig. Brigade; Brigadier.
Britt. Omn. (on coins) of all the Britains [L. *omnium*, of all].
B.R.M. British Racing Motors.
Bro. Brother.
Bros. Brothers (commercial).
B.S. Bachelor of Science; Bachelor of Surgery; British Standard.
B/S. Bill of Sale.
B.S.A. British South Africa; Birmingham Small Arms (Co.).
B.Sc. Bachelor of Science.
B.S.I. British Standards Institution.
B.S.T. British Summer Time.
Bt. Baronet.
b.t.m. euphemism for bottom.
B.T.U. Board of Trade Unit.
B.Th.U. British Thermal Unit.
B.U.P. British United Press.
B.V.M. Blessed Virgin Mary [L. *Beata Virgo Maria*].
B.W.T.A. British Women's Temperance Association.

C

C. centigrade; Conservative; Consul; Court.
c. cent; centigram; centime; centimetre; century; chapter; about [L. *circa*]; in cricket, 'caught.'
C.A. Chartered Accountant.
C.A.B. Citizens' Advice Bureau.
Cantab. *Cantabrigiensis*, of Cambridge.
Cantuar. of Canterbury, esp. in the signature of the Archbishop [L. *Cantuariensis*].
Capt. Captain.
C.B. Cape Breton (Canada); Cavalry Brigade; Companion of the Order of the Bath; confined to barracks; County Borough.
C.B.E. Commander of the Order of the British Empire.
C.B.S. Confraternity of the Blessed Sacrament; Columbia Broadcasting System (of America).
C.C. County Council; Cricket Club.
c.c. cubic centimetre.
C.D. Chancery Division; Civil Defence.
c.d. cum dividend.
C.E. Church of England; Civil Engineer; Christian Endeavour (Society).
Cent. centigrade.
cent. a hundred; 100; century [L. *centum*].
cert. certificate; certificated; certified.
cet. par. other things being equal [L. *ceteris paribus*].
C.E.T.S. Church of England Temperance Society.
C.F. Chaplain to the Forces.
cf. compare [L. *confer*]; in binding, calf.
c.f.i., cost, freight, and insurance.
cg. centigram.
C.G.M. Conspicuous Gallantry Medal.
C.G.S. centimetre-gramme-second (system or unit of measurement in science); Chief of the General Staff.
C.H. Companion of Honour.
Ch. Charles; Church.
Ch.B. Bachelor of Surgery [L. *Chirurgiae Baccalaureus*].
Ch.M. Master of Surgery [L. *Chirurgiae Magister*].
chq. cheque.
Chron. Chronicles (O.T.).
C.I.D. Committee of Imperial Defence; Criminal Investigation Department.
c.i.f. cost, insurance, and freight.
C.I.G.S. Chief of the Imperial General Staff.
C.-in-C. Commander-in-Chief.
cir. about [L. *circa, circiter*].
C.M. Master of Surgery [L. *Chirurgiae Magister*]; Certificated Master; (*Mus.*) common metre; Corresponding Member.
cm. centimetre.
Cmd. Command Paper.
C.M.G. Companion of (the Order of) St. Michael and St. George.
C.O. Colonial Office; Commanding Officer; conscientious objector; Crown Office.
Co. company; county.
c/o care of.
C.O.D. cash on delivery.
C. of E. Church of England.
C. of S. Church of Scotland.
Col. Colonel; Colossians (N.T.).
comp. comparative; compositor; compound.
con. against [L. *contra*].
Cons. Conservative; Consul.
cont. continued.
contr. contraction.
Co-op. Co-operative (Society).
Corp. Corporation; corporal.
cos. cosine.
cosec. cosecant.
cot. cotangent.
c.p. candle-power.
cp. compare.
C.P.S. Keeper of the Privy Seal [L. *Custos Privati Sigilli*].
Cpl. Corporal.
C.R. Keeper of the Rolls [L. *Custos Rotulorum*]; King Charles [L. *Carolus Rex*].
cr. credit; creditor; crown.
C.S. Chemical Society; Civil Service; Clerk to the Signet; Court of Session.
C.S.I. Companion of the (Order of the) Star of India.
C.S.M. Company Sergeant-Major.
ct. carat; cent.
C.T.C. Cyclists' Touring Club.
cub. cubic.
cum div. with dividend. Also **c.d.**

curt. current (month).
C.V.O. Commander of the (Royal) Victorian Order.
C.W.O. cash with order.
C.W.S. Co-operative Wholesale Society.
cwt. hundredweight(s).

D

d. date; day; deceased or died; denarius; (penny); diameter.
D.A. days after acceptance; deposit accounts; Diploma of Art; District Attorney.
D.A.D.M.S. Deputy Assistant Director of Medical Services.
D.A.D.O.S. Deputy Assistant Director of Ordnance Services. Also **DADOS.**
D.A.A.G. Deputy Assistant Adjutant General.
D.A.Q.M.G. Deputy-Assistant Quarter-master-General.
d.b. double-breasted (of a coat); decibel.
D.B.E. Dame Commander of the Order of the British Empire.
D.C. District of Columbia, District Court; Direct Current; (*Mus.*) repeat from the beginning [It. *da capo*].
D.C.L. Doctor of Civil Law.
D.C.M. Distinguished Conduct Medal.
D.C.V.O. Dame Commander of the Royal Victorian Order.
D.D. Doctor of Divinity.
d.d. given as a gift [L. *dono dedit*]; delivered.
D.D.D. gives, devotes, and dedicates [L. *dat, dicat, dedicat*].
D.D.S. Doctor of Dental Surgery.
D.D.T. dichloro-diphenyl-trichloro-ethane (an insecticide).
dec. deceased; declination; decorated; decorative.
decd. (*Law*) deceased.
del. delegate; delete; drawn by [L. *delineavit*].
dept. department; deponent.
Det.Insp. Detective Inspector.
Deut. Deuteronomy (O.T.).
D.F. Defender of the Faith; Dean of the Faculty; direction finder. Also **D/F.**
D.F.C. Distinguished Flying Cross.
D.F.M. Distinguished Flying Medal.
D.G. by the grace of God [L. *Deo gratia*]; thanks be to God [L. *Deo gratias*].
dim. (*Mus.*) diminuendo; diminutive.
Div. Division (Army).
D.L. Deputy-Lieutenant.
D.L.I. Durham Light Infantry.
D.Lit(t). Doctor of Literature.
D.Litt. Doctor of Letters.
D.L.O. Dead Letter Office.
D.L.P. Divisional Labour Party.
D.M. Doctor of Medicine; Deputy Master.
Dm. decametre.
dm. decimetre.
D.Mus. Doctor of Music.
D.N.B. Dictionary of National Biography.
do. (ditto) the same.
Dom. Lord; Master [L. *Dominus*]; Dominion.
D.O.M. to God the Best, the Greatest [L. *Deo optimo maximo*].
D.O.M.S. Diploma in Ophthalmic Medicine and Surgery.
D.O.R.A. Defence of the Realm Act.
doz. dozen.
D.P. Displaced Persons: Double Pole.
D.P.H. Diploma in Public Health.
D.Ph., D.Phil. Doctor of Philosophy (or Ph.d).
D.Q.M.G. Deputy Quartermaster-General.
Dr. Doctor; debtor.
dr. dram; drawer (bank).
dram. pers. characters of the play [L. *dramatis personae*].
d.s. days after sight (bill of exchange); (also **D/s**;) (*Mus.*) from the sign [It. *dal segno*].
D.Sc. Doctor of Science.
D.S.C. Distinguished Service Cross.
D.S.I.R. Department of Scientific and Industrial Research.
D.S.M. Distinguished Service Medal.
D.S.O. Distinguished Serice Order.
d.s.p. died without issue [L. *decessit sine prole*].
D.S.T. Double Summer Time.
D.Th. or **D.Theol.** Doctor of Theology.
D.V. God willing [L. *Deo volente*].
d.v.p. died during father's lifetime [L. *decessit vita patris*].
dwt. pennyweight [L. *denarius* (weight)].

E

E. East; Eastern.
E. and O.E. errors and omissions excepted.
Ebor. of York, esp. in the signature of the Archbishop [L. *Eboracensis*].
E.C. East Central (London Postal district); Established Church; Education Committee.
E.C.A. Economic Co-operation Administration.
Eccl., Eccles. Ecclesiastes (O.T.); Ecclesiastical.
Econ. Economics.
E.C.U. English Church Union.
Ed. editor.
ed., edit. edited; edition.
E.E. errors excepted; Envoy Extraordinary.
e.g. for example [L. *exempli gratia*].
E.I.S. Educational Institute of Scotland.
ejusd. of the same [L. *ejusdem*].
e.m.f. electromotive force.
E.P.T. Excess Profits Tax.
eq. equal; equivalent.
E.R. Queen Elizabeth [L. *Elizabeth Regina*].
E.R.P. European Recovery Programme.
E.S.P. extra-sensory perception.
esp. especially.
Esq. esquire.
est. established.
et al. and others [L. *et alia, et alii*]; and elsewhere [L. *et alibi*].
etc. and the rest [L. *et cetera*].
et seq., et seqq., et sq., et sqq. and the following [L. *et sequentes, et sequentia*].
E.T.U. Electrical Trades Union.
etym., etymol. etymology; etymological.
Ex., Exod. Exodus (O.T.).
Exc. Excellency.
exc. except; exception; engraved by [L. *excudit*].
exr., exor. executor.

F

F. Fahrenheit; Father (R.C.); Fellow; French; Friday.
f. farthing; fathom; filly; foot; franc; (*Mus.*) loudly [It. *forte*]; folio.
F.A. Field Artillery; Fine Arts; Football Association.
F.A.C.C.A. Fellow of the Association of Certified and Corporate Accountants.
Fahr. Fahrenheit.
F.A.I. Fellow of the Auctioneers' Institute.
F.A.N.Y. First Aide Nursing Yeomanry.
F.A.O. Food and Agriculture Organisation.
F.A.S. Fellow of the Antiquarian Society; Fellow of the Anthropological Society.
F.B.A. Fellow of the British Academy; Fellow of the British Association.
F.B.F. Federation of British Industries; Federal Bureau of Investigation (*U.S.*).
F.B.O.A. Fellow of the British Optical Association.
F.C.P. Fellow of the College of Preceptors.
F.D. Defender of the Faith [L. *Fidei Defensor*].
Feb. February.
fec. made by [L. *fecit*].
F.E.I.S. Fellow of the Educational Institute of Scotland.

ff. folios; following (pages); (*Mus.*) very loudly [It. *fortissimo*].
F.F.A. Fellow of the Faculty of Actuaries.
fff. (*Mus.*) as loudly as possible [It. *fortississimo*].
F.F.P.S. Fellow of the Faculty of Physicians and Surgeons.
F.G.S. Fellow of the Geological Society.
F.I.A. Fellow of the Institute of Actuaries.
F.I.A.C. Fellow of the Institute of Company Accountants.
F.I.A.S. Fellow Surveyor Member of the Incorporated Association of Architects and Surveyors.
Fid. Def. Defender of the Faith.
F.I.D.O. (*World War* 2) Fog Investigation Dispersal Organisation.
F.I.J. Fellow of the Institute of Journalists.
fin. at the end [L. *finis*, end]; financial.
F.I.S.A. Fellow of the Incorporated Secretaries' Association.
F.I.S.E. Fellow of the Institution of Structural Engineers.
F.L.A. Fellow of the Library Association.
Flt. Lt. Flight-Lieutenant.
F.M. Field-Marshal; Foreign Missions; frequency modulations.
F.M.S. Federated Malay States.
F.O. Field Officer; Flying Officer; Foreign Office; Food Office.
fo. firm offer; folio.
f.o.b. free on board.
F.P. fire-plug; former pupil.
f.p. foot-pound.
F.P.S. Fellow of the Philological Society; Fellow of the Philosophical Society.
Fr. Father; Frau; French; Friday.
F.R.A.M. Fellow of the Royal Academy of Music.
F.R.A.S. Fellow of the Royal Astronomical Society; Fellow of the Royal Asiatic Society.
F.R.B.S. Fellow of the Royal Botanic Society.
F.R.C.M. Fellow of the Royal College of Music.
F.R.C.O. Fellow of the Royal College of Organists.
F.R.C.P. Fellow of the Royal College of Physicians.
F.R.C.S. Fellow of the Royal College of Surgeons.
F.R.C.V.S. Fellow of the Royal College of Veterinary Surgeons.
F.R.G.S. Fellow of the Royal Geographical Society.
F.R.H.S. Fellow of the Royal Horticultural Society.
F.R.Hist.S. Fellow of the Royal Historical Society.
F.R.I.B.A. Fellow of the Royal Institute of British Architects.
F.R.Met.S. Fellow of the Royal Meteorological Society.
F.R.S. Fellow of the Royal Society.
F.R.S.A. Fellow of the Royal Society of Arts.
F.R.S.E. Fellow of the Royal Society of Edinburgh.
F.R.S. G.S. Fellow of the Royal Scottish Geographical Society.
F.R.S.L. Fellow of the Royal Society of Literature.
F.R.S.S.A. Fellow of the Royal Scottish Society of Arts.
F.S.A. Fellow of the Society of Antiquaries; Fellow of the Society of Arts.
F.S.A.(Scot.) Fellow of the Society of Antiquaries (Scotland).
F.S.A.A. Fellow of the Society of Incorporated Accountants and Auditors.
F.S.E. Fellow of the Society of Engineers.
F.S.S. Fellow of the Royal Statistical Society.
ft. foot; feet; fort; fortification.
fur. furlong.
f.v. on the back of the page [L. *folio verso*].
F.Z.S. Fellow of the Zoological Society of London.

G

g. gauge; genitive; gramme; guinea.
gal. gallon(s).
G.A.T.T. General Agreement on Tariffs and Trade, negotiated at Geneva in 1947.
G.B. Great Britain.
G.B.E. Grand Cross of the British Empire.
G.C. George Cross.
G.C.B. Grand Cross of the Bath.
g.c.f. greatest common factor.
G.C.I.E. Grand Commander of the Indian Empire.
G.C.M.G. Grand Cross of St. Michael and St. George.
G.C.S.I. Grand Commander of the Star of India.
G.C.V.O. Grand Cross of the Victorian Order.
G.H.Q. General Headquarters.
G.I. government issue; American private soldier (*U.S.*).
Gk. Greek.
gm. gramme.
G.M. George Medal; Grand Master.
G.M.C. General Medical Council.
G.M.T. Greenwich Mean Time.
G.O.C. General Officer Commanding.
G.O.M. Grand Old Man.
Gov. Governor.
G.P. general practitioner; Glory to the Father [L. *gloria patri*].
G.P.O. General Post Office.
G.P.U. the Soviet Russian Secret Political Police [*Gossudarstvennoye Polititcheskoye Upravlyeniye*].
G.W.R. Great Western Railway.

H

H.A.C. Honourable Artillery Company.
h. & c. hot and cold (water).
H.B. hard black (of a lead-pencil).
H.B.M. His (Her) Britannic Majesty.
H.C.F. or **h.c.f.** highest common factor.
hdqrs. headquarters.
H.E. high-explosive; His Eminence; His Excellency.
Heb. Hebrews (N.T.).
H.F. high frequency; Holiday Fellowship.
H.H. His (Her) Highness; His Holiness (the Pope); double hard (of a lead-pencil).
H.I.H. His (Her) Imperial Highness.
H.L.I. Highland Light Infantry.
H.M. His (Her) Majesty.
H.M.I.S. His (Her) Majesty's Inspector of Schools.
H.M.S. His (Her) Majesty's Service; His (Her) Majesty's Ship.
H.M.S.O. His (Her) Majesty's Stationery Office.
Hon. Honorary; Honourable.
Hon. Sec. Honorary Secretary.
h.p. hire purchase; horse-power.
H.Q. headquarters.
H.R.H. His (Her) Royal Highness.
H.S.H. His (Her) Serene Highness.
H.S.M. His (Her) Serene Majesty.
H.T. high tension.
h.w., ht. wkt. (*Cricket*) hit wicket.

I

ib., ibid. in the same place [L. *ibidem*].
i/c in charge of.
I.C.A. Institute of Chartered Accountants.
Ice., Icel. Iceland; Icelandic.
I.C.I. Imperial Chemical Industries.
id. the same [L. *idem*].
i.e. that is; namely [L. *id est*].
I.E.E. Institution of Electrical Engineers.
I.F., i.f. (*Radio*) intermediate frequency.
I.F.T.U. International Federation of Trade Unions.

I H S contracted form of the Greek word for Jesus (ΙΗΣΟΥΣ). Often, but incorrectly, said to be the initials of the Latin words, *In hoc signo* (*vinces*), 'In this sign thou shalt conquer,' or from *Jesus Hominum Salvator*, 'Jesus, Saviour of Men.'
I.L.O. International Labour Organisation.
I.L.P. Independent Labour Party.
I.M.F. International Monetary Fund.
Imp. Emperor; imperial [L. *imperator*].
imp. imperfect; imperative; let it be printed [L. *imprimatur*]; imported.
in. inch; inches.
Inc., Incorp. incorporated.
incog. unknown [L. *incognito*].
inf. below [L. *infra*]; infinitive; infantry.
I.N.I. in the name of Jesus [L. *in nomine Jesu*].
init. at the beginning [L. *initio*].
in loc. cit. in the place cited [L. *in loco citato*].
in pr. in the beginning [L. *in principio*].
I.N.R.I. Jesus of Nazareth, King of the Jews [L. *Jesus Nazarenus Rex Judaeorum*].
I.N.S. International News Service (*U.S.*)
Inst. Institute.
inst. instant, of the present month.
Inst. C.E. Institution of Civil Engineers.
Inst. E. E. Institution of Electrical Engineers.
in trans. in transit [L. *in transitu*].
inv. he designed, invented it [L. *invenit*].
I.O.O.F. Independent Order of Oddfellows.
I.O.R. Independent Order of Rechabites.
I.O.U. I owe you.
I.O.W. Isle of Wight.
I.Q. Intelligence Quotient.
I.R.A. Irish Republican Army.
ital. italics.
I.W.G.C. Imperial War Graves Commission.

J

J.C.D. Doctor of Civil Law [L. *Juris Civilis Doctor*]; Doctor of Canon Law [L. *Juris Canonici Doctor*].
J.D. Doctor of Laws [L. *Jurum Doctor*].
J.I.C. Joint Industrial Council; Junior Instruction Centre.
J.P. Justice of the Peace.
jr. junior.
J.T.C. Junior Training Corps.
Jud. Judges (O.T.); Judith; Judicial.
J.U.D. Doctor of both (Civil and Canon) Laws [L. *Juris utriusque Doctor*].
junr. junior.

K

K. King; Knight.
K.B. Knight of the Bath; Knight Bachelor; King's Bench.
K.B.E. Knight of the British Empire.
K.C. King's Counsel.
K.C,B. Knight Commander of the Bath.
K.C.I.E. Knight Commander of the Indian Empire.
K.C.M.G. Knight Commander of the Order of St. Michael and St. George.
K.C.S.I. Knight Commander of the Order of the Star of India.
K.C.V.O. Knight Commander of the Royal Victorian Order.
K.G. Knight of the Garter.
kg. kilogram(s).
K.G.C. Knight of the Grand Cross.
K.G.C.B. Knight Grand Cross of the Order of the Bath.
K.G.F. Knight of the Golden Fleece.
kil., kilom. kilometre(s).
kilo. kilogramme.
K.L.H. Knight of the Legion of Honour.
km. kilometre(s).
K.O.S.B. King's Own Scottish Borderers.
K.O.Y.L.I. King's Own Yorkshire Light Infantry.
K.P. Knight of St. Patrick.
K.R. King's Regulations.
K.S.I. Knight of the Star of India.
K.T. Knight of the Order of the Thistle.
kw. kilowatt.

L

l. lake; land; latitude; left; line; lira.
Lab. Labrador; Labour.
Lat. Latin.
L.B. Bachelor of Letters.
l.b. (*Cricket*) leg-bye.
lb. pound [L. *libra*].
l.b.w. (Cricket) leg before wicket.
l.c. (*Print.*) lower case; (*Stage*) left-centre; letter of credit.
L.C.C. London County Council.
L.C.I. Landing Craft, Infantry.
L.C.M. (or **l.c.m.**) least common multiple.
L.C.P. Licentiate of the College of Preceptors.
L.Cpl. Lance-Corporal.
L.D.S. Licentiate of Dental Surgery.
L.D.V. Local Defence Volunteers.
L.F. low frequency.
L.F.A.S. Licentiate of the Faculty of Architects and Surveyors.
L.F.P.S. Licentiate of the Faculty of Physicians and Surgeons.
L.G.U. Ladies' Golf Union.
l.h.d. left hand drive.
L.I. Long Island (U.S.A.); Light Infantry.
Lib. Library; Librarian; Liberal.
Lieut. Lieutenant.
lit. literal; literally; literary; literature; litre.
Litt.D. Doctor of Letters or Literature.
LL.B. Bachelor of Laws [L. *Legum Baccalaureus*].
L.L.C.M. Licentiate of the London College of Music.
LL.D. Doctor of Laws [L. *Legum Doctor*].
LL.M. Master of Laws [L. *Legum Magister*].
L.M.S. London Missionary Society; London, Midland, and Scottish Railway.
L.N.E.R. London and North Eastern Railway.
L.N.U. League of Nations Union.
loc. cit. in the place cited [L. *loco citato*].
log. logarithm.
loq. he speaks [L. *loquitur*].
L.P. Labour Party; letters patent.
l.p. long primer (*type*); low pressure.
L.P.O. London Philharmonic Orchestra.
L.P.T.B. London Passenger Transport Board.
L.R.A.M. Licentiate of the Royal Academy of Music.
L.R.C.M. Licentiate of the Royal College of Medicine.
L.R.C.P. Licentiate of the Royal College of Physicians.
L.R.C.S. Licentiate of the Royal College of Surgeons.
L.R.C.V.S. Licentiate of the Royal College of Veterinary Surgeons.
L.R.I.B.A. Licentiate of the Royal Institute of British Architects.
L.S.A. Licentiate of the Society of Apothecaries.
L.S.D. Lightermen, Stevedores, and Dockers.
L s. d. pounds, shillings, pence [L. *librae, solidi, denarii*].
L.S.O. London Symphony Orchestra.
L.T., l.t. low tension; long ton.
Lt. lieutenant.
L.T.A. Lawn Tennis Association.
Lt.-Col. Lieutenant-Colonel.
Lt.-Comm. Lieutenant-Commander (R.N.).
Ltd. Limited.

M

M. Monsieur (Fr.).
M. Majesty; Marshal; Master; Monday; 1000.
m. married; masculine; (*Mech.*) mass; medium;

meridian; metre; mezzo; middle; mile; mille (Fr.); minute; month; moon; morning; mountain.
M.A. Master of Arts.
mag. magazine.
Maj. Major.
M.A.P. Ministry of Aircraft Production.
math(s). mathematics.
matric. matriculation.
M.B. Bachelor of Medicine [L. *Medicinae Baccalaureus*].
M.B.E. Member of the Order of the British Empire.
M.C. Master of Ceremonies; Member of Council; Military Cross.
M.C.C. Marylebone Cricket Club; Middlesex County Council.
M.Ch. Master of Surgery [L. *Magister Chirurgiae*].
M.Comm. Master of Commerce and Administration (Manchester); Master of Commerce (Ireland).
M.C.P.S. Member of the College of Physicians and Surgeons; megacycles per second.
M.D. Doctor of Medicine [L. *Medicinae Doctor*]; mentally deficient.
Mdlle Mademoiselle (Fr.).
Mdm madame.
M. Ed. Master of Education.
mem. remember [L. *memento*].
memo. memorandum.
Messrs. the plural of Mr.
meth. methylated spirits.
M.F.H. Master of Fox Hounds.
mfr. manufacturer.
m.g. milligram; machine gun.
Mgr. Monsignor; Monseigneur.
M.I.5 Military Intelligence, Department 5.
M.I.C.E. Member of the Institution of Civil Engineers.
M.I.E.E. Member of the Institution of Electrical Engineers.
M.I.G. 15 Russian jet aeroplane.
M.I.Mech. E. Member of the Institution of Mechanical Engineers.
min. minute.
M.Inst.C.E. Member of the Institution of Civil Engineers.
misc. miscellaneous.
M.I.W.T. Member of the Institute of Wireless Technology.
Mlle(s) (Fr.) Mademoiselle; Mesdemoiselles.
M.M. Military Medal.
MM (Fr.) *Messieurs*, Gentlemen; Majesties.
mm. millimetre.
M.M.B. Milk Marketing Board.
Mme(s) Mesdames (Fr.).
M.N.I. Ministry of National Insurance.
M.O. Medical Officer; Money Order.
M.O.F. Ministry of Food.
M.O.H. Master of Otter Hounds; Medical Officer of Health; Ministry of Health.
M.O.I. Ministry of Information.
M.O.W.B. Ministry of Works and Buildings.
M.P. Member of Parliament; Military Police; Metropolitan Police; Mounted Police.
m.p.h. miles per hour.
M.P.S. Member of the Pharmaceutical Society; Member of the Philological Society.
Mr. Mister.
M.R.A.S. Member of the Royal Academy of Science; Member of the Royal Asiatic Society.
M.R.C.C. Member of the Royal College of Chemistry.
M.R.C.P. Member of the Royal College of Physicians.
M.R.C.S. Member of the Royal College of Surgeons.
M.R.C.V.S. Member of the Royal College of Veterinary Surgeons.
M.R.G.S. Member of the Royal Geographical Society.
M.R.P. Mouvement Républicain Populaire (France).
Mrs. Mistress.
M.R.S.L. Member of the Royal Society of Literature.
M.S. Master of Surgery; Sacred to the Memory [L. *Memoriae Sacrum*].
MS(S). manuscript(s).
M.S.S. Member of the Statistical Society.
M.Sc. Master of Science.
M.T.B. Motor Torpedo Boat.
M.T.C.P. Ministry of Town and Country Planning.
Mus.B(ac). Bachelor of Music.
Mus.D(oc). Doctor of Music.
M.V. Motor Vessel; subdued voice [It. *mezza voce*].
M.V.O. Member of the Royal Victorian Order.

N

N. North; Northern; New; National.
n. name; noun; born [L. *natus*].
n.a., n/a. (*Banking*) no account.
N.A.A.F.I. Navy, Army, and Air Force Institutes.
N.A.B.C. National Association of Boys' Clubs.
N.A.G.C. National Association of Girls' Clubs.
N.A.J. National Association of Journalists.
N.A.L.G.O. National and Local Government Officers (Association).
N.A.S. Nursing Auxiliary Service; National Association of Schoolmasters.
Nat. National; Nathaniel; Natural.
N.A.T.O. North Atlantic Treaty Organisation.
Nat.Phil. Natural Philosophy.
NAT.S.O.P.A. National Society of Operative Printers and Assistants.
N.B. New Brunswick; North British; note well [L. *nota bene*].
n.b. (*Cricket*) no ball.
N.C.B. National Coal Board.
N.C.C.L. National Council for Civil Liberties.
N.C.O. Non-commissioned officer.
N.C.S.S. National Council of Social Service.
n.d. no date.
N.D.C. National Defence Corps.
N.E. New England; North-East(ern).
nem. con. no one contradicting; unanimously [L. *nemine contradicente*].
nem. dis(s). no one dissenting [L. *nemine dissentiente*].
N.F.B.T.O. National Federation of Building Trades Operatives.
N.F.S. National Fire Service.
N.F.U. National Farmers' Union.
N.H.I. National Health Insurance.
N.L.I. National Lifeboat Institution.
N.O.I.C. Naval Officer in charge.
non-com. non-commissioned officer.
non seq. it does not follow [L. *non sequitur*].
Norvic. of Norwich, esp. in the signature of the Bishop [L. *Norvicensis*].
No(s). number(s) [L. *numero*].
n.s. not specified; not sufficient.
N.S.P.C.C. National Society for the Prevention of Cruelty to Children.
N.T. New Testament; Northern Territory (of Australia); National Trust.
N.U.C.A.W. National Union of Clerks and Administrative Workers.
N.U.G.M.W. National Union of General and Municipal Workers.
N.U.I. National University of Ireland.
N.U.J. National Union of Journalists.
num. number; numerals.
N.U.P.B.P. National Union of Printing, Bookbinding, and Paperworkers.
N.U.R. National Union of Railwaymen.
N.U.S. National Union of Seamen; National Union of Students.

N.U.T. National Union of Teachers.
N.V.M. Nativity of the Virgin Mary.
N.Z. New Zealand.

O

o/a. on account of.
Ob., Obad, Obadiah (O.T.).
ob. (he or she) died [L. *obiit*].
O.B.E. Order of the British Empire.
O.C. Officer Commanding.
o/c. overcharge.
O.C.T.U. Officer Cadet Training Unit.
O.E.C.D. Organisation for Economic Co-operation and Development.
O.E.D. Oxford English Dictionary.
O.F.C. Overseas Food Corporation.
O.F.S. Orange Free State (S. Africa).
O.H.M.S. On His (Her) Majesty's Service.
O.K. all correct; all right.
O.M. Order of Merit.
O.P. opposite prompter (side of stage); observation post.
o.p. out of print; overproof (of alcohol).
op. a work [L. *opus*].
op. cit. in the work quoted [L. *opere citato*].
O.T. Old Testament.
O.T.C. Officers' Training Corps.
O.U.D.S. Oxford University Dramatic Society.
Oxon. Oxford; Oxfordshire; of Oxford [L. *Oxoniensis*].
oz. ounce(s).

P

p. page; pint; (*Mus.*) soft [It. *piano*]; (new) pence.
P.A. Press Association.
p.a. per annum; by the year.
P. & O. Peninsular and Oriental (Steamship Company).
par. paragraph; parallel; parish.
P.A.Y.E. Pay As You Earn (Income Tax).
P.C. Parish Council; police constable; Privy Council; Privy Councillor.
p.c. per cent; post-card.
pd. paid.
P.E.N. Poets, Playwrights, Essayists, Editors and Novelists (Club).
per an. per year; yearly [L. *per annum*].
per pro., p.p. by proxy; by the agency of [L. *per procurationem*].
pf. (*Mus.*) soft becoming loud [It. *pianoforte*].
Ph.D. Doctor of Philosophy.
Phil. Philip; Philippians (N.T.).
P.L.A. Port of London Authority.
P.L.U.T.O. (*World War* 2) Pipe Line under the Ocean.
P.M. Past Master; Prime Minister; Postmaster; Provost Marshal.
p.m. after death [L. *post mortem*]; afternoon [L. *post meridiem*].
P.M.G. Paymaster-General; Postmaster-General. [Post Office.
P.O. Petty Officer; Pilot Officer; Postal Order;
P.O.W. Prisoner of War.
P.P. Parcel Post; Parish Priest; Past President; Post Paid.
p.p. on behalf of; by proxy [L. *per procurationem*].
pp. pages; (*Mus.*) very softly [It. *pianissimo*].
P.P.S. an additional postscript [L. *post postscriptum*].
P.R. Proportional Representation; the Roman People [L. *populus Romanus*].
P.R.A. President of the Royal Academy.
P.R.L. Republican Party of Liberty [Fr. *Parti républicain de la liberté*].
P.R.O. Public Relations Officer.
Prof. Professor.
prox. next; of the next month [L. *proximo*].
prox. acc. runner-up [L. *proxime accessit*].
P.R.S. President of the Royal Society.
P.S. paddle steamer; Privy Seal; prompt side (of stage).
P.S. or **PS** (pl. **PSS**) written after; a postscript [L. *post scriptum*].
Ps. Psalm(s) (O.T.).
P.T. Physical Training; post town.
Pte. (*Mil.*) Private.
P.T.O. Please turn over.

Q

Q. quart(s); Queen; question; quartermaster.
Q.A.I.M.N.S. Queen Alexandra's Imperial Military Nursing Service.
Q.A.R.A.N.C. Queen Alexandra's Royal Army Nursing Corps.
Q.A.R.N.N.S. Queen Alexandra's Royal Naval Nursing Service.
Q.B. Queen's Bench.
Q.C. Queen's College; Queen's Counsel.
q.d. as if he should say [L. *quasi dicat*].
q.e. which is [L. *quod est*].
Q.E.D. which was to be proved [L. *quod erat demonstrandum*].
q.s., quant. suf(f). as much as is required [L. *quantum sufficit*].
qto., 4to. quarto.
qu. query; question; as if [L. *quasi*].
quad. quadrangle; quadrant; quadrat.
quant. suf(f). See **q.s.**
quin. quintuplet.
q.v. which see [L. *quod vide*].

R

R. King, Queen [L. *rex, regina*]; Royal; River; Railway; take [L. *recipe*].
r. rupee; (*Cricket*) run(s).
R.A. Royal Academy; Royal Academician; Royal Artillery; Rear-Admiral.
R.A.A.F. Royal Australian Air Force.
R.A.C. Royal Armoured Corps; Royal Automobile Club.
R.A.C.D. Royal Army Chaplains' Dept.
Rad. Radical.
R.A.D.A. Royal Academy of Dramatic Art.
R.A.D.C. Royal Army Dental Corps.
R.Adm. Rear-Admiral.
R.A.E.C. Royal Army Educational Corps.
R.A.F. Royal Air Force.
R.A.F.R. Royal Air Force Regiment.
R.A.F.V.R. Royal Air Force Volunteer Reserve.
R.A.G.C., R. and A. Royal and Ancient (Golf Club), St. Andrews, Scotland.
rall. gradually more slowly [L. *rallentando*].
R.A.M. Royal Academy of Music.
R.A.M.C. Royal Army Medical Corps.
R.A.N. Royal Australian Navy.
R.A.O.C. Royal Army Ordnance Corps.
R.A.P.C. Royal Army Pay Corps.
R.A.S.C. Royal Army Service Corps.
R.A.V.C. Royal Army Veterinary Corps.
R.B. Rifle Brigade.
R.C. Roman Catholic; Red Cross.
r.c. right centre (of stage).
R.C.A. Royal College of Art; Railway Clerks' Association.
R.C.A.F. Royal Canadian Air Force.
R.C.M. Royal College of Music.
R.C.M.P. Royal Canadian Mounted Police.
R.C.N. Royal Canadian Navy; Royal College of Nursing.
R.C.O. Royal College of Organists.
R.C.P. Royal College of Physicians; Royal College of Preceptors.
R.C.S. Royal College of Surgeons; Royal College of Science; Royal Corps of Signals.
R.C.V.S. Royal College of Veterinary Surgeons.
R.D. Royal Dragoons; Rural Dean.
R.D., R./D. refer to drawer (of cheque).
R.D.C. Rural District Council.
R.E. Royal Engineers; Royal Exchange.
recit. (*Mus.*) recitative; recitation.

Ref. Referee.
ref. reference.
Reg. Queen [L. *regina*]; Reginald; Registrar.
Reg. Prof. Regius Professor.
Regt. Regiment; Regent.
Reliq. remains [L. *reliquiae*].
R.E.M.E. Royal Electrical and Mechanical Engineers.
Rep. Representative; Republican; Repertory.
ret(d). retired; returned; retained.
Rev. Revelations (N.T.); Reverend; Revised; Review; Revenue.
Revd. Reverend.
R.F. Royal Fusiliers; French Republic [Fr. *République Française*].
r.f. radio-frequency.
R.G.S. Royal Geographical Society.
Rgt. regiment.
R.H. Royal Highness.
R.Hist.S., R.H.S. Royal Historical Society.
R.H.S. Royal Horticultural Society; Royal Humane Society; Royal Historical Society.
R.I. Rhode Island (U.S.A.); Regimental Institute.
R.I.B.A. Royal Institute of British Architects.
R.I.C.S. Royal Institute of Chartered Surveyors.
R.I.I.A. Royal Institute of International Affairs.
R.I.P. may he (she) rest in peace [L. *requiescat in pace*].
R.I.P.H. Royal Institute of Public Health.
R/L., r/l. radiolocation.
R.M. Royal Marines; Royal Mail; Resident Magistrate; Riding Master.
R.M.P. Royal Military Police.
R.M.S. Royal Mail Steamer (Service).
R.N. Royal Navy.
R.N.A.S. Royal Naval Air Service (now Fleet Air Arm).
R.N.L.I. Royal National Lifeboat Institution.
R.N.R. Royal Naval Reserve.
R.N.V.R. Royal Naval Volunteer Reserve.
R.O.C. Royal Observer Corps.
R.P.C. Royal Pioneer Corps.
r.p.m. revolutions per minute.
r.p.s. revolutions per second.
R.Q.M.S. Regimental Quartermaster-Sergeant.
R.R. Right Reverend.
R.S.A. Royal Scottish Academy (Academician); Royal Society of Arts; Royal Society of Antiquaries.
R.S.A.A.F. Royal South African Air Force.
R.S.A.M. Royal Scottish Academy of Music.
R.S.F. Royal Scots Fusiliers.
R.S.F.S.R. Russian Socialist Federated Soviet Republic.
R.S.M. Regimental Sergeant-Major; Royal School of Mines; Royal Society of Medicine.
R.S.P.C.A. Royal Society for the Prevention of Cruelty to Animals.
R.S.S. Fellow of the Royal Society [L. *Regiae Societatis Socius*].
R.S.V.P. Please reply [Fr. *Répondez s'il vous plaît*].
R/T. Radio-Telegraphy.
R.T.C. Royal Tank Corps.
Rt.Hon. Right Honourable.
R.T.R. Royal Tank Regiment.
R.W.S. Royal Society of Painters in Water Colours.

S

S. South; Saint; Socialist; Society.
s. second; shilling; son; singular.
$. dollars.
S.A. South America; South Africa; South Australia; Salvation Army; Storm Troops; [Ger. *Sturm-Abteilung*]; (*Slang*) sex appeal.
S.A.A.A. Scottish Amateur Athletic Association.
s.a.e. stamped addressed envelope.
Sarum. of Salisbury, in signature of Bishop.
S.A.S. Fellow of the Society of Antiquaries [L. *Societatis Antiquariorum Socius*].
Sb antimony [L. *stibium*].
s.c., s.caps., sm. caps. small capitals.
Sc. Science.
S.C.A.P. Supreme Commander of the Allied Powers (in Japan).
S.C.A.P.A. Society for Checking the Abuses of Public Advertising.
Sc.B. Bachelor of Science [L. *Scientiae Baccalaureus*].
s.c.c. single cotton-covered (wire).
Sc.D. Doctor of Science [L. *Scientiae Doctor*].
S.C.M. State Certified Midwife; Student Christian Movement.
Scot. Scotland; Scottish; Scots.
sculp., sculps., sculpt. he (she) carved or engraved it [L. *sculpsit*].
S.C.W.S. Scottish Co-operative Wholesale Society.
S.D.F. Social Democratic Federation.
S.D.U.K. Society for the Diffusion of Useful Knowledge.
S.E.A.C. South-east Asia Command.
S.E.A.T.O. South-east Asia Treaty Organisation.
Sec. Secondary; Section.
Sec., Secy. Secretary.
sec. leg. according to law [L. *secundum legem*].
sec. reg. according to rule [L. *secundum regulam*].
Sen. Senate; Senator.
Sen., sen., senr. senior.
seq., seqq. the following [L. *sequens, sequentia*].
Serg., Sergt. Sergeant.
s.g. specific gravity.
Sgt. Sergeant.
sh. shilling(s).
S.H.A.E.F. Supreme Headquarters of the Allied Expeditionary Force.
S.H.A.P.E. Supreme Headquarters of the Allied Powers in Europe.
sin. (*Math.*) sine.
S.J. Society of Jesus (Jesuits).
S.J.A.A. St. John Ambulance Association.
S.M. Senior Magistrate; Sergeant-Major; short metre; Society of Mary.
S.M.M. Holy Mother Mary [L. *Sancta Mater Maria*].
Sn tin [L. *stannum*].
S.O.S. signal of distress (Morse).
sov. sovereign.
S.P. (*Betting*) starting price.
s.p. (*Law*) without issue [L. *sine prole*].
S.P.C.A. Society for the Prevention of Cruelty to Animals.
S.P.C.C. Society for the Prevention of Cruelty to Children.
S.P.C.K. Society for Promoting Christian Knowledge.
S.P.E. Society for Pure English.
S.P.G.B. Socialist Party of Great Britain.
sp.gr. specific gravity.
S.P.R. Society for Psychical Research.
sq(q). square(s); the following [L. *sequens*].
Sqd.Ldr. Squadron-Leader.
Sr. Senior; Sir.
S.R.I. Holy Roman Empire [L. *Sacrum Romanum Imperium*].
S.R.N. State Registered Nurse.
S.S. steamship; Straits Settlements; Nazi Defence Corps (Ger. *Schutz-Staffel*].
SS. Saints.
S.S.A.F.A. Soldiers', Sailors', and Airmen's Families' Association.
SS.D. Most Holy Lord (the Pope) [L. *Sanctissimus Dominus*].
S.S.U. Sunday School Union.
St. Saint; Strait; Street.
stet. (*Printing*) let it stand [L.].
stg. sterling.
Supt. Superintendent.
S.W.G. Standard Wire Gauge.
S.Y. steam yacht.
S.Y.H.A. Scottish Youth Hostels Association.

T

T.A. Territorial Army.
tan. (*Math.*) tangent.
t. and o. (*Betting*) taken and offered.
T.A.S.S. The official news agency of the U.S.S.R.
T.B. Torpedo-Boat; Tuberculosis.
T.B.D. Torpedo Boat Destroyer.
T.D. Territorial Decoration (Officer).
t.e.g. top edges gilt.
temp. in the time of [L. *tempore*].
Ter(r). Terrace; Territory.
Test. Testament; testamentary; testator.
tfer. transfer.
text. rec. the received, accepted text [L. *textus receptus*].
T.G.W.U. Transport and General Workers' Union.
T.H. Trinity House.
Th. D. Doctor of Theology.
Thess. Thessalonians (N.T.).
Tim. Timothy (N.T.).
Tit. Titus (N.T.).
T.N.T. trinitrotoluene (explosive).
T.O. Telegraph, Telephone Office; Transport Officer; turn over.
Toc H. Talbot House.
Treas. Treasurer.
trig. trigonometry.
T.S. Theosophical Society.
T.S.F.S.R. Transcaucasian Socialist Federal Soviet Republic.
T.T. total abstainer (teetotal); Tourist Trophy; torpedo tube; tuberculin-tested.
T.U. Trades Union; Transmission Unit.
T.U.C. Trades Union Congress.
T.U.C.G.C. Trades Union Congress General Council.
TV. television.

U

U. University; Unionist; Uncle; Upper.
U.A.B. Unemployment Assistance Board.
u.c. (*Print.*) upper case.
U.D.C. Union of Democratic Control; Urban District Council.
U.K. United Kingdom.
U.K.A. United Kingdom Alliance.
ult. in the preceding month [L. *ultimo*].
U.N.(O.) United Nations (Organisation).
U.N.A. United Nations Association.
U.N.C.F.A. United Nations Conference on Food and Agriculture.
U.N.E.S.C.O. United Nations Educational, Scientific and Cultural Organisation.
U.N.R.R.A. United Nations Relief and Rehabilitation Administration.
U. of S.A. Union of South Africa.
u.p. under proof.
U.S.A. United States of America.
U.S.D.A.W. Union of Shop and Distributive Workers.
U.S.S. United States Senate; United States Ship, Steamship (Also **U.S.S.S.**).
U.S.S.R. Union of Socialist Soviet Republics (Russia); Ukrainian Socialist Soviet Republic.
Ut. Utah (U.S.A.)

V

v. against [L. *versus*]; see [L. *vide*]; verb; verse; vice [L. *vice*, in place of]; volume.
V.I. German flying bomb [Ger. *Vergeltungswaffe No.* 1].
V.2. German rocket bomb [Ger. *Vergeltungswaffe No.* 2].
V.A.D. Voluntary Aid Detachment.
var. lect. variant reading (of MS., etc.) [L. *varia lectio*].
V.C. Vice-Chancellor; Victoria Cross.
V.D. Venereal Disease; Volunteer (Officers') Decoration.
Vet. Veterinary Surgeon.
V.H.F. very high frequency.
vid. see [L. *vide*].
V.I.P. (*Colloq.*) very important person.
Vis., Visc., Visct. Viscount.
viz. namely [L. *videlicet*].
vs. against; versus.
vv.ll. variant readings [L. *variae lectiones*].

W

W. West; Western; Welsh.
w. wicket; wide; wife; with.
W.A.A.C. Women's Auxiliary Army Corps.
W.A.A.F. Women's Auxiliary Air Force.
W.A.F.S. Women's Auxiliary Fire Service; Women's Auxiliary Ferrying Service (*U.S.*).
W.Aus. West Australia.
W.A.V.E.S. Women Appointed for Voluntary Emergency Service (*U.S.*).
W.C. West Central; Wesleyan Chapel; water-closet.
W.Comm. Wing-Commander.
W.C.T.U. Women's Christian Temperance Union.
W.D. War Department; Works Department.
W.E.A. Workers' Educational Association.
Wes.Meth. Wesleyan Methodist.
W.F.T.U. World Federation of Trade Unions.
w.g. wire gauge.
W.H.O. World Health Organisation.
W/L. wave-length.
W.L.A. Women's Land Army.
W.O. War Office; Warrant Officer.
Wor. Worshipful.
W.R.A.C. Women's Royal Army Corps.
W.R.A.F. Women's Royal Air Force.
W.R.I. Women's Rural Institute.
W.R.N.R. Women's Royal Naval Reserve.
W.R.N.V.R. Women's Royal Naval Volunteer Reserve.
W.R.N.S. Women's Royal Naval Service.
W.S. Writer to the Signet; weather ship.
W/T. wireless telegraphy.
wt. weight.
W.V.S. Women's Voluntary Services.

X

X. Christ [**X** = Gk. *Ch.* the initial letter in the Gk. form of the word].
Xmas Christmas.
Xt(ian). Christian.

Y

Y.H.A. Youth Hostels Association.
Y.L.I. Yorkshire Light Infantry.
Y.M.C.A. Young Men's Christian Association.
Y.W.C.A. Young Women's Christian Association.

Z

zoo. zoology.
Z.S. Zoological Society.

WEIGHTS AND MEASURES

TROY WEIGHT

24 grains	= 1 pennyweight.	
20 pennyweights	= 1 ounce (480 grains).	
12 ounces	= 1 pound (5760 grains).	

Diamonds and Pearls are weighed by Carats, of 4 grains each (equal only to 3·2 Troy grains). The Troy ounce is equal to 150 Diamond Carats. Gold, when pure, is said to be 24 carats fine; if it contains one part alloy it is said to be 23 carats fine, and so on.

AVOIRDUPOIS WEIGHT

Used for all General Merchandise

16 drams	= 1 ounce (437½ grains Troy).
16 ounces	= 1 pound (7000 grains Troy).
14 pounds	= 1 stone.
28 pounds	= 1 quarter.
100 pounds	= 1 cental.
4 quarters	= 1 hundredweight (112 pounds).
2000 pounds	= 1 short ton.
20 hundredweights	= 1 ton (2240 pounds).

Avoirdupois Pounds exceed Troy in the proportion of 17 to 14 nearly; Troy ounces are greater than Avoirdupois in the proportion of 79 to 72 nearly.

APOTHECARIES' WEIGHT

Used for Dispensing Drugs, etc.

20 grains	= 1 scruple.
3 scruples	= 1 dram.
8 drams	= 1 ounce.
12 ounces	= 1 pound.

MEASURE OF CAPACITY

Used for Liquids and Dry Goods

4 gills	= 1 pint.
2 pints	= 1 quart.
4 quarts	= 1 gallon.
2 gallons	= 1 peck.
4 pecks	= 1 bushel.
8 bushels	= 1 quarter.
5 quarters	= 1 load.
36 bushels	= 1 chaldron.

A bushel of wheat on an average weighs 60 pounds; of barley, 47 pounds; of oats, 40 pounds. The gallon contains 10 pounds avoirdupois of distilled water.

DECIMAL MEASURE OF CAPACITY

Pints		*Gall.*		*Cub. Ft.*		*Litres*
1	=	0·125	=	0·02	=	0·567
8	=	1·000	=	0·1604	=	4·541
16	=	2·000	=	0·3208	=	9·082

APOTHECARIES' FLUID MEASURE

60 minims	= 1 dram.
8 drams	= 1 ounce.
20 ounces	= 1 pint.
8 pints	= 1 gallon.

THE METRIC SYSTEM MEASURE OF LENGTH

10 Millimetres	= 1 Centimetre.
10 Centimetres	= 1 Decimetre.
10 Decimetres	= 1 Metre.
10 Metres	= 1 Dekametre.
10 Dekametres	= 1 Hectometre.
10 Hectometres	= 1 Kilometre.
10 Kilometres	= 1 Myriametre.

One Metre = 1·094 yards = 39·371 ins.

MEASURES OF LENGTH

Linear Measure

12 inches	= 1 foot.
3 feet	= 1 yard.
5½ yards	= 1 pole, rod, or perch.
4 poles	= 1 chain.
10 chains	= 1 furlong.
8 furlongs	= 1 mile (1760 yds.).
3 miles	= 1 league.

Other Linear Measures

3 barleycorns	= 1 inch.
3 inches	= 1 palm.
4 inches	= 1 hand.
7·92 inches	= 1 link.
9 inches	= 1 span.
18 inches	= 1 cubit.
30 inches	= 1 pace.
37·2 inches	= 1 Scottish Ell.
45 inches	= 1 English Ell.
5 feet	= 1 geometrical pace.
6 feet	= 1 fathom.
608 feet	= 1 cable.
10 cables	= 1 nautical mile.
6080 feet	= 1 nautical mile.
6087 feet	= 1 geographical mile.
22 yards	= 1 chain.
100 links	= 1 chain.
10 chains	= 1 furlong.
80 chains	= 1 mile.
1 knot	= speed of 1 nautical m.p.h.

SQUARE MEASURE

144 square inches	= 1 square foot.
9 square feet	= 1 square yard.
30¼ square yards	= 1 square pole.
40 square poles	= 1 rood.
4 roods	= 1 acre.
640 acres	= 1 square mile.

SOLID OR CUBIC MEASURE

1728 cubic inches	= 1 cubic foot.
27 cubic feet	= 1 cubic yard.
5 cubic feet	= 1 barrel bulk shipping.
40 cubic feet	= 1 ton shipping.
40 cubic feet	= 1 load hard timber.
50 cubic feet	= 1 load foreign fir.

MEASURE OF WEIGHT

10 Milligrams	= 1 Centigram.
10 Centigrams	= 1 Decigram.
10 Decigrams	= 1 Gram.
10 Grams	= 1 Dekagram.
10 Dekagrams	= 1 Hectogram.
10 Hectograms	= 1 Kilogram.
10 Kilograms	= 1 Myriagram.
1 Kilogram	= 2 Lbs. 3¼ ozs.
1 Pound Avoir.	= 0·4535 Kilogs.

MEASURE OF SURFACE

10 Centiares	= 1 Deciare.
10 Deciares	= 1 Are (100 sq. metres).
10 Ares	= 1 Dekare.
10 Dekares	= 1 Hectare.
100 Hectares	= 1 Sq. Kilometre.

One Hectare = 2 acres, 1 rood, 35 poles.

MEASURE OF CAPACITY

10 Millilitres	= 1 Centilitre.
10 Centilitres	= 1 Decilitre.
10 Decilitres	= 1 Litre.
10 Litres	= 1 Dekalitre.
10 Dekalitres	= 1 Hectolitre.
10 Hectolitres	= 1 Kilolitre.
1 Litre	= 1¾ pints.

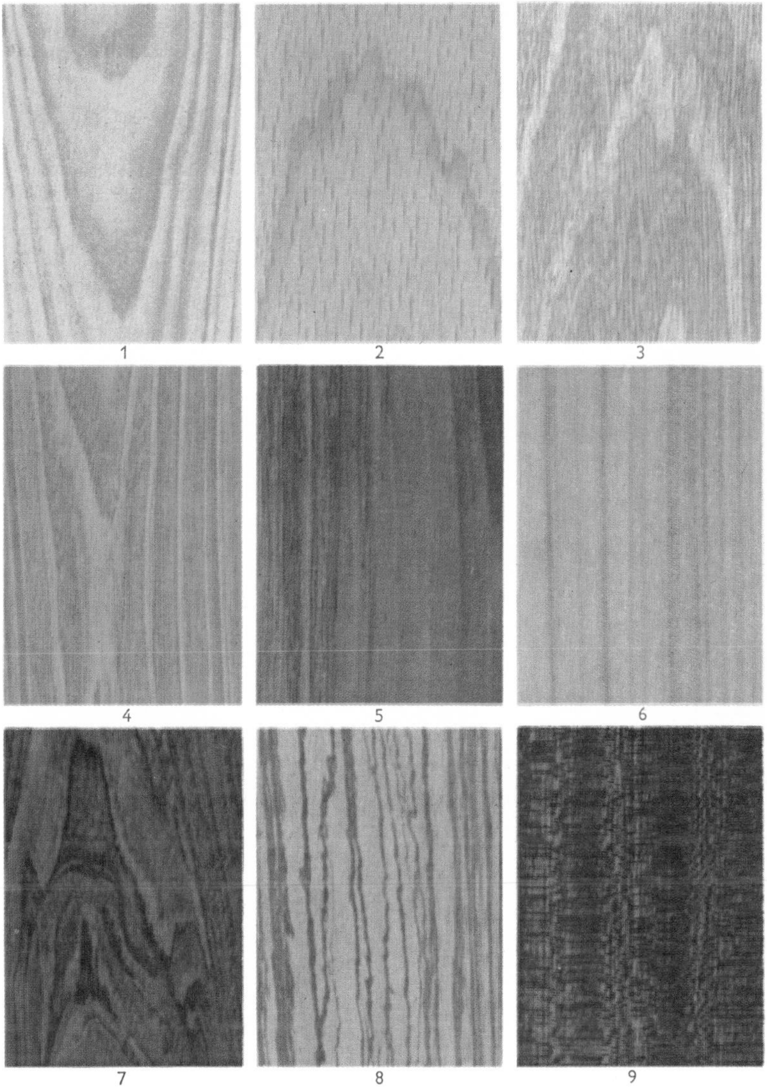

WOODS

1. pine   2. beech   3. oak   4. elm   5. walnut   6. cherry   7. rosewood   8. zebrawood   9. sapele

TWENTIETH CENTURY CRAFTS

Ring and pendant—1960

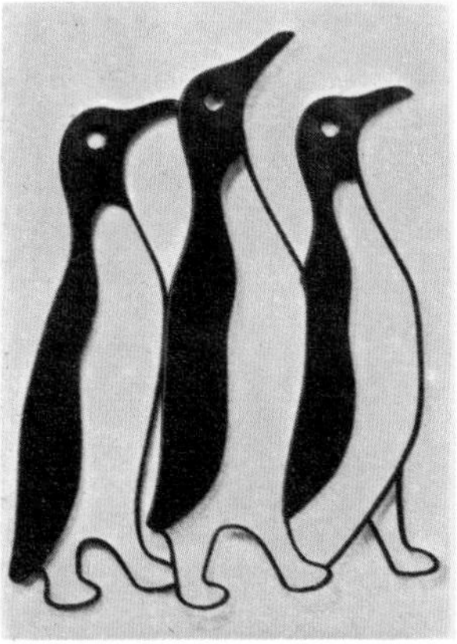

Penguins—wall decoration

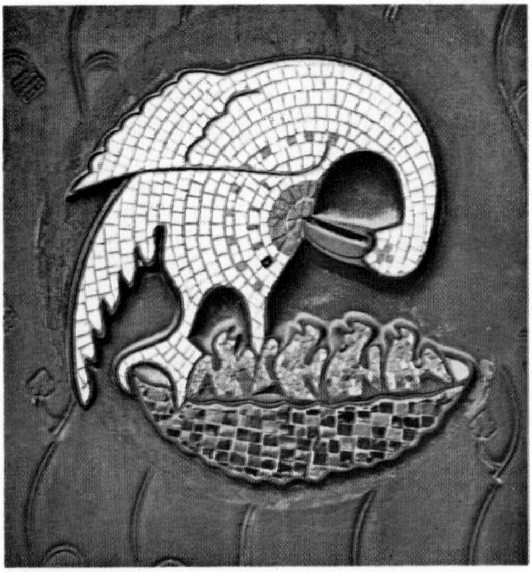

Pelican mosaic from the bronze door of Cologne Cathedral

ENCYCLOPEDIA

ENCYCLOPEDIA

ILLUSTRATED WITH LINE DRAWINGS

COLLINS
LONDON AND GLASGOW

GENERAL EDITOR: J. B. FOREMAN, M.A.

First published, 1966
Reprinted, 1966
Reprinted, 1968 (twice)
Reprinted, 1972

PRINTED IN GREAT BRITAIN BY COLLINS CLEAR-TYPE PRESS

PREFACE

An encyclopedia is a tool, and like all tools it must be designed with its function always in mind. Only in this way can it be really useful and satisfy the demands made of it. The first question that the editors of Collins National Encyclopedia had to ask themselves was—what is required of a new encyclopedia today?

First and foremost we believe that it should be comprehensive, and leave no field of useful knowledge unexplored. For biography this has meant selecting from the most interesting figures in the history of the world and reducing their lives to a general basic pattern, highlighting their achievements and works about them. The vital field of science is covered in the careers of scientists, with short entries on substances and processes as well as the developments in applied science that make up the history of technology. Religion, philosophy and art are, in the same way, covered in general entries and in biographies of important figures, carefully interrelated. World history, with its kings, battles and treaties, throwing long shadows into the political scene of today, has its place alongside the scientific assessments of mankind given by ethnography, sociology and economics. As the troubled political scene cannot be understood without history, it equally cannot be fully understood without geography, and we have included up-to-date articles on all the countries of the world with their most important cities and political divisions.

Politics and geography lead us to the second major requirement in a useful modern encyclopedia—impartiality. Never in the history of man, it seems, have accuracy and precision in the presentation of facts been more at a premium than now, when the mass media of communication disseminate facts and fallacies, problems and prejudices with equal enthusiasm. With this desperate world need in mind, the editors have tried at all times to report merely and to confine the expression of opinions and judgments to a minimum.

The crying need of our age is for facts. The changes that the last decade have made in the scope of what can be known have so stretched the limits of any one man's comprehension that he demands a guide he can trust. This we hope to provide, for we have kept rigidly to the rule of what we do not know we do not claim to know. We do not claim to read the future, so there will be no inspired guesses about the 'next step for the United Nations' such as you may find in any newspaper. When the next step has been taken we shall record it.

Our greatest problem has been to know what to exclude, since we had only a few hundred pages in which to cover all the world of human knowledge and interest. The basic difficulty was deciding how much space to give to the noisy topical event, the up and coming movements, new ideas and new scientific possibilities which man may soon be exploring, and how much to the past, to the accumulated wisdom and knowledge of the centuries. There can never be any absolute criterion on which to judge, and the ultimate decision is always a personal one.

Unlike a computer, which might have been able to tell us which entries were likely to be most in demand by scanning the history of some previous reference book, the editors have kept the human element very much in mind. We have remembered that there are two main types of reader using our encyclopedia. One is the person in a hurry, seeking specific information, knowing exactly what he is looking for and wanting it in less time that it takes to put the question. He will find that the essential information is presented in concise, meaty entries, simple, uncluttered and utilitarian in style. The other is the more leisurely person who can easily be induced to read on about Bicycles after he has satisfied his curiosity about Bicarbonate of Soda and can be just as interested in the Windward Islands as in Wine. He asks to be informed pleasantly about a variety of things, and for his sake we have tried not to make the text unpalatable through over-compression.

Nor has the lighter side of life been forgotten, for a person's hobbies are as vital to his well-being as his work. There had to be space for football and pottery, for chess and photography alongside aviation, space exploration and the great scourges of mankind—wars, diseases and natural calamities.

This new encyclopedia has been compiled by the staff of Collins Reference Book Department, of whom Miss Patricia Bascom, B.A., L.G.S.M., deserves special mention. We are confident that if you use Collins National Encyclopedia as a daily companion it will not only serve your needs well but will remind you of the great stores of knowledge in the world and encourage you to make use of them.

J. B. FOREMAN

ENCYCLOPEDIA

Contents

ABBREVIATIONS

USED IN THIS ENCYCLOPEDIA

(*A list of Customary Abbreviations will be found on pages 441-50*)

A.A. anti-aircraft
A.-S. Anglo-Saxon
acad. academy
adm. admiral
admin. administered, administration, administrative
agric. agricultural
alt. altitude
Amer. American
anat. anatomy
A.P. atmospheric pressure
approx. approximately
appt(d). appoint, appointed
Archbp. Archbishop
assoc. association, associated
astrol. astrology, astrological
astron. astronomy, astronomical
at. wt. atomic weight
atmos. atmospheric
Aust. Austria(n)
Austral. Australia(n)
autobiog. autobiography, autobiographical
av. average
b. born
Belg. Belgium, Belgian
betw. between
biog. biography, biographer
Brit. Britain, British
c. chapter
c. circa (about)
C. Central
C. of E. Church of England
Calif. California
cap. capital
capt. captain
cath. cathedral
Chanc. Chancellor
cent. century
chem. chemical
ch. church
circum. circumference
Co. Company; County
Coll. College
colloq. colloquial
comdr. commander
Commonw. Commonwealth
Cons. Conservative
cont. continental
corp. corporation
corresp. correspondence, correspondent
crit. critical
cr. crowned
cub. cubic
d. death; died
dept. department
diam. diameter
div. division
E. East, eastern, eastward
eccles. ecclesiastical
econ. economist
edit. edited
educ. educated, educational
Emp. Empire
Eng. English, England
esp. especially
est. estimated
estab(d) establish, establishment, established
exam. examination
exhib. exhibition
exhibd. exhibited
exped. expedition(ary)
Fed. Federal, Federatlon
Fr. France, French
ft. feet, foot
gen. general
geog. geographical
Gk. Greek
gov. governor
govt. government
Heb. Hebrew
hist. history, historical
hosp. hospital
ht. height
in. inch(es)
incl. including
Ind. India(n)

indep. independent (ce)
inf. infantry
inst. institute
internat. international
introd. introduced
Is. Island
Ital. Italian
Jap. Japanese
k. knots
L. Lake (when linked with name)
Lab. Labour
Lib. Liberal
lit. literature
m. mile(s)
mar. marriage, married
math. mathematical
med. medical, medicine
Med. Mediterranean
milit. military
Min. Minister, Ministry
min. minute(s)
mm. millimetre
mod. modern
mt. mountain, mount
myth. mythology
N. North, northern, northward
Napol. Napoleonic
nat. national
no. number
occup. occupied
orig. original(ly)
parl. parliament, parliamentary
phil. philosophical, philosophy
polit. political
pop. population
pres. president, presidential
prin. principal
prob. probably
prof. professor
prot. protectorate
prov. province
Pruss. Prussia(n)
pt. point
pub. publisher, published
q.v. which see
R.C. Roman Catholic
rec. received
regt. regiment
rel. religion
repub. republic, republican
ret. retired
rev. revolution
rly. railway
Rom. Roman
Russ. Russia(n)
s. shilling
S. South, southern, southward
Scot. Scotland, Scottish
Sec. secretary
sec. second
soc. society
Sp. Spanish
sp. speed
sp. gr. specific gravity
sq. square
St. Saint
sub-trop. sub-tropical
sym. symbol
Swed. Swedish
t. ton
temp. temperature
tr. translated, translation
trib. tributary
trop. tropical, tropics
univ. university
v. versus
var. variety
Visct. Viscount
vol. volume
W. West, western, westward
yd.(s) yard(s)
yr.(s) year(s)
zool. zoology

KEY TO PRONUNCIATION

VOWELS

a	as in m*a*n, m*a*rry	ew, yoo	as in f*ew* b*eau*ty	oo	as in m*oo*n
ȧ	„ f*a*ther	i	„ s*i*t	ow	„ n*ow*
ā	„ d*ay*	ī	„ h*i*gh	oi, oy	„ b*oy*
aw	„ p*aw*	o	„ n*o*t, s*o*rry	u	„ b*u*t, f*u*r
aï	„ f*ai*r	ō	„ n*o*	hl	Welsh sound used in words with Ll., *e.g.* Llanelly.
e	„ g*e*t, m*e*rry	o͞o	„ b*oo*k, p*oo*r		
ē	„ m*ee*t, b*ee*r				

A 'short' mark over a letter, thus: ă, ĕ, ŏ, ŭ, indicates the indeterminate vowel normally used in ide*a*, *a*bout, wat*e*r, etc.

CONSONANTS

b, d, f, h, k, l, m, n, p, r, s, t, v, w, z, have their normal English values.

ch	as in *ch*urch	zh	as in mea*s*ure	th	as in *th*in
ch	„ (Scottish) Lo*ch* (German) Bu*ch*	g	„ *g*et	th	„ *th*ere
sh	„ *sh*ut	ng	„ si*ng*er	j	„ *J*ack
				y	„ *y*es

FOREIGN SOUNDS

a(ng) represents the nasal vowel in French vin
u(ng) „ „ „ „ „ „ un
ȧ(ng) „ „ „ „ „ „ banc
ō(ng) „ „ „ „ „ „ bon

ö may be used to represent
1) vowel in French peu, German Schön
2) vowel in French coeur, German Götter

ü may be used to represent
1) vowel in French vu
2) vowel in German fünf

STRESS

The symbol ′ is used to indicate stress, and follows the syllable to be accented.
The symbol ˘ is used to indicate unstressed syllables.

A

A
1st letter and vowel in the Eng. alphabet derived from the Etruscan *a* through the Lat. alphabet. Early names were Alpha (Gk.) and Aleph or Alph (Heb.). In Eng. *a* represents at least 7 sounds as in *father, mat, mate, mare, many, ball, what,* besides being used in such digraphs as *ea* in *hear* and *oa* in *boat.*

AACHEN
[à'-chĕn] (*Fr.* **Aix-la-Chapelle**) Cath. city of W. Germany, in N. Rhine-Westphalia, *c.* 5 m. from the Belgian and Dutch frontiers. Stands on an important coalfield, has woollen and chem. manufactures. A. is assoc. with Charlemagne, who made it his cap. The treaty which ended the war of the Austrian Succession was signed at Aachen, 1748. Pop. 172,000.

AARDVARK
(*Orycterpus*) African earth-pig. A nocturnal, burrowing animal with hairy thick-set body, thick tail and long pig-like muzzle. It lives underground, and eats termites.

AARDWOLF
(*Proteles*) Wild animal resembling the hyaena, found chiefly in S. Africa. Has a grey-black-striped coat and bushy tail, and is largely insectivorous.

AARON
[air-'ŏn] (O.T.) Elder brother of Moses. High priest of Israelites during the exodus from Egypt. Set up Golden Calf on Mt. Sinai for the people to worship, and later rebelled against Moses. **Aaron's Beard.** Name for the plant, St. John's Wort and Mother of Thousands.

ABACUS
[ab'-a-kus] Apparatus of very ancient origin used by the Egyptians, Chinese, Gks. and Roms. for teaching children the elements of arithmetic and for visual calculation. It consists of a frame containing a number of parallel wires on which are strung rows of beads.

ABADAN
Town of Iran, on Abadan Is., in the Shatt-el-Arab at the N. of the Persian Gulf. Pop. 226,000.

ABBAS
Uncle of Mohammed and ancestor of the Abbasids; d. 652. His descendant Abul-Abbas was made caliph 750, a position retained by the Abbasids in Baghdad and then Cairo until the 16th cent. when the Ottoman sultans took the title themselves.

ABBEY
In the Christian Ch. building where a community of monks or nuns resides, ruled by an abbot or abbess respectively. Monastic life originated in the E. and in the W., St. Benedict founded the 1st abbey in A.D. 480.

ABBEY THEATRE
Opened in Dublin, 1904. Owed its origin to the co-operation of the playwrights George Russell (A. E.), W. B. Yeats and Lady Gregory with the actors W. G. and Frank Fay. Staged works by Yeats, Synge, Padraic Colum, Sean O'Casey.

ABBOT
Head of an abbey or monastery. A variant of the word *abba,* meaning father. An abbot must be in priest's orders and at least 25 yrs. old. Fem. form is *abbess;* she has the same powers, but cannot act as a priest.

ABDOMEN
Interior cavity of the trunk, bounded above by the diaphragm and below by the pelvis. It is enclosed by a muscular wall (and partly by the ribs) and is lined by the peritoneum. It contains the stomach, intestines, liver, spleen, pancreas and kidneys.

ABÉLARD, Peter
(1079-1142) Fr. scholastic philosopher. He and his pupil Héloïse rank among the great lovers in hist. He was castrated and became a monk, and Héloïse took the veil. A year later he resumed teaching, was cited for heresy, became a hermit at Nogent. He wrote *Historia Calamitatum* which drew from Héloïse the famous love letters.

ABELE
White poplar (*Populus alba*), a tree of S.E. Europe much planted in Brit. 60-100 ft. in ht. It has a smooth grey bark; leaves are covered underneath with a soft, white substance.

ABERCROMBIE, Lascelles
(1881-1939) Eng. poet and critic. *The Sale of St. Thomas* (1931) is his best known poem. He also wrote plays.

ABERDEENSHIRE
Maritime county of N.E. Scot. In the interior are the Grampian Mts. rising to 4,296 ft. The chief rivers are the Dee, Don and Ythan. Much is wooded; in the S. are Balmoral and Braemar, with the deer forests. The coast is rocky. Agriculture and fishing are important. Aberdeen is the county town; Aberdeenshire returns 4 members to Parl. (2 burgh constituencies). Pop. 520,385. **Aberdeen.** City and royal burgh of Aberdeenshire, at the mouth of the Dee. An important seaport, its chief industries are quarrying and granite working, fishing, engineering, chems., paper-making and textiles. A. possesses many beautiful buildings. Also notable are St. Machar's Cath., the city cross (17th cent.), Balgownie Bridge (18th cent.), and Dee bridge (16th cent.). It returns 2 members to Parl. Pop. 318,000.

ABERYSTWYTH
Borough, market town and seaside resort of Cardiganshire. The town contains the first Univ. Coll. to be opened in Wales (1872), and the Nat. Library of Wales. Pop. 10,480.

ABIDJAN
Port and cap. of Ivory Coast, W. Africa. Coffee, cocoa and timber are exported. Pop. 212,000.

ABOMINABLE SNOWMAN
Colloquial name for a creature, described by the Sherpas as half-man, half-beast (known as Yeti) said to live in the Himalayan mts. Tracks of its feet have been photographed in the snow.

ABORIGINES
The inhabitants of a country who are believed to be the orig. natives of the region. In Australia, specifically the native indigines.

ABORTION
(1) Law. Expulsion of contents of pregnant uterus at any period up to full term. (2) **Medicine.** Expulsion of the products of concep-

tion from the uterus before these are viable. During first 3 months of pregnancy this is abortion. After that and up to 28 weeks of pregnancy it is termed miscarriage and thereafter premature delivery. When induced by criminal means the term *criminal abortion* is used.

ABOUKIR
Port of Egypt, 10 m. N.E. of Alexandria. The bay was the scene of Nelson's victory in the Battle of the Nile, 1798.

ABRAHAM
or **Abram** (*c.* 2300 B.C.) (O.T.) Founder of the Jewish nation. With his father, his wife Sarah and his nephew Lot, he moved to Canaan. **Plains of Abraham.** Heights outside Quebec where the Brit. under Wolfe, beat the Fr. under Montcalm (1759).

ABRASIVE
A scouring and polishing material used in many manufacturing processes. High-grade abrasives are natural minerals, *e.g.*, emery, corundum, or artificial products of alumina or silicon-carbide, *e.g.*, carborundum. Low-grade abrasives are crushed quartz for sandpaper, etc., pumice powder, grindstones, whetstones, etc.

ABSALOM
(O.T.) David's favourite son; noted for his beauty and waywardness. When exiled he led a revolt: and was defeated in the ensuing battle. As he rode off on a mule his hair caught in a tree. He was found and killed, against orders, by Joab.

ABSCESS
Localised collection of pus occurring in the body. **Acute abscesses** form quickly and are assoc. with pain, increased pulse rate and rise in body temp. **Chronic abscesses** form slowly and are often assoc. with tuberculous disease. **Apical** abscess sometimes forms at root of decayed tooth and is often assoc. with chronic ill-health. **Abscess in the Ear.** Assoc. with severe pain and discharge.

ABSINTHE
[ab-sa(ng)t] Highly alcoholic, green liqueur, made from wormwood, anise, hyssop, angelica, mint, sweet-flag, etc.

ABSOLUTE ZERO
The lowest temp. which can possibly be realised. Its value is very nearly −273·2° C. or −459·8° F. At this temp. all molecular movement would cease and chem. reactions would be impossible.

ABYSSINIA *See* ETHIOPIA. **Abyssinian War.** In 1935, war broke out between Abyssinia, under Haile Selassie, and Italy, under Mussolini. The League of Nations declared Italy the aggressor and adopted sanctions against her, but proved too weak to apply them. Gas and high explosives were used. The poorly equipped Abyssinians gave way, and the country was annexed by Italy. This was recognised by the W. Powers in 1937. The country was liberated by Brit. in 1941.

ACACIA
Several shrubs and trees, one being the wattle of Australia. They grow chiefly in trop. countries and are usually found on the edges of deserts. The species found in Brit. gardens are *Robinia.*

ACADEMY
School of philosophy founded by Plato, so called after the garden of Academus near Athens, where his disciples assembled. **Académie Française** founded in 1635 was estabd. to purify Fr. language and to promote Fr. lit. Chief Brit. academies are the Royal Academy of Arts, which holds a yearly exhibition of pictures at Burlington House, London, and the Brit. Academy, founded 1900, for the promotion of historical, philosophical and philological studies.

ACANTHUS
Herb grown in S. Europe, and sometimes seen in Eng.

ACCENTOR
Small insectivorous birds—family Prunellidae. Includes the Brit. race of Hedge-sparrows or Dunnochs.

ACCESSORY
Law (1) *Accessory before the fact*: One who aids the perpetrator or who incites a person to commit a crime or assists in the execution of it. (2) *Accessory after the fact*: One who, knowing a crime has been committed, assists the perpetrator.

ACCIDENT
Law. Happening or event that is without premeditation, or deliberation. Industrial accidents are covered by the Nat. Insurance (Industrial Injuries) Act, 1946. Aircraft, railways and other Cos. that carry passengers for hire are liable to pay damages if persons are killed or injured through any negligence of the Cos.' servants unless there is a special contract excluding or limiting liability. Persons injured on the roads can obtain damages, if they can prove negligence, and motorists are obliged to insure against accidents to 3rd parties. Accidents on railways and in mines are investigated by officials of the Home Office; civil flying accidents by the Min. of Aviation.

ACCORDION
A musical instrument producing its sound by means of reed pipes supplied with wind from oblong pleated bellows operated between the player's hands. The right hand also operates buttons or a pianoforte-like keyboard, while the left hand controls buttons providing harmonic accompaniment.

ACCOUNTANT
One who specialises in the preparation, investigation and audit of accounts. Under the Companies Act, 1948, only those who are members of the recognised bodies of professional accountants or who hold a certificate of practice as a public accountant, may undertake the audit and certification of the accounts of limited liability Cos.

ACCRA
Cap. of Ghana, having road and rail communications with the interior. It has an internat. airport. Pop. 600,000.

ACCRINGTON
Borough and manufacturing town of Lancs. 23 m. N. of Manchester. Cotton, machinery and chems. are manufactured. A. sends 1 member to Parl. Pop. 38,940.

ACCUMULATOR
(secondary cell or storage battery). Device for storing electrical energy. In the simplest form a vessel filled with dilute sulphuric acid contains a pair of specially treated lead plates.

ACETIC ACID
$C_2H_4O_2$. Acid found in the juice of certain plants. It can be made by purifying the liquor obtained from the distillation of wood. Vinegar contains it. In a concentrated form the acid forms salts called acetates which are used in calico printing.

ACETONE
C_3H_6O. Colourless volatile liquid, obtained by distilling wood or by the dry distillation of acetates. It is used to make cordite, chloroform, etc., and as a solvent. As a solvent for acetylene it is a very powerful illuminant.

ACETYLENE
[-set'-til-in] Gas used for lighting purposes, obtained by mixing calcium carbide, which is made by fusing lime and coke together in an electric furnace, with water. It gives out a white, but powerful light about 15 times

stronger than commercial gas. With oxygen, acetylene is used to make an oxy-acetylene flame. It has a temp. of 3,500 deg. C. and is used for cutting iron and steel, and for welding metals.

ACHAEA
[-kē'-] Ancient division of Greece, often applied to the whole of Greece. The A. League was formed *c.* 280 B.C. to resist the Macedonians.

ACHILLEA
Genus of hardy perennial plants. *See* YARROW.

ACHILLES
[ă-kil'-ēz] Gk. hero, son of Peleus and Thetis. Homer's *Iliad* tells of his quarrel with Agamemnon and killing of Hector. **Achilles Tendon.** Tendon of the calf muscle leading to the back of the heel.

ACID
Chem. compounds containing hydrogen replaceable by metals to form salts; usually soluble in water. Acids are the opposites of alkalis.

ACIDITY
Term used to describe the symptoms of acid dyspepsia; sometimes used to denote heartburn.

ACNE
[ak'-ni] Skin disease occurring most often in young people. The disease is characterised by pimples, which are the obstructed sweat glands, and comedones or blackheads which are the obstructed ends of ducts of the sweat glands.

ACOMA
Indian village in New Mexico, 80 m. from Albuquerque, with the reputation of being the oldest inhabited place in the U.S.A.

ACONCAGUA
Highest mt. of S. Amer., alt. 22,835 ft. An extinct volcano in the Andes in Argentina.

ACONITE
[ak'-on-ĭt] Poisonous plant, commonly known as Monkshood (*q.v.*). All parts of the plant are poisonous.

ACOUSTICS
[-koos'-] Science of sound, dealing with the generation, propagation and detection of the various forms of audible vibrations.

ACRE
Brit. Land Measure. In medieval Eng. a field which could be ploughed by a yoke of oxen in one day. Subsequently the area was limited by statute to 40 by 4 poles, *i.e.* 4,840 sq. yards. In Scot. an acre formerly contained 6,150·4 sq.yds.; in Ireland 7,840 sq.yds. The Eng. acre is now the standard measure.

ACRE
Port of Israel, on the Bay of A. 80 m. N. of Jerusalem. Captured by the Crusaders, it was held for some years by the Knights of St. John.

ACRIFLAVINE
[-flāv'-ēn] Diamino-methyl-acridine chloride hydrochloride, it is a valuable antiseptic.

ACROPOLIS
[-krop'-] Highest part of a Gk. city, fortified and containing the citadel and temples. The most famous was at Athens, a rock 500 ft. high, on which stood the Parthenon.

ACT
(1) **Play.** A distinct main section of a play. (2) **Legal Act.** Act formally promulgated by a legislative or judicial body, *e.g.* an act of parliament (*q.v.*) (3) **Act of God.** An unpredictable and unexpected result of natural forces, not preventable by human foresight, *e.g.* an earthquake. (4) **Act of Grace.** A favour, esp. a pardon granted by a sovereign. (5) **Act of Parliament.** Decree of the Brit. legislature having the force of law. Introduced into parl, as a bill, the measure becomes an Act after passing the successive stages of first and second reading, committee and third reading in both houses and receiving the royal assent. The power to withhold assent (known as the *Royal Veto*) resides in the Sovereign but has not been exercised in the U.K. since 1707.

ACTINIC RAYS
Electromagnetic radiations which cause chem. changes in a photographic emulsion.

ACTINIUM
A radioactive element, occurring in pitchblende. Atomic No. 89. At. wt. 227.

ACTIUM
Headland of W. Greece where, in 31 B.C., Octavian, afterwards the Emperor Augustus, defeated Mark Antony and Cleopatra.

ACTS OF THE APOSTLES
5th book of the N.T. It may have been written by St. Luke *c.* A.D. 65. It relates the hist. of the Christian Ch. just after the Crucifixion and gives an account of the journeys and preachings of St. Paul.

ACTUARY
One who works out mathematical calculations dealing with the theory of probability as applied to life assurance, annuities, etc.

ADAM
First man, according to the Bible story (Gen. 1-5). The husband of Eve: the two became the parents of the human race. Similar stories are found in other ancient literatures. That part of the larynx bulging from the neck is called **Adam's Apple.**

ADAM, Robert
(1728-91) Scots architect. He built Lansdowne House, Osterley Park, Middlesex, Ken Wood, Hampstead, earning fame esp. for his staircases, chimney pieces and furniture.

ADAM DE LA HALLE
B. *c.* 1230. Fr. minstrel, a trouvère. He wrote the *Jeu de Robin et Marion.*

ADAMANT
Name given to emery from Naxos because of its unusual hardness.

ADAMNAN
(*c.* 624-704) Irish saint, Abbot of Iona. Best known for his *Life of St. Columba.*

ADAMS, John
(1735-1826) 2nd Amer. Pres. He was Amer. Min. in London 1785-88. From 1789-96 he was Vice-Pres. and in 1796 he was elected Pres. in succession to Washington; defeated by Jefferson, 1800. His son was **John Quincey A.** (1767-1848) 6th Pres. of U.S.A. From 1794-1802 he represented U.S.A. at several European capitals in turn. In 1817 he became Sec. of State under Monroe and in 1824 was elected Pres.

ADANA
[-dà-'] Town of Turkey, on the Sihun, *c.* 30 m. from the Medit. Cotton goods, wool and wine, are sent for export to the port of Mersin. Pop. 291,000.

ADDAX
Antelope found in the deserts of Arabia and N. Africa. It is *c.* 3 ft. high, has twisted horns, and in winter grows a beautiful mane.

ADDER *See* VIPER.

ADDIS ABABA
[ad'-is ab'-âbă] Cap. of Ethiopia in Shoa prov. on a plateau 8,000 ft. above sea level. Conquered by Itals. 1936. Addis Ababa was liberated by Brit. troops, 1941. Pop. 560,000.

ADDISON, Joseph
(1672-1719) Eng. writer. Became a Sec. of State (1717); wrote Lat. verses at Oxford, celebrated the victory of Blenheim (1704), wrote plays including *Cato, a Tragedy* (1713). He contributed essays to Steele's *Tatler* and largely to *The Spectator* (1711-12, 1714). The character of Sir Roger de Coverley was Addison's creation.

ADDISON'S DISEASE
Disease affecting supra-renal glands, first described in 1849 by Thomas Addison (1793-1860), a physician at Guy's Hospital, London.

ADELAIDE
Cap. of S. Australia standing on the Torrens near St. Vincent Gulf, sheltered to the E. and S. by hills of the Mt. Lofty Range. A. has an important trade in wheat, fruit, wool, wine and copper; industries include textiles and tanning. Pop. 596,800.

ADELAIDE
(1792-1849) Eng. queen, wife of William IV, daughter of the duke of Saxe-Coburg-Meiningen.

ADEN
Former Brit. protectorate in the S. of Arabia, on the Gulf of Aden. *See* SOUTH ARABIA, FEDERATION OF.

ADENAUR, Konrad
[ad'-en-owr] (1876-1967) First chanc. of the W. German Fed. Repub. During World War II he was twice imprisoned by the Nazis. In 1948 as chairman of the Christian Democratic Union, was appt. Pres. of the Bonn assembly. He was elected chancellor of the W. German repub. in 1949 re-elected in 1953, 1958 and 1961. Resigned 1963, succeeded by Prof. Ludwig Erhard.

ADENOIDS
Masses of lymphoid tissue situated in the area between nose and throat. In children, overgrowth with nasal obstruction is common and is often assoc. with chronic nasal infections.

ADIRONDACKS
Mts. in New York State, U.S.A., between Lake Champlain and the St. Lawrence. A popular holiday resort.

ADJUTANT
Officer in the Brit. army, responsible for secretarial duties. The **Adjutant Gen.** is the chief of the dept. which handles the supply of men, medical services, etc.

ADJUTANT
Bird like a stork, found chiefly in India, where because of its utility as a scavenger it is protected by law. It is *c.* 6 ft. high, has a wing span of 14-15 ft., a bald head and a hanging pouch.

ADLER, Alfred
(1870-1937) Psychologist and neurologist. B. Vienna, d. Aberdeen. He joined the Freudian circle of doctors in Vienna *c.* 1900 but diverged from Freud's teaching and developed his own Individual Psychology *c.* 1910.

ADMIRAL
High ranking naval officer. In the British navy the ranks are as follows: (1) *Admiral of the Fleet*, which is the highest rank that can be attained in the service. In general it is awarded on retirement for exceptional service. Alternatively it may be held by a member of the Royal Family. The three other ranks, which may be held by officers serving either in command of squadrons or in posts ashore, are: (2) *Admiral*, (3) *Vice-Admiral*, and (4) *Rear-Admiral*.

ADMIRALTY, Board of. *See* ROYAL NAVY ADMINISTRATION.

ADMIRALTY ISLANDS
Group of Is. in the Pacific, N.E. of New Guinea. Manus Is. the largest Is., Lorengau the chief town. Coconuts are the main product. They now form part of the Austral. trusteeship of New Guinea (*q.v.*). Pop. 18,835.

ADOPTION
Taking permanent charge of someone or something. Children can be adopted in Brit. but until 1926 there was no law on the subject. Since 1958 an adopted child can be put in exactly the same position as regards name, inheritance, etc., as a natural child but not so as to succeed to a title.

ADRENALIN
Discovered in 1901. Produced by the cortex of suprarenal glands of certain animals and also by synthesis. Its main action is to stimulate the autonomic nervous system.

ADRIAN
Name of 6 popes. **Adrian IV** (1154-1159) is noted as the only Englishman to be elected Pope. He was Nicolas Breakspear, b. Langley, Herts.

ADRIAN, Edgar Douglas, 1st Baron Adrian
O.M., F.R.S. (1889-) Physiologist. Educ. Camb. and St. Bartholomew's Hospital, he was Prof. of Physiology at Camb. Univ. 1937-51. Nobel Prize for Medicine, 1932; Gold Medal of the Royal Soc. 1950. Pres. of the Royal Soc. 1950.

ADRIATIC SEA
Branch of the Medit. Sea between the Ital. and Balkan peninsulas. The unbroken W. shore is Ital.; the E. or Dalmatian coast, fringed with numerous Is. is Yugoslav and Albanian.

ADVENT
(L. *adventus*) The 4 weeks before Christmas Day, *i.e.* the period before the birthday of Christ. It is reckoned from the Sun. nearest St. Andrew's Day (Nov. 30).

ADVOCATE
In Scot. a lawyer corresponding to the barrister in Eng. To become such, a man must join the Faculty of Advocates and pass certain exams.

AEGEAN SEA
[ē-jē'-ăn] A branch of the Medit. between Greece and Asia Minor.

AEGINA
[ē-jī'-nă] Is. of Greece, 20 m. S.W. of Athens.

AENEAS
[ē-nē-âs] Trojan hero and the subject of Virgil's *Aeneid*. According to the story, after the fall of Troy Aeneas escaped with his father and his son. Driven by a storm to Carthage he met Dido there. Later he mar. Lavinia, daughter of Latinus, King of Latium, and was regarded as the founder of the Rom. state.

AERIAL
Metallic conductor used for the transmission or reception of radio signals. A transmitting aerial consists of a wire, rod, or mast, supported above the ground and insulated from it. When an alt. current is caused to flow in the aerial, energy is radiated from it as an electromagnetic wave. A receiving aerial, placed in the path of this wave, absorbs a small amount of energy, which appears as an alt. current of the same frequency as that flowing in the transmitting aerial.

AERONAUTICS
The first accurately chronicled experiments in the theory of flight were conducted by Leonardo da Vinci, the Ital. artist and scientist, *c.* 1500. In 1783 Pilatre de Rozier ascended from Paris in a balloon filled with hot air. Numerous experiments with spherical balloons filled with

either hot air or hydrogen followed; in 1785 two balloonists crossed the channel, and in 1852 successful flights were made by a navigable airship driven by a steam engine. Aeroplanes developed later, a model glider being constructed by Sir George Cayley in 1804 and the first powered model being made by John Sttringfellow in 1848. *See* AVIATION.

AESCHYLUS
[ē'-skil-ŭs] (525-456 B.C.) Gk. tragic poet. B. Eleusis, near Athens; d. during a visit to Sicily. The creator of Gk. tragedy inasmuch as he made dialogue possible; latterly the rival of Sophocles; said to have written some 70 tragedies, of which 7 survive, *The Persians, The Suppliants, The Seven against Thebes, Prometheus Bound, Agamemnon, The Libation Bearers, The Furies.*

AESCULAPIUS
[ē-skew-lā'-piŭs] Gk. god of medicine.

AESIR
Collective name for chief gods in Scandinavian mythology. They lived in Asgard and fought against the powers of evil. They included Thor, Balder, Odin and Loki.

AESOP
Gk. fabulist (6th cent. B.C.). Orig. a slave. The reputed original author of the fables.

AESTHETICS
The science of the beautiful in nature and the fine arts. Its aim is to determine the nature of beauty and the laws governing its expression. On the nature of beauty there are two modes of thought *viz.* (1) the *Subjective,* which holds that beauty depends solely upon the perception of the beholder, and (2) the *Objective* which holds that beauty inheres in the external object. Attempts to formulate and elucidate the laws of Aesthetics were made by Plato, Aristotle, Hegel, Bosanquet, Croce, Santayana and others.

AFFIRMATION
Statement used legally as a substitute for an oath.

AFFORESTATION
Systematic planting of large areas of land with trees. The Forestry Commission, appointed under the Forestry Acts of 1919-51, is responsible in Brit.

AFGHANISTAN
Kingdom of Asia, bounded by Persia, the U.S.S.R., and Pakistan. It is a mountainous country, esp. in the N.E. where peaks of the Hindu Kush rise to over 24,000 ft. Two important Mt. passes, the Khyber and the Bolan, provide routes into Pakistan. The chief rivers are the Helmand, Kabul, Amu Darya and Hari Rud. The climate is dry, with great ranges of temp. In the valleys where the soil is fertile, wheat, barley, rice, millet and fruit are grown. Sheep are bred, and wool and skins are exported. Kabul is the cap. Admin. is by a king, assisted by 2 cabinets of mins. and 2 assemblies. During the 19th and early 20th cents. Brit. influence over the country was strong; in 1921 Afghanistan's indep. was recognised. Area: 250,000 sq.m. Pop. 13,800,000.

AFRICA
Continent surrounded by sea except in the N.E. where the Isthmus of Suez connects it with Asia. On the W. is the Atlantic Ocean, on the E. the Indian Ocean, on the N. the Medit., on the N.E. the Red Sea. Area is approx. 11,600,000 sq.m. The largest Is. off the coast is Madagascar. Features of the cont. are its unbroken coastline, its vast desert and its great rivers and lakes. The largest desert is the Sahara which divides the Medit. region from the rest of the cont. The Kalahari Desert lies in the S.W. The largest lakes are Victoria, Chad, Tanganyika, and Malawi. The principal rivers are the Nile, Congo, Niger, Zambezi and Limpopo. Much of Africa is occupied by a great plateau with bordering mt. ranges, *e.g.* the Atlas Mts. in the N., and the Drakensberg in the S.E. Mt. Kilimanjaro is 19,565 ft. and Mt. Kenya 17,058 ft. Since Africa lies chiefly within the tropics, temps. are generally high except in highland areas. Africa is rich in mineral wealth. Notable are the rich gold fields of the Transvaal and the copper deposits in Rhodesia. Products include coffee, cocoa, rubber, cotton, etc. The majority of the inhabitants are Negroes, others belonging to the Bushmen and Hottentot races. They are divided into 4 language groups, Bantu, Semitic, Hamitic and Sudanic. Arabs have settled in the N. and E., Indians in the E., and Brit. and Dutch in the S. From recent research it has been proved that man has lived on the continent since lower Pleistocene times though recorded history begins with the gradual development of the Nilotic civilisations. Later, the entire N. littoral became part of the Rom. Empire but in the 7th cent. fell to the forces of Islam. Brit. and other seamen followed Portuguese explorers of the 15th cent. and trading ports were established all round the coast, the Cape of Good Hope being especially important. Since trade was only in slaves for Amer., ivory, gold, etc., until the late 18th and early 19th cents., very little was known of the interior. During this period of some 75 years, explorers such as Mungo Park, James Bruce, Livingstone, Burton, Speke, Grant and Stanley discovered the main physical features. During the half-cent. preceding World War I almost the entire Continent was partitioned between the Brit., Fr., Germans, Itals., Belgians and Portuguese. Now the period of domination by European powers is rapidly drawing to a close. At the end of World War II the only indep. states were Egypt, Libya, Ethiopia, S. Africa and Liberia. Pop. 283,000,000.

AFRIKA CORPS
German army commanded by F.-M. Rommel (*q.v.*) which operated in the Western (Libyan) desert in World War II. Under F.-M. Montgomery the Brit. Army scored an overwhelming victory at El Alamein in Oct. 1942.

AFRIKAANS
Variety of Dutch (grammatical structure much simplified) spoken in S. Africa and Rhodesia.

AGA KHAN
Name given to the hereditary religious chief of the Ismailite sect of the Shia community of Islam. **Sultan Sir Mohammed Shah** (1877-1957) played an important part in the discussions of the future of India 1919-24, in 1930 and 1931. He was also well known as a racehorse-owner.

AGADIR
Seaport of Morocco, N. Africa, destroyed by earthquake, 1960: 12,000 killed.

AGAR AGAR
Malayan name for a seaweed widely used in the making of medicines, cosmetics, foodstuffs, photographic films, coated paper, etc.

AGATE
[ag'-āt] Amorphous (colloidal) form of silica usually presenting a banded structure. Coloured varieties are called cornelian, onyx, etc.

AGAVE
[ă-gā'-vi] Large flowering plant native to Mexico, with large, thick leaves, up to 5 ft. long. The stem which bears yellow-green flowers is sometimes 40 ft. high.

AGE OF CONSENT
(Marriage and Sex) In terms of the Age of Marriage Act, 1929, no minor under the age of 16 is permitted to marry. In Eng. young people of from 16 to 21 years of age can marry only with the consent of parent, guardian, or, in the last resort, by virtue of an Order obtained from

a Court of Law. In Scot. minors in the same age group can marry without the consent of parent or guardian. Minors of Eng. nationality may also marry in Scot. provided they have 15 days residence qualification. Throughout Gt. Brit. no girl of under 16 years of age is deemed capable in law of giving her consent to sexual intercourse.

AGESILAUS
King of Sparta from 398 B.C. when the kingdom was at the height of its power. In 371 when the Spartans were defeated by the Thebans at Leuctra, the efforts of Agesilaus saved their indep.

AGINCOURT
Village of N.E. Fr. *c.* 25 m. S.E. of Boulogne, where the Eng. under Henry V, defeated the Fr., Oct. 25, 1415.

AGNOSTICISM
Condition of not knowing. The word was first used in 1869 by T. H. Huxley to denote his attitude towards such matters as the existence of a personal God and the future life.

AGOUTI
[-goo'-tē] S. Amer. rodent of the genus *Dasyprocta.* It is similar to the rabbit, except that it lacks the long ears, and has 3 toes on each of the hind limbs.

AGRA
[ȧ'-] City of Uttar Pradesh, India, on the Jumna, *c.* 110 m. S.E. of Delhi. It trades in grain, cotton and sugar and was the cap. of the Mogul Empire for nearly a cent. The fortress contains the palace of the Shah Jahan, and the Taj Mahal. Pop. 462,020.

AGRICOLA, Gnaeus Julius
(A.D. 37-93) Rom. soldier. In 59-60 he was in Brit. Consul, 77; Gov. of Brit. 78-86. He defeated an army at Mons Graupius in the N.E.

AGRICULTURE
Science and practice of the cultivation of the soil. From the Iron Age to the 19th cent. there was little change in methods. In Eng. in the 17th cent. Jethro Tull secured a more thorough tilling of the soil and Robert Bakewell improved the breed of livestock. Root crops made it possible to keep cattle alive through the winter and another important change was an improved rotation of crops (*q.v.*). Agriculture may be divided into 3 great branches, (1) The production of cereals, rice, sugar, tea, coffee and other foodstuffs. (2) The rearing of livestock, including cattle for milk, and poultry. (3) The growing of fruit and vegetables (market gardening). Branches less easily classified include the growing of tobacco, the cultivation of hops, soya beans, the keeping of goats and bees. *See* FERTILISER; FOOD SUPPLIES.

AGRIMONY
Herbaceous perennial. It bears terminal spikes *c.* 2 ft. high of small yellow flowers. The root yields a yellow dye.

AGRIPPA
Name of 2 rulers of Judaea. **Agrippa I,** grandson of Herod the Great, is mentioned in *The Acts of the Apostles* and by Josephus. He was responsible for the d. of St. James and the imprisonment of St. Peter.

AGRIPPINA
(1) **The Elder,** granddaughter of the Emperor Augustus. She mar. Germanicus, and was the mother of Caligula and Agrippina the Younger. (2) **Agrippina the Younger** mar. 1st Gnaeus Domitius Ahenobarbus, and their child was the Emperor Nero. She mar. 2nd the Emperor Claudius, and by his influence secured the throne for Nero. She was put to d. by Nero.

AHASUERUS
Name of several kings of Persia mentioned in the O.T., one of whom, the husband of Esther, is usually identified with Xerxes.

AHMEDABAD
City of India, on the Sabarmati, 310 m. N. of Bombay. There are 2 large mosques and a Jain temple. Pop. 1,149,918.

AHURA MAZDA
or **Ormuzd.** The principle of good or light in Zoroastrianism. God of life, who will finally prevail over Ahriman the principle of darkness and evil.

AIDAN
(d. Bamborough 651) Brit. saint whose chief work was done in Northumbria.

AIDE-DE-CAMP
An officer who attends on an officer of high rank.

AINSWORTH, William Harrison
(1805-82) Eng. novelist. Wrote 39 novels, mostly hist. as *Jack Sheppard* (1839), *The Tower of London* (1840), *Old St. Paul's* (1841), *Windsor Castle* (1843).

AINTREE
[ān'-] District outside Liverpool, famous for its racecourse, over which the Grand Nat. Steeplechase is run.

AINU
[ī-noo] Language of a small white racial group in Hokkaido (N. Japan), apparently an early Nordic type surviving from the New Stone Age.

AIR TRAINING CORPS. *See* ROYAL AIR FORCE.

AIRBORNE FORCES
Troops carried to battle by aircraft and descending by parachute or glider. In World War II, the Germans used them to invade the Low Countries and Crete. Main Brit. airborne operations were in N. Africa (1942), in the invasion of Sicily (1943), and of Normandy (1944), in an unsuccessful attempt to secure the road bridge across the Rhine at Arnhem (*q.v.*) (1944) and at the crossing of the Rhine, Mar. 1945. All Airborne Forces are volunteers.

AIRCRAFT
Generic name for any airship, aeroplane or other flying machine. In Brit. as in other countries all aircraft must be registered, after being passed by the Min. of Aviation as airworthy. *See* AVIATION.

AIRCRAFT CARRIER
Warship designed to carry and service aircraft, which are housed in hangars in the ship and take off and land on a specially constructed flight deck. The first in the Brit. Navy were converted ships, *e.g. Argus* and the large light-cruisers *Furious, Glorious, Courageous,* which were still in commission on the outbreak of World War II. They served to give cover for convoy and land operations and played a vital part in major fleet actions, esp. the battle of Midway between the Amer. and Jap. fleets. During the War, Brit. completed *Illustrious, Victorious, Formidable, Indomitable, Implacable* and *Indefatigable* displacing 23,000-30,000 t. and accommodating *c.* 70 aircraft, and in 1951 the new *Eagle* was commissioned. Of 36,800 t. she carried 2 squadrons of jet aircraft. The world's largest carrier and ship is the U.S.S. *Enterprise,* with a full-load displacement of 85,800 tons, and a length of 1,102 ft. She is powered by 4 atomic reactors and can accommodate *c.* 100 aircraft. Recent Brit. inventions are the angled flight deck, which enables the deck to be used for parking aircraft and for taking off and landing at the same time, steam catapult and the mirror sight. *See* FLEET AIR ARM.

AIRE
River of Yorks. on which stands Leeds. It rises in the Pennines, passes through the Aire Gap, and crosses Yorks. flowing into the Humber near Howden. The valley through which the

Aire flows is called Airedale, which is the name of Brit. terrier dog. A large and strongly-built animal, it is a cross between the Otter-hound and the Irish or Welsh terrier. It has long legs and a hard, close coat.

AIRSHIP
Form of aircraft that depends for its support upon gas that is lighter than air. The first air-ships were balloons from which one or more cars for engines, fuel and crew were suspended. These were known as *non-rigid*. The Brit. Govt. built several. The first *rigid* airships were the German Zeppelins. They were giant cigar-shaped vessels with a rigid framework containing many balloons of gas. After the war several nations took up the building of airships. The Brit. Govt. constructed R33 and R34, and later R100 and R101, but the disaster to R101 in 1930 put a stop to further developments.

AITKEN, Robert Grant
(1864-1951) Amer. astronomer. His fame rests chiefly on his work on double stars, which he made his special study, and of which he himself discovered over 3,000. His book, *The Binary Stars* (1918), tabulates the results of 100,979 observations of stars.

AIX-LA-CHAPELLE
[ās-la-sha-pel′] *See* **Aachen.**

AIX-LES-BAINS
[ăks-lā-ba(ng)′] Town and resort of Fr. in Savoie, 8 m. N. of Chambéry, famous for its mineral waters. Pop. 15,000.

AJACCIO
[ă-jas′-iō, a yat′-chō] Cap. of Corsica, on the W. coast of the Is. The house in which Napoleon was b. still stands. Pop. 42,282.

AJANTA CAVES
Rock-cut shrines and monasteries at Ajanta, in N.W. Hyderabad, the walls of which contain astonishing wall paintings.

AJMER
[aj-mēr′] One of the principal cities of the state of Rajasthan. 220 m. S.W. of Delhi, it is an important railway centre with modern industries. Pop. 231,240.

AKHENATEN
[ak-en-ȧ′-ten] Egyptian 18th dynasty king who reigned 1656-25 B.C. He set up the worship of Aten as the state religion and built a new cap. on the E. bank of the Nile, 190 m. above Cairo, modern Tel-el-Amarna.

AKRON
City of Ohio, U.S.A., 30 m. S. of L. Erie. A rubber factory was estabd. 1870; now it is the largest rubber-manufacturing centre in the world. Pop. 273,300.

ALABAMA
[-bam′-] State in the S.E. of the U.S.A. except for a short coastline on the Gulf of Mexico, wholly inland. Lowland apart from the foot-hills of the Appalachian Mts. in the N.E., it is traversed by the Tennessee and Alabama rivers. Cotton is grown in the fertile Black Belt area. Montgomery is the cap. and Mobile the chief port. Birmingham is the centre of an important iron and steel industry. Alabama was first visited, 1540, and ceded to Brit. 1763; became a state, 1819; the institution of the Confederate States was proclaimed at Montgomery, 1861. Alabama sends 9 representatives to Congress. Area: 51,609 sq.m. Pop. (*c.* 35 % negro) 3,444,000.

ALABASTER
Massive translucent form of gypsum, found in Brit., suitable for domestic fittings and ornaments.

ALANBROOKE, Alan Francis
(1883-1963) 1st Visc. Brookeborough. Br. F.-M. Educ. abroad and at R.M.A. Woolwich. Joined R.F.A. 1902; served in Fr. during World War I, gaining D.S.O. and bar. C.-in-C. Home Forces 1940-41; C.I.G.S. 1941-46; F.-M. 1944; commanded the 2nd Corps of the B.E.F. 1939-40.

ALAND ISLANDS
[aw′-] Group of *c.* 300 Finnish Is. in Baltic. Industries are fishing, shipping and farming. Mariehamn is the chief town. Area: 572 sq.m. Pop. 22,144.

ALARIC
[a′lărik] (*c.* 370-410) King of the Visigoths. Became king in 395. He led his men through Italy to Rome, which he sacked in 410. Alaric II became king in 485. He was defeated by Clovis at Tours in 507.

ALASKA
State of the U.S.A. in the N.W. of N. Amer. including many Is. along the coast of Brit. Columbia, and the Aleutian Group. Bought by the U.S.A. from Russia, 1867, for *c.* 7,000,000 dollars, and made a territory in 1912. In 1958, it was created the 49th state. It is a cold, forested and largely mountainous region, the highest point being Mt. McKinley, 20,270 ft.; the Yukon is the chief river. The main industries are salmon fishing and canning, reindeer breeding, and the hunting and breeding of fur-bearing animals. Gold, copper, coal, uranium and other minerals are worked. Juneau is the cap. Alaska Highway links Juneau with Dawson City, Canada. An earthquake did much damage in 1964. Area: 586,400 sq.m. Pop. 302,200.

ALBANIA
(*Albanian*, **Shqiperia**) Repub. of S.E. Europe in the Balkan peninsula, bounded by Greece and Yugoslavia, with a coastline on the Adriatic Sea. Much of the country is mountainous, covered with dense forest. Along the coast is a fertile plain. Agriculture is the chief occupation. Tirana is the cap. There is no state religion, but the majority of the pop. is Mohammedan. A. was part of Turkey until it became an indep. state after the 1st Balkan War (1914). Itals. took possession of the country, 1917. A. became a repub. 1925, but in 1928 the pres. Ahmed Bey Zogu, became king as Zog I. Italy invaded the country in 1939, the Germans assuming control in 1941. After the liberation A. again became a Communist repub. with Gen. Enver Hoxha as Premier. Area: 11,100 sq.m. Pop. 1,965,000.

ALBANY
[awl′-] Cap. of New York State, U.S.A., 145 m. N. of New York, on the Hudson. Founded by the Dutch, Albany was named after James II, soon after it became Brit. in 1664, and made State cap. in 1797. Pop. 113,900.

ALBANY, Count of
[awl′-] Title assumed by the Young Pretender, Charles Edward. His wife, Louisa (1752-1824), was styled Countess of Albany. B. Mons, she mar. the Prince in 1772. In 1784 they separated.

ALBATROSS
Large sea bird found in the S. hemisphere. Its immense wings, up to 14 ft. from tip to tip, give it great power of flight. The bird is only found on land in the breeding season.

ALBENIZ, Isaac
[al-bā'-nith] (1860-1909) Sp. composer and pianist. He wrote operas and pieces for piano.

ALBERONI, Giulio
(1664-1752). Sp. statesman. In 1713 he was sent to Madrid as agent for the Duke of Parma and in 1714 Philip V made him his chief min. He filled the position for 6 years during which he improved the milit. and commercial condition of Spain.

ALBERT
or **Albert Nyanza.** Lake in Africa, on the boundary between Uganda and Congolese Rep. to the N.W. of L. Victoria. Discovered in 1864.

ALBERT
(1819-61) Francis Charles Augustus Albert Emanuel. Prince Consort and husband of Queen Victoria. Younger son of Ernest, Duke of Saxe-Coburg-Gotha. He mar. the Queen on Feb. 10, 1840, and was given the title of Prince Consort in 1857. He d. of typhoid fever, at Windsor Castle. The **Albert Memorial** was erected in Kensington Gardens, London, in his memory. In the Gothic style, it was designed by Sir Gilbert Scott, and was unveiled on Mar. 9, 1876. Opposite is the **Albert Hall.** Completed in 1871 it seats 10,000 people.

ALBERT MEDAL
Brit. decoration. Instituted in 1866. Orig. a reward for bravery in saving life at sea, since 1877 it has been conferred for similar deeds on land.

ALBERTA
Prov. of the Dominion of Canada. It stretches from the N.W. Territories to the U.S.A. frontier, with Brit. Columbia on the W. and Saskatchewan on the E. It is mainly flat, except in the S.W. where are the Rocky Mts. The prov. produces wheat and livestock. There are large supplies of coal and natural gas and immense forests. Edmonton is the cap. Alberta was made a prov. 1905. It is governed by an elected legislature of 1 house and a council, or cabinet. The lieut-gov. represents the Queen. It sends 6 senators and 17 representatives to the Parl. of the Dominion. Area: 255,285 sq.m. Pop. 1,400,000.

ALBIGENSES
Heretical sect. which appeared in Fr. *c.* 1180. The members had a mystical creed which was brought to Fr. from E. Europe.

ALBINO
Term applied to human beings and animals lacking the natural pigment of the skin, hair and eyes. Orig. used by the Portuguese to describe white negroes found in Africa. In human beings albanism is evidenced by white hair, transparency of skin, and pink feeble eyes. Partial albinism is a natural protective device in many winter adapted species, *e.g.* Ptarmigan, Stoat, Arctic Hare, Arctic Fox, etc.

ALBITE
['bīt] Sodium aluminium silicate, a soda-rich member of the plagioclase felspar series.

ALBUMEN
A nitrogenous substance, soluble in water, coagulating with heat, found only in plants and animals and classed as a protein.

ALBUQUERQUE
[al'-bŭ-ker-ki] Largest city of New Mexico, U.S.A., in the valley of the Rio Grande. Pop. 242,500.

ALCHEMY
[-kim-] Early form of chemistry, which originated in Alexandria about A.D. 100 and survived for 15 cents.

ALCIBIADES
[alsi-bī-ă-dēz] (*c.* 450-404 B.C.) Athenian statesman; educ. by his kinsman Pericles (*q.v.*), *c.* 422 he became leader of the party that favoured war with Sparta. His expedition against Syracuse had just sailed when he was accused of sacrilege. Recalled to Athens for trial, he escaped, but was sentenced to d. in his absence. In Sparta, Alcibiades became an implacable enemy of Athens. The Spartans began to distrust him and he fled to Persia. As leader of the Athenian army he won several battles over the Spartans. The failure of a further expedition led to his downfall and once again he was exiled (406). He was murdered by order of the Spartan Lysander.

ALCOHOL
C_2H_5OH. Name used for the liquid, ethyl alcohol, obtained by distilling a saccharine liquid, but it can be obtained synthetically from its elements, carbon, hydrogen and oxygen. Absolute alcohol is a colourless liquid with specific gravity ·79 and a boiling pt. of 78° F. It is the essential part of all spirits. Beer and wines also contain it, although in smaller proportions. The amount may be as low as 2 % in very light beer, or as high as 70 % in a powerful liqueur. Proof spirit contains 43 % alcohol. Alcohol is used in the manufacture of chloroform, ether, essences, perfumes, lotions, and as a solvent for oils, fats, resins and gums. It is also used as a source of power, in the form of methylated spirit. It can be made from potatoes, wheat, malt, rice, beetroot, molasses, honey, apples, etc. Methyl alcohol is distilled from wood and is much used commercially.

ALCOMETER
Scientific device which measures and records visually the amount of alcohol in the blood.

ALCOTT, Louisa May
(1832-88) Amer. writer. Wrote a number of books for young people; the best known are *Little Women* (1868) and *Good Wives* (1869).

ALDER
Small tree of the genus *Alnus* that grows freely in damp places in Brit., Europe, Asia and Amer. The tree is usually 30 or 40 ft. high. It bears rough oval leaves and 2 kinds of catkins. The bark is serviceable for tanning.

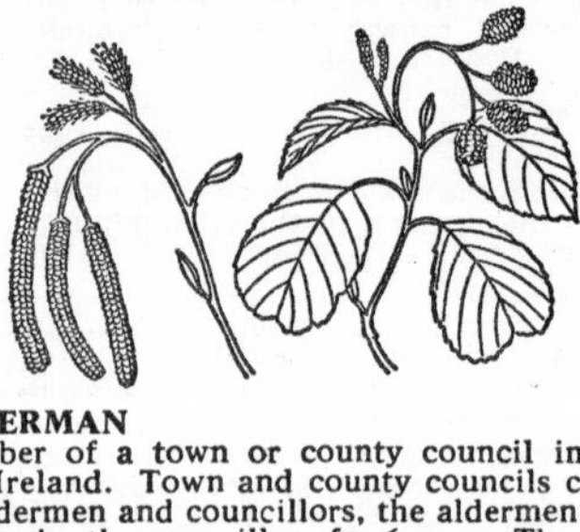

ALDERMAN
Member of a town or county council in Eng. and Ireland. Town and county councils consist of aldermen and councillors, the aldermen being chosen by the councillors for 6 years. The aldermen of the City of London are elected for life and from them the lord mayor is chosen. In Scot. the equivalent is bailie.

ALDERNEY
[awl'-] One of the Channel Is. 4 m. long, divided from the mainland of Fr. by the Race of A. The cap. is St. Anne, the only town. There is an air service to the Is. A. is noted for a breed of small cattle. Area: 3 sq.m. Pop. 1,449.

ALDERSHOT
[awl'-] Borough of Hants. 34 m. S.W. of London, the centre of the chief milit. camp in Eng. Pop. 32,810.

ALENÇON
[a-lä(ng)-sō(ng)'] Town of Fr. on the Sarthe, 56 m. S. of Caen. Cap. of Orne dept. the town gives its name to a variety of lace.

ALEPPO
City of N. Syria connected by railway with

Beirut (Lebanon) and Damascus. It was an important trading centre in the M.A. Pop. 563,000.

ALEUTIAN ISLANDS
[-loo'-shiăn] Group of mountainous volcanic Is. off Alaska, belonging to the U.S.A. Fishing is the chief occupation.

ALEXANDER
(the Great) (356-323 B.C.) King of Macedon. A son of King Philip II and his wife Olympias, he succeeded his murdered father in 336. Alexander decided to attack the huge Persian Empire, marched in 334 into Asia Minor and quickly mastered that country. He then conquered, with comparative ease, Phoenicia and Syria and overcame resistance at Tyre by the use of his fleet. Alexander next attacked Egypt which submitted without a struggle. Having founded the city of Alexandria, he passed through Syria into Persia and marched up the valley of the Tigris, through the country known as Mesopotamia. He captured Susa, Persepolis, Ecbatana and other wealthy Persian cities and advanced to the Caspian Sea. In 326 he crossed the Indus near Attock and gained a great victory. He returned to Persepolis, then set himself to organise his great empire. In the midst of this work he d. His d. prevented the consolidation of his empire, which fell rapidly to pieces.

ALEXANDER
(1888-1934) King of Yugoslavia, son of Peter of Serbia. In 1909 he became Crown Prince and Regent in 1914. He led the Serbian Army in World War I and in 1921 became king of the new state, Yugoslavia. Disorder led him, in 1929, to estab. a royal dictatorship. He was assassinated at Marseilles.

ALEXANDER
Name of 8 popes, of whom the most important was **Alexander VI.** Pope from 1492-1503, **Rodrigo Borgia** was b. near Valencia, Spain, in 1431. Passed his time in luxury and intrigue, chiefly in Rome, until elected pope. He was instrumental in bringing about the d. of Savonarola. *See* BORGIA. **Alexander III** (1159-81), ordered Henry II to do penance for the murder of Becket in 1170, and received at Venice in 1177 the homage of the Emperor Frederick I (Barbarossa).

ALEXANDER
Name of 3 Tsars of Russia. (1) **Alexander I** (1777-1825). The 1st years of his reign were occupied with war against Napoleon, interrupted by the Treaty of Tilsit (1807), by which Russia joined the Continental System. He took a leading part in the peace negotiations of 1814-15, esp. as the author of the Holy Alliance. (2) **Alexander II** (1818-81), son of Nicholas I, granted many important liberal reforms. In 1861 serfs were emancipated: local govt. and the judicial system were reorganised. This did not satisfy the Nihilists and Alexander was assassinated. (3) **Alexander III** (1845-94) son of Alexander II. He persecuted Jews and suppressed religious toleration and liberal thought.

ALEXANDER, Field-Marshal
(1891-1969) Harold Rupert Leofric George, Earl of Tunis, Brit. soldier. Educ. Harrow and Sandhurst; served in Fr. during World War I. From 1942-3 he was C.-in-C. Middle E. and from 1943-4 G.O.C. Allied Armies and Milit. Gov. of Sicily. As F.M. he was C.-in-C. Allied armies in Italy in 1944 and Supreme Allied Commander, Med. Theatre, 1944-5. Gov.-Gen. Canada 1946-52. Min. of Defence, 1952-54. K.G. 1946. P.C.

ALEXANDER, Samuel
(1859-1938) Philosopher. Prof. of Philosophy at Manchester, 1893. He is best remembered for his theory of Emergent Evolution.

ALEXANDER, Sir William, Earl of Stirling
(*c.* 1567-1640) Scots poet and statesman. His lyrics appeared as *Aurora* (1604).

ALEXANDER NEVSKI
(1218-63) Russ. grand duke. The early years of his life were spent in constant warfare with the Germans, Swedes and Lithuanians; the name Nevski derives from his victory over the Swedes on the banks of the Neva in 1248. On April 5, 1242 he overcame the Knights of the Teutonic Order on Lake Piepus.

ALEXANDRA
(1844-1925) Queen of Gt. Brit., consort of Edward VII whom she mar. in 1863. Daughter of Christian IX of Denmark.

ALEXANDRIA
Chief seaport of U.A.R. (Egypt) on a narrow strip of land between the Medit. Sea and L. Mareotis, connected by rail with Cairo and by canal with the Nile. A. has 2 harbours and handles most of Egypt's trade. Cotton, cottonseed oil, rice, cigarettes and phosphates are exported. Founded by Alexander the Great, 332 B.C., it was cap. of Egypt for over 1,000 years, and a centre of Hellenic culture. It contained the finest library in the world, numerous schools and 2 obelisks. Outside the city was the Pharos lighthouse, 480 ft. high, 1 of the 7 Wonders of the World. From 641 A.D. when Alexandria was taken by the Arabs, its importance declined. When Arabi Pasha rebelled, 1882, the city was bombarded by the Brit. fleet before being occupied by the Brit. forces. Pop. 1,801,000.

ALEXIUS
Name of 5 Byzantine, or E. Rom. emperors.

ALFALFA
(*Medicago sativa*) Species of medick, leguminous plant of the pea family grown for green fodder, and also found wild.

ALFONSO XIII
(1886-1941) King of Spain. In face of growing revolutionary feeling, he estabd. a royal dictatorship, but discontent increased, and in 1931 Alfonso went into exile. Sp. became a repub. Present Pretender to the throne is Alfonso's 3rd son, Don Juan.

ALFRED
(*c.* 849-901) King of Eng. called the Great, b. Wantage, a son of King Ethelwulf. In 871 Alfred was chosen king. The struggle with the Danes had intervals of peace which he used to organise the army and create something like a navy. In 878 Alfred was forced to take refuge in Somerset, but he soon collected an army and won a battle at Edington. The resulting Treaty of Wedmore divided the country between him and the Danish leader, Guthrum; Alfred received the S. and W. and was acknowledged by Guthrum as his lord.

ALGAE
A large and diverse class of plants known as seaweeds or waterweeds.

ALGERIA
Country of N.W. Africa, formerly part of the Fr. Repub. bounded by Morocco, Tunis and Libya, with a Medit. coastline. The chief physical features from N. to S. are the fertile coastal plain, the Atlas Mts. with the enclosed Plateau of the Shotts and the Sahara Desert. The chief exports are wine, fruit, cereals, sheep and oxen skins, zinc and iron ores. Algiers is the cap. and chief port. In 1954 an armed rebellion by the Moslem F.L.N. (*Front de Libération Nationale*) broke out. After 7 years of strife, peace talks took place at Evian in 1961, and despite disturbances by the illegal O.A.S. (*Organisation d'Armée Secrète*) led by Gen. Salan, indep. was achieved in 1962. The pop. is mainly Arab and Berber. Area: 919,637 sq.m. Pop. 11,786,000.

ALGIERS
Seaport and admin. centre of Algeria. There are 2 harbours and an extensive trade is carried on. Pop. 850,000.

ALGONQUIN *See* AMERICAN INDIANS.

ALI
(d. 661) Fourth caliph of Islam (656-61) and son-in-law of the Prophet Mohammed, whose daughter Fatima he mar. The period of Ali's reign was marked by continuous disharmony and civil war and the great schism between the Sunnites and the Shiites. Ali was murdered at Kufa by a band of fanatics. He is regarded by the Shiites as one of the great saints of Islam.

ALICANTE
[-kan'-] Sp. seaport and resort, cap. of A. prov. on the Medit. coast. Pop. 126,107.

ALICE SPRINGS
Town of N. Territory, Australia, in the MacDonnell Ranges. Pop. 4,000.

ALIEN
A person resident in a country of which he is not a subject by birth or naturalisation.

ALKALI
Name given to a group of compounds, oxides or carbonates, which are soluble in water and neutralise acids, forming salts. They turn red litmus blue. The common alkalis, ammonia, caustic soda, caustic potash, sodium and potassium carbonates are of great commercial importance.

ALKALOID
Group of very complex substances forming the active principles of certain plants. They are extracted by percolation with alcohol. Alkaloids act as bases, like ammonia, forming salts with acids. Typical alkaloids used in medicine are atropine, caffeine, cocaine, morphine, quinine and strychnine.

ALKMAAR
Town in N. Holland prov., the Netherlands, 24 m. N.W. of Amsterdam; an important market centre for cattle and cheese. Pop. 45,479.

ALL SAINTS' DAY
Ch. festival kept on Nov. 1. Formerly known as **All Hallows**, its Eve (Oct. 31), is still called Hallowe'en, esp. in Scot. **All Souls' Day.** Feast of R.C. Ch. on which the Ch. on earth prays for the souls of all the faithful departed still suffering in Purgatory.

ALLAH
Arabic name of God, used throughout Islam. He is One, Invisible, Eternal, Indivisible, Beneficent, Almighty, All-knowing, Omnipresent, Just, Merciful, Loving and Forgiving.

ALLAHABAD
City of Uttar Pradesh, India, at the confluence of the Jumna and Ganges. An important railway and trading centre. Yearly Moslem pilgrimages are made to the city. Pop. 411,995.

ALLEN, Bog of
Extensive peat bog in Ireland covering parts of Kildare, Offaly, and Laoighis.

ALLENBY, Viscount
Edward Henry Hyman, 1st Visct. Allenby of Meddigo and Felixstowe (1861-1936) Brit. soldier. Commanded the Cavalry Div. in Fr. (1914-15). As C.-in-C. Egyptian Exped. Force (1917-18), he invaded Palestine, captured Jerusalem, and ended Turkish resistance by the battle of Samaria (Sept. 1918). He was made a F.-M. and a viscount in 1919.

ALLERGY
[al'-er-ji] An exaggerated susceptibility possessed by some individuals to various substances or agents or stimuli which are harmless to normal persons.

ALLEYN, Edward
(1566-1626) Eng. actor; b. London. With his partner Philip Henslowe he managed the Rose Theatre and later built the Fortune. He founded Dulwich Coll.

ALLIANCE
A league or alliance between countries; sometimes used for an industrial league.

ALLIGATOR
Reptile of the same order as the crocodile, differing in having a shorter and broader head, very unequal teeth; the 4th tooth in the lower jaw fits into a pit in the upper jaw. The toes are incompletely webbed. Alligators are found in the warmer parts of the world. They are amphibious in habit and lay their eggs in the grass on the banks of rivers. The 2 surviving species come from N. Amer., *e.g.* Mississippi and other rivers, and from China.

ALLOA
[al'-ō-ă] Burgh, seaport and county town of Clackmannanshire, on the Firth of Forth, 6½ m. from Stirling. Pop. 13,902.

ALLOY
Material formed by the mixing of 2 or more metals. Some alloys are found in nature, but most of them are prepared artificially. Their purpose is to increase hardness, flexibility or toughness, to alter the colour, or to give a definite electric resistance. Iron is hardened by manganese; copper is toughened by arsenic and made more tenacious by aluminium. Gold is hardened for currency purposes by the addition of a baser metal. Some of the most useful alloys are brass, formed of copper and zinc; bronze, of copper and tin; gun metal, of copper and tin; German silver, of copper, nickel and zinc; Britannia metal, of tin, antimony and copper; and pewter, of tin and lead. *See* STEEL.

ALLSPICE
Spice, also called Jamaica pepper. It is made from the berries of a tree growing in the W. Indies, Mexico and parts of S. Amer. and is used for flavouring.

ALMA-ATA
[-ât-a] Important city of U.S.S.R., cap. of Kazakh S.S.R.. Pop. 634,000.

ALMA-TADEMA Sir Lawrence
[al-mă-tad'-ĕmă] (1836-1912) Eng. painter. B. Friesland, he studied painting at Antwerp. He settled in Eng. in 1870. Tadema's pictures are mainly scenes from Gk. and Rom. mythology.

ALMANAC
Orig. used of tables containing astron. data, covering a number of years; astrol. information, prophecies, and weather predictions were later added, and in more recent times the astron. and eccles. calendar is combined with statistical tables and general information. The *Nautical Almanac*, of astron. and navigational tables, is pub. by the Royal Observatory.

ALMANDINE
(or **Carbuncle**) Gem stone, a variety of garnet.

ALMOND
Tree that grows in S. Europe and in Eng. It bears white, pink or red flowers and blooms in the spring. It may be 10 ft. high and is very ornamental. The fruit seeds are dried and sold as a delicacy.

ALMONER
[âl'-] Originally, an officer of a religious establishment whose duty was the distribution of alms. The Brit. royal household has an hereditary grand almoner; the lord high almoner annually dispenses the Maundy Money (royal alms). **Hospital almoner** was formerly one associated with the assessment for payment towards their treatment by patients in hospital; now primarily a social worker and the name has been officially dropped.

ALOE
Trop. evergreen plant with thick fleshy leaves and many tubular flowers. From the dried juice of the leaves of many species the drug, **bitter aloes**, is obtained.

ALOPECIA
or **baldness.** [-pē-] Disease involving loss of hair. There is a natural loss of hair amongst certain men after middle life.

ALPACA
S. Amer. animal, really a domesticated form of the llama. It is bred in Peru and Bolivia for its wool. The hair, fine, silky, long, and black, brown or grey in colour, is used for making alpaca cloth.

ALPS
Mt. range in Europe. It extends from the Rhône in Fr. into Austria, and covers *c.* 80,000 sq.m. with a length of 600 m. and a breadth N. to S. varying from 50 to 150 m. The usual division of the Alps is into 3 parts, W., C. and E. The W. extends from the Medit. to Mt. Blanc; the C. from Mt. Blanc to the Brenner Pass, and the E. from the Brenner Pass into Austria. The general elevation of the range is between 5,000 and 7,000 ft. Above this are some hundreds of peaks, the highest being in the W. which include Mt. Blanc and Monte Rosa, the only two over 15,000 ft. The most famous of the Alpine peaks, apart from Mt. Blanc, are in Switzerland. Many rivers, including the Rhône, the Rhine and tributaries of the Danube, rise in the Alps. Between the mts. lie beautiful valleys and lakes. Of the lakes the most famous are those in Switzerland and Italy—Lucerne, Geneva, Constance, Thun, Garda, Como and Maggiore. The passes of the Alps are notable, esp. those leading into Italy.

ALSACE
District of Fr. in the Rhine Rift Valley, E. of the Vosges and N. of Switzerland. To the W. is a mountainous region but much of the land is fertile, and agriculture is the chief occupation. A. was part of Germany in the M.A. but was seized by Fr. in 1684. **Alsace-Lorraine**—Dist. of Fr. consisting of low-lying Alsace and the Vosges Mts. of Lorraine. It is the region taken from Fr. and added to Germany, 1871. Alsace-Lorraine was returned to Fr. 1919. Occupied by Germany in 1940, liberated by allies in 1944.

ALSATIAN
Orig. a German sheepdog from Alsace. It is a companion, guard and police dog. Ears should be erect, head and jaw strong and wt. *c.* 60 lb.

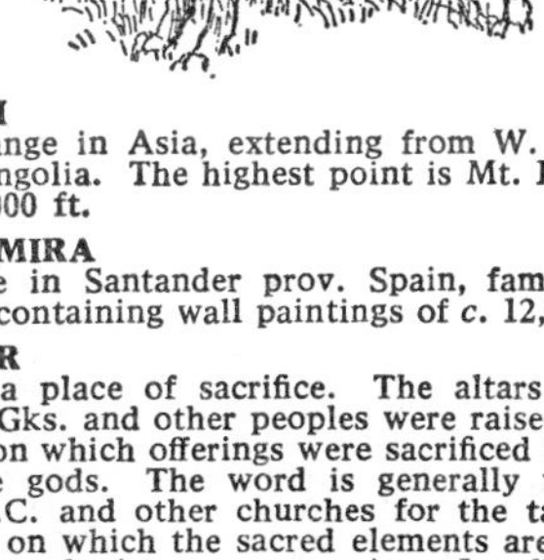

ALTAI
Mt. range in Asia, extending from W. Siberia to Mongolia. The highest point is Mt. Bieluka, *c.* 15,000 ft.

ALTAMIRA
Village in Santander prov. Spain, famous for caves containing wall paintings of *c.* 12,000 B.C.

ALTAR
Orig. a place of sacrifice. The altars of the Jews, Gks. and other peoples were raised structures on which offerings were sacrificed to God, or the gods. The word is generally used in the R.C. and other churches for the table, or stone, on which the sacred elements are placed at the eucharist, or communion. Legally there are no altars in the C. of E.; they are holy tables, or communion tables, and they must be movable and of wood.

ALTDORF
[ält'-] Cap. of Uri canton, Switzerland, S. of L. Lucerne, with a monument to William Tell.

ALTRUISM
Term first employed by the Fr. philosopher Auguste Comte (1798-1857), who founded the positivistic school of philosophy. Under the influence of Clotilde de Vaux, the doctrine that altruism must find expression in selfless service developed. The term was adopted by the Eng. positivists.

ALUM
White transparent mineral, the crystallised double sulphate of aluminium and potassium. The name also describes a similar substance obtained from ammonia, silver, sodium or thallium in which no aluminium is present, obtained from iron, chromium and manganese. Alum made from alunite is mixed with fuel in a furnace, roasted and exposed to the air. The rocks in which the mineral is present in large quantities are called alum shales.

ALUMINIUM
Bluish-white metallic element (at. wt., 27, at. no. 13, sp. gr. 2·7). It is widely distributed, constituting about 8 % of the earth's crust. The metal is usually extracted by an electrolytic process from bauxite. When exposed to the air, it quickly forms a protective layer of oxide, which preserves it from further attack. The lightness of the metal finds application in the transmission of electricity. **Alumina** (Al_2O_3) Oxide of aluminium. Occurs naturally in different forms as emerald, sapphire, ruby, emery and corundum. Also found as white powder, insoluble in water, and used extensively in the manufacture of clay articles. **Duralumin,** an alloy containing copper and magnesium, has great mechanical strength.

ALVA, Duke of
Fernando Alvarez de Toledo (1508-1582). Sp. gen. In 1567, Charles having abdicated, Philip sent Alva to the Netherlands as Gov.-Gen. For 6 years he tried to destroy the religious and polit. liberties of the people, but only succeeded in ruining the country and stiffening the resistance of the inhabitants.

ALYSSUM
Flowering plant with both annual and perennial species. The common sweet alyssum is an annual bearing white fragrant flowers in summer.

AMALEKITES
[a-mal'-e-kits] A roving Semitic people of the Sinai Peninsula and the areas S. of the Dead Sea and between Palestine and Egypt.

AMAZON
River of S. Amer. in vol. the largest in the world. Its sources are the headwaters of the Marañon, and its course from there to the ocean is *c.* 4,050 m. It has innumerable tributaries and drains some 2,700,000 sq.m. Its tributaries include the Negro, Purus, Madeira, Tocantins, Japura, Morona and Xingu. It is navigable by steamers as far as Iquitos, 2,500 m. from its mouth. With its navigable tributaries it supplies some 30,000 m. of waterway. It flows from Peru with an E. course across Brazil until it enters the Atlantic Ocean near Belem (Para). At its mouth it is 50 m. wide.

AMBASSADOR
One who represents his country in a foreign land. Ambassadors form the highest rank in the diplomatic service. They are *ordinary* when they reside permanently at a foreign court, or *extraordinary* when they are sent on a special occasion. *Ambassadors extraordinary* given full powers, *e.g.* of concluding peace, making treaties, etc. are called *plenipotentiaries.*

AMBER
Fossil resin, derived from coniferous trees. Used for ornamental purposes as it polishes

very easily. Colour golden with bluish tints, or transparent. Flies and other insects may be found in it. When rubbed, amber produces negative electricity, a quality known to the Gks. who, like other early peoples, used amber as an ornament. The powder obtained from amber can be distilled to give oil of amber which is used as a liniment and in scent.

AMBERGRIS
Waxy substance from the intestines of the Sperm Whale. It is much used in making scent on account of its suitability for mixing with substances of agreeable smell.

AMBULANCE
Vehicle used for transport of sick and injured. With the introduction of the Nat. Health Service, this service (formerly supplied by the Brit. Red Cross, St. John's and St. Andrew's Ambulance Assoc. and the local authority health and police depts.) became the responsibility of the local authority under the control of the Min. of Health and the Dept. of Health for Scot. Field ambulances, introduced after the Crimean War, are among the med. facilities of the Brit. Army. Ambulance is also used as a term for a surgical post accompanying troops. All ambulance transport is protected by the Geneva Convention and carries a red cross. *See* FIRST AID.

AMEN
(1) The Cosmic Logos, greatest of the gods of ancient Egypt. (2) **Amen-Ra** the Absolute manifested as the Solar Logos, the spiritual power which rules and governs our solar system. (3) Heb. word the exoteric meaning of which is *'so let it be.'* Prayers end with it.

AMENHOTEP III
[ä'-men-hō'-tep] Egyptian king (Reigned 1656-25 B.C.). His chief wife was Tiy, who was ambitious and a woman of strong character. She was the mother of Amenhotep IV (Akhenaten) (*q.v.*). The period of Amenhotep III was one of great prosperity. His building operations were enormous, and included the temple of Mut at Karnak, the greater part of the temple at Luxor, the great temple which the Gks. called the " Memnonium ".

AMERICA
Name of the great cont. which forms the land area of the W. hemisphere, the New World. It is named after Amerigo Vespucci, an Ital. Amer. occupies *c.* 17,000,000 sq.m. stretching from the Arctic circle to Cape Horn, some 7,000 m. It is usually divided into 2 conts. N. and S. Amer. linked by C. Amer. and includes the W. Indies. The orig. inhabitants of the cont. were Indians. They have since been called Amer. Indians. In S. Amer. the people are of Portuguese and Spanish ancestry; in N. Amer., Brit. and Fr. predominate. The word Amer. is used in a narrower and looser sense for the United States of Amer. *See* CENTRAL AMERICA, NORTH AMERICA, SOUTH AMERICA, UNITED STATES.

AMERICA'S CUP
Internat. yacht race. In 1851, when the Queen's Cup was offered by the Royal Yacht Squadron, the winner was the Amer. yacht *America*, hence the name. The race must be sailed in the waters of the successful country. In 1962 Australia entered a yacht, *Gretel*, for the first time but she was beaten. In 1964 a new Brit. yacht *Sovereign* was also beaten.

AMERICAN INDIAN LANGUAGES
(' Amerind '). It is doubtful whether these form a ' family '; but they are all polysynthetic, *i.e.* they string together several dependent ' words ' or particles into one locution.

AMERICAN INDIANS
Name given to the early inhabitants of the Amer. Cont. The word ' Indians ' was used by Columbus, *c.* 1493. Known also as the redman, or red-skin, the race is distinguished by its straight black hair, copper-coloured skin, aquiline nose, prominent jaw and pointed skull. The Indians are tall and strong. It is said that there are 1,500 tribes of Indians. It is possible to make certain generalisations about these people as they were in the time of Columbus. They worshipped spirits, who, they believed, watched over the tribe and its possessions. They had their own language. They knew something of weaving and spinning. They were very fond of music and dancing, and their songs have been collected. They used paint to adorn their bodies. Their food was obtained mainly by hunting. They knew something of agriculture, as they grew maize, and were continually at war with neighbouring tribes. The arrival of the Spanish in S. Amer., and the Brit. and Fr. in N. Amer. was followed by wars between the white men and the red men. The Spaniards introduced the horse to the Indians. In the 18th and 19th cents. many Indians were occupied in collecting furs, but in N. Amer. esp. the land over which they roamed was gradually occupied by the whites and the area left to them was steadily reduced. Today the remnants of the race in the U.S.A. and Canada, live in reservations. In Mexico, C. and S. Amer. they roam about much as of old.

AMERICAN LEGION
Organisation of World War veterans organised in Nov. 1919 and incorporated by Act of Congress. All honourably discharged ex-soldiers, sailors and airmen are eligible for admission to the Legion. The purpose of the legion is 'to uphold and defend the constitution of the United States; to maintain law and order; to foster and perpetuate 100 per cent Americanism.'

AMERICAN LOAN
Credit of £1,100 million from the U.S.A. to Brit. made in 1945. Negotiated for Brit. by Lord Halifax and Lord Keynes, the loan was designed to bridge the post-war transition and to maintain Brit. gold and dollar stocks. *See* MARSHALL PLAN.

AMETHYST
Gem stone. A purple, violet or blue variety of quartz, it owes its colour to impurities, prob. of manganese. It is found in India, Ceylon and S. Amer.

AMHARAS
[am-harr'-as] The ruling race of Ethiopia inhabiting Amhara, Tigré, Gojam and Shoa. Numbering *c.* 5,000,000, the Amharas are Coptic Christians.

AMIENS
[am-ya(ng)] City of N.E. Fr. cap. of Somme dept. 81 m. from Paris, on the Somme. It is a trading centre, with textile and chem. industries. A. in the M.A. was the cap. of Picardy. The battle of Aug. 1918, in which the Allies opened their final and victorious offensive, takes its name from the city. Pop. 109,869.

AMMAN
[am-man'] Cap. of Jordan, on the Hejaz rly. 30 m. E. of Jericho. Since Jordan became indep. in 1946 the city has grown considerably. Pop. 280,000.

AMMONIA
Colourless gas composed of nitrogen and hydrogen (NH_3), having a pungent suffocating odour. It is very soluble in water. It turns red litmus blue and combines with all acids to form salts. It is produced commercially in the manufacture of coal gas, and synthetically by combining nitrogen and hydrogen under great pressure. It is used in the preparation of dyes, also in medicine, and in liquefied form for refrigerating purposes.

AMNESIA
[-nē'-] Loss of memory or forgetfulness. Amne-

sia may result from disease of the brain, follow concussion or appear as a sign of psychological disorder.

AMOEBA
[amē'-] Organism belonging to the most primitive group of the animal kingdom, the protozoa. It consists of a minute fragment of protoplasm, and lives in ponds or streams. It feeds by engulfing suitable particles between 2 pseudopodia and drawing the material into its protoplasm. When grown to full size it can divide into 2 and so reproduce itself.

AMOS
(*c.* 760 B.C.) O.T. Prophet.

AMPHIBIA
Cold blooded vertebrate animals adapted for life either on land or in water. Placed between reptiles and fishes, they include frogs, toads, newts, salamanders, the axolotl, etc. Amphibia acquire the characteristics of the adult phase by stages. The eggs are usually laid in fresh water and hatch by the sun's heat. The larva that emerges is aquatic and possesses gills. Later, limbs and lungs develop and the adult stage is reached. Amphibia breathe partly through their moist skin even in the adult phase. They therefore inhabit damp situations.

AMPHITHEATRE
Rom. building used for public entertainments. Open to the sky, it consisted of an arena, in which beasts and gladiators fought, and tiers of seats for the spectators.

AMPHORA
[amf-] Vessel used by the Gks. and Roms. Made of earthenware, it had 2 handles and was used for holding wine and oil.

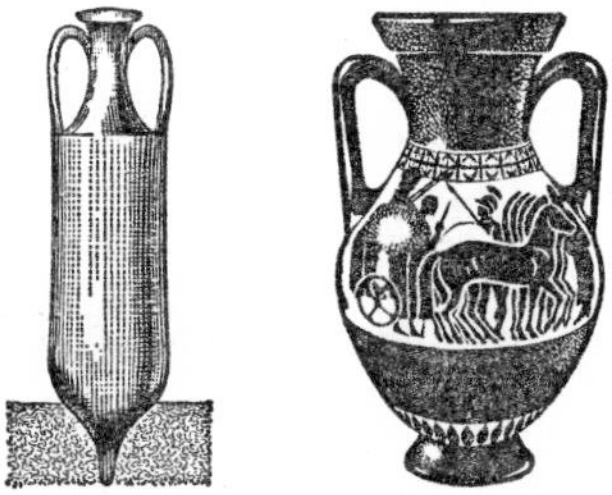

Roman and Greek amphorae

AMRITSAR
[um-rit'-sur] City of Punjab, N.W. India, with textile manufactures and a considerable trade. It is a sacred city of the Sikhs, containing the Golden Temple and a univ. Pop. 376,295.

AMSTERDAM
Cap. commercial centre, and largest city of the Netherlands, on the S.W. shore of the Ijsselmeer (Zuider Zee) at the mouth of the Amstel. Connected with Ijmuiden by the North Sea canal, A. is easily accessible to ocean shipping. Important industries include printing, fruit-canning, textiles, sugar-refining, cocoa and margarine manufacture. Diamond cutting is important, and A. is the world's chief diamond market. There are numerous canals. Although Amsterdam is the cap. the seat of govt. is at The Hague. Pop. 869,000.

AMU-DARYA
River of Asia, 1,400 m. long, known in ancient times as the Oxus. It rises in the Pamirs, on the frontier of India and Afghanistan, and flows N.W. across the U.S.S.R. into the Sea of Aral.

AMUNDSEN, Roald
[a'-mo͝on-sĕn] (1872-1928) Norwegian explorer, educ. Oslo. In 1897-9 he went to the Antarctic, and in 1901 to the Arctic. In 1910 in the *Fram* he sailed to the Antarctic and on Dec. 16, 1911, he reached the S. Pole. In 1926 he crossed the N. Pole in an airship and landed in Alaska. In 1928 he set out in a seaplane to rescue the Ital. explorer, Nobile, and d. on the expedition.

AMUR
River of E. Asia, 2,703 m. long. It runs along the boundary between Manchuria and the U.S.S.R. and then turns N. to enter the Sea of Okhotsk.

ANABAPTISTS
Fanatical Christian sect in 16th cent. It originated at Zwickau in Saxony and its leader was Thomas Münzer. The members did not believe in infant baptism, and became prominent because of their revolutionary ideas. They had a share in the revolt of the peasants in 1525.

ANACONDA
Large water and tree snake, found in Brazil and other parts of S. Amer. where it lives on the river banks and feeds upon birds and animals. Av. length 25-30 ft.

ANAEMIA
Condition in which blood lacks either proper constituents such as blood cells or iron, or in which blood volume has been reduced after a severe haemorrhage.

ANAESTHETIC
Drug acting either on the brain (*general anaesthetic*) or locally on the nerves (*local anaesthetic*) which reduces the appreciation of pain. Since early times man has tried to find anaesthetics. Hypnotism and mesmerism were tried. Modern anaesthetics were first introduced at the end of the 18th cent. Davy, in 1799, noticed the intoxicating effect of nitrous oxide (laughing gas). Farraday, in 1815, noted that ether had a similar effect, and in 1842 Long, in Amer. used ether at operation for the first time. In Brit. Liston, in 1846, was the first, and in 1847 in the Royal Infirmary at Edinburgh, Sir James Y. Simpson used chloroform. Today, anaesthetics such as ether and ethyl chloride are in common use. Novocaine is used as a local anaesthetic. **Analgesia** [-jē'-zi-a] The loss of sense of pain without loss of consciousness. The drugs in common use for this purpose are cocaine, certain of its derivatives and certain quinine derivatives.

ANANIAS
[a-na-nī'-as] Name of 3 Biblical characters mentioned in the Acts of the Apostles. Esp. convert who made a false declaration concerning the sale of a piece of land and who, when rebuked by Peter, fell dead.

ANARCHY
Gk. word meaning 'no govt.' It indicates the condition of a country without a govt. or with a govt. that is powerless to maintain order. **Anarchism** is a projected social revolution, the professed aim of which is the training of the individual so as to become a law to himself.

ANATOLIA
[-tō'-] Name used for Asia Minor (*q.v.*). It is a Gk. word meaning 'the east' and is used by the Turks.

ANATOMY
Science of the structure of the body as learned by dissection. Branches of this science include (1) **morbid anat.** or pathology (*q.v.*) (2) **comparative anat.** in which the anat. of various groups of animals is compared and (3) **microscopic anat.** as demonstrated by the microscope. Scientific study began in modern times with the discoveries of John Hunter.

ANCESTOR WORSHIP
Religion common to many ages and countries. Today it figures in the native religions of China and Japan, while the 'totem' pillar of

the Amer. Indians and the 'ancestor-tablet' of the Maoris are also symbolic of this cult.

ANCHORITES
[ang'-kor-] In the early Ch. a class of religious persons who withdrew themselves from the world and lived in cells, caves, or other habitations. They were most numerous in Egypt and Syria, where Christianity tended to merge with the philosophies of Egypt, Greece and the East.

ANCHOVY
Small coastal fish. It belongs to the herring family and is abundant in the Medit. and other European waters. Used for sauce and relishes.

ANCHUSA
Perennial flowering plant, also called alkanet.

ANCONA
Ital. city and seaport in the Marches, on the Adriatic Sea. Pop. 101,898.

ANDALUSIA
District of S. Spain, consisting of the 8 provs. Huelva, Cadiz, Seville, Malaga, Cordoba, Granada, Jaen, and Almeria, with a coastline on the Atlantic and Medit. Cadiz and Seville are the chief towns.

ANDAMAN ISLANDS
Indian owned group of Is. in the Bay of Bengal, 180 m. S.W. of Burma. There are 5 large Is. and *c.* 200 islets. Rubber and coconut are grown, and there are extensive forests. Port Blair on S. Andaman is the cap. and chief port. 1858 to 1945 they were used as a penal settlement by the Indian Govt. They form, with Nicobar Is. a centrally admin. territory; total pop. 63,548.

ANDERSEN, Hans Christian
(1805-75). Danish writer. Failing to become an opera-singer, took to writing, at first poetry and travels, then (1835-72) the fairy tales.

ANDERSON, Carl David
(1905-) Amer. physicist. He discovered the positron, for which he shared the Nobel Prize in physics with Victor F. Hess, 1936. In 1937, in collaboration with Seth Neddermeyer, he discovered the meson or mesotron, and photographed the meson in 1938.

ANDERSON, Elizabeth Garret
(1836-1917) First woman to qualify in Medicine. Pioneer with Dr. Sophia Jex-Blake for permission for women to enter med. profession. Estabd. dispensary in London in 1866 which became New Hosp. for Women.

ANDERSON, Sir John. *See* WAVERLEY, 1ST VISCOUNT.

ANDES
[-dēz] Mt. system of S. Amer. It stretches down the W. coast of the cont. from the Isthmus of Panama to Cape Horn, through Venezuela, Colombia, Bolivia, Brazil, Argentina, Ecuador, Peru and Chile. Its total length is 4,400 m. The average ht. of the system is stated to be 13,000 ft. The highest point is Aconcagua (22,835) ft.). Other peaks over 20,000 ft. in ht. are Chimborazo in Ecuador, Sorata and Illimani in Bolivia, and Huascaran in Peru. Many are active volcanoes. The Amazon and other great rivers of the cont. rise in the Andes, which are very rich in gold and other minerals.

ANDHRA PRADESH
State of India. Chief rivers are Godavari and Krishna. Cap. Hyderabad. Area: 106,286 sq.m. Pop. 35,978,000.

ANDORRA
Small repub. in the Pyrenees between Fr. and Sp. It is a region of narrow valleys and mt. peaks. The people live mainly by agriculture. Andorra la Vieja is the cap. and chief town. In 1278 Andorra was placed under the joint suzerainty of the Comte de Foix (Fr.) and the Bishop of Urgel (Spain). Area: 174 sq.m. Pop. 11,000.

ANDRADE, Edward Neville da Costa,
F.R.S. (1887-) Director of the Royal Inst. (*q.v.*), formerly Prof. of Physics at Univ. Coll., London. His researches have included atomic physics, sound, and crystal structure.

ANDREA DEL SARTO
[an-drā'-ā] (1486-1531) Ital. painter. B. Florence, he studied art and painted some famous frescoes now in Florence and various portraits and religious works.

ANDREW
(d. *c.* 70) Christian apostle and saint. Brother of Simon Peter, he followed John the Baptist, but later joined Jesus Christ. He is said to have been put to d. at Patrae on a cross in the shape of the letter X, since known as St. Andrew's cross. Patron saint of Scot.; his day is Nov. 30.

ANDREWS, Roy Chapman
(1884-1960) Amer. naturalist and explorer. Leader of the first Asiatic Expedition of the Amer. Mus. of Nat. Hist. to S.W. China in 1917 and to Mongolia and C. Asia, 1919, 1921-30. He discovered the first dinosaur eggs known to science.

ANEMOMETER
Instrument for measuring the velocity of the wind.

ANEMONE
Perennial flowering plants, also called windflowers, found in the temp. regions of Europe. There are many species. The wood anemone is a wild flower which grows freely in Eng. bearing white flowers. Name is also given to marine animals, the sea anemones, which are flowerlike in appearance.

ANEURISM
In human beings a dilatation of an artery which usually is filled with blood.

ANGEL
Supernatural being of Christian, Mohammedan and Jewish belief. Status, between God and man. A celestial hierarchy of 9 orders evolved by later Christian belief: *Seraphim, Cherubim, Thrones* who reflect God's glory; *Dominations, Virtues, Powers* who regulate the universe; *Principalities, Archangels, Angels* who minister to mankind.

ANGEL FALLS
Highest waterfall in the world (3,212 ft.). It was found in a V-shaped canyon in the N. face of Auyan-Tepui (Devil's Mountain), Venezuela, by James Angel, who, in 1935, was making a private survey of the area by air.

ANGEL FISH
or **Monk Fish.** Of the shark family it is found in warm waters, including the Medit. Some are very small, the trop. fish varying from a few inches to 2 ft.

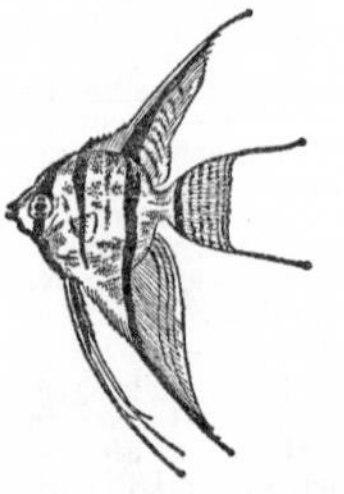

ANGELICA
Perennial herb of temp. zones. One species (*Angelica sylvestris*) grows in the woods of Brit. and reaches a ht. of 5 ft. The stalks are made into a sweetmeat.

ANGELICO, Fra
(1387-1455) Ital. painter. He took the name of Giovanni when he entered a Dominican monastery at Fiesole in 1407. Extant works include the frescoes in the monastery of San Marco at Florence.

ANGERS
[á(ng)-zhā] Cap. of Maine-et-Loire dept. Fr. on the Maine, 58 m. W. of Tours. The ancient cap. of Anjou, it has a fine cath. Pop. 115,252.

ANGEVINS
[an'-ji-vinz] (1154-1399) Eng. royal line founded by Henry of Anjou, who became Henry II of Eng. The other kings of this line were Richard Cœur-de-Lion, John, Henry II, Edward I, II and III, and Richard II. They were also known as Plantagenets.

ANGINA PECTORIS
[an-jī'-nă] Severe pain of sudden onset caused by exertion and usually localised over heart or down inside of left arm or either side of neck, with intense gripping sensation of the chest.

ANGKOR VAT
Ruins of the great temple of the Khmers, *c.* 1 m. S. of the ruined city of Angkor Thom, Cambodia, S.E. Asia.

ANGLER
Fish sometimes called **Frog Fish, Goose Fish,** etc. It belongs to the type called *Teleostei* or bony fishes, and the order *Pediculati*, distinguished by a head process which resembles bait. It is from 3-5 ft. in length and lives down to 200 fathoms.

ANGLES
Teutonic tribe living in Angleland, the modern Schleswig-Holstein. Some of them settled in Eng. *c.* A.D. 450, giving their name to E. Anglia.

ANGLESEY
County and Is. of Wales, separated by the Menai Strait from Caernarvonshire. Flat and fertile, A. is an agricultural area. The county town is Beaumaris and Llangefni the admin. centre. Holyhead stands on Holy Is. A. known as Mona, was a stronghold of the Druids, conquered by the Roms. in A.D. 78. A. sends 1 member to Parl. Area: 275 sq.m. Pop. 51,430.

ANGLICAN COMMUNION
Churches throughout the world that are in communion with the C. of E., *e.g.* Scot. Episcopal Ch., the Ch. of Ireland and Episcopal Churches of Amer. Worship is liturgical and is regulated by the Book of Common Prayer. **Anglicanism.** The teaching and practice of the C. of E. This has spread from Eng. to the various Brit. Dominions and Colonies. Each ch. has its own form of worship, its own prayer book and its own organisation, but all accept episcopacy and other fundamental beliefs of the C. of E. (*q.v.*).

ANGLING
Practice of catching fish with rod, line and bait, in rivers and lakes, and to a certain extent at sea. In Brit. the angler's favourite fish is the trout. Angling for salmon, chiefly in Scot., Norway and Brit. Columbia also requires considerable skill. The fish chiefly caught in Brit. inland waters are the roach, dace, gudgeon, perch, carp, pike, chub, tench, bream and rudd. There is a close season for these and other fish. In angling the 2 main divisions are: (1) *Bait fishing*. (2) *Fly fishing*. In *dry fly* fishing, the fly floats on the surface of the water: in *wet fly* fishing it is immersed. The interests of anglers are protected by the Anglers Assoc.

ANGLO-CATHOLIC
Term used for the 'High Ch.' party in the C. of E. which regards that ch. as a branch of the Catholic Ch. and claims that its fundamental beliefs should conform to those of that ch.

ANGLO-NORMAN
Form of Norman-Fr. used as the official langauge of Eng. after 1066. Eng. began to take its place in the 14th cent.: Parl. was opened by a speech in Eng. first in 1362. Anglo-Norman was the medium of much important lit. till *c.* 1450, and was the language of law till the 17th cent.

ANGLO-SAXON
See **Germanic; Middle Eng.** Name often given to Old Eng. (60-1100). Dialects: W. Saxon, standard medium of lit. from King Alfred's time; Kentish; Mercian or Anglian; Northumbrian. Old Eng. lit. includes the epic *Beowulf*, elegiac poems, heroic lays (*Waldere, Widsith, Finnsburh, Maldon, Brunanburh*), religious poems (*Dream of the Rood, Genesis, Exodus, Elene, Judith*); the *Anglo-Saxon Chronicle* (8th-12th cents.); homilies and lives of saints. **Anglo-Saxon Chronicle.** The annals which were compiled in Eng. at different monasteries (*e.g.* Winchester, Canterbury, Peterborough) between the 9th and the 12th cents. and which summarise the hist. of Eng. during that period and before it.

ANGOLA
Portuguese colony, first settled in 15th cent. between Congo Repub. and S.W. Africa, with 1,000 m. coast on Atlantic. There is a high plateau (3,000 ft.), divided by 3 rivers. Coffee, maize, sugar, palm oil and kernels are the chief products. Diamonds are mined. Chief towns are S. Paolo de Luanda, Novo Lisboa, Lobito and Benguela. Negroes are the predominant race. Area: 481,350 sq.m. Pop. 5,293,000.

ANGOSTURA
Bark of a tree that grows in Venezuela. It produces an aromatic drug of medicinal value.

ANGSTRÖM, Anders Jöns
[ang'-strŏm] (1814-74) Swedish physicist. He did notable work on the conduction of heat and on the solar spectrum. His name was given to the Angström Unit (A.U.), a unit of length (one hundredth-millionth of a centimetre) employed for measuring wavelengths of light.

ANGUS
(formerly **Forfarshire**) County of E. Scot. having a coastline on the N. Sea, with the Firth of Tay to the S. The Braes of Angus, spurs of the Grampian Mts. occupy the N.W. while the Sidlaw Hills lie to the S.W. Between them is the fertile Vale of Strathmore. Farming and fishing are important; also the manufacture of linen and jute. Forfar is the county town, but Dundee is larger. With Kincardine, Angus returns 4 members to Parl. (2 burgh constituencies). Pop. (excluding Dundee) 95,582.

ANHYDRITE
Anhydrous calcium sulphate $CaSO_4$.

ANILINE
$C_6H_5NH_2$. Colourless liquid used in the manufacture of aniline dyes. It boils at 183° C. and has a sp. gr. of 1·024 at 16°. It is poisonous.

ANIMAL
Term used in relation to living organisms apart from plant life. The distinction becomes one of great difficulty, as among the lowest types many of the characters usually assoc. with plants are shared by animals. The fundamental basis of all living organisms is protoplasm in which is inherent the vital activities of locomotion, respiration, food absorption, secretion and excretion, response to external stimuli, and reproduction. In the multicellular organisms specialisation of tissues for the carrying out of these functions occurs, giving rise to organs. Unlike plants, animals cannot build up their protoplasm from the simple elements. They search for food unless they are parasitic. Respiration consists of the absorption of oxygen and removal of carbon dioxide, the response to stimuli is performed by some form of nervous

system, digestion is characterised by preparation of organic and inorganic food materials for absorption in simpler form, with assoc. secretory and excretory organs, and reproduction occurs by simple or complex processes and organs. Some degree of consciousness is present.

ANIMISM
Attribution of a living soul to inanimate objects and natural phenomena. The present and generally accepted use of the term is due to E. B. Tylor, *Primitive Culture.*

ANISEED
Fruit of a perennial herb. An umbelliferous plant, the anise grows in S. Europe. Another variety, in China and Japan, belongs to the magnolia family. The anise is chiefly grown for its seeds which produce a fragrant essential oil used as a flavouring.

ANJOU
[â(ng)-zhoo] One of the provs. of Fr. before the Revolution. It was the district around Angers, its cap. and its chief river was the Maine. The duchy was lost by King John, 1203, and its later counts were members of the royal family of Fr. In 1360 the count was made a duke, and the dukes ruled it until 1584.

ANKARA
Cap. of Turkey on the Anatolian plateau, *c.* 200 m. S.E. of Istanbul. A. is a modern city, with industries and a transit trade. Pop. 650,067.

ANKLE
Part of the lower limb formed by the junction of the leg and foot. **Ankle joint.** Unites the leg with the foot and is composed of the lower end of the tibia and fibula with the talus and calcaneous bones. It is a hinge joint and its strength is dependent on the powerful ligaments that envelop the joint and the powerful leg muscles that pass along the side of the joint to their insertion into the foot.

ANNA
Name of 2 rulers of Russia. The 1st (1693-1740), a daughter of Ivan V, mar. the Duke of Courland in 1710. In 1730 she was chosen Empress of Russia. She ruled, aided by her favourite, Biren, under a system of terrorism, until her d.

ANNAN
Burgh and seaport of Dumfries, where the Annan river flows into Solway Firth. Site of Atomic Power Station. Pop. 5,572.

ANNAPURNA
26,492 ft. peak in the Himalayas. Summit first reached in 1950 by a Fr. exped. led by M. Herzog. **Annapurna Two,** 26,041 ft. the 2nd of A.'s 4 summits, was climbed in 1960 by an expedition led by Col. J. Roberts.

ANNE
(1665-1714) Queen of Brit. Younger daughter of James II and his wife Anne Hyde; b. London; mar. George, Prince of Denmark. Anne became Queen on d. of William of Orange, 1702, and reigned for 12 yrs. Her reign was made glorious by the victories of Marlborough and the writings of Addison and others. She had no surviving child, and her d. brought the rule of the House of Stuart to an end.

ANNE OF AUSTRIA
(1601-66) Daughter of Philip III of Spain, she mar. Louis XIII of France and was the mother of Louis XIV. On the d. of her husband she became regent, with Cardinal Mazarin as minister.

ANNE OF CLEVES
(1515-57) Henry VIII's 4th wife. The daughter of the Duke of Cleves, a Protestant, she was mar. to Henry, Jan. 1540. The union was dissolved in July, 1540.

ANNE OF DENMARK
(1574-1619) The queen of James VI and I, she was the daughter of the King of Denmark and Norway. She had 5 children.

ANNELID
Group of segmented worms, including Earthworms, Rag-worms, Lug-worms, and Leeches. The body is divided into a number of rings or segments. Many live in water, but some on land, where they burrow in soil or sand.

ANNIGONI, Pietro
(1910-) Ital. painter, known for his fashionable portraits.

ANNUNCIATION
Announcement of a forthcoming event. The word is used for tidings brought by the angel Gabriel to the Virgin Mary concerning the Incarnation (Luke, 1).

ANOUILH, Jean
(1910-) Fr. dramatist. Among his works are *Eurydice,* 1942; *Antigone,* 1946; *L'invitation au château,* 1948.

ANSELM
(*c.* 1033-1109) Eng. saint and prelate. Apptd. Archbp. of Canterbury 1093, but was soon at variance with William II. Refusal to do homage to the new king, Henry I, led to a 2nd exile. A compromise 1105, was made between the claims of ch. and state.

ANSON, Lord
(1697-1762) Eng. sailor. In 1740 he was given command of a squadron, Eng. being then at war with Spain. All his ships save 1 were lost, but in this he returned home with treasure worth £500,000. In 1747 he defeated the Fr. fleet off Cape Finisterre. As First Lord of the Admiralty (1751-62) he organised the Marines.

ANT
(or **Emmet**) Insect allied to bees and wasps. Belonging to the order Hymenoptera, there are *c.* 2,000 varieties. The White Ant, or Termite is *not* related to the ordinary ant. There are male, female and neuter ants and a queen. The neuters are sterile females who do the work. Only the males and females have wings. They mate while flying; soon afterwards the males die and the females, having shed their wings, lay eggs which are tended by the neuters. In a few days the eggs become pupae and in a few more, perfect insects. The homes of the ants are passages in the ground, or in the trunks of trees. They have stings which inject formic acid.

ANT LION
Larva of a neuropterous insect *Myrmeleon formicarius.* It is found in Europe, but not in Brit. It forms in the sand a small pit, into which ants and other wingless insects fall, to be seized by the ant lion lying at the bottom.

ANTANANARIVO *See* TANANARIVE.

ANTARCTIC, The
S. Polar cont. and the icebound sea surrounding it. Except for the outlying S. Georgia and S. Sandwich groups it lies within 60° latitude. In 1928 ' by virtue of discovery ', various parts of the cont. were included within the Brit. Empire. These included parts of Coats Ld., Enderby, Kemp, Queen Mary, Wilkes, King George V and Oates Lands. Now the cont. is divided into 6 sectors: the Brit. Antarctic Territory; the Norwegian A. Territory; the Austral. A. Territory; Adélie Land (Fr.); Ross Dependency (New Zealand) and the U.S. region of James Ellsworth and Marie Byrd Land. The **A. Circle** is the line of latitude drawn at 66½° S. **Antarctic Exploration.** The first man knowingly to cross the Antarctic circle was James Cook, 1773. In 1821 Bellingshausen first discovered land within the circle, at Peter I Is. and other expeditions, led by Weddell, Biscoe, Balleny, Ross and others followed. Ross, in

1839, made extensive discoveries including the volcanoes Erebus and Terror. In 1901 the *Discovery* expedition under R. F. Scott, found and named King Edward VII Land, and explored Victoria Land. Another expedition, led by W. S. Bruce, discovered Coats Land. In 1908, E. H. Shackleton led an expedition that got to within 100 m. of the pole. The first to reach the pole was Roald Amundsen, who, with a party on skis, arrived there on Dec. 16, 1911. A month later, using sledges, Scott, with 4 companions, reached it, but met his d. on the return journey. In 1929 an Amer. expedition was undertaken, in which Richard Byrd flew to the Pole from the Ross Ice Barrier. In 1955 an advance party from the U.K. led by Dr. Vivian Fuchs established Shackleton Base, in Vahsel Bay. Dr. Fuchs returned to the U.K. to complete the plans for the main expedition which left Britain in Nov. 1956, on the *Magga Dan*. This first journey of 2,200 m. across the A. Cont. began on 24th November, 1957, and ended with the arrival of Dr. Fuchs and his party at Scott Base, on the Ross Sea, on 2nd March, 1958. The New Zealand support party operated from Scott Base, and was led by Sir Edmund Hillary.

ANTEATER
Mammal feeding on termites and ants. The name chiefly indicates 3 quadrupeds inhabiting C. and S. Amer. The Great A. (*Myrmecophaga*), with a tubular muzzle and long viscid tongue, is a ground dweller measuring 7 ft. The

Cape Anteater, or Aardvark

Lesser (*Tamandua*) and the Pigmy (*Cycloturus*) are arboreal. Australia possesses the Banded A. (*Myrmecobius*), one of the pouchless marsupials, and the Spiny A. (*Echidna*) one of the 2 surviving oviparous mammals (*q.v.*). Others which feed mainly on termites are the Pangolins (*Manis*) of Africa, India, China, Borneo, etc., and the Aardvarks (*q.v.*), the Cape A.

ANTELOPE
Generalised name for hollow-horned ruminants. Asia possesses the Indian A. (Sasin), the Nilgai and 4-horned Chousingha, the Tartary Saiga, the Tibetan Chiru, and many gazelles. Most of the 150 species are confined to Africa, Arabia and Syria. Besides gazelles they include the Eland, Kudu, Bushbuck, Oryx, Addax, Springbok, Duiker, Hartebeest and Gnu.

ANTENATAL CLINIC
Clinic to provide medical advice and supervision for the expectant mother so as to ensure as far as possible her health during pregnancy and the safe delivery of her child. The first such clinic in Britain was estabd. at the Royal Hospital, Edinburgh, in 1902. The Maternity and Child Welfare Act of 1919 made such clinics the responsibility of the local authorities, and they continue to function under the aegis of the Nat. Health Service.

ANTHRACENE
[-sēn] Colourless crystals which belong to the group of aromatic hydrocarbons, have a blue fluorescence, and are used for making dye stuffs.

ANTHRACITE
Name given to that class of coal which contains the highest percentages of fired carbon, ranging from 90 % to 95 %. It is hard and dense and of brilliant lustre. It burns smokelessly with intense heat and barely luminous flame.

ANTHRAX
Commonly called wool-sorters' disease. Acute infectious fever caused by *Bacillus Antracis*. Disease common in Fr. and Russia but now rare in Brit. following legislation. In man it is characterised by large ulcer, usually situated on back of neck, or a type of pneumonia.

ANTHROPOID
Variety of ape. Of all the lower animals they are the most like men. There are 4 types: Orangs, Gibbons, Gorillas and Chimpanzees.

ANTHROPOLOGY
Science of man. Physical anthropology treats of the natural history of man. It seeks aid from palaeontology, which studies the fossil bones of early man and his organic contemporaries. Cultural anthropology, called by Herbert Spencer sociology, unfolds the story of civilisation. Ethnology is the study of racial origins and distribution.

ANTHROPOMORPHISM
Ascription to the deity of human attributes.

ANTHROPOSOPHY
[-pos'-of-i] System of religion, philosophy, science and art, founded by Rudolf Steiner (1861-1925). B. Austria, he had spiritual visions in childhood, and devoted much time to the study of science, educ., medicine, art, and social problems. An important item in anthroposophical teaching is the doctrine of reincarnation.

ANTIBES
[ȧ(ng)-tēb] Seaport and winter resort on the Fr. Riviera, dept. Alpes-Maritimes. Pop. 15,000.

ANTIBIOTIC
[-bī-o'-tik] The property of living organisms to produce in self-defence substances which retard the growth of, or destroy, unfriendly organisms. In 1929 Alexander Fleming discovered that the mould penicillin produced a substance destructive to staphylococcal germs. Other antibiotics are *streptomycin*, which is beneficial in tuberculosis; *chloramphenicol*, the first of the new antibiotics to be made synthetically. Highly satisfactory results have been obtained in the treatment of the enteric fevers, typhoid and paratyphoid, atypical virus pneumonia, Q-fever, and virus infections such as undulant fever, and psittacosis. The fact that there is now an effective treatment for typhus and similar fevers is a medical advance of prime importance. Aureomycin is specific for every common form of pneumonia. It is also of value in the treatment of venereal diseases. *See* PENICILLIN; STREPTOMYCIN.

ANTICYCLONE
Atmos. phenomenon. An area of high barometric pressure is caused by descending air, the pressure decreasing towards the edges of the area. The descending air becomes dry and warm and so transmits radiation freely. The centre of the system is calm, but from it winds blow out, in the N. hemisphere in a clockwise direction and in the S. in an anti-clockwise direction.

ANTIGUA
[-tē'-gȧ] Largest of the Leeward Is. lying N. of Guadeloupe. Sugar and molasses are the chief products. St. Johns is the cap. Barbuda and Redondo are dependencies. To be indep. state in assoc. with Brit. Pop. 62,000.

ANTILLES
Name collectively applied to the W. Indian Is. S. of the Bahamas. The **Greater A.** comprise Cuba, Jamaica, Haiti, Puerto Rico and some smaller Is. The **Lesser A.** include the Leeward and Windward groups, Trinidad, and the Dutch Is. of Curaçao, Aruba and Bonave.

ANTIMONY
Metallic element, sym. Sb., at. wt. 121·76. It is crystalline, brittle, lustrous, bluish-white, and melts at 630·5° C. The unrefined commercial metal called regulus is mainly derived from its sulphide stibnite, which is mined in China, Australia, Borneo, Fr. and Mexico. It is a constituent of alloys for sharp castings such as type metal, and anti-friction metals.

ANTIOCH
Town of Turkey, on the Orontes 60 m. W. of Aleppo. Founded *c.* 300 B.C. and named after Antiochus, King of Syria, it was a centre of the early Christians. The modern name is Antakya. Pop. 50,908.

ANTIPODES
Term denoting places diametrically opposite to each other on the earth's surface. A line joining them passes through the earth's centre.

ANTIRRHINUM
[-ī′-num] Genus of many-coloured flowering plants called snapdragon.

ANTI-SEMITISM
Opposition to the Jewish race. In its modern form the movement became conspicuous in Europe during the 19th cent. and was the cause of many brutal outrages in Russia and Hungary. The Dreyfus case is an illustration of Anti-Semitism in Fr. Under Hitler's rule in Germany the movement culminated in a deliberate policy of race-massacre in the concentration camps, and 6,000,000 Jews were put to d. *See* JEWS.

ANTISEPTIC
Substance which inhibits the growth of micro-organism. Their use in the antiseptic age of surgery was popularised by Joseph Lister (1827-1912). Largely superseded by asepsis. *See* DISINFECTANT.

ANTOFAGASTA
Seaport of Chile, *c.* 750 m. N. of Valparaiso. The chief industries are concerned with the silver and nitrates mined nearby. Pop. 214,090.

ANTONELLO DA MESSINA
(*c.* 1430-1479) Ital. painter who studied painting in oils in Bruges and is said to have taken the new medium to Italy.

ANTONINUS PIUS, Titus Aurelius Fulvus
(A.D. 86-161). Rom. Emperor of Gallic family. He was adopted by the Emperor Hadrian and succeeded him in 138. He brought peace to the Empire. The wall built between the Forth and the Clyde bears his name.

ANTRIM
Maritime county of N. Ireland, with a long coastline on the N. and E. The rivers Lagan and Bann, with Lough Neagh, form much of the S. and W. boundaries. Along the coast are the Antrim Mts. but inland the country is fertile, with some bogland. Flax and potatoes are grown, Antrim is the county town; others are Belfast, Carrickfergus, Larne and Ballymena. The county returns 2 members to Parl. Pop. (excluding Belfast) 278,600. **Antrim.** Market and county town of Co. A. on L. Neagh, 15 m. N.W. of Belfast. Pop. 1,700.

ANTWERP
City and chief seaport of Belgium, cap. of A. prov. on the right bank of the Scheldt, 27 m. N.E. of Brussels, and *c.* 50 from the N. Sea. A. is one of the great trading ports of Europe. Industries include shipbuilding and repairing, oil and sugar refining, and the manufacture of cloth, linen and textiles. In the 15th cent. A. replaced Bruges as the chief port of the Netherlands, and in the 16th cent. it was the greatest port in Europe. Its decline was caused by the Spanish invasion and its capture in 1585, and in 1648 the Scheldt was closed by the Treaty of Westphalia. After 1830, when Belgium became indep. it became once more a scene of great trading activity. It fell to the Germans during both World Wars. Pop. 647,060.

ANZIO
[an′-tsiō] Seaport in Lazio. Italy on the Tyrrhenian coast 30 m. South of Rome. During World War II, 40,000 Brit. and Amer. troops landed on a beach between Anzio and Nettuno, S.W. of Rome.

AORTA
Main artery of body. Beginning at left ventricle it slopes upwards to neck (*ascending Aorta*) and backwards to the spinal column (*arch of aorta*) where it becomes the *thoracic aorta*. Lies alongside spine and passes through diaphragm to become *abdominal aorta*. At lower end of back bone it divides into the *iliac arteries*, right and left. Other branches supply nearly all structures in chest and abdomen.

APACHE
[-pash′] Group of N. Amer. Indian tribes, who formerly ranged from Texas and Arizona S. to the Mexican state of Durango. They were at constant feud with the whites until 1886. The name was applied to hooligans of alien origin in Paris early in the 20th cent.

APARTHEID *See* SOUTH AFRICA, **Apartheid.**

APATITE
Mineral in which anhydrous calcium phosphate is assoc. with a variable proportion of the chloride or fluoride of the same metal. It appears as minute lustrous needles in igneous rocks or as hexagonal prisms in crystalline limestones.

APE
Word applied to the anthropoids, *i.e.* the Gorilla, Chimpanzee, Orang-utan, etc. *See* ANTHROPOID; MONKEY.

APENNINES
Chain of mts. forming the backbone of the Ital. peninsula. The highest peak is Mt. Corno, 9,583 ft.

APHIS
Insects known as plant lice or green fly, very common in Brit. They feed on plants and leave an excretion called honeydew, eaten by ants, but injurious to vegetation. They reproduce sexually once a year and in the spring the eggs hatch out into females. The eggs of this and of succeeding generations of females develop without fertilisation. The males are only developed in the autumn.

APHRODITE
[afrodī′-ti] Gk. goddess of love (**Venus**). By Ares she was the mother of Eros. Her worship, marked by excesses, was very widespread in the Gk. cities.

APOCALYPSE
[ă-pok′-a-lips) Form of religious writing. Emerged from the Jewish Hellenistic period. Classical O.T. example is Book of Daniel. The Book of Revelation (N.T.) is frequently referred to specifically as the Apocalypse.

APOCRYPHA
[ă-pok′-rif-a] Religious writings of Jewish origin not found in the Heb. canon of the O.T. There are 14 of these apocryphal books: *1 Esdras, 2 Esdras, Tobit, Judith, The Additions to Esther, The Wisdom of Solomon, Ecclesiasticus, Baruch, The Song of the Three Holy Children, The History of Susanna, Bel and the Dragon, The Prayer of Manasses, 1 Maccabees, 2 Maccabees.* N.T. apocrypha include *The Epistle of Barnabas, The Gospel of Peter* and *The Shepherd of Hermas.*

APOLLO
Gk. god, regarded later as the god of healing and the father of Aesculapius. He was also the god of song and music.

APOLOGETICS
Branch of theology which concerns itself with the grounds and defence of the Christian faith. It animated the work of Justin Martyr, Origen, Augustine, Anselm, Aquinas and Abélard, and was systematised in the 18th cent. by Butler and Paley. Modern apologetics emphasises the moral ideal.

APOPLEXY
Commonly called **stroke** or **seizure**, occurs after a haemorrhage into the brain or blockage of a cerebral vessel. Characterised by redness of the face, laboured breathing, loss of consciousness with unequal size and shape of pupils.

APOSTACY
Term generally employed to designate reproachfully the abandonment of a faith. In R.C. eccles. law it covers the renunciation of monastic vows, or of the clerical profession.

APOSTLE
Term, denoting messenger, adopted by Jesus Christ to designate the 12 men sent forth to preach the gospel (Luke, 6). The names of the 12 are: Simon Peter, Andrew, James, John, Philip, Bartholomew, Thomas, Matthew, James the Less, Thaddaeus, Simon the Canaanite and Judas Iscariot. After the betrayal by Judas Iscariot his place was allocated to Matthias. The title was claimed by St. Paul, the apostle to the Gentiles. **Apostle's Creed.** Confession of the Christian faith wrongly ascribed to the Apostles. **Apostolic Succession.** In Christianity, the doctrine that the episcopal power invested in the apostles by Christ passes in unbroken succession from them to the bishops of today. It is on this doctrine that the validity of the Sacraments rests, and it is held by the R.C. Ch. that, because of the schism caused by the Reformation, the consecration of bishops in the Ch. of England is not valid. Protestant nonconformist churches believe that the Apostolic faith is preserved in the Scriptures alone, and that belief in the Apostolic Succession is not essential to the discharge of episcopal functions and the transmission of the promised divine grace.

APOTHECARY
Person who mixes drugs. In Eng. the soc. of Apothecaries holds exams. and its degree of L.S.A. enables the holder to practise. **Apothecaries wt.** *See* TABLES, p. 453.

APPALACHIANS
Mt. system of N. Amer. extending for over 1,500 m. in the E. from Maine to Alabama.

APPEAL, Court of
Court of law in which the decisions of the lower courts can be reviewed, and, if necessary, reversed. In Eng., appeals from the county courts go to the Court of Appeal. Appeals from this court go to the House of Lords, which is the supreme court of appeal. In Scot., the inner house of the Court of Session hears appeals from the outer house; and from there appeals can be taken to the House of Lords. For criminal cases there is a Court of Criminal appeal estabd. in Eng. 1907, and in Scot. 1926.

APPENDICITIS
Disease of inflammatory character affecting vermiform appendix. It is usually acute in onset with pain commencing in region of umbilicus but eventually settling in right side of abdomen, with rise in temp. and vomiting.

APPLE
Malus pumila. Tree or bush bearing a popular fruit, very widely grown in Brit. Some well-known varieties are Blenheim, Cox's Orange Pippin (dessert), Bramley Seedling, Newton Wonder (cooking). Apples of a different kind are grown for making cider. Enormous quantities are grown in Calif., Canada, Australia, New Zealand and elsewhere.

APPLEBY
Borough and county town of Westmorland, on the Eden, 30 m. S.E. of Carlisle. Pop. 1,751.

APPLETON, Sir Edward Victor
K.C.B., F.R.S. (1892-1965) Brit. physicist. Educ. Camb. He discovered one of the conducting layers in the upper atmosphere—now called the Appleton layer—which are responsible for long-distance radio transmission. Nobel Prize for Physics in 1947. Princ. of Edinburgh Univ., 1949-65.

APPRENTICE
Person bound for a term of years to a master who instructs him in his trade. The system originated in Eng. in the 14th cent. As the apprentice is usually a minor the articles are signed on his behalf by his parent or guardian.

APPROVED SCHOOL
In Gt. Brit., in terms of the Children and Young Persons Act, 1933, any child or young person who has committed a crime, is refractory, or in need of care and protection, may be sent by a court of law to a school approved by the Home Sec.

APRICOT
Fruit tree. A native of Asia, introduced into Eng. in the 17th cent. It is cultivated in Fr. and Calif.

APTERYX *See* KIWI.

APULEIUS, Lucius
[a-pewl-ē′-us] Writer of African birth who lived in the 2nd cent. and wrote the *Golden Ass* or *Metamorphoses*, one of the few surviving examples of the Lat. novel.

AQUAMARINE
The finest variety of beryls of a sea-green or blue colour.

AQUEDUCT
Artificial channel used to convey water above the ground. The Roms. were great builders of aqueducts usually of stone, the water being carried in covered chambers lined with cement. In Eng. an aqueduct carries the Bridgwater Canal over the Manchester Ship Canal. In the U.S.A. the Catskill, 126 m. long, supplies New York with water. The longest is that running from Perth, W. Australia, to Kalgoorlie, 350 m.

AQUILEGIA
Genus of flowering plants of the family Ranunculaceae. The best-known is the columbine.

AQUINAS, Saint Thomas
(*c.* 1225-74) Ital. philosopher, founder of the system which became the official philosophy of the Catholic Ch.; entered Dominican order 1243. Commenced studies with Albertus Magnus, 1245. Avowedly Aristotelian in character, his philosophy teaches that while reason and faith differ as to the procedure, they cannot deny each other's findings. His greatest work is *Summa Theologica* (1267-73). He was canonised in 1323. His feast is on Mar. 7.

AQUITAINE
District of S.W. Fr. between the Garonne and the Pyrenees. Eleanor, the daughter of one of the ruling dukes, mar. Henry II of Eng.

ARAB
Semitic race, including all the Semites except the Jews, found in many parts of Asia and

Africa. They were settled in Arabia at the time of Mahomet, but his teaching induced them to invade Africa and later Spain, founding an empire in India and in Asia. Today they number *c.* 45,000,000, practically all Mohammedans. Math. and philosophy are prominent in their lit. and the Arab schools of learning at Baghdad and elsewhere have contributed much to human knowledge. **Arabic.** S. Semitic language known in Arabia from early times (Himyaritic and Thamudic inscriptions) and diffused throughout Middle E., and N. and W. Africa in 7th-8th cent. by Arab conquest and Islamic conversions. Arabic script is used throughout the Moslem world.

ARAB LEAGUE
Pan-Arab league of sovereign states founded in 1944 following the Alexandria Conference. The covenant was signed in Cairo by Egypt, Iraq, Saudi Arabia, Syria, Lebanon, Jordan, and Yemen. Lybia joined (1953); the Sudan (1956); Tunisia and Morocco (1958); Kuwait (1961); Algeria (1962). The League can mediate between any of the League states or a League state and a country outside the League. Since the founding of the U.A.R. its cohesion has lessened.

ARABI PASHA
(1839-1911) Egyptian nationalist leader. In 1882 he became Min. for War, and led a nationalist revolt against foreign influence and control.

ARABIA
Country of S.W. Asia, a peninsula bounded by the Persian Gulf, the Arabian Sea and the Red Sea. It consists of a plateau sloping from the S.W. towards the Euphrates valley in the N.E. In the S. running parallel to the Red Sea coast, and in the extreme E. on the Gulf of Oman, are mts. rising to over 7,000 ft. The interior is mainly sandy desert. The climate is hot and dry; rainfall is scanty. Many of the inhabitants are nomadic Bedouin Arabs. Since the 7th cent. Arabia has become the centre of Mohammedanism, and Mecca and Medina are visited by many pilgrims. Conquered by the Turks in the 16th cent. Arabia remained under Turkish rule until 1916, when the Sherif of Mecca, aided by Col. T. E. Lawrence, threw off Turkish authority. The Kingdom of Saudi Arabia (*q.v.*) was formed in 1926 by the union of Hejaz and Nejd (*qq.v.*). Other states are the Sheikhdom of Kuwait, the Sultanate of Muscat and Oman on the E. coast, the Yemen, Aden and the states of Bahrain, Qatar and Trucial Oman. Area: *c.* 1,200,000 sq.m. Pop. *c.* 10,000,000. *See* SAUDI ARABIA, SOUTH ARABIA, YEMEN, ETC.

ARACHNIDA
[-nē′-da] Class of arthropods. It includes spiders, scorpions and mites. They are chiefly carnivorous and have usually 6 pairs of limbs. They have no antennae; simple eyes vary in number from 2 to 12, and the head and thorax are fused together. *See* SPIDER.

ARAGON
Former kingdom of Spain, lying S. of the Pyrenees. It arose in the 11th cent. and was extended to include the Balearic Is., Naples, Sicily and Sardinia. In 1467 Aragon united with Castile.

ARAL, Sea of
Lake of Asia, in the U.S.S.R. *c.* 80 m. E. of the Caspian Sea. It covers some 26,035 sq.m.

ARAMAIC
Semitic language, with ancient Samaritan, Mandaean, Chaldee, Syriac as its varieties. It replaced Heb. as the language of the Jewish people 1st cent. B.C. and the Targums and Talmud are written in it. Aramaic phrases are quoted in the Gospels. Syriac is still spoken near Damascus. There is a 5th cent. B.C. Samaritan version of the Pentateuch.

ARAN
Group of Is. off the W. coast of Eire. Fishing is the main industry. Area 18 sq.m.

ARARAT
Mt. mass on the borders of Armenia (U.S.S.R.) and Turkey, an extinct volcano with 2 peaks, 16,945 ft. high. It is said to have been the resting place of the Ark after the flood.

ARBITRATION
Method of deciding disputes without resort to law, strikes, lock-outs or war. There are 3 kinds of arbitration: legal, industrial and international. **Industrial arbitration** is used in settling disputes between employer and employed. In Brit. there is an industrial court in the Min. of Labour. **Internat. arbitration** has been used many times. An internat. court was estabd. at The Hague in 1899.

ARBOR VITAE
[vē′-tī] Evergreen coniferous tree of 2 main species, the Amer. and the Chinese.

ARBUTUS
Evergreen tree with white or reddish flowers in clustered sprays.

ARCADIA
Mt. region in S. Greece. Its inhabitants were regarded as living a simple, rural life.

ARCHAEOLOGY
Study of the remains of the past. Sir Henry Layard examined the ruins of Nineveh and Babylon in the mid 19th cent. Unscientific explorations were done at Troy by T. Schliemann. Sir W. Flinders Petrie introduced more scientific methods in Egypt and Gen. Pitt Rivers in S. Eng. Sir Arthur Evans excavated in Crete and in 1922 Howard Carter opened the tomb of Tut-ankh-Amen. In Brit. evidence of occupation prior to the Rom. occupation has been revealed; digs in London and other Rom. cities have revealed much of Rom. life and at Sutton Hoo of the A.-S. invaders. Since World War II air photography has been used to identify and map sites. Their excavation has developed into a highly scientific process.

ARCHANGEL
[ark′-] Russian seaport and chief city of A. Region in the R.S.F.S.R. at the mouth of the Dvina, on the White Sea. The harbour is icebound in winter. Pop. 286,000.

ARCHBISHOP
High official in the Christian ch. The title first appeared in the 6th cent. In the C. of E. there are 2 archbishops, Canterbury ('Primate of All Eng.') and York ('Primate of Eng.').

ARCHDEACON
Official in the C. of E. Originally chief of the deacons attached to a cath. In time the archdeacons became almost indep. of the bishops, their duties being concerned with the financial and business side, but they are apptd. by the bishop.

ARCHER
(*Toxotes*) Small fish, found round the coasts of the E. Indies and Australia, so called because it can squirt water at its insect prey.

ARCHERY
The art of using the bow and arrow, formerly used in hunting and warfare, but today solely as a pastime. Archery was practised by the Egyptians, Persians, Gks., Roms., Arabs and Turks. Archery was the deciding factor in the battles of Hastings, Crécy and Agincourt. Late in the 18th cent. archery was revived in Eng. as a sport. In 1781 the Royal Toxophilite Soc. was founded. The pastime is now controlled by the Grand Nat. Archery Soc. founded 1861. In the N. of Eng. shooting for the Scorton Arrow has been going on with but few breaks since 1673. **The Royal Company of Archers** is a body of Scots noblemen and gentlemen founded 1676. It is the sovereign's bodyguard for Scot.

ARCHIMEDES
[-dēz] (*c.* 287-212 B.C.) Gk. mathematician. B. at Syracuse. He discovered the use of the lever and invented the Archimedean screw. He estabd. the principle that a body plunged in a fluid loses as much of its wt. as is equal to the wt. of the displaced fluid.

ARCHITECTURE
Art of designing and constructing buildings. Civil architecture is concerned with the building of structures of ordinary utility; eccles. deals with chs., and naval and milit. with the construction of ships and fortifications respectively. The beginnings of the art are seen in the primitive wattle huts of lake dwellings. The early flat roofs with horizontal beams gave place to the use of the arch which from a rounded form in time became the pointed arch of Gothic architecture. Classical archit. reached its peak in Greece. The classical tradition, in which the various columnar types fall into 5 'classical orders' *i.e.* Doric, Ionic, Corinthian, Tuscan and Composite each having its own rules of proportion, was formulated by Ital. architectural writers in the 16th cent. In earlier times the Greeks and Romans adhered to no set of rules and, except during the classical revival following the Renaissance, the same flexibility applies to most buildings which are modelled upon classical design. 20th cent. developments in building techniques have produced a remarkable freedom of shape as shown in the designs of Le Corbusier and others. **Architect.** Person who plans buildings and supervises their erection. Architects in Brit. must be registered before they can practise. The registration is controlled by the Royal Institute of Brit. Architects which holds exams.

ARCOT
City of Madras state, India, 65 m. S.W. of Madras, on the Palar. In 1751 the fort of Arcot was besieged by the Fr. and Clive beat off a series of attacks.

ARCTIC, The
Region surrounding the N. Pole, comprising for the most part the Arctic Ocean, which includes the Barents, White, and Kara Seas. It is connected by Davis Strait and other openings with the Atlantic, and by Bering Strait with the Pacific. The area of the **Arctic ocean** is regarded as approx. 5,440,000 sq.m. The **Arctic Circle** is the line of latitude 66½° N. **Arctic Exploration.** This began when sailors in the 15th cent. started on the search for a N.E. and a N.W. passage to the Pacific, and the earliest discoveries of land were made by Frobisher, Hudson, Davis, Baffin and others. Early in the 19th cent. the Brit. Govt. offered a prize for a further advance. Ross, Parry and others rediscovered the lands found by earlier navigators, and discovered others. In 1845, Sir John Franklin went out with the *Erebus* and *The Terror* but never returned. The existence of the N.W. passage to the Pacific was proved in 1878-9. Nordenskiold sailed through the N.E. passage. Exploration in the 20th cent. corrected the prevailing idea about the size and shape of Greenland. In the 19th cent. explorers had approached nearer the Pole, *e.g.* the Amers. Greely and Lockwood, in 1881-4 when 83° 24′ was reached. In 1893 Nansen left the *Fram* and made a dash for the pole, but failed. It was eventually reached on April 6, 1909, by Robert E. Peary. In 1926 Roald Amundsen flew over the pole, followed later by the Amer. Richard Byrd.

ARDENNES
[âr-den′] (1) Range of hills in N.E. Fr. extending into Belgium and Luxembourg. Scene of the last major German counter-attack, Christmas, 1944. (2) Dept. of N.E. Fr. Cap. Mézières.

ARECA
Genus of palm trees, grown in trop. Asia. *Areca catechu* is grown for its seeds, which are known as betel nuts.

AREQUIPA
[ar-ā-kē′-pa] City of Peru, situated at the foot of El Misti, an extinct volcano, at a ht. of 7,500 ft. Pop. 156,657.

ARGALI
Variety of wild sheep found on the steppes of Siberia and other parts of Asia.

ARGENTINA
[-tē′-] Repub. of S. Amer. extending from the Tropic of Capricorn S. to Cape Horn. It has a coastline on the S. Atlantic Ocean, and is separated from Chile on the W. by the Andes, which here include Aconcagua, 22,835 ft. the highest peak of S. Amer. The land slopes gently E. towards the plains of C. Argentina, around the estuary of La Plata. Of the chief rivers, the Parana, Paraguay and tributary Bermejo, Salado and Pilcomayo, flow into the Plata estuary. The S. rivers, the Colorado, Negro, Chubut and Chico, flow directly into the Atlantic. The most fertile area is the Pampas of C. Argentina. The Patagonian plateau in the S. is semi-desert, while the Chaco of the extreme N. is swampy and forested. Agriculture is the main industry, and cattle rearing, on the Pampas. Chilled and canned meat, wheat, maize, hides and wool are exported. Gold, coal, tin, copper and petroleum are mined. The cap. is Buenos Aires. The railway network covers the whole country, and there are river and coastal steamer services. The pop. is mainly of European descent, particularly Sp. and Portuguese, and the chief religion is R.C. Area: 1,084,120 sq.m. Pop. 20,959,000. The country was colonised by the Sp. in the 16th cent. and remained a Sp. possession for 300 years. In 1776 Buenos Aires was made cap. of a vast region, including Paraguay, Bolivia and Uruguay; in 1810 this area declared its indep. and war with Spain followed. Was governed by a Pres. with a legislature of 2 houses until 1966 when a military government took over. *See* PERÓN.

ARGENTITE
One of the commonest ores of silver. It contains *c.* 87 % of the metal. It is a soft, blackish-grey fusible mineral, soluble in nitric acid and usually occurring in massive form or as cubes.

ARGOL
Crust of impure cream of tartar or acid tartrate of potassium, deposited in wine casks or vats during the fermentation of the grape juice. From it is prepared commercial cream of tartar, tartaric acid and Rochelle salts.

ARGON
An inert gas which occurs in the atmosphere (about 0·9 % by vol.). Discovered by Rayleigh and Ramsay in 1894. Its principal use is in gas-filled lamps. Its density is 1·4 times that of air. Chem. sym. A.

ARGONAUTS
In Gk. legend the men who sailed in the ship *Argo* to fetch the golden fleece. Their leader was Jason and the fleece was at Colchis.

ARGOS
City of the Peloponnese, S. Greece, 25 m. S.W. of Corinth.

ARGYLL, Duke of
Scots. title borne by the family of Campbell. In 1457 Colin Campbell of Lochow was made Earl of Argyll. **Archibald,** 8th Earl of Argyll, made a Marquess, 1641, was prominent during the civil war. His son, **Archibald,** the 9th earl, was executed for leading a rising in conjunction with that of the Duke of Monmouth in 1685. **Archibald,** the 10th earl, organised, in 1692, the massacre of Glencoe. **John Douglas Sutherland Campbell** (1845-1914), 9th duke, mar. Louise, daughter of Queen Victoria. From 1878-83 he was Gov.-Gen. of Canada, being then known as the Marquess of Lorne. The 11th duke, **Ian Douglas Campbell** succeeded in 1949. Divorced his wife in 1963. The costly case attracted much publicity.

ARGYLLSHIRE
Maritime county of W. Scot. The coastline is indented, being 2,300 m. long, and there are many sea lochs. The great Kintyre peninsula is cut by the Crinan Canal. Much of the interior is mountainous, rising to over 3,000 ft. in Ben Cruachan (3,689 ft.), and Ben More (3,169 ft.). Of the Is., Mull, Islay, Jura, Coll, Tiree, Colonsay, Staffa and Iona are the largest. Industries include the rearing of sheep and cattle. Slate and coal are mined, and there are fisheries. Inveraray is the county town, but Lochgilphead is the admin. centre. Argyllshire returns 1 member to Parl. Pop. 60,226.

ARIES
[ā'-ri-ēz] (Lat. *ram.*) First sign of the Zodiac, operative from *c.* Mar. 21-April 21. It is a small constellation of stars.

ARIOSTO, Lodovico
(1474-1533) Ital. poet. His chief work is the romantic epic *Orlando Furioso,* pub. in 1510.

ARISTIDES
[-tē'-] (*c.* 529- *c.* 468 B.C.) Gk. statesman. He became known as an opponent of Themistocles and the people decided in 483, by vote, to expel or ostracise him. He took part in the war against Persia and commanded the Athenians at Plataea. In 477 he was responsible for the change by which any citizen of Athens could become an archon (magistrate).

ARISTOPHANES
[aris-tof'-ă-nēz] (*c.* 445-348 B.C.) Gk. comic dramatist. He wrote 54 plays, of which 11 are extant. These include *The Clouds, The Frogs* and *The Knights.*

ARISTOTLE
(384-322 B.C.), Gk. philosopher. In 367 he went to Athens to complete his educ. and there he remained for 20 years, much of his time being spent with Plato, whose greatest pupil he was. About 343 Aristotle was invited to Macedon by King Philip to supervise the educ. of his son Alexander. He remained there until Alexander became king, and in 335 returned to Athens. There he founded a school called the Peripatos. In a vol. called *Organon,* he discusses and expounds his ideas on logic, ethics, politics and philosophy. The *Politics* is the basis of much modern polit. philosophy; the *Ethics* is a treatise on the Gk. idea of virtue; the *Poetics* laid the foundation of modern aesthetics, and gave logic the form it has retained for 2,000 years.

ARIZONA
S.W. state of U.S.A. Its natural features are the Colorado River with its famous canyons and extensive deserts, and plateau, over 5,000 ft. high. The soil is not fertile. Cattle and sheep are reared, but the chief products are minerals. Phoenix is the cap. Arizona sends 2 representatives to Congress. Area: 113,909 sq.m. Pop. 1,773,000.

ARKANSAS
[-saw] S. state of the U.S.A. through which flow the Mississippi and the tributary Arkansas rivers. To the N.W. are the Boston and Ouachita Mts.; in the E. are fertile plains. Arkansas produces cotton, fruit, wheat and maize. Little Rock is the cap. Arkansas became a state in 1836, and now sends 7 representatives to Congress. Area: 53,104 sq.m. Pop. 1,923,300.

ARKWRIGHT, Sir Richard
(1723-92) Eng. inventor. He invented, with John Kay, a spinning frame. He began to work this at Preston, but popular feeling was against him and he moved to Nottingham. In 1771 he joined with Jedediah Strutt in opening a factory at Cromford. He was one of the first to use steam power in the factory.

ARLES
[ărl] Town of S. Fr. on the Rhône, 53 m. from Marseilles. Rom. remains include an amphitheatre, forum, palace, baths and aqueduct. Pop. 35,000.

ARLINGTON, Earl of
(1618-85) Eng. politician. Henry Bennet fought for the king during the civil war. In 1662 he was made Sec. of State and became a member of the group called the Cabal.

ARM
Upper limb in man which is divided anatomically into upper arm from shoulder to elbow, forearm from elbow to wrist, wrist, hand and fingers. *See* SHOULDER; ELBOW; WRIST; HAND.

ARMADA
Sp. word for an armed force, esp. the fleet sent by Philip II of Spain to invade Eng. in 1588. About 130 vessels left Cadiz on July 12, carrying, in addition to the crews *c.* 20,000 soldiers. To defend Eng. a fleet under Lord Howard of Effingham put to sea from Plymouth on July 19. The Eng. ships, most of them much smaller, attacked the Sp. in the Channel. The Sp. ships reached Calais Roads on July 27, where they were attacked by fireships. To escape these they put to sea, but were followed by the Eng. who sank or captured a number in a fight off Gravelines. On the journey home a gale wrecked many more.

ARMADILLO
S. Amer. mammal of the Dasipodidae family, so named because the body is protected by bones and scales like armour. The head and limbs are also protected and the animal can curl itself up like a hedgehog. It feeds on snakes and insects, and sometimes on carrion.

ARMAGH
[ăr-ma'] County of N. Ireland. The S. is hilly, but the N. grows flax, wheat and potatoes. The Bann, Blackwater and Newry are the chief rivers. Armagh is the county town; other places are Lurgan, Portadown, and Bessbrook. The county sends 1 member to Parl. Pop. 117,900. **Armagh,** county town of Armagh, 36 m. S.W. of Belfast. Pop. 9,950.

ARMENIA
Constituent republic of the U.S.S.R. S. of the

The Bosphorus

ASIA · 1

Fujiyama

Hindu temple, Bombay

Crocodile Temple, Bangkok

Manchuria: factory

R. Mindanao, Philippines

Yalta

Yangtsekiang bridge, Wuha

ASIA · 2

Mts. in Central Iran

The Sandia-Ghat, Benares

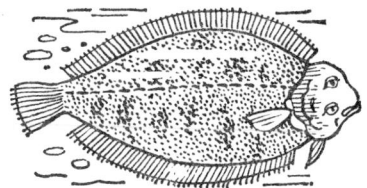

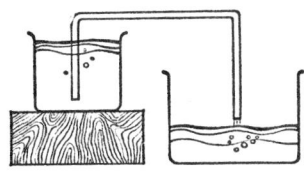

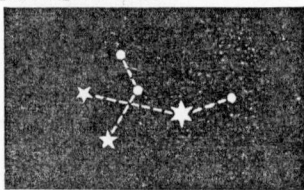

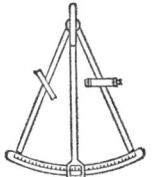

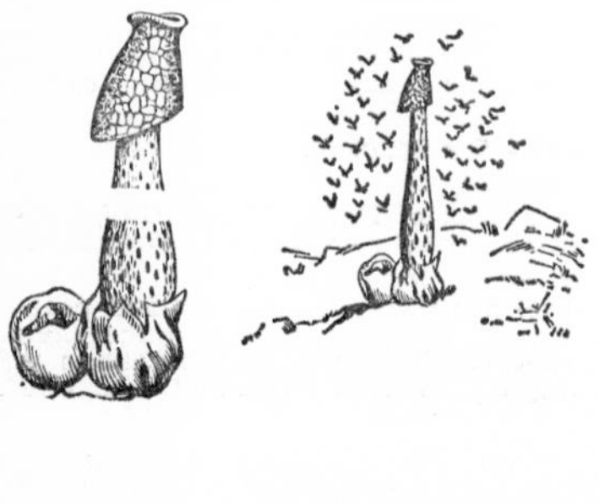

Palomar Observatory

Taj Mahal

Stonehenge

FAMOUS BUILDINGS · 1

Sydney Harbour Bridge

Lake Bridge, Lucerne

Doge's Palace, Venice

Palace of the Popes, Avignon

FAMOUS BUILDINGS · 2

Mexico Univ. Library

Kyoto Temple, Japan

BOOMERANG
Hardwood missile, chiefly of the Australian aborigines. It is a hunting weapon, 2-3 ft. long. A slight axial twist gives it an elliptical flight path and makes it possible for it to return to the thrower if it misses its mark.

BOOTH, William
(1829-1912) Founder of the Salvation Army (*q.v.*) B. Nottingham, he became an evangelistic preacher and in 1865 began work in the E. end of London. There he founded the Christian Mission. In 1878, after Booth had organised his followers on milit. lines, it was named the Salvation Army. Booth became the 1st general. Booth's eldest son, **William Bramwell B.** (1856-1929) recd. the C.H. for his social work. **Evangeline B.** (1865-1950) 7th child of Gen. Wm. B., became 3rd Gen. (1934-39).

BOOTLE
County borough of Lancs. on the Mersey near Liverpool. There are extensive docks. The chief industries are the smelting of tin and other metals, and engineering. B. returns 1 member to Parl. Pop. 83,220.

BORACIC (BORIC) ACID
(H_3BO_3) A colourless crystalline solid, greasy to the touch. Occurring in hot springs and lagoons in volcanic regions, such as the Lipari Islands, the Tuscan Maremma, and the Andean region of Atacama.

BORAX
Hydrated sodium pyroborate ($Na_2B_4O_7.10H_2O$), is a whitish crystalline salt. It comes chiefly from Calif. deposits and is used as a flux in soldering, in glass and enamel manufacture, and as an antiseptic food preservative.

BORDEAUX
[-dō′] City and seaport of S.W. Fr. 360 m. from Paris and 60 from the Bay of Biscay. The largest town of Aquitaine, it is connected with the Medit. by the Canal du Midi. Bordeaux possesses a fine natural harbour. The chief industry is the export of wine. The name **Bordeaux** is given to the white and red wines, including *Sauternes* and *Graves*, of the surrounding country. Pop. 254,122.

BORE
Tidal wave of great ht. and force which appears in certain rivers at the period of high, or spring tides. Rushing from the estuary along the gradually narrowing channel of the river, the impelling force resolves the water into a huge wall or wave. The bore, or eagre, appears in the Severn, the Trent and other Eng. rivers, and also in the Solway Firth, the Amazon and many rivers in the E.

BORGIA
[bor′-jà] Famous Ital. family. Alonso de Borja, Bishop of Valencia, was chosen pope as Calixtus III in 1455. The pope's sister was the mother of Rodrigo Borgia who became Pope Alexander VI. His son was **Cesare Borgia** (1476-1507). In 1492 his father was elected pope as Alexander VI, and Cesare was made an archbishop and a cardinal. As Captain-General of the papal forces, he showed great ability in bringing the States of the Ch. into submission, but his utter lack of pity or principle have made his name a synonym for evil. For some years he was in Spain, where he was killed in battle. His sister **Lucrezia** (1480-1519) had a reputation for learning and beauty.

BORN, Max
(1882-1969) Among the foremost math. physicists of the present time. Tait Prof. of Nat. Phil. at the Univ. of Edinburgh, 1936-53. In 1954 he was awarded the Nobel Prize for physics jointly with Prof. Walter Bothe of Heidelberg.

BORNEO
Large Is. in the E. Indies, lying across the equator. In the N. are the Malaysian states of Brunei, Sarawak and N. Borneo, while the S. and greater part of the Is. Kalimantan, forms part of the Republic of Indonesia (*q.v.*). The main mt. system runs parallel to the N.W. coast, terminating in Kinabalu (13,450 ft.). The pop. is chiefly Dyak, Malay, Negrito, Bugi and Chinese. Rubber, tobacco, rice, diamonds and oil are the most important products. Area: 287,400 sq.m. Pop. *c.* 4,500,000. **North Borneo.** N. part of the Is. of Borneo. The interior is mountainous, rising to 13,450 ft. in Mt. Kinabalu, and forested. Rubber is produced in the narrow coastal plain. Jesselton, Kudat and Sandakan are the chief towns. From 1942-5 it was occupied by the Japs. A Brit. colony until 1963 when it joined the Fed. of Malaysia as the State of Sabah. Area: 29,388 sq.m. Pop. 454,421.

BORODIN, Alexander
(1833-87) Russ. composer. He became a member of the Nationalist group, known as 'the Five'. His works include 3 symphonies (the 3rd unfinished), 2 string quartets and the opera *Prince Igor*, completed by Rimsky-Korsakov.

BORON
An element which occurs principally as the borates of sodium and calcium. Among its compounds are boric (boracic) acid H_3BO_3, and borax $Na_2B_4O_7.10H_2O$. Sp. gr. 2·5. Chem. sym. B.

BOROUGH
[bur′-rǎ] Orig. a fortified place, but now a town. The Scots. form is *burgh*. In the M.A. a borough was a place that had received a charter from a king or lord. A **county b.** which must either have been a county of itself or had 75,000 inhabitants, has the same privileges as a county and is indep. of the county in which it is situated. A **metropolitan b.** is 1 of the 32 boroughs in the County of London. A **parliamentary b.** is one that sends 1 or more members to Parl.

BORROW, George Henry
(1803-81) Eng. author. B. near E. Dereham, Norfolk; travelled in Europe and the E. acquiring languages and assoc. with the gipsies. Became an agent of the Brit. and Foreign Bible Soc.; 2 autobiog., novels, *Lavengro* (1851) and *The Romany Rye* (1857); *Wild Wales* (1862).

BORSTAL
Village of Kent, near Chatham. It gives its name to a system by which offenders, between the ages of 16 and 21, go to a **Borstal Institution,** where they are trained to earn an honest living. The system was introduced in 1902, but it only became possible in its present form after the passing of the Prevention of Crimes Act, 1908.

BORZOI
Russ. wolfhound. It ranks as a long-haired greyhound, slower but more powerful than the Eng. type, with longish jaws, narrow deep chest, and silky coat.

BOSPORUS
Strait connecting the Black Sea with the Sea of Marmara, and separating Asiatic and European Turkey. Istanbul stands on its W. shore.

BOSSUET, Jacques Bénigne
[bos-ü-ā] (1627-1704) Fr. writer and preacher. B. Dijon; educ. by the Jesuits; priest 1652; tutor to the Dauphin 1671; Bishop of Meaux 1681.

He was notable as a preacher, and as a controversialist against quietism, protestantism, and papal aggression.

BOSTON
Cap. of Massachusetts, and 10th city of the U.S.A. A great educ. centre, it has 2 univs. and contains some of the buildings of Harvard. It is also a lit. and musical centre, the B. Symphony Orchestra being particularly famous. B. is one of the largest ports in the country. Industries include machinery, textiles, shoemaking and fishing. Pop. 628,250.

BOSTON
Borough, seaport and market town of Lincs. near the mouth of the Witham. In 13th cent. B. was a flourishing port, but gradually the river was barred by silt. Pop. 24,930.

BOSWELL, James
(1740-95) Scot. writer. B. Edinburgh; educ. Edinburgh and Glasgow; met Samuel Johnson in London 1763; visited Voltaire and Rousseau; practised law in Scot. with frequent visits to London, where he frequented Johnson's circle; made a tour to the W. Isles with Johnson in 1773; succeeded to the family estate of Auchinleck in Ayrshire 1782; latterly resided much in London, working with Edmund Malone's help and counsel at the great *Life of Johnson* (pub. 1791). In recent years much light has been thrown on Boswell's extraordinarily complex character and talents by the pub. (1928-35) of his *Private Papers.*

BOSWORTH
Market town of Leics. The Battle of B. was fought on Aug. 22, 1485, between Richard III and Henry Tudor, Earl of Richmond; Richard was defeated and slain, Henry becoming king as Henry VII.

BOTANY
Study of plant life. *Plant morphology* deals with plant structures, *physiology* with the functions and living activities, *ecology* and plant geography with a plant's relation to its environment and its distribution, while the study of fossil plants forms a section of *palaeontology*.

BOTANY BAY
Inlet on coast of N.S.W. Australia, first sighted by James Cook, 1770. Arthur Philip arrived 1788, to found a penal colony, but went 13 m. farther N. to Port Jackson (Sydney Harbour).

BOT-FLY
Family of dipterous (2-winged) insects (Destridae). The Horse bot-fly (*Gastrophilus*) lays eggs on the skin which are licked off and become bots in the intestine. The Ox-bot (*Hypoderma*) forms tumour-like warbles in the skin. The Sheep bot-fly (*Oestrus ovis*) lays eggs in the nostrils and their larvae migrate to the sinuses where they remain until mature.

BOTHA, Louis
[bō'-ta] (1863-1919) Boer statesman and soldier. B. Natal; he settled in the Transvaal and served against the Zulus. In 1899 he opposed Brit., besieged them in Ladysmith and defeated them at Colenso. A prominent figure in the Transvaal, Botha accepted Brit. sovereignty and in 1907 became first premier of the Transvaal. In 1910 he became the 1st premier of the new Union of S. Africa, a position he held until his d. He led the S. African forces into German S.W. Africa, which was conquered.

BOTHWELL, Earl of
Scots. title which dates from 1489, and in 1559 came to James Hepburn (1536-1578) as the 4th earl. Although a Protestant, he became a strong partisan of Mary, Queen of Scots. Bothwell had a large share in the murder of Darnley, after which he carried the queen to Dunbar, and mar. her. The defeat at Carberry Hill put an end to the assoc. Bothwell sailed to Norway and remained a prisoner until his d. There is a village in Lanarkshire of this name, where the Battle of Bothwell Brig was fought in 1679.

BOTSWANA
See BECHUANALAND.

BOTTICELLI, Sandro
[-chel'-] (1444-1510) Ital. painter. He worked in the studio of Fra Filippo Lippi and soon showed signs of extraordinary gifts. Apart from his other paintings B. did frescoes for the Sistine Chapel and illustrations for Dante's works.

BOUGAINVILLE, Louis Antoine
[boo-ga(ng)-vēl'] (1729-1811) Fr. explorer. In 1763 his voyage round the world, the first made by a Frenchman, made him famous. The largest of the Solomon Is. was named after him; also the plant *Bougainvillea* native of S. Amer.

BOULOGNE
[bōō-loyn', bōō-lon'-yĕ] City and seaport of Pas-de-Calais dept., Fr. on the Eng. Channel, 157 m. N. of Paris. The old town contains the Cath. of Notre Dame, and the castle. Boulogne has a good harbour and is a fishing centre. There is a regular steamer service to Folkestone. Pop. 50,036.

BOULT, Sir Adrian Cedric
(1889-) Eng. conductor. Director of the Birmingham City Orchestra, 1924-30; music director of the B.B.C., 1930-42, conductor of the B.B.C. Symphony Orchestra, 1930-50, and conductor of the London Philharmonic Orchestra since 1950.

BOUNTY, Mutiny of the
Apr. 28, 1789, owing to the harsh conduct of their commander (Lieut. Wm. Bligh), the crew of H.M.S. *Bounty* mutinied. Bligh and the loyal members of the ship's Co. were turned adrift in the launch. Nine mutineers sailed for Pitcairn Is. accompanied by some native women. Next year, Capt. Edwards of H.M.S. *Pandora* captured 12 of the mutineers and hanged 3 of them. The fate of those who sailed for Pitcairn Is. remained unknown until 1808, when an Amer. vessel found the Is. inhabited by the children of the *Bounty* mutineers and their native wives, ruled by John Adams, last surviving Brit. sailor.

BOURBON
[boor-bō(ng)] European family that gave kings to Fr. and Spain. The name is taken from Bourbon l'Archambault not far from Vichy in C. Fr. These lands came by mar. to a son of St. Louis (Louis IX). Antony, a later duke, was the father of Henry who, in 1589, became the 1st Bourbon king of Fr. He and his descendants ruled until 1789 and again from 1814-48. The Bourbons were also kings of Spain from 1700 to 1931, ruled Naples, 1735-1860, and Parma, 1748-1859.

BOURGES
[boorzh] City of Fr., cap. of Cher dept. 144 m. S. of Paris. It has a Gothic cath. with fine stained glass. An agricultural centre, with engineering works. Pop. 54,000.

BOURNEMOUTH
County borough and seaside resort of Hants. on the Bourne. With Christchurch, Bournemouth returns 2 members to Parl. Pop. 149,530.

BOURNVILLE
Model village near Birmingham, founded, 1895, for the employees of Cadbury Bros. It is a garden city with ample facilities for recreation.

BOW
Suburb of E. London. A famous decorated earthenware was produced in the 18th cent. Bow Ch., built by Wren, is in Cheapside.

BOW-LEG
(or **Genu Varum**). A deformity affecting the lower limbs in which, on standing, the ankles

are together and the knees are widely separated. Rickets is the most common cause.

BOW STREET
London st. containing the chief police court for the London district. **The Bow Street Runners** were men employed on detective work until 1829.

BOWDLER, Thomas
(1754-1825) Eng. editor. B. Bath; engaged in prison reform: pub. (1818) *The Family Shakespeare,* in which the text was 'purged of all coarse and indecent expressions'.

BOWEL
That part of the digestive tract known as the intestine. In man it consists of the small and large intestines. The bowels serve to complete the digestion of food and to allow its absorption into the bloodstream. The useless food remains are gradually moved onwards, remaining in a liquid state until they reach the large bowel, but then they become, except in time of illness, a semi-solid mass of faeces and ready to be voided.

BOWER BIRD
Bird of Paradise. There are several species, all confined to Australia. The bowers are apparently places for social intercourse and recreation.

BOWLS
Apart from archery, the most ancient Brit. outdoor game, usually played on a bowling green 42 yds. sq. with 6 rinks and a ditch *c.* 6 in. wide all round. The requirements of the game are a jack and a few sets of bowls. The jack should not exceed 2½ in. in diam. nor more than 10 oz. in wt. The bowls are of lignum vitae, or other hard wood; they must not exceed 16½ in. in circumference and 3½ lb. in wt. and are made with a bias. There are many bowling clubs in Brit. and championship and internat. matches are played.

BOX
Shrub of the family Buxaceae. Found in many parts of the world, it grows freely in Brit. where there are 2 main varieties (1) a tree which may reach a ht. of 20 ft., (2) a dwarf, popular as an edging in gardens. The tree will keep any

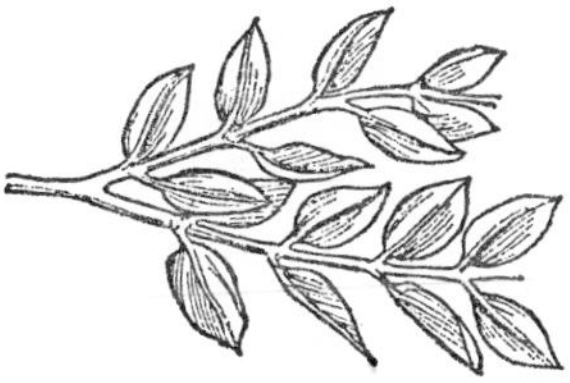

shape into which it is pruned. The wood is remarkable for its hardness and wt. and is used for musical and mathematical instruments. **B.** is also a large Austral. timber tree.

BOXERS
Organisation in China prior to 1900. Its aim was to drive exploiting foreigners from the country. In 1900 the 'boxers' marched on Peking, where they assailed the foreign legations. On Aug. 14 a relieving force entered Peking and the Rising was put down. The rebellion proved to the Chinese the necessity of reform, and China became a Republic, 1911.

BOXING
Art of fighting with gloves on the fists. Pugilism in which no gloves are worn is now illegal in Brit. but boxing is permitted by law. In pugilism there was no such thing as timed rounds, each fall marking the end of a round. Boxing superseded pugilism when the Queensberry Rules were drawn up by 8th Marquess of Queensberry in 1866. This provides that the ring shall be of a certain size. The rounds are of 3 min. each, with 1 min. interval between them. If a combatant is knocked down he must rise within 10 secs. or he loses the fight. It is won on pts. if neither combatant is knocked out. The gloves must weigh at least 4 oz. The Amateur Boxing Assoc. formed in 1884, governs Amateur Boxing. Professionalism is recognised in boxing and since 1929 has been governed by the Brit. Boxing Board of Control. There are contests for world, European, Empire, Brit. and other nat. championships.

BOY SCOUTS
Non-milit. non-polit. organisation for boys, founded by Sir Robert (later Lord) Baden-Powell, 1908. The boys wear a distinctive dress and their motto is *Be Prepared.* In Brit. the movement is divided into 4 groups, *i.e.* Wolf Cubs 8-11 years, Boy Scouts 11-15 years, Senior Scouts 15-18 years and Rover Scouts 18 and upwards. In addition to these age groups there are also specialised branches, *i.e.* Sea Scouts, Air Scouts and a branch catering for the physically handicapped boy. *See* BADEN-POWELL.

BOYLE, Robert
(1627-91) Eng. scientist. The 7th son of the 1st Earl of Cork. In Oxford he carried out experiments on the properties of air which resulted in his improved air pump, and his formulation of the celebrated law now known by his name. He was one of a group of natural philosophers who, in 1663, became known as the Royal Society. Boyle was the first to recognise the true nature of an element.

BOYNE
River of Eire, which rises in Kildare and enters the Irish Sea below Drogheda. In the battle fought in 1690, William III defeated James II and his Fr. allies.

BOYS' BRIGADE
A religious organisation for training boys, founded in Glasgow by Sir William Smith, 1883. It consists of Cos. formed in connection with chs. **The Boys' Life Brigade,** founded 1899, was united with the B.B. in 1926. The strength of the B.B. (inc. officers) is 150,000 and of **The Life Boys** 76,000.

BRACKEN
Species of fern (*Pteridium aquilinum*). Common in Brit. it has a creeping rootstock from which arise 2 ranks of leaves bearing on their margins linear groups of spore cases.

BRADFORD
City and county borough of the W. Riding, Yorks. 9 m. W. of Leeds. B. is a great centre of the woollen and worsted industry and has engineering works. B. returns 4 members to Parl. Pop. 296,220.

BRADLAUGH, Charles
(1833-91) Eng. freethinker and politician. M.P. 1880-91. An atheistical journalist, Bradlaugh was in 1876 tried and convicted, with Mrs. Annie Besant, for pub. a birth-control pamphlet. In 1880 he was elected a Radical M.P. but, as an atheist, was not allowed to take the oath. A long struggle ensued, ending in 1886, when he was allowed to take his seat.

BRADMAN, Sir Donald George
(1908-) Austral. cricketer. B. Cortamundra, New S. Wales. He was chosen to play for Australia, 1928, against Eng. He captained Australia in Test Matches 1935-7-8, '46-8. Only batsman to score 2,000 runs on each of 4 tours. Scored 27,984 runs in 366 innings for an average of 95·50. Hit 117 centuries (inc. 37 over 200).

BRAEMAR
[brā-mär'] Village and district of Aberdeenshire, 18 m. from Ballater, on the Dee. Balmoral and Abergeldie castles are in the neighbourhood, and a Highland gathering is held every year.

BRAGG, Sir William Henry
(1862-1942) B. Wigton, Cumberland, and educ. at Camb. His principal work, with his son, was in the application of X-rays to the study of crystal structure. F.R.S.; knighted, 1920; O.M. 1931; Pres. of the Royal Soc. 1935-40. His son is **Sir (William) Lawrence Bragg** (1890-1971) B. in Adelaide and educ. at Camb. In 1915 he was awarded a Nobel prize, jointly with his father.

BRAHE, Tycho
(1546-1601) Danish astronomer. B. Knudsting, Sweden. An eclipse of the sun in 1560 directed his attention to the study of Ptolemy's works. Brahe discovered that the positions of the planets did not coincide with those assigned them by accepted astronomical calculations. In 1572 he discovered the star, *Cassiopeia.* He pub. the first of his great astron. works, *De Nova Stella,* in 1573.

BRAHMA
[brăm'-ȧ] First person of the Hindu Trimurti (Brahma, Vishnu, Shiva), the Creator. **Brahmanism.** Hindu religion. It is a modification of Vedaism which is of very ancient origin. Its scriptures comprise 4 sacred inspired books, viz: the *Rigveda, Samaveda, Vajurveda* and *Atharvaveda.* Two fundamentals of doctrine are (1) *Karma* (causation) the law by which the individual reaps the results of his actions, good or evil; (2) *Reincarnation,* the doctrine of progressive re-birth, viz., that the soul uses not one but many physical bodies in its progress from savage to sainthood, and that reincarnation ceases only when the soul is merged in a greater consciousness.

BRAHMAPUTRA
[-poot'-] River of S. Asia, *c.* 1,700 m. long. It rises in a Tibetan glacier, at an altitude of 16,000 ft. and flows E. through Tibet, turning S. into Assam. Thence it flows W. and S. to the Ganges at Goalanda, in Pakistan, and enters the sea through the Meghna estuary.

BRAHMS, Johannes
(1833-97) German composer. In 1863 he settled in Vienna and devoted himself to composition. His works include 4 symphonies, 2 piano concertos, a violin concerto, a double concerto for violin and 'cello, the *German Requiem,* chamber and piano music and nearly 200 songs.

BRAILLE SYSTEM
System of characters for enabling the blind to read by touch. Letters of the alphabet, punctuation-marks, numerals and a certain number of common words, are represented by 6 or fewer dots embossed on paper. It was perfected (1834) by Louis Braille (1809-52), a professor at the Institution Nationale des Jeunes Aveugles in Paris.

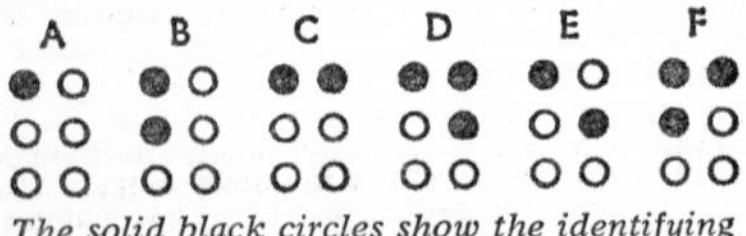

The solid black circles show the identifying portions of the first six letters of the Braille alphabet

BRAIN
Main centre of nervous system in man and higher animals. It is contained within skull, weighs 44-49 oz., and is composed of grey and white matter. The whole organ is covered by 3 membranes (1) the tough outer one under the skull called *dura mater,* (2) the spider web-like one called *arachnoid,* and (3) the soft inner one called *pia mater* covering the brain substance and acting as a coat for vessels penetrating the brain substance. The brain is composed of the cerebral hemispheres on top and the pons, medulla and cerebellum below. The medulla is continuous with the spinal cord.

BRAMBLE
(*Rubus fruticosus*) Plant of the rose family. The stems are thick and fleshy and covered with thorns, prickles and hairy bristles. The long stems frequently bend and re-root themselves in the soil, producing fresh plants. The commonest Brit. variety is the blackberry.

BRAMBLING
Small bird allied to the Chaffinch. A native of Scandinavia, Lapland and Siberia, it is a winter visitor to Brit. Head black, wings and tail chestnut brown, underparts white.

BRANDENBURG
Former state of E. Germany, containing Berlin. Potsdam was the cap. B. became a separate state *c.* 1130, and in 1356 the ruler became an elector. In 1701 the elector was made King of Prussia, and B. was a Prussian prov. until 1946. In 1952 it was split into 3 regions: Potsdam, Cottbus, Frankfurt. B. city is 36 m. W. of Berlin. Pop. 85,600.

BRANDT, Willy
(1913-), German statesman. In Scandinavia during war years. Mayor of West Berlin, 1957-66; Vice-Chancellor of West Germany, 1966- .

BRANDY
Distilled wine, or distilled and fermented fresh grape juice. Brandy, orig. colourless, becomes brown and golden from caramel and storage in oak casks. The alcoholic content is *c.* 53%. The best comes from Cognac, S.W. France.

BRAQUE, Georges
[bràk] (1882-1963) Fr. painter. B. Argenteuil-sur-Seine. He attended the Acad. Julian in Paris and associated with the orig. Fauve group. In 1908 he met Picasso and turned to Cubism. *See* FAUVES, CUBISM.

BRASILIA
City designed by Brazilian architect Otto Niemeyer. Inaugurated as new cap. of Brazil, in place of Rio de Janeiro, 1960. Pop. 142,000

BRASS
Yellow alloy of copper and zinc in varying proportions, with sometimes small quantities of lead, tin or iron. Brass is very malleable, fusible, ductile and readily cast and machined. Muntz or yellow metal is a variety of brass containing 60% of copper.

BRAZIL
The largest repub. of S. Amer. covering nearly ½ of the cont., bounded on 2 sides by the Atlantic and elsewhere by Guiana, and all the other repubs. except Ecuador and Chile. In the N.W. lies the vast Amazon basin, covered by dense forest, while in the S. is the Parana-Paraguay river system. The huge plateau forming the core of the country is traversed by 2 mt. chains. Itatiaya peak, in the Coast Range, reaches 9,820 ft. The climate is equatorial in the N., sub-trop. around Rio de Janeiro, and temp. in the extreme S. Coffee is the most important crop, *c.* 40 % of the world's supply being produced. Rubber is grown in the N. in the Amazon basin. Gold, manganese, coal and iron are worked in S. Brazil. The cap. is Brasilia (*q.v.*); other towns are Rio de Janeiro, São Paulo, São Salvador, Recife, Belem, Porto Alegre, Manaos and Bello Horizonte. The pop. is mixed; the white races of mainly Portuguese stock form *c.* 60 %. The language is Portuguese, and the religion predominantly R.C. Brazil was discovered in 1500, but was not colonised until 1532. 1815, the colony was declared a kingdom, and, 1889, became a repub. The Constitution is based on that of the U.S.A. In World War II Brazil declared war against the Axis powers. After an armed rising in Apr. 1964, Gen. Branco was elected Pres. with wide powers. Area: 3,286,000 sq.m. Pop. 85,655,000.

BRAZIL NUT
Seed of *Bertholletia excelsa,* a tree of the family Lecythidaceae, a native of Brazil. Each fruit

yields *c.* 20 triangular seeds with a hard woody cover. The nuts are edible and yield fine oil.

BREAD
Any cereal ground to a flour, made into a paste or dough with water and then baked, but specifically a wheaten flour product which has been subject to fermentation by means of an enzyme, such as yeast. In Brit., the Sale of Food and Drugs Act prescribe the materials which may be lawfully employed in its manufacture and prohibit its sale otherwise than by avoirdupois wt. Bread is now produced on a large scale.

BREAD FRUIT
(*Artocarpus incisa*) Large tree of the mulberry family (Moraceae) cultivated in trop. for its fruit which has the texture of bread.

BREAM
Fresh-water fish found in slow-running streams and ponds. There are 2 Brit. species, Common B. (*Abramis brama*) and White B. (*A. blicca*). B. is common in temp. parts of the N. hemisphere.

BREATHALYSER *See* ALCOMETER.

BRECHT, Bertold
(1898-1956) German playwright. Author of *Baal* (1922), *Threepenny Opera*, 1928, etc. Awarded the Stalin Peace Prize, 1954.

BRECKNOCKSHIRE
(or **Breconshire**) Inland mountainous county of S. Wales, bounded on the E. by Monmouth and Hereford. The chief rivers are the Wye and Usk, and the highest point is Pen-y-Fawr. It is an agricultural county. Brecon is the county town; others are Builth Wells and Hay. With Radnorshire, B. returns 1 member to Parl. Pop. 54,460. **Brecon** (or **Brecknock**) City, market and county town of Brecknockshire, on the Usk, 35 m. from Cardiff. The chief building is the cath. of the diocese of Swansea and Brecon. Christ's Coll., a public school for boys, dates from 1541. Pop. 5,830.

BREDA
[brā-dà'] Town in N. Brabant, the Netherlands, where Charles II stated, in the **Declaration of Breda** (1660), the terms upon which he accepted the crown of Eng. Pop. 113,193.

BREMEN
City and seaport of W. Germany, cap. of Bremen state, on the Weser, *c.* 60 m. from its mouth. The river has been deepened and there are 3 harbours. The old city has buildings dating from the time of the Hanseatic League. There is a cath. Pop. 557,000. The **State of Bremen**, formed 1946, comprises the city of Bremen and environs, and Bremerhaven, at the mouth of the Weser. Pop. 706,400. **Bremerhaven.** A fishing centre, the outport for the city of Bremen.

BRESLAU *See* WROCLAW.

BREST-LITOVSK
City of the U.S.S.R. at the confluence of the Bug and Muchavetz in White Russia. It was the scene of peace negotiations after the Bolshevik Revolution, 1917; treaties were signed by Russia and the Central Powers in Feb. 1918.

BREWING
Process by which various substances are fermented to produce an alcoholic liquor. Specifically the production of beer from an extract of malted barley and hops. The barley is prepared by allowing soaked grains to germinate under controlled conditions, so that the starch present is converted into sugar; the product is termed malt. An infusion of malt, known as wort, is boiled with hops and the mixture, when cool, is fermented with yeast. The resulting liquor, or beer, contains from 2-8 % of alcohol.

BRIDGE
Structure to carry a path, road, railway, or canal, across a river, other water, depressions in ground levels or across other roads or railways. Bridges are constructed of rope, wood, stone, metal or reinforced ferro-concrete, and come under 2 main classes, *i.e.*, fixed and opening in the general subdivisions as follows: *Bascule:* Tower Bridge, London; *Cantilever:* Forth Rly. Bridge (5,330 ft.); *Concrete Arch:* New Waterloo Bridge, London; *Drawbridge:* Monnickendam-Amsterdam, Holland; *Grass-rope Bridge:* over the Indus River in Tibet; *Masonry Arch:* London Bridge; *Roller:* Newport Docks Bridge, Montana; *Steel Arch:* Sydney Harbour Bridge; *Suspension:* Verrazano-Narrows, Brooklyn-Staten Is. U.S.A. (4,260 ft. long); *Swing:* Madison Avenue Bridge, Harlem River, New York; *Transporter:* Rouen Bridge, France; *Truss:* St. Louis Bridge, Mississippi River, Ohio; *Vertical Lift:* James River Highway, U.S.A. (23,178 ft. long). The world's 2 longest bridges are: (1) *Trestle:* S. Pacific Rly. Bridge, 20 m. over The Great Salt Lake, Utah, and (2) *Ferro-concrete:* Key-West Extension, Florida, where the rly. passes over 30 m. of open sea. The *Bailey Bridge* was used with great success in World War II. The Forth Road Bridge (*q.v.*), with a suspension span of 3,300 ft. was opened, 1964.

BRIDGE
Card game, played by 4 players with the full pack of cards. Each player has 13 cards and the aim of each pair is to make the highest possible number of tricks. Tricks in no trumps have the highest value; then follow in order spades, hearts, diamonds and clubs. From this game, introduced into London in 1894, *auction* and *contract* bridge have evolved.

BRIDGES, Robert
(1844-1930) Eng. poet. B. Kent; travelled; studied med., and practised until 1882, in London; poet laureate 1913; O.M. 1929. Interested in hymnology, spelling, handwriting, prosody. *Shorter Poems* (1873-93), *The Growth of Love* (sonnets) 1876 and later; plays; *The Testament of Beauty* (1929); *Milton's Prosody* (1893) revised 1921), *A Critical Introduction to Keats*, 1895; *The Yattendon Hymnal* (1899) and papers on chanting; *The Spirit of Man* (an anthology in Eng. and Fr.), 1916.

BRIDGET
(**Brigid or Bride**) **Saint** (453-523) A patron saint of Ireland. B. Fochart, Co. Louth. According to legend, her mother and she were sold to a wizard, whom Bridget converted to Christianity. She founded the great Ch. and Monastery of Kildare. Her body was interred in Downpatrick with those of St. Patrick and St. Columba.

BRIDGETOWN
Cap. and seaport of Barbados, W. Indies, on the shores of Carlisle Bay. Exports include sugar, molasses and rum. Pop. 11,289.

BRIDGWATER
Borough and river port of Somerset on the Parret, 12 m. from the Bristol Channel. The chief industry is brick and tile manufacture. Pop. 25,930.

BRIDIE, James
(Pseudonym of **Osborne Henry Mavor**) (1888-1951); Scots. dramatist. Educ. Glasgow Academy and Univ. He practised as doctor till 1938, and was prof. of Med. at Anderson Coll., Glasgow. *Some Talk of Alexander* (revue) 1926 was followed in 1928 by *The Sunlight Sonata.* Later plays include: *The Anatomist* (1931), *Tobias and the Angel*, *Sleeping Clergyman* (1933), *Susannah and the Elders* (1937), *The King of Nowhere* (1938) (on Fascism), *The Holy Isle* (or *The Queen of Ultima Thule*), *Mr. Bolfry* (1943), *Forrigan Reel* (1944), *Dr. Angelus* (1947), *John Knox*, *Gog and Magog* (1948), *Daphne Laureola* (1949), *Mr. Gillie* (1950), *The Queen's Comedy* (1950). Miscellanea: *British Drama* (pamphlets 1942, 1946), *A Small Stir*, 1949. His

autobiog. *One Way of Living*, appeared 1939. Bridie was a founder and director of Glasgow's Citizens' Theatre.

BRIER or BRIAR
Common name for the wild or dog rose, but also given to other varieties including the sweet brier or any shrub with wooded stems bearing thorns or prickles. It is also the name for the white heath (*Erica scoparia*), a Fr. shrub used in the manufacture of pipes.

BRIGHOUSE
Borough of the W. Riding, Yorks. on the Calder, 5 m. N. of Huddersfield. There are woollen and worsted manufactures. With Spenborough B. returns 1 member to Parl. Pop. 31,000.

BRIGHT, John
(1811-89) Eng. politician. M.P. (Lib.), 1843-57 and 1858-89. A great orator, with Cobden he led the agitation for the repeal of the Corn Laws. He was deeply opposed to warfare, denouncing the Crimean War and Gladstone's Egyptian policy. Over Irish Home Rule, Bright disagreed with Gladstone and followed the Lib. Unionists.

BRIGHTON
County borough and seaside resort of Sussex, 51 m S. of London. The Pavilion was built by George IV when he was Prince Regent. Brighton has railway shops and other industries, including some fishing. There is a racecourse at Kemp Town. It returns 2 members to Parl. Pop. 162,200.

BRIGHT'S DISEASE
Disease characterised by inflammation of kidneys (**nephritis** *q.v.*) first described by Dr. Richard Bright (1789-1858).

BRILL
(*Rhombus*) Flat fish closely allied to the Turbot, but smaller and smooth-skinned. Found around the coasts of Brit.

BRISBANE
Cap. and river port of Queensland, Australia, on the Brisbane river, over 10 m. from Moreton Bay. It is a commercial and banking centre, with an extensive overseas trade. Industries include food preserving, clothing, engineering, and tanning. Pop. 635,500.

BRISTOL
City, county borough and seaport of Gloucestershire, on the Avon, 9 m. from the Bristol Channel. There is a harbour on the Avon, with quays and warehouses, but for larger vessels the docks are at Avonmouth and Portishead. Industries include the manufacture of aircraft, tobacco, chocolate and shoes. The chief buildings are the cath. and St. Mary Redcliffe. There is a univ. opened 1909. Clifton Coll. is a public school. It returns 6 members to Parl. Pop. 434,260. **Bristol Channel.** Arm of the sea separating S. Wales from Somerset and Devon, outlet of Severn estuary. It receives in addition to the Severn the waters of the Towy, Taff, Usk, Wye, Avon, Parret, Tone, Taw and Torridge. Lundy Is. stands at the entrance to the Channel, off Hartland Pt. The Channel is remarkable for its high and rapid tides, which at the Severn estuary form the Severn bore.

BRITAIN
Name for Eng., Wales and Scot. from Rom. times to the coming of the Angles and Saxons in the 5th cent. It comes prob. from the Brythons, a Celtic people, and in the form Britannia was given to the land by the Roms. *See* ENGLAND; SCOTLAND; WALES; N. IRELAND. **Britain, Battle of.** German air offensive begun on August 8, 1940, against S.E. Eng. and London and intended to prepare the way for a seaborne invasion. The Brit. defending force was outnumbered, but the German air losses were so heavy that the operation was abandoned. Speaking in Parl. on Aug. 20, the P.M. (Winston Churchill), said: " Never in the field of human conflict was so much owed by so many to so few ". *See* WORLD WAR II.

BRITISH ACADEMY
The Society for the promotion of historical, philosophical and philological studies, granted a Royal Charter of incorporation in 1902. The members of the Academy, known as Fellows, must not now exceed 200 and from them are chosen a Pres. and council of 15 members elected for 3 years. The Annual Report was instituted in 1917. In 1924 the Govt. approved a subsidy of £2,000, with the proviso that no portion of it should be applied to the ordinary expenses of the Academy. The annual Govt. Grant, which has fluctuated, now stands at £5,000.

BRITISH ANTARCTIC TERRITORY *See* ANTARCTIC.

BRITISH ASSOCIATION
Soc. for the advancement of science, founded 1831. It holds a meeting every year at which an address is given by the pres., an eminent scientist, and sectional meetings are held for the discussion of matters of interest.

BRITISH COLUMBIA
W. prov. of Canada. It has an indented Pacific coastline and includes Vancouver, Queen Charlotte and other Is. A region of mts., river valleys and plateaux. Principal rivers are the Fraser, Columbia, Skeena and Finlay. Products include fish, fruit, timber, furs and silver, copper, lead, coal and other minerals. Victoria, on Vancouver Is. is the cap.; Vancouver is the largest city. In 1849 Vancouver Is. and in 1858 Brit. Columbia, were made Crown Colonies; they joined the Canadian Confed. 1871. It is administered by a legislative assembly, a ministry and a lieut.-gov. and sends 6 senators and 16 representatives to the Fed. parl. The univ. was founded in 1908. Area: 366,255 sq.m. Pop. 1,659,000.

BRITISH COMMONWEALTH OF NATIONS
The. An assoc. of countries owing allegiance to the sovereign of the U.K. The states of the Commonwealth may be divided into 4 groups: (1) The U.K. of Gt. Brit. and N. Ireland. (2) The dominions, Canada, Australia, New Zealand, India, Pakistan, Ceylon, Ghana, Nigeria, Cyprus, Sierra Leone, Tanganyika, W. Samoa, Jamaica, Trinidad and Tobago, Uganda, Zanzibar, Kenya, Malawi, Malta and Zambia. (3) Colonies, *e.g.* Hong Kong. (4) Protectorates, *e.g.* Solomon Is. **The dominions** are autonomous communities within the Commonwealth equal in status with U.K. and with one another. **Colonies** do not possess responsible govt. and may or may not have an elective legislature. **Protectorates** are areas over which the Brit. Govt. assumes control, but the chiefs are left to manage their internal affairs. The Queen is represented in each dominion and colony by a gov. or gov.-gen. The dominions have each a high commissioner in London. The indep. position of the dominions was fully recognised by the Statute of Westminster, 1931. A Commonw. P.M.'s Conference meets in London at intervals. **Commonwealth Office** is the current Brit. Govt. dept. responsible for relations with the self-governing members of the Commw. under the direction of a Sec. of State.

BRITISH EUROPEAN AIRWAYS CORPORATION
Commercial airline formed as a result of the Civil Aviation Act on Aug. 1, 1946. B.E.A. was the first airline in the world to use propeller-turbine airliners and the first to introduce regular passenger helicopter services. The route mileage of B.E.A. exceeds 26,000 m.

BRITISH GUIANA, now **Guyana**
Republic on the N. coast of S. America bounded by Venezuela, Brazil and Surinam

(Dutch Guiana). There are 3 distinct regions; the coastal lowland, a belt of forest and the hinterland of mts. and savannah. The chief rivers are the Berbice, Demerara and Essequibo. Sugar, rum, rice, timber, bauxite and balata are exported. Georgetown, at the mouth of the Demerara, is the cap. The area was settled by the Dutch *c.* 1620, captured by the Eng. 1796, and ceded to Gt. Brit., 1814. It is admin. by a Gov. with 2 councils. The movement towards indep. has been hindered by racial unrest, but B.G. became indep. state within Commonw. as **Guyana** in 1966, declared repub. 1970. Area: 83,000 sq.m. Pop. 603,000.

BRITISH HONDURAS
Crown colony on the Caribbean Sea, S. of Yucatan and N. of Guatemala. The coastal area is swampy, and the climate trop. The Belize is the chief river. Products include mahogany, logwood, bananas. chicle and citrus fruits. Belize (*q.v.*) is chief port; new cap. Belmopan is at geographic centre. Under 1964 constit. B.H. has more self-govt. with a view to indep. Area 8,900 sq.m. Pop. 120,000.

BRITISH ISLES
Gt. Brit., Ireland, and the adjacent Is. Its divisions are, Eng., Wales, Scot., N. Ireland, Eire, Isle of Man and the Channel Is. Area: *c.* 121,048 sq.m. Pop. *c.* 54,221,000.

BRITISH LEGION
Organisation instituted 1921 by the late Earl Haig to assist ex-servicemen and women of all wars. The funds are derived largely from the sale of poppies on Armistice Day, Nov. 11th. Activities include workshops, schools, homes and hospitals for members and dependants. There are *c.* 4,350 branches.

BRITISH MEDICAL ASSOCIATION
A world wide association of men and women with qualifications in medicine and surgery. It was founded in 1832 and its principal objects are to promote the medical and allied sciences and to maintain the honour and interests of the medical profession.

BRITISH MUSEUM
Nat. museum of Gt. Brit. It owes its origin to Sir Hans Sloane who d. in 1753 and by his will gave an option to Parl. to purchase for £20,000 his library, MSS. and collection of natural hist. specimens and other curiosities. The Act of Parl. by which the offer was accepted provided also for the purchase of the MSS. collected by Robert and Edward Harley, Earls of Oxford, and for the proper custody of the Cotton MSS. The development of the library and public reading room of the Museum was the work of Anthony Panizzi, apptd. keeper of printed books in 1837. Under the Copyright Act a copy of every book printed in the U.K. must be delivered to the Brit. Museum Library within a month of publication.

BRITISH OVERSEAS AIRWAYS CORPORATION
A commercial airline corporation wholly state-owned estabd. in Nov. 1939 under the provisions of the Brit. Overseas Airways Act and began operations in 1940.

BRITISH RAILWAYS
Name for the railways of the U.K. as from the date of their nationalisation, Jan. 1, 1948. Administered by the Brit. Rlwys. Board. There are 6 regions, namely: (1) *Southern* (formerly Southern Rly.), (2) *Western* (formerly G. Western Rly.), (3) *London Midland* (formerly Eng. section of the London-Midland and Scot. Rly.), (4) *Eastern* (formerly part of London and N. Eastern Rly.), (5) *North Eastern* (formerly part of London and N. Eastern Rly.), (6) *Scottish* (formerly Scottish sections of the L.M.S. and L.N.E. Rlys.). The former London Passenger Transport Board has become London Transport Board. Drastic reductions in services were postulated in the Beeching Report and some closures have been effected. The name Brit. Rail came into use 1964. *See* RAILWAY.

BRITISH STANDARDS
Specific standards of design, quality, method, etc. adopted by Brit. manufacturers fixed by the Brit. Standards Institution. In 1901 the Institutions of Civil, Mechanical and Electrical Engineers, together with the Iron and Steel Institute and the Institution of Naval Architects, formed a joint committee to deal, primarily, with the standardisation of steel girders. From

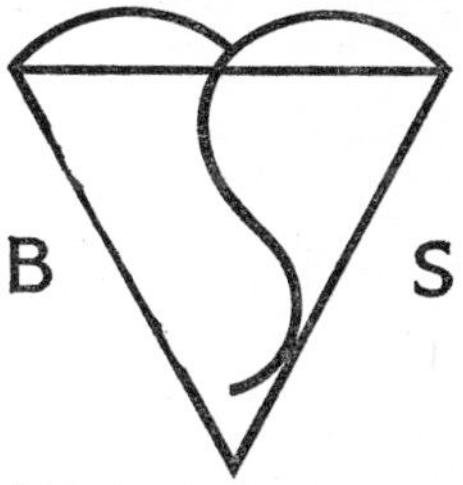

British Standards official mark

this developed the present Brit. Standards Inst. now covering over 60 major industries in the U.K. the main principles upon which it operates having been adopted by every other industrial country in the world. The Inst. is controlled by a Gen. Council with over 2,400 committees. These include producers, users, distributors, representatives from Govt. Depts.

BRITTANY
(*Fr.* **Bretagne**) Former prov. of Fr.; the modern depts. of Côtes-du-Nord, Ille-et-Vilaine, Loire-Inférieure, Morbihan and Finistère. It became known as Britannia Minor as a result of Brit. colonisation during the A.S. invasions of Eng. in the 5th and 6th cents. The Bretons speak a variant of the ancient Brit. tongue allied to Welsh. The people, who are mainly R.C.s. excel as fishermen and sailors. The soil is generally poor, and near the N. coast a manure of seaweed and shells is used to promote the growth of early vegetables for export. The chief towns are Rennes, Nantes, Brest and Lorient. Quimper is famous for its earthenware, and St. Malo and Dinard are resorts.

BRITTEN, Edward Benjamin
(1913-) Eng. composer. C.H. 1953. Studied pianoforte with Harold Samuel and composition with Frank Bridge, Arthur Benjamin and John Ireland. His works include the operas *Peter Grimes, The Turn of the Screw, Let's Make an Opera, Gloriana, A Midsummer Night's Dream*; song cycles with piano accompaniment; *War Requiem* (1962). See *Benjamin Britten* ed. by Donald Mitchell and Hans Keller (1953).

BRIXHAM
Resort and urban district of Devon, on Torbay, 32 m. S. of Exeter. Good harbour for the fishing and coasting trade. William III landed there in 1688. Pop. 10,870.

BROADCASTING
Word meaning to send out news to all men everywhere, but used today esp. for the sending out by wireless information, entertainment, etc. It began in Brit. in 1921. In 1922 the Brit. Broadcasting Co. was formed and in 1927 this became a Govt. Corp. It has a monopoly of broadcasting in Gt. Brit. and N. Ireland. Empire Broadcasts began in 1932. By 1944 services were directed to many European countries, and World War II these transmissions gave support throughout the world in 48 languages. During for 'underground' movements abroad. In 1945, peace time arrangements introduced a Home Service and the Light Programme and, in 1946,

the Third Programme. Network Three, introduced in 1957, caters for the specialist listener. Channels changed to Radio 1, 2, 3, and 4, 1967. Public television broadcasts, first introduced in 1936, were resumed in 1946. Commercial television under the control of I.T.A. was introduced in 1954. *See* B.B.C.; INDEPENDENT TELEVISION AUTHORITY.

BROADMOOR
Asylum for criminal lunatics, in Berks., since 1863.

BROADS, The
District of E. Anglia, mainly in Norfolk. It is so called from its numerous broads, or large shallow lakes. The district is intersected by the lower reaches of the rivers Yare, Bure, Ant and Waveney. The Broads are a very popular sporting holiday resort.

BROMIDE
Salts of hydrobromic acid, the commonest examples being the bromides of potassium and silver. Potassium bromide is used in medicine. Silver bromide is used to form bromide paper for photographic printing.

BROMINE
Non-metallic element. At. wt. 79·92, and chem. sym., Br. It exists as a heavy volatile liquid of a deep reddish-brown colour and has a suffocating irritant odour. Its chief source is the mineral carnallite from Stassfurt in Saxony. Bromine resembles chlorine and its compounds are used in medicine, photography and in the manufacture of aniline dyes.

BROMLEY
Borough of Greater London (1964), consisting of the former Beckenham, Bromley, Orpington, Penge and part of Chislehurst and Sidcup. Pop. 294,344.

BRONCHITIS
Acute or chronic disease affecting air tubes and characterised by tight feeling in chest and dry hard cough. Usually caused by bacteria and attack may be precipitated by cold, damp, irritating vapours, or as a complication of some other disease such as failing heart.

BRONTË, Charlotte
(1816-55) Eng. novelist. B. Thornton, Bradford; daughter of Rev. Patrick Brontë; educ. at a clergy daughters' school at Cowan Bridge, at Roehead, and at home; school-teacher and governess; with her sister Emily as pupil and teacher in Brussels (1842-3); lived in Haworth until her d.; *Jane Eyre* (1847), *Shirley* (1849), *Villette* (1853); mar. Rev. A. B. Nicholls, her father's curate, 1854. Her novels have a large autobiog. element. She also pub. with her sisters, some poetry (1846). All her work was, during her life-time, pub. under the pseudonym of **Currer Bell**. Her sisters were **Emily Jane** (1818-48) and **Anne** (1820-49). Emily, as **Ellis Bell**, pub. in 1847 *Wuthering Heights*. After her d. Charlotte pub. some of her poetry and revised the novel, part of which may have been written by their brother, **Patrick Branwell** (1817-48). As **Acton Bell**, Anne pub. *Agnes Grey* (1847) and *The Tenant of Wildfell Hall* (1848). See *The Brontë Story* by Margaret Lane (1953).

BRONZE
General name for copper-tin alloys, which include gun metal, bell metal and speculum metal. The colour and properties vary according to the proportions of the constituents, but ordinary bronze is harder and stronger than brass and is easily worked. **Bronze Age.** Period between the Stone Age and Iron Age when man used bronze for tools. In the E. it may have begun *c.* 5000 B.C., in W. perhaps *c.* 2000 B.C.; it continued until *c.* 1000 B.C.

BROOKE, Rupert
(Chawner) (1888-1915) Eng. poet. Educ. Rugby and King's Coll., Camb.; pub. *Poems* (1911); on outbreak of war, joined Royal Naval Div.; Antwerp; d. at Scyros in the Aegean.

BROOM
Leguminous shrub (*Sarothamnus scoparius*), native to Europe and N. Asia, growing on heaths and moors. The branches are green and furrowed, bearing compound leaves and yellow flowers.

BROUGHAM AND VAUX, Lord
[broom, vawks] **Henry Peter** (1778-1868) Eng. lawyer and politician. M.P. (Whig), 1810-12, 1816-30. He defended Queen Caroline, and estab. the Judicial Committee and the Central Criminal Court. He designed the carriage named after him.

BROWN, Ford Madox
(1821-93) Brit. artist. B. Calais, d. London. D. G. Rossetti worked under him and he was assoc. with the Pre-Raphaelites, writing for *The Germ*.

BROWN, John
(1800-59) Amer. abolitionist. B. Connecticut. On Oct. 16, 1859, with a few associates he seized the arsenal at Harper's Ferry. During the fighting he was wounded and captured. Tried, he was found guilty and was hanged at Charleston, Dec. 2, 1859. The opponents of slavery thought of him as a martyr and a song about him, *John Brown's Body*, became their battle chant.

BROWN, Lancelot
(Capability Brown) (1715-83) Eng. landscape gardener. He became gardener for the Duke of Buckingham, at Stowe. He designed gardens at Blenheim, and Kew.

BROWNE, Robert
(1550-1633). B. Stanford. Puritan leader, founder of the Brownists. Community founded in Norwich developed into modern Congregationalism.

BROWNE, Sir Thomas
(1605-82) Eng. writer. He studied med. at Oxford, Leyden, Montpellier. His interests were scientific, hist., archaeological. His statement of faith, *Religio Medici* (1642); later works include *Hydriotaphia* (Urn-Burial) (1658).

BROWNING, Elizabeth Barrett
(1806-61) Eng. poet. B. near Durham, daughter of Edward Barrett Moulton (Barrett); from 15 an invalid; had made some reputation as a poet when she eloped to Italy with Robert Browning, 1846; d. in Florence. Her works include *Poems* (1844), *Sonnets from the Portuguese* (1850), *Casa Guidi Windows* (1851), *Aurora Leigh* (1857).

BROWNING, Robert
(1812-89) Eng. poet. B. Camberwell; educ. privately; studied Gk. at Univ. Coll., London; after his marriage to Elizabeth Barrett lived mainly in Florence until her d.; d. in Venice. His output included *Pauline* (1832), *Paracelsus* (1833), *Sordello* (1840); collections of pieces, as *Bells and Pomegranates* (1841-6), *Dramatic Romances and Lyrics* (1845), *Men and Women* (1855), *Dramatis Personae* (1864), *Dramatic Idylls* (1879), *Christmas Eve and Easter Day* (1850), *The Ring and the Book* (1868-9). See *Robert Browning* by Betty Miller (1952).

BRUCE, James
(1730-94) Scot. explorer. In 1768 he set out from Alexandria and discovered the source of the Blue Nile in Abyssinia. He wrote *Travels to Discover the Source of the Nile.*

BRUCE, Robert
(1274-1329) King of Scot. After the capture of Wallace, Bruce became the leader of the Scots in the War of Indep. Crowned King in 1306, he kept up a bitter struggle, until the final defeat of Edward II at Bannockburn, 1314. Not until 1328 was Scot. recognised by the Eng. as

an indep. kingdom. Bruce d. of leprosy and was buried in Dunfermline Abbey. His grandson, Robert II, son of Margery Bruce and the High Steward, was the first Stewart King.

BRUCH, Max
(1838-1920) German composer of Jewish descent. He composed operas, works for chorus and orchestra, 3 symphonies, 2 violin concertos.

BRUCKNER, Anton
[brŏŏk′-] (1824-96) Aust. composer, organist and ch. musician. In 1868 he became Prof. at Vienna Conservatoire. His works include 9 symphonies, *Requiem*, *Te Deum*, a string quartet.

BRUEGHEL
(or **Breughel**) [bre′-gel] Dutch family of painters. **Pieter Brueghel** (1525?-69) known as Pieter the Elder, worked in Antwerp and Brussels, and is held in high esteem for his paintings depicting the life of the peasants. He left two sons—Pieter and Jan. **Pieter the Younger** (1564-1637) gained the name of 'Hell Brueghel' from the many scenes in which devils and witches appear. **Jan Brueghel** (1568-1625?), known as 'Velvet Brueghel', painted mostly landscapes.

BRUGES
[broozh] City of Belgium, cap. of W. Flanders prov., 9 m. from the N. Sea. The cloth trade made Bruges one of the richest cities of Europe in the M.A. but its importance declined with the growth of Antwerp. The chief buildings include the cath., 2 guild houses and city gates. Pop. 52,463.

BRUMMELL, George
(Beau) (1778-1840). Eng. dandy. An intimate of the Prince Regent, he was for some years the recognised arbiter of fashion. In 1816, having quarrelled with the Prince, he went to Fr. to escape his creditors. He d. in a hospital for the mendicant insane.

BRUNEI
[broo′-nī] Brit. protected state on the N.W. coast of Borneo. Exports include crude oil, rubber and sago. Brunei, the cap. is on B. Bay. During World War II B. was occupied by the Japs. It is administered by the Sultan with Privy and Executive Councils, and a Chief Min. with an Executive Council. Area: 2,226 sq. m. Pop. 92,000.

BRUNO, Giordano
(*c.* 1548-1600) Ital. philos. A Dominican monk. In 1576, having developed heretical opinions, he fled to Geneva. and afterwards to Paris where he lectured on philosophy. He visited England, where he became a close friend of Sir Philip Sidney. Returning to Italy in 1592 he fell into the hands of the Inquisition. Refusing to recant, he was burned in Rome, 1600.

BRUNSWICK
City of Lower Saxony, W. Germany, 32 m. S.E. of Hanover. A rly. junction, it has machinery and chem. manufactures and many fine buildings, including a 12th cent. cath. Pop. 249,000.

BRUNSWICK, Duke of
In 1780 **Charles William** became duke and in 1792 he led the Austrian and Prussian army that was defeated by the Fr. at Valmy. He held a high command in the Allied armies until he was wounded at Auerstadt. He d. of his wounds 1806. His name was given to the B. Manifesto (1792), which threatened the destruction of Paris if the King or Queen were harmed, thus inflaming the revolutionaries in Fr.

BRUSSELS
(*Fr.* **Bruxelles**) Cap. of Belgium on a tributary of the Scheldt, 25 m. S. of Antwerp. It is a great commercial centre with numerous manufactures and is famous for its art collections. In 1831, B. was made cap. of Belgium; during both World Wars it was occupied by the Germans. Pop. with suburbs 1,029,693. **Brussels, Treaty of.** Treaty of alliance signed at Brussels, on March 17, 1948, by Brit., Fr. and the Benelux countries (Belgium, Netherlands, Luxemburg). The purpose of this alliance, which is to last for 50 years, is the setting up of W. Union. In 1950 the milit. section was merged in N.A.T.O. (*q.v.*).

BRUSSELS SPROUTS
Vegetable grown in Brit. Belonging to the genus *Brassica*, it produces large compact edible buds upon the stem.

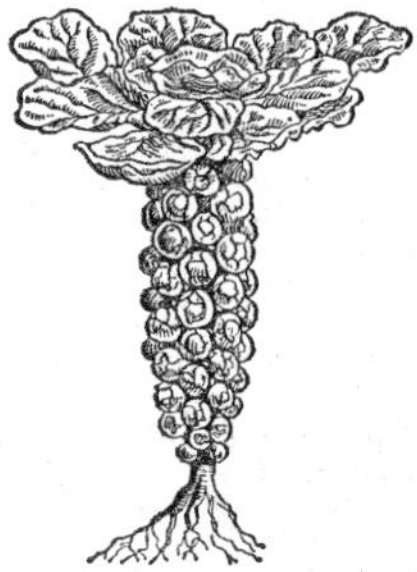

BRUTUS
[broo′-] Cognomen of several Roms. The word means fool, and was given to **Lucius Junius** because he pretended to be mad in order to save his life. He drove the unpopular Tarquin kings from Rome. He sentenced his own sons to d. for conspiring to restore the Tarquins. A later Brutus (**Marcus Junius**) was one of the murderers of Julius Caesar. When civil war broke out he sided with Pompey. Induced by Cassius to join in the plot against the dictator, he helped in the murder. He was one of the leaders of the force defeated by Caesar's friends at Philippi, and committed suicide (42 B.C.).

BRYONY
Name of 2 unrelated Brit. plants. The white bryony (*Bryonia dioica*), of the cucumber family, is common in hedgerows. The black bryony (*Tamus communis*), of the yam family, has a twining stem and heart-shaped leaves.

BUCHAN, John
1st Baron Tweedsmuir (1875-1940). Scot. writer, B. Peebles-shire; war corresp. World War I; gov.-gen. of Canada and peer 1935. Many books: some poetry; novels, as *John Burnet of Barns* (1898), *The Thirty-Nine Steps* (1915), *Witchwood*, *The Gap in the Curtain* (1932), biogs. as *Montrose* (1913); also an autobiog.

BUCHANAN, George
(1506-82) Scot. humanist and historian, b. Killearn, Stirlingshire. Having pub. satires on the Scots clergy, he was imprisoned but escaped and fled to Fr. He was classical tutor of Queen Mary and in 1567, Moderator of the Gen. Assembly.

BUCHAREST
(*Rum.* **Bucureşti**) [bew-kă-rest′] Cap. of Rumania, on a trib. of the Danube in a fertile plain. It deals with most of the country's trade. There is a univ. founded 1864, a R.C. cath. and several chs. Formerly the chief town of Wallachia, B. became cap. of Rumania, 1861. Occupied by the Hungarians, Germans and Russians in World War II. Pop. 1,511,000.

BUCHMAN, Frank Nathan Daniel
[book-] (1878-1961) Amer. evangelist. B. Pennsylvania. In 1928, he launched the campaign for Moral Rearmament (M R.A.), in London.

BUCKHOUND
A variety of staghound used for hunting the Buck Deer. Until 1901 Eng. sovereigns maintained a pack of buckhounds.

BUCKINGHAM
Borough of Bucks. on the Ouse, 61 m. from London. Once the county town and a centre of the wool trade, it has declined. Pop. 4,390.

BUCKINGHAM, Duke of
George Villiers (1592-1628) Eng. politician. On very friendly terms with James I and his son Charles. In 1623 he became Lord High Admiral, and led fruitless expeditions to Fr. and Spain. He was killed by John Felton at Portsmouth. His son was **George Villiers, 2nd Duke** (1628-87). Educ. with the children of Charles I and was with Charles II at Worcester. In 1657 he returned from exile and mar. a daughter of Lord Fairfax. He engineered Clarendon's fall and, 1667-73, was a leading member of the Cabal. He then assoc. with the Whigs and with the opposition to the govt.

BUCKINGHAM PALACE
Royal residence in London. George III bought it, 1761, and, 1825, its reconstruction was begun by Nash. Sir Aston Webb designed a new front, 1913.

BUCKINGHAMSHIRE
(Bucks) County of S. Eng. bounded on the S. by the Thames. The Chiltern Hills pass through the S. To the N. is the fertile Vale of Aylesbury. Chief rivers are the Ouse, Colne and Thames. It is principally an agricultural county. Aylesbury is the county town; others are Slough, High Wycombe, Chesham, Buckingham, Eton and Stowe. It returns 4 members to Parl. Pop. 505,130.

BUCKTHORN
Tall Brit. shrub (*Rhamnus carthartica*), with branches bearing sharp thorn-like points. The dense clusters of yellowish-green flowers are followed by small shining black fruits.

BUDAPEST
Cap., river port and rly. centre of Hungary, on the Danube. It consists of the twin cities of Buda and Pest, on opposite banks of the river, connected by several fine bridges. The commercial and financial centre of the country, Budapest has many manufactures. The kings of Hungary lived in Buda until 1526 and in 1867 it became a cap. city. They were formally united, 1873, and occupied by the Germans and Russians in World War II. Centre of the Hungarian revolution of 1956. *See* HUNGARY. Pop. 1,875,000.

BUDDHA, Siddhatha Gotama
[bo͝o'-dă] also called **Sakyamuni,** the founder of Buddhism. It is a generic title, for there have been many Buddhas, of whom Gotama was the latest, but not necessarily the last. He was the son of the Chief of the Sakyas, and was b. *c.* 621 B.C. At the age of 28 he experienced a profound religious change which caused him to leave his wife and child, and devote himself to a life of poverty and asceticism. He became a full Buddha in 592 B.C., began to teach and soon gained disciples. He d. *c.* 488 B.C. **Buddhism.** Religious system and philosophy taught by the Buddha (*q.v.*). The dominant religion of Ceylon, it is still found in parts of India, in the Lamaism of Tibet, in S.E. Asia, in China, and in Japan. Man is conceived to be an individualised self-conscious being linked irrevocably to the One Universal Cause. The aim of Buddhism is the achievement of *Nirvana* and the kernel of its ethics is the Buddha's Noble Eightfold Path, namely—(1) right comprehension (freedom from prejudices, illusions and superstitions), (2) right resolution (pressing forward to the higher goal), (3) right speech (kindly, faithful, true), (4) right conduct (peace-loving, honest, pure), (5) right living (harmless livelihood, hurting no living thing), (6) right effort (perseverance in well-doing), (7) right meditation (intellectual activity, always directed to Rule and Doctrine), (8) right rapture (intense reflection, the mind being wholly withdrawn from things of time and sense). As in Hinduism, the first of the two doctrines fundamental to Buddhism is that of *Reincarnation.* The second important doctrine is that of *Karma.* Thoughts and actions react upon the individual soul according to whether they are energised constructively or destructively, and rewards and punishments are of man's own making according to whether he serves the forces of good or evil.

BUDGERIGAR
Small, intelligent species of Austral, parrakeet. It breeds freely in captivity. Yellow, white, blue, green and mauve varieties are found.

BUDGET
In Brit. statement made by the Chanc. of the Exchequer to the Commons, sitting as the Committee of Ways and Means, about the nation's finances. In other countries a similar statement is made by the Min. of Finance. It consists of a statement of the actual revenue and expenditure for the past year; and an estimate of the revenue and expenditure for the coming year.

BUENOS AIRES
[bwā'-nos ī'-res] Cap. of Argentina, the largest city of the S. Hemisphere, on the W. bank of the Plate, 150 m. from the sea. B.A. has an enormous trade, handling half the commerce of Argentina, in cattle, meat and grain. There are many fine buildings, wide streets, beautiful parks. Pop. (Greater B.A.) 4,500,000.

BUFFALO
City of New York State, U.S.A., at the E. end of Lake Erie, 420 m. from New York City. A rail centre and lake port, it has miles of wharves. B. is the world's largest flour-milling centre. Pop. 532,759.

BUFFALO
Large mammal belonging to the Bovidae or ox family. The Indian water buffalo is a heavy black-haired animal with long, curved horns set on a straight head bearing small ears. The

American Bison

African species is not so heavy, and has a short neck, large ears and reddish hair. It lives in swamps and is fierce and untameable. The Amer. Bison belongs to a different genus and has a humped body and small horns, but is termed a Buffalo.

BUG
Insects belonging to the sub-order Heteroptera of the order Hemiptera. There are *c.* 8,000 varieties that live on land, besides many that live in the water. Some of them feed on plants and are harmful to vegetation. They have 4 wings and the mouth parts are arranged so that they can pierce the victim and draw blood or sap into the insect's body. The **Bed Bug** (*Cimex*) is frequent in dirty houses.

BUGANDA
[boo-] Native Kingdom under 'Kabaka', federated to Uganda and beneath overall control of the Ugandan C. Govt. Kampala became the seat of the C. govt. 1962.

BUGLE
A milit. wind instrument of brass or copper, similar to the trumpet. In its normal form it can produce only the notes of the harmonic series. Well-known calls are Reveille and the Last Post.

BUGLOSS
[bew'-] (*Lycopsis arvensis*) Plant of the borage family. It grows wild in fields to a ht. of *c.* 1 ft. bearing clusters of blue flowers.

BUKHARA
[-kà'-] Russ. town in Uzbek S.S.R., *c.* 60 m. W. Zarafshan. Once C. Asia's chief trading centre, and cap. of an indep. emirate. Pop. 50,400.

BULGARIA
Repub. of S.E. Europe, bounded by Rumania, Yugoslavia and Greece, with a coastline on the Black Sea. The country is traversed by the Balkan and Rhodope Mts. with the fertile plain of the Maritsa between the ranges. Other rivers are the Danube, forming the N. boundary, and the Struma. Bulgaria is mainly an agricultural country, producing cereals, sugar beet, tobacco, fruit and wine. Industrial development has been slow, although there are rich coal deposits. Sofia is the cap.; other towns are Plovdiv, Stalin, Ruschuk, Burgas and Pleven. The Gk. Orthodox is the country's traditional ch. From 1908 until 1918 Prince Ferdinand of Saxe-Coburg-Kohary reigned as Tsar. He abdicated in favour of his son Boris, who d. 1943. Bulgaria was invaded by Germany, 1941, and liberated by the Russ. 4 years later. A Communist repub. was set up in 1946, with a single chamber Nat. Assembly. By the peace treaty of 1947 the frontiers of 1941 were restored. Area: 42,818 sq.m. Pop. 7,798,000.

BULL
Term used for a pronouncement made by a Pope. Famous bulls include that of 1870 which asserted the infallibility of the Pope.

BULL-FIGHTING
Popular diversion of Spain and Sp. Amer. The combatants include: *picadores*, who fight on horseback; *chulos*, or *banderilleros*, foot-combatants, carrying banners; and, finally, the *matador*, who deals the animal the *coup de grâce*. At a given signal the bull is admitted to the arena. The *picadores*, stationing themselves near the animal, commence the attack with lances. The *chulos* draw the bull's attention with their cloaks. The *banderilleros* transfix the bull with their barbed darts. Finally the *matador* advances with a naked sword and a red flag. Attracting the bull's attention with the latter, he gives the fatal blow. In Portugal a milder form is practised. The bull's horns are truncated and padded, so that the men and horses are not seriously injured. The bull is never killed.

BULL-FROG
(*Rana catesbiana*) A large N. Amer. frog, 7-8 in. in length, whose croaks are like the bellow of a bull.

BULL TERRIER
Dog formerly bred for fighting and rat killing. It has a long wedge-shaped head with strong level jaws, small dark eyes and semi-erect ears. Its short body is usually white, and it has a broad chest, legs of medium length, and weighs from 15-50 lb.

BULLDOG
Breed of dog formerly used for bull-baiting. It is characterised by its massive body and short legs, short muscular neck, broad, square head with large wide nostrils, small ears and square jaws, the lower jaw projecting beyond the upper.

BULLFINCH
European bird 6 in. long; black and bluish-grey, red or grey-breasted according to sex. It haunts woodlands, and nests in May, laying 5 eggs.

BUMBLEBEE
Wild, loud-humming bee of the genus *Bombus*, of which numerous species are found throughout the world. That found in Brit. has a large, dark-coloured, hairy body, banded with yellow-orange. Each colony is founded in the late spring or early summer by a single fecundated queen mated in the previous summer or autumn. Each queen builds a small nest, in a hole in the ground or in a tuft of matted grass. The larvae which hatch from the eggs are fed progressively by the queen on nectar and pollen which she herself collects. The bees which emerge from these first cells are incapable of mating. These take over from the queen the duties of nest building, foraging for food and feeding her larvae. Towards the end of the summer a number of large female bumblebees which are sexually matured are produced and a number of males. The virgin queens and the males leave the nest in search of food and mates, the young queens of one colony mating with the drones of another. The young impregnated queens go off individually and remain quiescent until, in spring, they each attempt to found a new colony. *See* HUMBLE BEE.

BUNSEN, Robert William
[boon'-] (1811-1899) German scientist, who invented the gas burner which bears his name.

BUNTING
Group of small birds comprising the genus *Emberiza*, of the family Fringillidae, the finches. It includes the Common or Corn B., the Yellow-hammer, Reed B. and Snow B.

BUNYAN, John
(1628-88) Eng. religious writer. B. near Elstow, son of a tinker; served on the Parliament side in the Civil War; converted about 1650; preached as a nonconformist (Baptist); imprisoned 1660 for unlicensed preaching; 12 years in Bedford Jail, writing, and supporting his 2nd wife and 4 children by tagging laces; *Grace Abounding* pub. 1666; released 1672; again imprisoned 1675 for 6 months, beginning *The Pilgrim's Progress* (pub. 1678 and 1684); *Life and Death of Mr. Badman* (1680); d. in London.

BURBAGE, Richard
(1567-1619) Eng. actor; began acting as a boy. In 1597, he inherited a share in the Blackfriars Theatre, London. With his brother, he built the Globe Theatre, but his great claim to fame is his assoc. with Shakespeare.

BURBOT
or **Eel Pout** (Lota lota) The only fresh-water representative of the Cod family. Shaped like an eel, but shorter, with flat head; two small barbs on nose, another on chin.

BURDOCK
(*Arctium lappa*) Common plant of the family Compositae. It grows to *c.* 4 ft. in ht. and has large wavy leaves. The purple flower heads are succeeded by burrs covered with hooked scales.

BURGH
Scots word for a chartered town or borough (*q.v.*).

BURGHLEY, Lord
[bur'-li] **William Cecil** (1520-98) Eng. statesman. He became Sec. of State 1550. During Mary's reign (1553-8) he conformed to Catholicism; but he won the confidence of Elizabeth, and became Chief Sec. of State on her accession, responsible for Eng.'s foreign policy until his d.

BURGLARY
In Eng. law, crime of breaking into and entering the dwelling-house of another by night (de-

fined as between 9 p.m. and 6 a.m.) with intent to commit a felony. Same crime committed in daytime is called ' housebreaking '.

BURGOYNE, John
[-goin'-] (1722-92) Brit. Gen. in the War of Amer. Indep. Ill supplied and supported he was ambushed and defeated at Saratoga, 1777. This proved to be the turning-point in the struggle.

BURGUNDY
District of Fr. bounded to the S. by the Rhône, comprising much of the Saône Valley. Its chief towns are Châtillon-sur-Seine, Dijon, Le Creusot and Mâcon. The duchy lasted from 1032 to 1482. Its dukes, being also rulers of Flanders, became so powerful that they acted as indep. sovereigns. This was esp. true of Charles the Bold, but after he was killed, 1477, the king of Fr. found it possible to annex most of Burgundy and from then until 1789 it was a prov. The red and white wines produced in the district are called Burgundy.

BURKE and HARE
2 Irish murderers. Lived in Edinburgh where, 1827-28, they murdered *c.* 15 people, and sold their bodies to the anatomists. Burke was hanged on Hare's evidence in 1829.

BURKE, Edmund
(1729-97) Irish writer and statesman. After studying at Trinity Coll., Dublin, he went to London. In 1765 he was elected to the Commons as M.P. for Wendover. With his close friend, Charles James Fox, he supported reform of the govt. of the Amer. colonies and of India, Catholic Emancipation and Parl. Reform. His bitter opposition to the Fr. Revolution led to a quarrel with Fox. His writings include *Speeches on America* and *Reflections on the French Revolution.*

BURMA
Country of S.E. Asia, on the E. coast of the Bay of Bengal, bounded inland by Pakistan, India, Tibet, China, Laos and Thailand. There are 3 main physical divisions: the Arakan Hills and narrow coastal strip in the W.; the extensive valley of the Irrawaddy; and the Salween basin. The Irrawaddy, Chindwin, Sitting and Salween are the main rivers. Agriculture is the principal industry, but there are extensive forests and mineral wealth, including petroleum, rubies and wolfram. Rice and teak are the most important exports. Rangoon is the cap. and largest city; other centres are Mandalay, Moulmein and Bassein. The Irrawaddy is navigable to Bhamo. The Burmese are an Indo-Chinese race, closely akin to the Tibetans. There are large communities of Indian, Pakistani and Chinese immigrants. Buddhism is the religion of 85 % of the people. Burma formed part of Brit. India until 1937, when it became a separate state, with a certain amount of self-govt. The country was occupied by the Japanese, 1941. In 1944 General Wingate led his ' Chindits ' to liberate Burma. A constituent assembly was elected, 1947, and it was decided that Burma should become an indep. sovereign repub. outside the Brit. Commonwealth. This was ratified by treaty, Oct. 1947, and came into force, 1948. Admin. is by the Pres. assisted by a cabinet, but govt. control is limited and the country has been troubled by rebels since 1948. Proclaimed the first Buddhist state in 1961 when Buddhism was made the state religion. Area: 262,000 sq.m. Pop. 25,811,000.
Burma-Siam Railway. Line built by the Jap. in World War II, with prisoner-of-war labour. Running from the Burmese border to Ban Pong, it is now owned by the Govt. of Thailand (Siam).

BURNE-JONES, Sir Edward Coley
(1833-98) Eng. artist; b. Birmingham; educ. there and at Exeter Coll. Oxford, where he became assoc. with William Morris and Rossetti in the pre-Raphaelite (*q.v.*) movement.

BURNET, Gilbert
(1643-1715) Scots churchman and historian. Pub. *History of the Reformation of the Church of England* (1679, 1681, 1714); and *History of My Own Times* (1724 and 1734).

BURNEY, Fanny
Madame D'Arblay (1752-1840) Eng. novelist. B. King's Lynn; became a friend of Dr. Johnson; *Evelina* pub. anonymously 1778, with great success; *Cecilia* (1782); mar. 1793 an emigré general, Alexandre D'Arblay; *Camilla* (1796); her diary and letters (1778-1840) pub. 1842-6; her early diary was pub. 1889.

BURNLEY
County borough and manufacturing town of Lancs. on the Burn, where it joins the Calder, 16 m. N. of Manchester. A centre of the cotton industry. It returns 1 member to Parl. Pop. 80,540.

BURNS, Robert
(1759-96) Scots poet. B. Alloway, Ayrshire; eldest son of a cottar. After his father's d. 1784, farmed Mossgiel, Mauchline, with his brother. The ' Kilmarnock ' ed. of his poems, pub. 1786 made him famous, particularly in Edinburgh; a new ed., 1787. Mar. Jean Armour and took a farm at Ellisland near Dumfries, given up in 1791; contributed many songs to collections by Johnson and Thomson. D. in Dumfries. Many letters survive. His writing was perhaps the last first-class poetical work in vernacular Scots. See *Pride and Passion* by DeLancey Ferguson.

BURTON, Sir Richard Francis
(1821-90) Brit. explorer and orientalist. In 1853 he made his famous journey to Mecca and Medina, disguised as a Pathan Moslem. His account of his exploit, *The Pilgrimage to Al-Medinah and Meccah* created a great sensation (1855). In 1858 he discovered L. Tanganyika and the Victoria Nyanza. At Trieste he made his tr. of *The Arabian Nights* in 16 vols.

BURTON, Robert
(1577-1640) Eng. writer. B. Lindley, Leics. Vicar of St. Thomas's, Oxford, 1616, and rector of Segrave, Leicestershire, 1630. His chief work is *The Anatomy of Melancholy,* pub. ' by Democritus Junior ' in 1621.

BURTON-ON-TRENT
County borough of Staffs. on the Trent. The chief industry is brewing, which has been carried on for over 300 years. Other industries include engineering. It returns 1 member to Parl. Pop. 50,610.

BURUNDI
E.C. African state, cap. Bujumbura. Inhab. by Watutsi and Bahutu tribes. Belg. admin. 1921, indep. 1962. Area: 11,133 sq.m. Pop. 3,340,000.

BURY
County borough of Lancs. on the Irwell, 9 m. N. of Manchester, one of the centres of the cotton industry. With Radcliffe it returns 1 member to Parl. Pop. 60,000.

BURY ST. EDMUNDS
Borough and market town of Suffolk, on the Lark, 85 m. from London. An agricultural centre and the cap. of W. Suffolk. Of the great abbey only the tower and gateway remain. Pop. 21,680.

BUSHMEN
Nomadic hunters of S. Africa, living in the Kalahari Desert, of small stature, with yellow skins. The aboriginal race of S. Africa, they live in impermanent shelters.

BUSTARD
Large game bird of Europe, Asia and Australia. Same family as the Crane and the Plover. The Great B. may have a wingspan of 8 ft. and weigh over 30 lb. Other species are the little B. and the Australian B., sometimes called the Turkey.

BUTCHER BIRD
The Shrike, a family of strong-beaked birds which impale their prey, small birds, insects or animals, upon thorns. Several species occur in Europe, the largest being the Great Grey Shrike (*Lanius excubitor*).

BUTE
County of W. Scot. consisting of the Is. of Bute and Arran, Gt. and Little Cumbrae, Inchmarnock and Pladda. Rothesay is the chief town of the Is. and the county town. Bute unites with N. Ayrshire to send 1 member to Parl. Pop. 14,157.

BUTLER, Josephine Elizabeth
(1828-1906) Eng. social reformer, zealous promoter of the Mar. Women's Property Act of 1882. She led the agitation for the repeal of the Contagious Diseases Acts.

BUTLER, Samuel
(1612-80) Eng. poet. B. Strensham, Worcs.; page to the Countess of Kent. Pub. *Hudibras* (1663, 64, 78); pension from Charles II; said to have been neglected and to have d. poor. *Hudibras* is a satire on the Puritans.

BUTLER, Samuel
(1835-1902) Eng. writer. B. Langar, Notts.; educ. Shrewsbury and St. John's Coll., Camb. Sheep-farming in New Zealand; returned 1864 with a competence. *Erewhon* (1872); visited Canada (*A Psalm of Montreal*); travel-books, as *Alps and Sanctuaries* (1881); *The Authoress of the Odyssey* (1897). *Shakespeare's Sonnets Reconsidered* (1899); *Erewhon Revisited* (1901); *The Way of All Flesh* an autobiog. novel, 1903. Butler was a critic of orthodox Christianity and many accepted beliefs. See *Samuel Butler* by Philip Henderson.

BUTTER
Food made from the fat of milk by churning. It contains from 82 % to 87 % of milk fat, about 13 % of water and small proportions of casein, milk sugar and mineral matter. In the ripening process of butter pure cultures of lactic acid-forming bacteria are used. The colour is affected by the food of the cow yielding the milk. In Brit. food inspectors ensure that the butter offered for sale is unadulterated. **Buttermilk** is what remains after butter has been churned.

BUTTERFLY
One of the 2 great divisions of Lepidoptera, the other being moths. There are 6 families, Nymphalidae, Nemeobiidae, Lycaenidae, Pieridae, Papilionidae and Hesperiidae. Of these, Nymphalidae are most numerous, comprising over 4,000 species, including such well-known Brit. butterflies as the Red Admiral, Peacock, Tortoise-shell, Purple Emperor and the Fritillaries. To the Pieridae belong the common cabbage butterflies. The Papilionidae, or Swallowtails, include the most beautiful forms.

BUTTERWORT
(*Pinguicula vulgaris*) One of the few insectivorous plants found in Brit. It belongs to the family Lentibulariaceae, grows on wet ground and is stemless. It consists of a number of fleshy leaves with a sticky surface to capture small insects.

BUXTEHUDE, Dietrich
[bŏŏks'-tĕ-hoo-dĕ] (1637-1707) Swedish composer and organist. He wrote many works for organ and ch. cantatas. He had considerable influence on J. S. Bach.

BUXTON
Borough, winter resort and spa of Derbyshire, 22 m. S.E. of Manchester. Pop. 19,370.

BUZZARD
(*Buteo*) Bird of prey, resembling an eagle, but smaller. There are *c.* 20 species and they are found in most parts of the world, excluding Australasia and Oceania. The Common B. is, in Brit., confined to sea cliffs and woodlands and frequents other parts of Europe. It is black or brown in colour, measures *c.* 21 in., feeds chiefly on mice and small snakes. Other varieties of buzzard are found in Africa, Asia and Amer.

BY-LAW
Rule or law made by a corporation, council or company, county, city and district councils have power under Acts of Parl. to make by-laws on matters affecting the areas for which they are responsible.

BYRD, Richard Evelyn
(1888-1957) Amer. aviator and explorer. B. Winchester, Virginia, he entered the navy in 1912. In May, 1926, in a Fokker monoplane, he flew over the N. Pole, and in 1929 over the S. Pole. In 1946-7 he was again leader of an Antarctic expedition.

BYRD, William
(1543-1623) Eng. composer. In 1569, although a R.C., he was appointed Gentleman of the Chapel Royal and later organist. He wrote much ch. music for both the Latin and Eng. rites, 3 masses, 61 motets, 5 Anglican Services, 61 anthems. He wrote many fine madrigals, in addition to music for strings and virginal.

BYRON, Lord
George Gordon (1788-1824) Eng. poet. B. London, son of Capt. John Byron and his 2nd wife Catherine Gordon, whom he deserted. Educ. Aberdeen, Dulwich, Harrow, Trinity Coll., Camb. His early life was an unhappy one; he had a deformed foot and his mother was well-known for her flightiness. Pub. *Hours of Idleness* (1807); lived at Newstead Abbey, Notts. his ancestral home; *English Bards and Scotch Reviewers*, 1809; travelled to Greece by Spain; *Childe Harold's Pilgrimage*, Cantos i and ii, (1812); *The Giaour*, *The Bride of Abydos*, *The Corsair*. Mar. Anne Milbank 1815; a daughter, Augusta; left Eng. 1816, separated from his wife and pursued by scandal about his relations with his half-sister Augusta; estab. in Italy. *Childe Harold* iii and iv; assoc. with Shelley; lived with the Countess Guiccioli. *The Vision of Judgment* (1882); *Don Juan* (unfinished) 1819-24. Set out to help Gk. insurgents against the Turks 1823; d. of fever at Missolonghi; buried near Newstead at Hucknall Torkard.

BYZANTIUM
Ancient city on the Bosporus which formed the nucleus of Constantine's new cap. of the Rom. Emp. On the d. of Theodosius the Great in A.D. 395, the Emp. was divided between his sons, Arcadius and Honorious. Arcadius took the E. portion. His cap. was Byzantium, hence the use of term Byzantine for the E. Rom. Emp. The **Byzantine Emp.** lasted over 1,000 years, and the last remnant vanished with the capture of Constantinople by the Turks in 1453. The more memorable names in the long list of Byzantine emperors are **Justinian** (527-565), the famous legislator; **Isaac Comnenus,** the founder of a dynasty which ruled from 1057-1185; and **Michael Palaeologus,** whose family retained the sceptre from 1261 until the end. Byzantine art is a fusion of the Rom., Gk. and Persian cultures. Its supreme achievements were mosaics and frescoes, but metal work, ivory carving and silk weaving were also developed. The ch. of Santa Sophia, Constantinople, is the greatest example of B. architecture and there are famous mosaics at Ravenna and Venice. Byzantine lit. is the medium through which classical Gk. lit. has been preserved to modern times. The capture of Constantinople by the Turks, and the consequent flight of Byzantine scholars was one cause of the Renaissance or revival of learning.

C

C
3rd letter in the Eng. alphabet. It represents 2 sounds, *viz.* that of *k* before the vowels *a, o, u,* that of the *s* before the vowels *e, i,* and the semi-vowel *y.* It is sometimes mute as in *muscle,* and it also forms with *h* the digraph *ch* as in *church.*

CABBAGE
Vegetable of the cruciferous family, native of Brit. and other parts of Europe. Its varieties comprise borecole, Brussels sprouts, drumhead cabbage and savoy, cauliflower, sprouting broccoli, kohl-rabi and red cabbage.

CABINET
Council of mins. responsible for the govt. in Brit. and some other countries. The first Eng. cabinet came into existence in the time of Charles II, but cabinets in the modern sense did not appear until *c.* 1820. Usually the members belong to one polit. party—except when a coalition is formed—and that party must be able to rely on a majority of the House of Commons. The members are the heads of the depts. of state, and each must be a member of one of the Houses of Parl. The P.M. selects them, with the approval of the Monarch, and presides over their meetings.

CABOT, John
[kab′-] (*c.* 1450-98) Ital. explorer. In 1486 he settled in Eng. and was sent out by Henry VII to find a sea route to Cathay. He discovered and explored part of the coast of N. Amer. His son, **Sebastian** (1474-1557), went with his father on one or both of his voyages, and undertook a later voyage (1508-9), in search of a N.W. Passage. He prob. entered Hudson Bay.

CACHALOT
(*Physeter macrocephalus*) Toothed whale, also called the sperm whale. As much as 50 ft. long, ¼ comprises the massive head, with a cavity filled with fat or spermaceti, formerly much valued as an illuminant.

CACTUS
Group of succulent, fleshy-stemmed, prickly, and mostly leafless plants. Most of the 1,000 species, are natives of trop. Amer. The prickly pear, the most important economically, has become widespread in the Canary Is., the Medit. basin and Palestine. Many contain reserves of moisture which are utilised in deserts by man and beast.

CADBURY
Name of Eng. Quaker family of cocoa and chocolate manufacturers. The business was started in Birmingham in 1824 by **John Cadbury** and in 1879 removed from Birmingham to a rural site then beyond the city boundary. Here George C. carried out the town planning experiments now in the hands of the Bournville Village Trust which he founded, 1900.

CADDIS FLY
Moth-like insect belonging to the order Trichoptera. The larva (grub) lives in silk-lined tubes made of wood, leaves, shell or other substance. The larvae are used by anglers.

CADE, Jack
(d. 1450) Eng. rebel. In 1450, in the reign of Henry VI, Cade collected together the rebels, principally of Kent, and marched into London. He was declared a traitor and killed near Heathfield, Sussex, trying to escape.

CADIZ
City and seaport of S. Spain, cap. of C. prov. on the Gulf of C. 95 m. S. of Seville. C. flourished under the Roms. Taken by the Moors, it became important again on the discovery of Amer. Pop. 122,568.

CADMIUM
Soft, blue-white metal, discovered by Stromeyer in 1817. Cadmium rods are used as moderators to control the speed of reaction in nuclear energy piles.

CAEN
[kâ(ng)] Fr. city in Normandy, cap. of Calvados dept. on the Orne 9 m. from the Eng. Channel. William the Conqueror built an abbey there. Other notable buildings are the univ. founded by Henry VI when Caen was Eng., the town hall and law courts. During World War II it was the scene of bitter fighting. Pop. 91,336.

CAERLEON
[kar-lē′-] Urban district of Monmouth. on the Usk, 2 m. from Newport. An important Rom. city, it is connected in legend with King Arthur.

CAERNARVONSHIRE
County of N. Wales, lying S. of the Menai Strait, and connected with Anglesey by a bridge. The E. part is mountainous, and contains the Snowdon range. The chief rivers are the Conway and Ogwen. Agriculture is important in the W. Caernarvon is the county town; others are Bangor, Llandudno, Bethesda, Pwllheli, Beddgelert and Conway. It returns 2 members to Parl. Pop. 120,460. **Caernarvon.** [kar-nar′-] Royal borough, and market and county town of Caernarvonshire, on the Menai Strait. There is a 13th cent. castle. Pop. 9,030.

CAERPHILLY
[kar-fil′-] Market town and urban district of Glamorganshire, 7 m. N. of Cardiff. Noted for its white cheese. Pop. 36,230.

CAESAR
Branch of the *gens Julia,* or Julian family, which traced its descent from Julus (Ascanius), son of Aeneas. The most famous members were **Gaius Julius Caesar,** and his nephew **Augustus.** Later Emperors assumed it as a title; thus originated the words *Kaiser* (German) and *Czar* or *Tsar* (Russian). **Caesar, Gaius Julius** (102-44 B.C.) Rom. statesman, soldier and writer. He served with the army in the E. He was consul in 59 B.C. when with Pompey and Crassus he formed the 1st Triumvirate. His agrarian law made him popular with the poorer citizens and veterans. Made gov. of Gaul where he remained 10 yrs., he won great milit. successes, conquering most of Gaul and twice invading Brit. Caesar's successes created enemies, one being Pompey, and, after Caesar left Gaul and crossed the Rubicon into Italy, civil war ensued. Again elected consul, he crushed Pompey's army (48 B.C.) at Pharsalus. During this expedition he was in Egypt, where he was the lover of Cleopatra. He was assassinated in Rome on the Ides (15th) of Mar. 44 B.C. Caesar prepared the way for the great empire of his nephew Augustus.

CAESARIAN SECTION
[sē-zar'-i-an] Operation by which the child is removed from the mother by opening the abdomen and the uterus or womb. So called because it is believed Julius Caesar was b. in this way.

CAESIUM
Metallic element, discovered by Bunsen in 1860, used in the manufacture of light-sensitive surfaces for certain kinds of photo-electric cells.

CAFFEINE
Vegetable alkaloid: $C_8H_{10}O_2N_4.H_2O$. It is the active principle of coffee and tea. It stimulates heart action without subsequent depression.

CAGLIARI
[kȧl'-yȧ-rē] Cap. and commercial centre of Sardinia, on the Gulf of C. in the S. of the Is. Pop. 181,499.

CAIRN TERRIER
Small dog, probably the progenitor of the terriers of Scot. Wt. *c.* 15 lbs. Colours are grey, brindle or sandy.

CAIRNGORMS
Group of mts. in Scot. part of the Grampian range, on the borders of Inverness and Banff. Cairngorm itself is 4,084 ft.

CAIRO
Cap. of Egypt, on the Nile, 128 m. from Alexandria. There are various industries. C. is the largest city in Africa. Important historic buildings include the citadel built by Saladin, the cath. of St. Mark, and the mosques of El Hakim, Amru, Hasan, El Maayyad and Al Sunkur. The palace of Ismail, now a hotel, stands on the Gezirch, or Is. The univ. is in the rebuilt mosque of El Azhar. Pop. 3,346,000.

CAITHNESS
[kăth-] County of N.E. Scot. 3 parts surrounded by the sea. On the Sutherland border there are hills of over 2,000 ft. The Thurso is the chief river. John o' Groats and Duncansby Head are in the county. Farming is the main occupation. Wick is the county town. There is an atomic power station at Dounreay. With Sutherland it returns 1 member to Parl. Pop. 27,000.

CAJEPUT
[-i-po͝ot] (*Melaleuca leucadendron*) Evergreen myrtle-like shrub. A native of the E. Indies, it bears spikes of odourless flowers.

CALABASH
(*Crescentia cujete*) Evergreen tree of the family Bignoniaceae found in W. Africa, W. Indies and trop. Amer. The globular gourdlike fruit has a hard rind which is made into bottles, cups, pipes, etc.

CALABRIA
Region of Italy occupying the ' toe ' of the peninsula, separated from Sicily by the Strait of Messina.

CALAIS
[-lā] Seaport of Pas-de-Calais dept. N. Fr. 22 m. from Dover across the Eng. Channel, and 150 m. from Paris. An important packet station and fishing centre. C. was an Eng. possession between 1347-1558. Pop. 70,707.

CALAMINE
Brit. name for naturally occurring zinc carbonate. It is found in the Mendips and Pennines, in Belgium, in Spain and Missouri.

CALCEOLARIA
[-lair'-] Genus of herbs and shrubs of the snapdragon family. Native to the Pacific coast of S. Amer. Several species have been developed in Brit.

CALCITE
Native carbonate of lime, a white or colourless vitreous mineral which crystallises in many diverse forms, notably the double-refracting prisms of Iceland spar used in polariscopes.

CALCIUM
Hard, silvery metallic element, forming 3·5 % of the earth's crust. It was discovered by Davy in 1808. Calcium is an important constituent of bones, teeth and shells. Sp. gr. 1·5, Chem. Sym. Ca.

CALCULUS
Math. calculation which involves taking a limit, used to deal with speed, electrical currents, etc. Originated by Archimedes in 3rd cent. B.C. Descartes advanced the study in 17th cent. by illustrating how geometrical curves could be described and analysed by means of algebraic formulae. Fermat, Newton and Leibnitz further developed the study.

CALCUTTA
City and seaport of W. Bengal, India, on the Hooghly river, 90 m. from the sea. C. is a manufacturing centre with jute, rice and cotton mills, and native workers in brass and pottery. It is also a commercial centre with extensive docks. The city was founded as an E. India settlement in 1690. Pop. (Greater) 4,488,026.

CALDERÓN, Pedro
de la Barca (1600-81) Sp. dramatist. From 1636 he pub. some 120 plays, as *El Magico prodigioso. La Vida es Sueño*, and, after he became a priest, over 70 *autos sacramentales.*

CALEDONIA
[-dō'-] Rom. name for N. Brit. now used for Scot. as a whole. The **Caledonian Canal,** constructed between 1803 and 1822, extends from the Moray Firth on the E. to L. Linnhe on the W. and is 60 m. long. L. Ness, Oich, Lochy, and Dochfour were used for its course. Built by Thomas Telford.

CALENDAR
Systematic division of the year into months and days. Assuming a 365¼ day year, Julius Caesar introduced the Julian calendar in 45 B.C. distributing 365 days as at present and inserting an additional day every 4th year as did the ancient Egyptians. The solar year is actually short of this by 11¼ mins.; in 1582, therefore, the Old Style was inaccurate by 10 days. Gregory XIII then suppressed the surplus days and ordained that no closing year of a cent. should be bissextile unless divisible by 400. This Gregorian or New Style was adopted by Brit. in 1752. New calendars were introduced in the Fr. Revolution and in Russia in 1929. The Christian calendar starts from the alleged birth-year of Christ; the Mohammedan from the Hegira, or flight of Mahomet to Medina, in the 622nd year of the Christian era.

CALGARY
City of Alberta, Canada, on the Bow, at the foot of the Rocky Mts. 110 m. N.W. of Lethbridge. An important rly. centre, its industries include flour milling and meat packing. Pop. 323,000.

CALIFORNIA
W. state of the U.S.A. lying N. of the Mexican border and having a long Pacific coastline. Except for the S. where there is the Calif. Desert, there are 3 distinct physical divisions; the Sierra Nevada, which run the length of the state and rise to 14,500 ft. in Mt. Whitney, the highest peak in the U.S.A.; the Coast Range, a series of ranges, and the great C. Valley, containing the Sacramento and San Joaquin rivers, which unite and flow through the Golden Gate. Gold, silver, copper, lead and petroleum are produced. The film industry is very important. Sacramento is the cap. but Los Angeles and San Francisco are larger. Calif. was part of Mexico from its discovery until 1846, when it was claimed by the U.S.A. It became a state in 1850, following the increase in pop. and property caused by the gold rush of 1849. California sends 38 representatives to Congress. Area: 158,693 sq.m. Pop. 20,000,000.

CALIFORNIAN POPPY
(*Eschscholtzia californica*) Perennial herb of the poppy family from the Calif. coast, with finely cut leaves and bright-yellow, saffron-eyed 4-petalled blooms.

CALIGULA, Gaius Caesar
(A.D. 12-41) Rom. emperor. B. Antium, his parents being Germanicus and the elder Agrippina. He succeeded to the throne in A.D. 37. He developed megalomania which led to an orgy of cruelty and debauchery. Killed by a tribune.

CALIPH
[kā'-lif] Title applied first to Mahomet's successor Abu Bekr, as head of the Islamic state and defender of the faith, A.D. 632. Omayyad rulers in Spain, 755-1031, and Fatimide rulers in Egypt, 909-1171, called themselves caliphs. The title passed to Turkey *c.* 1362. In 1924 it was abolished by the nat. assembly at Ankara.

CALLAO
[kă-yá'-ō] Chief port of Peru, 8 m. W. of Lima. The old city was destroyed by an earthquake in 1746; in 1940, another earthquake caused great destruction. Pop. 234,000.

CALOMEL
(or **Subchloride of Mercury**) A dull, white, odourless and almost tasteless powder found in Spain, Bavaria and Czechoslovakia. Formerly used as a purgative and diuretic.

CALORIE
Metric unit of heat. The *large* calorie is the heat required to raise the temp. of 1 kilog. of water through 1° C. A *small* calorie is heat required to raise temp. of 1 gm. of water 1° C. *Large* calorie is used in biol.; *small* in physics.

CALVADOS
Dept. of N. Fr. in Normandy, between the Seine and the Cotentin Peninsula. Caen is the cap.

CALVARY
(1) Place where Christ was crucified. Traditionally identified with a spot beneath the Calvary chapel in the 5th cent. Ch. of the Holy Sepulchre. (2) Representations of the Passion erected in R.C. countries on wayside prominences or in churchyards.

CALVIN, John
(1509-64) Fr. theologian. B. Noyon, educ. for the priesthood in Paris. He became a Protestant and lived for a time in Paris and Basle. He settled in Geneva, 1536, where he became very active as a moral reformer, and in 1538 was banished, but, in 1541, was recalled to Geneva, where he d. For 13 years Calvin was the autocrat of Geneva. He aimed at making it a theocracy. Trade was fostered and educ. encouraged. **Calvinism.** Religious belief expounded by John Calvin. Its central idea is the doctrine of predestination, the idea of eternal salvation for some and eternal damnation for others. Calvinism was very strong among Protestants until the 19th cent. The Huguenots accepted it and it obtained a firm footing in Scot. and the Netherlands. The Puritans, both in Eng. and Amer. were Calvinists.

CAM
River of Cambridgeshire. Flows through the county for 40 m. until it meets the Ouse just below Ely. Above Cambridge it is also called the Granta.

CAMARGUE
[-marg] Silt-formed delta of the Rhône. The N. part has been reclaimed for vineyards and rice cultivation; the remainder is a salt marsh area used for cattle pasture.

CAMBODIA
[-bō'-] Repub. of Asia, formerly a Fr. protectorate, kingdom until 1970. Indep. declared in 1953, during war in Indo-China. It lies between Thailand and Vietnam. C. Cambodia, drained by the Mekong, is an important rice-growing area. An inland lake, Tonle Sap, 700 sq.m. in extent, supports a large fishing population. Rice and fish are the chief exports. Phnôm-Penh, the cap., is connected by railway with Bangkok. Area: 70,000 sq.m. Pop. 6,701,000.

CAMBRAI
[kā(ng)-brā] City of Nord dept., N.E. Fr. on the Escaut (Scheldt), 37 m. S. of Lille. Textiles are manufactured, and cambric is named after the town. During World War I, 2 battles were named after Cambrai. Pop. 30,000.

CAMBRIA
Lat. name for Wales. The mt. system running from the Black Mts. in Brecknockshire to Snowdonia is called the Cambrian.

CAMBRIDGE
City of Massachusetts, U.S.A., adjacent to Boston, the seat of Harvard Univ. and the Mass. Inst. of Technology. Pop. 107,716.

CAMBRIDGESHIRE
Inland county of E. Eng. in the fenland area. It is mostly low-lying, except for the chalk outcrop in the S., the Gog Magog Hills. The Ouse is the chief river. C. is an agricultural county, producing grain and fruit. Camb. is the county town; others are Wisbech, Ely, March and Newmarket. C. is divided into 2 admin. counties, Cambridgeshire and the Isle of Ely (County town, March). C. returns 2 members to Parl. (1 borough constituency). Pop. 279,025. *See* ELY. **Cambridge.** City and market town of Cambs. the county town and a univ. town on the Cam, 56 m. W. of London. Industries include the manufacture of radio, T.V. and scientific instruments. Camb. returns 1 member to Parl. Pop. 95,380. **Cambridge University.** One of the oldest European residential univ. There were 18 men's colls. A new coll., Churchill Coll., was founded 1960. There are 2 women's colls. Girton and Newnham. There are also several theological colls. There are many laboratories, including the Cavendish Physics Laboratory. No. of students in residence *c.* 9,040. There is a Chanc. but the acting head of the Univ. is the Vice-Chanc. who is elected for 2 years from among the masters of the colls. The discipline of the Univ. is the responsibility of the Proctors. There is a Univ. Press.

CAMEL
(*Camelus*) A hump-backed ruminant mammal with splay feet. Water cells in the stomach lining store a 3-day supply. The one-humped camel, *C. dromedarius,* comprises the swift racing breed called Dromedaries as well as baggage camels. Orig. Arabian, they now live in N. Africa, the Canaries, W. Asia and N.W. India, and have been introduced into Australia. The 2-humped Bactrian camel *C. bactriana,* inhabits the C. Asian steppes. The hair of the camel is used for making brushes and clothes.

CAMELLIA
(*Thea*) Genus of evergreen trees native in trop. and E. Asia. One sub-genus, with pendulous flowers and persistent sepals, is the tea plant. The other, with erect flowers and deciduous sepals, contains *c.* 8 species, of which *T. japonica,* a tree 20 ft. high, has laurel-like leaves and odourless red flowers.

CAMERA
Apparatus for throwing an image of an object through a lens upon a screen, for photographic record. The photographic camera is essentially a box holding a lens and sensitised glass plates or films.

CAMERON, Richard
(d. 1680) Scots. Covenanter. He became a preacher and a leader among those who disliked episcopacy. He joined the Sanquhar Declaration (1680) disowning allegiance to

Charles II, and was outlawed. His followers were called **Cameronians.** They refused to take the oath of allegiance to William III after the religious settlement of 1689-90. In 1876 most of them united with the Free Ch. of Scot.

CAMEROON
Indep. Repub. Former Fr. trusteeship, gained indep. 1960. Yaunde is cap., Duala the chief port. Area: 183,575 sq.m. Pop. 4,000,000.

CAMEROONS
District of W. Africa lying between Nigeria and Fr. Equatorial Africa, with a coastline on the Gulf of Guinea. Before World War I the area formed a German protectorate, but was placed under Fr. and Brit. mandate 1914-16. The former **Brit. Cameroons,** split up as a result of a plebiscite held in 1961, the N. joining Nigeria, the S. joining **Cameroon** (*q.v.*).

CAMOENS, Luis de
(*c.* 1524-80) Portuguese poet. Wrote poems and plays. Pub. 1572 *Os Lusiadas*, an epic poem in *ottava rima* on the descendants of Lusus and esp. on Vasco da Gama.

CAMOMILE
Genus of strongly-scented composite herbs in Europe, W. Asia, and N. Africa. The common camomile *Anthemis nobilis*, produces heads with yellow centres and white rays. Its bitter principle and aromatic oil are utilised as a stomachic, a tonic, and a purgative.

CAMPAGNA
[kam-pàn'-ya] Flat, marshy plain surrounding Rome and extending from the Sabine, Alban and Lepini hills to the coast. The area yields pasturage for horses, cattle, sheep and goats, was infested with malaria, but has been improved by drainage schemes.

CAMPANIA
Region of S. Italy on the Tyrrhenian coast. Naples is the chief town.

CAMPANULA
[-pan'-] (Bellflower) Genus of the family Campanulaceae which includes annuals, biennials, and perennials.

CAMPBELL, Sir Malcolm
(1885-1949) In 1924 he made a World record of 146·4 m.p.h. and continued to break records until at Daytona, in 1931, he beat Segrave's record with a speed of 245·7 m.p.h. On Coniston Water in 1939, he achieved 141·74 m.p.h. His son, **Donald** (1921-67) carried on his father's work on jet-powered speedboats and with *Bluebird* set up a world water speed record of 216·2 m.p.h. on Lake Mead, U.S.A., in 1955. Further attempts raised the record to 260·35 m.p.h. on Coniston Water in May, 1959. In 1964 on L. Eyre, Australia, he achieved a land speed record of 403 m.p.h.

CAMPBELL, Thomas
(1777-1844) Scot. poet. Pub. martial and patriotic lyrics, as *Ye Mariners of England*, and poems like *Lord Ullin's Daughter*; crit. and hist. work.

CAMPBELL-BANNERMAN, Sir Henry
(1836-1908) Scots. statesman. M.P. (Lib.) 1868-1908; Chief Irish Sec. 1884-5; War. Sec. 1886 and 1892-5; Leader of Lib. Party 1899-1908; P.M. 1905-8; knighted, 1895.

CAMPHOR
(*Cinnamomum camphora*) Species of tree. It grows in Formosa, Japan, and E. China. From its timber is distilled the hydrocarbon known as camphor.

CAMPION
Popular name for several plants of the pink-carnation family, common in Brit. N. Europe and Asia. Red campion is *Melandrium dioicum*; the night-flowering white campion is *M. album*. Meadow campion (ragged robin, *Lychnis floscuculi*), has dissected petals. Moss campion (*silene acaulis*) forms green cushions of close-set, hair-like leaves; bladder campion (*S. cucubalus*), with inflated calyx, is allied to sea campion (*S. maritima*).

CAMPION, Edmund
(1540-81) Eng. Jesuit. B. London. He went to Rome and joined the Jesuits, was sent to Eng. in 1581 with Robert Parsons, to strengthen the wavering Catholics. A year later he was captured, tried for treason, and hanged. Beatified, 1886.

CAMPION, Thomas
(*c.* 1567-1619) Eng. poet and composer. Composed poems in Lat. and Eng.; set his own verses to music; wrote on music and on poetical composition.

CAMUS, Albert
(1913-1960) Fr. author of *L'Etranger* (1942), *La Peste* (1947), *La Chute* (1956) and several essays. Nobel Prize for Literature 1957.

CAMWOOD
Red-wood obtained from a W. African leguminous tree (*Baphia*). Allied to barwood, it reaches 30 ft. in ht. and bears white flowers. The timber yields red dye.

CANAAN
(O.T.) Name of one of Noah's grandsons (Gen. 4), and of the land later called Palestine.

CANADA
A federal union of the provs. of Alberta, Brit. Columbia, Manitoba, New Brunswick, Newfoundland, Nova Scotia, Ontario, Prince Edward Island, Quebec and Saskatchewan; it also comprises the N.W. Territories and Yukon. Area of 3½ million sq.m. of land and ¼ million sq.m. of water stretches from latitude 42° to 70° N.; longitudinally it extends about 3,500 m. The pop. of 20,630,000 is mainly Brit. in origin with 5 million Fr. speaking Roman Catholics, 2½ million of other European origins, 66,531 Indians and Eskimos and 70,000 Asiatics. Discovered by Cabot in 1497, the Fr. took possession in 1534; the first permanent European settlements were Port Royal, Nova Scotia, 1605, and Quebec, 1608. Canada grew from a number of isolated settlements: (i) The Fr. penetrated along the St. Lawrence, exploring and organising the fur trade. (ii) The E. shores were of interest for fishing and naval purposes; Newfoundland was colonised by the Brit. in the 17th cent., Nova Scotia (then called Acadia), by the Fr. In 1713 the latter was ceded to Brit. and in 1784, New Brunswick was separated from it. Prince Edward Is. taken from the Fr. in 1758, was separated from Nova Scotia in 1769. (iii) The Hudson's Bay Co., from 1670, founded forts along Hudson Bay shores. (iv) Capt. Cook obtained furs from Vancouver Is. 1778, whereupon the Hudson's Bay Co. obtained a concession; the Is. became a Crown Colony in 1849. (v) After the Amer. War of Indep. loyal refugees settled in Ontario. Ontario was first known as Upper Canada to distinguish it from Lower Canada (Quebec). (vi) In 1812 the Red River Settlement was founded. Lower and Upper Canada and the Maritime Provs. were federated to form the Dominion of Canada in 1867; in 1869 the N.W. Territories were bought

from the Hudson's Bay Co. and out of them the prov. of Manitoba was formed in 1870. In 1871 Brit. Columbia agreed to join the Dominion on condition that a railway was built to link her with the E. This, the C.P.R., was completed from Vancouver to Montreal in 1885. By 1905 the great influx of settlers justified the formation of 2 new provs., Saskatchewan and Alberta. In 1949, Newfoundland and Labrador became the tenth province. Canada may be described in 5 major regions: *The Atlantic Provs.* to which Newfoundland may be added, are mountainous. Offshore, the shallow waters provide important fisheries. Rainfall is abundant in summer and snow in winter; the summers are warm, winters cool or cold. Mixed farming is carried on. Prince Edward Is. is intensively farmed. Lumbering is important. Coal is mined, chiefly in Cape Breton Is. and Newfoundland has large iron ore deposits. *Brit. Columbia*, about 3,000 m. W. of the Atlantic Provs. is also mountainous. The most lofty ranges are the Rockies, with numerous peaks over 11,000 ft. The climate is not unlike that of the Brit. Is. modified at high altitudes. The valley floors produce hay, oats, wheat and potatoes, and cattle, poultry and pigs are kept. Fruit is grown. Brit. Columbia produces over half the timber of Canada. Next to Ontario, Brit. Columbia is the chief mining prov. of Canada. Oil is available by pipeline from Alberta; pulp, newsprint and plywood manufacture have been extended. Between these coastal areas the principal inhabited regions are the *St. Lawrence* and *Great Lakes Lowlands* and the *Prairies*. The former lie S. and S.E. of the Canadian Shield. A narrow belt of lowland extends along the St. Lawrence from Quebec, broadening between Lakes Ontario, Erie and Huron. Mixed farming is general. Cheese is exported. Fruit is grown. The area lacks coal, yet developed as the first manufacturing region of Canada. Raw materials, timber, minerals and grain pass through en route for world markets. Hydro-electric power, developed at Niagara and from the rivers flowing from the Shield to the St. Lawrence, is widely distributed; the Great Lakes and their associated waterways provide cheap transport and direct connections with ocean transport by the St. Lawrence Seaway. Westwards, the coniferous forest is broken by bare rocky surfaces; the climate becomes increasingly severe. Beyond Winnipeg are the *Prairies*. The first section is the Manitoba, or Red River, Lowland. Extreme temperatures are experienced, ranging from well below 0° F. to about 75° F. Precipitation is slight but falls mainly in spring and early summer. This is now one of the great wheat growing areas of the world. In S. Alberta, irrigation is necessary and cattle ranching and sheep grazing replace extensive wheat cultivation. The Prairie region is also rich in minerals, bituminous coal, lignite, oil and natural gas are all important. N. of these populated areas lies a vast area of coniferous forest and lakes, beyond which again is tundra. This is sparsely populated, lacking agricultural possibilities, but rich in other resources. The forest is exploited for pulp and constructional timber, trapping remains important and there is a wide variety of minerals between the Great Bear, Great Slave and Athabaska Lakes in the W. and Labrador. A large percentage of the world's uranium reserves are found in the mines of N. Ontario. Canada owes its existence to the development of E.-W. rly. links, counterbalancing the strong natural attractions between each of the original separate colonies and the adjacent Amer. States. In the course of their construction many minerals were discovered; settlement of the prairies based on the growing of wheat for export depended on rail transport. The St. Lawrence, Ottawa and other rivers, the Great Lakes and the many other lakes, provided Canada with fine natural waterways which were improved by canal links. In 1959, the St. Lawrence Seaway between Montreal and L. Ontario was opened. Internal air lines are of great value in reducing effective distances and thus further promoting unity in Canada. The principal exports of Canada are wheat and wheat flour and wood pulp, sawn timber and newsprint. Minerals are less important. **Government.** The constitution is modelled on that of Brit.; the Queen is represented by a Gov.-Gen. and there is a Senate and House of Commons. The Gov.-Gen. appoints Lieut. Govs. in each Prov.; provincial self-govt. in most local matters is the rule.

CANAL
Artificial waterway used for transport. In a few canals the water is on the same level throughout, but in most of them locks are used for raising and lowering boats. Canals were made by the Chinese and the Persians in the days before Christ. In Gt. Brit. they were constructed for commercial purposes in the 18th cent. The world's ship canals include the Suez, Panama, Welland, Sault Ste. Marie, Kiel, Corinth, Manchester, Volga-Don and the Göta. *See* SUEZ CANAL; PANAMA CANAL.

CANALETTO, Antonio
(1697-1768) Ital. painter. B. Venice. In later life he twice visited Eng. His pictures are chiefly scenes of Venetian life.

CANARY
Popular songbird of the Finch family native to the Canary and Azores Is. In the 16th cent. it was domesticated, and since then has been bred in captivity. Of the many varieties the best singer is the Roller, bred in the Hartz Mts. Germany.

CANARY ISLANDS
Sp. archipelago in the N. Atlantic, 60 m. W. of Africa, of volcanic origin. The 7 larger Is. and 6 uninhabited islets form 2 provinces, Santa Cruz de Tenerife and Las Palmas. With a mild climate and fertile soil the Is. are noted for bananas. Area: 2,807 sq.m. Pop. 944,448.

CANBERRA
Cap. of Commonwealth of Australia, on fed. territory enclosed by New South Wales. It contains Parl. House, Austral. Nat. Univ., and Nat. Library. Pop. of city 63,313.

CANCER
Malignant tumour. Cause unknown. Occurs when tissue growth is overstimulated and the affected tissue overgrows. Almost any tissue in the body may become cancerous. Research is widespread and all large hospital areas have research centres. *See* LUNG CANCER.

CANCER
(1) Small constellation between the constellations Gemini and Leo. (2) The 4th sign of the Zodiac, symbolised by a crab, operative *c.* June 21st-July 21st.

CANCER, Tropic of
The line of latitude 23½° N. of the Equator showing the most N. position at which the sun appears to be directly overhead at noon. The tropic passes through the Sahara Desert, Arabia, S. China and Mexico.

CANDIA
or **Heraklion.** Largest city of Crete, on the N. coast. Pop. 63,458.

CANDLE TREE
C. Amer. tree of the bignonia family (*Parmentiera cerifera*). The large greenish flowers have sheath-like calyces from which grow fleshy, spindle-shaped fruits, nearly 4 ft. long.

CANDYTUFT
(*Iberis*) Hardy plant of annual and perennial varieties. The annual candytuft is *c.* 12 in. high with clusters of flowers. The perennial variety (*Iberis sempervirens*) is an evergreen.

CANEA
Cap. and principal port of Crete, on the N. coast of the Is. During World War II it was the scene of fierce fighting. Pop. 38,467.

CANKER
Plant disease caused by attacks of a fungus usually *nectria ditissima.* Growing tissues are destroyed and malformation of the cortical tissues ensues, a gaping wound being formed.

CANNABIS INDICA
Narcotic drug obtained from Indian hemp. Also called Bhang or Hashish.

CANNES
[kan] Resort in Alpes-Maritimes dept., Fr., on the Riviera coast, 120 m. E. of Marseilles. It is enclosed on the E. and W. by the Alps and the Estcrel Mts. Pop. 59,173.

CANNIBALISM
or **Anthropophagy.** The eating of human flesh by human beings. In most existing forms this practice is a religious ceremonial.

CANOE
Type of boat common to most primitive peoples. Propelled by either single or double-bladed paddles and used primarily on inland river and lake systems and on coastal areas containing island archipelagos. A common form is the *dug-out,* hollowed out from the trunk of a tree and shaped and pointed at both ends. Craft of this kind are common on the N. Pacific coast, the rivers of W. Africa and in the S. Sea Is. Some are of wood, but many are made of wooden frames covered with birch-bark or skins. The latter were much used by N. Amer. Indians. The *Kayak* of the Eskimos is of skin stretched over a driftwood or whale-bone frame. It holds a single paddler who wears a waterproof skin shirt which fits snugly over the cockpit and renders the boat completely watertight. The modern canvas canoe is modelled on the birch-bark canoe.

CANON
Orig. a rule or law ordered by eccles. authority; now, certain persons in holy orders. The rules were collected and became the Canon Law. The Apostolic Canons are a collection of ecclesiastical laws put together in the 8th cent. The Bible Canon is the list of books which have been declared canonical, *i.e.* included in the O.T. and N.T. The word canon, at one time used for all clergy now refers in the C. of E. to cath. clergy only.

CANONISATION
Act of making a person a saint, practised in the R.C. Ch. Since 1634, only the Pope has had authority to canonise.

CANOVA, Antonio
[-nō′-] (1757-1822) Ital. sculptor who lived and worked in Rome. He made a famous bust of Napoleon.

CANTERBURY
City and county borough of Kent and eccles. cap. of England on the Stour, 62 m. S.E. of London. It is a market town, trading in cattle, corn and hops. The chief building is the cath. built chiefly in the 12th and 14th cents. It is the site of the murder of Thomas à Becket. The archbishop has charge of the Diocese of Canterbury, is Primate of all Eng. and unofficial head of the Anglican Ch. Pop. 30,720.

CANTERBURY BELL
(*Campanula medium*) Genus of the family Campanulaceae, a biennial plant, 2-3 ft. high, bearing beautiful bell-like flowers.

CANTHARIDIN
[-thă′-rid-] Obtained from various species of beetles called Cantharis, or Mylabris—commonly called Spanish or Russian fly.

CANTON
Cap. and seaport of Kwangtung prov. China, on the Chukiang 80 m. from the sea. C. has a large river trade. Pop. 1,840,000.

CANUTE
Name of several Danish kings. **Canute I,** called the Great, became King of Denmark in 1014 and claimed the throne of Eng., won by his father, Sweyn. After a struggle with Edmund Ironside he became king.

CANVEY
Is. and urban district off the coast of Essex, 30 m. from London. Pop. 16,890.

CAPE BRETON
Is. of Canada, part of the prov. of Nova Scotia (*q.v.*). Agriculture, fishing, lumbering and coalmining are the chief occupations. The largest town is Sydney. In 1632 the Is. became Fr. It was ceded to Gt. Brit. 1763, and was united with Nova Scotia, 1819. Pop. 163,754.

CAPE HORN *See* HORN, CAPE.

CAPE OF GOOD HOPE
Headland of S. Africa, between Table and False Bays. Discovered by Bartholomew Diaz in 1488.

CAPE PROVINCE
Prov. of the Repub. of S. Africa occupying the most S. part of the cont. The interior consists of high plateau country, the veld, crossed by the Orange and tributaries. Rainfall is abundant in the extreme S.W. but inland desert conditions prevail. Agriculture is the chief occupation in the S. In the N.E. coal and diamonds are mined. Cape Town is the cap. and largest city; other centres are Port Elizabeth and E. London. The colony was founded by the Dutch, 1652. Taken by the Brit. 1795, it was officially ceded to Gt. Brit. 1814. It joined the Union of S. Africa, 1910. It includes the native territory of Transkei. Area: 278,465 sq.m. Pop. 5,342,720. **Cape Town.** Seaport, legislative cap. of the Repub. of S. Africa and cap. of Cape Prov. It stands on a coastal plain verging on Table Bay and backed by Table Mt. There is a fine, modern harbour and airport. Cape Town was founded, 1652, by the Dutch. Pop. 807,211.

CAPE VERDE ISLANDS
Portuguese possession in the Atlantic Ocean, 350 m. off Cape Verde in the most W. point of Africa. They consist of 10 Is. in 2 groups, Windward and Leeward. Praia on Sâo Thiago, is the cap. They were discovered by the Portuguese in the 15th cent. Area: 1,516 sq.m. Pop. 201,549.

CAPEK, Karel
(1890-1938) Czech playwright and novelist. His plays include *RUR* (' Rossum's Universal Robots ') (1921), *Insect Play* (1921), *The Mother* (1938). Wrote a trilogy of tragic novels; also short stories.

CAPER
(*Capparis spinosa*) Deciduous shrub found in the Med. lands. The flower buds are used in sauces.

CAPERCAILZIE
[kaper-kāl′-yi] (*Tetrao urogallus*) Wood grouse or **Cock of the Wood.** Game bird of N. Europe,

once indigenous in the Brit. Is. Equal in size to a small turkey, it weighs from 8 to 12 lb. The hen bird is smaller, with markings of red and black and an orange red tinge on the breast. She nests on the ground. It has been re-introduced into Scot.

CAPET
[ka-pā] A royal family of Fr. The first was Hugh Capet, who began to reign in 987. The Valois Bourbon kings were both descended from him. Louis XVI (*q.v.*) was tried under the name of Louis Capet.

CAPITAL PUNISHMENT
Infliction of d. as a punishment for crime. In Brit., it could be inflicted for stealing, and setting fire to the Royal Dockyards. In the 19th cent. laws were passed reserving the d. penalty for murder, treason and piracy. In other European countries it is also limited to serious offences and some have abolished it. In the U.K. the law was amended in 1957 and in 1969, the death penalty was finally abolished.

CAPITOL
Temple to Jupiter and citadel erected by Tarquin on the Capitoline Hill, one of the 7 hills of Rome.

CAPRI
Ital. Is. in the Bay of Naples, 21 m. S. of Naples, famous for its climate and scenery. Pop. 10,600.

CAPRICORN
10th sign of the Zodiac, operative *c.* Dec. 21-Jan. 19. In astrology this sign is often depicted as a figure having the forepart of a goat with the hind-quarters of a fish.

CAPRICORN, Tropic of
Line of latitude at 23½° S. showing the most S. position at which the sun appears to be directly overhead at noon. It passes through S. Africa, Australia, and central S. Amer.

CAPUCHIN MONKEY
Type of monkey found in the hot parts of Amer. The males are usually bearded.

CARACAL
(*Felis caracal*) A lynx found in Africa and S. Asia. It is small, fierce and carnivorous, *c.* 2 ft. long and averaging 10 in. high.

CARACAS
[kă-rȧ′-kăs] Cap. of Venezuela, 8 m. from the Caribbean and La Guaira, its port. It is on the S. slopes of the Coast Range, *c.* 3,000 ft. high. Pop. 1,257,515.

CARACTACUS
King of the Silures, a Brit. tribe. After defying Rome for 9 years, he was defeated near the Wrekin *c.* A.D. 50. He took refuge with the Queen of the Brigantes, who, however, gave him up.

CARAT
Standard of wt. for precious stones and of fineness of gold. The carat wt. is equal to 3·17 grains Troy, or 4 diamond or carat grains. Pure gold is said to be 24 carat, but standard gold for coinage, wedding rings, and so on contains a small percentage of base metal and is termed 22 carat.

CARAVAGGIO
[-vaj′-jō] **Michelangelo Amerighi Da** (1569-1609) Ital. painter. B. Caravaggio, in Lombardy; worked in Venice and Rome, and Naples, where he founded a school of painters influenced by the natural, as opposed to the ideal, way in which he treated his subjects.

CARAWAY
(*Carum carvi*) Biennial herbaceous plant of the family Umbelliferae, native to N. and C. Europe and Asia. The seeds are used in cooking and in the manufacture of the liqueur called kümmel.

CARBOHYDRATES
Group of organic substances containing carbon, hydrogen and oxygen. They are heat- and energy-forming foodstuffs of vegetable origin, the most important being the sugars and starch.

CARBOLIC ACID
Phenol, obtained from coal tar by distillation. A strong antiseptic and disinfectant, it is used in the manufacture of synthetic resins and plastics.

CARBON
An element which occurs in 3 forms (a) *diamond,* (b) *graphite,* (c) *amorphous carbon.* It is the principal constituent of coal and occurs in all living matter. Sp. gr. 2·2 (diamond), 1·9 (graphite), 4·8 (amorphous). Chem. sym. C.

CARBON MONOXIDE
Poisonous odourless gas produced by the burning of coke and also found in coal gas, the exhaust gases from a motor car and in coal mines. In cases of poisoning, get the victim to the fresh air; loosen clothing and perform artificial respiration. Get medical aid. On entering a room filled with coal gas to rescue a person, cover the mouth and nose with a damp cloth; open windows immediately; do not use a naked light.

CARBORUNDUM
Abrasive of extreme hardness, composed of silicon carbide and prepared by heating at a high temp. a mixture of sand, coke and sawdust.

CARBUNCLE
(1) A localised inflammation of the skin structures. The skin ulcerates and several cores or sloughs appear. (2) Garnet cut in a round or oval form.

CARBURETTOR
Apparatus used in motor cars and gas engines for converting petrol or other hydrocarbons into a gaseous or finely divided state to form with the air an explosive mixture.

CARCASSONNE
City of Aude Dept. S. Fr. 57 m. S.E. of Toulouse, on the Aude River and the Canal du Midi, famous for its medieval fortifications. Pop. 38,100.

CARDIFF
Cap. county borough and seaport of Wales, and county town of Glamorganshire, on the Bristol Channel at the mouth of the Taff, Ely and Rhymney. Cardiff's chief industry is shipping. There are also flour milling, steel, copper, zinc, lead, paper and chem. works. It contains the Univ. Coll. of S. Wales and the H.Q. of the Univ. of Wales. Llandaff with its cath. is within the city boundaries. The city returns 3 members to Parl. Pop. 260,640.

CARDIGANSHIRE
County of Central Wales, having a coastline on C. Bay. The rivers are the Dovey, Teifi, Ystwyth and Rheidol. Almost wholly an agricultural area. In the N. are mts. and some magnificent scenery. Cardigan is the county town, but Aberystwyth is the admin. centre. Cardiganshire returns 1 member to Parl. Pop. 55,390. **Cardigan.** Borough and market town of Cardiganshire, on the Teifi, 116 m. from Cardiff. Pop. 3,700.

CARDINAL
Amer. song bird of the Finch family and a popular cage bird. The male has a bright red plumage, black feet and pointed crest.

CARDINAL
Highest dignitary, save only the Pope, of the R.C. Ch. Cardinals are chosen by the Pope and together they form the Coll. of Cardinals who elect the pope.

CARIB INDIANS
Race of S. Amer. Indians. They inhabited the southern W. Indies at the time of Columbus (1492). Tall and of ruddy-brown complexion, they are now confined to the shores of the Caribbean Sea.

CARIBBEAN SEA
Part of the Atlantic Ocean, almost enclosed by the coasts of S. and C. Amer., Cuba and the W. Indian Is. The Strait of Yucatan connects it with the Gulf of Mexico and the Panama Canal leads from it into the Pacific Ocean. Area: 1,063,340 sq.m. **Caribbean Federation:** 1956-62 included Barbados, Jamaica, Trinidad and Tobago, Leeward Is. and Windward Is. In 1962 this was dissolved and replaced by the indep. states of Jamaica, Trinidad and Tobago, and the W. Indies Fed. consisting of Antigua, Barbados, Dominica, Grenada, Montserrat, St. Kitts, St. Lucia, and St. Vincent. A separate, independent, non-colonial relationship with Britain is under consideration for these territories, except Barbados, which is to achieve indep. separately in 1966.

CARIBOU
(or **Amer. Reindeer**) Reindeer found in Canada and Greenland. The Woodland is found in Canada proper and the Barren Ground in the Arctic regions.

CARLISLE
[-līl'] Borough and county town of Cumberland on the Eden, S. of the Scots. border. Industries include railway works, the making of biscuits and woollens. Carlisle returns 1 member to Parl. Pop. 70,800.

CARLISTS
In 1833, Ferdinand VII d. leaving an only daughter, Isabella. By the Salic law his brother Carlos claimed the throne, but Isabella was crowned. The Carlists started a civil war which lasted until 1839, but Isabella retained the crown. 1964, Princess Irene of the Netherlands m. Prince Carlos Hugo of Bourbon-Parma, the present claimant.

CARLOS I
(1863-1908) King of Portugal. In 1907 he suspended the constitution and the next year was murdered in Lisbon. His younger son, Manoel, was deposed in 1910, when a Repub. was proclaimed.

CARLOW
Co. of S.E. Eire, in Leinster prov. It is mainly flat, with hills in the S. The chief rivers are the Barrow and Slaney. Pop. 33,342. **Carlow** County town and urban district of Co. Carlow, Eire, on the Barrow, 56 m. S.W. of Dublin. There is a cath. Pop. 7,500.

CARLYLE, Thomas
(1795-1881) Scots. writer. B. Ecclefechan, Dumfriesshire. His important works appeared after he moved to London in 1831; *Sartor Resartus* (1833), *French Revolution* (1837); lectures on lit., hist. and *Heroes and Hero-Worship* (1841), *Past and Present* (1843), *Letters and Speeches of Cromwell*, *Life of John Sterling* (1851), *Frederick the Great* (1858-65). Carlyle mar. in 1826 Jane Baillie Welsh (1801-66).

CARMARTHENSHIRE
County of S. Wales, with a coastline on C. Bay. The Towy is the chief river. The county is mainly agricultural, but around Llanelly in the S.E. are coal mines. Carmarthen is the county town; others are Llanelly, Llandovery and Burry Port. C. returns 2 members to Parl. Pop. 167,736. **Carmarthen.** Borough and county town of Carmarthenshire, on the Towy, 8 m. from the sea.

CARNAC
Town in the dept. of Morbihan, Fr. near the largest group of megalithic monuments known. It consists of menhirs or prehistoric upright stones, dolmens and tumuli.

CARNEGIE, Andrew
[-nāg'-] (1835-1919) Scots. philanthropist. B. Dunfermline; taken to U.S.A. 1848; engaged in rly. work during Civil War; opened iron works at Pittsburg. In a few years he was the head of an enormous combine. He gave away during his lifetime nearly the whole of a fortune est. at £100,000,000. He founded the Carnegie endowment for internat. peace and built the Palace of Peace at The Hague. Estabd. a fund for aiding Univ. students in Scot. and founded pension funds and Carnegie Institutes at Washington and Pittsburg.

CARNELIAN
Variety of quartz. Typically bright orange-red, it varies from yellow to brown. Used as a semi-precious stone. Found in India, Brazil and Siberia.

CAROB
(*Ceratonia siliqua*) Algaroba or locust tree. Found in Medit. countries, its long fleshy pods, with hard bean-like seeds, used as cattle food.

CAROL
Name of 2 Kings of Rumania. **Carol I** (1839-1914). In 1866 he was elected Prince of Rumania and was made king, 1881. Was succeeded by his nephew **Ferdinand. Carol II** (1893-1953) the son of Ferdinand. He twice renounced his claim to the throne, mar. Princess Helen of Greece, 1921, of which was b. a son, **Prince Michael** (*q.v.*). In 1926 he again renounced the right to succession but changed his mind, returned to Rumania, 1930, deposing his son who had reigned since 1927, and was accepted King. He abdicated, 1940.

CAROLINE
Name of 2 Eng. queens. Caroline, daughter of the Margrave of Brandenburg-Anspach, was mar. in 1705 to George, Electoral Prince of Hanover, later George II of Gt. Brit. She d. 1737. **Caroline,** who mar. her cousin, George IV, when he was Prince of Wales in 1795, was a daughter of the Duke of Brunswick. They had 1 child, Charlotte, and after her birth they separated. In 1820 Caroline returned from Italy to assert her rights as queen, but George started proceedings against her in the House of Lords for adultery. However, the bill was abandoned. She d. in 1821.

CAROLINES
Group of *c.* 550 coral Is. in the W. Pacific, W. of the Marshall Is. Copra is the chief export. Pop. is mainly Malay, with some Jap. and Chinese. Placed under Jap. mandate in 1919, they were occupied by the Amers. in World War II. Under U.S. trusteeship to U.N. since 1947. Area: 380 sq.m. Pop. 57,352.

CAROLINGIANS
Rulers of the Franks (751-987) of the family founded by Pepin the Short, king of the Franks in 751. Most famous was Charlemagne, made Holy Rom. Emperor in 800. After 843 the empire was divided among his grandsons.

CARP
(*Cyprinus carpio*) Edible fish, from fresh waters. It can live to a great age.

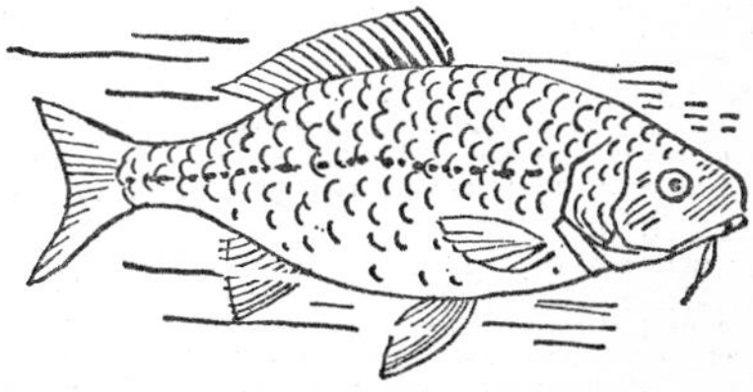

CARPATHIANS
Mt. range of Europe extending from near Bratislava, Czechoslovakia, to Rumania.

CARPENTARIA, Gulf of
Extensive inlet penetrating the N. coast of Australia, S. of the Arafura Sea.

CARPET
Floor covering made of woven or felted woollen, worsted or mixed fabrics. First used in E. countries. Fr. was the first European country to manufacture them, and the craft was brought to Eng. early in the 18th cent. The best are made in Turkey, Persia, India. Most seen in the houses of the W. world today are the inventions of Fr. workers. Brit. pile carpets are known as Wilton and Axminster. Carpets without a pile are called Kidderminster and are usually reversible.

CARRAGEEN
(or **Irish Moss**) (*Chondrus crispus*). Purplish cartilaginous seaweed found on the coasts of Europe and N. Amer. It is prepared with milk or water as a jelly.

CARRARA
[-rà'·] Town of Tuscany, W. Italy, 40 m. N. of Leghorn. Fine white marble is quarried nearby.

CARROLL, Lewis
Pseudonym of **Charles Lutwidge Dodgson** (1832-98) Eng. writer and math. Educ. Rugby and Christ Ch. Oxford; lecturer in maths until 1881; ordained deacon, 1861. *Alice in Wonderland*, pub. 1865; *Through the Looking Glass* (1871); *The Hunting of the Snark* (1876); also works on maths.

CARROLL, Paul Vincent
(1900-) Irish playwright. Lived in Dublin and Glasgow. Among his plays are *The Things that are Caesar's, Shadow and Substance, The Wise have not Spoken.*

CARROT
Root crop extensively cultivated for its strongly flavoured root, used for human food. Brought to Brit. from Holland in the 16th cent.

CARSE OF GOWRIE
Fertile plain, on the N. bank of the Tay, in Angus and Perthshire.

CARSON, Edward Henry, Baron
(1854-1935) Irish politician. M.P. (Unionist), 1892-1921. He led the Ulster Unionists in their resistance to Home Rule, and played a prominent part in the events of 1914.

CARTAGENA
Seaport of Colombia, on the Caribbean coast, W. of the Magdalena. It exports petroleum; conveyed by a pipeline, 325 m. from the Magdalena-Santander oilfield. Pop. 180,000.

CARTAGENA
[-je'-nà, -chā'-nà] City, seaport and naval base of Murcia prov. Spain, on the Medit. Silver and lead are exported. Pop. 128,047.

CARTHAGE
Ancient city of Africa, according to legend founded by Phoenicians from Tyre, led by Dido. About 300 B.C. Carthage was the centre of a great empire, including the Medit. coast of Africa, and the coast lands of Sp., Corsica and Sardinia and traded all over the known world. Carthage was Rome's great rival. The 3 Punic wars between them began over the possession of Sicily. Carthage was defeated in the 1st war, and also in the 2nd, but only after Hannibal had tried Rome's resources to the uttermost. In the 3rd war, the city was taken by Scipio and razed to the ground in 146 B.C.

CARTOGRAPHY
or **map-making.** Preparation of a plan or map of the earth's surface or a part of it. Areas are first surveyed and exact distances, contours and elevations obtained. Reduced to a scale, these are then accurately represented on paper. Maps are of many different kinds depending on the purpose in view, *e.g. political* maps, where countries, towns, etc. are shown; *physical*, representing natural features; *orographical*, exhibiting particularly the diversities of surface level. Nautical maps, or charts, concentrate on all marine features important in navigation.

CARTWRIGHT, Edmund
(1743-1823) Eng. inventor. B. Nottinghamshire, he went to Oxford and became a clergyman. While in a living in Leics., he invented a loom, since developed into the modern power loom.

CARUSO, Enrico
(1873-1921) Ital. operatic tenor; b. Naples. He made his début in *Faust* in 1895, and gradually attained to world eminence.

CARVER, George Washington
(*c.* 1864-1943) Negro scientist. Because of racial discrimination, he was unable to attend a white school, but he graduated as Master of Science at Iowa State Coll. 1892; became director of the dept. of agricultural research, Tuskegee Institute, Alabama, 1906, where he remained for the rest of his life.

CARVER, John
(*c.* 1575-1621) Eng. Puritan leader and first gov. of Pilgrim Fathers. He was the prime mover in planning the voyage and hiring and provisioning the *Mayflower* for the journey. He may have chosen the landing site at Plymouth, New Hampshire.

CARY, Joyce
(1888-1957) Eng. novelist. His works include *African Witch* (1936), *Mister Johnson* (1939), *The Horse's Mouth* (1944), *Except the Lord* (1953) and *Not Honour More* (1955).

CASABLANCA
Seaport of Morocco, on the Atlantic coast, 60 m. S. of Rabat. Grain, hides, wool and phosphates are exported. It is a popular tourist centre. Pop. 1,085,000.

CASALS, Pablo
(1876-) Sp. violoncellist, composer and conductor. B. Tarragona, he made his début in Eng. in 1898. He has composed symphonic choral and chamber music. In 1950 he founded at Prades, France, an annual festival of classical chamber music. *See* biography by Lillian Littlehales (1948).

CASANOVA, Giovanni Jacopo
[-ō'-va] (1725-98) Ital. adventurer. He early embarked on a career of intrigue. After various wanderings, he was apptd. to manage state lotteries in Paris.

CASCARA
Bark of the Calif. buckthorn, *Rhamnus purshiana.* From it are prepared solid and liquid extracts of **cascara sagrada,** one of the most useful tonic aperients. It is particularly useful in emptying the rectum.

CASEIN
Main constituent of cheese. An albumin, it is precipitated from skimmed milk by the enzyme in rennet, or by self-curdling with lactic acid. It yields a tasteless, amorphous, finely divided lime salt.

CASEMENT, Roger David
(1864-1916) Irish polit. B. Dublin, he entered the consular service. Becoming hostile to Brit. he went to Germany for help for the Irish rising of 1916, and was arrested on his return, when he landed from a German submarine. He was found guilty of treason and hanged. In 1965 his remains were taken for reburial to Ireland where he is regarded as a martyr-patriot.

CASHEL
Market town and urban district of Tipperary, Eire. It is famous for its rock, 300 ft. high, on which are the ruins of a cath. and 12th cent. round tower. Pop. 3,000.

CASHEW NUT
Hard-shelled fruit of a trop. gum tree, *Anacardium occidentale* which grows in the W. Indies.

CASPIAN SEA
Inland sea between Europe and Asia. The surface is 86 ft. below mean sea level, shallow in the N. where it freezes in winter, but deepening southward to 3,000 ft. Astrakhan and Baku are the chief ports. The world's largest inland sea, it is 680 m. long, and covers 163,800 sq.m.

CASSAVA
Name of several species of trop. euphorbiaceous plants. Bitter cassava yields from its fleshy root a starchy food, which when dried becomes tapioca.

CASSIA
Genus of leguminous plants of temp. and trop. regions outside Europe. *Cassia fistula* pods provide a mild laxative. Senna leaves come from the Alexandrian and Indian cassia shrub. **Cinnamomum cassia,** a species of aromatic laurel of trop. Asia, furnishes *cassia lignea,* a spice used in S. Europe.

CASSITERITE
[-it'-er-īt] Tin oxide, SnO_2, the commonest ore of tin. It is found in Cornwall and elsewhere.

CASSIUS LONGINUS, Gaius
Rom. gen. and politician. He led the conspiracy against Caesar and was present at his assassination, 44 B.C. Defeated by Antony at Philippi, he compelled his servant to slay him, 42 B.C.

CASSIVELAUNUS
[kasi-vĕ-law-nŭs] Brit. chief. He opposed the march of Julius Caesar during his 2nd Brit. campaign. He was defeated at a ford over the Thames and gave hostages to Caesar.

CASSON, Sir Lewis
(1875-1969) Actor and producer. B. Birkenhead, he made his first stage appearance, 1903. He acted with his wife, **Dame Sybil Thorndike** (*q.v.*). Director of Drama to C.E.M.A. (Arts Council) 1942-5.

CASSOWARY
(*Casuarius*) Ostrich-like bird. At least 10 species inhabit N. Australia, New Guinea and neighbouring Is. They are 3-toed with rudimentary wings and black plumage. They are forest dwellers and swift runners.

CASTANETS
Percussion instrument. They are shell-shaped, hinged together by a string, held between the fingers and clapped together by the hand. They are used by Sp. dancers, to accompany their dancing.

CASTE
Exclusive social group. Such a system prevails in India where the Hindu pop. is divided into: (1) The *Brahman*, sacerdotal, (2) the *Kshatriya*, warrior and governing, (3) the *Vaisya*, agricultural and merchant, and (4) the *Shudra*, labouring, castes. No member of any caste may marry outside it, while its rules may also regulate his occupation and even his diet.

CASTILE
[-tēl'] Former kingdom of C. Spain, comprising the 2 basins of the upper Douro, and the Tagus and Guadiana, separated by the Sierra de Guadarrama ranges. In 1469, Isabella of Castile mar. Ferdinand of Aragon, and the 2 kingdoms were united. From this the kingdom of Sp. developed. Burgos and Madrid are the chief towns. The **Castilian language** is the principal type of Sp. spoken.

CASTLE
Fortress erected for defence. The Roms. had castles on their camps. In feudal times strong buildings called castles sprang up in W. Europe. Notable examples were those erected by barons on the hills above the Rhine. In Brit. many castles were built by the Normans, consisting typically of an outer and an inner fort. The outer fort was protected by walls, round which was a moat, or ditch. The inner fort, or keep, served as a refuge.

CASTLEBAR
County town, urban district and market town of Co. Mayo, Eire. Pop. 4,900.

CASTLEREAGH, Viscount
Robert Stewart (1769-1822) M.P. (Irish), 1790-1801; (Brit.) 1794-98, 1800-21; War. Sec. 1805 and 1807-9; Foreign Sec. 1812-22; Leader of Commons, 1812-21; Marquess, 1821. As Foreign Sec. Castlereagh was responsible for the peace negotiations of 1814-15, and for Brit.'s participation in the Congress System. He d. by his own hand.

CASTOR OIL
Oil extracted from the seeds of the castor oil plant which grows in India. It is one of the oldest household remedies for constipation.

CASTRATION
The removal of the organs which make reproduction possible, *i.e.* the male testicles or the female ovaries.

CAT
Name, usually denoting domesticated breeds, derived from several small species of carnivorous mammals belonging to the family Felidae. Egyptian domesticated breed penetrated to S. Europe, crossing occasionally with European wild cats westward and Asiatic forms eastward. It reached Brit. during the Rom. occupation.

CAT-O'-NINE-TAILS
Short whip with 9 knotted lashes, used for corporal punishment. By the Criminal Justice Act, 1948, sentences of whipping were abolished except in cases of mutiny, incitement to mutiny, or gross violence to a prison officer.

CATACOMBS
[-koomz] Subterranean galleries excavated as burial places, beneath Rome, by the early Christians. Circular rooms served for families or distinguished martyrs. They were used for refuge and worship in times of persecution.

CATALEPSY
[kat'-] Psychological disorder characterised by sudden temporary loss, complete or partial, of will power and sensation with rigidity of muscles simulating d. Can be produced by hypnosis, or an infection, and is a symptom of hysteria.

CATALONIA
Former prov. of Spain, lying S. of the Pyrenees on the Medit. coast, and now comprising the provs. of Tarragona, Barcelona, Gerona and Lerida. The soil is fertile. Industrial development was stimulated by the World Wars, and now there are textile factories and mines. C. was given a large measure of home rule in 1931, when Sp. became a repub. During the Civil War, 1936–9, these privileges were lost. **Catalan.** Language spoken in Catalonia, Andorra, Fr. Pyrenees, Balearic Is.; akin to Provençal and imported into Spain about the 9th cent.

CATALPA
Genus of large-leaved ornamental trees of the bignonia family, natives of N. Amer. and E.

Asia. *C. bignonioides*, furnishes light, durable timber. *C. longissima*, Fr. oak, is rich in tannin.

CATAMARAN
Surf boat used on the Indian and S. Amer. coasts. Comprising 3 or more logs lashed together, 20-25 ft. long, the middle trunk, on which the 2 paddlers squat, is elongated for turning up as a prow. Double hulled yachts also called catamarans are becoming popular.

CATARACT
Disease of eye in which lens loses its transparency. Operation frequently brings relief.

CATARRH
[-tar'] Acute or chronic infection or irritation of mucous membrane giving rise to discharge. Affects any mucous membrane such as stomach (*see* GASTRITIS), bladder (*see* CYSTITIS), eyes (*see* CONJUCTIVITIS) and nose (*see* RHINITIS).

CATBIRD
(*Dumetella carolinensis*) (1) black-polled, slate-grey N. Amer. bird of the thrasher family, (2) type of Australian Bower-bird.

CATCHMENT AREA
The region made by its rainfall into a self-contained drainage basin. It is the area available for furnishing water at a specific point for a public water supply. In 1931, in connection with a scheme of land draining, Catchment Boards were set up in various parts of the country for each of the principal rivers.

CATECHISM
Instruction by question and answer, or a book containing such instruction, particularly in religious doctrine. The R.C. (Tridentine) 1566, is in Brit. replaced by The Penny Catechism. The catechism of the C. of E. is in the Book of Common Prayer. The Presbyterians have 2: the Shorter and the Longer, dating from 1648.

CATECHU (or CUTCH)
Tanning and dyeing extract, obtained from 2 Indian species of acacia. It also comes from the leaves of 2 Malayan species of cinchonaceous climbers.

CATERPILLAR
Popular name for the larva of a butterfly or moth. Its head bears strong biting mandibles, 3 simple eyes, 3 thoracic segments each with a pair of true jointed legs, and 10 abdominal segments.

CATFISH
(*Siluridae*) Numerous family of naked scaleless fish or fish with bony plates instead of scales. Almost all inhabit temp. and trop. freshwater, and include the largest European freshwater fish, the Wel (*Siluris glanis*) found only E. of the Rhine. Several species inhabit Amer. rivers and lakes, some travelling overland in dry seasons.

CATGUT
A material used in surgery for tying blood vessels and stitching wounds. Various types of catgut are used by anglers and in the making of tennis racquets, and strings for violins. It is manufactured from the intestines of sheep.

CATHEDRAL
Ch. in which a bishop has his seat. In the C. of E. most are controlled by a dean and a number of canons who are known as the dean and chapter. Notable examples abroad are St. Ambrose, Milan; St. Mark's, Venice; the Duomo, Florence; Seville; Notre Dame, Paris; Chartres; Rheims; Cologne. Modern examples are Westminster Cath. London, St. John the Divine, New York, and Coventry.

CATHERINE I
(1684-1727) Empress of Russia. She became the mistress of Peter the Great and in 1711 his wife. When Peter d. she was raised to the throne (1725). **Catherine II** (1729-96) Empress of Russia. In 1745 she mar. Peter, heir to the Russian throne. In 1761 Peter became Czar, but in 1762 was murdered and his widow took his place. Catherine greatly increased the area and power of Russia. She carried out many humanitarian reforms.

CATHERINE de Medici
(1519-89) Queen of Fr. Daughter of Lorenzo de Medici, in 1533 she mar. Henry, heir to the throne of Fr. He became king in 1544 and reigned for 15 years, after which 3 of their 4 sons were kings in turn. **Francis II,** reigned for only a year, but during the reigns of the other 2, **Charles IX** and **Henry III**, Catherine, as regent, was dominant in Fr. She assented to the Massacre of St. Bartholomew.

CATHERINE of Aragon
(1485-1536) Wife of Henry VIII. In 1501 she mar. Arthur, Prince of Wales. In 1502 he d. and the princess was betrothed to his brother Henry. He became king in 1509, and they were married. When Henry fell in love with Anne Boleyn he claimed that the union with Catherine had been illegal. The Pope refused a divorce and the result was the overthrow of the Papal authority in Eng. Cranmer then pronounced the mar. invalid. She was the mother of Mary Tudor, Queen of Eng. (*q.v.*).

CATHERINE of Braganza
(1638-1705) Wife of Charles II and daughter of John, King of Portugal. She mar. Charles in 1662, her dowry being Tangier, Bombay, and a large sum of money.

CATHODE
(or Kathode). Electrode from which the current leaves, or negative plate of a voltaic or electrolytic cell. In a vacuum tube or thermionic valve the electrons leave the cathode and flow to the anode. **Cathode-Ray Oscillograph.** Device for delineating wave-form of alternating quantity. Consists usually of a conical glass bulb with a fluorescent screen; inside, a beam of electrons is made to move over the screen. Cathode ray oscillographs are used in radar (*q.v.*) and in television (*q.v.*).

CATHOLIC EMANCIPATION
Term used for the removal of polit. and other disabilities under which R.C.'s suffered in Brit. from the time of the Reformation. Full emancipation dates from 1829. R.C.'s were permitted to sit in Parl., hold civil and milit. offices, and enter the professions.

CATILINE, Lucius Sergius
(*c.* 108-62 B.C.) Rom. politician and conspirator. Governed Africa in 67 B.C. and on his return conspired to seize the consulship. The conspiracy was defeated by Cicero, then consul.

CATMINT
Brit. flowering plant. *Nepeta cataria* bears blue flowers in dense whorls. The plant is aromatic and is supposed to attract cats.

CATO, Marcus Porcius
[kā'-tō] (234-149 B.C.) Rom. statesman, gen. and writer. In 184 he was chosen censor. Known for his enmity to Carthage, he coined the phrase *Delenda est Carthago* (Carthage must be destroyed). He wrote a book on agriculture, *De Re Rustica*.

CAT'S EAR
Popular name for a genus of composite plants (*Hypochaeris*). Inhabiting Europe, W. Asia and N. Africa are 30 species. Common cat's ear (*H. radicata*) found throughout Brit. has yellow heads.

CAT'S EYE
Gem which when cut convexly shows yellowish opalescence. The chrysoberyl, or true cat's eye, has a white gleam. Occidental cat's eye, also found in Ceylon, contains asbestos fibres. S. African cat's eye is a bluish stone with crocidolite fibres.

CAT'S TAIL
The club rush or reed mace (*Typha*). Growing throughout Brit. the broad-leaved has brown spikes from 6-12 in. long, the narrow-leaved being smaller. Cat's tail, or timothy grass (*Phleum*), is a useful fodder plant.

CATTLE
Cows and oxen used agriculturally for supplying beef, milk or labour. Most European strains descend from the extinct Aurochs. Among Brit. breeds Aberdeen Angus have provided high-priced pedigree stock the world over. Famous milkers are Devons, Ayrshires, Jerseys and Guernseys. Great continental milkers are Dutch, Swiss, Simmenthal, Norman, Breton and Danish.

CATULLUS, Gaius Valerius
(*c.* 84- *c.* 54 B.C.) Rom. poet. 116 poems survive, some concerned with his unhappy passion for 'Lesbia' others being satirical and defamatory and the rest lyrical or mythological.

CAUCASUS
[kaw'-] Mt. range between Europe and Asia, stretching for nearly 1,000 m. from the Black Sea to the Caspian. Its breadth varies from 30 to 140 m. Highest point is Mt. **Elbruz** (18,481 ft.). The oil wells of the Caucasus are important. **Caucasian Languages.** A small group (sometimes called Japhethic) having no other known affinities: Georgian, Lesghican, Avar, Circassian.

CAULIFLOWER
Variety of cabbage and a popular vegetable for the table. Its flowers have been mostly condensed while young into a succulent white head.

CAUSSES
[kōs] High limestone plateaux on the S. and S.W. edges of the Massif Central. The rivers Lot and Tarn cut deep valleys and there are underground streams, swallow holes, etc. Sheep are kept. Cheese is made from their milk, in the valleys, *e.g.* **Roquefort** and **Rocamadour.**

CAVALIER
Orig. one who could afford to own a horse; hence a knight or gentleman. Popularly applied to supporters of Charles I in the Civil War.

CAVALRY
Body of mounted soldiers. They are mentioned in the Bible and were used by the Persians, Carthaginians and Roms. The great age of cavalry in warfare was in medieval times. Their supremacy was challenged by the Eng. archers, esp. at Crécy (1346). Horsemen continued to be used for skirmishing and pursuit, till in the S. African war their place was taken by mounted infantry. In World War II all Brit. cavalry units were mechanised.

CAVAN
Co. of Eire, in Ulster Prov. S. of the N. Ireland border. The greater part is low lying. Chief rivers are the Erne and Blackwater. Agriculture is the main occupation; Cavan is the county town. Pop. 56,594.

CAVELL, Edith Louisa
[ka'-vil] (1865-1915) Brit. nurse. Became matron of a med. institute in Brussels, and during the German occupation harboured wounded and refugee soldiers, and aided their escape. Denounced by a renegade, she was tried by court-martial Oct. 7, 1915, and was shot 5 days afterwards.

CAVENDISH, Henry
(1731-1810) Eng. chemist and physicist. B. Nice. He discovered hydrogen, 1766, determined the constituents of water and atmospheric air, and combined oxygen and hydrogen into water, before 1784.

CAVIARE
[kav'-i-ar] Sturgeon roe prepared for table. The eggs are served as an hors d'oeuvre or savoury.

CAVOUR, Camillo Benso di
[kà-voor'] (1810-61) Ital. statesman. He worked for the polit., industrial, and agricultural development of Piedmont, and founded the newspaper *Il Risorgimento*. In 1848 he became an M.P. and by 1852 P.M. of Piedmont. He reorganised the country and played a dominating part in uniting it under Emmanuel of Piedmont.

CAVY
[kā'-vi] (*Cavia*) Small S. Amer. rodents living in burrows. *See* GUINEA PIG.

CAWNPORE
or **Kanpur.** City of Uttar Pradesh, India, on the Ganges, 40 m. S.W. of Lucknow. It is a centre of the grain trade. It was the scene of the massacre by Nana Sahib of surrendered Europeans during the Indian Mutiny, 1857. Pop. 1,112,000.

CAXTON, William
(*c.* 1422-91) Eng. printer and translator. Tr. a Fr. romance as *The Recuyell of the Historyes of Troy* and printed it at Bruges *c.* 1474. Returned to London in 1476 and set up a press in Westminster, printing about 80 books, as *The Canterbury Tales* and *Morte d' Arthur.*

CAYENNE
[-yen'] Cap. and seaport of Fr. Guiana, S. Amer. on the Is. of the same name. Exports include gold, balata and rosewood. It was the official H.Q. of the former Fr. penal settlement at the Ile du Diable. Pop. 13,000.

CAYENNE PEPPER
[kā'-yen] Condiment prepared from the dried and pounded pods of several species of *Capsicum*, a native of Cent. and S. Amer. The pungency arises from an active principle, capsicin, which is utilised in pharmacy.

CAYLEY, Sir George
(1774-1857) Eng. landowner, M.P. and experimenter in aviation. He built a glider and an 'aerial carriage', a cross between an aeroplane and a helicopter. Other inventions were a caterpillar tractor, breech-loading rifle and artificial limbs.

CAYMAN ISLANDS
Group of 3 Is. Grand C., Little C. and C. Brac, in the W. Indies, till 1962 admin. by Jamaica, *c.* 150 m. to the S.E. Turtle fishing is the chief industry. **Georgetown,** the cap. is on Grand C. Pop. 7,616.

CECIL OF CHELWOOD, Viscount
Edgar Algernon Robert Gascoyne (1864-1958) Eng. politician. M.P. (Cons.), 1906-10, and 1911-23; Foreign Under-Sec. 1915-16; Blockade Min. 1916-18. Played a large part in the founding (1919), and running of the League of Nations.

CECILIA
Ital. saint and martyr. Patron saint of music and the blind.

CEDAR
Name of various evergreen, coniferous trees, pre-eminently of the genus *Cedrus.* The cedar of Lebanon, *C. libani*, rises sometimes to 80 ft.

with horizontal branches. The silver cedar, *C. atlantica*, grows in the Atlas; a 3rd species, *C. deodara*, is the Himalayan deodar. Spanish cedars, and those used for cedar pencils, are *Juniperus*.

CEDRON
Pear-shaped fruit of a trop. Amer. tree (*Simaba cedron*) which contains a bitter, almond-shaped nut which is a remedy for snake bite, intermittent fever and hydrophobia.

CELANDINE
Name of 2 perennial yellow-flowered herbs. The greater (*Chelidonium majus*), of the poppy family, with much-divided leaves, bears umbels of 4-petalled flowers. The lesser (*Ranunculus ficaria*), of the buttercup family, is a short plant with scalloped leaves and stalks bearing single flowers with 8–12 petals.

CELÉBES
[sĕ-lē'-biz] or **Sulawesi.** Is. of Indonesia, E. of Borneo. The interior is mountainous, some volcanic peaks exceeding 10,000 ft. The inhabitants are chiefly Malayo-Polynesian. Products include timber, nutmegs and spices. C. was discovered in 1512 by the Portuguese, but was captured by the Dutch in 1660. Macassar is the chief town and port. Area: 73,000 sq.m. Pop. *c.* 7,000,000.

CELERY
A biennial umbelliferous herb (*Apium graveolens*). A native of Europe. W. Asia and N. Africa. Cultivated as a table vegetable, the heart and stems are blanched, and are eaten uncooked. Celery is also stewed and used in soups.

CELESTA
Keyboard instrument with a 4-octave compass and a tone like that of the Glockenspiel.

CELL
(Electricity) Single jar or unit used for interchanging chem. and electrical energy. Simple voltaic cells produce electric currents from electrodes, held in electrolytes.

CELLINI, Benvenuto
[che-lē'-ni] (1500-71) Ital. artist. B. Florence. Reaching Rome in 1519 he worked as a goldsmith for 20 years. In Florence, he produced the bronze casting of *Perseus, with the head of Medusa.*

CELLOPHANE
Proprietary name for the thin, transparent, flexible, non-poisonous, moisture-proof sheeting. The process was discovered by a Fr. textile worker, J. E. Branderberger, early 20th cent.

CELLULOID
Solid and highly inflammable substance made by mixing nitrated cellulose with camphor or a substitute. First produced in 1856 under the name xylonite. Unaffected by the atmosphere, water or dilute acids, it becomes plastic at 75° C. and can then be moulded. At ordinary temps. it is turned, sawn, cut or drilled, being used for pianoforte keys, combs, photographic films, etc. (Proprietary Name).

CELLULOSE
Essential constituent of all vegetable cells. A white, opaque carbohydrate, it is nearly pure in cotton, linen and hemp. Boiling with dilute sulphuric acid changes it into dextrose. Nitric acid converts it into nitrocellulose, the base of celluloid and collodion. With caustic soda and carbon disulphide it becomes the viscose which yields artificial silk.

CELTS
Appear as a distinct race in the Iron Age. 397 B.C. they sacked Rome and settled in Gaul and Spain. Landed in Brit. before 600 B.C. Their culture may be identified with Hallstadt and possibly La Tène. **Celtic Languages.** Branch of Indo-European, orig. spoken throughout W. Europe, as shown by names and inscriptions (*e*.g. Gallic). Divided into (a) Irish and Scot. Gaelic, Manx (b) Welsh, Cornish (extinct late 18th cent. but preserved in 5 late medieval miracle plays), Breton.

CENIS
[sĕ-nē'] Mt. of the Alps, on the border of Fr. and Italy, *c.* 7,000 ft. high, with a tunnel, opened 1871, on the line from Lyons to Turin.

CENSORSHIP
System of controls by which the circulation of any printed matter or the production of any play or film is prohibited unless official permission is granted. Until 1695, the Crown claimed a monopoly of all printing presses; since that date there has been no censorship of printed matter in Brit. During World Wars I and II censorship of the press extended only to milit. and defence matters. No play, however, may be acted or presented before it has been approved by the Lord Chamberlain (*Theatres Act*, 1843).

CENSUS
Official estimate of the population of a country, and of certain facts about them. Censuses of Jews, Roms. and other peoples were taken. Today, a census is taken in most countries every 5-10 years; in Brit. it has been taken every 10 years since 1801. Particulars asked for are name, age, sex, occupation, birthplace, marital condition and nationality.

CENTAURY
(*Centaurium umbellatum*) Annual herb which flowers from early summer to Sept. It is *c.* 12 in. high with oblong leaves joined at the base growing in pairs.

CENTIGRADE
Thermometer invented by Anders Celsius, a Swede, in 1742. The scale is divided into 100°. The lower point 0° C. is the melting pt. of ice and the higher pt. 100° C.

CENTIPEDE
Animal of the class Myriapoda. They resemble insects, but have no wings, and have from 15 to over 100 pairs of legs.

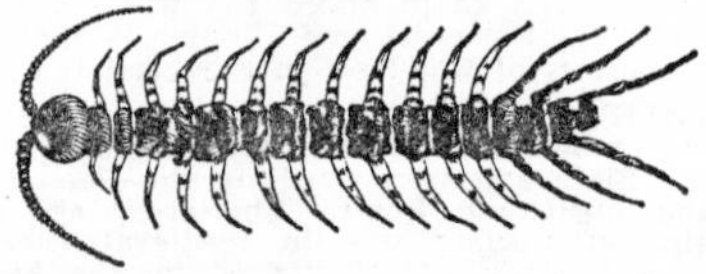

CENTRAL AFRICAN FEDERATION
Fed. in C. Africa set up in 1953 of the Brit. territories N. and S. Rhodesia. It broke up in 1963. *See* RHODESIA, MALAWI, ZAMBIA.

CENTRAL AFRICAN REPUBLIC
Former Fr. colony, N. of the Equator, between Cameroon and Sudan. It has a common boundary with Chad in the N. and the Congolese Repub. in the S. Indep. 1960. Cap. Bangui. Area: 238,000 sq.m. Pop. 2,088,000.

CENTRAL AMERICA
The isthmus connecting N. and S. Amer. containing the 6 repubs. of Guatemala, Costa Rica, Nicaragua, Honduras, Salvador and Panama, and Brit. Honduras. It is crossed in the S. by the Panama Canal. The area, excluding Panama, which was associated with Colombia, Venezuela and Ecuador, was Sp. from the 16th cent. until 1821.

CENTRAL CRIMINAL COURT
London court of law. It is in the Old Bailey and was set up in 1834. Here all treasons, felonies, and misdemeanours committed in the City of London, the former county of Middlesex, and parts of Essex, Kent and Surrey are heard. Usually a judge of the high court presides.

CEPHALONIA
[sef-] Largest of the Ionian Is. off the W. coast of Greece.

CEPHALOPODA
Class of marine, free-swimming molluscs with muscular tentacles and 2 or 4 plume-like gills. Two-gilled species include the Argonaut, 8-armed Octopoda, like the common octopus, 10-armed Decapoda, squids with horny pens, Cuttle fishes with calcareous bone, and Spirulas with coiled tubes. Of the 4-gilled order with external shells, only the pearly nautilus survives.

CERASTES
Genus of vipers ranging from Algeria to Arabia and Syria. The Horned Viper, *C. cornuta*, *c.* 2 ft. long, has small horn-like processes above the eyes. Its bite can cause d. in 30 m.

CEREAL
Grass cultivated for edible grains. As the chief source of breadstuffs cereals are of primary importance as food. Main temp. cereals are wheat, barley, oats and rye. Among trop. cereals rice and millet are staple foods.

CEREBRO-SPINAL FLUID
Clear, colourless fluid acting as cushion and source of nutriment for brain and spinal cord. Flows through ventricles to brain and spinal cord.

CERES
Largest and first discovered of the minor planets, observed by Piazzi at Palermo in 1801. Its diam. is 485 m. and it is invisible to the naked eye.

CERIUM
Silvery metal, occurring in a small number of minerals. Discovered by Berzelius in 1803, its oxide is used in the manufacture of gas mantles. An alloy of cerium with iron and certain rare metals is used as a flint in cigarette lighters.

CERVANTES, Miguel
(1547-1616) Sp. author. Captured by pirates 1575 and imprisoned in Algiers until 1580. Wrote poetry and plays; *Don Quixote*, 1605; 2nd part, 1615; *Novelas Exemplares* (1613) (short stories), and other works.

CESTODES
Tapeworms. Parasitic in the intestinal canals of vertebrates, they usually pass their larval and adult life in different hosts. The mature worm throws off whole egg-bearing segments that pass out and if swallowed, hatch and make their home in the second animal.

CETACEA
[si-tā'-shiă] Order of aquatic mammals. The main swimming organ is a fin-like horizontal 'fluke' instead of a vertical tail. The blubber is abundant and commercially valuable. Cetacea are divided into tooth bearing and whalebone types. The former include Porpoises, Dolphins and Sperm Whales. The latter bear sieves of whale-bone on their palates. These include the Right, Greenland, Southern Blue and Hump whales.

CETYWAYO
[seti-wā'-ō] (*c.* 1836-84) King of the Zulus. He became ruler in 1857 and king in 1872. War broke out between Brit. and the Zulus after Transvaal was annexed in 1877. The Zulus were beaten at Rorke's Drift and Ulundi and Cetywayo captured.

CÉVENNES
Range of mts. *c.* 330 m. long, in C. Fr. in the depts. of Lozère, Gard and Ardèche, dividing the Massif Central from the Rhône valley. The highest point is Mont de Lozère (5,650 ft.). Coal and other minerals are found, and in the S. are large forest areas.

CEYLON
Is. in the Indian Ocean, off the coast of Madras, a dominion of the Brit. Commonwealth. Much of the land is low-lying, rising in S. to *c.* 8,000 ft. in Pedrutalagala and Adam's Peak. The climate is trop. Agriculture is the principal occupation. Rice, tea, coconuts, rubber, cinnamon, cocoa and tobacco are cultivated. Minerals include sapphires, rubies, graphite and mica. The cap. and chief seaport is Colombo, on the W. coast; other centres are Jaffna, Galle and Kandy. The inhabitants are Sinhalese. The religion is Buddhism. C. was colonised by the Portuguese in 1505, but became Dutch some 150 years later. In 1796 the Brit. took over control. In 1947 the Dominion of Ceylon was estabd. with full responsible govt. Admin. is by gov.-gen. assisted by a cabinet, a senate and a house of representatives. Area: 25,332 sq.m. Pop. 10,168,000.

CÉZANNE, Paul
[sā-zan'] (1839-1906) Fr. painter. Influenced by Poussin and El Greco, and later by Manet and Pissarro, he sought to portray nature in subtle manifestations of light.

CHABLIS
[shah-blee] Town of Yonne dept., Fr., 11 m. E. of Auxerre. The name is used in Brit. for the Fr. dry white wines.

CHABRIER, Alexio Emmanuel
[shab'-ri-ā] (1841-94) Fr. composer. His works include the opera, *Le Roi malgré lui*, the orchestral rhapsody *España*, and *Marche Joyeuse*.

CHAD
Lake in northern C. Africa, between the Sudan and the Sahara. Area: *c.* 7,000 m. but it is steadily shrinking.

CHAD
Repub. of equatorial Africa, former Fr. possession. Indep. 1960. Cap. Fort Lamy. Area: 495,800 sq.m. Pop. 2,581,000.

CHADWICK, Sir James
F.R.S. (1891-) Physicist. Master of Gonville and Caius Coll., Camb. He discovered the *neutron* (*q.v.*).

CHAFFINCH
(*Fringilla coelebs*) Brit. songbird which breeds throughout Brit. and N. Europe. The ashy-brown female, usually migrates S. without the male. The male, 6 in. long, with reddish breast, forked tail-feathers, has sharp or sweet call notes.

CHAGALL, Marc
(1887-) Artist. B. Vitebsk, Russia. Went to Paris in 1907. He returned to Russia and started the revival of Jewish art there. Reached the U.S.A. as a refugee in 1941.

CHALCEDONY
[kal-sed'-ŏn-i] Semi-precious stone. A crypto-crystalline quartz mixed with opaline silica. This commonest of gem stones occurs as agate, bloodstone, carnelian, chrysoprase and onyx.

CHALDEA
[kal-] Biblical place name. It denoted in O.T. times the marshy sealand S.E. of Babylonia. Later a Chaldean or neo-Babylonian dynasty was estab. by Nabopolassar *c.* 625, and throughout this period, Chaldea denoted all Babylonia.

CHALIAPIN, Feodor Ivanovitch
[chal'-ya-pēn] (1873-1938) Russ. operatic singer. B. Kazan. First appeared in St. Petersburg in 1894. He won fame as the greatest of all Russ. singers.

CHALK
White, earthy variety of limestone, containing 94-98 % of calcium carbonate. It comprises mostly minute shells laid down in shallow waters across Europe during the Cretaceous period. It is burned for lime used in making Portland cement and, when levigated, whiting. The Downs and other hills in the S. of Eng. are of chalk.

CHALMERS, Thomas
(1780-1847) Scot. divine. In 1815 he removed to Glasgow, where he wrote his *Problems of Poverty.* A leader of the Disruption in 1843, he became the first moderator of the Free Ch.

CHÂLONS-SUR-MARNE
[sha-] Cap. of Marne dept. *c.* 100 m. E. of Paris, on the Marne. It is a centre of the champagne trade. Nearby in A.D. 451, the Huns, under Attila, were defeated by the Roms. and Visigoths. Pop. 36,800.

CHAMBERLAIN
Orig. the officer in charge of domestic affairs in royal households or monasteries. In Brit. the Lord Chamberlain is a court official who regulates the etiquette of the palace and acts as the official censor of plays.

CHAMBERLAIN, Joseph
(1836-1914) Eng. statesman. M.P. for Birmingham (Radical, later Unionist), 1876-1914; Pres. of Local Govt. Board, 1886; resigned to form Lib. Unionists; Colonial Sec. 1895-1903. Mayor of Birmingham, 1873-6, he did much for the development of the city. He broke with Gladstone over Irish Home Rule. In 1895 he became Salisbury's Colonial Sec. His action in declaring for Tariff Reform split the Unionist party, and he resigned in 1904. His son was **Arthur Neville** (1869-1940) Eng. statesman. M.P. (Cons.), 1918-40; Director of Nat. Service, 1916; Chanc. of the Exchequer, 1923-4 and 1931-7; P.M. 1937-40. On following Baldwin as P.M. in 1937 he had to deal with the threatening internat. situation. His negotiations with Hitler in 1938, and his general policy of 'appeasement' have been variously judged. His govt. fell in 1940, but for the remaining months of his life he served under Mr. Churchill.

CHAMBÉRY
Cap. of Savoie dept., E. Fr. A tourist centre, it manufactures silk and lace. Pop. 32,100.

CHAMELEON
Family of lizards differing from true lizards in their telescopic tongues, eyeballs moving independently, opposable toes and prehensile tails. They are famed for their power of changing colour according to the environment. The common species, 12 in. long, ranges the African and Asiatic Medit. coasts.

CHAMINADE, Cécile Louise Stéphanie
(1861-1944) Fr. composer, b. in Paris. Best-known compositions are her songs and piano pieces.

CHAMOIS
[sham'-wȧ] (*Rupicapra*) Animal of the Alps and other mt. areas of Europe and Asia Minor. Intermediate between antelopes and goats and remarkable for its jumping powers. Its average ht. is *c.* 2 ft. The skin is used for gloves etc.

CHAMPAGNE
[shȧ(ng)-pan'-yĕ] Prov. of Fr. before the Revolution, now comprising the depts. of Seine-et-Marne, Aube, Marne, Ardennes and Haute-Marne. The chief towns are Reims and Troyes. **Champagne** [sham-pān'] White sparkling wine produced from blended wines and grapes grown in the Champagne district of Fr. Fermentation takes place after the bottle has been sealed, hence the effervescence.

CHAMPLAIN
[shȧ(ng)-pla(ng)] Lake in the U.S.A. and Canada, between Vermont and New York States, discovered by the Fr. explorer Samuel de Champlain in 1609.

CHANCELLOR
Name of several high officials. The chanc. in Eng. became important about the time of Edward I, when he took the place of the justiciar as the chief min. When his duties were confined to legal matters he became Lord High Chanc. The exchequer had a chanc., at first a subsidiary official under the Lord High Treasurer. Other chancs. are those of the Duchies of Lancaster and Cornwall. The Chanc. of a Brit. Univ. is usually a man of distinction in public life, while its vice-chancellor is the acting head. **Chancery.** Court of the Lord Chanc. dating from the time of Edward the Confessor. In 1873 the court was made 1 of the present 3 divisions of the High Court of Justice. It has jurisdiction over actions in which redress cannot be obtained at common law.

CHANNEL ISLANDS
Group of Islands off N.W. Fr. comprising Jersey, Guernsey (*qv.*) Alderney, Brechou, Gt. and Little Sark, Herm, Jethou and Lihou. Formerly part of the Duchy of Normandy, they have been attached to Eng. since the Conquest (1066). They have a mild climate and fertile soil. Early flowers, fruit and vegetables are grown. Guernsey and Jersey cattle are famous. The chief towns are St. Helier (Jersey), St. Peter Port (Guernsey), and St. Anne's (Alderney). Fr. is the official language. Area: 75 sq.m. Pop. 104,398.

CHANNEL SWIMMING
The first man to swim the Eng. channel was Capt. M. Webb, an Englishman, who swam from Dover to Calais in 21 hrs. 45 mins. on Aug. 25, 1875. The first woman was Gertrude Ederle in Aug. 1926. First two-way Channel swim by Antonio Abertondo in 43 hrs. 5 mins. (1961).

CHANNEL TUNNEL
Proposed tunnel between Eng. and Fr. In 1876 a Co. was formed to carry out a similar idea, but the work was stopped in 1882. In 1930 a committee reported in favour of the project. The Govt. decided against it. New reports from Brit. and Fr. cos. were put before their respective govts. in 1964.

CHANTILLY
[shan-til'-i, shȧ(ng)-ti-yi] Town in Oise dept. Fr. 25 m. N.E. of Paris. It has a racecourse, on which the Fr. Derby is run. Pop. 5,000.

CHANTREY, Sir Francis
(1781-1841) Eng. sculptor. He left £150,000 (the **Chantrey Bequest**) which enables the Pres. and Council of the Royal Academy every year to buy pictures and sculptures for the nation.

CHAPEL
Place devoted to Christian worship. In caths. and large chs. a chapel is a part of the building railed off from the main part and provided with an altar. Places of worship in colls. and schools are also called chapels. At one time Nonconformists used the word chapel for their places of worship.

CHAPLAIN
Priest or min. officially discharging specific non-parochial duties. He may be attached to the sovereign, his representatives and defensive forces, or to institutions. There are 36 chaplains to the queen at the Eng. court, and she has chaplains in Scot. There are chaplains at schools and colls., at embassies and prisons. There are Anglican, R.C., and Free Ch. chaplains in the Brit. Navy, Army and Air Force.

CHAPLIN, Charles
(1889-) Film artist. B. London. Entered silent pictures in 1913 and formed his own Co. in 1918. He has produced many notable pictures including *The Kid, The Gold Rush, The Great Dictator, Limelight.*

CHAPMAN, George
(*c.* 1559-*c.* 1634) Eng. dramatist and poet. Continued Marlowe's *Hero and Leander* (1598); comedies, as (with Jonson and Marston) *Eastward Ho!* (1605); tragedies as *Bussy d'Ambois* (1607), *Revenge of Bussy d'Ambois* (1613). Tr. of the *Iliad* 1611, of the *Odyssey*, 1614-15.

CHAPTER
Permanent body of canons and prebendaries of a cath. or collegiate ch. presided over by the dean. It meets in the **Chapter House.**

CHAR
(*Salmo alphinus*) Salmon-like fish which frequents Eng. lakes and lochs in Scot. and Ireland. It is valued as a table fish.

CHARCOAL
Residue obtained when carbonaceous material of animal or vegetable origin is burnt or heated to remove volatiles. Wood charcoal, an impure, amorphous form of carbon containing at least 93 %, is a porous solid which, when burned as fuel, is flameless and smokeless. It is an ingredient in gunpowder, and serves also as a filter.

CHARLEMAGNE
[-mān] (*c.* 742-814) Frankish king, later Emperor. Elder son of King Pepin, in 771, he became King of all the Franks. He waged war successfully against the Saxons, Lombards and Magyars, less successfully against the Saracens in Spain. He was crowned in 800, at Rome, as the 1st 'Holy Rom. Emperor'. His *Life* was written by his friend and sec., Einhard.

CHARLEROI
[sharl-rwà'] Industrial town in Hainaut prov. Belgium, 22 m. E. of Mons, connected by canal with Brussels and N. Fr. Pop. 27,400.

CHARLES
Name of 7 rulers of the Holy Rom. Emp. The 1st was Charles the Great or **Charlemagne** (*q.v.*). The 2nd, his grandson, **Charles the Bald.** He obtained the W. part of the Frankish realm in 843. **Charles IV** (d. 1378) was also recognised as king in Germany and in 1355 was crowned emperor. **Charles VI (1685-1740)** was a son of Leopold I. In 1711 he succeeded his brother Joseph as Emperor (Maria Theresa (*q.v.*), was his daughter).

CHARLES
(1433-77) Last Duke of Burgundy, called the Bold. Son of Philip the Good, Duke of Burgundy. He waged war against the Fr. kings.

CHARLES V
(1500-58) Holy Rom. Emperor and King of Spain. B. Ghent, the elder son of Philip, son of the Emperor Maximilian, and Joanna, daughter of Ferdinand and Isabella of Sp. Became Emperor, 1520, the most powerful ruler in Europe. He crushed Francis of Fr. and once imprisoned the Pope. After attempts to reconcile the bitterness of the Reformation in Germany, he broke the power of the German princes. Abdicated 1556, leaving Spain to his son Philip II (*q.v.*). Don John, the hero of Lepanto, was an illegitimate son.

CHARLES
Name of 10 kings of Fr. The Emperor **Charlemagne** (*q.v.*), was the 1st and the Emperor **Charles the Fat** the 2nd. **Charles VI** reigned 1380-1422. In his reign, Henry V of Eng. conquered Fr. and succeeded Charles as king. **Charles VII,** d. 1464, was crowned king after the victories of Joan of Arc in 1439. **Charles VIII,** d. 1498, a son of Louis XI, became king in 1483. He tried to get possession of Naples and other parts of Italy. **Charles X** (1757-1836) was a brother of Louis XVI, and reigned from 1824-30, when he abdicated.

CHARLES
Name of 4 kings of Spain. **Charles II,** a son of Philip IV, was king 1665-1700. On his d. without heirs, a European war broke out for possession of his empire. **Charles III,** a son of Philip V, was king 1759-88. He was the 3rd of the Bourbon kings of Spain.

CHARLES
Name of 15 kings of Sweden. **Charles XII** (1682-1718) He defeated the Danes and Russians and made himself master of Poland and Saxony. In 1708 he invaded Russia, but in 1709 was routed at Poltava by Peter the Great. He was killed while attacking a fortress in Norway. In the reign of **Charles XIII,** Norway was united to Sweden. He d. 1818, having recognised the Fr. Marshal Bernadotte as his heir. **Charles XIV** (1764-1844) King of Sweden and Norway. B. **Jean Baptiste Jules Bernadotte,** he became a gen. in the Fr. army, attracting the notice of Napoleon. In 1810 he was offered the Swedish throne, and became king in 1818. The present royal family is descended from him.

CHARLES
(1771-1847) Aust. prince and soldier, younger son of the Emperor Leopold II. He won several victories over the Fr. 1796-9, but was defeated 1799, in Switzerland. In 1809 he defeated Napoleon at Aspern.

CHARLES
(1887-1922) Last emperor of Austria-Hungary. The murder of the Archduke Francis Ferdinand in June, 1914, made him heir and, on the d. of Francis Joseph in Nov. 1916, he succeeded. He abdicated at the end of World War I.

CHARLES I
(1600-49) King of Gt. Brit. and Ireland, 2nd son of James VI of Scot. (I of Brit.). In 1625 he became King and mar. Henrietta Maria, a Fr. R.C. princess. His wife's religion, his friends, extravagance and obstinacy and his attempts to force episcopacy on Scot. made him unpopular. From 1629-40 he ruled without Parl., raising money illegally. In 1642 civil war broke out and after defeat at Naseby, Charles gave himself up to the Scots. who handed him over to Parl. He was tried and beheaded.

CHARLES II
(1630-85) King of Gt. Brit. and Ireland, 2nd son of Charles I. Went into exile, 1646, on his father's defeat. In 1650, accepted the throne of Scot. and invaded Eng., was defeated and went again into exile. Issued the Declaration of Breda (1660) and returned to Brit. as king. He is remembered for his mistresses and his interest in art and science. Events included the Great Plague, and Fire of London.

CHARLES
Philip Arthur George, Prince of Wales, Duke of Cornwall and Duke of Rothesay (1948-). Son of H.M. Queen Elizabeth II and Prince Philip, Duke of Edinburgh. Invested Prince of Wales at Caernarvon Castle, 1969.

CHARLES EDWARD
(1720-88) Called **'Bonnie Prince Charlie.'** Stewart prince, known as the 'Young Pretender', and, to the Jacobites, as Charles III. Elder son of James Edward, the 'Old Pretender'. His attempt to recover the throne in 1745 failed, ending with defeat at Culloden.

CHARLES MARTEL
(*c.* 689-741) Frankish prince, son of Pepin, he became a soldier and real ruler of the Frankish kingdom, which he enlarged by conquest. In 732 he defeated the Saracens at Tours.

CHARLOCK
(Wild mustard, *Sinapsis arvensis*). Cruciferous

plant of the cabbage family. It is an annual, *c.* 2 ft. high with bright yellow 4-petalled flowers.

CHARLOTTETOWN
Seaport and cap. of Prince Edward Is., Canada. Pop. 17,956.

CHARTISM
Polit. movement of the 19th cent. In 1838 an organisation of reformers in London put forward a charter which contained 6 suggested Parl. reforms. Called Chartists, the advocates of these ideas soon became a powerful body. In 1840 they presented a petition to the House of Commons signed by over a million persons. There were riots in 1841 and 1842. 1849, the meeting at Kennington Common was a failure and a petition with 2,000,000 signatures was discredited. During the next 60 years, 4 of the 6 reforms were introd.

CHARTRES
[shartr] Cap. of Eure-et-Loir dept., Fr., 55 m. S.W. of Paris. The 13th cent. cath. is famous. Pop. 28,750.

CHARTREUSE
[shar-tröz'] Liqueur, made by a secret process from sweetened spirit mixed with extracts of various herbs. It was prepared orig. at the Grande Chartreuse Monastery near Grenoble.

CHATEAUBRIAND, François René Vicomte de (1768-1848) Fr. writer. In London as an emigré 1793-1800; diplomatist (ambassador in London 1822); d. Paris. He wrote *Essais sur les Révolutions* (1797); *Le Génie du Christianisme* (1802); *Atala* (1801) and *René* (1805); *Mémoires d'Outre-Tombe* (1848-50).

CHATHAM
Seaport, naval base and borough of Kent, on the Medway. There are barracks, arsenals, docks and shipyards. With Rochester it returns 1 member to Parl. Pop. 49,520.

CHATHAM, 1st Earl of William Pitt (1708-78) Brit. statesman. Entered Parl. in 1735 as a Whig, becoming an opponent of Walpole. From 1756, he was largely responsible for the policy followed during the 7 Years' War, but retired in 1761. He emerged in 1770 to denounce North's policy towards the N. Amer. colonists.

CHATTANOOGA
City of Tennessee, U.S.A. on the Tennessee River, 150 m. S.E. of Nashville, where in the Civil War, 1863, Grant defeated the Southerners. Pop. 113,000.

CHATTERTON, Thomas
(1752-70) Eng. poet. Produced what he said were writings of Rowley, 15th cent. monk, actually by himself. Came to London to make his living by lit. but sank into extreme poverty and despair, and poisoned himself.

CHAUCER, Geoffrey
(*c.* 1340-1400) Eng. poet. B. London; much employed on the king's business abroad. Controller of customs 1374; clerk of the king's works 1389. Chaucer's early work was influenced by Fr. models; he tr. *The Romaunt of the Rose*. Later he was inspired by Ital. models, as in *The House of Fame*, *The Parliament of Fowls*, and *Troilus and Criseyde*. His latest work is represented by the great unfinished cycle of 23 *Canterbury Tales*. In prose he tr. Boethius's *Consolations of Philosophy*, and wrote *The Parson's Tale*.

CHEDDAR
Village of Somerset, 2 m. S.E. of Axbridge. It is famous for its caves and its gorge. Also noted for cheese.

CHEESE
Nutritious article of food prepared from milk. With or without a lactic-ferment starter, the milk curd, or casein, is coagulated by rennet or an acid, separated from the serum or whey, and pressed into solid masses. Hard cheeses include the chief Eng. varieties, Gloucester, Stilton, Cheddar, Cheshire and Wensleydale, and also the Dutch, Canadian and Fr. Gruyère cheeses. Of soft or cream cheeses the best known is Camembert. Roquefort is made from the milk of ewes; some are made of goat's milk.

CHEETAH
(*Cynaelurus*) One of the Felidae, a cat-like carnivore. It has non-retractile, blunt claws, and catches its prey in chase. It is found in Africa, W. Asia, and India.

CHEKHOV, Anton Pavlovich
(1860-1904) Russ. author. He made a reputation as a writer of short stories and then as a dramatist. His plays include *The Seagull* (1896), *Uncle Vanya* (1899), *The Three Sisters* (1901), *The Cherry Orchard* (1904).

CHELMSFORD
City, borough and county town of Essex, 30 m. N.E. of London. Industries include corn-milling, brewing and the manufacture of wireless apparatus. Pop. 51,180.

CHELSEA
Borough of London, N. of the Thames between Westminster and Fulham. The chief buildings are the Royal Hospital for disabled soldiers (' Chelsea pensioners ') and the old ch. Chelsea returns 1 member to Parl. Pop. 48,550.

CHELTENHAM
Borough, market town and spa of Gloucestershire near the Cotswold Hills. C. returns 1 member to Parl. Pop. 73,770.

CHEMISTRY
Science dealing with the composition of matter, the laws of chemical change, and the relation between the properties and composition of substances. The experimental work of the alchemists led to many discoveries, and, in comparatively recent times, the pure science of chemistry emerged. **Inorganic chemistry** treats of the origin, properties and changes of all elements except carbon; **mineralogical chemistry** deals with the composition of minerals and rocks, while agricultural chemistry is concerned with the problems of soils, etc. **Organic chemistry**, treats of the innumerable compounds of carbon. **Biochemistry** is a highly specialised section concerned with the chem. problems of living things. **Physical chemistry** deals with physical properties of substances in relation to chem. changes. *See* INORGANIC CHEMISTRY; ORGANIC CHEMISTRY.

CHEOPS
[kē'-ops] Gk. name of *Khufu*, 2nd Egyptian king of the 4th dynasty (*c.* 4700 B.C.).

CHEQUERS
Official residence of the P.M. of Gt. Brit. 3 m. from Princes Risborough, Bucks. Sir Arthur Lee, in 1917, presented it to the nation.

CHERBOURG
[-boorg] Port and naval station of Fr., in Manche dept. on the N. of the Cotentin Peninsula. It has large docks and shipbuilding yards. Pop. 38,200.

CHEROKEE
Race of Amer. Indians of Iroquoian lineage, in the S. Allegheny Mts. Became U.S. citizens in 1906.

CHERRY
Tree of the rose family. A native of Europe and Asia, there are wild and cultivated varieties. **Cherry Brandy.** Liqueur made by steeping morello cherries in brandy.

CHERVIL
Biennial plant of E. Europe and W. Asia, used as a pot-herb for flavouring.

CHERWELL
[chär'-] Eng. river which rises at Charwelton in Northants. and flows into the Thames below Oxford.

CHESAPEAKE BAY
Largest inlet on the Atlantic coast of the U.S.A. in Maryland. It is *c.* 12 m. wide at the entrance, and widens to *c.* 40. Baltimore, Portsmouth and Norfolk are on its shores.

CHESHIRE
County of N. Eng. between Derbyshire and Wales, having a coastline on the Irish Sea. Low-lying area with moorland in the extreme E., watered by the Mersey, Dee and Weaver. In the centre are salt mines. The district between the Dee and the Mersey is called the Wirral. There are numerous industries, the chief centres of which are Birkenhead, Crewe, Stockport, Stalybridge and Hyde. Chester is the county town. The county returns 15 members to Parl. (6 borough constituencies). Pop. 1,392,220.

CHESS
Game played upon a checkered board divided into 64 squares, with 32 chessmen equally apportioned between 2 opposing players. Each player is equipped, in contrasting colours, light and dark. Each piece can be moved in a way peculiar to itself. The purpose of each player is to bring the opposing king into an exposed position from which he cannot retire; this checkmate ends the game.

CHEST
or **Thorax.** Upper compartment of body. Formed by diaphragm below, chest bone or sternum in front, back bone or spinal column behind. Heart, lungs and blood vessels are most important contents.

CHESTER
City, county borough and county town of Cheshire, on the Dee 16 m. S. of Liverpool. An important port in medieval times but with the silting up of the Dee declined. The 14th cent. walls completely surround the city. There is a city cross and remains of a castle. There are some manufacturing industries. Pop. 59,030.

CHESTERFIELD
Borough and market town of Derbyshire 12 m. S. of Sheffield. It has a Gothic ch. with a twisted spire. There are engineering works, textile factories and coal mines. It returns 1 member to Parl. Pop. 68,000.

CHESTERFIELD, 4th Earl of
Philip Dormer Stanhope (1694-1773) Eng. polit. and author. To his natural son, Philip Stanhope, he addressed a series of letters of advice (pub. 1774) which Dr. Johnson harshly criticised, but Johnson was prejudiced by Chesterfield's neglect of his Dictionary.

CHESTERTON, Gilbert Keith
(1874-1936) Eng. author. Poetry, journalism (ed. *G.K.'s Weekly*). Fiction, as *The Napoleon of Notting Hill* (1904), *The Man Who was Thursday* (1908), and the 'Father Brown' detective stories 1911-35. Lit. and art criticism, as *Charles Dickens* (1906), *Blake* (1910), *The Victorian Age in Literature* (1913). Theology, as *Orthodoxy* (1909). He became an R.C. 1922.

CHESTNUT
Fruit tree allied to the beech. The sweet or Sp. chestnut is widely grown and the trees reach to 100 ft. The nuts are eaten raw, roasted, boiled or as *marrons glacés*. The chestnut which grows freely in Brit. is the **horse chestnut.**

CHEVIOT HILLS
Range of hills extending for *c.* 40 m. along the borders of Eng. and Scot. The highest point is Cheviot (2,676 ft.). The hills are suitable for sheep rearing, and a special breed, famous for its wool, is reared.

CHIANG KAI-SHEK
(1887-) Chinese polit. In 1926 he led the Nanking forces to the capture of Peking. He became Pres. of the Executive Yuan, 1935-45; Pres. of China, 1943; re-elected in 1948. Director-Gen. of the Nationalist Kuomintang Party, 1938, he led the Chinese resistance to Jap. aggression, but was unsuccessful against the Chinese communist forces under Mao Tse-tung, 1951. He withdrew his forces from the mainland to Formosa in 1949. His wife, **Madame Chiang Kai-shek** (1887-) is a distinguished sociologist. Accompanied her husband on many of his military campaigns. She did much war relief work for women, refugees and the wounded. In 1943 she toured the U.S.A. and Canada making speeches, and took a prominent part in the conferences at Delhi in 1942 and Cairo in 1943.

CHIANTI
[kē-an'-] Popular Ital. wine. Made from grapes grown on the Chianti hills in C. Italy, particularly in Tuscany.

CHICAGO
[shi-kå'-gō] City of Illinois, U.S.A. the 2nd largest in the country, on the S. shore of L. Michigan. A railway and distributing centre of great importance, with several airfields and extensive docks. The most important industry is the preparation of foodstuffs, esp. meat-packing. It is a great wheat market. C. was built on the site of Fort Dearborn, estabd. 1804. Pop. 3,550,404.

CHICHESTER
City and borough of Sussex, 70 m. S.W. of London, and 2 m. from the sea. The cath. has a detached belfry. The cattle markets are important and there is a brewing industry. Pop. 19,540.

CHICKENPOX
(or **Varicella**) Acute infectious disease commonly occurring in childhood. It is caused by a virus and characterised by eruption of successive crops of vesicles. Usually occurring in epidemics, it is a self-limiting disease, and treatment is isolation and rest in bed.

CHICKPEA
Annual leguminous plant (*Cicer arietinum*). Cultivated in India, Egypt and the Medit. basin for food, it is also called gram. The peas are ground into bread flour, parched, boiled, or given to cattle.

CHICKWEED
Name of several weeds, mostly species of *Stellaria*, *Cerastium* and *Montia*, given as food to canaries and other cage birds.

CHICORY
Plant cultivated in Brit. and other European countries. It has a long fleshy root which is used to give bitterness, colour and body to coffee.

CHIFFCHAFF
(*Phylloscopus collybita*) Small song bird allied to the wood warbler. It is a common summer visitor to Eng. esp. the S.W. It frequents woods, pools and brooks where it feeds on insects and larvae.

CHIHUAHUA
[chē-wä'-wä] Cap. of C. state, N. Mexico, centre of silver-mining region. Home of smallest breed of dog. Pop. 159,430.

CHILBLAINS
Condition resulting from spasm of arterioles and sometimes small veins resulting in formation of small raised areas, white or red in colour, which throb and itch.

CHILD
The age at which a boy or girl ceases to be a child varies in different countries. In Brit. the Children Act of 1908 fixed it at 14, although for some purposes 16. Since the early 19th cent. special laws have been passed for the protection of children. Their hours of labour have been limited by Factory Acts, while Educ. Acts have made it compulsory for them to attend school. Other laws have made cruelty to children an offence and there is a soc. for the prevention of cruelty to children. The Children Act of 1908 increased the responsibilities of parents and guardians. It estabd. special courts to try cases where juvenile offenders are concerned. Children are not allowed to buy cigarettes, nor to enter public houses. It is possible, under a law passed in 1926, for a child to be legally adopted.

CHILDREN AND YOUNG PERSONS (Harmful Publications) Act
Popularly known as the 'Horror Comics Act', this legislation, introd. 1955, aims to prevent the dissemination to children and young persons of any printed matter "which consists wholly or mainly of stories told in pictures" which portray "commission of crimes, acts of violence or cruelty, or incidents of a repulsive or horrible nature" which, as a whole would "tend to corrupt" children or young persons.

CHILE
Repub. of S. Amer. consisting of a narrow strip, *c.* 2,800 m. long and 100 m. broad, on the Pacific coast. The country may be divided into 3 regions running parallel to the coast; the coastal range, the central valley, occupied in the N. by the Atacama desert, and the Andes Cordillera. S. of the Atacama desert, the central valley is intensively cultivated; further S. there are forests and sheep pastures. The rivers rise in the Andes and flow W. to the Pacific. Agriculture is the chief industry in the central zone. Chile is the chief mining country of S. Amer. Sodium nitrate is found in the Atacama Desert. Copper, iron and coal are also produced. Santiago is the cap.; other towns are Valparaiso, Concepcion, Antofagasta and Valdivia. The majority of the people are of mixed Sp. and Indian race. Sp. is the official language, and the R.C. religion is predominant. Chile was discovered by the Sp. in the 16th cent. and remained in their possession until the war of 1810-18, when a repub. was proclaimed. Chile is gov. by a Pres. with a legislature of 45 senators and 147 deputies. Area: 286,397 sq.m. Pop. 8,750,000.

CHILE PINE
Evergreen coniferous tree native to mt. regions in S. Chile (*Araucaria imbricata*). Popularly called monkey puzzle.

CHILLI
Fruit pod of a S. Amer. herb, the capsicum. It is used to make red, or cayenne, pepper, chilli vinegar, and chilli paste.

CHILLON
[shē'-lō(ng), shi-yō(ng)] Swiss castle, on an Is. of L. Geneva. It is now famous on account of Byron's poem, *The Prisoner of Chillon.*

CHILTERN HILLS
Range of hills in Oxon and Bucks., extending in a N.E. direction *c.* 45 m. into Beds. and Herts. **Chiltern Hundreds** *See* HUNDRED.

CHIMAERA
Fish allied to Rays. Found in European seas and off the Pacific coast of N. Amer. it is *c.* 4 ft. long with a formidable head, parrot-like jaws.

CHIMBORAZO
[-rä'-zō] Mt. of Ecuador, S. Amer. An extinct volcano, it is in the W. branch of the Andes Range and is 20,577 ft. high.

CHIMPANZEE
(*Anthropopithecus troglodytes*) Popular name of the smaller of the 2 African anthropoid apes, which most resemble man. 4½ ft. high, it dwells in forests, eating fruits and vegetables, and building large nests in the trees.

CHINA
Repub. of Asia, the most populous country in the world. Besides China proper it includes Manchuria, Inner Mongolia, Taiwan, Tibet, Yunnan and Sinkiang (*qq.v.*). In the N. of China proper is the Hwang-Ho, or Yellow River. The Yangtze-Kiang, the greatest of the 3 river systems, flows through C. China, entering the E. China Sea to the N. of Shanghai. The river of the S. is the Si-Kiang. There is naturally great variety in climate in so large an area, but the monsoon is the dominating feature. Winters are cold and dry, except in the extreme S.; summers are hot and wet, except in the interior. China is essentially an agricultural and pastoral country. Irrigation and rotation of crops are extremely important. Wheat, barley, maize, millet and other cereals are grown in the N. Rice, sugar and indigo are the chief crops in the S. Cotton, hemp, jute, flax, tea and silk are also produced in great quantities. Industries have developed in recent years. Peking is the cap.; other cities are Shanghai, Tientsin, Nanking, cap. 1928-49, Chungking, Hankow, Hangchow and Wenchow. There are numerous dialects, the chief of which is Mandarin. Area: *c.* 3,691,616 sq.m. Pop. *c.* 700,000,000. China has been ruled by emperors of many different dynasties. The last of these, the Manchus, ceased to rule, 1912. For some years the govt. was conducted from Peking, but in 1927 a group of nationalists from the S. transferred the cap. to Nanking. Chiang Kai-Shek (*q.v.*) was chosen as pres. 1928, and his party, the *Kuomintang*, achieved supremacy. Following war with Japan (1937-1945) disputes arose between the Govt. and the Communists. A new Constitution was adopted, Dec. 1946, and a new Nat. Assembly elected in Nov. 1947. Chiang Kai-Shek resigned as pres. Jan. 1949, and Communist troops advanced over the country. The Nat. Govt. now controls only Taiwan (Formosa). In 1949 the Communist leader, Mao Tse-Tung, assumed control of the newly formed People's Repub. This régime is at yet not recognised by the U.S.A. Recent dialectical differences have given rise to controversy with the U.S.S.R. and in China Mao's cultural revolution is meeting opposition.

CHINAWARE
Name originally applied to fine pottery produced in China, and later to any vitreous, trans-

Three Angels at Ravenna

Detail of the hand of the Empress Theodora at Ravenna

MOSAICS

Justinian at Ravenna

Adam and Eve from the Descent into Hell at Chios

FAMOUS CHURCHES

Norway: Stave Church

Barcelona: Sagrada Familia

Paris: Notre Dame

Moscow: St Basil's

lucent ware classed as porcelain. It excludes such fabrics as Wedgwood and all other stonewares and earthenwares. As invented in China it comprises a hardpaste body of china stone and kaolin or china clay, besides china stone and lime glaze, fired at one operation. Reproduced at Meissen in 1713. Meissen methods were imitated in Vienna in 1718, and Copenhagen in 1772. The best Fr. and Eng. chinaware is an artificial porcelain made of a soft paste of frit and white clay. Bone porcelain, which contains bone ash, was introduced by Spode in 1799, and all later Eng. china is of this kind.

CHINCHILLA
S. Amer. rodent, *c.* 10 in. long, found in the Alpine zones of the Andes from Peru to Chile. It has valuable soft, grey fur.

CHIOS
[kē'-] Gk. Is. in the Aegean Sea, 8 m. from the coast of Asia Minor. Birthplace of Homer. Pop. 62,090.

CHIPMUNK
Amer. ground squirrels belonging to the genus *Tamias.* The fur on their backs is marked by alternate light and dark bands.

CHIPPENDALE, Thomas
(1718-79) Eng. furniture maker. He borrowed ideas from Fr. but gradually developed his own style. In 1754 he pub. *The Gentleman and Cabinet Maker's Director.*

CHIPPENHAM
[chip'-nam] Borough and market town of Wilts. on the Avon, 13 m. N.E. of Bath, with cattle and cheese markets; other industries are bacon curing, flour milling and engineering. Pop. 17,930.

CHISLEHURST
[chiz'-] Residential dist. formerly in Kent, now in Greater London (1964). Beneath it are immense caves, open to the public. Pop. (U.D.) 88,560.

CHLORATES
Salts formed by the action of chloric acid upon bases. Potassium chlorate is used in medicine, also in the manufacture of fireworks, matches and detonators.

CHLORINE
Chem. sym. Cl. Greenish gaseous element, obtained from chlorides by electrolysis. Discovered by Scheele in 1774. It combines with most of the elements, forming chlorides, chlorates and hypochlorites. Its density is 2·5 times that of air.

CHLORODYNE
[klō'-rō-dīn] Tincture of chloroform and morphia with hydrocyanic acid and flavouring substances, used to promote sleep. This should be used with great care as it is habit-forming.

CHLOROFORM
(trichloromethane) Heavy colourless liquid with an agreeable odour and sweet taste. It is prepared by the action of bleaching powder upon alcohol or acetone, purified with sulphuric acid. It is a solvent of most resins, alkaloids and rubber. Once much used as an anaesthetic.

CHLOROPHYLL
[klo'-rō-fil] Green colouring matter of plants, extracted by ether or alcohol. It contains green and yellow pigments and chemically is related to the colouring matter of the blood.

CHOCOLATE
Preparation from the cacao bean and sugar. First sold in London in 1657. Acceptable chocolate for eating began to be made after the invention, in 1828, of the cocoa press, which enabled cocoa butter to be used for manufacture of chocolate. Milk chocolate contains in addition the solids of milk. In the 20th cent. chocolate became enormously popular.

CHOLERA
[kol'-er-ă] Acute infective disease caused by cholera vibrio and characterised by severe diarrhoea, muscular cramps, and rapid collapse. Epidemic in tropics usually occurring in autumn and attacking all ages.

CHOPIN, Frédéric François
[shō-pa(ng)] (1810-49) Polish composer and pianist. He settled in Paris in 1831. His first works for piano were pub. in 1832. He d. from consumption of the throat at the age of 38. He greatly extended the technical and expressive range of the pianoforte.

CHOREA
[kaw-rē'-] or **St. Vitus' Dance.** Disease most commonly found in children, characterised by irregular involuntary movements of any part of body. Cause unknown but closely assoc. with acute rheumatic heart disease.

CHOU EN-LAI
[choo'-en-lī] (1898-) Chinese statesman. He received a Western educ. at Tientsin. After the student riots of 1919 he was sent to prison. In Paris in 1921 took part in forming the first branch of the Chinese Communist Party abroad. In 1931 he joined the Red army in China and became vice-chairman of the Revolutionary Military Council, working with Mao Tse-tung. During the struggle against Japan he held office under Chiang Kai-shek in Chungking (1938-40). In 1949 Chou En-lai became Premier and Foreign Min. of the first all-China Communist govt. under Mao Tse-tung.

CHOUGH
[chuf] Bird of Crow family. It has red legs and glossy black plumage and is found in many parts of the Old World. The Cornish Chough, with its red curved beak, is now rare in Eng. but still lives in Europe and N. Africa.

CHOW CHOW
A type of dog which originated in China. It is unique because of its blue tongue. Red is usual colour, but there are also black, white, blue and cream varieties. With two coats, the dog is strong and compact.

CHRIST
Gk. name meaning 'the anointed'. *See* JESUS CHRIST.

CHRISTCHURCH
Borough of Hants. at the confluence of the Avon and Stour, 104 m. from London, with famous ch. Pop. 26,640.

CHRISTCHURCH
City of South Is. New Zealand, on the E. coast. Founded, 1850, by the Canterbury Assoc. of London, it is the market for the wool and meat of the C. plains. Pop. 232,700.

CHRISTIAN
Name of 10 kings of Denmark. **Christian IV** (1577-1648), who was King of Denmark and Norway, founded Christiania. **Christian X** (1870-1947) became king in 1912. During World War II he was virtually a prisoner of the Germans.

CHRISTIAN ERA
Era now almost universally employed in Christian countries to compute hist. dates, etc. It is supposed to begin with the year of the birth of Christ, but most N.T. scholars are of the opinion that Christ was born in 4 B.C. The era as now estabd. is computed from Jan. 1 in the 4th year of the 194th Olympiad, and the 753rd year from the building of Rome. Time before Christ is indicated by the letters B.C. (Before Christ); that after Christ by the letters A.D. (*Anno Domini*: in the year of our Lord).

CHRISTIAN SCIENCE
Religion founded by **Mary Baker Eddy** (*q.v.*).

CHRISTIANITY
Universal religion, originating in the life and

teachings of Jesus of Nazareth. He was a village carpenter, brought up in an atmosphere of Jewish ethical monotheism, and was crucified as a polit. malefactor. The Galilean disciples became the apostles of a movement which Paul of Tarsus, interpreted to the Greco-Rom. world. The story of Jesus and the apostolic age enshrined in the N.T. with the Heb. O.T. formed the potent scriptures of the new religion. The foundation of the emp. at Constantinople by Constantine in the 4th cent. coincided with the beginning of State recognition. In the 16th cent. growing demands for intellectual freedom introduced the Protestant Reformation. Something like a third of the inhabitants of the world own a nominal adherence to Christianity. Its largest branch, the R.C. Ch., numbers *c.* 550,357,000; the Gk. or E. Ch. 144,000,000, and the various Protestant communions 207,000,000.

CHRISTINA
(1626-89) Queen of Sweden. Only child of Gustavus Adolphus, as a minor she succeeded him on the throne in 1632. She assumed govt. in 1644. She had little polit. capacity and abdicated, 1654.

CHRISTMAS
Annual festival celebrating the birth of Jesus Christ, kept by most of the Churches in Christendom on Dec. 25, since *c.* 400. Dec. 25, or Christmas Day, and also the day following, called Boxing Day, are bank holidays; Christmas Day is also a quarter day in Eng. and Ireland.

CHRISTMAS
Name of 2 Brit. Is. One is in the Indian Ocean, 190 m. S. of Java. Annexed by Brit. in 1889, it became Austral. territory in 1958. The other is a large atoll in the Pacific Ocean, part of the Gilbert and Ellice Is. colony (*q.v.*), discovered by James Cook in 1777. Developed, with airstrip, roads, etc. for use as a test ground for Brit. nuclear weapons 1957-64. Area: 64 sq.m. Pop. 479.

CHRISTMAS ROSE
(*Helleborus niger*) Hardy perennial of the family Ranunculaceae, it has white blossoms. Varieties of *H. orientalis*, known as Lenten roses, have flowers of white, crimson and rose.

CHRIST'S THORN
(*Paliurus asculeatus*) Small thorny shrub with small, shining ovate leaves and yellowish-green flowers. It is common in S.E. Europe and Asia Minor.

CHROMITE
A black or brownish-black mineral composed of the chromates of iron, alumina and magnesia, and used as the chief ore of the metal chromium. **Chromium.** Metallic element, at. wt. 52·01, sym. Cr. A hard steel-grey metal, with high melting point, non-magnetic and resistant to corrosion by ordinary atmospheric agents. Readily alloys with other metals and its addition to steel gives great hardness.

CHROMOSPHERE
Rose-coloured gaseous envelope outside the photosphere or incandescent surface of the sun. The chromosphere, at least 5,000 m. thick, with irregular prominences, contains notably helium, hydrogen and calcium.

CHRONICLES
Two books of the O.T. which formed one book in the Hebrew canon, in which it is placed last. The book forms three parts: (1) genealogical tables; (2) the history of the reigns of David and Solomon; (3) the history of the kingdom of Judah from the separation under Rehoboam to the Babylonian captivity.

CHRYSANTHEMUM
Ornamental flower of the family Compositae. A hardy plant with both perennial and annual species, it came from China.

CHRYSOLITE
The yellow or green transparent forms of the mineral olivine, a silicate of magnesia and iron, and found in tabular crystals in igneous rocks.

CHUB
(*Leuciscus cephalus*) Fish of the same genus as Roach. Common in Eng. and other European countries, it often attains a length of 2 ft. and a wt. of 5-7 lbs.

CHUNGKING
City and commercial centre of Szechwan prov., China, and seat of govt. from 1937-46, in a remote area of W. China at the confluence of the Yangtze Kiang and Kialin Kiang. Pop. 2,121,000.

CHURCH ARMY
Relig. and philanthropic organisation, founded 1882, by the **Rev. Wilson Carlile** to spread the teaching of the C. of E. among the outcasts of Westminster and to estab. philanthropic and other organisations.

CHURCH ASSEMBLY
(or **National Assembly**) A body estabd. by Parl. 1919. Consists of a House of bishops, House of clergy, and House of laity. Has power to legislate concerning the C. of E.

CHURCH LADS' BRIGADE
Founded 1891 by **Col. Walter Mallock Gee.** Organisation on semi-milit. lines for the training of boys assoc. with the C. of E. It instils a regard for religion, health, good-fellowship and good citizenship.

CHURCHILL, Sir Winston Leonard Spencer
(1874-1965) Eng. statesman. M.P. (Cons.) 1900-6, (Lib.) 1906-22, (Cons.) 1924-64; Colonial Under-Sec. 1905-8; Home Sec. 1910-11; 1st Lord of the Admiralty, 1911-15; Munitions Min. 1917-18; War. Sec. 1919-21; Chanc. of the Exchequer, 1924-9; 1st Lord of the Admiralty, 1939-40; P.M. and Defence Min. 1940-45; Leader of the Opposition, 1945-51. P.M. 1951-55. In 1906 he left the Unionist Party over the question of Tariff Reform, returning in 1924, having been a successful Lib. min. During the '30's he gave constant warning of the German menace. In 1939 he returned to the Admiralty. On the development of the German W. offensive of 1940 and the Dunkirk Evacuation the Chamberlain Govt. was replaced by a Coalition under Churchill. He rallied the nation and led it to victory over Germany and Japan. Created K.G. April, 1953. He has written many books, these include *Lord Randolph Churchill* (1906); *Marlborough*, 4 vols. (1933-38); 6 vols. on World War II; and several vols. of speeches. Also *A History of the English-Speaking Peoples*, in 4 vols. pub. 1956-58. Awarded the Nobel Prize for literature (1953). U.S. Hon.-Citizen, 1963. Buried at Bladon, Oxon., after State funeral.

CIBBER, Colley
[sib'-] (1671-1757) Eng. playwright. He wrote some 30 plays, mostly comedies: *Love's Last Shift* (1696), *The Provoked Husband* (1728). Made poet laureate, 1730.

CICADA
[si-kā'- or si-kȧ'-] Large winged insect found in the tropics and noted for its long life. It is also famous for the loud shrill call of the males produced by muscle fibres inserted into a stiff membrane.

CICELY
[sis'-i-li] Perennial umbelliferous plant (*Myrrhis odorata*). The sweet cicely is native to Brit. growing 2-3 ft. high in mt. pastures, and used as a pot-herb.

CICERO, Marcus Tullius
[sis'-] (106-43 B.C.) Rom. orator, statesman and philosopher. He studied oratory in Greece and in 77 B.C. entered public life in Rome. Consul 63 B.C., crushing Cataline's conspiracy.

Supported Pompey in the Civil War. Denounced Antony after Caesar's murder and was proscribed and killed on Antony's orders. His writings founded a prose style used for 2,000 years.

CID, Roderigo Diaz de Bivar
[sēd, thēd] (*c.* 1040-99) Sp. nat. hero. Became a soldier of fortune and estabd. himself as a practically indep. ruler at Valencia. D. defending the city against the Moors.

CIDER
Fermented juice of apples. After fermentation in open casks it is filtered and freed from impurities. It may contain from 4 to 7 % of alcohol. In Eng. cider is made in Devon, Somerset, Herefordshire and Kent; also in Normandy and Brittany.

CIMABUE, Giovanni
[chima-boo′-ā] (*c.* 1240-1301) Ital. artist, b. Florence. Founder of the Florentine school, Giotto was his pupil.

CINCHONA
[sin-kō′-] Genus of rubiaceous evergreen trees, valuable for the medicinal qualities of the bark which contains quinine and other alkaloids.

CINCINNATI
[sinsi-nat′-i] City of Ohio, U.S.A. on the Ohio River, connected with Newport and Covington on the Kentucky bank. A centre of land, water and air routes, it is a manufacturing town, producing soap, machine tools, clothing and radios. There is a univ. Pop. 502,550.

CINEMATOGRAPHY
The art of photographing a moving object and projecting upon a screen a series of pictures in rapid sequence, giving an appearance of movement of the object. Edison, in 1889, demonstrated his kinetoscope, made possible by the use of a new photographic film. From this instrument, gradually evolved the modern apparatus. In 1928 the use of photo-electric apparatus made possible the reproduction of sound. The first experiments in colour were made in 1906. Much research has been done on stereoscopic film in the U.S. and Russia. The use of motion pictures has brought about special techniques in production different from those of the theatre. Apart from its use for recreation, the film has an important educ. and scientific value. The world's centre for film making is Hollywood, a suburb of Los Angeles in Calif.

CINERARIA
Flowering plant, 2 species of *Senecio* are cultivated, *S. cineraria* in the garden and *S. cruentus* in the greenhouse.

CINNABAR
HgS. Sulphide of mercury, the main source of mercury. It is mined in Spain, Italy, Hungary, California, Mexico, China and Peru.

CINNAMON
Inner bark of an evergreen tree, used as a spice in cooking and medicinally. The best cinnamon grows in Ceylon, where the bark is thin and smooth.

CINQUE PORTS
[sink] Group of seaports on the coast of Kent and Sussex, orig. Dover, Sandwich, Hastings, Romney and Hythe. Later Winchelsea and Rye were added. They were given certain privileges, retained until 1835, in return for supplying the king with ships in time of war.

CIRCLE
Closed curve which is everywhere at a constant distance from its fixed central pt. The linear relation of circum. to diam. is denoted by the sym. π and is 3·14159. The circumference of a circle is equal to π times its diameter. The area of a circle of radius R is πR^2. *See* Pi.

CIRCUMCISION
Religious rite. Performed on boys, usually in infancy, the foreskin being cut. It is practised by the Jews, Mohammedans and certain savage peoples for reasons of hygiene and has religious significance.

CIRCUMNAVIGATORS
Early navigators who sailed round the world. Magellan (*q.v.*) a Portuguese in the service of Spain, headed the first expedition round the globe. He was killed in the Philippine Is. in April 1521, Juan Sebastian del Cano continuing the voyage and reaching San Lucar in Sept. 1522. The principal early circumnavigators after Magellan, were Grijalva and Alvaradi (Sp.), 1537; Drake (Eng.), 1577-80; Cavendish, 1586-8; Le Maire (Dutch), 1615-17; Tasman (Dutch), 1642; Dampier, 1689; Cooke, 1708; Anson, 1740-4; Bougainville, 1766-9; Cook, 1768-71.

CIRCUS
Roman place of amusement, at first used for chariot races. The largest was the famous Circus Maximus at Rome, nearly 2,000 ft. long. In 18th cent. Eng. the chief attractions of the circus were feats of horsemanship; later acrobats and clowns were introduced. Astley's, which became Sanger's, Hengler's and Barnum's were notable.

CIRENCESTER
[sī′-ren-sester, *or* sis′-iter] Market town and urban district of Gloucs. 21 m. from Cheltenham. The chief industries are brewing, and bacon-curing. Pop. 12,600.

CIRRHOSIS
[si-rō′-] Replacement of specialised tissue cells by fibrous tissue. Cause unknown, but it is a reaction to disease process of bacterial or chem. origin.

CITRIC ACID
[sit-] Constituent of many fruit juices ($C_6H_8O_7$), esp. lemons. Readily soluble in water, it is used as an antidote for scurvy.

CITRON
[sit′-] Fruit of the citron tree, *Citrus medica.* The smooth-stemmed tree, with oval leaves, is cultivated in the Medit. basin, the W. Indies and elsewhere. It may grow to a ht. of 15 ft. and yields a large fruit whose rind is esteemed for candying.

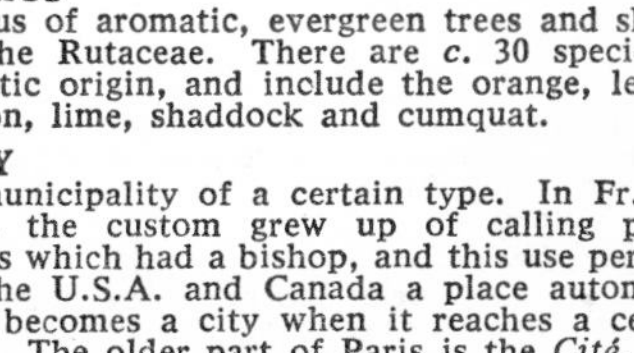

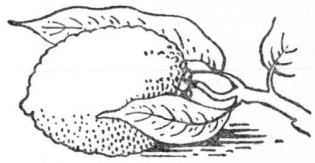

CITRUS
Genus of aromatic, evergreen trees and shrubs of the Rutaceae. There are *c.* 30 species of Asiatic origin, and include the orange, lemon, citron, lime, shaddock and cumquat.

CITY
A municipality of a certain type. In Fr. and Eng. the custom grew up of calling places cities which had a bishop, and this use persists. In the U.S.A. and Canada a place automatically becomes a city when it reaches a certain pop. The older part of Paris is the *Cité.* **The City.** Name applied to the business section of the City of London (*q.v.*).

CIUDAD TRUJILLO
[sew-dad′ troo-hē′-yō] *See* Santo Domingo.

CIVET
Fat musky substance from the perineal glands of Civet Cats (*Viverra*).

CIVIL DEFENCE
Organisation comprised of members of the civilian pop. to learn and co-ordinate protective measures against attack in wartime. In Gt. Brit. Civil Defence was estabd. under the Min. of Home Security in 1941, to support Air Raid Precautions set up by local authorities in 1937. The force was demobilised in 1945, but in 1949 recruiting was recommenced; a civil defence staff college and schools for instructors give leisure-time training in the principal features of modern warfare, esp. nuclear attack.

CIVIL LIST
Name given to the annual payments made to the sovereign and other members of the royal family. The civil list of H.M. the Queen amounts to £475,000. **Civil list pensions** are pensions granted to persons distinguished in science, art and lit. or their dependents.

CIVIL WAR
War between people of the same state or community. In Eng. hist. the name is usually applied to the struggle, from 1642-9, between Charles I and his supporters and Cromwell's Parliamentarians. In the Amer. Civil War (1861-5), the S. States fought to estab. a union separate from the N. States.

CLACKMANNANSHIRE
Smallest county of Scot. between the Firth of Forth and Perthshire. Its chief rivers are the Devon and Black Devon; in the N. are the Ochil Hills. Clackmannan is the county town; other places are Alloa, the admin. centre, Dollar, Alva and Tillicoultry. With E. Stirlingshire, C. returns 1 member to Parl. Pop. 41,636.

CLAM
Bivalve mollusc, found in the Atlantic off both the Amer. and European shores, it inhabits muddy regions close to the shore. It is a food, esp. in the U.S.A.

CLAN
Social group recognising a common ancestry. It was most developed in Scot. where in the Highlands and Is. the country was divided among the various clans. Each clan has its tartan and badge, which are worn ceremoniously today. The system decayed after the Jacobite defeats of 1715 and '45, and changing economic conditions.

CLARE
County of W. Eire in the prov. of Munster, having a long Atlantic coastline. The Shannon and its mouth form the N. and S. boundary. Much of Clare is lowland, with fringing mt. ranges. Lead and slate are worked. Ennis is the county town; Ardnacrusha, Kilrush and Killaloe are others. Pop. 73,702.

CLARE, John
(1793-1864) Eng. poet. Pub. *Poems descriptive of Rural Life and Scenery* (1820), *The Shepherd's Calendar* (1827), *The Rural Muse* (1835). He lost his reason 1837; d. in the Northampton County Asylum.

CLARENCE HOUSE
Royal mansion in London. Originally part of St. James's Palace, it was remodelled by John Nash, 1825-7. The official residence of the Queen Mother.

CLARENDON
Village of Wilts. near Salisbury, the home of the early Eng. kings. The Constitutions of Clarendon were issued in the 12th cent. These were intended to curb the privileges of the clergy, but Henry II withdrew them after the murder of Becket.

CLARENDON, 1st Earl of
Edward Hyde (1609-74) Eng. statesman and historian. In exile with Prince Charles. In 1661, after the Restoration, he was created Earl, and Lord Chanc. He wrote his *History of the Great Rebellion* during his exile. **Clarendon Code.** Four laws passed between 1661-5, while the Earl of Clarendon was chief adviser of Charles II, to strengthen the position of the C. of E. (1) **The Corporation Act** of 1661; (2) **The Act of Uniformity** of 1662; (3) **The Conventicle Act** of 1664; (4) **The Five Mile Act.**

CLARET
Eng. name for the red wines of Bordeaux; from *c.* 60 vineyards in the Médoc district of the Gironde.

CLARINET
A woodwind instrument with a single reed: invented later than the other orchestral woodwind, it did not estab. its place in the orchestra until after the middle of the 18th cent.

CLARK, Mark Wayne
(1896-) Amer. Gen. Educ. U.S. Milit. Acad. 1917; graduated Army War Coll. 1937. C.-in-C. Ground Forces in Europe, July, 1942; Comdr. 5th Army in invasion of Italy, 1943-4; Commanding Gen. 15th Army Group, Dec. 1944; Commanding Gen. U.S. Forces in Austria, July, 1945. Succeeded Gen. Ridgeway as U.N. Supreme Commander, Korea, 1952.

CLAUDE LORRAIN
Fr. landscape painter (1600-82). B. in Lorraine. His landscapes are in the Ital. classical tradition, and have beautiful light and cloud effects.

CLAUDEL, Paul
(1868-1955) Fr. dramatist and poet. B. Champagne. His work is Symbolist (*q.v.*); it includes *Partage de Midi* (1906); *L'Echange* (1893); odes and other poems, and crit. essays.

CLAUDIUS
(10 B.C.-A.D. 54) Rom. Emperor. Nephew of Tiberius, he was proclaimed Emperor by the praetorian guards on the murder of Caligula in 41. He was much under the influence of Messalina his wife. On her execution he mar. his niece Agrippina who poisoned him to ensure the throne for her son, Nero.

CLAUSEWITZ, Karl von
[klow'-zē-vitz] (1780-1831) Pruss. gen. In Pruss. service, he fought in the Waterloo campaign.

CLAUSTROPHOBIA
Type of anxiety neurosis in which the predominant feature is a fear of enclosed spaces.

CLAVICHORD
A small oblong keyboard instrument. The strings are arranged parallel to the keyboard, and are sounded by being struck by a flat piece of metal.

CLAY
Earthy hydrous aluminium silicate. It is tenacious, plastic when wet, and when heated to 300° C. loses its plasticity irrecoverably. Of economic importance are the fireclays, pipe clays, pottery clays and clays for brick-making.

CLAYTON, Philip Thomas Byard
(1885-) *See* Toc H.

CLEFT PALATE
Congenital defect due to failure of 2 develop-

mental halves of palate to unite before birth. Operative repair and constitution of normal appearance is possible, and most successful if begun in early infancy.

CLEMATIS
Genus of hardy and half-hardy plants of climbing habit of the family Ranunculaceae. The wild clematis is called traveller's joy or old man's beard. Hybrid varieties are mostly derived from *C. viticella,* a native of S. Europe and parts of Asia, and *C. lanuginosa,* a large flowered lilac-coloured species of Chinese origin.

CLEMENCEAU, Georges Eugène Benjamin
[-ä(ng)-sō'] (1841-1929) Fr. statesman. In 1871, a member of the extreme Left, he entered the Nat. Assembly. He supported Dreyfus. Became a senator (1902), Min. of the Interior (1906), then Premier (1906-9). His ministry opposed German claims in Morocco and furthered the Entente Cordiale with Brit. In opposition until 1917, he became Premier to win the 1st World War. He presided over the peace conference at Versailles.

CLEMENT
Properly **Titus Flavius Clemens,** commonly known as *Clement of Alexandria.* Famous teacher of the Christian Ch. in the 2nd and at the beginning of the 3rd cent.

CLEOPATRA
(69-30 B.C.) Queen of Egypt. She became, in 51 B.C. joint ruler of Egypt. In 48 B.C. she was driven out, but Caesar restored her. After his d. she became the mistress of Mark Antony. This was one of the causes of the war between Antony and Octavian. After Antony's defeat and d. Cleopatra killed herself. **Cleopatra's Needles** are 2 obelisks erected at Heliopolis *c.* 1500 B.C. In 1878 one of these was brought to London and erected on the Victoria Embankment.

CLERGY
The collective term applied to ordained men as distinct from the laity. Bishops, priests and deacons date back to the time of the Apostles; minor orders of the clergy have been admitted later. In the 12th cent. the See of Rome promulgated the theory which elevated the rank of Pope to a position superior to all other bishops. **Benefit of Clergy.** An obsolete but once important feature in Eng. criminal law. Benefit of Clergy began in the 12th cent. with the claim by the eccles. authorities that every *clericus* should be exempt from the jurisdiction of temporal courts and be subject to spiritual courts alone. Abuse of the privilege was widespread. The practice was not finally abolished by statute until 1827.

CLERIHEW
A loose mock-biog. quatrain, viz.

When Alexander Pope
Accidentally trod on the soap
And came down on the back of his head—
Never mind what he said.

Invented by **Edmund Clerihew Bentley** (1875-1956) Eng. journalist.

CLERMONT-FERRAND
Industrial city, cap. of Puy-de-Dôme dept. Fr. *c.* 80 m. W. of Lyons. Its industries include the manufacture of cars, engineering machinery and textiles. There is a beautiful cath. Pop. 160,000.

CLEVELAND
Largest city of Ohio, U.S.A., on the S. shore of L. Erie, 375 m. E. of Chicago. Iron ore is brought from the Lake Superior dist. for coal from Pennsylvania, and important iron and steel industries have developed. Pop. 739,000.

CLEVELAND, Stephen Grover
(1837-1908) Amer. pres. B. New Jersey. He was twice elected to the presidency as a Democrat (1885-9, 1893-7). During his second term of office the trouble with Gt. Brit. over the boundary of Venezuela occurred.

CLIMATE
Average succession of atmospheric conditions which, regarded individually, constitute weather. These conditions embrace variations of temperature, moisture and pressure which are governed by latitude, the position relative to oceans, and local geog. conditions. The sun's ecliptic path delineates 5 climatic zones: the torrid or tropical, between the tropics $23\frac{1}{2}$° N. to $23\frac{1}{2}$° S.; the arctic, N. of the circle, $66\frac{1}{2}$° N.; the antarctic S. of the circle $66\frac{1}{2}$° S.; and the intermediate N. and S. temp. zones.

CLINTON, Sir Henry
(1738-95) C.-in-C. of the Brit. forces in the Amer. War of Indep. He played a conspicuous part in the Battle of Bunker Hill. In 1779 he took Charleston in S. Carolina. He was too late to help Cornwallis at Yorktown (1781), whose fall marked the end of the war.

CLIVE, Robert
Baron Clive of Plassey (1725-74) Eng. gen. and statesman. In 1743 went to Madras as a writer in the E. India Co. In 1751 he captured Arcot and estabd. the power of Brit. in that region. He was sent to regain Calcutta after the tragedy of the 'Black Hole' and in 1757, won his greatest victory at Plassey. He ruled the country until 1760, when he returned to Eng. In 1765-7 he was again in India as Gov. for the E. India Co. On his return, criticisms of his conduct of Indian affairs, and a threat of impeachment, drove him to suicide.

CLOCKS
The Babylonians invented the water clock, in which time was indicated by the level of a float in a vessel filled with water at a uniform rate. Mechanical clocks, with gear wheels driven by springs or weights, appeared in the 14th cent. In 1657 Huyghens added a pendulum to regulate the rate at which the gears were driven. The first accurate timekeeper was Harrison's Chronometer (1671) which included an accurate escapement for transferring the energy of the spring to the movement of the clock. Recent developments have included electric clocks and clocks controlled by radio-frequency oscillators.

CLONMEL
County town of Tipperary, Eire, on the Suir, 28 m. from Waterford. Pop. 10,640.

CLOTH
Woven fabric. The materials may be animal, vegetable or asbestos fibre and metallic wires. The manufacture of cloth, orig. a domestic industry, is now highly mechanised. Some fabrics may be moth-proofed or waterproofed during finishing.

CLOUD
Masses of minute water particles condensed by cooling air from water vapour, which float in the atmosphere. Distinguished from fog or mist by the ht. at which they occur. Clouds are classified according to the ht. at which they travel. **Cirrus** and **Cirro-stratus** clouds occur at *c.* 30,000 ft. The former consist of minute ice-specks and appear as feathery wisps, sometimes called mare's tails. **Cirro-cumulus** occur in rounded tufts; **Alto-cumulus,** are similar but larger; **Alto-stratus,** are heavy, grey Cirro-stratus clouds. All 3 are found between 10,000-24,000 ft. **Strato-cumulus** (up to 7,000 ft.), are dull, grey clouds, producing heavy skies, but not necessarily rain. **Nimbus** clouds are dark, shapeless rain clouds, at a similar height. The **Cumulus** and **Cumulo-nimbus** are produced by diurnal ascending currents. The former have a flat base at *c.* 4,500 ft., while the upper dome-shaped part reaches *c.* 6,500 ft. Cumulo-nimbus often extend as high as 20,500 ft. Heavy rain showers and thunder

often accompany them. **Stratus** clouds, below 3,500 ft., appear as a horizontal layer of mist.

CLOUDBERRY
(*Rubus chamaemorus*) Species of wild berry resembling a mulberry. The plant has rough, erect stems *c.* 8 in. high. The fruit is orange-yellow and slightly acid. Found in N. Europe and other cold regions.

CLOUGH, Arthur Hugh
(1819-61) Eng. poet. He pub. *The Bothie of Toper-na-Fuosich* in Eng. hexameters and (1849, with Thomas Burbridge) *Ambarvalia*, and had written *Dipsychus*; *Amours de Voyage*, pub. in Amer. 1858.

CLOVE
(*Eugenia carophyllata*) Pungent aromatic spice, the dried bud of an evergreen shrub of the family Myrtaceae. The volatile oil of cloves is used medicinally. Supplies come from Zanzibar and the W. and E. Indies.

CLOVER
Genus of leguminous herbs (*Trifolium*) native to N. temp. regions. Of the 170 species 18 are native to Brit. Several are cultivated for fodder, esp. red. *T. pratense;* white or Dutch, *T. repens*, crimson or Ital., *T. incarnatum*; and alsike or Swedish, *T. hybridum*. Important in the rotation of crops as they add nitrogen to the soil.

CLOVIS
(466-511) Frankish king. A son of Childeric I, he was the founder of the Frankish realm, of which he made Paris the cap.

CLUB FOOT
(or **Talipes**) Usually a congenital deformity affecting the ankle and foot. In early cases much can be done by orthopaedic manipulations, but in advanced cases orthopaedic surgery gives good results.

CLUNY
[kloo-] Town in Saône-et-Loire dept., E. Fr., 12 m. from Mâcon, where, in 910, a Benedictine abbey was founded.

CLYDESDALE
Valley of the Clyde, a district in Lanarkshire. It is fertile, famous for its orchards and tomato-growing, and a breed of cart-horses.

COAL
Carbonaceous material forming stratified deposits in the earth. It represents the remains of ancient land vegetation which has undergone slow chem. change, reducing the oxygen and increasing the carbon content up to 75-90 %. Common coal is black, and contains 75-85 % of carbon. Steam coals are less bituminous, burn well with a large flame and little smoke. Anthracite, the most mineralised of coals, consists almost entirely of carbon. There are believed to be enormous deposits untouched in Canada, S. Africa, China, Japan and elsewhere. Coal has been worked in Eng. since Rom. times, but it was not until end 18th cent. that it became the basis of Brit. industry. At that time, output was 10,000,000 t.; in 1949 *c.* 215,124,000 t.; in 1962 *c.* 197,425,000 t. In 1946 the Coal Industry Nationalisation Act received the Royal Assent and the Nat. Coal Board was instituted, 1946, to administer the nationally-owned mines. **Coal-gas** is obtained as one of the products when coal is heated to about 1,000° C. in the absence of air. The illuminosity is due to the ethylene, and all of the components, except nitrogen, are readily inflammable. Coal gas usually has a calorific value of about 500 Brit. Thermal Units per cub. ft. When coal is distilled, volatile products evolve, leaving coke. Coal-gas and coal-tar are 2 of these. **Coal-Tar.** Dark, viscid oil. Benzol is obtained up to 140° C. Two more redistillations, up to 170° C. produce solvent and burning naptha. From 170°-230° naphthalene and carbolic acid are given. From 230°-270°, creosote oil and lubricating oil are formed, and later, anthracene oil, anthracene, lamp-black, pitch and coke. These are used largely in the making of drugs, perfumes, explosives, dyes, disinfectants, and fuel for internal combustion engines.

COALITION
In politics, a working arrangement between two or more parties, made either to carry on the govt. or to challenge the party in power. In Brit. there was a coalition govt. between Fox and Lord North in 1783; in 1895 the Cons. and Lib.-Unionists formed a permanent coalition. During World War I a coalition govt. was formed under Asquith in 1915, with a successor under Lloyd George, 1916-22. The Churchill Govt. of 1940-5 was another.

COATBRIDGE
Burgh of Lanarkshire, 9 m. E. of Glasgow. Centre of a great iron and steel industry. With Airdrie it returns 1 member to Parl. Pop. 54,594.

COATI-MUNDI
Racoon-like mammal found in S. and C. Amer. with long body, banded tail and elongated snout.

COBALT
Mining centre of Ontario, Canada, 270 m. N. of Toronto, producing silver, cobalt and nickel. Pop. 2,367.

COBALT
Metallic element, chem. sym. Co, at. wt. 58·95. Widely distributed in assoc. with nickel, copper and arsenic. Cobalt is a greyish-white, hard, tenacious and malleable metal important in alloys and compounds. **Cobalt Steel** is used in magnets and the valves of internal combustion engines.

COBB, John
(1900-52) Brit. racing motorist. He reached a record speed of over 400 m.p.h. at Bonneville, Utah, U.S.A. in 1947.

COBBETT, William
(1762-1835) Eng. writer, soldier, farmer, journalist. Besides *Weekly Political Register* (1802-35), *Parliamentary Debates* (1803, passing to Hansard 1812) etc.; his works are: *Rural Rides* and *Advice to Young Men* (1830).

COBDEN, Richard
(1804-65) Eng. politician. M.P. (Radical), 1841-57; 1859-65. With John Bright, Cobden led the agitation against the Corn Laws culminating in their repeal in 1846.

COBRA
(*Naja*) Venomous snakes able to dilate the neck into a hood. The Indian Black Snake, *N. tripudians*, bears a binocular mark on the neck. The King Cobra, or Hamadryad (*N. bungarus*) is larger and fiercer. The African *N. haje* is the Cape Spitting Snake.

COCA
(*Erythroxylon coca*) Bolivian and Peruvian shrub of the flax order. The leaves produce a tingling sensation when chewed, followed by deadening of the sensation of hunger. The plant yields the alkaloid **cocaine.** First separated in 1860, the hydrochloride serves as a local anaesthetic in dentistry and minor operations. Even a small dose may induce the habit of taking the drug.

COCHABAMBA
City of Bolivia, at a height of 8,400 ft. An agricultural centre, it is the 2nd city of the Repub. Pop. 76,500.

COCHINEAL
[-eel'] Dye used in cooking for crimson tints. It is obtained from the female cochineal, an insect which inhabits Mexico and Peru.

COCK FIGHTING
Sport of pitting gamecocks against one another to fight; breeding and training them for the purpose. It was popular in ancient India, China and Persia, and spread to Greece and Rome. It was introduced to Eng. by the Rom. The cocks wore steel spurs from 1½ to 2½ ins. long and usually fought until one was killed. Cock fighting was abolished in Brit. by law in 1849.

COCK OF THE ROCK
(*Rupicola*) Perching birds of the chatterer family, also called Rock Manikin. The 3 species, inhabiting Peru and Ecuador have compressed semi-circular, helmet-like crests.

COCKATOO
Parrots inhabiting Australia and the Malay Archipelago. They have recurved crests which can be erected. They are usually white, tinged with yellow or red.

COCKCHAFER
(*Melolontha*) Popular name of a genus of lamellicorn beetles. The brown elytra make a whirring sound in flight. Destructive Brit. species incl. the Common Cockchafer (*M. vulgaris*). The Rose Chafer (*Cetonia aurata*) is green.

COCKCROFT, Sir John Douglas
O.M. K.C.B. F.R.S. (1897-1967) Director of the Atomic Energy Research Estab. until 1958. Chief Supt. of the Air Defence Research and Development Estab. 1941-4, and with the Nat. Research Council in Montreal, 1944-6. With E. T. S. Walton, developed in 1931 a high-voltage apparatus with which the first artificial transmutations of the elements were accomplished. Nobel Prize for Physics, 1951. O.M. 1957. First Master of Churchill Coll. Cambridge, 1960.

COCKER SPANIEL
Small variety of spaniel. Show favourite and pet. Will work well with the gun. It has pendant ears, silky coat and colours are black, golden, roan and parti. Wt. 20–25 lbs.

COCKLE
Bivalve mollusc. The typical genus, *Cardium*, has equal convex shells, heart-shaped in profile, with radial ribs and scalloped edges. The common Brit. *C. edule*, is collected from sand at low water.

COCKROACH
(*Blatta orientalis* and *Periplaneta americana*) Reddish-brown orthopterous insect, short-winged, flat-bodied, with leathery integuments and long antennae. The cockroach is voracious and odoriferous, frequenting places with warm temperature and food.

COCOA
Corruption of *cacao*, the name of a trop. tree. The seeds (cacao beans) provide the raw material from which cocoa powder and chocolate (*q.v.*) are manufactured.

COCONUT PALM
(*Cocus nucifera*) Tree of economic importance, cultivated in many trop. countries. The outer husk of the fruit furnishes coir for matting, ropes, etc. The kernel is edible, and, when dried, forms copra, the source of coconut oil used in making soap, candles and margarine.

COCOS-KEELING ISLANDS
Group of *c.* 20 coral Is. in the Indian Ocean, 1,200 m. from Singapore. Copra, coconut-oil and nuts are exported. Annexed by Gt. Brit. 1857. Control was transferred to Australia in 1955. Pop. 615.

COCTEAU, Jean
(1891-1963) Fr. playwright. Author of *La Voix Humaine* (1930), *La Machine Infernale* (1931), *Les Monstres Sacrés*, *La Machine à Écrire* (1941). Also film scripts, ballets, novels, essays.

COD
(*Gadus morrhua*) N. Atlantic fish. It averages

3 ft. in length, but sometimes reaches 6 ft. It is a valuable food. Chiefly found off Newfoundland and in the N. Sea. The liver yields cod liver oil.

CODE NAPOLÉON
Official name given to the first code of Fr. civil law. Its compilation began in 1800 and was promulgated in 1803. The final revision of the original code appeared in 1816.

CODY, Samuel Franklin
(1862-1913) Brit. airman. In 1908 he flew in a machine he had made and stayed in the air for 27 mins.

COELACANTH
[sē'-la-kanth] Species of fish which is believed to have existed 300,000,000 years ago and which at one time was thought to have been extinct for at least 50,000,000 years. In 1938 a living coelacanth was found off E. London, S. Africa. Another, caught in 1953 off Anjouan, was preserved intact for examination.

COFFEE
Genus of evergreen trees and shrubs. They produce berries, the beans of which are ground to make a beverage. The first coffee came from Arabia, but Brazil is now the main source of the world's supply.

COGNAC
[ko-nyak] Town of W. Fr. in Charente dept., 23 m. W. of Angoulême. It has given its name to a famous type of brandy. Pop. 19,000.

COLBERT, Jean Baptiste
[-bair] (1619-83) Fr. statesman. Chief Min. to Louis XIV. He created a shipbuilding industry and a great navy, and fostered the arts and sciences.

COLCHESTER
Borough and market town of Essex on the Colne. It was a Rom. city called Camulodunum. Chief city of the Trinovantes, taken by the Roms. and rebuilt as Camulodunum. There are corn and cattle markets, and engineering, printing and clothing industries. There are oyster beds. Nearby is Univ. of Essex (1964). Pop. 67,010.

COLEOPTERA
Order of insects comprising the beetles. The fore wings are modified into a pair of stiff, horny sheaths called elytra encasing the transparent hind-wings. Many beetles lack hind-wings altogether. About 150,000 species are named.

COLERAINE
[kōl-rān'] Borough and seaport of Londonderry, N. Ireland, on the Bann, 4 m. from its mouth. It is a centre of salmon fishing and linen is manufactured. Pop. 12,550.

COLERIDGE, Samuel Taylor
(1772-1834) Eng. writer. After meeting Wordsworth (1797) wrote the *Ancient Mariner* for their *Lyrical Ballads* (1798); *Kubla Khan* (1797) and *Christabel* 1798-1800 (pub. 1816). About this time he began taking opium. He gave courses of lectures on Shakespeare and wrote *Essays on the Fine Arts* (1814), *Biographia Literaria* (1817), *Treatise on Method* (1818), *Aids to Reflection* (1825); and plays, *e.g.* *Fall of Robespierre* (1799), *Remorse*. Much of his critical work was pub. posthumously: *Table Talk* (1835), *Lectures on Shakespeare*, etc.,

Essays on his Own Times, Philosophical Lectures (1949).

COLERIDGE-TAYLOR, Samuel
(1875-1912) Eng. composer, remembered for settings of passages from Longfellow's *Hiawatha* and the suite *Othello*.

COLET, John
(*c.* 1467-1519) Divine and humanist. Ordained, 1496, and lectured at Oxford. Represents reaction against scholastic tradition and influenced Erasmus. Founder of modern biblical exegesis.

COLIC
Severe spasmodic abdominal pain due to spasm of muscles in bowel wall and assoc. with presence of irritating substance in bowel. Sometimes a symptom of lead poisoning.

COLIGNY, Gaspard de
[-lē-nyē′] (1519-72) Huguenot leader. B. of a noble Burgundian family, he led the Huguenots in the civil war. He was one of the victims of the massacre of St. Bartholomew.

COLITIS
[-lī′-] Inflammation of the colon characterised by diarrhoea containing blood and mucus, and assoc. with infectious disease, or certain deficiency diseases, or poisoning. *See* ENTERITIS.

COLLECTIVISM
Term first used when Mikhail Bakunin described himself as a collectivist anarchist. A congress at Havre in 1880 adopted a collectivist programme, demanding the state ownership of all means of production, to secure for the community as a whole an equitable distribution of the fruits of their assoc. labour.

COLLEGE OF ARMS (Heralds' College)
Corporation of Eng. heralds endowed by Richard III in 1483. It deals with all matters affecting the grants and use of coats of arms and armorial bearings.

COLLEGE OF JUSTICE
The supreme civil court of Scotland (*i.e.* the Court of Session), composed of the lords of council and session (the judges), together with the advocates (barristers), clerks of session, and Writers to the Signet.

COLLIE
Breed of sheep-dog. Lighter than the old Eng. breed, with small ears whose tips fold back, it is keen-witted, trained to herd sheep. The rough-haired variety has a thick, soft undercoat and neck frill; the smooth-haired a short, stiff, flat coat.

COLLINGWOOD, Baron
(1750-1810) Eng. Admiral. Cuthbert Collingwood fought in the Amer. War of Indep., and during the Fr. Revolutionary Wars in the 'Glorious First of June', and at St. Vincent. As Nelson's 2nd in command at Trafalgar, he led the 2nd line and on Nelson's d. took command of the fleet.

COLLINS, Lawton
(1896-   ) Amer. Gen. He commanded with conspicuous success an inf. div. at Guadalcanal. In Europe he directed his 7th Corps in the capture of Cherbourg. He was Chief of Staff of the Amer. Army, 1949-53.

COLLINS, Michael
(1890-1922) Irish politician. In 1916 he was imprisoned for sharing in the Easter Rebellion. He was head of the repub. army during the warfare of 1920-21. In 1921 he helped to negotiate the treaty with Brit. As C.-in-C. of the Free State Army he was killed in the war against the rebels.

COLLINS, William Wilkie
(1824-89) Eng. novelist. B. London; called to the Bar, 1851; took to lit., wrote: *The Woman in White* (1860), *Armadale* (1866), *The Moonstone* (1868). He remains one of the great exponents of the novel of mystery.

COLMAR
Cap. of Haut-Rhin dept., N.E. Fr. in the district of Alsace. Except 1871-1914, when it belonged to Germany, Colmar has been Fr. since 1673. Centre of viticulture in Alsace. Pop. 54,264.

COLOGNE
[-lōn′] City and river port of N. Rhine-Westphalia, W. Germany, on the Rhine. Of Rom. origin, Cologne is the 4th city of Germany. It has a large river trade and numerous industries. There are many fine buildings, including the cath. and univ. Pop. 795,183.

COLOMBIA
[-lom′-] Repub. of northern S. Amer. having coastlines on the Caribbean and Pacific. The W. is traversed by the 3 great Andean ranges which run N.-S., parallel to the Pacific coast. In the E. lie the plains of the headwaters of the Orinoco and Amazon systems. Of the agricultural products, coffee and bananas are the most important. Coffee is grown at heights of 2,000-7,000 ft. Bananas are produced in the N. Colombia is the chief emerald producing country of the world; platinum, gold and silver, and petroleum are also produced. Bogotá is the cap.; other towns are Medellin, Cartagena and Barranquilla. The pop. consists of mixed races. The nat. language is Sp. and the state religion R.C. Inland transport is difficult, but air services have solved the problem. Colombia was discovered by the Sp. in the 16th cent. In 1819 Simon Bolivar created the Repub. of Colombia; Colombia, Panama, Venezuela and Ecuador. Later the provs. split up. Venezuela and Ecuador leaving the assoc. 1830, and Panama 1903. The Constitution of 1886 was revised, 1945. There is a Pres. and normally a congress of 2 houses but in 1953 the armed forces seized power and the country is now gov. by decree. Area: 439,525 sq.m. Pop. 19,215,000.

COLOMBO
[-lum′-] Cap. and chief port of Ceylon, on the W. coast, with a fine artificial harbour and extensive coal and oil depots. The industries are chiefly concerned with the preparing and marketing of tea. Pop. 502,700.

COLON
City of Panama, near the Caribbean entry to the Panama Canal. U.S. town of Cristobal adjoins it. Combined pop. 90,100.

COLON
Part of the bowel or large intestine which extends from the caecum on the right side of the abdomen to the anus and rectum on left side of abdomen. The 1st part is called *caecum* where large and small intestine join. As it descends again into the pelvis it is called the *pelvic colon* and that passes into the *rectum* which communicates with outside by an opening called the *anus*.

COLONISATION
Act of founding settlements abroad. In the ancient world the great colonising races were the Phoenicians and the Gks. who estabd.

colonies round the Medit. The Roms. did a certain amount. A new era in colonisation began with the discovery of Amer. In this movement the Fr., Brit., Dutch, Sp. and Portuguese nations took the largest part. Fr. and Sp. in the course of time lost their empires, and Portugal lost most of hers. The Netherlands retained a good deal, and Brit. became the owner of the greatest colonial empire ever known. In the 19th cent. Fr. acquired a vast colonial empire in Africa, where Brit. gained also.

COLORADO
W. state of the U.S.A. in the Rocky Mts. containing some of the highest peaks of the country. Numerous rivers rise in the mts. the chief being the Colorado, S. Platte and Arkansas. Coal, gold, silver, copper, molybdenum, lead and petroleum are mined. Agriculture is becoming important, sugar-beet, wheat, maize and oats being the chief crops. There are several Nat. Parks. Denver is the cap. and largest town; others are Pueblo, Colorado Springs and Greeley. C. became a state, 1876, now sending 4 representatives to Congress. Area: 104,200 sq.m. Pop. 2,207,300. **Colorado River** rises in N. Colorado, and flows through the arid plateau between the Rocky Mts. and the Sierra Nevada before falling into the Gulf of Calif. It is 1,400 m. long and is famous for the gorges in its course. These have a total length of 1,000 m. the chief being the Grand Canyon in Arizona.

COLORADO BEETLE
(*Leptinotarsa decemlineata*) Beetle now general in the U.S.A. It completely destroyed potato and other solanaceous crops until controlled by poisonous powders dusted or sprayed on the foliage.

COLOSSIANS, Epistle to the
One of the 4 captivity epistles written to the Colossians by the apostle Paul from Rome. The epistle contains a summary of Christian doctrine and a series of practical exhortations.

COLOSSUS
Statue, esp. of gigantic proportions. The Colossus of Rhodes, the figure of Apollo raised by Chares, *c.* 280 B.C., and overthrown by earthquakes, *c.* 224 B.C., was one of the 7 Wonders of the World.

COLOUR
Sensation or class of sensations arising from stimulation of the optic nerve. This is effected normally by light rays emanating from luminous bodies or reflected from non-luminous bodies. These light rays, varying in wavelength, furnish in combination the white colour of sunlight, which when refracted through a prism, is spread out into a spectrum, each part of which corresponds to a particular wavelength. At the long-wave end are the red radiations; at the short-wave end, the violet. **Colour Blindness.** An incurable defect of vision, reducing ability to distinguish one colour from another. There are several forms, *e.g.* Daltonism, *i.e.* inability to discriminate red from green.

COLTSFOOT
(*Tussilago farfara*) Herb of the composite family, native to Europe, W. Asia and N. Africa. Its yellow heads appear before the leaves.

COLUMBA
(521-597) Irish St. Settled in Iona *c.* 563, where he founded a monastery from which monks were sent out to convert Scot. and the N. of Eng. to Christianity.

COLUMBIA
River of the U.S.A. which rises in the Canadian Rocky Mts. and flows through Washington state into the Pacific.

COLUMBIA
Cap. of S. Carolina, U.S.A. on the Congaree. It is a manufacturing and educ. centre. Pop. 96,700.

COLUMBIA District of
Seat of the U.S.A. Govt. containing the fed. cap. Washington. The land was ceded by Maryland to the U.S.A. 1790. Area: 69 sq.m. Pop. 756,500.

COLUMBINE
(*Aquilegia vulgaris*) Perennial herb of the buttercup family. Native to N. temp. regions, its stem bears finely divided leaves and panicles of flowers, with 5 petaloid sepals and 5 short-spurred petals.

COLUMBUS
Cap. of Ohio, U.S.A. on the Scioto. A railway centre, it has many manufactures. It is the seat of Ohio State Univ. Pop. 533,500.

COLUMBUS, Christopher
(1451-1506) Reputed discoverer of Amer. B. Genoa. Financed by Spain, he led an expedition to find the W. route to India and reached the W. Indies in 1492. Columbus made 3 other voyages to Amer. In 1492 he took 1,500 men to the W. Indies; in 1498 he landed in S. Amer. and in 1503 he was in C. Amer. and the W. Indies, where Sp. settlements had been made.

COLZA
A semi-drying oil, extracted from the crushed seeds of a cruciferous plant. It is an important lubricant. The cake, left after the oil has been expressed, is a cattle food.

COMA
Stuporose condition from which patient cannot be roused. Breathing loud and deep, heart beat thudding in character, limbs and body limp. Results from concussion, cerebral haemorrhage or thrombosis, overdosage of drugs, untreated diabetes and kidney failure.

COMBINATION ACTS
Passed by Pitt the Younger (1799-1800), during the wars against Fr. they punished all combinations of wage-earners and so made Trade Unionism illegal. They were repealed in 1824. *See* TRADE UNION.

COMEDY
Strictly, a form of drama evolved in early 5th cent. Gk. '*Old Comedy*' (5th cent. B.C.; Aristophanes) is largely social satire; '*Middle Comedy*' (4th cent.), myth. burlesque; '*New Comedy*' (from 320 B.C.; Menander, imitated by the Rom. Plautus and Terence) has a love-motive, and many stock characters and situations. In M.A. it meant a story beginning sadly, ending happily, *e.g. Divine Comedy*.

COMET
(1) Luminous celestial body moving about the sun. Bright comets contain a nucleus, an enveloping haze or coma, and usually a tail of luminous matter. Some return at calculable intervals, ranging from the 3½ yrs. of *Encke's* to the 76 yrs. of *Halley's*; others, moving parabolically, may never return. (2) Earliest Brit. passenger steamship. Built by Henry Bell (1767-1830) at Greenock in 1811, it plied between Glasgow and Greenock.

COMET
Originally the name of the de Havilland D.H. 88 racing aeroplane which in 1934 flew from Mildenhall to Melbourne in 71 hrs., it was later applied to the same company's D.H. 106 jet airliner which first flew in July 1949. Unfortunately, in Jan. and April 1954, Comets vanished without trace off Italy, and investigations showed evidence of metal fatigue (*q.v.*). After extensive redesign the Comet 4 entered the B.O.A.C. service in October 1958, and versions of this aircraft are now widely used.

COMFREY
[kum′-] Genus of rough, erect, tuberous-rooted perennial herbs of the Boraginaceae, native to Europe and W. Asia. The common Brit. comfrey (*Symphytum officinale*) has been naturalised in N. Amer.; the other (*S. tuberosum*) is cultivated ornamentally.

COMINFORM
Information and co-ordination centre set up in Belgrade in 1947 by the Communist parties of E. Europe; intended as a countermove to the Marshall Plan and aimed primarily at creating a new Communist organisation to co-ordinate the party's internat. activities.

COMMANDO
Brit. Army raiding unit raised in World War II by Admiral Sir Roger Keyes and were trained for marauding invasions into enemy-held territory, *e.g.* the Dieppe Raid in 1942, the Battle of Normandy, Rhine Crossing, etc.

COMMISSION
Act of placing a charge or trust upon a person. It describes the charge entrusted, and the document setting forth the authority. A body of persons appointed to act for another person or body is called a commission. Such are the **royal commissions** appointed to report to the king or queen upon a certain matter. The magistrates of the counties and boroughs of Eng. who are appointed by a commission from the king or queen, are known collectively as the **commission of the peace.** Also the authority by which an officer of the navy, army or air force holds his position. Commissions are granted by the Queen, through the Sec. of State or other official, to qualified persons.

COMMODORE
(1) **Royal Navy:** Rank between Capt. and Rear-Admiral. A Commodore may command a light-cruiser squadron or a flotilla of destroyers, or hold other appointments afloat or ashore. (2) **Merchant Navy:** Title sometimes given to the senior capt. in the service of a maritime company. (3) The commander of a yacht club or squadron.

COMMON LAW
Law common to the whole of the kingdom. Many of its rules have been estabd. by ancient usage and depend on precedent.

COMMON MARKET
European Economic Community estabd. by the Treaty of Rome, signed in 1957, in force 1958, consisting in 1962 of Germany, Italy, France, Belgium, the Netherlands, Luxembourg (the original signatories) and Greece (1961). The Common Market has three main aims: to remove all barriers against free flow of goods, labour, capital, services; to replace national tariffs with a common external tariff; to apply common policies to transport, external trade and exchange rates, and also to agriculture. U.K. negotiations in 1961, 1967 broke down after French veto; application accepted by E.E.C. 1971; other E.F.T.A. countries (Irish Repub., Norway) may apply for membership.

COMMON PRAYER, Book of
C. of E. service book, based largely upon the Rom. Breviary. First Book of Common Prayer in Eng. was pub. 1549. Revised Prayer Book issued, 1559, based upon that of 1549. Suppressed by parl. 1645, but restored, 1660. A Revised Book approved by Ch. Assembly, 1927, rejected by House of Commons.

COMMONS
In Brit., land that is owned by the public. Orig. land on which villagers had right of grazing, attached to their village or manor. In 15th and 16th cents. much was enclosed by landowners; in 18th cent. by Acts of Parl. In 1866 enclosures were forbidden in the London area, and in 1876 elsewhere. Today commons are supervised by the local authorities.

COMMONS, House of
In Brit. and Canada the name given to the House of Parl. elected directly by the people. In Eng., the House began in the 14th cent., when the representatives of the counties and boroughs separated themselves from the Lords, and were called the Commons. By reason of their control of finance, the Commons gradually asserted themselves, fighting a long struggle with the Crown in the 17th cent. and later with the Lords, culminating in the Parl. Act of 1911. For practical purposes the Commons are omnipotent in legislation. Only a defeat in the Commons can force a Govt. to resign. The number of members in the Brit. House of Commons was at one time 670; in 1950 after a redistribution, 625 members were returned, and after the 1955 redistribution, the number was increased to 630. Women have been eligible for election since 1918. The Pres. of the House is the Speaker. The control of business is in the hands of the P.M. and his assistants.

COMMUNE
Word meaning much the same as municipality or corporation. In Fr. today the commune is an administrative district, with a council elected by all adults and presided over by a mayor.

COMMUNION, Holy
Participation in the sacrament of the Lord's Supper (1 Cor. 10). In the R.C. Ch. it takes the form of the Mass. In the High C. of E. it is called the Eucharist. High Churchmen, like R.C.'s, believe in the doctrine of the real presence. To Lutherans, Nonconformists and others the taking of the communion is symbolic only.

COMMUNISM
Orig. the doctrine of the common ownership of all property, the term now means that form of revolutionary socialism based on the writings of Karl Marx (*q.v.*), and esp. strong in E. Europe. It forms the Govts. of Russia, Poland, China, etc. Its principles include the nationalisation of the means of production, distribution and exchange. In Russia, strict control of the country's economy was maintained by means of Five Year Plans. During World War II, Communists worked with the Resistance Movements in the occupied countries, and after the war gained power in countries within the Russian sphere of influence. The Communist parties in W. Europe sought election to Parl. In the Brit. election of 1945, 2 members were returned and in 1964 and 1966 none.

COMO
[kō′-mō] City and tourist centre of Lombardy, N. Italy on the S. shore of L. Como at the foot of the Alps. The chief industry is silk manufacture. Pop. 76,800.

COMORO ARCHIPELAGO
Group of Is. belonging to Fr., N.W. of Madagascar. The Is. now have admin. and financial autonomy, and send deputies to Fr. The chief products are vanilla, sisal, sugar and copra. Cap. Dzaoudzi. Area: *c.* 838 sq.m. Pop. 183,133.

COMPANION OF HONOUR
Brit. order. Instituted in 1917, it is limited to 65 members, and is conferred for conspicuous nat. service. Companions use C.H. after their names. The badge, a plaque with mounted knight, and an oak-tree supporting the Royal Arms, centres an enamelled blue oval bearing the motto *In action faithful and in honour clear*, affixed to a crown suspended on a gold-edged carmine ribbon.

COMPENSATION
Reparation for loss or injury, which must be paid if property is damaged by riot. If property is taken by a local authority, compensation must be paid and it can also be obtained if a man's business is damaged in this way. Com-

pensation can be obtained also if a person or his property is injured while travelling in a public vehicle. Legislation has been introduced to provide compensation for the victims of crimes of violence.

COMTE, Auguste
(1798-1857) Fr. philosopher. He came under the influence of St. Simon, and in 1830 pub. vol. 1 of his *Cours de Philosophie Positive.*

CONCENTRATION CAMPS
Prison camps set up by the Nazis to contain German and other nationals opposed to the Nat. Soc. régime or considered to be politically suspect. Camps of the kind were in existence prior to World War II (1939-45), but during hostilities enormous numbers of men, women and children of all ages were incarcerated in such camps without trial. These included Jews, Socialists, Communists and people of liberal and pacifist convictions, both Catholic and Protestant, from all over Europe. The majority of such prisoners underwent incredible hardships. Millions were murdered by shooting, hanging, gassing, etc. When Germany was invaded, the Allies found 80,000 prisoners at Buchenwald, 30,000 at Belsen and 32,000 at Dachau. Thousands were found to be suffering from dysentery, typhoid, tuberculosis and other diseases. It is estimated that at the Polish camp of Oswiecim more than 4,000,000 people, men, women and children, were put to death in gas-chambers, and medical experiments were carried out on living persons.

CONCORD
(1) Cap. of New Hampshire, U.S.A. on the Merrimack. Pop. 29,600. (2) Town of Mass. U.S.A. 17 m. N.W. of Boston. The scene of the first hostilities in the War of Indep., 1775.

CONCRETE
Constructional material of broken brick, stone, etc., mixed with sand and a cementing agent in definite proportions, in water. It furnishes, when set, a durable, strong artificial stone. In reinforced concrete the mass is formed round cores of steel rods, corrugated or expanded bars, wire mesh or netting.

CONCUSSION
State of being concussed or dazed which follows injury to head. May be assoc. with loss of memory, unnatural actions, hallucinations or unconsciousness.

CONDÉ
[-dā] Town in Nord dept., Fr. near the Belgian frontier. It gave its name to a famous family, a branch of the Bourbons. Louis de Bourbon, first Prince of Condé, was a prominent Huguenot. His grandson, Louis (1621-86), called the Gt. Condé, was a soldier. He won several victories over the Spaniards, rebelled against his king and entered Sp. service. Later he returned to Fr.

CONDOR
(*Sarcorhampus gryphus*) Amer. vulture of the Andes. Among the largest birds of flight, spanning 10 ft., it has black plumage with a white band round the neck.

CONDY'S FLUID
Solution of potassium permanganate in water. It is reddish purple in colour and is a potent disinfectant and deodoriser owing to its oxidising action.

CONEY ISLAND
Pleasure resort of New York, lying off Long Is. part of the borough of Brooklyn. Of the 3 beaches, W. Brighton is perhaps the most popular resort in the world.

CONFESSION
(1) Disclosure of sin to a priest in order to receive absolution. Auricular confession prevails in the R.C. and Gk. Chs. The Council of Trent declared it essential. The Protestant ch. rejects confession, but the Anglo-Catholic party in the C. of E. favours it. (2) A **confession of faith** is a statement of belief, or creed. Such are the Westminster Confession and the Confession of Augsburg. (3) In law a confession is a statement by an incriminated person acknowledging guilt, directly or indirectly.

CONFIRMATION
Religious ceremony administered by a bishop in Episcopal and Lutheran chs. after instruction. In the R.C. Ch. it ranks as a sacrament.

CONFUCIANISM
[-foosh'-] System of teaching based on ancient Chinese classics. The precepts were ed. or transmitted by K'ung-fu-tsze, 551-478 B.C., whose name was Latinised as Confucius.

CONGER
(*Conger vulgaris*) Marine eel with large eyes and of wide distribution, found off the Scandinavian coast and off the W. coast of Brit. Its life-hist. is similar to that of the common eel.

CONGO
River of C. Africa, one of the longest in the world, 2,900 m., with a drainage basin of 1,425,000 sq.m.

CONGO
(formerly Fr.) Repub. on the Equator between Gaboon and the Congolese Repub. Proclaimed indep. 1960. Brazzaville is the capital. Area: 132,000 sq.m. Pop. 900,000.

CONGOLESE REPUBLIC
Formerly the Belgian Congo, indep. June, 1960. Occupies the greater part of the Congo basin. The centre is occupied by extensive swamps and forests. The land rises in the E. and S. to Mt. Ruwenzori (16,794 ft.). Palm oil, timber, cotton, cocoa, rubber and coffee are important products. Copper, radium and zinc are mined. Kinshasa is the cap.; other towns are Matadi, Lubumbashi, Kisangani and Jadotville. Since independence, some states have tried to become autonomous, notably Katanga and S. Kasai, and U.N. troops had to be called in. This has led to a disruption of economic life and trade and disorders continue. Area: 905,582 sq.m. Pop. 13,650,000.

CONGREGATIONALISM
Protestant religious body. Originated in Eng. *c.* 1550. Early in the 17th cent., owing to persecution, some of them fled to the Netherlands, and thence to N. Amer. In Eng. in 1662, the Act of Uniformity ejected many clergymen from the estabd. ch. and a number of these became mins. of indep. congregations. In the 19th cent., these became known as Congregationalists. In 1832 the Congregational Union of Eng. and Wales was founded.

CONGRESS
Chief legislative body of the U.S.A. and other countries. In the U.S.A. it consists of 2 houses sitting at Washington, the House of Representatives, which consists of 435 members elected by the states according to pop. and the Senate of 100 members, 2 from each state.

CONGREVE, William
(1670-1729) Eng. playwright and poet. He wrote

comedies *The Old Bachelor* (1693), *The Double-dealer* (1694), *Love for Love* (1695), *The Way of the World* (1700).

CONJUNCTIVITIS
[-ī'-tis] A disease affecting conjunctiva or white part of eye with redness, inflammation, and yellow discharge.

CONNAUGHT
W. Prov. of Eire, consisting of the 5 counties of Galway, Mayo, Sligo, Leitrim and Roscommon. Bounded on the E. by the Shannon, it has a long Atlantic coastline to N. and W.

CONNECTICUT
[-net'-] New. Eng. state of the U.S.A. with a coastline on the Atlantic, on Long Is. Sound. It is mainly lowland. Tobacco and fruit are grown, but it is mainly industrial. Hartford is the cap. and largest town; others are New Haven, the home of Yale Univ., Bridgeport and Waterbury. Connecticut was settled in 1635. It was one of the orig. 13 states of the Union, and now sends 6 representatives to Congress. Area: 5,009 sq.m. Pop. 3,032,250.

CONNEMARA
[-mă'-rà] District of W. Galway, Eire. Wild, mountainous country, with rugged coastline.

CONRAD, Joseph
(1857-1924) Eng. novelist (**Jozef Teodor Konrad Nalecz Korzeniowski**), b. Ukrainian Poland. Served in Fr. and Brit. ships. Naturalised as a Brit. subject. His stories and novels deal largely with the sea and seamen; *The Nigger of the Narcissus* (1897), *Lord Jim* (1900), *Typhoon* (1903), *Nostromo* (1904), *Suspense* (1925); *The Mirror of the Sea* (1906) and *A Personal Record* (1912) are autobiog.

CONSCIENCE
Sense or knowledge that one's conduct is right or wrong. According to one theory it is the eternal moral law acting on the mind of the individual. A **conscience clause** is a clause in an Act of Parl. which allows persons liberty of conscience in religious and other matters. It allows persons who object to vaccination to obtain exemption from the law compelling the vaccination of children. A **conscientious objector** is one who objects to milit. service because war is contrary to his religious or other beliefs.

CONSCRIPTION
Enrolment for milit. purposes *by lot* was introduced into Eng. 1757 and into Fr. 1792. Reintroduced into Fr. in 1818, it was replaced after 1872 by universal compulsory milit. service, and this became the estabd. practice in almost all European states. During World War I compulsory milit. service was introduced in Brit. for single men between the ages of 18 and 41 in Jan. 1916, and for mar. men 2 months later. In Brit. in April, 1939, all men aged 20 became liable to 6 months milit. training and the Nat. Service Act (Sept. 1939) brought in all men between 18 and 41. In 1941 women also became liable to be called up for the Women's Services. Conscription was abandoned in Brit. at the end of World War II but from 1946 men reaching the age of 18 were liable for a period of service in the armed forces until 1960.

CONSERVATIVE
In Brit. politics a member of the Right or Cons. party. Cons. policy includes belief in free enterprise (subject to the supervisory control of nat. policy), distrust of state intervention, conservation of the estabd. order in crown and ch. As a party title, the name took the place of 'Tory' in the time of Sir Robert Peel; towards the end of the cent. the accession of the Liberal-Unionists resulted in 'Unionist' displacing it, but after World War I 'Conservative' returned to use. In 1951 the Cons. were returned to power with 320 seats and in 1955 increased their majority, with a total of 344 seats. In 1959, they were returned with a total of 365 seats. In 1964 (303 seats) and in 1966 (253 seats) they were defeated. Re-elected, 1970.

CONSISTORY
Court for trying eccles. causes. Appeals from its decisions lie to the court of the archbishop and the Privy Council. Under the Clergy Discipline Act, 1892, clerical offences against morality are tried by special consistories with assessors to assist.

CONSORT
In Eng. constitutional law, term denoting the husband or wife of the reigning monarch. Under Brit. law, the queen consort is a subject but has certain privileges, particularly as regards the law of treason. The position of the husband of the queen regnant (*q.v.*) is estabd. by statute in each individual case.

CONSTABLE
Title derived from the late Rom. count of the stable. The Lord High Constable of Eng. was one of the great officers of state in the M.A. but the office has now no significance save at coronations. Term now designates members of the police force. Special constables are civilians who assist the police in times of special need.

CONSTABLE, John
(1776-1837) Eng. painter. B. East Bergholt, Suffolk. A great landscape painter, he also painted some portraits.

CONSTANTINE
(288-337) Rom. emperor called **the Great.** His father was Constantinus Chlorus, on whose d. he became emperor after dealing with his rivals. Christians were tolerated, the emperor himself became attached to their faith. By defeating Licinius at Adrianople in 324 Constantine became ruler of the whole Rom. Emp. and in 330 transferred the cap. from Rome to Byzantium.

CONSTANTINOPLE
Former name of the Turkish city now called Istanbul (*q.v.*).

CONSTELLATION
Group of fixed stars usually assoc. with an imaginary figure. The Gks. recognised 48 such groupings, including the 12 zodiacal signs. The S. sky was similarly mapped out by 16-18th cent. astronomers. There are now recognised 28 Northern, 12 zodiacal and 49 Southern constellations.

CONSTIPATION
Incomplete or irregular evacuation caused by disease of bowel, general debility or, most important, failure to adopt regular daily habits.

CONSTITUTION
Assemblage and union of the essential parts of a body or system. It may be of natural origin, as with the universe stars and living bodies, or a system of principles and rules, either recognised by prescriptive usage or written, governing a state or assoc. **The Brit. constitution** which is unwritten, comprises the collective principles of public policy whereby Brit. is governed. The **Constitution of the U.S.A.** is contained in a document, the terms of which cannot be changed without special procedure.

CONSUL
(1) Ancient Rome's 2 chief magistrates. Holding office for a year, they presided over the senate. Under the emp. their authority declined, but the office lingered until A.D. 541. In 1799 Napoleon was styled 1st Consul in France. (2) Official commissioned by a state to protect the interests of its subjects in a foreign country. Brit. consuls report to the Foreign Office, rendering services also to the mercantile marine for the Board of Trade. The general division comprises consuls-gen., consuls, vice-

consuls, consular agents and attachés. Like an embassy, a consulate is regarded as being on the soil of the country there represented.

CONTAGION
Communication of disease to person by the inhalation of small particles of saliva sprayed into the air by infected persons and containing micro-organisms. Other method of contagion is by contact with crockery and cutlery used by the patient, his clothes and bed linen which contain germs.

CONTEMPT OF COURT
A legal term meaning any disobedience of the orders of a court of law. All forms of it can be punished with a prison sentence.

CONTRABAND
In time of war, materials and commodities which internat. law forbids subjects of neutral states to supply to belligerents. Materials of direct application to hostile use are absolute contraband and are distinguished from articles fit for such use, conditional contraband.

CONVENTICLE
Term used before and after the Reformation for a secret or unauthorised gathering for religious worship, or for its place of meeting.

CONVENTION
Term denoting a formal meeting, or formal agreement after a conference. The meetings of the polit. parties that choose the candidate for the U.S.A. presidency are called conventions. Agreements between states on matters of non-polit. interest are usually called conventions.

CONVOCATION
Assembly summoned by constituted authority. At Oxford Univ. it is the governing body. The convocations of Canterbury and York are assemblies for eccles. purposes.

CONVOLVULUS
Genus of twining herbs. Gardeners cultivate the European *C. althaeoides* and *C. tricolor*, calling the latter *Convolvulus minor*. The trop. Amer. *Ipomaea purpurea* or morning glory, is called *Convolvulus major*.

CONWAY
Borough and market town of Caernarvonshire, at the mouth of the Conway river, 13 m. W. of Bangor. It is famous for its castle. Pop. 11,100.

COOK, James
(1728-79) Eng. seaman and explorer. He surveyed and charted the estuary of the St. Lawrence, the coasts of Newfoundland, Labrador and New Zealand and surveyed the whole E. coast of Australia. On his second voyage (1772-5) he practically completed the exploration of the S. hemisphere, determined the position of Easter Is., discovered New Caledonia, Norfolk Is. and the Isle of Pines. On his last voyage to discover a N. passage from the Pacific to the Atlantic, he discovered the Hawaiian Is. and surveyed the W. coast of N. Amer. to beyond the Bering Strait. He returned to Hawaii, where he was killed by the natives.

COOK, James Wilfrid
F.R.S. (1900-) Regius Prof. of Chemistry in the Univ. of Glasgow, 1939-54. Was responsible, with Kennaway, for discovering and elucidating cancer-producing hydrocarbons.

COOK ISLANDS
Group of Is. in the S. Pacific Ocean, comprising 6 large and numerous small Is. Citrus fruits, tomatoes, copra and arrowroot are exported. The group was discovered by Capt. Cook, 1777, Brit. protectorate, 1888 and annexed by New Zealand, 1901. Internal self-govt. has been introduced, 1964. Pop. 23,000.

COOLGARDIE
Mining town of W. Australia, *c.* 350 m. E. of Perth, famous for the Coolgardie goldfields. Pop. 2,000.

COOLIDGE, John Calvin
(1872-1935) Gov. of Mass. in 1919, he became Republican Vice-Pres. of the U.S.A. in 1921, and Pres. in 1923. He was re-elected for 1925-9 when portions of the nat. debt were paid off and income-tax was reduced.

COOPER, James Fenimore
(1789-1851) Amer. author. He wrote more than 30 novels, such as *The Last of the Mohicans* (1826), *The Pathfinder* (1840).

CO-OPERATION
Acting together for mutual benefit. Co-operation in agriculture, which takes the form of setting up creameries, bacon factories, etc., to deal with the produce of a group of farmers, is one form. In the narrower sense co-operation is used for the movement started by Robert Owen in 1821. His idea was that a body of consumers should band themselves together to supply their own wants and so eliminate the capitalist. In 1844 a few of his followers opened a store in Rochdale. Similar stores were opened in Leeds, Derby, Oldham, and are movement spread to the S. Management was in the hands of committees elected by the members. In Brit. in 1962 the membership of the Co-op Retail Trading Socs. reached 12,893,000 with total assets for that year at £497,142,000, while the wholesale and productive socs. had assets totalling £185,556,000.

COOT
(*Fulica atra*) Water fowl belonging to the Rail family. It is widely dispersed throughout N. Europe and Asia. The plumage is black.

COOTE, Sir Eyre
(1726-83) Brit. soldier. In 1759 he commanded the forces at Madras, and next year defeated the Fr. under Lally at Wandiwash.

COPAL
[kop′-] Resin used in the manufacture of varnish. Obtained from various sources, including *Trachylobium hornemannianum*

COPE, Sir John
(d. 1760) Eng. soldier. During the Jacobite rebellion in 1745 he was C.-in-C. of the Eng. forces and met the rebels at Prestonpans.

COPENHAGEN
(*Danish* **Kjobenhavn**) Cap. of Denmark, on the adjacent Is. of Zealand and Amager. With a fine harbour, Copenhagen is the centre of Denmark's shipping trade. Industries incl. the manufacture of textiles, watches and porcelain, and brewing, distilling and sugar refining. There is a univ. founded 1479, a cath. and several palaces. Copenhagen began to assume importance in the 12th cent. but it was not until the middle 15th cent. that it became the cap. The Germans occupied Copenhagen from May, 1940, until May, 1945. Pop. 1,378,000.

COPERNICUS, Nicolaus
(1473-1543) Polish astronomer. From 1505-12 he lived at Heilsberg, and later Frauenberg, where he elaborated his treatise *De Revolutionibus. Orbium Coelestium*, which first suggested that the Earth moves round the Sun and not, as was then believed, the other way round.

COPLAND, Aaron
(1900-) Amer. composer. A pupil of Nadia Boulanger. His works include ballets. *e.g.*

Billy the Kid, 3 symphonies, *El Salon Mexico*, chamber music, and music for films.

COPPER
Chem. sym. Cu. Bright reddish-brown metallic element, known since prehistoric times. It occurs free and in many ores. It is very ductile and malleable and is a good conductor of heat and electricity. Sp. gr. 8·9.

COPPERHEAD
Poisonous snake of N. Amer. During the Amer. Civil War name applied by Lincoln's supporters to Northerners who advocated an agreed peace with the S. Hence a nickname for the Democratic party.

COPTS
Christian sect in Egypt, descended from the ancient race of Egypt. The Coptic Ch. has an ancient ritual, not unlike that of the Gk. Ch. Its head is the patriarch of Alexandria under whom are bishops in Egypt and Abyssinia. **Coptic.** Hamitic language of ancient Egypt so called when it came to be written in Gk. alphabet in the 2nd cent. A.D. It became extinct in the 16th cent. but it is still the liturgical language of the Coptic Ch.

COPYRIGHT
The sole right to reproduce a book, play, picture, photograph, piece of music, or any other artistic work, or any substantial part thereof. In Brit. the Copyright Act of 1956 retained certain important provisions of the Act of 1911 but abandoned others. The copyright of a book still exists for the lifetime of the author and 50 yrs. after his d. One of the main benefits of the new Act was that it enabled the U.K. to ratify the Berne-Brussels Convention and the Universal Copyright Convention, thereby securing copyright for Brit. books in the U.S.

COR ANGLAIS
[-lā] A double-reed woodwind instrument. It has a small metal tube bent back towards the player's mouth and at the other end a pear-shaped bell. Its compass is of *c.* 2½ octaves from the E below middle C.

CORAL REEF
Chain of rocks formed by the accumulation of skeletons of the coral polyp (*q.v.*) near the surface of the sea. There are 3 types of coral reef, fringing reefs, barrier reefs and atolls. **Fringing reefs** are built on the shores of conts. or Is., forming a platform at low-water level. **Barrier reefs** are separated from the shore by a wide and deep lagoon, *e.g.* the Gt. Barrier Reef which extends for *c.* 1,200 m. down the N.E. coast of Australia, some 60 m. from the mainland. **Atolls** are ring-shaped reefs often surrounded by islets.

CORANTOS
First Eng. news-sheet (1621-41), containing foreign news; succeeded (1641-65) by the 'Newsbooks' of 8 pp.

CORBY
Urban district of N. Northants. 8 m. N. of Kettering, on the Northants. ironfield. There are iron and steel industries. Pop. 39,460.

CORDILLERA
Name specifically used for the mt. systems between the Rocky Mts. and the Sierra Nevada.

CORDOBA
City of Sp., cap. of C. prov. on the Guadalquivir, 80 m. N.E. of Seville. Founded by the Carthaginians, and developed by the Moors. Pop. 207,009.

CORFU
Northernmost of the greater Ionian Is. off the coasts of Albania and Greece. It is mountainous in the N. rising to 3,000 ft. Olives, pomegranates, figs and grapes are grown. Pop. 27,000.

CORGI
Welsh breed of dog. Pembrokeshire var. have short tails and red, or red and white colouring. Cardiganshire var. have longer tails and may be black, brown, brindle or red.

CORIANDER
Fruit of an umbelliferous plant found in S. Europe, Asia Minor and parts of Eng. The plant has pinkish flowers and its fruit is used as a flavouring.

CORINTH
City of Greece, 3 m. from the Gulf of C. on the isthmus between the mainland and Peloponnesus. Prob. founded *c.* 1000 B.C., it was a great trading centre. The city's most famous building was the Acrocorinth, on a hill 2,000 ft. high. The rivalry between Athens and Corinth led to the Peloponnesian War in 431. After being under Byzantine and Turkish rule it was destroyed by an earthquake, 1858. New Corinth was erected on the gulf.

CORINTHIANS, Epistles to the
2 epistles addressed to the Ch. at Corinth *c.* A.D. 57 or 58, which have been admitted as genuine writings of St. Paul. They are instructive from the insight which they furnish into the character of St. Paul.

CORK
Co. of S. Eire in the prov. of Munster. The chief rivers are the Blackwater, Lee and Bandon. The soil is very fertile and the county is noted for its dairy produce. Oats, potatoes and barley are grown. Cork is the chief town; other places are Cobh (Queenstown), Fermoy, Youghal, Bandon, Mallow, Skibbereen, Clonakilty and Kinsale. Pop. 330,443. **Cork.** City, county borough, and seaport of Eire, also the county town. It stands on the Lee, 11 m. from its entrance into Cork harbour. The city has a considerable import and export trade. Brewing, distilling and bacon curing are industries. Pop. 77,980. **Cork Harbour** is 8 m. broad and 1 m. wide at the entrance.

CORK
Evergreen oak of the Medit. region (*Quercus suber*), grown in Sp., Portugal and parts of Fr. The bark is useful as it is impervious, compressible and elastic.

CORMORANT
Diving birds with all 4 toes webbed (*Phalacrocorax*). The Black C. (*P. carbo*) known in Brit. and all round the N. hemisphere, is 36 in. long. The Green C. or Shag (*P. aristotelis*), is somewhat smaller. Cormorants have been trained to catch fish in the Far East from time immemorial, the fish being stored in the throat pouch.

CORN COCKLE
(*Agrostemma githago*) Herb of the carnation-pink family. Native to Europe and W. Asia, it has been introduced into N. Amer. Common in Brit. cornfields.

CORN LAWS
Parl. Statutes concerning the importation and exportation of corn. In 1773 Burke introduced a duty on foreign corn, when the home price was high. In 1815 the law forbidding foreign corn to be imported when the price of native corn was under 80s. per quarter, caused great distress. Peel tried, in 1836-43, to right matters with a sliding scale but was converted to Free Trade by Cobden and Bright in 1849, and corn laws were abolished.

CORNCRAKE
(or Landrail) (*Crex crex*) Bird of the Rail family.

Essentially migratory, it spends the summer in the N. and the winter in Africa. Its plumage is tawny-brown, and it utters a harsh cry.

CORNEILLE, Pierre
(1606-84) Fr. dramatist. B. Rouen; studied law; took to writing plays: *Le Cid* (1636), *Horace* (1641), *Cinna* (1643), *Polyeucte* (1643) etc.; his most famous comedy was *Le Menteur* (*The Liar*) 1644; patronised by Richelieu.

CORNELL
Amer. Univ. at Ithaca, New York, founded 1865, and named after Ezra Cornell, one of the chief subscribers. Students numbered 12,687 incl. 3,206 women in 1962.

CORNET
A brass instrument similar in shape to the trumpet, but shorter and with less brilliant tone.

CORNFLOWER
Herb of the composite family (*Centaurea cyanus*). It is a showy, hardy annual and grows to *c.* 2 ft. high.

CORNS
Localised overgrowths of the horny or top layers of the skin, resulting from friction and pressure of ill-fitting shoes in the case of feet, and tools in the case of hands. *Hard corns* are horny elevations of skin which occur chiefly on the top of the toes. *Soft corns* occur in the spaces between the toes.

CORNWALL
Peninsular county of S.W. Eng. including the Scilly Is. Much of it is hilly, the highest point being Brown Willy, on Bodmin Moor. The coast, esp. on the N. is extremely rugged and incl. Plymouth Sound and Mount Bay, the Lizard and Land's End. The chief rivers are the Camel, Fowey, Tamar, Looe, Fal and Lynhor. Early fruits, vegetables and flowers are grown. Tin and china clay are mined, as is some copper. Fishing and tourism are important. Bodmin is the county town and Truro the admin. centre. Falmouth, St. Ives and Newquay are resorts. Cornwall has a distinct life of its own, and at one time had its own language. There are castles and ruins at Tintagel, Launceston and elsewhere. The county returns 5 members to Parl. Pop. 340,880.

CORNWALLIS, Charles
1st Marquess (1738-1805) Brit. gen. in the Amer. War of Indep. who had to surrender at Yorktown (1781). Lord-Lieut. of Ireland, 1798-1801, suppressing the rebellion of 1798 and helping to carry through the Act of Union.

CORONA
[-ō'-] (1) Inner appendage to the floral envelope in some flowering plants. (2) Silvery aureole enveloping the sun's chromosphere. Imperceptible to the naked eye, except during total eclipses, it is observable spectroscopically.

CORONARY THROMBOSIS
[kor'-on-ar-i] The blocking of a branch of the coronary artery by means of a small blood clot. The thrombosis is manifested by acute heart pain and shock, breathlessness, and sometimes sickness. The pain is accompanied by an intense feeling of constriction.

CORONATION
Ceremony of crowning the sovereign. The rulers of the restored Rom. Emp. were crowned by the Pope. Since the A.-S. Eng. kings have been crowned in Westminster Abbey. Scots kings were crowned at Scone, Charles II, in 1651, being the last. Seated in the chair of St. Edward, the sovereign takes the coronation oath. The Archbp. of Canterbury places the crown upon his head. He is anointed and is then invested with the robes and emblems of high office. The **Coronation Stone** is a stone placed under the seat of St. Edward's chair. It was used at Cashel at the coronations of the King of Munster and later taken to Scone (near Perth). In 1296 Edward I took it to Westminster, where it remained, until Dec. 1950, when it was smuggled into Scot. It was replaced in the Abbey on April 13th, 1951.

CORONER
Eng. official. The conditions relating to the office were revised by the Coroners' Amendment Act, 1926. This requires coroners to be barristers, solicitors or legally qualified med. practitioners of at least 5 years' standing. His duties are to inquire into the cause of all deaths occurring in his district from violence, unnatural or unknown causes. If, at the inquest, any one is found guilty of murder or manslaughter, the coroner commits him for trial. They retain the right to inquire into cases of treasure trove. In Scot. similar duties are discharged by the procurator fiscal.

COROT, Jean-Baptiste Camille
[kor-ō'] (1796-1875) Fr. artist. In 1857 was made an officer of the Legion of Honour. He was one of the founders of the Barbizon School.

CORPORAL PUNISHMENT
Punishment on the body. Legally this can be given by parents, teachers and others to children, but if the person punished is injured, the parent or teacher can be brought before a magistrate and punished. In most boys' schools corporal punishment can be inflicted. Corporal punishment by the cat-o'-nine-tails could formerly be ordered by a judge in certain cases but was abolished in 1948.

CORREGGIO
[ko-rej'-jō] (1494-1534) Ital. painter thus named from his birthplace. His sensitive perception of beauty is specially shown in his treatment of children. He painted a fresco in the cath. at Parma.

CORSICA
Fr. dept., an Is. in the Medit. Sea, S.E. of Nice, separated from Sardinia by the Strait of Bonifacio. It is mountainous, the highest point being Mt. Cinto, *c.* 8,800 ft. Sheep are kept inland; fruit, vines, wheat and olives are grown in the lower coastal areas. Ajaccio is the cap.; other towns are Calvi, Bastia, Aleria and Bonifacio. The Corsicans were formerly noted for their vendettas and lawlessness. The Is. was sold to Fr. by Genoa, 1768, but in 1793 the Fr. were driven out. Brit. governed it for 2 years, when it again passed to Fr. Pop. 275,465.

CORTES
[-tes] Parl. of Sp. It consisted of 2 houses: senate and congress. In 1923 it was dissolved, its place being taken by a nat. assembly which has consultative powers only. The Cortes was recalled in 1930, and in 1931 a constituent Cortes was elected. It was suspended during the Civil War but restored in 1942.

CORTES, Hernando
[-tes] (1485-1547) Sp. conquistador. Went to Hispaniola in 1504 and in 1518 was sent with a small force to Mexico. He soon had Montezuma, the Aztec ruler, in his power, and, with his Indian allies took Mexico City. Made Gov.-Gen. of the territory, but in 1528 returned home.

CORUNDUM
Native alumina (Al_2O_3). Next to diamond in hardness, appears in crystals which, tinted by metals, furnish ruby, sapphire and other gems. Its common form is emery.

CORUNNA
or **La Coruña.** Sea-port and cap. of Corunna prov. N.W. Sp. There are important sardine fisheries. At the Battle of Corunna, 1809, the Fr. were defeated by the Eng. under Sir John Moore, who was killed. Pop. 190,213.

CORVETTE
[-vet'] (1) A full-rigged sloop of war which

carried 20 guns on the upper deck. (2) A small warship of modified trawler design, equipped with guns and anti-submarine devices. They did work on convoy escort duties, etc. in World War II.

COSGRAVE, William Thomas
(1880-1965) Irish politician. Became a Sinn Fein M.P. in 1917. He was the first Pres. of the Free State Executive, holding the position until his defeat in the election of 1932.

COSMIC RAYS
Rays consisting of high-speed electrical particles of extra-terrestrial origin which enter the earth's atmosphere at very high velocities and have enormous energy. It has been found that they penetrate water, concrete, lead, etc. Many experiments have been carried out since those initiated by V. F. Hess in 1910.

COSMOLOGY
The cosmologist takes over from the astronomer and endeavours to fit the facts revealed by astron. (*q.v.*) into his conception of the universe, but this is now conceptual and mathematical. Einstein's Cosmos is finite and curved in a 4-dimensional manner into a closed spherical structure. A rocket travelling in a ' straight line ' in space would never reach a boundary, and would not go on into infinity, but would eventually return to the point from which it started. The alternative theories are (1) that the universe is expanding. This was asserted by Eddington, who reasoned that in future ages the galaxies would be so remote from one another that the Cosmos would cease to exist as a unity. (2) The theory advanced by Richard Tolman, working from Lemaître's theory that a universe of constant size would be unstable, and having affinities with the Ancient Hindu teaching of the ' Great Breath ', is that there are 2 fundamental forces at work in the universe, one of *repulsion*, from the orig. explosion of a single compact super-atom, and one of *attraction* deriving from clots of matter in space, and that expansion will go on until the forces balance each other. The universe will then fall in upon itself with increasing velocity until another super-atom is created and the process starts all over again.

COSSACK
Russ. name for a lightly armed horseman. The cossacks were formed into a milit. organisation and settled in the district around the Don and the Dnieper.

COSTA RICA
[rē'-ka] Repub. of Amer. bounded by the Pacific Ocean and the Caribbean Sea, and the repub. of Nicaragua and Panama. Much of the country is a high plateau, traversed by 2 volcanic ranges. The San Juan, which drains L. Nicaragua, is the chief river. Coffee, bananas, cacao and sugar are produced. Gold and silver are mined. San José is the cap.; other towns are Limon, Cartago, Heredia and Puntarenas. The Pan-Amer. Highway passes through the country. Sp. is the official language, and R.C. the chief religion. C.R. once part of Sp. Amer. became indep. 1821. Governed by a Pres. From Apr. 1948, a revolutionary junta governed until Nov. 1949, when a new constitution was formed under a Pres. to remain in office for a period of 4 years. Area: 19,633 sq.m. Pop. 1,598,000.

COSTELLO, John Aloysius
(1891-) Irish politician. B. Dublin. He was attorney-gen. under Cosgrave, 1926-32; T.D. Co. Dublin, 1933-7; Dublin Townships, 1937-43 and 1944-8. Leader of the Fine Gael party, he was P.M. 1948-51, and 1954-7.

COSWAY, Richard
(1742-1821) Eng. miniature painter. B. Tiverton, Devon; studied art in London. Elected A.R.A. 1770; R.A. 1771.

COTENTIN
Peninsula in the N.W. of Fr. comprising the dept. of Manche. It is a flat, marshy area famed for cattle. Cherbourg is the largest town.

COTMAN, John Sell
(1782-1842) Eng. artist, b. Norwich. Notable for his skill in draughtsmanship and painting.

COTONEASTER
[-ni-as'-ter] Genus of rosaceous shrubs or trees.

COTOPAXI
Volcano of the Andes, in the N. of Ecuador. The highest of the active volcanoes of the world, it is 19,612 ft. high.

COTSWOLD HILLS
Range of hills in Gloucs. running for *c.* 50 m. from the Worcs. border, through Gloucs. almost to the Avon. The highest pt. is Cleeve Hill, 1,344 ft.

COTTON
White fibrous material clothing the seeds of trop. shrubs of the mallow order (*Gossypium*). Generally bushy plants from 3 to 6 ft. high, their capsular bolls comprise compartments containing from 7 to 9 seeds each. Cultivated in pre-Christian times, cotton grows anywhere between 43° N. and 33° S. Separated from the

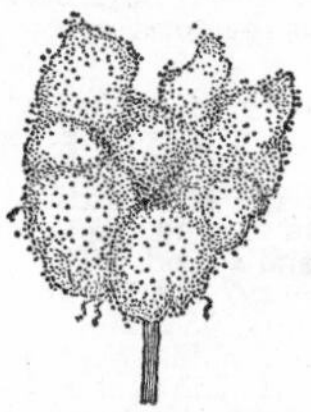

Boll of cotton showing hairs

seed by ginning, the lint, weighing *c.* $\frac{1}{3}$, is compressed into bales and as such is sent to the cotton mills for conversion into yarn. The unspinnable fibres, pure cellulose, become paper. Cotton is grown chiefly in the S.E. states of the U.S.A., the U.S.S.R., in Egypt, the Sudan, E. Africa and parts of the Brit. Commonwealth. **Cotton Cake.** Foodstuff for cattle, obtained by compressing cotton seeds after the extraction of their oil.

COTTON GRASS
(*Eriophorum*) Genus of perennial, sedge-like herbs, of some 12 species, spread over the N. temp. regions. The common and the sheathing cotton sedges grow in Brit. bogs. The former bears tufts of white bristles which can be spun into thread.

COUCH GRASS
Perennial grass with stout, creeping rootstock (*Agropyron repens*). With stems growing to 4 ft. high, it is a weed on arable land. A maritime ally, *A. junceum*, is a useful binder on sand dunes.

COUGH
Reflex action caused by irritation of larynx or trachea by particles of foreign substance. Sudden explosive expiration to clear airways of irritating substances.

COULOMB, Charles Augustin de
(1736-1806) Fr. physicist. B. Angoulême. His name is preserved in the **coulomb**, the unit used in describing quantity of electricity.

COUNCIL OF EUROPE
Organisation for political and economic consultation set up in 1949. It includes Belgium, Denmark, France, Italy, Luxembourg, Netherlands, Norway, Sweden, the U.K., Eire, Greece, Turkey, Germany and Austria.

COUNSEL
Word used in Eng. and Scot. for a barrister when acting for a client. Queen's Counsel are barristers who enjoy special privileges.

COUNTESS
Title in the Brit. peerage. Most of its holders are the wives of earls (*q.v.*) but some are countesses in their own right.

COUNTY
Division of a country for purposes of local govt. The old Eng. word is shire. Eng. was divided into counties after the Norman Conquest. Wales, Scot. and Ireland were divided later. Eng. has 40 counties, including London and Monmouth. Wales has 12, Scot. 33, and N. Ireland 6. Some counties, called counties palatine, had special privileges. **County Council.** Largest of our local govt. units, a body of persons estabd. in every admin. county of Eng., Wales and Scot. by the Local Govt. Acts of 1888 and '89. Each consists of councillors, elected by the ratepayers, who hold office for 3 years and of aldermen or bailies elected by the councillors for 6 years. Their powers include the admin. of educ., the maintenance of roads and bridges, town and country planning. **County Court.** In Eng. and Wales and N. Ireland a court of law for the trial of civil cases. In 1846 Eng. and Wales were divided into districts and in each of these a number of county courts were set up. A judge was appointed for each district. He holds sittings in various towns in his district and hears cases in which £200, or less, is at stake. He can also hear chancery cases in which the amount is not more than £500, and the exam. and discharge of bankrupts is under his control. In Scotland the equivalent is the **Sheriff Court.**

COUPERIN, François
[-a(ng)] (1688-1733) Fr. composer. In 1693 he was organist to Louis XIV. His compositions include organ pieces, suites for strings and harpsichord, chamber sonatas, ch. music.

COURBET, Gustave
[koor-bā'] (1819-77) Fr. painter. B. Ornans. Studied in Paris at the school of David d'Angers. Reacted against classicism and romanticism to begin (with Manet) the ' realist ' movement in painting. *See* IMPRESSIONISM.

COURSING
Pursuit of hares by greyhounds by sight not scent. It is an old field sport, popular in Eng. In each event 2 dogs, each held by a man called a slipper, compete against one another. When released they pursue the hare and earn pts. according to their skill in catching and killing it. The controlling body in Eng. is the Nat. Coursing Club. *See* GREYHOUND RACING.

COURT
Orig. a house, esp. the king's house. It came to mean his followers and, as he was the nation's judge, was used for the place where law cases were tried, hence the various kinds of law courts. The court means the sovereign and attendants, and so ' the court ' is described as being wherever they are residing. Parl. is the High Court of Parl. **Court Circular.** Official record of the daily doings of the Queen and the Royal Family, prepared by the Lord Chamberlain's dept. and issued to the Press every evening.

COURT MARTIAL
Court for trying soldiers, sailors and airmen, both officers and men, for offences incidental to their profession. A court is composed of officers and the procedure is much more direct than in the civil courts. Milit. courts martial are either regimental, district or general. Officers can only be tried by a general court martial, which can inflict sentence of d. The others deal with minor offences.

COUSTEAU, Capt. Jacques-Yves
(1910-) Fr. Naval officer who developed the ' aqualung ', a device which does away with heavy diving equipment and allows freedom of movement. *The Silent World* gives an account of his experiences.

COVENANT
[kuv-] Mutual compact. Agreements, sometimes made binding by ritual oaths, occur in the Bible between men or nations, and between God and His chosen people, the Old and New Covenants being called in Eng. and other versions the O. and N.T. In the Treaty of Versailles, 1919, the covenant created the League of Nations. In the autumn of 1949 a petition, known as a **Covenant,** for Scots. self-govt., was sponsored by an all-party committee. **Covenanters.** Scots who signed the *National Covenant* to uphold the Presbyterian religion in 1581, and the *Solemn League and Covenant* of 1643. The Episcopalian Ch. was restored in Eng. and an attempt was made to impose it in Scot. Many of the Covenanters refused to accept its authority. Their meetings were broken up by soldiers in Galloway, their stronghold.

COVENTRY
City and county borough of Warwicks. on the Sherbourne, 19 m. S.E. of Birmingham. In the 14th cent. Coventry was one of the richest places in Eng. After a period of decline it became in the 19th cent. a manufacturing centre. Motor cars, cycles, sewing machines, watches and artificial silk are among its products and there are engineering works and dyeworks. The reconstruction of Coventry Cath. was completed 1962. Designed by Sir Basil Spence, it includes a baptistery window by John Piper and a tapestry ' Christ in Glory ' by Graham Sutherland. C. returns 3 members to Parl. Pop. 310,640.

COVERDALE, Miles
(1488-1569) Eng. divine. He tr. the Bible into Eng. This was printed in Zürich and was the 1st Eng. tr. He was largely responsible for both the Bibles assoc. with the name of Cranmer.

COVERLEY, Sir Roger de
Fictitious character in *The Spectator*, the creation of Addison and Steele.

COW PARSNIP
(*Heracleum*) Biennial or perennial herb of the umbelliferous family, native to the N. temp. zone. The Brit. species, *H. sphondylium*, has stout, hollow stems, with broadly-sheathed stalks to the leaves.

COWARD, Sir Noel
(1899-) Eng. dramatist, actor, composer. Among his plays are *The Vortex, Hay Fever, Bitter Sweet, Private Lives, Cavalcade, Blithe Spirit, Present Laughter, I'll Leave It To You.* The films he has written include *In Which We Serve* and *Brief Encounter*. Knighted, 1970.

COWBANE
(or **Water Hemlock**) Perennial umbelliferous herb, with a poisonous rootstock. The European *Cicuta virosa*, has stout, furrowed stems, much-divided leaves and many-rayed umbels with minute white flowers.

COWBERRY
(*Vaccinium vitis-idaea*) Evergreen shrub of the family Vacciniaceae, native to N. Europe, N. Amer. and N. Africa. Its berries are red and acid in flavour.

COWES
Seaport and urban district in the N. of the Is. of Wight, on the Medina. Cowes is the headquarters of the Royal Yacht Squadron and its regatta is the chief event in the yachting world. Pop. 17,000.

COWLEY, Abraham
(1618-67) Eng. poet and essayist. In Civil War

took royalist side. Returned to Eng. after the Restoration. He wrote poetry and plays; *The Mistress* (1647); *Miscellanies* (1656). In prose he wrote a tract on *The Advancement of Experimental Philosophy* (1661). He was one of the founders of the Royal Soc. (1662).

COWPER, William
[koo'-] (1731-1800) Eng. poet. Agitation at the prospect of public examination for a clerkship in the House of Lords led to madness and an attempt at suicide 1763; confined until 1765. He contributed to *Olney Hymns* (1779) and pub. a collection of poems 1782. *John Gilpin* and *The Task* were pub. 1785; a tr. of Homer 1791; *The Castaway* (1798).

COWRY
Shell of a univalve mollusc of the family Cypraeidae. There are *c.* 200 species. One (*Cypraea moneta*) found in the Indian and Pacific Oceans is used for money and decoration in parts of Asia and Africa. It was venerated in the Aegean Is. *c.* 2000 B.C. and was used in trading there and in China.

COWSLIP
(*Primula veris*) Perennial herb of the primrose family, native to Europe and W. Asia. It bears stalked umbels of drooping flowers with buff-yellow funnel-shaped corolla.

COYOTE
[koy-ō'-ti] N. Amer. prairie wolf (*Canis latrans*). Ranging from Canada to Guatemala, it is smaller than the grey or timber wolf, with a hairier coat and a bushier tail.

COYPU
(*Myopotamus coypu*) S. Amer. water rat. It is one of the largest members of the order Rodentia, being *c.* 2 ft. long. Its fur is used under the name Nutria.

CRAB
Stalk-eyed, short-tailed crustaceans with the reduced abdomen folded beneath the combined regions of the head and thorax. The first pair of prominent limbs have pincer-like claws, the others are walking legs. The common European Edible Crab is *Cancer pagurus*.

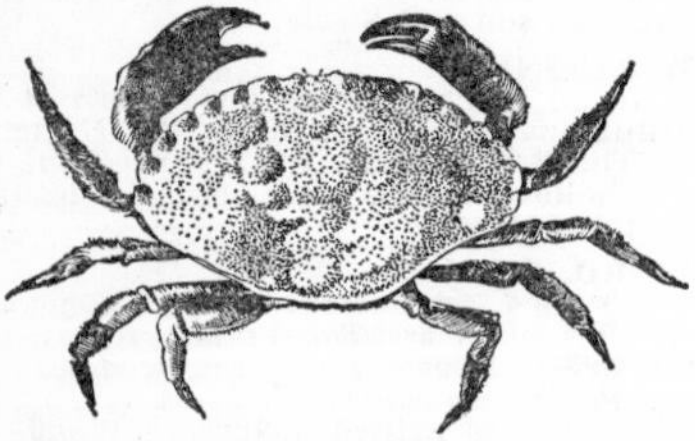

CRAB APPLE
Small tree of the rose order. A native of Europe and W. Asia (*Malus pumila*), its few pink-tinged white flowers bear yellow acrid fruit. It is an ancestor of the cultivated apple.

CRABBE, George
(1754-1832) Eng. poet. His poems describe country and sea-coast life, esp. among the poor. They include *The Library* (1781), *The Village* (1783), *The Borough* (1810), *Tales of the Hall* (1819).

CRACOW
[krak'-] City of Poland on the Vistula, 45 m. S.E. of Katowice. C. was cap. of Poland 1305-1596. Of the many fine buildings the cath., castle and univ. (1364) are important. Pop. 490,000.

CRAIG, Edward Gordon
(1872-1966) Eng. actor; son of Ellen Terry. In 1900 he began a series of productions involving new scenic ideas. His ideas are set out in *The Art of the Theatre* (1905 and 1911); *Towards a New Theatre* (1913), etc.

CRAKE
Various species of short-billed stout-bodied birds of the Rail family. The Spotted Crake, *Porzana porzana*, breeds in Brit. laying buff spotted eggs among reeds. Two other species, the Little Crake and Baillon's Crake, are stragglers from N. Africa, where all crakes winter. *See* CORNCRAKE.

CRAMP
Painful spasmodic involuntary muscle contraction. Assoc. with over exertion of muscle power in badly trained athletes, arteriosclerotic subjects or may be due to excessive salt depletion resulting from heat or neurosis (*q.v.*).

CRANBERRY
(*Oxycoccus*) Genus of creeping evergreen shrubs of the heath order, native to the N. temp. regions. The European *O. quadripetalus* has rose-coloured flowers bearing dark-red berries. The larger Amer. *O. macrocarpus* is cultivated in Massachusetts and New Jersey.

CRANE
Long-necked, long-legged wading bird found everywhere except in S. Amer. The European *Grus cinerea* was formerly bred in Eng. but is now a rarity.

CRANE, Hart
(1899-1932) Amer. poet. B. Ohio. His chief work was *The Bridge* (1930).

CRANE'S BILL
Popular name of 11 species of *Geranium*. Natives of Brit., they are distributed throughout the N. temp. regions. They are distinguishable from the *Pelargonium* in having regular flowers and no spurred sepals.

CRANMER, Thomas
(1489-1556) Eng. prelate. In 1533 he was made Archbp. of Canterbury. He pleased Henry VIII in securing his divorces and mar., and in rejecting the authority of the Pope. Instrumental in introducing into Eng. the ideas of the reformers. During the reign of Edward VI, Cranmer introduced the 2 prayer books and made other changes. With Mary's accession, 1553, his power ended. Accused of treason, sentenced to death and burned for heresy.

CRAYFISH
Name given to a number of fresh water Crustacea resembling lobsters but much smaller. Those of the N. and S. hemispheres represent different families. The Brit. *Astacus pallipes* is greenish-brown above and yellowish-brown beneath. *A. fluviatilis,* found from Fr. to Russia, is esteemed for the table.

CREAM
Rich surface of milk which has been allowed to stand for a time. It abounds in vitamins and is highly nutritious. **Devonshire Cream,** or clotted cream, may contain as much as 75 % of fat, but has much less sugar than ordinary cream, making it suitable for sufferers from diabetes.

CRÉCY
[krā'-si] Village of Fr. in the dept. of Somme, 12 m. N.E. of Abbeville, where, in 1346, Edward III, and his son, the Black Prince, defeated the Fr.

CREED
Concise expression of a religious faith. The chief creed of Christendom is the Apostles' Creed, accepted by the Rom., Gk. and Anglican Chs. The Nicene is an elaboration of the Apostles'. Both are in the Anglican Prayer Book.

CREMATION
Burning of human corpses as an alternative to burial, practised by many ancient peoples in

Asia and Europe, but forbidden by the R.C. Ch. owing to the belief in the resurrection of the body. In the 19th cent. it was revived in Europe, and in 1874 a cremation soc. was formed in Eng. Before a body can be cremated, 2 med. certificates must be obtained and other formalities complied with.

CREMONA
City of Lombardy, N. Italy, on the Po, 45 m. S.E. of Milan. C. was the home of the violin makers, Amati and Stradivarius. Pop. 71,800.

CREOSOTE
Product derived from the distillation of wood, coal, and shale. It is medicinally useful in bronchial complaints. **Creosote Oil,** used to preserve timber, is that part of coal tar distillate which boils between 200° and 300° C.

CRESS
Name denoting various salad vegetables of the cruciferous family. Of garden cress, *Lepidium sativum*, only the seed leaves are eaten. Curled or Normandy cress is *Barbarea verna*; water cress is *Nasturtium officinale;* rock cress is *Arabis.*

CRETE
Gk. Is. in the Medit., S. of the Aegean Sea. It has a mountainous interior rising to 8,195 ft. in Mt. Ida. The valleys are very fertile. Candia and Canea, the cap., both on the N. coast, are the chief towns. The people speak a Gk. dialect; the E. Orthodox Ch. predominates. Crete is famous as the home of one of the oldest of the world's civilisations. Before 2000 B.C. the people had attained a high degree of artistic achievement. Cretan civilisation is called Minoan, after Minos, one of the kings. Its chief centre was Knossos (*q.v.*). This civilisation declined when the cities of Greece rose to importance. In 1669 it was taken by the Turks, who retained it until 1913, when it was given to Greece. During World War II it was the scene of bitter fighting when the Germans invaded the Is. on May 20, 1941. Area: 3,240 sq.m. Pop. 483,258.

CRETINISM
[kret'-] Condition assoc. with absence, or disease, of thyroid gland characterised by onset in infancy of defective mental and body development, treated by daily doses of thyroid extract.

CREWE
Borough and industrial town of Cheshire, now an important railway junction with rly. works. Pop. 53,580.

CRICKET
Orthopterous insects allied to grasshoppers. The male chirps by rubbing together the 2 outer wings. The hearing organs are on the legs. Brit. species are the House Cricket, *Gryllus domesticus*; Field Cricket, *G. campestris*; the Tiny Wood Cricket, *Nemobius sylvestris*; and the Mole Cricket, *Gryllotalpa vulgaris.*

CRICKET
Eng. nat. summer game. Mod. cricket dates from the forming of the Hambledon Club in Hampshire in 1750, but became a great nat. game only with the foundation of Lord's Cricket Ground and the formation of the Marylebone Cricket Club (M.C.C.), now the world governing body of cricket. Lord's, first estabd. in Dorset Square in 1787, has been at St. John's Wood since 1814. The first Oxford v. Camb. match took place in 1827. County cricket, resulting in the county championship at the end of the season dates from 1850. Cricket is played extensively in the Brit. Commonwealth. Eng. teams first visited Australia 1862-78 and the first Austral. team to visit Eng. came in 1878 and defeated the M.C.C. by 9 wickets. Test matches between Eng. and Australia were first played in 1880.

CRIMEA
Peninsula of the U.S.S.R. on the N. coast of the Black Sea. The Crimea consists of steppeland except for the fertile coastal strip in the S. which has a Medit. climate and is a popular tourist area. In the E. is the barren Kerch peninsula, an area with rich oil and iron deposits. The cap. is Simferopol; other centres are Sevastopol, Feodosiya, Kerch and Yalta. **The Crimean War** was fought between Brit. and Fr. as allies of Turkey, against Russia. In Mar. 1854, the allied fleets sailed into the Black Sea and bombarded Odessa. In Oct. the Brit. made their famous cavalry charges at Balaklava (*q.v.*) and on Nov. 5 their camp at Inkerman was attacked by the Russ. Army. The attack was beaten back. Other events of the war incl. the bombardment of the Aaland Is. and the destruction of Kimburn, a fortress opposite Odessa, by the Fr. Peace was signed Mar. 30, 1856.

CRIMINAL APPEAL
Eng. court of law set up in 1907. Before then a convicted criminal could not appeal against his sentence. The court consists usually of 3 judges of the Queen's Bench Division; in addition to upsetting the verdict they can increase or reduce the sentence.

CROATIA
[krō-ā'-shă] Fed. unit of N. Yugoslavia, with a coastline on the Adriatic Sea. Much of the area is mountainous. Agriculture is the chief occupation. Zagreb on the Sava, is the cap. Croatia was formerly a kingdom of the Austro-Hungarian Empire. Became part of the Yugoslav repub. 1918.

CROCE, Benedetto
[krō'-chā] (1866-1952) Ital. philosopher. An opponent of Fascism, he became Min. in Badoglio's Cabinet as Min. Without Portfolio, April, 1944, but resigned in July. He holds that ideas do not *represent* but *are* reality. Art is the expression of a Creative Mind outside of which nothing exists; thus reality is hist. and all knowledge historical knowledge. Of his works the best known are *Aesthetics as Science of Expression* and *General Linguistics.*

CROCODILE
Large reptiles forming a separate order. True Crocodiles differ from Caimans and Alligators by their interlocked upper and lower teeth, and from Gavials by their rounder snouts. Some have broad, short snouts like alligators, *e.g.* the Indian Mugger, *Crocodilus palustris*; others have narrow, long ones like Gavials, *e.g.* the *Gavialis gangeticus* of India. The Nile *C. niloticus*, survives only in its upper waters. All crocodiles are carnivorous. They can swim rapidly. The largest, the Estuarine C. has been known 33 ft. long.

CROCUS
Genus of hardy perennial plants of the iris family, native to Europe and W. Asia. The scaly remains of last season's leaves cover a swollen corm from which the new leaves and flowers shoot. *C. vernus* and *C. versicolor* yield white, purple and striped garden varieties; the yellow blooms are Dutch developments from *C. aureus*. The Brit. *C. nudiflorus* found wild in the Eng. Midlands is bright purple. *C. sativus* yields saffron.

CROME, John
(1768-1821) Brit. artist. Called Old Crome, he founded the Norwich School of Painting.

CROMPTON, Samuel
(1753-1827) Eng. inventor. In 1779 he invented a new kind of spinning jenny, which was a combination of the ideas of Hargreaves and Arkwright, and was called the *mule.*

CROMWELL, Oliver
(1599-1658) Eng. soldier. In 1628 he became an M.P. In the Civil War he took the Parl. side,

raised the troop which became known as the Ironsides. Organised the New Model Army and led it to victory at Naseby. In 1648-9 he crushed further Royalist resistance at Preston, and was one of those who condemned Charles I. Eng. was proclaimed a repub. In 1649-50 he crushed his opponents in Ireland, defeated the Scots. at Dunbar and the forces of Charles II at Worcester. In 1653 he dismissed the Long Parl. and was made Lord Protector. As a dictator ruling by a milit. organisation, he restored Eng. prestige abroad. His son was **Richard** (1626-1712) Second Lord Protector of Eng. In 1658 he succeeded his father as Lord Protector. In May, 1659, he gave up the office.

CROMWELL, Thomas
(*c.* 1485-1540) Eng. politician. As Wolsey's sec. helped to suppress the smaller monasteries. On Wolsey's fall Cromwell was for 11 years Henry VIII's chief adviser. He carried through the measures that finally separated Eng. from Rome. His fall followed the marriage he brought about between Henry and Anne of Cleves. He was charged with high treason and beheaded.

CROOKES, Sir William
O.M. F.R.S. (1832-1919) Eng. scientist. B. London, he was trained at the Royal Coll. of Chemistry. Among his inventions are the Crookes tube and the radiometer. He discovered thallium and enlarged our knowledge of radium.

CROQUET
[krŏ′-ki] Outdoor game introduced to this country from Fr. in the 1850's. The aim of each player is to send his own ball and that of his partner, if he has one, through the hoops and to hit the posts in regular order, and to prevent his opponents from so doing.

CROSS
Symbol of very ancient origin which also became the symbol of the Christian faith.

CROSSBILL
A bird of the family Fringillidae (Finches), characterised by a peculiar bill, the 2 sheaths of which are crossed obliquely. This formation enables the birds to extract seeds from fruit and fir cones. The Crossbill has a plumage of rich colours.

CROUP
Condition found mainly in children, assoc. with spasm of larynx following inflammation, high temp. and difficulty in breathing. An alarming condition which is seldom fatal.

CROW
Bird of the family Corvidae, usually black, found all over the world. It includes the Raven, Jackdaw, Jay, Chough, Magpie and Rook, as well as the Hooded Crow and the Carrion Crow.

CROWBERRY
(*Empetrum*) Dwarf shrub, found on bogs or moors in Brit. Its wiry trailing branches bear leathery leaves rolled into closed tubes.

CROWN
Headgear worn by kings and queens as a sign of sovereignty. Usually of precious metals and precious stones, crowns are only worn today on ceremonial occasions. The Eng. kings have had crowns since A.-S. days. The present imperial crown was made for Queen Victoria. The act of placing it on the sovereign's head is called the coronation (*q.v.*).

CROWN, The
The central and oldest part of the British constitution. The Queen is the supreme head of the state. Without her assent Parl. cannot be assembled or dissolved, no Minister can be appointed, and no measure can become law. She is also the supreme head of the Eng. Ch. Since Magna Carta (1215) there has been no absolute exercise of the royal prerogative. As a result of the passing of the Statute of Westminster in 1931, the Crown has been the chief link in the Brit. Commonwealth of Nations.

CROWN ESTATES
In U.K., properties formerly known as Crown Lands, the remains of estates once owned by the monarchy. George III surrendered his interest in the Crown Lands in return for an annual income from the civil list, and later sovereigns have done the same. The Crown Estates, since 1956, are admin. by Crown Estate Commissioners.

CROWN JEWELS
or **Regalia** (1) **Crowns.** In Brit. the sovereign has 3 crowns, *viz.* (*a*) *St. Edward's Crown*, which was made for the coronation of Charles II in 1662. It is the crown of Eng. and is used at coronation ceremonies. (*b*) *The Imperial State Crown* was made for Queen Victoria in 1838. It contains the ruby owned by the Black Prince and worn by Henry V at the Battle of Agincourt, the Stuart sapphire, the second largest portion of the Star of India diamond weighing 309 carats, the pearl ear-drops of Queen Elizabeth I, and the sapphire from the coronation ring of Edward the Confessor. (*c*) *The Imperial Crown of India* was made for the ceremony of crowning King George V as emperor of India at Delhi. (2) **Queen's Crowns or Diadems.** (*a*) *The Crown of Queen Mary of Modena*, consort of James II; (*b*) the *diadem* of the same queen; (*c*) *the State Crown of Queen Mary*, consort of George V. (3) **Sceptres.** (*a*) the *king's royal sceptre* with the cross, which dates from the period of Charles II, and has at its head the principal Star of India; (*b*) the *king's sceptre* with the dove; (*c*) the *queen's sceptre* with the cross; (d) the *queen's sceptre* with the dove; (*e*) the *queen's ivory rod.* (4) **Orbs.** (*a*) the *king's orb*, and (*b*) the *queen's orb*. The former is held in the left hand by Brit. sovereigns at their coronation, and is symbolic of the dominion of the Christian religion. (5) **St. Edward's Staff.** This is also known as the *Rod of Justice and Equity* and is of gold, 4 ft. 7 in. (6) **Ampulla** and **Anointing Spoon.** These are of ancient workmanship and are used for the anointing of the sovereign at the coronation ceremony. (7) **Swords.** These are 5 in number, *viz.* (*a*) the *sword of state*, a long two-handled sword carried before the sovereign on all State occasions. (*b*) the *jewelled sword of state* used only at the coronation, when the sovereign lays it, together with the *Golden Spurs of St. George*, on the altar, thus symbolising that his or her military power is placed at the service of the church. (*c*) the *Curtena*, or *sword of Mercy*, the point of which has been broken off, (*d*) the *sword of justice, spiritual*, (*e*) the *sword of justice, temporal*. (8) **Armillas** or **Bracelets.** A pair of bracelets of gold.

CROYDON
County borough of Greater London (1964) formerly in Surrey. The borough, which includes Norbury, Addiscombe, Addington, Thornton Heath and Norwood, returns 3 members to Parl. Pop. 327,125.

CRUCIFIX
Cross bearing an image of Christ. From the 6th to the 12th cent. crucifixes showed Jesus triumphant and clothed. Since then, they have stressed His suffering.

CRUIKSHANK, George
(1792-1878) Eng. artist. Illustrated the works of Fielding and Dickens and Grimm's *Fairy Stories*, and magazines such as *Bentley's Miscellany*.

CRUISER
Warship having less fighting power and thinner armour than the battleship, but greater sp. They are used to screen the battle fleet, for recon., convoy duties, etc. Prior to World War

II, cruisers were grouped in 3 main categories, *viz.*, Light, Heavy and Battle Cruisers.

CRUSADE
Milit. expedition sent under the banner of the cross, esp. those sent out from Europe to recover Palestine for the Christians. Palestine was overrun by the Saracens in the 7th cent. but Christians were allowed to make pilgrimages to the Holy Places at Jerusalem. In the 11th cent. the Turks occupied the country and pilgrims were maltreated. This gave rise to the **First Crusade**, preached by Peter the Hermit and ordered by Pope Urban II at Clermont in 1095. Some European princes raised an army in 1097 and this took Antioch, and in 1099 captured Jerusalem, where a kingdom was set up under Godfrey of Bouillon. In 1187 Jerusalem was retaken by Saladin and the **Third Crusade** was organised. In this Richard I, Frederick Barbarossa and Philip Augustus of Fr. took part. It ended in 1192 in a treaty allowing the pilgrims to visit the Holy Places.

CRUSTACEA
[-tā'-shiă] Class of the Phylum Arthropoda. The body is segmented and has jointed limbs; the head is fused with some of the thoracic segments. The rest of the body segments are usually divided into 2 regions, and the whole animal is covered with a chitinous cuticle. The head bears a pair of stalked eyes, 2 pairs of sensory antennae and modified jaws.

CRYSTAL
Solid body of regular shape bounded by symmetrically disposed plane surfaces, and possessing definite internal structure and properties. Crystals arise from solidification of chem. elements or compounds. **Crystallography** is the study of the geometric forms of crystals. The science involves the consideration of the relation between crystal faces and their axes, the measurement of the interfacial angles, the identification of similar faces, and the classification into different grades of symmetry.

CRYSTAL PALACE
Pleasure resort at Sydenham, London, gutted by fire in 1936. It was designed by Sir Joseph Paxton, erected 1854, and became public property in 1920. In 1951 the property was transferred to the L.C.C. and in 1964 a nat. youth and sports centre covering 36 acres was opened.

CUBA
Is. repub. of the W. Indies, one of the Greater Antilles, situated across the entrance to the Gulf of Mexico. Long, narrow, with wooded mts. in the extreme S., Cuba is principally an agricultural country, producing sugar and tobacco. Fruit and vegetables are grown. About one sixth is forest land. Copper, manganese and iron are worked. Havana is the cap. and largest town; others are Santiago, Camaguey, Holguin, Santa Clara, Cienfuegos and Matanzas. There is a central rail system, good roads, and numerous harbours. There is no state religion. The pop. is mainly of Sp. origin. Cuba was discovered by Columbus, 1492, and conquered by the Spaniards, 16th cent. After a civil war, the U.S. govt. intervened, and the Sp. were forced to leave the country. With U.S. help, Cuba achieved indep. (1902). In 1959 Dr. Fidel Castro overthrew the existing dictatorship and estabd. a quasi-Communist govt. The Cuban crisis of Oct. 1962 arose from the U.S.A.'s discovery of offensive Soviet missile sites on the island. Area: 44,219 sq.m. Pop. 8,033,000.

CUBISM
Form of Fr. painting, originated *c.* 1907, with Picasso, Braque, Gris, Léger and others. The style shows a tendency to rectangular treatment of forms.

CUCKOO
(*Cuculidae*) Family of birds of widespread distribution. The Common Cuckoo (*Cuculus canorus*) is one of the earliest spring visitants to Brit. Eggs are laid singly and deposited in the nests of smaller birds. The young cuckoo will often eject its weaker companions from the nest. The name cuckoo is taken from the cry of the male bird.

CUCKOO PINT
(*Arum maculatum*) Brit. wildflower. It has tuberous roots and arrow-shaped leaves. The flower stalk bears a large green rolled-up leaf which withers, leaving a spike of scarlet berries.

CUCKOO SPIT
Froth-like spume produced by Frog hoppers (*q.v.*).

CUCUMBER
(*Cucumis sativus*) Cultivated trailing herb of the gourd family. Male and female flowers are distinct; the ovaries become cucumbers without fertilisation.

CUDWEED
Popular name of several species of composite herbs (*Gnaphalium*). The commonest Brit. form is *G. sylvaticum*. It is densely cottony, with narrow leaves and small flower heads enclosed by scales which usually persist.

CULLODEN
Moor about 7 m. from Inverness, scene of the final defeat of the Jacobites under Charles Edward, by the Duke of Cumberland (April 16, 1746).

CUMAE
[kew'-mē] Ancient town, the first Gk. colony in Italy, it was founded by the Chalcidians of Euboea. First taken by the Campanians and then by the Roms. it became a municipal town in 339 B.C.

CUMBERLAND
County of Eng. S. of the Scot. border. In the N. are peaks of the Pennine range; in the S. are the mts. of the Lake District, Scafell, Helvellyn and Skiddaw, the 3 highest in Eng. The lakes include Derwentwater, Thirlmere, Buttermere and Wastwater. The rivers are the Eden, Derwent and Esk. There is fertile soil in the dales and sheep are reared on the hills. Around Whitehaven is a coalfield. Carlisle is the county town. Other towns are Whitehaven, Workington, Keswick, Cockermouth and Penrith. Cumberland sends 4 members to Parl. (including the borough constituency of Carlisle). Pop. 294,130.

CUMBERLAND, Duke of
Eng. title held by several members of the royal family. In 1726 William Augustus (1721-65), a son of George II, was made Duke of Cumberland. He routed the Jacobites at Culloden. In 1766 Henry Frederick, a brother of George III, was made duke. In 1799 the dukedom was revived for Ernest Augustus, son of George III. In 1837 he was succeeded by his son, George, whose son, Ernest Augustus (1843-1923) was also known as the Duke of Cumberland.

CUMIN
Herbaceous annual (*Cuminum cyminum*) of the Umbelliferae, cultivated in the E. and around the Medit. for its fruit which contains an essential oil.

CUNEIFORM
Writing which consists of wedge-shaped and of rectangular marks, *e.g.* in Ninevite sculptures. Sir Henry Rawlinson deciphered 3 forms. *Babylonian*, *Median* and *Persian*.

Assyrian cuneiform script

CUNNINGHAM, Viscount of Hyndhope, Andrew Browne (1883-1963) Brit.

Adm. of the Fleet. Entered R.N., 1898; served in World War I, gaining triple D.S.O. C.-in-C. Med. 1939-42; C.-in-C. Allied Naval Forces, Med. 1943; Adm. of the Fleet and first Sea Lord, 1943. As 1st Sea Lord, he was responsible for the operational policy of the Navy during the later stages of the War.

CUPAR
[koo′-păr] Royal burgh and county town of Fife, on the Eden. Pop. 5,861.

CUPID
Lat. god of love. Identical with the *Eros* and *Amor* of Gk. and Lat. writers, he was the son of Venus (Aphrodite).

CURAÇAO
[kew-ră-sō′] Group of Dutch Is. in the W. Indies, 40 m. N. of Venezuela, comprising Curaçao, Aruba, Bonaire, St. Eustatius and Saba and part of St. Martin: an integral part of the Kingdom of the Netherlands. Salt and guano phosphates are exported. The liqueur Curaçao is now made elsewhere. Willemstad is the chief town and seat of govt. Area: 394 sq.m. Pop. 187,041.

CURARA
(or **curare**) [koo-rah′-ri] Arrow poison used by the S. Amer. Indians. Prepared from various plants, principally species of *Strychnos*, and used to some extent in medicine. From it is obtained the active principle, curarine, in the form of a yellowish-brown powder which paralyses the muscles if injected beneath the skin.

CURIA
One of the 30 divisions of the Rom. people. It also designates the *curia Romana*, the institutions whereby the Vatican governs the R.C. Ch.

CURIE, Pierre
[kü-rē′] (1859-1906) Fr. scientist. B. Paris, educ. the Sorbonne. He became Prof. of Physics there, and married Marie Sklodowska, who assisted him in his researches. They discovered *polonium* and *radium* in 1898. For this they were awarded a Nobel prize in 1903. **Marie Curie** (1867-1934) succeeded her husband as Prof. at the Sorbonne. In 1911 she received a Nobel prize for chem. **Irène** (1897-1956) daughter of the above, mar. (1932) **Frédéric Joliot.** In 1935 they were jointly awarded the Nobel Prize for chemistry research which led to the discovery of neutrons.

CURLEW
(*Numerius*) The Common Curlew (*N. arquata*), breeds in Brit.; the Jack Curlew, or Whimbrel (*N. phoeopus*), only in the N. of Scot.; and the Eskimo Curlew (*N. borealis*), is rare. The Stone Curlew, or Norfolk Plover, is of another family. They are birds of the Plover family with marled brown plumage and long downwardly curved beaks. Female is larger than male.

CURLING
Game popular in Scot. It is played on ice with large stones fitted with handles. The aim is to place the stones as near as possible to a fixed mark called a tee. The legislative body is the Royal Caledonian Curling Club, formed in 1838.

CURRANT
Fruit of various shrubs of the Grossulariaceae. *Ribes sativum* yields cultivated red currants, and in another variety, white currants; *R. nigrum* yields black currants. The Amer. red-flowered *R. sanguineum* is a shrubbery plant. A currant is also the dried seedless fruit of a grape grown esp. in the Ionian Is.

CURRENCY
Money that passes current in a country. It may consist of coins of gold, silver, bronze or nickel, or be paper money. The name **currency notes** is used sometimes for the notes for £1, £5, etc., issued in Brit. since the 1st World War. At first issued by the Treasury, they have been issued by the Bank of Eng. since 1928.

CURRENT
Movement of a fluid in a determined direction. Air currents caused by the earth's rotation are affected by differences of density and temperature . Every prevalent wind causes oceanic drift currents. Thus the Atlantic equatorial currents, drifted W. by the trade winds, unite in the Gulf of Mexico, creating the Gulf Stream, which flows N.

CUSTARD APPLE
Fruit of trop. trees (*Anona reticulata* and *squamosa*). Its brown berries contain reddish-yellow pulp.

CUSTOMS
Taxes levied on imported goods since the reign of Richard I. Customs duties are levied on many articles imported into Brit. Dutiable articles inc. tea, sugar, tobacco, wines and spirits. Collections of duties is controlled by the Board of Customs and Excise.

CUTCH
(or **Kutch**) Former state of India on the coast of the Arabian Sea, S. of Sind, Pakistan. Became a prov. of Gujarat in 1960.

CUTTER
Single-masted sailing vessel with mainsail, fore-staysails, and jib set to the bowsprit end.

CUTTLEFISH
(*Sepia*) Marine molluscs with internal calcareous shell. Unlike the 8-armed octopus, they and the squids have 2 long, additional tentacles with suckers, and ink-sacs for darkening water as a protection. 3 species inhabit Brit. waters, S. Asia and the Medit. region.

CUTTY SARK
The most famous sailing ship of the type known as clipper. She was built at Dumbarton in 1869 and engaged in the Australian wool trade. The Cutty Sark Preservation Soc. and an appeal for funds were launched in Apr. 1953, to restore the ship and set up and maintain a fund to help boys who wish to be trained for the Merchant Navy.

CUXHAVEN
[kooks′-hă-fen] Seaport of Lower Saxony, W. Germany, at the mouth of the Elbe, 60 m. N.W. of Hamburg, for which it is the outport. Pop. 47,000.

CUYP, Albert
[koip] (1620-91) Dutch painter; b. Dordrecht, known for his landscapes, and pictures of horses and people on horseback. He was the son of **Jacob Gerritsz C.** (1594-1652), a landscape and portrait painter.

CUZCO
City of S. Peru, in a small valley, 11,400 ft. above sea level, connected by rly. with La Paz and Mollendo, on the coast. Once the cap. of the Inca Emp. it was taken by the Sp. 1533. Pop. 72,120.

CYANAMIDE
White crystalline solid (NH_2CN), melting at 42° C. It forms metallic derivatives, in which the 2 hydrogen atoms are replaced by an atom of a metal. The chief metallic derivative is calcium cyanamide.

CYANIDE
Compound of cyanogen with an element or radical; also a salt of hydrocyanic acid, especially potassium cyanide. In metallurgy, the cyanide process is a method of extracting gold and silver from their ores.

CYCLADES
[sik′-] Group of *c.* 200 Gk. Is. in the Aegean Sea. S.E. of Euboea Pop. 99,931.

CYCLING
Riding a bicycle or tricycle. Towards the end of the 19th cent. when the bicycle invented by Kirkpatrick Macmillan in 1839 was developed, the sport was very popular. The interests of Brit. cyclists are looked after by the Cyclists' Touring Club. For the sport, the controlling authority is the Nat. Cyclists' Union. On the Continent road cycle racing enjoys enormous popularity, a major race being the *Tour de France* (3,250 m.). *See* BICYCLE.

CYCLONE
Region of low atmospheric pressure. There are 2 types, the cyclone of temperate latitudes, usually called a *depression*, and the smaller, more violent *tropical* cyclone. In both cases, the pressure is lowest in the centre, with winds rotating anti-clockwise in the N. hemisphere but clockwise in the S.

CYCLOPS
Small freshwater Crustacea of the order Copepoda. They have enlarged feelers, used as oars. There is a single eye in the head. The female carries 2 oval egg-sacs externally; the larvae hatch without the full number of appendages.

CYMBELINE
(or **Cunobelinus**) Brit. king. He was called by Suetonius king of the Britons. The plot of Shakespeare's *Cymbeline* is devoid of hist. truth.

CYMMRODORION
Soc. for preserving Welsh literature and nationality. Estabd. for instructing the ignorant and relieving distress in 1751, it ceased in 1781. Revived for promoting lit. study in 1820, it lasted to 1843. Reconstituted as the Hon. Soc. of Cymmrodorion of London in 1877. A similar soc. estab. in 1792 led to the revival of the national Eisteddfod.

CYNEWULF
(lived *c.* 750) O.E. poet. Four poems—*Juliana, The Fates of the Apostles, Elene, The Ascension*—have passages containing Cynewulf's name in runes.

CYNICS
[sin'-] Sect of Gk. philosophers founded by Anisthenes, who regarded virtue as the only good, consisting in avoiding evil and wanting nothing. From the Cynics developed the Stoics (*q.v.*).

CYPRESS
Genus of evergreen shrubs and trees of the coniferous order, natives of S. Europe, Asia and N. Amer. (*Cupressus*). The common cypress, *C. sempervirens*, grown around the Medit., in antiquity was regarded as a symbol of the dead. One variety, *C. fastigiata*, grows like the Lombardy poplar.

CYPRUS
Is. in the E. Medit. *c.* 40 m. from the coast of Asia Minor. Products include wheat, barley, olives and citrus fruits. Sheep and goats are reared; iron, copper and asbestos are mined. Nicosia is the cap.; other towns are Larnaca, Limassol, Famagusta and Kyrenia. The Cypriots are predominantly of Gk. ancestry (*c.* 20 % Turkish). Cyprus was occupied by the Gks. and Phoenicians and Roms. Conquered by Turkey, 1571. Following an agreement with the Sultan, 1878, the Is. was admin. by Brit. and became a colony, 1925. On the withdrawal of Brit. troops from the Suez Canal zone, 1954, the H.Q. of the Brit. M.E. land and air forces was set up in the island. Serious rioting broke out in 1954 when a section of the people demanded union of Cyprus with Greece. During 1955-56 outbursts of terrorism against Brit. rule caused considerable damage and many deaths. After talks between Sir John Harding, Gov.-Gen. and Archbp. Makarios, head of the Enosis (union with Greece) movement, had failed to produce agreement, Archbp. Makarios was arrested by the Brit. authorities and deported from Cyprus in March, 1956; released April, 1957. After 3 years of hostilities the London agreement was reached in Feb. 1959. Archbp. Makarios became Pres. of the new repub. 1960. Christmas 1963 saw the beginning of renewed hostilities between the Gk. and Turkish communities. U.N. troops were sent in to deal with a situation approaching civil war. Area: 3,572 sq.m. Pop. 574,000.

CYRENAICA
[sīrĕ-nā'-ikă] Territory of Libya (*q.v.*). Benghazi, Derna and Tobruk, the chief towns, were the scene of fighting in World War II.

CYRIL and **METHODIUS**
Christian saints. Brother apostles of the Slavs in the 9th cent. Believed to have invented the Cyrillic alphabet still used among the Serbs, Bulgars and Russians.

CYRUS
Names of 2 rulers of Persia, **Cyrus the elder,** called the Great, was the founder of the Persian Empire. He captured Babylon, united the Medes and Persians and made Susa his cap. **Cyrus the Younger** was the 2nd son of Darius, King of Persia. He led an army of Gks. from Asia Minor into Persia and was killed at the Battle of Cunaxa in 401 B.C.

CYST
[sist] Any localised swelling in body with a lining membrane around a collection of fluid.

CYSTITIS
[sis-tī'-] Inflammation of urinary bladder caused by infection with micro-organisms.

CZECH
[chek] People of Slavic stock inhabiting Bohemia and Moravia. They form, with Poles, Wends and Slovaks, the W. branch of the Slavs, prob. migrating from the Upper Vistula in the 5th cent. Their speech became differentiated and was kept alive by John Hus, and by the Moravian Brethren. They are closely akin to the Slovaks but have a very different hist.

CZECHOSLOVAKIA
[chek-] Repub. of C. Europe N. of Austria and Hungary, and S. of Poland. It consists of 2 areas, the ancient Bohemian plateau in the W. and the Carpathian Mts. of Slovakia, divided by the Morava valley. The former, drained by the Elbe and Vltava, is well developed and densely populated, whilst the E. is more backward. Crops incl. cereals, sugar beet and hops. Czechoslovakia is rich in minerals, coal, iron, silver, copper and lead. Numerous industries have developed, particularly in Bohemia; there are engineering and metallurgical works, glass, leather and textile manufactures, and breweries at Pilsen. Wood pulp and paper are produced in forested Slovakia. Prague is the cap. of Czechoslovakia and of Bohemia; other towns are Brno, Moravska, Ostrava, Bratislava and Pilsen. Czechoslovakia became an indep. repub. 1918, after the break up of the Austro-Hungarian Empire. It was formed of Bohemia, Moravia, Slovakia, and parts of Silesia and Ruthenia, the latter being ceded to the U.S.S.R., 1945. First pres. was Prof. T. Masaryk (*q.v.*). In 1939 Nazi troops invaded Czechoslovakia in violation of the Munich Conference. After the liberation, 1945, German and Hungarian minorities were expelled, and there was a large scale nationalisation programme. In 1948 the Communists won complete control of the govt. In 1968, after liberal reforms had been inaugurated, Warsaw Pact armies entered the country in an attempt to prevent the changes. Area: 49,359 sq.m. Pop. 13,742,000.

D

D
4th letter of the Eng. and Lat. alphabets. It represents a soft dental sound (made with tongue and teeth), the corresponding hard sound being *t*. Cap. D is the Rom. numeral symbol for 500.

D.D.T.
Dichloro-Dipheny-Trichlorethane. Powerful insecticide powder highly lethal to flies, mosquitoes, sandflies, lice and fleas. Has proved valuable in helping to combat diseases caused by those pests esp. malaria, yellow fever, plague, and typhus. It was discovered by Swiss firm J. R. Geigy in 1940. *See* TYPHUS FEVER.

DAB
(*Pleuronectes limanda*) Flat fish of Brit. coastal waters and brackish estuaries, it is *c.* 12 in. long, with rough skin, light-brown above and white beneath.

DABCHICK
Popular name of the **Little Grebe** (*Podiceps rufficollis*). It has a dark brown back and in summer the male has cheeks, sides and front of neck chestnut red.

DACCA
Chief city of E. Pakistan, on the Buhri Ganga, a trib. of the Meghana. There are numerous industries and a univ. Pop. 556,712.

DACE
Freshwater fish of the Carp family (*Leuciscus vulgaris*). Black-brown with silvery sides, it is 8-9 in. long and up to 1 lb. in wt. Swims in shoals in running streams in Fr., Germany and S. Eng.

DACHSHUND
[-hoont] A German breed originally used for badger hunting. Good watch-dog with a loud bark. Has short legs, long cylindrical body and long pendulous ears. Normal dogs weigh *c.* 20 lb. and miniatures *c.* 10 lb. Coats are smooth, wiry or long-haired.

DAFFODIL
Hardy bulbous plant of various species of *Narcissus* of the Amaryllis family, native to Europe. The Brit. Lent lily (*Narcissus pseudonarcissus*), whose flowers have crimped trumpet-shaped coronas, comprises many varieties, including the Tenby and Sp. daffodil.

DAGENHAM
Former Essex borough, now part of Greater London (1964) on the N. side of the Thames. It is the site of the Eng. works of the Ford Motor Co.

DAHLIA
[dā′-] Genus of herbaceous plants of the family compositae. In 1784 brought to Europe from Mexico and cultivated by Dahl, a Swedish botanist, whence its name.

DAHOMEY
Repub. in W. Africa, between Togoland and Nigeria, bounded on the N. by the Niger. D. has only 78 m. of coast, but there is a large hinterland, much of it forested. Palm kernels and oil are the chief products. Porto Novo is the cap. and Kotonu the chief port. Formerly Fr., D. became fully indep., 1960. Area: 44,697 sq.m. Pop. 2,508,000.

DAIL EIREANN
[doil air′an] House of the legislature of the Repub. of Ireland.

DAISY
(*Bellis perennis*) Genus of hardy herbaceous perennial plants of the family compositae, native to Brit. and Europe. **Marguerites,** or oxeye daisies, are *Chrysanthemum leucanthemum.*

DALAI LAMA
Chief pope of Lamaism (*q.v.*).

DALCROZE, Émile-Jacques
[-ōz′] (1865-1950) B. Vienna of Swiss parentage, he estabd. in 1910, a school of eurhythmics near Dresden. **Dalcroze Eurhythmics.** Method by which the appreciation and expression of music are taught through movement.

DALI, Salvador
[dȧ′-lē] (1904-) Sp. painter. B. Figueras. He studied in Madrid and experimented in Impressionism and Pointillism. Influenced by Picasso and Miro and by Surrealism of which he is now an outstanding exponent.

DALLAS
City of Texas, U.S.A., an important centre of communications. Its industries include meat-packing, cotton manufacturing and flour-milling. Scene of assassination of Pres. Kennedy, 1963. Pop. 836,200.

DALMATIA
Narrow coastal region of Yugoslavia 200 m. long, between Bosnia-Herzegovina and the Adriatic. Most of the interior is mountainous. The chief towns are Sibenik, Split and Kotor. In 1920 it was given by treaty to Yugoslavia, except for the cap. Zadar, which became Ital. In 1947 the latter was ceded to Yugoslavia. **Dalmatian** [-mā-] This breed is the carriage dog of Victorian days. Coat is white and spotted all over in either black or liver spots. Sleek in appearance and suggestive of the pointer; wt. *c.* 50 lb.

DALTON, John
(1766-1844) Eng. scientist. In 1794 Dalton, himself colour blind, pub. the first scientific account of that defect, often called **Daltonism.** Dalton also laid down 2 laws: (1) The pressure exerted by, and the quantity of, a vapour which saturates a given space are the same for the same temps. whether the space is a vacuum or is filled with gas. (2) (**Dalton's Law**) The pressure of a mixture of gases is the sum of the pressures exerted separately by the several constituents if each alone were present.

DAMASCUS
Cap. of Syria, in the Anti-Lebanon foothills, 57 m. S.E. of Beirut. It is a great commercial centre. D. belonged in turn to Assyria, Persia and Rome, and from 661-750 was the cap. of the Caliphate. In 1516 the Turks captured it and in Oct. 1918, the Brit. entered it. Later, it became part of the new Repub. of Syria. Pop. 600,000.

DAMPIER, William
(1652-1715) Eng. navigator, buccaneer and hydrographer. B. Somerset; buccaneered in S. Amer. waters, 1679-86; reached Guam 1686, sighted Australia 1688, and was marooned on the Nicobar Is., reaching Eng. 1691. He ex-

plored the Austral. coast from Shark's Bay to Dampier Archipelago and discovered New Brit. He pub. *Voyages and Descriptions* (1690) and *A New Voyage Round the World* (1697).

DAMSON
Fruit of a rosaceous species (*Prunus insititia*), grown largely in Shropshire, Cheshire, Worcestershire and Kent. Smaller than the plum, and oval-shaped, the damson is usually dark blue.

DANCING
Rhythmical steps and movements of the body. Primarily it is an expression of strong emotion, religious or social, and is illustrated in Stone Age art. Primitive peoples manifest it variously. The sound for measuring the rhythm enhances the emotional appeal, even if it is only hand clapping. The morris dance round a maypole survives in the games of modern children. From Spain came the pavane, fandango, bolero and saraband. Fr., besides elaborating the gavotte, minuet and quadrille, adapted the C. European polka, schottische and waltz. Amer. barn dances of negro origin, governed by jazz band syncopation, were introduced into Europe and developed into the two-step, one-step and foxtrot. Popular modern dances are gen. short lived.

DANDELION
Perennial herb of the Compositae family (*Taraxacum officinale*), native to temp. and cold regions. Its long black tap root bears hollow

flower stalks with solitary heads of yellow strap-shaped florets. The seeds radiate white pappus hairs.

DANDIE DINMONT
Breed of dog. Introd. in Teviotdale, largely through a farmer; it is a long-backed, short-legged terrier. With deep muzzle, the dog is muscular and plucky, averaging 18 lb. The silky coat is slate-blue, pepper or mustard in colour.

DANDRUFF
Condition affecting the skin and assoc. with scurf, which forms on the head and comes off in scales.

DANES
Rovers from the Scandinavian countries who raided Eng. before 1066, also called Northmen. From 790 to 851 raids were frequent and great damage was done by the invaders, who sailed up rivers in search of plunder. In 851 the Danes began to settle in Eng. and Alfred the Great handed over the **Danelaw** to them. About 922 the Danish ravages began again. Ethelred the Unready raised money, the **Danegeld**, to buy them off. In 1013 Sweyn, King of Denmark, conquered the N. and in 1016 his son, Canute, became King of Eng. He reigned until 1035, and his sons, Harold and Hardicanute, until 1042, when the Danish rule ended.

DANEWORT
Popular name for the dwarf elder (*Sambucus ebulus*). A native of Europe, W. Asia, and N. Africa, it is a many-stemmed herb, with pink-tipped, white, bell-shaped flowers.

DANTE, Alighieri
(1265-1321) Ital. poet. B. (probably) at Florence; d. Ravenna. Engaged in city politics and was banished 1301; led a wandering life. In the *Vita Nuova*, written after the d. of Beatrice (*q.v.*), Dante celebrated the exalted love of his boyhood and youth. In *The Commedia*, begun about 1300, he records his journey through Hell, Purgatory and Paradise.

DANTON, Georges Jacques
(1759-94) Fr. revolutionary leader. B. Arcis-sur-Aube. In 1790 he commanded the Nat. Guard. He became a member of the Paris Commune (1791). He sat in the Convention as a leader of the Mountain, voted for the king's d., was a member of the Committee of Public Safety, but was not willing to follow Robespierre further. Consequently he was arrested and guillotined.

DANUBE
The most important river of S. Europe. It rises in Baden-Württemberg, Germany, and flows 1,750 m. through Bavaria, Austria, Czechoslovakia, Hungary, Yugoslavia and Rumania to the Black Sea. It has over 300 tribs. and on it are 3 caps., Vienna, Budapest and Belgrade. Other towns are Ulm, Regensburg, Passau, Bratislava and Orsova with the Iron Gates. Navigable by large vessels to Braila and by barges to Ulm, it is connected with the Rhine via the Main and a system of canals. An international river, it was governed by an international commission set up in 1919. This was dissolved, 1940, and in 1948 a new commission was set up of some of the Danubian states and Russia. In 1955 Austria's rights were restored and the Danube opened to all vessels of commerce.

DANZIG *See* GDANSK.

DAR-ES-SALAAM
Seaport and cap. of United Repub. of Tanzania. Sisal hemp, coffee, cotton and minerals are exported. Pop. 190,000.

DARDANELLES
Strait between Europe and Asia, uniting the Sea of Marmara with the Aegean. The classical Hellespont, it is 47 m. long and *c.* 4 m. broad. The channel was crossed, between Sestos and Abydos, on boat bridges by the armies of Xerxes, 480 B.C. and Alexander, 334 B.C. Russian policy from 1774 was to obtain control of the straits, but Brit. and Fr. supported Turkey. The straits were internationalised, but the Treaty of Lausanne, 1923, largely restored them to Turkish control. Almost complete Turkish sovereignty was conceded by the Montreux Convention, 1936. **Dardanelles Campaign.** During World War I, the forts were bombarded by Brit. and Fr. warships and an attempt to force the straits failed. These operations preceded the Gallipoli landing.

DARIEN
[dair'-] Name formerly applied to the E. part of the Isthmus of Panama. The Serrania del Darien is an Andean range on the Colombian frontier. **The Darien Scheme** was a plan to start a Co. in Scot. to trade with the W. Indies, authorised in 1695 by the Scots. Parl. In 1698 settlers were sent out to Darien, but they found it impossible to remain there owing to the climate and Sp. hostility. Eng. traders' jealousy and lack of co-operation, to which the Scots. attributed their failure, caused bad feeling between the 2 countries.

DARJEELING
Town of W. Bengal, India, *c.* 7,000 ft. up on the S. slopes of the Himalayas, 360 m. N. of Calcutta. There are many tea plantations. Pop. 26,000.

DARLING
River of Australia, 1,700 m. long, which rises in the Great Dividing Range in Queensland

and flows across N.S.W. until it joins the Murray, of which it is the largest trib.

DARLING, Grace
(1815-42) B. Bamborough, daughter of keeper of the lighthouse on the Longstone, Farne Is. On Sept. 7, 1838, the steamer *Forfarshire* was driven on the rocks about a mile from the Longstone. Traditionally, Grace Darling persuaded her father to help her in their rescue.

DARLINGTON
County borough and industrial town of S. Durham, on a trib. of the Tees, 23 m. from Durham. The industries include engineering works, iron works and woollen mills. It returns 1 member to Parl. Pop. 84,400.

DARNEL
(*Lolium temulentum*) Annual grass related to rye grass, native to Europe, temp. Asia and N. Africa.

DARNLEY, Lord
(1545-67) Scots noble. Henry Stuart, b. Temple Newsam, the eldest son of the Earl of Lennox. Through his mother, he was descended from Henry VII. In 1565, he mar. Mary, Queen of Scots. Their only child became James I of Gt. Brit. Darnley was killed whilst lying ill in Edinburgh, 1567.

DARTFORD
Borough of Kent, on the Darent, 17 m. S.E. of London. Cement and paper are made, and there are engineering and chemical works and flour mills. It returns 1 member to Parl. Pop. 46,180.

DARTMOOR
Moorland district in S.W. Devon. High Willhays and Yes Tor are the highest peaks, both just over 2,000 ft. The Dart, Tavy, Teign and Okement rise on the moor.

DARTMOUTH
Borough and seaport of S. Devon, on the W. bank of the Dart, 30 m. from Exeter. It is a yachting centre. Pop. 6,360. **Dartmouth Royal Naval Coll.** was opened, 1905, to train officers for the navy.

DARWIN
Port and cap. of N. Territory, Australia, in N.W. Arnhem Land. Port of entry for European and Asian passenger air services. Mother-of-pearl fishing is important. Pop. *c.* 15,000.

DARWIN, Charles Robert
(1809-82) Eng. naturalist. B. Shrewsbury; educ. there and at Edinburgh and Camb. In 1839 he mar. Emma Wedgwood. The next 20 years were spent in scientific research. The results were pub. in *The Origin of Species*, 1859, and in *The Descent of Man*, 1871. He believed that man is related to the lower animals and that in animal life there is a struggle for existence which leads to the natural selection of those qualities most useful to continue the life of the species. This is the doctrine of the survival of the fittest, or natural selection. Four of his 5 sons became prominent in the world of science. **Sir George Howard D.** (1845-1912) was Prof. of Astron. at Camb. (1883-1912). **Sir Francis D.** (1848-1925) was reader in botany at Camb. **Leonard D.** (1850-1943) became pres. of the Eugenics Soc. **Sir Horace D.** (1851-1928) became the head of a scientific instruments firm at Camb. **Charles Galton D.** (1887-1963) son of Sir George Howard D. was prof. of Nat. Phil. at Edinburgh Univ. 1923-36.

DARWIN, Erasmus
(1731-1802) Eng. scientist. His most noted scientific work was his *Zoonomia*, 1794. He anticipated much of the Lamarckian idea of evolution. Grandfather of Charles Darwin and Francis Galton.

DATE
Fruit of a tree of the palm order, native to N. Africa and S.W. Asia (*Phoenix dactylifera*). Cultivated in India. It is straight-stemmed, with feather-like leaves, the male and female flowers being on separate trees. It grows to 100 ft. and bears dates in bunches. The natives of N. Africa use the date-palms for building huts, for fibre cloth, ropes, etc.

DATELINE, International
A hypothetical line which follows the meridian of long. of 180° from Greenwich, except where it diverges to include the Aleutian Is. with Alaska, and some S. Sea Is. with Australia. It is used by mariners and airmen as the most convenient place to adjust their clocks, the reason being that, as compared with sun time, a day (one hour for every 15°) is lost in making a complete circumnavigation of the globe.

DAUPHIN
[daw'-fin] Title borne by the eldest son of the kings of Fr. Formerly the title of certain nobles, one of whom, the Dauphin of Vienne, sold his lands to the prince who became King Charles V. He gave these lands to his son, and from that time the eldest son was called the Dauphin. His inheritance, the district round Grenoble, became known as Dauphiné, now the depts. Isère, Drôme and Hautes Alpes.

DAVENANT, Sir William
(1606-68) Eng. poet. He wrote comedies and tragedies; became poet laureate 1638; supported the King in the Civil War and was imprisoned by the Parliamentarians. His production of *The Siege of Rhodes*, a musical play, 1656, when ordinary dramatic performances were forbidden, helped to estab. Eng. opera.

DAVID
(O.T.) Youngest son of Jesse of Jerusalem, a shepherd and famed for his skill on the harp. Samuel, the prophet, anointed him as Saul's successor. Having killed the giant Goliath, he became the friend of Saul's son, Jonathan, but Saul's enmity drove him into the wilderness. The d. of Saul, and Jonathan, in battle against the Philistines, followed, and David became King of Judah. He is regarded as the founder of the royal line to which Jesus Christ belonged.

DAVID
(lived *c.* 550) Patron saint of Wales. According to legend a grandson of King Ceredig, uncle of King Arthur. Became Bishop of Menevia, now St. David's. He moved the seat of eccles. govt. from Caerleon to Menevia. Canonised by Calixtus II, 1120, **St. David's Day** is March 1.

DAVID, Jacques Louis
[da-vēd'] (1748-1825) Fr. painter. B. Paris. Under Napoleon he was given official recognition, but was afterwards exiled and d. in Brussels. As a member of the convention he voted for the d. of Louis XVI.

DAVIE, Cedric Thorpe
(1913-) Scots. organist and composer. B. Blackheath. Master of Music, St. Andrews Univ. Studied under Vaughan Williams, R. O. Morris and Gordon Jacob. Works include musical settings of *Gammer Gurton's Needle*, *The Forrigan Reel*.

DAVIES, Sir Henry Walford
(1869-1941) Eng. organist, teacher and composer. Master of the King's Musick from 1934. Wrote choral works, orchestral pieces, the *Solemn Melody* for organ and strings, ch. music, chamber music and songs.

DAVIES, William Henry
(1871-1940) Eng. poet. B. Newport, Mon.; led a vagrant life in Brit. and Amer. Wrote: poetry, *The Soul's Destroyer* (1907), *The Birth of Song* (1936); prose, *The Autobiography of a Super-Tramp* (1908).

DA VINCI, Leonardo
(1452-1519) Ital. painter, phil., mathematician, scientist and engineer. B. Vinci, near Florence. About 1470 he worked in the studio of Veroc-

chio and later was in Egypt as an engineer. In 1500 he was architect and engineer to Cesare Borgia in Florence, and in 1506 he went to Fr. He d. near Amboise. Among his paintings are *The Last Supper* and *La Gioconda* (the Mona Lisa). In physics he was probably the first to understand the principle of inertia. He understood the wave nature of sound and light and appears to have understood the circulation of the blood (a cent. before Harvey).

DAVIS, Jefferson
(1808-89) Amer. statesman and Pres. of the Confederacy. He was in the Army (1828-35), and in Congress (1845). He served in the Mexican War (1846-7), and became a Senator; Sec. for War (1853). In 1861, when the S. States seceded, he was elected their Pres. When the war ceased he was accused of treason and imprisoned, but released in 1867.

DAVIS, John
(*c.* 1550-1605) Eng. navigator sometimes called John Davys. In 1585-6 and 7 he went in search of the N.W. Passage. Unsuccessful, he discovered the Falkland Is. (1592). He invented a quadrant. **Davis Strait,** the channel connecting Baffin Bay with the Atlantic is named after him.

DAVIS CUP
Colloq. name for **Dwight Davis International Bowl,** a lawn tennis trophy, competed for annually. Presented by Dwight Filley Davis (1879-1945) in 1900. He took part in the first two contests.

DAVOS
[dä'-] 2 resorts in Grisons canton, Switzerland, in the Landwasser Valley (5,150 ft.).

DAVY, Sir Humphry
(1778-1829) Eng. chemist. He investigated the properties of gases, and discovered laughing gas (nitrous oxide). Prof. of chemistry at the Royal Inst. London, 1802. In 1810 Davy demonstrated the true nature of chlorine, and his discovery by electrolytic methods of the metals sodium and potassium was followed by the isolation of boron, and the invention of the Davy safety lamp. He was knighted (1812), received a baronetcy (1818) and (1820) was made pres. of the Royal Society.

DAY-LEWIS, Cecil
(1904-) Eng. poet. Exhibitioner at Wadham Coll. Oxford. Clark Lecturer at Camb, 1946 (*The Poetic Image*); Prof. of Poetry at Oxford, 1951-6. He ed. *Oxford Poetry*, 1927, with W. H. Auden. Pub. 10 vols. of poems, 1925-48, including *Transitional Poems*, 1929. He tr. Virgil's *Georgics* (1940). Created Poet Laureate (1968) in succession to Masefield.

DAYS OF THE WEEK
A day (in Solar time) is the time taken by the earth to make one revolution on its axis. A day begins at midnight and is divided into 24 hours, each of 60 minutes, each minute containing 60 seconds. The hours from midnight to noon, when the sun crosses the meridian, are designated A.M. (*ante meridiem*); those from noon to midnight P.M. (*post meridiem*). A modern practice is the use of the 24 hour clock on the basis of which the hours are numbered 0 to 23 from midnight to midnight. The week is a period of seven days. Sunday (Rom. *Sol*), Monday (Rom. *Luna*). Tuesday (Scand. *Tiw*, the god of war), Wednesday (Scand. *Woden* or *Odin*), Thursday (Scand. *Thor*), Friday (Scand. *Frig.* wife of Odin), Saturday (Rom. *Saturnius*).

DEACON
In the Anglican and Rom. Ch. a member of a clerical order. The 1st deacons, of whom Stephen, the 1st Christian martyr was one, were appointed soon after the d. of Jesus Christ (*Acts*, 6). In the C. of E. a man cannot be ordained deacon until he is 23 years of age. In certain Nonconformist chs. deacons are laymen elected to manage the affairs of the ch. The office of **deaconess** existed in the early ch. They are now found in the C. of E. and various Nonconformist chs.

DEAD MEN'S FINGERS
(*Alcyonium digitatum*) A zoophyte frequently cast up on Brit. coasts. The pink, spongy-looking masses are studded with tentacled polyps. Name also refers to the Spotted Orchis, *O. maculata*, or Marsh Orchis, *O. latifolia*, with pale hand-like tubers.

DEAD NETTLE
(*Lamium*) Genus of annual and perennial hairy herbs of the Labiatae, native to temp. Europe, Asia and N. Africa. The commonest Brit. species are the red flowered *L. purpureum*, white flowered *L. album*, yellow flowered *Galcobdolon luteum*, the henbit, *L. amplexicaule*, and the spotted *L. maculatum*, with striped leaves.

DEAD SEA
Lake of the M.E. 47 m. long, almost surrounded by Jordan territory, with the S.W. shore forming the Israeli boundary. It receives the waters of the Jordan, and lies *c.* 1,300 ft. below sea level. There is no outlet to the sea, and the water contains a concentration of mineral salts. **Dead Sea Scrolls,** *see* HEBREW.

DEADLY NIGHTSHADE *See* BELLADONNA.

DEAFNESS
Lack of hearing which may be partial or complete. Among the common causes of deafness is wax in the ear. In all cases of deafness med. advice should be obtained. **Occupational deafness** occurs in certain industries such as boiler-making, coopering, caisson workers and artillerymen and is due to degeneration of cochlear apparatus. **Word deafness** is due to disease affecting brain in the area controlling sight and hearing. **Deaf Mutism.** Condition in which speech is absent owing to a high degree of deafness, congenital or acquired. Is usually due to abnormalities of the inner ear although a few cases are assoc. with brain disease. Educ. of the child is of great importance either by lip reading or finger spelling. Educ. of deaf mutes is compulsory.

DEAN
Eccles. and coll. official. Most of the Eng. caths. have a dean who is the head of the chapter and responsible for looking after its affairs. In the Oxford and Camb. Colls., the dean is responsible for matters of discipline.

DEATH
End of physical life. Legally d. must be certified by a med. practitioner after exam. of the body. He then issues a d. certificate. In cases of sudden d., or where violence is suspected, an inquest must be held by the coroner in Eng., or an inquiry by the Procurator-Fiscal in Scot. Before disposal of a body the d. must be registered with the registrar of births, marriages and deaths. **Death duties** are duties charged on the property left by a deceased person. **Death**

Rate. Annual number of deaths per 1,000 of a country's population.

DEATH WATCH BEETLE
A small beetle (*Xestobium rufovillosum*) which lives in wood, and makes a ticking noise.

DEBRETT, John
[-bret′] (*c.* 1752-1822) Eng. publisher. In 1781 he took over the business of John Almon, who had already issued, 1754, a *New Peerage.* This was turned by Debrett into *Debrett's Peerage and Baronetage.*

DEBUSSY, Claude Achille
[dĕ-bûs′-] (1862-1918) Fr. composer. His 1st work of importance was a setting of a Fr. version of Rossetti's *Blessed Damozel* (1888). His music can be regarded as the counterpart of Impressionism in painting. His works include the opera *Pelléas et Mélisande,* and many orchestral pieces.

DECIMAL
In arithmetic, a fraction having 10 or some power of 10 as a denominator. It is represented by a point, thus ·4 means 4-10ths and 62·5 means 62½. To divide or multiply by 10 and multiples of 10 the point is moved in one way or the other, and if necessary noughts are added, thus, 33·412 divided by 1000 is ·033412. The decimal system of coinage has been adopted in many countries. There are proposals to introduce it into Brit. when a suitable basis has been worked out. A standard unit is taken for reference, such as the franc in Fr. and the dollar in the U.S.A. In the metric or decimal system of weights and measures the metre is the standard unit of length, the gramme of weight and litre of capacity. U.K. decimal currency, 100p=£ sterling introduced 1971.

DECLARATION
Formal statement of any kind. Outstanding examples are the Declaration of Indulgence, 1687; the Declaration of Rights, 1689; the Amer. Declaration of Indep., 1776 (*q.v.*); the Declaration of Paris, 1856, and the Declaration of London, 1908-9, both on maritime warfare. In Eng. law, solemn declarations before authorised persons sometimes replace affidavits. A death-bed declaration respecting cause of d. may be valid evidence. In Scots law prisoners may make signed declarations before magistrates within 48 hours of arrest. **Declaration of Independence.** The formal declaration by the 13 orig. Amer. colonies of their polit. separation from Gt. Brit. adopted July 4, 1776. Drafted by a committee of 5, including Thomas Jefferson, Benjamin Franklin and John Adams. July 4 is now the chief Amer. patriotic holiday, known as **Indep. Day.** *See* UNITED STATES.

DECREE
Authoritative decision having the force of law. The term designates such decisions by Rom. emperors, and by eccles. councils. Decrees are now called judgments, except in the divorce court, which makes decrees for restitution of conjugal rights, judicial separation or divorce.

DEE
Name of several Brit. rivers. The Welsh Dee rises in Bala Lake and flows to Chester where it enters the sea. Another Dee is in Aberdeenshire; it passes Balmoral and is famous for its salmon.

DEE, John
(1527-1608) Eng. mathematician, alchemist and astrologer. In the reign of Mary he was imprisoned on suspicion of practising the 'black art'; but Elizabeth is said to have sought his advice. He wrote many works of a scientific and occult character.

DEER
(*Cervidae*) Family of solid-horned ruminants. They are found all over the world except the Ethiopian Region (E., W. and S. Africa) and Australia. Their horns or antlers, which are shed and renewed every year, are borne by the stags. Exceptions to this are Reindeer, in which both sexes bear antlers, and the hornless Musk Deer. Three varieties are found in Brit., the Red, Roe and Fallow deer. The Red deer is found wild in the Scot. Highlands and on Exmoor. The flesh of the deer is called venison.

DEERHOUND
A rough-haired, stoutly-built variety of Scot. greyhound, used in deerstalking. Brindled, fawn or blue, it has long tapering head. Quick-running, and keen-scented, it averages 90 lbs. The almost extinct Irish deerhound has reappeared by careful breeding.

DEFENDER OF THE FAITH
Fidei Defensor, a title conferred on Henry VIII of Eng. by Pope Leo X in 1521 in token of the tract against Luther entitled, *On the Seven Sacraments, against Martin Luther the Heresiarch by the Illustrious Prince Henry VIII.* It appears on Brit. coins in the form *Fid. Def.*

DEFOE, Daniel
(*c.* 1661-1731) Eng. writer. B. London, d. in Moorfields. Took part in Monmouth's rebellion; joined William in 1688; pilloried for his pamphlet *The Shortest Way with Dissenters* (1702). While in prison started his newspaper 'The Review' (1704), which appeared thrice weekly until suppressed 1713. Employed by Govt. as an agent in Scot. and elsewhere; pamphleteer against the Jacobites. *Robinson Crusoe* (1719); novels such as *Moll Flanders* (1722), *Roxana* (1724); *Journal of the Plague Year* (1722). Defoe was an early master of the realistic novel.

DEGAS, Hilaire Germain Edgar
[de-gȧ] (1834-1917) Fr impressionist painter, b. Paris. He studied law there, but abandoned it in order to join the École des Beaux-Arts, where he came under the influence of Ingres. He was esp. remarkable for his draughtsmanship.

DE GASPERI, Alcide
(1881-1954) Ital. statesman. B. in Aust. prov. of Trento; educ. Univ. of Vienna. Sat in Diet as a deputy. When Trento became Ital. he sat in Parl. as a member of the Catholic Popular Party. Imprisoned by the Fascist Govt. 1943, Became P.M. 1945 in Coalition Govt.

DE GAULLE, Charles André Joseph Marie
(1890-1970) Fr. gen. and statesman. Served in World War I and II. Brig.-Gen. commanding tank brig. 1940. Escaped after Dunkirk and organised Free Fr. Movement. Pres. of Fr. Committee for Nat. Liberation, 1943-4. Head of Provisional Govt. 1944. Retired from public life, 1946. Became P.M. 1958 and Pres. 1959, concentrating power in his own hands. Opposed entry of Brit. into European Common Market. His memoirs, *The Call to Honour,* were pub. 1955. Retired after referendum defeat (1969).

DEIRA
[dē′-] Ancient Anglian kingdom between the Humber and Tyne. It was united with Bernicia to form Northumbria.

DEISM
Belief in a personal God, detached from the

world and recognised by the light of reason, denying Christianity and the supernatural authority of the Scriptures. It emerged in Eng. through the teachings of Lord Herbert of Cherbury, and of Blount, Tindal, Toland, Collins and Bolingbroke. Their influence reached Voltaire, Rousseau and Diderot in Fr., Eberhard, Reimarus and Lessing in Germany. Eng. deism encountered the strength of the evangelical revival, provoked Butler's *Analogy of Religion*, and passed into the scepticism of Hume.

DEKKER, Thomas
(*c.* 1570-*c.* 1641) Eng. playwright and pamphleteer. He wrote nearly 40 dramas. Best known are his comedies *Shoemaker's Holiday* (1599) and *Old Fortunatus* (1600). Of his pamphlets, the best-known is *The Gull's Hornbook* (1609).

DELACROIX, Ferdinand Victor Eugène
[-krwà] (1798-1863) Fr. historical painter. The leader of the Romantic school. His output of oil paintings, water colours, crayons and etchings was enormous, and he was also a master of mural painting.

DE LA MARE, Walter
O.M. C.H. (1873-1956) Eng. poet. B. Charlton, Kent. Poems, as *Songs of Childhood* (1902), *The Listeners* (1912), *Peacock Pie* (1913), *The Burning Glass and other Poems* (1945), *The Traveller* (1946). Novels, as *Memoirs of a Midget* (1921); short stories, as *The Riddle* (1923), *On the Edge* (1930), *A Beginning and Other Stories* (1955). Studies, as *Ding Dong Bell* (1924), *Desert Islands* (1930), *Early One Morning* (1935). Essays and criticism, as *Pleasures and Speculations* (1940), *Private View* (1953). Anthologies, *Come Hither* (1923), *Love* (1943), *O Lovely England* (1953).

DELAWARE
Atlantic state of the U.S.A., W. of D. Bay. It produces maize, wheat, fruit and vegetables. Dover is the cap. but the only large town is Wilmington. One of the orig. 13 states, D. was settled, 1631. It sends 1 representative to Congress. Area: 2,060 sq.m. Pop. 548,100.

DELFT
Dutch town in the prov. of S. Holland, 5 m. S.E. of The Hague. Since the 17th cent. D. has been famous for its porcelain. Pop. 75,125.

DELHI
City and cap. of the Republic of India, and of D. state, and former cap. of the Indian Emp. (1912-47), on the Jumna, 110 m. N. of Agra. The old city was built in the 17th cent. by Shah Jehan, and contains his fort, with the Lahore Gate, and the Mosque. New Delhi stands 5 m. S.W. of the old city. Planned as the H.Q. of the Indian Govt. There are modern industries, flour milling and cotton spinning, and older crafts, such as metal work, ivory carving and weaving. Pop. 2,061,758. **Delhi.** A Union Territory of N. India. Area: 570 sq.m. Pop. 2,658,612.

DELIBES, Leo
[dĕ-lēb'] (1836-91) Fr. composer. His works include operas, *e.g.* *Lakmé*, but perhaps best known are his ballets *Sylvia* and *Coppélia*.

DELIUS, Frederick
(1862-1934) Eng. composer. While in Florida in 1884, he received help from a local organist Thomas Ward. From 1889 he lived in Fr. and in 1922 he was attacked by paralysis. He wrote operas, *Koanga, A Village Romeo and Juliet*; orchestral music. He also wrote works for chorus and orchestra, concertos for piano, for violin and for cello, and chamber music.

DELLA ROBBIA
Family of Florentine artists. **Luca della Robbia** (1399-1482) perfected the art of enamelling terra cotta. His nephew, **Andrea** (1435-1525) produced enamelled reliefs adapted to friezes and medallions.

DELPHI
(now **Kastri**) In ancient geography, a town in Phocis, on the slope of Parnassus. Seat of the oracle of the Pythian Apollo, and supposed to be the centre of the earth. Gk. cities and foreign princes sent rich presents to Delphi.

DELPHINIUM
Genus of hardy ranunculous plants, both biennial and perennial.

DELTA
Tract of coastal land bounded by the most divergent branches of a river's mouth. It is a triangular area formed from the silt brought down in suspension by a muddy river and deposited when the river's current becomes ineffective. Deltas include the Ganges-Brahmaputra, Mississippi (*q.v.*), Danube, Rhône and Nile. The name was orig. applied by the Gks. to the alluvial tract of the Nile, because it resembled the 4th letter, Δ in their alphabet. **Deltoid.** Having the shape of the Gk. letter delta Δ. Deltoid muscle is the large muscle covering the shoulder which raises the arm from the side.

DEMERARA
River of Guyana, S. America, 180 m. long, which rises in the highlands of the interior, and flows N. into the Atlantic at Georgetown. D. sugar is produced in D. county.

DEMOCRACY
A form of Govt. in which supreme power is vested in the people collectively, whether administered by them directly or through their appointed officials. The earliest democracies were the Gk. states, small enough for every citizen to take a part in the deliberations. Teutonic and A.-S. tribal custom also gave a place to the assembly of all members and it was from these two traditions that the representative system was evolved. So far, democracy has reached its highest development in W. Europe.

DEMOCRATIC PARTY
Amer. polit. party. It arose soon after the formation of the Republic, and the pres. from 1801-61 were nearly all Democrats. The party split over secession, and, as most Democrats found themselves on the side of the S. during the Civil War, from 1861 to 1932 only two, Cleveland and Wilson, secured election. Led by Franklin Roosevelt and Harry Truman the party was in power from 1932; defeated by the Republicans when Dwight D. Eisenhower was elected Pres. in 1952, it returned with John F. Kennedy, 1960-3.

DEMOCRITUS
(*c.* 460-370 B.C.) Gk. philosopher, called the 'father of physics', b. at Abdera in Thrace. He propounded an atomic energy theory of the universe.

DEMOSTHENES
[-ēz] (384-322 B.C.) Athenian orator. He employed all his energies in opposing Philip of Macedon. He fought in the Athenian army at Chaeronea in 338. After the d. of Philip in 336 he opposed his son Alexander. In 322 he led an expedition against Antipater of Macedon. This was beaten at Crannon and Demosthenes committed suicide on the islet of Calauria. Many of his speeches have survived.

DENBIGHSHIRE
County of N. Wales, with a short coastline on the Irish Sea. The interior is mountainous, and is penetrated by the fertile Vale of Clwyd. The chief rivers are the Dee, Conway and Clwyd. Agriculture is important in the lowland areas. Ruthin is the admin. centre; towns are Wrexham, Llangollen and Colwyn Bay. Returns 2 members to Parl. Pop. 174,180. **Denbigh.** [den'-bi] Borough and county town of Denbighshire, 30 m. from Chester. There are ruins of a

castle and a priory, and a trade in agricultural produce. Pop. 8,130.

DENMARK
Kingdom of N.W. Europe, comprising the greater part of the Jutland peninsula and numerous Is. The Is. except Bornholm in the Baltic, are separated by channels from the Danish mainland and Sweden. D. is part of the N. European plain, the highest point is 565 ft. In the W. of Jutland is a belt of sandy dunes, but the remaining soil is fertile. Intensive methods of cultivation are used. The co-operative system is used in marketing the dairy produce, eggs, bacon and meat. Fishing is important, and there are some localised industries. Copenhagen is the cap. and largest town. Others are Aarhus, Odense and Aalborg. Esbjerg is an important port on the W. coast of Jutland. Ferry services connect the Is. with the mainland, and with Sweden. The people are mainly Lutheran in religion; there are two univs. Denmark's early hist. is very closely connected with that of the other Scandinavian counties, and at one time all were under the same ruler. The union was dissolved, 1448, when Denmark chose a king of the house of Oldenburg. In 1947 Frederick IX became king. After a referendum, a new constitution was created, June 5, 1953, which revoked the law forbidding the succession of women to the throne. It also lowered franchise age from 25 to 23, and changed the status of Greenland (*q.v.*), formerly a colony, which became a part of Denmark. The parl. or Rigsdag, consists of 1 elected house, the Folketing, and a cabinet. Denmark was invaded by Germany in April, 1940, and occupied until 1945. Area: 16,600 sq.m. Pop 4,585,000.

DENTIST
Person who has specialised in care and treatment of teeth and diseases of the mouth. Dental Board in London is the controlling body who grant, after a period of study at a Univ. or Dental School, the diploma of L.D.S. **Dentistry.** Science dealing with the care of the teeth. With the aid of anaesthetics and advance in understanding of disease it is now accepted as a profession. Fillings first appeared in the 9th cent., gold foil treatment in the 16th, the universal use of anaesthetics in the early part of this cent. and operative dental surgery after the 1st World War. The preventative aspects of dental care are being developed, *e.g.* in school and industrial dental services. **Dentition.** Arrangement of the teeth in vertebrate animals. In fishes the teeth are all alike and are very numerous since they are borne in the roof of the mouth as well as on the jaws. Accessory palate teeth are also found in some reptiles, *e.g.* snakes. In birds teeth are absent. In mammals the number of teeth varies in the different orders. They may be all alike (homodont) as in porpoises, or are divisible according to their position and function into incisors, canines, premolars and molars (heterodont). Those in the front of the jaw, usually one-rooted, are incisors; those in the jaw proper generally include on each side a long, pointed, one-rooted canine and several grinding teeth usually with 2 or more roots called molars.

DENVER
City and cap. of Colorado, U.S.A. on the slopes of the Rocky Mts. It is the commercial and industrial centre of the W. and has a univ. Pop. 494,000.

DEODAR
[dē'-ō-dar] Coniferous evergreen tree, similar to the cedar. It forms extensive forests in the Himalayas at an altitude above 7,000 ft. and also grows in Baluchistan and Afghanistan. It sometimes reaches a ht. of 200 ft.

DEPTFORD
[det'-] Part of Lewisham, borough of Greater London (1964). It has a short frontage on the Thames. It had a naval dockyard and a victualling yard in the 16th cent.

DE QUINCEY, Thomas
(1785-1859) Eng. writer. B. Manchester, educ. there and, after a vagrant life in London and elsewhere, at Worcester Coll. Oxford, where he began to take opium. Lived in the Lake District, coming to know Wordsworth and his circle, until 1828, when he moved with his family to Edinburgh, where he d. His fame rests on his *Confessions of an English Opium-Eater* (1822) and on scattered pieces of imaginative prose and criticism, as *Suspiria De Profundis* (1845), *Reminiscences of the Lake Poets* (1834 onwards), *On the Knocking at the Gate in 'Macbeth'* (1823), and *On Murder considered as one of the Fine Arts* (1827).

DERBY, Earl of
[dar'-] Eng. title borne by the family of Stanley since 1485. **James,** the 7th earl, was Lord of the Isle of Man, and his wife, **Charlotte,** was famous for her defence of Lathom House during the Civil War. The direct line d. out in 1736. **Edward George Geoffrey Smith Stanley,** 14th Earl, (1799-1869) Eng. statesman. M.P. (Cons.) 1820-44; P.M. 1852, 1858-9, and 1866-8. **Edward George Villiers Stanley,** 17th Earl (1865-1948) in 1916-18 was Min. for War. The method of voluntary recruitment (1916) for war service, was known as the 'Derby Scheme'. Derby Day is the day on which the race for the Derby stakes, the most important horse race in Eng., is run. Estabd. by the 12th Earl of D. in 1780, it takes place at Epsom in May or June.

DERBYSHIRE
Midland county of Eng. divided into 2 portions. In the N. is the mt. Peak district, while in the S. is a level, fertile region. Chief rivers are the Derwent, Trent and Dove. Coal and iron are mined in the S. where dairying is also important. Derby is the county town. Industrial centres include Alfreton, Belper, Chesterfield, Glossop and Ilkeston. Buxton, Bakewell and Matlock are pleasure resorts, and the county contains Chatsworth, Haddon, Hardwick and many beauty spots in the Peak district. The county returns 10 members to Parl. (3 borough constituencies). Pop. 890,180. **Derby** [dar'-] County borough and county town of Derbyshire, on the Derwent. There are motor car and other engineering works. Other products are lace, hosiery, silk, chems. and chinaware. Derby gives its name to porcelain known as Crown Derby, first made, 1750. Derby returns 2 members to Parl. Pop. 132,000.

DERMATITIS
An inflammation of the skin. The term is widely applied to include all such inflammations, irrespective of their causes, which include drugs such as bromides, sulphonamides, gold salts; animal parasites such as scabies and lice; rays such as X-rays; bacteria such as streptococcus in erysipelas; chems. such as lime, cement, and turpentine; vitamin deficiencies such as pellagra. Occupational dermatitis occurs in many industries such as dyeing, chrome plating, printing ink manufacture.

DERVISH
Moslem devotee. Throughout Islam the word denotes a monk; in Turkey and Persia a wandering mendicant, called in Arabic-speaking countries a fakir. Thirty fraternities include the *Kalandarite, Rifalite,* or howling dervishes, *Mevlevite,* or dancing dervishes, and the modern *Senussi.*

DESCARTES, René
[dā'-kart] (1596-1650) Fr. philosopher, mathematician and scientist. B. La Haye, Touraine; educ. Jesuit Coll. of La Flèche and Univ. of Poitiers; served in the army of Prince Maurice of Nassau (1616-21). In 1628 he retired to Holland where he studied for some 20 years. In 1649 he was invited to Sweden by Queen Chris-

tina, and d. at Stockholm. Discarding the authoritarian system of the schoolmen, he began with universal doubt, but doubt itself cannot be doubted, hence his famous postulate *Cogito, ergo sum* (I think, therefore, I am). His works include *Discourse on Method* (1637) and *Principia philosophiae* (1664).

DESERT
Region where, on account of intense cold or insufficient rain, few forms of life and little, or no, vegetation can exist. Deserts are characterised by intense heat, as in the Sahara, or by great cold, as in the Arctic and Antarctic wastes.

DESERTION
The voluntary forsaking of a duty imposed by legal or moral obligation. It applies esp. to desertion from the services (punishable by d. during war-time); or from the merchant navy; or of a husband or wife from his or her spouse or children. Under the *Matrimonial Causes Act*, 1937, desertion by a husband or wife for a period of not less than 3 yrs. immediately preceding the presentation of a petition, is made a ground for divorce.

DESSALINES, Jean Jacques
[de-sa-lēn] (*c.* 1758-1806) Emperor of Haiti. B. a negro slave, he served under Toussaint L'Ouverture in the wars of liberation. In 1802 he served under Leclerc, but later joined the enemy. Although Toussaint was captured and Leclerc's army decimated by yellow fever, Dessalines again changed sides, led another revolt, and in 1803 the Fr. invaders were defeated. In the following year Haiti declared her indep. and set up her own govt. with Dessalines as emperor.

DESTROYER
Designed orig. in the 1890's to destroy torpedo boats. Their primary duties are to torpedo the enemy's ships, screen the battle fleet, and hunt down and destroy enemy submarines. They are also used for reconnaissance, for patrol, for escorting convoys of merchant ships, etc. Typical modern Brit. examples are (1) *Daring* Class, *c.* 2,610 t.; armament: 6-4·5 in. guns and 10-21 in. T-tubes; 1 anti-sub. squid; speed over 30 k. (2) *Weapon Class*: (fleet anti-sub escort vessels), *e.g. Battleaxe, c.* 2,280 t.; armament: 4-4 in. guns and 10-21 in. T-tubes; 2 anti-sub. squids; speed 34 k. (3) *County* Class: guided missile destroyers, over 5,000 t.; 4-4·5 in. guns; *Seaslug* and *Seacat* missiles.

DETROIT
City of Michigan, U.S.A. on the D. river near the Canadian frontier. Formerly a Fr. trading station, it is now an industrial centre and headquarters of the Ford motor works. Pop. 1,670,000.

DEUTERONOMY
Fifth book of the O.T. The title, ' second law ', is a Septuagint mistranslation of a Heb. word meaning copy of the law.

DE VALERA, Eamon
[-lair'-ă] (1882-) Irish politician, M.P. (Sinn Fein), 1918-22. Of Sp.-Irish parentage, and b. in New York, de Valera was educ. in Ireland and became an active Sinn Feiner. Refusing to accept the treaty of 1921, he led the Republican insurrection. After a year in prison he entered the Dail as leader of the Repub. Party. In World War II he maintained a policy of neutrality. In 1948, de Valera was replaced by John A. Costello, but returned to power in 1951. In 1954 he was defeated, but became P.M. once more, 1957-9. Pres. of Eire, 1959-.

DE VALOIS, Dame Ninette
[-wȧ] (1898-) Dancer; b. Ireland; studied under Cecchetti. She toured Europe with the Diaghileff Russ. Ballet, 1923-5; produced ballets at the Old Vic, 1928-30 and was apptd. director for the Vic-Wells Ballet in 1931. Retired, 1963.

DEVIL
Evil spirit, pre-eminently the Hebraic chief of the powers of darkness. The doctrine of a personal devil does not emerge clearly in Heb. thought until after the Exile, when a personality called Satan was conceived. This conception, passing into Christian phil. became very powerful in the M.A. The doctrine of a malignant power who must be withstood is officially recognised by Roman Catholicism.

DEVONPORT
District of Plymouth, on estuary of the Tamar. It is one of the chief stations of the Brit. Navy, and at Keyham is the R.N. Engineering Coll. A dockyard was first opened, 1691.

DEVONSHIRE
S.W. maritime county of Eng. between the Bristol and Eng. Channels, with irregular coastlines N. and S. In the N. is the barren expanse of Exmoor while to the S. lies Dartmoor. The rest of the county is lowland, generally with a rich red soil. The rivers are the Dart, Teign, Exe, Tavy, Tamar and Plyn. Lundy Is. is in Devonshire. It is an agricultural county, famous for its cream, while fishing and the tourist industry are important. The county town is Exeter; other towns and resorts are Plymouth, Bideford, Brixham, Dartmouth, Barnstaple, Tiverton, Honiton and Torquay. Devonshire returns 10 members to Parl. (4 borough constituencies). Pop. 823,000.

DEW
Moisture deposited on the earth's surface at night, when radiation from the earth has cooled the lower layers of the atmosphere and the water vapour has condensed into drops.

DEWBERRY
(*Rubus caesius*) Species of bramble with fruit resembling a blackberry. The drupes of the berry, which are larger and fewer than those of the blackberry, are covered with a bluish bloom.

DE WET, Christian Rudolf
[vet] (1854-1922) Boer soldier. From 1885-97 he was a member of the legislature of the Orange Free State. When war broke out, he was one of the Boer leaders and in 1900 he was made C.-in-C. of the Free State army. In 1907 de Wet entered the legislature of the Orange River Colony.

DEWEY, John
(1859-1952) Amer. philosopher and educator. Prof. of Phil. at Columbia Univ. His philosophy, generally called *instrumentalism*, is opposed to all forms of absolutism. Reality is not something static, but undergoes continual growth and change; hence it was inevitable that he should take a lively interest in education, social welfare and political reform. His books include: *Psychology* (1887), *Democracy and Education* (1916), *Culture and Freedom* (1939).

DHOLE
[dol] Indian wild dog. It inhabits the jungles of the Deccan, is somewhat larger than the jackal and differs from true dogs in lacking the last lower molars. In colour it is bay with darker mottlings. It hunts in packs of 50.

DHOW
Vessel of *c.* 150 or 200 t. burden much used in the Arabian Sea and along the coast of E. Africa.

DIABETES
Diabetes mellitus. Condition due to deficiency of internal secretion of the pancreas, characterised by upset of carbohydrate digestion with passage of large quantities of urine containing sugar and acetone. Insulin is used in conjunction with diet in successful treatment. *See* INSULIN.

DIAGHILEFF, Sergei Paulovitch
[di-ăg'-i-] (1872-1929) Russ. artist. About 1907 he went to Paris where he produced operas and plays. His ballets were a landmark in the hist. of stage dancing.

DIALECTIC
(Dialectics) Philosophic method by which, in the ancient schools, teaching was imparted by means of question and answer. A notable example is that of the Dialogues of Plato in which Socrates is the chief interlocutor. Aristotelian dialectic treats of the universal laws of reasoning. In the philosophy of Kant (1724-1804) the word has a special connotation, but in that of Hegel (1770-1831) it reverts to its Socratic sense.

DIAMOND
Crystalline form of carbon, found in nature as water-worn pebbles, or grains, in river gravels and other alluvial deposits, also in conglomerates and sandstones in S. Africa, India, Brazil, Borneo and elsewhere. The crystals belong to the cubic system and occur in octahedra and dodecahedra often with curved faces. They are usually white, but other colours also occur. One of the most popular of gem stones, owing to its lustre. It is used as an abrasive because of its extreme hardness. Two of the finest diamonds ever found are the Koh-i-Noor and the Cullinan, both Brit. crown jewels.

DIANA, Temple of
Temple at Ephesus, Asia Minor, the vastness and grandeur of which placed it among the Seven Wonders of the World. It was dedicated to the Gk. *Artemis* (Roman *Diana*) and held the right of sanctuary until the advent of Christianity. It was finally closed by the Rom. Emperor Theodosius (*c*. 346-395).

DIANTHUS
Genus of herbs of the carnation-pink family, native to the N. temp. regions and to S. Africa. Of 70 species, several grow wild in Brit. The Medit. clove pink originated all the garden varieties of carnation.

DIAPHRAGM
[dī'-a-fram] Large dome-shaped layer of muscle separating chest from abdomen. It is the main muscle responsible for respiration. By contraction and relaxation it increases and decreases air volume in chest and brings about change of air in lungs.

DIAZ, Bartholomew
[dē'as] (d. 1500) Portuguese navigator; first European to round the Cape of Good Hope (1486-8). This voyage opened up the sea-route to India.

DIAZ, Porfirio
[dē'-as] (1830-1915) Mexican Pres. A lawyer. He led the Mexican Army in the struggle against the Emperor Maximillian and in 1877 was elected Pres. Under his rule, order and prosperity were restored, although the poor were neglected.

DI CHIRICO, Giorgio
(1888-) B. Volo, Greece, of Ital. parents. Studied art at Athens and Munich. In Paris 1911-15, he met Picasso and took an active part in the Surrealist movement.

DICKENS, Charles
(1812-70) Eng. novelist. B. near Portsmouth, son of a govt. clerk; childhood spent in Chatham and London; became a shorthand reporter and journalist. *Sketches by Boz,* collected 1836. The rest of his life was busy with successful novel writing, varied by amateur theatricals on a large scale, visits to Fr. and Italy, and in 1842 and 1867-8, the U.S.A. He was prominent in philanthropic activities; he worked himself to d. His novels incl. *Pickwick Papers* (1837), *Oliver Twist* (1838), *Nicholas Nickleby* (1839), *A Christmas Carol* (1843), *Martin Chuzzlewit* (1844), *Dombey and Son* (1848), *David Copperfield* (1850), *A Tale of Two Cities* (1859), *Great Expectations* (1861), *Our Mutual Friend* (1865), *Edwin Drood* (1870) (unfinished). See Edgar Johnson's *Charles Dickens* (1953).

DICKINSON, Emily Elizabeth
(1830-86) Amer. poet. B. Amherst (Mass.). She lived quietly and wrote poems (over 1,000 lyrics) secretly.

DICTATOR
Orig. the name of an office under the Rom. Repub. Its holder was a magistrate appointed in times of great difficulty and invested with wide powers. The name is now applied to an individual who secures absolute power in a state. The S. Amer. States have had dictators at various times and after World War I they arose in several European countries. Since gaining independence several former colonies have become dictatorships.

DIDEROT, Denis
[dē'-de-rō] (1713-84) Fr. philosopher, encyclopedist, and author. B. Langres; educ. by the Jesuits; worked for a bookseller. A materialistic atheist, he was nevertheless ardent and dynamic, ever striving for new aspects of truth, and had an influence third only to that of Voltaire and Rousseau. The best of his energy was expended on the *Encyclopédie* (17 vols. 1751-65). He influenced the development of drama and pioneered art criticism. He was a friend of Grimm, quarrelled with Rousseau, and paid a visit to Catherine the Great.

DIE
Term having the primary significance of a small cube used for gaming, dice being the collective form. Each side is marked with a black spot or spots numbering 1-6. Poker dies have each side marked with either 9, 10, Jack, Queen, King or Ace. There are 5 such dies in a set of poker dice.

DIEFENBAKER, Rt. Hon. John George
(1895-) Canadian politician. K.C. 1929. Member of Canadian House of Commons since 1940. Leader of federal Cons. Party, 1956; Leader of Opposition, 1957. After elections of June, 1957, he became P.M. In 1963 his party was defeated by the Liberals and he resigned.

DIEPPE
[dē-ep'] Port in Seine-Inférieure dept. Fr. at the mouth of the Arques. It has a steamer service with Newhaven. Pop. 26,400.

DIESEL ENGINE
Type of internal combustion engine invented by Rudolf Diesel (1858-1913). Air is drawn into the cylinder and compressed to about 500 to 600 lb. per sq.in. so that it becomes greatly heated. The heat of the air charge then ignites the liquid fuel which has been sprayed through a jet into the cylinder.

DIET
Name used for the representative body of the Holy Rom. Emp. and of similar bodies elsewhere. Its power gradually diminished and after 1648 little was heard of it. The word was also used for the parl. of the Germanic Fed. and other states and provinces of C. Europe, *e.g.* Poland.

DIGESTION
The process of preparing food for absorption from the bowel and subsequent utilisation and storage by the body. The process may be divided into 3 stages (1) that occurring in the

EUROPE · 1

Galway, Ireland

Hammerfest, Norway

Heidelberg

Mont Blanc

EUROPE · 2

Monaco

Cathedral and Tower, Pisa

Dunes, Sylt

Trafalgar Square, London

mouth, or salivary digestion (2) that occurring in the stomach, or gastric digestion, and (3) that occurring in the small bowel, or intestinal digestion. In the mouth, food mixes with salivary juices which contain ptyalin, that acts on the starch particles and changes them to sugars. The chewing action of the jaw and tongue breaks up the food into smaller pieces. The stomach or gastric juice containing hydrochloric acid acts on the proteins producing amino-acids. In the small bowel the bile, pancreatic and bowel juices complete the digestive process. Bile emulsifies fat. Pancreas produces ferments (lipase and trypsin), the bowel juice the succus entericus. As the food moves into the distant parts of the bowel absorption of the material now called chyme begins. When the food residue reaches the large bowel or colon, only water and waste products are left. Sugars, salts and amino-acids are absorbed into the blood and carried to the liver where they are stored.

DIGITALIS
[-tā′-] Genus of plants belonging to the family Scrophulariaceae, native to Brit., Europe, N. Africa and Asia. The foxglove, *D. purpurea*, is a well-known species. Its leaves yield the poisonous alkaloid digitalin. Both the leaves themselves and various preparations are used in certain forms of heart disease, and dropsy.

DIJON
[dē′-zhō(ng)] Cap. of Côte d'Or dept. S.E. Fr. It is a route centre with a trade in wine and agricultural produce. D. once a cap. of the Duchy of Burgundy, has a univ. Pop. 141,104.

DILL
(*Peucedanum graveolens*) Annual umbelliferous plant found in Asia and S. Europe. It has small yellow flowers and flat brown fruits or seeds. From these is prepared dill water, and the leaves are used for flavouring.

DIMENSION
In maths. the term has 2 common meanings: (a) the power to which an expression is raised, thus x is of one dimension, x^2 of 2 dimensions, x^3 of 3 dimensions, etc. and (b) a direction of measurement, thus a point has no dimensions, a *line* has 1 dimension (L), and *area* has 2 (LxB) and a *volume* 3 dimensions (LxBxH). The 3 dimensions of space are length, breadth and thickness. *See* FOURTH DIMENSION.

DINGO
So-called ' wild dog ' of Austral. It is stoutly built, short-legged, with bushy tail, and foxy appearance. It is believed to have been introduced by man, and related to the S. Asian pariah dogs. It is very destructive to flocks, and is systematically destroyed.

DINGWALL
Burgh and county town of Ross and Cromarty on the Cromarty Firth, 18 m. N.W. of Inverness. Pop. 3,851.

DINOSAUR
[dī′no-sawr] Order of extinct 4-footed reptiles of the mesozoic era. Mostly small-brained, they dominated by bulk; some laid eggs; others produced living young. At least 4 sub-orders: (1)

Lizard-footed herbivores, as *Atlantosaurus*, 100 ft., *Diplodocus*, 80 ft., *Cetiosaurus* and *Brontosaurus*, 60 ft.; (2) Armour-plated herbivores, as *Stegosaurus*, 25 ft., and 3-horned *Triceratops*, with 6 ft. head; (3) Bird-footed herbivores, as *Iguanodon*, 30 ft.; (4) Beast-footed carnivores, as *Megalosaurus*, 20 ft., and *Tyrannosaurus*, 40 ft.

DIOCESE
District under the authority of a bishop. The whole of Gt. Brit. is divided into dioceses and there are dioceses wherever the Anglican Ch. works. The R.C. Ch. is also divided into dioceses. A group of dioceses forms a prov. There are now 43 in Eng., 30 in the prov. of Canterbury and 13 in the prov. of York. Wales has 6.

DIOCLETIAN
[dī-ŏ-klē′-shiăn] (245-313) Rom. Emperor. **Gaius Aurelius Valerius Diocletianus**, a soldier, who in 284 was proclaimed emperor. He divided the empire with his colleague, Maximian, and later, in 292, with Galerius and Constantius Chlorus. Nicomedia was his cap. He persecuted the Christians.

DIOGENES
[dī-oj′-i-nēz] Gk. cynic philosopher (412-323 B.C.). B. Sinope, he early emigrated to Athens, became a pupil of Antisthenes, the founder of the Cynics.

DIONYSIA
[dīŏ-niz′-iă] Gk. festivals in honour of Dionysus. The greater or city Dionysia were celebrated at Athens. On the 1st day there was a grand procession to the altar of the god, a feast, and a choral dance; on the 2nd day dithyrambs were sung; and on the last 3, contests of tragedy and comedy were held in the great theatre of Dionysus.

DIONYSUS
Gk. name for the god **Bacchus** (*q.v.*).

DIPHTHERIA
Highly infectious disease caused by Klebs-Loeffler bacillus. Infection arises from another infected person by droplet infection or from infected articles such as crockery or from people called carriers or by infected milk. Incubation period usually 2 to 5 days and duration of illness may be from 3 weeks to several months. A very serious condition. Disease can be prevented or modified by immunisation which is provided free by all local authorities.

DIPPER
or **Water-ouzel** (*Cinclus gularis*) 7 in. semi-aquatic song bird. Brownish, white-breasted with short rounded wings, it haunts mt. streams. It dives and swims, using its wings under the water.

DIPTERA
Order of insects, with 2 membranous wings, usually transparent, not folded at rest, the posterior pair present in other insect orders is reduced to a pair of drumstick-like balancers or halteres. With short antennae and 2 large compound eyes, the mouth parts form a probiscis for piercing and sucking. Eggs hatch into legless larvae which in turn form pupae. Upwards of 40,000 species have been named. Nearly 3,000 are recognised in Brit. They include Crane Flies, Mosquitoes, House Flies, Tsetse and Bot Flies, Gnats and ' Daddy Long Legs '.

DIRAC, Paul Adrien Maurice
F.R.S. (1902-) Mathematical physicist, largely responsible for the development of quantum mechanics, and was awarded the Nobel Prize for Physics in 1933.

DIRECTORY
Committee of 5 men who governed Fr. 1795-9. The Convention framed a constitution and entrusted the executive power to the Directory.

Its 1st members were Barras, Carnot, Lépeaux, Letourneau and Rewbel. Under the Directory Napoleon conducted campaigns in Italy, Egypt and Germany. Napoleon ended the Directory Nov. 9, 1799, and made himself First Consul.

DISCUS
Round wood and metal missile used in athletic contests. Throwing it was one of the games of ancient Greece. It is now an event at most athletic meetings. The discus weighs 4 lb. 6⅜ oz.

DISINFECTANT
A substance which is used to kill micro-organisms or germs. **Disinfection** can be carried out by physical or chem. means. Physical means include the application of heat, boiling, steaming or flaming. Sunlight, certain types of rays and osmotic pressure are also used. Chem. means include the use of hydrogen peroxide, chlorine, iodine and bromine compounds as well as acids and alkalies.

DISNEY, Walter
(1901-66) Amer. artist and film producer. His famous Mickey Mouse cartoons began in 1928. In 1932 colour was introduced in *Flowers and Trees*. Shortly before World War II he produced the first feature-length cartoon, *Snow White and the Seven Dwarfs*. Disney turned his attention to the combination of human and cartoon figures, as in *Cinderella, Alice in Wonderland, The Sword in the Stone*. He has also made full-length nature films.

DISRAELI, Benjamin
[-rā'-] **1st Earl of Beaconsfield** (1804-81) Brit. statesman and writer. B. London. He was educ. as a lawyer, and in 1817-31 travelled in S. Europe and the Near E. Beginning with *Vivian Grey* (1826) he pub. a series of clever novels. In 1837 he became Tory M.P. for Maidstone. He became a spokesman of the ' Young England ' group of Tories, who believed that the Crown and Ch. are the natural protectors of the industrial and agricultural labouring classes. In 1846 Disraeli led Tory opposition to Peel and in 1852 became Chanc. of the Exchequer and Leader of the Commons under Derby. In 1868 when Derby retired, he became Prime Min. After Gladstone's defeat in 1874, Disraeli again became Premier. He bought shares in the Suez Canal, made Queen Victoria Empress of India, and attended the Congress of Berlin. He resigned in 1880.

DISSENTER
In Gt. Brit. one who separates from the Estabd. Ch. for reasons of doctrine, discipline or ritual. The word was applied to those who declined to accept the Act of Uniformity of 1662, but it denotes more particularly the Protestant dissenters referred to in the Toleration Act of 1689. Members of the Episcopal Ch. of Scot. are technically dissenters from the Estabd. Ch. of Scot.

DISTAFF
Cleft stick *c*. 36 in. long, for holding fibre in hand spinning. The cotton, wool or flax was wound loosely upon it in readiness for the spinning. It was held under the left arm and the right hand drew out the fibre and twisted it on its way to the weighted spindle.

DISTEMPER
Canine distemper or plague is specific infectious fever, chiefly affecting young animals, characterised by fever, catarrh of mucous membranes with upsets of nervous system. Caused by a virus, disease can be prevented by immunisation. Mortality in dogs not immunised is 30-50 %.

DISTILLING
Converting a substance or its volatile constituents into vapour condensable into liquid drops. Distillation is used in the extraction of essential or volatile oils from plants, mineral oils from coal tar, fresh water from sea water, and alcoholic spirit from fermented liquids. Brandy is distilled from wine. Rum is distilled from sugar cane and molasses. Whisky is distilled from starchy materials, such as barley, rye, oats, wheat and maize. Industrial alcohol is distilled from beet and molasses, also from potatoes and sawdust. Distilling is a considerable industry in Scotland, where most of the world's best whisky is made.

DIVER
Diving birds, family Colymbidae. Of the 4 species, 3, the Great Northern (*Colymbus immer*), with glossy black head and neck, the Red-throated (*C. stellatus*), with reddish-grey throat patch, and, very rarely, the White-billed (*C. adamsi*), are winter visitors to Brit. but breed inland in more N. regions. The Black-throated (*C. arcticus*), breeds in the Hebrides.

DIVINATION
Quest of the unknown by non-rational methods. The processes observed are subjective, as in dreams, crystal-gazing, trance speaking, dowsing and necromancy; or objective, depending upon inference from observed facts. Their interpretation developed schools of empirical deduction, traceable among Chaldean soothsayers and prevalent in ancient Rome.

DIVING
(1) Act of plunging into water adopted as the means of obtaining pearls and sponges from the sea bed in shallow waters. A diver can remain for only 2 to 3 min. under water. For recovery of treasure and other purposes in deeper waters, the diving dress consists of a flexible waterproof or metal garment and copper helmet, provided with air tubes, signal line, telephone and outlet air valves. Recently the aqualung was developed by Capt. Cousteau (*q.v.*) of the Fr. Navy, which allows the diver greater freedom of movement and longer periods of time beneath the water. (2) Diving is also an internat. competitive sport which figures in the Olympic Games.

DIVINING ROD
Fork twig used in searching for something hidden. This is still employed by professional dowsers in searching for metalliferous deposits or water springs. Timber twigs, usually hazel, or metal wires and springs are used.

DIVORCE
Legal ending of the marriage tie. Divorce was allowed on very slender grounds by the Roms. but became much more difficult to obtain when Christianity was estabd. in Europe. At the time of the Reformation some countries, *e.g.* Scot. began to allow it in cases of adultery. In Eng., until 1857, a divorce could only be obtained by a special Act of Parl. and so it was confined to the rich. In 1857 a law was passed which allowed a husband to apply for a divorce if his wife had committed adultery. A wife could only obtain a divorce if adultery was coupled with desertion or cruelty. Divorce could also be obtained for bigamy. A divorce court was set up and is now part of the probate, divorce and admiralty division of the high court. Divorce is obtainable by either husband or wife on the following grounds: adultery, desertion persisted in for 3 years, cruelty, incurable insanity and by wife against husband on ground of criminal sexual offences committed by him. In Eng. except in exceptional circumstances no petition for divorce will be entertained until spouses have been mar. for 3 years. In other countries the law varies greatly.

DJAKARTA
Jakarta (formerly **Batavia**). City on the N. coast of Java, cap. of the Repub. of Indonesia, with its harbour at Tanjong Priok, 6 m. distant. D. is connected by rly. with the rest of the Is. During World War II it was occupied by the Japanese from 1942-5. Pop. *c*. 3,000,000.

DNIEPER
[dnē'-] River of the Ukraine, U.S.S.R. rises in the Valdai Hills, *c.* 150 m. W. of Moscow, and enters the Black Sea just below Kherson. Over 1,420 m. long, it is linked by canals with other rivers.

DOCK
Genus of biennial and perennial herbs of the polygonum family (*Rumex*), native to all temp. climates. They have tapering rootstocks, alternate leaves, and whorled clusters of small greenish flowers bearing leathery 3-sided fruits.

DOCK
Enclosure, usually in a port, for the reception of vessels. It is made by enclosing some part of a harbour or river with strong walls. The usual division of docks is into wet and dry. Dry docks are divided into graving docks, slip docks and floating docks. The **floating dock** is a movable repairing dock. In the large ports, certain docks are set aside for certain classes of merchandise. The King George V dock, opened in 1921, one of the largest in the world, covers 186 acres.

DOCTOR
Title given to a person who holds the degree of doctorate of a univ. but also applied as a courtesy title to med. practitioners who may or may not hold such a degree. The univs. give the degree of doctor in most faculties.

DODECANESE
Group of Is. in the Aegean Sea belonging to Greece, comprising some 50 Is. The chief are Rhodes, Kos and Kalimnos. The town of Rhodes is the cap. and seat of govt. The majority of the pop. is Gk. adhering to the Orthodox Ch.

DODO
(*Didus ineptus*) Large flightless bird. Prob. a kind of pigeon. Found in Mauritius when discovered by the Portuguese in 1507, it is known to have survived to 1681, but is now extinct.

DOG
Domesticated quadruped, derived from one or more canine flesh-eating mammals. The systematic name, *Canis familiaris*, is a conventional, not a zoological, classification. Its nearest congener is the wolf, their crossing producing fertile offspring. Dogs may have domesticated themselves in mesolithic times. Classed as sporting, non-sporting and toy, there are many kinds, widely different in size and other qualities. Dogs are chiefly kept for companionship, but they are still useful for guarding houses and property. In the Arctic regions they are used for drawing sledges. In Brit. a licence of 7s. 6d. a year must be taken out for a dog unless it is kept by a shepherd or a blind person.

DOG DAYS
Period beginning between July 3 and Aug. 15, and lasting for 30 to 54 days. The heat and unhealthiness of these days in ancient Egypt were held to be due to the rising of the dog star. Now the period is generally considered to last from July 3 to Aug. 11. *See* DOG STAR.

DOG-FISH
Various small sharks found in packs in temp. and trop. waters. Brit. species include the Large-spotted Nurse Hound (*Scyllium catulus*) and the Small-spotted Rough Hound (*Scyliorhinus canicula*). They are marketed as Rock Salmon. The most abundant species in N. latitudes (*Squalus acanthias*) is the Spiny Dogfish which produces the young alive. The other species produce them from eggs contained in leathery egg cases, the so-called mermaids' purses. The fish are 3-5 ft. in length.

DOG ROSE
Prickly bush of the rose family, native to Europe, Siberia and N. Africa (*Rosa canina*). Brit's. largest wild rose, it has white or red flowers bearing crimson hips.

DOG STAR
Alternative name for Sirius, the brightest star in the heavens, found in the constellation *Canis Major*.

DOGE
[dōj] Title of the chief magistrate in the Venetian and Genoese repubs. In Venice in the 8th cent. city tribunes were replaced by a single *dux*. The office lasted until the overthrow of the repub. in 1797. In Genoa the doge first appeared in the 16th cent.

DOGGER BANK
Sandbank in the N. Sea, between Brit. and Denmark, famous as a fishing ground. A naval engagement took place here in 1915 between Brit. and German battle-cruiser squadrons.

DOGGETT, Thomas
(d. *c.* 1721) Irish actor; b. Dublin. In 1715 he founded the annual young watermen's race from London Bridge to Chelsea for Doggett's Coat and Badge, to celebrate the accession of George I.

DOGS, Isle of
District in Poplar, London. Formerly a peninsula jutting out into the Thames, opposite Greenwich, it became an Is. when the docks were built.

DOGWOOD
Genus of shrubs and small trees of the cornaceous family native to temp. and sub-trop. regions. The common *Cornus sanguinea* has egg-shaped leaves and cream flowers bearing black-purple berries. The berry-bearing alder (*Rhamnus frangula*) is sometimes called black dogwood.

DOHNÁNYI, Ernö von
[doch'-nán-yi] (1877-1960) Hungarian composer and pianist. His works include operas, symphonies and chamber music.

DOLLFUSS, Engelbert
[-foos] (1892-1934) Aust. politician. Chanc. in 1932-4, he led the nationalist totalitarian movement. Opposition from the Nazis inside Austria led to considerable tension with Germany and in 1934 Dollfuss was murdered.

DOLMEN
Megalithic chambers incorrectly called cromlechs or druid altars. It consists of an unhewn capstone poised on 2 or more unhewn uprights. They originated in neolithic times. They are found in Europe, Asia and N. Africa.

DOLOMITE
Mineral composed of carbonate of lime and carbonate of magnesia. Brittle and lustrous, it is used in the production of steel. It is found in Brit., in the Alps, Canada and the Transvaal. It is named after the Fr. geologist D. G. de Dolomieu (1750-1801). The name is also given to magnesian limestone. A division of the Alps is called **the Dolomites.**

DOLPHIN
(*Delphinus delphis*) Cetacean mammal found in Medit. and temp. Atlantic waters. Dolphins follow ships in large herds. With sharp snouts and toothed jaws they are *c.* 7 ft. long. Varieties include the Bottle-nosed, White-beaked and

White-sided. Several freshwater dolphins of another family occur in the Ganges, Amazon and La Plata rivers.

DOMESDAY BOOK
[doomz'-] Survey of Eng. Drawn up by order of William the Conqueror in 1086. It states for each county, except those in the N., who are the holders of the land, what each holding is worth, and what it was worth under Edward the Confessor. Other details given are the names of the landholders, the numbers of villeins, cottars and others on each holding, the numbers of oxen, pigs, etc.

DOMINIC
(1170-1221) Sp. saint. B. Calaruega. Ordained in 1195, and sent by Innocent III to fight the Albigensian heresy. He founded the order of preaching friars, the Dominicans, in 1215 and lived to see it flourishing. Canonised, 1234.

DOMINICA
[-nē'-] Island in the West Indies, N. of Martinique. The Is. is mountainous, but the soil is fertile; tropical fruits are grown. Roseau, on the S.W. coast, is the chief town. D. was transferred to the Windward Is. group in 1940. Is to have separate non-colonial relationship with Brit. Area: 300 sq.m. Pop. 59,000.

DOMINICAN REPUBLIC
Republic of the West Indies, occupying the eastern two-thirds of the Island of Hispaniola. It is a mountainous region, reaching 10,310 ft. with a narrow coastal plain. Agriculture is the chief occupation; sugar, cocoa, tobacco, maize and bananas are produced. Some minerals, gold, copper and iron, are worked. Santo Domingo is the cap. The pop. is of mixed European, African and Indian blood. Sp. is the official language, and R.C. the state religion. The Is. was discovered by Columbus in 1492. The Fr. occupied it *c.* 1795-1808, when Sp. resumed control. In 1821 the Is. became indep. It is is governed by a Pres. assisted by a senate of 52 deputies. Affairs remain unsettled following milit. revolt and intervention by O.A.S., 1965. Area: 19,300 sq.m. Pop. 3,889,000.

DOMINION STATUS
Polit. status of certain of the members of the Brit. Common. of Nations.

DOMREMY LA PUCELLE
[dō(ng)-rā'-mē-] A small Fr. village, Dept. of Vosges, birthplace of Joan of Arc.

DON
River of the R.S.F.S.R. rising *c.* 110 m. S. of Moscow, and flowing S. into the Sea of Azov. It is 1,222 m. long and is much used, except in winter, for the transport of grain and cattle.

DON JUAN
Legendary character. He is first found in written lit. in a Sp. play of *c.* 1630, and became the type of the blasphemous sensualist.

DONATELLO
(*c.* 1386-1466) Ital. sculptor and painter. B. and d. in Florence. He executed many fine statues in marble and bronze. His masterpiece, *David*, is at the Bargello, Florence.

DONCASTER
County borough of the W. Riding, Yorks., on the Don. There are engineering works, railway shops, and manufactures of glass, artificial silk, etc. The town is a famous racing centre. It returns 1 member to Parl. Pop. 86,460.

DONEGAL
N.W. county of Eire, in the prov. of Ulster. It has a long coastline on the Atlantic Ocean. The scenery is wild and mountainous. Erigal is the highest peak, Derg the largest lake, and Foyle the longest river. Aran Is. are included in the county. The people are chiefly engaged in agriculture and fishing. Lifford is the county town. Pop. 113,842. **Donegal.** Market town of D. on D. Bay, an opening of the Atlantic. Pop. 1,100.

DONIZETTI, Gaetano
[-tset'-] (1797-1848) Ital. composer of operas. Some of the best known are *L'Elisir d'Amore*, *Lucia di Lammermoor*, and *Don Pasquale*.

DONNE, John
[dun] (1571-1631) Eng. poet and divine. Lost his position as sec. to Sir T. Egerton, lord-keeper, because of his secret mar. 1601, to Anne More, niece of the lord-keeper's wife. An R.C. in earlier life, he took Anglican orders in 1615. Dean of St. Paul's, 1621, until his d. His poetry, satirical, elegiac, erotic, religious, is ' metaphysical '. His prose is mainly contained in the 160 sermons.

DOOLITTLE, Hilda
(1886-1961) Amer. poet known as **' H.D.'** B. Pennsylvania. She was the chief Imagist poet. Her vols. of poems include *Sea Garden* (1916), *Hymen* (1921).

DORCHESTER
Borough and county town of Dorset. There are breweries and an agricultural trade. The town has connections with Thomas Hardy. Pop. 12,750.

DORE, Gustave
[do-rā'] (1833-83) Fr. artist, b. Strasbourg. He painted many religious and historical works but his fame rests upon his remarkable skill as a draughtsman and illustrator.

DORIAN
One of the 4 great divisions of the Hellenic race, the others being the *Aeolian*, *Ionian* and *Achaean*. After considerable wandering, they finally migrated to the Peloponnese.

DORMOUSE
Family of small arboreal rodents (*Myoxidae*), widely distributed from Brit. to Japan. Dormice hibernate in nests in which nuts are stored. The Eng. D. (*Muscardinus avellanarius*) is tawny in colour, *c.* 3 in. long, has a hairy tail, prominent eyes and untufted ears. It eats insects, hazel nuts and corn.

DORNOCH
Royal burgh and county town of Sutherland on D. Firth, 58 m. from Inverness. Pop. 1,014. **D. Firth** is an inlet of the N. Sea between Sutherland and Ross and Cromarty. It is 22 m. long and is a noted fishing area.

DORSET
County of S. Eng. with a coastline on the Eng. Channel. Portland Bill is a feature of the coast. It is almost wholly agricultural although famous for its stone, esp. Portland and Purbeck; fishing is an industry. Dorchester is the county town. Poole, Weymouth, Swanage and Lyme Regis are resorts. Places of historic and other interest are Bridport, Sherborne, Shaftesbury and Blandford. The county contains Corfe Castle and is the scene of Hardy's novels. It returns 4 members to Parl. (1 borough constituency). Pop. 319,800.

DORTMUND
W. German industrial town in the Ruhr valley, N. Rhine-Westphalia, 36 m. N.E. of Düsseldorf. The industries include the manufacture of iron and steel goods. Pop. 630,000.

DORY
Edible, marine spiny-finned fish. The best known is the John Dory (*Zeus faber*). Found in Brit., Medit. and Austral. waters, it is olive-brown in colour, with two dark patches on the sides. The body is much compressed, the head is very large and the gape wide.

DOSTOIEVSKY, Fyodor Mikhailovitch
[dos-tō-yef'-ski] (1821-81) Russ. novelist. B. Moscow. Arrested for polit. activities and sent to Siberia, 1849, for 5 years of hard labour. After his return in 1859, worked at journalism and writing novels including *Crime and Punishment* (1866), *The Idiot* (1866), *The Brothers Karamazov* (1880). *The House of the Dead*

(1861-2) is autobiog. See *Dostoievsky: His Life and Art* by Avraham Yarmolinsky (1957).

DOTTEREL
Bird of Plover family. Rare in Eng. it still breeds in Scot. It is *c.* 9 in. long, its plumage being brown with black and white markings. It is found in mt. areas.

DOUAI
[doo'-ā] Town in Nord dept., Fr., on the Scarpe, 20 m. S. of Lille. It was an educ. centre, and the Douai Bible was issued, 1610. Pop. 50,104.

DOUBLE-BASS
The largest and lowest member of the violin family, supplying the bass of the string orchestra, often playing an octave below the 'cellos. It normally has 4 strings: it differs from other members of the violin family in that it retains the flat back and sloping shoulders of the viol.

DOUGHTY, Charles Montagu
(1843-1926) Eng. traveller and writer. Educ. Camb.; learned Arabic in Damascus and travelled in Arabia and Asia (1876-8). *Travels in Arabia Deserta* (1888) is his account of his journeyings.

DOUGLAS
Cap. of the Is. of Man on Douglas Bay, on the E. coast. It is connected by steamer with Liverpool, Barrow-in-Furness, Belfast, Glasgow and Fleetwood. On Prospect Hill are the buildings of the govt. of the Is. Pop. 18,837.

DOUGLAS
Scot. family, powerful from the early 13th cent. **Sir James Douglas,** called the Black Douglas, was one of the associates of Robert Bruce and is immortalised by Scott. One is mentioned in *Ballad of Chevy Chase*. In Scot. the power of the Douglases became almost equal to that of the king, so in 1440 **William,** the 6th earl, was put to d. A Douglas was made **Marquess of Queensberry** in 1681 and the dukes of Queensberry were Douglases. In addition to the marquess, the family is represented today by the Duke of Buccleuch, the Duke of Hamilton, who bears the title of Marquess of Douglas, the Earl of Morton. Sir Alec Douglas-Home is a Douglas of the female line.

DOUGLAS, Alfred
Lord (1870-1945) 3rd son of the 8th Marquess of Queensberry. His close association with Oscar Wilde led ultimately to Wilde's imprisonment. His relationship with Wilde he discussed in his autobiography (1929), and *Oscar Wilde, A Summing Up* (1940).

DOUGLAS, Gawain
(or **Gavin**) (1474-1522) Scot. poet. His chief poems are the allegories *Palace of Honour* and *King Hart* and his tr. of Virgil's *Æneid*.

DOUGLAS, Stephen Arnold
(1813-61) Amer. politician. A member of the House of Representatives, 1843-7, and a Senator, 1847-61, he is chiefly remembered for his Kansas-Nebraska Bill of 1854, relating to slavery. In 1858 he won Lincoln's seat in the Senate for the Democrats, but was decisively beaten by him in the presidential election of 1860.

DOUGLAS, William Sholto
Lord (1893-1969) Brit. Marshal of the R.A.F. He was 2nd Lieut. R.F.A., Aug. 1914. Was granted permanent commission as Squadron Leader, 1920. Wing-Commdr. 1925. Became Director of Staff Duties, Air Min. 1936. Deputy Chief and Air-Marshal, 1940. C.B., 1940; K.C.B., 1941. Marshal of the R.A.F., 1946. Milit. Gov. Brit. Zone of Germany, 1946-7. During World War II had successive charge of Fighter, Middle E., and Coastal Commands. Created 1st baron Douglas of Kirtleside, 1948. Chairman of B.E.A. 1949-64.

DOUGLAS FIR
N. Amer. evergreen tree of the cone-bearing order (*Pseudotsuga taxifolia*). Also called Oregon pine, it forms great forests from Brit. Columbia to Mexico. The most valued timber tree of the Pacific region. It grows 300 ft. high.

DOULTON
[dōl'-] Brand of ware made at Doulton Pottery Works, Lambeth. **Sir Henry Doulton** (1820-97) entered his father's potteries in 1835, and introduced the use of a good enamel glaze. The manufacture of sanitary and drainage ware was started 11 years later, and in 1870 the production of art pottery began.

DOUNREAY
Ham. near Thurso, Caithness. Site of World's largest fast nuclear reactor. First generated electricity for the nat. grid, 1962. *See* ATOM.

DOURO
River of Spain and Portugal. It rises in Old Castile, Sp. and flows W. The boundary between the 2 countries for *c.* 60 m., it flows across Portugal and enters the sea S. of Oporto.

DOVE
Any bird of the Pigeon family. In popular usage it generally designates the Ring D. or Wood Pigeon, Stock D., Rock D. and the Turtle D.

DOVER
Borough, seaport and market town of Kent, on the Strait of Dover, 77 m. S.E. of London. It is the chief port for communication with Fr. being only 21 m. from Calais. The port has 2 harbours. Both have been improved to accommodate large vessels. D. was one of the Cinque Ports (*q.v.*) and has been important from Rom. times. Pop. 35,650. **Dover, Strait of.** Stretch of water connecting the N. Sea and the Eng. Channel. It is 21 m. across from Dover to Calais. The Strait was swum by Capt. Matthew Webb, 1875, and this has now often been achieved.

DOWAGER
Used for the widow of the holder of a title which has passed to another. Thus, the widow of a duke is the dowager duchess, to distinguish her from the wife of the present duke.

DOWDING, Hugh Caswall T.
(1882-1970) Air Chief Marshall. Educ. Winchester and R.M.A. Woolwich. Served with R.A. until 1914, and with R.F.C. in Fr., 1914-18. Commanded Fighter Area, Air Defence of Brit. Member of Air Council for Supply and Research, 1930-6. Was A.O.C.-in-C. Fighter Command, 1936-40. Air Chief Marshall, 1937, and later received G.C.V.O. and for war services, the G.C.B. On retired list Oct. 21, 1941. Created Baron D., 1943.

DOWLAND, John
(1563-1626) Eng. composer and player of the lute.

DOWN
County of N. Ireland, with a long coastline on the Irish Sea. Belfast Lough is to the N. The rivers are the Bann, Lagan and Newry. The soil is fertile; in the S. are the Mourne Mts. Agriculture is the main industry, but fine linen is manufactured. Downpatrick (*q.v.*) is the county town. Others are Lisburn, Newry and Bangor. Newcastle and Donaghadee are resorts. It returns 2 members to Parl. Pop. 270,200.

DOWNPATRICK
County town of Down, N. Ireland, 25 m. S.E. of Belfast. Is reputed to be the burial place of St. Patrick. Pop. 3,400.

DOWNS
Two ranges of chalk hills in S. Eng. between which is the Weald. The N. Downs are in Kent and Surrey, the highest point being Leith Hill. The S. Downs run from Hants. through Sussex, terminating in Beachy Head.

DOYLE, Sir Arthur Conan
(1859-1930) Eng. author. B. Edinburgh. Educ. Stoneyhurst and Edinburgh (M.B.); practised as a physician. Hist. romances such as *The White Company* (1890), *Brigadier Gerard* (1896); novels and short stories about Sherlock Holmes, *A Study in Scarlet* (1887), *The Adventures of S. H.* (1891), *The Hound of the Baskervilles* (1902), and others; hist. studies and works on politics and spiritualism.

D'OYLY CARTE, Richard
(1844-1901) Eng. theatrical manager, producer of the Gilbert and Sullivan operas.

DRACHM
[dram] Unit of weight. It is 1-16th of an oz. avoirdupois. Drugs are still compounded and prescriptions made up by apothecaries' wt. except in the Brit. Pharmacopoeia, where avoirdupois wt. is used. *See* TABLES p. 453.

DRACO
[drā'-] Magistrate at Athens. He lived *c.* 600 B.C. and codified the laws. These were severe, and since then the word draconian has been used for severity.

DRAGON
Fabulous monster. It was a huge reptilian quadruped breathing fire, *e.g.* the monster killed by St. George. It is one of the nat. emblems of Wales, and appears in the heraldry of China and Japan.

DRAGON FLY
Winged insects comprising the Order Odonata. Of world-wide distribution, and 2,200 species; only 50 are Brit. Large-headed and strong-jawed, with 2 enormous compound eyes and short antennae, these insects are slender-bodied, with 4 large, transparent, membranous wings. The eggs are deposited in water. The larva preys on other water organisms, and reaches a nymphal stage of continued activity before completing the metamorphosis.

DRAGON TREE
Genus of trees of the lily family, native to the warmer parts of Africa, Asia and Polynesia. It has long leaves, usually lance-shaped. Its small whitish flowers bear berries. The dragon tree (*Dracaena draco*) of the Canary Is. attains great size and age.

DRAGONET
(*Callionymus*) Brilliantly coloured spiny-finned fishes inhabiting temp. and trops. seas. The Brit. *C. lyra* is smooth-skinned with pointed mouth and upturned eyes. In the breeding season the male is adorned with coloured stripes.

DRAKE, Sir Francis
(*c.* 1540-96) Eng. navigator and admiral. B. near Tavistock. In 1567 he sailed with his cousin, John Hawkins, to Amer. and in 1570 he again crossed the Atlantic and attacked Sp. settlements and ships. In 1577, with 5 ships, Drake set out upon a voyage round the world. He was away for 3 years and lost all his vessels except the *Golden Hind*, but fulfilled his purpose and was the first Englishman to circumnavigate the globe. In 1587 he led an expedition to Cadiz. In 1595 Drake left Plymouth on his last voyage. He reached the W. Indies where he d.

DRAMA
The hist. of drama can be summed up in the following periods:—(1) *Gk. drama* originating from the Dionysian festivals matured in the 5th cent. B.C. into the great tragedies of Aeschylus, Sophocles and Euripedes and the comedies of Aristophanes. (2) *Roms.* e.g. Plautus, Terence and Seneca, borrowed from the Gks. (3) *Eng. ch. drama* of the M.A.; (4) *The renaissance* forerunners of Shakespeare; Lyly, Peele, Greene, Kyd and Marlowe. (5) *Shakespeare* and his contemporaries Jonson, Beaumont and Fletcher, Webster and Massinger. (6) *The Ital. comedians*; their influence felt by Molière and later the Eng. restoration dramatists. (7) *Restoration*; the patent theatres of Davenant and Killigrew; dramatists Congreve, Wycherley, Farquhar and Vanbrugh. (8) *18th cent.*; dramatists Goldsmith, Sheridan; the advent of Garrick. (9) *19th cent.*; Robertson headed the revolt against unreality, followed by Pinero and Jones. (10) *Ibsen's* revolutionary influence; disciples in other countries, notably Bjornson (Norway), Chekhov (Russia), and Strindberg (Sweden). (11) *20th cent. dramatists*; Galsworthy, Shaw, O'Casey, Eliot, O'Neill, Becket, Ionesco, Pinter.

DRAVIDIAN
Family of agglutinative languages spoken in S. India.

DRAWING
The pictorial representation of objects or ideas on any surface. The portrayal of lines and masses (with the aid of perspective and shading if realism is desired) may be carried out with chalk, charcoal, pencil, pen and ink, brush or many other media including scraper and etching needles. Drawing is older than writing. Other arts such as painting, sculpture, and architecture are based upon drawing, and it is also used as a means of diagrammatic representation in mechanics and engineering.

DRAYTON, Michael
(1563-1631) Eng. poet. B. Warwickshire. His extensive output comprises religious poems, pastorals, sonnets (*Idea's Mirror*, 1594), hist. poems (*The Barons' Wars*, 1603), epistles and topographical verse (*Polyolbion*, 1622).

DREAM
Dreams occur whenever the human body is in the state called sleep. They are rarely remembered on waking but experiments indicate that they are an essential part of sleep. They often concern material already present in the mind, and some have been interpreted by Freud as the fulfilment of unsatisfied desires. The ancients attributed considerable importance to their interpretation.

DRESDEN
E. German city, cap. of Saxony, on the Elbe, 100 m. S. of Berlin. It is a famous art centre. Industries include textiles, machinery, and metallurgy, and the city is a banking and financial centre. D. china, first made in 1709, is produced at Meissen, farther down the river. Pop. 494,588.

DREYFUS, Alfred
(*c.* 1859-1935) Fr. artillery officer. He was falsely charged (1893) with selling milit. secrets, court-martialled, degraded and sent to Devil's Is. The case dominated Fr. politics for over a decade and the prejudices aroused, particularly anti-Semitic, made efforts to free him for a long time unsuccessful. Reinstated 1906.

DRINKWATER, John
(1882-1937) Eng. poet and dramatist. Wrote *Abraham Lincoln* (1918) and other plays, biog., criticism and verse.

DROGHEDA
[draw'-ĕ-dă] Urban district and seaport of Louth, Eire, on the Boyne, 4 m. from the sea and 32 from Dublin. Captured by Cromwell in 1649, it surrendered to William III, following the Battle of the Boyne. Pop. 17,085.

DROITWICH
Borough, spa and market town of Worcs. 6 m. from Worcester. D. is famous for its brine baths. Pop. 8,100.

DROMEDARY
(*Camelus dromedarius*) Name applied to racing breeds of camel as distinguished from baggage animals. They are thoroughbreds expressly raised for riding purposes. They are one-humped Arabian species. Two-humped Bactrian camels of Turkestan also have breeds of superior speed. *See* CAMEL.

DRONE *See* BEE.

DROPSY
or **Oedema.** Morbid accumulation of straw-coloured liquid beneath the skin and in the body cavities—skull, abdomen and chest. It may result from poisoning of the capillary walls from toxic substances accumulating in the body when the kidney function has failed, as in nephritis.

DROPWORT
Perennial herb (*Filipendola hexapetala*) of the rose family, native to Europe, N. Asia and N. Africa, it has smooth leaves and an erect stem, with panicles of small flowers, white or rosy outside. These distinguish it from the taller willow-leaved dropwort (*Spiraea salicifolia*).

DROUGHT
Condition of dryness of an area due to lack of rainfall, sufficiently prolonged to cause serious deficiency in water supplies. Meteorologically, *absolute drought* is 15 consecutive days with rainfall less than ·01 in.; *partial drought* is 29 consecutive days with an average rainfall of less than ·02 in. Deserts occur where permanent drought exists, *e.g.* the Sahara in Africa and the Gobi in Asia. Australia is subject to periodical drought, but this is being overcome by artesian wells, the barrage system of conserving water, and irrigation.

DROWNING
State of suspended animation following submersion in water. *Treatment.* Send for med. aid and apply art. resp. immediately. To clear air passages lay body on face, stand astride, raise abdomen so that all liquid in the lung will run out of the mouth. Lower after 30 secs., turn face to side, pull forward tongue, commence art. resp. Keep body warm. *See* ARTIFICIAL RESPIRATION.

DRUG
Any substance of vegetable, animal or mineral origin used to compound or prepare a med. preparation. Opium is obtained from the unripe capsules of the poppy. Quinine comes from the bark of the Cinchona tree, digitalis from the leaf of a species of foxglove. Other drugs are obtained by chem. processes; of this group aspirin, menthol and the sulphonamides are every day examples. **Antibiotic drugs.** The latest group to be introduced for treatment of illness in man include *penicillin* and *streptomycin* which are extracted from cultures in which those moulds grow. Many drugs in use today are harmful poisons and are carefully controlled by various laws passed by Parl. and by Internat. bodies. *See* POISON. **Drug Addiction.** There is always the possibility of addiction when drugs with central nervous activity (*i.e.* affecting the brain itself) are taken for any reason. Opinions differ on what causes susceptibility to addiction; lack of maturity and intelligence have been suggested. Opiates, which cause euphoria, are particularly liable to cause it: as for example the groups which are derivatives of morphine, cocaine, amphetamine, barbiturate, etc. The symptoms produced by such drugs include slowing of reaction times, impaired motor co-ordination and personality changes. Usage may be intermittent or continuous and the need to continue varies in intensity: it is overpowering with the morphine group. Withdrawal of the drug, in addition to causing craving, can lead to abstinence illness with symptoms including nausea, anxiety and sometimes convulsions. Treatment involves weaning the patient from the drug and providing psychotherapy to treat the mental disturbances of which drug addiction was the expression, in order to minimise chances of relapse.

DRUID
Priest of the Celts of Gaul, Brit. and Ireland. The oak was regarded as of sacred significance and oak groves were places of worship.

DRUM
Instrument composed of a skin stretched over a frame and struck with a stick or with the hands. In the orchestra the most important are the *kettle-drums*, where the skin is stretched over a hemispherical basin of copper. On these drums variable notes of definite pitch can be sounded. The orchestra normally includes 3

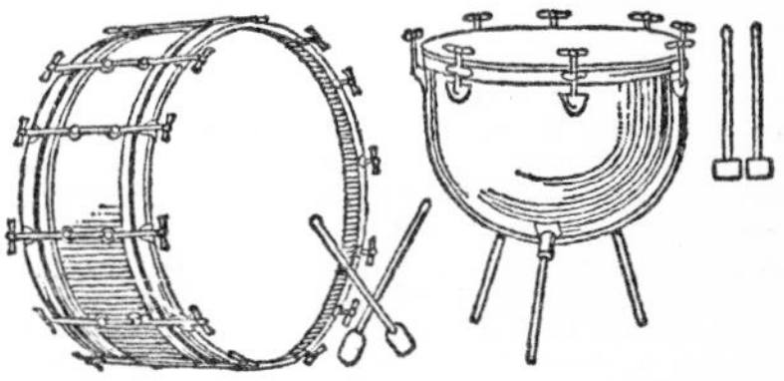

kettle-drums (or Timpani) played with wooden sticks with felt heads. The *Side Drum* or *Snare Drum*, the normal milit. drum is a small cylindrical drum with 2 heads; the upper one is played with 2 hard-wood sticks, the lower one has gut strings, ' snares ', stretched across it. The *Bass Drum*, the larger of the drums with 2 heads, is struck with a heavy stick with a felt head.

DRUMMOND, William
of **Hawthornden** (1585-1649) Scot. poet and writer. B. Hawthornden, near Edinburgh. Wrote on politics (as a royalist), and hist. and a meditation on death, religious, elegiac and amatory verse, and sonnets. His notes of his conversations with Ben Jonson at Hawthornden in 1619 were pub. in 1842.

DRUNKENNESS
Condition of being intoxicated or inebriated due to consumption of a drug such as alcohol, opium or cocaine, in which person is mentally confused, unsteady in gait or muscular movements. Chronic drunkards or habitual drug addicts can be treated in special hospitals. To be drunk and disorderly is an offence in Brit. law and punishable by law.

DRYBURGH
Ruined abbey of Scot. now nat. property, in Berwickshire on the Tweed, 4 m. from Melrose. An aisle, in which Sir Walter Scott and Earl Haig are buried, remains.

DRYDEN, John
(1631-1700) Eng. poet. B. Aldwinkle, Northants. Wrote *Heroic Stanzas* on the d. of Cromwell, *Astraea Redux* on the Restoration; comedies and tragedies; *Marriage à la Mode* (1673), *Aurengzebe* (1676), *All for Love* (1678). Poet Laureate, 1670. The poetry which has made him famous, satires and elaborate ' pindaric ' odes, belong to the years after 1680; *Absalom and Achitophel* (1681), *MacFlecknoe* (1682, '84), *The Hind and the Panther* (1687), *Alexander's Feast* (1697). His prose *Essay on Dramatic Poesy* (1668), and his many prefaces constitute a valuable body of criticism.

DU BARRY, Marie Jeanne Bécu
(1743-93) Fr. adventuress. She mar. Jean, Comte

du Barry, and in 1769 became mistress of Louis XV. She was banished in 1774, and went to Eng. 1792, to raise money on her jewels, but was accused on her return, 1793, of conspiring against the repub. and guillotined.

DUBLIN
County of Eire in the prov. of Leinster, with a coastline on the Irish Sea. The Liffey is the chief river. Agriculture is important. Dublin is the cap. and chief town. Dun Laoghaire is the only other large town. Lambay and other Is. are included in the county. **Dublin (Baile Atha Cliath).** Cap., port and county borough of Eire, at the mouth of the Liffey on D. Bay, 6 m. from its outport, Dun Laoghaire. The chief industries are the manufacture of stout, biscuits and whisky. It is also a banking and distributing centre. The buildings include the castle, the mansion house, art galleries, the nat. museum, the city hall, the fine cath. of St. Patrick and Christ Ch. The Four Courts is where the courts of law sit. Charleville House, a beautiful specimen of 18th cent. architecture, is now an art gallery. Phoenix Park contains the zoological gardens. Dublin is also an educ., lit. and artistic centre. In it are the hist. univ. called Trinity Coll. and Univ. Coll. belonging to the newer nat. univ. The Abbey Theatre is famous. Pop. 537,448.

DUCAT
Medieval coin, generally of gold. First minted *c.* 1140 by Roger II of Sicily for his duchy. Adopted by Florence in 1252, and Venice in 1283.

DUCK
Aquatic bird of the family Anatidae. The male is called the drake. There are 40 genera and 160 species of freshwater ducks found all over the world. All Brit. domesticated breeds, including the Aylesbury, are descended from the common wild duck, the Mallard. Flat-billed and short-legged, usually with 3 front toes completely webbed, they include Gadwalls, Shovellers, Widgeons, Pintails, Sheldrakes, Teal and Mandarin Ducks. Sea ducks or diving ducks include Scaups, Pochards, Canvas-Backed and Eider Ducks. The whistling Teal are tree ducks.

DUCKBILL
(*Ornithorhynchus anatinus*) Egg-laying aquatic mammal. Occurring only in Australia and Tasmania, it is also called the Duck-billed Platypus. With toothless, horny, duck-like beak, inconspicuous eyes and glossy dark-brown fur, it burrows in river banks and stores its food, which consists of insects, molluscs and worms, in the pouches of its cheeks.

DUCKWEED
Family of minute, annual, floating, green, scale-like, flowering plants, allied to the arum family. They grow in all standing waters. Eaten by ducks and geese, they comprise oval structures called fronds, with or without thread-like roots.

DUDLEY
County borough of Worcs. 8 m. N. of Birmingham in the Black country. The industries are chiefly engineering and iron founding. With Stourbridge it returns 1 member to Parl. Pop. 61,748.

DUEL
Single combat. It was usually arranged by challenge and fought with deadly weapons under conventional rules, to settle a personal quarrel, or decide a point of honour. They were very common in Fr., Italy and other countries during the 16th-17th cent., and efforts to stop them failed. In Germany duels among army officers were fairly common before World War I, and duels of students were a feature of univ. life. In Eng. as elsewhere, it was a development of the old combats of the knights. It began in the 16th cent. and duels were fairly frequent in the 17th-18th cents.

DUFY, Raoul
(1877-1953) Fr. artist. B. Le Havre. He began to paint as a hobby. In 1901 he went to Paris and studied there until 1905. His best work was in water colour and designs for tapestries, ceramics or textiles.

DUGONG
[doo'-] (*Halicore*) Aquatic mammal found in the Indian Ocean and along the coasts of Australia. From 7-9 ft. long with flippers, it has no hind limbs. It is allied to the Manatee, with which it constitutes the mammalian order Sirenia, or sea cows. The appearance of the Dugong is supposed to have originated the stories of mermaids.

DUKAS, Paul
[dü-kas'] (1865-1935) Fr. composer. Teacher of composition at the Paris Conservatoire. He wrote opera, a symphony in C and other orchestral works, among them the scherzo *L'Apprenti Sorcier.*

DUKE
Eng. title. Lat. *dux*, a milit. leader. Later it was used in Germany for the ruler of a large district. In Eng. Edward, the Black Prince, was made a duke in 1337. The first Scot. dukedom dates from 1398. Duke is the highest rank in the Brit. peerage. The Duke of Norfolk is the premier duke of Eng.; the Duke of Hamilton of Scot. A duke's heir is a marquess. *See* PEERAGE.

DULLES, John Foster
(1888-1959) Amer. lawyer and statesman. B. Washington, D.C. U.S. deleg. to U.N. Gen. Assembly, 1946, 1947, 1950. Sec. of State 1953-9. Received Medal of Freedom shortly before his d.

DULSE
Fleshy seaweed of the florideous order (*Rhodymenia palmata*). It serves in parts of Scot., Ireland and Iceland as a food relish, either stewed or dried.

DULWICH
[dul'-ich] Suburb of S.E. London, mainly in the borough of Camberwell. **Dulwich College** was founded by Edward Alleyn, the actor, in 1619.

DUMAS, Alexandre
[doo-mà'] (1803-70) Fr. novelist, known as **Dumas père.** B. Villers-Cotterets, d. Puys. Assisted Garibaldi. Among his best-known works is the series devoted to *The Three Musketeers* from 1844 onwards; others are *Le Comte de Monte Cristo* (1844), *La Tulipe Noire* (1850). His son was **Alexandre** (1824-95) Fr. writer, known as **Dumas fils.** Known for *La Dame aux Camélias*, a novel (1848).

DU MAURIER, George
(1834-96) Eng. artist and author. B. and educ. in Paris. Joined 'Punch' in 1864 and regularly contributed both satirical drawings and writings. Pub. 3 novels; *Peter Ibbetson* (1891), *Trilby* (1894), *The Martian* (1896), posthumously. His son was **Sir Gerald** (1873-1934) Eng. actor; educ. Harrow. His daughter, **Daphne** (1907-) has written a study of him, also many successful novels, which have been filmed, and *The Infernal World of Branwell Brontë* (1960).

DUMBARTON
Burgh and county town of Dunbartonshire, on the Clyde estuary at the mouth of the Leven, 15 m. N.W. of Glasgow. A castle stands on the famous Rock. There are shipbuilding yards and engineering works. Pop. 26,461.

DUMBNESS *See* DEAF MUTISM.

DUMFRIESSHIRE
County of S.W. Scot. with a coastline on the Solway Firth. The chief rivers are the Annan, Nith and Esk, which divide the county into 3 districts or dales. Chief hills are the Lowthers. Cattle and sheep are reared. Towns are Moffat, Sanquhar, Annan, Lockerbie and Langholm.

The county returns 1 member to Parl. Pop. 88,113. **Dumfries** [-frēs'] Royal burgh and county town of Dumfriesshire, 74 m. S.W. of Glasgow. The manufactures include cloth and hosiery, and there is an agricultural trade. Pop. 27,042.

DUN LAOGHAIRE
Seaport and borough of Dublin, Eire, on Dublin Bay, with steamer services to Holyhead. Pop. 47,792.

DUNBAR, William
(*c.* 1460-*c.* 1514) Scot. poet. Travelled in Fr. and Eng. on diplomatic missions. He celebrated the mar. of James IV and Margaret Tudor in *The Thrissil and the Rois* (1503). Besides religious, meditative, and allegorical poems like *The Dance of the Sevin Deidly Sins*, there are satirical and personal poems like *The Flyting of Dunbar and Kennedie*. He is one of the ' Scottish Chaucerians '.

DUNBARTONSHIRE
County of W. Scotland with a coastline on the Firth of Clyde. On its borders are Loch Lomond and Loch Long. Chief rivers are the Leven and Kelvin. Dumbarton is the county town; other towns are Clydebank, Kirkintilloch and Helensburgh. County returns 2 members to Parl. Pop. 190,138.

DUNCAN, Isadora
(1878-1927) Amer. dancer, b. San Francisco. She won a great reputation in Europe appearing in London, Paris and other capitals. Her work led to a revival of classical dancing.

DUNCANSBY HEAD
Promontory of Scot. in Caithness, on which are 3 rocks called the Stacks.

DUNDEE
City and seaport of Angus, on the N. side of the Firth of Tay, crossed by the Tay Bridge. It is a centre of jute manufacture. Other industries are engineering, shipbuilding, dyeing, publishing and printing. It is famed for its marmalade. There is a good harbour and the port has a large trade in timber. The buildings incl. Queen's Coll., part of the Univ. of St. Andrews. A road bridge is being built across the Firth of Tay. Dundee returns 2 members to Parl. Pop. 183,560.

DUNDEE, Viscount John
(1649-89) Scot. soldier. Son of Sir William Graham of Claverhouse, he went to the Univ. of St. Andrews; became a soldier. In 1678 he was sent to Scot. to put down the Covenanters. In 1688 he was made a viscount, and was killed at Killiecrankie leading the force he had raised for the Stuarts against William III.

DUNEDIN
City and seaport of New Zealand, on the S.E. coast of S. Is. Industries incl. refrigerating works, iron and brass foundries, and woollen manufactures; wool, meat and dairy produce are exported. Founded 1848, under the auspices of the Free Ch. of Scot. Now the seat of Otago Univ. Pop. 107,400.

DUNFERMLINE
[-lin] Royal burgh of Fifeshire, on the Firth of Forth, 15 m. N.W. of Edinburgh. It stands on the Fife coalfield, and industries incl. the manufacture of linen and linoleum. The birthplace of Andrew Carnegie. With Cowdenbeath, Inverkeithing, and Lochgelly, it returns 1 member to Parl. Pop. 48,863.

DUNKIRK
Port of Nord dept., N. Fr., on the Strait of Dover, near the Belgian frontier. Shipbuilding and fishing are important. **Dunkirk Evacuation.** On May 10, 1940 Germany invaded Holland, Belgium and Luxemburg. The capitulation of the Dutch Army was signed on May 15 and that of the Belgian Army at midnight on May 27. The navy, helped by numerous ' little ships ' placed at the disposal of the Admiralty, began the evacuation of the Brit. army on May 28. It continued until the night of June 2-3 by which time 224,585 Brit. and 112,546 Fr. and Belgian troops had been evacuated. 6 destroyers and 24 smaller war vessels were lost.

DUNLIN
(or **Red-backed Sandpiper**) An abundant wader, haunting sandy shores, estuaries, mud-flats, etc. Plumage variable, grey-backed in winter, red-brown above in summer.

DUNLOP, John Boyd
(1840-1921) Brit. inventor. B. Dreghorn, Ayrshire. In 1887 he devised a pneumatic tyre which he patented 1888. In 1890 Dunlop sold his patent to William Harvey Du Cros and a company was formed for its commercial exploitation.

DUNMOW
[-mō] Two places in Essex. **Great D.** is a market town on the Chelmer, 8 m. W. of Braintree and 40 from London. **Little D.** is *c.* 2 m. away. Noted for the custom of giving a flitch of bacon to any couple who can publicly prove that, having been mar. for a year and a day, they have not regretted the union.

DUNOIS, Jean
[dü-nwa'] (1403-68) Fr. gen. He was a natural son of Louis, Duke of Orleans, a brother of Charles VI, and was known as the Bastard of Orleans. He became a soldier, was given a high command. He defended Orleans until it was relieved by Joan of Arc. In 1450 he finally expelled the Eng. from Normandy and later from Guienne.

DUNS SCOTUS
Friar. B. at Duns, Scot. he became a teacher at Merton Coll. Oxford. He became a Franciscan and went to Paris. He d. in Cologne, Nov. 8, 1308. Scotus was the founder of Scotism, metaphysical doctrines which long struggled for the mastery against Thomism, the theological doctrines of St. Thomas Aquinas.

DUNSTABLE
[dun'-stăbl] Borough and market town of Bedfordshire, 4 m. W. of Luton. Nearby are Dunstable Downs and Whipsnade Zoo. Pop. 26,480.

DUODECIMAL
arithmetic. Method of computation based upon the division of a scale into 12 equal parts. A foot is divided into 12 in. or primes, these into 12 parts or seconds, and similarly into 3rds or 4ths.

DUPLEIX, Joseph François
[dü-pleks] (1697-1763) Fr. colonial statesman. *c.* 1720 he settled in India and became an official of the Fr. E. India Co. In 1742, as Gov. of Pondicherry, became the head of Fr. India, with the aim of making Fr. influence paramount. War with Brit. in 1744 gave him an opportunity. He was checked by the rise of Robert Clive (*q.v.*) and in 1754 recalled and disgraced.

DURBAN
or **Port Natal.** Chief seaport and commercial cap. of Natal, S. Africa, on D. Bay. It has a

modern harbour, and is linked by rly. with the Transvaal and Orange Free State. Chief industries are connected with shipping and distributing trades. Founded in 1824, and named after its first gov. Sir B. d'Urban. Pop. 659,934.

DÜRER, Albrecht
(1471-1528) German artist. B. and d. at Nuremberg. He assisted his father, a goldsmith, but soon began to study under Michael Wohlgemut. Afterwards he spent some years in travel, visiting Venice and meeting Raphael. Towards the end of his life he went to the Netherlands where Charles V made him a court painter. His engravings on copper reveal a remarkable power of drawing in detail and richness of invention, seen esp. in *The Knight, Death and the Devil* and *The Arms of Death.* His woodcuts are scarcely less notable, but his portrait paintings are somewhat hard and severe.

DURHAM
County of N.E. Eng. between the Tyne and the Tees, with a coastline on the N. Sea. The W. is hilly, with Pennine moorland and peaks; the centre and E. is a densely populated industrial area with rich coal mines. The chief rivers are the Tees and Wear. Durham is the county town, but Gateshead, S. Shields and Stockton are larger. Sunderland and the Hartlepools are large seaports. Other places are Jarrow, Darlington, Bishop Auckland and Barnard Castle. 18 members are returned to Parl. (9 borough constituencies). Pop. 1,530,170. **Durham.** City and county town of Durham, on the Wear, 14 m. S. of Newcastle. The chief buildings are the cath. and the castle, both standing high on land almost surrounded by the river. The castle, now used by the univ., was once the residence of the prince bishops of Durham. Durham has some manufactures. Pop. 22,010.

DURHAM, Earl of
John George Lambton (1792-1840). Brit. statesman. In 1813 he became M.P. for Durham, and was known as ' Radical Jack '. In 1830 he became Lord Privy Seal and was one of the 4 framers of the Reform Bill of 1832. In 1838 he was Gov.-Gen. of Canada where, because of the revolt of the Fr., the constitution was suspended. His famous Report advocated responsible self-govt. for Canada, and she became the first Dominion (1867).

DURIAN
Tree of the mallow family, native to Malaya, where it is widely cultivated for its fruit.

DUSE, Eleonora
[doo'-zā] (1859-1924) Ital. actress: b. near Venice, she made her first success 1878. She performed in Europe and the U.S.A., achieved internat. fame in *Camille,* and in plays by Ibsen; also as Paula in *The Second Mrs. Tanqueray.*

DÜSSELDORF
W. German industrial city in N. Rhine-Westphalia on the Rhine, 24 m. N. of Cologne. It is a great river port and commercial centre. The manufactures include iron and steel goods and chemicals. Pop. 664,000.

DUTCH GUIANA
or **Surinam.** Territory on the N. coast of S. Amer. between Fr. and Brit. Guiana, an integral part of the Netherlands Kingdom. Exports include rum, coffee, bauxite and timber. Paramaribo is the cap. and chief port. Area: 55,143 sq.m. Pop. 330,000.

DUTCH WARS
Naval wars between Eng. and the United Provinces. The 1st and 2nd, 1652-4 and 1664-7, were purely trade wars resulting from rivalry in N. Sea and E. Indies. In the 1st, Admiral Tromp considerably injured Eng. naval prestige, until Admiral Blake defeated him in 1653. The wars ended with the Treaty of Westminster (1654) and the Peace of Breda (1667) respectively. The 3rd War (1672-4) was bound up with continental politics, and the Dutch, under William of Orange, eventually forced Eng. to make peace.

DVOŘÁK, Antonin
[dvor'-zhak] (1841-1904) Czech composer. Between 1892-5 he was director of the Nat. Conservatoire in New York. His symphony No. 5 (*From the New World*) was written as a result. His music is strongly flavoured with the folk music of Bohemia. He wrote operas, 9 symphonies, symphonic poems, Slavonic dances, concertos for piano, for violin and for 'cello, chamber music, ch. music, pianoforte works and songs.

DWARF
Term applied to men, animals or plants which do not attain normal ht. Dwarfism is normal in Pigmy races of C. Africa, or Bushmen of S. Africa. It also occurs in cretinism, where thyroid secretion is deficient, or where cartilage growth of long bones is stunted. Dwarf trees which may bear flowers and fruit are cultivated in China and Japan.

DYAKS
Aboriginal people of Borneo. Some of them still live in pile huts made of bamboo and use blow guns. They were chiefly known as head hunters, but this practice has now been suppressed.

DYEING
Art of imparting colour to textile and other materials. Various substances of vegetable origin have been used, but these are more or less fugitive. The introduction of coal tar derivatives has led to the disuse of most natural dyes as the synthetic products give a wider range of tints and great permanency. The chief vegetable dyes are indigo, fustic, logwood, archil and annatto.

DYKE
An embankment erected on a river bank or on the sea shore to prevent the flooding of the adjacent land. These are seen in low-lying countries. In Holland the sea dykes are of great size.

DYNAMITE
Powerful explosive. Used chiefly for blasting purposes, it consists of 75 % of nitro-glycerine and 25 % of kieselguhr, the latter being used as an absorbent.

DYNAMO
Generator of electric current in which mechanical energy is converted into electrical energy. The essential parts are the magnets and the armature with which are connected the commutator, and stationary brushes. The armature consists of a series of wires or conductors arranged around an iron core mounted on a shaft. It is rotated near the poles of a powerful permanent or electro-magnet, and the current generated is carried from the armature by brushes of copper wire or carbon rubbing on the commutator.

DYSENTERY
[dis'-en-] Infectious disease caused by the group of bacteria, *Bacillus dysenteriae,* and assoc. with an acute inflammatory condition of the bowels. The disease can be spread by faecal material of patients suffering from disease or by water, milk, foodstuffs contaminated by an infected person or by flies. The symptoms are profuse, watery bowel motions which may contain blood and mucus, assoc. with fever, malaise and sickness. In the tropics another type of dysentery is seen (Amoebic Dysentery), caused by parasites.

DYSPEPSIA
[dis-pep'-] Symptom assoc. with gastric disease esp. chronic gastritis or gastric ulcer. Functional or nervous dyspepsia is assoc. with prolonged overwork and worry. *See* GASTRITIS.

E

E
2nd vowel and 5th letter of the Eng. alphabet, occurring more frequently in Eng. words than any other letter of the alphabet. It possesses 2 principal sounds, long as in *here* and *me*, short as in *men* and *set*. It has besides a sound like *a* in *bare*, as in *there*, *where*, etc. and the obscure sound which is heard in *her*. In *clerk*, *Derby*, *e* has the sound (in England) of *a*. Combined with other vowels or half-vowels, *e* makes diphthongs, as in *ear*, *beauty*, *sleigh*, *deuce*.

E.E.C. *See* COMMON MARKET.

E.F.T.A.
European Free Trade Association. U.K., Sweden, Norway, Denmark, Austria, Switzerland and Portugal, 1960. Finland joined 1961. Aimed to abolish internal tariffs and quotas by 1970.

EAGLE
Large bird of prey. Its feather-clad head, short sharply-hooked bill and habit of killing its prey distinguish it from the unfeathered head and longer bill of the vulture. The Golden Eagle, rarely seen in Eng. comes from Scot. or Ireland, where it builds its nest on inaccessible cliffs. It will attack young lambs, though usually it feeds on rabbits and hares. The Sea-eagle or White-tailed eagle breeds in Scot.

EAGLE
Heraldic symbol. It dates from Egyptian, Persian and Roman times, and was used by Charlemagne. Russia, as the successor of the Gk. Empire, and Austria used a double-headed eagle. Germany, which took the symbol in 1871, a single-headed one. In Amer. the eagle was used by the Indians, and adopted by the U.S.A. as a nat. emblem, with a single head and in its talons arrows and an olive branch.

EALING
Borough of Greater London (1964) consisting of the former Ealing, Acton and Southall. Formerly in Middlesex, it was made a borough in 1901. It returns 2 members to Parl. Situated at Ealing are the first British film studios to be built for sound film production (1931).

EAR
Organ of hearing. The human ear consists of 3 parts, outer, middle and inner. The outer ear is composed of the pinna or auricle. The middle ear is a small space in the temporal bone communicating with the naso-pharynx by the Eustachian tube, and with the mastoid air cells through the tympanic antrum. The inner ear consists of the labyrinth or balancing apparatus and the cochlea or organ in which the nerve of hearing has its end filaments. *See* DEAFNESS.

EARL
Title of the Brit. peerage. It ranks 3rd but historically is the oldest. An earl's wife is called a countess. An earl's eldest son bears his father's 2nd title; the other sons use the word honourable, and the daughters, lady, before the Christian name. The Earl of Arundel, a title of the Duke of Norfolk, is the premier Eng. earl; the Earl of Crawford and Balcarres is the premier Scots. earl.

EARTH
Fourth largest of the 9 planets, lies between Venus and Mars in the solar system, with 1 satellite, the moon. It has 3 motions: that of rotation round its axis once a day; that of revolution round the sun (93,000,000 m. distant) in an orbit which it completes once a year; and that through space with the whole solar system. Its diam. at the equator is 7,900 m. and its circum. 24,900. Its area is 196,500,000 sq.m. of which only 55,500,000 are land.

EARTHQUAKE
Movement of the earth's crust. It may be caused by volcanic eruptions or by folding and faulting of rock strata. Earthquakes may cause a change of surface level, but generally the only visible sign is the damage to buildings, etc. owing to the shaking. Large earthquakes are often followed by other shocks; where the earthquake occurs near or beneath the sea, large waves are formed which may cause considerable damage by flooding. There are 3 main regions of activity: (1) a belt of the Pacific Ocean, including Japan, the Philippines and the E. Indies, (2) a belt across S. Europe and S. Asia, through the Medit. to the Himalayas, and (3) the W. coast of N. and S. Amer.

EARTHWORM
Annelid worms living in the soil. Their cylindrical bodies, tapering at both ends, comprise segmented rings each bearing 4 pairs of minute bristles. They swallow soil for its organic contents and void the mineral matter as worm casts. Reproduction is hermaphroditic.

EARWIG
(*Forficula*) Insect with short, horny, beetle-like forewings which protect thin, membranous underwings folded fanwise and crosswise. The pincer-like appendages at the end of the abdomen are quite innocuous.

EAST ANGLIA
District of E. Eng., the counties of Norfolk, Suffolk, Camb. and Huntingdon, and part of Essex.

EAST INDIA COMPANY
Co. formed for the purpose of trading between Brit. and India and the E. Indies. The Brit. Co.'s charter was granted 1600. It became powerful and conquered much territory, esp. under Clive, Hastings, Richard Wellesley. Acts of 1773 and 1784 estabd. a measure of govt. control, but its admin. power lasted until after the Mutiny, 1857-8.

EAST INDIES
Name given to the Is. archipelago which includes Sumatra, Java, Borneo, New Guinea, Celebes and the Philippines, and Malaya on the mainland. Now comprises mainly the Repub. of Indonesia (*q.v.*).

EAST LONDON
Port of Cape Province, S. Africa

EAST LOTHIAN
(formerly **Haddingtonshire**). County of S.E. Scot. with a coastline on the N. Sea and Firth of Forth. It is chiefly agricultural, but there are collieries, and fishing is important. The Lammermuir Hills are in the S. and the Tyne is the chief river. Haddington is the county town. With Berwick, it returns 1 member to Parl. Pop. 51,814.

EAST PAKISTAN
Dist. of Pakistan with a coastline on the bay of Bengal, bounded inland by the Indian states of W. Bengal, Tripura and Assam, and Burma. It comprises the E. territories of the former prov. of Bengal and the former Assam dist. of Sylhet. It is watered by the Ganges and the Brahmaputra and contains *c.* ½ of the pop. of Pakistan. Rice, hemp, oilseeds, sugar, silk, tea and coal are the chief products. Cap. is Dacca. Disastrous flooding, 1970, affected 3 millions; 200,000 killed Civil War, 1971. Area: 55,134 sq. m. Pop. 50,844,000.

EAST RIDING
One of the 3 admin. divisions of Yorks. (*q.v.*).

EASTBOURNE
County borough and resort of Sussex, on the Eng. Channel. Pop. 61,250.

EASTER
Eccles. festival, instituted *c.* A.D. 68, commemorating the resurrection of Christ. The name is derived from that of the A.-S. goddess of spring. It is governed by the lunar calendar. Now it is, briefly, the 1st Sun. after the full moon following the vernal equinox, falling between Mar. 22nd and Apr. 25th.

EASTER ISLAND
Is. in the S. Pacific, belonging to Chile, from which it is 2,300 m. away. Discovered on Easter Day, 1722, by a Dutch sailor, it is chiefly famous for a remarkable collection of stone figures.

EASTERN CHURCH
Shortened name of the Holy Orthodox Catholic Apostolic E. Ch. Representing the Christendom estabd. by Constantine in the E. Rom. Empire, it accepts the general ch. councils down to the Gt. Schism and comprises pre-eminently the Gk. and Russian, besides the Armenian and Coptic Chs.

EASTMAN, George
(1854-1932) Amer. inventor. B. Waterville, New York. In 1880 he perfected a process for making sensitive gelatine dry plates. In 1884 he patented a photographic roll film and in 1888 a Kodak camera. His gifts for charitable purposes are estimated at £15,000,000.

EAU DE COLOGNE
[ō'-dĕ-kŏ-lōn'] Celebrated perfume, first prepared by Johann Maria Farina at Cologne soon after 1700. The essential oils of citron, orange, bergamot, neroli, rosemary are used.

EBBSFLEET
Hamlet on the coast of Kent, 3½ m. from Ramsgate, the traditional landing place of Hengist and Horsa, 449. St. Augustine landed 597.

EBBW VALE
[eb'-boo] Urban district of Monmouthshire, on the S. Wales coalfield. It has important iron and tinplate industries. Pop. 28,350.

EBONY
Tree of the family Ebenaceae. There are several species and in some the fruit is edible. The tree grows only in trop. areas, notably in India, Ceylon and Africa. Its wood is extraordinarily hard and is used for math. instruments, etc.

ECCLESIASTES
Book of the O.T. It comprises the discourses and aphorisms of a despondent sage. His reflections culminate in the assertion 'all is vanity'.

ECCLESIASTICAL COMMISSION
Body apptd. in 1836 to manage the property of the C. of E. The property of the Ch. of Scot. is also managed by an ecclesiastical commission at Edinburgh.

ECCLESIASTICAL LAW
The laws governing the rights and obligations of a ch. estabd. by law. Its jurisdiction deals only with ecclesiastical matters.

ECCLESIASTICUS
Alternative title of an apocryphal O.T. book.

ECHIDNA
[ek-] Spiny ant-eater. Egg-laying mammals, found in Australia and New Guinea. Their 2 eggs are hatched in a pouch beneath the body. There are 5-toed and 3-toed forms. The head and body bear stiff hairs and short, thick spines.

ECHO
Repetition of a sound a short time after its production. An echo occurs when sound can reach the listener by 2 paths of different length; thus a handclap made in front of a cliff will be heard first by sound which has travelled directly from the hand to the ear, and later by sound which has travelled to the cliff and has been reflected from it. If the cliff is 100 ft. away, the interval between the sound and its echo will be $\frac{200}{1120}=0{\cdot}18$ sec. (since the speed of sound is about 1,120 ft. per sec. and the extra distance travelled by the sound forming the echo is 200 ft.). **Echo Sounding.** Method by which ships determine the depth of water in which they are sailing. An instrument records the time taken by a sound wave to travel to and return from the sea bed.

ECLIPSE
In astronomy, the obscuring of one celestial body by another. Eclipses are either partial or total. Partial eclipses of both the sun and the moon occur every year; total eclipses occur about once every 2 years. A solar eclipse can occur only at the time of the new moon, and even then, only when it is near one of the nodes of the ecliptic. The laws of solar and lunar eclipses were known to the astronomers of ancient Egypt. Only 2 total eclipses of the sun were visible in the 18th cent. None were visible in the 19th cent. A number fall in the 20th cent. including (1) that of June 30, 1954 which was a total eclipse in the track of the moon's shadow where it crossed the U.S.A., Canada, the Shetlands, Norway, Sweden, and Russia, and (2) that which will occur on July 10, 1972, and will be visible in N. Canada and Alaska.

ECONOMICS
Orig. the science of household management. The term polit. economy came into use to denote the production, distribution and consumption of wealth. This was first discussed in Fr. early in the 17th cent. The foundation of the science is usually attributed to Adam Smith, who, in 1776, pub. *The Wealth of Nations.* This was followed by the writings of John Stuart Mill, David Ricardo, and many Fr. and German economists. Early economists regarded polit. economy as free from all social and ethical considerations. Towards the end of the 19th cent. economists began to take account of educ. and housing, even pleasure and recreation. Polit. economy became economics and its scope was widened. In the 20th cent. the study was revolutionised by Lord Keynes. Economics is a subject of study at all univs. The London School of Economics is an important centre.

ECUADOR
[ek-wā-dor'] Repub. of S. Amer. in the W. of the cont. lying across the Equator. The Andes

traverse the country from N. to S. rising to over 20,000 ft. in Chimborazo. In the W. is the coastal plain, which produces trop. crops. From this the land rises rapidly to the W. Cordillera of the Andes, which is separated from the E. Cordillera by a plateau. To the E. lies the Oriente, the land descending to the plains of the Amazon; this is inhabited by Indians. There is great diversity of climate, depending on the altitude. Agriculture is the chief occupation, and cacao is the principal crop. It is grown in the coastal region, on large estates. Ivory, nuts, rubber, coffee, tobacco and fruits are also produced. Oil production has increased in recent years. The cap. is Quito. Ecuador was conquered by the Incas in the late 15th cent. and by the Sp. a cent. later. With Colombia, Venezuela and Panama it formed the repub. of Columbia of Simon Bolivar, but became indep. 1830. In March 1966 Pres. Indaburo's govt. replaced the military junta. The **Galapagos Is.** forming the prov. of Colon, were annexed, 1832, and are governed by a territorial chief. Area: 109,000 sq.m. Pop. 5,508,000.

ECUMENICAL COUNCIL
In Christianity, a convocation of duly constituted authorities *of the whole Church.* In the Rom. Ch. the proceedings are considered to be inspired by the Holy Ghost, hence its pronouncements on faith and morals are regarded as infallible. The councils recognised as ecumenical by the R.C. Ch. number 21, ranging from the Council of Nicaea, 325, to the Vatican Council of 1962. In Brit. other churches hold ecumenical conferences.

ECZEMA
[ek'-simă] Skin disease characterised by the eruption of small watery vesicles which burst and discharge a thin watery fluid, assoc. with much irritation. Cause is unknown, but there may be some relation between this disease and sensitivity of the body to certain materials.

EDAM
Dutch town in the prov. of N. Holland, 13 m. N.E. of Amsterdam, near the shore of the Ijsselmeer; it is famous for the round red Edam cheese. Pop. 9,000.

EDDA
Norse name for 2 collections of Icelandic lit. the elder poetry, and the younger prose. **Brynjulf Sveinsson,** an Icelandic bishop, discovered the elder in 1643. The younger, in 3 parts, was compiled by **Snorri Sturluson** (1178-1241).

EDDINGTON, Sir Arthur Stanley
O.M. F.R.S. (1882-1944) Eng. astron. B. Kendal, educ. Owens Coll. Manchester, and Trinity Coll. Camb. He was chief assistant at the Royal Observatory, Greenwich. Eddington did valuable work in developing the theory of relativity and gravitation.

EDDY, Mary Baker
(1821-1910) Founder of Christian Science and author of its text-book, *Science and Health with Key to the Scriptures.* B. Bow, New Hampshire, Mrs. Eddy was deeply religious by nature. In 1866 her reading of Matt. 9, 2-8, led to her recovery from an accident, and the discovery in the Bible of the scientific law which underlay the healing works of Christ Jesus. This she named **Christian Science.**

EDELWEISS
[ā'-dĕl-vīs] (*Leontopodium alpinum*) Hardy perennial plant found in Switzerland. The hairy leaves have a whitish appearance; flowers are greyish-white.

EDEN, Anthony
Earl of Avon (1897-) Eng. politician. P.M. 1955-57. M.P. (Cons.) for Warwick and Leamington, 1923-57. Educ. Eton and Christ Church, Oxford. In 1935 he became Min. for League of Nations Affairs, and Foreign Sec. Resigned in 1938 as a protest against appeasement. At the outbreak of war he returned to the Cabinet and became Foreign Sec. 1940-5. Leader of the House of Commons, 1942-5. Appointed Sec. of State for Foreign Affairs and Deputy P.M. 1951-5. He became Premier in succession to Sir Winston Churchill in April, 1955. Resigned from polit. life, Jan. 1957, as result of prolonged ill-health. Earl of Avon 1961. See *Sir Anthony Eden* by Lewis Broad (1955).

EDGAR
Eng. prince called the Atheling. B. in Hungary, son of Edward the exile, and grandson of Edmund Ironside. In 1066 he was proclaimed king in the N. of Eng. in opposition to William I. The risings were unsuccessful and he made peace with the Conqueror. He lived in Normandy for many years, went on a Crusade and became a prisoner after the Battle of Tinchebrai in 1106.

EDINBURGH
Cap. of Scotland on the S. shore of the Firth of Forth. The city is dominated by the castle which is of great historic interest. The site of the old town is the 'Royal Mile' from the Castle to Holyroodhouse, a Royal residence at the foot of Arthur's Seat. The Mile contains many famous buildings, *e.g.* The Cathedral Ch. of St. Giles, the old Parliament House, now used as the Law Courts, the Advocates' Library (now the National Library), John Knox's House, etc. Other famous buildings are the Royal Scottish Museum, the Scottish Nat. Gallery and the Nat. Portrait Gallery. Edinburgh is famous as a centre of education. The Univ. dates from 1583. Public schools include Fettes Coll., Loretto and Merchiston Castle. Edinburgh is a banking and insurance centre, and its leading industries include printing and publishing, brewing, distilling, biscuit making, chemicals and the preparation of rubber. An Internat. Festival of Music and Drama has been held annually since 1947. The city is gov. by a Council under a Lord Provost and sends 7 members to Parl. Pop. 475,338.

EDINBURGH, Duke of
Brit. title created by Queen Victoria for her son, Prince Alfred. It lapsed when he became hereditary Grand Duke of Saxe-Coburg-Gotha and relinquished his Brit. titles. Conferred, Nov. 1947 on Lieut. Philip Mountbatten, husband of Princess Elizabeth along with the titles Baron Greenwich of Greenwich and Earl of Merioneth. In February 1957 the Queen conferred the title of Prince on her husband, who was henceforth to be known as 'His Royal Highness the Prince Philip, Duke of Edinburgh'. *See* PHILIP, PRINCE.

EDISON, Thomas Alva
(1847-1931) Amer. electrician and inventor. B. Milan, Ohio, of Dutch and Scots descent. His inventions included the phonograph, from which the gramophone was developed; the first practicable automatic repeater for telegraphic messages; an electric storage battery of a new type; and the carbon filament used in early electric lamps.

EDMONTON
Cap. of Alberta, Canada on the N. Saskatchewan, 180 m. N. of Calgary. It is the commercial and distributing centre. Pop. 281,027.

EDMUND
(d. 870) Eng. saint and King of E. Anglia. In 870 he was taken prisoner by the Danes and martyred. The city which grew up round his shrine was named after him, Bury St. Edmunds.

EDMUND
(980-1016) Eng. king, called Ironside. Son of Ethelred the Unready, he succeeded his father in 1016. He fought bravely against the Danes, but was beaten and agreed to divide the kingdom with Canute.

EDUCATION
Term for mental and physical training, esp. of the young. Modern educ. began with the Gks. With the estab. of Christianity in Europe, educ. became the province of the Ch. The Ch. was responsible for the early schools and univs. Educ. was given to a very few boys by monks in schools connected with the monasteries. The Renaissance gave considerable impetus to educ. and the 15th and 16th cents. witnessed the founding of many univs. and schools. In the 19th cent. educ. was taken over by the State. Women were included. Elementary education was distinguished from secondary. Technical educ. was introduced. The old univs. were reorganised, and new ones were created. Brit. educ. was made compulsory by an Act of 1870, and schools, called board schools, later council schools, were set up by the side of the existing ch. schools. For the wealthier classes, the public school system was extended. In 1891 educ. in the elementary schools was made free; prior to this, payment had been based on the parents' income. In 1918 the leaving age was raised to 14, in 1930 to 15 (enforced 1947). **Elementary Education.** After the Nursery School, the child will proceed to the Infant and Primary School and thence in some cases to the Secondary Modern School, where he will remain until he is 15 or older. Facilities are provided for further technical and commercial training, and evening classes may be attended. The Secondary Grammar School is attended after the Primary School from the age of 11 or more. Scholarships are now freely obtainable by exam. which will pay the full fees for secondary educ. to the age of 19, and in special cases some contribution towards maintenance. Children are accepted in preparatory and private schools at 5-7 years of age, and they usually remain until they are 12 or 13. **Public Schools.** For entrance to most of the public schools it is necessary to arrange the matter many years before the child is of age. The age for entrance to a public school is usually from 12 to 14 years, and the leaving age is 18 to 19. **Preparatory Schools.** The child for whom a Public School educ. has been planned will usually begin in either a private or a preparatory school. Pupils in Secondary Schools in Eng. and Wales may sit for exams leading to the General Certificate of Education (G.C.E.), papers being set at 3 levels, ordinary, advanced and scholarship. This is being introduced in Scot. After leaving school specialised training may take the form of an apprenticeship or attendance at Business, Technical or Training Colleges, in some of which a degree may be taken for such purposes as teaching. **The Universities.** Every univ. publishes an annual 'calendar', which contains full particulars of entrance, scholarships and tuition. 2 important White Papers on educ. were pub. in 1963. The Newsom Rep. on Secondary Educ. recommended raising the leaving age to 16, among other things. The Robbins Rep. on Higher Educ. recommended 6 new univs. (at least 1 in Scot.), 5 Special Inst. for Science and Technology, Colls. of Advanced Technology which would be technological univs. conferring their own degrees, and developments in all fields of Further Education.

EDWARD
(1005-66) Eng. king called the Confessor, son of Ethelred the Unready. In 1041 he crossed over to Eng. and was chosen king in succession to his half-brother, Hardicanute. He reigned for 25 years. He built the 1st abbey at Westminster, and was canonised in 1161.

EDWARD I
(1239-1307) King of Eng., eldest son of Henry III. He fought against the rebellious barons and in 1265 defeated Simon de Montfort at Evesham. Later he went on a crusade and during his absence in 1272 became king. He conquered Wales and made war on Scot. but won his most enduring fame by calling the Model Parl. of 1295.

EDWARD II
(1284-1327) King of Eng. Son of Edward I, b. at Caernarvon, and created Prince of Wales in 1301, the 1st Eng. prince to bear that title. Coming to the throne in 1307, he made peace at once with Scot. His reign of 20 years was marked by the dominance of favourites and revolts of the nobles. The king was eventually deposed and murdered in Berkeley Castle.

EDWARD III
(1312-77) King of Eng., son of Edward II. He became king in 1327, and in 1330 put an end to the usurped authority of his mother Isabella, and Roger Mortimer. His reign was chiefly occupied with the Fr. war and was marked by the victories of Crécy and Poitiers. His reign was notable for constitutional developments, the Black Death (1348), the Statute of Labourers (1351) and the preaching of Wycliffe.

EDWARD IV
(1442-83) King of Eng., the eldest son of Richard, Duke of York. He began to fight for the Yorkists, and in 1460, on his father's d. became their leader. In 1469, owing to the desertion of the Earl of Warwick, he left Eng. but returned and crushed his foes at Barnet and Tewkesbury. In 1464 Edward mar. Elizabeth Woodville. Their son was **Edward V** (1470-83). In April, 1483, he became king, with his uncle, the Duke of Gloucester, afterwards Richard III, as his guardian. With his brother he was imprisoned in the Tower, where both were murdered.

EDWARD VI
(1537-53) King of Eng. Son of Henry VIII and Jane Seymour, he became king in 1547, and reigned for 6 years. The chief event was the estab. of the Protestant Ch.

EDWARD VII
(1841-1910) King of Gt. Brit. and Ireland, eldest son and 2nd child of Queen Victoria and Albert of Saxe-Coburg. He was created Prince of Wales and Duke of Cornwall soon after his birth. In 1863 Albert Edward mar. Alexandra, daughter of the prince who afterwards became King Christian IX of Denmark. Because of the queen's retirement, the Prince and Princess of Wales were for many years the acknowledged leaders of Eng. society. The Prince entered into every form of social activity, but his mother did not allow him any considerable share in affairs of State. On Jan. 22, 1901, the Prince became King and Emperor.

EDWARD VIII
(1894-   ) King of Gt. Brit. and Ireland, 1936. Eldest son of George V and Queen Mary, he was created Prince of Wales in 1911. He had a naval training at Osborne and Dartmouth, studied at Paris and Magdalen Coll. Oxford, and was on active service during World War I. He succeeded to the throne in Jan. 1936. His wish to marry the Amer. Mrs. Simpson roused such opposition that he abdicated in Dec. of that year. He mar. Mrs. Simpson in 1937 and received the title of **Duke of Windsor.**

EDWARD
(The Black Prince) (1330-76) Eng. prince. Eldest son of Edward III.

EDWIN
(*c.* 585-633) King of Northumbria, son of Ella, King of Deira. Driven out by the King of Bernicia, in 617 he killed his foe in battle, and united Bernicia and Deira into the Kingdom of Northumbria. He mar. Ethelburga of Kent, and in 627, under her influence and that of Paulinus, became a Christian. He was killed in battle against Penda, King of Mercia.

EEL
Soft-rayed fishes with long snake-like bodies. They lack ventral fins and external scales. Widespread in temp. fresh waters, the common European Eel, *Anguilla vulgaris*, is greenish-brown and silvery beneath. The female, which anglers call the Sharp-nosed, measures 3-4 ft., the male, called the Broad-nosed, is much smaller. The females inhabit rivers and ponds, where they live for many years. Eventually

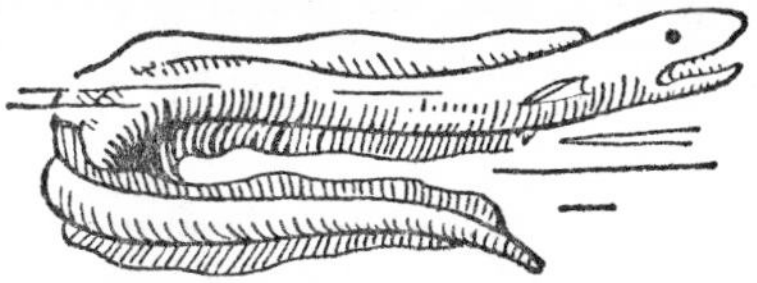

they descend seawards and spawn in the deep waters off Bermuda; the males do not return. The eggs produce tiny ribbon-like creatures. These larval forms, from which elvers of eel fry are derived, float E. in the Gulf Stream. The Leptocephali grow in transit and change in form to cylindrical elvers when entering the river estuaries. The elvers ascend and estab. themselves in the rivers and ponds where they grow to the adult fish.

EGG
A single cell which by dividing builds up the whole structure of a living organism. They remain inactive until fertilised by union with a male sperm cell, except in parthenogenetic animals, (*e.g.*, Aphis), where they proceed to divide as soon as they are fully mature. Its size is governed by the amount of nutritive yolk it contains and this is dependent on the method of feeding the developing embryo. Thus, in all mammals, with the exception of the platypus and the spiny ant-eater, the egg is minute, yolk is wanting and the embryo early develops in intimate connection with the maternal circulation. The young develop in the body of the mother and are born. In most other animals the more or less yolk-laden eggs are shed after fertilisation. The embryos grow at the expense of the food material available as yolk and they finally hatch. Most of the reptiles, including crocodiles, lay eggs, as do all birds. Many eggs are enclosed in a hard shell, but those of fishes, frogs, etc. that are laid in the sea or in wet places, are not. The most familiar kind of egg is that laid by the bird. These vary much in size and colour, but all possess the hard shell. Brit. law forbids the taking of the eggs of wild birds at certain seasons. The egg of the ordinary fowl is a popular and nutritious article of food. At Milford, Surrey, is a farm where, under the auspices of the Nat. Utility Poultry Soc. egg-laying tests are held, to determine the laying qualities of the various breeds.

EGLANTINE
Poetic name for the sweet briar (*Rosa eglanteria*). It is of bushy growth, the branches being thickly set with hooked prickles and bristles; the flowers are small and pink, and the foliage fragrant.

EGRET
[ē'-] Small white herons, with long, narrow, loose-webbed plumes. Populate inland waters, esp. in India, and are also found in S. Europe and Asia.

EGYPT (now **United Arab Republic**)
Repub. of N.E. Africa, bounded by Libya and the Sudan, with coastlines on the Medit. and Red Seas. The only fertile area is that through which the great rivers flow, some 13,600 sq.m., for rain is infrequent. The Nile is over 4,090 m. long with a delta mouth on the Medit. and the Arabian and Libyan deserts to E. and W. By means of irrigation cotton, rice, sugar cane, maize, cereals, beans and lentils are grown. Oil has been found in Sinai. Manufactures include textiles, pottery, leather and luxury goods. Cap. is Cairo. State religion is Mohammedanism. Area: 386,000 sq.m. Pop. 3,907,000. Egypt had a high degree of civilisation by *c.* 5510 B.C. The next 4,500 years up to the d. of Cleopatra saw the flourishing of a unique culture symbolised by such great works as the pyramids and the temples of Karnak and Luxor. After 30 B.C. Egypt became a Rom. prov. and in 642 was conquered by the Arabs. From 1517 until 1798 it was a prov. of Turkey. Napoleon was defeated by the Brit. who restored Turkish rule. This was confirmed between 1841 and 1875 and the Suez Canal was built by Brit. and Fr. enterprise. A further period of unrest terminated in 1905 when Brit. rule was accepted by the European powers. In 1922 Egypt was granted indep. under King Fuad I, but Brit. troops remained until the Treaty of Alliance, 1936, after which they stayed only in the Canal Zone. In Oct. 1951, *c.* 6,000 Brit. troops flew into the Canal Zone. The Egyptian Cabinet, under Nahas Pasha, decided in Dec. to dismiss all Brit. officials in the Egyptian Govt. service. Relations with Brit. remained strained and in May of that year Brit. Govt. claimed £1,750,000 compensation for damage to property and deaths of Britons in Cairo riots. On 29th May Hussein Sirry Pasha was appointed P.M. after resignation of Hilaly Pasha, who was later recalled and agreed to form Govt. on 21st June. Two days later the Egyptian Govt. resigned as a result of a *coup d'état* by the army led by Maj.-Gen. Neguib Mohammed which occupied Cairo to end instability of govt. and corruption. King Farouk was forced by the Army to abdicate in favour of his infant son Ahmed Fuad. In Sept. Aly Maher resigned and Neguib formed a new Ministry. All polit. parties were dissolved in Jan. 1953 and the duration of Neguib's special powers was extended. On Feb. 12th an Anglo-Egyptian agreement was signed concerning the future of the Sudan. In June, 1953, Egypt declared herself a repub. and Neguib became P.M. and the first Pres. He retained these positions until Feb. 25th, 1954, when, on failing to obtain the power of veto over the Revolution Council decisions, he was forced to resign all his official posts. Col. Nasser assumed full control, becoming Prime Min. Demonstrations and riots resulted and Gen. Neguib was restored as Pres. of the Egyptian Parl. Repub. with Col. Nasser still in the posts of P.M. and chairman of the council of revolutionary command. On the 6th March, Nasser became Milit. Gov. of Egypt and the milit. régime of Egypt undertook to return to parl. govt. as soon as possible, and intimated their readiness to resume talks on the Suez Canal issue if the Brit. Govt. was willing. At the end of March the Egyptian Govt. cancelled their earlier statement permitting the restoration of polit. parties. After prolonged negotiations with the Brit. Govt. an agreement on the Suez Canal issue was signed on 19th Oct. 1954. Brit. evacuation of the Canal Zone was to be completed by June 1956. Former Brit. bases in the zone were to be kept in efficient working order. This agreement was to last for 7 years, the position to be reviewed in the final year. Gen. Neguib was removed from the office of President in 1954 by a mil. coup. In 1956 Nasser became Pres. and soon announced the nationalisation of the Canal. He remained adamant despite French and British pressure and losses to the Israeli army. A U.N. police force was finally accepted by both sides and a settlement was reached. In Feb. 1958 Syria and Egypt announced their union under the name of United Arab Republic, however, in 1961 Syria seceded, but Egypt retains the name. In June 1967, Egypt closed the Strait of Tiran to Israeli shipping and demanded the withdrawal of the U.N. troops in Sinai. In spite of support from the

U.S.S.R. and Arab countries she was driven beyond the Suez Canal within 5 days. The U.N. established a cease-fire, but the situation remains tense and there have been outbursts of shelling since. *See* SUEZ CANAL, UNITED ARAB REPUBLIC.

Egyptology. Study of Egyptian antiquities. Modern archaeological investigation began with the work of Rhind and Mariette in the mid-19th cent. and was developed by Naville, Maspero, Petrie, Breasted, Budge and other scholars. The work consists of the excavation of tombs, temples, towns, etc., the trans. of papyri and reconstruction of the religious, polit., social, economic, literary and artistic life of Ancient Egypt. Of the many tombs excavated throughout the years, almost all had been plundered. The exception was that of the 18th dynasty Pharaoh Tut-ankh-amen (*q.v.*). The Egypt Exploration Soc., founded 1882, the Brit. School of Archaeology in Egypt, founded 1896, and learned socs. and univs. in Europe and the U.S.A. further Egyptological research. *See* AKHENATEN, PYRAMIDS.

EIDER DUCK
(*Somateria*) Sea ducks which line their nests with down. Dwelling on N. Atlantic coasts, the Common Eider Duck, *S. mollissima*, lays green eggs in nests on the ground. The down, valued for stuffing quilts, etc. is collected in Iceland and other localities. Eider ducks breed in the Farne Is., Hebrides and Donegal.

EIFFEL, Alexandre Gustave
[ef-fel'] (1832-1923) Fr. engineer. B. Dijon, he was one of the 1st engineers to use compressed air caissons for building bridges. His works include the Eiffel Tower, completed 1889.

EIGG
[egg] Is. of the Inner Hebrides, in Inverness-shire, half-way between the Is. of Rhum and the mainland.

EINSTEIN, Albert
(1879-1955) German scientist, b. Ulm and educ. Munich and Zurich. He was appointed Prof. at Zurich Univ. (1909). In 1915 he produced his theory of relativity. Awarded the Nobel prize for physics 1921. Became Prof. of Theoretical Physics at the Institute for Advanced Study, Princeton, U.S.A. He showed that energy and matter and space and time are part of a single reality. In 1949 he announced that he had developed a unified or generalised field theory which integrates gravitation and electro-magnetism. See *The Meaning of Relativity*, 1953.

EIRE *See* IRELAND, REPUBLIC OF.

EISENHOWER, Dwight David
(1890-1969) Pres. of U.S. 1952-60. He graduated from U.S. Milit. Acad. W. Point, 1915, and after Staff appointments was given command of the U.S. forces in Brit. 1942. Under his supreme command, 1944-5, the Allied Exped. Forces invaded Normandy from Eng., liberated German-occupied countries, and defeated Germany on her own soil. He became Commander Amer. Occup. Zone, Germany, 1945; Chief of Staff, U.S. Army, 1945-8; Supreme Comdr. N. Atlantic Treaty Forces in Europe, 1950-2; retired 1952. Elected Pres. 1952-6, 1956-60.

EISTEDDFOD
[i-steth'-vŏd] Welsh bardic congress held annually in different towns for encouraging nat. music and lit. Sprung from the Gorsedd or Nat. Assembly, it is mentioned in early records. It was held in 1567, and has been held almost annually since 1819. The chief bard is crowned, and prizes awarded for choral singing, harping, and lyrical compositions and essays.

EL ALAMEIN
[-mān] Town of N. coast of Egypt, 70 m. W. of Alexandria, site of important World War II battle.

EL GRECO
(Domenico Theotocopuli) (1542-1614) B. Crete. In *c.* 1566 he went to Venice and studied under Titian. He was profoundly influenced by Tintoretto and Michelangelo. He left Italy in 1576 and is next heard of in Spain in 1577, when he arrived in Toledo. Mainly a religious painter. He was hailed by 19th cent. experimental painters and has greatly influenced modern art.

ELAN
River of S. Wales, which rises in Cardiganshire and flows into the Wye below Rhayader. The valley is now a reservoir supplying Birmingham.

ELAND
Taurotragus oryx. African antelopes. The largest, also called the Cape Elk, has a tufted forelock and can stand *c.* 6ft. at the withers. The screwlike horns occur in both sexes. Except on reserves in Natal the eland has disappeared from S. Africa. Herds still roam N. of the Zambesi.

ELBA
Ital. Is. in the Medit. Sea, 6 m. from the mainland. Porto Ferraio is the cap. Napoleon lived in exile from May, 1814 to Feb. 1815. Pop. 32,200.

ELBE
River of Europe, 706 m. long, rises in Czechoslovakia and enters the N. Sea near Cuxhaven. On it stand Prague, Dresden, Magdeburg and Hamburg.

ELBOW
Area of junction of the arm and forearm. Elbow joint composed of humerus, radius and ulna, as a bony skeleton with muscles, vessels and nerves. It is a combination of hinge joint and ball and socket joint.

ELBURZ
Mt. range of Persia, S. of Caspian Sea. Mt. Demavend, a dormant volcano, is the highest peak (18,600 ft.).

ELDER
Genus of deciduous shrubs and trees (*Sambucus*) allied to the guelder rose, native to all temp. regions except S. Africa. The common *S. nigra* is a rapidly growing tree, normally *c.* 10 ft. with cream-coloured flowers in flat clusters. The purplish-black berries are used for home-made wine.

ELDER
Ruler in some civil and ecclesiastical systems of govt. It is analogous to the Rom. senator and the Eng. alderman. The term was used by the Jews. In the Presbyterian ch. elders elected by each ch. form the ruling body. Members of the Corporation of Trinity House are called **elder brethren.**

ELEANOR
Name of 3 Eng. queens including the daughter of William, Duke of Aquitaine, who in 1137 mar. Louis VII of Fr. The marriage being dissolved, she became the wife of Henry II of Eng. She was the mother of Richard I and John, and d. 1204. **Eleanor,** a daughter of Ferdinand III, King of Castile. In 1254 she mar. Edward, later Edward I, and with him went on crusade. She d. 1290.

ELECTION
In politics, the act of choosing a representative or the holder of a particular office, usually by ballot. Elections are of several kinds. In one the electors choose their representatives directly; in another they vote for persons who in turn choose the representatives. The Pres. of the U.S.A. and the aldermen of Eng. county and town councils are examples of indirect election. A **general election** occurs when all the representatives on a body are elected at once; a **by-election** is held to replace a representative who has resigned or d. *See* VOTE.

ELECTRIC FISH
Three kinds of fish which store electrical energy and can release a sufficient potential at will to give a considerable shock under water. They are: the Electric Eel (*Gymnotus electricus*), a native of the rivers of Brazil and Guiana; Electric Catfish (*Malapterurus electricus*), a native of the larger African rivers; and the Torpedo, or Electric Ray, found widely in warm seas.

ELECTRIC POWER
The use of electrical energy for the production of heat or motion. Electrical energy can be easily transported over great distances. The power is usually produced in electric generators driven by either steam or water turbines. In the U.K. prior to 1947, electric power was generated and distributed to consumers by municipalities and companies. To link producers and distributors, the Nat. Electricity Grid was estabd. under the Central Electricity Board in 1926 by Act of Parl. The electric power-producing industry was nationalised in 1947 under the Central Electricity Authority.

ELECTRIC SHOCK
To rescue: Disconnect current or short circuit wire by earthing with metal rod, and remove patient. If it is impossible to disconnect current, rescuer must be protected if possible with rubber gloves or a thick dry material such as sacking to cover hands. A dry board, piece of asbestos, rubber mat or dry sacking must be used to stand on.

ELECTRICITY
Among the ancient Gks. Thales recorded the attraction of light bodies by a piece of amber. In the 16th cent., Gilbert showed that other bodies also possessed this property. With the Leyden jar, invented 1745, came an understanding of the principles of induction, and 7 years later, Franklin demonstrated the identity of lightning with the electric spark. In 1800 Volta discovered a new source of electricity in the contact of 2 dissimilar metal plates immersed in acidulated water. This discovery led to the foundation of **electro-chemistry.** The work of Faraday, Oersted and Ohm resulted in the enunciation of the laws governing electrolysis, the principles of electro-magnetism and the idea of electrical resistance. The researches of Hertz and others have further increased our knowledge of the working of electrical forces, and the work of J. J. Thomson culminated in the discovery of the atomic nature of electricity and the elaboration of the electron theory.

ELECTROCUTION
Method of inflicting the d. penalty adopted in the U.S.A. It consists of the passage of a current of electricity of very high voltage through the body of the criminal. It is claimed to be more nearly instantaneous and less revolting than other methods.

ELECTRON
Unit of electric charge. The electron may be regarded as a small particle of diam. *c.* 10^{-13} cms, mass 9×10^{-28} gram and negative charge $1{\cdot}6 \times 10^{-19}$ coulombs. A movement of electrons constitutes an electric current. *See* ATOM.

ELECTRONICS
Term for that branch of science which is based on the study of electro-magnetic waves. The thermionic valve, in one of its many forms, is the basic unit in all electronic apparatus. Recent developments include radar (*q.v.*). Some other applications of electronics are to be found in the electron microscope, the radio telescope (*q.v.*), television, dielectric heating, computers, etc.

ELECTRUM
An alloy of gold (70-80 %) and silver, used in jewellery.

ELEMENT
A material which cannot be decomposed by a chem. process into other materials. 92 elements occur in nature and 9 more have been made in the laboratory.

ELEPHANT
(*Elephas*) Mammals including the largest existing quadrupeds. They are sometimes 8 to 11 ft. high. The nose forms a flexible, double-barrelled proboscis or trunk, often 4-5 ft., the sensitive tip of which can pick up small objects. The teeth include upturned upper incisors or tusks, the source of ivory. Large tusks may

African and Indian elephants

measure up to 9 ft. and weigh 100 lb. The 2 living species of elephant are the Asiatic or Indian, with concave forehead and small ears, and tusks of female generally much reduced, and the taller African species with convex forehead and large flapping ears, in which the size of the tusks of both sexes is approximately the same. A dwarf race, standing 5½ ft. occurs in the Congo basin. Tamed Asiatic elephants serve for ceremonial, timber and other transport; they rarely breed in captivity. White elephants are albinos.

ELEPHANTIASIS
[-tī'-] Disease characterised by swelling of a chronic type assoc. with increased fibrous tissue. Blockage of lymphatic vessels, abnormal conditions of the arteries and in trop. countries infection with parasitic worm called filaria are causes.

ELGAR, Sir Edward
(1857-1934) Eng. composer. Largely self-taught, he played the bassoon and violin. In 1889 he mar. and moved to London. In 1890 the *Froissart* overture was played at the 3 Choirs Festival. In 1905 he became Prof. of Music at Birmingham. Elgar is at his greatest in his orchestral music which includes 2 symphonies, many overtures and suites, the *Enigma Variations*, Concertos for violin and for 'cello, 3 oratorios, chamber music and smaller choral works. See *Elgar O.M.* by Percy M. Young (1955).

ELGIN
[el'-gin] Royal burgh and county town of Moray, 67 m. N.W. of Aberdeen. There is a ruined cath. and remains of a castle. Pop. 12,000.

ELGINSHIRE *See* MORAYSHIRE.

ELIA *See* CHARLES LAMB.

ELIJAH
(O.T.) Heb. prophet (1 Kings 17-21; 2 Kings 1-3). He led the life of a hermit, emerging to proclaim the wishes of God. Finally he disappeared in a fiery chariot.

ELIOT, George
(1819-80) Pen-name of **Marian** or **Mary Ann Evans**, Eng. novelist. B. near Nuneaton. She went to Coventry, 1841; London, 1849; widely read, she replaced her early evangelical faith with an agnostic and positivistic morality. Lived with **G. H. Lewes** from 1854 until his d. Her works include: *Scenes of Clerical Life* (1858), *Adam Bede* (1859), *The Mill on the Floss* (1860), *Silas Marner* (1861), *Romola* (1862-3),

Felix Holt the Radical (1866), *Middlemarch* (1871-2), *Daniel Deronda* (1874-6). See *Marian Evans and George Eliot* by L. and E. Hanson (1952).

ELIOT, Thomas Stearns
(1888-1965) Anglo-Amer. poet and critic. B. St. Louis, Mo.; educ. Harvard, Oxford, Paris; settled in Eng. 1915 (naturalised 1927). Has pub. poetry: *Prufrock and other Observations* (1917), *The Waste Land* (1922), *The Hollow Men* (1925), *Poems* (1909-25), *Four Quartets* (1944), poetic dramas, *Murder in the Cathedral* (1935) and *The Family Reunion* (1939); *The Cocktail Party* (1949), and *The Elder Statesman* (1958); much criticism, such as *The Sacred Wood* (1920), *Dante* (1929), *The Idea of a Christian Society* (1939), *On Poetry and Poets* (1957). Awarded O.M. 1948, Nobel Prize for Lit. 1948, and the 'Ordre pour le Mérite' in arts and sciences in Bonn (1959).

ELISABETHVILLE
Principal town of Katanga prov., Congolese Repub. Renamed Lubumbashi. Pop. 183,000.

ELIZABETH
(1709-62) Empress of Russia, daughter of Peter the Great and Catherine I, she appeared in 1741 at the head of the party that deposed the young Tsar, Ivan VI. She became empress and ruled Russia until her d. Much of her reign was occupied in fighting against Frederick the Great. She founded the Univ. of Moscow.

ELIZABETH
Eldest daughter of James I, mar. Frederick, later King of Bohemia. Mother of Sophia whose son was George I.

ELIZABETH, Woodville *See* EDWARD IV.

ELIZABETH
(1533-1603) Queen of Eng. and Ireland, daughter of Henry VIII and Anne Boleyn. She succeeded to the throne in 1558. The first part of her reign was occupied with the estab. of the C. of E. Then hostility between Eng. and Sp. became open war. Plots were discovered to kill the Queen and replace her by Mary, Queen of Scots. The execution of Mary in 1587 put an end to one danger, and the defeat of the Sp. Armada in 1588 made Eng. supreme on the seas. The last years of the reign were troubled by risings in Ireland and by the queen's reluctance to name a successor. She refused to mar. Philip II of Sp.; she toyed with the idea of marrying Henry III of Fr. or a Fr. prince, but these were only moves in the polit. game. See Neale's *Queen Elizabeth* and Lytton Strachey's *Elizabeth and Essex*.

ELIZABETH
(1900-) Queen of Gt. Brit. Lady Elizabeth Bowes-Lyon, daughter of 14th Earl of Strathmore, mar. April 26th, 1923, Prince Albert Frederick Arthur George, Duke of York, 2nd son of King George V. On the abdication of Edward VIII, 1936, the Duke and Duchess of York became King and Queen.

ELIZABETH
(1926-) Queen of Gt. Brit. **Elizabeth Alexandra Mary**, the elder daughter of George VI and Queen Elizabeth. She first undertook public duties at the age of 16, and in the 2nd World War she served in the A.T.S. She mar. Lieut. Philip Mountbatten, Duke of Edinburgh, in Westminster Abbey in Nov. 1947. They have 4 children: Prince Charles, Prince of Wales, b. in Nov. 1948, Princess Anne, b. in Aug. 1950, Prince Andrew, b. in Feb. 1960, and Prince Edward, b. March 1964. Became Queen, Feb. 6th, 1952, upon death of her father. Crowned Queen, June 2nd, 1953.

ELK
(*Alces machlis*) Largest species of deer, native to N. Europe, Siberia and Amer. where it is called the Moose. The Alaskan Elk is a gigantic

animal, with broad, palmate antlers weighing 50-60 lb. Americans give the name Elk to the Wapiti deer, *Cervus canadensis*.

ELLIS, Henry Havelock
(1859-1939) Brit. psychologist. B. Croydon. After teaching in N.S. Wales, he took his med. degree in London. He soon afterwards abandoned his practice for lit. and scientific work. His works include: *Man and Woman* (1894-1904), *The Task of Social Hygiene* (1912), *Essays in Wartime* (1916), *Essays of Love and Virtue* (1931). His greatest work is *Studies in the Psychology of Sex* (7 vols.).

ELM
Genus of trees and shrubs (*Ulmus*), native to N. temp. regions. The common *U. procera*, a tree growing up to 130 ft. rarely perfects its winged, 1-seeded fruits in Brit. The hard, tough, close-grained timber serves for keels, tackle-blocks, coffins, wheel-naves and common turnery. The indigenous Scotch or wych elm, *U. glabra*, which is almost as tall, yields timber for boat building. Elms are subject to a disease which causes the tree to die back.

ELSINORE *See* HELSINGOR.

ELY, Isle of
District of N. Cambridgeshire, an admin. county with its cap. at March. Ely is the chief town. It is an agricultural region, famous for its market gardens. Ely returns 1 member to Parl. Pop. 89,420. **Ely.** City and market town of Cambridgeshire on the Ouse, 16 m. N. of Camb. It is the chief town of the Is. of Ely and has an agricultural trade. Ely is famed for its cath. Pop. 9,815.

EMBOLISM
Med. term denoting obstruction of artery by clump of bacteria, clot of blood or droplets of fat or air, none of which originated at the site of obstructions but were carried there by bloodstream. *See* THROMBOSIS.

EMBRYOLOGY
Science relating to the development of an animal or plant from the egg to the mature organism. The individual plant or animal usually starts its life cycle in the union of 2 germ cells or gametes, one the sperm cell or spermatozoon, the other the ovum or egg cell. The ovum, after fertilisation, undergoes cell division, resulting in the formation of tissues and organs. The details of these early stages showing the plastic nature of the earliest cells and the changes undergone as they come to form organised tissues is part of the subject matter of experimental embryology. Further, the nuclear characteristics of the fertilised egg determine its heredity, *i.e.* the type of organisation it is capable of developing, and provides the starting point for the science of genetics.

EMERALD
Precious stone, the green beryl. It is a silicate of beryllium and aluminium, the colour being due to a minute proportion of chromium compounds and varying from a grass-green with a yellowish tinge to a deep emerald green. The lustre of the emerald is vitreous with a velvety

effect in the finest gem stones. The finest stones are found in Colombia.

EMERSON, Ralph Waldo
(1803-82) Amer. author. B. Boston, Mass.; educ. Boston and Harvard; taught; visited Europe. Returned to U.S.A. and settled at Concord; preached and lectured, ed. *The Dial* (1842-4), and wrote both prose and poetry, becoming identified with *Transcendentalism*, an idealist philos. leaning towards a mystical naturalism. His reputation was based mainly on his lectures and essays: *Nature* (1836), *Essays* (1841), *The Conduct of Life* (1860), *Society; Solitude* (1870), *Letters and Social Aims* (1876).

EMERY
Dark brown or greyish-black variety of corundum, composed of alumina mixed with the iron oxides, magnetite and haematite, used as an abrasive on account of its extreme hardness. It is found in crystalline limestones assoc. with metamorphic rocks in Naxos in the Aegean Sea, but its chief commercial sources are Ontario, New York State and the Transvaal.

EMIGRATION
Act of leaving one's native country in order to settle in another. Emigration in the modern sense began in the 17th cent. when Europeans crossed the Atlantic to settle in Amer. In the 19th cent. emigration to N. Amer. reached enormous proportions. Australia and parts of S. Africa were also peopled by European emigrants. After a time the new countries began to place restrictions on immigrants. Still more drastic measures were taken in the U.S.A., Australia, Canada and elsewhere to keep out coloured immigrants. In order to assist emigration, the Brit. Govt. has an Overseas Settlement Dept. at Caxton House, Westminster. In 1948, 157,290 emigrants left the Brit. Is., the total for 1962 being 91,200.

EMPEROR
(1) Word used for a ruler more powerful than a king. Julius Caesar called himself *imperator* which then meant C.-in-C. and his nephew, Augustus, assumed the power permanently, and was thus the first Emperor. The title was used by those who claimed to be the successors of the Roman emperors. *See* EMPIRE. (2) A large butterfly found in the S. of Eng. is called the emperor, or purple emperor, on account of the purple lustre on the male. There is also an emperor moth which is found in Britain.

EMPIRE
Term used loosely for a state of the most powerful kind used by the Roms. for their Empire and for the Egyptian, Assyrian, Persian, Babylonian and other states. The Rom. Empire (*q.v.*) was continued by the Byzantine and the medieval empires, and on the ruins of the latter arose the Austrian and German Empires in 1804 and 1871. Both these disappeared in 1918, while the Russian Empire was destroyed a year earlier. The title 'Emperor of the Fr.' was taken by Napoleon in 1804 and Fr. was an Empire for 10 years. The 2nd (Fr.) Empire under Louis Napoleon lasted 1852-71. On the unification of Germany under Prussia, the King of Prussia became the first Emperor of the Germans in 1871. In the 19th cent. the term began to be used for the lands under the King of Gt. Brit. and Ireland. India was made an Empire when the title of Empress was given to Queen Victoria in 1876. In Amer. 2 empires, Brazil and Mexico arose. The only empires in the world since 1918 were the Brit. and the Indian, the one within the other, and the Japanese; but India is now a Republic within the Commonwealth, and after defeat in World War II Japan was driven back into the 4 main islands. **The Holy Roman Empire** (800-1806) was created by Charlemagne, who was crowned Emperor in Rome by the Pope. It consisted of the lands under his rule, *i.e.* the present Fr. and Germany, part of Italy and other European lands. Divided after his d., it fell to pieces in the 9th and 10th cents. It was, however, revived in 962 by Otto the Great, Duke of Saxony who, like Charlemagne, was crowned in Rome by the Pope. His Empire consisted of Germany and Italy. In 1062 the Saxons were succeeded as Emperors by the Franconian or Salian line, who ruled till 1124. The Franconian Emperors were succeeded by the Swabian house of Hohenstaufen. Rudolph of Habsburg was elected German King in 1273. In 1346, Charles, King of Bohemia became ruler of Germany and later became Emperor. Charles was followed by his sons, Wenceslaus and Sigismund, and on the d. of the latter, Albert of Habsburg secured the throne. From then until 1806, in practice though not in theory, the Empire was the possession of that great family. One after another its members were elected, but, esp. after 1648, the Empire was but a loose collection of rival states over which the Emperor had little authority. The greatest Habsburg Emperor was Charles V, and the last was Francis, who resigned in 1806.

EMPLOYER
One who engages another to work for him or her at a wage or salary, either temporarily or permanently. An employer must observe the laws concerning the relations between master and servant. Between the employer and employed there is a contract. At common law an employer is liable to pay damages to a servant who is injured in the course of his employment. This was dealt with in detail in the **Employers' Liability Act** of 1880, and in the various Workmen's Compensation Acts. The Nat. Insurance (Industrial Injuries) Act, 1946, supersedes these.

EMPLOYMENT EXCHANGES
Local agencies for estab. contact between employers requiring labour and workers seeking employment. They were instituted under the *Labour Exchanges Act*, 1909. The *Unemployment Insurance Act* of 1912 placed on the exchanges the task of paying unemployment benefits. During and after World War II, they were responsible for the registration of men and women for National Service.

EMS TELEGRAM *See* FRANCO-PRUSSIAN WAR.

EMU
(*Dromaeus*) Large bird found only in Australia and the adjacent Is. Though smaller, it resembles the ostrich, having only rudimentary wings. It can run very fast and swim well. Emus live in flocks in uninhabited parts and feed chiefly on native plant life and grasses. The male is smaller than the female and incubates the eggs, which are green.

ENCYCLOPAEDIA BRITANNICA
The 1st edition begun in 1768 was completed in Edinburgh in 1771. Edited by Wm. Smellie (1740-95) it had 2,670 pages. The 9th ed. was completed in 1889. It consisted of 29 vols., its contributors including distinguished men of letters and science *e.g.* Lord Macaulay, C. Kingsley, Robert Chambers. In 1901 Messrs. H. Hooper and W. M. Jackson bought all rights and began the 11th edit. sponsored by Camb. Univ. and issued by the Univ. press in 1910-11 in 29 vols. In 1920 the E.B. was bought by Sears, Roebuck & Co. of Chicago. A brand new edit. the 14th, containing contributions from *c.* 3,500 famous men and women, was pub. in 1929. The E.B. is now pub. with the editorial advice of, and consultation with, the faculties of the Univ. of Chicago. The first vol. of the *Britannica Year Book* was pub. in 1938.

ENCYCLOPÉDIE
Encyclopedia issued in Fr. (1751-76, 35 vols.), begun as tr. of Ephraim Chambers' *Encyclopaedia* (1728). It was ed. by Diderot and d'Alembert and had Voltaire, Rousseau, Buffon, Montesquieu and others as contributors. It was typical of the 18th cent.'s aim of co-ordinated

and national knowledge, but vigorously opposed Ch. and State and helped to prepare intellectuals for the ideas of the Fr. Revolution.

ENDOCRINE GLANDS
Collection of glands concerned with body metabolism, growth and reproduction. Because these glands have no ducts communicating with other structures they are called ductless glands. Principal glands are thyroid, pituitary, thymus, suprarenal, parts of pancreas, testes and ovary (*q.v.*). **Endocrinology.** Study of endocrine glands and their secretion and effects on body.

ENFIELD
Borough of Greater London (1964), consisting of the former boroughs of Edmonton, Enfield and Southgate. Pop. 273,637.

ENGELS, Friedrich
(1820-95) German socialist. On completing an apprenticeship in Germany he was sent to his father's factory near Manchester in 1842 and became interested in the Owenite and Chartist movements. His assoc. with Karl Marx began in Paris in 1844, and from then onwards they strove to organise an internat. socialist movement and collaborated in the *Communist Manifesto*.

ENGLAND
Kingdom of Europe, occupying the S. part of the Is. of Gt. Brit. Bounded by Scot. and Wales on the N. and W., it has a long coastline on the N. Sea, the Eng. Channel, the Atlantic Ocean and the Irish Sea. The N., W. and S.W. of the country is hilly. From N. to S. the main regions of high ground are the Cheviot Hills, the Cumberland Mts., the Pennine Chain, with the Yorkshire Moors to the E., the Cotswold Hills, and Dartmoor and Exmoor in the W. country. The highest peak is Scafell Pike (3,210 ft.) in the Lake District. In the lowland region of Eng. are the Chilterns, the N. and S. Downs and the Weald. The chief rivers are the Thames, Severn, Trent, Tyne, Tees, Mersey. Round the coast are many excellent harbours and ports, *e.g.* London, Liverpool and Bristol. Eng. includes several smaller Is. such as the Is. of Wight, the Scilly Is. and the Is. of Man (*q.v.*). The climate is temp. Agriculture is carried on over most of the country, but is mainly important in the lowland region of the S. and E. E. Anglia produces wheat, barley and beet sugar; Kent is famous for its orchards and hop fields; Devon, Hereford and Worcester also produce fruit. Agriculture does not provide sufficient food for the population, and many foodstuffs are imported. Industry is much more important. There are extensive coalfields, and around these great industrial centres have developed. These include the iron and steel regions of Birmingham and Sheffield; the shipbuilding of the N.E. coast; the cotton and woollen districts of Lancs. and Yorks. Fishing is carried on round all the coasts. London is the cap. and largest city; other great cities are Birmingham, Liverpool, Manchester, Sheffield, Leeds, Bristol, Newcastle-upon-Tyne (*q.v.*). The Eng. people on the whole are descended from the Anglo-Saxons and Danes, who invaded the country, but there have been many additions to the racial composition during the cents. The Celtic strain is dominant in the S.W. Eng. is divided into 40 geographical counties, excluding Monmouthshire. Area: 50,332 sq.m. Pop. *c.* 44,017,660. **England, Church of.** Nat. Ch. of Eng. and the recognised parent of the Anglican Ch. throughout the world. It dates from the 6th cent. when St. Augustine settled at Canterbury and it was soon organised into dioceses under bishops. Under Henry VIII the C. of E. broke away from Rome. Its doctrines were reformed under Edward VI, and since the time of Elizabeth there have been no fundamental changes. The C. of E. is organised in 2 provinces, Canterbury and York, each under an archbishop. The 2 archbishops and 22 bishops sit in the House of Lords. The C. of E. is controlled by the state, and no alterations can be made in its doctrines, or its form of worship, without the sanction of Parl. Under Parl. it is governed by a nat. assembly, a body set up in 1920 and consisting of 3 houses, bishops, clergy and laity. There is an annual ch. congress.

ENGLISH CHANNEL
Arm of the sea, between Eng. and Fr. On the W. it connects with the Atlantic Ocean and on the E. with the N. Sea. It is narrowest bet. Dover and Calais (21 m.).

ENNISKILLEN
Market and county town of Fermanagh, N. Ireland, on an Is. in the narrowest part of Lough Erne. Pop. 7,530. Enniskillen or Inniskilling, a great Protestant centre in the time of William III, gives its name to 2 regiments of the Brit. Army. These are the 27th Foot, known as the Royal Inniskilling Fusiliers and the Royal Inniskilling Dragoons.

ENSIGN
The flag carried by a ship as the insignia of her nationality or the nature of her duties. Brit. has 3 ensigns: the white of the Royal Navy, the blue of the Royal Naval Research and the red of the Merchant Navy. Ships of the Royal Yacht Squadron have the privilege of flying the White Ensign. Each flag has the Union Jack in the 1st quarter and the White Ensign bears in addition the cross of St. George. An ensign for civil aircraft was authorised in 1931. It is light blue with a dark blue cross, edged with white, and has the Union Jack in the 1st quarter. The R.A.F. ensign is similar to the Blue Ensign with, in addition, a small red circle surrounded by circles of white and blue.

ENTERITIS
[-ī'tis] Inflammatory disease affecting mucous membrane of bowel. Usually assoc. with infection such as dysentery but occurring as an indication of general toxaemia in pneumonia, nephritis, tuberculosis and many other diseases, including poisons. *See* TYPHOID FEVER; DYSENTERY; COLIC.

ENTOMOLOGY
Branch of zoology that deals with insects. Now restricted to the true or 6-legged insects.

ENZYME
[-zim] Active principle of a ferment. Enzymes belong to the class of catalysts, or substances whose mere presence induces chem. changes in other molecules, but an enzyme will usually act on one or a few closely related chem. compounds only, and will refuse to touch any molecule coming outside its own limited range of specificity.

EOCENE
[ē'-ō-sēn] Oldest division of the Tertiary system of geological deposits, the period of the dawn of mammal life following the Cretaceous period. Eocene strata usually rest upon the denuded surface of the underlying beds of white chalk and often form basin-like areas showing, by their character and fossil contents, their origin in estuaries and shallow seas. The beds consist of sands, clays and marls.

EOLITH
[ē'-ō-] Name given to certain very early flint

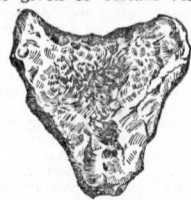

implements. Eoliths are generally flat on one surface and chipped to form a scraping edge or notches.

EPAMINONDAS
(*c.* 418-362 B.C.) A Theban general and statesman. In 371 he was one of the generals at the Battle of Leuctra; in 370 he invaded Peloponnesus, where he founded Messene and Megalopolis. In 362 he invaded it for the 4th time, and was killed gaining a brilliant victory over the Lacedaemonians at Mantinea.

EPHEMER
(*Ephemeroptera Optera*) Order of insects popularly called May-flies. They have a long, jointed abdomen, with 3 bristle-like tails. The aquatic larvae, living in ponds and sluggish streams, pass into a chrysalid stage which, in *Ephemera vulgata* and *E. danica*, 2 of the commonest of Brit.'s 50 species, furnish the bait anglers call Green Drake and Grey Drake. The perfect insects do not eat and are short-lived.

EPHESUS
In ancient geog. the chief of the 12 Ionian cities on the coast of Asia Minor. It has numerous interesting ruins, including the famous temple of Diana (Artemis) built in the 6th cent. B.C. **Ephesians, Epistle to the.** Tenth book of the N.T. Written during St. Paul's first imprisonment in Rome, A.D. 62, it was apparently a circular letter addressed to the churches of Asia Minor.

EPHRAIM
[ēf-] Younger son of the patriarch Joseph. His descendants formed 2 of the tribes of Israel estabd. in N. Palestine. Ephraim led the tribal opposition against the kingdom of Judah which resulted in the formation of the separate kingdom of Israel.

EPIC
The story of a momentous action conceived and told with some grandeur. A distinction is made between **'primary epic'** (*Iliad, Odyssey, Beowulf, Nibelungenlied, Irish epic, Kalevala, Gilgamesh*), close to popular legend, a natural growth, and **'secondary epic'** or **art-epic** (Virgil's *Æneid*, Camoens' *Lusiads*, Milton's *Paradise Lost*, Ronsard's *Françiade*), the conscious imitation of the first in a more sophisticated society.

EPICUREANISM
Gk. school of philosophy founded by Epicurus (341-270 B.C.). B. Samos, he taught in Athens from 306 B.C. His method is condensed in 4 canons. (1) Seek pleasure that produces no pain. (2) Reject pleasure that produces pain. (3) Reject pleasure that prevents the enjoyment of greater pleasure or produces greater pain. (4) Endure pain that averts greater pain or secures greater pleasure.

EPIGLOTTIS
[-glot'-] Flap-like structure of cartilage with a covering of mucous membrane, situated behind the tongue and above the opening of the larynx or upper windpipe. It prevents food and fluids from passing into air passages.

EPILEPSY
Disorder of nervous system characterised by sudden attacks of unconsciousness of short or long duration accompanied on occasions by convulsive movements and loss of control of bladder and bowel. Attacks of epilepsy with convulsions are called *grand-mal*, attacks with momentary loss of consciousness are called *petit-mal*. The cause of epilepsy is unknown but is assoc. with hereditary influences, and may follow meningitis. *Treatment* of a grand-mal is mainly directed to preventing patient injuring himself by knocking his body against hard objects or falling into fire. The air passages should be kept cleared and tongue protected by introducing a handle of a spoon or piece of stick between the teeth. Since 1970 in Britain, driving licences are issued to those epileptics who, on med. evid., have been free from day attacks for at least 3 years.

EPIRUS
Geog. division of N.W. Greece. It flourished under Pyrrhus (295-272 B.C.), and later formed part of the Rom. Emp.

EPISCOPACY
Form of ch. govt. of which bishops are the head. It grew up in the 2nd cent. and has since been the rule in the R.C. Ch. which claims for its bishops an unbroken descent from those times. The Anglican and Gk Chs. are both episcopal. Bishops can be ordained only by other bishops; thus the apostolic succession is maintained.

EPISCOPAL CHURCH IN SCOTLAND
The old Ch. of Scot. Catholic and Apostolic. Disestabd. 1690 when the Scot. Bishops refused to break their oath of allegiance to James II. In full Communion with the C. of E. provinces of the Anglican Communion, and the Old Catholic Ch. The first Bishop of the Amer. Episcopal Ch. was consecrated by the Scot. Bishops, 1784. The Scot. Episcopal Ch. consists of 14 Dioceses grouped under 7 bishops (1 of whom is elected as Primus).

EPPING FOREST
District occupying *c.* 6,000 acres between the Lea and Roding. Acquired by the corporation of the city of London and opened in 1882, it is a popular beauty spot.

EPSOM
Borough (with Ewell) of Surrey, 14 m. S.W. of London. On the nearby Downs the Derby, Oaks and other horse races are run. Pop. 70,380.

EPSOM SALTS
Magnesium sulphate in the form of white crystals. It is used medicinally as a purgative. The name is derived from a mineral spring at Epsom from which it was at one time obtained.

EPSTEIN, Sir Jacob
[ep'-stīn] (1880-1959) Brit. sculptor of Russo-Polish parentage. B. New York; studied art there and in Paris, where he was influenced by Rodin. His large sculptured pieces, *e.g. Genesis, Day and Night, Lazarus.*, etc. provoked lively criticism. His last great religious work was a bronze, *St. Michael and the Devil*, for the new Coventry Cathedral.

EQUATION
In algebra, a statement or formula expressing the equality of 2 quantities. The 2 parts of the equation are separated by the sign of equality, as, *e.g.* $3x=21$. The term **chemical equation** is used for the symbolic representation of a chem. reaction, the symbols of the reacting substances being placed on the left and those of the substance produced by the reaction on the right, as in $H_2+Cl_2=2\ HCl$.

EQUATOR
Imaginary line drawn round the earth equally distant from the poles. Its plane cuts the earth's axis at right angles and it divides the globe into 2 halves, the N. and S. hemispheres. Latitude is measured N. and S. of the equator by small circles parallel to it, the equator being regarded as 0° of latitude. The sun is directly over the equator at noon twice a year, the *vernal* and *autumnal equinoxes* (*q.v.*).

EQUATORIAL GUINEA
See SPANISH GUINEA

EQUINOX
Period when the equator lies in the plane of the earth's orbit and day and night are equal in length in all parts of the world. The vernal or spring equinox occurs on Mar. 21-22, the autumnal on Sept. 21-22. The vernal equinox also marks the point in the heavens where the sun crosses the equator.

ERASMUS, Desiderius
(1466-1536) Dutch humanist. B. Rotterdam, d. Basel. Travelled; visited Eng. (first in 1496)

and 1511-14 taught Gk. at Camb. He was a friend of Sir Thomas More and assoc. with the 'Oxford Reformers'. Erasmus's ed. (text with Lat. tr. and comment) of the N.T. 1516, and his *Encomium Moriae* (*Praise of Folly*) 1509, influenced the Reformation, but he wrote against some of Luther's views. His *Colloquia* (*Dialogues*) *and Adagia* (*Proverbs*) are well known, and the vast collection of his letters (over 3,000) is an important Renaissance document. See *Erasmus of Rotterdam* by J. Huizinga (1953).

ERASTIANISM
Theory that the Ch. should be subordinate to the State. Name derived from **Thomas Erastus** (1524-83), a German-Swiss theologian.

ERFURT
Town of Thuringia, E. Germany, on the Gera, 64 m. S.W. of Leipzig. It is a market town with numerous manufactures. Pop. 174,600.

ERGOSTEROL
Chem. substance which occurs in small quantities in the skin and other tissues of the body. When exposed to ultra-violet radiation (*e.g.* in sunlight) it becomes Vitamin D. *See* VITAMINS.

ERGOT
(*Claviceps purpurea*) Fungus which attacks the flowers of cereals and grasses. It shows 3 well-marked stages in its life hist. (1) The **honey dew**, or *Sphacelia*, stage consists of a network of threads ramifying through the ovary and producing spores and honey dew; (2) The **winter**, or sclerotium, stage forms a hard curved purplish body (ergot) and (3) The **spring**, or ascospore, stage which forms thread-like spores. Ergot of rape is used in medicine as a haemostatic and peristaltic agent.

ERICSSON, Leif
(*c.* A.D. 1000) Norse coloniser of Greenland, and discoverer of America.

ERIE
[ē'-rē] City of Pennsylvania, U.S.A., S. of Lake Erie. There is much shipping and some manufactures. Pop. 138,440. Erie. One of the Gt. Lakes of N. Amer. connected with Lake Ontario by the Niagara River. The Welland Canal enables shipping to pass between these lakes, and the Erie Canal connects up with the Hudson. Area: 9,889 sq.m.

ERITH
[ĕr'-] Part of Bexley, borough of Greater London (1964). Formerly in Kent. There are dockyards and engineering works.

ERITREA
[-trā'-] Former Ital. colony in E. Africa, with a coastline on the Red Sea, bordered inland by Ethiopia and the Repub. of the Sudan. There is a narrow coastal plain, with mts. in the interior. In 1950, Eritrea was federated with Ethiopia. Federation was dissolved 1962, Eritrea becoming an integral part of Ethiopia. Area: 45,000 sq.m. Pop. *c.* 1,000,000.

ERMINE
(*Mustela erminea*) White fur, with black-tipped tail. It is the winter coat of the stoat, which is native in Brit. and in temp. and subarctic regions. It is largely used on state and judicial robes. In heraldry symbolised by black arrow-heads crowned with 3 dots on a white ground.

Shields showing heraldic ermine

ERNST, Max
(1891-1969) German painter. B. in Bruhl near Cologne. Studied at the Univ. of Bonn, 1909-14. Served in World War I. Was with the Surrealist group in Paris in 1922. In 1926 collaborated with Miro in designs for Diaghileff. Went to U.S.A. in 1941. Fr. citizen, 1958.

ERVINE, St. John Greer
(1883-) Irish novelist, playwright and dramatic critic. B. Belfast. His name is assoc. with Dublin Abbey Theatre. His plays include *Jane Clegg* (1911), *First Mrs. Fraser* (1928), *Robert's Wife* (1938), *Friends and Relations* (1940), *Private Enterprise* (1947), *Ballyfarland's Festival* (1953). Among his novels are *Mrs. Martin's Man* (1914), *Sophia* (1941).

ERYSIPELAS
Acute infectious disease caused by the streptococcal group of bacteria and assoc. with patches of inflammation on the skin, fever and general body upset. The areas are red and raised and most often seen on the face.

ESBJERG
2nd seaport of Denmark, in W. Jutland, connected with Copenhagen by railway and ferries. Fishing is an important industry; exports include bacon, dairy produce, and beef. Pop. 55,171.

ESCURIAL
Palace-monastery in Spain. Designed for Philip II in 1563-84, it is situated amid the mts. 26 m. S. of Madrid. In the centre is a fine ch. and the Pantheon where the kings and queens of Spain are buried. Among the buildings are also a convent and a library.

ESDRAS, Books of
First 2 apocryphal books of the O.T. The Vulgate calls the canonical books Ezra and Nehemiah, 1 and 2 Esdras, making these apocryphal scriptures 3 and 4 Esdras.

ESHER
[ē'-sher] Urban district of Surrey, on the Mole, 15 m. S.W. of London. The gateway of Esher Palace, which was once owned by Wolsey, still stands. Sandown Park racecourse is nearby. Pop. 60,970.

ESKIMO
N. Amer. Indian people who inhabit the Arctic coast from E. Greenland westward across the Bering Strait to Siberia. They number *c.* 30,000, and live by hunting the musk ox, reindeer and seal. They occupy in summer conical skin tents, in winter, igloos. They use 1-man skin canoes (kayaks) and larger cargo or women's boats (umiaks). **Eskimo Dog** (*Husky*) Used as a draught animal by the Eskimos, they are tamed rather than domesticated. They are trained to pull sledges, and usually work in teams.

ESPARTO GRASS
(*Stipa tenacissima*) Tall perennial grass native to S. Spain and N. Africa. Also called halfa, its grey-green tufts serve when young as cattle food, but after several years furnish a very tough and tenacious fibre, useful for making cables, baskets, matting, sandals and paper. *Lygeum spartium* also supplies esparto fibre, an important ingredient in paper making.

ESPERANTO
Artificial, internat., auxiliary language. Invented by Dr. Zamenhof, a Polish oculist, and pub. in 1887. Phonetically spelt, it has about 2,500 word-roots, with 30 word-forming prefixes and suffixes, logically applied.

ESQUIRE
Orig. a shield-bearer attendant on a knight; thus a title of dignity next in degree below that of knighthood. In Brit. the title is properly given to the following: (1) all sons of peers during their fathers' lives, and the younger sons after their fathers' deaths; the eldest sons of peers' younger sons, and their eldest sons forever. (2) Noblemen of all other nations. (3) Companions and Commanders of the Orders of

Knighthood. (4) The eldest sons of baronets and knights. (5) Persons entitled to bear arms and to the title of esquire by letters patent. (6) Barristers at law. (7) Justices of the Peace and Mayors. (8) Lieutenants and Deputy Lieutenants of counties or cities. (9) Holders of a superior office under the crown.

ESSEN
W. German industrial city in N. Rhine-Westphalia, centre of the coal-mining, and iron and steel industries of the Ruhr. Krupps steelworks produced armaments there during World War II. Pop. 727,000.

ESSEX
County of S.E. Eng. with coastline on the Thames estuary and the N. Sea. It includes Canvey and Mersea. Epping forest lies on the W. boundary. The chief rivers are the Colne, Stour and Crouch. The Thames divides it from Kent and the Lea from Hertford. Chelmsford is the county town. Resorts include Southend, Westcliff, Clacton, Frinton and Dovercourt. Univ. of Essex was opened near Colchester, 1964. In 1964 it lost 9 boroughs to Greater London, which halved its pop. It is mainly agricultural, but there are oil installations at Shellhaven and Thames Haven. Pop. 1,105,983.

ESSEX, Earl of
(1566-1601) Eng. courtier. Robert Devereux, favourite of Queen Elizabeth. He was sent to Ireland as gov.-gen. in 1599. Executed for his part in a rebellion. His son, **Robert Devereux** (1591-1646) was restored to the earldom in 1604. In 1642 he was C.-in-C. of the parl. army.

ESTERHAZY
of Galantha. Noble Hungarian family. **Nicholas** (1582-1645) fought long to free Hungary from the Turks. His son, **Paul** (1635-1713) helped to deliver Vienna from the Turks in 1683, was a devoted supporter of the Habsburgs, and was made a prince of the Holy Roman Empire in 1712. **Nicholas** (1765-1833), a great art collector, raised troops and fought against Napoleon. He was offered the kingship of the Magyars in 1809, but refused it. **Paul Anthony** (1786-1866) was foreign minister in the first responsible Hungarian ministry. Another Esterhazy, **Ferdinand Walsun** (1847-1923), Fr. army officer, was discovered in 1896 to be the real criminal in the Dreyfus Case.

ESTHER, Book of
Book of the O.T. It narrates an episode at the court of the Persian king Ahasuerus (Xerxes) in Susa, 5th cent. B.C. The royal consort Vashti was deposed, and her place taken by Esther, related to a Jewish exile, Mordecai. Esther and Mordecai frustrated the plots of the grand vizier, Haman, against the Jewish people, whose deliverance was thereafter commemorated by the Purim festival.

ESTONIA
Repub. of the U.S.S.R. in the extreme W. with coastlines on the Gulf of Finland, the Baltic and the Gulf of Riga. It is a low-lying region bounded on the E. by Lake Peipus. Agriculture and dairy farming are the chief industries. There are extensive forests. Shale is mined, the gas produced from it being sent by pipe line to Leningrad. Manufactures include textiles, paper and engineering. The cap. is Tallinn. There is a univ. at Tartu. Orig. Swedish, Estonia was part of Russia, 1721-1917. It was proclaimed an indep. repub. 1918, and admitted to the U.S.S.R. 1940. In 1941 Estonia was overrun by German forces and was recaptured by the Russians in 1944. Area: 17,413 sq.m. Pop. 1,196,000.

ETHELRED
Name of 2 Eng. kings. **Ethelred II** (968-1016) was a son of King Edgar. He began to reign when only 10, and was on the throne for nearly 40 years. His inability to deal with the Danish peril won for him the name of the Unready. He began the payment of Danegeld.

ETHEREGE, Sir George
(1635-91) Eng. dramatist. He served as diplomat, and wrote comedies: *She Would if She Could* (1668), *The Man of Mode* (1676) (with Sir Fopling Flutter as character).

ETHERS
Series of chem. compounds having similar structures. The term *ether*, as commonly used, refers to diethyl ether $(C_2H_5)_2O$, which is used as an anaesthetic. It is also a useful solvent for fats, oils, resins, etc.

ETHICS
Science of moral values. Zeno of Citium in Cyprus, in the 3rd cent. B.C. set up a scientific system of ethics. Virtue is the only good and baseness the only evil. The correct knowledge of virtue is acquired by *phronēsis* (practical wisdom), and the aim of life should be 'to live in complete agreement with nature.'

ETHIOPIA
or **Abyssinia.** Indep. empire of N.E. Africa, entirely surrounded by the Sudan, Kenya, and Somalia. It is a region of high plateaux and mts., several peaks rising to 14,000 ft. in the centre and N. The chief river is the Blue Nile, issuing from Lake Yana, the largest lake. The climate of the low-lying land is hot; that of the higher plateaux, pleasant. Agriculture and cattle rearing are the principal occupations; sugar cane, cotton, cereals, coffee, tobacco and various fruits are grown. The chief exports are coffee, hides and skins. Addis Ababa is the cap. and largest city. Other centres are Harar, Diredawa, Gondar, Gambela and Magdala. Most of the Christians belong to a branch of the Coptic Ch. from Egypt, but the Danakil are Mohammedans. There is also a number of Jews. In 1868 a Brit. army invaded Abyssinia, because the Emperor Theodore imprisoned some Brit. officials. Theodore was soon defeated, and after a time, 1889, Menelek, King of Shoa, became emperor. He made Abyssinia really indep. Menelek d. in 1913, and there was a certain amount of disorder. The new ruler was deposed, 1916, and Menelek's daughter was declared empress. A regent, Ras Tafari, was appointed to govern and to succeed when she d. In 1928 the regent was crowned king. The Ital. conquered the country in an arduous war in which gas was used 1935-36. The King of Italy assumed the title Emperor of Abyssinia. Brit. troops liberated the country, occupying Addis Ababa in April, 1941, when the Emperor Haile Selassie was restored. Eritrea (*q.v.*) became part of Ethiopia in 1962. Area: 400,000 sq.m. Pop. *c.* 21,800,000.

ETHYL
C_2H_5. Organic radical, or group of atoms capable of behaving like an element. It forms a number of important compounds, such as ethyl alcohol, ethyl chloride and ethyl nitrate.

ETHYLENE
Colourless gaseous hydrocarbon prepared by strongly heating alcohol with sulphuric acid. It is very inflammable, burns with a luminous flame and is explosive when mixed with oxygen. A considerable quantity is present in coal gas.

ETNA
Volcano near E. coast of Sicily, 10,740 ft. The base covers over 400 sq.m. Over 80 eruptions have been recorded since those described by Pindar, 476 B.C.

ETON
[ē'-] Urban district of Bucks. on the Thames opposite Windsor, 21 m. W. of London. With Slough it returns 1 member to Parl. Pop. 67,000. **Eton College.** One of Eng.'s public schools. Founded by Henry VI in 1440. The governing body consists of a provost apptd. by the Queen and 10 fellows.

ETRURIA
Ancient district of Italy, now known as Tuscany (*q.v.*) once inhabited by a people, the Etruscans. The Etruscans were skilled artists, esp. in iron, bronze and gold, and produced beautiful pottery. They introduced the vine and olive, and improved agriculture.

EUBOEA
[yŏŏ-bē'-ă] Largest of the Gk. Is. in the Aegean Sea. Mt. Delphi, 5,725 ft. rises from fertile lowlands producing corn, wine and fruit. Khalkis is the cap. Area: 1,430 sq.m. Pop. 165,758.

EUCALYPTUS
Genus of evergreen trees and shrubs of the family Myrtaceae. The blue gum, *E. globulus*, yields an aromatic oil with antiseptic qualities and grows chiefly in Australia and Tasmania. There are about 600 species.

EUCHARIST
The sacrament of the Lord's Supper. The word, denoting thanksgiving, was applied to the consecrated elements, and then to the whole celebration, which passed into the sacrifice of the Mass. At the Reformation, the Anglican Ch. adopted the term Holy Communion; some other Protestant chs. adhere to the orig. name, the Lord's Supper. The R.C. Ch. and high Anglican Ch. use the term Eucharist.

EUCLID
Gk. mathematician. He taught at Alexandria *c.* 300 B.C. Other extant works are *Data*, 95 geometrical propositions, and an astronomical treatise *Phaenomena.*

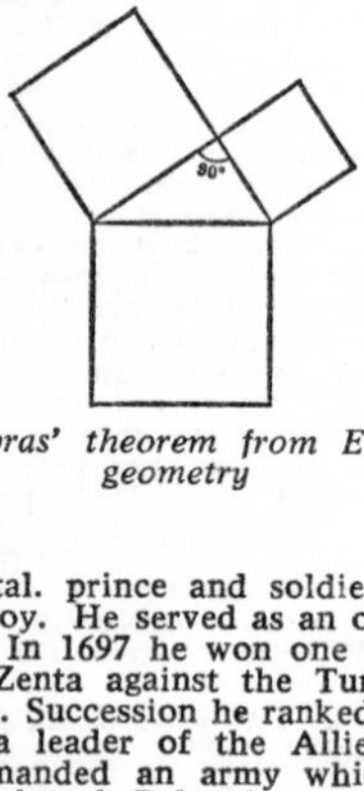

Pythagoras' theorem from Euclid's geometry

EUGÈNE
(1663-1736) Ital. prince and soldier, son of a prince of Savoy. He served as an officer in the Aust. army. In 1697 he won one of his great victories at Zenta against the Turks. In the war of the Sp. Succession he ranked with Marlborough as a leader of the Allies. In 1716 Eugène commanded an army which defeated the Turks, and took Belgrade.

EUGENICS
Study of the factors which may improve or impair the physical and mental racial qualities of future generations. The modern science owes its inception to Sir Francis Galton. A further advance was made by the Mendelian research into the laws governing the transmission of hereditary physical characters. See *Eugenics* by C. P. Blacker (1953).

EUGÉNIE
[ö-zhen-ē'] (1826-1920) Empress of the Fr. She mar. Napoleon III in 1853. From 1853-70 she was the centre of a brilliant and luxurious court; from 1871 she was an exile in Eng.

EUPHRATES
[-frā'-] River of the M.E. which flows through Turkey and Syria into Iraq, where it joins the Tigris to form the Shatt-el-Arab. Formed by the union of 2 streams in E. Asia Minor, the Karu Su and Murad Su, the Euphrates has a total length of 1,700 m. Babylon stood upon its banks.

EURHYTHMICS *See* DALCROZE.

EURIPIDES
[yŏŏ-rip'-i-dēz] (*c.* 485-406 B.C.) Gk. dramatist. B. Salamis. He composed 92 dramas, of which 19 survive, including *Alcestis, Medea, Hippolytus, Helen, Orestes, Iphigenia at Aulis, Andromache, The Children of Heracles, Iphigenia in Tauris, Ion.*

EUROPE
Continent bounded on 3 sides by the sea and on the other by the Ural Mts. which separate it from Asia. The seas are the Arctic, Atlantic Ocean and the Medit. A short land boundary is formed by the Caucasus Mts. in the S.E. The length of the continent from Cape St. Vincent in Spain to the Urals is *c.* 3,200 m. From Cape Matapan in Greece to the North Cape in Norway it is *c.* 2,400 m. There are 3 major divisions: (1) the Scandinavian Highlands in the extreme N., (2) the N. European Plain, which extends from the W. coast of Fr. across the continent, and (3) the mts. of C. and S. Europe, including the Pyrenees, Alps, Carpathians and Apennines and the Balkan Mts. The highest mts. are the Alps. There are many rivers, *e.g.* the Rhine, Danube and Volga. The chief lakes are Vener, Vetter and Onega in the N., and Geneva, Constance, Lucerne and Zurich in the Alps. The climate is temp. maritime in the W. increasing in continentality eastwards and inland. The soil is on the whole fertile. There are rich deposits of the basic metals so that many industries have grown up and in certain areas the density of pop. is extremely high. Europe was orig. peopled from the M.E. and Asia. From the time of the Gks., Europe has led the world in Science and Art, and there has been a series of emp. building countries *viz.* the Gks., Rom., Fr., Brit., Germans and Russians. Much of Europe was included in the Rom. Empire, on the fall of which separate states began to rise. Between these states there were constant wars and frequently changes of boundary. The smaller states were gradually joined to form large ones. Later 5 countries ranked as the Gt. Powers. They were Brit., Fr., Germany, Austria and Russia, joined later by Italy. Austria and Germany claimed to be the successors of the Holy Rom. Empire. The most important movement in Europe during the last cent. was the rise of Prussia and the formation of the German Empire in 1871. Germany's ambitions provoked the world conflict of 1914-18, and were responsible for the War of 1939-45. The influence of the Soviet Union spread further and further W. The tendency for countries to form themselves into Republics was marked, and the left-wing movement became increasingly prominent throughout Europe. Area: *c.* 3,750,000 sq.m. Pop. 572,000,000.

EUTHANASIA
Comfortable or painless death. Long advocated for people suffering from incurable diseases assoc. with great pain, but no legislation has yet been introduced to legalise any such procedure.

EVANGELICAL
Pertaining to the Christian evangel or gospel. The term may denote the first 4 books of the N.T. The principles conformable thereto, *i.e.* evangelical doctrine, or communions governed by scripture alone, *i.e.* Protestant evangelical ch. In 18th cent. Eng. an evangelical revival developed a Low Ch. movement within the Anglican Ch. and occasioned John Wesley's Methodist movement.

EVANS, Sir Arthur
(1851-1944) Eng. archaeologist. B. Herefordshire; educ. Harrow and Brasenose Coll. Ox-

ford, and Göttingen. Between 1900-8 he excavated the palace of Minos at Knossos and did other valuable work. From 1884 to 1908 he was keeper of the Ashmolean Museum, Oxford, and he was twice Pres. of the Brit. Assoc.

EVE
(O.T.) Name given by Adam to his wife, because she was 'the mother of all living' (Gen. 3, 20). Her sons were Cain, Abel and Seth.

EVELYN, John
(1620-1706) Eng. writer and diarist. B. Wotton House, near Dorking, Surrey; educ. Balliol Coll. Oxford. He was one of the founders of the Royal Soc. (Sec. 1673). He wrote on agriculture, forestry, engraving, but is famous for the Diary which covers his life from 1641 until 3 weeks before his d. at Wotton.

EVENING PRIMROSE
Biennial herb (*Oenothera biennis*), of the family Onagraceae, a native of the U.S.A. It has flower stems 4-5 ft. high, bearing spikes of large yellow flowers which only open towards sunset.

EVEREST, Mount
Peak, 29,028 ft. high, of the Himalayas, the highest mt. in the world, on the borders of Nepal and Tibet. It was named after Sir George Everest, 1st Surveyor-General of India. In 1922 Brigadier-General C. G. Bruce led an expedition in an attempt to reach the summit of Everest. Mallory, Somervell and Norton reached 27,000 ft. without using oxygen. In 1924 Norton and Somervell attained an altitude of 28,000 ft. A day later Mallory and Irvine set out on a determined effort to reach the summit. They were last seen by Odell. For the next 9 years Tibet was closed to all white men, but in 1933, 2 planes flew over the summit, for the first time. No further exped. was possible during World War II and after the Communist occupation of Tibet, but in 1951 permission was granted by the Maharajah of Nepal for a new approach from the south, to a Brit. exped. led by **Eric Shipton.** A Swiss exped. under **Wyss-Dunant** in 1952, reached the highest point yet attained, 28,215 ft. and in 1953 the Brit. exped. under **Col. H. C. J. Hunt** was successful, E. P. Hillary, a New Zealander, and Sherpa Tensing Bhutia reaching the Summit on May 29. See *The Ascent of Everest* by John Hunt (1953).

EVIL EYE
Faculty of influencing persons or things to their harm by looking at them. Belief in the evil eye was common to the Hebs., Gks. and Egyptians and was rife throughout Europe in the M.A. Most savage races have been found to believe in it. Charms and amulets are supposed to avert it.

EVOLUTION
Process by which plants and animals have developed by gradual modification from previously existing forms of life. It is only by reference to the fact of evolution that the resemblances and differences of structure in various groups of plants and animals can be satisfactorily explained. It elucidates the appearance of features, permanent in lower forms, in the development stages of the higher animals, *e.g.* fish-like characters and reptilian characters in the early stages of the embryo of a mammal. Fossil remains, though necessarily incomplete, supply many indications of the evolution of complex types from simpler ones.

EXCHEQUER
In Brit. the govt. dept. which deals with monies received and paid on behalf of the public services of the country.

EXCISE
[-siz'] Duties levied on goods produced within a country, as distinct from customs duties levied on goods entering a country. Under a system of Free Trade every customs duty is counterbalanced by a corresponding excise duty. In Eng. the earliest excise duties date from the 17th cent. In the 18th cent. they became very numerous and their collectors, the excisemen, were detested. In the 19th cent. many excise duties were removed and today are levied only on beer, spirits, entertainments, sugar, matches, table waters, British wines, liquor licences, dog, gun and game licences, and a few other minor articles and licences.

EXCOMMUNICATION
Exclusion of offending members from the rights and privileges of a religious communion. It may be temporary or permanent, partial or total. It is based upon synagogue practice, involving congregational assent, but bishops gradually assumed the prerogative of excluding offenders from the sacraments for heresy, immorality or disobedience. Pope Gregory VII first deposed a monarch by excommunicating the Emp. Henry IV, 1077; Innocent III placed Eng. itself under an interdict and excommunicated King John.

EXE
Eng. river which rises on Exmoor, Somerset, and flows S. across Devon, entering the Eng. Channel by a navigable estuary 6 m. long.

EXECUTION
One kind is a distraint on the goods of a person who has not paid a debt after being ordered to do so by a court. Another form of execution is putting a person to d. after sentence has been passed. This is done in Brit. by hanging; in Fr. by the guillotine; and in parts of the U.S.A. by the electric chair. Until 1868 executions in Eng. were public. Soldiers, sailors and airmen sentenced to d. under military law, are shot.

EXETER
City, county borough and county town of Devon, on the Exe. It is the agricultural and commercial centre for a wide district. The chief building is the cathedral dedicated to St. Peter. The Guildhall dates from Elizabethan times. Parts of the city walls still stand. There is a Univ. Coll. founded 1865, and a public school, Exeter School, 1633. Exeter returns 1 member to Parl. Pop. 80,000.

EXHIBITIONISM
(Psychology) Behaviour designed to attract attention. It may stem from an inferiority complex or the desire to find compensation for what the subject believes to be lack of appreciation of his personality, mind or work. In children it may develop from a sense of being neglected or unwanted.

EXISTENTIALISM
Philosophical system propounded, esp. after World War II, by the Fr. philosophers J.-P. Sartre, Simone de Beauvoir and Albert Camus. Its main tenet is that in all important matters 'Facts come before the idea', and it insists on facing the facts of man's nature. Sartre ignores the religious element and is himself an atheist Existentialist.

EXMOOR
Moorland tract in N. Somerset and Devon. It covers 20,000 acres of wild and beautiful scenery. Dunkery Beacon, 1,708 ft. is the highest point. Simonsbath is the centre of the moor, and on its borders are Minehead and Dulverton. Much of it belongs to the Nat. Trust.

EXODUS, Book of
Second book of the O.T. Describes the release of the Hebrews from their Egyptian bondage, the preparation of Moses, the ten plagues, the passover, and the flight across the Red Sea to Sinai (c. 1-18). The remainder records the prolonged sojourn in the Sinai wilderness, the promulgation of the Ten Commandments, and the Book of the Covenant (c. 19-40).

EXPLOSIVE
Material capable of rapid conversion into a large volume of gas, usually by detonation. The original explosive, gunpowder, has become superseded by dynamite, gun cotton and cordite. Owing to obvious dangers in the manufacture, storage and conveyance of explosives, the industry is strictly regulated by the Explosives Act, 1875, and other legal restrictions.

EXPORTS
Goods sent out of a country. In Brit. they are valued by the authorities at the custom houses. The difference between a country's exports and imports is the *balance of trade* (*q.v.*). Invisible exports are sums paid for shipping, insurance, etc. Re-exports are goods imported in order to be sent to another part of the world. In 1913 Brit's. exports were valued at £634,800,000. In 1938, they were valued at £470,755,320. In direct consequence of the War, with the disappearance of many of Brit's. overseas assets, the imperative need of exports has become evident. The value of exports in 1963 amounted to approx. £4,080,076,444, but the improvement is largely due to inflation.

EXPRESSIONISM
The term given to an approach to painting which is essentially emotional. Expressionist painters aim at conveying a state of mind rather than a naturalistic representation. Early masters were El Greco, Bosch, Goya and Grunewald. At the end of the 19th cent. Edvard Munch, a Norwegian, led a group of painters in Berlin. Other artists who may be termed expressionists are Ernst Josephson, Oskar Kokoschka, Rouault, Chagall, Jack Yeats, Soutine, van Dongen and Kandinsky.

EXTRA-SENSORY PERCEPTION
Evidence shows that: (1) Some people can become directly aware of events taking place in the minds of others. (2) Some have knowledge of events taking place remotely from them. (3) Some can become aware of events, either mental or physical, which have not yet taken place. (4) Some are capable of *telekinesis*, *i.e.* they can influence the behaviour of matter at a distance by means beyond the range of the senses. (5) Some have the power of *clairvoyance*, *i.e.* they ' see ' things which may exist in states of matter the rates of vibration of which are beyond those of normal vision, or, with no help from sense impressions, can give information about events taking place in the outside world. (6) Some have the power of *clairaudience*, *i.e.* they hear sounds which are beyond those of normal hearing. (7) Some possess the power of *psychometry*, *i.e.* by the ' feel ' of an article which has been carried or worn by an individual, they can tell a great deal about the life, health, etc. of the person.

EXTREME UNCTION
A sacrament of the R.C. Ch. consisting of anointing the dying with oil. Olive oil, blessed by a bishop, is used, and is applied by a priest to the eyes, ears, nostrils, mouth, hands, feet, loins.

EYCK, Hubert Van
[īk′] (*c.* 1370-1426) Flemish painter, b. in Holland. About 1420 he began *The Adoration of the Lamb*, finished by his brother **Jan** (*c.* 1390-1441) famous for his *John Arnolfini and his Wife*.

EYE
Organ of vision comprising eye-ball 1 in. in diameter set in hollow of skull called orbit. The eye structure comprises the eye muscles, the eye-ball and the optic nerve. Eye-ball consists of 3 coats. An outer which is transparent in front and called *cornea* and opaque at back and is called *sclera*; a vascular tissue called *choroid* which lines inner aspect of sclera, and a nerve tissue part called *retina* which lines inside of choroid and is developed from the optic nerve which pierces sclera and choroid. Other structures of eye include lens which is a bi-convex solid translucent disc suspended between iris and vitreous body and is enclosed in a glossy elastic capsule. Vitreous body occupies ⅘ of space at back of eye, with retina on its outer aspect. Composed of soft transparent jelly-like body.

EYEBRIGHT
Annual herb (*Euphrasia officinalis*), of the family Scrophulariaceae, a native of N. temperate regions growing throughout Brit. It is parasitic upon grass roots and has egg-shaped or lance-shaped leaves, and small white or lilac flowers stained with purple, the lower lip's mid-lobe being yellow.

EYRA
[ā′-rǎ] Wild cat of S. Amer. (*Felis eyra*) inhabiting the region between S. Brazil and N. Mexico. Preys on poultry.

EYRE
[air] Large salt lake of C. Australia into which drain numerous intermittent rivers. It is dry for much of the year. Named after its discoverer, the Eng. explorer, **Edward John Eyre** (1815-1901).

EZEKIEL, Book of
Prophetical book of the O.T. Ezekiel was a priest of Jerusalem, exiled to Babylon by Nebuchadnezzar, 597 B.C. The book gives a vision of the ideal theocracy.

EZRA, Book of
Historical book of the O.T. Ezra was a Jewish scribe living in captive exile in Babylon under Artaxerxes Longimanus. Recording Cyrus's decree for rebuilding the Jerusalem Temple, the book describes the return of the first company of exiles under Zerubbabel, and the rebuilding (c. 1-6), then Ezra's return and the reforms he effected (c. 7-10).

F

F
6th letter of the Eng. and Lat. alphabets. A labio-dental articulation, it is formed by the passage of breath between the lower lip and the upper teeth. The figure of the letter F is the same as that of the ancient Gk. digamma, and in words derived from Gk. the sound of *f* is represented by *ph*, *e.g. philosophy*.

FACTORY ACTS
19th cent. Acts of Parl. to regulate hours, conditions of work, safety and sanitary provisions.

FAEROES, The
Group of *c.* 20 Is. belonging to Denmark, in the N. Atlantic, 200 m. N.W. of the Shetland Is. The largest are Strömö, containing the cap. Thorshavn, and Syderö. Fishing is the most important industry. In 1946 the people voted for separation from Denmark, but subsequently reversed this decision. They now have a certain measure of self-govt. The legislative body is the Lagting; representatives are sent to the Danish Rigsdag in Copenhagen. Area: 540 sq.m. Pop. 35,000.

FAHRENHEIT, Gabriel Daniel
(1686-1736) German physicist, b. Danzig. He devised, *c.* 1726, the thermometric scale in which the freezing pt. of water is fixed at 32° and the boiling pt. at 212°, the intervening space being divided into 180 equal degrees. In the centigrade scale freezing pt. is 0° and boiling pt. 100°. Conversion is effected as follows:

$$°C=5(°F-32)\div 9. \quad °F=(°C\times 9\div 5)+32.$$

FAIR ISLE
Is. of Scot. one of the Shetland Is., 16 m. S. of Mainland, and midway between the Shetland and Orkney groups. The inhabitants engage in sheep rearing and fishing, and in making woollen garments, including the celebrated Fair Isle jerseys. In 1954 the Is. was taken over by the Nat. Trust for Scotland to provide a permanent foundation for research into migratory bird life.

FAIRFAX, Baron
(1612-71) Thomas Fairfax, Eng. soldier. He joined the Parl. forces at the outbreak of the civil war. Fairfax was made C.-in-C. in 1645 and was partly responsible for the victory at Naseby. He refused to attend as one of the judges apptd. to try Charles I. Later he aided Monk in placing Charles II on the throne.

FAITH HEALING
In the Christian Ch. the tradition of faith healing dates from the earliest days of Christianity. In the Reformation faith healing proper was performed by the Moravians and Waldenses and Luther and other reformers practised faith cures in the 16th cent. In the 17th and 18th cents. Baptists', Quakers' and Methodists' faith cures were recorded and it is practised today. The miracles of Lourdes, the tombs of St. Louis and St. Francis of Assisi are products of faith healing. Christian Science (*q.v.*) holds that pain is an illusion and seeks to cure by instilling this fact into the mind of the patient.

FAKIR
Religious devotee. The term is used chiefly in India, where they number over 1,000,000. They are partly orthodox ascetic mendicants of the dervish orders, partly irresponsible nomads and also Hindus. Some of the latter pertain to the yogi orders.

FALAISE
Town of Calvados dept. Fr. 20 m. S. of Caen, birthplace of William the Conqueror. Pop. 5,600.

FALCON
Birds of prey having stout, hooked beaks, and long, sickle-shaped claws. Resident Brit. forms include the Black-crowned Peregrine (*Falco peregrinus*) male 15 in., female 18-20 in., formerly trained for hawking; the Kestrel (*Falco tinnunculus*) 13 in. long; and the still smaller Merlin (*Falco columbarius*). The Hobby (*Falco sulbuteo*) is a summer visitor; the Norway Gyrfalcon and Iceland and Greenland Falcons are rarer.

FALKIRK
[fawl-'] Burgh and industrial town of Stirlingshire, 22 m. N.E. of Glasgow. There are coal mines and iron works, distilleries and chem. works. With Stirling and Grangemouth it returns 1 member to Parl. Pop. 38,000.

FALKLAND ISLANDS
Group of Is. in the S. Atlantic, 300 m. E. of the Straits of Magellan. A crown colony, it consists of 2 large Is., E. and W. Falkland, and numerous adjacent islets. By the Antarctic Treaty signed in 1959 the Dependencies include only those islands north of Latitude 60° S. *i.e.* S. Georgia and S. Sandwich Is. Sheep farming and whaling are the chief occupations. Stanley, on E. Falkland, is the cap. and only town. The colony is admin. by a Gov. and a council. Area: 6,067 sq.m. Pop. *c.* 2,233. **Battle of the Falkland Islands.** On Dec. 8, 1914, a naval battle was fought near the Falkland Is. between Brit. and German forces.

FALLA, Manuel de
[fal'-ya] (1876-1946) Sp. composer of nationalist outlook, his work making abundant use of Sp. folk-music and its idiom. He lived all his life in Sp. until the Sp. Civil War when he migrated to S. Amer. His works include operas, ballets, a concerto for harpsichord, chamber music and songs.

FALLOW DEER
A small European deer commonly found in Eng. deer parks.

FALMOUTH
Borough and seaport of S. Cornwall, 12 m. from Truro, at the mouth of the Fal. The port is a fishing and yachting centre. Pop. 17,330.

FAMILY
Unit. of soc. consisting of father, mother, and their offspring. It is used also for a larger unit, brothers, sisters, and their offspring. Scholars agree that it goes back to the beginnings of human soc. The family was mainly patriarchal and under the rule of the father. In many countries it included his children by various wives and concubines. In some socs. it was matriarchal, the mother being the recognised head. In the western world, protected by the power of the Christian Ch. it took the form which it now retains.

FAMINE
General scarcity of food leading to starvation

and frequently d., caused by the failure of the crops, which in its turn may have been due to drought, war, or pestilence. They have been most terrible in the densely populated countries of the E. where any serious decrease in production quickly brings about a famine. Famines are mentioned in the Bible. There was a terrible European famine in 1162 and a potato famine in Ireland in 1846-7. The Thirty Years' War, and, to some extent, World War I led to famines. The severity and frequency of famines has been greatly mitigated by irrigation and modern methods of farming, improved means of transport, methods of preserving food, and attacks on the diseases that destroy food crops.

FARADAY, Michael
(1791-1867) Eng. chemist, and physicist. B. London, he was apprenticed to a bookbinder, but found time to study science and in 1813 became assistant to Sir Humphry Davy. In 1827 he succeeded Davy as Prof. of Chemistry at the Royal Inst. Faraday's researches in electrolysis laid the foundations of electro-chemistry. In 1831, he showed that the motion of a conductor in a magnetic field led to the generation of an electric current.

FARNBOROUGH
Urban district of Hants. 33 m. S.W. of London, near Aldershot. On F. Common is the Royal Aircraft Establishment. Pop. 33,430.

FARNE
Group of Is. off the coast of Northumberland. On Longstone is the lighthouse assoc. with Grace Darling (*q.v.*).

FARNESE
[-nā'-zā] Ital. ducal house of Parma. In 1493 Pope Alexander VI created Alexander Farnese a cardinal. In 1534 Alexander became Pope as Paul III. He had a family and to one of his sons he gave the Duchy of Parma. One duke of Parma, Alexander, was the Sp. soldier who led the army that was intended to invade Eng. in 1588. Paul III was responsible for the **Farnese Palace,** one of the finest buildings in Rome.

FAROUK I
[fā-rōōk'] (1920-65) King of Egypt, 1936-52, who succeeded his father, Fuad I while still a minor. He mar. (1) Farida, daughter of Zulficar Pasha, 1938, and divorced her 1949; (2) Narriman Sadek, 1951, by whom he had a son, Achmed Fuad (1952-). In July 1952, he abdicated in favour of his son, Fuad II, and left the country. Egypt was declared a repub. 1953. *See* EGYPT.

FARQUHAR, George
(1678-1707) Eng. playwright. Educ. Trinity Coll. Dublin. He wrote comedies: *Twin-Rivals* (1703), *The Recruiting Officer* (1706), *The Beaux' Stratagem* (1707).

FARRAR, Frederic William
(1831-1903) Eng. author and divine. Schoolmaster at Marlborough (headmaster 1871-6) and Harrow. He wrote several school-stories for boys, including *Eric, or Little by Little,* 1858.

FASCISM
Political and social movement, strongly nationalist in character, in which the state is paramount and militant. Strongly opposed to Communism and Socialism, the movement is fiercely anti-Semitic. In Italy it began *c.* 1919 amongst those who were dissatisfied with the conduct of affairs after World War I. Mainly composed of men who had served in the War, the movement grew rapidly. Fascism was at first republican and socialistic in its aims. Benito Mussolini soon stood out as a leader. They became known as opponents of Communism, then strong in Italy, and in several towns there were riots. In Oct. 1922, there took place the march on Rome. The city was entered by 200,000 armed Fascists, the govt. was overthrown and a new one under Mussolini set up. Thereafter Fascism was supreme in Italy until milit. defeat in World War II brought about its collapse in 1943. Although Fascism undoubtedly developed Italy's material prosperity, it was at the price of ruthless suppression of constitutional liberty. During the inter-war period there existed a **Brit. Union of Fascists,** led by Sir Oswald Mosley (*q.v.*) but the Nazi movement in Germany was the most notorious derivative.

FASTING
Abstention from food. The Mosaic law imposed an annual fast on the ' day of the atonement ' and the Jews still observe this and other fast days. Moslems fast from sunrise to sunset in the month of Ramadan. The Anglican Ch. prescribes days of fasting or abstinence during the 40 days of Lent, Ember days, Rogation days, all Fridays except Christmas Day, and the vigils of various festivals. The R.C. Ch. makes fasting compulsory. Its most usual form is to eat no meat on Fridays. R.C.'s and High Anglicans must take Holy Communion fasting. Fasting is sometimes resorted to as a means of public protest.

FASTNET
Rocky islet off the coast of Cork, S. Ireland, site of a lighthouse.

FATES
In classical myth, 3 goddesses ruling over human destiny. The Rom. name was **Parcae.**

FATHER
A male parent. In Eng. law a father is responsible for the maintenance of his offspring until they can maintain themselves. By analogy the word is used for God, esp. as the 1st person of the Trinity. Christianity teaches the doctrine of the fatherhood of God. Father is used for priests and members of monastic orders in the R.C. Ch. and to some extent in the Anglican Ch.

FAULKNER, William Harrison
(1897-1962) Amer. novelist. His novels include: *The Sound and the Fury* (1929), *As I Lay Dying* (1930), *Knight's Gambit* (1951). He also pub. several vols. of poems and short stories. He was awarded the Nobel Prize for Lit. in 1949. *Requiem for a Nun* appeared as a novel in 1953, as a play in 1955; *A Fable,* pub. in 1954, won a Pulitzer Prize, 1955.

FAURÉ, Gabriel
[faw-rā'] (1845-1924) Fr. composer. In 1896 he was apptd. Prof. of composition at the Paris Conservatoire and 9 years later became Director until 1920. His compositions include an opera, incidental music, much chamber music and pianoforte works, a Requiem for soloists, chorus and orchestra and over 90 songs.

FAUSTUS
Historical figure, Dr. Johan Faust, who lived in Germany in the early 16th cent., the subject of legends which attributed to him a pact with the devil. The Faust legend has inspired much lit. and music. A collection of tales about him, pub. in German in 1587, inspired Marlowe's *Doctor Faustus.* Goethe's *Faust* inspired music by Berlioz, Liszt, Schumann, Wagner, Gounod, Busoni. Another *Faust* by Nikolaus Lenau (1802-50) inspired music by Liszt. Thomas Mann's *Doktor Faustus* (1947) is a contemporary German adaptation of the theme.

FAUVES, Les
(wild beasts) Term given in derision to a group of painters who exhibd. in Paris, 1906. Their chief exponent was Henri Matisse, 1869-1954. With him were grouped Braque, Vlaminck, Dorain, Dufy, Marquet, Friesz and van Dongen.

FAWKES, Guy
(1570-1606) Eng. conspirator. He enlisted in the Sp. army in Flanders, returning to Eng. in 1604. To Fawkes was left the actual execution

of the plot to blow up the Houses of Parl. and he was arrested at his post, Nov. 4, 1605, the day before Parl. was due to meet. He confessed under severe torture, and with other conspirators was hanged. *See* GUNPOWDER PLOT.

FEDERAL BUREAU OF INVESTIGATION
(F.B.I.) Detective branch of the U.S. dept. of justice. Estabd. in 1908 to investigate crimes against federal law, as distinct from those against the laws of individual states, the F.B.I. enforces laws against espionage, white-slave traffic, blackmail, racketeering, etc. During World War II, F.B.I. detachments accompanied U.S. armed forces on counter-espionage duties, and since 1945 the bureau has been prominent in anti-Communist activities. The detectives are known as G-men from the dept.'s code letter " G ".

FEDERATION OF BRITISH INDUSTRIES
Non-polit. assoc. for the encouragement, promotion and protection of Brit. Industries. It was founded in 1916 and granted a Royal Charter in 1923. Its two main functions are: (1) to promote policies serving Brit. Industry as a whole, and (2) to supply its individual members with information and practical assistance. The membership, which is confined to non-nationalist industries, exceeds 6,600 firms, and thousands more are represented by affiliated trade associations. The Federation deals with some 30,000 inquiries each year, and these cover questions on almost every subject having to do with industrial productivity other than labour relations. The Federation has ready access to Mins. and Govt. Depts. and gives evidence to all official committees or Royal Commissions reviewing industrial questions.

FEISAL
[fī'-] (1885-1933) King of Iraq, 2nd son of Hussein, Sharif of Mecca (*q.v.*). Educ. in Constantinople, he was one of the group that deprived Abdul Hamid II of his throne in 1909. In 1918 he helped the Brit. to conquer Palestine and Syria, and he attended the Peace Conference in Paris in 1919. In August, 1921, he was elected and proclaimed King of Iraq. Until 1932 Iraq was governed in assoc. with Brit. along mandatory lines. He was succeeded by his son Ghasi (1912-39) and by his grandson **Feisal II** (1935-58), who was assassinated. *See* IRAQ.

FELO DE SE
One who commits suicide (*q.v.*).

FELONY
Class of crime in Eng. law. All crimes are either felonies or misdemeanours, the more serious ones falling into the former category. Felony includes such crimes as murder, manslaughter and burglary.

FELSPAR
Group of minerals found in most eruptive rocks. They consist of silicates of aluminium with varying proportions of lime, soda or potash, hence the names of potash felspar, soda felspar, etc. They vary in colour and form, but have almost the same hardness and specific gravity and similar crystalline shape.

FENCING
Pastime in which the 2 combatants use a light weapon either a foil, sabre or épée. In the 15th and 16th cents. a knowledge of swordsmanship was part of the educ. of a gentleman. In the 16th cent. light swords began to be used and in this way fencing originated, being practised with blunt or protected weapons, as a preparation for the real combat. In Eng. fencing died out when pistols became the regular duelling weapons. As a pastime fencing was taken up in Eng. in the 19th cent. and prospered greatly from *c.* 1900. To avoid injury the fencers are masked and wear a guard over the head, whilst the weapon is fitted with a button on the point. A little later women began to fence,

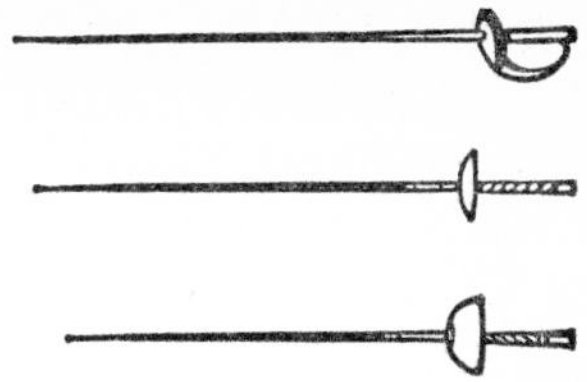

Sabre (top), épée (middle) and foil (bottom)

and the Olympic games recognised fencing with foil, épée and sabre as events. There are championships confined to Eng. fencers, one being for women. The Amateur Fencing Assoc. is the controlling body in Brit. Competitions are held regularly.

FENIANS
[fē'-] Patriotic secret society founded in the U.S.A. *c.* 1860 to make Ireland an indep. repub. In 1867 they attacked a prison van to release 2 colleagues, and killed a policeman; 3 of them were executed, and they are known to the Irish as the ' Manchester Martyrs '. The executions bred terrorism, which forced the Brit. Govt. to give attention to Irish affairs.

FENNEC
(*Vulpes zerda*) Small, large-eared African fox, found in all the coastlands of N. Africa from Egypt to Senegambia.

FENNEL
Name of various perennial umbelliferous herbs, esp. the aromatic *Foeniculum vulgare*, native to Brit. Varieties are cultivated in Europe, Amer. and India for their seeds, which yield fennel water.

FERDINAND
Name of 7 kings of Spain. **Ferdinand V** (1452-1516) became King of Aragon, 1470. Previously he had mar. Isabella, who became Queen of Castile, 1474. Under their rule Spain became a single kingdom with an immense empire overseas, as the Moors were crushed and the New World discovered. His grandson was the Emperor Charles V.

FERMANAGH
[-man'-nă] Inland county of N. Ireland, in Ulster prov., containing Lough Erne. It is mainly lowland, and agriculture and fishing are the chief industries. Enniskillen is the county town. Other places are Newtown Butler, Lisnaskea and Rosslea. With S. Tyrone it returns 1 member to Parl. Pop. 52,400.

FERMI, Enrico
[fairmi] (1901-54) Ital. nuclear physicist, b. Rome. He was prof. of physics in Rome and Columbia Univ. and in 1942 constructed the first atomic pile. Nobel Prize for physics, 1938.

FERN
Group of flowerless plants. Mostly perennial herbs with fibrous roots or creeping root stocks, a few have woody trunks. They reproduce by means of microscopic spores; these develop into a green, leaf-like scale or prothallus, beneath which male and female elements, simulating floral anthers and ovaries, produce sexually another spore-bearing plant. The 2,500 species of ferns are cosmopolitan, preferring humid temp. and trop. regions.

FERNANDEZ, Juan
(1536-1602) Navigator. B. Cartagena, he observed the course of the trade winds and the currents off the W. coast of S. Amer. He discovered, in the S. Pacific, the islands now bearing his name, one of which became famous as the residence of Alexander Selkirk.

FERNANDO PÓO
Sp. Is. in the Bight of Biafra, W. Africa, part of the colony of Sp. Guinea (*q.v.*). It is moun-

tainous but the soil is fertile. Discovered by Portugal in 1471, ceded to Spain in 1788. Area: 800 sq.m. Pop. 34,200.

FERRET
(*Putorius furo*) Half-tamed variety of the pole-cat. Originating in N. Africa or Spain, and used in Italy for rabbit hunting, it has been known in Brit. for 6 cents. where it is employed for hunting rabbits and rats.

FERRY, Jules François Camille
[-rē′] (1832-93) Fr. statesman and lawyer. In 1869 he was elected republican deputy for Paris and was responsible for the govt. of Paris during the seige of 1870. He was twice Premier, 1880-1 and 1883-5.

FERTILISER
Agric. term for plant food added to the soil, such as guano from Peru, potash salts from Germany and nitrate of soda from Chile. It is also used in connection with the artificial manures. Deposits of calcium phosphate occur in many places and the material is treated to form superphosphate of lime. Sulphate of ammonia is a by-product from gas works. More recently the huge supplies of nitrogen in the atmosphere have been drawn upon for the manufacture synthetically of nitrogenous fertilisers.

FERTILITY
The ability to procreate children. About 10 % of marriages in Brit. are childless without the wishes of the partners concerned. Contrary to popular idea, infertility is common in the male. Infertility in the male can be established by examination of the seminal fluid. In the female, fertility varies within wide limits; failure to conceive may also be due to some defect or disease of the reproductive organs. Research is now going on in the science of fertility. For twins, the chance is estimated at once in eighty-eight births, for triplets, once in seven thousand five hundred births, and for quadruplets, once in six hundred thousand births.

FETISHISM
[fet′-] Form of magico-religious belief. It holds that the services of a 'spirit' may be appropriated by possessing its material embodiment. A fetish may be an animal, plant or stone, and may house a disembodied soul.

FEUDALISM
Social and economic system that existed in much of W. Europe from the 11th to the 16th cents. The chief principle of the system was the holding of land in return for services. The king was regarded as the holder of all the land, but much of this he let out to barons, who were his tenants-in-chief and who agreed to perform certain services, usually to provide him with soldiers in time of war. These tenants-in-chief, in their turn, let out land to others on like conditions. In Fr. and elsewhere, although not to the same extent in Eng., feudalism was a danger to the king, as his vassals could make war on him. In Eng. the minor or mesne tenants, as well as the tenants-in-chief, owed allegiance to the king. Feudalism finally broke down in Eng. in the 14th cent. Trade increased, towns grew up, methods of warfare changed, and it became more convenient to pay cash than to render services. It was not until Charles II that the feudal payments were abolished. In Fr. relics of feudalism persisted until they were completely swept away by the Revolution.

FEVERFEW
Wild perennial plant (*Chrysanthemum parthenium*) allied to camomile. It has branched stems, broad, deeply-toothed leaves, and clusters of daisy-like flowers. The plant has an aromatic odour and tonic properties.

FEZ
City of Morocco, in a valley N. of the Middle Atlas range, *c.* 100 m. from Rabat. Fez is a sacred Mohammedan city. Silk and cotton goods are manufactured. Pop. 216,133.

FIBRE
Thread-like filament of mineral, plant or animal derivation. Plant fibres are of diverse origin and composition; the hairs of cotton and the fibres of flax and ramie represent nearly pure cellulose; in jute, esparto and sisal, lignin is present, and in raffia and hemp, cutin is a constituent. The hair or fur of animals supplies wool, mohair and other textile fibres, the silk-worm provides silk, and the mineral asbestos forms an incombustible fibre. Artificial fibres have chemical structures similar to those of the natural fibres. *See* TERYLENE.

FIBROSITIS
[-sī′-] Painful condition affecting muscles due to inflammation at their insertions into bone or of the fibrous sheaths binding the muscle tissue together. Affects both sexes and all ages and is characterised by sudden onset of pain and tender areas in muscles.

FICHTE, Johan Gottlieb
[fi<u>ch</u>′-tă] (1762-1814) German philosopher who re-shaped the Kantian Philosophy. B. Remeneu, studied Theology at the Univs. of Jena and Leipzig. His first book *Critique of all Revelation* was written after a visit to Kant. He was Prof. at Jena (1794) but was dismissed on a charge of atheism. He was subsequently appointed Prof. at Erlengen and finally at the Univ. of Berlin. The philosophy of Fichte is a system of pure subjective idealism.

FIDEI DEFENSOR *See* DEFENDER OF THE FAITH.

FIELD MARSHAL
Highest rank in the Brit. army. It dates from 1736. A Field-marshal carries a baton as a sign of his rank. The equivalent rank in the navy is Admiral of the Fleet, and in the air force Marshal of the R.A.F.

FIELD MOUSE
Several small rodents which include the long-tailed *Mus sylvaticus*, and a number of voles, all very destructive to field and forest produce.

FIELDFARE
(*Turdus pilaris*) Bird breeding in N. Europe in pine and birch forests; multitudes spend autumn and winter in Brit. They nest in colonies, and feed on grubs, slugs and berries.

FIELDING, Henry
(1707-54) Eng. novelist. B. Somerset; educ. Eton; studied law at Leyden. Wrote for the stage. Called to Bar 1740; J.P. for Westminster, 1748, where he vigorously put down crimes of violence. His first novel was *Joseph Andrews* (1742), followed by *Jonathan Wild the Great* (1743), *Tom Jones* (1749), *Amelia* (1751). See *Henry Fielding: His Life, Work and Times* by F. Homes Dudden (1953).

FIFE
Peninsular county of E. Scot. between the Firths of Forth and Tay. It is hilly in the N.W.; the chief rivers are the Eden and Leven. The county has rich coal-mines and there is much fishing. Cupar is the county town; other places are Dunfermline, Kirkcaldy, St. Andrews, Buckhaven and the new town of Glenrothes. The county returns 4 members to Parl. (2 borough constituencies). Pop. 321,000.

FIFTH COLUMN
Collaborationist group, native to one country but working for another. The term dates from the Spanish Civil War. During World War II, the Germans made use of such groups.

FIG
Genus of fruit-bearing trees (*Ficus*). The common *F. carica*, cultivated from antiquity in the Medit. region, bears pear-shaped receptacles containing nearly closed cavities within which

the flowers are fertilised. It was introduced into Eng. in Tudor times.

FIGARO
Character in comedies by Beaumarchais; a witty and resourceful servant and satirist of the privileged classes.

FIJI
Indep. dominion of Commonwealth in Pacific Ocean; former Brit. crown colony, 1874-1970. Comprises *c.* 322 Is. of volcanic origin; *c.* 106 are inhabited. The largest are Viti Levu, and Vanua Levu. The soil is fertile. There are various industries, including, timber-, sugar-, rice- and oil-milling. Suva, on the S. coast of Viti Levu, is the cap. The Is were discovered by Tasman, 1643, and visited by Capt. Cook, 1769. The new govt. has 52-member house of representatives (with equal representation of Fijians and Indians), with P.M., and Gov. General. Area: 7,055 sq.m. Pop. 519,000.

FILBERT
Fruit of cultivated varieties of hazel (*Corylus avellana*). A leathery husk encloses the nutshell. It grows esp. in Kent, and is much esteemed in Amer. Larger varieties are known as cobs.

FILM
In photography the flexible material used in the making of negatives. It was first introduced for general photographic work by the Eastman Co. in 1891. The particular value of the film for cinematographic work was soon recognised by Edison, who used it first in his kinetoscope. Celluloid was originally used as the material of films, but owing to its inflammability a non-inflammable film made from cellulose acetate is now in use. *See* CINEMATOGRAPHY.

FINCH
Various small perching birds (*Fringillidae*). Members of family are distributed over all temp. regions except Australasia. Common Brit. resident species include Bullfinch, Goldfinch, Greenfinch and Hawfinch. The Snow Bunting is mainly a winter visitor. The Siskin, Yellow Bunting, House Sparrow, Linnet, Redpoll and the migrant Brambling are also finches.

FINGER
Terminal part of the hand composed of 3 bones called phalanges, except in case of thumb where there are only 2. Joint between each phalanx is called interphalangeal joint and that between finger and hand is called metacarpal phalangeal joint. Interphalangeal joints depend for stability on fibrous capsule and on muscle tendons. Nerves and blood vessels run down each side of finger. **Finger-Print.** Impression of the surface ridges of the human finger. As a method of establishing identity, no 2 finger-prints being exactly alike, it was introduced into the Bengal law courts in 1858. A system of classifying impressions was devised by Sir E. Henry and accepted as evidence by Brit. law courts in 1901. Police identification by finger-prints is now universal.

FINISTERRE, Cape
Most W. point of Spain in Corunna prov. scene of Anson's victory over the Fr. 1747.

FINLAND
Repub. of N. Europe, between Sweden and the U.S.S.R. and N. of Latitude 60°, with a long coastline on the Gulfs of Bothnia and Finland. The Aland Is. form a dept. It consists of a low plateau; half of the surface is covered by lakes and bogs. The winters are severe, and most of the coast is icebound for several months each year. Forests cover much of the country, with tundra in the extreme N. Agriculture is the chief occupation, particularly in the S. Livestock are reared, and dairying is developing. Lumbering is also important, and the industries of the S. are related to the resources of timber and water power. Manufactures include paper, matches, plywood and textiles. The important towns are Helsinki, the cap., Turku, Tampere, Oulu and Pori. The pop. mainly Finnish-speaking, is predominantly Lutheran in religion. There are 3 univs. F. was an integral part of Sweden from the 12th cent. until 1809, when the country was ceded to Russia. In 1917 the Finnish indep. repub. was proclaimed, with a Pres., council of state and house of representatives, elected by universal suffrage. Area: 130,000 sq.m. Pop. 4,446,000.

FINN
(or **Fionn**) Legendary hero assoc. with both Ireland and Scot.

FINNISH *See* URAL-ALTAIC.

FINSBURY
Part of Islington, borough of Greater London (1964), includes Clerkenwell.

FIORD
[fyord] Steep-sided, narrow inlet in the sea coast found in Norway, Greenland, W. Scot., and S. Island, New Zealand.

FIR
General name for various resinous cone-bearing trees yielding useful timber. The silver fir, *Abies alba*, abounds in C. and S. Europe, often reaching 90 ft. The Norway spruce fir, *Picea abies*, may reach 170 ft. Other genera yield the hemlock, Douglas and Jap. parasol firs. The needle-like leaves of firs grow singly on the shoots, not in sheathed clusters, as in larches and pines: the Scotch fir is *Pinus sylvestris*.

Douglas fir cone

FIRE BRIGADES
All large towns and cities maintain, from public funds, trained fire brigades equipped with mobile appliances. The first scientifically organised fire-fighting brigade in Gt. Brit. was set up in 1833. Prior to 1833 fire brigades were maintained by Insurance Companies for protection of properties insured by them against fire. During World War II fire-fighting was an important part of the defence organisation against air raids in Gt. Britain. Local brigades were strengthened in men and equipment, known during 1941-7 as the Nat. Fire Service. Since World War II great advances have been made in fire-fighting and fire prevention.

FIRE DAMP
Term applied by miners to methane or marsh gas, in coal mines. When mixed with air it explodes with great violence in contact with a naked flame, hence the necessity for the use of safety lamps.

FIREFLY
Name of certain types of beetles which possess luminous organs. The firefly of trop. Amer. belongs to the group of click beetles and is remarkable for the brilliance of the light it emits.

FIREWORKS
Devices or preparations of an explosive or inflammable nature used chiefly for purposes of display. Pyrotechny has been known in the E. from remote times. Pyrotechnic compositions

consist of substances such as charcoal and sulphur, which ignite or explode in contact with an oxygen yielding substance, such as nitre or chlorate of potash. Their manufacture is supervised by the Home Office, and is carried on under strictly controlled conditions.

FIRKIN
Measure used in Scot. for liquids, chiefly beer. It equals 9 gallons. A firkin of butter weighs 56 lb.

FIRST AID
Term used for treatment or repair given in case of sudden illness, accident or mechanical breakdown which will allow of work to be continued or transportation to more suitable surroundings where full scale remedies can be applied. As the result of wars, knowledge of First Aid to the injured is widespread and its further development and teaching is fostered by St. John Ambulance Assoc., Brit. Red Cross Soc. and St. Andrews Ambulance Soc.

FIRST OFFENDER
In Eng. and Scots. law, a criminal who has committed only one offence. In 1887 a law was passed empowering magistrates to bind over such persons to be of good behaviour instead of sending them to prison for minor offences. Today first offenders are often put in charge of a probation officer as provided for by an Act of 1907.

FIRST REPUBLIC *See* FRANCE.

FISH
Loosely applied to include marine mammals, *e.g.* Whales, Dugongs; amphibia such as Newts; and a number of invertebrates, *e.g.* Cuttle-fish, shell-fish, and star-fish, it properly denotes a class of cold-blooded vertebrates living in water and breathing through gills. The body is usually covered with scales and the limbs, when present, are represented by paired fins. Reproduction is mainly by eggs fertilised after being spawned. The preservation of fish for food purposes is a large industry. At Yarmouth and elsewhere in Brit. the curing of herrings is carried out on a large scale. Salmon and other fish are canned, an important industry in Brit. Columbia and California. Cod is cured in Newfoundland and Norway. Sardines and anchovies are prepared and packed in oil in Fr., Italy and Spain. To conserve the supply of fish, hatcheries have been estabd. for several freshwater species in Brit.

FISHER, Geoffrey Francis
(1887-) Archbp. of Canterbury (1945-61). Took holy orders, 1913. Headmaster of Repton, 1914-32. Became Archbp. of Canterbury, 1945, in succession to Dr. Temple. Ret. May 1961. Life Peerage conferred, he took the title of Lord F. of Lambeth.

FISHER, John
(*c.* 1469-1535) Eng. prelate. In 1527 he refused his assent to the declaration that the mar. of Henry VIII to Catherine of Aragon was unlawful, and in 1534 refused to swear to the Act of Succession. He was beheaded for refusing to recognise Henry as head of the ch. and beatified, 1886.

FISHGUARD
Urban district and port of Pembrokeshire, 12 m. N. of Haverfordwest. There is a steamer service with Cork, Waterford and Rosslare, Ireland. Pop. 4,880.

FITZGERALD, Edward
(1809-83) Eng. tr. and poet. B. Woodbridge in Suffolk. Lived quietly in Suffolk; a friend of Carlyle and Tennyson, his celebrity is due to his study of Persian and tr. of *Rubáiyát* of Omar Khayyám, pub. anonymously (1859, and 68, 72, 79, with considerable variations).

FITZROY
River of Queensland, Australia, formed by the union of the Dawson and Mackenzie. Rockhampton stands at the head of navigation.

FIUME
[fewm-, fem'-mā] or **Rijeka.** Seaport and city of Yugoslavia, on the E. coast of the Istrian peninsula, 40 m. S.E. of Trieste. There are some manufactures but the chief industry is shipping. Until 1914 it was part of Austria-Hungary. In 1920 it was made an indep. state, but was ceded to Italy 4 years later. After World War II it was occupied by Yugoslavia and ceded to her by the treaty of 1947. Pop. 100,000.

FIVES
Game of handball for 2 or 4 players. It is played in a court enclosed completely or on 3 sides; the ball is played with the hand. The game dates from the 14th cent. In Brit. the game is played mostly at public schools.

FLAG
Popular name of various flowering herbs, with sword-shaped leaves. Several species of iris are known as flags, *e.g.* the yellow flag, common throughout Brit. and the blue and white flags, equally common in C. and S. Europe. The **sweet flag,** *Acorus calamus,* is rare in Eng. and naturalised in Scot. and Ireland. The **corn flag** is a *Gladiolus,* the **cat-tail flag** is the reed mace.

FLAG
Piece of material, usually oblong, with a distinctive design, flown as a symbol or sign. Each country has its national flag. The Union Jack is the nat. flag of Brit., and the Tricolour of Fr. It is customary to fly them at half-mast on the d. of an important person. Nat. flags are also flown over embassies and consulates. A sovereign has his standard or flag which is flown over the house in which he is at the time residing. Every ship, merchantman or warship, shows her nationality by her flag. The flag of the Brit. Navy is the White Ensign; ships of the Royal Naval Reserve and the Royal Yacht Squadron wear the Blue Ensign; the mercantile marine flies the Red Ensign. In the army the flags of regts. are known as colours. *See* ENSIGN.

FLAGSHIP
A warship from which an admiral commands a squadron of ships and which wears a distinctive flag to denote his presence. The *Victory* was Nelson's flagship at Trafalgar; the *Iron Duke* Jellicoe's at Jutland. A flagship, like any other vessel, has her own capt. and officers.

FLAGSTONE
Hard, fine-grained sandstone capable of being split into thin slices. It has a close texture, great durability and a non-slippery surface, and is used for paving stones, steps, etc. York stones, comprises stones varying in colour from whitish to blue, brown and mottled. The Craigleith flagstone from Scot. is a whitish grey.

FLAMBOROUGH HEAD
Chalk promontory on the coast of the E. Riding, Yorks. with a lighthouse and numerous caves.

FLAME
Burning gaseous matter. Normally due to its union with oxygen in the air, when the temp. is raised sufficiently. In a coal fire the temp. of the flame is seldom above 1,000° C. A Bunsen burner may reach 1,800° C. and an oxy-acetylene flame 3,500° C.

FLAME FLOWER
Perennial flowering herb. Also called the red-hot poker, it is native to S. Africa, but flourishes in Brit.

FLAMINGO
Tall wading birds intermediate between ducks and storks. They are widely distributed in the warmer regions except Australia, and are long-

FLAGS · 1

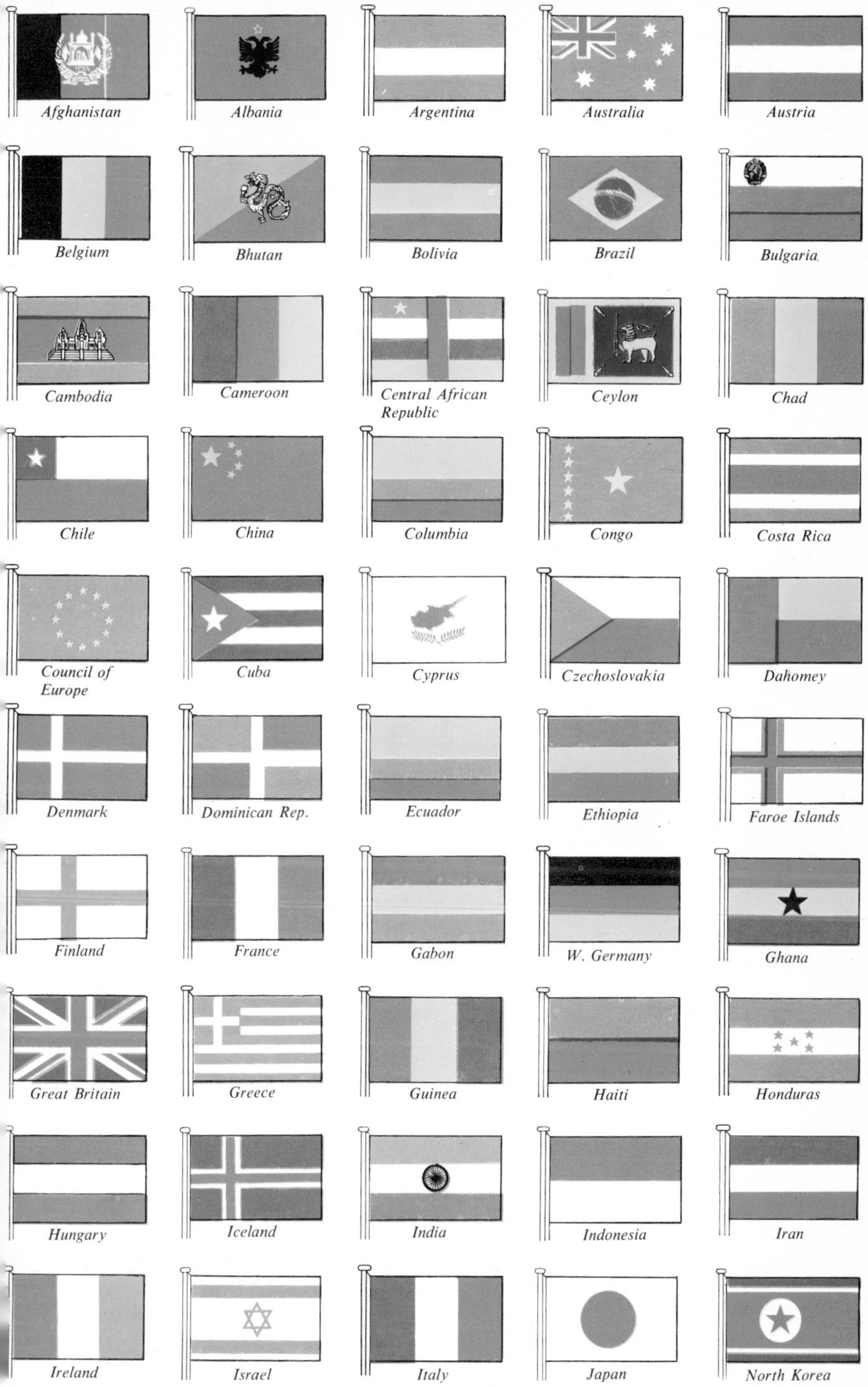
Afghanistan
Albania
Argentina
Australia
Austria
Belgium
Bhutan
Bolivia
Brazil
Bulgaria
Cambodia
Cameroon
Central African Republic
Ceylon
Chad
Chile
China
Columbia
Congo
Costa Rica
Council of Europe
Cuba
Cyprus
Czechoslovakia
Dahomey
Denmark
Dominican Rep.
Ecuador
Ethiopia
Faroe Islands
Finland
France
Gabon
W. Germany
Ghana
Great Britain
Greece
Guinea
Haiti
Honduras
Hungary
Iceland
India
Indonesia
Iran
Ireland
Israel
Italy
Japan
North Korea

FLAGS · 2

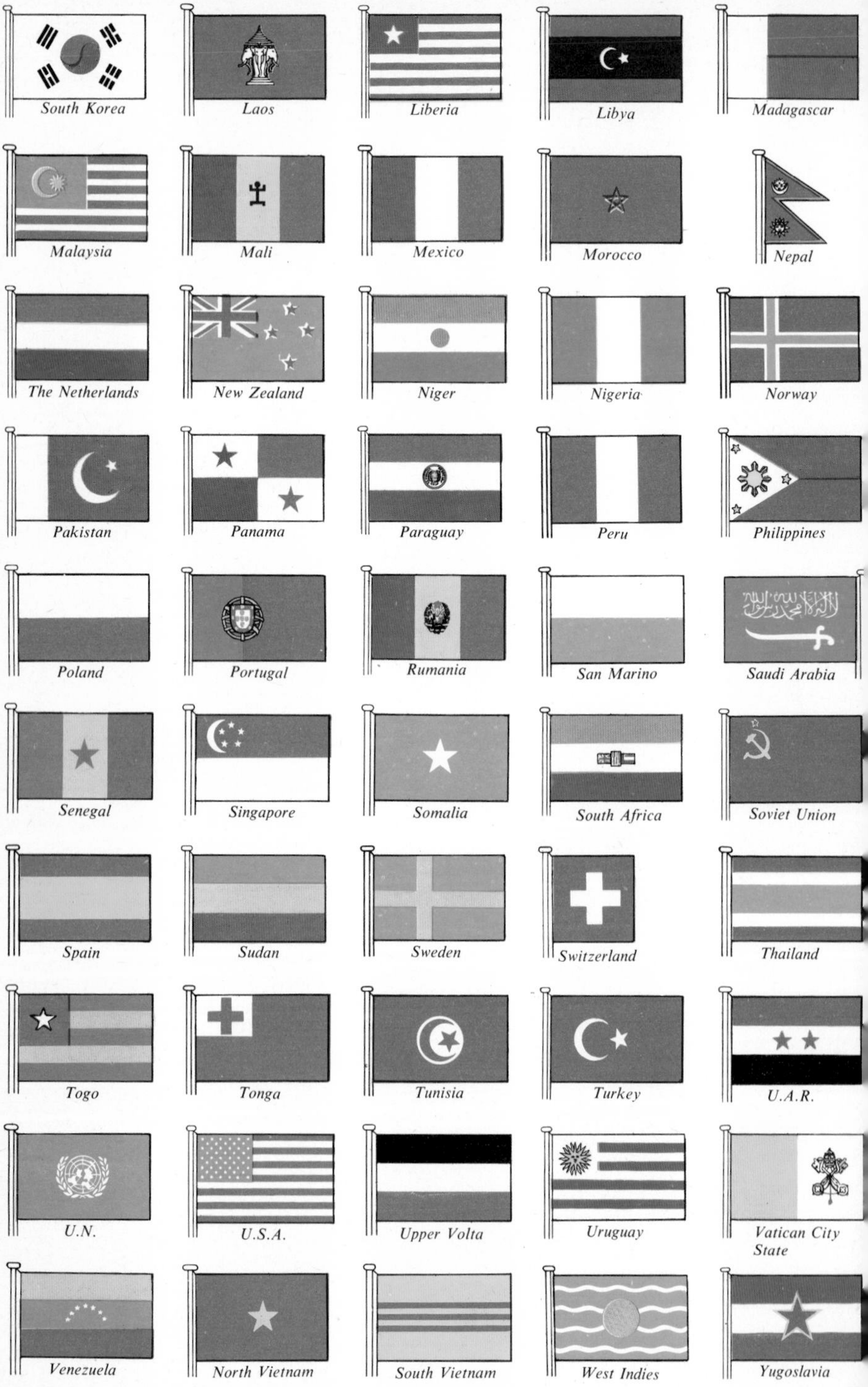

South Korea · Laos · Liberia · Libya · Madagascar

Malaysia · Mali · Mexico · Morocco · Nepal

The Netherlands · New Zealand · Niger · Nigeria · Norway

Pakistan · Panama · Paraguay · Peru · Philippines

Poland · Portugal · Rumania · San Marino · Saudi Arabia

Senegal · Singapore · Somalia · South Africa · Soviet Union

Spain · Sudan · Sweden · Switzerland · Thailand

Togo · Tonga · Tunisia · Turkey · U.A.R.

U.N. · U.S.A. · Upper Volta · Uruguay · Vatican City State

Venezuela · North Vietnam · South Vietnam · West Indies · Yugoslavia

necked and long-legged. Their beaks serve as scoops when the head is twisted upside down. They are found in great flocks, particularly near the great lakes in C. Asia. The European *Phoenicopterus roscus* breeds in the Medit. region, and makes conical mud nests. The plumage is rosy white, with black marks on the wings.

FLAMSTEED, John
(1646-1719) Eng. clergyman and 1st Astron. Royal. B. Denby, Derbyshire, and educ. at Camb. On the estab. of the Royal Observatory at Greenwich in 1675 he was apptd. Astron. Royal by Charles II. He pub. his catalogue of the fixed stars.

FLANDERS
Name given to a district of the Low Countries now comprising Nord and Pas de Calais depts. in Fr. E. and W. Flanders prov. in Belgium and the S. part of Zeeland in the Netherlands. From 1385 to 1477 it was part of Burgundy and later a Sp. possession. In the 17th cent. Fr. acquired a portion and in 1830 the remainder became the kingdom of Belgium. In both World Wars there was heavy fighting in Flanders.

FLAT-FISH
Fishes like plaice, dab, sole, etc. with compressed and flattened bodies, the eyes and nostrils twisted round to the upper side, and the mouth awry. The fish swims on one side, and the under side is colourless; the other, darkly pigmented, changes colour protectively. The transparent and perfectly symmetrical young gradually acquire the asymmetrical form of the adult. Almost all flat-fishes are marine. Common edible species include turbot and halibut.

FLAUBERT, Gustave
(1821-80) Fr. novelist. B. Rouen; studied law; travelled. Pub. 1856, *Madame Bovary*, for which he and his pub. were prosecuted for 'an offence against morals' but were vindicated; *Salammbô* (1862); *L'Education Sentimentale* (1869); *Bouvard et Pécuchet* (unfinished 1881). He was an invalid after 1843. See *Flaubert* by Philip Spencer (1952).

FLAX
Fibre used for linen thread and the plant which produces it. The annual herb, *Linum usitatissimum*, has narrow lance-shaped leaves and purplish-blue flowers. Flax grows in Europe, notably in Russia, also in Ulster, Yorkshire and elsewhere. The tissues of the stems when woven form linen. The seed yields linseed oil, the residue being useful cattle food.

FLEA
Small wingless insects, mostly parasitic on mammals and birds. The mouth parts are adapted for piercing and sucking and the adult insect lives on blood, its bite being troublesome. Owing to the length of its hind legs, the flea is able to leap, in some species, 200 times its own length. The human flea, *Pulex irritans*, breeds in dirty houses. Rat fleas, *Xenopsylla*, convey plague.

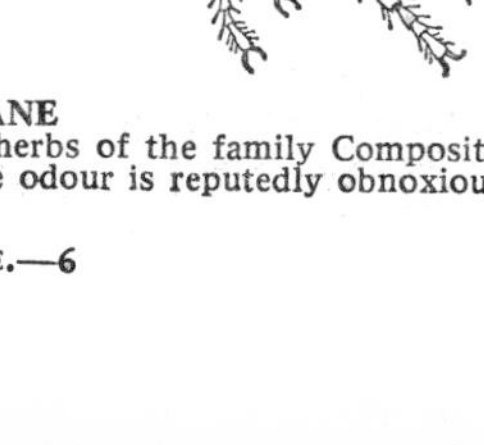

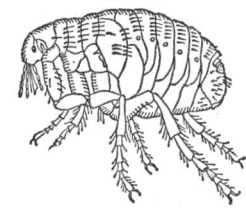

FLEABANE
Several herbs of the family Compositae. Their soap-like odour is reputedly obnoxious to fleas. Two Brit. species of *Pulicaria* extend to India. There are 3 Brit. species of *Erigeron*, and the Canadian species, *E. canadensis*, is naturalised in Brit. Another fleabane, *Inula conyza*, is ploughman's spikenard.

FLECKER, James Elroy
(1884-1915) Eng. poet and dramatist. Educ. Uppingham and Oxford; consular service; d. of tuberculosis at Davos, Switzerland. His works include: *The Golden Journey to Samarkand* (1913) and a play *Hassan* (pub. 1922).

FLEECE
Coat of the living sheep removed at one shear ing. Fleece wools are distinguished from dead wools, which are not derived from the living animal. The fleece, after the shearing with hand or power implements, is roughly trimmed and bundled together ready for baling.

FLEET
River of London, now merely an underground stream. It rose at Hampstead and flowed into the Thames at Blackfriars. It gives its name to **Fleet St. Fleet Prison,** a historic London prison taking its name from the Fleet stream. It is as a prison for debtors that its chief claim to notoriety lies. It was destroyed twice, rebuilt in 1782, and finally sold to the corporation of the city (1844) and pulled down.

FLEET AIR ARM
It originated in 1912 as the Naval Wing of the Royal Flying Corps and was renamed Royal Naval Air Service in 1914. In 1918 the R.F.C. and R.N.A.S. were merged to form one service, the R.A.F. controlled by the Air Ministry. In 1937, ship-borne aircraft were placed under the Admiralty and the Naval air service was named Fleet Air Arm. In World War I, aircraft, mostly seaplanes, were used for reconnaissance, etc. at sea on a limited scale. When World War II began in Sept. 1939, *Hermes*, the first specially designed carrier was in service. *Ark Royal*, the first carrier of post-war design, joined the Fleet in 1939, and was torpedoed off Gibraltar, 1941. During World War II the regular fleet carriers, specially designed light-carriers, and many ships converted for the purpose and equipped with aircraft adapted for use at sea, gave continuous protection to fleets at sea, to convoys and to invading forces.

FLEETWOOD
Borough, port and resort of Lancs. 9 m. from Blackpool. There are steamer services to the Is. of Man. Pop. 28,330.

FLEMING, Sir Alexander
(1881-1955) Brit. bacteriologist and discoverer of penicillin. B. Loudoun, Ayrshire; graduated London; F.R.S. 1943; knighted, 1944; in 1945 shared the Nobel Prize for Medicine with Sir Howard Florey; Prof. of Bacteriology, Univ. of London, from 1928-48; Rector, Edinburgh Univ. 1951. In 1928 a spore of the mould of *penicillium notatum* came through the window of his laboratory. This was found to be deadly to bacteria on his slide. *See* PENICILLIN.

FLEMING, Sir John Ambrose
F.R.S. (1849-1945) Electrical physicist. B. Lancaster, he was Prof. of Electrical Engineering at Univ. Coll. London, 1885-1926. His invention of the thermionic valve, patented in 1904, led to the development of telecommunications, electric light, radio, television, and electronics.

FLEMINGS
Inhabitants of Flanders (*q.v.*). Many of them settled in E. Eng. They brought with them the weaving industry. In the 12th cent. Henry I settled some of them in Pembrokeshire. Today Belgium is inhabited by Flemings, who speak Flemish and inhabit Flanders and other parts in the N.W., and Walloons who speak Fr. and live in the S.E. **Flemish.** W. Germanic language descended from the speech of the Salic Franks settled at mouth of the Scheldt in 1st

cent. B.C. It is spoken by 5,000,000 Belgians and by 200,000 French.

FLETCHER, John
(1579-1625) Eng. dramatist. B. Rye, Sussex. He wrote 30-odd plays, about 15 of them in collaboration with **Francis Beaumont** (1584-1616) and some others with Massinger and Rowley and other dramatists: *The Faithful Shepherdess* (printed by 1610) is his own; *The Knight of the Burning Pestle* (1609), *The Maid's Tragedy* (1611) with Beaumont; *The Two Noble Kinsmen* was pub. in 1634 as by Fletcher and Shakespeare.

FLINDERS, Matthew
(1774-1814) Eng. naval capt. 1795-9, he carried out numerous explorations, made surveys of the Austral. coasts and circumnavigated Tasmania.

FLINT
Opaque cryptocrystalline form of silica, it is dark grey or dark brown, breaks with a shell-like fracture, and occurs in nodules, tabular masses and veins, in the chalk formations of Brit. and W. Europe. Flint was employed for buildings in medieval times. Starting in prehistoric times, flints were struck with iron pyrites to produce fire. The artificial flaking of flints by sharp blows of hammer stones gave rise to flint implements, characteristic of the Stone Age.

FLINTSHIRE
County of N. Wales, between the estuary of the Dee and Denbighshire. It is mainly lowland and is watered by the Dee and Clwyd. Coal and lead are mined; iron and steel, artificial silk, flannel, cement are manufactured, and agriculture is important. Mold is the county town; other towns are Rhyl, Flint, Holywell, Buckley and Prestatyn. F. returns 2 members to Parl. Pop. 150,430. **Flint.** Borough and market town of Flintshire on the estuary of the Dee 12 m. N.W. of Chester. It was an important seaport before the estuary silted up with sand, and was formerly the county town. Industries include chemicals, lead and coal-mining. Pop. 13,790.

FLODDEN
One of the Cheviot Hills, 3 m. from Coldstream and near the Till. A battle was fought here between the Eng. and the Scot. Sept. 9, 1513. The Eng. gained a great victory, James IV and his bodyguard of nobles being among the slain. Flodden was one of the most disastrous events in the hist. of Scot.

FLOOD
Inundation of low-lying ground. Generally caused by an overflow of water from a river. In the case of great rivers such as the Mississippi, Hwang-ho and Nile, floods have played an important part in modifying the features of surrounding areas. Ancient Egyptian, Babylonian and other ancient lits. refer to floods in which whole civilisations perished.

FLORENCE
(*Ital.* **Firenze**) City of Tuscany, Italy, on the Arno, 55 m. from its mouth in the Ligurian Sea. A manufacturing and railway town, it is chiefly a centre of culture, having assocs. with Dante, Boccaccio, Machiavelli, Michelangelo and the Medici family. Among the fine buildings is the great cath. with the campanile by Giotto. Founded by the Roms., Florence became a rich trading town, and from 1250 an independent and powerful city. It was disturbed by the struggle between the Guelphs and Ghibellines. Great prosperity followed, and Florence ruled over most of Tuscany, with Pisa as its seaport. In the 15th cent. the rich family of the Medici (*q.v.*) became masters of Florence. Florence remained the cap. of the grand duchy of Tuscany until 1860, when it was included in the Kingdom of Italy. From 1865-71, Florence was the cap. of Italy. Pop. 438,138.

FLOREY, Sir Howard Walter
(1898-) Pathologist. B. Adelaide, Australia. Became Prof. of Pathology at Oxford 1935. He shared the Nobel Prize for Medicine with Sir A. Fleming (*q.v.*) in 1945.

FLORIDA
State of the U.S.A. in the extreme S.E. It consists mainly of a peninsula between the Atlantic Ocean and the Gulf of Mexico. In the S. is a swampy region, the Everglades. Agriculture is the chief industry, and sugar, rice, cotton, tobacco and trop. fruits are grown. Fishing is important, and there are valuable forest reserves. Tallahassee is the cap. but Jacksonville and Tampa are larger. Miami is a famous resort on the S.E. coast. F. was discovered in 1513, and was bought by the U.S.A. from Spain, 1819, becoming a state in 1849. It sends 12 representatives to Congress. Area: 58,560 sq.m. Pop. 6,789,500.

FLOUNDER
Small flatfish (*Pleuronectes flesus*) allied to the plaice. It is also called the fluke. It inhabits N. European coasts from the Eng. Channel to Iceland, dwelling in river waters and descending to the sea to breed. It rarely exceeds 12 in. in length and 1½ lb. in wt.

FLOUR
Term denoting esp. the ground contents of the wheat seed. Similar meals from other grasses and from non-cereal plants usually bear qualifying or variant names, *e.g.* cornflour, oatmeal and arrowroot. The wheat kernel, which is nine-tenths of the seed, the remainder being skin and germ, consists of starchy matters (73·5 %), gluten and other proteins (11 %), fats and minerals (3·5 %) and water (12 %). *See* WHEAT.

FLOWER
Part of a plant containing the reproductive organs. It is composed, in its most complete form, of 4 distinct whorls of modified leaves. (1) The outer whorl or *calyx* consists of sepals, usually green. (2) The *corolla* consists of petals, often coloured and sometimes forming a tube, their length, form and odour often being adapted to assist insect fertilisation;

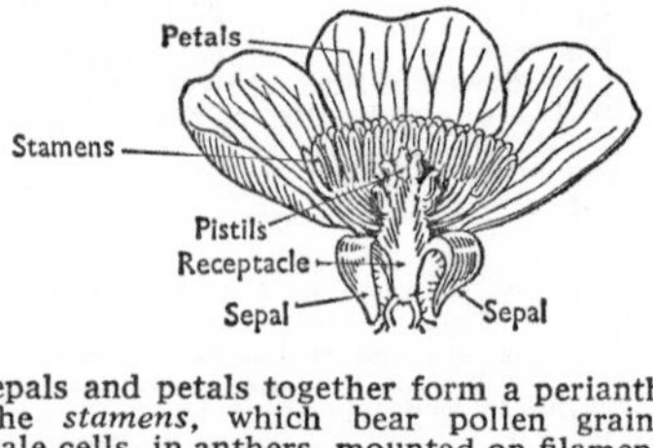

sepals and petals together form a perianth. (3) The *stamens*, which bear pollen grains, or male cells, in anthers, mounted on filaments. (4) The *pistils*, in which ovules, or female cells, in ovaries are surmounted by styles bearing stigmas. Stamens and pistils are essential to reproduction, although in some cases each plant bears flowers of one sex only.

FLUKE
Flat sucker-bearing parasitic worms. The Common Liver Fluke, *Fasciola hepatica*, passes its adult life in the livers of sheep, producing an incurable rot.

FLUORESCENCE
Conversion of short-wavelength radiation (such as X-rays or ultra-violet) into radiation of longer wavelengths (such as visible light). Materials displaying fluorescence include zinc orthosilicate, barium sulphide, calcium tungstate and others. Fluorescent screens are used in cathode-ray oscilloscopes, television sets and in radiography.

FLUORINE
A pale yellow gaseous element, which attacks and decomposes materials, forming fluorides. Discovered by Scheele in 1771. Its density is 1·3 times that of air. Chem. Sym. F.

FLUORSPAR
[floor'-] Mineral consisting of fluorine and calcium, found in veins and often assoc. with lead ore. It may be colourless, yellow, blue, green or violet. In Derbyshire it is known as Blue-John.

FLUSHING
Seaport and resort of the Netherlands, in the Scheldt estuary, with cross-channel services. Pop. 20,600.

FLUTE
A woodwind instrument, consisting of a cylindrical tube *c.* 2 ft. long with a hole in the side, across which the player blows. There are a number of holes opened and closed by the fingers and an elaborate key mechanism. It has an upward compass of 3 octaves from middle C. The smaller flute, the **Piccolo,** has a compass extending an octave above that of the Flute. The **Bass Flute** extends downwards to the G below middle C.

FLY
Name widely used, with or without prefix, for the winged state of many insects. Apart from Butterflies, Dragon flies, May flies and Caddis flies, strictly pertains to the 2-winged order, **Diptera,** and includes Crane flies, House flies, Bot flies, Mosquitoes, Tsetse flies, etc. The mouth parts form a proboscis for piercing and sucking. Some flies are blood-suckers; many others have a destructive maggot state; in some the larvae are parasitic, in some aquatic. The widespread House fly, *Musca domestica,* is a disease carrier and, because of its rapid breeding, a dangerous pest.

FLYCATCHER
Large family of small insectivorous perching birds. They pursue their prey on the wing, and abound in the trop. regions of the world. The Spotted Flycatcher, *Muscicapa striata,* is a summer visitor to Brit. The Pied F., *M. hypoleuca,* frequents hilly, well-wooded districts. The Paradise Flycatchers of E. Asia have brilliant plumage.

FLYING BOAT
Aircraft with a buoyant boat-shaped body which floats in the water. Much used for patrol work by the R.A.F. Coastal Command during World War II.

FLYING BOMB *See* V. WEAPONS.

FLYING DOCTOR SERVICE
Austral. service designed to give speedy aid to anyone taken ill in isolated areas. The system is based on the use of *transceivers* capable of transmitting and receiving vocal messages for distances exceeding 400 m., by means of which cases are discussed and treatment indicated.

FLYING FISH
Name denoting 2 genera of trop. and sub-trop. marine fishes. They are the Flying Herrings, *Exocoetus,* and Flying Gurnards, *Dactylopterus,* Their long pectoral fins, acting when distended as parachutes, sustain them in the air against the wind, sometimes for 500 ft. They fly to escape the attacks of predatory fishes.

FLYING FOX
(*Pteropus*) Fruit bat of the tropics of the old world. The largest is the Javanese Kalong, *P. edulis,* with a wing-spread of 4-5 ft.; others, in India and Queensland, damage gardens. Nocturnal in their habits, they slumber by day head downwards.

FLYING SAUCERS
Colloq. name for mysterious objects mostly of circular shape and of varying sizes. Observers state that they are noiseless, travel at enormous speeds and that they can remain stationary in the air. Reports were at first received with scepticism but there is a growing body of opinion that they have an extra-terrestrial origin.

FLYING SQUID
(*Ommastrephes*) Widespread cuttle-fish, esp. common in the warmer seas of the world. Long and tapering, they leap, by means of their large lateral fins, high out of the water. The Sea Arrow (*O. sagittatus*), frequent in Scot. firths, is a common cod bait off Newfoundland, and an important food of Sperm Whales. It may be 4 ft. in length.

FOCH, Ferdinand
(1851-1929) Fr. soldier. On the outbreak of war in 1870 he joined the army. In 1894 he was appointed Prof. of Milit. Hist. at the Staff Coll. In World War I, Foch became head of the 9th army, which had a great share in the victory of the Marne (Sept. 1914). He was prominent in directing the operations on the Somme, July, 1916. In the following Mar. 1918 he was apptd. generalissimo of all the armies on the W. front, Fr., Br., Amer. and Belgian. In that capacity he controlled the movements of the final advance.

FOG
Atmos. condition of low lying cloud or thick mist, due to the presence of dust particles around which a film of water is deposited when the temp. falls suddenly below dew point. These drops, in the absence of wind, may remain in suspension for a long time and thus form the white fogs of the countryside and the dense black fogs of large towns where sooty particles predominate. Over the sea a current of warm air passing over a cooler layer, or over icy waters, causes condensation to occur, resulting in thick fogs, as off Newfoundland. *See* SMOG.

FOLK-DANCING
Dancing uninfluenced by urban or professional tendencies and peculiar to a particular people, nation or country. The preservation of folk-dancing in Eng. is largely due to the work of Cecil Sharp who founded the Eng. Folk Dance Soc. in 1911. It may be classed under 2 heads (1) social, when it is danced purely as a pastime by all; (2) ceremonial, when performed by selected performers to mark a definite occasion.

FOLKESTONE
Borough, port and resort of Kent, on the Eng. Channel. There is a steamer service with Boulogne. Pop. 44,390.

FONTAINEBLEAU
[-blō'] Fr. town in Seine-et-Marne dept. *c.* 37 m. S.E. of Paris. It is famous for the magnificent palace built by Francis I and improved by later kings.

FONTEYN, Dame Margot
(Peggy Hookham) (1919-) B. Reigate, Surrey. Made her début in 1934 with Sadler's Wells in *The Haunted Ballroom.* As Brit. prima ballerina, she has appeared in most well-known ballets. Mar. Dr. Roberto Arias, Feb. 1955. Undoubtedly owes much of her success to Ninette de Valois (*q.v.*).

FOOD
That which nourishes the body of man and other members of the animal world. Man's food may be divided into 2 classes: the flesh of animals and the produce of the soil. Today, except for certain fruits, nearly all the food eaten by man is cooked or prepared. In general, those who live in cold latitudes require more food, esp. that containing fat. Improved methods of treating the soil, esp. with artificial fertilisers, and new strains of plants have increased output. There is, however, the problem of feeding a constantly increasing population. *See* FOOD AND AGRICULTURAL ORGANISATION. **Diet.** The essentials of a proper diet are

that it should provide for growth and the replacement of waste, that it should furnish the heat and energy required by the body, and also a measure of stimulation to metabolism. Analysis shows that foods are made up of proteins or nitrogeneous substances, carbohydrates, fats, salts, vitamins and water. The proteins, together with mineral matter and water, make good the loss of tissue due to the wear and tear of living; they also go to the making of the secretions of the body. A growing person requires a liberal allowance of proteins, contained in flesh, fish and fowl and also in wheat and other vegetable foods. Proteins also furnish a certain amount of heat and energy, but the proper sources of these are carbohydrates and fats. The amount of heat is calculated according to a unit known as a calorie. The mineral matter in foodstuffs include salts of iron, calcium, magnesium, sodium and potassium, which are necessary in tissue building. Iron is a necessary constituent of the red blood corpuscles, while sodium chloride is a constituent of blood, etc. and the source of hydrochloric acid in the gastric juice. **Regulations and Control.** In Brit. and other civilised countries steps are taken to see that the food sold in the shops is pure. The sale of diseased and unsound food is forbidden and laws prescribe a certain standard of purity. These laws are actively enforced in each county, city or district by inspectors who have power to visit shops and take samples for analysis and, if these are found to be adulterated, the vendors are prosecuted. During World War I (1914-18), the German submarine campaign and the Allied counter-blockade created an acute shortage of food which was rationed in all of the belligerent countries. During World War II rationing was again introduced in Brit. Consumption of meat, tea, sugar, butter, cooking-fats, cheese, milk and bacon was limited, each person being provided with a ration book necessary for the purchase of these foods. A system of ' points ' was worked out in 1940 for the purchase of dried fruit, breakfast cereals, some tinned foods, biscuits, etc. In the yrs. following the war, the food shortage throughout the whole of Europe was acute.

FOOD AND AGRICULTURAL ORGANISATION
Organisation set up by the U.N. in Rome in 1945 to work out a programme for achieving adequate world distribution of food, now has 105 members and associates. A survey in 1946 indicated that ½ world's pop. was underfed, hence production must be doubled. Extensive programmes of research and technical aid have been initiated.

FOOL
A medieval court jester; he wore motley and carried a bauble. At the Feast of Fools (about 1st Jan.) lower clergy of medieval Fr. and Eng. cathedrals burlesqued ch. services.

FOOT
Portion of lower limb below ankle joint. Has a similar construction to that of the hand with 5 metatarsal bones corresponding to 5 metacarpal bones and 14 phalanges corresponding to those of the hand. The most common foot troubles are corns, bunions, blisters, ingrowing toe nails and flat foot. The *treatment* of those conditions falls into the province of the chiropodist.

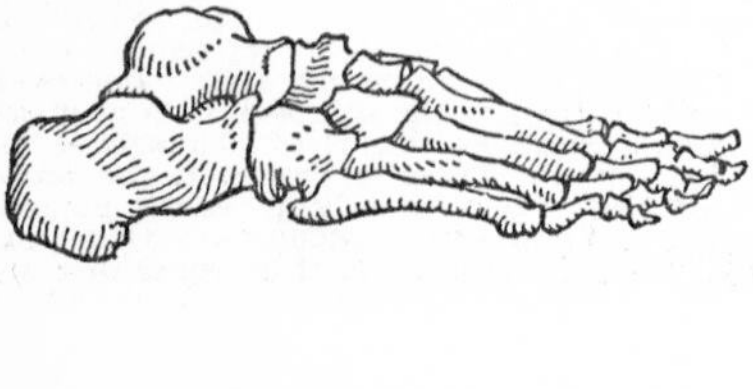

FOOT AND MOUTH DISEASE
Acute contagious fever affecting cattle, sheep, goats and swine and characterised by vesicular lesions of the mouth or feet or both. Disease is scheduled under the Diseases of Animals Act and all diseased animals and those in immediate contact must be slaughtered.

FOOTBALL
Popular ball game at first played by 2 teams of men, without any definite rules. Each side tried by sheer force to get the ball past its adversaries. The public schools each played it according to their own rules, survivals being the wall and field games at Eton and the games at Winchester and Harrow. In the 19th cent. the game was organised and rules drawn up. Of its 2 popular forms the first is the Association game. This is played with a round ball by 11 players on each side. Except by the goalkeeper the hands must not be used, the ball being propelled by the feet or head. Each match is decided by the number of goals scored, these being obtained by kicking the ball between the goal posts. **Association Football,** or soccer, owes its name to the fact that, 1863, a Football Assoc. was formed to draw up a set of rules. In 1871 a challenge cup was presented for competition between the clubs. There are also Scots, Irish and Welsh Assocs. each of which offers a cup. The first players were all amateurs, but soon professionalism was introduced, legalised in 1885. In 1888 a league was formed. Internat. matches are played between the 4 home countries, the players are usually professionals. The 2nd form, **Rugby Union Football,** is played with an oval ball and is a development of the orig. game as played at Rugby School. In 1823 William Webb Ellis picked up the ball and ran with it, and in 1841 this was recognised in the rules. Soon clubs were formed to play the game according to the Rugby rules. The Eng. Rugby Union then came into existence and similar unions were formed in other countries. It has also spread to Fr., Australia, N. Zealand and S. Africa. It is strictly an amateur game. Rugby is played with 15 players a side. There are several methods of scoring, the chief of which is to score a try by grounding the ball behind the opponent's back line. This counts 3 pts. and enables the side gaining it to kick at goal without interference, if the ball goes over the bar and between the posts a further 2 pts. are added. If, while the ball is in play, a dropped goal is scored, 3 pts. are awarded. Internat. matches are played between the 4 home countries, and Fr. From time to time teams from S. Africa, N. Zealand and Australia come to Brit., and Brit. teams go overseas. A 3rd form of football is the **Rugby League game.** This came into existence in 1895 when the Rugby Union refused to allow professionalism. Some Rugby clubs in Lancashire and Yorkshire then broke away, formed the N. Union and began to play a slightly different kind of game. The number of players was reduced from 15 to 13 and other changes made for a more open and spectacular game. This game is much played in Australia, Fr. and N. Zealand. The Rugby League Assoc. now controls the game. Further purely domestic variations of the game have been evolved in the U.S.A., Australia and Canada. Gaelic football (Ireland) is played with a round ball. **Football Pools.** In Brit. some 10,000,000 people participate in this form of gambling. The money thus invested reaches an annual total of *c.* £60,000,000.

FORD, Henry
(1863-1947) Amer. manufacturer. B. Greenfield, Michigan, he became interested in mechanics and experimented in motor car manufacture. In 1903 he started the business that grew into the Ford Motor Co. There are factories at Manchester and Cork, and extensive works at Dagenham. Succeeded as Pres. of Co. by

grandson Henry Ford II, son of Edsel Ford (d. 1943).

FORD, John
(1586-1640) Eng. dramatist. His tragedies include *'Tis Pity She's a Whore* (1633), *Perkin Warbeck* (1634).

FOREIGN LEGION
Corps of the Fr. Army. Trained very rigorously and cut off from European life, the legion has won great reputation as a fighting corps.

FOREIGN OFFICE
Department of the Brit. govt. responsible for all political affairs concerning other countries and which controls all ambassadors and other official representatives abroad. Its head is a sec. of state, usually a cabinet min.

FOREST
Word used orig. for a tract of woodland wherein wild beasts lived. In Europe these were used by the kings for hunting, and forest laws were passed to prevent any interference with this sport. The area under forest is now much reduced. Eng. has very few, the largest being the New Forest. Fr., Germany and other countries have more, while Scot. has extensive areas of deer forests. There are also vast forest areas in Canada, India and other countries, used for timber and state owned. *See* AFFORESTATION.

FORFAR
Burgh and county town of Angus, 15 m. N. of Dundee. There are linen and other manufactures. Pop. 10,319.

FORFARSHIRE *See* ANGUS.

FORGERY
In Eng. and Scots law, the uttering of a false document, or material alteration therein, without authority: also counterfeiting a seal or die. The forging of documents, such as wills, deeds or bank notes is a felony and can be punished by imprisonment for life.

FORGET-ME-NOT
Various annual or perennial herbs (*Myosotis*). Native to temp. regions, the common *M. scorpioides* has rather stout, flexible stems, and sky-blue flowers. The wood forget-me-not, *M. sylvatica*, has bright blue flowers; the Alpine sub-species is a dwarf.

FORMALDEHYDE
HCHO. Simplest of the aldehydes, oxidation products of alcohols. Formaldehyde is produced by passing methyl alcohol vapour over heated platinum. A 40 % solution in water (**formalin**) is a disinfectant, an antiseptic, and renders gelatine insoluble in water. Formaldehyde is of great importance in the manufacture of synthetic resins and plastics.

FORMIC ACID
HCOOH. Simplest of the fatty acids. First obtained from ants by distillation with water, it is now obtained by the distillation of sodium formate with a mineral acid. It has a pungent odour and a blistering effect upon the skin. It is used in dyeing.

FORMOSA *See* TAIWAN.

FORT DE FRANCE
Cap. and chief commercial town of the Is. of Martinique, Fr. W. Indies. Pop. 60,600.

FORT SUMTER
Fort in S. Carolina, U.S.A. on an Is. off Charleston. Its bombardment by the Southerners on Apr. 12, 1861, opened the Amer. Civil War.

FORT WILLIAM
Town and resort of Inverness-shire, 65 m. from Inverness, on the banks of Loch Linnhe. Built 1665, it lies near the S. end of the Caledonian Canal, at the foot of Ben Nevis. Pop. 2,759.

FORTH
River and estuary of S.E. Scot. The river rises in Perthshire and flows to Alloa, where the firth or estuary is said to begin. Stirling stands on its banks, and tributaries include the Teith, Devon and Allan Water. It is navigable by small vessels to Stirling. The estuary from Alloa to the N. Sea at Fife Ness is *c.* 50 m. long. On its banks are Leith, Granton, Grangemouth, Burntisland and Methil. **The Forth Railway Bridge** carries the line from S. Queensferry in W. Lothian to N. Queensferry in Fife. Designed by Sir W. M. Arrol (1839-1913), the bridge was begun in 1883 and opened for traffic in 1890. It is 1 mile 972 yds. long and consists of a S. Viaduct (10 spans) a N. approach viaduct (8 spans) and 2 great central spans. The clearance above high-water mark is 150 ft.; the piers are 340 ft. high. The cost was £3,000,000. The **Forth Road Bridge**, opened 1964, is a suspension bridge with a span of 3,300 ft. The two 24-ft. carriageways, with cycle tracks and footpaths, stand 150 ft. above the highest tide marks.

FORTRESS
Place suitable for defence protected by some artificial works, *e.g.* walls, ditches, etc. Orig. a mound with wood fences, stone fortresses were used by the Gks., *e.g.* at Troy. The medieval castle was a highly developed form, rendered useless by the invention of artillery.

FORUM
[faw'-] In Rom. times any open place devoted to public business. It was the official centre of a city's public and corporate life, and was usually surrounded by its chief public buildings, and often ornamented with statues.

FOSSIL
Traces of plants or animals in the earth's crust, where they have been embedded by geological agencies. The dating of strata by fossils is fundamental in geological research. The effect of time may be to alter the form or chem. constitution of buried organisms by petrifaction. Thus, molluscan shells may be preserved unchanged, may be converted into silica, or may disappear, leaving only an external or internal cast. Rocks may perpetuate traces of footprints and even rain drops.

FOTHERINGHAY
Village of Northants. on the Nene, 4 m. N.E. of Oundle. In the castle Mary Queen of Scots was tried and executed (1587).

FOUCHÉ, Joseph
Duke of Otranto (1763-1820) Fr. statesman. Elected to Nat. Convention, 1792; voted for execution of Louis XVI. From 1799-1815, though with interruptions, was Min. of Police. Pres. of Council under Louis XVIII, with whom he intrigued before Napoleon's fall.

FOURTH DIMENSION
The three dimensions of length, breadth (or width) and thickness are generalisations or abstractions founded on our normal sense-perceptions. The mathematician postulates a 4th dimension and this has been confirmed, esp. in the work of Einstein, who, in his theory of relativity, suggests a dimension which welds indivisibly the 3 spatial dimensions with that of time to form a curved 'continuum', *i.e.* space-time.

FOWEY
[foy] Borough and resort of Cornwall, on the estuary of the Fowey, 10 m. S. of Bodmin. There is a good harbour, with some shipping and fishing. Pop. 2,090.

FOX
(*Vulpes alepex*) The common Brit. fox averages 4 ft. in length, including the tail, is 14 in. high, weighs from 15-22 lb. and is reddish-brown with white-tipped hairs. The female is known as a vixen and the young as cubs. The N. Amer. Silver or Black Fox yields a silver-tipped, black fur. The Arctic Fox, *V. lagopus*, is entirely white in winter or may be slaty-blue

throughout the year. **Foxhunting.** Brit. sport at least 300 years old. Foxes are hunted chiefly in the Shires of Leicester, Northampton and Warwick in Eng. Among the most famous Hunts are the Pytchley, Buccleuch, Beaufort, Quorn and Belvoir. A pack of foxhounds usually numbers approx. 35-couple. Conventional rules of conduct on the hunting field are strictly observed.

FOX, Charles James
(1749-1806) Eng. politician. M.P. (Whig), 1769-1806. Fox favoured the reform of Parl., Catholic emancipation, and Amer. indep. His support for the Fr. Revolution and opposition to Pitt cost him Burke's friendship and much support.

FOX, George
(1624-91) Founder of the Soc. of Friends. He became a shoemaker, but gave his time to preaching. He believed in the guidance of the inner light. He soon had followers in many places. These met regularly for worship and were called Quakers.

FOX TERRIER
House dog with smooth or wire-haired coat. Both smooth and rough-coated are black and white or liver and white in colour. Fox terriers are compact, clean-legged, cat-footed and straight-fronted. Excellent ratters, they weigh *c.* 16 lb.

FOXE, John
(1516-87) Eng. martyrologist. Soon after the accession of Mary he went to Frankfurt, where he met Knox. In 1562-3 he pub. his great work, popularly known as *The Book of Martyrs.*

FOXGLOVE
Genus of hardy biennial or perennial herbs (*Digitalis*), natives of Europe, W. Asia and N. Africa. The only Brit. foxglove, *D. purpurea*, has spikes of drooping, thimble-shaped pink flowers, spotted inside. The leaves yield digitalin used in medicine.

FOXHOUND
Breed of hound maintained for fox hunting. It averages 20 or 22 in. in ht. It is notable for fleetness, strength, fine scent, endurance and subordination.

FRACTION
In maths. any part of a unit. In common or vulgar fractions the number above the bar is termed the numerator and the number beneath the bar the denominator. Thus in the fraction $\frac{3}{8}$, 3 is the numerator and 8 the denominator. In decimal fractions, the denominator is 10 or some power of 10, a dot or decimal point being placed before the number. Thus ·1 represents 1-tenth, ·325 equals 3-tenths plus 2-100ths plus 5-1,000ths. *See* DECIMAL.

FRAGONARD, Jean Honoré
[frag-ō-nar'] (1732-1806) Fr. artist. B. Grasse, he made a reputation with pictures of contemporary life and landscapes.

FRANCE
Repub. of W. Europe stretching from the Eng. Channel to the Pyrenees and the Medit., and from the Atlantic E. to the land frontiers of Belgium, Germany, Switzerland and Italy. The N. and W. of the country is lowland, broken only by the hills of Brittany and Normandy; the S. and E. is highland, including the great plateau of the Massif Central, the Cévennes and Fr. Alps, the Jura and Vosges Mts. The chief rivers are the Loire and Garonne, flowing W. to the Bay of Biscay, the Seine and Somme entering the Eng. Channel, and the Rhône flowing S. into the Medit. The climate is of a maritime type, modified to the E. by the mts. In the extreme S. the climate is Medit. Fr. is a great agricultural country. A great quantity of wine is produced and exported, *e.g.* in the Bordeaux, Burgundy and Champagne districts. Fruits are grown. There are many industrial centres, such as Paris and Lyons and the district in the N.E. where there is a valuable field of coal and iron ore. Large quantities of silk and cotton goods, iron, steel and chems. are exported. The fisheries are valuable. Paris is the cap. and largest city. Next in size are Marseilles, the great seaport, Lyons, Toulouse, Bordeaux, Nice, Nantes, Lille, St. Etienne and Strasbourg. Before the Revolution, Fr. was divided into provs. and some of these retain something of their old indep. life. Today the country is divided into 90 depts., including the Is. of Corsica. The head of the govt. is the Pres. who is elected for 7 years by direct universal suffrage according to the 1962 amendment to the Constitution. (In 1965 General de Gaulle was re-elected by this method.) He presides over the Council of Ministers and appoints the P.M. Pop. 46,520,000. Area: 212,919 sq.m. As part of the Rom. Empire, Fr. was one of the most civilised regions of Europe. Later it was conquered by the Franks and became part of the empire founded by Charlemagne. Early in the 11th cent. it had its own kings, but much of the land was under powerful dukes and counts. In the later M.A. the hist. of Fr. is largely one of wars with Eng. This period ended in the 15th cent. and then Fr. under the Valois and later the Bourbon kings, became the most centralised monarchy in Europe. The kingdom reached the height of its glory under Louis XIV (1643-1715), when it led the social life of Europe. It was at that time a great milit. nation, and enjoyed a great flowering of intellectual life, but there was also extravagance and corruption and great injustice towards the poor. The Revolution destroyed the monarchy and set up a repub. in 1790. Then came the empire of Napoleon which ended in 1815, after which the Bourbon monarchy was restored. This lasted until 1830, when Louis Philippe became king; he was overthrown in 1848 and a 2nd repub. estabd. From this Louis Napoleon emerged as the Emperor Napoleon III and reigned until 1870. The 3rd Repub. was created after the Franco-Prussian War in 1871. It carried through to World War I and when peace was achieved, turned to the task of restoring and strengthening Fr. It was allied with Brit. in 1939 and overrun by the Germans in 1940, being partially occupied. The Govt. under Marshal Pétain, was transferred from Paris to Vichy. Gen. de Gaulle formed a provisional Nat. Govt. in Eng. and estabd. the Free Fr. movement. The country was liberated in 1944. A new constitution was accepted in 1946 and Vincent Auriol became pres. of the 4th Repub. This was dissolved in 1958 and the 5th Repub. inaugurated under Gen. de Gaulle. *See* FRENCH REVOLUTION.

FRANCE, Anatole
(**Jacques Anatole Thibault**) (1844-1924) Fr. novelist. B. Paris. Noted as a free-thinker, socialist, polit. satirist. *Jocaste et le Chat Maigre* (1879), *L'île des Pingouins* (1908), *La Révolte des Anges* (1914); and crit. works.

FRANCIS
Name of 2 Emperors. **Francis II** (1768-1835) Emperor of Austria and the Holy Rom. Empire, was the brother of Marie Antoinette, and from 1792-1814 was often at war with Fr. His daugh-

ter, Marie Louise, became Napoleon's wife, but in 1813 he joined the allies and assisted in the final defeat of the emperor. Francis was the last emperor of the Holy Rom. Empire, which was dissolved in 1806, and the first Emperor of Austria.

FRANCIS
Name of 2 kings of Fr. **Francis I** (1494-1547) mar. in 1514, Claude, daughter of Louis XII, and succeeded to the throne in 1515. His reign was largely occupied by his wars against the Emperor Charles V. His son became Henry II. **Francis II** (1541-60) Eldest son of Henry II and Catherine de Medici. He mar. Mary Stuart in 1558 and in 1559 succeeded as king.

FRANCIS of Assisi, St.
(1182-1226) B. at Assisi in Umbria. A serious illness led to his conversion, and he devoted his life to poverty, self-denial, and the service of the poor. He formed a brotherhood which received papal sanction in 1210 and became the great *Franciscan Order* devoted to poverty, work and service. Some missions still survive.

FRANCIS FERDINAND
(1863-1914) Aust. archduke, nephew to the emperor Francis Joseph. On the d. of the Crown Prince (1889) he became heir-apparent. Whilst on a visit to Bosnia, he and his wife were assassinated at Sarajevo, an event which precipitated World War I.

FRANCIS JOSEPH
(1830-1916) Emperor of Austria and king of Hungary. He was the eldest son of the Archduke Francis, a grandson of the Emperor Francis II and a member of the house of Habsburg. His 60 years' reign was one of nat. and personal misfortune. The defeat of Austria by Prussia in 1866 was the end of her long dominance in German affairs. With innate stubbornness the emperor held on, and towards the end took the fatal step of attacking Serbia, after the murder of his nephew and heir, **Francis Ferdinand.**

FRANCK, César Auguste
[frā(ng)k] (1822-90) Belgian composer. He settled in Paris in 1844. He was a prolific composer but his works are uneven in quality. He wrote organ music, a symphony, Prelude, Chorale and Fugue for Piano, a sonata for Violin and Piano, and a Piano Quintet.

FRANCO, Francisco
(1892-) Sp. gen. and dictator. Chief-of-Staff, 1935; organised milit. revolt, July, 1936, and proclaimed himself Caudillo and C.-in-C. Oct. 1936. Revolt threw Spain into Civil War (1936-9) in which Franco was aided by Mussolini and Hitler. Joined Anti-Comintern Pact, 1939; during World War II Spain maintained neutrality but had Fascist sympathies. Form of govt. is authoritarian, and the 'Falange' (Sp. Fascist Party) is the sole permitted polit. organisation.

FRANCO-PRUSSIAN WAR
Struggle in 1870-1 between Fr. and Prussia. There was some tension because Napoleon III, then ruling Fr., objected to the selection of a German prince as king of Spain. Bismarck, who wished to weaken Fr., precipitated the struggle by altering and publishing a telegram from Ems which made it appear that the King of Prussia had insulted the Fr. Ambassador. War was declared by Fr. on July 19. German victories forced a large Fr. army to take refuge in Metz. The decisive Battle of Sedan ended in the surrender of Napoleon and his army. The Germans then besieged Paris from Sept. 20 until its surrender in Jan. 1871. Fr. agreed to surrender Alsace-Lorraine and to pay a huge indemnity. At Versailles, Jan. 18, 1871, William I of Prussia was declared Emperor.

FRANKFURT-ON-MAIN
W. German city and river port in Hessen, 22 m. N.E. of Mainz. It early became a free city; it was the meeting place of the diet of the German Confederation, from 1816-66 when it became part of Prussia. Before World War II it was a banking and rly. centre, with considerable river trade and numerous industries. Pop. 674,079.

FRANKFURT-ON-ODER
City of E. Germany near the Polish frontier, 50 m. S.E. of Berlin. It belonged to the Hanseatic League in the M.A. and is now a shipping and manufacturing centre. Pop. 76,000.

FRANKLIN, Benjamin
F.R.S. (1706-90) Amer. politician and scientist. B. Boston. In 1723 he settled in Philadelphia but soon went to London. Returning to Philadelphia he became owner of *The Pennsylvania Gazette*, and in 1732 started the popular *Poor Richard's Almanac.* In 1757, Franklin went to London, and remained there until 1762 and from 1764-75. In 1776 he helped to draw up the Declaration of Indep. and went to Paris where he arranged for the help of Fr. in the struggle with Brit. He was Pres. of the State from that time until he retired in 1788, and helped to draw up the constitution of the U.S.A. Much of his time was spent in scientific research, particularly on electricity.

FRANKLIN, Sir John
(1786-1847) Eng. explorer. In 1845 he set out in search of the N.W. Passage, and for many years nothing was heard of him. In 1859 a paper was found giving some record of the voyage and of the d. of Franklin and the entire expedition. It proved also that he had actually discovered the N.W. Passage.

FRANKS
Name given to some European tribes, first heard of in the 3rd cent. along the lower courses of the Rhine. By the 4th cent. these were collected into 2 groups, the *Ripuarian Franks* and the *Salian Franks.* Under the leadership of Clovis, the Salian Franks moved into what is now Fr. and in 481 he was made their king. In the 9th cent. when their land had extended in all directions, the Franks again broke into 2 divisions. The W. Franks remained in Fr. whilst the E. Franks founded what later became Germany.

FRASER
River of Brit. Columbia, Canada, which rises in the Rocky Mts. near the Yellowhead Pass, and follows a 750 m. course before entering the sea near Vancouver. Famous for its salmon and scenery.

FRAY BENTOS
[frī-] Port of Uruguay, cap. of Rio Negro dept. 120 m. from Buenos Aires, famous for its meat packing industry. Pop. 18,000.

FRAZER, Sir James George
(1854-1941) Brit. scholar. B. Glasgow; educ. privately. His life was spent in studying comparative religion and its assocs. with folklore and mythology and this led to publication in 1890 of *The Golden Bough.*

FREDERICK
Name of 2 Holy Roman Emperors. **Frederick I** (1124-90) known as **Barbarossa** (Redbeard) belonged to the Hohenstaufen family. In 1155 he was crowned Emp. in Rome. To Germany he was a strong and resolute ruler, crushing the Dukes who opposed him. In Italy he was involved in quarrels with the Papacy. In 1189 he set out on a Crusade, and was drowned. **Frederick II** (1194-1250) son of the Emperor Henry VI, was chosen German King in 1196. In 1212 he was crowned king, but had to fight to estab. his position. In 1220, in Rome, he was crowned Emperor by the Pope, and in 1228, having spent some years in Sicily, he went on

a Crusade and was crowned King of Jerusalem. His sons, Henry and Conrad had in turn risen against him. Brilliantly versatile, he was known as *Stupor Mundi*—Wonder of the World.

FREDERICK
(1596-1632) King of Bohemia. Son of Frederick IV, Elector Palatine of the Rhine. In 1613 he mar. Elizabeth, daughter of James I, and in 1619, being a Protestant, he was elected King of Bohemia. His enemies were too strong for him. From 1623 until his d. Frederick was an exile. Among his children were Sophia, Electress of Hanover, mother of George I.

FREDERICK IX
(1899-) King of Denmark, son of Christian X; succeeded to the throne 1947. He mar. Ingrid, granddaughter of Gustavus V of Sweden, and has 3 daughters, the eldest of whom is the heir to the throne, the Salic Law having been revoked, 1953.

FREDERICK II
(1712-86) King of Prussia called **the Great.** B. Berlin, son of Frederick William I. He had a very unhappy childhood, and was a virtual prisoner for some years. Later he mar. a princess of Brunswick, corresponded with Voltaire, read much in Fr. In 1740, Frederick became king, and almost at once made war on Austria. His aim was to obtain Silesia. In 1756 the Seven Years' War began. The odds against Prussia, aided only by Brit. were immense, but her king performed miracles both as general and administrator. His country was utterly exhausted when peace was made in 1763. For the rest of his reign, ruling as an absolute monarch, he did much to restore its prosperity. The king wrote a great deal, always in Fr., and his writings have been pub. in 33 vols.

FREDERICTON
Cap. of New Brunswick, Canada, on the St. John, 80 m. from the Bay of Fundy. Industries include lumbering and shipping. Pop. 18,000.

FREE CHURCH OF SCOTLAND
Formed by opponents of private patronage at the disruption of the Ch. of Scot. in 1843. They formed a new ch., joined in 1876 by the Reformed Presbyterian Ch. In 1900 the Free Ch. and the United Presbyterian Ch. were united as the **United Free Church of Scot.,** and in 1939 there was a union of this body and the estabd. ch. The present Free Ch. of Scot. consists of those members of the original Free Ch. who refused to unite with the United Presbyterian Ch. The Ch. has its own Theological Coll. in Edinburgh. The curriculum is recognised by Scot. Universities, and Free Ch. students are eligible for the Degree of B.D.

FREEMAN
One who is not a slave. In early soc. there was a sharp distinction between freemen and slaves, this being the case in Greece and Rome, as well as among the Germanic tribes, the freemen forming the fighting and governing class. Gradually, as slaves became free, the distinction disappeared. By the end of the 15th cent. serfdom had disappeared in Brit. In other European countries the same process took place, but at a slower rate. The word freeman was then used in Eng. for a man who had the right to take part in the govt. of the city or borough in which he lived. These privileges were greatly abused, and in 1835 they were swept away. London was an exception, and there freemen still remain. A 3rd kind of freeman came into existence in the 19th cent. These are men of distinction who are given the honorary freedom of a city or borough, now a popular way of recognising distinguished services to the state or community.

FREEMASONRY
Secret brotherhood which flourished in ancient Egypt and was known throughout the ancient world. It teaches by use of ritual, allegory and symbol the practice of every moral and social virtue, esp. that of charity. The ritual has changed, but the spiritual principles remain unchanged, and have been transmitted in unbroken succession via Egypt, Greece, Rome and the M.A. The first Grand Lodge was estabd. in Eng. in 1717, in Ireland in 1730 and in Scot. in 1736. The date of its advent in the U.S.A. is uncertain, but a lodge was estabd. in Boston in 1733. The organisation consists of a no. of lodges each with its own Master and elected office bearers. Regular meetings are held at which with impressive ceremonial, degrees are conferred on candidates. The lodges are united under Provincial Grand Masters. Over all is the United Grand Lodge. On the continent Freemasonry has frequently become involved in politics, and this has occasionally led to its suppression. It is condemned as a 'secret soc.' by the R.C. ch.

FREETOWN
Cap. of Sierra Leone, W. Africa. A naval and commercial port, F. has rly. connections with the interior. Pop. 85,000.

FREEZING POINT
Temp. at which a liquid changes to the solid state. For water at atmos. pres. it is 0° C. (32° F.). Under great pressures, the freezing pt. is lowered about 1° C. for a pressure of 130 atmospheres.

FREMANTLE
Principal seaport of W. Australia, 12 m. below Perth. It handles most of the trade of the state, exporting wheat and wool. Pop. *c.* 27,000.

FRENCH GUIANA
[gē-ā'-nă] Fr. overseas dept. on the N. coast of S. Amer. with Dutch Guiana on the W. and Brazil on the E. and S. Under the admin. of Fr. Guiana is a group of islands known as Iles du Salut. There are extensive forests. The chief crops are rice, cocoa and sugar. Gold mining is important. Cayenne is the cap. Area: 35,000 sq.m. Pop. 33,000.

FRENCH GUINEA *See* GUINEA.

FRENCH POLYNESIA
Fr. overseas territory in the E. Pacific consisting of the Society Is., Marquesas, Tuamotu group, Leeward Is. and the Gambier, Austral and Rapa Is. The most important Is. is Tahiti, chief town Papeete. Area: 1,545 sq.m. Pop. 85,000.

FRENCH REVOLUTION
Overthrow of the estabd. monarchical govt. of Fr. in 18th cent. Main causes were: distressed state of the country as a whole, out of date admin., hopeless confusion of financial system causing heavy taxation of the poor which the rich escaped, widespread corruption and extreme hardship of the poor. The ideas of Voltaire and Rousseau stirred up intellectual discontent with this state of affairs. The actual movement began in 1789 when the States Gen. was called together, for the first time since 1614, and a Nat. Assembly was called. On July 14, 1789, the mob destroyed the Bastille, and there were risings all over the country. The Nat. Assembly turned itself into an assembly for the preparation of a constitution. Many of the nobles fled to Eng. and elsewhere, but the king, Louis XVI, still had many supporters. In June, 1791, he escaped from Paris, but was brought back. The Assembly then decided to make Fr. a constitutional monarchy. Several foreign rulers were now alarmed at the course of events in Fr. and the exiled nobles were urging them to interfere. The Emperor of Austria, brother of Marie Antoinette, the wife of Louis XVI, issued a declaration, demanding that Fr. should restore Louis XVI. The Republican party was gaining strength, foreign interference only added to its influence. In March, 1792, Fr. de-

clared war on Austria. Prussia hastened to the side of Austria, but the Fr. troops defeated the Prussians at Valmy. A Nat. Convention took over the control of affairs. The extremists were now supreme, their leaders being Danton, Robespierre and Marat. A republic was estabd. and on Jan. 21, 1793, after a trial, Louis was executed. In 1793, a Committee of Public Safety was estabd. under Robespierre, and the Reign of Terror began, to exterminate prospective collaborationists. Hundreds of aristocrats and politicians were sent to the guillotine. On Oct. 16, 1793, Marie Antoinette was executed. The revolutionary leaders disagreed among themselves; Robespierre brought about the execution of Danton on April 5, 1794, and himself suffered the same fate on July 28. The Reign of Terror came quickly to an end, but it was not until Oct. 1795, that the Directory was estabd. and the period described as that of the Fr. Revolution was over. See J. H. Thompson's *French Revolution.*

FRENCH SOMALILAND
Former name of Fr. Territory of the Afars and the Isaas on N.-E. coast of Africa. Voted to remain Fr., 1967. Jibuti is the capital. Area: 8,500 sq.m. Pop. 81,000.

FRESHWATER
Resort in the W. of the Is. of Wight, on the Yar, 1½ m. from Yarmouth.

FREUD, Sigmund
[froid] (1856-1939) Austrian scientist. His investigations into neurotic diseases led to his becoming Prof. of the Therapeutics of Neurotic Diseases and of Neurology in Vienna (1902). He explained such phenomena as the mind of the individual being influenced by repressions in the unconscious mind which are subconsciously seeking an outlet. His method of approach, called psycho-analysis, is propounded in many works, *e.g. Delusion and Dream, The Psychopathology of Everyday Life.* See *Sigmund Freud* by E. Jones (1953).

FRIESE-GREENE, William Edward
(1855-1921) Eng. inventor, b. Bristol. He gave his first demonstration of cinematography in 1885 and was the first to appreciate the value of celluloid film. In 1889 his invention was granted a patent.

FRIGATE
Orig. a small, swift, undecked Medit. vessel, using oars or sails. Adopted by Portugal in the 16th and 17th cents. for naval purposes in the Indies, it became a fast, 3-masted, full-rigged scouting and cruising craft, carrying from 24 to 50 guns. In World War II the name was given to a large sloop of *c.* 100 ft. designed for escort and anti-submarine duties.

FRIGATE BIRD
(*Fregala*) Trop. sea fowl, allied to Gannets. The Common *F. aquila* has a small, slender, short-necked body, a straight bill with a hooked tip and a dilatable throat pouch. Its swallow-like tail and great wing spread make it very swift in flight.

FRISIAN ISLANDS
Chain of Is. off the N.W. coast of Europe, extending from the Netherlands to S. Denmark. There are 3 groups, the N., E and W., divided between Denmark, Germany and the Netherlands. **Frisian.** The Germanic language closest to Eng.; spoken in Friesland and Frisian Is.

FRITILLARY
(1) A flowering plant allied to the lily with only one species, *Fritillaria meleagris*, endemic in Brit. It is plentiful in E. and S. England. (2) Name also given to various butterflies *Euphydryas, Hamearis, Argynnis,* etc.

FROBISHER, Sir Martin
[frō'-] (*c.* 1535-94) Eng. navigator. In 1576 he set out on the first of his 3 unsuccessful voyages in search of a N.W. passage to China.

FROEBEL, Friedrich
[frö'-] German educ. reformer. His book, tr. as *The Education of Man*, appeared 1826. Froebel held that children should grow up naturally, and that play was of the utmost importance.

FROG
(*Rana*) Tailless amphibian. Popularly the name includes toads which with true frogs are widely distributed in temp. and trop. regions. The eggs, usually laid in fresh water, adhere together in jelly-like masses. They develop into

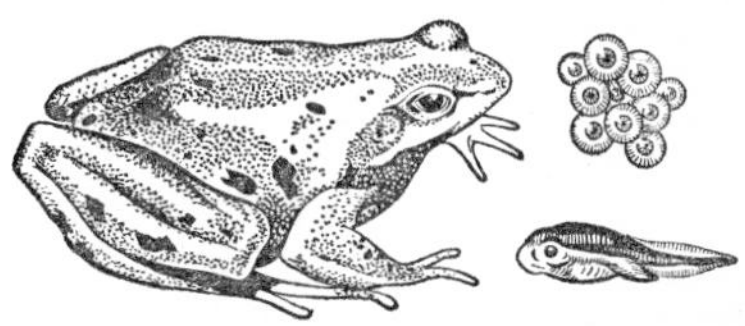

tailed legless tadpoles which breathe oxygen dissolved in water by means of gills. There follows gradual growth to the 4-legged tailless adult form with lungs for breathing atmospheric air. The tongue, rooted in the front of the mouth, is sticky and used for seizing the worms and insects upon which it feeds. Besides the common *R. temporaria*, the edible *R. esculenta* and the N. Amer. Bull Frog, there are many other species, *e.g.* the ½ in. Guppy of the Solomon Is. and the 11 in. Goliath Frog, of the Cameroons.

FROG HOPPER
Family of homopterous insects (*Cercopidae*). The greyish or greenish adults have 4 stiff opaque wings and hind legs strengthened for vigorous leaping. The larvae surround themselves with white froth called cuckoo spit.

FROGBIT
Small, floating aquatic herb (*Hydrocharis morsus-ranae*). Native to Europe and N. Asia, it has roundish kidney-shaped leaves, reddish beneath, which support the male and female flowers on separate plants.

FROISSART, Jean
(*c.* 1337-*c.* 1410) Fr. chronicler. B. Valenciennes; visited Eng. 1356. He travelled much, visiting Scot., Italy, Flanders, collecting material for his *Chroniques*, which deal with the period 1325-1400 in W. Europe. They were pub. in 3 versions during his lifetime and first printed *c.* 1495 in Paris, and tr. into Eng. 1523-5, by Lord Berners.

FRONDE
[frō(ng)d] Civil war that took place in Fr. (1648-53). The first Fronde was due to a quarrel between Mazarin and the Parl. of Paris about taxation. Helped by troops under the great Condé, Mazarin put down the rising and peace was made in March, 1649. The second Fronde was a rising in 1652-3. Condé had quarrelled with Mazarin and raised a revolt which Mazarin quelled.

FRONTENAC, Comte de
(1620-98) Fr. statesman. Louis de Buade became a soldier and in 1672 went to Canada as gov.

FROST
Weather condition which prevails when the air temp. falls to, or below, 0° C. (32° F.), the freezing point of water. Frosts may be roughly divided as follows: (1) *Hoar Frost:* fine ice crystals which condense from the air on objects on or near the ground when low temps. prevail. (2) *Rime:* ice crystals which are formed when, in severe weather, drops of water are driven by the wind against, or over, exposed surfaces. (3) *Glazed Frost:* when rain freezes on trees, etc., and on road surfaces. (4) *Black Frost:* (*a*) Intense cold, without crystallisation. (*b*) Frost of

exceptional severity encountered in sub-Arctic latitudes by fishing vessels, etc.

FROST, Robert Lee
(1874-1963) Amer. poet. B. San Francisco; worked in bobbin factory and as shoemaker, teacher, farmer. First poems, *A Boy's Will*, pub. in Eng. (1913), where he lived 1912-15. *North of Boston* (1914) brought him fame; then *New Hampshire* (1923), *Collected Poems* (1939 and 1950). He was awarded the Pulitzer Prize for Poetry four times.

FRUIT
Part of a flowering plant that contains the seed, esp. such as is used for human food. It may be divided into tree fruit, *e.g.* apples, and bush fruit or small fruit, *e.g.* strawberries. It may also be classified as pip fruit, *e.g.* oranges; stone fruit, *e.g.* plums; berries, *e.g.* currants; or shell fruit, *e.g.* walnuts. Grapes belong to the berry class; bananas and pineapples are allied to it. Fruit is a popular and important article of food. It contains much water, but also acids which are good for health. Sugar is an important content and many fruits contain vitamins. The grape is cultivated in the warmer part of the world. Oranges and lemons are largely grown in the Medit. region. Calif., S. Africa, Brit. Columbia and Australia are great fruit-growing countries. Figs, raisins and other fruits are dried and exported from Greece and neighbouring lands; also from Australia. Brit. imports tinned and dried fruit, but of the hardier fruit much is produced at home. In Somerset, Devon and Hereford a special kind of apple and pear is grown for making cider and perry. The blackberry still grows wild on a large scale.

FRY, Christopher
(1907-) Eng. playwright. B. Bristol; educ. Bedford. Taught, then became an actor. His verse plays include *The Boy with the Cart* (1937), *A Phoenix Too Frequent*, *The Lady's Not for Burning* (1948), *Venus Observed* (1950), *The Dark is Light Enough* (1954), *Curtmantle* (1963).

FRY, Elizabeth
(1780-1845) Eng. prison reformer, daughter of John Gurney, the Quaker banker. In 1800 she mar. Joseph Fry and settled in London. In 1813 she visited Newgate Prison, and, horrified by the terrible conditions, at once set to work to reform them. The family to which Joseph Fry belonged is known for its assoc. with the cocoa business in Bristol. This was founded in the 18th cent. by an earlier Joseph Fry.

FRY, Roger
(1866-1934) Eng. painter and art critic. Slade Prof. of Fine Art, Camb. 1933-4, author of *Vision and Design* (1920) and *Transformations* (1926). In 1911 he brought the first Post-Impressionist exhib. to London.

FUCHSIA
[few'-shă] Genus of flowering shrubs and small trees, named after the 16th cent. botanist, Leonhard Fuchs. There are some 50 species, mostly natives of Mexico and the Andes region.

FUJIYAMA
[foo-jē-yà'-] Mt. of Japan, 12,389 ft. on Honshu 60 m. S.W. of Tokyo. A sacred mt., it last erupted, 1707.

FULHAM
Part of Hammersmith, borough of Greater London (1964). It has a long river frontage on the Thames. Fulham Palace is the residence of the bishops of London. There is a large power station.

FULLER, Thomas
(1608-61) Eng. divine. B. Aldwinkle, Northants.; educ. Camb.; chaplain in the Civil War in royalist forces; preacher at the Savoy; chaplain extraordinary to the king. Wrote *Worthies of England* (Pub. 1662).

FULLER'S EARTH
Soft, dull, greenish-brown or grey variety of clay. It consists of impure hydrous silicate of alumina. Unlike ordinary clays, it falls to a powder in water. It is still used as an absorbent for grease.

FUMITORY
Small annual plant (*Fumaria officinalis*). The rose-coloured flowers are borne in erect spikes upon slender brittle stems bearing much-divided leaves. The plant has a bitter saline taste.

FUNCHAL
[foon-shàl'] Cap. of the Portuguese dist. of Madeira on the S. coast of the Is. Pop. 37,000.

FÜNEN
or **Fyn.** Is. of Denmark, in the Baltic Sea, between Slesvig and Zeeland. Agriculture is important. Odense is the cap.

FUNGUS
Large group of the lowest division of plants, the thallophyta, distinguished by an absence of chlorophyll and starch and the special characters in their structure and life hist. The plant body, or mycelium, consists of a mass of filaments, or hyphae, sometimes forming false tissues, the cell walls being composed of fungal cellulose. In their nutrition fungi obtain their food materials from dead or living organic matter, and consequently some are parasites, such as rust and mildews, others are saprophytes, living on decaying matter, as toadstools and mushrooms. Fungi have no flowers, but reproduce by asexual spores or, in some, by a sexual process. Some, *e.g.* mushrooms, are edible; others are highly poisonous.

FUR
Undercoat of short, fine, soft hair, intermingled with longer overhair, found on the skin of certain mammals. It is often used for clothing. The animals chiefly valued for their fur are the Musquash, Chinchilla, Ermine, Skunk, Mink, Wolverine, Sable, Beaver, Seal and Bear. The skins of the Mole, Fox, Rabbit and Squirrel are also used. Most of these animals are caught in the wild state in Canada and Siberia and to a lesser extent in Australia, but foxes are now bred for the purpose on special farms.

FURZE
Genus of spiny, leguminous plants (*Ulex*), native to C. and W. Europe and N.W. Africa. The common species (*U. europaeus*) also called gorse or whin, grows from 2-6 ft. high, has terminal spines besides branched spines on the stems and bears sweet-scented, 2-lipped yellow flowers.

FUSION BOMB
Bomb which works on the principle that, given a sufficiently high temperature, the nuclei of an element will fuse to form another element, coupled with an enormous release of energy.

FUTURISM
Form of art, which arose in Italy, *c.* 1910. Marinetti and his disciples claimed that the new movement introduced into painting a dynamic state, whereby a picture not only depicted a scene, but also indicated the emotions and ideas of the artist together with those of the person portrayed.

FYNE
[fīn] Sea loch of Argyllshire, extending from above Inverary to the Kyles of Bute. Famous for herring fisheries.

G

G
7th letter of the Eng. and Lat. alphabets. In Eng. it has 2 sounds: *g hard* is a guttural sound, as in *gate, good*, etc.; the *soft g* is a palatal sound the same as that of *j*, as in *gender, ginger*, etc. Before *n*, it is mute as in *gnat, reign*; it may lengthen the preceding vowel, as in *resign*. Initial *gh* is sounded as *hard g*, as in *ghost;* when medial it is mute, as in *thought*. When final it is silent, as in *plough*, or has the sound of *f*, as in *enough, cough*, etc.

G.A.T.T.
(General Agreement on Tariffs and Trade) An agreement drawn up in 1947 by 23 nations to eliminate all forms of discriminatory treatment in international commerce and to reduce tariffs and other trade barriers. The original signatories were: Australia, Belgium, Brazil, Burma, Canada, Ceylon, Chile, China, Cuba, Czechoslovakia, France, India, Lebanon, Luxemburg, the Netherlands, New Zealand, Norway, Pakistan, S. Rhodesia, Syria, the Union of S. Africa, U.K. and the U.S.A. By 1952 China, Lebanon and Syria had withdrawn; by 1955, 35 countries were contracting parties to the G.A.T.T., including Japan who entered into formal membership in 1955.

GABON
Former Fr. colony in Equatorial Africa on the Gulf of Guinea, between Cameroon and the former Fr. Congo Republic. Fully indep. 1960. Cap. Libreville. Area: 101,400 sq.m. Pop. 473,000.

GAD FLY
(*Tabanus bovinus*) 2-winged insect belonging to the order Diptera. It is *c.* 1 in. long, a blackish colour above and reddish beneath and on the sides. Its larvae live in damp soil. The female Gad Fly is a blood sucker and is troublesome to horses and cattle in hot weather.

GAEL
[gāl] Member of the Gaelic branch of the Celtic-speaking peoples. The Gaels, who arrived in Scot. and Ireland from the cont. of Europe, used an older form of speech characterised by the Q sound, which survives in Erse, or Irish Gaelic, Scot. Gaelic and Manx. A younger form, using P. appears in Welsh, Cornish, and Breton. The term **Gaelic** is used for the national speech, lit., customs, etc. that are peculiar to the Gaelic peoples in Ireland and the Scot. Highlands. Some of the univs. have professorships and lectureships in Gaelic. In Ireland the govt. of Eire has made Erse a compulsory language.

GAINSBOROUGH, Thomas
(1727-88) Eng. painter. B. Sudbury, Suffolk. In 1745 he mar. and settled at Ipswich. He moved to Bath in 1759, but in 1774 returned to London. In 1768 he was elected an orig. member of the R.A. He is remarkable both for his landscapes and his portraits.

GALAPAGOS
[gala-pā′-gos] Group of volcanic Is. in the Pacific, on the Equator, *c.* 500 m. W. of Ecuador, of which they form a prov. San Cristobal is the cap.

GALASHIELS
[-shēlz′] Burgh of Selkirkshire, on Gala Water, S.E. of Edinburgh. It is a centre of the woollen industry, particularly tweeds. Pop. 12,262.

GALATIA
Ancient district of Asia Minor, named from the Galatae, Gauls who settled there *c.* 300 B.C. At the time of Augustus it became part of the Rom. Empire. **Galatians, Epistle to the.** 9th book of the N.T. In it the apostle Paul vigorously deplores defections from Gospel freedom among his Galatian readers in favour of Jewish formalism.

GALEN
[gā′-] (130-200) B. Pergamum in Asia Minor, he studied medicine in Greece and Egypt. In 163 he went to Rome where he became physician to the Emperors Marcus Aurelius and Commodus. He wrote a great deal on med. and his influence remained for many cents.

GALENA
Chief ore of lead, found in N. Amer., Australia, Sp. and Germany. It is a sulphide of the metal and occurs in veins and pockets, assoc. with quartz, fluor, and ores of copper, zinc and silver.

GALICIA
Former kingdom and prov. of Spain, N. of Portugal; the modern provs. of Corunna, Lugo, Orense, and Pontevedra. The Gallegos are a hardy people, devoted to agriculture and fishing. Their dialect, called **Galician,** forms, with Portuguese, a branch of Romance speech distinct from Castilian Sp.

GALILEE, Sea of. *See* TIBERIAS, LAKE.

GALILEE
Rom. prov. of Palestine in N.T. times. It lies N. of Samaria and W. of the Jordan, its cap. being Tiberias. It was Christ's home in boyhood.

GALILEI, Galileo
[gal-i-lā′-ē/-lā-ō] (1564-1642) B. Pisa, Italy. He made the first systematic experiment in mechanics and laid a foundation for the work of Newton. His work included the invention of the thermometer, the discovery of the law governing the vibrations of a pendulum, the first attempts to measure the speed of light and to weigh air, and the first experiments on the production of a vacuum. In 1609, he made the first astronomical telescope. He was able to overthrow the accepted doctrine that the Earth was the centre of the Universe and to estab. the ideas of Copernicus concerning the solar system.

GALL STONES
Hard concretions formed in gall bladder, assoc. with chronic inflammatory condition. Predisposing causes are over-eating and lack of exercise.

GALLEON
Large Sp. vessel of the 15th-17th cents. It served both for warfare, as in the Sp. Armada, and for transporting treasure from the Indies.

GALLEY
(1) Long, narrow boat propelled by oars. Such vessels were largely employed in the Medit. until the 16th cent. They had *c.* 50 oars, each worked by 5 men, usually captives or convicts.

(2) 6-oared boat on a warship, devoted to the capt.'s use.

GALLIPOLI
(now **Gelibolu**) Peninsula which forms European shore of Dardanelles, part of Turkish Republic since 1936. **Gallipoli Campaign, 1915.** In World War I, this was an attempt to force the Dardanelles and sever German-Turkish collaboration. Brit. and Fr. failed to dislodge the Turks. Severe casualties resulted both from battle and from the insanitary conditions. A gallant part was played by the Australian and N. Zealand Army Corps (ANZAC). The campaign was abandoned and Gallipoli was evacuated, 1916. See *Gallipoli* by Alan Moorehead (1956).

GALLIUM
Hard, white, ductile and malleable metal. It was discovered in 1875 by de Boisbaudran in zinc-blende from the Pyrenees. Its symbol is Ga, at. wt 69·7 and melting pt. 86° F. It softens by pressure of the fingers, and once melted remains in liquid form at low temperatures.

GALSWORTHY, John
(1867-1933) Eng. novelist and dramatist. B. Coombe, Surrey; educ. Harrow and New Coll. Oxford; barrister 1890. His novels include *The Man of Property* (1906), *The White Monkey* (1924), *The Silver Spoon* (1926). His plays deal with social problems and include *The Silver Box* (1909), *Strife* (1909), *Justice* (1910), *Loyalties* (1922). He received the O.M., 1929 and the Nobel Prize, 1932.

GALWAY
[gawl'-] County of Eire, in the prov. of Connaught, with an Atlantic coastline and many lakes. Much of the country is lowland, rising to the Connemara Mts. in the W. and the Slieve Aughty in the S. The chief rivers are the Shannon, Clare and Suck. Occupations include agriculture, fishing and quarrying. Galway is the county town. Galway includes the Aran Is. in Galway Bay. Pop. 149,887. **Galway.** Seaport, county town and urban district of Galway, Eire, on Galway Bay, at the mouth of the Corrib. Shipping and fishing are the industries. Pop. 22,028.

GAMA, Vasco da
[gà'-mă] (*c.* 1460-1524) Portuguese navigator, he rounded the Cape of Good Hope, discovered and named Natal, and crossed the Indian Ocean to Calicut. D. at Cochin. He was the first European to round the Cape and to reach India by sea.

GAMBIA, The
W. African repub. within Brit. Commonwealth, on either side of the Gambia river, surrounded by Fr. territory. The country comprises Bathurst, the cap. of Gambia, and some adjoining land. The climate is unhealthy during the rainy season, June to Oct. Ground-nuts are the chief export. Gambia was discovered, but not settled, by Portuguese sailors. In the 17th cent. a Brit. trading post was estabd., controlled from Sierra Leone. It was made a crown colony in 1888, was admin. by a Gov. and 2 councils until 1970. Full internal self-govt. since 1963, indep. 1965, declared repub. 1970. Area: 3,977 sq.m. Pop. 315,500.

GAMBIER, Baron
(1756-1833) Eng. admiral. James Gambier joined the navy at the age of 11. In command of the Channel fleet in 1809, he refused to support Lord Cochrane in his attempt to destroy the Fr. fleet in the Basque Roads and was court-martialled, but acquitted.

GAMMA RAYS
Electromagnetic radiations emitted from radioactive materials. They are similar in properties to X-rays. The biological effects of radium are due to gamma rays emitted by its products, radium B and C (*q.v.*). *See* RADIOACTIVITY.

GANDER
Airport in E. Newfoundland, Canada, *c.* 130 m. N.W. of St. John's, on the transatlantic route.

GANDHI, Mohandas Karamchand
(1869-1948) Hindu polit. leader and saint (Mahatma). Barrister-at-Law, Inner Temple, London. He practised passive resistance in India after World War I in order to overthrow Brit. rule, and was frequently imprisoned. Pres. and chief influence in Indian Nat. Congress, 1924-33. Very influential because of asceticism and popularity. Undertook several fasts to end communal riots after partition of India (1947). He was killed by a Hindu fanatic, 1948.

GANGES
River of India which rises in the Himalayas, 14,000 ft. above sea level. It is first called the Bhagirathi, taking the name of Ganges after the Alaknanda joins it. It flows S.E. to Allahabad, where it receives the Jumna, then turns E. past Varanasi and Patna. S. of its confluence with the Brahmaputra the vast delta begins. It enters the sea by several mouths, one being the Hooghly, on which Calcutta stands. The Ganges is 1,560 m. long and drains an area of *c.* 390,000 sq.m. It is subject to floods which cover an immense area. To the Hindus the Ganges is a sacred river, and they come in thousands to bathe in her waters.

GANNET
Widespread family of web-footed sea-fowl (*Sulidae*). The N. Solan Goose, *Sula bassana*, 34 in. long, with a 6 ft. wing-spread, haunts the Atlantic coasts of Europe and N. Africa and feeds on fish. It is white-plumaged, with a yellow-tinged neck, and black wing feathers. Its breeding grounds include the Hebrides, Ailsa Craig, Lundy Is. and Bass Rock.

GARDEN CITY
Residential district incorporating parks, gardens and cultural centres within the town area. The first garden city in Eng. was planned at Letchworth, in 1903, on 6 sq. miles of land to house 35,000 people. Other garden cities followed, one being at Welwyn. The movement has greatly influenced 20th cent. town planning.

GARDENIA
Genus of evergreen trees and shrubs, named by Linnaeus after the botanist Alexander Garden, F.R.S. Native to S. Africa and trop. Asia, several species are cultivated, esp. the Chinese, *G. jasminoides*, popularly called Cape-jasmine, and the Japanese, *G. radicans.*

GARDINER, Stephen
(*c.* 1493-1555) Eng. prelate and statesman. In 1528 he was sent by Henry VIII to Italy to secure the consent of the Pope to the divorce of Catherine of Aragon. On the accession of Mary in 1553, was made Lord Chancellor.

GARFIELD, James Abram
(1831-81) 20th Pres. of the U.S.A. B. Orange, Ohio, he distinguished himself as a soldier during the Civil War. In 1880 he was chosen Pres. but in July, 1881, he was shot at Washington, and d. in September.

GARIBALDI, Giuseppe
[gari-bal'-di] (1807-82) Ital. patriot. B. Nice, he early came under the influence of Mazzini. In 1848 he fought for the King of Sardinia and defended Rome against the Fr. After the peace

of Villafranca, he led a small army of volunteers, his 'red shirts', into Sicily, which he captured from the Bourbon King of Naples. He then captured the Neapolitan territory on the mainland and handed both to Victor Emmanuel thus helping him to become the first King of united Italy. In 1862 and 1867, Garibaldi made unsuccessful attempts to take Rome.

GARLIC
Pungent perennial bulbous herb (*Allium sativum*) of the lily family, native to Asia. It has long been a favourite condiment in S. Europe and Asia, and was introduced into Eng. in Tudor times. The bulb has membranous scales whose axils bear 10 or 12 smaller bulbs called cloves. Medicinally, it is a stimulant and stomachic. *A. ursinum* is bear's garlic or ramsom; other Brit. species are crow, wild, and field garlic.

GARNET
Group of complex silicates of various oxides used as gemstones. They crystallise in 12- or 24-sided forms. Lime alumina garnets are red, yellow, or green, a gemstone of this class being the cinnamon stone of Ceylon. Iron-alumina garnet, or almandine, is purplish red; the common red garnet is a magnesia-alumina variety.

GARRICK, David
(1717-79) Eng. actor; b. Hereford; educ. Lichfield. He there met Samuel Johnson, who took him as a pupil, and in 1737 the pair set out together for London. Garrick first appeared on the stage in London in 1741. He played at Drury Lane, in Dublin, and at Covent Garden, and in 1747 became joint manager of Drury Lane, where he remained until 1776.

GARTER, The Most Noble Order of the
Eng. order of knighthood, founded in 1348 by King Edward III. It is a religious and milit. fraternity. The fraternity comprised 26 knights and held its convocations in St. George's Chapel, Windsor, rebuilt by Edward IV. There are now 5 officers of the order: the Prelate, Registrar, Usher, Chancellor, and the Garter King of Arms. The Sovereign head of the order is H.M. Queen Elizabeth. Membership of the order is now limited to 25 knights and to members of the royal family and of foreign royal families. The knights wear below the left knee a garter of dark blue velvet bearing the motto in gold (*honi soit qui mal y pense*). They also wear a blue velvet mantle, surcoat, and hood with a collar of Tudor roses, from which the George, a figure of St. George, and a star are suspended.

GAS
State of matter in which the cohesion between the material particles is at its minimum, producing a condition of perfect fluidity. By cooling, a gas may be liquefied and solidified. Gases readily diffuse into one another, are soluble in many liquids, and their properties of viscosity in flow and compressibility are well marked characters. *See* COAL GAS; NATURAL GAS; POISON GASES. **Gas Engine.** Type of internal combustion engine. The power is obtained from the combustion of an explosive mixture of gas and air in a cylinder. The first engine of this type was invented in 1860 by Lenoir, who used coal gas as fuel. Improved upon by Otto introducing the 4-stroke cycle. A 2-stroke cycle is used for many large engines since it gives a greater output of power.

GAS TURBINE *See* TURBINE; JET PROPULSION.

GASCONY
Former prov. of S.W. Fr. between the Garonne and the Pyrenees. In the M.A., Gascony became part of Aquitaine, and was included in the dowry of Eleanor, wife of Henry II of Eng. It remained an Eng. possession until *c.* 1453.

GASKELL, Elizabeth Cleghorn
(1810-65) Eng. novelist. B. London, the daughter of a Unitarian minister. Mar. 1832, W. Gaskell, a Unitarian minister in Manchester. Pub. *Mary Barton* anonymously, 1848, giving a view of industrial conditions in the N. Wrote a series of papers pub. 1853 as *Cranford.* Mrs. Gaskell also wrote the controversial *Life of Charlotte Brontë* (1857).

GASTEROPODA
Mollusca that crawl on a broad, muscular, disc-like foot beneath the body. A univalve shell, never a bivalve, is generally developed in the larval form; it is sometimes reduced or absent in the adult. All gasteropods possess rasping 'tongues', or radulae, the mouth being situated in the foot. Over 16,000 species are known, and they are found on land, or in fresh or salt water.

GASTRITIS
[-trī′-] Inflammation of the stomach which results from indiscretions in diet, over-consumption of alcohol, poisoning or infection. The chronic type is assoc. with longstanding incorrect feeding.

GATESHEAD
County borough and seaport of Durham, on the Tyne, opposite Newcastle. The industries include engineering works, railway shops and chem. manufactures. It returns 2 members to Parl. Pop. 103,000.

GATUN
Town of C. Amer. in the Panama Canal Zone, under U.S. jurisdiction.

GAUGUIN, Paul
[gō-ga(ng)′] (1848-1903) Fr. painter. B. Paris. Encouraged by Pissarro, he began painting, joining the Post-Impressionist group, and later started the Synthesist movement. After painting in Brittany and S. Fr. he worked in Tahiti from 1891-3. After visiting Paris, he returned to Tahiti in 1895, and removed to Dominiha in 1901, where he d. See *The Gold of their Bodies* by Charles Gorham (1955).

GAUSS, Karl Friedrich
(1777-1855) German mathematician. He demonstrated that by elementary geometry a circle can be divided into 17 equal arcs, and made the notable discovery of *the principle of least squares*, which is still the basic method used for the reduction of observations in astronomy, etc. On Jan. 1, 1800, he observed the small hitherto unknown planet which he named *Ceres*. At the age of 30 he was apptd. Prof. of Astronomy at Göttingen, and estabd. the world's first regular magnetic observatory there in 1833. This led to discoveries in the mathematical theory of electricity and, in 1851, to the realisation that magnetic changes were closely linked with magnetic storms, and that both of these were linked with the sun-spot cycle of *c.* 11 years. The unit of intensity of a magnetic field is named after him (the *Gauss unit*).

GAUTIER, Théophile
(1811-72) Fr. author. B. Tarbes, d. Paris. Educ. Paris. A 'Romantic'. Among his novels are *Mlle. de Maupin* (1835) and *Le Capitaine Fracasse* (1863). His poetry includes *Émaux et Camées*.

GAY, John
(1685-1732) Eng. poet and dramatist. B. Barnstaple. He wrote poems, pamphlets, plays; *Trivia* (1716), *Fables* (1727). *The Beggar's Opera* (1728), a ballad-opera, had an immense success. Gay also wrote ballads and the libretto of Handel's *Acis and Galatea* (1732).

GAZA
[gȧ′-ză] Town of N. Egypt, near the Israeli frontier. Gaza was the scene of 2 battles in World War I. The **Gaza Strip** was occupied by Egyptian forces, 1948, and is a source of frequent strife between Egypt and Israel. Pop. 37,800.

GAZELLE
[-ell′] Small antelopes. Native to N. Africa

and Asia, they form large herds on the desert borders. They are graceful, swift and slender limbed, and are mostly under 30 in. high at the shoulder. The male of the Dorcas Gazelle has lyre-shaped, ringed horns, *c.* 13 in. long.

GDANSK
(formerly **Danzig**) City and port of Poland, on the W. arm of the Vistula, *c.* 4 m. from its mouth. As Danzig it was the cap. of E. Prussia, and in 1919 became a free city. Occupied by Germany from 1939-45, when it was taken by Poland and renamed Gdansk. Pop. 324,000.

GDYNIA
[gdin′-yă] Polish seaport on the Gulf of Danzig, 12 m. N.E. of Gdansk. During World War II the port was destroyed by the Germans, but since 1945 it has been rebuilt. Pop. 148,000.

GEDDES, Sir Patrick
(1854-1932) Scottish biologist, sociologist and town-planner. Prof. of Botany, Dundee, 1883-1920; Prof. of Sociology and Civics, Bombay. Geddes had a world-wide influence on town planning and on social, educ. and economic reform.

GEELONG
City and port of Victoria, Australia, 45 m. S.W. of Melbourne, on an inlet of Port Phillip Bay. Shipping is important, and there are woollen mills. Pop. 90,000.

GEIGER-MÜLLER COUNTER
Device used for detecting nuclear radiations and particles.

GEIKIE, Sir Archibald
[gē′-ki] (1835-1924) Scots geologist. B. and educ. in Edinburgh. An F.R.S. in 1865, he was knighted in 1891, and given the Order of Merit in 1914. His many works include *Scenery of Scotland*, 1865; *Outlines of Field Geology*, 1882; and *Text Book of Geology*.

GELATINE
Purified form of glue. The purest form, isinglass, is a fish glue. It is used for culinary purposes, in the preparation of photographic plates and films, in bacteriology and dyeing.

GELIGNITE
High explosive. A modification of gelatine dynamite containing about 65 % of nitro-glycerine, collodion cotton, nitrate of potash and wood meal. Standard explosive for blasting.

GEMSBOK
(*Oryx gazella*) Antelope, a native of S.W. Africa. It is about the size of a stag, with maned neck, tufted tail and a neutral coat marked black and white.

GENE
[jēn] A unit of hereditary material incorporated in the chromosomes of reproductive cells. The gene is a self-producing unit of living substance common to all groups of animals and plants including bacteria. **Genetics.** The science of inheritance and study of the factors involved in the variation of organisms.

GENERAL ASSEMBLY
Name given to the governing body of the Ch. of Scot. and other Presbyterian chs. in Ireland, Canada, Australia and elsewhere. The Scot. general assembly meets annually in Edinburgh in May, and consists of mins. and laymen sent as representatives by the presbyteries. The queen is represented by a High Commissioner appointed each year. The assembly is presided over by a min. elected to the office, called the Moderator.

GENESIS
First book of the O.T. Its Gk. name, meaning 'origin', is that of the Septuagint version. After an account of the creation of the world it surveys the early hist. of mankind (11), and in fuller detail that of the patriarchs Abraham, Isaac and Jacob (12-50).

GENEVA
[je-nē-vă] City of Switzerland, cap. of Geneva canton at the W. end of the Lake of Geneva. A financial and intellectual centre, its chief industries are the manufacture of watches and light machinery. There is a univ. and a cath. Other fine buildings include the tower of the bishop's palace and Palace of the Nations, the former headquarters of the League of Nations. The internat. Labour Office and the Internat. Red Cross are still centred in the city. It became a republic and remained so until the Fr. Revolution. In 1815 it became part of Switzerland. Pop. 181,400. **Geneva.** Canton of S.W. Switzerland, bounded by Vaud and 3 Fr. depts. Cap. Geneva. Area: 110 sq.m. Pop. 291,000. The **Geneva Convention** (1906) provides for better treatment of the wounded in war and forbids any misuse of the Red Cross flag. **Geneva, Lake of** (*Fr.* **Lac Léman**) lake between Switzerland and Fr. It is 45 m. long, and covers *c.* 225 sq.m.

GENOA
[jen′-ō-a] (*Ital.* **Genova**) City and seaport of Liguria, N. Italy, 75 m. S. of Milan. It is the chief port for the Lombardy Plain, importing raw materials for industrial cities such as Milan and Turin. Industries include shipbuilding and engineering. The city has a univ. founded in 1243, a 10th cent. cathedral and numerous historic buildings, many of which suffered from Allied bombing in World War II. Genoa became a flourishing seaport, *c.* A.D. 1000, and monopolised, with Venice, the sea trade between Asia and Europe. In 1815 it was given to Sardinia and then became part of Italy. Pop. 775,107.

GENTIAN
[jen′-shian] Genus of annual or perennial herbs (*Gentiana*). The funnel-shaped corollas, usually blue, are adapted for various kinds of insect visitors; the small vernal gentian for butterflies, the marsh gentian for bumble-bees, etc. The yellow *G. lutea* contains a bitter principle, used medicinally. Native of temp. and alpine regions; of the 300 species only 5 are Brit.

GEOFFREY OF MONMOUTH
(*c.* 1100-54) Eng. historian. Studied at Oxford; became Bishop of St. Asaph, 1152. First recorded Arthurian legends.

GEOGRAPHY
Science dealing with the surface configuration of the earth in relation to man. **Commercial Geography** deals with economic products of the earth. **Oceanography,** the study of the sea. **Historical Geography** is the study of changing space relationship, with a changing knowledge of the world, and of the development of nations, empires, industries and transport.

GEOLOGY
Science dealing with the constitution and hist. of the earth's crust. *Mineralogy*, the study of the mineral constituents, and *Petrology*, the study of rock structure, form important sections of the science. *Physical* geology is concerned with the evolution of land forms. *Stratigraphical* geology deals with the historical sequence of the rocks and strata, and *Palaeontology* with the fossils. The foundation of modern geology dates from the publication of James Hutton's *Theory of the Earth* in 1788, in later years of William Smith, Sedgwick, Murchison, Geikie, Lyell and others. **Geological history.** Knowledge of the rate of decay of uranium to lead has enabled an approximate absolute time scale to be compiled for the sequence of events since the cooling of the earth's crust some 2,000 million years ago.

GEOMETRY
Science dealing with measurement and the properties of space. Plane or 2-dimensional geometry is concerned with the properties of plane figures, while solid geometry deals with

solid figures of 3 dimensions. The science flourished among the Gks., especially at Alexandria. Thales, ' the father of geometry ', was followed by Pythagoras, Hippocrates, and later, Euclid.

GEORGE I
(1660-1727) King of Gt. Brit. and Ireland. His mother, a granddaughter of James I of Gt. Brit. was made heir to the throne in 1701, and George became king of Brit. on the d. of Queen Anne in 1714. He spoke no Eng. and left the admin. of the country to his ministers, a practice which initiated the system of Cabinet Govt.

GEORGE II
(1683-1760) King of Gt. Brit. and Ireland. Son of George I, he was created Prince of Wales in 1714. In 1727 he succeeded to the throne, and followed his father's policy of ruling through his ministers, esp. Sir Robert Walpole, the first P.M. In 1743 he led his army against the Fr. at Dettingen. During his reign occurred the Jacobite Rebellion of 1745, and war with Fr. His family consisted of 2 sons and 5 daughters, but as his eldest son Frederick, Prince of Wales, d. before him, he was succeeded by Frederick's son, as George III.

GEORGE III
(1683-1760) King of Gt. Brit. and Ireland. Son father d. in 1751. In 1760, George succeeded his grandfather, George II. In 1762 he made Bute P.M., but in 1763 the earl resigned. In 1770, having formed in Parl. a party known as the King's Friends, he was able to put Lord North at the head of affairs. For 12 years George and North were responsible for the govt., a period marked by the loss of the Amer. colonies. In 1788, the king's mind gave way, and his son George was appointed regent. He became permanently insane in 1811, and for the rest of the reign his son was regent. George mar. in 1761, Charlotte, princess of Mecklenburg-Strelitz and had 15 children, 7 of the 9 sons survived.

GEORGE IV
(1762-1830) King of Gt. Brit. and Ireland, eldest son of George III, he was made Prince of Wales in 1762. In 1795 he mar. Caroline of Brunswick but soon quarrelled with his wife. As Prince of Wales, George was notorious for his extravagance and profligacy. He became the central figure of the Whig opposition to the govt., Fox and Sheridan being among his friends. He acted as regent during his father's insanity in 1788. In 1811 he was again regent, and retained the office until he became king in Jan. 1820. Mrs. Fitzherbert was his morganatic wife from 1785 until her d. 1813.

GEORGE V
(1865-1936) King of Gt. Brit., Ireland and the Brit. Dominions beyond the Seas, and Emperor of India. B. in London, he was the 2nd son of Edward VII, then Prince of Wales, and his wife Alexandra. In 1893 mar. Mary, the only daughter of the Duke of Teck. He was Duke of Cornwall when his father succeeded to the throne in 1901. Opened 1st Parl. of new Commons. He had between 1901 and 1910 made journeys through the Empire. On May 6, 1910, George became king, and on June 22, 1911, he was crowned in Westminster Abbey. The King and Queen had 6 children, of whom 2 survive. Five were sons, viz. Edward, Duke of Windsor, Albert, King George VI, d. 1952, Henry, Duke of Gloucester, George, Duke of Kent, d. 1942, and John, d. 1919. The only daughter, Mary, Countess of Harewood became Princess Royal in 1932 and d. 1965.

GEORGE VI
(1895-1952) King of Gt. Brit. **Prince Albert Frederick Arthur George**, 2nd son of King George V. In 1923 he mar. Lady Elizabeth Bowes-Lyon. They had 2 daughters, Elizabeth (b. 1926), who became Queen on her father's death, and Margaret Rose (b. 1930). In 1936 Edward VIII abdicated a few months after his accession, and the Duke of York succeeded. His steadfastness won the devotion of his peoples everywhere. With the Queen he paid State visits to France (1938), Canada and U.S.A. (1939), and to S. Africa (1947). In Sept. 1951 he underwent a lung operation, and d. suddenly in Feb. 1952.

GEORGE
(1902-42) Brit. prince, 4th son of King George V. He served with the Navy and then in the Foreign Office. In 1934 he mar. Princess Marina of Greece and Denmark (b. 1906), and became Duke of Kent. During World War II he served with the R.A.F. and was killed in a flying accident. There are 3 children, **Prince Edward,** Duke of Kent (b. 1935), **Princess Alexandra** (b. 1936) and **Prince Michael** (b. 1942).

GEORGE
Made patron saint of Eng. 1349. He may have been a Christian soldier in Cappadocia, put to d. at Nicomedia, 303. The popular legend is that he killed a dragon and then became a preacher of Christianity. His festival is on Apr. 23.

GEORGE CROSS
Decoration intended to mark acts of the greatest courage by men and women in all walks of civil life. The Award was also conferred on the Is. of Malta in 1942. The *George Medal* is awarded for similar acts of a less exceptional nature. Both awards instituted 1940.

GEORGIA
Constituent repub. of the U.S.S.R. in the Caucasus between the Black Sea, the Caucasas Mts. and Armenia. Agriculture is the chief industry; tea, citrus fruits and tobacco are grown in the sub-trop. coastal area and grapes and silk are produced inland. The production of oil, manganese and other minerals is important. The cap. is Tbilisi. The Georgians form *c.* ⅔ of the pop. Its people were indep. until 1801 they placed themselves under the protection of Russia. In 1918 a repub. was set up in G. and in 1921 the Soviet form of govt. was adopted. In 1922 it united with Azerbaijan and Armenia to form the Trans-Caucasian Fed. of Socialist Soviet Repubs. In 1936 the G.S.S.R. was formed; it includes the Abkhazian and Adzharian, autonomous repubs. Area: 27,570 sq.m. Pop. 4,000,000.

GEORGIA
S. state of the U.S.A., 1 of the 13 orig. members of the union. It has a coastline on the Atlantic and is lowland, except for the Appalachian Mts. in the N.W. The state produces cotton, maize, tobacco and fruit, and there are forests; there are important fisheries and mines. Atlanta is the cap.; other towns are Savannah, Augusta, Macon and Columbus. Georgia was settled in 1738. It entered the union in 1788 and now sends 10 representatives to congress. Area: 59,876 sq.m. Pop. 4,589,600.

GERANIUM
Genus of herbs native to temp. regions, with regular flowers generally rosy, purplish-red or blue in colour, and divided leaves; 12 native Brit. species are popularly called crane's bill. Allied herbs, with irregular flowers, varying in colour from scarlet to white, form the distinct genus *Pelargonium.*

GERARD, David
(1450-1523) Flemish painter, the last great artist of the Bruges school.

GERMAN
Properly High German; distinct from Plattdeutsch or Low German of the N. Old High German has lit. from 8th cent. *e.g.* epic fragment *Hildebrandslied.* Middle High German (1100-1500) includes much epic and romance, *e.g. Nibelungenlied.*

GERMAN, Edward
(1862-1936) Eng. composer. His light operas, particularly *Merrie England* and *Tom Jones,* are well-known.

GERMAN BOXER
Dog native to Munich. A companion and guard dog, its wt. is *c.* 60 lb. ht. *c.* 23 ins. at the shoulder. Colours are brindle and fawn with white markings on chest and paws. The muzzle is deep, broad and undershot.

GERMAN MEASLES *See* RUBELLA.

GERMANIC LANGUAGES
A branch of Indo-European, originating in C. and N. Europe. Divisions: (a) **E.:** *Gothic,* extinct (b) **N.:** *Icelandic* and *Norwegian, Swedish, Danish* (c) **W.:** *German, Low German; Dutch,* and *Flemish*; *Eng.* (*see* ANGLO-SAXON), and *Frisian. Lombard* belonged with latter to lower Elbe (from A.D. 5) but migrated to N. Italy and yielded to Ital.

GERMANY
Country of Europe, bounded on the E. by Poland and Czechoslovakia, and on the W. by the Netherlands and Belgium, with short coastlines on the N. and Baltic Seas. Physically it may be divided into 4 regions: the extensive N. German Plain; the C. German region of block mts.; the Rhine Rift Valley and the assoc. highlands of the Black Forest, and the Alpine foreland of Bavaria, with a few peaks over 9,000 ft. high. The chief rivers are the Rhine, with tribs. Main, Moselle, Ruhr; the Ems, Weser, Elbe, Danube. Cattle are reared in C. Germany, where sugar beet is also important. Areas around Berlin and Hamburg specialise in market gardening. Tobacco, hops and vines are grown in the Rhine valley. Forestry is conducted on scientific lines. The fisheries of the N. Sea are important. Certain parts of Germany are rich in minerals, and great manufacturing centres have developed. Coal is mined in N. Rhine-Westphalia, the Saar Basin (which is now re-united with Germany). Iron and steel industry is in the Ruhr; Saxony is the centre for the production of cotton, woollen and other textiles. Berlin specialises in electrical instruments, while glass, porcelain and earthenware are manufactured mainly in Saxony and Thuringia. Berlin is the largest city, and Hamburg the chief port; other important towns are Munich, Cologne, Essen, Frankfurt, Dresden and Leipzig. About ⅔ of the pop. are Protestant in religion. There are 23 univs. **History.** For cents. Germany was divided into hundreds of states. In the 17th cent. this area was ravaged by the 30 Years' War. In 1815 a federation of the German states was estabd. which lasted until 1866. Its place was then taken by the N. German Confederation, in which Bavaria and the states of the S. had no part. In 1871 the German Empire was founded, the king of Prussia becoming emperor. It fell to pieces as a result of World War I. In 1918, the monarchy was overthrown, and a republic formed. The country was in a deplorable condition, politically and financially. An improvement began in 1923 when Gustav Stresemann became chancellor. Reform of the currency was followed by the signing of the Pact of Locarno and the entry of Germany into the League of Nations. In 1925 Hindenburg was elected pres. In 1929, Germany was badly hit by the economic depression. She declared herself quite unable to make reparation payments and there was polit. unrest. Under Adolf Hitler the Nazi Party became strong. Hitler became Chancellor in 1933. In 1935 he estabd. conscription, and annexed Austria (1938) and Czechoslovakia (1939). World War II commenced with his invasion of Poland in Sept. 1939. Following Germany's unconditional surrender in 1945, the country was divided into 4 zones of occupation, administered by Gt. Brit., the U.S.A., Fr. and the U.S.S.R. Greater Berlin was occupied by forces of each of the 4 Powers, and adjustments were made to boundaries, particularly in the E. 2 republics were estabd. **W. Germany.** The W. German Federal Repub. comprises the area covered by the Fr., Brit., and Amer. zones. Bonn, on the Rhine, 15 m. from Cologne, is the cap. The 1st pres. was Theodor Heuss; 1st Chancellor, Dr. Konrad Adenauer. In May 1955 Germany attained her sovereignty within the structure of the W. European Union, and was formally inducted as the 15th member of N.A.T.O. (*q.v.*). Area: 95,700 sq.m. Pop. 57,247,200. **E. Germany.** The German Democratic Repub. consists of the territory of the Russian zone, parl. meeting in the Russian sector of Berlin. Wilhelm Pieck was elected the 1st pres. Area: 41,400 sq.m. Pop. 17,135,867.

GESTAPO
[ges-tà′-pō] Abbreviated form of **Geheime Staats-Polizei** (Secret State Police) during the Nat. Soc. régime in Germany. Founded (1933), consolidated (1936) under Himmler. It became notorious for its methods of torture and extermination and was indicted as a body at the Nuremberg war-crimes trial (1945-6).

GETHSEMANE
Plantation at the foot of the Mt. of Olives, to which Christ retired across the Kidron after the Last Supper with His disciples.

GETTYSBURG
[get′-iz-] Town of Pennsylvania, U.S.A. 70 m. from Washington. Near Gettysburg on July 1-3, 1863, one of the decisive battles of the Amer. Civil War was fought. In Nov. 1863, part of the battlefield was dedicated as a national cemetery. On this occasion Lincoln made a memorable speech.

GEUM
Genus of hardy rosaceous perennials. The wild herb bennet, or wood avens, *G. urbanum,* has small yellow flowers and its aromatic root possesses medicinal qualities.

GEYSER
[gē′-] Intermittent hot spring, characterised by eruptions of steam and boiling water. They are due to the gradual heating of water under high pressure in cavities and fissures in the rock.

GHANA
State of W. Africa having a 340 m. coastline on the Gulf of Guinea. Attached to it are the districts of Ashanti and N. Territories, with the Trusteeship of Togoland. Mainly low-lying, traversed by rivers, the chief of which is the Volta. There are dense forests near the coast, but inland, savanna predominates. Accra is the cap. The whole area became Brit. in the 19th cent. In Mar. 1957, it became a self-governing state within the Brit. Commonwealth and changed its name from Gold Coast to Ghana. Area: 92,100 sq.m Pop. 8,143,000.

GHATS
Mt. ranges of India, enclosing the Deccan tableland. The E. Ghats, average ht. of 1,500 ft. extend along the Madras coast from Orissa to the Nilgiri hills. The W. Ghats, averaging 3,000 ft. stretch from the Tapti valley S. for 800 m. to the Palghat gap. The term ghat is also applied in India to flights of steps along a river's bank. Such are frequently seen along

the Ganges, where the burning ghats are used for cremation.

GHENT
(*Fr.* **Gand**) City and river port of Belgium, cap. of E. Flanders prov. at the confluence of the Lys and Scheldt, 32 m. N.W. of Brussels. Industries include glass, cotton and linen manufactures, engineering and sugar refining. It was a flourishing trading centre in the 13th cent. Since the 19th cent. it has become an important commercial centre. Pop. 228,986.

GHETTO
The quarter of a town set apart by law for the residence of Jews. The first Ghetto was estabd. in Rome, in 1555, by the order of Pope Paul IV. The practice was revived by the Nazis during World War II.

GHOST
Disembodied spirit, or etheric element from physical body of dead person.

GIANT'S CAUSEWAY
Columnar basalt formation on the N. coast of Antrim, N. Ireland. It is composed of polygonal pillars.

GIBBON
(*Hylobates*) Manlike or anthropoid apes. Native to the Indo-Malay region and 3 ft. high, they are tailless, with arms reaching to the ankles. They are tree dwellers and are gregarious and agile. The largest is the Sumatra Siamang. Although readily tamed, they do not live long in Europe.

GIBBON, Edward
(1737-94) Eng. historian; b. Putney; educ. at Westminster, in 1752 he went to Oxford for a short time. From 1753-8 he lived at Lausanne. In 1763 Gibbon visited Rome and there decided to write *The Decline and Fall of the Roman Empire*. The first vol. was not pub. until 1776. The last 3 vols. were pub. in 1788. Gibbon's *Decline and Fall* is one of the world's great books.

GIBBONS, Grinling
(1648-1721) Eng. wood carver. B. Rotterdam, he early came to London. John Evelyn introduced him to Charles II. He worked for Wren, carving the choir stalls in St. Paul's Cathedral.

GIBBONS, Orlando
(1583-1625) Eng. composer. He wrote much ch. music. He also wrote madrigals, 30 fantasies for viols and much music for the virginals.

GIBRALTAR
[ji-brawl'-] Brit. colony, consisting of a rocky peninsula S. of Spain. It is a fortress and naval base guarding the narrow entrance to the Medit. It is a free port. The colony is administered by a Gov. and 2 councils. For some cents. after 711 it belonged to the Moors. Previously Moorish, it was captured from Spain in 1704 by a Brit. and Dutch fleet under Sir George Rooke. The Fr. and Spaniards tried to regain it, notably by the siege of 1779-83. Pop. 24,502. **Straits of Gibraltar.** Straits between Spain and N. Africa. At the narrowest point the straits are 9 m. across. The Rock of Gibraltar and Mt. Abyla, on the African coast, were known as the Pillars of Hercules.

GIDE, André
(1869-1951) Fr. author. B. Paris. Writings include *Les Nourritures Terrestres* (1897), *Symphonie Pastorale* (1919), *Si le Grain ne Meurt* (autobiog.) (1921), *Voyage au Congo* (1928). See Notes on *André Gide* by Roger Martin du Gard (1953).

GIELGUD, Sir John
(1904-) Eng. actor and producer. B. London. Roles include Richard II, Macbeth, John Worthing in *The Importance of Being Earnest*, King Lear, and his most famous role, Hamlet, He has appeared also in films. His autobiog., *Early Stages*, was pub. 1939. Knighted 1953.

GIGLI, Beniamino
[zhē'-lē] (1890-1957) Ital. tenor. B. in Recanati, Italy, and educ. there. Studied music under Prof. Enrico Rosati at the Rome Conservatory, making his début at Rovigo, near Venice, in 1914. He sang in all the principal cities of Europe and the U.S. and became one of the world's foremost tenors.

GILBERT, Sir Humphrey
(1539-83) Eng. navigator. B. Dartmouth and educ. Eton and Oxford. In 1583 he took possession of Newfoundland, where he founded a settlement. Drowned on return journey.

GILBERT, Sir William Schwenck
(1836-1911) Eng. dramatist; b. London. Graduated at London Univ. He contributed to *Fun*, for which he wrote his *Bab Ballads*. In 1871 he began to work with **Sir Arthur Sullivan** (*q.v.*), the composer, and during 1875-96 they produced a series of topical comic operas. They include *Patience, Iolanthe, The Mikado, The Yeomen of the Guard* and *The Gondoliers*. See *The Gilbert and Sullivan Book* by Leslie Baily (1952).

GILBERT AND ELLICE ISLANDS
Brit. colony in the Pacific Ocean comprising the Gilbert, Ellice and Phoenix groups, with Christmas, Fanning, Washington and Ocean Is., all coral atolls with the exception of Ocean Is. Pandanus fruit and coconuts are the chief crops. The colony, annexed in 1915, is administered by the High Commissioner for the W. Pacific, but most of the Is. have a native govt. Area: 135 sq.m. Pop. 47,500.

GILGAMESH
Ancient epic allegorical poem. It was known to the Assyrians and Babylonians *c.* 2000 B.C.

GILL, Eric Rowland
(1882-1940) Eng. sculptor, typographer and author. B. Brighton. He became an R.C. 1913, and was commissioned to execute the *Stations of the Cross* for Westminster Cathedral. His many other sculptures include *Madonna and Child, St. Sebastian,* and the sculptures on Broadcasting House, London.

GILLOW, Robert
Eng. craftsman. About 1730 he began to make furniture. His sons continued the business and were the leading furniture makers of the time. Hepplewhite and Sheraton designed pieces for them.

GIN
Spirit distilled from malt and maize grain in a patent still, and flavoured with juniper berries or other aromatic substances such as orris root, cardamoms, cassia and coriander seeds. The percentage of alcohol varies from 40 to 50.

GINGER
Rootstock of a perennial reed-like herb (*Zingiber officinale*). Cultivated in antiquity as a spice. The irregular hand-like pieces, washed and dried, form coated or black ginger; washed, scraped and bleached they become white ginger. Young green rootstocks are preserved in syrup, or in crystallised sugar. In powdered form it is widely employed to flavour cakes, confectionery and ginger ale.

GINSENG
[jin'-] (*Panax schin-seng*) Root of a shrub of the ivy family, reputed by the Chinese to possess rejuvenating properties. Amer. exports the variety called *P. quinquefolius* to China as a substitute.

GIORGIONE, Giorgio
[jor-jō'-nā] (1477-1510) Venetian painter. B. at Castelfranco, pupil of Bellini. Painted many works of great beauty.

GIOTTO DI BONDONE
[-dō'-nā] (*c.* 1266-1336) Ital. artist. B. near Florence. A series of his frescoes are preserved in the Ch. of St. Francis at Assisi and at Padua.

GIRAFFE
(*Giraffa camelopardis*) Ruminant hoofed mammal. A native of Africa, S. of the Sahara. The tallest of all animals, it may attain to a ht. of 18 or 19 ft. and is tawny coloured with brown blotches. Its relatively short body and long limbs and neck are characteristic. Its ears are large and pointed, and it has skin-covered, horn-like appendages, and a tufted tail. It feeds on leaves. Timid and swift-moving, giraffes are rapidly disappearing.

GIRAUDOUX, Jean
(1882-1944) Fr. dramatist. B. Haute-Vienne; educ. Ecole Normale Supérieure and became a diplomat. *Suzanne et le Pacifique* (1921), *Bella*, are novels. His plays include *Siegfried* (1928), *Electra* (1937).

GIRL GUIDES
Youth organisation founded by Lord Baden-Powell and his sister, Agnes, to give girls a training corresponding to that of the Boy Scouts. It was incorporated by charter in 1915 and granted a Royal Charter in 1923. Membership of *c.* 3,000,000 includes *c.* 500,000 in the Brit. Is.

GIRONDINS (Girondists) *See* FR. REVOLUTION.

GIRTIN, Thomas
(1775-1802) Eng. painter. B. London; produced a number of water colours. Turner paid tribute to his powers.

GISSING, George Robert
(1857-1903) Eng. novelist. B. Wakefield, d. St. Jean de Luz. Mar. early and moved to Amer. where he was very poor. Pub. *Demos* (1886), *New Grub Street* (1891), *Born in Exile* (1892), *The Odd Women* (1893), *The Private Papers of Henry Ryecroft* (1903) (to some extent autobiog.).

GLACIER
Stream of ice which flows slowly down a mt. valley towards the sea. It is formed above the snowline, where the lower layers of the accumulated snow become, by pressure, converted into ice. When the glacier reaches a certain level, the ice melts about as fast as it advances, so that the base is usually nearly stationary. Much of now temperate Europe is marked by signs of retreated glaciers, evidence of the last Ice Age (*q.v.*). In Arctic and Antarctic regions great masses of ice break off and form icebergs.

GLADIOLUS
Genus of flowering plants of the iris family, native mostly to the Mediterranean region and S. Africa. They grow from seed or from bulbous offsets of old corms.

GLADSTONE, William Ewart
(1809-98) Brit. statesman. B. Liverpool, educ. Eton and Oxford. In 1832 he was elected Tory M.P. for Newark; Greenwich 1868-80; and Midlothian, 1880-95. In 1845 he resigned rather than agree to a grant for R.C. education. He was Chancellor of the Exchequer, 1852-55. During the next 6 years he was responsible for the great financial reforms. From 1868-74, as P.M. and leader of the Liberal Party, he introduced reforms, including voting by ballot, the disestablishment of the Irish Ch. and reforms in education. On the Lib. defeat in 1874 Gladstone proposed to retire from public life. In 1880, he led the Libs. into power and became P.M. The Third Reform Act was passed in 1884, but in 1885 Gladstone, having become convinced of the necessity for Irish Home Rule, resigned and was re-elected 1886. The defection of the Liberal Unionists, such as Bright, Chamberlain and Hartington, led to his resignation. In 1892, after 6 years as leader of the Opposition, he became P.M. for the fourth time. Home Rule failed once more, and Gladstone resigned from office. Gladstone was a great parliamentarian, with a magnificent record both as administrator and orator. He was profoundly religious and an outstanding classical scholar. See Morley's *Life of Gladstone*, and *Gladstone*, a biography by Philip Magnus (1954).

GLAMIS
[glàmz] Village of Angus, 6 m. S.W. of Forfar. Near is Glamis Castle.

GLAMORGANSHIRE
County of S. Wales, with a long coastline on the Bristol Channel. In the N. are the Welsh Mts. but in the S. is the Vale of G. The chief rivers are the Taff, Tawe, Rhondda and Ogwr. Coal is mined extensively in Rhondda, Merthyr Tydfil, and Aberdare. Tin plating and other metal industries are important. Cardiff is the county town. Glamorganshire returns 16 members to Parl. (9 borough constituencies). Pop. 1,236,980.

GLANDERS
Acute infectious disease mainly affecting horses and caused by *Bacillus Mallei*. *Treatment* is destruction of all infected animals.

GLASGOW
[glàz'-] Largest city, port and royal burgh of Scot. and 3rd city of the U.K. Lying on the Clyde, it is the principal commercial centre of Scot. and has numerous industries. These include shipbuilding, the manufacture of machinery, locomotives and various forms of iron and steel ware, chems., tobacco and textiles. Printing, distilling and dyeing are also important. There are extensive docks, wharves and warehouses. The cath. has parts dating from the 12th cent. The Mitchell Library and the Art Gallery are notable. The univ. was founded in 1451. A tunnel under the river was opened 1965. There are many public parks and a botanic garden. The city is governed by a lord provost and a town council, and sends 15 members to Parl. Pop. 1,049,115.

GLASS
Non-crystalline, transparent or semi-transp. inorganic substance. Commercial glass is obtained by the fusion of silica with alkalis. Glass was known to the ancients and certainly in Egypt from remote times. Modern glass varies in composition according to the purpose for which it is intended. Glass fibres, less than 1,000th of an in. thickness, can be woven into silk-like fabrics used for many purposes.

GLASSWORT
Genus of leafless herbs (*Salicornia*) of the goosefoot family, native to saline soils throughout the world. The stems of the marsh samphire when burnt produce barilla formerly used for glass making.

GLASTONBURY
Borough and market town of Somerset, on the Brue, 37 m. S.W. of Bath. There is a ruined abbey, once one of the largest and richest in Eng. Pop. 5,940.

GLAUCOMA
[glaw-kō'-mă] A systematic disease assoc. with symptoms appearing in the eye. **Primary glaucoma.** Characterised by pain, coloured haloes round lights, dilatation of pupil, cloudiness of vision with swelling of eyelids and conjunctiva.

Secondary glaucoma results from perforation of cornea, wounds of lens, tumour of the eye and haemorrhage into eye.

GLAZUNOV, Alexander
[glaz′-ōō-nof] (1865-1936) Russian composer. Studied with Rimsky-Korsakov, 1880-1. He settled in Paris in 1928. His output includes 8 symphonies, ballets, symphonic poems, a violin concerto, 2 piano concertos, 5 string quartets, songs and cantatas.

GLENCOE
Valley of the Coe river, N. Argyllshire, where, in 1692, the Macdonalds of Glencoe were massacred by the Campbells. The order was signed by William III, but the extent of his responsibility is still a matter of controversy.

GLENDOWER, Owen
(*c.* 1359-1416) Welsh rebel. After the accession of Henry IV he proclaimed Welsh independence, with himself as Prince of Wales, and for the remainder of his life was in active warfare with Eng.

GLIDING
The science and sport of moving through air in a heavier-than-air machine not provided with an engine. The glider depends on gravity for its forward motion and upon upward air-currents for attaining altitude.

GLINKA, Michael Ivanovitch
(1803-57) Russian composer. He founded the Russian Nat. School. He wrote operas, orchestral pieces, chamber music, pianoforte works, ch. music and songs.

GLOBE FISH
Various trop. and sub-trop. genera of fish. They have the power of swallowing air, thereby making themselves more or less globular. Varying in length up to 2 ft. they include the small spined, brilliantly coloured and poisonous *Tetrodon,* found in the Nile, in Brazilian and Indian rivers, and occasionally in Brit. seas, and the sea hedgehogs, *Didon.*

GLOBE FLOWER
Genus of the buttercup family. The Brit. form has incurved, yellow, petal-like sepals with tiny linear petals.

GLOCKENSPIEL
A musical instrument composed of a series of steel bars, which are struck with wooden hammers, giving a bright bell-like sound.

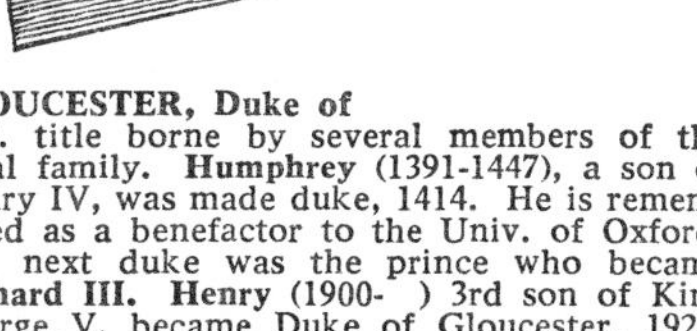

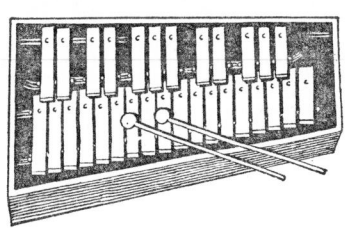

GLOUCESTER, Duke of
Eng. title borne by several members of the royal family. **Humphrey** (1391-1447), a son of Henry IV, was made duke, 1414. He is remembered as a benefactor to the Univ. of Oxford. The next duke was the prince who became **Richard III. Henry** (1900-) 3rd son of King George V, became Duke of Gloucester, 1928. B. Sandringham, he was educ. at Broadstairs and Eton. A knight of the Garter and P.C.

GLOUCESTERSHIRE
(Glos.) County of W. Eng. round the Severn estuary. The Cotswold Hills cross the E. part, with the fertile Vale of Gloucester to the N.W. The chief rivers are the Severn, Wye and Avon. It is predominantly an agricultural county. Coal is mined in the Forest of Dean. Late in the M.A. Glos. was a centre of the woollen industry. Gloucester is the county town, and Bristol is the largest city; other towns are Cheltenham, Tewkesbury, Cirencester and Stroud. Glos. returns 12 members to Parl. (8 borough constituencies). Pop. 1,013,740.
Gloucester [glos′-ter] City, county borough, also market and county town of Gloucestershire, on the Severn. The industries are carriage and aircraft building, engineering, flour-milling and other manufactures. Its cattle market is important. The cathedral has fine cloisters and stained glass. Gloucester was a settlement in Rom. times. Gloucester returns 1 member to Parl. Pop. 70,180.

GLOW-WORM
Name given to beetles of the genus *Lampyris.* Both sexes, and larva have phosphorescent organs on the underside of the abdomen.

GLOXINIA
(*Sinningia speciosa*) Popular variety of sinningia, a genus of the order *Gesneriaceae.* A tuberous rooted plant with bell-like flowers.

GLUCK, Christoph Willibald
[glŏŏk′] (1714-88) German composer. He wrote nearly 40 serious operas, including *Orfeo,* as well as comic operas, ballets and instrumental music.

GLUCOSE
[gloo′-kōz] Form of sugar also known as grape sugar or dextrose.

GLUE
Impure form of gelatine. Made from the skins and bones of animals. For the weaker glues bones are used, and the skins of codfish and other fishes yield a tenacious fish glue.

GLUTTON
Largest carnivorous mammal (*Gulo luscus*), of the weasel family.

GLYCERINE
$C_3H_5(OH)_3$. Trihydric alcohol. It forms a thick colourless liquid with a sweet taste. It is used in medicine and in explosives.

GLYNDEBOURNE
[glīn′-bōrn] Eng. private opera house. The theatre, which seats 600, was built, and the Glyndebourne Opera founded, by John Christie in 1934 as a tribute and memorial to his wife, Audrey Mildmay.

GNAT
[nat] Two-winged insects of a family collectively called mosquitoes (*Culicidae*). The female has a piercing and sucking proboscis. Brit. species include the Common House Gnat, *Culex pipiens,* and the larger Banded, *C. annulatus.* All have aquatic larvae.

GNOSTICISM
[nos′-] Spiritual and metaphysical system antecedent to Christianity, but esp. active during the first 3 cents. of the Christian era.

GNU
[noo′] (*Connochaetes gnu*) Hottentot name for large, white-tailed antelope, called by the Boers the Black Wildebeest. It is 4 ft. high and heavy-headed, with a wide muzzle and a long mane. Both sexes have cylindrical horns, curving downward and then upward.

GOA
Former **Portuguese India,** consisting of Goa proper, the settlements of Damao and Diu and several small Is. Occupied by India, Dec. 1961. Panjim (Goa) is the cap. Area: 1,426 sq.m. Pop. 626,978.

GOAT
(*Capra*) Hollow-horned ruminants. The bucks are usually chin bearded. Domesticated, in neolithic times by lake dwellers, the ancestral

form came from the Medit. region and Persia. Wild species include the Ibex and Markhor. The so-called Rocky Mountain Goat is a goat antelope.

GOAT'S BEARD
Biennial herb (*Tragopogon pratensis*) of the Compositae family, common in Brit. Is.

GOAT'S RUE
Tall perennial leguminous herb (*Galega officinalis*), cultivated for fodder.

GOBELIN
[gō'-bla(ng)] Family of Fr. dyers. Gilles and Jean estabd. themselves in Paris *c.* 1440. In 1601 a tapestry works was started in the same place, and took the name of Gobelin. Louis XIV bought the factory, and it became a state inst.

GOBI
[gō'-] Desert of Asia, in E. and S. Mongolia, forming a plateau nearly 4,000 ft. high. Buried towns and fossils have been found.

GOBY
Various spiny-finned fishes. Their ventral fins form a sucker-like disk for clinging to rocks. Dwelling off trop. and temp. coasts, the largest Brit. species, the Black *Gobius niger*, 10 in. long, is common in rock pools. The Spotted *G. minutus*, a smaller fish, abounds in the Thames estuary.

GOD
The Supreme Being, the creator of the universe, omnipotent and eternal.

GODETIA
[-dē'-shă] Annual plant (*Oenothera*) native to California and Chile and related to the evening primrose.

GODIVA
Wife of Leofric, Earl of Mercia. She lived in the 11th cent. and legend describes her as having ridden naked through Coventry's streets, a condition imposed by her husband for securing for its citizens relief from his exactions.

GODUNOV, Boris Fedorovich
[god'-ŏŏ-nof] (*c.* 1551-1605) Tsar of Muscovy. On the d. of Ivan the Terrible he was apptd. guardian of his son. He put down all rebellion. His rule was strong and wise. On the d. of Theodore, he was elected Tsar.

GODWIN
(d. 1053) Eng. earl. He helped to secure the succession of Edward the Confessor and until 1051 was the most powerful man in Eng. In that year he quarrelled with Edward and was exiled. He returned in 1053, but d. the same year. Harold and Tostig were 2 of his sons.

GODWIN, Mary
(1759-97) Eng. writer, b. **Mary Wollstonecraft.** Mar. William Godwin (*q.v.*) 1797; d. giving birth to Mary (later Mary Shelley). She pub. *Thoughts on the Education of Daughters* (1787), *Vindication of the Rights of Women* (1792).

GODWIN, William
(1756-1836) Eng. writer. B. Wisbech; educ. Norwich and Hoxton; dissenting minister; gave up the ministry on becoming an atheist and radical. *An Enquiry concerning Political Justice* (1793) made him well known and gave him influence over such writers as Shelley and Wordsworth. Mar. 1797 Mary Wollstonecraft (see above). Wrote novels. Mar. a widow, Mrs. Clairmont (1801).

GODWIN-AUSTEN
or **K2.** Mt. 28,250 ft., in the W. Himalayas, It was named in 1888 after Lieut.-Col. H. H. Godwin-Austen (1834-1923). The summit was not reached until 1954.

GOEBBELS, Paul Joseph
(1897-1945) Nazi leader, b. Rhineland. Min. of Propaganda, 1933. He and his family committed suicide at Hitler's side, 1945.

GOERING, Herman Wilhelm
(1893-1946) Nazi leader, b. Bavaria. Joined Nazi party 1922. In 1936 he became director of the 4-year plan for war preparation and later commander of the Luftwaffe. Tried as a war criminal at Nuremberg and condemned to death, he d. by taking poison while in prison.

GOETHE, Johann Wolfgang von
[gö'-tė] (1749-1832) German writer. B. Frankfurt. Educ. at the Univs. of Leipzig and Strasburg; wrote *Die Leiden des Jungen Werthers* (1774). He settled in Weimar, 1775, and became the friend and adviser of Carl August, Duke of Saxe-Weimar. During this period he began his association with Christiane Vulpius, whom he mar. 1806. *Hermann und Dorothea* (1798); pub. 1808 *Faust* (Part I), on which he had been working since 1770 (Part II pub. 1833); *Aus meinem Leben, Dichtung und Wahrheit*, an autobiog. 1811-14 and 1831; poems; dissertations on scientific questions. Fell in love with Ulrike von Levetzow 1822. Ed. his *Correspondence with Schiller* (1828-9).

GOGH, Vincent Van
[goch] (1853-90) Dutch painter. First influenced by Millet, then by the Impressionist School, later became with Cézanne and Gauguin, one of the great leaders of the Post-Impressionists.

GOGOL, Nikolai Vassilievitch
(1809-52) Russ. novelist. B. Sorochintsky, d. Moscow. His works, which are humorous and satirical, include: *Taras Bulba* (1834); *The Government Inspector* (a comedy) (1836); *Dead Souls* (1842).

GOITRE
Chronic enlargement of the thyroid gland.

GOLD
One of the elementary precious metals. Chem. sym. *Au* from the Lat. *aurum*; at. wt. 197·2; spec. gr. 19·32. In 1962 S. Africa produced £318,291,000 of gold. Other producing countries are the U.S.A., Canada, Russia, Mexico, Australia, Rhodesia. **Gold Standard.** Introduced officially into Brit. in 1816 and during the course of the 19th cent. there was a significant co-relation between prices and the quantity of gold. The value of gold increases with falling prices and falls when prices rise. Between 1820-48 the price level fell by 25 % because the supply of gold was insufficient to counterbalance the expanding vol. of trade. Prices rose between 1848-73 as a result of the discovery of gold in Calif. and Australia. The drain on Brit.'s gold resources became so great that she had to suspend gold payments in 1931. The system now takes 3 forms (1) the gold specie standard depending on the use of gold coins as current exchange. (2) The gold exchange standard in which notes or token coins are used as medium of exchange, in relation to gold, govt.-controlled. (3) The gold bullion standard in which gold bullion is bought and sold without restriction at fixed prices. This system is in existence when a country is unable otherwise to discharge its balance of debt abroad. At present Brit. operates on a system combining (2) and (3).

GOLDCREST *See* WREN.

GOLDEN ROD
Genus of composite herbs (*Solidago*). *S. virgaurea*, common on Brit. waysides, bears a wandlike spike of tiny yellow flower-heads.

GOLDFINCH
(*Carduelis carduelis*) Brit. resident song bird. Its length is *c.* 5 in. and it has black, yellow and white wings, and bright red throat. Lays reddish-spotted blue and white eggs.

GOLDFISH
Small fish allied to the Carp, brought to Eng. from China or Japan *c.* 1700. The orig. fish was brown, the gold tints having since been produced by breeding.

GOLDSMITH, Oliver
(1728-74) Irish writer. Educ. Trinity Coll. Dublin. Studied med. in Edinburgh. Lived in London, supporting himself by med. and lit. hack-work. He came to know Percy and, by 1761, Johnson; *The Vicar of Wakefield* (1766), was written some years earlier and, with Johnson's help, sold for pub. Later *The Good-natured Man* (1762), a comedy; *The Deserted Village* (1770) (a poem); *She Stoops to Conquer* (1773), (another comedy).

GOLF
Popular outdoor game played upon links, or courses. Each course consists of a number of stretches with a small hole at the end of it. The aim of each player is to drive his ball into this hole in as few strokes as possible. Each player has a number of clubs, each adapted for a particular kind of stroke. A game is played by 2 or 4 players. The oldest club is the Royal and Ancient Golf Club of St. Andrews (*q.v.*). The chief event is the Open Championship, for both amateurs and pros. There are also amateur championships for men and women, for Eng., Scot., Ireland, Fr. and other countries.

GONDOLA
[gon′-] Boat used on the canals and lagoons of Venice. It has a prow and stern high above the water, and in the middle is a cabin. It is propelled by standing gondoliers, and is used for conveyance of passengers all over the city. Many persons have their own gondolas.

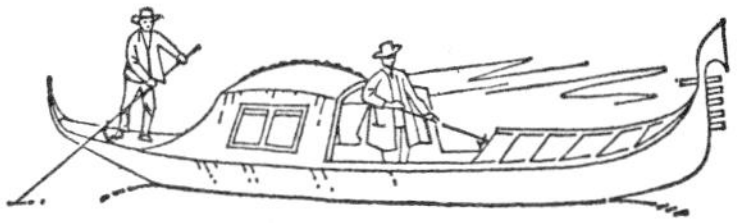

GONORRHOEA
[-rē′-ă] Disease acquired most often by sexual intercourse with a person suffering from the disease. Characterised by inflammation of the urethra and pain on micturition with yellow discharge from penis in male and in the female pain on micturition with profuse vaginal discharge. *Treatment* should be obtained immediately from the venereal disease clinics or from the family doctor.

GOOD FRIDAY
The Friday before Easter and the day set apart in the Christian Ch. to observe the anniversary of Christ's death on the cross. From very ancient times it has been a day of mourning, of penance and of fasting.

GOODWIN SANDS
Sandbank off the coast of Kent, *c.* 6 m. from the coast of Deal, and extending *c.* 10 m. N. to S. There are several lightships.

GOODWOOD
Seat of the dukes of Richmond and Gordon, 3 m. N.E. of Chichester. It is chiefly celebrated for its racecourse and the nearby motor racetrack, which is no longer in use.

GOOSE
Web-footed bird of the family *Anatidae* (Geese, Swans, Ducks). The male is called the gander, the young, goslings. There are *c.* 40 species among them being the Grey Lag, Bean, Laughing, Brent and Barnacle. Of these, the Grey Lag breeds in Scot. and Ireland, but others are only visitors to Brit.

GOOSEBERRY
Fruit of a shrub related to the saxifrages (*Ribes grossularia*), cultivated for its fruit. Fruit growers have produced many varieties. The fruit is somewhat acid, but is eaten both raw and cooked.

GOOSSENS, Eugène
(1893-1962) Eng. composer. His works include operas, 2 symphonies, an oboe concerto, pianoforte works and songs. His brother **Léon** (1897-), oboist, has promoted the oboe to the rank of a solo instrument.

GOPHER
['-fer] Small N. Amer. rodents. They include Ground Squirrels.

GORDON, Charles George
(1833-85) Brit. gen. B. Woolwich, d. Khartoum. Joined R.E. in 1852, served in the Chinese war of 1860. Gordon was besieged by the Mahdi's army in Khartoum and was killed 2 days before the arrival of the relief force. Khartoum had fallen after a 10-month siege.

GORDON RIOTS
Rising in London, June, 1780. The R.C.'s in Brit. lived under serious disabilities, some of which were removed in Eng. in 1778. In 1779, to oppose this removal, a Protestant Assoc. was formed, and **Lord George Gordon** (1751-93) became its leader. On June 2, 1780, he marched with a petition to Westminster at the head of 60,000 persons. In the ensuing disorder some R.C. property was damaged. There was further rioting on the 4th. George III ordered the military to put down the rioters. Lord George Gordon was tried, and acquitted as being insane, but 21 others were executed.

GORGONZOLA
Town of Lombardy, Italy, 12 m. N.E. of Milan, famous for its cheese.

GORILLA
Largest man-like or anthropoid ape, native to W. Equatorial Africa. Allied to the chimpanzee, it differs in having an elongated head, nasal grooves, arms reaching to the knee, small thumbs, and beetling brow ridges. The males are as much as 5½ ft., the females 4½ ft. in ht.

GORKY, Maxim (orig. A. M. Peshkov)
(1868-1936) Russ. writer. B. Nizhni Novgorod (now called Gorki); wrote stories which reflected his knowledge of Russ. poverty. *The Lower Depths* (1903), a drama. Wrote a 3-part autobiog. Supported Bolsheviks 1917. Stayed in Italy 1913-17, 1921-8. Returned to Russia 1928. Most famous novel *The Mother* (1907).

GOSHAWK
One of the Falcons, the European Goshawk, *Astur palumbarius*, is the largest, short-winged hawk used in falconry, the female being flown at rabbits, and the smaller male at partridges.

GOSPEL
Word used esp. for the first 4 books of the N.T. Together they give practically all the known facts about the life and teaching of Jesus Christ. The first 3, written by Matthew, Mark and Luke, are called, from their similar structure, the synoptic gospels. Wycliffe's followers were called **gospellers,** and later the term **'hot gospellers'** was given to fanatical preachers.

GÖTEBORG
or **Gothenburg.** City and largest seaport of Sweden. Pop. 410,681. The **Göta Canal** is a ship canal connecting Göteborg with the Baltic at Mem.

GOTHIC
In philology: the earliest preserved Germanic language—in tr. of Bible by Wulfila (Ulfilas), b. 311, Bishop of N. Danubian Goths, 341.

GOTHS
Teutonic people, who prob. came from N. Europe. They were dwelling on the shores of the Baltic in the 1st cent. Soon they were divided into 2 branches, in the E. the **Ostrogoths** and in the W. the **Visigoths.** They were converted to Christianity by the preaching of Ulfilas. *c.* 400, under Alaric, a warlike and

ambitious leader, they began to move. They marched W., reached Italy, and in 410 captured and plundered Rome. In a short time they estabd: a Gothic kindom in Fr. and Sp.; first king was Theodoric. In Fr. they were overthrown by the Franks under Clovis early in the 6th cent. In Spain they conquered the Vandals and occupied a dominant position until their last king, Roderic, was killed in battle with the Moors in 711. After the Visigoths had moved W. the Ostrogoths were temporarily conquered by the Huns. About 520 they marched into Italy, as the emissaries of the Empire at Byzantium. They estabd. themselves there under their leader, Theodoric, who made Ravenna his capital. Soon after his d. in 526, Justinian sent Belisarius against the Ostrogoths. A long struggle took place, ending only when Narses, the successor of Belisarius, destroyed the power of the Ostrogoths.

GOTTWALD, Klement
[-vald] (1896-1953) Czech politician and one of the founders of the Czechoslovak Communist party. B. Dedice; d. Prague. He became P.M. 1946 under the Presidency of Dr. Benes, whom he succeeded in Feb. 1948, and was also Chairman of the Czech Com. Party and C.-in-C. of the Army. He was succeeded by **Antonin Zapotocky** as Pres. in 1953.

GOUDA
[gow'-] Dutch town in S. Holland prov. 12 m. N.E. of Rotterdam, famous for its cheese. Pop. 37,600.

GOUNOD, Charles
[goo'-nō] (1818-93) Fr. composer. At the Paris Conservatoire he won the Prix de Rome. On his return to Paris he became an organist. His greatest success was his opera *Faust*, 1859. His output of music of all kinds, ch. music, operas, symphonies, pianoforte works, was enormous.

GOURD
Succulent fruit of various trailing herbs (*Cucurbita*) of the pumpkin family. Mostly of Asian or Mexican origin, they are mentioned in the Bible. The most valuable is the S. European globular yellow gourd derived from the species *C. maxima*, which sometimes weighs 240 lb. Other edible forms are the pumpkin and the marrow.

GOUT
A disorder of metabolism affecting purine bodies which are assoc. with protein digestion. Attacks are assoc. with deposits of crystals of uric acid in joints. Main symptoms in acute attack are intense pain in joint which is swollen, shiny, red and tender. *Treatment* is by diet of simple meals.

GOVERNMENT
System or method of governing; also the persons who form the governing body of a country. Govts. were classified by Aristotle according to whether they were directed by the one, the few or the many. We may call these monarchy or tyranny, aristocracy or oligarchy, and democracy. In addition, there were govts. such as the Jewish, in which the priests played a large part, called theocracies. Representative govt. arose in the M.A. from the fusion of primitive Teutonic and Ch. influences, but the representation was that of only a small class in the community. Govt. rested on the consent of the governed, though that consent was passive rather than active. The great age of democracy began with Rousseau and the ideas of the Fr. Revolution. In the 20th cent. women were given the vote in many countries. This made these govts. for the first time real democracies, as all adults had a part therein. But democracy has not fulfilled expectations. It may be that the modern state is too vast, that the individual, one only among millions, feels himself unimportant. After World War I, authoritarian govts. based on the identification of an individual or a polit. party with the state, arose in many countries in contradistinction to democracy. A govt., *i.e.* the body of men who occupy the offices of state in a democracy, is liable to lose power as a result of an adverse vote by the electorate. Authoritarian govts. are not subject to such constitutional limitations.

GOWER, John
(*c*. 1330-1408) Eng. poet. His 2 chief works are *Speculum Meditantis*; *Confessio Amantis*.

GOYA Y LUCIENTES
[goy'-a ē looth-yen'-tes] **Francisco José de** (1746-1828) Spanish painter. B. in Aragon he went to Saragossa to study art. He designed many tapestries for the royal tapestry factory at Santa Barbara. He became court painter, and painted portraits of 4 Sp. sovereigns, as well as members of the court. He also produced fine etchings.

GRACCHUS
Name of 3 famous Romans. **Tiberius Sempronius Gracchus**, twice consul in the 2nd cent. B.C., mar. Cornelia, daughter of Scipio Africanus. They had 2 sons, and Cornelia's devotion to them, together with her high character have made her one of the most renowned of Rom. matrons.

GRACE, William Gilbert
(1848-1915) Eng. cricketer. B. Downend, Gloucs. He was a doctor. In 1863 he began to play in first-class cricket matches. He was a member of the Gloucestershire team from 1870 until 1899. He then became manager of the London County Cricket Club, continuing to play cricket almost until his d. In first-class cricket he scored over 54,000 runs and took over 2,800 wickets. He captained Eng. in test matches against Australia.

GRAHAM, Dr. William
(Billy Graham) (1918-) Amer. evangelist. B. near Charlotte, Carolina; attended Wheaton Coll. Illinois. His first major campaign in the U.S.A. was in Grand Rapids, 1947. In 1950 his campaign was enlarged to include the coast-to-coast radio broadcast ' Hour of Decision ' on 124 stations; by 1955 this number had reached 400, with, in addition, 50 foreign stations, and consistently earned the highest audience ratings ever recorded for a religious broadcast. Visited Eng. 1954, Scot. 1955, and again in 1966.

GRAMOPHONE
Instrument for the reproduction of sound. A recent major technical development has produced **Stereophonic sound,** a method of recording and reproducing on record which gives a 3-dimensional effect. **Stereophonic records** are played on special gramophones with more than one loudspeaker. *See* TAPE-RECORDER.

GRAMPIANS
Mt. range of Scot. extending from Aberdeenshire to Dunbartonshire and Argyllshire. The highest point is Ben Nevis.

GRAMPUS
(*Orca gladiator*) Cetacean of the Dolphin family. Ranging from Greenland to the Antarctic, it sometimes attains a length of 21 ft., is black above and white beneath, with rounded flippers and formidable teeth in the upper jaw only. Fierce and voracious, it is called the Killer Whale, preys on porpoises, seals and small dolphins, and in packs hunts larger whales.

GRANADA
[-nà'-] Moorish kingdom of S. Spain which grew up around the city of G. It became indep. *c*. 1238, and was captured by the Spaniards in 1492. **Granada.** City of Sp., cap. of G. prov. 63 m. N.E. of Malaga, the centre of a fruit growing district. Pop. 157,663.

GRAND ALLIANCE, War of the
(1688-97) Known also as the war of the League of Augsburg, it was the third of the wars

waged by Louis XIV against Spain, the Empire, Brit. and Holland. In 1688 Louis sent his troops into Germany. The League of Augsburg took up the challenge and, converted into the 'Grand Alliance' by the addition of new members in 1689, waged war against Louis. Treaty of Ryswick ended the war.

GRAND BANK
Part of the N. Atlantic Ocean, off Newfoundland, covering *c.* 500,000 sq.m. It is a noted fishing ground esp. for cod.

GRAND NATIONAL
Eng. steeplechase run annually since 1839 (except 1916-18). It takes place in Mar. or April. at Aintree, near Liverpool. The course is about 4½ m. long and is very arduous. Recognised as the greatest steeplechase in the world.

GRANGEMOUTH
Burgh and seaport of Stirlingshire, S. of the Firth of Forth. There are large docks and its trade is chiefly in coal, iron ore, and oil. Pop. 19,249.

GRANITE
Acid plutonic igneous rock of equigranular texture, composed typically of quartz, felspar and mica. Minute quantities of other minerals such as zircon, apatite and rutile are usually present. Granites vary in texture and colour, and are used largely as building stones, for paving, etc.

GRANT, Ulysses S.
(1822-85) Amer. soldier and statesman. B. Ohio, educ. for the army at West Point. In the Civil War he took Fort Henry and Fort Donelson, and in 1862 fought the Battle of Shiloh. He took Vicksburg, after a long resistance, won the Battle of Chatanooga. In 1864 he was appointed C.-in-C. Grant defeated Lee who surrendered, 1865. In 1868 Grant, as a Republican, was elected Pres. and again in 1872. His terms of office saw the settlement of the *Alabama* Dispute with Brit. **Grant's Tomb,** overlooking the Hudson is a prominent New York landmark.

GRANTHAM
Borough and market town of Lincs. on the Witham, 25 m. S. of Lincoln. The chief industries are engineering and the manufacture of agricultural implements. Pop. 25,170.

GRANVILLE-BARKER, Harley
(1877-1946) Eng. playwright. After producing, he wrote a series of plays incl. *Madras House* (1910); works on drama; *The Function of Drama* (1945), and finally 5 vols. of *Prefaces to Shakespeare* (1923-46).

GRAPE
Fruit of various shrubs of the vine family. The grape vine (*Vitis vinifera*) indigenous to the Medit. region, has always been cultivated for its clustered, edible berries. There are 1,500 varieties, most grown for wine-making. Some are seedless, *e.g.* sultanas. They are raised under glass in Brit. and outside in Fr., Italy, and in Africa, Australia, Canada, Argentina and the U.S.A. Several native N. Amer. vines are cultivated.

GRAPEFRUIT
(*Citrus decumana*) Large, smooth-rinded fruit, with pleasantly acid pulp, grown in the W. Indies, Florida, S. Africa, New Zealand, etc.

GRAPHITE
Form of carbon. It occurs as a soft, black mineral, greasy to the touch, with a metallic lustre. Used as a lubricant, for stove polish and for making pencils and crucibles. Graphite occurs in schistose, slaty and igneous rocks in Cumberland, Ceylon, Madagascar and Canada.

GRASS
All plants belonging to the family *Gramineae*, incl. many cereals. More usually the herbage that grows in fields and on open spaces, and farmers distinguish between grassland, used for pasture, and arable, sown with wheat and other crops.

GRASS SNAKE
(*Tropidonotus natrix*) Non-venomous snake found in Europe and Brit. esp. in the S. Olive-brown, greyish brown beneath with a light neckband; sometimes called the *ring snake.* It averages 3-4 ft. in length and lives on frogs and fish.

GRASSHOPPER
Straight winged, orthopterous insect, whose hindmost legs are adapted for leaping. The chirp is made in the long-horned g. by friction of the wings; in short-horned g. by friction of wings and hind legs.

GRAVES, Robert Ranke
(1895-   ) Eng. writer. B. London. Educ. Charterhouse and St. John's Oxford. His autobiog. *Goodbye to All That* (1929) made him famous; hist. novels include *I, Claudius* (1934), *The White Goddess* (1948) is a work of anthropology. More recent works include *Occupation: Writer* (1950), *Poems and Satires* (1951). Became Prof. of Poetry at Oxford, 1961.

GRAVESEND
River port and borough of Kent, S. of the Thames, 24 m. E. of London. Connected by ferry with Tilbury, and is an important pilot centre. Pop. 51,950.

GRAY, Thomas
(1716-71) Eng. poet. B. London, educ. Eton and Peterhouse, Camb. Settled at Camb., LL.B., 1743. His poems include *On a Distant Prospect of Eton College*, *On Adversity*, and the *Elegy written in a Country Churchyard.* D. Camb.; buried Stoke Poges.

GRAYLING
(*Thymallus*) Freshwater fishes related to salmon. A small-mouthed, large-scaled fish and its enlarged dorsal fin has from 20 to 24 rays. The iridescent *T. vulgaris,* which frequents clear Eng. streams, has been introduced into Scot. Usually under 4 lb. in wt. they spawn in spring. Mar. to June is the close season.

GRAY'S INN
One of the 4 inns of court in London. The buildings are in the angle formed by Holborn and Gray's Inn Road. The library has a valuable collection of books and manuscripts. The sign of the inn is a griffin.

GRAZ
[grāts] 2nd city of Austria, cap. of Styria prov. on the Mur, 90 m. S.W. of Vienna. There is a univ.; industries include metallurgy, paper and textiles. Pop. 237,080.

GREAT BARRIER REEF
Coral reef *c.* 1,200 m. long, off the E. coast of Australia. Between the reef and the mainland is a channel, in some places 30 m. wide, in which are numerous Is.

GREAT BRITAIN
Name in general use for the Is. that contains Eng., Wales and Scot. It is thus the larger

part of the U.K. of Gt. Brit. and N. Ireland, and the headquarters of the Brit. Commonwealth. The name was first used officially in 1603, when James I called himself King of Gt. Brit. *See* ENGLAND; SCOTLAND; WALES.

GREAT DANE
Classed as a German Boarhound, it is the largest European mastiff. Stands about 30 in. high and weighs from 120-170 lb. Gracefully built, it carries the head high, is long-tailed and sleek-coated; in colour bluish-grey, black or black-and-yellow. It has developed in Brit. since 1870, as companion and show dog.

GREAT FIRE
London conflagration, Sept. 2-6, 1666. Starting in a bakery in Pudding Lane, in 4 days it devastated 400 streets and lanes, 13,200 houses, St. Paul's Cathedral, and other public buildings. 200,000 people were made homeless, but casualties were few.

GREAT FISH
Canadian river, which rises in L. Sussex, N. of L. Aylmer, and flows N.E. for 560 m. into the Arctic Ocean at Elliot Bay.

GREAT LAKES
Name given to the 5 great lakes, Superior, Michigan, Huron, Erie and Ontario, between Canada and the U.S.A., connected by canals.

GREAT PLAGUE
Epidemic of bubonic plague which ravaged London in 1665. Many periodical visitations occurred after Saxon times—including the Black Death. Total number of deaths for 1665 reached 68,596, two-thirds of the pop. of 460,000 having fled from the city.

GREAT SALT LAKE
Lake in Utah, into which flow 3 rivers. Salts accumulate, mostly sodium chloride and sodium sulphate, at times as much as 20 %.

GREBE
[grēb] Family of diving birds (*Podicops*). Found in temp. regions, 2 species occur in lakes and ponds in Brit., the Great Crested G. nearly 2 ft. in length and has a coloured ruff in the breeding season, and the Little G. or Dabchick, which may be 10 in. long. The Rednecked, Horned and Back-necked breed in Brit.

GREECE
Kingdom of Europe, in the S. of the Balkan Peninsula. Bounded on the N. by Albania, Yugoslavia, Bulgaria and Turkey, it has a long, indented coastline fringed with numerous Is. Greece is mountainous, but in the valleys and coastal plains the soil is very fertile. Cereals, olives, tobacco and fruit are grown; there are mineral deposits. Industries are developing. Athens is the cap. and largest town. There are many ports. Most of the pop. belong to the Gk. Orthodox Ch., the state religion; there are 2 univs. at Athens and Thessaloniki. Area: 50,534 sq.m. Pop. 8,389,000. **History.** Many cents. B.C. Mycenae in Crete was a powerful city. About 1000 B.C. the people of Greece were called Hellenes and from Greece their settlements spread to Asia Minor, Italy and Sicily, the Is. of the Aegean Sea, and almost all round the European and Asiatic coasts of the Medit. This is the Greece pictured by Homer. By the 6th cent. B.C. Greece, or Hellas, consisted of a number of independent states, ruled by 'tyrants' or dictators. Trade was active, most of it done by sea. Among the city states Athens, Sparta, Corinth, Thebes were prominent. Among these people, art and lit. began to flourish as never before. This civilisation reached its zenith in Athens in the time of Pericles, the 5th cent. B.C. This was also the time when Greece was engaged in the unequal struggle with Persia. At Marathon, on land, and at Salamis, on sea, the Persians were utterly defeated. Only with great difficulty and in the presence of great danger, had the city states united together. In 431 B.C. Athens and Sparta entered upon the Peloponnesian War, which ended in 404 with the defeat of Athens. Sparta for a short time, and then Thebes was the most powerful of the city states. Macedonia passed, in 359, under the rule of Philip. He became the most powerful man in Greece, and, when he d. was succeeded by Alexander the Great. He exercised a kind of sovereignty over Greece. The position of Macedonia in the 2nd cent. B.C. was challenged by Rome and in 146 B.C. Greece became part of the Rom. Empire which borrowed greatly from its civilisation. Later the E. Empire was Gk. and not Lat. in speech and customs. In 1204, on the collapse of the Byzantine Empire, Greece became part of the Lat. kingdom of Rumania. In the 15th cent. it was conquered by the Turks, who dominated it until the 19th cent. In 1821 the Gks. revolted against Turkish misrule. In 1833, Otto, a prince of Bavaria, became king, but was expelled in 1862. The throne was then offered to a Danish prince who, in 1863, became George I, King of the Hellenes. His son and successor, Constantine, was dethroned in 1917, Constantine's son, Alexander, then had a short reign which ended in his d. and in his father's return. In 1924 Greece became a repub. under Venizelos. The monarchy was restored in 1935 after a plebiscite, and George II returned. He supported the dictatorship of General Metaxas from 1936 until 1941. Italy attempted to invade Greece in 1940. The Germans occupied Greece from 1941 until 1944. Civil war between the royalists and left-wing parties following the liberation, resulted in a royalist victory. The King returned; he was succeeded on his d. in 1947 by his brother, Paul I (d. 1964). Succeeded by his son, Constantine. In 1947 Communist guerilla disturbances placed the country in a state approaching civil war, which continued until the summer of 1949. Peaceful conditions were sufficiently restored to enable a general election to be held in Mar. 1950. In 1967 a military junta siezed power, Constantine left country and a regent was appointed.

GREEK
Branch of Indo-European, known from before 1000 B.C. in Aegean neighbourhood. Dialects: (a) *Aeolic* (Lesbos), (b) *Doric* (Peloponnese, Crete, Sicily, etc.), (c) *Ionic* (Ionia, Aegean Is., etc.), used by Archilochus, Herodotus, etc.; (d) *Attic* (Athens, etc.), refined form of Ionic, became standard lit. language 500-300 B.C., (e) *Koine*, common speech of Hellenistic world from 323 B.C. There are today 2 forms of the language. One is that spoken at Constantinople. It lost its official status in 1453, but continued to be spoken in a somewhat altered form to the present day. Classical Gk. in which the masterpieces of lit. are written was a dormant tongue for over 1,000 years. At the revival of learning its wonderful treasures were discovered by scholars and since then it has been one of the 2 classical languages of the univs. and schools of Europe. **The alphabet** consists of the following letters:—

Α	*Β*	*Γ*	*Δ*	*Ε*	*Ζ*	*Η*	*Θ*	*Ι*	*Κ*	*Λ*	*Μ*	
Ν	*Ξ*	*Ο*	*Π*	*Ρ*	*Σ*		*Τ*	*Υ*	*Φ*	*Χ*	*Ψ*	*Ω*
α	β	γ	δ	ε	ζ		η	θ	ι	κ	λ	μ
ν	ξ	ο	π	ρ	σ	(ς)	τ	υ	φ	χ	ψ	ω

GREEK CHURCH
Name sometimes used for the E. or Orthodox Ch. Separation from Rome was effected, 1054, when the 2 chs. differed about a clause in the Nicene Creed and Pope Leo IX excommunicated the patriarchs of Constantinople.

GREENAWAY, Kate
(1846-1901) Eng. artist. B. London; studied art at the Slade School; exhibited in 1877 at the

R.A. One of her books, *Under the Window*, 1879, had a large sale in Eng., Fr. and Germany.

GREENE, Graham
(1904-) Eng. novelist. Worked on *The Times*, *Spectator* (1936-41), and for Foreign Office, in W. Africa (1941-4). His novels include *Brighton Rock* (1938), *The Power and the Glory* (1940), *The Heart of the Matter* (1948), also stories, travel and essays. Recent works include *Loser Takes All* (1955), *The Quiet American* (1956), *The Burnt-Out Case* (1961), *The Comedians* (1968).

GREENE, Robert
(*c.* 1560-92) Eng. writer. B. Norwich; educ. Camb. His plays include *The Honourable History of Friar Bacon and Friar Bungay.*

GREENFINCH
(*Chloris chloris*) Common Brit. resident song bird. Stoutly-built, it is *c.* 6 in. long, yellowish-green and yellow in colour, with black wing and tail tips; the hen is of soberer hue.

GREENFLY
Popular name for various plant lice or Aphis. Several generations of living young develop asexually by parthenogenesis. The Brit. Apple Aphis includes Amer. Blight.

GREENGAGE
Small, round, dessert variety of plum, native to Fr. It is named after Sir William Gage, who introduced it into England *c.* 1725.

GREENHEART
Valuable timber tree (*Nectandra rodiaei*) of the laurel family (Lauraceae). Native of Guyana, it reaches 60-70 ft. in ht. The wood is heavier than teak, and it is extensively used in shipbuilding.

GREENLAND
Island, part of the Danish kingdom, in the Arctic Ocean, N.W. of Iceland and separated from the Canadian Baffin Is. by Davis Strait. Only the S. part is outside the Arctic regions. The coast is rugged and an extensive ice sheet covers the mountainous interior. Most of the inhabitants, of mixed Danish and Eskimo stock, live on the S. and W. coasts. The chief settlements are Godthaab and Godhavn. The main products are fish, whale and seal oil and furs. In the 19th and 20th cents., Nansen and other explorers examined the interior of the country. By the agreement of April, 1941, the U.S.A. acquired the right to construct bases for the defence of Greenland. In 1953 Greenland was declared part of the Danish Kingdom, with 2 representatives in the Folketing at Copenhagen. Area: *c.* 840,000 sq.m. Pop. 41,000.

GREENOCK
[grē′-] Burgh and seaport of Renfrewshire, S. of the Firth of Clyde. Industries include shipbuilding, engineering and sugar refining. Birthplace of James Watt. It returns 1 member to Parl. Pop. 74,607.

GREENSHANK
(*Tringa nebularia*) Wading bird. Allied to the Sandpipers, it is slender and is *c.* 14 in. long, with long, olive-tinted legs, a long neck and slightly uptilted black bill. It migrates in summer to Brit. and breeds in Scot. Its primitive groundnest shelters 4 dark-blotched greyish eggs.

GREENWICH
[grin′-ich] Borough of Greater London (1964), which includes the former Greenwich and port of Woolwich. The Blackwall Tunnel links it with the N. side of the river. Buildings include Greenwich Hospital, now the Royal Naval Coll. Greenwich Hospital, begun in the 17th cent. contains Nelson relics. Greenwich Park is now public property. Standard time was reckoned from the Royal Observatory which stood on the zero meridian (1672-1956) hence Greenwich mean-time. Greenwich returns 1 member to Parl. Pop. 84,730.

GREGORY
Name of 16 popes. **Gregory I** (*c.* 540-604) Pope, called the Great. B. Rome. In 574 he became a monk and later was one of the 7 deacons who looked after the Christians in Rome. In 590 he was elected pope. He was zealous in spreading the faith and caring for the unfortunate. His best-known actions are the sending of Augustine to Eng. in 596, and the invention of Gregorian chant. **Gregory VII. Hildebrand** (d. 1085) Pope 1073-85. In 1054 he declined to become pope, but was elected in 1073 and he took the name of Gregory VII. He reigned for 12 years. He forbade the investiture of clerics by lay rulers, and this brought on his famous quarrel with the Emperor Henry IV, who submitted at Canossa in 1077. After 3 years the quarrel was renewed. Henry took possession of Rome, after a long siege, in 1084, and set up a rival pope. **Gregory XII**, 1406-15, abdicated as ordered by the Council of Constance and thus helped to end the Gt. Schism. **Gregory XIII**, pope 1572-85, reformed the calendar, called after him the Gregorian Calendar.

GREGORY, Augusta, Lady
(1852-1932) Irish playwright. Her works include: *Cuchulain of Muirthemne* (1902), *The Image* and other plays (1923).

GRENADA
[grĕ-nā′dă] Volcanic island of the West Indies, the most S. of the Windward Is. St. George's is the cap. and chief port. Governed by an Administrator and 2 Councils. Brit. since 1783. Previously Fr. Area: 130 sq.m. Pop. 89,000. **Grenadines.** Group of small Is. in the W. Indies, administered by Grenada and St. Vincent (*qq.v.*).

GRENOBLE
Cap. of Isère dept. S.E. Fr. Industries include the making of gloves, paper and fancy goods. There is a univ. Pop. 162,704.

GRENVILLE, George
(1712-70) Eng. statesman. In 1763 he became P.M. for 2 years. His govt. was responsible for the prosecution of John Wilkes and for the Stamp Act of 1765.

GRENVILLE, Sir Richard
(*c.* 1541-91) Eng. sailor. A Sp. fleet of 53 vessels attacked a squadron of 16 under Sir Thomas Howard off Flores. Half Howard's men being ill of the scurvy, he fled from the Sp., Grenville in his flagship the *Revenge* being somehow separated. Attempting to break through the Spanish line, the valiant ship fought the entire fleet for 15 hours, but was eventually captured, Grenville dying of his wounds a few hours later.

GRESHAM, Sir Thomas
(1519-79) Eng. merchant and financier. A member of the Mercer's Co. to whom he gave money to found Gresham College. His name is associated with the principle now known as **Gresham's law:** 'bad money drives out good money.' It arose from the fact that the actual coins in circulation varied considerably from the standard of wt. and fineness prescribed. The good coins were more valuable for foreign trade where money passed by wt. rather than tale, and disappeared from circulation where bad coins predominated.

GRETNA GREEN
Village of Dumfriesshire just across the river Sark that divides Eng. from Scot. As first village over the border, couples still come here from Eng. to be married.

GREUZE, Jean Baptiste
[gröz] (1725-1805) Fr. artist. B. near Mâcon; when 30 years of age was elected to the Paris Academy.

GREY, Earl
Charles (1764-1846) Eng. politician. P.M. 1831-4. Advocate of polit. and social reform, as Leader of the Reform Ministry, Lord Grey was responsible for the passing of the 1st Reform Act of 1832.

GREY, Sir George
(1812-98) Brit. administrator. Gov. of Cape Colony 1854. Gov. of New Zealand 1846 and 1861-7. P.M. 1877-84. He had a great interest in the Maoris.

GREY, Lady Jane
(*c.* 1537-54) Queen of Eng. for 9 days. B. Leicester, eldest daughter of Henry Grey, Duke of Suffolk, her mother was a granddaughter of Henry VII. The Duke of Northumberland mar. her in May, 1553, to his son and then sought to alter the succession in her favour. After the d. of Edward VI on July 6th, she was, against her will, proclaimed queen, but Mary's friends were too strong. She was arrested, tried, sentenced to d. for high treason, and beheaded on Tower Hill.

GREY OF FALLODEN, Edward, Viscount
(1862-1933) Eng. statesman. Foreign Sec. 1905-16. He conducted the negotiations which led to Brit.'s entry into World War I. He resigned with Asquith in 1916.

GREYHOUND
A tall, slenderly built, long-limbed hound, it is smooth-haired and in colour uniformly grey or sandy. Very fleet, it is kept for coursing hares by sight. The old Eng. greyhounds were heavier than the modern breed. Rough-haired Scotch, Persian, Afghan and Russ. breeds exist and Ital. greyhounds are miniature pets. **Greyhound Racing.** Sport held on circular enclosed tracks. It is a form of coursing but mechanical, not real, hares are used. It began in the U.S.A. and the first track was opened in Eng. in 1925. The sport affords ample opportunity for betting, and bookmakers attend the meetings. Tracks are controlled by the Nat. Greyhound Racing Assoc.

GRIEG, Edvard
[grēg'] (1843-1907) Norwegian composer and pianist. Studied at the Leipzig Conservatoire from 1858-62. He studied the folk music of his country. Among his works are the music to *Peer Gynt* and a Piano Concerto.

GRIERSON, Sir Herbert
(1866-1960) Brit. scholar, critic and historian. Educ. King's Coll., Aberdeen and Christ Ch. Oxford. Prof. of Rhetoric and Eng. at the Univ. of Edinburgh 1915-35. His many vols. of lit., history and criticism include *Lyrical Poetry from Blake to Hardy* (1928), *Milton and Wordsworth* (1937), *The English Bible* (1944).

GRIEVE, C. M. *See* Hugh McDiarmid.

GRIFFITH, Arthur
(1872-1922) Irish journalist and politician. Founder of the *United Irishman*, he was an early Sinn Feiner. During de Valera's absence in the U.S.A. 1920-1, he had a prominent share in the settlement of 1921. Elected head of the Free State executive, he d. shortly afterwards.

GRIFFON
Breed of dog. Used for hunting game birds, it is somewhat taller than a setter and has a rough coat of a grizzly, liver colour. The Brussels G. is a Belgian toy dog of terrier extraction, introduced into Brit. in 1895.

GRIMALDI, Joseph
(1779-1837) Eng. clown; b. London; began his theatrical career at Drury Lane when an infant. He performed until 1828.

GRIMM
Name of 2 brothers, German philologists and folklorists. **Jacob Ludwig Carl** (1785-1863) and **Wilhelm Carl** (1786-1859). Profs. in Berlin 1840. They collaborated in much of their work, *e.g.* in the great series of *Kinder- und Hausmärchen* 1812-22 (tr. as *German Popular Stories and Fairy Tales* (1823-6)).

GRIMSBY
County borough and seaport of Lincs., 15 m. S.E. of Hull, near the mouth of the Humber. Fishing port with trade in coal and timber. It returns 1 member to Parl. Pop. 96,780.

GRINDELWALD
[-valt] Pleasure resort in Berne canton, Switzerland, in a valley S.E. of Interlaken. Nearby are the Wetterhorn, Schreckhorn, Eiger and 2 glaciers.

GRISONS
[grē-zō(ng)] or **Graubünden.** Largest canton in Switzerland, in the E. Enclosed by mts. it is a popular tourist region, with resorts St. Moritz and Davos. Cap. Chur.

GRIZZLY
(*Ursus horribilis*) N. Amer. bear, found in Alaska, through the Rocky Mts. to Mexico and still common in Brit. Columbia. It has yellowish-brown fur, and is formidable when attacked or hungry.

GROAT
Eng. silver coin, first coined by Henry III in 1249, and by Edward III in 1351.

GROSBEAK
Various stout-billed birds. Most of them are of the Finch and Weaver Bird families. Except the Hawfinch, only stragglers reach Brit.

GROSSMITH, George
(1847-1912) Eng. actor and entertainer. His brother, **Weedon Grossmith** (1852-1919), wrote *The Diary of a Nobody* for *Punch.*

GROSZ, George
[grōz] (1893-1959) Amer. artist, b. Berlin. Assoc. with the Berlin Dadaists in 1917 and 1918. While in Germany he produced a series of bitter, ironical drawings attacking German militarism and the middle classes. He fled to the U.S.A. 1932.

GROTIUS, Hugo
[grō'shus] (1583-1645) Dutch jurist, b. Delft. In 1619, for polit. activities, he was put in prison, but in 1620 he escaped to Fr. Grotius is known as the author of *De Jure Belli et Pacis*, pub. in 1625, which laid the foundations of internat. law.

GROUND-NUT
Fruit of an annual leguminous herb (*Arachis hypogaea*), native to S. Amer. It is now cultivated in most warm countries for its oil. The flower stalk twists downward and buries the immature fruits in the soil, where they ripen. These are called monkey-nuts or peanuts in Brit. and peanuts in U.S.A.

GROUNDSEL
Common herbaceous plant (*Senecio vulgaris*) of the Compositae. Found in all parts of Brit. it has deeply cut leaves and small yellow flowers succeeded by white fluffy seed heads.

GROUSE
In Brit. used for the Red Grouse or Moor-fowl (*Lagopus scoticus*), a form of the Willow Grouse. The grouse is preserved for shooting, and in Scot. and N of Eng. large moorland areas are devoted to it. The season lasts from Aug. 12 to Dec. 10. The hen bird lays 7-10 eggs. Other species of grouse are the Wood G. or Capercailzie, the Snow G. or Ptarmigan, the Spruce or Canadian G. and the Sage G.

GRUNDY, Mrs.
In *Speed the Plough* (1798), a play by Thomas Morton (*c.* 1764-1838). Dame Ashfield is always wondering what Mrs. G. (a neighbour, who never appears) will think or say. Mrs. G. has become the symbol of public prudery and conventional morality.

GRUYÈRE
[grü-yair'] Town in Fribourg canton, Switzerland, famous for the Gruyère variety of cheese.

GUADALQUIVIR
[gwȧ-dal-kĕ-vĕr'] River of S. Spain, which rises in the Sierra de Segura and flows W. into the Gulf of Cadiz.

GAUDELOUPE
[gwȧd-loop'] Fr. W. Indian overseas dept. in the Lesser Antilles, consisting of the two Is. They lie between Antigua and Dominica. Coffee, sugar, rum, bananas and other trop. products are exported. Cap. Basse Terre; the chief port and largest town is Pointe-à-Pitre. With dependencies the area is 688 sq.m. Pop. 282,000.

GUAM
[gwȧm] Is. in the Pacific Ocean, belonging to the U.S.A. the largest of the Ladrone or Marianas Is. Agana is the cap. and Piti the chief port. Coconuts, copra and sugar are grown and there are large forests. Devastated by a typhoon, 1962. Area: 209 sq.m. Pop. 67,044.

GUANACO
[gwă-nȧ'-kō] Wild S. Amer. llama which lives in herds in the mts. It is *c.* 4 ft. high at the shoulder.

GUANO
[gwȧ'-] Accumulated excrement of sea-fowl. Deposits 50 or 60 ft. thick, found on Is. off Peru, have been used for manure since *c.* 1841 because of their ammonia and phosphorus.

GUARDIAN
Person who looks after another, usually a minor, or a person of weak intelligence. A child's natural guardian is the father or mother, but when they are d., 1 or 2 guardians are usually appointed by will. Sometimes, when disputes arise, a guardian is appointed by the Court of Chancery, and to this court a guardian can appeal if in a serious difficulty with his ward. In Scot. the terms are *Tutor* for infants and *Curator* for minors.

GUARDS
Name given to milit. units with special qualifications. The Rom. emperor had the Praetorian Guard and the Kings of Fr. had regts. of guards. In Eng. apart from the Yeomen of the Guard, guards first appeared in the time of Charles II. There are 2 regts. of horse guards in the Brit. Army, the Life Guards and the Royal Horse Guards; they form the sovereign's escort on ceremonial occasions. Of foot guards there are 5 regts., Grenadiers, Coldstream, Scots, Irish and Welsh.

GUATEMALA
[gwȧ-tĕ-mȧ'-lă] Repub. of C. Amer. bounded by Mexico, Brit. Honduras, Salvador and Honduras. It has coastlines on the Gulf of Honduras, and the Pacific Ocean. In the W. and S.W. high volcanic mts. rise up from the coastal plains. The chief rivers are the Usumacinta and the Motagua. An agricultural country, producing coffee, maize, bananas, sugar cane, chicle gum and cotton. Sulphur is obtained from the volcanoes. The cap. and commercial centre is Guatemala City. About ½ of the pop. are Indians, the remainder are of mixed Spanish-Indian descent. R.C. is the state religion, and Sp. the commercial language. G. was a Sp. possession from the 16th cent. until 1821. In 1839 it became a repub. In 1963 the Army seized power, with Gen. Azurdia as Head of Government. Area: 42,000 sq.m. Pop. 4,017,000. **Guatemala City.** Cap. and largest city of Guatemala, 80 m. from the Pacific coast, at an altitude of 4,880 ft. The previous 3 cities of this name were destroyed by earthquakes, the last in 1918. Pop. 417,218.

GUAVA
[gwȧ'-] Small W. Indian tree, with white

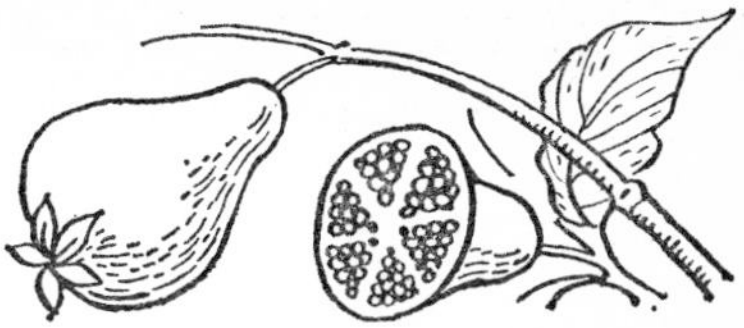

flowers and edible fruit. It has an acid taste, but is sweeter than the lemon.

GUAYAQUIL
[gwī-ya-kēl'] Chief port and commercial town of Ecuador, on the estuary of the Guayas, connected by rail with Quito. Exports include rice, bananas and cacao. Pop. 506,037.

GUDGEON
(*Gobio fluviatilis*) Small freshwater fish. Common throughout Europe, it is found in rivers and streams of the Brit. Is.

GUELDER ROSE
(*Viburnum opulus*) Small tree of the honeysuckle family, native to Brit. and temp. and colder N. regions. Its roundish clusters of small creamy flowers are ringed by larger white sterile corollas, and are succeeded by scarlet fruits. It grows 7-8 ft. high.

GUELPHS
[gwelfs] and **Ghibellines** [gib'-] Opposing political factions in the later M.A. The struggle spread to Italy, where the members of the papal party were known as Guelphs, and those of the aristocratic and imperialist party as Ghibellines. The rivalry ruined Italy. The rulers of Brunswick, Hanover, and since 1714, Gt. Brit. were of Guelphic descent.

GUERNSEY
[guern'-zē] 2nd largest of the Channel Is. (*q.v.*). The chief industry is market gardening, fruit, flowers and vegetables being grown. Its breed of cattle is famous and fishing is carried on. There is a regular service of steamers from Southampton and Weymouth. The cap. and largest town is St. Peter Port. The Is. has its own govt. with a gov. and for this purpose includes Herm and Sark. Pop. 45,150.

GUESCLIN, Bertrand du
(1320-80) Constable of Fr. B. Britanny, he made a name for himself fighting the Eng. He took part in the war against Pedro the Cruel in Spain, and in 1367, was taken prisoner by the Black Prince. In 1370 he was made Constable of Fr. by Charles V, later recovering much territory from the Eng. armies.

GUIANA *See* BRITISH, FRENCH AND DUTCH GUIANA.

GUIDED MISSILE
A projectile which can be directed on to its target by remote (*i.e.* radio) control. Propulsion is usually by a rocket motor. Guided missiles may be directed at land targets, *e.g.* the German V1 and V2 weapons used against the British Is. in World War II. Other types have an anti-aircraft role and may be launched and directed from the ground or from an aircraft. Guided missiles of various types are now standard armament.

GUILD
(or **Gild**) Assoc. of men in a common employment or cause. The members subscribed to the guild, the money being used for the assistance of the poorer brethren, also for feasts and Masses for the dead. The earliest guilds appeared in the 12th cent. and in a short time they became very powerful. In some cases they secured a charter and became the council or governing body of the town. Other guilds remained craft guilds, or assocs. of workers in the same trade. These controlled the trade, regulated the supply of apprentices and acted

much as modern trade unions do. In London they remain as the city livery companies. In the 19th cent. the word was revived for a voluntary assoc. of workers and also for a religious assoc.

GUILDFORD
Borough and county town of Surrey, on the Wey, 29 m. S.W. of London. The new cath. was consecrated 1961.

GUILLEMOT
[gil′-ĕ-mot] (*Uria*) Short-tailed, long-billed diving birds abundant on rocky Brit. coasts in the breeding season. The common *Uria aalge* shows variation between the N. and S. races. The upper parts of the adult are chocolate to black, depending on the race and the season, the under parts white. The single egg is usually laid on an open ledge of a cliff.

GUILLOTINE
[gil′-ō-tēn] Instrument for decapitating criminals, adopted in Fr. during the Revolution. It consists of an upright frame in which is suspended a heavy triangular blade which, when released by a cord, falls upon the neck of the victim.

GUINEA
Repub., formerly Fr., fully indep. 1958. The chief products are rice, bananas, palm nuts, rubber and coffee. The cap. is Conakry. Area: 95,000 sq.m. Pop. 3,702,000.

GUINEA
[gin′-i] Eng. gold coin. It was first minted in 1663 from gold from the Guinea coast and was then worth 20s. In 1717 its value was fixed at 21s.

GUINEA FOWL
(*Numida meleagris*) A game bird with short bill, red wattle and a fleshy casque. The Portuguese brought it from Africa to Europe in the 16th cent. It lives in large flocks in Africa and parts of Europe. The bird is used for the table and its eggs are eaten.

GUINEA PIG
Small domesticated rodent. A descendant of the cavy of Peru, it was introduced from Guiana into Europe in the 16th cent. The animals, which are very prolific, are kept as pets and for experimental purposes.

GUINEVERE
Wife of King Arthur. She was unfaithful to him. This led to the break-up of Arthur's court and the d. of the king.

GUISE
[gēz] Famous Fr. family. The countship of Guise was held by a junior branch of the ruling family of Lorraine. **Mary de Guise** was the mother of Mary, Queen of Scots. The 2nd duke was **François** (1519-63) who became, under Francis II, the virtual ruler of Fr. **Henri**, the 3rd duke (1550-88) played a conspicuous part in the massacre of St. Bartholomew, 1572. He conspired against Henry III, who had him murdered.

GUITAR
A stringed instrument of the same family as the lute, but with a flat back. The 6 strings are tuned a fourth apart from each other and are plucked with the fingers. Its playing is cultivated in Spain.

GULF STREAM
Ocean current which flows from W. of Cuba through Florida Straits, is 100 m. wide and has speed of approx. 3 k. It then takes a N.E. course, broadens and weakens, and is known as the N. Atlantic Drift. Thereafter some flows N. reaching the Barents Sea, but the larger part flows S.E. and has a modifying influence on the climate of N.W. Europe.

GULFWEED
Coarse, olive-brown seaweed (*Sargassum natans*) of the bladderwrack family. It grows in the Gulf of Mexico and is carried N. by the Gulf Stream, sometimes reaching Brit. waters. It collects in the Atlantic, in the Sargasso Sea. Its branches bear stalked bladders which keep it afloat over large areas.

GULL
Family of web-footed sea birds, Laridae. The upper bill bends down over the lower. The tail is usually square. White or grey in colour, they are strong swimmers and powerful and swift in flight. They move in flocks and many nest on cliffs, their eggs are edible. Of regular Brit. residents the Sea-mew or Common Gull (*Larus canus*), a miniature Herring-gull, is frequently seen inland. Black-headed Gull (*L. ridibundus*) is common in London; Herring-gull (*L. argentatus*) mostly seen at the S. coast.

GUM
Name of various trees. Chiefly found in Australia, they grow to an enormous ht. and girth. Specimens over 500 ft. high and 80 ft. in circumference have been known. The timber and the bark are both valuable. The blue gum tree, which grows in Europe, produces a powerful antiseptic oil. Gum trees also grow in N. Amer.

GUM
Substance exuding from certain plants and hardening on exposure to the air. It is tasteless, odourless, amorphous carbohydrate, yielding an adhesive liquid, and is either soluble in water, as gum arabic, swelling up and forming a mucilage, as gum tragacanth, or partly soluble, partly mucilaginous, as cherry gum. The basic ingredient of chewing gum is chicle gum, obtained from a trop. Amer. tree. Gum resins are vegetable juices combining gum, soluble in water, and resin, soluble in alcohol. When powdered they form emulsions in water, *e.g.* myrrh.

GUM
Fleshy tissue, covered by mucous membrane, connected with the membrane enveloping the jaw bones. It forms a raised collar round the base of each tooth. Scurvy or neglected teeth may cause inflammation; abscesses, resulting from carious teeth or chill, may break through and form gumboils. Disease producing pus in tooth socket is called pyorrhoea.

GUN
General term for various kinds of firearms. It includes all varieties from the sporting gun, rifle, revolver, etc. to the heavy gun of artillery and naval ordnance. In rifles, machine-guns, artillery and naval ordnance, guns are rifled, the rifling imparting a spin to the projectile when in flight. Modern naval guns have been designed up to calibres of 18 in. Guns used in the Brit. Army range from small arms, automatic weapons, anti-tank guns, and field-guns to large howitzers. The modern trend would seem to be in the direction of the gun being superseded by recoilless rocket type weapons.

GUNMETAL
Bronze alloy. Consisting typically of 90 % of copper and 10 % of tin, it approximates to the composition of ancient bronze. It was used formerly for making cannon. Usually the composition of modern gun-metal averages *c.* 86 % of copper, 10 % of tin and 4 % of zinc.

GUNPOWDER
Oldest known explosive; a mixture of saltpetre, charcoal and sulphur, in varying proportions, according to its purpose. It is still used for blasting purposes and in some kinds of sporting cartridges. **Gunpowder Plot.** Plot to blow up the Houses of Parl. on Nov. 5, 1605, when James I was to open Parl. The conspirators were discontented R.C.s. One sent a message to a friend in Parl. which led to the discovery

of Guy Fawkes (*q.v.*). With others he was tried and executed. The plot made a great impression in the country and since then Nov. 5 has been commemorated by bonfires and firework displays.

GURKHA
Name of certain tribes who live in Nepal, where they settled in the 16th cent. Owing to their fighting qualities they were recruited for the Indian Army and retained in the Brit. Army today.

GURNARD
Fishes allied to the Bullheads. They have spiny, armoured heads, crawl over the sea floor on 6 sensitive, finger-like feelers, and emit a grunt-like sound when captured. Brit. coasts yield the Red G., the Grey G. and the great Sapphirine and Piper G. which can weigh up to 5 lb.

GUSTAV V
(1858-1950) B. and d. Stockholm. King of Sweden, son of Oscar II, whom he succeeded, 1907. He mar. in 1881, had 2 sons, **Crown Prince Gustav Adolf** and **William.** A democratic king, he refused to wear his crown and was never crowned.

GUSTAV VI
(1882-) King of Sweden, son of Gustav V, whom he succeeded, 1950. Mar. (1) Margaret, daughter of the Duke of Connaught, who d. 1920. (2) In 1923, Lady Louise Mountbatten, Queen Louise of Sweden (d. 1965). Eldest son, **Prince Gustav Adolf,** was killed in a Copenhagen air crash, 1947. Grandson, **Prince Charles Gustav** (b. 1946), is the Crown Prince.

GUSTAVUS ADOLPHUS
(1594-1632) Gustavus II, King of Sweden. A son of Charles IX, he succeeded his father in 1611. Though much of his reign was spent in warfare he found time to improve the state of his then very poor country. He made the Swedish Army into a most efficient instrument, winning back Swedish land from Denmark, and defeating Russia and Poland. In 1630 he entered the 30 Years' War on the side of the Protestants. For 2 years he dominated the scene. His greatest victories were Breitenfeld, 1631, and Lutzen, 1632, but in the latter battle he was killed. His only child, Christina (*q.v.*), succeeded him.

GUT
Tough, semi-transparent material prepared from the intestines of sheep and other animals. The intestines, after being cleaned, scraped and washed, form coverings for sausages, are used for violin strings, cords for tennis rackets, and in a specially fine spun and sterile form for surgical ligatures. Silkworm gut, employed for fishing tackle, is prepared from glutinous secretions of the silkworm. Nylon is now sometimes used as a substitute.

GUTENBERG, Johann
(*c.* 1397-1468) German printer. B. Mainz, he worked in Strasbourg on an idea for the printing of books from movable type. Returning to Mainz in 1448, he set up a printing press.

GUTTA PERCHA
A brownish-red substance from the stems of certain Malayan trees. Formerly *Palaquium gutta* was the chief source but, owing to reckless destruction, it is now rare, gutta percha being obtained from the allied *Payena leerii.* It is tough, inelastic, plastic at 149° F. and less resilient and durable than rubber.

GUY, Thomas
(*c.* 1645-1724) Eng. bookseller and founder of Guy's Hospital. His charities included gifts to Tamworth and to St. Thomas' Hospital and Christ's Hospital, London. He set apart nearly £250,000 for the hosp. that bears his name.

GUYANA *See* British Guiana.

GWYNN, Nell
(1650-87) Eng. actress. She was an orange girl at the Theatre Royal, Drury Lane, London. She became the mistress of Charles II, and gave birth, May 8, 1670, to a son, Charles.

GYNAECOLOGY
[gī-nĕ-kol'-] Branch of med. science covering ailments confined to women. For over 3,000 years this has been a specialised branch of medicine and in modern times many specialised hospitals have been opened.

GYPSIES
Nomadic people, believed to be of Indian origin, who entered Europe early 15th cent. Now found in most of the countries of S. Europe. There are some thousands of them in Eng. They live in caravans and earn a livelihood as tinkers, makers and sellers of basketware. Many of the women tell fortunes. They have their own customs, speech and superstitions.

GYPSOPHILA
[jip-sof'-i-la] Hardy plant also known as chalk plant or gauze flower, with slender stems and sprays of tiny white flowers.

GYPSUM
Mineral, a hydrous calcium sulphate, occurring in nature in several different forms. In the massive state, it is a soft, white material, or reddish brown in impure varieties. It occurs in Eng. in large beds in Triassic marls, and in Tertiary strata near Paris. It also occurs as alabaster, a semi-crystalline variety, or in fine crystals, as selenite, and in fibrous form, as satin spar. It is used for making plaster of Paris and as a top dressing for soils. When processed and moulded, gypsum can be made as strong as concrete, and is used in the building industry.

GYPSY MOTH
(*Porthetria dispar*) A European moth which was introduced into the New World. It became a pest in Massachusetts *c.* 1885. The larvae sometimes defoliate the plants, but can be controlled.

GYROSCOPE
Instrument which consists essentially of a heavy disc spinning at high speed (5,000-10,000 r.p.m.). If the axis of the disc is displaced, a restoring movement is developed which returns it to the initial direction.

H

H
8th letter of the Eng. and Lat. alphabets. The sound that distinctively belongs to it is that which it has when preceding a vowel at the beginning of a syllable, as in *hard, heavy*. In Eng. the initial *h* is silent in such words as *honour, hour* and *honest*. The letter *h* is very commonly joined to other consonants to represent sounds for which there are no special letters, as in the digraphs *ch, sh, th* (*child, ship, that*). It is also used to give a hard sound in certain words, generally of foreign origin, as in *chemistry, ghetto*, etc.

HAAKON
[haw'-] Name of 7 kings of Norway. **Haakon VII** (1872-1957) was a son of Frederick VIII, King of Denmark. In 1905, on the separation of Norway from Sweden, he was chosen king and crowned in June, 1906. In 1940, having refused to surrender to the invading German forces, he fled to Eng. and led the Norwegian fight from London. He was succeeded by his son, **Olav V** (1903-).

HAARLEM
Town and river port of the Netherlands, in N. Holland prov., 15 m. W. of Amsterdam. It is a centre of the bulb industry. Pop. 169,000.

HABSBURG
[haps'-] Name of European family, taken from a castle near the union of the Aar and the Rhine. In 1273 one of them, Rudolph, was chosen German king. He secured Austria and Styria, and his descendants were archdukes of Austria. In 1438, when **Albert,** Archduke of Austria, a descendant of Rudolph, was German King, he inherited by right of his wife the kingdoms of Bohemia and Hungary. Until 1806, the Habsburgs were German kings and Rom. emperors, though they were descended from **Frederick,** who became German king in 1440. Frederick's son was Maximilian I, who was succeeded by a grandson, **Charles V.** Charles had a brother, **Ferdinand,** who became King of Bohemia and Hungary. The Aust. Habsburgs descended from Ferdinand and the Sp. Habsburgs descended from Charles's son **Philip II.** The Sp. Habsburgs became extinct when **Charles II** d. in 1700; the Aust. Habsburgs, when **Charles VI** d. in 1740. The later Habsburgs are descended from the Empress **Maria Theresa,** daughter of Charles VI, and **Francis,** Duke of Lorraine. **Francis II,** a grandson of Maria Theresa, resigned the imperial crown in 1806, and the Holy Rom. Emp. came to an end. In 1804 he had declared himself Emperor of Austria, and his descendants, notably **Francis Joseph,** kept this dignity until 1918.

HADDOCK
(*Gadus aeglefinus*) N. Atlantic fish with black patches above the breast fins and black lateral lines. It averages 4 lb. in wt. but may reach 17 lb. It is eaten, either freshly cooked or split, dried and smoked, when it is called Findon, or Finnan haddock.

HADRIAN
[hā'-] (76-138) Rom. emperor. A soldier and administrator selected by his friend and patron, the Emperor Trajan, as his successor. He visited Brit. where he was responsible for the wall called after him. **Hadrian's Wall.** Defensive wall extending from the Solway Firth across Eng. to Wallsend-on-Tyne. It was built *c.* A.D. 122, was 73 m. long and its course may still be traced.

HAEMOPHILIA
[hēmō-fil'-iă] Hereditary abnormality of the blood, limited to males but transmitted by females, characterised by tendency to excessive bleeding from slight injuries and to lack of faculty of blood to clot.

HAEMORRHAGE
The escape of blood from a blood vessel. When an artery is damaged (arterial Haemorrhage) the blood is bright red and may flow in regular spurts synchronising with the heart beat. When a vein is damaged (venous haemorrhage) the blood is darker red and usually flows at a steady rate. Internal haemorrhage is hidden bleeding and usually occurs into the brain or lungs or abdomen and is characterised by a faint feeling, pallor, thirst, rapid irregular soft pulse and increased respiration.

HAEMORRHOIDS
[hem'-or-] (or **Piles**) Dilatation of lower rectal veins which may protrude through the anus or rupture and bleed after a bowel movement.

HAGGAI
One of the minor prophets of the O.T.

HAGGIS
Scots dish of Fr. origin. It consists of the heart, lungs and liver of a sheep, finely minced, to which are added onions, suet, lemon juice, oatmeal, seasoning and gravy.

HAGUE, The
[hāg] (Dutch, **'s Gravenhage**) Admin. centre and seat of the Govt. of the Netherlands, cap. of S. Holland prov., 3m. from the N. Sea and 14 N.W. of Rotterdam. The legislature meets in the Binnenhof. There are printing works and various manufactures. The Hague was damaged by air raids in World War II. Pop. 604,112.

HAHN, Otto
(1879-1968) German chemist. He succeeded in splitting the uranium atom nucleus in 1939 and, in 1944, was awarded the Nobel Prize in chemistry. He was given Allied protective custody in 1945, and reports of his experiments given to Amer. scientists were instrumental in the development of the atomic bomb.

HAIFA
[hī'-fă] Seaport of Israel, situated on the Bay of Acre, at the foot of Mt. Carmel. It has oil-refineries and a flourishing export trade. Pop. 182,007.

HAIG, Earl
Douglas (1861-1928) Brit. soldier. Commanded 1st Army in Fr. 1914-15. Succeeded French as C.-in-C., 1915, being responsible for the Battle of the Somme (1916), the indecisive engagements of 1917, and the final offensive (1918), which ended World War I, He was made a field marshal, 1917, an Earl, 1919, given the O.M., voted £100,000. See *Douglas Haig: The Educated Soldier* (1963).

HAILE SELASSIE
[hī'-lē-se-las'-ē] (1892-) Emperor of Ethiopia. Through his influence many reforms were carried out, including the modernising of the

educ. system, and the abolition of slave-trading. In 1930, he was officially crowned Emperor. In 1935 Ethiopia was invaded by Italy and overwhelmed. Haile Selassie strongly protested to the League of Nations against the Ital. aggression, but it was not until the outbreak of World War II that liberation became possible. In 1936 he escaped to Eng. He recovered his throne in 1941. Since the war he has finally abolished slavery and set up an advisory two-chamber Parl. *See* ABYSSINIAN WAR.

HAILSHAM
Viscount (1872-1950) Eng. lawyer. **Douglas McGarel Hogg** was the eldest son of the philanthropist Quintin Hogg. In 1922 he became Cons. M.P. for Marylebone. From 1922-4 and 1924-8 he was Att.-Gen. In 1928-9 and again in 1935-38 he was Lord Chanc. Joined the Nat. Govt. in 1931, he was War Sec. until 1935. His son **Quintin McGarel Hogg** (1907-) was Cons. M.P. for Oxford, 1938-50. In 1957 became Lord Pres. of the Council and Chairman of Cons. Party. First Min. of Science and Technology, 1959-64. Renounced title under Peerage Act, 1963.

HAINAUT
[ā'-nō] Prov. of S.W. Belgium, on the Fr. border, drained by the Scheldt and Sambre. The people are mainly Walloons. Mons is the cap. and Charleroi and Tournai are important towns.

HAIR
Filamentous outgrowth from the skin, forming the coat of mammals. The word is loosely applied also to analogous outgrowths from the bodies of plants, insects and other organisms. Each hair is formed by a single papilla in a skin follicle, with fat-producing glands, and comprises a bulbous root, shaft and point. Commercially, hair is much used. The finer kinds, such as the hair of goats, etc. are used for making garments. The hair of horses, being coarser, is used as a stuffing and padding for furniture. The hair of the cow is used for making felt.

HAITI
[hā'-] Repub. of the W. Indies, occupying the W. part of the Is. of Hispaniola. Coffee, cocoa, cotton, bananas and sisal are exported. There are mineral resources of gold, silver, copper and iron. Port-au-Prince is the cap. and chief port. Fr. is the official language, and R.C. the state religion. The majority of the pop. are negroes and mulattoes. Haiti was a Fr. colony from 1677-1801 when it became indep. From 1820 it has been a repub. with a pres. and nat. assembly of senators and deputies. Area: 10,700 sq.m. Pop. 4,000,000.

HAKE
(*Merluccius vulgaris*) Resembling the cod, this fish has no barbels and fewer dorsal and anal fins. It may reach 3 ft. in length and over 30 lb. in wt. It is a valued food fish.

HAKLUYT, Richard
[hak'-lo͞ot] (*c.* 1552-1616) Eng. writer. B. Herefordshire, educ. Westminster School and Oxford. In 1582 he pub. *Divers Voyages Touching the Discovery of America.* Hakluyt's chief work is the collection called *Principal Navigations, Voyages and Discoveries of the English Nation.*

HALDANE
Famous Scots family. **Robert Haldane of Cloan,** a lawyer, mar. **Mary Burdon Sanderson.** Their eldest son was **Viscount Haldane** (1856-1928) Brit. statesman. Became a barrister and 1885 Lib. M.P. In 1905, Sec. for War, created the Territorial Army and organised the force that took the field in 1914. After the war joined Lab. Party. Ranked as one of leading philosophers. His ideas are expressed in *Pathway to Reality.* **John Burdon Sanderson H.** (1892-1964), a grandson of Robert H., made a reputation as a scientist. In 1927 he was apptd. head of the genetical dept. of the John Innes Horticultural Inst. From 1932-7 he was Prof. of Genetics and since 1937 Prof. of Biometry in London Univ. He became Chairman of the Editorial Board of the *Daily Worker* in 1940 but later stated that he thought that communist orthodoxy was mistaken and in 1956 went to India where he found Hindu philosophy and religion congenial.

HALIBUT
(*Hippoglossus vulgaris*) The largest flatfish. It is sometimes more than 8 ft. long and 200 lb. in wt. The eyes and dark coloration are on the right, the upper, side. The fish is a popular food.

HALIFAX
County borough and market town of the W. Riding, Yorks. 7 m. S.W. of Bradford. Industries include the making of carpets and woollen goods. It returns 1 member to Parl. Pop. 96,150.

HALIFAX
Cap. of Nova Scotia and the chief winter port of Canada, with ice-free harbour. It is the terminus of both the transcontinental railways. Apart from shipping, the chief industries are shipbuilding, oil-refining and fishing. Pop. 179,000.

HALIFAX, Earl of
Edward Frederick Lindley Wood (1881-1959) Eng. statesman. M.P. (Unionist), 1910-25; Viceroy of India, 1926-31; Min. of Educ. 1932-5; Foreign Sec. 1938-40; Ambassador to the U.S.A. 1940-6. As Foreign Sec. he was in office during the events which led to the outbreak of war in 1939.

HALIFAX, Marquess of
George Savile (1633-95) Eng. statesman and writer. Chief adviser to Charles II, 1681-5. Lord Pres. of Council under James II but resigned. As Lord Pres. formally offered crown to William and Mary. From the middle course he pursued, earned the name of '*The Trimmer.*'

HALIOTIS
The 'Ormer' of N. Brittany and the Channel Is. A flat-shelled marine gasteropod mollusc, it is esteemed as a delicacy. The nacreous internal lining of the shell is thick mother-of-pearl. *Haliotis,* alternatively *Abalone,* adheres to the rocks like a limpet.

HALL MARK
A set of marks stamped on gold and silver articles at the Goldsmith's Hall, London, and at Assay Offices or Halls throughout the country to attest the genuineness of the metal and the year of testing. The marks are: (1) Makers' initials. (2) Standard marks of Assay Office—Lion or Thistle for Silver—Carat marking for Gold. (3) Stamp of Assay Office or Hall; Leopard's Head for London, Crown for Sheffield, Anchor for Birmingham, 3 Wheat Sheaves for Chester, City Coat of Arms for Glasgow, Castle (or 3 turrets) for Edinburgh. (4) Letter signifying year of Hall marking. This letter is common to all Assay Offices and is changed annually.

HALLAM, Henry
(1777-1859) Eng. historian. His works include: *The Constitutional History of England from the Accession of Henry VII to the d. of George II.* His son was **Arthur Henry** (1811-33) Eng. writer. He was Tennyson's friend and is lamented in *In Memoriam.*

HALLE
City of E. Germany, cap. of Saxony-Anhalt, on the Saale, 21 m. N.W. of Leipzig. There is a univ. founded 1694. Pop. 278,049.

HALLÉ, Sir Charles
(1819-95) Eng. musician. B. Germany. In 1848 he settled in London and became naturalised. Hallé won a reputation by his concerts in Lon-

don and by his work for music in Manchester, where he founded the Royal Coll. of Music and in 1857 the Hallé orchestra.

HALLEY, Edmund
(1656-1742) Eng. astron. In 1703 he was made Savilian Prof. of Geometry at Oxford, and in 1720 Astron. Royal at Greenwich. **Halley's Comet.** In 1682 Halley observed the movement of the comet which is named after him. Its period is 75 or 76 years.

HALLSTADT
Village of Austria, on H. lake, 32 m. S.E. of Salzburg. Salt mining is the chief industry, but H. is important for the prehistoric cemetery unearthed, 1846. The name has been given to the first part of the Iron Age (*c.* 850-400 B.C.).

HALS, Franz
[hȧls] (1580-1666) Dutch painter, b. Antwerp, his life was spent mainly at Haarlem, where he painted and taught painting. A great master of portraiture, his work greatly influenced the Dutch school.

HAMBURG
W. German city and seaport, cap. of H. state, on the Elbe estuary, 75 m. from its mouth and 56 N.E. of Bremen. In 1939 H. was the largest port of Germany. In the M.A. Hamburg was a leading member of the Hanseatic League. It was made a free city, 1510, and joined the German Confed. 1815. Pop. 1,847,000. The **State of H.** was formed, 1938, by the amalgamation of the city and certain neighbouring Prussian districts. It is now a state of W. Germany.

HAMELN
W. German town in Lower Saxony, on the Weser, 23 m. S.W. of Hanover. It is famous for the legend of the Pied Piper. Pop. 51,200.

HAMILTON, Duke of
Scots title, the senior of its kind. **James,** the 2nd marquess, was made a duke in 1643. In 1648 he led an army into Eng. to help Charles I, but was defeated at Preston, and in 1649 was executed. In 1660, **William Douglas, Earl of Selkirk,** having mar. the heiress of the last duke, was made Duke of Hamilton. **Alexander,** the 12th duke, d. without sons in 1895, when a kinsman, **Alfred** (1862-1940) inherited the titles and the estates in Lanarkshire.

HAMILTON, Emma
(1765-1815) Mistress of Lord Nelson. In 1781 she became the mistress of the Hon. Charles Greville, leaving him in 1786 for Sir William Hamilton. At Naples, in 1793, she met Nelson. Their child, Horatia, was b. in 1801.

HAMMARSKJÖLD, Dag Hjalmar Agne Carl
[ham'-ar-shöld] (1906-61) Swed. internationalist. Sec. Gen. of the U.N. 1953-61. D. in air crash while conducting negotiations on Congo. Awarded Peace Prize posthumously.

HAMMERFEST
Town and fishing port of N. Norway, on an Is. A centre of the cod fisheries, the most N. town of Europe.

HAMMERHEAD
(*Scopus*) (1) A heron, brown in colour, and *c.* 2 ft. long. It is found near lakes, as it feeds on fish and frogs. The feathers on the head give it a certain resemblance to a hammer. (2) Hammerhead **Shark** (*Zygaena*) Large species of shark from temp. and trop. seas. The extended head lobes with the eyes at their extremities account for the popular name.

HAMMURABI
(*c.* 2100 B.C.) King of Babylon. He dominated the Sumerian and Akkadian city states, and made Babylonia a single monarchy. He left valuable letters, and a Semitic code of laws.

HAMPDEN, John
(1594-1643) Eng. statesman. He became M.P. for Grampound in 1621, then for Wendover and then for Buckinghamshire. His fame rests on his opposition to Ship Money (*q.v.*). Refused to pay this tax, and finally won his case. Hampden was one of the 5 members whom Charles I tried to arrest.

HAMPSHIRE
(Hants.) County of S. Eng. with a coastline on the Eng. Channel. It includes the Is. of Wight, which is a separate admin. county. The rivers include the Itchen, Test, Hamble, Avon and Lymington. There are Downs in the N. and around Winchester; sheep farming is one of the chief industries. The county contains the New Forest and other forest areas. Winchester is the county town, but Southampton, Portsmouth and Bournemouth are larger. Portsmouth Harbour is the headquarters of the navy, and Southampton Water is a great commercial harbour. Hampshire returns 13 members to Parl. (8 borough constituencies). Pop. 1,384,030.

HAMPSTEAD
Part of Camden, borough of Greater London (1964), lying S. of Hendon. **Hampstead Heath.** Public recreation ground *c.* 430 ft. high. It was once noted for its fairs and is still a popular resort on bank holidays.

HAMPTON
District on the Thames, 15 m. S.W. of London. **Hampton Court.** Palace on the Thames, erected by Cardinal Wolsey and enlarged by Henry VIII. Further additions were designed by Wren. The larger apartments are open to the public.

HAMSUN, Knut
(1859-1952) Norwegian novelist. B. Gudbrandsdal. He won the Nobel Prize in 1920. His first novel, *Sult* (*Hunger*) appeared in 1890.

HAND
(1) Prehensile extremity of the fore limb. Skeleton composed of 5 metacarpal bones—1 for each finger—which articulate with the wrist or carpal bones above and phalanges or finger bones below. There are 14 phalanges—3 for each finger and 2 for thumb. The development of hands is peculiar to man and arose from the withdrawing of the fore limbs from the function of support and locomotion and endowing them with the faculty of grasping by means of mobilising thumb joints. (2) A unit of length used in measurement of horses. Orig. roughly the breadth of a man's hand it is standardised at 4 inches.

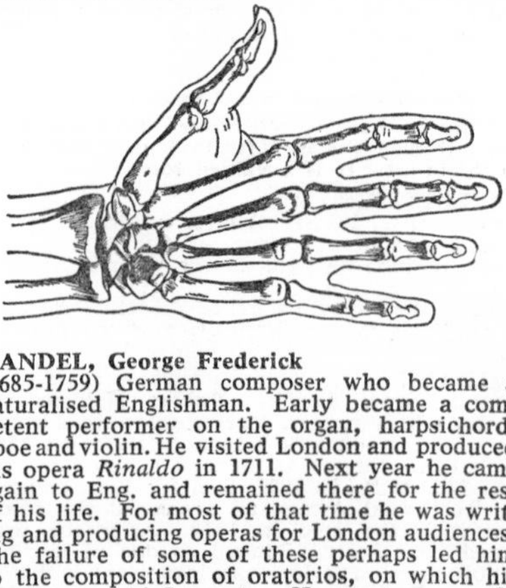

HANDEL, George Frederick
(1685-1759) German composer who became a naturalised Englishman. Early became a competent performer on the organ, harpsichord, oboe and violin. He visited London and produced his opera *Rinaldo* in 1711. Next year he came again to Eng. and remained there for the rest of his life. For most of that time he was writing and producing operas for London audiences. The failure of some of these perhaps led him to the composition of oratorios, on which his fame now chiefly rests. He wrote some 30 operas, *c.* 18 oratorios including *Messiah,* 1741, ch. music, 12 concerti grossi for strings, 6 for

HERALDRY

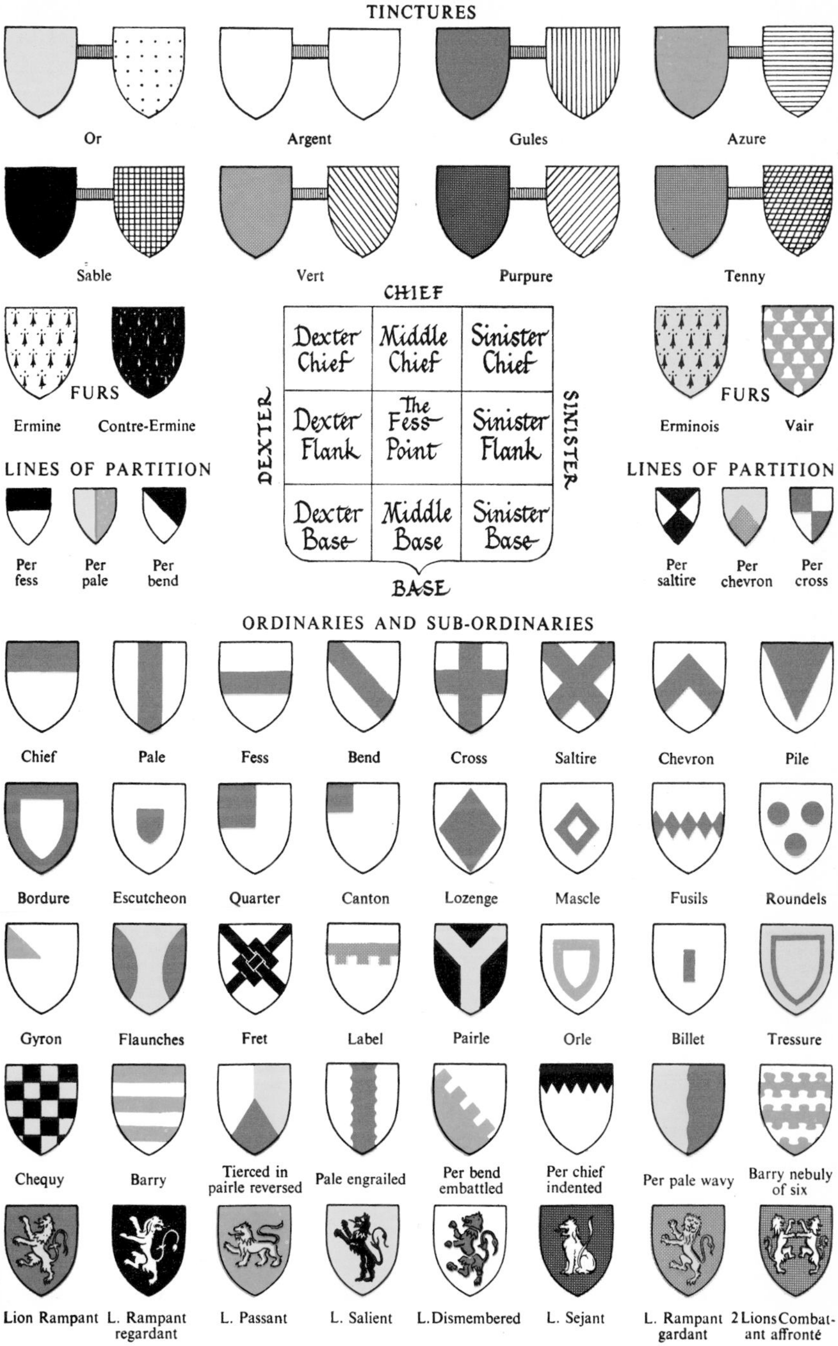
TINCTURES
Or
Argent
Gules
Azure
Sable
Vert
Purpure
Tenny
FURS
Ermine
Contre-Ermine
Erminois
Vair
CHIEF
Dexter Chief
Middle Chief
Sinister Chief
Dexter Flank
The Fess Point
Sinister Flank
Dexter Base
Middle Base
Sinister Base
DEXTER
SINISTER
BASE
LINES OF PARTITION
Per fess
Per pale
Per bend
Per saltire
Per chevron
Per cross
ORDINARIES AND SUB-ORDINARIES
Chief
Pale
Fess
Bend
Cross
Saltire
Chevron
Pile
Bordure
Escutcheon
Quarter
Canton
Lozenge
Mascle
Fusils
Roundels
Gyron
Flaunches
Fret
Label
Pairle
Orle
Billet
Tressure
Chequy
Barry
Tierced in pairle reversed
Pale engrailed
Per bend embattled
Per chief indented
Per pale wavy
Barry nebuly of six
Lion Rampant
L. Rampant regardant
L. Passant
L. Salient
L. Dismembered
L. Sejant
L. Rampant gardant
2 Lions Combatant affronté

COATS OF ARMS of NATIONS

Australia · *Austria* · *Belgium* · *Bolivia* · *Brazil* · *Bulgaria* · *China*

Cuba · *Czechoslovakia* · *Denmark* · *Ethiopia* · *Finland* · *France* · *W. Germany*

Ghana · *Great Britain* · *Greece* · *Iceland* · *India* · *Ireland* · *Israel*

Italy · *Japan* · *Mexico* · *The Netherlands* · *New Zealand* · *Norway* · *Pakistan*

Panama · *Peru* · *Poland* · *Portugal* · *Soviet Union* · *Spain* · *South Africa*

Sweden · *Switzerland* · *Thailand* · *United Nations* · *United States* · *Vatican City State* · *Yugoslavia*

wind and strings, organ concertos and instrumental music.

HANKOW
City and port of Hupeh prov. China, at the confluence of the Han and Yangtze-Kiang. With Hanyang and Wuchang, it forms a great commercial and industrial centre, Wuhan. Total pop. 2,146,000.

HANNIBAL
(*c.* 247-183 B.C.) Carthaginian soldier, son of Hamilcar Barca. In 229, he took command of the Carthaginian forces and restarted open war by the capture of the Sp. Rom. city of Saguntum in 218. He then set out for Italy and led his army on a costly journey across the Alps to avoid the enemy on the coast. He won a first victory over the Roms. at Ticinus, then had 3 important victories at the R. Trebia, L. Trasimene (217), and Cannae (216). Many think that Rome would have fallen to him had he attacked the city. Hannibal chose to pass the winter at Capua to the S. of Rome. After 10 years of indecisive warfare he was defeated at Metaurus in 207. Utterly defeated by Scipio in 202 at Zama, he went into exile.

HANOI
Chief town of N. Vietnam repub., formerly cap. of Tong King, on the Red River (Song-koi), *c.* 80 m. from the sea. Pop. 800,000.

HANOVER
Cap. of Lower Saxony, W. Germany, on the Leine, 65 m. S.E. of Bremen. Printing machinery, textiles and chems. are the chief industries. Pop. 576,600.

HANOVER
Former prov. of Prussia. The duchy of Lüneburg-Celle was ruled, 1692, by Ernest Augustus, who was made Elector of Hanover. From 1714-1837 the Electors were also Kings of Gt. Brit. and N. Ireland. In 1837 Hanover was separated from Gt. Brit. In 1946 it became part of the new State of Lower Saxony. **House of Hanover.** Eng. royal house. The succession to the throne was claimed through Sophia, granddaughter of James I, wife of the Elector Ernest Augustus. The Act of Settlement, 1701, made their son, George of Hanover, heir to Queen Anne, to exclude the Catholic Stuart line. Hanoverian monarchs were George I, George II, George III, George IV and William IV.

HANSEATIC LEAGUE
Union of towns, chiefly in N. Europe, for trading purposes. In the 12th cent., merchants formed themselves into a *hansa* or assoc. for the purpose of securing privileges. Later, these *hansa* united themselves together for the same purpose. In forming this league Lübeck, Hamburg and Bremen took the leading part, and in the 14th cent. they had made it into a great confederation. Most of the seaports on the Baltic and the E. side of the N. Sea were members. Its H.Q. was at Lübeck. The 14th cent. was the most flourishing period of the League's hist. Its membership meant valuable privileges, and protection for merchants, for the League kept an army. In the 15th cent. the power of the League declined.

HARBOUR
Stretch of water, where ships can anchor in safety. There are natural harbours and artificial harbours. The best natural harbours are found where the sea penetrates the land by a somewhat narrow entrance. The entrance to New York makes a fine natural harbour. The mouths of rivers may make harbours, but these are more liable to be silted up with sand or débris. **Artificial harbours** are made in suitable places by the construction of breakwaters and other works of that kind. Dover, Southampton, and Buenos Aires are examples. Two **Mulberry Harbours,** used in the Normandy landings of June, 1944, were floated across the Channel. *See* MULBERRY.

HARDIE, James Keir
(1856-1915) Scots politician. M.P. (Lab.), 1892-95 and 1900-15. For many years Hardie ed. Lab. journals, and founded the Indep. Lab. Party.

HARDING, Warren Gamaliel
(1865-1923) 28th Pres. of the U.S.A. B. Ohio, he started life as a schoolmaster, but soon became a printer. As a Republican he was elected to the U.S. Senate in 1914, and opposed Pres. Wilson's policy in World War I. In 1920 Harding was nominated for the presidency and he won a signal victory. The chief event of his term of office was the calling of the Washington Conference, but he d. before the expiration of his term. His admin. was one of the most corrupt in U.S. history.

HARDY, Thomas
(1840-1928) Eng. writer. B. near Dorchester, Dorset. His first novel *Desperate Remedies,* appeared in 1871 and *Under the Greenwood Tree* in 1872. Then came *A Pair of Blue Eyes* (1873), *Far from the Madding Crowd* (1874), *The Return of the Native* (1878), *The Mayor of Casterbridge* (1886), *Tess of the D'Urbervilles* (1891), *Jude the Obscure* (1895), and *The Well-Beloved* (1897). Violent criticism of his last written novel, *Jude,* decided Hardy to devote himself to poetry, and 7 vols. of lyrics appeared 1898-1925, and his great dramatic poem on the Napoleonic Wars, *The Dynasts* (1904-8). *Collected Poems* (1919). In 1910 he was awarded the O.M.

HARDY, Sir Thomas Masterman
(1769-1839) Eng. admiral. In 1796 began his friendship with Nelson. They fought at the Battle of the Nile in the same ship, and at Trafalgar. Hardy was capt. of the *Victory* when Nelson addressed to him his dying words.

HARE
In Brit. a common rodent, the Brown Hare (*Lepus europaeus*). It is *c.* 2 ft. long and weighs 7-8 lb. It has a short tail, long ears and a cleft upper lip. It runs swiftly by leaps, and lives in grassy furrows. The young is called the leveret. The hare is used in coursing and is also hunted by harriers and beagles.

HAREBELL
Name of the Scots bluebell (*Campanula rotundifolia*) distinct from the wild hyacinth, or Eng. bluebell. The flowers are bell-like and of a clear colour, nodding on stiff-angled stems. It is found on heaths and meadow-land from July to Sept.

HARFLEUR
Port of N. France in Seine Inférieure dept. to the N. of the Seine estuary, 6 m. E. of Le Havre. Captured by Henry V, 1415. Pop. 5,000.

HARGREAVES, James
(1745-1778) Eng. inventor. B. Lancs. he became a weaver at Standhill near Blackburn. There *c.* 1764, he built the spinning jenny, a great improvement on the existing machinery.

HARLECH
Town of Merionethshire, 10 m. N.W. of Barmouth. Once the county town, it is now a small pleasure resort. There are ruins of a castle.

HARLEY, Robert
1st Earl of Oxford and Earl Mortimer (1661-1724) Eng. statesman and lawyer, Whig M.P. 1690. He was member of the commission for the union with Scot. 1706. He tried to undermine Marlborough's influence with Queen Anne. He brought the war with Fr. to an end. The intrigues of Bolingbroke (St. John), caused his fall (1714). The valuable collection of books and manuscripts, the *Harleian Mss.,* made by him and his son Edward, is in the Brit. Museum.

HARMONIUM
A small portable reed organ of 1 or 2 manuals originating early 19th cent. Wind is supplied from bellows worked by the player's feet.

HAROLD
Name of 4 kings of Norway. **Harold I** reigned 872-930. He was at first a chieftain, one of several, in Norway, but succeeded in bringing the whole land under his own rule. **Harold III,** called Hardrada, invaded Eng. in 1066 and was killed at Stamford Bridge.

HAROLD I
(d. 1040) Eng. king called **Harefoot.** A son of Canute the Great, he claimed the throne on his father's d. 1035. It was also claimed by his half-brother, Hardicanute. **Harold II** (*c.* 1022-66) Eng. king, son of Earl Godwin. In 1051 Godwin and his sons were banished. By 1053 Harold had returned and succeeded his father as Earl of Wessex. In 1066, on Edward's d. the Witan chose him as king and he was crowned at Westminster. Shortly afterwards, Harold, King of Norway, together with Tostig, a rebellious brother of the Eng. king, invaded Eng. Harold II defeated them at Stamford Bridge, Sept. 25, and then led his army S. where William of Normandy had landed to claim the crown. At Hastings he met the Normans and there he was killed.

HAROUN AL-RASCHID
[hà-roon'ăl-rà-shēd'] (763-809) Abbasid Caliph of Baghdad. A son of Mohammed Mahdi. In 786 he became caliph in succession to his brother. His life at Baghdad is immortalised in *The Arabian Nights*.

HARP
One of the most ancient instruments known to man, dating from *c.* 3000 B.C. The ancient harp had few strings, all with notes of fixed pitch; the modern double-action harp invented by Erard in 1810 has a range of 6 octaves and a 5th. The normal tuning is the diatonic scale of C flat major.

HARPOON
Dart-like barbed weapon used for killing whales, orig. thrown by hand from an open boat. The older form is superseded now by the shot-harpoon which is fired from a gun, and carries an explosive charge.

HARPSICHORD
A keyboard instrument in use from the 16th to 18th cents. It is similar in shape to the modern grand pianoforte, differing from it chiefly in that the sound is produced by the mechanical plucking of the strings by plectra instead of by striking them with a felt-headed hammer.

HARRIER
Breed of dog maintained for hunting hares by scent. The dogs, smaller than fox-hounds, may be 20 in. high and have large pointed ears.

HARRIS
S. part of the Is. of Lewis in the Outer Hebrides, forming part of Inverness-shire. The soil is very poor. The district gives its name to a type of tweed. Tarbert, on the coast, is the chief town.

HARRISON, Julius
(1885-1963) Eng. composer. His works include a Mass in C for soloists, chorus and orchestra, 'cello concerto, rhapsody for violin and orchestra, chamber music and songs.

HARROGATE
Borough and inland spa of W. Riding, Yorks. 15 m. N. of Leeds. Pop. 56,000.

HARROW
Borough of Greater London (1964). Formerly in Middlesex. **Harrow School.** Eng. public school founded by John Lyon in 1571. Towards the end of the 18th cent. it became one of the chief schools in the land, rivalling Eton and Winchester. Among its pupils were Byron, Sheridan, Peel, Palmerston and, more recently, Baldwin, Galsworthy and Winston Churchill.

HARTEBEEST
One of the swiftest African antelopes. It is *c.* 4 ft. high and reddish-brown in colour. It is disappearing rapidly from S. Africa.

HARTFORD
Cap. of Connecticut, U.S.A. on the C. River, midway between New York and Boston. It has light industries and is a centre of the insurance business. Pop. 161,200.

HARTY, Sir Hamilton
(1879-1941) Irish composer, conductor and pianist. From 1920-33 he conducted the Hallé Orchestra. His compositions include a symphonic poem, a violin concerto and songs.

HARVARD UNIVERSITY
Senior univ. and oldest educ. inst. of the U.S.A. at Camb. Founded 1636, by John Harvard. Its first Pres. was Nathaniel Eaton, and it was strongly sectarian. To the orig. Harvard Coll., med. and law schools were added in 1782 and 1817. Its students, which include *c.* 1,000 women, number 12,413.

HARVEST MITE
Familiar name for 6-legged larval forms of a family of velvety ticks, not insects; also called the harvest bug. In Brit. the common crimson-haired *Microtrombidium autumnale* infests grass and herbage, and burrows into the skin of man and other animals.

HARVEY, William
(1578-1657) He became physician to St. Bartholomew's Hospital and lecturer at the Royal Coll. of Physicians. His chief discovery was the circulation of the blood.

HARWELL
Site of the Atomic Energy Research Estab. in Berks. instituted in 1946.

HARWICH
[har'-ich] Seaport and borough of Essex on the estuary of the Orwell and Stour. There is a steamer service with Amsterdam, the Hook of Holland, Hamburg and Zeebrugge. Pop. 13,570.

HASHISH
or **Bhang.** A harmful, habit-forming narcotic drug. It produces voluptuous visions and hallucinations. Use of the drug is controlled by an internat. organisation and in many countries its use is prohibited by law.

HASTINGS
[hā'-] County borough and resort on the S. coast of Sussex. H. is one of the Cinque Ports. H. returns 1 member to Parl. Pop. 66,640. **Battle of Hastings.** Battle fought between the Norman invaders and the A.-S. on Oct. 14, 1066. William, Duke of Normandy, who claimed the Eng. crown on the d. of Edward the Confessor, landed at Pevensey. Having just defeated the Norwegians at Stamford Bridge, Harold hurried S. to meet him. He took up a position on a hill, about 6 m. from Hastings. The battle was stubbornly contested, but after a time William tricked the Saxons into breaking their ranks. Shooting in the air, the Norman archers killed a number of them, including Harold.

HASTINGS, Warren
(1732-1818) Eng. admin. In 1750 he went to India as a writer with the E. India Co. He became Pres. at Murshidabad, 1758, member of the Council of Bengal, 1761-64, and of Madras, 1768. In 1772 he became Pres. of the Council of Bengal, and in 1773 the first Gov.-Gen. of India. During his period of office Hastings did much to consolidate Brit. authority in India. He was unscrupulous in his means of raising money. For this reason he met with opposition on the Council, and, on his return to Eng. 1784, a demand for impeachment. His chief accusers were Burke, Fox and Sheridan. See *Warren Hastings* by Keith Feiling (1954).

HATFIELD
Town and rural district of Herts. on the Lea, 17 m. N. of London. H. House is a fine example

of Jacobean style. Pop. 22,500. *See* WELWYN GARDEN CITY.

HATHAWAY, Anne
(1556-1623) Wife of William Shakespeare. On Nov. 28, 1582, she mar. the poet, whom she survived. She had 4 children, but only 2 daughters attained maturity.

HATTON, Sir Christopher
(1540-91) Eng. courtier and lawyer, chiefly known as one of Elizabeth's favourites. **Hatton Garden**, a London thoroughfare in which he lived, has become the centre of the diamond merchant trade.

HAUPTMANN, Gerhart Johann
(1862-1946) German author. In 1889 he pub. *Vor Sonnenaufgang*, a realistic play which had great influence. He also wrote novels, and a poem *Ihma.*

HAUSA
[how'-] Negroid people of W. Africa, living chiefly in the Sudan and Nigeria. Their language is Hamitic and is the *lingua franca* of the Sudan.

HAVANA
Cap. of Cuba, on the N. coast, on a fine natural harbour. H. is famous for its manufacture of tobacco and cigars, whilst sugar is another staple industry. H. was founded, 1514, and still bears traces of its Sp. origin. Pop. 787,765.

HAVELOCK, Sir Henry
(1795-1857) Eng. gen. In 1823 he went to India. When the Mutiny began he led a force from Allahabad to Cawnpore. After fighting 8 battles he was forced to fall back until reinforcements arrived. With these he made his way to Lucknow, but was besieged until relieved by Sir Colin Campbell.

HAVRE, Le
[âvr] Port of N. Fr. in Seine-Inférieure dept. on the estuary of the Seine, 55 m. from Rouen. There is a regular steamer service to Southampton. The seat of the Belgian Govt. 1914-18, Le Havre was severely damaged in World War II. Pop. 223,000.

HAWAII
[hăwī'-ē] State of the U.S.A. consisting of a chain of Is. in the N. Pacific Ocean. The group is of volcanic origin, Mauna Kea (13,820 ft.), is the highest volcano. The climate is trop. and the vegetation luxurious. Crops include rice, sugar, pineapples, coffee and bananas. Honolulu, on Oahu, is the cap. and Pearl Harbour is a U.S. naval station. The Is. were discovered by Capt. Cook, 1778, and were known as the Sandwich Is. At first they were an indep. kingdom and from 1873 a repub. They were finally annexed by the U.S.A. 1898, and became the 50th state, 1959, with 2 representatives in Congress. Area: 6,400 sq.m. Pop. 769,900.

HAWFINCH
(*Coccothraustes vulgaris*) A stout-billed Finch distributed over Europe, Asia and N. Africa, and common in Eng. 7 in. long.

HAWICK
Burgh and market town of Roxburghshire, on the Teviot, 50 m. S.E. of Edinburgh. The town is a centre of the wool industry. Pop. 16,000.

HAWK
Diurnal birds of prey not being vultures or eagles. The term comprises a sub-family, incl. the harriers, represented in Brit. by the Goshawk and the Sparrow Hawk. **Hawking.** Sport of hunting game with hawks or falcons, also called *falconry*. Of very ancient origin, it has been practised throughout the world. In Eng. falconry was practised by the A.-S. and for some 7 cents. it was the chief sport of the richer classes. The birds used in hawking were the peregrine falcon, gyrfalcon, merlin and

Goshawk

others belonging to the long-winged class, and the sparrow hawk, goshawk and others of the short-winged class. When fully trained and ready for the field, the hawk's eyes were hooded, and the bird was carried on the wrist of the falconer. When the game was sighted the hawk was unhooded and loosed by the falconer. In the 20th cent. there is a revival of the sport.

HAWKBIT
(*Leontodon*) Genus of biennial or perennial herbs of the Compositae family. The yellow flower-heads appear on numerous simple or branched milk-juiced stalks springing from the root stock.

HAWKINS, Sir John
(1532-1595) Eng. seaman. B. Plymouth, he went to sea when a boy. He fought his own ship, the *Victory*, against the Spaniards in 1588, and was knighted. His son **Richard** (1562-1622) sailed under Drake and commanded a ship against the Armada.

HAWKWEED
(*Hieracium*) Large genus of milk-juiced perennial herbs of the Compositae family, native to N. temperate and Arctic regions. Among many Brit. species is the mouse ear, *H. pilosella.*

HAWTHORN
Small tree found in Brit. and other temp. regions. It bears fragrant white or red flowers in large clusters. Hawthorn, also called may, bears berries called haws. It belongs to the family Rosaceae.

HAWTHORNE, Nathaniel
(1804-64) Amer. writer. B. Salem, Mass., d. Plymouth, New Hampshire. In 1841 he joined the Brook Farm community, a Socialist experiment. From 1853-7 he was consul at Liverpool, then travelled in Europe. His novels, which use the New Eng. background, include: *The Scarlet Letter* (1850), *The House of the Seven Gables* (1851). Also many short stories for children.

HAY
Grass, clover and other herbage mown and dried for use as fodder. It is derived from rotation crops or permanent meadow and pasture. Sun-drying reduces the moisture from ¾ in the green plants to ½ in the dry. A ton or load of hay comprises 36 trusses, each weighing 56 lb. of old, or 60 lb. of new hay. **Hay Fever.** Affection of nose, throat, upper air passage and eyes, caused by over-sensitivity to pollen and certain plants. Characterised by sneezing, eye irritation, copious flow of tears and nasal discharge, headache and general depression.

HAYDN, Franz Joseph
[hī'] (1732-1809) Aust. composer. In 1761 he was apptd. musical director to the Esterhazy family. He has been called the father of the symphony and the founder of the string quartet. He visited London, 1790-2, when he performed 12 specially commissioned symphonies. His oratorio *The Creation* was produced in Vienna in 1798. His immense output includes 104 symphonies, 84 string quartets, much other chamber music, 42 piano sonatas, many works for the stage, 12 Masses and other ch. music.

HAZEL
Genus of shrubs or trees related to the birch family. The common *Corylus avellana* yields a useful wood. Cultivated varieties furnish cobs, filberts and Barcelona nuts. The tree is found in Europe and Asia; in Brit. it may reach 30 ft.

HAZLITT, William
(1778-1830) Eng. writer. Son of a Unitarian minister; b. at Maidstone. He lived in Paris and painted portraits, but soon turned to writing, settling in London in 1812. He worked for *The Morning Chronicle, The Edinburgh Review* and the *London Magazine*. His critical work includes *Characters of Shakespeare's Plays, Lectures on the English Poets, Dramatic Literature of the Age of Elizabeth.* His essays include *Table Talk*.

HEALTH
Soundness of body and mind. In recent years much thought has been given to preventive medicine and the result is seen in increased longevity, the fall in maternal death rate, infantile morbidity and mortality, etc. With the passing of the Health Act in 1947 the State has now complete control over all med. facilities and is empowered by Acts of Parliament to provide all med. services necessary for use of civil population. Maternity and Child Welfare, School Med. Service, and Health Service allow of complete supervision from the antenatal period onwards with ancillary services, *e.g.* dental service, health visitors, school meals, and industrial med. services.

HEALY, Timothy Michael
(1855-1931) Irish politician. M.P. (Nationalist) 1880-1918. He was a firm R.C. and opposed Parnell after the split in the Party. He was the 1st Gov.-Gen. of the Irish Free State.

HEARING
One of the 5 senses. Consists of outer ear, tympanic membrane, tympanic ossicles, internal ear with cochlea, blood vessels and nerves. A sound is perceived, or heard, when a wave strikes the tympanic membrane, setting up oscillations which travel to the hearing centre in the brain. Man is capable of perceiving vibrations ranging from 30-50,000 per sec. *See* DEAFNESS.

HEART
A 4-chambered organ which maintains the circulation of the blood by virtue of the muscular tissue in its walls. Situated mainly in the left side of the thorax with its right border along the outer edge of the sternum, between the 2nd and 4th ribs. *See* ANGINA PECTORIS; CORONARY THROMBOSIS; ARTERIO-SCLEROSIS.

HEARTSEASE
Species of violets, esp. *V. tricolor* and its subspecies *V. lutea*, whose mingling of purple, white and golden-yellow in the same flower distinguishes it from 1-coloured violets and 2-coloured pansy violets.

HEAT
A form of energy, which may be obtained from, or converted into, the other forms, *e.g.* mechanical energy, electrical energy, chemical energy. Radiant Heat is an electromagnetic vibration of wavelength longer than that of visible light. It travels through empty space without any loss, but on encountering water of any form it may be converted to molecular heat which is simply an agitation of the molecules of the body which possesses it. The distinction between heat and temp. is important. The temp. of a body is a property which indicates whether heat flows from the body to its surroundings or from the surroundings into the body. The effects which may be produced by the application of heat to a body are (1) increase of temp., (2) increase of volume (or expansion), (3) changes of state, *e.g.* from solid to liquid or liquid to vapour. The unit of heat on the Brit. System is the Brit. Thermal Unit, which is the quantity of heat required to raise the temp. of 1 lb. of water through 1° F. The metric unit is the calorie, which will raise the temp. of 1 gram of water through 1° C. The Specific Heat of a substance is the quantity of heat required to raise unit mass through a temp. of 1°. The Latent Heat of a substance is the quantity of heat absorbed or released when unit mass experiences a change of state. It is measured in calories per gram on the metric system, and B.Th.U. per lb. on the Brit. System.

HEATH
Rigid, evergreen shrub (*Erica*), native to Europe, N. Asia and Africa. Brit. species include the fine-leaved *E. cinerea*, the cross-leaved *E. tetralix*, and others characteristic of S.W. Europe.

HEATH, Edward Richard George
(1916-) Brit. Cons. statesman. P.M. (1970-). Lord Privy Seal (1960-3), headed Brit. delegation at Common Market negotiations (1961-3). Elected leader Cons. party (1965) and led it to victory in Gen. Election (1970).

HEATHER
(or Ling) (*Calluna*) Shrub of the heath family, native to Europe, Siberia and Greenland. It grows widely in Scot. and Ireland. The flowers are usually purple, but there is also a white variety.

HEAVY WATER
Water containing deuterium instead of hydrogen. Its properties differ slightly from those of water (sp. gr. 1·1, freezing pt. 3·8° C.). Heavy water is concentrated by electrolytic decomposition of water, when the ordinary water breaks up more readily, leaving a residue rich in the heavy form. Used in nuclear reactors and for preparing deuterium.

HEBREW
W. Semitic (Canaanite) language, revived among Palestinian Jews, and the official language of Israel. The Books of the O.T. were written in Hebrew (*c.* 760-168 B.C.). A modified Heb. alphabet is used by Yiddish speakers. **Dead Sea Scrolls.** Ancient scrolls and fragments of scrolls discovered by a Bedouin in a rocky hillside cave 2 km. from the N. end of the Dead Sea, in 1947. The scrolls were variously dated by experts as belonging to periods varying from *c.* 200 B.C.-A.D. 100. The Syrians possess 5 scrolls. The Heb. Univ. Jerusalem also possesses 5, viz. a complete *Isaiah, Wars of the Sons of Light and the Sons of Darkness, Praises of the Lord*, etc. Prof. Sukenik assigned the scrolls to the Maccabean, Dr. Ginsburg to the Herodian period. See *The Scrolls from the Dead Sea* by Edmund Wilson (1955).

HEBRIDES
[he'-bridēz] Group of *c.* 500 Is. off the W. coast of Scot. only *c.* 100 of which are inhabited. They form parts of the counties of Ross and Cromarty, Argyll and Inverness. They are divided into 2 groups, Outer and Inner, separated by the Minch and Little Minch. The

Inner Hebrides include Skye, Islay, Jura, Mull, Colonsay, Rhum, Tiree, Staffa and Iona. The Outer Hebrides comprise Lewis-Harris, Taransay and Benbecula, N. and S. Uist, Barra, the Flannan Is., etc. St. Kilda, now uninhabited, is the most westerly. The soil is poor. Sheep rearing and fishing are the main occupations. The Is. were ruled by the Kings of Norway until 1266, when they were ceded to Scot. Many islanders speak Gaelic and are R.C.s.

HEDGE MUSTARD
(*Sisymbrium*) Large genus of annual or biennial herbs of the cruciferous family, native to temp. and cold regions.

HEDGEHOG
(*Erinaceus*) Insect-eating nocturnal mammals. They are natives of Europe and parts of Asia and Africa. All are able to roll themselves into balls and also to erect a protective armour of short, prickly spines.

HEGEL, George William Frederick
[hā'-] (1770-1831) German philosopher. B. Stuttgart. In 1816 he was chosen Prof. of Philosophy at Heidelberg. In 1818 he went to Berlin as prof. at the univ. He was one of the foremost exponents of idealism. He taught that the world of objects can be nothing more than the manifestation or revelation of intelligence. God himself is just the self-development of the Absolute. The universal principle is the idea; being and the idea are identical.

HEIDELBERG
[hī'-dĕl-] W. German town in Baden-Württemberg, on the Neckar 48 m. S. of Frankfurt. The univ., founded 1385, is the oldest in Germany. Pop. 127,000.

HEINE, Heinrich
(1797-1856) German poet. B. Düsseldorf. After 1831 he lived in Paris and became a leader of the democratic movement. Heine was, by birth, a Jew, but in 1825 became a Christian. His fame rests chiefly upon his lyrics (1822-7).

HEIR
One who inherits anything. Heirs are usually created by will, but in Eng. law the heir is one who succeeds to an estate, not by will, but by a settlement. The heir to a title is usually the eldest son of the holder, but, if there is no son, it may be a daughter or a nephew. An heir is called an heir apparent; an heir presumptive is the heir provided a nearer heir is not b.

HEISENBERG, Dr. Werner Karl
[hī'-zĕn-bairg] (1901-) German physicist and founder of quantum mechanics and of the principle of indeterminacy in physics.

HEJIRA
Arabic word used for the flight of Mahomet from Mecca to Medina, in 622. From it the Mohammedans date their era and their year, which begins on July 16.

HELENA
(*c.* 248-328) Saint and Rom. empress. Her son was Constantine the Great. In her old age she made a pilgrimage to Jerusalem. A legend says that she discovered the Holy Sepulchre and the true cross.

HELICOPTER
A heavier-than-air aircraft supported in flight by the reactions of the air on one or more power-driven rotors. The first helicopter capable of lifting itself was built in 1907 by Louis Breguet and Prof. Richet. The pioneer of the successful helicopter was the exiled Russ., Igor Sikorsky, whose first machine flew in Amer. early in 1940. By the end of World War II several types were in production in Amer. The first use of such machines on a large scale took place during the Korean War. Civil applications include scheduled passenger and freight transport, agricultural operations, etc.

HELIGOLAND
German Is. in the N. Sea, *c.* 40 m. from the mouth of the Elbe. In 1807 the Is. was taken by Brit. from Denmark, and ceded to Germany, 1890.

HELIOTROPE
Large genus of herbs and shrubs of the borage family (*Heliotropium*). They bear alternate leaves, and clusters of small, white or lilac salver-shaped flowers.

HELIUM
Inert, colourless, gaseous element, occurring in certain minerals, discovered in 1868 by Lockyer and isolated in 1895 by Ramsay. Used for filling balloons, its density is 0·14 times that of air. Chem. sym. He.

HELIX
Widely distributed genus of air-breathing, gasteropod molluscs of the land snail family. They can withdraw entirely into their spiral shells. Among 25 Brit. species are the Common Garden Snail, *H. hortensis*, and the Edible Snail, *H. pomatia*.

HELL
Place or state of retribution for impenitent sinners after death. The A.V. of the Eng. Bible frequently uses the word for the Heb. *Sheol* and the Gk. *Hades*, denoting the abode of the departed, as well as for *Gehenna* and *Tartarus*.

HELLEBORE
[-i-bawr] Genus of perennial herbs of the buttercup family. The stinking hellebore *Helleborus foetidus*, and the bear's foot (*H. viridis*) grow wild in Brit. The Medit. black hellebore (*H. niger*) is the Christmas rose of Eng. gardens.

HELMHOLTZ, Hermann von
(1821-1894) German physicist and physiologist. He developed a theory of colour vision; in acoustics he developed the resonance theory of hearing. He invented the Ophthalmoscope (1851).

HELPMANN, Sir Robert Murray
(1909-) Brit. actor and dancer. B. Mt. Gambier, S. Australia, he first appeared at the Theatre Royal, Adelaide, 1923. He made his London début in the ballet of *Job* in 1931 and was principal dancer at Sadler's Wells, 1932-46. He has appeared in several films, and in Shakespeare at the Old Vic.

HELSINGOR
(formerly **Elsinore**) Seaport of Denmark, in N.E. Zealand. It is the reputed scene of Shakespeare's *Hamlet*.

HELSINKI
(formerly **Helsingfors**) Cap. city and seaport of Finland, on the Gulf of Finland, 250 m. W. of Leningrad. The harbour is kept open by icebreakers. There is a considerable shipping trade, and numerous industries, and a univ. Pop. 679,000.

HELSTON
Borough and market town of Cornwall, 11 m. S.W. of Falmouth. It is noted for its annual festival on May 8, when the Floral Dance is danced. Pop. 7,000.

HELVETII
[-vet'-ē] Name of a Teutonic tribe. They lived in the district now called Switzerland and around Avranches. The repub. set up in Switzerland by the Fr. in 1798 was called the **Helvetic Republic.** It lasted only until 1803.

HEMINGWAY, Ernest Millar
(1898-1961) Amer. novelist and short-story writer. He served in the Ital. Army in World War I and went to Spain as a war correspondent during the Sp. Civil War. His novels include: *The Sun also Rises* (1926), *Farewell to Arms* (1929), *For Whom the Bell Tolls* (1940).

He also wrote *Death in the Afternoon* (1932), on bullfighting, and *The Green Hills of Africa* (1935), a book on big game hunting. *The Old Man and the Sea* (1953), was awarded the Pulitzer Prize in the U.S.A. and the Nobel Prize for Literature for 1954.

HEMLOCK
Biennial umbelliferous herb, native to Europe, Asia, and N. Africa, and common in Brit. It is poisonous, and in Greece a decoction of it was given to those sentenced to d. Today the alkaloid prepared from it, **conine**, is used in med.

HEMP
(*Cannabis sativa*) The fibre of a herb of the nettle family, used for making rope. The best is grown in Italy, and a little in Eng. and Ireland. It also produces a resinous secretion, made into the drugs known as bhang and hashish. Two other plants bearing the name are the **hemp agrimony** and the **hemp nettle.**

HENBANE
(*Hyoscyamus niger*) Herb of the nightshade family, native to warm and temp. Europe, Asia and Africa, and poisonous to domestic fowls. It is foetid and viscid, with a stout stem, large leaves and funnel-shaped, purple-veined yellow flowers. Both leaves and seed yield alkaloid poisons, hyoscyamine and hyoscine, used as sedatives and anodynes.

HENDERSON, Arthur
(1863-1935) Brit. politician. M.P. (Lab.), 1903-18, 1919-22, 1923, and 1924-31; Home Sec. 1924; Foreign Sec. 1929-31; Pres. of World Disarmament Conference, 1932. He resigned, 1931 and became leader of the Lab. Party in opposition to MacDonald's Nat. Govt.

HENDON
Part of Barnet, borough of Greater London (1964). On the Brent, Hendon became a flying centre. Within the borough is the Metropolitan Police Coll., the London Univ. Observatory, and Mill Hill public school.

HENGIST
A.-S. leader. In A.D. 449, with his brother, Horsa, he landed at the head of a force of Angles at Ebbsfleet in Kent. He defeated the Britons and settled in Kent.

HENLEY-ON-THAMES
Borough of Oxon. on the Thames, 36 m. W. of London. Pop. 9,270. **Henley Regatta.** Principal rowing event in Eng. It is held every July. The first was in 1839.

HENRIETTA MARIA
(1609-66) Eng. queen, wife of Charles I, daughter of the Fr. king, Henry IV. In 1625, she and Charles were mar. by proxy in Paris. A strong R.C., Henrietta took part in public affairs and her bigotry added to the difficulties of her husband. At the outbreak of the Civil War, she got a little help for Charles in Fr. and the Netherlands, but in 1644 she left Eng. and they never met again.

HENRY
Name of 7 German kings. **Henry IV** (1050-1106) became king in 1056. In 1069 he began to rule as well as reign, and he passed a long life mainly in a quarrel with the Ch. In 1074 he submitted to Gregory VII at Canossa, but the struggle was soon renewed.

HENRY
Name of 4 kings of Fr. **Henry I** was a grandson of Hugh Capet. He ruled from 1031-60, fighting William, Duke of Normandy, and other of his vassals. **Henry II**, a son of Francis I, reigned from 1547-59. He is known as the husband of Catherine de Medici and the father of 3 kings, Francis II, Charles IX and Henry III. His daughters mar. Philip of Spain and Henry IV of Fr. He was also the lover of Diane de Poitiers. **Henry IV** (*q.v.*) reigned from 1589-**1610.**

HENRY
(1394-1460) Prince of Portugal, called the Navigator, son of John I and a grandson of John of Gaunt. He provided money for voyages of exploration to the Asian and African coasts.

HENRY I
(1068-1135) King of Eng., 4th son of William I. In 1100, after his brother, William II's d., he ascended the throne. He reigned for 35 years and is regarded as the founder of the Eng. system of justice. He also quarrelled with the ch. Henry mar. Matilda, daughter of Malcolm, King of Scot. His only legitimate son, William, was drowned in the White Ship in 1120; consequently he left the throne to his daughter, Matilda or Maud.

HENRY II
(1133-89) King of Eng., son of Matilda, daughter of Henry I. In 1153 a treaty was made by which Henry was recognised as Stephen's successor on the throne. He became king in 1154, 2 years after he had mar. Eleanor, Duchess of Aquitaine, the divorced wife of Louis VII of Fr. In Eng. he restored order after the anarchy under Stephen and introduced legal reforms. This led him into a quarrel with the Ch. and Thomas à Becket, whose murder led to the king's humiliation. In Fr. Henry was chiefly occupied in fighting King Louis and his own rebellious nobles. In 1173 he had to face a rebellion in Eng. in which his eldest son, Henry, took part. His other sons, Richard I, John and Geoffrey, also rebelled against him.

HENRY III
(1207-72) King of Eng., son of King John and Isabella of Angoulême. He was only 9 years old when he became king. As a ruler he was influenced by favourites and his mar. in 1236 with Eleanor of Provence led to the arrival of many needy foreigners. The barons, in 1258, compelled Henry to hand over the govt. to themselves, with Simon de Montfort as their leader. War broke out, Henry was defeated and made prisoner at Lewes in 1264. In 1265 his son Edward defeated the barons at Evesham.

HENRY IV
(1367-1413) King of Eng. Eldest son of John of Gaunt, Duke of Lancaster. In 1398, he was sent into exile by Richard II and on Gaunt's d. the king seized his lands. Henry returned, collected a small army in Yorkshire, and Richard being in Ireland, he had no difficulty in securing the throne. His title to it was admitted by Parliament and he began to reign in 1399. The reign, which lasted for 13 years, was marked by rebellions.

HENRY IV
(1553-1610) King of Fr., son of Jeanne d'Albret, Queen of Navarre. Although a Protestant he was educ. at the court in Paris and in 1572, just before the Massacre of St. Bartholomew, he mar. Margaret, daughter of the King, Henry II. In 1572, also, he became King of Navarre. In 1589, when Henry III was murdered, he was crowned King. He defeated the Catholic faction in battle at Ivry and Arques, took Paris and then declared himself a R.C. In 1598 he granted the Protestants toleration by the Edict of Nantes.

HENRY V
(1387-1422) King of Eng., eldest son of Henry IV. He was made Prince of Wales in 1399 and began to take part in public affairs. In 1413 he became king and claimed the throne of Fr. and went with an army to make good his right. In 1415, he won the great victory of Agincourt, and between then and 1420 he conquered the whole of Normandy. In 1420 the Fr. king agreed to the Treaty of Troyes, by which Henry was made regent, or recognised as the next king. He mar. Catherine, a daughter of the King of Fr. and left an only son, Henry VI.

HENRY VI
(1421-71) King of Eng. Only son of Henry V, he became King of Eng. and Fr. in 1422. In 1445 he mar. Margaret of Anjou, but before then the faction fights which led to the Wars of the Roses had begun. Henry was quite unable to keep order between the factions, esp. after 1453, when he became insane. Richard, Duke of York was named protector and in 1455 the civil war began. The cause of Henry was championed by his wife, but in 1460 he was made a prisoner. York then claimed the throne, but it was decided that Henry should rule during his lifetime, his rival and not his son, succeeding. War was soon renewed. York was killed at Wakefield and his son made himself king in 1461 as Edward IV. In 1465 Henry was again taken prisoner, but in 1470, by a sudden reversal of fortune, due to Warwick, he was restored for a few months. Edward IV returned from his exile, crushed the Lancastrians and put Henry to d.

HENRY VII
(1457-1509) King of Eng., son of Edmund Tudor and Margaret Beaufort, a descendant of John of Gaunt, Duke of Lancaster. In 1485 he claimed the throne. He collected an army, defeated Richard III at Bosworth and was crowned. Parl. accepted him and he mar. Elizabeth, daughter of Edward IV. He laid the foundation of the Tudor monarchy, by husbanding his revenues, keeping the peace, and crushing the last remnants of baronial indep. His sons were Arthur and Henry VIII. His daughter, Margaret, mar. James IV, of Scot. and their great-grandson became first king of Gt. Brit. in 1603.

HENRY VIII
(1491-1547) King of Eng. 2nd son of Henry VII. He became heir to the throne when his brother, Arthur d. 1502. He became king in 1509 and at once mar. **Catherine,** daughter of Ferdinand and Isabella of Spain, and widow of his brother Arthur. The emperor, Charles V, and Francis I of Fr. both sought his aid, and he defeated the Scots at Flodden in 1513. At this time Henry had for his adviser Thomas Wolsey, Archbishop and Cardinal. *C.* 1526, Henry fell in love with **Anne Boleyn.** To marry her he had to divorce Catherine, which could only be done at the expense of a breach with Rome. In 1529 a Parl. met, which made Henry supreme head of the Ch. in Eng. The work of reform was completed by the dissolution of the monasteries. This led to the abortive rising called the Pilgrimage of Grace. In 1536, Anne Boleyn, charged with crimes against the king, was executed and Henry mar. **Jane Seymour.** She d. very soon, and he took for his 4th wife **Anne** of Cleves. She was soon divorced, this leading to the execution of the king's adviser, Thomas Cromwell, in 1540. Henry's 5th wife was **Catherine Howard,** a niece of the Duke of Norfolk, who was beheaded for infidelity. The 6th was **Catherine Parr,** who survived him. Henry left 3 children, Edward VI, Mary and Elizabeth, children of Jane Seymour, Catherine of Aragon and Anne Boleyn resp.

HENRYSON, Robert
(*c.* 1430-*c.* 1506) Scots poet. One of the first members of Glasgow Univ. (1462). His poems, in the Chaucerian tradition, include *The Testament of Cresseid* (1593).

HEPPLEWHITE, George
(d. 1786) Eng. cabinet-maker, apprenticed to George Gillow. His work is characterised by delicacy, grace and lightness of workmanship. See illustration at foot of next column.

HERACLITUS
Gk. philosopher. The founder of metaphysics, he pronounced the theory that fire, the 1st principle, is a rational element governing the universe from which all things evolve and to which they ultimately return.

HERALD
Officer entrusted in time of war with messages to the enemy. Such existed in Gk. and Rom. times. They were allowed to come and go unharmed. Heralds were employed in the wars of the M.A. and in the days when knighthood flourished were given new duties, connected with the bearing of arms. **College of Heralds.** In Eng. Richard III, in 1483, made the heralds into a coll. also called the Coll. of Arms. It is presided over by the Earl Marshal who has under him 3 kings-of-arms, 6 heralds, Windsor, Lancaster, York, Somerset, Chester and Richmond and 4 pursuivants. **Heraldry.** Generally all the business of heralds, specifically the art and science of genealogy, precedence, hon. distinctions and armorial bearings. In the M.A. after knights assumed them, personal devices extended rapidly.

HERB PARIS
Herb of the lily family (*Paris quadrifolia*) indigenous to Europe and Asia, found in woodland in Brit.

HERB ROBERT
(Stinking Crane's Bill) Annual herb of the geranium family (*Geranium robertianum*), indigenous to temp. and Arctic Europe and Asia, and N. Africa. It is abundant in Brit.

HERBERT, Sir Alan P.
(1890-) Eng. writer. M.P. for Oxford Univ. 1935-45. He was knighted for promoting the Mar. Bill 1942. He has written *The Water Gipsies, Uncommon Law.* Comic operas include *Bless the Bride, Made for Man.*

HERBERT, George
(1593-1633) Eng. poet. B. Montgomery. Ordained, he held livings in Huntingdonshire and at Bemerton near Salisbury. Herbert's poems appeared in *The Temple* (1633). See *George Herbert* by Margaret Bottrall (1954).

HERBERT OF LEA
Sidney, Baron (1810-61) Eng. politician. In 1845-6, and 1852-5, he was Sec. for War, and was held responsible for the mismanagement of the campaign in the Crimea.

HERCULES
[-lēz] Lat. name of **Heracles,** son of Zeus and Alcmene. **Pillars of Hercules.** Ancient name for Calpe (Gibraltar) and Abyla (Ceuta), the rocky headlands guarding the Medit. outlet to the Atlantic.

HERDER, Johann Gottfried Von
(1744-1803) German writer. Influenced by Kant and Goethe. His *Ideas on the History of Mankind* suggests the theory of evolution.

HEREFORDSHIRE
County of W. Eng. on Welsh border. In the E. are the Malvern Hills, and in the S. the Black Mts. The chief rivers are the Wye, Lugg and Frome. The county is almost entirely given up to agriculture, and is esp. famous for

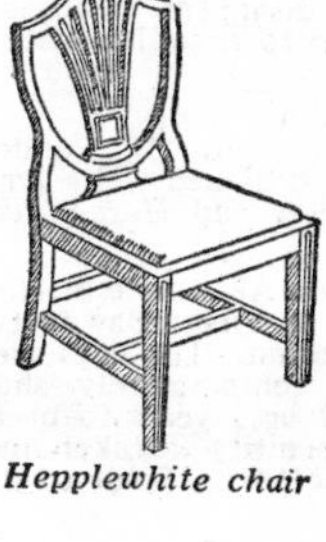

Hepplewhite chair

its cider and its cattle. Hereford is the county town; other towns are Leominster, Ross and Ledbury. Its historic interest centres in the border castles. Herefordshire returns 2 members to Parl. Pop. 132,670. **Hereford** [her'-i-fŏd] City on the Wye. The principal building is the 12th cent. cath. Every 3 years a musical festival is held, given by the choirs of Hereford, Gloucester and Worcester. These counties also hold an agricultural show in Herefordshire every 3rd year. Pop. 41,300.

HERESY
Opinion or doctrine at variance with recognised standards of theological belief and procedure. The first heresies were largely of Gnostic origin, and were vigorously contested in early ch. councils. Later the Albigenses, Lollards and others were treated as heretics, and many persons were put to d. for holding heretical opinions.

HERMAPHRODITE
[her-maf'-rō-dīt] Individual capable of producing both spermatozoa and ova, and therefore possessing the function of both sexes. The condition is normal in plants whose flowers contain stamens and pistils, although self-fertilisation is less usual than cross-fertilisation. Earthworms are hermaphrodite.

HERNIA
or **Rupture.** A protrusion of a viscus or part of a viscus through an opening or weak spot in the wall of the cavity in which the organs lie.

HEROD
(74-4 B.C.) King of the Jews, termed **the Great.** Rebuilt the Temple at Jerusalem. Matthew states that he ordered the slaughter of all infants in Bethlehem to ensure the d. of Christ, his rival. His son, **Herod Antipas** was tetrarch of Galilee and Peraea, 4 B.C.-A.D. 39. Ordered execution of John the Baptist.

HERODOTUS
Gk. historian (*c.* 484-424 B.C.) B. Cappadocia in Asia Minor. The hist. of Herodotus is in 9 books. It deals with the early hist. of Persia, Lydia and Egypt, but its main theme is the struggle between the Gks. and the Persians. See *Herodotus* by J. L. Myres (1953).

HEROIN
A drug obtained from morphine and used in the same way.

HERON
Sub-family of birds allied to the Bitterns. The common grey species, *Ardea cinerea*, with long legs and neck, great wings and pointed bill, is the only one now breeding in Brit. It is *c.* 3 ft. long. The birds breed in colonies, usually high up in trees.

HERPES
Skin disease characterised by crops of blisters. Common areas affected are lips, eyes and body. Caused by virus. **Herpes Zoster.** Acute inflammation of nerve endings, usually occurring on face, chest, abdomen or legs, characterised by intense pain followed by a crop of papules which later become vesicles. These rapidly crust over and disappear. Caused by a filterable virus allied to organism causing chicken-pox.

HERRICK, Robert
(1591-1674) Eng. poet. B. London, went to Camb. and was ordained. His lyrics appeared in *Noble Numbers* and *Hesperides* (1648).

HERRING
(*Clupea harengus*) Abundant in N. waters, esp. in the N. Sea, the fish spawns twice a year, summer and autumn. The eggs are laid on the sea bottom in comparatively shallow water. The fish takes 2 or 3 years to become mature. An enormous quantity is taken into the ports on the E. coast of Brit. Some of these are sold

fresh, but the greater part are salted and dried to become bloaters, or smoked to become kippers, giving rise to a large industry, esp. in Yarmouth.

HERSCHEL, Sir Frederick William
(1738-1822) Eng. astron. He discovered the planet Uranus (1781), the planet's satellites, many double stars and numerous nebulae. In 1800 he discovered the infra-red component in the Sun's radiation. **John Frederick William Herschel** (1792-1871), his only son, was senior wrangler at Camb. and he there gave his time to studying astronomy. He mapped the stars in the N. Hemisphere.

HERTFORDSHIRE
County of S. Eng. N. of London. The chief rivers are the Lea and Colne. Agriculture and market gardening are important, except in the S. which is in greater London. Hertford is the county town; other places are St. Albans, Letchworth and Watford. Hertfordshire returns 7 members to Parl. (including the borough constituency of Watford). Pop. 857,200. **Hertford** [har'-fŏd] Borough and county town of Herts. on the Lea, 24 m. N. of London. Industries include brewing, printing and milling, and there is an agricultural trade. Pop. 16,670.

HERTZ, Heinrich Rudolf
(1857-94) German scientist, b. Hamburg. Studied the experimental production of electro-magnetic (' Hertzian ') waves.

HERTZOG, James
(1866-1942) S. African statesman. B. Cape Colony. Gen. in S. African War and in 1910 Min. of Justice. In 1913 he formed the Nationalist party and in 1924 became M.P. He opposed participation in both World Wars and resigned in 1939 to ally himself with Malan's Nationalists.

HESIOD
[hē'-si-od] Gk. epic poet who flourished during the 8th cent. B.C. Some claim that the name was given to a school of Boeotian poets distinct from the Homeric school. Of the poems ascribed to him 3 are extant.

HESS, Dame Myra
(1890-1965) Brit. pianist. Studied R.A.M. made her début, 1907. The concerts she organised in the Nat. Gallery, London, during World War II met with great success.

HESS, Walter Richard Rudolph
(1896-) German Nazi leader. Joined Nazi Party, 1920; apptd. Hitler's deputy, 1932. In 1941, he landed by parachute near Glasgow, with peace proposals to the Duke of Hamilton and Lord Simon. Held P.O.W. till 1945, he was tried at Nuremberg in company with other German war criminals. Sentenced to life imprisonment.

HEYSHAM
[hēsh'-] Seaport and resort of Lancs. 5 m. from Lancaster. There are steamer services to Belfast, Douglas and Londonderry. Pop. (borough) 41,000.

HEYWOOD, John
(*c.* 1497-*c.* 1580) Eng. playwright. He was a friend of Sir Thomas More, but is best-known for his interludes: *The Pardoner*, etc., *The Four P's* (1533-45).

HEYWOOD, Thomas
(*c.* 1575-1641) Eng. dramatist. His plays include: *The Four Prentices of London*, *A Woman Killed with Kindness* (1603). He also wrote poems, masques and pageants.

HIAWATHA
[hī-ā-woth'-ă] (1) Red Indian chief of the Onondaga tribe. He lived about A.D. 1500 and reconciled warring tribes. (2) Legendary being who taught the arts of peace to the Red Indians.

HIBISCUS
Herbaceous plant of the family Malvaceae (mallows). They consist of *c.* 200 varieties of trop. and sub-trop. herbs and shrubs, and are prized for their large, brilliantly-coloured blossoms.

HICCOUGH
Spasm of diaphragm muscle. Assoc. with irritation of stomach following eating of indigestible food. Also found in cases of intestinal obstruction, alcoholic intoxication and pleurisy of diaphragm.

HICKORY
(*Carya*) Genus of N. Amer. trees of the walnut family. They include the shellbark, the pecan, the white-heart and the pig-nut.

HIGH COMMISSIONER
The title given to a Dominion representative living in London, or to Brit. representative in a part of the Commonwealth or mandated territory. A Lord High Commissioner is apptd. by the Queen each year to represent her at the annual **General Assembly of the Ch. of Scot.** in Edinburgh.

HIGH COURT OF JUSTICE
Eng. court of law. In 1873, when the judicial system was reformed, the high court was estabd. It is in 3 divisions: chancery; queen's bench; probate, divorce and admiralty. The judges sit in London, at the law courts in the Strand, except those on circuit.

HIGH PRIEST
Chief priest, specifically in the ancient Jewish ch. He kept the anointing oil and entered alone, in white linen, into the Holy of Holies on the Day of Atonement.

HIGH SHERIFF
The sheriff of a county in Eng. and Wales. He is appointed for a year from among the landowners in the county, and discharges duties connected with the admin. of justice.

HIGHLANDS
Term used for elevated land, but esp. for the N. of Scot. N.W. of a line joining Stonehaven, on the E. coast, and Ardmore, on the Clyde. It has mountain scenery, with moors, forests and desolate uplands alternating with fertile valleys. Inverness is regarded as the cap. **Highland sports** are seen at the various Highland games held every year in different centres. The district has its own music in which the bagpipes play an important part.

HIGHWAYMAN
Robber on the public way, esp. in the 17th and 18th cents. and in the 19th until the building of rlys.

HILL, Sir Rowland
(1795-1879) Eng. reformer. B. Kidderminster. It was mainly through his efforts that the penny post was introduced in 1840.

HILLARY, Sir Edmund
(1919-) B. Wellington, New Zealand. First, with Sherpa Tensing, to reach summit of Everest, 1953. Knighted, 1953. Leader of New Zealand support party in Commonwealth Trans-Antarctic Expedition, 1957-8.

HIMALAYA
Range of mts. in Asia containing the highest peaks in the world. They are between India and Tibet and stretch for *c.* 1,600 m. from Afghanistan to Burma; *c.* 200 m. wide, they consist of several ranges. There are passes through the mts. but these are all above 15,000 ft. The highest peak is Everest, 29,145 ft. The Ganges, Indus, Brahmaputra, Sutlej and other rivers rise in the range. *See* EVEREST, GODWIN-AUSTEN.

HIMMLER, Heinrich
(1900-45) Nazi leader, b. Munich. Joined Nazi party; became leader of its S.S. 1939. Promoted in 1936 to command of all German police forces, and became Hitler's deputy. In 1945 he tried unsuccessfully to negotiate a conditional surrender of Germany. He was captured and committed suicide.

HINDEMITH, Paul
[hin'-dĕ-mit] (1895-1963) German composer. Under the Nazi régime, his works were banned. In 1939 he emigrated to the U.S.A. H. has attempted to produce a system of teaching composition, divorced from a classical harmonic background. His works include operas, a symphony in E, chamber music, 5 string quartets, choral music and pianoforte works.

HINDENBURG, Paul von
(1847-1934) German soldier. B. Posen, entered Prussian Army as an officer, 1865. Retired 1911, but recalled to active service in 1914 and given command of the German forces in E. Prussia. Won Battle of Tannenberg, and became idol of the German people. He was promoted Aug. 1916, to succeed Falkenhayn as head of all German Armies. He remained in command throughout 1917-18. In 1925, was elected Pres. of the Republic, and re-elected on April 10, 1932. In 1933 he was reduced to a virtual figurehead when Hitler became Chanc.

HINDUISM
Social and religious organisation in India. It is a development of *Brahmanism.* There are some 230,000,000 Hindus in India. Modern Hinduism, based on the *Puranas,* gives less prominence to *Brahma* than to his associates *Vishnu,* the preserver, and *Shiva,* the destroyer and regenerator.

HINDUSTANI
Name given to Hindi and Urdu, languages spoken by 65,000,000 in N. India. Hindi has many Sanskrit forms; Urdu has borrowed from Persian and Arabic, under Moslem influence. Hindi is being developed as the nat. language of India.

HIPPOCRATES
[-pok'-ră-tēz] (*c.* 460-377 B.C.) Gk. physician, b. *c.* 460 B.C. in the Is. of Cos. Regarded as the father of modern med., his oath, the H. oath, is still admin. to graduates in med. in many Brit. and Amer. univs.

HIPPOPOTAMUS
Large mammal now only found in trop. Africa. The ordinary *H. amphibius,* is *c.* 14 ft. long and may weigh 4 tons. It lives by the side of rivers. Its naked, almost hairless skin, is brown or slate. Its skin and ivory are valuable.

HIROHITO
[hirō-hē'-tō] (1901-) Emperor of Japan. He became a constitutional monarch, May, 1946, by order of the Occupying Powers, and renounced war. He signed the treaty ending the state of war between Brit. and Japan in 1951. *See* JAPAN.

HIROSHIMA
City and seaport of Japan, on S. coast of Honshu, 160 m. W. of Osaka. On Aug. 6, 1945, an atomic bomb, the first used in warfare, was dropped on the city. Most of H. was devastated, there being 129,558 casualties, including 78,150 killed, out of a pop. of 343,970.

HISPANIOLA
Is. of the W. Indies, lying between Puerto Rico and Cuba, divided into 2 repubs., **Haiti** and **Dominica** (*qq.v.*).

HITLER, Adolf
(1889-1945) German dictator. B. Austria; corporal in World War I. Joined German Workers' Party, 1919, and became its leader in 1921, renaming it the National Socialist German Workers' Party. In 1923 he was sentenced to 9 months in prison where he wrote *Mein Kampf*. In 1932 he polled 7 million votes against Hindenburg in the pres. election. On the fall of Papen's govt. in 1933 he became Chanc. and soon seized dictatorial powers. His policy was that of world domination. He became Führer and Head of the State in 1934. The Rome-Berlin Axis became an official alliance in 1937. Germany signed a non-aggression pact with Russia on Aug. 21, invaded Poland on Sept. 1 and World War II began on Sept. 3, 1939. Denmark, The Netherlands, Belgium, France and Norway were overrun. On June 22, 1941, Germany attacked Russia and by Dec. German troops were within 25 m. of Moscow. The German armies were finally driven from Russia in the great offensive of 1943. The Allied landing in Normandy on June 5-6, 1944, sealed the fate of the German forces. By April, 1945, the Russians were occupying a large part of Berlin. Hitler and his wife committed suicide on April 30, 1945, and their bodies were burned in the garden of the Chancellory. See *Hitler* by Alan Bullock (1952).

HITTITES
Ancient people in Asia Minor. The Biblical names Heth and Hittite indicate a people almost unknown until exploration from 1870 onwards revealed distinctive monuments. Prof. Sayce announced in 1880 the discovery of a Hittite empire. Their federation took place about 1400 B.C. They disappeared about 1200 B.C. **Hittite Language.** Prob. branch of Indo-European with which it shares vocabulary and inflectional system. Found in hieroglyphic clay-tablet archives at Boghazkeui (Turkey), prob. of the 2nd millennium B.C.

HOBART
Cap. of Tasmania on the S. side of the Is. with harbour on the Derwent. Founded 1804, it is the commercial centre of Tasmania, with extensive docks and wharves, and flour milling and fruit preserving industries. Pop. 118,828.

HOBBEMA, Meindert
[hob'-] (1638-1709) Dutch artist, b. and d. in Amsterdam.

HOBBES, Thomas
(1588-1679) Eng. philosopher. B. Malmesbury; educ. Oxford. He spent some years as tutor with the Cavendish family, assoc. with Bacon, Ben Jonson and other men of note. He returned to Eng. in 1651, and lived quietly under the Commonwealth and then under Charles II. His fame rests upon *The Leviathan*, pub., 1651. It is a cogent argument for absolute sovereignty and has had enormous influence on polit. thought.

HOCK
German white wine, esp. Rhenish. The name is really Hochheimer, a still or sparkling wine produced at Hochheim, near Mainz.

HOCKEY
Outdoor game played by men and women. The implements are a hard ball weighing not more than 28 oz. and a stick with a curved end, the object being to drive the ball through the goal 12 ft. wide, 7 ft. high. The ground should be 100 yds. long and 55 or 60 yds. wide with a centre and two 25 yd. lines. Only the goal-keeper may kick the ball. A Hockey Assoc. was founded in 1875 and the rules were drawn up in 1883 by the Wimbledon Club. The game is played in schools, univs., clubs, and Internat. matches are played. Infringements of rules are countered by a free-hit or a penalty-bully.

HOGARTH, William
(1697-1767) Eng. painter and engraver. B. London. Under Sir James Thornhill he studied painting, and his numerous portraits show remarkable technical skill and power of expression. His most famous pictures are those in which he satirised the life of his time. See *Hogarth's Progress* by Peter Quennell (1955).

HOGG, James
(1770-1835) Scots poet. Called the Ettrick Shepherd. In 1801 he became known to Sir Walter Scott, who included in his *Border Minstrelsy* several ballads supplied by Hogg. His first vol. of verse, *The Mountain Bard*, was pub. in 1803.

HOHENZOLLERN
[hō-ěn-tsol'-ern] German family. In 1415 Frederick of Hohenzollern was made Margrave, or Elector, of Brandenburg, and his successors esp. Frederick William, called the Great Elector, made this into an important state. In 1871 King William I was made head of the new German Empire and the Hohenzollerns played a great part in European hist. until William II abdicated in 1918. A branch of the Hohenzollerns ruled until 1848 over a principality in S. Germany. One of them, Carol, was made King of Rumania in 1881, and the family ruled till 1947.

HOKKAIDO
[-kī'-dō] Most N. of the 4 chief Is. of the Jap. Emp., separated from Sakhalin in the N. by Soya Strait, and from Honshu by Tsugaru Strait. Student riots, 1969. Area: 30,077 sq.m.

HOKUSAI, Katsushika
[hoo-koo-sī-ē] (1760-1849) Japanese painter. He became the most famous artist of the popular school.

HOLBEIN, Hans
[-bīn] (1497-1543) German painter and engraver. B. Augsburg. At an early age he showed great promise esp. in engraving, designing of stained glass and decorative work. In 1516 he removed to Basle and later visited Eng. where in 1536 he was apptd. court painter to Henry VIII. He painted Henry VIII, Anne of Cleves, Jane Seymour, Erasmus and many others.

HOLINSHED, Raphael
(d. *c.* 1580) Eng. chronicler, translator and printer. He compiled *The Chronicles of England, Scotland and Ireland* (1577), used by Shakespeare.

HOLLAND
District of the Netherlands, on the coast between the Waal mouth and Ijsselmeer. In the 15th cent. it became part of the great empire of Charles V, until several provs. revolted, and formed the Dutch Repub. Since then the term has been applied to the **Kingdom of the Netherlands** (*q.v.*) N. and S. Holland are 2 modern Dutch provs.; caps. Haarlem and The Hague.

HOLLY
(*Ilex*) Large genus of shrubs and trees of the holly family, native to every continent but mostly found in C. and S. Amer. The common Brit. and European *I. aquifolium* is an ever-

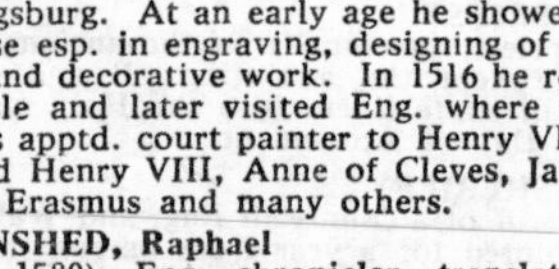

green with ashy bark, wavy, spiny, glossy, smooth leaves, and small white flowers bearing scarlet berries. The leaves and berries are largely used as a decoration at Christmas time. It grows to 30-40 ft. high.

HOLLYHOCK
Hardy perennial herb of the mallow family (*Althaea rosea*). It is a tall plant with lobed leaves and a flower spike 8-10 ft. high.

HOLLYWOOD
Centre of the Amer. film industry, in Calif., W. of Los Angeles (*q.v.*).

HOLM OAK
Evergreen species of oak tree (*Quercus ilex*). Native in the Medit. region. It has glossy, dark-green leaves, usually with prickles; its acorns are short-stalked

HOLST, Gustav
(1874-1934) Eng. composer. A pupil of Stanford. In World War I he organised musical activities among troops serving in and around Salonica. His *Planets* Suite and the ballet music from *The Perfect Fool* are frequently heard. He wrote operas, ballets, a choral symphony, a tone poem, a concerto for 2 violins, part songs and songs.

HOLY ISLAND
Name of several Is. in the Brit. Is. One is off the coast of Anglesey and on it stands Holyhead. Another, also called Lindisfarne, is off the coast of Northumberland.

HOLYOAKE, Rt. Hon. Keith J.
(1904-) New Zealand politician. Succeeded S. G. Holland as P.M. 1957. He lost the election of that year, but returned to power in 1960. P.C. 1954. C.H. 1963.

HOLY ROMAN EMPIRE
A revival of the Ancient Rom. emp. of the W. founded by Charlemagne in 800, under the sanction of the Pope. The epithet Holy was first annexed to the title by Frederick Barbarossa in 1156. Rudolph, the first Hapsburg Emp., was elected in 1273, and thereafter the empire was a German institution. After the 30 Years' War, its centre shifted to Austria (1648), and it was dissolved in 1806 by the resignation of Francis II, Emp. of Austria following the unsuccessful struggle against Napoleonic France.

HOLY SEPULCHRE, Church of the
Christian ch. in Jerusalem, a place of pilgrimage, as it contains the traditional tomb of Christ. The tomb is covered by a small Greek chapel, but many doubt the authenticity of the site. The first Christian ch. to occupy the site was that ordered to be built by the Roman Emperor Constantine (306-337) in 326.

HOLY SPIRIT
Third person of the Trinity. Genesis mentions the Spirit of God; the Psalms and Isaiah use the epithet Holy. The N.T. witnessing Christ's advent as God's incarnate Son, also emphasises the function of the Holy Spirit, described as the Spirit of Truth and as the Paraclete or Comforter. The early Ch. believed that the Holy Spirit proceeded from the Father; the insertion of *filioque*, ' and the Son ', in the Nicene creed caused the Grand Schism between E. and W. Christendom.

HOLYHEAD
[hol'-i-] Market town, seaport and urban district of Anglesey, on Holy Is. It is connected by steamers with Dublin. Pop. 10,320.

HOLYROOD
(Holyroodhouse) Royal palace in Edinburgh, originally an abbey founded in 1128 by King David I. It belonged to the Augustinian Canons and was destroyed in the 16th cent. Near the abbey James IV built a palace and this was a residence of the Scots. kings. Here Mary was mar. to Darnley, Rizzio murdered, Charles I crowned, and Charles Edward held court.

HOME, Sir Alexander Frederick Douglas-
[hūm] (Douglas-Home) (1903-) Cons. politician. Unionist M.P. for S. Lanark, 1931-45; Cons. M.P. for Lanark Div. of Lanarkshire, 1950-1; Parl. Private Sec. to P.M. 1931-9. He was apptd. Sec. of State for Commonw. Relations, 1955; For. Sec. 1960. Renounced title under Peerage Act (1963) to become P.M. (1964). Elected M.P. for Kinross and W. Perthshire. Led Cons. opposition after defeat 1964-5.

HOME GUARD
Brit. defence organisation founded May, 1940, against invasion. A well-equipped and highly efficient force *c.* 2,000,000 strong, it rendered invaluable service in guarding places of strategic importance, etc.

HOME RULE
Movement for granting Ireland self-govt. It began *c.* 1870. Members pledged to secure some measure of self-govt. were sent to Parl. by the Irish constituencies. Called Nationalists, they were led in turn by Isaac Butt, C. S. Parnell and J. Redmond. Gladstone introduced the first Home Rule Bill, 1886, but it was defeated in the House of Commons. In 1893, he introduced the 2nd Home Rule Bill, which was defeated in the House of Lords. The 3rd Bill was introduced by the Lib. ministry under H. H. Asquith in 1912. It became law in Sept. 1914, although serious opposition was offered to it in Ulster. By that time, World War I had begun, so its operation was postponed. Then the position entirely changed with the rise of the Sinn Fein Party. A settlement was made in 1921, by which the Irish Free State was formed as a self-governing dominion of the Brit. Commonwealth, N. Ireland remained part of the U.K. *See* IRELAND, REPUBLIC OF.

HOMER
Gk. poet who lived between 1200 and 850 B.C. Seven cities claimed to be his birthplace: Chios, Smyrna, Rhodes, Argos, Athens, Colophon and Salamis in Cyprus. Homer wrote two epics; the *Iliad* describes the concluding weeks of the Siege of Troy by the Gks.; the *Odyssey* describes the wanderings of Ulysses (Odysseus) after the fall of Troy.

HOMICIDAL MANIA
[hō-mi-sīd-al] State of mental abnormality in which there is an obsessional and irresistible impulse to kill or take human life.

HOMOEOPATHY
[hō-mi-op'-] A system of medicine introduced by Hahnemann, a German physician, in 1796. It is based on the belief that ' like cures like ' and that the action of drugs are potentiated by dilution.

HOMOSEXUALITY
Abnormality in which adults are attracted sexually to members of their own sex. Causes are disputed, but may possibly be glandular as when physical abnormality is present, or possibly due to arrested emotional development when the individual has not progressed beyond a normal homosexual phase.

HONDURAS
Repub. of C. Amer. bounded by Guatemala, Salvador and Nicaragua, with a long coastline on the Caribbean Sea, but only 40 m. on the Pacific. The interior is mountainous and forested, and the coastal plains are very fertile. There are numerous rivers. Bananas, coconuts, coffee and timber are exported. Silver is an important export. Tegucigalpa is the cap. Spanish is the official language and R.C. the predominant religion. Honduras, once part of Sp. Amer. became an indep. repub. 1838. It is governed by a Pres. with a chamber of 56 members. Area: 43,000 sq.m. Pop. 1,883,000.

HONEGGER, Arthur
[hon'-ĕ-ger] (1892-1955) Swiss composer. A member of the group known as ' Les Six '. His

HONESTY
Annual or biennial cruciferous herb (*Lunaria annua*), native to C. and W. Asia. It has toothed, heart-shaped leaves, and stems bearing flowers, usually purple. It grows in Brit.

HONEY
A sweet viscid liquid, elaborated by honey bees from nectar collected by them from flowers and transported to the hive to be deposited in the cells of the honeycomb. This serves as food for the bees esp. during the winter months. Bees are kept for the honey they produce and they can be made to produce honey greatly in excess of their own needs. Honey consists mainly of sugar in the form of levulose and dextrose and takes on its flavour according to the flowers which the bees work.

HONEY EATER
(*Meliphaga*) Slender-billed singing bird related to the Sun Bird about the size of a thrush. The brush-like tips of the long tongue extract insects and nectar from flowers. They are found in Australasia.

HONEYSUCKLE
(*Lonicera*) Genus of erect or climbing shrubs of the elderberry family with fragrant flowers, found in warm and temp. parts of the N. hemisphere. The plant is found wild, but can be cultivated.

HONG KONG
Brit. crown colony on the S. coast of China, comprising the Is. of Hong Kong, the Kowloon peninsula and several small Is. and the New Territories. The Is. has a magnificent harbour; it is a free port with a great entrepôt trade. The cap. is Victoria, on the S. side of the harbour. A univ. was opened, 1912. Hong Kong was ceded to Brit. 1842; Kowloon was acquired, 1860. Admin. is by a Gov. and 2 councils. The colony was occupied by the Japanese, 1942-5. In 1967, the colony was disturbed by Chinese agitation. Area: 1,125 sq.m. Pop. 3,527,000.

HONITON
[hon'-] Borough and market town of Devon, on the Otter, 16 m. N.E. of Exeter, famous for its lace and its pottery. Pop. 4,550.

HONOLULU
Cap. and port of the Hawaiian Is. on Oahu Is., tourist resort and shipping centre. Pop. 294,194.

HONSHU
or **Mainland.** Most important Is. of Japan. It is crossed by a mt. range and a group of volcanoes. Of these the chief are Fujiyama (*q.v.*), 12,389 ft., and Asamayama. Tokyo, the cap., Kyoto, Nagoya, Yokohama, Osaka and Kobe are the principal cities. Area: 88,000 sq.m.

HOOCH, Pieter de
[hōch] (1629-83) Dutch painter. B. Rotterdam. He was essentially a painter of interiors.

HOOD, Thomas
(1799-1845) Eng. poet and humorist. B. London. He ed. *The Gem*, and from 1830-9 issued yearly a *Comic Annual*. His best-known poems are *Faithless Nelly Gray*, *Song of the Shirt*, *The Bridge of Sighs*, *Eugene Aram*.

HOOK OF HOLLAND
Port of the Netherlands, 17 m. W. of Rotterdam, with steamer services to Harwich.

HOOKER, Richard
(1554-1600) Eng. divine. Hooker is famous as the author of a unique *Treatise on the Laws of Ecclesiastical Polity*, which sets out the fundamental principles of Protestantism and esp. of the C. of E.

HOOKWORM
(*Ancylostoma*) Parasite causing ankylostomiasis in man. It is common in many trop. countries where the larva matures in the small intestine. Ova voided in the excreta infect the soil.

HOOPOE
(*Upupa*) Beautifully coloured bird, which visits Europe and Siberia in summer and winters in Africa and India. Its golden-buff head and neck bear a semi-circular crest of erect plumes with white-bordered black tips.

HOOVER, Herbert Clark
(1874-1964) 31st Pres. of the U.S.A. During and after World War I he organised relief measures in Europe. Standing as a Republican, became Pres. in 1929. His admin. had to face the economic crisis of 1931, and in 1932 he was defeated by Roosevelt.

HOPKINS, Gerard Manley
(1844-89) Eng. poet. B. Essex. He became an R.C. 1866, a Jesuit 1868, and parish priest, prof. of Gk in Dublin (1884), Bridges pub. 11 of his poems in *Poets and Poetry of the Century* (1893) and an ed. of the *Poems* (1918). Only with the 2nd ed. of these (1930) did Hopkins's originality in rhythm, imagery, syntax, attract attention widely and influence poets. His *Letters* (1935-8) and *Notebooks and Papers* (1937) contain valuable comments on poetry. *Poems* 3rd ed. appeared 1948.

HOPPNER, John
(1758-1810) Eng. portrait painter. B. Whitechapel, London, of German parentage.

HOPS
Cone-like catkins of female flowers of the hop plant *Humulus lupulus*, used chiefly for flavouring beer. The plant is a perennial climbing herb with rough twining stems bearing either male flowers or female flowers.

HORACE
Lat. poet (65-27 B.C.) **Quintus Horatius Flaccus,** b. Venusia. About 38 B.C. Virgil introduced him to Maecenas, who gave him a farm. His works include: *Satires* (2 books), *Odes* (4 books), *Epistles* (2 books), *The Art of Poetry* and *Carmen Seculare*. The *Satires* and *Epistles* were much imitated by Pope and his contemporaries.

HOREHOUND
Name of 2 plants found in Brit. and other temp. zones. White horehound has stems and leaves covered with down and bears whorls of white flowers in the summer. Black horehound has also downy and wrinkled leaves, but its flowers are purple.

HORMONES
Secretions of the ductless glands. These include the pituitary, thymus, thyroid, parathyroids, pancreas, ovaries and testes. *See* DUCTLESS GLANDS.

HORN, Cape
Most S. point of the S. Amer. cont. on the Chilean Is. of Tierra del Fuego, *c.* 1,400 ft. high.

HORN
A brass wind instrument, usually known as the **French horn.** The 19th cent. invention of valves enables the player to achieve a fully chromatic range of over 3 octaves.

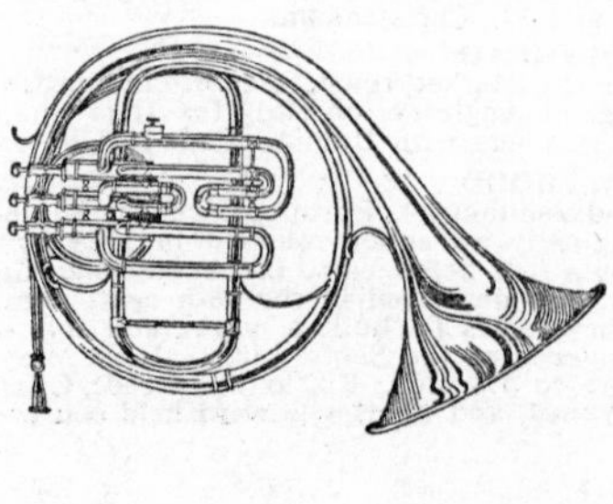

HORNBEAM
Tree of the birch order (*Carpinus betulus*), indigenous to Europe and W. Asia and grows sometimes 70 ft. high in Brit. Its dull, doubly-toothed leaves, hairy underneath, and winged fruit, distinguish it from the beech. Its heavy, close-grained wood is difficult to split.

HORNBILL
Fruit-eating birds allied to the Hoopoes. They inhabit Africa, India and Malaya, and have horn-like helmets, hollow or solid, surmounting large bills.

HORNET
(*Vespa crabro*) Brit. wasp. About 1 in. long and distinguished from the common wasp by its ruddier hue, it builds paper nests, chiefly of rotten wood.

HOROSCOPE
In astrology a circular map of 12 houses or signs of the Zodiac, in which is marked the disposition of the sun and planets at a given time and place. By this means astrologers are enabled to assess their influences on the subject at the time of birth. In ancient times in, for example, India, Egypt, Babylonia, Greece, etc., astrology and astronomy formed one science and many great minds were devoted to its study.

HORSE
(*Equus caballus*) Hoofed mammal of great value to man, distinguished by having only 1 toe on each foot, and seen in shades of red, brown, black, white and piebald. The horse was hunted for food by primitive man, was known to the Egyptians and Assyrians, and by the time it was mentioned in the Bible it had been domesticated. The Arabs showed its capability in speed and beauty. The Rom. chariot was drawn by horses and later the horse became an essential part of the knight's equipment. Until World War I the horse played an important part in warfare. When the roads were bad goods were conveyed on pack horses; as they improved, horses were used to draw coaches and carts over them. In agricultural work horses replaced oxen in many countries, while every gentleman learned to ride. The finest animal in existence is prob. the Eng. thoroughbred racehorse, in which there is an Arab strain. For agricultural and draught purposes the chief breeds are the Shire, Clydesdale and Suffolk Punch. Wild horses are still found in Asia. The Mustang of Amer. is the wild descendant of the domesticated horse. **Horse Racing.** Sport very popular in England, Ireland, Australia, Fr., the U.S.A., and to a lesser extent in other countries. 'Eclipse' (1769-70) was the greatest racehorse on record. Racing in Eng. is controlled by the Jockey Club. The chief centre is Newmarket. In Ireland the chief racing centres are the Curragh and Leopardstown. The 5 classic races are the Derby and Oaks at Epsom, the St. Leger at Doncaster, the Two Thousand Guineas and the One Thousand Guineas at Newmarket. The courses vary from half a m. to over 2 m. In addition to flat racing, hurdle races and steeplechases are held at various centres. The chief of these is the Grand Nat.

HORSE CHESTNUT
(*Aesculus*) Genus of large trees of the soapwort family, native to Europe, India and N. Amer. The common *A. hippocastanum* bears pyramidal spikes of showy blossoms. It grows 60 ft. high.

HORSE FLY
Name loosely indicating 2-winged insects of various families, annoying to horses, *e.g.* (1) The large brownish-black *Tabanus bovinus*, and other blood-sucking species of the Gadfly family. (2) The parasitic yellowish-brown *Hippobosca equina*, or Horse-tick. *See* BOT-FLY.

HORSE LEECH
(*Aulostoma gulo*) Blackish-green leech with a particularly narrow fore part of the body bearing the mouth which contains only 3 small teeth. It is voracious and lives chiefly on earthworms, snails, grubs and other leeches.

HORSE MACKEREL
Several unrelated marine fishes, particularly *Caranx*, abounding in almost all trop. and temp. seas. The Brit. *C. trachurus* is also called the Scad.

HORSERADISH
Perennial herb of the cruciferous family (*Cochlearia amoracia*). Its pungent root serves grated as a condiment with beef.

HORTHY de Nagybanya, Nicholas
[hor'-ti] (1868-1957) Hungarian leader. A naval officer, he was given command of the Austro-Hungarian fleet in 1918. During the troubles in Hungary which followed the War, he collected a force which drove the Communist Bela Kun from the country and restored order. Became Regent in 1920. Hungary joined the Axis, 1941. Horthy asked for Armistice, Oct. 1944. In protective custody, but released, Oct. 1946.

HOSPITAL
Building for the care of the sick and injured. Such places have existed since the earliest times and are mentioned in Egyptian and Gk. lit. With the coming of Christianity the Ch. accepted responsibility for them, and in R.C. countries and Mission settlements, still does. In Brit. nationalisation of hosp. systems has taken place and in Aug. 1948, all voluntary hosps. came under control of the Min. of Health and the Dept. of Health for Scot. Special hosps. for the treatment of Eye, Ear, Nose and Throat, Heart, Lung, Children's, Women's, Nervous and Venereal diseases have been developed. *See* QUARANTINE; CONTAGION; HEALTH.

HOTTENTOT
Primitive people living in S. Africa. With a negroid strain in them, they are also allied in blood to the Bantus and Bushmen.

HOUGHTON, Baron
[how'-] (1809-85) Eng. scholar and politician. **Richard Monckton Milnes** was a son of a Yorks. landowner. Dicky Milnes, as he was called, was a champion of liberal ideas, and a friend of most of the great literary men of his day.

HOUSE
Dwelling of a permanent kind. Today they usually contain one or more living rooms for meals and daily life and adequate sleeping accommodation. In the W., brick, stone or wood are materials chiefly used, but concrete, gypsum, asbestos, etc., are also being tried.

HOUSE FLY
(*Musca domestica*) Two-winged insect belonging to a family of the order Diptera which includes the Blowfly or Bluebottle. It has a sucking proboscis and walks on ceilings and windows by sucker-like feet. Its eggs produce, in a day, legless maggots which reach adult life in a month. It is a carrier of disease germs.

HOUSE LEEK
(*Sempervivum*) Genus of succulent herbs or undershrubs of the stonecrop family, native to Europe, Asia and N. Africa. The Brit. hardy perennial, *S. tectorum*, frequently forms rosettes of fleshy leaves on cottage roofs and walls.

HOUSMAN, Albert Edward
[how'-] (1859-1936) Eng. scholar and poet. In 1911 made Fellow of Trinity and Prof. of Lat. at Cambridge. He pub. 2 vols. of poetry, *The Shropshire Lad* (1896) and *Last Poems* (1922). His brother was **Laurence H.** (1865-1959) Eng. author and artist. He won a reputation by his book illustrations. In 1893 he pub. a book on William Blake; *Prunella, or Love in a Dutch Garden* (with H. Granville-Barker) 1907; *Little Plays of St. Francis*; *Victoria Regina*.

HOUSTON, Samuel
(1793-1863) Amer. politician. B. Virginia, he entered the army, but soon turned to politics. In 1835, when Texas revolted against Mexico, he was chosen as the leader of the Texas army, and in 1836, he won a crushing victory. This made Texas indep. and Houston was its pres. until 1845, when it was annexed by the U.S.A. In 1859 he was apptd. gov. but was deposed in 1861.

HOVERCRAFT
Vehicle first introduced to the public in 1959, in the U.K. Employs a revolutionary means of suspension, riding on a cushion of air, which allows it to operate over land or water. Vehicles as large as 37¼ ft. with speeds up to 80 m.p.h. have been demonstrated.

HOWARD, Catherine
(*c.* 1522-42) Wife of Henry VIII and daughter of Lord Edmund Howard. On July 28, 1540, Henry mar. her secretly as his 5th wife. Within 2 years she was accused of misconduct before and after her mar., found guilty and beheaded.

HOWARD, John
(1726-90) Eng. philanthropist. He inherited an estate in Beds. in 1742. In 1773, when high sheriff, he noticed the terrible conditions of the prisons and prisoners. He wrote *The State of the Prisons*, which drew public attention to the matter and led to considerable reforms. The **Howard League** carries on his work.

HOWE, Earl
Richard (1726-99) Eng. admiral. In 1794 he gained a great victory over the Fr. on the Glorious First of June. He suppressed the mutiny at Spithead in 1797.

HOWELLS, Herbert
(1892-) Eng. composer; a pupil of Stanford. He has written much chamber, choral and orchestral music, a piano concerto and songs.

HOYLE, Fred
(1915-) Brit. astronomer. Educ. Camb. Fellow of St. John's Coll. and Univ. lecturer, 1945. His controversial book *The Nature of the Universe* was pub. 1950. Wrote *Frontiers of Astronomy* (1955), *Man and Materialism* (1957).

HUCKLEBERRY
Fruit of several N. Amer. shrubs. They resemble cranberries.

HUDDERSFIELD
County borough and market town of the W. Riding, Yorks., on the Colne 16 m. S.W. of Leeds. The making of woollen goods is the principal industry. It returns 2 members to Parl. Pop. 131,000.

HUDSON
River of the U.S.A. which rises in the Adirondack Mts. and flows through New York State to the Atlantic. Towards its mouth the Hudson flows between New York and New Jersey. Its valley was the chief trading route between New York and Canada.

HUDSON, Henry
(*c.* 1550-1611) Eng. explorer. He made several voyages in search of the N.E. and N.W. Passages. In 1610, in the *Discovery*, he entered Hudson Bay. During the winter the crew mutinied; Hudson was put in a small boat with 8 companions and set adrift, and nothing more was heard of him.

HUDSON BAY
Sea of Canada, connected with the Arctic Ocean by several channels, and with the Atlantic by the Hudson Strait. It receives many rivers, incl. the Churchill, Nelson, Rupert, Albany and Severn. Navigation is impeded by ice in winter. Area: 475,972 sq.m. **Hudson's Bay Company.** Trading Co. in Canada. It dates from 1670 when Charles II gave a charter to Prince Rupert and others, bestowing upon them the lands around Hudson Strait and the sole trading rights therein. Trading stations were built and a trade in furs was carried on with the Indians. In 1821 it was united with a rival Co. and received a new charter. By this the Co. secured the sole right of trading with the Indians in Brit. Columbia. The area under its control was *c.* 2,300,000 sq.m. In 1869 the new Dominion of Canada decided to take over the vast area of land owned by the Co. It then became a limited liability Co.

HUGHES, Thomas
(1822-96) Eng. writer. From 1865-74 he was a Lib. M.P. and assoc. with the Christian Socialist movement. He is best known for *Tom Brown's Schooldays* (1857).

HUGO Victor Marie
(1802-85) Fr. writer. B. Besançon. He wrote poems, stories, then dramas: *Cromwell, Hernani, Rigoletto, Ruy Blas.* His romances began with *Notre Dame de Paris* (1831) then *Les Misérables, Quatre Vingt Treize.* Also wrote books dealing with the events of his own time, and autobiog. works. In 1848 and 1849, he was elected to the constituent and the legislative assemblies and, in 1851, having opposed the designs of the future emperor, he fled to Brussels, and finally to Guernsey.

HUGUENOTS
[hew'-gĕ-nō] Frenchmen who accepted the reformed religion in the 16th cent. Their leader was Henry of Navarre who later turned R.C. They were persecuted and their resistance led to religious wars. In 1598, by the Edict of Nantes, they were granted civil and religious liberty, but this was revoked in 1685, and many emigrated.

HULL
(Kingston-upon-Hull) City, county borough and seaport of the E. Riding, Yorks., situated where the river Hull enters the Humber estuary, 22 m. from the N. Sea. It is the 3rd port and the chief fishing port of the U.K. The docks cover *c.* 250 acres. There are large flour mills and numerous manufactures. Hull was damaged during World War II. It returns 4 members to Parl. Pop. 301,640.

HUMBER
Estuary on the E. coast of Eng. formed by the Trent and Ouse. On its banks are Hull and Grimsby.

HUMBLE BEE
(*Bombus*) Humble, or Bumble bees (*q.v.*) live in communities. The females and the neuters help to construct the nest, where honey is stored for the females, who alone survive in the winter.

HUME, David
(1711-76) Scot. writer and thinker. B. Edinburgh, educ. there and in Fr. by the Jesuits. In 1737 wrote *A Treatise of Human Nature,* and in 1751 *Inquiry into the Principles of Morals.* In 1752 he wrote his *Political Discourses.*

HUMERUS *See* ARM.

HUMMING BIRD
Amer. birds allied to Swifts. They make a humming sound when vibrating the wings in rapid flight. There are *c.* 500 species, found in trop. regions.

HUMPERDINCK, Engelbert
[hŏŏm'-] (1854-1921) German composer. Assistant to Wagner at Bayreuth, 1880-1. His most outstanding work is his opera *Hansel und Gretel* produced in 1893.

HUNCHBACK
Deformity of the spine usually assoc. with old standing tuberculous disease. Richard III and Alex. Pope were notable personalities who bore this deformity. *See* DWARFISM.

HUNDRED
Name used for a division of many Eng. counties. It goes back to A.-S. times. Best known example left is the Chiltern Hundreds. When an M.P. wishes to resign his seat, he applies for Stewardship of the Chiltern Hundreds. As this is counted an office of profit under the Crown, he cannot hold it and sit in the Commons.

HUNDRED DAYS
Name given to the period between Napoleon's escape from Elba and his surrender after Waterloo, March 20, to June 28, 1815.

HUNDRED YEARS' WAR
(1337-1453) Struggle between Eng. and Fr. It began when Edward III claimed the throne of Fr. The Eng. won victories at Crécy and Poitiers, and in 1360 peace was made at Bretigny. The war began again in 1369 and lasted until 1396. By the treaty of 1396 the Eng. lost many of their possessions. In 1415 Henry V claimed the throne of Fr. He won the Battle of Agincourt, conquered Normandy, and in 1420 was recognised as Regent and future King of Fr. Part of the nation refused to submit and the war went on until 1429, when the tide turned on the arrival of Joan of Arc. The Eng. then steadily lost ground and the struggle ended in 1453, all Fr., except Calais, being lost.

HUNGARY
Repub. of C. Europe, N. of Yugoslavia and W. of Rumania. Across the plains flow the Danube, Tisa and Drava. Balaton is a large shallow lake. The soil is very fertile, and agriculture is the chief occupation. Cereals, grapes, tobacco and sugar beet are grown, and livestock are reared. Wines are manufactured in the W. and N.E. (Tokay). Budapest is the cap.; other towns are Szeged, Debrecen and Miskolc. The people are predominantly Magyar in race and R.C. in religion; there are 4 univs. Hungary became an indep. kingdom *c.* 1000, with Stephen, now the patron saint, as King. In 1526 Turkish forces occupied the S. part of the country. The remaining part was united with Austria from 1867 until 1918. In 1918 a repub. was proclaimed. Hungary was occupied by Russian troops, 1945. A Communist repub. was proclaimed in 1946, during occupation of the country by Soviet armed forces. In Nov. 1956, Russ. troops were sent into Hungary to suppress a popular rising. Many refugees fled and were given asylum in W. Europe, Amer. and the Commonwealth. The rising was ruthlessly crushed. In Budapest more than 25,000 perished in the fighting and as a result of starvation. The U.S.S.R. overthrew Premier Nagy's moderate Communist régime and replaced it with a puppet govt. Area: 35,900 sq.m. Pop. 9,971,000.

HUNS
Horde of Asiatics who invaded Europe in the 4th cent. After a career of conquest under Attila they were defeated in 451 at Châlons by Theodoric, King of the Visigoths and disappeared.

HUNT, James Henry Leigh
(1784-1859) Eng. writer. In 1821 he went to Italy to visit Shelley and Byron. With his wife and 7 children he returned to London in 1825, and lived in poverty there until his d. at Putney. He wrote essays, poems and novels. *The Feast of the Poets, Wit and Humour*, and *Imagination and Fancy*, contain some of his best work.

HUNT, William Holman
(1827-1918) Eng. painter. In 1848 he assisted D. G. Rossetti, John E. Millais and others to found the Pre-Raphaelite brotherhood.

HUNTER, John
(1728-1793) B. Long Calderwood, Lanarkshire. In 1745, he began to study medicine and assist in his brother William's surgical work. One of the most famous names in medicine, a skilled surgeon and a brilliant anatomist, he founded the museum in the Royal Coll. of Surgeons. He pub. works on geology and other branches of science.

HUNTINGDONSHIRE
County of E. Eng., W. of Cambs. The chief rivers are the Ouse and Nene; the land is flat and fertile. Wheat and barley are grown, and market gardening is important. Huntingdon is the county town; other towns are St. Neots, St. Ives and Godmanchester. The county returns 1 member to Parl. Pop. 85,520. **Huntingdon.** Borough, county and market town of Huntingdonshire, on the Ouse, 15 m. N.W. of Camb. Notable buildings are the George Inn and Cromwell House. Pop. (with Godmanchester), 9,800.

HURDLE
Interlaced frame of twigs or sticks. Hurdles are used to make pens for sheep and for other such purposes or for games. Races over hurdles 2 ft. 6 in.-3ft. 6in. in ht. are events at most athletic sports.

Technique of hurdling

HURON
Lake of Canada and the U.S.A., part of the Great Lakes system. It is connected by Sault Ste. Marie Canal with L. Superior, and by St. Clair and Detroit rivers with L. Erie. Area: 23,860 sq.m.

HURRICANE
Violent trop. storm accompanied by sudden changes of the wind with a velocity of over 75 m.p.h., common in the W. Indies. Changing weather conditions have now put the entire N. Atlantic seaboard in a hurricane area. In the China Sea similar storms are called typhoons (*q.v.*).

HURSTMONCEUX
[-soo'] Village of Sussex, 9 m. E. of Hailsham. The restored 15th cent. castle has been converted for occupation by the Royal Observatory. Now spelt **Herstmonceux.**

HUSBAND
Mar. man. Until recent times husband and wife were in very different positions before the law of Eng., as they were, and to some extent are, in other countries. Since 1870 a mar. woman's property has been distinct from that of her husband. The grounds on which divorce can be obtained are now the same for both sexes. Until 1923 a wife could not obtain a divorce for adultery unless it was accompanied by cruelty or some other matrimonial offence. A husband is responsible for his wife's debts and for maintaining her in her station in life.

HUSS, John
(*c.* 1373-1415) Bohemian reformer. His preaching of Wycliffe's doctrines angered the authorities, and he was charged with heresy. In 1412 he retired from Prague and wrote his chief work, *De Ecclesia*. In 1414 the Emperor Sigismund gave Huss a safe conduct to attend the Council of Constance. He went and was at once arrested as a heretic, tried, condemned on July 5, and burned. **Hussites.** Followers of John Huss. After his martyrdom in 1415, his followers became important politically. They made war for several years on the Emperor Sigismund. Now known as the *Bohemian Brethren.*

HUSSEIN, Ibn Ali
[hoo-sān'] (1856-1931) An Arab chief. In 1916, assisted by Gt. Brit., he declared himself indep. His troops entered the war against Turkey, and Hussein was recognised as King of the Hejaz (1917). His 2nd son, **Feisal** (*q.v.*), was king of Iraq 1921-33; his 3rd, **Abdullah,** was King of Transjordan 1946-51. Abdullah was assassinated in 1951. His grandson, **Hussein** (1935-) became King of the Hashemite Kingdom of The Jordan on the deposition of his father, King Talal, in 1952. Mar. 1961 Miss Toni Gardner (Muna al Hussein). Son b. 1962.

HUXLEY, Aldous
(1894-1963) Eng. novelist. Novels include *Crome Yellow, Antic Hay, Point Counterpoint, Brave New World, The Genius and the Goddess.* Also essays, stories, poems, anthologies. His elder brother is **Sir Julian Sorell H.** (1887-). From 1925-7 he was prof. of zool. at King's Coll. London, and in 1926 was made Fullerian prof. of physiol. at the Royal Institution; Dir. Gen. UNESCO, 1946-8. Author of *Religion Without Revelation* (1957).

HWANG-HO
[hwong'-] or **Yellow River.** River of China, 2,900 m. long, which rises in Tibet and flows through China to the Gulf of Pohai, where it enters the sea by a great delta. Its chief tributary is the Wei-Ho. Floods are frequent and the river has changed its course several times.

HYACINTH
Hardy bulbous herb of the lily family, cultivated, esp. in Holland, since the 16th cent. It was derived from a Levantine plant, *Hyacinthus orientalis.* **Hyacinth** (or **Jacynth**) Transparent red variety of the mineral zircon. It is valued as a gemstone.

HYAENA
Carnivorous mammals allied to the Civets. They are shaggy, with powerful jaws and short tails. The hind limbs are shorter than the fore limbs. The Striped, or Laughing Hyaena is found in Asia and Africa; the Brown and Spotted in Africa only. Hyaenas feed at night on carrion.

HYDE, Edward
Earl of Clarendon (1609-74) Eng. statesman and historian. He took Charles I's side in the Civil War, the subject of his *History of the Great Rebellion.*

HYDERABAD
[hi'-dra-bad'] One of the former States of India, watered by the Rivers Godavari and Kistna. The ruling dynasty of this Hindu state was Moslem. In 1947 the Nizam declared Hyderabad's indep. of both India and Pakistan, but following the occupation by Indian troops, 1949, the state became part of the Indian Repub.

HYDRA
Small freshwater organism or 'polyp'. Belonging to the class Hydrozoa, it is common in ponds and streams, where it attaches itself by a sticky secretion to weeds, etc. Hydra consists of a soft tubular body, ¼ to ½ in. in length, with a circle of 6 to 8 hollow tentacles round the mouth.

HYDRANGEA
Genus of flowering shrubs of the saxifrage family. Several are grown in Brit. notably *H. paniculata* and *H. macrophylla.*

HYDROCEPHALUS
[-sef'-] Pathological condition in which fluid is retained within the skull. Popularly known as water on the brain.

HYDROCHLORIC ACID
Aqueous solution of the gaseous compound hydrogen chloride (HCl), it was formerly called muriatic acid. It is prepared by heating common salt with sulphuric acid, the gas being collected in water. The crude impure acid, often termed spirits of salt, is used for cleaning metal work.

HYDROCYANIC ACID
HCN. Highly poisonous acid, also known as prussic acid, found in bitter almonds and laurel leaves. With bases it forms a series of salts known as cyanides. It is very volatile and has a characteristic smell of bitter almonds. Its poisonous action is rapidly fatal.

HYDRO-ELECTRIC POWER
Electrical energy obtained from generators driven by water-turbines. The initial source of power may be natural, as in waterfalls, or artificial, as in river-damming. The first large hydro-electric installation was completed at Niagara in 1892, and since then plants have been set up in many other parts of the world where water power is available.

HYDROFOIL
Boat fitted with hydrofoils. When the boat is at rest or moving slowly, the hydrofoils extend down into the water, but when it gathers speed, the water impinging on the hydrofoils exerts greater pressure on the bottom than on top. As the hydrofoils rise, so does the hull, which rides along as if on stilts. Boats of this type virtually eliminate friction of the water on the hull. The first hydrofoil patents are dated 1905, and the Wright Brothers experimented with a boat of this type in 1907. In recent times, every navy of importance has renewed its experiments with boats of this kind.

HYDROGEN
Colourless gaseous element, a constituent of water and of nearly all organic materials. It is the lightest element, having a density 0·07 times that of air. It was first recognised as a distinct substance by Cavendish in 1766. **Hydrogen Bomb.** Nuclear weapon that derives its energy largely from nuclear fusion, *i.e.* the joining together of light elements. Very high temperatures are required, provided initially by the fission of heavy elements such as uranium and plutonium. The first was exploded by U.S. forces, 1952.

HYDROGEN PEROXIDE
Colourless, odourless, water-like liquid which gives off oxygen on coming in contact with organic tissues. Hence it is a valuable antiseptic and bleaching agent.

HYDROMETER
Instrument for determining the relative densities of liquids.

HYDROPLANE
Type of boat constructed to skim over the surface of water when driven at a high speed.

HYKSOS
or **Shepherd Kings.** Name given to the leaders of a group of Semitic tribes who seized power in Egypt after the downfall of the 13th dynasty, *c.* 2300 B.C. and were expelled when the Theban kings regained the ascendency. *c.* 1829 B.C.

HYMENOPTERA
[hī'-] Large order of insects. Possessing 2 pairs of membranous wings, and mouth parts adapted for biting and sucking, they are represented by the ants, bees, wasps, and gall flies. In the female the abdomen is provided with an ovipositer modified for sawing, piercing or stinging.

HYMN
Song of praise and thanksgiving to God. Hymns were introduced into Christian worship at an early date and developed from the Psalms. The earliest were in Lat.

HYOSCINE
or **Hyoscine Hydrobromide** or **Scopolamine.** Drug used to dilate pupil of the eye and as a

sedative. Combined with morphia it is used occasionally to produce the 'twilight sleep' for childbirth.

HYPERTENSION
Sign of arterial and heart disease occurring in adults of all ages but principally in later life. The sign is assoc. with generalised arteriosclerosis.

HYPNOSIS
[hip-nō'-sis] Special form of sleep induced under the influence of an operator. The hypnotic state presents 3 phases which merge into each other. The first is that of catalepsy or trance in which the limbs though rigid may be moulded at the will of the operator; the second is that of lethargy in which the whole body appears placid and the subject unconscious; the third is that of artificial somnambulism in which the subject is extremely susceptible to suggestion. In this last phase the subject may be made to perform actions which were impossible to him in his waking state; also he may be enabled to remember incidents which previously were beyond recall. Suggestions given in the hypnotic state are carried out subsequently when awake but without cognisance of the reason of their performance or of the existence of the hypnotic command. The condition is induced in a variety of ways. The subject must co-operate with the operator. Once hypnotism is estabd. it is an easy matter to hypnotise on subsequent occasions. *See* MESMERISM.

HYPNOTIC
[hip-not'-ic] Term applied to drugs which promote sleep. Other terms used are soporific and narcotic. There are a large number of hypnotic drugs, the most commonly used being the barbiturates, chloral hydrate and paraldehyde. Bromides are sedative and so indirectly lead to sleep. Morphia and opium (laudanum) tend to lead to drowsiness, but they are primarily pain-relieving drugs. Great care should always be exercised in their use. There is always the danger of habit formation.

HYRAX
[hī'-] Tailless quadrupeds of the genus *Procavia* allied to the hoofed mammals. They are about the size of a rabbit and have short fur. The toes have nails except 1 digit in the forefoot which has a curved claw; and the upper lip is cleft. They are found in Africa and Asia.

HYSSOP
Small perennial aromatic plant (*Hyssopus officinalis*) with bluish flowers and lance-like leaves, native to the Medit. The hyssop of the Bible was probably a species of thyme.

HYSTERIA
Symptoms of a group of conditions called psycho-neurosis or functional nervous diseases which show no evidence of pathological changes in the organs concerned.

I

I
9th letter and 3rd vowel of the Eng. alphabet. It represents several vowel sounds and also the consonantal sound of *y*. The 3 principal sounds are: the long *i* as in *machine, intrigue;* the short sound in *pit, sin, fit;* the diphthongal sound, as in *mine, fine, wine,* etc. It also has several other sounds when in combination with certain vowels, as in *brief, grief,* or in the endings — *-tion, -sion,* etc.

IBEX
[ī'beks] Wild alpine goat. It has long, curved horns and its average measurement is 4½ ft. Naturalists recognise allied forms called Himalayan, Arabian and Abyssinian.

IBIS
[ī'-bis] Slender-billed wading birds related to the storks. They have bald, black heads and necks and are found nearly all over Africa. Allied species live in Japan and Australia. *Ibis religiosa* was sacred to the Egyptians.

IBN SAUD
[sowd'] **Abdul Aziz Ibn Rahman Al Feisal,** G.C.B., G.C.I.E. (1880-1953) King of Saudi Arabia. Originally rulers of Nejd, Ibn Saud's family was deposed and took shelter at Kuwait; he won his capital Rijadh, with 40 followers (1901); was king of Hejaz and Nejd (1927); changed name of kingdom to Saudi Arabia in 1932. Ibn Saud took a leading part in founding the Arab League, 1945. He was succeeded by his eldest son, Emir Saud (1953), who abdicated in favour of his brother Faisal, 1964.

IBSEN, Henrik
(1828-1906) Norwegian author. He lived abroad, mainly in Germany, till 1891. His chief plays include *Brand, Peer Gynt, A Doll's House, Ghosts, The Wild Duck, Hedda Gabler, The Master Builder, John Gabriel Borkman.*

ICE
Solid state of water. It is a colourless substance crystallising in the hexagonal system, of which hoar-frost, snow and hail are forms. The temp. 0° C. (32° F.) is defined as the temp. of melting ice. Water expands when freezing, and ice floats on cold water. Sp. gr. 0·92. The latent heat of fusion of ice is 80 calories per gram. **Ice Age.** Period of intense cold occurring after the deposition of the tertiary beds. Glaciation spread over N.W. Europe to parts of S. Europe and over the N. area of N. Amer. The deposits of this period are boulder clays and tills. There are indications that man was contemporary with the later part of the ice age.

ICE HOCKEY
Game played on ice between 2 teams of 6 players, first played in Canada in 1867. The playing area is 185 by 85 ft. All players wear protective clothing. Although popular in Brit., the game is played most in Canada, U.S.A., and Scandinavia.

ICEBERG
Mass of ice floating in the sea which has broken off a glacier or ice barrier. The latter are characteristic of the Antarctic. Icebergs from Greenland are carried S. by the Labrador current, and may endanger shipping in the N. Atlantic.

ICELAND
Repub. of Europe, Is. in the Atlantic Ocean, *c.* 200 m. S.E. of Greenland, just S. of the Arctic circle. The highest mt. is over 6,000 ft. high, and there are some active volcanoes, notably Hekla. Iceland is also famous for its hot springs, or geysers. The S. has a cool maritime climate. The pop. is mainly concentrated in the S.W. Hay is the chief crop, and sheep and cattle are reared. Fishing is the principal occupation. Reykjavik is the cap. and chief port. The people are Lutherans. From 930 to 1264 Iceland was an indep. repub., with an assembly, the *Althing,* the oldest parl. in the world. In 1263 the rule of the King of Norway was recognised. Both countries passed to Denmark in 1381. I. obtained indep. in 1918, being united with Denmark only through the common sovereign. Occupied by Allied Forces during World War II (1940-5). I. was declared an indep. repub. in 1944. Area: 40,500 sq.m. Pop. 183,000.

ICELAND MOSS
Lichen (*Cetraria islandica*), growing abundantly in Arctic and Antarctic climates and in the higher mt. regions of Brit. It grows *c.* 3 in. high. It forms a starch used for sizing.

ICELANDIC *See* NORSE.

ICHNEUMON
[-new'-] (1) (*Herpestes*) Small carnivorous mammal common in the valley of the Nile. It preys on snakes and crocodiles' eggs. (2) **Ichneumon Fly,** a small hymenopterous insect, is parasitic in its larval stage upon caterpillars.

IDAHO
State of U.S.A. in the N.W. Mainly mountainous, much of Idaho is arid, and irrigation is widely practised. The Snake is the chief river. Agriculture is the chief industry. Dairying is carried on in the valleys. Minerals include gold, silver, zinc and copper. Boise is the cap. Idaho was organised as a Territory, 1863, and became a state, 1890. 2 representatives are sent to Congress. Area: 83,560 sq.m. Pop. 713,000.

IDEALISM
In metaphysics a doctrine that the only real existence is the idea, the intellectual perception, and that the material substance is dependent upon the idea. The theory was elaborated by Descartes with his dictum, *I think, therefore I exist.* Adopting this central principle, a school of philosophers arose, among whom Berkeley and Hegel were prominent.

IDOLATRY
Worship of images or other objects as representing super-human personalities. More advanced than animism and nature worship. Modern Judaism, Christianity and Islam regard as idols all objects of worship, public, family or personal, in polytheistic systems.

IGUANA
[i-gwä'-nä] Family of lizards, mainly Amer., but found in Madagascar and Fiji. The trop. Amer. *I. tuberculata,* with spiny crest along the back and large dewlap, is an herbivorous tree dweller. *C.* 6 ft. long, its flesh and eggs are edible.

IJSSELMEER
Lake in the Netherlands, between the provs. of

N. Holland and Friesland, and separated from the N. Sea by a 20-m. dam, completed 1932. The lake was formed in the 13th and 14th cents. Since the 17th cent. much land has been reclaimed from the Zuider Zee.

ILE DE FRANCE
[ēl] Old prov. of Fr. with Paris as its cap. Also name of Mauritius 1715 to 1815.

ILEX
Large genus of shrubs and trees of the holly family, widely distributed in both hemispheres, esp. in S. Amer. The most important economically is *I. paraguariensis* which yields maté, or Paraguay tea. The common holly is *I. aquifolium*; others in cultivation are the inkberry and winterberry of N. Amer.

ILFORD
Part of Redbridge, borough of Greater London (1964). Photographic materials are manufactured. It returns 2 members to Parl.

ILKLEY
Urban district and resort of the W. Riding, Yorks., on the Wharfe, 16 m. N.W. of Leeds. Beauty spots nearby include Ilkley Moor, Wharfedale and Bolton Abbey. Pop. 18,360.

ILLINOIS
[-noy'] State of the U.S.A., S.W. of L. Michigan, bounded on the W. and S. by the Mississippi and Ohio rivers. I. is mainly agricultural. Slaughtering and meat packing are the chief industries. Coal is the most important mineral. Springfield is the cap. but Chicago is the largest city. I. was discovered by Fr. explorers in the 17th cent. and ceded to Brit. in 1763. In 1783 it became Amer. and was admitted as a state, 1818. It sends 26 representatives to Congress. Area: 56,400 sq.m. Pop. 11,114,000.

ILLYRIA
Prov. of the Rom. Empire in S.E. Europe, covering the district now known as Bosnia, Herzegovina, Dalmatia and Montenegro. There was a prov. of Illyria in Austria, 1815-48.

ILMENITE
Iron titanate forming the principal ore of the metal titanium. It contains iron and titanium oxide and occurs in Norway and Canada.

IMAGE
In optics, the optical counterpart or picture of an object produced by reflection from a mirror or by refraction by a lens. An image may be either real or virtual. In the former case rays of light actually pass through the image, while in a virtual image they only appear to do so. To the eye, there is no difference, but a real image may be thrown on to a screen, while a virtual image cannot.

IMMIGRATION
Entrance of people into a foreign country for the purpose of settling there. Considerable immigration into the N. Amer. cont. in the 19th cent. led to steps being taken to restrict it. At first these were directed against the coloured races whose standard of living was lower than that of the white man. Today almost every country takes measures to keep out all who are considered undesirable, either on grounds of poverty or disease. Immigration into U.S.A. occurs on a large scale, the figures rising to 8,500,000 in 1900-10. Since 1920, the Austral. Govt. has given financial aid to Brit. subjects seeking settlement in Australia, a facility which has been revived since World War II.

IMMORTALITY
Condition or quality of being exempt from d. or annihilation. Confidence in the continuance of human existence beyond the grave is traceable to primeval man. The pantheistic view of reabsorption in the universal life, or that of the Buddhist Nirvana, and the positivist view of corporate rather than individual survival, do not satisfy those who regard immortality as essentially involving perpetuation of the personal consciousness. The Christian doctrine looks for fellowship with the Eternal through the resurrection of Jesus Christ.

IMMUNITY
The power of the animal body to resist infection. **Acquired immunity** results after the natural recovery from an illness and may be a permanent feature as after smallpox, or temporary as after pneumonia. **Active artificial immunity** is obtained by inoculation of a germ altered in its disease-producing properties so that it produces a modified attack of the disease by which in many cases the patient is not upset at all. **Passive immunisation** is produced by injecting blood or serum from an actively immunised animal or from a person who has recovered from the disease.

IMPERIALISM
Term used for the movement aiming at the strengthening of the Brit. Empire. It was much used towards the close of the 19th cent., its opposite being Little Englander. Lord Beaconsfield was regarded as a great imperialist.

IMPORTS
Goods coming into a country by way of trade, opposed to exports, which are goods sent out to foreign countries. In Brit. and most other countries the value of imports is calculated by officials at the ports of entry. Most countries levy duties on imported goods, Brit. joining the number in 1932 after almost a cent. of Free Trade. In Brit. the value of imports is always considerably greater than that of exports. The difference—the balance of trade—has been generally paid by invisible exports, such as shipping dues and insurance charges, but since World War II the aim has been to reduce imports and to balance them by increased exports. In Brit. the value of imports for 1963 was £4,820,165,241. *See* BALANCE OF TRADE; EXPORTS.

IMPRESSIONISM
School of painting originating in Fr. about 1870, assoc. with Edouard Manet and Claude Monet. Other painters of this school were Boudin, Degas, Renoir, Pissarro, Morisot and Sisley. The Impressionists claimed freedom from conventional academic methods of lighting and composition. For later developments, *see* SEURAT, CÉZANNE, GAUGUIN.

INCAS
People of a very ancient Peruvian civilisation possibly reaching back to 12,000 B.C. who possessed an empire which covered the modern Peru and part of Bolivia and Chile, an area 2,000 m. long and *c.* 500 wide. It was overthrown by Pizarro in 1533. The Incas achieved a high level of culture, as is evidenced by their social system, agriculture, road-making, ceramics, textiles, and buildings.

INCARNATION
Act of embodying in flesh, but specifically the assumption by the Godhead of human form and nature in the person of Jesus Christ.

INCENSE
Blend of sweet smelling spices burned in a thurible, etc. In the R.C. Ch. its use is general, but in the C. of E. it is used by a few high churchmen only.

INCEST
Intercourse between persons so closely related that they are debarred from contracting legal marriage. An Act of 1908 made it a misdemeanour for a male to have intercourse, or attempt to procure it, with his mother, sister, daughter, or granddaughter. A female over 16 who, knowing the relationship, permits such intercourse, is guilty.

INCOME TAX
A tax on income introduced by Pitt in 1799, removed in 1816 and reimposed in 1842 on all

income arising in Brit. and N. Ireland. Numerous later acts were consolidated by the passing of the Income Tax Act, 1918, and later revised in 1945. Later acts were consolidated in the Income Tax Act of 1952. Tax is levied under 4 schedules according to the nature of the income. Sch. 'B' covers occupiers of land. Sch. 'C' covers income from abroad. Sch. 'D' which is divided into 6 classes charges the profits of all trades and professions and other income not taxed directly at the source. Sch. 'E' is in respect of income from employment which is collected under P.A.Y.E. The standard rate of income tax is decided by Parl. when the Chancellor of the Exchequer presents his budget.

INCUBATION
(1) In zoology the process by which birds stimulate the development of their eggs by the heat of the body of the parents, who sit on the eggs until their young are hatched. (2) In pathology, **incubation** is the period between the infection and the appearance of the symptoms of a disease.

INDEPENDENCE
The **Declaration of I.** is the document by which the U.S.A. declared themselves independent of Brit. It was drawn up by Congress and accepted by the representatives of the 13 orig. states on July 4, 1776. The 13 states were Massachusetts, New York, New Jersey, Virginia, Pennsylvania, Maryland, N. Carolina, S. Carolina, New Hampshire, Rhode Island, Delaware, Connecticut and Georgia.

INDEPENDENT LABOUR PARTY
Brit. polit. organisation, founded at Bradford in 1893. It helped to found the Labour Party. The I.L.P. gradually lost its influence. In 1932, under the leadership of James Maxton, the I.L.P. severed all connection with the Lab. Party, and entered into an alliance with the Communist Party. However, many branches and individual members left the I.L.P. and formed the Soc. League, which secured affiliation to the Lab. Party.

INDEPENDENT TELEVISION AUTHORITY
Public Corporation established by the Television Act 1954 to provide television services additional to those of BBC for a period of 10 years, renewed for further 12 years, 1964. The Authority operates transmitting stations but studios are the responsibility of the programme companies appointed by the ITA. These companies are completely responsible for the programmes, and legal obligations concerning standards of programmes and advertising are laid down in their contracts, while the ITA is responsible to Parliament. The system is financed by the sale to programme companies of restricted amounts of advertising time. Sponsored programmes supplied by advertisers are prohibited. Provisions of the Television Act governing programmes include: (1) nothing must be broadcast which is offensive to good taste or decency, (2) news must be accurate and impartial, (3) due impartiality must be preserved in matters of political or industrial controversy, or relating to current public policy. The ITA receives no public money, its revenue and capital needs being supplied from rentals paid by programme companies. The first ITA transmitter went on the air at Croydon in 1955. By 1966 30 transmitters were in operation serving 98% of the population. The country is divided into 13 areas served by 14 independent companies. After July 1968 14 areas will be served by 15 companies.

INDEX LIBRORUM PROHIBITORUM
Official list of books the reading of which was forbidden to the faithful of the R.C. Ch. Drawn up by a Committee of the Council of Trent, it received papal approval and was first pub. in 1564. The office of the Congregation of the Index was finally abolished in 1965.

INDIA
The partition of the Indian subcontinent in 1947 gave the new Dominion of India 77 % of the area and 81 % of the pop. In 1950 the new state proclaimed itself a Repub. In 1956 the

26 states then existing were replaced by 14 states and 6 centrally administered territories or union states. Each state of the union has a Gov. appointed by the Pres. who is himself elected by a college consisting of members of the state legislative assemblies and members of the union's House of States and House of the People. Nagaland became the 16th State of the Indian Union in 1962. **Physical Geography.** The peninsula of India is a block of old igneous, metamorphic and sedimentary rocks. The W. half is covered with lava sheets (Deccan Traps) whereon lies a black soil highly suited to cotton. There is also an E. line of Ghats through which flow the rivers Mahanadi, Godavari, Kistna and Cauvery forming large deltas on entering the Bay of Bengal. In the extreme N. are the Himalayas, comprising 3 main ranges, the Siwaliks, the Lesser Himalayas and the Greater Himalayas. Between these ranges and the peninsular block is a sediment-filled trough drained by the Indus and the Ganges and their tributaries. The hottest and driest period of the year is Feb.-May. During June heavy monsoon rains sweep over India and continue until Oct. During this season the Ghats and the land to seaward receive well over 40 ins. while the W. interior gets only 20 ins. or less. The coast of Madras receives rain also from Oct. to Dec. from the retreating monsoon. **Ethnic and Social History.** India has received many waves of immigrants. The Himalayas held back the Mongolian peoples but entry was made by the N.W. passes and the Arabian Sea. An early immigrant group was Dravidian-speaking and their tongue still persists S. of the Godavari. There followed after 1500 B.C. speakers of an Indo-European tongue whose influx is recorded in the Rig-Veda. Their descendants (Hindus) occupy India. Other invasions were those of the Gks., Persians and Scythians after 500 B.C., of the Huns in the 5th cent. A.D. and of the Arabs from the 8th to the 16th cents., leading to the dissemination of Islamic culture. European traders and missionaries established themselves on the W. coast from the end of the 15th cent. The Brit. E. India Co. and the Brit. Army ousted Fr. rivals. In 1858 the E. India Co. was wound up and direct govt. by Brit. replaced dual control. From that time, by a series of Acts, mainly those of 1861, 1909, 1919 and 1935, greater responsibility was given to the Indians. This process culminated in indep. and partition in 1947. Social practice, peace, famine control and health measures have allowed a great increase in pop. which has rapidly outrun the country's own food supply. India is predominantly an agricultural country. Where water is sufficient, rice is the chief crop, elsewhere, millet forms the staple food. India exports much cotton, tea, spices, linseed and sugar. Mod. industry began its growth at the end of the 19th cent., largely at the ports of Bombay, Calcutta and Madras. In 1947 six industries—cotton spinning and weaving, jute manufacturing, ordnance factories, general engineering, railway workshops and cotton gin-

ning—each employed over 100,000 workers. Four industries—sugar milling, iron and steel manufacture, tea factories and rice mills—each employed between 50,000 and 100,000. The Damodar Valley is becoming a region of heavy industry. Since 1953 a programme of rural development is in hand.

INDIAN INK
Ink of an intense black colour used by artists and draughtsmen, sometimes called Chinese ink.

INDIAN MILLET
Cereal grass yielding, after rice, the most extensively grown grain in the Old World. It is derived from *Sorghum vulgare*, and varieties produce durra in Egypt and the Sudan, and Guinea and Kaffir corn in Africa.

INDIAN MUTINY
(1857-59) Revolt against Brit. rule in India, attributed partly to an order stating that in future Bengali soldiers were liable to service overseas, and partly to the annexation of Oudh in 1856. The mutiny proper began at Meerut on May 10. There, some native regts. murdered their officers with their families, marched to Delhi, and restored the old Mogul Empire. Other centres of revolt were Cawnpore and Lucknow, and at both places Brit. garrisons were besieged. On June 27, Cawnpore surrendered, and, in spite of a safe conduct, all men, women and children were murdered by order of Nana Sahib. Sir Henry Havelock fought several battles on his way to Cawnpore. From there he marched towards Lucknow which he reached on Sept. 23. The mutiny at Delhi had meanwhile been crushed. Sir Colin Campbell with reinforcements from Brit. reached Cawnpore, and then with 8,000 men relieved the garrison at Lucknow. The capture of Jhansi and Gwalior in the summer of 1858 marked the end of the major operations.

INDIAN OCEAN
One of the 5 great oceans. It stretches from Africa to the E. Indies and Australia and from Asia to the Antarctic. Area: 28,360,000 sq.m.

INDIANA
State of the U.S.A. lying S.E. of L. Michigan, bounded in the S. by the Ohio River. The land is mainly devoted to agriculture. Coal, petroleum, and iron are mined. Indianapolis is the cap. Indiana was settled in 1732, and became a state in 1816; 11 representatives are sent to Congress. Area: 36,290 sq.m. Pop. 5,193,700.

INDIANAPOLIS
Cap. of Indiana, U.S.A., 110 m. N.W. of Cincinnati. Industries include the manufacture of agricultural implements and the preparation of canned foods. Pop. 742,700.

INDIARUBBER
Name of *Ficus elastica*, a tall evergreen tree growing in the damp forests of N. India, Assam and Burma. A favourite pot plant in Brit. *See* RUBBER.

INDIGO
Important blue dyestuff, prepared from several leguminous plants of the genus *Indigofera*, chiefly *I. tinctoria* and *I. suffruticossa*, cultivated in India, Java and Natal. Natural indigo is largely superseded by the synthetic product, a derivative of naphthalene.

INDO-EUROPEAN
Family of inflectional languages, originating prob. in C. or N. Europe or S.W. Asia before 2000 B.C., and including the languages of N. India, Persia, and Europe (except *Hungarian, Finnish, Lapp, Estonian*—all *Ural-Altaic*—*Basque*, and ancient *Etruscan, Pictish*, etc.). Branches: *Indo-Ayran, Iranian, Armenian, Albanian, Baltic, Slavic, Gk., Italic, Celtic, Germanic.*

INDONESIA
Ethnological term for groups of Is. in the Indian and Pacific oceans. Included are the Java group, part of the Malay Peninsula, Borneo, Celebes, the Philippines and the Pacific groups. **The Repub. of I.** State of the E. Indies comprising the Is. of Java, Madura, Sumatra, Banka, Belitong, part of Borneo, Celebes, the Moluccas, the Riouw-Lingga group, Bali and Lombok, and W. Timor. Much of the region was under Dutch rule from the 17th cent. Following World War II, a nationalistic movement arose, and intermittent fighting occurred between the Dutch forces and the Indonesians, until sovereignty was transferred by the Netherlands, Dec. 1949. General elections were held in 1955. The Repub. of I. is divided into 10 provs.: W., C. and E. Java; N., C. and S. Sumatra; Borneo, Celebes, Lesser Sunda Is. and the Moluccas. Djakarta (Batavia) on the N.W. coast of Java, is the federal cap. Govt. is by a pres. (Dr. Sukarno became the first pres. 1949) and council of mins. with a senate and house of representatives. Area: 736,532 sq.m. Pop. *c.* 97,085,000.

INDUS
River of Pakistan, which rises in the Himalayas in Tibet, at 18,000 ft. Flowing N.W. through the Kashmir gorges, it turns S.W. near Bunji, receives the Kabul near Attock and collects the Punjabi streams at Mithankot, below which it traverses the plain of Sind to its delta on the Arabian Sea. The fall to Attock, 900 ft. above sea level, below which it is navigable, causes flooding, but this has been reduced by a dam and vast irrigation works. The length of the river is *c.* 1,900 m. and its drainage area is 372,000 sq.m. **Indus Valley Civilisation.** Beginning in 1922, 3 principal sites, Mohenjo-Daro, Harappa, and Chanhu-Daro were explored along the Indus river. Ruined cities were discovered which gave abundant evidence of a highly advanced civilisation which reached its climax about 2500 B.C. In the city of Mohenjo-Daro the domestic and civic architecture bears evidence of an elaborate system of drainage. Correspondence in pottery design and decoration, and the presence of actual beads from ancient Egypt, confirms that there was trade between Egypt and the Far East.

INDUSTRIAL DISEASE
A disease wholly or partly attributable to conditions pertaining at work, such as *dermatitis* in chem. industry, *nystagmus* in miners, *silicosis* in stone masons, *lead poisoning* in printers and painters and *anthrax* in wool sorters. A workman contracting any disease signified as an industrial or occupational disease can claim compensation under the Nat. Ins. (Industrial Injuries) Act, 1946.

INDUSTRIAL REVOLUTION
Term used for the social and economic changes marking the transition from self-supporting agricultural village life and domestic industry to the capitalist factory system and modern industrialism. It generally refers to the period 1750-1850 in Brit.

INFANT
Person under 21 years of age. In Eng. law an infant cannot bring an action at law, but must sue, if and when it is necessary, through a next friend. An infant cannot generally enter into a contract. In Scot. an infant is called a **pupil** while under 14 if male and 12 if female. From these ages until 21 the child is a **minor.** The murder of very young children is known as **infanticide. Infant Mortality.** Term used for the death rate per 1,000 live births of children under 1 year old. This rate varies in each country and the rate in Brit. compares unfavourably with the Scandinavian countries.

INFANTILE PARALYSIS *See* POLIOMYELITIS.

INFECTION
Conveyance of disease into the body by matter infected with micro-organisms. Infection may

be spread by droplets, *i.e.* small particles of moisture containing germs which are coughed or sneezed around; by drinking germ-contaminated water, or eating contaminated food; by bites of insects such as the mosquito; by "carriers", *i.e.* people who may have suffered from a disease but still retain the causal germs in their body; and lastly by direct touch or contagion as in the case of the venereal diseases. **Infectious Disease.** Disease capable of being spread by an infected person to another person in various ways. *See* INFECTION. In Brit. certain diseases so classified are notifiable by law to the local Med. Officer of Health, so that certain measures may be taken to prevent their spread. Smallpox, scarlet fever and tuberculosis are amongst those so classified. The local authority has power to include any disease in this list for its own local area.

INFERIORITY COMPLEX
State of lack of confidence in one's ability to compete with others frequently demonstrated by diffidence, or dissatisfaction with one's achievements. May be compensated by a bold, over-confident, self-satisfied or even pompous demeanour.

INFLAMMATION
Reaction of an area of the body which is the seat of bacterial invasion. The affected part is congested with blood cells, and large quantities of lymph are poured out by the affected tissues in an attempt to wash the invading organisms away. *See* SEPTICAEMIA.

INFLUENZA
Acute infectious disease attacking nose, throat and lungs. The virus was isolated in 1933. Chief symptoms are headache, generalised body aches and pains, fever, catarrh of larynx and trachea with cough and spit, fever, and in severe cases prostration, cyanosis and bronchopneumonia.

INFRA-RED RAYS
Electro-magnetic waves or heat rays. They are below the red rays of the visible spectrum and are invisible to the human eye. Infra-red rays emit heat. They are used to elucidate molecular structures; and to photograph through fog and mist or at distances invisible to the human eye. The rays are also used in medical treatments. *See* PHYSIOTHERAPY.

INGE, William
(1860-1954) Eng. divine. B. Yorkshire; educ. Eton and King's Coll. Camb. In 1911 he was made Dean of St. Paul's. During his years at St. Paul's, he became a very popular writer on the problems of the modern world.

INGELOW, Jean
(1820-97) Eng. poet. B. Boston, Lincs. A volume of her verse attracted attention in 1863.

INGRES, Jean Auguste Dominique
[a(ng)-gr] (1780-1867) Fr. painter. He was awarded the Grand Prix in 1801. He painted portraits and classical subjects.

INJECTION
Method employed in medicine for administering certain drugs. Types of injection in use are *subcutaneous* or under the skin, *intramuscular* or into the muscle, *intravenous* or into the vein.

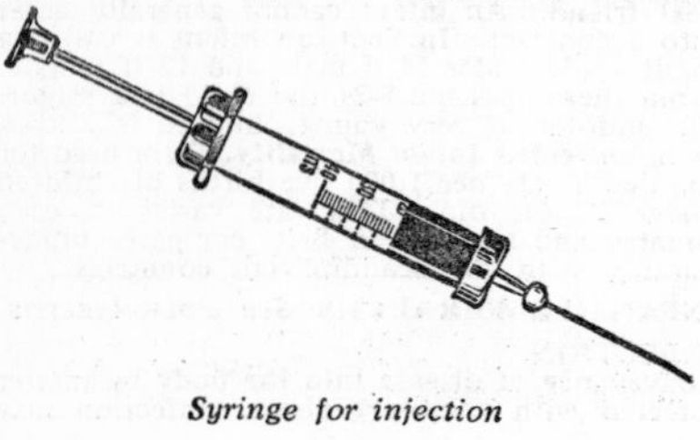

Syringe for injection

INK
Ordinary **writing inks** were formerly made from ferrous sulphate and an infusion of gall-nuts with gum, but are now mainly made from aniline dyes. **Copying ink** contains glycerine to prevent drying. **Printing inks** are made from lampblack or other pigments mixed with drying oils. **Ballpoint pen inks** are essentially printing inks. **Marking inks** are preparations of silver nitrate or aniline dyestuffs.

INKERMAN
A ridge in the Crimea (U.S.S.R.) overlooking Sebastopol Harbour, where, in the final battle of the Crimean War, Nov. 1854, the Russians were defeated by the Brit. and Fr.

INNOCENT
Name of 13 popes. **Innocent III** (1160-1216) Lothaire Conti, the nephew of Pope Clement III, b. at Anagni; educ. in Paris and Bologna. In 1198 he was chosen pope. In Germany his influence helped Otto IV and then Frederick II to secure the imperial throne; he forced John of Eng. to a humiliating surrender. Innocent called the council of the Lateran, which in 1215 proclaimed a crusade, and he was responsible for the crusade against the Albigenses.

INNS OF COURT
In Eng. 4 socs. that alone have the right of admitting men and women to practise as barristers. They are Lincoln's Inn, Gray's Inn, Inner Temple and Middle Temple. In Dublin there is an inn of court and one has existed since 1922 for N. Ireland at Belfast. In Scot. a similar work is performed by the Faculty of Advocates.

INNSBRUCK
[-brŏŏk] Austrian town, cap. of the Tirol, on the Inn *c.* 60 m. S. of Munich. A tourist centre, I. controls the railway over the Brenner Pass. Pop. 100,695.

INOCULATION
Term used in medicine when certain materials producing an immunity to disease are given by injection. Many diseases can be prevented by inoculation such as smallpox, typhus fever, diphtheria, whooping cough, rabies, yellow fever and tetanus.

INORGANIC CHEMISTRY
The chemistry which is concerned with the elements and non-carbon compounds. In the pre-Christian era elements such as gold, silver, tin, iron, lead and copper had been discovered and used by the ancient Chinese, Hindus, Egyptians and Greeks, together with some of the simpler alloys. By about the middle of the 17th cent. the alchemists were familiar with most of the common metals, their alloys and metallic salts, and some of the acids, alkalis, medicinal minerals and non-metallic elements. Robert Boyle (1627-91) might be considered the first of the modern chemists because of the insistence on experimental method. The discoveries of cobalt (1733) and nickel (1750) were followed by Henry Cavendish's recognition of elementary hydrogen in 1766, the isolation of nitrogen by Daniel Rutherford in 1772, oxygen by Joseph Priestley and chlorine by K. Scheele in 1774. In 1784 Cavendish discovered that water is composed of two volumes of hydrogen to one of oxygen; and in 1789 Klaproth detected uranium in the mineral pitchblende, which led to the discovery of the radioactive compounds of polonium and radium by Marie and Pierre Curie in 1898. The beginning of the 19th cent. witnessed the discovery of a most powerful means of analysing compounds and their elements, *viz.* electrolysis. This enabled Sir Humphry Davy to decompose the supposed elements soda and potash and in 1808 he isolated the

metals sodium and potassium. The spectroscopic method of analysing discovered in 1859 has led to great advances in physical knowledge of the structure of atoms. In 1922, Prof. Juroslav Heyrovsky discovered the polarographic method of analysis. In 1910 it was observed that certain of the radio-elements were identical in chemical behaviour and could only be distinguished by their radioactive constants; and when their atomic weights were determined these were found to be different. This led to the conclusion that chemical analysis may separate matter into types of matter and not into elements. These types, although identical chemically, may be found to be made up of more than one element when examined by other methods. Frederick Soddy gave the name *isotopes* (*q.v.*) to these chemically identical elements. *See* ELEMENT; ORGANIC CHEMISTRY.

INQUEST
Inquiry of any kind. In Eng. today the word is confined to inquiries held by a coroner. These concern persons for whom a doctor will not give a certificate stating the cause of death. Since 1927 he need only summon a jury if he thinks that the death was due to violence, such as murder or manslaughter, or to a street accident. *See* CORONER.

INQUISITION
Any inquiry, but chiefly the inquiry known in the R.C. Ch. as the Holy Office. It was founded in 1248 by Pope Innocent IV, for the suppression of heresy. The first tribunal was set up at Toulouse, and it was introduced into Italy, Spain, the Netherlands, Portugal, and taken to the New World. It lasted until the 19th cent. but its great age was the 15th cent., and the country where it was most active was Spain where it was closely connected with the State. Under Inquisitors-General, the most notorious of whom was Torquemada, it had an elaborate organisation. Torture was freely used to extract confessions, and the condemned were usually burned with great ceremonial.

INSANITY
State of having an unsound mind, in that one commits actions foreign to accepted social behaviour. Insanity is usually assoc. with disease of brain or derangement of mental process of thought and reason. In severe cases where patient is a danger to himself or to the community he is placed in the care of a mental hospital after certification of mental state by a doctor. *See* LUNACY.

INSECT
Class of the Arthropoda, a major division or phylum of invertebrate animals. They have jointed appendages, and consist of a larger number of species than any other class of arthropods. Insects are characterised by having the body divided into head, thorax and abdomen, the head provided with antennae, mandibles and other appendages. The thorax bears 3 pairs of legs and in most cases 2 pairs of wings; the abdomen is limbless but may have an ovipositor or its modification. The exo-skeleton is of uncalcified chitin, and may be of considerable thickness. Insects are air-breathers. The sexes are separate, and development is usually in 3 stages involving a larva which metamorphoses into a pupa and this in turn metamorphoses into the chrysalis.

INSULIN
Preparation used in medicine containing specific anti-diabetic principles of mammalian pancreas. The drug is given hypodermically and controls body use of sugar.

INSURANCE
The cover received in exchange for a stated premium paid to secure peace of mind and immunity from loss which might arise from causes beyond the insured's control. The first insurance policies recorded were on foreign trading vessels and their cargoes and Insurance Cos. began to be formed in the late 17th cent.

INTELLECT
Inherent faculty of the mind in reference to the power of understanding and reasoning, the power of perception and thought. In occultism the intellect is synonymous with the Higher (as compared with the Lower) Mind, the vehicle of the egoic consciousness.

INTELLIGENCE DEPARTMENT
Dept. which collects and interprets the information obtained by Intelligence officers of the army, navy and air force regarding an actual or potential enemy. In Brit. there is an intelligence division at the admiralty, a director of intelligence at the air ministry, and in the army a recognised unit, the Intelligence Corps, which was estabd. 1940.

INTELLIGENCE QUOTIENT TESTS
(I.Q.) Tests given to determine the powers of memory, vocabulary, reasoning power and mathematical ability. They were originated in Paris in 1904, when Binet, director of the psychological laboratory at the Sorbonne, made a survey of the intelligence of children in elementary schools. The investigators compiled a list of test questions and the answers enabled them to estab. standards for the average child of each age. The I.Q. figure is determined thus: if a child of 8 years gives results comparable with those of a child of 12 years, his mental age is rated 50 % above his chronological age, and his I.Q. is 150. Many industrial and commercial organisations use intelligence and aptitude tests as part of their procedure for selection and promotion.

INTERLAKEN
[in'-ter-là-kin] Swiss tourist centre for the Oberland district, Berne canton, on the Aare, between lakes Thun and Brienz. Pop. 5,000.

INTERNATIONAL, The
Name given to a number of Socialist and Labour organisations. **The 1st International** was founded in London in 1864 and accepted a programme drawn up by Karl Marx. The **2nd (Socialist) International**, constituted in 1889, a federation of Nationalist and Socialist Parties, was affiliated to the Labour Party in 1908. **The 3rd (Communist) International** (commonly called the Comintern) was founded in Moscow in 1919. It sought to win the support of the European proletariat and colonial, semi-colonial, and oriental peoples. When Hitler came to power (1933) it sought to estab. a "popular front" in which Communists, Socialists and Liberals would be ranged against Fascism.

INTERNATIONAL COURT OF JUSTICE
Organisation set up in 1921 by Treaty of Versailles to settle disputes on matters of internat. law and the interpretation of treaties. It was replaced in 1945 by a similar institution created under the charter of the U.N.

INTERNATIONAL GEOPHYSICAL YEAR
The period July 1957-Dec. 1958 was devoted to a programme of internat. research into the weather and other natural phenomena. An important project was the launching and subsequent tracking of earth satellites by the U.S.A. in conjunction with the U.S.S.R., for the measurement of pressures and temperatures as well as for observations of cosmic rays, micrometeorites, the geomagnetic field and solar radiation. Another project was the measuring of the level of nuclear radiation on a worldwide basis by a network of stations. For the purposes of meteorological radiation research a new standard scale for expressing measurements of solar energy was adopted generally. Antarctic expeditions included the Commonwealth Trans-Antarctic Expedition. *See* ANTARCTIC EXPLORATION.

INTERNATIONAL LABOUR ORGANISATION
Intergovernmental agency related to the United Nations and estabd. at Geneva. The office organises conferences, dealing with labour matters, at which govts., employers' and workers' organisations are represented, with the object of raising the standard of lab.

INTERNATIONAL LAW
Body of law regulating the relations between nations, esp. in time of war. It differs from other bodies of law in that there exists no power to enforce its decisions. The Roms. recognised something like internat. law in what they called *jus gentium.* In the M.A. and later, certain customs were observed, and to give clarity to these, Hugo Grotius in 1625 wrote his *De Jure Belli et Pacis.* This founded modern international law. It is contained in customs, treaties and declarations, and deals with such matters as the treatment of prisoners and wounded, contraband and blockade, the rights of neutrals and the special conditions of maritime and aerial warfare. International law is administered by the prize courts and the international court of justice (*q.v.*).

INTERNATIONAL MONETARY FUND
Estabd. after Bretton Woods Conference, 1944, to promote internat. monetary co-operation. *See* UNITED NATIONS.

INTERNATIONAL POLAR YEAR
Name given by scientists to year devoted to polar meteorological research. The first was 1882-3. This was brought about by the Internat. Meteorological Committee which, in 1879, appointed a special commission to organise temporary observatories in the N. polar region for one year. During the **second Polar Year,** these researches were extended to include the importance of the ionosphere in radio communications. A **third Polar Year,** held from July 1957 to Dec. 1958, was known as *The International Geophysical Year* (*q.v.*).

INTERPOL
(International Criminal Police Commission) Internat. police organisation designed to counter the growing internationalism in crime and to abolish national frontiers in pursuit of the criminal. Founded in Vienna in 1923. The central radio station is situated near Paris and every year the police chiefs of the member states meet to co-ordinate new methods of detection and prevention.

INTESTATE
Person who dies without making a will. In such cases Eng. law provides that the property shall pass according to certain rules. If a mar. man or woman dies, the surviving spouse takes all the furniture and personal effects and £5,000 free of death duties. If there are children, or a child, the remainder is divided into 2 equal parts. One is put in trust and the income paid to the surviving spouse, passing on his, or her, death to the child or children. The other half passes to the children, if they attain 21 years of age. If an unmar. person, or a widow or widower, without children, dies the property passes to the parents. If they are dead it passes to the brothers and sisters in equal shares, and if there are none, to more distant relatives. If there are no relatives within certain limits the estate passes to the crown.

INTESTINE
Part of alimentary canal beginning at exit of stomach and ending at anus. It is a long continuous muscular tube which receives the various digestive juices—and secretes its own juice. The process of digestion is completed, waste products are collected for voiding at next bowel movement. There is a small intestine or proximal part which connects duodenum with large intestine or distal part. The parts of the large intestine are described under **colon** (*q.v.*).

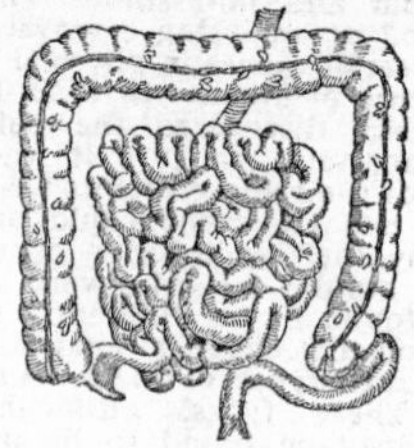

Diagram showing human intestines

INTUITION
In Eng. philosophy the term is sometimes used to denote a spiritual inspiration which enables us at once to know the distinction between what is correct and incorrect, or right or wrong. The German philosopher Kant (1724-1804) distinguished between the two modes of perception, calling the first *empiric intuitions, i.e.* those conveyed to the senses from external objects, and the second *pure intuitions.* In the philosophy of Henri Bergson (1859-1951) intuition is that sympathetic attitude to the reality without us that makes us seem to enter into it, to be one with it, to live it.

INVERGORDON
Burgh and seaport of Ross and Cromarty, on Cromarty Firth, 13 m. N. of Dingwall. It was a naval base in both world wars.

INVERNESS-SHIRE
Largest county of Scot. with an indented coastline on the W. It consists of 2 portions, the mainland, and Skye, Harris, N. Uist, S. Uist and many other Is. of the Hebrides. The Caledonian Canal, traversing Glen More, cuts the mainland area in 2. The shire contains wild and beautiful scenery. The soil is infertile and most of it is devoted to deer forests and grouse moors, with only a small portion for sheep rearing. The chief rivers are the Spey, Ness and Beauly. In the county are Ben Nevis and other mts. Inverness is the county town; Fort William is the only other town of importance. With Ross and Cromarty, the county returns 3 members to Parl. Pop. 82,264. **Inverness.** Burgh and county town of Inverness-shire. The recognised cap. of the Highlands, Inverness stands on the N. side of the Ness near the point where it flows into the Moray Firth. Industries include distilling, shipbuilding, tweed manufacture and railway works. Pop. 29,603.

IODINE
Bluish solid element, volatile at ordinary temps., producing an irritating vapour. Discovered by Courtois in 1811, it occurs as iodides in sea water and seaweed. By far the greater part of the world's supply is extracted from caliche —a natural form of sodium nitrate. Iodine is added to table salt and animal feeding-stuffs.

ION
[ī'-] Electrically charged atom. When, *e.g.* copper sulphate. $CuSO_4$, is dissolved in water, or in a solution of organic salts, most of its molecules break up into 2 ions, one being Cu—a copper atom with 2 units of positive charge, and the other SO_4—the remainder of the molecules with 2 units of negative charges. In a gas, ions may be formed by such agencies as X-rays and fast atomic particles. *See* ELECTROLYSIS.

IONA
One of the Inner Hebrides, off the W. coast of Mull, Argyll. Fishing and sheep and cattle breeding are the principal occupations. St. Columba landed there in A.D. 563 and laid the foundations of his monastery, which developed into the most famous centre of Celtic Christianity, whence missionaries were sent to Scot.

and N. Eng. The cath. church of St. Mary dates from the 13th cent. Restoration work has been done by the Iona Community.

IONIAN
[ī-ō'-niăn] Name of one of the chief races that settled in Greece in ancient times. They may have arrived as early as 1500 B.C. About the 11th cent. B.C., many of them settled on the coast of Asia Minor, where a district was named after them. The Homeric poems are in the Ionian dialect. **Ionian Islands.** Is. of Greece, off the W. coast in the Ionian Sea. The chief are Corfu, Cephalonia, Zante and Levkas. The chief town is Corfu. From 1814-64 they were under Brit. protection, being then handed over to the new kingdom of Greece. The islands have frequently suffered from earthquakes. The most violent occurred in 1953, when over 400 people were killed and *c.* 3,000 left homeless. The ports of Argostoli and Lixouri were completely destroyed. Area: 750 sq.m. Pop. 212,573. **Ionian Sea.** Part of the Medit., lying S. of the Adriatic Sea and bounded on E. and W. by Greece and Italy.

IOWA
Prairie state of the U.S.A. lying between the Mississippi and Missouri rivers. It is chiefly an agricultural state. Maize, wheat, barley, rye, soya beans and potatoes are grown, and livestock are kept in great numbers. Coal is mined. Des Moines is the cap. Iowa was settled in 1788, and became a state in 1846. There are 8 representatives in Congress. Area: 56,290 sq.m. Pop. 2,825,100.

IPECACUANHA
[ipi-kakew-ā'-nă] Dried, knotted roots of *Uragogo ipecacuanha,* native to Brazil, exported chiefly from Rio de Janeiro. The drug has an acrid, bitter taste and faint odour, and is used as a powerful emetic and expectorant.

IPSWICH
County borough and county town of E. Suffolk, on the Gipping. The industries include engineering works, tobacco factories and chem. works. Clothing and agricultural implements are made. It returns 1 member to Parl. Pop. 118,410.

IRAN *See* PERSIA.

IRANIAN LANGUAGES
Branch of Indo-European, including *Avestic, Achaemenian* (inscriptions 520-350 B.C.), *Pahlavi,* and modern *Persian, Kurdish, Baluchi, Pushtu, Ossetic.*

IRAQ
[i-rāk'] Country of the M.E. bounded by Saudi Arabia, Jordan, Syria, Turkey and Persia, with a short coastline on the Persian Gulf. Most of the country consists of the fertile alluvial plain of the Tigris and Euphrates. The soil is rich, but there are extensive areas where irrigation is necessary. Dates, cotton, wheat and barley are grown, and wool produced. There are oilfields. Baghdad is the cap. and Basra is the chief port. Iraq became a state in 1919 under Brit. mandate. The mandate was terminated in 1932. In Feb. 1958, Iraq and Jordan united to form the Arab Federal State, but this was disbanded the same year after the murder of King Feisal II and the Regent. Brig. Kassem was P.M. 1958-1963, killed in a milit. *coup.* Col. Abdul Salam Arif was Pres. 1963-1966, died in plane crash. In April 1966 he was succeeded as Pres. by his brother Abdul Rahman Arif. In 1964 Iraq and Egypt signed a polit. agreement with a view to eventual union. Area: 169,240 sq.m. Pop. 8,338,000.

IRELAND
Is. of Europe, lying W. of Gt. Brit. In 1922 it was divided into two states: Eire, comprising the provs. of Leinster, Munster and Connaught, and N. Ireland, which includes most of the prov. of Ulster. The mts. of Ireland are peripheral, surrounding a central plain which is flat and boggy. There are enormous areas covered with peat, used as fuel. The chief river is the Shannon, which is used to generate electric power. There are many lakes. The few Is., chiefly of the W. coast, include the Aran and Achill groups. The W. coastline of Ireland is indented, the bays forming some of the finest harbours in the world. Notable are Cork and Waterford on the S. coast. The climate is mild and damp, with heavy rainfall in the mt. or extreme W. districts. Area: 32,408 sq.m. Pop. *c.* 4,243,803. In early times Ireland was the centre of Christianity and learning. It was ruled by a number of kings and chiefs, who were more or less subject to a king at Tara. In the 8th cent. and later, it suffered from the inroads of Scandinavian pirates, until their decisive defeat at Clontarf by Brian Boru in 1014. In the reign of Henry II Ireland became definitely assoc. with Eng. Much land was taken from the native inhabitants and given to the Eng. settlers, and there grew up side by side 2 distinct classes, one dominant and landowning, the other servile and landless. The Eng. were predominantly Protestant, and the Irish R.C. The Eng. lived within the district around Dublin called the Pale, and there filled the offices of state and controlled the parl. The antagonism between the 2 races and creeds grew steadily worse, and in the time of Elizabeth there were constant and terrible wars in Ireland. In the 17th cent. James I settled, or planted, Scotsmen in Ulster. This caused a rising, and in 1642 there was another orgy of massacre and ruin, this time in the N. This was put down and at the end of the civil war came the conquest of Ireland by Cromwell. The struggle between William III and James II was fought out in Ireland, and when it was over a new period of Protestant ascendancy began, with the introduction of the Penal Code. R.Cs. could hold no offices whatever, nor even possess land in their own country. Restrictions on commerce forbade anything that might possibly compete with Eng. traders. After 1750 there was some relaxation. The laws against R.Cs. were made less severe, and the trading restrictions removed. In 1782 Ireland was given legislative indep. but the right to vote and sit in Parl. was still confined to Protestants. In 1798, with Brit. at war with Fr., there was a rising in Ireland, but this was crushed at Vinegar Hill. In 1800 the parl. was abolished and the U.K. of Gt. Brit. and Ireland came into being. R.C. emancipation was delayed until 1829. Conditions seemed somewhat better when the terrible potato famine broke out in 1845. The pop. was reduced by starvation and emigration to *c.* ½. For the rest of the cent. the hist. of Ireland was one of agitation against Eng. rule, except in Ulster, where the Eng. connection was valued. Members, called nationalists, were elected to Parl. to work for some degree of indep. for their country and Gladstone 3 times tried to give Ireland Home Rule. He failed to convince the Eng. people of the wisdom of this policy, which was opposed bitterly by the Protestants of Ulster. In 1914 a measure of Home Rule was granted, but the outbreak of war prevented its operation. When the struggle ended, a new party (called Sinn Fein) dominated the country. They set up an Irish Repub., a step which was followed by 2 or 3 years of terrorism. Finally a treaty was signed in 1921 by which the Irish Free State was created, and the counties which refused to be separated from Brit. were formed into a separate state known as N. Ireland. In 1949 the Repub. of Ireland Act came into operation. By this the Irish Repub. was declared a sovereign, indep. state. *See* IRELAND, REPUBLIC OF; NORTHERN IRELAND.

IRELAND, John
(1879-1962) Eng. composer. A pupil of Stanford. He wrote many pianoforte pieces and songs.

His works include a piano concerto, symphonic rhapsody for chorus and orchestra, and chamber music.

IRELAND, CHURCH OF
St. Patrick made his first missionary visit A.D. 432. Opposition to papal claims ceased after the Synods of Kells, 1152, and Cashel, 1172. The Dissolution of the Irish Monasteries took place 1528-38. The Act of Catholic Emancipation was passed in 1829, and the Act of Disestablishment in 1869.

IRELAND, REPUBLIC OF
Formerly known as Eire or the Irish Free State. The chief occupations are agriculture and fishing. Dairying is becoming increasingly important. Crops include cereals, potatoes, turnips and mangolds, sugar beet and flax. There are various manufacturing industries. The cap. and largest town is Dublin; other towns are Cork, Dun Laoghaire, Limerick and Waterford. Erse is the national language, but Eng. is also used. There are steamer services with Gt. Brit. to Glasgow, Liverpool and Fishguard. Shannon Airport lies on the trans-Atlantic route. The Irish Free State, a republic, was created Dec. 1921. The first general election was held in Dec. 1922. William T. Cosgrave's party was successful, and for 10 years he remained pres. of the executive. The elected members of the Repub. party refused at first to take the oath of allegiance, but later under Eamon de Valera (*q.v.*) took their seats and became the official opposition. In Feb. 1932, the Republican party secured a majority in the Dail and de Valera took Cosgrave's place as pres. His ministry decided to abolish the oath of allegiance and then refused to remit to Gt. Brit. the interest due on the money borrowed for the purchase of land. In 1937 a new constitution was approved, under which links with the Brit. Commonwealth were loosened. During World War II, Eire remained neutral. In 1949 the Repub. of Ireland Act declared Eire a sovereign, indep. state outside the Commonwealth. The head of state is the pres., who serves for 7 years. Parl. consists of 2 houses, a house of representatives (*Dail Eireann*) and a senate (*Seanad Eireann*). Area: 26,600 sq.m. Pop. 2,818,341.

IRETON, Henry
(1611-51) Eng. soldier. Originally a lawyer, in 1642 he joined the parl. army. He was closely assoc. with Cromwell. In 1645 he was elected an M.P. and later, as one of the judges of Charles I signed the death warrant.

IRIS
Genus of hardy flowering plants, of 2 sorts, bulbous and non-bulbous. There are many varieties of each, known as Spanish, Japanese, Eng. and Dutch irises.

IRIS
Membranous contractile curtain surrounding the pupil of the eye of vertebrate animals. It dilates or contracts to regulate the amount of light entering the eye through the pupil.

IRISH LITERATURE
Early hymns, religious poems, romances, etc., are preserved in MS. miscellanies called the 'Books' of Armagh (807), Leinster (*c.* 1100), Lecan (1407): Ballymote (*c.* 1400), Lismore, Fermoy, Maine (*c.* 1350), the *Lebor ma h'uidre* (11th cent.), *Leabhan Creac.* Most important are the romances: (1) the Ulster cycle, represented esp. by the great epic *Tain Bo' Cualuge*, prob. first written in 7th cent. and telling of the hero Cuchulinn, Ailill and Medb (Maeve) of Connaught (*c.* 1st cent. A.D.); (2) the later S. or Leinster-Munster cycle of Finn or Fionn (d. *c.* A.D. 283) leader of the warriors Fianna and father of Ossian.

IRISH SEA
Arm of the sea between Gt. Brit. and Ireland. It is connected with the Atlantic Ocean by St. Patrick's Channel in the N. and St. George's Channel in the S.

IRISH TERRIER
Believed to have originated from the old broken-haired black and tan terrier. Rather aggressive. Red and gold in colour; wt. *c.* 23 lb. Excellent for vermin destruction.

IRON
Silvery metallic element, widely distributed as oxides, and forming 5 % of the earth's crust. The manufacture of iron was in Eng. in the time of the Roms., charcoal being used to smelt the ore. Today pig or cast iron is made by mixing the ore with coal, coke and limestone, and passing is through a blast furnace. Iron is easily magnetised and is a fairly good conductor. Sp. gr. 7·9. Chem. sym. Fe.

IRON AGE
In archaeology a cultural phase marked by the use of iron. In Europe and W. Asia it usually followed the copper-using or bronze-using phase or age; in Africa it directly succeeded the stone age. In Europe ironworking became general in the Med. region *c.* 1000 B.C. The two periods are characterised esp. by finds at Hallstadt and La Tène respectively.

IRON CROSS
German order founded in Prussia 1813. Divided into a civil and milit. division, there are 3 grades.

IRON GATES
Name given to a narrow passage, *c.* 2 m. long, in the course of the Danube, near Orsova, Rumania.

IRON LUNG
Apparatus used in pulmonary medical treatment. The first was designed by Dr. Philip Drinker of Harvard Medical School, U.S.A. in 1935, and is now in use throughout the world for patients whose chest muscles have been incapacitated by disease, *e.g.* poliomyelitis.

IRRAWADDY
River of S.E. Asia, which has 2 sources on the borders of Tibet, and flows S. through the centre of Burma to enter the Bay of Bengal in a delta.

IRRIGATION
Means by which water is conveyed to semi-arid areas from rivers or wells to increase the fertility of the land. Where rivers are the sources of the water supply, weirs (or, on a large scale, barrages) are used to raise the level of the water to that of the irrigation canals. In many instances, to conserve the supply and regulate the flood waters of a river, huge reservoirs are built, as in N. Amer., Egypt, the Sudan, India and Australia. In Arizona, India and Australia, artesian wells are used. The value of irrigation was recognised in ancient times, and there remain evidences of its use in Mesopotamia, Egypt, Italy, Spain and other countries.

IRVING, Edward
(1792-1834) Scot. divine. Preached the nearness of the 2nd advent. His ch. found him guilty of heresy. He then joined the group of men who founded the Catholic Apostolic Ch., sometimes called after him **Irvingites.**

IRVING, Sir Henry
(1838-1905) Eng. actor-manager; **John Henry Brodribb** took the name of Irving. In 1878 he began to play in Shakespearean and other plays with Ellen Terry. His successes were numerous. In 1895 he was knighted, at that time an unusual honour for an actor.

ISABELLA
(1292-1358) Queen of Edward II of Eng. A daughter of Philip IV of Fr., she mar. Edward in 1308. The union was not happy, and *c.* 1324, having become the lover of Roger Mortimer, she escaped to Fr. In 1326 they returned and secured the throne for her son, Edward III, Edward II being murdered.

ISABELLA
Name of 2 queens of Spain. **Isabella I** (1451-1504) was a daughter of John of Castile. In 1469 she mar. Ferdinand. The two conquered the Moors and united Spain into a single monarchy. **Isabella II** (1830-1904) was a daughter of King Ferdinand VII. In 1843 she began to reign and in 1846 mar. for reasons of state, a cousin, Francis. After a series of insurrections, the queen was deposed in 1870, her son, Alphonso XII, becoming king.

ISAIAH
Greatest of the O.T. prophets. The **Book of Isaiah** contains long passages of incomparable beauty. It is in 2 parts, of which ch. 1-39 were apparently rearranged to bring together the prophecies against foreign nations.

ISHERWOOD, Christopher
(1904-) Eng. novelist. Educ. Corpus Christi Coll. Camb., taught Eng. in Berlin, 1930-3; with W. H. Auden (*q.v.*). He became a U.S. citizen in 1946. His publications include *Mr. Norris Changes Trains* (1935), *Prater Violet*; wrote plays *Ascent of F6* (1937), *On the Frontier* (1938) with W. H. Auden.

ISIS
Grecian form of name of Egyptian goddess, the Mother-divinity, wife (or sister) of *Osiris* and mother of *Horus*. One of her symbols is the moon.

ISLAM
(1) The corporate body of those of the Mohammedan faith. (2) The religion taught by Mohammed whom Muslims regard as a prophet divinely inspired. The Muslim conception of God is that he does not assume and must not be represented in human form. Muslims believe in the immortality of the soul and the accountability for human actions in another existence, but each soul must work out its own salvation.

ISLAY
[ī'-lă] One of the Inner Hebrides, in the county of Argyll, separated from Jura by the Sound of Islay. Bowmore is the chief town; other places are Bridgend and Port Ellen.

ISMAILIA
[is-mī-lē'-ă] Town of Lower Egypt, *c.* halfway between Port Said and Suez.

ISMAY, Lord
Hastings Lionel (1887-1965) 1st Baron. Brit. Gen. Educ. Charterhouse and at R.M.C. Sandhurst. Commissioned, 1905; Sec. Committee of Imp. Defence, 1938. Chief of Staff to P.M. in his capacity as Min. of Defence during World War II. Sec. of State for Commonwealth Relations, Oct. 1951. Sec-Gen. N.A.T.O. 1952-57, P.C.

ISOBAR
Term used in meteorology for a line upon a map running through places where the atmos. pressure is the same at a stated time. Isobars are shown on weather maps, drawn usually for every 1-10th of an in. The barometric gradient is shown by the nearness or distance between the isobars.

ISOTHERM
Line drawn upon a map passing through places where the temp. of the air is the same at a stated time, or where the average temp. over a certain period is the same.

ISOTOPES
Varieties of atom having substantially the same chemical properties, but different atomic weights. Every element possesses isotopes. In 1948 an Isotope Division was formed at the Atomic Research Establishment at Harwell for the production and distribution of radioactive materials. These are employed to control industrial processes, and in biology, biochemistry and medicine.

ISRAEL
Jewish national state, bounded by Lebanon, Syria, Jordan and Egypt, with a coastline on the Medit. It occupies the greater part of the territory formerly known as Palestine (*q.v.*). The country consists of 4 zones: the coastal plain and the plain of Esdraelon; the inland plateau; the Negev, a semi-desert area in the S.; parts of the Jordan Valley, including Lake Merom, Lake Tiberias and the S.W. shore of the Dead Sea. The summers are hot, rain falling mainly from Oct. to April. Much of the country is fertile. Crops include citrus fruits, olives, wheat, barley, pulses and millet. Dairying is becoming important. Oil was discovered at Heletz in 1955. The chief towns are Jerusalem, the cap. (*q.v.*), Tel-Aviv, Jaffa, and Haifa, the chief port. The majority of the people are Jews. Hebrew is the official language, and there is a Hebrew univ. founded 1925. The State of Israel was formed May, 1948, when the Brit. mandate ended. On the next day the frontier was crossed by troops of Lebanon, Syria, Jordan and Iraq. Hostilities ceased Jan. 1949. Under armistice agreements, Israel retained most of her territory, and Jerusalem was divided between Israel and Jordan. Border fighting between Israel and Egypt broke out, and in Oct. 1956, Israeli troops pushed the Egyptians across the Sinai Desert to the Suez Canal. Fr.-Br. mil. intervention and later a U.N. police force prevented spread of war. By June 1967, the situation became intolerable to both sides. U.N. troops withdrew and fighting broke out. After 4 days Israel had driven U.A.R. forces beyond the Suez Canal. A cease-fire was accepted, June 10, but the situation remains tense. *See* EGYPT. Israel is governed by a pres., an executive council and a constituent assembly. Area: *c.* 7,993 sq.m. Pop. 2,330,000.

ISTANBUL
(formerly **Constantinople**) Largest city, seaport and former cap. of Turkey, on the Sea of Marmara and the W. shore of the Bosphorus. Its harbour is formed by the Golden Horn. The Gks., Jews and Armenians have their districts. I. controls the sea route from the Medit. to the Black Sea, and stands on an important rail route. Interesting buildings include the Mosque of St. Sophia and the palaces once occupied by the sultans. I. stands where the Gks. built the city of Byzantium. It was chosen as cap. of the Rom. Empire by Constantine the Great, *c.* 330. On the division of the Rom. Empire it became the cap. of the E. part, and from 1204-61 was the cap. of a Lat. kingdom founded by the Crusaders. It was the Turkish cap. from 1453 until after World War I. Pop. 1,882,092.

ITALIC
Branch of Indo-European languages found orig. in Italy: (a) *Lat.* and *Faliscan*, (b) *Oscan* (*Samaitic*), *Umbrian*, *Volscian*, absorbed and replaced by Lat. from 3rd cent. B.C. From Vulgar or spoken Lat. spring the modern Romance languages: *Italian*, *Provençal*, *Fr.*, *Spanish*, *Portuguese*, *Rumanian*, *Rumansh* (*Ladin*), *Logudorese-Campidanese* (*Sardinia*), *Catalan*, *Galician*.

ITALY
Repub. of Europe, bounded in the N. by Fr., Switzerland, Austria and Yugoslavia. The greater part of the country forms a long peninsula, extending S.E. into the Medit. Included in the republic are the Is. of Sicily and Sardinia (*qq.v.*). Italy proper consists of (1) the extensive N. Plains, surrounded on 3 sides by the Alps and Apennines, and drained by the Po and its tributaries and by the Adige and Piave. There are many lakes, including Maggiore, Como, Garda, Lugano; (2) the long narrow peninsula, bounded by the Adriatic, Ionian, Tyrrhenian and Ligurian seas. The Apennine Mts. form the backbone of the peninsula. The Arno, Tiber and Volturno are the most important rivers. The lowlands of the W. particularly near the Arno and around Naples, are extremely fertile. The climate over most of the country is Medit. with mild, wet winters and hot, dry summers. The N. Plains, shut off by mts. from sea influences, have a more continental type of climate. Italy is an agricultural country. Mulberries are cultivated for the silkworm industry; cotton and flax are also grown. Sheep and goats are reared; the dairying industry is primarily concerned with the manufacture of cheese. Sulphur production and marble quarrying are important. Hydro-electric power is important. Manufactures include textiles, iron and steel goods, chem. products and agricultural machinery. Rome is the cap.; other towns are Milan, Naples, Turin, Genoa, Florence, Bologna, Venice, Verona and Leghorn. By a treaty between the Holy See and Italy in 1929, the R.C. religion was estabd. as the state religion. Italy became a repub. in June, 1946, and a new constitution came into force in Jan. 1948. The pres. is elected for a term of 7 years; parl. consists of 2 houses, a chamber of deputies and a senate. For admin. purposes the repub. is divided into 19 regions. Area: *c.* 116,280 sq.m. Pop. 50,464,000. Until modern times Italy was merely a geographical expression. Rome was the heart of a great Rom. empire and when Rome fell Italy was overrun by barbarians. In 800 it became part of the empire founded by Charlemagne, and was nominally included in the Holy Rom. Empire until its dissolution in 1806. In reality it was divided into a number of indep. states. Some were repubs. such as Venice and Genoa; some like Naples, kingdoms. In addition there were the Papal States. Among the important rulers in Italy was the Count of Savoy, who in 1418 obtained Piedmont. In the 19th cent., the King of Sardinia was the centre of the movement for the union of Italy. Lombardy was secured in 1859, Tuscany and other areas in 1860, and in 1861 Victor Emmanuel, King of Sardinia, was declared King of Italy. He secured Venice in 1866 and the Papal States, except the Vatican itself, in 1870. The difficulty with the Vatican was not adjusted until 1928. In 1915, Italy entered the war on the side of Gt. Brit. and Fr. and carried on campaigns against Austria. The period after the war was one of economic and social unrest which led to the establishment of a Fascist govt. under Benito Mussolini. Under this régime, great economic progress was made, the great debts were liquidated and much colonial development took place. Great strides in internal reform and social services took place between 1924-43. In 1935 Italy declared war on Ethiopia. In 1937 Hitler and Mussolini exchanged visits and the Rome-Berlin ' Axis ' was formed. War was declared on the Allies in June, 1940, and on the U.S.A. in Dec. 1941. Defeats by the Allies in N. Africa were followed by the invasion of Sicily in 1943. Mussolini was overthrown and a democratic govt. estabd. In 1945, Mussolini was captured by partisans while trying to flee the country, and shot. The king, Victor Emmanuel III, abdicated in favour of his son, Umberto II in 1946. The king's reign was short, however, a repub. being estabd. in June, 1946.

IVAN
Name of 4 rulers of Russia. **Ivan III, called the Great,** reigned 1462-1505. He made his territory indep., extended its areas, issued laws, made treaties with rulers and took as his emblem the Rom. Eagle. **Ivan IV,** who reigned 1547-84, was the first to take the title of Tsar. He earned the epithet of ' Terrible ' by his cruelties. It is said that he d. of sorrow for his eldest son, Ivan, whom he killed, 1580.

IVORY
Hard white material of which the teeth of certain animals are composed. The finest ivory comes from the tusks of the African and Indian elephant. It is used as a medium for carving, esp. in China and India.

IVORY COAST
Rep. of W. Africa formerly Fr. between Liberia and Ghana. Gained independence 1960. Rice, rubber, cocoa, coffee and palm oil are produced. Abijan is the cap.; other towns are Bouaké and Grand-Bassam. Area: 189,000 sq.m. Pop. 3,300,000.

IVY
Evergreen shrub of the family Araliaceae, found in Europe, Asia and N. Africa. It climbs by means of aerial roots.

IZMIR
(formerly Smyrna) City of Turkey, on the W. coast of Asia Minor. It was captured by the Turks, 1424. As a result of World War I, the city was admin. by Greece for some time, but in 1922 the Turks drove the Gks. out. Pop. 286,310.

J

J
10th letter of Eng. and Lat. alphabets. The sound corresponds exactly with that of *g* in *genius*, and is classed as a palatal. As a character it was formerly used interchangeably with *i*, and the two were not separated in Eng. dictionaries until the 17th cent.

JABIRU
(*Xenorhyncus asiaticus*) Austral. bird with long neck, up to 5 ft. high, common in swamps and coastal waters.

JACANA
[-kȧ′-] (*Parra*) Brazilian name for certain birds resembling water hens. The extraordinary length of their toes enables them to walk with ease over other plants of lakes and rivers. They are also found in Africa, India, Ceylon, Australia and China.

JACKAL
Wild dog found in S.E. Europe, Africa, and Asia. Often hunting in packs, jackals feed on living prey, carrion, and fruits. The common jackal (*Canis aureus*) is 2-2½ ft. long, and 15 in. high. The N. African variety is larger, and the so-called ' Egyptian Wolf ' larger still.

JACKDAW
(*Corvus monedula*) Bird of the Crow family. Smaller than the Rook, may be distinguished by its white eyes, smaller beak and grey neck. It can be easily tamed, but is a very mischievous pet. It is common in Brit.

JACKSON, Andrew
(1767-1845) 7th Pres. of the U.S.A. He led the Amer. forces against the Brit. in the war of 1812. In 1821-3 he was Gov. of Florida. In 1828 he was elected Pres. and was re-elected in 1832. He left office in 1836.

JACKSON, Thomas
(1824-63) Amer. soldier. B. W. Virginia, he was, after Lee, the most renowned of the S. gens. during the Civil War, winning the name of ' Stonewall Jackson '.

JACOB, Gordon
(1895-) Eng. composer, a pupil of Stanford and Charles Wood. He has written 2 symphonies, concertos for piano, for oboe, for bassoon, chamber music and part songs.

JACOB, Sir Ian
(1899-) Hon. Lieut.-Gen. of the Brit. Army, and Director-Gen. B.B.C. 1952-60. During World War II was one of 3 personal staff officers serving the P.M. He joined the B.B.C. 1946. In 1952 he was given leave of absence from the B.B.C. in order to become chief staff officer to Gen. Ismay at N.A.T.O. but returned Dec. 1952, on his appointment as Director-Gen.

JACOBINS
Fr. political clubs which arose during the Fr. Revolution, consisting of men who wished for constitutional reform of a moderate kind. Affiliated clubs were formed in most of the cities. Later its members became more extreme in their views, and carried out the reign of terror, but its power ended in 1794 with the execution of Robespierre.

JACOBITES
Name given to those who, after 1688, refused to acknowledge William and Mary (and afterwards the Georges) as rulers, believing that James II and his descendants were the rightful kings. The Jacobites were strong in the Highlands of Scot. and in Ireland, but the movement faded after the rising of 1745 had been crushed.

JACQUARD, Joseph Marie
[-qwar′] (1752-1834) Fr. inventor. B. Lyons, he invented a loom which enabled figured patterns to be woven.

JACQUERIE
[zhak-rē′] Rising of the Fr. peasantry in 1358, when, as the result of the 100 Years' War and other circumstances, the condition of the peasants was critical. Soon suppressed.

JADE
Very hard compact variety of the mineral tremolite. White jade is found in China, and green jade, or greenstone, in New Zealand. A similar soda-containing mineral, jadeite, is often confused with true jade. Both minerals are used as ornamental stones.

JAGUAR
(*Felis onca*) Large cat found in both N. and S. Amer. It corresponds to the Leopard of the old world, but has a bigger head. It averages 4 ft. The colouring is a rich tan with small black spots and black-spotted rosettes.

JAINISM
Religion professed by *c.* 1,500,000 Hindus. Its sacred books record the teachings of **Mahavira** (599-527 B.C.). B. Vessati, he became an ascetic, 569. The code of ethics of the Jains is based on sympathy and compassion and there is no deity.

JALAP
A drug used in medicine, obtained from the tubers of the plant species *Ipomaea*, which grows in Mexico.

JAMAICA
[jă-mā-kă] Largest Is. of the W. Indies, *c.* 100 m. S. of Cuba. It is traversed by a mt. range, culminating in the Blue Mts. (7,388 ft.) in the E., but the soil is extremely fertile. Sugar, rum, coffee, citrus fruits and bananas are the chief products, and tourism is important. Kingston is the cap. and principal seaport. J. was discovered by Columbus in 1494, and taken by Sp. 1509. Cromwell sent out an expedition, 1655, and the Is. was ceded to Brit. 1670. J. became an indep. dominion, 1962. Dependencies of J. include the Morant and Pedro Cays. Area: 4,411 sq.m. Pop. 1,766,000.

JAMES
Name of 6 kings of Scot. **James I** (1394-1437) was son of Robert III. **James III** (1451-88) was the eldest son of James II. In 1488, urged on by the nobles, his young son rebelled against him, and after a fight near Stirling, the king was killed. **James IV** (1473-1513) became king on his father's d. He mar. Margaret, daughter of Henry VII, had a comparatively peaceful reign of 25 years, and d. at Flodden. **James V** (1512-42) became king when under 2 years old. In 1530 he began to rule for himself. In 1542 the Eng. defeated his troops at Solway Moss and on Dec. 14 of that year he d. at Falkland. James mar. Mary, daughter of the Duke of Guise, and their only child was Mary, Queen

of Scots. Her son was **James VI**, who later became **James I** of Gt. Brit. (*q.v.*).

JAMES I
(1566-1625) King of Gt. Brit. B. Edinburgh, the son of Mary, Queen of Scots, and Lord Darnley, he was proclaimed King as James VI in 1567. His minority, marked by struggles for his person among the nobles, ended in 1583, and for 20 years he ruled Scot. In March, 1603, James became also King of Eng. and the rest of his life was passed in that country. His religious ideas were disliked by both Puritans and R.Cs. His quarrels with parl. had a bearing on the troubles of the next reign. His eldest son, Henry, d. in 1612, and the 2nd, Charles, succeeded him. From his daughter, Elizabeth, the present royal family is directly descended. James was a thinker, and in *The True Law of Free Monarchies* he set out his ideas on govt. He also wrote *Counterblaste to Tobacco.*

JAMES II
(1633-1701) King of Gt. Brit. The 2nd surviving son of Charles I. In 1660, as Lord High Admiral, he commanded the fleet in battles with the Dutch. Later in Scot. he took part in the suppression of the Covenanters. His conversion to the R.C. Ch. led to the formation of a strong party determined to exclude him from the throne, but in 1685 he became king. The rebellion led by Monmouth having been crushed, James endeavoured to make Eng. a R.C. country. Only 3 years after his succession, an invitation was sent to William of Orange to come and take the crown. James found himself unable to defend his throne and fled to Fr. In 1690 he was in Ireland, where, despite Fr. help, he was defeated at the Battle of the Boyne. James mar. Anne Hyde, daughter of the Earl of Clarendon. Their children were Mary, who mar. William of Orange (1677), and Anne. His 2nd wife was Mary, daughter of the Duke of Modena, by whom he had a son, James Edward, known as the Old Pretender.

JAMES
Saint and apostle. Son of Zebedee and Salome, he and his brother John were Galilean fishermen whom Jesus called to be his disciples. He was beheaded by Herod Agrippa. He is the patron saint of Spain.

JAMES, Henry
(1843-1916) Anglo-Amer. novelist. B. New York. *Roderick Hudson*, his first novel, appeared 1876; then *Portrait of a Lady*, *Europeans*, *The Bostonians*, *Ivory Tower*, and shorter stories like *Aspern Papers*, *What Maisie Knew*, *Spoils of Poynton*. Last came *The Ambassadors*, *The Golden Bowl* (1903-5). In 1915 James became a naturalised Englishman and received the O.M. in 1916. He d. at Chelsea. His brother was **William** (1842-1910) Amer. philosopher. B. New York; educ. Harvard. He passed his life in the study of philosophy and psychology. He was the founder of the philosophy of pragmatism. His books include *The Principles of Psychology*, *Varieties of Religious Experience* and *The Meaning of Truth*.

JAMES, Epistle of
Book of the N.T. Its superscription ascribes it to our Lord's brother, Jerusalem's first bishop.

JAMES FRANCIS EDWARD
(1688-1766) Brit. prince, known as the Old Pretender, the son of James II. The news that James had a son decided his enemies to act against him, and the result was the loss of the crown by the Stewarts. The young prince was sent to Fr. He became nominally King of Gt. Brit. as James III, 1701. In 1708 and 1715 he went to Scot. to try to win the throne, on the latter occasion leading a rising—the '15. In 1715, when peace was made between Brit. and Fr. he went to Bar-le-Duc in Lorraine and later to Rome. He mar. Clementina, daughter of John Sobieski, King of Poland, and had 2 sons, Charles Edward and Henry.

JAMESON, Sir Leander Starr
(1853-1917) Brit. administrator. B. Edinburgh. He went to Kimberley where he made friends with Cecil Rhodes and in 1895 led the ill-fated attack of Brit. settlers on the Transvaal. For this he was tried and imprisoned in Eng. but soon released. In 1900 he became a member of the legislature of the Cape and from 1904-8, he was P.M.

JAMESTOWN
Eng. settlement in the U.S.A., the first of its kind. It is on the James River in Virginia, *c.* 30 m. from its mouth, and dates from 1607.

JAMMU AND KASHMIR
Territory in the Himalayas lying N. of India and Pakistan, bounded also by Afghanistan, the U.S.S.R. and China. It is traversed by the Himalayas and Karakoram range, with the fertile Indus valley between. Agriculture is the chief industry, and much of the land is forested. Srinagar is the cap.; Jammu is the winter residence. The people are chiefly Moslems. In the M.A. Kashmir was a flourishing indep. state. From 1846-1947, when the Maharajah acceded to the Dominion of India, it was under Brit. protection. Following a dispute between India and Pakistan, the future of Kashmir was referred to the U.N. In 1952, became a Repub. War broke out, 1965, but, following the ceasefire, agreement in principle was reached under Soviet auspices, Jan. 1966. Area: 86,024 sq.m. Pop. 5,000,000.

JAN MAYEN
[yan-mī'-en] Is. in the Arctic Ocean, between Greenland and Norway, officially incorporated into the Norwegian state in 1929-30.

JANÁČEK, Leoš
[yan'-à-chek] (1854-1928) Czech composer. He made a study of his native folk-music, using it freely in his composition, which include 10 operas, *e.g. Jenufa*, many choral works, including a Slavonic folk-mass, chamber music and folk-song arrangements.

JANSENISM
The teaching of **Cornelius Jansen** (1585-1638), a Dutchman. His *Augustinus* was pub. in 1640. It influenced a group of thinkers, including Pascal, who lived at Port Royal and called themselves Jansenists.

JAPAN
Country of Asia, an empire off the N.E. coast of the cont. from which it is separated by the Sea of Japan. It consists of 4 main Is., Honshu, Kyushu, Shikoku, Hokkaido and *c.* 1,000 smaller Is. The Is. are volcanic and mountainous, Fujiyama (12,389 ft.), on Honshu, being the most famous mt. The climate is diverse, as Japan extends through many degrees of latitude. Typhoons, earthquakes and tidal waves cause much damage. The vegetation is rich and varied, and agriculture is the chief industry; rice, wheat, barley, rye, tobacco and tea are the main crops. Mineral reserves include gold, silver, copper, lead, zinc, iron, sulphur and petroleum. Manufactures include textiles, paper, glass, earthenware, lacquered ware, ships and chems. Tokyo is the cap. and largest city; other centres are Isaka, Kyoto, the ancient cap. Nagoya, Yokohama, Kobe, Fukuoka and Kitakyushu City. The principal religions are Shintoism and Buddhism. The Japanese language is one of the Altaic group. The Japanese Emp. dates from 660 B.C. From the 12th to the 19th cents. it was ruled by Shoguns, but in 1871, after a civil war, the emperor regained his authority. In 1894 Japan was victorious in a struggle with China, and in 1904-5 her armies defeated the Russ. An alliance with Brit. was concluded, and as an ally Japan entered the 1914-18 war against Germany. She

secured a sphere of influence in Manchuria, which in 1931-2 led to the war with China, July, 1937, until 1945. Japan joined the Axis Powers, 1940, and attacked the U.S. base, Pearl Harbour, Dec. 1941. A large part of S.E. Asia was occupied by the Japanese troops. After 2 atom bombs had been dropped on Hiroshima and Nagasaki (Aug. 1945), Japan surrendered unconditionally. A new constitution, by which the Emperor is divested of his divinity, came into force, May, 1947. The *Diet* is composed of a house of representatives and a house of councillors. The Peace Treaty was signed Sept. 1951. Area: *c.* 142,730 sq.m. Pop. 99,920,000.

JAPONICA
Certain plants growing in Japan. In Brit., gardeners use it for the Japanese quince, *Chaenomeles lagenaria* and other flowering shrubs, *e.g. Skimmia* or *Kerria.*

JARRAH
Reddish hardwood, from the mahogany gum tree, *Eucalyptus marginata,* of W. Australia.

JARROW
Borough and river port of Durham, on the Tyne, 4 m. S.W. of S. Shields. Chief industries are shipbuilding and iron smelting. Pop. 29,000.

JASMINE
Large genus of shrubs of the olive family, native to the warmer regions. Two vars. grow in Brit. One bears white flowers in summer (see below), and the other, the **winter j.,** is an evergreen with yellow flowers.

JASPER
Impure form of silica. It consists of an intimate mixture of quartz and red and yellow iron oxides or clay.

JAUNDICE
Yellow discoloration of skin and white of eyes. Assoc. with obstruction of normal flow of bile from liver to intestine but also occurs in liver and blood diseases. Epidemic jaundice or acute infective hepatitis is an acute infectious disease affecting liver, caused by a virus.

JAVA
[jä'-vä] Is. in the Repub. of Indonesia, between Sumatra and Bali. A volcanic mt. range traverses the Is. rising to 12,000 ft. in Sameru. The soil is fertile, and the climate hot and wet. There are extensive forests; crops include sugar, tobacco, tea, coffee and rubber. Tin is mined. Djakarta (formerly Batavia), is the chief town and fed. cap. Early in the 16th cent. the Portuguese discovered Java, which was later taken by the Dutch. By the agreement of 1946, Java became part of the Indonesian Repub. Area: 51,000 sq.m. Pop. 63,000,000.

JAVELIN
Kind of throwing and thrusting spear, used in ancient times by both infantry and cavalry. When thrown it had a range up to *c.* 40 yds. Javelin throwing is an event in certain athletic sports. The standard javelin is now 8 ft. 6 in. long, and weighs 1 lb. 12½ oz.

JAY
(*Garrulus glandarius*) Perching bird related to the crows. The common jay of Brit. and Europe is about 14½ in. long and has blue barred wings and a black-and-white crest.

JAZZ
Orig. the music of the Amer. Negro, characterised by its frequent use of syncopated rhythm and improvisation. In the 20th cent. it has been commercialised in various forms.

JEANS, Sir James
O.M. F.R.S. (1877-1946) Eng. mathematician, astrophysicist, and cosmogonist. From 1905-9 he was prof. at Princeton Univ. and in 1909 he returned to Camb. as lecturer in Applied Maths. Best known for his lucid and skilful popular expositions of recent scientific theories, as in *The Mysterious Universe* and *The Stars in their Courses.*

JEDBURGH
Burgh and county town of Roxburghshire, 50 m. S.E. of Edinburgh. The chief industry is the making of tweeds. Pop. 3,630.

JEFFERSON, Thomas
(1743-1826) 3rd Pres. of the U.S.A. B. in Virginia. He helped to draw up the Declaration of Indep. in 1776. He went to Paris to help to make the peace treaty with Brit. in 1784. In 1797 he was elected Vice-Pres. and in 1801, Pres. He was again elected Pres. in 1805, but retired in 1809. During his term of office, Louisiana was bought from Fr. (1803).

JEFFREYS, Lord
(1648-89) Eng. judge. George Jeffreys, a barrister, in 1677 was made serjeant of the city of London, and in 1678 its recorder. He made himself notorious by the severity with which he punished those implicated, or said to be implicated, in the rebellion of the Duke of Monmouth, when he sentenced over 300 persons to d. at the 'bloody assizes'.

JEHOVAH'S WITNESSES
In 1884 there was formed a corporation named Watch Tower Bible and Tract Soc. Members are known as *Jehovah's Witnesses.*

JELLICOE, Earl
John Rushworth (1859-1935) Brit. admiral. From 1914-16 he was C.-in-C. of the Grand Fleet, which he commanded in the Battle of Jutland, May 31st-June 1st, 1916. Admiral of the Fleet, 1919, and Gov.-Gen. of N. Zealand from 1920-4.

JELLY FISH
Popular name given to the medusa stage of certain marine organisms. The common jelly fish, *Aurelia aurita,* has a shallow umbrella-like body, whose soft translucent substance contains 95 % of water.

JENGHIZ (or **Genghis**) **Khan**
[jen-giz] Mongol emperor (1162-1227). He was proclaimed khan, or emperor of Mongolia in 1206. He led his armies into China, Turkestan, Persia, India and Russia.

JENKINS'S EAR, War of
(1739-41) Struggle between Brit. and Spain for supremacy in trade and at sea. Robert Jenkins, a master mariner, was supposed to have had his ear cut off on the orders of a Sp. commander. This roused public opinion and Walpole unwillingly declared war.

JENNER, Edward
(1749-1823) B. Berkeley, Gloucs., he studied under John Hunter in London. Famous for his work on smallpox, he made the first successful practical experiment in inoculation for this disease in 1796. Despite violent opposition, he successfully developed the idea.

JERBOA
(*Dipus deserti*) **'Desert rat,'** a leaping rodent with long naked ears, long tufted tail and 3-

toed hind limbs six times the length of its short 5-toed fore limbs.

JEREMIAH
(O.T.) One of the 4 major prophets and author of the book called after him. His writings covered 40 years, from the time of Josiah to that of Hezekiah and the Exile.

JEREZ DE LA FRONTERA
Town of Cadiz prov. S. Spain, 16 m. N.E. of Cadiz. It gives its name to sherry, made from vintage grapes of the surrounding vineyards. Pop. 134,400.

JERICHO
Ancient city of Israel, in the valley of the Jordan, 17 m. N.E. of Jerusalem and 5 m. N. of the Dead Sea. It was the first Canaanite settlement reduced by the Israelites.

JEROME
(*c.* 340-420) Saint and scholar of the Christian ch. B. Strido. He lived as a hermit in the deserts of Syria and studied Heb. He built a monastery, and completed his tr. of the Bible (*The Vulgate*).

JERSEY
Largest of the Channel Is. (*q.v.*), 13 m. from the coast of Fr. The soil is fertile, and the climate equable. Its breed of cattle is famous. The tourist industry is important. St. Helier is the cap. and the chief port. The Is. is gov. by a lieut.-gov. and the official language is Fr. Pop. 57,200.

JERUSALEM
Cap. of Israel and chief city of the Holy Land, 33 m. from Tel-Aviv-Jaffa, *c.* 15 m. from the Dead Sea. Nearly 4,000 ft. above sea level, it was inhabited in ancient times. It was captured by David *c.* 1000 B.C. and became the national centre of the Jews. Temples were built by Solomon, Zerubbabel and Herod. It witnessed the d. of Christ and was destroyed by Titus A.D. 70. In 135 the Emperor Hadrian rebuilt the city, and *c.* 200 years later Constantine the Great built a ch. on the site of the Holy Sepulchre. This attracted thousands of pilgrims from Europe, and for the next 300 years it was a prosperous Christian city. In 637 it was taken by the Arabs, and to recover the Holy Places, the first crusade was organised. In 1099 Jerusalem was taken and until 1187 was the cap. of a Lat. kingdom. In 1517 it became a Turkish possession. It remained part of the Turkish realm until Brit. troops entered it in 1917, and a Brit. mandate was estabd. Following the partition of Palestine (*q.v.*) 1948, and the hostilities between Israel and Jordan, Jerusalem was made a U.N. Area. The city has been divided between the two states, and, 1950, the Israeli parl. proclaimed it cap. of Israel. Two hills, Zion and Moriah, are in the S., overlooking the valley of Himmon. The main objects of Christian veneration are the Holy Places. The Mosque of Omar is the chief of several mosques. The Wailing Wall is sacred to the Jews. The Jordanian part occupied by Israeli forces in 1967 War. Pop. 240,000.

JESUITS
Popular name for the religious order known as the Soc. of Jesus. It dates from 1543. The order soon became very influential. Whilst retaining its orig. purpose of converting the heathen, its members concerned themselves with polit. affairs, esp. in the 16th and 17th cents. Paraguay came under the rule of the order, one of the few instances in the world's hist. of a theocracy. In N. Amer. the labours of the Jesuits are among the most heroic in the annals of missionary work. In the 18th cent. the polit. work of the Jesuits was suspect in several countries. In 1759 they were expelled from Portugal. Fr. and Spain followed this example, and in 1773 the Pope suppressed the order, which, however, was revived in 1814.

JESUS CHRIST
(4 B.C.-A.D. 29 or 30) The central figure of Christianity. Jesus is the Greek form of the Hebrew Joshua, meaning saviour. Christ is a Gk. title, 'anointed', representing the Hebrew Messiah. Nothing is known of Christ's early life beyond what is contained in the 4 gospels. According to these He was b. in the stable of an inn at Bethlehem. His parents were Jews, Mary and Joseph, the latter a carpenter of Nazareth, but the accepted Christian belief, based on passages in the gospels of St. Matthew and St. Luke, is that Mary was a virgin. The date was fixed in the 6th cent. as the year 1, but modern calculations have placed it in 4 B.C. Dec. 25 is kept as the natal day. Only one event of His boyhood is recorded. When 12 yrs. old He went to Jerusalem with His parents and was found by them debating with the doctors in the Temple. He worked as a carpenter until He was 30 yrs. old. When He entered upon His life work, He was baptised by a relative, John, in the Jordan, and passed 40 days in retirement in the wilderness, where He was tempted by Satan. He then gathered around Him 12 followers or disciples and spent nearly 3 yrs. teaching and preaching. Of His teachings, many take the form of parables; they are summarised in the Sermon on the Mount. He performed many miracles, mainly deeds of healing. His teaching lays stress upon the love of God to man and contains sayings of infinite wisdom and universal application. He claims for Himself the position of the Son of God and the interpreter to man of the divine will. After nearly 3 yrs. of teaching, the officials decided to stop His activities. He was at Jerusalem and had just taken His last supper with His disciples, when, through the agency of one of the 12, Judas Iscariot, He was seized and tried before Pontius Pilate who found Him guiltless, but after some hesitation sentenced Him to d. He was then crucified, on a hill called Calvary, between 2 thieves, dying on a day since commemorated as Good Friday. His body was moved to a tomb by one Joseph of Arimathea. The Christian Ch. believes that after 2 days in the tomb He rose from the dead and appeared to various followers. After 40 days He made in their presence His final ascension into Heaven.

JET
Black lustrous form of lignite resembling cannel coal, but harder and blacker. It is light in wt., easily cut, and takes a high polish. It is used for making ornaments, etc.

JET PROPULSION
The theory of jet propulsion is to be found in Newton's second Law of Motion which states that the change in momentum of a system is equal to the external forces applied to the system. This is used in aircraft jet engines where the incoming air is compressed, heated, greatly accelerated by the turbine and ejected as a high speed jet forcing the aircraft to move forward. The pure-jet engine, or turbojet, consists of a combustion space in which fuel is mixed with compressed air and burnt, an air compressor, a turbine wheel and a pipe through which the products of combustion are ejected. The function of the turbine is to extract sufficient energy from the flow of exhaust gases to drive the compressor. Sometimes fuel is burnt in the jet-pipe to provide additional power at

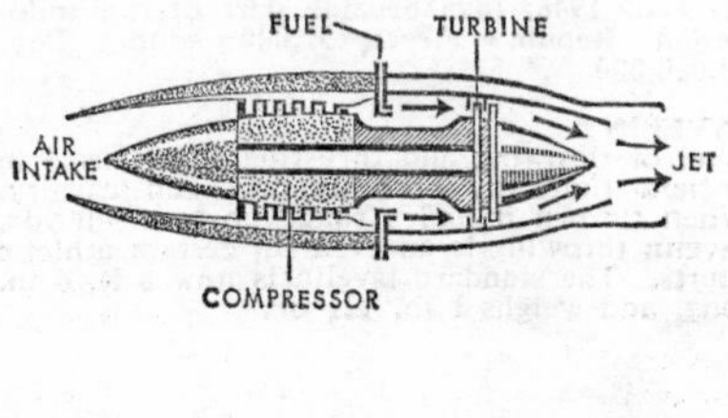

Sahara in Libya

AFRICA · 1

Khartum, Sudan

R. Niger in Mali

Congo landscape

Kilimanjaro, Tanzania

AFRICA · 2

Congo: House in Katanga Province

Capetown harbour, with Table Mt. behind

Zanzibar: copra plantation

take-off, or in combat. This is known as after-burning or reheat. Turboprops are basically similar to turbojets, but deliver very little jet thrust. In the turboprop, the turbine extracts practically all the energy from the stream of gases. Power surplus to that required to drive the compressor is taken forward by means of an extended drive-shaft, to a propeller. Owing to the fact that the turboprop and propeller handle an enormous mass of air at a relatively low velocity, the propulsive efficiency is very high up to speeds of approximately 450 m.p.h. At greater speeds the turbofan or by-pass turbo-jet is more efficient, this in effect being a turbojet driving a 'fan' which can either be thought of as an enlarged axial compressor or as a multi-stage shrouded propeller discharging atmospheric air around the hot parts of the engine. At speeds greater than that of sound, the straight turbojet is more efficient. *See* ROCKET.

JEWS
Race of Semitic origin. The word Jew (corrupted from Yahudim) means a man of Judea, or of Judah. A synonym is Hebrew. The early hist. of the Jews is narrated in the O.T., the facts being supplemented and corrected from other sources and by the results of archaeological research. They appear to have migrated from Mesopotamia to Palestine *c.* 2000 B.C., led by the patriarch Abraham. Some 250 years later they moved with their flocks into Egypt. Some 430 years later (*c.* 1320 B.C.) they fled the country under the leadership of Moses and spent 40 years wandering in the wilderness. Entering Canaan, the modern Palestine, the Jews conquered the tribes there. They divided it among their 12 tribes named after the sons, or grandsons, of Jacob, also called Israel, one of their patriarchs. The priestly functions were allotted to the family of Aaron of the tribe of Levi. The Jews were ruled at first by judges, but later they took a king called Saul. He was succeeded by David and then by Solomon. At Jerusalem, their cap., Solomon built a magnificent temple which served as the centre of the national life. Soon after the d. of Solomon, the Jewish kingdom was divided into two, Judah in the S. and Israel in the N. These came to an end in 586 and 721 B.C. respectively, and for a time the Jews were captives in Babylon. After the overthrow of the Babylonian Emp. by the Persians, Ezra and Nehemiah led the tribes of Judah and Benjamin back to Jerusalem. The temple was restored in 520 and (*c.* 444) Ezra promulgated his famous legal code. Later the Jews came under the dominance of the Egyptian Ptolemies and the Syrian Seleucids. The priest kings, or Maccabees revolted and won freedom in 165 B.C. At the time of Christ the land was part of the Rom. Empire. In A.D. 70 the Emperor Titus destroyed their temple and soon they were driven out of Palestine and scattered. Since the dispersion, or diaspora, the Jews have been found in almost every country in the world and have suffered almost continuous persecution. They were expelled in the 12th cent. from Eng. but allowed to return in the 17th. In the 19th they were granted equality with other citizens. Successive persecutions, restrictions and expulsions deprived them of settled occupations and threw them into money-lending, in which, in time, they excelled. Where freedom and full citizenship was accorded they made contributions to Philosophy, Science and Art, *e.g.* Bergson, Spinoza, Heine, Einstein, Mahler, Bloch, Epstein. In the 19th cent. there arose a movement called Zionism, to get the Jews back to Palestine. It received an impetus, when, as a result of World War I, Palestine was taken from the Turks and Mr. A. J. Balfour, Brit. Foreign Sec. declared that the Govt. would use its best endeavours to estab. in Palestine a national home for the Jewish people. Between the World Wars some progress was made but, under Hitler, European Jewry suffered tortures more terrible than any in recorded hist. It is estimated that from 1939-45, 6,000,000 Jews lost their lives. When World War II ended, Palestine was still being governed under a Brit. Mandate. For a time Jewish subversive forces carried on guerilla warfare against Brit. troops and police, which resulted in the steady deterioration of Anglo-Zionist relations, loss of life, etc. The question of the future of Palestine was referred by Brit. to U.N.O. in 1947 and when, in May, 1948, the Mandate was handed back to U.N.O. and Brit. troops left the country, the Jews in Palestine proclaimed the state of Israel (*q.v.*). In 1949, the migration of Jews from all over the world, rich and poor alike, reached the figure of 300,000. **Religion.** Jewish religion is composed of 2 elements, theology and ethics. Theologically, the main tenet is adherence to monotheism. Ceremonial in synagogue is conducted in Heb. and rabbis regularly expound and discourse on Mosaic Law. Ethics, laid down in the *Talmud*, provide a complete guide to the good life. The Jewish year begins in Sept. or Oct. and has 12 or 13 lunar months varying as between ordinary and leap years. Fast days or festivals are widely observed. The literary language of the Jews is Heb. The spoken language is Heb. in the land of Israel, but elsewhere, in addition to the language of the country of residence, Yiddish is spoken. This is a Germanic dialect interspersed with Heb., Aramaic and Slavonic words.

JIDDA
Chief port of Saudi Arabia, in Hejaz on the Red Sea. A pilgrim port, connected by road with Mecca, it exports hides, carpets and coffee. Pop. 150,000.

JOAD, Cyril E. M.
(1891-1953) Eng. philosopher. From 1941 he became a public figure because of his broadcasts as a member of the 'Brains Trust'. His works include *Guide to Philosophy* (1936), *The Recovery of Belief* (1952) and *Folly Farm* (1954), pub. posthumously.

JOAN OF ARC
(1412-31) Fr. saint. B. Domrémy, the daughter of a peasant. She imagined she heard voices telling her to save Fr., then under the Eng. She procured an introduction to the uncrowned King Charles VII. By him she was given a troop of soldiers to lead to the relief of Orleans, besieged by the Eng. Her faith infused new courage into her countrymen and the siege was raised. In July, 1429, Charles was crowned at Rheims. In 1430, Joan was taken prisoner by the Burgundians and sold to the Eng. By them she was tried at Rouen, and on May 30, 1431, having been found guilty of sorcery and heresy, was burned to death. In 1920 she was canonised.

JOB
O.T. book. Its prose prologue describes an opulent Arabian emir in the patriarchal age suffering loss of his children and possessions, yet ascribing no wrong to God. Job is finally humbled by God's majestic response.

JOCKEY
Rider in a horse race. In Brit. before they can ride in a race they must obtain a licence either from the Jockey Club or from the Nat. Hunt Committee. The body that controls racing on the flat in Brit. is called the Jockey Club. It has power to suspend jockeys and trainers for infringements of its rules. Its affairs are managed by 3 stewards and its H.Q. are at Newmarket.

JOEL
Second of the 12 minor prophets of the O.T. Peter effectively quoted at Pentecost Joel's promise of the Holy Spirit.

JOFFRE, Joseph Jacques Césaire
[zhofr'] (1852-1931) Fr. soldier. In 1914 he took command of the Fr. armies on the W. front. His plans failed to check the German advance and his offensives in 1915 were not very successful, but he must be credited with some share in the victory of the Marne.

JOHANNESBURG
Largest city of S. Africa, in the Transvaal, 30 m. S. of Pretoria. Founded in 1886 when gold was discovered in the Witwatersrand, it is now the chief mining and industrial centre of the Rand. Pop. 1,110,905.

JOHN
(1167-1216) King of Eng., youngest of the 5 sons of Henry II. He revolted against his father, and was also disloyal to his brother Richard. In 1199 John's disastrous reign began. A war with Fr. ended in the loss of Normandy; a quarrel with the Pope brought on an interdict and a humiliating surrender; the wrath of the barons forced him to sign Magna Carta in 1215. He left 2 sons, Henry III and Richard, Earl of Cornwall.

JOHN
(1529-79) Sp. soldier. Usually known as Don John of Austria, he was the natural son of Charles V and Barbara Blomberg. He commanded the fleet which smashed the Turks at Lepanto in 1571.

JOHN
Name of 24 popes and anti-popes. **John VIII,** 872-82, combated the Saracens, sought the conversion of the Slavs and crowned as Emperor, first, Charles the Bald and then Charles the Fat. **John XIII,** an anti-pope during the Great Schism, was elected by the Pisans, 1410. He convoked, 1414, the council of Constance which deposed him. **John XXIII** (1881-1963) elected Pope in Oct. 1958 on the death of Pius XII (*q.v.*). He encouraged liberal and ecumenical movements in the Ch.

JOHN
Saint and apostle. He and his brother James were Galilean fishermen whom Jesus called to be His disciples. John attended the trial of Christ and stood by the Cross. He is commemorated on Dec. 27. According to tradition he lived his later life at Ephesus and d. at a great age.

JOHN, Gospel of St.
4th book of N.T. The writer designs to prove that Jesus is the Christ, the son of God. **Epistles of John.** Three letters in the N.T. usually regarded as written by St. John the Evangelist, but the second and third are contested by certain scholars.

JOHN, Augustus Edwin
(1878-1961) Eng. painter. He studied art at the Slade School, London, showing a special gift for portraiture. He was elected R.A. 1928, Pres. of the Nat. Portrait Soc. 1948-53.

JOHN BULL
First used as the designation of the typical Englishman, in Arbuthnot's *History of John Bull* (pub. 1712).

JOHN OF GAUNT *See* LANCASTER, DUKE OF.

JOHN O'GROAT'S
Place on the N. coast of Caithness. Figuratively, the most N. point of Gt. Brit. it is 1½ m. W. of Duncansby Head.

JOHN THE BAPTIST
Christian saint. He was, through his mother, Elizabeth, a cousin of the Virgin Mary. The last of the prophets, he led an ascetic life in the wilderness beyond Jordan, preaching the coming of the Messiah. He baptised Jesus Christ, recognising and acknowledging Him. He was executed by Herod, *c.* A.D. 38.

JOHNSON, Amy
(1904-41) British airwoman. She was the first woman to make a solo flight from Eng. to Australia (May 1930). She also made record solo flights to Tokio (1931) and to Cape Town and back (1932).

JOHNSON, Andrew
(1808-75) 17th Pres. of the U.S.A. B. N. Carolina. In 1864 he was elected Vice-Pres. and, on Lincoln's murder in the next year, he became automatically Pres. He followed the same policy, endeavouring by conciliation and concession to re-unite the nation. Serious troubles arose and he was impeached, but was acquitted.

JOHNSON, Hewlett
(1874-1966) English divine. After serving his apprenticeship in his father's cotton mill he went to Wadham Coll. Oxford, and studied theology. He became Dean of Manchester, 1924, and Dean of Canterbury, 1931. A professed Communist, he has frequently visited Soviet Russia and China.

JOHNSON, Lyndon Baines
36th Pres. of U.S.A. B. 1908, Stonewall, Texas. Worked his way through college. Elected Democratic Senator, 1949. Became Vice-Pres. under Kennedy (*q.v.*), 1961; succeeded as Pres. after assassination of Kennedy in 1963. Re-elected, 1964. Did not seek re-election, 1968.

JOHNSON, Samuel
(1709-84) Eng. writer. B. Lichfield, son of a bookseller; educ. Pembroke Coll. Oxford. In 1735 he mar. a widow Elizabeth Porter, and opened a school at Edial, Garrick being a pupil. With him he went to London in 1737. He wrote *London,* an imitation of Juvenal's Satires. Having secured financial support, in 1747 he began to work on his dictionary, pub. in 1755. In 1759, to pay for his mother's funeral, he wrote a novel, *Rasselas.* In 1762, after imprisonment for debt, he was granted a pension of £300 a year by the state. About this time his circle of friends began to grow: Sir Joshua Reynolds, Burke, Goldsmith, Boswell, the Thrales, later Gibbon. In 1765 his ed. of Shakespeare appeared; *Journey to the Western Islands,* 1775; 1779-81, *Lives of the Poets* contributed as prefaces to a collection. Johnson was devoutly religious. His lively and robust talk is reported in Boswell's *Life,* in Mrs. Thrale's *Anecdotes of S.J.* (1786), etc.

JOHORE
State of the Fed. of Malaya (*q.v.*) in the extreme S. The land is low-lying and fertile; the main products are rubber, palm-oil and pineapples. Johore Bahru is the cap. Area: 7,330 sq.m. Pop. 1,084,351.

JONAH
Heb. prophet. He announced to Jeroboam II forthcoming victories over the Aramaeans. A book of the O.T. bearing his name professedly narrates an episode in his life.

JONES, Henry Arthur
(1851-1929) Eng. playwright. His plays include *The Silver King* (1882), *Saints and Sinners* (1891), *The Lie* (1914).

JONES, Inigo
(1573-1652) Eng. architect. B. London. He studied architecture and came under the patronage of the Earl of Pembroke, who enabled him to visit Italy and Fr. Jones was the first to introduce pure Renaissance architecture into Eng., adapting Ital. ideas, esp. those of Palladio, to Eng. requirements.

JONES, John Paul
(1749-92) Amer. sailor. B. Kirkcudbrightshire. He settled in Virginia. In 1775, the colonies being at war with Brit. he was given command of a ship and for some years he harried Brit. shipping.

JONQUIL
Hardy perennial bulbous herb of various species of narcissus of the amaryllis family.

JONSON, Ben
(1573-1637) Eng. dramatist and poet. His first comedy, *Every Man in His Humour* (1598) was followed by *Cynthia's Revels, The Poetaster* and *Sejanus.* His greatest comedies are *Volpone, Epicoene, The Alchemist, Bartholomew Fair.* He also wrote 30 court masques. James I granted him a pension.

JORDAN
River of Israel and the Jordan, which rises on Mt. Hermon and flows through lakes Huleh and Tiberias into the Dead Sea, *c.* 1,300 ft. below sea level.

JORDAN, The Hashemite Kingdom of the
State of the M.E. bounded by Israel, Syria, Iraq and Saudi Arabia. It comprises 2 areas, E. and W. Jordan, united, 1950. The W. includes the districts of Hebron and Jerusalem, the Jordan river and the Dead Sea, and is generally fertile. Much of E. Jordan is arid steppe. The majority of the people are Sunni Moslems. Amman is the cap. and largest town. Jordan is gov. by a king, assisted by a council of mins. and a legislative council. The country was admin. as a Brit. mandate until 1946, when Emir Abdullah was proclaimed king. He was assassinated, 1951. The Crown Prince Talal acceded to the throne in Sept. but was deposed, 1952, and his son, Hussein, proclaimed king. Area: *c.* 36,715 sq.m. Pop. *c.* 2,145,000. *See* IRAQ.

JOSEPH
Husband of the Virgin Mary and foster father of Jesus. The gospels recount his betrothal to Mary and his life as a carpenter at Nazareth.

JOSEPH OF ARIMATHEA
Rich and influential Jew mentioned in the 4 gospels. A secret supporter of Christ, he went to Pilate after the Crucifixion and asked for the body of Jesus which he prepared for burial and laid in a tomb.

JOSEPHINE
(1763-1814) Empress of the Fr. B. Martinique. In 1779 she mar. the Vicomte de Beauharnais. In 1794 her husband was guillotined. In 1796 Josephine mar. Napoleon Bonaparte. In 1809 she was divorced.

JOSHUA
(O.T.) Successor of Moses as leader of the Israelites into Canaan. He was one of those sent to spy out the land of Canaan. He took Jericho and divided the land among the tribes. **The Book of Joshua,** the 6th book of the O.T., describes his exploits.

JOULE, James Prestcott
(1818-89) Eng. physicist. He showed that heat and work are interconvertible, with a constant rate of exchange, and was the first to measure this, the *Mechanical Equivalent of Heat.*

JOYCE, James
Irish writer (1882-1941) B. Dublin. His works have exercised a strong influence. They are *Pomes Penyeach,* and other poems; the play *Exiles* (1918); *Dubliners* (short stories) (1914); and his novels *Portrait of the Artist as a Young Man* (1917), *Ulysses* (1922), *Finnegan's Wake* (1939).

JUAN FERNANDEZ
[hwàn] Group of Is. in the S. Pacific, 400 m. from Valparaiso, belonging to Chile. It was discovered *c.* 1565 by Juan Fernandez, and was inhabited, 1704-9, by Alexander Selkirk.

JUAREZ, Benito
[hwà'-reth] (1806-72) Mexican statesman. In 1864-7 came the Fr. attempt to set up a Mexican Empire under the Austrian Maximilian. Juarez was supported in his resistance by the Mexican people, and the Empire fell. In 1867 and '71 he was re-elected, and tried to carry many far-reaching reforms.

JUDAISM
The system of Jewish religious beliefs, practices and rites: an ethical monotheism based on the unity and spirituality of God. During the post-exilic period Judaism developed into that system of rigid obedience to the Law and priestly sacrificial worship, which existed in the days of Christ. The roots of Christianity are fixed deep in Judaism. *See* JEWS.

JUDAS ISCARIOT
One of Christ's 12 disciples who afterwards betrayed him. He was the only apostle who was not a Galilean. He acted as purse-bearer to the group.

JUDAS TREE
Small tree of the leguminous family (*Cercis siliquastrum*) native to the Medit. region. The flowers impart an acid flavour to salads.

JUDE, Epistle of
Book of the N.T. Its superscription attributes it to a brother of James. Some think that it was written at a later date. It borrows from the Apocrypha, and most of it is contained in the 2nd epistle of Peter.

JUDGE
High legal official who hears cases and tries criminals. Every judicial system has its judges, who are invariably lawyers of considerable experience. Each is attached to a court. In Eng., the highest are the Lord Chanc. and the law lords who sit in the House of Lords. Then come the lords justices who form the court of appeal, and then the judges of the high court. The judges of the court of appeal are recruited from the judges of the high court. There are also in Eng. **county court judges,** one to each circuit. They must be barristers of at least 7 years' standing and are appointed by the Lord Chancellor. In Scot. judges are attached to the 2 houses of the court of session. In both parts of Ireland the courts are staffed by judges on the Eng. model. The **Judge-Advocate-General** is an official of the Brit. Army and Air Force. He acts in advisory capacity to the crown on milit. law, especially concerning courts martial. He is assisted by a deputy judge-advocate-general. Similar duties are performed for the Navy by the Judge-Advocate of the Fleet. **The Judges** of the Bible were the men who ruled over the Jews before Saul was chosen king. Among them were Gideon and Samson.

JUDGES, Book of
(O.T.) With its companion *Ruth* it is found between the Joshua story of Israel's settlement in Canaan and the books of *Samuel* and *Kings.*

JUDITH
Heroine of the book of Judith, in the Apocrypha. Judith visited the besieging Assyrian camp at Bethulia, feasted with Holofernes, and beheaded him.

JUGGERNAUT
Name of the Hindu solar lord, Vishnu, as wor-

shipped at Puri in Orissa. The symbolic image on certain festivals is taken out and dragged in a huge car through the streets.

JU-JITSU
(or **Jiujitsu**) Japanese method of offence and defence without weapons. It has developed into a national system of physical culture for both sexes. Early in the 20th cent., schools arose in Brit., Europe and the U.S.A.

JUJUBE
Small tree, *Zizyphus vulgaris*, a native of China, now grown in Medit. countries. The plant bears leathery leaves and small greenish flowers followed by red or black sub-acid fleshy fruits.

JULIAN
[joo′-liăn] (331-63) Rom. emperor, nephew of Constantine the Great. In 355 his cousin, the Emperor Constantine, made him joint ruler.

JULIAN CALENDAR
Calendar as revised and modified by Julius Caesar in 46 B.C. It was in use in W. Europe until A.D. 1752. The Julian Year was 365¼ days, with a leap year of 366 days every 4th year, and the intervening 3 years of 365 days.

JULIANA
(1909-) Queen of the Netherlands. She mar. Prince Bernhard of Lippe-Biesterfeld. After a year as Regent, Juliana became Queen, 1948, when her mother, Wilhelmina, abdicated.

JUMNA
River of India, 850 m. long, which rises in the Himalayas and flows through Uttar Pradesh to join the Ganges at Allahabad. Delhi, Agra and Muttra are on its banks.

JUMPING HARE
(*Pedetes caffer*) S. African rodent. It averages 2 ft. in length with rather longer tail, and is a burrowing night feeder. It can cover as much as 30 ft. at a single bound.

JUMPING MOUSE
(*Zapus*) Small rodent *c.* 3 in. long, found in N. Amer. and China. It lives in forests, feeds upon seeds and leaves, and makes its home in clefts in the rocks. Its jumping powers are remarkable, sometimes as much as 10 ft.

JUNEAU
Cap. of Alaska, in the S.E. The centre of a gold mining region, it is also a fishing, lumbering and trading centre. Pop. 6,797.

JUNG, Carl Gustav
(1875-1961) Swiss physician and psychologist. He was a disciple of Freud, but later disagreed with many of his theories. He divided mankind into 2 main groups, *introverts* and *extroverts*, and assigned 4 primary functions to the mind; thinking, feeling, sensation and intuition.

JUNGFRAU
[yŏŏng′-frow] Mt. in the Bernese Oberland, Switzerland. It is 13,670 ft. high, and was first climbed by the Meyer brothers, 1811.

JUNIPER
Genus of evergreen trees or bushes of the *Cupressus* family. They grow in the temp. and colder parts of the N. hemisphere. The fruit of the juniper is used to flavour gin and as a diuretic. The wood is hard and smells of turpentine.

JUNK
Type of sailing vessel used by the Chinese and Japanese. Has a high stern and forecastle, usually 3 masts having square sails of matting.

JUNO
Chief Rom. goddess. (Gk. **Hera.**) Worshipped by women at all life's crises.

JUPITER
Chief diety of the Roms. also called **Jove,** the son of Saturn and Rhea and the husband and brother of Juno. He was also the god of thunder and rain, justice, and hospitality. The equivalent of the Gk. **Zeus,** he was armed with thunderbolts and attended by eagles.

JUPITER
The 5th known planet, distant from the sun *c.* 483,900,000 m. It is the largest of the major planets, almost 1,320 times that of the earth. Its diameter is *c.* 88,770 m.; it makes one revolution on its axis in *c.* 9 hrs. 55 mins., and revolves round the sun in *c.* 11 yrs. 315 days. It has 12 known satellites, and its surface temp. has been computed at minus 200° F. During the period of its orbit, the surface of the planet would seem to undergo considerable changes.

JURA
[zhü-ra] European mt. range. It separates the Rhine and Rhône valleys and forms part of the frontier between Fr. and Switzerland. About 150 m. long and 40 m. broad, the mts. have an average ht. of 2,400 ft. with peaks of over 5,000 ft.

JURA
[jŏŏ′-ră] Is. of the Inner Hebrides, in Argyllshire, separated from the mainland by the Sound of Jura. A rugged and bleak Is., the hills rise to 2,500 ft. Cattle and sheep are reared, and there are deer forests.

JURY
In Eng. a body of persons chosen to give a verdict in trials of importance, both civil and criminal. Trial by jury is a very old custom in Eng. Today there are 2 kinds of jury. (1) **Petty jury** consists of 12 persons and these, having heard the case, are responsible for the verdict. It must be unanimous; if it is not, the jury is discharged and a fresh one called. In Scot. a jury can return a verdict of not proven; in Eng. it must be either guilty or not guilty. In civil cases the jury decides on the amount of damages, if any. (2) **Coroner's jury.** At one time there was a jury for every inquest, but since 1927 it has not been necessary to have one except in cases of d. by violence. Any man or woman, between the ages of 21 and 60, with certain exemptions, is liable to be called to serve on a jury and must serve unless a good reason for absence is given. In important cases the greatest care is taken to keep the jury from outside influences.

JUSTICE OF THE PEACE
In Brit. a man or woman apptd. to keep the peace and often called a magistrate. These justices are appointed by the Lord Chanc. for the various counties and such cities and boroughs as have a commission of the peace. Their duties include holding magistrates' courts, where minor offences are tried. Justices first appeared in the 13th cent. and since 1919 women have been eligible to serve.

JUSTINIAN
Name of 2 E. Rom. emperors. **Justinian I** (483-565) was a nephew of Justin I, who reared him. In 527 he became emperor at Constantinople. His reign was marked by the victories of Belisarius and Narses over the Persians, Vandals and Ostrogoths. His wife was the Empress Theodora. Justinian is remembered for the codification of Rom. law which he organised. Its influence on the development of the legal systems of Europe can hardly be exaggerated.

JUTE
Cordage and textile fibre obtained from 2 annual species of the genus *Corchorus.* This grows 10-15 ft. high in parts of E. Bengal, Orissa and Bihar. Jute fibre is used for cheap tapestries and carpets, also bags, packing canvas, cordage, etc.

JUTES
Teutonic tribe. Their country of origin may have been Jutland. Invading Eng. in the 5th

cent., they settled in Kent and the Isle of Wight. They are mentioned by Bede.

JUTLAND
Peninsula forming a prov. of Denmark. Aarhus is the chief town. It became part of Denmark, 10th cent. **Jutland, Battle of (World War I).** Naval battle fought May 31-June 1, 1916, between the Brit. and German fleets.

JUVENAL
Rom. satirist (60-140). He served in the army and wrote 16 Satires, bitterly attacking conditions in Rome.

JUVENILE COURTS
Separate children's courts set up originally in 1908 and considerably modified in accordance with the Children and Young Persons Act, 1933, which in turn has been subject to amendment. The probation system figures prominently and beneficiently in the work of these courts. In Scot. the operation of these courts is governed by a similar Codifying Act of 1937. Further reforms are under consideration.

JUVENILE DELINQUENCY
Term given to offences by juveniles of both sexes under the age of 17 yrs. including those punishable in an adult by imprisonment, *e.g.* burglary, common assault; those confined to children, *e.g.* truancy; and those not offending against specific legal enactments, *e.g.* continual disobedience. An immense amount of research is given to the study of the physical, intellectual, emotional and social factors, and to methods of correction and psychiatric treatment.

K

K
11th letter of the Eng. alphabet. It represents a guttural articulation in Eng. and has the sound of hard *c*; before *n* it is mute, as in *knee*. The common combination *ck*, was originally *kk*; modern Eng. uses *ck* even when final as in *stick, deck*, etc.

KABBALAH
(Cabala) Extremely ancient system of esoteric philosophy and the science of numbers. By virtue of this, which was almost certainly known to the Jews prior to the Babylonian exile, the Rabbis interpret the mystic sense of the Heb. scriptures.

KABUKI
A Japanese form of drama, a mixture of singing, dancing and acting. Over 300 years old it contains elements that are very much older. The acting is formal and very stylised. The faces of the actors are set and immobile and make-up is heavy and strictly conventional. Kabuki plays deal mainly with historical dramas, tales of everyday life in ancient Japan, legendary demons and witches. Musical accompaniments consist of flutes, small drums and three-stringed Jap. guitars, with singers chanting a commentary on the action.

KABUL
[kȧ'-bool] Cap. of Afghanistan, on the Kabul river, a tributary of the Indus, in the E. It is an important market centre. Pop. 439,000.

KAFFIR
Name adopted by Dutch and Brit. settlers for African negroid peoples who constitute, with the Zulus, the Zulu-Kaffir division of the S. Bantu peoples. Following a war in 1809 there was almost constant trouble breaking out into serious wars in 1834, 1836, 1850-3, 1858 and finally 1877-8. The Kaffirs form a considerable element in the population of S. Africa, and are largely employed on the land, in the gold mines, etc. **Kaffir Bread.** Native farinaceous food, derived from the spongy pith of the stems of a S. African cycad, *Encephalartos caffer*.

KAFKA, Franz
(1883-1924) German-Jewish writer. His works (novels and allegorical stories) bear evidence of his mystic temperament, his interest in phil. and religion. Except *Metamorphosis* (1916) and *In the Penal Settlement*, they were pub. after his d. from tuberculosis, by his friend and biog. Max Brod, they include *The Trial* (1925), *The Castle* (1926), *America* (1927).

KAISER
[kī'-zer] Title of the Holy Rom. emperors, and until 1918, of the rulers of Austria and Germany. It was first used in 800 for the Emperor Charlemagne. In 1871, the King of Prussia also took the title.

KAISER, Georg
(1878-1945) German playwright, leader of the expressionist school. His numerous plays included *Von Morgens bis Mitternachts*, produced in London, 1926.

KAKA
(*Nestor meridionalis*) New Zealand parrot. Smaller than the Kea, olive-brown. It feeds on insects and nectar. The eggs are laid in tree hollows. It can be tamed as a pet.

KAKAPO
(*Stringops habroptilus*) New Zealand parrot. It nests in burrows, and is nocturnal. The wings are not well adapted for flight.

KALAHARI
[kală-hȧ'-rī] Desert of S. Africa, stretching across much of Botswana.

KALGOORLIE
W. Austral. gold-mining town, 375 m. from Perth. Pop. *c*. 23,000.

KANCHENJUNGA
Peak of the Himalayas, 28,146 ft. high, in Sikkim, 75 m. from Everest. In 1930 an internat. expedition reached an altitude of 24,400 ft. In 1955 the Royal Geographical Soc. sponsored an expedition which reached the summit.

KANDINSKY, Vasily
(1866-1944) Russ. painter. B. Moscow. Lived in Fr. from 1934.

KANDY
Town of Ceylon, 60 m. N.E. of Colombo, famous for the Buddhist Temple of the Tooth. Pop. 70,400.

KANGAROO
Pouched mammals indigenous to Australasia and New Guinea. The Great Grey Kangaroo (*Macropus giganteus*) has a small head and large ears, with massive hindquarters and long legs. It measures *c*. 5 ft. in length and can leap 30 ft. It is herbivorous and lives in herds. The female rears 1 young at a time in a pouch from a very early foetal stage. There are also Brush, Rock, Tree and Rat kangaroos.

KANO
Town of N. Nigeria, W. Africa. It is the terminus of a railway from Lagos and of Sahara caravans. Pop. 295,000.

KANSAS
C. state of the U.S.A. to the S.W. of the Missouri. A prairie state, it is watered by the Kansas and Arkansas rivers, and is agricultural. Wheat farming is mechanised, and K. produces the largest crop of the U.S.A. Topeka is the cap., but Kansas City and Wichita are larger. K. was settled, 1727, and became a state, 1861, sending 6 representatives to Congress. Area: 82,280 sq.m. Pop. 2,249,100.

KANSAS CITY
(1) Largest city of Kansas, U.S.A., at the junction of the Kansas and Missouri rivers. Pop. 166,700. (2) City and port of Missouri, U.S.A., on the Missouri, opposite Kansas City, Kansas. It is an important distributing centre, with meat packing, milling, and the manufacture of agricultural implements. Pop. 495,500.

KANT, Immanuel
(1724-1804) German philosopher, b. Königsberg. In 1755 he was appointed lecturer in the univ., becoming in 1770 Prof. of Philosophy. Kant ranks as one of the most influential of modern philosophers. His teaching is contained in 3 books, *The Critique of Pure Reason, The Critique of Practical Reason* and *The Critique of Judgment*.

KAOLIN
[kā'-ō-lin] Silicate of aluminium sometimes

called China Clay, it is a soft whitish powder. When given internally, it acts as a protective to the membranes of the stomach and intestines, and it absorbs toxins. It is also used as a poultice.

KAPOK
Tall evergreen tree of the family Bombaceae, found in the W. Indies. It has a prickly stem and its leaves are divided into lance-shaped leaflets. The woody capsules are filled with silky hairs attached to the seeds. These filaments are used as stuffing.

KARACHI
[-rä'-] City and seaport of Sind, and cap. until 1960 of Pakistan; on the coast of the Arabian Sea, N. of the Indus delta. Wheat is the chief export. Pop. *c.* 1,916,000.

KARAGEORGE
(1766-1817) Serbian peasant, and leader of his people against the Turks. He captured Belgrade in 1806 and in 1808 became hereditary chief of Serbia.

KARAKORAM
Mt. range of C. Asia, extending for over 400 m. across N.E. Kashmir, and connecting the Himalayas with the Hindu Kush. In it is Godwin-Austen or K2, 28,250 ft., the second highest mt. in the world.

KAREN STATE
Former name of a territory of the Union of Burma, in the E. bounded by the Shan State and Siam. It has been extended and renamed **Kawthoolei.** The Karens number *c.* 1,200,000.

KARNAK
Village in Upper Egypt, near the town of Luxor. It contains some of the most famous ruins in the world.

KARROO, Great and Little
Semi-arid tableland in Cape Prov., S. Africa.

KASHMIR *See* JAMMU AND KASHMIR.

KATANGA
Prov. in the Congo. Chief town, Elisabethville. When the Congo gained its indep., Pres. Tshombe tried to create an autonomous repub. of Katanga, which led to much strife, and the intervention of the U.N.O.

KATCHIN STATE
Territory of the Union of Burma in the extreme N. The country is very hilly. The Katchins number *c.* 150,000.

KATMANDU
[kȧt'-mȧn-doo'] Cap. of the Himalayan kingdom of Nepal. Pop. 195,000.

KATTEGAT
Sea passage between Jutland, Denmark, and S. Sweden, linking the North Sea with the Baltic.

KATYDID
Name for certain grasshoppers found in N. Amer.

KAURI PINE
New Zealand tree which reaches 100 ft. with a straight trunk up to 10 ft. in diameter. It gives excellent timber. Fossil gum is used for varnish making.

KAZAKHSTAN
Constituent repub. of the U.S.S.R., N. of the Caspian Sea, bounded by the R.S.F.S.R., Uzbekistan and Kirghiz, and China. It is a region of steppes, rising from the plains of the W. to the mts. on the S.E. boundary. The main rivers are Ural, Upper Irtish, Ishim and Sir Darya. L. Balkhash lies within the republic. Cotton, sugar beet, rice, tobacco and grapes are produced and stock are reared. There are extensive mineral deposits. Alma Ata is the cap. Area: *c.* 1,060,000 sq.m. Pop. 11,300,000.

KAZAN
[-zȧn'] Russ. city, cap. of the Tartar A.S.S.R. on a trib. of the Volga. It is an industrial town and a great trading centre. Pop. 725,000.

KEA
[kā'-ă] (*Nestor notabilis*) New Zealand parrot. Seventeen in. long with dull black-edged, olive-green plumage and bright red patches below the wings. It is fond of mutton fat and will attack living animals.

KEAN, Edmund
(1787-1833) Eng. actor; b. London. In 1814 he appeared on the London stage. He was prob. the greatest tragic actor of his day. He visited the U.S.A. where he had a great reception.

KEATS, John
(1795-1821) Eng. poet. B. London. He met Hazlitt, Leigh Hunt, Shelley, and other men of letters. In 1816 two of his sonnets appeared in *The Examiner;* in 1817 he pub. his first vol. of *Poems*; in 1818 the long narrative poem *Endymion*, which was savagely reviewed; in 1819 *Ode to a Nightingale*; in 1820 *La Belle Dame sans Merci*; and a vol. containing the narrative poems *Lamia, Isabella, The Eve of St. Agnes, Hyperion.* Keats d. of tuberculosis in Rome. Lawn Bank, his home in Hampstead (1817-20), is now a museum. His *Letters*, valuable for the light they throw on his conception of poetry, were pub. by Monckton Milnes, 1848.

KEBLE, John
(1792-1866) Eng. poet and divine. B. Fairford, d. Bournemouth. Educ. Corpus Christi Coll., Oxford. Vicar of Hursley, near Winchester. He was a prof. of poetry at Oxford 1831-41. He wrote *The Christian Year* (1827) which contains some very popular hymns. He was one of the founders of the Oxford Movement. Keble Coll., Oxford, was founded in his memory in 1870.

KEDAH
State of the Fed. of Malaya, on the N.W. coast. The S. part consists of undulating land, occupied by rubber plantations, while the N. coastal region is a fine rice growing area. Alor Star is the chief town. Area: 3,660 sq.m. Pop. 794,086.

KEIGHLEY
[kēth'-li] Borough of the W. Riding, Yorks., 9 m. N.W. of Bradford. Industries include the manufacture of woollen and worsted goods, textile machinery and sewing machines. It returns 1 member to Parl. Pop. 56,000.

KELANTAN
[ke-lan'-tan] State of the Fed. of Malaya, on the E. coast, N. of Pahang. The fertile coastal plain produces rice, coconuts and fruit; to the S. in the hilly country are rubber estates. Kota Bharu is the cap. Area: 5,780 sq.m. Pop. 579,246.

KELLER, Helen Adams
(1880-1968) Amer. blind and deaf mute. Anne Sullivan taught her to read by the deaf and dumb alphabet. In 1890 she learned to speak. She graduated with honours at Radcliffe Coll. Cambridge, Mass., and wrote *The Story of My Life* (1902), and travelled widely.

KELLS, Ceannanus Mor
Urban district of Meath, Eire, on the Blackwater, 10 m. N.W. of Navan. The site of a monastery built by St. Columba, in the 6th cent. The **Book of Kells,** written in the 8th cent., is now in Trinity Coll., Dublin.

KELLY, Grace
Princess Grace of Monaco (1929-) Wife of Prince Rainier III of Monaco. Formerly an Amer. film actress, she was b. in Philadelphia. She appeared in *Dial M for Murder, The Country Girl, The Swan, High Society.* She mar. Prince Rainier in Monaco in 1956. They have three children: Caroline, b. 1957, Albert, b. 1958 and Stephanie, b. 1965. *See* MONACO.

KELP
Name given to the porous ash obtained by burning seaweed slowly. From it is obtained iodine and alkaline salts.

KELVIN, Baron
O.M. F.R.S. (1824-1907) Scot. physicist. **William Thomson** b. Belfast. In 1846 he was made Prof. of Nat. Phil. at Glasgow. He made important contributions to hydrodynamics and to heat, where his greatest achievement was the development of the laws of thermodynamics and of the absolute temp. scale. In electricity he laid the foundation for the work of Maxwell in electro-magnetic theory, and in magnetism he perfected the mariner's compass. He was largely responsible for the successful completion of the Atlantic Cable in 1858.

KEMAL ATATÜRK
Mustapha Kemal (1881-1938) Turkish Gen. and statesman. B. Thessalonica. The Sultan was overthrown in Nov. 1922 and Kemal was elected 1st Pres. of the Turkish Repub. He became the virtual dictator of his country and shaped its complete redevelopment on W. lines. In politics his aim was the formation of a Balkan Federation.

KEMBLE, Charles
(1775-1854) Eng. actor, brother of Sarah Siddons. He appeared in London, mainly in comedy. His brother was **John Philip** (1757-1823). He made his first appearance at Wolverhampton, 1776. He made his London début as Hamlet at Drury Lane Theatre. He achieved great popularity as a tragedian, esp. in Shakespeare.

KEMPIS, Thomas à
(1380-1471) German writer, *c.* 1400 entered an Augustinian monastery near Zwolle. He made a copy of the Bible, and wrote sermons, hymns, and mystical works, including *The Imitation of Christ.*

KENDAL
Market town and borough of Westmorland, on the Kent, 21 m. N. of Lancaster. Pop. 18,630.

KENILWORTH
Urban district of Warwick., 4 m. N. of Warwick, famous for its castle. Pop. 15,330.

KENNAWAY, Sir Ernest Laurence
F.R.S. (1881-1958) Pathologist who worked with J. W. Cooke on cancer-producing hydrocarbons.

KENNEDY, John Fitzgerald
(1917-63) 35th Pres. of U.S.A. B. Boston, Mass. Torpedo boat commander in Pacific (Navy medal and Purple Heart). Democratic representative (1947) and Senator (1952) for Mass. 1960 became first Catholic and youngest Pres. Assassinated in Dallas, Texas, Nov. 1963, near end of 1st term of office during which he had blocked Russ. attempts to fortify Cuba and had helped to bring about the nuclear test ban treaty. His brother, Robert, was assassinated in June 1968 in Los Angeles, while running for nomination as Pres. candidate.

KENNINGTON, Eric Henri
(1888-1960) Eng. sculptor, painter and designer. Exhibd. R.A. and Leicester Gall. *The Costardmongers*, and *The Kensingtons at Laventie*, are 2 of his best-known paintings.

KENSINGTON
Part of Royal Borough of Kensington and Chelsea in Greater London (1964). The chief buildings include the Victoria and Albert Museum, the Natural Hist. Museum, the Commonwealth Institute and the Albert Hall. It returns 2 members to Parl. Pop. 172,020. **Kensington Gardens** adjoining Hyde Park, contain the Albert Memorial and a statue of Peter Pan. Overlooking the gardens is K. Palace, the birthplace of Queen Victoria, now home of Princess Margaret and the Earl of Snowdon.

KENT
County of S.E. Eng., with a long coastline on the Thames estuary and the Strait of Dover, and with Surrey and Sussex on its inland borders. It is a fertile and, in the main, a level county, with the N. Downs running W. to E. across it. The chief rivers are the Medway, Darent and Stour. The Weald is an important agricultural area, with market gardens, orchards and hop fields. Maidstone is the county town, and Canterbury the eccles. cap. of Eng. Along the estuary of the Thames and on the Medway is a great industrial area, with Dartford, Gravesend, Chatham, Rochester and Gillingham. Chatham is also a naval station. Round the coast are resorts, Herne Bay, Whitstable, Margate, Broadstairs, Ramsgate, Dover, Folkestone, Deal and Romney. Dover and Folkestone are also seaports for continental traffic. Inland towns include Tunbridge Wells, Sevenoaks, Ashford, Faversham and Sittingbourne. 'Kentish Men' are those born W. of the Medway. Persons of the E. part are 'Men of Kent'. Kent returns 18 members to Parl. (6 borough constituencies). Pop. 1,701,000.

KENT, Duke of
Eng. title. In 1799, George III made his 4th son, **Edward Augustus** (1767-1820), Duke of Kent. He was the father of Queen Victoria. **George** (*q.v.*), youngest son of King George V, became Duke of Kent in 1934, and on his d. in 1942, his son **Edward** succeeded. He m. 1961, Miss Katharine Worsley. A son, Earl of St. Andrews, b. 1962. A daughter, 1964.

KENTIGERN, ST. *See* MUNGO, ST.

KENTUCKY
State of the U.S.A. between the Appalachian Mts. and the Ohio. A level and fertile region, it produces great quantities of wheat, tobacco, and maize. Stock raising is important, and it is famous for its horses. The cap. is Frankfort, but Louisville, Covington and Lexington are larger. It was orig. part of Virginia, became a state, 1792, and sends 7 representatives to Congress. Area: 40,400 sq.m. Pop. 3,219,400.

KENYA
Indep. repub. of Brit. Commonwealth in E. Africa between Ethiopia and Tanganyika on the Indian Ocean. The N. is arid and unproductive. The S. region, which is more important economically, comprises a coastal plain and a volcanic plateau, which rises to over 17,000 ft. in Mt. Kenya. The chief river is the Tana. Crops include coffee, tea, maize, wheat, cotton and sisal. Timber is produced, and there are minerals. The cap. is Nairobi, but Mombasa, the chief port, is larger; other towns are Kisumu and Nakuru. The pop. is predominantly African. There are 5 provs. and 1 district. Since World War II a 10-year development plan has been put into operation, with schemes for the conservation of water, production of ground-nuts, etc. Brit. influence in Kenya dates from 1895, and the crown colony from 1920. Terrorist activities by the Mau Mau necessitated a state of emergency being proclaimed in 1952, which did not end till Jan. 1960. A constitution conferring self-govt. was brought into force, June 1963, and full indep. was achieved, Dec. 1963. Area: 224,960 sq.m. Pop. 8,626,000.

KENYATTA, Jomo
[jō′-mō ken-yat′-ă] (*c.* 1889-) P.M. of Kenya. African nationalist. He came to Brit. in 1929. From 1931 he studied anthropology, journeyed in Europe, and m. an Eng. woman. A member of the Kikuyu tribe in Kenya he was one of those accused of managing the Mau Mau risings (*q.v.*) and sentenced to 7 years' imprisonment in 1953. Released 1961, he joined Mr. Mboya as leader of the K.A.N.U., the Kenya African Nationalist Party, and entered the govt.

KEPLER, Johann
(1571-1630) German astron. In 1594 he went to

Graz as Prof. of Mathematics and Astronomy, and in 1601 he succeeded Tycho Brahe at Prague. His chief title to fame arises from his 3 laws of planetary motion.

KERALA
State of India formed from former state of Travancore Cochin with part of coastal area of Madras state. Cap. Trivandrum. Area: 15,005 sq.m. Pop. 16,903,715.

KERENSKY, Alexander Feodorovitch
[ker'-ĕn-ski] (1881-1970) Russian lawyer and politician. In 1917, when the Revolution broke out, he joined the govt. Later he became P.M. and then Pres. The Bolshevists soon proved too strong for him and he escaped from Russia. In 1919 he pub. *The Prelude to Bolshevism.*

KEROSENE
Mineral illuminating oils, esp. those derived from petroleum, commonly known as paraffin oil. Kerosene is a mixture of liquid hydrocarbons, sp. gr. from *c.* 0·780 to 0·830.

KERRY
Co. of Eire in S.W. Munster. The N. part is lowland, but in the S. are the highest mts. of Ireland, rising to 3,414 ft. in Macgillycuddy's Reeks. Of the many lakes, Killarney is the best known. Agriculture is the chief industry. Tralee is the county town; other towns are Killarney, Listowel and Dingle. Pop. 116,458.

KESTREL
(*Falco*) Small birds of prey. The Common K. (*F. tinnunculus*), also called the Windhover, is found in Brit. and other parts of Europe and Asia. The bird resembles the Falcon, av. 13 in. in length, and feeds on mice, insects and sometimes on young birds.

KESWICK
[kez'-ik] Market town and urban district of Cumberland, on the Greta, near Derwentwater. It is a centre for visitors to the Lake District. Pop. 4,590.

KETT, Robert
(*c.* 1500-49) Eng. agitator who took the lead against the enclosure of common lands. In 1549 he marched with the rebels to Norwich where he held courts and heard complaints from the people around. They got possession of Norwich, but were defeated. Kett was taken and hanged.

KETTERING
Borough and market town of Northants, 14 m. N.E. of Northampton. Industries include iron smelting, the manufacture of boots and shoes and hosiery. Pop. 38,650.

KEW
Suburb of London, 10 m. S.W. of London. At Kew is the observatory maintained by the Meteorological Office. **Kew Gardens** are the chief botanical gardens in Eng.

KEYES, Lord
Roger John Brownlow (1872-1946) Eng. Admiral of the Fleet. He was Chief of Staff to the Naval C.-in-C. in the operations against the Dardanelles. He was Director of Combined Operations, 1940-1; toured the Pacific theatre 1944-5.

KEYNES, Lord
[kānz] **John Maynard** (1883-1946) Eng. economist. He represented the Treasury at the Peace Conference in 1919, but soon after left the service. He then pub. his *Economic Consequences of the Peace,* a criticism of the conference. In 1943 he took part in the monetary negotiations at Bretton Woods. He helped to negotiate the Anglo-Amer. Loan Agreement of 1945. Keynes' teachings had great influence.

KEYS, House of
One of the 2 branches of the legislature of the Isle of Man. It consists of 24 members, who are elected by men and women electors, for 7 years. With the council or upper house, it forms the parl. of the Is. called the Court of Tynwald.

KHARKOV
Industrial city of the Ukraine, U.S.S.R., in the steppes, 250 m. E. of Kiev. Manufactures include textiles, felt, soap, sugar, farm machinery, locomotives and motor vehicles and electrical apparatus. Intellectual and admin. centre of the Ukraine. Pop. 1,070,000.

KHARTOUM
[-toom'] Cap. of the Repub. of the Sudan and of Khartoum prov., at the confluence of the Blue and White Nile, *c.* 1,100 m. S. of Cairo. It is an important trading centre. Khartoum was founded 1822, and destroyed during the Dervish rebellion of 1885, when Gen. Gordon was killed. Pop. 124,000.

KHYBER PASS
Rocky defile 33 m. long, leading from Afghanistan into Pakistan. It is now the main road from Kabul into the N.W. Frontier Prov.

KICKING HORSE PASS
Pass over the Rocky Mts., Canada, on the borders of Brit. Columbia and Alberta, 100 m. N.W. of Calgary. It is 5,340 ft. high, and is crossed by the C.P.R.

KIDD, William
(*c.* 1645-1701) Scot. pirate. In 1696 he obtained command of a privateer to prey upon Fr. commerce, but soon turned pirate and, in the *Adventure*, did a great deal of damage to Eng. and other shipping.

KIDDERMINSTER
Borough and market town of Worcs. on the Stour, 15 m. N. of Worcester. The chief industry is the manufacture of carpets. Pop. 42,470.

KIDNEY
Highly complex structures, bean shaped and reddish-brown in colour, lying in abdomen just under diaphragm, concerned chiefly with filtration of waste products from blood, and their concentration and excretion as urine via ureters to urinary bladder.

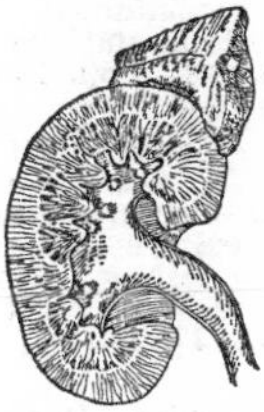

KIEL
[kēl] W. German seaport, cap. of Schleswig-Holstein on Kiel Bay, 60 m. N. of Hamburg. Later the **Kiel Canal** was constructed linking the N. Sea with the Baltic; 61 m. long, it is open to ships of all nations. Kiel has docks, shipyards and numerous industries. Pop. 271,000.

KIERKEGAARD, Søren Aaby
[ker'-kĕ-gawr] (1813-55) B. Copenhagen. Son of a Jewish merchant; converted to Christianity, 1848. For Kierkegaard the Individual Self is the ultimate and only human reality. This doctrine lies at the base of the philosophical conception, *Existentialism* (*q.v.*). Among best-known works are *Either—Or, Training in Christianity.*

KIEV
[kē-ef'] Cap. of the Ukrainian S.S.R. at the confluence of the Dnieper and Desna. It is a great route centre and commercial city, with

metallurgical and chem. works, railway repair shops and various food industries. It was taken by the Russ. 1868. Pop. 1,248,000.

KILDARE
Inland co. of Eire, in Leinster, W. of Dublin. The rivers are the Liffey, Boyne and Barrow. In the N. are bogs, part of the Bog of Allen, but in the E. and S. oats and potatoes are grown. Naas is the county town; other towns are Maynooth, Kildare and Athy. Pop. 64,420.

KILIMANJARO
[-jà'-] Extinct volcano in Tanganyika, E. Africa, the highest mt. in Africa, 19,565 ft.

KILKENNY
Inland county of Eire, in Leinster, E. of Tipperary. The rivers are the Barrow, Suir and Nore. The county is level except for a few hills in the N. and the soil is mainly fertile. Agriculture is the chief industry. Pop. 45,069. **Kilkenny.** County town and urban district of K. county on the Nore, 80 m. S.W. of Dublin. Pop. 10,159.

KILLARNEY
Market town and urban district of Kerry, near the Lakes of Killarney. Nearby are the Gap of Dunloe and Macgillycuddy's Reeks. Pop. 6,300.

KILMARNOCK
Burgh and market town of Ayrshire, 22 m. S.W. of Glasgow. Industries include engineering, carpets, woollen and leather manufactures and pottery. Pop. 48,000.

KILO
Prefix in the metric system denoting 1,000 units. *See* TABLES, p. 450.

KILT
Traditionally the national dress of Scotsmen, esp. Highlanders. It consists of a tartan skirt heavily pleated at the back and reaching to the knee. The kilt is worn by officers and men of Highland regts. of the Brit. Army and by pipers of Lowland regts. It is also part of the Irish national dress.

KIMBERLEY
Diamond-mining centre in Cape Prov. S. Africa, 90 m. N.W. of Bloemfontein. The first mine was opened in 1870, and the town grew up around the workings. Pop. 79,031.

KINCARDINESHIRE
or **The Mearns.** County of E. Scot. with a coastline on the N. Sea. In the N. are deer forests and grouse moors, and in the W. are the Grampians. Agriculture is the chief industry, but there is some fishing. Stonehaven is the county town. With N. Angus it returns 1 member to Parl. Pop. 25,538.

KING
Name given to a ruler. It was given to the rulers of the little states in Eng. in Anglo-Saxon times. There were kings in Greece and Rome and later many European countries called their rulers by an equivalent of this word. The early kings were elected, but later the office became hereditary in Eng., Scot., Fr., Spain, Portugal, Hungary and Bohemia. Poland retained an elective king. In 1700 the ruler of Brandenburg was made King of Prussia. A king was given to the Netherlands in 1815 and later in the 19th cent. kings arose in Greece, Rumania, Bulgaria and other parts of the Balkan area, and in Italy. The German Kaiser was deposed and exiled after World War I and in 1931 the King of Spain was deposed. Tribal rulers in Ireland were referred to as kings.

KING BIRD
Name of various Amer. flycatchers. The commonest are the ashy-grey *Tyrannus carolinensis*, a summer migrant to Canada, and the grey, W. Indian Petchery *T. griseus dominicensis.*

KING CHARLES SPANIEL
Toy dog which became fashionable in Charles I's reign. Derived from the Cocker spaniel, it has a short muzzle, wide eyes, upturned nose, domed head, long, silky coat and drooping ears.

KINGFISHER
Large family of birds allied to the Hornbills. With large heads, long, straight bills and small feet, they are often brilliantly coloured. The Common K. *Alcedo ispida*, is Brit.'s handsomest bird. The round, white eggs are laid in unclean nests of disgorged fishbones burrowed in river banks.

KING, Martin Luther
(1929-1968) Outstanding Amer. negro leader in campaign to end segregation in U.S. B. Atlanta, Georgia. Awarded Nobel Peace Prize, 1964, and in April 1968, was assassinated.

KINGS, Books of
Two books of the **O.T.** They give a history of the Jewish kings from the time of Solomon to the end of the monarchy. The author is unknown.

KING'S CUP
Challenge cup presented by King George V to be awarded annually to the winner of an aeroplane race organised by the Royal Aero Club.

KING'S LYNN
Borough and seaport of Norfolk, near the mouth of the Great Ouse. Industries include shipping, fishing. Pop. 27,460.

KING'S MESSENGER
(or **Queen's**) Officials in the royal household, whose duties are to carry despatches to ambassadors and other persons in high position.

KINGSLEY, Charles
(1819-75) Eng. writer. B. Holme, Devon. In 1860-9 he was Prof. of Mod. Hist. at Camb. His novels include *Westward Ho!* (1855), *Hereward the Wake* (1866). *Hypatia* (1853), deals with social and religious problems. He also wrote poetry and 2 books for children, *The Heroes* and *The Water Babies* (1863). He was assoc. with the Christian Socialist movement, and wrote many articles under the name of Parson Lot.

KINGSTON
Cap. of Jamaica, with a good harbour on the S.E. coast. In 1907 damaged by earthquake. Pop. 445,797.

KINGSTON-UPON-THAMES
Royal borough of Greater London (1964), formerly in Surrey, on the Thames. Industries include brewing, and it is a favourite boating centre. The Saxon kings were crowned at Kingston.

KINKAJOU
(*Cercoleptes caudivolvulus*) Small cat-like mammal. Belongs to the Raccoon family. A native of C. and S. Amer. with soft, short, yellow-brown fur, and long, prehensile tail.

KINROSS-SHIRE
County of Scotland between Fife and Perthshire. In the county is Loch Leven, and the Devon is the chief river. Agriculture is the main occupation. Kinross is the county town. With W. Perthshire Kinross-shire returns 1 member to Parl. Pop. 10,579.

KIPLING, Rudyard
(1865-1936) Eng. writer. B. Bombay, educ. at Westward Ho. In 1882 he returned to India. He pub. *Plain Tales from the Hills, Soldiers Three, Wee Willie Winkie. The City of Dreadful Night* revealed Indian life to Eng. readers in a new light. *The Light that Failed* (novel) appeared 1891. His verses include *Barrack Room Ballads, The Years Between. Kim* (novel) appeared 1901, the *Just So Stories*, 1902. His 2

Jungle Books, Puck of Pook's Hill, Rewards and Fairies were written for children. Later came *The Day's Work, Debits and Credits, A Diversity of Creatures, Stalky and Co.* Nobel Prize for literature in 1907.

KIRGHIZIA
Constituent repub. of the U.S.S.R. in C. Asia, bounded by Kazakhstan, Tajik and Sinkiang (China). It is a mountainous country. Agriculture is carried on in the valleys. Sheep, goats and cattle are reared on the mt. pastures. There are various mineral deposits. Frunze is the cap.; K. was formed 1936. Area: 76,642 sq.m. Pop. 2,063,000.

KIRKCALDY
[kir-kaw′-di] Burgh and seaport of Fifeshire, on the Firth of Forth, 26 m. N. of Edinburgh. Industries include the manufacture of linoleum, oilcloth and linen. With 4 burghs it returns 1 member to Parl. Pop. 52,697.

KIRKCUDBRIGHTSHIRE
County of S.W. Scot. with a long coast-line on the Solway Firth. The Dee, Cree, Ken and Ure are the chief rivers. Agriculture is the principal occupation. It unites with Wigtownshire to send 1 member to Parl. Pop. 28,305. **Kirkcudbright** [kir-koo′-bri] Burgh and county town of Kirkcudbrightshire at the mouth of the Dee, 30 m. S.W. of Dumfries. Pop. 2,421.

KIRKWALL
Burgh, seaport, and county town of the Orkney Is. on Mainland. Pop. 4,414.

KIRRIEMUIR
Burgh of Angus, 8 m. N.W. of Forfar, the birthplace of Sir J. M. Barrie. Pop. 3,477.

KITCHENER, Earl
Horatio Herbert (1850-1916) Brit. field-marshal. Defeated the Mahdi at Omdurman, 1898, thereby gaining control of the Sudan. Helped to win Boer War; Sec. for War, Aug. 7, 1914, until lost in cruiser *Hampshire* which struck a mine off the Orkneys on passage to N. Russia, June 5, 1916. Responsible for expansion and re-organisation of Brit. Army 1914-16.

KITE
Birds of prey, particularly the Common Glede or Red K. of Europe and N. Africa, which has reddish-brown plumage. It is *c.* 24 in. long and feeds on carrion.

KITTIWAKE
White gull with a yellow bill. Length 15-16 in. It is found chiefly in the N. Atlantic, breeding in Greenland, Spitsbergen and in the Brit. Is., esp. Scot. It feeds on fish and nests on precipitous cliffs. A variety with red legs is found in the N. Pacific.

KIWI
[kē′-wē] Rare New Zealand bird (*Apteryx*), there are 3 species, *A. mantelli, A. australis* and *A. oweni*. They are nocturnal birds, brown in colour with long beak and rudimentary wings.

KLEE, Paul
(1879-1940) Swiss painter. Became Prof. at the Bauhaus, an institution devoted to experimental art. Noted for the child-like nature of his fantasies in drawing.

KLIPSPRINGER
Small variety of antelope. It is found in Africa, esp. in rocky districts, and is an exceptionally good climber.

KLONDIKE
River of the Yukon Territory, Canada. In 1896 gold was discovered but now silver is more important.

KNAPWEED
(*Centaurea nigra*) Perennial plant of the family Compositae, found in waste places and on dry meadowland it is 2 or 3 ft. high.

KNEE JOINT
Joint formed by lower end of femur and upper end of tibia and by the patella or kneecap with

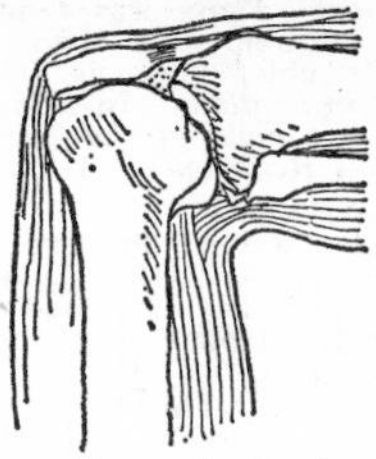

powerful ligaments and muscles to maintain its stability.

KNELLER, Sir Godfrey
(1646-1723) Eng. painter. B. Lübeck. He was apptd. court painter by Charles II, and painted portraits of the ladies of the court of Charles II and his successors to George I.

KNIGHT
One who has received the honour of knighthood. The earliest knights were members of an order, such as the Knights of the Hospital of St. John and the Knights Templars. Others were made knights for deeds of valour. There are 10 classes of knights, all created by the sovereign. Three belong to the great orders of knighthood, *Garter, Thistle* and *St. Patrick*. Six other orders, Bath, Star of India, St. Michael and St. George, Indian Emp., Royal Victorian Order and Order of the Brit. Emp. consist of knights and members of lower rank. The knights are called 'sir' and use letters indicating the order and rank. The equivalent of knight in the orders that admit women to membership is dame. The 10th class consists of **knights bachelor.** Persons knighted for services of a civic nature are usually made knights bachelor. Knighthood is not hereditary. Some Irish chiefs are called, by courtesy, knights, *e.g.* **The Knight of Kerry.**

KNIGHT, Dame Laura
(1877-) Eng. artist. In 1903 she mar. a portrait painter, Harold Knight. She was elected A.R.A. 1927; R.A. 1936; and her pictures deal chiefly with theatrical and circus life.

KNOCK-KNEE
or **Genu Valgum.** A deformity of the knees resulting in the knees knocking on walking. Rickets is cause, but lax muscles in a debilitated patient may produce the same result.

KNOSSOS
Ancient city of Crete, 3 m. from Candia, with ruined palace of Minos. *See* CRETE.

KNOT *See* TABLES, p. 452.

KNOT
(*Calidris canutus*) Wading bird of the Plover family. Related to the Sandpiper, it breeds in the Arctic regions and visits Brit. in autumn and winter.

KNOX, John
(*c.* 1515-72) Scot. reformer. His friendship with George Wishart led him to join the reformers just after the murder of Cardinal Beaton, 1546. He was taken prisoner by the Fr. In Feb. 1549, he was released, at the instance of Edward VI, and during that king's reign he lived in Eng. He assisted in the preparation of the Prayer Book. Edward d. in 1553 and Knox went to Dieppe and then to Geneva, where he made a name as a preacher. He returned to Scot. in 1558. He won many adherents by his preaching, and was equally zealous as a politician. Made a treaty with Eng. now under Elizabeth, and proceeded to make Protestantism the religion of Scot. In 1561 the young Queen Mary returned to Scot. and soon came into conflict with Knox. When Mary fled to Eng. Knox and his friends were

again dominant. Knox was twice mar., first to Marjory Bowen and then to Margaret Stewart. His chief book is *History of the Reformation in Scotland.* In 1558 at Geneva he wrote *The First Blast of the Trumpet Against the Monstrous Regiment of Women.*

KNOX, Ronald
(1888-1957) Eng. writer. Protonotary Apostolic 1951-7. He became fellow and lecturer at Trinity Coll. and, having joined the R.C. Ch. was later made chaplain to the R.C. students in the Univ. of Oxford. His books include *A Spiritual Aeneid* (1918), *The Viaduct Murder, Essays in Satire, Caliban in Grub Street, The Belief of Catholics.* His tr. of the Bible appeared 1947-9.

KOALA
[kō-ä'-lă] (*Phascolarctus cinereus*) Native name of a marsupial mammal. Found only in Australia, it is stout and clumsy, tailless, with ashy-grey fur and tufted ears. Living in eucalyptus trees, it feeds on their leaves and tender shoots.

KOBE
Seaport and industrial city of Japan, on the S. coast of Honshu Is., 20 m. W. of Osaka. Pop. 1,149,000.

KOBLENZ
City and cap. of Rhineland-Palatinate, W. Germany, at the confluence of the Moselle and Rhine. Pop. 100,649.

KOCH, Ludwig
(1881-) German naturalist, author and lecturer. After World War I he helped with the repatriation of Allied p.o.w. He made the first out of door recordings of songs of wild birds in 1928. On coming to Brit. 1936, he joined the B.B.C. He has written on the songs and language of birds and animals.

KOCH, Robert
(1843-1910) German scientist. In 1882 he discovered the bacillus of tuberculosis, and a little later the bacilli of cholera and phthisis. Tuberculin, or the lymph cure for tuberculosis, was another of Koch's discoveries. Nobel prize for medicine in 1905.

KODÁLY, Zoltán
[kod'-ī] (1882-1967) Hungarian composer. He made researches into Hungarian folk-song and joined Bartok in collecting examples. His works include the comic opera *Háry János*, chamber music and songs.

KOH-I-NOR
[-noor] Famous diamond, it orig. weighed 186 carats. Formerly in the possession of the Mogul emperors, it was presented to Queen Victoria in 1849, recut to 106 carats.

KOLA
Nut of an African evergreen tree, about the size of a walnut and is very bitter to the taste. It contains caffeine and is eaten as a stimulant.

KORAN
or **Quran.** The Sacred book of the Mohammedans, claimed as a divine revelation, communicated through the angel Gabriel at intervals over 23 years to the Prophet Mahomet.

KOREA
Country of E. Asia, consisting for the most part of a peninsula extending S. from Manchuria. It is bounded by the Yellow Sea and the Sea of Japan. The land is forested and mountainous. Rice, barley, wheat, beans, tobacco and cotton are grown and cattle are reared. Gold, copper, iron ore and coal are mined to a slight extent. The chief towns are Seoul (Keijo), Pusan (Fusan), Pyongyang (Heijo), Taegu (Taikyu), and Inchon (Chemulpo). Korea, whose troubled hist. goes back 1,000 years B.C. was an indep. kingdom in the 10th cent. After the devastating invasion of the Japanese in 1592-8, it was until recent times nominally under Chinese suzerainty. After the Russo-Japanese War of 1904-5 Korea was formally annexed by Japan, 1910. At the end of World War II, Korea was occupied by troops of the U.S.A. and U.S.S.R. and the 38th parallel was chosen as the line of demarcation of the zones of occupation. N. Korea was governed by a People's Repub. under the aegis of Russia and S. Korea became a repub. under the aegis of the U.N. On June 25, 1950 the N. Korean govt. staged a surprise attack against the S. Koreans, and their armed forces crossed the 38th parallel. The U.N. Security Council, with the backing of Pres. Truman, decided to oppose this unprovoked aggression by sending assistance to the S. Korean forces. Gen. Douglas MacArthur was apptd. supreme commander of the S. Korean forces. On Sept. 15, large U.N. forces made landings at Inchon and an offensive began which ousted the invaders from S. Korea and drove them at one point to the Manchurian border. On Nov. 26, some 200,000 Chinese crossed the Manchurian Border to aid the N. Korean forces and developed an offensive which forced the U.N. troops to fall back to a line which approximated the 38th parallel. In July, the Soviet U.N. representative proposed a conference to discuss an armistice. Cease-fire began at Kaesong on July 10, but the Communists suspended the peace talks on Aug. 23. The cease-fire agreement was resumed on Oct. 22. On Mar. 14, the Soviet accused the U.S. of using germ warfare and on Oct. 21 the proposed talks broke down on the p.o.w. issue. Negotiations for an armistice went on, and this was reached at Panmunion on July 27, 1953. Throughout the war the U.N. forces suffered one great disadvantage, viz. that except at the risk of extending the war, they could not invade Chinese soil or bomb the airfields which the enemy used as their fighting bases. Had Chinese territory been violated, the terms of the Russia-Chinese treaty were such that Russia would have been compelled to enter the conflict. Three years of war resulted in heavy milit. and civilian casualties and in the almost complete devastation of the aggressor's territory without any compensating gain. N. Korea—Area: 48,000 sq.m. Pop. 12,700,000. S. Korea—Area: 37,000 sq m. Pop. 30,010,000.

KOSCIUSKO
[kozi-us'-kō] Second highest mt. in Australia, in the Snowy Mts., N.S.W., reaching 7,305 ft.

KOSCIUSKO, Tadeusz
[kosh-choos'-ko] (1746-1817) Polish nat. hero. He served in the Fr. Army and led the Poles against the Russ. Following the partition of 1794, he set up a govt. in Warsaw, but was defeated by both Pruss. and Russ.

KOSSUTH, Lajos (Louis)
[kosh'-oot] (1802-94) Hungarian leader. In 1832 he was elected a member of the diet at Presburg, and advocated polit. and social reform. In 1847, he became a member of the diet of Hungary, and in 1848 was leader of the party that demanded indep. His energy raised a nat. force, and the Diet declared for an indep. repub. The movement failed and in 1849 Kossuth resigned his office and went to Turkey.

KREBS, Sir Hans Adolf
F.R.S. (1900-) Biochemist. Whitley Prof. of Biochem. Univ. of Oxford, 1954- . Director of Medical Research Council Unit for Research in Cell Metabolism since 1945. Joint winner, Nobel Prize for Medicine, 1953. K.B. 1958.

KREFELD URDINGEN
[krā-] Town in N. Rhine-Westphalia, W. Germany, near the Rhine, 32 m. N.W. of Cologne. Famous for its silk and velvet manufactures. Pop. 216,310.

KREISLER, Fritz
[krī'-zler] (1875-1962) Austrian composer and violinist. B. Vienna. He became one of the world's great violinists. As a composer he was best known for his smaller pieces for the violin, *e.g. Caprice Viennois, Liebesfreud.*

KREMLIN
Citadels or fortresses built in various towns in Russia during the feudal period. The most famous is that of Moscow, now the polit. and admin. centre for the U.S.S.R.

KRUGER, Stephanus Johannes Paulus
(1825-1904) Boer politician. As a boy he settled in the Transvaal. In 1880 he was a leader in the revolt against Brit. annexation. In 1883 he was elected Pres., an office he still held when difficulties arose between Brit. and the Transvaal in 1899. Stubbornly hostile to concession of any kind, he must bear some of the responsibility for the war that followed. **Kruger National Park.** Game reserve in the E. of the Transvaal, S. Africa.

KRUPP
[kro͝op] German family. **Friedrich Krupp** (1787-1826) started in business at Essen as a maker of iron and steel in 1812. His son **Alfred** developed the concern. He d. 1887 and left it to his son **Friedrich Alfred,** who d. 1902. The **Krupp works** were best known as armament works. After 1919 the works continued to manufacture arms in secret. In 1945 the firm was taken over by the Allied Milit. Govt. and placed under Brit. control. In 1953, the break-up of the organisation was ordered by the W. High Commissioner. It still survives and prospers.

KRUSHCHEV, Nikita Sergheyevich
[kroosh-chov'] (1894-) Russian polit. Son of a coal-miner, he joined the Communist Party in 1918. In 1932 he was apptd. Sec. of the Moscow city committee of the Comm. Party. In March 1939 he was apptd. by Stalin to full membership of the **Politburo.** After Stalin's d. in 1953, he succeeded Malenkov as Sec. Gen. of Cen. Comm. Party. In 1954 he began a series of foreign visits, including the 1955 visit to the U.K. He was apptd. Chairman of the Council of Ministers, 1958. In Nov. 1964 he was replaced as P.M. by Mr. Kosygin, and as 1st Sec. of the Communist Party by Mr. Brezhnev.

KUALA LUMPUR
[kwä'-lă-lo͝om'-per] Cap. of Selangor and of the Fed. of Malaysia. It is an important trading centre. Pop. 316,230.

KUBELIK, Jan
[koob'-e-lēk] (1880-1940) Czech violinist. His youngest son **Rafael K.** (1914-) is a conductor. In 1942 he became the chief conductor of the Czech Philharmonic Orchestra. During the Communist *coup d'état* in Prague in 1948 K. left Czechoslovakia and the following year was invited to succeed Sir Adrian Boult as conductor of the B.B.C. Symphony Orchestra. Musical director of the Covent Garden Opera House, 1955-8.

KUBLAI KHAN
[koo'-blī] (*c.* 1216-94) Mongol Emperor of China, the grandson of Jenghiz Khan. His great work was the conquest of China. He then became head of a great Mongol Empire with his cap. at Peking. Under him Buddhism became the State religion. He was the patron of Marco Polo.

KUDU
African antelope, *Strepsiceros capensis.* Tawny with vertical white stripes on the sides and reaching 5 ft. at the shoulder. The horns, present only in the male, are spirally twisted.

KUIBYSHEV
(formerly **Samara**) Chief city of the K. Region, Russ. S.F.S.R. on the Volga, 180 m. S. of Kazan. Now an industrial centre, with metallurgical and chem. industries. Pop. 901,000.

KU KLUX KLAN
Founded in Tennessee in 1865, it developed into an elaborate movement to maintain the purity of the white race and its domination of the negro. It spread widely, and soon degenerated as its lower members turned to terrorism and looting. As a result of this the official Ku Klux Klan was disbanded, and 1871-2, laws were passed against such secret socs. Subsequent outbursts of racial terrorism have been attributed in part to the Klan, including some of the most recent.

KUN, Bela
[koon] (1886-*c.* 1937) Hungarian agitator of Jewish extraction. He set up a Bolshevist repub. in Hungary. He later went to Russia, but was again in Hungary in 1927. During the Communist party purges of the 1930's he was interned in Russia, and d.

KUOMINTANG
Polit. party in China. Composed of the followers of Sun Yat Sen it stands for a policy of 'China for the Chinese'. Under Chiang Kai-Chek it then monopolised the govt. of the Repub. but attempts to present a united front against the Jap. invasion failed and since the war the Communists have completely taken over the country.

KURD
[koord] People of mixed stock inhabiting the region called Kurdistan now divided among Turkey, Persia and Iraq. Kurds are partly nomadic. They number *c.* 1,500,000 and are mainly Mohammedans.

KUWAIT
[koo-wāt'] Indep. state on the N.W. Persian Gulf, allied to U.K. since 1961, previously (since 1914) a protectorate. Bounded by Iraq and Saudi Arabia, it is mainly desert inhabited by nomadic Bedouin. There are rich oil wells in the S. The cap. and chief port is Kuwait. Pop. 321,621.

KWANGTUNG
[kwong'-to͝ong'] Prov. of S. China with a long coastline on the S. China Sea. It includes the Luichow peninsula and Hainan Is. The chief river is the Si Kiang, at the mouth of which stand Hong Kong and Macao (*qq.v.*). Canton is the cap. Pop. 37,960,000.

KYD, Thomas
(*c.* 1557-95) Eng. dramatist. Author of *The Spanish Tragedy* (1589).

KYOTO
City and ancient cap. of Japan, on Honshu Is. 27 m. N.E. of Osaka. It is an industrial centre. Univ. student riot, 1969. Pop. 1,396,000.

L

L
12th letter of the Eng. alphabet. It is one of the two liquid consonants. *L* has only one sound in Eng. as in *lit*, *leaf*, but in many words it is mute before another consonant, *e.g. would*, *psalm*, *half*, *talk*. In Roman numerals *L* is 50.

LABOUR PARTY
Polit. party in Brit. and elsewhere. Standing for socialism and the interests of the working classes, it arose during the 19th cent. In Brit. it was first represented in Parl. in 1900. In 1923 became the official Opposition in the House of Commons, and in 1924 it formed a Ministry. A 2nd Lab. Ministry was in power, 1929-31. The party then split, the majority, under Arthur Henderson, forming the Nat. Govt. of Ramsay MacDonald. In 1945 it had an overwhelming majority, and formed a govt. under Mr. Attlee. In 1950 it was again returned but this time with a majority of 6 seats, and in 1951 lost power to the Cons. Returned to power in 1964 (317 seats) and in 1966 (363 seats, a majority of 99). Defeated, 1970.

LABRADOR
District of N.E. Canada, part of the prov. of Newfoundland (*q.v.*). The most E. part of the cont., it stretches along the Atlantic Ocean, from the strait of Belle Is. to Hudson Strait. The coastline is *c.* 1,000 m. long. The interior is mountainous, the climate cold and the soil infertile. The pop. mainly consists of Eskimos, and the industry is fishing. There are considerable unexploited natural resources of timber and minerals. The ports include Battle Harbour. Area: *c.* 110,000 sq.m.

LABURNUM
Genus of hardy herbs of the leguminous family native to S. Europe. The common *L. anagyroides* bears pendulous sprays of yellow pea-like flowers. Purple L. is a hybrid.

LACCADIVE ISLANDS
Group of Is. in the Indian Ocean, 200 m. W. of the Malabar coast, forming with the Amindivi Is. a centrally admin. territory of India. Pop. 24,108.

LACE
Ornament of silk or cotton used on clothing and for other purposes. Handmade lace has been produced for cents., and various kinds were called after European cities specialising in their manufacture, *e.g.* Venetian, Mechlin. **Point lace** is like embroidery, the lace pattern being worked upon a fabric foundation. **Pillow lace** is made by plaiting the threads around bobbins placed on a pillow or frame. Lace was first made by machinery in the 18th cent. and in the 19th this became a staple industry of Nottingham, Devon and parts of Scot. Other centres were Calais and Plauen.

LACROSSE
Outdoor ball game originated by the Red Indians and adopted by Canadians. Introduced to Eng. 1867. The stick is furnished at the end with a net, and the aim of the player is to catch the rubber ball in this and then to carry, or hurl, it forward towards the goal.

LACTIC ACID
Organic acid, $CH_3.CHOH, CO_2H$, formed in the fermentation of sour milk.

LADOGA
Lake of the U.S.S.R., E. of the boundary of Finland. It is 125 m. long and covers 7,000 sq.m.

LADYBIRD
Large family of beetles (Coccinellidae), *c.* 2,000 species; the most familiar Brit. are the red or yellow 2-spot and 7-spot. They and their larvae consume scale insects and plant lice.

LADY'S SMOCK
(*Cardamine pratensis*) Perennial plant of the cruciferous family, found in Brit. in swampy places in spring. Its flowers are of the palest lilac or pinkish purple on stems 12-18 in. high. The upper leaves are pinnate with small narrow leaflets; the lower leaves are more rounded.

LADYSMITH
Town of Natal, S. Africa, on the Klip, 190 m. N.W. of Durban. Besieged by the Boers from Nov. 1899 to Feb. 1900, in the S. African War. Pop. 28,000.

LAFAYETTE, Marquis de
(1757-1834) Fr. statesman. In 1777 went to help the Amer. colonists in their struggle with Brit. In 1789, being again in Fr. he was elected to the States-General, but soon quarrelled with the Jacobins and fled the country.

LA FONTAINE, Jean de
(1621-95) Fr. poet. B. Chateau-Thierry. His chief works are the *Fables* (1668-94) based on Phaedrus, Aesop, etc. which revived the fable as a poetic form; and the *Contes et Nouvelles* (1665-74).

LAGOS
[lă'gos] Seaport and cap. of Nigeria, W. Africa, on a small Is. in L. lagoon. There is a good harbour. Pop. 665,000.

LAHORE
City of Pakistan, on the Rav, *c.* 30 m. S.W. of Amritsar. A railway centre, L. has various industries and an agricultural trade. Pop. *c.* 1,297,000.

LAKE
Expanse of water in a depression in the land surface. They may form in rock basins or be caused by an obstruction such as ice or moraine accumulations in a river valley; or by the upheaval or subsidence of land, or old volcanic craters. The Caspian Sea and Lake Superior are the largest in the world. **Lake District.** Area in N. Eng. in the counties of Cumberland, Westmorland and N. Lancs. Centres are Keswick, Ambleside, Grasmere and Windermere, and in the district are the 3 highest mts. of Eng., Scafell, Helvellyn and Skiddaw. The lakes include Windermere, Derwentwater, Ullswater, Coniston and Grasmere. It was made popular by the poems of Wordsworth, Coleridge and Southey, the Lake poets. **Lake Dwelling.** Habitation supported on piles or fascines, usually found on shallow lake margins. Remains found in C. Europe, esp. in Switzerland, yielded many objects belonging to the stone, bronze and early iron ages.

LALO, Édouard
[là-lō] (1823-92) Fr. composer of Sp. origin. His early studies were mainly devoted to violin and 'cello. Became a successful composer of operas and orchestral music.

LAMAISM
[lā'-ma-izm] Religious system prevalent in Tibet, Mongolia and Sikkim. The first Tibetan Monastery was founded by the Indian monk Padmakara (Padmasambhava) near Lhasa in 749. The head of the order is the *Dalai Lama* (*q.v.*) until 1959 residing in the Potala Palace, Lhasa. He is said to be of divine origin and receives divine honours.

LAMARTINE, Alphonse de
(1790-1869) Fr. writer and polit. B. Mâçon, educ. Lyons. In 1820 he pub. poems called *Méditations*, and these with later vols. marked the revival of romantic poetry. His books include *La Chute d'un Ange, Histoire des Girondins.*

LAMB, Charles
(1775-1834) Eng. writer. B. London; in 1792 became a clerk in the E. India Co. Best-known for his *Essays of Elia*, which appeared, 1823. With his sister, Mary, he wrote *Tales from Shakespeare*, and he himself wrote other books for children, as well as *Selections from Elizabethan Drama*, and poems. His *Letters* were ed. by E. V. Lucas 1935. His domestic life was clouded by the periodical madness of his sister, who in one of her attacks killed their mother.

LAMBETH
Borough of London on the Thames opposite Westminster. **Lambeth Palace** has been for 700 years a res. of the archbps. of Canterbury. A decennial meeting of bishops of the Anglican Ch. is held at L. and called the L. Conference.

LAMENTATIONS, Book of
(O.T.) Ascribed to Jeremiah, it consists of 5 dirges, 4 of which are written acrostically, beginning with the successive letters of the Heb. alphabet.

LAMMAS DAY
Name given to Aug. 1, a Scots and formerly also an Eng. quarter day. In medieval times it marked the end of the wheat harvest. When the calendar was altered, it became Aug. 12.

LAMPREY
Aquatic vertebrates lower than normal fishes. Scaleless and jawless, they cling to rocks or prey by their characteristic round mouths. They are found in all temp. waters.

LANARKSHIRE
Inland county of S.W. Scot. The chief rivers are the Clyde, Cart and Kelvin. Market gardening and the rearing of stock are important. There are coalfields, and industries, including shipbuilding and textiles. Lanark is the county town. Burghs incl. Glasgow, Rutherglen, Motherwell, Hamilton and Airdrie. L. returns 22 members to Parl. (16 burgh constituencies). Pop. 1,606,787. **Lanark.** Burgh and county town of Lanarkshire, on the Clyde, 31 m. S.E. of Glasgow. Cotton and other textiles are manufactured, and there is an agricultural trade. Pop. 8,406.

LANCASHIRE
(Lancs.) County of N.W. Eng. with a long coastline on the Irish Sea. The W. part is low-lying, but the Pennines traverse the E. The rivers include the Mersey, Irwell, Ribble, Lune, Calder and Darwen. Much of Lancs. is a thickly populated area, and a centre of the coal-mining, chemical and cotton industries. Liverpool and Manchester are the chief industrial towns, and the principal seaports, Manchester being linked with the sea by a ship canal. Lancaster is the county town, and Preston the admin. centre. Blackpool and Southport are resorts. L. returns 64 members to Parl. (48 borough constituencies). Pop. 5,160,660.

LANCASTER
City and county town of Lancs. on the Lune, 7 m. from the sea. The chief industries are manufactures of linoleum and engineering works. Univ. founded 1964. Pop. 48,480.

LANCASTER, Duke of
(1340-99) Eng. prince. John of Gaunt, so called because he was b. at Ghent, the 4th son of Edward III. 1359, he mar. Blanche, heiress of the Duke of Lancaster, and so gained that title. When his father's health failed he became active in Eng. politics, and remained so in reign of his nephew, Richard II. Leader of the party that favoured Wycliffe, his son became Henry IV. By his 3rd wife, Catherine Swynford, he was father of the Beauforts whose descendant became Henry VII in 1485.

LANCASTER, House of
Family that provided kings of Eng. from 1399 to 1461. Its founder was Edmund, a son of Henry III. Henry, son of John of Gaunt (*see above*) claimed the throne, and in 1399 landed in Eng. and was crowned Henry IV, Richard II being deposed. He, his son Henry V, and his grandson Henry VI were kings in turn. Richard, Duke of York, claimed the crown in opposition to Henry VI, and the Wars of the Roses began. Henry VI was deposed 1461, and murdered, 1471. His son had already been killed and the house of Lancaster became extinct in the male line.

LANCELET
(*Amphioxus*) Found in sand near the coast of most warm countries, it is sickle-shaped and *c.* 2 in. long. It belongs to the class Cephalochorda, one of the lowest of the chordate animals, regarded as a link between vertebrates and invertebrates.

LAND CRAB
Widespread family of trop. crustacea. Their modified gill cavities, acting as lungs, enable them to live on land. They spend the day in burrows inland, migrating to the coast collectively in the breeding season.

LANDES
[lā(ng)d] Dept. in S.W. Fr. on the Bay of Biscay. The W. part consists of sandy plains, with dunes along the coast. Pines have been planted to fix the sand and make the land suitable for sheep pasture. Cap. Mont de Marsan.

LANDING CRAFT
Vessels designed to land on enemy beaches the personnel, equipment and stores necessary for the sustained occupation of enemy territory.

LANDOR, Walter Savage
(1775-1864) Eng. writer. His poetry, *Hellenics, Italics* (1846-8), his *Imaginary Conversations* (1824-9), *Pericles and Aspasia*, 1836, and the dramatic trilogy *Andrea of Hungary*, etc. (1839-40), reflect his interest in classical and hist. themes.

LANDRAIL
Alternative name for the Corncrake (*q.v.*).

LAND'S END
Extreme W. point of Eng. in Cornwall, 9 m. S.W. of Penzance.

LANDSEER, Sir Edwin Henry
(1802-73) Eng. artist. Elected A.R.A., 1826; R.A., 1830; knighted, 1850. Landseer became very popular as an animal painter. He designed the lions for the Nelson column in Trafalgar Square, London.

LANFRANC
(*c.* 1005-89) Eng. prelate. B. Pavia. In 1041 he became a Benedictine monk at Bec. Through the influence of William of Normandy, he became Archbishop of Canterbury in 1070. He was one of William's most trusted advisers.

LANG, Andrew
(1844-1912) Scots. writer. He pub. vols. of poetry, (*Grass of Parnassus*), tr., (*Iliad, Odyssey*), and books on Mary, Queen of Scots and the rising of 1745. His books on folklore include *Custom and Myth, Magic and Religion, Perrault's Fairy Tales.*

LANG, Cosmo Gordon
(1864-1945) Brit. prelate. He entered the Ch. and became (1909) Archbishop of York. In 1928 he was apptd. Archbishop of Canterbury.

LANGLAND, William
(*c.* 1330-1400) Eng. poet. His *Piers Plowman* is a religious and moral allegory, with vivid glimpses of 14th cent. life.

LANGSIDE
District of Glasgow, where in 1568 the forces of Mary, Queen of Scots, were beaten by those under the Regent Moray.

LANGTON, Stephen
(*c.* 1150-1228) Eng. prelate. In 1206 he was made a cardinal and in 1207 was apptd. Archbp. of Canterbury. Best-known as one of the leaders of the barons who compelled John to sign Magna Carta.

LANGUEDOC
[là(ng)'-gĕ-dok] A prov. of S. Fr. before 1789; situated N. of the Pyrenees and W. of the Rhône delta. The chief town was Toulouse.

LANOLIN
Hydrous wool fat. It is a yellowish white tenacious substance derived from the skin of the sheep. It is absorbed readily by the skin and used as the basis of many ointments.

LANSING
Cap. of Michigan, U.S.A., 80 m. N.W. of Detroit, on Grand R., a manufacturing centre. Pop. 107,807.

LAOIGHIS
or Leix [lā'-ish]. Inland co. of Repub. of Ireland, in the prov. of Leinster. The chief rivers are the Barrow and Nore. Agriculture is the principal occupation. Port Laoighise (Maryborough) is the county town. Pop. 45,069.

LAOS
Former Fr. protectorate of Asia. Despite negotiations at Geneva between Fr., Brit., Russ., U.S. and China, political unrest continues. Country is mountainous, watered by the Mekong, surrounded by Thailand, Burma, China, Vietnam and Cambodia. There are extensive forests in the N.; tin, rice, coffee and tea are produced. Vientiane is the admin. cap. Area: 91,431 sq.m. Pop. 2,200,000.

LA PAZ
[pàs] City of Bolivia, the seat of the govt., 12,400 ft. high in the mts., 30 m. from L. Titicaca. Founded in 1584, La P. is a prosperous trading centre, and has a univ. Pop. 352,912.

LAPIS LAZULI
[lap'-is laz'-yew-lī] Blue mineral. A sodium-aluminium silicate, with calcium sulphur and chlorine. Valued as an ornamental stone from ancient times.

LAPLAND
District of Europe, in N. Sweden, Norway, Finland and U.S.S.R. The Lapps, who are of short stature, with high cheek bones, lead a nomadic life, hunting and fishing. There is a colony of them in Alaska; in Europe they number *c.* 30,000.

LA PLATA
[plà'-tă] Cap. of Buenos Aires prov., Argentina. Its chief industry is the preparation and export of meat. Pop. 330,310.

LAPP *See* URAL-ALTAIC.

LAPWING
Green Plover or Peewit (*Vanellus vanellus*) found in Europe and Asia, winters in India and Africa and is recognised by glossy black crest on the head. It feeds upon insects, worms, and vegetable matter. It frequents moorland.

LARCH
Genus of deciduous cone-bearing trees (*Larix*). The common larch, *L. decidua,* native in the

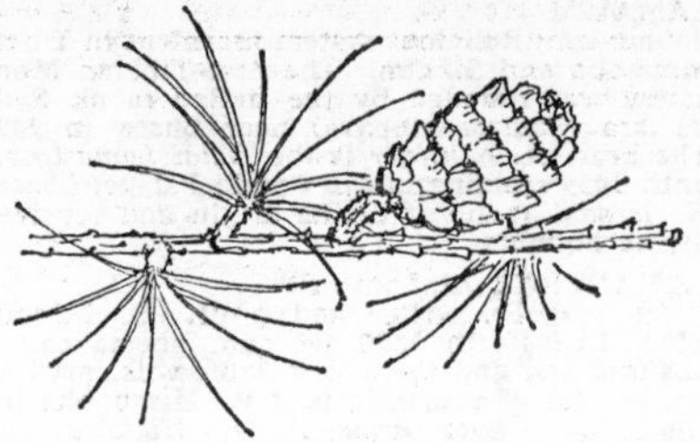

Alps, is 80-140 ft. high, with needle-like leaves and small cones. It provides tough timber and turpentine and bark for tanning.

LARK
Family of birds (*Alaudidae*) A few are seen in Brit., *viz.* the Skylark and Wood L.

LA ROCHEFOUCAULD, Duc de
(1613-80) Fr. writer. B. Paris. His *Réflexions, ou Sentences et Maximes Morales* appeared 1665. He also wrote *Mémoires,* valuable for the history of the time.

LARVA
Stage in life hist. of many animals where the body of the animal that hatches from the egg differs from the adult. Among the amphibia some adult forms are terrestrial, their larvae aquatic.

LARYNX
Part of the air passages between the pharynx and the bronchus. Composed mainly of cartilage and muscles. The entrance or glottis is guarded by the epiglottis and the larynx contains the vocal cords. **Laryngitis.** Inflammation of larynx characterised by cough, hoarseness or loss of voice, choking sensation, and difficulty in breathing. Often accompanies common cold or bronchitis but may be produced by excessive smoking or inhalation of irritating gases.

LA SALLE, Sieur de
[-sal] (1643-87) Fr. explorer. He made several voyages along the St. Lawrence and traced the Mississippi to its mouth in the Gulf of Mexico (1682). The vast Mississippi region he annexed as a Fr. possession and was apptd. its gov.

LASCAR
Indian word applied to Asiatic seamen, esp. Ind., it is officially recognised by the Merchant Shipping Acts as excluding non-Ind., *e.g.* Malays and Chinese.

LAS PALMAS
[las pal'-mas] Seaport and resort of the Canary Is. (*q.v.*) cap. of the Sp. prov. of L.P. There is a good harbour. Pop. 178,000.

LATAKIA
Seaport of Syria, 70 m. N. of Tripoli. It occupies the site of Laodicea, and excavations have revealed remains of the earlier city. Pop. 105,400.

LATERITE
[lat'-] Deposit of yellowish or reddish coloured clay, found in India, the Sudan and S. Amer. These are extensive and thick, and result from the decomposition of rocks rich in iron minerals by weathering under trop. conditions.

LATIMER, Hugh
(*c.* 1490-1555) Eng. bishop. B. near Leicester. In 1535 he was made Bishop of Worcester, but in 1539 he was imprisoned for not accepting the Six Articles. During the reign of Edward VI he assisted Cranmer in furthering the Reformation. In Sept. 1555, he was found guilty of heresy and was burned with Ridley in Oxford.

LATIN
The Italic (*q.v.*) language of ancient Latium,

disseminated throughout W. Europe by Rome's power. After the fall of Rome, Lat. lived on as the language of the W. Ch. learning and lit. till *c.* 14th cent. Little lit. work has been done in Lat. since the mid-18th cent. *Classical Lat.* is that of the Augustan period (Virgil, Horace, Ovid, Livy, Cicero); followed in 1st cent. A.D. by *Silver Lat.*; then *late* and *medieval Lat.*; *Renaissance Lat.* is a deliberate return to classical idiom; much poetry was written in it, *e.g.* Petrarch's epic *Africa*, early poems of Milton. The prose includes More's *Utopia* (1516).

LATTER DAY SAINTS
Formal and correct name of the body known more usually as Mormons.

LATVIA
Constituent republic of the U.S.S.R. bounded by Estonia, Lithuania, White Russ. and the R.S.F.S.R. with coastlines on the Baltic and Gulf of Riga. The chief river is the Dvina. The soil is fertile, and agriculture the main occupation. There are shipbuilding, engineering and chemical industries. Riga is the cap.; other towns are Liepaja, Daugavpils, Jelgava and Ventspils. L. was an indep. repub. 1918-46, when the country was occupied by Russ. troops and incorporated in the Soviet Union. It was occupied by the Germans, 1941-4. Area: 25,590 sq.m. Pop. 2,190,000.

LAUD, William
(1573-1645) Eng. archbishop. Entering the Ch. he was made chaplain to James I. His advancement was rapid and in 1633 he became Archbishop of Canterbury. The king's eccles. policy in Eng. and Scot. was inspired by Laud. It aimed at establishing uniformity of worship and caused much unrest, esp. in Scot. In 1641 Laud was impeached, and under a bill of attainder beheaded on Tower Hill.

LAUDANUM
Tincture of opium, a dark, reddish-brown liquid, standardised to contain 0·75 % of anhydrous morphine, used as an anodyne and soporific.

LAUDER, Sir Harry
(1870-1950) Scots comedian. His songs, which he wrote himself, include *I Love a Lassie*, *Roamin' in the Gloamin'* and *Stop yer Ticklin', Jock.*

LAUDERDALE, Duke of
(1616-82) Scots politician. He became a leading spirit among the Covenanters but soon changed sides, and in 1650 returned to Scot. with Charles II. With Charles II on the throne Lauderdale became member of the Cabal and Sec. of State for Scot. was responsible for persecution of the Covenanters between 1672-80.

LAUGHING GAS
Nitrous oxide. A colourless, transparent gas with a sweet taste, when inhaled it produces insensibility, hence its use as an anaesthetic. *See* ANAESTHETICS.

LAUGHING JACKASS
Austral. name for the largest of the kingfisher family (*Dacelo gigas*). It has a strident laugh.

LAUNCESTON
[làn'-ston] Borough of Cornwall at the confluence of the Kensey and Tamar. Pop. 4,510.

LAUNCESTON
[lon'-ses-tŏn] City and river port of Tasmania, on the Tamar. Industries include shipping, smelting and wool-spinning. Pop. 49,300.

LAUREL
Diverse evergreen shrubs and trees. The laurel of antiquity was prob. the Medit. bay tree (*Laurus nobilis*). The cherry laurel (*Prunus laurocerasus*) and the Portuguese laurel contain hydrocyanic acid. Brit's. only native laurel is the spurge (*Daphne laureola*).

LAUSANNE
[lō-zan'] Cap. of Vaud canton, Switzerland, on the hills N. of L. Geneva. L. is an educ. and tourist centre. Pop. 132,500.

LAVAL, Pierre
(1883-1945) Fr. politician. P.M. 1931-2 and 1935-6; Colonial Min. 1934; Foreign Min. 1934-5; Head of Govt. 1942-4. After the fall of Fr. in 1940, Laval co-operated with the Germans and eventually secured complete control of the Vichy Govt. He was tried and executed by his countrymen in 1945.

LAVENDER
(*Lavandula*) Genus of perennial herbs or shrubs of the labiate family. *L. officinalis* bears mauve flowers, from which an aromatic oil is distilled.

LAVOISIER, Antoine Laurent
[la'-vwa-siā] (1743-94) Fr. scientist who showed that the gain in wt. on burning is due to combustion with oxygen from the air.

LAW
Word meaning rule or order. It is used in two main senses. The first is for an inevitable order of the universe, as the laws of motion or the laws of cause and effect. In the second it refers to a rule laid down for human action, disobedience of which is likely to be followed by some penalty or inconvenience. Laws appeared at a very early stage in human hist. Religion played a great part, and early laws were regarded as the commands of a god. This idea in modern times is partly responsible for what is known as the moral law. Among primitive peoples custom was an important factor, and many early codes of law, *e.g.* the laws of Eng. before Norman times, are merely collections of accepted customs. The lawgivers of ancient times, such as Hammurabi and Moses, did not make laws; they restated those already existent. The Gks. had a developed system of law, but modern law owes its greatest debt to the Roms. They divided law into the civil, or national law, and the law of nations, which is the basis of internat. law. Another division of law is into the civil law, and the canon or eccles. law, and another is into the common, or unwritten law and the statute law, a classification familiar in Eng. The unwritten law is called case law, or law as interpreted by the judges. In Eng. as in other countries, the criminal law has been separated from the civil law. Today every country has its own legal system. Each system has 3 essentials; an individual, or body, with power to make laws; a body of judges to declare them, and another body to enforce them. Internat. law must be excepted from these statements, because as yet no power to enforce its orders has been created. Lawyers are divided into several classes, but entrance to each is everywhere a privilege guarded by educ. and other tests. **Law Lord.** Name given in Eng. to the 9 Lords of Appeal in Ordinary. They sit in the House of Lords as life peers. *See* BARRISTER; SOLICITOR.

LAWES, Henry
(1596-1662) Eng. composer. Gentleman of the Chapel Royal 1626-33. Wrote music for Milton's *Comus* and a coronation anthem *Zadok the Priest* for Charles II.

LAWN TENNIS
Outdoor game played by both sexes. It was developed from real tennis and is played with racquets and balls on a court 78 ft. long and 36 ft. wide for doubles and 24 ft. for singles. The court is divided into 2 equal parts by a net 3½ ft. high at the posts and 3 ft. at the centre and further into sections by white lines. Both grass courts and hard courts of gravel, cement or asphalt are used. The great event of the Lawn Tennis year is the internat. meeting at Wimbledon (*q.v.*). The Davis Cup is contended for by male teams from the various countries. The Wightman Cup is fought out between

women players from Brit. and the U.S.A. The game in Brit. is gov. by the Lawn Tennis Assoc. formed in 1888. Pros. are recognised for coaching but are strictly debarred from matches and competitions.

LAWRENCE, David Herbert
(1885-1930) Eng. writer. B. Eastwood, son of a coal-miner. In 1911 he pub. his first novel, *The White Peacock*, and in 1913 he made his name with *Sons and Lovers*, a realistic story of life among the coal-miners. His other novels include *The Plumed Serpent*, *Women in Love* (1921), *Aaron's Rod* (1922). *Lady Chatterley's Lover* was pub. in Paris 1928; this was pub. in G.B. in 1960 after a court decision that it was not an obscene publication.

LAWRENCE, Sir Thomas
(1769-1830) Eng. artist. B. Bristol, he painted portraits when only a child. In 1792 he was made painter to the king. In 1820 he was chosen Pres. of the Royal Academy. Lawrence was the most fashionable portrait painter of his day.

LAWRENCE, Thomas Edward
(1888-1935) Brit. soldier and statesman. B. Wales. Educ. Oxford. During World War I he organised an Arab revolt against the Turks. He was greatly loved by the Arabs. His account of the Arab revolt, *The Seven Pillars of Wisdom*, was pub. in 1926.

LAWYER
Member of any branch of the legal profession. In Eng. and elsewhere it includes barristers and solicitors; in Scot., advocates, writers to the signet and law agents. *See* BARRISTER; SOLICITOR; LAW.

LAYARD, Sir Austen Henry
(1817-94) Eng. scholar. His excavations of Nineveh (1845-7) and Babylon were recorded in his *Nineveh and its Remains* (1849).

LE CORBUSIER
(Charles Edouard Jeanneret) (1887-1965) Swiss architect. He lived in Fr. after 1916. His designs used reinforced concrete constructions of extreme simplicity, with the maximum of fresh air and light. He planned the cities of Buenos Aires, Stockholm, Antwerp, Algiers, Bogotá, Chandigarh, etc., and acted as consultant for town and country planning for govts. in Europe, Africa, Amer. and Asia.

LEA
River of Eng. which rises in Beds. and flows into the Thames near Blackwall.

LEAD
Bluish-grey, soft metallic element, very malleable and ductile, it occurs chiefly as the sulphide in galena. It is widely used in sheets and pipes and is a constituent of many alloys. Sp. gr. 11·4. Chem. sym. Pb. **Lead Poisoning.** Disease attacking workers using lead compounds. Formerly common in pottery-glazing, painting, printing, plumbing and other industries. Attacks must now be notified, workers must be medically examined and adequate ventilation and cleanliness maintained in the works.

LEAF
Outgrowth from the stem of a plant forming a lateral expansion of varying form and function. The mesophyll is traversed by veins, continuous with those of the stem, and it contains the chlorophyll grains which colour the leaf and function in carbon assimilation under the action of sunlight. A typical foliage leaf consists of a leaf base, stalk or petiole, and blade or lamina. **Leaf insect.** A large class of straight-winged insects (*Orthoptera*). The body is comparatively large and flat and the legs resemble bits of stick or a leaf.

LEAGUE OF NATIONS
International organisation. It came into existence Jan. 10, 1920, as part of the treaty that followed World War I, and was finally wound up in 1945. Its headquarters were at Geneva. It had over 50 members, including all the leading countries of the world except the U.S.A., Russia, Mexico and Brazil. The Covenant of the League contained fundamental clauses on the prevention and settlement of disputes. 2 depts. are now parts of UNO; the permanent **Court of International Justice** at The Hague; and the **International Labour Office** at Geneva. The failure of the League to hold its members together in action against aggressor nations (*e.g.* Japan in Manchuria and Italy in Abyssinia), coupled with the withdrawal of these nations from membership, caused its abandonment. *See* UNITED NATIONS ORGANISATION.

LEAMINGTON
[lem'-] Borough and spa of Warwicks. on the Leam, 2 m. E. of Warwick. Pop. 43,000.

LEAP YEAR
Year of 366 days occurring every 4 years. It was introduced by Julius Caesar in 46 B.C. in the Julian calendar, to adjust the calendar year to the solar year, which is not quite 365¼ days. The slight over-correction is put right by omitting leap year at long intervals.

LEAR, Edward
(1812-88) Eng. writer of Danish descent. He exhibited regularly at the R.A. In 1846 he pub. *The Book of Nonsense*, then *More Nonsense Rhymes* and *Laughable Lyrics*.

LEATHER
Hides are the skins of larger animals such as the horse, cow and bull. The term skin is usually applied to calfskins, pig skins, sheep- and goatskins, but skins are also got from seals, and from crocodiles and other reptiles. These are subjected to the processes of curing, dehairing, fleshing and tanning. Chamois leather is prepared from the flesh split of a sheepskin.

LEATHERWOOD
(*Dirca*) (1) Sole Amer. genus of shrubs of the spurge-laurel family. (2) The close-grained timber of a tree of the saxifrage family that grows in New S. Wales.

LEBANON
Repub. on the Medit. coast, bounded by Syria on the N. and E. and Israel on the S., 120 m. long and *c.* 30 m. wide. Most of the country is hilly, except for the depression, the Beqaa, and the narrow coastal strip. The L. and Anti-L. ranges run parallel to the coast. The chief rivers are the Orontes and Litani. Fruit, tobacco, silk and cotton are the chief products. Beirut is the cap. and largest town; other centres are Tripoli, Sidon and Tyre. Until 1918 when it became a Fr. mandate with Syria, L. was part of the Ottoman Emp. It became an indep. repub. in 1944. Area: 4,015 sq.m. Pop. 1,750,000.

LECHIC LANGUAGES
Polish, Kashubian, Polabian. *See* SLAVIC.

LEE, Nathaniel
(*c.* 1653-92) Eng. dramatist. His tragedies include *Nero* (1675), *Sophonisba* (1676), *The Rival Queens* (1677), *Mithridates* (1678), *Constantine the Great* (1684). Confined in Bedlam 1684-9.

LEE, Robert E.
(1807-70) Amer. soldier. B. Virginia, he served in the war against Mexico (1846), and against the Indians. In 1861, on the outbreak of the Civil War, Lee threw in his lot with the Southerners and commanded a force sent to the confederate army from Virginia. In 1863 he won a great victory at Chancellorsville, and, although defeated at Gettysburg, he managed to hold his own against superior forces. On April 9, 1865, he was surrounded and forced to surrender at Appomattox Court House, and in a short time was pardoned.

LEECH
Segmented or annelid worms possessing suckers at both ends and feeding on the blood of animals. The best known Brit. species are the horse leech and the smaller leech much used at one time in med. The latter is *c.* 2 in. long.

LEECH, John
(1817-64) Eng. artist. B. London; educ. Charterhouse. In 1841 he joined the staff of *Punch.* He illustrated *The Christmas Carol* by Dickens.

LEEDS
City and county borough of the W. Riding, Yorks. on the Aire, connected by rail and canal with the Humber and Mersey. The chief industry of L. is the manufacture of cloth and clothing. Others are engineering, leather, printing works, and the manufacture of shoes, chemicals and glass. It returns 7 members to Parl. Pop. 514,640.

LEEK
(*Allium porrum*) Hardy bienniel bulbous herb of the lily family. The root is cooked and eaten as a vegetable. The leek is the national emblem of Wales and is worn on Mar. 1, St. David's Day.

LEEWARD ISLANDS
[lē'-wărd] N. group of the Lesser Antilles, W. Indies. The Leeward Islands include Antigua (with Barbuda and Redonda), St. Kitts-Nevis-Anguilla, Montserrat and the Virgin Is. (*q.v.*). Fully indep. 1962. Area: 420 sq.m. Pop. 133,350.

LEG
Limb supporting and moving the body. Most vertebrates have 2 pairs. Insects have normally 3 pairs; spiders, 4; higher crustacea, 5; some millipedes more than 100 pairs. The human leg or shank contains the tibia or shin bone, which enters into the knee joint and into the ankle joint.

LEGHORN
(*It.* **Livorno**) City and seaport of Tuscany, Italy, on the Ligurian coast, 12 m. S. of Pisa. There is a harbour, enlarged in the 20th cent. Shipping, shipbuilding, and the manufacture of glass and straw hats are the chief industries. Pop. 159,973.

LEGION
Unit of the Rom. Army, consisting of from 5-6,000 men.

LEGION OF HONOUR
Fr. order, founded by Napoleon in 1802. The Pres. of the repub. is the grand master.

LEHÁR, Franz
[lā'-har] (1870-1948) Hungarian composer. Composed light operas, which had tremendous success. They include *The Merry Widow, The Land of Smiles, Frederica.*

LEIBNITZ, Gottfried Wilhelm
[līb'-nits] (1646-1716) German scholar. B. Leipzig. He discovered a new method of the calculus, which led to a dispute with Sir Isaac Newton. He invented a calculating machine. As a philosopher, he expounded a system in which substance consists of atoms, or monads, each self-contained and individual, the whole forming a perfect harmony with its centre and creator, God.

LEICESTER, Earl of
(1532-88) Eng. courtier. **Robert Dudley** was a younger son of John Dudley, Duke of Northumberland. In 1560 Amy Robsart, whom he mar. in 1550, d. in suspicious circumstances. In 1573 he mar. Lady Shenfield and in 1578 he bigamously mar. Lettice, Countess of Essex, but all the time he was paying his addresses to Elizabeth. In 1585 he was sent with an army to the Netherlands, and in 1588 he commanded the force at Tilbury gathered to meet the Sp.

LEICESTERSHIRE
Midland county of Eng. It is mainly level, with the hills of Charnwood Forest and the Wolds in the N. and E. The chief rivers are the Soar, Avon and Welland. Agriculture is the principal industry, and there is some coal mining. Leicester is the county town. Other places are Loughborough, Market Harborough, Coalville and Ashby-de-la-Zouch. L. returns 8 members to Parl. Pop. 691,530. **Leicester** [les'-ter] City, county borough and county town of Leics. The making of hosiery, boots and shoes, and cotton goods are the chief industries. L. occupies the site of the Rom. station, Ratae. L. returns 4 members to Parl. Pop. 272,500.

LEIDEN
Town of S. Holland, S.W. Netherlands, 9 m. N.E. of The Hague. L. is famous for its univ. founded 1575. It was besieged by the Sp. (1574). Pop. 98,013.

LEINSTER
[lin-] Prov. of Repub. of Ireland, and covering the E. and S.E. part of the country. It contains 12 counties—Carlow, Dublin, Kildare, Kilkenny, Laoighis, Longford, Louth, Meath, Offaly, W. Meath, Wexford and Wicklow.

LEIPZIG
City in Saxony, E. Germany, 68 m. N.W. of Dresden and 100 S.W. of Berlin. Famous as a musical and educ. centre, L. has museums and theatres, and the univ. founded 1409. It is a route centre and market town. In 1813, Napoleon was defeated by Russ., Aust. and Pruss. forces at L. Pop. 587,226.

LEITH
[lēth] Part of Edinburgh, on the Firth of Forth, 2 m. N. of the city. It has a large harbour, enlarged just before World War I, and extensive docks. The chief industry is shipping; others are distilling, paper-making and the manufacture of chems.

LEITRIM
[lē'-] Co. of Repub. of Ireland, in the prov. of Connaught. There are hills in the N. and E. and the Shannon flows along its S. border. Lough Allen is the largest lake. Agriculture is its staple industry. Carrick-on-Shannon is the county town. Pop. 44,600.

LELY, Sir Peter
[lē'-li] (1618-80) Eng. painter. B. near Utrecht, he settled in London in 1641, became Eng. subject and was made Court Painter by Charles II.

LEMMING
Rodent of the Vole family, *c.* 5 in. long and yellowish-brown, found in Europe, Asia and N. Amer. It lives in the ground like the rabbit and feeds on grass. It is very common in Norway, and migrates periodically. The animals move across country, until they reach the sea, where hosts of them perish by drowning.

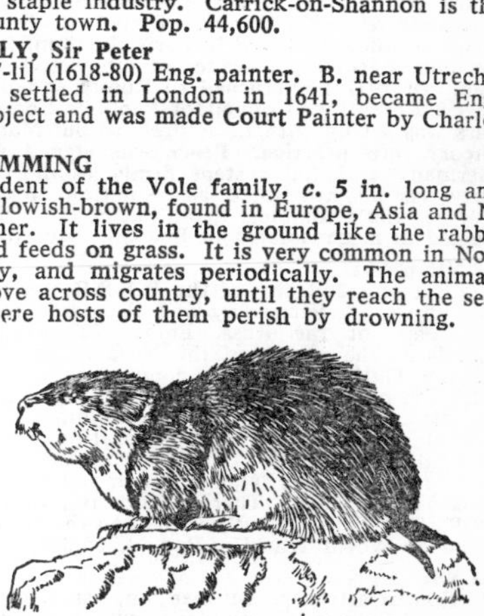

LEMNOS
Gk. Is. in the Aegean Sea, 45 m. from the entrance to the Dardanelles. Fruit and tobacco are grown.

LEMON
Oval fruit of an evergreen tree, a variety of citron (*Citrus medica*). Grown in Italy, Spain, Greece, California, Florida and S. Africa, its yellow rind furnishes candied peel and an essen-

tial oil; its juice is used for lemonade and citric acid, and for cooking and med. purposes.

LEMON GRASS
Tall aromatic grasses, cultivated in the tropics for their essential oils. That sold as E. Indian is distilled from *Andropogon flexuosus*, indigenous to Cochin and Tinavelly; W. Indian comes from *Cymbopogon citratus*, also produced in Ceylon and Malaya.

LEMON SOLE
Flat fish allied to the dab, extensively caught off N. Europe. It is smaller but wider than the ordinary sole. It spawns in the spring and early summer.

LEMUR
[lē'-] Monkey-like mammals with tails, confined to Madagascar and the Comoro Is., once common in Europe and Africa. The head resembles that of the fox and the appearance is something between a cat and a monkey. They live in trees and sleep during the daytime.

LENA
[lā'-nă] River of Siberia, U.S.S.R., 2,648 m. long, which rises in the mts. W. of L. Baikal, and flows N. into the Laptev Sea, a branch of the Arctic Ocean.

LEND-LEASE
Act signed by Pres. Roosevelt (1941), which gave him power to sell, transfer, lend or lease necessary war supplies to nations whose defence was vital to that of the U.S.A. Repayment was to be ' in kind or property, or any other direct or indirect benefit which the Pres. deems satisfactory '. The Lend-Lease Act was extended by Congress in 1943, 1944 and 1945. After the U.S.A. entered the war, ' reverse lend-lease ' in the form of goods, services, shipping and real estate was given to Amer. forces overseas, under the terms of a Reciprocal Aid Agreement (Sept. 3, 1942) of the U.S.A. with Gt. Brit., Australia, N. Zealand and the Free Fr.

LENIN
(1870-1924) Name taken by the Bolshevist leader **Vladimir Ilyich Ulyanov.** Exiled to Siberia while a student. Lived in Paris, London, Switzerland, becoming a leader of internat. socialism. In 1917 he returned to Russia and overthrew Kerensky. Council of People's Commissars was set up with L. as Pres. to put Marxist theory into practice. Peace was signed with Germany and the system firmly estabd. He survived an attempted assassination in 1918 but became a complete invalid after 1922. He is buried in a mausoleum in Red Sq., Moscow.

LENINGRAD
Seaport and 2nd city of the U.S.S.R. formerly known as St. Petersburg and Petrograd (1914-24), cap. of the Russ. Emp. 1703-1918. It stands at the mouth of the Neva at the head of the Gulf of Finland, connected by canal with the port, Kronstadt, and L. Ladoga. Shipbuilding, metallurgy, textiles, tanning, brick and glass-making and food preparations are the principal industries. L. has some fine buildings, including the famous winter palace overlooking the Neva. There is a univ., founded 1819. The city heroically withstood the German siege of World War II. Pop. 3,300,000.

LENS
Portion of a transparent medium, usually glass, enclosed between 2 boundaries which are parts of spherical or plane surfaces. In passing through a lens light rays are refracted and become more convergent or divergent according to the type of lens. *Convex lenses* cause light to converge and *Concave lenses* produce divergence. The image produced by a single lens has 2 important defects: (a) *Spherical aberration*, which causes straight lines to be curved in the image, and (b) *chromatic aberration*, due to the fact that light of different colours forms images at different points. These can be corrected by the use of 2 or more lenses.

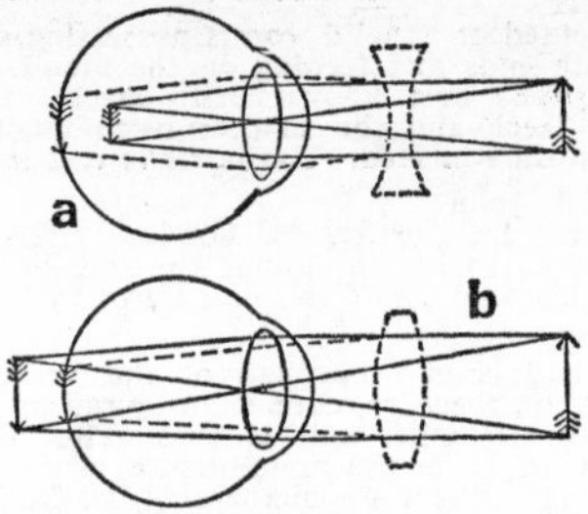

Showing effect of (*a*) *concave and* (*b*) *convex lenses*

LENT
In the Christian year the 40 days just before Easter. It begins on Ash Wed. and is a time of abstinence.

LENTIL
Annual herb of the family *Leguminosae*, growing in the Mediterranean region and bearing single pale-blue flowers.

LEO
(1) Name of one of the constellations, beneath the feet of the Great Bear, it contains important stars, such as Regulus, or α Leonis; the blue star, Denebola, or β Leonis; and the double star, Algieba. (2) In Astrology the 5th sign of the Zodiac (The Lion) operative from July 22-Aug. 21.

LEO I
Leo the Great, Pope 440-461. He combated heresies and strengthened the authority of Rome. He saved the city from Attila and later protected it when it was captured by Genseric and the Vandals.

LEO X
(1475-1521) Pope 1513-21. A son of Lorenzo the Magnificent, of the Medici family, b. Rome, he was chosen Pope in 1513. He was the typical Pope of the Renaissance. His chief interests were art and lit. The Reformation began during his reign.

LEÓN
[lā-on'] Former kingdom of N.W. Sp. which united with Castile, 1230. Its cap. was L. and it included the cities of Salamanca and Valladolid. Modern León is a prov. S. of the Cantabrian Mts. **León.** City and cap. of L. prov. in mountainous country, *c.* 175 m. N.W. of Madrid, with a fine Gothic cath. (1199). Pop. 77,430.

LEON, Luis de
(1527-1591) Sp. poet and mystic. He joined the Augustinian order. He was denounced to the Inquisition and imprisoned, 1572-6, then released with admonition.

LEONCAVALLO, Ruggiero
[lā-on-ka-val'-ō] (1858-1919) Ital. composer. *I Pagliacci*, produced in Milan in 1892, had an enormous success, never attained by any other of his works.

LEONIDAS
[lē-on'-] King of Sparta, leader of the small band of Spartans who defended the Pass of Thermopylae against the Persians. He was killed in the pass in 480, with *c.* 1,000 followers.

LEOPARD
Felis pardus. One of the ' great cats ' of Africa and Asia, notable for its spots. The average length is *c.* 4 ft. The leopard preys by night on dogs, goats and monkeys, but does not usually attack man. It can climb trees. In India, the

true leopard is called panther; the word leopard is reserved for the cheetah.

LEOPOLD I
(1790-1865) King of the Belgians. Son of the Duke of Saxe-Coburg-Gotha, he became a soldier and fought against Napoleon. In 1816 he mar. Charlotte, only child of George IV. In 1831 he was chosen the 1st King of the Belgians. He reigned for 34 years and did much to make Belgium peaceful and prosperous. He was on friendly terms with Queen Victoria.

LEOPOLD II
(1835-1909) King of the Belgians. The elder son of Leopold I, b. in Brussels, he served in the army. He became king in 1865 and ruled, on the whole, successfully, although his management of the Congo Free State was not universally approved. Succeeded by his nephew.

LEOPOLD III
(1901-) King of the Belgians. Son of King Albert (*q.v.*), he mar. Princess Astrid of Sweden 1926 (d. 1935), and succeeded to throne 1934; as C.-in-C. Belgian Armed Forces, May, 1940, he capitulated to the Germans. Throne held by brother, Prince Charles acting as Regent, until Mar. 1950, when Leopold returned to Belgium. Forced by Govt. to abdicate in favour of his son Baudouin, 1951.

LEOPOLDVILLE
River port and cap. of the Congolese Rep. on the Congo. Renamed Kinshasa. Pop. *c.* 900,000.

LEPIDOPTERA
Order of insects characterised by butterflies and moths, having 4 wings covered with imbricating scales, and sucking mouth parts. Larvae called caterpillars emerge from the eggs. The caterpillars change into immobile pupae or chrysalises frequently protected by webs. The image or perfect insect emerges from the pupa.

LEPIDUS, Marcus Aemilius
(*c.* 74-13 B.C.) Rom. soldier and triumvir. Supported Caesar, who made him Dictator of Rome and Consul. In 43, after Caesar's murder, he ruled with Mark Anthony and Octavian.

LEPROSY
A chronic infectious disease caused by a germ called *mycobacterium leprae* (discovered in 1874 by Hansen). Mosaic law has references to it. In the M.A. leper houses were provided in Europe and Asia for sufferers with the disease. The disease is found nowadays in Egypt, Asia, Africa, W. Indies and in the Pacific Is. Leper colonies have been estabd. where patients are treated. Two forms of the disease exist—the *nodular* type which affects the skin and the *nervous* type which attacks the nerves. It is spread by intimate contact, but it can affect any organ of the body.

LERWICK
[ler′-wick] Chief town and seaport of the Shetland Is. on mainland, with a fishing industry. Pop. 5,977.

LESOTHO
See BASUTOLAND.

LESSEPS, Ferdinand de
(1805-94) Fr. engineer. In 1849 he began his work on the Suez Canal, and supervised the work until the opening in 1869.

LESSING, Gotthold Ephraim
(1729-81) German author and critic. B. Saxony, son of a Lutheran clergyman. Set down his ideas on poetry in *Lakoon*, and on drama in *Hamburg Dramaturgy*. Apptd. playwright to theatre at Hamburg, 1767. His plays include *Nathan the Wise*, *Minna von Barnheim*, etc.

LETCHWORTH
Urban district of Herts. near Hitchin. The first Eng. garden city was laid out, 1903. Pop. 26,000.

LETTUCE
Hardy annual herb. Cultivated as a vegetable, it was brought to Eng. from Flanders in the 16th cent.

LEUCITE
[loo′-] Rock-forming mineral. It consists of a silicate of potassium and aluminium and is found in lavas in the vicinity of Vesuvius, Capo di Bove, near Rome, and in the basaltic rock of the Eifel.

LEUCOTOMY, PREFRONTAL
[lew-kot′-o-mi] Brain operation performed to give relief in certain serious mental disorders, esp. severe schizophrenia.

LEVANT
Name used for the coastal regions of the E. Med. counties, *i.e.* Turkey, Syria, Lebanon and Israel.

LEVELLERS
Polit. and religious party that arose in Eng. during the Civil War. Their leader was John Lilburne and their radically democratic ideas were set out in *The Agreement of the People.*

LEVERHULME, Viscount
[-hyōōm] **William Hesketh Lever** (1851-1925) Eng. manufacturer and philanthropist. B. Bolton. Started the Lever soap business which became a £50,000,000 concern. Estabd. the town of Port Sunlight and was Lib. M.P. for Wirral (1906-10). In 1918 bought Is. of Lewis but failed to estab. a fishing industry there.

LEVERRIER, Urbain Jean Joseph
(1811-77) Fr. astron. With John C. Adams he discovered the planet Uranus.

LEVITES
One of the 12 tribes of Israel. Its male members were set aside to assist the priests in the service of the temple. No definite piece of territory was allotted to them in the Promised Land.

LEVITICUS
Book of the O.T. It comprises the legal and ceremonial institutions regulating the sanctuary service of the Israelites.

LEWES
[loo′-is] Borough and county town of E. Sussex, on the Ouse, 50 m. S. of London, it is an agricultural centre and has a racecourse. Pop. 14,000.

LEWIS
Largest Is. of the Outer Hebrides, Harris (*q.v.*) being in the S.; 30 m. from the mainland. The surface is chiefly moorland with sea lochs; some hills in the S. rise to a height of 1,750 ft. The coast is rugged. Fishing is important, and oats and potatoes are grown. Stornoway is the chief town and port.

LEWIS, Clive Staples
(1898-1963) Eng. writer. Fellow of Magdalen Coll. 1925. He wrote critical works on Eng. Lit. (*The Allegory of Love*, 1936, *Preface to Paradise Lost*, 1942), and much popular theology, some in allegorical form.

LEWIS, Matthew Gregory
(' Monk ') (1775-1818) Eng. writer, best-known for the horrific novel *The Monk* (1796); also *Tales of Terror* and *Tales of Wonder*.

LEWIS, Wyndham
(1884-1957) Author and artist. Founder and leader of Vorticist movement, which arose out of Cubism. Controversial writer on philosophic and polit. themes.

LHASA
[lā′sa] Cap. of Tibet, 12,000 ft. above sea level, 390 m. N.E. of Darjeeling. The sacred city of Lamaism, it is called the Forbidden City and until 1904 only one Englishman had visited it. Pop. *c.* 25,000.

LIANA
General name for long climbing plants in trop. and sub-trop. forests. Usually woody and rooted in the ground, they attach themselves by aerial roots and tendrils to other vegetation.

LIBEL
Writing or otherwise issuing anything that may damage a person's business or reputation. In Eng. law it is also a libel to pub. anything of a seditious nature.

LIBERAL
In politics, one who is in favour of wide individual freedom and against concentration of power. In Brit. the **Liberal Party** developed from the Whigs and took the name early in the 19th cent. In the 50 years after the Reform Bill of 1832 it was the dominant party. Its leaders were Earl Grey, Earl Russell, Lord Palmerston and W. E. Gladstone. In 1885 the party was divided over Home Rule for Ireland and was out of office, except during 1892-5, until 1905. It then had a spell of office lasting 10 years and covering the early days of World War I. When the war ended the Lib. party was weak and divided, but its work was, for the time, done; many of the reforms on its programme had been carried out. Its decay was hastened by the growth of the Lab. party which, in 1922, supplanted it as the official opposition. The Lib. party has since steadily declined and has suffered from defections. In 1932 those who stayed with the Nat. Govt. became the **Nat. Libs.**, acting in alliance with the Cons. party. Over 470 candidates stood for parl. in the 1950 election, but only 8 were returned, in 1964, 9 and, in 1966, 12 were returned.

LIBERIA
Indep Negro repub. of W. Africa on the Atlantic coast, between Sierra Leone and the Ivory Coast. The land rises from the narrow coastal plain to a forested plateau. Rice, cassava, sugar cane and coffee are cultivated. Rubber, palm oil and crude gold are the chief exports. Monrovia is the cap. and chief seaport. L. was founded, 1820, by the Amer. Colonisation Soc. as a home for freed Negro slaves, and has been indep. since 1847. It is gov. by a Pres. and council of mins. with a legislature of 2 houses. Eng. is the official language. Amer. influence is strong; during World War II air bases were constructed by the U.S. Area: 43,000 sq.m. Pop. 1,300,000.

LIBERTY, STATUE OF
Bronze figure (height *c.* 150 ft.; wt. *c.* 225 tons) on Bedloe's Island in New York harbour. Made by Bartholdi, it was presented by the people of France to the people of the U.S. on the hundredth anniversary of Amer. indep., 1886.

LIBRA
(1) Seventh zodiacal constellation, represented by the Roman scalebeam, indicating equal nights and days at the autumnal equinox. (2) Astrology (The Balance), sign operative from Sept. 22-Oct. 22.

LIBYA
Country of N. Africa with a coastline on the Medit. bounded on the W. by Algeria and Tunisia, and on the E. by Egypt. There are 3 regions; the Medit. coastal zone, the sub-desert, and the desert of the interior. Rainfall is uncertain. Agriculture can be practised only in the coastal region, although there are fertile oases inland. Sheep, goats, cattle and camels are reared, and cereals, dates, lemons, oranges and olives are produced. Sponge and tunny fishing, and the preparation of tobacco and salt are important. The chief towns are Tripoli, Benghazi, Misurata and Homs, all on the coast. Inland, caravans are the chief means of transport. L. was a Turkish possession from 1835 until 1911, when Ital. forces occupied the area. After the Axis troops were expelled in 1943, Tripoli and Cyrenaica were placed under Brit. milit. admin. The U.K. of Libya was proclaimed an indep. sovereign state on 24th Dec. 1951, with Idris el Senussi, Emir of Cyrenaica, as king. In 1963 Beida on the coast became cap. Proclaimed socialist repub., 1969, after overthrow of king by military junta. Area: 679,358 sq.m. Pop. 1,700,000.

LICENCE
Permission by the state to enjoy a certain privilege. Today it is the usual way by which the state controls trades and privileges, and is a source of revenue. The word has a special connection with the sale of intoxicating liquors, which must be only by licence. Licences are necessary to enable one to keep a dog, drive a motor car, sell tobacco, possess a wireless receiving or television set, act as a moneylender or pawnbroker and own a gun.

LICHEN
[lī'-ken] Compound plant organism consisting of 2 symbiotic partners, a fungus and an alga. The fungal element belongs to the Ascomycete group; green algal cells become enveloped in the fungal threads. Form incrustations, foliaceous or branching masses on rocks, etc.

LICHEN
A disease affecting the skin, sometimes called 'dry itch' because of the extreme itch and burning sensation which is present.

LICHFIELD
City and borough of Staffs., an agricultural centre. The cath. was begun in the 12th cent. Pop. 15,350.

LIDGETT, John Scott
(1854-1953) Eng. divine. He entered the Wesleyan ministry in 1876. He assisted in the foundation of the Bermondsey Settlement, 1891. He was Leader of the Progressive Party on the L.C.C. 1918-28. Pres. of the Uniting Conference of the Methodist Churches and first Pres. of the United Church, 1932.

LIE, Trygve
[lē] (1896-1968) Norwegian politician and lawyer. B. Oslo. An active member of the L. Party and a Trade Unionist, he was the first Sec. Gen. of the U.N. 1946-53.

LIECHTENSTEIN
[lēch'-] Small principality of Europe on the Upper Rhine between Aust. and Switzerland. It is an agricultural country. Vaduz is the cap. Before World War I, L. was closely assoc. with Aust. but since 1924 it has been included in the Swiss Customs' Union. The language is German. Area: *c.* 62 sq.m. Pop. 18,000.

LIÈGE
[le-e'-zh] City of Belg., cap. of L. prov. on the Meuse, 55 m. S.E. of Brussels, a centre of iron and steel manufacturing. Pop. 446,414.

LIFE PEERS
The Life Peerage Act of 1958 empowered the Sovereign to confer a barony for life which entitles the recipient to sit and vote in the House of Lords, and expires on his or her d.

LIFEBOAT
Boat designed for saving life at sea. It is exceptionally seaworthy, and frees itself automatically of any water that comes aboard. A lifeboat built of glass fibre was perfected in 1957. The first lifeboat was that of Henry Greathead, built 1789. By 1824, when the Royal Nat. Lifeboat Inst. was founded, there were 40 boats in use. The first steam lifeboat was put into service in 1890; the first motor lifeboat in 1904. The Royal Nat. Lifeboat Inst., supported by voluntary contributions, controls the lifeboat service of the country, and operates 200 boats. The term is also used for open boats carried for emergency use on ships, and for the easily inflated rubber dinghy carried for the same purpose by aircraft.

LIFFEY
River of Ireland, on which Dublin stands. It rises in the mts. of Wicklow and flows through counties Kildare and Dublin to the sea.

LIGHT
Electro-magnetic vibration of wavelength between 4,000 and 8,000 Å.U. approx. It causes the sensation of sight by its action upon the eye. The speed at which light travels is about 186,000 m. per sec. Newton was the first to demonstrate that a beam of sunlight, when transmitted through a prism, is broken up into a spectrum, the colours being red, orange, yellow, green, blue, indigo and violet. It is now known that beyond the red end of the spectrum are invisible heat or **infra-red** rays, and similarly beyond the violet end, other invisible ultra-violet rays. For measuring the distance of the stars from the earth, a **light year** is taken as the unit. This is the distance travelled by light in a year and is calculated at 6 million million miles (6,000,000,000,000). *See* RELATIVITY.

LIGHTHOUSE
Building provided with powerful illumination to guide ships in dangerous waters. Lighthouses are built either on the coast or on a rock, and usually take the form of a tower or high building surmounted by a 'lantern'. **Lightship.** Vessel used for giving warning of sandbanks and other dangers to navigation on the coast. Moored in shoal water it bears at its masthead a form of lantern as a warning signal.

LIGHTING
For purposes of illumination, candles, rush lights and oil lamps were early devices. With the invention of the Argand burner in 1783 and the introduction of petroleum, greater efficiency was obtained. From the 19th cent. coal gas was used; the invention of the Welsbach incandescent mantle in 1886 giving a marked increase in lighting power. A further advance came with the use of electric arc lamps and the introduction of the incandescent electric bulb by Edison and Swan in 1879 and 1880. *See* ELECTRICITY; COAL GAS; FLUORESCENT LIGHTING.

LIGHTNING
Flash due to an electrical discharge between 2 clouds or between clouds and the earth. *Sheet lightning* is a reflection of a distant discharge or of lightning below the horizon. *Ball lightning* is a slower moving globular form. **Lightning Conductor.** Appliance attached to buildings for discharging gradually the electrification of clouds, thereby avoiding a lightning stroke to the building.

LIGNUM VITAE
[-vē′-tī] Trop. Amer. evergreen tree *Guaiacum officale* called 'wood of life', because of its med. repute. The tough, unsplittable, greenish-black heartwood contains ¼ resin.

LIGURIA
Region of N. Italy S. of Piedmont, adjacent to Fr., with a coastline on the Ligurian Sea.

LILAC
Genus of hardy deciduous shrubs of the olive family, natives of S.E. Europe and temp. Asia (*Syringa*).

LILLE
[lēl] City of N. Fr., cap. of Nord dept. on the Deule, 115 m. N. of Paris. Industries include the manufacture of iron and steel goods and textiles. Pop. 195,000.

LILY
(*Lilium*) Genus of herbs with scaly bulbs. Natives of N. temp. regions, the flowers comprise 6 free perianth-segments, the anthers being on slender filaments. One of the oldest in cultivation is the Medit. white Madonna lily; the E. Asian dark-spotted, orange-red, tiger lily is either single or double flowered; the Japanese yellow-banded white *L. auratum* may be 6-10 in. across. The S. European purple martagon or turk's cap and the Bermuda white Easter lily are other favourites. *See* DAFFODIL.

LILY OF THE VALLEY
(*Convallaria majalis*) Perennial plant of the family Liliceae. The white bell-like flowers spring on erect stems from oval green leaves and have a delicious fragrance.

LIMA
[lē′-mǎ] Cap. of Peru, on a fertile plain 7 m. from its port, Callao. Once the cap. of Sp. S. Amer., Lima has a univ. Pop. 1,715,971.

LIME
Oxide of calcium, or quicklime. It is a white substance obtained by heating to redness limestone or marble. It readily absorbs water, evolving heat, and finally crumbles to a soft bulky powder known as slaked lime or calcium hydroxide, which is soluble in water. Lime is used in the making of mortar and cements, and as a soil dressing in agriculture.

LIME
(*Tilia*) Genus of timber trees of the lime family, natives of N. temp. regions. The leaves are heart-shaped, oblique and saw-toothed; the nectared flowers attract bees. Small-leaved and taller large-leaved subspecies grow wild in Brit. The common European lime or linden, *T. europaea*, furnishes useful white wood.

LIME FRUIT
Yellow, round or oval, thin-rinded fruit of 2 cultivated varieties of the citron, native to Asia. Sour limes, regarded as *Citrus medica*, var. *acida*, yield commercial lime-juice, citric acid and an essential oil, W. Indian being preferred.

LIMERICK
Co. of Eire, in the prov. of Munster. It is mainly level, with the Galtee Mts. in the S.E. Farming is the main occupation. The chief rivers are the Shannon, which forms the N. boundary, and its tribs. Limerick, the county town and chief port on the W. coast, exports dairy produce. Pop. 133,339.

LIMESTONE
Rocks whose chief constituent is carbonate of lime. When pure, a limestone is white. Examples of limestones are chalk, dolomite and marble.

LIMOGES
[lē-mōzh] City of Fr., cap. of Haute-Vienne dept., *c.* 250 m. S. of Paris, on the Vienne, famous for its porcelain. Pop. 120,596.

LIMPET
Widely distributed marine gasteropod molluscs with conical shells. The common limpet (*Patella*) clings to rocks with its sucker-like foot. It feeds upon seaweed. Millions are collected annually for bait. *See* GASTEROPODA.

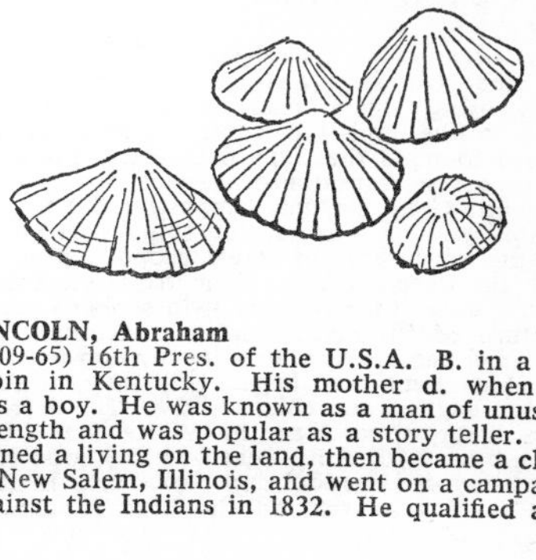

LINCOLN, Abraham
(1809-65) 16th Pres. of the U.S.A. B. in a log cabin in Kentucky. His mother d. when he was a boy. He was known as a man of unusual strength and was popular as a story teller. He earned a living on the land, then became a clerk at New Salem, Illinois, and went on a campaign against the Indians in 1832. He qualified as a

lawyer in 1836, and began to practise at Springfield in 1837. In 1834 he was elected to the legislature of Illinois, where he became leader of his party. In 1847 he was elected to the House of Representatives at Washington. The Republican party was formed to prevent any extension of the slave holding area; Lincoln soon became its leader in Illinois and continued a series of debates with Stephen A. Douglas, begun in 1839-40. He was nominated for the presidency and in 1860 was elected. In 1861 the S. States seceded and the Civil War began, the N. States being under Lincoln's direction. In 1863 he announced the emancipation of the slaves. In 1864 he was again elected Pres. In April, 1865, Lee surrendered, and the N. was finally victorious. The Union was saved and Lincoln's aim in going to war was achieved. Only 5 days later he was shot by J. Wilkes Booth, when at the theatre.

LINCOLNSHIRE
County of Eng. with a long coastline on the N. Sea, from the Humber to the Wash. The principal rivers are the Trent, Witham and Welland. The county is flat and the soil is fertile. Fishing is an industry. In the N. is a coal and iron field, while in the S.E. is the fen district and much reclaimed land round the Wash. Lincoln is the county town; other towns are Grimsby, Boston, Grantham and Sleaford. The whole county returns 9 members to Parl. (2 borough constituencies). Pop. 743,383. **Lincoln.** City, county borough and county town of Lincs. on the Witham. Industries include engineering works and flour mills. The Gothic cath. is magnificent. L. was a Rom. city. It returns 1 member to Parl. Pop. 76,930.

LINDBERGH, Charles
(1902-) Amer. airman. He entered the Airmail Service of the U.S.A. In May, 1927, he was the first to make a W.-E. solo-crossing of the Atlantic, for a prize of £5,000. His monoplane, *The Spirit of St. Louis,* flew from New York to Paris in 33 h. 50 m. Pub. *The Spirit of Saint Louis* (1953), awarded the Pulitzer Prize for 1954.

LINDISFARNE *See* HOLY ISLAND.

LINDSAY, Sir David
of the Mount (1490-1555) Scot. poet. His poems satirise eccles. and polit. abuses of his day: *Ane Satyre of the Three Estaits* (play) (1540), *Dialog betwixt Experience and Ane Courteour* (1552).

LINEN
Textile material made from the fibres of the flax plant, *Linum usitatissimum.* The flax fibres represent the hard bast of the stem and are prepared by retting. The retted straw is broken or scutched in mills. By passing through hackling mills, the short fibres or tow are separated from the long fibres or line which are then spun into yarn for making linen. The chief seat of the industry is N. Ireland.

LINER
Large ocean-going passenger-carrying ship. In 1825 the steamship *Enterprise* reached India. Ships using steam made Atlantic crossings prior to the mid-19th cent. In 1840 Samuel Cunard founded the Cunard Line and there began a regular transatlantic service. In 1844 the iron-built *Great Britain* demonstrated both the suitability of this metal for ship construction and the advantages of screw propulsion. Later came the development of the triple expansion engine, water tube boilers, twin screws and, at the turn of the cent., turbine machinery. By then steel had replaced iron in ship construction and experiments had begun with internal combustion engines and electric drive. The first express luxury liner was the White Star Liner *Oceanic* (*c.* 3,707 tons; speed 14·75 knots) running between Liverpool and New York. In 1893 the Cunard Line secured the Blue Riband of the Atlantic with the *Campania* and *Lucania,* which had a gross tonnage of 12,950 and a speed of 22 k. The Cunard company's *Lusitania* and *Mauretania* were epoch-making ships. Built on the Clyde and Tyne respectively, and launched in 1907, their gross tonnage was *c.* 31,500, and direct coupled turbines driving quadruple screws gave a s.h.p. of 68,000 and a speed of 26·5 k. The *Lusitania* was torpedoed and sunk by a German submarine in 1915, and 1,198 persons lost their lives. The *Mauretania* won the Blue Riband in 1907 and held the honour for 22 years. At the end of World War I (1918) the general trend in designing was towards ships of moderate size and speed, *e.g.* the 5 Cunarders of the *Franconia* type which had a gross tonnage of 20,000 and a speed of 17 k. In 1926, the Compagnie Générale Transatlantique built the *Ile de France* of 43,548 t., s.h.p. 52,000, speed 24 k. The climax of express passenger ships of huge dimensions was reached with the Cunard White Star Line *Queen Mary* and *Queen Elizabeth.* The former was ordered in Dec. 1930. She was launched by Queen Mary in 1934 and entered service in 1936. Of 81,237 t. gross, she is 1,019 ft. long and is driven by geared turbines which give an av. speed of 28·5 k. She has accommodation for 704 first class, 751 cabin and 583 tourist passengers. In Aug. 1938 she made a record W. to E. Atlantic crossing, 2,938 m. in 3 days, 21 hrs. 48 min. at an av. speed of 30·99 k. The return trip was done at an av. speed of 31·69 k. During World War II she served as a troopship, carrying up to 10,500 men per voyage. Her sister ship was launched in 1938 and made a secret voyage to New York in 1940. For 5 years she too served as a troopship. Both ships are now employed on the Southampton-New York service. The fastest liner commissioned since the end of World War II, and the largest ever built in the U.S.A. is the U.S. Line *United States* employed on the New York-Havre-Southampton service. Built in a graving dock, she was floated out in 1951 and sailed from New York on her maiden voyage on July 3rd, 1952. On her outward trip she covered the distance between Ambrose Light and Bishop Rock in 3 days, 10 hrs. 40 min. at an av. speed of 35·59 k., thus winning the Blue Riband of the Atlantic. She is 990 ft. long, has a g.t. of 53,329 and is powered by 4 high pressure steam turbines developing 165,000 h.p. She carries 2,000 passengers and a crew of 1,000. Liners over 20,000 t. built since 1939 include: 1939: *America* (U.S.A.), 26,314 t., *Oranje* (Dutch), 20,166 t.; 1940: *Queen Elizabeth* (Brit.), 83,674 t.; 1952: *United States* (U.S.A.), 53,329 t.; 1961: *Canberra* (Brit.), 45,270 t., *France* (Fr.), 66,000 t.; 1963: *Michelangelo* and *Raffaello* (Ital.), 43,000 t. A new Cunard liner of 58,000 t. is being built on the Clyde.

LING
(*Molva vulgaris*) Food-fish, of the cod family, ranging from Iceland to the Eng. Channel. Dark-grey, lighter beneath, 4-6 ft. long, it is a ground-fish, trawled at 50-100 fathoms in the N. Sea, and line-fished in winter. Salted or dried as Lenten stockfish for C. and S. Europe.

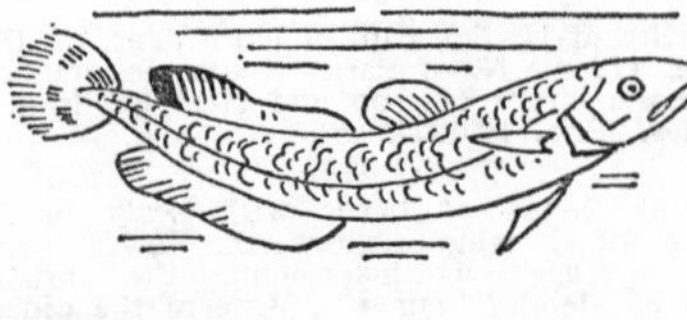

LINLITHGOW
Burgh and county town of W. Lothian, 17 m. W. of Edinburgh. The palace was the birthplace of Mary, Queen of Scots. Pop. 4,562.

LINNAEUS, Carl
[li-nē'-us] (1707-78) Swedish botanist. B. Rashult in Smaland. In 1735 he gained his doctor's degree in Holland, but from 1741 until his d. he was Prof. of Botany at Uppsala. In his most famous works, the *Systema Naturae, Genera Plantarum* and *Bibliotheca Botanica*, Linnaeus laid the foundations of modern botanical nomenclature.

LINNET
Common Brit. resident songbird of finch family, *Carduelis cannabina*. Stout-billed, 5¾ in. long, it is grey, brown or rose according to sex and season. It ranges Europe and W. Asia, wintering southward.

LINSEED
Ripened and dried flax seeds. From the cotyledons are expressed 40 % of a drying oil used for paint, varnish, linoleum, soap and printer's ink. The residual 60 % is pressed into oil-cake for cattle food. Argentina is the world's largest producer.

LINZ
[lints] Cap. of Upper Aust. on the Danube, 95 m. W. of Vienna. An old bridge town with routes running N. and S. across the Danube. Pop. 195,978.

LION
(*Felis leo*) Largest of the great cats, sometimes reaching 10 ft. overall, and surpassing 500 lb. The shaggy mane on the male's head and shoulders distinguishes it from other large Old World cats. Lions prey on Antelope, Zebra and other large mammals, also on cattle and pigs; man-eating is rare. They are found in Africa and parts of Asia, including India.

LIP
Name of fleshy structures above and below the mouth, covering teeth in man and many animals. **Lip Reading.** Interpretation of the speech of others by observing the movements of lips, tongue and facial expression. Mastery of this aid to hearing requires special instruction by experienced personnel over a period of 6 to 12 months. Of very little service in aiding deaf mutes. The Brit. Nat. Inst. for the Deaf recognises as one of its objects the re-educ. of partially deaf people through lip-reading. *See* DEAFNESS; HARE-LIP.

LIPARI
[lē'-pari] Group of Ital. Is. *c.* 20 m. off the N. coast of Sicily. Of volcanic origin, the largest are Lipari, Vulcano, Salina and Stromboli. Sulphur and pumice are produced. Pop. *c.* 25,000.

LIPPI, Fra Filippo
(1412-69) Ital. painter. B. Florence, he became a monk. Living at Padua, Florence, Prato, where he was chaplain in a convent, and elsewhere, he did some painting. His son, **Fra Filippino Lippi** (1460-1504) was equally famous as a painter.

LIQUEUR
[li-kyoor'] Potable spirit, usually sweetened with a distinctive flavouring. Well-known varieties include Kirsch and Maraschino, flavoured with cherries; Kümmel, flavoured with caraway seeds, Bénédictine and green or yellow Chartreuse utilise secret monastic recipes. Apricot, cherry, orange and peach brandy, and sloe gin, are prepared by steeping the fruits.

LIQUORICE
[lik'-ŏris] Brittle, blackish substance (*glycyrrhiza*). It comprises juice from the woody roots of a perennial Medit. leguminous herb. Both this stick liquorice and the peeled root serve as a mild laxative, sweetmeat and flavouring for medicines.

LISBON
[liz'-] (*Port.* **Lisboa**) Cap. city and seaport of Portugal, on the estuary of the Tagus. Situated on low hills, it has a pleasant climate. Interesting buildings include the cath., univ. (1911) and palace, and a marble aqueduct at Alcantara. L. has a fine harbour, and is the financial and distributing centre of the repub. with an important fishing industry. Pop. 1,397,213.

LISTER, Joseph
(1827-1912) A Quaker, b. at Upton House near Plaistow. In 1860 he was elected to the Chair of Surgery in Glasgow and began his work on sepsis, which culminated in the introduction of antiseptic surgery. Later he was elected to the Chair of Surgery in Edinburgh and in 1877 he became Prof. of Clinical Surgery at King's Coll. London. He was elected Pres. of the Royal Soc. (1865) and Pres. of the Brit. Assoc. (1866). He was one of the orig. members of the Order of Merit instituted at the coronation of King Edward VII.

LISZT, Franz
[list] (1811-86) Hungarian composer. In 1848 he became director of music to the Duke of Weimar. All his life he continued to teach and play in every part of Europe. He made many transcriptions for pianoforte as well as writing orig. works for the instrument. Other compositions include symphonic poems, a title he was the first to use, 2 symphonies, 2 piano concertos, choral works, songs and works for organ.

LITHIUM
A soft white element, the lightest known metal, discovered by Arfvedson in 1817. Sp. gr. 0·53. Chem. sym. Li.

LITHUANIA
Constituent repub. of the U.S.S.R. on the Baltic coast, bounded by Latvia, White Russ., and Poland. It is low-lying, with lakes and swamps. The main river is the Niemen. The chief industries are agriculture and forestry. Vilna (Vilnius) is the cap., other large towns are Kaunas and Memel. L. became a grand duchy in the 14th cent.; in 1569 it was united with Poland, and divided between Russ. and Prussia in the 18th cent. In 1918 it became an indep. repub. but entered the U.S.S.R. in 1940. It was occupied by German forces during World War II, 1941-4. Area: 26,173 sq.m. Pop. 2,713,000.

LITMUS
Colouring matter obtained from various lichens, used as a chem. test for acids and alkalis, as its natural purplish-blue colour is turned red by acids and restored by alkalis.

LITRE *See* TABLES, p. 451

LIVER
Biggest organ in body, wt. 50-60 ozs. It is situated under diaphragm on right side of abdomen and protected by ribs. Main storehouse and cleansing area in body. Rich blood supply from intestinal canal by portal circulation. This circulation carries all products of digestion. The liver stores substances such as glucose, renders harmless poisonous materials and prepares them for excretion. Bile and blood formation are also part of its functions. *See* BILE; JAUNDICE.

LIVER FLUKE
(*Fasciola*) A flat worm which is harmful to sheep and occasionally to horses, cattle and dogs. It causes serious disease called liver rot.

LIVERPOOL
City, county borough and seaport of Lancs. on the estuary of the Mersey. The city grew with the growth of the Amer. colonies and the importation of raw cotton. Now the main industry is shipping, with cotton the chief import. Other industries are the manufacture of cement and chemicals, flour milling, sugar refining and engineering. The univ. was founded 1903. L. returns 9 members to Parl. Pop. 745,230.

LIVERWORT
Flowerless plant of a class (*Hepaticae*) closely allied to mosses.

LIVINGSTONE
Town of Zambia, Africa, North of the Victoria Falls on the Zambezi. Named after the explorer, L. was the admin. cap. of N. Rhodesia until 1935.

LIVINGSTONE, David
(1813-73) Scots missionary and traveller. B. Low Blantyre, Lanarkshire. In 1840, under the auspices of the London Missionary Soc. he went to Bechuanaland, S. Africa. In 1849 Livingstone began his explorations. He travelled down the Zambezi, discovered the Victoria Falls, Nyasa and other lakes. In 1871, he was rescued at Ujiji by Stanley. He d. at Ilala.

LIVY
(59 B.C.-A.D. 17) Rom. historian, b. in Padua. His *History of Rome* was in 142 books, and the 35 books extant cover the period from the founding of the city (753 B.C) until 9 B.C.

LIZARD, The
Most S. point of Eng. in Cornwall, 10 m. S.E. of Helston.

LIZARD
Reptiles belonging to the suborder Lacertilia, found in all temp. and trop. regions. They differ from snakes by having normally 4 limbs, movable eyelids, and united mandibles. The 1,700 species are carnivorous or herbivorous, mostly terrestrial and arboreal, producing either eggs or living young. The Gila monster is the only venomous form. Geckos, chameleons and true lizards form suborders. Of Brit.'s 4 species, the common *Lacerta vivipara*, 7 in. long, and the snake-like Blindworm produce living young; the Sand-lizard, 9 in., is egg-laying.

LLAMA
[lä'-] S. Amer. 2-toed ruminant. Related to Old World camels, but smaller, humpless and woolly-haired. 2 breeds:—*Llama glama* Pre-Columbian Amer. domesticated, now unknown in the wild state, and *L. pacos* the Alpaca.

LLANBERIS
[hlan-ber'-is] Village of Caernarvonshire, 9 m. E. of Caernarvon, near the foot of Snowdon. The Pass of L. rises to over 1,100 ft.

LLANDAFF
[lan'-] Cath. city of Glamorgan. in the county borough of Cardiff, on the Taff.

LLANDUDNO
[hlan-did'-nō] Resort and urban district on the N. coast of Caernarvon. where the Conway flows into the sea. Pop. 17,170.

LLEWELLYN
[loo-el'-in] Name of several Welsh princes. **Llewellyn the Great** (1194-1239) was constantly at war with King John and his son, Henry III. His grandson was the **Prince Llewellyn II** who fought against Edward I. He was beaten and made prisoner, 1276, but later released.

LLOYD GEORGE, David
(1863-1945) **Earl L.G. of Dwyfor.** Welsh statesman. M.P. (Lib.) 1890-1945; Chanc. of Exchequer, 1908-15; Munitions Min. 1915-16; War Sec. 1916; P.M. 1916-22; Earl, 1945. His 1909 budget led to the quarrel with the Lords and to the Parl. Act. He was a supporter of the declaration of war on Germany, but in 1916, dissatisfied with the conduct of the war, resigned and brought Asquith's coalition to an end. He became Premier in a new coalition, which prosecuted the war vigorously, and also negotiated the peace settlement of 1919. He was confirmed in power by an election in 1919, but the withdrawal of the Cons. in 1922 broke up his coalition and left him without a party. Thereafter, Lloyd George was never again in power. His son **Gwilym** (1894-) was a Lib. M.P. 1922-4, 1929-50; Lib.-Cons. M.P. 1951-7; Min. of Food from 1951-4. He was Min. for Welsh Affairs, 1954-7. His daughter **Lady Megan** (1904-66) was a Lib. M.P. 1929-51; deputy leader of Lib. Party, 1949-51; joined Lab. Party in 1955. Lab. M.P. for Carmarthen from 1957.

LLOYDS
An assoc. of underwriters covering marine risks. They distribute shipping intelligence through Lloyds List which is the second oldest paper in Europe. The name is derived from the coffee house kept by Edward Lloyd in the 17th cent.

LOACH
(*Nemachilus barbatulus*) Small fresh water fish of the carp family, which frequents clear shallow streams. It occurs in Eng. and S. Scot. and elsewhere in Europe. There are six barbels on the upper jaw. The **spined loach** or **groundling** (*Cobitis taenia*) is found in Eng.

LOAD LINE
Plimsoll mark placed amidships on the sides of a vessel to show the limit to which loading may be carried. *See* PLIMSOLL.

LOANDA, S. Paulo de
[lō-an'-] or Luanda. Cap. and seaport of Angola (Portuguese W. Africa). Pop. 40,000.

LOBELIA
Large genus of perennial and annual plants, mostly herbs, allied to the Campanulaceae, natives of temp. and warmer regions. The dwarf, *L. erinus*, came from S. Africa.

LOBSTER
Large edible marine crustacean. The head and thorax encased in a skeletal unit. Foremost pair of limbs in the thoracic region developed as pincer-like claws. The common *Homarus*, deep blue in colour when living, bright red after boiling, averages 8-12 lb.; the Amer. var. sometimes reaches 20-23 lb. The larger clawless rock-l. or crawfish, *Palinurus vulgaris*, has a spiny carapace. The smaller Norway-l, *Nephrops norvegicus*, has slender pincers.

LOBWORM
Free-living marine segmented worms found in seashore mud and sand. The common European *Arenicola marina* is a favourite angler's bait.

LOCARNO
Town of Switzerland, on the N. shore of L. Maggiore. **Locarno Pact.** 7 conventions concluded in 1925 by Czechoslovakia, Poland, Germany, Fr., Brit., Belg. and Italy. In the major treaty, the powers individually and collectively guaranteed the common boundaries of Germany, Belgium and Fr. as determined by the Treaty of Versailles; a section of the Rhineland was demilitarised; and these countries agreed not to resort to war against each other unless (1) in self-defence, (2) in the event of a violation of the demilitarisation formula, (3) as a result of action by the League of Nations. The signatories also bound themselves to aid the defending power in case of aggression by another state violating the Pact.

LOCH
Term applied to lakes in mountainous districts and to fiord-like inlets of the sea on the coast

of Scot. By submergence of the lower reaches of the valley the loch may become an inlet of the sea.

LOCKE, John
(1632-1704) Eng. philosopher. B. Wrington, Somerset. He was a Commissioner of the Board of Trade, 1696-1700, when he retired. Locke's philosophical ideas are set out in his *Essay Concerning the Human Understanding*. In this he argues that all our knowledge is the result of experience; our beliefs in good or evil arise largely from the assoc. of ideas. In *On Civil Government* he developed the principle that sovereignty depends upon contract.

LOCKJAW
Popular name for TETANUS (*q.v.*).

LOCOMOTIVES
The steam locomotive has served the world's rlys. for 130 years but is now being replaced by electric and diesel traction. By 1965 the majority of Brit.'s main line trains were hauled by diesel or electric locos. It was in Brit. that the steam loco was first developed. The first public rly. in the world, opened betw. Stockton and Darlington in 1825, was first operated by a Geo. Stephenson loco. As early as 1904 a G.W.R. loco, the 4-4-0 'City of Truro', reached 102·3 m.p.h. near Taunton. In 1937, a streamlined Gresley loco, 'Coronation', hauling the 'Coronation Scot' train between Glasgow and London, attained 114 m.p.h. near Crewe and averaged nearly 80 m.p.h. over the 185 m. between Crewe and Euston. On July 3, 1938, the L.N.E.R. A4 'Mallard' was taken up to a max of 126 m.p.h. for 5 consecutive miles between Peterborough and Grantham, setting an unbroken world record for steam locos. When the rlys. of Gt. Brit. were nationalised after World War II over 400 loco designs were replaced by 11, the largest of which were the 'Britannia' 4-6-2 and the Heavy Freight 2-10-0. Steam locos are generally classed by their wheel arrangements. Thus a loco with a leading four-wheeled bogie, six-coupled driving wheels, and no carrying wheels at the trailing end is a 4-6-0. Among the best known types are: Pacific: 4-6-2; Atlantic: 4-4-2; Mogul: 2-6-0; Prairie: 2-6-2; Consolidation: 2-8-0; Baltic: 4-6-4; and Beyer-Garratt: 2-6-0+0-6-2. An electric loco is a power unit receiving its power either from a third rail or from overhead wires. Diesel train traction usually depends on the use of diesel engines to drive dynamos which make electric current for electric motors which drive the axles as on an electric train. Electric traction on rlys. began towards the end of the 19th cent. Its advantages over steam traction include more rapid acceleration and the elimination of smoke. Many European countries which have steep gradients and cheap hydro-electric power available have built large networks of electric rlys. There are now more than 1,000 daily runs in Fr. at over 62 m.p.h. In March, 1955, 2 Fr. electric locos both attained a max. speed of 205·6 m.p.h. for a new world rail speed record. The luxurious Ital. 'Settebello' runs from Rome to Milan, 393 m., at an av. speed of 67·5 m.p.h. The fastest electric train of all is that from Tokyo to Osaka where electric 'bullet trains' maintain a 100 m.p.h. schedule. By 1967 3,300 h.p. electric locos will be hauling the principal expresses between Liverpool, Manchester, the Midlands and London at up to 100 m.p.h. and, as in other highly populated countries, Brit. has made use of electrification on busy suburban lines. On less heavily-trafficked lines, Gt. Brit. has replaced steam traction by diesel. The diesel 'blue riband' in Brit. is held by the 3,300 h.p. 'Deltic' diesel-electric locos which haul the principal expresses on E. coast routes between London and Edinburgh, maintaining a 6-hour schedule over 393 m. Multiple-unit diesel trains are widely used on suburban and inter-city services. In Amer. diesel traction is used on a large scale. As early as 1935, the 'Comet', a streamlined diesel-electric train of the New York, New Haven and Hartford Railroad exceeded 110 m.p.h. and a 6-car streamlined aluminium diesel-electric train covered the 3,259 m. between Los Angeles and New York in 56 hours, cutting the steam record by over 17 hours. On many of today's long-distance diesel and electric trains, the rlys. are countering the attraction of airliner speeds with comfort and luxury impossible in the air with lounges, bars, restaurants, domed compartments for better visibility and a wide variety of sleeper accommodation.

LOCUST
Name used for several kinds of large short-horned grasshoppers that in a certain phase of their life become gregarious and migrate in large swarms. Among the best known are the African migratory *Locusta migratoria*, the Desert Locust *Schistocerca gregaria* of Africa and Asia, and various species of *Melanoplus* in N. Amer. The adults may carry out a migratory flight of many hundreds of miles, usually in dense clouds. Both the hoppers and the adults are extremely destructive to crops of many kinds. Locust control is one of the most important aspects of economic entomology.

LOCUST BEAN
Pod of the carob tree, grown in Asia Minor and Italy, remarkable for the large proportion of sugar it contains.

LODGE, Sir Oliver Joseph
F.R.S. (1851-1940) Eng. scientist. B. Penkhull, Staffs. As a physicist Lodge was among the first to demonstrate the possibility of wireless communication. Later he gave much attention to the phenomena of spiritualism. His books include *Modern Views of Electricity, Ether and Reality* and *Relativity*.

LODGE, Thomas
(*c.* 1558-1625) Eng. writer of romances (*e.g. Rosalind*, 1590, on which Shakespeare based *As You Like It*).

LOESS
[lō′-es] Yellowish fine-grained, sandy and calcareous loam. It covers large areas in C. and S.E. Europe and China. In the Rhine Valley the deposits are of fluviatile origin, but those in N. China appear to be due to the action of wind.

LOFOTEN
[lŏ-fō′-tēn, loo′-footēn] Group of Is. off the N.W. coast of Norway. The chief occupation is cod-fishing.

LOGANBERRY
Hardy, prickly shrub of the Rosaceae. Derived from the European raspberry and a Calif. blackberry, it was hybridised by Judge Logan, 1881.

LOGARITHMS
(Gk. *Account-number*) Mathematical tabular system invented and compiled in 1614 by the Scot. mathematician John Napier. Logarithms simplify complex arithmetical computations. Thus the operations of multiplication, division, involution or the finding of roots, are changed to those of addition, subtraction, multiplication and division respectively. Logarithms are of 2 kinds. *Common* (which have a *base* of 10) for general use, and *Napierian* (which have a base denoted by small *e*).

LOGIC
Science of reasoning, or the science of the laws of thought. The earliest and most influential system was that laid down by Aristotle in his *Organon*. The study was revived by Abelard and other early scholars and logic has been taught in the univs. since their day. A new direction was given to it by the *Novum Organum* of Francis Bacon.

LOIRE
[lwâr] The longest river of Fr., rising in the Cévennes and flowing past Orléans, Blois, Tours and Nantes to the Atlantic at St. Nazaire. Over 600 m. long, it is famous for the châteaux on its banks.

LOLLARDS
Followers of John Wycliffe. They arose towards the end of the 14th cent., objected to prayers for the dead, celibacy and other ch. ordinances, attacked the wealth and indolence of the clergy and became a polit. party. During the reigns of Richard II and of Henry IV, they were persecuted and some put to d.

LOMBARDS
People of Europe. Their first home was in Germany, but *c.* 470, they conquered much of Italy including the district still called Lombardy. They formed an indep. kingdom, their kings wearing the famous iron crown.

LOMBARDY
Region of N. Italy. It contains lakes Garda, Como, Maggiore and Iseo, and the rivers Po, Oglio and Adda. A fertile area, L. produces flax, wheat, sugar beet and wine. Milan, Bergamo and Cremona are the chief towns. **Lombardy Poplar** (*Populus italica*) Tall ornamental tree of the willow family. Inhabiting Persia and N.W. India from remote ages, reaching 100-150 ft., Lombardy apparently received it in post-classical times.

LOMOND
[lō'-] Largest loch of Scot. in Stirling and Dunbartonshire, overlooked by Ben L., 3,192 ft.

LONDON
Cap. of Eng. and of the Brit. Commonwealth of Nations, a seaport and a financial, manufacturing and trading centre. It stands on the Thames, and has taken over the former County of Middlesex and extends into Surrey, Kent, Herts., Essex and Bucks. The orig. London, still called the City (*q.v.*), occupied *c.* 1 sq.m. on the N. side of the river. Around it is the admin. county of L., now organised as 32 boroughs under the Greater London Council. Manufactures include fancy goods, furniture, clothing and foodstuffs, as well as motor cars and heavy goods. The centre of the country's railway system, it has also an underground system of electric railways. The river below the Tower Bridge has tunnels for foot passengers and vehicles. Important buildings include St. Paul's Cath., Westminster Abbey, Southwark Cath., the R.C. Cath. at Westminster, and St. Margaret's, Westminster. The Houses of Parl. built 1840-50, the orig. House was destroyed by bombs in 1941 but a new chamber was opened in 1950. The Tower of London is unique. Buckingham and St. James's palaces are in the heart of London. The H.Q. of the Bank of Eng., the Guildhall, the Mansion House, the Charterhouse, and other historic buildings are in the city. The largest of the central open spaces is Hyde Park. Hampstead Heath is the largest of scores of open spaces under the control of the L.C.C. A series of bridges across the Thames. London is a great educ. centre. It has a univ. L. is the broadcasting centre of the Brit. Isles. Pop. 7,984,387. L. was first mentioned in A.D. 61, by the Rom. writer Tacitus. In Saxon times it was a small indep. state with its own council. William the Conqueror granted a charter to the burgesses. In 1191 the first mayor was appointed. By a clause in *Magna Carta* L. retained its old privileges. The **City of L.** is governed by the Corporation of L. acting through the Common Council, which consists of the Lord Mayor, 25 other Aldermen and 159 Common Councilmen. Area: 677 acres. Pop. 4,610. The **County of London** includes the City of L. and 32 metropolitan boroughs created under the London Government Act, 1963.

LONDON, University of
Founded 1836, it was an examining body only. Later it became a teaching body also and in 1900 was reorganised. In 1878 it threw open all degrees to women, the first Brit. univ. to do so.

LONDON GAZETTE
The organ of the Brit. Govt. The first Brit. newspaper, it came into existence under the title *Oxford Gazette* while the court was resident in Oxford during the Great Plague of London (1665-6) and took its present title when the court returned to London. The *Gazette* is the official publication for state proclamations, orders in council, diplomatic and other appointments, and advertisements required by Statute.

LONDON MISSIONARY SOCIETY
Formed 1795 by **Thomas Haweis** and **David Bogue**, Congregationalists. Socs. in Edinburgh and Glasgow followed, 1796, and in the Netherlands, 1797.

LONDON PRIDE
Hardy perennial herb of the Saxifragaceae, native in Ireland and S.W. Europe (*Saxifraga umbrosa*). Naturalised throughout Brit.

LONDONDERRY
Co. of N. Ireland, in the prov. of Ulster, with a coastline on the N. The land is fairly level except in the S. The Roe, Foyle and Bann are the chief rivers. Londonderry is the county town; other towns are Coleraine, Limavady and Dungiven. The old name of the county was Derry, London was prefixed to it, 1609. L. returns 1 member to Parl. Pop. 113,600. **Londonderry.** County town on the Foyle, 95 m. N.W. of Belfast. Industries include flour milling, and linen manufacturing. It resisted the troops of James II, 1689. Scene of politic.-relig. disturbances 1969- . Pop. 55,000.

LONDONDERRY, Marquess of
Title held by the family of Vane-Tempest-Stewart. The best-known holder was **Viscount Castlereagh** (*q.v.*).

LONG ISLAND
Is. of the U.S.A. forming part of New York state. It lies off the E. coast, separated from the mainland by L.I. Sound, and is chiefly a pleasure resort for New York. On it are Brooklyn and Coney Is.

LONGFELLOW, Henry Wadsworth
(1807-82) Amer. poet. B. Portland, Maine. In 1836 he became prof. of modern languages at Harvard. His narrative poems are *Evangeline* (1847), *The Golden Legend* (1851), *Song of Hiawatha* (1855).

LONGFORD
County of Eire, in the prov. of Leinster. The Shannon and L. Ree form its boundary, and the chief river is the Camlin. The soil is fertile except in the N. where there are bogs; cattle and horses are reared. Pop. 30.643. **Longford.** County town 75 m. N.W. of Dublin, on the Camlin. Pop. 4,000.

LOOM
Machine used for weaving textile fabrics. In the simplest form of weaving, one set of threads running the whole length of the fabric and known as the warp, is manipulated so as to pass alternately over and under a crosswise set known as the weft. The power loom was introduced by Cartwright in 1785-7, and a further improvement was effected when automatic action was introduced by Jacquard, *c.* 1801.

LOOSESTRIFE
Perennial herbaceous plant of the family Lythraceae. The purple l. (*Lythrum salicaria*) is common on river banks and in marshy places. Another genus *Lysimachia vulgaris* (Primulaceae) is the yellow loosestrife.

LORCA, Federigo Garcia
(1899-1936) Sp. poet. B. Fuente Vaqueros; friend of composer De Falla. He pub. poems 1921-30: *Lament for the Death of a Bull-Fighter* (1935); and tragedies *Yerma* (1934). *Doña Rosita la Soltera* (1935).

LORD ADVOCATE
Chief law officer of the crown in Scot. His office is in Edinburgh and he is responsible for public prosecutions in Scot.

LORD CHAMBERLAIN
Officer in the royal household of Gt. Brit. He ranks immediately next to the lord steward. The lord chamberlain also acts as the censor of plays.

LORD CHIEF JUSTICE
Pres. of the queen's bench division of the high court of justice. He ranks next to the lord chancellor. In the U.S.A. the supreme court is under a chief justice.

LORD LIEUTENANT
Official who represents the sovereign in each of the counties of Eng., Wales, Scot. and N. Ireland. Formerly they raised men for defending the country. He is appointed for life. He is also the keeper of the records, or *custos rotulorum*, for the county.

LORD MAYOR
Title of the chief magistrate in London, York, and other cities of Eng. and Wales. London has had a lord mayor since early times; he is elected every year from among the aldermen. During his term of office he lives at the Mansion House. The day of his instalment, Nov. 9, is marked by a procession through the streets of London, called the Lord Mayor's Show, which has been held since 1215.

LORD OF THE ISLES
Title borne by the rulers of the W. Isles of Scotland. It was first conferred by David I of Scot. on Somerled of Argyll, 1135. The title passed to the MacDonalds of Islay in 1346, was forfeited to the Scot. crown in 1493.

LORDS, House of
Upper House of the legislature of Brit.; also the supreme court of law. It arose from the council of barons summoned by the king to advise him on affairs of state. After a time the greater barons separated themselves from the lesser barons and the commons, and with the bishops and abbots became the House of Lords. Today the house consists of two classes, the lords temporal and the lords spiritual. The former are divided into dukes, marquesses, earls, viscounts and barons. The latter consists of the 2 archbishops and 24 bishops. In addition there are a few law lords who are peers for life only and Life Peers and Peeresses created under the Life Peerages Act, 1958. The basis of membership is heredity, but there are also 16 representative Scots peers, chosen by their fellows, and 28 Irish peers, whose places are not filled as they die. Each other member, save only the bishops and the law lords, is the holder of an hereditary title, which carries with it the right to a seat in the House of Lords. Under the Peerage Act, 1963, peers may renounce their titles. The speaker, or chairman of the House, is the Lord Chancellor. In 1911, by the Parl. Act, the House was made subordinate to the House of Commons. Now it can only delay, not utterly reject, legislation passed by the Commons.

LORD'S
Cricket ground in St. John's Wood, London, which belongs to the M.C.C. (Marylebone Cricket Club) and is regarded as the H.Q. of the game.

LORD'S PRAYER
Model of prayer given by Jesus to his disciples (Matt. 6, Luke 11). The R.V. omits Matthew's doxology, a liturgical addition of Jewish origin. The prayer appeared in early Christian liturgies.

LORETO
Famous place of pilgrimage in Italy, 15 m. S. of Ancona.

LORIENT
[lori-â(ng)'] Port and naval station of W. Fr. in Morbihan dept., 30 m. W. of Vannes. Formed in 1664 by the Fr. E. Ind. Co. Pop. 63,924.

LORRAINE
District of E. Fr. between Luxembourg and Alsace. It formed part of the district of Alsace-Lorraine (*q.v.*) L. owes its name to Lothair who was its first king, in the 9th cent. It was seized by Fr. but later became part of Germany. Soon it passed under the control of Fr. and its dukes were subject to the King of Fr. Their line died out 1736, when Stanislaus, the exiled King of Poland and the father-in-law of Louis XV, was made duke. He d. 1766, and the duchy passed to Fr. who retained it until 1871. The chief town is now Metz, and the chief river the Moselle.

LORY
Subfamily of Austromalayan brush-tongued parrots. The purple-capped, red-tailed *Lorius domicella* of the Moluccas, with yellow gorget, fruit-eating and honey-eating, is frequently tamed for its unrivalled ventriloquism.

LOS ANGELES
[an'-ji-lēz] City of S. Calif. on the coastal plain, backed by mts. Water is brought by aqueduct from the hills, and electricity is generated. It is the 4th city of the U.S.A. and is known chiefly for the film industry centred in Hollywood. There is a large trade in fruit. There is a univ. Pop. 2,479,000.

LOTHIAN
District of Scot. which stretched from the Cheviot Hills to the Forth. The Lothians now include the 3 counties of Linlithgow or West L., Edinburgh or Midlothian and Haddington or East L.

LOTUS
Classical name of various plants, *e.g.* the jujube tree assoc. with the lotus-eaters, and the sacred water lilies, *Nymphaea lotus*, of Egypt and *Nelumbium speciosum* of India. It is also the name of a large cosmopolitan genus of leguminous herbs and undershrubs.

Egyptian Lotus

LOUIS
[loo'-ē] Name of 3 kings of Bavaria, also known as Ludwig. **Louis II** (1845-86) became king in 1864. Interested in art and music, he neglected affairs of state. He was the patron of Wagner. Later his mind gave way, and in 1886 a regent was apptd. **Louis III** (1845-1921) a son of the regent, Luitpold, succeeded his father as regent for the insane king Otto (1912), and in 1913 became king. Compelled to abdicate in 1918.

LOUIS
Name of 18 kings of Fr. The first 5 were de-

scendants of Charlemagne. Louis VII, of the Capet family, reigned 1137-80. He was the rival of Henry II of Eng., who mar. his divorced wife, Eleanor of Aquitaine. **Louis IX** (1214-70) called St. Louis. He was a son of Louis VIII and Blanche of Castile. In 1226 he became king. When he came of age he went to war with Henry III of Eng. From 1248-54 he was absent on a crusade. In the next 16 years he won his reputation as a law giver and a saint, having estabd. the Sorbonne Univ. in Paris, issued a new code of laws and set up courts of justice. He was canonised in 1290. **Louis XI** (1423-83) Son of Charles VII, he became king in 1461 and reigned for 22 years. At home he made the crown stronger and the nobles weaker; abroad he was occupied with wars and intrigues with Charles the Bold and Edward IV of Eng. In 1468 he was taken prisoner by Charles, but released 3 days later. Louis has won fame as one of the craftiest of kings. **Louis XII** (1462-1515) Son of Charles, Duke of Orléans. He mar. a daughter of Louis XI, and took some part in politics and in war, being later recognised as heir to the childless king Charles VIII, whom he succeeded in 1498. Louis reigned for 16 years, some of which were spent warring in Italy. Louis mar., as his 2nd wife, Anne, Duchess of Brittany, and as his 3rd, Mary, daughter of Henry VII of Eng. He left no sons, and his successor was Francis I. **Louis XIII** (1601-43) A son of Henry IV and Mary de Medici, he became king at the age of 9. His mother acted as regent. In his personal reign of over 25 years he was overshadowed by his min. Richelieu, who took office in 1624 and directed the affairs of state. Risings of the Huguenots were put down firmly. Later, Fr. went to the help of the Protestants in the Thirty Years' War. Louis mar. Anne, daughter of Philip III of Spain. Their sons were Louis XIV and Philip, Duke of Orléans. **Louis XIV** (1638-1715) A son of Louis XIII and Anne of Austria, he came to the throne in 1643. In his long reign of 72 years he exercised enormous influence upon politics, art, lit. and fashion. During the earlier part of his reign he greatly extended the area of Fr. He surrounded himself with pomp and was called 'le roi soleil' and 'le grand monarque'. He built Versailles. Louis mar. Maria Theresa, a Spanish Princess, and after her d., Madame de Maintenon. He was succeeded by his great-grandson Louis XV. **Louis XV** (1710-74) Son of Louis, Duke of Burgundy, who was a grandson of Louis XIV. For much of his reign Fr. was at war with Brit. and other European powers. The king exercised little influence on affairs of state; and inefficiency of the governmental machinery, plus reckless extravagance and the expense of wars, brought Fr. to the verge of bankruptcy and revolution. He had many mistresses, notably Madame de Pompadour. **Louis XVI** (1754-93) B. Versailles, he was a son of the dauphin Louis who d. in 1765. In 1774 he succeeded his grandfather as king, having 4 years before mar. Marie Antoinette, a member of the great Hapsburg family. In 1789 the revolution began. In June, 1791, he escaped from Paris to Varennes, but was captured and brought back. Until Sept. 1792, he reigned as a constitutional king, but the office was then abolished and Louis was tried, condemned and guillotined as Louis Capet. The king left a son, known as Louis XVII, and a daughter. **Louis XVII** (1785-*c*. '95) King of Fr. in name only. A son of Louis XVI. He was put in prison with the other members of the royal family. He was alleged to have d. in the Temple, Paris, then a prison, June 8, 1795. Several pretenders came forward, claiming to be the dauphin. **Louis XVIII** (1755-1824) A brother of Louis XVI. In 1795, when the prince, nominally Louis XVII, d. he proclaimed himself king. In 1814 as the head of the Bourbons he was recalled to Fr. and became king, but was soon forced to flee; in 1815 he returned and reigned until his d. His successor was his brother, Charles X.

LOUIS PHILIPPE
[loo′-ē] (1773-1850) Eldest son of the Bourbon, Philip, Duke of Orléans, known as Egalité. When the Fr. Revolution began he followed his father in renouncing his titles and joining the revolutionary army. In 1794, he fled from the country. In 1815 he returned to Fr. and in 1839 on the deposition of Charles X, was chosen King. He was known as the Citizen King. At first his rule was successful, but the Industrial Revolution stimulated a demand for reform. This he refused to grant. The trouble came to a head in 1848 when the king abdicated and fled to Eng.

LOUISIANA
S. state of the U.S.A. with a coastline on the Gulf of Mexico. The chief river is the Mississippi, which forms part of the E. boundary, before entering the sea by a large delta. It is a fertile area, with forests, sulphur mines and oil deposits. The industries are assoc. with the products of the state, petroleum, sugar, cottonseed and lumber. Baton Rouge is the cap. but New Orleans is the largest town. L. became a state, 1812, and sends 8 representatives to Congress. Area: 48,520 sq.m. Pop. 3,643,200. L. was the name given by the Fr. to a great district which they acquired in 1682. It included the whole of the C. part of the present U.S.A. from the Gt. Lakes to the Gulf of Mexico and from the Eng. colonies to the Rocky Mts., Texas being excluded. In 1803 this area, over 1,100,000 sq.m. in extent, was sold by Fr. to the U.S.A. for £3,000,000, a deal known as the 'L. Purchase'.

LOURDES
[loord] Town of S.W. Fr. in Hautes-Pyrénées dept., 22 m. S.E. of Pau. It is famous for its grotto, visited every year by thousands of pilgrims. Pop. 16,000.

LOURENÇO MARQUES
[lō-ren′-sō marks′] Cap. of Mozambique, with a large harbour and extensive docks. It has a large import trade. Discovered, 1502, and settled 1544. Pop. 48,000.

LOUSE
Name denoting unrelated groups of small invertebrate animals, esp.: (1) wingless parasitic suctorial insects infesting the hair of human and mammalian hosts; (2) another wingless order having biting mouth-parts, parasitic on birds and mammals, called *Bird-lice*; (3) Degraded parasitic crustaceans called *Fish-lice* and *Whale-lice*; (4) plant-sucking green 'fly' and their larvae, called *Plant-lice*. *See* WOODLOUSE.

LOUSEWORT
Large genus of herbs, mostly perennial, of the figwort family, native to N. temp. regions (*Pedicularis*). Parasitic on roots, the common Brit. heath l., *P. sylvatica*, bears rose-coloured, 2-lipped flowers. The marsh l., *P. palustris*, is an annual, with dull-pink flowers.

LOUTH
Co. of Eire, in Leinster prov., with a coastline on the Irish Sea. The Boyne forms its S. boundary and is the only navigable river. Agriculture is the chief industry. Dundalk is the county town; others are Drogheda, Greenore, Carlingford and Louth. Pop. 63,378.

LOUVAIN
[loo-va(ng)] City of Brabant prov., Belg., on the Dyle, 19 m. E. of Brussels. Chiefly famous for its univ., founded 1426. Pop. 32,474.

LOUVRE, The
Museum and art gallery in Paris, long one of the chief palaces of Fr. kings. The present building was begun in the 16th cent. by Francis

I and added to by Louis XIV and Napoleon. The palace has been a museum since the time of Napoleon.

LOVAGE
Genus of smooth perennial umbelliferous herbs (*Ligusticum*), natives of N. temp. regions. Scotch lovage, *L. scoticum*, has a stout, branched, aromatic and pungent rootstock.

LOVE-IN-A-MIST
(*Nigella damascena*) Annual ranunculaceous plant. The flowers are blue or white, surrounded by filmy leaves.

LOVE-LIES-BLEEDING
(*Amaranthus*) Annual plant bearing red flowers on long drooping stems. Princes' feather (*A. hypochondriacus*), of the same genus, is slightly taller with red flowers.

LOVEBIRD
Various small parrots. They include the African short-tailed genus *Agapornis*, of which the Rosy-faced, 6½ in., is a favourite cage-bird, and some trop., Amer. and Papuan pygmy parrots. The Austral. budgerigar or lovebird, *Melopsittacus undulatus*, is a long-tailed grass-parrot.

LOVELACE, Richard
(1618-57) Eng. poet. He fought on the Royalist side in the Civil War, and served in the Fr. Army, then came back to Eng. where he was in prison in 1648-9. His lyrics appeared as *Lucasta* (1649).

LOWE, Sir Hudson
(1769-1844) Brit. soldier. In 1815 he was made Gov. of St. Helena and therefore responsible for the custody of Napoleon.

LOWESTOFT
Borough, seaport and resort of Suffolk, at the mouth of the Waveney. It is a great fishing port with a large fish market. Pop. 46,340.

LOYOLA, Ignatius de
(1491-1556) Sp. saint and founder of the Soc. of Jesus. He was b. at Loyola. In Mar. 1522, he dedicated himself to the service of the ch. He was canonised in 1622. *See* JESUITS.

LÜBECK
[lü'-] Seaport in Schleswig-Holstein, W. Germany, on the Trave, 10 m. from its mouth. It was one of the chief towns of the Hanseatic League, and has several fine buildings, of which the 13th cent. town hall and the Gothic cath. are good examples. Pop. 234,766.

LUCAN
Roman poet (39-65) (**Marcus Annaeus Lucanus**). B. Spain. He was concerned in a plot to murder Nero, and on this being discovered, he committed suicide. He wrote an epic, *Pharsalia*, dealing with civil war between Caesar and Pompey.

LUCERNE
[loo-sern'] Tourist centre of C. Switzerland, cap. of L. canton, situated where the Reuss leaves the L. of Lucerne. Industries include the manufacture of machinery and furniture. Pop. 72,400.

LUCERNE
[loo-sern'] Perennial leguminous herb of the Medit. region, also called purple medick (*Medicago sativa*). Cultivated in antiquity, it grows widely nowadays in temp. climates, including western N. Amer. which calls it **Alfalfa.**

LUCKNOW
Cap. of Uttar Pradesh, Ind., on the Gumti, 40 m. N.E. of Kanpur. The siege of L. was an outstanding incident in the Indian Mutiny. Pop. 740,000.

LUCULLUS
[lo͝o-kul'-ŭs] (*c.* 110-57 B.C.) Rom. epicure. In 65 he retired from active service as a soldier and during the next 9 years gave feasts of unsurpassed profusion and splendour.

LUDDITES
Men who caused disturbances in the Midland counties of Eng., 1811-12. The Luddites, believing that machinery was the cause of their unemployment and distress, went about destroying it.

LUDENDORFF, Erich
(1865-1937) German soldier. In Aug. 1914, he took part in the attack on Liège. When, in Aug. 1916, Hindenburg took command of all the German forces, he remained his chief adviser. L. was responsible for the defeat of Rumania. He directed the German campaigns of 1917-18. He was in control until the end came, but could not avert final defeat.

LUGANO
[loo-gä'-nō] Resort and largest town of Ticino canton, Switzerland, on the N. shore of Lake L., lying between lakes Maggiore and Como. The lake, on the Swiss-Ital. frontier, 50 m. N. of Milan, is famous for its beauty. Pop. 18,000.

LUKE
Saint and evangelist, and traditional author of the 3rd gospel and the Acts of the Apostles in the N.T. Traditionally he d. in Bithynia. He is commemorated on Oct. 18. **Luke, The Gospel of St.** Third book of the N.T. Written after the Matthew and Mark gospels, and addressed to the Gentile world.

LULLY, Jean Baptiste
(1632-87) Fr. composer of Ital. origin. In 1672 his first opera, *Cadmus et Hermione*, appeared and before his d. he had written 20 operas. He collaborated with Molière in producing comedy ballets and wrote music for his comedies.

LUMPSUCKER
(*Cyclopterus*) Fish found round the coasts of Brit. and N. Europe. It is about 12 in. long, and has the power of attaching itself to the rocks by means of its sucker.

LUNACY
State of being unable to control one's actions or the state of being insane. Such people are usually treated in a mental hospital to which they may go voluntarily, which is preferable, or after certification by a med. practitioner. If a patient enters a mental hospital as a voluntary patient he retains full civic rights and may leave such a hospital if he wishes on giving 3 days' notice to the person in charge.

LUNDY
Is. in the Bristol Channel, off the N. coast of Devon.

LUNÉVILLE
[lü'-na-vēl'] Town of Meurthe-et-Moselle dept. N.E. Fr., 20 m. S.E. of Nancy. A garrison town, it has engineering and textile industries. The **Peace of Lunéville** was signed, 1801, between Fr. and Aust. Pop. 25,000.

LUNG
In man and animals organ of respiration. Man has 2 lungs situated in the chest or thorax—]

on each side of middle line. The left one is lobes. Main bronchus or air tube from each lung fuses and forms trachea, which passes into larynx and to outside air. **Lung Cancer.** Carcinoma which attacks the lung. In recent years much research has been undertaken esp. in Brit. and Amer. in attempts to identify the cause. Many experts assoc. it with heavy cigarette smoking and have produced statistics in support of this, while others have identified carcinogens in polluted town air. Still another factor under review is the possible relationship betw. all types of cancer and certain synthetic divided into 2 lobes and the right one into 3 food dyes and preservatives, many of which have consequently been banned. *See* PLEURISY; PNEUMONIA; TUBERCULOSIS.

LUNG FISH
Surviving descendants of possibly transitional stages between fishes and amphibia. *Protopterus* and *Lepidosiren* are eel-like. Both come to the surface to take air into the lungs and hibernate in the dry season. *Protopterus* survives almost complete desiccation. *Lepidosiren* withdraws into a deep U-shaped burrow which it plugs, and thus retains a moist atmosphere about it during the period of intense drought.

LUNGWORT
(*Pulmonaria longifolia*) (or **Jerusalem Cowslip**). Perennial rough-haired herb of the borage family, the funnel-shaped flowers change from pink to blue. *P. officinalis,* has broader root-leaves, and the blooms are sometimes white. It is a native of Europe.

LUPIN
[loo′-] Genus of annual and perennial leguminous herbs and undershrubs, native to the Medit. region and temp. Amer. The best-known hybrid is the Russell lupin, developed by George Russell, a Yorkshire jobbing gardener.

LUPUS
Skin disease occurring in 2 forms: *Lupus vulgaris* and *herpes erythematoses.* **Lupus vulgaris** is caused by the bacillus of tuberculosis.

LURCHER
Cross between a greyhound and a collie sheep dog or retriever. They are useful for hunting hares and rabbits and for retrieving game.

LUSAKA
[loo-sá′-kă] Cap. of Zambia, on the railway, *c.* 30 m. N. of Kafue. Pop. 83,900.

LUTE
A plucked stringed instrument. It was widely played in the 16th and 17th cents.

LUTHER, Martin
(1483-1546) German reformer. In 1508 he went to Wittenberg as a lecturer at the univ. He had worked out a doctrine of salvation, different from that taught by the ch. and in 1517 he became a national figure. He challenged John Tetzel, a friar who was selling indulgences, to a discussion and drew up 95 theses as a basis for the debate. These he fixed on a ch. door at Wittenberg on Oct. 31, 1517, an event which is usually regarded as marking the opening of the Reformation. His action created violent controversy in Germany, and he soon had a considerable following. In 1520 the Pope issued a bull condemning his views, but this was publicly burned by the reformer at Wittenberg and his breach with the ch. was complete. To save him from violence he was carried off to a fortress, the Wartburg, and there he lived under the protection of the Elector of Saxony. Much of his later life was passed in organising the Reformed Ch. in Germany. He trans. the Bible and wrote hymns. **Lutheranism.** Form of religion founded by Martin Luther. Its creed is contained in the confession of Augsburg. L. is strong in Germany where it now forms a united ch. to which more than half of the population nominally belong and is the state religion in Norway, Sweden and Denmark, and is strong in the U.S. It is governed by its mins., by elected courts and by synods.

LUTINE BELL
Bell in the rostrum of Lloyds which is rung by the Caller before important announcements—2 strokes if good news, 1 if bad. The bell was salvaged in 1859 from the wreck of H.M.S. *Lutine*, which had foundered in Oct., 1799.

LUTON
[loo′-] Borough and market town of Beds., 30 m. from London. The chief industry is the manufacture of motor cars. L. returns 1 member to Parl. Pop. 134,820.

LUTYENS, Sir Edwin Landseer
(1869-1944) Eng. architect. He designed the Cenotaph in Whitehall.

LUXEMBOURG
Grand duchy of W. Europe, an indep. state between Belg., Fr. and Germany. The Moselle forms the S.E. boundary. Iron ore is mined around Esch, on the Fr. border, but agriculture is the chief occupation. The city of L. on the Alzette is the cap. The majority of the people are R.C. In the M.A. Luxembourg was a county with powerful rulers. In 1354 their land became a duchy, and, 1443, a part of Burgundy. Later it belonged to Sp., then Austria. In 1839 it was divided between Belg. and the Netherlands. In 1890 when the king of the Netherlands d., L. again became a separate state with Adolph, Duke of Nassau, as grand duke. He was succeeded by a son, William, after whose d., 1912, his daughter, Marie, became grand duchess. In 1919 Marie abdicated in favour of her sister, Charlotte, who abdicated in favour of her son, Prince Jean, in 1964. In 1922, an economic union with Belg. was made; later (1947) a customs union was set up with the Netherlands and Belg. (Benelux). L. is a constitutional monarchy with a council of mins. and a chamber of deputies. Area: 999 sq.m. Pop. 324,000.

LUXOR
Town in Upper Egypt, on the right bank of the Nile, 400 m. S. of Cairo. It is a tourist centre. Pop. *c.* 20,000.

LUZON
[loo-zon′] Largest Is. of the Philippines in the extreme N. Tobacco, sugar and hemp are grown. Manila, on the W. coast, is the chief town; Quezon City, the new cap. of the Republic (*q.v.*) lies to the N.E. Area: 40,420 sq.m. Pop. 12,526,000.

LYDDA
or **Ludd.** Town of Israel, *c.* 11 m. S.E. of Tel-Aviv-Jaffa, with an internat. airport.

LYDGATE, John
(*c.* 1370-1451) Eng. poet. Henry IV made him court poet. His many long poems include *The Troy Book, The Fall of Princes, The Temple of Glass.*

LYDIA
Kingdom of W. Asia Minor before the Christian era. It came into existence after 700 B.C. and was most flourishing under the rule of Croesus.

LYELL, Sir Charles
(1797-1875) Brit. geologist. Pres. Brit. Assoc. 1864. His *The Principles of Geology* is a standard work on the subject. He also wrote *The Geological Evidences of the Antiquity of Man.*

LYLY, John
(1553-1606) Eng. writer. For 20 years he was responsible for the entertainments at court. His *Euphues* 1579-80 is a prose romance in 2 parts.

LYNCH LAW
Name given to the system by which people take the law into their own hands. It appears to

Veratrum album

Lilium margaton

ALPINE FLOWERS

Gentian

Azalea

Edelweiss

Soldanella alpina

Cyclamen

Etroplus Maculatus

Platypoecilus maculatus

AQUARIUM FISH

Cynolebias nigripinis

Carassius auratus

Betta splendens

Tetrodon fluvialitis

Colisa lalia

Hyphessobrycon innesi

Xyphophorus helleri

flourish where racial antagonism is strong and authority somewhat weak.

LYNX
A large cat found in Europe, Asia and N. Amer. At one time it lived in Eng. The animal is heavier than the cat, has a short tail and bearded cheeks, and feeds on birds and small mammals.

LYONESSE
A belief widely held in Cornwall and S.W. Britain is that there existed at one time a land of this name which lay between Cornwall and the Scilly Isles, some 30 m. away.

LYONS
(*Fr.* **Lyon**) City of E. Fr., cap of Rhône dept., at the confluence of the Rhône and Saône. The 3rd largest town of Fr. Silk, the chief industry, has developed rapidly since 1450. The cath. was begun, 12th cent. Pop. 471,000.

LYRE
A stringed instrument used by the ancient Gks., similar in shape to the harp, but smaller and with fewer strings, plucked with a plectrum.

LYRE BIRD
Perching birds, found only in Australia. Resembling the pheasant in size, the males, after the 3rd year, develop in the breeding season handsome tails, which are displayed peacock-wise in the form of stringed lyres.

LYTTLETON
Port for Christchurch, S. Is., New Zealand. It has been dredged to accommodate large liners and exports lamb, mutton and wool.

LYTTON, Baron
Edward George Earle Lytton Bulwer (1803-73) Entered Parliament, became Sec. for the Colonies, and a baron in 1866. His chief novels are *Falkland* (1827), *Eugene Aram* (1832), *Last Days of Pompeii* (1834), *Last of the Barons* (1843), *Harold* (1848), *The Caxtons* (1849), *The Coming Race* (1871). He also wrote plays, poems and shorter tales.

M

M
13th letter of the Eng. alphabet. It is a voiced labial, formed by the closing of the lips, and always has the same sound in Eng., that of *m* in *rim, mother*. It is silent in the initial combination of *mn* in words derived from Gk., *e.g. mnemonic* but both letters are sounded when the combination is medial, as in *hymnal*. When combined with *b*, only the *m* is sounded, as in *dumb, numb*. In Rom. numerals *M* represents 1,000.

MABINOGION
11 prose tales found in the Welsh (*q.v.*) *Red Book of Hergest*. Lady Charlotte Guest ed. and tr. the collection (1838-49); new tr. by G. and T. Jones, 1949.

MABUSE
[ma-büs'] **Jan Gossaert de** (*c.* 1472-1532) Flemish painter. He was in the service of the Duke of Burgundy.

McADAM, John
(1756-1836) Scot. engineer. B. Ayr, he introduced the use of firmly embedded layers of small pieces of granite or similar material for road surfaces, known as *macadamising*.

MACAO
[ma-kȧ'-ō] Portuguese colony in China, comprising M. Is. at the mouth of the Canton river and the Is. of Taipa and Colône. The Portuguese who settled, 1557, hold the colony by treaty of 1887. Area: 6 sq.m. Pop. 475,000.

MacARTHUR, Douglas
(1880-1964) Amer. soldier. Though retired from the Army (1937), he returned to command Amer. armed forces in the Far East. After the Jap. attack on Pearl Harbour (1941) he led the Philippine defence until he left for Australia to command Allied forces in the S.W. Pacific. From there he launched the New Guinea campaign. As Supreme Commander for Allied Powers, he directed the Allied occupation of Japan. Also directed the Allied campaign in Korea (1950-1). Relieved of all commands, 1951.

MACASSAR
Seaport and chief town of Celebes, S.W. Indonesia. It exports timber, coffee, copra, rubber, etc. Pop. 450,000.

MACAULAY, Lord
(1800-59) Eng. historian. His early home was at Clapham where his parents were members of the Evangelical sect. A convinced Whig, Macaulay was returned as M.P. for Calne (1830) and Leeds (1833). In 1839 he was elected M.P. for Edinburgh, and joined the Whig ministry. His chief writings are *Essays*, including *Milton, Addison, Johnson, Clive, Hastings*, etc.; his *History of England*, in 5 vols., 1849-61; his poems *Lays of Ancient Rome* (1842); *Speeches* (1854).

MACAW
Long-tailed S. Amer. parrot (*Ara*). Distinguished by gorgeous plumage, they are gregarious forest birds and incorrigible screamers.

MACBETH
(d. *c.* 1057) King of the Scots. He became king in 1040, by murdering Duncan. He was killed during a battle with Duncan's son, Malcolm. The story as told by Holinshed in his *Chronicle* served as the basis of Shakespeare's tragedy.

MACCABEES
[mak'-ă-bēz] Jewish family distinguished in the revolt against Syrian tyranny, 2nd cent. B.C. Judas Maccabaeus re-took Jerusalem, restored the Temple service and was slain in battle 161 B.C. The O.T. Apocrypha include 2 historical books on this period, 1 and 2 Maccabees.

McCARTHY, Joseph
(1909-57) Amer. politician. During World War II he served with distinction as a Marine flyer. His campaigns against Communism and those suspected of Communist sympathies in Amer. aroused the opposition of many.

McCORMACK, Count John
(1884-1945) Irish tenor singer. A chorister in Dublin R.C. Cath.; went to Milan to study with Sabbatino. Made his début in London, 1907. Became Amer. citizen, 1917; papal count, 1928.

McDIARMID, Hugh
Pen-name of **Christopher Murray Grieve** (1892-) Scots poet. His works include *Sangschaw, Penny Wheep, To Circumjack Cencrastus* (verse), *Lucky Poet* (1942) (autobiog.). A founder of the Scots Nat. Party.

MACDONALD, Flora
(1722-1790) Scots heroine. In 1746 Prince Charles Edward escaped to the Hebrides after Culloden. Flora succeeded in taking him to Portree, so enabling him to escape to Fr.

MacDONALD, George
(1824-1905) Scot. writer. His novels (of Scots life) include: *David Elginbrod, The Marquis of Lossie*. For children he wrote *At the Back of the North Wind.*

MacDONALD, James Ramsay
(1866-1937) Scots statesman. B. Lossiemouth, he joined the I.L.P. 1894, and was a Lab. M.P. 1906-18, 1922-35 and 1936-7. Sec. of the Lab. Party, 1900-12, and the Leader of the Party in the House of Commons, 1911-14 and 1922-9. He was P.M., 1924, 1929-31 and 1931-5. During World War I he held pacifist views and lost his seat in 1918. He led both the inter-war Lab. Govts. On the financial crisis of 1931 MacDonald and a few colleagues went against the majority of their Party and joined with the other 2 parties to form a Nat. Govt. The general election of Oct. 1931 confirmed nat. support for this govt. and until 1935 MacDonald led it.

MACEDONIA
District in the Balkan Peninsula across the Yugoslav-Gk. border to the Aegean Sea. Under Philip and Alexander the Gt. it held sway over the rest of Greece. It was part of the Bulg. emp. from 800-1000, and fell to the Turks, 1689. From 1875 there were constant revolts of the Christian Bulg. against the Turks, culminating in a great massacre, 1903. After World War I, M. was divided between Greece and Yugoslavia.

MACHIAVELLI, Niccolo
(1469-1527) Ital. writer. *Il Principe* (*The Prince*), which maintains the absolute supremacy of the ruler, was very influential in Europe for two centuries.

MACHINE GUN
Firearm provided with automatic mechanism for the rapid and continuous discharge of rifle bullets or small shells.

MACKENZIE
River of the N.W. Territories, Canada, which flows from Gt. Slave Lake to M. Bay in the Arctic Ocean. Length with Peace R., 2,635 m.

MACKENZIE, Sir Compton
(1883-) Brit. author. B. W. Hartlepool. He served in the S. African and 1st World Wars. He has written *The Passionate Elopement* (1911), *Sinister Street* (1913-14), *The Four Winds of Love* (1937-41), *Whisky Galore* (1947), *Hunting the Fairies* (1949), and vol. of broadcast talks *Echoes* (1954). Kt. 1952.

MACKENZIE KING, William Lyon
(1874-1950) Canadian politician. P.M., 1921-6, 1926-30, 1935-8. Leader of the Lib. Party from 1919, his leadership contributed very largely to Canada's prosperity.

MACKEREL
(*Scomber scombrus*) Marine food-fish related to the tunny, abundant in the N. Atlantic. The slightly compressed body, *c.* 10-12 in. long, mostly covered with minute scales, is black-barred, bluish-green above and silvery beneath.

McKINLEY, William
(1843-1901) 24th Pres. of the U.S.A. B. Ohio. In 1876 he was sent to Congress by the electors of Ohio, and sponsored the high tariff of 1890 (**McKinley Tariff**). In 1896 he was elected Pres. His 2nd term had only just begun when he was murdered. Succeeded by the Vice-Pres. Theodore Roosevelt.

MACMAHON, Marie Edmé Patrice Maurice de
(1808-93) Fr. soldier of Irish descent. Was head of army that, 1864, defeated the Aust. at Magenta. Made prisoner at Sedan. After his release he put down the Commune and estabd. the Repub. This led, in 1873, to his election as Pres.

MACMILLAN, Harold
(1894-) Cons. polit. P.C. P.M. 1957-63. Unionist M.P. for Stockton-on-Tees, 1924-9, and 1931-45. During World War II, he held office in the Coalition govt. In 1951, he became Min. of Housing and Local Govt., Min. of Defence 1954, Sec. of State for Foreign Affairs from April to Dec. 1955, when he was apptd. Chanc. of Exchequer. M.P. for Bromley 1945-63. Succeeded Sir Anthony Eden as P.M. Jan. 1957. Resigned because of ill-health and withdrew from polit. life, 1963.

M'NAUGHTEN RULES
Rules which may be used by the prosecution or the defence in determining whether or not a person arraigned on a capital charge was insane when the crime was committed. Formulated following the acquittal on the grounds of insanity of Daniel M'Naughten, who, in 1843, shot dead Sir Robert Peel's private secretary. In 1922 the Atkin committee was set up to examine and report upon the Rules. This recommended that, with one exception, the Rules should continue to form the basis of assessment of the sanity or insanity of the prisoner in criminal trials. The advances made in psychiatric med. during the past 30 years have made revision necessary again.

MacNEICE, Louis
(1907-63) Brit. poet. B. Belfast. B.B.C. feature-writer (1941-9). He pub. 8 vols. of poems, 1927-48. He wrote the verse play *Out of the Picture* (1937), and many others for radio; *Ten Burnt Offerings* (1953), and *Autumn Sequel* (1954). C.B.E. 1958.

MÂCON
[mä-kō(ng)] Cap. of Saône-et-Loire dept., E. Fr., on the Saône 45 m. N.E. of Lyons. It gives its name to a popular Burgundy. Pop. 21,000.

MACPHERSON, James
(1736-96) Scot. writer. In 1760 he pub. *Fragments of Ancient Poetry Collected in the Highlands of Scotland*, then two more 'translations' from Gaelic, the epics *Fingal* (1762) and *Temora* (1763). Their authenticity was doubted and a committee decided that Macpherson had expanded and modified traditional Gaelic poems a great deal. *See* OSSIAN.

MADAGASCAR
Is. in the Ind. Ocean, forming the Malagasy Repub.; formerly Fr. Ind. 1960. It is a mountainous country, reaching *c.* 9,000 ft. in the peak Ankaratra, with coastal low lands. The climate is tropical. There are valuable forests and mineral resources. Agriculture and cattle raising are the chief industries. Tananarive is the cap.; other towns are Tamatave, Majunga and Diégo Suarez. M. was discovered by the Portuguese, 1500, and became a Fr. possession 1896. The last native sovereign, Queen Ranavalona III, d. 1916. Area: 229,812 sq.m. Pop. 5,658,000.

MADDER
Pigment from the roots of the madder plant, *Rubia tinctorum*, a perennial, growing in S. Europe and Asia Minor. It forms a series of richly-coloured, transparent lakes used as water colours.

MADEIRA
or **Funchal**. Is. group in the N. Atlantic, a district of Portugal. M., the largest Is., containing the cap. Funchal (*q.v.*) is a popular resort. Wine and fruit are produced. Area: 270 sq.m. Pop. 270,000.

MADISON, James
(1751-1836) 4th Pres. of the U.S.A. B. Virginia, he helped to frame the Amer. constitution. At first he sided with Alexander Hamilton but later, with Jefferson, tried to limit the power of the central govt. When in 1801, Jefferson became Pres., Madison was made Sec. of State. He was elected Pres. (1809), re-elected in 1812 and retired in 1817.

MADRAS now **Tamil Nadu**
[mă-drás'] State of S. India. It has a long coastline on the Bay of Bengal, and is bounded inland by Andhra Pradesh and Mysore and in the S.W. is Kerala. The chief rivers are the Kistna, Godavari and Cauvery; irrigation is practised in the fertile river deltas. Rice, cotton, millet, oilseeds, spices, tobacco and tea are produced. Madras is the cap. Most of the people are Hindus. The state is admin. by a gov. and council. Area: 50,132 sq.m. Pop. 33,686,953. **Madras.** Cap. of M. state and chief port on the E. coast of India. There are cotton mills, iron foundries and engineering works, and overseas trade. Founded in 1640 by the E. Ind. Co., M. has a univ. estabd. 1857. Pop. 1,729,141.

MADRID
Cap. city of Spain and of M. prov. on the Manzanares. It stands on a plateau over 2,000 ft. above sea level. Captured by the Moors in the 10th cent., it became the cap. of Philip II's kingdom (1560). It is now the seat of the repub. parl. The univ. and the Prado Art Gall. are notable buildings. M. has many industries, including the manufacture of leather, pottery, carpets, soap and paper. Pop. 2,599,000.

MAECENAS, Gaius Cilnius
[mī-sē'-] (d. 8 B.C). He was the intimate friend of the Emperor Augustus. Famous as a patron of men of letters, notably Virgil and Horace.

MAES, Nicholas
[mās] (1632-93) Dutch painter. B. Dordrecht, he studied under Rembrandt, worked as a portrait painter, and d. at Amsterdam.

MAETERLINCK, Maurice
Comte (1862-1949) Belgian playwright. Influenced by the Symbolists (*q.v.*). His poetic plays include *Les Aveugles* (1890), *Pelléas et Mélisande* (1892), *L'Oiseau Bleu* (1909). Nobel Prize in 1911.

MAFEKING
Town in the Cape of Good Hope prov., Repub. of S. Africa. Under Baden-Powell it withstood a siege of 217 days (1899-1900) during the Boer War. The rejoicing in Gt. Brit. over its relief has become proverbial.

MAFIA
[maf′-yă] Secret soc. in Sicily. It arose early in the 19th cent. The members, called Mafiosi, were pledged to carry out ruthlessly the orders given to them and were responsible for a great number of outrages. Attention has recently been drawn to their activities by the work of Danilo Dolci and others.

MAGDALENIAN
Uppermost stage of the palaeolithic period in Europe. Named from La Madeleine rock-shelter near Les Eyzies, Dordogne.

MAGELLAN, Ferdinand
(*c.* 1480-1521) Anglicised name of the Portuguese sailor, Ferñao de Magalhães. In 1517 he took service with the King of Spain and in 1520 discovered the strait which was named after him. He was killed in a fight on one of the Philippine Is. but one of his ships completed the 1st voyage round the world. **Magellan, Straits of.** [-gel′-] Arm of the sea, linking the Atlantic and Pacific Oceans. At the extremity of S. Amer., it is between Chile and Tierra del Fuego.

MAGGOT
Popular name applied indefinitely to a grub or insect larva, esp. when pale-hued and legless. Found in decaying animal and vegetable matter.

MAGINOT LINE
[mazhi-nō′] Highly fortified area on E. and N.E. boundary of Fr., built 1927-35. The Germans successfully took the line at Sedan, 1940. Fr. faith in its invulnerability was an important psychological cause of their collapse.

MAGISTRATE
Official appointed to administer justice. In Brit. magistrates are of 2 kinds. Unpaid magistrates are appointed for the counties and certain boroughs and collectively form the commission for the peace. Certain officials, *e.g.* a mayor or the chairman of an urban district council, are magistrates because of their office. **Paid** or **Stipendiary Magistrates** sit in the London police courts and in certain large towns. They can sit alone as they have the powers of 2 ordinary magistrates.

MAGNA CARTA
Charter of privileges signed by King John at Runnymede, near Staines, June 15, 1215. It was a statement of the laws or customs of the land, it became the symbol of the supremacy of the constitution over the king, and was interpreted in later ages as a guarantee of liberties.

MAGNESIA
MgO. Magnesium oxide, a white powder produced by burning the metal or calcining the carbonate. **Magnesia alba** is a mixture of the carbonate and hydroxide used in pharmacy.

MAGNESITE
[-nēz′-] Mineral consisting of magnesium carbonate. It is assoc. usually with serpentine and allied rocks occurring in Silesia, Norway and N. Amer. M. is used in preparing Epsom Salts.

MAGNESIUM
A white, hard metal, which forms *c.* 2 % of the earth's crust. It was discovered in 1829 by Bussy. In ribbon or powder form, it burns brilliantly in air and was used for flashlight photography. Sp. gr. 1·7. Chem. sym. Mg.

MAGNET
Substance having the property of attracting iron, and in a lesser degree, nickel and certain other metals. A **permanent magnet** is a straight or horseshoe shaped steel bar magnetised by contact with a similar magnet or an **electro magnet,** the latter consisting of a soft iron bar surrounded by insulated wire coils and then temporarily magnetised by an electric current. **Magnetic Poles.** Places on the Earth's surface at which a compass needle points vertically downward. The N. Magnetic Pole, which is at about lat. 70° 40′ N., long. 96° 30′ W., can be reached by following the direction indicated by a compass needle from any point on the earth. The S. Magnetic Pole is at about lat. 71° 10′ S., long. 150° 45′ E.

MAGNETITE
Fe_3O_4. Black mineral with metallic lustre. It consists of the magnetic oxide of iron. The lodestone of the ancients, it is a natural magnet.

MAGNOLIA
Genus of hardy and half-hardy trees and shrubs related to the tulip tree. Native to sub-trop. Asia and N. Amer., they bear large, fragrant, solitary flowers. The earliest to reach Brit. was the Amer. evergreen shrub *M. glauca,* in 1688.

MAGPIE
(*Pica pica*) Perching birds of the Crow family. Stout-beaked, lustrous-black, relieved by white on wings and breast, the common magpie, 18 in. long, is wary when wild, and is a thief when domesticated.

MAGYARS
The dominant race of Hungary, of Finno-Ugrian stock, who moved W. into the Hungarian plains in the 9th cent. After 1919 the pop. of Hungary became almost entirely Magyar.

MAHARASHTRA
Indian state, formed 1960 from S. part of Bombay State. Chief town, Greater Bombay. Area: 118,741 sq.m. Pop. 39,504,294.

MAHDI, El
The Moslem Messiah. Best known was **Mohammed Ali of Dongola** (1843-85), who successfully opposed Egyptian rule in the E. Sudan, defeated an Egyptian Army led by Hicks Pasha, 1883 and in 1885 captured Khartoum, where General Gordon (*q.v.*) was killed.

MAHLER, Gustav
(1860-1911) Austrian composer. From 1908 he was chief conductor of the Metropolitan Opera House in New York. His works include 9 symphonies, a setting of Chinese poems for mezzo-soprano, tenor and orchestra, and over 40 songs.

MAHOGANY
Compact timber, distinguished as Spanish or Cuban. It is derived from a Central Amer. and W. Indian tree (*Swietenia mahagoni*). Reaching Brit. early in the 18th cent. it acquired favour for domestic furniture.

MAHON
Chief town and port of Minorca. Sp. Balearic Is. Pop. 17,000.

MAIDENHAIR FERN
(*Adiantum*) Large genus of ferns, natives of temp. and trop. regions. The common *A. capillus-veneris,* whose fronds have spreading hair-like branches, occasionally occurs wild in the W. of Eng., Wales and Ireland.

MAIDSTONE
County town and borough of Kent, on the Medway. Industries include the manufacture of agricultural implements, paper and cement. Pop. 60,570.

MAIMONIDES, Moses
(Moses Ben Maimon) (1135-1204) B. Cordoba, Jewish codifier and phil. His Code of Jewish Law is known as the *Mishneh Torah.*

MAINE
N.E. state of the U.S.A. with a rugged Atlantic coastline. It lies E. of New Hampshire. Agriculture, fishing, forestry and quarrying are the main occupations. The cap. is Augusta, but Portland, Lewiston and Bangor are larger. M. was settled 1624, became part of Mass. and entered the union as a state, 1820, sending 3 representatives to Congress. Area: 33,220 sq.m. Pop. 993,700.

MAINE
Prov. of Fr. before 1789, S. of Normandy, around the town of Le Mans, its cap.

MAINTENON, Madame de
[ma(ng)t-nō(ng)] (1635-1719) 2nd wife of Louis XIV of Fr. She became governess to the children of Louis XIV and Madame de Montespan. In 1678 she became a marquise and was prob. the King's mistress. They mar. *c.* 1685. She had great influence, and was a patroness of lit. and the arts.

MAINZ
[mīnts] City and river port in Rhineland-Palatinate, W. Germany, at the confluence of the Rhine and Main, 22 m. S.W. of Frankfurt. M. has a wine trade and numerous manufactures. There is a cath. Pop. 137,613.

MAIZE
Stout, annual grass. Next in importance to rice as a cereal food, it is native to trop. Amer. It is raised in U.S.A., Canada, Mexico, Argentina and Brazil, and is naturalised in S. Africa, India, China, S. Europe and Australia. The grain is roasted or boiled; coarsely milled it becomes hominy or polenta, deprived of gluten it yields cornflour.

MAJORCA
(*Sp.* Mallorca) Sp. Is. in the Medit., largest of the Balearics (*q.v.*), 115 m. S. of Barcelona. Products include fruit, wine and pottery. Palma is the cap.

MAKARIOS, Archbishop
(1913-) Pres. of Cyprus since indep. 1960. Deeply involved in struggle for indep. Exiled to Seychelles by Brit. govt., 1956-7. Took part in negotiations leading to London agreement (1959).

MALACCA
State of the Fed. of Malaya, part of Malaysia, on the S.W. coast. Occupied by the Portuguese, 1511, it was incorporated with Singapore and Penang as the Straits Settlements crown colony, 1867-1946. Rubber is the chief export. M. is the cap. and port of the territory. Area: 640 sq.m. Pop. 355,279.

MALACHI
Name assigned to the last book of the O.T. in the Eng. Bible.

MALACHITE
[-kīt] Green mineral composed of the basic carbonate of copper. It occurs in the Ural Mts., Australia, Fr. and Brit. When cut and polished it is used as a gemstone.

MALAGA
City and seaport of Sp., cap. of M. prov. on the Medit. 65 m. N.E. of Gibraltar. Wine and raisins are exported. Founded by Phoenician merchants, it passed into Rom., Visigothic and Moorish hands, becoming Christian, 1487. Pop. 307,162.

MALAGASY REPUBLIC *See* MADAGASCAR.

MALAN, Dr. Daniel François
[mă-lun'] (1874-1959) S. African politician. P.M. of the Union of S. Africa and Min. for External Affairs 1948-54. An ordained clergyman of the Dutch Reformed Ch. he preached continuously for a free repub., denouncing both Smuts and Botha, who had agreed to work with Brit. Between 1910 and the start of World War II 1939, he became successively editor of *Die Burger*, 1915; member of Parl. 1919; Min. of the Interior, Health and Educ. under Hertzog; leader of the extreme Nationalists, 1933. He was against S. Africa's entry into the War, and it was at this time that he assumed leadership of all the Nationalists. From then his policy was one of *apartheid* (racial segregation), which he instituted in 1950, and which calls for strict White Supremacy. *See* SOUTH AFRICA.

MALARIA
Intermittent fever caused by parasite conveyed by female mosquito of Anopheles group. Disease is world-wide but most common in trop. and sub-trop. areas. Prior to 1925 the specific remedy was quinine. This was followed by the

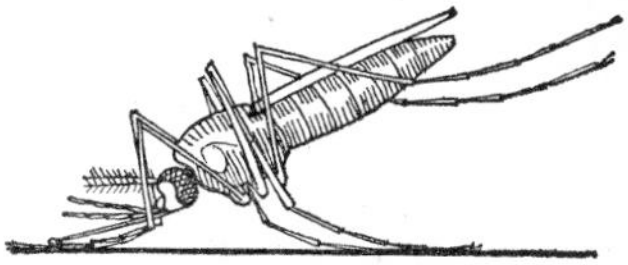

Anopheles mosquito

synthetic compounds *pamaquin* and *mepacrine.* Efforts to find an effective and less toxic drug resulted in the discovery of *paludrine* in the I.C.I. research laboratories. *See* BLACKWATER FEVER.

MALAWI
C. African repub. bounded by Zambia and E. Africa. Part of C. African Fed. of Rhodesia and Nyasaland, 1953-63. Consists mainly of table land over 3,000 ft. Tobacco, tea, cotton, pulses and tung are grown. Lilongwe is to be the cap. Nyasaland achieved self-govt. in Feb. 1963 with Dr. Hastings Banda as P.M. and in Dec. the Fed. was dissolved. In July 1964, N. became an indep, sovereign state in the Commonwealth with the name of Malawi. Area: 36,686 sq.m. Pop. 4,130,000.

MALAY
People of Mongoloid stock dominant in the Malay Peninsula and the E. Ind. Is. A shortish, round-headed, straight-haired, olive-brown race, of an easygoing temperament. First arriving in Sumatra and Malacca, they became islamised in the 13th-16th cents. and underwent ethnic admixture with their Ind. and Melanesian neighbours. Their language is the *lingua franca* of the E. Indies.

MALAYA, Fed. of
State of Malaysia (*q.v.*) S.E. Asia, member of Brit. Commonwealth, crossed by a mt. ridge, with peaks rising to over 7,000 ft. Much of the interior is covered by dense forest, and there are extensive coastal swamps. The chief rivers are the Pahang, Kelantan, Perak, Trengganu and Kemaman. The climate is very hot and the humidity is high. Rainfall is gen. in the form of torrential showers, with thunder and lightning. The tin mining and rubber industries are of great importance. Other products are rice, palm oil and kernels, and tea; fishing is carried on. The cap. of the Fed. is Kuala Lumpur. The pop. is predominantly Malay (*q.v.*), with Chinese, Ind., Eurasians and Europeans. The Fed. consists of 11 states; the former Fed. Malay States of Perak, Selangor, Negri Sembilan and Pahang; the former Unfederated States of Johore, Kedah, Perlis, Kelantan and Trengganu; and the 2 Brit. Settlements of Penang and Malacca (*qq.v.*). Area: 50,680 sq.m. Pop. 8,580,000.

MALAYSIA, Fed. of
Member of Brit. Commonwealth, formed 1963 by union of Fed. of Malaya, State of Singa-

pore, colonies of N. Borneo (renamed Sabah) and Sarawak. Fed. cap. Kuala Lumpur. Tunku Abdul Rahman is 1st P.M. Pres. Sukarno of Indonesia has claimed that this Fed. is a threat to I. and guerilla warfare is being carried on. Singapore withdrew from Fed., 1965.

MALDIVE ISLANDS
Group of coral atolls in the Ind. Ocean, indep. Sultanate to the S.W. of Ceylon. Coconuts, millet and fruit are produced. The people are Moslems, and many are fishermen and traders. Malé, on King's Is., is the cap. Pop. 90,000.

MALENKOV, Georgi Maximilianovitch
[mal-ĕn-kof] (1902-) Russ. politician. He joined the Communist Party, 1920. He impressed Stalin and was taken into the Chancellery, becoming a member of the important Central Committee, and eventually Stalin's private secretary. As a result of his wartime services, he became a full member of the Politburo, 1946. Forming a clique with Beria (*q.v.*) and Krushchev (*q.v.*) he manoeuvred into position and upon the d. of Stalin became P.M. Fell from power in July, 1957.

MALHERBE, François de
(1555-1628) Fr. poet. He started a reaction against the artificialities of Ronsard and the Pléiade.

MALI
Republic of N.W. Africa, a former Fr. colony. Indep. since 1960. Cap. Bamanako. Chief rivers: Niger, Senegal. Main exports: groundnuts, cotton. Area: 465,000 sq.m. Pop. 4,900,000.

MALINES
or **Mechlin.** City of Antwerp prov., Belgium, 13 m. N.E. of Brussels. Famous for its lace and its cath. Pop. 63,200.

MALLARD
Common wild duck of Brit. and the N. hemisphere (*Anas platyrhyncha*). The drake, 24 in. long, has glossy-green head and neck, white-ringed, purplish breast and greyish-white underparts; the duck is brown with buff markings.

MALLOW
Genus of herbs, natives of the N. hemisphere (*Malva*). The common blue-flowered mallow, the lilac-flowered dwarf, or round-leaved, and the musk-mallow grow wild in Brit. *See* MARSH MALLOW.

MALMÖ
Seaport of Sweden, 16 m. S.E. of Copenhagen, Denmark. Industries are connected with the production of tobacco, sugar and textiles. Pop. 237,517.

MALMSEY
[mâm'-] Sweet high-flavoured wine produced from grapes grown in the M.A. in the Ægean. The Fr. name, Malvoisie, is also used. Its modern representative is produced at Santorin.

MALNUTRITION
Condition of impaired bodily health with loss of vitality of the tissues, as a consequence of inadequate food, or an inability from disease to utilise the food even though it is adequate. Malnutrition may be the forerunner of numerous serious diseases.

MALORY, Sir Thomas
(lived *c.* 1470). Eng. writer. He compiled a collection of Arthurian Stories from Fr. romances. Caxton pub. it as *Morte d'Arthur* (1484).

MALPLAQUET
[mal'-plă-kā] Village of Nord dept. Fr., 10 m. from Mons, where in 1709 the Brit. and Aust. under Marlborough and Pr. Eugene, defeated the Fr.

MALRAUX, André
(1901-) Fr. writer. His works include *La Condition Humaine* (1933), *Le Temps du Mépris* (1935), *La Psychologie de l'Art* (1949), *Les Voix du Silence* (1951).

MALT
Partially germinated grain of various cereals, chiefly barley. The barley is steeped first in water, then the soaked grain is allowed to germinate up to a certain stage. During this process the ferment diastase is formed and converts the starch present into maltose and dextrin. The 'green malt' is dried in a kiln and finally cured at a greater heat without free circulation of air until the mass becomes friable, brown in colour, and develops a distinctive flavour. *See* BREWING.

MALTA G.C.
Is. in the Medit. 55 m. S. of Sicily, forming an indep. member of the Brit. Commonw. with the Is. of Gozo and Comino, and several islets. The climate is hot in summer and the Is. are intensively cultivated. Fishing is carried on. There is a fine harbour and extensive naval dockyards. The cap. and chief town is Valletta. There is a cath. in Mdina, the former cap. and a univ. The people, who speak Maltese and Eng., are R.C. Malta was ruled in turn by the Phoenicians, Gks., Carthaginians, Rom. and Arabs. It was part of the emp. of Charles V, who gave it to the knights of St. John. They fortified and ruled it until 1798, when it was seized by Napoleon. In 1814 it was formally handed over to Brit. During World War II, M. was an important Brit. base. Heavily damaged by air raids, it was awarded the George Cross, 1942, in recognition of the courage of its inhabitants. The colony was granted responsible govt. 1921, but this was suspended following a dispute between the state and the Ch. of Rome. In April, 1959, a new constitution came into force, whereby the island was administered by an Executive Council with Br. and Maltese members. After protracted negotiations indep. agreement was signed July 1964, to take effect from Sept. Area: 120 sq.m. Pop. 329,000.

MALTESE TERRIER
Ancient form of lap-dog. It resembles a toy Skye terrier, with long, white, silky coat and thickly-haired tail curling over the back.

MALTHUS, Thomas Robert
(1766-1834) Eng. economist. In 1798 he pub. anonymously his *Essay on the Principle of Population*, which set out to prove that increase of population was dependent upon the presence of warmth and food, and would only be checked by the lack of these things, or by such checks as disease, epidemics, wars and plagues.

MALVERN
[mawl'-] Inland resort and urban district of Worcs. on the Malvern Hills. The town has medicinal waters. Pop. 27,040. **Malvern Hills.** Range of hills in England chiefly in Worcs. and Hereford. The chief hill is Worcester Beacon, *c.* 1,395 ft.

MAMMAL
Highest class of the animal kingdom. Mammals are air-breathing warm-blooded vertebrates with hair, and with the exception of the lowest group, the monotremes, are viviparous and suckle their young. The foetus undergoes a gestation period during which it is nourished by an organic connection or placenta between the foetal membranes and the uterine wall. The spinal column is characterised by having intervertebral discs between the centra. The skull possesses 2 condyles. The lower jaw or mandible is a single bone articulated directly to the skull. The brain differs from that of the lower vertebrates by having a band of transverse fibres, the *corpus callosum*, between the 2 hemispheres.

MAMMARY GLAND
or **Breast.** In the male the structure is rudi-

mentary, but in the female the organ develops with onset of puberty. With the onset of pregnancy there is a further temporary increase in size and a secretion of milk.

MAMMOTH
Extinct elephant of N. latitudes in glacial and pre-glacial times. In build it closely resembled the Indian elephant, but had a thick, hairy coat over a woolly undercoat, and its long, slender tusks curved upwards and outwards. It was depicted in drawings by primitive man.

MAN
or **Mona.** Is. in the Irish Sea, almost equidistant from Eng., Scot. and Ireland. The highest point, Snaefell, is 2,034 ft. Dairy farming, lead mining and fishing are industries. It is a popular tourist centre. In the summer steamers ply regularly to Douglas from Liverpool, Barrow, Glasgow and other ports. Douglas is the cap.; other places are Peel, Ramsey, Castletown, Port Erin and Laxey. Man is a part of the Brit. Commonw. but has its own constitution. This consists of a council and a House of Keys, an elected body of 24 members. A Lieut.-Gov. represents the Queen. It has its own legal system, but its ch. under the Bishop of Sodor and M. is part of the C. of E. The Manx lang., a Celtic one, is still spoken. Edward I secured it for Eng. and, 1406, Henry IV gave it to the Stanley family. The Stanleys were Lords of M. until 1736, when the Dukes of Atholl succeeded to the title. In the 19th cent. the Is. of M. obtained home rule. Area: 220 sq.m. Pop. 48,150.

MAN
Homo: a genus of biped mammals belonging to the order Primates. Biologically similar to the other members of the order, apes, monkeys and baboons; differences include perfectly opposable thumbs on the hands, erect posture, arms relatively shorter and legs relatively longer and stronger progression on the soles of the feet, brain relatively larger and more complex than in any other animal, and capacity for articulate speech and educ. Modern man is regarded as a single species, *Homo sapiens.*

MANATEE
Aquatic mammals of the order Sirenia. They inhabit estuaries and rivers on the trop. Atlantic coasts of Amer. and Africa. They are inoffensive, thick-skinned, 8 ft. long, with hand-like fore-paddles and no hind limbs.

MANCHESTER
City and county borough of Lancs. on the Irwell, 189 m. N.W. of London. It is the headquarters of the cotton manufacture in Eng. The M. Ship Canal connects the city with the Mersey. The univ. grew out of Owens Coll. and the city is famous as a mus. centre, with a Royal Coll. of Mus. and the Hallé Orchestra. Its leading newspaper, the *Guardian*, is known throughout the civilised world. M. is gov. by a Lord Mayor, and returns 9 members to Parl. Pop. 659,170.

MANCHU
People of Tungus stock in E. Asia. Tall, slender, medium-headed, level-eyed, they peopled Manchuria and ruled China A.D. 1644-1912.

MANCHURIA
District of E. Asia, a territory of the Chinese Repub. the E. of Mongolia. It is bordered by the U.S.S.R. and Korea, the Amur and Yalu rivers forming parts of the N. and S. boundaries. Much of the surface is lowland, and the soil is fertile. Soya bean, wheat, barley and millet are grown; coal, oil and iron are produced. Shenyang (Moukden), Harbin, Changchun (Hsinking), Yingkow, Kirin, Dairen and Port Arthur are the chief towns. Russ. obtained a footing in the country, but, 1905, her rights were transferred to Japan. After World War I there was lawlessness in the prov. in which Jap. troops remained. In 1932 the indep. of M. was proclaimed, and the former Emp. of China was installed in March as ruler of Manchukuo. In 1945 upon the collapse of Japan in World War II, Manchuria was returned to China, and no longer exists as an admin. unit.

MANDALAY
Chief city of Upper Burma, on the Irrawaddy, *c.* 400 m. from Rangoon. Pop. 322,000.

MANDARIN *See* SINO-TIBETAN.

MANDARIN DUCK
(or **Chinese Teal**) Small freshwater duck of E. Asia (*Aix galericulata*). The drake has purple, green and chestnut plumage, with long, silky, erectile crest.

MANDEVILLE, Sir John
The Voyage and Travel of Sir John Mandeville is a compilation of geog. lore. The orig. Fr. version was prob. by **John de Bourgoyne** (*c.* 1313-65) of Liège.

MANDOLINE
The only surviving representative of the lute family of instruments.

MANDRAKE
(*Mandragora*) Genus of perennial herbs of the potato family. They are stemless plants with thick, fleshy roots. Source of drug *Mandragora.*

MANDRILL
(*Papio maimon*) Species of baboon, native of W. Africa. It is remarkable for its bright colouring, the muzzle being bright red with blue on either side, and the hinder parts purplish.

MANET, Edouard
[-ā] (1832-83) Fr. painter and greatest exponent of the Impressionist school. B. Paris, he studied under Couture. His work, notably *The Garden* and *Olympia*, aroused much hostility.

MANGANESE
A greyish metal, hard and brittle, forming 0·09 % of the earth's crust, discovered in 1774 by Gahn. It is a constituent of alloys. Sp. gr. 7·2. Chem. sym. Mn.

MANGE
Skin disease affecting domestic animals such as the horse, ass, mule, ox, sheep, goat, pig, camel, dog, cat and fowl. Disease is notifiable under Diseases of Animals Acts.

MANGEL WURZEL
Cultivated variety of *Beta vulgaris*, a biennial herb of the goose-foot family. Red and yellow forms serve as winter fodder for livestock.

MANGO
Tall, evergreen tree of the cashew family, native to the E. Indies and Malaya (*Mangifera indica*). 30 or 40 ft. high, it is cultivated in trop. Asia, Africa and Amer. for its fruit.

MANGOSTEEN
Evergreen tree (*Garcinia mangostana*). It grows in Malaya and the E. Indies and produces a luscious fruit.

MANGROVE
Various trees abounding in trop. coastal swamps. The common mangrove (*Rhizophora mangle*) with thick, smooth leathery leaves and large 4-petalled flowers, sends down from the trunk and branches spreading stilt-like roots.

MANHATTAN
Is. of the U.S.A. at the mouth of the Hudson R.; borough of New York City. Pop. 1,698,281.

MANICHAEISM
[-i-kē'-] Religious system founded by the Persian Mani, or Manichaeus, in the 3rd cent. A.D. It spread to Mesopotamia, C. Asia, W. Christendom and N. Africa, long resisted Islamic opposition, and influenced the Albigenses.

MANILA
Chief city and seaport of the Philippines, on the W. coast of Luzon at the mouth of the Pasig. There is a 16th cent. cath. and a univ. founded 1857. Pop. 1,356,000.

MANILA HEMP
(or **Manilla**) Fibre of great strength, tenacity and lightness, obtained from *Musa textilis*, a plant of the banana family. It is used for making cordage, muslins and other fabrics, also as a binding material for plaster.

MANIN, Daniele
(1804-57) Ital. statesman; leader of the Venetian revolution against Aust. domination (1848-9). He was imprisoned for treason, but released by the revolutionaries and became Pres. of the Republic of St. Mark.

MANITOBA
Prov. of the Dominion of Canada, between Ontario and Saskatchewan with a coastline on Hudson Bay. It is one of the prairie prov. The lakes cover 20,000 sq.m. Grain is produced in large quantities and there is a good deal of dairy farming. Coal, gold, silver, copper, nickel and zinc are mined. Winnipeg is the cap. The prov. was formed, 1870, from land bought from the Hudson's Bay Co. Before 1870 it was called the Red River Settlement. The prov. has a legislative assembly and a lieut.-gov. It sends 6 senators and 14 representatives to Ottawa. The Univ. was founded 1877. Area: 251,000 sq.m. Pop. 921,686.

MANN, Thomas
(1875-1955) German writer. His major novels are *Buddenbrooks* (1900); tetralogy on Jacob and Joseph (1933-44); *Lotte in Weimar* (1939); *Dr. Faustus* (1948). He moved to Amer. (1938). He was awarded the Nobel Prize for Lit. in 1929 and the Goethe Prize in 1949. *Der Erwählte* (*The Chosen*) was pub. 1951.

MANNA
Saccharine exudation, obtained from incisions in the stems of *Fraxinus ornus*, a native of S. Europe. Similar exudations are derived from a number of trees, the manna of the Bible probably being that from the tamarisk.

MANNERHEIM, Baron Karl Gustav Emil
(1867-1951) Finnish soldier. He commanded Finnish resistance to the Bolshevists in 1918, and was Regent of the newly-freed country in 1918-19. Recalled to command the army against the Russ. attack of 1939, he conducted a masterly defence, and afterwards remained in command in the 2nd Russ. War of 1941-4. He was Pres. of Finland, 1944-6.

MANSFIELD, Katherine
(1888-1923) Pseudonym of **Katherine Beauchamp**, Brit. writer. B. New Zealand. Her best work is in *Bliss* (1920), *The Garden Party* (1922), *The Dove's Nest* (1923), *Something Childish* (1924); collected works, 1945.

MANSLAUGHTER
In Eng. law the unlawful killing of another without premeditation. It may be due to an accident or done in the heat of the moment, or as an act of self-defence. It may be the result of neglect, as when a failure to call in a doctor results in death. Maximum punishment is imprisonment for life. Manslaughter is not recognised in Scots law.

MANTEGNA, Andrea
[man-tān'-yă] (1431-1506) Ital. painter. B. Vicenza; settled in Mantua. A series of 9 of his pictures, called *The Triumph of Julius Caesar*, are in Hampton Court Palace.

MANTIS
Orthopterous insects not unlike locusts. Sometimes called the Praying Mantis because the forelegs assume an attitude of prayer.

MANTUA
City of Lombardy, Italy, on the Mincio, 24 m. S.W. of Verona, the birthplace of Virgil (*q.v.*). Pop. 58,000.

MAORI
[mow'-ri] People of Polynesian stock in New Zealand. Estimated at 167,000, mostly in N. Is., fifth being half-caste, they are tall and muscular, black-haired, with oval faces of Caucasian type. Traditionally arriving from Rarotonga *c.* 1350, they encountered still earlier Polynesian immigrants intermingled with indigenous Papuans. Remarkable cultural developments occurred. When Gt. Brit. undertook sovereignty, 1840, conflicts with the natives developed, 1843-7 and 1861-71. They have now native representative on the executive council, and 4 elected members in the Parl. of N.Z.

MAO TSE-TUNG
[mow' tsē-tŏŏng'] (1893-) Chinese communist leader. B. Hunan, in 1918 went to Peking Univ. He helped to form the Communist Party in Shanghai, 1921, and took part in the Nationalist-Communist march, 1926, and in the ill-fated Nanchang rising, 1927, when he set up the first Chinese Soviet Repub. He gained full control of the Party in 1935. A truce was brought about in 1936 which lasted during the course of the Jap. War but in 1946 civil war was renewed and the Communists under Mao won the whole Chinese mainland. In 1959 resigned his gov. though not his party chairmanship. *See* CHINA.

MAPLE
(*Acer*) Genus of deciduous trees, native to N. temp. regions. The fruits are ash-like 2-winged 'keys'. Many species are planted for their valuable timber, sugary product or variegated foliage. Brit.'s native small-leaved maple is *A. campestre*; the false sycamore or great maple, *A. pseudo-platanus*, 40-60 ft. high, has long been naturalised.

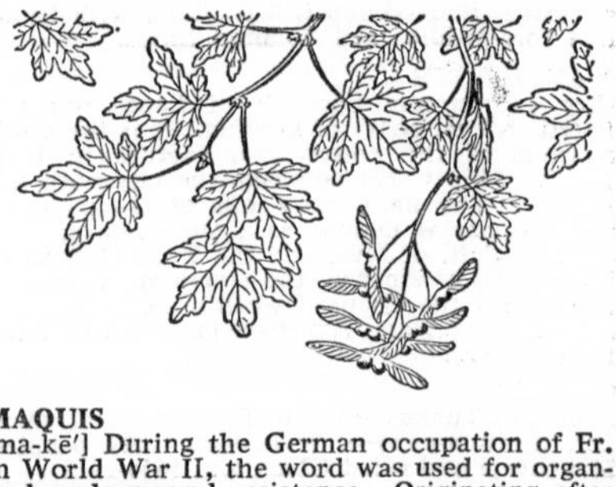

MAQUIS
[ma-kē'] During the German occupation of Fr. in World War II, the word was used for organised underground resistance. Originating after Pierre Laval's introduction of compulsory labour service (1943), the **maquis** took to the countryside, were supplied with weapons from the air by the Allies and formed part of the Allied forces after June 6, 1944.

MARABOU
Central African Stork (*Leptoptilus*). Its undertail coverts were formerly collected for trimmings.

MARAT, Jean Paul
[mar-rȧ'] (1743-93) Fr. revolutionary leader. In 1789 he started a polit. paper *L'Ami du Peuple*,

which attacked those in authority. He engaged in a bitter struggle with the Girondins, which led to his assassination in his bath by Charlotte Corday.

MARATHON
Plain of Greece, 25 m. N.E. of Athens. It is famous for the battle fought there in 490 B.C. The Persians invaded Greece and encamped on a plain near the sea. There they were attacked by a Gk. army, chiefly composed of Athenians, directed by Miltiades. The Gk. victory was conveyed to Athens by Pheidippides an Olympic champion runner, who fell d. as he entered the city.

MARBLE
Term for any rock capable of taking a high polish. Strictly it means a hard limestone used for ornamental purposes. The colour varies. Statuary marble is quarried at Carrara, Italy, onyx marble in Algeria, green serpentinous marbles in Ireland, Italy and Greece.

MARCH, Earl of
(*c.* 1287-1330) Eng. soldier. **Roger Mortimer** was one of the group that followed Thomas, Earl of Lancaster, in his rebellion against Edward II. Put in prison, in 1324 he escaped and went to Fr. There he became the lover of Isabella, the wife of Edward II, and in 1327 the pair returned to Eng., took the king prisoner and had him put to d. Mortimer then helped the queen to rule in the name of her son, Edward III, for 3 years.

MARCONI, Guglielmo
(1874-1937) Italian inventor. B. Bologna, he took out the first wireless telegraph patent on June 2, 1896. In 1901 Marconi succeeded in transmitting and receiving signals between Newfoundland and Cornwall. In 1914 he began experiments with short waves, which led to the 'beam' system of long distance and directed wireless transmission. Nobel Prize for Physics in 1909.

MARCUS AURELIUS
[-rē'-] (121-180) Rom. emperor and Stoic philosopher. He became co-emperor in 161 and sole emperor in 169. He re-estabd. discipline, ameliorated the conditions of slaves, reformed the civil laws and carried out long and successful wars against the barbarians. His *Meditations* show him to have been, at a time of universal corruption, self-denying, just and unaffected.

MARE'S TAIL
(*Hippuris vulgaris*) Water plant of the family Haloragaceae. It has a creeping root stock and the whorls of narrow leaves encircle the joints of the slender stems.

MARGARET
(*c.* 1045-93) Saint and Queen of Scot. In 1067 she was mar. at Dunfermline to Malcolm III. In 1093 her husband was killed, and the same year the queen d. leaving 3 sons, Edgar, Alexander I and David I, who all became kings. She was canonised 1250.

MARGARET
(1283-90) Queen of Scot. called the Maid of Norway. She was the daughter of Eric, King of Norway, and a granddaughter of Alexander III of Scot. In 1290 on the d. of Alexander she was sent for to become Queen, but, on her way to Scot., d. at the Orkney Is. The appearance of 13 claimants to the throne led to the intervention of Edward I of Eng. and to the War of Indep.

MARGARET OF ANJOU
[ā(ng)-zhoo'] (1430-1482) Queen of Henry VI, whom she mar. in 1445. Her politics helped to rouse discontent ending in a quarrel for the throne, claimed by Richard, Duke of York. In 1455 began the Wars of the Roses, and Margaret actively supported the claims of her husband and young son. After Tawton (1461), she went to Fr. for help, but defeat at Tewkesbury (1471) ended Lancastrian hopes.

MARGARET ROSE, Princess
(1930-) B. Glamis Castle, Scot., she is the younger daughter of Queen Elizabeth the Queen Mother, and of the late King George VI, and the sister of H.M. Queen Elizabeth II. In 1960, mar. Anthony Armstrong-Jones (created Earl of Snowdon, 1961). Son, David, Viscount Linley, b. 1961; daughter, 1964.

MARGARINE
Name given to a butter substitute. It was made orig. from beef fat digested in a weak alkaline solution with pepsin.

MARGAY
Brazilian name of a small tiger-cat, *Felis tigrina.* A forest dweller, 24 in. long, with 12 in. tail, its harsh grizzly-grey fur is variously spotted and ringed.

MARGUERITE
Composite flowers of various hardy perennial herbs of the type of the ox-eye daisy, *Chrysanthemum leucanthemum.* A shrubby form from Tenerife, *C. frutescens,* and a yellow variant, are garden favourites. *See* DAISY.

MARIA THERESA
(1717-80) Empress of Austria. Daughter of Charles VI. As her father had no sons, he named her as his successor and persuaded the Powers to agree to this. When he d. a Bavarian prince was elected emperor, and Frederick the Great invaded Silesia. The result was a European war which lasted until 1748, and then the Seven Years' War, 1756-63. Maria Theresa lost Silesia, but in 1748 she secured the election of her husband, Francis, Duke of Lorraine, as Holy Rom. Emperor. Her large family included the Emperor Leopold II and Marie Antoinette.

MARIANAS
or **Ladrones.** Group of Is. in the Pacific Ocean, *c.* 1,500 m. N.E. of the Philippines. Formerly gov. by Japan, they are now under U.S. occupation. Area: 250 sq.m. Pop. 44,000.

MARIE ANTOINETTE
(1755-93) Queen of Louis XVI of Fr. A daughter of Maria Theresa and Francis I. In 1770, she mar. the dauphin, who in 1774 became King of Fr. Her frivolity made her most unpopular. In 1792, with Louis, she was arrested. At her trial in Oct. 1793, she defended herself with dignity and spirit, but sentence of d. was passed Oct. 16, 1793, and she was guillotined. *See* LOUIS XVI.

MARIE DE MEDICI
[mā'-di-chi] (1573-1642) Queen of Fr., wife of Henry IV. B. Florence and mar. Henry in 1600. After the murder of her husband in 1610, she was made Regent for her son, Louis XIII and was at war with him, 1617-20.

MARIE LOUISE
(1791-1847) Empress of the Fr.; daughter of the Emperor Francis II. In 1810 she became the 2nd wife of Napoleon. In 1814 she returned to Austria. She had a son by Napoleon, and several children by her lover, Count von Neipperg, whom she mar. in 1822.

MARIGOLD
Annual composite herb with orange or lemon-coloured flowers. The common pot-marigold is *Calendula officinalis,* from S. Europe: an allied Cape marigold, white-rayed with purple disk, called *Dimorphotheca.* Mexican species of *Tagetes* furnish so-called African and Fr. marigolds. The corn marigold is *Chrysanthemum segetum. See* MARSH MARIGOLD.

MARINE
Soldier who serves on board ship. Marines were first raised in Eng. in 1664, but the Royal Marines in its present form dates from 1755.

From them have been formed the Royal Marine Commandos. The Amer. Marines correspond in status to the Brigade of Guards in Brit.

MARINER'S COMPASS
Instrument to show the course of a vessel. The compass is contained in a case or binnacle and is placed usually in the wheelhouse and above the bridge. Errors caused by the magnetisation of the steel in the ship are adjusted by correctors placed in the binnacle.

MARITAIN, Jacques
[mà-rē-ta(ng)'] (1882-) Fr. philosopher. A convert to Catholicism, he led the neo-scholastic movement of the 1930's-40's.

MARIUS, Gaius
(157-86 B.C.) Rom. soldier and politician. He quarrelled violently with Sulla, and civil war ensued, 88. Marius escaped for a time to Africa, but returned in triumph when Sulla was in the E., held a 'proscription' (or purge) of his enemies and had just been elected consul for the 7th time when he d.

MARJORAM
Genus of perennial aromatic herbs or under-shrubs (*Origanum*), native to N. temp. regions. Wild marjoram, 1-3 ft. high, is purple-flowered. Sweet and pot marjoram are 2 cultivated culinary forms.

MARK
One of the 4 evangelists. He was a Jew, probably from Cyprus. Known as John Mark, he accepted Christianity and went on a missionary journey with St. Paul, and his own cousin, Barnabas. Patron saint of Venice, his day is April 25. **Mark, The Gospel of St.** Second book of the N.T. As early as A.D. 130 Papius recorded that Mark, having become Peter's interpreter, wrote down all he remembered. The work is a brief, rugged narrative, dealing with the acts rather than the sayings of our Lord. It was the framework for the other 2 synoptic gospels.

MARK ANTONY
(83-30 B.C.) Rom. statesman, a kinsman of Julius Caesar. He helped Caesar to defeat Pompey at Pharsalus in 48 B.C. After Caesar's murder, Antony, with Octavian, the future emperor, and Lepidus, formed the triumvirate to restore order. Antony and Octavian destroyed the army of Brutus and Cassius at Philippi. Antony went to Egypt, where he became the lover of Cleopatra. He quarrelled with Octavian, and the final struggle came in 31 B.C. The naval fleets met off Actium. Antony's ships were scattered or destroyed, but with Cleopatra he managed to get back to Egypt, where both committed suicide.

MARKOVA, Alicia
(Alice Marks) (1910-) Brit. ballerina. Was a member of Diaghilev's Russian Ballet Co. Formed a Co. with Anton Dolin. Awarded C.B.E. 1958. Retired from stage, 1963.

MARLBOROUGH, Duke of
John Churchill (1650-1722) Eng. soldier. After the revolution of 1688 he joined William of Orange. In 1702 he was given the command of the Eng. forces in the war of the Sp. Succession. M. saved Austria from invasion by the Fr. by his victory at Blenheim in 1704, and foiled Louis XIV's schemes for the invasion of Holland by the victories of Ramillies (1706), Oudenarde (1708) and Malplaquet (1709). His wealth and unscrupulousness gained him many enemies who obtained his recall in 1711. He was accused of peculation, and dismissed, but reinstated for a time by George I.

MARLOWE, Christopher
(1564-93) Eng. dramatist. B. Canterbury. He was killed by Ingram Frizar in a Deptford tavern. His plays were written for the Earl of Nottingham's Company: *Tamburlaine*, 2 parts (1587), *Dr. Faustus* (1588-9), *The Jew of Malta*, *Edward II*, etc. He adapted the *Hero and Leander* of Musaeus in rhyming couplets. His contribution to Eng. drama was his phil. conception of tragedy and his use of blank verse.

MARMOSET
Small monkey about the size of a squirrel, with a long tail and thick fur. There are 2 genera, *Midas* and *Hapale*, inhabiting Brazil and Columbia respectively.

MARMOT
(*Arctomys*) Rodents inhabiting N. temp. regions. They are stout, burrowing vegetable-feeders, generally hibernating. Besides the Alpine M., 15-25 in. long, with short, bushy tail, inhabiting the Pyrenees, Alps and Carpathians, the Bobac, 15 in. long, ranges from E. Germany to Siberia; other species occur in the Himalayas and C. Asia. N. Amer. marmots include the woodchuck, 14½ in. long, with 7 in. tail, ranging from Manitoba to Carolina.

MARNE
Name of 2 depts. in Fr. (1) **Marne** lies in the N.E. and is a famous champagne district. Cap. Châlons-sur-Marne. (2) **Haute Marne,** lies S.E. of Marne. Cap. Chaumont. Both are watered by the river M. **Marne, Battles of the.** Decisive battles of World War I. The first, Sept. 6-9, 1914, checked the great German advance. The 2nd Battle, July 15, 1918, marked the limit of Germany's last big offensive. Pushing on to reach Paris, they crossed the Marne E. of Rheims. Foch sent a Franco-Amer. force against them and defeated them at Seringes.

MARQUESAS
[-kā'-sas] Fr. group of Is. in the S. Pacific, midway between New Guinea and S. Amer. The 2 largest Is. are Nukahiva and Hivaoa. Area: 480 sq.m. Pop. 3,000.

MARQUESS
Title in the Brit. peerage, ranking next below that of duke. In Eng. the first marquess was created in 1385. The senior marquess is the Marquess of Winchester. The coronet bears 4 strawberry leaves and 4 pearls. A marquess is styled 'the most honourable'.

MARRAKESH
City of Morocco, *c.* 140 m. S. of Casablanca, and 90 m. from the coast. One of the traditional capitals, M. is a trading centre. Pop. 243,134.

MARRIAGE
Union between man and woman recognised by law or custom, to enforce responsibility of parentage and determine ownership of property. Among primitive peoples various forms of polygamy have been found. Christianity has helped estab. monogamy. Today in Eng. no one under 16 years of age can be legally mar. and before 18 consent of parents must be obtained. Mar. between near relatives is forbidden. In Eng. marriages can be celebrated either in ch. or registrar's office, by certificate, licence or banns. In Scot. the law differs considerably. Consent of parents is not required under 18 and marriages by habit and repute are legal. Scots living outside Scot. may marry in Scot. without 15 days residence qualification provided a surviving parent still lives in Scot.

MARRYAT, Frederick
(1792-1848) Eng. author. His books include *Peter Simple*, *Jacob Faithful*, *Mr. Midshipman Easy*, *Masterman Ready*, *The Children of the New Forest.*

MARS
The 4th known planet in order of distance from the sun (*c.* 141,700,000 m.). It has a diameter of *c.* 4,220 m. and its mass is one-tenth that of the earth. Its solar orbit takes *c.* 687 days, and its period of axial rotation

is *c.* 24 hrs. 37 mins. 23 secs. It has 2 small satellites. The climate on the surface of Mars is an extreme version of our continental climate. The atmosphere must contain far less oxygen and water than that of the earth, but there is a high concentration of carbon dioxide.

MARSALA
[-sà'-] Seaport of W. Sicily, 19 m. S. of Trapani. It is the centre of a wine-producing region. Pop. 76,000.

MARSEILLES
[mar-sā'] Chief seaport of S. Fr., cap. of Bouches-du-Rhône dept. on the Gulf of Lyons. It has extensive docks, and is connected by canal with the Rhône. Industries include oil-refining, and the manufacture of soap, margarine and flour. Pop. 783,738.

MARSH MALLOW
(*Althaea officinalis*) Perennial herb of the mallow family, native in temp. regions. Occurring on Brit. maritime marshlands, it is a downy plant 2-3 ft. high, with large, thick, oval leaves and rose-coloured 1-2 in. flowers. The root was formerly used for making sweetmeats.

MARSH MARIGOLD
(*Caltha palustris*) Perennial herb of the buttercup family, native in N. temp. regions. Its fleshy, creeping rootstock bears large kidney-shaped leaves and showy golden 1-2 in. flowers.

MARSHAL
At first the earl marshal was something like master of the horse to the king. Today in Eng. he is one of the great officers of state. As a milit. title, marshal originated in Fr. and was given to famous soldiers by Louis XIV. Napoleon made great use of the dignity as a reward for services in the field. It was revived in 1916. The Brit. Army equivalent is Field Marshal and Marshal of the R.A.F. is the highest rank in that service.

MARSHALL
Group of Is. in the Pacific Ocean, E. of the Caroline Is. Copra is the chief product. Taken by Germany, 1885, they were under Japanese mandate after World War I. Now under U.S. occupation. Area: 160 sq.m. Pop. 17,363.

MARSHALL, George Catlett
(1880-1959) Amer. soldier and statesman. Chief of Staff, 1939-47, U.S. Ambassador to China, 1945, and later U.S. Sec. of Defence, resigning 1951. He was responsible for the plan for economic rehabilitation in W. Europe. Awarded the Nobel Peace Prize, 1953. **Marshall Plan.** Proposals put forward in 1947, for a long-term plan for Amer. financing of Europe (including Brit.) reconstruction. A conference of European nations was held at Paris to work out a programme of needs, but the E. Europe countries refused to attend. Legislation went before the Amer. Congress and was passed in 1948. Marshall Aid was suspended Dec. 14, 1950.

MARSTON, John
(*c.* 1575-1634) Eng. dramatist. His chief plays are revenge tragedies, *Antonio's Revenge* (*c.* 1600); *Sophonisba* (1606); comedies, *The Malcontent, The Dutch Courtesan* and (with Jonson and Chapman) *Eastward Ho.*

MARSUPIAL
Sub-class of mammals intermediate in structure between the primitive egg-laying species and placental mammals. The young are b. in an immature condition and continue development in an abdominal pouch. The group includes the Opossums, Wombats, Kangaroos, etc.

MARTELLO TOWER
Round fort. Many were constructed on the Eng. coast and in the Channel Is. at the time of the threatened invasion by Napoleon.

MARTEN
(*Mustela* or *Martes*) Various arboreal carnivorous mammals of the N. hemisphere. The European pine-marten, 18 in. long, with 9-12 in. tail, still lingers in Brit. The white-breasted beech-marten is widely distributed in C. Europe and W. Asia.

MARTHA
A sister of Lazarus and Mary, at whose village home in Bethany, near Jerusalem, Jesus was an honoured guest.

MARTIAL
(43-104) Rom. epigrammatist. His witty epigrams were much imitated after *c.* 1550.

MARTIAL LAW
Law administered by the milit. authorities in times of danger or disorder.

MARTIN
Perching birds of the swallow family. The black and white house martin, *Delichon urbica*, 5¼ in. long, makes rough mud-built, swallow-like nests. The lighter-hued sand martin, *Riparia riparia*, 4¾ in. long, forms nesting colonies in sandstone cliffs.

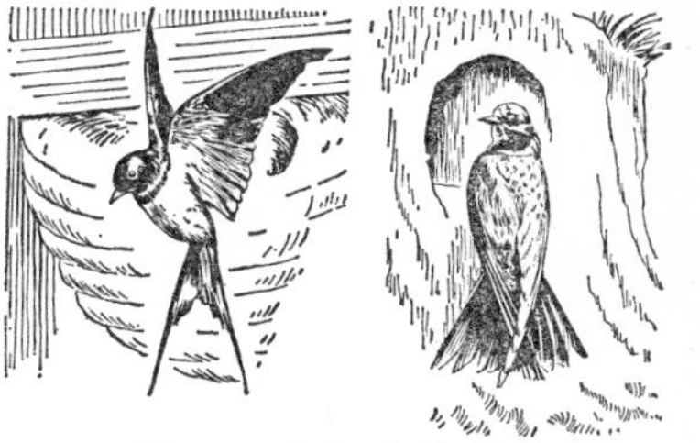

House and Sand Martins

MARTINIQUE
[-ti-nēk'] Fr. Is. and overseas dept. in the W. Indies, between Dominica and St. Lucia, in the Lesser Antilles. Sugar, tobacco, rum and coffee are produced. Fort de France is the cap. and chief port. Area: 285 sq.m. Pop. 291,000.

MARTYR
Term denoting a witness esp. one who willingly suffers d. rather than surrender his religious faith. The first Christian martyr was the deacon Stephen. Under the Rom. Emp. many Christian confessors suffered persecutions and, if to the d., were remembered as saints and martyrs. Both Catholics and Protestants have martyrs.

MARVELL, Andrew
(1621-78) Eng. poet. B. Winestead, Yorks. Besides vigorous pamphlets and satires he wrote many lyrics (pub. 1682).

MARX, Karl Heinrich
(1818-83) German social economist of Jewish descent. A journalist, his advanced views led to his expulsion from Germany and then from Paris. After 1848 he went to London, where he d. Marx exercised an enormous influence on the Socialist and Communist movements. In 1847, at Brussels, he and Engels issued the *Communist Manifesto*, in which are the ideas more fully developed in *Das Kapital* (1867).

MARY
Mother of Jesus, cousin of Elizabeth, John the Baptist's mother. Mary attended the mar. feast in Cana, was committed by Christ to John's care at the Crucifixion, and traditionally d. at Jerusalem.

MARY
(1542-87) Queen of Scots. Mary became Queen when only a week old owing to the d. of her

father after the battle of Solway Moss. To avoid a forced betrothal to Prince Edward of Eng. she was taken to Fr. (1548). In 1558 she mar. the Dauphin and became Queen of Fr. the next year. She was also heiress to the Eng. throne as next of kin to Elizabeth Tudor. In 1560, her husband d. and she returned to Scot., 1561. The Presbyterian Ch. was ousting the R.C. faith, but Mary sought only toleration for herself and others of her faith. Nevertheless she was constantly engaged in conflict with John Knox, the Protestant leader, and her half-brother James Stewart. In 1565 she mar. Lord Darnley. The mar. was unhappy, and before the birth of their son (1566) Darnley became jealous of an Ital. sec., Rizzio, and had him murdered. In 1567, however, Darnley was himself murdered, prob. by the Earl of Bothwell. Mary came under suspicion of connivance, and when she mar. Bothwell the nobles revolted. She was imprisoned in Lochleven Castle and her son was proclaimed king, with Moray as Regent. She escaped, and fled to Eng. Elizabeth kept her in prison, for 19 years. There Mary became a centre for R.C. plots to depose Elizabeth, and was finally accused of being implicated in one of them (1586). She was convicted mainly on the evidence of the Casket Letters and executed on a charge of high treason at Fotheringay Castle. Her son, James, became 1st king of Brit., 1603.

MARY
(1867-1953) Queen of George V (*q.v.*). Only daughter of the Duke and Duchess of Teck. In 1891 she was betrothed to Albert Victor, Duke of Clarence. He d. early in 1892 and in May, 1893, the princess was betrothed to George, Duke of York. On July 6, 1893, they were mar. in London. In 1910 George became king. When the king d. in 1935 Queen Mary retired to live in Marlborough House.

MARY
(1897-1965) Princess of Gt. Brit., 3rd child and only daughter of King George V and Queen Mary. On Feb. 28, 1922, the princess mar. Viscount Lascelles who in 1929 became Earl of Harewood. He d. in 1947. Their sons are **George Henry Hubert,** b. 1923, and **Gerald David,** b. 1924. In 1932, the princess was created *Princess Royal.*

MARY I
(1516-58) Queen of Eng. Daughter of Henry VIII and Catherine of Aragon. In July, 1553, her half-brother, Edward VI, d. The plan to make Lady Jane Grey his successor failed and Mary was proclaimed queen. In 1554 she mar. Philip II, King of Spain. Mary's short reign was marked by the restoration of the R.C. religion in Eng. and the persecution of the Protestants. She was succeeded by her half-sister Elizabeth.

MARY II
(1662-94) Queen of Eng., daughter of James II, and his 1st wife, Anne Hyde. In 1677 she mar. William, Prince of Orange. In 1688 William was invited to take the Brit. throne, and after James II had fled, he and his wife became joint rulers of Gt. Brit. She had no children.

MARYLAND
State of the U.S.A. on the Atlantic Coast, bounded by Pennsylvania, Delaware and Virginia. Chesapeake Bay, a long arm of the Atlantic, divides it in two. Much of the area is agricultural. There is mining in the W. hilly regions. Steel manufacture and copper smelting are the chief industries. The cap. is Annapolis, but Baltimore, Cumberland and Hagerstown are larger. One of the orig. 13 states, M. was settled, 1634. It sends 8 representatives to Congress. Area: 10,580 sq.m. Pop. 3,922,400.

MARYLEBONE, St.
Borough of N.W. London. N. of Westminster. In it are St. John's Wood, Harley St. and Lord's Cricket Ground. It returns 1 member to Parl. Pop. 68,070. **Marylebone Cricket Club.** Cricket club, regarded as the governing body of the game. Popularly known as the M.C.C., its headquarters are at Lord's Cricket Ground.

MASAI
[-sī′] People of Hamitic-negro stock in E. equatorial Africa. Now nomadic herdsmen in Kenya and N. Tanzania.

MASARYK, Thomas
[maz′-] (1850-1937) Czechoslovak politician. During World War I he organised, in Brit., the Czechoslovakian Movement for Indep. After the Armistice he was Pres. of the new state, 1918-35. His son, **Jan M.** (1886-1948), diplomat and patriot. On the occupation of Czechoslovakia by the Germans, 1939, he became Foreign Min. in the exiled govt. in London under Benes. When the Communists came to power, Feb. 1948, he agreed to co-operate with them but later committed suicide.

MASCAGNI, Pietro
[mas-kȧn′-yi] (1863-1945) Ital. composer. He won 1st prize in a competition with his opera *Cavalleria Rusticana.*

MASEFIELD, John Edward
(1878-1966) Eng. poet. He became an officer in the merchant service. In 1902 he pub. *Salt Water Ballads*; then *The Everlasting Mercy* (1911), *The Widow in the Bye Street, Dauber, Reynard the Fox.* In 1930 he was apptd. poet laureate. His dramas include *The Trial of Jesus* and *The Coming of Christ.* Among his novels are *Captain Margaret, Multitude and Solitude, Sard Harker.* He has written crit. essays.

MASHONALAND
The E. portion of Rhodesia, inhabited by the Mashona tribes. It contains the famous ruins of Zimbabwe (*q.v.*) near Ft. Victoria, Salisbury is the chief town.

MASON-DIXON LINE
Boundary between states of Pennsylvania and Maryland, surveyed by the astronomers Charles Mason and Jeremiah Dixon, 1763-7. Popular for the dividing line between 'North' and 'South', *i.e.* between free and slave states.

MASS
The celebration of the Holy Eucharist according to the rites of the R.C. Ch. It is a commemoration of the Passion, a propitiatory sacrifice, a service of praise and thanksgiving and a means of grace to all its participants and celebrants. A Requiem mass is celebrated for the soul(s) of the dead.

MASSACHUSETTS
[-choo′-] New Eng. State of the U.S.A. with a coastline on the Atlantic. The interior is hilly, rising to over 3,000 ft. The Merrimack and Connecticut are the chief rivers. M. is mainly an industrial state. Boston is the cap. and largest town. M. was founded, 1620, by the Pilgrim Fathers, and, 1780, became 1 of the orig. 13 states. It now sends 14 representatives to Congress. Area: 8,260 sq.m. Pop. 5,689,200.

MASSÉNA, André
[-sā-nȧ′] (1758-1817) Fr. soldier. Considered to have been Napoleon's greatest gen. He distinguished himself at the battles of Rivoli, Zürich, the siege of Genoa, Essling and Wagram. In 1810 he fought against Wellington in Spain.

MASSANET, Jules Émile Frédéric
(1842-1912) Fr. composer. His easy attractive style won him great success as a composer of operas.

MASSEY, Vincent
(1887-1967) Canadian administrator and politician. Gov.-Gen. of Canada, 1952-9. P.C.

B. Toronto, he was Min. to the U.S., 1926-30 and High Commissioner to Brit., 1935-46.

MASSINGER, Philip
(1583-1640) Eng. dramatist. His best-known plays are the comedies *The City Madam* (1632) and *A New Way to Pay Old Debts* (1633).

MASTIC
Gum resin obtained from incisions in the bark of a small tree, *Pistacia lentiscus*, common in S. Europe. Becoming plastic when heated, it is used for making a varnish for paper.

MASTIFF
Powerful, round-muzzled, short-coated, small-eyed, and thin-tailed dog with pendulous upper lips. Brindled or fawn-coloured, it has ears and muzzle of black. The old Eng. strain is now used as a watch-dog. The modern mastiff is 29 in. high, with pendent ears.

MASTODON
Extinct elephant closely allied to the mammoth. It was covered with thick woolly hair, and it existed from the Miocene age to the Pleistocene in Europe and N. Amer.

MASTOID
Name given to part of temporal bone lying behind the external ear. It contains a number of hollow cells or cavities often the seat of inflammation in ear infections.

MATAPAN
Most S. cape of Greece.

MATCHES
Match heads contain phosphorus sulphide (P_4S_3), potassium chloride and ground glass. The heat produced by friction on striking ignites the mixture. Safety matches contain potassium chlorate, potassium dichromate, etc., but no phosphorus.

MATÉ
[mà'-tā] Roasted and powdered leaves of an evergreen shrub of the holly order, growing wild in Paraguay and S.E. Brazil, and cultivated in plantations (*Ilex paraguensis*).

MATHEMATICS
The science of numbers and abstract quantities. Another definition, due to Russell, regards it as 'the science concerned with the logical deduction of consequences from the general principles of reasoning'. *Pure maths.* includes geometry, algebra and related branches; *applied maths.* comprises the mechanics of solids and fluids and parts of astron., actuarial maths., theoretical physics, etc.

MATILDA
Name of 2 Eng. queens. **Matilda or Maud** (1102-67) was the daughter of Henry I, heiress to the Eng. throne. When Henry d. in 1135 his nephew, Stephen, seized the throne, Matilda being then in Fr. In 1141 she defeated Stephen and was crowned queen. The civil war continued until 1153 when peace was made and Matilda's son, afterwards Henry II, was recognised as heir. The other **Matilda** was the wife of William the Conqueror. She mar. William in 1053, and was crowned queen of Eng. in 1068. She died in 1083, and was buried at Caen.

MATISSE, Henri
[ma-tēs'] (1869-1954) Fr. artist. He studied in Paris. He was one of the orig. Fauvists and his style is noted for its simplicity, its rather violent colouring and its vigorous calligraphic manner of brushwork.

MATTERHORN
Mt. of Switzerland in the Pennine Alps on the Ital. frontier, 6 m. S.W. of Zermatt. 14,782 ft. high, it was first climbed 1865.

MATTHEW
Saint and apostle. A Jewish customs officer, he became one of Christ's 12 disciples. **Matthew, The Gospel of St.** First book of the N.T. traditionally attributed to the apostle. Mod. scholarship tends to hold that Matthew's personal contribution comprised certain logia which he compiled in Hebrew. Designed for the Jewish community, the book takes for granted the authority of the O.T.

MATTHEWS, Sir Stanley
(1915-) Eng. footballer. Has played for Eng. more than 50 times. First cap at 19. Kt. 1965.

MAU MAU
E. African secret society, powerful among the Kikuyu who number over 1,000,000. Bound by religious ritual, the society demanded exacting obedience to its oath and enforced it by ruthless terrorism.

MAUGHAM, William Somerset
(1874-1965) Eng. writer. C.H. 1954. His novels include *Liza of Lambeth* (1897), *Of Human Bondage* (1915), *The Moon and Sixpence* (1919), *The Razor's Edge* (1944), also short stories and essays. His best-known plays are *The Circle* (1921), *The Breadwinner*, *Home and Beauty* (1909), *Our Betters* (1923).

MAUNDY
Name given to the Thur. of Holy Week. It also refers to the ceremonial ablutions, gift of money and Eucharistic celebration proper to the day. In Eng. maundy money is still given to the poor, usually at Westminster Abbey.

MAUPASSANT, Henri de
(1850-93) Fr. novelist. Best known for his short stories.

MAURITANIA
Repub. former Fr. colony of W. Africa, on the Atlantic coast, S. of Sp. Sahara and N. of Senegal. Salt, sheep and cattle are the chief exports. Fully indep. 1960. Area: 419,400 sq.m. Pop. *c.* 1,000,000.

MAURITIUS
Mountainous Is. in Indian Ocean, 500 m. E of Madagascar; until 1968 a Brit. colony. Sugar is principal export. Port Louis is cap. and chief port. Settled by the Dutch (1598). It became Fr. 1715, and was ceded to Brit. 1814. A former Brit. colony, gained independence, 1968. Area: 805 sq.m. Pop. 750,000.

MAXIMILIAN
(1832-67) Emperor of Mexico. A son of Francis Charles, Archduke of Austria. In 1863 he accepted the throne of Mexico and was crowned in 1864. The Fr. left him to struggle with his recalcitrant subjects. He was betrayed to them, and shot.

MAXIMILIAN I
(1459-1519) Holy Rom. Emperor. Son of Frederick III. He became Emperor in 1493. Much of his reign was occupied with warfare against the Fr. in Italy and the Turks in the valley of the Danube. By the mar. of his son Philip to Juana, heiress of Ferdinand and Isabella of Spain, he brought about the succession of the Habsburgs to the vast Spanish dominions, while

the mar. of his grandson Ferdinand to Anna of Hungary brought Hungary and Bohemia.

MAY, Phil
(1864-1903) Eng. artist. He developed an extraordinary genius for caricature, and later he became a popular cartoonist.

MAY FLY *See* EPHEMER.

MAYA
[mī'ya] Amer. Indian people with a highly developed culture which lasted for at least 2,000 years. The Maya still form the majority of the inhabitants of Yucatan, and some 400,000 live in Mexico. Evidence of their culture is widespread, including great temples and cities in Guatemala, S. Mexico, Honduras and Yucatan. Their culture was based on agriculture, corn being the chief grain. They had knowledge of mathematics and astronomy. The Maya perfected a system of writing, and erected carved stelae to record chronology in a glyphic script. The break-up of Mayan civilisation began *c.* A.D. 800 when they were invaded by Mexican tribes. By the time of the Sp. invasion in the 16th cent. the Maya had splintered into numbers of separate nations.

MAYFLOWER
Sailing vessel carrying the Pilgrim Fathers (*q.v.*) *c.* 102 men, women and children, from Plymouth, Devon, in Sept. 1620. It reached Plymouth, Mass. on Dec. 21.

MAYO
Co. of the Repub. of Ireland, in the prov. of Connaught, with a long coastline on the Atlantic. Achill, Clare and other Is. lie off the W. coast, and Clew Blacksod and Killala Bays are openings of the sea. The chief occupation is fishing. Castlebar is the county town; other places are Ballina, Killala and Westport. Pop. 123,330.

MAYOR
The chief magistrate of a city or corporate town in England, Ireland and the U.S.A. The Scot. equivalent is *provost*. The mayor is elected by the aldermen or councillors, holds office for a given period and may be re-elected.

MAYWEED
(*Matricaria inodora*) Plant of the family Compositae, of branching growth with narrow finely-cut leaves and daisy-like scentless flowers. Stinking mayweed (*Athemis cotula*) has a malodorous juice which causes skin irritation.

MAZARIN, Jules
[ma'-za-ra(ng)] **Cardinal** (1602-61) Fr. statesman, of Ital. origin, chief min. of Louis XIII and Louis XIV. He brought the 30 Years War to a conclusion, negotiated the Peace of the Pyrenees (1659) with Sp., and the mar. of Louis XIV to the Infanta, Maria Theresa.

MAZEPPA
(1644-1709) Cossack trader. Belonged to a noble Polish family. He went to the Ukraine and joined the Cossacks. In 1687 he became their leader or hetman. He helped Peter the Great against Turkey and Sweden, but in 1708 transferred his services to Peter's enemy Charles XII. The enmity of the Tsar was fatal and Mazeppa's power was soon broken.

MAZZINI, Giuseppe
[ma-tsē'-ni] (1805-72) Ital. patriot and author, b. at Genoa. For 40 years (1830-70) he laboured for Ital. unity. Banished from Italy in 1830. He vigorously supported Cavour and Garibaldi in 1859-60.

MEAD
Alcoholic beverage of medieval Eng. It is made by boiling honey in water with spices and adding a yeast or other ferment.

MEADOW-GRASS
Hay and pasture grasses of the genus *Poa*, abounding in cold and temp. regions. They include the smooth *P. pratensis*, the blue grass of Kentucky, the rough *P. trivialis*, and the wood meadow-grass *P. nemoralis*.

MEADOW RUE
Large genus of perennial herbs of the buttercup family, natives of N. temp. and frigid regions (*Thalictrum*).

MEADOW SAFFRON
(*Colchicum autumnale*) Bulbous plant of the family Liliaceae. It is a hardy perennial. The leaves are large and fleshy and appear in the spring, dying down before the purple flowers appear. The plant is poisonous and contains the drug colchicum.

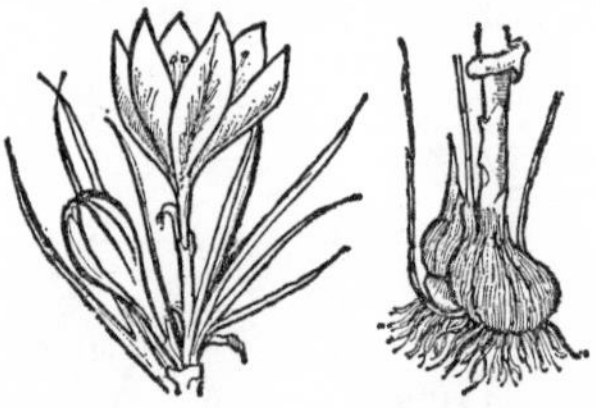

MEADOW SWEET
(*Filipendula ulmaria*) Perennial herb of the Rosaceae, indigenous to N. Europe, Asia Minor and N. Asia. Common in waterside meadows in Brit.

MEASLES
Acute infectious disease occurring commonly in epidemics and affecting mainly children. Caused by a virus and characterised by blotchy rash preceded by running nose and eyes, with rise in temp., and lassitudes.

MEATH
Co. of Repub. of Ireland, in the prov. of Leinster, with a short coastline on the Irish Sea. The chief rivers are the Boyne and Blackwater. The soil is fertile and the country level, and farming is the main industry. Trim is the county town. Pop. 65,132.

MECCA
Sacred city of Saudi Arabia, cap. of Hejaz, 70 m. E. of Jiddah on the Red Sea. The birthplace of Mahomet. Pop. 200,000.

MEDES
People closely assoc. with the Persians, who lived in Asia Minor and Persia, where they gave their name to a district called Media, which corresponds roughly to modern Persia. Their greatest king was Darius, who is mentioned in the Bible.

MEDICI
[mā'-di-chi] Famous Ital. family. **Giovanni de Medici** was a trader and banker in Florence in the 13th and early 14th cents. In 1424 **Cosimo** was recalled to Florence and until his d., 1464, was the real ruler of the repub. **Lorenzo,** called the Magnificent, fully earned the epithet by the way he spent his wealth in beautifying the city and encouraging artists and poets. In 1530 **Alessandro** was recognised by the Emperor as Duke of Florence. Other notable members of the house were Catherine and Maria (*q.v.*), both queens of Fr.

MEDICINE
Science of healing. First practised by primeval man with magico-religious methods, it developed during ancient Euphrates, Indus and Nile civilisations into empirical systems making use of remedial herbs. In early Greece rational cure first arose under the Gk. physician Hippocrates, *c.* 500 B.C., whose writings influenced

med. theory and practice for nearly 2,000 years. Knowledge was further advanced by Galen and by the study of anat. at Padua med. school. With the Renaissance came the teachings of Paracelsus. Later Harvey, an Eng. physician, discovered the circulation of the blood and with the discoveries of Hunter, Laennec, Bell, Abercromby, Darwin, Koch, Pasteur, Wassermann, Erlich, Curie and Lister, modern scientific medicine was firmly estabd.

MEDICINE HAT
Town of Alberta, Canada, on the S. Saskatchewan, 165 m. S.E. of Calgary. It is the distributing and trading centre for a large district. Pop. 24,621.

MEDICK
(*Medicago falcata*) Perennial leguminous herb. Stalks bearing clusters of yellow, or violet flowers, rise from the axils of the leaves which are trifoliate. Native to Europe, the herb is found also in India and parts of Asia. Other species include the **Black medick** (*M. lupulina*) and Lucerne.

MEDINA
City of Saudi Arabia, in Hejaz, 240 m. N. of Mecca. It was the home of Mahomet for a time. M., the res. of early caliphs, is much visited by pilgrims, and ranks after Mecca as a holy city. Pop *c.* 50,000.

MEDITERRANEAN SEA
Largest enclosed sea in world. Over 2,000 m. long, it divides Europe from Africa, with Asia on the E. At the W. end is the Strait of Gibraltar. Connected with the Black Sea by the Dardanelles and Sea of Marmara, and with the Red Sea by the Suez Canal, it has the Adriatic, Ionian, Tyrrhenian and Aegean seas in the N. There are many is., the largest being Sicily, Crete and Cyprus. There is no regular tide. Area: *c.* 966,757 sq.m.

MEDLAR
(*Mespilus germanica*) Hardy tree of the Rosaceae, indigenous to Greece and W. Asia. In Brit. it grows as a much-branched spiny tree, bearing roundish ½-1 in. fruits. The **Japanese medlar** is the Loquat.

MEDOC
A wine-growing district of W. France in the dept. of Gironde, producing red Bordeaux.

MEDWAY
River of S.E. Eng. which rises in Sussex and flows through Kent to the Thames Estuary.

MEERUT
City of Uttar Pradesh, Ind., 40 m. N.E. of Delhi. The place where the Ind. Mutiny began, 1857. Pop. 200,470.

MEGALITHIC AGE
Archaeological term for the culture period characterised by the building of massive structures and monuments, and coinciding with the later Stone and Bronze Ages. In Brit. the remains of the great stone circles at Avebury and Stonehenge are examples.

MEGALOSAURUS
Extinct carnivorous reptile of the order Dinosauria. Fossil remains are found in Jurassic and Cretaceous formations in Europe, Asia and N. Amer. It was *c.* 20 ft. in length and assumed the erect posture, support being given by its long thick tail.

MEGATHERIUM
Extinct giant sloth. Its remains are found in Pleistocene deposits in S. Amer. Prob. contemporaneous with early man, it was *c.* 20 ft. long.

MEISSEN
City in Saxony, E. Germany, on the Elbe, 15 m. below Dresden. M. is famous for its china. Pop. 45,000.

MEKONG
River of Asia, which rises in W. China and flows for 2,600 m. to S. China Sea. It crosses China, and later forms the border between Thailand and Laos.

MELANCHOLIA
Symptom of mental upset characterised by depression of all body functions. Lethargy, listlessness, and emotional instability are assoc. features.

MELANCHTHON, Philip
(melangk'-thon] (1497-1560) German Protestant reformer and theologian. He assisted Luther in preparing his German tr. of N.T. Composed the Augsburg Confession, 1530.

MELANESIA
One of the 3 divisions of Oceania, S. of Micronesia and E. of New Guinea: New Hebrides and New Caledonia, and the Solomon and Ellice Is.

MELBOURNE
Cap. of Victoria, Australia, on the Yarra Yarra, overlooking Port Phillip Bay. Founded, 1835, the city developed rapidly after the discovery of gold, 1851. There are numerous industries, and an important shipping trade. Pop. 1,956,400.

MELBOURNE, Viscount
William Lamb (1779-1848) Eng. statesman. **M.P.** (Whig), 1806-12, 1816-25 and 1827-8; **P.M.** 1834 and 1835-41. Personally indolent, Melbourne was unable as P.M. to keep his party together. His greatest work was done in his relations with the young Queen Victoria.

MELON
(*Cucumis melo*) Annual trailing herb of the gourd family, indigenous to S. Asia. It provides important crops in all trop. and subtrop. lands, being raised for some European markets under glass. **Water melons,** the fruit of the allied *Citrullus vulgaris*, are usually larger and coarser-fleshed.

MELROSE
Burgh of Roxburghshire, on the Tweed, 37 m. S.E. of Edinburgh. The abbey was assoc. with Sir Walter Scott. Pop. 2,143.

MELTON MOWBRAY
Urban district of Leics., 14 m. N.E. of Leicester. M. is famous for pork pies, and as a hunting centre. Pop. 16,000.

MELVILLE, Herman
(1819-91) Amer. author. He went to sea when 17 in a whaler, eventually joined a man-of-war. He pub. *Typee* (1846) and *Omoo* (1847), tales of life among the cannibals. In 1850 came *White Jacket*, which led to the abolition of corporal punishment in the navy. In 1851 he pub. his masterpiece, *Moby Dick*, a tale of whaling. *Billy Budd* was not pub. till 1924.

MEMEL
or **Klaipeda.** Seaport of Lithuania, U.S.S.R., on the Baltic, with a fine harbour and a trade in grain and timber. Prior to World War I a port of E. Pruss., incorporated in Lithuania, 1924. Pop. 68,000.

MEMLINC, Hans
(*c.* 1430-94) Flemish religious painter, b. Mainz. He had an orig. style, powerful yet simple.

MEMORY
Unconscious faculty in which mental impressions are retained and reproduced in the mind. Memory consists of 4 processes (1) *learning*, (2) *retention*, (3) *recall*, and (4) *recognition of facts*. Memory process depends on the assoc. of ideas, objects and events with other facts.

MEMPHIS
Ancient city of Egypt, on the Nile, 14 m. S. of Cairo. It contained magnificent buildings, and a colossal statue of Rameses II.

MENDELISM
Theory of heredity based upon the experiments made by the Abbé Gregor Mendel, an Austrian scientist (1822-84). Mendel found that certain characters are inherited by hybrids, and these he termed *dominant*, others were not shown by hybrids but occur in their offspring, and these are known as *recessive* characters.

MENDELSSOHN -Bartholdy, Felix
(1809-47) German composer. He wrote his 1st symphony at the age of 15 and the overture to *A Midsummer Night's Dream*, 2 years later. His large output is of varied worth, but his music for *A Midsummer Night's Dream*, the *Hebrides Overture*, the *Scottish* and *Italian Symphonies*, the violin concerto, and many of the *Songs without Words* for piano testify to his greatness.

MENDÈS-FRANCE, Pierre
[mā(ng)'-dez-] (1907-) Fr. politician. P.M. from June 1954-Feb. '55. During World War II he enlisted in the Fr. Air Force Reserve. He was captured on the defeat of Fr. but escaped and joined the Free Fr. Air Force. In 1943 he was apptd. Commissioner for Finance by Gen. de Gaulle in his 'Liberation Committee'. He resigned 7 months later. In June 1953 he tried to form a Cabinet but failed to obtain a majority. In June 1954 he promised to end the 7 years war in Indo-China within one month. He obtained a large majority and by skilful negotiating at the Geneva Conference brought this about. He was forced to resign in Feb. '55 when defeated over his policy in N. Africa.

MENDIP HILLS
Range of hills in Somerset, from Wells to the Bristol Channel. Water action has led to the formation of caves (Cheddar) and swallow holes, in the carboniferous limestone.

MÉNIÈRE'S DISEASE
[mān-yairz] Disease of ear first described in 1861 by Fr. physician Ménière. Characterised by acute dizziness, ringing in ear, nausea, vomiting and deafness.

MENINGITIS
[men-in-jī'-tis] Disease affecting the meninges or covering of the brain and spinal cord and producing an inflammation.

MENOPAUSE
Period in female life which marks end of reproductivity. Age of onset varies considerably from 40 onwards. Reproductive organs atrophy and ovarial activity ceases.

MENTAL DEFECTIVE
Person whose mind has failed to develop and who as a result has an intelligence quotient of 70 to 50. Of those a proportion are capable of benefiting by educ. at a special school.

MENTAL HOSPITALS
Formerly known as lunatic asylums, the mental hospitals of today are evolving into true hospitals. Doctors and nurses are specially trained. Consultant specialists are attached to the staffs. Much attention is devoted to cultural and occupational amenities with a view to rehabilitating patients. The majority of sufferers from mental disease enter the hospitals in the voluntary category. At least two-thirds of patients admitted to mental hospitals are able to be discharged. Entrance to a mental hospital is obtained either by direct presentation of the patient at the hospital, or by recommendation of the patient's doctor or from a Nerve Clinic. Under the *Mental Treatment Act*, 1930, patients may be admitted in the 'temporary category' if they are neither willing nor unwilling to receive treatment. This procedure requires two doctors' certificates and the patient may remain in hospital for six months. Amendments to the Act were introduced, 1959 and 1960.

MENTHOL
White crystalline substance from *Mentha arvensis* or *piperascens* and *glabra*, growing in Japan and China. It is used as a local anaesthetic.

MENUHIN, Yehudi
[men'-yew-in] (1916-) Violinist. B. New York of Jewish parents. He is regarded as one of the world's leading players. K.B.E. (Hon.) 1965.

MENZIES, Sir Robert Gordon
(1894-) Austral. politician. Commonwealth Attorney-Gen. 1935-9; Treasurer, 1939-40; P.M. 1939-41; Min. for Trade, Information and Munitions, 1940; Leader of Opposition, 1943; P.M. 1949-66. P.C.

MERCATOR, Gerardus
[-kā'-] (1512-94) Flemish geographer, employed by the Emp. Charles V to draw maps. In 1568 he first used the system of projection, since known by his name.

MERCHANT NAVY
Originated under Henry VIII and Elizabeth as the Merchant Service. Trade followed the flag to India (The E. India Co.), and N. Amer. (Hudson's Bay Co.), and the E. and W. Indies. World War I caused the loss of 3,400 vessels and 16,000 men. An official uniform was created in 1919, and in 1922 King George V bestowed on the service the name Merchant Navy. The Merchant Navy played a large part in World War II by carrying food, war materials and troops under the constant threat of enemy U-boats, warships, mines and the Luftwaffe. The Admiralty announced on June 13, 1945, that between Sept. 1939 and May 8, 1945 (V.E. Day), 4,280 Allied merchant vessels were sunk, over half of which were Brit. *See* ATLANTIC, BATTLE OF.

MERCHANT TAYLORS
London livery company. It is one of the 12 great cos. and dates from *c.* 1300. **The Merchant Taylors' School** was founded by the Co. in London in 1561.

MERCIA
[-shia] A.-S. kingdom of Eng. between the Thames and Trent. Under Offa, who d. 795, it was the most powerful of the Eng. kingdoms, but in the 9th cent. was conquered by Wessex.

MERCURY
Planet which is believed to be nearest to the sun, the smallest of the major planets so far discovered. Its mean distance from the sun is 36 million m., its diameter 3,100 m., its mass *c.* one twenty-seventh that of the earth. Its period of revolution round the sun is 88 days.

MERCURY
A silvery liquid metallic element, occurring chiefly as the sulphide. It dissolves many metals, forming amalgams. Sp. gr. 13·6. Chem. sym. Hg.

MEREDITH, George
(1828-1909) Brit. novelist and poet. Of mixed Irish and Welsh origin. Among his novels are *The Ordeal of Richard Feverel* (1859), *Beauchamp's Career* (1875), *The Egoist* (1879) (his best), and *Diana of the Crossways* (1885) recalling the story of the Hon. Mrs. Norton. His verse includes *Modern Love* (1862) (sonnets) and *Poems and Lyrics of the Joy of Earth* (1883).

MERGANSER
[-gan'-] Genus of aquatic birds belonging to the duck family. The commonest Brit. species are the Red-breasted Merganser (*mergus serrator*) and the goosander (*M. merganser*). The Smew (*M. albellus*) is native to the northern part of the Old World, wintering in Brit., the Medit., N. India, China and Japan. There are two N. Amer. species *Americanus* and the Hooded M. (*lophodytes cucullatus*).

MÉRIMÉE, Prosper
(1803-70) Fr. novelist. He is best known for his *Colomba* (1841) and *Carmen* (1846). His *Lettres à une Inconnue* show society during the Second Empire in Fr.

MERINO
Sp. name for a breed of sheep producing fine white wool. Imported by Louis XVI to Rambouillet, 1783, that and other improved breeds have reached S. Africa, Australia, N. Zealand, Argentina and U.S.A.

MERIONETHSHIRE
[meri-on'-ĕth-shīr] Maritime county of Wales, between Caernarvon and Montgomery. Agriculture is the chief industry. Dolgellau is the county town; on the coast are Barmouth, Towyn and Harlech. M. returns 1 member to Parl. Pop. 38,360.

MERIT, Order of
Brit. order founded in 1902. Its membership is limited to 24, but it gives neither title nor precedence. Letters O.M. signify membership.

MERLIN
(*Falco columbarius*) Small bird of prey inhabiting Europe and Asia. The smallest of Brit. falcons, 10-12 in. long.

MEROVINGIANS
Line of Frankish kings. They began to rule *c.* 500 in the person of Clovis and remained on the throne until 751.

MERSEY
River of Eng. formed by the union of the Goyt and Tame at Stockport. It flows between Lancs. and Cheshire to the Irish Sea.

MERTHYR-TYDFIL
[-ther tid'-vil] County borough of Glamorganshire, on the Taff, 24 m. N.W. of Cardiff. Industries are coal-mining and iron and steel manufacturing. M.-T. returns 1 member to Parl. Pop. 59,000.

MESMERISM
A doctrine, called after the German physician **Friedrich Anton Mesmer** (1733-1815), which stated that any one person can exercise influence over the will of another by virtue of emanations proceeding from him. The practice was popular at the end of the 18th cent. and used as a means of lessening sensitivity to pain.

MESOPOTAMIA
Region of Asia, the basin drained by the Tigris and the Euphrates. Hist. records go back to the 4th millenium B.C. and the oldest civilisation was that of the Sumerians. Successive Semitic invasions gradually overwhelmed the Sumerian dynastics, the emp. of Akkad, opening the era of consecutive hist. which witnessed the rise of Babylon, the great succession of Babylonian dynasties, the conquests of the Assyrians and the passing of Babylonia under the sway of Persia. Conquered by Alexander the G., M. passed by degrees under the rule of the Parthians and briefly was part of the Rom. Emp. Reconquered by Persia, it fell to the Arabs shortly after the rise of Islam. It was the scene of a struggle between Turks and Persians and M. remained in Turkish possession till the growth of Arab nationalism led to its liberation during World War I and its reconstitution into the kingdom of Iraq (*q.v.*). M. is rich in archaeological remains and ancient monuments.

MESSINA
City and seaport of N.E. Sicily, 55 m. N.E. of Catania on the Strait of M. Pop. 251,423.

METAL
Larger of the 2 groups of chemical elements. Iron and aluminium in the form of oxides and silicates, with calcium and magnesium as carbonates, form a considerable portion of rocks, while sodium and potassium compounds are abundant in sea-water and certain deposits. The characteristic physical properties of metals are their lustre and opacity, density, malleability, ductility and fusibility. **Metal Fatigue.** Structural change brought about in metal by repeated applications of stress. In light alloys, cyclic application of even very small stresses is liable to result in eventual failure. Steels and certain other metals have a 'fatigue limit' of stress below which any number of reversals can be sustained. Fatigue did not involve critical engineering problems until post-war civil aircraft began to use new alloys. Fatigue in light alloy structures cannot be abolished, and the designer's aim is to prevent its occurrence within the required life of the aircraft.

METAXAS, Yanni
(1870-1941) Gk. soldier and politician. Chief of the Gen. Staff, 1913-16. He assumed autocratic powers in 1936, and until his d. led the govt., refusing to accept the Ital. ultimatum of 1940.

METEMPSYCHOSIS
Belief that the human soul passes through a series of incarnations in a physical body. It was taught in ancient Egypt and by Plato, Pythagoras and other Gk. philosophers, and is fundamental to theosophy, and to the Hindu and Buddhist faiths.

METEOR
Small, solid body moving in a regular orbit in space. Meteors usually occur in swarms which, on entering the earth's atmosphere at a great velocity, become incandescent and visible as so-called shooting stars.

METEORITE
Metallic or non-metallic body occasionally found on the earth's surface and having its origin in interplanetary space. Meteorites vary in size from small grains to large masses found in Greenland and S. Africa, weighing 50 to 60 t.

METEOROLOGY
Science dealing with the study of atmospheric conditions in relation to the weather and climate. It is based upon regular and systematic observations. Uniformity in recording these necessitates a central office where deductions are made and charts drawn up, enabling weather forecasts to be made. *See* WEATHER FORECAST.

METHANE
CH_4. Simplest of the paraffin series of hydrocarbons, known also as marsh gas or fire-damp. It is a colourless, odourless gas, which burns with a faintly luminous flame. Methane is a constituent of coal gas and is given off from decaying vegetable matter.

METHODISM
Religious communions arising from the 18th cent. evangelical revival. John Wesley began evangelistic work in London, 1739, instituted lay-preaching, 1741, and in 1744 held a conference of his followers. Wesley and his helpers took up open-air preaching, and the movement spread. Immigrant local preachers of N. Amer. from 1760, developed a movement resulting in a conference in Philadelphia, 1773. Coke's adoption of the title 'bishop' started the

Amer. Methodist Episcopal Ch. An Enabling Act, 1930, empowered the Wesleyan, Primitive and United Methodist Chs. to combine as the Methodist Ch. 1933.

METHYL
CH_3. Organic radicle or group of atoms which does not exist alone, but has many derivatives.

METHYL ALCOHOL
CH_3OH. Simplest of the alcohol series of organic compounds. In its commercial form it is known as wood spirit; it may also be made directly by interaction of hydrogen and carbon monoxide in the presence of catalysts. **Methylated Spirit.** Form of industrial spirit. It consists of a mixture of rectified spirit and wood naphtha or methyl alcohol with pyridine or petroleum.

METRIC SYSTEM
Weights and measures system having a decimal scale of numeration and based upon the metre as the unit. *See* p. 451.

METTERNICH, Prince Clemans Lothar Wenzel
(1773-1859) Austrian diplomat and statesman. He negotiated the mar. of Napoleon and Marie Louise. In 1814 he took a prominent part in the Congress of Vienna, and from 1815 was the most influential European diplomat, advocating suppression of all popular constitutional movements.

METZ
Cap. of Moselle dept. N.E. Fr. on the Moselle R. It was taken by the Germans in 1870, and made cap. of Lorraine. The Fr. recovered it in 1919. Pop. 147,000.

MEUSE
[mös] Dept. of N.E. Fr. bounded by Belg. Cap. Bar-le-Duc. The **River M.** rises near Langres, flows N. past Verdun to Givet, where it enters Belg. and then past Liège into the Netherlands. The Dutch name is Maas.

MEXICO
Fed. repub. of C. Amer., S. of the U.S.A. and N. of Guatemala and Brit. Honduras. The greater part consists of a high plateau, with an average altitude of 6,000 ft., flanked by 2 cordillera. Pica de Orizaba (18,000 ft.), and Popocatepetl (17,880 ft.) are the highest mts. There are numerous lakes, the largest being Chapala. There is a great range of climate, and 3 types may be defined: trop. in Yucatan and the low-lying areas, temp. on the plateau, and cold above 6,000 ft. Agriculture is the chief industry. Coffee, tobacco, cotton, maize, wheat, fruit and vegetables are the chief crops. Irrigation is widely practised. Oil, silver, gold, lead, copper, zinc and vanadium are produced. Industries are mainly dependent on hydro-electricity. M. City is the cap.; other important towns are Guadalajara, Monterrey, Merida, León, Tampico and Vera Cruz. Sp. is the official language, and R.C. the predominant religion. M. was annexed by the Sp. in the 16th cent. when Cortes conquered the Aztecs. A repub. was set up, 1824, and Texas separated from M. 1837. Following the 1846-8 war, Calif. and New Mexico were given to the U.S.A. The Aust. Ferdinand Maximilian, ruled as emp. from 1864-7, when the present repub. was proclaimed. Mexico is gov. by a Pres. with a congress of senators and deputies. Area: 760,396 sq.m. Pop. 45,671,000. **Mexico City.** Cap. and largest city of Mexico, *c.* 7,400 ft. above sea level. It is the oldest city of N. Amer. built on the remains of the Aztec cap. Tenochtitlan. Pop. 3,353,000.

MEYERBEER, Giacomo
[mī'-er-bir] (1791-1864) Composer. B. Berlin, d. Paris. He went to Paris in 1826 and there produced *Robert le Diable* (1831), *Les Huguenots* (1836), *Le Pardon de Ploermel* (*Dinorah*, 1858).

MIAMI
[mī-am'-i] City of S. Florida, at the mouth of the M. river, and on Biscayne Bay. A popular pleasure resort. Pop. 292,000.

MICA
Group of mineral silicates of aluminium and potassium, sodium, lithium, or iron and magnesium, characterised by a pearly lustre and cleavage into thin elastic sheets. The colourless varieties are used for lamp chimneys and stove doors.

MICAH
(O.T.) Minor Heb. prophet. Writings denounce oppression and pray for a religion of justice and mercy.

MICHAEL
(1921-) King of Rumania, son of **Carol II** (*q.v.*). He was recognised as heir apparent when Carol renounced his rights in 1925. Carol returned and was recognised as king in 1930. In 1940 Carol once more left Rumania and Michael became king. The Communists forced him to abdicate, 1947.

MICHELANGELO
(Michelangelo Buonarotti) (1475-1564) Ital. painter, sculptor, architect and poet. He worked under the patronage of Lorenzo de Medici and Popes Alexander VI, and Julius II. His verse ranks high in Ital. poetry.

MICHIGAN
[mish'-] N. State of the U.S.A., 2 peninsulas between lakes Superior, Michigan and Huron. Once an agricultural state, M. is now predominantly industrial. Coal, petroleum, iron ore, cement and gypsum are produced and there are forests. Lansing is the cap. although Detroit, Grand Rapids, Flint and Saginaw are larger. First settled, 1668, and became a state, 1837; it sends 19 representatives to Congress. Area: 96,720 sq.m. including 39,700 sq.m. inland water. Pop. 8,875,100. **Lake Michigan.** One of the Gt. Lakes, lying wholly within the U.S.A. Chicago and Milwaukee are lakeside cities. Area: 22,400 sq.m.

MICRONESIA
One of the 3 divisions of Oceania, N.E. of New Guinea. It comprises the Caroline, Marshall, Gilbert and Mariana groups.

MICROPHONE
Device for converting sound vibrations into electric currents. In the moving coil microphone, a small coil, attached to a paper or metal cone, is caused by the sound to move in the field of a permanent magnet.

MICROSCOPE
Optical instrument used for examining minute objects by magnification. **Electron microscope.** An instrument in which electrons and electromagnetic fields replace light rays and glass lenses. It is much more powerful than the optical microscope. **Ion Microscope.** The pictures are formed by atoms of helium gas which have lost an electron (*i.e.* have become ionised) through proximity to the electrode.

MIDDLE ENGLISH
Period 1100-1450, in which O.E. inflections of nouns, adjectives, verbs are levelled, the vowels modified, the vocabulary increased by large borrowings from Fr. and the London dialect becomes Standard Eng.

MIDDLESBROUGH
County borough of the N. Riding, Yorks., on the Tees estuary. Founded early in the 19th cent., it has extensive docks. The chief industries are the production of iron, steel and chemicals. It returns 2 members to Parl. Pop. 157,690.

MIDDLESEX
Former county of S. Eng. lying N.W. of London, which has ceased to exist as an admin. unit, being taken into the new Greater London area (1964-5).

MIDDLETON, Thomas
(1570-1627) Eng. dramatist. He wrote *A Mad World, My Masters*; *Women Beware Women*; *The Spanish Gypsie*. He collaborated with Thomas Dekker in *The Honest Whore* and *The Roaring Girle*.

MIDGE
Delicate flies with mouth parts adapted for piercing in only a few genera. They swarm near water. The piercing Black Midge, *Culicoides*, causes much annoyance. The harmless *Chironomus* is notable because it does not feed at all in adult life. Its larvae are called 'blood worms '.

MIDI
District of S. Fr. around Toulouse, once ' middle land ' between Fr. and Sp.

MIDLOTHIAN
County of Scot. with a short coastline on the Firth of Forth. In it are the Pentland and Moorfoot Hills. Its rivers are the Leith, Gala, and Almond. The county is chiefly agricultural. Edinburgh is the county town. M. returns 1 member to Parl. with Peebles and 7 members for Edinburgh. Pop. 580,000.

MIDNIGHT SUN
Phenomenon seen in high latitudes around midsummer, when the sun is above the horizon for the full 24 hours.

MIDWAY
Group of Is. in the N. Pacific, *c.* 1,200 m. from Hawaii, administered by the U.S. Navy Dept. Scene of World War II battle when U.S. fleet and aircraft inflicted crushing defeat on Japs. Area: 2 sq.m. Pop. *c.* 2,356.

MIDWIFE
A professional nurse, trained in obstetrics, who attends a mother during childbirth. She may assist, or take the place of, a qualified medical practitioner. The controlling body is the Central Midwives Board in London, who grant the certificate of C.M.B., a specialist qualification obtained after a period of study and examination by a state registered nurse.

MIGNONETTE
[min-yŏ-net′] Genus *Reseda* of annual herbs of the Resedaceae, natives of the Medit. region and W. Asia. The fragrant *R. odorata* reached Chelsea from Egypt, 1752.

MIGRAINE
[mē′-] Condition characterised by intense headache, assoc. with disorders of vision and nausea with occasional vomiting. Condition in severe form is disabling, lasting several hours.

MIGRATION
Periodic mass-movement of animals, esp. birds, from one seasonal habitat to another. The primary stimulus is the food-quest. In the N. hemisphere most birds exhibit mass-movements between summer quarters for nesting and breeding and winter quarters for feeding and resting. Birds breed in the colder area of their range. The collective movement is remarkably uniform, punctual and constant in direction.

MILAN
City of Lombardy, Italy, on the Olona river in the Lombardy plain. The 2nd city of Italy, a commercial and financial centre, it commands the Simplon and St. Gotthard routes across the Alps. M. has many famous buildings, including the cath., the Castello Sforza and the monastery of Sta. Maria delle Grazie. Pop. 1,580,978.

MILDEW
Group of epiphytic and parasitic fungi belonging to the *Erysiphae*. *Erysiphe tuckeri*, the mildew of the grapevine, attacks the leaves and fruit damaging the vine.

MILE
The Rom. m. was 1,000 paces of 5 ft. The Eng. statute m. is 1,760 yds. The *geographical* m. is 6,076·8 ft.; the *nautical* m. is 6,080 ft. (2,026⅔ yds.).

MILHAUD, Darius
[mē′-yō] (1892-) Fr. composer. Pupil of Widor and d'Indy, joined *Les Six*, 1920; emigrated to the U.S.A. 1940. His large output includes operas, ballets, 4 symphonies, 15 string quartets and other chamber music.

MILK
Fluid secreted in the mammary glands for the nourishment of the young animal. It is an emulsion, minute fat globules being held in suspension in a liquid which consists of water containing, in solution, albuminoids, lactose and mineral salts. Cow's milk consists of *c.* 87 % water, 3·5 % fat, 3·0 % albuminoids, 4·5 % lactose or milk sugar, and 0·7 % ash.

MILKWORT
(*Polygala*) Large genus of temperate and trop. perennial herbs. The common Brit. *P. vulgaris* has wiry stems, leathery leaves and small flowers.

MILKY WAY
The starry belt seen on a clear night, esp. in autumn, when it stretches E. and W. close to the zenith. With the aid of the telescope it is seen to consist of a dense belt of stars. It is the universe of which the solar system forms part and has a rotation independent of other more distant universes or nebulae.

MILL, John Stuart
(1806-73) Eng. economist, publicist and philosopher, son of **James Mill,** who was the founder, with Jeremy Bentham, of the Utilitarian philosophy. J. S. Mill became the foremost exponent of Utilitarianism, but later adjusted his views on more altruistic lines. He advocated universal suffrage and franchise, and wrote *On Liberty*, *Principles of Political Economy*, etc.

MILLAIS, Sir John
[-lā] (1829-96) Eng. artist. B. Southampton. One of the founders of the Pre-Raphaelite Brotherhood.

MILLET
Cereal grasses. Common m. *Panicum miliaceum*, and little m. *P. miliare*, are grown largely in India for food. Ital. m. comes from *Setaria italica*, German m. is a dwarf variety.

MILLET, Jean François
[′-lā] (1814-75) Fr. painter. B. Gréville, Normandy. In 1849 he settled at Barbizon and became famous for his paintings of peasant life.

MILLIPEDE
(*Julus terrestris*) Arthropod belonging to the class Myriapoda. The body is long, rounded and segmented; each segment, with the exception of the first four, bears 2 pairs of legs.

MILNE, Alan Alexander
(1882-1955) Eng. novelist and playwright. The poems and prose written for his son Christopher Robin are still popular esp. the stories concerning Winnie the Pooh.

MILTON, John
(1608-74) Eng. poet. B. London. He studied systematically to fit himself to be a great poet. His earliest poems are Lat. elegies; in Eng. are *Ode on the Morning of Christ's Nativity, L'Allegro, Il Penseroso, Lycidas* (1637), and the masque of *Comus*. After a tour abroad Milton turned to polit., writing in defence of liberty in Ch. (*The Reason of Church Government*) in mar. (4 divorce tracts), in the Press (*Areopagitica* 1644). In the Civil War espoused the Parliamentary cause; in 1649 he became Lat. sec. to the Commonwealth, and in 1655 sec. to Cromwell. He became blind in 1652. After his retirement from public life came his long poems *Paradise Lost* 1667, *Paradise Regained* 1671, *Samson Agonistes* 1671.

MILWAUKEE
[-waw'-] City and port of Wisconsin, U.S.A. on the W. shore of L. Michigan, 85 m. N. of Chicago. Industries include steel manufacture, flour milling and tanning. Pop. 709,600.

MIMOSA
Large genus of leguminous plants, natives of the warmer regions of Africa, Asia and Amer. The leaves are in many species sensitive, closing when touched, *e.g.* the Brazilian *M. pudica*.

MIMULUS
Cultivated variety of musk (*Mimulus moschatus*) of the Scrophulariaceae.

MIND
The brain is the essential organ of mind. As the chief focus of the nervous system, the brain, with its vast number of cells closely interlinked, is related to all the tissues and organs of the body by means of nerves. The reception by the brain cells of messages from the various sense organs arouses what is called *sensation*, and consciousness, from a physiological point of view, is simply awareness of sensation. All mind functioning is therefore primarily dependent on sensation and sensation is dependent on efficient sense organs and healthy nerves to transmit impulses when these sense organs are stimulated. In turn, consciousness depends upon the integrity of the brain cells and should these cells be injured, as in concussion from a blow or damaged by the poisons of alcohol or disease, then consciousness may be reduced or completely suspended. All forms of mental activity use up energy in the nerve cells and this need is met with by an increased flow of blood containing nutriment to the brain.

MINDANAO
Second largest Is. in the Repub. of the Philippines (*q.v.*) in the S. of the group. Zamboanga is the chief town. Area: 36,540 sq.m.

MINING
Art of extraction of metallic ores and mineral substances of economic value from the earth, also the methods of prospecting or searching for minerals. Prospecting entails some knowledge of the principles of geology, acquaintance with mineralogy and some practical knowledge of chem. analysis. In surface mines, excavators, steam navvies and hydraulic jets may be used, while in deeper mines mechanical haulage is needed for transport of material.

MINK
(*Mustela*) Name of several semi-aquatic carnivorous mammals of the weasel family. Comprising the European mink or marsh-otter, the Siberian, and the Amer. *M. vison*, they are trapped for their furs.

MINNEAPOLIS
Port and largest city of Minnesota, U.S.A. on the Mississippi. It is a great trading centre, esp. in wheat, and its industries include flour milling and meat packing. Pop. 432,000.

MINNESOTA
[-sō'-] N. state of the U.S.A., W. of L. Superior, and S. of the Canadian boundary. The chief rivers are the Mississippi, which rises in the C. highlands, Red and Minnesota. M. is mainly an agricultural state. Milk, milk powder and butter are important. Iron ore is mined. St. Paul is the cap. and Minneapolis the largest town. M. was settled in the early 19th cent. and became a state, 1858, sending 8 representatives to Congress. Area: 84,070 sq.m. Pop. 3,805,100.

MINNOW
(*Leuciscus phoxinus*) Small freshwater fish similar to Carp, common in Brit. and European rivers and brooks. Normally 3-4 in. long.

MINORCA
(*Sp.* **Menorca**) One of the Balearic Is. (*q.v.*) in the Med. Mahon is the cap. Fruit and wine are produced.

MINOS
[mi'-] Legendary king of Crete, son of Zeus by Europa. It is probable that there was such a person and that the labyrinth at Knossos was his palace.

MINT
Place where money is coined under govt. authority. Formerly there were mints in Eng. at York, Norwich, Chester, Bristol and Exeter, but now money is coined only at the Royal Mint at Tower Hill, London.

MINT
Genus of perennial labiate herbs (*Mentha*), distributed throughout N. temp. regions. 10 Brit. species include peppermint, pennyroyal and horsemint. From this apparently came the garden spearmint, *M. spicata*, grown for culinary purposes.

Spearmint and Peppermint

MIRABEAU, Honoré Gabriel Requetti, Comte de
[mē'-ra-bō] (1749-91) Fr. politician. He lived precariously in writing until he was elected by Marseilles to the *Tiers État* of the States-General. Tried to put the king at the head of the Revolution, by forming a new govt. on the Eng. plan, but failed, largely through intervention of Marie Antoinette.

MIRAGE
[-rázh'] Optical phenomenon that arises from the reflection and refraction of light in unusual circumstances, seen chiefly at sea or in deserts where there is calm air that is either extremely hot or cold.

MISSAL
Lat. book containing all the liturgical forms prescribed for the due celebration of the R.C. Mass throughout the year. After the Council of Trent it was enjoined universally. At the Reformation the Anglican Prayer Book, 1549, superseded the ancient Sarum missal.

MISSEL THRUSH
(*Turdus viscivorous*) Largest Brit. songbird, abundant throughout Europe and some parts

of W. Asia. It is partial to mistletoe berries. The male, 11 in., is greyish-brown above, black-spotted white beneath.

MISSIONS
Organised efforts for the spread of a religion. The Acts of the Apostles records the progress of Christianity from Judaea into Europe under the leadership of Paul. Later missionaries went throughout Europe. In the R.C. Ch., missionary activity has been carried on by the Dominican, Franciscan and Jesuit orders. In the Protestant chs.. of Brit., the closing years of the 18th cent. witnessed a great outburst of missionary enthusiasm.

MISSISSIPPI
River of the U.S.A. It rises in a lake in Minnesota and flows S. to the Gulf of Mexico. The chief tributaries are the Missouri, Ohio, Arkansas, Red, Illinois, Des Moines, and Yazoo. It enters the sea by a large delta. Floods occur in the lower course, and embankments (levees) have been built. The M. is navigable as far as Minneapolis. Length with Missouri (*q.v.*) 3,760 m.

MISSISSIPPI
S. state of the U.S.A. lying E. of the Mississippi river near its mouth, with a short coastline on the Gulf of Mexico. It is one of the cotton growing states. Jackson is the cap. It was settled, 1716, and became a state, 1817, sending 7 representatives to Congress. Area: 47,720 sq.m. Pop. 2,217,000.

MISSOLONGHI
[mis-ō-long'-gē] Town of Greece. It is notable for its resistance to Turkish armies in 1821 and 1825-6. Byron d. there in 1824.

MISSOURI
[mi-zoo'-ri] River of the U.S.A., the chief tributary of the Mississippi. It rises in the Rocky Mts. in Montana, and joins the Mississippi above St. Louis. It is navigable for over 2,000 m. of its course.

MISSOURI
State of the U.S.A. bounded on the E. by the Mississippi. M. produces maize, winter wheat, oats, potatoes, cotton and tobacco; there are great numbers of livestock. Lead, zinc and coal are mined. Meat packing is the chief industry. Jefferson City is the cap. but St. Louis and Kansas City are larger. M. was settled in 1764 and became a state, 1821, sending 10 representatives to Congress. Area: 69,670 sq.m. Pop. 4,677,400.

MISTLETOE
(*Viscum album*) Evergreen parasitic shrub of the family Loranthaceae, indigenous to Europe and N. Asia. The smooth yellowish-green stem, 1-4 ft., bears forking branches with oval lance-shaped leaves, small green flowers and round, white berries. The Brit. host-plants include the apple, black poplar, hawthorn, lime and willow. Associations with early Celtic druidical ritual survive in modern Christmas celebrations.

MITE
Small 8-legged invertebrate creatures of the class Arachnida. It forms with ticks the widely distributed order Acari. Many are parasitic, such as those causing itch, mange and scab. Gall-mites cause big-bud disease in fruit trees; ' Red Spiders ' form a family injurious to cultivated plants.

MITHRA
Ancient Iranian solar deity whose rites were incorporated in the *Mithraic Mysteries*, introduced into the Rom. emp. and esp. favoured by the legions from the 1st cent. B.C. onwards. Wherever they went, they built temples to Mithra; hence large numbers of these were erected in Italy, N. Africa, Southern France, right across Europe from the Caspian to the N. Sea and in the chief Rom. centres in Brit. The cult received a set-back during the period of Constantine (272-337) and virtually ended with the victory of Theodosius in A.D. 394.

MITHRIDATES
[-dă'-tēz] *VI Eupator* (*c.* 131-63 B.C.) King of Pontus and great soldier known as Mithridates the Great. His conflict with the Rom. repub. resulted in the *1st Mithridatic War* (88-84 B.C.). In 88 B.C. M. conquered virtually the whole of Asia Minor. In 85 B.C. Fimbria's victorious attack in Asia Minor coincided with the destruction of M's army in Greece. The *2nd Mithridatic War* (83-81 B.C.) was between M. and the Roman L. Murena. Murena was defeated and was superseded by A. Gabrinius, who made peace with M. The Roman decision to annex Bithynia led to the *3rd Mithridatic War* (74-63 B.C.). Lucullus was sent against M. In 66 B.C. Lucullus was superseded by Pompey who quickly drove M. E. to the Crimea, the last of his provs.

MOA
Maori name for a family of flat-breasted flightless birds formerly abundant in New Zealand, and now extinct. They are known from remains collected from beds of Pleistocene age. They ranged from the Giant Moa, *Dinornis maximus*, 12 ft. high, down to one 3 ft. high.

MOAB
Region anciently occupied by the Moabites. It is a lofty tableland E. of the Dead Sea and lower Jordan valley, bounded N. by Ammon and S. by Edom, and confronts the E. desert.

MOCCASIN SNAKE
Venomous N. Amer. snake; (1) the upland copperhead, *Ancistrodon contortrix*, 3 ft. long; (2) the fish- and frog-eating water-moccasin, *A. piscivorus*, 5 ft. long, dreaded by negroes in the rice-fields.

MOCHA
[mō'-kă] Seaport of Yemen, once important for the export of M. coffee.

MOCKING BIRD
Various birds with exceptional powers of mimicry. The common N. Amer. perching song-bird, *Mimus polyglottus*, 10 in. long, is intermediate between the Wrens and the Babblers.

MODERATOR
Word used in the Presbyterian chs. for a presiding min. Each year a distinguished min. is elected moderator by the Gen. Assembly that meets in Edinburgh. In Eng. the Congregational ch. has moderators, each in charge of a district.

MODIGLIANI, Amedeo
[mod-il-yá'-ni] (1884-1925) Ital. painter and sculptor. B. Leghorn. Influenced by Negro sculpture, Ital. primitives, Picasso and Lautrec.

MOHAIR
The hair of the Angora goat, a native of Asia Minor. The hair is used extensively, often in conjunction with wool, silk or cotton yarns.

MOHAMET
(*c.* 570-632) Founder of Mohammedanism (*q.v.*). B. Mecca. He lived with an uncle and was employed in tending camels and sheep. In 610 Mohamet began to regard himself as chosen by God to preach a new faith. He denounced idolatry and declared there was only one God, Allah, and that Mohamet was his prophet. His few followers were persecuted, his wife d. and he himself in 622 was obliged to leave the city. He went to Medina, where the new faith was soon firmly estabd. Mohamet raised an army and entered Mecca as a victor in 630 and before his d. in Medina, had subdued all Arabia. His sayings were collected together to form the Koran. **Mohammedanism.** Religion founded by Mohamet. When Mohamet d. 632,

his faith had a considerable hold in Arabia and Asia Minor. His successor carried on his policy of converting unbelievers by force. In 654 Mohamet's son-in-law, Ali, became caliph, and the adherents were divided into 2 great branches, **Sunnites and Shiites.** During its first 2 cents. or thereabouts, Mohammedanism spread into Africa and Europe, esp. Spain. In the 11th and 12th cents. Asia Minor was almost completely Mohammedan, and the faith spread over India. It was accepted by the Turks and inspired them to the conquests which were such a menace to Europe in the 15th, 16th and 17th cents. In the 18th cent. they lost ground and at the end of World War I Turkey almost ceased to be a European power. The faith of Islam is contained in the sentence coined by Mohamet, 'There is no God but Allah, and Mohamet is his prophet.'

MOHAWKS
N. Amer. Ind. tribe of Iroquoian stock found between the St. Lawrence and the Catskills. Becoming the leaders of the Six Nations confederacy, they sided with Eng. in the War of Indep.

MOHS' SCALE
[mōz] A method of classification of minerals according to hardness. It was devised by the German mineralogist, Friedrich Mohs (1773-1839) in 1820. The ten test substances chosen are: (1) talc; (2) gypsum; (3) calcite; (4) fluorite; (5) apatite; (6) orthoclase; (7) quartz; (8) topaz; (9) corundum; (10) diamond.

MOISEIWITSCH, Benno
[moi-zā'-vich] (1890-1963) Pianist. He was a child prodigy. Aged 19, he made his début at the Queen's Hall, London. In 1937 he took Brit. nationality. One of the world's greatest pianists, he toured very extensively. Awarded the C.B.E. in 1946.

MOLDAVIA
Constituent republic of the U.S.S.R. in the extreme S.W. bounded by the Ukraine and Rumania. There are flat steppes in the N. and S. with wooded hills in the centre. The Dniester is the chief river. Agriculture is the main occupation, and there are state fruit- and vine-growing farms. Industries such as food preserving, wine-making have been developed. Kishinev is the cap. There is a univ., estabd. 1946. The Moldavian republic was formed 1940, after Rumania had returned Bessarabia to Russ. Area: 13,012 sq.m. Pop. 2,880,000.

MOLE
(*Talpa*) Common burrowing insectivorous mammal with very small eyes, concealed ears and close fur.

MOLECULE
Smallest particle of matter composing a compound and consisting of a group of atoms having an independent existence and yet possessing the special properties of the substance in question.

MOLIÈRE, Jean Baptiste Poquelin
(1622-73) Fr. dramatist. He became the leading Fr. playwright. His greatest comedies are *L'Avare, Le Médecin Malgré Lui, Le Malade Imaginaire, Tartuffe, Le Misanthrope, Le Bourgeois Gentilhomme.*

MOLLUSCA
Invertebrate phylum including such forms as cuttlefishes, oysters, whelks and snails. They are soft-bodied, cold-blooded, and lack segments, limbs and internal skeletons, being mostly protected by a shell of one or more pieces. *See* BIVALVES, CEPHALOPODA, GASTEROPODA.

MOLOTOV, Vyacheslav Mikhailovich
(1890-) Russ. politician. He became Commissar for Foreign Affairs in 1939, and at the reorganisation of 1946, Foreign Min. He retained his position of Foreign Min. after the d. of Stalin, 1953, but resigned May, 1956. Dismissed from office, July, 1957. Expelled from Party, Nov. 1961.

MOLTKE, Helmuth, Count von
[-kă] (1800-91) Pruss. gen. From 1858-88 he was Chief of the General Staff in Berlin, and was largely responsible for the Pruss. success in the Seven Weeks' War with Austria (1866). In the Franco-Pruss. war he planned the concentration of the Pruss. armies on Metz, which resulted in the Fr. capitulation at Sedan and the investment of Paris.

MOLUCCAS
Group of Is. in Indonesia, lying between Celebes and New Guinea. They include Ternate, Halmahera, Serang, Buru, Banda, Timor-Laut and Amboina. Spices are produced. Amboina is the chief town.

MOLYBDENUM
Hard silvery metal. It is a constituent of several steels. Sp. gr. 10·2. Chem. sym. Mo.

MOMBASA
[-bȧ'-să] Seaport of Kenya, E. Africa, on M. Is. With its new harbour, Kilindini, it controls the foreign trade of Kenya. Pop. 180,000.

MONA LISA
(**La Gioconda**) Painting by Leonardo da Vinci, now in the Louvre, Paris. It dates from *c.* 1503 and is a half-length portrait of Lisa di Anton Maria di Noldo Gherardini.

MONACO
[mon'-ă-kō] Principality of Europe, on the Medit., 9 m. E. of Nice, surrounded by Fr. territory. It is gov. by Prince Rainier III, who in 1956 mar. Miss Grace Kelly, An heir, Prince Albert was b. 1958. The cap. is M. town. Pop. 20,000.

MONAGHAN
[mon'-ă-hăn] Inland co. of the Repub. of Ireland. The Blackwater and Finn are the chief rivers. The land is hilly, with many bogs and lakes. Linen is manufactured. Monaghan is the county town. Pop. 47,088.

MONARCHY
Form of govt. in which supreme power is vested in a single individual. It may be absolute, independent of all other authority; or constitutional, subject to a form of constitution, written or unwritten. The Brit. monarchy is constitutional.

MONASTICISM
System of corporate life adopted by persons who retire from the world into religious seclusion. The monastic life is exemplified in Buddhism and among the Essenes. In Egypt in the 2nd cent. solitary asceticism was practised by many hermits, one of whom, St. Anthony, organised corporate hermitages, *c.* 305, and founded Christian monasticism. These practices spread W., notably to Ireland, until Europe's unregulated asceticism was replaced by the ordered life of self-denial introduced by St. Benedict at Monte Cassino, *c.* 529. His rule, based on poverty, chastity, and obedience to a superior, governed all W. monasticism.

MONET, Claude
[-ā] (1840-1926) Fr. painter, and one of the founders of the Impressionist school. He was particularly interested in the effect of light on his subjects.

MONEY
Primarily coins used for the purchase of commodities. The term also includes pieces of impressed paper used for the same purpose and has been extended to cheques, bills of exchange, etc. Metallic money was first used, it is said, in Lydia, 7th cent. B.C. The right of coinage soon became the monopoly of the State.

MONEYWORT
(*Lysimachia nummularia*) Perennial creeping herb of the primrose family, allied to the yellow pimpernel, a native of Europe.

MONGOL *See* URAL-ALTAIC.

MONGOLIA
Repub. of C. Asia, bounded by the U.S.S.R., China proper, Sinkiang and Manchuria. The N.W. is a high plateau, watered by the head-waters of the Irtish and Yenisei, with many lakes. The S. includes the *Gobi* (Desert). The chief industry is sheep and cattle raising, wool and hides being exported. Ulan Bator (Urga) is the cap. and chief town. The people are mainly nomads. M. became indep. of China, 1915, and 1924 a repub. was estabd. China recognised its complete indep., 1945. Area: *c.* 592,681 sq.m. Pop. *c.* 1,018,000. **Inner Mongolia.** Territory of the Chinese Repub. S.E. of Mongolia. Agriculture is being developed, particularly near the Hwang-Ho. Area: *c.* 360,000 sq.m. Pop. *c.* 9,200,000.

MONGOLS
Yellow-skinned race from the plains E. of L. Baikal. In the 12th cent. Genghis Khan (1162-1227) made himself master of the whole of C. Asia. In 1234 a Mongol emperor seized the throne of China and one of his descendants was Kublai Khan (1216-94). Another branch pushed W. as far as Moravia and Hungary and founded the empire over which Tamerlane (1336-1405) held sway. A 3rd was that from which came Baber (1483-1530) founder of the Mogul empire of India.

MONGOOSE
Small weasel-shaped carnivorous mammals. They form a family of the Civet tribe and are indigenous to Africa and S. Asia. The Indian *Herpestes mungos*, 15-18 in. long, with 15 in. tail, is frequently tamed for destroying snakes and rats. The somewhat larger Egyptian M. or Ichneumon, devours crocodile eggs.

MONITOR
(*Varanus*) Fork-tongued lizard inhabiting S. Africa, S. Asia and Australasia. Long bodied, with uncrested back and frequently with flattened tails, the head is covered with small scales.

MONK, George
(or **Monck**) **1st Duke of Albemarle (1608-70)** Eng. soldier and politician. He first supported Charles I in the Civil War. Later he joined the Parl. side, helped to subdue the Irish, and in 1651, the Scots. After Cromwell's d. he marched on London, dissolved the Rump, and called a new Parl. (1660). He then invited Charles II to return, and after the issue of the Declaration of Breda, the monarch was recognised by Parl.

MONKEY
Mammals of the order Primates except man and the anthropoid apes. Distributed throughout the warmer regions.

MONKEY FLOWER
(*Mimulus*) Genus of perennial herbs of the figwort family, native to extra-trop. Amer. and Australasia.

MONKEY PUZZLE TREE. *See* CHILE PINE.

MONKSHOOD
(*Aconitum napellus*) Genus of hardy perennials of the Ranunculaceae. The leaves are dark green and the flowers dull blue. Another species (*A. bicolor*) has violet, blue and white blossoms. The whole plant is poisonous.

MONMOUTH, Duke of
James Scott (1649-85) Son of Lucy Walter and Charles II. He was created Duke of Monmouth, but as a result of the Rye House Plot he was exiled in 1683. He returned to Eng. in 1685 and led a revolt against James II. He was defeated and captured at Sedgemoor and executed on Tower Hill.

MONMOUTHSHIRE
County of Eng. on the borders of Wales, with which it is assoc. for admin. purposes. It has a coastline on the Severn estuary, and is bounded on the E. by the Wye. The Usk, Ebbw and Rhymney are the chief rivers. The N. and N.W. is hilly. Near the coast agriculture is important. Coal is mined in the W. Monmouth is the county town, and Newport the admin. centre. M. returns 6 members to Parl. (including the borough constituency of Newport). Pop. 449,370. **Monmouth.** Borough and county town of Monmouthshire, at the confluence of the Monnow and Wye, 19 m. S. of Hereford. Pop. 5,780.

MONOPOLY
Exclusive right to trade in a particular commodity. A modern use of the term is for a grouping of firms in the one industry.

MONOTHEISM
System of religious thought and practice which recognises only one God.

MONROE, James
(1758-1831) 5th Pres. of the U.S.A. In 1790 he was elected to the Senate. In Paris, as ambassador, he arranged the purchase of Louisiana by the U.S.A. In 1816 and 1820 he was elected Pres. He retired from public life in 1825. Monroe is chiefly known as the author of the **M. doctrine.** In 1823 he recognised the indep. of the repubs. in S. Amer. previously under Sp. rule, and he declared that the Amer. continents 'are henceforth not to be considered as subjects for future colonisation by any European power'.

MONROVIA
Cap. and seaport of Liberia, at the mouth of the St. Paul, on the Atlantic coast. Founded 1822. Pop. 70,000.

MONS
Chief town of Hainaut prov., Belg. A coal mining centre. M. was several times taken and retaken during wars with Fr. Pop. 27,062. **Mons, Battle of.** Battle between the Brit. and the Germans, Aug. 23, 1914.

MONSOON
Seasonal wind blowing from the Indian Ocean over S.E. and E. Asia bringing heavy rain. The summer monsoon of India is S.-W. and blows strongly across the Ind. Ocean, becoming S.-E. up the Ganges Valley giving heaviest rainfall in the valley of Assam.

MONT BLANC
Mt. in the Pennine chain of the Alps on the frontiers of Fr. and Italy. It is the loftiest in Europe, rising to 15,781 ft. above sea-level.

MONTAGU, Lady Mary Wortley
(1690-1762) Eng. letter writer, famous for her beauty and wit. Introduced inoculation against smallpox into Brit., 1718.

MONTAIGNE, Michel de
(1533-92) Fr. writer, philosopher and moralist.

In the *Essais* he studies his own nature and that of humanity as a whole, he was particularly interested in the apparently contradictory elements of human nature.

MONTANA
[-tan′-ă] N.W. state of the U.S.A. on the Canadian border. The W. part is traversed by ranges of the Rocky Mts., while there are prairies in the E. The chief rivers are the Missouri and Yellowstone. The raising of sheep and cattle is important. Gold, silver, copper and lead are mined. Helena is the cap. but Butte, Gt. Falls and Billings are larger. M. became a state in 1889, sending 2 representatives to Congress. Area: 147,140 sq.m. Pop. 694,500.

MONTCALM
[-kàm] (1712-59) Fr. soldier. M. was finally routed in battle by Wolfe on the Plains of Abraham, Quebec, and was mortally wounded.

MONTE CARLO
Pleasure resort of Monaco, on the Med. coast, 9 m. E. of Nice. Its chief building is the casino. A long-distance car trial, **The M.C. Rally,** has been a yearly event since 1911. Pop. 11,000.

MONTE CASSINO
Ital. mt. (1,700 ft.) in the N. of Campania, 75 m. S.E. of Rome on which stood the monastery founded by St. Benedict in A.D. 529. In 1886, it became a national monument. In the course of World War II the town and mt. were part of the German Gustave line defending Rome. The monastery was bombed by the Allies in 1944 and razed to the ground.

MONTENEGRO
Fed. unit of S. Yugoslavia, with a coastline on the Adriatic Sea. The cap. is Cetinje. M. began *c.* 1390 as a principality nominally part of the Turkish Emp. until 1878 when it became indep. When World War I began, Montenegro took the side of Serbia. The Montenegrins in 1918 deposed Nicholas and united with Yugoslavia (*q.v.*).

MONTERREY
[-tā-rā′] Cap. of Nuevo Leon state, Mexico, with considerable industrial development. Pop. 821,000.

MONTESPAN, Marquise de
[mon-te-span′] **Françoise Athenais** (1641-1707) mistress of Louis XIV. She attracted the king's attention soon after her appearance at court. Mme. de Montespan bore the king 8 children. She exercised great power over the king and in public affairs until *c.* 1679, when his growing attachment to Mme. de Maintenon led to their final estrangement.

MONTESQUIEU
[mō(ng)-tes-kyö′] **Charles de Secondat, Baron de la Brède et de** (1689-1755) Fr. polit., philosopher. His *De l'Esprit des Lois* was pub. at Geneva in 1748. His admiration for the Eng. constitution influenced the 1st part of the Fr. Revolution.

MONTESSORI, Maria
[-saw′-] (1870-1952) Ital. teacher. In 1898 she became head of an institution for the educ. of children of weak intellect. The **Montessori system** aims at developing the child's individuality.

MONTEVERDI, Claudio
[mon-ti-vair′-di] (1567-1643) Ital. composer. He adopted successfully the new harmonic style. He made great advances in the use of the orchestra. His works include operas, ballets, ch. music, canzonetti and more than 250 secular madrigals.

MONTEVIDEO
[monti-vi-dā′-ō] Cap. and seaport of Uruguay, on the La Plata estuary. Founded, 1726, M. is now a prosperous trading centre. There is a univ. and a cath. Pop. 1,173,114.

MONTEZUMA
[-ti-zoo′-] Name of 2 Aztec emperors. **Montezuma II** (*c.* 1466-1520) greatly enlarged his empire. In 1519 the Spaniards, under Cortes made the emperor a virtual prisoner. In 1520 Montezuma tried to prevent the Mexicans from attacking the Sp. but was killed.

MONTFORT, Simon de
(*c.* 1206-1265) At first a great friend of Henry III of Eng. Sent to Gascony to quell a rebellion, he returned in 1253 to find the barons in revolt. He led the barons in attempts to make Henry rule wisely, and in 1265 called a parl.

MONTGOMERY
Cap. of Alabama, U.S.A. on the Alabama R. Scene of the formation of the Confederate States, where Jefferson became the 1st Pres. of the Confederation. Pop. 129,400.

MONTGOMERY, Viscount of Alamein, Bernard Law (1887-) Brit. Field Marshal. Served in World War I. As a Maj.-Gen. he took part in the Dunkirk evacuation. In 1942 he took command of the 8th Army in Libya, won the battle of El Alamein, drove Rommel from N. Africa. Commanded Allied armies at D. Day and later, under Eisenhower, took part in the liberation of N. Europe. He was in charge of the Brit. occupation army till 1946, when he became C.I.G.S. Created Field Marshal in 1944. On creation of N.A.T.O. he became Deputy Supreme Commander, Europe, 1951-8.

MONTGOMERYSHIRE
Inland county of N. Wales, W. of Salop. It is mountainous, with the Plynlimmon range in the S.W. The rivers include the Severn, Dovey, Vyrnwy and Wye. The soil is used chiefly for the rearing of sheep. Welshpool is the admin. centre. M. returns 1 member to Parl. Pop. 43,690. **Montgomery.** Borough and county town of M., 6 m. S. of Welshpool. Pop. 950.

MONTMARTRE
[mō(ng)-màtr′] The Bohemian quarter of Paris. The chief building is the Sacré Coeur.

MONTPELLIER
[mō(ng)pel-yā′] Cap. of Hérault dept., S. Fr. and 31 m. S.W. of Nîmes. The univ. founded 1125, was a famous med. school in the M.A. Pop. 124,000

MONTREAL
[-trē-awl′] Largest city and commercial cap. of Canada, on an Is. at the confluence of the St. Lawrence and Ottawa, in Quebec prov. Shipping is the principal industry, the St. Lawrence being connected with L. Erie by St. Lawrence Seaway (*q.v.*). Milling, paper and shoe manufactures, textiles and steel are other important industries. There are 2 univs. M. was founded, 1642, by the Fr. Pop. (City) 1,191,062.

MONTROSE
Royal burgh and seaport of Angus, 31 m. N.E. of Dundee, at the mouth of the S. Esk. The chief industries are flax spinning and fruit preserving. Pop. 10,702.

MONTROSE
[-trōz] Scots title held by the family of Graham. In 1505 **William, Lord Graham,** a title dating from 1445, was made Earl of Montrose. **James,** the 5th earl (1612-50) was the soldier who was made a marquis in 1644, started his career by defending the Covenant which he had helped to draw up, but later went over to the Royalists. He returned in 1644 to rally the Highlanders for King Charles. At first successful, he was defeated at Philiphaugh. He was betrayed to the Scots govt. and publicly hanged in Edinburgh.

MOON
Satellite of the earth. It revolves round the earth in 27 days 7 hrs. 43 mins. and its average distance is *c.* 238,840 m. The moon's diam. is

c. 2,160 m. and its mass is est. at 1-80th that of the earth. It shines by reflected light from the sun and when opposite the sun is called full moon; a fortnight later when between the earth and sun it is nearly invisible and is called new moon. First manned landing by U.S. spacecraft *Apollo XI*, July, 1969.

MOONSTONE
Precious stone: a translucent, colourless variety of orthoclase intergrown with albite felspar.

MOONWORT
(*Botrychium lunaria*) Fern of the adder's-tongue family, native to Brit., cold and temp. regions.

MOOR HEN
(*Gallinula chloropus*) Waterfowl. Common in Brit. on rivers, ponds, etc.

MOORE, Henry Spencer
(1898-) Eng. sculptor. Awarded Internat. Sculpture prize, Venice, 1948. Work is based on the hypothesis that every material (stone, wood, cement), has its own individual qualities. C.H. 1955. Hon. D.Litt. 1961.

MOORE, Sir John
(1761-1809) Scots soldier. He was sent to Sp. in 1808 at the head of an army. He marched from Lisbon into Sp. but the advance of a large Fr. army forced him to fall back on Corunna. The retreat was a difficult march of 250 m. but Moore, on reaching Corunna, was able to defeat the pursuing Fr. During the battle he was fatally wounded.

MOORE, Thomas
(1779-1852) Irish poet. His works include *Irish Melodies* (1807), *Lalla Rookh* (1817) and *Life of Byron* (1830).

MOORS
Name of a people who live in N. Africa. They are descended from the Berbers and Arabs, and gave their name to Morocco. Some of them crossed into Sp. and set up a kingdom which lasted from 711-1492; the S. parts of Sp. still bear extensive traces of their influence, esp. in architecture. Other Moors helped to people Algeria and Tunisia.

MOOSE
The World's largest deer (*Alces machlis*) Ranking as an Amer. variety of the Elk of N. Europe and Siberia, it formerly ranged from 43° N. lat. northward to the so-called Arctic barren-grounds. It is still found in Alaska and in N.W. Canada, being protected in Alberta and elsewhere. *See* ELK.

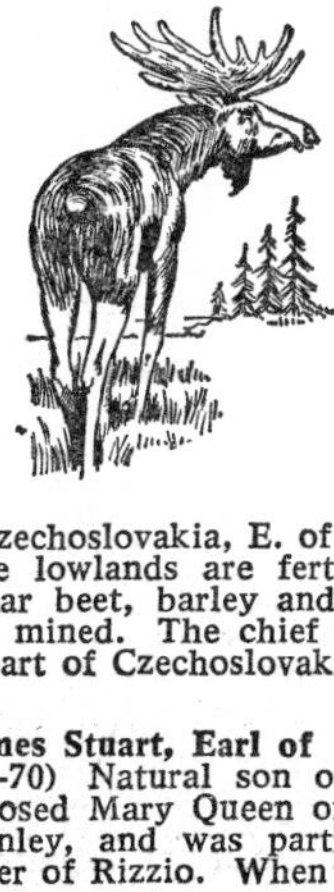

MORAVIA
District of Czechoslovakia, E. of the Bohemian plateau. The lowlands are fertile, producing crops of sugar beet, barley and wheat. Coal and iron are mined. The chief town is Brno. M. became part of Czechoslovakia after World War I.

MORAY, James Stuart, Earl of
[mur'-] (1531-70) Natural son of James V of Scot. he opposed Mary Queen of Scots in her mar. to Darnley, and was partly responsible for the murder of Rizzio. When Mary was imprisoned on Loch Leven, Moray was apptd. Regent. He did much to restore civil and religious peace in Scot.

MORAY FIRTH
[mur'-ri] Arm of the sea, on the N.E. coast of Scot. lying between Tarbat Ness and Lossiemouth. It is an important fishing area.

MORAYSHIRE
(formerly **Elginshire**) County of Scot. bounded by Banff, Nairn and Inverness, with a coastline on the N. Sea. The chief rivers are the Spey, Lossie, and Findhorn. Whisky is distilled. Elgin is the county town. With Nairn, M. returns 1 member to Parl. Pop. 50,322.

MORE, Sir Thomas
(1478-1535) Eng. scholar and lawyer. B. London. Thomas Wolsey appointed him Treasurer of the Exchequer and Chanc. of the Duchy of Lancaster, while the Commons chose him as Speaker. In 1529, succeeded Wolsey as Lord Chanc. In 1532 he resigned that office and in 1534, for refusing to recognise the king as head of the ch. he was accused of high treason and executed. Beatified in 1886. He wrote a *History of Richard III* as well as *Utopia.*

MORLAND, George
(1763-1804) Brit. painter. He painted chiefly country subjects, remarkable for their beauty of conception and harmony of colouring.

MORLEY, Thomas
(1557-*c.* 1603) Eng. composer. In 1597 he pub. his famous treatise *A Plaine and Easie Introduction to Practicall Musick*. In 1601 he pub. a collection of madrigals in praise of Queen Elizabeth.

MORMONS
Religious organisation entitled the Ch. of Jesus Christ of Latter-day Saints, founded by Joseph Smith in New York State, 1830. So-called divine revelations included a hist. of primitive Amer., *The Book of Mormon*, claimed as of equal authority with the Jewish and Christian scriptures. In 1843 the prophet received a 'revelation' permitting polygamy; during the 'Gentile' indignation thereby aroused, he was shot. Brigham Young, who succeeded, led the ch. in 1847 to Gt. Salt Lake.

MORNING GLORY
Popular name of various twining herbs of the bindweed family, the trop. Amer. *Ipomoea purpurea* which gardeners also call *Convolvulus major*. *Ipomoea* includes also the sweet potato.

MOROCCO
(**Maghreb el Aksa**) Kingdom of N.W. Africa, N. of the Sahara Desert, with a coastline on the Medit. and Atlantic. It is crossed by the Atlas Mts., 5 parallel ranges enclosing fertile plains; the N. slopes are wooded, while the S. slopes are generally arid. The climate is mainly healthy. Agriculture is the principal industry; cereals, fruits and wine are produced. Minerals include phosphates, iron, gold, silver, coal and gypsum. The largest towns are Casablanca, Marrakesh, Fez, Tangier and Tetuán. Rabat is the cap. The pop. consists largely of Berbers and Arabs. Mohammed ben Youssef, Sultan Mohammed V, was succeeded in 1961 by his son, as King Hassan II. M. is a constitutional monarchy. Constit. was approved by a referendum in 1962. Area: *c.* 171,305 sq.m. Pop. *c.* 14,140,000. The former territory of **Fr. M.** occupied the greater part of the country. From 1912 it was admin. by a Fr. Resident-Gen. In 1947 many reforms were introduced, giving a greater measure of control to the Sultan and his council and in 1956 Morocco regained full indep. with its own diplomatic corps and army. Formerly, **Sp. M.** occupied the N. part of the country. In April, 1956, one month after the Franco-Moroccan Declaration of Indep., the Sp. Govt. concluded a similar agreement with M.

MORPHIA
or **Morphine Hydrochloride.** An alkaloid obtained from opium, isolated 1816. It is a white powder with a bitter taste. Used largely in medicine because of its powerful analgesic and hypnotic action, it is an important member of the habit-producing group of drugs. Its use is controlled by nat. and internat. legislation. *See* POISON, DRUG.

MORRIS, William
(1834-96) Eng. writer. In 1858 appeared the poem *The Defence of Guenevere*, followed by others. He promoted the revival in decorative art in Eng., was one of the chief exponents of the art of staining glass in the 19th cent., started the Kelmscott Press (1890).

MORRISON, Herbert Stanley
(1888-1965) Baron M. of Lambeth, Eng. politician. Before entering the House of Commons he led the Lab. group in the L.C.C. M.P. (Lab.) S. Hackney, 1923-4, 1929-31, 1935-45. Home Sec. 1940-5. In 1945 he became Lord Pres. of the Council and Leader of the House of Commons; Foreign Sec. 1951; created C.H. 1951. Retired from the House of Commons in 1959 and was created a life peer. P.C.

MORSE CODE
System of signalling. It was devised by Samuel F. B. Morse, in collaboration with Alfred Vail, 1837, for telegraphic purposes, and consists of a series of dot and dash symbols representing letters of the alphabet, numerals, punctuation marks and conventional phrases.

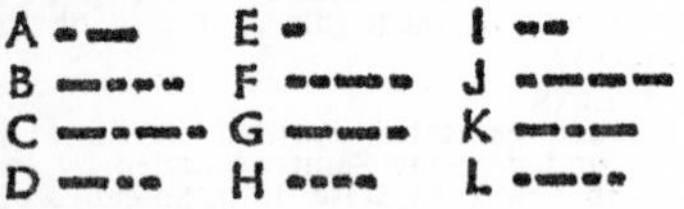

MORTAR
Type of muzzle-loaded cannon. First used in Italy in 15th cent.; brought to Eng. 16th cent. The barrel was thick-walled with a smooth bore. The 3 in., 4 in. and 6 in. mortars of World War I were superseded by the 2, 3 and 4·2 in. of World War II. These are all muzzle-loading, smooth-bore weapons firing streamlined fin-stabilised bombs.

MORTLAKE
District of London on the Thames, near Richmond. It is the finish of the Oxford and Cambridge boat race.

MOSCOW
[mos'-kō] Cap. and largest city of the U.S.S.R. on the Moskva, 400 m. S.E. of Leningrad. It has developed into a great commercial and industrial city. Industries include textiles, dyeing, the manufacture of clothing and footwear, food processing, metallurgy, tanning, engineering, printing and paper-making. The city is built round the great citadel, the Kremlin, on the N. bank of the river. There are numerous parks and gardens and fine buildings, *e.g.* Cathedral of St. Basil on Red Square, where stands the Mausoleum of Lenin, the Tower of Ivan Veliki, the Uspenski cath. Founded *c.* A.D. 1147, M. became in the 15th cent. cap. of Russ. Peter the Gt. transferred his cap. to St. Petersburg, 1703, but M. again became cap. 1918. During World War II the Germans reached the city's outer defences. Pop. 6,354,000.

MOSELLE
[mō-zel'] Dept. of N.E. Fr. bounded in N.E. by Luxembourg and the Saar. Cap. Metz. The **River M.** rises in the Vosges Mts., flows through M. dept. into Germany, and joins the Rhine at Koblenz. Canalisation of this section was opened, 1964, giving Fr. access to the sea at Rotterdam. A light wine takes its name from the M. Valley.

MOSES
(*c.* 15th cent. B.C.) Heb. law giver and leader. According to the O.T. he was adopted by Pharaoh's daughter, educ. as an Egyptian prince. He became the leader of the Israelites, and after the Exodus, accompanied them to the outskirts of Canaan, and d. near Mt. Pisgah. Posterity ascribed to him the first 5 O.T. books and the legislative code embodied therein.

MOSQUE
Mohammedan house of prayer. Normally an open quadrangular court, surrounded by an arcaded sanctuary, with a wall-niche indicating the direction of Mecca, a pulpit and sometimes a lectern.

MOSQUITO
Insects belonging to the Culcidae or gnat family. A number occur in Brit. These insects pass their larval stage in stagnant water, and only the female has biting mouth parts. The trop. genus, *Anopheles*, is a carrier of the malarial parasite.

MOSS
Group of cryptogramic plants forming a division of the class *Bryophyta* and closely related to the liverworts. Like the ferns, alteration of generations occurs, the moss plant representing the sexual stage bearing the sexual elements or ' gametes ', with the spore capsule borne upon the moss stem as the asexual generation.

MOSS, Stirling
(1929-) Brit. racing motorist. First Brit. driver to win Italian Mille Miglia (1955), Brit. Grand Prix, Aintree (1955) and Monaco Grand Prix (1956). O.B.E. 1959. A serious crash in 1962 led to his retiral, 1963.

MOSUL
City of N. Iraq, on the Tigris, 220 m. N. of Baghdad. Near are the ruins of Nineveh. Muslin is a corruption of the name. Pop. 341,000.

MOTH
Lepidopterous or scale-winged insect of the division Heterocera. It has variously-shaped feelers, as distinct from a butterfly of the division Rhopalocera, with club-like feelers. Moths usually fly during twilight or at night, but this is not invariable. Most have the fore and hindwing linked in flight by a bristle and catch, the frenulum, which butterflies lack. The most important economically are those whose larvae produce silk.

MOTHER-OF-PEARL
Inner lining of the shell of the Pearl Oyster, used for buttons, ornamental articles and for inlaying. White mother-of-pearl from Thursday Is. and the Great Austral. Barrier Reef is the best.

MOTHER OF THOUSANDS
Popular name applied to 2 unrelated flowering herbs. (1) The European ivy-leaved Toad-flax of the Scrophulariaceae (*Linaria cymbalaria*). (2) The Creeping-sailor from E. Asia (*Saxifraga sarmentosa*), is a favourite cottage-window plant.

MOTOR CAR
Self-propelled road vehicle driven by a petrol engine. Steam-driven vehicles came into use in the early 19th cent. but the invention of the petrol motor in 1884 resulted in a new type of engine. Prototypes of jet propelled cars are indicative of the power units of the future. Basically the motor car consists of a streamlined watertight body, under the bonnet of which an internal combustion engine is situated, either at the front or rear. The power from the engine is transmitted to the wheels through a gear box and propeller shaft. Cars are now among Britain's most important exports. *See* AUTOMOBILE ASSOCIATION. **Motor Racing.** Competi-

tions for motor vehicles started in 1894. Among the first were the Gordon-Bennett races for teams of touring cars, first run in 1899 over a 350 m. course. The Grand Prix was estabd. in Fr. in 1906, to enable individual makes to compete with one another but rather gave way to the Le Mans 24 hr. race started in 1923. The Monte Carlo and Lisbon Rallies are popular endurance tests on the Continent, and the Grand Prix d'Europe, Ital. Mille Miglia road race, Grand Prix (Belgium) are important races. Drivers such as R. Parnell, Stirling Moss (*q.v.*), R. Mays, Mike Hawthorn, Jim Clark helped to increase Brit. prestige since World War II. The chief **motor cycle** races in Brit. are the Senior, Junior and Lightweight T.T. races in the Isle of Man, the Manx Grand Prix and the Ulster Grand Prix.

MOUFFLON
[moof'-] Wild sheep now confined to Corsica and Sardinia (*Ovis musimon*). 28 in. at the withers, it has short, non-woolly hair, abundant under-wool. It was prob. the ancestor of the domesticated sheep.

MOUNTAIN
Term used for an elevation of the earth's crust. There are 2 types: tectonic mts., due to accumulation or deformation of the earth's crust, and subsequent or relict mts., the remains of ancient elevated areas. In Gt. Brit. the name is applied to peaks over 2,000 ft. high. The highest mt. in the world is Mt. Everest (*q.v.*) 29,145 ft. **Mountaineering.** The climbing of mountains as a pastime or adventure. It developed in the 19th cent. when Frenchmen, Englishmen and others began to climb some of the peaks of the Alps. The Alpine Club was founded in 1857. Mountaineers went to Africa and Amer. where mountains of over 20,000 ft. were climbed: these included Aconcagua, Mt. St. Elias and Kilimanjaro. After several attempts to climb Everest, 29,145 ft., a Brit. expedition was successful in 1953. *See* EVEREST.

MOUNTBATTEN, Lord Louis
Earl Mountbatten of Burma (1900-) P.C. Gov-Gen. of India, 1947-8, last Viceroy of India. He is the younger son of Admiral of the Fleet 1st Marquess of Milford Haven and Princess Victoria. Their name was changed from Battenberg to Mountbatten in 1917. Entered the Navy in 1913. He was Chief of Combined Operations (1942-3). From 1943-6 he was Supreme Allied Commander in S.E. Asia. Viceroy of India, Mar.-Aug. 1947. He submitted a plan for the partition of India which was accepted both by the Brit. Govt. and Indian leaders. First Sea Lord and Chief of Naval Staff (1955-9). Promoted Admiral of the Fleet, Oct. 1956. Chief of Defence Staff (1964-5).

MOUNTEVANS, Lord
Edward Radcliffe Carth Russell Evans (1881-1957) Eng. sailor and explorer. He accompanied Scott on his expedition (1909) and took charge after Scott's d. He was London Regional Commissioner for S. Defence, 1939-46. He was raised to the peerage as 1st Baron Mountevans, 1945. He wrote *South with Scott, The Desolate Antarctic.*

MOUSE
Small rodents. Brit. species include the house-mouse (*Mus musculus*), the tiny nest-building harvest-mouse (*Micromys minutus*) and the long-tailed field-mouse.

MOUSSORGSKY, Modeste Petrovich
[-sorg'-] (1839-81) Russ. composer. He was a member of the Five (the Russ. Nationalist group of composers). His greatest work is the opera *Boris Godounov.* Other well-known works include the orchestral tone-poem *Night on the Bare Mountain.*

MOUSTERIAN
Middle Palaeolithic culture. It is derived from the cave of Le Moustier in Dordogne, where flint implements, as well as bones of the mammoth, woolly-haired rhinoceros, cave-bear and musk-ox were found.

MOUTH
Median opening in the head of an animal leading into the mouth cavity which is continuous with the alimentary canal through the oesophagus, and the lungs through the trachea.

MOVABLE FEASTS, Christian
(1) *Ash Wednesday*: the first day in Lent. (2) *Easter Day*: Held on the first Sunday after the first full moon of the calendar which happens on or next after Mar. 21. (3) *Ascension Day*: Can fall on any day from April 30 to June 3 (inclusive) according to calendar. (4) *Whit Sunday*: Can fall on any day between May 10 and June 13 (inclusive) according to calendar. (5) *Rogation Sunday*: Sunday which comes before *Holy Thursday*, i.e. *Ascension Day*. (6) *Trinity Sunday*: Sunday following *Whit Sunday*. (7) *Corpus Christi*: falls on the Thursday following *Trinity Sunday*. (8) *Advent Sunday*: Sunday nearest to Nov. 30.

MOZAMBIQUE
Portuguese overseas territ. betw. Tanganyika and S. Africa, opposite Madagascar. Discovered by Vasco da Gama, 1498; settled 1505. Chief rivers are Zambesi and Limpopo. Products include sugar, maize, cotton, copra and sisal; also gold, silver and coal. Cap. is Lourenço Marques. Area: 302,250 sq.m. Pop. 6,593,000.

MOZART, Wolfgang Amadeus
[mōt'-sart] (1756-91) Austrian composer. As a child he showed remarkable ability both as a performer and as a composer. In London Mozart met J. C. Bach and wrote his 1st symphony and violin sonatas. His 1st opera *La Finta Semplice* was written when he was 12. 1769-71 he was in Italy and had some counterpoint lessons from Padre Martini at Bologna. On his return to Salzburg in 1779 as Konzertmeister and organist to the court and cathedral he wrote a great deal of music, including his opera *Idomeneo*, produced at Munich in 1781. He estabd. a reputation as a performer and composer. He d. in poverty. His output of over 600 works is almost all of high quality. He wrote 23 string quartets, 5 string quintets, a clarinet quintet, and piano concertos, etc. Among his 19 operas *Le Nozze di Figaro, Don Giovanni, Cosi fan Tutte,* and *Die Zauberflöte* are outstanding.

MUDFISH
Name given to certain fishes which bury themselves in the mud during a dry season. Among these are the Bowfin (*Amia calva*) of N. Amer., and the Dipnoi or lung-fishes, which have lung-like organs for breathing air.

MUFTI OF JERUSALEM
Islamic official. From 1921-48, post was held by Haj Emin el Husseini (1899-). Organiser of opposition to Jewish colonisation and of the Arab revolt 1936-9; took refuge with Hitler, 1941-5; captured as War criminal but escaped from prison in Fr., 1945.

MUGWORT
Perennial compositae herb indigenous to Europe, Asia and N. Africa (*Artemisia vulgaris*). Woolly, aromatic, with erect stems, 2-4 ft. high, it has reddish-yellow flower-heads.

MUKDEN
[mook'-den] City of N.E. China cap. of Liaoning prov. A walled city, 10 m. in circumference. It has railway workshops, engineering works, blast furnaces, machine-tool shops, coal-washing plant. Pop. 2,411,000.

MULBERRY
Genus of deciduous trees or shrubs, allied to the nettle family, natives of the N. hemisphere (*Morus*). The **black m.**, of Persian origin, with purplish-black fruit, was brought to Tudor Eng. The **Chinese white m.**, with white fruit, whose

leaves silkworms prefer, grows extensively in Medit. lands. The **N. Amer. red m.**, 40-70 ft. high, with red fruit, yields useful timber.

MULBERRY
Code name for artificial harbours constructed during World War II to facilitate allied landing in N.W. Europe.

MULE
The hybrid offspring of a male ass and a mare, of considerable strength and hardiness.

MULE
Cotton spinning machine invented by Samuel Crompton in 1779, a cross between the spinning jenny of Hargreaves and the throstle of Arkwright.

MULL
Second largest Is. of the Inner Hebrides, Argyllshire, 7 m. W. of Oban. Tobermory is the chief town. The interior is mountainous, up to 3,000 ft. high.

MULLET
Two unrelated food fishes. 2 forms of each occur on Brit. coasts. Of Red mullets (*Mullus*), the Striped or Surmullet, 6-16 in. long, is commoner than the smaller Plain-red. Of Grey mullets (*Mugil*), the thin-lipped, 12-20 in. long, is commoner than the smaller thick-lipped.

MULLINGAR
Co. town of Westmeath, Repub. of Ireland, 50 m. N.W. of Dublin. Pop. *c.* 5,600.

MUMBLES
Watering place of Glamorganshire, on Swansea Bay, famous for its lifeboat station.

MUMMY
Dead body prepared for burial in ancient Egypt. To postpone natural decay it was at first soaked in crude natron. From the 21st dynasty onwards, brain and entrails were removed, the body-cavities repacked, the whole enswathed in smeared linen bandages and enclosed in a mummy-case. It ceased *c.* A.D. 700.

MUMPS
Infectious disease caused by virus, commonest in childhood, occurring in epidemics and characterised by swelling of salivary glands, slight fever, and malaise. Incubation period 12-25 days.

MUNCH, Edvard
(1863-1944) Norwegian artist who worked in Paris and later in Berlin. After contact with impressionism he led the movement of 'Expressionism'.

MÜNCHHAUSEN
The Narrative of the Marvellous Travels of Baron von Münchhausen, a collection of tall stories, was pub. (1785) by a German writer, **Rudolph Erich Raspe.**

MUNGO
(518-603) Scot. saint, Bishop of Glasgow. Known also as **St. Kentigern,** he is the patron saint of Glasgow.

MUNICH
(*Ger.* **München**) City and cap. of Bavaria, W. Germany, on the Isar, 40 m. S.E. of Augsburg. It is an important art centre. The univ. was founded, 1472. Industries include brewing, the manufacture of machinery and scientific instruments, and wood carving. M. was closely assoc. with the Nazi party. Pop. 1,080,000. **Munich Agreement.** Agreement made in Sept. 1938, between Brit., Fr., Germany and Italy, whereby German claims on Czechoslovakia for Sudeten territory were conceded. Fr. and Brit. guaranteed the truncated Czech state against further aggression.

MUNNINGS, Sir Alfred
(1878-1959) Eng. painter of horses and hunting scenes and portraits. P.R.A. 1944.

MUNSTER
Prov. of S.W. of Repub. of Ireland: 6 counties, Clare, Kerry, Cork, Tipperary, Limerick and Waterford.

MURAT, Joachim
[mü-rä'-] (1767-1815) King of Naples. He distinguished himself as cavalry general under Napoleon who made him King of Naples in 1808. Murat abandoned Napoleon in 1814, to ally himself with Austria and Eng. but was himself abandoned later by his allies. He was captured and shot.

MURILLO, Bartolomé Esteban
[-rēl'-yō] (1617-82) Sp. painter. B. Seville, he saved sufficient money to visit Madrid where he became a pupil of Velasquez. He interpreted religious subjects with homely realism.

MURMANSK
Seaport of the Russ. S.F.S.R., *c.* 75 m. S.E. of Pechenga (Petsamo). The only ice-free port on the Arctic coast of the U.S.S.R., M. has a trade in timber and phosphates. Pop. 254,000.

MURRAY
Austral. river, which rises in the Austral. Alps and flows W. forming the boundary between Victoria and N.S.W. to enter the sea through L. Alexandria. The chief tributaries are the Darling and Murrumbidgee. The water is used for irrigation. Length with the Darling 2,310 m.

MURRY, John Middleton
(1889-1957) Eng. critic. In 1913 mar. **Katherine Mansfield** (*q.v.*). His works include *Dostoievsky* (1917), *The Problem of Style* (1922), *Countries of the Mind* (1922-31); works on Shakespeare, Blake, Keats and D. H. Lawrence.

MUSCAT and OMAN
Now **Sultanate of Oman** in E. Arabia with long coast on the Gulf of O. and Arabian Sea. The interior mts. and plateau are barren, but the fertile coastal plain produces dates, sugar cane and fruit. The cap. and seat of govt. is Muscat; Matrah, Sohar and Sur are ports. The pop. is chiefly Arab, with negro, Indian and Baluch elements. Area: 82,000 sq.m. Pop. 550,000.

MUSCATEL
General name for wines derived from muscat and similar grapes. Sometimes red, but mostly white, they are produced in Languedoc and other Fr. wine-growing districts and elsewhere.

MUSCLE
The parts of the body whose function is to produce movement, which contain cells which have the property of contraction and relaxation. Muscles under control of the will are called *voluntary m.* and those not under control *involuntary m.*

MUSHROOM
Name for several of the larger fungi, esp. if edible. The common edible mushroom or agaric (*Psalliota campestris*), comprises a cylindrical stalk supporting an umbrella-shaped cap, 3-5 in. across, with coloured gills beneath which ultimately blacken. A toadstool (*Amanita phalloides*) causes 9-10ths of all deaths from so-called mushroom-poisoning.

MUSIC
Music is the art or science of arranging sounds in melodies and rhythms to give a desired pattern or effect. It is thought that the music of the Christian Ch., in which much W. music has its origins, was derived from Gk. and Heb. At the beginning the M.A. the introduction of organum or diaphony, and later descant, was accompanied by a system of notation by *neumes.* While the W. was progressing along polyphonic and harmonic lines, E. musicians explored the subtleties of melody and rhythm. The end of the M.A. was marked in Europe by the evolution of notation into its modern form. Choral music reached its peak at the end of the

16th century at the same time as opera emerged and the equivalent of an orchestra. Oratorios, concertos, and operatic overtures paved the way for symphonic compositions. Since the beginning of the 19th cent., every great composer has added to orchestral resources. Chamber music and **lieder** provide an important contrast to the symphony. Folk song has made many contributions to serious music, and in our own day ragtime and jazz music owe their origin to negro folk rhythms.

MUSK
Perennial herb of the figwort family, native of Oregon (*Mimulus moschatus*) with nearly regular yellow flowers, diffuse hairy stems, and thin oblong leaves, with a musky odour, a favourite house plant.

MUSK DEER
(*Moschus moschiferus*) Small ruminant inhabiting the mts. of C. Asia. Clumsily-built, 20 in. high at the shoulder, the males have projecting sabre-like upper-jaw tusks 3 in. long and an abdominal gland containing perfume or musk, used as a basis for perfume. Neither sex bears antlers.

MUSK OX
(*Ovibos moschatus*) Arctic Amer. ruminant, sharing ox-like and sheep-like characters, the male horns being wide and flattened. It resembles a large, hairy ram, with long, thick, brownish coat; its flesh has a musky odour.

MUSLIM
Mohammedan; one who accepts the Revelation of the Koran. No baptism or formal ceremony of conversion is necessary. *See* MOHAMMEDANISM.

MUSQUASH
(*Fiber zibethicus*) N. Amer. rodent. Also called Musk-rat, a musky-smelling gland being present in both sexes. Twelve in. long, with compressed 10-in. tail, and partly-webbed hind feet, it is amphibious. Its fur is extensively used by furriers.

MUSSEL
Popular name for bivalve molluscs of world-wide distribution. The Common Sea-mussel of Brit. coasts, *Mytilus edulis*, as well as being human food, is also a valuable bait. Brit. fresh-water mussels include River-mussel and Pearl-mussel, *Unio*, and the Swan-mussel, *Anodonta*.

MUSSET, Alfred de
(1810-57) Fr. writer. He was the lover of **George Sand** (*q.v.*), 1833-5. His poems include *Les nuits* (1835-40). His plays include *Caprices de Marianne* (1833), *Il ne faut jurer de rien* (1836).

MUSSOLINI, Benito
(1883-1945) Ital. dictator, b. Romagna, d. near Como. Founded *Fasci di Combattimento* in 1919. M. became P.M. 1922, assuming dictatorial powers in 1925. He remodelled the entire State on Fascist lines. In 1935-6 there was a successful invasion of Abyssinia and this was followed by Ital. intervention in the Sp. Civil War, 1936-9, and the conquest of Albania. In 1940 she entered the war. This was not a success, and continuous defeats destroyed Mussolini's prestige; he was compelled to resign in July, 1943. He was captured by partisans in 1945, and shot on April 28.

MUSTARD
Name of several species of annual plants of the genus *Brassica*, belonging to the Cruciferae, native to Europe, Asia, and N. Africa. The dark brown seeds of the black mustard, *B. nigra*, are ground with those of the white mustard, *B. alba*, to form the condiment. **Mustard Gas.** Name given to a noxious gas—dichloridethyl sulphide—used in World War I. It caused blistering of the skin, damage to the eyes and severe inflammation of the lungs.

MYCENAE
[sē′-nē] Ancient Gk. city in the **Peloponnesus**, 15 m. N.E. of Argos, where Bronze Age immigrants developed a remarkable civilisation. After the fall of Knossos this civilisation dominated the E. Medit. The city was destroyed 468 B.C. Explored by archaeologists, innumerable gold and silver ornaments, utensils, weapons and pottery objects have been revealed.

MYRRH
[mer] Gum resin, exuded from the stem of trees, *Commiphora*, growing in Arabia and Abyssinia. It is used medicinally as a tonic.

MYRTLE
Evergreen shrub of Asiatic origin, long naturalised in the Medit. region, and hardy in S.W. Eng. (*Myrtus communis*). Its thick, shining, opposite leaves and fragrant white flowers, largely used in perfumery, yield an aromatic medicinal oil; the berries are used in cookery.

MYSORE
State of S. India. Agriculture is the main occupation, the state forests are important. Textiles and other industries have been developed. Mysore is the cap. but Bangalore is the chief city. Area: 74,191 sq.m. Pop. 23,586,772.

MYSTICISM
Mode of religious faith dependent upon personal spiritual experience of God as the ultimate reality. Element common in Hinduism, Buddhism, Islam, Christianity. First introduced into W. Europe through Neo-platonism (*q.v.*). William Blake and William Law are the great mystics of the 18th cent. Revival in 20th cent. in the works of W. B. Yeats, Aldous Huxley, etc.

MYTILENE
or **Lesbos**. Gk. Is. in the Aegean, off the coast of Turkey. Olives, grain and fruit are grown. Sappho, Alcaeus, Theophrastus and other famous writers lived on the Is. Pop. 140,144.

MYXOEDEMA
[mik-sō-dē′-mă] Condition resulting from lack of secretion of the thyroid gland, assoc. with lethargy, obesity, loss of hair and general lassitude.

MYXOMATOSIS
[mik-sō-ma-tōs′-is] A contagious and highly fatal rabbit disease. It is caused by a virus, spread by direct contact, and by biting insects. In Australia, the rabbit pest is such a menace that myxomatosis was deliberately introduced. Many areas in the U.K. were cleared entirely of rabbits by it. Remarkable improvements in crop yields resulted. But attenuated strains of the disease have appeared and rabbits have developed a resistance and numbers are increasing again.

N

N
14th letter of the Eng. alphabet. It represents a dental nasal sound, frequently combining with *g*, as in *ring, sung*, etc. The usual sound is that in *can, nap, not.* It is silent when final after the letter *m*, as in *solemn.*

N.A.T.O.
North Atlantic Treaty Organisation. The N. Atlantic Treaty was concluded in 1949 and signed by U.S.A., Canada, and 10 European nations—Brit., Fr., Belgium, Netherlands, Luxembourg, Norway, Denmark, Iceland, Italy, Portugal. This Treaty linked the nations for 20 years in a defence alliance. The N. Atlantic Council estabd. in article 9 of the Treaty, held its first meeting in Washington on Sept. 17, 1949. It set up a defence committee, a milit. committee, a standing group and 5 regional planning groups. Of the original planning groups only one now remains, the Canadian-U.S.A. Planning Group. The functions of 3 of the remainder have been taken over by SHAPE and its regional commands, and later the fourth has been absorbed in the Atlantic Command. In 1966, when France left NATO, there were still 14 countries in the organisation.

NAGASAKI
Seaport of Kyushu, Japan, on the W. coast. On Aug. 9, 1945, an atomic bomb was dropped on the city, causing severe damage and over 50,000 casualties.

NAHUM
O.T. minor prophet. His book predicts the fall of Nineveh, which occurred in 612 B.C.

NAIL
Modified epidermis with production of a horny layer, growing on the tips of fingers and toes and corresponding to claws and hoofs in birds and animals.

NAIRNSHIRE
County of Scot. with a short coastline on the Moray Firth. The rivers are the Findhorn and Nairn. The chief industry is the rearing of sheep. Nairn is the county town; other towns are Auldearn and Cawdor. With Moray, N. returns 1 member to Parl. Pop. 8,296. **Nairn.** County town and burgh of Nairnshire, on the Moray Firth, 15 m. N.E. of Inverness. Pop. 4,867.

NAIROBI
City and cap. of Kenya, E. Africa, on a high plateau, 280 m. N.W. of the port of Mombasa. It has a cath. and govt. offices. Pop. 297,000.

NANCY
[nà(ng)'-sē'] Town of N.E. Fr. Cap. of Meurthe-et-Moselle dept. Once the cap. of Lorraine. Pop. 133,532.

NANKING
City and river port of Kiangsu prov. China, on the Yangtze Kiang, *c.* 200 m. from the sea. There are numerous manufacturing industries and an important shipping trade. Pop. 1,650,000.

NANSEN, Fridtjof
(1861-1930) Norwegian explorer. After the first crossing of Greenland in 1888, he attempted, unsuccessfully, in 1893 to reach the N. Pole by letting his ship freeze in the ice and drift with a current setting towards Greenland. His work as high commissioner for refugees to the League of Nations earned him a Nobel Peace Prize in 1922.

NANTES
[nà(ng)t] Port of W. Fr. Cap. of Loire-Inférieure dept. on the Loire. There is considerable trade. The **Edict of Nantes** was signed in 1598. Pop. 246,227.

NAPHTHA
One of the derivatives of petroleum coal tar or wood. **Petroleum n.**, a product of the distillation of petroleum, has a sp. gr. *c.* 0·700 and is used as a solvent and cleaning material. **Coal tar n.** or ' light oil ' is the first product of coal tar distillation, and is used for dissolving rubber. **Wood n.** is a form of methyl alcohol. **Naphthalene** is solid hydrocarbon which crystallises out from the ' middle oils ' formed in the distillation of coal tar. Naphthalene is used as an antiseptic, for enriching water-gas and coal-gas, and it forms the basic substance for intermediate dyestuffs. **Napthol, Alpha and Beta.** Solid hydrocarbon derivatives of naphthalene, used as basic substances in the preparation of aniline dyestuffs.

NAPIER of Magdala, Baron
Robert Cornelius N. (1810-90) Brit. field-marshal. He was present at the relief of Lucknow. In 1867 he commanded the Abyssinian expedition and was given a peerage for his brilliant storming of Magdala.

NAPIER, John
(1550-1617) Scot. mathematician. His principal work was the invention of logarithms, 1614.

NAPLES
City and seaport of Italy, on the beautiful Bay of N., 120 m. S.E. of Rome. The centre of a productive district, Naples is the 3rd city of the country. In addition to shipbuilding and engineering, it has manufacturing industries, based on hydro-electric power. On the N. shore of the bay are the sites of Herculaneum and Pompeii, overshadowed by Vesuvius, while to the S. are the Is. of Ischia and Capri. In the 12th cent. it was made cap. of the Kingdom of Naples, passing under Aust. rule in 1713. After Garibaldi's liberation of Italy it became part of the Sardinian kingdom (1860). Pop. 1,179,608.

NAPOLEON I, Bonaparte
(1769-1821) Emperor of the Fr. B. Ajaccio in Corsica. In 1796 he was in command of the Fr. army in Italy. After a brief campaign in Egypt he returned, and by the *coup d'état* of 18 Brumaire (Nov. 9, 1799), made himself 1st Consul. He contrived to make himself Consul for life in 1802. In 1804 he became Emperor as Napoleon I. He overcame Austria at Austerlitz (1805), Prussia at Jena (1806), threatened Brit. with invasion and blockade, and came to terms with Russia in the treaty of Tilsit (1807); but his ambition brought about his downfall, beginning with the unsatisfactory campaign in Spain, and later the disastrous march into Russia and the retreat from Moscow (1812). The end came with the battle of Leipzig and the invasion of Fr. by the Allies, which resulted in his abdication (1814) and exile to Elba. On Feb. 26, 1815, he returned to Fr. and was decisively beaten at Waterloo on June 18, 1815.

Surrendering to the Brit., he was exiled to St. Helena. He was mar. to Josephine de Beauharnais, whom he divorced in 1809 in favour of Marie Louise of Austria.

NAPOLEON III
Charles Louis Napoleon Bonaparte (1808-73) Emperor of the Fr., nephew of Napoleon I. After the Revolution of 1848 he accepted the Repub. and was elected Pres. In 1851, by a *coup d'état*, he dissolved the Constitution, and became Emperor. He carried out a policy of administrative centralisation and remodelled Paris. His foreign policy was unsuccessful. When the Franco-Prussian War, into which he was driven by Bismarck, resulted in the total defeat of the Fr. and the collapse of the 2nd Empire, the Emperor sought refuge in Eng. His son, the Prince Imperial, was killed in 1879, fighting against the Zulus.

NARCISSUS
Genus of bulbous herbs of the Amaryllidaceae, native to C. Europe and the Medit., one species extends E. to Japan. The special feature of the tubular perianth is the cup springing from the base of the flower-segments. *See* DAFFODIL.

NARVIK
Seaport of N. Norway, at the head of Lofoten Fiord. It exports iron-ore from the Gallivare and Kiruna mines. Pop. 13,506.

NARWHAL
(or **Sea-unicorn**) (*Monodon monoceros*) Scandinavian name of cetacean of the Dolphin family, inhabiting the Arctic regions. The male possesses a tapering ivory tusk, spirally grooved, which may be 8 ft. long. The N. is black-grey above, white beneath. It frequents polar seas, usually in schools of 15-20.

NASEBY
[nāz'-bi] Village of Northants, 7 m. S.W. of Market Harborough, where Charles I was defeated, June 1645.

NASH, Paul
(1889-1946) Brit. painter. It was not until 1918 when his work as an official war artist (1917-18) was shown, that he attracted attention. He also produced woodcuts, and book illustrations.

NASSAU
[nas'-o] Principal city and seaport of New Providence and cap. of the Bahama Is., W. Indies. Sponge-gathering used to be the chief industry; now tomatoes are cultivated for export. Other main exports include prunes, crayfish, salt, sisal and lumber. Pop. 57,858.

NASSER, Gamal Abdel
(1918-70) Egyptian army officer and politician. During World War II he served in the W. desert and in 1942 founded the secret Free Officer's Movement. In 1952 he approached Major-Gen. Mohammed Neguib to offer him the leadership of the planned revolution. After the successful *coup d'état* of July 1952 Neguib became the head of state and later Pres. of the Repub. and Premier. When in Nov. 1954 Neguib was relieved of his office, Nasser assumed the duties of head of state, and became Pres. in 1956. One of the chief advocates of Arab unity, he resigned the Presidency after the disastrous result of the 1967 war with Israel, but he was at once reinstated by popular demand. *See* EGYPT; SUEZ CANAL; UNITED ARAB REPUBLIC.

NASTURTIUM
[-shĕm] (1) Genus of Brit. and N. temp. cruciferous herbs, called watercress. (2) Popular name for a genus of S. Amer. herbs of the geranium order, *Tropaeolum*.

NATAL
Prov. of the S. African Repub., N.E. of Cape Prov.; it includes Zululand. Along the coast is a fertile plain, while the land rises inland to the Drakensberg range on the W. border. The Tugela and Buffalo are the chief rivers. Sugar, coffee, fruit and tobacco are grown. Pietermaritzburg is the cap.; Durban the chief port. Natal was discovered by Vasco da Gama on Christmas Day, 1497. It formed part of Cape Colony, 1844-56. In 1910 it became part of the Union. Area: 33,578 sq.m. Pop. 2,979,920.

NATIONAL GALLERY
Any collection of pictures belonging to the state, but particularly the one in Trafalgar Square, London. This dates from 1824. Connected with it is the Nat. Gallery at Millbank, founded by Sir Henry Tate and usually called the **Tate Gallery.** It was opened in 1897 and is chiefly used for Brit. pictures. The **Nat. Portrait Gallery** adjoins the Nat. Gallery in Trafalgar Square. There is a **Nat. Gallery of Scot.** at the Mound, Edinburgh.

NATIONAL INSURANCE
A scheme of State Insurance inaugurated on July 5, 1948, under the Nat. Insurance Act, 1946, and the Nat. Insurance (Industrial Injuries) Act, 1946, whereby all employed, self-employed and non-employed persons are insured for: (1) Unemployment Benefit (except self- and non-employed persons); (2) Maternity Benefit (except non-employed persons); (3) Widows' Benefits; (4) Guardian's Allowance; (5) Retirement Pension (payable to women at age 60 and men at 65); (6) Death Grant; (7) Sickness Benefit (except non-employed persons). Every person so insured receives a card to which is affixed weekly and cancelled with the date, a stamp, obtainable from any Post Office, representing the contribution for that week. Contributions are normally payable in part by the employer and in part by the employee.

NATIONAL TRUST
Founded in 1895, to promote the permanent preservation of beautiful and historic places, for the benefit and access of the people. **National Trust for Scot.** was founded 1931.

NATIVITY
For Christ's Nativity, commemorated on Dec. 25, *see* CHRISTMAS. **Nativity, Church of the.** Famous church at Bethlehem, in W. Jordan, which, according to tradition, occupies the site where Jesus was b. The first Christian ch. to occupy the site was that built by St. Helena (*c.* 250-330) mother of the Emp. Constantine, in 325. When Palestine was conquered by the Moslems, the Caliph Omar (*c.* 581-644) ordered that the ch. be given special protection, and it remained in Moslem hands until 1947. Now in the care of representatives of the Gk., Latin and Armenian Churches.

NATRON
[nā'-] Natural form of sodium carbonate, occurring usually in white or greyish efflorescent incrustations near certain lakes in Egypt, in Kenya, and in Brit. Columbia.

NATTERJACK
(*Bufo calamita*) Toad indigenous to W. Europe. Found in Brit., it is smaller than the common toad, with shortened hind limbs, short and nearly webless toes, and a yellow line down its back.

NATURAL GAS
Various gaseous hydrocarbons in rocks of varied geological age in Canada, the U.S.A., the N. Sea, and elsewhere, due to the natural destructive distillation of carbonaceous rocks. Accumulations of the gas are, in U.S.A., tapped by deep borings and collected for illumination and heating. In 1964 the Brit. Govt. licensed the drilling of areas of the N. Sea for gas and oil.

NATURAL HISTORY
Term formerly used for the study of nature, now generally restricted to the science of zoology. The **Natural History Museum,** opened in 1881, is in S. Kensington, London.

NAURU
[now'-roo] Small coral Is. in the Pacific *c.* 26 m. S. of the Equator, in longitude 166° E. Discovered in 1798, annexed by Germany in 1888, it was taken by Austral. troops in 1914, admin. under U.N. trusteeship, 1914-68; indep. member of Commonwealth, 1968. Pop. 4,475.

NAUTICAL MILE
One sixtieth of a degree of lat. It varies from 6,046 ft. at the Equator to 6,092 ft. in lat. 60° N. or S.

NAUTILUS
Cephalopod mollusc having affinities with the extinct Ammonites. Of the 3 or 4 species, confined to Indo-Pacific waters, the best-known is the Pearly N. The female of the 2-gilled *Argonauta* makes a shell-cradle.

NAVARRE
[na-var'] Former kingdom between Fr. and Sp. with a coastline on the Bay of Biscay. It arose in the 11th cent. and, after 1284, was ruled by the kings of Fr. In 1316 the two were again separated, and Navarre had a queen, the daughter of Louis X. After being connected with Aragon, Navarre came to another queen, Catherine de Foix. She was the grandmother of the Henry who became King of N. and later, 1589, King of Fr. as Henry IV.

NAVIGATION
Art of sailing or directing a ship on its course from one port to another. For this purpose charts for determining the course, and plotting the position of the vessel at any given point, are necessary, as well as the mariner's compass for taking bearings. From the time of Cromwell onwards a number of laws known as the **Navigation Acts** were made for the regulation of shipping and the fostering of Brit. trade.

NAVY
Ships and personnel of a nation, used for purposes of war. The 1st Eng. navy was built by Alfred the Great to fight the Danes. Under Henry VIII and the Stuarts the navy was greatly improved, but received little further impetus till the time of Nelson. Marked improvements are comparatively modern—the introd. of iron, first as a protection and, *c.* 1860, for constructional purposes and later replaced by steel, and the introd. of steam propulsion. The development of the water-tube boiler, oil fuel, turbine, electric and hydraulic power have revolutionised shipbuilding. Scientific devices have helped to maintain efficiency and to improve living conditions in the ships. *See* ROYAL NAVY.

NAXOS
Gk. Is., the largest of the Cyclades.

NAZARETH
Town of Israel, in a hollow of the hills midway between the Medit. and the Sea of Galilee. Its assoc. with Christ's early life made it a place of pilgrimage from early times.

NAZARITES
(or **Nazirites**) Name denoting certain Jews under a personal vow. This included abstinence from wine and strong drink, from cutting of the hair and from contact with the dead.

NAZI
[nât'-sē] A member of the German Nat. Soc. Party. Organised by Hitler, the Party came to the forefront during the years of depression. When Hitler became Chanc. in 1933 the Party soon wielded a dictatorship over Germany, leading the country into the aggressive policy which ended in war and disaster. On the collapse of Germany in 1945 the Nazi organisation disintegrated.

NEAGH, Lough
[nā] Lake of N. Ireland, the largest in the Brit. Is.

NEANDERTHAL MAN
Extinct palaeolithic race which inhabited Pleistocene Europe during the Mousterian period. Fossilised remains were found in the

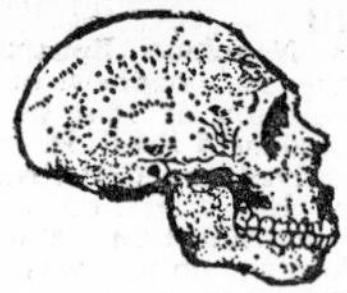

Neanderthal ravine near Düsseldorf, 1856. The race is generally considered to be unrelated to modern or Aurignacian man.

NEBRASKA
State of the U.S.A. between the Rocky Mts. and the Mississippi. The Bad Lands occupy much of the W. part, but the E. is an agricultural area producing great quantities of cereals. It is also a stock raising area. Lincoln is the cap. It was reached by the Sp. 1541, became Fr. and was eventually bought by the U.S.A. in the Louisiana Purchase, 1803. Nebraska became a state in 1867, and sends 3 representatives to Congress. Area: 77,227 sq.m. Pop. 1,483,800.

NEBUCHADNEZZAR
Name of 3 Babylonian kings. Nebuchadnezzar II reigned 604-561 B.C. He took Jerusalem, carrying many Jews into captivity, 586 B.C.

NEBULA
In astron. any one of the many dark or luminous masses which are situated in our own galaxy (the Milky Way) or in extra-galactic systems. They may be classified as follows (1) *Planetary Nebulae* (regular). These are oval or circular in shape, well defined, frequently with a star at the centre surrounded by outlying rings or shells. (2) *Bright Diffuse Nebulae* (irregular). These vary greatly in size and shape and are immense masses of luminous matter, at enormously high tempts. which may be stars in the making. (3) *Dark Nebulae.* Masses of non-luminous matter which are found in and far beyond the Milky Way. They cut off the light of stars beyond them and sometimes parts of the bright Nebulae. (4) *Variable Nebulae.* These change in form and fluctuate in luminosity and are occasionally assoc. with variable stars. (5) *Extra-Galactic Nebulae.* Giant conglomerations of stars and gaseous nebulous material, the so-called 'Island Universes' of stars, etc., outside our system. Nebulae would seem to be an essential part of all galaxies. The nebula to which our Sun belongs contains *c.* 200,000 million stars and occupies a volume of space the diameter of which is *c.* 70,000 light years.

NECK
That portion of the animal's body joining the head to the trunk and having in all mammals, with few exceptions, 7 cervical vertebrae. The carotid arteries and jugular veins are the chief blood vessels and internally there is placed the oesophagus, trachea, larynx and the thyroid glands.

NECKER, Jacques
(1732-1804) Fr. financier. B. Geneva, he became a banker in Paris. In 1777 he was made a director-general of finance, but too late to save the country from bankruptcy. His policy was one of reform and retrenchment and equal taxation, which made him hated by the nobles and Court Party. His dismissal in 1789 was the signal for the storming of the Bastille.

NECTARINE
Smooth-skinned variety of peach. The skin of the ripe fruit is more crimson-tinted: the flesh is firmer. They sometimes grow side by side on the same tree.

Gold

Copper ore

MINERALS and GEM-STONES

Galena

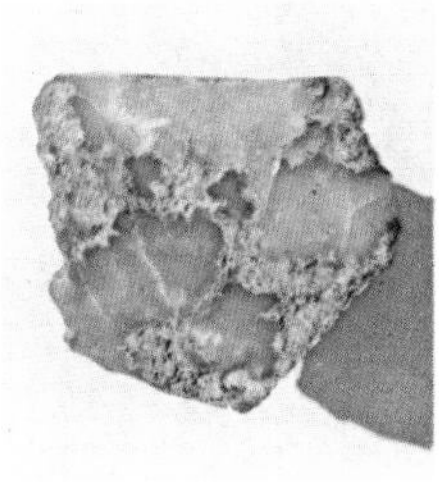

Chrysophrase

Rock Crystal

Rose Quartz

Serpentine

Amethyst

COLOUR PRINTING

The following is an account of colour printing by letterpress method. First, the coloured original (in this case a photographic transparency) is photographed four times, using a series of filters to separate the colours into yellow, red, blue and black negatives. These filters are complementary to each colour required, i.e. a blue filter is used to obtain the yellow negative, green for the red negative, and red for the blue negative, black being obtained by a combination of filters, depending on the original and the result required.

At the same time that this separating process is taking place, the image on each negative is split up into a great many very small dots or solids by taking the photographs through a "half-tone" screen made of glass and engraved with many fine intersecting lines. In light areas of the original picture these half-tone dots are small and widely spaced; in the dark or solid areas they are larger and closer together. In this way a realistic gradation of tone and colour is obtained. The screen dots in the accompanying illustration can be seen quite clearly through a magnifying glass.

The colour-separated negatives are photographically printed on to metal, usually copper, and the non-printing area is chemically etched away, leaving the printing surface in relief. In the actual printing, these plates pass under inking rollers and the ink adheres to the raised surface with which paper is then brought into contact and an impression taken. The illustrations on this page show the progressive build-up and range of colours obtained by this method.

(The illustration is a small portion of one of the plates from W. B. Turrill's *British Plant Life* in Collins *New Naturalist Series.*)

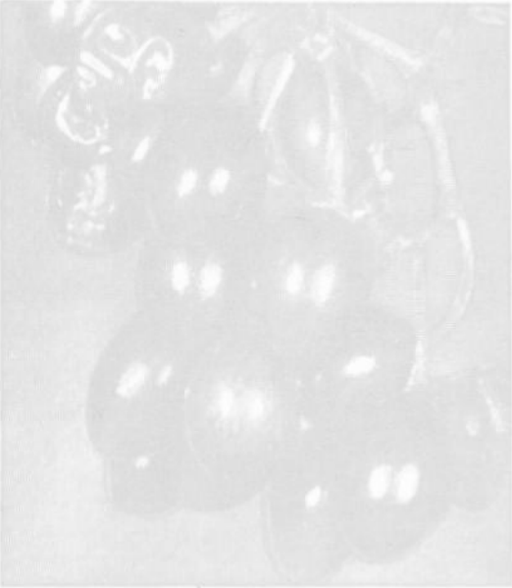

Yellow

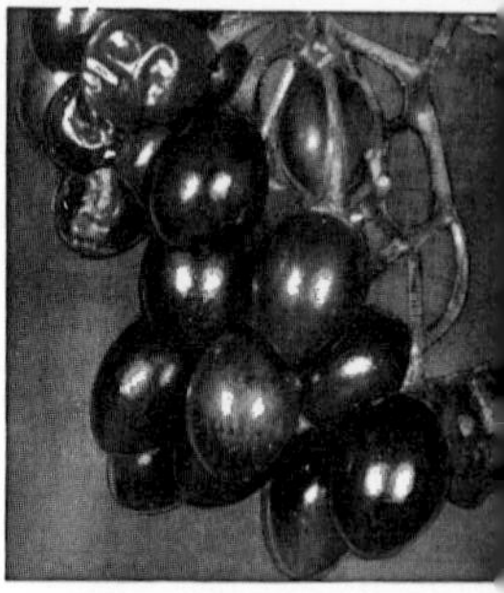

Black print of Yellow

Red

Red on Yellow

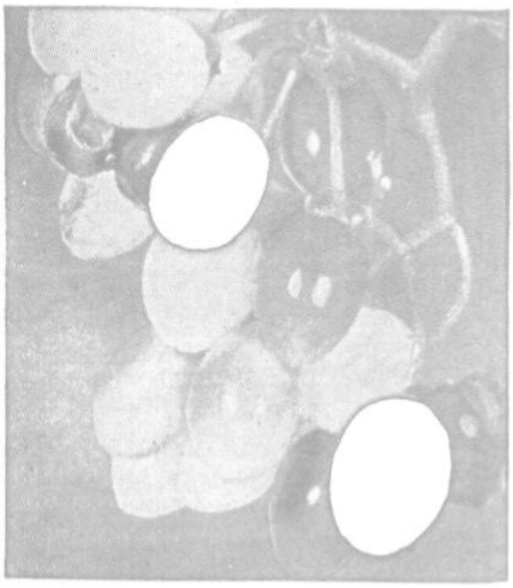

Blue

Blue on Red and Yellow

Black

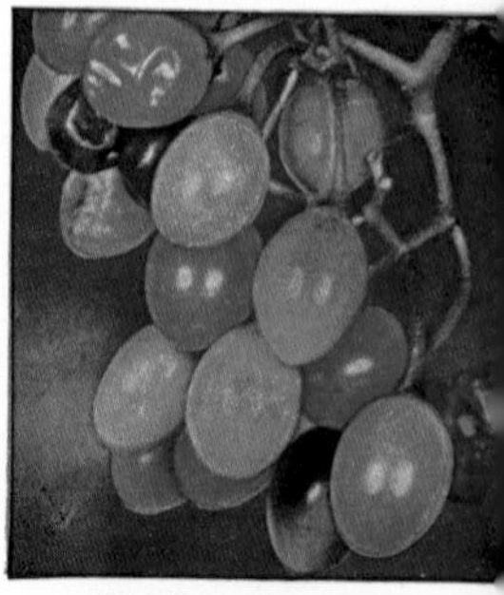

Black on Blue, Red and Yellow

NEEDLES, The
Three rocks off the W. coast of the Is. of Wight, with a lighthouse.

NEGRI SEMBILAN
[-sĕm-bē'-lăn] State of the Fed. of Malaya on the W. coast of the peninsula, N. of Malacca. Area: 2,580 sq.m. Pop. 430,227.

NEGRITO
Diminutive peoples of the black race in S.E. Asia, and equatorial Africa. Dark-skinned and black-haired, the Asiatic section comprises the Andamanese of the Bay of Bengal, the Semang of Malaya, the Aeta of the Philippines and the Tapiro of W. New Guinea. The African pygmies include the Bambute, Akka and Batwa.

NEGRO
Name denoting dark-skinned, woolly-haired African peoples. A branch of the Negroid division of mankind which includes the E. Asiatic Papuo-Melanesians, the pure Negro race inhabits W. Africa, S. of the Sahara; an E. or Nilotic section extends from the E. Sudan to the Kenya coast. They have narrow heads, broad noses, prominent jaws, large teeth and thick lips. There are large pops. of Negroes in the W. Indies and Amer. **The American Negro.** The Negroes in Amer. now number over 18,000,000. Until 1863, they were all slaves in the N. and S. In 1865-9 laws were passed giving full civic rights to the Negro, although since then the Negro in the S. has become more or less disenfranchised and is treated as a separate race. A Commission on Civil Rights in 1963 reported on racial discrimination in voting rights, public facilities, educ., employment, etc. Attempting to remedy this, the Kennedy admin. introd. the Civil Rights Bill (became law under Pres. Johnson). Integration and attempts to prevent it have led to serious disturbances in the U.S. **Negro Languages.** This family is divided into: (1) **Sudanese-Guinean,** spoken across W. and C. Africa, S. of Sahara (*Nubian, Yoruba, Mandingo, Masai, Hausa*); (2) **Bantu,** spoken throughout Africa S. of Gulf of Guinea (*Swahili, Ruanda, Zulu, Umbundu*); (3) **Hottentot-Bushman,** spoken in S.W. Africa.

NEHRU, Pandit Motilal
(1861-1931) Indian Swarajist leader. In 1919 he founded the *Independent,* an aggressively nationalist paper. He supported Gandhi in his non-co-operative campaign, and was imprisoned. He was pres. of the Swaraj party in 1928, presided over the 'All-Parties Conference' at Bombay, which formulated a scheme for Dominion status for India. His son was **Pandit Jawaharlal** (1889-1964) Pres. of the Congress Party in 1929, 1936, 1937, and 1946. A strong adherent of Indian indep., he became the 1st P.M. of the Repub. of India when it was set up in 1947, and a dominant influence in world affairs. His daughter, **Mrs Indira Gandhi,** became P.M. on d. of Mr. Shastri, 1966.

NELSON, Horatio
Viscount (1758-1805) Brit. admiral. B. Burnham Thorpe, Norfolk, he entered the navy in 1770, saw continuous service until 1787 when he mar. and retired. Returning to the navy in 1793, he fought in the Medit. and lost his right eye at Calvi. He continued his service in the Medit. and as Commodore was responsible for the victory off Cape St. Vincent in 1797. In the same year he lost his right arm at Santa Cruz. In 1798 he won an overwhelming victory over the Fr. in Aboukir Bay (*see* NILE, BATTLE OF THE). He formed in this year a liaison with Emma, Lady Hamilton, which lasted until his d. In 1801 he won another victory at Copenhagen, and in Oct. 1805, Nelson, now a viscount and C.-in-C. sailed to his last victory. The Battle of Trafalgar ended in the annihilation of the Fr.-Sp. fleet, but Nelson was mortally wounded.

NEOLITHIC
Term denoting the highly finished and polished stone implements of the later prehistoric Stone Age, contrasted with the earlier or palaeolithic phase. During this cultural stage mankind developed agriculture, animal domestication, pottery, basketry and weaving. The grinding of stone edge-tools led to carpentering, improved navigation, megalith building, settled homes, etc.

NEON
[nē'-ŏn] Inert gas, discovered in 1895 by Ramsay and Travers. It is used in electric discharge lamps, and for illuminated signs in different colours. Its density is 0·67 times that of air. Chem. sym. Ne.

NEO-PLATONISM
Last school of pagan philosophy. It was influenced by the philosophy of Philo and the Gnostics. It emerged in 3rd cent. in Alexandria and was profoundly remodelled by Plotinus. It influenced Clement, Origen, Augustine and others.

NEPAL
[-pawl'] Kingdom of Asia on the S. slopes of the Himalayas, between Tibet and Ind. The country is mountainous in the N. and includes Everest (29,145 ft.), and Dhaulagiri (26,810 ft.), Rice, wheat and other crops are grown in the fertile valleys, and there are forests. Katmandu is the cap. and chief city. The people are of Mongolian origin, mainly Buddhists or Hindus. The state, which became indep. 1923, is gov. by a king and by a P.M. Area: 54,600 sq.m. Pop. 10,500,000.

NEPHRITE
[nef'-] A compact variety of 2 allied minerals of the amphibole group. Nephrite or jade is white or green in colour, very hard and tough. White nephrite consists of silicate of calcium and magnesium.

NEPHRITIS
[nĕ-fri'-] Inflammation of the kidneys. The causes are many.

NEPTUNE
The 8th known planet in order of distance from the sun (*c.* 2,797,000,000 m.). It was discovered in 1846 by Galle of Berlin. The planet has a diameter of *c.* 30,900 m. and its mass is over 17 times that of the earth. The period of its solar orbit is *c.* 164 yrs. 288 days.

NERNST, Walter
(1864-1941) German physicist and chemist. He discovered absolute zero is not the zero point of motion (energy), but of *entropy.* He was awarded the Nobel Prize for Chemistry, 1920.

NERO
(37-68) Rom. emperor, the last of the Caesars. Adopted by the Emperor Claudius in 50, and succeeded him in 54. His reign was marred by a series of murders attributed to him. His mother and 2 successive wives were among the victims. He blamed the Christians for the burning of Rome, and had many put to d.

NERVE
Anatomical structure whose special properties allow of transmission of impulses along its substance from brain to muscles. *Motor nerves* are those that carry impulses from brain to muscle; *sensory nerves* are those that carry sensation from skin to brain for interpretation.

NESS, Loch
Lake of Inverness-shire, forming part of the course of the Caledonian Canal. It is connected by the river Ness with the Moray Firth. Reputed to be inhabited by a 'monster'.

NESTORIANS
Influential Christian sect of W. Asia, so called from their founder Nestorius, a 5th cent. Syrian divine. It was founded in the 5th cent., is perpetuated in Mesopotamia, Syria, Persia, India, etc. and recognises 3 sacraments only, Baptism, The Lord's Supper and Ordination.

NET-BALL
Had its origin as an indoor game in the U.S.A. in 1892, though in Brit. it is played outdoors on a court 95 ft. long; at each end is a goal consisting of a small bottomless net suspended on posts 10 ft. high. The aim is to throw the ball through the opponents' net.

NETHERLANDS
or **Low Countries.** Former designation of the area now comprising Belg. and the Kingdom of the Netherlands. The Netherlands has had a stormy and heroic hist., being a long struggle against Sp. William the Silent was the dominating figure of the struggle. The Dutch Repub. emerged from the struggle at the end of the 16th cent. and for the next cent. was a maritime and commercial power of prime importance. At the end of the 18th cent. it became the Batavian Repub. and the modern kingdom came into being, 1814. Belg. became a separate kingdom, 1831. *See* BELGIUM; NETHERLANDS, KINGDOM OF THE.

NETHERLANDS, Kingdom of the
Country of W. Europe, commonly known as Holland, bounded by Germany and Belg. with a long coastline on the N. Sea. The country is low-lying, with large areas in the W. and N. below sea-level, and is drained by the Rhine, Maas (Meuse) and Scheldt. The Ijsselmeer (Zuider Zee) has been separated from the sea by a dam, and partially reclaimed. Dykes have been constructed to protect the country from inundation by the sea. Off the coast are 2 groups of Is.; across the mouths of the Rhine and Scheldt are Walcheren, Schouwen and Over Flakkee, while farther N. are the Frisian Is. The country is primarily agricultural. Bulbs are grown on a large scale for export, and there are important fisheries. Industries include shipping, the manufacture of machinery, textiles, pottery and glass. Diamond cutting is carried on in Amsterdam. The Hague is the seat of govt. of the Netherlands, but Amsterdam is the commercial cap.; other towns are Rotterdam, Utrecht, Haarlem. There are univs. at Amsterdam, Groningen, Leiden, Nijmegen and Utrecht. Area: 12,997 sq.m. Pop. 11,890,000. In World War II the Netherlands were invaded by Germany, and much of the land was flooded during the fighting. In 1947 the Netherlands, Belg. and Luxembourg formed a customs union, known as Benelux. The country is ruled by a constitutional monarch, and the States-Gen. consisting of 2 chambers. Overseas possessions include Surinam (or Dut. Guiana) and Curaçao in the W. Indies (*q.v.*).

NETTLE
(*Urtica*) Typical genus of herbs of the nettle family, scattered over temp. and sub-temp. regions. The stem and leaves bear stinging hairs. Of the 3 Brit. species the tender shoots of the great perennial downy *U. dioica*, 2-4 ft. high, are used as a pot-herb.

NETTLE TREE
(*Celtis autralis*) Tree of the elm family, indigenous to the Medit. region E. to China. It is straight-trunked, 30-40 ft. high, with toothed, lance-shaped leaves and small, sweet blackberries. The allied N. Amer. *C. occidentalis* is the hackberry.

NETTLERASH *See* URTICARIA.

NEUCHÂTEL
[nö-shä-tel'] Cap. of the Swiss canton of N. on the W. shore of L. Neuchâtel. The castle is the seat of the cantonal govt. and assizes. Pop. 27,600.

NEUROSIS
[new-rō'-] Functional disorder of the mind not assoc. with any demonstrable pathological changes in brain or spinal cord. **Occupational neurosis** manifests itself in production of signs assoc. with occupation, such as writers' cramp, miners' nystagmus.

NEUTRON
One of the types of minute particles which make up the nucleus (*q.v.*) of an atom. It carries no electrical charge. With the proton, the neutron is present in all atomic nuclei, the two conforming to the laws of quantum mathematics. The discovery that neutrons could split uranium atoms led eventually to the creation of the atomic bomb and to the harnessing of atomic energy for power.

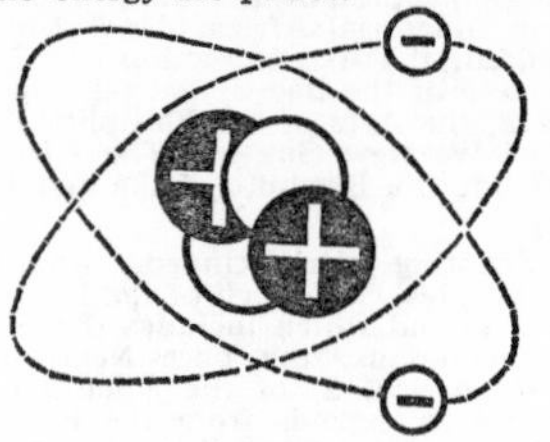

Atom of helium showing neutrons (white circles)

NEVADA
W. state of the U.S.A., a plateau area between the heights of the Rocky Mts. and the Sierra Nevada on the W. The soil is infertile, and the climate arid, but irrigation has improved it. Mining is important; gold, silver, copper, lead and zinc are worked. Carson City is the cap. N. became a state, 1864, and sends 1 representative to Congress. Area: 110,540 sq.m. Pop. 488,800.

NEVIS
One of the Leeward Is., S. of St. Kitts. Sugar, coconuts and cotton are exported. Charlestown is the chief town. Pop. 57,000.

NEW BRITAIN
Largest Is. in the Bismarck Archipelago (*q.v.*) in the W. Pacific, forming part of the Austral. trust territory of New Guinea. Kokopo is the admin. centre. *See* PAPUA AND NEW GUINEA.

NEW BRUNSWICK
Maritime prov. of the Dominion of Canada, in the E. Bounded by Nova Scotia, Quebec and Maine (U.S.A.), it has coastlines on the Gulf of St. Lawrence and the Bay of Fundy. There are hills rising to 1,500 ft. in the N.W. Much of the area is forested, and lumbering is important. Agriculture, fishing and mining are other occupations. Fredericton is the cap. but St. John and Moncton are larger. New B., once part of Acadia, was ceded to Brit. by Fr. 1713. It was settled, 1764, and joined the Confed. 1867. It is admin. by a lieut.-gov. and a legislative assembly, and sends 10 senators and 10 representatives to the Fed. parl. Area: 27,000 sq.m. Pop. 614,000.

NEW CALEDONIA
Fr. Is. in the S. Pacific, 700 m. E. of Queensland. Noumea is the cap. Discovered by Cook, 1774, annexed by Fr. in 1854. Area: 7,200 sq.m. Pop. 82,500.

NEW ENGLAND
Name given to 6 N.E. states of the U.S.A. They are Maine, New Hampshire, Connecticut, Massachusetts, Rhode Is. and Vermont.

NEW FOREST
District of S.W. Hants. Beaulieu Abbey and the Rufus Stone are objects of interest. The forest has its own breed of ponies.

NEW GUINEA
Is. of the W. Pacific S. of the Equator. It is traversed by mt. ridges which rise to over 16,000 ft. in the Nassau Mts. in the W. The largest river is the Fly. Much of the interior is densely forested. The climate is hot and humid. Exports include rubber, timber, copra,

pearls, cocoa and coffee. There are gold, copper and phosphate reserves, but transport difficulties have limited exploitation. The inhabitants are mainly Papuan negroes with mixtures of Malay and Polynesian blood. The W. half of the Is., once Dutch, in 1963 became part of Indonesia. Transferred from U.N. to Indonesian control, 1963, becoming known as W. Irian. Area: 317,000 sq.m. Pop. 2,621,000. *See* PAPUA AND NEW GUINEA.

NEW HAMPSHIRE
New Eng. state of the U.S.A. It is mountainous, and is crossed by the Connecticut and Merrimack rivers. There is much forest land and some agriculture. The chief industries are shoe manufacturing and cotton goods. Concord is the cap. and Manchester is the largest town. One of the orig. 13 states, N.H. sends 2 representatives to Congress. Area: 9,300 sq.m. Pop. 737,700.

NEW HEBRIDES
Group of Pacific Is. *c.* 500 m. W. of Fiji, admin. jointly by Brit. and Fr. Copra, cocoa, coffee and timber are exported. Area: 5,700 sq.m. Pop. 60,000.

NEW JERSEY
State of the U.S.A., S. of New York State, with a long Atlantic coastline. The state is largely agricultural, producing market garden crops. Trenton is the cap. but Newark, Jersey City and Paterson are larger. Settled in 1600, N.J. was 1 of the orig. 13 states; it now sends 15 representatives to Congress. Area: 8,204 sq.m. Pop. 7,168,200.

NEW MEXICO
S.W. state of the U.S.A. bounded by Texas, Colorado, Arizona and Mexico. Much of the area is a high plateau, with mts. reaching 13,000 ft. in the N.; the chief rivers are the Rio Grande, Pecos, and Canadian. An agricultural state, growing maize, wheat, potatoes, cotton and fruit. There are extensive forests, and gold, silver and copper are worked. Santa Fé is the cap. but Albuquerque is the largest town. Following the war between Mexico and the U.S.A. it became Amer. territory, and was made a state, 1912. It sends 2 representatives to Congress. Area: 121,670 sq.m. Pop. 1,016,000.

NEW ORLEANS
Port and chief commercial city of Louisiana, U.S.A. on the Mississippi, *c.* 100 m. from the mouth. It is the great cotton mart of the country. The principal industry, after shipping, is sugar refining. Settled by the Fr. in 1718, N.O. was ceded to Sp. 1763. It fell to Fr. 1800 and was purchased with Louisiana by the U.S.A. 1803. Pop. 585,800.

NEW SOUTH WALES
(N.S.W.) State of the Commonwealth of Australia, in the S.E. between Queensland and Victoria. The narrow coastal strip is separated from the inland plains by the Gt. Dividing Range, which rises to 7,305 ft. in Mt. Kosciusko. The W. is watered by the Murray-Darling river system. N.S.W. lies within the temp. zone; wheat, maize, oats, rice, sugar cane, tobacco and fruit are grown, and sheep farming is important. There are rich deposits of gold and other minerals. Sydney is the cap. and chief port. Other centres are Newcastle, Wollongong and Broken Hill. First colonised, 1788, N.S.W. was given responsible govt. 1855, and federated with the other states, 1901. Admin. is by a Gov. and 2 houses. Area: 309,430 sq.m. Pop. 4,086,293.

NEW TESTAMENT
One of the 2 divisions of the Bible. The books record the life and teaching of Jesus Christ and the foundation of the Christian Ch. The 2nd cent. gradually formed an authoritative list of those recognised by orthodox and heretic alike.

NEW YORK
E. state of the U.S.A. stretching from the Canadian border to the Atlantic; it includes Manhattan Is. on which N.Y. City stands, and Long Is. In the E. are the Adirondack and Catskill Mts.; the chief river is the Hudson. Agriculture is important. There is some mining, and industries include clothing manufacture and printing. Albany is the cap. but New York, Buffalo, Rochester, Syracuse and Yonkers are larger. At first a Dutch possession, N.Y. was under Eng. rule until the War of Indep. It was one of the orig. 13 states, and now sends 41 representatives to Congress. Area: 49,200 sq.m. Pop. 18,190,800. **New York.** City of the U.S.A., the financial and commercial cap. It has a magnificent harbour formed by the rivers Hudson and North, at the entrance to which stands the Statue of Liberty. New York centres on Manhattan Is. Bowery is the Jewish and Harlem the negro quarter. Ferries connect Manhattan Is. with Brooklyn and Hoboken, 4 great bridges cross the East R. to Brooklyn and the Verrazano-Narrows Bridge joins Long Is. and Staten Is. The city has several airports, including La Guardia and Kennedy. Famous buildings include the Emp. State Building (1,472 ft.). Amusements and theatres centre on Broadway, and also at Coney Is. Central Park has 840 acres; Bronx Park contains the great N.Y. Zoo. Long Is. has a garden suburb. N.Y. is the chief shipping port of the world; it has *c.* 770 m. of waterfront. A great manufacturing centre, its industries include chemicals, clothing, tobacco and sugar and oil refining. Wall St. is the financial centre. The city is gov. by a mayor, 5 borough pres. and a city council. Pop. 7,799,000.

NEW ZEALAND
The Dominion of N.Z. lies 1,200 m. south-east of Australia and 5,000 m. W. of S. Amer. A little smaller (104,000 sq.m.) than the Brit. Is. it supports a pop. of about 2½ million. It administers certain W. Pacific Is. and Ross Dependency in Antarctica. The principal parts of the Dominion are the N. and S. Is. of N.Z. extending between latitudes 34° and 48° S.; about 1,000 m. in a N.E.-S.W. direction but less than 300 m. wide. The Is. are mountainous, particularly S. Is., where Mt. Cook reaches 12,349 ft. North Is. has plains around Hauraki Gulf, where Auckland, the largest city, is situated, and in the S.W. and S.E.; S. Is. has the Canterbury Plains in the E. There are many areas of hill country (1-2,000 ft.) formerly forested but now important for grazing. In N. Is. there are active volcanoes and hot springs. Climatically there is a general likeness between New Zealand and the Brit. Is. The prevailing winds are W. at all seasons and bring heavy precipitation to the W. coast and mts., especially in S. Is. Over a thousand plants are peculiar to N.Z. Tree ferns up to 50 ft. in height are abundant. The evergreen sub-trop. rain forest, characteristic below 4,000 ft., has been largely cleared for agriculture. **History.** First discovered in 1642 by Tasman, the coast was explored by Capt. Cook in 1769, 1773, 1774 and 1777. Sealers and whalers, chiefly from Australia, were the first Europeans to settle, and a timber trade developed. In 1840, the sovereignty of Queen Victoria was proclaimed. In that year the N.Z. Islands' first permanent settlement, Wellington, was founded. The Free Ch. of Scot. sponsored that at Dunedin (S. Is.) in 1848 and the Ch. of Eng. the Canterbury settlement in 1850; in 1907 the Dominion of N.Z. was estabd. After the Maori Wars in 1845-8 and 1860-70 the natives settled peacefully and now take an increasing part in life and govt. In the present cent. their numbers have more than doubled and there are now 170,000 mainly in N. Is. There is no colour bar. About two-thirds of the farm products are exported and these represent over 90 % of the total exports.

Before refrigeration N.Z. could put only non-perishable commodities on the world market—wool, wheat, and some flax—but meat and dairy produce are more profitable. Adequate moisture with mild temperatures all year round favour grass. About 18 million acres of native forest have been cleared and replaced by grass, in addition to which there are about 14 million acres of native tussock grass. Type of farming varies with altitude and soil: generally, the moister lowlands are dairying areas, particularly in N. Is., and the drier areas and uplands carry sheep. Small, intensively and scientifically worked farms are characteristic. Marketing is also well organised. Gold was once important but the annual value of production is now less than £1 m. Coal is mined. With a pop. of only 2½ million the home market for manufactured goods is small. The processing and manufacture of meat, butter and cheese accounts for much of the industry, but more and more consumer goods, for home use, are made. Coal is the chief source of power but hydro-electric power is being developed. Clothing, footwear, motor car bodies, electrical equipment, farm machinery and fertilisers are produced and there is a substantial saw-milling industry. N.Z. is a self-governing dominion; the Gov.-Gen. is apptd. by the Crown. The House of Representatives is elected by all adults; the Maori pop. (having a separate electoral roll) has 4 members of a total of 80. N.Z. has been a pioneer of social legislation. Social services are well organised. Educ. is compulsory and free. The Univ. of New Zealand consisted of Univ. Colls. at Auckland, Wellington, Christchurch and the Univ. of Otago, now separate univs.

NEWBOLT, Sir Henry
(1862-1938) Eng. poet. The ballads *Admirals All* (1897) were followed by other sea poems, *e.g. Drake's Drum*. In 1920 he pub. his *Naval History of the Great War*.

NEWBURY
Borough and market town of Berks. on the Kennet, 17 m. S.W. of Reading. Chief trade is in agric. prod. and sheep. There were 2 battles of N. in the Civil War, 1643 and 1644. Pop. 20,700.

NEWCASTLE-UPON-TYNE
City, county borough and port of Northumberland, on the Tyne, 8 m. from the sea. It is an important colliery and shipbuilding centre, with engineering, electrical works and chemical manufactures. Orig. a Rom. station, N. has a castle built by Henry II, and its cath. dates from the late 14th cent. The univ. separated from that of Durham, 1963. N. sends 4 members to Parl. Pop. 263,360.

NEWFOUNDLAND
[new-fŏnd-land'] Prov. of the Dominion of Canada, comprising the Is. of Newfoundland and the territory of Labrador (*q.v.*). The Is. is triangular, with Capes Bauld, Race and Ray at the angles. There are mts. in the W. and N.W. rising to over 2,600 ft. and many lakes. Much of the land is infertile and unproductive, and most of the inhabitants live near the coasts or the lakes. Timber, pulp, newsprint, minerals and fish are the chief products. The only large city is the cap., St. John's. Gander is an internat. airport. N. was discovered by John Cabot, 1497, and annexed by Sir Humphrey Gilbert, 1583, for Eng. In 1948 N. voted to enter the Canadian fed. thus becoming the 10th prov. There is a lieut.-gov. and a legislative assembly. Area (excluding Labrador): 42,730 sq.m. Pop. 481,000. **Newfoundland Dog.** Imported into Brit. in the 18th cent. Broad-backed, deep-chested, it has a massive head, muscular hind-quarters and thick, well-covered tail. Dogs should average 27 in. in ht., bitches 25 in. The shaggy, oily coat is usually black.

NEWHAVEN
Urban district and seaport of Sussex. The most direct sea route between London and Paris is from Newhaven to Dieppe. Pop. 8,520.

NEWMAN, John Henry
(1801-90) Eng. Cardinal, theologian and writer. Educ. Trinity Coll. Oxford, where he formed a friendship with Pusey, Hurrell, Froude and others. After ordination he became one of the leaders of the Oxford Tractarian or High Ch. Movement which resulted in the conversion of many to Rom. Catholicism, including himself. He was made a cardinal in 1879. Of his works, his *Apologia pro Vita Sua*, a hist. of his own religious life, is the best known. He wrote the hymn 'Lead Kindly Light'. His epic poem, *The Dream of Gerontius*, was set to music by Elgar.

NEWMARKET
Urban district and market town of Suffolk, 13 m. N.E. of Camb. It is a great centre of horse racing. Pop. 11,200.

NEWPORT
County borough and market town of Monmouthshire, near the mouth of the Usk, 12 m. N.E. of Cardiff. It has extensive docks and a large shipping trade. Other industries are the manufacture of iron and steel, chems. and glass. N. returns 1 member to Parl. Pop. 108,550.

NEWPORT
Borough, market town and cap. of the Is. of Wight, on the Medina, 7 m. from Ryde. Pop. 19,000.

NEWT
A tailed amphibian comprising 18 species, of which 3 are known natives of Brit. The Common N. or Eft, *Molge vulgaris*, is *c.* 3 in. long.

NEWTON, Sir Isaac
(1642-1727) Eng. mathematician, astron. and philosopher. In 1666, it is said, the fall of an apple suggested to him the law of gravitation. He is also remembered for his work on the spectrum, his statement of the laws of motion, the construction of telescopes, his work in geometry and the differential calculus. His two chief works are *Principia* and *Optics*.

NEY, Michel
(1769-1815) Fr. soldier. He enlisted in 1788, and distinguished himself at Jena, Eylau, and Friedland, and esp. in the Russ. campaign of 1812. Louis XVIII made him peer of Fr. but, sent to oppose Napoleon on his return from Elba, he rejoined him, and fought bravely at Waterloo.

NIAGARA FALLS
Waterfall on the Niagara R., N. Amer. The river flows between the U.S.A. and Canada, and the Falls are divided between the two countries. The Amer. falls are 167 ft. high and are separated by Goat Is. from the Canadian or Horseshoe Falls, 158 ft. high. The latter are 3,100 ft. across, but the Amer. falls are only 1,080 ft.

NICAEA
[nī-sē'-ă] Ancient city of Asia Minor, in Bithynia. A famous ch. council was held, 325. This condemned the teaching of Arius, formulated the Nicene creed and fixed the date of Easter.

NICARAGUA
Repub. of C. Amer. between Honduras and Costa Rica, with coastlines on the Pacific Ocean and Caribbean Sea. The interior mts. are healthy and fertile but the E. coast is trop. and swampy. In the W. are 2 large lakes, connected by the R. Tipitapa. Nicaragua is an agricultural country. Mahogany and cedar are

grown and gold is mined. Managua is the cap. Corinto, on the Pacific, and Bluefields, on the Caribbean, are the chief ports. It was discovered by Columbus, and was a Sp. possession until 1821. The Constitution of 1951 provides for a congress of 15 senators and 55 deputies. Area: *c.* 57,143 sq.m. Pop. 1,559,000.

NICE
[nēs] Cap. of Alpes-Maritimes dept. S. Fr., and resort on the Riviera coast. Pop. 294,976.

NICHOLAS
Patron saint of Russia. The widespread making of gifts on St. Nicholas' Eve, afterwards transferred to Christmastide, accompanied early Dutch colonists to the U.S.A., where the name was corrupted to Santa Claus.

NICHOLAS I
(1796-1855) Tsar of Russia and son of Paul I, he succeeded his brother Alexander I as Emperor in 1825. In 1848, during the ' Revolutionary Year ', he assisted in quelling the Hungarian revolt against Austria. His rule was despotic and reactionary.

NICHOLAS II
(1868-1918) Tsar of Russia, he succeeded his father, Alexander III in 1894. He formed an alliance with Fr. and an Entente Cordiale with Gt. Brit. At home he opposed the growth of social democracy. Early in World War I he took over the command of the army and left the conduct of home affairs to the Empress, who was dominated by Rasputin (*q.v.*). In Mar. 1917, he was forced to abdicate and was later shot, with his family.

NICKEL
Hard, white metal showing magnetic properties and occurring chiefly in Canada. Discovered by Cronstedt in 1751, it is a constituent of many steels and other alloys. Alloyed with copper and other metals it is used to make condenser tubes and coins, while with zinc and copper it forms nickel silver. Sp. gr. 8·9. Chem. sym. Ni.

NICOBAR ISLANDS
Indian-owned group of 19 Is. in the Bay of Bengal, S. of the Andaman Is. Coconuts are the main product. They form a centrally admin. territory. Acquired by the Brit. 1869, the Is. were occupied by the Japs. 1942-5. Pop. 14,500.

NICOSIA
Cap. of Cyprus, near the centre of the Is. and connected by railway with its port, Famagusta. Pop. 95,343.

NICOTINE
Colourless volatile liquid alkaloid obtained from the leaves of the tobacco plant, *Nicotiana tabacum*. About 2·7 % is present in tobacco. Nicotine is highly poisonous.

NIETZSCHE, Friedrich Wilhelm
[nē'-chă] (1844-1900) German philosopher. He is the author of several philosophical works beginning in 1878, which stated that man should concentrate on the development of vital energy and develop into a ' superman '. This seemingly anti-Christian doctrine has been wrongly interpreted as meaning ' Might is Right '.

NIGER
River of Africa, 2,600 m. long, rising in the highlands on the borders of Sierra Leone and Fr. Guinea. It flows N.E. past Timbuktu, then S.E. through Nigeria, to the Gulf of Guinea.

NIGER TERRITORY
Repub., former Fr. colony of W. Africa N. of Nigeria, indep., 1960, consisting of a Sahara region in the N., a wooded strip in the centre, and an agricultural zone in the S. Salt and gum arabic are exported. Niamey, the cap., and Zinder are the termini of 2 trans-Sahara motor routes. Area: 489,200 sq.m. Pop. 3,117,000.

NIGERIA
Indep. W. African Rep. within the Commonwealth. Nigeria comprises a narrow coastal strip in the S.W., surrounding Lagos. Bounded on the S. by the Gulf of Guinea, on the W. and N. by Dahomey and Niger, and on the E. by the Cameroon Repub. Geographically, Nigeria consists of 4 areas. Along the coast is a strip, some 20 m. deep, of swamp and mangrove swamp. N. of this lies a belt of dense forest, merging gradually into savanna. The greater part of the country, N. of the Niger and Benue, the chief rivers, is occupied by a plateau. There are 2 seasons, ' rainy ', characterised by the S.W. monsoon, and ' dry ', with the dust-laden N.E. wind, the Harmattan. Crops include cotton, cocoa, ground-nuts, kolanuts and maize. Cattle are reared in the N., hides and skins being exported. Palm oil and kernels, bananas, timber, tin, coal and rubber are also produced. The chief towns are Ibadan, Lagos, the seat of govt., Kano, Ogbomosho and Iwo. In 1886 the colony and protectorate of Lagos was estabd.; in 1900 the protectorates of N. and S. Nigeria were formed, the latter uniting with Lagos, 1906. Nigeria became a Fed. in Oct. 1954, and fully indep. 1960, and a repub. in 1963. In 1966 there was a series of military *coups*, the Federation of regions became a republic of 4 provinces. Lt.-Col. Y. Gowon is the head of state. Secession of the Biafran region, 1967, resulted in civil war. Area: 356,669 sq.m. Pop. 61,450,000.

NIGHTINGALE
(*Luscinia megarhyncha*) A passerine bird ranging over Europe, Asia and N. Africa, reaching S.E. Eng. about mid-April, the males utter their melodious song by night and day.

NIGHTINGALE, Florence
(1820-1910) Eng. nurse and hospital reformer. She went out during the Crimean War with a staff of 38 women to nurse the wounded. In 4 months the death-rate in the hospitals was reduced from 42 % to 2 %. She founded hospital schools of nursing.

NIGHTJAR
(*Caprimulgus europaeus*) Migratory bird belonging to a numerous cosmopolitan subfamily resembling the Swifts. It breeds in Brit. and Europe, spending the N. winter at the Cape.

NIGHTSHADE
Several species of Brit. plants. Common N., *Solanum nigrum*, bears black berries. The Bittersweet or Woody N., *S. dulcamara*, bears scarlet berries. The Deadly N., *Atropa belladonna*, highly poisonous, bears black berries, cherry-sized. Enchanter's N., *Circaea lutetiana* bears tiny fruit.

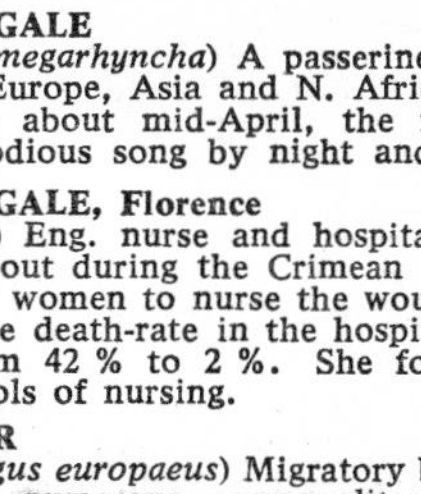

NIHILISM
[nī'-i-lizm] Term used in the 19th cent. for a movement in Russia aimed at overturning the existing order. The Nihilists were responsible for the murder of the tsar Alexander II, in 1881.

NIJINSKY, Vaslav
[ni-jin'-ski] (1890-1950) Russ. ballet dancer and choreographer. Appeared with the Diaghileff

Co. Turned to choreography 1912, creating *L'Après-midi d'un Faune* and *Le Sacre du Printemps*.

NIJMEGEN
[nī'-mā-gěn] Dutch town in Gelderland prov. on the Waal near the German frontier. There are numerous manufactures and a univ. Pop. 130,000.

NILE
Longest river of Africa, which rises in L. Victoria, 3,700 ft. above sea level, and flows N. for 4,090 m. entering the Medit. by a wide delta. From L. Victoria the river flows over rocky country. After leaving L. Albert the Nile flows across marshy lowland, and is joined, below Khartoum, by the Blue Nile which rises in L. Tana. Below Cairo the river divides into a delta of 8,500 sq.m. The Nile is the source of Egyptian prosperity. The Aswan Dam, completed 1902, has since been enlarged. Work on the A. High Dam, 5 m. upstream, has begun. **Nile, Battle of the.** Naval engagement, fought Aug. 1, 1798, in Aboukir Bay. The Fr. ships were found by Nelson, who attacked them, and won a conspicuous victory.

NILGAI
[-gī'] (*Boselaphus tragocamelus*) Indian antelope *c.* 5 ft. high. The horns of the male are short and straight.

NÎMES
[nēm] Town of S. France, cap. of Gard dept. Famous for extensive Rom. remains. Pop. 89,100.

NINEVEH
Ancient city of Assyria, on the left bank of the Tigris, opposite Mosul. The Medes brought about its fall, 612 B.C.

NITRE
Common name for potassium nitrate or saltpetre which occurs in nature as a white incrustation or as crystals in porous soil. Nitre is used in the preparation of gunpowder, for salting meat and in medicine.

NITRIC ACID
HNO_3. Compound of nitrogen with hydrogen and oxygen, commonly known as aqua fortis. It is very corrosive.

NITROGEN
Gaseous element which forms about 4-5ths of the atmosphere and occurs in all living material. It was isolated in a pure state by Rutherford in 1772. Its density is 0·97 times that of air. Chem. sym. N.

NITROGLYCERIN
Explosive substance prepared by treating glycerin with a mixture of cold concentrated nitric and sulphuric acids. It explodes violently by concussion or when quickly heated.

NIXON, Richard Milhous
(1913-) Amer. statesman, Repub. Pres. (1969-). Vice-Pres. under Eisenhower (1953-61). Narrowly beaten (1960) by J. F. Kennedy. Elected (1968).

NKRUMAH, Dr. Kwame
(1909-) African statesman. Formed Convention People's Party in Gold Coast, 1949. Elected P.M. 1952. P.M. of Ghana after indep. 1957. Became Pres. 1960, deposed 1966. P.C.

NOAH
O.T. patriarch. Son of Lamech, and father of Shem, Ham and Japheth, he built the Ark in which he, his family, and some representative animals were saved from the flood.

NOBEL, Alfred Bernhard
(1833-96) Swedish chemist and inventor of dynamite. B. Stockholm. **Nobel Prizes.** On his death Nobel left a fortune of £2,000,000 most of which he ordered to be used to found the 5 Nobel prizes awarded annually for the most important discoveries and works for the benefit of humanity in physics, chemistry, medicine, literature and the furtherance of peace in the world.

NONCONFORMITY
Dissent from the practices and doctrines of the Estabd. Ch. In Brit. the first secession was made in 1563 by the Puritans. After the restoration, however, they suffered severe penalties under the Act of Uniformity (1662), the Conventicle Act (1664), the Five Mile Act (1665), and the Corporation Act (1661). The movement received fresh strength about 1760 through the secession of the Methodists. In 1892 the Nat. Council of the Evangelical Free Chs. was estabd. to protect the rights of the Nonconformists.

NORE, The
Sandbank at the mouth of the Thames, 3 m. from Sheerness. It has a lightship and is famous for the mutiny in the navy that took place, 1797.

NORFOLK
Australian Is. in the S. Pacific, *c.* 930 m. N.E. of Sydney. Discovered by Cook, 1774. From 1914 it has been admin. by the Commonwealth Govt. Pop. 1,877.

NORFOLK
County of E. Eng. with an extensive coastline on the N. Sea. The county is mainly flat, esp. round the Wash. The chief rivers are the Ouse, Yare, Waveney and Bure. In the E. are the Broads, famous as a yachting area. Agriculture is extremely important. Livestock are kept, and the Norfolk turkeys are famous. The fishing industry is centred in Yarmouth. Norwich is the county town. Norfolk and Suffolk were the most densely populated counties in Eng. at the time of the Domesday Survey, and were the centre of a flourishing woollen industry. Norfolk returns 8 members to Parl. (2 for Norwich). Pop. 568,420. **Norfolk, Duke of.** Eng. title held since 1483 by the family of Howard. It is the senior dukedom in the peerage. **John Howard** (1430-85) was granted the title but lost it because of his support of Richard III. **Thomas Howard,** 3rd duke (1473-1554) Defeated Scots at Flodden. Rewarded by restoration of dukedom. Succeeded his father, 1542, and led opposition to Wolsey. Favoured mar. of Ann Boleyn to Henry VIII. Put down the rising called The Pilgrimage of Grace. **Thomas Howard,** 4th duke (1536-72) intrigued with Spain so that he might marry Mary, Queen of Scots, but this was discovered and he was beheaded.

NORMAN
Inhabitant of Normandy, one of the Northmen who settled in N. Fr. and also in Italy and Sicily. In 1066 there was a Norman invasion of Eng. in which William, Duke of Normandy, overcame the Saxons and ruled Eng.

NORMANDY
District of N. Fr., formerly a prov., now divided into depts. of Seine Inférieure, Eure. Orne, Calvados and Manche. The chief towns are Rouen, the old cap., Dieppe, Le Havre, Caen. Bayeux, Cherbourg and Mont St. Michel. **Normandy, Allied Landing (World War II).** On the night of June 5-6, 1944, Allied airborne

troops made landings behind the German defences in Normandy. On June 6 (D-Day) Allied naval forces supported by strong air forces began landing Allied armies between Cherbourg and Le Havre.

NORSE
The N. Germanic or Scandinavian language, esp. Old Norse (*c.* 700-1530). The Vikings carried it to Iceland (where sagas were composed *c.* 1000-1300; *see* EDDA) to Greenland, the Faroes, Caithness, Sutherland, Orkney and Shetland, to Normandy, to Ireland, and to N. Eng.

NORTH, Lord
Frederick (1732-92) Brit. politician. He entered parl. in 1754, becoming Chanc. of the Exchequer, 1767, and P.M. 1770-82. He is best known as the leader of the admin. during the Amer. War of Indep.

NORTH AFRICA, War in
When Italy entered World War II (June 10, 1940), N. Africa became an active theatre of war, in which the aims of both sides were (1) control of the Suez Canal and (2) control of the Medit. The great desert war began in Aug. 1940, and was waged along the whole coast of Libya and Egypt. After reverses in 1942 Gen. Montgomery launched a powerful attack on the Germans under Rommel. Tripoli was captured by the Brit. (Jan. 23, 1943). On Nov. 7-8, 1942, a large-scale amphibious force under Gen. Eisenhower (*q.v.*) made a landing at Algiers, Oran and Casablanca and moved rapidly towards Tunisia. The Germans were now encircled. On May 7 the Amers. took Bizerta and the Brit. occupied Tunis. 5 days later the Axis forces in N. Africa capitulated.

NORTH AMERICA
Term applied to the whole of the N. of the Amer. cont. including the U.S.A., Canada and Mexico. The chief physical features are the Laurentian Plateau in the N. of Canada, the hilly Appalachian area from Newfoundland to Alabama, the W. highlands which include the Rocky Mts. and the vast central plains or prairies. Important rivers are the Mississippi, St. Lawrence, Mackenzie, Columbia, Colorado and Hudson. Gold is plentiful in many districts; oil, coal, iron, uranium and most of the essential minerals are found. Fur-bearing animals are a source of considerable wealth, and large stretches of country have rich agricultural land. The orig. inhabitants were the Amer.-Ind. of different tribes. The hist. of the cont. starts with its discovery by Columbus, 1492, though earlier voyagers had sighted parts of it, and there had been European settlers in Greenland. From the 17th cent. there have been many immigrants, predominantly European. Area: *c.* 8,000,000 sq.m. Pop. *c.* 233,000,000.

NORTH CAROLINA
S. state of the U.S.A. with an Atlantic coastline. The W. contains the ranges of the Appalachian Mts. but the E. is low-lying. The chief agricultural products are maize, cotton, tobacco, peanuts and sweet potatoes. Raleigh is the cap. N.C. was settled, 1653, and was 1 of the orig. 13 states. It sends 11 representatives to Congress. Area: 52,712 sq.m. Pop. 5,082,100.

NORTH DAKOTA
[-kō′-] N. state of the U.S.A., S. of the Canadian border in the Great Plains. Agriculture is the chief occupation, with large-scale farms. Horses and cattle are reared. Bismarck is the cap. but Fargo, Grand Forks and Minot are larger. Settled *c.* 1800. N.D. became a state, 1889, and sends 2 representatives to Congress. Area: 70,660 sq.m. Pop. 617,800.

NORTH ISLAND
More N. of the 2 chief Is. of New Zealand (*q.v.*). It is famous for its sheep and cattle. The principal cities are Auckland and Wellington. Area: 44,280 sq.m. Pop. *c.* 1,820,118.

NORTH POLE
N. terminus of the axis of the earth. *See* ARCTIC.

NORTH RHINE-WESTPHALIA
State of W. Germany, bounded on the N.W. by the Netherlands. It is traversed by the Rhine, and contains the great industrial area of the Ruhr. Düsseldorf is the cap. Pop. 15,901,700.

NORTH RIDING
One of the 3 admin. divisions of Yorks. (*q.v.*) constituting a separate county; chief town, Northallerton. It returns 6 members to Parl. (2 borough constituencies). Pop. 565,080.

NORTH SEA
Sea bounded by the coasts of Brit., Norway, Denmark, Germany and the Netherlands, with the Arctic Sea and Strait of Dover to N. and S. It is shallow, averaging *c.* 60 fathoms, and slopes from N. to S. One of the most important fishing grounds in the world.

NORTH-WEST PASSAGE
Route from the Atlantic to the Pacific round the N. of Canada. In 1714 Parl. offered a reward of £20,000 to the first discoverer of the passage. There were many attempts, including that of Sir J. Franklin in 1845. It was navigated by Amundsen, 1903-5. 1st navigated by commercial vessel (SS Manhattan) 1969.

NORTHWEST TERRITORIES
Admin. district of Canada. Orig. Rupert's Land and the N.W. Territory, it was purchased from the Hudson's Bay Co. 1867, by the Dominion Gov. It now consists of the mainland W. of Hudson Bay, E. of the Rockies and N. of latitude 60° N. including the Northern archipelago. There are numerous lakes, of which the largest are the Gt. Bear and Gt. Slave. The principal rivers are the Mackenzie, Coppermine and Dubawnt. Mining is important, gold, radium and petroleum being found. The only other industry is the fur trade. The pop. consists mostly of Ind. and Eskimos. For administrative purposes the territories are sub-divided into districts governed by a commissioner, deputy-commissioner and 5 councillors. Area: 1,253,000 sq.m. Pop. 30,000.

NORTHALLERTON
Urban district, market town, and administrative centre of the N. Riding, Yorks. 30 m. N.W. of York. Pop. 8,610.

NORTHAMPTONSHIRE
(Northants.) Midland county of Eng. which stretches from Oxfordshire to Lincs. The land is hilly; in the N.E. round Peterborough, is reclaimed fenland. The chief rivers are the Welland, Nene and Great Ouse. Agriculture is important. Iron is mined, and boots and shoes manufactured. Northampton is the county town. Northants., with the Soke of Peterborough, returns 5 members to Parl. (incl. the borough constituency of Northampton). Pop. 405,870. **Northampton.** County borough and county town of Northants., on the Nene. Famous for the manufacture of shoes, it has also tanning and textile works, breweries, iron foundries, brick works. Pop. 105,000.

NORTHCLIFFE, Viscount
(1865-1922) Eng. journalist. **Alfred Charles William Harmsworth** was b. in Dublin. In 1888 he founded a weekly paper, *Answers.* Other papers were started and the foundation was laid of the Amalgamated Press. He and his brother **Harold** bought, 1894, *The Evening News*, a London daily paper. Founded *The Daily Mirror*, 1903, and, 1905, bought *The Observer.* In 1908 Harmsworth became chief proprietor of *The Times.* In 1911 he sold *The Observer* and later *The Daily Mirror* but he kept control of *The Daily Mail* and *The Times.* In 1918 he became director of propaganda in enemy countries.

NORTHERN IRELAND
Country of the U.K. of Gt. Brit. and N.I. Under the Govt. of Ireland Act, 1920, it consists of the 6 Ulster cos. of Antrim, Armagh, Down, Fermanagh, Londonderry and Tyrone (*qqv.*). It occupies the extreme N.E. of Ireland. Much of the land is hilly, with the Mts. of Antrim, and the Mourne and Sperrin Mts. rising to over 1,800 ft. In the centre is the fertile lowland of Lough Neagh. The chief rivers are the Bann, Lagan and Derg. Agriculture is important. Industries are centred in the N.E. around Belfast, and include the manufacture of linen, rope and machinery, and aircraft and shipbuilding. Belfast is the cap.; other towns are Londonderry, Lisburn, Bangor, Ballymena and Newry. N.I. has a House of Commons and Senate. The Gov. represents the Queen, and N.I. sends 12 members to the H. of Commons at Westminster. Area: 5,461 sq.m. Pop. 1,435,000.

NORTHERN TERRITORY
Part of the Commonwealth of Australia, between Queensland and W. Australia, with a coastline on the Gulf of Carpentaria and the Arafura Sea. Much of the interior is plateau, with the MacDonnell and Musgrave ranges. It lies almost entirely within the tropics, is dry and sandy, except in the extreme N. Most trop. crops can be grown, but pastoral farming is the chief industry. Gold, wolfram and mica are mined, and mother-of-pearl fishing is carried on. Darwin, the admin. centre, has a good harbour and airport. N.T. was taken over by the Commonwealth from S. Australia, 1911. Area: 523,620 sq.m. Pop. 40,000.

NORTHUMBERLAND
Most N. county of Eng., separated from Scot. by the Cheviot Hills and the Tweed. The coastal region is lowlying, rising to moorland and mts. (the Cheviot 2,676 ft.). The Tyne and Tweed are the chief rivers. Sheep are reared, and oats and barley grown. The county is rich in coal, and a large industrial area is centred on the Tyne. Newcastle-upon-Tyne is the county town; other towns are Alnwick, Berwick-on-Tweed, Wallsend and Hexham. The county has numerous Rom. remains, including Hadrian's Wall. The county returns 10 members to Parl. (7 borough constituencies). Pop. 825,650.

NORTHUMBERLAND, Duke of
John Dudley (*c.* 1502-53) Eng. statesman. In 1550 he was created Duke of Northumberland and opposed the Duke of Somerset, who was executed 1552. He mar. his son, Lord Guildford Dudley, to Lady Jane Grey, and proclaimed her queen. Forced to surrender to Mary Tudor, he was executed for high treason.

NORTHUMBRIA
One of the kingdoms of Eng. in A.-S. times. It came into existence *c.* 600. For a time it was the strongest of the Eng. kingdoms, but in less than a cent. it was subordinate to Mercia or Wessex.

NORWAY
Kingdom of N. Europe, the W. portion of the Scandinavian Peninsula, bounded on the E. by the U.S.S.R., Sweden and Finland it has a long coastline on the Arctic and Atlantic Oceans, the N. Sea and the Skagerrak. It is composed of a mt. mass of ancient rocks. The highest peaks, Galdhopig and Jötunheim, exceed 8,000 ft. Numerous short, swift streams are a source of electricity. The coastline is indented with fiords. The climate is tempered by the N. Atlantic Drift and S.W. winds, and the coasts are ice-free all year round. At N. Cape there is continuous daylight from May until July; in winter there is a corresponding period without sun. Industry is the chief occupation. Cultivation is limited to the sheltered areas. Cattle are reared. There are important fisheries, and much frozen and canned fish is exported. Whaling is important in the N. Valuable forests provide abundant timber. There are mineral resources, including pyrites and ore. Oslo, the cap., and Bergen, are the largest towns; others are Trondheim and Stavanger. The Lutheran religion is predominant. The present kingdom dates from 1905 when the union with Sweden was terminated. Prince Charles of Denmark was elected king, as Haakon VII. The legislative assembly, the Storting, has 2 houses, elected by universal suffrage. Occupied by the Germans in April, 1940, a puppet Govt., under Quisling, was set up, and the King escaped to London. A new govt. was elected in Oct. 1945. King Olav V came to the throne in 1957 on the d. of his father. Area: 125,065 sq.m. Pop. 3,654,000. Norwegian overseas possessions are Spitsbergen Bear Is. and Jan Mayen in the Arctic Ocean; Bouvet Is. (S. Atlantic), Peter the First Is. (Antarctic Ocean) and a dependency on the Antarctic Continent.

NORWICH
[nor'-ich] City, county borough and county town of Norfolk. It was a Rom. settlement. Industries include the manufacture of boots, shoes, textiles, mustard and starch; foundries and breweries. Near is the Univ. of E. Anglia (1962). N. returns 2 members to Parl. Pop. 119,760.

NOSE
Facial prominence above mouth in man and higher apes. Divided by a plate of cartilage into 2 nostrils.

NOTARY
Official, usually a solicitor or other law agent, who attests or certifies documents. There is a Soc. of Notaries in London. In Scot. the **Notary Public** fulfils tasks analogous to those of Commissioners for Oaths in Eng.

NOTTINGHAMSHIRE
(Notts.) Inland county of Eng. in the N. midlands. The E. part is lowlying, but, in the W. are hills of 600 ft. and a woodland district, called the Dukeries, which includes the remains of Sherwood Forest. The chief rivers are the Trent and Idle. The county is mainly agricultural in the E. and industrial in the W. The chief industries are the manufacture of lace, hosiery and bicycles; there are also iron foundries and cotton and woollen mills. N. is the county town; other towns are Newark, Mansfield and Worksop. Notts. returns 10 members to Parl. Pop. 916,520. **Nottingham.** City, county borough and county town of Nottinghamshire, on the Trent, 15 m. E. of Derby. The univ. received its charter in 1948. N. returns 4 members to Parl. Pop. 314,360.

NOVA
A variable star which suddenly, at long intervals of time, assumes a luminosity many times greater than that of its normal condition, to be followed by a gradual and fluctuating fall in brightness.

NOVA SCOTIA
Maritime prov. of the Dominion of Canada comprising a peninsula and an Is. Cape Breton (*q.v.*) in the extreme E. There are numerous rivers and lakes. Agriculture is the most important industry. Minerals include coal, gold, gypsum and salt. Iron and steel are manufactured at Sydney in C. Breton Is. The cod and lobster fisheries are also important. Halifax is the cap. and largest city. First settled by the Fr., Nova Scotia passed to Eng. 1621; its possession was contested until 1713, when, by the Treaty of Utrecht, it was ceded to Brit. It is gov. by a lieut.-gov. and a legislative assembly. The prov. sends 10 senators and 12 representatives to the Dominion Parl. Area: 21,068 sq.m. Pop. 723,000.

NOVAYA ZEMLYA
Group of Russ. Is. in the Arctic Ocean, con-

sisting of 2 large Is. and several smaller ones, between Barents Sea and Kara Sea. Used by Russians as nuclear test area. Area: 30,000 sq.m.

NOVOCAINE
Crystalline salt, very soluble in water, known also as ethocaine hydrochloride. It is a complex substance prepared from glycol bromohydrin, and used as a local anaesthetic in dentistry.

NUBIA
Region of N.E. Africa from the Red Sea to the Nile and from Egypt to Ethiopia. Important in ancient times, it now lies in the Repub. of the Sudan.

NUCLEAR PHYSICS
In 1911 Rutherford demonstrated that the atom was constructed of electrons revolving round a positive nucleus. In 1913 Bohr showed how such an atom could radiate and absorb energy in the same way as do the stars. Einstein announced his general theory of relativity in 1915. In 1925 there were formulated the fundamental principles of quantum mechanics. In 1929 there was estabd. the phenomenon of the expansion of the universe. In 1938 there was worked out the mechanism by which stellar energy is thought to be generated. In 1939 came the first realisation that hydrogen is overwhelmingly the most abundant element in the universe. In 1948 the idea of the continuous creation of fundamental particles of matter was first introduced into a systematic scheme of evolution of the universe. The year 1950 brought Mr. Fred Hoyle's contribution. This caused much controversy and is contained in his book *The Nature of the Universe*.

NUCLEAR POWER
The U.K. Atomic Energy Authority are responsible for developing nuclear power stations. In the Calder Hall station the fuel consists of natural uranium metal rods enclosed in magnesium alloy cans. These are set in channels in a cylindrical structure of pure graphite enclosed in a steel pressure vessel. A controlled nuclear-fission chain reaction produces heat in the fuel and is cooled by carbon dioxide gas under pressure. To obtain a higher gas outlet temperature a reactor using uranium in powder form and stainless steel as a canning material has been developed. Known as the Advanced Gas-Cooled Reactor, a prototype is being operated at Windscale, adjoining Calder Hall. Other countries, esp. the U.S.A. have developed reactors cooled by water and the A.E.A. have one under construction at Winfrith, Dorset. One feature common to all these reactors is that during the nuclear reaction some of the uranium in the fuel is converted to plutonium, itself a valuable fuel. This may be used in the Fast Reactor, and research into Fast Reactor technology is endeavouring to make use of the stocks of plutonium now accumulating as a by-product. An experimental Fast Reactor at Dounreay in N. Scot. has been generating electricity for some time. It is also possible to obtain energy from the joining together or fusion of light elements such as hydrogen. Stars obtain their energy in this form, as does the hydrogen bomb. The problem of achieving a controlled reaction producing energy in an economically useful form is immense, but research is being undertaken on this aspect at Culham, Berks.

NUCLEUS
Central core of an atom, containing most of its mass, and bearing a positive charge of electricity. *See* NEUTRON; PROTON.

NUFFIELD, William Richard Morris, Viscount
(1877-1963) Brit. industrialist and philanthropist. He became an apprentice in a small bicycle shop in Oxford, 1894. In 1912 he began to produce the Morris Oxford light car. After World War I mass-production methods of manufacturing motor cars gained him a large fortune, £2 m. of which he has distributed for medical research, hospitals, scientific and industrial research, social studies, and the care of aged persons.

NUMBERS, Book of
Fourth book of the O.T. The title indicates its statistical records of 2 nat. censuses, beginning and ending the wilderness wanderings.

NUMERAL
Figure used to express a number. The use of letters was adopted by the Gks. and later by the Roms., who used the 7 letters—M. D. C. L. X. V. I. From about the 12th cent. European nations adopted the so-called Arabic system of notation.

NUNEATON
Municipal borough of Warwickshire, on the Anker, 9 m. N. of Coventry. Pop. 58,770.

NÜRNBERG
or **Nuremberg.** City in Bavaria, W. Germany, on the Pegnitz, 95 m. N.W. of Munich. An ancient town, with many fine old buildings, including the 11th cent. castle and the city walls. Toys, optical and electrical apparatus, and pencils are manufactured. In 1945-6 the major German war criminals were tried here by an Allied tribunal, found guilty of war crimes and crimes against humanity and sentenced to d. or long periods of imprisonment. Pop. 454,221.

NURSING
Tending the sick and injured. Modern concept of nursing was introduced in Germany in the 19th cent. and furthered in this country by Florence Nightingale during the Crimean war. Since then special branches have come into being, *e.g.* children's, fever, mental, tuberculosis and public health in the school and maternity clinics, as well as in child welfare clinics. Industrial nursing has developed rapidly since 1932.

NUTCRACKER
(*Nucifraga caryocatactes*) Bird belonging to the same family as the crow with brown and white plumage, the beak is long and nearly straight. Common in N. Europe and Asia.

NUTHATCH
(*Sitta europaea*) Bird with stout beak, slaty grey upper-parts, white throat and rufous under-parts. The Brit. race of these widely distributed birds is practically confined to Eng. and Wales, esp. the S. counties.

NUTMEG
Seed-kernel of the fleshy fruit of a bushy evergreen tree (*Myristica fragrans*) indigenous to the Dutch E. Indies. It is used as an aromatic condiment; the fibrous network enclosing the nutshell is the spice called Mace.

NUX VOMICA
Disk-shaped seeds of a deciduous tree of the strychnos family (*Strychnos nux-vomica*), indigenous to India, growing also in N. Australia, Burma, Thailand and Indo-China. They yield most of the bitter alkaloid poisons, strychnine and its derivatives, employed medicinally as tonics and heart stimulants.

NYASALAND
[ne-as'-a-land'] Former Brit. Protectorate in C. Africa, on the W. and S. shores of L. Malawi now called **Malawi** (*q.v.*).

NYERERE, Julius Kambarage
(1922-) African statesman. Formed Tanganyika African Nat. Union in 1954. Became P.M. of T. in 1961, and first Pres. of repub. on indep. in 1962. Negotiated union with Zanzibar in 1963 and became Pres. of Tanzania.

NYLON
Generic name for a class of polymers which can be spun into silk-like fibres.

O

O
15th letter and 4th vowel of the Eng. alphabet. Its form was derived from the Semitic alphabet. It has two main sounds in Eng., the long *o* as in *note*, the short *o* as in *hot*. It is used in combinations with other vowels: to form the long *o* in *boat, foe; the oo* sound in *food, soon* and the short *u* sound in *flood, blood;* combined with *u* it has various sounds—long, as in *through* and in *dough*; short, as in *cough, thought*, etc.

O.E.E.C.
Organisation for European Economic Co-operation set up in 1948 by Aust., Belg., Denmark, Eire, Fr., Greece, Iceland, Italy, Luxembourg, the Netherlands, Norway, Portugal, Sweden, Switzerland, Turkey, U.K. and the U.S.A. (*See* MARSHALL PLAN). A conference in 1957 paved the way for a free trade area in Europe. *See* COMMON MARKET.

OAK
(*Quercus*) Genus of deciduous or evergreen trees, and shrubs of the beech family, natives of N. temp. regions. Their nuts, called acorns, have cup-like receptacles. Of nearly 300 species 2 only, *Q. robur* and *Q. petraea* are native to Brit.; they may be 120 ft. high. The timber was used in 16th-18th cent. Brit. for shipbuilding, roof-construction, wall-panelling and furniture. Oak bark is a source of tannin, acorns a swine food. *See* CORK. **Oak Gall.** Excrescence on the surface tissues of oak trees. Varying in size and form, they occur on leaves, flower-stalks, bark and rootlets. They are mostly due to gall-wasps, *Cynips*, whose eggs are deposited with an irritant fluid which occasions the abnormal cell-growth.

OAKLEY, Annie
(1860-1926) Amer. folk heroine. B. Darke County, Ohio. She was probably the greatest woman marksman of all time.

OASIS
[ō-ā'-sis] A fertile area in a desert; it is due to the presence of wells or subterranean water, or to the sinking of artesian wells in N. Africa and Australia.

OATES, Lawrence Edward Grace
(1880-1912) Eng. explorer. Educ. Eton and served with the cavalry in S. Africa (1901-2). In 1910 he went with Scott on the expedition to reach the S. Pole. On Mar. 17, 1912, Capt. Oates, crippled with frost-bite, walked out into the open and d. in order to make the task of his comrades easier.

OATES, Titus
(1649-1705) Eng. conspirator. He took Anglican orders, and posed as an R.C. in order to get inside knowledge of supposed Catholic plots. He concocted the false story of a 'Popish plot'. Charles II did not believe it, but the populace did, and acclaimed him as saviour of the country.

OATH
Solemn declaration attested by the name of God. In Eng. Law nearly all evidence must be given on oath, save that, since the Oaths Act of 1888, anyone who objects to an oath on the ground of religious belief may make an affirmation instead.

OATS
Annual cereal grass (*Avena sativa*), apparently first cultivated in bronze-age Europe. It is grown exclusively in C. and N. Europe, Russia, the U.S.A., Canada, Argentina and elsewhere. Mostly grown for horse-fodder, oats are also an important human food.

OB
River of Asiatic Russ. which rises in the Altai Mts. and flows N. through the R.S.F.S.R., entering the Arctic Ocean by the Gulf of Ob. Length with its trib. the Irtysh 3,460 m.

OBAN
[ō'-băn] Burgh and seaport of Argyllshire, 113 m. N.W. of Glasgow, on the Firth of Lorne. It is a tourist and yachting centre. Pop. 6,758.

OBERAMMERGAU
Village of Upper Bavaria, Germany. Situated in the Ammer valley, 45 m. S.S.W. of Munich. After a plague in 1633 the villagers vowed to present every 10th year, as an act of devotion, a living representation of Christ's Passion. Pop. 5,000.

OBESITY
Pathological condition of the body resulting in the over-accumulation of fat, which is deposited in the abdomen, around the various organs, in the thighs and neck. The cause may be due to over-eating, esp. of starchy foods and to lack of outdoor exercise. Disease of the endocrine glands is assoc. with excessive obesity.

OBOE
A woodwind instrument with a double reed fixed to the upper end of a conical tube *c.* 2 ft. long. It has an upward compass of 2 octaves and a 6th from the B flat below Middle C.

O'BRIEN, William Smith
(1803-64) Irish nationalist. He entered parl. in 1826 and though a Protestant he supported the Catholic claims as a Whig. In an endeavour to effect a rising in Tipperary in 1848, O'Brien was arrested, tried and sentenced to death. In 1854 he was released on condition of not returning to Ireland, and, 1856, received a free pardon.

OBSCENE PUBLICATIONS ACT
This Act, introduced in 1959, revised the test of obscenity first laid down by Lord Chief Justice Cockburn in 1868, by requiring that no article shall be deemed obscene unless 'its effect is, *if taken as a whole*, such as to deprave and corrupt persons who are likely, *having regard to all relevant circumstances*, to read, see or hear' it. The Act provides that publication may be justified if it is 'in the interests of science, literature and art or learning', and that evidence to this end by qualified experts may be admitted. The Act had its first important test in October 1960, when Penguin Books Ltd. defended 'Lady Chatterly's Lover', which was vindicated. The 'Fanny Hill' case in 1964 invoked the provisions of the Act for seizure under warrant, leading to the book being banned in limited areas. The Act was amended in 1964 to allow search and seizure of goods potentially held for sale, allowing no automatic right of appeal to jury in such cases. Several books were seized for local prosecution during the year. *See* CHILDREN AND YOUNG PERSONS (HARMFUL PUBLICATIONS) ACT.

OBSERVATORY
There are 2 royal observatories in Britain, at Hurstmonceaux Castle (Sussex), and Edinburgh. In addition there are some 30 others all over the Commonwealth. The finest astronomical observatories in the world are those of the U.S.A. Among them are the Lick Obser. in Calif., the Lowell Obser. in Arizona, the Carnegie Solar Obser. on Mt. Wilson, Calif., and the Obser. on Mt. Palomar, Calif. (*q.v.*). The radio telescope of Manchester Univ. is the largest in the world. *See* ASTRONOMY; RADIO ASTRONOMY; TELESCOPE.

OBSTETRICS
Specialised branch of med. science concerned with the care of mother and child before birth (ante-natal), at birth (natal), and after birth (post-natal period).

O'CASEY, Sean
(1884-1964) Irish playwright. B. Dublin. Author of *Juno and the Paycock* (1925), *The Plough and the Stars* (1926), *Within the Gates* (1933), *The Bishop's Bonfire* (1955), and several autobiog. books. *The Green Crow* (essays and stories), 1957.

OCCULTISM
The study of esoteric religion, philosophy and science. The main purpose is the development of spiritual powers which will enable the individual to be of service to mankind. This is known as ' white magic '. The same powers used against morality or religion are termed ' black magic '.

OCCUPATIONAL THERAPY
Term originally used to denote the occupational methods adopted for the relief and treatment of nervous and mental illness, but has now come to include the methods adopted for the same purpose for *all* illness where it is likely to expedite recovery. Apart from physical occupations such as weaving, raffia and basket work, toymaking, bookbinding, clay modelling, reading and debating circles, educational film shows, and gramophone and music recitals are organised. *See* MENTAL HOSPITALS.

OCEAN
Geographical name for the largest expanses of water which together occupy *c.* 72 % of the earth's surface. Of these the Pacific is the largest, being equal to *c.* ⅜ of the total oceanic area and having the greatest depths. *See* ATLANTIC, PACIFIC, INDIAN, ARCTIC OCEANS. **Oceanology** is the study of ocean currents, temperatures, salinity, etc. and deep-sea expeditions have discovered a great deal about life in the oceans. The first real deep-sea enterprise was the British *Challenger* expedition of 1872-6, when animals were found at depths down to 3,000 fathoms. This estabd. that life could exist in the oceans at great depths. The next important expedition was that organised jointly by the Royal Danish Navy and the Univ. of Copenhagen. The naval frigate *Galathea*, carrying some 20 scientists and technicians, set off in Oct. 1950 for a world cruise. They explored the Philippine Trench, the Sunda Trench S. of Java, the Banda Deep W. of New Guinea, the Solomon Trench and the Tonga-Kermadec Trench. The expedition demonstrated that life exists at the bottom of the deepest ocean, under a pressure of 1,000 atmospheres. When brought to the surface, all the animals were dead, but several species of bacteria, taken from the bottom clay, survived. Fishes, sea-urchins, star-fishes, crabs, etc. have not yet been found at depths below 4,000 fathoms.

OCEANIA
Name applied to the Is. in the Pacific Ocean. The main divisions of the region are the 3 large Is., Australia, Tasmania and New Guinea, and 3 Is. groups, Melanesia, Micronesia, and Polynesia (*q.v.*).

OCELOT
(*Felis pardalis*) Amer. tiger-cat, ranging from Arkansas to Paraguay. Normally tawny-yellow, spotted with black-edged, fawn-coloured markings. A forest animal, of savage disposition, it preys on small mammals and birds.

OCHRE
[ō'-ker] Certain earthy or clay varieties of the oxides of iron. Yellow and brown ochres are forms of the hydrated oxide, limonite, whilst red ochre, or reddle, is a variety of the peroxide haematite.

O'CONNELL, Daniel
(1775-1847) Irish politician. M.P. 1828-47. Entering Parl. when the Catholics were emancipated, O'Connell organised the agitation for the repeal of the Union, forming the ' Catholic Association '.

O'CONNOR, Feargus
(1794-1855) Irish politician. M.P. 1832-5 and 1847-52. At first a follower of O'Connell, O'Connor broke with him and joined the Brit. working-class movement, being assoc. with the Chartist movement.

OCTOPUS
Widespread group of 8-armed Cephalopod molluscs. They have no shell, lurk in shallow waters and prey chiefly on other molluscs and on crustacea.

ODENSE
[ō'-dĕn-sĕ] City and port of Denmark, on Fünen I., 27 m. W. of Copenhagen. A ship canal connects it with the fiord of O. O. was the birthplace of Hans Andersen. Pop. 111,145.

ODER
River of Europe, 500 m. long, which rises in Czechoslovakia, and flows through Poland in a N.W. and N. direction.

ODESSA
Seaport of the Ukraine, U.S.S.R. on the N.W. coast of the Black Sea, 25 m. from the mouth of the Dniester. It is an important commercial centre. Pop. 709,000.

ODIN
The supreme deity of Scandinavian myth.

OEDIPUS
[ē'-di-pŭs] In Gk. legend, son of Laius, King of Thebes, and Jocasta. Unwittingly he slew his father and wedded his own mother. The gods demanded the discovery of the king's slayer, and the investigation led Jocasta to hang herself and Oedipus to blind himself.

OFFA
(d. 796) King of Mercia. Of royal blood, he elected a rival and obtained the crown, 757. He restored Mercia's prosperity, and secured virtual control of Brit. S. of the Humber. **Offa's Dyke.** Ancient earthwork forming a boundary between Mercia and the Welsh. Built by King Offa, *c.* 779.

OFFALY
Inland county of Repub. of Ireland, in the prov. of Leinster. The Shannon, Brosna and Barrow are the principal rivers. There are hills in the S. and in the E. the Bog of Allen. Agriculture is the main occupation. Tullamore is the county town; other places are Birr and Banagher. Pop. 51,533.

OFFENBACH, Jacques
[of'-ĕn-bach] (1819-80) German-Fr. composer. Studied 'cello and composition at the Paris Conservatoire. He wrote many operettas but only one large-scale opera, *Les Contes d'Hoffmann*, which he left unfinished at his d.

OFFICIAL SECRETS ACT
Act of the U.K. parl. declaring it to be a felony for any person, whether in war or peace, to engage in spying or similar offences. It is unlawful for any unauthorised person to enter

a prohibited area, for purposes prejudicial to the State, or to communicate any such information as is likely to be useful to an enemy.

OGHAM
(or **Ogam**) 20-letter alphabet of strokes and dots found in ancient Brit. inscriptions.

O'HIGGINS, Bernardo
(1776-1842) Chilean soldier and statesman. He fought against the Royalists, but had to flee to Mendoza. His meeting with José de San Martin resulted in the decisive victory of Chacabuco (1817). In 1822 O'Higgins called a congress, which adopted a constitution giving him dictatorial powers. Discontent and risings occurred, and in 1823 O'Higgins resigned.

OHIO
[ō-hī'-ō] State of the U.S.A. S. of Lake Erie, and bounded on the S. by the O. river. It is an agricultural state. There are extensive mineral resources, such as coal, iron ore and petroleum. Columbus is the cap.; Cleveland, Cincinnati, Toledo and Dayton are other important towns. By an oversight, the formal resolution admitting Ohio to the Union in 1803 was neglected and this was only rectified, 1953. It sends 24 representatives to Congress. Area: 41,220 sq.m. Pop. 10,652,100. The **Ohio River** is formed by the confluence of the Monongahela and Allegheny near Pittsburgh, and flows into the Mississippi at Cairo. It is an important routeway, and is 950 m. long.

OHM, Georg Simon
[ōm] (1787-1854) German physicist. In 1827 he promulgated what is known as 'Ohm's Law' in electricity. **Ohm.** Practical unit of electrical resistance defined as the resistance offered to an unvarying current by a column of mercury 106·3 cms. long, of a constant area in cross-section, and weighing 14·4521 grams at the temp. of melting ice.

OIL
Viscous fluid substance of either min., veg. or animal origin. The **mineral oils,** consisting of hydrocarbons, are derived from the decomposition of organic matter in rocks and are represented by petroleum (*q.v.*) and its derivatives. The **vegetable oils** consist of fixed or fatty oils and essential or volatile oils, the former being again divided into drying and non-drying oils. The fixed oils, composed of mixtures of glycerides of fatty acids, vary in consistence, some being solid fats above 68° F. and others which remain liquid at ordinary temps. and consequently are used in paint and varnish manufacture. Such oils are linseed, poppy, cottonseed and rape. The non-drying oils such as olive, palm, coconut and almond oils are used as lubricants, edible oils, and in soap manufacture. Essential oils are volatile odorous liquids distilled from plants and used in pharmacy and perfumery. The **animal oils** are fish and whale oils, seal oils, tallow, butter, etc., and are used as food, in soap, or as lubricants.

OKAPI
[ō-kȧ'-pi] (*Okapia johnstoni*) African ruminant of the giraffe family discovered by Sir Harry Johnston near Lake Albert in 1901. It stands 5 ft. high at the shoulder.

O'KELLY, Sean Thomas
(1882-1966) Pres. of the Repub. of Ireland 1945-59. He was one of the founders, with Arthur Griffith, of the Sinn Fein.

OKLAHOMA
[ōklă-hō'-mă] State of the U.S.A. in the S. to the N. of Texas. It is an agricultural region. Petroleum, coal, and gypsum are produced. Oklahoma City is the cap.; other towns are Tulsa and Muskogee. O. was admitted into the Union, 1907, and now sends 8 representatives to Congress. Area: 69,920 sq.m. Pop. 2,559,300. **Oklahoma City.** Cap and commercial centre of O. state, on the N. Canadian R. Pop. 363,300.

OLD AGE PENSION
(now **Retirement Pension**) In Brit. and other countries a pension paid by the State to all persons who are insured and who reach a certain age. On July 5, 1948, the Contributory Pensions Acts were superseded by the provisions of the Nat. Ins. Act, 1946. An insured man aged 65 or an insured woman aged 60, who has retired from employment and has paid sufficient contributions, is entitled to a retirement pension. Full rate of retirement pension is paid when a man reaches 70 or a woman who is herself insured 65, whether the pensioner continues to work or not. **Non-Contributory Pensions** are payable as heretofore to a man or woman who has reached 70 years of age and fulfils the necessary conditions or to a Blind Person who has attained the age of 40.

OLD TESTAMENT
Collection of 39 books of the Bible, recording Jewish hist. and religion from the beginning down almost to the times of Christ and his apostles. Written between the 8th and 2nd cents. B.C., in Heb. or Aramaic, the Jewish grouping, Law, Prophets and Writings, marks the stages which estabd. the Heb. canon. *See* APOCRYPHA.

OLDCASTLE, Sir John
(d. 1417) Leader of the Lollards. He served in the fighting on the Welsh marches. He was condemned as a heretic in 1413.

OLDHAM
County borough of Lancs. on the Medlock, 6 m. N.E. of Manchester. Textiles are produced; there are engineering works and collieries nearby. It returns 2 members to Parl. Pop. 115,000.

OLEANDER
(*Nerium oleander*) Evergreen shrub of the dogbane family, native to the Medit. The stems bear willow-like leaves which exude a poisonous milky juice when bruised.

OLEASTER
Genus of deciduous or evergreen shrubs and small trees (*Elaeagnus*) akin to the spurge laurel family, native to Europe, Asia and N. Amer. The common oleaster, *E. angustifolia*, 15-30 ft. high, is grown round the Medit. for its edible berries.

OLIVE
Small evergreen tree typical of the olive order (*Olea europaea*). It abounds in the Medit. region. The ripe pericarp yields under pressure 60-70 % of an edible oil which replaces in S. Europe butter and animal fats.

OLIVES, Mt. of
Ridge E. of Jerusalem. Rising about 300 ft. above the city beyond the Kidron valley, it was closely assoc. with the final scenes of Christ's life.

OLIVIER, Sir Laurence
(1907-) Eng. actor. He made his début in 1922. Among his great successes have been *Hamlet*, *Henry V*, *Macbeth* and *Coriolanus* with the Old Vic Co. His film career commenced in 1930: he directed and played the title roles in *Henry V*, *Hamlet* and *Richard*

III. A leader of the Brit. stage and screen, he was knighted in 1948. Apptd. first Director of the Nat. Theatre, 1962.

OLIVINE
[ol′-i-vēn] Olive-green mineral, occurring in basic igneous rocks, such as gabbro and basalt, and in certain meteorites. It is a magnesium iron silicate with a hardness above that of felspar. Transparent olivine, known as *chrysolite* (*q.v.*) is used in jewellery.

OLYMPIA
Religious centre of ancient Greece, scene of the Olympic games, on the banks of the Alpheus in the Peloponnesus. **Olympic Games.** Athletic contests held at O. in Greece in ancient times. The festival took place every 4 years and had a religious basis. The games were open to competitors from all Greece, and the contests included chariot racing, horse racing, running, wrestling, boxing, and the pentathlon, a contest involving jumping, quoit-throwing, javelin-throwing, running and wrestling. The modern 4-yearly contests represent a revival of the old Gk. games, were first held at Athens in 1896, and have been restaged every 4 years since, except during the 2 World Wars. The 18th Modern Olympic Games were held at Tokyo in 1964. The Winter Olympic Games were first held in 1924.

OLYMPUS
Mt. range in Greece, separating Thessaly from Macedonia. Highest point *c.* 10,000 ft.

OMAGH
[ō′-mă] Urban district, market and county town of Tyrone, N. Ireland, 34 m. S. of Londonderry. There are flour mills and linen factories. Pop. 8,240.

OMAHA
[ō-mă-hà′] Largest city of Nebraska, U.S.A. on the Missouri above its confluence with the Platte. It is a railway centre with many industries, including meat-packing. Pop. 327,800.

OMAN *See* MUSCAT AND OMAN.

OMAR KHAYYÁM
(d. 1123) Persian mathematician, astronomer and poet. Edward FitzGerald (*q.v.*) tr. a number of his 'Rubáiyát' (quatrains).

OMDURMAN
Town of the Sudan, on the Nile, opposite Khartoum. An important native market, it was formerly the Dervish cap. In 1898, an Anglo-Egyptian force under Kitchener defeated the Dervishes, and avenged Gen. Gordon. Pop. 116,000.

ONAGER
[on′-ă-jer] (*Equus onager*) Name of several races of wild ass ranging from Syria and Persia to N.W. India. Eleven hands high, chestnut-coloured and broadly striped along the back.

ONEGA
Lake of the U.S.S.R. 2nd largest lake of Europe after Ladoga, 100 m. to the W., it is connected by canal with the White Sea and Gulf of Finland. Area: 3,800 sq.m.

O'NEILL
Ancient Irish family, descended from King Niall of the Nine Hostages, who were Lords of Tyrone. **Shane O'Neill** (*c.* 1530-67) the 2nd earl of Tyrone, nominally paid allegiance to Elizabeth. He fought against the Scots, and continually against the O'Donnells. **Phelim O'Neill** was the leader of the insurrection against the Eng. and Scots settlers in Ulster, in which occurred the Ulster massacre of 1641.

O'NEILL, Eugene
(1888-1953) Amer. dramatist, b. New York. He wrote *Emperor Jones* (1920), *Strange Interlude* (1928), and the trilogy *Mourning Becomes Electra* (1931). For his last play, *Long Day's Journey into Night* (1956), he was posthumously awarded a Pulitzer prize. Nobel Prize for Lit. in 1936.

ONION
(*Allium cepa*) Hardy bulbous biennial herb of the Lillaceae, now widely grown for culinary purposes. The Welsh, a bulbless form of Siberian origin introduced into medieval Europe, is grown for spring salads. *See* LEEK, SHALLOT.

ONTARIO
Prov. of the Dominion of Canada, which extends from Detroit, U.S.A. to Hudson Bay. It includes part of Lakes Ontario, Erie, Huron and Superior. The chief rivers are the St. Lawrence in the E., the Abitibi and Albany. The area known as the Lakes Peninsula is the most thickly settled region. It has the greatest output of any prov. in manufactures, mining and agriculture. Gold is the most valuable metal mined. Petrol is found. There are very large timber resources. Electric power is obtained from Niagara and other natural sources. Toronto, on L. O. is the cap.; Ottawa is the Dominion capital; Hamilton, Windsor, London and Fort William are other towns. Champlain was the first European to visit O. It became Brit. 1763, and 1774 became part of the prov. of Quebec. In 1791 it was separated from Quebec, becoming the prov. of Upper Canada with its own legislature. John Graves Simcoe was the first gov. During the war of 1812, the Amers. took and burned the cap. York (now Toronto). Following a rebellion in 1837-8, it was once again united with Quebec under a common parl. in 1842, remaining thus till the Confederation, 1867. Since then the prov. has been gov. by its own legislature under a lieut.-gov. assisted by an executive council. It sends 24 senators and 85 representatives to the Federal parl. Area: 412,582 sq.m. Pop. 6,321,000. **Ontario.** Lake of N. Amer. on the Canadian-U.S.A. border, the smallest and most E. of the 5 Gt. Lakes. The waters of L. Erie are carried to it by the Niagara, and thence the St. Lawrence Seaway opens into its E. end.

ONYX
[on′-iks] Name of certain kinds of agate in which there is a parallel banded structure, the milky white layers alternating with dark or coloured chalcedony. In the sardonyx the coloured bands are red, consisting of carnelian or sard.

OOLITE
[ō′-o-līt] (1) Name given to aggregates of small spherical grains of calcium carbonate which are formed from saturated sea water in constant motion depositing the layers successively around a nucleus. (2) Geological term for the upper and middle divisions of the Jurassic system.

OPAL
Mineral consisting of amorphous hydrated silica and occurring as layers, nodules and stalactitic masses. In the precious opals there is a remarkable play of colours due to reflection and diffraction of light from thin laminae.

OPHTHALMIA
[of-thal′-] Inflammation of the eye characterised by redness, pain, increased tear flow, increased sensitivity to light and purulent discharge. Gonorrhoea, pneumococcal and streptococcal infections are the commonest causes. Notifiable disease.

OPIUM
Narcotic drug obtained from the white poppy. It contains the alkaloids morphine, codeine, narcotine and narceine. The opium poppy is grown in the East. **Opium—Eating and Smoking.** When eaten or smoked as a narcotic, the first effect of opium is stimulation of the mind, followed by sleep. The after-effects are un-

pleasant and harmful, and the habit, once acquired, is very difficult to relinquish.

OPORTO
Second city of Portugal, cap. of O. district, near the mouth of the Douro. It is the centre of the port wine trade. There is a univ. founded 1911. Pop. 303,424.

OPOSSUM
Marsupial mammals which inhabit C. and S. Amer., except the largest, the cat-sized Virginian Opossum which ranges northwards. The pouch is generally rudimentary, the tail often long, scaly and prehensile. They are nocturnal and arboreal, except the web-footed Vapok or Water-opossum. Austral. Phalangers, also marsupials, but allied to the vegetarian herbivorous species are called Opossums.

OPPENHEIMER, J. Robert
[-hī-mer] (1904-67) Amer. scientist. B. New York, and educ. Harvard. He studied at the Cavendish Laboratory at Cambridge. In 1928 he returned to the U.S.A. to the Calif. Inst. of Technology and the Univ. of California. Assoc. Prof. 1931-3; Prof. 1933-47. From 1942-5 he was director of the Los Alamos Laboratory, New Mexico, concerned with the production of the first atom bomb. Chairman of the General Advisory Committee of the Atomic Energy Committee, 1947-52. He was the principal scientific adviser on the scheme for internat. control of atomic energy which later became known as the Baruch Plan. He delivered the Reith lectures of 1953 in Gt. Brit., pub. as *Science and the Common Understanding* (1954).

OPTICS
Science of light and the principles underlying the phenomena of light and vision. In physical optics a study is made of the nature of light, colour, refraction, reflection, interference, diffraction and polarisation, while geometrical optics is concerned with the laws governing these phenomena, the formation of images, etc. *See* LIGHT.

ORAN
[-ràn'] Seaport of Algeria, *c.* 220 m. S.W. of Algiers. Produces grass, used in paper manufacture. O. was the scene of a landing during the N. African invasion, World War II. Pop. 430,000.

ORANGE
Fruit of an evergreen tree (*Citrus aurantium*). Introduced into S.W. Asia before the 9th cent., and thence into Spain. It is now cultivated in many localities including S. Africa, the W. Indies, Florida, California and Australia. The sweet or China orange *C. sinensis* occurs in many forms, including Malta blood-oranges and flattened thin-peeled mandarins and tangerines. It is rich in mineral salts and vitamins A, B, and esp. C.

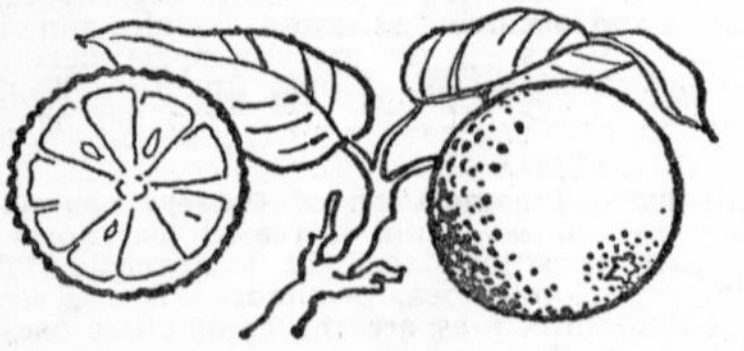

ORANGE
Fr. family settled in the Netherlands. William the Silent and his descendant who became William III of Gt. Brit. belonged to this family. Another branch is now represented by the Queen of the Netherlands.

ORANGE FREE STATE
Prov. of the S. Afr. Rep. lying S. of the Transvaal, bounded on the E. by the Drakensberg range, and on the N. and S. by the Vaal and Orange rivers. Much of the land consists of plateaux, over 4,000 ft. above sea level. Stock rearing and mining are important. The cap. is Bloemfontein; other towns are Harrismith, Kroonstad and Odendaalsrust. In 1899 it joined the S. African repub. (Transvaal) in the war against Brit. It was annexed as a colony, 1900, and entered the Union of S. Africa in 1910 as a prov. Area: 49,866 sq.m. Pop. 1,386,000.

ORANGE SOCIETY
Irish polit. soc. Founded in 1795, the first lodge was formed at Armagh, and the movement spread rapidly. The professed objects were the defence of the Protestant faith and succession. The soc. was named after William III. *See* IRELAND.

ORANG-OUTANG
['-ootan'] (*Simia satyrus*) Malay name for the ape of Borneo and Sumatra. Powerfully built, standing 4 ft. 4 in., when erect, the long arms almost touch the ground. The males often have warty cheek callosities and enormous pouch-like neck distensions. Inhabiting low-lying forests, which they traverse from tree to tree, they construct family sleeping-platforms 20-25 ft. above the ground.

ORCHID
[or'-kid] Herb of an extensive family of plants with 1 seedleaf, growing in all climates except the very cold. The 1 or more flowers have perianths of 6 coloured segments, that forming the lip being sometimes spurred. There are about 40 Brit. species including the Bee Orchis, Twayblade, and Lady's-slipper.

ORDINATION
Ecclesiastical ceremony for the setting apart of Christian mins. to their life-work. In the Gk., R.C. and Anglican chs. the rite is carried out by a bishop. In the Free Chs. it is administered by one or a number of senior mins.

ORDNANCE
Term for weapons of 1 in. calibre and over from which a missile is projected from the barrel by the pressure of gases resulting from an explosion. It is confined to guns, howitzers and mortars, and includes tank guns, anti-aircraft guns and naval guns of all calibres. Modern guns of all calibres have barrels in which helical grooves (rifling) impart a rotary motion to the projectile, which has a driving band of soft metal which engages with the rifling of the gun. The calibre of a gun is the diameter of the bore, and the length of the bore is expressed in calibres: *e.g.* a 45 cal. 15 in. gun is a weapon 56·25 ft. long. It would seem that guns are likely to be superseded by weapons of the rocket type and radar-guided missiles.

ORDNANCE SURVEY
The Ordnance Survey was formed in 1791 to make an official map of Gt. Brit. for defence purposes, at a scale of 1 in. to 1 m. It was entrusted to the Board of Ordnance; hence the title. Control was transferred from the War Office to the Board of Agriculture. The whole of Gt. Brit. is mapped at a scale of 2½ in. to 1 m. With the assistance of the R.A.F. air photography is being used in a 20 yr. programme, begun in 1950, of mapping the urban areas of Gt. Brit. at a scale of 50 in. to 1 m. Infra-red photography will also be used to estab. low tide marks on the coasts.

OREGON
Pacific state of the U.S.A. between Washington and Calif. It is divided into 2 regions by the Cascade Range. To the W. is a fertile region; to the E. on the plateau, irrigation is necessary. The main rivers are the Columbia and Willamette. Lumbering and fishing are important, and gold, silver and copper are mined. Salem is the cap. O. was admitted to the Union,

1859, and now sends 4 representatives to Congress. Area: 96,980 sq.m. Pop. 2,091,400.

ORGAN
Keyboard wind instrument of pipes, bellows, etc. The depression of keys on a keyboard (the complete set of keyboards, pedals, stops, etc., is called the console) admits air to certain pipes according to the stops drawn, each stop operating a set of a given pitch and tonal quality. These range from less than 2 ft. to 32 ft. Very large instruments may have a 64 ft. stop. The stops (or push-buttons) are usually arranged according to depts. on either side of the manuals, or above the top manual. Each has its own group of stops. There is also a pedal organ which is played with the feet. By a system of manual pistons great flexibility is exercised in obtaining a wealth of tone colour, by linking one dept. to another. Balanced swell pedals, operated by the right foot, open and close louvres on the boxes which contain the pipes of the Swell and (frequently) Choir depts., thus obtaining the splendid crescendo-diminuendo effect so typical of this instrument. Most modern organs have electric mechanism. Outstanding examples of large Brit. instruments are the Willis 5-manual organ in Liverpool Cathedral, and the Harrison 4-manual in the Royal Albert Hall.

ORGANIC CHEMISTRY
Orig. the chem. of living materials, but now the study of all compounds containing carbon. Antoine Laurent Lavoisier (1743-94) established the composition of many natural products, and showed that nearly all vegetable substances were composed of carbon, hydrogen and oxygen, while animal substances contained these three elements, with nitrogen and sometimes phosphorus and sulphur in addition. Today, organic chemistry covers a very wide range of substances, from the simple hydrocarbons to the complex starches, proteins, etc. Many synthetically prepared organic compounds do not occur in nature.

ORIGEN
(*c.* 185-254) Gk. father of the ch. B. Alexandria, of Christian parentage. He influenced the course of ch. hist. for cents., formulating its dogmas and founding Biblical criticism. He d. at Tyre. His works include *On First Principles*, the earliest attempt to form a Christian phil.

ORINOCO
River of Venezuela, rising in the Parima Mts. on the Brazilian borders. *C.* 1,500 m. long, it reaches the sea by a large delta near Trinidad.

ORIOLE
['-ri-ōl] Family of perching birds, natives of temp. and trop. regions of the Old World. The Golden O. *Oriolus*, 9 in. long, with brilliant male yellow plumage and black wings and tail, is an irregular summer resident in S. Brit. It breeds in Europe and S.W. Asia and winters in Africa.

ORKNEY
Insular county of Scot. off the N.E. coast of Caithness, from which it is separated by the Pentland Firth. The Is. are divided into 3 groups: S. Isles, Mainland and N. Isles. The most important Is. are Mainland (the largest), Hoy, N. and S. Ronaldsay, Stronsay, Sanday, Westray and Shapinsay. Fishing is of great importance; there is also agriculture and whisky distilling. Kirkwall, on Mainland, is the county town; Stromness is the only other town of importance. O. unites with Zetland (Shetland Is.) to send a member to Parl. Pop. 18,531. The O. Is. were annexed by Norway in the 9th cent. and, 1468, were attached to Scot. as a pledge for the dowry of Margaret of Denmark, who mar. James III. They became Scots, 1590.

ORLÉANS
[or-lā-ō(ng)] Cap. of Loiret dept. Fr. on the right bank of the Loire, S.W. of Paris. It is a commercial centre, with hosiery and textile manufactures. Famous for its assoc. with Joan of Arc, who raised the siege, 1429. Pop. 84,233.

ORLÉANS, House of
[or-lā-ō(ng)] Fr. noble family of royal blood. The title Duke of Orléans was created by Philip VI, who conferred it on his natural son **Philip** in 1344. On the accession of the 3rd Duke to the throne in 1498 as Louis XII, the title lapsed. Louis XIV conferred the dukedom on his brother **Philippe** in 1660. The latter's grandson, of the same name, who succeded to the title, was regent of Fr. during the minority of Louis XV. **Louis Philippe Joseph** (1747-93) Cousin of Louis XVI, leader of a discontented faction against the govt. As a member of the States-General, he led the group of nobles who joined the 3rd Estate (June, 1789), to form the Nat. Assembly. Voted for Louis' execution, but, suspected of wanting the crown, he was guillotined.

ORNITHORHYNCHUS
[or-nith-ō-ring'-kŭs] Generic name of the Duck-billed Platypus, a mammal restricted to S. and E. Australia and Tasmania. It forms with Echidna the lowest sub-class of mammals and has many primitive structural characters which display their affinity with reptiles. Both are oviparous.

ORPINGTON
Part of Bromley, borough of Greater London (1964), formerly in Kent.

ORRIS-ROOT
Rhizome, or underground stem, of various species of iris, which when dried has a delicate violet-like smell.

ORTHOCLASE
One of the potash felspars, a common rock-forming mineral consisting of potassium aluminium silicate. It occurs in monoclinic prisms of a lustrous white, grey or reddish colour in granites and other crystalline igneous rocks. Its pearly variety, moonstone, is cut *en cabochon* for use as gem stones.

ORTHOPAEDICS
That branch of surgery which concerns itself with the diagnosis and treatment of injuries, deformities and diseases of the bones, joints, ligaments, muscles and nerves. Has developed rapidly since the discovery of X-rays (*q.v.*) and owes much to pioneers like Thomas and Robert Jones, and more recently to Böhles of Vienna and Watson Jones of London, and to progress during the 2 World Wars.

ORTOLAN
(*Emberiza hortulana*) Species of Bunting. It spends the summer in Europe and W. Asia, wintering in Africa. The male, 6½ in. long, is attractively plumaged.

ORWELL, George
(1905-50) Eng. novelist. He served as war correspondent and wrote satirical novels: *Road to Wigan Pier* (1937), *Animal Farm* (1945), *Nineteen Eighty-Four* (1949); also critical and other essays.

OSAKA
City of Honshu, Japan, on the Bay of O. at the mouth of the Yodo. Industries include sugar refineries, iron works and cotton spinning mills; there is a trade in tea and rice. Among its buildings are the univ. and temples. Pop. 3,140,000.

OSCAR
Name of 2 kings of Norway and Sweden. **Oscar I** (1799-1859), the son of Gen. Bernadotte, who afterwards became Charles XIV, became king in 1844 and estabd. the freedom

of the Press. In 1848 he supported Denmark against Germany. **Oscar II** (1829-1907) a son of Oscar I, succeeded his brother, Charles XV, in 1872. His remarkable intelligence and great diplomacy resulted in Gt. Brit., Germany and the U.S.A. requesting him to appoint the chief justice of Samoa in 1889, and he became umpire in the Anglo-Amer. Arbitration Treaty of 1897. In 1905, Norway became indep. and Oscar abdicated from the Norwegian throne.

OSCAR
Gold plated statuettes awarded by the U.S. Motion Picture Academy to a director, actor, script-writer, etc., for the year's best work in the different spheres of the motion picture industry.

OSIER
[ō-zher] The native or cultivated forms of willow trees and shrubs whose tough, flexible branches serve for basketry and wickerwork. Besides the common osier, *Salix viminalis*, with 40 varieties, Brit. osier-beds also contain the brown or Fr. willow, *S. triandra*, the red *S. purpurea*, and the golden osier.

OSIRIS
Gk. form of the name of the most beloved of the gods of Ancient Egypt. The ' husband ' of *Isis* and ' brother ' of *Set*, by whom he was slain.

OSLO
Cap. city of Norway, on the S.E. coast at the head of O. Fiord. It has rail connections with Sweden and the rest of Norway. Industries include iron foundries and the manufacture of paper, textiles, matches and tobacco. The city was rebuilt by Christian IV, 1624, and renamed Christiania. The Danish name was changed to Oslo, 1925. Pop. 482,495.

OSMIUM
Hard, bluish-white crystalline metal. Discovered by Tennant in 1803. Sp. gr. 22·5. Chem. sym. Os. At. No. 76. At. wt. 190·2.

OSPREY
or **Fish-hawk** (*Pandion haliaetus*). Cosmopolitan bird of prey, related to the Falcons, it feeds solely on fish. The male, 24 in. long, has dark-brown plumage laced with white, and white underparts. 2-3 red-blotched eggs are laid.

OSSA
or **Kissavos.** Mt. of Greece, 6,400 ft. high, in Thessaly near Olympus.

OSSIAN
Legendary Irish hero and bard. Assoc. with Fionn and other 3rd-cent. warriors at the court of Tara. His literary work has disappeared, unless it be embodied in *Works of Ossian* (1765), which James Macpherson (*q.v.*) (1736-96) claimed to have discovered.

OSTEND
Seaport and resort of Belg. in W. Flanders prov. Manufactures include linen and sail-cloth, and there are docks. Pop. 56,811.

OSTEO-ARTHRITIS
Disabling condition arising in joints assoc. with injury, exposure to wet and cold over prolonged period, old age and various body diseases.

OSTEOPATHY
System of med. treatment with a main theory that proper mechanical adjustment of the body structure, esp. the alignment of the spinal column, is more important than chem. or drug intake in maintenance of health.

OSTIA
Ancient town and harbour of Lazio, at the mouth of the Tiber, 14 m. S.W. of Rome.

OSTRICH
(*Struthio camelus*) Two-toed flightless bird with keelless breastbone, indigenous to Africa and S.W. Asia. It is the largest living bird. They still occur wild in Africa, and are reared on farms in S. Africa, Kordofan, Argentina, California and elsewhere.

OSTROGOTHS
E. branch of the Goths. They flourished in the 4th and 5th cents. *See* GOTHS.

OSWALD
(*c.* 605-42) King of Northumbria. He succeeded his brother as king of Bernicia in 635. He was successful as a soldier and united Bernicia and Deira into the kingdom of Northumbria. He was killed at Oswestry in a battle against Penda, king of Mercia, and was made a saint.

OTHO, Marcus Salvius
(32-69) Rom. emperor. In 69 he supported Galba in a revolt against Nero. He next rose against Galba, who was slain, and proclaimed himself Emperor. When he had reigned only 3 months, Vitellius completely overthrew his forces, and he committed suicide.

OTTAWA
Cap. of the Dominion of Canada, on the Ottawa R. between the Chaudière and Rideau Falls. O. numbers among its important buildings, the Parl. buildings, Royal Mint, Nat. Museum and Nat. Art Gallery. The chief industry is lumbering, paper and pulp being produced in great quantities. No settlement was attempted, owing to the hilly nature of the district, until the 19th cent. when a canal was built from the Chaudière Falls to L. Ontario. This settlement soon developed into an important factor in the lumber trade. Ottawa was incorporated as a city, 1854, and in 1858 was chosen as the cap. of Canada. Pop. 286,206.

OTTER
Widely distributed carnivorous mammal of the Weasel family. The common European River-otter, *Lutra vulgaris*, 27 in. long with 15 in. tail, has short limbs, rounded webbed feet, and small external ears. The larger Amer. *L. canadensis* furnishes the most valuable of N. Amer. furs. The Sea-otter forms a distinct sub-family.

OTTER-HOUND
Breed of dog maintained for otter-hunting. It is distinguishable from the Rough Welsh Harrier only by its broad, splayed feet and its abundant oily undercoat. Standing 23 in. high, with sweeping ears, deep-set eyes and long neck, it is essentially a water-dog. Several packs exist in W. Eng.

OTTO
Four Holy Rom. Emperors. **Otto I** (912-73) called **the Great**, was the son of Henry I, and crowned German King in 936. His 1st wife was Edith, daughter of Edward the Elder; his 2nd wife, Adelaide, Queen of Lombardy. **Otto II** (955-83) son of Otto the Great, was crowned German King in 961 and joint Emperor of Rome in 973. **Otto III** (980-1002) called ' The Wonder of the World ', the son of Otto II, was chosen king as his father's successor and crowned in 983. His mother, Theophano, governed until her d. in 991, and he took over the govt. in 996. **Otto IV** (1174-1218), the son of Henry the Lion, was chosen German King, 1208, and

crowned Emperor in Rome, 1209. He quarrelled with the Pope who excommunicated him, and in 1212 declared him deposed, upholding Frederick II in opposition to him.

OTTO I
(1815-67) King of Greece, son of Louis I of Bavaria. Elected by the Conference of London to occupy the newly created throne of Greece when only 17. In 1861 the nation revolted after an attempt to murder Queen Amalie, and in 1862 Otto and Amalie were forced to leave Greece and return to Bavaria.

OTTOMAN
Name of a Turkish people. Osman, or Othman (1259-1326) was the leader of a tribe called the Ottoman Turks, who in 1453 took Constantinople. **Ottoman Empire** *See* TURKEY.

OTWAY, Thomas
(1652-85) Eng. dramatist. Educ. Winchester and Christ's Ch. Oxford. He tr. Racine's *Bérénice* and Molière's *Cheats of Scapin*. His greatest tragedy is *Venice Preserved* (1682).

OUDENARDE
or **Audenarde.** Town of E. Flanders prov. Belg. on the Scheldt, 17 m. S. of Ghent, the scene of Marlborough's victory over Louis XIV in 1708.

OUNCE
(or **Snow Leopard**) (*Felis uncia*) Large spotted cat inhabiting the mountainous regions of C. Asia. Obtuse-muzzled, 7 ft. long, including 3 ft. tail, the long, woolly fur, greyish above, pure white beneath, has large irregular spots. It preys on wild sheep, goats and rodents.

OUNDLE
[own'-] Urban district and market town of Northants. on the Nene, 13 m. S.W. of Peterborough. O. School, founded 1556, is a public school. Pop. 3,350.

OUSE
[ooz] Name of several rivers in Brit. (1) **The Great O.** rises in Northants. and flows N.E. into the Wash N. of King's Lynn. The Cam, Little O. and Ouzel are tributaries. (2) **The Yorkshire O.** formed by the union of the Ure and Swale at Boroughbridge, joins the Trent to form the Humber estuary. (3) **The Sussex O.** rises near Horsham and flows past Lewes into the Eng. Channel at Newhaven.

OUZEL [oo'zl] *See* DIPPER.

OVARY
Endocrine gland situated at upper edge of pelvis one on each side. It produces female germ cells or ova, and has a part in controlling female sex characteristics by its action on other endocrine glands (*q.v.*).

OVID
(43 B.C.-A.D. 17) Rom. poet **Publius Ovidius Naso.** B. Sulmo, in the Paeligni. His *Metamorphoses* is a collection of stories from Gk. myth. His elegiac poems are the *Amores, Ars Amatoria, Remedia Amoris, Heroides, Tristia, Fasti*.

OVIEDO
[ov-yā'-dō] City of N. Spain, cap. of O. prov. 15 m. S. of the Bay of Biscay, the centre of an important coal and iron mining district. Pop. 137,000.

OWL
(*Strigidae*) Family of nocturnal birds of prey. They have large heads, shortened faces, hooked bills and large forward-looking eyes, usually set in a ruff of feathers, many with feathered ear-tufts or horns. Of about 200 species, several, including the Barn, the Tawny and the Long-eared, are resident in Brit. Two others, the Short-eared, an irregular nesting resident, and the Snowy, a regular winter visitor, are commonly recognised.

OX-BOW LAKE
Lake which is formed when a meandering river, bent almost in a complete circle, takes a new and quicker path, leaving a backwater. This eventually becomes separated from the river. Such are common in the lower Mississippi valley where they are known as *bayous*.

OXALIC ACID
Organic acid occurring in the wood sorrel, *Oxalis acetosella*, and in rhubarb leaves. It is a white crystalline and poisonous substance, prepared commercially by fusing sawdust with a mixture of caustic soda and potash.

OXFORD AND ASQUITH, Earl of
Herbert Henry A. (1852-1928) Eng. statesman. M.P. (Lib.), 1886-1918 and 1920-4; P.M. 1908-16; War. Sec. 1914; Earl, 1925. His premiership covered the Parl. Act struggle, the Ulster controversy, and the outbreak of World War I. His conduct of the war was subject to criticism in 1915-16, and as a result both his Lib. ministry and its coalition successor fell. In 1926 he quarrelled with Lloyd George over the General Strike. See *Asquith* by R. Jenkins, 1964.

OXFORD GROUP
Religious movement in the C. of E. Founded by Rev. Frank Buchman (*q.v.*), Amer. Methodist. min., it first took root in Eng. at Oxford. Stress is laid upon confession, self-dedication and guidance. The movement spread rapidly over Brit. and Amer.

OXFORD MOVEMENT
Movement for the reform of the C. of E. also known as the Tractarian movement. The Rev. E. B. Pusey is usually regarded as its founder. It aimed at bringing more reverence and order into the worship of the church.

OXFORD UNIVERSITY
Oldest residential univ. in Brit. There are 21 men's coll.; the oldest is Univ. Coll. (1249), the newest, St. Catherine's (1962). There are 5 women's coll. At the head of the univ. is the chanc. but the acting head is the vice-chanc. The univ. legislates through Convocation, controlled by the Hebdomadal Council. The disciplinary officer of a coll. is the dean. The Bodleian Library is one of the 4 libraries in the country which has a claim on any book pub. in the country. The new Bodleian buildings were opened 1946.

OXFORDSHIRE
Inland county of S. Eng. with the Thames as its S. boundary. The Chiltern Hills cross the county in the S. while in the N.W. are hills rising to 800 ft. It is a well-wooded county and agriculture is the main occupation. Oxford is the county town; others are Banbury, Bicester, Henley, Woodstock and Witney. It also contains Blenheim, Nunsham and other places of interest. O. returns 3 members to Parl. including the member for Oxford. Pop. 317,880. **Oxford.** City, county borough and county town of Oxfordshire, on the Thames, 51 m. W.N.W. of London. In Saxon times it was an important milit. fortification. From the 13th cent. O. played a prominent part in Eng. hist. Several Parl., notably the Mad Parl., were held at O. The establishing of the Morris Motor Works at Cowley has made O. an important industrial centre. It returns 1 member to Parl. Pop. 105,560.

OXIDE
In chemistry, a compound formed by the combination of an element with oxygen. All the non-metallic elements, except hydrogen, form oxides which combine with water to produce acids, these being termed acidic oxides. Metals when burnt in air or oxygen form basic oxides, which, uniting with water, produce hydroxides.

OXLIP
(*Primula elatior*) Perennial herb of the prim-

rose family, native of Europe and Siberia. The scentless flowers form a stalked umbel, the corolla limbs being broader and flatter than in the primrose.

OXYGEN
A colourless gas discovered by Priestley in 1774. The most abundant element, it forms 46·5 % of the earth's crust. Liquid oxygen is blue in colour and shows magnetic properties. The density is 1·43 times that of air. Chem. sym. O.

OYSTER
(*Ostrea*) Cosmopolitan genus of bivalve molluscs. The common edible *O. edulis* of Brit. and European coasts is very prolific. The larvae or 'spat' settle on a suitable bank or reef, metamorphose into young oysters attached by the flattened valve, and there remain until dislodged. During the spawning period, May-Aug. they are out of season. Pearl oysters form a distinct family.

OYSTER-CATCHER
(*Haematopus*) Genus of wading birds of the plover tribe. The European *H. ostralegus*, 16½ in. long, is resident in Brit. It has a long coral-red bill, black and white plumage and pink feet; 3-4 blotched clay-coloured eggs are laid in hollows near the shore. It feeds on mussels, limpets, etc.

OZOKERITE
[ō-zō'-ker-it] Wax-like hydrocarbon found with petroleum. When pure it is transparent, pale yellow to greenish in colour, with an odour like benzine, and of the hardness of beeswax. Purified with sulphuric acid, ozokerite forms a white wax known as ceresin used in candles and boot polishes, and as an insulating material.

OZONE
O_3. Gas having a distinctive odour, and formed in dry oxygen or air subjected to a series of sparks from an electrical machine. It is a powerful oxidising agent, bleaching vegetable dyes and destroying organic matter, and is used on a large scale in purifying drinking water, bleaching, and for deodorising the air in crowded places. The characteristic effluvium of seaside areas is probably produced by other agencies, *e.g.* seaweed.

P

P
16th letter of the Eng. alphabet. It is a labial or lipsound normally pronounced as in *pip*. In words derived from the Gk. it is often silent when combined with another consonant as in *psychology*, *psalm*. The combination *ph* is sounded as *f*, *e.g. philosophy*, *pharmacist*.

PACIFIC, War in the
On Dec. 7, 1941, Pearl Harbour (*q.v.*), the Philippine Is. and Malaya were attacked without warning and war was declared on Japan by U.S.A., Gt. Brit., Holland, Australia, Canada, New Zealand and some Lat. Amer. nations. Burma was invaded from Siam on Dec. 14. Brit. forces were pushed out by May 17, 1942, and the Burma road was cut. The Japanese occupied Java, then New Guinea, Gilbert Is., New Brit. and the Solomon Is. The first setback suffered by the invaders was the battle of the Coral Sea when they were prevented from moving farther S. towards Australia. In June, 1942, the Japanese navy was decisively defeated at the battle of Midway Is. Lt.-Col. Doolittle made a daring bombing raid on Japan itself (April 18, 1942). In Aug. 1942 Guadalcanal was invaded by the Amers. under Gen. MacArthur. In Dec. 1942 Brit. forces under Gen. Wavell thrust into Burma, and Gen. Wingate's ' Chindit ' raiders had inflicted heavy losses behind the enemy lines. Late in 1943 Gen. Joseph W. Stilwell began his advance into N. Burma, while a Japanese counterthrust to the S. moved into India and threatened Imhal and Kohima (Spring, 1944). The Japanese failed in their objective and Amer., Chinese and Brit. forces took the offensive from the N., E. and W. In Sept. 1944, the Allies had launched a 2-pronged attack towards Japan through the Pacific Is.: the 1st prong through New Guinea, New Brit. and the Philippine Is. (Oct. 1944) and the 2nd through the Gilbert Is. (Nov. 1943), the Marshall Is. (Jan. 1944), the Marianas (June 1944) and the Caroline Is. (Sept. 1944). The use of the atomic bomb on Hiroshima (Aug. 6, 1945) and Nagasaki (Aug. 9, 1945) and the entry of Russia (Aug. 9, 1945) into the Pacific war made the actual invasion of Japan unnecessary.

PACIFIC ISLAND TRUSTEESHIP
U.S. trusteeship set up by U.N. Security Council in 1947. 96 islands of Mariana (excluding Guam), Caroline and Marshall groups. Pop. 81,000.

PACIFIC OCEAN
Largest ocean of the world, with an area of *c.* 63,800,000 sq.m. containing many Is. In the N. it is bounded by the Aleutian Is. but on the S. it is widely open, and its mean depth is much greater than that of the Atlantic. The greatest depth known is 36,198 ft. in the Marianas trench.

PADEREWSKI, Ignaz Jan
[-ef'-ski] (1860-1941) Polish pianist and statesman. After a long career as teacher and concert pianist he became 1st Pres. of the Polish Repub. 1919.

PADUA
City of Veneto, N. Italy, 25 m. W. of Venice. Famous buildings include the Palazzo della Ragiane, and the univ. founded by Frederick II, 1238. Pop. 198,403.

PAEONY
or **Peony.** Genus of perennial herbs (*Paeonia*) native to Europe, Asia and N.W. Amer. The carmine flowers of the common paeony occur in single and double-flowered cultivated forms.

PAGANINI, Niccolò
[pagă-nē'-ni] (1780-1840) Ital. violinist and composer. He vastly extended the range and capabilities of his instrument. His works include 2 violin concertos, concert pieces for violin and orchestra.

PAHANG
[pă-hung'] E. coast state of Malaysia. The surface is mountainous in the W. The seat of govt. is at Kuala Lipis. Area: 13,873 sq.m. Pop. 359,739.

PAINT
Preparation of a pigment mixed with an appropriate vehicle. Some pigments are of mineral origin; others are derived from plants. A few are of animal origin, while many synthetic dyestuffs are used as pigments. **Painting.** The art dates back to palaeolithic times when early man made drawings on the walls of caves. In later times in Egypt and Greece mineral and some organic pigments were used. In medieval Italy the artists painted in fresco and tempera. Then with the Renaissance came the beginnings of perspective, the pioneer artists being Masaccio, Uccello, Mantegna and Leonardo. With the Van Eycks in the Netherlands originated **oil painting,** later carried to a high level of excellence by the Dutch and Flemish schools under Rubens, Rembrandt, Hals and others. In Italy the new method was taken up by Leonardo, Perugino and others, and used by the Venetian School under Tintoretto and Veronese. A further development came with the rise of **water-colour painting** in Eng. during the 18th cent.

PAISLEY
[pāz'-] Burgh of Renfrewshire, on the Cart, 7 m. S.W. of Glasgow; the centre of cotton thread manufacture. There is also an abbey, partly restored. P. returns 1 member to Parl. Pop. 96,670.

PAKISTAN
Country comprising 2 parts. *c.* 1,000 m. apart. W. Pakistan is much larger than E. Pakistan but the density of pop. is very much less, the former having 41 million people and the latter 51 million. W. P. consists of the former provinces of Sind, W. Punjab, Baluchistan, the N.W. Frontier Prov., Bahawalpur and Khairpur, while E. Pakistan comprises E. Bengal and most of the former Assamese district of Sylhet. 86% of the Pakistanis are Moslems and gained indep. from Brit. rule on such a religious basis in 1947. The cap. was removed to Rawalpindi, 1960. In March, 1956, P. became ' The Islamic Repub. of Pakistan ', but the Constituent Assembly decided that the country should remain in the Brit. Commonwealth. In 1958 the constitution was abrogated, and P. came under martial law, with Ayub Khan as Pres. (resigned 1969). **E. Pakistan** is bordered to the E. by the Chittagong Hills and the Shillong Plateau. In the N. it reaches almost to the Himalayas but at almost every point it is surrounded by Indian territory The main artery

is the Ganges, the Brahmaputra and the Meghna rivers. The rivers, which flood widely during the monsoon period, have created large alluvial and deltaic areas. The rainfall is confined almost entirely to the summer monsoon period but there are preceding rains in April and May which bring the total in the S. and E. to over 100 in. per year. E. Pakistan is predominantly agricultural. The region is particularly suited to the growing of rice, and of jute. Commercial agriculture and communications were centred on Calcutta but the partition boundary has cut across the railways and divided the raw material from the industry. E. Pakistan had no industry except some jute-baling, cotton spinning and weaving and sugar milling. Textile mills are now being built in and near Dacca, the only large city. There is no coal, oil, or iron in E. Pakistan, but there is a large hydro-electric potential which is being developed on the Karnafuli river. The Ganges and other rivers are important highways. P. has proved itself a viable state largely owing to the jute of E. Pakistan which brings in nearly twice as much as the cotton of W. Pakistan. In the N., **W. Pakistan** is bordered by the wooded ranges of the Himalayas and stretches in the W. over the ridged plateaux of Baluchistan to the borders of Iran and Afghanistan. The most important part is the sediment-filled basin of the river Indus. In the S., where the E. state boundary crosses the Thar Desert, the Indus passes through a region with less than 5 ins. of rain per year. As compared with E. Pakistan and India, the onset of the monsoon rains are later, the preceding months are hotter and the winters colder, except in the extreme S. Winter wheat is the chief cereal crop of W. Pakistan. The chief cash crop is cotton which depends almost entirely on perennial irrigation. The Punjab and Sind have canal and barrage schemes built by Brit. capital. The amount of water within the drainage area is not sufficient to meet the needs. Mineral wealth consists of salt from the Salt Range and oil from the Potwar Plateau to the north of it. Claim by E. Pakistan of independence as Bangla Desh led to Civil War, 1971.

PALAEOLITHIC
Term denoting the rudely chipped and flaked flints and other implements produced by man during the older phase of the prehistoric stone age.

PALE, The *See* IRELAND.

PALERMO
Cap. and seaport on the N. coast of Sicily. Orig. a Phoenician colony of 8th-6th cents. B.C., it was also an important Carthaginian centre until acquired by Rome, 254 B.C. Pop. 587,063.

PALESTINE
The Holy Land of Christianity and the scene of most of the events of Biblical hist. Conquered by the Turks in the 16th cents., P. was taken by the Brit. under Gen. Allenby, 1917. It was gov. by Brit. under mandate from the League of Nations from 1928-48. Now occupied by the State of Israel, and the Kingdom of Jordan (*q.v.*).

PALESTRINA
[-trē′-nă] **Giovanni Pierluigi da** (1525-94) Ital. composer. In 1577 he was entrusted by Pope Gregory XIII with the revision of the Gradual. He wrote 94 masses, over 250 motets and other ch. music, madrigals, etc.

PALI
Language and form of script of Buddhist sacred books. It was the living tongue of cultured India from the 7th cent. B.C. onwards, being ultimately displaced as Brahmanism regained its hold.

PALLADIO, Andrea
[pa-lăd′-yō] (1518-80) Ital. architect and founder of the Palladian style of architecture, he pub. in 1570 *Quattro Libri dell' Architettura.* This greatly influenced Inigo Jones who introduced the Palladian style into Eng.

PALLADIUM
Rare metallic element, Chem. sym. Pd and at. wt. 106·7. P. is silvery white in colour and like platinum is unaltered by exposure to air, but is slowly attacked by nitric acid.

PALLAS
(astronomy) One of the minor planets (or asteroids) revolving round the sun between Mars and Jupiter. It was discovered by Olbers at Bremen in 1802. Its orbit is inclined 35° to the ecliptic, and it revolves round the sun in 4·61 years. Its diameter has been estimated at *c.* 350 m.

PALM
(*Palmaceae*) Family of endogenous plants, mostly large trees, natives of trop. and sub-trop. regions. Estimated at 600-1,000 species. The coconut's seed-kernels, the date-palm's pulpy fruit, the sago-palm's farinaceous pith, and the cabbage-palm's terminal buds are edible. Other species yield palm-sugar or jaggery, palm-wine or toddy, candle wax, oil, vegetable ivory, fans, rattans, leaf-stalk fibre, leaves for thatch, and the like. The only European species, *Chamoerops humilis*, the Medit. fan-palm, is used for basketry, hats and vegetable horse hair. **Palm Oil.** Fatty substance from the fruits of several palms, pre-eminently the W. African oil palm, *Elaeis quineensis.* The boiled pericarp yields an orange-red fat, which melts at 80·5° F. Palm kernels yield a white oil used in making margarine. *See* DATE.

PALM SUNDAY
Sun. before Easter; 1st day of Holy Week. In the R.C. Ch. palm branches are carried in commem. of Christ's entry into Jerusalem.

PALMERSTON, Viscount
Henry John Temple (1784-1865) Eng. statesman, M.P. 1807-65; P.M. 1855-7, 1857-8 and 1859-65. Best remembered for his vigorous foreign policy. He was forced to resign in 1851 but soon returned, and as P.M. in 1855, vigorously prosecuted the Crimean War. He met his match in Bismarck, and was worsted in the Schleswig-Holstein episode of 1865.

PALMYRA
Ancient city of Syria in a desert oasis, 120 m. N.E. of Damascus. Under the Rom. Emp. it was important because of its position on the Euphrates caravan route. Under Hadrian it enjoyed indep. in the 3rd cent. Modern P. is a town on the oil pipeline to the Medit.

PALOMAR OBSERVATORY
On Mt. P., Calif. U.S.A. it houses the Hale reflecting telescope, the largest in the world, having a 200-in. mirror and a range of a billion light-years.

PAMIRS
Region of lofty tablelands in C. Asia, on the borders of Tajik (U.S.S.R.) and Sinkiang (China). It is a treeless desert area crossed by mt. ranges, Hindu Kush and Tien Shan.

PAMPAS
Plains of Argentina, from the Andean foothills to the Parana and the Atlantic coast. Prior to the coming of settlers the plains were one vast sea of Pampas grass (*Cortaderia argentea*). As a result of the work of pioneers and their descendants in the last 80 years, the Pampas is no longer a treeless and uncultivated area. Wire fencing encloses fertile fields, and there are trees of many kinds to prevent soil erosion and to provide shade for cattle during the summer. Herds spend their time on the rough pastures of open range all the year round.

PAN
In Gk. myth. the god of shepherds, huntsmen and rural people, protector of flocks and herds, wild beasts and bees.

PANAMA
Repub. of C. Amer. between Costa Rica and Colombia, on the isthmus of P. It has long coastlines on the Pacific Ocean and Caribbean Sea, and is crossed at its narrowest part by the P. Canal Zone. Mt. ranges run parallel to the coasts, enclosing numerous valleys and plains. Much of the land is forested; agriculture is primitive. Sp. is the official language, and R.C. the state religion. The pop. is mixed. P. was formerly part of the Repub. of Colombia, but became indep. 1903. There is a Pres. and a chamber of 51 deputies. Area: 28,576 sq.m. Pop. 1,329,000. **Panama City.** Cap. of the Repub. of Panama, near the Pacific entrance to the Canal. Built in the 17th cent. P. has a cath. with mother-of-pearl domes, and a univ. Pop. 334,000.

PANAMA CANAL
Canal connecting the Atlantic and Pacific Oceans. It was constructed as the result of a treaty (1903) between the U.S.A. and Panama.

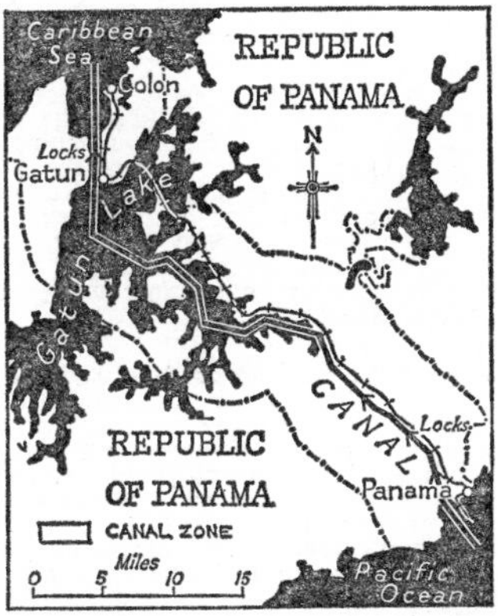

The canal is *c.* 50 m. long, with 12 locks. The width is from 300 to 1,000 ft. and the min. depth 41 ft. The average time of passage is 7 to 8 hours. It was informally opened to traffic Aug. 15, 1914. The official opening was on June 12, 1920. The Hay-Pauncefote Treaty provides for the use of the canal under equal terms by vessels of all nations. The suggestion that a canal should be cut was first made in the 16th cent., but it was not until 1876 that work started.

PANCREAS
Glandular organ situated in upper part of abdomen. Secretes digestive substances which act on carbohydrates, fats and proteins.

PANDA
(or **Wah**) A mammal (*Ailurus fulgens*) found in the woody parts of the mts. of N. India. In size it is approx. equal to a large cat, is chestnut brown in colour, feeds mostly on vegetable food.

PANDIT, Mrs. Vijayalakshmi
[pun'-] (1900-) Indian politician. The daughter of Motilal Nehru and sister of Pandit Jawaharial Nehru. Her public career began with service on the Allahabad City Council; thereafter she was elected to the Legislature of the United Provs. and held ministerial office. She was Pres. of U.N. 1953-4. Indian High Commissioner to Gt. Brit. 1954-61.

PANGOLIN
(or **Scaly Anteaters**) (*Manis*) Toothless mammals occurring in S. Asia and trop. Africa. Short-legged, with lizard-like bodies and tails protected by overlapping horny scales, they roll into a ball when disturbed.

PANKHURST, Emmeline
(1858-1928) Brit. suffragist. She helped to found the **Women's Franchise League** (1889). In 1903 she was instrumental, with her daughter, Christabel, in founding the **Women's Social and Political Union.** 3 times imprisoned for her activities.

PANSY
Perennial herb of the violet order (*Viola tricolor*), native to Europe, N. and W. Asia and N. Africa.

PANTHER
Large carnivorous mammal of the cat family, indistinguishable from the Old World Leopard. In N. Amer. the name colloquialised as ' painter ', denotes the Puma which in S. Amer. is sometimes called the Cougar.

PAPACY, The
Term employed in 2 senses (1) eccles., denoting the system under which the Pope, as successor of St. Peter and Vicar of Christ, governs the Catholic Ch. as its supreme head, and (2) historical, signifying the papal influence as a polit. force. Under Innocent III in the 13th cent. the Pope became a sort of emperor. A temporal Papal State grew up with an area of 17,000 sq.m. After the Austro-Ital. War of 1859 nearly ⅔ of this territory was added to the kingdom of Italy, Rome and its environs being preserved for the Pope by the Fr. In 1870 Rome was adopted as the seat of govt. of united Italy, and the Papacy restricted to the Vatican. In 1929, by the Treaty of Feb. 11, the full and indep. sovereignty of the Holy See in the city of the Vatican was recognised.

PAPAW
Small evergreen tree akin to the passion flower order of S. Amer. origin (*Carica papaya*). Now widely naturalised in the tropics, its long-stalked 7-lobed leaves, 2 ft. across, shelter melon-shaped yellow fruits 10 in. long.

PAPER
Substance manufactured from vegetable fibres of different lengths and sizes, fitted together to form a sheet or web. The art of making paper from rags is credited to a Chinese named Tsai-lun (*c.* A.D. 105) and paper was in general use in China, for *c.* 500 years before its method of manufacture became known to the Moors and Arabs (*c.* 751). The first Eng. paper mill was estabd. by John Tate at Stevenage, Herts. in 1489. Other important years in the chronology of papermaking are 1809, when a machine for making paper in a continuous web was invented by the Frenchman, Louis Robert; 1840, which saw the production of mechanical pulp by Keller; the introduction of esparto grass by Routledge, 1857; the invention of the process of wood pulp by Tilghmann, 1866. The 5 main types of fibre used in papermaking are cotton, linen, esparto, straw and wood. Esparto papers are distinguished for their bulk, opacity and their close, uniform surfaces and are thus eminently suitable for fine printing.

PAPHOS
[pā'-fos] Ancient city of S.W. Cyprus, where Aphrodite is reputed to have risen from the sea.

PAPUA AND NEW GUINEA
2 territories in the E. half of the Is. of New Guinea (*q.v.*), since 1949 uniting for admin. purposes. Port Moresby is the seat of govt. **Papua.** Austral. territory consisting of the S.E. portion of New Guinea, with the Woodlark, Trobriand, D'Entrecasteaux and Louisiade groups of is. Copra, gold and rubber are the main exports. Port Moresby is the chief town. The territory was annexed by Queensland, 1883, and became a Brit. protect. In 1901 the Austral. Fed. Govt. took over control, and the name was changed to Papua 5 years later. Area: 90,540 sq.m. **New Guinea.** Austral. mandated territory comprising N.E. New Guinea, with the ad-

jacent Is., the Bismarck Archipelago, Admiralty Is. and the 2 northernmost Solomon Is. (*qq.v.*). The chief centres on the mainland are Lae, Madang and Aitape. The mainland of N. G. and many of the adjacent Is. were German until 1914. An Austral. mandate was estabd. 1921; now the territory is under the trusteeship system of the U.N. Area: 93,000 sq.m. Combined pop. 2,025,000.

PAPYRUS
Kind of paper used by the ancient Egyptians. It was prepared by cutting into long strips the central pith of the stems of the paper-rush, *Cyperus papyrus*, laying others across, moistening, pressing, drying and polishing.

PARABOLA
Curved figure formed by the intersection of a cone and a plane parallel to one side.

PARACELSUS
(*c.* 1493-1541) Swiss physician, alchemist and mystic. His revolutionary ideas aroused much antagonism, but he was an orig. thinker and investigator and his theories and treatments had a lasting influence on the science of medicine.

PARACHUTE
Life-saving apparatus used to descend safely from a ht. In its usual form it consists of an umbrella with cords attached at the circumference, and fastened to straps on the shoulders. It is carried in a bag fastened to the body and is released either automatically or by means of a rip-cord. The first successful descent with one was made in 1797 by the Fr. aeronaut, Garnerin. **Parachute Regiment.** Unit of the Brit. Army formed in 1941 for the purpose of landing behind the enemy lines.

PARAFFIN
In organic chemistry a large series of hydrocarbons. More generally the term is used for a burning oil obtained from petroleum (*q.v.*) and shales, also for the solid wax-like substance from the same source.

PARAGUAY
[-gwī] Repub. of S. Amer. bounded by Brazil, Bolivia and Argentina, and having no coastline. It is divided in 2 by the P. river, a tributary of the Paraná on the E. border. In the W. there are the grassy plains of the Gran Chaco, well adapted to stock rearing; the E. half, the most populous, is rolling, forested country. P. has a sub-tropical climate, with a hot summer and 2 rainy seasons. An agricultural country, producing livestock, timber, tannin, tobacco, cotton and yerba maté, P. also has large mineral deposits. Asunción, on the P. River, is the cap. The people are bilingual, speaking Sp. and Guarani; R.C. is the estabd. religion. P. was visited by Sebastian Cabot in 1527, and was a Sp. possession, 1535-1811. Then followed a succession of despots, and a disastrous war with Brazil. The Pres. is assisted by a council of state. Area: 157,000 sq.m. Pop. 2,167,000.

PARALLAX
The apparent change in position of a celestial body caused by a change in position of the observer, and esp. applied to the amount of apparent motion due to this displacement. By observing the apparent direction of the sun from different places on the earth—or from the same point at different times of day—the solar parallax may be found.

PARALYSIS
Loss of power of muscular action or function of any part of body. Assoc. either with hysteria (functional paralysis) or organic disease of brain, spinal cord or nerves. *See* POLIOMYELITIS.

PARAMARIBO
[pārā-ma'-ribō] Port and cap. of Dutch Guiana, at the mouth of the Surinam. Pop. 120,000.

PARASITE
Term used in biology to indicate any organism which obtains its nourishment at the expense of another organism, upon which or within which it lives. **Parasitic Diseases.** Diseases produced by the action of any animal or plant on the human body. The term is generally confined to diseases produced by parasites visible to the naked eye, *e.g.* tape-worm, trichina, guinea-worms, louse, acarus, etc. **Parasitic Plants.** Plants that grow on others and from which they receive their nourishment. They include many fungi such as the rusts, smuts and mildews. Among the larger parasites is the mistletoe. Parasites are distinguished from *epiphytes*, which, though they grow upon other plants, are not nourished by them.

PARCHMENT
Writing material used for documents of a permanent character. Ordinary parchment is made from the skins of the sheep and goat. Vellum from the skins of the calf, kid or lamb, a tough variety for book-binding from pigskin, and a parchment for drums from asses' skins.

PARENT
Father or mother. The parents of a child are its natural guardians till it attains the age of 21, or unless it marries before reaching that age. The primary right resides in the father, but custody of the child may be granted to the mother. Parents' liability for maintenance of their children is governed by the Nat. Assistance Act, 1948. Educ. of children, and parents, responsibility for it is regulated by various Educ. Acts. *See* EDUCATION.

PARIS
Cap. city of Fr. situated on 2 Is. and on both banks of the Seine, 110 m. from the sea. It is an important commercial centre and river port, with a variety of manufactures, *e.g.* clothing, food products, footwear and jewellery. Famous buildings include the Louvre, and the Bastille; the cath. of Notre Dame (1163-1230); the Palais Royal, Champs Élysées and Palais de Justice; the Conciergerie; Bibliothèque Nationale and Hôtel des Invalides, the Arc de Triomphe, the Palais du Luxembourg, the Opéra, Champ de Mars, and the Eiffel Tower. The chief educ. inst. is the Univ. of Paris, including the Sorbonne. More than 30 bridges cross the Seine. Its historical importance dates from A.D. 508, when Clovis built his cap. on the Ile de la Cité. The decay of feudalism and the rise of the guilds in the 11th cent. hastened the city's growth. In 1422 the Eng. took P. and held it against Joan of Arc (1429). After 1559 the city was the residence of the kings of Fr. Modern Paris dates from the Renaissance; Catherine de Medici began to build the Tuileries in 1564. Quays were constructed and the city spread, esp. under Louis XIV. Besieged and captured by the Pruss. in 1870, it narrowly escaped a 2nd capture in Sept. 1914. It was occupied in 1940 and liberated in Aug. 1944. Pop. 2,790,091. **Paris Conference.** Meeting of the victorious powers in World War II, at which the peace treaties with Italy, Rumania, Hungary, Bulgaria, and Finland, were drawn up, and the Free State of Trieste brought into being.

PARIS
Small genus of perennial herbs of the Liliaceae, native to temp. Europe and Asia. Their short unbranched stems, rising from creeping rootstocks, bear a whorl of 4-9 leaves with a single yellow-green flower.

PARK, Mungo
(1771-1806) Scot. doctor and explorer. His services were accepted in 1795 by the African Assoc. and, starting from Senegal, he reached the Niger at Segu. He traced the course of the river for some distance. In 1805, starting from Pisania on the Gambia, he reached the Niger, but was attacked by natives and drowned.

PARLIAMENT
Word used for the legislature of Brit. and other self-governing parts of the Brit. Commonw. The Eng. Parl. has been developed from the Witan of the A.-S. kings, and the King's Council of the Normans. In the 13th cent. knights of the shire and representatives from the towns joined the barons, abbots and bishops and parl. in the modern sense began. Both Simon de Montfort and Edward I have been credited with the decisive step, but the development was gradual. Early in the 14th cent. it was divided into two, a form it has since retained, the House of Lords and House of Commons. The Lords were much more powerful, the Commons' assent being usually taken for granted, but gradually the Commons made themselves equal and in the 19th cent. became the dominant partner. The Tudor sovereigns made their parls. register their will, but in the time of the Stuarts the memorable struggle between king and parl. became a civil war. Having asserted in the Bill of Rights, 1689, their control of the raising of finance, Parl. in 1694 passed a Triennial Act which stated that not more than 3 years should pass without the calling of a parl. In 1715 a Septennial Act was passed by which a parl. could sit for 7 years, and this remained the law until 1911, when the Parl. Act reduced the period to 5 years. Nevertheless, parl. being a sovereign body, can prolong its own existence as it did during both World Wars. The Parl. Act of 1911 made the House of Lords subordinate to the House of Commons. It could delay the passing of a Bill into law, but has no control over money Bills. If the Commons, under the required conditions, pass a measure 3 times that Bill becomes law, whether the Lords oppose or not. A parl. is called together by the sovereign. Its sittings are divided into sessions. Each session is prorogued, but a parl. is dissolved. This is done on the advice of the P.M. and a Gen. Election must follow. The parls. in Canada, Australia, and elsewhere follow very largely the Brit. model, except that their 2nd chambers contain no hereditary elements and have rather more power than the House of Lords. *See* COMMONS, HOUSE OF; LORDS, HOUSE OF.

PARMA
City of Emilia, Italy, in the Plain of Lombardy, 75 m. S.E. of Milan. Considerable trade is carried on. Univ. was founded 1601. Pop. 152,995.

PARMENIDES
[-men′-i-dēz] Gk. philosopher. He flourished about the middle of the 5th cent. B.C., and was head of the Eleatic school.

PARNASSUS
Mt. 8,000 ft. high in C. Greece, in Gk. myth the home of the Muses.

PARNELL, Charles Stewart
(1846-91) Irish Nat. politician. M.P. 1875-91. He and his followers acquired considerable influence and, after wrecking the 1st Salisbury Govt., contracted an alliance with Mr. Gladstone in the hope of achieving Irish Home Rule. An entanglement in a divorce case led to his withdrawal into private life.

PAROTID GLAND
[-rot′-] Main salivary gland situated in front of ear and below angle of jaw. Inflammation of gland gives rise to mumps (*q.v.*).

PARR, Catherine
(1512-48) Sixth and last wife of Henry VIII of Eng. He was her third husband. After the d. of the King in 1547, she mar. Lord Thomas Seymour, but she d. the following year in childbed.

PARRAKEET
Various small parrots, often with long and slender tails. Among aviary favourites are the red-billed genus *Palaeornis*. Austral. Budgerigars and other Grass-parrakeets are favourite cage-birds.

PARROT
Order of birds of high intelligence and organisation, inhabiting trop. and sub-trop. regions (*Psittaci*). Of 500 species S. Amer. has most, followed by the E. Indies, Australia and Polynesia; there are a few in Asia and Africa, and 1 in N. Amer. Many have gorgeous colouring. Some readily learn to talk.

PARRY, Sir Charles Hubert Hastings
(1848-1918) Eng. composer. His best works are his choral compositions. With Stanford he may be considered one of the prime movers in the revival of Eng. music at the turn of the cent.

PARSEES
(or Parsis) Religious community in India and parts of Persia. In the 7th cent. Arab conquest many Persians who refused to embrace Islam fled to Gujarat, taking with them their Zoroastrian faith.

PARSLEY
Biennial umbelliferous herb (*Petroselinum crispum*). Its crisp, curled, mossy leaves are used when fresh for garnishing, and either fresh or dried for flavouring.

PARSNIP
Biennial umbelliferous herb, native of Europe and Siberia (*Pastinaca sativa*). Wild in Brit. its thin, woody root has become palatable and nutritious. A milk-producing cattle-food. *See* COW PARSNIP.

PARSONS, Sir Charles Algernon
(1854-1931) Brit. engineer and inventor of the steam turbine.

PARTHENON
Temple at Athens dedicated to Pallas Athene, begun *c.* 450 B.C. under the direction of the sculptor, Phidias. Some of the sculpture was removed by Lord Elgin in 1812. These are in the Brit. Museum.

PARTHIA
In ancient geog. a country S.E. of the Caspian and E. of Media. The Kingdom of P., which had previously belonged to the emp. of the Seleucidae, lasted from *c.* 250 B.C. to *c.* A.D. 190.

PARTRIDGE
Game-birds of the pheasant sub-family. The Brit. Grey Partridge, *Perdix perdix*, extends throughout Europe, being assoc. in Asia with related forms. The Red-legged or Fr. partridge, *Alectoris rufa*, a native of S.W. Europe introduced into Brit. *c.* 1770, is now common. Partridge-shooting in Brit. and Ireland is legal from Sept. 1 to Feb 1.

PARTRIDGE, Sir Bernard
(1861-1945) Eng. artist. Worked 1880-4 in stained glass designing and decorative painting, subsequently in book and press illustration. He joined the staff of *Punch* in 1891.

PASCAL, Blaise
(1623-62) Fr. philosopher, mathematician and scientist. At Rouen he came into close touch

with the Jansenists, with whose doctrines he became identified. His famous *Provincial Letters*, an ironical exposition of Jesuit moral theology (1656-7), created a profound sensation. His *Pensées* was pub. posthumously in 1669.

PASSION, The
Term denoting the sufferings of Christ from the agony in the Garden to the d. on the Cross. The recital of these sufferings in the early ch. at Passiontide was accompanied by the chanting of the narrative portions by male voices, and choral representation of the crowds.

PASSION FLOWER
Large genus of climbing herbs and shrubs (*Passiflora*) natives of trop. S. Amer. The common blue passion flower, *P. caerulea*, is hardy in Brit.

PASSOVER
Jewish festival. It was traditionally instituted by Moses to commemorate the passing over of the Heb. thresholds when Egypt's firstborn were smitten at the time of the Exodus.

PASSPORT
A permission to travel necessary in the case of most foreign countries, and, when granted, ensuring some measure of protection. Passports are granted by the Foreign Office to natural-born Brit. subjects, and to persons naturalised in the U.K., in the Brit. Dominions and the Colonies. Brit. passports are only available for travel to the countries named thereon, but may be endorsed for additional countries. They must be renewed after 5 years from date of issue, and expire absolutely after 10 years from the date of issue.

PASTERNAK, Boris
(1890-1960) Russ. poet. His novel, *Dr. Zhivago* (1958) won internat. fame. He was awarded the Nobel Prize for Lit. but refused it under Communist pressure.

PASTEUR, Louis
(1822-95) Fr. chemist. In 1867, became Prof. of Chem. at the Sorbonne. He showed that living micro-organisms are responsible for fermentation and for disease, and was the first to use inoculation for the prevention of disease.

PATAGONIA
Region of S. Amer. S. of latitude 40° S. discovered by Magellan in 1520. Since 1881 it has been divided politically between Chile and the Argentine. The W. part, consisting of the Andes, is damp and forested; sheep are reared in the dry E. plateau. Cap. Punta Arenas.

PATENT
Grant from the Crown by Letters Patent to an inventor of the sole right of making, using or selling his invention during a specified period. It is essential to the validity of the patent that the subject-matter of it should be an invention, that the invention should be new, and that it should fulfil the purpose for which it was designed by the patentee.

PATER, Walter Horatio
(1839-94) Eng. critic. His works include *Studies in the History of the Renaissance* (1873); *Imaginary Portraits* (1887); *Appreciations* (1889) of Lamb, Wordsworth, Coleridge and others, *Miscellaneous Studies* (1895).

PATHAN
[pă-tàn'] Iranian peoples of the former N.W. Frontier Prov., Pakistan and related trans-frontier tribes in E. Afghanistan. They are Moslems and speak Pushtu.

PATMOS
Gk. Is. in the Dodecanese group, off the W. coast of Asia Minor. It formerly belonged to Turkey. St. John is supposed to have lived in exile on P. *c.* A.D. 90, and to have seen the visions described in the Book of Revelations.

PATRIARCH
Head of a family or tribe. The name denotes specifically various O.T. figures. Applied to the head of the Jewish Sanhedrin, it denoted in early Christianity outstanding metropolitan bishops.

PATRICK
Patron saint of Ireland. B. 387, he was captured by Irish raiders, escaped to the continent and studied at Tours. Pope Celestine I consecrated him bishop, entrusting him with Ireland's conversion. Landing in Wicklow, he estabd. missionary settlements. He is commemorated on March 17.

PATTI, Adelina
(1843-1919) B. Madrid, she made her operatic début in 1859 in *Lucia di Lammermoor*. She first appeared in London in 1861.

PAU
[pō] Town of S.W. Fr.; cap. of Basses-Pyrenées dept., a winter health resort. Pop. 48,300.

PAUL
(*c.* A.D. 3-64) Saint and Apostle. B. Tarsus in Asia Minor, he was trained as a Rabbi under Gamaliel at Jerusalem. He took an active part in the persecution of Christ's followers, but on his way to Damascus, he saw Christ in a vision and was converted. After 3 years' preparation he revisited Jerusalem, and then embarked on his 1st mission tour in Cyprus, Pisida, Pamphilia and Lycaonia. On his return he engaged in a controversy with St. Peter concerning the admission to the Christian Ch. of Gentiles, to whom his subsequent missionary efforts were devoted. Tried at Caesarea for causing disturbances he was sentenced to imprisonment and, appealing to Caesar, was sent to Rome where, after 2 years' captivity, tradition says, he was executed under Nero. **Paul, Epistles of.** *See* ROMANS, CORINTHIANS, GALATIANS, EPHESIANS, PHILIPPIANS, COLOSSIANS, THESSALONIANS, TIMOTHY.

PAUL I
(1901-64) King of the Hellenes. He mar. Princess Fredericka of Brunswick in 1938. Their son, Constantine (1940-) succeeded on his father's d.

PAUL I
(1754-1801) Tsar of Russia, 2nd son of Peter III and the Empress Catherine II, at whose d. in 1796 he succeeded to the throne. He rapidly became unpopular by reason of his violent temper. His nobles conspired to compel him to abdicate, and he was strangled.

PAUL VI
(1889-) **(Giovanni Battista Montini)** Succeeded Pope John XXIII, 1963, like him having liberal sympathies. Has sanctioned use of vernaculars in Mass, admitted women to debates of Ecumenical Council (1964); and went on pilgrimage to the Holy Land and to a conference in India. Made plea for world peace at U.N., 1965.

PAVIA
[pă-vē-ă] Town of Lombardy, Italy, on the Ticino, 2 m. above its confluence with the Po. There are iron foundries and engineering works.

PAVLOVA, Anna
(1885-1931) Russ. dancer; b. St. Petersburg; entered the Imperial Ballet School at the age of 10; became the prima ballerina of the Marianski Theatre, St. Petersburg (1901). First visited London with Michael Mordkin in 1910.

PEA
Annual climbing leguminous herb (*Pisum sativum*). Field peas preceded the garden forms. The sweet-pea (*Lathyrus*) is closely allied.

PEACH
Fruit-tree of the Rosaceae (*Prunus persica*). The roundish fleshy drupes, 2-3 in. across, covered with down, ripen in Brit. in favourable

situations. Large market supplies are grown in Fr., Delaware and Calif.

PEACOCK
(*Pavo*) Male bird of a game-fowl, indigenous to India and S.E. Asia and allied to Pheasants. In the breeding season, its upper tail-coverts develop spray-like webs interspersed with glittering ' eyes ', the whole train being displayed vertically in a semi-circle. The Common *P. cristatus* of India and Ceylon was domesticated in antiquity; albino examples occur.

PEACOCK, Thomas Love
(1785-1866) Eng. writer. He was a friend of Shelley; his essay *The Four Ages of Poetry* (1820) prompted Shelley's *Defence of Poetry.* He is best known for his satiric romances: *Headlong Hall* (1816), *Nightmare Abbey* (1818), *Crochet Castle* (1831), *Gryll Grange* (1860).

PEAK DISTRICT
Mt. area of Derbyshire, in the S. Pennines. Kinder Scout, 2,088 ft. is the highest point.

PEAR
Fruit-tree of the rose order (*Pyrus communis*), native from E. Europe to W. Asia and the Himalayas. There are innumerable varieties. Fermented pear-juice furnishes the alcoholic beverage called ***perry.***

PEARL
Calcareous secretion formed in many bivalve molluscs, but chiefly in the so-called pearl oysters, *Meleagrina*, and the freshwater mussels of the genus *Unio*. A pearl consists of extremely thin concentric layers of calcium carbonate deposited around some foreign object or parasite. Pearls vary in colour from white to pink or black. The principal fisheries are in the Persian Gulf, the Gulf of Manaar in Ceylon, the S. Pacific and the Gulf of Mexico.

PEARL HARBOUR
Naval base of the U.S. fleet on the S. coast of Oahu Is., Hawaii, and the scene of the treacherous attack by Jap. carrier-borne aircraft on December 7, 1941. The attack brought the U.S.A. into World War II. Casualties to naval personnel included 2,117 killed.

PEARY, Robert
(1856-1920) Amer. explorer. He joined the Amer. Navy. In 1891-2 he led a sledging expedition towards the N. Pole, a journey of 1,300 m., succeeded in discovering the N. Pole, 1909.

PEASANTS' REVOLT
(1381) Although the Black Death caused a labour shortage, the Statute of Labourers (1351) fixed wages at pre-plague standards. This, heavy taxes, and the breakdown of the feudal system, caused unrest among the labourers. Led by Wat Tyler and John Ball, the rebels seized Canterbury, entered London, took the Tower and executed their worst enemies. At Smithfield, Tyler met Richard II, and was killed by the Lord Mayor. The rebellion was then quickly suppressed.

PEASANTS' WAR
(1524-6) Rising of German peasants and poor artisans. Feudal lords were becoming autocratic and extortionate. The revolt began at Stühlingen, and spread quickly, peasants demanding the abolition of serfdom, relief from lesser tithes, impartial courts, restoration of common lands, abolition of d. duties. It was ruthlessly suppressed. The preaching of Luther had helped to undermine respect for authority, but Luther was violently against the peasants in this war.

PEAT
Partially decomposed vegetable matter found on or near the surface in many of the cooler parts of the world in swampy places. Its carbon content is sufficiently high to enable it to be used for fuel.

PECCARY
(*Dicotyles*) Hoofed mammal constituting the indigenous swine of Amer. They have the upper tusks directed outwards and only 3 toes on the hind feet. The Collared P., 3 ft. long, ranges from Texas to Patagonia, and somewhat larger White-lipped var. from Brit. Honduras to Paraguay.

PEDIATRICS
[pēd-i-at'-riks] The special branch of medical practice which is concerned with the diseases of children and their treatment.

PEDICULOSIS
or **Phthiriasis.** An infection of the skin and hair-bearing areas of the body. It is caused by lice.

PEEBLESSHIRE
County of S. Scot. known as Tweeddale. It is mountainous, and is watered by the Tweed and its tributaries. Sheep rearing is the main industry. Woollens are manufactured at Peebles, Innerleithen and Walkerburn. With Midlothian it returns 1 member to Parl. Pop. 14,000. **Peebles.** Burgh and county town of Peeblesshire, on the Tweed, 23 m. S. of Edinburgh. Pop. 5,305.

PEEL, Sir Robert
(1788-1850) Brit. statesman, M.P. (Tory), 1809-50; P.M. 1835, 1839 and 1841-6. Best remembered for his formation of the police force and for his repeal of the Corn Laws in 1846. His *Tamworth Manifesto* of 1835 laid the foundations of the modern Cons. Party.

PEERAGE
Peers as a body and also all members of their families. Only countries with a hereditary ruler possess a peerage. Eng. peers and representative peers from Scot. and Ireland sit in the House of Lords. There are 5 ranks in the Brit. peerage, duke, marquess, earl, viscount and baron. Bishops are considered to be peers, because they sit in the House of Lords by right of succession. Peers have the right to be tried, when necessary, by their peers. A peerage is created by letters patent, and this states how the title shall descend. Since 1963 titles may be renounced. *See* LIFE PEER.

PEKINESE DOG
Lap-dog of Chinese origin, it has a flat skull and tail curved over the loins. Wt. should not exceed 10 lbs. It is heavy in front, with short broad muzzle, falling away lion-like behind. It is light-red or yellow, mottled with white.

PEKING
Cap. city of China, in Hopei prov. *c.* 100 m. from the Gulf of Pohai. Estabd. as cap. of the Chinese Emp. 1264, by Kublai Khan, it consists of the Chinese city and the Tartar city. Inside the latter is the Imperial City, containing the Forbidden City. In 1928, the name was changed to Peiping and Chiang-Kai-Shek's govt. moved the cap. to Nanking. Pop. 4,010,000.

PELARGONIUM
Genus of herbs of the geranium family. Often half-shrubby, they have stalked umbels of flowers with irregular corollas and upper sepals spurred. *See* GERANIUM.

PELICAN
(*Pelecanus*) Waterfowl allied to Cormorants, of

trop. and sub-trop. regions. Their long furrowed beaks have extensible pouches attached to the lower mandible for collecting fish-food. The hook which terminates the bill is red; this is reputed to be the origin of the fable that the P. feeds its young with blood from its own breast. The Common P. (*P. onocrotalus*) 5 ft. long, inhabits S.E. Europe, S.W. Asia and N.E. Africa.

PELOPONNESUS
or **Morea.** Gk. peninsula connected with the mainland by the Isthmus of Corinth. **Peloponnesian War.** The war between Athens and Sparta, 431-404 B.C. In the 1st period, which was concluded by the Peace of Nicias (421 B.C.), both sides had their successes. In the 2nd, Sicily was the centre of hostilities; in the 3rd, Sparta had the advantage.

PELVIS
Name given to the bony frame work which forms a basin-like cavity at the lower part of the abdomen and contains important organs such as part of the bowel, bladder and in the female the sex organs. The pelvis proper consists of 2 innominate bones each consisting of 3 parts fused together called the *ilium*, *ischium* and *pubis*.

PEMBROKESHIRE
Maritime county of S.W. Wales, with coastline on St. George's Channel. Its chief river is the Teifi. Agriculture is important; coal, lead and iron are mined. Pembroke is the county town, and Haverfordwest the admin. centre. P. returns 1 member to Parl. Pop. 94,000. **Pembroke.** Municipal borough, seaport and county town of Pembrokeshire, on a navigable creek of Milford Haven. Pop. 12,220.

PENANG
State of the Fed. of Malaya. George Town is the cap. and chief port. Before the inauguration of the Fed., 1948, P., Malacca and Singapore formed the colony of the Straits Settlements. Area: 400 sq.m. Pop. 651,899.

PENGUIN
Flightless sea-birds inhabiting S. temp. and antarctic regions. The backward position of the short legs, the webbed feet, stiff tails and erect station on land give them an ungainly appearance; the wings are transformed into paddles. From Antartica they extend N. to the Cape of Good Hope, Australia, N. Zealand, Falklands and other Is. The largest are the King and Emperor P., *Aptenodytes.* Medium-sized species include the Adele, Gentoo and Ring P. *Pygoscelis.*

PENICILLIN
An antibiotic drug obtained by culture of the mould *Penicillin notatum.* It acts by preventing the germs increasing in number in the blood stream and so allows the body defences to kill off the invaders. In 1928 Sir A. Fleming noticed this effect in his laboratory.

PENINSULAR WAR
(1808-14) Fought against Fr. in the Iberian Peninsula by Gt. Brit., Spain and Portugal. The Allied forces were under the command of Sir Arthur Wellesley, afterwards Duke of Wellington, and outstanding victories were won at Vimiero, Albuera (1811), and Salamanca (1812).

PENN, Sir William
(1621-70) Brit. admiral. He fought on the Parl. side in the Civil War, but in 1660 accompanied Montagu to bring Charles II back. His son, **William** (1644-1718), was a prominent Quaker. He suffered imprisonment because of his faith. In 1681 granted territory in N. Amer. which became Pennsylvania.

PENNEY, Sir William
(1909-) Brit. physicist. Worked with the Min. of Home Security and Admiralty, 1940-4; Director Atomic Weapons Research Estab. Aldermaston, 1953-9; Chairman of the U.K. Atomic Energy Authority since 1963.

PENNINE CHAIN
Mt. range running from the Cheviots to the Vale of Trent, incl. the Peak tableland of Derbyshire. The chief heights are Cross Fell, 2,930 ft., Mickle Fell, 2,591 ft., Ingleborough, 2,373 ft. and Penyghent, 2,231 ft.

PENNSYLVANIA
N.E. state of the U.S.A. S. of New York State, traversed by the Allegheny Mts. and watered by the Delaware, Susquehanna and Allegheny. Agriculture, market gardening and forestry are important, but P. has rich deposits of minerals. P. is the greatest steel-producing state and Pittsburgh is the industrial centre. Harrisburg is the cap. but Philadelphia is the largest city. P. was first settled in the 17th cent. and is named after William Penn. It was one of the original 13 states, and now sends 27 representatives to Congress. Area: 45,330 sq.m. Pop. 11,794,000.

PENNYROYAL
Perennial labiate herb (*Mentha pulegium*), native of Europe and W. Asia. Abundant in Eng., its branched prostrate leafy stem, 12 in. long, bears dense whorls of hairy, tubular, lilac flowers.

PENNYWORT
(*Umbilicus pendulinus*) Species of the family, Crassulaceae, known also as navelwort. It has succulent leaves depressed in the centre and greenish yellow flowers borne on erect spikes.

PENRITH
Market town of Cumberland, Eng., 18 m. S.E. of Carlisle. There are ruins of a castle and a 14th cent. grammar school. Pop. 11,000.

PENSION
Retiring Allowance, or a grant made to an aged or needy person. A pension may be non-contributory, as those granted to members of the fighting forces and to civil servants after a certain term of service, or contributory, as when it is given as a superannuation provision. For the State Scheme introduced by the Nat. Ins. Act, 1946, *see* HEALTH INSURANCE; OLD AGE PENSION, etc. **Civil List Pensions** are granted by the Crown to necessitous persons who have attained distinction in art, literature or science, or to their dependents.

PENTATEUCH
Gk. ' five-volume book ', used since the 2nd cent. A.D. for the first 5 O.T. books, Genesis, Exodus, Leviticus, Numbers, Deuteronomy.

PENTECOST
Gk. ' fiftieth ', used in the Gk. N.T. to denote the Jewish harvest festival or feast of weeks. It acquired a supreme significance to the Christian Ch. because on that day, called in Eng. Whit-Sunday, the Holy Spirit descended on the apostles.

PENTLAND FIRTH
Strait off N. coast of Scot. between Caithness and the Orkneys. It connects the N. Sea with the Atlantic and is 14 m. long.

PEPPER
Perennial climbing shrub (*Piper nigrum*) typical of the pepper order, indigenous to the Malabar coast of India. Cultivated in Malaya, as well as the Philippines, W. Indies and other trop. lands, it produces a black or white spice derived from the dried fruits. *See* CAYENNE PEPPER.

PEPPERMINT
European perennial labiate herb (*Mentha piperita*). Growing wild in Brit. with creeping rootstock, opposite coarsely-toothed leaves and loosely-spiked flowers, it is cultivated in Brit., continental Europe and the U.S.A. for its pungent essential oil, which contains menthol.

PEPYS, Samuel
(1633-1703) Eng. diarist and Sec. of the Admiralty during the Stuart Restoration (1673-88). He secured a post in the Navy office and held several important public appointments. His shorthand diary (1659-69) gives a picture of his times and is a revelation of his character.

PERAK
[pē'-rā] State of the Fed. of Malaya, on the W. coast. Rubber and tin are the main products. The chief towns are Ipoh, in the centre of the rich tin-producing Kinta valley, and Kuala Kangsar. Area: 7,980 sq.m. Pop. 1,470,478.

PERCH
(*Perca*) The common perch (*P. fluviatilis*), seldom exceeding 3 lb., inhabits rivers and lakes in Brit. and elsewhere.

PERFUME
Substance which has a pleasant sweet-smelling odour, as in the case of certain gums, essential oils of plants, some animal products and synthetic compounds. For incense, odoriferous gums such as frankincense or olibanum, and gum benzoin are used, along with sandalwood. Musk, civet and ambergris are animal perfumes, and the essential oils include otto of roses, the oils of lavender, rosemary, etc.

PERICLES
(*c.* 495-429 B.C.) Athenian statesman. He distinguished himself as a gen. as well as a statesman. Under his admin. the naval power of Athens was built up, the city was developed and embellished, and under his patronage the sculptor Phidias worked. His policy during the Peloponnesian Wars was one of concentration in Athens.

PERIDOT
The transparent olive-green and bottle-green varieties of the mineral olivine, used as gemstones.

PERIM
Small Brit. Is. in the Straits of Bab-el-Mandeb at the S. end of the Red Sea, admin. as part of the State of Aden. Pop. 283.

PERISCOPE
Optical instrument used in trench warfare and in submarines for enabling an observer to see surrounding objects from a lower level.

PERITONEUM
Thin translucent membrane lining cavity of abdomen and covering coils of bowel and abdominal organs. In the female the Fallopian tubes pass through it. Inflammation is called *peritonitis.*

PERIWINKLE
(1) Genus of perennial evergreen herbs or trailing undershrubs of the dogbane order (*Vinca*), natives of temp. Europe, Asia and N. Africa. Long naturalised in Brit., the greater, *V. major*, and lesser *V. minor*, with bluish-purple, salver-shaped corollas, are cultivated in gardens. (2) Also, popularly, *Littorina littorea* the largest and most widely spread species of Sea Snail.

These gasteropod molluscs occur on every rocky shore in profusion.

PERLIS
State of the Fed. of Malaya in the N.W. on the borders of Siam. Rice is grown; rubber and tin are also produced. Kangar is the chief town. Area: 310 sq.m. Pop. 106,980.

PERMANGANATES
The salts derived from permanganic acid, the most important being *permanganate of potash* which is readily decomposed with evolution of oxygen when in contact with organic matter.

PERÓN, Juan Domingo
(1896-) Pres. of the Argentine Repub. 1946-55. Orig. a leader of the group of the pro-fascist army officers which seized power in 1943; elected Pres. June, 1946. After considerable unrest Perón was forced to resign and flee the country in 1955. In 1945 he mar. **Maria Eva Duarte** (1922-52).

PERSIA now **Iran**
Country of W. Asia, bounded on the N. by the Caspian Sea and on the S. by the Persian Gulf. It is mainly an arid tableland, encircled, except. in the E., by mt. ranges which rise to 18,600 ft. in the Elburz Mts. of the N. The E. and C. portion is an extensive salt desert. Persia is predominantly an agricultural country. Sheep and goats are reared and the wool used for the manufacture of carpets. Dates, cereals, fruit and cotton are grown in the S. and there are extensive forests in the N. and W. Chief export is crude oil. March, 1951, the oil industry was nationalised. The Brit. Govt. refused to recognise the position and the dispute reached internat. proportions. This was not settled until 1954 when a consortium of 8 Cos. was formed to handle Persian oil, and compensation of £25,000,000 was awarded to Anglo-Iranian Oil Co. Tehran in the N. is the cap.; other towns are Tabriz, Isfahan (the old caps.), Meshed and Shiraz. Bushire is the chief port. The people are mainly Shi'ah Moslems, but some are Sunnites, Zoroastrians, Jews, and Armenian and Nestorian Christians. Persia has a long and interesting hist. beginning with the Sumerians, continuing through the Medes to Alexander the Great, and the Arab, Turkish and Mongolian conquests: the periods of the two great warriors **Tamerlane** (1336-1404) and **Nadir Shah** (1668-1747), and the Safavid and Qajar dynasties, 1499-1736 and 1795-1925 respectively. In 1921, **Riza Khan Pahlavi**, a former army officer and P.M. seized power, was elected Shah, 1925. In 1941 following the German invasion of the U.S.S.R., Brit. and Soviet forces entered the country and expelled the Axis agents, who had been active there. Shah Riza, who had shown Axis sympathies, abdicated in favour of his son and left the country. His son, **Mohammed Riza**, the present Shah, had to flee the country in Aug. 1953, when a move to arrest the P.M., Dr. Moussadek, who was attempting to overthrow the régime, failed. A few days later the Royalist faction gained control by a *coup d'état*, arrested Moussadek, and recalled the Shah. In 1967, the Shah crowned himself and his wife, Queen Farah. His Heir, Prince Reza (b. 1960). Area: 636,000 sq.m. Pop. 26,284,000. **Persian Gulf.** Arm of the Ind. Ocean, lying between Persia and Arabia. The Shatt-el-Arab flows into the gulf, which is *c.* 550 m. long.

PERSIMMON
(or **Date-plum**) Deciduous tree of the ebony family (*Diospyros virginiana*). It produces a sweet, orange-yellow plum.

PERSPIRATION
Process by which water is excreted by the sweat glands on to the surface of the skin from which it evaporates. The heat required for the evaporation comes almost entirely from the body, and so perspiration is a means possessed by the body to control its temp.

PERTH
Cap. of W. Australia, 12 m. from its port, Fremantle. P. was founded 1829, but did not

develop until the discovery of gold there, 1891. Now a busy commercial centre. Pop. 431,000.

PERTHSHIRE
Midland county of Scot. In the N. are the Grampian Mts. rising to over 3,000 ft., *e.g.* Ben Lawers (3,984 ft.). The Ochils and Sidlaw Hills cross the county in the S.E. To the N. of these lies the fertile Vale of Strathmore. The chief rivers are the Tay and Forth; Katrine, Tay and Ericht are the largest lochs. Agriculture is important in the lowlands, esp. the Carse of Gowrie, and cattle are reared. Perth is the county town. With Kinross-shire, P. returns 2 members to Parl. Pop. 124,441. **Perth.** City and county town of Perthshire, on the Tay. It has large industries, of which dyeing is the chief. Perth was the cap. of Scot. until the 15th cent. Pop. 41,000.

PERU
[-roo′] Repub. of S. Amer. on the Pacific coast. It may be divided into 3 regions, the narrow coastal plain, the Andes and the Montana, comprising the E. slopes of the mts. and the Amazon lowlands. The W. Cordillera of the Andes is the highest, containing Huascaran (22,000 ft.), and from it many rivers flow into the Pacific. In the S. on the Bolivian border, is L. Titicaca, the largest lake in S. Amer. The climate varies according to altitude; along the coast it is semi-trop. Agriculture is of great importance, esp. in the coastal strip. Cotton, sugar, rice, wheat, vegetables and fruits are grown. Peru is rich in minerals. In addition, guano, a govt. monopoly, is worked on the Lobos and other Is. Industries have developed, such as textiles, flour milling, and meat packing. Lima is the cap. Sp. is the official language and R.C. is the state religion. Peru was the centre of the great Inca civilisation subjugated by the invading Sp. in the 16th cent. For nearly 300 years Peru was under Sp. rule: in 1821 its indep. was proclaimed, and a revolutionary war followed. According to the Constitution of 1933, the Pres. governs with the aid of a senate, and a chamber of deputies. Area: 496,093 sq.m. Pop. 12,385,000

PERUGINO
[-jē′-nō] (*c.* 1446-1524) Ital. painter. In 1480 Pope Sixtus IV commissioned him to work on the decoration of the Sistine Chapel. Raphael was among his pupils.

PERUVIAN BARK
The bark of various species of *Cinchona*, natives of Peru, Bolivia and Ecuador, from which quinine and allied alkaloids are extracted. Grown in Java, Sikkim, Ceylon, Jamaica and elsewhere.

PESTALOZZI, Johann Heinrich
(1746-1827) Swiss educ. reformer. Trying to apply Rousseau's theories, he evolved his own philosophy, that social reform can best be brought about by moral and intellectual training of the individual child. Froebel was one of his pupils, and Robert Owen was influenced by his ideas.

PÉTAIN, Henri Philippe
(1856-1951) Fr. soldier and politician. He rose to prominence by his defence of Verdun in 1916. In 1940 he was Vice-Premier and led the party who wished to capitulate to Germany after the collapse. On Reynaud's resignation he became P.M. and then Chief of the State in the Vichy Govt. of unoccupied Fr. He was captured and tried by the Fr. Govt. after the liberation, and sentenced to d. for treason, but sentence was commuted to life imprisonment.

PETER
One of the 12 apostles. Named Simon, son of Jonas, and orig. a Galilean fisherman, he was one of Christ's earliest disciples. His confession concerning the Messiahship of Jesus, the bestowal of his 2nd name Cephas or Peter, and the risen Lord's commission to 'feed My sheep', prepared him for a dominant place in the infant ch. He was traditionally martyred under Nero in Rome.

PETER I
(1672-1725) Tsar of Russia, known as **the Great.** He became tsar in 1682. He devoted himself to the reorganisation of his army and navy. In 1696 he went to war with Turkey, winning Azov, and in 1700 with Sweden acquiring the Baltic provs. and part of Finland after the victory at Poltava (1709). His wife eventually succeeded him as Catherine I. In 1703 he founded St. Petersburg.

PETERBOROUGH
City of Northants., on the Nene. Industries include the manufacture of agricultural implements. The cath. is largely Norman. Pop. 63,430.

PETERHEAD
Burgh and port of E. Aberdeenshire, on P. Bay. Besides the herring fishery, there is a granite polishing industry. Pop. 12,698.

PETRA
Ancient stronghold of Edom, Israel, on the Wadi Musa in a valley between the Dead Sea and the Gulf of Aqaba.

PETRARCH
(Francesco Petrarca) (1304-74) Ital. poet. Became an enthusiastic classical scholar, esp. of Cicero and Virgil. After he returned to Avignon (1327) he met Laura, who was to become his inspiration. Her identity is unknown. He is remembered for his lyrics, esp. sonnets.

PETREL
Oceanic birds of powerful flight with prominent tubular nostrils. The Fulmar (*Fulmarus glacialis*), 19 in long, is resident chiefly on N. coast of the Brit. Is. The Storm-petrel or Mother Carey's Chicken (*Hydrobates pelagicus*), 6 in. long, breeds locally on islets off W. and N. coasts of Brit. from the Shetlands to the Scillies.

PETRIE, Sir W. M. Flinders
(1853-1942) Eng. Egyptologist. His work included the unearthing of important papyri in the Fayum (1888-9), and the investigation of the city of Lacnish (1890) and Naucratis.

PETROLEUM
Mineral oil whose formation is believed to have begun as early as 400 million years ago and whose source material was marine animal and plant life remains that were buried, prior to decomposition, in the mud of ocean beds. Subsequent pressures converted the mud into rock, while chemical reaction converted the organic remains into crude oil. In certain places where non-porous rock halted the oil's percolation, the mineral accumulated to form an oilfield. Chief oil-producing areas of the world are N. Amer., the Caribbean, the M.E., the Caspian-Volga-Ural districts of Russia, Indonesia and Borneo. Major oil-producing countries include the U.S.A., Venezuela, Kuwait, Saudi Arabia, Iraq, Persia, Canada, and

Mexico. Total world crude oil production (including natural gasoline) in 1955 was 795,300,000 metric t., figures for 1962 showing that the 1,200 million t. mark was clearly exceeded, and the oil industry is planning to meet an eventual world oil demand in excess of 1,500 million metric t. annually. Sea transportation of oil has become one of the most important tasks of the world's mercantile marine: oil tankers now comprise over one-fifth of all merchant tonnage in service. Research and improved refining techniques have broadened the range of finished petroleum products now in everyday domestic and industrial use. U.K. annual refining capacity is now of the order of 30 million metric t. Of great importance to industry generally has been the post-war development of petroleum-chemical production. These chemicals enter into the manufacture of synthetic detergents, artificial textiles, plastics, insecticides, medicines, drugs and toilet requisites, kitchen-ware and motor tyres. Chief finished petroleum derivatives are gasolines (petrols), kerosenes (paraffins and vaporising oils), gas oils and diesel oils, lubricating oils, paraffin waxes, heavy fuel oils and bitumens.

PETTY SESSIONS
In Eng. the sitting of a court of summary jurisdiction. It consists of 2 or more justices of the peace or of a stipendiary magistrate. Such a court can deal summarily with numerous offences, but its powers of punishment are restricted.

PETUNIA
Genus of perennial ornamental herbs of the deadly nightshade family, chiefly S. Amer.

PEWTER
Alloy of lead and tin used for making flagons, jugs, plates, etc. The common metal consists of 80 % tin and 20 % lead, but the finest pewter is mostly tin.

PHARISEE
Religious party among the Jews originating in the Maccabean age. Their teaching upheld the precise observance of the Mosaic law, both canonical and traditional; they believed in the resurrection of the body and the existence of angels.

PHARMACY
Art of preparing drugs and medicines. Now has a scientific background as the action of most drugs has been investigated by experiment. The science of pharmacy is controlled by the Pharmaceutical Soc., estabd. in 1841, which is also responsible for the exam. and granting of a certificate, to all pharmaceutical chemists under the Pharmacy Acts.

PHAROS
Small Is. off the N. coast of Egypt, near Alexandria, on which stood the lighthouse, erected by Ptolemy I, 260 B.C. It was one of the Seven Wonders of the World.

PHARYNX
[fa'-rinks] Cavity at back of mouth extending above from back of nose to opening of the oesophagus and the larynx below. The eustachian tubes open into it.

PHEASANT
(*Phasianus*) Game bird, with short, slightly-curved bill, short wings and long tail. Introduced to Brit. from the Caucasus, the common *P. colchicus* is now distributed in all parts of the country except the Shetlands and Orkneys. They are preserved. The shooting season lasts from Oct. 1 to Feb. 1.

PHILADELPHIA
Largest city of Pennsylvania, U.S.A. on the Delaware, *c.* 100 m. from the sea. It is a great industrial and educ. centre. Founded by Wm. Penn, 1682. There is a univ. Industries include textiles, tanning, chemicals and food preparation. The 'Declaration of Indep.' was signed in P. 1776. Pop. 2,003,000.

PHILATELY
The study of postage stamps. This originated in Fr. in 1862, *i.e.* 22 yrs. after the introduction of the penny post in Brit. There is an abundance of lit. on stamp-collecting, and clubs or societies have been formed in most cities of the world.

PHILIP
Name of 6 kings of Fr. **Philip II** (Philip Augustus, 1165-1223) estabd. a strong monarchy. He took from the Eng. kings the greater part of their lands in Fr. and secured his possession by victory over the combined forces of John and the Emperor Otto IV at Bouvines in 1214. **Philip IV** (1268-1314) was involved in a struggle with Pope Boniface VIII, in which he gained the victory, again strengthening the authority of the Crown. In the reign of **Philip VI** (1328-50) the Hundred Years' War with Eng. began.

PHILIP
Name of 5 kings of Spain, of whom the most important was **Philip II** (1527-98) who succeeded his father, the Emperor Charles V (*q.v.*) in 1556. His 2nd wife was Mary, Queen of Eng. An ardent Catholic, his aim was to restore the supremacy of the Ch., overthrown by the Reformation. He carried on a long struggle with Elizabeth of Eng.

PHILIP, Prince
Duke of Edinburgh (1921-) B. Corfu. Great-great-grandson of Queen Victoria. Spent early life at home of his uncle, Earl Mountbatten, in Hants. Served with distinction in R.N. during World War II. Became Brit. citizen, Feb. 1947. Married H.R.H. Princess Elizabeth, Nov. 20, 1947, being previously created Duke of Edinburgh. A son, Charles, Prince of Wales, Duke of Cornwall, was b. 1948, and a daughter, Princess Anne, in 1950. A 2nd son, Prince Andrew, was b. 1960 and a 3rd, Prince Edward, in 1964. In Feb. 1957, the Queen conferred the title of Prince on the Duke of Edinburgh.

PHILIP of Macedon
(382-336 B.C.) King of Macedonia. He made himself ruler of the whole of Greece. Against his ambitious designs the Athenian orator, Demosthenes (*q.v.*), directed his famous *Philippic* orations. He laid the foundations for the conquests of his son, Alexander.

PHILIPPI
City of E. Macedonia founded by Philip of Macedon, where Octavian and Antony defeated Brutus and Cassius, 42 B.C. St. Paul founded a ch. at P. **Philippians, Epistle to the.** N.T. book comprising the last letter of St. Paul now extant. Its authenticity is fully estabd.

PHILIPPINES
Repub. of Asia, a group of Is. N.E. of Borneo between the S. China Sea and the Pacific. The largest Is. are Luzon, Mindanao, Samar, Negros, Palawan, Panay, Mindoro, Leyte, Cebu, Bohol and Masbate. Other Is. number more than 7,000. They are mountainous and there are several volcanoes. The principal exports are coconut products, sugar, lumber and timber, tobacco and Manila hemp. Manila, on the W. coast of Luzon, is the most important city. A new cap., Quezon City, has been built N.E. of Manila. The inhabitants, Filipinos, are predominantly Malay, with Sp. and Chinese mixture in some areas. The Is. were discovered, 1521, by the Portuguese (Magellan), and conquered by the Sp. in the later 16th cent. The Is. remained a Sp. possession until 1898, when they were ceded to the U.S.A. Invaded and overrun by the Japanese, 1942, the Philippines were subject to heavy fighting. Following the re-conquest by Amer. forces under Gen. MacArthur, an indep. repub. was estabd. 1946. Area: 115,000 sq.m. Pop. 34,656,000.

PHILISTINES
Ancient people occupying the Palestine coastlands S. of Joppa. Their confederacy came into conflict with Israel under Samson, Samuel and David.

PHLOX
Genus of herbs, mostly perennials, allied to Jacob's Ladder, of N. Amer. origin. Many garden forms have come from the perennial *P. paniculata* and *P. maculata*, and the dwarf moss-pink, *P. sabulata*.

PHNOM PENH
Cap. of Cambodia, on the Mekong, S. of Tonle Sap. Pop. 404,000.

PHOENICIA
[fi-nēsh'-] Strip of coastland between the mts. of Lebanon and the Medit. The Phoenicians founded Carthage (*q.v.*). Tyre and Sidon were their principal cities, and the Tyrian purple, a rich dye, one of their main objects of commerce. They penetrated as far as Cornwall and the Scilly Isles. Tyre fell to Alexander the Gt., 332 B.C., and ended Phoenician power. **Phoenician.** W. Semitic (Canaanite) language spoken in ancient Tyre and diffused along N. African coast. The Phoenician alphabet is the ancestor of those used by most Indo-European and Semitic languages.

PHOENIX
[fē'-] Fabulous bird. According to Ovid, when it has lived 500 years it builds a nest. This it ignites and so dies. From the body of the parent a young Phoenix issues forth.

PHONETICS
Study of speech-sounds. The human voice, inarticulate or articulate, results from the passage of air through the larynx. Modified by the vibrating vocal cords and the relation of the mouth-parts to the mouth and nose-cavities, the volume and resonance of the sounds produced are determined by physiological principles.

PHOSPHATES
Compounds of phosphoric acid and various bases. In commerce it means, chiefly, phosphates of lime, occurring as mineral deposits and used as fertiliser. The impure massive form of the mineral apatite known as phosphorite consists of calcium phosphate, fluoride and chloride, and is an important source of phosphates.

PHOSPHORESCENCE
Power possessed by certain animals, minerals and plants of emitting light. It occurs in the glow worm, firefly and many marine creatures, esp. the deep sea fauna. The phosphorescence of the sea is often due to swarms of minute protozoa (*Noctiluca*).

PHOSPHORUS
An element which forms 0·12 % of the earth's crust, chiefly in the form of phosphates and is an essential constituent of all living cells. It was discovered by Brandt in 1669 and occurs in 3 forms—yellow, red and black. Yellow phosphorus is the base of many rat poisons. Black phosphorus is obtained from the red variety under high pressure at a temp. of 200° C. During the last 40 years the industrial applications of phosphorous and its derivatives have greatly increased. Sp. gr. 1·8 (yellow), 2·2 (red), 2·8 (black). Chem. sym. P.

PHOTO-FINISH
Method of determining the winner of a race. On a racecourse a ray is projected between the judges' box and the finishing post, and received in a photo-electric cell. The interruption of the ray opens the shutter of a cine-camera and a photograph is taken.

PHOTOGRAPHY
Reproduction in permanent form of an optical image. Stages in the process are as follows:—(1) **Exposure:** a plate or film, coated with an emulsion of silver bromide in a gelatine base, is exposed in a camera to light constituting an image of the scene or object to be photographed. (2) **Development:** the plate is immersed in a solution of chems. which reduce to silver the bromide in regions where light has fallen, but have no effect on the rest of the emulsion. (3) **Fixing:** the negative is immersed in a solution of hypo (sodium thiosulphate) which removes, as soluble compounds, the unexposed silver bromide, leaving clear patches between the black silver areas. (4) **Printing:** the negative formed by these processes is now placed in contact with a sheet of paper bearing silver bromide emulsion and 1, 2 and 3 are repeated, producing finally (on the paper) a representation of the orig. scene. In *Colour photography* it is necessary to superpose 3 photographs, corresponding to the blue, green and red components of the orig. scene. This may be done by using a film which has the red, green and blue filters permanently attached to it as a regular grid of colour dots in front of the silver bromide layer. If the dots are very small, examination of the negative, or of a positive made from it on the same material, will show a coloured image.

PHYLLOXERA
Insects belonging to the family of Aphides or Plant-lice. *Phylloxera vastatrix*, a native of N. Amer., is the most dreaded insect pest of the grape vine. It appeared in Fr. *c.* 1860 and spread over Europe, ruining the vineyards. *See* APHIS.

PHYSICIAN
Person who specialises in the science of medicine and who, in addition to his ordinary degrees, has obtained the higher degree of Doctor of Medicine (M.D.), or the diploma of Membership of the Royal Coll. of Physicians (M.R.C.P.). Doctors who are accepted as eminent physicians are elected as Fellows of the Royal Coll. of Physicians (F.R.C.P.). The Coll. was estabd. in the 16th cent.

PHYSICS
(or **Natural Philosophy**) The science which deals with the study of natural phenomena, their causes and effects, and the laws and forces governing them. Its branches include heat, light, sound, at. physics, electricity, magnetism and parts of mechanics.

PHYSIOTHERAPY
The treatment of disease and injury by physical means instead of drugs or surgery. Methods employed include massage, exercise, and the application of heat rays and various forms of electricity.

PI
(π) A number which occurs in many branches of mathematics, *e.g.* it is the ratio of circumference to diameter of a circle. Value 3·1416.

PIANOFORTE
A keyboard instrument in which the strings are struck by felt-covered hammers when the keys are depressed. The pianoforte has 2, sometimes 3, pedals. The right pedal raises all the dampers, so allowing the sound to continue after the key is released. The left pedal shifts the keyboard action so that the hammers now strike 2 instead of 3 strings tuned to each note and, in lower part of the instrument, 1 instead of 2; this is the case on the horizontal (' grand ') piano; on an upright, the depression of this pedal brings the hammers closer to the strings.

PICARDY
Prov. of Fr. before the Rev. now comprising the dept. of Somme and portions of Aisne, Oise and Pas de Calais. Its principal city was Amiens, on the Somme. The prov. was annexed to the crown of Fr., 1477.

PICASSO
[pi-kà'-sō] (1881-) Name taken by **Pablo Ruiz,** Sp. painter. B. Malaga, he came to Paris and was assoc. with Braque (1906-12) becoming known for his cubist works. Later the abstract nature of his paintings aroused much controversy, which still continues.

PICCOLO
A small flute *c.* 2 ft. long with similar shape and technique to the ordinary flute, and a compass extending an octave higher.

PICTS
People occupying E. Scot. from pre-Rom. times onwards. First mentioned in Constantius Chlorus' campaigns, 296 and 306, their subsequent incursions S. of Hadrian's Wall helped the Scots to harass the Roms.

PIEDMONT
Region of N. Italy, bordered on the W. and N. by Fr. and Switzerland, with the Apennines to the S. The Po and its tributaries water the fertile land which produces fruit, olives, rice and wine. Turin is the cap. It became part of the Ital. kingdom in 1859.

PIETERMARITZBURG
[pēter-ma'-rits-] Cap. of Natal, S. Africa, 40 m. N.W. of the port of Durban. Founded by the Boers, 1839. Pop. 129,000.

PIG
Mammal belonging to the family Suidae, order Artiodactyla. The group comprises, besides the true pig, the Wart-hog, Bush Pig and Babirussa. Domesticated pigs are derived from the Wild Boar *Sus scrofa.* Principal Brit. breeds include the Large White, Landrace, Wessex, Essex, Tamworth, Large Black, Lincoln and Berkshire.

PIGEON
In general, all birds belonging to the order Columbiformes (true Pigeons, Doves and certain extinct birds, *e.g.* the Dodo). In its more limited meaning the name is given to members of the genus *Columba*, representing *c.* 70 species of Pigeons. Widely distributed over all but the coldest regions, the genus is particularly numerous in Australia, Malay Archipelago, New Guinea and adjacent Is. Brit. species include the Wood Pigeon, Stock Dove, Blue Rock and various domesticated birds.

PIKE
Freshwater fishes inhabiting N. temp. regions. The Common P., *Esox lucius*, of Brit. and Europe, prefers lakes and sluggish reaches. Its long compressed body, up to 30 lb. and more, is covered with small scales. It is an exceptionally voracious species.

PILATE, Pontius
Rom. procurator of Judaea, Samaria and Idumaea, under whom Christ suffered crucifixion. His attitude during the trial of Jesus has in all ages been variously interpreted.

PILCHARD
(*Sardina pilchardus*) An abundant marine food fish related to the herring, in the Medit. and Atlantic coasts of N. Europe to the Eng. Channel. The Sardines of the W. coast of Fr. 5-7½ in. long, are immature fish of the same stock.

PILEWORT *See* CELANDINE.

PILGRIM
One who, from religious motives, journeys to a place held sacred. Christian pilgrimage, esp. to Palestine, developed after Constantine. Medieval Europe also fostered visiting the tombs of saints, as those in Rome, St. James of Compostela, Becket at Canterbury; while curative pilgrimages are still made to Lourdes. **Pilgrim Fathers.** Specifically the first company of emigrants who sailed from Plymouth, Devon, in the *Mayflower*, reaching Plymouth Rock, Mass., 1620.

PILOT
One who navigates a ship or controls an aircraft. A licensed pilot is employed to navigate a ship into or out of a port or harbour, through a river, channel or road. When a vessel wishes to enter, *e.g.* a port, a recognised signal is made and a local pilot goes out to board the vessel for the purpose. The master or mate, however, may be a qualified pilot. Licensing is carried out by the local chief officer of customs. Pilots of aircraft are certificated after completing specified training and passing tests.

PILOT FISH
(*Naucrates ductor*) Sub-trop. marine fish of the Horse-mackerel family. About 12 in. long, spindle-shaped, steel-blue with dark vertical bars, it often accompanies sharks and ships.

PILSEN
or **Pizen.** City of Bohemia, Czechoslovakia, 59 m. S.W. of Prague; there are important breweries, and the Skoda works. Pop. 137,673.

PILTDOWN SKULL
Fossil parts of a skull found at Piltdown, Sussex, 1911-15. In 1953 experts asserted that a modern ape's jaw-bone had been fitted to the cranium and the whole skull was described as ' an elaborate and skilful hoax '.

PIMIENTO
(or **Jamaica Pepper**) Dried fruit of a W. Indian evergreen tree of the myrtle order (*Pimenta officinalis*), widely grown in Jamaica and C. Amer. Also called allspice.

PIMPERNEL
(*Anagallis*) Genus of herbs of the primrose family, natives of Europe, Asia and N. Africa. The wheel-shaped corollas of *A. arvensis*, scarlet in Brit., blue in continental Europe, expand in clear forenoons.

PINCHBECK
Reddish-yellow alloy of copper formerly much used in cheap jewellery, its composition varying from 80 to 93 % copper, with 20 to 7 % zinc.

PINDAR
Gk. lyric poet (522-442 B.C.) B. near Thebes, His *Epinicia* are divided into 4 books dealing respectively with the Olympian, Pythian, Nemean and Isthmian games.

PINE
(*Pinus*) Genus of large evergreen cone-bearing trees, widely distributed in the N. hemisphere. They have needle leaves clustered in two's to five's. The only species native to Brit. is *P. sylvestris*, 70-100 ft. high, popularly called the Scotch fir. It yields turpentine, resin and tar.

PINEAPPLE
S. Amer. perennial herb of the Bromeliaceae (*Ananas comosus*). The edible fruit consists of the flower-spike consolidated into a richly perfumed succulent mass. In Europe, it is raised in hothouses, while large canning and export industries have arisen in Singapore, the Azores, Fiji, Hawaii and Natal.

PINERO, Sir Arthur Wing
(1855-1934) Eng. dramatist. His best-known

works are *The Weaker Sex, The Second Mrs. Tanqueray* (1893), *His House in Order* (1906).

PINK
Cultivated forms of various species of *Dianthus*. The pinks of Eng. gardens derive from a Medit. form, *D. plumarius*. Some tufted rock-plants come from the native Cheddar and Maiden pinks.

PINKERTON, Allan
(1819-84) Amer. detective. He emigrated to Amer. in 1842, and opened a detective agency in Chicago in 1850. In 1861 he organised the U.S. Secret Service, and was Lincoln's guard.

PINKIE, Battle of
Fought Sept. 10, 1547, near Musselburgh. The purpose was the enforcement of a treaty of mar. between Edward VI and Mary, Queen of Scots. The Scots were defeated, but the mar. never took place.

PIPE-FISH
A family of long, slender, tuft-gilled fishes akin to the sea-horse, generally found off trop. and temp. sea-coasts. Five Brit. species include the Sea-adder, 2 ft. long, and the Worm Pipe-fish, 6 in. The commonest Brit. species is the Great Pipe-fish, *Syngnathus acus*, 18 in. long.

PIPIT
Widespread song-birds akin to the Wagtails (*Anthus*). Of Brit. species the commonest, the Meadow-pipit or Tit-lark, is partly resident, partly migratory. The Tree-p., a summer visitor, is called the Woodlark in Scot. The Rock P. is a coastal resident. The Water P. is a summer visitor.

PIRAEUS
[pī-rē′-ŭs] Seaport of Greece, on the Gulf of Aegina, 6 m. S.W. of Athens. It is an industrial town, with shipyards, iron foundries, and various factories. Pop. 183,000.

PIRANDELLO, Luigi
(1867-1936) Ital. dramatist and novelist. In 1910 he began to write plays, *e.g. Right You Are If You Think So* (1922), *Six Characters in Search of an Author* (1921), *Henry the Fourth* (1922). Nobel Prize in 1934.

PISA
[pē′-] City of Tuscany, Italy, on the Arno, 45 m. W. of Florence. Buildings include the Gothic cath. (1063-1118), and the Leaning Tower (1174-1350). Pop. 84,600.

PISANO
[pē-zä′-nō] **Andrea** (*c.* 1290-1349) Ital. sculptor and architect. He decorated, in relief, a set of bronze doors for the baptistry at Florence. **Niccola Pisano** (*c.* 1225-85), produced the sculptured pulpit in the baptistry of Pisa. **Giovanni**, his son (*c.* 1250-after 1314) built the tomb of Benedict XI at Perugia. **Vittore Pisano or Pisanello** (*c.* 1395-1455), was an artist and medallist.

PISCES
[pīs′-ēz] (Lat. *fishes*) Twelfth sign of the Zodiac, operative *c.* Feb. 19-Mar. 20. The constellation from which the sign takes its name is described as 2 fishes.

PISSARO, Camille
(1830-1903) Son of a Fr.-Jewish father and Creole mother. A leading figure in the Impressionist movement, generally linked with Monet and Sisley.

PISTACHIO NUT
Kernels of fruit borne by the *Pistachio verae*. They are bright-green in colour.

PISTOL
Small firearm invented at the beginning of the 16th cent. Introduction of the percussion cap for larger firearms in the early 19th cent. led to its use in pistols thus superseding the older methods.

PITCAIRN
Small Is. in the Pacific, equi-distant from Lima, Peru and Auckland, N.Z. Discovered in 1767, it was occupied by the mutineers of H.M.S. *Bounty* (1790). The colony is admin. by the Governor of Fiji through a council of elected and appointed members. Pop. *c.* 100.

PITCH
Black viscous substance obtained from coal tar as a residue after fractional distillation, and from the distillation of oils and coal tar. Mineral pitch is the name often given to natural asphalt or bitumen.

PITCHBLENDE
Mineral consisting of a mixture of uranium oxides with oxides, sulphides and arsenides of lead, iron and other metals. It is the chief ore of uranium and radium as well as various rare metals. Pitchblende occurs in small veins in Cornwall, Norway, Bohemia, and N. Amer.

PITCHER PLANT
Insectivorous plant, with pitcher-shaped leaf-organs: *e.g.* a large genus of shrubs, *Nepenthes*, found in E. trop. forests, and the Amer. side-saddle plant, *Sarracenia*.

PITLOCHRY
Village and resort of Perthshire, on the Tummel, 28 m. N.W. of Perth, near the Pass of Killiecrankie and Loch Tummel. A festival of drama is held annually.

PITMAN, Sir Isaac
(1813-97) Inventor of a system of shorthand.

PITT, William
(1759-1806) Brit. statesman. Elected M.P. for Appleby, 1781. In Dec. 1783 Pitt formed a govt. in which he had to face the opposition of a large parl. majority. In 1793, Brit. went to war with revolutionary Fr. Pitt built up the European coalitions against her and fought her in India, Amer. and the W. Indies. He suppressed the Irish Rebellion of 1798 and effected the union of the 2 parls. by the Act. of 1800. He had intended to include a measure for R.C. emancipation, but abandoned this and resigned office, 1801. Hearing the tidings of Napoleon's success at Austerlitz, Pitt, then in poor health, returned from Bath to London, where he d.

PITT-RIVERS, A. H. Lane-Fox
(1827-1900) Archaeologist. He studied archaeology and anthropology and organised scientific excavations of local antiquities in Wilts.

PITTSBURGH
[-burg] 2nd city of Pennsylvania, U.S.A., situated where the confluence of the Allegheny and Monongahela rivers forms the Ohio. It is one of the chief iron and steel centres of the world. Andrew Carnegie set up his iron and steel works, 1848. Pop. 604,000.

PITUITARY GLAND
[-tew′-it-] Small gland situated under surface of brain. It has secretions which control activity of sex glands, thyroid gland, development of the skeleton, and control blood pressure.

PIUS
Name of 12 Popes. **Pius XI**, b. 1875, was chosen Pope in 1922, on the d. of Benedict XV. The notable achievement of his pontificate was the re-establishment of the temporal power of the papacy in 1929. **Pius XII** (Eugenio Pacelli), b. 1876. Crowned Pope, 1939. Before and during World War II he was untiring in his efforts for peace, and protested strongly against anti-Semitism. A redoubtable opponent of atheistic communism. D. 1958.

PIZARRO, Francisco
[pi-thä′-rō, -sä-rō] (*c.* 1478-1541) Sp. conqueror of Peru. The conquest of Mexico (1520) aroused in P. the desire to secure Peru. He made a voyage there in 1526, but it was not till 6 years

Alice Springs

Mt. Cook

AUSTRALIA and NEW ZEALAND

Barrier Reef near Hannibal Island

Sheep in New South Wales

South Pole: Ross Ice Sheet

THE PACIFIC OCEAN

New Guinea: natives on the way to market

Waikiki, Hawaii

later that he landed at Tumbez. Cuzco was taken in 1533 and on Jan. 6, 1535, Pizarro founded the city of Lima as the new cap.

PLAGUE
Specific infective disease caused by *bacillus pestis* carried by rat fleas and characterised by sudden onset with headache, backache, high fever, enlarged glands, haemorrhages from skin, lungs and stomach. A severe and prolonged illness with high mortality. Cycles of the disease include the famous Black Death epidemic which occurred in the 14th cent.

PLAICE
(*Pleuronectes platessa*) Marine food fish inhabiting N. European waters, from Iceland to S. of Brit. Allied to the Dab and Flounder, but orange-spotted, it may attain 8-10 lb., measuring 30 in. or more. *See* FLAT FISH.

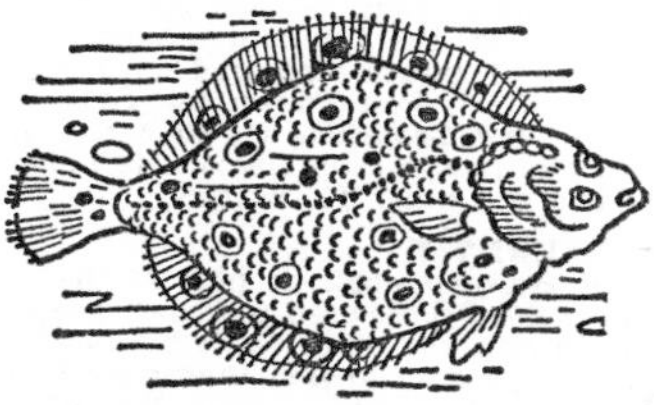

PLANCK, Max
(1858-1947) German physicist. Awarded Nobel prize for physics for his Law of Radiation, 1918; F.R.S. 1926; from 1930 Pres. of Kaiser Wilhelm Institute. Achieved universal fame as originator of Quantum Theory which laid the foundations of the modern theory of atomic processes. Unlike the charge of the electron, the unit of radiant energy is different for every wavelength on which it is emitted, Planck worked out these fundamental new relationships in terms of a universal constant, now called Planck's Constant.

PLANE
Genus of large trees (*Platanus*), natives of N. temp. regions. They have large deciduous palm-shaped leaves and smooth, whitish bark, scaling off annually in patches. The W. plane or buttonwood, N. Amer's. tallest deciduous forest-tree, reached Stuart Eng. The London Plane, *P. acerifolia*, is a hybridised derivative.

PLANET *See* SOLAR SYSTEM.

PLANKTON
Microscopic floating animal and plant life of the sea, rivers and lakes. In temp. seas there are commonly 2 seasonal outbursts.

PLANTAGENET
Surname applied to the Angevin kings of Eng. The house included Henry II, Richard I, John, Henry III, Edward I, II, III, Richard II, Henry IV, V, VI, Edward IV, V and Richard III. At the d. of Richard II the house of Plantagenet became divided into the branches of Lancaster and York, so that the line may be regarded as ending with his d. in 1399. The name is derived from the *planta genista*, or broom plant, the badge of the house.

PLANTAIN
[-tin] (*Plantago*) Genus of herbs, mostly noxious weeds with brownish-white flowers, distributed over all temp. regions. There are 5 Brit. species. Water plantains (*Alisma*) grow in marshland.

PLASTER
Cementing material used for making casts of objects and for covering walls and other parts of buildings with a protective and binding layer. For internal walls, ceilings, mouldings, etc., plaster of Paris and various modifications are used, the aim being to obtain a plaster whose setting is slow enough to be easily worked and which will take paint quickly. **Plaster of Paris.** Form of cement composed of calcined gypsum or sulphate of lime. The gypsum, when burnt at a moderate temp. forms a cement which, on the addition of water rapidly sets or solidifies.

PLASTICS
A group of materials. There are 2 principal divisions (1) *thermoplastic materials,* which can be softened by heating and remoulded repeatedly; (2) *thermosetting plastics,* which undergo chem. changes during the heating and forming process and cannot be resoftened by heating. This group includes bakelite. Thermoplastics are of 2 main types: (1) the *cellulose derivatives,* including celluloid, cellulose acetate, cellophane and rayon (artificial silk); (2) the *polymers,* consisting of organic substances with molecules in the form of long chains which are formed by the repetition of smaller groups of atoms. Among these are polystyrene, polyethylene (or polythene), polyvinyl chloride and methyl methacrylate (perspex).

PLATINUM
White metal, widely used for electrical contacts where its freedom from corrosion is important. It was discovered by Wood in 1741.

PLATO
(427-347 B.C.) Gk. philosopher. He came under the influence of Socrates and *c.* 387 founded an institute for the study of philosophy. His works have come down to us in the form of dramatic dialogues in which the chief speaker is Socrates, into whose mouth Plato put theories developed after the former's d. Of these dialogues, 35 remain, the most important being the *Gorgias*, the *Protagoras*, the *Phaedo*, the *Symposium*, the *Laws* and the *Republic*. His philosophy is social, and according to him, justice and the good can only be completely attained in the social sphere. It was the source of that great body of **Platonism,** and profoundly influenced Christian thought.

PLATYPUS
Generic name of the egg-laying 'Water-mole' of Australia and Tasmania. It was changed to *Ornithorhynchus* but is still popularly called the Duck-billed Platypus. *See* DUCKBILL.

PLAUTUS, Titus Maccius
(251-184 B.C.) Rom. comic poet. He is said to have been responsible for 130 comedies. They are brisk adaptions from Gk. originals 'New Comedy' (Menander); *Amphitruo, Trinummus, Miles, Mercator, Mostellaria, Menacchmi.*

PLEIADES
[plī-ă-dēz] Conspicuous group of stars in the shoulder of the constellation of Taurus the Bull. The pleiades form an open cluster of over 2,000 stars.

PLEURISY
[ploo'-] Inflammation of pleura or serous membrane lining lung or pleural cavity. Usually occurs in acute form and often assoc. with pneumonia.

PLIMSOLL, Samuel
(1824-98) Brit. politician. In 1868 he became M.P. for Derby and endeavoured to prevent the use of overladen and unseaworthy ships. The Merchant Shipping Act, 1878, made compulsory the affixing to a Brit.-owned merchant vessel a maximum load line, the **Plimsoll Mark.**

PLINY
(The Elder, 23-79) Rom. writer. (**Gaius Plinius Secundus**). He d. in the eruption of Vesuvius which buried Herculaneum and Pompeii. His *Natural History* deals also with such arts as sculpture, painting, etc. **Pliny the Younger** (62-113) (**Gaius Plinius Caecilius Secundus**). Nephew and adopted son of Pliny the Elder. He wrote a panegyric on the Emperor Trajan. His fame rests on his *Letters*.

PLOTINUS
(*c.* 203-270) Founder of the Neo-Platonic School of Philosophy. B. in Egypt, prob. of Rom. descent, he studied Indian and Persian philosophy in the E. His theories are Platonic in their origin but they suggest a way of mystical escape from the concrete world rather than a fulfilment of what is best in it.

PLOUGH
Agricultural implement used for turning over the soil, thereby loosening and pulverising it, and exposing the new surface to the air in preparation for sowing seed.

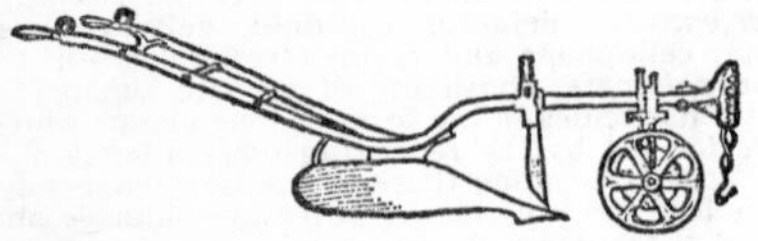

PLOVER
[pluv'-er] Widely-distributed family of birds which are typically Waders. Brit. species include the Lapwing, Ringed Plover, Golden Plover, Dotterel, Avocet, Turnstone, Stilt, Oyster Catcher, etc.

PLUM
Fruit of the cultivated plum-tree. Derived from one or more species of *Prunus*, of the Rosaceae, the main European varieties originated from the wild plum, *P. domestica*, including the Victoria, Magnum Bonum and Greengage. A Japanese species furnished not only Japanese and Californian but also S. African varieties. *See* GREENGAGE; PRUNE.

PLUTARCH
(46-120) Gk. biographer. After travels in Greece and Egypt, he opened a school at Rome. He is notable for his parallel biogs. of eminent Gks. and Roms. Sir T. North's tr. (1579-95) was popular in Elizabethan Eng. and is the source of Shakespeare's Rom. plays.

PLUTO
The 9th known planet in order of distance from the sun (*c.* 3,670,000,000 m.); it was discovered in 1930 at Lowell Observatory, Arizona. The diameter of the planet is *c.* 3,650 m. and it takes *c.* 247 yrs. 255 days to make one revolution round the sun.

PLUTONIUM
One of the elements made for the first time during work on the atomic bomb. If uranium 238 is bombarded by neutrons it changes into uranium 239, and then into unstable neptunium 239, and finally into plutonium 239. *See* NUCLEAR POWER, NEUTRON.

PLYMOUTH
[plim'-ŭth] City, county borough and seaport of S. Devon, on P. Sound at the mouth of the Plym. It includes Devonport and Stonehouse, and is an important port. Devonport is a naval station, with dockyards and barracks. There is a large fishing industry. The Pilgrim Fathers sailed from P. in the *Mayflower* in the 17th cent. It returns 2 members to Parl. Pop. 209,900.

PLYMOUTH
Seaport of Mass. U.S.A., S.E. of Boston, where the Pilgrim Fathers landed from the *Mayflower* (*q.v.*), 1620.

PLYMOUTH BRETHREN
Evangelical Christian community formed by John Nelson Darby at Plymouth in 1830. He assoc. in Dublin with certain persons calling themselves 'Brethren'. Removing to Plymouth he estabd. similar self-contained communities, who commemorate the Lord's Supper every Sun, but reject all eccles. organisation.

PLYWOOD
Name given to thin boards made of layers of wood, cemented or glued together under pressure. Plywood is less liable to warp or split than ordinary boards.

PNEUMONIA
[new-] Inflammation of lung substance by bacteria usually pneumococcus, tuberculosis, streptococcus or staphylococcus. Acute lobar pneumonia begins with rigor and is characterised by cough, fever, bloodstained spit and breathlessness.

PO
Longest river in Italy, which rises on Monte Viso, near the Fr. border, and flows across the Lombardy Plain, entering the Adriatic Sea by a large delta.

POE, Edgar Allan
(1809-49) Amer. writer. He wrote for Baltimore journals and ed. the *Southern Literary Messenger*. Vols. of poems appeared in 1827, 1829 and 1831. He is best known for *Tales of the Arabesque and Grotesque* (1840) and *Tales of Mystery and Imagination* (1845). He influenced Baudelaire and other Fr. writers.

POET LAUREATE
Office of crowned poet, or poet at the Court. The Gks. and Roms. used to crown poets with laurel. In Eng. the office really began with the giving of a pension to Ben Jonson by James I. Dryden was the first to have the title. In modern times the laureateship has been held by Wordsworth, Tennyson, Robert Bridges, and C. Day Lewis.

POINCARÉ, Jules Henri
[pwa(ng)-kà-rā] (1854-1912) Apptd. Prof. of mathematical physics at the Sorbonne, 1886, and of celestial mechanics, 1896. In 1889 he won the prize offered by the King of Sweden with a memoir on the problem of three bodies. His researches covered practically the whole range of mathematics and mathematical physics and he was equally distinguished as a philosopher.

POINCARÉ, Raymond Nicolas Landry
(1860-1934) Fr. statesman. Entered Chamber of Deputies, 1887. Premier and Min. of Foreign Affairs, 1912, resigning on his election as Pres. of the Repub. 1913. His term of office ended in 1920. He brought about the stabilisation of the franc, 1928, and resigned the premiership, 1929.

POINTER
Sporting dog introduced from 17th-cent. Spain. The Eng. Pointer is close-haired, 24 in. high, and usually parti-coloured. It hunts by body-scent, and when it scents game stands stiffly with muzzle and tail outstretched, and one foot raised.

POISON
An agent which will produce a morbid, nervous and dangerous or deadly effect on living tissue. Poisons may be *corrosive, irritant, hypnotic* or *metabolic*. The latter is produced in the body by a faulty utilisation by tissues of products of catabolism. Corrosive poisons cause burning of the tissues and include caustics and acids. Hypnotic poisons include morphia and barbitone. Irritant poisons cause acute inflammation of body tissues and include arsenic and certain vegetable poisons. The use of such substances in med. is controlled by the Dangerous Drugs Act, 1932, by the Pharmacy and Poisons Act, 1933, and the Poisons Rules. *See* DRUG.

POISON GASES
The poisonous gases may be divided into the following classes: (1) *tear gases*, which are poisonous only in large amounts. (2) *nose irritants.* (3) *lung irritants*, including Chlorine and Phosgene. (4) *blister gases*, including Mustard Gas and Lewisite. Chlorine, Phosgene and

blister gases were employed as lethal or incapacitating agents in World War I, but not in World War II. In the course of World War II, the Germans experimented with two gases, Sarin and Soman, which paralyse the nervous system of the individual, thus rendering him incapable of defensive action.

POITIERS
[pwȧ-tyā′] Cap. of Vienne dept. W. Fr., *c.* 60 m. S. of Tours. Its trade, apart from wine, is mainly agricultural. Founded in pre-Rom. times, P. fell to the Franks, 507; an Eng. possession, 1356-73. There are some Rom. remains, a cath. and a univ., founded 1431. Pop. 66,222. **Poitiers, Battle of.** Edward the Black Prince defeated the Fr. under King John II, in 1356.

POKER
Card game played for money stakes. Introduced into Amer. from Fr. *c.* 1830, it became the now prevalent draw-poker, using 52 cards, *c.* 1860.

POLAND
Repub. of C. Europe, bounded by E. Germany, Czechoslovakia and the U.S.S.R., with a coastline on the Baltic. Most of the land is gently undulating. In the S. are the Carpathian and Sudeten ranges. The chief rivers are the Vistula, Bug, Oder and Neisse. Before World War II P. was primarily an agricultural country, but now industries are equally important. There are extensive forests and important mineral resources. Textiles, iron and steel goods, chemicals and glass are the chief manufactures. Warsaw, on the Vistula, is the cap. Szczecin, Gdansk (Danzig) and Gdynia are the chief ports. Area: *c.* 120,362 sq.m. Pop. 31,994,000. The state of P. was formed *c.* the 6th cent. Sobieski, elected king, 1674, is famous for his relief of Vienna (1683), besieged by the Turks. The partitions of 1772, 1793 and 1795 divided P. between Aust., Russ., and Pruss. Stanislaus, the last king, abdicated at Grodno, 1795. During World War I, P. was seized by Aust.-German forces and indep. proclaimed 1916. A repub. was proclaimed at Warsaw, 1918, and its indep. confirmed by the Peace Treaty of 1919. Pilsudski became first pres. and Paderewski premier. Threatened by Russ. invasion, 1921, the Soviet armies were repulsed. In 1926, Pilsudski instituted a dictatorship, which lasted until the outbreak of World War II, 1939. Russ. and German forces occupied the country. The Germans terrorised the pop. Following the liberation of P. by the Russ. armies in 1945, provisional frontiers were drawn up at Potsdam. Poland gained a portion of Germany, and most of E. Prussia, losing half of Galicia and White Russia to the U.S.S.R. The govt., dominated by the Communist Party, consists of a Diet, a Council of State and a Cabinet. In Oct. 1956, a surge of anti-Russian feeling in the country resulted in the removal from power of the Russian-appointed C.-in-C. and the restoration of Wladyslaw Gomulka to the position of first Sec. of the Polish Communist Party.

POLE
In geog. a term applied to the ends of the earth's axis. The magnetic poles are the ends of the earth's axis regarded as a great magnet, and lie near the poles of rotation. **Pole Star.** Nearest conspicuous star to the N. celestial pole. It is the second magnitude star *alpha* in the 'Little Bear' constellation. The hindmost wheels of Charles's Wain, the *alpha* and *beta* of the 'Great Bear' are the pointers; a line through them prolonged 4½ times northwards indicates its whereabouts.

POLECAT
(*Putorius putorius* or *P. foetidus*) Carnivorous mammal of the Weasel family, native to Europe and found in Brit. A pouch under the tail contains a fetid-smelling yellowish substance. It is 18 in. long. It usually breeds in rabbit-burrows. Furriers call the fur Fitch or Fitchet.

POLICE
A civil force organised by Sir Robert Peel, while P.M. 1841-6, for prevention and detection of crime, and from whom the popular names 'Bobbies' or 'Peelers' are derived. Police forces are now controlled by Local Authorities throughout the U.K. and N. Ireland with overall control by the Home Sec., Sec. of State for Scot., and N. Ireland Min. of Home Affairs respectively. By virtue of the Police Act of 1919 and amendments, conditions of service and ranks are standardised. A specially trained Detective Branch is maintained by all police forces and the Women's Police Dept. deals with crimes involving women and young girls.

POLICE COURT
Court of summary jurisdiction, now called Magistrates' Courts (except in London). In London they are presided over by a stipendiary (paid) magistrate, as in certain other towns. Generally, however, it is Justices of the Peace (unpaid) who act as judges. *See* MAGISTRATE.

POLIOMYELITIS
[-mī-i-lī′-] (or **Infantile Paralysis**) Acute infective disease most frequently affecting children. Caused most probably by a virus affecting the brain and spinal cord and characterised by fever, headache, pain in limbs, vomiting and later paralysis. In 1955-6 a most effective anti-poliomyelitis vaccination was introduced.

POLL
Voting or taking of votes at an election, applied also to the register of those entitled to vote.

POLL TAX
Tax levied on every head. In ancient Athens a poll tax was paid by resident aliens and others. Charles II imposed a capitation tax, all subjects being assessed by rank. In U.S.A. the term means a tax to be paid before one can vote. It is also imposed on black people in S. Africa.

POLLACK
(*Gadus poliachius*) A marine food fish belonging to the same genus as Cod. Akin to the Coalfish, it is taken in the Channel and on Scot. and Irish coasts up to 25 lb.

POLLEN
Fine dust produced in the anthers of flowering plants. Each grain contains a male element whose union with the female element in an ovule originates the embryo constituting the seed.

POLO
Ball game played on horseback, mallets being used to hit a ball. Of Persian origin, the game has long been played in E. countries. In India it became popular among Eng. Army officers and residents, and was brought to Eng. in 1869. The game is played on turf, the ground being 300 yds. by 160 yds. The goals are 250 yds. apart.

POLO, Marco
(1254-1324) Ital. traveller. In 1271, accompanied his father on a journey to the court of Kublai. Marco was given a governorship by the Khan and sent on missions to India and China.

POLYANDRY
Plurality of husbands. There are cases among the S. Amer. Ind., in N. Amer. among the Eskimos, in the Marshall Is. and Marquesas, in Tibet and S. India.

POLYANTHUS
Hardy perennial herb of the primrose family with an umbel of numerous flowers on a leafless stem. *See* NARCISSUS.

POLYGAMY
Term denoting plurality of consorts. Polygamy is most common among primitive nomadic peoples. It was regulated among the early Semites and permitted in Aryan India and was retained by Mohammedanism. Mormon polygamy ceased in 1890.

POLYGON
[pol′-i-gon] A plane figure having more than 4 sides. It is regular when all of its sides and all of its angles are equal. Regular polygons are named according to the number of sides from 5 to 12 as follows: *pentagon, hexagon, heptagon, octagon, nonagon, decagon, undecagon, duodecagon.*

POLYNESIA
One of the 3 divisions of Oceania. It includes the Samoan, Fiji, Hawaiian and Marquesas Is. and the Society, Tuamotu, Phoenix, Tokelau and Manahiki groups. Polynesians are brown-skinned, tall and well developed.

POLYPORUS
Large widely-distributed genus of fungi found on living trees or timber.

POLYPUS
[pol′-i-pus] Cyst-like formation of mucous membrane. Most commonly found in nostrils, ears, bowel and bladder.

POLYTHEISM
Doctrine of a plurality of divine beings, superior to man. Conceived as possessing animal, human or superhuman forms and attributes, they represent a system of worship observable in ancient civilisations and in modern India.

POMEGRANATE
[pom′-gran-it] Tree (*Punica granatum*), long naturalised in the Medit. and other sub-trop. regions. The fruit, containing pulp-covered seeds, has a golden-red rind containing an astringent used in pharmacy, dyeing and tanning.

POMERANIA
District of N. Germany, on the Baltic coast. Before World War II, P. covered a much larger area, extending E. almost to Gdansk (Danzig). Now all P. to the E. of the Oder is Polish.

POMERANIAN DOG
Called in Germany the Spitz, akin to the Eskimo and other Arctic breeds, it is strongly-built, scaling 20 lb. and more, long-haired, with sharply-pointed muzzle and bushy, back-curled tail. Miniature breed is shown below.

POMPADOUR, Marquise de
Jeanne Antoinette Poisson (1721-64) Favourite of Louis XV of Fr. She had great influence over the king, and brought about the alliance with Austria in the Seven Years' War.

POMPEII
[pom-pā′-ē] Ancient ruined city of Italy, at the foot of Mt. Vesuvius, 13 m. S.E. of Naples. In A.D. 79 Pompeii was buried by a great eruption of the volcano and has since been excavated.

POMPEY, Gnaeus
(106-48 B.C.) Rom. triumvir. His E. campaign (65-62 B.C.) resulted in a great extension of Rom. sovereignty. As Caesar's influence increased, Pompey's declined, and when the inevitable civil war broke out, Pompey was defeated at Pharsalus in Greece (48 B.C.), and afterwards murdered in Egypt.

POMPIDOU, Georges Jean Raymond
(1911-) Fr. statesman. Pres. (1969-) As P.M. (1962-8) supported de Gaulle and elected Pres. after his resignation.

PONTEFRACT
or **Pomfret.** Borough and market town of the W. Riding, Yorks., 13 m. S.E. of Leeds, noted for its liquorice cakes. It returns 1 member to Parl. Pop. 27,960.

PONY
A small horse. Technically those ranging from 13 hands high downwards are called ponies, those from 13 to 13·3 hands high, galloways and those above, horses. In popular usage the dividing line between ponies and horses is 14 hands; on the N. Amer. prairies hardy mustangs, broken in by Indians, are called ponies. The rough-coated ponies bred in N.W. Europe are of the domesticated Celtic stock.

POODLE
Breed of dog of Fr. origin. Weight up to 45 lb.; height up to 18 in. at shoulders. Miniature poodles are not more than 15 in. high at shoulders; toy poodles weigh 4-5 lb.

POOLE
Borough and seaport of Dorset, on a peninsula in P. Harbour, 5 m. W. of Bournemouth. Pottery is made. P. returns 1 member to Parl. Pop. 92,920.

POOR LAWS
Local provision in Brit. for the indigent, dates from an enactment of Elizabeth, 1601. A **Poor-Law Board** was apptd. in 1849. The duties were taken over in 1871 by local govt. boards, and in 1919 the Min. of Health came into existence, and took over the admin. In 1948 an Act was passed abolishing the last vestiges of the Poor Law.

POPE, The
Head of the R.C. Ch. The title was used generally for bishops until 1073, when it became restricted to bishops of Rome. A new pope is elected on the d. of the reigning pontiff, by the Coll. of Cardinals. He has supreme authority in matters of faith, and his infallibility when speaking, *ex cathedra*, on matters of faith and morals was declared by a Vatican council in 1870. *See* PAPACY; VATICAN.

POPE, Alexander
(1688-1744) Eng. poet. His *Essay on Criticism* (1711), the mock heroic *Rape of the Lock* (1712, 14), brought him into contact with Gay, Arbuthnot, Addison and Swift. His best work is the satiric poetry of his later years: *The Dunciad* (1728-43), *Epistle to Dr. Arbuthnot, Moral Essays* (1731-5), *Imitations of Horace* (1731-8), *The Essay on Man* (1733).

POPERINGHE
Town of Belg. in W. Flanders, 6 m. W. of Ypres. *See* TOC H.

POPISH PLOT *See* OATES, TITUS.

POPLAR
(*Populus*) Genus of trees of the willow family. Their leaves are usually preceded by male and female flowers in separate catkins. Black, white, grey Lombardy and aspen, besides balsam and cottonwood, are in cultivation. *See* LOMBARDY POPLAR.

POPPY
(*Papaver*) Large genus of herbs. Their milky sap, with narcotic properties, is absent from the seeds, which yield an edible oil. The most important economically is the annual opium poppy.

POPULATION
Term applied to the number of living human inhabitants of the world. It is almost impossible to arrive at an accurate estimate. The pop. of the whole world has been estimated at over 3,069,000,000, giving a density of over 55

per sq.m. Of the continents, Europe has the greatest density, with Asia next. Two types of region favour density of pop. One is the moist, warm climate, where rice, the cheapest form of food, can be produced in large quantities, as in China and Japan. The other is in temp. climates, on the great coal and mineral fields, as in W. Europe and U.S.A. Numerically, the largest pops. are found in China, India and Africa. The pop. of China has been put at over 700,000,000.

PORCUPINE
Widespread rodents. The Porcupine of S. Europe and N. Africa, *Hystrix cristata*, 27 in. long, has long, black-and-white quills or spines.

PORCUPINE GRASS
(1) Spinifex, a coarse grass of various species of *Triodia*, growing in inner Australia. The stiff, spiny leaves, 3-4 ft. high, cause much suffering to man and beast. (2) *Stipa spartea*, a grass abounding in some Amer. prairies. The awns become fixed in sheep's skin, eventually causing d.

PORK
Uncured flesh of swine as food. The flesh of the pig is forbidden to Jews and Mohammedans, being regarded as unclean. *See* PIG.

PORPHYRY
[por'-fer-i] Geological term for various igneous rocks, with large, conspicuous crystals in a fine-grained ground mass. Many are used as ornamental stones.

PORPOISE
(*Phocaena*) Cetacean mammal of the N. seas. The Common P., *P. communis*, 5 ft. long, abounds off Brit. coasts. It is killed mainly for its oils.

PORT ARTHUR
Grain port of Ontario, Canada, on the N. shore of L. Superior. Now, with Port William, known as **Thunder Bay**. Comb. Pop. 106,000.

PORT-AU-PRINCE
[-ō-prins] Seaport and cap. of Haiti, W. Indies. It has a good harbour, and exports coffee and cacao. Pop. 250,000.

PORT ELIZABETH
Seaport of Cape Prov. S. Africa, on Algoa Bay, 410 m. E. of Cape Town. Wool and fruit are exported. Pop. 274,180.

PORT LOUIS
or **Isle of France.** Seaport and cap. of the Is. of Mauritius, on the N.W. coast. Pop. 92,400.

PORT MORESBY
Seaport of Papua, and the admin. centre of Papua and New Guinea, on the S.E. coast of the Is. Pop. *c.* 3,000.

PORT OF SPAIN
Cap. and seaport of Trinidad in the W. Indies, on the W. coast. Pop. 93,954.

PORT SAID
[sīd] Seaport of Egypt at the N. end of the Suez Canal. Founded, 1859, it is now an important fuelling station with modern dockyard facilities at Port Fuad. Occupied by Brit. and Fr. forces, Nov. 1956, following the Israel attack on Egypt. Pop. 244,000.

PORT SUNLIGHT
Town of Cheshire, 3 m. S.E. of Birkenhead, founded in 1888 by Lord Leverhulme.

PORT TALBOT
Borough and seaport of Glamorganshire, on Swansea Bay, 11 m. S.E. of Swansea. There are docks and vast steel works. Pop. 51,150.

PORT WINE
Rich red wine from grapes grown in the Douro Valley, Portugal, and shipped from Oporto. Its alcoholic content is 17-25 %. Tawny port usually comprises blends of different years, kept in cask in Oporto until shipped.

PORTAL, Viscount
Charles Frederick Algernon, of Hungerford (1893-) Marshal of the R.A.F. Became observer in R.F.C. 1915; graduated as pilot, 1916. Commanded No. 7 (Bomber) Squadron in 1927 and Brit. Forces in Aden, 1934-5. Air Marshal, 1939; Air Member for Personnel on Air Council, 1939-40. A.O.C.-in-C. Bomber Command, Mar.-Oct. 1940; Chief of the Air Staff, 1940-5.

PORTLAND
Peninsula of Dorset, called the Is. of P. At its S. extremity is Portland Bill, with a lighthouse.

PORTLAND
(1) Largest city of Oregon, U.S.A. on the Willamette. It has a large trade in wheat and lumber. Pop. 375,200. (2) Largest town of Maine, U.S.A. on Caxo Bay. Pop. 64,400.

PORTREE
Chief town of Skye, on P. bay, 120 m. by sea from Oban. Pop. 2,100.

PORTRUSH
Urban district and seaport of Antrim, N. Ireland, 67 m. N.W. of Belfast; tourist resort. The Giant's Causeway is 7 m. away. Pop. 4,300.

PORTSMOUTH
County borough, seaport and naval station of Hants. on the peninsula of Portsea Is., 27 m. S.E. of Southampton. Ferries link P. with the Is. of Wight. The premier Brit. naval base, P. has extensive dry docks and building slips. P. returns 3 members to Parl. Pop. 226,670.

PORTUGAL
Repub. of S.W. Europe, in the Iberian peninsula, bounded S. and W. by the Atlantic, and N. and E. by Sp. The chief rivers are the Minho, Guadiana, Douro and Tagus. N. of the Douro, the Cantabrian Mts. run to the coast near Oporto. The climate is Medit. type, with heavy winter rainfall. Agriculture is important, the chief crops being wheat, maize, flax, vines. olives and citrus fruits. There are extensive forests and lumbering is an important industry. Textiles and metal goods are manufactured. Fishing is carried on round the coast, sardines being the chief fish for export. Lisbon is the cap.; other towns are Oporto, Setubal, Funchal (Madeira), Coimbra. From the 11th cent. until 1910 P. was a monarchy. An armed rising brought about the establishment of a repub. The country is governed by a pres. and a single-chamber national assembly. For admin. purposes the P. repub. include the Is. of Madeira and the Azores (*qq.v.*), in the N. Atlantic. Area: 35,341 sq.m. Pop. 9,440,000.

PORTUGUESE GUINEA
Colony on the W. African coast. The chief products are rice, palm oil, hides and ground nuts. The towns are Bissau, cap. since 1942, and Bolama, on an Is., the former cap. Area: 36,125 sq.m. Pop. 544,184.

POSSUM
Phalanger of arboreal habit unique to Austral., unrelated to the Amer. opossum.

POST OFFICE
In Brit. the P.O. is a State inst. with the sole right of carrying letters, and dates from 1657. In 1840, Rowland Hill introduced the penny post system, under which a letter could be sent to any part of the kingdom for a charge of 1d. per ½ oz. Adhesive stamps came into use in 1841. In 1870, ½d. postcards were introduced, and in 1881 postal orders. The parcel post came into operation in 1883, and imperial penny postage in 1898. The P.O. took over all existing telegraphs in 1870 under an Act which gave it the sole right of transmitting telegrams. The same Act enabled it to obtain control of the telephone system, which in 1911 came entirely under P.O. as, at a later date, did wire-

less telegraphy and telephony. The P.O. issues local taxation licences; pays family allowances, and old-age, widows', and war pensions, and naval and milit. allowances; also issues health and pensions ins. stamps.

POTASH
Common name for potassium carbonate K_2CO_3. Caustic potash is potassium hydroxide KOH.

POTASSIUM
A soft silvery metal, occurring chiefly as the chloride in certain minerals and in the sea. It was discovered in 1807 by Sir Humphry Davy who prepared it by electrolysis of caustic potash. Potassium salts (potash) are essential to agriculture.

POTATO
Tuber of a perennial herb of the nightshade family (*Solanum tuberosum*). It reached 16th-cent. Sp. from Peru, and later Ireland from Virginia, 1585-6. Its cultivation in Brit. dates from 17th-cent. in Lancs. Now extensively grown in all temp. and sub-trop. regions, it ranks next to cereal grains as a food-plant for man and cattle. *See* SWEET POTATO.

POTSDAM
Town in Brandenburg, E. Germany, 16 m. S.W. of Berlin on an Is. in the Havel. Buildings include the former palaces of the Hohenzollern family. Pop. 115,257. **Potsdam Agreement.** Decisions reached at a conference in 1945 at Berlin between Brit., the U.S.A. and the U.S.S.R. By it Poland was provisionally given territory in E. Germany, a Council of Foreign Mins. was set up to draft peace treaties, and an Allied Control Council was set up in Germany.

POTTERY
Art of making vessels and other objects from clays air-dried or fired. In its earlier stage a vessel was built up by hand and fired on an open hearth. Later the potter's wheel and kiln were introduced. In medieval times the Moors brought enamelled ware into Spain, and in the 12th cent. a soft coarse ware was introduced from Majorca into Italy. In Fr. from the 16th cent. the making of soft porcelain followed by hard porcelain marked a further advance, and other improvements were made in Eng. by Josiah Wedgwood.

POULENC, Francis
[poo-la(ng)k'] (1899-1963) Fr. composer. A member of ' les Six ', the Fr. modernist group.

POULTRY
Name used for domestic fowls, ducks, geese and turkeys. The fowl is derived from the wild Indian Jungle Fowl. The many varieties are classed roughly as layer, utility, table and fancy breeds. *See* DUCK; GOOSE; TURKEY.

POUND
(1) Brit. unit of weight. It is divided into 16 oz. avoirdupois or 7,000 grains. (2) Brit. monetary unit, equivalent to 100 new pence. The pound sterling was orig. 5,760 grains of silver. In 1816 gold replaced the silver pound. *See* GOLD STANDARD.

POUND, Ezra Loomis
(1885-) Amer. poet, ed. and lit. critic. From 1908 onwards he lived in Europe. From 1910 he led new groups, *e.g.* Vorticists and Imagists; Joyce and Eliot were his disciples. His vols. of poems include *Exaltations* (1909), *Homage for Sextus Propertius*, *Quia Pauper Amavi* (1918) containing Cantos I-III of a long poem which has occupied him ever since. His prose works include *Noh* (on Japanese drama 1917), *Instigations* (1920), *ABC of Reading* (1934), *Culture* (1938). During World War II he held an official position under Mussolini and broadcast to the U.S.A.

POUSSIN, Nicholas
[poo-sa(ng)] (1593-1665) Fr. painter. From 1640-2 he was in Paris as court painter to Louis XIII, returning thereafter to Rome, where he worked until his d. Poussin's brother-in-law, **Gaspard Dughet** (1613-75) took the name of **Poussin,** and became famous for his landscapes.

POWER
The rate at which work is done in a system—*i.e.* the rate of consumption of energy. Units of power are the horse-power and the kilowatt (1,000 watts). The practical unit of energy in the Brit. system is the foot-pound, representing the work done in lifting a 1 lb. wt. through a vertical distance of 1 ft. 1 H.P. is a rate of working of 550 ft.-lbs. per sec. and is approx. 0·75 of a kilowatt. The kilowatt-hour, which is the Board of Trade unit of electrical energy, is the energy required to maintain a power of 1 kilowatt for 1 hour.

PRAETOR
In ancient Rome, a magistrate next in importance to a consul. The praetor was first elected in 366 B.C. Later more praetors were apptd., to govern new provs. or take charge of depts. of the state. The **Praetorian Guard** was a body of troops whose duty was to guard the emperor.

PRAGUE
[prāg] (*Czech.* **Praha**). Cap. city of Czechoslovakia and chief town of Bohemia, on the Vltava. It is a route centre, with extensive river traffic, and numerous industries. There is a univ. (1348) and a Gothic cath., (1344). Pop. 1,003,341.

PRAIRIE
The grassy, almost flat plains of central N. Amer. covering the S. regions of Alberta, Saskatchewan and Manitoba in Canada, and extending from the Rockies to L. Michigan in the U.S.A. **Prairie Dog** (*Cynomys*) (or **Prairie Marmot**) N. Amer. burrowing rodent. Stout, squat, 12 in. long with 4 to 5 in. tail, reddish-grey and paler beneath, they live gregariously on the plains. **Prairie Squirrel** (or **Gopher**) Name for several N. Amer. rodent animals of the genus Spermophilus, found in the prairies in great numbers. They live in burrows and not in trees. They subsist on prairie plants and have cheek-pouches.

PRASAD, Dr. Rajendra
[-shȧd'] (1884-1963) Indian statesman and first Pres. of the Repub. of India 1950-62. He became a follower of Gandhi and was a prominent member of various committees working towards indep. and Pres. of Congress, 1947-8.

PRAWN
Shrimp-like Crustacea. Mostly marine, 2-12 in. long. The Brit. edible *Palaemon serratus*, 3-4

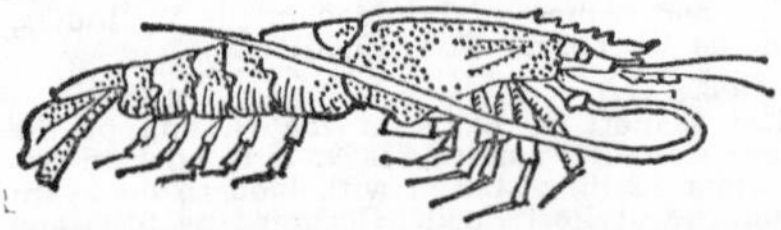

in. long, is usually taken in hand ring-nets or osier basket-traps. Some trop. species rival lobsters in size, *e.g.* the W. Indian prawn, *P. jamaicensus.*

PRAXITELES
[-sit'-ĕ-lēz] (*c.* 400-330 B.C.) Gk. sculptor. He lived at Athens. His works are known mostly by copies, *e.g.* the Aphrodite of Cnidus, Eros, Satyr, Apollo, and others.

PRAYER
Address of supplication, adoration, confession or thankfulness to a divine power. R.C. and Gk. chs. sanction prayer to the Virgin, angels and saints, but Protestant chs. limit prayer to God alone.

PRECEDENCE
Priority of place to which titled and official persons or officers of the Services are entitled by the rank conferred on them by the crown. There is an official table of precedence. The sovereign is at the head, followed by the Prince of Wales and other sons, brothers, uncles and nephews of the sovereign, and ambassadors. Next come the Arch. of Canterbury, Lord Chanc., Arch. of York, P.M., Lord Pres. of the Council, Speaker of House of Commons, Lord Privy Seal, Lord Great Chamberlain, Lord High Constable, Earl Marshal, Lord Steward of the Household, and Lord Chamberlain. Then follow dukes, marquesses, earls, viscounts, bishops, secs. of state (if barons), barons, certain officers of the household, secs. of state not barons, Knights of Garter, Privy Councillors, Chanc. of Exchequer, Chanc. of Duchy of Lancaster, Lord Chief Justice, Master of Rolls, Appeal Justices, Lords of Appeal, other Judges, baronets, members of orders of knighthood, County Court judges, companions, members and officers of various orders, gentlemen entitled to bear arms.

PRECESSION of the Equinoxes
A slow motion of the line of intersection of the celestial equator or equinoctial and the ecliptic, which causes the positions occupied by the sun at the equinox to move backward or westward at the mean rate of 50·26 secs. per year. This motion of the equinox along the ecliptic carries it, with reference to diurnal motion, continually in advance upon the stars. This sweeping round in the heavens of the equinoctial line indicates a motion of the axis of rotation of the earth, such that it describes circles round the poles of the ecliptic in 25,791 years.

PREDESTINATION
Theological term denoting the Divine predetermining of human destiny. It may stand for belief in fate, the conception that all that is to be is eternally and changelessly decreed, or, specifically, that each individual is destined beforehand to everlasting weal or woe. *See* AUGUSTINE; CALVIN.

PREGNANCY
The state of a woman who is with child. Nine calendar months, ten lunar months, or 280 days, is the time calculated for human pregnancy, but this is only an approximation and the actual time of the child's development in the womb may be longer or shorter than this period by several weeks. The actual date of delivery is difficult to predict, and the duration of pregnancy should be calculated from the first day of the last menstrual period. A common practice is to add 7 days and count forward 9 calendar months. Labour will probably commence a day or two before or after this date. The calculation should be checked by the date of the 'quickening' which occurs about 22 weeks before labour is due.

PRE-RAPHAELITES
Group of Eng. artists who, in 1848, broke away from the conventional art of their day with the idea of returning to the primitive outlook of the early Ital. painters. The founders were Holman Hunt, Rossetti and Millais.

PRESBYTER
Elder of the early Christian Ch.; the name is also used for a priest. In the Presbyterian denominations a presbyter is an elder or a member of a presbytery, the latter being an official court of a district, composed of pastors and elders. **Presbyterianism.** Form of ch. govt. by presbyters or elders. Claiming to be a N.T. institution, in continuation of Jewish synagogue practice, it developed into the prelatic form of rule of medieval Christendom. At the Reformation, presbyterianism emerged once more, notably under Calvin's forceful influence. Destined to prevail in Scot., it acknowledges the govt. of each ch. by elders, including the preaching elder or min. *See* SCOTLAND, CHURCH OF.

PRESIDENT
Elected head of a republic, who discharges the functions performed in a monarchy by a king. The powers of the office vary from country to country. The Amer. Pres. has control of the administration of the country, and is equal in authority with Congress.

PRESS GANG
Men formerly engaged in compulsory recruiting for the army or navy. By an act of 1835 the period of compulsory service for men impressed for the navy was limited to 5 years.

PRESTER JOHN
Legendary 12th cent. Christian ruler of a kingdom in the Far E.

PRESTON
County borough and port of Lancs., 31 m. N.W. of Manchester, on the estuary of the Ribble, 12 m. from its mouth. P. is the centre of the cotton spinning industry. P. was the scene of a battle 1648, between Parliamentarians and Royalists. P. returns 2 members to Parl. Pop. 112,130.

PRESTONPANS
Village of E. Lothian on the Firth of Forth, 9 m. E. of Edinburgh, famous for the Battle of 1745, which the Jacobites won against the royal troops.

PRESTWICK
Town of Ayrshire, on the Firth of Clyde, 38 m. S.W. of Glasgow, with internat. airport. Pop. 13,000.

PRETORIA
Cap. of Transvaal prov. and admin. cap. of Repub. of S. Africa, 35 m. N. of Johannesburg. Named after Pretorius, first pres. of the S. African repub. (Transvaal). Pop. 416,000.

PRICKLY PEAR
(*Opuntia vulgaris*) A plant of the natural order Cactaceae and native of trop. Amer. whence it has been introduced into Europe, Syria, Arabia, China, etc. The opuntia which has a ht. of 7 or 8 ft., is a fleshy and succulent plant destitute of leaves, covered with clusters of spines. The fruit, purplish in colour and covered with fine prickles, is edible.

PRIESTLEY, John Boynton
(1894-) Brit. author. Novels include *The Good Companions* (1929), *Angel Pavement*, *The Magicians* (1954). His plays include *Dangerous Corner* (1932), *Johnson over Jordan*, *Time and the Conways*, *They Came to a City*. Later novels include *Lost Empires* (1965).

PRIESTLEY, Joseph
(1733-1804) Brit. chemist. Among his discoveries were oxygen, nitric oxide, hydrochloric acid, and sulphur dioxide.

PRIMATE
Title of the Archbishops of Canterbury (Primate of all Eng.) and York (Primate of Eng.). An analogous title, primus, is held by the bishop who presides over the Synod of the Episcopal Ch. of Scot.

PRIME MINISTER
Chief min. of the Brit. sovereign and people, also known as the Premier. He must be a member of Parl. and since 1902 has been a member of the House of Commons. He is selected by the sovereign, but must enjoy the support of a majority of the members. He selects the members of the Cabinet, advises the sovereign on all matters of importance, heads the govt. and is the leader of his own polit. party. **Prime Ministers of the 20th cent.: 1902-5** A. J. Balfour, **1905-8** Sir H. Campbell-Bannerman, **1908-16** H. H. Asquith (Earl of Oxford), **1916-22** D. Lloyd-George, **1922-3** A. Bonar Law,

1923-4 Stanley Baldwin, **1924** J. Ramsay MacDonald, **1924-9** Stanley Baldwin, **1929-35** J. Ramsay MacDonald, **1935-7** Stanley Baldwin, **1937-40** Neville Chamberlain, **1940-5** Winston S. Churchill, **1945-51** Clement R. Attlee, **1951-5** Sir Winston S. Churchill, **1955-7** Sir Anthony Eden, **1957-63** Harold Macmillan, **1963-4** Sir A. Douglas-Home, **1964-** Harold Wilson.

PRIMITIVE METHODISTS
Evangelical community. From 1807 onwards open-air revival meetings, held under Wesleyan Methodist protection, were esp. fostered by Hugh Bourne and William Clowes who adopted the Primitive Methodist title, 1812. Organic union with other Methodist communions was authorised by Parl. 1933. *See* METHODISM.

PRIMROSE
Herbaceous perennial of the genus *Primula*, of which there are 250 species. **Primrose League.** Cons. polit. organisation. Founded in 1883, its name is an allusion to a favourite flower of the Earl of Beaconsfield.

PRIMULA
Large genus of perennial herbs of the primrose family. The Brit. species are the common, bird's-eye and Scots primroses, cowslip and oxlip.

PRINCE EDWARD ISLAND
Prov. of the Dominion of Canada, in the Gulf of St. Lawrence. Agriculture is the principal industry. Silver foxes are reared on farms. The cap. is Charlottetown, on Hillsborough Bay. The Is. was colonised by the Fr. *c.* 1720, became a Brit. possession, 1763, and entered the Confederation, 1873. It is admin. by a lieut.-gov. and a legislative assembly; it sends 4 senators and 4 representatives to the Federal parl. Area: 2,180 sq.m. Pop. 106,000.

PRINCE OF WALES
Title borne first by the son of Edward I and since conferred on the eldest son of the sovereign. The badge is a plume of 3 ostrich feathers enfiled by a coronet, the motto being *I serve.*

PRINCE RUPERT
City and seaport of Brit. Columbia, Canada. Pop. 11,987.

PRINCETON
Town of New Jersey, U.S.A. 10 m. from Trenton. The univ. was founded as a coll. at Elizabethtown, 1746, and moved to Princeton, 1756.

PRINCETOWN
Village of Devon on Dartmoor, 22 m. N.E. of Plymouth. Dartmoor prison is near.

PRINTING
The art or practice of impressing letters or illustrations on paper or other material by mechanical means. The Chinese early printed from movable blocks, but in Europe, apart from block-printing from single pieces of wood, which can be traced back to the 12th cent., the art originated in the mid-15th cent. Laurens Janszoon Coster of Haarlem was probably the inventor of movable types (*c.* 1420-30). The first book printed from such was probably *Speculum Nostrae Salutis.* The 42 line Bible known as Gutenberg's appeared in 1455. From Mainz the art spread to Nuremberg, Cologne and Augsburg. Sweynheim and Pannartz estabd. a press first at Subiaco and then at Rome. The Frenchman, Jenson, inventor of Roman type, began printing at Venice in 1470. In 1475 the Eng. Caxton, after work at Bruges, set up his press at Westminster. Caxton was succeeded by Wynkin de Worde (d. 1535). Modern printing is divided into 3 main categories, *i.e. letterpress, lithography and photogravure* (intaglio). Letterpress printing (printing from raised surfaces) comprises the composition and assembling of type (and blocks) and thence machining.

PRISM
A solid whose 2 ends are equal, similar and parallel plane figures, and whose sides are parallelograms. The axis joins the centres of the 2 ends, and a right prism has its axis perpendicular to its ends.

PRISON
Place of detention. The modern system dates from the early 19th cent. John Howard pub. in 1777 his powerful plea for reform. In 1813 Elizabeth Fry began her work for the Newgate prisoners. Jeremy Bentham's 'Panopticon' was the model for Millbank penitentiary (1816). Pentonville (1842) was part of the scheme recommended by the House of Lords in 1835. Dartmoor, built for Fr. war prisoners in 1806, was made into a convict prison in 1850. *See* BORSTAL; TRANSPORTATION.

PRIVET
(*Ligustrum*) Genus of shrubs or low trees of the olive family, with simple entire leaves and clustered white funnel-shaped flowers, yielding small globular berries.

PRIVY COUNCIL
Council to advise the sovereign on matters of state. Since the adoption of cabinet govt. this body has lost much of its former power, and now deals mainly with certain formal matters. Thus on the d. of the ruler it is summoned to proclaim the new sovereign. The council is composed of distinguished persons, including the royal princes, the Archbishops of Canterbury and York, officers of State and of the Household, the Speaker of the House of Commons, etc. Its members are styled 'The Right Honourable' and take precedence after Knights of the Garter.

PRIVY PURSE
In Brit. the allowance from the civil list for the personal use of the sovereign.

PROBATE
Legal proving of a will. The will, with a copy, is taken to a probate registry, and also an affidavit stating particulars of the testator's estate, and another proving his d. etc. Upon the will being admitted to probate a copy (the probate copy) is issued, which is legal evidence of the will, the orig. being filed at the registry where it can be inspected. *See* WILL.

PROBATION
Judicial system under which offenders, instead of being fined or committed to prison upon being convicted, are placed under the supervision of a probation officer for a specified period. *See* BORSTAL.

PROCURATOR FISCAL
Scots law officer apptd. by the Lord Advocate. He inquires into cases of crime and conducts investigations into cases of sudden d.

PROHIBITION
Term esp. applied to the prohibition of the manufacture, sale, and transportation of intoxicating liquors for beverage purposes. The U.S.A. imposed a prohibition measure, 1919.

As a war measure, control was imposed in several other countries. Various provinces of Canada from 1915-17 introduced prohibition until Quebec alone remained outside, and in that territory a great area had adopted it under local option. In the U.S.A. an illicit liquor trade quickly developed. Because of growing disrespect for the law and the difficulty of enforcement the measure was finally repealed, 1933.

PROKOFIEV, Sergei
[prō-kof'-yef] (1891-1953) Russ. composer. His opera *The Love of Three Oranges* was produced in Chicago in 1921. He wrote for Diaghilev's Russian ballet in Paris. In 1934 he settled in Moscow. His works include operas, ballets, 5 symphonies, 5 piano concertos, 2 violin concertos, chamber music, choral works, piano works and film music.

PROPORTIONAL REPRESENTATION
System of voting. It aims at securing representation of minority bodies according to their numerical proportions. By the best-known method, when a constituency returns several representatives the voter records also a 2nd or 3rd choice, according to the number of those seeking election. A definite quota of votes is necessary to procure election, the quota being determined after the ballot, according to the number of votes polled and the number of vacancies to be filled. When, on the first count, one or more candidates secure election by polling the requisite number of votes, any surplus votes above the quota are apportioned among the other candidates according to the second choice shown on the ballot papers.

PROSTITUTION
Promiscuous sexual intercourse for gain by a woman known as a prostitute. Regulated prostitution has existed since ancient times. In Brit. importuning by a prostitute is a punishable offence.

PROTECTOR
Former Eng. title of state, borne by one who governed during the minority or absence of the king. In 1216 the Earl of Pembroke was protector; in 1422, Humphrey, Duke of Gloucester; in 1547, the Duke of Somerset; and in 1549, Dudley, Duke of Northumberland. Cromwell (1653), held the office of Lord Protector of the Commonw. *See* REGENT.

PROTEINS
A large group of chem. compounds. Proteins contain carbon, hydrogen, oxygen and nitrogen. They occur in egg white, egg yolk, milk, flour, meat and many vegetables. They are an important constituent of diet, forming almost the only source of nitrogen and of sulphur. In the body, proteins occur in bones, skin, hair and nails. Animal proteins are widely useful as wool, silk and other fibres, leather, parchment, catgut, etc.

PROTESTANTISM
Faith of those who protest against the Ch. of Rome. The name **Protestants** was given to those followers of Luther who protested against the decrees of the Second Diet of Spires (1529). It soon came to be applied to any religious body which had separated from the Rom. Ch. To Protestants the Bible is the supreme and ultimate authority. The relation of the soul to God is direct and personal, needing no intermediary, such as a priest; and sacraments, though recognised, are not essential to salvation. **Protestant Episcopal Church.** Official title of the Episcopal Ch. of Amer. in communion with the See of Canterbury, *i.e.* the Anglican Ch. in Amer. The Ch. was organised as a separate denomination in 1789.

PROTON
A particle carrying one unit of positive electrical charge found in the nuclei of all atoms. Its mass is almost equal to that of a hydrogen atom. *See* ATOM; NUCLEUS; NEUTRON.

PROUST, Marcel
(1871-1922) Fr. novelist. His series of novels *À la Recherche du Temps Perdu* was pub. in 15 vols. 1913-26; *Sodome et Gomorrhe, La Prisonnière, Albertine Disparue, Le Temps Retrouvé* and *Jean Santeuil* which was first pub. in 1952.

PROVENCE
[-vá(ng)s] Former prov. of Fr. now comprising the depts. of Basses-Alpes, Vaucluse, Var, Bouches-du-Rhône, and part of Alpes Maritimes. The cap. was Arles, on the Rhône. **Provençal.** Language of Provence, going back to Languedoc. Lit. begins in 11th cent. and, through the Troubadours, deeply influenced all medieval poetry in the W.

PROVERBS, Book of
Book of the O.T. A manual of practical life, placed after the devotional manual, the Psalms. Finally welded in the post-exilic age, the whole was attributed to Solomon in accordance with the literary usage of the time.

PROVOST
In Scot. the chief magistrate of a burgh, equivalent of an Eng. mayor. The provosts of Aberdeen, Dundee, Edinburgh, Glasgow and Perth are entitled Lord Provost.

PRUNE
Dried fruit of several varieties of the cultivated plum-tree. The finest, grown in the Loire valley, are called Fr. plums.

PRURIGO
[proo-rī'-gō] Skin disorder characterised by the development of very itchy pimples.

PRUSSIA
Former state of Germany which was divided between the U.S.S.R. and Poland after World War II. It was formed in the 17th cent. by the union of the Mark of Brandenburg and the State of the Teutonic Order in Prussia. Frederick the Gt. laid the foundations of Pruss. greatness. The peak of its supremacy as a monarchy was reached under William I and Bismarck (1840-90).

PRUSSIC ACID *See* HYDROCYANIC ACID.

PSALMS, Book of
Book of the O.T. It comprises 150 'praise-songs' set to music, primarily for Temple use. In the Heb. Bible it constitutes 5 books. Nearly half—73—were traditionally assoc. with David. Mostly of post-exilic date, some clearly reflect the Maccabean age. **Psalter.** Book containing the O.T. Psalms. The Anglican prayer-book psalter contains the Great Bible version of 1539. The metrical psalms still persist in Scot.

PSITTACUS
[sit'-] African genus of parrots. The best-known is the Grey Parrot, *P. erythacus*, with ashy-grey plumage and short red tail, ranging from the Guinea coast to L. Malawi. A familiar cage-bird in Europe for cents., it is remarkable for its ability to repeat words.

PSYCHIATRY
[sīkī'-a-tri] The scientific study of all aspects of the human mind in states of ill-health or disease. It includes the study of the neuroses, the psychoses, mental deficiency, the problem of the nervous or maladjusted child, delinquency and criminality, etc. *See* NEUROSIS.

PSYCHICAL RESEARCH
Systematic investigation into phenomena, regarded as appertaining to the spiritual sphere. In 1882 was founded the Soc. for Psychical Research, whose object is the investigation of apparitions, hauntings, clairvoyance, spiritualistic manifestations, etc.

PSYCHOANALYSIS
[sī'-kō-] Method of treatment of mental disease.

Based on theory of Sigmund Freud and Jung who believed that such functional conditions as hysteria and neurosis originate from mental conflicts between conscious and unconscious control. *See* FREUD.

PSYCHOLOGY
[sī-kol′-] Science of mental phenomena. It investigates psychical processes or states and the conditions under which they arise. Its main methods of approach are introspection and inference. Another line of study is the exam. of the mental life of others, *e.g.* the child from infancy to adult life. **Social psychology** deals with the mental phenomena of communities; industrial psychology with the special problems of factory life, etc.

PTARMIGAN
[tä′-] (*Lagopus mutus*) Game bird *c.* 15 in. long, allied to Grouse but having feathered feet and nearly white winter plumage, with black outer tail-feathers. It ranges over Scot. moors above 2,500 ft.

PTERODACTYL
[ter-o-dak′-til] Extinct order of flying reptiles found fossil in Mesozoic rocks in Europe and N. Amer. Long-tailed or tailless, large-headed, wide-mouthed, toothed or toothless, with flexible necks, they had smooth 'bat-like' membranes.

PTOLEMY
[tol′-] Name of a dynasty of Egyptian kings (305 B.C.-A.D. 40). The legitimate line ended in 80 B.C. when **Ptolemy X** was assassinated, the crown going to a natural son of **Soter II (Ptolemy VIII)**. He was named Auletes, or 'the flute player'. Auletes' son, **Philopator,** succeeded in 51 B.C. reigning jointly with his sister, **Cleopatra,** as **Ptolemy XII.** On his d. in 47 B.C. his younger brother became **Ptolemy XIII** and reigned also with Cleopatra. The last kings of the dynasty were son and grandson of Cleopatra, **Ptolemy XV** dying in A.D. 40.

PTOLEMY
[tol′-] Egyptian astronomer and geographer. His system, the Ptolemaic, represented the earth as the fixed centre of the universe, the sun, moon, other planets and stars revolving about it from E. to W. in separate zones.

PUBERTY
A period in both male and female which is marked by the functional development of the generative system. In males it usually takes place between the ages of 13 and 16; in females it may occur earlier. In very warm climates puberty is reached sooner than in temp. zones. In males, puberty is marked externally by the deepening of the voice, the first appearance of the beard, greater firmness and fullness of body, etc.; in females, by the enlargement of the breasts, and the commencement of menstruation.

PUCCINI, Giacomo
[po͝o-chē′-ni] (1858-1924) Ital. composer. His first triumph was with his opera *Manon Lescaut* in 1893. Thereafter followed a series of successful operas, nearly all remain favourites in the operatic repertoire—*La Bohème, Madame Butterfly, La Tosca, Turandot.*

PUERPERAL FEVER
Notifiable disease occurring in women after childbirth and caused by septic infection of birth canal. In former years it caused many deaths, but maternity nursing and med. services have reduced incidence markedly.

PUERTO RICO
[pwair′-tō rē′-kō] Is. possession of the U.S.A. in the Greater Antilles, W. Indies, E. of Hispaniola. Cocoa, coffee, sugar, bananas, cotton and tobacco are produced, and cattle are reared. San Juan is the cap. The pop. is mainly white, of Sp. descent, and Eng. is the official language. P.R. was discovered by Columbus, and was a Sp. possession until 1898, when it was ceded to the U.S.A. The Gov. is elected, as also are the 27 senators and 51 representatives. P.R. is represented in Congress by a Resident Commissioner. Area: 3,420 sq.m. Pop. 2,513,000.

PUFF ADDER
(*Bitis arietans*) Venomous viper of Africa. The large flattened head and thick body, 4-5 ft. long, are covered with scales. When irritated, its indrawn breath, visibly swelling the body, gradually escapes.

PUFFIN
(*Fratercula*) The Common Puffin, *F. arctica*, is a sea-bird 12 in. long, with black-and-white plumage, reddish feet, and brilliantly coloured bill, red, orange and bluish-grey, with horny sheath-like plates that moult. Common on the rocky Atlantic coasts of Europe and the coasts of the Brit. Is.

PUG DOG
Toy dog of the Mastiff group. It was introduced from Holland and much esteemed in the 18th cent.

PUGLIA
Region of S. Italy, E. of the Apennines. The soil is porous and irrigation is essential. Brindisi, Bari and Taranto are important ports.

PULITZER PRIZES
[pool′-] Set up in terms of a bequest by Joseph Pulitzer (1847-1911) Amer. journalist and proprietor of the *New York World.* 12 prizes of $500 are given every year to Amer. citizens who win distinction in various aspects of journalism.

PULSE
Intermittent distension of arterial walls caused by vol. of blood passing under increased pressure after heart beat towards distant parts of body. In a normal healthy person the pulse rate at rest is regular at 70-80 beats per min. but varies with age and sex.

PUMA
(*Felis concolor*) Large Amer. cat ranging from Brit. Columbia to Patagonia. Called the Amer. Lion, Panther or Painter, Catamount and Cougar, it measures 3½ ft. with 2 ft. tail. The head is relatively small and maneless, with flesh-coloured nostrils, the tail dark-tipped and untufted.

PUMICE
Light spongy form of volcanic glass, usually a greyish, froth-like scum formed on molten lava by the escape of vapours and rapidly solidified. It is a useful polishing and smoothing stone.

PUMPS
Machines to raise or move fluids. Examples are: *centrifugal pumps* which are efficient in dealing with large volumes, and are capable of pumping against any pressure up to 1,500 lb. sq. in.; *reciprocating pumps,* useful where small volumes under high heads are to be handled; *pumps of the rotary type,* well adapted for working over a wide range of speeds and comparatively low head; *gas pumps* raising water by the direct action of the pressure accompanying the explosion and expansion of an air-gas mixture.

PUMPKIN
(*Cucurbita pepo*) Trailing annual herb of the gourd family. Each plant bears male and female flowers separately, the latter developing into the fruit, sometimes weighing 80 lb. and more. Varied forms, including vegetable marrows, are widely grown in Europe, N. Amer. and elsewhere.

PUNJAB
[pun′-jäb′] **(India)** State of India, bounded by Pakistan, Tibet, and the states of Kashmir, Uttar Pradesh and Rajasthan. Cap. is Chandi-

garh. Rainfall is slight, and agriculture is dependent on irrigation. Wheat, millet, barley, sugar, oilseeds and cotton are the chief crops. Area: 47,304 sq.m. Pop. 20,306,812. **Punjab (Pakistan).** By an Act of 1955, the former prov. of (W.) Punjab became incorporated with the prov. of W. Pakistan. The district is agricultural, growing wheat, rice, cotton, etc. Principal city of the region is Lahore. *See* PAKISTAN.

PUPIL *See* EYE.

PURBECK
Peninsula of Dorset, 12 m. long, between Poole Harbour and the Frome and the Eng. Channel. Swanage and Corfe Castle are on the peninsula.

PURCELL, Henry
[pur'-sēl] (1659-95) Eng. composer. He composed much ch. music. He was a prolific writer of music for the theatre; *e.g.* his most famous opera, *Dido and Aeneas* and the half-masques—*The Faery Queen, King Arthur, The Tempest.* He wrote fantasies for strings and sonatas of great beauty for 2 violins and continuo, harpsichord suites and songs.

PURCHASE TAX
Tax first levied in Brit. 1940, by the *Finance Act* (No. 2). It affected the majority of goods other than raw materials, food, and drink. The yield in the financial year 1962-3 was £571,308,394.

PURGATORY
Place or state, according to R.C. belief, in which souls after d. are purified from venial sins and rendered fit for heaven. Protestant Reformers rejected the doctrine.

PURIM
[pŏŏ'-] Jewish festival commemorating the preservation of the Jews in Persia from the destruction threatened them by Haman. (*Esther*, 9). It is observed on the 14th and 15th of Adar (March).

PURITANS
In Eliz. Eng. advanced Protestant clergy who advocated stricter manners and simpler worship than generally obtained after the severance from Rome. The Puritan spirit long prevailed in New England, U.S.A.

PUSEY, Edward Bouverie
(1800-82) Eng. divine. Regarded as founder, or restorer, of the High Ch. movement in the Ch. of E. Its principles are contained in his sermons and writings, including *The Doctrine of the Real Presence* and one of the *Tracts for the Times*.

PUSHKIN, Alexander Sergeyevitch
(1799-1837) Russ. poet. His first notable success came in 1820 with *Ruslan and Lyudmila*; this was followed by *The Tzigani* (1827), *Boris Godunov* (1825), *Poltava* (1829), and in 1831 his autobiog. poem, *Eugène Onegin*.

PYGMY
Name for a human being naturally diminutive. The pygmy races nowadays comprise specifically Asiatic Negritos and African Negrillos, 4 ft. 11 in. down to 3 ft. 6 in. and less. *See* DWARF.

PYM, John
(1584-1643) Eng. statesman and patriot. He entered Parl. in 1614, supported the Petition of Right in 1628, led the Short Parl. of 1640 and the impeachment of Strafford in that year, and shared in the Grand Remonstrance in 1641. He was one of the 5 members who escaped arrest by Charles I.

PYONGYANG
[pyong'-yang'] Town of Korea, cap. of the People's Repub. on the railway connecting Seoul and Shenyang (Moukden). Pop. 940,000.

PYORRHOEA
[pī-rē'-ā] A condition of the teeth where the tooth sockets and gums become infected and inflammation with pus formation results.

PYRAMIDS, The
Ancient Egyptian pyramidal structures, the largest of which (The Great Pyramid) was one of the 7 wonders of the world. They are built of stone, generally on a square base, with sloping sides meeting at the apex. Most are royal tombs having a tomb-chamber for the Sarcophagus and a chapel for the performance of the ritual connected with the Ka.

PYRENEES
Mt. range of S.W. Europe, which divides Fr. from Sp. The highest point is in the Maladetta, 11,169 ft. It extends from the Medit. to the Bay of Biscay, some 270 m. Popular resorts include Pau, Lourdes, Bagnères-de-Luchons and St. Jean de Luz.

PYRETHRUM
Several composite perennial herbs of the chrysanthemum genus when ranked as a sub-genus. An ornamental large-flowered garden species from Asia Minor is akin to forms grown commercially in Dalmatia and Japan for the insect-killing pyrethrum powder.

PYRITES
[pī-rī'-tēz] Minerals containing sulphide of iron (iron pyrites) or sulphides of copper and iron (copper-pyrites). Iron pyrites is a brass-yellow hard mineral crystallising in the cubic system and is a source of sulphuric acid and iron sulphate. Marcasite is a form of iron pyrites. Copper-pyrites, an imported copper ore, occurs in yellow tetragonal crystals or in massive form.

PYTHAGORAS
[-thag'-] (*c.* 582-507 B.C.) Gk. philosopher and the greatest mathematician, geometer and astronomer of his age. In *c.* 539 B.C. he settled at Crotona where he estabd. a school of Initiates. The central idea of his philosophy was that Number was the First Principle of the universe: on numbers depended the harmonies which estabd. it and which sustain it in ordered motion. Pupils were instructed in natural studies, in geometry, the heliocentric system, the doctrine of reincarnation, etc.

PYTHON
Non-venomous snakes of the Boa family, inhabiting trop. Asia, Africa and Australia. The prey is crushed by the snake's powerful coils and swallowed from the head downwards. Pythons include the largest of all snakes except Anacondas. Averaging 10 to 20 ft., the Netted Python of Indo-China and the Rock-snake of India and Ceylon sometimes attain 30 ft. The female is oviparous.

Q

Q
17th letter of the Eng. alphabet. It is a consonant and has the same sound as that of *k* or hard *c*. In Eng. it is always followed by *u*, the combination having the sound *kw*, except at the end of words, when it has the sound of *k*, *e.g. arabesque, opaque*. Exceptions are words like *quay* (*kee*).

QATAR
Arab sheikhdom in the Persian Gulf. The inhabitants are Bedouin tribesmen, and there are few towns. Q. has been in alliance with Brit. since 1882. Area: 8,000 sq.m. Pop. *c.* 60,000.

QUADROON
Word of Sp. origin denoting offspring of a mulatto and a white. In early Sp. Amer. before negro immigration began, it denoted the offspring of an Amer.-Indian half-breed and a white.

QUAGGA
Extinct variety of the Zebra. The light-red upper parts bore irregular chocolate-brown stripes. It was slaughtered by the Boers for its hide.

QUAIL
(*Coturnix*) Small Old World game-birds of the Pheasant family. The Migratory Q. (*C. communis*), 7½ in. long, is a summer resident in Brit., fluctuating a great deal in numbers. Vast numbers, crossing the Medit. in spring and autumn, are netted for food in S. Europe.

QUAKE GRASS
(or **Dodder Grass**) Genus of perennial or annual grasses (*Briza*), natives of temp. Europe, Asia and Africa. Slender-stalked, many-flowered pyramidal clusters bear large compressed tremulous spikelets.

QUAKER
(1) Colloquial name for a member of the Soc. of Friends (*q.v.*). (2) **Quaker Bird,** another name for the Sooty Albatross.

QUAMASH
[kwom-] Genus of perennial herbs of the lily order (*Camassia*), natives of N.W. Amer. The best known, *C. esculenta,* 1-3 ft. high, produces stout-stemmed spikes, of 10-20 blue 2-in. flowers.

QUANTUM
Unit of radiant energy. **Planck's** (*q.v.*) quantum theory (1901) leads to the conclusion that radiant energy does not exist in a continuous distribution, but only in multiples of a small unit—the *quantum*. The quantum for energy of frequency n is hn, where h is Planck's constant $= 6{\cdot}6 \times 10^{-27}$ erg. cms.

QUARANTINE
Preventative detention in special areas such as hospitals, hospital ships or quarantine stations of individuals, animals and birds reaching this country from abroad who may be carriers of disease, the incubation period of which is longer than the time spent on the journey. Also applied to persons suffering from infectious diseases as a precaution against further spread to the general population.

QUARTER DAYS
The last day upon which rent or interest becomes due for payment. In Eng. and Ireland they are: Lady Day, Mar. 25; Midsummer, June 24; Michaelmas, Sept. 29; Christmas, Dec. 25. In Scot. they are: Candlemas, Feb. 2; Whitsun, May 15; Lammas, Aug. 1; Martinmas, Nov. 11.

QUARTER SESSIONS
In Eng. a court of law held 4 times a year but in some places more frequently. The judges are the magistrates for the county sitting with a jury, and the cases are those sent on to them from the courts of petty sessions. Certain cities and towns also have a court of quarter sessions which is presided over by a legally qualified judge called a recorder.

QUARTZ
Widely distributed mineral consisting of silica and forming a constituent of sands and many rocks. It occurs in masses or as crystals forming hexagonal prisms and pyramids having a vitreous lustre and great hardness. Quartz is colourless (rock crystal) or white, yellow, brown or violet.

QUASSIA
A substance used in medicine and obtained from the stem wood of a S. Amer. trop. tree, *picraena excelsa* or *Jamaica quassia.*

QUATRE BRAS
[kåtr brå] Village of Belg., 19 m. S.E. of Brussels, where, 2 days before Waterloo, Wellington defeated the Fr. under Ney.

QUAY
[kē] Landing-place on the side of a river, harbour or docks, for receiving and discharging cargoes from ships.

QUEBEC
Prov. of the Dominion of Canada, extending from the U.S. boundary, S. of the St. Lawrence, to Hudson Strait. The S. is fertile, but much of the N. between Hudson Bay and Labrador is covered by coniferous forest and tundra. The chief rivers are the St. Lawrence, Ottawa and St. Maurice. Wheat, barley, milk, butter and fish are produced. The forests supply pulp for paper and there are mineral deposits, including gold and asbestos. There is abundant hydro-electricity. Quebec is the cap. but Montreal is the largest city and seaport. There are 4 univs., 2 Protestant and 2 R.C. The inhabitants are mainly R.C.s of Fr. descent. Quebec, or Lower Canada, is the oldest settled part of the country. 1791-1841, it was a prov. under Brit. rule. In 1841 it was united with Upper Canada, and in 1867 became a prov. of the Dominion. It is gov. by a lieut.-gov. and legislature of 2 houses with a ministry responsible to it. It sends 24 senators and 75 representatives to the Fed. parl. Area: 594,860 sq.m. Pop. 5,366,000. **Quebec.** Cap. city and seaport of the prov. of Quebec, Canada, on the N. shore of the St. Lawrence. It stands on a tableland rising to 333 ft. above the river 180 m. from Montreal. Beyond the citadel are the Plains of Abraham (*q.v.*) where Wolfe defeated Montcalm (*q.v.*). The city has a fine harbour, with a govt. grain elevator. New wharves have been constructed at Wolfe's Cove. Pulp and paper manufacture is the chief industry, but machinery, cutlery, ropes and steel are also made. The city is well supplied with hydroelectric power. Founded by Champlain, 1608,

on the site of an Ind. settlement, Q. was taken by the Eng. 1629, restored to the Fr. 1632, and held by them till its capture by Wolfe, 1750. Pop. 171,979.

QUEEN
The wife of a reigning monarch. A queen has unique privileges, and has a household of her own. She is crowned with solemnities similar to those used for a king. The **queen dowager** is the widow of the deceased king. The **queen mother** is the mother of the reigning sovereign, and a **queen regnant** is a sovereign princess, reigning in her own right, with all the powers of a king, whose husband is her subject.

QUEEN CHARLOTTE IS.
Group of Is. off the W. coast of Canada, forming part of Brit. Columbia. Coal is mined and there is some fishing.

QUEEN'S BENCH DIVISION
In Eng. one of the 3 divisions of the High Court of Justice. It was the court held by the king and was held at first wherever he happened to be, but after a time was fixed at Westminster. Judges from this court went round the country to try offenders in the king's name, as they do today in the Queen's name. All criminal cases of importance come before these judges.

QUEEN'S PRIZE
Annual prize for rifle shooting, open to members of the forces throughout the Commonwealth. It was first given 1860; since 1890 it has been at Bisley.

QUEEN'S REGULATIONS
The rules issued under the authority of the Queen, which refer to the Brit. navy, army and air force, covering their organisation, seniority, leave, ceremonies, discipline, correspondence, financial and other returns, relations with authorities in foreign places and in the Dominions, etc.

QUEEN'S SPEECH
Address with which the Queen or her deputy opens each session of Parl. It is prepared by the Govt. and outlines their programme for the coming session. It is read to both Houses assembled in the House of Lords and, after debate, an address of thanks is sent to her Majesty.

QUEENSBERRY, Marquess of
Scot. title held by the family of Douglas. The 8th marquess, a noted sportsman, was responsible for the **Queensberry Rules** which govern boxing contests.

QUEENSFERRY
Burgh of W. Lothian, on the S. shore of the Firth of Forth, 9 m. N.W. of Edinburgh. The Forth Rail and Road Bridges traverse the Forth at Q. Pop. 2,997. *See* FORTH BRIDGE.

QUEENSLAND
State of the Commonwealth of Australia, lying N. of N.S.W. with a long coastline on the Coral Sea and the Gulf of Carpentaria. The chief rivers are the Flinders, Mitchell, Burdekin, Brisbane, Fitzroy and Warrego. The coastal regions are warm and moist, but in the far W. rainfall is scanty. Cattle and sheep are reared, and sugar cane, maize, potatoes, and fruit are produced. There are extensive forests and rich deposits of minerals. The cap. is Brisbane; other towns are Rockhampton, Townsville, Toowoomba and Cairns. Q. became a separate colony in 1859, having previously formed part of N.S.W. Admin. is by a Gov. and an assembly. Area: 670,500 sq.m. Pop. 1,542,629.

QUERN
Hand-mill for grinding corn. Its most usual form is that of two circular flat stones the upper of which is pierced in the centre and revolves around a wooden or metal pin inserted in the lower.

QUETZAL
Mexican name for the Trogon, *Pharomacrus mocinno*, a trop. picarian bird ranging from Guatemala to Panama. About magpie size, the crested male is handsomely plumaged in brilliant metallic green, with deep blood-red underparts. Frequently represented in Maya art, the bird appears in the arms of the Guatemala repub. and gives its name to the local dollar.

QUEZON CITY
New cap. of the Philippines, situated to the N.E. of Manila on Is. of Luzon. Pop. 482,000.

QUICKLIME
Commercial name for calcium oxide, obtained by calcining chalk or limestone, the carbon dioxide being driven off in the process. It is a valuable dressing for clay soils and is used in making mortar and cements. Slaked or hydrated lime is employed in making lime-water and in tanning and sugar industries.

QUICKSILVER *See* MERCURY.

QUILLWORT
Genus of stemless rush-like vascular cryptograms, *Isoetes*, chiefly found in N. temp. and warm regions. Merlin's grass, *I. lacustris*, growing on subalpine lake bottoms in Brit. and elsewhere, has a filbert-sized corm producing a tuft of 10-20 rigid awl-shaped tubular leaves.

QUILTER, Roger
(1877-1953) Eng. composer, mainly of songs of great charm and skilful craftsmanship.

QUINCE
Genus of shrubs and small trees of the Rosaceae. *Cydonia*, akin to the pear, is indigenous to Asia. Common quince, *C. oblonga*, of Persian origin, bears yellow astringent pear-shaped or apple-shaped fruits, used for flavouring. *See* JAPONICA.

QUININE
Chief alkaloid contained in cinchona bark. Its salts, which have a very bitter taste, are used medicinally as a tonic, pre-eminently for treating malaria.

QUINOA
[kē′-nō-a] Annual herb of the goosefoot family, *Chenopodium quinoa*, indigenous to the Pacific slopes of the Andes.

QUINSY
Med. term applied to an acute inflammation, with abscess formation, of the tonsil and soft palate.

QUISLING, Vidkun
[kwiz′-] (1887-1945) Norwegian fascist leader. He helped Germany to prepare the conquest of Norway (1940). He was made Premier (1942) by the invaders and remained in power till 1945. He was convicted of high treason and shot. From his name has come the word ' quisling ', meaning traitor.

QUITO
[kē′-tō] Cap. of Ecuador, situated at an altitude of 9,500 ft. in a basin in the Andes. There are some textile manufactures. Pop. 384,151.

QUOITS
[koyts] Pastime consisting in throwing flattened iron rings at a distant mark.

QUORUM
Minimum number of persons necessary to constitute a meeting. In public Companies and socs. the articles of assoc., or the rules, state the number necessary for a quorum. In the House of Lords it is 3, and in the House of Commons 40. In the Congress of the U.S.A. a quorum is a majority of the members.

R

R
18th letter of the Eng. alphabet. It is classed as a liquid consonant. *R* has two principal sounds: the hard initial sound, in *rat, rag, rot* and the soft medial sound in *tart, hard.* In S. Eng. the final *r* is often inaudible, and lengthens a preceding vowel, *e.g. hear, car.*

R.S.F.S.R.
(Russian Soviet Federated Socialist Republic) Largest of the constituent repubs. of the U.S.S.R. extending from the Gulf of Finland to the Sea of Japan. In the S.W. it is bounded by the Black Sea; in the S.E. by Mongolia and Manchuria. There are 3 major physical divisions: the plain of the W. lying on either side of the Ural Mts.; the region stretching from the Yenisei to the Pacific; the mt. area in the S. on the Mongolian and Manchurian frontiers. Rivers include the Volga, Pechora, Don, Ob, Irtish, Yenisei, Lena and Amur. L. Baikal is in E. Siberia. The climate is very varied, ranging from the Arctic type of the N. to the subtropical in the Caucasus area. There is great variety in agriculture. In the S.W. in the Crimean region, cotton, tobacco and vines are cultivated. The mineral deposits are of great importance. Moscow and Leningrad are 2 of the older centres, the Urals and Kuzbas newly developed centres. Moscow is the chief city; others are Leningrad, Gorky, Volgograd, Sverdlovsk, Novo Sibirsk, Kazan, Kuibyshev. About 83 % of the pop. is Russ. Area: 6,593,391 sq.m. Pop. 124,800,000.

RABAT
[rá-bàt'] Seaport and cap. of Morocco, the chief res. of the Sultan, on the Atlantic coast, 60 m. N. of Casablanca. Pop. 353,000.

RABBI
Hon. title for the Jewish scribes after Herod's day. Applied to learned persons, the N.T. mentions Christ as so addressed by his disciples and the common people. It designates modern Jewish clergy.

RABBIT
(*Oryctolagus cuniculus*) A burrowing rodent. The wild form is smaller, greyer and less speedy than the Hare, to which it is allied, and breeds abundantly. Naturalised in Brit. and elsewhere, notably in Australia, it is useful for food, its fur being felted for hats and, disguised as Coney, used by furriers. Game-laws regulate rabbit-shooting. *See* MYXOMATOSIS.

RABELAIS, François
(1483-1553) Fr. writer. B. Chinon; was successively a monk, a teacher at Montpellier, and a priest. He wrote *Gargantua et Pantagruel* (1532-4) a huge comic narrative.

RABIES
or **Hydrophobia.** An acute fatal disease of the nervous system characterised by convulsions, and later paralysis of all muscles. Caused by a virus transmitted to man through the saliva of an infected animal, such as dog, fox or wolf. Pasteur introduced a vaccine capable of curing the disease.

RACCOON
(*Procyon*) Amer. carnivorous mammals related to the oriental Pandas. The common grey N. Amer. tree-dwelling 'Coon', *P. lotor.* 24 in. long with 10-in. ringed tail, feeds by night, habitually dipping its prey into water before eating.

RACHEL, Elizabeth Rachel Felix
[rá-shel'] (1821-58) Fr. tragedienne of Jewish extraction. On June 12, 1838, she appeared at the Théâtre Français. Soon she became the greatest tragic actress of her day.

RACHMANINOV, Sergei Vassilievitch
[ràch-man'-i-nofl] (1873-1943) Russ. pianist and composer. He toured widely in Europe and Amer. He left Russia in 1917 and lived mainly in Amer. He wrote music of all kinds.

RACINE, Jean Baptiste
[ra'-sēn] (1639-99) Fr. dramatist. After making the acquaintance of Boileau and Molière, he began to write for the stage. Plays include *Andromaque, Les Plaideurs* (1668), *Britannicus* (1669), *Bérénice* (1670), *Iphigenie* (1674) and *Phèdre* (1677). He retired from the theatre for 12 years, until, at the request of Madame de Maintenon he wrote *Esther* (1689), and *Athalie* (1691).

RACKETS
Ball game played on walled-in courts. The game consists in hitting the ball against the end wall, above a certain line, with the racket.

RADAR
A process of determining the position of distant objects by radio waves. Radar stands for *R*adio *D*irection *A*nd *R*ange. In 1935, Sir Robert Watson-Watt and a team of Brit. scientists began work on the adaptation of radiolocation to milit. purposes. In 1939 Brit. already had stations estabd. for the detection of aircraft and development went on throughout World War II. The apparatus consists of a transmitter and receiver. The energy transmitted by the former is reflected back to its starting point as a luminous 'response' on a cathode-ray oscilloscope. Long Range Navigation ('Loran') employs long radio waves and a similar principle has been applied to weather prediction and the location of fish.

RADHAKRISHNAN, Sir Sarvepalli
[rà-da-krish'-nan] (1888-) Vice-Pres. of the Republic of India 1952-62, Pres. 1962. He was Spalding Prof. of E. Religions and Ethics at Oxford, 1936-52. From 1946-52 he was leader of the Indian Delegation to U.N.E.S.C.O. and Pres. of the General Conference, 1952-4. In 1949 he was apptd. Indian ambassador to the U.S.S.R., a post which he relinquished in 1952 to become Vice-Pres. of India. Knighted in 1931. O.M. 1963.

RADIANT HEAT
(or **Infra-Red Rays**) Heat which is produced artificially from electric light bulbs or electric radiators, and which is used for the relief of chronic rheumatic affections and muscular strains. Radiant heat is composed of infra-red rays which have some penetrative power in the body, causing dilatation of blood-vessels and an increase of blood-supply in the part exposed.

RADIATION
A term which embraces electro-magnetic waves, in particular X-rays and gamma rays as well as streams of fast moving charged particles such as electrons, protons, mesons, neutrons, *i.e.* all

the ways in which energy is given off by the atom. Radioactive dust, or fallout, is radioactive material that resettles to earth after a nuclear explosion. It takes 2 forms: firstly as local fallout composed of denser particles produced by the explosion, which descend to earth in a short time near the site of the detonation and in an area extending downwind for some distance. The other form, world-wide fallout, consists of lighter particles which reach the upper troposphere and stratosphere and are distributed by the winds over a wide area of the earth, coming to rest eventually through the action of rain and snow. **Radiation sickness.** Small doses of radiation produce no immediate visible effects. Long-term effects (such as genetic damage or leukemia) are not yet fully understood. Exposure to large amounts of radiation (*e.g.* after an atomic bomb explosion or nuclear accident) produces radiation sickness characterised by nausea, vomiting and diarrhoea and a fall in the number of white blood cells. Later stages may include anaemia, loss of appetite and fever.

RADIO ASTRONOMY
Research into this aspect of astronomical science resulted from enquiries into the origin of the short-wave radio noise which reaches us from space. The strength of radio waves from different parts of our own galaxy (the Milky Way), was mapped in detail and it was discovered that it came not from the shining stars, but from dark stars. These dark stars may be clouds of hydrogen which are slowly becoming light stars; alternatively they may be burnt-out light stars which have collapsed to dwarfs. Their emissions are studied by means of Radio Telescope. *See* ASTRONOMY.

RADIO COMMUNICATION
The basic principle of radio communication is that the passage of alternating current through a conductor causes a loss of energy as electromagnetic radiation from the wire. The electromagnetic, or radio wave, travelling with the speed of light (*c.* 186,000 miles per sec. in air) induces, in any conductor placed in its path, an alt. current similar to that which originally flowed in the transmitting aerial. This current may be amplified and made perceptible by the use of an appropriate receiver.

RADIOACTIVE ISOTOPES
Those of chemical elements exist naturally, but many more can now be made artificially either by bombardment of material by sub-nuclear particles in a nuclear reactor or by means of a particle accelerator. In such isotopes the atoms are unstable and disintegrate at variously differing rates during which process energy is released in the form of radiation. In medicine, the isotope of iodine can be used to determine the concentration of iodine in the thyroid gland. Medical instruments can be sterilised by exposing them to bacteria-killing radiation from radio-active cobalt. In industry many automatic processes, such as control of thickness of material by recording the attenuation of radiation passing through it, can be carried out by the use of radioisotopes. The manufacture of radioisotopes is carried out by the Atomic Energy Authority at the Radiochemical Centre, Amersham, Bucks., while research into their application is undertaken at the Isotope Research Division, Wantage, Berks.

RADIOACTIVITY
Spontaneous and uncontrollable breaking up of the nucleus, which occurs principally in a number of heavy elements occupying positions from 82 and upwards in the periodic table. The breaking up is followed by emanation of 3 kinds (1) *alpha rays* which are streams of alpha particles (helium nuclei), (2) *beta rays*, which are streams of electrons, (3) *gamma rays*, which are an electromagnetic radiation of very short wavelength—next below X-rays. *See* RADIUM; RUTHERFORD, ERNEST; NEUTRON.

RADIOLOGY
Study and use of X-rays in medicine. In 1895 Röntgen discovered that X-rays passing through human tissues could be used photographically to differentiate between easily penetrable tissues and bone.

RADISH
(*Raphanus*) Genus of annual or biennial cruciferous herbs, natives of Europe and temperate Asia. The garden radish, *R. sativus*, has an agreeably pungent fleshy root, olive-shaped or turnip-shaped, usually whitish or reddish, and is eaten uncooked as salad.

RADIUM
Radioactive element having chem. sym. Ra and at. wt. 226·05, discovered in 1898 by Madame Curie. It is present in pitchblende, carnotite and other ores assoc. with uranium, from which it is derived by radioactive decay. Radium compounds are used extensively in surgery in the treatment of certain diseases.

RADNORSHIRE
Inland county of Wales; rising to 2,180 ft. in Radnor Forest. The chief river is the Wye. Farming is important, sheep rearing in particular. Presteign is the county town. With Brecknock, R. returns 1 member to Parl. Pop. 18,000.

RAEBURN, Sir Henry
(1756-1823) Scots portrait painter. He taught himself to paint, and was helped by David Martin, a leading Edinburgh portrait painter.

RAGGED ROBIN
Perennial crimson-flowered wild plant (*Lychnis flos-cuculi*) of the pink family. It is a slender herb growing *c.* 1½ ft. high and common in Brit.

RAGLAN, Lord
Fitzroy James Henry Somerset (1788-1855) Brit. soldier. As C.-in-C. in the Crimean War, he was unjustly blamed for the soldiers' privations in 1854-5.

RAGWORT
A perennial composite herb (*Seneccio jacobaea*). The stems 1-4 ft. high, with much-divided leaves, bear dense clusters of bright-yellow flower heads.

RAHMAN PUTRA, Tunku Abdul
(1903-) Malayan statesman. Leader of Malaya Alliance Party, 1954; P.M. of Malaya, 1957-63. Prime mover in creation of Malaysia, 1963, and first P.M. Has stood firm in face of Indonesian threats.

RAIKES, Robert
(1735-1811) Founder of Sunday Schools. B. Gloucester. In 1780 he started a Sun. School, which taught the poor children of the town to read and to learn the catechism.

RAIL
Name orig. denoting 2 related birds, **Land-rail** and **Water-rail**, now extended to all members of a numerous and cosmopolitan family. The common European Water-rail (*Rallus aquaticus*) 11½ in. long, short-tailed and long-legged, is distinguishable by its long bill, and black and white barred flanks. The Land-rail or Corncrake (*Crex crex*) is a summer resident in most parts of the Brit. Is.; wedge-shaped, short-billed, with yellowish brown upper parts and paler barred flanks.

RAILWAY
Permanent way, on which locomotives and the rolling stock drawn by them can travel. The power employed is either steam, electricity or diesel oil. The first railways were rough constructions designed for carrying coal wagons drawn by horses or ponies. The invention of steam, 1804, made it possible for the steam locomotive to replace the horse. The first rail-

way line was opened between Stockton and Darlington in 1825. Accommodation for passengers passed from rude open wagons to comfortable carriages, with dining, sleeping and other facilities. In the great cities, overhead and underground railways were made. In Brit. the large number of railway Cos. that arose in the 19th cent. was gradually reduced, leaving the Midland, Gt. Western, Gt. Northern, and Gt. Eastern. Scot. had the Caledonian, Glasgow and S. Western, N. British and others. In 1921, *c.* 250 separate Cos. were welded into 4 systems: London, Midland, Scottish, 7,464 m.; Gt. Western, 3,765 m.; London and N.E., 6,464 m.; and Southern, 2,129 m. In 1948 these were nationalised and became known as *British Railways,* divided into 6 Regions.

RAIN
Fall of condensed atmospheric vapour in drops of water owing to the lowering of the temp. below dewpoint. Condensation first forms minute drops which float in masses as cloud, and as the process continues these drops coalesce, forming larger drops, whose weight causes them to fall as rain. **Rain-making.** Production of rain by mechanical or other means. There is now definite evidence that under suitable conditions cloud-seeding does produce rain. **Rainbow.** Coloured arch seen in the sky away from the sun when rain is falling during sunshine. It is due to the reflection and refraction of light in the raindrops, causing the breaking-up of the white light into the 7 colours of the spectrum.

RALEIGH, Sir Walter
[raw′-li] (*c.* 1552-1618) Elizabethan explorer and writer. He became a favourite of Queen Elizabeth and in 1584 founded the new colony of Virginia. In 1596 his advice gained Eng. the triumph of Cadiz. Raleigh was condemned to d. for treason, but was instead imprisoned in the Tower, where he wrote his *History of the World.* In 1616 he made a disastrous expedition to the Orinoco in search of gold, and on his return was condemned to d. on the old charge, and beheaded.

RAMADAN
Ninth month of the Mohammedan year, invested with special sanctity by the Koran and observed by faithful Moslems as a period of fasting.

RAMEAU, Jean Philippe
[ram′-ō] (1683-1764) Fr. composer and theorist. Wrote an important *Traité de l'harmonie.* In 1722 he moved to Paris and estabd. himself as a successful composer of operas.

RAMESES
[ram′-i-sēz] Gk. form of name of 11 kings of the 19th and 20th Egyptian dynasties. The most famous was **Rameses II** called **the Great,** who reigned 1558-1491 B.C. A prolific builder: he was responsible for the temple of Abu Simbel and the Ramesseum at Thebes.

RAMIE
Name of Malay origin for the bast fibre of a stingless nettle (*Boehmeria tenacissima*), called in Assam **thea.** This is a variety of *B. nivea,* the source of China-grass. Now grows in the S. parts of Africa, Fr., Eng. and U.S.A.

RAMILLIES
[ram′-i-lēz] Village of Belg., 13 m. N. of Namur, famous for the battle, May 23, 1706, when Marlborough defeated the Fr. in the War of the Sp. Succession.

RAMPION
Name of several perennial herbs of the bell-flower family, natives of Europe and W. Asia. (1) The genus *Phyteuma* includes the Brit. *P. spicatum.* (2) *Campanula rapunculus,* also Brit. has a spindle-shaped fleshy root.

RAMSAY, Allan
(1686-1758) Scot. poet. *The Gentle Shepherd* 1725, and *Fables,* are his chief works. He ed. *Evergreen* (old songs), 1724. His son **Allan** (1713-84) was appointed portrait-painter to George III in 1767.

RAMSAY, Sir Bertram
(1883-1945) Brit. Admiral. Entered R.N. 1898, retired 1938, but rejoined at the commencement of World War II. He organised the Allied landings in N. Africa, Sicily, Italy and Normandy. He organised the evacuation from Dunkirk.

RAMSAY, Sir William
(1852-1916) Scot. chemist. In 1895 he obtained helium for the first time.

RANDALL, John Turton
F.R.S. (1905-) Was responsible for the development of many of the successful applications of radar during World War II. Prof. of Biophysics, King's Coll. 1961- .

RANGOON
Cap. and principal seaport of Burma on the R. River, *c.* 20 m. from the Gulf of Martaban. The principal building is the Shwe Dagon Pagoda. Pop. 740,000.

RANJITSINHJI, Kumar Shri
(1872-1935) Indian prince, and a cricketer. In 1895 he settled in Sussex and began to play cricket for that county. He played for Eng. against Australia. In 1906 Ranji became Maharajah of Nawanagar.

RANKL, Karl
(1898-) Austrian conductor and composer. Educ. Vienna. Came to Brit. following Nazi occupation of Czechoslovakia. Musical Director, Covent Garden, 1946-51. Principal Conductor, Scottish Nat. Orchestra, 1952-7.

RAPE
In law, the crime of having carnal knowledge of a woman by force, against her will. Since 1861 has been punishable in Eng. by penal servitude (since 1949, imprisonment), for life.

RAPE
Cultivated varieties of several cruciferous herbs of the cabbage genus, notably *Brassica napus* and *B. campestris.* They are grown extensively in Europe and India for green forage; the seeds, used for feeding poultry, yield an oil, known commercially as **colza.**

RAPHAEL SANZIO
[raf′-ā-ĕl sant′-siō] Ital. painter (1483-1520). B. Urbino. His work falls into 3 periods: (1) *Perugian* (1500-4), during which he worked in co-operation with Perugino; (2) *Florentine* (1504-8), when he came under the influence of Leonardo da Vinci and Michelangelo; (3) *Roman* (1508-20) during which he decorated the state apartments in the Vatican for Pope Julius II.

RAPHIA PALM
Genus of palm-trees indigenous to trop. Africa and Amer. Important species are the Amazon jupati palm and the W. African bamboo, or wine-palm, yielding a fermentable sap and a bass.

RASPBERRY
Shrub of the rose family (*Rubus idaeus*). Its perennial stool produces shoots which bear, in the 2nd year, scarlet or yellow fruits. Cultivated varieties are used for dessert, jam, wine, etc. *See* LOGANBERRY.

RASPUTIN, Gregory Efimovitch
(1872-1916) Russ. monk. In 1904 he left his family, and practised religious exercises, adopting the attitude that it was necessary to sin in order to obtain forgiveness. He appeared at court, and exercised a malign influence on Ch. and State, until he was shot d.

RAT
Various rodents, specifically the larger species of the genus *Mus.* The long-tailed Black **rat**

(*Mus rattus*), 7 in. long with 8-9 in. tail, of Asiatic origin, which reached 13th cent. Europe, and became estabd. in Brit., is the progenitor of domesticated forms. Later came the Brown or Norway rat, 8-9 in. long, which swam the Volga, 1727, reached Brit. in E.-Indiamen, *c.* 1730, and ousted its smaller congener. *See* MUSQUASH.

RATEL
Genus of burrowing carnivores of the Weasel family (*Mellivora*), inhabiting India and Africa.

RATIONING
Apportioning of a share of supplies, usually of food. During World War I the entire pop. of Brit. was rationed, from June, 1917, in fats, sugar and meat. The Ministry of Food, estabd. in 1939, was responsible for the maintenance and distribution of food supplies. The rationing introduced in Dec. 1939, included bacon, butter, sugar and subsequently, meat, tea, margarine, jam, cheese, milk, sweets, biscuits and bread.

RATTLESNAKE
(*Crotalus*) Amer. venomous snakes of the Pit Viper sub-family. Measuring 4-8 ft. there are several N. Amer. species; one extends S. of Panama. They produce living young. The rattle comprises several loose-jointed horny pieces attached to the tail's end.

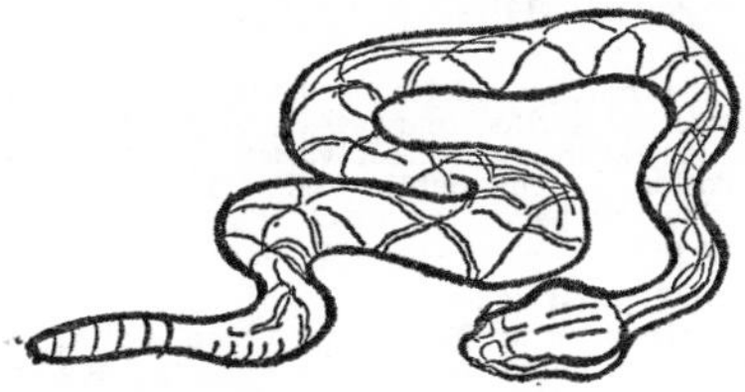

RAVEL, Maurice
[ra-vel'] (1875-1937) Fr. composer. At the age of 22 his *Pavane pour une Infante défunte* for piano appeared. His first great success came with the ballet *Daphnis et Chloe*, 1909.

RAVEN
(*Corvus corax*) Largest bird of Crow family. Normally 25 in. long, strong-billed, strong-flying, harsh-voiced, with ebony-black bill, legs and plumage. It breeds in hilly districts and rocky coasts in Brit., in Lakeland, Wales, the Pennines and parts of Scot. Easily tamed, it makes an intelligent but thievish pet.

RAVENNA
City of Emilia, N. Italy, 70 m. S. of Venice, famous for its ecclesiastical archit. of 5th to 8th cents. It is one of the oldest Ital. towns. Pop. 115,205.

RAWALPINDI
Temporary cap. of Pakistan on N.W. Frontier, 90 m. S.E. of Peshawar. Pop. 340,175.

RAWSTHORNE, Alan
(1905-71) Eng. composer. His first major work was his *Theme and Variations* for two violins, 1938. Since then have appeared *Symphonic Studies* for orchestra, concertos for piano and for violin, a symphony, etc. C.B.E. 1961.

RAY
Flat, cartilaginous fish with broad and fleshy pectoral fins. Of true rays (*Raia*), Brit. forms include the Short-snouted Thornback, the Spotted, Starry and Sandy rays. Allied families include the Electric ray or Torpedo, Sting-ray, Eagle-ray and Ox-ray.

RAZOR SHELL
(or **Razor Fish**) Sand-burrowing bivalve molluscs with long, narrow, parallel-sided shells.

RAZORBILL
(*Alca torda*) Sea-bird of the Auk family, inhabiting arctic and N. regions. Resident in Brit., 17 in. long, it has a glossy blackish plumage which is white underneath. The massive deeply-furrowed bill has a hooked tip.

READE, Charles
(1814-84) Eng. novelist and dramatist. He began writing plays in 1850, but it was as a novelist that he achieved fame: *e.g. It is Never Too Late to Mend* (1856), *The Cloister and the Hearth* (1861).

READING
County borough and county town of Berks., 36 m. W. of London, at the confluence of the Kennet and the Thames. Famous for its biscuits and seeds; it is an agricultural and railway centre and has engineering works. The univ. was constituted in 1926. R. returns 2 members to Parl. Pop. 121,420.

RECHABITES
(1) Heb. religious community. They dwelt in tents, and avoided wine, vine-planting and grain-growing (2 Kings, 10). (2) **Independent Order of Rechabites,** a total abstinence Friendly Soc. founded 1835.

RECORD OFFICE
Public building in London. In it the state papers and other historical documents are kept.

RECORDER
A woodwind instrument. It has a whistle mouthpiece at one end.

RECORDER
In Eng. a judge. Certain cities and towns have the right to hold courts of quarter sessions and to preside over them, a barrister, called a recorder, is appointed.

RECTOR
Lat. word meaning 'ruler'. In the C. of E. a rector is one who holds a living in which all the tithes belong to him. It is also used for the headmaster of some Scot. schools. The title is also held by certain ecclesiastics who are engaged in teaching in the R.C. Church.

RED CROSS
Internat. agency for the alleviation of human suffering, esp. for giving relief to the sick and wounded in time of war. Its origin may be dated from a meeting held at Geneva on Feb. 9, 1863, to discuss the suggestions contained in a booklet by Henri Dunant entitled *Un Souvenir de Solferino*. An internat. conference at Geneva accepted the principle of giving protection in war to the personnel of milit. hospitals and authorised as the symbol of such protection the red cross on a white background. The Internat. Red Cross Committee at Geneva acts as a clearing house for all nat. units.

RED DEER
(*Cervus elaphus*) A large deer widely distributed in temp. Europe, W. Asia and N. Africa. The male, 4 ft. high at the withers, is called a Stag, becoming in the 6th year a Hart; the female is the Hind, the young the Fawn. The male develops finely-branched antlers each breeding season. *See* DEER.

RED SEA
Inland sea separating N.E. Africa from Arabia. It is *c.* 1,400 m. in length, from Suez in the N. to the Strait of Bab-el-Mandeb in the S. which connects it with the Ind. Ocean. Its greatest breadth is 250 m. The completion of the Suez Canal in 1869 restored it as a great commercial highway. Area: 169,073 sq.m.

REDMOND, John Edward
(1856-1918) Irish politician. M.P. 1881-1918. Redmond's aim was not separation, but a 'free Ireland within the Empire', and he expressed his abhorrence of the rebellion of April, 1916.

REDPOLL
Song-bird of the Finch family, distinguished by the male's crimson crown and rosy breast. The name applies loosely to the Cock Linnet in summer plumage and to the Mealy R. *Carduelis linaria*, with white-marked wings, a winter visitor to Brit. The Lesser R., *C. cabaret*, is resident.

REDSHANK
(*Tringa totanus*) Brit. shore-bird akin to the Sandpipers and ranging over Europe, Asia and N. Africa. Measuring 11 in. with greyish-brown plumage, whitish beneath, long bright red legs and black-tipped dusky red bill. The slightly larger Spotted R. with more mottled plumage, is a bird of passage in E. Eng.

REDSTART
Song-birds of the Thrush sub-family, natives of Europe, Asia and Africa. The Common European (*Phoenicurus Phoeniarus*) with white forehead and black throat, habitually flirts the chestnut tail; the male, $5\frac{1}{4}$ in. long, has a bright bay breast. The female is brownish with paler underparts. The Black R. (*P. ochrurus*) visits S. Eng. autumnally.

REDWING
(*Turdus musicus*) Small species of Thrush. The male, $8\frac{3}{4}$ in. long, with reddish-orange under wing-coverts and axillaries, is distinguishable from the song-thrush by a white streak over the eye.

REDWOOD
Name of several unrelated trees. The Calif. redwood, *Sequoia sempervirens*, a cone-bearing evergreen growing 130-140 ft. high, with a trunk 8 to 25 ft. across, yields light durable timber much used in Europe. Baltic redwood is the Scots pine.

REED
Various tall perennial water-loving grasses. The common broad-leaved reed, *Phragmites communis*, 6-10 ft. high, abounds in Brit. The sea-reed or marram grass, *Ammophila arenaria*, is extensively planted for binding sand-dunes.

REED
The sound-producing agent of certain wood-wind instruments. It consists of a small piece of thin cane fastened at one end with the other end free to vibrate. It may be a single reed fastened to and vibrating against the mouth-piece as in the clarinet and saxophone; or a double-reed, 2 pieces of cane bound together to form the mouthpiece and vibrating against each other, as in the oboe and bassoon. These are *beating reeds*; there are also *free reeds*; in the case of the harmonium, mouth organ and accordian, metal tongues vibrate to and fro through a slot.

REEDBUCK
Several allied African antelopes, esp. *Cervicapra arundinea*. It is 3 ft. high at the shoulders, short-tailed, pale-fawn, orange-tinted on the head, and dingy-white underneath.

REFERENDUM
Method in politics by which the people decide in favour of or against a certain proposal. It has long been used in Switzerland and in the U.S.A. but never as yet in Brit.

REFORMATION, The
Religious and polit. movement in Europe in the 16th cent. which ended in the establishment of the Protestant Chs. Its causes were the abuses prevalent in the R.C. Ch., the new critical spirit, fostered by the Renaissance, and the growing force of nationalistic feeling. In 1517, Martin Luther nailed to the church-door at Wittenberg his famous 95 theses, in which he attacked the sale of indulgences. He resisted attempts made by the Pope to suppress him, and was excommunicated in 1520. His followers received the name of 'Protestant' from their protest made at the Diet of Spires against a decree which enacted that no change should be made in Ch. practice and doctrine. The name **Reformed Churches** was given to the bodies estabd. as a result of the Calvinistic teaching, including the Huguenots in Fr. and the Presbyterian Ch. in Scot. The **Counter-Reformation** was the attempt of the R.C. Ch. to reform itself in the 16th cent. and to stem the flow of Protestantism, exemplified in the Council of Trent.

REFRIGERATION
Process of artificially lowering the temp. below that of the atmosphere. **Quick-freezing,** *i.e.* reducing the temp. to 30° below zero almost instantly, preserves the flavour and vitamins of fruit, vegetables, indefinitely. It is common to chill flesh-foods within 10° F. Flowers, and blood plasma for surgical use, can also be preserved by refrigeration.

REGENT
One who rules on behalf of a sovereign. When a sovereign is a minor, or is insane or in any other way incapable of ruling, it is usual to appoint a regent to act for him.

REGINA
Cap. city of Saskatchewan, Canada, 350 m. W. of Winnipeg. It has an extensive trade in wheat and manufactures agricultural machinery. Pop. 112,141.

REGISTRATION
(1) The official entries in books kept by a registrar of births, marriages and deaths, and also for recording a great variety of other information for the public use. (2) The act of insuring, by paying an extra fee, the safe delivery of letters, articles and luggage.

REGIUS PROFESSOR
The title given at Oxford and Camb. univs. to a prof. appointed to a 'chair' dating back to the time of Henry VIII. In Scot. the term signifies the holder of a professorship created by the Crown.

REGULUS, Marcus Atilius
(d. 250 B.C.) Rom. general. Victorious over the Carthaginians several times, he was defeated by them in 255 B.C. and held in captivity. In 250 B.C., according to tradition, the Carthaginians sent him under parole to sue for peace. He strongly advised the Senate to reject their proposals, and went back to Carthage, where he was put to d.

REINCARNATION
The return of the soul to another physical body after d. The doctrine of progressive rebirth is of very ancient origin, and is a cardinal tenet of Hinduism, Buddhism and theosophy.

REINDEER
(*Cervus* or *Rangifer trandus*) Sole species of deer antlered in both sexes. Standing 4 ft. high at the shoulders, swift-footed, it is brownish-grey, with whitish face and neck; the antlers are more or less palmate. The European form has long been domesticated, esp. by the Lapps, large herds being maintained for their milk, flesh and hides.

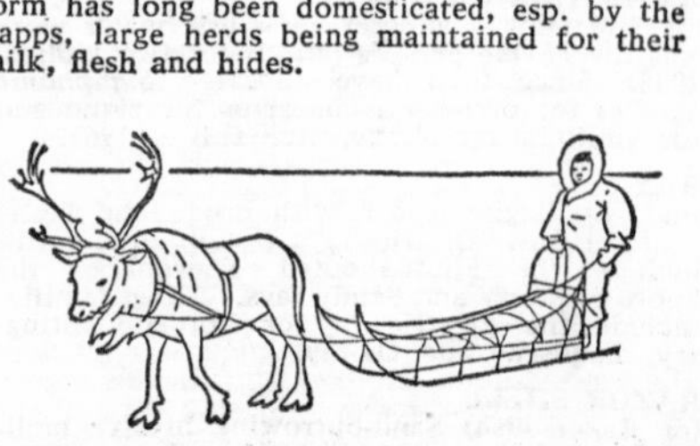

REINDEER MOSS
(*Cladonia rangiferina*) A widespread species of lichen, native of Brit. and esp. abundant in high altitudes. Comprising an intermingled mass of much-branched tubular structures, 2-12 in. high, it covers barren plains in Lapland and elsewhere.

REITH, John Charles Walsham, Baron
(1889-1971) A Scotsman. Qualified as a civil engineer. First Gen. Manager, latterly first Director-Gen. of the B.B.C. During the early years of the B.B.C. he maintained its intellectual and spiritual standards of polit. integrity and independence. Lord Reith was chairman of Imperial Airways (now B.O.A.C.), 1938-40; Min. of Information and of Transport (1940), of Works and Planning, 1940-2; chairman of the Colonial Development Corp., 1950-9.

RELATIVITY
Mathematical theory of the universe first put forward by Einstein in 1905. In it he postulated: (1) that absolute motion has no observable effect upon physical phenomena, *i.e.* that all physical phenomena are so constituted that it is not possible to observe absolute motion by their means; (2) that the rate of travel of light is the same in all directions at a given place, and its value is constant for all places in the universe, no matter what may be the relative movements of the earth or other system of reference involved. *See* EINSTEIN.

RELIGION
The term may be said to indicate an attitude of reverence to the Supreme Being, together with the resulting system of behaviour, including worship. Fundamentally religion embraces three ideas, *i.e.* of the soul, the world and the diety. In primitive cultures, man's religion is centred in nature worship. Objects are regarded as possessing mysterious powers or spirits, which require to be propitiated by worship and sacrifice. Thus arose polytheism. Monotheism is fundamental to Judaism, Islam and Christianity, and the religion of ancient Egypt was rooted in Monotheism.

REMBRANDT
Rembrandt Harmensz van Rijn (1606-69) Dutch painter. Studied painting from an early age, and began as an etcher. His output was enormous, and there remain *c.* 600 paintings, 2,000 drawings, and 300 etchings. He was the leader of the reaction against Ital. influence in the Dutch school.

RENAISSANCE
Revival of art and letters in Europe during the 15th and 16th cents. In 1453 Constantinople was captured by the Ottoman Turks. Their advance accelerated the migration to Italy of Gk. scholars, who gave a strong impetus to the new learning. The lit. of ancient Greece and Rome was studied. The movement was aided by the invention of printing (*q.v.*). In Eng. the Renaissance was assoc. esp. with Sir Thomas More, John Colet, and Erasmus.

RENFREWSHIRE
County of S.W. Scot., bounded on the N. by the Clyde. Other rivers are the Cart and Gryfe. The land is hilly in the S. and S.W. Agriculture is carried on; also coal and iron mining, and cotton and flax spinning. Renfrew is the county town, but Paisley is the admin. centre. R. returns 4 members to Parl. (2 burgh constituencies). Pop. 342,938. **Renfrew.** Burgh and county town of Renfrewshire on the Clyde, 5 m. W. of Glasgow. Pop. 18,000.

RENI, Guido
[rā'-ni] (1575-1642) Ital. painter, b. near Bologna. He went to Rome and painted there his famous *Aurora and the Hours*. He was famous also as an etcher, and is noted particularly for the accuracy of his drawing.

RENNES
[ren] Cap. of Ille-et-Vilaine dept. in N.W. Fr. Connected by canal with St. Malo. Pop. 157,692.

RENNET
Substance contained in the membranous lining of an unweaned calf's fourth stomach. It is used for curdling milk, esp. in cheesemaking. It comprises gastric juices including a ferment, rennin, which affects the coagulation.

RENO
[rē'-nō] City of Nevada, U.S.A., near the Calif. border. Divorces can be obtained after only 6 weeks' residence in the town. Pop. 51,470.

RENOIR, Auguste
[ren-wår] (1841-1919) Fr. artist. He studied art at the École des Beaux-Arts and met Monet and Sisley. In 1865 he exhibd. at the Salon and in 1874 took part in the first Impressionist Exhib.

RENT
Payment made for the use of land or buildings, made by the tenant to the landlord, weekly, monthly, quarterly or as arranged. Arrears of rent are recoverable by process of law. A payer of rent is entitled to deduct the income, or property, tax paid by him from the amount handed over to the landlord. In theory rent is fixed by an economic law. It is the amount which one will pay for land that is of greater value than no-rent land as it is called.

REPARATIONS
Payments made in money and kind, esp. by Germany as compensation for the damage done by her troops during World War I. The principle was laid down in the Treaty of Versailles. In 1921, at a conference held in London, the amount was fixed at £6,600,000,000. A payment was made, but the scheme soon proved impossible, and a moratorium was granted to Germany. In 1923 a committee was appointed to inquire into the subject and the **Dawes Plan** was agreed upon. Payments were regularly made until 1928, when it broke down. Another committee then met and the **Young Plan** was evolved, fixing the total sum. The economic and financial paralysis of 1930-2 made this plan inoperative, and in 1931 a moratorium of one year was granted to Germany. Before the end of this period Germany stated that she was unable to meet her liabilities and in 1932 a European conference met at Lausanne to effect a permanent settlement. This decided to abolish reparations. Thereafter the subject lapsed. By the peace treaties of 1947 Italy and the other allies of Germany in World War II were bound to pay substantial reparations.

REPRESENTATION
In politics, to take the place of other persons. Today all civilised countries possess representative institutions, as they are called. Under this system the people, unable, owing to their numbers, to rule themselves directly, elect certain persons to do this for them. These representatives are responsible to those who elect them because the latter can refuse to re-elect them at the end of their term of office. The system arose in Eng. in the M.A. when districts were asked to send men to the county courts to state who owned certain land, or who had committed a certain crime. From this type of representation arose the element of the Commons in Parl. The Fr. Revolution saw the beginning of representative govt. on the Continent, and in the 19th and 20th cents. is has spread widely. The progress has not been unchecked. Authoritarian govts., although retaining representative assemblies, have stripped them of power; examples of this can be seen in Soviet Russia, and formerly in Nazi Germany and Fascist Italy.

REPRESENTATIVES, House of
Name of the lower house of Congress of the U.S.A. and of the Parl. of the Commonwealth of Australia. The former consists of 435 members, elected for 2 years and paid salaries, as well as 2 delegates and a resident commissioner from territories outside the U.S.A. Its Pres. is the Speaker. Shares all legislative powers with Senate (*q.v.*). All legislation needs its assent. The Austral. House consists of 123 members who are paid salaries and elected for 3 years, or less. It is under a Speaker and resembles the Brit. House of Commons.

REPRODUCTION
Process by which animals perpetuate their own species or race. Reproduction may take place by either or both of 2 chief methods, (1) *Sexual* in which the elements of sex are concerned, since in this process male and female cells are united, and (2) *Asexual* in which no elements of sex are concerned. The *sexual* process includes (a) *Hermaphrodite* parents possessing male and female organs in the same individual; and (b) *Dioecious* parents which may be Oviparous (*e.g.* fishes, birds, etc.), Ovo-viviparous (*e.g.* some amphibians and reptiles), or Viviparous (*e.g.* mammals). The *asexual* reproductive process includes the processes of (a) Gemmation or budding, and (b) Fission. *See* EMBRYOLOGY.

REPTILE
Class of vertebrate animals ranking above amphibia and fishes but below birds and mammals. All bear epidermal layers of scales. They are cold-blooded, breathe by lungs, never by gills, and bear eggs, sometimes hatched within the female's body. Except for some tortoises, all are carnivorous. There are 4 orders: (1) lizards and snakes, (2) crocodiles, (3) tortoises, (4) now represented solely by the *Tuatera* of New Zealand. Several other orders, which flourished in the mesozoic age, are extinct. Known only from their fossil remains, they include Dinosaurs, Ichthyosaurs, Plesiosaurs and Pterodactyls.

REPUBLIC
State in which there is no monarchical head. Most of the Gk. states were repubs. as was Rome until Augustus. Repubs. were rare from that date until the revolt of the Amer. colonies and the Fr. Revolution, Venice and the United Provs. of the Netherlands being the exceptions. Fr. was a repub. for a short time after the deposition of Louis XVI, and in 1848-52, 1871-1940, 1946-58, and a 5th was constituted in 1958. A number of new ones emerged after World War I, including Germany, Austria, Turkey and in a sense Russia. Spain was added to the number in 1931; India, 1950; Egypt, 1953; the Sudan and Pakistan, 1956; and many of the emergent nations since.

REPUBLICAN
One who believes in a republic, but more exactly a member of one of the 2 great polit. parties in the U.S.A., the other being the Democratic (*q.v.*). The party is descended from the anti-federalists of Washington's time, and after the Civil War was dominant until 1932, save for Wilson's Presidency. From 1932 until 1952 it went out of office until it returned under Eisenhower. Harding, Coolidge and Hoover were all Republicans. The party stands for high protection and an extension of the power of the Nat. Govt.

RESIN
Substance exuded from some plants. Resins are insoluble in water, but soluble in alcohol and some oils, and are very inflammable. The soft resins are malleable and are used in medicine as ointment ingredients, while the hard resins are used chiefly as varnishes.

RESPIGHI, Ottorino
[res-pē′-gi] (1879-1936) Ital. composer. At the age of 21 he was 1st viola in the orchestra of the St. Petersburg Opera and was able to study with Rimsky-Korsakov. His works include operas, ballets, orchestral works, chamber music, piano pieces and songs.

RESPIRATION
Process in living matter whereby oxygen is obtained and waste products such as carbon dioxide are removed. In the unicellular organisms such interchange takes place over the entire body surface, but in the higher types special organs have been developed such as gills in fishes, lungs in mammals. **Respiratory System.** Lungs, bronchial tubes, trachea, larynx, mouth and nose constitute the respiratory system in man. Air is drawn into the lungs through the windpipe mainly by the muscular movements of the chest and diaphragm.

REST HARROW
Perennial pink-flowered shrub (*Ononis spinosa*), of the leguminous family. The taller growth is spiky, the lower covered with viscid hairs.

RESURRECTION
Belief in the rising again of the human body. The doctrine of immortality, which is of very ancient origin, was fundamental to the Osirian system in Ancient Egypt and some traces of it are found in the O.T. In modern times ideas about the resurrection can be divided into 4 categories. (1) That the bodies of the dead will be resurrected at the ' last day ' when all will be judged according to their deeds, good or bad. Linked with this is the belief based on Christ's teachings and promise as found in the N.T. (2) Many regard the physical body as the ' house ' which the soul inhabits on earth. (3) Spiritualists aver that there is a great body of evidence to prove the survival of the personality in a post mortem existence. (4) Rationalists and agnostics hold that faith and dogma are insufficient proof of survival, and that d. brings about the extinction of the individual.

RESURRECTIONISTS
(Body Snatchers) Persons who, during the latter half of the 18th and the first half of the 19th cents., stole newly-buried corpses from graveyards and sold them to teachers of anatomy. Prior to the passing of the first Anatomy Act (1832), this was highly remunerative. The famous case of Burke and Hare brought to light the fact that unscrupulous resurrectionists would not stop at murder to supply corpses.

RETRIEVER
Sporting dog. There are 4 varieties. The flat haired is hybrid between a Setter and a Welsh Collie sheep dog. The Curly Haired has a Poodle strain. The Golden Haired is highly ornamental and has all retriever qualities. The Labrador, besides being an excellent gun dog, is popular as house dog and pet.

RÉUNION
[rā-ü-nyō(ng)] or **Bourbon.** Fr. overseas dept., an Is. in the Ind. Ocean, 420 m. E. of Madagascar. Sugar, rum and manioc are produced. The cap. is St. Denis. Discovered by the Portuguese early in the 16th cent. it was annexed by Fr. in 1649, and occupied by Brit. between 1810 and 1814. Area: 1,000 sq.m. Pop. 347,000.

REUTER, Paul Julius, Baron von
[roi′-ter] (1816-99) B. Germany, became a naturalised Brit. subject in 1851. He founded Reuters Telegraph Agency which was developed into a world wide service for the collection and dispensing of internat. news. It has an unrivalled reputation for unbiased accuracy.

REVELATION, Book of
Last book of Bible. It is the only example contained in the N.T. of an extensive Jewish apocalyptic lit.

REVOLVER
A small firearm evolved from the pistol. In 1835 Col. Samuel Colt invented the type which has one fixed barrel and a revolving cylinder containing a number of chambers for cartridges which are fired in turn by a one-lock mechanism.

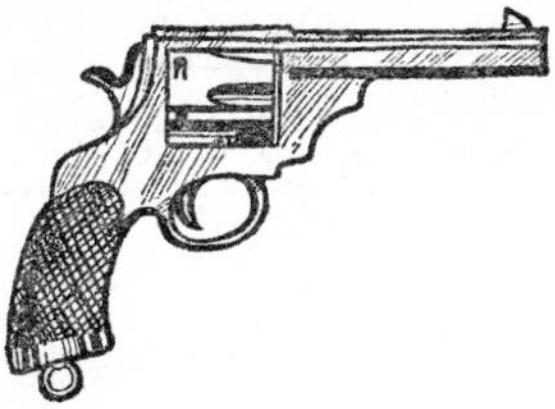

REYKJAVIK
[rā′-kyă-vik] Cap. of Iceland, on the S.W. coast of the Is. It is the seat of the Althing or parl. The chief port of Iceland, it exports fish, fish oil and skins. Hot springs form a natural hot water supply. Pop. 89,000.

REYNAUD, Paul
(1878-1966) Fr. politician. He succeded Daladier as P.M. in 1940. When Fr. collapsed before the German attack in the early summer Reynaud attempted to continue resistance, but was overborne and gave place to Pétain. Imprisoned by the Germans.

REYNOLDS, Sir Joshua
(1723-93) Eng. painter. B. Plympton, Devon. 1st Pres. of the Royal Academy, 1768. The following year he was knighted, and in 1784 received the appointment of painter-in-ordinary to George III. His friends included Burke, Johnson and Goldsmith.

RHEA
[rē′-ă] Amer. ostrich, represented by 3 species, all found in the pampas of S. Amer. It has 3 toes on the feet, and is smaller than the African O. The eggs are laid in a shallow excavation on the ground.

RHEIMS
[rēmz] (*Fr.* **Reims** [ra(ng)s]). City in Marne dept. N.E. Fr. *c.* 90 m. from Paris. Centre of the woollen industry. Founded in pre-Rom. times. Many Fr. kings were consecrated in the cath., including Charles VII, at the instigation of Joan of Arc, 1429. Pop. 138,576.

RHESUS FACTOR
[rē′-zus] In 1940, it was found that the red blood cells of 85 % of the white population reacted to antibodies that developed in rabbits' blood when rabbits were injected with red cells of rhesus monkeys. Individuals who reacted were regarded as Rh-positive and the remaining 15% Rh-negative. Further research revealed that all human blood contained an Rh factor, the form of which was determined genetically by grouping of a number of genes. When an Rh-negative person is transfused with Rh-positive blood, he may develop antibodies which will cause clotting or breaking of the red cells of subsequent transfusions of Rh-positive blood. An Rh-negative mother may develop similar antibodies in response to an Rh-positive foetus.

RHEUMATISM
Popular name for a variety of diseases resulting from different causes, all being characterised by pain and stiffness. **Rheumatic Fever** or **Acute Rheumatism.** Acute infection of unknown origin characterised by multiple inflammation of joints and disease of heart valves. **Rheumatoid Arthritis.** Condition of unknown cause most often seen in adult females but sometimes in children and characterised by attacks of pain affecting fingers and wrists with later swelling of those joints as well as those of hands, feet, ankles and knees. Disease may progress with wasting of muscles and deformities of affected limbs. *See* FIBROSITIS; OSTEO-ARTHRITIS; GOUT.

RHINE
River of Europe. It rises in Switzerland and flows through the Lake of Constance to Basle. Thence it turns N. between the Black Forest and Vosges Mts. in a wide rift valley. At Bonn the river enters the N. European plain, and flows N.W. into the N. Sea near Rotterdam; the Waal, Lek, Ijessel and Old Rhine are the distributaries. It has always been an important routeway. Canals connect it with C. and S. Fr. and N. Germany. The main tributaries are the Neckar, Main and Ruhr; Mainz, Bonn, Cologne, Düsseldorf and Nijmegen are towns on its banks.

RHINITIS
[rin-ī′-] Inflammation of mucous membrane of nose. Dust, irritating fumes, bacterial infection and pollen of grasses or flowers are the most common causes. Commonly called catarrh, treated by removing cause.

RHINOCEROS
Ungulate mammal of the order Perissodactyla. A clumsy, heavily built animal 5-6 ft. high at the shoulders, it is timid and nocturnal, frequenting swampy regions. There are 1 or 2 horns, on snout or forehead. In the Indian species the thick warty skin is disposed in folds and there is 1 horn. The white rhinoceros, 6 ft. high, is the largest, and, with the black species, is native to Africa.

RHODE ISLAND
Smallest state of the U.S.A. on the Atlantic coast, between Connecticut and Massachusetts. There is little agriculture, but manufacturing is important, esp. textiles. Providence is the cap. Became a separate Eng. colony in 1663. It was of the orig. 13 states, and now sends 2 representatives to Congress. Area: 1,214 sq.m. Pop. 949,800.

RHODES
Is. of the Dodecanese group in the Aegean Sea, 12 m. S. of the coast of Asia Minor. Vines and fruits are grown, and kaolin is mined. A great centre of Gk. culture, it formed part of the Rom. and Byzantine emp. Assigned to Italy as a result of World War I, the Is. was ceded to Greece, 1946. Pop. 61,800.

RHODES, Cecil John
(1853-1902) Eng. statesman. He was sent to S. Africa for his health. He amassed a fortune at Kimberley, came home, and entered Oriel Coll., Oxford. In 1889 he formed the Brit. S. Africa Co. to penetrate N. He was P.M. of Cape Colony, 1890-6, his ministry ending owing to his connection with the Jameson Raid (*q.v.*). Turned his attention to the development of Rhodesia, to which he devoted the rest of his life. In his will he bequeathed £6,000,000 for the founding of **Rhodes Scholarships** at Oxford.

RHODESIA
Territory in S. Africa stretching from the Transvaal N. to Tanganyika and the Congolese Repub. The N. and S. regions joined with Nyasaland (*see* MALAWI) in the C. African Fed. (1953-63) *q.v.* In 1888 the Brit., through Cecil Rhodes made a treaty with the Matabele king, Lobengula, for the right to seek and work minerals. The Brit. S. Africa Co., formed by Rhodes, began settlement of the country, interrupted by the Matabele War, the Jameson Raid and the S. African War. S. R. was annexed as a crown colony in 1923, while N. R. was separately admin. from 1911, being taken over by the Brit. govt. 1924. N. R. became indep. 1964 and S. R. became Rhodesia. *See* ZAMBIA. Negotiations between the Brit. and S. R. govts. over constitutional changes broke down, 1965.

Led by Mr. Ian Smith, R. made unilateral declaration of indep. It became repub., 1970, formally severing ties with Brit. Maize, cotton, tobacco, sheep and cattle, copper, gold, coal and diamonds are produced. Salisbury is the cap., Bulawayo is larger. Area: 150,330 sq.m. Pop. 5,090,000

RHODIUM
Silvery metallic element discovered by Wollaston in 1804. It occurs free in nature, often assoc. with platinum.

RHODODENDRON
Genus of ornamental flowering shrubs and trees of the family Ericaceae.

RHONDDA
[ron'-thă] Borough of Glamorgan 16 m. N.W. of Cardiff. It returns 2 members to Parl. Pop. 100,000.

RHÔNE
[rōn] River of Switzerland and Fr. which rises on the slopes of Mt. St. Gotthard, 6,000 ft. high. It flows through the Lake of Geneva to Lyons, where it is joined by the Saône, and then S. to the Medit.

RHUBARB
Herbaceous plant of the genus *Rheum* and family Polygonaceae. A native of Siberia, it is widely cultivated in other countries for its edible stalks, which are stewed and used as preserves.

RHUM
[rum] Is. of the Inner Hebrides, Scot., 15 m. N.W. of Ardnamurchan.

RHYMER, Thomas (the)
A half-legendary Scot. poet of the 13th cent. who lived in Erceldoune in Berwickshire.

RIB
Bone, of which there are 12 pairs, forming the box-like structure called the thorax. Behind they are all attached to the spinal column. In front the upper 7 are attached to the sternum the 3 upper ones of the remaining 5 fuse together and the last 2 are free.

RIBBENTROP, Joachim von
(1893-1946) German Nazi leader. During World War I he was a secret agent in the U.S.A. He joined the Nazi party in 1932. German ambassador to Brit. 1936-8, and Foreign Minister (1934-43). Responsible for the annexation of Austria and the occupation of Czechoslovakia (1938-9); he negotiated the pact with Russia in 1939, and delivered the ultimatum to Poland which precipitated World War II. He was taken by the Brit. in 1945, tried at Nuremberg as a war criminal, 1946, and executed.

RIBBON FISH
Deep-sea fish from the Atlantic, Medit. and Pacific. The thin, narrow, elongated body bears a dorsal fin strengthened with longer rays at the head end.

RIBBON GRASS
(*Phalaris arundinacea*: var. *picta*) Cultivated variety of tall grass with broad, striped leaves of green and white.

RIBOFLAVIN
[rib-ō-flā'-vin] Name given to vitamin B2. It is naturally present in milk and the whole wheat grain. *See* VITAMINS.

RICARDO, David
(1772-1823) Brit. political economist. In 1799 his interest in political economy was awakened by Adam Smith's *Wealth of Nations*. His chief work, *The Principles of Political Economy and Taxation* appeared in 1817.

RICE
Dressed grain of the annual grass, *Oryza sativa*. Grown extensively in the E. as the principal food, it is also cultivated in the U.S.A., Africa, S. Europe and elsewhere. Grown chiefly in wet land, the young plants are set out actually under water which subsequently dries.

RICHARD I
(1157-99) King of Eng. 3rd son of Henry II. Succeeded Henry as king in 1189. He reigned for 10 years, but passed only a few months in Eng. He took a leading part in the Crusades. In 1192 he was taken prisoner in Germany and ransomed in 1194. Known as Coeur de Lion (Lionheart) he was killed in battle at Chaluz. He mar. Berengaria, daughter of the King of Navarre, but left no legitimate children. His successor was his brother John.

RICHARD II
(1366-1400) King of Eng. Son of the Black Prince, he succeeded his grandfather Edward III, in 1377. His reign was full of trouble. Taxation was heavy, and risings took place in many parts of the country, the most serious being that of Wat Tyler (1381). The preaching of the Lollards (*q.v.*) helped to increase discontent. Henry of Lancaster forced him to abdicate in 1399.

RICHARD III
(1452-85) King of Eng. Throughout the reign of his brother, Edward IV, he gave him loyal assistance, but on his d. he usurped the crown from his nephew, Edward V, whom he is believed to have had murdered in the Tower. He d. fighting Henry of Richmond at Bosworth.

RICHARDS, Sir Gordon
(1905-) Eng. jockey. Champion jockey 26 times in 34 years. Has ridden 4,870 winners. Knighted in 1953. He pub. his autobiog. *My Story* in 1955.

RICHARDSON, Samuel
(1689-1761) Eng. novelist. *Pamela* (1740) is the first Eng. ' novel '. Richardson also wrote *Clarissa* (1748), *Sir Charles Grandison* (1754).

RICHELIEU, Duc de
[rēsh-ē'-loo, -lö] **Armand Jean du Plessis** (1585-1642) Fr. cardinal and min. of Louis XIII. Made cardinal in 1622, chief min. in 1624. Founded Fr. Academy, 1635. His policy aimed at the suppression of the Huguenots, the vindication of the royal authority, and the security of Fr. against the Habsburgs.

RICHMOND
Borough of Greater London (1964) on the Thames, formerly in Surrey. It includes Kew. R., with Barnes, returns 1 member to Parl. Pop. 41,000.

RICHMOND
Seaport and cap. of Virginia, U.S.A. at the mouth of the James, 115 m. from Washington. It is a great tobacco centre. Pop. 219,958.

RICHMOND and Gordon, Duke of
Brit. title. Henry VIII created his natural son **Henry Fitzroy,** Duke of Richmond. Charles II's natural son, **Charles Lennox,** created by him Duke of Richmond, was the ancestor of the present Duke of Richmond and Gordon.

RICHTER, Jean Paul Friedrich
[rich'-ter] (1763-1825) German writer. His early books, *Selection from the Devil's Papers* (1789), *The Invisible Lodge* (1793), *Hesperus* (1795), and the humorous idyll *The Life of Quintus Pixlein* (1796), earned great praise. In general, his works are cast in the form of the novel, but they are deeply philosophical and analytical in character. He himself regarded *The Titan* (1800-3) as his masterpiece.

RICKETS
A nutritional disease occurring where there is deficiency of vitamin D. It is seen most often in infancy but can occur in later life, esp. during pregnancy. The chief signs of the disease are failure of growth and softening of bone.

RIDGWAY, Matthew B.
(1895-) Amer. Gen. Served in World War II under F.-M. Montgomery. He succeeded Gen. MacArthur as C.-in-C. U.N. forces in Korea, Dec. 1950. Supreme Allied Commander Europe (1952-3), when he returned to U.S. as Army Chief of Staff. Retired, 1955.

RIDLEY, Nicholas
(*c.* 1500-55) Eng. bishop and martyr. Leader of the reformed faith and one of the compilers of the Eng. Prayer Book (1548). When Mary became queen, he was arrested and tried for heresy. He was burned at the stake in Oxford.

RIEMANN, Georg Friedrich Bernhard
[rē′-män] (1826-66) German mathematician. Best remembered for his epoch-making discoveries in non-Euclidean geometry.

RIENZI, Cola di
[rē-en′-zi] (1313-54) Rom. statesman. His aim was to restore the former glory of Rome. In 1347 he led a successful rising against the nobles. Encouraged by this triumph, he essayed to unite all Italy in a great repub. with Rome as cap. He was killed in a popular rising.

RIF
Mt. district of Morocco. It is chiefly known because its inhabitants, of Berber stock, were constantly at war with Spain.

RIFLE
Firearm with a grooved barrel which gives a rotary motion to the bullet. The *Enfield* with a percussion lock was introduced into the Brit. Army in 1855. The revolving chamber was invented by the Amer. Samuel Colt (1814-62). The *Lee-Metford* (1888), was the first Brit. magazine rifle with bolt action, followed by the *Lee-Enfield*, with a calibre of ·303 and a range up to 2,800 yds. This was replaced by the ·30 calibre in 1954.

RIG VEDA
[-vā′-] The most important and the oldest of the 4 extant collections of Hindu Scriptures. The date is believed to be *c.* 1000 B.C. but it is probably much earlier.

RIGA
[rē′-] Seaport and cap. of Latvia, U.S.S.R. on the Dvina, 7 m. from its mouth in the Gulf of R. Founded, 1158, it was a member of the Hanseatic League. It fell to Poland, 1561, was taken by Sweden, 1621, and finally by Russ. 1710. From 1919-40 it was cap. of the indep. Latvian repub. Pop. 605,000.

RIGHT OF WAY
The right of the public to pass over land in private ownership. If a way over land has existed without interruption for 20 years, it is for ever a right of way. Many landlords close the footpaths on their estates for one day in 7 years, or some other period, in order to prevent a right of way being estabd.

RIGOR MORTIS
[rī′-gor mor′-tis] The general stiffening of the muscles which sets in after d. It is caused by a coagulation of the muscle-plasma. The time of onset varies; it is seldom sooner than 10 minutes or later than 7 hours. The duration is also variable.

RILKE, Rainer Maria
(1875-1926) German poet. B. Prague, he wrote *Lay of Love and Death of Cornet Christopher Rilke, Notes of Malte-Laurids Brigge.*

RIMBAUD, Arthur
(Jean Nicolas) (1854-91) Fr. poet; author of *Une Saison en Enfer* (1873). *See* SYMBOL.

RIMSKY-KORSAKOV, Nicholas Andreievich
(1844-1908) Russ. composer. A member of the ' Five ', the Russian nationalist group of composers under Balakirev, he made skilful use of Russian folk music. He wrote over a dozen operas. He was a master of orchestration. Prob. his best known orchestral piece is the symphonic suite *Scheherazade.*

RINDERPEST
(or **Cattle Plague**) An acute contagious disease chiefly affecting cattle, characterised by fever and inflammatory lesions of mucous membranes. Disease is world wide in temp. climates. Not now seen in Brit. due to adequate measures at the ports to deal with imported livestock.

RING DOVE
(*Columba palambus*) Largest species of the common Wood Pigeon. Common in Brit. and Europe, it frequents open spaces in cities, as well as the countryside, assembling in flocks. It causes much damage to crops in its quest for food.

RING OUSEL
(*Turdus torquatus*) Species of mountain song bird of Thrush family. Common in Scandinavia and other parts of Europe, it is a summer visitor to Brit. It breeds in the N. in the Peak district, Devon and Cornwall. Somewhat larger than the Common Blackbird, the plumage is black with greyish margins and a crescent of white on the breast.

RINGWORM
Highly contagious disease caused by a species of bacteria of the fungus group. Scalp infection is most common in school years, beards and pubic region in later life, but body ringworm is found at all ages.

RIO DE JANEIRO
[jă-nā′-rō] Former cap. and seaport of Brazil, on the W. side of the Bay of Rio de J. At the entrance to the bay is the Sugar Loaf Mt. Rio de J. was founded 1555, and became cap. 1822, when Brazil became indep. When Brasilia (*q.v.*) was built, Rio became the 21st state of Brazil, known as Guanabara. It is the centre of a federal district. Pop. 3,909,000.

RIO GRANDE
River of N. Amer. 1,800 m. long. It rises in the Rocky Mts. in S.W. Colorado, flows across New Mexico, forms the boundary between the U.S.A. and Mexico and eventually flows into the Gulf of Mexico.

RIPON
Cath. city and borough of the W. Riding, Yorks. on the Ure, 24 m. N. of Leeds. An agricultural centre. Pop. 10,540.

RIVER
Stream of water flowing in a natural channel to the sea, a lake or other river. The water percolates slowly through the soil and may be supplemented in wet weather by the actual run off from the land, sometimes causing floods. River water carries much material in suspension. When the current is checked, as happens during flooding, much of the suspended material is deposited on the flood plain, to give rise ultimately to a greater fertility. Suspended material may result in delta formation.

RIVER HOG
(*Potamochaerus*) One of the pigs (fam. *Suidae*) native in W. Africa and Madagascar. It ranges in herds among swampy forest regions. Its natural food is roots and herbage, but the herds raid plantations and cause great damage.

RIVERINA
Region of N.S.W. Australia, between the Murray and Murrumbidgee rivers. Wheat, wool and fruit are produced.

RIVIERA
[riv-yair'-ă] Name given to a strip of land in Fr. and Italy on a branch of the Medit. It extends for *c.* 140 m. and is noted for its wonderful climate and scenery. Resorts include Cannes, Nice, Monte Carlo, Antibes (Fr. Riv.), Rapallo and Bordighera (Ital.).

RIYADH
Cap. of Saudi Arabia and of Nejd. A station on the caravan route from Mecca to Hasa. Pop. 225,000.

RIZZIO, David
[rit'-siō] (*c.* 1533-66) Ital. musician, who became Sec. to Mary, Queen of Scots. Lord Darnley, after his mar. to the queen, had R. dragged from her presence and murdered.

ROACH
(*Leuciscina rutilus*) Freshwater fish. Of a deep and silvery colour and 10-15 in. long, it is common in N. Europe.

ROARING FORTIES
Area of the S. oceans between 40° and 60° S. The name was given in the days of sailing ships because strong W. gales prevail.

ROB ROY
(1671-1734) Scots outlaw, whose orig. name was Robert Macgregor. In 1712 he raided the estate of the Duke of Montrose, who, he alleged, was unfairly pressing him for debt. After a long career as a freebooter, he was arrested and imprisoned, but afterwards pardoned.

ROBERT
Name of 2 dukes of Normandy. **Robert I** (d. 1035), called the Devil, was the father of William the Conqueror. **Robert II** (*c.* 1055-1135) the eldest son of William, succeeded him as Duke of Normandy (in 1087) but not as King of Eng.

ROBERT
Name of 3 kings of Scot. The first is more generally known as **Robert the Bruce** (*q.v.*). **Robert II** (1316-90) was a son of Walter the Steward and a grandson of Robert Bruce. He was the first of the Stewart kings.

ROBERTS, Earl
(1832-1914) Eng. soldier. B. Cawnpore, Frederick Sleigh Roberts served in the Indian Army throughout the Mutiny, winning the V.C. in 1858. In 1880, Roberts made his famous march through Afghanistan to the relief of Kandahar. From 1885-93 he was C.-in-C. in India. He was sent to S. Africa to retrieve the situation after the early Boer victories. He retired in 1904, but during World War I visited the troops in Fr., contracted pneumonia, and d. at St. Omer.

ROBERTSON, Thomas William
(1829-71) Eng. actor and dramatist. His fame was definitely estabd. by *Ours* (1866). Other successful plays followed, including *Caste* (1867), *Home* (1869), and *Dreams* (1869).

ROBESON, Paul
(1898-) Negro actor and vocalist. He is famous as a bass singer, specialising in negro spirituals.

ROBESPIERRE, Maximilien
[rōbz-pyair] (1758-94) Fr. revolutionary leader. He became the leader of the Jacobins. As member of the Convention, he demanded the establishment of a repub. and the d. of the king. He was a member of the Committee of Public Safety, and connected with the Reign of Terror. The Convention, in fear, turned on him as soon as the invasion threat was removed and he was guillotined.

ROBIN
(*Erithacus rubecula*) Small, brown bird common in Gt. Brit. The adult male has a bright red breast. The Amer. robin is a member of the Thrush family.

ROBIN HOOD
Eng. legendary hero represented in a series of old ballads as a chivalrous outlaw living in Sherwood Forest.

ROBINSON, William Heath
(1872-1944) Eng. artist. His humorous drawings were a popular feature of many Eng. and Amer. periodicals.

ROCHDALE
County borough of Lancs. on the Roch, 11 m. N.E. of Manchester, starting place of the co-operative movement. R. returns 1 member to Parl. Pop. 86,000.

ROCHELLE, La
[-shell'] Fr. town, cap. of Charente-Maritime dept. on the W. coast opposite the Ile de Ré. As a shipping centre it is connected with the Newfoundland fishing industry. A Huguenot centre in the 16th and 17th cents. Pop. 68,445.

ROCHESTER
Cath. city and borough of Kent on the Medway, 33 m. from London. Cement and machinery are manufactured. With Chatham, R. sends 1 member to Parl. Pop. 51,010.

ROCHESTER, Earl of
John Wilmot (1648-80) Eng. poet. B. near Woodstock, educ. Oxford. He was a courtier and wit, and wrote brilliant satires and lyrics.

ROCK
Mineral aggregate of which the earth's crust is composed. From their origin rocks may be classified into sedimentary, metamorphic and igneous. Sedimentary rocks are usually laid down under water, and may be fragmental, such as conglomerates, sandstones and shales, chem., such as inorganic limestones and beds of rock salt or gypsum, organic, such as the normal fossiliferous limestones and coal seams, or they may be pyroclastic, *e.g.* volcanic ashes. Metamorphic rocks have undergone alteration by high temps. and pressures, into schists and gneisses. Igneous rocks are those which have solidified from a molten state, or possibly re-crystallised from ultra-metamorphism.

ROCKALL
Small Atlantic Is. some 70 ft. high and 83 ft. wide. On Sept. 18, 1955, a party from H.M.S. *Vidal* took possession of the island. The Admiralty announcement of Sept. 21 said: 'A flagstaff was erected on the island, the Union Jack was broken, and a commemorative plaque was cemented to the rock. The annexation of this island was necessary since it is within the sector of the sea which is likely to come within the orbit of the projected guided weapons range in the Hebrides.' Rockall first appeared on maps less than 400 years ago.

ROCKEFELLER, John Davison
(1839-1937) Oil magnate and philanthropist. B. Richford, N.Y., he became, at the age of 50, the richest man in the world. He distributed *c.* $600,000,000 of his wealth, most of it for the establishment of: (1) **The Rockefeller Institute for Medical Research,** 'to conduct, assist and encourage investigations in medicine, surgery and allied subjects.' (2) The **Rockefeller Foundation,** 'to promote the well-being of mankind throughout the world.' (3) The General Education Board. (4) The **Laura Spelman Rockefeller Memorial.**

ROCKET
A propulsive system in which thrust is obtained from the rapid expansion of a jet of hot gas through a suitably profiled nozzle. The reaction is obtained solely from the change in momentum of the molecules which constitute the jet as they pass through the nozzle. In no sense does the jet impinge upon the air; indeed, in a vacuum, the absence of back-pressure on the nozzle results in increased thrust and efficiency. Unlike the jet engine, the rocket contains all the material needed to support the combustion which produces the jet. Thus it can function in outer space, where oxygen to support the normal burning of fuel is completely absent. The earliest recorded rockets were fireworks used for pyrotechnic purposes by the Chinese more than 2,000 years ago. By the 12th century the Chinese had evolved warlike missiles with rocket propulsion, and similar devices were used by the native Indian rulers against the British in the 18th cent. and by the British forces early in the 19th cent. By the beginning of the 20th cent. rockets were widely used not only as fireworks but also to carry life-saving lines to ships in distress. During World War II the German and Soviet armies used rocket propelled missiles in an artillery rôle on a large scale, and simple rocket projectiles were widely employed in Britain for anti-aircraft purposes. Of an entirely different nature was the German missile popularly known as V-2. This was a streamlined ballistic shape, 46 ft. long and about 65 in. maximum diameter, provided with four tail fins and propelled by a single-chamber rocket engine developing a sea-level thrust of 60,000 lb. This engine was fed with liquid propellants. The complete missile was arranged to take off vertically and could deliver a 2,230 lb. warhead over a range of about 190 miles. The speed at burnout of the engine was approximately 3,470 m.p.h. A total of 12,000 of these great missiles were manufactured; some 4,300 were launched, roughly half being aimed at London. In all, 1,050 impacted on the city, causing 2,754 deaths. Their modern successors are the ICBMs (inter-continental ballistic missiles), such as Polaris with a weight of 222,000 to 265,000 lb., launch thrust of 300,000 to 389,000 lb., and the ability to deliver a thermo-nuclear warhead over a range of from 6,300 to 12,000 m., with a probable impact error of less than 2 m. Other rocket-propelled guided weapons are used against aircraft, surface targets, submarines and all other kinds of military target, the smallest such missiles being those designed to be carried by infantrymen and fired against tanks. Rocket-propelled vehicles are used for space exploration (*q.v.*). *See* SATELLITE.

ROCKET, The
The first locomotive invented by George Stephenson, which ran on the Manchester and Liverpool Railway in 1830. It is now in the Science Museum, S. Kensington, London.

ROCKET
(*Hesperis*) Genus of plants of the family Cruciferae, including annual and perennial varieties.

ROCKHAMPTON
Port of Queensland, Australia, at the mouth of the Fitzroy. Dairy produce and minerals are exported. Pop. 44,500.

ROCKY MOUNTAINS
American mt. range, or system of ranges. It is the watershed of the Amer. continent, reaching from the Yukon R. in Alaska to New Mexico in the S., a distance of 2,200 m. In Colorado there are more than 40 peaks over 14,000 ft.

RODIN, Auguste
[rō-da(ng)] (1840-1917) Fr. sculptor. His first exhibition in the Salon was the *Bronze Age*, 1877. His famous *Burgesses of Calais* was exhibited in 1889, and *The Kiss* in 1898. His best known work in Eng. is *Le Penseur*, purchased for the nation in 1904.

RODNEY, Baron
(1719-92) Brit. admiral. One of his most brilliant victories was at Cape St. Vincent in 1780, when he defeated the Spanish fleet. In 1782 he drove the Fr. fleet from the Atlantic.

ROE-DEER
(*Capreolus*) Small deer widely distributed in Europe, including Brit. About 2 ft. high at the shoulders, it has a reddish coat (brown in winter) and a white rump. The antlers are short, nearly vertical, with 2 or 3 tines.

ROHAN, Duc de
[rō-ā(ng)] **Henri** (1579-1638) Fr. soldier and Protestant leader. He joined the court of Henri IV and on the d. of the king became chief of the Huguenots. After the fall of La Rochelle (1628), and the peace of 1629, he left France. In 1638 he joined the Protestant army on the Rhine, and d. of wounds at Rheinfelden.

ROLAND
Frankish hero. A soldier in Charlemagne's army, he was killed at Roncesvalles in 778. **The Song of Roland** (1066-99) is the oldest of the *chansons de geste* and deals with the conquest of Sp. by Charlemagne.

ROLLER
Family of European birds related to Woodpeckers, with brilliant plumage. The Common Roller, *Coracias garrula*, with brown and blue plumage, visits Brit. in the autumn. The male bird has the curious habit, during the breeding season, of rolling over when in flight. The word Roller is also used for certain Tumbler Pigeons.

ROLLS-ROYCE
Two Englishmen developed the most famous motor car in the world. The **Hon. C. S. Rolls** (1877-1910) was an intrepid pioneer in ballooning, motor-racing and flying. He met Royce in Manchester in May 1904 and was so impressed by the performance of the 10 h.p. 2-cylinder Royce car that he agreed to be responsible for the sale of all Royce's future products. He was successful in racing these cars. The Company of Rolls-Royce was founded in 1907 for the purpose of building cars; aero-engines followed during the early part of the 1914-18 war. In 1910 Rolls was the first to fly the Eng. Channel both ways without stopping. **Sir Frederick Henry Royce, Bt.** (1863-1933) was the son of a miller in the Fen country. At 17, he found a job in a machine-tool shop at Leeds. At 21, he was in business for himself. His first car was built in Manchester in 1904. His aim was to produce the finest car in the world, and he succeeded. Many British fighter and bomber pilots in both World Wars owed their lives to the Rolls-Royce tradition, and this is being maintained with the same degree of superb technical excellence in the engines built by the firm for cars and planes, including those designed for jet propulsion (*q.v.*).

ROMAN CATHOLIC CHURCH
Numerically the largest body in Christendom. According to its own definition it is not *a* ch. among chs. but *the* Ch. It claims to be (*a*) ' One ' in doctrine, sacraments and government. (*b*) ' Holy ' with a sanctity of life and character arising esp. out of the sacramental system. (*c*) ' Catholic ' because its members are found in every part of the world. (*d*) ' Apostolic ', through an unbroken succession going back to the Apostle Peter. Among the distinctive R.C. doctrines are the authority of eccles. tradition, the 7 sacraments, transubstantiation, the sacrificial aspect of the Mass, purgatory, the infallibility of the Pope and the immaculate conception of the Virgin Mary. The principal act of worship is the celebration of the Mass. The supreme council of the Ch. is the Coll. of Cardinals, which acts as adviser to the Pope and at his d. elects a successor. The total R.C. pop. of the world is reckoned at over 550,000,000.

ROMAN EMPIRE
Empire of the ancient world. It grew up around the city of Rome. Traditionally the city was founded in 753 B.C. by descendants of fugitives from Troy, led by Aeneas. In 529 Tarquin, last of the 7 kings, was exiled, and the city became a repub. The chief officials were 2 consuls, who served for a year. Under them many conquests were made, with the result that in *c.* 200 years after Tarquin's expulsion almost the whole of Italy was ruled by Rome. In 264 B.C. the first of Rome's wars with Carthage began. During this struggle, Rome made her first acquisition of territory outside the mainland. Sicily and then Corsica and Sardinia were acquired, and a little later Greece was invaded. Spain and then Gaul were brought within the Rom. sphere of influence and possessions in Africa were extended. Meanwhile the constitution of the city was being slowly altered. The conquest of Gaul was largely the work of Julius Caesar. In 46 B.C. Caesar made himself dictator, but in 44 he was murdered. His heir was his nephew, Octavian, who, as Augustus, became the first of the Rom. emperors after crushing Antony and his other rivals. Soon after the d. of Augustus the Roms. invaded Brit. and settled in its S. half. The Empire centred in the Medit. and included S. and N.W. Europe, Asia Minor and a fringe of Africa. The Augustan age was one also of great literary activity in which Virgil, Horace, Livy and other great writers flourished. Augustus was followed in A.D. 14 by Tiberius. The last of the Julio-Claudian Emperors was Nero. The best of the later rulers were Trajan, Hadrian and the Antonines. With the d. of Marcus Aurelius the decline began. His son Commodus was killed by the soldiers, who nominated Emperors in quick succession, while the barbarians became more and more menacing. The decline was arrested by the efforts of Claudian, Aurelian, and above all Diocletian. In A.D. 323 Constantine the Great became emperor and in 330 he moved his capital from Rome to Byzantium. After his term there was one ruler in the E. and another in the W. and most of them were fully occupied in resisting the barbarians. Italy was overrun and Rome itself was sacked by Alaric, 410. In 455 the last emperor of the W., Romulus Augustulus, resigned and the Rom. empire ceased to exist.

ROMANES, George John
(1848-94) He carried out extensive research supporting the Darwin theory. In 1890 he settled in Oxford where he founded the **Romanes lectureship.**

ROMANOFF
Family name of the Tsars of Russia. It means ' son of Roman ', a Russian noble of the 16th cent. The male line d. out in 1730. The later Romanoffs are descended from Anna, daughter of Peter the Great and her husband, and they ruled until the abdication of the Tsar Nicholas II in 1917. *See* NICHOLAS II.

ROMANS, Epistle to the
First of the Pauline epistles in the N.T. Canon. It was probably written at Corinth at the close of Paul's third missionary expedition.

ROMANY
Language of the Gipsies, belonging to N.W. (Dardic) group of Indo-Aryan languages. 3 main dialects: (a) *Asiatic*, (b) *Armenian*, (c) *European*. *Parlyaree* (language of showmen, tinkers, etc.), has a Romany base.

ROME
Cap. of the Ital. Repub. on the Tiber, 16 m. from its mouth in the Tyrrhenian Sea. R. grew up round the ' seven hills ' which rose above the flood level. These hills are still enclosed by the Aurelian Wall, 21 m. long. R. is a polit. cap. rather than a commercial or industrial centre. It is a great tourist and pilgrim resort. Of the many ruined buildings, the most impressive are the Colosseum, a vast amphitheatre, the Baths of Caracalla, and the Forum. There are numerous palaces of the Renaissance period, and many fine chs. of which the most famous is St. Peter's. It was the chief city of a small kingdom, then of a powerful repub. (510 B.C.-30 B.C.), and finally of a vast emp. (*q.v.*). From that time until 1872, when the Ital. kingdom was estabd., R. was cap. of the Papal States and seat of the Popes. The Vatican City (*q.v.*) lies within the city. Pop. 2,485,000.

ROMFORD
Borough of Greater London (1964) formerly in Essex, on the Rom. There are cattle markets and engineering works. It returns 1 member to Parl. Pop. 115,600.

ROMMEL, Erwin Eugen Johannes
(1891-1944) German field-marshal. B. Swabia he served in World War I, later joining the Nazi party. As commander of the Afrika Korps (*q.v.*) in Libya, 1941-2, he gained a reputation as a skilful and formidable general before being defeated at the Battle of El Alamein (*q.v.*). Oct. 1944 it was reported that he had d. His chief-of-staff later revealed that he had been involved in the German Generals' Plot of July 20, 1944, and committed suicide.

ROMNEY, George
(1734-1802) Eng. painter. B. Dalton-in-Furness. After a period as a cabinet-maker, he studied painting, became a portrait painter and came to London in 1762.

ROMNEY MARSH
District near the S. Kent coast, covering *c.* 44,000 acres, noted for its sheep.

ROMULUS
Founder of Rome and its first king. Legend says that in infancy, Romulus and his twin brother, Remus, were thrown into the Tiber by their uncle, but the trough in which they were placed went aground. The children were suckled by a wolf and brought up by a shepherd. While they were building walls a quarrel arose and Remus was killed. Romulus became king of Rome.

RONALD, Sir Landon
(1873-1938) Eng. conductor and composer. Apptd. Prin. Guildhall S.M., London, 1910; knighted 1922. His works include incidental music; *Birthday Overture* for orch., piano pieces, songs, etc.

RONSARD, Pierre de
(1524-85) Fr. poet. After spending his youth as page and courtier, he became deaf and turned to study and poetry. He formed a group of 7 poets (' La Pléiade ') with Joachim du Bellay, Belleau, etc. to reform Fr. poetry by classical standards.

RÖNTGEN, Wilhelm Konrad von
[rönt'-gān] (1845-1923) German physicist. His most famous work was the discovery of the X-rays (**Röntgen rays**) in 1895. Röntgen demonstrated that these rays would pass through the body and print a shadow picture of the bones on a sensitive plate. Nobel Prize for physics in 1901.

ROOK
(*Corvus frugilegus*) Gregarious bird of the Crow family. In Brit. it remains through the year; farther N. it is a migrant. It nests in colonies. The plumage is black, with a bare patch at the base of the bill.

ROOSEVELT, Franklin Delano
(1882-1945) 32nd Amer. Pres. In 1932, as a Democratic candidate for the Presidency, he defeated Herbert Hoover and during his term of office the gold standard was abandoned and the dollar devalued. He introduced the Utilities Act and the Social Securities Act in 1935. He defeated Alfred Landon in 1936. Soon after the outbreak of war he launched a vast rearmament programme and introduced conscription. He was re-elected in 1940 and introduced his ' lease-lend ' plan for the supply of war materials to the Allies. In 1941 he drew up the Atlantic Charter with Mr. Churchill. From the time of the attack on Pearl Harbour he concerned himself solely with the conduct of the war. He was re-elected in 1944 but d. suddenly on April 12, 1945, having fought a continual battle against polio since 1921. His wife **(Anna) Eleanor Roosevelt** (1884-1962) actively helped him in his polit. life and did much social welfare work. She was U.S. representative to the U.N. General Assembly 1945-52.

ROOSEVELT, Theodore
(1858-1919) 26th Pres. of the U.S.A. Gov. of New York State in 1898, he was elected as Republican Vice-Pres., 1900. On McKinley's assassination in 1901 he became Pres. and was re-elected in 1904. A split in the Republican vote between Roosevelt and Taft caused his defeat by the Democrat Wilson in 1912.

RORKE'S DRIFT
Place in Zululand, successfully held against a Zulu onslaught by a handful of Brit. soldiers, Jan. 22, 1879.

RORQUAL
[ror'kwal] (*Balaenoptera musculus*) Related to the Blue Whale but smaller, the Common R. is a whalebone whale of the Arctic and Atlantic oceans.

ROSA, Carl August Nicolas
(1842-89) German musician. The Opera Co. which bore his name was formed in 1875 with the object of encouraging Eng. composers and producing their works.

ROSA, Salvator
(1615-73) Ital. artist. B. Renella, near Naples. He studied under Ribera and Falcone. His reputation rests mainly upon his landscapes.

ROSARY
String of beads used by Rom. Catholics as an aid to memory during devotional exercises. The devotions themselves are sometimes called rosaries.

ROSCOMMON
Inland county of Eire, in the prov. of Connaught, bounded by the Shannon and Suck. Cattle, sheep and pigs are reared, esp. on the plain of Boyle, and oats and potatoes are grown. Roscommon is the county town. Pop. 59,217.

ROSE
Flowering tree or shrub of the family Rosaceae. From the wild rose, *Rosa canina*, numerous strains have been developed. The main groups are ramblers. climbing roses, bush and standards, each with many varieties.

ROSE OF JERICHO
(*Anastatica hierochuntica*) Cruciferous plant of S. Europe with small, white flowers. After flowering the plant withers and the stems curve inward, forming a dry, shrivelled ball.

ROSEBERY, Earl of
Archibald Philip Primrose (1847-1929) Scots statesman. Foreign Sec. 1886 and 1892-4; P.M. 1894-5. He was a keen sportsman, his horses winning the Derby 3 times.

ROSEMARY
(*Rosmarinus officinalis*) Hardy evergreen perennial shrub of the Labiate family; 2 or 3 ft. in ht., it has fragrant green leaves from which an aromatic oil is extracted.

ROSES, Wars of the
(1455-85) Civil war in Eng. Richard, Duke of York, claimed the throne when Henry VI became insane. Henry's supporters, the Lancastrians, took a red rose as their symbol, and the Yorkists a white. At the Battle of Northampton, 1460, Henry was made prisoner and in 1461, York was killed at the Battle of Wakefield. The Lancastrians were defeated at Towton and their cause was hopeless until the Earl of Warwick changed sides in 1470. Henry was then released from prison and restored to the throne. At Barnet and Tewkesbury in 1471, the Lancastrian armies were crushed and the war was virtually over, although it is usually regarded as ending with the Battle of Bosworth, 1485, where Henry Tudor, defeating his enemies, became King Henry VII.

ROSETTA
Town of Lower Egypt on the Nile, 100 m. N.W. of Cairo, where the Rosetta stone was found, 1799. Pop. 28,700.

ROSS, Sir Ronald
(1857-1932) He discovered the part played by the mosquito in malaria. He became Director-Gen. of the Ross Institute and Hospital for Trop. Diseases in London. Nobel Prize for Medicine, 1902; knighted, 1911.

ROSS AND CROMARTY
County of N. Scot. which stretches from the E. to the W. coasts and includes Lewis and other Is. of the Hebrides. The coasts are indented with sea lochs, Dornoch, Cromarty and Beauly on the E., Broom and Torridon on the W. It is a mountainous area with peaks rising to 3,800 ft. Fishing is important; whisky is distilled. Dingwall is the county town; other towns are Stornoway, Cromarty, Tain and Invergordon. R. and C. with the W. Is. division of Inverness, returns 2 members to Parl. Pop. 57,388.

ROSS SEA
Antarctic sea, discovered by and named after, Capt. J. C. Ross, R.N., in 1839.

ROSSETTI, Dante Gabriel
(1828-82) Eng. poet and painter. B. London. His poem *The Blessed Damozel* was written before he was 20. In art he was influenced by Ford Madox Brown and became one of the founders of the Pre-Raphaelite Brotherhood,

1848. A collection of poems, after being buried with his wife (Elizabeth Siddal, d. 1862), was disinterred and pub. in 1870. His sister was **Christina Georgina R.** (1830-94). Among her works are *Goblin Market* (1862), *Prince's Progress* (1866), *The Face of the Deep* (1892).

ROSSINI, Gioacchino
[ro-sē′-ni] (1792-1868) Ital. composer. His best-known work *Il Barbiere di Siviglia* was produced unsuccessfully when he was only 24. He wrote a series of over 40 operas until 1829 when *Guillaume Tell* was produced. Thereafter he wrote little music apart from the *Stabat Mater* and the *Petite Messe Solennelle*.

ROSSLARE
Seaport of Wexford, Eire, 6 m. S.E. of Wexford, the terminus of the Fishguard steamer service.

ROSTAND, Edmond
(1868-1918) Fr. dramatist; b. Marseilles. He is the author of numerous plays, including *Les Romanesques, Cyrano de Bergerac, L'Aiglon.*

ROSYTH
[rō-sīth′] Seaport of Scot. on the N. of the Firth of Forth. The dockyards and other works were begun, 1909, and much used during World War I and II.

ROTARY INTERNATIONAL
The first fellowship Club was founded in Chicago in 1905, and grew out of the conception that one man from each trade or profession should form a group which would meet at each other's business premises according to a weekly rota. Soon the movement spread throughout the U.S.A. and was introduced into Gt. Brit. (1911). There are now some 8,500 clubs in 90 countries with a total membership of 390,000; 790 in Brit. and Ireland. The fundamental principle of ' one man one job ' has been adhered to—one architect, doctor, plumber, and so on. A spectacular achievement of Rotarians during World War II was the establishment of the committee that was destined to become the United Nations Educational, Scientific and Cultural Organisation—UNESCO.

ROTHAMSTED
Village of Herts. near Harpenden. Sir John Bennet Lawes (1814-1900) carried out valuable agricultural experiments there. His work has been carried on by the Lawes Agricultural Trust.

ROTHENSTEIN, Sir William
[-stīn] (1872-1945) Eng. artist. During World War I was made one of the official painters. In 1920 he was apptd. Prin. of the Royal Coll. of Art, S. Kensington, London. He pub. his *Reminiscences* in 1932. His son, **Sir John Rothenstein** (1901-)—Director and Keeper of the Tate Gallery, London, 1938-64.

ROTHERHAM
County Borough of the W. Riding, Yorks., 6 m. N.E. of Sheffield, on the Don and Rother. It has glass and pottery manufactures, iron, steel and chemical works. It returns 1 member to Parliament. Pop. 86,220.

ROTORUA
Town of N. Is., New Zealand. It is famous as a beauty spot and health resort, and the centre of the remarkable volcanic hot spring district. Pop. 28,100.

ROTTERDAM
City and most important seaport of the Netherlands in S. Holland prov. at the confluence of the Rotte and New Maas, 22 m. from the sea. It has extensive docks, and is accessible to the largest vessels. Industries include shipbuilding, iron works, chemicals, and tobacco and margarine manufacture. Pop. 730,963.

ROUAULT, Georges
[roo′-ō] (1871-1958) Fr. artist. B. Paris. He was apprenticed to a stained glass artist. His early subjects were mainly landscapes in the academic style. He later painted subjects from the theatre and street scenes.

ROUEN
[roo′-ā(ng)] River port of N. Fr. Cap. of Seine-Inférieure dept. on the Seine, 87 m. below Paris. The chief oil and coal port of Fr., its industries include oil refining. R. was the old cap. of the Duchy of Normandy, and contains many hist. buildings, including the 13th cent. Gothic cath. Pop. 123,474.

ROULETTE
[roo-let′] Fr. game of chance, a feature of the gambling rooms of Monte Carlo. The roulette table, covered with a green cloth, is made up of 2 similar halves with a space in the middle for the wheel.

ROUND TABLE
Legendary table used by King Arthur and his knights. It was made round so that there should be no jealousies about precedence.

ROUNDERS
Outdoor game played with a stick and a ball. The members of one side strike the ball in turn, when it is tossed to them, each as he does so running to first base. If possible he runs round to the striking post, passing all the bases. *See* BASEBALL; CRICKET.

ROUSSEAU, Henri
(1844-1910) Fr. artist. His first dated paintings are 1880. Exhibd. at the Salon des Indépendants 1886-1910.

ROUSSEAU, Jean Jacques
(1712-78) Fr. writer and phil. After a vagabond career, he went to Paris, and achieved fame with *La Nouvelle Héloise* (1760), *Du Contrat Social* (1762) (which paved the way for the Revolution), and *Confessions* (1782).

ROUSSEAU, Théodore
[roos-ō′] (1812-67) Fr. artist. In 1848 he settled at Barbizon, and was a leading member of the group there.

ROWE, Nicholas
(1674-1718) Eng. poet and playwright. He edited Shakespeare (1709), and wrote *Tamerlane* (1702), *The Fair Penitent* (1703), *Jane Shore* (1714), *Lady Jane Grey* (1715). Poet laureate, 1715.

ROWING
Art of propelling a boat by means of oars. In sport the most famous rowing race is that held annually between the univs. of Oxford and Camb. (*see* BOAT RACE). In other races the crews number 4 or 2, an even number being essential as each man pulls a single oar. In sculling, a man uses 2 sculls. A rowing crew usually carries a cox for steering the boat, but races between coxswainless fours are held. A great event of the rowing year in Eng. is the regatta at Henley-on-Thames.

ROWLANDSON, Thomas
(1756-1827) Eng. artist. B. and d. London. He studied art there and in Paris. His fame rests upon his caricatures. These dealt with current polit. events and occupied him from 1784.

ROXBURGHSHIRE
County of S. Scot. on the Eng. border. It contains peaks of the Cheviot and Eildon Hills. The chief river is the Teviot; others are the Tweed, Liddel, Ale and Jed. R. is famous for its sheep, and woollens, tweeds and blankets are manufactured. Jedburgh is the county town and Newtown St. Boswells is the administrative centre. Together with Selkirkshire, it sends 1 member to Parl. Pop. 43,000.

ROYAL ACADEMY OF ARTS
An institution founded in London, 1768, by

George III to encourage painting, sculpture and architecture. The Academy is gov. by a council of 10 academicians. The Pres., Keeper and Treasurer are *ex-officio* members. Academicians (R.A.s) and associates (A.R.A.s) are elected by academicians and associates together. An exhibition of the works of contemporary artists is held at Burlington House every summer. The first Pres. was Sir Joshua Reynolds.

ROYAL ACADEMY OF MUSIC
Founded London, 1822, for musical training in all branches. Open to students of both sexes.

ROYAL AIR FORCE
On April 1, 1911, there came into force an army order creating an Air Battn. of the Royal Engineers. A year later it became the **Royal Flying Corps.** The R.F.C. was composed of 2 wings, *i.e.* milit. and naval. Later, the naval wing became the **Royal Naval Air Service.** The role of the R.F.C. was at first confined to reconnaissance but, as the war progressed, new designs and techniques made possible combats with enemy aircraft, the bombing of milit. objectives and attacks on troops. On April 1, 1918, the R.F.C. and the R.N.A.S. were united to form the **R.A.F.** In spite of the formation of the **R.A.F. Volunteer Reserve** in 1936, the R.A.F. was greatly outnumbered by the enemy when World War II was declared in Sept. 1939. That the spirit of the pilots and the excellence of their machines made up for this deficiency in numbers was clearly shown in the Battle of Britain (*q.v.*). In 1964, control of the Air Force became a responsibility of the Unified Min. of Defence. Under it, the Air Force board administers 4 depts. (1) *Air Staff*, which deals with Policy and Operations. (2) *Personnel*, which handles all Service Personnel, Recruiting, Mail Services, Reserves and Cadet Forces. (3) *Supply and Organisation*, covering Equipment, Organisation, Airfields, and all technical services. (4) *Permanent under Sec. of State*, who deals with Secretarial, Financial and Public Relations. Commands are functional at home (Bomber, Fighter, Flying Training, etc.), and geographical overseas (Middle E.A.F., Far E.A.F., etc.). Officers enter the R.A.F. either through the ranks or by direct entry through univs. or the R.A.F. Coll. The **Women's Air Force** was formed on April 1, 1918, and disbanded in Mar. 1920. On June 28, 1939 the **Women's Auxiliary Air Force** was formed. In 1948 the name was changed once more to the **Women's Royal Air Force. R.A.F. Regiment:** Up to 1942 airfield security was the job of Ground Defence personnel of the R.A.F. in conjunction with Army units. In Feb. 1942, the R.A.F. Regt. was formed and by Sept. had taken over all airfield defence in the U.K. **Royal Observer Corps,** formed in 1925 and manned by Special Constables, was taken over by the Air Min. on Jan. 1, 1929. The 'Royal' prefix was granted on April 11, 1941, in recognition of the part played by the Corps in the Battle of Brit. The main duty of the Corps is tracking and reporting aircraft, esp. low-flying aircraft over the U.K. The **Air Training Corps** was formed in Feb. 1941, and is organised as follows: (1) *Univ. Air Squadrons.* (2) *School Units* (age 11-12). (3) *Local Units*, raised under the leadership of civil authorities. (Age 16 upwards).

'ROYAL AND ANCIENT'
Golf club in St. Andrews, Fife, Scotland. On May 14, 1764, 'Twenty-two Noblemen and Gentlemen' met together to subscribe for a silver club and to form the Society of St. Andrews' Golfers. In 1834 King William IV consented to the Club being named 'Royal and Ancient' and became its patron, an office now held by H.M. the Queen. It is the traditional authority and arbiter on the rules of the game, and it manages the Brit. Open and Amateur Championships.

ROYAL AUTOMOBILE CLUB
The R.A.C. was founded in 1897 under the name of the Automobile Club of Gt. Brit. and Ireland, as a Soc. of Encouragement for the motoring movement in the Brit. Empire. In 1907 the title was changed by Royal Command to The Royal Automobile Club. The Patron of the Club is H.M. the Queen. Candidates for full membership must be proposed and seconded by 2 members and are subject to election by the Committee. They have the use of the Clubhouses in Pall Mall and at Woodcote Park and all the facilities accorded to Associate Members. Associate Membership is open to any person owning or using a private car or motor cycle and includes the benefits of all R.A.C. road services, *e.g.* Road Patrols throughout Gt. Brit. and N. Ireland; Roadside Telephone Boxes; 'Get-You-Home' Service; Free Legal Defence for motoring offences; Technical Advice; Home and Foreign Touring facilities; R.A.C. Guide and Handbook.

ROYAL HORTICULTURAL SOCIETY
Founded in 1804, this is the oldest horticultural society in the world. The Society was granted a Royal Charter a few years later and held fortnightly meetings in Regent St., London. The H.Q. are now in Vincent Square, Westminster, where fortnightly exhibitions are held, as well as a spring show at the Royal Hosp. Gardens, Chelsea, in May.

ROYAL HOUSEHOLD
The attendants of the sovereign. In Eng. it consists of the Lord Steward's, Lord Chamberlain's, and Master of the Horse depts. There is also a Privy Purse dept. consisting of the Queen's personal staff.

ROYAL NAVY
Administration. The control of the Navy is vested in a board of 11 members. The Sec. of State for Defence is chairman of the Admiralty Board. Members of the Board are: Min. of Defence for the R.N. (formerly 1st Lord of the Admiralty), Parl. Under-Sec. for the R.N., the chief of the Naval Staff and 1st Sea Lord and his staff. The Naval Staff divides into various bodies, *e.g.* Naval Intelligence, Plans, Local Defence, Trade, Operations, Training and Naval Air Arm. Since World War II, Brit. naval forces have been considerably reduced in the light of strategy based on nuclear weapons, guided missiles and the greatly increased potential of submarines. The Navy's first nuclear-powered submarine came into service in 1963. The Fleet Air Arm (*q.v.*) is the front line defence of the Navy against air attack. Aircraft carriers now provide the main striking power of the fleet. Carrier borne aircraft include single-seat strike/fighter aircraft, low-level strike aircraft, all-weather day-and-night fighters, airborne early-warning aircraft and helicopters. **Personnel.** The General List is the main body of officers of the R.N. serving on permanent commissions. The various branches in which ratings may serve are: Seaman, Communications, Engineering, Fleet Air Arm, Electrical, Supply and Secretariat, Sick Bay,

Artificers and Regulating. **The Royal Marines.** The primary rôle of the Royal Marines has always been to fight on land and this Corps enables the Fleet to deal with troubles ashore or to establish a foothold for further operations. The R.M. Commando Brigade is a highly trained and powerful unit, at immediate readiness to move anywhere. The special commando ships now in service carry helicopters for putting the assault force ashore and can also provide all the equipment necessary for their support. **The Women's Royal Naval Service (W.R.N.S.)** carries out a wide range of important tasks. Officers undertake admin. duties and may also specialise in secretarial work, personnel selection, educ., safety equipment, technical work, etc. Ratings serve as airframe and radio mechanics, radar plot operators, meteorological assistants, drivers, signallers, switchboard operators, typists, stores assistants, cooks, etc. Naval hospitals are staffed by the **Queen Alexandra's Royal Naval Nursing Service**, at home and overseas. **Reserves.** The aim of the **Royal Naval Reserve** is to provide a single force of volunteers to meet the Navy's additional manpower requirements in an emergency.

ROYAL OBSERVER CORPS *See* ROYAL AIR FORCE.

ROYAL SOCIETY
Eng. learned soc. Founded in 1645, and received a charter from Charles II in 1660. The soc. holds meetings, gives medals and in other ways encourages scientific research. Its membership (F.R.S.) is a coveted distinction.

ROYAL YACHTS
Royal yachts have been part of the British Navy since the time of the Stuarts, when a yacht was presented to Charles II by the Dutch. Other nations have Royal or Presidential yachts, notably Denmark, Yugoslavia, Rumania. During 1954 a new Royal yacht, *Britannia*, entered service, the first to be completed for the Navy since 1907. Of *c.* 4,000 tons displacement, and 21 knots speed, she can undertake long sea voyages. She is designed to be used as a hosp. ship if necessary.

RUANDA
Indep. state, part of former Belgian trusteeship **Ruanda-Urundi.** Gained its indep. in 1962. The cap. is Kigali. The other half of the trusteeship took the name Burundi.

RUBBER
Elastic substance, derived from the milky latex of various trop. trees, the chief commercial kind, Para rubber, being from a species of *Hevea.* Ceará rubber is derived from *Manihot*, while Assam rubber is chiefly the latex of *Ficus elastica.* Rubber chemically consists of a mixture of resins, hydrocarbons, water and other substances. Formerly S. Amer. was the chief source, but *Hevea* trees are cultivated now in Malaya, the E. Indies, Ceylon and other countries. The trees are tapped when *c.* 5 years old by making incisions in the bark, the latex being collected in cups. The crude rubber is formed into sheets or crepe for export. **Synthetic Rubbers** are produced from chemicals, *e.g.* crude petroleum, alcohol, acetylene, etc.

RUBBRA, Edmund
[rub-ră] (1901-) Eng. composer. Studied at Reading Univ. under Holst and at the Royal Coll. of Music under Vaughan Williams. He has written 5 symphonies, a sinfonia concertante for piano and orchestra, chamber music, cantatas for chorus and orchestra. C.B.E. 1960.

RUBELLA
Popularly called German measles. Mild specific infection characterised by rose tint rash affecting face, trunk and arms, and by enlarged glands in neck. Disease is distinct from both measles and scarlet fever.

RUBENS, Peter Paul
[roo'-binz] (1577-1640) Flemish artist. He worked under several great painters, and spent some years in Venice, Rome, Milan and other Ital. cities. In 1608 he returned to Antwerp where he lived until his d. He was the greatest painter of his day.

RUBICON
[roo'-] Small river of Emilia, Italy, at one time the boundary between Italy and Gaul. In 49 B.C., Caesar crossed it and so gave the signal for war. Today the phrase 'crossing the Rubicon' is for a decisive step.

RUBINSTEIN, Anton Gregorovitch
[roo'-bin-shtīn] (1829-94) Russ. musician. As a boy he attracted the attention of Chopin and Liszt. In 1858 the Tsar appointed him court pianist. He toured Eng. and the U.S.A.

RUBY
Transparent variety of corundum coloured red by ferric oxide. When pure in colour and flawless, the ruby comes next in value to the diamond, and is of greater value when of large size and of the shade known as 'pigeon's blood'. The best are found in Burma, also in gem gravels in Ceylon and Siam.

RUDD
or **Red-eye** (*Leuciscus erythropthalmus*) Small freshwater fish with red fins and eyes. Common in Brit. rivers, weighs about 1 lb.

RUE
(or **Herb of Grace**) (*Ruta graveolens*) Perennial plant of shrub-like growth, it has clusters of yellowish flowers. The leaves contain an oil used in medicine.

RUFF
(*Philomachus pugnax*) Bird found in Europe and Asia. It is migratory, moving S. to the Medit. region in the cold weather. The Ruff is *c.* 12 in. long. In the breeding season the male grows tufts of feathers on both sides of the head, and a broad ruff of feathers on the throat. The female, called the Reeve, lays its eggs in a nest of coarse grass among rushes.

RUGBY
Borough of Warwickshire, on the Avon, 30 m. S.E. of Birmingham. It is a railway junction, and there are engineering works. R. School was founded 1567. Pop. 53,510.

RUGBY LEAGUE and UNION *See* FOOTBALL.

RUHR
[roor] German river which rises in the Sauerland, in N. Rhine-Westphalia, and flows W. across an extensive coalfield, joining the Rhine at Ruhrort. In the vicinity are the mining and industrial cities of W. Germany. The R. was occupied by Fr. and Belg. 1923-5. It was the centre of German war industries in World War II.

RULE OF THE ROAD
Regulations laid down by convention or sometimes by law, to facilitate the movement of traffic. In Brit. the rule for vehicles is to keep to the left and to pass a vehicle in front on the right. In Europe and the U.S.A. the rule is

to keep to the right. At sea the rule is for ships to pass port to port, port being the left-hand side.

RUM
Spirit distilled from diluted cane sugar molasses fermented by the action of a yeast. It is coloured with caramel or by storing in sherry casks, and its aroma increases with age. Jamaica, Demerara and Martinique are the chief centres of manufacture.

RUMANIA
Repub. of S.E. Europe, bounded by the U.S.S.R., Hungary, Yugoslavia and Bulgaria, with a coastline on the Black Sea. It is traversed by the Carpathian Mts. and Transylvanian Alps. To the W. the land slopes towards the Hungarian plains. Rivers are the Danube, Prutul, on the Russ. border, Argesul, Muresul and Somesul. Agriculture is the main industry. Oil is obtained in the Transylvanian Alps, near Ploesti, and conveyed by pipe-line to Constanta on the Black Sea. Other minerals are salt, lignite, iron and copper. Flour milling, brewing and distilling are important industries. The chief town is Bucharest, the cap. There are minorities of non-Rumanian peoples, Magyars, Turks and Bulgars. Moldavia and Wallachia, part of Turkey, were united, 1859, under a lord who ruled as a vassal of Turkey. R. became indep. of Turkey, 1878, and 3 years later Carol, a Hohenzollern prince, took the title of king. R. entered World War I on the side of the Allies. In 1940 R. ceded Bessarabia and N. Bukovina to the U.S.S.R., S. Dobruja to Bulgaria and part of Transylvania to Hungary. The latter area was restored to R. after the armistice. Carol II abdicated in favour of his son Michael, who was forced to abdicate, 1947, and the Rumanian People's Repub. was proclaimed. Govt. consists of a single chamber, almost entirely Communist, and a council of min. Area: 91,600 sq.m. Pop. 18,681,000. **Rumanian.** Italic language dating from Rom. occupation of Dacia, A.D. 101-7, but much influenced by Slav, Hungarian, Albanian, Turkish. There are 4 dialects. Literature dates from 1550.

RUMANSH
(Also **Ladin** or **Rhetian**) One of Switzerland's 4 official languages, with Fr., Ital., German. Spoken in Engadine, Grisons, Italy, Tyrol, Friuli.

RUNNING
Form of sport and exercise since very early times. The Gks. included it among the contests at the Olympic Games. Today is divided into the following: (*a*) The sprint, or short distance, (*b*) Middle distances. (*c*) Long distances, which may be anything from 3 m. and upwards, and where a high level of training and a knowledge of timing are essential.

RUNNYMEDE
Field near Egham, in Surrey, on the Thames, where, it is believed, King John sealed the Magna Carta, 1215. The field is the property of the National Trust and is the site of the Commonwealth Air Force Memorial and John F. Kennedy Mem.

RUPERT
(1619-82) German prince and soldier. A son of the elector palatine Frederick V and Elizabeth, daughter of James I. In 1642 came to Eng. to assist Charles. He made a reputation as a cavalry leader. In 1648 Rupert went to sea in command of the fleet, but was defeated by Blake off Malaga in 1650. He left his mark in 2 spheres of activity—the colonisation of the great area of Canada named after him, Rupert's Land, and the introduction into Eng. of the mezzotint process of engraving.

RUSH
(*Juncus*) Genus of plants, mainly perennials. They grow in temp. and cold climates and in wet sandy soil, and are distinguished by their long, straight, smooth stems. The stems are either hollow or filled with a white pith.

RUSKIN, John
(1819-1900) Eng. writer. His autobiog. *Praeterita*, tells the story of his early days. From 1869-79 he was Slade prof. of art at Oxford. *The Seven Lamps of Architecture* and *Stones of Venice* deal with art. Ruskin later turned to polit. econ., myth., etc. His mar. with Effie Gray (1848) was annulled in 1855.

RUSSELL, Bertrand Arthur William, Earl
(1872-1970) Eng. philosopher, mathematician. Grandson of the first Earl Russell. He settled in London and devoted himself to social and political work. He was a pacifist during World War I, for which he incurred 6 months' imprisonment, during which he wrote *Introduction to Mathematical Philosophy* (1919). He visited the U.S.S.R. and China, went to the U.S.A. in 1935. His works include *Principia Mathematica* (1910), *Problems of Philosophy* (1911), *Principles of Social Reconstruction* (1917), *History of Western Philosophy* (1945). His shorter works include *The A.B.C. of Relativity*, *Why I am not a Christian*, *Marriage and Morals*, *Human Society in Ethics and Politics*. His ideas in all these fields may be described as revolutionary. He was awarded the Nobel Prize for Lit. 1950; O.M. 1949.

RUSSELL, Lord John
(**Earl Russell**) (1792-1878) Eng. statesman. M.P. (Whig), 1813-61; P.M. 1846-52 and 1865-6; Earl Russell, 1861. One of the main architects of the Reform Bill of 1832, he supported Peel over the repeal of the Corn Laws in 1846.

RUSSIA *See* U.S.S.R.

RUSSIAN REVOLUTION
Many yrs. of revolutionary propaganda culminated in open rebellion on Mar. 12, 1917. The army refused to deal with food rioters in Petrograd and the navy joined the strikers. The Duma elected a provisional govt. and on Mar. 15 the Tsar abdicated. Lenin returned from exile, and the struggle for mastery was won by the Bolshevists. On Nov. 7 they seized Petrograd, deposed the Kerensky govt. and obtained complete power. On Mar. 3, 1918, they concluded the Peace of Brest-Litovsk with the C. Powers, the Tsar and his family were assassinated, the Ch. repressed and the Nat. debt repudiated. Lenin was Dictator and Trotsky Foreign Secretary. By the end of 1921 all opposition had been suppressed. Lenin d. in 1924 and was succeeded by Stalin. That there was dissension within the Communist party was evident from the exile of Trotsky to Siberia in 1927, and from purges and mass trials of 'counter revolutionaries'. Meanwhile, educational, industrial and scientific development went on in the U.S.S.R., and the Red army and air force became ever more powerful. The avowed object of the Russ. rulers is world Communism.

RUSSO-JAPANESE WAR
War (1904-5) caused by the clash of Jap. and Russ. interests in the Pacific. It was begun by Japan, with a successful attack on the Russ. fleets at Chemulpo and Port Arthur. The Russ. resistance was finally broken in May, when her fleet under Rozhdestvensky was routed by Admiral Togo in the battle of Tsushima. Peace was signed, Sept. 5, 1905, at Portsmouth, U.S.A.

RUSSO-TURKISH WARS
Several wars between Turkey and Russia, mainly caused by the treatment of Christian subject peoples by the Sultan, and the desire of Russia for domination of the Black Sea and for an outlet to the Medit. The first in 1696 gave Russia Azov. The war of 1827-9 rose out of Mahmud II's cruel treatment of rebel Gks.,

which united Brit. Fr. and Russia against him. The Turkish fleet was destroyed at Navarino, 1827, and the Treaty of Adrianople, 1829, gave indep. to the Gks. The Crimean War (1854-6) lost Russia her Danube possessions and naval power in the Black Sea. Treaty of Berlin, 1878, practically ended the Turkish Emp. in Europe but alienated Russia from Austria and Germany.

RUTHENES
[roo-thēnz'] Ukrainians found in E.C. Europe. Before World War I they were under Russ. and Austro-Hungarian rule. Ruthenia was part of Czechoslovakia until World War II, when it was ceded to the U.S.S.R.

RUTHERFORD, Ernest
Baron Rutherford of Nelson O.M., F.R.S. (1871-1937) B. Nelson, N. Zealand, he studied at the Univ. of N.Z. and at Camb. where he returned in 1919 as Cavendish Prof. of Experimental Physics. In 1899 he showed the existence of 2 components—the *alpha* and *beta* rays—in the radio-active emanation from uranium, and in 1902, with Soddy, he estabd. the general nature of radio-activity and initiated research into the radio-active series. In 1908 he showed the identity of the alpha particles with helium ions and in 1911 he propounded the theory of at. structure. In 1919 he found evidence of the disintegration of nitrogen by collision of its atoms with alpha particles which initiated subsequent developments in at. physics.

RUTLAND
Smallest county of Eng., wholly inland, surrounded by Leics., Lincs. and Northants. The land is fairly level, watered by the tributaries of the Welland, which forms the S.E. border. Agriculture is important. Oakham is the county town. With the Stamford division of Lincs. it sends 1 member to Parl. Pop. 26,390.

RUYSDAEL, Jakob van
[rois'-dål] (1628-82) Dutch painter. His pictures are chiefly of rural scenes.

RUYTER, Michael de
[roi-] (1607-76) Dutch admiral. In 1666 he defeated the Eng. off the N. Foreland and sailed up the Thames and the Medway.

RYDE
Borough and resort of the Is. of Wight, *c.* 7 m. N.E. of Newport. It is a yachting centre, and has regular steamer services with Portsmouth. Pop. 20,000.

RYDER CUP
Cup presented by Samuel Ryder (d. 1936) for competition between teams of professional golfers from Gt. Brit. and U.S.A. Since 1927 matches for the trophy have been played every second year (except 1939-45) alternately in the U.S.A. and in Gt. Brit.

RYE
One of the 5 cereals. It will flourish on a poorer soil than any other and is much grown as cattle food. The ears are also ground into flour and black bread is made from it. The world's yearly production averages 1,500 to 1,800 million bushels. This is chiefly produced in N. Amer. **Rye grass** is grown for permanent pasture.

RYLANDS, John
(1801-88) Eng. merchant. B. St. Helens. He joined his father and brother in a cotton manufacturing business at Wigan. Head of the firm from 1847, John became a millionaire. In 1888 Mrs. Rylands bought the magnificent library of Earl Spencer at Althorp. To house it she erected in Manchester the John Rylands Library, which contains one of the most valuable collections of books and MSS. in Brit.

ARTS in ANTIQUITY · 3

Mural: Pompeii

Ancient Egyptian coffin painting

Castel St Angelo

Temple of Concordia, Sicily

Amphora: Hercules and Cerberus

Amphora: Dionysus

GREEK ART · VASES

Attic oil jar

Attic water jug

S

S
19th letter of Eng. alphabet, descriptively classed as a sibilant with 2 sounds: unvoiced in *sing, sit;* voiced in *rose.* When followed by *u,* it sometimes has the sound *zh,* as in pleasure.

S.E.A.T.O.
South-East Asia Treaty Organisation. A defence treaty signed 15 Sept., 1954, by 8 countries committing them to united action against aggression in S.E. Asia or the S.W. Pacific. The treaty was signed in Manila by the representatives of Gt. Brit., U.S.A., Fr., Australia, New Zealand, Pakistan, the Philippines and Siam.

S.H.A.P.E.
Supreme Headquarters Allied Powers in Europe. Org. under N.A.T.O. (*q.v.*) for co-ordinating the armed forces of the N. Atlantic Treaty Powers.

S.P.C.K.
Society for Promoting Christian Knowledge. Founded 1689. Oldest missionary organisation in C. of E.

SAARLAND
[sär-] State in W. Germany. It is an industrial region, with iron and coal mines. It was admin. after 1919 by a League of Nations Commission. The inhabitants voted in a plebiscite, 1935, to return to Germany. In 1947 they voted for economic union with Fr., but on 1st Jan. 1957, S. was officially reunited with Germany. Pop. 1,096,600. **Saarbrücken.** Cap. of the Saarland, W. Germany, 75 m. S.W. of Mainz. Pop. 132,711.

SABINES
[sa′-binz] (or **Sabini**) An ancient people allied to the Latins, widely distributed in C. Italy, incorporated with the Rom. state in 290 B.C.

SACCHARIN
[sak′-] A coal tar derivative, 300 to 500 times sweeter than sugar. It is used instead of sugar esp. by diabetics.

SACHEVERELL, Henry
[sash-] (*c.* 1674-1724) Eng. clergyman. He attacked the Whig. govt. as the enemy of the Ch. (1709).

SACKVILLE
Famous Eng. family. Richard Sackville was a Kentish landowner in the time of Henry VIII. His son, **Thomas,** was made Earl of Dorset in 1604. **Victoria Sackville-West** (1892-1962), daughter of the 3rd baron won the Hawthornden Prize in 1927 with a poem, *The Land.*

SACRAMENT
In religion, and esp. in Christianity, a sacred ceremony. There are 2 views of the sacrament. One, held by the R.C., the Gk., and the official Anglican Chs., is that without the reception of certain sacraments the believer cannot attain salvation. The other view is that they are symbolic only, beneficial to the believer because of his belief in the verities of which they are the sign. The Gk. and Rom. Chs. recognise 7 sacraments: baptism, confirmation, marriage, penance, ordination, the eucharist and extreme unction. The Anglican Ch. insists that only two of these are necessary for salvation, baptism and the holy communion.

SACRAMENTO
Cap. of Calif. U.S.A. on the Sacramento river, 90 m. inland from San Francisco. Pop. 191,667.

SACRIFICE
Offering to God, or to a god. Animal sacrifices were common among the Jews, Gks., and Roms. as well as among less cultured peoples. In many religions, human beings were sacrificed, a practice now almost extinct. The idea of human sacrifice passed from Jewish into Chr. thought, and the voluntary d. of Jesus Christ is regarded as the supreme sacrifice; by it the human race is redeemed. *See* ATONEMENT.

SADDUCEES
Jewish sect. They were priests whose religious opinions differed from those of the Jews in general. They did not believe in the resurrection of the dead or in the existence of spirits. They opposed the teaching of the Pharisees.

SADLER'S WELLS
The mineral spring from which it received its name was discovered in 1683 and was exploited by Sadler, who built a music house there. It became a music hall and then a cinema and in 1915 was closed. Rebuilt, it was opened in 1931, and closed again in 1968.

SAFFLOWER
Herb found in Europe, Asia and Africa which bears orange-coloured flowers used for dyeing.

SAFFRON
Perennial herb, *Crocus sativus,* growing in Europe and Asia. The flowers are purple with orange coloured stigmas. The herb is used in medicine and cooking.

SAFFRON WALDEN
Borough and market town of Essex, 44 m. N.E. of London. Pop. 7,810.

SAGA *See* NORSE.

SAGE
Herb which grows to a ht. of *c.* 1 ft. and bears purple flowers and oblong leaves. It is much used as a flavouring in cookery.

SAGITTARIUS
[saj-i-tār-i-us] (Lat. *archer*) Ninth sign of the Zodiac, operative *c.* Nov. 21-Dec. 20.

SAGO
Farinaceous foodstuff prepared from the starchy pith of palms of the genus *Metroxylon* growing in Malaya and the Dutch E. Indies.

SAHARA
Desert of Africa, the largest in the world. It contains lofty mountains and deep valleys. Area: 3,500,000 sq.m.

SAIGON
Cap. and seaport of S. Vietnam. Pop. 1,400,000.

SAINFOIN
Leguminous plant, with long leaves and pink flowers. It is grown in the warmer parts of Eng., and in Fr., for grazing purposes and hay.

SAINT
Holy person, one consecrated to the divine service. More exactly it refers to persons who have been canonised by the Christian Ch. and are recorded as saints in its calendar. Christian countries and socs., as well as professions and

charities, have each their patron saint, *e.g.* England—St. George (Apr. 24); Scot.—St. Andrew (Nov. 30); Ireland—St. Patrick (Mar. 17); and Wales—St. David (Mar. 1). St. Dunstan is patron saint of the blind.

ST. ALBANS
City and market town of Herts. on the Ver, 21 m. N.W. of London. The cath., restored in 1856, was once an abbey. Its Gothic nave is the longest in Eng. Remains of the Rom. city of Verulamium include the forum, theatre, and a hypocaust. Pop. 50,000.

ST. ANDREWS
Burgh and resort of Fifeshire, on a bay, 12 m. S.E. of Dundee. There are ruins of a castle and a cath. The Univ. dates from 1411. St. Andrews is the headquarters of the Royal and Ancient Golf Club (*q.v.*). Pop. 10,149.

ST. ASAPH
or **Llanelwy.** Cath. city and market town of Flintshire, 5 m. N. of Denbigh. Pop. 2,238.

ST. BARTHOLOMEW, Massacre of
An attempt, organised by Catherine de Medici and the Duke of Guise, to crush the Huguenots or Fr. Protestants; *c.* 30,000 perished.

ST. BERNARD, Great
The second highest pass over the Alps on the Swiss-Ital. frontier. The pass is known for the Hospice at the summit, famous for its hospitality to travellers. **St. Bernard.** A kind of mastiff kept at the St. Bernard Hospice for finding lost travellers and also by private persons as pets.

SAINTE-BEUVE, Charles Augustin
(1804-69) Fr. critic. He wrote weekly critical essays, later collected as *Causeries du Lundi, Nouveaux Lundis, Premiers Lundis.*

ST. CLOUD
[sa(ng) kloo'] Town in Seine-et-Oise dept. Fr., on the Seine, below Paris. Its palace, built *c.* 1600, was once the residence of Napoleon. Pop. 20,700.

ST. CYR
[sa(ng)-sēr] Village of Fr., 13 m. W. of Paris, famous for its military college, founded by Napoleon, 1806.

ST. DAVID'S
Cath. city of Pembrokeshire, 15 m. N.W. of Haverfordwest, on St. Bride's Bay.

ST. DENIS
[sa(ng)-dè-nē'] Town in Seine-et-Oise dept. Fr., 4 m. N. of Paris, famous for its ch. in which most of the Fr. kings were buried. Pop. 95,072.

ST. DUNSTAN'S
Institution or hostel in London for training the blind. It was founded by Sir Arthur Pearson for soldiers blinded in World War I.

ST. ELMO'S FIRE
Silent electrical discharge between the atmosphere and such structures as masts of ships, flagstaffs and trees.

SAINT-EXUPÉRY, Antoine de
(1900-44) Fr. author and aviator. B. at Lyons he was killed on a flight over France. *Terre des Hommes* (1939) is his chief work.

ST. GALLEN
[gal'-] Cap. of St. G. canton, in N.E. Switzerland, *c.* 10 m. S. of L. Constance. Pop. 77,100.

ST. GEORGE'S CHANNEL
Opening of the Atlantic Ocean between Ireland and Wales.

ST. GOTTHARD
Pass over the Alps in cantons Uri and Ticino, *c.* 7,000 ft. high.

ST. HELENA
Small Is. of volcanic origin in the Atlantic Ocean, *c.* 1,200 m. from the coast of Africa, forming a Brit. colony. From 1815-21 it was Napoleon's prison. Area: 47 sq.m. Pop. 4,624.

ST. HELIER
Seaport and chief town of Jersey, Channel Is. on the S. side of the Is. Pop. 26,500.

ST. IVES
Seaport and borough of W. Cornwall, on St. I. Bay, 8 m. N. of Penzance. Pop. 8,870.

ST. JAMES'S PALACE
Royal palace in London. Built 1530, it was a royal residence until the time of George III, when it was replaced by Buckingham Palace.

SAINT JOHN
Seaport of New Brunswick, Canada, at the mouth of the St. J. river on the Bay of Fundy. Pop. 55,155.

ST. JOHN of Jerusalem, Order of
Charitable religious order. Founded in Jerusalem *c.* 1048, for the relief of Christian pilgrims to the Holy Land.

ST. JOHN'S
Cap. and chief seaport of Newfoundland, on the E. coast. Pop. 90,833.

ST. JOHN'S WORT
Perennial evergreen plant (*Hypericum*), 1-2 ft. high, with branching stems and clusters of large yellow flowers.

ST. KILDA
Most W. Is. of the Outer Hebrides, part of Inverness-shire, 40 m. W. of N. Uist.

ST. KITTS
Is. of the Leeward group, W. Indies, 50 m. N.W. of Antigua. Discovered by Columbus in 1493, it was the first Brit. W. Ind. possession to be colonised (1623). Pop. 38,291.

ST. LAWRENCE
River of N. Amer. which forms, with the Great Lakes, a river system nearly 2,000 m. long. The St. L. proper issues from L. Ontario and flows N.E. into the Atlantic Ocean. Near Anticosti it is 100 m. wide. **St. Lawrence Seaway.** Canal and hydro-electric complex mainly between Prescott and Montreal, financed and built jointly by U.S.A. and Canada. Opened 1959. *See* CANADA.

ST. LOUIS
Chief city of Missouri, and 10th city of the U.S.A., on the Mississippi below its confluence with the Missouri. Pop. 750,000.

ST. LUCIA
Is. in the Windward group, W. Indies to the S. of Martinique. Discovered by Columbus in 1502, the island finally became Brit. in 1803. Area: 240 sq.m. Pop. 94,718.

ST. MARTIN
Is. of the W. Indies in the N. of the Lesser Antilles group.

ST. MARY'S
Largest of the Scilly Isles, 27 m. from Land's End.

ST. MICHAEL and St. George
Eng. order of knighthood, founded in 1818 for persons from the Ionian Is. and other Brit. possessions of the Medit. Later it became an order for those who serve the crown in the overseas parts of the Commonwealth.

ST. MICHAEL'S MOUNT
Islet in Mount's Bay, Cornwall, 3 m. from Penzance.

ST. MORITZ
Swiss winter sports centre in the Upper Engadine.

ST. NAZAIRE
[na-zair'] Seaport of Loire-Inférieure dept. W. Fr. Brit. commandos, in World War II, blocked the harbour, used as a submarine base by the Germans. Pop. 59,181.

ST. OMER
[ō-mair'] Town in Pas-de-Calais dept. Fr., 25 m. S.E. of Calais. From Oct. 1914 to March 1916, St. O. was the Brit. H.Q. in Fr.

ST. PATRICK, Order of
Irish order of knighthood, founded in 1788.

ST. PAUL
Cap. of Minnesota, U.S.A. on the Mississippi. Industries include the manufacture of clothing and hardware. Pop. 313,000.

ST. PAUL'S CATHEDRAL
Cath. ch. of the diocese of London. The first was burned down in 1086 and the second in 1666 during the Great Fire. The present one was built between 1675 and 1710 by Sir Christopher Wren.

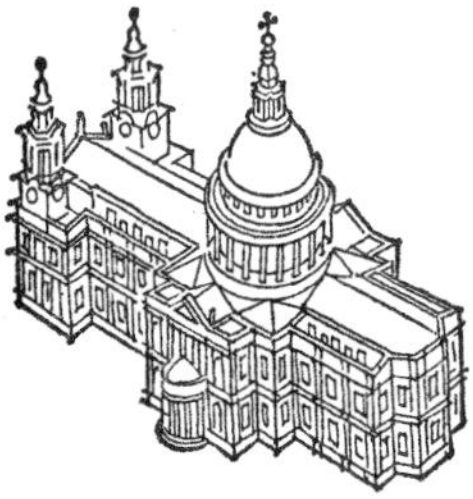

ST. PETER PORT
Chief town of Guernsey, Channel Is., on the E. coast. Pop. 18,000.

ST. PETER'S, ROME
Largest and grandest ch. in the world. It was begun in 1450, and consecrated by Pope Urban XIII in 1626. The building was designed by Bramante and Michelangelo, with a piazza of 284 columns by Bernini.

ST. PIERRE AND MIQUELON
Fr. overseas territory consisting of 2 groups of Is. off the S. coast of Newfoundland. Area: 90 sq.m. Pop. 4,900.

ST. QUENTIN
[sa(ng)-ka(ng)-ta(ng)] Town in Aisne dept. Fr., 85 m. N.E. of Paris, on the Somme. Pop. 62,597.

SAINT-SAËNS, Charles Camille
[sa(ng)-sa(ng)s] (1835-1921) Fr. composer. He wrote music of all types, the best known of his dozen operas being *Samson et Dalila.*

SAINT-SIMON, Duc de
(1675-1755) Fr. writer. **(Louis de Rouvroy Saint-Simon)** In 1714 he became a member of the council of regency for Louis XV. His *Memoirs* are a valuable source for the history of the time.

ST. VINCENT, Earl of
John Jervis (1735-1823) is best known for his victory over a Sp. fleet off Cape St. Vincent in Feb. 1797.

ST. VINCENT
Is. in the Windward group, W. Indies, an Associated State since 1969. Kingstown is the cap. Became Brit. in 1783. Area: 150 sq.m. Pop. 80,042.

ST. VITUS'S DANCE
Popular name for chorea (*q.v.*).

SAINTSBURY, George Edward Bateman
(1845-1933) Eng. scholar. His works include *A History of Criticism, A Short History of English Literature, A Short History of French Literature.*

SAKI
Monkey found only in S. Amer. They have white and yellow faces and the body is covered with thick hair.

SAKKARA
[sa-kà'-ra] Egyptian village near the Nile and 10 m. S. of Cairo, with interesting ruins.

SAL AMMONIAC
Common name for ammonium chloride. A white fibrous substance when sublimed, it is used as a charge for electric batteries, in galvanising iron, as a flux in soldering, and in medicine.

SALADIN
(1137-93) Sultan of Egypt, he won renown fighting in Egypt against the Christians. Saladin is best known for his campaigns against the Lat. kingdom of Jerusalem in the 3rd Crusade, which began in 1187. He captured Jerusalem and other places, but was checked by Richard I.

SALAMANCA
Town of W. Sp., cap. of S. prov. on the Tormes, 172 m. N.W. of Madrid. Pop. 93,130. Scene of important victory over Fr. under Marmont won by Wellington in Peninsular War (1812). Both opposing forces were *c.* 42,000, but the Fr. lost *c.* 8,000 men, and 7,000 prisoners, and Wellington marched into Madrid.

SALAMANDER
Amphibia found in Europe and W. Asia, with 4 fingers and 5 toes. *Salamandra maculosa,* the Fire or Spotted Salamander, is *c.* 6 in. Its young are b. as larvae. *S. atra* bears only 2 well-developed young at once. These complete their development at the expense of other developing young.

SALAMIS
Is. of Greece, near Athens, where the Persian fleet was defeated by the Athenians in 480 B.C.

SALEM
City of Massachusetts, U.S.A., 16 m. N.E. of Boston, on Mass. Bay. It was dominated by the Puritans in the 17th cent. Pop. 41,800.

SALERNO
City and seaport of Campania, Italy, 30 m. S.E. of Naples. S. was the beachhead of the Allied landings in Italy in World War II. Pop. 121,625.

SALFORD
City and county borough of Lancs. on the Irwell, opposite Manchester. The industries include engineering works, cotton mills and chemical factories. It sends 2 members to Parl. Pop. 152,570.

SALICYLIC ACID
Complex organic acid occurring in nature in oil of wintergreen (*Gaultheria procumbens*). It is a white crystalline substance with strong antiseptic properties. Its salts are used in medicine.

SALISBURY
Cath. city and county town of Wilts., 84 m. S.W. of London, on the confluence of the Avon, Bourne and Wylye. The 13th cent. cath. has the highest spire (404 ft.) in Eng. Salisbury has a large agricultural trade. Old Sarum lies on a hill N. of the city. Pop. 35,000. **Salisbury Plain.** Chalk plain, 10 m. from N. to S. in S.E. Wilts., rising to 770 ft. in Westbury Down, and crossed by the Avon. It contains Stonehenge and Amesbury with their prehistoric monuments. Most of it is used for milit. purposes.

SALISBURY
Cap. of Rhodesia (*q.v.*). Pop. 314,200.

SALISBURY, Earl of
(*c.* 1565-1612) Eng. statesman. Robert Cecil, youngest son of the 1st Lord Burghley, succeeded his father in 1598 as sec. and chief adviser to Queen Elizabeth. Created Earl of Salisbury in 1605, in 1608 he was made Lord Treasurer and solely responsible for the conduct of the realm. **Salisbury, Robert Arthur**

Talbot Gascoyne-Cecil, 3rd Marquess of (1830-1903) Eng. statesman. M.P. (Cons.) 1853-68; Foreign Sec. 1878-80; P.M. 1885-6, 1886-92 and 1895-1902. Mainly concerned throughout his career with foreign affairs. The **5th Marquess, Robert Arthur James Gascoyne-Cecil** (1893-) sat in the Commons from 1929-41, when he was cr. Baron Cecil. Lord Pres. of the Council, 1952-7 and Leader of the House of Lords, 1951-7. Resigned from Govt. 1957, in protest against release of Archbishop Makarios (*q.v.*).

SALLUST
(86-34 B.C.) Rom. historian (**Gaius Sallustius Crispus**). He became Gov. of Numidia, where he amassed wealth by extortion; then retired in luxury and wrote his histories.

SALMON
Food fish (*Salmo*) of the family Salmonidae. It attains a length of 5 ft. and a wt. of 40 lb. The adult fish ascends the rivers where the ova are deposited and fertilised. In the 2nd year the young fish journey to the sea, staying there 2, 3 or more years till they in turn mature and migrate to the river spawning grounds to breed.

SALOME
[să-lō'-mi] Daughter of Herodias (the wife of Herod Antipas) by a former husband. Urged on by her mother, she asked Herod for the head of John the Baptist. John was accordingly beheaded and the head given to her.

SALT LAKE CITY
Cap. of Utah, U.S.A., the home of the Mormons (*q.v.*) One of the main centres in the W. for agricultural produce, printing, meat-packing and mining. Pop. 176,800.

SALTPETRE
[-pē'-ter] Common name for nitre or potassium nitrate, used in the manufacture of gunpowder, nitric acid, fertilisers, and for salting meat.

SALTS
Compounds formed by the chem. union of acids with bases. Thus, hydrochloric acid and sodium hydroxide combine to give sodium chloride.

SALTWORT
Species of herb (*Salsola kali*) common on the seashore in Brit.

SALVADOR, El
Repub. of C. Amer., S. of Guatemala and Honduras, on the Pacific Ocean. The smallest and most populous of the C. Amer. repubs., S. is intensively cultivated, producing coffee, sugar, maize, indigo, rice and balsam. San S. is the cap. Sp. is the official language and R.C. the religion. Govt. is by a Pres. and a congress of 42 deputies. Area: 8,000 sq.m. Pop. 3,151,000.

SALVATION ARMY
Religious organisation founded 1877 by William Booth (*q.v.*) for the revival of religion among the masses. The movement was organised on a milit. model and at first met with much opposition. The Salvation Army is now active in 82 countries; uses 100 different languages.

SALVIA
Genus of the Labiatae, widely spread in temp. and warmer areas.

SALWEEN
River of Asia, 1,750 m. long, which rises in Tibet and flows S.E. into Burma.

SALZBURG
[salts'-bŏŏrg] City of Austria. It was the birthplace of Mozart (1756). Pop. 108,114.

SAMARIA
Ancient district of Palestine, now lying across the borders of Israel and Jordan. **Samaritans.** Jewish sect to which references are found in the Bible. Outlawed from orthodox Judaism by Ezra in the 5th cent. B.C., they developed their own fundamental doctrine based on the Pentateuch.

SAMARKAND *See* ZARAFSHAN.

SAMBRE
[som'-br] River of Fr. and Belgium which rises in Fr. and flows N.E. joining the Meuse at Namur, Belgium. The **Battle of the S.** ended with the armistice on Nov. 11, 1918.

SAMBUR
(*Cervus aristotelis*) Deer living in the forests of India and Ceylon. Its average ht. is 4½ ft.

SAMOA
or **Navigators' Islands.** Group of Is. in the Pacific, N.E. of the Fiji group. Discovered in the 18th cent. by the Dutch. Area: 1,130 sq.m. **Western Samoa,** indep. state, member of Brit. Commonw. since 1970. Exports copra. Area: 1,097 sq. m. Pop. 131,400. **American Samoa,** U.S. territory since 1899. Exports canned fish. Cap. is Pago Pago. Area: 80 sq. m. Pop. 20,000.

SAMOS
Greek Is. in the Aegean Sea, 1 m. from the coast of Asia Minor. Pop. 52,034.

SAMOYED
[sam'-ō-yed] Primarily a sledge-dog, but is much in favour as house dog and pet. They should be between 18 and 22 in. high.

SAMPHIRE
Perennial herb (*Crithmum maritimum*) of the family Umbelliferae, found in many parts of Europe, usually on rocks near the sea.

SAMSON
(O.T.) The Book of Judges (*c.* 13-16) represents him as an Israelitish hero of vast strength.

SAMUEL
Prophet of the Israelites. As a child he became an attendant to Eli, the high priest. The **Books of Samuel** are 2 historical books of the O.T. covering roughly 100 years during which Israel emerged from the state of anarchy described in the Book of Judges.

SAN FRANCISCO
City and seaport of Calif. U.S.A. on the Bay of San F.; one of the world's finest natural harbours, it is entered from the Pacific by a channel, the Golden Gate. Founded in 1776 by Sp., San Francisco was seized by the U.S.A. in 1848, from which year the gold rush brought a great increase of pop. Pop. 742,855. **San Francisco Conference.** The conference opened on April 25, 1945, the Co-ordinating Committee completed the text of the Charter of the United Nations on June 23, and this was signed by the delegates, June 26. The World Security Charter was signed by 50 nations on June 26 and approval was given to the Statute of the Court of Internat. Justice and the estab. of the Preparatory Commission of the U.N.

SAN JUAN
[hwàn] Cap. and seaport of Puerto Rico, on a small Is. off the N. coast. Pop. 451,658.

SAN MARINO
Repub. of Europe, in the Apennines, 12 m. S.W. of Rimini, entirely surrounded by Ital. territory. Area: 24 sq.m. Pop. 17,000.

SAN SALVADOR
Cap. of Salvador, C. Amer., connected by rail with the port of La Libertad, 25 m. away. Pop. 255,744.

SAND
Natural fine-grained material resulting from the disintegration of granite and other highly siliceous rocks. While essentially of quartz grains, other minerals may be present.

SAND, George
(1804-76) Pen-name of **Amantine Lucile Aurore Dupin,** Fr. novelist. She formed a liaison with the poet Alfred de Musset, and later with Chopin (*q.v.*). Her novels include *Jacques, Jeanne, La Mare au Diable* (1847) (her best), *Nanon* (1872).

SAND GROUSE
Small game bird. Unlike Grouse, but related to the Pigeon, it is distinguished from Brit. birds by peculiar feet, feathered to the claws.

SAND HOPPER
(*Orchestia*) Small shrimp-like crustacea, occurring in large numbers on the seashore and of a pale yellowish colour.

SAND LIZARD
(*Lacerta agilis*) Found in Brit. frequenting sandy districts. It is *c.* 7 in. long. The male is bright green, the female brownish.

SANDALWOOD
Fragrant wood from a small evergreen tree (*Santalum album*), growing in India and the E. Indies.

SANDERLING
Small bird, *Calidris arenaria,* allied to the Plover, which it resembles. It is a winter visitor to the shores of seas and lakes in Brit.

SANDHURST
Village of Berks., 4 m. S.E. of Wokingham, famous for the Royal Milit. Academy, founded 1799.

SANDPIPER
Small bird allied to the Snipe, Curlew and Plover. The Common S. (*Tringa hypoleucos*) is a very common summer resident in Brit.

SANDRINGHAM
Estate in Norfolk, the property of the Queen, 6 m. N.E. of King's Lynn.

SANDSTONE
Sedimentary rock, consisting of sand grains cemented together, used as building and paving material.

SANDWICH
Borough and market town of Kent., 5 m. S.W. of Ramsgate, on the Stour. Pop. 4,370.

SANDWICH ISLANDS *See* HAWAII.

SANDWORT
Genus (*Arenaria*) of Alpine plants of the family Caryophyllaceae.

SANHEDRIN
[san′-i-drin] Council of the Jews. It was powerful in the time of Christ and held power of life and death.

SANITATION
Carrying out of health measures, usually the responsibility of a special sub-division of the local Health Dept. Concerned mainly with water, sewage disposal, drainage and refuse disposal.

SANSKRIT
The ancient Indian language, which preserves closely the original Indo-European consonant system.

SANSOVINO, Andrea
[-vē′-nō] (1460-1529) Ital. sculptor. He was responsible for the Sforza monument in the church of S. Maria del Popolo, Rome.

SANTA CRUZ
Group of Is. in the Pacific Ocean, 100 m. N. of the New Hebrides, part of the Brit. Solomon Is. Protectorate (*q.v.*).

SANTA CRUZ DE TENERIFE
Cap. and seaport of the Sp. prov. of the same name, Canary Is. Pop. 141,557.

SANTA FÉ
[fā] Town of Argentina, on the Parana. Cap. of S.F. prov. and centre of a fertile region. Pop. 260,000.

SANTA FÉ
City and cap. of New Mexico, U.S.A. on the S.F. river. Pop. 34,676.

SANTANDER
Sp. seaport and resort, cap. of S. prov. on the Bay of Biscay. Pop. 122,630.

SANTAYANA, George
[-yà′-nă] (1863-1952) Sp. philosopher and poet. His works include *Scepticism and Animal Faith* (1923), *Background of My Life* (1945), and *The Middle Span* (1948). *My Host the World* (1953) was pub. posthumously by the author's request.

SANTIAGO
[santi-à′-gō] Cap. of Chile, 1,700 ft. above sea level. Founded 1541 by Pedro de Valdivia. Pop. 1,169,481.

SANTIAGO
City of N.W. Spain in Galicia, 33 m. S. of Corunna. Pop. 56,000.

SANTO DOMINGO
Cap. of the Dominican Repub. on the S. coast of the mouth of the Ozama, founded by the Sp. 1496. Renamed **Ciudad Trujillo** but reverted to orig. name after assassination of Gen. Trujillo. Pop. 447,782.

SÃO PAULO
[sowng pow′-loo] Largest city of Brazil, cap. of São P. state, the world's coffee centre. Pop. 3,825,351.

SAONE
[sōn] River of Fr. which rises in the Vosges Mts. and flows S. to join the Rhône at Lyons.

SAPPHIRE
Precious stone. A transparent variety of corundum, blue to lilac. It is found in Siam, Burma, the river gravels of Ceylon and in granites in Kashmir.

SAPPHO
(lived *c.* 610 B.C.) Gk. poetess known as the 'tenth muse'. Only fragments of her odes survive.

SARAGOSSA
City of N.E. Sp., cap. of the prov., on the Ebro. Cap. of the former kingdom of Aragon, it is now a manufacturing and market centre. Pop. 343,468.

SARAJEVO
[sà-rà-yā′-vō] City of Yugoslavia, and cap. of Bosnia, with a pop. of 198,914. The assassination there, on June 28, 1914, of the Archduke Ferdinand, precipitated the First World War.

SARATOV
Chief city of the Saratov Region, Russian S.F.S.R. on the Volga, 210 m. S.W. of Kuibyshev. It is an iron and steel manufacturing centre. Pop. 644,000.

SARAWAK
[să-rà′-wak] Former Brit. colony in N.W. Borneo, became a state in Federation of Malaysia (1963). Oil is produced at Miri and Bakong, and there are considerable deposits of coal. The chief town is Kuching, on the Sarawak river, in the extreme S.W. The territory was obtained by Sir James Brooke from the Sultan of Brunei, in 1841, and was placed under Brit. protection in 1888. Area: *c.* 50,000 sq.m. Pop. 903,000.

SARD
Variety of chalcedony of a brownish-red colour and horny lustre.

SARDINE
Small fish preserved in oil. In Brit. the word is used only for pilchards when immature, preserved and tinned. Sardines are a popular food.

SARDINIA
Ital. Is. in the Medit. S. of Corsica. Agriculture is the chief occupation, and stock are raised. Tunny fishing is important. Cagliari is the cap. and chief port. From 1478 it was governed as a Sp. vice-royalty until 1708, when it became an Austrian possession. In 1848 the Is. was united politically with Piedmont. In 1947 the Region of Sardinia was granted autonomous government. Area: 9,300 sq.m. Pop. 1,413,289.

SARDONYX
Variety of red-banded onyx, consisting of alternate layers of cornelian or sard and chalcedony.

SARGASSO SEA
Section of the Atlantic Ocean, S.E. of Bermuda, distinguished by the masses of brown seaweed that float therein.

SARGENT, Sir Harold Malcolm Watts
(1895-1967) Brit. conductor. Chief conductor of the B.B.C. Symphony Orchestra, 1950-7; conductor of the Huddersfield Chorale Society since 1932. Conductor-in-Chief, Prom. Concerts.

SARGENT, John Singer
(1854-1925) Eng. artist. B. Florence, of Amer. parentage. His fame rests upon his portraits.

SARK
Channel Is. 6 m. from Guernsey. The chief harbour is Masseline on the E. coast. It has an indep. feudal govt. under the Seigneur. The industries are fishing and the tourist trade. Pop. 556.

SAROYAN, William
(1908-) Amer. writer. He wrote many novels: *The Daring Young Man* (1934), *The Laughing Matter* (1953), and plays.

SARSAPARILLA
Dried rhizome and roots of various species of *Smilax*, esp. *S. officinalis*, climbing plants native to C. America, credited with diuretic properties.

SARTRE, Jean-Paul
(1905-) Fr. novelist and dramatist. Leader in Fr. of the Existentialist school. He wrote plays; novels *La Nausée* (1937), *Les Chemins de la Liberté* (1944-5), *Lucifer and the Lord* (1953), *Existentialism and Humanism* (1949), *The Psychology of Imagination* (1951).

SASKATCHEWAN
One of the prairie provs. of Canada, between Manitoba and Alberta, and extending from the N.W. Territories to the border of the U.S.A. It is the chief wheat growing prov. of Canada, and its live stock industries are of great importance. Minerals include gold, silver and cadmium. Regina is the cap. and largest town. The prov. was formerly part of the N.W. Territories, until it entered the Confederation, 1905. Admin. is carried on by a lieut.-gov., a council of ministers and a legislative assembly. It sends 6 senators and 17 representatives to the Dominion parl. Area 251,700 sq.m. Pop. 925,181.

SASKATOON
City of Saskatchewan, 150 m. N.W. of Regina. Industries include the manufacture of agricultural machinery, bricks and clothing. Pop. 103,623.

SASSAFRAS
Deciduous tree (*S. officinale*). The bark has aromatic and tonic properties.

SATELLITE
In astronomy a term for a companion body to a planet, round which it revolves. All the planets, with the exception of Venus, Pluto and Mercury, have satellites. On October 4, 1957, the first artificial Earth Satellite (Sputnik 1) was successfully placed into an orbit by Russ. scientists. The first Amer. satellite was launched on 17th March, 1958. Since then many satellites have been launched. These include, besides the man-carrying satellites, meteorological satellites, early-warning military satellites and communication satellites (*e.g.* *Telstar*). A Brit. satellite was launched by a U.S. rocket, 1962.

SATURN
[sat'-] The 6th known planet in order of distance from the sun (*c.* 887,100,000 m.). It has a diameter of 74,200 m., the period of its orbit is 29 yrs. 167 days, and that of its mean rotation *c.* 10 hrs. 13 mins. A remarkable feature of Saturn is the horizontal flat rings which surround it in the manner of an outer belt at equatorial level.

SAUDI ARABIA
Kingdom of Arabia (*q.v.*), covering the greater part of the peninsula. Pilgrimages are made to Mecca, the birthplace of Mohammed, and Medina, where lies his tomb. Exports include dates, livestock, hides and fruit. Oil is found near Dhahran on the Persian Gulf. In 1916 Hussein, Grand Sherif of Mecca, was recognised as king of the Hejaz, and in return fought for Gt. Brit. against Turkey. In 1919 he became involved in a struggle with his hereditary enemy, Ibn Saud. Defeated by him, Hussein abdicated in 1924. Ibn Saud captured Mecca in 1924, and 2 years later Gt. Brit. recognised him as King of the united kingdom of Hejaz and Nejd. Ibn Saud d. in 1953, and was succeeded by his eldest son, Emir Saud, deposed in favour of his brother Faisal (1964). Area: 600,000 sq.m Pop. 6,870,000.

SAUERKRAUT
[sow'-er-krowt] Popular German dish. It consists of shredded cabbage placed in a cask with alternate layers of salt and spices and left till fermented.

SAUTERNE
[sō-tairn'] District in Gironde dept., S.W. Fr., S. of Bordeaux. It gives its name to the local white wines.

SAVANNAH
City and seaport of Georgia, U.S.A., on the Savannah river, 18 m. from its mouth. Pop. 149,245.

SAVONAROLA, Girolamo
(1452-98) Ital. religious and polit. reformer, a Dominican monk. After the d. of Lorenzo the Magnificent, in 1492, he led his party in the new republic, and ruled Florence as a Christian commonwealth. He was accused of heresy by Rome, excommunicated, and burned.

SAVOY
Name of the family of which the ex-King of Italy was the head. In 1034, a certain Humbert became Count of Savoy. Savoy itself was ceded to Fr. 1860, but the king was more than compensated when, 1870, he became King of Italy.

SAW FLY
Hymenopterous insects of 4 different families, formerly grouped as one, in which the egg-laying appendage (ovipositor) of the female is saw-like.

SAXIFRAGE
Genus of herbs of the family Saxifragaceae, with over 150 recognised species.

SAXONS
Teutonic group of races. They lived in modern Schleswig-Holstein, and *c.* A.D. 300 appeared as pirates. Later they spread into what are now Fr. and Germany, and crossed to Eng. where many of them settled.

SAXONY, Lower
State of W. Germany bounded on the W. by the Netherlands, with a coastline on the N. Sea. The chief rivers are the Elbe, Weser, and Ems. Hanover is the cap. Pop. 6,731,600.

SAXOPHONE
A single reed wind instrument invented by Adolphe Sax in 1840. Its mouthpiece is similar to that of the clarinet, but its tube is of metal. It is built in 7 sizes, has a compass of 2½ octaves, and is extremely agile and flexible.

SCABIES
[skā'-] Skin disease due to infection with parasite, *sarcoptes scabei* or itch mite, from infected persons. Disease is only spread by direct contact of skin to skin. Main symptom is intense itch.

SCABIOUS
[skā'-biŭs] (or **Pin-cushion Flower**) Annual and perennial herb of the genus *Scabiosa*. The colours range from blue, through shades of red, to white.

SCAFELL
[skaw'-fel] Mt. of Cumberland, the highest peak in Eng. (3,210 ft.) at the E. end of Wastwater.

SCALIGER, Julius Caesar
(*c.* 1484-1558) Fr. physician, soldier, scholar and writer. His 10th child, **Joseph Justus** (1540-1609) was perhaps the greatest scholar of the M.A. He founded a new school of classical criticism and revolutionised the study of ancient chronology.

SCALP
Outer covering of the cranium. The scalp is formed of several layers, the outermost being the skin bearing sweat and sebaceous glands and hair follicles, next the superficial fascia, a fibrous layer connecting the skin to the underlying occipitofrontal muscle and its aponeurosis, which covers in turn a layer of loose areolar tissue.

SCANDINAVIA
Collective name for the peninsulas of N. Europe consisting of Norway and Sweden, and Denmark.

SCAPA FLOW
Natural anchorage in the Orkney Is. surrounded by the islands of Pomona, Burray, S. Ronaldsay, Walls and Hoy. It is 15 m. long and 8 m. wide. It was the chief strategic base of the Brit. Grand Fleet in World War I, and equally important in World War II (1939-45).

SCAPEGOAT
Term used among the early Hebs. for the goat driven out into the wilderness on the Day of Atonement symbolically bearing the sins of the people.

SCARAB
General name for an Egyptian amulet representing the sacred beetle, *Scarabaeus sacer*, symbol of Khepe-Ra.

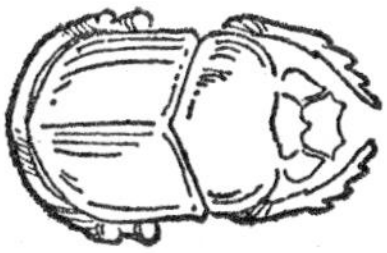

SCARBOROUGH
Borough and resort of the N. Riding, Yorks., 42 m. N.E. of York. Pop. 41,900.

SCARLATTI, Alessandro
[-lat'-i] (1660-1725) Ital. composer. He helped to estab. the form of the chamber cantata of which he wrote over 600 examples. His son was **Domenico Scarlatti** (1685-1757) Ital. composer. A brilliant harpsichordist, he met Handel in Rome in 1708. He considerably developed harpsichord technique and wrote for the instrument 500 Esercizi, now referred to as Sonatas.

SCARLET FEVER
Acute infectious disease characterised by red rash appearing on 2nd or 3rd day, sore throat, and fever. Caused by *streptococcus scarlatinae*. On 6th day temp. falls, symptoms subside and peeling of skin begins.

SCAUP
[skawp] (*Nyroca marila*) A wild duck residing in small numbers in Scot., a passage migrant or winter visitor to other coasts of Brit. and Ireland.

SCENT
In plants scent serves as a protection against insects or in flowers for the attraction of insects in pollination. **Scent glands** occur in many animals and serve as a defence against enemies, a means of recognition of their own species, or for sex attraction.

SCEPTICISM
The philosophical theory of those who deny (1) current or customary beliefs, or (2) the possibility of knowing reality. In modern times Pascal is a representative of a scepticism which depreciates the value of scientific knowledge, while on the other hand Hume's scepticism takes its stand on physical science.

SCHAFFHAUSEN
[shaf-howz'-] Cap. of S. canton, in N. Switzerland, near the Rhine Falls. Industries include the manufacture of watches and machinery. Pop. 25,900.

SCHARNHORST
Notable air and naval action of World War II which resulted in severe damage to the German battle-cruisers *Scharnhorst* and *Gneisenau* and the heavy cruiser *Prinz Eugen*.

SCHELDT
River of W. Europe, 250 m. long, which rises in Fr. and flows through Belgium to enter the N. Sea at Antwerp.

SCHELLING, Friedrich Wilhelm
(1775-1854) German philosopher. His philosophy consists of 3 main divisions. (1) The Philosophy of Nature, (2) The Philosophy of Identity, (3) The Antithesis of Positive and Negative Philosophy.

SCHIAPARELLI, Giovanni Virginio
[shē-ap'-a-rel'ē] (1835-1910) Ital. astronomer. In 1877 came his report that he had detected on the surface of the planet Mars the channels (' canals ') which were subsequently photographed by Lowell.

SCHIEDAM
[skē'-dăm] Town of S. Holland prov., the Netherlands, with chemical and glass industries. Pop. 81,100.

SCHILLER, Johann Christoph Friedrich
(1759-1805) German poet. B. in Marbach, Württemberg. His first play, *Die Räuber*, appeared in 1782 and created a sensation by its revolutionary sentiments.

SCHIPPERKE
[ship'per-ki] Small dog bred orig. in Flanders. It is black with short hair.

SCHIST
[shist] A fine-grained foliated rock of meta-

morphic origin found in areas where great earth movements have taken place and where large igneous intrusions have baked the surrounding sediments.

SCHIZOPHRENIA
[skid-zō-frēn'-i-a] Disorder of the mind characterised by confusion of thought, hallucinations, delusions, etc. The disease usually reveals itself in predisposed persons between the ages of 15 and 30 years.

SCHLESWIG-HOLSTEIN
[schles'-vig] State of W. Germany, S. of Denmark, with coastlines on the North and Baltic Seas. Agriculture is the chief occupation, although there is some shipbuilding and engineering. Pop. 2,351,300.

SCHLIEMANN, Heinrich
[shlē'-] (1822-90) German archaeologist. He excavated the Mycenaean Troy at Hissarlik, mistaking it for the Homeric one.

SCHOLASTICISM
Teaching of the scholastics or schoolmen of the M.A. who examined the doctrines of the Ch. in the light of philosophic ideas. Scholasticism took on a new form when the writings of Aristotle came to be studied.

SCHÖNBERG, Arnold
[shön'-bairg] (1874-1951) Austrian composer. Largely self-taught, he developed orig. harmonic theories and *c.* 1910, he evolved the *Twelve-note technique.*

SCHOOL
The schools of Europe in the M.A. were adjuncts to the monasteries. Then in Eng. came the **grammar schools,** a product of the Reformation, and similar schools in Scot., Germany and other protestant countries. The **public schools** grew out of the grammar schools and in the 19th cent. public schools for girls were founded on the same lines. For elementary education, schools were provided by the Ch. of E. and the R.C. Ch., in 1871, when educ. was made compulsory, schools were built out of public funds. *See* EDUCATION.

SCHOPENHAUER, Arthur
(1788-1860) German philosopher and exponent of systematic pessimism. His principal work *The World as Will and Idea,* 1819, teaches a pantheism of the will.

SCHUBERT, Franz
[shoo'-bairt] (1797-1828) Austrian composer. His output was enormous and his melodies have a marvellous freshness and spontaneity that has never been equalled, and his songs are among the loveliest in the world.

SCHUMANN, Robert
[shoo'-] (1810-56) German composer. He pub. his 1st piano compositions in 1830. Apart from a vast quantity of piano music and songs he wrote a fine piano quintet, a piano concerto, and 4 symphonies.

SCHUSCHNIGG, Kurt von
(1897-) Aus. politician. Min. for Justice in 1932, he succeeded Dollfuss as Chanc. in 1934. After the end of Aust. indep., S. was imprisoned by the Nazis.

SCHWEITZER, Albert
[shvīt'-ser] (1875-1965) Alsation theologian, philosopher, organist, and medical missionary. He took a medical degree, 1913, and went to Gabon, Fr. Equatorial Africa, as a missionary. With the help of his wife, he founded the hospital at Lambaréné, which he maintained on the proceeds of his books, by organ recitals on his infrequent visits to Europe, and by charitable gifts. Awarded the Nobel Peace Prize for 1952; apptd. hon. member of Order of Merit, Feb. 1955.

SCHWYZ
[shvits] Canton of C. Switzerland which formed, with Uri and Unterwalden, the Confederation of 1291, the nucleus of modern Switzerland.

SCIATICA
[sī-at'-] Term applied to pain of any origin distributed down back of leg.

SCILLY ISLES
[sill'-] Group of Is. in Cornwall, 25 m. S.W. of Land's End. 5 are important; St. Mary's, Tresco, St. Martin's, St. Agnes, and Bryher. The climate is mild. Flowers and vegetables are raised for the Eng. market. The cap. is Hugh Town, on St. Mary's.

SCIPIO, Publius Cornelius
(*c.* 234-183 B.C.) Surnamed *Africanus.* His decisive victory over Hannibal at Zama, N. Africa, 202 B.C., ended the 2nd Punic war.

SCIPIO AEMILIANUS, Publius Cornelius
(185-129 B.C.) Surnamed *Africanus Minor.* He took part in the 3rd Punic war. In 147 he took Carthage by storm and, by order of the Senate, levelled it to the ground.

SCLEROSIS
[sklē-rō'-] Term used in pathology indicating an invasion of tissue by small cells. Sclerosis of organs is a physiological change in old age.

SCONE
[skoon] Burgh of Perthshire, on the Tay, 2 m. N.E. of Perth. In the 8th cent. it became the cap. of the kingdom of the Picts, and in the abbey, destroyed 1559, the kings were crowned on the Stone of Destiny. This is now kept in Westminster Abbey.

SCORPIO
Eighth sign of the Zodiac, operative *c.* Oct. 23-Nov. 21.

SCORPION
An arthropod of the class Arachnida. It has claws resembling a lobster's but formed from head appendages and a jointed flexible abdomen terminating in a sting. The poison of the smaller species is generally more virulent than that of the larger kinds.

SCORPION FLY
Insect so named from the fact that the last few segments of the body in males are curved upwards somewhat like a scorpion's tail.

SCOT, Michael
(*c.* 1175-*c.* 1232) Scots mathematician and astrologer. Scot was an able scholar, educ. at Oxford, Paris and Bologna. He translated part of Aristotle and the commentaries from Arabic into Latin.

SCOTCH TERRIER
Small rough-haired dog. It is very hardy, highly intelligent, a first-rate companion.

SCOTER
[skō'-] or **Black-duck** (*Oidemia nigra*) It has dark plumage, the males blacker than the females, which are rusty brown. Resident in N. Scot., otherwise a passage migrant or winter visitor.

SCOTLAND
Kingdom of Gt. Brit. occupying the N. part of the Is. and including the Inner and Outer

Hebrides, the Orkney and Shetland groups and many other Is. It is bounded on the E. by the N. Sea, on the W. by the Atlantic. The coastline is much indented, particularly on the W. There are 3 main physical divisions: (1) the S. Uplands, which lie N. of the Cheviot Hills and rise to over 2,600 ft.; (2) the C. Lowlands, a rift valley which includes the valleys of the Clyde, Forth and Tay, and (3) the N. Highlands, which occupy the greater part of the country. The Highlands are divided into a N. and S. system by the Gt. Glen. In the S. region are the Grampian Mts. with Ben Nevis (4,406 ft.), the highest point in the Brit. Is., Ben Macdhui (4,296 ft.), and Ben Lawers (3,984 ft.). The chief river of Scot. is the Clyde, which flows N.W. through Glasgow, entering the N. Channel by the Firth of Clyde. The Tweed, Forth, Tay, Dee and Spey flow into the N. Sea. Of the many lochs, the largest are Lomond, Awe, Tay and Rannoch in the Grampians, Ness, Ericht, Lochy, Shin and Maree farther N. Much of the soil is unproductive, particularly in the mts. where cattle and sheep are bred. The S.W. specialises in dairy farming. Sheep are kept over most of the country. The principal crops are oats, barley, wheat and root crops. Certain areas, such as the Carse of Gowrie, specialise in fruit farming. Fishing is an important industry, the chief centres being Aberdeen, Peterhead, Wick and Stornoway. There are coalfields in the Lowlands around which heavy industries have developed. Glasgow, Motherwell, Coatbridge, Airdrie and Kilmarnock are centres of the iron and steel and engineering industries. Shipbuilding is important at Clydebank, linoleum at Kirkcaldy, cotton textiles at Paisley and jute at Dundee. Whisky and woollen goods are also produced. Edinburgh is the cap. but Glasgow is much larger. Most of the inhabitants are descendants of the original Celts; the Norse influence is strong in the extreme N. The people are mainly Presbyterians, belonging to the Ch. of Scot., but there are many R.Cs. The country has 6 univs., St. Andrews, Aberdeen, Glasgow (2), Edinburgh (2), Dundee and Stirling (1966). In early days the Highlands were inhabited by Gaelic tribes living in clans under their own chiefs and the Lowlands were populated by people not unlike those living in the N. of Eng. About 900 a king of the Scots arose. Gov. at first only a small district in the S., he gradually extended his power until there was a kingdom of Scot. covering the whole country. Edward I conquered Scot. and made its king subject to him. After the Battle of Bannockburn, Scot. regained its indep., which it retained under its own kings until 1603, when James VI became James I of Gt. Brit. In 1707 the parl. of the two countries were united. In some respects Scot. remains apart from Eng. Its laws are different and it has its own judicial system. The local govt. system has been made very much like that of Eng. There are 33 counties. Scot. affairs are controlled by a Sec. of State and for certain purposes there are special govt. depts in Scot. Area: 30,410 sq.m. Pop. 5,178,490. **Scotland, Church of.** Presbyterian in doctrine and govt., it has been the estabd. ch. since 1560. In 1929 it united with the United Free Ch. of Scot. The ch. has approx. 1,281,559 members in 2,200 congregations. The controlling body is the Gen. Assembly.

SCOTLAND YARD
Headquarters of the Metropolitan Police in London.

SCOTS
Lowland Scots is the descendant of the Northumbrian dialect of O.E.; *Middle Scots* has a rich poetry: John Barbour's *Bruce* (14th cent.), James I's *Kingis Quair*, Henryson, Dunbar, Gavin Douglas (15th cent.), Sir David Lindsay. **Lallans.** Word to distinguish a form of Scots developed by modern Scot. writers who are striving to give fresh life to the Scots tongue in literature and in the theatre.

SCOTS GREYS
Cavalry regt. known officially as the 2nd Dragoons. It traces its origin to certain mounted troops added to the Scot. Establishment in 1678, which, after serving under Graham of Claverhouse, were regimented as the Royal Scots Dragoons.

SCOTS GUARDS
Regt. of foot guards. Orig. formed in Scot. in Nov. 1660, they became the Scots Fusilier Guards under William IV. The ancient title of Scots Guards was restored to the regt. by Queen Victoria in 1877.

SCOTT, Sir George Gilbert
(1811-78) Brit. architect. After 1840 he threw himself into the Gothic revival, and built or restored 26 caths., over 500 chs. and numerous monuments. His grandson was **Sir Giles Gilbert Scott** (1880-1960) Brit. architect. His design for the new Ch. of E. Liverpool Cathedral, embodying his dream of a Gothic revival, was accepted in 1903. His work was chiefly ecclesiastical.

SCOTT, Robert Falcon
(1868-1912) Eng. explorer. S. Pole expedition in the *Terra Nova* set out in June 1910. In Jan. 1912, Scott reached the Pole with 4 companions, Oates (*q.v.*), Wilson, Bowers, and P.O. Evans, to find that the Norwegian explorer Amundsen had been there 3 weeks before. On the terrible return journey Evans d. Scott, Wilson and Bowers perished within a day's march of One Ton Depot where supplies were waiting. His son, **Peter Markham Scott** (1909-), is an artist, particularly noted for his paintings of birds. He is a Director of the Severn Wild Fowl Trust.

SCOTT, Sir Walter
(1771-1832) Scot. poet and novelist. B. Edinburgh. He wrote long narrative poems: *The Lay of the Last Minstrel* (1805), *Marmion*, *The Lady of the Lake*, *Rokeby* (1813). His first novel *Waverley* appeared anon. in 1814; then *Guy Mannering*, *Rob Roy*, *The Heart of Midlothian*, *The Bride of Lammermoor*, *Ivanhoe*, *The Monastery* (28 in all); also stories. He ed. *Minstrelsy of the Scottish Border* (1802-3), wrote *Lives of the Novelists* (1821), works on demonology, romance, Scots hist.

SCOTTISH NATIONAL PARTY
The first Scot. Home Rule Assoc. was formed in 1886, and The Young Scots Soc. was estabd. in 1900. In 1918 certain members of the Y.S.S. formed the 2nd S.H.R.A. In 1928, the S.H.R.A. joined forces with the Scot. Nat. League and the Scot. Nat. Movement to form the Nat. Party of Scot. In 1934 the N.P.S. amalgamated with the Scottish Party (founded 1932) to form the present Scottish Nat. Party. Scot. nationalists have no desire to sever their connection with the crown, but they firmly believe that an essential condition of Scots economic prosperity is that Scot. should have its own parl.

SCOUTING
Primarily a military term denoting observation of an enemy's movements, actual or intended, by individuals or parties, pushed out in advance of the main fighting force. Nowadays reconnaissance is done chiefly from the air, photography playing a large part in this work. *See* Boy Scouts.

SCRIABIN, Alexander Nicholaevich
[skri-à'-bin] (1872-1915) Russ. composer. His works were bound up with a mystical philosophy.

SCRIBES
Jewish group of priests and laymen. Devoted themselves to studying law of Moses and sat in the Sanhedrin.

SCROFULA
or **King's Evil.** Form of tuberculous disease affecting glands of neck which enlarge, break down and ulcerate, leaving a chronic sore. Said to disappear upon a touch from the hand of the king.

SCULLING
Art of propelling a boat with a pair of sculls shorter and lighter than rowing oars, and without a cox. For the world's pro. sculling championship the Thames course is from Putney to Mortlake, a distance of 4¼ m. Another famous sculling event is the **Diamond Sculls** at Henley.

SCULPTURE
One of the oldest arts, it represents an object, real or imaginary, in material and 3 dimensional form.

SCURVY
Nutritional disease caused by lack of Vitamin C in diet and assoc. with dryness of skin, anaemia, swelling of gums and haemorrhages. Formerly a very common disease esp. among sailors. Prevented completely by adequate diet, containing fresh fruit and vegetables.

SCYTHIA
[sith'-] Name used by the ancients for a region around the Black Sea. It received its name from the Scythians, a people from upper Asia who occupied it in the 7th cent. B.C.

SEA ANEMONE
Marine animals of the order Anthozoa, related to the corals. They commonly occur in rock-pools and in form have a flower-like appearance.

SEA BASS
Carnivorous fish, chiefly marine, forming one of the largest families (Serranidae) of fishes. It occurs occasionally off Brit. shores, and weighs up to 15 lb.

SEA-DRAGON
(*Pegasus draco*) Small teleostean fish found in Indian seas.

SEA-EAGLE
Name given to several members of the eagle family but esp. to the white-tailed eagle or erne (*Haliaetus albicilla*) found in most parts of the Old World. The bird, which breeds in Shetland and the Hebrides, is some 3 ft. and has a wing-spread of 6-7 ft.

SEA HEATH
Perennial herb (*Frankenia laevis*). It grows on land impregnated with salt, and is found in W. Europe, Asia and Africa.

SEA HOLLY
Perennial herb (*Eryngium maritimum*), found on sandy sea coasts.

SEA HORSE
(*Hippocampus*) Small fish allied to the Pipe Fishes. They range from 2-12 in. long, and are found mostly in trop. seas, but one species, *H. antiquorum*, is common in the Medit.

SEA KALE
Perennial herb (*Crambe maritima*) of the family Cruciferae, common on the coasts of Europe and grown in Brit. as a vegetable.

SEA LAVENDER
Genus of plants (*Limonium*) of the family Plumbaginaceae. They are common on temp. shores, and have bluish-purple flowers.

SEA LION
Another name for the Fur Seal. Sea Lions differ from the true Seals in having a more pointed muzzle. They spend more time out of the water than the true Seals.

SEA MOUSE
(*Aphrodite aculeata*) A polychaete worm often found cast up by the sea along Brit. coasts.

SEA OTTER
(*Latax*) Carnivorous mammal allied to, but larger and more massive than, the true Otter. The beautiful brown fur is very valuable. The Sea Otter occurs on the shores of the N. Pacific, notably the Aleutian Is. and Alaska.

SEA PERCH
(*Serranus cabrilla*) Fish allied to the Sea Bass. About 10 in. long, it is sometimes found off the S. coasts of Eng. It also occurs in the Medit. and the Red Sea. Some are normally hermaphrodite.

SEA-PINK
(*Armeria maritima*) Small plant common to all the coasts of Brit. which is also found in many mountain regions.

SEA-ROBIN
or **Red** or **Cuckoo Gurner** (*Trigla cuculus*) Brit. acanthopterous fish. It is about a foot long and bright red in colour.

SEA SERPENT
Large marine reptilian animal, with affinity to the plesiosaurs, which has been seen at sea from time to time. Eye-witnesses' descriptions suggest a creature having a reptilian head, a long, snake-like neck, a long, thick body and a tapering tail. *See* LOCH NESS.

SEA-SICKNESS *See* TRAVEL SICKNESS.

SEA SNAKE
Trop. aquatic snakes (Hydrophiinae) occurring in the Indian and Pacific Oceans. Ranging from 3 to 8 ft. in length, they are marked with bands of bright colours. Their bite is very poisonous. All are viviparous.

SEA SQUIRT
Ascidians or Sea Squirts belong to the class Urocharda or Tunicata. They eject 2 fine jets of sea water from their sac-like gelatinous bodies, if touched when in the expanded state.

SEA URCHIN
(*Echinus*) Marine invertebrate belonging to the Echinodermata. The Common Sea Urchin (*E. esculentis*) is valued as food in the Medit. The stony case enclosing its body is studded with long spines.

SEA-WATER
The salt water of the sea or ocean which contains chlorides and sulphates of sodium, magnesium, and potassium, with bromides and carbonates, chiefly of potassium, and calcium. The salts amount to *c.* 3·5 % of the total wt., sodium chloride being by far the most abundant.

SEA-WOLF
(**Sea-Cat** or **Swine-Fish**) (*Anarrhichas lupus*) A genus of spiny-finned teleostean fishes of the Blenniidae family. Its mouth is armed with sharp, strong teeth of large size. The Brit. variety attains a length of from 5 to 6 ft.

SEAL
Carnivorous sea mammals, having long tapering bodies and short limbs equipped with paddles. Seals are found chiefly in Arctic and Antarctic waters, but many species are visitors to, and residents on, Brit. coasts.

SEALYHAM
[sē'-liăm] A breed of wire-haired terriers named after the place in Pembrokeshire.

SEAPLANE
Type of heavier-than-air craft so constructed as to be able to land on, or arise from, the water.

SEARCHLIGHT
A powerful electric lamp, the light being reflected from a parabolic mirror, thus giving minimum dispersion of the intense beam. In World War II they were used principally to find and illuminate enemy aircraft for anti-aircraft guns and night-fighters. Rendered obsolescent by radar (*q.v.*).

SEATTLE
[sē-at'-] City and seaport of Washington, U.S.A. between L. Washington and Elliot Bay. The seat of Washington Univ. Pop. 563,000.

SEAWEED
General name for a large number of the spore-bearing plants known as algae, which grow on the sea bottom at distances ranging from high-water mark to a depth of some 600 ft. There are no roots, many parts of the plant body having the power of taking in nutriment.

SECOND EMPIRE
Period in the hist. of Fr. extending from Dec. 2, 1852, when Louis Napoleon, after overthrowing the Second Repub., became emperor as Napoleon III, to Sept. 4, 1870, 3 days after the Battle of Sedan, when the 3rd Repub. was set up.

SECRET SERVICE
Intelligence dept. of a State which procures information about naval, milit., air, polit. and other matters. In connection therewith is usually a system of secret agents in other lands, who furnish intelligence as required by their employer. In war time this work becomes of enhanced importance, and the domiciled agents are supplemented by men and women detailed for espionage and secret service in enemy or neutral countries.

SECRETARY BIRD
(*Serpentarius sagittarius*) Long-legged, long-tailed African bird allied to the vultures. In appearance resembling the Heron, it feeds chiefly on snakes. The plumage is grey, black, and white. It takes its name from the tufts at the back of its head, which look not unlike quill pens stuck behind the ear.

SECRETARY OF STATE
Title given to the officials in charge of various Brit. govt. depts. The name was first used in the reign of Elizabeth I for 2 officials who assisted the sovereign.

SECURITY COUNCIL
U.N. council charged with the primary responsibility of maintaining internat. peace and security. It consists of 5 permanent members, viz: China, Fr., U.S.S.R., Brit. and the U.S.A., and 6 non-permanent members elected for 2 years. Security Council decisions are made by the affirmative vote of 7 members including the concurring vote of the 5 permanent members—hence the use and abuse of the power of veto. The S.C. has authority to settle disputes by calling upon members of the U.N. to take any measures it thinks fit. Its permanent seat is in New York, but meetings can be held anywhere. It has the power to set up *ad hoc* committees and commissions as required.

SEDAN
[si-dan', sĕ-dà(ng)'] Town in Ardennes dept. N.E. Fr. In 1870 Napoleon III surrendered to the Germans with 86,000 of the Fr. Army. Pop. 19,000.

SEDBERGH
Market town of the W. Riding, Yorks., near the Westmorland border, 28 m. S.E. of Penrith. Sedbergh School, founded 1551, became a public school in 1874. Pop. 3,900.

SEDGE
Plant of the genus *Carex*, found in many temp., Alpine and Arctic areas, *e.g.* the common bull-rush.

SEDGEMOOR
Place in Somerset, near Bridgewater, where in 1685, the Protestant rising against James II led by the Duke of Monmouth, was crushed.

SEED
Term for the part of higher plants from which a new individual arises. It consists of an embryo and a supply of food, developed during the life of the parent plant and subsequently becoming detached, when it is capable of germinating to form a new plant.

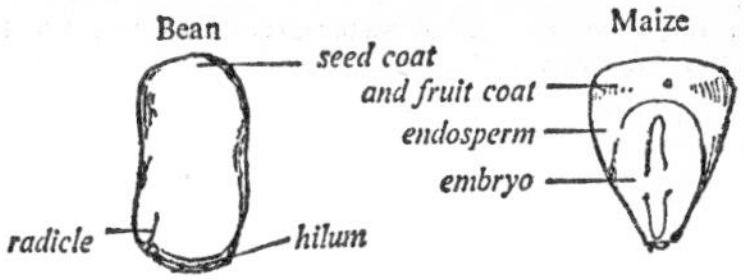

SEINE
[sān] River of Fr. which rises near Dijon, and flows in a N.W. direction, entering the Eng. Channel by an estuary at Le Havre. Commercially the most important river of Fr., it flows past Troyes, Paris and Rouen, and gives its name to 4 depts.

SEINE NET
[sen] Type of net used for catching fish such as Mackerel, Herring, Pilchards, Bass, etc. The extended net is kept vertical by means of cork floats secured at the top and leads attached to the bottom, the 2 ends finally being drawn together.

SEISMOMETER
An apparatus for measuring and recording earthquake shocks.

SELANGOR
State of the Federation of Malaya. Most of the country consists of a fertile plain, rising inland to the main mt. ridge, where tin is mined. Kuala Lumpur is the seat of govt. of the State and the Federation. Area: 3,160 sq.m. Pop. 1,221,661.

SELBORNE
Village of Hants., 5 m. from Alton, the home of Gilbert White, author of *The Natural History of Selborne.*

SELBY
Urban district in the W. Riding, Yorks, on the Ouse, 14 m. S. of York, famous for its abbey church. Pop. 10,500.

SELENIUM
A grey, crystalline element, having some, but not all of the properties of a metal. Sp. gr. 4·81. Chem. sym. Se.

SELKIRK
Burgh and county town of Selkirkshire, on Ettrick Water, 40 m. S.E. of Edinburgh. The manufacture of woollen goods is the chief industry. Pop. 5,634.

SELKIRK, Alexander
(1676-1721) Scots sailor. B. Largo. In 1703 he went to the S. Seas under William Dampier, but for insubordination was put ashore at Juan Fernandez. He was there for over 4 years, and from his stay Defoe obtained the idea for *Robinson Crusoe.*

SELKIRKSHIRE
Inland county of S.E. Scot., a hilly district once covered by the forest of Ettrick. The rivers are the Tweed and Yarrow, and among the lochs is St. Mary's. Sheep rearing and woollen manufactures are the chief industries. Selkirk is the county town, but Galashiels is larger. With Roxburghshire, Selkirkshire returns 1 member to Parl. Pop. 21,000.

SEMANTICS
Orig. the study of the changes of meaning in words. Since the 1920's, emphasis has shifted to the nature of meaning, the relation of behaviour and belief to language, the language of signs in general.

SEMAPHORE
Signalling apparatus consisting of an upright post with 2 arms turned on pivots. The system

may also be used by a signaller holding a flag in each hand. The different positions of the arms indicate letters of the alphabet.

SEMITE
Name given orig. to any descendant of Shem, Noah's son. The anthropological classification is made more by language than by race, and includes Arabs and Jews, of modern races.

SENATE
(1) Governing body of ancient Rome, which orig. comprised 100 members, all patricians. This number increased in time and was fixed by Augustus at 600. (2) In the modern world the name Senate has been adopted by various states for the upper houses of legislatures. (3) Governing body of a univ. or other learned institution.

SENECA, Lucius Annaeus
(*c.* 4 B.C.-A.D. 65) Statesman and philosopher; one of the noblest characters of his times. He was the author of several tragedies, but is better known for his phil. dissertations.

SENEGAL
[senĕ-gawl'] Rep. of W. Africa, formerly Fr., fully indep. 1960. Agriculture is the principal source of wealth, and the chief exports are groundnuts, oil and gums. St. Louis is the cap., Dakar the chief port. Area: 66,100 sq.m. Pop. 3,100,000.

SENNA
Medicinal shrubs and herbs of the family Leguminosae. The drug, useful as a purgative, is made from the dried leaves. The plants grow mainly in trop. climates.

SENNACHERIB
[-nak'-] (d. 681 B.C.) King of Assyria. He reigned *c.* 702-681 B.C. Events during his reign are somewhat obscure, but he conquered Phoenicia, ravaged Judaea and unsuccessfully besieged Jerusalem. He was responsible for great public works.

SENNAR
Town of the Repub. of the Sudan, on the Blue Nile, 160 m. S.E. of Khartoum. The S. Dam, opened 1926, provides water for the irrigation of the Gezira Plain.

SENSITIVE PLANT
Trop. Amer. herbaceous perennial (*Mimosa*) of the family Leguminosae. It is sensitive to contact, and the leaflets into which the leaves are divided fold together at the slightest touch.

SENUSSI
Moslem sect founded in 1835 by **Sidi Mahomed ben Ali es Senussi,** who d. 1859. Its tenets are an attempt to return to the simple doctrines of the Koran.

SEOUL
[sōl] Cap. of the Repub. of S. Korea, *c.* 20 m. from the W. coast. Pop. *c.* 2,445,402.

SEPIA
Generic name of the Cuttle-fishes. Allied to the Octopus, they differ in having 10 arms with stalked suckers and a large flat internal shell—the ' cuttle bone '. Their inkbag was the orig. source of the brown pigment known as sepia.

SEPTICAEMIA
[-ti-sē'-] Condition resulting from invasion of blood stream by large numbers of organisms without local abscess formation.

SEPTUAGESIMA
Word derived from Latin ' seventieth '. Septuagesima Sun. is the 3rd before Ash Wed.

SEPTUAGINT
Gk. tr. of the O.T. It is traditionally ascribed to 70 or 72 scholars working under the patronage of Ptolemy Philadelphus at Alexandria in the first half of the 3rd cent. B.C.

SEQUOIA
[si-kwoi'-ă] Genus of the Coniferae, found on the W. coast of N. Amer., comprising the redwood of California (*S. sempervirens*) and the ' big trees ' of the Sierra Nevada (*S. gigantea*).

SERANG
or **Ceram.** Is. of the Molucca Archipelago, E. Indonesia, between Buru and New Guinea. The densely forested interior is peopled by head-hunting Papuans, while on the coast Malays grow tobacco, sago, rice and sugar.

SERBIA
Federal unit of Yugoslavia. The N. part is mainly forest, but further S. wheat and maize are grown. In the Vardar valley grapes and tobacco are cultivated. Belgrade is the cap. On the conclusion of peace in 1918 the reconstituted kingdom was united with Montenegro and became the principal part of Yugoslavia (*q.v.*).

SERJEANT-AT-ARMS
Officer of the Houses of Parl. He is usually the mace-bearer and his duty is to precede certain dignitaries.

SERPENT
Name applied to the reptiles of the sub-order Ophidia comprising the snakes. Popularly, it denotes the larger species.

SERPENTINE
[-tīn] A mineral consisting essentially of magnesium silicate, and regarded as a decomposition product of igneous rocks rich in ferro-magnesian silicates. Serpentine occurs in massive form.

SERUM
[sēr'-] (1) The thin transparent part of the blood, liquid in character, straw coloured or greenish yellow in colour and containing in solution, mineral salts, protein substances and sugar, as well as substances protecting the body against attacks of germs. (2) Name applied to therapeutic substances used in the treatment of certain diseases. *See* DRUG.

SESAME
[ses'-ă-mi] Annual herbaceous plant of the genus *Sesamum*, being the most important species (*S. indicum*). It is cultivated in India and other E. countries. Popular for cooking purposes.

SESSION, Court of
In Scot. the supreme court of law. It deals with civil cases only and sits at Parl. Square, Edinburgh. Its judges are senators of the Coll. of Justice. They sit in 2 houses, Inner and Outer, the Inner being a court of appeal from the Outer. The Inner house sits in 2 divisions, presided over by the Lord Pres. and the Lord Justice Clerk respectively.

SESSION
Literally, a sitting. It is applied to the sittings of the Parl. of Brit. and other legislatures. It is finally ended by a dissolution. The **kirk session** is the term used in the Ch. of Scot. and other Presbyterian chs. for the meetings of the min. and elders of an individual church.

SETTER
Large gun dog. There were orig. 2 species, the pure white Eng. Setter and the chestnut brown Irish Setter.

SEURAT, George Pierre
[sö-rà] (1859-1891) Fr. artist. B. Paris. He evolved a style of painting in coloured dots called Pointillism. His work is linked with Impressionism.

SEVASTOPOL
Black Sea port of the Russ. S.F.S.R. on the S.W. coast of the Crimea. Old Sebastopol was destroyed during the siege of 1854-5. Pop. 169,000.

SEVEN WONDERS
of the World. In the ancient world 7 works of man: the Colossus of Rhodes, the hanging gardens of Babylon, the Pharos at Alexandria, the Pyramids of Egypt, Pheidias' statue of Jupiter at Olympus, the temple of Diana at Ephesus, and the mausoleum at Halicarnassus.

SEVEN YEARS' WAR
(1756-63) War fought by an alliance of Austria, Fr. and Russia against Eng. and Prussia (under Frederick the Gt.). It had 2 aspects: (1) colonial, arising out of Anglo-Fr. rivalry for colonies and trading areas in Amer. and India; (2) continental, due to the struggle between Austria and Prussia for Silesia. Brit., under the energetic leadership of Pitt, began to gain the upper hand, and 1759 was a year of many victories, including the capture of Quebec by Wolfe. The war resulted in the ceding of Silesia to Prussia, and of Canada to Brit., the foundation of the Brit. Indian Empire and the establishment of her naval supremacy.

SEVENTH DAY ADVENTISTS
Religious sect, mainly Amer. They hold Saturday as the Sabbath Day.

SEVERN
River of Brit. which rises on the E. slopes of Plynlimmon, Montgomeryshire, and flows for 210 m. before entering the Bristol Channel. Gloucester and Worcester are cities on its banks, and its principal tribs. are the Wye, Avon and Teme. The **Severn Bridge** connects Bristol and Cardiff.

SEVERUS, Alexander
(205-235) Rom. emperor. He was virtuous in an age when vice reigned almost supreme, and although a pagan, respected the doctrines of Christianity.

SEVERUS, Lucius Septimius
(146-211) Rom. emperor. B. in Africa, and after the murder of Pertinax (193) was proclaimed emperor. Going to Brit. in 208 to crush a rebellion, he repaired and added to Hadrian's wall, and d. at Eboracum (York).

SÉVIGNÉ, Marquise de
Marie de Rabutin Chantal (1626-96) Fr. letter-writer. She is best known for her *Letters* to her daughter, the Countess of Grignon.

SEVILLE
[sev'-] City of S.W. Sp.; cap. of Seville prov., on the Guadalquivir. It was a centre of Moorish Sp. There is a Gothic cath., a Moorish palace, the Alcazar, and a univ. Manufactures include chocolate, soap, perfumes, and silks; wine and oil are exported. Pop. 459,786.

SÈVRES
Town in Seine-et-Oise dept. Fr., on the Seine, noted for its famous porcelain factory estabd. in 1756. Pop. 17,100.

SEWAGE
House refuse carried by sewers. In urban areas sewage is carried by drains to the sewer system, and thence to a disposal works, where it is treated and purified and the effluent rendered fit for discharge into a river or the sea, or for use as a fertiliser. In the absence of a sewer system the sewage is treated in septic (bacterial) tanks, or collected in cesspools.

SEX
The male and female qualities exhibited in most organisms, both plant and animal. In the male the germ cells are spermatozoa in animals, antherozoids in the lower plants; in the female ova or egg-cells. In most animals there are further differences in the form and size of the body, functional and mental qualities, and in the minute structure of the germ cells themselves. In the Aphis, unfertilised development of eggs is a normal method of reproduction and is known as parthenogenesis.

SEXTANT
Optical instrument used in navigation for measuring angular distances between objects at a distance, particularly the altitude of the sun at noon for calculating the ship's latitude.

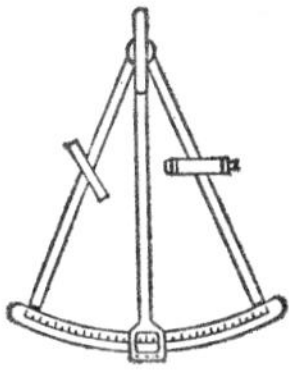

SEYCHELLES
[sā-shel'] Brit. colony consisting of a group of 92 Is. in the Ind. Ocean, N.E. of Madagascar. The principal Is. is Mahé, on which the cap. Victoria stands. Coconuts, vanilla, cinnamon and guano are exported. They became a colony in 1903. Area: 150 sq.m. Pop. 43,750.

SEYMOUR
Eng. family, whose present representatives are the Duke of Somerset and the Marquess of Hertford. **Jane Seymour** (*c.* 1509-37) was the third wife of Henry VIII and the mother of Edward VI.

SFORZA, Count Carlo
(1873-1952) Ital. diplomat and politician. He became Foreign Under-Sec. in 1919, rising to Foreign Min. in 1920. He went into exile in 1926, but returned to public affairs with the Armistice in 1944. He became Foreign Sec. and held office until 1951.

SHACKLETON, Sir Ernest Henry
(1874-1922) Brit. explorer. He accompanied Scott in his Antarctic expedition of 1901-4. In 1908 he sailed from New Zealand in the *Nimrod* and got within 100 m. of the South Pole. In 1914-16 he made an unsuccessful attempt to cross the Antarctic continent.

SHAD
Three food fishes, all belonging to the genus *Clupea*. The Amer. Shad is found in the seas and some of the rivers of N. Amer. The Allice and the Twaite Shad are found in the waters of Brit. and other parts of Europe, and in the Nile.

SHAFTESBURY, Earl of
Title borne by family of Ashley Cooper. **Anthony Ashley Cooper,** 1st Earl (1621-83), was a Royalist who went over to Parl. in 1644. He rejoined the Royalists, and after the Restoration was Chanc. of the Exchequer, 1661-72, and Lord Chanc. 1672-3. He led the attempt to exclude the R.C. James of York from the succession to the throne. **Anthony Ashley Cooper,** 7th Earl (1801-85) M.P. 1826-51, was the leading spirit in the movement for reform of working conditions in factories.

SHAKERS
Religious sect. Founded by Ann Lee, they migrated to Amer. in 1772, and settled at New Lebanon, New York. They were derived from Quakers.

SHAKESPEARE, William
(1564-1616) Eng. dramatist. B. and d. Stratford-on-Avon, son of John Shakespeare and Mary Arden. He mar., 1582, Ann Hathaway: children, Susanna (1583), Hamnet and Judith (1585). He went to London in mid-1580's, becoming playwright to Pembroke's Men, then (1594) joined the Lord Chamberlain's Men. He was a sharer in the Globe (1599) and Blackfriars Theatres (1608). He bought New Place at Stratford, where he retired in 1611. His poems *Venus and Adonis* and *The Rape of Lucrece* appeared 1593-4; his *Sonnets* 1609; *Taming of*

the Shrew (1590-2), *Richard III* (1592-3), *Midsummer Night's Dream* (1595), *Merchant of Venice* (1595), *Romeo and Juliet* (1595), *Richard II* (1595), *Much Ado About Nothing* (1598-9), *Julius Caesar* (1598-9), *Henry V* (1599), *As You Like It* (1599), *Hamlet* (1600), *Twelfth Night* (1601), *Othello* (1602), *Macbeth* (1606), *King Lear* (1606), *Antony and Cleopatra* (1607), *Tempest* (1611).

SHALE
Laminated rock. Shales vary greatly in character. Bituminous shales are worked for oil, alum shales for alum and copperas, and clay shales for firebricks.

SHALLOT
Plant of the onion family, *Allium ascalonicum*. The small edible bulbs are less strongly flavoured than ordinary onions.

SHAMANISM
[shà'-man-] Primitive religion, practised among certain tribes of C. and W. Asia, the Turanian peoples of Siberia, some Amer. Indians, etc.

SHAMROCK
Colloquial name for the trefoil plant, which is the national emblem of Ireland.

SHAN STATE
Territory of the Union of Burma, a mt. region in the E. on the borders of China, Laos and Thailand. The Shans number *c.* 1,000,000.

SHANGHAI
City and seaport of Kiangsu prov., China, 10 m. S. of the Yangtze-Kiang estuary. S. has a large export trade in silk, tea, cotton, sugar, hides and woollen goods. Pop. 6,900,000.

SHANKLIN
Resort of the S.E. Is. of Wight. There is a famous ravine and medicinal springs. Pop. (U.D.) 13,250.

SHANNON
River of Ireland, dividing Connaught from Leinster and Munster. It rises in Cavan, and flows through Loughs Allen, Ree and Derg, entering the Atlantic below Limerick. The waters have been harnessed to supply hydro-electricity. **Shannon Airport.** Transatlantic airport at **Rineanna,** on the Shannon estuary, 15 m. W. of Limerick.

SHARK
Large carnivorous marine cartilaginous fish allied to the Dog-fish. The larger Sharks inhabit warm sea. The lower jaw is exceedingly powerful, the mouth being large and provided with rows of sharp teeth. Being powerful swimmers and voracious feeders, they are a serious danger to bathers, or to shipwrecked persons. The Man-eater (*Carcharodon rondeleti*) approaches 40 ft. in length. The blue and white Sharks span up to 18 ft. Shagreen is the prepared skin.

SHASTRI, Shri Lal Bahadur
(1904-1966) Indian statesman. Educ. Benares. Imprisoned for political activities with non-violent non-cooperative movement. Member of United Provs. Legislative Assembly, 1937. Gen. Sec. Indian Nat. Congress, 1951. Became P.M. after d. of Jawarhalal Nehru (*q.v.*), 1964.

SHAW, George Bernard
(1856-1950) Irish dramatist. B. Dublin; came in 1876 to London, where he struggled as a journalist for 9 years. He worked as a musical, lit. and art critic. He joined (1884) the Fabian Soc. for whom he wrote tracts. *The Quintessence of Ibsenism* helped to popularise Ibsen in Brit. His plays included *Mrs. Warren's Profession* (1893), *Candida* (1894), *Devil's Disciple, Caesar and Cleopatra, Man and Superman* (1903), *The Doctor's Dilemma, Androcles and the Lion, Pygmalion.* His later work includes *Back to Methuselah, Saint Joan* (1923).

SHEATHBILL
(*Chionis alba*) S. Amer. bird about the size of a pigeon. The plumage is white and the bill yellow or pink. A horny sheath encloses the bill.

SHEBA
Ancient kingdom of Arabia; possibly the modern Yemen.

SHEEP
Ruminant mammals belonging to the genus *Ovis*. Wild sheep are found in Europe, Asia, Africa, and N. Amer. The domesticated breeds are grouped according to the type of wool yielded. Long-wool breeds include Cotswold, Devon, Kentish, and Wensleydale; short-wool the Clun Forest, Dorset, Hampshire, Southdown, and Suffolk breeds. Mountain breeds include Black-face, Cheviot, Exmoor and Welsh. They are horned, as are also the Dorset short-wool sheep. Ewes bear the first lambs at 2 years old, in Brit. during winter, from Oct. to April, according to the variety.

SHEEP-DOG
The bob-tailed Old Eng. Sheep-dog. It is also a useful breed for gun work, and good in the water. For the work of rounding up sheep, many other breeds are also suitable, esp. the Scotch Collie.

English Sheep-dog

SHEEPSHEAD
Amer. fish of the family Sparidae allied to Perches.

SHEERNESS
Urban district, seaport and naval station of Kent in the Is. of Sheppey, on the Medway. Pop. 13,620.

SHEFFIELD
City and county borough of the W. Riding, Yorks., 42 m. S.E. of Manchester. Sheffield is the centre of the special steel and cutlery trade. Industries include the manufacture of alloy steel, cutlery, instruments, bicycles, engines and glass. There is a univ. Sheffield became a city in 1893, and returns 7 members to Parl. Pop. 495,290. **Sheffield Plate.** Articles made of copper plated with silver either by fusion or soldering. The manufacture of Sheffield plate was begun about 1743 by Thomas Bolsover.

SHELDRAKE
(or **Sheld-drake**) (*Tadorna tadorna*) Sea duck resident in the Brit. Is. and chiefly confined to mud flats and estuaries. About 25 in. long, its head and neck are a glossy green, the wings and body black and white, a chestnut band on breast and back, and a brown or black line on the white underpart.

SHELL
The exoskeleton of certain animals such as the Molluscs, Crustaceans, etc., also the hard outer covering of eggs, and the carapace of the Turtle and Tortoise. Shells of certain Molluscs and the horny covering of tortoise-shell are of economic value.

SHELL
A deadly projectile used in naval, milit. and

air warfare and discharged from guns of many calibres. A shell contains explosive and filling according to the nature of the projectile.

SHELL-FISH
Various types of bivalves and other Mollusca used for food, including Oysters and Cockles, as well as Lobsters, Crabs, Shrimps, etc.

SHELL SHOCK
Name formerly given to the symptoms resulting from exposure to bombardment or other violent concussion.

SHELLEY, Mary Wollstonecraft
(1797-1851) Eng. author. Daughter of William Godwin and Mary Wollstonecraft, and 2nd wife of Shelley (*q.v.*). Wrote a ghost story (*Frankenstein*), pub. in 1818; she edit. Shelley's poems and letters.

SHELLEY, Percy Bysshe
(1792-1822) Eng. poet. B. Field Place, Sussex; educ. Eton and Oxford whence he was expelled for writing a pamphlet *The Necessity of Atheism*. Shelley was accidentally drowned off Leghorn. His poems include *Adonais* (on Keats' d.), *Alastor, Prometheus Unbound, The Cenci* (tragedy), *The Revolt of Islam, Ode to the West Wind.*

SHENYANG
(formerly **Moukden**) City and important trading centre of Manchuria, *c.* 320 m. S.W. of Harbin. Near the city, the Japanese gained a decisive victory over Russia in 1905. Pop. 2,411,000.

SHEPPARD, Jack
(1702-24) Eng. robber and highwayman.

SHEPPEY
Is. off the N. coast of Kent, at the mouth of the Thames, separated from coast by the Swale. Chief towns are Sheerness and Queenborough.

SHERATON, Thomas
(1751-1806) Eng. furniture designer. His style may be described as one in which ornamentation was generally subordinated to utility.

SHERBORNE
Urban district and market town of Dorset, 18 m. N. of Dorchester. It is famous for its abbey, and its school, founded 1550. Pop. 7,140.

SHERIDAN, Richard Brinsley Butler
(1751-1816) Irish dramatist and polit. Coming to London, he produced *The Rivals, The Critic, The School for Scandal.* M.P. for Stafford in 1780, he became Foreign Sec. in 1782, and took part in the impeachment of Warren Hastings.

SHERIFF
Public official, the descendant of the reeve, or governor, of the shire, an office which existed in Eng. before the Conquest. Now the county official is known as the high sheriff and is nominated on Nov. 12 every year. In Scot. the sheriff has legal duties and is himself a lawyer.

SHERIFFMUIR
Battlefield on the slopes of the Ochils, Perthshire, between the Jacobites under the Earl of Mar, and the Hanoverians under the Duke of Argyll, in 1715.

SHERRINGTON, Sir Charles Scott
(1857-1952) Physiologist, philosopher and poet. B. in London. Wrote *The Integrative Action of the Nervous System* (1906). Won the Nobel prize for his researches on the nervous system.

SHERRY
Name of certain Spanish white wines made in the neighbourhood of Xeres near Cadiz.

SHERWOOD FOREST
Woodland district of W. Notts. assoc. with Robin Hood.

SHETLAND
or **Zetland.** Insular county of Scot., 50 m. N.E. of Orkney. Sheep and cattle are reared, and also ponies. Woollen goods are knitted, and fishing is important. The inhabitants are mostly of Norwegian descent. Lerwick is the county town. Shetland unites with Orkney to send 1 member to Parl. Pop. 18,000.

SHETLAND PONY
(or **Shelty**) Small breed of pony from the Shetland Is. It is the smallest in Brit.

SHIELD
(1) Protective armour. Roman shield was oblong and convex; made of wood, it was covered with leather. The Gk. shield was often round with leather apron, the Norman was kite-shaped. (2) (Her.) The escutcheon or field on which coats of arms are placed or blazoned.

SHIITES
Mohammedan sect. Their special tenet is additional reverence for Ali, cousin of Mahomet.

SHIKOKU
Smallest of the 4 principal Japanese Is., lying S. of Honshu and E. of Kyushu. Area: 7,250 sq.m.

SHINGLE
Shore deposit consisting of pebbles formed by wave action upon the base of a cliff.

SHINGLES
A virus disease affecting nerve endings. *See* HERPES ZOSTER.

SHINTOISM
State religion of Japan. The goddess of the sun, Amaterasu, is the chief deity. The book of Shintoism is the *Kojiki* (A.D. 712).

SHINTY
Form of hockey, played in Ireland and the Highlands of Scot.

SHIP MONEY
Tax for the upkeep of the navy and coastal defences. The writs issued by Charles I in 1634 and 1635 levying ship money in time of peace and on inland as well as maritime counties and towns aroused the opposition of John Hampden. It was expressly declared illegal in 1641.

SHIP-WORM
Colloquial name for a bivalve mollusc distinguished by the elongation of the respiratory 'siphons'. It has 2 three-lobed valves of small size and globular shape situated at its anterior extremity.

SHIPS
As early as 5,000 B.C. sailing ships were used on the Nile and the Gks. and Roms. used galleys with sails, and having 2, 3, 4 or 5 banks of oars, manned by slaves. The Viking long-ships used a single large sail and up to 60 oars. Brit. sea power began when King Alfred built oak 60-oared ships to fight the Danes. In the 15th cent. came the *Great Harry*, the first double-decked Eng. warship. Typical of the 17th cent. was the E. Indiaman, a useful cargo and fighting vessel of *c.* 600 t., trading with India and China. By the end of the 18th cent. a ship of the line had reached a length of 250 ft., displaced *c.* 3,000 t. and carried 100 guns. Famous in the 19th cent. were the Brit. and Amer. sailing clippers which travelled 300 m. a day. The Brit. *Cutty Sark* (*q.v.*) made the voyage from Sydney to London in 75 days. The first Brit. ironclad was built in 1860. One of the first paddle wheelers was the *Charlotte Dundas*, built by Symington in 1802. In 1812 Henry Bell's *Comet* ran on the Clyde. In 1838 the *Great Western* crossed the Atlantic under steam alone. The screw propeller was invented by Capt. John Ericsson. In 1894 *Turbinia* was equipped with turbine engines invented by Sir Charles Parsons and reached a speed of 34 k. Improved hull construction kept pace with increased engine power and ships became larger and larger. For passenger ships *see* LINER. Many cargo vessels of from 2,500-8,000 t. are also employed on set routes or on tramping.

Ships of the Merchant Navy designed for special purposes include oil tankers, which carry bulk oil, whalers, iron ore, grain, and refrigerated meat and fruit vessels. The trend in shipbuilding is towards mechanisation of cargo handling, and greater facility of remote-control. The world's first nuclear-powered submarine, the Amer. *U.S.S. Nautilus* (3,000 t.) was launched in 1954 and is capable of speeds above 20 k. when submerged. The application of atomic power to merchant shipping should provide fuel economies of 50 % to be set against high capital cost of installation; also nuclear energy becomes cheaper the larger the scale on which it is used, hence its usefulness for long-distance, large capacity oil tankers.

SHIRAZ
City of S. Persia, founded in the 7th cent., 120 m. N.E. of Bushire. Besides the wine industry there is a trade in cotton, spices and perfumes. Pop. 170,659.

SHIRE
Territorial division of Brit., the equivalent of county (*q.v.*).

SHIRE HORSE
Heaviest breed of horse used for farm and traction work.

SHITTIM
(*Dalbergia*) Allied to acacia. It grows in Palestine, esp. in the neighbourhood of the Dead Sea. Its wood was used by the Jews for the Ark of the Covenant and the Tabernacle.

SHIVA
(or **Siva**) The 3rd 'person' of the Hindu Trimurti (trinity) *i.e.* **Brahma** (Creator), **Vishnu** (preserver), **Shiva** (destroyer).

SHOCK
State resulting after severe body injury in which all vital processes are depressed. The patient is cold, pale, beads of sweat appear on the brow, pulse is rapid and difficult to feel, breathing slow and shallow.

SHOREDITCH
Borough of N.E. London; centre of the furniture and cabinet making trade of London. The first London theatre was built by James Burbage in Shoreditch. With Finsbury it sends 1 member to Parl. Pop. 40,000.

SHOSTAKOVITCH, Dmitri
[-kō'-] (1906-) Russ. composer. He has written 13 symphonies, a concerto, operas, ballets and chamber music.

SHOULDER
Part of the body to which the upper limb is attached. Composed of bones, muscles and ligaments. Shoulder joint composed of the head of the humerus, parts of the scapula and one end of the clavicle or collar bone.

SHOVEL, Sir Cloudesley
(*c.* 1650-1707) Eng. admiral. As rear-admiral he assisted in the capture of Barcelona, but attacked Toulon unsuccessfully.

SHOVELLER
(*Spatula clypeata*) A native duck of Europe, Asia, N. Africa and N. Amer. and a winter visitor to Brit., breeding in the E. counties, in Ireland, and in parts of Scot. The bill is broad. The male plumage is striking, head and neck, green; back, brown; wings, white and brown; breast, chestnut; shoulders, light blue; underparts, chestnut. The bill is black and the legs orange.

SHREW
Small, mouselike, insectivorous mammal. A long snout, small, rounded ears, and the specialised teeth are characteristics. The Common Brit. Shrew (*Sorex vulgaris*) is nearly 3 in. long with a shorter tail, the fur being brownish to reddish-grey above and lighter beneath. Besides insects, it eats worms and snails.

SHREWSBURY
[shrōz'-] Municipal borough and county town of Salop, on the Severn, 43 m. N.W. of Birmingham. Shrewsbury School, founded by Edward VI in 1552, is a famous public school. Pop. 50,000.

SHRIKE
[shrīk] Bird of the family Laniidae. 4 of the shrikes, including the Woodchat (*L. rutilus*), visit Brit. in winter, but only 1 species, the Red-backed Shrike (*L. Collurio*), or Butcher Bird, breeds here occasionally.

SHRIMP
Small marine Crustacea of the sub-order *Macrura*, in particular the so-called edible Brown Shrimp (*Crangon vulgaris*). When alive the Brown Shrimp is greyish-green, spotted with brown; it turns pinky-brown when cooked.

SHROPSHIRE
or **Salop.** County of Eng. on the Welsh border, E. of Montgomeryshire. The Severn divides the county in two. To the N. and E. the land is low-lying, except for the Wrekin (1,335 ft.). The S.W. is hilly. Mainly agricultural, Shropshire produces barley and oats, and rears sheep and cattle. Iron and coal are mined. Shrewsbury is the county town. Shropshire returns 4 members to Parl. Pop. 297,000.

SHROVE TUESDAY
Day before Ash Wed. It was so called from the fact that in former times it was customary for people to be shriven, *i.e.* to make their confessions, on that day, in preparation for Lent. The eating of pancakes is a survival of the old Shrove Tuesday feasting.

SHUTE, Nevil
(1899-1960) Pseudonym of **Nevil Shute Norway,** Brit. novelist. His novels include *Ruined City* (1938), *Pied Piper* (1942), *The Chequer Board* (1947), *No Highway* (1948), *A Town like Alice* (1949), *Round the Bend* (1951), *On the Beach* (1957).

SI KIANG
River of S. China, which rises in the mts. of the Yunnan-Kwangsi boundary and flows into the S. China Sea. Canton and Hong Kong are situated to the E. of its mouth.

SIAMANG
[sē'a-] (*Hylobates syndactylus*) Gibbon of Sumatra and the Malay archipelago. It stands about 3 ft. in ht. and has a slender body, with long legs and arms.

SIAMESE TWINS
First recorded instance of this condition occurred in 1811 in Siam when a Chinese woman gave birth to male twins joined together by a fold of skin stretching from the breast of one to that of the other. In 1953 S. twins were born to a Nigerian woman and separated in a London hospital. One d. shortly after the operation but the other returned to Nigeria to live a normal life.

SIBELIUS, Jean
[-bā'-li-o͞os] (1865-1957) Finnish composer. Much of his work was inspired by the legends and

scenery of his native land. He wrote 7 symphonies, a violin concerto, many orchestral pieces, a string quartet, as well as lesser pieces and songs.

SIBERIA
The Asiatic region of the U.S.S.R., stretching from the Ural Mts. to the Bering Strait. More specifically, Siberia is used for 2 areas of the R.S.F.S.R., E. and W. Siberia which lie E. of the Ural Mts. and Kazakhstan and W. of Yakutsk A.S.S.R., with a coastline on the Arctic. The land is either steppe or forest, and there are vast mineral resources.

SIBYL
Name given by the Roms. to prophetesses, generally reckoned to be 10 in number and supposed to be inspired by Apollo.

SICILY
Ital. Is. in the Medit. separated from the ' toe ' of Italy by the Strait of Messina. Mt. Etna, a volcano 10,740 ft. high, is the highest point. S. Sicily is infertile and relatively unproductive; in the extreme S. are limestone rocks, in the E. the marshy and malarial plain of Catania. Sicily is an important source of sulphur. Palermo is the cap. The Phoenicians and Gks. planted colonies; it was then dominated successively by Roms., Goths, Saracens and Normans, and later was ruled by Angevin, Hapsburg and Bourbon dynasties, until liberated by Garibaldi. It became a part of united Italy in 1861, and in 1947 was granted autonomous govt. as a region of Italy. Area: 9,930 sq.m. Pop. 4,711,783.

SICKERT, Walter
(1860-1942) Eng. painter and etcher. Studied under Whistler at Chelsea.

SIDDONS, Sarah
(1755-1831) Considered by many to be Eng.'s greatest tragic actress. She made her London début at Drury Lane as Portia but was a failure. She then toured Eng. for 6 years and returned to Drury Lane to make an immediate success. Joining her brother, John Kemble, at Covent Garden in 1803, she acted there until her formal farewell, as Lady Macbeth, in 1812.

SIDERITE
[sī-dĕ-rīt] Iron carbonate. In its impure form as clay ironstone it forms one of the most valuable ores of iron in England.

SIDGWICK, Henry
(1838-1900) Eng. philosopher who took an active part in the provision of higher educ. for women, Newnham Coll. being the outcome of his efforts.

SIDI BARRANI
Settlement on the Medit. coast of Egypt, the scene of heavy fighting in World War II.

SIDNEY, Sir Philip
(1554-86) Eng. author and soldier, nephew of the Earl of Leicester, killed at Zutphen. His chief works are *Arcadia, Astrophel and Stella,* and the *Apologie for Poetrie.*

SIDON
or **Saida.** Seaport of the Lebanon, on the E. coast of the Medit. between Tyre and Beirut. It was an important Phoenician city, famous for its glass and linen, purple dye and perfumes. Pop. 22,000.

SIEGFRIED LINE
[sēg'-frēd] Line of defences in depth erected by Germany along her W. border. Its construction began in 1936. The Allies finally broke through the entire line in Mar.-April 1945.

SIEMENS, Sir William
[sē'-] (1823-83) German scientist and inventor. Settled in Eng. 1844, naturalised 1859, knighted 1883. His regenerative furnace practically revolutionised the methods of steel production. He was also a pioneer in electric tramways.

SIENA
City of Tuscany, Italy, 32 m. S. of Florence. There is a 13th cent. univ. and a Gothic cath. Pop. 53,200.

SIERRA LEONE
[-lē-ōn'] Former Brit. colony and protectorate in W. Africa between Guinea and Liberia, with an Atlantic coastline. Indep. 1961. The area comprises the S. L. peninsula, Tasso Is. and York Is., Banana Is. and Bonthe township on Sherbro Is. Palm kernels and oil, rubber, diamonds, iron and chrome are exported. Freetown is cap. and chief port. The state is divided into 3 provs., N., S.E. and S.W. Total area is about 28,000 sq.m. Total pop. 2,183,000.

SIGHT
or **Light Sense.** Impressions of degrees of light are received on retina of eye, interpreted by rods and cones which in turn send stimuli along optic nerve to sight centre in occipital part of brain.

SIGNALLING
Term applied to the system of transmitting signals to greater or lesser distances. The signals may be of the nature of flags, lamps, heliographs, smoke, sound signals such as bells and sirens, semaphores, and also telegraphy and telephony including wireless transmission. The Morse code and its modifications are commonly used in signalling.

SIGNET, Writer to the
Member of the principal class of solicitors in Scot. who form a soc. presided over by the Keeper of the Signet, apptd. by the Crown.

SIKH
[sēk] Member of a great Ind. community, mostly distributed throughout the Punjab. Sikhism was founded in the 15th cent. by a teacher named Nanak. Under Govind Singh in the 17th cent., the Sikh community began to cherish milit. ambitions, which were fostered later by Ranjit Singh (1780-1839). The d. of Ranjit Singh was followed by 2 Sikh wars with Gt. Brit. and Brit. annexation of the Punjab.

SIKKIM
Small state to the S. of the Himalayas, bounded by Nepal, Tibet and Bhutan. Rice, millet and fruit are grown. Gangtok is the cap. S. is under the protection of the Repub. of India. Area: 2,750 sq.m. Pop. 161,080.

SIKORSKY, Wladyslaw
(1881-1943) Polish soldier and politician. After World War I he was Chief of the Gen. Staff, 1921, P.M. 1922, and War Min. 1924-5. When Poland was overrun in 1939 he organised Polish refugee forces in Fr., becoming Premier and C.-in-C. of the Repub. in exile.

SILESIA
District of E. central Europe, divided between Poland and Czechoslovakia after World War II. Much of the area is rich in coal, iron and zinc, and important metallurgical and engineering industries have developed.

SILICON
A brown or black non-metallic element. It is widely distributed in sand, clay, quartz, granite and many other rocks, and forms 27·6 % of the earth's crust. It was first prepared in 1823 by Berzelius.

SILICONES
Branch of the glass family manufactured from coal, oil or glass, and sand. The first silicone compound was created in Germany in 1863. In the U.S.A., Dr. J. Franklin Hyde discovered a silicone resin which would hold glass fibres together. Other products include white enamels that do not dull, water-repellants, stain-resistants, fluids that pour at −120° C., silicone oils for lubrication, ointments for skin therapy, etc.

SILK
Fabric orig. manufactured solely from the filament spun into cocoons by silkworms. Silk is known to have been made in China cents. before the Christian era. The first silk weaving factory in Europe was estabd. in the 6th cent. A.D. at Constantinople. China and Japan lead in the production of raw silk. Since 1863 the manufacture of artificial silk from nitro-cellulose has progressed steadily. **Silkworm.** Silk-spinning caterpillars. The most common is *Bombyx mori*, a native of N. China, *c.* 3 in. long, and of a yellowish-grey colour. It spins a yellow or white cocoon round itself, then metamorphoses into a chrysalis, which again metamorphoses into the egg-laying moth.

SILURES
People inhabiting the area now covered by the Welsh and Eng. counties of Glamorgan, Brecknock, Monmouth, Radnor and Hereford. They were prob. of non-Aryan origin, and they offered a fierce resistance to the Roms. until subdued *c.* A.D. 80.

SILURIAN
[sī-lew'-riăn] Geological formation consisting of the rocks lying between the Ordovician below and the Devonian above.

SILVER
A white metal found chiefly as the sulphide, often in assoc. with antimony. The best known conductor of heat and electricity, it is very malleable and ductile. Its principal uses are in electroplating, photography, mirrors and in coinage.

SILVER FIR
Tall evergreen tree (*Abies alba*). Growing to a ht. of 150 ft. or more with a diameter of over 6 ft., it is a native of C. and S. Europe. The cones, 6 in. long, are erect and cylindrical.

SIMENON, Georges
(1903-) Belgian novelist. B. Liège. He has written a great many detective novels, including *The Maigret* series 1930-5, *The Man Who Watched Trains Go By*, *Blind Path*, etc.

SIMLA
Chief city of Himachal Pradesh, India, a hill station on a spur of the Himalayas, at a height of 7,000 ft.

SIMNEL, Lambert
(*c.* 1475-1535) Eng. impostor. He was persuaded to impersonate Warwick, gained a large following, and was crowned as Edward VI. Landing in Eng. at Furness in 1487, he marched to Stoke, where Henry VII defeated his adherents.

SIMON, John Allsebrook
1st Viscount (1873-1954) Eng. lawyer and statesman. Lib. M.P. for Walthamstow, 1906, became Solicitor-General, 1910, Attorney-General, 1913 and Home Sec., 1915. In 1916 he resigned in protest against conscription. In 1918 he lost his seat but was re-elected in 1922, for Spen Valley. From 1927-30 he was Chairman of the Statutory Commission on India which issued the 'Simon Report'. He was leader of the Nat. Libs. in Parl., Home Sec., 1935-7, Chanc. of the Exchequer, 1937-40 and Lord Chanc., 1940-5.

SIMOON
Name given to desert sandstorms of N. Africa.

SIMPLON
[sa(ng)-plō(ng)] Pass over the Alps, rising to *c.* 6,500 ft. A great trade route in the M.A. The **S. Tunnel,** 12½ m. long, runs from Brig to Iselle, east of the Pass.

SIMPSON, Sir James Young
(1811-70) Specialising in obstetrics he introduced chloroform anaesthesia into the practice of this med. science and brought about its general use in this country. *See* ANAESTHETIC.

SIN
(1) Guilt before God or the gods. Some doctrine of sin and of escaping its penalties forms part of most religions. It is not defined in the Scriptures, but appears as the element in man which puts him at enmity with God and requires the work of a Redeemer for its atonement. The 7 'mortal' or 'deadly' sins are anger, lust, gluttony, sloth, pride, envy and avarice. (2) **Original sin** is the Christian doctrine that all mankind fell with Adam's first sin, but that the whole world was redeemed by the sacrifice of Christ.

SINAI
[sī'-nī] Peninsula of Egypt between the Gulfs of Suez and Aqaba, at the head of the Red Sea. The **Mount Sinai** of the Bible is identified with Gebel Katherina, in the S. of the peninsula.

SINCLAIR, Upton Beall
(1878-1968) Amer. novelist His works include *The Jungle* (1906), *World's End* (1940), *Between Two Worlds* (1941), *One Clear Call* (1948), *O Shepherd Speak* (1951), *A Personal Jesus* (1952).

SIND
District of W. Pakistan on the Ind. frontier, with a coastline on the Arabian Sea, N. of Cutch. It is watered by the Indus and Nara, and is primarily an agricultural region. The area under cultivation has been increased by vast irrigation schemes. There are cotton mills and other industries. Karachi is the chief city.

SINGAPORE
Is. at the S. tip of the Malayan peninsula with air and naval base. There are extensive docks, and large tin-smelting works. The city of Singapore was founded as a trading settlement by Sir Stamford Raffles, in 1819. 5 years later, the Is. was ceded to Gt. Brit. and in 1826 united with Penang and Malacca to form the colony of the Straits Settlements. A year later Singapore became a separate crown colony admin. by a Gov. and 2 councils. In 1957 agreement was reached on the establishment of an autonomous State of Singapore. Joined Fed. of Malaysia, 1963, and withdrew after disagreements, 1965. Area: 220 sq.m. Pop. 1,913,000.

SINGER, Isaac Merritt
(1811-75) Amer. inventor, who improved Howe's orig. sewing machine and founded the Singer Company.

SINGING
The controlled use of the voice for the production of melodious sounds in musical succession. The power to sing is normally present in every human being. The average compass of the voice is about one and a half octaves; a mixed choir will offer a range of about three octaves and three notes.

SINN FEIN
[shin-fān] Gaelic meaning 'Ourselves alone' adopted by the Irish Nat. movement at the beginning of the 20th cent. Orig. it referred to the revival of the Irish language and lit. but later it grew into a determination to throw off the Brit. yoke. This culminated in the Easter rebellion of 1916. At the election of Dec. 1918, the party was returned in Ireland with a large majority. After the setting-up of the Free State in 1922 many Sinn Feiners refused to recognise the new govt. and civil war followed. *See* IRELAND, REPUBLIC OF.

SINO-JAPANESE WARS
(1894-5) War which resulted from the rivalry of China and Japan over Korea. The capture of Port Arthur in Nov. 1894, and of Wei-hai-wei, brought the war to an end. China was forced, in April, 1895, to sign the Treaty of Shimonoseki, ceding the Liao-Tung peninsula, the Is. of Formosa and the Pescadores Is. **(1937-45)** War which started, 1937, as a skirmish between Jap. and Chinese troops on the outskirts of Peking, N.E. China. By Oct. 1938,

Jap. troops were in possession of the 7 largest cities, all the larger ports and most of the railways of China, and had forced the Nationalist Army under the leadership of Chiang Kai-Shek (*q.v.*) to the W., where they set up govt. at Chungking. The Jap. attack on Brit. and the U.S.A., 1941, and her invasion of Indo-China and Burma, cut Free China's supply route from the W. The deadlock ended with Russia's entry into the war, Aug. 1945. By the time Japan had surrendered formally to the Allies, Chiang Kai-Shek had regained most of occupied China and the Jap. commander surrendered all Jap. forces in China, Formosa, and parts of Fr. Indo-China, on Sept. 9, 1945.

SINO-TIBETAN
Family of languages having uninflected monosyllabic words and using different tones. It includes *Siamese* (*Thai*), *Tibeto-Burmese*, *Chinese*.

SINOPE
Turkish port on the Black Sea. It was the most important of all the Gk. colonies. Pop. 15,700.

SINUS
[sī′-] Med. term for any cavity with an exit on to skin of mucous membrane which contains either air, blood or pus.

SIOUX
[soo] N. Amer. Ind. tribe of the Dakota family.

SIPHON
Curved or rectangular tube or pipe, with arms of unequal length, which is used to transfer liquid first vertically over an obstruction, or over the edge of a containing vessel, and then to a lower level. A soda-water siphon does not operate on the true siphon principle, the liquid being expelled through the nozzle by the operation of a lever which controls the gas pressure with which the liquid is charged.

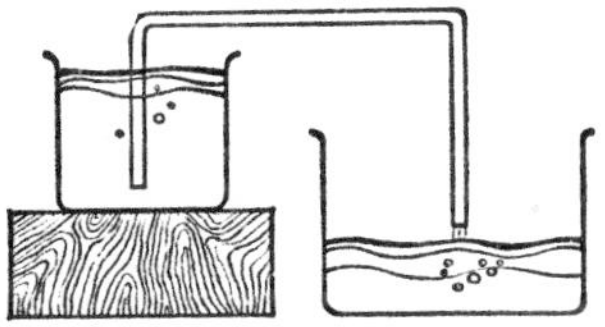

Apparatus to show basic principle of the siphon

SIRIUS
The dog star. The brightest star in the sky, whose light is 26 times more powerful than that of the sun. Its distance from the earth is *c.* 9 light years.

SIROCCO
Hot, dry S. wind experienced in N. Africa, Sicily and the N. Medit.

SISKIN
Species of small finch (*Carduelus spinus*) which is distributed over all temp. regions. It breeds in Scot., parts of Eng. and in Ireland, and large flocks from the continent winter in Brit. The plumage of the male is olive-green with yellow patches, the chin and crown being black.

SISTINE CHAPEL
Pope's private chapel in the Vatican. It was built by Sixtus IV in 1480, and is decorated with frescoes by Michelangelo and other famous artists. Raphael designed the tapestries.

SITWELL, Dame Edith
(1887-1964) Eng. poetess. B. Scarborough. She led a new movement in poetry in 1916 against outworn forms. She pub. *Façade* (1922), *Bucolic Comedies* (1923), *Gardeners and Astronomers* (1953), and several collected ed. (1930), *The Canticle of the Rose* (1949), also critical and historical works, anthologies, and a novel. Created D.B.E. in 1954. Her brother is **Sir Osbert Sitwell** (1892-1969). His *Collected Poems and Satires* were pub. 1931; also stories, novels, essays and an autobiog.—*Left Hand Right Hand, Great Morning, Noble Essences* (1945-50) and a travel book, *The Four Continents* (1954). Created C.H. 1958. His brother **Sacheverell** (1897-   ) writes books on art, hist. and travel.

SKATE
(*Raia*) Food fish of the class Elasmobranchii. One of the cartilaginous fishes, its body is flattened in the dorso-ventral plane, and there is a long tail. The snout is triangular, the mouth being on the ventral side. There are several Brit. species.

SKATING
Ice Skating. Popular sport using specially designed steel blades fitted to skating boots.

SKELTON, John
(*c.* 1460-1529) Eng. poet. B. Norfolk. He was tutor to Prince Henry (Henry VIII). His poems are *Philip Sparrow, The Bowge of Court, Colin Clout.* His satires obliged him to take sanctuary in Westminster, where he d.

SKI-ING
Method of travel, and sport. The word is derived from the Norwegian snow shoes or 'ski'. The skis are strips of wood some 9 ft. long and 4 ins. wide, curved in front and strapped to the foot. Poles with a circular piece of metal at the end to prevent them from sinking into the snow are carried for steering and braking.

SKIN
Tissue covering entire body surface, composed of two main layers. Top or outer layer composed of masses of scaly-like cells and called *epidermis.* Under layer called *dermis* composed of blood vessels, sweat glands, hair follicles and muscle fibres as well as nerves.

SKITTLES
Game resembling ninepins. A cheese-shaped bowl weighing *c.* 10 lb. is hurled at 9 skittles, with the object of knocking them over.

SKOPLJE
[skop′-lyā] Cap. of Macedonia, Yugoslavia, on the Vardar. Disastrous earthquake, 1963, killed 1,200 people, and destroyed greater part of the city. Now being rebuilt.

SKUA
[skew′-ă] (*Stercorarius*) A Robber Gull which obtains its food by victimising other sea-fowl.

SKULL
The skeleton of the head of the higher animals. In man, it consists of the 8 bones of the cranium enclosing the brain, and the 14 bones of the face. The cranial bones protect the brain.

SKUNK
(*Mephitis*) Carnivorous mammal allied to Badgers, etc. Skunks can project a malodorous secretion from two glands situated near the tail. *M. mephitica,* common in C. and N. Amer. is about the size of a domestic cat. The fur is thick and soft and handsomely marked in black and white.

SKYE
Largest Is. of the Inner Hebrides, in the county of Inverness. The Is. is wild and beautiful, the Cuillins rising to over 3,300 ft. Farming and fishing are the main occupations. Portree, the chief town and port, has steamer connections with Oban.

SKYE TERRIER
Was orig. bred in Skye where it was used for hunting. It has a long, silky coat of a silvery blue-grey, with short legs and a long, low body.

SKYLARK
Passerine bird (*Alauda arvensis*) native of Europe and Asia. Plumage is warm brown above, with black streakings; yellowish-white beneath. The length is 7 in. The lark is noted for its pleasing song, uttered as it hovers high in the air.

SLADE, Felix
(1770-1868) Eng. collector. He left money to found Chairs of fine arts at Oxford, Camb. and London, Slade School.

SLATE
Compressed shale. Split into thin sheets, it is used mostly for roofing purposes.

SLAV
[slåv] Peoples of E. Europe. The classification of the group is by language including such peoples as Russians, Poles, Czechs, Slovaks, Yugoslavs, all of whom speak dialects of the Slavonic sub-family of Indo-European languages. *See* SLAVIC.

SLAVE TRADE
The exploitation of the Negro as a slave by Spain, Portugal, Gt. Brit. and other European countries, and later U.S.A. African villages were raided, and the inhabitants carried off, usually to the New World. They were introduced into the Brit. settlements in 1619. At the end of the 18th cent. the growth of humanitarianism caused an attack on the slave trade, led in Eng. by Wilberforce, Clarkson, Zachary Macaulay and Brougham. The slave trade in the Empire was abolished 1807, and slavery itself in 1833.

SLAVIC
(or Slavonic) **languages.** Branch of Indo-European, including (a) **East:** *Russian, White Russian, Ukrainian;* (b) **South:** *Bulgarian, Serbo-Croatian, Slovene, Macedonian;* (c) **West:** *Slovak, Czech* (lit. from 13th cent.), *Sorabian* or *Wendish, Polish, Kashubian, Polabian.*

SLEEP
Phase of body life in which a state of unconsciousness prevails. During this phase certain body processes cease and others have their activity reduced so that a period of rest results. In man this varies considerably but the usual is 6-8 hours daily. Children and young people require very much more.

SLESVIG
District of S. Denmark, officially called S. Jutland Provs., which became Danish in 1920 as the result of a plebiscite. Formerly Danish, it was taken by Aust. and Pruss., 1864, and was Pruss. prov. until 1920.

SLIGO
[slī'-gō] County of N.W. Eire, in Connaught prov., with a coastline on the Atlantic Ocean. The chief industries are cattle rearing, potato growing and fishing. Pop. 53,561. **Sligo.** Seaport and county town of Sligo, Eire, at the mouth of the Garrogue. Fishing is extremely important. Pop. 15,000.

SLIM, William Joseph
1st Viscount (1891-1970) Field-Marshal. During World War I, he served in Gallipoli, Fr. and Mesopotamia. In World War II he commanded the 10th Indian Div. in Syria, Persia and Iraq; the 1st Burma Corps in Burma; and finally the 14th Army. In 1948 he became C.I.G.S. Created F-M., retired from C.I.G.S., Nov. 1952; Gov.-Gen. of Australia, 1953-60.

SLOANE, Sir Hans
(1660-1753) He travelled extensively collecting plants, books and curiosities which at his d. were purchased for the nation and formed the nucleus of the Brit. Mus.

SLOE
(or **Blackthorn**) *Prunus spinosa,* and its fruit, which resembles a miniature plum and when ripe is a rich black.

SLOTH
Arboreal mammals of S. Amer. There are 2 species, *Bradypus and Choloepus.* Both are found in forest regions, where they feed on leaves, fruit and young shoots. They hang inverted from branches.

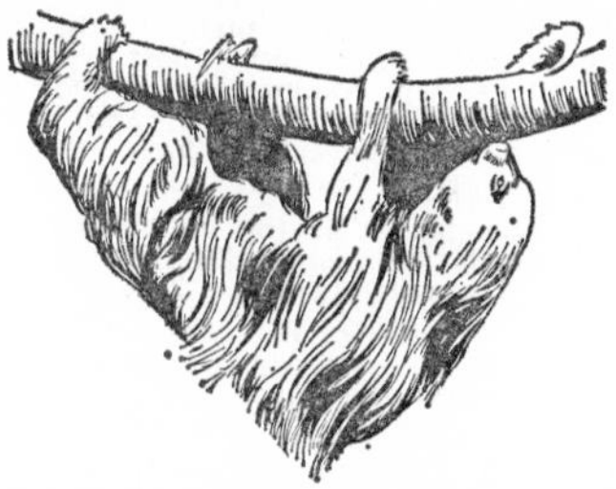

SLOUGH
Borough of Bucks., 2 m. N. of Windsor. There are numerous industries. With Eton, Slough sends 1 member to Parl. Pop. 82,700.

SLOVAK
[slō'-] People of Slav race found chiefly in Czechoslovakia (*q.v.*). Before 1919, the Slovaks were under Hungarian rule. They number *c.* 3,000,000. **Slovakia.** Prov. of Czechoslovakia (*q.v.*) to the E. of Moravia. It consists mainly of highland, the Carpathian Mts., but there is lowland in the S. around Bratislava, the cap. From 1939-45 Slovakia was an indep. state, allied with Germany.

SLOW-WORM
(*Anguis fragilis*) Small legless lizard, brownish-black in colour and common in Brit.

SLUG
(*Limax*) Snail-like land gasteropod mollusc, usually lacking a visible shell. Many feed on lichens and fungi. During the winter they rest under stones or in the ground.

SMALLPOX
(Variola) Dangerous infectious fever characterised by the eruption of a rash which, after passing through stages, dries up and leaves permanent scarring of the skin. Spread is favoured by overcrowding and unhygienic surroundings, but protection is afforded to a community by vaccination.

SMELL
One of the special senses possessed by man and certain animals. The sense is highly developed in animals and in primitive races, and is composed mainly of nerve filaments of the nerves of smell or olfactory nerve which is situated in upper part of nose.

SMELT
(*Osmerus*) Genus of small sea fish belonging to Salmon family. The best known species, and the only one found in European waters, is the Common Smelt (*O. eperlanus*), abundant in Brit.

SMETANA, Bedrich
[smet'-ă-nă] (1824-84) Czech composer. He helped to estab. the Nat. Theatre in Prague in 1862. The best known of his 8 operas is *The Bartered Bride.*

SMITH, Adam
(1723-90) Brit. economist. A friend of David Hume, he pub. his *Theory of the Moral Sentiments* in 1759. Turning to economics, he pub. in 1776, *The Wealth of Nations,* which, as the first scientific exposition of the principles of polit. economy, had a far-reaching influence.

SMITH, John
(1579-1631) He was one of the early settlers of Virginia. His most famous adventure was his rescue from d. by Pocahontas, a 13-year-old Indian girl.

SMITH, Sydney
(1771-1845) Eng. clergyman, Whig, author and wit. In 1802 he began, with Jeffrey and Brougham, the *Edinburgh Review*.

SMITH, Walter Bedell
(1895-1961) Amer. General. First U.S. Sec. Combined Chiefs of Staff, 1941-2; Chief of Staff at SHAEF, 1942, for planned invasion of Fr. Brig.-Gen., 1943; U.S. ambassador to U.S.S.R., 1946-9. Army retired list, 1953. U.S. Under-Sec. of State, 1953-4.

SMITH, William
(1769-1839) Eng. geologist. He became convinced that the age of each stratum could be determined by the fossils which it contained. Smith has been described as 'The father of English geology'.

SMITH, Sir William Sidney
(1764-1840) Brit. admiral. He entered the navy at 11 and was captain at 18. In 1799, after capturing the Fr. ships, he compelled Napoleon to raise the siege of Acre and subsequently served in Egypt, Sicily, Naples, etc.

SMITHSONIAN INSTITUTION
Amer. scientific institution, founded in Washington, D.C. under the will of James Macie Smithson (1765-1829). Activities include the research work of the Weather Bureau, the Nat. Museum, the Bureau of Ethnology, the Nat. Zoological Park, the Langley Aerodynamical Lab. and the Aerophysical Lab.

SMOKE
Volatile matter formed by the imperfect combustion of wood, coal or other fuels, and consisting largely of particles of carbon and hydrocarbons along with various gaseous products. Combined with fog it produces the harmful compound called **Smog.** The need for the abatement of smoke has brought about regulations under Public Health Acts.

SMOLENSK
City of the Russ. S.F.S.R., cap. of S. Region, on the Dnieper, 240 m. S.W. of Moscow. Pop. 170,000.

SMOLLETT, Tobias George
(1721-71) Brit. novelist. B. Dunbartonshire. His novels are *Roderick Random* (1748), *Peregrine Pickle* (1751), *Humphry Clinker* (1771).

SMUGGLING
Breach of the revenue laws, whether by importing or exporting prohibited goods, or by evading customs duties.

SMUT
Disease of cereals and various herbs and grasses. It is also the name of the fungi that cause it.

SMUTS, Jan Christiaan
(1870-1950) S. African statesman. During the Boer War he commanded the Boer forces in Cape Colony. He was Min. of the Interior 1910-12; Finance Min. 1912-13, and Defence Min. 1910-20. In World War I he commanded in E. Africa. He succeeded Botha as P.M. 1919-24. He led the revolt against Hertzog's neutrality policy in 1939, and was again P.M. 1939-48 when, his party being defeated by the Nationalist Party under Dr. Malan, he became Leader of the Opposition.

SMYTH, Dame Ethel Mary
(1858-1944) Eng. composer. Her *Mass in D* was heard at the Albert Hall in 1893. Her works include the opera *The Wreckers*, chamber, orchestral, and choral music. She was a militant suffragette, and was awarded the D.B.E. in 1922.

SMYTHE, Francis Sydney
(1900-49) Mountaineer. B. in Maidstone, he took part in the 1930 Kangchenjunga, 1931 Kamet and 1933, '36 and '38 Everest expeds.

SMYTHE, Patricia Rosemary
(1928-) Brit. horsewoman. Member of the Brit. Show Jumping Team, she first went abroad with the Brit. Team in 1947. She estabd. a ladies' record for the high jump (2 m. 20 cm.) in the Bruxelles Puissance in 1954. Member Brit. Olympic Team, 1960.

SNAIL
Various gasteropods. They have an external shell and respire air directly through part of the mantle. Some live in fresh or salt water, others on land.

SNAKE
Limbless reptile. With a long cylindrical body furnished with overlapping scales, it belongs to the sub-order Ophidia of the order Squamata. Snakes slough their skins from time to time. Venom is secreted in a modified salivary gland. The only poisonous kind in Brit. is the Adder.

SNAKE-ROOT
Plants used as an antidote for snake bite, esp. the mongoose plant (*Ophiorrhiza mungos*) of the E. Indies.

SNAPDRAGON
(*Antirrhinum majus*) Perennial herb. Of the family Scrophulariaceae, the bag-shaped flower can be made to open by squeezing sideways. One species, *A. orontium*, grows wild in Brit.

SNEEZEWORT
Perennial herb (*Achillea ptarmica*) of the family Compositae, found in Europe, Asia Minor and Siberia. It has a strong pungent smell.

SNIPE
(*Capella gallinago*) Allied to the Plover, it is a marsh frequenting long-beaked bird, resident in Brit. The best known is the Common Snipe, about 10 in. long, and is mottled brown and black. The other Brit. species are the Jack Snipe (*Lymnocryples minimus*), which is slightly smaller, and the Solitary or Great Snipe (*C. major*).

SNORING
Flapping of the soft palate, which frequently arises from the habit of sleeping with the mouth open, especially when lying on the back.

SNOW
(1) Frozen water-vapour precipitated in soft white flakes. (2) **Snow-line.** Ht. above which snow always lies. It varies with latitude and elevation.

SNOW, Charles Percy, Baron Snow
(1905-) Eng. writer and Lab. politician. His sequence of novels began with *Strangers and Brethren* (1940), *The Light and the Dark* (1947), *The Masters* (1951), *Corridors of Power* (1964). Created Lord Snow, 1964, to serve as Parl. Sec. Min. of Technology. Ret. from this office 1966.

SNOW BUNTING
(*Plectrophenax nivalis*) Song-bird of N. Europe and Siberia. It visits the N. of Brit. in winter. The wings are noticeably pointed, and the hind claws very long. The bird has black and white plumage.

SNOWDEN, Philip, Viscount
(1864-1937) Brit. politician. M.P. (Lab.), 1906-18 and 1922-31; Chanc. of Exchequer, 1924 and 1929-31; Lord Privy Seal, 1931-2; Viscount, 1931. In 1931 he went against his party by joining the Nat. Govt. in which he was Chanc. of the Exchequer and responsible for the abandonment of the gold standard.

SNOWDON
Highest mt. in Wales, in Caernarvonshire, 10 m. S.E. of Caernarvon. Of the 5 peaks, Y Wyddfa, 3,560 ft. is the highest.

SNOWDON, Earl of *See* ARMSTRONG-JONES.

SNOWDROP
(*Galanthus nivalis*) Perennial herb of the family Amaryllidaceae, it grows wild in Europe and Asia and sometimes in Brit. The plant grows from a bulb, has 2 tapering leaves, and 1 pendent white flower on a tall stem.

SOANE, Sir John
[sōn] (1753-1837) Eng. architect. He secured appointments as architect to the Bank of Eng. and St. James's Palace.

SOAP
Sodium or potassium salt of certain organic acids, palmitic, oleic, stearic and others. Made by boiling an oil or a fat, with caustic soda, or caustic potash.

SOBIESKI, John
(1624-96) King of Poland, known as John III. He was a soldier, who in 1668 was made C.-in-C. He conspired against the king, who was consequently forced, in 1672, to cede the Ukraine to the Turks. Sobieski defeated the Turks in 5 battles and, the king having d. in 1673, secured his own election as king in 1674.

SOCIAL PSYCHOLOGY
Branch of psychology which deals with the modification of perception and emotion, idea and action, in so far as these are the result of social environment.

SOCIALISM
Polit. and economic theory. It aims at the state ownership of the means of production, distribution and exchange, and that the opportunities of life and the rewards of labour be apportioned equitably. To many it stands for an opposition to capitalism. Among its foremost exponents were Karl Marx, Robert Owen and George Bernard Shaw (*q.v.*). In the 19th and 20th cents. it made great advances over almost all the world. Some countries instituted greater state control over conditions of labour, state provision for old age and sickness, state ownership of public utilities and state interference with unrestricted competition. The refusal of others *e.g.* Czarist Russia, to make any concessions assisted the growth of Social parties in those countries. In the polit. sphere Socialism became very strong in the 20th cent. In Brit., Australia and New Zealand the Lab. Party became responsible for govt. It was less powerful in the U.S.A. and Canada, but attained enormous strength in Germany and Fr. After World War I some of the republics that arose were definitely named Socialist. Other countries have gone far in putting Socialist principles into operation.

SOCIETY ISLANDS
Fr. archipelago in the S. Pacific Ocean. The largest Is. are Tahiti, on which is the cap. Papeete, and Moorea. Exports include phosphates and copra. Area: 650 sq.m. Pop. 68,245.

SOCIETY OF FRIENDS
Christian body, also known as the Quakers, formed in the middle of the 17th cent. under the leadership of George Fox. The Friends do not take the oath in courts of law, are averse to milit. service, and are noted for their philanthropy.

SOCINUS
[sō-sī'-nŭs] Name of heresiarchs of Ital. origin. **Lelius Socinus** (1525-62) and **Faustus Socinus** (1539-1604), were uncle and nephew. The teachings of Lelius approximated closely to modern Unitarianism. Persecuted, he fled to Fr., Eng., Holland, Germany and Poland, dying in Zurich. Some years after his d. his nephew vigorously resumed his work.

SOCIOLOGY
The study of human behaviour in society. The mod. term was first used by Compte in 1834. Others who have made notable contributions to the subject include Herbert Spencer, J. S. Mill, William James, Max Weber and Emile Durkheim. Sociology as a science studying the development, nature and laws of human society covers a wide field including social psychology, social philosophy, social and economic history, statistical methods and anthropology. It helps man to understand the society he lives in and through this knowledge maximise his limited resources in the correct channels.

SOCRATES
(469-399 B.C.) Gk. philosopher. He devoted his later life to the pursuit of philosophy, and gathered around him a number of pupils, the two most famous being Xenophon and Plato. He taught that self-knowledge is more important than speculation about the universe; that truth (or wisdom) and virtue are inextricably connected, and that vice arises from ignorance.

SODA
Sodium carbonate. This is known also as soda ash, washing soda, or soda crystal. It occurs naturally and is also manufactured from common salt. **Baking soda** is sodium bicarbonate obtained by the action of carbon dioxide upon the carbonate and is used for baking powders, and as an antacid.

SODA WATER
Aerated water. Prepared by charging ordinary water with carbon dioxide gas under pressure.

SODDY, Frederick
(1877-1956) Brit. physicist and chemist. He did research on radioactivity with Sir Ernest Rutherford; worked with Sir Wm. Ramsay at Univ. Coll., London till 1904 when he was apptd. lecturer in physical chemistry and radioactivity at the Univ. of Glasgow. He suggested that certain elements could exist in 2 or more forms having different atomic weights but chemically indistinguishable and inseparable. He received the Nobel Prize for chemistry in 1921.

SODIUM
A soft silvery metal, best known as the chloride, NaCl (common salt) it is used in certain aluminium alloys.

SODOM
Former city of the Dead Sea region, one of the 5 'cities of the plain' proverbial for their wickedness, and destroyed by 'fire and brimstone' (Gen. xix).

SODOR AND MAN
Anglican diocese of the Isle of Man. The diocese of Sodor, formed in 1154, was included in the prov. of Trondheim in Norway; it comprised, besides the Is. of Man, several Is. W. of Scot. The Norwegian connection ended in 1266 but the name remained.

SOFIA
Cap. of Bulgaria at the base of the Vitosha Mts., 80 m. N.W. of Plovdiv. It is an important trading centre. Sofia was in the hands of the Turks from 1382 until 1878. Pop. 801,000.

SOIL
Surface layer of earth. Supplying nourishment for the growth of plants, a soil is formed by the weathering of rocks or may result from transport of disintegrated material by rivers or glaciers. The mineral constituents may be either sand, clay or calcium carbonate, with various carbonates, sulphates, phosphates and nitrates.

SOLAR GENERATOR
Apparatus which converts solar light into electrical energy.

SOLAR SYSTEM
Name given to designate collectively the Sun and the group of bodies which revolve round it. These consist of planets, comets and meteors. The planets are comparatively cool and dense bodies which shine by reflecting the light of the Sun. 9 major planets are known (see Table below).

	Distance from Sun (millions of miles)	*Revolution Period* Yrs.	Days	*Diameter in miles*
1. Mercury	36·0	—	88	3,100
2. Venus	67·3	—	225	7,700
3. Earth	93·0	1	0	7,927
4. Mars	141·7	1	322	4,220
5. Jupiter	483·9	11	315	88,770
6. Saturn	887·1	29	167	74,200
7. Uranus	1785	84	6	32,400
8. Neptune	2797	164	288	30,900
9. Pluto	3670	247	255	7,900

The largest planet, *Jupiter*, weighs more than double all the other planets combined, but the Sun's mass exceeds that of all the planets by more than 700 times. As *Pluto* revolves at *c.* 3,700,000,000 m. from the Sun, the planetary system measures at least 7,400,000,000 m. across. It is generally accepted that the material which formed the Sun, planets, comets and meteors was once extended in a widely diffused nebulous form, and that it slowly became aggregated into the large masses of the Sun and planets. The Sun is travelling constantly at the rate of *c.* 12 m. per sec. in a direction approx. towards the bright star Vega. *See* ASTRONOMY, UNIVERSE, TELESCOPE.

SOLDER
Alloy used in joining metals. *Soft solder* is 60 % lead and 40 % tin, with a little antimony. *Plumbers' solder* is 70 % lead and 30 % tin. *Silver solder* is an alloy of copper, zinc and silver.

SOLE
(*Solea*) Flat-fish much valued for food. The Common or Dover Sole (*S. vulgaris*) averages 12 in., but sometimes exceeds 2 ft. in length. The so-called Lemon Sole is a kind of dab.

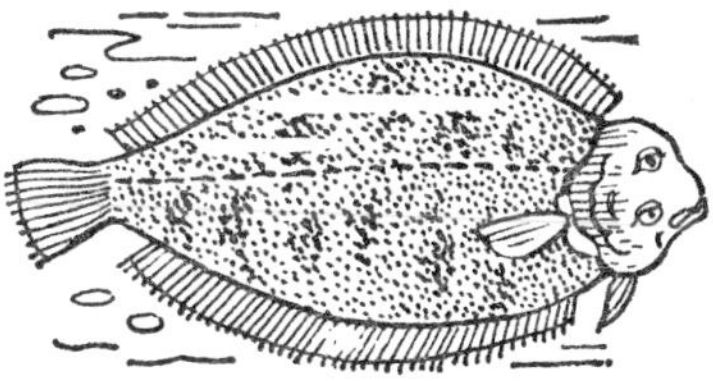

SOLENT
Strait in the Eng. Channel, between Hants. and the Is. of Wight.

SOLOMON
(reigned *c.* 974-937 B.C.) King of Israel. A son of David and Bathsheba, he succeeded his father *c.* 974 B.C. and reigned for nearly 40 years. His reign was peaceful and prosperous. Solomon built the first temple at Jerusalem. The O.T. book known as the **Song of Solomon** is now considered a secular poem, falsely attributed to him.

SOLOMON, Solomon Joseph
(1860-1927) Brit. painter. He was the originator of camouflage in World War I.

SOLOMON ISLANDS
Group of Is. in the W. Pacific to the E. of New Guinea. The 2 northernmost Is., Bougainville and Buka, and the adjacent Is. form part of the Australian trust territory of New Guinea (*q.v.*). The remaining Is. constitute the **British Solomon Is. Protectorate.** Ebony, sandalwood, pearl shells and copra are exported. The seat of govt. is Honiara, on Guadalcanal. The Is. were the scene of hard fighting against the Japanese in World War II. Area: 11,500 sq.m. Pop. 124,400.

SOLON
(*c.* 639-*c.* 559 B.C.) Athenian lawgiver. He ranks as one of the 'Seven Sages'.

SOLSTICE
The point in the ecliptic at which the sun is at its greatest distance from the equator and consequently at the turning point in its apparent path. *See* SUMMER, WINTER.

SOLWAY FIRTH
Inlet of the Irish Sea between England and Scot. Rivers flowing into it include the Annan, Nith, Esk, Derwent and Eden. There is a tidal bore (*q.v.*).

SOLYMAN
[soo-lā-] (or **Suleiman**) (1496-1566) The greatest Turkish sultan, known as 'the Magnificent'. He began his reign by making extensive reforms which earned him in Turkey the name of 'the Lawgiver'.

SOMALIA
Repub. of E. Africa, consisting of former Brit. and Ital. colonies of Somaliland. Gained indep. 1960. Cattle raising is the main occupation, and there is a modest export trade in live cattle, skins and hides. The cap. and chief port is Mogadishu. The pop., largely nomadic, is estimated at 2,660,000. Area: *c.* 246,000 sq.m.

SOMALILAND
[-mà'-] Region of E. Africa lying E. of Ethiopia with a long coastline on the Ind. Ocean and Gulf of Aden. Once divided into Fr., Brit. and Ital. colonies, only the Fr. portion now remains under colonial rule. **Fr. Somaliland** lies between Somalia and Eritrea. *See* FRENCH SOMALILAND, SOMALIA.

SOMERSET
Maritime county of S.W. Eng. with a coastline along the Bristol Channel and Severn Estuary. The chief rivers are the Avon, Parrett, Exe and Axe. Crops include wheat, barley and cider apples; cattle and sheep are raised. Cheddar cheese is produced. The county town is Taunton; other towns include Bath, Weston-Super-Mare, Bridgwater, and Yeovil. S. returns 7 members to Parl. Pop. 609,410.

SOMERSET, Duke of
(*c.* 1506-52) Protector of Eng. In 1536 Henry VIII mar. Jane, his sister, and Seymour was created Earl of Hertford on the b. of Edward VI. On the d. of Henry in 1547 Hertford, now Duke of Somerset, was chosen as protector. He disagreed with the council and was sent to the Tower in 1549. Released in 1550, he was again imprisoned in 1551, was condemned on a technical charge and executed.

SOMERSET HOUSE
Brit. Govt. building between Victoria Embankment and the Strand, built in 1776. Offices in S.H. include the registrars of wills and probate, and that of the Registrar-Gen. of births, marand deaths for Eng. and Wales.

SOMERVELL, Sir Arthur
(1863-1937) Eng. composer. He taught composition in the Royal Coll. of Music, London. His works include 2 masses, an oratorio, *The Passion of Christ* and chamber music. Perhaps most notable are his song cycles.

SOMME
Dept. of N. Fr. taking its name from the river Somme which rises near St. Quentin and flows into the Eng. Channel near St. Valéry. Cap. Amiens. **Somme, Battles of the.** The first lasted from July to Nov. 1916. Brit. and Fr. made repeated attacks on strong German positions,

using tanks for the first time. In the great German spring offensive of 1918 (Mar. 21-28), they failed to obtain their objective of breaking through the Allied line. The final allied advance over the Somme area was carried out during Aug. 1918.

SOMMERVILLE, Sir James Fownes
(1882-1949) Brit. Admiral of the Fleet. Served in Dardanelles operations in World War I; deputy to Vice-Admiral, Dover, 1939-40, he took part in the evacuation from Dunkirk. Later he commanded Force H operating from Gibraltar and carried out the attack on the Fr. Fleet at Oran on July 3, 1940.

SONG THRUSH
(or Mavis) Brit. bird (*Turdus musicus*). This thrush is known by its spotted breast of an olive-brown colour, and is one of the most melodious of song-birds.

SOPHIA
(1630-1714) Electress of Hanover, youngest child of Elizabeth, daughter of James I, and Frederick V, Elector Palatine. Her son (George I), succeeded to the throne of Eng. in 1714.

SOPHISTS
Name given to the itinerant professional teachers of Greece, who flourished from about the middle of the 5th century B.C. to the middle of the 4th.

SOPHOCLES
(*c.* 496-405 B.C.) Athenian dramatist. Out of over 100 tragedies, 7 survive: *Œdipus Rex, Œdipus Coloneus, Antigone, Electra, Trachineae, Ajax, Philoctetes.* He was the first to use a third actor.

SORBONNE
[sor-bon'] Educ. institution of Paris. It was founded in 1252 by Robert de Sorbon, chaplain to Louis IX. It became famed as a centre for theological studies. It is now the seat of the Univ. of Paris.

SORGHUM
The species, *S. vulgare,* with many varieties is cultivated as a cereal and forage plant in many parts of the world under the names of Kaffir corn, dhurra, Guinea corn and Indian millet.

SORREL
Genus of plants of the family Polygonaceae. Several of them will grow in Brit. esp. the sheep's sorrel and the common sorrel (*Rumex acetosa*). Its leaves are used for salad, soup and for purée.

SORRENTO
Ital. resort in Campania, on the S. shore of the Bay of Naples, 10 m. N.E. of Capri.

SOUL
The doctrine of the immortality of the soul was promulgated in Ancient Egypt, India and elsewhere. Christian theology teaches a man as a reflection of the Trinity possessing a spirit, soul and body, and of the immortality of the soul.

SOULT, Nicolas Jean de Dieu
[soolt'] (1769-1851) Fr. soldier. He held a command at Austerlitz, and other of Napoleon's victories. In 1808 he was sent to Spain where he remained in command of the Fr. forces until 1813. He won some successes, but was finally beaten by Wellington. He was exiled after the defeat of Napoleon at Waterloo, but was allowed to return to Fr. in 1819.

SOUND
A sensation produced in the brain by the action on the eardrum of airborne or other vibrations. Sources of sound consist usually of strings, membranes or air columns in vibration. The pitch of a sound depends on the number of vibrations per sec.; of these the human ear can perceive sounds up to *c.* 16,000. The speed of sound in air at 15° C. is about 1,120 ft. per sec.

SOUND FILMS
The sound is photographically recorded along the edge of the motion picture film. Talking pictures were first produced *c.* 1928, revolutionising film production and technique. *See* CINEMATOGRAPHY.

SOUSA, John Philip
(1854-1932) Amer. bandmaster who wrote many popular milit. marches.

SOUTH AFRICA, Republic of
Consists of 4 provs. and S. W. Africa (*q.v.*):

	Area (*sq. m.*)	*Population*
Cape of Good Hope ...	278,500	5,362,853
Natal	33,600	2,979,920
Transvaal	109,600	6,273,477
Orange Free State ...	49,900	1,386,547
S.W. Africa	318,300	526,004

The 4 provs. occupy the S. section of the great African plateau which here has a rim of uplands and mts. surrounding the basin of the Orange River and the Kalahari desert. In the extreme S. a series of E.-W. ridges form a very broken belt of country behind which lies the Great Karroo (2-4,000 ft.). In the extreme west these meet short N.-S. ridges. The greater part lies in the path of the S.E. trade winds, thus the E. coast receives heavy rain, especially in summer. In the interior rainfall is restricted to the summer period and the amount decreases westwards. The uplands of S.W. Africa have slightly more rainfall and sheep may be grazed. The Cape region lies in the path of W. winds in winter and thus receives winter rainfall. Temperature varies from about 50° F. to about 70° F. The Dutch established a station at Table Bay in 1652 to supply their ships passing to and from the E. Indies; their descendants are Afrikanders, speaking Afrikaans, a language closely related to Dutch. In 1814 the Cape became Brit. The new rule provoked opposition from the Afrikanders. In 1838 the Boers trekked over the Great Escarpment on to the veld. Meanwhile, in 1824, new Eng. settlement had begun on the coast of Natal. The trek Boers settled in N. Natal, the remainder crossed the Vaal river, defeated the Zulus and in 1852 formed the S. African Repub. (Transvaal). 2 years later the Orange Free State was similarly established. By the mid-19th cent. S. Africa had 2 Brit. colonies and 2 Boer repubs. The discovery of diamonds at Kimberley in 1867, and later, of gold on the Witwatersrand, led to much non-Afrikaan immigration. Differences arose, culminating in the Boer War, 1899-1902. The Repubs. were annexed but were soon given responsible govt. Botha and Smuts tried to eradicate the legacy of bitterness and in 1910, the 4 colonies became the Union of S. Africa. S.W. Africa was mandated to the Union in 1919. In 1960 a referendum held among white voters decided by a narrow majority in favour of making S. Africa a Repub. On May 31, 1961, S. Africa became a Repub. and withdrew from the Commonwealth, Mr. C. R. Swart becoming Pres. The preponderance of non-Europeans is very great. Figures are (1961): European, 3,067,638; Bantu, 10,807,809; Asiatic, 477,414; Others, 1,488,267. Temporary migrant native labour has long been the basis of S. African economy, particularly in gold mines. Increasing pressure of population has led to decline in fertility of arable and pasture land, and many natives have moved townwards in search of a permanent living. Large squatters' townships have grown up, often appalling slums. The idea of separating the white and black races of S. Africa presented itself at the beginning of the 19th cent. The Emancipation of Slavery Act, 1833, led to the forming of two groups with widely divergent opinions. By 1910, the subject of the segregation of native from white peoples was being hotly disputed. The S. African Party under Smuts opposed the idea; the S. African Labour Party under Walter Madeley supported the Nationalists in their policy of segregation. In 1948 the Smuts Govt. was defeated and the Nat. Govt. came into power. As the chief pointer in the election manifesto, the Nat. used the slogan 'Apartheid', segregation of all coloured races, socially, polit. and physically, *i.e.* a native peasantry living on its own land, in reserves, from which men migrate temporarily for employment in European areas. The policy of introducing *apartheid legislation* into the Union was continued by Dr. Verwoerd. Among his restrictive legislation was the Bantu Educ. Act, which estabd. the principle of complete segregation in educ. Widespread dissatisfaction among coloured people led to disturbances culminating in the deaths of 72 people during riots at Sharpesville. Diamonds, gold, coal and iron are the chief minerals. The chief gold mines are on the Witwatersrand, centred on Johannesburg. The Rand has produced over £1,000,000,000 of gold. Uranium extraction plants have recently been set up. Mining is a great source of government revenue. Besides which it supports a large population which, in turn, provides an important market for farmers. In the E. Rand is coal, which, with iron ore, has led to the rise of steel works. **Administration.** There is a Senate, 11 members of which are apptd. by the Govt. and the remaining 43 are elected. Proportional representation was reintroduced in 1960 but Native representation was excluded. The House of Assembly consists of 160 elected members and 41 members representing the coloured voters in the Cape Prov. B. J. Vorster became P.M. on Dr. Verwoerd's death in 1966.

SOUTH AMERICA
One of the world's greatest continents. In the W. hemisphere, it is joined to N. Amer. by the narrow isthmus of Panama and extends to the S. for *c.* 4,500 m. The greatest breadth is 3,200 m. and the total area is *c.* 7,000,000 sq.m. In the extreme W. the great mt. ranges of the Andes run parallel to the Pacific coast, rising to peaks of 20,000 ft. The E. part of the continent consists of the Guiana and Brazilian Highlands. Between these mt. regions lie the great plains through which flow the 3 largest rivers of S. Amer., the Amazon, Orinoco and Parana-Paraguay systems. The Equator passes through the continent just S. of the Amazon. There is thus a great range of climate, and vegetation, from the desert of the Atacama to the dense forests of Brazil. The native inhabitants are Indians but with the introduction of negro and European stock, the pop. is very mixed. Apart from Brit., Fr. and Dutch Guiana in the N., the continent is divided politically into 10 repubs. Brazil and Argentina are the largest; the others are Bolivia, Chile, Colombia, Ecuador, Paraguay, Peru, Uruguay and Venezuela (*qq.v.*).

SOUTH ARABIA, Fed. of
Protectorate formed in 1962 of Arab states in the Aden penin. Cap. Al Attihad. Area: 60,000 sq.m. Pop. (est.) 712,500. In 1963 the crown colony of Aden acceded to the Fed. Separate Orders in Council have been made for the Is. of Kemara, Perim and Kuria Maria. Aden town is an important fuelling station for ships passing through Suez. Salt is exported. A Fed. of all the states of S.A. should achieve indep. by 1968.

SOUTH AUSTRALIA
State of the Commonwealth of Australia, with a coastline on the Great Australian Bight. The only important river in the state is the Murray, in the S.E. Wheat and wool are the chief products, but fruit, wine and brandy are produced, and iron, gypsum and salt are mined. There is an iron and steel industry at Whyalia. Adelaide is the cap. Admin. is by a Gov., a council and an assembly. Area: 380,070 sq.m. Pop. 1,107,000.

SOUTH CAROLINA
S. state of U.S.A., with an Atlantic coastline. Chief rivers are the Savannah and Santee. It is an agricultural state, producing maize, oats, sweet potatoes, cotton and tobacco. Columbia is the cap. Negroes form *c.* 35 per cent. of the pop. S.C. was settled in 1670, and was one of the orig. 13 states. It sends 6 representatives to Congress. Area: 31,060 sq.m. Pop. 2,590,600.

SOUTH DAKOTA
[-kō'-] N. state of the U.S.A. in the Great Plains region. Of the many rivers, the Missouri and James are the most important. Large scale farming is practised. Gold, silver and lignite are mined, and the chief industries are meat-packing and butter-making. Pierre is the cap., Sioux Falls the largest town. It sends 2 representatives to Congress. Area: 77,050 sq.m. Pop. 666,300.

SOUTH GEORGIA
Is. in the S. Atlantic, 800 m. E. of the Falkland Is. It is an important centre of the whaling industry. Area: *c.* 1,000 sq.m. Pop. 430.

SOUTH ISLAND
One of the 2 principal Is. of New Zealand (*q.v.*).

SOUTH SEA BUBBLE
A disastrous financial scheme by which the South Sea Co. offered in 1719 to take over the Nat. Debt in exchange for concessions, causing vast speculation in its shares. The Co. went bankrupt in 1720 and thousands were ruined.

SOUTH SHIELDS
County borough and seaport of Durham, on the S. bank of the Tyne, 8 m. E. of Newcastle. It returns 1 member to Parl. Pop. 109,300.

SOUTH WEST AFRICA now **Namibia**
Mandated territory of S. Africa, bounded on the N. by Angola, on the S. by the Cape of Good Hope, on the E. by Bechuanaland, and on the W. by the Atlantic. Most of the region is barren, with the Kalahari Desert in the E. Cattle, sheep and goats are raised; wheat and tobacco are among the crops grown; and copper and diamonds are mined. The cap. is Windhoek. It was annexed by S. Africa, 1915, and 4 years later was placed under the mandate of the Union. It was granted a constitution, 1925. Fundamental changes in the constitution were introduced in 1949. In the House of Assembly of the Rep. of S.A. the Territory is represented by 6 members. Area: 318,300 sq.m. Pop. 526,000.

SOUTHAMPTON
County borough, city and seaport of Hants., on S. Water. It is the most important passenger port in Eng. It returns 2 members to Parl. Pop. 207,220. **Southampton Water.** Sea inlet of the Eng. Channel, 10 m. long, protected from the open sea by the I. of Wight. It has 4 tides daily.

SOUTHEND-ON-SEA
County borough and resort of Essex, on the estuary of the Thames, 36 m. from London. Southend returns 2 members to Parl. Pop. 166,130.

SOUTHERN CROSS
(Crux Australis) Constellation of the S. heavens which corresponds to the Great Bear in the N. heavens. Its 5 principal stars form a rough, irregular cross.

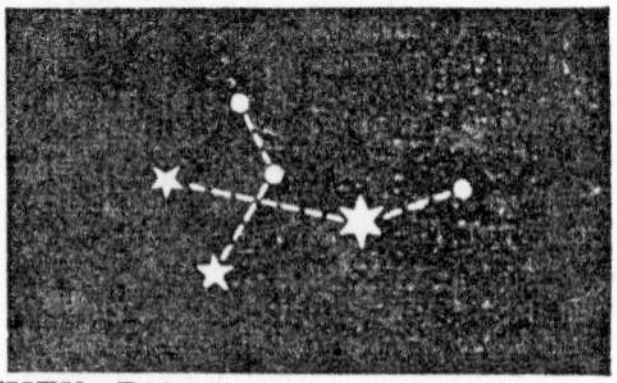

SOUTHEY, Robert
(1774-1843) Eng. poet. B. Bristol. He settled at Keswick and became friendly with Coleridge and Wordsworth. He wrote histories, long narrative poems, and a *Life of Nelson*. He was made poet laureate in 1813.

SOUTHPORT
County borough and resort of Lancs. on the estuary of the Ribble, 18 m. N. of Liverpool. It returns 1 member to Parl. Pop. 80,730.

SOUTHWARK
[suth'-ăk] Borough of London, on the S. side of the river, just oposite the City. The area along the river is the Bankside of Shakespeare's day. It returns 1 member to Parl. Pop. 86,440.

SOUTHWELL
Cath. city of Notts., 16 m. N.E. of Nottingham. The cath. dates from the 12th cent. Pop. 4,301.

SOVIET
System of govt. existing in Russia, based fundamentally on the small soviet in workshop, factory, village or town, which themselves elect delegates to similar congresses covering larger areas, the system culminating in the All-Russian Congress of Soviets which delegates its powers to a Central Executive Committee. The supreme executive is the Council of People's Commissaries, drawn from this committee, and its chairman is the titular head of the state. *See* U.S.S.R.

SOVIETSK
(formerly **Tilsit**) Town in the Russ. S.F.S.R., on the Niemen, 65 m. N.E. of Kaliningrad. Part of E. Prussia, it was ceded to the U.S.S.R. by Germany after World War II. Pop. 57,000.

SOYA BEAN
Herb of the family Leguminosae, native to Asia and grown for its food value. The beans are in pods. The bean is grown on a vast scale in Manchuria, from where it is exported. From it an oil is obtained, used in the making of margarine.

SPA
Place where mineral springs are found, the water of which is supposed to have some medicinal properties. Situated all over Europe, the better-known are at Wiesbaden, Aix-les-Bains, Contrexeville, Bath, Harrogate and Buxton.

SPACE EXPLORATION
Navigation of spacecraft in the regions beyond the earth's atmosphere, to increase information about the solar system. From a scientific viewpoint, interplanetary travel is viable as, once beyond the earth's field of gravity, little power is needed for flight. The first artificial earth satellite, *Sputnik I*, was put into orbit, 1957; the first U.S. satellite, *Explorer I*, 1958, proved the existence of the Van Allen radiation belts. The first man to orbit the earth was Yuri Gagarin, 1961. The *Apollo* project of the U.S. National Aeronautic and Space Admin. (N.A.S.A.) aimed at putting man on the moon. Neil Armstrong and Edwin Aldrin of *Apollo XI* were the first men on the moon, 21 July 1969. In 1970, the Soviet unmanned *Luna 16* landed on the moon to collect rock samples; and *Luna 17* transported the lunar vehicle, *Lunokhod I*. 3 Russian astronauts died as *Soyuz II* re-entered the earth's atmosphere after 24 days in space (1971). Other extended missions undertaken include unmanned probes to Venus and Mars, to determine the composition of the atmosphere, and the presence of water.

SPACE-TIME
The work of the German geometer, Riemann (1826-66), the Polish mathematician, Minkowski (d. 1908), the Dutch physicist, Lorentz (1853-1928) may be said to have culminated in the work of the great German physicist, Albert Einstein (1879-1955) whose Theory of Relativity wrought fundamental changes in the basic theories of the universe held by physicists, and in their conceptions of space and time. Space and time are conceived as inseparable, and the universe cannot be understood except in terms of a uniform four-dimensional continuum, three of space and one of time. Everything in motion is constantly changing its state and position relative to every other thing. If we assume a hypothetical observer of one of our hydrogen bomb explosions to be situated on the star Sirius, what is ' past ' for us becomes ' future ' for the observer; because Sirius is 9 light years distant from the earth, he will perceive the explosion 9 years after the event. In this connection, past, present and future, and time, are relative. Furthermore, the Newtonian Theory of Gravitation, *i.e.* that a body travels in a straight line until halted or deflected by some force outside itself, is now proved false. In Einstein's cosmos, which is finite, and curved in a four-dimensional way by the matter within it into a closed, spherical structure, all bodies whether planets in the solar system or electrons in the atom, move as they do because they cannot do other—they must conform to the ' shape ' of the continuum. See *The Meaning of Relativity* by Albert Einstein (1953).

SPAIN
State of S.W. Europe, forming the greater part of the Iberian peninsula. It has a long coastline on the Bay of Biscay, the Atlantic Ocean and the Medit. Sea. The country has the Cantabrian Mts. and Pyrenees in the N., and the Sierra Nevada in the S. Most of the interior is occupied by an extensive tableland, the Meseta, crossed by several ranges. The chief rivers are the Ebro and Jucar, flowing into the Medit. and the Guadalquivir, Guadiana, Tagus, Douro and Minho, entering the Atlantic. The plateau has a wide range of temps. and light rainfall; the N.W. has a mild climate with heavy rain, while the E. and S.E. coastlands have a Medit. climate. Sp. is an agricultural country, although there are valuable deposits of tin, silver, lead, copper, coal and iron. Fishing is an important industry in the N.W. and sardines are canned for export. The main industrial region is centred on Barcelona. Madrid is the cap.; other cities are Barcelona, Valencia, Seville, Malaga and Bilbao. R.C. is the state religion. For admin. purposes the Balearic and Canary Is. form provs. of Sp. Area: 197,000 sq.m. Pop. 31,339,000. Its recorded hist. begins with the settlement of the Phoenicians. Later the Gks. and the Carthaginians arrived and then the Roms. made it part of their emp. From *c.* 530 to 730, the Visigoths had a kingdom in Sp. A Moorish one followed it, covering the S. of Sp., with its cap. at Cordoba. In the N., *c.* 1,000 A.D., Christian kingdoms emerged, the chief of them

being Castile, Aragon, Leon and Navarre. In 1479 Ferdinand of Aragon mar. Isabella of Castile. Two great events marked this joint reign; Columbus discovered Amer. and founded there a great Sp. emp., and the kingdom of the Moors in Sp. was destroyed. During the 16th cent., Sp. was the greatest country in Europe. Its ruler (1516-65) was Emp., Charles V; then came his son, Philip II. In 1580 the king united Portugal with Sp. In 1700 the last Hapsburg king d., and, 1714, after the War of the Sp. Succession, a Bourbon, Philip V, was recognised as king. Sp. played a considerable part in European politics in the 18th cent., until dominated by Napoleon. Early in the 19th cent. the countries in S. Amer. made themselves independent of Sp. and at the end of the cent., Cuba and the Philippine Is. were lost after a war with the U.S.A. In 1833 and again in 1868 there was civil war. Finally the queen, Isabella, a daughter of Ferdinand VII, secured the throne and her opponents, called Carlists, were defeated. In 1886 Alphonso XIII became king and he reigned until 1931. His reign, esp. after World War I, was marked by considerable unrest. The king was forced to leave the country, 1931, and a socialist repub. was set up. Strikes and general polit. disorder led to the rise of the Sp. Fascist Party. In July, 1936, Civil War broke out, beginning with army mutinies, and Gen. Franco assumed the leadership of Nationalist Sp. in Oct. The war between Republicans and Nationalists was marked by startling ruthlessness and by foreign intervention on both sides. In 1939 the Nationalists were finally victorious. Gen. Franco assumed the leadership of the State and estabd. a Fascist dictatorship. During World War II Sp. remained neutral, although friendly towards Axis powers.

SPALDING
[spawl'-] Urban district of Holland, Lincs., on the Welland, 14 m. S.W. of Boston. It is an agricultural centre famed for its bulbs and potatoes. Pop. 14,940.

SPANIEL
Group of dogs used for retrieving game. Spaniels are characterised by the broad skull with high forehead and large pendulous lobe-shaped ears.

SPANISH GUINEA now **Equatorial Guinea**
Indep. repub. in W. Africa, former Span. colony, comprising the Is. of Fernando Póo, Annobon, Corisco, and Great and Little Elobey, with Rio Muni on the mainland. Cocoa, coffee and sugar are exported. The cap. is Santa Isabel. Called Equatorial Guinea since indep., 1968. Area: *c.* 10,000 sq.m. Pop. 183,377.

SPANISH SAHARA
Colony of W. Africa, consisting of 2 zones, Rio de Oro and Sekia el Hamra.

SPARROW
(*Passer domesticus*) Really a Finch, this common bird is found in most settled parts of the world. About 7 in. long, it has the short strong beak of the Finch family.

SPARROW HAWK
(*Accipiter*) The genus has several species of which *A. nissus* is the common Brit. example. It lives in the woods and kills game.

SPARTA
City of ancient Greece, also known as Lacedaemon. It stood on the banks of the Eurotas in the Peloponnese. The Spartans of hist. were Dorian invaders. The training of citizens was strictly milit. Sparta played a leading part in the Graeco-Persian Wars but her greatest struggle took place against Athens in the Peloponnesian war (*q.v.*) in which she was finally victorious.

SPEAKER
Pres. of the Brit. House of Commons and of similar legislative bodies. The first Speaker was Sir Thomas Hungerford in 1377. The Speaker is elected by the members from among their number at the beginning of each Parl. The tradition has grown up that the Speaker must not vote nor express any opinion on controversial questions.

SPEAR
One of the oldest weapons used by man. It consists of a shaft and a head which in early times was of flint or other stone or bone. Later it was made of iron.

SPEARMINT
(*Mentha spicata*) Perennial herb of the family Labiatae. The creeping root throws off numerous underground runners. The stems are square and erect, with opposite deep green aromatic leaves. It is used as a flavouring.

SPECIAL CONSTABLE
Man sworn in to assist the police in times of emergency.

SPECIFIC GRAVITY
Ratio of the density (weight of unit volume) of a substance to that of water or other standard substance. In the case of gases, air or hydrogen is taken as the standard; for liquids and solids, water at 4° C.

SPECTRUM
Series of images, usually of a narrow slit, each formed by 1 wavelength (*i.e.* 1 colour) in a beam of light including several wavelengths. A white light source contains all of the visible wavelengths and its spectrum is a continuous band of colour.

SPEECH
Ability to utter articulate sounds or words. The sounds are produced by the passage of air between the vocal chords and are modified by use of the tongue, teeth and lips. *See* PHONETICS.

SPEEDWAY RACING
Motor-cycle races held on oval courses of dirt or cinders. The sport originated in Australia, was brought to Brit. in 1928. The tracks have their own teams and were organised in divisions each of which ran league matches. In 1965 these amalgamated to form the British League. There is also an Individual Riders World Championship open to all countries.

SPEEDWELL
Flowering herb, of the family Scrophulariaceae and the genus *Veronica*, growing in Europe and Asia. Several species are found in Brit. They have bright blue flowers.

SPEKE, John Hanning
(1827-64) Eng. explorer. He travelled extensively in Asia and in 1854, with Sir Richard Burton, explored Somaliland and the region around L. Tanganyika. He discovered the source of the Nile in the Victoria Nyanza.

SPELEOLOGY
The scientific study of caves.

SPELLING
The present conventions in Eng. spelling date from the late 17th cent. The basis is largely the writing of Eng. by Anglo-Norman scribes of the 12th-13th cent. Initial capitals for nouns ceased in the late 18th cent.; so did italics for proper names.

SPENCE, Sir Basil Urwin
(1907-) Architect. Particularly well known for his work on Festival of Britain buildings (1951) and for Coventry Cathedral. K.B., 1960. R.A., 1960. O.M., 1962.

SPENCER, Herbert
(1820-1903) Eng. philosopher. In 1848 he became Assistant Ed. of *The Economist*, and thenceforward devoted himself to developing his system of philosophy. He wrote *First Principles, Principles of Biology, Principles of*

Psychology, *Principles of Sociology*, and *Principles of Ethics*.

SPENCER, Sir Stanley
(1891-1959) Brit. painter. B. Cookham. His religious works are a modern interpretation of the Bible.

SPENDER, Stephen Harold
(1909-) Eng. poet. He ed. *Horizon* (1939-41) with Cyril Connolly; pub. 7 vols. of poems (1929-49); verse-play *Trial of a Judge* (1938); *The Destructive Element* (1936); *The Making of a Poem* (1955); *World Within World* (1951) (autobiog.); several novels. C.B.E. 1962.

SPENGLER, Oswald
[speng′-gler] (1880-1936) German philosopher. His interpretation of history as a series of identical cultural cycles the last 8 of which pertain to W. civilisation which, he averred, is now on the decline, created interest in Germany, esp. among the Nazis.

SPENSER, Edmund
(1552-99) Eng. poet. He pub. *The Shepheards Calender* in 1579. His unfinished allegorical epic *The Faerie Queene* was pub. 1590-6. He also wrote *Epithalamion*; *Amoretti* (sonnets).

SPERM
Alternative name for the Cachalot Whale. Sperm oil is a complex oleate. *See* CACHALOT.

SPERMACETI
[-set′-i] A pearly-white, glistening, crystalline, wax-like solid obtained from the sperm oil present in the head cavities of the sperm whale (*Physeter macrocephalys*).

SPERMATOZOA
Mobile male germ cells or microgametes produced in the testes. In the higher forms of animal life they are extremely minute structures, somewhat tadpole-like in form.

SPHENODON
(*Sphenodon punctatus*) Lizard-like reptile found in New Zealand. It is the only remaining representative of the order Rhynchocephalia.

SPHINX
[sfingks] (1) Name applied by Greek travellers to sphinx-headed figures resembling the sphinx of Theban legend, which propounded riddles and strangled those who failed to solve them. (2) Huge sculptured recumbent human-headed lion at Gizeh, a short distance S.E. of the Great Pyramid.

SPICE
Vegetable substance, aromatic to smell and pungent to taste. It is obtained from certain plants, esp. those that grow in hot countries, and is used for flavouring, etc. Examples are pepper, ginger, nutmeg and cinnamon.

SPIDER
Arthropod of the order Araneidae belonging to the class Arachnida. In some trop. countries it attains a length of over 2 in. and spins a net capable of capturing birds. The spider's spinnerets are contained in its abdomen and the foot is provided with a comb which helps in drawing the silken thread out of the spinneret.

SPIKENARD
Perennial herb, native to the Himalayas. The root is very fragrant and from it a perfume is prepared.

SPINACH
Edible herb of the family Chenopodiaceae, introduced to Brit. in the 16th cent. and now a popular table vegetable.

SPINDLE TREE
Tree found in woods and hedges in Brit. It bears glassy lance-shaped leaves and clusters of small, greenish flowers followed by crimson fruit. It is *c.* 20 ft. high.

SPINE
Bony skeleton which plays an important part in body architecture. Consists of numerous small bones called vertebrae built one on top of the other and firmly held in position by ligaments and muscles.

SPINEL
Group of minerals typified by common spinel, a mineral composed of magnesia and alumina.

SPINOZA, Benedict
(1632-77) Dutch philosopher. B. Amsterdam. By birth a Jew, later he left that faith. He embodied his ideas in his *Ethica* and other works pub. after his d. His *Tractatus Theologico Politicus* is an expansion of the ideas of Descartes. Spinoza's philosophy is pantheistic.

SPIRAEA
[spī-rē′-ă] Genus of plants of the family Rosaceae and sub-family Spiraeoideae. Two of the herbaceous species, dropwort and meadow sweet, are native to Brit.

SPIRIT
God as the *supreme* Cosmic Reality. The term is also used for (1) the animating, non-material, divine element in man that gives life and reason; (2) the Soul, the immortal individuality; (3) will and intelligence divorced from a physical body; and (4) loosely, for ghosts, apparitions, etc.

SPIRITUALISM
Belief in the possibility of intercommunication between the living and the dead. The intercourse is usually carried out with the help of mediums who submit to the direction of spirits acting as agents for the spirit world. Seances for the purpose of getting into touch with the departed, held in the presence of scientific investigators, have revealed remarkable phenomena. These are recorded by the Soc. for Psychical Research.

SPITHEAD
Roadstead at the entrance to Portsmouth Harbour.

SPLEEN
Soft, fleshy, dark-blue organ situated near back bone. Main function concerned with formation of white cells called lymphocytes and the destruction of old red cells.

SPLEENWORT
Any form of the genus *Asplenium* of the family Polypodiaceae. The commonest Brit. form is *Ceterach officinarum*, which grows on rocks and masonry.

SPODE
[spōd] Chinaware first made by Josiah Spode, at Stoke in 1799.

SPOKANE
City of Washington, U.S.A. The 2nd city of the state, it is a mining and lumbering centre. Pop. 184,000.

SPONGE
Animal belonging to the Phylum porifera or parazoa. In its simplest form consists of an individual organism, having a cylindrical or vase-shaped body, forming a 3-layered sac, pierced by numerous pores through which water passes into the inner cavity, whose walls are lined with flagellate cells.

SPOONBILL
Bird allied to the Ibis, it is the only European species of *Platalea leucorodia*. Formerly a resident in Brit. but now only an occasional visitor, it is white in colour with a tinge of pink or buff, and has a remarkably long, flat bill much dilated at the tip.

SPORADES
Gk. archipelago in the Aegean Sea.

SPORE
(1) (**Biology**) Non-sexual reproductive cell found in the flowerless plants and capable of giving rise to a new plant which may or may not resemble the parent. (2) (**Zoology**) Hard-coated reproductive cells produced in some of the lower animals, esp. the Protozoa.

SPOROZOA
Class of parasitic protozoa which reproduce by the formation of spores. One of them, the parasite of red blood cells, *Plasmodium*, is the cause of malaria the greatest killing disease of man.

SPRAT
(*Clupea sprattus*) A small fish of the Herring family. It abounds along the Brit. coasts.

SPRING
(1) The first of the 4 seasons. In the N. Hemisphere it commences at the Vernal Equinox when the Sun enters the Zodiacal sign Aries, *c.* Mar. 21-22, and crosses the Equator. At this period of the year day and night are of equal duration throughout the world. Spring terminates at the Summer Solstice, *c.* June 21-22. (2) Natural outflow of water from the earth. Water percolates through a permeable bed such as sandstone or limestone until it reaches one that is impermeable. Here it accumulates, ultimately finding its way by fissures or joint-planes to the surface.

SPRINGBOK
(*Antidorcas*) Kind of Gazelle, found in S. Africa, and famed for its power of springing when running.

SPRINGFIELD
Cap. of Illinois, U.S.A., *c.* 180 m. S.W. of Chicago. Home of Abraham Lincoln. Pop. 83,271.

SPRINGTAIL
Small wingless insects of the order Collembola. The name is derived from a forked organ under the abdomen which, on being released, acts as a spring, throwing the insect into the air.

SPRUCE
Genus of the Coniferae inhabiting cold and temp. regions of the N. hemisphere. *Picea abies* (Common spruce), important timber tree in N. Europe and Asia.

SPURGE
Genus of plant. Of the family Euphorbiaceae, mostly herbaceous, but some woody; *c.* 12 species are natives of Brit.

SPY
One who unlawfully collects secret information. By internat. law a spy, if caught, may be shot.

SQUASH RACKETS
A development of the game of rackets. The earliest courts were built at Harrow School. The court has 4 walls, the floor 32 by 21 ft. The front wall 15 ft. high, back wall 7 ft. and the side walls sloping from 15 ft. to 7 ft. A soft hollow rubber ball and a light racket 7-8 in. diam. and 27 in. long is used. The ball is played alternately by each player. It is allowed to bounce once and has to hit the front wall during the flight.

SQUATTER
One who settles on land that is unoccupied. In Eng. law if such a person has not been disturbed in his possession for a period of years he becomes the owner of the land.

SQUID
Calamary or Cuttle-fish. The name is more particularly applied to the small variety (*Loligo vulgaris*) found along the Brit. and Fr. coasts. It carries a reservoir of inky fluid which it squirts out in order to baffle an enemy.

SQUINTING
(**Strabismus**) Squinting is due to some muscle weakness causing the 2 eyes not to look in the same direction at the same time. It may be hereditary or may arise from muscle strain resulting from optical error. Paralysis, resulting from disease within the brain or affecting one of the nerves supplying the eye muscles, may lead to squinting.

SQUIRREL
Small rodent of the family Sciuridae. Mostly arboreal and found nearly everywhere except in Australia, the Brit. variety (*Sciurus vulgaris*) measures 18 in. long, including an 8 in. tail.

SRINAGAR
Cap. and chief city of Jammu-Kashmir, on the Jhelum. Pop. 285,257.

STAËL, Madame de
[stâl] **Anne Louise Germaine** (1766-1817). She achieved fame as a writer, a conversationalist, and a society woman. She wrote *Corinne*, *Delphine*, *De L'Allemagne* and *De la Littérature* (1800).

STAFFA
Is. of the Inner Hebrides, Scot., in Argyll, 6 m. N. of Iona. It is famous for its basalt caves.

STAFFORDSHIRE
(**Staffs.**) Midland county of Eng. The chief river is the Trent. In the N. are the Potteries, embracing Hanley, Burslem and Stoke-on-Trent. In the S. is the Black Country, in which, at Wolverhampton and Walsall, all types of iron are manufactured. Burton-on-Trent is renowned for its breweries. It returns 18 members to Parl. (12 borough constituencies). Pop. 1,734,000. **Stafford.** Borough and county town of Staffs., 23 m. N.W. of Birmingham. Industries include boot factories and engineering works. It returns 1 member to Parl. Pop. 48,000.

STAG
Male of the red deer. Stags in Scot. are stalked, and shot with a rifle. On Exmoor, in the New Forest, and in Ribblesdale, Yorks., they are hunted.

STAGE COACH
Vehicle that formerly carried passengers and goods. It was drawn by 2, 4 or more horses, and had seats inside and outside. It appeared in the 17th cent. and was in favour until superseded by railways.

STAGHOUND
Breed of dog used for hunting stags. The modern staghound is a large foxhound, different from the staghound of old which was a bloodhound.

STAINED GLASS
Glass coloured by fusing metallic oxides into it, or burning pigment into its surface. There are many fine examples of the 13th and 14th cents., *e.g.* at Chartres Cathedral, Canterbury, York Minster. In the 19th century, William Morris and Burne-Jones (*qq.v.*) revived the art.

STALACTITE
Calcareous growth, usually cylindrical or conical in shape and formed by the steady drip-

ping of water from the roofs of caves. Each drop when it evaporates leaves behind it a tiny speck of calcium carbonate deposited from solution. There are examples in Eng. in the caves at Cheddar and the Peak cavern in Derbyshire. **Stalagmites** are of similar formation, but are found on the floors of caves, built from the ground upwards.

STALIN, Iosif Vissarionovich
(Djugashivili) (1879-1953) Russ. statesman. Pres. of the Council of People's Commissars. B. Georgia. He was active in the plot to overthrow Kerensky in 1917 and subsequently became Sec. of the Russian Communist Party. On Lenin's d. Stalin assumed his place and removed all opposition, including Trotsky (*q.v.*). As dictator of Russia he inspired his country to fight against the Germans in World War II and co-operated to some extent with the W. Powers. After 1945, however, the 'Iron Curtain' dropped on Russia and her satellites and any real co-operation between the U.S.S.R. and the W. Powers proved impossible. After his d. the 'anti-Stalin cult' developed in U.S.S.R.

STALINGRAD *See* VOLGOGRAD.

STAMFORD
Borough of Kesteven, Lincs., partly in Northants. Pop. 12,310.

STAMP, Charles Josiah
1st Baron S. (1880-1941) Brit. economist who sat on the royal commission on income tax, 1919, the N. Ireland finance arbitration committee, 1923-4, the committee on taxation and nat. debt, and the Dawes Committee, 1924. He was a member of the court of enquiry into the coal industry, 1925, and of the Young Committee on reparations, 1929. In 1939-41 he was an economic adviser to the govt.

STAMP ACT
Measure requiring all legal documents in the Amer. colonies to bear a revenue stamp. Passed by Parl. in 1765, the act was violently opposed in Amer. on the ground that Parl. had no right to impose taxation unless representation went hand-in-hand with it.

STAMP DUTY
Form of indirect taxation. Duties are collected by means of stamps affixed to legal and other documents by which property is transferred or other privileges are secured. Among documents requiring to be stamped are insurance policies, bills of exchange, contract notes, patent specifications.

STANFORD, Sir Charles Villiers
(1852-1924) Irish composer. He was conductor of the London Bach Choir, and teacher of composition at the Royal Coll. of Music in London. He wrote operas, 7 symphonies, 3 piano concertos, choral music, much ch. music and chamber music, also over 100 songs.

STANHOPE, James
1st Earl (1673-1721) Eng. general and statesman. C.-in-C. of the Brit. forces in Spain, 1708. He captured Port Mahon. On the accession of George I (1714) he was made a Sec. of State. He directed the suppression of the Jacobites, 1715. **Lady Hester Lucy S.** (1776-1839) Eng. traveller, daughter of the 3rd Earl of Stanhope. From 1803-6 she lived with her uncle, William Pitt.

STANLEY
Chief town of the Falkland Is. Prot. on the E. coast of E. Falkland. Pop. *c.* 1,074.

STANLEY, Sir Henry Morton
(1841-1904) African explorer. Orig. named John Rowlands he was b. in Wales. He made his famous journey in 1871-2 in search of David Livingstone and found him near L. Tanganyika. His works include: *How I Found Livingstone, Through the Dark Continent, The Congo,* and *In Darkest Africa.*

STAR
Heavenly body other than a planet. The aspect of the heavens in regard to stars varies according to the annual motion of the sun, one half of the heavens being visible at midnight in June, and exactly another half at midnight in Dec. Some stars, called 'variables', undergo changes of brilliance, and have to be ranked at different times under different magnitudes. There are numerous double and binary stars, and in particular parts of the sky there are clusters, such as the Pleiades, Hyades, etc., which are quite distinct from nebulae. The *stellae fixae* or fixed stars appear to the eye to be stationary, but are in fact moving at enormous speeds (*c.* 10 m. per sec.) but are so distant that no change in their relevant positions is perceptible. For example, *Sirius* is 9 light years distant and other fixed stars visible to the naked eye are from 10-100 light years away. These stars send no detectable radio waves. However, strong radio signals received by radar led to experiments which began in 1924 revealing that in addition to the light stars there exist radio or dark stars which transmit radio waves, but no detectable light waves. With this discovery there began a new science of radio astronomy (*q.v.*).

STAR CHAMBER
Eng. law court. Regulated in 1487 by Henry VII to deal with the nobles who were too powerful to be punished by the ordinary courts. It was operative under the Tudors and Stuarts, and became very much hated in the time of James I and Charles I owing to its arbitrary procedure. It was abolished in 1641.

STAR OF BETHLEHEM
Bulbous-rooted plant, of the family Liliaceae, bearing from 6-9 large white fragrant flowers, it is native to Fr., Germany, Switzerland and other parts of Europe. The common star of Bethlehem (*Ornithogallum umbellatum*) is a garden flower in Eng.

STARCH
A carbohydrate occurring in the cells of plants. Starch is insoluble in cold water but on boiling gelatinises, forms a paste, and when boiled with diluted acids is changed into glucose, or by dry heat into dextrine or Brit. gum.

STARFISH
Echinoderms belonged to the class Asteroidea. In the Pacific some starfish attain a great size: *Pycnopodia helianthorides*, *c.* a yd. in diameter with over 20 arms. The Common Brit. starfish (*A. rubens*) is found at low tide.

Brittle Star

STARLING
(*Sturnus*) A passerine bird, family Sturnidae. The Common Starling (*S. vulgaris*) is abundant throughout Brit., migrating from district to district in search of food, breeding twice in a season and laying from 4-7 pale blue eggs in a rudely built nest. In autumn Starlings form flocks in which they fly about before roosting.

STARS AND STRIPES
Nat. flag of the U.S.A. Its 7 horizontal red and 6 horizontal white stripes, represent the orig. 13 seceding states. It had a blue canton emblazoned with 50 stars, representing the 50

states of the union. The flag, as orig. designed in 1777, had only 13 stars.

STATEN
Is. of New York, at the mouth of the Hudson, separated from Manhattan by the Narrows.

STATES GENERAL
Estates of the realm. The name was formerly used in Fr., Spain and other countries for the precursors of the modern legislatures. They consisted usually of 3 classes, clergy, nobility and commons. In Fr. they never obtained much power. They met from time to time until 1614. Their meeting in 1789 proved the prelude to the Revolution. The Dutch repub. possessed a states general and this is the name of the legislature of the present kingdom of the Netherlands.

STATISTICS
Numerical or pictorial statements of facts produced and arranged so as to make clear the relationship between each group of figures.

STAVANGER
Port of Norway, 105 m. S. of Bergen on the S. Fiord. Fishing and shipping are the chief industries. Pop. 53,000.

STEAM ENGINE
The first recorded steam engine was that of Hero of Alexandria (130 B.C.), but no real progress was made prior to the 18th cent. when the Scot, James Watt (1736-1819), hit upon the idea of a separate condenser in 1763. In 1796 Richard Trevithick (1771-1833) invented the first steam-propelled road vehicle. George Stephenson (1781-1848) constructed his first locomotive in 1814, and William Symington (1763-1831) devised an early form of steam engine for ships and for road locomotion.

STEEL
Alloy of iron with carbon, manganese and sometimes small amounts of other materials. The **carbon steels,** containing less than 2 % of carbon, comprise the mild steels (0·1 to 1·5 % carbon), and the tool steels (0·6 to 1·5 % carbon). The metal produced is tough and greyish-white with great tenacity and tensile strength, these characters adapting it to constructional work.

STEELE, Sir Richard
(1672-1729) Eng. writer. B. Dublin. In 1709 he founded the *Tatler*; it was followed by the *Spectator* and the *Guardian,* Addison co-operating in all.

STEEN, Jan
[stān] (1626-79) Dutch painter. B. Leiden. His best known works are *Domestic Life, Work and Idleness* and *Bad Company.*

STEEPLECHASING
Horse racing over hedges, ditches and other obstacles set up on a regular course. The Grand Nat., the great steeplechasing event of the year, was instituted in 1839. It is held at Aintree in March, the course being 4½ m. with 30 jumps.

STEIN, Heinrich Friedrich Karl, Baron von
[shtīn] (1757-1831) Prussian statesman, who achieved the regeneration of Prussia after Jena (1806) and Tilsit (1807). He abolished serfdom, caste and the relics of feudalism, enabled peasants to buy land, reformed local govt. and civil service.

STEIN, Sir Mark Aurel
(1862-1943) Brit. archaeologist. His researches and excavations in C. Asia, Persia and Baluchistan, revealed the existence of great civilisations, hitherto almost unknown.

STEINBECK, John Ernst
(1902-68) Amer. novelist. His chief works are: *Tortilla Flat* (1935), *Of Mice and Men* (1937), *The Grapes of Wrath* (1939), *Cannery Row* (1944), *East of Eden* (1952), *The Short Reign of Pippin IV* (1957). Awarded Nobel Prize for Lit., 1962.

STEINBOK
(*Raphicerus campestris*) S. African antelope (Dutch; Stone Buck). It is under 2 ft. high and of a stone colour. It has upright horns *c.* 4 in. long.

STELLENBOSCH
Town of Cape Prov., S. Africa, 31 m. E. of Capetown. One of the first Dutch settlements in Africa. Pop. 10,738.

STENDHAL
[sta(ng)'-dal] (1783-1842) Pseudonym of the Fr. novelist **Marie Henri Beyle.** B. at Grenoble; became a soldier in the wars of Napoleon. Beyle wrote 4 novels: *Armance* (1827), *Le Rouge et le Noir* (1830), *Lucien Leuwen* (unfinished), and *La Chartreuse de Parme* (1839).

STEPHEN
(*c.* 977-1038) King of Hungary. Crowned as king by the Pope in 1000, he mar. a princess from Bavaria and did much to convert his people to Christianity. He is regarded as the patron saint of Hungary.

STEPHEN
(*c.* 1097-1154) King of Eng., the 3rd son of Stephen, Count of Blois, and Adela, daughter of William I. On the d. of Henry I in 1135, he usurped the crown, the rightful heiress being Henry's daughter, Matilda (Maud). His reign was marked by frequent internal wars, during one of which Matilda took him prisoner. She was acknowledged as queen, but soon alienated the people and left Eng., Stephen agreeing to appoint her son Henry as his successor.

STEPHEN, Sir Leslie
(1829-1904) Eng. author. He wrote for the *Saturday Review*; helped to found the *Pall Mall Gazette*; ed. the *Cornhill*, 1871-82; ed. the *Dictionary of National Biography.* Virginia Woolf (*q.v.*) was his daughter.

STEPHENSON, George
(1781-1848) Eng. engineer. B. near Newcastle. In 1821 he constructed the Stockton and Darlington Railway, and in 1829 a line from Liverpool to Manchester. His 'Rocket' did 35 m.p.h.

STERILISATION
(1) Rendering free of all bacterial contamination. Milk is sterilised in bulk by pasteurisation. (2) Surgical operation for removal of sexual organs (ovary and testes).

STERLING
Legal tender of the U.K. During and since World War II the word has been much used in connection with the existence of the 'sterling area' namely that portion of the world in which sterling is a common medium of exchange.

STERNE, Laurence
(1713-68) Eng. novelist. B. Clonmel, Ireland, of Eng. parentage. *Tristram Shandy* appeared in 9 vols. (1759-67); *A Sentimental Journey* (1768).

STETHOSCOPE
Instrument invented by Lainnec, used in med. diagnosis for hearing sounds in heart and lungs.

STETTIN *See* SZCZECIN.

STEVENAGE
Urban district of Herts., 28 m. N. of London, site of the first 'New Town'. Pop. 55,000.

STEVENSON, Robert Louis
(1850-94) Scots novelist, essayist and poet. B. Edinburgh. He pub. articles in the *Cornhill Magazine* (1874). He d. of tuberculosis while working on his unfinished novel *Weir of Her-*

miston. His fiction includes the *New Arabian Nights* (1882), *Treasure Island* (1883), *Dr. Jekyll and Mr. Hyde*, *Kidnapped* (1886), *The Master of Ballantrae* (1889), *Catriona* (1893). His vols. of essays include *Travels with a Donkey* (1879). *A Child's Garden of Verses* (1885) and *Underwoods* (1887) are books of poetry.

STEWART
Great Scot. family, later sometimes spelt Stuart. In *c.* 1100 King David I made a certain Walter, steward of Scot., and the office became hereditary. A descendant, Walter, mar. Marjorie, daughter of Robert Bruce, and their son, Robert, became King of Scot. in 1371. The royal line became extinct on the male side in 1542 when James V d. but his daughter, Mary, mar. Lord Darnley, who was also a Stuart, and their son, James VI, became King of Scot. and then of Eng. His male descendants ruled Brit. until James II was deposed in 1688. After this the Stuarts maintained a claim to the throne until the d. of the last male, Henry Benedict, cardinal and Duke of York, July 13, 1807. *See* CHARLES I; JACOBITES.

STEWART, Dugald
(1753-1828) Scot. philosopher. B. Edinburgh. He wrote *Elements of the Philosophy of the Human Mind* and *The Philosophy of the Active and Moral Powers.*

STICK INSECT
(*Phasmidae*) Orthopterous insects modified so as to imitate sticks, grass stems, etc. Some linear specimens attain a length of 9-13 in. Usually the female is large, sluggish, wingless; the male small, active and winged.

STICKLEBACK
(*Gasterosteus*) Small fish in which the dorsal fin is replaced by strong spines. There are only 3 Brit. species, 3-spined and 9-spined Freshwater and a Marine Stickleback.

STILT
(*Himantopus*) Wading bird of the Snipe family. It is so called from the length of its legs which is almost equal to that of its body. *H. candidus* breeds in Holland and S. Europe.

STILTON
Village of Huntingdonshire, 6 m. S.W. of Peterborough. It gives its name to cheese.

STILWELL, Joseph Warren
(1883-1946) Amer. general. In World War II he served in China, becoming Chief of Staff to Chiang Kai-Shek, March 1942; commanded U.S. troops in China-Burma-India areas, and organised forces for the counter attack against the Japs, 1943-4. In command of Army Ground Forces Jan.-June, 1945.

STING
Sharp-pointed hollow spine. Present in certain insects for defence or other purposes, it is a modified ovipositor provided with a poison gland.

STINKHORN
Fungus (*Phallus impudicus*). It grows *c.* 7 in. high and is surmounted by a conical cap containing an olive-green slime with a disgusting smell.

STINT
(*Calidris minuta*) Small shore bird. A passage migrant to Brit. coasts chiefly in autumn. About 6 in. long, with a black bill.

STIPENDIARY
Recipient of a stipend. A stipendiary magistrate is one who is paid, as distinct from a justice of the peace who serves voluntarily. Stipendiary magistrates are appointed by the crown, and must be barristers or solicitors of at least 7 years standing.

STIRLINGSHIRE
County of C. Scot. bordering on the Firth of Forth and Loch Lomond. The land in the E. is fertile and cultivated, but further W. it rises to the Campsie Fells (1,896 ft.) and Ben Lomond (3,192 ft.). The main river is the Forth. There is coal and iron mining, and agriculture. Stirling is the county town. With Clackmannanshire, it returns 3 members to Parl. (1 borough constituency). Pop. 195,957. **Stirling.** Burgh and county town of Stirlingshire, on the Forth, 40 m. N.W. of Edinburgh. It has been a royal burgh since 1100. With Falkirk and Grangemouth it sends 1 member to Parl. Pop. 27,599.

STITCHWORT
(or **Starwort**) Perennial herbaceous plant (*Stellaria holostea*) common in hedgerows. *S. media* is known as the chickweed.

STOAT
(or **Ermine**) Small carnivorous mammal (*Mustela erminea*) related to the Weasel. It is widely distributed over N. regions, and common in Brit. The total length is *c.* 15 in. including the black-tipped tail. The pelt is reddish-brown above. In N. latitudes it adopts a white winter coat. The fur is much valued as Ermine (*q.v.*).

STOCK
(*Matthiola*) Popular annual and biennial flowering plants of the cruciferous family. The annual night scented stock (*M. tristis*) has insignificant flowers which give out a delicious fragrance in the evening.

STOCKHOLM
Cap. city and important port of Sweden, situated on the mainland and 13 islands, at the outlet of L. Malar on the Baltic Sea. The docks are well equipped, but Stockholm is ice-bound for part of the year. Of the industries, iron and steel, engineering and shipbuilding are the most important. Stockholm is the king's residence and seat of govt. Pop. 807,127.

STOCKPORT
County borough, chiefly in Cheshire but partly in Lancs., on the Mersey, 6 m. from Manchester. It is a cotton manufacturing centre. It returns 2 members to Parl. Pop. 142,570.

STOCKTON-ON-TEES
Borough and river port of Durham, 4 m. W. of Middlesbrough. There are machine shops, iron foundries and shipbuilding yards. It returns 1 member to Parl. Pop. 82,890.

STOICISM
School of philosophy. Its name is derived from the porch (*Stoa*), where its founder, Zeno (340-270 B.C.), taught at Athens. Later Stoicism had great influence in the Rom. world.

STOKE-ON-TRENT
City and county borough of Staffs., 16 m. N. of Stafford, the centre of the china and earthenware industry. It returns 3 members to Parl. Pop. 266,130.

STOMACH
Bag-like structure at lower end of the oesophagus. Food accumulates here after swallowing and the process of gastric digestion takes place. After digestion, food is passed by muscle action through the pylorus into the duodenum.

Buddha statue, Sarnath

EASTERN ART

Hiroshige: Cloudburst

Chinese Painting

TAPESTRY and CARPETS

Tapestry—1948

Tapestry—mid 15th c.

Bayeux Tapestry—11th c.

Persian carpet—16th c.

STONE AGE
A primitive stage of human development before man was acquainted with metal. The Stone Age is divided into 4 periods: (1) Eolithic, the dawn of hist.; (2) Palaeolithic, the old Stone Age when tools were fashioned by chipping; (3) Mesolithic, a transitional stage; (4) Neolithic, the new Stone Age, when tools were fashioned by grinding or polishing. **Stone Circles.** Upright pillars which are monoliths of unhewn stone, generally set up to form one or more concentric circles. Circles of this kind are very widely distributed, being found in S. Spain, Portugal, Brittany, W. England, Wales, Ireland, W. and N.E. Scotland and Scandinavia. Many contain a subterranean chamber at the centre. Experts are divided as regards the age, origin and purpose of such constructions. *See* STONEHENGE; CARNAC.

STONECHAT
(*Saxicola torquata*) Small bird found on Brit. moorlands and commons. It is *c.* 6 in. long, the plumage black with a brownish tinge on the back and white markings on the neck, wings and tail.

STONEHAVEN
Burgh, county town and resort of Kincardineshire, 16 m. S. of Aberdeen. Pop. 4,500.

STONEHENGE
Prehistoric monument on Salisbury Plain: an outer and an inner circle of stones. In the former 16 of the 30 are still standing. The inner circle is less complete. The largest stones are 21½ ft. high and were brought, it is believed, from Pembrokeshire.

STOPES, Marie Carmichael
(1880-1958) D.Sc., Ph.D. Brit. scientist and writer. She was the first woman to be apptd. to the Science Staff at Manchester Univ. in 1904. The author of widely read books on sexual hygiene. Her works include *Married Love* (1918), *Radiant Motherhood* (1920).

STORK
Family of large wading birds (*Ciconiidae*) related to the Heron. Protected in some C. European countries, it nests on the house-tops and acts as a scavenger. The White Stork (*Ciconia alba*) attains a length of 40 in. The black species (*C. nigra*), a little smaller, has black plumage, except that the lower parts are white. Both are migrants, wintering in Africa.

STORK'S BILL
(*Erodium cicutarium*) Herb of the family Geraniaceae. Related to the crane's bill, its fern-like leaves have deeply cut leaflets.

STORMONT
Castle and estate of Down, N. Ireland, near Belfast. It was bought in 1921 for the H.Q. of the Govt. of N. Ireland. In the grounds the Houses of Parl. were built.

STORNOWAY
Burgh and fishing port of Lewis, in Ross and Cromarty, 180 m. N.W. of Oban. Pop. 5,221.

STOWE, Harriet Elizabeth Beecher
(1811-96) Amer. writer. The horrors of slavery she saw in Kentucky led her to write *Uncle Tom's Cabin* (1851-2) which roused anti-slavery feeling.

STRACHEY, Giles Lytton
(1880-1932) Eng. essayist and biographer. His first book, *Landmarks in French Literature,* appeared in 1912. Others are *Eminent Victorians* (1918), *Queen Victoria* (1921), *Elizabeth and Essex* (1928).

STRADIVARI, Antonio
[stradi-vá′-ri] (*c.* 1644-1737) A pupil of Amati and father of a family of violin makers.

STRAFFORD, Earl of
Thomas Wentworth (1593-1641) Eng. statesman. After supporting the Petition of Right in 1628, he transferred his allegiance to Charles I (*q.v.*). His policy was to strengthen the monarchy and put down opposition with a firm hand. Accused by the Long Parl. of high treason during the Scot. Rebellion of 1640, he was beheaded in the Tower.

STRANRAER
[-rár′] Burgh and seaport of Wigtonshire. There is a regular service of steamers to Belfast and Larne. Pop. 9,000.

STRASBOURG
[-boorg] Cap. of Bas-Rhin dept., N.E. Fr., in the Middle Rhine plain. It manufactures beer, leather and locomotives. From 1870-1918 it was German. It was selected H.Q. of the Council of Europe, 1949. Pop. 228,971.

STRATFORD-ON-AVON
Borough and market town of Warwickshire, 24 m. S.E. of Birmingham. It is chiefly famous as the birthplace of Shakespeare. The Shakespeare Memorial Theatre, renamed the Royal Shakespeare Theatre in 1961, was opened in 1932. Pop. 16,700.

STRATHMORE
District of Scot. in the counties of Perth and Angus. The title of Earl of S. and Kinghorne has been held since 1677 by the family of Lyon, later Bowes-Lyon. The 14th earl was the father of Queen Elizabeth, the Queen Mother.

STRATOSPHERE
(or **Isothermal Layer**) The outer layer of the earth's atmosphere. The layer's distance from the earth's surface varies according to latitude: the Equator *c.* 9 m.; middle latitudes *c.* 6 m.; Poles *c.* 2 m. The upper limits of the stratosphere have not been accurately determined. From the surface of the earth to the stratosphere the temp. falls by *c.* 1° F. per 300 ft. The first ascent by man into this region was made by Piccard in 1931, and on Nov. 11, 1935 a huge manned balloon (' Explorer II ') reached an altitude of 72,395 ft.

STRAUSS, Johann
[strows] (1825-99) Austrian composer. The son of a successful conductor and composer. Against his father's wishes he entered upon a very similar musical career. He wrote a number of waltzes and other dances, as well as 16 operettas, the best known of which is *Die Fledermaus.*

STRAUSS, Richard
[strows] (1864-1949) German composer. He wrote 16 operas. Perhaps the most delightful is the comedy *Der Rosenkavalier.* Equally famous are his tone poems, *e.g. Don Juan* and *Till Eulenspiegel.*

STRAVINSKY, Igor
[-vin′-] (1882-) Russ. composer; became an Amer. citizen, 1945. He was commissioned by Diaghilev to write *The Firebird* and it appeared in 1910. A year later he wrote the ballet *Petrouchka,* and in 1913 *The Rite of Spring.* He left Russia in 1914. Controversy that raged round his early works still continues about his more recent compositions. Awarded Gold Medal of the Royal Philharmonic Society, 1954.

STRAWBERRY
(*Fragaria*) Perennial herb belonging to the family Rosaceae, valued for its delicious fruit. The small wild strawberry (*F. vesca*) is native to Brit.

STRESEMANN, Gustav
(1878-1929) German politician. A Nat. Lib., in 1917 he became leader of his party. Chanc. in 1923, he was also Foreign Min., 1923-9. He played a large part in bringing about the Locarno Pact and the entrance of Germany into the League of Nations.

STRIKE
Combination among employees in industry or trade to cease work in order to rectify a griev-

ance or enforce a demand. Strikes are commonly organised by Trade Unions who distribute strike pay while the stoppage lasts. In 1926 there was a general strike in support of the miners, for the first time in Brit. The Govt. took prompt steps to safeguard essential supplies such as food and water, and in a few days the strike collapsed. A feature of industrial life after World War II is the unofficial strike, when workers stop work without or against the orders of their Union leaders.

STRINDBERG, Johann August
(1849-1912) Swedish playwright. The poverty of his early days helped to embitter him; as did his unhappy marriages. He wrote 53 plays including *The Father* (1887), *Countess Julie*, *Easter* (1901).

STROMBOLI
One of the Ital. Lipari Is., N. of Sicily, famous for its volcano, 3,040 ft. high.

STROMNESS
Port on the S.W. coast of Mainland, Orkney Is. Pop. 1,600.

STRONTIUM
Metallic element having the sym. Sr and at. wt. 87·63. Strontium occurs as a sulphate in the mineral celestine and as a carbonate in strontianite.

STROUD
Urban district of Glos., 9 m. S. of Gloucester. An early centre of the woollen industry. Pop. 17,000.

STRYCHNINE
A drug obtained from *nux vomica.* It is used as a stimulant in heart failure and in paralysis of breathing. It is a poisonous drug and its use is controlled by law.

STUD
Establishment for horse-breeding. Pedigrees of thoroughbred horses have been systematically filed since 1791 and are pub. at intervals in stud-books.

STURDEE, Sir Frederick Charles Doveton
(1859-1925) Brit. admiral. Admiral of the Fleet, 1921. Is chiefly remembered for his defeat of a German squadron off the Falkland Is., 1914.

STURGEON
Largely cartilaginous fish without teeth, the surviving sturgeons form an isolated remnant of the family Acipenseridae. The Common Sturgeon (*A. sturio*) has a long narrow body and snouted head. The length of an adult fish is 6-9 ft. In Eng. the sturgeon is traditionally a royal fish belonging, when captured in a river, to the Queen.

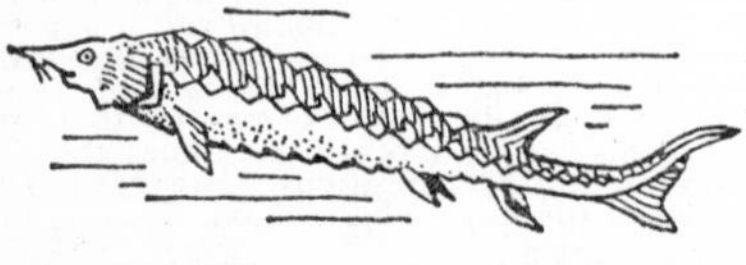

STURT, Charles
(1795-1869) Australian explorer. In 1828 he was the leader of an expedit. to the interior of Australia and discovered the Macquarie, Castlereagh and Darling rivers. Subsequently he explored the Murrumbidgee and discovered the Murray (1830).

STUTTGART
City of W. Germany, cap. of Württemberg-Baden, 40 m. S.E. of Karlsruhe. Pop. 634,000.

STYRIA
Prov. of Austria. It is mountainous and forested; iron, coal, salt and zinc are mined. Graz is the chief town.

SUBMARINE
War vessel which can be navigated on the sea surface, but is capable of being submerged and of moving under water. The first Brit. submarine was launched in 1901. Its principle weapon is the torpedo. The Schnorkel device, which allows a supply of air to be drawn from the surface, now enables the submarine to stay under water for very long periods of time and to recharge her accumulators without surfacing. In 1953, a Brit. submarine was able to stay submerged during her entire voyage from N. Amer. to Brit. *U.S.S. Nautilus* (launched Jan. 21, 1954) was the first ship to be driven by nuclear energy. Brit.'s first nuclear submarine, *H.M.S. Dreadnought*, was launched in Oct. 1960. Ships of this class have a surface displacement of over 3,000 t., an underwater speed of 25 knots, and can remain below water for very long periods. They can circumnavigate the world (*c.* 25,000 m.) without refuelling. The *Nautilus* sailed under the N. Pole in 1958. **Midget Submarine.** During World War II, small submarines of *c.* 30 t. and carrying a crew of 3, were employed on numbers of occasions. *See* ATLANTIC, BATTLE OF.

SUBMARINE CABLE
A cable, armoured on the outside, and containing insulated conductors for the transmission of telegraphic or telephonic messages. The first was laid in 1850 from Dover to Calais; the first successful trans-Atlantic telegraphic cable was laid in 1866. The earliest submarine *telephone* cables were laid 1891. In 1956 the first trans-Atlantic telephone cable linked America with the U.K. *See* TELEPHONE.

SUBSIDY
Formerly a term applied to parl. grants to the Crown, but it is now used chiefly to denote assistance lent either by one Power to another, or by the State to various trades or industries. From time to time various Brit. industries have been subsidised. In order to keep food prices down for the consumer during and after World War II the Brit. Govt. subsidised certain foodstuffs.

SUCKING FISH
Fish with suckers which enable them to attach themselves to objects. The Shark Sucker *Remora* has a special sucker on its head and habitually attaches itself, temporarily, to large sharks.

SUCKLING, Sir John
(1609-42) Eng. poet, courtier and soldier. His lyrics appeared in *Fragmenta Aurea* (1646).

SUCRE
[soo'-krā] City of Bolivia, legal cap. of the repub., 320 m. S. of La Paz. Pop. 32,000.

SUDAN
[soo-dän'] Country of N. Africa extending from the N. borders of Uganda and Congo, to the S. boundary of Egypt, and having a coastline on the Red Sea. The Nile flows through the Sudan in a N. direction. The S. part of the territory is well-watered and forested, but the N. is predominantly desert. The Sudan is the chief source of gum arabic. Other products are dura (great millet), dates, sesame and cotton, produced in the Gezira Plain irrigation area between the Blue and White Nile. Khartoum is the cap. The pop. consists of Arabs, Negroes and Nubians. The majority are Moslems. The rule of Egypt in the Sudan was interrupted in 1882 by the Mahdist revolt. After the Battle of Khartoum, 1898, the country recovered and was placed under Anglo-Egyptian admin. In 1955 the Sudan House of Representatives unanimously voted a declaration that the Sudan was a fully indep. sovereign state; the Repub. was proclaimed on Jan. 1, 1956, and the military regime seized power in 1958. Area: 967,500 sq.m. Pop. 14,355,000.

SUDBURY
Town of Ontario, Canada, 210m. N.W. of Toronto. World's greatest nickel-mining centre, also has copper and platinum. Pop. 80,120.

SUERBRUCH, Ferdinand
[sōō'-er-brooch] (1875-1951) German surgeon. In 1904, he demonstrated to the Berlin Surgical Congress a method of successfully opening the chest cavity and operating upon the lungs, thus achieving one of the most significant developments in the history of surgical science.

SUEZ CANAL
Artificial waterway connecting the Medit. and Red Seas. Projected by Ferdinand de Lesseps, it was started in 1859 and opened on Nov. 17, 1869. In 1873 Gt. Brit. received a controlling interest in the canal through the purchase of the shares of the Khedive of Egypt. The canal is 100 m. long, has a minimum depth of 34 ft. and a minimum width of 198 ft. The average time of passage is 11 to 12 hours. In July 1956 Pres. Nasser announced that the Egyptian Govt. had nationalised the Suez Canal Co. When in Nov. 1956, Brit. and Fr. forces intervened in Egypt, the Egyptian Govt. ordered the sinking of blockade ships in the Canal. The U.N. intervened, however, and the Brit. and Fr. troops withdrew. In the fighting of June 1967 the Canal was once again blocked.

SUFFOLK
Maritime county of E. Eng. The land is undulating, with a flat coastline, broken by the estuaries of the Stour, Orwell and Deben. Agriculture is the main occupation. Horsebreeding is important. Newmarket is a racing centre; Lowestoft is a centre of the herring fisheries. Ipswich is the county town. It returns 5 members to Parl. Pop. 473,000.

SUFFRAGE
[-frij] Right to vote in local and Parl. elections. The need for reform became acute with the Industrial Revolution, as many large new towns, *e.g.* Manchester, had no representation. In 1832 the position was regularised by Earl Grey's Reform Act, and large numbers of the new middle classes received the right to vote for the first time. In 1918, after a long agitation by Suffragettes, women were given the right to vote, so that only peers, lunatics and felons are now debarred from voting. The Representation of the People Act of 1948 abolished plural voting. Voting is by ballot.

SUGAR
Generic term for a group of carbohydrate foodstuffs present in plant tissues and in milk. The sugars contain carbon, hydrogen and oxygen, and are sweet crystalline substances very soluble in water. There are 2 groups: the monosaccharoses, having 6 carbon atoms; the disaccharoses, having 12 carbon atoms, include maltose in malt, lactose in milk and sucrose, the sugar of commerce, present in the sap of the sugar cane and the sugar beet.

SUICIDE
Act of killing oneself. In Eng. law until 1961 it was a felony. Act of 1961 made suicide no longer a crime but a person who aids or abets the suicide or attempted suicide of another is committing a crime.

SUKARNO, Achmed
(1900-70) Indonesian statesman. Proclaimed Repub. of Indonesia, 1945 (President 1945-49). Pres. of United States of Indonesia, 1949-67. (Repub. of I., 1950). P.M. 1959-66.

SULLIVAN, Sir Arthur Seymour
(1842-1900) Eng. composer In 1871 began collaboration with W. S. Gilbert which lasted for 25 years. They wrote 13 operettas. He wrote one serious opera, ch. music, songs.

SULLY, Duc de
[sü-l'ē] **Maximilien de Bethune** (1560-1641) Fr. statesman, famous as the counsellor of Henry IV of Fr. His first task was to repair the ruinous financial condition of the kingdom. After Henry IV's assassination, he was obliged to resign.

SULPHATES
A series of salts formed by the action of sulphuric acid upon various bases. Common examples are Epsom salts, Glauber salts, and gypsum.

SULPHONAMIDES
A group of drugs recently introduced into medicine. The first to be used was *Prontosil rubrum* by Domack in 1935. Their action is mainly to prevent the germs multiplying in the blood. Their use has greatly increased the rate of cure in puerperal fever, gonorrhoea, pneumonia, dysentery.

SULPHONIC ACIDS
A group of compounds formed by the action of strong sulphuric acid upon benzene or other organic compounds. They render organic dyestuffs soluble in water.

SULPHUR
A yellow, brittle element, widely distributed in nature, both free and in sulphides and sulphates of many metals. Sp. gr. 2·0. Chem. sym. S. **Sulphuric Acid.** Oil of vitriol. It is made on a large scale in Brit. and other countries, chiefly from sulphur dioxide. Chem. Sym. H_2SO_4.

SUMATRA
Is. of the Malay Archipelago, separated from the Malay Peninsula by the Malacca Straits and by the Sunda Strait from Java. It forms part of Indonesia. The soil is fertile and sugarcane, rice, coffee, pepper and tobacco are grown for export. The mts. are heavily forested. Gold and coal are mined. The chief towns are Padang and Palembang. Area: *c.* 182,860 sq.m. Pop. 15,700,000.

SUMMER
The second of the 4 seasons. In the N. Hemisphere it commences at the Summer Solstice when the Sun attains its greatest N. declination and enters the zodiacal sign Cancer, *c.* June 21-22. The season of Summer terminates (astronomically) at the Autumnal Equinox, Sept. 21-22.

SUMMONS
In Eng. and Scots law a document ordering a person to appear in a court of law to answer a charge.

SUN
The central body of the solar system around which the planets revolve in their orbits and from which their light and heat is derived. The average distance of the sun from the earth is *c.* 93,000,000 m. and its diameter is calculated at 864,000 m. Its radiating surface or photosphere is finely mottled and in certain positions are to be seen dark sunspots. Above the photosphere is the solar atmosphere. Beyond this lies the bright-red incandescent chromosphere, and above that the extremely tenuous gaseous corona, which is seen only during a total eclipse of the sun.

SUN BEAR
(or **Honey Bear**) (*Ursus malayanus*) Small bear inhabiting forest regions in the Malay Archipelago. The fur is short and black. The animal feeds on honey and insects.

SUN-BIRD
Birds of the family *Nectariniidae.* Found in trop. Africa, Asia and Australia, they resemble Humming Birds in size and coloration. The long slender bill and long tongue are adapted to the diet of insects, nectar of flowers, etc.

SUN FISH
(*Mola*) Bony fishes allied to the Globe-fishes.

The body is short, deep and compressed, with a very short tail. Sometimes met with in Brit. waters, it may reach 7-8 ft. in length.

SUNDA ISLANDS
Name given to the E. Ind. Is. archipelago, stretching from the Malay Peninsula to the Moluccas. The Greater Sunda Is. include Sumatra and Java.

SUNDAY SCHOOL
Voluntary agency for the religious training of young people. The origin of the Sun. School in its present form is ascribed to Robert Raikes (*q.v.*).

SUNDERLAND
County borough and port of Durham, on the estuary of the Wear, 12 m. N. of Durham. The town is situated on the Durham coalfield. Industries include ship-building, machinery and chemicals. S. returns 2 members to Parl. Pop. 190,580.

SUNDEW
(*Drosera rotundifolia*) Insectivorous plant found in bogs or marshy hollows on heath or moorland.

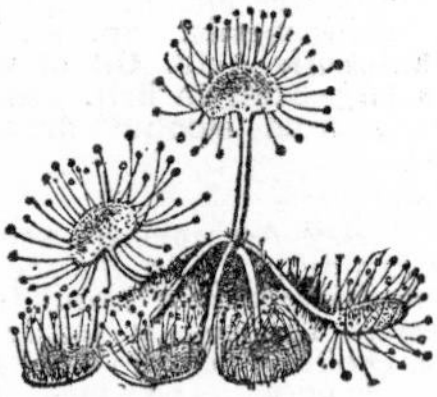

SUNDIAL
Instrument by which the time of day is shown from the sun's shadow thrown by an upright upon a flat surface. A simple type of shadow clock was used in ancient Egypt.

SUNFLOWER
Annual and perennial plant, a genus of the family Compositae. Sunflowers are of very vigorous growth with erect stems several ft. high, the flowers being brilliant yellow.

SUNNI
Orthodox Mohammedan believer. The sect of the Sunnis (or Sunnites) arose together with others on the d. of Mohammed, as he left no authorised successor.

SUNSPOT
Black irregular area seen on the photosphere of the sun. Their diameter varies; but often measures many thousands of miles. They consist of a black central nucleus surrounded by a less dark penumbra. Their nature is not definitely known. Their numbers vary but reach a maximum every 11 years, when the propagation of radio waves is affected.

SUNSTONE
A reddish variety of oligoclase felspar showing a golden sparkle.

SUPERHEATING
In a steam engine, steam entering the cylinder usually carries with it some condensed water. If the steam is superheated to a temp. much above its boiling pt. it can expand (and cool) considerably without any condensation occurring, and can therefore do more work. Super heated steam is steam heated above the normal boiling point, *i.e.* 100° C. or 212° F. Above 374° C. (' critical temp.') steam cannot be condensed to liquid water. At 100° C. pressure is 14·7 lb. per sq. in., at 215° C., 300 lb. per sq. in.

SUPERIOR
Lake of N. Amer., the largest of the Great Lakes. It lies between Canada and the U.S.A. and is connected by the St. Mary R. with L. Huron. The chief port on the Amer. side is Duluth and on the Canadian side Port Arthur; from these ports ships can pass to the St. Lawrence Seaway (*q.v.*). Area: 32,483 sq.m.

SUPERNATURALISM
Belief in a power or powers transcending the known forces of nature. In this is found the raw material of magic as well as religion, which as it rose to higher planes was mingled with gratitude and changed into reverence.

SUPERNOVA
Rare type of star which explodes with great violence and then fades. Chinese astronomers recorded a stellar explosion which occurred in A.D. 1054 and which left the gas cloud known as the *Crab Nebula*. A remnant of a supernova observed by Kepler in 1604 was discovered by Walter Baade in 1942.

SUPERSONIC SPEED
Speed greater than that of sound. At sea-level this is *c.* 760 m.p.h., decreasing with altitude until at 40,000 ft. it is only 600 m.p.h. It remains constant above that ht. *See* AVIATION.

SUPPÉ, Franz von
[soop'-ā] (1819-95) Aust. composer of Belgian origin. He was a conductor of many theatre orchestras and a successful composer of light operas.

SUPRA-RENAL GLANDS
One of the ductless or endocrine glands. Small flattened yellowish bodies situated on top of kidneys and producing *adrenalin* and *cortin. See* ADRENALIN.

SURABAYA
[soo-rǎ-bī'-yǎ] Indonesian port on the N.E. coast of Java, opposite Madura Is. An important naval base, with shipyards and various industries. Pop. 1,008,000.

SURGEON
Person who specialises in the practice of surgery. Such people in addition to their ordinary med. degree have usually obtained the specialised degree of Master of Surgery (M.Ch.), or the diploma of F.R.C.S. (Fellow of the Royal Coll. of Surgeons). Such are designated Mr. and not Dr. The **Royal Coll. of Surgeons of Eng.,** estabd. 1800, has its main H.Q. in Lincoln's Inn Fields, London.

SURGERY
The art and practice of treating diseases, wounds, injuries, deformities, etc. by manual operation. The art of surgery was highly developed in ancient Egypt. In the middle ages surgical methods were crude. In the 18th and 19th centuries epochal contributions were made by men such as Hunter, Pasteur, Lister, Simpson and others, and with the development of new methods of diagnosis, better operative technique, the introduction of modern antiseptics, anaesthetics, radiology, etc. the scope of surgery is now such that no single tissue in the body is beyond the reach of this science. *See* MEDICINE; HUNTER; LISTER.

SURINAM
River of Dutch Guiana, S. Amer., which enters the Atlantic Ocean near Paramaribo. It is also another name for Dutch Guiana (*q.v.*).

SURREALISM
[su-rē'-al-] A trend in 20th cent. art and literature; an attempt to portray dreams, both waking and sleeping, and the unfathomable realms of the subconscious, by means of symbols. The surrealists were much influenced by Freud, and by the paintings of Giorgio de Chirico, an Italian (1888-) and Marc Chagall, a Russian (1889-). Notable surrealists include Salvador Dali (1904-), Max Ernst (1891-), and Paul Klee (1879-1940).

SURREY
Inland county of S. Eng., S. of the Thames. The N. part is included in the county of London and much of it is a residential area. The S., where the N. Downs cross the country, is very beautiful. The chief rivers are the Wey, Mole, Wandle and Eden. Guildford is the county town. Surrey returns 19 members to Parl. (9 borough constituencies). Pop. 904,197.

SURREY, Henry Howard, Earl of
(*c.* 1517-47) Eng. poet and courtier. Son of 3rd Duke of Norfolk. He is best known for his lyrics from Ital. models (*e.g.* sonnets) in *Tottel's Miscellany* (1557). He was arrested and beheaded on a charge of treason by Henry VIII.

SURTEES, Robert Smith
(1803-64) Eng. novelist. He is famous for the creation of Jorrocks, a sporting Cockney grocer in *Jorrocks' Jaunts and Jollities* (1832-4). *Handley Cross* (1843) is the best known of his other works.

SURVEYING
The art by which the boundaries and size of an area of the earth's surface are determined for purposes of map-making and the various requirements of civil and other depts. of engineering. The survey of Brit. is carried out by the Ordnance Survey (*q.v.*).

SUSA
Cap. city of Susiana (Elam, Persia). It was the chief residence of Darius I and his successors. It has been the scene of much modern excavation, the code of Hammurabi (*q.v.*) being discovered there.

SUSSEX
Maritime county of S. Eng., between Hants. and Kent. It is crossed by the chalk S. Downs, which terminate at the coast in Beachy Head. The chief rivers are the Arun, Adur, Rother, Ouse and Cuckmere. Agriculture is important. For admin. purposes the county is divided into E. and W. Sussex with Lewes and Chichester the county towns. The largest towns are coast resorts such as Brighton, Eastbourne, Hastings and Worthing. It returns 11 members to Parl. (5 borough constituencies). Pop. 1,076,000.

SUTCLIFFE, Herbert William
(1894-) Eng. cricketer. B. near Harrogate, he first played for Yorks. in 1914. His batting averages in test matches are unique; in 1930 it was 87·2 and he scored 7 centuries against Australia. In 1930 he scored 3,006 runs. In June, 1932, Sutcliffe and Holmes estabd. a record by scoring 555 runs in a first wicket partnership for Yorks. against Essex, Sutcliffe's score being 313. His 50,000th run was made in 1939 and he retired in 1945.

SUTHERLAND, Graham
(1903-) Brit. landscape painter and designer. He combines ' neo-romanticism ' with abstract tendencies. Designed the tapestry behind the altar in Coventry cath., the biggest tapestry ever made.

SUTHERLAND
Maritime county of N. Scot. The S. is a mountainous area with a number of lochs. The soil is infertile. Rivers include the Oykell, Helmsdale and Brora. Dornoch is the county town. With Caithness it sends 1 member to Parl. Pop. 13,442.

SUTTON COLDFIELD
Borough of Warwickshire, 8 m. N.E. of Birmingham. A television station was opened in 1950. Pop. 75,220.

SVALBARD
Norwegian territory in the Arctic Ocean between Novaya Zemlya and Greenland. It comprises several Is., the chief being W. Spitsbergen, N.E. Land, Prince Charles Foreland and Edge and Bear Is. They are mountainous and barren, and sparsely populated. Coal is the main export. S. officially became a Norwegian possession in 1925. Area: *c.* 22,300 sq.m.

SVERDLOVSK
City of the Sverdlovsk Area, in the Russ. S.F.S.R., E. of the Ural Mts. and 120 m. N. of Chelyabinsk. There are blast furnaces; machine tools and electrical apparatus are made. Pop. 777,000.

SWAHILI
[-he'-] People of E. Africa, inhabiting the coastal lands of Kenya and Tanganyika. They are Bantus who have intermarried with others of African and Arab blood. The Swahili language is the *Lingua Franca* of much of C. and E. Africa.

SWALLOW
Migratory passerine insectivorous bird (*Hirundo rustica*) of the family Hirundinidae. It is characterised by the short, wide beak, forked tail and long, narrow wings. It is distinguished from the House Martin by length of tail feathers and absence of white rump. Native to Africa, Asia and Europe, it visits Brit. during the summer months, making its nest in the roofs of buildings.

SWAN
(*Cygnus*) Large aquatic birds widely distributed. Of the family Anatidae, they are related to the Geese, etc. The Mute Swan (*C. olor*) 1 of 3 varieties which come to Brit. in winter, is the tame Swan of our rivers and lakes. It is entirely white, the bill orange with black basal patch and tubercles. The neck is long and curved, the legs short, the body *c.* 54 in. long.

SWAN, Sir Joseph Wilson
(1828-1914) Eng. physicist and electrician. In 1860 he produced the first carbon electric lamp, and was the first to produce photographic dry plates and bromide printing paper.

SWANSEA
City (since 1969) of Glamorganshire, 45 m. W. of Cardiff. Tinplate is an important manufacture, and various metals are smelted. S. returns 2 members to Parl. Pop. 169,150.

SWASTIKA
Ancient religious symbol which consists of a Gk. cross with the arms bent to right angles. In Germany the Nazi party under Adolf Hitler adopted the swastika as an anti-semitic symbol.

SWAZILAND
Kingdom of S. Africa, bounded by the Transvaal, Natal, and Portuguese E. Africa. Indep. 1968, after 65 years as Brit. Prot. Cattle, sheep, maize, tobacco, ground-nuts, asbestos and tin are produced. Mbabane is the cap. Area: 6,700 sq.m. Pop. 269,500.

SWEATING SICKNESS
Epidemic disease which spread over the greater part of Europe during the 15th and 16th cents. It first appeared in Eng. in 1485, when 20,000 persons d. in London.

SWEDEN
Kingdom of N.W. Europe, comprising the E. part of the Scandinavian pensinsula, with a long coastline on the Baltic Sea and Gulf of Bothnia. There are 4 main regions: Norrland, N. of Lat. 60°; the lowland area surrounding lakes Venner and Vetter; the Småland Plateau; and fertile Scania in the extreme S. The Gota is the most important river. Oland and Gottland are large islands in the Baltic. The Baltic coast is frozen for several months in winter. Agriculture is chiefly important in the S. where cereals, potatoes and sugar beet are produced, and dairy cattle reared. In the N. are extensive forests and valuable mineral deposits, iron ore, zinc, silver, lead and copper. Hydro-electric power is important as there is no coal. Industries include textiles, flour milling, iron and steel works, also matches, paper and elec-

trical manufactures. The chief towns are Stockholm the cap., Göteborg, Malmö, Norrköping and Hälsingborg. The Lutheran church is the state religion, and there are univs. at Uppsala (1477) and Lund (1668). Sweden became a kingdom *c.* 10th cent. and accepted Christianity a little later. In the 17th cent. Sweden, under Gustavus Adolphus and Charles XII, was one of the great powers of Europe. The rise of Russia deprived Sweden of her dominant position among the Baltic states. In 1810 Napoleon secured the choice of his marshal, Bernadotte, as heir to Charles XIII, and in 1818, Bernadotte became king as Charles XIV. He also ruled over Norway, which was united with Sweden from 1814 to 1905. Sweden is governed by a parl. (Riksdag) consisting of 2 houses, with a council of state. Area: 173,400 sq.m. Pop. 7,542,459.

SWEDENBORGIANISM
Name applied to the religious system of **Emanuel Swedenborg** (1688-1772).

SWEEPSTAKE
Form of gambling, in which chance or skill wins the combined subscriptions of the competitors. The commonest form is organised on horse races, in which the horses are drawn by lottery, the prize money being distributed to the winners according to the placing of the horses in the race.

SWEET FLAG
Perennial herbaceous plant (*Acorus calamus*), of the family Araceae. It grows in marshy places.

SWEET PEA
Annual leguminous plant (*Lathyrus odoratus*) cultivated for its handsome flowers. The butterfly-like blossoms are borne in clusters of 2-4 on long stalks.

SWEET POTATO
(or **Batata**) Perennial herbaceous plant (*Ipomaea batatas*) of the family Convolvulaceae. It has large funnel-shaped white and purple flowers. A native of S. Amer. it is grown for its edible tubers.

SWEET WILLIAM
Perennial herb (*Dianthus barbatus*) of the family Caryophyllaceae. A popular garden plant, it is treated as a biennial.

SWEETBREAD
Term commonly used to denote certain glands of animals when used for food.

SWEETBRIER
(*Rosa rubiginosa*) Species of rose with prickly stems and serrated leaves. The small rose-pink flowers are single and borne in small sprays, followed by red or orange hips in the autumn.

SWIFT
(*Apus apus*) Insectivorous, gregarious bird of Europe, Asia and Africa, a summer visitant to Brit. It is 7 in. in length with long narrow wings, and forked tail. The claws are hooklike, enabling the bird to cling to walls, etc. The nest, placed usually under the eaves, is made of straw, grass, etc. cemented together with saliva. The Swift's plumage is sooty black, with a greyish white throat patch.

SWIFT, Jonathan
(1667-1745) Eng. writer. B. Dublin of Yorkshire parentage. The revolution of 1688 drove him to Eng. He became sec. to Sir William Temple, under whose roof he met 'Stella' (Hester Johnson), and wrote *The Tale of a Tub.* His gifts as a satirist made him a valuable ally of the Tory party. *The Drapier's Letters* (1724) attacked the grant of a patent to William Wood for supplying a copper coinage to Ireland. In 1726 appeared *Gulliver's Travels*, a satire on faction, humbug, and human depravity.

SWIMMING
Self-propulsion in water. As a pastime it has developed greatly in recent years. Competitions for speed, fancy diving, back strokes, etc., figure prominently in the Olympic Games.

SWINBURNE, Algernon Charles
(1837-1909) Eng. poet, was assoc. with the Pre-Raphaelite Brotherhood. In 1865 appeared his verse play *Atalanta in Calydon*; *Poems and Ballads* (1866), *Songs Before Sunrise* (1871).

SWINDON
Borough of Wilts., 77 m. W. of London, sending 1 member to Parl. New Swindon grew up after 1849 around the railway works. Pop. 94,560.

SWINE FEVER
Highly contagious febrile disease affecting swine.

SWITHUN
(*c.* 800-862) Eng. saint, commemorated on July 15. It is a common belief that if it rains on that day it will rain for 40 days afterwards.

SWITZERLAND
Repub. of W. Europe, between Fr., Austria, Italy and Germany. The most mountainous country of Europe, it has 3 distinct divisions; the Jura in the N.W.; the fertile midland plateau strewn with lakes, and the high Alps in the S. covering more than half the country. The chief rivers are the Rhine, the Rhône, Ticino and Inn. Lakes include Geneva, Constance, Neuchatel, Zurich and Lucerne. The Alpine peaks are perpetually covered in snow. Agriculture is the chief occupation in the valleys; cattle rearing and dairying are important, and many of the food products are exported. Industries, many of them based on the hydro-electricity of the Alps, include the manufacture of machinery, textiles, chemicals, watches and clocks. In addition there is the tourist industry. Berne is the cap.; other cities are Zurich, Basle, Geneva, Lausanne, St. Gallen and Lucerne. Of the passes, the Julier, St. Gotthard, Simplon and Gt. St. Bernard are of greatest importance for internat. traffic. German is the dominant language in 16 cantons, Fr. in 5, and Ital. in 1. 58 % of the pop. is Protestant, *c.* 40 % R.C. Switzerland originated 1291, when the 3 cantons of Uri, Schwyz and Lower Unterwalden formed a defensive league around the Holy Roman Emp. By 1353 there were 8 members of the league. In 1648 the league became formally indep. of the Holy Rom. Emp. In 1798 the Helvetic Repub. was formed under Fr. influence. Napoleon Bonaparte gave the Swiss a new constitution, 1803, and increased the number of cantons to 19. In 1815 Swiss neutrality was recognised by Austria, U.K., Russ., Portugal and Pruss. New constitutions were drawn up in 1848 and 1878. Under the latter which is still in force, Switzerland is gov. by the Federal Assembly, which comprises a council of states and a nat. council, the Federal Council, elected by the assembly and the Pres. Area: 15,950 sq.m. Pop. 6,050,000

SWORD
Offensive weapon. It consists of a steel blade with 1 or 2 cutting edges, and fitted with a hilt for grasping. Ancient swords were usually short with a broad pointed blade, but in medieval types the sword was long and often cross-hilted.

SWORD FISH
Oceanic bony fish of the family Xiphidae, found in the Atlantic, Pacific and Medit. From 3-14 ft. long, it is fierce and powerful, with a sword-like prolongation of the upper jaw which serves as a weapon.

SYCAMORE
Large timber tree (*Acer pseudo-platanus*) long naturalised in Brit. The sycamore grows 60 ft. high. The clusters of drooping greenish flowers appear in May and are succeeded by winged fruit.

SYDNEY
Port and cap. of New South Wales; the oldest and largest city of Australia. It has one of the finest harbours in the world, spanned by the famous Sydney bridge. It is the banking, commercial and shipping centre of the country, with extensive wharves and docks. Pop. 2,215,970.

SYMBOL
A sign by which one knows or infers a thing; an *emblem*. It is generally a definite visible figure intended to represent or stand for something else, as in the case of the common *astronomical symbols*, which are signs conveniently representing astronomical objects, phases of the moon, etc. and astronomical terms. The symbols for the chief heavenly bodies are as follows: Sun, ⊙, Mercury ☿, Venus ♀, Earth ⊕, and ♁, Moon ☽, Mars ♂, Jupiter ♃, Saturn ♄, Uranus ♅, Neptune ♆, Comet ☄, Star ✳. *Lunar phases*: ● Moon in conjunction, or *new*; ☽ Moon in E. quadrature, or *first quarter*; ○ Moon in opposition, or *full*; ☾, Moon in W. quadrature, or *last quarter*. **Chemical symbols** are merely the first letters of the names of the chemical elements; or, when the names of two or more elements begin with the same letter, two letters are used as the symbol, one of which is always the first letter of the name of the element. **Mathematical symbols** are letters or characters used to denote numbers, functions, operations, and relations. Sometimes a letter is used for a definite number, as *e*, or π; more usually the use of a letter for a number indicates that the number is not restricted to have one special value. Similarly, when a letter is used as a symbol for a *function*, it may stand either for one special function, or for any function at all. The symbols γ, π, J, for example, are invariably understood to stand for the gamma, pi, and first Bessel Function respectively. Symbols other than letters, such as +, −, ×, ÷, √, ∴, =, ⊳, ⊲, are also in general use.

SYMBOLISM
Representation of a thing, person or idea by means of a sign, drawing, symbol, etc. which being recalls that which by analogy it is intended to represent. Sacred emblems, etc., many of which have an esoteric significance, have been, and are, used in many religious, occult and mystic fraternities throughout the world. Many orders and fraternities (Catholic, Rosicrucian, Masonic, Political, Educational, etc.) employ symbols for initiatory and other purposes. **Symbolism** was a movement in Fr. poetry (*c.* 1870-1920) which exploited the music and suggestiveness of words rather than their meaning.

SYNAGOGUE
Meeting place for Jewish worship. There is no certain reference to the synagogue in the O.T. but in the time of Christ it was already an old-estabd. and widespread institution (Acts, 15, 21) not only in Palestine but throughout the Dispersion.

SYNCOPE
[sin'kōpi] or **Fainting.** A sudden loss of consciousness. It results from failure of the heart action and resultant reduction in oxygen supply to the brain. Failure of the heart action may be produced psychologically by nauseating smells or unpleasant sights.

SYNDICALISM
Theory of trade unionism, prevalent in particular in Fr. before World War I, where it led to the great railway strike of 1910. Its primary features were open reliance on class-warfare and violence.

SYNGE, John Millington
(1871-1909) Irish playwright, assoc. with the Lit. movement of the Irish Renaissance. His plays are *The Shadow of the Glen* (1903), *Riders to the Sea* (1904), *The Playboy of the Western World* (1907), *Deirdre of the Sorrows* (1910).

SYPHILIS
An infectious and contagious disease contracted by sexual intercourse with an infected person or passed from an infected mother to her unborn child. Usually the first sign is a small red area on the male genital organ. In the female this area may be inside the vagina and invisible except at special exam. The red area breaks down and an ulcer or chancre with a yellow centre forms. During this period the person is very infectious. During the next 2 or 3 years the general health is poor. This is the secondary stage of the disease and the discharge from the throat or skin during this time is highly infective. In the third or final stage the disease may affect the heart and blood vessels, or the brain and spinal cord or bone and skin. Congenital syphilis resulting from infection passed from the mother to her unborn child causes deformities of the teeth and bones, lack of development of the brain with early mental deficiency, blindness, deafness and other conditions.

SYRACUSE
Seaport of E. Sicily, 35 m. S.E. of Catania. The city has a cath. and remains of an amphitheatre. There is a trade in salt, wine, olive oil and fruit. Founded *c.* 732 B.C., it was the most important Gk. city in Sicily. Pop. 86,000.

SYRIA
Repub. in the Levant, bounded by Turkey, Iraq, Jordan, Israel and Lebanon, with a short coastline on the Medit. Except for Mt. Hermon and the Anti-Lebanon range on the Lebanese border, the country consists of a desert plateau drained by the upper Euphrates and tributaries, and the Orontes. Wheat, barley, tobacco and cotton are the chief crops, and leather goods, wool and silk are produced. The oil pipe-line from Kirkuk, in Iraq, to Tripoli, crosses the country. Damascus, the cap., Aleppo, Homs and Hama are the chief towns. Latakia is the principal port. The Arabic speaking population is mainly Moslem. The Syria of ancient times stretched along the Medit. from Egypt as far as the Taurus Mts. From 64 B.C. until A.D. 634 it was part of the Rom. Emp. It remained in the hands of the Ottoman Turks from 1516 until 1918, when they were expelled by the Brit. Fr. interests in Syria were recognised by the assignation of a mandate for the country to Fr. from 1920 to 1941. Complete indep. was achieved in 1946, when all foreign troops were withdrawn. In 1949 the govt. was overthrown by a *coup d'état*, and a temporary dictatorship followed. This ended when the Pres. was arrested and shot. A new constitution formulated, 1950. In 1951, there followed another *coup d'état*, the P.M. becoming also the head of state, but in Feb. 1954 a new Pres. took over control. On Feb. 1st, 1958, it was announced

that Syria and Egypt had united to form the United Arab Republic (*q.v.*). In 1961 a military *coup d'état* took place in Syria, and Syria withdrew from the U.A.R. in Sept. In 1963, a mutual defence agreement was signed by Egypt and Syria. Area: *c.* 71,000 sq.m. Pop. 5,500,000.

SYRIAC *See* ARAMAIC.

SYRINGA
[-ring'-gă] Genus of deciduous shrubs of the order *Oleaceae*, including the common lilac (*S. vulgaris*). The name is applied to the mock orange, a shrub of the Hydrangeaceae.

SZCZECIN
[sh-chet'-sin] (formerly **Stettin**) Town and river port of N.W. Poland, on the Oder, 80 m. N.E. of Berlin. Before World War II, S. was a German port. Pop. 269,000.

SZECHWAN
[sech'-wăn'] Prov. of W. China, bounded on the W. by the mountains of Sikang. Most of the prov. consists of the Red Basin, the basin of the Yangtze-Kiang and its tributaries. Chengtu, the cap., and Chungking, seat of the govt. from 1937-46, are the chief towns. Pop *c.* 85,000,000.

Quebec: Chateau Frontenac

Alaska: Mt. McKinley

THE AMERICAN CONTINENT · 1

Colorado: Grand Canyon

Florida: Daytona Beach

THE AMERICAN CONTINENT · 2

Brazil: Rio de Janeiro

Ecuador: Guanijo district

Brazil: Iguaçu Falls

Brazil: Bahia harbour

Inca Temple near Cuzco

T

T
20th letter of the Eng. alphabet. It is a dental with a sharp sound made by contact of tongue with teeth. The normal sound is that of *t* in *tip, top*; with *ia*, and *io*, it has the sound of *sh*, *e.g. satiate, diction*. When combined with *h*, it may be voiced as *th*, in *this, them*, or unvoiced as *thin, think*.

TABERNACLE
Portable sanctuary set up by Moses for the worship of Jehovah in the wilderness. It was divided into two parts, the holy place, and the 'holy of holies'. The **Feast of Tabernacles** is a Jewish autumn festival.

TABLE MOUNTAIN
Mt. of S. Africa, 3,550 ft. high, near the Cape of Good Hope, overlooking Cape Town.

TABLE TENNIS
Game introduced *c.* 1901 and played on a table 9 ft. by 5 ft., 2 ft. 6in. above the floor, divided by a net 6¾ in. high, into 2 courts. Lightweight bats and a small celluloid ball are used.

TABRIZ
City of Iran, cap. of Azerbaijan prov. Founded in 791, T. is a trading centre, with carpet manufactures. Pop. 290,000.

TABU
(or **Taboo**) Custom of prohibiting contact with certain persons or things. It is a practice widespread among primitive peoples in all parts of the world. Some people or things are inherently tabu, on others tabu may be imposed temporarily or permanently by priests or rulers.

TACITUS, Publius Cornelius
(58-120) Rom. historian. His extant writings are the *Life of Agricola*, a biography of his father-in-law; the *Germania*; the *Annales*, the hist. of the Rom. emp. from Tiberius to Nero (14-68), and the *Historiae* (69-97).

TADPOLE
Undeveloped aquatic larva of a frog or toad. It leaves the water when the tail vanishes and legs appear. *See* FROG.

TAFT, William Howard
(1857-1930) 27th Pres. of the U.S.A. Apptd. Civil Gov. of the Philippines, 1901, where he established an admin. to cope with the effect of Spanish misrule. Pres. T. Roosevelt made him Sec. for War, and supported his successful candidature in the presidential elections of 1909. Taft continued Roosevelt's policies, but in 1912 the ex-Pres. broke with him. Roosevelt was nominated for the Pres. and this schism was directly responsible for the victory of the Democrats in 1912, when Woodrow Wilson became Pres. During World War I he favoured a policy of Amer. neutrality, but when the U.S. entered the war in April 1917, he gave his support to Allied propaganda. Later he urged the U.S. to join the League of Nations.

TAGORE, Sir Rabindranath
(1861-1941) Indian poet and mystic. B. in Calcutta. In 1901 he founded a school at Santinikitan, Bengal. In 1913 he was awarded a Nobel Prize for literature.

TAGUS
[tā'-] River of Sp. and Portugal, which rises in E. Sp. and flows W., entering the Atlantic Ocean near Lisbon.

TAHITI
[ta-hē'-ti] One of the Society Is. (*q.v.*). Area: 600 sq.m. Pop. 52,068.

TAILOR BIRD
(*Orthotomus sutorius*) Small bird of the order Sylviidae, found in Asia, which fastens the edges of large leaves together with vegetable fibres to form a pouch for its nest.

TAIWAN
or **Formosa.** Chinese Is. in the Pacific, separated from the S.E. coast of China by Formosa Strait. The E. part is mountainous, rising to over 13,000 ft. In the W. plain rice, sugar and tea are grown. There are supplies of timber, and minerals. Taipeh is the cap. T. was ceded to Japan in 1895, and returned to China in 1945. After the resignation of Pres. Chiang Kai-Shek in 1949, the authority of the Chinese Nationalist Govt. rapidly declined, and by 1950, the Nationalists retained control only in Taiwan and Hainan. Area: 13,890 sq.m. Pop. 13,188,000.

TAJ MAHAL
[tȧj'-măh-ȧl'] Mausoleum at Agra, India, built in 1632 by the Emp. Shah Jahan for his favourite wife.

TAJIKISTAN
Repub. of the U.S.S.R. in C. Asia, bounded by Uzbekistan, Kirghizia, Afghanistan and Sinkiang (China). The Pamirs in the E. rise to 24,000 ft. Cotton growing is the principal industry. Dushambe is the cap. Area: 54,019 sq.m. Pop. 2,535,000.

TAKORADI
Chief port of Ghana in W. Africa, W. of Sekondi, with an artificial deep-water harbour.

TALC
Soft mineral with greasy feel and pearly lustre, composed of magnesium silicate, and occurring in silvery-white or greenish foliated masses. The name talc is applied commercially to mica.

TALIESIN
(or **Taliessin**) (*c.* 550) Welsh bard. He and Aneirin are assoc. with the N. Welsh Cycle legends of 6th cent. heroes.

TALLEYRAND-PÉRIGORD, Charles Maurice de
[talā-rȧ(ng)'-pā-ri-gor'] (1754-1838) Fr. statesman and diplomat. Exiled during the Terror, he returned in 1796 and helped Napoleon Bonaparte to plan his *coup d'etat* of 1799, and served him as Foreign Min. though he intrigued after 1808 with the Bourbons. He represented Fr. at Vienna, 1814, and secured the restoration of Louis XVIII.

TALLINN
(formerly **Reval**) Cap. and seaport of Estonia, U.S.S.R., S. of the Gulf of Finland. Pop. 322,000.

TALLIS, Thomas
(*c.* 1505-85) Eng. composer. He wrote a great deal of ch. music, most of it for the R.C. Ch. and a number of anthems for the use of the Reformed Ch.

TALLOW TREE
Chinese tree (*Sapium sebiferum*); family Euphorbiaceae. The seeds are covered with a tallowy grease. The African tallow tree (*Pentadesma buturacea*) is of the family Guttiferae.

TALMUD
Book of Rabbinical writings. It consists of 2 parts, the *Mishnah*, a collection of laws and traditional duties, and the *Gemara*, a kind of commentary.

TAMARIN
Name given to certain squirrel-monkeys of S. Amer.

TAMARIND
Tropical leguminous tree (*Tamarindus indica*), native of the E. and W. Indies. The pods and bark are used medicinally.

TAMARISK
Evergreen tree (*Tamarix anglica*), of the family Tamaricaceae. About 10-12 ft. high, it is used extensively for hedges in seaside places in S. Eng. There are over 60 species of trees and shrubs in the genus.

TAMATAVE
[tama-tāv'] Chief port of Madagascar, on the E. coast. Pop. 39,627.

TAMBOURINE
[tam-bo͞o-rēn'] A small single-headed drum, in the rim of which are fitted pairs of small circular metal plates called jingles.

TAMERLANE
(1336-1405) Mongol conqueror. In 1358 he began a series of conquests which took him from his kingdom in Turkistan as far as the Caspian Sea, the Urals, the Volga, through Persia, to Egypt and India. Samarkand was his chief city.

TAMPERE
Town of Finland, on L. Nasi, 95 m. N.W. of Helsinki. Textiles are manufactured. Pop. 188,000.

TAMPICO
[tam-pē'-kō] Port and chief commercial centre in N. Mexico, 7 m. up the Panuco. Situated near oil fields, it has numerous refineries. Pop. 122,535.

TANAGER
Finch-like passerine birds, natives of Amer. The plumage is brilliant and the conical bill is notched towards the end. *Tanagra rubra*, the Scarlet T., has brilliant scarlet plumage with black wings and tail.

TANANARIVE
(now **Antananarivo**) Cap. of Madagascar on the hills *c.* 100 m. from E. coast. Connected by rail with its port, Tamatave. Pop. 322,000.

TANGANYIKA
Indep. repub. within the Commonwealth in E. Africa, with a coastline on the Ind. Ocean, between Kenya and Portuguese E. Africa. Part of German E. Africa until 1918. T. was a mandate under the League of Nations until 1946, when it came under U.N. trusteeship. Most of the country is a plateau, rising to 19,565 ft. in Mt. Kilimanjaro in the N.E. and 9,000 ft. in the S.W., on the borders of Lakes Victoria, T. and Malawi. There are extensive forests and much fertile land. Gold, tin, diamonds, lead and other minerals are worked. Dar-es-Salaam is the cap. and chief seaport. The native pop. are mainly of mixed Bantu race, speaking Swahili. Pres. is Head of State and of the govt. In 1964 an Act of Union was signed uniting T. with the Repub. of Zanzibar (*q.v.*) and the name Tanzania was adopted. Area: *c.* 343,000 sq.m. Pop. 12,231,000. **Tanganyika, Lake.** Lake of E. Africa, between Congolese Rep. and Tanganyika. Discovered in 1858, the lake is *c.* 450 m. long. Area: *c.* 12,700 sq.m.

TANGIER
Seaport of Morocco (*q.v.*) on the Strait of Gibraltar. The port belonged to Eng. for some 22 years until captured by the Moors, 1683. In 1923 T. was made an internat. zone. In 1941 Spain suppressed the internat. admin. At the end of World War II the internat. régime was restored. After the declaration of Morocco's indep. in 1956 T. was incorporated into Mor. Terr. 1960. In 1962 it was decreed that T. would be the summer cap. of Mor. Pop. 110,000.

TANK
Armoured fighting vehicle carrying a large gun in a turret, and machine guns. First used by the Brit. Army during the Battle of the Somme, 1916. They incorporated the caterpillar track to enable them to deal with trenches and rough terrain. At the beginning of World War II tank warfare as demonstrated by the German Panzer Divs. revolutionised the art of land warfare. Among the many types of tanks produced during World War II were the Brit. *Churchill* and *Cromwell* and the Amer. *Grant* and *Sherman*. The most powerful German tank was the *Tiger*, the largest model of which weighed 70 t. and carried an 88-mm gun. Brit. was particularly successful in producing tanks for special purposes. These included Bulldozer tanks to clear away obstacles; Flail tanks to clear pathways through minefields; and amphibious tanks which could swim ashore under their own power.

TANNENBERG
Village in E. Poland, 85 m. S. of Kaliningrad, celebrated for 2 battles. In 1410 the Teutonic Knights were defeated by the Poles, and in 1914, the Russ. were beaten by the Germans.

TANNIN
Alternative name for tannic acid. Present in gall nuts, it is an amorphous astringent powder very soluble in water, less so in alcohol. An analogous series of tannins is found in many plants, such as tea, oak, bark, and catechu. It is used in making inks, and in medicine.

TANNING
Process by which leather is made from the skins of animals. In vegetable tanning the process depends upon the action of tannic acid upon the skin, and the materials used are oak, wattle and mangrove barks, sumach, etc.

TANSY
Genus of perennial herbaceous plants (*Tanacetum*) of the family Compositae. *T. vulgare*, the native Brit. species, has a creeping rootstock, green, feathery leaves and golden yellow flowers.

TANTALUM
Hard metallic element, discovered in 1802 by Ekeberg. It is also resistant to most corrosive agents and is used in many applications as a substitute for platinum. Sp. gr. 16·6. Chem. sym. Ta.

TANZANIA Repub. (1964) *See* TANGANYIKA. ZANZIBAR.

TAOISM
[tā'-ō-izm] Chinese philosophical system which was developed into a popular religion. Its origins are obscure but Lao-tzu (6th cent. B.C.) wrote the *Tao-Teh-King* which provides the basis of the system.

TAPE RECORDER
Records of speech and music are made by the magnetisation of a plastic tape impregnated with iron oxide. In 1953 a method of video-recording on magnetic tape was introduced, which makes possible an immediate reproduction of films, and also TV programmes. *See* GRAMOPHONE.

TAPESTRY
Fabric coverings of furniture, floors and walls,

characterised by the way the pattern is woven across the warp threads. The tapestries of Gobelins, Beauvais and Bayeux are famous.

TAPEWORM
A flat worm resembling tape. The body is divided into segments, the head minute and provided with suckers and in many species with hooks also. Tapeworms are parasites inhabiting the alimentary canal of warm-blooded vertebrates.

TAPIOCA
(*Manihot utilissima*) Trop. plant of the order *Euphorbiaceae*. It is several ft. high, of shrubby growth, and has a large fleshy root which contains an acrid milk juice, which is extracted by pressure and purified. Its root also yields a starchy substance which is dried to form tapioca for use at the table.

TAPIR
[tā′-] (*Tapirus*) A short-haired medium sized odd-toed mammal. Found in C. and S. Amer. and Malaya. On the front feet there are 4 digits, on the hind feet 3. A shy nocturnal animal, inhabiting forest regions near water, it is vegetarian.

TAR
Dark brown or black viscid liquid with a peculiar aromatic odour, obtained when wood, coal or similar substances are subjected to destructive distillation. By distillation coal tar yields numerous substances from which aniline dyes are derived. Tar is used also as a protective coating for wood and iron, for road making and also in medicine.

TARA
[tä′-rä] Village of Meath, Eire, on the Boyne, 6 m. S. of Cavan. The Hill of Tara (507 ft.) is the legendary site of the crowning of the kings of Ireland.

TARANTULA
Several species of large spider, esp. *Lycosa tarantula* found near Taranto in Italy.

TARPAN
A species of wild horse at one time found in large numbers in the Asiatic Steppes.

TARPON
(*Megalops atlanticus*) Fish of the Herring family. Abundant in S. Atlantic waters, it often weighs over 112 lb. It is a food fish and affords good sport.

TARQUINIUS, Lucius
[tär-kwin′-] Surnamed **Superbus** (the Proud) seventh and last of the traditional kings of Rome. He greatly extended the Rom. power. He completed the Capitol, built the temple of Jupiter, and acquired the Sibylline books (*see* SIBYL). He was driven from Rome, following the outrage perpetrated by his son Sextus on Lucretia.

TARRAGON
Perennial herb (*Artemisia dracunculus*), native to Spain, Italy and other Medit. countries. It is used to flavour vinegar, pickles and sauces.

TARSIER
Rare animal of the genus *Tarsius*, resembling the Lemur, inhabiting the E. Archipelago. It is about as big as a squirrel, inhabits trees, and feeds on lizards and insects.

TARSUS
Town of Turkey, 12 m. from the mouth of the Cydnus in S. Asia Minor, the birthplace of St. Paul.

TARTAN
Material chequered or cross-barred with threads of various colours. Orig. of wool or silk, and used in Scot. where each clan had its own particular patterns, it is now made of all materials. After the 1745 rising in Scot. the wearing of tartan was prohibited by law from 1746-82, under the Highland Garb Act.

TARTAR
Crude potassium hydrogen tartrate (KH $C_4H_4O_6$). Wines when fementing deposit a crystalline crust (argol), which, when purified, yields **Cream of T.** This is used in making tartaric acid, silver cleaning, wool dyeing and in the preparation of baking powder.

TARTARY
Area inhabited by the Tartars in the M.A. It was partly in Europe and partly in Asia.

TARTINI, Giuseppe
[-tē′-] (1692-1770) Ital. composer. In 1728, he estabd. a school of violin playing at Padua. His works include over 100 violin concertos and many sonatas including the famous *Devil's Trill*.

TASHKENT
Cap. of Uzbekistan, U.S.S.R. and the largest city of Asiatic Russ., 300 m. N.E. of Bukhara. Scene of 1966 conference betw. India and Pakistan resulting in T. Declaration. Pop. 1,073,000.

TASMANIA
Is. S. of Victoria, forming a state of the Commonwealth of Australia, with the Furneaux Group and King Is. The Is., separated from the mainland by Bass Strait, is mountainous in the interior. The Tamar and Derwent are the largest rivers. T. has moderate temperatures and sufficient rainfall. Forestry is important, and copper, zinc, tin, silver and lead are mined. There are numerous industries, based on hydro-electricity. Hobart, the cap. and Launceston, are the only large towns. T. was first settled by the Brit. in 1803, and obtained responsible govt. in 1856. Admin. is by a Gov. and 2 houses. Area: 26,220 sq.m. Pop. 361,000.

TASMANIAN DEVIL
(*Dasyurus*) A nocturnal marsupial mammal found only in Tasmania. It is *c.* 21 in. long, with a 7 in. tail, and generally bear-like appearance.

TASSIGNY, Jean de Lattre de
(1890-1952) Fr. gen. During World War II he escaped to Eng. and in 1943 became Chief of the Fr. Expedit. Force. In 1950 he went to Fr. Indo-China to oppose the Viet-Minh rebels there. Appointed C.-in-C. Land forces under S.H.A.P.E. (*q.v.*), 1951.

TASSO, Torquato
(1544-95) Ital. poet. He became attached to the ducal court at Ferrara, and wrote the epics *La Gerusalemme Liberata* and *Rinaldo*.

TASTE
The sense of taste lies in the mouth, principally in the tongue, but also on the surface of the palate, epiglottis, and throat. Certain distinctions are dependent on the sense of smell.

TATE, Nahum
(1652-1715) Eng. poet. He wrote tragedies, made an adaptation of *King Lear* (1681) and, with Nicholas Brady, a metrical version of the *Psalms* (1690).

TATE GALLERY
Brit. Nat. Art Gallery at Millbank, Westminster, London. It is named after Sir Henry Tate (1819-99), Brit. sugar merchant, who gave to the nation his collection of 65 paintings, together with £80,000 for a building. A Turner wing was added by Sir Joseph Duveen in 1910, and his son, Sir Joseph, presented the Sargent gallery in 1926. The scope of the collection has been widened to include modern foreign works.

TATTERSALLS
Horse Auction Mart in London famous throughout the world for nearly 200 years. The firm was founded by Richard Tattersall in 1766 to deal in horses and hounds, carriages and harness.

TAUBER, Richard
[tow′-] (1891-1948) Singer, conductor, and composer. B. Linz, Austria, he first appeared on the stage in 1912. His Eng. successes included *Old Chelsea* which he composed.

TAUNTON
Borough and county town of Somerset, on the Tone. An important agricultural centre and has manufactures of gloves, shirts, cider and agricultural machinery. Pop. 36,230.

TAUPO
[taw′-] Lake in the centre of N. Is., New Zealand, in a region of geysers and hot springs. Area: *c.* 240 sq.m.

TAURUS
[taw′-rus] (Lat. *bull*) Second sign of the Zodiac, operative *c.* April 21-May 20. The constellation of this name contains the first magnitude star Aldebaran, the Pleiades and the Hyades, and the Crab nebula.

TAVISTOCK
Urban district and market town of Devonshire, on the Tavy, 16 m. N. of Plymouth. Pop. 6,310.

TAXATION
Method of raising money from a people for the maintenance of the state. **Income Tax** (*q.v.*), a certain proportion of each person's income, is the most obvious type of direct taxation. Indirect taxes are derived from a general payment on some commodity or activity (*e.g.* Purchase Tax and Entertainment Tax).

TAY
River of Scot. which rises in the hills of W. Perthshire, and enters the sea in the Firth of Tay. **The Firth of T.** is crossed by a railway bridge. The first, opened in 1878, was destroyed by a storm 2 years later. The existing bridge was built between 1882 and 1887, and in 1966 a new road bridge was opened.

TAYLOR, Jeremy
(1613-67) Eng. divine. B. Camb.; entered Caius Coll. His *Holy Living* and *Holy Dying* are fine examples of devotional literature.

TAYLOR, Tom
(1817-80) Eng. playwright. B. in Sunderland, educ. Glasgow and Camb. He wrote more than 100 plays, *e.g. The Ticket of Leave Man* and *Our American Cousin.* In 1874 he edited *Punch.*

TBILISI
(formerly **Tiflis**) Cap. of Georgia, U.S.S.R., on the Kura, S. of the Caucasus Mts. It stands on the railway and oil pipe-line from the Caspian to the Black Sea. Pop. 794,000.

TCHAIKOVSKY, Peter Ilich
[chī-kof′-ski] (1840-93) Russ. composer. He was not a member of ' the Five ', the nationalist group, and his music is that of a Romantic cosmopolitan. His works include 8 complete operas, ballets, *The Swan Lake, The Sleeping Beauty, The Nutcracker,* 6 symphonies, 3 piano concertos, a violin concerto, some chamber music and nearly 100 songs.

TEA
The prepared leaf of the plant (*Thea sinensis*), long grown in China and introduced to Eng. by the Dutch in 1645. India, Ceylon and China provide most of Brit.'s tea.

TEAK
Asiatic timber tree (*Tectona grandis*), of the family Verbenacae. The wood is extremely hard and durable.

TEAL
(*Anas crecca*) Small duck of Europe and Asia. It is common throughout the year on Brit. inland waters.

TEASEL
(*Dipsacus fullonum*) Common Brit. biennial plant of the Dipsacaceae. The flower stems are 5-6 ft. high, rough and spiny with cylindrical flower heads of purple flowers. It is cultivated for use by cloth manufacturers for raising the nap of cloth.

TECHNICAL EDUCATION
Special training to equip the student to take his place in a trade or profession, given in a technical school or college. Modern technical educ. dates from the T. Instruction Act (1889). With the founding of the Imperial Coll. of Science and Technology in 1907, T.E. reached univ. status. The Robbins Report (1963) examined the whole structure of higher educ. and recommended considerable expansion of technical facilities. *See* EDUCATION.

TEDDER, Arthur William
(1890-1967) **1st Baron.** Marshal of the R.A.F. Entered Dorset Regt. as 2nd Lieut. 1913. Seconded to R.F.C. 1916. Granted permanent commission in R.A.F. as Squadron Leader, 1919. In 1934 he became Air Commodore and Director of Training. In 1938 he became Director-Gen. of Research and Development, and in 1940 Deputy Air Member for Development and Production (Min. of Aircraft Production). As Deputy Supreme Comm. under Gen. Eisenhower, 1943-5, was largely responsible for the initial success of the Normandy landings. Became Marshal of the R.A.F. 1945, Chief of Air Staff, 1946. He was made a Gov. of the B.B.C., 1950.

TEETH
A tooth is composed of dentine with a covering of hard chem. resisting material called enamel, usually white in colour. Each tooth is attached to the bone of the jaw by roots. Each person in a life-time has 2 sets of natural teeth. The first begin to appear at the 6th month and the set of 10 above and below is complete by the age of 2½ years. The second or permanent teeth begin to appear at 6 years and in the process of eruption push the milk teeth out. There are 32 permanent teeth. The common arrangement of teeth is 2 incisors, 1 canine and 2 molars in the first dentition, and 2 incisors, 1 canine, 2 bicuspids or pre-molars and 3 tricuspids or molars. The eruption of the permanent teeth is complete by the age of 20 years. *See* DENTIST.

TEHRAN
[tair-rán′] Cap. of Persia, S. of the Elburz Mts., 70 m. from the Caspian Sea. Carpets and cotton goods are manufactured. Pop. 1,900,000.

TEL-AVIV-JAFFA
[telă-vēv-] Largest port of Israel, on the Medit., *c.* 50 m. S. of Haifa. Pop. 386,612.

TEL-EL-AMARNA
Modern name given to an ancient site of ruins and rock tombs, on the Nile, 58 m. N. of Asyut. *See* AKHENATEN; AMENHOTEP III.

TELEGRAPH
Electrical apparatus devised to transmit messages to a distance. The first needle telegraph was patented by Cooke and Wheatstone in 1836. The Morse code is used for telegraphic mes-

sages. Recording is made automatically on a tape. In submarine telegraphy a siphon recorder invented by Lord Kelvin acts as a receiving instrument. The wireless telegraph is based upon similar principles, the messages being transmitted by electro-magnetic radiations.

TELEPATHY
Transference of thought from one person to another. The earliest recorded experiments were conducted by Sidgwick in 1871.

TELEPHONE
Electrical instrument by which sound is transmitted and reproduced at a distance. The first telephone capable of reproducing speech was invented by Graham Bell and exhibited at the Philadelphia Exhib. 1876. Improvements were made by Edison, and a carbon transmitter or microphone was devised by Prof. Hughes. The wireless telephone uses electromagnetic radiations for transmission. The first trans-Atlantic telephone cable service was formally opened in Sept. 1956.

TELESCOPE
Optical instrument for viewing distant objects. The simplest form of astron. telescope consists of 2 lenses placed one at each end of a tube. For astronomical observation a reflecting type is used. The two largest reflectors in the world are the 100-in. at Mt. Wilson and the 200-in. Halo at Mt. Palomar, Calif. In 1925 the former first showed the immensity of the universe and the latter has revealed a galaxy 1 million light yrs. distant. *See* ASTRONOMY, RADIO ASTRONOMY, RADIO TELESCOPE, COSMOLOGY.

TELEVISION
Transmission and reception of visual images using electro-magnetic radiation. At the transmitter an image of the scene to be televised is projected by lenses on to a sensitive surface consisting of a mosaic of tiny photo-electric elements each comprising a caesium globule. Electrons are emitted from the globules in proportion to the light falling on them. Periodically a beam of electrons is swept across the mosaic, touching each photo-element in turn and replenishing it with electrons; in this way a current is caused to flow in an external circuit connected to the mosaic. This is used to modulate a high-frequency carrier wave. At the receiver, the amplified signal is used to vary the intensity of another electron beam sweeping across a fluorescent screen exactly in step with that at the transmitter. *See* BROADCASTING; B.B.C.; INDEPENDENT TELEVISION AUTHORITY.

TELFORD, Thomas
(1757-1834) Scot. engineer. B. Eskdale. He was chosen by the Govt. to report on the Scots roads, and became engineer for the Caledonian Canal. He was also responsible for many hundred m. of roads, numerous bridges and harbours.

TELL, William
Swiss legendary hero. According to tradition he was compelled to shoot an apple from his son's head and led a popular rising against the tyranny of Austria.

TELLURIUM
Non-metallic element having the sym. Te and at. wt. 127·6. Related to sulphur and selenium. It is found chiefly as a telluride in combination with bismuth, gold, silver, etc.

TELSTAR *See* SATELLITE.

TEMPERANCE
Movement which aims at reducing or ending the consumption of alcohol as a beverage. It originated in 1826. *See* PROHIBITION.

TEMPERATURE
Condition of hotness or coldness of a body that determines the transfer of heat energy to other bodies. Two bodies are at the same temp. when the mutual interchange of heat is the same, but if the one body transmits more heat than it receives from the other, the first is said to be at a higher temp. The thermal range is measured in units or degrees of temp. by means of a thermometer. The human body in health is about 98·4° F. but in fevers may rise to 106° F., or higher, while in collapse it may fall to 80° F. or lower.

TEMPLE
Building for worship. The earliest Jewish temple was that built by Micah, but the most famous was that of Solomon, the centre of Jewish nat. worship at Jerusalem. The Mosque of Omar now occupies the site; only the 'Wailing Wall' remains. Egyptian temples reached their apogee in Karnak. Later came rectangular Gk. and Rom. temples.

TEMPLE, William
(1881-1944) Eng. archbishop. Headmaster of Repton School. He was Rector of St. James's, Piccadilly, 1914, and Archbp. of Canterbury, 1942.

TENCH
(*Tinca vulgaris*) Freshwater fish related to the carp, a native of Europe and Asia Minor. It grows to a length of 16 in. and a wt. of 4 lb. It frequents the muddy bed of rivers and passes the winter buried there.

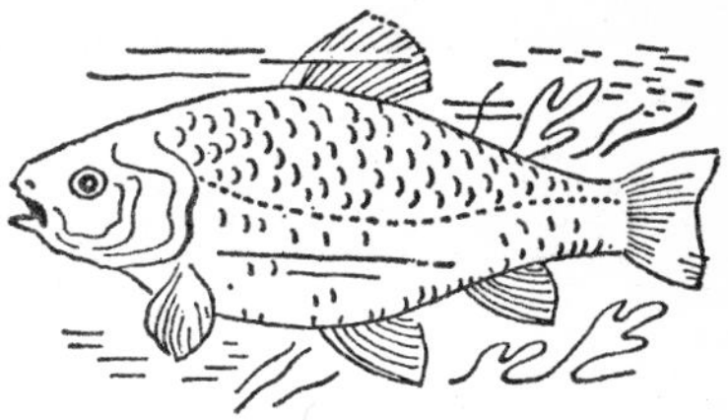

TENERIFE
Largest of the Canary Is. (*q.v.*) in the Sp. prov. Santa Cruz de T.

TENIERS
[ten'-yerz] Family of Flemish painters of the 17th cent. **David T. the Elder** (1582-1649) was a pupil of Rubens. His canvases are either mythological or rustic in subject. **David T. the Younger** (1610-90) was a greater painter than his father.

TENNESSEE
S. state of the U.S.A. bounded by the Mississippi and the Appalachian Mts. and Kentucky in the N. In the E. there is the Cumberland Plateau, while the W. is lowland. The T. river rises in Virginia, and flows through the state to join the Ohio. Agriculture is important, the chief crops include cereals, cotton and tobacco. There are extensive forests, and lumbering is carried on. Nashville is the cap. but Memphis is the largest town. T. first settled in 1757, became a state in 1796, now sending 9 representatives to Congress. Area: 42,250 sq.m. Pop. 3,924,200.

TENNIEL, Sir John
(1820-1914) Eng. caricaturist. He became world-famous through his long connection with *Punch* (1850-1901). He also illustrated *Alice in Wonderland, Through the Looking Glass*, the *Ingoldsby Legends*, etc.

TENNIS
Ball game. It is played in a walled court divided by a net, and from it the modern game of lawn tennis has developed. Henry VIII built a court at Hampton Court. The game is still played. *See* LAWN TENNIS.

TENNYSON, Alfred, Lord
(1809-92) Eng. poet. B. at Somersby, Lincs. In 1827 *Poems, by Two Brothers* (Alfred and Charles) appeared; then *Poems, Chiefly Lyrical*

(1830), and *Poems* 1832, 1842. In 1850 he succeeded Wordsworth as poet laureate and pub. *In Memoriam* (on his friend Arthur Hallam, *q.v.*). *Maud* was pub. 1855, *The Idylls of the King* in instalments in 1859, '60, '72; *Tiresias*, *Locksley Hall* (1886); also plays.

TENZING NORKAY
(1914-) Nepalese mountaineer. Porter on many Brit. Everest expeditions, culminating in 1953, when on Col. John Hunt's expedition he and Edmund Hillary (*q.v.*) were the first men to reach the summit.

TEREBINTH
(or **Chian Turpentine**) Tree (*Pistacia terebinthus*), of the family Anacardiaceae. It is a native of S. Europe and the Levant. An oleoresin from the trunk is used in medicine.

TEREDO
[-rē'-] Molluscs found in the submerged timber of ships, piers, etc. The young estab. themselves in timber, forming burrows by the action of their 2 small shell valves. These run in all directions and render infected timbers useless.

TERENCE
(195-159 B.C.) Latin comic poet. (**Publius Terentius Afer**). He was a slave, but his talents gained him his freedom. His extant comedies include *Andria*, *Eunuchus*, *Phormio*, *Adelphi*.

TERMITE
Insect of order *Isoptera*. It is not an ant although it is colloq. called White Ant. Termites are social in habit. Colonies consist of kings and queens, wingless workers of both sexes, and soldiers. The insects build galleries in wood and can cause enormous damage to houses, furniture, etc. Many species are found in Amer. In Africa they build galleried mounds which may reach 20 ft. high and extend the same distance below ground.

TERN
Sea bird of the Gull family (*Sterna hirundo*). The Common T. has a black head and nape of neck, grey, black, white rump and underparts. The legs are short, the wings long and pointed. It is a summer visitor to Brit. inland and coastal waters.

TERRA COTTA
Variety of reddish bricklike earthenware. It was used for decorative purposes by the Gks., in Italy during the M.A., and in Eng. during the 19th cent.

TERRAPIN
Various amphibious Tortoises. One species, *Malacoclemmys terrapin*, found in the salt marshes of the E. shores of N. Amer. is used as food. *See* TORTOISE, TURTLE.

TERRIER
Breed of dog. Light and nimble, with short muzzles and relatively large heads, they are intelligent and brave. Popular breeds include Eng. Smooth Coat 'Fox' Terrier; the Rough-haired Scotch Terrier; the Skye Terrier, with long body and large ears; the small Maltese Terrier; and the Bull Terrier.

TERRITORIAL ARMY
Part of the Brit. Army, estabd. under the Territorial and Reserve Forces Act of 1907 by Lord Haldane. In 1965 amalgamation with Army Emergency Reserve to form 50,000-strong force known as Terr. Reserve was proposed.

TERRITORIAL WATERS
Belt of sea surrounding the coast of a state and subject to its jurisdiction. Recent internat. legislation has increased national limits.

TERROR
Extinct volcano of Ross Is., Antarctica, 11,000 ft. high.

TERRY, Dame Ellen Alicia
(1848-1928) Eng. actress. In 1875 she made a sensation as Portia, under the Bancrofts. In Dec. 1878 there began her assoc. with Irving at the Lyceum.

TERTIARY
[ter'-sher-i] Geological group of systems of strata, lying above the Cretaceous rocks. During the Tertiary age mammals finally approached existing genera.

TERTULLIAN
(*c.* 155-222) Christian theologian. He was the founder of a Christian Lat. lit. and influenced Cyprian and Augustine.

TERYLENE
Synthetic fibre, first produced in Brit. in 1941. The main raw materials which are used are paraxylene, ethylene glycol and methanol. (Protected Trade Name).

TESTES
Male sex glands situated in pouch or scrotum.

TETANUS
[tet'-ăn-ŭs] Infective disease caused by toxins of *Bacillus* (*Clostrudium*) *tetani*, popularly called lock-jaw. Infection occurs chiefly by the contamination of wounds with soil. This disease has a mortality of 45-70%.

TETRADYMITE
['-im-īt] Mineral consisting of bismuth telluride and sulphide occurring in assoc. with gold.

TETTRAZZINI, Luisa
[-tra-tsē'-] (1871-1940) Ital. soprano. B. Florence. She studied with Ceccherini there, and made her début in Florence, 1895. She first appeared in London in 1907, and in the U.S.A. in 1908.

TETZEL, Johann
(*c.* 1455-1519) Dominican monk. In 1517 he travelled in Germany, selling indulgences to assist Pope Leo X in raising funds for the building of St. Peter's, Rome. Luther nailed his famous 95 theses on the ch. door at Wittenberg, attacking this abuse and others. Indirectly this led to the Reformation in Germany.

TEWKESBURY
Borough and market town of Gloucs., on the Avon, 8 m. N. of Cheltenham, famous for its abbey church. Pop. 5,880.

TEXAS
Largest and most S. state of the U.S.A., on the Mexican border with a coastline on the Gulf of Mexico. The chief rivers are the Rio Grande, Colorado, Pecos, Brazos and Red. It is an important agricultural state. Minerals include petroleum, lignite and cement. Austin is the cap. but Houston, Dallas, San Antonio, Fort Worth and El Paso are larger. Once part of Mexico, T. became indep. in 1836, and entered the Union, 1846, sending 23 representatives to Congress. Area: 267,340 sq.m. Pop. 11,197,000.

TEXEL
Dutch Is. the most W. of the Frisian group, off the coast of N. Holland prov. Burg is the chief town.

THACKERAY, William Makepeace
(1811-63) Eng. writer. He took up, successively, law, journalism and art (in Paris). *The Professor* and *Yellowplush Papers* appeared in 1837. He joined *Punch* in 1842. *Vanity Fair* was pub. in monthly parts (1847-83). *Pendennis* and *Henry Esmond* followed. *The Newcomes* appeared in 1853-5. He ed. *The Cornhill Magazine* 1860-62.

THAILAND
(formerly **Siam**) Kingdom of S.E. Asia, bounded by Burma and Laos and Cambodia and extending S. into the Malay Peninsula. The land slopes S. from the mts. of the interior

to the wide plain of the Menam and its tributaries. Rice, rubber, teak and tin are the chief products of the country. There are numerous rice mills but few industries. Tin, wolfram, rubies and sapphires are mined. Bangkok, on the Menam delta, is the cap. and largest city. The predominant religion is Buddhism. T. is a sovereign indep. state gov. by a king. During World War II Thailand was allied with Japan. Area: *c.* 198,000 sq.m. Pop. 30,000,000.

THALES
[thā'-lēz] (*c.* 640-550 B.C.) Gk. philosopher. B. Miletus, and regarded as one of the 7 wise men of Greece.

THALLIUM
Rare metallic element; sym. Tl; at. wt. 204·39. It is widely diffused in small quantities in iron pyrites, chalcopyrites, mica and lepidolite. It is a soft, heavy, white metal resembling lead and readily tarnishes on exposure to air.

THAMES
[temz] River of Eng. which rises in several head streams in the Cotswold Hills and flows in an E. direction to its estuary in the N. Sea. From Lechlade in Glos. to the Nore it is 210 m. long, the last 60 being from London Bridge to the open sea. It flows past Oxford, Reading, and other places, and is crossed by a number of bridges, esp. in the London area. The lowest is Tower Bridge. Below this the banks are linked by tunnels, and by ferries. At London Bridge the river is 300 yds. wide and at the Nore 6 m. It is tidal to Teddington; from there to Oxford it is given up almost entirely to boating and angling. Below Teddington it is a commercial river controlled by the Port of London Authority. Below London Bridge there are many docks handling great quantities of cargo.

THANET
District, sometimes called an Is. of N. Kent. On it are Margate, Ramsgate, Broadstairs and Ebbsfleet.

THEBES
[thēbz] Ancient city of Boeotia (Greece). It appears very early as a flourishing city, with 7 gates, the rival of neighbouring Athens. In 371 B.C. at the Battle of Leuctra, T. defeated Sparta.

THEBES
[thēbz'] Gk. name for an ancient city of the Upper Nile. It reached the zenith of its greatness in the 18th and 19th Dynasties under Rameses II. It has a giant necropolis, the colossus of Rameses II, the temples of Karnak and Luxor, and the colossi of Memnon.

THEISM
Belief in the existence of God, and in His influence upon the world. Theism corresponds to the natural theol. of the Roms. and, in its exclusion of polytheism, has been extensively meditated through the ages.

THEMISTOCLES
(*c.* 525-*c.* 460 B.C.) Athenian general and statesman, polit. leader in Athens after the ostracism of Aristides (482). In 480 B.C. he inflicted a crushing defeat near the Is. of Salamis on the Persians under Xerxes. This victory and others made Athens the foremost maritime power of the period.

THEOBALD, Lewis
(1688-1744) Eng. writer. Attacked Pope's ed. of Shakespeare (*Shakespeare Restored* 1726). His own ed. of Shakespeare 1734 has many valuable emendations.

THEOCRITUS
Gk. bucolic poet (*c.* 276 B.C.). Prob. of Syracuse. His extant work consists of *c.* 30 Idylls, poems and epigrams.

THEODORA
(*c.* 508-548) Byzantine empress. The mistress and then the wife of Justinian I, over whom she exercised much influence.

THEODORIC the Great
(*c.* A.D. 454-526). He led the E. Goths from Pannonia over the Alps in 487, defeated Odoacer at Aquileia and Verona, and after the capture of Ravenna in 493 founded the Ostrogoth Empire.

THEODOSIUS I
(The Great) (*c.* A.D. 346-395) Rom. Emperor. After the d. of Gratian and Valentinian II he became (the last) sole ruler. Soon after his d. began the barbarian invasions which eventually led to the overthrow of the empire.

THEOSOPHY
[thē-os'-] Various ancient and modern systems of *esoteric* religion and philosophy. In general the teaching is that *all* exoteric religions are expressions of one esoteric Truth.

THERAPEUTICS
Medical term applied to the science and treatment of disease. *See* MEDICINE, SURGERY, etc.

THERESA, Saint
(1515-82) Spanish nun. Teresa de Cepeda was b. in Avila, and educ. at the Augustinian convent there. When 18, she entered the Carmelite convent of the Incarnation. In 1554 while she was at prayer in the oratory she was overcome by an image of the wounded Christ. From then onwards she began to experience conditions of trance which persisted throughout the remainder of her life. She was also instrumental in re-establishing the severe discipline which prevailed when the Order was first instituted. She was canonised by Pope Gregory XV in 1622.

THERMIDOR
11th month of Fr. revolutionary calendar (July).

THERMIT
Mixture of aluminium powder and a metallic oxide, usually that of iron, used for producing high localised temps. for welding iron or steel rails, etc.

THERMOMETER
Instrument for measuring variations in temperature by the expansion or contraction of a liquid or gas. The thermometric scale used in English-speaking countries was that of Fahrenheit with the freezing pt. of water as 32° and its boiling pt. at 212°, but the Centigrade scale with 0° as freezing pt. and 100° as boiling pt. is being substituted. See below.

THERMOPYLAE
Pass of Greece between the mountains and the sea on the E. coast. Here, in 480 B.C. *c.* 300 Gks. under Leonidas, King of Sparta, defended the pass against a Persian army. The Persians, by treachery, got to the rear of the Gks. who were all killed.

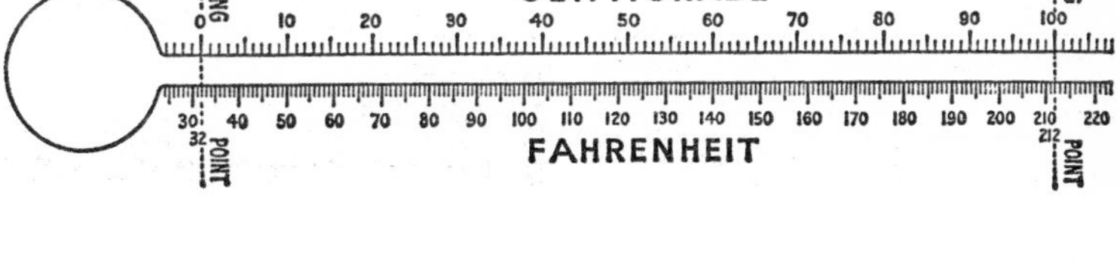

THESEUS
Legendary hero of Attica. The son of Egeus, King of Athens, he performed many marvellous feats.

THESPIS
Gk. dramatist of the 6th cent. B.C. Regarded as the founder of the drama, as he introduced an actor to assist the chorus in the festivals held in honour of Bacchus.

THESSALONIANS, Epistles to
Two N.T. books. They appear to have been written by Paul to the Ch. at Thessalonica.

THESSALONIKI
(formerly **Salonika**) Gk. city and seaport in Macedonia, at the head of the Gulf of Thermai, E. of the Vardar delta. Industries include the manufacture of tobacco, leather and cotton goods and brewing. The scene of bitter fighting in World War II. Pop. 250,000.

THIERS, Louis Adolphe
(1797-1877) Fr. statesman and writer. Between 1823-7 he wrote his *Histoire de la Revolution Française*. Elected Deputy for Aix in 1830, he became Pres. of the Council. Resigning in 1836, in 1840 he was again Pres. of the Council and Foreign Min. Exiled for a year after Louis Napoleon's *coup d'état*, after the fall of the empire in 1870, he negotiated for peace. From 1871-3 he was Pres. of the Repub.

THIRTY-NINE ARTICLES
Creed of the Ch. of E. They were adopted by the united convocations in 1563 and became law by Act. of Parl. 1571. Since 1604 no change has been made in them.

THIRTY YEARS' WAR
(1618-48) A general European war, mainly fought in Germany. The offer of the Bohemian crown to the Lutheran prince, Frederick, Elector Palatine, son-in-law of James I of Gt. Brit. was followed by the defeat of Frederick and the seizure of his lands by the Emperor Ferdinand. The German Protestant princes and Gustavus Adolphus of Sweden then carried on the struggle for Protestantism against Catholicism but after the d. of Gustavus the war became a polit. struggle between the Habsburgs and Spain on the one side, and Fr. on the other. It ended in 1648 with the signing of the Treaty of Westphalia (*q.v.*).

THISTLE
Name of many plants with prickly stems, leaves, etc. They belong chiefly to the genus *Carduus* of the family Compositae. Some of the varieties are the spear thistle, specially assoc. with Scot., the dwarf thistle and the musk thistle. **Order of the T.** Scots order of knighthood founded by James II in 1687 and dedicated to St. Andrew. The motto is *Nemo*

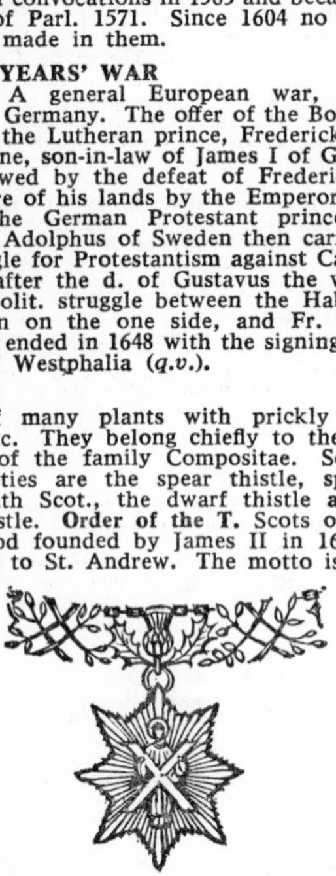

me impune lacessit. The chapel is in St. Giles' Cath., Edinburgh.

THOMAS
Called Didymus (*the twin*); 1 of the 12 apostles. He is known as 'doubting Thomas', on account of his disbelief in Christ's resurrection until he had received personal proof.

THOMAS, Ambroise
(1811-96) Fr. composer. He studied at the Paris Conservatoire, 1828, became its director, 1871. His compositions include ballets, cantatas, and songs.

THOMAS, Dylan Marlais
(1914-53) Welsh poet. Worked as reporter, then radio and film script-writer. His works, *18 Poems* (1934), *Portrait of the Artist as a Young Dog* (stories) (1940), *Deaths and Entrances* (1946), and verse for documentary film *Our Country* (1945), *Collected Poems of Dylan Thomas* (1952). *Under Milk Wood* (play) was pub. posthumously (1954).

THOMPSON, Francis
(1859-1907) Eng. R.C. poet. In 1885 he went to London, began to take opium, became destitute but found good friends in Wilfrid and Alice Meynell. In 1893 his masterpiece, *The Hound of Heaven* was pub. with other poems.

THOMSON, James
(1700-48) Scot. poet. B. Ednam near Kelso, went to London 1725. *The Seasons* appeared in 4 parts (1726-30), *The Castle of Indolence* (1748).

THOMSON, Sir Joseph John
O.M. F.R.S. (1856-1940) Eng. scientist. From 1884-1918 he was Cavendish Prof. of Experimental Physics in Camb. He was awarded the Nobel Prize for Physics in 1906. His work included the discovery of the electron (1897) and the first experiment on mass spectra (1912).

THOREAU, Henry David
(1817-62) Amer. writer. For several years he lived with Emerson. *Walden, A Life in the Woods* (1854) is a description of 2 years spent alone in a shanty in the forest. His other works include *Excursions* (1863), and essays.

THORIUM
A rare metallic element, important in atomic physics as one of the materials capable of fission (*q.v.*). Sp. gr. 11·2. Chem. sym. Th.

THORNDIKE, Dame Sybil
(1882-) Eng. actress. She studied for the stage at Ben Greet's Academy and made her début in *The Merry Wives of Windsor*. She was a prominent member of Miss Horniman's Co. in Manchester. Her London début was in 1908 at the Scala. She was awarded the D.B.E. 1941. She is mar. to **Sir Lewis Casson** (*q.v.*).

THORNYCROFT, Sir William Hamo
(1850-1925) Eng. sculptor. Among his many statues, or memorials, are *Queen Victoria*, at the Royal Exchange; *General Gordon*, in Trafalgar Square; *John Bright*, in Rochdale.

THREE ESTATES, The
In terms of the constitution of Gt. Brit., the 3 estates are the *Lords Spiritual*, the *Lords Temporal* and the *Commons*. Edmund Burke (1729-97) introduced the term *The Fourth Estate* for the Brit. Press.

THREE RIVERS
River port of Quebec, Canada, at the confluence of the St. Lawrence and St. Maurice, 70 m. S.W. of Quebec. Pop. 53,477.

THRIFT
Perennial plant (*Armeria vulgaris*) of the family Plumbaginaceae, also known as the *sea pink*. The soft, rosy flower heads rise on slender, hairy stems from the tufts of leaves.

THROAT
Front part of neck from chin above to collar bone below. Contains pharynx, larynx, trachea and oesophagus as well as muscles, blood vessels and nerves.

THROMBOSIS
Clotting of blood in artery or vein resulting in blockage of vessel and d. of surrounding tissues.

THRUSH
or Throstle (*Turdus*) Birds allied to which are the Ousel, Stonechat, Robin and Hedge-sparrow. Inhabiting the Brit. Is., their eggs are sea green with black spots.

THRUSH
Infectious disease of mouth and throat common in debilitated babies and old people.

THUCYDIDES
Athenian historian (*c.* 471-399 B.C.). His *History of the Peloponnesian War* (423-403 B.C.) is remarkably impartial and scholarly.

THURSDAY ISLAND
Smallest of the Prince of Wales group in the Torres Strait, 30 m. N.W. of Cape York, Queensland. It is the centre of the pearl-shell fisheries. Pop. 1,100.

THURSO
Burgh and seaport of N. Caithness, 154 m. from Inverness, terminus of the steamer route to the Orkney and Shetland Is. Pop. 8,713.

THYLACINE
(*Thylacinus*) Nearly extinct nocturnal Tasmanian marsupial, with dog-like head. It is destructive to sheep.

THYME
[tīm] Genus of small, aromatic shrubs (*Thymus*) of the family Labiatae. The wild thyme (*T. serpyllum*) is found on downs and hillsides. *T. vulgaris*, the garden thyme, is used for flavouring food.

THYMOL
Crystalline substance of the phenol group, present in the volatile oil of thyme and forming 50 % of oil of ajowan. It is an antiseptic and germicide.

THYMUS GLAND
Ductless gland, thought to influence the stimulation of growth, and to influence the central nervous system.

THYROID GLAND
One of the group of endocrine glands. Situated in the neck with one half on either side of trachea. Lack of secretion of this gland results in cretinism in children and myxoedema in adults, conditions which can be cured by thyroid extract. Over-secretion produces thyrotoxicosis or toxic goitre. *See* CRETINISM; MYXOEDEMA; GOITRE.

TIBER
[tī'-] River of C. Italy on which Rome stands. It rises in the Apennines and flows S. for 240 m. entering the Tyrrhenian Sea near Ostia.

TIBERIAS
Lake of Israel, 65 m. N. of the Dead Sea, 680 ft. below sea level.

TIBERIUS
(42 B.C.-A.D. 37) Rom. Emperor. Son of Tiberius Claudius Nero and Livia. By Livia's influence, Tiberius succeeded in A.D. 14. His reign was prosperous for the Empire.

TIBET
Country of C. Asia between India and China. It is a mountainous area, bounded by the Himalayas on the S. and the Kun Lun Mts. in the N. The country contains the source of the Indus, Sutlej, Brahmaputra, Salween and Mekong. Rice, barley and fruit are grown, and yaks, sheep and pigs are reared. The chief city is Lhasa. Lamaism is the religion. T. came under the influence of Mongolia and China in the M.A. Early in the 18th cent. the Emp. of China invaded the country and T. remained under Chinese authority until *c.* 1912. In 1950 Communist China claimed T. and sent troops to the E. part of the country. In 1959 there was a revolt against the Communist régime and the Dalai Lama fled to India. Area: *c.* 470,000 sq.m. Pop. *c.* 6,000,000.

TICKS
The largest members of the order of mites (Acarida). They are parasitic animals having oval or rounded bodies and possess a piercing and sucking proboscis.

TIDE
Regular ebb and flow of the oceans, due to the attraction of moon and sun. The lunar force predominates. The waters are drawn into a long wave, whose crests (high tide) are antipodal with corresponding troughs (low tide) between them. The highest, *spring tides*, occur at, or near, new and full moon. The lowest, or *neap tides*, occur when the moon is in the 1st or 3rd quarter.

TIENTSIN
City and port of Hopei prov. China, where the Grand Canal joins the Peiho, *c.* 70 m. S.E. of Peking. Pop. 3,220,000.

TIERRA DEL FUEGO
[tyair'-a del fwā'-gō] Group of Is. at the extreme S. of S. Amer. Divided between Chile and Argentina, the Is. are separated by the Straits of Magellan from the mainland. They were discovered by Magellan in 1520. The S. point is C. Horn.

TIFLIS *See* TBILISI.

TIGER
(*Felis tigris*) Large carnivore of the family Felidae. Widely distributed throughout Asia, it inhabits jungle and forest regions, preying on smaller mammals. The body is 6 ft. long with a 3-ft. tail, and at the shoulder the adult Tiger stands 3 ft. high. The fur is reddish-brown above, with black striping on head, limbs, body and tail.

TIGER-BEETLE
(*Cicindela campestris*) A species of swift and active beetles which preys upon other insects.

TIGER-LILY
(*Lilium tigrinum*) Bulbous plant of the family Liliaceae. It is a Chinese variety of lily, 3 or 4 ft. high, with handsome orange-red blooms.

TIGER-MOTH
(*Arctia caja*) Red and brown moth whose caterpillars are popularly named ' woolly bears '.

TIGRIS
River of the M.E. which rises in the mts. of Kurdistan, and flows S.E. for *c.* 1,150 m. through Iraq, joining the Euphrates to form the Shatt-el-Arab. Mosul and Baghdad are on its banks.

TILBURY
Urban district of Essex, having important docks on the Thames, 22 m. from London. Pop. 18,387.

TILE
Thin, flat slab of marble, stone or baked clay, glazed or unglazed, and used in the structure or decoration of a building.

TILSIT *See* SOVIETSK.

TIMBUKTU
Town in Mali, on the S. edge of the Sahara. Pop. 7,000.

TIME
Primitive peoples observed that Nature had her own times and seasons, *i.e.* that day, lunar month, and year were units of measurement. The sun appears to rise in the E. at dawn, to cross the sky, and to set in the W., and in the middle latitudes it was observed that the day was long or short according to the period of the solar year. Furthermore men observed that there was correspondence between the spring and autumn equinoxes and the summer and winter solstices. A sundial keeps time by solar days, but these are not absolutely uniform in length. They would be so only if there were no variations in the inclination of the earth's

axis, nor of the speed of its motion in its orbit. Such variations are overcome by *Greenwich Mean Time*. The zero of the Greenwich Mean Time scale is the instant at which the ' mean sun ', which is sometimes ahead of and sometimes behind the real sun, is on the geographical meridian of Greenwich. At intervals throughout the day the B.B.C. broadcasts 6 pips, the last of which is the exact moment of G.M.T. and ships' chronometers are regulated by this signal. Midway in the Pacific Ocean, where time differs from G.M.T. by 12 hours, is the ' International Date Line ' where ships proceeding W. lose a day (by putting the date forward) and ships moving E. lose a day (by putting the date back).

TIMES, The
London newspaper, regarded as the country's premier journal. It was founded in 1785 by John Walter and was called *The Daily Universal Register* till 1788.

TIMOR
E. Ind. Is. lying between Flores and N. Australia, divided in 1859 between Portugal and Holland. The E. portion, with neighbouring Is. forms a Portuguese colony, cap. Dili. Area: 7,300 sq.m. Pop. 517,079. The remainder of the Is. is part of the Repub. of Indonesia (*q.v.*).

TIMOTHY
Saint and companion of St. Paul. He helped to found chs. in Macedon and did important missionary work in Corinth, Thessaloniki and Philippi, and later in Asia minor. **Epistles to T.** 2 books of the N.T. The traditional view that they were written by the apostle Paul has not been disproved.

TIMOTHY-GRASS
(*Phleum pratense*) A hard, coarse grass, with cylindrical spikes from 2-6 ins. long and usually mixed with other grasses for permanent pasture.

TIMPANI *See* DRUM.

TIN
A silvery metallic element, occurring chiefly as the oxide. Its principal use is as a protective coating for metal containers and plates, because of its resistance to corrosion. Sp. gr. 5·75, 6·6, 7·3. Chem. sym. Sn.

TINTAGEL
Village of Cornwall. On T. Head are the ruins of a castle which legend associates with King Arthur.

TINTERN
Village of Monmouthshire, on the Wye, 5 m. N. of Chepstow, famous for the ruins of its abbey.

TINTORETTO
Jacopo Robusti. Ital. painter (1518-94). B. Venice; studied under Titian. His skill in portraiture, in composition, drawing, colour and general conception caused Ruskin to rank him among the ' five supreme painters '.

TIPPERARY
Inland county of Munster, Eire. In it are the Galtee Mts. and other ranges of hills, but in the centre and the W. is the fertile Golden Vale. The Shannon, Suir and Nore are the chief rivers. Milk and butter are produced, and there is a little coal mining. Clonmel is the county town. Pop. 123,822. **Tipperary.** Urban district and market town of Tipperary, Eire, 110 m. S.W. of Dublin. It is a centre for the sale of farm produce. Pop. 5,300.

TIPPETT, Sir Michael
(1905-) Eng. composer. One of his most moving compositions is his cantata, *A Child of Our Time*. Among other works are a symphony, 3 string quartets, and a concerto for double string orchestra, etc.

TIPPU SAHIB
(1753-99) Sultan of Mysore. His invasion of Travancore in 1789 led to a 3 years' sanguinary war. His implacable hatred of the Brit. led him to stir up further strife, and he was killed during the storming of his cap. Seringapatam.

TIRANA
[-rä'-] Cap. of Albania. Pop. 140,300.

TIREE
[tī-rē'] Is. of the Inner Hebrides, in Argyllshire, 19 m. N.W. of Iona.

TIROL
Alpine prov. of Aust., bounded by Germany and Italy. It is mountainous and forested. The Inn is the chief river, and Innsbruck the cap.

TIRPITZ,
(1) **Alfred Friedrich von** (1849-1930) German admiral. Became Lord High Admiral 1911. His aim was to make Germany a great naval power. He commanded the navy from Aug. 1914 to Mar. 1916. He entered the Reichstag in 1921 as a nat. deputy. (2) One of the 2 most powerful battleships built by Germany and commissioned during World War II.

TISSOT, James Joseph Jacques
[tē-sō] (1836-1902) Fr. painter. During the war of 1870-1 he left Paris for London, where he soon attracted attention by his caricatures in *Vanity Fair*.

TIT
Small passerine bird of the family Paridae. Natives of N. Europe and Asia, some 7 species are found in Brit. They are tree-living birds.

Blue and Crested Tits

The Tomtit or Blue T. (*Parus coeruleus*) is *c.* 4½ in. long. The heads, wings and tail are blue, upper parts greenish-yellow, yellowish beneath, throat being black. The Long-tailed, Bearded and Marsh T. are common; the Great T. is general in the Brit. Is. except in the far N.; the Crested T. is confined to a few districts in Scot.

TITANIC DISASTER
The mammoth White Star liner, *Titanic*, 46,000 tons, 852 ft. long, struck an iceberg near Cape Race on April 14, 1912, during her maiden voyage. She sank with the loss of 1,600 lives.

TITANIUM
A white metal, one of the few which will burn in air, and the only one which will burn in nitrogen. It is a constituent of a few alloys. It was discovered in 1789 by Gregor, and forms about 0·6 % of the earth's crust. Sp. gr. 4·5. Chem. sym. Ti.

TITHE
Ancient tax, being a levy of 1-10th of a man's estate, *i.e.* its produce, payable to the Ch.

TITIAN
[tish'-] **Tiziano Vecelli** (*c.* 1490-1576) Ital. painter. Was sent as a child to Venice. There he became the pupil of Giovanni and Gentile Bellini, and Giorgione. He is one of the greatest portrait painters and colourists in the hist. of art.

TITICACA
[titi-kä′-kă] Lake in the Andes, on the boundary between Peru and Bolivia. At an altitude of over 12,600 ft., it covers 3,200 sq.m.

TITO
[tē′-tō] **Josip Broz, Marshal** (1892-) Pres. of Yugoslavia since 1953. A Communist agitator, he spent some time in Russia and fought on the Repub. side in Sp. After the German invasion of Yugoslavia he organised the Partisan Nat. Army of Liberation, which fought a guerrilla war against the occupying forces. After the liberation he became Min. of Nat. Defence and virtual dictator. He governed on Communist lines, in close assoc. with Russia, until in 1948 he was expelled from the Cominform for 'nationalist deviation'.

TITUS
(A.D. 40-81) Rom. Emperor **T. Flavius Sabinus Vespasianus,** son of Vespasian (*q.v.*). The terrible eruption of Vesuvius occurred during the first year of his reign. He completed the Colosseum.

TIVERTON
Borough of Devon, 12 m. N. of Exeter, on the Exe. An agricultural centre, it has breweries, flour-mills and a silk industry. Blundell's School, founded in 1604, is outside the town. Pop. 12,770.

TOAD
(*Bufo*) Toads resemble Frogs in the metamorphosis, etc. but their skin is dry, with glands exuding an acid secretion; there are no teeth and the legs are shorter. After the larval stage Toads are land dwellers. Brit. species are the Common Toad (*B. vulgaris*), which has a wrinkled, warty skin; and the Natterjack (*B. calamita*) of sandy regions.

TOAD FLAX
Genus of plants (*Linaria*) of the family Scrophulariaceae. The yellow toad flax (*L. vulgaris*) has a creeping rootstock, tufts of long, narrow leaves and bright yellow flowers resembling the snapdragon. The ivy toad flax (*L. cymbalaria*) has slender trailing stems, dark-green leaves and purple-blue blossoms.

TOADSTOOL
Mushroom-like fungi other than the mushroom (*q.v.*) itself. Some species are definitely known to be poisonous; others may be innocuous.

TOBACCO
Plant of genus *Nicotiana,* extensively used as a narcotic in chewing, snuff and smoking through cigars, pipes and cigarettes. Natives smoking cigars were seen by Columbus in 1492 and tobacco chewing was observed in 1502, in Amer. Tobacco was first brought to Europe by Francisco Fernandes. The U.S.A. still yields the largest supply, but Mexico, Germany, Russia, China and Turkey produce large quantities for export. Tobacco is an important source of revenue, high duty being paid in Brit.

TOBAGO
Is. in the W. Indies, 21 m. N.E. of Trinidad (*q.v.*) with which it forms an indep. state of the Brit. Commonw. Copra, cocoa, livestock and vegetables are exported. Scarborough is the chief town. Area: 120 sq.m. Pop. 33,333.

TOBIT, Book of
Apocryphal book of the O.T. It is thought to date from *c.* 250 B.C.

TOBOGGANING
Winter sport. It was prob. copied from the devices of Amer. Indians for sliding down steep snow-covered hills. It has been perfected in Switzerland, where specially prepared runs, such as the Cresta at St. Moritz, are available for annual championships.

TOBRUK
Seaport on coast of Libya. During World War II it was taken by the Allies in 1941, besieged for a year and taken by the Axis in June, 1942. Finally captured by S. Africans in Nov. 1942.

TOC H
Organisation of Christian fellowship and social service incorp. by royal charter in 1922. It originated during World War I at Poperinghe, where Talbot House, founded by the **Rev. P. T. B. Clayton,** served as a club and a ch. for soldiers from Dec. 1915.

TOGO
Repub. of W. Africa, once Fr., indep. 1960, cap. Lomé. Area: *c.* 20,000 sq.m. Pop. 1,724,000. Formerly a German colony. **Brit. T.,** the W. portion, was attached to the Gold Coast for admin. purposes. In 1957 Gold Coast became indep. as Ghana (*q.v.*) In 1960 Repub. of T. was set up as an indep state. A new constitution was adopted and Mr. Olympio was elected Pres. A milit. *coup* in 1963 resulted in the assass. of the Pres. and the overthrow of his govt.

TOKAY
Town of N.E. Hungary, famous for wine. **Imperial T.** is a liqueur made from the juice of over-ripe grapes.

TOKYO
Cap. city of Jap. Emp. in Honshu Is. on the Sumida. The city contains the imperial palace, the univ., numerous temples and Govt. buildings. Founded in the 16th cent. and called Yedo until 1868, T. suffered severely from an earthquake in 1923. Pop. 8,893,000.

TOLEDO
[tō-lā′-dō] City of C. Sp., cap. of T. prov. on the Tagus, 45 m. S. of Madrid. It was a Rom., Gothic and Moorish centre, and later the Castilian cap. Pop. 42,100.

TOLPUDDLE MARTYRS
Six labourers who lived in Tolpuddle in Dorset, and who had formed a 'friendly society of agricultural labourers' through which they hoped to obtain a weekly wage of 10/-, were charged with 'administering unlawful oaths'. This would be trade union activity today, but they were convicted at Dorchester and, on Mar. 19, 1834, sentenced to 7 years' transportation.

TOLSTOY, Count Leo Nikolaevitch
(1828-1910) Russ. author, social reformer and mystic. After marrying (1862) he settled on his estates, devoting himself to the interests of the peasantry. His chief works are the novels *War and Peace* (1865-72), *Anna Karenina* (1875-6), *The Kreutzer Sonata* (1889). During the last few years of his life he shared the life of the peasants, and d. in a railway station.

TOLTEC
The precursors of the Aztecs (*q.v.*), a vigorous, highly cultured and war-like people.

TOLUENE
[tol′-ew-ēn] Clear liquid with a pleasant aromatic odour. It occurs in the light oils distilled from coal tar and separated by further distillation; the source of trinitrotoluene (*q.v.*).

TOM THUMB
Name given to the Amer. dwarf **Charles Sherwood Stratton.** B. Bridgeport, Conn., 1838. He was 2 ft. 7 in. in ht.

TOMATO
(*Lycopersicom esculentum*) S. Amer. climbing plant of the Solanaceae, with red or golden fruit, and a popular article of food. They are grown extensively in Brit.

TOMSK
City of the W. Siberian Area of the Russ. S.F.S.R. on the Tom, 25 m. above its confluence with the Ob. Pop. 292,000.

TONBRIDGE
Urban district and market town of Kent, on the Medway, 29 m. S.E. of London. Pop. 23,310.

TONE, Theobald Wolfe
(1763-98) Irish patriot. Wishing to make Ireland independent, he enlisted the help of the Fr. In 1798 he embarked with a small Fr. squadron, which was captured. He was condemned to be hanged for treason but committed suicide in prison.

TONGA
[tong'-ă] or **Friendly Islands.** Indep. Polynesian kingdom (under Brit. protection, 1900-70), in the S. Pacific, 300 m. E. of the Fiji group. Nukualoaa, on Tonjotabu, is the seat of govt. The main group was discovered by Tasman, 1643, and was visited, 1773, by Capt. Cook. The country is gov. by a Legislative Assembly, elected triennally, and a hereditary monarch. The climate is mild and healthy, malaria being unknown. Copra is the chief export. The Tongans are Christian. Area: 270 sq.m. Pop. 65,620.

TONGUE
Fleshy outgrowth from floor of the mouth, fixed at the back, but free at the sides and front. It aids mastication by mixing food; speech by consonant formation and taste by means of taste buds.

TONIC SOL-FA
A system of musical notation developed in Eng. during the 19th cent. by *John Curwen.* It simplifies the sight-reading of single lines of music, but less useful the more advanced harmonically the music becomes.

TONSIL
Name given to 2 collections of lymphoid tissues situated one on either side of throat at level of back of tongue. Their main function is protective trapping and destroying of some of the germs passing in with food or air into stomach or lungs.

TOOTHACHE
Pain in a tooth, the seat of dental decay. Treatment by a qualified dentist should be obtained as quickly as possible. *See* ABSCESS.

TOOWOOMBA
Town of Queensland, Australia, *c.* 70 m. W. of Brisbane. It is the marketing centre for the surrounding country. Pop. 51,000.

TOPAZ
A fluosilicate of aluminium. Used as a gem stone, its characteristic colour is yellow, varying from a pale tint to a deep orange.

TORNADO
Type of whirlwind which travels at an av. rate of 20-40 m.p.h. from 5 to 30 m. wide and devastates the country as it goes. It is seen as a funnel-shaped cloud.

TORONTO
Cap. of Ontario and 2nd largest city of Canada, on the N. shore of L. Ontario, 220 m. S.W. of Ottawa. It has a fine harbour and is the industrial and commercial centre of the country. Pop. (City) 665,000.

TORPEDO
A cigar-shaped missile invented by Robert Whitehead (1823-1905) in 1866. It is the main offensive armament of submarines (*q.v.*). It has its own engines, driven by compressed air, and its speed, depth of running and direction are determined prior to firing. **Torpedo Boat.** Vessel built to carry and fire torpedoes, now superseded by the destroyer. *See* DESTROYER.

TORQUAY
Borough, seaport and resort of Devon, on Tor Bay, 26 m. S. of Exeter. William of Orange landed at T. in 1688. T. returns 1 member to Parl. Pop. 51,700.

TORQUEMADA, Thomas de
[tor-kwi-mä'-] (*c.* 1420-98) Sp. Inquisitor. In his zeal for the destruction of heresy he induced the pope to create the Holy Office of the Inquisition. His ruthless methods have made his name a by-word for cruelty.

TORRENS, Sir Robert Richard
(1814-84) Austral. statesman. In 1840 he went to S. Australia, became premier in 1867 and replaced the cumbrous system of conveyancing by public registration of land.

TORRES STRAIT
Channel, 90 m. wide, between Queensland and New Guinea, discovered by Torres in 1606, noted for its pearl fisheries.

TORTOISE
Land-living reptiles of the order Chelonia which includes also Turtles and Terrapins. It is characterised, like these, by a box-like armour, beneath which head, limbs and tail can be withdrawn for security, formed of bony plates and over which lies a horny outer covering or tortoise shell. Tortoises belong to warm regions. There are 5 European species. The mottled tortoise shell of commerce is obtained from a turtle, the Hawksbill (*C. imbricata*).

TORTOISESHELL BUTTERFLY
Name given to 2 Brit. butterflies because of their colouring. They are the small t. (*Vanessa urticae*) and the large t. (*V. polychloros*).

TORTURE
Extreme physical pain inflicted for judicial purposes. In ancient times it was inflicted either as part of punishment or to extort a confession. During the Hitler régime in Germany, torture was used on Jews and other so-called enemies of the Reich, and during World War II it was used on members of resistance movements by the Nazis.

TORY
Name of an Eng. polit. party. Employed as a term of contempt in Eng. for the supporters of Charles II. It became the accepted name of the party opposed to the Whigs, and remained so until about 1832. *See* CONSERVATIVE; UNIONIST.

TOSCANINI, Arturo
[toskă-nē'-ni] (1867-1957) Ital. conductor. He conducted at La Scala, Milan, 1898-1908, the Met. Opera House, New York, 1908-15 and the Phil. Symphony Soc. of New York, 1926-36. He was a guest conductor at Bayreuth, Salzburg, Vienna, Paris, Israel and London. Last visited London to conduct at the Festival Hall, 1952.

TOTALITARIANISM
Despotic form of govt. which permits of no opposition of any kind, and unites all the functions of the state in the hands of a dictator, clique, or party. The outstanding examples in recent times have been Fascist Italy and Nazi Germany, but the same principle is now in force in the U.S.S.R. and in the Communist countries of E. Europe.

TOUCAN
[too'-] Bird of family Rhamphastidae, of trop. S. Amer. Allied to the Barbets, T. have vividly

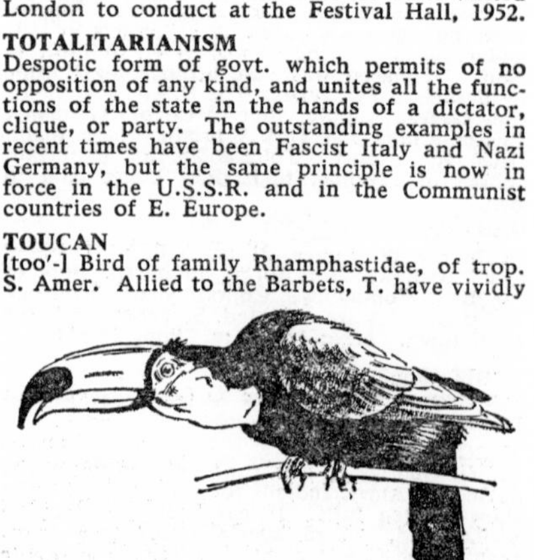

coloured bill and plumage. They inhabit forest regions; feed on fruit, insects, etc.

TOUCH-ME-NOT
(*Impatiens nolitangere*) Brit. plant, a species of balsam.

TOUCHWOOD
(*Polyporus igniarius*) Fungus growing on forest trees. It smoulders if ignited.

TOULON
[too-] Seaport in Var. dept., S. Fr. on Medit. 30 m. S.E. of Marseilles. With a fortified harbour, T. is the H.Q. of the Fr. Medit. Fleet; in 1942, the fleet was scuttled to prevent capture by the Germans. Pop. 221,000.

TOULOUSE
[-loos'] Cap. of Haute-Garonne dept., S. Fr., on the Garonne. There are woollen and iron manufactures, and the national tobacco factory. A Rom. town, T. was the ancient political and intellectual centre of S. Fr. In 1814 Wellington's army defeated the Fr. under Soult. Pop. 329,000.

TOULOUSE-LAUTREC, Henri de
(1864-1901) Fr. artist. In 1889 he first exhibd. at the Salon des Indépendants, and found his subjects in the café night life of Paris and the circus. His work in poster art and lithography raised it to a high level.

TOURMALINE
Mineral sometimes used as a gem stone. Found in Ceylon, Brazil, Burma and Siberia, its colour varies from almost colourless through yellow, red, green to blue.

TOURNAI
[-nā'] City in Hainaut prov., Belgium, on the Scheldt, near the Fr. border. Pop. 33,346.

TOURNEUR, Cyril
(or **Turner**) (*c.* 1575-1626) Eng. playwright. Author of *The Revenger's Tragedy* (*c.* 1607) and *The Atheist's Tragedy* (*c.* 1611).

TOURS
[toor] Cap. of Indre-et-Loire dept. Fr., on the Loire *c.* 130 m. S.W. of Paris. Manufactures include silk and steel, and there is a considerable trade in wine and fruit. At the **Battle of Tours**, in 732, Charles Martel checked the Moorish advance into W. Europe. Pop. 151,000.

TOUSSAINT L'OUVERTURE
[too-sa(ng) loo-ver-tür] (1746-1803) W. Indian negro patriot, who took part in the negro rebellion in Haiti in 1791. In 1795 the Fr. Convention made him commander of the army in the Is. When Napoleon proclaimed the re-establishment of slavery, and he refused to obey, he was treacherously seized and taken to Fr. where he d. in prison.

TOWER BRIDGE
Lowest bridge across the Thames, in London. Opened in 1894, it consists of 2 towers with a roadway and foot bridges.

TOWER OF LONDON
Fortress in London on N. bank of Thames built by the Normans, later added to and used as a palace and state prison. The orig. Norman keep, the White Tower, still stands and other towers house the Crown Jewels and other objects of interest.

TOWN COUNCIL
In Brit. a body elected to manage the affairs of a city, borough or burgh. Created in 1835, it consists of councillors and aldermen. Councillors are elected by the ratepayers and serve for 3 years; aldermen or baillies (Scot.) are elected by the councillors and serve for 6. The council elects a mayor or provost (Scot.) who is the official head of the town. Each has a paid official called the town clerk, and a staff of officials.

TOXAEMIA
[tok-sē'-mi-a] Condition of blood-poisoning due to the presence in the blood of toxins or poisons produced by disease germs or the abnormal function of certain organs within the body.

TOYNBEE, Arnold
(1852-83) Eng. social reformer. Believing that only those could help the poor who lived among them, he took lodgings in Whitechapel. **T. Hall** was opened in 1884 as a memorial to him. It is a coll. and social centre, where univ. men go into residence, provide facilities for educ. and recreation, and formulate plans for promoting the general welfare of the poorer classes. **Arnold Joseph Toynbee** (1889-) nephew of above, Brit. historian. From 1925 Research Prof. of Internat. Hist. at London Univ.; retired 1955. Author of *A Study of History*.

TRABZON
Turkish port on the S.E. coast of the Black Sea. Founded by the Gks., it was a station on the caravan route from Asia to Europe. Pop. 53,039.

TRACHEA
[-kē'-ă] or **Windpipe.** Extends from larynx in the throat to the bronchi which lie behind at a level half-way from top breast bone or sternum. A rigid tube containing rings of cartilage and muscle with a lining of ciliated mucous membrane, it acts as an airway between larynx and lung.

TRADE MARK
Distinctive mark placed upon goods offered for sale. If the mark is a word it must be invented, not one in general use or the name of a place or person. They are protected by law provided they are registered. *See* PATENT.

TRADE UNION
Assoc. of workers in a particular trade formed principally for the purpose of collective bargaining. In their modern form Trade Unions date in Brit. from 1824 when the laws passed in the 18th cent. forbidding combinations of masters and workmen, were repealed. In 1868 the first Trade Union Congress was held. In 1889 the General Federation of Trade Unions was set up. The first election of trade unionists to Parl. was in 1874. Another development was 'industrial unionism' in which all employees of one firm are in one organisation, *e.g.* the Nat. Union of Railwaymen, in contrast with craft unions. With the repeal of the Trade Dispute Act, 1946, T.U.s were freed from legal restrictions imposed after the General Strike, 1926. The polit. side of the T.U. Mov. has overshadowed their work as friendly socs. They pay out sums to members during times of illness and unemployment. In 1963 there were in Brit. about 8,315,332 members in the 176 unions, affiliated to the T.U.C. There are powerful unions in the U.S.A., Germany, Australia, etc. **Trade Union Congress.** Organisation of Brit. trade unions, representing the industrial side of the Lab. movement. The C. is made up of delegates from the affiliated unions on the basis of 1 delegate for every 5,000 members. The Annual Congress elects a Gen. Council to observe all industrial developments and legislation affecting labour.

TRADE WIND
Persistent wind blowing from the sub-trop. belts of high pressure towards the low pressure region of the Equator. In the N. hemisphere it blows from the N.E., in the S. from the S.E. In the days of sailing ships it was of the greatest importance to trade. It prevails in the Atlantic and Pacific, and has considerable influence upon climatic conditions.

TRAFALGAR
A low, sandy headland (Cape T.) on the S.W. coast of Spain, at the W. entrance to the Strait of Gibraltar. Off this area on October 21, 1805, there occurred one of the most famous naval battles in history, when a Brit. fleet under Nelson defeated the combined fleets of Fr. and Sp. Of the 33 ships of the Franco-Spanish fleet involved, 15 were destroyed. No Brit. ships were lost but 499 men were killed, including Nelson himself. *See* NELSON. **Trafalgar Square.** Area in London, laid out to celebrate the victory at Trafalgar. In it is the Nelson Column, 145 ft. high.

TRANSISTOR
A semiconductor device operating on a very small amount of power, giving striking improvements in reliability and length of life of electrical apparatus with considerable reduction in size.

TRANSPORTATION
Punishment for criminals. By this they are sent to a penal settlement in a distant land. From Eng. prisoners were sent to work on the plantations in Amer., a practice which lasted until the indep. of the U.S.A. in 1783. In 1788 convicts were first sent to Botany Bay in Australia, but this ceased in 1840. From then until 1853, when transportation ceased entirely, they were sent to Tasmania. Banishment merely sends the offender out of the country. Transportation sends him to a definite place for a definite period under supervision.

TRANS-SIBERIAN RAILWAY
Line of the U.S.S.R. running from Moscow to Vladivostok on the Pacific coast, via Omsk, Novo Sibirsk, Krasnoyarsk, Irkutsk and Khabarovsk. Begun in 1891 and finished 1904.

TRANSUBSTANTIATION
Theological term. It denotes the belief held by the R.C. Ch. that ' the whole substance ' of the Eucharistic bread and wine are changed into the body and blood of Christ.

TRANSVAAL
Prov. of the S. African Repub., bounded by the Limpopo and Vaal on the N. and S. respectively, with Portuguese E. Africa and Swaziland on the E. It consists of high plateaux traversed by the Crocodile and Olifants, and other tribs. of the Limpopo. In the S. is the High Veld, bordered by the Witwatersrand range, with the Low Veld farther N. Cattle and sheep are reared, and there is good agricultural land. The chief asset of the prov. is its mineral wealth, esp. gold and diamonds. Pretoria is the cap.; other towns are Johannesburg, Germiston and Brakpan. The territory was first settled by Boer farmers from the Cape in 1836. It became a repub. in 1852, but was annexed by Brit. in 1877. Self govt. was recognised in 1881, but the country was again annexed in 1902. Responsible govt. was granted in 1906, and 4 years later the T. became a prov. of the Union of S. Africa. Area: 110,450 sq.m. Pop. 6,273,477.

TRANSYLVANIA
District of Rumania, bounded by the Carpathian Mts. and Transylvanian Alps. It consists of a plateau, rising to over 6,000 ft. in the Bihar Mts. Much is forested, and there are mineral resources. Wheat and corn are grown in the lowlands; grapes and fruits on the hillsides. Towns include Brasoy and Cluj. T. was part of Hungary until 1918.

TRAPPIST
Member of a branch of the Cistercian religious order. It was founded by Dominique A. J. le B. de Rancy, who lived from 1626-1700.

TRAVEL SICKNESS
The vibrations and movements produced by travelling in ship, train, car or aeroplane can cause nausea and actual sickness, in susceptible persons. It is due to stimulation of the labyrinth of the internal ear, but psychological factors are also significant. For the prevention of seasickness, careful tests, prior to the Normandy landing in World War II, proved that hyoscine hydrobromide is the most effective preparation.

TRAVELLERS' CHEQUES
Issued by banks and the larger tourist agencies for the use of customers travelling abroad.

TRAVELLER'S JOY
(*Clematis vitalba*) Eng. wild climbing plant of Ranunculaceae. It is a perennial shrub with tough stems and leaf stalks by means of which it climbs. Numerous stamens surround the styles which in autumn elongate into white plumy tails, *i.e.* **' Old man's beard '.**

TRAVELLER'S TREE
(*Ravenala madagascariensis*) Plant of Madagascar allied to the banana and resembling a palm. Rain water collects in a cavity at the base of each leaf stalk; and flour prepared from the ground seeds is used as food.

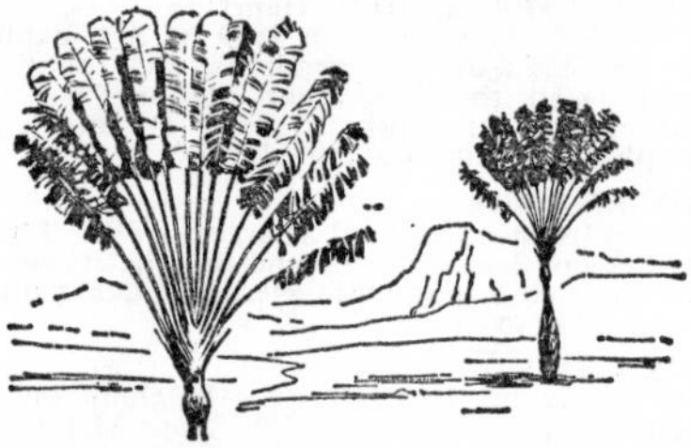

TREASURE TROVE
Any gold or silver, in coin, plate or bullion, found hidden in a house or in the earth, or other private place, the owner thereof being unknown. It belongs by law to the crown. Anyone who finds treasure trove and does not disclose the fact may be prosecuted.

TREASURY
Dept. of the Brit. Govt. It supervises the nat. revenue and expenditure. The Chanc. of the Exchequer is its head. The permanent head is the Sec. to the Treasury, the official head of the Civil Service.

TREATY
Agreement contract or league between 2 or more nations. Treaties are made by diplomatists and other representatives of the various countries, but before they are valid they need ratification by legislative or other authority in the several countries.

TREE
Woody stemmed plant, differing from a shrub in size only and perennial in habit. Trees are either deciduous, as the oak and elm, or evergreen like the pine.

TREE, Sir Herbert Beerbohm
(1852-1917) Eng. actor-manager. He managed the Haymarket Theatre, 1887-97, when he opened Her Majesty's Theatre, where he staged elaborate Shakespearean productions. In 1904 he founded the Academy of Dramatic Art.

TREE-CRAB
Crab of the genus Brigus and a species of land crab. This crustacean climbs the coco-palm, perforates the soft spot in the shell of the coco-nut, breaks open the shell and feeds upon the soft pulp of the nut.

TREE-CREEPER
Small bird (*Certhia familiaris*) widely spread in the temp. regions of Europe, N. Amer., Asia, and N. Africa. It climbs on the bark of trees in search of insects.

TREE-FERNS
Tropical ferns which attain the size of trees, *e.g. Alsophila vestita.* The trunk of *Cyathea medullaris* contains a pulp used extensively for food in Polynesia and N. Zealand.

TREE FROG
Family (*Hylidae*) of tree-living Frogs. The digits of both pairs of limbs are furnished with adhesive pads. The male has a vocal sac. *Hylva arborea* is common in S. Europe.

TRELAWNY, Sir Jonathan
(1650-1721) Cornish bishop. He was one of the 7 bishops accused by James II in 1688 of seditious libel, and is the subject of the famous ballad *And shall Trelawny die?*

TRENCH
In warfare, an excavation in the earth used to protect soldiers from enemy fire. Early in 1915 trenches were dug on both sides which reached from the Belgian coast to Switzerland. They became very elaborate with deep dug-outs. The period of trench warfare lasted for nearly 4 years. Casualties were heavy.

TRENCHARD, Hugh Montague
(1873-1956) **1st Visct.** Marshal of the R.A.F. Entered the Army as 2nd-Lieut., Royal Scots Fusiliers, 1893. In Aug. 1914, appointed O.C., R.F.C. (Milit. Wing). Transferred to Fr. as Wing-Cdr., Nov. 1914. Became Chief of Air Staff in Jan. 1918, on formation of R.A.F. and Air Min. In 1919 he reorganised the R.A.F. and in 1922 became Air Marshal. On Jan 1, 1927, he became the first Marshal of the R.A.F. He was Commissioner of the Metropolitan Police, 1931-5.

TRENGGANU
[-gá'-] State of the Fed. of Malaya on the E. coast of the peninsula, S. of Kelantan. Kuala T. is the seat of govt. and residence of the Sultan. Area: 5,027 sq.m. Pop. 320,431.

TRENT
River of Eng. which rises in Staffs. and flows through Derbyshire, Notts. and Lincoln, joining the Humber near Alkborough. It is 180 m. long and has a bore. Towns on its banks are Stoke, Burton, Nottingham, Newark and Gainsborough.

TRENT, Council of
Ecumenical council set up in 1545 to define the position and creed of the Ch. of Rome in opposition to the doctrines and claims of the Churches of the Reformation.

TRENTO
Ital. town in Venezia, Tridentina, on the Adige, 45 m. N. of Verona. Industries include marble quarrying. Austrian prior to World War I. Pop. 64,200.

TRENTON
Cap. of New Jersey, U.S.A. on the Delaware, 34 m. from Philadelphia. There are manufactures for which hydro-electric power is generated. Pop. 114,167.

TRESCO
Scilly Is. which contains the residence of the lord proprietor. *See* SCILLY ISLANDS.

TREVELYAN, Sir George Otto
(1838-1928) Eng. historian and politician. He wrote *Early History of Charles James Fox, Life and Letters of Lord Macaulay,* and *The American Revolution.* His son, **George Macaulay** (1876-1962) from 1927-44 Prof. of Modern Hist. at Camb. and 1944-51 Master of Trinity Coll. His works include *History of England, England under the Stuarts.*

TREVITHICK, Richard
(1771-1833) Eng. inventor. B. Cornwall. He built high-pressure non-condensing steam engines and in 1801 a locomotive which carried passengers along a road.

TRIANGLE
In music, a steel bar bent in the shape of a triangle, open at one corner and struck with a metal beater.

TRIANON
[trē'-] Royal palaces built in 1670 and 1766, in the great park of Versailles.

TRIASSIC SYSTEM
Geological system overlying Permian. Gypsum, alabaster and salt are mined.

TRIBE
Clan or body of people believed to be descended from the same ancestor. The Jews were divided into 12 tribes, descendants of the sons of Jacob, and the Amer. Indians are still divided into tribes. In Athens and Rome, the social organisation was based on that of the early tribes.

TRIER
(*Fr.* Trèves) German city on the Moselle, in the Rhine Palatinate. It contains a Rom. amphitheatre and palaces, and a cath.

TRIESTE
[trē-est'] Seaport, and its surrounding territory, on the Adriatic. Formerly an Ital. city, T. was constituted a ' free territory ' in 1947 as a compromise between the claims of Italy and Yugoslavia. The area was divided into 2 zones admin. by a Gov. apptd. by the U.N. and an Assembly. This arrangement was not a success, and in 1954 the territory was partitioned between Italy and Yugoslavia. Ital. T. has an area of about 90 sq.m. and pop. of 296,229. The Yugoslav part has an area of 200 sq.m. with a pop. of *c.* 74,000.

TRILOBITES
Class of fossil marine Arthropoda. Peculiar to the Palaeozoic rocks and esp. abundant in the Cambrian and Silurian periods, the oval flattened body was covered with a hard trilobed exoskeleton.

TRIM
County and market town of Meath, Repub. of Ireland, on the Boyne, 30 m. N.W. of Dublin. Pop. 1,400.

TRINIDAD
Is. of the W. Indies, forming an Indep. state of the Brit. Commonwealth (1962) with Tobago (*q.v.*). It lies off the coast of Venezuela, N. of the Orinoco delta. The land is undulating, rising to over 3,000 ft. in the N. and the soil is fertile. Sugar, cocoa, molasses, rum and copra are the chief products. In the S.W. is the famous Pitch Lake, an important source of asphalt. Petroleum is also produced. The cap. and chief port is Port of Spain on the N.W. coast. T. was discovered by Columbus in 1498, colonised by Sp. and ceded to Brit. in 1802. Area: 1,864 sq.m. Pop. 850,000.

TRINITROTOLUENE
High explosive for shells. Formed by the action of nitric acid upon toluene, it is also known as trotyl or T.N.T.

TRINITY, The Holy
Theological term. It denotes the Christian belief in the union of 3 ' persons ' (Father, Son and Holy Spirit) in one Godhead.

TRIPOLI
City and seaport of Libya, N. Africa, chief town of the district of Tripolitania and former cap. of Ital. Libya. Pop. 214,000.

TRIPURA
Union Territ. of E. India, bounded by Assam and Pakistan. Agartala is the cap. Area: 4,050 sq.m. Pop. 1,143,000.

TRISTAN
In romantic legend, the nephew of King Mark of Cornwall and lover of his uncle's wife, Iseult.

TRISTAN DA CUNHA
[koo′-nă] Three Brit. volcanic islands in the S. Atlantic Ocean, *c.* 2,000 m. W. of the Cape of Good Hope. Discovered in the 16th cent. by the Portuguese. Following a volcanic eruption, 1961, the 300 islanders were evacuated to Brit. 1963 saw the beginnings of resettlement. Area: *c.* 50 sq.m. Pop. 280.

TRITOMA
Genus of herbaceous plants, also known as Kniphofia, natives of S. Africa. One species, the red-hot poker plant, has a long spike of scarlet flowers.

TRIUMVIRATE
Govt. in Rom. Repub. consisting of 3 men. The 1st, formed in 60 B.C. by Pompey, Caesar and Crassus ended with Civil War between the 2 former; the 2nd 43 B.C., of Octavian, Antony and Lepidus after the murder of Caesar, did likewise, leaving Octavian, later Augustus, supreme.

TRIVANDRUM
Cap. city of Kerala state, India, on the S.W. coast. Pop. 239,815.

TROLLOPE, Anthony
(1815-82) Eng. novelist. He worked in the Post Office 1841-67. The 'Barsetshire Novels' *The Warden* (1855), *Barchester Towers* (1857), *The Small House at Allington* (1864), *Last Chronicle of Barset* (1867) made him famous. His 52 novels (many of them polit.) also include *Can You Forgive Her?* and *Phineas Finn.*

TROMBONE
A brass instrument with a cupped mouthpiece and a cylindrical tube. The sounding length of the tube can be increased by means of a slide mechanism.

TROMP, Martin Harpertzoon van
(1597-1653) Dutch admiral. In May, 1652, he was worsted by Blake, but in Nov. he defeated him in the Straits of Dover. The final struggle was July 31, 1653, off the coast of Holland, where the Dutch lost 30 vessels, and van Tromp was killed.

TROMSÖ
Seaport of N. Norway, on T. Is., an important centre of the cod fisheries and whaling. Pop. 12,448.

TRONDHEIM
[tron′-yem] City, seaport and former cap. of Norway, on T. Fiord, 250 m. N. of Oslo. Shipbuilding and saw-milling are among the industries. Pop. 59,000.

TROPICS
Term used for part of the earth's surface, the region lying N. and S. of the Equator between the Tropics of Cancer and Capricorn (*qq.v.*). It is the region in which the sun is overhead twice a year.

TROSSACHS, The
Mt. pass of Perthshire, extending from Loch Katrine to Loch Achray, noted for its scenery. Overlooking the pass are Ben Venue, 2,393 ft. and Ben A'an, 1,850 ft.

TROTSKY, Leon Davidovich
(1879-1940) Russ. politician. In the Oct. Revolution he became Foreign Commissar, reorganised the army and stemmed the Counter-Revolution. After Lenin's d. a struggle developed between Trotsky and Stalin for power, which ended in 1927 with Trotsky's expulsion from the Communist Party. He was murdered in Mexico City by a Communist.

TROUT
Freshwater fish of the family Salmonidae. The Common T. (*Salmo fario*) is found in streams and rivers of N. Europe. Coloration is generally olive green above and paler beneath.

TROY
Ancient city on the N.W. promontory of Asia Minor, 3½ m. from the Hellespont (Dardanelles). Excavation has revealed the remains of 9 cities from the Stone Age to Rom. times. The 6th has been estabd. as the Troy of Gk. legend. This was the scene of the Trojan War. The Gks. finally captured the city by the stratagem of the wooden horse.

TROYES
[trwà] Cap. of Aube dept., Fr. in the Champagne country S.E. of Paris. Pop. 59,000.

TRUCE
Word used for a cessation of war for a definite time. It differs from an armistice, which is a cessation of war preparatory to the negotiation of a peace treaty.

TRUCIAL STATES
Territory on the S. shore of the Persian Gulf, between Muscat and Oman and Qatar, divided between 7 sheikhdoms which have treaty relations with Brit. Dubai and Sharjah are the ports. Pearls and dried fish are exported. Area: *c.* 32,000 sq.m. Pop. 110,000.

TRUFFLE
Genus of edible fungi of the division *Ascomyceteae,* found just below the soil. The best known variety (*Tuber aestivum*), looks like a potato, usually oblong or irregularly globose, with a dark, warty, hard exterior. A Fr. species (*T. melausporum*) is especially valued.

TRUMAN, Harry S.
(1884-) 33rd Pres. of the U.S.A. A Senator since 1934, Truman was elected as Roosevelt's Vice-Pres. in 1944, and on the latter's d. in 1945 became Pres. following his policy of participation in world affairs and support for the European democracies. In 1948 he was re-elected. During his 2nd term of office Truman dealt vigorously with the war in Korea. Pres. Truman continued to support Aid for Europe. In 1952 he nominated Adlai Stevenson as his successor. The latter was defeated by Gen. Dwight D. Eisenhower (*q.v.*).

TRUMPET
A brass instrument with a cup-shaped mouthpiece and a mainly cylindrical tube, expanding slightly at the bell.

TRURO
City, borough and market town of Cornwall, 12 m. N. of Falmouth. The cath. was built between 1880 and 1910. Pop. 13,620.

TSAR
[zar] Title of the pre-1917 rulers of Russia.

TSETSE FLY
[tset′-si] (*Glossina*) Blood sucking Dipterous flies, natives of trop. Africa. They inhabit low-lying bush or forest regions near water, and transmit the parasites of sleeping sickness, and of a cattle disease.

TSUSHIMA
[tsoo′-shē-mà] A Japanese island (area 274 sq.m.) situated between Korea and Kyushu, *c.* 50 m. off the Korean coast. In 1905 the Russ. fleet was intercepted by a Jap. fleet under Admiral Togo, outmanoeuvred, outgunned and virtually annihilated.

TUAM
Market town of Galway, Repub. of Ireland, 20 m. N.E. of Galway. It is an important eccles. centre. Pop. 4,000.

TUAREG
Arab name for Saharan Berber peoples. The men wear the veil day and night, the women never.

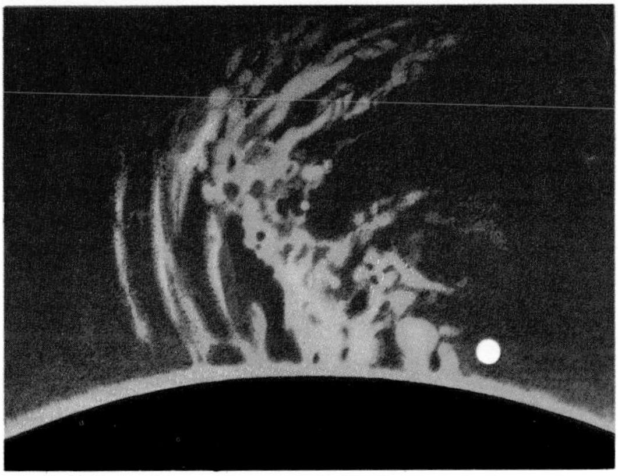

Solar prominence

THE SOLAR SYSTEM

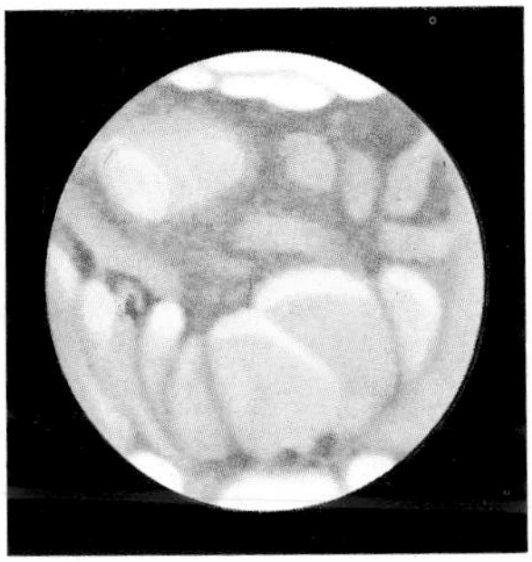

Mars

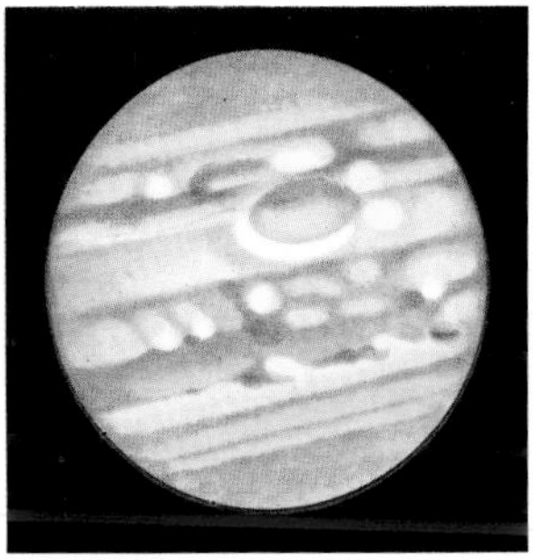

Jupiter

Saturn

Cumulonimbus formation with rainbow

CLOUD FORMATIONS

Cumulonimbus and stratus formation

Cumulus

Cirrostratus

Cirrocumulus

Large stratocumulus after rain

TUBA
A brass instrument with a cup-shaped mouthpiece; its tube has a conical bore like the horn.

TUBERCULOSIS
Infectious disease caused by the micro-organism bacillus *tuberculosis*. This disease was known to the Gks. and to Hippocrates and Galen. Koch who, in 1882, discovered the germ, and Erlich his assistant who discovered a method of demonstrating the germ by the staining method are assoc. with the description of the disease and the discovery of the cause. The disease is contracted in man from the spit or droplets from the mouth of infected people, or by drinking the milk of infected cows. It usually affects the lungs, but can affect any part of the body and its onset is characterised by loss of energy, night sweats, loss of weight and appetite and in the later stages by anaemia, fever and cough. In India a survey in 1952 showed that ½ million people die of T.B. each year. A 7-year campaign was instituted with the help of the World Health Organisation and U.N.I.C.E.F. The W.H.O. is helping governments to set up tuberculosis control centres and to organise educ. programmes for more sanitary living conditions and pure food supplies. Statistics show that the mortality from lung T.B. has declined by 50 % in 21 nations in 12 years. The drop reached 72 % in Sweden, 74 % in Norway, 50 % in France and 64 % in the U.S.A. Regular medical check-ups and mass radiography methods as well as vaccination play a vital part in eradicating the disease.

TUBEROSE
(*Polianthes tuberosa*) Plant originally brought from the E. and now extensively cultivated under glass throughout Europe.

TUCSON
[too-son'] Winter resort and industrial town S.E. Arizona, U.S.A. in an agric. and cattle-raising area. Pop. 233,000.

TUDOR
Surname of an Eng. dynasty. A Welshman, Owen Tudor, mar. Catherine of Fr., widow of Henry V. His eldest son was Edmund, Earl of Richmond, who mar. Margaret, daughter of John Beaufort, Duke of Somerset, whose son was afterwards Henry VII. Henry VIII, Edward VI, Mary and Elizabeth were **Tudor** monarchs.

TUG-OF-WAR
Event at sporting and athletic meetings. Two sides, each consisting of 8 men, pull against each other with a rope. The object of each is to pull the other team over the midway line.

TUILERIES, Palais des
[twē'-lĕ-rē] Palace founded by Catherine de Medici and Henry IV, and for long the residence of Louis XIV, in whose reign the gardens were laid out by André Le Nôtre. On June 20, 1792, the palace was invaded by the mob, and again on Aug. 20. This second onslaught resulted in the capture and imprisonment of Louis XVI.

TULA
R.S.F.S.R. (1) Region on upper Don and Oka. Chiefly agric. also coal and iron-ore industries. (2) Manufacturing town, cap. of Tula region. Founded in the 12th century, it received in 1595 the first ordnance factory in Russia, built by Boris Godunov. Pop. 360,000.

TULIP
Genus of bulbous plants of the family Liliaceae. Natives of Asia and the E. Medit., they were introduced into Eng. from Holland in the 16th cent.

TULIP TREE
(*Liriodendron tulipifera*) N. Amer. flowering timber tree. A species of magnolia, it sometimes reaches 180 ft.

TULL, Jethro
(1674-1741) Brit. agricultural reformer. Chiefly known for the invention of a drill which sowed the seeds in rows.

TULLAMORE
Urban district and county town of Offaly, Repub. of Ireland, 58 m. W. of Dublin. Pop. 5,900.

TULLE
Formerly **Tutela**, cap. of Corrèze, dept. of central Fr., 58 m. from Limoges. Industrial, with textile and armament industries. Pop. 16,000.

TUMOUR
New tissue formation. It originates and grows a similar tissue in the body, and serves no useful purpose. It may be *simple*, when it is localised and harmless, or *malignant*, when it spreads and death results. *See* CANCER.

TUNBRIDGE WELLS
Borough and market town of Kent, 35 m. S.E. of London. A popular spa in the 17th and 18th cents. Royal borough since 1909. Pop. 40,000.

TUNDRA
Cold desert area of N. Eurasia and N. Amer. It lies within the Arctic circle, and during the winter is ice and snow covered. In summer only the surface becomes thawed, the temp. being even then *c.* 48°-50° F. A treeless region with lichen mosses and low shrubs, supporting caribou and reindeer.

TUNGSTEN
A hard, brittle metallic element sometimes called Wolfram. It was discovered in 1783 by d'Elhujar. It is a constituent of many steels and other alloys, and, because of its high melting pt. (3,370° C.), it is used for electric lamps and thermionic valve filaments. Sp. gr. 18·7. Chem. Sym. W.

TUNIS
Seaport and cap. of Tunisia, on the Gulf of T. Occupied by the Fr. in 1881, the town has a mixed Fr. and Moslem pop. There are textile manufactures and a considerable trade. Pop. 680,000.

TUNISIA
Formerly a Fr. protectorate of N. Africa, between Algeria and Libya. In the N. is a fertile coastal plain, with mt. ranges inland. To the S. are the Shott Djerid and Shott el Rharsa, 2 large salt lakes, and an extensive desert. The country is mainly agricultural, producing cereals, olives, dates and citrus fruits. Native industries include spinning, weaving, leather-work and embroidery. Lead, zinc and iron are mined, and phosphates are exported. Tunis is the cap. T. was occupied by the Fr. in 1881 but in 1956 became an indep. sovereign state, but remained within the 'franc zone' and maintained the customs-union with Fr. The P.M. heads the government and a Constituent Assembly was set up in April, 1956. In July, 1957, the Assembly decided to abolish the monarchy and proclaimed a repub. Area: 45,000 sq.m. Pop. 4,198,000.

TUNNEL
Passage cut through a hill or under a river, for traffic purposes, to convey water to power stations, etc. The earliest tunnels were made to take railway lines through hills, but later were much used for relieving the congestion of the traffic in large cities, *e.g.* the London Underground. Tunnels also run beneath the Thames and many other rivers. For transport purposes the first in Eng. was made under the Bridgwater Canal *c.* 1760. St. Bernard tunnel (opened 1964) links Switzerland and Italy by road.

TUNNY
(*Thynnus*) Large marine fish of the family

Scombridae related to the Mackerel. Found abundantly in the Medit. and less commonly off S. Brit. coasts. It is a useful food fish.

TUPPER, Martin Farquhar
(1810-89) Eng. writer. Of his 40 works only the verse *Proverbial Philosophy* is well-known.

TURBINE
The history of the turbine dates back to the time of Hero of Alexandria (1st cent. A.D.). However all efforts to produce a satisfactory prime mover in this form proved unsuccessful until Sir Charles Parsons (1854-1931) developed the steam turbine into the most powerful, most reliable, most adaptable and efficient single generator of primary power output, based on the 2 properties of jets of steam, *impulse* and *reaction*. Many types of ships use propelling machinery of the turbine type. *See* LINER. On land most power stations are now equipped with turbo-alternators for the generation of electric current for industrial and household use. **Water Turbines** are machines of both impulse and reaction type which convert a large mass of water flowing at high velocity into h.p. Experiments with **Gas Turbines** began as far back as 1791. The principle is that compressed air is heated at constant pressure by oil fuel, and the expanded air impinges upon the vanes of the turbine, causing the shaft to revolve. Gas turbines are now used for ship propulsion, in power stations, in aircraft, railway traction, etc. An aviation gas turbine was first fitted to a 'Gloster' aircraft powered by a Whittle jet-propulsion gas turbine in 1941. There are 3 main types of aviation gas turbine. (1) *The jet-propulsion unit* or *turbo-jet* in which all the air for combustion and propulsion passes through the engine; (2) the *ducted-fan engine* (which is a turbo-jet incorporating the multi-bladed turbine type of fan or propeller enclosed in a duct) in which part of the air flows through and part over the engine; (3) the *propeller-turbine* in which the ratio of the turbine to compressor is such that sufficient power is available to drive a propeller in addition to that absorbed by the compressor. Gas turbines have replaced piston engines in most modern civil and fighting aircraft, *e.g.* The Bristol *Britannia*, De Havilland *Comet*, Gloster *Javelin*, etc., and developments continue. Experiments are proceeding with gas turbines for road vehicles and they have been installed in some naval craft. *See* AVIATION, JET PROPULSION.

TURBOT
(*Rhombus*) Flat popular food fish, family Pleuronectidae, common in N. Brit. waters.

TURENNE, Vicomte de
[tür-] **Henri de la Tour d'Auvergne** (1611-75) Fr. general. In 1641 Richelieu entrusted him with the supreme command of the Fr. troops engaged in the Thirty Years' War, during which, with Condé, he gained several notable victories. During the civil wars of the Fronde, T. fought against Condé. He conquered parts of the Sp. Netherlands, advanced into Germany, but was killed at Salzbach.

TURGENEV, Ivan Sergeievitch
(1818-83) Russ. novelist and poet. *Fathers and Sons* (1862) is his best work; others are *The Duellist* (1846), *A Lear of the Steppe* (1870), *Virgin Soil* (1876). After imprisonment in 1852 he lived chiefly in Baden-Baden and Paris.

TURIN
(*It.* **Torino**) City of Piedmont, N. Italy, at the foot of the Alps, on the Po. A route centre controlling the Mt. Cenis Pass, T. has numerous industries. T. was cap. of the kingdom of Sardinia until 1860, and of Italy, 1860-5. Pop. 1,019,230.

TURKESTAN
Area of C. Asia. West T. includes the N. prov. of Afghanistan. East T. is Chinese T., officially included in the prov. of Sinkiang. The Pamir district occupies a large part of the area, and much is desert. The pop. is almost entirely nomadic, trading in skins, furs and horses. The mulberry tree is extensively cultivated.

TURKEY
Repub. partly in Europe and partly in Asia, occupying Asia Minor and having a long coastline on the Black, Aegean and Medit. Seas. European T. is separated from the rest by the Bosphorus, the Sea of Marmara and the Dardanelles. Asiatic T. comprises the extensive Anatolian plateau, with a narrow coastal plain. The land rises to the S. in the Taurus Range, and towards the Persian and Russ. boundary on the E. The soil of Asia Minor is fertile, but agriculture is primitive. Cereals, tobacco, fruit, cotton, nuts, beet sugar and olives are grown. Livestock include sheep, goats and cattle. Chrome, zinc, manganese, copper, coal and silver are mined, and various types of timber are produced. Ankara is the cap. and Istanbul the largest city. The people, who are of Mongolian origin, are mainly Moslems. T. is a repub. with a pres. and council of mins. and a nat. assembly. Area: 294,500 sq.m. Pop. 33,823,000. The Turks enter European hist. when Amurath I estabd. his cap. at Adrianople (Edirne). His son, Bajazet I, annihilated the combined hosts of Hungary and Poland at Nicopolis (1396) and Ottoman aggression continued till it reached its limit under Solyman the Magnificent (1520-66) who humiliated Vienna and marched against Germany. By the Battle of Lepanto (1571) Sp. taught Europe that the Turk was not invincible. In 1730 began the long series of Russo-Turkish wars. The Crimean War saw Eng. and Fr. united in protecting the Sultan's Emp. against Nicholas I. In the war of 1877 and the resultant Berlin Treaty, it was foreign interference which saved the 'sick man of Europe' from Russ. domination. The Young Turk Reform Party drove Abdul Hamid from his throne in 1908. In World War I the Turks stayed the allied attempts to force the Dardanelles (1915). A Nationalist revolution (1919), resulted in the estab. of a separate govt. at Ankara. In 1922 the sultanate was abolished, and T. was declared a repub. with Mustapha Kemal Atatürk. (*q.v.*) as pres. In 1945 T. declared war on Germany and Japan, and has since joined N.A.T.O. Now involved in Cyprus in the struggle between Gk. and Turkish Cypriots.

TURKEY
(*Meleagris*) Large game bird extensively bred for the table. A native of N. Amer., there are 2 species. The common domesticated birds are derived from *M. gallopavo*. The male bird may weigh up to 34 lb. with metallic bronze plumage and fan-like expansible tail. The neck and head are reddish or bluish, nearly bare, with a wattle on the throat.

TURKISH *See* URAL-ALTAIC.

TURKMENISTAN
Constituent repub. of the U.S.S.R. in C. Asia, E. of the Caspian Sea, bounded on the S. by Persia and Afghanistan. Much of the country is a plain, fringed by hills in the S. The Qara Qum desert occupies most of the repub. Agri-

culture and stock-rearing are carried on with the aid of irrigation. Industries are being developed. Ashkhabad is the cap. Formed 1924, the repub. entered the Union, 1925. Area: 187,900 sq.m. Pop. 1,893,000.

TURKS AND CAICOS ISLANDS
Dependency of Jamaica until reverted to U.K. admin. 1962, consisting of some 30 small Is. S.E. of the Bahamas. Pop. 5,716.

TURKU
City and seaport of Finland on the Gulf of Bothnia, 95 m. W. of Helsinki. Pop. 138,299.

TURNER, Joseph Mallord William
(1775-1851) Eng. landscape painter. B. and d. in London. Studied under Reynolds. He was an ascetic by nature, never mar. and shunned all soc. His early pictures are sober in colouring. The works of his middle and late period are marked by splendour of colour and brilliance of light.

TURNIP
(*Brassica campesirts*) Edible tuber of the family Cruciferae. Native to Europe and Asia, it grows freely in Brit. where it is cultivated as a food for human beings and cattle. It reaches 2 ft. and has bristly leaves and yellow flowers. The white turnip is grown for the table and the gold turnip or swede as a cattle food.

TURNSTONE
(*Arenaria interpres*) Small shore bird allied to the Lapwing. It is *c.* 9 in. in length. The plumage is black and white, with reddish-brown shading. It frequents the shores of Brit. from Aug. to April.

TURPENTINE
Liquid used for cleaning and industrial purposes. It is obtained by distilling a resin which exudes from pine and other coniferous trees.

TURPIN, Dick
(1705-39) Eng. highwayman. Hanged for murder in York.

TURQUOISE
Mineral used as a gem stone. It is a hydrated aluminium phosphate found in the rocks of Persia, Arabia and the U.S.A. The best comes from Persia. In colour the turquoise varies from blue to green, the best being blue.

TURTLE
(*Chelonidae*) Aquatic reptile of the Tortoise family. The limbs are modified into paddles adapted for swimming. The Hawksbill T. (*Chelone imbricata*) yields tortoiseshell. The edible Green T. (*C. midas*) is used for making turtle soup. *See* TERRAPIN.

TURTLE DOVE
A native of N. Africa and parts of Asia, the Common T. D. (*Streptopelia turtur*) is a summer visitor to Brit., nesting in coppices and woods. It is a pest of grain crops. The plumage is ashen blue on head, wings, rump and back; wing coverts rufous; brownish tail, margined with white; there is a white and black patch on each side of the neck. The length is 11-12 in.

TUSCANY
Region of N.W. Italy with the coastline fringed by the Is. of Elba, Monte Cristo, Pianosa and Giglio. The valley of the Arno is the most fertile area, the rest being hilly and forested. Florence, Pisa, Siena and Leghorn are the chief towns. The Tuscan language was adopted as the literary language of Italy.

TUSSAUD, Madame Marie
(1760-1850) She learned the art of wax modelling in Paris. In 1802 she estabd. herself in London, gradually building up the famous waxwork show in Baker St.

TUSSORE
[tus'-ŏr] Fabric first made from Tussah silk obtained from the cocoons of the Tussah (or Tussar) moth, native to India and Pakistan. *Shantung*, a similar but stronger, coarse-surfaced cloth, is still made in China and India, but an imitation of this also is now extensively produced.

TUT-ANKH-AMEN
[toot-] Egyptian king of 18th dynasty who reigned from 1595-86 B.C. His tomb was found at Luxor by the Earl of Carnarvon in 1923. It was virtually intact and contained his mummified body and magnificent treasures.

TUVA
Autonomous prov. of the R.S.F.S.R. in C. Asia, N.W. of Mongolia. It broke away from Chinese suzerainty, 1911, and was incorporated into the Soviet Union, 1944. Pop. 198,660.

TWAIN, Mark
(1830-1910) Pen-name of **Samuel Langhorne Clemens**, Amer. writer. By turns printer, river pilot, miner and journalist, he gained immediate fame with *The Celebrated Jumping Frog of Calaveras County* (1865). Pub. *The Innocents Abroad* in 1869. *Tom Sawyer* (1876), *Huckleberry Finn* (1884), *A Connecticut Yankee in King Arthur's Court* (1889), are humorous tales.

TWEED
River of Gt. Brit. which rises in Peebles and flows through Selkirk and Roxburghshire, entering the sea in Northumberland at Tweedmouth. Below Kelso it forms the boundary between Eng. and Scot. It is noted for its fishing and is famous in stories and legends of the border country.

TWELFTH DAY
12th day after Christmas, Jan. 6. On it the feast of the Epiphany is held to commemorate the bringing of gifts to Jesus Christ by the wise men.

TWELVE TABLES, The
Code of Rom. law, drawn up in 449 B.C. by a body of 10 chosen for the purpose, after a long struggle between patricians and plebeians.

TWICKENHAM
Part of borough of Richmond-on-Thames (formerly in Middlesex) on the Thames. In the borough is the Rugby Union football ground. Alexander Pope is buried in the ch.

TWILIGHT SLEEP
Form of hypnosis used during childbirth and obtained by using drugs, hyoscine and morphia. *See* HYOSCINE.

TYBURN
Small tributary of the Thames, which gave its name to the gallows formerly standing at the end of Oxford St. The last execution there took place in 1783.

TYLER, Wat
Leader of the Peasants' Revolt in 1381. He gathered a following in Kent and Essex, and marched to London. On arrival at Smithfield the rebels were met by Richard II and the Lord Mayor, and the latter killed Tyler.

TYNDALE, William
(*c.* 1492-1536) Eng. writer. In 1525 he began to print his Eng. tr. of the N.T. at Cologne. He tr. the Pentateuch and other portions of the Bible (1530). He was strangled and burned at the stake in Antwerp as a heretic.

TYNE
River of Eng. formed by the union of the N. and S. Tyne, at Hexham. The former rises in the Cheviot Hills and the latter near Crossfell. On its banks are Jarrow, Wallsend, S. Shields, Gateshead and Newcastle. It flows into the N. Sea at Tynemouth.

TYNEMOUTH
County borough and seaport of Northumberland, at the mouth of the Tyne, 6 m. below

Newcastle. Chief industry is shipping. With Whitley Bay, T. returns 1 member to Parl. Pop. 71,390.

TYNWALD
Legislative body of the Isle of Man, consisting of (1) the Lieut.-Gov. appointed by the Crown for 7 yrs., (2) a Legislative Council, (3) the House of Keys comprising 24 members, (4) the Tynwald Court composed of the Leg. Council and the House of Keys sitting together under the presidency of the Lieut.-Gov. but voting separately. It transacts all administrative business and levies, and appropriates all taxes.

TYPE
A small rectangular block of metal or wood, having on its upper end a raised letter, figure, punctuation mark or other character, for use in printing. Among Eng. typefounders of earlier centuries, two are outstanding, Wm. Caslon (1692-1766) and John Baskerville (1706-75). In Fr., Pierre Simon Fournier (1712-68) invented the system of typographic points for determining the sizes and proportions of types, a system which was perfected by F. A. Didot (1730-1804). Francesco Griffo designed the typeface known as *Bembo* in Italy in 1495, and Giambattista Bodoni of Parma designed the type which bears his name, *c.* 1800. Modern designs include *Perpetua*, a beautiful book face designed by Eric Gill in 1929, who also designed the *Gill Sans Serif*; *Fontana*, founded upon a design by Alexander Wilson, a Scot. typefounder of the 18th cent. and designed by Hans Mardersteig for the exclusive use of the publishing firm of Wm. Collins Sons & Co. Ltd. in 1936. In 1952 a Swiss, Adrian Frutiger, started work on the Sanserif type which he later developed as *Univers*.

TYPHOID FEVER
Highly infectious and dangerous disease characterised by ulceration and inflammation of the bowel with generalised toxaemia, wasting and prolonged convalescence. Caused by *Bacillus typhosus*. Main features are high and prolonged fever, rose-coloured eruption, diarrhoea or constipation, enlargement of the spleen and acute abdominal pain.

TYPHOON
Violent cyclonic hurricane, on land or sea, but esp. one occurring in the China Sea from July to Nov.

TYPHUS FEVER
Acute, highly contagious disease caused by virus *Richettsia* and conveyed by lice. Common in C. Europe. Characterised by sudden onset of rigor, headache, nausea, delirium and fever followed by rash on 4th and 5th day. Incubation period 12 days. General mortality 20 % d. resulting mainly from toxaemia. Disease is prevalent in war, famine and poverty.

TYRANT
Orig. a despotic ruler. The term was applied in particular to rulers over the Gk. city states in the 7th and 6th cents. B.C., such as Hiero of Syracuse, etc. The derogatory sense is modern.

TYRE
Phoenician seaport founded in the 15th cent. B.C. now in the Lebanon. Orig. a colony of Sidon (*q.v.*). Captured by Alexander the Great in 332 B.C. is was destroyed by the Muslims after the fall of Acre. In Rom. times Tyre was famous for its purple dye and silk. Pop. 12,000.

TYRE
A band of wood, metal, rubber, etc. which is made to fit firmly the outer circumference of a wheel. The wheels of locomotives and other railway rolling stock are given rolled-steel tyres, which are shrunk when white-hot on to the cast iron wheel. The invention of the *Pneumatic Tyre* in 1888 is generally attributed to John Boyd Dunlop, a Scot. veterinary surgeon. A pneumatic tyre consists of an inner tube filled with air which is pumped through a nozzle, thus inflating the tyre to whatever pressure per square inch is desired, and an outer cover of compounded rubber, reinforced with cotton, nylon or steel. The outer surface of the tyre has an incised pattern, thus ensuring that the vehicle is given the greatest possible grip on the road surface, etc. The most important modern development in tyre manufacture occurred in 1954 when *Tubeless Tyres* were made available.

TYRONE
Co. of N. Ireland, S. of Londonderry. The chief rivers are the Foyle, Blackwater and Derg. With the exception of the E. plain the county is hilly. Cattle are raised, and oats, flax and potatoes are the chief crops. Linens, woollens and earthenware are manufactured. The county town is Omagh, Clogher, once important eccles., has an 18th cent. cath. With Fermanagh and S. Londonderry, T. returns 2 members to Parl. Pop. 134,500.

TYRRHENIAN SEA
Branch of the Medit. Sea, bounded by Corsica, Sardinia, Sicily and Italy.

U

U
21st letter and 5th vowel of the Eng. alphabet. It was not until the 19th cent. that *u* and *v* were definitely separated in Eng. Its primary sound was the *oo* sound in *truth, flute,* etc. The short *u* is pronounced in *nut, but*; *u* has the sound of short *i* in *busy*. In Eng. *q* is invariably followed by *u* to give *kw* sound, but *u* is occasionally mute, as in *liquor, opaque*.

U.N.R.R.A.
United Nations Relief and Rehabilitation Administration. Estab. 1943. Its greatest achievement was the saving of Greece. It ended in 1947 from lack of financial help.

U.S.S.R.
(Union of Soviet Socialist Republics) Country in Eur. and Asia, formed after the revolution of 1917. Until World War II the U.S.S.R. comprised 11 repubs., the R.S.F.S.R., Ukraine, White Russ., Armenia, Azerbaidjan, Georgia, Turkmenistan, Uzbekistan, Tajikistan, Kazakhstan and Kirghizia. In 1940 Estonia, Latvia, Lithuania, Moldavia, and Finno-Karelia became constituent repubs. Eur. Russ. extends from the Arctic Ocean to the Caucasus, and from Poland to the Urals. Asiatic Russ. includes Siberia, stretching from the Urals to the Pacific Ocean. Moscow (*q.v.*) is the fed. cap. The U.S.S.R. is gov. by the Supreme Soviet, which consists of 2 chambers. It delegates its power to the *Presidium*, a collective leadership. A council of ministers is apptd. by the Supreme Soviet. Educ. is compulsory. Russ. was formerly primarily an agricultural country, but the Five Year Plans are fostering industry. Farming is carried on by the collective system and in state farms. Foreign trade is a monopoly of the state. The Russ. empire began as a collection of principalities with Moscow as its cap. The first to take the title of Tsar was Ivan, 1547. Of his successors the greatest were Peter, who founded St. Petersburg, and Catherine II. Catherine and her successors greatly extended the area of Russ., first in Eur. and then by acquiring Siberia and other districts of Asia. Since the Napoleonic age the country has ranked as one of the Great Powers. Dissatisfaction with the sufferings caused by World War I brought matters to a head, and in Mar. 1917, a socialist republic was estabd. *See* RUSSIAN REVOLUTION. In Sept. 1939, Soviet forces invaded Poland, which had already been overrun by German troops. In Dec., Finland was invaded, and in 1940 the Baltic states were occupied. Germany invaded the U.S.S.R. in 1941 and in 1942 the U.S.S.R. signed a treaty with the Allies. After the war ideological differences between the U.S.S.R. and the W. became more apparent, the former adopting a hostile attitude at U.N. meetings. Diplomatic relations became increasingly strained, but were slightly improved after the d. of Stalin (*q.v.*) in 1953, when Malenkov succeeded him as chairman of the Council of Ministers. Malenkov was succeeded by Marshal Nicolai Bulganin. He was succeeded by N. S. Krushchev (*q.v.*) in 1957, who was succeeded by Kosygin and Brezhnev in 1964. The Communist Party is the governing, and only, polit. party in U.S.S.R. Area: 8,649,859 sq.m. Pop. *c.* 229,000,000. *See* RUSSO-JAPANESE WAR; RUSSO-TURKISH WARS; BOLSHEVISM; COMMUNISM.

U-BOAT
Abbreviation for *Unterseeboot* the German name for a submarine. *See* SUBMARINE; ATLANTIC, BATTLE OF.

UGANDA
State of E. Africa, N. of L. Victoria, and bounded on the W. by L. Albert and Edward. The country forms part of the C. African plateau. The White Nile, which flows N. from L. Victoria through L. Kioga and Albert, is the chief river. U. is an agricultural country. There are mineral reserves, and salt is produced. Kampala, which succeeded Entebbe as cap. 1962, and Jinja are the commercial centres. U. is divided into 4 provs. The country was first visited in 1862 and came under Brit. influence in 1890. U. became an indep. state within the Commonwealth, 1962. In 1963, the Kabaka of Buganda became 1st Pres. Deposed 1966. Area: 93,981 sq.m. Pop. 7,934,000.

UIST
Two islands of the Outer Hebrides, in Inverness-shire. The chief place of N. Uist is Lochmaddy; on S. Uist it is Lochboisdale. The inhabitants are engaged in cattle and sheep rearing and fishing.

UKELELE
[yoo-ki-lā'-li] Hawaiian guitar with 4 gut strings.

UKRAINE
Constituent repub. of the U.S.S.R. in the S.W. The chief rivers are the Dnieper, Dniester, Bug and Donets, and the main feature of the country is its steppe land. The Carpathian Mts. cross the S.W. part. Agriculture is the most important industry, the Ukraine being the principal cereal-growing district of Russ. Stock raising is carried on and flour milling, sugar and oil refining, leather and textiles are important. The minerals include salt and coal, iron, manganese and mercury. The metallurgical, chemical and other industries contribute a large proportion of Russia's output. There is considerable hydro-electric development on the rivers. The cap. is Kharkov and Odessa is the principal port. The Ukrainian S.S.R. was estabd. 1919, and entered the Union, 1923. In 1939 and 1940 W. Ukraine and N. Bukovina were incorporated in the repub. During World War II the U. was occupied by the Germans. Area: 225,000 sq.m. Pop. 41,893,000.

ULAN BATOR
(formerly Urga) Cap. of the Mongolian Repub. on the Tola. It is the Mongol holy city. Pop. 195,000.

ULCER
Break in continuity of a covering surface, the result of inflammatory reaction to bacterial infection causing d. of tissues followed by their disintegration and sloughing of surface tissues.

ULSTER
One of the 4 provs. of Ireland. It consists of the 6 cos. of N. Ireland, *i.e.* Londonderry, Antrim, Tyrone, Fermanagh, Armagh and Down, with Cavan, Donegal and Monaghan in the Repub. of Ireland.

ULSTER KING OF ARMS
The chief heraldic official in Ireland. He is registrar of the Order of St. Patrick.

ULTRA-VIOLET RAYS
Radiations of a wavelength next to and shorter than the visible rays. They are present in sunlight and are used for treatment of rickets, their beneficial action being due to the formation in the skin of vitamin D.

ULYSSES
(Odysseus) One of the heroes of the Trojan war. Homer's *Odyssey* describes his 10 years' adventures on the way home after the destruction of Troy.

UMBER
Brown earth containing iron and manganese oxides, used as a pigment.

UMBILICAL CORD
Fleshy cord containing 2 arteries and a vein which unites an unborn infant's abdomen with the placenta within the womb of the mother. The cord is severed at birth and the resulting scar is known as the umbilicus or navel.

UNCONSCIOUS
(1) Term used to denote a state of being in which there is inability to appreciate events in one's surroundings. It may be caused by injury to the brain, by drugs or by hypnosis. (2) In psychology, it denotes a mental state in which repressed memories come to the surface and are experienced as living events. The unconscious state of mind harbours thoughts, ideas and memories which may be out of place in society and are repressed to allow a person's behaviour to conform to accepted codes. **Unconsciousness.** Loss of sensibility assoc. with poisoning, apoplexy, haemorrhage, heart attacks, coma of diabetes and kidney failure etc.

UNEMPLOYMENT
Absence of livelihood-producing employment. The conditions of modern industry, mass production, fashion, machinery, the credit system and other factors produced mass unemployment after World War I. Destruction caused by World War II resulted in the temporary disappearance of unemployment, but automation and the decay of certain industries have caused it to recur significantly in the last decade.

UNESCO
(United Nations Educational, Scientific and Cultural Organisation) Organisation set up in 1945 under the Charter of the U.N. designed to promote respect for justice, law, and human rights by educ., scientific, and cultural collaboration between nations. H.Q. Paris.

UNIAT
Name used for Christian Chs. that are Gk. in practice, but have accepted the authority of the Ch. of Rome. They are found in the Balkan area and other parts of Europe and Asia Minor.

UNICORN
Fabulous animal with head and body of a horse and a horn in the middle of its forehead. The Scot. royal arms are supported by 2 unicorns.

UNIFORMITY
Acts of U. have been passed from time to time to enforce a set form of religious worship. In Eng. they were passed in 1549, 52 and 59. The last, passed in 1662, ordered all clergymen to be properly ordained, to accept the 39 articles and to use the Book of Common Prayer.

UNION, ACT OF
Name of 2 Acts of Parl. By the first, passed in 1707, the Eng. and Scots Parls. were united. By the 2nd, passed in 1801, the Brit. and Irish Parls. were united.

UNION JACK
British nat. flag, composed of the banners of St. George (white with a red cross), St. Andrew (a white saltire or diagonal cross on a blue field), and St. Patrick (white with a red saltire), representing Eng., Scot., and Ireland. The banners of Eng. and Scot. were combined, 1603 and confirmed, 1707. St. Patrick's flag was added, 1801, at the union with Ireland.

UNIONIST
Polit. party in Brit. Originated in 1885 when Gladstone proposed to give Home Rule to Ireland. A number of Libs., led by the Marquis of Hartington and Joseph Chamberlain, left the party and called themselves Lib. Unionists because they were determined to maintain union between Eng. and Ireland. In 1895 they joined the Cons. party in forming a govt. After World War I there was a return to the name Cons. The name Unionist, however, is still used, esp. in Scot. *See* CONSERVATIVE; TORY.

UNITARIANISM
Denotes belief in one God and is generally used to designate the faith held by those Protestants, who, while denying the doctrine of the Trinity and other beliefs of orthodox Christianity, accept the pre-eminence of Jesus Christ as a religious teacher and prophet.

UNITED ARAB REPUBLIC
Name given to the union of Egypt and Syria announced on Feb. 1, 1958. Pres. Nasser of Egypt was acclaimed pres. of the repub. on Feb. 21st by a plebiscite held in both countries. He obtained the right of nominating his cabinet, and the first was composed of 24 Egyptians and 14 Syrians. On March 9 the Yemen joined the U.A.R. in a fed. to be known as the United Arab States, but this agreement was abrogated by the U.A.R. 1961. After a Syrian *coup*, 1961 S. seceded. Since 1963 title has been confined to Egypt, negotiations with Syria and Iraq proving inconclusive.

UNITED FREE CHURCH OF SCOTLAND
Came into existence in 1900 by the Union of the United Presbyterian and the Free Ch. of Scot. In 1929, the majority of the U.F. Ch. of Scot. joined with the Ch. of Scot. A minority of some 13,000 members and 41 congregations carried on the U.F. Ch. of Scot.

UNITED KINGDOM
Name given in 1800 to the kingdom of Gt. Brit. and Ireland. The parl. of Eng. and Scot. were united in 1707, and those of Gt. Brit. and Ireland in 1801. The latter union was dissolved in 1922. *See* ENGLAND; N. IRELAND; SCOTLAND; WALES.

UNITED NATIONS ORGANISATION
The successor to the League of Nations, set up at the San Francisco Conference in 1945, comprising 110 States. The essential organs of U.N.O. are the *General Assembly, Security Council, Economic and Social Council, Trusteeship Council*, and the *International Court of Justice;* of these the Security Council is the most important, as it concentrates upon the peaceful settlement of disputes and the prevention of aggression. The Assembly has wide powers of discussion and recommendation, but cannot intervene in a dispute already being handled by the Security Council. The sessions of the Assembly and Security Council have not revealed a high degree of unity, and the use of the veto has created much disharmony. An 'internat. police force' made up of small detachments of troops from some member states was set up by UNO for the first time in 1956, following milit. intervention by Brit. and Fr. to separate the armies of Israel and Egypt. A similar force was sent to the Congo in 1960 and to Cyprus, 1964. UNO works through its Specialised Agencies such as the United Nations Educ., Scientific and Cultural Organisation (UNESCO); Food and Agriculture Organisation (FAO); Internat. Labour Organisation (ILO) etc. (*See* p. 466 U.N. structure.)

UNITED STATES OF AMERICA
The U.S.A. has an area of 3,615,316 sq.m., almost all of which is on the Amer. continent.

Her overseas possessions are mainly small Pacific islands (Guam, Samoa, etc.) plus Puerto Rico and the Panama Canal Zone. There are 50 states and one Fed. Dist., created as a site for the Fed. Cap., Washington, and known as the Dist. of Columbia. In latitude, U.S.A. stretches from 25° N. to 49° N. Longitude is 67° W. to 124° 30′ W. Her pop. in 1970 was 204,766,000. The U.S.A. has 4 clearly defined physiographic regions. (1) The *W. Cordillera* consists of high ranges parallel to the Pacific Coast culminating in the Rocky Mts. on the E. with peaks of 13,000 and 14,000 ft. It is an extensive mt. area occupying approximately ⅓ of the area of U.S.A. and is 1,000 m. broad between the states of Calif. and Colorado. It is drained principally by the Columbia R. and its tributaries in the N. and the Colorado R. in the S. Between the Rockies and the high W. ranges of the Cascade Mts. and Sierra Nevada are higher intermontane basins and plateaux. W. of the Cascade Mts. and Sierra Nevada and separated from the Pacific by coastal ranges is a deep, broad trough. It is at its widest in Calif. where it is drained by the Sacramento and San Joaquin rivers which enter the sea forming the natural harbour of San Francisco. (2) The *C. Lowlands* represent the drainage basin of the Mississippi-Missouri system and the smaller area in S.W. U.S.A. which drains to the Gulf of Mexico. The W. and N. of this area consists of the High Plains which fall gradually from 3,000 ft. near the Rockies to 600 ft. near the Mississippi. W. these Gulf coast lowlands become narrower towards Mexico. (3) E. they continue into the *Atlantic Coastal Plain* which extends along the entire Atlantic coast northwards to New York and is 150-200 m. wide. (4) It is backed by the *Appalachians*, a ridge of high land (3,000 ft.) trending from S.W. to N.E. and dividing the plain from the Middle Mississippi basin. The high land continues into New England where the S.W.-N.E. trend is broken by the N.-S. valleys of the Hudson, Connecticut and Merrimac Rivers. W. winds bring rain to the seaward slopes of the Coast Ranges, Cascade Ranges and Sierra Nevada, but the C. Lowlands are in the rainshadow of the Cordillera. In the lee of the Rockies cattle ranching is the main type of farming. Even the intermontane basins and the Great Valley of Calif. within the Cordillera are effectively shielded from the rain-bearing winds by the high coastal ranges, and irrigation is necessary. Aridity increases southwards, and the deserts of U.S.A. lie in the S.W. states. The Great Valley of Calif. has a Medit. climate receiving 15-20 in. of rain from the westerlies in winter but having drought in summer. The Appalachians form a much less sharp barrier to rainfall spreading inland from the Atlantic and in summer rain-bearing winds from the Gulf of Mexico are drawn N. along the Mississippi valley. The N. part of the C. Lowlands suffers from extremes of temperature, *e g.* Chicago 26° F. Jan., 74° F. July. The part S. of Cairo is sufficiently near the tropics and the Gulf of Mexico to experience mild winters with virtually no frost. When the 13 Eng. colonies of the E. seaboard declared their indep. in 1776 they formed the original United States of Amer. The pop. was then about 3 millions and has risen to 190 millions by natural increase and immigration. The territory of the U.S.A. was increased by colonisation, annexation and purchase until it stretched from the Atlantic to the Pacific. Colonisation spread W. across the Appalachians into the Ohio valley and the Mississippi Lowlands. In 1803 the Louisiana Purchase was made from Fr. The N.W. territories (Washington, Oregon and Idaho) were occupied between 1804 and 1811, and the S.W. territories from Calif. to Texas were acquired by conquest, purchase or annexation from Mexico in 1845-8. Most of the immigrants before 1880 were from N.W. Europe. For the next 40 years most came from E. and S. Europe and provided a cheap labour force for rapidly extending industry. Since 1914-18 immigration has been carefully controlled, each country having a quota and preference being given to those from N.W. Europe. The negro slave was introduced to carry farming W. into the sub-trop. lands of the Lower Mississippi valley and the Gulf Coast, and made possible the extensive cultivation of cotton (*q.v.*). The 15 million negroes remain the only substantial element in the pop. which is not absorbed. Colour prejudice remains very strong although the negroes were freed as a result of the Civil War between N. and S. States. The only other national groups remaining in the Amer. nation are the 300,000 native Indians who live on special reservations and some 200,000 Chinese and Japanese on the Pacific coast. U.S.A. can be divided into 2 halves along the meridian 100° W. which coincides with the 20 ins. isohyet. *West* of this line, except along the Pacific coast, aridity and high relief make cattle ranching the predominant farming type. New irrigation projects have brought additional areas of land into intensive cultivation, *e.g.* the lower Colorado Valley (Boulder and Parker Dams) and the valley of the Salt R. (Roosevelt Dam), and here subtropical crops are grown. Wheat can be grown in the high plateaux and basins using dry farming techniques, and is important on the rich volcanic soils of the Columbia plateau in the N. *East* of this line adequate rainfall and extensive lowland have led to intensive agricultural development: crops vary from temp. to sub-trop. There are 6 crop belts. From the N. these are: (*a*) *Spring wheat belt* stretches from the high plains of Montana through the Dakotas to the Mississippi valley in Minnesota. It is a continuation of the Canadian Prairies. (*b*) *Hay and Dairying belt* stretches round the S. shores of the Great Lakes and across N.E. U.S.A. into New England. The predominance of grass and fodder crops results from a climate with rain all the year round and the demand for dairy produce. (*c*) *Maize belt* lies S. of the spring wheat belt, from Omaha on the Missouri to the Appalachians and reaching S. to St. Louis. Summers are longer and hotter than in the wheat belt and a rainfall of 4-5 in. in July ensures swelling of the grain. (*d*) *Maize and Winter Wheat belt* lies S. of the Maize belt and stretches across to the E. coast between Cape Hatteras and the head of Chesapeake Bay. Wheat can be sown in autumn and harvested in early summer before the maize is ripe. Tobacco is very important in Virginia and Maryland. (*e*) *Cotton belt* lies S. of the Maize and Winter Wheat belt and stretches from the 20 ins. isohyet on the W. to the Atlantic coast on the E. (*f*) *Sub-trop. belt* lies along the coastline of the Gulf of Mexico and includes Florida. Rice and sugar cane are important. Florida specialises in pineapples and citrus fruit. U.S.A. is particularly rich in supplies of coal and oil. The most important coalfields are those in the Appalachians, notably in Pennsylvania and Alabama. The Pennsylvania field has high quality coal and is easily worked by mechanised methods. The main oilfields are in Oklahoma, Texas and Louisiana in the S.W. C. Lowlands and near Los Angeles in Calif. U.S.A.'s big iron deposits were at the W. and S. side of L. Superior, but as they are gradually worked out they may be replaced by Canadian ores. The W. Cordillera has always been an important source of copper. Gold caused the rush to Calif. in 1849 but is no longer important. The N.E. is responsible for ⅔ of U.S.A.'s manufactures. It has a dense and long settled pop., local supplies of coal and water power and some iron, and cheap transport on the Great Lakes. The principal industries are: (1) iron and steel; (2) textiles. The iron and steel industry is based (*a*) at Pittsburgh on the Pennsylvania coalfield, (*b*) at the ports on the Lakes Erie and Ontario (Cleveland, Erie and Buffalo). Associated with it is the shipbuilding industry of the E. coast ports (Philadelphia, Baltimore), the motor car industry of Detroit, the engineering at Buffalo and Detroit and the manufacture of small metal goods in New England. The textile industry is in New England and manufactures cotton, wool and silk goods of a high quality. The iron and steel industry is also found at Birmingham, Alabama, and at Gary, near Chicago; the textile industry is springing up particularly in the Tennessee valley, at the N. edge of the cotton belt. Meat packing is important, particularly at Chicago and St. Louis; aluminium smelting at St. Louis (bauxite from Arkansas); pulp and paper mills in New England and the Pacific north-west; fruit drying and canning in California and Florida.

Communications. Rlys. were built in the 19th cent. There are 4 main transcontinental lines: (1) The N. Pacific, linking Chicago and Minneapolis-St. Paul with the N.W. Pacific states. (2) The Union Pacific, linking Chicago with Omaha, Salt Lake City and San Francisco. (3) The Santa Fé railway, linking Chicago and Kansas City with Santa Fé and Los Angeles. (4) The S. Pacific, linking New Orleans with Los Angeles via El Paso. Chicago is a great rly. junction because it is at the S. end of L. Michigan and all routes from N.E. U.S.A. to N.W. U.S.A. have to pass round the S. end of the lake. There is a very good system of main roads and extensive bus services. Internal air transport has been developed in the last 20 years to link all the principal cities. The U.S.A. is a Fed. Repub. consisting orig. of 13 states, but now of 50 and one Fed. Dist. The written constitution of 1787 has seen various amendments. Executive power is in the hands of a Pres. elected for 4 years by electors from each state who are themselves chosen by direct vote. The number of electors for each state is equal to its Senators and representatives in Congress. Electors are nominated by the various parties. The vice-pres. is elected similarly. The Pres. is ex-officio C.-in-C. of the Army, Navy and Air Force; he appoints Cabinet officers and a great many officials; he conducts foreign policy, and he has the power of veto (unless out-voted by a $\frac{2}{3}$ majority of both Houses). *Legislative* power is in the hands of Congress, consisting of the Senate and the House of Representatives. Each state has two Senators, elected for 6 years; one-third of the Senators retire every second year. The numbers of representatives is allocated to the states in proportion to the pop. of each and elected for two-year terms. Each state has its own constitution, with a Gov. and a Legislature of 2 Houses (only one in Nebraska); the states deal with all matters except general taxation, foreign affairs (including commerce), defence, postal services, and a few others.

UNIVERSE

The whole system of created things. In the West, until the 16th cent., the earth was considered as the centre, with the sun, moon and stars revolving round it. In the 17th cent. it became clear that the earth moved round the sun, and the work of Newton and Kepler led to the accurate forecasting of the movement of planetary bodies. The improvement of the telescope led to the discovery of more and more stars, and spectroscopy enabled their distance and constitution to be investigated. Now, astronomers estimate that the universe contains *c.* 30,000 million stars, the nearest being *c.* 50 million million miles from the earth. The extent of the universe had caused much philosophical difficulty. Einstein's theory of relativity led to experimental proof that light travels in a curved path, which if prolonged far enough, will return to its starting point, and it is in this sense that the universe is now considered finite but boundless. As a result of discoveries made at the Mt. Palomar observatory in 1953, the universe is now said to be twice as large and twice as old as previously supposed, the revised estimate of its age being *c.* 4,000 million years. See *The Nature of the Universe* by Fred Hoyle.

UNIVERSITY

Corporation of men and women devoted to the teaching and studying of the higher branches of learning. A primary function of univs. is research; univs. have the authority to confer degrees on the completion of a prescribed course of study and/or on the satisfactory passing of certain exams. The first European univ. was the Univ. of Salerno founded in the 9th cent. for the study of medicine. The revival of legal studies in the 12th cent. led to the foundation of univs. at Bologna, Padua and elsewhere, while in the 13th cent. the schools of dialectic in Paris developed into the Sorbonne. The first Scot. foundation at St. Andrews, was founded in the 15th cent. The earliest Eng. univs. were Oxford and Cambridge which date from the 12th and 13th cent. and here colls. were first estabd. as places of residence for students. The Robbins Report on Higher Educ. (1963) recommended the founding of 6 new univs. and Colls. of Higher Technology which would be technol. univ. conferring their own degrees. More than 12 new univs. have already been started in Brit. since 1952. *See* WORKERS' EDUCATIONAL ASSOCIATION.

UPAS TREE

[yew'-] Tree found in Java and in trop. Africa.

UPPSALA

City of Sweden, on L. Mälar, 40 m. N. of Stockholm, with the oldest univ. (1477) in Sweden. The cath. was begun in 1287. Pop. 79,308.

UR

Ancient Sumerian city. The biblical ' Ur of the Chaldees ' is generally identified with it. It was situated on the Euphrates, *c.* 150 m. S.E. of Babylon. Excavations have revealed the great temple (*c.* 2300 B.C.) with its *ziggurat* or stage tower.

URAL

Range of mts. running from the Arctic to the Caspian Sea, forming a boundary between Europe and Asia. The range is important for its timber, its salt-mines and deposits of gold, platinum, copper, iron and coal. The area has been extensively industrialised. Important centres are Molotov, Magnitogorsk, Chelyabinsk and Sverdlovsk.

URAL-ALTAIC

Family of agglutinative languages found in Finland, etc., and in Soviet Asia and Mongolia. Branches: (a) **Finno-Ugrian**; (b) **Altaic.**

URANIUM

Metallic element first obtained by Klaproth in 1798. It is one of the elements which undergo fission (*q.v.*), Sp. gr. *c.* 19. Chem. sym. U.

Uranium has a number of isotopes, with atomic wts. varying from 227 to 240.

URANUS
[yoo'-ra-nus] The 7th known planet in order of distance from the sun (*c.* 1,783,000,000 m.). It was discovered by Sir Wm. Herschel in 1781. It has a diam. of *c.* 32,400 m. and its mass is *c.* 15 times that of the earth. It completes one revolution of its orbit in *c.* 84 yrs. 6 days and its period of rotation has been estimated to be *c.* 10 hrs. 49 mins. It has at least 5 satellites.

URBAN DISTRICT
In Eng. and Wales an area set up, for purposes of local government, in 1894. Each U.D. has a council, elected by the people for 3 years and presided over by a chairman. The U.D.s are represented on the county councils.

URBINO
Small town in Italy, 25 m. S. of Rimini. The birthplace of Raphael.

URDU *See* HINDUSTANI.

URINE
The secretion of the kidney. Urine is composed of many by-products of the body which are extracted by the kidneys from the circulating blood. The most common constituents are water, urea, uric acid, hippuric acid and bile pigments.

URTICARIA
or **Nettle Rash.** A skin condition arising usually as the result of some bodily upset.

URUGUAY
[oor-oo-gwī'] Smallest repub. of S. Amer. on the N. bank of La Plata estuary, bounded by Argentina and Brazil. The Uruguay R. forms the W. border. Climate and soil make U. an agricultural country. Meat products and wool account for *c.* 80 % of the exports, wool being by far the most valuable. Montevideo is the cap. There are good road and rail systems and the Uruguay is an important highway. The pop. is almost entirely white; Sp. is the official language, and R.C. the dominant religion. U. was taken by the Portuguese in the 17th cent. and 100 years later by the Sp. It was captured by the Argentine Govt. in 1814. Later it became a prov. of Brazil. War followed between Brazil and Argentina, and U. became an indep. state in 1828 and a repub. in 1830. The Pres. governs with a cabinet, a senate of 30 members and a chamber of deputies, with 99 members. Area: 72,172 sq.m. Pop. *c.* 2,590,158.

USKUDAR
(formerly **Scutari**) District of Istanbul, on the E. of the Bosporus. The scene of Florence Nightingale's work in the Crimean War.

USURY
Orig. any premium paid for the use of money; nowadays, the practice of demanding an exorbitant premium or interest. Attempts were made by the Roms. to provide maximum rates of interest. Later, usury was condemned by the Ch. and was allowed to fall into the hands of the Jews.

UTAH
W. state of the U.S.A. in the Rocky Mts. It contains the Great Salt and Utah lakes, and is traversed by the Colorado. The state is rich in minerals, copper, silver, lead, coal and salt. Irrigation is used in the valleys. Salt Lake City is the cap. U. was settled by Brigham Young and his Mormons in 1847, but was not admitted to the Union until polygamy was abolished in 1896. It sends 2 representatives to Congress. Area: 84,920 sq.m. Pop. 1,059,300.

UTERUS
Female organ found only in mammals in which the fertilised ovum or embryo becomes embedded and develops during pregnancy.

UTRECHT
[-trecht] Dutch city, cap. of U. prov. on the Old Rhine, 24 m. S.E. of Amsterdam. Industries include machine shops, printing, clothing and chemicals. Pop. 261,043. The **Treaty of U.** (1712-13) terminated the War of the Sp. Succession.

UTRILLO, Maurice
(1883-1955) Fr. artist. B. Paris. His work falls into 3 periods: Impressionism, an intermediary period and a ' white ' period.

UVULA
Small extension of soft palate hanging down between tonsils.

UZBEKISTAN
Repub. of the U.S.S.R. in C. Asia bounded by the Kazakh, Turkmen, Tajik and Kirgiz S.S.Rs. and Afghanistan. The W. is a low-lying, waterless plain, with oases. In the E. the land rises towards the Pamirs. The chief river is the Amu Darya. The climate is dry, and irrigation is necessary. Cotton is the principal product. Minerals include oil, coal, copper and sulphur. Tashkent is the cap.; other cities are Bukhara and Samarkand. The repub. was formed 1924 and entered the Union 1925. Area: 158,069 sq.m. Pop. 9,700,000.

V

V
22nd letter of the Eng. alphabet. In classical Lat. *v* represented both the vowel sound *u* and the consonant *v*. In Eng. *v* is related to the unvoiced *f*, but is always a sonant lip-sound, *e.g. vain, value, venom*, etc.

V.H.F. BROADCASTING
Very High Frequency Broadcasting, introduced to improve reception. In 1955 V.H.F. stations to reinforce transmissions of the Home, Light and Third programmes on long and medium waves came into operation at Wrotham, Kent. Operating on frequencies around 90 megacycles per sec., which is equivalent to a wavelength of a little more than 3 metres.

V. WEAPONS
Vergeltungswaffen *i.e.* the **Flying Bomb (V.1)** and the **Rocket (V.2)**, pilotless projectiles used by the Germans against London and the S. of Eng., Antwerp, etc. in World War II. The V.1 was a jet-propelled, winged bomb which carried a powerful charge of explosive and, when the engine cut out, fell to earth and exploded. Launching sites were constructed along the Channel coast and over 8,000 V.1s were launched from June till Aug. 1944. During the last 2 weeks of June, 2,000 flying bombs were released. Of these, 661 were destroyed by fast Brit. fighter aircraft and A.A. defences, and barely half reached London. The attack imposed a severe strain on the civil pop. but casualties averaged only 1 per bomb. **Rocket-Bomb (V.2)**. A giant rocket-propelled bomb, fired from sites in The Hague. It was 50 ft. long, carried a ton of explosive, attained a speed of 2,500 m.p.h. and reached a ht. of 60 m. The first V.2s landed in London on Sept. 8, 1944, and attacks were kept up until the sites were captured by the Allied invading forces in Mar. 1945.

VACCINATION
Protective inoculation of a vaccine. Commonly applied to the inoculation of calf lymph in the prevention of smallpox, vaccination was first practised in Eng. by Jenner in 1796. Following its introduction the incidence of smallpox has fallen very considerably throughout the world. In terms of the Health Bill of 1947, vaccination is now voluntary. Vaccination against poliomyelitis has had considerable success.

VACUUM
Space devoid of matter. The perfect vacuum is not attainable, methods of exhaustion always leaving some residual gas. A vacuum is a non-conductor of heat and will not transmit sound waves. Heat, light and other electro-magnetic radiation are transmitted readily. The vacuum flask is a container with a vacuum interspace to prevent the conduction of heat. The contents are thus retained for long periods at their orig. temp.

VAGINA
[va-jī′-na] The vagina, or birth canal, is the passage leading from the womb to the exterior of the body. The external genitalia consist of two pairs of folds, called the labia, which enclose the vaginal opening, the urethral opening from the bladder, and a vestigal organ in front named the clitoris, which corresponds to the male penis.

VALENCIA
City of E. Spain, cap. of V. prov., near the mouth of the Turia. There is a univ. and a cath. 3rd largest city of Spain, V. manufactures textiles, leather and pottery, and exports fruits. Pop. 503,358.

VALENTINE
Christian martyr under the Emperor Claudius, *c.* 270. Commemorated on Feb. 14. The ancient custom of sending valentines or love tokens on this day is said to be a survival of Rom. Lupercalian custom.

VALENTINIAN
Rom. Emperor (364-75) who succeeded Jovian in 364. He was intolerant in religious matters, but made useful laws. He divided the empire into E. and W. and ruled the W. division.

VALERIAN
[-lēr′-] Perennial herbaceous plant (*Valeriana officinalis*) of the family Valerianaceae. The root is used medicinally. Another variety, the small marsh valerian (*V. dioica*) is found in boggy places.

VALÉRY, Paul
(1871-1945) Fr. poet. His poems (Symbolist) include *La Soirée avec M. Teste* (1896), *Le Cimetière Marin* (1920), *Album des Vers Anciens* and *Odes, Charmes* (1922). His critical essays include *Pièces sur l'Art* (1934), *Regards sur le Monde Actuel* and a work on Leonardo da Vinci.

VALLADOLID
[valȧ-dō-lid′] Sp. city, cap. of V. prov., with a cath. and univ. It was the home of Cervantes. Linen, silk and pottery are manufactured. Pop. 159,135.

VALLETTA
Cap. of Malta, an important port and a Brit. naval base. Founded in 1566, V. is built on a spur of rock projecting into the bay. Most of the fine buildings, such as the lodges of the Knights of St. John, were damaged by bombing in World War II. Pop. 18,202.

VALOIS
[val-wȧ] Former royal house of Fr. Members of the house of V. were kings of Fr. from 1328-1589 . **Marguerite de Valois**, daughter of Henry II and Catherine de Medici, mar. Henry of Navarre, and was one of the best memoir writers of the 16th cent.

VALPARAISO
[val-pȧ-rī-zō] City and seaport of Chile, cap. of V. province, 90 m. N. of Santiago. The chief port of the Pacific coast of S. Amer. Pop. 259,241.

VAMPIRE
According to ancient belief, the soul of a dead man, which leaves the body by night in the form of a bat, bird or spider to suck the blood of the living, who slowly decline and die.

VAMPIRE BAT
Blood sucking bat. 2 such inhabiting S. and C. Amer. were discovered by Darwin. The commoner type, *Desmodus rufus*, is some 3 in. in length, reddish-brown, with large sharp incisor teeth.

VAN DE VELDE
Family of Dutch painters. **Jan** (1593-1642), **Willem** (1611-93) and his son **Willem** (1633-1707) were engaged by Charles II and James I to paint naval actions.

VAN DIEMEN'S LAND
[dē'-] Name given to Tasmania (*q.v.*) by the Dutch explorer, Tasman, who discovered it in 1642.

VAN DYCK, Sir Anthony
(1599-1641) Flemish portrait painter. In 1615 he entered the workshop of Rubens and was invited by Charles I to London, where he became court painter. He painted many of the distinguished personalities of his day and a number of religious pictures.

VANADIUM
A rare earth, Sym. V., at. no. 23, at. wt. 50·95. Discovered by Berzelius in 1831, the metal, which is of a light colour, belongs to the phosphorus group and has 5 oxides. It dissolves in nitric acid and improves the resistance of steel.

VANBRUGH, Dame Irene
(1872-1950) Eng. actress. She began her career at Margate in *As You Like It* (1888). She appeared in London and the U.S.A., also in S. Africa, Australia and New Zealand with her husband **Dion Boucicault** (1859-1929).

VANBRUGH, Sir John
(1664-1726) Eng. architect and dramatist. He finished Greenwich Hosp. (1695), Castle Howard in Yorks. (1702), and Blenheim Palace (1705). He wrote *The Relapse* and *The Provok'd Wife* (1697).

VANCOUVER
Canadian Is. in the Pacific; part of Brit. Columbia, separated from the mainland by the Strait of Georgia. Discovered in 1592 by Juan de Fuca. It united with the mainland colony of New Caledonia in 1866, to form Brit. Columbia. Victoria, the prov. cap., is on the S. coast. Area: *c.* 12,400 sq.m.

VANCOUVER
City and chief seaport of Brit. Columbia, Canada. The terminus of the C.P. Railway, it has a natural harbour and an important shipping trade. Industries include lumbering, paper-pulp and canning. V. was founded in 1886. Pop. 410,000.

VANDALS
Tribe, first appearing in E. Germany. In A.D. 400, began to move W., coming into contact with the Goths and Franks. Under Gunderic they crossed the Pyrenees; in 428, 80,000 Vandals under Genseric crossed to N. Africa. They formed bands of pirates and in 455 captured Rome by surprise. Their cruelty to the Christians gave rise to the word **Vandalism.**

VANE, Sir Henry
(1613-62) Eng. statesman. During the Civil War he was the civil leader but quarrelled with Cromwell and was imprisoned. After the Restoration, he was beheaded on Tower Hill for high treason. He was a promoter of the Solemn League and Covenant.

VANILLA
Flavouring material obtained from the seed pod of the vanilla plant (*Vanilla planifolia*), a native of C. Amer. It has green flowers, long slender seed pods, and belongs to the *Orchidaceae.*

VARANASI
Formerly **Benares.** Sacred city of the Hindus, in the state of Uttar Pradesh, India, on the Ganges, 79 m. E. of Allahabad. Along the river bank are the flights of steps called *ghats* (*q.v.*) by which the pilgrims can reach the water; also the Hindu cremation ground. Pop. 471,258.

VARICOSE VEINS
Dilated veins of lower limb, often assoc. with aching of legs and cramp after exercise. If symptoms are severe, injection or ligation of the vein may be required and may give relief.

VARIOLITE
Basaltic rock, found in the tertiary dykes in Ireland, in Skye and Argyllshire. It has a glassy matrix containing felspathic fibres.

VARNISH
A liquid applied as a thin coating, which dries to form a hard, shining layer. Alcohol or volatile varnishes contain amber resins; these varnishes dry very quickly giving a hard, glossy surface which is liable to crack. Oil varnishes contain copal gum and non-volatile oils, such as linseed-oil; the oil does not evaporate, so that the film is tough and pliable and unlikely to crack. By introducing a pigment into varnish, paint is obtained.

VARNISH TREE
(*Aleurites moluccana*) Chinese tree. The seeds contain lac, a resinous secretion exuded by certain insects, to which the tree owes its name.

VASA
Swedish Royal House which was founded by **Gustavus Vasa** (1523-60).

VATICAN
Pontifical palace, Rome; largest palace in the world, covering an area of 882,817 sq.ft. Pope Gregory XI, on his return from Avignon in 1377, chose the palace as his residence, and it has remained the home of the popes and the centre of the R.C. Ch. The Sistine Chapel, where the pope is crowned, erected by Sixtus IV, in 1473, is famous for its masterpieces by Michelangelo. The Vatican Library contains over 220,000 vols. including many ancient MSS. The Lateran Treaty between Italy and the Holy See was ratified there in 1929. By it the state of **Vatican City** came into being; it has an area of 108 acres in Rome. Foreign powers are represented at the court of the Vatican, and the city has its own broadcasting station, postage stamps, coinage, flag, etc.

VAUGHAN, Henry
(1622-95) Brit. metaphysical poet, disciple of George Herbert. *Silex Scintillans* (religious poems, (1650-5), *Thalia Rediviva, the Pastimes and Diversions of a Country Muse,* are his chief vols.

VAUGHAN WILLIAMS, Ralph
[vawn] (1872-1958) Eng. composer. His works include *London Symphony, Sea Symphony, Sixth Symphony, Sinfonia Antarctica, This Day* and choral works, several operas, a ballet, *Job,* chamber music, ch. music and songs.

VEDAS
[vā'-] Collections of hymns and rituals which form the earliest scriptures of the Aryans of India.

VEGA Carpio, Lope Felix de
(1562-1635) Sp. dramatist. He is said to have written over 520 plays, including comedies and hist. dramas.

VEGETABLE MARROW
The commonest of the gourds. The fruit is of oblong-elliptical shape, 9-18 in. long.

VEGETARIANISM
Dietetic custom (or injunction) that human beings must not partake of any kind of animal food. The rule was fundamental to certain orders of the priesthood in ancient Egypt, is practised by Hindus and Buddhists, and by the adherents of certain other religions. Some vegetarians reject all animal food. Others allow the use of butter, milk, eggs and cheese. Fruitarians partake of nothing but fruit, nuts, etc. The advantages urged for Vegetarianism are: the avoidance of the taking of life; the

beneficial effect on physical health and moral character; the greater freedom of wholesome fruit and vegetables from the germ of disease.

VEIN
Blood vessel formed by union of several small veins. Large veins such as those in legs have simple valves which prevent backward flow of blood. Main venous system consists of 3 parts. (1) *General system* carrying blood from limbs, head, neck and face to heart. (2) *Portal system* carrying blood with nutrient material from bowel to liver and by a second relay to general system. (3) *Pulmonary circulation* bringing oxygenated blood back from lungs to the left side of the heart for distribution to remainder of body.

VELASQUEZ
[vi-las′-kwiz] **Diego de Silva y** (1599-1660) Philip IV made him his private painter, and he painted many portraits and studies of court life.

VELVET
Silk fabric. It is woven with a short, thick pile on one side only. In medieval times Genoa was the source of the finest velvet.

VENDÉE, La
[vá(ng)-dā] Dept. of Fr. on the Atlantic coast, important in revolutionary hist. The Vendeans caused civil strife from 1793-6.

VENEREAL DISEASES
Group of diseases arising from infection contracted at sexual intercourse. Gonorrhoea, syphilis, lymphogranuloma venereum granuloma inguinale and chancroid. Immediate and prolonged med. treated is essential for cure. *See* GONORRHOEA; SYPHILIS.

VENEZUELA
[-iz-wā′-] N. repub. of S. Amer. with a coastline on the Caribbean Sea, bounded by Colombia, Brazil and Brit. Guiana. There are 4 regions. In the centre are the llanos, plains of the Orinoco basin, bounded on the S.E. by the Guiana Highlands, and on the N.W. by the Andean ranges. Coastal plains surround L. Maracaibo. There are 3 climate zones, torrid, temp. and cold, according to the height above sea level. Coffee, sugar, cotton, cocoa and tobacco are produced and exported; sheep and cattle are raised on the llanos. Of the minerals produced, petroleum is the most important. Gold is mined in the E. in the Ciudad Bolivar area. Caracas is the cap. and La Guaira the chief port. The pop. is mainly of mixed Sp. and Ind. descent; the language is Sp. and the religion R.C. V. became a repub. in 1830, after seceding from the Repub. of Colombia. There is a Pres., who presides over a Coalition Gov. Area: 352,140 sq.m. Pop. 9,352,000.

VENICE
Ital. city, seaport and naval base in Veneto, 25 m. E. of Padua on the Gulf of V. at the head of the Adriatic Sea. It is built on some 100 islets, with canals as the main thoroughfares. The harbour is well equipped; industries include the manufacture of glass, tapestry and lace. V. has many fine buildings, *viz.*: the Palace of the Doges, the cath. of St. Mark, the Bridge of Sighs, and numerous chs. To the S.E. of the city is the Lido, a famous resort. Pop. 336,184. The ancient repub. of V. was a maritime power of great importance until the capture of Constantinople by the Turks in 1453, and the discovery of the Cape Route to the Indies. In 1866, after the defeat of Austria by Prussia, V. became part of United Italy.

VENIZELOS, Eleutherios
[ven-i-zā′-los] (1864-1936) Gk. statesman. He took part in the Cretan rising, 1896, becoming Pres. of the Assembly in 1897, and Min. for Foreign Affairs. In 1909 he went to Athens, and became P.M. of Greece in 1910. At the outbreak of World War I his sympathies, contrary to those of his sovereign, were with the Allies, and he resigned in 1915. After the dethronement of King George in 1917, he was again P.M. until 1920.

VENUS
The 2nd known planet in order of distance from the sun (*c.* 67,300,000 m.). It is slightly smaller than the earth, having a diam. of 7,700 m. and its mass is 0·83 that of our planet. Its rotation period has been estimated as *c.* 68 hrs. and it completes one revolution round the sun in *c.* 225 days. V. is almost permanently screened from view by its cloud-laden atmosphere, but it presents to the earth phases like those of the moon. In Oct. 1967 the Russ. Venus IV made a soft landing and the Amer. Mariner flew past.

VENUS'S LOOKING GLASS
(*Specularia speculum*) Annual herbaceous plant of the family Campanulaceae. It is *c.* 12 in. high with vivid purple flowers.

VERA CRUZ
[kroos] City and seaport of Mexico, on the Gulf of M. It dates from 1520, following the advent of Cortez. Pop. 186,000.

VERBENA
[-bē′-] Genus of shrubs, mostly native to Amer. One variety is known as Lemon-grass and yields a fragrant oil.

VERDI, Giuseppe
[vair′-di] (1813-1901) **Ital.** composer. With the production of *Nabucco* in 1842 his success was assured. 3 of his best known operas, *Rigoletto, Il Trovatore* and *La Traviata,* were written in a single year. *Aïda* was commissioned to celebrate the opening of the Suez Canal. His last opera, *Falstaff*, was written when he was almost 80. Of his other works the most popular is the *Requiem* written in 1873.

VERDUN
Town in Meuse dept. N.E. Fr., on the Meuse. Of Rom. origin, the town capitulated to the Germans in 1789, after the Revolution, and in 1870. In both World Wars, V. was the scene of heavy fighting. Pop. 18,800.

VEREENIGING
Town of the Transvaal, S. Africa, on the Vaal, 35 m. S. of Johannesburg, where the treaty was signed between Brit. and Boer leaders which ended the S. African War (1899-1902).

VERLAINE, Paul
(1844-96) Fr. poet. B. Metz. Author of *Poèmes Saturniens* (1866), *Fêtes Galantes* (1869), *Sagesse* (1881), *Parallèlement* (1890).

VERMEER, Jan
[ver-mēr′] (1632-75) Dutch painter, b. Delft. He prob. studied under Fabritius, a pupil of Rembrandt. He was forgotten until 1866, when he was ' discovered ' by Theophile Thore, and V. is now considered the most perfect in technique of the Dutch masters.

VERMIN
Word used for a noxious animal, or one destructive to crops and game. Rats, mice, moles, foxes, polecats and weasels are vermin. In Brit., by a law passed in 1919, persons who fail to destroy rats and mice on their land, wherever it is reasonably possible to do so, can be fined. The word is also used for lice, fleas and other insects.

VERMONT
New England state of the U.S.A., S. of the Canadian border and bounded on the E. by the Connecticut R. Agriculture is the chief industry. There are deposits of asbestos. Montpelier is the cap. but Burlington and Rutland are larger. V. became a state in 1791, and sends 1 representative to Congress. Area: 9,610 sq.m. Pop. 445,000.

VERMOUTH
[vur′-mooth] Apéritif prepared from distilled white wines. It is made in Fr. and in Italy.

VERNE, Jules
(1828-1905) Fr. writer. *Round the World in Eighty Days* and *Twenty Thousand Leagues under the Sea* are imaginary travel-tales.

VERONA
City of Veneto, N. Italy, on the Adige, 90 m. E. of Milan. A market centre with varied industries, V. has a cath. and remains of a Rom. amphitheatre. Pop. 221,138.

VERONESE, Paola
[vair-ō-nā′-zi] (1528-88) Venetian painter, b. Verona. He settled in Venice in 1555. He visited Rome in 1563, the result being a greater dignity and grace in his work.

VERONICA
Genus of plants, shrubby and herbaceous, of the family Scrophulariaceae. *Veronica longifolia*, a popular garden variety is *c.* 2 ft. high and bears spikes of blue flowers. *V. spicata*, 18 in., has varieties bearing rose, blue or white blooms, and another *V. rupestris* is of dwarf growth. *V. chamaedrys*, the germander speedwell, is the best known of the 16 Brit. species, and is often called Bird's eye, or Cat's eye. *V. agrestis*, the field speedwell, has small blue blooms.

VERROCCHIO, Andrea del
[ve-rok′-yō] (1435-88) Florentine artist. He worked under Donatello. He was a sculptor, goldsmith, architect, painter and musician. Leonardo da Vinci was his pupil.

VERSAILLES
[vair-sī′] Fr. town, cap. of Seine-et-Oise dept., 11 m. S.W. of Paris. It is chiefly famous for its royal palace, erected by Louis XIII, and enlarged by Louis XIV. The **Treaty of V.**, which fixed the terms of peace after World War I was signed on June 28, 1919. It contained 15 parts; Part I dealt with the Covenant of the League of Nations (*q.v.*); II and III with territorial dispositions, Germany losing Alsace and Lorraine to Fr., several frontier districts to Belg., Denmark, Poland and Lithuania; the Saar basin was placed under an internat. commission, with Germany's colonial possessions which were ceded to the chief Allied Powers; Part V restricted her armaments while VIII and IX dealt with Reparations (*q.v.*) and finance. Other parts dealt with economic restitution, shipping, the Rhine zone, prisoners, war graves, etc.

VERSE
Language in which the logical or syntactical progression takes place against a *metrical* background, of lines and perhaps stanzas of fixed structure. The principle of the verse may be (1) **quantitative,** *i.e.* based on the *length* of syllables, (2) **syllabic,** *i.e.* the *number* of syllables, (3) **accentual,** *i.e.* the *weight* or *stress* on syllables (as in O.E.).

VERWOERD, Hendrick
(1901-66) S. African statesman. Exponent of the strict racial policy of apartheid. Elected P.M. by national parl. caucus. After criticism of his policy at Commonw. P.M.'s conference, 1961, S.A. left the Commonwealth. Dr. Verwoerd was assassinated, 1966; succeeded by B. J. Vorster as P.M. of South Africa.

VESPASIAN
(A.D. 9-79) Rom. emperor. Served in Brit. under Aulus Plautius. In 69 he was declared emperor and seized Rome from Vitellius.

VESPUCCI, Amerigo
[-poo′-chi] (1451-1512) Ital. explorer. When 50 years old he explored the coasts of Venezuela. His name, Amerigo was given to the 2 continents through the erroneous belief that he had discovered the mainland the year before Columbus.

VESUVIUS
Volcano in Campania, Italy, some 4,000 ft. above the Bay of Naples. In A.D. 79 a tremendous explosion destroyed Pompeii (*q.v.*) and Herculaneum.

VETCH
Plant of the genus *Vicia*, also known as tares. Certain vetches belong to other genera, *i.e.* horse-shoe Vetch (*Hippecrepis*), and milk-vetch (*Astragalus*). The vetches are reddish-purple, annual herbs and form a valuable forage crop.

Common Vetch

VETERINARY SURGEONS
Persons who have studied the science which deals with the health and disease of animals. The first Vet. Coll. was estabd. at Lyons, Fr. in 1762. The controlling body is the Royal Coll. of Vet. Surgeons who grant the diploma of M.R.C.V.S.

VETO
The power which one branch of the legislature of a State has to negative the resolutions of another branch; or the right of the executive branch of Govt., such as King, Pres. or Gov. to reject the bills, measures, or resolutions proposed by other branches. In Brit. the power of the Crown is confined to a veto, a right of rejecting and not resolving, rarely exercised, the last occasion being in 1707; while the power of the House of Lords to veto bills which had passed the Commons was curtailed by the Parl. Act, 1911, *i.e.* the Lords have now power to delay but not to reject legislation. In the U.S. the Pres. may veto all measures passed by Congress, but after that right has been exercised, the rejected bill may become law by being passed by two-thirds of each of the Houses of Congress. *See* UNITED NATIONS ORGANISATION.

VICAR
(1) In the Ch. of E. the rector of a parish is, in theory, the owner of the tithes, and the *vicar* is his deputy. The term *vicar* is used for any incumbent of a parish (other than a rector) who is sanctioned to solemnise marriages, etc. (2) **Vicar (R.C. Ch.)** (*a*) One of the titles of His Holiness the Pope is *Vicar of Christ*. (*b*) In general a *vicar* is an ordained priest who acts as the deputy of a ch. official of higher rank. (*c*) **Vicar-Apostolic.** Formerly one to whom the Pope delegated some distant portion of his jurisdiction. Also used of titular bishop appointed by the Vatican for service in a country where there are no Sees, or one exercising temporary authority in a vacant See. (3) **Vicar-Gen.** (*a*) In the Ch. of E. a lay official who represents the bishop; a chanc. of a diocese. (*b*) In the R.C. Ch. an official who performs the duties of an archdeacon.

VICHY
[vē′-shē] Town in Allier dept., C. Fr. During the German Occupation of Fr. in World War II, it was the cap. of Pétain's govt. Pop. 30,400.

VICTOR EMMANUEL II
(1820-78) King of Sardinia, afterwards King of Italy. With the help of his army and

Garibaldi, and by diplomacy with the help of his min., Cavour, he was the real creator of a united Italy. **Victor Emmanuel III** (1869-1947) King of Italy, son of Umberto I, he came to the throne in 1900. He refused to oppose Fascist occupation of Rome and became Mussolini's tool. He abdicated in 1944, in favour of his son, Umberto.

VICTORIA
(1819-1901) Queen of the U.K. of Gt. Brit. and Ireland and Empress of India, only child of Edward, Duke of Kent, 4th son of George III. She succeeded William IV in 1837, and mar. her cousin, Prince Albert of Saxe-Coburg-Gotha, in 1840. Her long reign saw more changes than any other in Brit. hist. The Emp. was considerably enlarged; the greater colonies achieved self-govt.; successive reform bills extended the franchise; the Corn Laws were repealed, and Free Trade was adopted. Educ. was made compulsory; rlys., the telegraph and telephone came into being; penny postage was inaugurated; and many measures for improvement in working class conditions were passed. Gt. Brit.'s interests abroad involved her in several wars. In the E. she waged war in China and Afghanistan; her rule in India involved her in the Indian Mutiny, 2 Sikh wars and 2 Burmese wars, and in Africa the Zulu and Boer Wars. In Europe she took part in the Crimean War. Among the Queen's P.M.s were Melbourne, Peel, Palmerston, Disraeli, Gladstone and Salisbury. She followed the policy indicated by them, but made her influence felt. She celebrated her Diamond Jubilee in 1897.

VICTORIA
or **V. Nyanza.** Lake of C. Africa, in Kenya, Uganda and Tanganyika. The S. shore was discovered in 1856 by Speke who also found the N. outlet, in 1861. The principal source of the White Nile, it is 3,717 ft. above sea level. Area: *c.* 26,800 sq.m.

VICTORIA
Cap. of Brit. Columbia, Canada, on the S. coast of Vancouver Is. V. became cap. of the prov. in 1866. It is a fine city with a good harbour. Pop. 154,152.

VICTORIA
State of the Commonwealth of Australia, S.E. corner of the continent. The Austral. Alps and Gt. Dividing Range run from E. to W., dividing the lowland into 2 regions, the fertile coastal plain and the Murray basin in the N. The Murray, the chief river, forms the boundary between V. and N.S.W. Wheat and wool are the most important products; others are dairy produce, fruit and wine. Coal and gold are mined, and industrial development has increased considerably since World War II. Irrigation is of great importance. Melbourne is the cap. and largest city; other towns are Geelong, Ballarat and Bendigo. Orig. part of N.S.W., V. became a separate colony in 1851, receiving responsible govt. 4 years later. Admin. is by a Gov., a ministry, and a parl. of 2 houses. Area: 87,880 sq.m. Pop. 3,013,447.

VICTORIA CROSS
Brit. decoration awarded to officers and men of the fighting services for individual gallantry in the face of the enemy. It was instituted at the suggestion of Queen Victoria. It was authorised by Royal Warrant on Jan. 29, 1856, and the first investiture took place in Hyde Park in 1857. The first V.C. was Lieut. C. D. Lucas, R.N. who won the cross during the bombardment of a Russian fortress in the Baltic on June 21st, 1854. The reward carries, for non-commissioned ranks only, a yearly pension of £100, plus an addition of 6d a day to the recipient's pension. In 1920, the V.C. Warrant was revised and brought up-to-date to include the R.A.F. and Nursing Services, and to civilians of either sex regularly or temporarily under the orders, direction or supervision of the Naval, Military or Air Forces of the crown. From 1854-1954, 1,347 V.C's were awarded.

VICTORIA FALLS
Falls on the Zambezi in Rhodesia, 800 m. from the sea. Discovered by Livingstone in 1855, the falls consist of a single drop of 256-355 ft. Now called Mosi-Oa-Toenja.

VICTORIAN ORDER, Royal
Brit. order of knighthood instituted 1896. Its members are divided into 5 classes, viz.: Knight Grand Cross (G.C.V.O.), Knight Commander (K.C.V.O.), Commander (C.V.O.), and Members, in 2 classes (M.V.O.). Women are eligible and if of the rank of knight are Dames (D.V.O.), also Dame Commander (D.C.V.O.).

VICTORY
Eng. wooden warship, launched at Chatham in 1765. In 1803 she became the flagship of Nelson, in which he fought at Trafalgar.

VICUNA
Species of llama found in Peru and Chile. It is *c.* 2½ ft. in ht. The hair, soft and fine in texture, and of a pale yellowish brown shading to white underneath, is used in the manufacture of a fine cloth. *See* LLAMA.

VIENNA
Cap. city of Austria, on the Danube, in a rich agricultural region. A natural focus of routes, V. is a leading commercial city, with an extensive transit trade. Besides manufacturing optical instruments, machinery and chemicals, it has a large film industry. A Rom. garrison town named Vindobona, the city became the cap. of the Duchy of Aust. in 1156 and the centre of the Hapsburg power in the 13th cent. After World War I, V. became cap. of the Aust. Repub. In 1945, V. became the seat of the Allied Council, and the city was divided in 4 zones, occupied by the U.K., U.S.A., Fr. and U.S.S.R. In 1955 the Aust. State Treaty was signed in V. by which Aust. was recognised as a sovereign, indep. and democratic state. Pop. 1,627,566. **Vienna, Congress of.** (1814-15) Congress of all European Powers except Turkey, called to adjust frontiers and settle Europe after the fall of Napoleon. Chief Powers were Aust. (Metternich), Pruss. (Blücher), Brit. (Castlereagh), Russ. (Alexander I) and Fr. (Talleyrand).

VIETNAM
[vyet'-nam] Until 1954 a Repub. in the Fed. of Indo-China within the Fr. Union. According to the armistice agreement of 1954, drawn up at Geneva between Fr. Union and Communist forces, Vietnam was divided into two approx. equal zones along the 17th parallel, but bitter fighting continues, in which the U.S.A. has played a controversial part, supporting S. Vietnam against attacks from the North. **N. Vietnam,** ruled by a Communist admin. in Hanoi, lies to the S. of China with a coastline on the Gulf of Tong King. Products include rice, maize, sugar, coffee, coal and silk. Area: *c.* 59,935 sq.m. Pop. 20,100,000. **S. Vietnam** has now been recognised as an indep. Repub., proclaimed under Pres. Diem in 1955. The country has a long coastline on the S. China Sea. Rice, haricots, soya, sugar and cotton are the main crops. The cap. is Saigon. Area: *c.* 65,950 sq.m. Pop. 16,973,000.

VIGNY, Alfred de
(1797-1863) Fr. poet, playwright, novelist. His first poems appeared in 1822. He wrote the tragedy *Chatterton* (1835), and the novels *Cinq Mars* (1826) and *Servitude et Grandeur Militaires* (1835).

VIKING
Name given to seafarers of Scandinavian origin. *The Saga of Eric the Red*, 1320, tells of the voyage of Eric from Iceland to Greenland and

of his son Leif's voyage to what must have been N. Amer. at least 500 years before Columbus. The Vikings conquered and settled in the Hebrides, Orkneys, Shetlands and Faroes, made many raids on the Brit. Isles and the shores of Europe, and colonised the coast of Fr. They made Iceland a repub. A.D. 930, and estabd. a parl, which is still in existence.

Viking ship

Their principal gods were Thor and Odin; honour, courtesy and hospitality were paramount virtues; poetry, music and literature were the chief creative arts.

VILLENEUVE, Pierre de
[vēl-nöf] (**Charles Jean Baptist Sylvestre**) (1763-1806) Fr. admiral. In the Battle of the Nile he saved the rear division of the Fr. navy. He gave battle to Nelson at Trafalgar in 1805, and was defeated.

VILLON, François
[vē-lō(ng)] (1431-*c.* 1463) Fr. poet. B. Paris. He was arrested for complicity in murders and robberies, and was sentenced to be hanged in 1462. This was commuted to banishment for 10 years. His poems are highly personal.

VILNA
or **Vilnius**. Cap. of the Lithuanian S.S.R. V. is rich in hist. assoc. and possesses 2 caths. Formerly inhabited by the Lithuanians, it was ceded to Russ. 1795. After World War I it was claimed by the Lithuanians, but the Poles took possession of it. In 1940 Lithuania became part of the U.S.S.R. and Vilna became its cap. Pop. 271,000.

VINCENT, Earl of St.
John Jervis (1734-1823) Brit. admiral. Entered the navy as a boy. On 14th Feb. 1797, when in command of the Medit. squadron of 15 sail, he defeated 27 Spanish ships of the line off Cape St. Vincent.

VINE
Climbing plant of the family Vitaceae. It has sturdy woody stems, which cling by means of tendrils to a wall or any other support. The large leaves have tooth-like edges and the small green flowers are clustered in racemes. The berries, or grapes, contain hard seeds. The grape varies from dark purple to a very light green, almost white. The chief areas for growing are the Medit. countries, Australia, S. Africa and parts of U.S.A. Viticulture is most flourishing in the Rhineland in Germany, in the S. parts of Fr., in Italy, Sp., Portugal, Hungary, etc.

VINEGAR
Sour liquid used for flavouring and preserving. It is acetic acid and is usually made in Brit. from malted barley, which is fermented. It can be made from alcoholic liquors and in Europe is obtained from white wine. In U.S.A. it is made from cider.

VINEGAR PLANT
A slimy gelatinous mass found on the surface of alcoholic fluids during fermentation, and composed of filaments of bacteria and fungi. The action of these converts the alcohol into vinegar.

VIOL
A group of stringed instruments of the 16th and 17th cents. They were superseded by the violin family and lack their brilliance and agility.

VIOLA
The second member of the violin family, its 4 strings being tuned a 5th lower than the violin, the lowest being the C below middle C and the others upward in 5ths, G, D and A. Its compass is *c.* 3 octaves.

VIOLET
Genus of herbs of the family Violaceae. They are perennials of low growth, 7 species being Brit. The sweet violet, *V. odorata*, is found wild in S. and E. Eng. The leaves are broad and heart-shaped and the blossoms purple or white. Other varieties include the dog violet, *V. canina* and *V. silvestris*, and the wood violet. The genus includes the heartsease or wild pansy, *Viola tricolor*.

VIOLIN
A stringed instrument, developed at the same time as the viol in the middle of the 16th cent. from medieval types of fiddle. Brought to perfection by Amati and Stradivari in the 17th and early 18th cents. it has been little modified since. Its 4 strings are tuned in 5ths upwards from the G below middle C. Its compass is *c.* 4 octaves.

VIOLONCELLO
The *'cello* is of the same general construction as the violin. Its 4 strings are tuned upwards in 5ths from the C, 2 octaves below middle C: it has a compass of *c.* 3½ octaves. It was first made in the middle of the 16th cent. and in the 17th and early 18th cents. was used mainly to supply the bass, but later developed as a solo instrument.

VIPER
Venomous snakes of the group, Viperidae, found in Europe, Africa and Asia. The Brit. species is known as the Adder. True vipers (*Vipera*) have a characteristic flattened triangular head and relatively short, thick body. Russell's Viper of India causes many d. each year. Rattlesnakes are included in the normal meaning of the term.

VIPER'S BUGLOSS
[bew'-] (*Echium vulgare*) Annual or biennial herbaceous plant of the family Boraginaceae. The tall stem and the leaves are covered with short bristly hairs. The flowers are borne in a long panicle.

VIRGIL
(70-19 B.C.) Rom. poet. (**Publius Vergilius Maro**). B. Mantua, in Gaul. He enjoyed the patronage of Maecenas and others, whose munificence gave him the leisure to write the *Aeneid*, the *Georgics* and 10 *Eclogues*.

VIRGIN ISLANDS
Group of *c.* 100 Is. in the W. Indies, E. of Puerto Rico. Several are linked with Brit., the majority are Amer., purchased from Denmark in 1917. The chief Brit. town is Road Town. Of the Amer. Is., St. Thomas, St. Croix and St. John are the largest, and Charlotte Amalie is the principal town. Products include sugar and rum.

VIRGINAL
A 16th cent. type of harpsichord, at first box-like in shape and placed on the table or in the player's lap.

VIRGINIA
State of the U.S.A. having a coastline on Chesapeake Bay, with Pennsylvania on the N. and the Carolinas on the S. The valley of V.,

enclosed by the Alleghenies and the Blue Ridge range, is extremely fertile. Rivers include the Potomac, Rappahannock, York and James. Tobacco is grown, as well as maize and cereals. There are coalfields and quarries and oyster fisheries. The cap. is Richmond. The state contains the oldest European settlements in the country, dating from 1607. It was one of the 13 orig. states of the Union and it retains many traces of Eng. influence. It sends 10 representatives to Congress. Area: 40,820 sq.m. Pop. 4,648,500.

VIRGINIA CREEPER
(*Parthenocissos vitacea*) Hardy climbing shrub of the family Vitaceae. The leaves are large and green, turning in autumn to vivid scarlet and russet. *P. tricuspidata*, a Jap. species, has smaller short-stemmed leaves which adhere closely to any wall or support.

VIRGO
[ver′-gō] 6th sign of the Zodiac, operative *c.* August 22-Sept. 21. The constellation from which it takes its name contains the first magnitude star Spica and the spiral nebula, Messier 99.

VIRUS
An infective organism comparable with, but very much smaller than, ordinary microbes. Nearly all are invisible with an ordinary microscope. The electronic microscope has recently demonstrated their presence to the human eye. *See* BACTERIA.

VISBY
Seaport of Sweden, on Gottland Is. 150 m. S.E. of Stockholm. In the M.A. one of the wealthiest of the Hanseatic towns.

VISCOUNT
Title in the peerage of the U.K. It originated in Fr. It ranks 4th in the peerage, between earl and baron.

VISHNU
[vish′-noo] The 2nd of the 3 ' persons ' of the Hindu Trimurti (Trinity).

VISIGOTH *See* GOTHS.

VITAMINS
Organic compounds normally present in foodstuffs, and which are required in the diet in very small amounts to maintain life and health. When these are lacking, deficiency diseases appear. *Vit. A.* is esp. necessary for maintaining the mucous membranes in a healthy condition. *Vit. B complex*. Vit. B_1 (aneurin) is essential for the well-being of the nervous system and digestion. Vit. B_2 (riboflavin) promotes growth and healthy skin and eyes. Vit. B_3 (pantothenic acid) is essential for carbohydrate metabolism. Vit. B_6 (pyridoxine) is important in maintaining a healthy skin and nervous system. Vit. B_{12} (cyanocobalamin) prevents pernicious anaemia. The P-P factor (nicotinic acid) is responsible for maintaining the health of the skin and the intestinal tract. Folic Acid is a vitamin in the B-complex vital for the correct functioning of the blood-forming organs. *Vit. C* is the anti-scurvy vitamin and occurs in fresh fruit and green vegetables. *Vit. D* promotes the formation of strong bones and teeth. Its lack in children produces rickets. *Vit. E* is important for normal pregnancy and in men may produce sterility if deficient. It is present in wheat, cereals, peas and lettuce. *Vit. K* is essential for the process of clotting.

VIVALDI, Antonio
[-val′-] (*c.* 1675-1741) Ital. composer. He wrote nearly 50 operas as well as choral music, but is chiefly known for his 124 violin concertos.

VLADIVOSTOK
Town of the extreme eastern U.S.S.R. on the Sea of Japan. It is the Pacific terminus of the Trans-Siberian Railway, with a harbour. Pop. 338,000.

VODKA
Name of a spirituous liquor. It is made in Russia by distilling rye or potatoes.

VOLCANO
[-kā′-] An opening in the crust of the earth, through which superheated matter is expelled, forming a hill with a crater. The chief volcanic centres are Italy and Sicily, the S. Andes, E. Indies and Japan. Volcanoes may be many years in repose, but the longer their repose the greater their violence in eruption. The eruptions are succeeded by dense clouds of vapour and lava.

VOLE
(*Microtus*) Small herbivorous rodents of the family Arvicolidae. The Field V. (*M. agrestis*) has a short tail, brown fur above and lighter beneath. The Water V., 8 in. long without its tail, has reddish or yellowish-brown fur.

VOLGA
Russ. river, 2,290 m. in length, which rises in the Valdai plateau, and enters the Caspian Sea at Astrakhan. Gorki, Kazan, Kuibyshev, Saratov and Volgograd are on its course. In 1953 the 60 m. long Volga-Don canal was completed, thus connecting navigable waterways from the Baltic to the Black Sea.

VOLGOGRAD
(formerly **Stalingrad**) River port and chief city of V. region of the Russ. S.F.S.R. on the Volga. A market town, it has saw-mills, chem. factories, etc. Pop. 684,000.

VOLOS
Town and seaport of Thessaly. Industries include flour-milling and cigarette manufacture. Pop. 49,221.

VOLTAIC REPUBLIC
(Formerly **Upper Volta**) Former Fr. colony: indep. 1960. Exports include livestock, fish and groundnuts. Cap. Ouagadougou. Area: 103,000 sq.m. Pop. 4,400,000.

VOLTAIRE, François Marie Arouet de
(1694-1778) Fr. writer. Educ. by the Jesuits. He visited Berlin, where he was the close friend of Frederick II; quarrelled with him and spent the remainder of his life at Ferney on L. Geneva. He wrote tragedies, satires and epigrams, studies of Charles XII of Sweden and of the age of Louis XIV, stories (*Candide*, *Zadig*) and an epic, *La Henriade*.

VOLVOX
Colonial flagellate infusorians found in freshwater ponds. They are green in colour with one dominating chromatophore or chloroplast. Having chlorophyll, *Volvox* is able to synthesise its food requirements like a plant. It reproduces both by the asexual method of forming daughter colonies by division and sexually after the union of gametes.

VOODOO
Body of primitive beliefs and practices of African origin found among the natives of the W. Indies, notably the repub. of Haiti, and the negroes of the southern U.S. The rites are secret and of the nature of black magic.

VOROSHILOV, Kliment Efremovich
(1881-1969) Marshal of the U.S.S.R. Led workers of Lugansk in 1905 and Oct. 1917 Revolutions. Met Lenin and Stalin at Stockholm Congress of Bolshevik Party, 1906. Arrested, exiled and escaped several times between 1907-14. Member of C. Committee of Communist Party, 1921. Member of Supreme Soviet and Polit. Bureau since 1926. On the d. of Stalin (*q.v.*) 1953, he was apptd. Pres., a post he held until 1960.

VORTICISM
The vorticists originated in 1913 from a soc. which included P. Wyndham Lewis and the poet Ezra Pound. Their theory was that

modern art should be based on the principles of an industrial civilisation. Vorticism had much in common with *Futurism* and *Cubism.*

VOTE
Expression of a will or an opinion, esp. at an election. For important purposes, such as the election of members to parl. and county and other councils, it is done by ballot. In Brit. before 1873 open voting was usual at elections for Parl. Each country has its own laws stating who is entitled to vote. The privilege is confined to adults, and for long to men only, but in the 20th cent. most countries gave to women the right to vote.

VULGATE
Lat. version of the Bible based on the *Septuagint,* which was written in Gk. and incorporated translations of certain Heb. writings not included in the early canon. The Vulgate was trans. by St. Jerome (331-420) and 2 cents. after its completion it was universally adopted in the W. Chr. Ch. as authoritative for both faith and practice. The *Vulgate* is still the authorised Lat. version of the R.C. Ch., its use having been sanctioned by the Council of Trent, 1545-63. An important Catholic translation of the Bible from the *Vulgate* was made by Ronald A. Knox, pub. 1944-50. In translating the O.T. books, constant reference was made to the Heb. text, and to that of the *Septuagint.* Furthermore a definitive multi-volume edition of the *Latin Vulgate* is also in the course of preparation. The *Vulgate* is not accepted as canonical by Protestant Chs.

VULTURE
Birds of prey belonging to the families Vulturidae and Cathartidae, the latter being Amer. They resemble the Eagles, but almost all have a bare head and neck. They feed on dead animals. The Black V. (*Vultur monachus*) and the Griffin V. (*Gyps fulcus*), are large birds of the Medit. region and S. Europe respectively. Amer. V. include the Condor and Turkey Buzzard.

W

W
23rd letter of the Eng. alphabet. The character is formed by doubling the *u* or *v*. It represents a consonantal sound and at the end of words or syllables it is either silent, as in *low*, or it modifies the preceding vowel as in *new*.

WAGGA WAGGA
[wog'-ă] Town of N.S.W. Australia, on the Murrumbidgee. It is a business centre for the district of the Riverina. Pop. 22,840.

WAGNER, Richard
[vag'ner] (1813-83) German composer. His first successes came with the production of *Rienzi* in 1842 and *Der fliegende Holländer* a year later. In 1864 he was befriended by Ludwig II of Bavaria and commissioned to complete his opera-cycle, *The Ring*. Later Wagner planned a festival theatre at Bayreuth for *The Ring*. The 4 operas of the cycle were produced there in 1876. Wagner achieved a new type of opera which he called Music Drama; in it everything was to forward the main purpose of the drama.

WAGRAM
[vag'-] Village near Vienna, Austria, where in July, 1809, Napoleon defeated the Aust. under the Archduke Charles.

WAGTAIL
(*Motacilla*) Insectivorous, passerine birds of the Old World related to the Pipits. They are easily recognised by bright plumage and lively movement of their long tails as they run about. The Yellow, Grey and Pied W. are common in Brit.; the White W. is a summer visitor.

WAHHABI
Mohammedan sect, followers of the Abe-el-Wahab, who, at the beginning of the 18th cent. taught the necessity of complete obedience to the Koran. They are prominent in Saudi Arabia.

WAKE ISLAND
Small Is. in the N. Pacific, 2,000 m. W. of Hawaii. A U.S. naval base.

WAKE ROBIN
Perennial wild plant (*Arum maculatum*) familiarly known as lords and ladies, cuckoo pint or starchwort. The flower's stem bears a pale-green folded wrapper which reveals a purple column. As the plant withers, the flowers are succeeded by pale scarlet poisonous berries.

WAKEFIELD
City and county borough of Yorks., the county town of W. Riding, on the Calder, 9 m. S. of Leeds. In 1460, the Lancastrians defeated the Yorkists. Hosiery and woollen goods are manufactured, and coal is mined. It returns 1 member to Parl. Pop. 60,430.

WALCHEREN
[val'-] Is. in Zeeland prov., the Netherlands, in the Scheldt estuary. Dairying is the main industry. Middelburg and Flushing, the chief towns, are connected by rly. with the mainland.

WALDENSES
Religious sect, founded by Peter Waldo, a Lyons philanthropist; *c.* 1114, they denounced the Ch. of Rome. Persecuted, they disappeared from the S. of Fr. and lived in the valleys of Piedmont, S.W. of Turin.

WALES
Principality of Gt. Brit., W. of Eng. with a long coastline on the Irish Sea and the St. George's and Bristol Channels. Off the N.W. coast, separated from the mainland by the Menai Strait is the Is. of Anglesey. The Cambrian Mts. cover most of the interior; they include Snowdon (3,560 ft.), the highest point in Eng. and Wales; Plynlimmon (2,468 ft.); Cader Idris (2,927 ft.); Brecon Beacons and the Black Mts. The rivers Severn and Wye rise on the slopes of Plynlimmon and flow N.E. and S.E. respectively, crossing the border into Eng. The shorter ones—Dee, Conway, Dovey, Teify, Towy, Taff, Ogmore and others—are wholly Welsh. Much of the country is agricultural. Sheep are reared in the hilly districts; cattle are reared in the lowlands, where cereals and root crops are grown. There is an extensive coalfield in the S. in Glamorgan, around which a great industrial area has developed. The more important mining centres are Rhondda, Merthyr-Tydfil, Pontypridd, Abertillery and Maesteg. Iron and steel, chemical and tinplate industries have grown up in Swansea, Llwchwr, Port Talbot and Tredegar. The tourist industry is of great importance in the N. Cardiff is the cap.; Llandudno, Rhyl and Colwyn Bay, are seaside resorts on the N. coast. Fishguard and Holyhead are connected by steamer with Ireland. The earliest recorded inhabitants of Wales were Celts; they were subdued by the Roms. and Normans, but not completely, and lived in their own way under their own princes for many cents., carrying on constant war with Eng. In the time of Edward I Wales was really conquered by Eng., and an Eng. prince was made Prince of Wales. By the Act of Union (1536) Eng. law was made current in Wales, and Welsh representatives were admitted to Parl. Wales now sends 36 members to Parl. The Welsh have a language and lit. of their own. In the 18th cent. there was a considerable revival of national feeling. Welsh is taught in the schools. This nat. feeling has been kept alive by the Eisteddfod which has been held annually for at least 800 years. The Eng. Ch. was for long estabd. in Wales, but in the 18th and 19th cents. the majority of the people became Nonconformists. The Univ. of Wales, founded in 1893, consists of coll. at Aberystwyth, Bangor, Cardiff and Swansea. Monmouth, although nominally part of Eng. is generally included in Wales for admin. purposes. Area (including Mon.); 8,000 sq.m. Pop. 2,641,000.

WALL OF CHINA, Great
Wall in N.W. China *c.* 1,500 m. long, 25 ft. wide at the base, 15 ft. at the top and having an average ht. of 20 ft. A defence against the N. Mongols, the work was begun in 215 B.C.

WALLABY
Small Kangaroo-like animal from which it differs only in size and coloration. Confined to Australia.

WALLACE, Sir William
(1270-1305) Scots national hero. He became the leader of the fight for indep. and had driven the Eng. from Scot. by 1297. In 1298 he was defeated by Edward I at Falkirk, and

in 1305 was treacherously handed over to the Eng. king, who had him executed.

WALLASEY
County borough of Ches. on the Mersey estuary, opposite Liverpool. It returns 1 member to Parl. Pop. 103,000.

WALLER, Edmund
(1606-87) Eng. poet. B. Coleshill, Bucks. He is chiefly known for his lyrics.

WALLFLOWER
Perennial flowering plant (*Cheiranthus cheiri*) of the family Cruciferae. The orig. wild variety bears single yellow blooms.

WALLOON
Race found in certain parts of Belg. and N. France. Their language is a Romance dialect akin to mod. Fr. The Walloons number *c.* 3,000,000.

WALMER
Urban district and resort of Kent, 3 m. S. of Deal. The 16th cent. castle is the residence of the Lord Warden of the Cinque Ports. Pop. 5,300.

WALNUT
Tree (*Juglans regia*) grown in Brit. since the 15th cent. A green fleshy case encloses the seed, or nut, in its hard, wrinkled shell. The unripened fruits are used for pickling, and a fine oil from the matured nut is employed in paint and varnish making. The ripe nut of the walnut is a popular dessert fruit. The wood is valuable for furniture and cabinet-making.

WALPOLE, Sir Hugh Seymour
(1884-1941) Eng. novelist. B. Auckland, N.Z.; educ. King's School, Canterbury, and Camb. His novels include *The Wooden Horse* (1909), *Mr. Perrin and Mr. Traill* (1911), *Jeremy* (1919), *The Cathedral* (1922), *The Fortress* (1932), and the *Herries* tetralogy (1930-3).

WALPOLE, Sir Robert
(1676-1745) Eng. statesman. Entered Parl. in 1701 and became Sec. for War in 1708. Out of office 1717-21, his handling of the crisis occasioned by the S. Sea Bubble (*q.v.*) brought him back to power. For the next 21 years he was virtually P.M. His Whig principles secured him the support of the Whig landowners, his policy of peace ensured that of the commercial classes. He was opposed to the War of Jenkin's Ear and to Eng. participation in the Aust. Succession War, and resigned in 1742. His 4th son was **Horace** (1717-97) Eng. man of letters. He bought a villa at Strawberry Hill near Twickenham in 1748, and rebuilt it as a Gothic mansion. He wrote on painters; a 'Gothic' novel *The Castle of Otranto* (1765); but is best known for his correspondence.

WALRUS
(*Odobaenus*) Large marine mammal allied to the Seals, characterised by the prolongation of the upper canine teeth into tusks. Inhabiting the N. polar regions, its flesh is eaten by the Eskimos, and the oil, hide and ivory are valuable.

WALSALL
County borough of Staffs., 9 m. N.W. of Birmingham. Leather goods, clothing and hardware are manufactured. W. returns 1 member to Parl. Pop. 120,590.

WALSINGHAM, Sir Francis
(*c.* 1530-90) Eng. statesman. Burghley sent him on diplomatic missions. So successful was he that Burghley recommended Elizabeth to appoint him one of her secs. of state. He was an enemy of Mary, Queen of Scots, intercepted her letters, and had spies among her entourage. His activities prepared the way for her execution.

WALTON, Ernest T. S.
(1903-) In 1931 he made, with J. D. Cockcroft, the first artificial disintegration of atomic nuclei. Received Nobel Prize for Physics (with J. D. Cockcroft) in 1951.

WALTON, Izaak
(1593-1683) Eng. writer. B. Stafford. *The Compleat Angler* was pub. 1653-55. Walton wrote *Lives* of Donne (1640), Wotton (1651), Hooker (1665), Herbert (1670) and Sanderson (1678).

WALTON, Sir William Turner
(1902-) Eng. composer. His 1st string quartet was performed at Salzburg in 1923, and in the same year he produced *Façade*. His *Belshazzar's Feast* is an outstanding oratorio. He has written film music, a string quartet, 1947, and the opera *Troilus and Cressida* (1954).

WALVIS BAY
Chief port of S.W. Africa, 170 m. W. of Windhoek. It is admin. as a portion of S.W. Africa. Pop. 2,600.

WANTAGE
Urban district of Berks., 26 m. N.W. of Reading, in the Vale of the White Horse. It was the birthplace of Alfred the Great. Pop. 5,940.

WAPITI
Deer (*Cervus canadensis*) found in N. Amer. It is larger than the red deer and has very fine antlers. The hide makes excellent leather.

WAR OF 1812
War between Gt. Brit. and the U.S.A. The war, declared by Congress, was caused by the rigorous exercise on the part of Brit. of her rights of search over neutral (in this case Amer.) vessels. In 1814 a Brit. force under Ross captured Washington and burnt the White House, but a 2nd contingent under Pakenham was repulsed at New Orleans in 1815, by Andrew Jackson, with great loss.

WAR, First World
(1914-18) Internat. struggle which raged over nearly all the Old World between Aug. 1914 and Nov. 1918. It began with Austria's attack on Serbia in July 1914, following the murder of the Archduke Francis Ferdinand at Sarajevo. Russia came to the help of Serbia, and Germany to that of Austria. War was then declared on Fr. as Russia's ally and the invasion of Belg. involved Brit. Germany and Austria, a little later, secured the aid of Turkey and then of Bulgaria. Fr., Russ. and Brit., the strongest members of the group called the Allies, with Belg. and Serbia on their side, were joined by Japan and Italy in 1915, and by Rumania in 1916. The last to join the group was the U.S.A. in April, 1917. The main theatres of war were in Europe where, on the W. Front, Fr. and Brit. confronted Germany, while on the E. Front Austria and Germany confronted Russia. The operations on the Ital. frontiers may be regarded as an extension of the W. Front, and those in the Balkans as an extension of the E. one. The Turkish Empire afforded 2 other theatres, the Gallipoli Peninsula and Mesopotamia. Second in importance only to the struggle on the W. Front was the command of the sea by the Brit. and Allied fleets. The German fleet was penned in its harbours although raiding cruisers in the outer seas caused havoc to allied shipping until they were rounded up and destroyed. German ports were successfully blockaded, but the German fleet was not destroyed. It remained in being even after the indecisive Battle of Jutland, and this had an important bearing on the course of the war. The German submarine campaign against Allied shipping caused serious losses, esp. in 1916-17, only narrowly failing to achieve its purpose. In 1914 the Germans nearly reached Paris, and the Russ. invaded E. Prussia and Austria, but both advances were driven back. The chief engagements were on the Marne and the Aisne in the

W. and at Tannenberg in the E. In the W. 1915 was a year of trench warfare, from the Belg. coast to Switzerland. Attacks were made by the Brit. at Neuve Chapelle and Loos, while the Germans attacked at Ypres. The Brit. attacked the Turks on the Gallipoli Peninsula, but withdrew before the end of the year. The Russ. were driven back, and Poland was overrun. Events of 1916 included the costly Battle of the Somme, the desperate fighting between the Fr. and Germans for the possession of Verdun, and the German conquest of Rumania. Russia was weakening, Italy was making no progress, and the Brit. suffered a serious reverse in Mesopotamia. On land the stalemate seemed complete when 1917 opened. The fierce and costly fighting in the W. led to no definite result. The year's main events were the entry into the war of the U.S.A. and the collapse of Russia, who made peace with Germany at Brest Litovsk early in 1918. After the Ital. defeat at Caporetto, Brit. and Fr. troops were sent to that country. The Brit. regained the upper hand in Mesopotamia, and Allenby entered upon his successful campaign in Palestine. Early in 1918 a last German offensive gained ground against Brit. forces at St. Quentin and the Fr. were driven back on Paris as in 1914; but with Amer. armies in the field a marked change was soon seen. The Allies drove the Germans from the ground they had held for years in Fr. and Belgium. The Itals. defeated the Austrians, the Turkish armies were routed everywhere, and the advances from Salonika crushed the Bulgarians. The enemy one by one called for an armistice, and fighting ended with that granted to Germany on Nov. 11, 1918. Terms of peace were arranged in Paris and embodied in the Treaty of Versailles (*q.v.*).

WAR, Second World
(1939-45) Internat. conflict involving most countries in the world. The first move by the Fascist powers in Europe was the open re-creation of the German army in 1935. Italy overpowered Ethiopia (1935-6) and both Germany and Italy sent forces to assist the rebels in Spain. Japan, engaged in conflict with China since 1931, drew towards a partnership with the Rome-Berlin Axis, later formalised in the Pact of Berlin (Sept. 1940). Hitler (*q.v.*) sent his troops to occupy Austria in Mar. 1938, and in the summer threatened Czechoslovakia. Brit. and Fr. reacted with ultimate ' appeasement ' in the Munich Pact (Sept. 1938). In the spring of 1939, Germany absorbed Bohemia and Moravia, and Italy invaded Albania. Brit. and Fr. then began to prepare an ' anti-aggression front '. In the summer Germany threatened Poland and signed a non-aggression pact with Russia (Aug. 1939). Poland was attacked on Sept. 1, and 2 days later Brit. and Fr. declared war on Germany. The German air and land ' Blitzkrieg ' soon overpowered Poland, Russia defeated Finland (1939-40) and meanwhile, during a winter of inactivity, the Brit. and Fr., behind the Maginot Line, faced the fortified German Siegfried Line. In April, 1940, Germany made a surprise attack on Denmark and Norway; the former offered no resistance and Norway was overpowered by June. Meanwhile, German forces had (May 10) overrun Luxembourg, invaded Holland and Belg. and penetrated into Fr. at Sedan. German columns moved to the Channel, cut off Flanders, and the Allies were evacuated from Dunkirk (*q.v.*). The battle of Fr. ended on June 22, with the Fr. surrender. Gt. Brit. remained the only Allied power, attacked by Italy in N. Africa (*see* NORTH AFRICA, CAMPAIGNS IN) and by German air bombardment at home. The Brit. Is. withstood the air attack, winning the Battle of Brit. (began July 1940) causing the abandonment of Hitler's plan to invade Brit, and the war in Africa was undecided. In Oct. 1940, Italy invaded Gr. In the spring of 1941 Germany rapidly conquered Yugoslavia and Gr. and seized Crete. Brit. began to receive Amer. lend-lease aid and she was joined by a new ally when Hitler invaded Russia. German advances on Moscow and Leningrad were stopped in Dec. 1941, and a drive to the Caucasus was halted at Stalingrad. The Jap. attack on the U.S. fleet at Pearl Harbour occurred also in Dec. and the U.S. declared war on Japan. Extensive operations in the Pacific followed, involving Brit. and Amer. forces. In Oct. 1942, the Brit. victory at El Alamein (*q.v.*) was the turn of the African fighting and on Nov. 7-8, 1942, Amer. forces, at war since Pearl Harbour (*q.v.*) invaded N. Africa. While fighting was still going on there, an entire German army surrendered at Stalingrad. Victory in Tunisia (May 12, 1943), the invasion of Italy, the capture of Sardinia and Corsica caused the surrender of the Itals. The Allies, who had signed the U.N. Declaration (Jan. 1, 1942), were drawn more closely together by the Moscow Conferences, the Cairo Conference, and the Teheran Conference. Aug. 1942, Amer. bombers raided airfields in Holland and later joined in attacks on targets in Germany as well as occupied countries. An invasion of Normandy was begun on June 6, 1944 (' D-Day '). Hard-won battles at Cassino and Anzio furthered the campaign against the Germans in Italy and Rome fell, June 4, 1944. By Sept. victory in Fr. and Belg. was almost complete, despite the setbacks of Arnhem (*q.v.*) and the Ardennes, and of the German use of V-1 and V-2 missiles against the Brit. Isles. In 1944, the Red Army overran the Baltic States, E. Poland, White Russia and the Ukraine, causing the collapse of Rumania (Aug. 23), Finland (Sept. 4), and Bulgaria (Sept. 9). The Russ. forces entered E. Prussia, E. Czechoslovakia and overran Germany to the Oder. The Allies crossed the Rhine on Mar. 7, and when the W. and Russ. armies met, German collapse was complete and Hitler d. in Berlin. Unconditional German surrender was signed at Rheims, May 7, 1945 and ratified at Berlin, May 8. The war against Japan continued. After warnings, the 1st atomic bomb was dropped on Hiroshima on Aug. 6th and the 2nd on Nagasaki on Aug. 9th. Japan accepted Allied demand for unconditional surrender on Aug. 14th. **War Casualties (World War II)** On May 29, 1945, Mr. Churchill announced that the total casualties in the Armed Forces of the Brit. Commonwealth and Empire from Sept. 3, 1939, to end of Feb. 1945, were 1,128,315, of which 307,210 were deaths. On July 29, 1945, it was stated that German casualties on all fronts from the beginning of the war to the end of Nov. 1944, were 4,064,438, of whom 1,119,300 were killed.

WAR CRIMES
The idea that the defeated side in war could be held criminally responsible for their actions during the war was first embodied at the U.N. War Crimes Commission in 1943. War Criminals included many generals, etc., whose connection with ' atrocities ' was indirect. At Nuremberg, 21 Nazi major war criminals were tried, 18 found guilty, 11 condemned to d. and 9 executed. Major Japanese criminals were tried in Tokyo.

WAR OFFICE
Former dept. of the Brit. Govt. responsible for the control of the army, now combined with Admiralty and Air Min. in unified Min. of Defence.

WARATAH
(*Telopea speciosissima*) Austral. shrub of the family Proteaceae, one of the nat. emblems.

WARBECK, Perkin
(1474-99) Native of Tournai who posed as

Richard, Duke of York, said to have been murdered in the Tower by Richard III. Recognised by Charles VIII of Fr., he landed in Brit. in 1495 and was accepted by James IV of Scot. Surrendering at Beaulieu, Hants. he was imprisoned and eventually hung.

WARBLER
Migratory insectivorous birds of the family Sylvidae. Among Brit. species are the Garden W. (*Sylvia corin*); Dartford W. (*S. undata*); White Throat (*S. communis*); Blackcap (*S. atricapilla*); Chiffchaff (*Phylloscopus collybita*); Wood W. (*P. sibilatrix*); Reed W. (*Acrocephalus scirpaceus*); Sedge W. (*A. schoenobaenus*).

WARD, Mary Augusta
(Mrs. Humphry Ward) (1851-1920) Eng. novelist. Matthew Arnold's niece; in 1872 she mar. Thomas Humphry Ward. Among her novels are *Robert Elsmere* (1888), *David Grieve* (1892), *The Marriage of William Ashe* (1905).

WARLOCK, Peter
(1894-1930) Eng. composer (real name **Philip Heseltine**). Besides songs, his works include the *Capriol* suite, the *Old Song and Serenade* for string orch., and the *Serenade for Strings*.

WARRINGTON
County borough of Lancs., on the Mersey, 18 m. E. of Liverpool. Cotton, hardware, soap and glass are manufactured. It sends 1 member to Parl. Pop. 76,000.

WARSAW
(*Polish* **Warszawa**) Cap. of Poland, on the Vistula, 175 m. S.E. of Gdansk. Before World War II it was an important industrial centre, but was almost destroyed by the Germans in 1939 and during the rising of Aug. 1944. Since its liberation in Jan. 1945, most of the city has been rebuilt. Pop. 1,232,000.

WARSHIPS
Information on types of fighting ships, *e.g.* battleship, cruiser, destroyer, etc., will be found under the respective main entries. The lessons of World War II have resulted in a trend away from battleships and towards heavy and light fleet aircraft carriers, guided missile carriers, rocket ships and ships specially equipped to deal with submarine attack, mines, etc. *See* ROYAL NAVY.

WART
Localised growth of skin tissue commonly found on hands and neck but also in other parts of the body.

WART DISEASE
Notifiable in Brit., occurring on potatoes. It produces on the surface of the tuber large irregular warts which are caused by a parasitic fungus (*Synchytrium endobioticum*).

WART HOG
(*Phacochoerus*) African pigs of 2 species. The boar has 4 large tusks. *P. africanus* is found over most of the continent; *P. aethiopicus* in the S.E. regions.

WARWICK, Earl of
(1428-71) Eng. soldier called the 'King Maker'. Son of Richard, Earl of Salisbury, Richard Neville became Earl of Warwick by his wife's inheritance. At Northampton (1460) he took Henry VI prisoner, placing Edward IV on the throne in 1461. In 1464, Edward mar. secretly, in opposition to Warwick, who ultimately was forced into revolt. In 1470 he landed from Calais with the Lancastrians, and restored Henry VI to the throne, but the next year Edward returned, and Warwick was killed at Barnet.

WARWICKSHIRE
Midland county of Eng. The land is undulating, watered by the Avon, Leam and Tame. In the N. is the Forest of Arden. Agriculture is practised, and there are extensive coalfields. Warwick is the county town, but Birmingham, Coventry, Rugby and Sutton Coldfield are larger. Warwicks. returns 22 members to Parl. (16 members for Birmingham and Coventry). Pop. 2,023,000. **Warwick.** Borough and county town of Warwicks., 21 m. S.E. of Birmingham. The chief building is the 14th cent. castle. Pop. 16,000.

WASH, The
Arm of the N. Sea, between Lincoln and Norfolk, into which flow the Gt. Ouse, Nene, Welland and Witham.

WASHINGTON
N.W. state of the U.S.A. on the Canadian border, with a Pacific coastline. It is chiefly mountainous, except for the valley of the Columbia and the coastal plain of the W. Agriculture is the chief occupation. Coal, gold, silver and copper are mined, and there are extensive forests. Industries include shipbuilding and food processing. Olympia is the cap. W., formerly part of Oregon, became a state in 1889, and now sends 6 representatives to Congress. Area: 68,190 sq.m. Pop. 3,409,200.

WASHINGTON, D.C.
Cap. city of the U.S.A., *c.* 230 m. from New York, on the Potomac. It stands in fed. territory called the Dist. of Columbia. W. was founded *c.* 1790 as the seat of govt. and contains public buildings. Chief among them are the Capitol, with accommodation for the 2 houses of Congress, the White House, the 4 univs. and the Lincoln and Washington Memorials. Pop. 746,200. **Washington Conference, First.** The Anglo-Amer. War Council held its inaugural meeting in W. on Dec. 22, 1941. Mr. Churchill, accompanied by Lord Beaverbrook, had crossed the Atlantic in the battleship *Duke of York* to discuss full Allied co-ordination. It was decided that the entire milit. and economic resources of the 2 nations should be pooled under the direction of a common command, the Combined Chiefs of Staff.

WASHINGTON, George
(1732-99) Amer. soldier and statesman. B. Virginia, he became a tobacco planter. Elected a member of the House of Burgesses in 1758; he came to the front as a champion of colonial liberties, 1770. He did not favour Amer. Indep. but in 1775 he was chosen to command the colonial forces. In 1776 he succeeded in occupying Boston. Defeated in 1777 at Brandywine Creek, he wintered at Valley Forge, fought an indecisive battle at Monmouth in 1778, and in 1781 received the surrender of Cornwallis at Yorktown. In 1787 as representative of Virginia he presided at the Federal Convention in Philadelphia and in 1788 was chosen first Pres. of the U.S.A.

WASP
Hymenopterous insect of the family Vespidae, including both social and solitary genera. Social wasps of the genus *Vespa* are represented in Brit. by 6 species. The colony is begun by a female (queen) of the previous summer's brood, who lays eggs in a few cells made of pulped wood fibre, in a burrow made in the ground. In due course males and workers appear, then

females nurtured in larger cells, who are the 'queens'. The colonies exist for a single season only. Males and workers perish in the autumn and only the fertilised females hibernate to start new colonies.

WASSERMANN, August von
[vas'-] (1866-1925) Famous for many discoveries in medicine—the best-known being his test **Wassermann reaction** for syphilis by which a blood exam. will reveal presence of this disease at all stages. *See* SYPHILIS.

WATCH
Portion of time during which sailors are on duty:

first watch	8 P.M. to midnight
middle watch	midnight to 4 A.M.
morning watch	4 A.M. to 8 A.M.
forenoon watch	8 A.M. to 12 noon
afternoon watch	12 noon to 4 P.M.
first dog-watch	4 P.M. to 6 P.M.
second dog-watch	6 P.M. to 8 P.M.

WATER
H_2O. Colourless liquid, a chem. compound of hydrogen and oxygen. When pure it is clear, tasteless and chemically neutral. Its freezing and boiling pts. under normal atmos. pres. are used as standards in measuring temp. defining 0° C. (32° F.) and 100° C. (212° F.) respectively. It reaches its maximum density at 4° C. and expands on freezing (which causes the bursting of pipes), and when converted into steam it expands *c.* 1,700 times. It is a poor conductor of heat and electricity. Water covers 72 % of the area of the earth, forms two-thirds by wt. of the human body, and is indispensable to the existence of life. *See* HYDRO-ELECTRIC POWER; WATER POWER.

WATER-BEETLE
Various species of water-beetles including *Dytyscus marginalis*, found in Brit. ponds. Their legs are adapted for swimming.

WATER COLOUR
Method of painting. Water colour paints are mixed with some adhesive substance and applied with water. The art is of considerable antiquity and is still the most popular method for sketching and other rapid work.

WATER CRESS
Edible perennial aquatic herb (*Nasturtium officinale*), of the family Cruciferae. It inhabits brooks and streams in Europe and parts of Africa and Asia.

WATER-GLASS
Popular name for sodium silicate. It is made by fusing together soda ash and clean sand under strong heat. Its most common use is for preserving eggs.

WATER LILY
Aquatic plant of the family Nymphaeaceae, found in temp. to trop. regions. Mostly with broad floating leaves, and red, yellow or white flowers, they range from the Brit. white (*Nymphaea alba*), and yellow (*Nuphar lutea*) lilies to the giant Brazilian lily (*Victoria regia*).

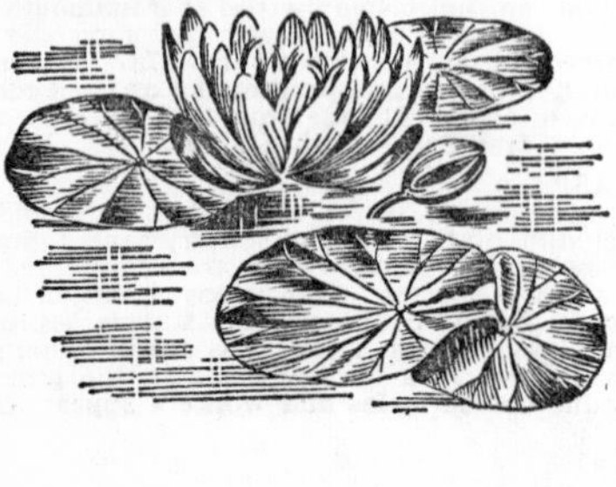

WATER MITE
Small freshwater mites, family Hydracarina, with legs having long, closely packed hairs adapted for swimming.

WATER POLO
Ball game played by swimmers. The game consists of propelling an inflated rubber ball into a goal. The pitch is 30 yds. long by 20 yds. wide.

WATER POWER
Energy obtained from moving water. The introduction of electricity increased the use of water power, as it could be employed to drive turbines to generate electricity. *See* TURBINE (WATER).

WATER SCORPION
Hemipterous insects of ponds and other stagnant waters. The flat, thin body is furnished with a tail-like breathing tube, which is protruded from the water when the insect takes in air.

WATER THYME
Water weed (*Elodea canadensis*), with long, jointed stems which root at every joint.

WATER VIOLET
Water plant (*Hottonia palustris*); family Primulaceae. The long roots are suspended in the water. The flower stem rises about a ft. above the water bearing whorls of salver-shaped flowers.

WATERBOATMAN
(*Notonecta*) Insect commonly seen on the surface of stagnant pools. It swims on its back, which is shaped like a boat; it dives readily and takes below surface supplies of air in between the wings.

WATERBUCK
(*Cobus ellipsiprymnus*) A large game antelope standing up to 53 in. at the shoulder. Coat colour grizzled grey roan, with graceful horns, in the male, *c.* 3 ft. long. It lives in swamps and boggy places in S. and E. Africa.

WATERFALL
Sudden fall of water, caused generally by the existence of a bed of hard rock in a river's course, overlying softer rocks. The highest in the world is the Angel Falls, Venezuela, S. Amer., with a drop of 3,212 ft.

WATERFORD
Maritime county, Irish Repub. in Munster prov. In the N. are the Comeragh and Knockmealdown Mts. but the E. is flat and marshy. The chief rivers are the Suir and Blackwater. Agriculture and fishing are important. Pop. 71,439. **Waterford.** Borough and county town of Waterford, Eire, at the confluence of the Suir and Barrow, 94 m. S.W. of Dublin. It trades in dairy produce and glass. Pop. 28,216.

WATERLOO
Village of Belgium, *c.* 11 m. S. of Brussels, it gives its name to a battle between the Brit. and their allies, and the Fr., on June 18, 1815. The army of Napoleon came into touch with the allied forces near Brussels. On the 16th there were 2 indecisive battles at Quatre Bras, where a mixed force of Dutch, Belgians and Brit. drove back the Fr., and at Ligny, where the Pruss. were forced to retreat. The Brit., under Wellington, fell back to Waterloo, followed by the Fr. In the battle which began on the 18th, the Brit. held the Château of Hougomont, and the Brit. infantry made a desperate stand against Fr. cavalry charges. The arrival of the Pruss. under Blücher turned the scale. The battle finally ended Napoleon's attempt to regain the Fr. throne.

WATFORD
Borough of Herts. on the Colne, 18 m. N.W. of London. There are brewing, milling and printing works. It returns 1 member to Parl. Pop. 76,000.

WATSON-WATT, Sir Robert
C.B. F.R.S. (1892-) Was largely responsible for the development of radar in the 1939-45 War. Superintendent of the Radio Dept. of the Nat. Physical Lab. 1936-8. Director of Communications Devel. Air Min. 1938-40 and Scientific Adviser on Telecommunications to the Air Min. 1940-6.

WATT, James
(1736-1819) Scots inventor. His experiments led to the evolution of the modern steam engine.

WATTEAU, Antoine
(1684-1721) Fr. painter. He excelled as a painter of pastoral scenes, fêtes galantes, etc.

WATTLE
Acacia that grows in Australia. Sprigs of it are worn on Australia Day.

WATTS, George Frederick
(1817-1904) Eng. painter and sculptor. Famous people sat for him, and there is a collection of his symbolical pictures in the Tate Gallery.

WATTS, Isaac
(1674-1748) Eng. hymn writer and divine. In 1702 became min. of the indep. Ch. in Mark Lane. His hymns include *O God our help in ages past*, *When I survey the wondrous cross* and *Jesus shall reign where'er the sun.*

WAVE
A travelling electrical or mechanical disturbance, which repeats itself at regular intervals in space and time. In sound and water waves, the particles of the medium create quite small vibrations to and fro, and do not travel forward with the wave. The distance between successive crests is the *wavelength* and the interval of time between the appearance of 2 successive crests at one point is the *period*. The number of periods per sec. is the *frequency*.

WAVELL, Earl
Archibald Percival (1883-1950) British F.-M. Served in Fr. 1914-16; served with Egyptian Exped. Force 1917-20. Gen. 1940; F.-M. 1943. C.-in-C. M.E. 1939-41, he achieved notable success in the N. African War against Italy, 1940-1, and in Ethiopia. Supreme Comdr. S.W. Pacific, 1942. He succeeded Lord Linlithgow as Viceroy of India, 1943-7, and was involved in the negotiations for indep. which resulted in India and Pakistan becoming self-governing Repub. and Dominion respectively. He was succeeded as Viceroy by Earl Mountbatten of Burma (*q.v.*).

WAX
Name given to various substances of animal, vegetable or mineral origin, usually consisting of esters of monohydric alcohols, being thus distinguished from oils and fats which are glycericides. *Animal waxes* include beeswax, which is prepared from melted honeycomb and is used for polishes, unguents, cosmetics, church candles, etc.; that from any of the wax-insects; spermaceti and sperm-oil from the sperm-whale; wool fat or wax, from sheep's wool, etc. *Vegetable waxes* include certain waxes obtained from S. American wax-palm trees, wax-trees such as the Japanese Sumac, the wax-myrtle, etc. *Mineral waxes* include certain hydrocarbons of mineral origin, *e.g.* paraffin wax, which is obtained from shale oil, petroleum and brown coal, and is used for the making of unguents, candles, etc. There are of course many other types of waxes, *e.g.* that found in the human ear; that used to seal letters, etc.

WAX PALM
Palm tree (*Copernicia cerifera*) of trop. S. Amer. Its trunk is coated with wax (*q.v.*). Another wax palm is *Ceroxylon andicola*, a native of Colombia.

WAX TREE
(or American Gamboge) Shrub (*Vismia guianensis*) of trop. S. Amer. It exudes a resinous juice with properties similar to those of Garcinia, the gamboge of Siam. It belongs to the family Guttiferae.

WAXBILL
Small bird, order Estreldinae, related to the Weaver Birds. They are found in Africa, Australia and parts of Asia, and have translucent, often vividly-coloured bills.

WAXWING
(*Ampelis garrulus*) Bird which breeds in the extreme N. of Europe and is a winter visitor to Brit. It is *c.* 7½ in. long, with a short, stout body. The plumage is brownish-grey and crested head and throat are black, the wings and tail black with white and yellow markings. The secondary wing feathers have wax-like vermilion tips.

WAYLAND THE SMITH
In German myth. a demi-god. He was apprenticed to Mimir, the famous smith. There are local traditions of him in Westphalia and S. England.

WAZIRISTAN
Mt. region of former N.W. Frontier, Pakistan. The Waziri tribes were fierce and warlike.

WEALD, The
[wēld] District in S.E. Eng., in Kent, Sussex and Surrey, between the N. and S. Downs. It was formerly a great forest, famous for the ironworks of Rom. and A.-S. times.

WEASEL
(*Putorius vulgaris*) Small carnivorous mammal. It is a native of Europe, parts of Asia, and N. Amer. The body is *c.* 6 in. long, the pelt being reddish-brown above and white below. It preys on rats, mice and small game. The coat colour of the larger Stoat (*P. erminea*) turns white in winter except for the black tail tip.

WEATHER FORECAST
Weather Ships. Vessels moored in a chain across the Atlantic Ocean for the purpose of reporting navigational and meteorological conditions to aircraft and ships. Balloons record barometric pressure. By means of radar, air liners are supplied by continuous bearings. The 6 nations now operating the 10 stations are U.S.A., Brit., the Netherlands, Fr., Scandinavia and Belg. In addition 6 ocean weather ships are located in the N. Pacific, operated by U.S.A., Canada and Japan. *See* METEOROLOGY.

WEAVER BIRD
Small bird which constructs an elaborate nest of woven grass. Some, such as *Philataerus* of S. Africa, make a common nest in which each pair has a separate cavity with its own entrance.

WEBB, Sir Aston
(1849-1930) Eng. architect. He designed the Victoria Memorial, the Admiralty Arch and the new front of Buckingham Palace.

WEBB, Matthew
(1848-83) Eng. swimmer. B. Dawley, Salop. He swam the Channel in 1875 in 21¾ hrs. On July 24, 1883, he attempted to swim the Niagara River below the Falls, and was drowned.

WEBB, Sidney, Lord Passfield
(1859-1947) Eng. politician and sociologist. M.P. (Lab.), 1922-9; Pres. Board of Trade 1924; Dominion Sec. 1929-30; Colonial Sec. 1930-31. Author with his wife **Beatrice**, of *English Local Government* (1906-22), and *History of English Poor Law* (1927-9).

WEBER, Carl Maria von
[vā´-] (1786-1826) German composer. After a conductorship at Breslau he became conductor in Prague, and then at Dresden. Weber was one of the leaders of the Romantic movement in Germany. He wrote also choral music,

orchestral works, 2 piano concertos, 2 clarinet concertos, chamber music and piano works.

WEBERN, Anton von
[vā-] (1883-1945) Aust. composer. A pupil of Schönberg. He was a distinguished composer in the *Twelve Note* technique. His works include chamber works and 2 symphonies.

WEBSTER, Daniel
(1782-1852) Amer. statesman. B. Salisbury, New Hampshire. Unsuccessful candidate for the Pres. in 1836 and 1848. Under Pres. Harrison, he was apptd. Sec. of State, 1841, and helped to arrange the Ashburton Treaty of 1842. He opposed the admission of Texas as a slave state, and the Mexican War.

WEBSTER, John
(*c.* 1580-1625) Eng. dramatist. His chief tragedies are *The White Devil* (1608), *The Duchess of Malfi* (1614).

WEBSTER, Noah
(1758-1843) Amer. lexicographer. His reputation rests upon his *Dictionary of the English Language* (1806).

WEDDELL SEA
Bay of Antarctica. Discovered by James Weddell in 1823, it lies between W. Antarctica and Coats Land. Shackleton's ship, *Endurance*, was crushed and sunk by ice there in 1915.

WEDEKIND, Frank
(1864-1918) German playwright. His plays include *Der Erdgeist, Die Büchse von Pandora, Schloss Wetterstein* (1910).

WEDGWOOD, Josiah
(1730-95) Eng. potter. B. Burslem, he came of a family of potters. After being apprenticed to his brother in 1744, he began work on his own account in 1759. He improved the cream-coloured earthenware, and later, inspired by discoveries of ancient Gk. and Rom. vases, made classic shapes, with figures raised upon them.

WEEVIL
Beetle belonging to the largest natural family, Curculionidae, in the animal kingdom. They are characterised by the prolongation of the head into a snout, with the mouth at the apex. Vegetable feeders, they are often injurious to crops.

WEIMAR
[vī'-mär] Former cap. of Thuringia, E. Germany, 13 m. E. of Erfurt. It was the cap. of the duchy of Saxe-Weimar until 1919, and was the home of Goethe, Schiller, Herder and Wieland. Pop. 65,500.

WEINBERGER, Jaromir
[vīn'-] (1896-) B. Prague. He won fame with his opera *Schwanda der Dudelsackpfeifer* (1927). When the Nazis invaded Czechoslovakia he went to Calif. (1939).

WEISMANN, August
[vīs'-] (1834-1914) German biologist, b. Frankfurt-on-M. In 1882 he pub. *Studies in the Theories of Descent*, but is best-known as the author of the germplasm theory of heredity.

WEIZMANN, Dr. Chaim
[vīts'-man] (1874-1952) Zionist leader. B. Russia; naturalised Brit. citizen. Interested Balfour in the Zionist cause, and 1921-46 was almost continually Pres. of the Jewish Agency and was throughout his life a moderating influence in Zionist Councils. He was sworn in as first Pres. of Israel, 1949; re-elected, 1951.

WELL
Artificial excavation that brings fluid, usually water, from between the rock or soil through which it penetrates. Wells are usually circular in shape, and are often lined with brick or concrete, to keep out pollution from the top layers of earth. The best wells in Europe are

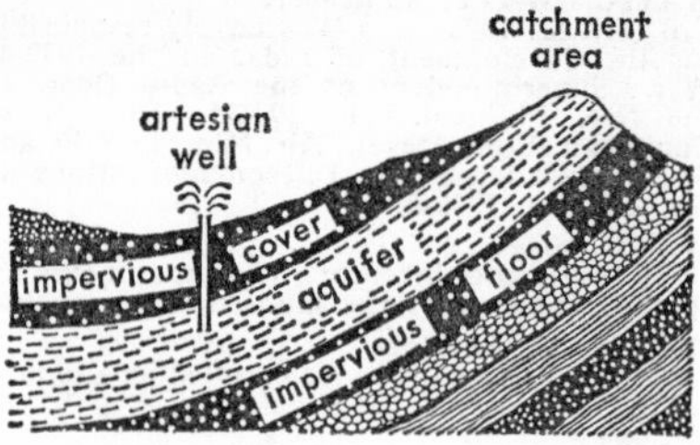

in chalk, and the poorest in igneous rocks. **Artesian Wells** obtain underground water by sinking a bore of relatively small diameter through impervious strata to tap water-bearing strata below (see above).

WELLAND SHIP CANAL
Waterway of Canada, linking L. Erie and Ontario, W. of Niagara Falls. Completed, 1931, the canal is *c.* 27 m. long.

WELLINGTON
Cap. city of New Zealand, on land-locked harbour on the S. coast of N. Is. First settled, 1839, it became the seat of govt. in 1865. It is the business centre and chief port of N.Z., with various industries. Pop. 143,000.

WELLINGTON, Duke of
Arthur Wellesley (1769-1852) Eng. soldier and politician. B. Dublin, entered the army in 1787. In 1796 he went to India, where he was the victor in the Mahratta War of 1803. In 1808, he was sent to the Peninsula and won the Battle of Vimiero. Given full command after the Battle of Corunna (*q.v.*), he drove the Fr. from Oporto, and in July, 1809, won a victory at Talavera. He withdrew to the lines of Torres Vedras. In 1812 he took Ciudad Rodrigo and Badajoz, won a great victory at Salamanca and entered Madrid. In 1813 he overwhelmed the Fr. at Vittoria, and in 1814 at Orthes. In 1815 he won his greatest victory at Waterloo (*q.v.*). With Castlereagh, he represented the U.K. at the Congress of Vienna. Returning to politics, he became P.M. in 1828. He favoured Catholic emancipation, but opposed Parl. Reform. *See* PENINSULAR WAR; WATERLOO.

WELLINGTONIA
(*Sequoia gigantea*) Giant evergreen tree of California of the Coniferae.

WELLS
Cath. city and market town of Somerset, 20 m. S. of Bristol. Pop. 6,960.

WELLS, Herbert George
(1866-1946) Eng. writer. B. Bromley; a draper's asst., then grad. at Royal Coll. of Science in 1888; taught till 1893. *The Time Machine* appeared in 1895. His novels include *Kipps* (1905), *Love and Mr. Lewisham* (1900), *The History of Mr. Polly* (1910), *Tono Bungay* (1909). His scientific romances include *The Invisible Man* (1897), *The Food of the Gods* (1904), and *The First Men in the Moon* (1901). Among his general works are *First and Last Things* (1908), *New Worlds for Old* (1908), *The Outline of History* (1920), and *The Shape of Things to Come* (1933).

WELSH *See* CELTIC. Early Welsh poetry and romances are preserved in the Four Ancient Books of Wales: *Black Book of Carmarthen* (1170-1230), *Book of Aneirin* (1250), *Book of Taliessin* (1275), *Red Book of Hergest* (1375-1425). The 11th-13th cents. is the age of the court-poets (*Gogynfeirdd*). The 14th cent. produced Dafydd ap Gwilym, chief bard of Glamorgan, author of love poems and of satires. Welsh poetry was revived by Gronwy Owen (1723-69).

WELSH POPPY
(*Meconopsis cambrica*) Hardy perennial. The pale yellow or orange flowers rise on tall, erect stems.

WELWYN GARDEN CITY
Urban district of Herts., 5 m. N. of Hatfield. The town was planned in 1920, between Welwyn proper and Hatfield. Combined with Hatfield for joint development, 1948. Industries include chemicals and electrical engineering. Pop. 38,000.

WEMBLEY
Part of Brent, borough of Greater London (1964). It was formerly in Middlesex. It is best known for its exhibition grounds and stadium, where the F.A. cup final is played annually. W. returns 2 members to Parl. Pop. 125,000.

WENLOCK
Borough of Salop, 14 m. S.E. of Shrewsbury. To the S.W. is a famous beauty spot, W. Edge. Pop. 15,000.

WESLEY, John
(1703-91) Eng. divine. B. Epworth, Lincs.; educ. Charterhouse and Christ Ch. Oxford, he took orders in 1725. Returning to Oxford in 1729, he joined a group of undergraduates who had received the nickname of 'Methodists' because of their religious way of life. On his return from a mission to Georgia, he took the lead in a similar soc. which met near Moorfields, London, and began his campaign of field-preaching. At his d. his followers numbered 100,000. His brother was **Charles** (1707-88) Educ. Westminster School and Christ Ch. Oxford, he helped his brother to found the Methodist movement. He took part in evangelistic work, but is best remembered as one of the great hymn writers of the 18th cent. His best-known hymn is *Jesus, Lover of My Soul*. **Wesleyan Methodist Church.** Non-conformist denomination. The Wesleyan Methodists were the orig. body founded in 1739 by John and Charles Wesley. *See* METHODISTS.

WESSEX
Kingdom of the W. Saxons, estabd. in the 6th cent. by the Saxon invaders. It covered the district S. of the Thames between Sussex and Devon, with its cap. at Winchester. In 802 Egbert became King of Wessex and later overlord of Eng. Today Wessex is used as a general term for the counties of Dorset, Hants. and Somerset.

WEST BENGAL
[-gawl'] State of Ind. on the Pakistan frontier. It is a fertile region, watered by the Ganges and its distributaries. Coal is mined, and there are cotton and jute mills. Calcutta, the chief city, and Howrah, the jute manufacturing centre, stand on the Hooghly. Admin. is by a Gov. with a cabinet and legislature. Area: 33,928 sq.m. Pop. 34,926,279.

WEST BROMWICH
County borough of Staffs., on the Tame, 6 m. N.W. of Birmingham. Its manufactures include machinery, tools and bricks. It sends 1 member to Parl. Pop. 173,000.

WEST HARTLEPOOL
County borough and port of Durham, 2 m. S. of Hartlepool. Industries include shipping, shipbuilding, engineering, iron and steel smelting. With H. it returns 1 member to Parl. Pop. 78,600.

WEST INDIES
Fertile trop. Is. discovered by Columbus. They form a chain from Florida and Mexico to Venezuela, enclosing the Caribbean. The W. is. except for the Bahamas, are large, the E. ones quite small, except for Trinidad. First colonised by Sp. they have been the scene of much strife. They now comprise the repubs. of Dominica, Cuba and Haiti, the dominions of Jamaica, Trinidad and Tobago, and dependencies of the U.S.A., France, the Netherlands and Gt. Brit. *See* CARIBBEAN.

WEST IRIAN
(Formerly **Netherlands New Guinea**) Territory comprising W. half of the Is. of New Guinea. Under U.N. control 1962-3, when it was taken over by Indonesia. Cap. is Djajapura. Area: 160,000 sq.m. Pop. *c.* 700,000.

WEST LOTHIAN
(formerly **Linlithgowshire**) County of S.E. Scot., with a coastline on the Firth of Forth. The Avon and Almond are the chief rivers. Coal and iron are mined, and there are paper mills. Linlithgow is the county town. The county returns 1 member to Parl. Pop. 93,000.

WEST POINT
Milit. Coll. for U.S. Army. Founded in 1802, it stands on the Hudson, 50 m. from New York City.

WEST RIDING
One of the 3 admin. divisions of Yorks., constituting a separate county, chief town Wakefield. It returns 45 members to Parl. (31 borough constituencies). Pop. 3,641,000.

WEST VIRGINIA
E. state of the U.S.A., E. of the Ohio and W. of Virginia. The Allegheny Mts. run through the E. half. The chief rivers are the Ohio, Monongahela and Kanawha. Cereals, tobacco and fruit are grown, and coal and oil mined. Charleston is the cap. W.V. entered the Union as a state in 1863, after Virginia had seceded. It sends 5 representatives to Congress. Area: 24,180 sq.m. Pop. 1,744,300.

WESTERHAM
Market town of Kent, 5 m. W. of Sevenoaks. Chartwell, home of the late Sir Winston Churchill, is near. Pop. 3,100.

WESTERN AUSTRALIA
State of the Commonwealth of Australia consisting of that part of the continent W. of 129° E. The interior is hilly, though Mt. Bruce (4,024 ft.) is the highest point known. The chief rivers are the Fortescue, Ashburton, Gascoyne, Murchison and Swan, flowing W. into the Ind. Ocean. Inland are extensive deserts and numerous small salt lakes. Agriculture is limited to the S.W. coastal districts, where wheat, fruit and wine are produced. Sheep are grazed over a large area, and there are hard-wood forests in the Medit.-type region of the S.W. The mines of Coolgardie and the adjacent goldfields are still being worked, and there are deposits of other minerals. Perth is the cap. and largest city. First settled by the Brit. in 1829, W.A. was granted responsible govt. in 1890. It is admin. by a Gov. and a parl. of 2 houses. Area: 975,920 sq.m. Pop. 864,000.

WESTERN DESERT BATTLES *See* NORTH AFRICA, WAR IN.

WESTMEATH
Inland county of Eire, in the prov. of Leinster. The country is undulating, except for some bogs in the S., with some fine loughs. The Shannon, Brosna, Inny and Boyne are the chief rivers. Agriculture and dairy farming are the principal occupations; woollens are manufactured. Mullingar is the county town. Pop. 54,900.

WESTMINSTER
City and borough of Greater London (1964), consisting of the former borough of the City of Westminster and Paddington (*q.v.*). It occupies a considerable area to the N. of the river and contains, in addition to the Abbey, R.C. cath. and School, the Houses of Parl. the govt. offices in Whitehall, the Cenotaph, St. James's and Buckingham Palaces, the Nat. Galleries,

Law Courts, and Burlington House; Westminster, Charing Cross and St. George's hospitals; Charing Cross and Victoria stations. Of the chs. the most famous are St. Margaret's, and St. Martin's in the Fields. The Thames is crossed by W. Bridge. With the City of London it returns 1 member to Parl. Pop. 86,110. **Westminster Abbey.** Once the abbey church of a Benedictine monastery, now having the status of a Nat. shrine. Several chs. had already occupied the site when *c.* 1050, Edward the Confessor built the Norman ch., the reconstruction of which was begun by Henry II in 1245. The cloisters, abbot's house and principal monastic buildings were added in the 14th cent. The Nave is 15th cent. and Henry VIII finished and dedicated to his predecessor the superb chapel in the perpendicular style, now called the chapel of Henry VII. The 2 western towers date from 1722-40 and are the work of Hawkesmoor and Wren. The coronation of every Eng. monarch since William the Conqueror, and every Brit. sovereign since the Union of Crowns, has taken place in Westminster Abbey. The bodies of 13 Brit. kings, 5 queens and many distinguished persons have been interred in the ch. since the 14th cent. **Westminster Cathedral.** Chief and largest of R.C. Chs. in London and Brit. and seat of the Cardinal Archbishop. Built (1895-1903) of brick in the Byzantine style, the chief feature is a square campanile which rises 273 ft. **Westminster Hall.** This was orig. built by William Rufus and finished in 1099. The timbered roof was added in 1394. It was the scene of many famous trials, including those of Richard II, Charles I, and Queen Caroline.

WESTMORLAND
County of N.W. Eng. with a short coastline on Morecambe Bay. It contains part of the Lake District and magnificent mt. scenery (Helvellyn, 3,118 ft.). The lakes include Windermere, Ullswater, Grasmere and Haweswater. Sheep rearing and dairy farming are the chief occupations. Appleby is the county town, but Kendal is the admin. centre. W. returns 1 member to Parl. Pop. 67,222.

WESTPHALIA
District of Germany to the S.E. of the Netherlands, now part of the state of N.-Rhine-Westphalia (*q.v.*). It was ruled by the electors of Cologne until 1803. In that year it was given to Hesse-Darmstadt, and in 1815 to Pruss. **Treaty of W.** Peace, signed in 1648, which ended the Thirty Years' War.

WEXFORD
County of S.E. Eire, in Leinster prov. with a coastline on St. George's Channel and the Atlantic. The surface is hilly with mts. on the Carlow and Wicklow boundaries (Mt. Leinster, 2,610 ft.). The Slaney and Barrow are the principal rivers; agriculture and fishing the staple industries. Pop. 83,308. **Wexford.** County town, seaport and urban district of Wexford, Eire, on the estuary of the Slaney, 87 m. S. of Dublin. Pop. 14,000.

WEYGAND, Maxime
[vā-gà(ng)'] (1867-1965) Fr. gen. He was in command of the Fr. armies at the time of the collapse in 1940.

WEYMOUTH
[wā'-müth] Seaport and market town of Dorset, 8 m. S. of Dorchester. There is a steamer service to the Channel Is. Pop. 41,000.

WHALE
Marine mammal of the order Cetacea. They comprise 3 groups: (1) *Archaeoceti*. Their teeth consist of three incisors, 1 canine, 4 pre-molars and 3-2 molars on either side of each jaw. (2) *Mystacoceti*, or Whalebone whales in which the mouth contains fine plate-like structures supported by the palate in place of teeth, and (3) *Odontoceti*, or Toothed Whales, which include sperm whales, dolphins and porpoises. The most prized species is the Blue whale, the largest of all animals, which is found chiefly in the Antarctic Ocean. It reaches a length of 100 ft. and a wt. of at least 120 t. Blue, Fin, and Humpback whales enter the Antarctic in summer and feed on vast shoals of an oceanic shrimp some 2½ in. long. In winter they frequent the warmer latitudes to breed. The Sperm Whale is the largest toothed whale. It attains a length of 60 ft. Fin and Humpback whales may reach lengths of 65 and 50 ft. respectively. Whales are warm blooded, breathe air and have lungs. They conserve body heat by immense layers of blubber from which whale oil is produced. The bulk of this is processed into margarine, but there are many useful by-products, *e.g.* frozen whalemeat, meat meal, meat extracts, bone meal, liver oil and vitamin extracts. Whales bear their young like land mammals. Statistics on the whaling industry are compiled annually by the Norwegian Committee for Whaling Statistics. After World War II, the Internat. Whaling Commission was formed. The major field for whaling is the Antarctic. There are comprehensive regulations for whaling in all parts of the world. Early whaling was carried out by means of harpoons flung by men in small boats. Now a gun is employed which fires a harpoon with an explosive head. The gun is mounted in the bows of a fast whale catcher sent out either from a shore-based factory or, as one of a team, based on a large ocean-going whale factory ship with a crew of 400.

WHEAT
Grain of the genus *Triticum* with a dense 4-sided spike and flowering glumes bearded or beardless. Within the glumes are the florets, each bearing a grain which is the edible part of the grass. When ground it yields a fine white flour. Wheat has been widely grown for food since prehistoric times. In the 19th cent. experiments in fertilisers, etc. resulted in a great improvement in its quality. The largest producers are Ukraine, U.S.A., Canada, India, Argentina, Fr., Australia and Italy.

WHEATEAR
(*Oenanthe*) Small bird allied to the Stonechat and the Whinchat, found in N. Europe, Asia and Amer. It is seen in Eng. during the summer. Bluish-grey on the back, the bird has a light buff breast, and a white rump.

WHEELER, Sir Charles
(1892-) Brit. sculptor. Trustee of the Tate Gallery, 1942-9. F.R.B.S. 1935 (Pres. 1944-9); elected R.A. 1940; Pres. of the Royal Academy, 1956-66.

WHEELER, Sir R. E. Mortimer
(1890-) Archaeologist. Served in World War I. Keeper and sec. of the London Mus. 1926-44, and Director-Gen. of Archaeology in India, 1944-8. He served in World War II. He directed excavations in England, Wales, France, India and Pakistan. From 1948-55 he was prof. of the archaeology of the Rom. Provs. Univ. of London.

WHELK
(*Buccinum*) Common gasteropod mollusc with a high spiral shell. Found over a wide area

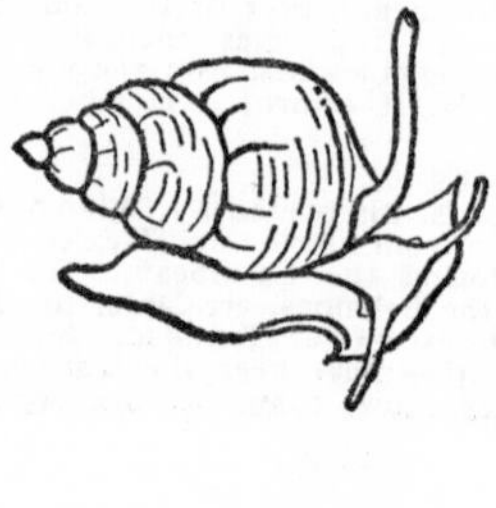

from the N. Atlantic to the Bay of Biscay, and from the coast of Amer. to Siberia, the Whelk is carnivorous.

WHIG
Term applied 1660-88 to the polit. party supporting the power of Parl. opposed to the Tory court party. It remained the party name until after 1832, when it gave way to the term 'Liberal'. The Whigs, strengthened by the 1688 Revolution, supported the Protestant George I, and were in power until the time of George III. They regained power in 1830, as the party pledged reform and religious toleration. Their outstanding leaders were Walpole, Chatham, Burke, Fox, Grey, Russell and Palmerston.

WHINCHAT
(*Saxicola rubetra*) Small bird. It resembles the Stonechat, but is distinguished by white streaks on the head and neck.

WHIPPET
Dog used for coursing and racing. It resembles the Greyhound, but is smaller, and was prob. derived by crossing terriers and Ital. Greyhounds.

WHIP-POOR-WILL
(*Antrostomus vociferus*) Nightjar of N. Amer. It is 9-10 in. long, with brown plumage mottled with black and cream. The name is derived from the characteristic call.

WHIRLWIND
Violent or light wind which revolves round a vertical axis. On a miniature scale they may be seen as dust-whirls in very dry weather. On a larger scale they occur mostly in the tropics and sub-tropics. In desert regions they may become quite formidable and extend some hundreds of ft. upwards.

WHISKY
Spirit made by the distillation of the fermented extracts from malted or unmalted cereals, potatoes or any starch-yielding material. The best whisky is *Scotch*. The liquid must be matured for some years in wooden casks before it is ready for drinking.

WHIST
Eng. card game. It originated *c.* 1621, from a combination of several older games and is played by 4 persons, 2 sets of 2 partners each, with a full pack of 52 cards equally divided, the last card dealt being turned up and declared trumps.

WHISTLER, James Abbott McNeill
(1834-1903) Amer. artist. B. Lowell, Mass. His outstanding portrait is *The Artist's Mother*, See *The Man Whistler* by Hesketh Pearson (1953).

WHITE, Gilbert
(1720-93) Eng. naturalist. He is remembered chiefly by his *Natural History and Antiquities of Selborne* (1789).

WHITE HELLEBORE
[hel'-i-] (*Veratrum album*) Perennial European herb also called false hellebore. It has long vertical leaves and panicles of white flowers. The rootstock is poisonous, yielding a substance used medicinally.

WHITE HORSE, Vale of the
Valley of the Ock, N. Berks., which takes its name from the figure of a horse, 374 ft. high, cut out in the hillside. According to tradition, it commemorates the victory of Alfred over the Danes.

WHITE HOUSE
Name given to the Executive Mansion or official residence of the Pres. of the U.S. in Washington, D.C. It stands on a site chosen by George Washington who laid the cornerstone in 1792.

WHITE LEAD
Carbonate of lead. A dense white powder, it is insoluble in water, but is easily dissolved in dilute nitric acid or acetic acid. Its manufacture is a hazardous occupation due to a risk of poisoning, and laws have been passed to protect the health of its workers.

WHITE RUSSIA
or **Byelorussia.** Constituent repub. of the U.S.S.R. in the W. Bounded by Poland, Latvia, Lithuania, the Ukraine and the R.S.F.S.R. A lowland area with many lakes, marshes and swamps, it is crossed by the Dnieper, Dvina, Niemen, Berezina and Pripet. There are extensive forests. The Pripet Marshes occupy the S. area. Minsk is the cap. The repub. was estabd. 1919. Area: 81,090 sq.m. Pop. 8,400,000.

WHITE SEA
Branch of the Arctic Ocean between the peninsulas of Kanin and Kola, over 300 m. long. Its chief port, Archangel, is connected with the Caspian and Black Seas by canal, but owing to ice is open only in the summer.

WHITEBAIT
Fry of Sprats and Herrings taken in bag-nets at the mouth of the Thames and in other estuaries during the months Mar. to Aug.

WHITEFIELD, George
(1714-70) Eng. religious leader. B. Gloucester. At Oxford he met John and Charles Wesley. He went to Amer. to join Wesley, who was establishing missions there. His Calvinistic views led to a breach with the Wesleys.

WHITEFISH
(*Coregonus*) Fish related to the salmon, and found chiefly in large inland lakes. It is a native of N. Amer. and the cold to temp. regions of Europe and Asia.

WHITEHEAD, Alfred North
(1861-1947) Eng. philosopher and mathematician. His works include *Principia Mathematica* (with Bertrand Russell) 1910, *Science and the Modern World*, 1926, and *Adventures of Ideas*, 1933.

WHITETHROAT
(*Sylvia communis*) Migratory bird of the family Sylviidae. It is 5½-6 in. long with greyish or reddish-brown plumage above, and white beneath. A common summer visitor to Brit.

WHITGIFT, John
(1530-1604) Eng. prelate. Ordained in 1560, he became Archbishop of Canterbury, 1583. He vigorously supported Elizabeth's policy of religious uniformity.

WHITHORN
Small royal burgh and ancient eccles. centre of Wigtownshire. Its first charter was granted by King Robert the Bruce. The place is connected with St. Ninian (or Ringan), the first Christian missionary to Scot. who, in 397, landed at the Is. of W. and built what is thought to have been the first stone ch. in Brit.

WHITING
(*Gadus merlangus*) Marine food fish related to the Cod. It is usually 1½ lb. or so in wt. and is esteemed for the table.

WHITLEY, John Henry
(1866-1935) Eng. politician. M.P. (Lib.) 1900-28; Speaker, 1911-28. As chairman of the committee on 'Relations between Employer and Employed' (1916), he began his development of the Whitley Councils.

WHITMAN, Walt
(**Walter**) (1819-92) Amer. poet. His first work was *Franklin Evans* (1842). He wrote the free-verse *Leaves of Grass* (1855), *Drum Taps* (1865) and many other vols. His prose works include numerous short stories.

WHITSTABLE
Urban district and resort of Kent, on the Thames estuary, 6 m. N.W. of Canterbury. The chief industry is oyster fishing. Pop. 19,280.

WHITSUNDAY
Feast of the Chr. Ch. celebrated 6 weeks after Easter Sun. in memory of the descent upon the disciples of the Holy Ghost.

WHITTINGTON, Richard
(1358-1423) Allegedly, the Dick Whittington of legend. He became apprenticed to Sir John Fitz-Warren, eventually marrying his daughter. He was Mayor of London in 1398, 1406, and 1419.

WHITTIER, John Greenleaf
(1807-92) Amer. poet. B. Haverhill, Mass. He wrote the ballads *Barclay of Ury* and *Barbara Frietchie* and religious poems and hymns, reflecting his Quaker thought.

WHITTLE, Sir Frank
Air Commodore, K.B.E. F.R.S. (1907-) Brit. engineer and pioneer in the application of jet propulsion to aircraft. He became test pilot at the Marine Aircraft Experimental Establishment, R.A.F. 1931-2. He was apptd. Hon. Technical Adviser, Jet Development, B.O.A.C. 1948-52. The first flights of the Gloster jet-propelled aircraft powered by a Whittle engine took place in 1941. *See* JET PROPULSION.

WHOOPING COUGH
Specific infectious disease characterised by catarrh of the respiratory tract and paroxysms of coughing terminating in a ' whoop '. Caused by *Bacillus pertussis* first described in 1906 by Bordet-Gengou. Incubation period 6 to 18 days. Symptoms begin with generalised catarrh, followed later by cough, vomiting, fever, loss of appetite.

WHYMPER, Edward
(1840-1911) Brit. mountaineer. After 7 vain attempts, he was the first to reach the summit of the Matterhorn, in July, 1865.

WICK
Burgh, seaport and county town of Caithness. There is a steamer service to the Orkney and Shetland Is. Pop. 7,555.

WICKLOW
Co. of Eire, in the prov. of Leinster, S. of Dublin and having a coastline on the Irish Sea. The surface is mountainous, with the Wicklow Mts. rising to 3,039 ft. The Slaney, Avoca and Liffey are the chief rivers. Minerals are worked, and sheep reared. Wicklow is the county town; other towns are Bray and Arklow. Pop. 58,473. **Wicklow.** County town and resort of W. Eire, 28 m. S. of Dublin. Pop. 3,300.

WIDGEON
(*Anas penelope*) Species of wild duck which abounds in Europe and N. Asia. The drake has a chestnut head and neck, buff forehead, grey flanks, and green and black wings.

WIESBADEN
[vēs'-bȧ-den] Cap. of Hesse, W. Germany, in the Taunus Mts. near the Rhine. There are mineral springs and a trade in wine. Pop. 240,000.

WIGAN
County borough of Lancs., 18 m. N.W. of Manchester. There are cotton mills and clothing factories, also engineering works. Coal is mined. W. returns 1 member to Parl. Pop. 78,780.

WIGHT, Isle of
Is. and admin. county off the coast of Hants. Chalk downs cross the Is. culminating in the Needles off the W. coast. The chief river, the Medina, rises near the S. coast and flows due N. The Is. is predominantly a holiday resort with centres at Ventnor, Freshwater, Sandown, Shanklin and Ryde. Newport is the admin. centre, and Cowes the chief port. The Is. returns 1 member to Parl. Pop. 95,479.

WIGTOWNSHIRE
County of S.W. Scot. in Galloway, with a long coastline on the Irish Sea. The rivers are the Cree and Luce. Agriculture is the chief occupation. Wigtown is the county town, and Stranraer the admin. centre and chief port. With Kirkcudbright, it returns 1 member to Parl. Pop. 29,000.

WILBERFORCE, William
(1759-1833) Eng. politician and philanthropist. M.P. 1780-1825. Most notable for his campaign for the abolition of the slave-trade.

WILDE, Oscar Fingall O'Flahertie Wills
(1854-1900) Irish-born author, assoc. with the aesthetic cult. His plays are *Lady Windermere's Fan* (1892), *An Ideal Husband, The Importance of Being Earnest*; among his stories are *The Portrait of Dorian Gray*, and *Lord Arthur Savile's Crime. Poems* appeared in 1881 and 1892, and he also wrote and pub. reviews and crit. essays. In May, 1895, Wilde was sentenced to 2 years' imprisonment for immoral practices. He wrote *The Ballad of Reading Gaol*, and the prose *De Profundis*.

WILFRID
Eng. saint (*c.* 634-709). About 665 he was made Bishop of York, but he disagreed with the Archbp. of Canterbury and went to Compiègne. In 668 he returned to Northumbria, and was restored to his see, only to be driven out by King Egfrith. In 685 he was again restored, but was again expelled in 691.

WILHELMINA
[vil-hel-mē'-nă] (1880-1962) Queen of the Netherlands. She succeeded to the throne in 1890. During the German occupation of 1940-4 she conducted her govt. from London. In 1948, for reasons of health she abdicated in favour of her daughter, Juliana.

WILHELMSHAVEN
[vil'-helmz-hȧ-fen] Seaport in Lower Saxony, W. Germany, 40 m. N.W. of Bremen. Before World War II it was Germany's chief naval base on the N. Sea. Pop. 100,485.

WILKES, John
(1727-97) Eng. journalist and politician. M.P. 1757-90. Expelled from Parl. in 1764 for a libel in his journal, Wilkes was 3 times returned as Member for Middlesex in 1768 and 1769, but was not allowed to take his seat until 1774.

WILKIE, Sir David
(1785-1841) Scots painter. In 1806 he settled in London, where his *Village Politicians* and *Blind Fiddler* gained him his R.A., 1811.

WILL
Document by which a person called a testator disposes of property on death. By Eng. law wills must be in writing and all signatures of the testator witnessed by 2 persons. The witnesses should be persons who have no interest in the will. In Scots law a will need not be witnessed if it is in the handwriting of the testator. No person under 21 years of age can make a will. A will becomes invalid if a later will is made revoking the former or disposing of all the testator's property, or if the testator marries, unless the will has been made in contemplation of that marriage. A will must name one or more executors or trustees, whose duty it is to have it proved and to carry out its provisions. The property of persons who die without making a will, is dealt with by taking out letters of administration.

WILLIAM I
(1027-87) King of Eng. surnamed the Conqueror, the natural son of Robert II, Duke of Normandy, he succeeded to the dukedom in

1035. He invaded Eng. in 1066, landing at Pevensey and defeating the Eng. army under King Harold at Senlac, near Hastings, on Oct. 14. He had to quell insurrections in Eng. and later in Normandy. He carried out a complete survey of his Eng. realm, the results of which are preserved in the Domesday Book (*q.v.*). **William II, Rufus** (c. 1058-1100) King of Eng., 3rd son of William I. He gained milit. successes in Normandy and Scot. but his cruelty and profligacy earned the hatred of his subjects. He was found in the New Forest slain by an arrow.

WILLIAM III
(1650-1702) King of Gt. Brit., posthumous son of William II, Prince of Orange and Mary, daughter of Charles I. As Capt.-Gen. of the Dutch forces, he carried on the struggle of the Dutch against Louis XIV. In 1677 he mar. Mary, daughter of James II. In 1689 after the deposition of James II (*q.v.*) he and Mary became joint rulers of Brit. His last years were occupied with negotiations concerning the Sp. Succession (*see* SPAIN), and war had just been declared when he d.

WILLIAM IV
(1765-1837) Brit. king, 3rd son of George III. After a term of service in the navy, he was created Duke of Clarence in 1789. His 20 years' assoc. with Mrs. Jordan was broken when he mar. Adelaide of Saxe-Meiningen, but he had no issue. He succeeded George IV in 1830. The Reform Act of 1832 was the outstanding measure of his reign.

WILLIAM I
(1797-1888) King of Prussia and German Emperor. He took part in the final campaigns of the Napoleonic Wars. He supported repression of the revolutionary movement of 1848. In 1861 on the d. of his brother, he became king. He worked in harmony with Bismarck (*q.v.*) in carrying out the policy which led to the formation of the German Emp. During the Franco-Pruss. War he was in command of the Pruss. forces. He was proclaimed German Emperor at Versailles, 1871.

WILLIAM II
(1859-1941) German Emperor and King of Prussia. B. Berlin, the eldest son of the Crown Prince Frederick (afterwards Frederick III), and of Victoria (eldest daughter of Queen Victoria). Within 2 years of his accession (1888) Bismarck was dismissed, and the Emperor went ahead with his policy of expanding Germany's power. At the beginning of World War I he directed operations in person. On Oct. 9, 1918, he abdicated and crossed the Dutch frontier to reside at Doorn Castle where he d. in exile.

WILLIAM the Silent
(1533-84) Prince of Orange-Nassau. Philip II made him Stadtholder (gov.) of Holland, Zeeland and Utrecht. In 1567 he espoused the cause of the Netherlanders against Sp. rule, and of Protestantism against the Rom. Ch. He failed to unite all the Netherlands provs., but in 1579 the Union of Utrecht estabd. the 7 Protestant United Provs.

WILLIAMS, Sir George
(1821-1905) He took an active interest in religious work, and on June 6, 1854, with 12 others he founded the Y.M.C.A.

WILLIAMS, Tennessee
(1912-) Amer. playwright. B. Missouri, Ohio; educ. Washington; Rockefeller Fellowship in drama, 1941. He wrote *Glass Menagerie* (1944), *A Street Car Named Desire* (1947), *Summer and Smoke* (1948), *The Roman Spring of Mrs. Stone* (1950) (novel).

WILLOW
A tree or shrub of the genus *Salix*, varying in ht. from a few ins. to 120 ft. The leaves are narrow, the flowers are borne on catkins. Male

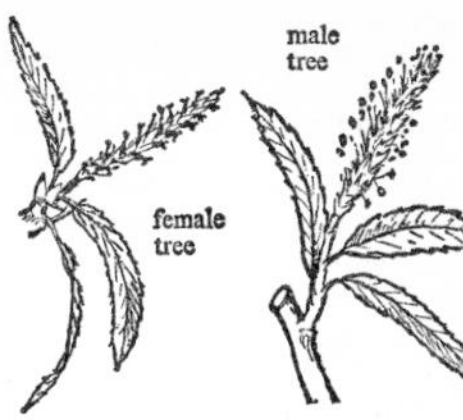

and female catkins grow on separate trees, and cross-pollination is effected by insects and the wind. Willow is used as timber and wood pulp, and for wicker and basket-making. The timber of one variety is used for cricket bats.

WILLOW PATTERN Ware
Chinaware bearing a design which copies the orig. blue china of Nanking. It was introduced into Eng. porcelain by Thomas Turner of Caughley, *c.* 1700.

WILSON, (James) Harold
(1916-) Lab. statesman. Educ. Jesus Coll. Oxford. Lecturer in economics. Pres. Board of Trade, 1947-51. M.P. for Huyton, Lancs. (1950-). Chairman Lab. Party Exec. Committee, 1961-2. Leader of Lab. Party (1963-). Led party to victory in Gen. Election, 1964, and became P.M. Defeated, 1970.

WILSON, Thomas Woodrow
(1856-1924) 28th Pres. of the U.S.A. B. Virginia. In 1912, owing to a split in the Repub. vote between Roosevelt and Taft, he was elected Pres. At the outbreak of World War I he favoured neutrality, and he was re-elected in 1916. The continued ruthless submarine campaign forced W. to join the Allied cause in April, 1917. He took a leading part in the peace negotiations, and suggested the formation of the League of Nations. The rejection of the Versailles Treaty by the U.S. Senate and his own rejection in the presidential contest of 1920 led to his complete retirement.

WILTON
Borough of Wilts., on the Wylye, 2 m. W. of Salisbury, famous for a type of carpet that is made in the town. Pop. 3,930.

WILTSHIRE
(Wilts.) Inland county of Eng. There are hills in the N. and in the S. Salisbury Plain. The main rivers are the Avon, Nadder and Kennet. An agricultural area, the county is noted for its bacon and cheese. Woollens and carpets are manufactured, and there are locomotive works at Swindon. Salisbury is the county town, but Trowbridge is the admin. centre. Stonehenge and Avebury have famous prehistoric monuments. Wiltshire returns 5 members to Parl. Pop. 422,753.

WIMBLEDON
Part of Morden, borough of Greater London (1964), formerly in Surrey. Famous for its Lawn Tennis ground, the Courts of the All Eng. Tennis Club and centre of the Brit. Amateur Open Lawn Tennis Championships. The Centre Court can take *c.* 16,000 spectators.

WINCHELSEA
Town of Sussex, 8 m. N.E. of Hastings. It was one of the flourishing Cinque Ports.

WINCHESTER
City and county town of Hants., on the Itchen, 66 m. S.W. of London. It has an agricultural trade. The cath., first completed in the 7th cent. and rebuilt *c.* 1080, is notable for its long nave. In the Shire Hall is the so-called table of King Arthur. Of Rom. origin, it was the cap. of Wessex, and for *c.* 200 years before the Norman Conquest was the cap. of Eng. Pop.

29,000. **Winchester College.** Eng. public school, founded by William of Wykeham, 1388.

WIND
Air in natural motion. Winds are caused by differences of atmospheric pressure. Air flows to a low-pressure region from one where a higher pressure exists. *See* BEAUFORT SCALE.

WINDERMERE
Urban district of Westmorland, near the E. side of L. Windermere, 4 m. S.E. of Ambleside. The lake is the largest in Eng. Pop. 6,640.

WINDHOEK
[-hoŏk] Cap. of S.W. Africa, 170 m. E. of Walvis Bay and 5,500 ft. above sea level. Pop. 36,051.

WINDSOR
Borough of Berks., on the Thames, 22 m. W. of London. It is connected by bridges with Eton. Pop. 28,350. **Windsor Castle.** Chief residence of the Brit. sovereign. It stands above the town of Windsor. The first castle was built by William I, but the present one dates from the 14th cent. with additions made in the 18th and 19th. The gem of the building is St. George's Chapel, restored 1922-3. The keep, or round tower, is in the centre of the castle, and the grounds cover 12 acres. Around is the Home Park, and beyond the Great Park covering 3 sq.m.

WINDSOR
City and port of Ontario, Canada, on the Detroit R. It is an important centre for the manufacture of motor vehicles. Pop. 192,000.

WINDSOR, Edward, Duke of. *See* EDWARD VIII.

WINDSOR, House of
Name of the Brit. royal family. King George V is regarded as the founder of the House of Windsor, having, in 1917, abandoned for himself and his family all German titles. In 1960 H.M. the Queen declared that all her descendants would use the name **Mountbatten-Windsor** except those males bearing royal style and title.

WINDWARD ISLANDS
Group of Is. in the West Indies. As indep. territories, Grenada, St. Vincent and St. Lucia form part of the W. Indies assoc. states. Area: 829 sq.m. Pop. 329,786.

WINE
Fermented juice of certain fruits. Beverage wines are made from ripe grapes, and the juice allowed to ferment naturally, and fine wines are from perfect grapes, perfectly fermented. Fortified wines contain a certain proportion of spirit distilled from wine, added to raise the alcoholic strength. Still wines are those which have been allowed to lose their carbon dioxide during the process of fermentation, and sparkling wines have been kept bottled up until used. *See* VINE.

WINGATE, Charles Orde
(1903-44) Brit. Brigadier. Joined Wavell's staff in M.E. during early part of World War II; later was moved to the Far E. where he commanded the 3rd Indian Div. engaged in guerilla warfare behind the Jap. lines in Burma. W. was noted for his audacious exploits with this Div., his men being known as the ' Chindits '.

WINNIPEG
Cap. city of Manitoba, Canada, S. of L. W. at the confluence of the Red and Assiniboine rivers. It is an important rly. and commercial centre, with a large grain market. Pop. 257,000

WINTER
4th of the 4 seasons. In the N. Hemisphere it commences at the Winter Solstice when the Sun enters the Zodiacal sign Capricornus, *c.* Dec. 21-22, although in Brit. the winter months are popularly considered to be Nov., Dec. and Jan. The Winter Solstice corresponds with the Summer Solstice. Day and night are of equal duration.

WINTER CHERRY
(*Physalis*) Hardy herbaceous plant of Chinese origin. The orange-coloured calyx becomes enlarged and distended, hence its familiar name of Chinese lantern.

WINTER-MOTH
Moth (*Chuimatobia brumata*) which appears in its perfect state in the beginning of winter. The larvae are very injurious to fruit trees.

WINTERGREEN
Genus of small herbaceous evergreen plants (*Pyrola*) of the order Ericales. *Pyrola rotundifolia*, a Brit. species, has small round leaves and white flowers. The Amer. wintergreen (*Gaultheria procumbens*), is a low-growing aromatic plant. **Oil of w.**, used for flavouring and also in unguents for external application, is obtained from the leaves.

WIREWORM
Larva of the Click-beetles (*Elsteridae*) About 3 in. in length, and yellow in colour. It has 3 pairs of jointed legs and very powerful jaws.

WISBECH
[bēch] Borough and river port on the Is. of Ely, Cambridgeshire, on the Nene, 15 m. S.W. of King's Lynn. It is the centre of a rich market gardening district. Pop. 17,500.

WISCONSIN
N. state of the U.S.A. with coastline on L. Superior and Michigan, and bounded by the Mississippi on the W. It is the leading dairy state of the Union. Iron ore and zinc are mined, and there are manufacturing industries on the L. Michigan shore. Madison is the cap. but Milwaukee is the largest town. It was settled by Fr. traders in 1670, and ceded to the U.S.A. in 1783. It became a state in 1848, and sends 10 representatives to Congress. Area: 56,150 sq.m. Pop. 4,418,000.

WISEMAN, Nicholas
(1802-65) Eng. Cardinal. In 1850, he was made Cardinal Archbp. of Westminster. Wiseman's pastoral aroused fears in Eng. of ' papal aggression ', but his *Appeal to the English People*, and his tact and moderation enabled him to outlive the hostility.

WISTARIA
[-tair'-] Genus of leguminous climbing shrubs (*W. sinensis*). The soft blue flowers grow in long drooping racemes. *W. japonica* is white.

WITAN
Short name for the **witenagemot**, an assembly in Eng. in A.-S. times. Its members were called together by the king when he wanted advice. It consisted of members of the royal family, the archbps., bps., abbots and thegns. It lasted until the Norman Conquest, when it was replaced by the feudal Great Council.

WITCH
Woman who practised sorcery, and was supposed to have dealings with the devil. In medieval times, witches were generally women who foretold the future, and practised *white magic*—the gathering and brewing of herbs to cure people; or *black magic*, when these things were done to work harm. Witches usually had ' familiars '—supposedly the devil in the disguise of a dog, cat, toad, etc. Witchcraft was sternly put down from the 15th cent. by all zealous members of the Christian Chs. and witches were hanged, burned, and drowned.

WITCH HAZEL
N. Amer. shrub (*Hamamelis virginica*), resembling the hazel. The bark and leaves have an astringent property.

WITT, Jan de
(1625-72) Dutch repub. statesman. He opposed William II of Orange, and later the young prince (afterwards William III). Apptd. Grand Pensionary of Holland while the Dutch were

at war with Eng., he concluded peace in 1654. Again in 1667 he negotiated peace with Eng. by the Treaty of Breda, and next year brought about the Triple Alliance between Eng., Holland and Sweden. Louis XIV's invasion of the United Provs. brought about his fall.

WITTENBERG
Town of Saxony-Anhalt, on the Elbe, 50 m. S.E. of Magdeburg. The centre of the Reformation, W. contains the tombs of Martin Luther and Melancthon. Pop. 28,000.

WOAD
(1) A cruciferous plant (*Isatis tinctoria*) formerly extensively cultivated in Brit. for the blue dye extracted from its pulped and fermented leaves. The ancient Britons are said to have coloured their bodies with this dye. (2) **Wild Woad** (**weld** or **wold**) a Brit. plant (*Reseda luteola*), yields a beautiful yellow dye.

WOKING
Urban district of Surrey, on the Wey, 24 m. S.W. of London. Nearby is the cemetery and crematorium of the London Necropolis. Pop. 70,610.

WOLF
Wild member of the Dog family. Found in N. countries, its colour is usually grey. Wolves run down their quarry and are killers of sheep, but when hunting in packs can overcome deer and antelopes. They have been extinct in Brit. for 200 years.

WOLF, Hugo
(1860-1903) Aust. composer. For 4 years he was music critic to the Vienna *Salonblatt* in which he attacked Brahms and championed Wagner. He is now chiefly remembered for more than 250 songs.

WOLF-FERRARI, Ermanno
[volf-fè-ra'-ri] (1876-1948) Ital.-German composer. He is best known as a composer of light operas.

WOLFE, Charles
(1791-1823) Irish poet. Educ. Trinity Coll. Dublin, and it was during that period (1817) that there was pub. the poem for which he is best remembered—*Ode on the Burial of Sir John Moore at Corunna.*

WOLFE, James
(1727-59) Eng. soldier. He took part in the battles of Dettingen, Culloden and Laffeldt. His crowning achievement was the taking of Quebec, 1759. Having scaled the heights at night, he routed the Fr. under Montcalm, the result being that Canada, in 1760, became Brit.

WOLFHOUND
Name given to a variety of dogs used to hunt the Wolf. The Irish, the Borzoi and the Alsatian Wolfhounds are examples.

WOLFRAM
Ore from which tungsten is extracted. It is found in Malaya, Spain, Australia and Colorado, and is a mixture of iron tungstate ($FeWO_4$) and manganese tungstate ($MnWO_4$).

WOLLONGONG
Seaport of N.S.W., Australia, 50 m. S. of Sydney. Coal is mined, and there are iron and steel works. Pop. 142,170.

WOLSEY, Thomas
(*c.* 1475-1530) Eng. cardinal. His rise under Henry VIII was rapid. In 1515 he was made cardinal. Apptd. Chanc. the same year, he did valuable admin. work, and was one of the leading European diplomatists. He used some of his wealth to found the coll. of Christ Church, Oxford, and to build Hampton Court. He failed to obtain for Henry a divorce from Catherine of Aragon. In 1529 he was deprived of his chancellorship and arrested for high treason. He d. on his way to trial.

WOLVERHAMPTON
County borough of Staffs., 13 m. N.W. of Birmingham. A centre of the hardware manufacture, it has also engineering works. It returns 2 members to Parl. Pop. 267,000.

WOMBAT
(*Phascolomys*) Austral. marsupial. They have large flat heads, small eyes, sharp teeth, a vestigial tail, short, stout legs, with broad, naked-soled feet. They can drive tunnels in almost any terrain. They sleep during the day in holes and burrows, and at night go out in search of vegetable food.

WOMEN'S LAND ARMY
Organisation which functioned during both World Wars. Entrants received training in farm or horticultural duties, and were sent to work for individual farmers or market gardeners. They were issued with a suitable uniform and received a weekly wage.

WOMEN'S SUFFRAGE
Exercise of the vote in parl. and municipal elections by women. Advocated in the middle of the 19th cent. by Cobden, Mill, and Disraeli, the socs. formed to promote it were united in a Nat. Union in 1887 under Mrs. Henry Fawcett. The Women's Social and Polit. Union was formed, 1903, under Mrs. Pankhurst (*q.v.*) and developed militant tactics. In 1906 the Lib. party came into power under Asquith, a violent opponent of the cause. Suffragettes heckled M.P.'s and held demonstrations. When sent to prison they went on hunger-strike. During World War I they showed such ability that in 1916 a conference decided that women over 30 years old who were householders or wives of householders should be allowed to vote, and this was secured in 1918, when the Act making women eligible to sit in Parl. was passed. In 1928 a Bill was passed giving complete electoral equality to women.

WOOD
Solid part of trees and plants, used to transport water and dissolved salts from the roots to the growing parts. Commercially it is classified into wood and timber. Timber is wood of large dimensions only; wood includes thin branches, twigs, etc. Timber is of 2 kinds—soft woods, derived from conifers, and hardwood produced by dicotyledonous trees such as oak, ash, beech, teak, etc. Soft woods are used in the manufacture of wood pulp and paper, artificial silk and other cellulose industries, while the finer hardwoods are used for cabinet-making, etc.

WOOD, Sir Henry
(1869-1944) Eng. conductor and founder of the London Prom. concerts. B. London, he began conducting when 19, and at 25 conducted the first series of Queen's Hall Prom. concerts.

WOOD SORREL
(*Oxalis acetosella*) Perennial wild herb native to Brit. The rootstock is creeping, the heart-shaped leaves grow in threes, resembling the clover leaf. The seed capsule at the slightest touch discharges the seeds forcibly.

WOODCOCK
(*Scolopax rusticola*) Wild bird found in many parts of Europe and Asia. It has a long bill which is used in digging for insects. It is grey, buff or mottled black in colour. The bird nests in a hollow on the ground and moves about at night. It is *c.* 14 in. long and is very like the snipe.

WOODFORD
Part of Redbridge, borough of Greater London (1964). Sir Winston Churchill was M.P. 1945-64.

WOODLOUSE
(*Oniscus*) A small crustacean belonging to the order Isopoda. It feeds on decaying vegetation. The body has 7 free thoracic segments, each with a pair of legs.

WOODPECKER
Climbing birds of the family Picidae. The feet are adapted to arboreal life, and the long, barbed and sticky tongue is employed to get insects out of crevices in the bark, etc. The nest is made in a deep hole dug in the tree trunk. A common Brit. species, the Green W. (*Picus viridis*) is *c.* 12½ in. long, the plumage olive green, yellow to grey on rump and underparts. The head and nape of neck are crimson, with a black cheek. Others found less abundantly in Brit. are *Dryobates major* and *minor*, the Greater and Lesser Spotted W., 9 in. and 6 in. in length respectively.

WOODRUFF
Wild herb (*Asperula odorata*) of the family Rubiaceae. The slender erect stems, *c.* 12 in. high, bear whorls of bright, smooth leaves, surmounted by a flowerhead of very small funnel-shaped white blooms.

WOODRUSH
Genus of perennial plants (*Luzula*). They have short, grass-like leaves, with a hairy edge, and clusters of brown flowers borne in small sprays. Other varieties include the field woodrush (*L. campestris*), and the mountain species (*L. spicata* and *L. arcuata*).

WOODWORM
Larvae of certain beetles, which feed on wood. To destroy the worms, brush the wood with a solution of formalin. A more efficient method is to fumigate the affected piece of furniture, using cyanide.

WOOKEY HOLE
Cavern in Somerset, 2 m. W. of Wells.

WOOL
Fibrous coat of sheep, which differs from the hair of other animals in being rougher and more hooked, so that it binds or felts together very readily. In cold and temp. climates it is the chief material for clothing, owing to its resistance to damp and to the warmth which it gives by being a good insulator of heat. Most of the world's finest wool comes from the Merino sheep, but the name is also given to the fibrous covering of the llama, angora goat, etc.

WOOLF, Virginia
(1882-1941) Eng. writer. Her work includes novels *The Voyage* (1912), *Jacob's Room* (1922), *Mrs. Dalloway* (1925), *To the Lighthouse* (1927), *The Waves* (1931), *Between The Acts* (1941); short stories *Monday or Tuesday* (1921), *A Haunted House* (1943); biog. *Roger Fry* (1940); essays *The Common Reader* (1925-32); *The Captain's Death-Bed* (1950).

WOOLTON, Earl
Frederick James Marquis (1883-1964) Eng. administrator and politician. Food Min. 1940-3; Min. of Reconstruction, 1943-5; Chairman of Cons. and Unionist Central Office, 1946-55; Viscount, 1953. Woolton took charge of food organisation in 1940, a task which he accomplished with great success.

WOOLWORTH, Frank Winfield
(1852-1919) Amer. merchant. He conceived the idea of stores in which inexpensive but attractive goods would be put on display and purchased for cash. After two failures, he opened a 5 and 10 per cent store in New York State. Within a few years he had hundreds of branches throughout the U.S.A. He d. worth $7,000,000.

WORCESTERSHIRE
W. Midland county of Eng. in the Severn basin. The land is undulating, with hills in the N.E. and S.W., the Malvern Hills rising to 1,395 ft. The chief rivers are the Severn and its tributaries, the Avon, Stour and Teme. Fruit growing and market gardening are important, esp. in the Vale of Evesham. The N. part of the county lies within the Black Country. Worcester is the county town; other centres are Kidderminster, Stourbridge and Malvern. It returns 6 members to Parl. (3 borough constituencies). Pop. 581,270. **Worcester.** City, county borough and county town of Worcs., on the Severn, 22 m. S.W. of Birmingham. The chief building is the cath. The chief industries are the making of gloves, boots, vinegar and sauces. The porcelain works, estab. 1751, are well known. In 1651 Cromwell defeated the Scots under Charles II, outside the town. With Droitwich, it returns 1 member to Parl. Pop. 669,000.

WORDSWORTH, William
(1770-1850) Eng. poet. In 1790 he visited the continent, spent a year in Fr. He sympathised with the Revolution. *An Evening Walk* and *Descriptive Sketches* (1793) opened his poetic career. *Lyrical Ballads* (with Coleridge) appeared 1798: with a Preface on poetry 1800. He settled at Grasmere, Westmorland, and in 1843 succeeded Southey as poet laureate. His finest work was done before 1807; the *Ode on Intimations of Immortality*; *The Prelude*, a poetic autobiog., pub. 1850; the Lucy poems, *Tintern Abbey*, *Resolution and Independence*.

WORKERS' EDUCATIONAL ASSOC.
Non-sectarian fed. of educ. and workers' organisations founded by Albert Mansbridge in 1903. The W.E.A. soon became the centre of the workers' educ. movement in Brit. As univ. tutorial classes were estabd. the assoc. expanded rapidly.

WORKMEN'S COMPENSATION
In Brit. a system by which workmen and their families receive compensation for d. or accident during employment, regulated by various Acts of Parl.

WORLD COUNCIL OF CHURCHES
Formally constituted at an assembly of representatives from Anglican, E. Orthodox, Protestant and Old Catholic Chs., Amsterdam, 1948. H.Q. are at Geneva.

WORMS
[vorms] Town of the Rhineland-Palatinate, Germany. One of the most ancient towns of Germany, on the Rhine, 13 m. N. of Ludwigshafen. It has a Romanesque Cath. In 1521, the Imperial Diet meeting there judged Martin Luther. Pop. 51,900.

WORMWOOD
Herbaceous perennial plant (*Artemisia absinthium*) with strongly aromatic properties. 1-3 ft. high, the stems are rough and branching, the silky leaves are segmented and flat at the edge. Common to many countries, it grows wild in Brit.

WRATH
Cape of Sutherlandshire, 370 ft. high, the most N.W. point of Gt. Brit.

WREN
(*Troglodytes*) Small song bird. Native of European and Asiatic countries, and common

in Brit. The feathers are shaded brown, the short tail erect and the movements quick and restless. The domed nest has an aperture at the side.

WREN, Sir Christopher
(1632-1723) Eng. architect. He showed great aptitude for mathematics and science. After the Great Fire of 1666 he built a new St. Paul's Cath. and furnished plans for over 50 other chs. He also drew up elaborate plans for the improved rebuilding of the entire city.

WRESTLING
Form of athletics. A favourite pastime among the Gks. and Roms. and still a regular feature of the Olympic Games. The art of Ju-Jitsu has been practised by the Japanese from the earliest times.

WRIGHT, Orville
(1871-1948) Amer. aviator. B. Dayton, Ohio. With his brother, **Wilbur** (1867-1912) he succeeded in making the first flight in a heavier-than-air machine on Dec. 17, 1903, at Kitty Hawk, N. Carolina. The brothers, on Sept. 12, 1908, estabd. a 2nd record by remaining in the air for 75 min.

WRIST
Part of upper limb between hand and forearm. Wrist joint or carpus is composed of a series of joints between the radius and ulna above, and the metacarpals below and contains 8 small bones called carpals held together by ligaments and tendons.

WRITING
The writing of ideographs on stone and other materials, *e.g.* wood, prob. began many millenia B.C.; then came clay tablets (Babylonian, Egyptian, Hittite); papyrus, and reed- or quill-pen; wax-tablets and pointed *stilus*, for jottings; parchment, in a roll (*volumen*) or book-form (*codex*); paper, and steel-pen in 19th cent. Book-hand developed in the M.A. out of the separate capitals of Rom. inscriptions, etc. It was imitated in early printing in Black Letter—still used in Germany, but replaced elsewhere (by the late 16th cent.) by Rom. type, based on a hand used in Italy *c.* 1420 as a deliberate revival of ancient forms. In the 17th cent. 'Italian' hand replaced the older Eng. cursive script. *See* CUNEIFORM.

WROCLAW
[vrot'-sláf] (formerly **Breslau**) City and river port of Poland, on the Oder, 95 m. S. of Poznan. There is an extensive trade in coal, timber and iron; machinery, railway stock and textiles are manufactured. It was a German city until World War II, when the W. boundary of Poland was extended to the Oder-Neisse line. Pop. 477,000.

WRYNECK
(*Jynx torquilla*) Bird of Woodpecker family. It is insectivorous and its name is derived from its habit of twisting its neck about in feeding. It is 7 in. long, the plumage being grey above, mottled and streaked with black, the underparts yellowish with darker arrow-like markings.

WÜRTTEMBERG
[vür'-] Former kingdom of Germany, W. of Bavaria, in Dec. 1946, divided between the two W. German states of Württemberg-Baden and Württemberg-Hohenzollern. (1) **W.-Baden,** on the lower course of the Neckar, mainly lowland. (2) **W.-Hohenzollern,** traversed by the upper Danube and bounded in the S. by the L. of Constance, mainly mountainous. In 1952, as the result of a plebiscite, both were merged with Baden to form Baden-Württemberg (*q.v.*).

WYAT, Sir Thomas
(1503-42) Eng. diplomat and poet. Favourite of both Henry VII and Henry VIII. He was the first to tr. the sonnets of Petrarch. His son, **Thomas** (1520-54) saw milit. service on the continent. In 1554, in opposition to Mary's mar. to Philip of Sp., he roused a rebellion and attacked London. He failed and was executed.

WYCHERLEY, William
(1640-1716) Eng. dramatist. Educ. in Fr. and at Oxford. His chief plays are *The Country Wife* (1672), *The Plain Dealer* (1674).

WYCLIFFE, John
(*c.* 1324-84) Eng. Reformer. A scholar and theologian, he attacked the abuses in the Ch. The first complete tr. of the Bible into Eng. is assoc. with his name. He influenced considerably the teaching of John Huss (*q.v.*). His followers were called Lollards and their preaching fomented the popular discontent which showed in the Peasants' Revolt of 1381.

WYE
River of Gt. Brit. which rises in Montgomeryshire on Plynlimon, flows through Radnorshire and Herefordshire and forms the boundary between Mon. and Glos., entering the Severn estuary at Chepstow.

WYKEHAM, William of
(1324-1404) Eng. bishop and chanc. B. Wickham, Hampshire. He founded New Coll. Oxford, 1380, and in 1388-94, Winchester School. Between 1394 and 1404 he added to Winchester Cath. and was buried in the chantry.

WYOMING
[wī-ō'-] W. state of the U.S.A. in the Rocky Mts. It is a semi-arid region, and agriculture is only possible with irrigation. Alfalfa, cereals and sugar beet are grown, and livestock kept. Large quantities of coal are mined. Cheyenne is the cap. and largest town. There are 2 nat. parks, the Yellowstone and Grand Teton. It was settled in 1834, and became a state in 1890, sending 1 representative to Congress. Area: 97,910 sq.m. Pop. 332,500.

X

X
24th letter of the Eng. alphabet. It is usually pronounced as a double consonant, having the sound *ks*, as in *wax*, *tax*, or the sound *gz*, as in *exhaust*, *exert*. At the beginning of words (often derived from the Gk.) it is pronounced like the English *z*, *e.g. xylophone*.

X-RAYS
(or **Röntgen Rays**) Invisible penetrative rays discovered by W. K. Röntgen (*q.v.*) in 1895. Produced by passing an electric current of high potential through a vacuum tube, the rays penetrate many substances opaque to light, and, by their effect of casting a shadow of bony parts, are of great value in the diagnosis of fractures, joint disorders, etc. Irradiation by the Röntgen rays is a method of treating cancerous growths, skin disorders, etc. When first introduced, the beneficial effects of X-rays were universally applauded, but with increasing knowledge the dangers associated with repeated exposure to X-rays have become more apparent. The accumulation of small doses of radiation could be dangerous.

XENOCRATES
[zen-ok′-rȧ-tēz] Gk. philosopher. He became a disciple of Plato. 339 B.C. he succeeded Speusippus as Pres. of the Old Academy. He modified the Platonic system by introducing the Pythagorean doctrine of numbers.

XENON
[zen′-on] Zero-valent chemical element discovered by Sir W. Ramsay and M. W. Travers (1898), who liquified it at −109° C. and solidified it at −140° C. One of the rare gases present in the atmosphere, in the proportion of one part in 20,000, it is colourless, odourless, tasteless, heavy and inert. Symbol Xe or X; atomic no. 54; at. wt. 131·3.

XENOPHON
(*c.* 435-355 B.C.) Athenian writer. A pupil of Socrates, fought in the army of Cyrus of Persia and fought for the Lacedaemonians against the Athenians at Coronea, 394 B.C. He retired to Scillus, near Olympia, where he wrote his *Anabasis* recounting the retreat of Cyrus' Gk. force to the Black Sea (401). His *Cyropaedia* is a romance embodying his ideas on educ. His brilliant dialogue, the *Symposium*, gives us a picture of Socrates and his table-talk. He died at Corinth.

XERXES
[zerk-sēz] King of Persia (485-465 B.C.). Son of Darius I, he led the 2nd Persian expedition against Greece in 480 B.C. The Persians defeated the Gks. at Thermopylae, and were then defeated on sea at Salamis. A further defeat at Plataea in 479 led X. to abandon his attempt to conquer the Gks. He was assassinated.

XYLOPHONE
[zī′-lō-fōn] A percussion instrument composed of a series of wooden bars with a complete chromatic compass of 3 octaves from middle C upwards. It is played with wooden hammers.

Y

Y
25th letter of the Eng. alphabet. It is both a vowel and a consonant. In mod. Eng., at the beginning of syllables and when followed by a vowel it is consonantal, *e.g. yellow, yacht*; when medial or at the end of words it is a vowel, having the short *i* sound in words like *system*, the long *y* sound in *deny, cry, shy*, etc.

YACHTING
Racing or cruising in yachts. The Royal Cork Yacht Club dates from 1720, and matches were sailed at Cowes in 1780. The Royal Yacht Squadron, then the Yacht Club, was estabd. at Cowes in 1812. In 1851 the *America* won a cup given by the Royal Yacht Squadron, the cup passing to the New York Yacht Club and becoming 'The America Cup', for which Sir Thomas Lipton 5 times challenged unsuccessfully. Internat. rules were first introduced in 1906. The present internat. rules date from 1920. The principal regattas in Brit. are held at Cowes, Ryde, Torquay, Plymouth, Lowestoft, Harwich, Belfast, the Clyde and elsewhere.

YAK
(*Bos grunniens*) Bovine mammal of Tibet and neighbouring regions. Kept for its milk and flesh, and used as a beast of burden. A heavy, bulky animal with short legs, it has long shaggy hair. The male stands *c.* 5½ ft. at the shoulders.

YALE UNIVERSITY
Amer. Univ. at New Haven, Conn. founded in 1701 (at Saybrook), by 10 ministers as the Collegiate School of Amer. When in 1718, the first building was begun on the present campus, the Coll. was renamed in honour of Elihu Yale. It became a Univ. in 1887, and is now world famous. Students number *c.* 8,300, incl. 649 women.

YALTA CONFERENCE
Conference held at Yalta in Crimea, Feb. 4-11, 1945, attended by Mr. Churchill, Pres. Roosevelt and Marshal Stalin, with their foreign mins. and Chiefs of Staff. Complete agreement was reached on milit. operations. It was also decided to call a conference at San Francisco on April 25, to prepare Charter of U.N. Organisation.

YAM
Genus of trop. climbing plants of the Dioscoreaceae. Native to the E. Indies, yams are much cultivated in the W. Indies and China. The large tuberous roots form a valuable food.

YANGTZE-KIANG
Longest river of China, 3,430 m. long, which rises in Tibet and flows E. through C. China.

YARMOUTH, Great
County borough, resort and market town of Norfolk, at the mouth of the Yare, 19 m. E. of Norwich. It is a fishing port and has associations with Nelson. Pop 52,450.

YARROW
Perennial plant (*Achillea millefolium*); family Compositae. The leaves are slender and segmented. The large flower head has pink or white blossoms with a yellow central disc.

YAWS
Trop. disease, occurring in the E. and W. Indies, Africa, Amer. and S. Pacific Is.

YEAR
Unit of time marked by the revolution of the earth in its orbit round the sun. The solar year is 365 days, 5 hrs. 48 mins. 49·7 secs. The sidereal year is 19 min. longer. For practical purposes the year may be taken at 365¼ days. It is therefore fixed at 365 days with an extra day every 4th year, which is called a leap year. The leap years are those which are divisible by 4 without remainder. These arrangements follow the Gregorian Calendar introd. in 1582. In this cal. the years are calculated from the birth of Jesus Christ which was termed Anno Domini, and written A.D. 1, the years before that event being numbered backwards as B.C. (Before Christ). The Jewish year varies in length between 353 and 385 days. The Mohammedan Year is one of 354 or 355 days only, consequently it loses some days each year by comparison with the Gregorian dates. Year 1 to the Mohammedan is A.D. 622. *See* CALENDAR.

YEAST
Minute fungi of the *Saccharomyces*. In the presence of sugar, yeasts, by the enzyme known as zymase which promotes fermentation, produce alcohol and carbon dioxide. They are used in brewing and baking.

YEATS, William Butler
(1865-1939) Irish poet. Son of Jack B. Yeats, artist. In Paris he came under the influence of the Symbolists (*q.v.*). He pub. vols. of poems, 1889-1937; *Last Poems and Plays* (1940). His plays include *The Countess Kathleen, The Land of Heart's Desire* and *Deirdre*. In 1923 he was awarded a Nobel Prize for lit. His interest in an Irish Theatre led him and Lady Gregory (*q.v.*) to found the Abbey Theatre, Dublin, in 1904.

YELLOW FEVER
Infectious disease transmitted by a mosquito. Characterised by jaundice, bleeding from stomach (black vomit), fever, and pains in body and limbs. Disease is epidemic in W. Africa and W. Indies. Vaccine produced to combat disease in troops during World War II has given very satisfactory results.

YELLOW-HAMMER
(*Emberiza citrinella*) Yellow Bunting of N. Europe. It is a common Brit. bird, 6½ in. long, the plumage yellow-brown above.

YELLOW SEA
Branch of the Pacific Ocean. It lies between China, Manchuria and Korea. Its greatest width is *c.* 400 m.

YELLOWSTONE
River of the U.S.A. which rises in the Rocky Mts. in Wyoming, and flows through the Y. Lake and a canyon to the Missouri. The river gives its name to the **Yellowstone National Park** in Wyoming which covers 3,350 sq.m.

YEMEN, Peoples Democratic Republic of
State of S.W. Arabia with a coastline on the Red Sea. Although mountainous, Y. contains the most fertile part of Arabia. Coffee, food grains, hides and raisins are exported. Sana is the cap. and Hodeida the chief port. The Iman was recognised as king by Brit., 1934. In Sept.

1962 Col. Sallal set up Revolutionary Council. Area: 75,290 sq.m. Pop. 4,500,000.

YEW
(*Taxus baccata*) Evergreen tree of the Coniferae, from 15-50 ft. high, it is of spreading growth. The twigs are many and thickly leaved. The wax-like vivid red berries are cup-shaped with a central seed. The wood is hard but pliable, and is commercially valuable.

YEZD
Industrial city of Persia, 170 m. N.E. of Isfahan, a considerable route centre. Pop. *c.* 60,000.

YGGDRASIL
Ash tree in Norse mythology which binds together heaven, earth and hell.

YIDDISH
Composite language spoken by Jews throughout Europe, with borrowings from German, Slav, Eng. and written in Heb. characters.

YOGA
A strict spiritual discipline the ultimate aim of which is to attain union with the Universal Spirit. The 3 principle stages are (1) *Meditation*, (2) *Contemplation*, and (3) *Absorption*. The physical discipline entails controlled posture and breathing, diet, continence. Yoga is described in the *Aphorisms of Patanjali*, *The Bhagavad Gita*, etc.

YOGHOURT
A nutritious and refreshing type of fermented milk, popular in Bulgaria. It is produced from the milk of the cow, goat, or buffalo by the inoculation of pasteurised milk with a certain bacterium.

YOKOHAMA
Seaport and city of Honshu Is. Japan, on Tokyo Bay, 15 m. S. of Tokyo. It possesses a large modern harbour, from which silk and coal are exported. Pop. 1,789,000.

YONGE, Charlotte Mary
(1823-1901) Eng. novelist. *The Heir of Redclyffe* (1853) brought her enough money to provide the schooner for Bp. Selwyn's Melanesian mission.

YORK, House of
Branch of the Brit. Royal Family. It traces its origin to Edward III, through his 5th son, Edmund, Duke of York. **York, Duke of** (1411-60) **Richard,** Duke of York was the son of Richard, Earl of Camb. and Anne Mortimer, being thus descended on both sides from Edward III. He was the father of Edward IV and Richard III. Protector of Eng. during the mental incapacity of Henry VI, it was his claim to the succession that started the Wars of the Roses. His claim descended to his eldest son, who became Edward IV in 1461.

YORK, Duke of
(1763-1827) Frederick Augustus, 2nd son of King George III. In 1784 he was created Duke of York. In 1793 and 1799 he commanded Eng. contingents against the Fr. He did good work, carrying out army reforms.

YORKSHIRE
County of N. Eng. lying between the Humber, Durham and Lancs. The largest county of Eng., it is divided into 3 Ridings, N., E. and W. (*qq.v.*). It contains some peaks of the Pennines in the W., the York Moors and Wolds and the Cleveland Hills. Between the ridges of the Pennines are beautiful valleys or dales. The chief rivers are the Ouse and its tributaries, Wharfe, Aire, Nidd, Swale, Ure, Don and Derwent. In the N. are the Tees and Esk. A great industrial area centres on Sheffield, Leeds and Bradford, known for its coal mines and woollen mills. Around Doncaster the coalfield has been developed in the 20th cent. There are also industrial areas around Hull and Middlesbrough, but elsewhere agriculture remains the dominant industry. Y. was famous for its Cistercian abbeys; Fountains and Kirkstall are outstanding examples. The county returns 57 members to Parl. Pop. 4,723,000. **York.** City, county borough and county town of Yorks., on the Ouse, 188 m. N.W. of London. In Rom. times it was a fort called Eboracum. The walls and gateways of the med. city remain. Y. Minster is one of the finest Gothic chs. in Eng. The Archbp. of Y. is Metropolitan of the N. Prov. and Primate of Eng. Y. is a rly. junction and milit. centre, with railway and printing works, flour mills and confectionery factories. It returns 1 member to Parl. Pop. 104,000.

YORKSHIRE TERRIER
Small terrier with black nose, long straight, silky hair, steel blue on the back, legs and head a light fawn.

YORKTOWN
Town of S.E. Virginia, U.S.A., where British forces under Cornwallis were besieged in 1781 by Americans under Washington and where Cornwallis surrendered.

YOSEMITE VALLEY
Famous valley in C. Calif., U.S.A., in Yosemite Nat. Park with outstanding mountain scenery including waterfalls.

YOUNG, Brigham
(1801-77) Amer. Mormon leader. He organised the settlement of the Mormons in Utah, in 1847, and was the founder of Salt Lake City, where he d., survived by 17 wives and *c.* 50 children.

YOUNG, Edward
(1683-1765) Eng. poet. Became a clergyman at Welwyn (1730). He wrote satires 1725-8, and *The Complaint or Night Thoughts on Life, Death and Immortality* (1742-5).

YOUNG MEN'S CHRISTIAN ASSOCIATION
Founded in 1844 by (Sir) **George Williams** with the purpose of uniting young men in an endeavour to improve themselves physically, mentally and intellectually. There are over 75,000 members in Eng., Ireland and Wales, and the World Alliance, constituted in 1855, comprises more than 50 nat. movements. **Young Women's Christian Association.** Formed on the lines of the Y.M.C.A. in 1855, it has a Brit. membership of over 45,000.

YOUNGHUSBAND, Sir Francis
(1863-1942) Brit. soldier and explorer. He explored the mts. between Kashmir and China and accompanied the Brit. mission to Tibet in 1902. Among his many books are *Heart of a Continent* (1898), and *The Epic of Everest* (1927).

YOUTH HOSTELS ASSOCIATIONS
Brit. network of organisations founded 1930-1 and modelled on the former German *Wandervögel*. There are 3 such assocs. serving Eng. and Wales, Scot. and N. Ireland. Their object is to enable young people of limited means, and of both sexes, to enjoy the countryside by providing them with inexpensive accommodation when on hiking or cycling expeditions.

YPRES
[ēpr] Town of W. Flanders prov., 26 m. S. of Ostend. It was famous for its silk and lace. During World War I it suffered severely. There were 3 **Battles of Ypres** during World War I. The first took place in 1914; the second, in spring 1915 was the first occasion that the Germans used poison gas, and the third formed part of the Allied offensive in Flanders, 1917.

YUCATAN
[yoo-kă-tän'] Peninsula of C. Amer. covering parts of Mexico, Guatemala and Brit. Honduras. It was the seat of Maya civilisation with many magnificent ruins of cities, temples,

pyramids, etc., dating from the period 100 B.C. to A.D. 1200.

YUGOSLAVIA
Repub. of S.E. Europe in the Balkan Peninsula S. of Hungary, with an indented coastline on the Adriatic Sea. Except for the area round the Danube and its tributaries, the country is mountainous. More than half the land surface is under cultivation, and there are large areas of forest. Mineral resources include iron, copper, lead and chrome ores. Industries are mainly connected with agriculture. The cap. is Belgrade, on the Danube. Three languages are recognised, Slovene, Macedonian, and Serbo-Croat, the latter being in official use. Y. became an indep. state in 1918, after the fall of the Austro-Hungarian empire. Alexander I, who succeeded King Peter in 1921, took dictatorial powers from 1929 to 1934, when he was assassinated in Marseilles. His son Peter II assumed the royal power in 1941 when Y. was invaded by Germany. After World War II, a Communist repub. was proclaimed. The Fed. People's Repub. of Y. comprises the 6 repubs. of Serbia, Croatia, Slovenia, Montenegro, Macedonia and Bosnia-Hercegovina. Parl. composed of 2 chambers, elects the pres. The dominating figure is Marshal Josip Broz Tito, 1st Pres. of Yugoslavia. Area: 98,725 sq.m. Pop. 19,958,000.

YUKON
Territory of the Dominion of Canada, N. of Brit. Columbia and E. of Alaska. It occupies the basin of the Yukon river, and has a short coastline on the Arctic Ocean. It contains Mt. Logan (19,850 ft.), the highest peak in Canada. The area is forested; mining is the chief industry. Gold was discovered in the Klondike, and the pop. rose to 27,000. By 1931 it had declined to 4,100. The seat of govt. is Dawson. It is gov. by a commissioner and a council, and sends 1 representative to the Dominion parl. Area: 207,100 sq.m. Pop. 14,628.

Z

Z
26th letter of the Eng. alphabet. It is a sibilant consonant and represents a vocal or sonant *s*. It has precisely the same sound as that of *s* in *rose*, etc. Almost all Eng. words beginning with *z* are of foreign origin, mostly Gk.

ZAGAZIG
Town of Egypt on a branch of the Nile, 40 m. N.E. of Cairo. It is the centre of a district producing Ashmauni cotton. Pop. 124,000.

ZAGREB
(formerly **Agram**) Cap. of Croatia, Yugoslavia, on the Sava. There is a 15th cent. Gothic cath., a univ. and manufacturing industries. Pop. 457,499.

ZAMA
Numidian town, *c.* 75 m. S.W. of Carthage, where Scipio Africanus Major defeated Hannibal in 202 B.C. and ended the 2nd Punic War.

ZAMBEZI
River of Africa, 1,650 m. long, which rises in N.W. Rhodesia near the frontier of the Congolese Rep. and flows S. and E. into the Ind. Ocean near Chinde, Port E. Africa.

ZAMBIA
Former Brit. S. African Territory of N. Rhodesia. Became indep. 1964 a year after dissolution of C. African Fed. (N. and S. Rhodesia and Nyasaland). It consists of a high plateau traversed by the valleys of the Zambezi Kafue, Luangwa and Luapula and includes L. Bangweulu. Cattle are reared but tsetse fly is a pest. Maize, tobacco, cotton and coffee are grown. Minerals include copper, lead, zinc and gold. Lusaka is the cap. Area: 290,323 sq.m. Pop. 3,947,000.

ZANZIBAR
Repub. of E. Africa, comprising the Is. of Z. and Pemba, and several small islets. The land is low-lying and fertile, the climate humid. Cloves, copra and sugar are the chief products. Z. town is the cap. The pop. is predominantly African, of Moslem religion. In the 19th cent. Z. was an Arab state under a sultan, whose lands included a large area on the mainland. In 1890 it was declared a Brit. protectorate, the sultan retaining his position on the Is. In Dec. 1963, Z. became indep. and in Jan. 1964, the sultanate was overthrown. In Apr. Z. united with Tanganyika to form the repub. of Tanzania. Area (Zanzibar): 1,020 sq.m. Pop. 325,000. **Zanzibar.** Port and cap. of Zanzibar Is. on the W. coast. Pop. 45,000.

ZÁPOTOCKY, Antonin
[zà-pŏ-tot-ski] (1884-1957) Communist Pres. of Czechoslovakia 1953-7. When the Germans entered Prague, 1938, he was arrested while trying to escape to Russia and spent World War II in concentration camps.

ZARAFSHAN
(Samarkand) Cap. of Uzbekistan, U.S.S.R., 150 m. E. of Bukhara. As Samarkand, the town was the cap. of the Mongol prince, Tamerlane. It came under the dominion of China, being taken by Russ. in 1868. Pop. 226,000.

ZEALAND
Largest Is. of Denmark, separated from Sweden by the Sound, and from Fünen by the Great Belt. On it are Copenhagen and Helsingor.

ZEBRA
(*Hippotigris zebra*) Striped animal of horse family (Equidae), a native of Africa and resembles the Ass in the shape of its ears, its tufted tail and erect mane. The tawny, or white, coat is striped with black on the head, limbs and body.

ZEBRA CROSSING
The name given to pedestrian road crossing in Gt. Brit. The crossing is marked by black and white stripes and there is a lighted winking beacon at either end.

ZEBU
Domesticated animal of the Ox family found in Asia. It is used as a draught animal. About the size of a bull, the animal is white or grey, horned and has a hump on the back.

ZECHARIAH
(O.T.) Heb. minor prophet. A contemporary of Haggai, he shared with him the task of inducing the people to rebuild the Temple.

ZEDOARY
[zed′-ō-à-ri] Herbaceous E. Ind. plant (*curcuma zedoaria*) with aromatic tuberous root-stocks. *C. longa*, provides turmeric, a spice used for pickling and in curry powder.

ZEEBRUGGE
[zā-broog′-gė] Seaport of Belg., 8 m. N. of Bruges. On April 23, 1918, during World War I, a Brit. force under Adm. Keyes sealed the entrance to the harbour by sinking three block ships.

ZEELAND
Prov. of S.W. Netherlands in the Scheldt estuary. It includes Walcheren and other islands. Middelburg is the cap.

ZEND-AVESTA
Parsee religious work. Traditionally ascribed to Zoroaster, the orig. is said to have been destroyed when Persia was invaded by Alexander.

ZENITH
That point of the heavens vertically above the observer, one of the two poles of the horizon, the other being the *nadir*. If the earth were a homogeneous and non-rotating sphere, the zenith of a place would be exactly in the straight line from the earth's centre through the place, but because of the elliptic nature of the globe, and the fact that it rotates, the zenith is slightly nearer to the celestial pole.

ZENO
Founder of the Stoic philosophy. B. Citium, Cyprus, prob. early in the 14th cent. B.C. he went to Athens, where he started his own school in the *stoa poikile* or ' painted porch ' whence the name Stoic.

ZENOBIA
Queen of Palmyra. On the d. of her husband she took the name Augusta and claimed to be Queen of the E. Her subjugation of Egypt caused the Emperor Aurelian to lead an exped. against her in A.D. 271.

ZEPHANIAH
Heb. minor prophet. He appears to have prophesied in the reign of Josiah, King of Judah (639-608 B.C.).

ZEPPELIN
Type of rigid airship invented by **Ferdinand, Count Zeppelin** (1838-1917), a German. He produced his first in 1906. From his plans many others were constructed for the German Govt. and during World War I they dropped bombs on London and other cities. After World War I a monster Zeppelin, the *Graf Zeppelin*, was built. *See* AIRSHIP.

ZETLAND
Alternative name for the Shetland Is. (*q.v.*), generally applied to the admin. county.

ZEUS
[zews] The chief deity of the Gks. whose principal seat of worship was Mt. Olympus in Thessaly.

ZIMBABWE
[zim-bab'-wi] Massive ruins in Rhodesia which include walls in varying states of preservation, buildings enclosing a cluster of granite rocks, two turrets, and are built in solid granite. P. S. Nazaroff in 1931 identified them as Persian: the *dakhmas* of the Mazdaists, who practised the religion of Zarathustra (Zoroaster). At some period in history the ancient Persians arrived in this part of Africa, bringing with them their culture, their religion and plants. They became the dominating element among the native population, spread their influence over an extensive area, laid out towns and villages and introduced the mining of reef gold.

ZINC
(or **Spelter**) Chem. element, with the sym. Zu, at. no. 30, and at. wt. 65·38. A bluish white metal, with a melting pt. of 786° F., it is found chiefly as the carbonate, calamine and the sulphide, zincblende. It is used for the plates of electric batteries and for roofing, galvanising, etc. Applied as a protective coat to iron, it prevents rusting. Alloyed with copper, it forms brass. The chloride is used as a flux for soldering.

ZINNIA
Genus of the family Compositae. They are perennial herbs, natives of the S. U.S.A.

ZINOVIEV, Grigori Evseevich
(1883-1936) Russ. revolutionary leader. Joined Bolshevik Party 1903; in exile, 1907-17; returned to Russia with Lenin, 1917; Pres. of Comintern, 1919-26. In 1924 the famous 'Zinoviev Letter', the authenticity of which was denied by the Soviet Govt., was sent to the Russ. chargé d'affaires in London. It is alleged to have urged intensive revolutionary propaganda in Brit. and was largely responsible for the overthrow of the first Lab. Govt.

ZION, Mount
One of the hills on which Jerusalem was situated. The name is used for the whole hill, for Jerusalem itself, and for the Jewish people. **Zionism.** Jewish nationalist movement. In 1897 the Zionist organisation was estabd. 'to create for the Jewish people a home in Palestine secured by public law', but not till 1920 was the definite step taken of setting up in Palestine a nat. home for the Jews. With the setting up of the state of Israel in 1948, Zionist hopes were fulfilled.

ZIRCONIUM
Chem. element; sym. Zr, at. no. 40, at. wt. 91. One of the rare earth elements, it is found in zircon and is used in tool steels.

ZITHER
An instrument found in Bavaria and Austria, consisting of a flat wooden soundbox over which are stretched 30 to 40 strings; 4 or 5 melody strings are played with a plectrum, the remainder, used for accompaniment, are plucked by the fingers.

ZODIAC
In astronomy, imaginary belt or zone in the heavens extending 9° on each side of the ecliptic and divided into 12 'signs', each of 30°. It contains the apparent paths of the Sun, Moon and chief planets. The 12 signs are: Aries, the Ram (♈); Taurus, the Bull (♉); Gemini, the Twins (♊); Cancer, the Crab (♋); Leo, the Lion (♌); Virgo, the Virgin (♍); Libra, the Balance (♎); Scorpio, the Scorpion (♏); Sagittarius, the Archer (♐); Capricornus, the Sea-Goat (♑); Aquarius, the Water-bearer (♒); Pisces, the Fishes (♓). *See* EQUATOR, EQUINOX.

ZOGU, Achmet
(or **Zog**) (1895-1961) Ex-king of Albania. After serving in the Aust. Army during World War I, he became P.M. 1922. He was elected Pres. of the Albanian Repub. 1925 and proclaimed king, 1928. Defeated by Mussolini in 1939.

ZOLA, Émile
(1840-1902) Fr. author. B. Paris, he engaged in clerking, then journalism. *L'Assommoir*, dealing with drunkenness, created a sensation. In 1898 he successfully espoused the cause of Capt. Dreyfus in his letter to *L'Aurore*, beginning *J'accuse*.

ZOOLOGICAL GARDENS
Enclosure in which living wild animals are kept for exhibition. In Eng. the chief is in Regent's Park, maintained by the **Zoological Society**.

ZOOLOGY
Study of living animals. Its chief branches are Morphology dealing with form and structure, position and relation of organs and parts; Embryology, dealing with development from the ovum to maturity; Physiology, which treats of the functions of organs; and Ecology or inter-relationship between animals and their environment.

ZOROASTER
Religious teacher, who is also known as **Zarathustra**, the most recent lived *c.* 800 B.C. and founded a religion which was the faith of the Persians from the 6th cent. B.C. to the 7th cent. A.D. His followers are now represented in India by the **Parsees**.

ZUIDER ZEE
[zi'-der-] An inlet from the N. Sea, it extended S. into the heart of the Netherlands with the islands of Ameland, Terchelling, Vlieland and Texel across the sea opening. Originally forest land on which the sea encroached in 12th-14th cent., reclamation started in 17th cent. A 20-m. long dyke across the opening to the N. Sea was completed in 1932 and drainage of the whole embarked upon. Much ground has been reclaimed and the work is still going on. Now known as the *Ijsselmeer* (*q.v.*).

ZULULAND
District of Natal, S. Africa, lying N. of the Tugela river, with a coastline on the Ind. Ocean. The land is chiefly inhabited by Zulus, who possessed a powerful kingdom in the 19th cent. Between them and the Boers there was perpetual dissension, and in 1879 there were also serious difficulties with Brit., the result being the Zulu War. At Ulundi on July 4, 1879, the Zulus were defeated and their king, Cetawayo, was made prisoner. Zululand was then annexed and in 1897 was made part of Natal. Area: 10,430 sq.m.

ZÜRICH
[tsü'-rich] Univ. town of N. Switzerland, at the N. end of the Lake of Z. on the Linnet, in Z. canton. It is the most important centre of trade, banking and industry in Switzerland. Pop. 440,800.

ZWINGLI, Ulrich
(1484-1531) Swiss Protestant. B. St. Gall. Became minister in Zürich, 1518. Opposed Luther's teaching of Communion.

ACKNOWLEDGEMENTS

The publishers gratefully acknowledge the assistance of the following in the preparation of this Encyclopedia:

The United Kingdom Atomic Energy Authority

The Technology Editor, Science Journal

The Secretary of The Publishers Association

The Regional Physics Department, Western Regional Hospital Board

The Assistant Librarian of the Royal Geographical Society

William A. Porter, Esq.